THE BREATHE LIFE BIBLE

PRESENTED

to

____

by

____

on

____

THE BREATHE LIFE BIBLE

THE BREATHE LIFE BIBLE

Thomas Nelson NKJV

THOMAS NELSON
Since 1798

www.ThomasNelson.com

Published in Nashville, TN, by Thomas Nelson.
Thomas Nelson is a registered trademark of HarperCollins Christian Publishing, Inc.

Library of Congress Control Number: 2023938317

Printed in India

24 25 26 27 28 29 30 31 32 33 /BPI/ 15 14 13 12 11 10 9 8 7 6 5 4 3 2 1

FOREWORD

THE BIBLE THAT FOLLOWS IS like no other Bible you have read. It has all the words of the New King James Version, but the contributors have provided you with a helpful perspective to put those words into action in your family, in your community, in your nation, and in the world. *The Breathe Life Bible* is about making real the Beloved Community where everyone is valued and cared for. We all have a part to play in that. I have spent my life trying to play my part in living up to the words "Love your neighbor." But there is plenty of work still to do.

The continuing questions are "How do we do this in a world gone wrong? How do we do this in the face of injustice and oppression?" Jesus was sent to set at liberty those who are oppressed. If we are His hands and feet, then we should take an active hand in standing against injustice and oppression. But we are to do that with God's authority and, to the extent possible, at peace and in unity with all of God's children. This may seem to be a tall order, but nothing is impossible if we have faith in God and are obedient to His Word. The answers can be found in the Bible, and I hope that the articles and commentary that follow give you guidance and breathe life into your heart, mind, and life.

Peace and Blessings,
Ambassador Andrew Young
United Nations, 1977–1979

CONTENTS

Foreword v
Acknowledgments from the General Editors x
Contributors xii
Preface xiii
The Guide
The Breathe Life Bible Highlights xv
The Prayer xviii
The Call xix
The Insight
My Peace I Give to You xx
The Way: *Jesus Saves* xxii
The Sky
Faith: *The Faith That the Dark Past Has Taught Us* xxv
In: *The Power and Spirit of "In"* xxvii
Action: *Working Out Our Faith* xxix

The Books of the Old Testament

Genesis 1
Exodus 63
Leviticus 114
Numbers 152
Deuteronomy 204
Joshua 250
Judges 281
Ruth 313
1 Samuel 320
2 Samuel 360
1 Kings 395
2 Kings 435
1 Chronicles 473
2 Chronicles 509
Ezra 552
Nehemiah 567
Esther 588
Job 600
Psalms 642
Proverbs 750
Ecclesiastes 791
Song of Solomon 805
Isaiah 815
Jeremiah 898
Lamentations 977
Ezekiel 988
Daniel 1052
Hosea 1076
Joel 1093
Amos 1102
Obadiah 1115
Jonah 1120
Micah 1126
Nahum 1138
Habakkuk 1144
Zephaniah 1150
Haggai 1158
Zechariah 1162
Malachi 1180

The Books of the New Testament

Matthew 1191
Mark 1237
Luke 1267
John 1314
Acts 1349
Romans 1392
1 Corinthians 1412
2 Corinthians 1431
Galatians 1447
Ephesians 1457
Philippians 1468
Colossians 1476
1 Thessalonians 1484
2 Thessalonians 1491
1 Timothy 1496
2 Timothy 1505
Titus 1512
Philemon 1517
Hebrews 1521
James 1538
1 Peter 1547
2 Peter 1556
1 John 1562
2 John 1571
3 John 1575
Jude 1578
Revelation 1582

Contributor Biographies 1607
Index to Articles 1611
Table of Monies, Weights, and Measures 1615
The Parables of Jesus Christ 1617
The Miracles of Jesus Christ 1618
Prayers of the Bible 1619
Concordance 1622

ABBREVIATIONS

Book Abbreviations

in alphabetical order by abbreviation
OT = Old Testament
NT = New Testament

1 Chr.	1 Chronicles	OT	Hos.	Hosea	OT
1 Cor.	1 Corinthians	NT	Is.	Isaiah	OT
1 John	1 John	NT	James	James	NT
1 Kin.	1 Kings	OT	Jer.	Jeremiah	OT
1 Pet.	1 Peter	NT	Job	Job	OT
1 Sam.	1 Samuel	OT	Joel	Joel	OT
1 Thess.	1 Thessalonians	NT	John	John	NT
1 Tim.	1 Timothy	NT	Jon.	Jonah	OT
2 Chr.	2 Chronicles	OT	Josh.	Joshua	OT
2 Cor.	2 Corinthians	NT	Jude	Jude	NT
2 John	2 John	NT	Judg.	Judges	OT
2 Kin.	2 Kings	OT	Lam.	Lamentations	OT
2 Pet.	2 Peter	NT	Lev.	Leviticus	OT
2 Sam.	2 Samuel	OT	Luke	Luke	NT
2 Thess.	2 Thessalonians	NT	Mal.	Malachi	OT
2 Tim.	2 Timothy	NT	Mark	Mark	NT
3 John	3 John	NT	Matt.	Matthew	NT
Acts	Acts	NT	Mic.	Micah	OT
Amos	Amos	OT	Nah.	Nahum	OT
Col.	Colossians	NT	Neh.	Nehemiah	OT
Dan.	Daniel	OT	Num.	Numbers	OT
Deut.	Deuteronomy	OT	Obad.	Obadiah	OT
Eccl.	Ecclesiastes	OT	Phil.	Philippians	NT
Eph.	Ephesians	NT	Philem.	Philemon	NT
Esth.	Esther	OT	Prov.	Proverbs	OT
Ex.	Exodus	OT	Ps.	Psalms	OT
Ezek.	Ezekiel	OT	Rev.	Revelation	NT
Ezra	Ezra	OT	Rom.	Romans	NT
Gal.	Galatians	NT	Ruth	Ruth	OT
Gen.	Genesis	OT	Song	Song of Solomon	OT
Hab.	Habakkuk	OT	Titus	Titus	NT
Hag.	Haggai	OT	Zech.	Zechariah	OT
Heb.	Hebrews	NT	Zeph.	Zephaniah	OT

Special Abbreviations

Arab. Arabic

Aram. Aramaic

Bg. Bomberg, the 1524–25 edition of the Hebrew Old Testament published by Daniel Bomberg

cf. compare

ch., chs. chapter, chapters

DSS Dead Sea Scrolls

e.g. for example

f., ff. following verse, following verses

fem. feminine

Gr. Greek

Heb. Hebrew

i.e. that is

Kt. Kethib (literally, in Aramaic, "written"), the written words of the Hebrew Old Testament preserved by the Masoretes (see "Qr." below)

Lat. Latin

lit. literally

LXX Septuagint, an ancient translation of the Old Testament into Greek

M Majority Text

masc. masculine

ms., mss. manuscript, manuscripts

MT Masoretic Text, the traditional Hebrew Old Testament

NU the modern eclectic, or "critical," text of the Greek New Testament, published in the twenty-seventh edition of the Nestle-Aland Greek New Testament (N) and in the fourth edition of the United Bible Societies' Greek New Testament (U)

pl. plural

Qr. Qere (literally, in Aramaic, "read")—certain words read aloud, differing from the written words, in the Masoretic tradition of the Hebrew Old Testament (see "Kt." above)

Sam. Samaritan Pentateuch, a variant Hebrew edition of the books of Moses used by the Samaritan community

sing. singular

Syr. Syriac

Tg. Targum, ancient Aramaic paraphrase of the Old Testament

TR Textus Receptus or Received Text

v., vv. verse, verses

vss. versions, ancient translations of the Bible

Vg. Vulgate, an ancient translation of the Bible into Latin, translated and edited by Jerome

ACKNOWLEDGMENTS FROM THE GENERAL EDITORS

WHAT FOLLOWS IS DEDICATED TO those who have faced the pain of injustice and still held tight to the hem of His garment.

After the public killing of George Floyd in 2020, something broke in me. At first I thought, surely everyone would now clearly see how racism has infested our society. But I soon lost heart because so many refused to see. As that year progressed, I witnessed division in the church on many social issues. I took my sorrow to the Lord, starting with my own repentance and asking Him, "Lord, what shall we do?" These questions continued to burn deep within me as the Lord made me dig deep for answers. I am thankful that my editorial partner, Stephanie Perry Moore, listened to my heartache and suggested that we wrestle through these issues together and write about them. She continues to be my true sister in faith.

For twenty-six years, my husband and I have been members of Liberty Church in Marietta, Georgia, a multicultural "on purpose" church. I serve alongside some of the most loving ambassadors of Christ, particularly co-pastors Chuck and Katrina Campbell and our senior pastors, John and Beth Fichtner. They have prayed for us and walked with us through many struggles. I am thankful to the elders with whom we serve: the Baines, Baileys, Bekkers, Davises, Wynnes, and Sheelah Gault, all of whom prayed over the project and encouraged me. I want to acknowledge my family Bible study members—Henry Howard, Karen Clark, Jerome Yates, Douglas Harris, Simone Harris, and Suzen Witcher—who have been steadfast, meeting weekly to walk through Scripture with me and help bring clarity to many passages. Much of what we learned I carried into this work. I also want to thank the women who have been meeting with me every day for two years to read and share about the Word of God. Thank you, Bernadine Bryant and Felicia Roberts, for convening the group.

I would like to thank all our contributors and editors for answering the call and pouring out what God has deposited in them, particularly Brenda Noel and Dawn Sherrill-Porter (ECHO Creative Media), who spent many late nights editing. Thank you to the HarperCollins Christian Publishing Group and the Thomas Nelson Bibles team for trusting us to say what we needed to say, particularly Brian Dembowczyk, who listened, sought to understand, and encouraged us through the process. Bob Sanford, I know you have moved on, but you are the friend who first believed in me in the world of Christian publishing; for that I remain thankful. Thank you to my husband, Kym, who did not complain as he watched me disappear into my office every night for months and not emerge until the wee hours. Last, but always first in my life, thank You, Lord, for laying this on our hearts and giving us this assignment.

Michele Clark Jenkins

I WAS BORN IN 1969, the year after my hero, Dr. Martin Luther King Jr., was senselessly slain. My parents and the village that raised me in Petersburg and Ettrick, Virginia, made certain I was keenly aware of the importance of his sacrifice. I was part of the realization of his dream that one day kids of color would go to schools with others outside our race. He gave so much, and he was gone too soon, but his life has instilled in me the need to keep shaking the tree so that others can eat the fruit. More importantly, to live a life that breathes for God. However, breathing for the Lord and daily walking with Him might be easy until the inhumanity and violence of humanity causes pain and heartbreak. After the deaths of Trayvon Martin, Breonna Taylor, George Floyd, and many others, the only thing that kept me going was my faith and the red blood of Jesus running through my soul. Thus, I felt a calling to do more. That is what led me to this project, created to be a road map of how we can allow the Father to lift the weight of this world off the oppressed.

The Lord truly blessed me with being a Bible editor, and I thank Him so much for His love and covering. I offer a special thank-you to the others who have helped put my faith in action: my parents, Dr. Franklin and Shirley Perry, whose faith helped groom mine; my publisher, Thomas Nelson, especially, Mark Schoenwald, Doug Lockhart, Philip Nation, and Brian Dembowczyk, whose faith in this project allowed us the opportunity to reach an underserved market and make a difference; Jim and Deen Sanders, whose faith to help people of a different color has blessed my life. I also want to thank my extended family—brother, Dennis Perry; godparents, Rev. Walter and Marjorie Kimbrough; mother-in-law, Ann Redding; nephew, Franklin Perry III—whose faith helped me see God's love working in the hearts of people. I am thankful for the project team, especially the ECHO Creative Media and the dynamic contributors. Your faith in our cause will affect people and change lives.

I am also thankful to friends: Jackie Butts, Adrienne Brown, Saundra Forrest, Jenell Clark, Melissa Mims, Gloria London, Vickie Davis, Vanessa Griggs, Lorenne Fey, Cedric Pendleton, Jay Spencer, Malik Yoba, Dr. Lakeba Williams, Ruth Watson, Dayna Fleming, Victoria Murray, Yolanda Howsie, and Deborah Bradley. My pastor and first lady, Rev. Dr. Eric and Meik Lee, whose faith charges me to live a life that pleases Him. Mel Banks Jr., whose vision helped show Michele and me the Bible publishing world. My children—Dustyn, Sydni, and Sheldyn—whose faith in God touches my soul. My husband, Derrick, whose faith in me keeps me dreaming and working for Christ. My editorial partner, Michele Clark Jenkins, whose faith is steadfast and has carried us through. Finally, I especially appreciate you, the reader. Your faith to read this Bible is a blessing that I pray will bless you in return and help you to Breathe Jesus in your daily life.

Stephanie Perry Moore

CONTRIBUTORS

MICHELE CLARK JENKINS, GENERAL EDITOR

STEPHANIE PERRY MOORE, GENERAL EDITOR

The Air Book Introductions

Old Testament Dr. Charrita Danley Quimby

New Testament Rev. Dr. Eric W. Lee

We Speak

Michele Clark Jenkins

Inhale-Exhale

Inhale Stephanie Perry Moore

Exhale Min. Derrick Moore

Release

Believe Dr. Arthur Satterwhite

Reconcile Pastor Debra L. Morton

Exalt Pastor Tommy Kyllonen

Act Rev. Dr. Helen Delaney

Trust Pastor Tommy Stevenson

Hope Bishop Vashti McKenzie

Elevate Bishop Marvin Sapp

#Oxygen

Believe Dr. Franklin Perry Sr.

Reconcile Rev. Dr. LaKeesha Walrond

Exalt Antonio Neal Phelon

Act Elder De'Leice R. Drane

Trust S. James Guitard

Hope Dr. Lakeba H. Williams

Elevate Rev. Dr. Walter L. Kimbrough

Life Support

Life Jekalyn Carr

Support Jamell Meeks

Editorial services provided by Brenda Noel and Dawn Sherrill-Porter of ECHO Creative Media.

PREFACE TO THE NEW KING JAMES VERSION®

TO UNDERSTAND THE HEART BEHIND the New King James Version, one need look no further than the stated intentions of the original King James scholars: "Not to make a new translation . . . but to make a good one better." The New King James Version is a continuation of the labors of the King James translators, unlocking for today's readers the spiritual treasures found especially in the Authorized Version of the Holy Bible.

While seeking to maintain the excellent *form* of the traditional English Bible, special care has also been taken to preserve the work of *precision* which is the legacy of the King James translators.

Where new translation has been necessary, the most complete representation of the original has been rendered by considering the definition and usage of the Hebrew, Aramaic, and Greek words in their contexts. This translation principle, known as *complete equivalence*, seeks to preserve accurately all of the information in the text while presenting it in good literary form.

In addition to accuracy, the translators have also sought to maintain those lyrical and devotional qualities that are so highly regarded in the King James Version. The thought flow and selection of phrases from the King James Version have been preserved wherever possible without sacrificing clarity.

The format of the New King James Version is designed to enhance the vividness, devotional quality, and usefulness of the Bible. Words or phrases in italics indicate expressions in the original language that require clarification by additional English words, as was done in the King James Version. Poetry is structured as verse to reflect the form and beauty of the passage in the original language. The covenant name of God was usually translated from the Hebrew as LORD or GOD, using capital letters as shown, as in the King James Version. This convention is also maintained in the New King James Version when the Old Testament is quoted in the New.

The Hebrew text used for the Old Testament is the 1967/1977 Stuttgart edition of the *Biblia Hebraica*, with frequent comparisons to the Bomberg edition of 1524–25. Ancient versions and the Dead Sea Scrolls were consulted, but the Hebrew is followed wherever possible. Significant variations, explanations, and alternate renderings are mentioned in footnotes.

The Greek text used for the New Testament is the one that was followed by the King James translators: the traditional text of the Greek-speaking churches, called the Received Text or Textus Receptus, first published in 1516. Footnotes indicate significant variants from the Textus Receptus as found in two other editions of the Greek New Testament:

(1) NU-Text: These variations generally represent the Alexandrian or Egyptian text type as found in the critical text published in the twenty-seventh edition of the Nestle-Aland Greek New Testament (N) and in the United Bible Societies' third edition (U).

(2) M-Text: These variations represent readings found in the text of *The Greek New Testament According to the Majority Text*, which follows the consensus of the majority of surviving New Testament manuscripts.

The textual notes in the New King James Version make no evaluation, but objectively present the facts about variant readings.

THE GUIDE

THE BREATHE LIFE BIBLE HAS been developed for those who feel they need God's help simply to breathe in today's suffocating world. It is for everyone—but it has been especially crafted with people of color in mind. We need God's wisdom and guidance in every area of our complex lives. Reading this Bible is intended to help you grow in your Christian walk and put your faith in action. Within the pages of this Bible, then, you will find seven features with answers and insights designed to help you apply the truth of God's Word to the realities of your life:

1. **The Sky** consists of three motivational articles that dive more deeply into this Bible's subtitle of "Faith in Action." Through the Word of God, you are empowered to live a fruitful, abundant life, fully engaged in the pursuit of healthy relationships with God and others. Each article offers wisdom to help you find the deeper meaning of each of these three words of the subtitle.

2. **The Air** provides an enriching introduction and overview of each book of the Bible, allowing you to get acquainted with its content and themes. In addition, insight has been added on how each book is relevant to the hearts of people of color today and how it will help you breathe in today's world.

3. **We Speak** offers you a chance to look at life through the eyes of forty-nine people in the Bible. These inviting, first-person accounts allow you to relate to the joys, sorrows, victories, and defeats of these individuals from long ago so that you might find insight in how to live today.

4. **Life Support** focuses on ten passages in Scripture and is presented in two parts. Part 1 addresses the question of what we can do to put our faith into action based on what we read in the

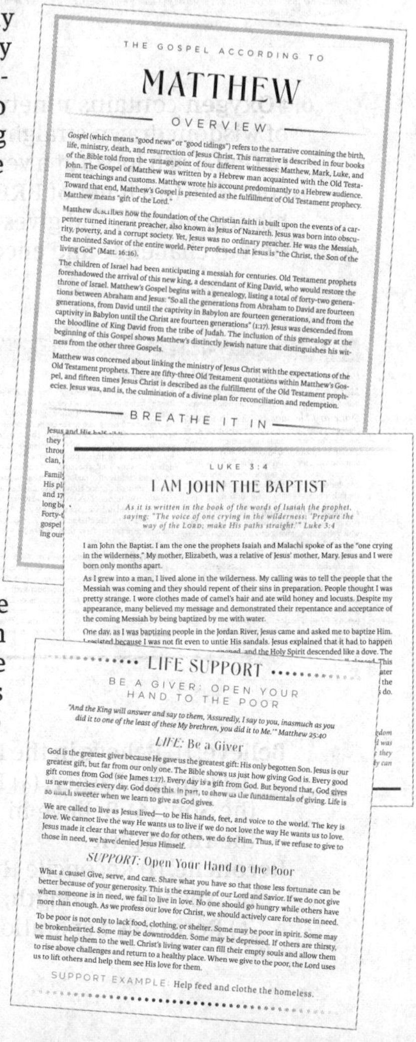
THE GOSPEL ACCORDING TO

MATTHEW

OVERVIEW

Gospel (which means "good news" or "good tidings") refers to the narrative containing the birth, life, ministry, death, and resurrection of Jesus Christ. This narrative is described in four books of the Bible told from the vantage point of four different witnesses: Matthew, Mark, Luke, and John. The Gospel of Matthew was written by a Hebrew man acquainted with the Old Testament teachings and customs. Matthew wrote his account predominantly to a Hebrew audience. Toward that end, Matthew's Gospel is presented as the fulfillment of Old Testament prophecy. Matthew means "gift of the Lord."

Matthew describes how the foundation of the Christian faith is built upon the events of a carpenter turned itinerant preacher, also known as Jesus of Nazareth. Jesus was born into obscurity, poverty, and a corrupt society. Yet, Jesus was no ordinary preacher. He was the Messiah, the anointed Savior of the entire world. Peter professed that Jesus is "the Christ, the Son of the living God" (Matt. 16:16).

The children of Israel had been anticipating a messiah for centuries. Old Testament prophets foreshadowed the arrival of this new king, a descendant of King David, who would restore the throne of Israel. Matthew's Gospel begins with a genealogy, listing a total of forty-two generations between Abraham and Jesus: "So all the generations from Abraham to David are fourteen generations, from David until the captivity in Babylon are fourteen generations, and from the captivity in Babylon until the Christ are fourteen generations" (1:17). Jesus was descended from the bloodline of King David from the tribe of Judah. The inclusion of this genealogy at the beginning of this Gospel shows Matthew's distinctly Jewish nature that distinguishes his witness from the other three Gospels.

Matthew was concerned about linking the ministry of Jesus Christ with the expectations of the Old Testament prophets. There are fifty-three Old Testament quotations within Matthew's Gospel, and fifteen times Jesus Christ is described as the fulfillment of the Old Testament prophecies. Jesus was, and is, the culmination of a divine plan for reconciliation and redemption.

BREATHE IT IN

LUKE 3:4

I AM JOHN THE BAPTIST

As it is written in the book of the words of Isaiah the prophet, saying: "The voice of one crying in the wilderness: 'Prepare the way of the LORD; make His paths straight.'" Luke 3:4

I am John the Baptist. I am the one the prophets Isaiah and Malachi spoke of as the "one crying in the wilderness." My mother, Elizabeth, was a relative of Jesus' mother, Mary. Jesus and I were born only months apart.

As I grew into a man, I lived alone in the wilderness. My calling was to tell the people that the Messiah was coming and they should repent of their sins in preparation. People thought I was pretty strange. I wore clothes made of camel's hair and ate wild honey and locusts. Despite my appearance, many believed my message and demonstrated their repentance and acceptance of the coming Messiah by being baptized by me with water.

One day, as I was baptizing people in the Jordan River, Jesus came and asked me to baptize Him. I resisted because I was not fit even to untie His sandals. Jesus explained that it had to happen

LIFE SUPPORT

BE A GIVER: OPEN YOUR HAND TO THE POOR

"And the King will answer and say to them, 'Assuredly, I say to you, inasmuch as you did it to one of the least of these My brethren, you did it to Me.'" Matthew 25:40

LIFE: Be a Giver

God is the greatest giver because He gave us the greatest gift: His only begotten Son. Jesus is our greatest gift, but far from our only one. The Bible shows us just how giving God is. Every good gift comes from God (see James 1:17). Every day is a gift from God. But beyond that, God gives us new mercies every day. God does this, in part, to show us the fundamentals of giving. Life is so much sweeter when we learn to give as God gives.

We are called to live as Jesus lived—to be His hands, feet, and voice to the world. The key is love. We cannot live the way He wants us to live if we do not love the way He wants us to love. Jesus made it clear that whatever we do for others, we do for Him. Thus, if we refuse to give to those in need, we have denied Jesus Himself.

SUPPORT: Open Your Hand to the Poor

What a cause! Give, serve, and care. Share what you have so that those less fortunate can be better because of your generosity. This is the example of our Lord and Savior. If we do not give when someone is in need, we fail to live in love. No one should go hungry while others have more than enough. As we profess our love for Christ, we should actively care for those in need.

To be poor is not only to lack food, clothing, or shelter. Some may be poor in spirit. Some may be brokenhearted. Some may be downtrodden. Some may be depressed. If others are thirsty, we must help them to the well. Christ's living water can fill their empty souls and allow them to rise above challenges and return to a healthy place. When we give to the poor, the Lord uses us to lift others and help them see His love for them.

SUPPORT EXAMPLE: Help feed and clothe the homeless.

passage. Part 2 takes a deeper look at how we can put our faith into action. These two interwoven parts provide true action steps to help you apply the truth of God's Word to your life.

Several articles and commentary notes in *The Breathe Life Bible* focus on seven tenets derived from the acronym **BREATHE**: Believe, Reconcile, Exalt, Act, Trust, Hope, and Elevate.

> BELIEVE IN THE SON
>
> **INHALE**
>
> The Bible tells of Jesus answering many requests and meeting many needs. He healed the sick, turned water to wine, fed five thousand people with only two fish and five loaves of bread, and above all, raised the dead! Well, I need Him to act in my life now. My mortgage has increased, but my income has not. On top of that, my parents are aging, and they always seem to need financial assistance. Now, my spouse has a chronic illness. I have saved for my kids' college fund, but I have had to dip into that just to live from day to day. In just a couple of months, I'm going to be flat broke. Does God still act in our lives and meet our urgent needs? If He does, why hasn't He shown up for me?
>
> **EXHALE**
>
> God is a need-meeting God. Notice that I did not say that He *was* a need-meeting God! He is unchanging. So, the same God who provided lunch for over five thousand people can provide for your needs too. The challenge for us, though, is that while God can grant any and all requests, He is not obligated to. We see this in the life of Jesus, don't we? He healed and fed many people—but there were still others who were sick and hungry in His day. Sometimes He walked on water. At other times, He rode in a boat.
>
> The problem we often face is thinking that we can figure out the mind of God. Or that we know what He should do. We can't and we don't. But one thing we see clearly in the Bible is God's love for people. All of Jesus' miraculous actions were done for two key reasons. First, they revealed that He is the Son of God. He did what normal people cannot do. Second, though, His actions revealed His deep love for people. He had love and compassion for the sick and hungry. And He has that same love and compassion for us.
>
> God knows every detail of our problems. It can seem like He disregards our problems, but that is simply not true. This is a fallen world, and we will still have difficulties. But God cares about everyone, and God will answer in the way that is best for us. Matthew 7:7 says, "Ask, and it will be given to you; seek, and you will find; knock, and it will be opened to you." Jesus cares for you.

5. **Inhale-Exhale** features questions and answers that address some of the most difficult situations life can bring your way. Based on the truth of Scripture and incorporating the seven tenets of BREATHE, answers are provided that remind you that it is possible to rise above the challenges of life. God wants you to succeed, and you can in His power.

> #OXYGEN
>
> MARK 4:39
>
> *Reconcile Chaos with Peace*
>
> The winds and waves of life are often chaotic, but do not fear. Your current situation is not your final destination. Embrace calm over chaos.
>
> In spite of it all, **breathe** and **reconcile chaos with peace.**

6. **#Oxygen** contains ninety-eight snippets of wisdom drawn straight from the Word of God. Each looks at a verse of Scripture, connects to a tenet of BREATHE, presents biblical insight, and gives personal resolution to challenge and encourage you.

> RELEASE // RECONCILE CHAOS WITH PEACE
>
> *Do Not Allow Unbelief to Steal Your Peace*
>
> *Mark 9:23* // Jesus said to him, "If you can believe, all things are possible to him who believes."
>
> *Summary Message* // A father brought his child who was suffering from convulsions to Jesus' disciples for them to heal him, but they could not. The father, in turn, told Jesus of his son's condition and what had happened with the disciples. Jesus' response was, "If you can believe, all things are possible to him who believes" (Mark 9:23). When the father believed, the son was healed.
>
> *Practical Application* // Many of us have become well acquainted with crises in our lives, which often visit us without our invitation or compliance. The child in Mark 9 had a condition that wreaked havoc on his body and in his family. We will experience many issues—such as health challenges, job loss, death of loved ones, and divorce—that can overwhelm us and sometimes cause us to question God. We wonder, "God, if You want only good things for me, then why is this bad thing happening?" This question, and perhaps God's nonimmediate answer to it, can cause our faith to falter and the situation to overwhelm us. In these chaotic and overwhelming situations, like the father in Mark 9, our response should be to turn to the Lord in faith, knowing His will for us is good and He is able to see far beyond what we can know or understand. In the account of the child in need of healing, the father responded to Jesus' words by saying: "Lord, I believe; help my unbelief!" (Mark 9:24). The father had a mixture of belief and some level of doubt or unbelief. Consequently, he had no peace. He was as tortured as his son. When we find our lives in chaos and we need a touch from the Lord, we must turn to Jesus to help us build our faith. Unbelief will destroy our peace, but a piece of faith is more than enough for Jesus to work with and grow.
>
> *Fervent Prayer* // Father, because You know all things, You know when our faith is weak. Please, help us today. Holy Spirit, please remind us that faith can move confusion and bewilderment out of our lives when chaotic situations descend. We ask You to enable us to speak peace over every chaotic situation we face. We trust the power You have given to us through simply believing. In Jesus' name we pray. Amen.

7. **Release** is a series of devotions developed by Christian leaders who are seeking hope and guidance in God's Word, as are you. These pastors and teachers share their hearts and their understanding of God's Word in ways that directly address your life. You will find forty-nine devotional articles throughout the pages of this Bible, each focusing on one of the tenets of BREATHE:

Believe: (1) Believe in the Promise; (2) Believe in Prayer; (3) Believe in the Father; (4) Believe in Forgiveness; (5) Believe in the Son; (6) Believe in the Resurrection Life; (7) Believe in the Holy Spirit

Reconcile: (1) Reconcile Hurt with Healing; (2) Reconcile Weaknesses with Strength; (3) Reconcile Wrongs with Rights; (4) Reconcile Separation with Reunion; (5) Reconcile Chaos

with Peace; (6) Reconcile Sins with Righteousness; (7) Reconcile Darkness with Light

Exalt: (1) Exalt His Guiding Light; (2) Exalt His Amazing Omnipresence; (3) Exalt His Awesome Mercy; (4) Exalt His Splendid Omnipotence; (5) Exalt His Immutability; (6) Exalt His Mighty Name; (7) Exalt His Splendid Omniscience

Act: (1) Act in Faith; (2) Act When He Calls; (3) Act out of Selflessness; (4) Act as He Does; (5) Act in Confidence; (6) Act with Self-Control; (7) Act Like His Chosen

Trust: (1) Trust in His Word; (2) Trust in His Will; (3) Trust in His Ways; (4) Trust in His Wisdom; (5) Trust in His Wonder; (6) Trust in His Warmth; (7) Trust in His World

Hope: (1) Hope for Today; (2) Hope for Peace; (3) Hope for the Salvation of the Lost; (4) Hope for True Judgments; (5) Hope for Deliverance; (6) Hope for What We Do Not See; (7) Hope for the Lord

Elevate: (1) Elevate the Stands You Take; (2) Elevate How You Serve Others; (3) Elevate Your Way of Thinking; (4) Elevate the Steps You Take; (5) Elevate Your Identity; (6) Elevate the Love You Share; (7) Elevate Your Time with Him

To enrich your spiritual journey the most, be sure to take the time first to read the Scripture that each feature in this Bible is based on, meditate on what is shared in the feature, and consider your own life in light of the truth presented. You have much to gain through the treasures contained in the living and powerful Word of God. May *The Breathe Life Bible* bless and encourage your soul and inspire you to put your faith in action.

THE PRAYER

BY HEZEKIAH WALKER

Dear Reader,

God has been gracious to give me talents to share His Word through gospel music. Many of the songs He has given me align with the message of *The Breathe Life Bible*. Therefore, as in those songs, may each of you give God "Every Praise" and say to Him, "I Feel Your Spirit" and "You're All I Need." I pray that every one of you raises your own voice to shout, "Wonderful Is Your Name," because only in Jesus will you find true peace.

Although sometimes life can weigh heavy and mistakes can be made, I want you to know that we serve the God who gives us a "Second Chance." I hope that you find life in this Bible by knowing that there is "No Defeat," for we were "Born to Win." "What a Mighty God We Serve!"

May each of you come to a place where you recognize that you need Jesus to keep you "Moving Forward." Regardless of the past, do not go back, but keep moving ahead. Know that all things are made new when you surrender your life to Christ. So I lift each of you up before the Lord and pray:

Heavenly Father,

What an honor and privilege it is to be able to seek Your blessing on every reader of *The Breathe Life Bible*. This Bible's purpose resonates with my heart. Life on this side of heaven can sometimes be so suffocating that we feel unable to breathe. Thankfully, Your Word reminds us that You are there, especially in the tough times, and that You care.

May those who read *The Breathe Life Bible* **Believe** that it can help them **Reconcile** everything that is weighing heavy in their lives and find freedom when they **Exalt** and uplift Your name. May they use this word to **Act** righteously and **Trust** that You are guiding their footsteps. I pray this Bible gives them **Hope** in every area of their lives and will ultimately **Elevate** them to become all that You have made them to be.

Lastly, I pray that every reader of this Holy Bible will be uplifted and grateful for the things that You have done. Through it all, may they reach a place where they can be grateful for the victories won. Though much can be hard, may they see Your works and praise You, Lord. You love us, and You will forever help us to breathe!

In Jesus' name, I pray.
Amen and Amen!

THE CALL

TO A GREAT DEGREE, BLACK Americans are loyal and consistent in their Christian beliefs with a rich history of faith preserved under fire. Because of the history of slavery and societal discrimination, the faith of Black people has been intimately tied to uplifting the human condition. Every Sunday, out of the pulpits of Black churches across America comes a message to move the community forward and the challenge to rise above in excellence.

In many ways, the killing of George Floyd in May 2020 changed the way America viewed the issue of race. For some, there seems to have been a change of heart and an acknowledgment that silence on racial injustice is no longer an option. The subsequent protests and demonstrations were an outpouring of generations of frustration, anger, and weariness, not only by Black people but also by those who see racial injustice as a stain on our society. The results were like a replay of the 60s with the "voice of the unheard" speaking out night after night on the evening news.

But, as a good portion of America was just waking up to the existence of racial injustice and societal racism, many Black Americans viewed the death of George Floyd as a last straw. They felt a continued weariness of Black lives being devalued time after time and the resulting calls for justice falling on deaf ears time after time also. Many wondered, then, if this time would be any different from the others that had come before. There were clues that perhaps it would, as more individuals and institutions seemed to take note and take action.

The Slave Bible of the nineteenth century, as it was called, was used to teach those who were slaves about the Christian faith, but its publisher purposely omitted passages that might inspire these men, women, and children to seek freedom. They were taught to praise God, accept their condition, and serve their masters. So how should Black Christians respond to the human condition in 2020 and beyond? As Dr. Martin Luther King Jr. asked, "Where Do We Go from Here: Chaos or Community?"

Unlike the Slave Bible, *The Breathe Life Bible* navigates the Word of God to bring light to the issues of today through articles and commentary providing biblical and timely wisdom and guidance. This Bible offers you a Christ-centered alternative to the stifling environment that gave rise to George Floyd's (and before him, Eric Garner's) heartbreaking statement "I can't breathe." It seeks to replace fear, anxiety, confusion, and anger with God's peace and promises. It replaces helplessness with active faith. The goal of *The Breathe Life Bible* is to connect Scripture to personal experience and biblical truth to daily life so you can answer the divine call to put your faith in action.

THE INSIGHT
MY PEACE I GIVE TO YOU

BY REV. DR. BERNICE A. KING

Blessed are the peacemakers, for they shall be called sons of God.
Matthew 5:9

Peace I leave with you, My peace I give to you; not as the world gives do I give to you. Let not your heart be troubled, neither let it be afraid.
John 14:27

For the earnest expectation of the creation eagerly waits for the revealing of the sons of God.
Romans 8:19

OFTEN, WHEN WE REFER TO a "piece," we speak of some sort of weapon. In another sense, we might say that we want to give somebody a "piece" of our minds. These expressions capture two of the most dangerous weapons we can wield: guns and our tongues. If we are going to have true peace in the world and nonviolence is going to be our way, then we are going to have to exchange our "piece" for the peace of Jesus Christ.

But we must first have peace with God before we can even begin to be peacemakers. You cannot give something you do not have. Peace is a gift from God. There is no true peace unless its source is God. So, if you do not have peace with God, who is the ultimate Peacemaker, then it is impossible for you to be a vessel of peace with your neighbor. You cannot gain peace from any source but from the Peacemaker. You cannot manufacture peace. Peace is a by-product of a right relationship with Christ, who says, "My peace I give to you."

My father, the apostle of nonviolence, was only successful because he had peace with God. There is nothing else to which we can ascribe the reason he was such a great man of God. Oh yes, he was an awesome orator. He obtained the highest degree a person can receive from our educational system. He was an avid reader and a preacher, born and reared in the Baptist tradition. But what made Dr. Martin Luther King Jr. great was that he understood he could not change the world merely by his impressive oratory skills, education, and leadership. He knew peace in the world only comes through peace with God.

On January 27, 1956, a call came to my parents' home. The caller said, "Dr. King, if you don't get out of town in three days, we're going to blow up your home and kill your baby and your wife." That was the most troubling call my father had ever received. That night, my father began to reflect over his life and his upbringing to draw peace from them, but he could not find any. He thought of his father and how he was not afraid to confront systems—how his father was a block and shield for him

as he was growing up—but he could not find peace. He thought of his beautiful wife and child and tried to find peace and comfort in them, but not even that gave him peace in that turbulent moment.

He said, "God, I'm down here trying to do the right things, but I am at the end of my powers." Suddenly a voice came, speaking to him like the one that spoke when Jesus was baptized and came up out of the water, or the one heard by the disciples on the Mount of Transfiguration, saying, "Martin Luther King Jr.! Stand up for justice! Stand up for freedom! Stand up for righteousness! And lo, I will be with you until the end." A weight was lifted from my father's shoulders.

Sure enough, three nights later, that house was bombed with my mother and my sister, Yolanda, inside. My mother, a unique woman, remained amazingly calm through it all. Even more amazing was what transpired at the end of the evening. My mother and father went out to the front porch. Angry people had gathered with all kinds of weapons, ready to handle business. But the flesh of man did not rule that day. My father stood firmly with my mother by his side, and the peace of God spoke. Though moved by their loyalty, my father told each of those people to put down his or her "piece," take up God's peace, and go home. He said, "We're going to fight this with Christian love."

From that day forward, the movement led by my father was driven and defined by nonviolence. Nonviolence is for courageous people who are willing to step out, trusting that God always has their backs. Doing what is right is not always going to be "peaches and cream." You will come against resistance, but you must be ready from the inside out. It does not happen from the outside in. If you do not have that still small voice of the Holy Spirit inside you to steady your mind, heart, and hands, you will break.

The world in which we live will not change until we, the people of God, get in line to give up our "piece" (our prerogative, our desires) and surrender to His peace (His prerogative and His desire). Nothing else but God's peace will transform lives and nations.

THE WAY
JESUS SAVES

THE BREATHE LIFE BIBLE FOCUSES on faith in action. But it makes a very big presumption that you are starting from a position of faith. If you have not accepted Jesus Christ as your Lord and Savior, then what is presented on the following pages will be like sitting in the driver's seat of a big, powerful automobile without a key to start the engine. The words of Scripture have horsepower under the hood that you cannot even imagine. They will take you on the adventure of a lifetime and into eternity. They will never get rusty or run out of gas; there will never be a new model to take their place. However, without that little key, you will never know their power. The "key" is Jesus.

If you have not met Jesus, the key to salvation, now is the perfect time for an introduction. Jesus is God, one with the Father and Holy Spirit, but He also came to earth as a man and became one of us. Though He could have chosen to come to earth as royalty, He did not. He did not have money or fine clothes. He had no position and no beauty of form. He did not even have a place to lay His head. Instead, He lived as a lowly carpenter before beginning His ministry, which led to Him being despised by those He came to serve and rejected by the ruling elite. Certainly, no one can boast that Jesus does not know what it is to be a man who is downtrodden and oppressed.

When Jesus came into the world, the world was already condemned because it had been overtaken by sin. People had forgotten or rejected God and were living their own way. Sin separates us from God, our Father, so Jesus came into this fallen world to save us from that sin. That is how much He loves us.

Those who were attracted to Jesus were drawn not by His worldly attributes—again, there were none—but because of what He spoke and did. They heard and saw God in Him. Jesus lived a perfect life, but He did not come into the world just to live; He came into the world also to die—to become the sacrifice for our sin. He was crucified on the cross and became sin in our place. He became every sin ever committed and every sin that will ever be committed. He did this so that our relationship with the Father that was torn away in the Garden of Eden might be restored.

Three days after Jesus died on the cross, He was resurrected, and the power of sin and death in the lives of those who put their trust in Him was destroyed forever. No other person, power, or religion can claim such triumph over death; only Jesus can! Now, He has ascended into heaven, and He sits at the right hand of our Father God. However, He is soon coming back for those who love Him.

We want you to get to know this Jesus the Bible speaks of and we proclaim. We want you to encounter Him for yourself, experience forgiveness and freedom of sin, and have a relationship like no other with

"Help! Help! Save me!" the girl cried with glazed eyes as she began to bob up and down in the water. But all of the other kids seemed frozen and merely began to scream, "Somebody do something!" One of the supervisors heard the shrieks and jumped into the pool in an attempt to rescue the young girl. Unfortunately, he approached her from the front, only to be met with a death grip around his neck as she reached out choking and spitting water. In a few seconds, they both began to go down. The would-be rescuer now shared the look of fear and panic that gripped the drowning girl. Death seemed to be clawing at both of them. Then an older teen gathered his wits, dove into the water, and came up behind the girl. He pried her off the supervisor and pulled her to the side of the pool while the supervisor swam to safety.

Spiritual salvation is like this water rescue. It begins when you realize you are in danger of disaster, destruction, and spiritual death. You are drowning in the waters of life, cannot save yourself, and recognize it. Your first response might be to call out. Maybe in the frustration and discouragement of your life, you have called out for help. That calling is important, but what is even more important is the One you call to. Maybe you called out to a friend. Maybe you called out to drugs. Maybe you called out to someone in the dark of a bedroom whose name you barely knew. In the end, you were just like the girl in the pool. The person you called out could not help you, no matter how much you tried to hold on. There is no one, no name you can call that can save you except the name of Jesus (Acts 4:12).

Excerpt from "Help! Save Me!"
by Bishop Kenneth Ulmer

Him. There is nothing you can do to earn salvation. It is given freely by God. All you have to do is accept it. It is God's desire that everyone would come to know Him. Are you ready to know Him?

If you are ready to commit your life to Him, you can do it wherever you are. The Bible says, "If you confess with your mouth the Lord Jesus and believe in your heart that God has raised Him from the dead, you will be saved" (Rom. 10:9). So, stop now and admit to God that you have sinned against Him. You have gone your own way instead of His way. Acknowledge that you believe Jesus is who He claimed to be—the Son of God—and that you recognize that He died in your place for your sins. Ask God to forgive your sins. Invite Christ into your life. Let Him know that you do not want to live without Him anymore.

You can tell God these things through prayer that can go something like this:

"God, I come in the name of Jesus. I know I have sinned, and I ask You to forgive me. I know that my life is not what it was meant to be. I now turn from a life outside Your will and turn toward You. I know that I cannot do this on my own. I surrender to You, God. I give my heart to You, Lord. Come into my life. I receive You as my Lord and Savior. Thank You, Lord, for saving me. Amen."

If you have just made Christ Lord of your life, you may not feel any different from how you felt before, but know that you have already been transformed. God has made you a new person in Christ (see 2 Cor. 5:17). You are fully forgiven and accepted and loved by God beyond measure for all eternity. Furthermore, you are already taking your first steps of faith that will help you live your new identity in Christ and carry you for eternity. But be sure to get into a Bible-believing church where you can be discipled and serve. Now you can win the battles in your life, whatever they are, because God dwells within you.

THE SKY: FAITH
THE FAITH THAT THE DARK PAST HAS TAUGHT US

BY REV. MATTHEW WESLEY WILLIAMS

"Sing a song full of the faith that the dark past has taught us."
James Weldon Johnson, "Lift Every Voice and Sing"

> Now faith is the substance of things hoped for, the evidence of things not seen.
>
> Hebrews 11:1

> Without faith it is impossible to please [God].
>
> Hebrews 11:6

> And all these, having obtained a good testimony through faith, did not receive the promise.
>
> Hebrews 11:39

THESE VERSES FROM THE LETTER to the Hebrews were written to a people struggling to breathe. The community who originally read this book was a group of Jewish followers of the Way of Jesus who were living in the Roman Empire. This empire would come to persecute them for pledging allegiance to Christ rather than Caesar.

This Christian community endured brutality from the Roman police force and unjust imprisonment by a criminal injustice system. Their resources had been robbed by Roman financiers in cahoots with public officials and Jewish religious leaders. Suffocating under the knee of a brutal empire, the people were on the verge of giving up.

To this community, the writer of Hebrews said, "Now faith . . ."

This would be a puzzling prescription if we read the anemic faith of popular American culture into it. However, this Hebrew community understood that faith is not (1) a cure-all that if activated makes everything in your life instantly better; (2) an escape hatch to avoid reckoning with injustice; (3) a passive belief in personal piety—a set of endless dos and don'ts; or (4) a genie's lamp that we rub to get God to give us our every wish.

So, what is faith?

Dr. Joe Samuel Ratliff once observed that if you really want to understand what this text says about faith, replace the word *faith* with the word *risk*, and read the passage again:

> Now [risk] is the substance of things hoped for, the evidence of things not seen.
>
> Hebrews 11:1

> But without [risk] it is impossible to please [God].
>
> Hebrews 11:6

> And all these, having obtained a good testimony through [risk], did not receive the promise.
>
> Hebrews 11:39

Hebrews 11 describes faith as an ancestral inheritance of courage that we take hold of ourselves. The writer of the Book of Hebrews bolstered the faith of the original recipients by reminding them of their ancestors who acted in faith in the face of their own challenging circumstances. They took great risks to fulfill God's purpose and serve God's people. Those first readers of Hebrews were to do the same.

We, too, are heirs to a faith that reminds us of this powerful truth. Our ancestral inheritance is not just about what has been done to us; it is about what God has done through us. Our ancestors' risks opened paths and possibilities from which we now benefit. However, we do not get to rest on those risks of our forebearers. This inheritance is a debt that must come due. We repay this debt by risking our comfort and convenience to ensure that all people have access to the abundant life Jesus came to bring. The faith of our ancestors found its future in us, and our faith ought to facilitate a future far beyond our years. Our work is to become ancestors whose names can be called by future generations in the roll of those who modeled this kind of faith.

THE SKY: IN
THE POWER AND SPIRIT OF "IN"

BY DR. THELMA THOMAS DALEY

For as we have many members in one body, but all the members do not have the same function, so we, being many, are one body in Christ, and individually members of one another.

Romans 12:4–5

AS A LITTLE GIRL GROWING up in Maryland, I was in awe and disbelief of the newborn Jesus being placed in a manger and wrapped in swaddling cloth when I heard this taught in Sunday school and dramatized at our Christmas programs. How could this be when every night I was in a pretty, little bed all snuggled in a pink, wool blanket? According to Psalm 84:3, "even the sparrow has found a home, and the swallow a nest." Yet, Jesus had so little. And the very next verse in Psalm 84 tells us that "blessed are those who dwell in [God's] house."

These thoughts caused me to realize the power of always living our lives *in* Christ. The little word *in*—sometimes a preposition, sometimes an adjective, sometimes a noun, and even at other times an adverb—can be easily overlooked. But it means everything to how we live and breathe and have our being *in* Him (see Acts 17:28). We are not just devotees of Christ; we are *in* Him, and He is *in* us. We are one. Even more, if we are living *in* Christ, we are one with each other. That means that we look out for each other and serve one another so not one of us is without.

Have you ever stopped to think just how the word *in* penetrates almost everything in our daily lives? We drive *in*, sleep *in*, dine *in*, pray *in*, live *in*, negotiate *in*, swim *in*, fly *in*, and learn *in*. We are *in* our churches, *in* our organizations, *in* the hallowed pages of the Bible, and *in* God's world and mercy. Now, try putting the word Christ after each of those "ins" of our lives. That is the key. All things are done *in* Christ Jesus. The world should see Jesus in each of us because we are His hands and feet and His ambassadors to the world.

This is why organizations like the National Council of Negro Women (NCNW) walks each day *in* its powerful mission to embrace and serve women of African descent and their families. Its myriad of programs and projects touch the hearts and lives of more than two million women in the United States and its territories and in foreign lands. The organization's spiritual roots are strong and undergirded *in* Christ. Believing *in* God, the NCNW realizes the value of all people and the challenges that inspired Black women like Bethune, Height, Hamer, and our mothers never to give up or give in. Their foresight reminds us ever to embrace the young and the experienced, the powerful and the powerless, the weak and the strong and, *in* Christ, never to leave anyone behind.

Moving forward with respect, love, kindness, dignity, vision, power, and the recognition of God in our endeavors, the spirit and power of "in" will never be broken. Each of us has an impenetrable God-given "in" to be used for the goodness of others.

The power of "in," coupled with its spirit, is unquenchable and indestructible! "If we live *in* the Spirit, let us also walk *in* the Spirit" (Gal. 5:25, emphasis added).

THE SKY: ACTION
WORKING OUT OUR FAITH

BY DERRICK JOHNSON

RACIAL JUSTICE AND SOCIAL JUSTICE are not new concepts. In 1908, after the race riots in Springfield, Illinois, a multicultural coalition of social activists formed the National Association for the Advancement of Colored People (NAACP) to stand up for the equality of all people. Since then, the NAACP has fought against injustice and oppression wherever it is found. God is not a respecter of persons, and neither should we be.

Although the NAACP is not a faith-based organization, many of its founders followed their faith in its establishment, like W. E. B. Du Bois, who believed that the church was the central change agent for the Black community and fought against heretical religious concepts that deemed Black people incompatible with the divine. Founder, Ida B. Wells-Barnett, followed her faith in fighting for racial and gender equality and spoke boldly against the lynch laws. She is considered prophetic in the church by connecting Christ to the hope of the oppressed.

We know that without faith it is impossible to please God. But we also know that faith without works is dead. It is important that we follow Christ's example as we experience the grace of God. When we ask, "What did Jesus do?" we know that He was anointed to preach the gospel to the poor, heal the brokenhearted, proclaim liberty to the captives, recover the sight of the blind, and set at liberty those who are oppressed (see Luke 4:18). Faith, then, is not a passive concept. We are all called to put our faith into action, just as Jesus did. Jesus saves, and we become His hands and feet in a world of injustice.

When we serve the least of these, we are doing the will of God. When one is lifted up, all of society is lifted up to a better place for all of us. This is how we perfect our faith, by serving one another in love. The Bible speaks of unity of the body and the premise that we should leave no one behind. All of us should move forward together. First Corinthians 12:26 says, "If one member suffers, all the members suffer with it; or if one member is honored, all the members rejoice with it." We look forward to rejoicing with all our brothers and sisters.

The NAACP and I personally will continue to take action on behalf of those who are marginalized or forgotten, standing shoulder to shoulder with those who want to see equality for all. Our faith for the future is that we act today so that all people are valued.

OLD TESTAMENT

THE FIRST BOOK OF MOSES CALLED

GENESIS

OVERVIEW

Scholars commonly believe the prophet Moses wrote the Book of Genesis between 1450 and 1410 BC as a historical text for the people of Israel. It is the first book of the Pentateuch (the first five books of the Bible, as a collective unit). Genesis is often called the "book of origins" for two primary reasons: (1) It describes the creation of the world and the beginning of humankind. (2) The word *genesis* means "beginning," "origin," or "creation."

Genesis opens with God speaking the world into existence and breathing life into humankind (chs. 1–2). It describes the world as God made it and intended it to be. As a result of the fall of humankind, however, the earth was cursed and death was introduced (ch. 3). The remainder of the Book of Genesis describes sin's effect on the world and reveals God's desire and plan to redeem people (chs. 4–50).

Genesis contains many of the most well-known Bible figures and stories. The compelling lives of those whom God chose to complete specific tasks (such as Noah, Abraham, Isaac, Jacob, and Joseph) are highlighted. Popular stories like Cain and Abel (see 4:1–15), Noah's ark (chs. 6–9), the Tower of Babel (see 11:1–9), Abraham's willingness to sacrifice his son Isaac (see 22:1–19), Jacob's deception of his father and brother (see 27:1–40), and Joseph's journey from prison to power (chs. 37–41) all appear in the Book of Genesis. Through these people and their stories, God's connection to humankind is made evident.

Focusing primarily on the people of Israel, Genesis conveys their ancestry and chronicles God's relationship with them. God's character is revealed through these relationships and interactions with His chosen people. Genesis tells of God's grace, His promises, His works, His expectations for His people, and the introduction of His plan for salvation. It also shows the wrath and the judgment of God; yet even that is motivated by a holy and unquestionable love. In summary, Genesis gives readers insight into God's creation of the world and humankind, as well as His relationship with and commitment to those whom He created.

BREATHE IT IN

When God breathed life into Adam and Eve, He desired a peaceful existence for them that would extend to all humanity. But when sin came into the world, all kinds of evil came with it. Just one generation from perfection, Cain killed his brother Abel. When God asked Cain where his brother was, Cain defiantly asked, "Am I my brother's keeper?" (Gen. 4:9). Thus began humanity's inhumanity. By the end of Genesis, the people of Israel were enslaved by the Egyptians. This vile practice of slavery has continued in various forms throughout history.

Institutional slavery began before 1612 in the colonies that would become the United States. During the early days of our nation, Southern economies were heavily built upon slave labor. In order to rationalize slavery, Black people were reduced to chattel. In 1857, the Supreme Court of the United States in *Dred Scott v. Sandford* determined Black people "[were] so far inferior, that they had no rights which the white man was bound to respect; and that the negro might justly and lawfully be reduced to slavery for his benefit." Even after the Thirteenth, Fourteenth, and

Fifteenth Amendments to the Constitution (called the Civil Rights Amendments) legally ended slavery and established citizenship and the right to vote for Black people, those rights were abridged for the next one hundred years through the legal concept of "separate but equal" and "Jim Crow" laws. Many would say we are still fighting the same battles to end racism, poverty, and political disenfranchisement.

As a result of discrimination, people of color and their supporters have protested in the streets about social injustices. In the 1960s, these protests were part of the civil rights movement. In the 2020s, protestors reemerged as part of the I Can't Breathe movement (named in memory of Eric Garner's and George Floyd's last words before they died). The statement is also a metaphorical reference to African Americans' collective response to the weight of the remnants of slavery that too many still bear.

So where is God in the midst of injustice? The better question is where are we? God is the same God today as He was during the days of Genesis. He asks the same question of each of us that He asked of Cain: "Where is your brother?" Our responsibility is to rescue our brother, leaving no one behind. Our responsibility is to bring the good news of Jesus Christ to the poor, heal the brokenhearted, proclaim freedom for the captives, and set the prisoners free.

So, if hatred, unrest, and violence continue to be blights upon our nation, we must all look to our Creator. God is with us just as He was with the people of Israel. True justice will not come from humanity but will come only from the Lord.

†

THE FIRST BOOK OF
MOSES CALLED

GENESIS

The History of Creation
(Gen. 2:4–9; Job 38:4–11; John 1:1–5)

1 In the [a]beginning [b]God created the heavens and the earth. 2 The earth was [a]with-
out form, and void; and darkness *was*[1] on
the face of the deep. [b]And the Spirit of God
was hovering over the face of the waters.
3 [a]Then God said, [b]"Let there be [c]light";
and there was light. 4 And God saw the
light, that *it was* good; and God divided
the light from the darkness. 5 God called
the light Day, and the [a]darkness He called
Night. So the evening and the morning
were the first day.
6 Then God said, [a]"Let there be a firmament in the midst of the waters, and let it
divide the waters from the waters." 7 Thus
God made the firmament, [a]and divided the
waters which *were* under the firmament
from the waters which *were* [b]above the firmament; and it was so. 8 And God called the
firmament Heaven. So the evening and the
morning were the second day.
9 Then God said, [a]"Let the waters under
the heavens be gathered together into one
place, and [b]let the dry *land* appear"; and it
was so. 10 And God called the dry *land* Earth,
and the gathering together of the waters He
called Seas. And God saw that *it was* good.
11 Then God said, "Let the earth [a]bring
forth grass, the herb *that* yields seed, *and*
the [b]fruit tree *that* yields fruit according to its kind, whose seed *is* in itself, on
the earth"; and it was so. 12 And the earth
brought forth grass, the herb *that* yields
seed according to its kind, and the tree
that yields fruit, whose seed *is* in itself according to its kind. And God saw that *it was*
good. 13 So the evening and the morning
were the third day.
14 Then God said, "Let there be [a]lights in
the firmament of the heavens to divide
the day from the night; and let them be
for signs and [b]seasons, and for days and
years; 15 and let them be for lights in the
firmament of the heavens to give light on
the earth"; and it was so. 16 Then God made
two great lights: the [a]greater light to rule
the day, and the [b]lesser light to rule the
night. *He made* [c]the stars also. 17 God set
them in the firmament of the [a]heavens to
give light on the earth, 18 and to [a]rule over
the day and over the night, and to divide
the light from the darkness. And God saw

#OXYGEN

GENESIS 1:3

Believe in the Promise

When life gets dark and you cannot see your way through, do not get frustrated. God can shine light on any situation.

So, just **breathe** and **believe in the promise.**

1:1 [a] Ps. 102:25; Is. 40:21; [John 1:1–3; Heb. 1:10] [b] Gen. 2:4; [Ps. 8:3; 89:11; 90:2]; Is. 44:24; Acts 17:24; Rom. 1:20; [Heb. 1:2; 11:3]; Rev. 4:11 1:2 [a] Jer. 4:23 [b] [Gen. 6:3]; Job 26:13; Ps. 33:6; 104:30; Is. 40:13, 14 [1] Words in italic type have been added for clarity. They are not found in the original Hebrew or Aramaic. 1:3 [a] Ps. 33:6, 9 [b] 2 Cor. 4:6 [c] [Heb. 11:3] 1:5 [a] Job 37:18; Ps. 19:2; 33:6; 74:16; 104:20; 136:5; Jer. 10:12 1:6 [a] Job 37:18; Jer. 10:12; 2 Pet. 3:5 1:7 [a] Job 38:8–11; Prov. 8:27–29 [b] Ps. 148:4 1:9 [a] Job 26:10; Ps. 104:6–9; Prov. 8:29; Jer. 5:22; 2 Pet. 3:5 [b] Ps. 24:1, 2; 33:7; 95:5 1:11 [a] Ps. 65:9–13; 104:14; Heb. 6:7 [b] 2 Sam. 16:1; Luke 6:44 1:14 [a] Deut. 4:19; Ps. 74:16; 136:5–9 [b] Ps. 104:19 1:16 [a] Ps. 136:8 [b] Deut. 17:3; Ps. 8:3 [c] Deut. 4:19; Job 38:7; Is. 40:26 1:17 [a] Gen. 15:5; Jer. 33:20, 25 1:18 [a] Jer. 31:35

that *it was* good. 19So the evening and the
morning were the fourth day.

20Then God said, "Let the waters abound
with an abundance of living creatures, and
let birds fly above the earth across the face
of the firmament of the heavens." 21So [a]God
created great sea creatures and every living thing that moves, with which the waters abounded, according to their kind, and
every winged bird according to its kind.
And God saw that *it was* good. 22And God
blessed them, saying, [a]"Be fruitful and multiply, and fill the waters in the seas, and let
birds multiply on the earth." 23So the evening and the morning were the fifth day.

24Then God said, "Let the earth bring
forth the living creature according to its
kind: cattle and creeping thing and beast of
the earth, *each* according to its kind"; and
it was so. 25And God made the beast of the
earth according to its kind, cattle according to its kind, and everything that creeps
on the earth according to its kind. And God
saw that *it was* good.

26Then God said, [a]"Let Us make man in
Our image, according to Our likeness; [b]let
them have dominion over the fish of the
sea, over the birds of the air, and over the
cattle, over all[1] the earth and over every
creeping thing that creeps on the earth."
27So God created man [a]in His *own* image;
in the image of God He created him; [b]male
and female He created them. 28Then God
blessed them, and God said to them, [a]"Be
fruitful and multiply; fill the earth and
[b]subdue it; have dominion over the fish of
the sea, over the birds of the air, and over
every living thing that moves on the earth."

29And God said, "See, I have given you
every herb *that* yields seed which *is* on the
face of all the earth, and every tree whose
fruit yields seed; [a]to you it shall be for food.
30Also, to [a]every beast of the earth, to every [b]bird of the air, and to everything that
creeps on the earth, in which *there is* life, *I
have given* every green herb for food"; and
it was so. 31Then [a]God saw everything that
He had made, and indeed *it was* very good.
So the evening and the morning were the
sixth day.

2 Thus the heavens and the earth, and
[a]all the host of them, were finished.
2[a]And on the seventh day God ended His
work which He had done, and He rested on
the seventh day from all His work which
He had done. 3Then God [a]blessed the seventh day and sanctified it, because in it He
rested from all His work which God had
created and made.

4[a]This *is* the history[1] of the heavens and
the earth when they were created, in the
day that the LORD God made the earth and
the heavens, 5before any [a]plant of the field
was in the earth and before any herb of the
field had grown. For the LORD God had not
[b]caused it to rain on the earth, and *there
was* no man [c]to till the ground; 6but a mist
went up from the earth and watered the
whole face of the ground.

7And the LORD God formed man *of* the
[a]dust of the ground, and [b]breathed into his
[c]nostrils the breath of life; and [d]man became a living being.

Life in God's Garden

8The LORD God planted [a]a garden [b]east-
ward in [c]Eden, and there He put the man
whom He had formed. 9And out of the
ground the LORD God made [a]every tree
grow that is pleasant to the sight and good
for food. [b]The tree of life *was* also in the
midst of the garden, and the tree of the
knowledge of good and [c]evil.

10Now a river went out of Eden to water
the garden, and from there it parted and
became four riverheads. 11The name of the
first *is* Pishon; it *is* the one which skirts
[a]the whole land of Havilah, where *there is*
gold. 12And the gold of that land *is* good.
[a]Bdellium and the onyx stone *are* there.
13The name of the second river *is* Gihon;
it *is* the one which goes around the whole
land of Cush. 14The name of the third river
is [a]Hiddekel;[1] it *is* the one which goes toward the east of Assyria. The fourth river
is the Euphrates.

1:21 [a] Ps. 104:25–28 **1:22** [a] Gen. 8:17 **1:26** [a] Gen. 9:6; Ps. 100:3; Eccl. 7:29; [Eph. 4:24]; James 3:9 [b] Gen. 9:2; Ps. 8:6–8 [1] Syriac reads *all the wild animals of.* **1:27** [a] Gen. 5:2; 1 Cor. 11:7 [b] Matt. 19:4; [Mark 10:6–8] **1:28** [a] Gen. 9:1, 7; Lev. 26:9 [b] 1 Cor. 9:27 **1:29** [a] Gen. 9:3; Ps. 104:14, 15 **1:30** [a] Ps. 145:15 [b] Job 38:41 **1:31** [a] [Ps. 104:24; 1 Tim. 4:4] **2:1** [a] Ps. 33:6 **2:2** [a] Ex. 20:9–11; 31:17; Heb. 4:4, 10 **2:3** [a] [Is. 58:13] **2:4** [a] Gen. 1:1; Ps. 90:1, 2 [1] Hebrew *toledoth,* literally *generations* **2:5** [a] Gen. 1:11, 12 [b] Gen. 7:4; Job 5:10; 38:26–28 [c] Gen. 3:23 **2:7** [a] Gen. 3:19, 23; Ps. 103:14 [b] Job 33:4 [c] Gen. 7:22 [d] 1 Cor. 15:45 **2:8** [a] Is. 51:3 [b] Gen. 3:23, 24 [c] Gen. 4:16 **2:9** [a] Ezek. 31:8 [b] [Gen. 3:22; Rev. 2:7; 22:2, 14] [c] [Deut. 1:39] **2:11** [a] Gen. 25:18 **2:12** [a] Num. 11:7 **2:14** [a] Dan. 10:4 [1] Or *Tigris*

15 Then the LORD God took the man and
put him in the garden of Eden to tend and
keep it. 16 And the LORD God commanded
the man, saying, "Of every tree of the garden you may freely eat; 17 but of the tree of
the knowledge of good and evil [a]you shall
not eat, for in the day that you eat of it [b]you
shall surely [c]die."

18 And the LORD God said, "*It is* not good
that man should be alone; [a]I will make him
a helper comparable to him." 19 [a]Out of the
ground the LORD God formed every beast
of the field and every bird of the air, and
[b]brought *them* to Adam to see what he
would call them. And whatever Adam called
each living creature, that *was* its name. 20 So
Adam gave names to all cattle, to the birds
of the air, and to every beast of the field.
But for Adam there was not found a helper
comparable to him.

21 And the LORD God caused a [a]deep sleep
to fall on Adam, and he slept; and He took
one of his ribs, and closed up the flesh in
its place. 22 Then the rib which the LORD
God had taken from man He made into a
woman, [a]and He [b]brought her to the man.

23 And Adam said:

"This *is* now [a]bone of my bones
And flesh of my flesh;
She shall be called Woman,
Because she was [b]taken out of Man."

24 [a]Therefore a man shall leave his father
and mother and [b]be joined to his wife, and
they shall become one flesh.

25 [a]And they were both naked, the man
and his wife, and were not [b]ashamed.

The Temptation and Fall of Man
(Rom. 5:12–21)

3 Now [a]the serpent was [b]more cunning
than any beast of the field which the
LORD God had made. And he said to the
woman, "Has God indeed said, 'You shall
not eat of every tree of the garden'?"

2 And the woman said to the serpent,
"We may eat the [a]fruit of the trees of the
garden; 3 but of the fruit of the tree which
is in the midst of the garden, God has said,
'You shall not eat it, nor shall you [a]touch
it, lest you die.'"

4 [a]Then the serpent said to the woman,
"You will not surely die. 5 For God knows
that in the day you eat of it your eyes will
be opened, and you will be like God, knowing good and evil."

6 So when the woman [a]saw that the tree
was good for food, that it *was* pleasant
to the eyes, and a tree desirable to make
one wise, she took of its fruit [b]and ate. She
also gave to her husband with her, and he
ate. 7 Then the eyes of both of them were
opened, [a]and they knew that they *were* naked; and they sewed fig leaves together and
made themselves coverings.

8 And they heard [a]the sound of the LORD
God walking in the garden in the cool of the
day, and Adam and his wife [b]hid themselves
from the presence of the LORD God among
the trees of the garden.

9 Then the LORD God called to Adam and
said to him, "Where *are* you?"

10 So he said, "I heard Your voice in the
garden, [a]and I was afraid because I was naked; and I hid myself."

11 And He said, "Who told you that you
were naked? Have you eaten from the tree
of which I commanded you that you should
not eat?"

12 Then the man said, [a]"The woman
whom You gave *to be* with me, she gave
me of the tree, and I ate."

13 And the LORD God said to the woman,
"What *is* this you have done?"

The woman said, [a]"The serpent deceived
me, and I ate."

14 So the LORD God said to the serpent:

"Because you have done this,
You *are* cursed more than all cattle,
And more than every
beast of the field;
On your belly you shall go,
And [a]you shall eat dust
All the days of your life.

2:17 [a] Gen. 3:1, 3, 11, 17 [b] Gen. 3:3, 19; [Rom. 6:23] [c] Rom. 5:12; 1 Cor. 15:21, 22 2:18 [a] 1 Cor. 11:8, 9; 1 Tim. 2:13 2:19 [a] Gen. 1:20, 24 [b] Ps. 8:6 2:21 [a] Gen. 15:12; 1 Sam. 26:12 2:22 [a] Gen. 3:20; 1 Tim. 2:13 [b] Heb. 13:4 2:23 [a] Gen. 29:14; Eph. 5:28–30 [b] 1 Cor. 11:8, 9 2:24 [a] Matt. 19:5; Eph. 5:31 [b] Mark 10:6–8; 1 Cor. 6:16 2:25 [a] Gen. 3:7, 10 [b] Is. 47:3 3:1 [a] 1 Chr. 21:1; [Rev. 12:9; 20:2, 10] [b] 2 Cor. 11:3 3:2 [a] Gen. 2:16, 17 3:3 [a] Ex. 19:12, 13; Rev. 22:14 3:4 [a] John 8:44; [2 Cor. 11:3; 1 Tim. 2:14] 3:6 [a] 1 John 2:16 [b] 1 Tim. 2:14 3:7 [a] Gen. 2:25 3:8 [a] Job 38:1 [b] Job 31:33; Jer. 23:24 3:10 [a] Gen. 2:25; Ex. 3:6; Deut. 9:19; 1 John 3:20 3:12 [a] [Prov. 28:13] 3:13 [a] Gen. 3:4; 2 Cor. 11:3; 1 Tim. 2:14 3:14 [a] Deut. 28:15–20; Is. 65:25; Mic. 7:17

15 And I will put enmity
Between you and the woman,
And between [a]your seed
and [b]her Seed;
[c]He shall bruise your head,
And you shall bruise His heel."

16To the woman He said:

"I will greatly multiply your sorrow
and your conception;
[a]In pain you shall bring forth children;
[b]Your desire *shall be* for your husband,
And he shall [c]rule over you."

17Then to Adam He said, [a]"Because you
have heeded the voice of your wife, and
have eaten from the tree [b]of which I commanded you, saying, 'You shall not eat of it':

[c]"Cursed *is* the ground for your sake;
[d]In toil you shall eat *of* it
All the days of your life.
18 Both thorns and thistles it
shall bring forth for you,
And [a]you shall eat the
herb of the field.
19 [a]In the sweat of your face
you shall eat bread
Till you return to the ground,
For out of it you were taken;
[b]For dust you *are,*
And [c]to dust you shall return."

20And Adam called his wife's name [a]Eve,
because she was the mother of all living.
21Also for Adam and his wife the LORD
God made tunics of skin, and clothed them.
22Then the LORD God said, "Behold, the
man has become like one of Us, to know
good and evil. And now, lest he put out
his hand and take also of the tree of life,
and eat, and live forever"— 23therefore the
LORD God sent him out of the garden of
Eden [a]to till the ground from which he was
taken. 24So [a]He drove out the man; and He
placed [b]cherubim [c]at the east of the garden
of Eden, and a flaming sword which turned
every way, to guard the way to the tree of
[d]life.

Cain Murders Abel
(Luke 11:51; Heb. 11:4; 12:24)

4 Now Adam knew Eve his wife, and she
conceived and bore Cain, and said,
"I have acquired a man from the LORD."
2Then she bore again, this time his brother
Abel. Now [a]Abel was a keeper of sheep, but
Cain was a tiller of the ground. 3And in the
process of time it came to pass that Cain
brought an offering of the fruit [a]of the
ground to the LORD. 4Abel also brought
of [a]the firstborn of his flock and of [b]their
fat. And the LORD [c]respected Abel and his
offering, 5but He did not respect Cain and
his offering. And Cain was very angry, and
his countenance fell.
6So the LORD said to Cain, "Why are you
angry? And why has your countenance
fallen? 7If you do well, will you not be accepted? And if you do not do well, sin lies
at the door. And its desire *is* for you, but
you should rule over it."
8Now Cain talked with Abel his brother;[1]
and it came to pass, when they were in the
field, that Cain rose up against Abel his
brother and [a]killed him.
9Then the LORD said to Cain, "Where *is*
Abel your brother?"
He said, [a]"I do not know. *Am* I [b]my
brother's keeper?"
10And He said, "What have you done?
The voice of your brother's blood [a]cries out
to Me from the ground. 11So now [a]you *are*
cursed from the earth, which has opened
its mouth to receive your brother's blood
from your hand. 12When you till the ground,
it shall no longer yield its strength to you.
A fugitive and a vagabond you shall be on
the earth."
13And Cain said to the LORD, "My punishment *is* greater than I can bear! 14Surely
You have driven me out this day from the
face of the ground; [a]I shall be [b]hidden from

3:15 [a] John 8:44; Acts 13:10; 1 John 3:8 [b] Is. 7:14; Luke 1:31, 34, 35; Gal. 4:4 [c] Rom. 16:20; [Rev. 12:7, 17] 3:16 [a] Is. 13:8; John 16:21 [b] Gen. 4:7 [c] 1 Cor. 11:3; Eph. 5:22; 1 Tim. 2:12, 15 3:17 [a] 1 Sam. 15:23 [b] Gen. 2:17 [c] Gen. 5:29; Rom. 8:20–22; Heb. 6:8 [d] Job 5:7; 14:1; Eccl. 2:23 3:18 [a] Ps. 104:14 3:19 [a] 2 Thess. 3:10 [b] Gen. 2:7; 5:5 [c] Job 21:26; Eccl. 3:20 3:20 [a] 2 Cor. 11:3; 1 Tim. 2:13 3:23 [a] Gen. 4:2; 9:20 3:24 [a] Ezek. 31:3, 11 [b] Ex. 25:18–22; Ps. 104:4; Ezek. 10:1–20; Heb. 1:7 [c] Gen. 2:8 [d] Gen. 2:9; [Rev. 22:2] 4:2 [a] Luke 11:50, 51 4:3 [a] Num. 18:12 4:4 [a] Num. 18:17 [b] Lev. 3:16 [c] Heb. 11:4 4:8 [a] Matt. 23:35; Luke 11:51; [1 John 3:12–15]; Jude 11 [1] Samaritan Pentateuch, Septuagint, Syriac, and Vulgate add *"Let us go out to the field."* 4:9 [a] John 8:44 [b] 1 Cor. 8:11–13 4:10 [a] Num. 35:33; Deut. 21:1–9; Heb. 12:24; Rev. 6:9, 10 4:11 [a] Gen. 3:14; Deut. 11:28; 28:15–20; Gal. 3:10 4:14 [a] Ps. 51:11 [b] Deut. 31:18; Is. 1:15

Your face; I shall be a fugitive and a vagabond on the earth, and it will happen *that*
[c]anyone who finds me will kill me."
15 And the LORD said to him, "Therefore,[1] whoever kills Cain, vengeance shall
be taken on him [a]sevenfold." And the LORD
set a [b]mark on Cain, lest anyone finding
him should kill him.

The Family of Cain

16 Then Cain [a]went out from the [b]pres-
ence of the LORD and dwelt in the land of
Nod on the east of Eden. 17 And Cain knew
his wife, and she conceived and bore Enoch.
And he built a city, [a]and called the name of
the city after the name of his son—Enoch.
18 To Enoch was born Irad; and Irad begot
Mehujael, and Mehujael begot Methushael,
and Methushael begot Lamech.
19 Then Lamech took for himself [a]two
wives: the name of one *was* Adah, and the
name of the second *was* Zillah. 20 And Adah
bore Jabal. He was the father of those who
dwell in tents and have livestock. 21 His
brother's name *was* Jubal. He was the father of all those who play the harp and
flute. 22 And as for Zillah, she also bore Tu-
bal-Cain, an instructor of every craftsman
in bronze and iron. And the sister of Tubal-
Cain *was* Naamah.
23 Then Lamech said to his wives:

"Adah and Zillah, hear my voice;
Wives of Lamech, listen to my speech!
For I have killed a man for
wounding me,
Even a young man for hurting me.
24 [a]If Cain shall be avenged sevenfold,
Then Lamech seventy-sevenfold."

A New Son

25 And Adam knew his wife again, and
she bore a son and [a]named him Seth, "For
God has appointed another seed for me instead of Abel, whom Cain killed." 26 And as
for Seth, [a]to him also a son was born; and
he named him Enosh.[1] Then *men* began [b]to
call on the name of the LORD.

The Family of Adam
(1 Chr. 1:1–4; Luke 3:36–38)

5 This is the book of the [a]genealogy of
Adam. In the day that God created
man, He made him in [b]the likeness of
God. 2 He created them [a]male and female,
and [b]blessed them and called them Mankind in the day they were created. 3 And
Adam lived one hundred and thirty years,
and begot *a son* [a]in his own likeness, after his image, and [b]named him Seth. 4 After he begot Seth, [a]the days of Adam were
eight hundred years; [b]and he had sons and
daughters. 5 So all the days that Adam lived
were nine hundred and thirty years; [a]and
he died.
6 Seth lived one hundred and five years,
and begot [a]Enosh. 7 After he begot Enosh,
Seth lived eight hundred and seven years,
and had sons and daughters. 8 So all the
days of Seth were nine hundred and twelve
years; and he died.
9 Enosh lived ninety years, and begot
Cainan.[1] 10 After he begot Cainan, Enosh
lived eight hundred and fifteen years, and
had sons and daughters. 11 So all the days of
Enosh were nine hundred and five years;
and he died.
12 Cainan lived seventy years, and begot
Mahalalel. 13 After he begot Mahalalel, Cainan lived eight hundred and forty years,
and had sons and daughters. 14 So all the
days of Cainan were nine hundred and ten
years; and he died.
15 Mahalalel lived sixty-five years, and
begot Jared. 16 After he begot Jared, Mahalalel lived eight hundred and thirty years,
and had sons and daughters. 17 So all the
days of Mahalalel were eight hundred and
ninety-five years; and he died.
18 Jared lived one hundred and sixty-two
years, and begot [a]Enoch. 19 After he begot
Enoch, Jared lived eight hundred years, and
had sons and daughters. 20 So all the days
of Jared were nine hundred and sixty-two
years; and he died.
21 Enoch lived sixty-five years, and begot
Methuselah. 22 After he begot Methuselah,

4:14 [c] Gen. 9:6; Num. 35:19, 21, 27 4:15 [a] Gen. 4:24; Ps. 79:12 [b] Gen. 9:6; Ezek. 9:4, 6 [1] Following Masoretic Text and Targum; Septuagint, Syriac, and Vulgate read *Not so.* 4:16 [a] 2 Kin. 13:23; 24:20; Jer. 23:39; 52:3 [b] Jon. 1:3 4:17 [a] Ps. 49:11 4:19 [a] Gen. 2:24; 16:3; 1 Tim. 3:2 4:24 [a] Gen. 4:15 4:25 [a] Gen. 5:3 4:26 [a] Gen. 5:6 [b] Gen. 12:8; 26:25; 1 Kin. 18:24; Ps. 116:17; Joel 2:32; Zeph. 3:9; 1 Cor. 1:2 [1] Greek *Enos* 5:1 [a] Gen. 2:4; 6:9; 1 Chr. 1:1; Matt. 1:1 [b] Gen. 1:26; 9:6; [Eph. 4:24; Col. 3:10] 5:2 [a] Gen. 1:27; Deut. 4:32; Matt. 19:4; Mark 10:6 [b] Gen. 1:28; 9:1 5:3 [a] 1 Cor. 15:48, 49 [b] Gen. 4:25 5:4 [a] 1 Chr. 1:1–4; Luke 3:36–38 [b] Gen. 1:28; 4:25 5:5 [a] Gen. 2:17; 3:19; 6:17; [Heb. 9:27] 5:6 [a] Gen. 4:26 5:9 [1] Hebrew *Qenan* 5:18 [a] Jude 14, 15

Enoch [a]walked with God three hundred
years, and had sons and daughters. 23So all
the days of Enoch were three hundred and
sixty-five years. 24And [a]Enoch walked with
God; and he *was* not, for God [b]took him.

25Methuselah lived one hundred and
eighty-seven years, and begot Lamech.
26After he begot Lamech, Methuselah lived
seven hundred and eighty-two years, and
had sons and daughters. 27So all the days of
Methuselah were nine hundred and sixty-
nine years; and he died.

28Lamech lived one hundred and eighty-
two years, and had a son. 29And he called
his name [a]Noah, saying, "This *one* will
comfort us concerning our work and the
toil of our hands, because of the ground
[b]which the LORD has cursed." 30After he
begot Noah, Lamech lived five hundred
and ninety-five years, and had sons and
daughters. 31So all the days of Lamech were
seven hundred and seventy-seven years;
and he died.

32And Noah was five hundred years old,
and Noah begot [a]Shem, Ham, [b]and Japheth.

The Wickedness and Judgment of Man

6 Now it came to pass, [a]when men began
to multiply on the face of the earth,
and daughters were born to them, 2that the
sons of God saw the daughters of men, that
they *were* beautiful; and they [a]took wives
for themselves of all whom they chose.

3And the LORD said, [a]"My Spirit shall
not [b]strive[1] with man forever, [c]for he *is* indeed flesh; yet his days shall be one hundred and twenty years." 4There were giants
on the earth in those [a]days, and also afterward, when the sons of God came in to the
daughters of men and they bore *children*
to them. Those *were* the mighty men who
were of old, men of renown.

5Then the LORD[1] saw that the wickedness
of man *was* great in the earth, and *that* every [a]intent of the thoughts of his heart *was*
only evil continually. 6And [a]the LORD was
sorry that He had made man on the earth,
and [b]He was grieved in His [c]heart. 7So the
LORD said, "I will [a]destroy man whom I
have created from the face of the earth,
both man and beast, creeping thing and
birds of the air, for I am sorry that I have
made them." 8But Noah [a]found grace in the
eyes of the LORD.

Noah Pleases God

9This is the genealogy of Noah. [a]Noah
was a just man, perfect in his generations.
Noah [b]walked with God. 10And Noah begot
three sons: [a]Shem, Ham, and Japheth.

11The earth also was corrupt [a]before God,
and the earth was [b]filled with violence. 12So
God [a]looked upon the earth, and indeed it
was corrupt; for [b]all flesh had corrupted
their way on the earth.

The Ark Prepared

(Heb. 11:7; 1 Pet. 3:20)

13And God said to Noah, [a]"The end of all
flesh has come before Me, for the earth is
filled with violence through them; [b]and
behold, [c]I will destroy them with the earth.
14Make yourself an ark of gopherwood;
make rooms in the ark, and cover it inside
and outside with pitch. 15And this is how
you shall make it: The length of the ark *shall*
be three hundred cubits, its width fifty cubits, and its height thirty cubits. 16You shall
make a window for the ark, and you shall
finish it to a cubit from above; and set the
door of the ark in its side. You shall make it
with lower, second, and third *decks.* 17[a]And
behold, I Myself am bringing [b]floodwaters
on the earth, to destroy from under heaven
all flesh in which *is* the breath of life; everything that *is* on the earth shall [c]die. 18But I
will establish My [a]covenant with you; and
[b]you shall go into the ark—you, your sons,
your wife, and your sons' wives with you.
19And of every living thing of all flesh you
shall bring [a]two of every *sort* into the ark,
to keep *them* alive with you; they shall be

5:22 [a] Gen. 6:9; 17:1; 24:40; 48:15; 2 Kin. 20:3; Ps. 16:8; [Mic. 6:8]; Mal. 2:6; 1 Thess. 2:12; [Heb. 11:39] 5:24 [a] 2 Kin. 2:11; Jude 14 [b] 2 Kin. 2:10; Ps. 49:15; 73:24; Heb. 11:5 5:29 [a] Luke 3:36; Heb. 11:7; 1 Pet. 3:20 [b] Gen. 3:17–19; 4:11 5:32 [a] Gen. 6:10; 7:13 [b] Gen. 10:21 6:1 [a] Gen. 1:28 6:2 [a] Deut. 7:3, 4 6:3 [a] Gen. 41:38; [Gal. 5:16, 17]; 1 Pet. 3:19, 20 [b] 2 Thess. 2:7 [c] Ps. 78:39 [1] Septuagint, Syriac, Targum, and Vulgate read *abide.* 6:4 [a] Num. 13:32, 33; Luke 17:27 6:5 [a] Gen. 8:21; Ps. 14:1–3; Prov. 6:18; Matt. 15:19; Rom. 1:28–32 [1] Following Masoretic Text and Targum; Vulgate reads *God;* Septuagint reads *LORD God.* 6:6 [a] Gen. 6:7; 1 Sam. 15:11, 29; 2 Sam. 24:16; Jer. 18:7–10; Zech. 8:14 [b] Ps. 78:40; Is. 63:10; Eph. 4:30 [c] Mark 3:5 6:7 [a] Gen. 7:4, 23; Deut. 28:63; 29:20; Ps. 7:11 6:8 [a] Gen. 19:19; Ex. 33:12, 17; Luke 1:30; Acts 7:46 6:9 [a] Gen. 7:1; Ezek. 14:14, 20; Heb. 11:7; 2 Pet. 2:5 [b] Gen. 5:22, 24; 2 Kin. 23:3 6:10 [a] Gen. 5:32; 7:13 6:11 [a] Deut. 31:29; Judg. 2:19; Rom. 2:13 [b] Ezek. 8:17 6:12 [a] Ps. 14:2; 53:2, 3 [b] Ps. 14:1–3; Is. 28:8 6:13 [a] Is. 34:1–4; Jer. 51:13; Ezek. 7:2, 3; Amos 8:2; 1 Pet. 4:7 [b] Gen. 6:17 [c] 2 Pet. 2:4–10 6:17 [a] Gen. 7:4, 21–23; 2 Pet. 2:5 [b] 2 Pet. 3:6 [c] Luke 16:22 6:18 [a] Gen. 8:20—9:17; 17:7 [b] Gen. 7:1, 7, 13; 1 Pet. 3:20; 2 Pet. 2:5 6:19 [a] Gen. 7:2, 8, 9, 14–16

male and female. 20 Of the birds after their kind, of animals after their kind, and of every creeping thing of the earth after its kind, two of every *kind* [a]will come to you to keep *them* alive. 21 And you shall take for yourself of all food that is eaten, and you shall gather *it* to yourself; and it shall be food for you and for them."

22 [a]Thus Noah did; [b]according to all that [c]God commanded him, so he did.

The Great Flood
(Luke 17:26, 27)

7 Then the [a]LORD said to Noah, [b]"Come into the ark, you and all your household, because I have seen *that* [c]you *are* righteous before Me in this generation. 2 You shall take with you seven each of every [a]clean animal, a male and his female; [b]two each of animals that *are* unclean, a male and his female; 3 also seven each of birds of the air, male and female, to keep the species alive on the face of all the earth. 4 For after [a]seven more days I will cause it to rain on the earth [b]forty days and forty nights, and I will destroy from the face of the earth all living things that I have made." 5 [a]And Noah did according to all that the LORD commanded him. 6 Noah *was* [a]six hundred years old when the floodwaters were on the earth.

7 [a]So Noah, with his sons, his wife, and his sons' wives, went into the ark because of the waters of the flood. 8 Of clean animals, of animals that *are* unclean, of birds, and of everything that creeps on the earth, 9 two by two they went into the ark to Noah, male and female, as God had commanded Noah. 10 And it came to pass after seven days that the waters of the flood were on the earth. 11 In the six hundredth year of Noah's life, in the second month, the seventeenth day of the month, on [a]that day all [b]the fountains of the great deep were broken up, and the [c]windows of heaven were opened. 12 [a]And the rain was on the earth forty days and forty nights.

13 On the very same day Noah and Noah's sons, Shem, Ham, and Japheth, and Noah's wife and the three wives of his sons with them, entered the ark— 14 [a]they and every beast after its kind, all cattle after their kind, every creeping thing that creeps on the earth after its kind, and every bird after its kind, every bird of every [b]sort. 15 And they [a]went into the ark to Noah, two by two, of all flesh in which *is* the breath of life. 16 So those that entered, male and female of all flesh, went in [a]as God had commanded him; and the LORD shut him in.

17 [a]Now the flood was on the earth forty days. The waters increased and lifted up the ark, and it rose high above the earth. 18 The waters prevailed and greatly increased on the earth, [a]and the ark moved about on the surface of the waters. 19 And the waters prevailed exceedingly on the earth, and all the high hills under the whole heaven were covered. 20 The waters prevailed fifteen cubits upward, and the mountains were covered. 21 [a]And all flesh died that moved on the earth: birds and cattle and beasts and every creeping thing that creeps on the earth, and every man. 22 All in [a]whose nostrils *was* the breath of the spirit[1] of life, all that *was* on the dry *land,* died. 23 So He destroyed all living things which were on the face of the ground: both man and cattle, creeping thing and bird of the air. They were destroyed from the earth. Only [a]Noah and those who *were* with him in the ark remained *alive.* 24 [a]And the waters prevailed on the earth one hundred and fifty days.

Noah's Deliverance

8 Then God [a]remembered Noah, and every living thing, and all the animals that *were* with him in the ark. [b]And God made a wind to pass over the earth, and the waters subsided. 2 [a]The fountains of the deep and the windows of heaven were also [b]stopped, and [c]the rain from heaven was restrained. 3 And the waters receded continually from the earth. At the end [a]of

6:20 [a] Gen. 7:9, 15 6:22 [a] Gen. 7:5; 12:4, 5; Heb. 11:7 [b] Gen. 7:5, 9, 16 [c] [1 John 5:3] 7:1 [a] Matt. 11:28 [b] Matt. 24:38; Luke 17:26; Heb. 11:7; 1 Pet. 3:20; 2 Pet. 2:5 [c] Gen. 6:9; Ps. 33:18; Prov. 10:9; 2 Pet. 2:9 7:2 [a] Lev. 11; Deut. 14:3–20 [b] Lev. 10:10; Ezek. 44:23 7:4 [a] Gen. 7:10; Ex. 7:25 [b] Gen. 7:12, 17 7:5 [a] Gen. 6:22 7:6 [a] Gen. 5:4, 32 7:7 [a] Gen. 6:18; 7:1, 13; Matt. 24:38; Luke 17:27 7:11 [a] Matt. 24:39; Luke 17:27; 2 Pet. 2:5; 3:6 [b] Gen. 8:2; Prov. 8:28; Is. 51:10; Ezek. 26:19 [c] Gen. 8:2; Ps. 78:23 7:12 [a] Gen. 7:4, 17; 1 Sam. 12:18 7:14 [a] Gen. 6:19 [b] Gen. 1:21 7:15 [a] Gen. 6:19, 20; 7:9 7:16 [a] Gen. 7:2, 3 7:17 [a] Gen. 7:4, 12; 8:6 7:18 [a] Ps. 104:26 7:21 [a] Gen. 6:7, 13, 17; 7:4 7:22 [a] Gen. 2:7 [1] Septuagint and Vulgate omit *of the spirit.* 7:23 [a] Matt. 24:38, 39; Luke 17:26, 27; Heb. 11:7; 1 Pet. 3:20; 2 Pet. 2:5 7:24 [a] Gen. 8:3, 4 8:1 [a] Gen. 19:29; Ex. 2:24; 1 Sam. 1:19; Ps. 105:42; 106:4 [b] Ex. 14:21; 15:10; Job 12:15; Ps. 29:10; Is. 44:27; Nah. 1:4 8:2 [a] Gen. 7:11 [b] Deut. 11:17 [c] Gen. 7:4, 12; Job 38:37 8:3 [a] Gen. 7:24

the hundred and fifty days the waters decreased. 4Then the ark rested in the seventh
month, the seventeenth day of the month,
on the mountains of Ararat. 5And the waters decreased continually until the tenth
month. In the tenth *month,* on the first *day*
of the month, the tops of the mountains
were seen.
6So it came to pass, at the end of forty
days, that Noah opened [a]the window of the
ark which he had made. 7Then he sent out
a raven, which kept going to and fro until
the waters had dried up from the earth. 8He
also sent out from himself a dove, to see
if the waters had receded from the face of
the ground. 9But the dove found no resting place for the sole of her foot, and she
returned into the ark to him, for the waters *were* on the face of the whole earth.
So he put out his hand and took her, and
drew her into the ark to himself. 10And he
waited yet another seven days, and again
he sent the dove out from the ark. 11Then
the dove came to him in the evening, and
behold, a freshly plucked olive leaf *was* in
her mouth; and Noah knew that the waters had receded from the earth. 12So he
waited yet another seven days and sent
out the dove, which did not return again
to him anymore.
13And it came to pass in the six hundred
and first year, in the first *month,* the first *day*
of the month, that the waters were dried up
from the earth; and Noah removed the covering of the ark and looked, and indeed the
surface of the ground was dry. 14And in the
second month, on the twenty-seventh day
of the month, the earth was dried.
15Then God spoke to Noah, saying, 16"Go
out of the ark, [a]you and your wife, and your
sons and your sons' wives with you. 17Bring
out with you every living thing of all flesh
that *is* with you: birds and cattle and every
creeping thing that creeps on the earth, so
that they may abound on the earth, and
[a]be fruitful and multiply on the earth."
18So Noah went out, and his sons and his
wife and his sons' wives with him. 19Every
animal, every creeping thing, every bird,
and whatever creeps on the earth, according to their families, went out of the ark.

God's Covenant with Creation

20Then Noah built an [a]altar to the LORD,
and took of [b]every clean animal and of every clean bird, and offered [c]burnt offerings on the altar. 21And the LORD smelled [a]a
soothing aroma. Then the LORD said in His
heart, "I will never again [b]curse the ground
for man's sake, although the [c]imagination
of man's heart *is* evil from his youth; [d]nor
will I again destroy every living thing as I
have done.

22"While the earth [a]remains,
Seedtime and harvest,
Cold and heat,
Winter and summer,
And [b]day and night
Shall not cease."

9 So God blessed Noah and his sons, and
said to them: [a]"Be fruitful and multiply, and fill the earth.[1] 2[a]And the fear of you
and the dread of you shall be on every beast
of the earth, on every bird of the air, on all
that move *on* the earth, and on all the fish
of the sea. They are given into your hand.
3[a]Every moving thing that lives shall be
food for you. I have given you [b]all things,
even as the [c]green herbs. 4[a]But you shall
not eat flesh with its life, *that is,* its blood.
5Surely for your lifeblood I will demand *a*
reckoning; [a]from the hand of every beast I
will require it, and [b]from the hand of man.
From the hand of every [c]man's brother I
will require the life of man.

6 "Whoever [a]sheds man's blood,
By man his blood shall be shed;
[b]For in the image of God
He made man.
7 And as for you, [a]be fruitful
and multiply;
Bring forth abundantly in the earth
And multiply in it."

8:6 [a] Gen. 6:16 8:16 [a] Gen. 7:13 8:17 [a] Gen. 1:22, 28; 9:1, 7 8:20 [a] Gen. 12:7; Ex. 29:18, 25 [b] Gen. 7:2; Lev. 11 [c] Gen. 22:2; Ex. 10:25 8:21 [a] Ex. 29:18, 25; Lev. 1:9; Ezek. 20:41; 2 Cor. 2:15; Eph. 5:2 [b] Gen. 3:17; 6:7, 13, 17; Is. 54:9 [c] Gen. 6:5; 11:6; Job 14:4; Ps. 51:5; Jer. 17:9; Rom. 1:21; 3:23; Eph. 2:1–3 [d] Gen. 9:11, 15 8:22 [a] Is. 54:9 [b] Ps. 74:16; Jer. 33:20, 25 9:1 [a] Gen. 1:28, 29; 8:17; 9:7, 19; 10:32 [1] Compare Genesis 1:28 9:2 [a] Gen. 1:26, 28; Ps. 8:6 9:3 [a] Deut. 12:15; 14:3, 9, 11; Acts 10:12, 13 [b] Rom. 14:14, 20; 1 Cor. 10:23, 26; Col. 2:16; [1 Tim. 4:3, 4] [c] Gen. 1:29 9:4 [a] Lev. 7:26; 17:10–16; 19:26; Deut. 12:16, 23; 15:23; 1 Sam. 14:33, 34; Acts 15:20, 29 9:5 [a] Ex. 21:28 [b] Gen. 4:9, 10; Ps. 9:12 [c] Acts 17:26 9:6 [a] Ex. 21:12–14; Lev. 24:17; Num. 35:33; Matt. 26:52 [b] Gen. 1:26, 27 9:7 [a] Gen. 9:1, 19

8Then God spoke to Noah and to his sons
with him, saying: 9"And as for Me, [a]behold,
I establish [b]My covenant with you and with
your descendants[1] after you, 10[a]and with
every living creature that *is* with you: the
birds, the cattle, and every beast of the
earth with you, of all that go out of the ark,
every beast of the earth. 11Thus [a]I establish
My covenant with you: Never again shall all
flesh be cut off by the waters of the flood;
never again shall there be a flood to destroy the earth."
12And God said: [a]"This *is* the sign of the
covenant which I make between Me and
you, and every living creature that *is* with
you, for perpetual generations: 13I set [a]My
rainbow in the cloud, and it shall be for the
sign of the covenant between Me and the
earth. 14It shall be, when I bring a cloud
over the earth, that the rainbow shall be
seen in the cloud; 15and [a]I will remember
My covenant which *is* between Me and you
and every living creature of all flesh; the
waters shall never again become a flood to
destroy all flesh. 16The rainbow shall be in
the cloud, and I will look on it to remember [a]the everlasting covenant between God
and every living creature of all flesh that *is*
on the earth." 17And God said to Noah, "This
is the sign of the covenant which I have established between Me and all flesh that *is*
on the earth."

Noah and His Sons

18Now the sons of Noah who went out
of the ark were Shem, Ham, and Japheth.
[a]And Ham *was* the father of Canaan.
19[a]These three *were* the sons of Noah, [b]and
from these the whole earth was populated.
20And Noah began *to be* [a]a farmer, and
he planted a vineyard. 21Then he drank of
the wine [a]and was drunk, and became uncovered in his tent. 22And Ham, the father
of Canaan, saw the nakedness of his father,
and told his two brothers outside. 23[a]But
Shem and Japheth took a garment, laid *it*
on both their shoulders, and went backward and covered the nakedness of their
father. Their faces *were* turned away, and
they did not see their father's nakedness.
24So Noah awoke from his wine, and
knew what his younger son had done to
him. 25Then he said:

[a]"Cursed *be* Canaan;
A [b]servant of servants
He shall be to his brethren."

26And he said:

[a]"Blessed *be* the LORD,
The God of Shem,
And may Canaan be his servant.
27 May God [a]enlarge Japheth,
[b]And may he dwell in the
tents of Shem;
And may Canaan be his servant."

28And Noah lived after the flood three
hundred and fifty years. 29So all the days
of Noah were nine hundred and fifty years;
and he died.

Nations Descended from Noah
(1 Chr. 1:5–27)

10 Now this *is* the genealogy of the
sons of Noah: Shem, Ham, and Japheth. [a]And sons were born to them after
the flood.
2[a]The sons of Japheth *were* Gomer, Magog, Madai, Javan, Tubal, Meshech, and
Tiras. 3The sons of Gomer *were* Ashkenaz, Riphath,[1] and Togarmah. 4The sons
of Javan *were* Elishah, Tarshish, Kittim,
and Dodanim.[1] 5From these [a]the coastland *peoples* of the Gentiles were separated
into their lands, everyone according to his
language, according to their families, into
their nations.
6[a]The sons of Ham *were* Cush, Mizraim, Put,[1] and Canaan. 7The sons of Cush
were Seba, Havilah, Sabtah, Raamah, and
Sabtechah; and the sons of Raamah *were*
Sheba and Dedan.
8Cush begot [a]Nimrod; he began to be a
mighty one on the earth. 9He was a mighty

9:9 [a] Gen. 6:18 [b] Is. 54:9 [1] Literally *seed* **9:10** [a] Ps. 145:9 **9:11** [a] Gen. 8:21; Is. 54:9 **9:12** [a] Gen. 9:13, 17; 17:11 **9:13** [a] Ezek. 1:28; Rev. 4:3 **9:15** [a] Lev. 26:42, 45; Deut. 7:9; Ezek. 16:60 **9:16** [a] Gen. 17:13, 19; 2 Sam. 23:5; Is. 55:3; Jer. 32:40; Heb. 13:20 **9:18** [a] Gen. 9:25–27; 10:6 **9:19** [a] Gen. 5:32 [b] Gen. 9:1, 7; 10:32; 1 Chr. 1:4 **9:20** [a] Gen. 3:19, 23; 4:2; Prov. 12:11; Jer. 31:24 **9:21** [a] Prov. 20:1; Eph. 5:18 **9:23** [a] Ex. 20:12; Gal. 6:1 **9:25** [a] Deut. 27:16; Josh. 9:23, 27 [b] Josh. 9:23; 1 Kin. 9:20, 21 **9:26** [a] Gen. 14:20; 24:27; Ps. 144:15; Heb. 11:16 **9:27** [a] Gen. 10:2–5; 39:3; Is. 66:19 [b] Luke 3:36; John 1:14; Eph. 2:13, 14; 3:6 **10:1** [a] Gen. 9:1, 7, 19 **10:2** [a] 1 Chr. 1:5–7 **10:3** [1] Spelled *Diphath* in 1 Chronicles 1:6 **10:4** [1] Spelled *Rodanim* in Samaritan Pentateuch and 1 Chronicles 1:7 **10:5** [a] Gen. 11:8; Ps. 72:10; Jer. 2:10; 25:22 **10:6** [a] 1 Chr. 1:8–16 [1] Or *Phut* **10:8** [a] Mic. 5:6

[a]hunter [b]before the LORD; therefore it is
said, "Like Nimrod the mighty hunter before the LORD." 10[a]And the beginning of his
kingdom was [b]Babel, Erech, Accad, and Cal-
neh, in the land of Shinar. 11From that land
he went [a]to Assyria and built Nineveh, Rehoboth Ir, Calah, 12and Resen between Nineveh and Calah (that *is* the principal city).
13Mizraim begot Ludim, Anamim, Lehabim, Naphtuhim, 14Pathrusim, and
Casluhim [a](from whom came the Philistines and Caphtorim).
15Canaan begot Sidon his firstborn, and
[a]Heth; 16[a]the Jebusite, the Amorite, and the
Girgashite; 17the Hivite, the Arkite, and the
Sinite; 18the Arvadite, the Zemarite, and
the Hamathite. Afterward the families of
the Canaanites were dispersed. 19[a]And the
border of the Canaanites was from Sidon as
you go toward Gerar, as far as Gaza; then as
you go toward Sodom, Gomorrah, Admah,
and Zeboiim, as far as Lasha. 20These *were*
the sons of Ham, according to their families, according to their languages, in their
lands *and* in their nations.
21And *children* were born also to Shem,
the father of all the children of Eber, the
brother of Japheth the elder. 22The [a]sons
of Shem *were* Elam, Asshur, [b]Arphaxad,
Lud, and Aram. 23The sons of Aram *were*

GENESIS 10:15–18

I AM CANAAN

Canaan begot Sidon his firstborn, and Heth; the Jebusite, the Amorite, and the Girgashite; the Hivite, the Arkite, and the Sinite; the Arvadite, the Zemarite, and the Hamathite. Afterward the families of the Canaanites were dispersed. Genesis 10:15–18

I am Canaan, the son of Ham. My father was a son of Noah, along with his brothers, Shem and Japheth. It is through my family that the whole world was repopulated. But what our family is probably most known for is a curse. My father sinned greatly after my grandfather got drunk and passed out naked. My father went into Noah's tent and looked at Noah's nakedness and did nothing to cover him. Instead, he reported his father's unfortunate state to his brothers. His brothers immediately went into their father's tent with a garment. Walking backward so they would not see their father's nakedness, they covered him. When Noah awakened and found out what Ham had done and the disrespect he had shown, Noah cursed my family—a curse that lasted for generations. The curse sentenced us to be the lowest of slaves to the nations that came from Noah's other two sons.

After this, my family scattered throughout the land that God had given to Abraham as the Promised Land. But eventually, my family was driven out of the land by the Israelites, not because of this curse, but because of the wickedness of our people.

†

There is no curse of Ham on black and brown people as has been erroneously taught. First, Ham was not cursed; the curse was upon his son Canaan (see Gen. 9:25). Second, this was not because he was black or brown but because the Canaanites did evil in the sight of God. Generational curses are certainly real. They are often perpetuated when families pass down sinful behaviors and wrong thinking from generation to generation. These curses cause many of the ills of society to continue. Praise God, though, that Jesus took all curses upon Himself so we would all be free.

10:9 [a] Jer. 16:16; Mic. 7:2 [b] Gen. 21:20 10:10 [a] Mic. 5:6 [b] Gen. 11:9 10:11 [a] Gen. 25:18; 2 Kin. 19:36; Mic. 5:6 10:14 [a] 1 Chr. 1:12
10:15 [a] Gen. 23:3 10:16 [a] Gen. 14:7; 15:19–21; Deut. 7:1; Neh. 9:8 10:19 [a] Gen. 13:12, 14, 15, 17; 15:18–21; Num. 34:2–12
10:22 [a] Gen. 11:10–26; 1 Chr. 1:17–28 [b] Gen. 10:24; 11:10; Luke 3:36

Uz, Hul, Gether, and Mash.[1] 24Arphaxad
begot [a]Salah,[1] and Salah begot Eber. 25[a]To
Eber were born two sons: the name of one
was Peleg, for in his days the earth was divided; and his brother's name *was* Joktan.
26Joktan begot Almodad, Sheleph, Hazarmaveth, Jerah, 27Hadoram, Uzal, Diklah,
28Obal,[1] Abimael, Sheba, 29Ophir, Havilah,
and Jobab. All these *were* the sons of Joktan. 30And their dwelling place was from
Mesha as you go toward Sephar, the mountain of the east. 31These *were* the sons of
Shem, according to their families, according to their languages, in their lands, according to their nations.

32[a]These *were* the families of the sons
of Noah, according to their generations, in
their nations; [b]and from these the nations
were divided on the earth after the flood.

The Tower of Babel

11 Now the whole earth had one language and one speech. 2And it came
to pass, as they journeyed from the east,
that they found a plain in the land [a]of Shinar, and they dwelt there. 3Then they said
to one another, "Come, let us make bricks
and bake *them* thoroughly." They had brick
for stone, and they had asphalt for mortar.
4And they said, "Come, let us build ourselves a city, and a tower [a]whose top *is* in
the heavens; let us make a [b]name for ourselves, lest we [c]be scattered abroad over the
face of the whole earth."
5[a]But the LORD came down to see the
city and the tower which the sons of men
had built. 6And the LORD said, "Indeed
[a]the people *are* one and they all have [b]one
language, and this is what they begin to
do; now nothing that they [c]propose to do
will be withheld from them. 7Come, [a]let
Us go down and there [b]confuse their language, that they may not understand one
another's speech." 8So [a]the LORD scattered
them abroad from there [b]over the face of
all the earth, and they ceased building the
city. 9Therefore its name is called Babel,
[a]because there the LORD confused the language of all the earth; and from there the
LORD scattered them abroad over the face
of all the earth.

Shem's Descendants

(1 Chr. 1:17–27; Luke 3:34–36)

10[a]This *is* the genealogy of Shem: Shem
was one hundred years old, and begot Arphaxad two years after the flood. 11After he
begot Arphaxad, Shem lived five hundred
years, and begot sons and daughters.

12Arphaxad lived thirty-five years, [a]and
begot Salah. 13After he begot Salah, Arphaxad lived four hundred and three years,
and begot sons and daughters.

14Salah lived thirty years, and begot Eber.
15After he begot Eber, Salah lived four hundred and three years, and begot sons and
daughters.

16[a]Eber lived thirty-four years, and begot
[b]Peleg. 17After he begot Peleg, Eber lived
four hundred and thirty years, and begot
sons and daughters.

18Peleg lived thirty years, and begot Reu.
19After he begot Reu, Peleg lived two hundred and nine years, and begot sons and
daughters.

20Reu lived thirty-two years, and begot
[a]Serug. 21After he begot Serug, Reu lived
two hundred and seven years, and begot
sons and daughters.

22Serug lived thirty years, and begot Nahor. 23After he begot Nahor, Serug lived
two hundred years, and begot sons and
daughters.

24Nahor lived twenty-nine years, and begot [a]Terah. 25After he begot Terah, Nahor
lived one hundred and nineteen years, and
begot sons and daughters.

26Now Terah lived seventy years, and
[a]begot Abram, Nahor, and Haran.

Terah's Descendants

27This *is* the genealogy of Terah: Terah
begot [a]Abram, Nahor, and Haran. Haran
begot Lot. 28And Haran died before his

10:23 [1] Called *Meshech* in Septuagint and 1 Chronicles 1:17 **10:24** [a] Gen. 11:12; Luke 3:35 [1] Following Masoretic Text, Vulgate, and Targum; Septuagint reads *Arphaxad begot Cainan, and Cainan begot Salah* (compare Luke 3:35, 36). **10:25** [a] 1 Chr. 1:19 **10:28** [1] Spelled *Ebal* in 1 Chronicles 1:22 **10:32** [a] Gen. 10:1 [b] Gen. 9:19; 11:8 **11:2** [a] Gen. 10:10; 14:1; Dan. 1:2 **11:4** [a] Deut. 1:28; 9:1; Ps. 107:26 [b] Gen. 6:4; 2 Sam. 8:13 [c] Deut. 4:27 **11:5** [a] Gen. 18:21; Ex. 3:8; 19:11, 18, 20 **11:6** [a] Gen. 9:19; Acts 17:26 [b] Gen. 11:1 [c] Deut. 31:21; Ps. 2:1 **11:7** [a] Gen. 1:26 [b] Gen. 42:23; Ex. 4:11; Deut. 28:49; Is. 33:19; Jer. 5:15 **11:8** [a] Gen. 11:4; Deut. 32:8; Ps. 92:9; [Luke 1:51] [b] Gen. 10:25, 32 **11:9** [a] 1 Cor. 14:23 **11:10** [a] Gen. 10:22–25; 1 Chr. 1:17 **11:12** [a] Luke 3:35 **11:16** [a] 1 Chr. 1:19 [b] Luke 3:35 **11:20** [a] Luke 3:35 **11:24** [a] Gen. 11:31; Josh. 24:2; Luke 3:34 **11:26** [a] Josh. 24:2; 1 Chr. 1:26 **11:27** [a] Gen. 11:31; 17:5

father Terah in his native land, in Ur of the
Chaldeans. 29 Then Abram and Nahor took
wives: the name of Abram's wife *was* [a]Sarai,
and the name of Nahor's wife, [b]Milcah, the
daughter of Haran the father of Milcah and
the father of Iscah. 30 But [a]Sarai was barren;
she had no child.
31 And Terah [a]took his son Abram and
his grandson Lot, the son of Haran, and his
daughter-in-law Sarai, his son Abram's wife,
and they went out with them from [b]Ur of
the Chaldeans to go to [c]the land of Canaan;
and they came to Haran and dwelt there.
32 So the days of Terah were two hundred
and five years, and Terah died in Haran.

Promises to Abram
(Acts 7:2–5)

12 Now the [a]LORD had said to Abram:

"Get [b]out of your country,
From your family
And from your father's house,
To a land that I will show you.
2 [a]I will make you a great nation;
[b]I will bless you
And make your name great;
[c]And you shall be a blessing.
3 [a]I will bless those who bless you,
And I will curse him who curses you;
And in [b]you all the families of
the earth shall be [c]blessed."

4 So Abram departed as the LORD had
spoken to him, and Lot went with him. And
Abram *was* seventy-five years old when he
departed from Haran. 5 Then Abram took
Sarai his wife and Lot his brother's son, and
all their possessions that they had gathered, and [a]the people whom they had acquired [b]in Haran, and they [c]departed to go
to the land of Canaan. So they came to the
land of Canaan. 6 Abram [a]passed through
the land to the place of Shechem, [b]as far as
the terebinth tree of Moreh.[1] [c]And the Canaanites *were* then in the land.
7 [a]Then the LORD appeared to Abram and
said, [b]"To your descendants I will give this
land." And there he built an [c]altar to the
LORD, who had appeared to him. 8 And he
moved from there to the mountain east of
Bethel, and he pitched his tent *with* Bethel
on the west and Ai on the east; there he
built an altar to the LORD and [a]called on the
name of the LORD. 9 So Abram journeyed,
[a]going on still toward the South.[1]

Abram in Egypt

10 Now there was [a]a famine in the land,
and Abram [b]went down to Egypt to dwell
there, for the famine *was* [c]severe in the
land. 11 And it came to pass, when he was
close to entering Egypt, that he said to Sarai his wife, "Indeed I know that you *are* [a]a
woman of beautiful countenance. 12 Therefore it will happen, when the Egyptians see
you, that they will say, 'This *is* his wife'; and
they [a]will kill me, but they will let you live.
13 [a]Please say you *are* my [b]sister, that it may
be well with me for your sake, and that I[1]
may live because of you."
14 So it was, when Abram came into
Egypt, that the Egyptians saw the woman,
that she *was* very beautiful. 15 The princes
of Pharaoh also saw her and commended
her to Pharaoh. And the woman was taken
to Pharaoh's house. 16 He [a]treated Abram
well for her sake. He [b]had sheep, oxen, male
donkeys, male and female servants, female
donkeys, and camels.
17 But the LORD [a]plagued Pharaoh and
his house with great plagues because of
Sarai, Abram's wife. 18 And Pharaoh called
Abram and said, [a]"What *is* this you have
done to me? Why did you not tell me that
she *was* your wife? 19 Why did you say, 'She
is my sister'? I might have taken her as
my wife. Now therefore, here is your wife;
take *her* and go your way." 20 [a]So Pharaoh
commanded *his* men concerning him; and
they sent him away, with his wife and all
that he had.

11:29 [a] Gen. 17:15; 20:12 [b] Gen. 22:20, 23; 24:15 **11:30** [a] Gen. 16:1, 2; Luke 1:36 **11:31** [a] Gen. 12:1 [b] Gen. 15:7; Neh. 9:7; Acts 7:4 [c] Gen. 10:19 **12:1** [a] Gen. 15:7; Acts 7:2, 3; [Heb. 11:8] [b] Gen. 13:9 **12:2** [a] [Gen. 17:4–6]; 18:18; 46:3; Deut. 26:5; 1 Kin. 3:8 [b] Gen. 22:17; 24:35 [c] Gen. 28:4; Zech. 8:13; Gal. 3:14 **12:3** [a] Gen. 24:35; 27:29; Ex. 23:22; Num. 24:9 [b] Gen. 18:18; 22:18; 26:4; 28:14; Ps. 72:17; Matt. 1:1; Luke 3:34; Acts 3:25; [Gal. 3:8] [c] Is. 41:27 **12:5** [a] Gen. 14:14 [b] Gen. 11:31 [c] Gen. 13:18 **12:6** [a] Heb. 11:9 [b] Deut. 11:30; Judg. 7:1 [c] Gen. 10:18, 19 [1] Hebrew *Alon Moreh* **12:7** [a] Gen. 17:1; 18:1 [b] Gen. 13:15; 15:18; 17:8; Deut. 34:4; Ps. 105:9–12; Acts 7:5; Gal. 3:16 [c] Gen. 13:4, 18; 22:9 **12:8** [a] Gen. 4:26; 13:4; 21:33 **12:9** [a] Gen. 13:1, 3; 20:1; 24:62 [1] Hebrew *Negev* **12:10** [a] Gen. 26:1 [b] Ps. 105:13 [c] Gen. 43:1 **12:11** [a] Gen. 12:14; 26:7; 29:17 **12:12** [a] Gen. 20:11; 26:7 **12:13** [a] Gen. 20:1–18; 26:6–11 [b] Gen. 20:12 [1] Literally *my soul* **12:16** [a] Gen. 20:14 [b] Gen. 13:2 **12:17** [a] Gen. 20:18; 1 Chr. 16:21; [Ps. 105:14] **12:18** [a] Gen. 20:9, 10; 26:10 **12:20** [a] [Prov. 21:1]

Abram Inherits Canaan

13 Then Abram went up from Egypt, he and his wife and all that he had, and [a]Lot with him, [b]to the South.[1] 2 [a]Abram *was* very rich in livestock, in silver, and in gold. 3 And he went on his journey [a]from the South as far as Bethel, to the place where his tent had been at the beginning, between Bethel and Ai, 4 to the [a]place of the altar which he had made there at first. And there Abram [b]called on the name of the LORD.

5 Lot also, who went with Abram, had flocks and herds and tents. 6 Now [a]the land was not able to support them, that they might dwell together, for their possessions were so great that they could not dwell together. 7 And there was [a]strife between the herdsmen of Abram's livestock and the herdsmen of Lot's livestock. [b]The Canaanites and the Perizzites then dwelt in the land.

8 So Abram said to Lot, [a]"Please let there be no strife between you and me, and between my herdsmen and your herdsmen; for we *are* brethren. 9 [a]*Is* not the whole land before you? Please [b]separate from me. [c]If *you take* the left, then I will go to the right; or, if *you go* to the right, then I will go to the left."

10 And Lot lifted his eyes and saw all [a]the plain of Jordan, that it *was* well watered everywhere (before the LORD [b]destroyed Sodom and Gomorrah) [c]like the garden of the LORD, like the land of Egypt as you go toward [d]Zoar. 11 Then Lot chose for himself all the plain of Jordan, and Lot journeyed east. And they separated from each other. 12 Abram dwelt in the land of Canaan, and Lot [a]dwelt in the cities of the plain and [b]pitched *his* tent even as far as Sodom. 13 But the men of Sodom [a]*were* exceedingly wicked and [b]sinful against the LORD.

14 And the LORD said to Abram, after Lot [a]had separated from him: "Lift your eyes now and look from the place where you are—[b]northward, southward, eastward, and westward; 15 for all the land which you see [a]I give to you and [b]your descendants[1] forever. 16 And [a]I will make your descendants as the dust of the earth; so that if a man could number the dust of the earth, *then* your descendants also could be numbered. 17 Arise, walk in the land through its length and its width, for I give it to you."

18 [a]Then Abram moved *his* tent, and went and [b]dwelt by the terebinth trees of Mamre,[1] [c]which *are* in Hebron, and built an [d]altar there to the LORD.

Lot's Captivity and Rescue

14 And it came to pass in the days of Amraphel king [a]of Shinar, Arioch king of Ellasar, Chedorlaomer king of [b]Elam, and Tidal king of nations,[1] 2 *that* they made war with Bera king of Sodom, Birsha king of Gomorrah, Shinab king of [a]Admah, Shemeber king of Zeboiim, and the king of Bela (that is, [b]Zoar). 3 All these joined together in the Valley of Siddim [a](that is, the Salt Sea). 4 Twelve years [a]they served Chedorlaomer, and in the thirteenth year they rebelled.

5 In the fourteenth year Chedorlaomer and the kings that *were* with him came and attacked [a]the Rephaim in Ashteroth Karnaim, [b]the Zuzim in Ham, [c]the Emim in Shaveh Kiriathaim, 6 [a]and the Horites in their mountain of Seir, as far as El Paran, which *is* by the wilderness. 7 Then they turned back and came to En Mishpat (that *is,* Kadesh), and attacked all the country of the Amalekites, and also the Amorites who dwelt [a]in Hazezon Tamar.

8 And the king of Sodom, the king of Gomorrah, the king of Admah, the king of Zeboiim, and the king of Bela (that *is,* Zoar) went out and joined together in battle in the Valley of Siddim 9 against Chedorlaomer king of Elam, Tidal king of nations,[1] Amraphel king of Shinar, and Arioch king of Ellasar—four kings against five. 10 Now the Valley of Siddim *was full of* [a]asphalt pits; and the kings of Sodom and Gomorrah

---

13:1 [a] Gen. 12:4; 14:12, 16 [b] Gen. 12:9 [1] Hebrew *Negev* 13:2 [a] Gen. 24:35; 26:14; Ps. 112:3; Prov. 10:22 13:3 [a] Gen. 12:8, 9 13:4 [a] Gen. 12:7, 8; 21:33 [b] Ps. 116:17 13:6 [a] Gen. 36:7 13:7 [a] Gen. 26:20 [b] Gen. 12:6; 15:20, 21 13:8 [a] 1 Cor. 6:7; [Phil. 2:14, 15] 13:9 [a] Gen. 20:15; 34:10 [b] Gen. 13:11, 14 [c] [Rom. 12:18] 13:10 [a] Gen. 19:17–29; Deut. 34:3 [b] Gen. 19:24 [c] Gen. 2:8, 10; Is. 51:3 [d] Gen. 14:2, 8; 19:22; Deut. 34:3 13:12 [a] Gen. 19:24, 25, 29 [b] Gen. 14:12; 19:1 13:13 [a] Gen. 18:20, 21; Ezek. 16:49; 2 Pet. 2:7, 8 [b] Gen. 6:11; 39:9; Num. 32:23 13:14 [a] Gen. 13:11 [b] Gen. 28:14 13:15 [a] Gen. 12:7; 13:17; 15:7, 18; 17:8; Deut. 34:4; Acts 7:5 [b] 2 Chr. 20:7; Ps. 37:22 [1] Literally *seed,* and so throughout the book 13:16 [a] Gen. 22:17; Ex. 32:13; Num. 23:10 13:18 [a] Gen. 26:17 [b] Gen. 14:13 [c] Gen. 23:2; 35:27 [d] Gen. 8:20; 22:8, 9 [1] Hebrew *Alon Mamre* 14:1 [a] Gen. 10:10; 11:2 [b] Is. 11:11; 21:2; Dan. 8:2 [1] Hebrew *goyim* 14:2 [a] Gen. 10:19; Deut. 29:23 [b] Gen. 13:10; 19:22 14:3 [a] Num. 34:12; Deut. 3:17; Josh. 3:16 14:4 [a] Gen. 9:26 14:5 [a] Gen. 15:20 [b] Deut. 2:20 [c] Num. 32:37; Deut. 2:10 14:6 [a] Gen. 36:20; Deut. 2:12, 22 14:7 [a] 2 Chr. 20:2 14:9 [1] Hebrew *goyim* 14:10 [a] Gen. 11:3

fled; *some* fell there, and the remainder
fled [b]to the mountains. 11Then they took
[a]all the goods of Sodom and Gomorrah,
and all their provisions, and went their way.
12They also took Lot, Abram's [a]brother's
son [b]who dwelt in Sodom, and his goods,
and departed.

13Then one who had escaped came and
told Abram the [a]Hebrew, for [b]he dwelt by
the terebinth trees of Mamre[1] the Amorite,
brother of Eshcol and brother of Aner; [c]and
they *were* allies with Abram. 14Now [a]when
Abram heard that [b]his brother was taken
captive, he armed his three hundred and
eighteen trained *servants* who were [c]born
in his own house, and went in pursuit [d]as
far as Dan. 15He divided his forces against
them by night, and he and his servants [a]at-
tacked them and pursued them as far as
Hobah, which *is* north of Damascus. 16So
he [a]brought back all the goods, and also
brought back his brother Lot and his goods,
as well as the women and the people.

17And the king of Sodom [a]went out to
meet him at the Valley of Shaveh (that *is*,
the [b]King's Valley), [c]after his return from
the defeat of Chedorlaomer and the kings
who *were* with him.

Abram and Melchizedek
(Heb. 7:1, 2)

18Then [a]Melchizedek king of Salem
brought out [b]bread and wine; he *was* [c]the
priest of [d]God Most High. 19And he blessed
him and said:

[a]"Blessed be Abram of God Most High,
[b]Possessor of heaven and earth;
20 And [a]blessed be God Most High,
Who has delivered your
enemies into your hand."

And he [b]gave him a tithe of all.

21Now the king of Sodom said to Abram,
"Give me the persons, and take the goods
for yourself."

22But Abram [a]said to the king of Sodom,
"I [b]have raised my hand to the LORD, God
Most High, [c]the Possessor of heaven and
earth, 23that [a]I *will take* nothing, from a
thread to a sandal strap, and that I will not
take anything that *is* yours, lest you should
say, 'I have made Abram rich'— 24except
only what the young men have eaten, and
the portion of the men who went with me:
Aner, Eshcol, and Mamre; let them take
their portion."

God's Covenant with Abram
(Heb. 11:8–10)

15 After these things the word of the
LORD came to Abram [a]in a vision,
saying, [b]"Do not be afraid, Abram. I *am* your
[c]shield, your exceedingly [d]great reward."

2[a]But Abram said, "Lord GOD, what will
You give me, [b]seeing I go childless, and the
heir of my house *is* Eliezer of Damascus?"
3Then Abram said, "Look, You have given
me no offspring; indeed [a]one born in my
house is my heir!"

4And behold, the word of the LORD *came*
to him, saying, "This one shall not be your
heir, but one who [a]will come from your own
body shall be your heir." 5Then He brought
him outside and said, "Look now toward
heaven, and [a]count the [b]stars if you are able
to number them." And He said to him, [c]"So
shall your [d]descendants be."

6And he [a]believed in the LORD, and He
[b]accounted it to him for righteousness.

7Then He said to him, "I *am* the LORD,
who [a]brought you out of [b]Ur of the Chaldeans, [c]to give you this land to inherit it."

8And he said, "Lord GOD, [a]how shall I
know that I will inherit it?"

9So He said to him, "Bring Me a three-
year-old heifer, a three-year-old female
goat, a three-year-old ram, a turtledove,
and a young pigeon." 10Then he brought all
these to Him and [a]cut them in two, down
the middle, and placed each piece opposite
the other; but he did not cut [b]the birds in

14:10 [b] Gen. 19:17, 30 14:11 [a] Gen. 14:16, 21 14:12 [a] Gen. 11:27; 12:5 [b] Gen. 13:12 14:13 [a] Gen. 39:14; 40:15 [b] Gen. 13:18 [c] Gen. 14:24; 21:27, 32 [1] Hebrew *Alon Mamre* 14:14 [a] Gen. 19:29 [b] Gen. 13:8; 14:12 [c] Gen. 12:5; 15:3; 17:27; Eccl. 2:7 [d] Deut. 34:1; Judg. 18:29; 1 Kin. 15:20 14:15 [a] Is. 41:2, 3 14:16 [a] Gen. 31:18; 1 Sam. 30:8, 18, 19 14:17 [a] 1 Sam. 18:6 [b] 2 Sam. 18:18 [c] Heb. 7:1 14:18 [a] Ps. 110:4; Heb. 7:1–10 [b] Gen. 18:5; Ex. 29:40; Ps. 104:15 [c] Ps. 110:4; Heb. 5:6 [d] Acts 16:17 14:19 [a] Ruth 3:10 [b] Gen. 14:22; Matt. 11:25 14:20 [a] Gen. 24:27 [b] Gen. 28:22; Heb. 7:4 14:22 [a] Gen. 14:2, 8, 10 [b] Dan. 12:7 [c] Gen. 14:19 14:23 [a] 2 Kin. 5:16; Esth. 9:15, 16 15:1 [a] Gen. 15:4; 46:2; 1 Sam. 15:10; Dan. 10:1 [b] Gen. 21:17; 26:24; Is. 41:10; Dan. 10:12 [c] Deut. 33:29; Ps. 3:3; 84:11; 91:4 [d] Num. 18:20; Ps. 58:11; Prov. 11:18 15:2 [a] Gen. 17:18 [b] Acts 7:5 15:3 [a] Gen. 14:14 15:4 [a] 2 Sam. 7:12; Gal. 4:28 15:5 [a] Gen. 22:17; 26:4; Deut. 1:10; Ps. 147:4 [b] Jer. 33:22 [c] Ex. 32:13; Rom. 4:18; Heb. 11:12 [d] Gen. 17:19 15:6 [a] Gen. 21:1; Rom. 4:3, 9, 22; Gal. 3:6; James 2:23 [b] Ps. 32:2; 106:31 15:7 [a] Gen. 12:1 [b] Gen. 11:28, 31 [c] Gen. 13:15, 17; Ps. 105:42, 44 15:8 [a] Gen. 24:13, 14; Judg. 6:36–40; 1 Sam. 14:9, 10; Luke 1:18 15:10 [a] Gen. 15:17; Jer. 34:18 [b] Lev. 1:17

RELEASE // BELIEVE IN THE PROMISE

The Gift of Belief

Genesis 15:5–6 // Then He brought him outside and said, "Look now toward heaven, and count the stars if you are able to number them." And He said to him, "So shall your descendants be." And he believed in the LORD, and He accounted it to him for righteousness.

Summary Message // Amid the chaos of this world, it can be difficult to hold on to the promises God has made to us. Yet, Scripture reminds us that we can always trust in God's promises.

In Abram's story found in Genesis 15, we realize the road to what we have been promised is rarely easy. However, God's gift to each of us is that holding on to God's promises will enable us to endure anything and achieve things beyond our greatest expectations.

Practical Application // Throughout the Bible, we find countless promises: promises God made to specific individuals, promises God made to specific communities (e.g., the Israelites), even promises to future generations—to those who would humbly, faithfully, and obediently follow God wherever He would lead them. The trials, tribulations, pain, and injustices we face can easily leave us feeling as if the promises of God are far from us, maybe even impossible to experience. But that is not the character of our God. All things are possible with God.

Abram is an example to help us understand where God is in these distant promises. In Genesis 15, we find Abram (not yet Abraham) in the middle of one of those moments when he wondered if he had rightly heard God. He was an old man, and his wife was well beyond her childbearing years. Yet, God told him he would be the father of nations. But Abram was at a crossroads and questioned whether God would be faithful to the promises He had made. Abram had already left his country, his family, and everything he had known on the strength of God's promise. Though doubt assailed him, God reassured him of a few things:

- God had his back (see v. 1).
- God is always faithful to His promises (see vv. 2–4).
- God's promises are always better than our plans for ourselves (see vv. 5–6).

In reality, the things we face on any given day can easily begin to squeeze the life and breath out of us. The trials and difficulties of life can cause us to lose sight of God and even our faith in God and His promises. However, God extends the invitation to trust Him through the difficult times. Belief in God's faithfulness to keep His promises will enable us to endure. Like Abram, if we hold on to this belief and trust that God will do what He has promised, we will find that His vision, hope, and intent for our lives is sure.

Fervent Prayer // Abba Father, help us today in our disbelief. You have shown time and again, throughout Your Word and our lives, that You are faithful and true to what You have promised. Yet, life sometimes feels like it is controlling us rather than the other way around. The hurt we have experienced, the pain we have suffered, and even the busyness of life often feel overwhelming. In moments of doubt, we sometimes question what You have promised. Did You mean it? Is it possible? Did we understand You? Help us, Lord, to remember. Help us, God, to hold on to the truth that You love us. Because of that love, You will always stay true to the promises You have given us. Help us to breathe, especially when everything around us seems to strangle the life out of us. In Jesus' name we pray. Amen.

---

two. 11And when the vultures came down
on the carcasses, Abram drove them away.
12Now when the sun was going down, [a]a
deep sleep fell upon Abram; and behold,
horror *and* great darkness fell upon him.
13Then He said to Abram: "Know certainly
[a]that your descendants will be strangers in
a land *that is* not theirs, and will serve them,
and [b]they will afflict them four hundred
years. 14And also the nation whom they
serve [a]I will judge; afterward [b]they shall
come out with great possessions. 15Now
as for you, [a]you shall go [b]to your fathers in
peace; [c]you shall be buried at a good old

15:12 [a] Gen. 2:21; 28:11; Job 33:15 15:13 [a] Ex. 1:11; Acts 7:6 [b] Ex. 12:40 15:14 [a] Ex. 6:6 [b] Ex. 12:36 15:15 [a] Job 5:26 [b] Gen. 25:8; 47:30 [c] Gen. 25:8

age. 16But [a]in the fourth generation they
shall return here, for the iniquity [b]of the
Amorites [c]*is* not yet complete."
17And it came to pass, when the sun went
down and it was dark, that behold, there
appeared a smoking oven and a burning
torch that [a]passed between those pieces.
18On the same day the LORD [a]made a covenant with Abram, saying:

[b]"To your descendants I have given this
land, from the river of Egypt to the great
river, the River Euphrates— 19the Kenites,
the Kenezzites, the Kadmonites, 20the Hittites, the Perizzites, the Rephaim, 21the Amorites, the Canaanites, the Girgashites, and
the Jebusites."

Hagar and Ishmael

16 Now Sarai, Abram's wife, [a]had borne him no *children.* And she had [b]an
Egyptian maidservant whose name was
[c]Hagar. 2[a]So Sarai said to Abram, "See now,
the LORD [b]has restrained me from bearing
children. Please, [c]go in to my maid; perhaps I shall obtain children by her." And
Abram [d]heeded the voice of Sarai. 3Then
Sarai, Abram's wife, took Hagar her maid,
the Egyptian, and gave her to her husband
Abram to be his wife, after Abram [a]had
dwelt ten years in the land of Canaan. 4So
he went in to Hagar, and she conceived.
And when she saw that she had conceived,
her mistress became [a]despised in her eyes.
5Then Sarai said to Abram, "My wrong
be upon you! I gave my maid into your embrace; and when she saw that she had conceived, I became despised in her eyes. [a]The
LORD judge between you and me."
6[a]So Abram said to Sarai, "Indeed your
maid *is* in your hand; do to her as you
please." And when Sarai dealt harshly with
her, [b]she fled from her presence.
7Now the [a]Angel of the LORD found her
by a spring of water in the wilderness, [b]by
the spring on the way to [c]Shur. 8And He
said, "Hagar, Sarai's maid, where have you
come from, and where are you going?"

She said, "I am fleeing from the presence of my mistress Sarai."
9The Angel of the LORD said to her, "Re-
turn to your mistress, and [a]submit yourself
under her hand." 10Then the Angel of the
LORD said to her, [a]"I will multiply your descendants exceedingly, so that they shall
not be counted for multitude." 11And the
Angel of the LORD said to her:

"Behold, you *are* with child,
[a]And you shall bear a son.
You shall call his name Ishmael,
Because the LORD has heard
your affliction.
12 [a]He shall be a wild man;
His hand *shall be* against every man,
And every man's hand against him.
[b]And he shall dwell in the presence
of all his brethren."

13Then she called the name of the LORD
who spoke to her, You-Are-the-God-Who-
Sees; for she said, "Have I also here seen
Him [a]who sees me?" 14Therefore the well
was called [a]Beer Lahai Roi;[1] observe, *it is*
[b]between Kadesh and Bered.
15So [a]Hagar bore Abram a son; and
Abram named his son, whom Hagar bore,
Ishmael. 16Abram *was* eighty-six years old
when Hagar bore Ishmael to Abram.

The Sign of the Covenant
(Ex. 12:43—13:2)

17 When Abram was ninety-nine years old, the LORD [a]appeared to Abram
and said to him, [b]"I *am* Almighty God; [c]walk
before Me and be [d]blameless. 2And I will
make My [a]covenant between Me and you,
and [b]will multiply you exceedingly." 3Then
Abram fell on his face, and God talked with
him, saying: 4"As for Me, behold, My covenant is with you, and you shall be [a]a father
of many nations. 5No longer shall [a]your
name be called Abram, but your name
shall be Abraham; [b]for I have made you a
father of many nations. 6I will make you

15:16 [a] Gen. 15:13; Ex. 12:41 [b] Gen. 48:22; Lev. 18:24–28; 1 Kin. 21:26 [c] 1 Kin. 11:12; Matt. 23:32 **15:17** [a] Jer. 34:18, 19 **15:18** [a] Gen. 24:7 [b] Gen. 12:7; 17:8; Ex. 23:31; Num. 34:3; Deut. 11:24; Josh. 1:4; 21:43; Acts 7:5 **16:1** [a] Gen. 11:30; 15:2, 3 [b] Gen. 12:16; 21:9 [c] Gal. 4:24 **16:2** [a] Gen. 30:3 [b] Gen. 20:18 [c] Gen. 30:3, 9 [d] Gen. 3:17 **16:3** [a] Gen. 12:4, 5 **16:4** [a] 1 Sam. 1:6, 7; [Prov. 30:21, 23] **16:5** [a] Gen. 31:53; Ex. 5:21 **16:6** [a] 1 Pet. 3:7 [b] Gen. 16:9; Ex. 2:15 **16:7** [a] Gen. 21:17, 18; 22:11, 15; 31:11 [b] Gen. 20:1; 25:18 [c] Ex. 15:22 **16:9** [a] [Titus 2:9] **16:10** [a] Gen. 17:20 **16:11** [a] Luke 1:13, 31 **16:12** [a] Gen. 21:20; Job 24:5; 39:5–8 [b] Gen. 25:18 **16:13** [a] Gen. 31:42 **16:14** [a] Gen. 24:62 [b] Gen. 14:7; Num. 13:26 [1] Literally *Well of the One Who Lives and Sees Me* **16:15** [a] Gal. 4:22 **17:1** [a] Gen. 12:7; 18:1 [b] Gen. 28:3; 35:11; Ex. 6:3; Job 42:2 [c] 2 Kin. 20:3 [d] Gen. 6:9; Deut. 18:13 **17:2** [a] Gen. 15:18; Ex. 6:4; [Gal. 3:19] [b] Gen. 12:2; 13:16; 15:5; 18:18 **17:4** [a] [Rom. 4:11, 12, 16] **17:5** [a] Neh. 9:7 [b] Rom. 4:17

exceedingly fruitful; and I will make [a]na-
tions of you, and [b]kings shall come from
you. 7And I will [a]establish My covenant between Me and you and your descendants
after you in their generations, for an everlasting covenant, [b]to be God to you and
[c]your descendants after you. 8Also [a]I give
to you and your descendants after you the
land [b]in which you are a stranger, all the
land of Canaan, as an everlasting possession; and [c]I will be their God."

9And God said to Abraham: "As for you,
[a]you shall keep My covenant, you and your
descendants after you throughout their
generations. 10This *is* My covenant which
you shall keep, between Me and you and
your descendants after you: [a]Every male
child among you shall be circumcised; 11and
you shall be circumcised in the flesh of
your foreskins, and it shall be [a]a sign of
the covenant between Me and you. 12He
who is eight days old among you [a]shall be
circumcised, every male child in your generations, he who is born in your house or
bought with money from any foreigner who
is not your descendant. 13He who is born
in your house and he who is bought with
your money must be circumcised, and My
covenant shall be in your flesh for an everlasting covenant. 14And the uncircumcised
male child, who is not circumcised in the
flesh of his foreskin, that person [a]shall be
cut off from his people; he has broken My
covenant."

15Then God said to Abraham, "As for Sarai your wife, you shall not call her name
Sarai, but Sarah *shall be* her name. 16And I
will bless her [a]and also give you a son by
her; then I will bless her, and she shall be *a*
mother [b]*of* nations; [c]kings of peoples shall
be from her."

17Then Abraham fell on his face [a]and
laughed, and said in his heart, "Shall *a child*
be born to a man who is one hundred years
old? And shall Sarah, who is ninety years
old, bear *a child?*" 18And Abraham [a]said to
God, "Oh, that Ishmael might live before
You!"

19Then God said: "No, [a]Sarah your wife
shall bear you a son, and you shall call his
name Isaac; I will establish My [b]covenant
with him for an everlasting covenant, *and*
with his descendants after him. 20And as
for Ishmael, I have heard you. Behold, I
have blessed him, and will make him fruitful, and [a]will multiply him exceedingly.
He shall beget [b]twelve princes, [c]and I will
make him a great nation. 21But My [a]cov-
enant I will establish with Isaac, [b]whom
Sarah shall bear to you at this [c]set time next
year." 22Then He finished talking with him,
and God went up from Abraham.

23So Abraham took Ishmael his son, all
who were born in his house and all who
were bought with his money, every male
among the men of Abraham's house, and
circumcised the flesh of their foreskins
that very same day, as God had said to him.
24Abraham *was* ninety-nine years old when
he was circumcised in the flesh of his foreskin. 25And Ishmael his son *was* thirteen
years old when he was circumcised in the
flesh of his foreskin. 26That very same day
Abraham was circumcised, and his son Ishmael; 27and [a]all the men of his house, born
in the house or bought with money from
a foreigner, were circumcised with him.

The Son of Promise
(Heb. 13:2)

18 Then the LORD appeared to him by
the [a]terebinth trees of Mamre,[1] as he
was sitting in the tent door in the heat of
the day. 2[a]So he lifted his eyes and looked,
and behold, three men were standing by
him; [b]and when he saw *them,* he ran from
the tent door to meet them, and bowed
himself to the ground, 3and said, "My Lord,
if I have now found favor in Your sight, do
not pass on by Your servant. 4Please let
[a]a little water be brought, and wash your
feet, and rest yourselves under the tree.
5And [a]I will bring a morsel of bread, that
[b]you may refresh your hearts. After that
you may pass by, [c]inasmuch as you have
come to your servant."

17:6 [a] Gen. 17:16; 35:11 [b] Matt. 1:6 17:7 [a] [Gal. 3:17] [b] Gen. 26:24; 28:13; Lev. 11:45; 26:12, 45; Heb. 11:16 [c] Rom. 9:8; Gal. 3:16 17:8 [a] Gen. 12:7; 13:15, 17; Acts 7:5 [b] Gen. 23:4; 28:4 [c] Ex. 6:7; 29:45; Lev. 26:12; Deut. 29:13; Rev. 21:7 17:9 [a] Ex. 19:5 17:10 [a] John 7:22; Acts 7:8 17:11 [a] Ex. 12:13, 48; [Rom. 4:11] 17:12 [a] Lev. 12:3 17:14 [a] Ex. 4:24–26 17:16 [a] Gen. 18:10 [b] Gen. 35:11; Gal. 4:31; 1 Pet. 3:6 [c] Gen. 17:6; 36:31; 1 Sam. 8:22 17:17 [a] Gen. 17:3; 18:12; 21:6 17:18 [a] Gen. 18:23 17:19 [a] Gen. 18:10; 21:2; [Gal. 4:28] [b] Gen. 22:16; Matt. 1:2; Luke 3:34 17:20 [a] Gen. 16:10 [b] Gen. 25:12–16 [c] Gen. 21:13, 18 17:21 [a] Gen. 26:2–5 [b] Gen. 21:2 [c] Gen. 18:14 17:27 [a] Gen. 18:19 18:1 [a] Gen. 13:18; 14:13 [1] Hebrew *Alon Mamre* 18:2 [a] Gen. 18:16, 22; 32:24; Josh. 5:13; Judg. 13:6–11; Heb. 13:2 [b] Gen. 19:1; 1 Pet. 4:9 18:4 [a] Gen. 19:2; 24:32; 43:24 18:5 [a] Judg. 6:18, 19; 13:15, 16 [b] Judg. 19:5; Ps. 104:15 [c] Gen. 19:8; 33:10

They said, "Do as you have said."

6 So Abraham hurried into the tent to Sarah and said, "Quickly, make ready three measures of fine meal; knead *it* and make cakes." 7 And Abraham ran to the herd, took a tender and good calf, gave *it* to a young man, and he hastened to prepare it. 8 So [a]he took butter and milk and the calf which he had prepared, and set *it* before them; and he stood by them under the tree as they ate.

9 Then they said to him, "Where *is* Sarah your wife?"

So he said, "Here, [a]in the tent."

10 And He said, "I will certainly return to you [a]according to the time of life, and behold, [b]Sarah your wife shall have a son."

(Sarah was listening in the tent door which *was* behind him.) 11 Now [a]Abraham and Sarah were old, well advanced in age; *and* Sarah [b]had passed the age of childbearing.[1] 12 Therefore Sarah [a]laughed within herself, saying, [b]"After I have grown old, shall I have pleasure, my [c]lord being old also?"

13 And the LORD said to Abraham, "Why did Sarah laugh, saying, 'Shall I surely bear *a child,* since I am old?' 14 [a]Is anything too hard for the LORD? [b]At the appointed time I will return to you, according to the time of life, and Sarah shall have a son."

15 But Sarah denied *it,* saying, "I did not laugh," for she was afraid.

And He said, "No, but you did laugh!"

Abraham Intercedes for Sodom

16 Then the men rose from there and looked toward Sodom, and Abraham went with them [a]to send them on the way. 17 And the LORD said, [a]"Shall I hide from Abraham what I am doing, 18 since Abraham shall surely become a great and mighty nation, and all the nations of the earth shall be [a]blessed in him? 19 For I have known him, in order [a]that he may command his children and his household after him, that they keep the way of the LORD, to do righteousness and justice, that the LORD may bring to Abraham what He has spoken to him." 20 And the LORD said, "Because [a]the outcry against Sodom and Gomorrah is great, and because their [b]sin is very grave, 21 [a]I will go down now and see whether they have done altogether according to the outcry against it that has come to Me; and if not, [b]I will know."

22 Then the men turned away from there [a]and went toward Sodom, but Abraham still stood before the LORD. 23 And Abraham [a]came near and said, [b]"Would You also [c]destroy the [d]righteous with the wicked? 24 Suppose there were fifty righteous within the city; would You also destroy the place and not spare *it* for the fifty righteous that were in it? 25 Far be it from You to do such a thing as this, to slay the righteous with the wicked, so [a]that the righteous should be as the wicked; far be it from You! [b]Shall not the Judge of all the earth do right?"

26 So the LORD said, [a]"If I find in Sodom fifty righteous within the city, then I will spare all the place for their sakes."

27 Then Abraham answered and said, "Indeed now, I who *am* [a]*but* dust and ashes have taken it upon myself to speak to the Lord: 28 Suppose there were five less than the fifty righteous; would You destroy all of the city for *lack of* five?"

So He said, "If I find there forty-five, I will not destroy *it.*"

29 And he spoke to Him yet again and said, "Suppose there should be forty found there?"

So He said, "I will not do *it* for the sake of forty."

30 Then he said, "Let not the Lord be angry, and I will speak: Suppose thirty should be found there?"

So He said, "I will not do *it* if I find thirty there."

31 And he said, "Indeed now, I have taken it upon myself to speak to the Lord: Suppose twenty should be found there?"

So He said, "I will not destroy *it* for the sake of twenty."

18:8 [a] Gen. 19:3 **18:9** [a] Gen. 24:67 **18:10** [a] 2 Kin. 4:16 [b] Gen. 17:19, 21; 21:2; Rom. 9:9 **18:11** [a] Gen. 17:17; Luke 1:18; Rom. 4:19; Heb. 11:11, 12, 19 [b] Gen. 31:35 [1] Literally *the manner of women had ceased to be with Sarah* **18:12** [a] Gen. 17:17 [b] Luke 1:18 [c] 1 Pet. 3:6 **18:14** [a] Num. 11:23; Jer. 32:17; Zech. 8:6; Matt. 3:9; 19:26; Luke 1:37; Rom. 4:21 [b] Gen. 17:21; 18:10; 2 Kin. 4:16 **18:16** [a] Acts 15:3; Rom. 15:24 **18:17** [a] Gen. 18:22, 26, 33; Ps. 25:14; Amos 3:7; [John 15:15] **18:18** [a] [Gen. 12:3; 22:18]; Matt. 1:1; Luke 3:34; [Acts 3:25, 26; Gal. 3:8] **18:19** [a] [Deut. 4:9, 10; 6:6, 7] **18:20** [a] Gen. 4:10; 19:13; Ezek. 16:49, 50 [b] Gen. 13:13 **18:21** [a] Gen. 11:5; Ex. 3:8; Ps. 14:2 [b] Deut. 8:2; 13:3; Josh. 22:22; Luke 16:15; 2 Cor. 11:11 **18:22** [a] Gen. 18:16; 19:1 **18:23** [a] [Heb. 10:22] [b] Ex. 23:7; Num. 16:22; 2 Sam. 24:17; Ps. 11:4–7 [c] Job 9:22 [d] Gen. 20:4 **18:25** [a] Job 8:20; Is. 3:10, 11 [b] Deut. 1:16, 17; 32:4; Job 8:3, 20; 34:17; Ps. 58:11; 94:2; Is. 3:10, 11; Rom. 3:5, 6 **18:26** [a] Jer. 5:1; Ezek. 22:30 **18:27** [a] [Gen. 3:19]; Job 4:19; 30:19; 42:6; [1 Cor. 15:47, 48]

32Then he said, [a]"Let not the Lord be angry, and I will speak but once more: Suppose ten should be found there?"
[b]And He said, "I will not destroy *it* for
the sake of ten." 33So the LORD went His
way as soon as He had finished speaking
with Abraham; and Abraham returned to
his place.

Sodom's Depravity

19 Now [a]the two angels came to Sodom
in the evening, and [b]Lot was sitting
in the gate of Sodom. When Lot saw *them,*
he rose to meet them, and he bowed himself with his face toward the ground. 2And
he said, "Here now, my lords, please [a]turn
in to your servant's house and spend the
night, and [b]wash your feet; then you may
rise early and go on your way."
And they said, [c]"No, but we will spend
the night in the open square."
3But he insisted strongly; so they turned
in to him and entered his house. [a]Then he
made them a feast, and baked [b]unleavened
bread, and they ate.
4Now before they lay down, the men of
the city, the men of Sodom, both old and
young, all the people from every quarter,
surrounded the house. 5[a]And they called to
Lot and said to him, "Where are the men
who came to you tonight? [b]Bring them out
to us that we [c]may know them *carnally.*"
6So [a]Lot went out to them through the
doorway, shut the door behind him, 7and
said, "Please, my brethren, do not do so
wickedly! 8[a]See now, I have two daughters
who have not known a man; please, let me
bring them out to you, and you may do to
them as you wish; only do nothing to these
men, [b]since this is the reason they have
come under the shadow of my roof."
9And they said, "Stand back!" Then they
said, "This one [a]came in to stay *here,* [b]and
he keeps acting as a judge; now we will deal
worse with you than with them." So they
pressed hard against the man Lot, and
came near to break down the door. 10But the
men reached out their hands and pulled
Lot into the house with them, and shut the
door. 11And they [a]struck the men who *were*
at the doorway of the house with blindness,
both small and great, so that they became
weary *trying* to find the door.

Sodom and Gomorrah Destroyed
(Matt. 11:23, 24; Luke 17:28–32)

12Then the men said to Lot, "Have you
anyone else here? Son-in-law, your sons,
your daughters, and whomever you have
in the city—[a]take *them* out of this place!
13For we will destroy this place, because
the [a]outcry against them has grown great
before the face of the LORD, and [b]the LORD
has sent us to destroy it."
14So Lot went out and spoke to his sons-
in-law, [a]who had married his daughters,
and said, [b]"Get up, get out of this place; for
the LORD will destroy this city!" [c]But to his
sons-in-law he seemed to be joking.
15When the morning dawned, the an-
gels urged Lot to hurry, saying, [a]"Arise, take
your wife and your two daughters who are
here, lest you be consumed in the punishment of the city." 16And while he lingered,
the men [a]took hold of his hand, his wife's
hand, and the hands of his two daughters,
the [b]LORD being merciful to him, [c]and they
brought him out and set him outside the
city. 17So it came to pass, when they had
brought them outside, that he[1] said, [a]"Escape for your life! [b]Do not look behind you
nor stay anywhere in the plain. Escape [c]to
the mountains, lest you be destroyed."
18Then Lot said to them, "Please, [a]no, my
lords! 19Indeed now, your servant has found
favor in your sight, and you have increased
your mercy which you have shown me by
saving my life; but I cannot escape to the
mountains, lest some evil overtake me and
I die. 20See now, this city *is* near *enough* to
flee to, and it *is* a little one; please let me
escape there (*is* it not a little one?) and my
soul shall live."
21And he said to him, "See, [a]I have favored you concerning this thing also, in
that I will not overthrow this city for which

18:32 [a] Judg. 6:39 [b] James 5:16 **19:1** [a] Gen. 18:2, 16, 22 [b] Gen. 18:1–5 **19:2** [a] Gen. 24:31; [Heb. 13:2] [b] Gen. 18:4; 24:32 [c] Luke 24:28 **19:3** [a] Gen. 18:6–8; Ex. 23:15; Num. 9:11; 28:17 [b] Ex. 12:8 **19:5** [a] Is. 3:9 [b] Judg. 19:22 [c] Gen. 4:1; Rom. 1:24, 27; Jude 7 **19:6** [a] Judg. 19:23 **19:8** [a] Judg. 19:24 [b] Gen. 18:5 **19:9** [a] 2 Pet. 2:7, 8 [b] Ex. 2:14 **19:11** [a] Gen. 20:17, 18 **19:12** [a] Gen. 7:1; 2 Pet. 2:7, 9 **19:13** [a] Gen. 18:20 [b] Lev. 26:30–33; Deut. 4:26; 28:45; 1 Chr. 21:15 **19:14** [a] Matt. 1:18 [b] Num. 16:21, 24, 26, 45; Rev. 18:4 [c] Ex. 9:21; Jer. 43:1, 2; Luke 17:28; 24:11 **19:15** [a] Ps. 37:2; Rev. 18:4 **19:16** [a] Deut. 5:15; 6:21; 7:8; 2 Pet. 2:7 [b] Ex. 34:7; Ps. 32:10; 33:18, 19; Luke 18:13 [c] Ps. 34:22 **19:17** [a] 1 Kin. 19:3; Jer. 48:6 [b] Gen. 19:26; Matt. 24:16–18; Luke 9:62; Phil. 3:13, 14 [c] Gen. 14:10 [1] Septuagint, Syriac, and Vulgate read *they.* **19:18** [a] Acts 10:14 **19:21** [a] Job 42:8, 9; Ps. 145:19

you have spoken. 22Hurry, escape there. For [a]I cannot do anything until you arrive there."

Therefore [b]the name of the city was called Zoar.

23The sun had risen upon the earth when Lot entered Zoar. 24Then the LORD rained [a]brimstone and [b]fire on Sodom and Gomorrah, from the LORD out of the heavens. 25So He overthrew those cities, all the plain, all the inhabitants of the cities, and [a]what grew on the ground.

26But his wife looked back behind him, and she became [a]a pillar of salt.

27And Abraham went early in the morning to the place where [a]he had stood before the LORD. 28Then he looked toward Sodom and Gomorrah, and toward all the land of the plain; and he saw, and behold, [a]the smoke of the land which went up like the smoke of a furnace. 29And it came to pass, when God destroyed the cities of the plain, that God [a]remembered Abraham, and sent Lot out of the midst of the overthrow, when He overthrew the cities in which Lot had dwelt.

The Descendants of Lot

30Then Lot went up out of Zoar and [a]dwelt in the mountains, and his two daughters were with him; for he was afraid to dwell in Zoar. And he and his two daughters dwelt in a cave. 31Now the firstborn said to the younger, "Our father *is* old, and *there is* no man on the earth [a]to come in to us as is the custom of all the earth. 32Come, let us make our father drink wine, and we will lie with him, that we [a]may preserve the lineage of our father." 33So they made their father drink wine that night. And the firstborn went in and lay with her father, and he did not know when she lay down or when she arose.

34It happened on the next day that the firstborn said to the younger, "Indeed I lay with my father last night; let us make him drink wine tonight also, and you go in *and* lie with him, that we may preserve the lineage of our father." 35Then they made their father drink wine that night also. And the younger arose and lay with him, and he did not know when she lay down or when she arose.

36Thus both the daughters of Lot were with child by their father. 37The firstborn bore a son and called his name Moab; [a]he *is* the father of the Moabites to this day. 38And the younger, she also bore a son and called his name Ben-Ammi; [a]he *is* the father of the people of Ammon to this day.

Abraham and Abimelech

20 And Abraham journeyed from [a]there to the South, and dwelt between [b]Kadesh and Shur, and [c]stayed in Gerar. 2Now Abraham said of Sarah his wife, [a]"She *is* my sister." And Abimelech king of Gerar sent and [b]took Sarah.

3But [a]God came to Abimelech [b]in a dream by night, and said to him, [c]"Indeed you *are* a dead man because of the woman whom you have taken, for she *is* a man's wife."

4But Abimelech had not come near her; and he said, "Lord, [a]will You slay a righteous nation also? 5Did he not say to me, 'She *is* my sister'? And she, even she herself said, 'He *is* my brother.' [a]In the integrity of my heart and innocence of my hands I have done this."

6And God said to him in a dream, "Yes, I know that you did this in the integrity of your heart. For [a]I also withheld you from sinning [b]against Me; therefore I did not let you touch her. 7Now therefore, restore the man's wife; [a]for he *is* a prophet, and he will pray for you and you shall live. But if you do not restore *her,* [b]know that you shall surely die, you [c]and all who *are* yours."

8So Abimelech rose early in the morning, called all his servants, and told all these things in their hearing; and the men were very much afraid. 9And Abimelech called Abraham and said to him, "What have you

---

19:22 [a] Ex. 32:10; Deut. 9:14 [b] Gen. 13:10; 14:2 **19:24** [a] Deut. 29:23; Ps. 11:6; Is. 13:19; Jer. 20:16; 23:14; 49:18; 50:40; Ezek. 16:49, 50; Hos. 11:8; Amos 4:11; Zeph. 2:9; Matt. 10:15; Mark 6:11; Luke 17:29; Rom. 9:29; 2 Pet. 2:6; Jude 7; Rev. 11:8 [b] Lev. 10:2 **19:25** [a] Ps. 107:34 **19:26** [a] Gen. 19:17; Luke 17:32 **19:27** [a] Gen. 18:22 **19:28** [a] Rev. 9:2; 18:9 **19:29** [a] Gen. 8:1; 18:23; Deut. 7:8; 9:5, 27 **19:30** [a] Gen. 19:17, 19 **19:31** [a] Gen. 16:2, 4; 38:8, 9; Deut. 25:5 **19:32** [a] [Mark 12:19] **19:37** [a] Num. 25:1; Deut. 2:9 **19:38** [a] Num. 21:24; Deut. 2:19 **20:1** [a] Gen. 18:1 [b] Gen. 12:9; 16:7, 14 [c] Gen. 26:1, 6 **20:2** [a] Gen. 12:11–13; 26:7 [b] Gen. 12:15 **20:3** [a] Ps. 105:14 [b] Job 33:15 [c] Gen. 20:7 **20:4** [a] Gen. 18:23–25; Num. 16:22 **20:5** [a] 1 Kin. 9:4; 2 Kin. 20:3; Ps. 7:8; 26:6 **20:6** [a] Gen. 31:7; 35:5; Ex. 34:24; 1 Sam. 25:26, 34 [b] Gen. 39:9; 2 Sam. 12:13 **20:7** [a] 1 Sam. 7:5; 2 Kin. 5:11; Job 42:8; James 5:14, 15 [b] Gen. 2:17 [c] Num. 16:32, 33

done to us? How have I offended you, [a]that
you have brought on me and on my kingdom a great sin? You have done deeds to
me [b]that ought not to be done." 10 Then
Abimelech said to Abraham, "What did
you have in view, that you have done this
thing?"

11 And Abraham said, "Because I thought,
surely [a]the fear of God *is* not in this place;
and [b]they will kill me on account of my
wife. 12 But indeed [a]*she is* truly my sister.
She *is* the daughter of my father, but not
the daughter of my mother; and she became my wife. 13 And it came to pass, when
[a]God caused me to wander from my father's
house, that I said to her, 'This *is* your kindness that you should do for me: in every
place, wherever we go, [b]say of me, "He *is*
my brother."'"

14 Then Abimelech [a]took sheep, oxen, and
male and female servants, and gave *them* to
Abraham; and he restored Sarah his wife to
him. 15 And Abimelech said, "See, [a]my land
is before you; dwell where it pleases you."
16 Then to Sarah he said, "Behold, I have
given your brother a thousand *pieces* of silver; [a]indeed this vindicates you[1] [b]before all
who *are* with you and before everybody."
Thus she was rebuked.

17 So Abraham [a]prayed to God; and God
[b]healed Abimelech, his wife, and his female
servants. Then they bore *children;* 18 for the
LORD [a]had closed up all the wombs of the
house of Abimelech because of Sarah,
Abraham's wife.

Isaac Is Born
(Heb. 11:11)

21 And the LORD [a]visited Sarah as He
had said, and the LORD did for Sarah
[b]as He had spoken. 2 For Sarah [a]conceived
and bore Abraham a son in his old age, [b]at
the set time of which God had spoken to
him. 3 And Abraham called the name of his
son who was born to him—whom Sarah
bore to him—[a]Isaac. 4 Then Abraham [a]cir-
cumcised his son Isaac when he was eight
days old, [b]as God had commanded him.
5 Now [a]Abraham was one hundred years old
when his son Isaac was born to him. 6 And
Sarah said, [a]"God has made me laugh, *and*
all who hear [b]will laugh with me." 7 She also
said, "Who would have said to Abraham
that Sarah would nurse children? [a]For I
have borne *him* a son in his old age."

Hagar and Ishmael Depart
(Gal. 4:21–30)

8 So the child grew and was weaned. And
Abraham made a great feast on the same
day that Isaac was weaned.

9 And Sarah saw the son of Hagar [a]the
Egyptian, whom she had borne to Abraham, [b]scoffing. 10 Therefore she said to
Abraham, [a]"Cast out this bondwoman and
her son; for the son of this bondwoman
shall not be heir with my son, *namely* with
Isaac." 11 And the matter was very displeasing in Abraham's sight [a]because of his son.

12 But God said to Abraham, "Do not let
it be displeasing in your sight because of
the lad or because of your bondwoman.
Whatever Sarah has said to you, listen to
her voice; for [a]in Isaac your seed shall be
called. 13 Yet I will also make [a]a nation of
the son of the bondwoman, because he *is*
your seed."

14 So Abraham rose early in the morning, and took bread and a skin of water;
and putting *it* on her shoulder, he gave *it*
and the boy to Hagar, and [a]sent her away.
Then she departed and wandered in the
Wilderness of Beersheba. 15 And the water
in the skin was used up, and she placed
the boy under one of the shrubs. 16 Then
she went and sat down across from *him* at
a distance of about a bowshot; for she said
to herself, "Let me not see the death of the
boy." So she sat opposite *him,* and lifted her
voice and wept.

17 And [a]God heard the voice of the lad.
Then the [b]angel of God called to Hagar out
of heaven, and said to her, "What ails you,
Hagar? Fear not, for God has heard the

20:9 [a] Gen. 26:10; 39:9; Ex. 32:21; Josh. 7:25 [b] Gen. 34:7 20:11 [a] Gen. 42:18; Neh. 5:15; Ps. 36:1; Prov. 16:6 [b] Gen. 12:12; 26:7 20:12 [a] Gen. 11:29 20:13 [a] Gen. 12:1–9, 11; [Heb. 11:8] [b] Gen. 12:13; 20:5 20:14 [a] Gen. 12:16 20:15 [a] Gen. 13:9; 34:10; 47:6 20:16 [a] Gen. 26:11 [b] Mal. 2:9 [1] Literally *it is a covering of the eyes for you* 20:17 [a] Num. 12:13; 21:7; Job 42:9; [James 5:16] [b] Gen. 21:2 20:18 [a] Gen. 12:17 21:1 [a] 1 Sam. 2:21 [b] Gen. 17:16, 19, 21; 18:10, 14; [Gal. 4:23, 28] 21:2 [a] Acts 7:8; Gal. 4:22; Heb. 11:11, 12 [b] Gen. 17:21; 18:10, 14; Gal. 4:4 21:3 [a] Gen. 17:19, 21 21:4 [a] Acts 7:8 [b] Gen. 17:10, 12; Lev. 12:3 21:5 [a] Gen. 17:1, 17 21:6 [a] Gen. 18:13; Ps. 126:2; Is. 54:1 [b] Luke 1:58 21:7 [a] Gen. 18:11, 12 21:9 [a] Gen. 16:1, 4, 15 [b] [Gal. 4:29] 21:10 [a] Gen. 25:6; 36:6, 7; Gal. 3:18; 4:30 21:11 [a] Gen. 17:18 21:12 [a] Matt. 1:2; Luke 3:34; [Rom. 9:7, 8]; Heb. 11:18 21:13 [a] Gen. 16:10; 17:20; 21:18; 25:12–18 21:14 [a] John 8:35 21:17 [a] Ex. 3:7; Deut. 26:7; Ps. 6:8 [b] Gen. 22:11

voice of the lad where he *is.* 18 Arise, lift up
the lad and hold him with your hand, for
[a]I will make him a great nation."
19 Then [a]God opened her eyes, and she
saw a well of water. And she went and
filled the skin with water, and gave the lad
a drink. 20 So God [a]was with the lad; and he
grew and dwelt in the wilderness, [b]and became an archer. 21 He dwelt in the Wilderness of Paran; and his mother [a]took a wife
for him from the land of Egypt.

A Covenant with Abimelech

22 And it came to pass at that time that
[a]Abimelech and Phichol, the commander
of his army, spoke to Abraham, saying,
[b]"God *is* with you in all that you do. 23 Now
therefore, [a]swear to me by God that you will
not deal falsely with me, with my offspring,
or with my posterity; but that according to
the kindness that I have done to you, you
will do to me and to the land in which you
have dwelt."
24 And Abraham said, "I will swear."
25 Then Abraham rebuked Abimelech
because of a well of water which Abimelech's servants [a]had seized. 26 And Abimelech said, "I do not know who has done this
thing; you did not tell me, nor had I heard
of it until today." 27 So Abraham took sheep
and oxen and gave them to Abimelech, and
the two of them [a]made a covenant. 28 And
Abraham set seven ewe lambs of the flock
by themselves.
29 Then Abimelech asked Abraham,
[a]"What *is the meaning of* these seven ewe
lambs which you have set by themselves?"
30 And he said, "You will take *these* seven
ewe lambs from my hand, that [a]they may
be my witness that I have dug this well."
31 Therefore he [a]called that place Beersheba,[1] because the two of them swore an
oath there.
32 Thus they made a covenant at Beersheba. So Abimelech rose with Phichol, the
commander of his army, and they returned
to the land of the Philistines. 33 Then *Abraham* planted a tamarisk tree in Beersheba,
and [a]there called on the name of the LORD,
[b]the Everlasting God. 34 And Abraham
stayed in the land of the Philistines many
days.

Abraham's Faith Confirmed
(Heb. 11:17–19)

22 Now it came to pass after these
things that [a]God tested Abraham,
and said to him, "Abraham!"
And he said, "Here I am."
2 Then He said, "Take now your son,
[a]your only *son* Isaac, whom you [b]love, and
go [c]to the land of Moriah, and offer him
there as a [d]burnt offering on one of the
mountains of which I shall tell you."
3 So Abraham rose early in the morning
and saddled his donkey, and took two of his
young men with him, and Isaac his son;
and he split the wood for the burnt offering,
and arose and went to the place of which
God had told him. 4 Then on the third day
Abraham lifted his eyes and saw the place
afar off. 5 And Abraham said to his young
men, "Stay here with the donkey; the lad[1]
and I will go yonder and worship, and we
will [a]come back to you."
6 So Abraham took the wood of the burnt
offering and [a]laid *it* on Isaac his son; and
he took the fire in his hand, and a knife,
and the two of them went together. 7 But
Isaac spoke to Abraham his father and said,
"My father!"
And he said, "Here I am, my son."
Then he said, "Look, the fire and the
wood, but where *is* the lamb for a burnt
offering?"
8 And Abraham said, "My son, God will
provide for Himself the [a]lamb for a [b]burnt
offering." So the two of them went together.
9 Then they came to the place of which
God had told him. And Abraham built an
altar there and placed the wood in order;
and he bound Isaac his son and [a]laid him
on the altar, upon the wood. 10 And Abraham stretched out his hand and took the
knife to slay his son.
11 But the [a]Angel of the LORD called to

21:18 [a] Gen. 16:10; 21:13; 25:12–16 **21:19** [a] Gen. 3:7; Num. 22:31; 2 Kin. 6:17; Luke 24:31 **21:20** [a] Gen. 28:15; 39:2, 3, 21 [b] Gen. 16:12 **21:21** [a] Gen. 24:4 **21:22** [a] Gen. 20:2, 14; 26:26 [b] Gen. 26:28; Is. 8:10 **21:23** [a] Josh. 2:12; 1 Sam. 24:21 **21:25** [a] Gen. 26:15, 18, 20–22 **21:27** [a] Gen. 26:31; 31:44; 1 Sam. 18:3 **21:29** [a] Gen. 33:8 **21:30** [a] Gen. 31:48, 52 **21:31** [a] Gen. 21:14; 26:33 [1] Literally *Well of the Oath* or *Well of the Seven* **21:33** [a] Gen. 4:26; 12:8; 13:4; 26:25 [b] Gen. 35:11; Ex. 15:18; Deut. 32:40; 33:27; Ps. 90:2; 93:2; Is. 40:28; Jer. 10:10; Hab. 1:12; Heb. 13:8 **22:1** [a] Deut. 8:2, 16; 1 Cor. 10:13; Heb. 11:17; [James 1:12–14; 1 Pet. 1:7] **22:2** [a] Gen. 22:12, 16; John 3:16; Heb. 11:17; 1 John 4:9 [b] John 5:20 [c] 2 Chr. 3:1 [d] Gen. 8:20; 31:54 **22:5** [a] [Heb. 11:19] [1] Or *young man* **22:6** [a] John 19:17 **22:8** [a] John 1:29, 36 [b] Ex. 12:3–6 **22:9** [a] [Heb. 11:17–19; James 2:21] **22:11** [a] Gen. 16:7–11; 21:17, 18; 31:11

him from heaven and said, "Abraham,
Abraham!"
So he said, "Here I am."
12And He said, [a]"Do not lay your hand
on the lad, or do anything to him; for [b]now
I know that you fear God, since you have
not [c]withheld your son, your only *son*,
from Me."
13Then Abraham lifted his eyes and
looked, and there behind *him was* a ram
caught in a thicket by its horns. So Abraham went and took the ram, and offered
it up for a burnt offering instead of his
son. 14And Abraham called the name of
the place, The-LORD-Will-Provide;[1] as it is
said *to* this day, "In the Mount of the LORD
it shall be provided."
15Then the Angel of the LORD called to
Abraham a second time out of heaven,
16and said: [a]"By Myself I have sworn, says
the LORD, because you have done this
thing, and have not withheld your son, your
only *son*— 17blessing I will [a]bless you, and
multiplying I will multiply your descendants [b]as the stars of the heaven [c]and as the
sand which *is* on the seashore; and [d]your

BELIEVE IN THE PROMISE

INHALE

I was raised in the church and taught that all of God's promises are "Yes and Amen." To me, that has always meant that God has promised always to be with me and that everything in my life would be positive and good. Well, my life is anything but that. Right now, I am struggling just to hold on. Now, I have no idea what that means. Am I being punished for something I have done? Is God mad at me because I do not make it to church every week? I am just so unhappy, hurt, and confused. I feel like God has abandoned me. Real talk . . . where is God right now? Does He even care?

EXHALE

God is omnipresent, meaning He is everywhere. So, God is surely with you, even if it might not feel that way. In creation, God was present in bringing everything from nothing, life from lifelessness, and order from disorder. He did not do that from afar; He did it from being present in what He created. And just as God moved upon the face of the waters, He moves upon the despair and chaos in our lives. God is with you. He always is and always will be. This is a promise you can always count on.

Just as God is always with you, He is always good to you. All of God's promises being "Yes and Amen" certainly means that God's purpose in all that He does is indeed for our good. But Genesis 3 describes how humanity rebelled against God and broke what He had made. Because of this, we experience hardship and pain that God did not intend. Consider Abraham. God chose Abraham to play a significant part in His plan of redemption. That didn't mean that Abraham's life was easy, though. But through it all, God kept encouraging him to remember the promise He had made to bless him, even when life didn't make sense. We see this immediately following the near sacrifice of Isaac: "By Myself I have sworn, says the LORD, because you have done this thing, and have not withheld your son, your only son—blessing I will bless you, and multiplying I will multiply your descendants as the stars of the heaven and as the sand which is on the seashore; and your descendants shall possess the gate of their enemies" (Gen. 22:16–17).

"Yes and Amen" doesn't mean we are immune to pain; rather, it means that God will use our pain—that He has a plan for it. Just as God brought the greatest good from the greatest pain ever of Jesus on the cross, He can bring beauty from ashes in our lives too. Do not doubt God's forever promises based on your temporary pain.

22:12 [a] 1 Sam. 15:22 [b] Gen. 26:5; James 2:21, 22 [c] Gen. 22:2, 16; John 3:16 22:14 [1] Hebrew *YHWH Yireh* 22:16 [a] Ps. 105:9; Luke 1:73; [Heb. 6:13, 14] 22:17 [a] Gen. 17:16; 26:3, 24 [b] Gen. 15:5; 26:4; Deut. 1:10; Jer. 33:22; Heb. 11:12 [c] Gen. 13:16; 32:12; 1 Kin. 4:20 [d] Gen. 24:60

descendants shall possess the gate of their enemies. 18 [a]In your seed all the nations of the earth shall be blessed, [b]because you have obeyed My voice." 19 So Abraham returned to his young men, and they rose and went together to [a]Beersheba; and Abraham dwelt at Beersheba.

The Family of Nahor

20 Now it came to pass after these things that it was told Abraham, saying, "Indeed [a]Milcah also has borne children to your brother Nahor: 21 [a]Huz his firstborn, Buz his brother, Kemuel the father [b]of Aram, 22 Chesed, Hazo, Pildash, Jidlaph, and Bethuel." 23 And [a]Bethuel begot Rebekah.[1] These eight Milcah bore to Nahor, Abraham's brother. 24 His concubine, whose name was Reumah, also bore Tebah, Gaham, Thahash, and Maachah.

Sarah's Death and Burial

23 Sarah lived one hundred and twenty-seven years; *these were* the years of the life of Sarah. 2 So Sarah died in [a]Kirjath Arba (that *is,* [b]Hebron) in the land of Canaan, and Abraham came to mourn for Sarah and to weep for her.

3 Then Abraham stood up from before his dead, and spoke to the sons of [a]Heth, saying, 4 [a]"I *am* a foreigner and a visitor among you. [b]Give me property for a burial place among you, that I may bury my dead out of my sight."

5 And the sons of Heth answered Abraham, saying to him, 6 "Hear us, my lord: You *are* [a]a mighty prince among us; bury your dead in the choicest of our burial places. None of us will withhold from you his burial place, that you may bury your dead."

7 Then Abraham stood up and bowed himself to the people of the land, the sons of Heth. 8 And he spoke with them, saying, "If it is your wish that I bury my dead out of my sight, hear me, and meet with Ephron the son of Zohar for me, 9 that he may give me the cave of [a]Machpelah which he has, which *is* at the end of his field. Let him give it to me at the full price, as property for a burial place among you."

10 Now Ephron dwelt among the sons of Heth; and Ephron the Hittite answered Abraham in the presence of the sons of Heth, all who [a]entered at the gate of his city, saying, 11 [a]"No, my lord, hear me: I give you the field and the cave that *is* in it; I give it to you in the presence of the sons of my people. I give it to you. Bury your dead!"

12 Then Abraham bowed himself down before the people of the land; 13 and he spoke to Ephron in the hearing of the people of the land, saying, "If you *will give it,* please hear me. I will give you money for the field; take *it* from me and I will bury my dead there."

14 And Ephron answered Abraham, saying to him, 15 "My lord, listen to me; the land *is worth* four hundred [a]shekels of silver. What *is* that between you and me? So bury your dead." 16 And Abraham listened to Ephron; and Abraham [a]weighed out the silver for Ephron which he had named in the hearing of the sons of Heth, four hundred shekels of silver, currency of the merchants.

17 So [a]the field of Ephron which *was* in Machpelah, which *was* before Mamre, the field and the cave which *was* in it, and all the trees that *were* in the field, which *were* within all the surrounding borders, were deeded 18 to Abraham as a possession in the presence of the sons of Heth, before all who went in at the gate of his city.

19 And after this, Abraham buried Sarah his wife in the cave of the field of Machpelah, before Mamre (that *is,* Hebron) in the land of Canaan. 20 So the field and the cave that *is* in it [a]were deeded to Abraham by the sons of Heth as property for a burial place.

A Bride for Isaac

24 Now Abraham [a]was old, well advanced in age; and the LORD [b]had blessed Abraham in all things. 2 So Abraham said [a]to the oldest servant of his house, who [b]ruled over all that he had, "Please, [c]put your hand under my thigh, 3 and I will make

---

22:18 [a] Gen. 12:3; 18:18; 26:4; Matt. 1:1; Luke 3:34; [Acts 3:25, 26]; Gal. 3:8, 9, 16, 18 [b] Gen. 18:19; 22:3, 10; 26:5 **22:19** [a] Gen. 21:31 **22:20** [a] Gen. 11:29; 24:15 **22:21** [a] Job 1:1 [b] Job 32:2 **22:23** [a] Gen. 24:15 [1] Spelled *Rebecca* in Romans 9:10 **23:2** [a] Gen. 35:27; Josh. 14:15; 15:13; 21:11 [b] Gen. 13:18; 23:19 **23:3** [a] Gen. 10:15; 15:20; 2 Kin. 7:6 **23:4** [a] [Gen. 17:8]; Lev. 25:23; 1 Chr. 29:15; Ps. 39:12; 105:12; 119:19; [Heb. 11:9, 13] [b] Acts 7:5, 16 **23:6** [a] Gen. 13:2; 14:14; 24:35 **23:9** [a] Gen. 25:9 **23:10** [a] Gen. 23:18; 34:20, 24; Ruth 4:1, 4, 11 **23:11** [a] 2 Sam. 24:21–24 **23:15** [a] Ex. 30:13; Ezek. 45:12 **23:16** [a] 2 Sam. 14:26; Jer. 32:9, 10; Zech. 11:12 **23:17** [a] Gen. 25:9; 49:29–32; 50:13; Acts 7:16 **23:20** [a] Jer. 32:10, 11 **24:1** [a] Gen. 18:11; 21:5 [b] Gen. 12:2; 13:2; 24:35; Ps. 112:3; Prov. 10:22; [Gal. 3:9] **24:2** [a] Gen. 15:2 [b] Gen. 24:10; 39:4–6 [c] Gen. 47:29; 1 Chr. 29:24

you [a]swear by the LORD, the God of heaven and the God of the earth, that [b]you will not take a wife for my son from the daughters of the Canaanites, among whom I dwell; 4[a]but you shall go [b]to my country and to my family, and take a wife for my son Isaac."

5And the servant said to him, "Perhaps the woman will not be willing to follow me to this land. Must I take your son back to the land from which you came?"

6But Abraham said to him, "Beware that you do not take my son back there. 7The LORD God of heaven, who [a]took me from my father's house and from the land of my family, and who spoke to me and swore to me, saying, [b]'To your descendants[1] I give this land,' [c]He will send His angel before you, and you shall take a wife for my son from there. 8And if the woman is not willing to follow you, then [a]you will be released from this oath; only do not take my son back there." 9So the servant put his hand under the thigh of Abraham his master, and swore to him concerning this matter.

10Then the servant took ten of his master's camels and departed, [a]for all his master's goods *were in* his hand. And he arose and went to Mesopotamia, to [b]the city of Nahor. 11And he made his camels kneel down outside the city by a well of water at evening time, the time [a]when women go out to draw *water.* 12Then he [a]said, "O LORD God of my master Abraham, please [b]give me success this day, and show kindness to my master Abraham. 13Behold, *here* [a]I stand by the well of water, and [b]the daughters of the men of the city are coming out to draw water. 14Now let it be that the young woman to whom I say, 'Please let down your pitcher that I may drink,' and she says, 'Drink, and I will also give your camels a drink'—*let* her *be the one* You have appointed for Your servant Isaac. And [a]by this I will know that You have shown kindness to my master."

15And it happened, [a]before he had finished speaking, that behold, [b]Rebekah, who was born to Bethuel, son of [c]Milcah, the wife of Nahor, Abraham's brother, came out with her pitcher on her shoulder. 16Now the young woman [a]*was* very beautiful to behold, a virgin; no man had known her. And she went down to the well, filled her pitcher, and came up. 17And the servant ran to meet her and said, "Please let me drink a little water from your pitcher."

18[a]So she said, "Drink, my lord." Then she quickly let her pitcher down to her hand, and gave him a drink. 19And when she had finished giving him a drink, she said, "I will draw *water* for your camels also, until they have finished drinking." 20Then she quickly emptied her pitcher into the trough, ran back to the well to draw *water,* and drew for all his camels. 21And the man, wondering at her, remained silent so as to know whether [a]the LORD had made his journey prosperous or not.

22So it was, when the camels had finished drinking, that the man took a golden [a]nose ring weighing half a shekel, and two bracelets for her wrists weighing ten *shekels* of gold, 23and said, "Whose daughter *are* you? Tell me, please, is there room *in* your father's house for us to lodge?"

24So she said to him, [a]"I *am* the daughter of Bethuel, Milcah's son, whom she bore to Nahor." 25Moreover she said to him, "We have both straw and feed enough, and room to lodge."

26Then the man [a]bowed down his head and worshiped the LORD. 27And he said, [a]"Blessed *be* the LORD God of my master Abraham, who has not forsaken [b]His mercy and His truth toward my master. As for me, being on the way, the LORD [c]led me to the house of my master's brethren." 28So the young woman ran and told her mother's household these things.

29Now Rebekah had a brother whose name *was* [a]Laban, and Laban ran out to the man by the well. 30So it came to pass, when he saw the nose ring, and the bracelets on his sister's wrists, and when he heard the words of his sister Rebekah, saying, "Thus

24:3 [a] Gen. 14:19, 22 [b] Gen. 26:35; 28:2; Ex. 34:16; Deut. 7:3; 2 Cor. 6:14–17 24:4 [a] Gen. 28:2 [b] Gen. 12:1; Heb. 11:15 24:7 [a] Gen. 12:1; 24:3 [b] Gen. 12:7; 13:15; 15:18; 17:8; Ex. 32:13; Deut. 1:8; 34:4; Acts 7:5 [c] Gen. 16:7; 21:17; 22:11; Ex. 23:20, 23; 33:2; Heb. 1:4, 14 [1] Literally *seed* 24:8 [a] Josh. 2:17–20 24:10 [a] Gen. 24:2, 22 [b] Gen. 11:31, 32; 22:20; 27:43; 29:5 24:11 [a] Ex. 2:16; 1 Sam. 9:11 24:12 [a] Gen. 24:27, 42, 48; 26:24; 32:9; Ex. 3:6, 15 [b] Gen. 27:20; Neh. 1:11; Ps. 37:5 24:13 [a] Gen. 24:43 [b] Ex. 2:16 24:14 [a] Judg. 6:17, 37; 1 Sam. 14:10; 16:7; 20:7; 2 Kin. 20:9; Prov. 16:33; Acts 1:26 24:15 [a] Is. 65:24 [b] Gen. 24:45; 25:20 [c] Gen. 22:20, 23 24:16 [a] Gen. 12:11; 26:7; 29:17 24:18 [a] Gen. 24:14, 46; [1 Pet. 3:8, 9] 24:21 [a] Gen. 24:12–14, 27, 52 24:22 [a] Gen. 24:47; Ex. 32:2, 3; Is. 3:19–21 24:24 [a] Gen. 22:23; 24:15 24:26 [a] Gen. 24:48, 52; Ex. 4:31 24:27 [a] Gen. 24:12, 42, 48; Ex. 18:10; Ruth 4:14; 1 Sam. 25:32, 39; 2 Sam. 18:28; Luke 1:68 [b] Gen. 32:10; Ps. 98:3 [c] Gen. 24:21, 48 24:29 [a] Gen. 29:5, 13

the man spoke to me," that he went to the
man. And there he stood by the camels at
the well. 31 And he said, "Come in, [a]O blessed
of the LORD! Why do you stand outside? For
I have prepared the house, and a place for
the camels."

32 Then the man came to the house. And
he unloaded the camels, and [a]provided
straw and feed for the camels, and water
to [b]wash his feet and the feet of the men
who *were* with him. 33 *Food* was set before
him to eat, but he said, [a]"I will not eat until
I have told about my errand."

And he said, "Speak on."

34 So he said, "I *am* Abraham's servant.
35 The LORD [a]has blessed my master greatly,
and he has become great; and He has given
him flocks and herds, silver and gold, male
and female servants, and camels and donkeys. 36 And Sarah my master's wife [a]bore
a son to my master when she was old; and
[b]to him he has given all that he has. 37 Now
my master [a]made me swear, saying, 'You
shall not take a wife for my son from the
daughters of the Canaanites, in whose land
I dwell; 38 [a]but you shall go to my father's
house and to my family, and take a wife for
my son.' 39 [a]And I said to my master, 'Perhaps the woman will not follow me.' 40 [a]But
he said to me, 'The LORD, [b]before whom I
walk, will send His angel with you and prosper your way; and you shall take a wife for
my son from my family and from my father's house. 41 [a]You will be clear from this
oath when you arrive among my family;
for if they will not give *her* to you, then you
will be released from my oath.'

42 "And this day I came to the well and
said, [a]'O LORD God of my master Abraham,
if You will now prosper the way in which I
go, 43 [a]behold, I stand by the well of water;
and it shall come to pass that when the
virgin comes out to draw *water,* and I say
to her, "Please give me a little water from
your pitcher to drink," 44 and she says to
me, "Drink, and I will draw for your camels also,"—*let* her *be* the woman whom the
LORD has appointed for my master's son.'

45 [a]"But before I had finished [b]speaking
in my heart, there was Rebekah, coming out
with her pitcher on her shoulder; and she
went down to the well and drew *water.* And
I said to her, 'Please let me drink.' 46 And she
made haste and let her pitcher down from
her *shoulder,* and said, 'Drink, and I will give
your camels a drink also.' So I drank, and
she gave the camels a drink also. 47 Then I
asked her, and said, 'Whose daughter *are*
you?' And she said, 'The daughter of Bethuel, Nahor's son, whom Milcah bore to
him.' So I put the nose ring on her nose
and the bracelets on her wrists. 48 [a]And I
bowed my head and worshiped the LORD,
and blessed the LORD God of my master
Abraham, who had led me in the way of
truth to [b]take the daughter of my master's
brother for his son. 49 Now if you will [a]deal
kindly and truly with my master, tell me.
And if not, tell me, that I may turn to the
right hand or to the left."

50 Then Laban and Bethuel answered and
said, [a]"The thing comes from the LORD; we
cannot [b]speak to you either bad or good.
51 [a]Here *is* Rebekah before you; take *her* and
go, and let her be your master's son's wife,
as the LORD has spoken."

52 And it came to pass, when Abraham's
servant heard their words, that [a]he worshiped the LORD, *bowing himself* to the
earth. 53 Then the servant brought out [a]jew-
elry of silver, jewelry of gold, and clothing,
and gave *them* to Rebekah. He also gave
[b]precious things to her brother and to her
mother.

54 And he and the men who *were* with
him ate and drank and stayed all night.
Then they arose in the morning, and he
said, [a]"Send me away to my master."

55 But her brother and her mother said,
"Let the young woman stay with us *a few*
days, at least ten; after that she may go."

56 And he said to them, "Do not hinder
me, since the LORD has prospered my way;
send me away so that I may go to my master."

57 So they said, "We will call the young

24:31 [a] Gen. 26:29; Judg. 17:2; Ruth 3:10; Ps. 115:15 **24:32** [a] Gen. 43:24; Judg. 19:21 [b] Gen. 19:2; John 13:5, 13–15 **24:33** [a] Job 23:12; John 4:34; Eph. 6:5–7 **24:35** [a] Gen. 13:2; 24:1 **24:36** [a] Gen. 21:1–7 [b] Gen. 21:10; 25:5 **24:37** [a] Gen. 24:2–4 **24:38** [a] Gen. 24:4 **24:39** [a] Gen. 24:5 **24:40** [a] Gen. 24:7 [b] Gen. 5:22, 24; 17:1; 1 Kin. 8:23 **24:41** [a] Gen. 24:8 **24:42** [a] Gen. 24:12 **24:43** [a] Gen. 24:13 **24:45** [a] Gen. 24:15 [b] 1 Sam. 1:13 **24:48** [a] Gen. 24:26, 52 [b] Gen. 22:23; 24:27; Ps. 32:8; 48:14; Is. 48:17 **24:49** [a] Gen. 47:29; Josh. 2:14 **24:50** [a] Ps. 118:23; Matt. 21:42; Mark 12:11 [b] Gen. 31:24, 29 **24:51** [a] Gen. 20:15 **24:52** [a] Gen. 24:26, 48 **24:53** [a] Gen. 24:10, 22; Ex. 3:22; 11:2; 12:35 [b] 2 Chr. 21:3; Ezra 1:6 **24:54** [a] Gen. 24:56, 59; 30:25

woman and ask her personally." 58Then they called Rebekah and said to her, "Will you go with this man?"

And she said, "I will go."

59So they sent away Rebekah their sister [a]and her nurse, and Abraham's servant and his men. 60And they blessed Rebekah and said to her:

"Our sister, *may* you *become*
[a]*The mother of* thousands
of ten thousands;
[b]And may your descendants possess
The gates of those who hate them."

61Then Rebekah and her maids arose, and they rode on the camels and followed the man. So the servant took Rebekah and departed.

62Now Isaac came from the way of [a]Beer Lahai Roi, for he dwelt in the South. 63And Isaac went out [a]to meditate in the field in the evening; and he lifted his eyes and looked, and there, the camels *were* coming. 64Then Rebekah lifted her eyes, and when she saw Isaac [a]she dismounted from her camel; 65for she had said to the servant, "Who *is* this man walking in the field to meet us?"

The servant said, "It *is* my master." So she took a veil and covered herself.

66And the servant told Isaac all the things that he had done. 67Then Isaac brought her into his mother Sarah's tent; and he [a]took Rebekah and she became his wife, and he loved her. So Isaac [b]was comforted after his mother's *death.*

Abraham and Keturah
(1 Chr. 1:32, 33)

25 Abraham again took a wife, and her name *was* [a]Keturah. 2And [a]she bore him Zimran, Jokshan, Medan, Midian, Ishbak, and Shuah. 3Jokshan begot Sheba and Dedan. And the sons of Dedan were Asshurim, Letushim, and Leummim. 4And the sons of Midian *were* Ephah, Epher, Hanoch, Abidah, and Eldaah. All these *were* the children of Keturah.

5And [a]Abraham gave all that he had to Isaac. 6But Abraham gave gifts to the sons of the concubines which Abraham had; and while he was still living he [a]sent them eastward, away from Isaac his son, to [b]the country of the east.

Abraham's Death and Burial

7This *is* the sum of the years of Abraham's life which he lived: one hundred and seventy-five years. 8Then Abraham breathed his last and [a]died in a good old age, an old man and full *of years,* and [b]was gathered to his people. 9And [a]his sons Isaac and Ishmael buried him in the cave of [b]Machpelah, which *is* before Mamre, in the field of Ephron the son of Zohar the Hittite, 10[a]the field which Abraham purchased from the sons of Heth. [b]There Abraham was buried, and Sarah his wife. 11And it came to pass, after the death of Abraham, that God blessed his son Isaac. And Isaac dwelt at [a]Beer Lahai Roi.

The Families of Ishmael and Isaac
(1 Chr. 1:29–31)

12Now this *is* the [a]genealogy of Ishmael, Abraham's son, whom Hagar the Egyptian, Sarah's maidservant, bore to Abraham. 13And [a]these *were* the names of the sons of Ishmael, by their names, according to their generations: The firstborn of Ishmael, Nebajoth; then Kedar, Adbeel, Mibsam, 14Mishma, Dumah, Massa, 15Hadar,[1] Tema, Jetur, Naphish, and Kedemah. 16These *were* the sons of Ishmael and these *were* their names, by their towns and their settlements, [a]twelve princes according to their nations. 17These *were* the years of the life of Ishmael: one hundred and thirty-seven years; and [a]he breathed his last and died, and was gathered to his people. 18[a](They dwelt from Havilah as far as Shur, which *is* east of Egypt as you go toward Assyria.) He died [b]in the presence of all his brethren.

19This *is* the [a]genealogy of Isaac, Abraham's son. [b]Abraham begot Isaac. 20Isaac was forty years old when he took Rebekah

---

24:59 [a] Gen. 35:8 **24:60** [a] Gen. 17:16 [b] Gen. 22:17; 28:14 **24:62** [a] Gen. 16:14; 25:11 **24:63** [a] Josh. 1:8; Ps. 1:2; 77:12; 119:15, 27, 48; 143:5; 145:5 **24:64** [a] Josh. 15:18 **24:67** [a] Gen. 25:20; 29:20; Prov. 18:22 [b] Gen. 23:1, 2; 38:12 **25:1** [a] 1 Chr. 1:32, 33 **25:2** [a] 1 Chr. 1:32, 33 **25:5** [a] Gen. 24:35, 36 **25:6** [a] Gen. 21:14 [b] Judg. 6:3 **25:8** [a] Gen. 15:15; 47:8, 9 [b] Gen. 25:17; 35:29; 49:29, 33 **25:9** [a] Gen. 35:29; 50:13 [b] Gen. 23:9, 17; 49:30 **25:10** [a] Gen. 23:3–16 [b] Gen. 49:31 **25:11** [a] Gen. 16:14 **25:12** [a] Gen. 11:10, 27; 16:15 **25:13** [a] 1 Chr. 1:29–31 **25:15** [1] Masoretic Text reads *Hadad.* **25:16** [a] Gen. 17:20 **25:17** [a] Gen. 25:8; 49:33 **25:18** [a] Gen. 20:1; 1 Sam. 15:7 [b] Gen. 16:12 **25:19** [a] Gen. 36:1, 9 [b] Matt. 1:2

as wife, [a]the daughter of Bethuel the Syrian
of Padan Aram, [b]the sister of Laban the Syrian. 21 Now Isaac pleaded with the LORD for
his wife, because she *was* barren; [a]and the
LORD granted his plea, [b]and Rebekah his
wife conceived. 22 But the children struggled together within her; and she said, "If
all is well, why *am I like* this?" [a]So she went
to inquire of the LORD.

23 And the LORD said to her:

[a]"Two nations *are* in your womb,
Two peoples shall be separated
from your body;
One people shall be stronger
than [b]the other,
[c]And the older shall serve the younger."

24 So when her days were fulfilled *for her*
to give birth, indeed *there were* twins in her
womb. 25 And the first came out red. *He was*
[a]like a hairy garment all over; so they called
his name Esau.[1] 26 Afterward his brother
came out, and [a]his hand took hold of Esau's
heel; so [b]his name was called Jacob.[1] Isaac
was sixty years old when she bore them.

27 So the boys grew. And Esau was [a]a skillful hunter, a man of the field; but Jacob was
[b]a mild man, [c]dwelling in tents. 28 And Isaac
loved Esau because he [a]ate *of his* game, [b]but
Rebekah loved Jacob.

Esau Sells His Birthright
(Heb. 12:16)

29 Now Jacob cooked a stew; and Esau
came in from the field, and he *was* weary.
30 And Esau said to Jacob, "Please feed me
with that same red *stew,* for I *am* weary."
Therefore his name was called Edom.[1]

31 But Jacob said, "Sell me your birthright
as of this day."

32 And Esau said, "Look, I *am* about to
die; so [a]what *is* this birthright to me?"

33 Then Jacob said, "Swear to me as of
this day."

So he swore to him, and [a]sold his birthright to Jacob. 34 And Jacob gave Esau bread
and stew of lentils; then [a]he ate and drank,
arose, and went his way. Thus Esau [b]de-
spised *his* birthright.

Isaac and Abimelech

26 There was a famine in the land, besides [a]the first famine that was in
the days of Abraham. And Isaac went to
[b]Abimelech king of the Philistines, in Gerar.

2 Then the LORD appeared to him and
said: [a]"Do not go down to Egypt; live in
[b]the land of which I shall tell you. 3 [a]Dwell in
this land, and [b]I will be with you and [c]bless
you; for to you and your descendants [d]I
give all these lands, and I will perform [e]the
oath which I swore to Abraham your father.
4 And [a]I will make your descendants multiply as the stars of heaven; I will give to
your descendants all these lands; [b]and in
your seed all the nations of the earth shall
be blessed; 5 [a]because Abraham obeyed My
voice and kept My charge, My commandments, My statutes, and My laws."

6 So Isaac dwelt in Gerar. 7 And the men of
the place asked about his wife. And [a]he said,
"She *is* my sister"; for [b]he was afraid to say,
"*She is* my wife," *because he thought,* "lest
the men of the place kill me for Rebekah,
because she *is* [c]beautiful to behold." 8 Now
it came to pass, when he had been there
a long time, that Abimelech king of the
Philistines looked through a window, and
saw, and there was Isaac, showing endear-
ment to Rebekah his wife. 9 Then Abimelech
called Isaac and said, "Quite obviously she
is your wife; so how could you say, 'She *is*
my sister'?"

Isaac said to him, "Because I said, 'Lest
I die on account of her.'"

10 And Abimelech said, "What *is* this you
have done to us? One of the people might
soon have lain with your wife, and [a]you
would have brought guilt on us." 11 So Abimelech charged all *his* people, saying, "He
who [a]touches this man or his wife shall
surely be put to death."

12 Then Isaac sowed in that land, and

25:20 [a] Gen. 22:23; 24:15, 29, 67 [b] Gen. 24:29 25:21 [a] 1 Sam. 1:17; 1 Chr. 5:20; 2 Chr. 33:13; Ezra 8:23; Ps. 127:3 [b] Rom. 9:10–13 25:22 [a] 1 Sam. 1:15; 9:9; 10:22 25:23 [a] Gen. 17:4–6, 16; 24:60; Num. 20:14; Deut. 2:4–8 [b] 2 Sam. 8:14 [c] Gen. 27:29, 40; Mal. 1:2, 3; Rom. 9:12 25:25 [a] Gen. 27:11, 16, 23 [1] Literally *Hairy* 25:26 [a] Hos. 12:3 [b] Gen. 27:36 [1] Literally *Supplanter* 25:27 [a] Gen. 27:3, 5 [b] Job 1:1, 8 [c] Heb. 11:9 25:28 [a] Gen. 27:4, 19, 25, 31 [b] Gen. 27:6–10 25:30 [1] Literally *Red* 25:32 [a] Matt. 16:26; Mark 8:36, 37 25:33 [a] Heb. 12:16 25:34 [a] Eccl. 8:15; Is. 22:13; 1 Cor. 15:32 [b] Heb. 12:16, 17 26:1 [a] Gen. 12:10 [b] Gen. 20:1, 2 26:2 [a] Gen. 12:7; 17:1; 18:1; 35:9 [b] Gen. 12:1 26:3 [a] Gen. 20:1; Ps. 39:12; Heb. 11:9 [b] Gen. 28:13, 15 [c] Gen. 12:2 [d] Gen. 12:7; 13:15; 15:18 [e] Gen. 22:16; Ps. 105:9 26:4 [a] Gen. 15:5; 22:17; Ex. 32:13 [b] Gen. 12:3; 22:18; Gal. 3:8 26:5 [a] Gen. 22:16, 18 26:7 [a] Gen. 12:13; 20:2, 12, 13 [b] Prov. 29:25 [c] Gen. 12:11; 24:16; 29:17 26:10 [a] Gen. 20:9 26:11 [a] Ps. 105:15

reaped in the same year [a]a hundredfold;
and the LORD [b]blessed him. 13The man [a]be-
gan to prosper, and continued prospering
until he became very prosperous; 14for he
had possessions of flocks and possessions
of herds and a great number of servants. So
the Philistines [a]envied him. 15Now the Philistines had stopped up all the wells [a]which
his father's servants had dug in the days
of Abraham his father, and they had filled
them with earth. 16And Abimelech said to
Isaac, "Go away from us, for [a]you are much
mightier than we."

17Then Isaac departed from there and
pitched his tent in the Valley of Gerar, and
dwelt there. 18And Isaac dug again the wells
of water which they had dug in the days of
Abraham his father, for the Philistines had
stopped them up after the death of Abraham. [a]He called them by the names which
his father had called them.

19Also Isaac's servants dug in the valley,
and found a well of running water there.
20But the herdsmen of Gerar [a]quarreled
with Isaac's herdsmen, saying, "The water
is ours." So he called the name of the well
Esek,[1] because they quarreled with him.
21Then they dug another well, and they
quarreled over that *one* also. So he called
its name Sitnah.[1] 22And he moved from
there and dug another well, and they did
not quarrel over it. So he called its name
Rehoboth,[1] because he said, "For now the
LORD has made room for us, and we shall
[a]be fruitful in the land."

23Then he went up from there to Beersheba. 24And the LORD [a]appeared to him
the same night and said, [b]"I *am* the God
of your father Abraham; [c]do not fear, for
[d]I *am* with you. I will bless you and multiply your descendants for My servant Abraham's sake." 25So he [a]built an altar there
and [b]called on the name of the LORD, and
he pitched his tent there; and there Isaac's
servants dug a well.

26Then Abimelech came to him from
Gerar with Ahuzzath, one of his friends,
[a]and Phichol the commander of his army.
27And Isaac said to them, "Why have you
come to me, [a]since you hate me and have
[b]sent me away from you?"

28But they said, "We have certainly seen
that the LORD [a]is with you. So we said, 'Let
there now be an oath between us, between
you and us; and let us make a covenant
with you, 29that you will do us no harm,
since we have not touched you, and since
we have done nothing to you but good and
have sent you away in peace. [a]You *are* now
the blessed of the LORD.'"

30[a]So he made them a feast, and they ate
and drank. 31Then they arose early in the
morning and [a]swore an oath with one another; and Isaac sent them away, and they
departed from him in peace.

32It came to pass the same day that
Isaac's servants came and told him about
the well which they had dug, and said to
him, "We have found water." 33So he called
it Shebah.[1] [a]Therefore the name of the city
is Beersheba[2] to this day.

34[a]When Esau was forty years old, he
took as wives Judith the daughter of Beeri
the Hittite, and Basemath the daughter of
Elon the Hittite. 35And [a]they were a grief of
mind to Isaac and Rebekah.

Isaac Blesses Jacob

27 Now it came to pass, when Isaac was
[a]old and [b]his eyes were so dim that
he could not see, that he called Esau his
older son and said to him, "My son."

And he answered him, "Here I am."

2Then he said, "Behold now, I am old. I
[a]do not know the day of my death. 3[a]Now
therefore, please take your weapons, your
quiver and your bow, and go out to the field
and hunt game for me. 4And make me savory food, such as I love, and bring *it* to me
that I may eat, that my soul [a]may bless you
before I die."

5Now Rebekah was listening when Isaac
spoke to Esau his son. And Esau went to
the field to hunt game and to bring *it*. 6So

26:12 [a] Matt. 13:8, 23; Mark 4:8 [b] Gen. 24:1; 25:8, 11; 26:3; Job 42:12; Prov. 10:22 **26:13** [a] Gen. 24:35; [Prov. 10:22] **26:14** [a] Gen. 37:11; Eccl. 4:4 **26:15** [a] Gen. 21:25, 30 **26:16** [a] Ex. 1:9 **26:18** [a] Gen. 21:31 **26:20** [a] Gen. 21:25 [1] Literally *Quarrel* **26:21** [1] Literally *Enmity* **26:22** [a] Gen. 17:6; 28:3; 41:52; Ex. 1:7 [1] Literally *Spaciousness* **26:24** [a] Gen. 26:2 [b] Gen. 17:7, 8; 24:12; Ex. 3:6; Acts 7:32 [c] Gen. 15:1 [d] Gen. 26:3, 4 **26:25** [a] Gen. 12:7, 8; 13:4, 18; 22:9; 33:20 [b] Gen. 21:33; Ps. 116:17 **26:26** [a] Gen. 21:22 **26:27** [a] Judg. 11:7 [b] Gen. 26:16 **26:28** [a] Gen. 21:22, 23 **26:29** [a] Gen. 24:31; Ps. 115:15 **26:30** [a] Gen. 19:3 **26:31** [a] Gen. 21:31 **26:33** [a] Gen. 21:31; 28:10 [1] Literally *Oath* or *Seven* [2] Literally *Well of the Oath* or *Well of the Seven* **26:34** [a] Gen. 28:8; 36:2 **26:35** [a] Gen. 27:46; 28:1, 8 **27:1** [a] Gen. 35:28 [b] Gen. 48:10; 1 Sam. 3:2 **27:2** [a] [Prov. 27:1; James 4:14] **27:3** [a] Gen. 25:27, 28 **27:4** [a] Gen. 27:19, 25, 27, 31; 48:9, 15, 16; 49:28; Deut. 33:1; Heb. 11:20

Rebekah spoke to Jacob her son, saying,
"Indeed I heard your father speak to Esau
your brother, saying, 7'Bring me game and
make savory food for me, that I may eat it
and bless you in the presence of the LORD
before my death.' 8Now therefore, my son,
[a]obey my voice according to what I command you. 9Go now to the flock and bring
me from there two choice kids of the goats,
and I will make [a]savory food from them for
your father, such as he loves. 10Then you
shall take *it* to your father, that he may eat
it, and that he [a]may bless you before his
death."

11And Jacob said to Rebekah his mother,
"Look, [a]Esau my brother *is* a hairy man, and
I *am* a smooth-*skinned* man. 12Perhaps my
father will [a]feel me, and I shall seem to be a
deceiver to him; and I shall bring [b]a curse
on myself and not a blessing."

13But his mother said to him, [a]"*Let* your
curse *be* on me, my son; only obey my voice,
and go, get *them* for me." 14And he went and
got *them* and brought *them* to his mother,
and his mother [a]made savory food, such
as his father loved. 15Then Rebekah took
[a]the choice clothes of her elder son Esau,
which *were* with her in the house, and put
them on Jacob her younger son. 16And she
put the skins of the kids of the goats on his
hands and on the smooth part of his neck.
17Then she gave the savory food and the
bread, which she had prepared, into the
hand of her son Jacob.

18So he went to his father and said, "My
father."

And he said, "Here I am. Who *are* you,
my son?"

19Jacob said to his father, "I *am* Esau
your firstborn; I have done just as you told
me; please arise, sit and eat of my game,
[a]that your soul may bless me."

20But Isaac said to his son, "How *is it*
that you have found *it* so quickly, my son?"

And he said, "Because the LORD your
God brought *it* to me."

21Isaac said to Jacob, "Please come near,
that I [a]may feel you, my son, whether you
are really my son Esau or not." 22So Jacob
went near to Isaac his father, and he felt
him and said, "The voice *is* Jacob's voice,
but the hands *are* the hands of Esau." 23And
he did not recognize him, because [a]his
hands were hairy like his brother Esau's
hands; so he blessed him.

24Then he said, "*Are* you really my son
Esau?"

He said, "I *am.*"

25He said, "Bring *it* near to me, and I will
eat of my son's game, so [a]that my soul may
bless you." So he brought *it* near to him,
and he ate; and he brought him wine, and
he drank. 26Then his father Isaac said to
him, "Come near now and kiss me, my son."
27And he came near and [a]kissed him; and
he smelled the smell of his clothing, and
blessed him and said:

"Surely, [b]the smell of my son
Is like the smell of a field
Which the LORD has blessed.
28 Therefore may [a]God give you
Of [b]the dew of heaven,
Of [c]the fatness of the earth,
And [d]plenty of grain and wine.
29 [a]Let peoples serve you,
And nations bow down to you.
Be master over your brethren,
And [b]let your mother's sons
bow down to you.
[c]Cursed *be* everyone who curses you,
And blessed *be* those who bless you!"

Esau's Lost Hope
(Heb. 12:17)

30Now it happened, as soon as Isaac
had finished blessing Jacob, and Jacob
had scarcely gone out from the presence
of Isaac his father, that Esau his brother
came in from his hunting. 31He also had
made savory food, and brought it to his father, and said to his father, "Let my father
arise and [a]eat of his son's game, that your
soul may bless me."

32And his father Isaac said to him, "Who
are you?"

So he said, "I *am* your son, your firstborn, Esau."

27:8 [a] Gen. 27:13, 43 **27:9** [a] Gen. 27:4 **27:10** [a] Gen. 27:4; 48:16 **27:11** [a] Gen. 25:25 **27:12** [a] Gen. 27:21, 22 [b] Gen. 9:25; Deut. 27:18 **27:13** [a] Gen. 43:9; 1 Sam. 25:24; 2 Sam. 14:9; Matt. 27:25 **27:14** [a] Prov. 23:3; Luke 21:34 **27:15** [a] Gen. 27:27 **27:19** [a] Gen. 27:4 **27:21** [a] Gen. 27:12 **27:23** [a] Gen. 27:16 **27:25** [a] Gen. 27:4, 10, 19, 31 **27:27** [a] Gen. 29:13 [b] Song 4:11; Hos. 14:6 **27:28** [a] Heb. 11:20 [b] Gen. 27:39; Deut. 33:13, 28; 2 Sam. 1:21; Ps. 133:3; Prov. 3:20; Mic. 5:7; Zech. 8:12 [c] Gen. 45:18; Num. 18:12 [d] Deut. 7:13; 33:28 **27:29** [a] Gen. 9:25; 25:23; Is. 45:14; 49:7; 60:12, 14 [b] Gen. 37:7, 10; 49:8 [c] Gen. 12:2, 3; Zeph. 2:8, 9 **27:31** [a] Gen. 27:4

33 Then Isaac trembled exceedingly, and
said, "Who? Where *is* the one who hunted
game and brought *it* to me? I ate all *of*
it before you came, and I have blessed
him—[a]*and* indeed he shall be blessed."
34 When Esau heard the words of his father, [a]he cried with an exceedingly great
and bitter cry, and said to his father, "Bless
me—me also, O my father!"
35 But he said, "Your brother came with
deceit and has taken away your blessing."
36 And *Esau* said, [a]"Is he not rightly
named Jacob? For he has supplanted me
these two times. He took away my birthright, and now look, he has taken away my
blessing!" And he said, "Have you not reserved a blessing for me?"
37 Then Isaac answered and said to Esau,
[a]"Indeed I have made him your master,
and all his brethren I have given to him as
servants; with [b]grain and wine I have sustained him. What shall I do now for you,
my son?"
38 And Esau said to his father, "Have
you only one blessing, my father? Bless
me—me also, O my father!" And Esau lifted
up his voice [a]and wept.
39 Then Isaac his father answered and
said to him:

"Behold, [a]your dwelling shall be
of the fatness of the earth,
And of the dew of heaven from above.
40 By your sword you shall live,
And [a]you shall serve your brother;
And [b]it shall come to pass, when
you become restless,
That you shall break his yoke
from your neck."

Jacob Escapes from Esau

41 So Esau [a]hated Jacob because of the
blessing with which his father blessed him,
and Esau said in his heart, [b]"The days of
mourning for my father are at hand; [c]then
I will kill my brother Jacob."
42 And the words of Esau her older son
were told to Rebekah. So she sent and
called Jacob her younger son, and said
to him, "Surely your brother Esau [a]com-
forts himself concerning you *by intending*
to kill you. 43 Now therefore, my son, obey
my voice: arise, flee to my brother Laban
[a]in Haran. 44 And stay with him a [a]few days,
until your brother's fury turns away, 45 until
your brother's anger turns away from you,
and he forgets what you have done to him;
then I will send and bring you from there.
Why should I be bereaved also of you both
in one day?"
46 And Rebekah said to Isaac, [a]"I am
weary of my life because of the daughters
of Heth; [b]if Jacob takes a wife of the daughters of Heth, like these *who are* the daughters of the land, what good will my life be
to me?"

28

Then Isaac called Jacob and
[a]blessed him, and charged him,
and said to him: [b]"You shall not take a wife
from the daughters of Canaan. 2 [a]Arise, go
to [b]Padan Aram, to the house of [c]Bethuel
your mother's father; and take yourself a
wife from there of the daughters of [d]Laban
your mother's brother.

3 "May [a]God Almighty bless you,
And make you [b]fruitful
and multiply you,
That you may be an
assembly of peoples;
4 And give you [a]the blessing
of Abraham,
To you and your descendants with you,
That you may inherit the land
[b]In which you are a stranger,
Which God gave to Abraham."

5 So Isaac sent Jacob away, and he went to
Padan Aram, to Laban the son of Bethuel
the Syrian, the brother of Rebekah, the
mother of Jacob and Esau.

Esau Marries Mahalath

6 Esau saw that Isaac had blessed Jacob
and sent him away to Padan Aram to take
himself a wife from there, *and that* as he

27:33 [a] Gen. 25:23; 28:3, 4; Num. 23:20; Rom. 11:29 **27:34** [a] [Heb. 12:17] **27:36** [a] Gen. 25:26, 32–34 **27:37** [a] 2 Sam. 8:14 [b] Gen. 27:28, 29 **27:38** [a] Heb. 12:17 **27:39** [a] Gen. 27:28; Heb. 11:20 **27:40** [a] Gen. 25:23; 27:29; 2 Sam. 8:14; [Obad. 18–20] [b] 2 Kin. 8:20–22 **27:41** [a] Gen. 26:27; 32:3–11; 37:4, 5, 8 [b] Gen. 50:2–4, 10 [c] Obad. 10 **27:42** [a] Ps. 64:5 **27:43** [a] Gen. 11:31; 25:20; 28:2, 5 **27:44** [a] Gen. 31:41 **27:46** [a] Gen. 26:34, 35; 28:8 [b] Gen. 24:3 **28:1** [a] Gen. 27:33 [b] Gen. 24:3 **28:2** [a] Hos. 12:12 [b] Gen. 25:20 [c] Gen. 22:23 [d] Gen. 24:29; 27:43; 29:5 **28:3** [a] Gen. 17:16; 35:11; 48:3 [b] Gen. 26:4, 24 **28:4** [a] Gen. 12:2, 3; 22:17; Gal. 3:8 [b] Gen. 17:8; 23:4; 36:7; 1 Chr. 29:15; Ps. 39:12

blessed him he gave him a charge, saying, "You shall not take a wife from the daughters of Canaan," 7and that Jacob had obeyed his father and his mother and had gone to Padan Aram. 8Also Esau saw [a]that the daughters of Canaan did not please his father Isaac. 9So Esau went to Ishmael and [a]took [b]Mahalath the daughter of Ishmael, Abraham's son, [c]the sister of Nebajoth, to be his wife in addition to the wives he had.

Jacob's Vow at Bethel

10Now Jacob [a]went out from Beersheba and went toward [b]Haran. 11So he came to a certain place and stayed there all night, because the sun had set. And he took one of the stones of that place and put it at his head, and he lay down in that place to sleep. 12Then he [a]dreamed, and behold, a ladder *was* set up on the earth, and its top reached to heaven; and there [b]the angels of God were ascending and descending on it.

13[a]And behold, the LORD stood above it and said: [b]"I *am* the LORD God of Abraham your father and the God of Isaac; [c]the land on which you lie I will give to you and your descendants. 14Also your [a]descendants shall be as the dust of the earth; you shall spread abroad [b]to the west and the east, to the north and the south; and in you and [c]in your seed all the families of the earth shall be blessed. 15Behold, [a]I *am* with you and will [b]keep you wherever you go, and will [c]bring you back to this land; for [d]I will not leave you [e]until I have done what I have spoken to you."

16Then Jacob awoke from his sleep and said, "Surely the LORD is in [a]this place, and I did not know *it*." 17And he was afraid and said, "How awesome *is* this place! This *is* none other than the house of God, and this *is* the gate of heaven!"

18Then Jacob rose early in the morning, and took the stone that he had put at his head, [a]set it up as a pillar, [b]and poured oil on top of it. 19And he called the name of [a]that place Bethel;[1] but the name of that city had been Luz previously. 20[a]Then Jacob made a vow, saying, "If [b]God will be with me, and keep me in this way that I am going, and give me [c]bread to eat and clothing to put on, 21so that [a]I come back to my father's house in peace, [b]then the LORD shall be my God. 22And this stone which I have set as a pillar [a]shall be God's house, [b]and of all that You give me I will surely give a tenth to You."

Jacob Meets Rachel

29 So Jacob went on his journey [a]and came to the land of the people of the East. 2And he looked, and saw a [a]well in the field; and behold, there *were* three flocks of sheep lying by it; for out of that well they watered the flocks. A large stone *was* on the well's mouth. 3Now all the flocks would be gathered there; and they would roll the stone from the well's mouth, water the sheep, and put the stone back in its place on the well's mouth.

4And Jacob said to them, "My brethren, where *are* you from?"

And they said, "We *are* from [a]Haran."

5Then he said to them, "Do you know [a]Laban the son of Nahor?"

And they said, "We know him."

6So he said to them, [a]"Is he well?"

And they said, "*He is* well. And look, his daughter Rachel [b]is coming with the sheep."

7Then he said, "Look, *it is* still high day; *it is* not time for the cattle to be gathered together. Water the sheep, and go and feed *them*."

8But they said, "We cannot until all the flocks are gathered together, and they have rolled the stone from the well's mouth; then we water the sheep."

9Now while he was still speaking with them, [a]Rachel came with her father's sheep, for she was a shepherdess. 10And it came to pass, when Jacob saw Rachel the daughter

---

28:8 [a] Gen. 24:3; 26:34, 35; 27:46 **28:9** [a] Gen. 26:34, 35 [b] Gen. 36:2, 3 [c] Gen. 25:13 **28:10** [a] Gen. 26:23; 46:1; Hos. 12:12 [b] Gen. 12:4, 5; 27:43; 29:4; 2 Kin. 19:12; Acts 7:2 **28:12** [a] Gen. 31:10; 41:1; Num. 12:6 [b] John 1:51; Heb. 1:4, 14 **28:13** [a] Gen. 35:1; 48:3; Amos 7:7 [b] Gen. 26:24 [c] Gen. 13:15, 17; 26:3; 35:12 **28:14** [a] Gen. 13:16; 22:17 [b] Gen. 13:14, 15; Deut. 12:20 [c] Gen. 12:3; 18:18; 22:18; 26:4; Matt. 1:2; Luke 3:34; Gal. 3:8 **28:15** [a] Gen. 26:3, 24; 31:3 [b] Gen. 48:16; Num. 6:24; Ps. 121:5, 7, 8 [c] Gen. 35:6; 48:21; Deut. 30:3 [d] Lev. 26:44; Deut. 7:9; 31:6, 8; Josh. 1:5; 1 Kin. 8:57; Heb. 13:5 [e] Num. 23:19 **28:16** [a] Ex. 3:5; Josh. 5:15; Ps. 139:7–12 **28:18** [a] Gen. 31:13, 45 [b] Lev. 8:10–12 **28:19** [a] Judg. 1:23, 26 [1] Literally *House of God* **28:20** [a] Gen. 31:13; Judg. 11:30; 2 Sam. 15:8 [b] Gen. 28:15 [c] 1 Tim. 6:8 **28:21** [a] Judg. 11:31; 2 Sam. 19:24, 30 [b] Deut. 26:17; 2 Sam. 15:8 **28:22** [a] Gen. 35:7, 14 [b] Gen. 14:20; [Lev. 27:30]; Deut. 14:22 **29:1** [a] Gen. 25:6; Num. 23:7; Judg. 6:3, 33; Hos. 12:12 **29:2** [a] Gen. 24:10, 11; Ex. 2:15, 16 **29:4** [a] Gen. 11:31; 28:10 **29:5** [a] Gen. 24:24, 29; 28:2 **29:6** [a] Gen. 43:27 [b] Gen. 24:11; Ex. 2:16, 17 **29:9** [a] Ex. 2:16

of Laban his mother's brother, and the
sheep of Laban his mother's brother, that
Jacob went near and [a]rolled the stone from
the well's mouth, and watered the flock of
Laban his mother's brother. 11Then Jacob
[a]kissed Rachel, and lifted up his voice and
wept. 12And Jacob told Rachel that he *was*
[a]her father's relative and that he *was* Rebekah's son. [b]So she ran and told her father.
13Then it came to pass, when Laban
heard the report about Jacob his sister's
son, that [a]he ran to meet him, and embraced him and kissed him, and brought
him to his house. So he told Laban all these
things. 14And Laban said to him, [a]"Surely
you *are* my bone and my flesh." And he
stayed with him for a month.

Jacob Marries Leah and Rachel

15Then Laban said to Jacob, "Because
you *are* my relative, should you therefore serve me for nothing? Tell me, [a]what
should your wages *be?*" 16Now Laban had
two daughters: the name of the elder *was*
Leah, and the name of the younger *was* Rachel. 17Leah's eyes *were* delicate, but Rachel
was [a]beautiful of form and appearance.
18Now Jacob loved Rachel; so he said, [a]"I
will serve you seven years for Rachel your
younger daughter."
19And Laban said, "*It is* better that I give
her to you than that I should give her to
another man. Stay with me." 20So Jacob
[a]served seven years for Rachel, and they
seemed *only* a few days to him because of
the love he had for her.
21Then Jacob said to Laban, "Give *me* my
wife, for my days are fulfilled, that I may [a]go
in to her." 22And Laban gathered together
all the men of the place and [a]made a feast.
23Now it came to pass in the evening, that
he took Leah his daughter and brought her
to Jacob; and he went in to her. 24And Laban gave his maid [a]Zilpah to his daughter
Leah *as* a maid. 25So it came to pass in the
morning, that behold, it *was* Leah. And he
said to Laban, "What is this you have done
to me? Was it not for Rachel that I served
you? Why then have you [a]deceived me?"
26And Laban said, "It must not be done
so in our country, to give the younger before the firstborn. 27[a]Fulfill her week, and
we will give you this one also for the service which you will serve with me still another seven years."
28Then Jacob did so and fulfilled her
week. So he gave him his daughter Rachel
as wife also. 29And Laban gave his maid
[a]Bilhah to his daughter Rachel as a maid.
30Then *Jacob* also went in to Rachel, and
he also [a]loved Rachel more than Leah. And
he served with Laban [b]still another seven
years.

The Children of Jacob

31When the LORD [a]saw that Leah *was* unloved, He [b]opened her womb; but Rachel
was barren. 32So Leah conceived and bore
a son, and she called his name Reuben;[1] for
she said, "The LORD has surely [a]looked on
my affliction. Now therefore, my husband
will love me." 33Then she conceived again
and bore a son, and said, "Because the
LORD has heard that I *am* unloved, He has
therefore given me this *son* also." And she
called his name Simeon.[1] 34She conceived
again and bore a son, and said, "Now this
time my husband will become attached to
me, because I have borne him three sons."
Therefore his name was called Levi.[1] 35And
she conceived again and bore a son, and
said, "Now I will praise the LORD." Therefore she called his name [a]Judah.[1] Then she
stopped bearing.

30 Now when Rachel saw that [a]she bore
Jacob no children, Rachel [b]envied
her sister, and said to Jacob, "Give me children, [c]or else I die!"
2And Jacob's anger was aroused against
Rachel, and he said, [a]"*Am* I in the place of
God, who has withheld from you the fruit
of the womb?"
3So she said, "Here is [a]my maid Bilhah;
go in to her, [b]and she will bear *a child* on

29:10 [a] Ex. 2:17 29:11 [a] Gen. 33:4; 45:14, 15 29:12 [a] Gen. 13:8; 14:14, 16; 28:5 [b] Gen. 24:28 29:13 [a] Gen. 24:29–31; Luke 15:20 29:14 [a] Gen. 2:23; 37:27; Judg. 9:2; 2 Sam. 5:1; 19:12, 13 29:15 [a] Gen. 30:28; 31:41 29:17 [a] Gen. 12:11, 14; 26:7 29:18 [a] Gen. 31:41; 2 Sam. 3:14; Hos. 12:12 29:20 [a] Gen. 30:26; Hos. 12:12 29:21 [a] Judg. 15:1 29:22 [a] Judg. 14:10; John 2:1, 2 29:24 [a] Gen. 30:9, 10 29:25 [a] Gen. 27:35; 31:7; 1 Sam. 28:12 29:27 [a] Gen. 31:41; Judg. 14:2 29:29 [a] Gen. 30:3–5 29:30 [a] Gen. 29:17–20; Deut. 21:15–17 [b] Gen. 30:26; 31:41; Hos. 12:12 29:31 [a] Ps. 127:3 [b] Gen. 30:1 29:32 [a] Gen. 16:11; 31:42; Ex. 3:7; 4:31; Deut. 26:7; Ps. 25:18 [1] Literally *See, a Son* 29:33 [1] Literally *Heard* 29:34 [1] Literally *Attached* 29:35 [a] Gen. 49:8; Matt. 1:2 [1] Literally *Praise* 30:1 [a] Gen. 16:1, 2; 29:31 [b] Gen. 37:11 [c] 1 Sam. 1:5, 6; [Job 5:2] 30:2 [a] Gen. 16:2; 1 Sam. 1:5 30:3 [a] Gen. 16:2 [b] Gen. 50:23; Job 3:12

my knees, [c]that I also may have children
by her." 4Then she gave him Bilhah her
maid [a]as wife, and Jacob went in to her.
5And Bilhah conceived and bore Jacob a
son. 6Then Rachel said, "God has [a]judged
my case; and He has also heard my voice
and given me a son." Therefore she called
his name Dan.[1] 7And Rachel's maid Bilhah
conceived again and bore Jacob a second
son. 8Then Rachel said, "With great wres-
tlings I have wrestled with my sister, *and*
indeed I have prevailed." So she called his
name Naphtali.[1]

9When Leah saw that she had stopped
bearing, she took Zilpah her maid and [a]gave
her to Jacob as wife. 10And Leah's maid Zilpah bore Jacob a son. 11Then Leah said, "A
troop comes!"[1] So she called his name Gad.[2]
12And Leah's maid Zilpah bore Jacob a second son. 13Then Leah said, "I am happy, for
the daughters [a]will call me blessed." So she
called his name Asher.[1]

14Now Reuben went in the days of wheat
harvest and found mandrakes in the field,
and brought them to his mother Leah. Then
Rachel said to Leah, [a]"Please give me *some*
of your son's mandrakes."

15But she said to her, [a]"*Is it* a small matter that you have taken away my husband?
Would you take away my son's mandrakes
also?"

And Rachel said, "Therefore he will lie
with you tonight for your son's mandrakes."

16When Jacob came out of the field in the
evening, Leah went out to meet him and
said, "You must come in to me, for I have
surely hired you with my son's mandrakes."
And he lay with her that night.

17And God listened to Leah, and she conceived and bore Jacob a fifth son. 18Leah
said, "God has given me my wages, because
I have given my maid to my husband." So
she called his name Issachar.[1] 19Then Leah
conceived again and bore Jacob a sixth
son. 20And Leah said, "God has endowed
me *with* a good endowment; now my husband will dwell with me, because I have
borne him six sons." So she called his name
Zebulun.[1] 21Afterward she bore a [a]daughter,
and called her name Dinah.

22Then God [a]remembered Rachel, and
God listened to her and [b]opened her womb.
23And she conceived and bore a son, and
said, "God has taken away [a]my reproach."
24So she called his name Joseph,[1] and said,
[a]"The LORD shall add to me another son."

Jacob's Agreement with Laban

25And it came to pass, when Rachel had
borne Joseph, that Jacob said to Laban,
[a]"Send me away, that I may go to [b]my own
place and to my country. 26Give *me* my
wives and my children [a]for whom I have
served you, and let me go; for you know my
service which I have done for you."

27And Laban said to him, "Please *stay,* if
I have found favor in your eyes, *for* [a]I have
learned by experience that the LORD has
blessed me for your sake." 28Then he said,
[a]"Name me your wages, and I will give *it.*"

29So *Jacob* said to him, [a]"You know how
I have served you and how your livestock
has been with me. 30For what you had before I *came was* little, and it has increased
to a great amount; the LORD has blessed
you since my coming. And now, when shall
I also [a]provide for my own house?"

31So he said, "What shall I give you?"

And Jacob said, "You shall not give me
anything. If you will do this thing for me,
I will again feed and keep your flocks:
32Let me pass through all your flock today, removing from there all the speckled and spotted sheep, and all the brown
ones among the lambs, and the spotted
and speckled among the goats; and [a]*these*
shall be my wages. 33So my [a]righteousness
will answer for me in time to come, when
the subject of my wages comes before you:
every one that *is* not speckled and spotted among the goats, and brown among
the lambs, will be considered stolen, if *it*
is with me."

34And Laban said, "Oh, that it were according to your word!" 35So he removed
that day the male goats that were [a]speckled

30:3 [c] Gen. 16:2, 3 30:4 [a] Gen. 16:3, 4 30:6 [a] Gen. 18:25; Ps. 35:24; 43:1; Lam. 3:59 [1] Literally *Judge* 30:8 [1] Literally *My Wrestling* 30:9 [a] Gen. 30:4 30:11 [1] Following Qere, Syriac, and Targum; Kethib, Septuagint, and Vulgate read *in fortune.* [2] Literally *Troop* or *Fortune* 30:13 [a] Prov. 31:28; Luke 1:48 [1] Literally *Happy* 30:14 [a] Gen. 25:30 30:15 [a] [Num. 16:9, 13] 30:18 [1] Literally *Wages* 30:20 [1] Literally *Dwelling* 30:21 [a] Gen. 34:1 30:22 [a] Gen. 19:29; 1 Sam. 1:19, 20 [b] Gen. 29:31 30:23 [a] 1 Sam. 1:6; Is. 4:1; Luke 1:25 30:24 [a] Gen. 35:16–18 [1] Literally *He Will Add* 30:25 [a] Gen. 24:54, 56 [b] Gen. 18:33 30:26 [a] Gen. 29:18–20, 27, 30; Hos. 12:12 30:27 [a] Gen. 26:24; 39:3; Is. 61:9 30:28 [a] Gen. 29:15; 31:7, 41 30:29 [a] Gen. 31:6, 38–40; Matt. 24:45; Titus 2:10 30:30 [a] [1 Tim. 5:8] 30:32 [a] Gen. 31:8 30:33 [a] Ps. 37:6 30:35 [a] Gen. 31:9–12

and spotted, all the female goats that were
speckled and spotted, every one that had
some white in it, and all the brown ones
among the lambs, and gave *them* into the
hand of his sons. 36Then he put three days'
journey between himself and Jacob, and Jacob fed the rest of Laban's flocks.

37Now [a]Jacob took for himself rods of
green poplar and of the almond and chestnut trees, peeled white strips in them, and
exposed the white which *was* in the rods.
38And the rods which he had peeled, he
set before the flocks in the gutters, in the
watering troughs where the flocks came
to drink, so that they should conceive
when they came to drink. 39So the flocks
conceived before the rods, and the flocks
brought forth streaked, speckled, and spotted. 40Then Jacob separated the lambs, and
made the flocks face toward the streaked
and all the brown in the flock of Laban; but
he put his own flocks by themselves and did
not put them with Laban's flock.

41And it came to pass, whenever the
stronger livestock conceived, that Jacob
placed the rods before the eyes of the livestock in the gutters, that they might conceive among the rods. 42But when the flocks
were feeble, he did not put *them* in; so the
feebler were Laban's and the stronger Jacob's. 43Thus the man [a]became exceedingly
prosperous, and [b]had large flocks, female
and male servants, and camels and donkeys.

Jacob Flees from Laban

31 Now *Jacob* heard the words of Laban's sons, saying, "Jacob has taken
away all that was our father's, and from
what was our father's he has acquired all
this [a]wealth." 2And Jacob saw the [a]counte-
nance of Laban, and indeed it *was* not [b]*favorable* toward him as before. 3Then the
LORD said to Jacob, [a]"Return to the land of
your fathers and to your family, and I will
[b]be with you."

4So Jacob sent and called Rachel and
Leah to the field, to his flock, 5and said to
them, [a]"I see your father's countenance,
that it *is* not *favorable* toward me as before;
but the God of my father [b]has been with me.
6And [a]you know that with all my might I
have served your father. 7Yet your father
has deceived me and [a]changed my wages
[b]ten times, but God [c]did not allow him to
hurt me. 8If he said thus: [a]'The speckled
shall be your wages,' then all the flocks bore
speckled. And if he said thus: 'The streaked
shall be your wages,' then all the flocks bore
streaked. 9So God has [a]taken away the livestock of your father and given *them* to me.

10"And it happened, at the time when the
flocks conceived, that I lifted my eyes and
saw in a dream, and behold, the rams which
leaped upon the flocks *were* streaked,
speckled, and gray-spotted. 11Then [a]the
Angel of God spoke to me in a dream, saying, 'Jacob.' And I said, 'Here I am.' 12And
He said, 'Lift your eyes now and see, all the
rams which leap on the flocks *are* streaked,
speckled, and gray-spotted; for [a]I have seen
all that Laban is doing to you. 13I *am* the
God of Bethel, [a]where you anointed the pillar *and* where you made a vow to Me. Now
[b]arise, get out of this land, and return to
the land of your family.'"

14Then Rachel and Leah answered and
said to him, [a]"Is there still any portion or
inheritance for us in our father's house?
15Are we not considered strangers by him?
For [a]he has sold us, and also completely
consumed our money. 16For all these riches
which God has taken from our father are
really ours and our children's; now then,
whatever God has said to you, do it."

17Then Jacob rose and set his sons and
his wives on camels. 18And he carried away
all his livestock and all his possessions
which he had gained, his acquired livestock
which he had gained in Padan Aram, to go
to his father Isaac in the land of [a]Canaan.
19Now Laban had gone to shear his sheep,
and Rachel had stolen the [a]household idols
that were her father's. 20And Jacob stole
away, unknown to Laban the Syrian, in that
he did not tell him that he intended to flee.

30:37 [a] Gen. 31:9–12 30:43 [a] Gen. 12:16; 30:30 [b] Gen. 13:2; 24:35; 26:13, 14 31:1 [a] Ps. 49:16 31:2 [a] Gen. 4:5 [b] Deut. 28:54 31:3 [a] Gen. 28:15, 20, 21; 32:9 [b] Gen. 46:4 31:5 [a] Gen. 31:2, 3 [b] Gen. 21:22; 28:13, 15; 31:29, 42, 53; Is. 41:10; Heb. 13:5 31:6 [a] Gen. 30:29; 31:38–41 31:7 [a] Gen. 29:25; 31:41 [b] Num. 14:22; Neh. 4:12; Job 19:3; Zech. 8:23 [c] Gen. 15:1; 20:6; 31:29; Job 1:10; Ps. 37:28; 105:14 31:8 [a] Gen. 30:32 31:9 [a] Gen. 31:1, 16 31:11 [a] Gen. 16:7–11; 22:11, 15; 31:13; 48:16 31:12 [a] Gen. 31:42; Ex. 3:7; Ps. 139:3; Eccl. 5:8 31:13 [a] Gen. 28:16–22; 35:1, 6, 15 [b] Gen. 31:3; 32:9 31:14 [a] Gen. 2:24 31:15 [a] Gen. 29:15, 20, 23, 27; Neh. 5:8 31:18 [a] Gen. 17:8; 33:18; 35:27 31:19 [a] Gen. 31:30, 34; 35:2; Judg. 17:5; 1 Sam. 19:13; Hos. 3:4

21 So he fled with all that he had. He arose
and crossed the river, and [a]headed toward
the mountains of Gilead.

Laban Pursues Jacob

22 And Laban was told on the third day
that Jacob had fled. 23 Then he took [a]his
brethren with him and pursued him for
seven days' journey, and he overtook him
in the mountains of Gilead. 24 But God [a]had
come to Laban the Syrian in a dream by
night, and said to him, "Be careful that you
[b]speak to Jacob neither good nor bad."

25 So Laban overtook Jacob. Now Jacob
had pitched his tent in the mountains, and
Laban with his brethren pitched in the
mountains of Gilead.

26 And Laban said to Jacob: "What have
you done, that you have stolen away unknown to me, and [a]carried away my daughters like captives *taken* with the sword?
27 Why did you flee away secretly, and steal
away from me, and not tell me; for I might
have sent you away with joy and songs, with
timbrel and harp? 28 And you did not allow me [a]to kiss my sons and my daughters.
Now [b]you have done foolishly in *so* doing.
29 It is in my power to do you harm, but
the [a]God of your father spoke to me [b]last
night, saying, 'Be careful that you speak
to Jacob neither good nor bad.' 30 And now
you have surely gone because you greatly
long for your father's house, *but* why did
you [a]steal my gods?"

31 Then Jacob answered and said to Laban, "Because I was [a]afraid, for I said, 'Perhaps you would take your daughters from
me by force.' 32 With whomever you find
your gods, [a]do not let him live. In the presence of our brethren, identify what I have
of yours and take *it* with you." For Jacob
did not know that Rachel had stolen them.

33 And Laban went into Jacob's tent, into
Leah's tent, and into the two maids' tents,
but he did not find *them.* Then he went
out of Leah's tent and entered Rachel's
tent. 34 Now Rachel had taken the household idols, put them in the camel's saddle,
and sat on them. And Laban searched all
about the tent but did not find *them.* 35 And
she said to her father, "Let it not displease
my lord that I cannot [a]rise before you, for
the manner of women *is* with me." And he
searched but did not find the household
idols.

36 Then Jacob was angry and rebuked Laban, and Jacob answered and said to Laban:
"What *is* my trespass? What *is* my sin, that
you have so hotly pursued me? 37 Although
you have searched all my things, what part
of your household things have you found?
Set *it* here before my brethren and your
brethren, that they may judge between us
both! 38 These twenty years I *have been* with
you; your ewes and your female goats have
not miscarried their young, and I have not
eaten the rams of your flock. 39 [a]That which
was torn *by beasts* I did not bring to you;
I bore the loss of it. [b]You required it from
my hand, *whether* stolen by day or stolen by
night. 40 *There* I was! In the day the drought
consumed me, and the frost by night, and
my sleep departed from my eyes. 41 Thus
I have been in your house twenty years;
I [a]served you fourteen years for your two
daughters, and six years for your flock, and
[b]you have changed my wages ten times.
42 [a]Unless the God of my father, the God of
Abraham and [b]the Fear of Isaac, had been
with me, surely now you would have sent
me away empty-handed. [c]God has seen my
affliction and the labor of my hands, and
[d]rebuked *you* last night."

Laban's Covenant with Jacob

43 And Laban answered and said to Jacob, "*These* daughters *are* my daughters,
and *these* children *are* my children, and
this flock *is* my flock; all that you see *is*
mine. But what can I do this day to these
my daughters or to their children whom
they have borne? 44 Now therefore, come,
[a]let us make a covenant, [b]you and I, and let
it be a witness between you and me."

45 So Jacob [a]took a stone and set it up *as*
a pillar. 46 Then Jacob said to his brethren,

31:21 [a] Gen. 46:28; 2 Kin. 12:17; Luke 9:51, 53 31:23 [a] Gen. 13:8 31:24 [a] Gen. 20:3; 31:29; 46:2–4; Job 33:15; Matt. 1:20 [b] Gen. 24:50; 31:7, 29 31:26 [a] 1 Sam. 30:2 31:28 [a] Gen. 31:55; Ruth 1:9, 14; 1 Kin. 19:20; Acts 20:37 [b] 1 Sam. 13:13 31:29 [a] Gen. 28:13; 31:5, 24, 42, 53 [b] Gen. 31:24 31:30 [a] Gen. 31:19; Josh. 24:2; Judg. 17:5; 18:24 31:31 [a] Gen. 26:7; 32:7, 11 31:32 [a] Gen. 44:9 31:35 [a] Ex. 20:12; Lev. 19:32 31:39 [a] Ex. 22:10 [b] Ex. 22:10–13 31:41 [a] Gen. 29:20, 27–30 [b] Gen. 31:7 31:42 [a] Gen. 31:5, 29, 53; Ps. 124:1, 2 [b] Gen. 31:53; Is. 8:13 [c] Gen. 29:32; Ex. 3:7 [d] Gen. 31:24, 29; 1 Chr. 12:17 31:44 [a] Gen. 21:27, 32; 26:28 [b] Josh. 24:27 31:45 [a] Gen. 28:18; 35:14; Josh. 24:26, 27

"Gather stones." And they took stones and
made a heap, and they ate there on the
heap. 47Laban called it Jegar Sahadutha,[1]
but Jacob called it Galeed.[2] 48And Laban
said, [a]"This heap *is* a witness between you
and me this day." Therefore its name was
called Galeed, 49also [a]Mizpah,[1] because he
said, "May the LORD watch between you and
me when we are absent one from another.
50If you afflict my daughters, or if you take
other wives besides my daughters, *although*
no man *is* with us—see, God *is* witness between you and me!"

51Then Laban said to Jacob, "Here is
this heap and here is *this* pillar, which I
have placed between you and me. 52This
heap *is* a witness, and *this* pillar *is* a witness, that I will not pass beyond this heap
to you, and you will not pass beyond this
heap and this pillar to me, for harm. 53The
God of Abraham, the God of Nahor, and
the God of their father [a]judge between us."
And Jacob [b]swore by [c]the Fear of his father
Isaac. 54Then Jacob offered a sacrifice on
the mountain, and called his brethren to
eat bread. And they ate bread and stayed all
night on the mountain. 55And early in the
morning Laban arose, and [a]kissed his sons
and daughters and [b]blessed them. Then Laban departed and [c]returned to his place.

Esau Comes to Meet Jacob

32 So Jacob went on his way, and [a]the
angels of God met him. 2When Ja-
cob saw them, he said, "This *is* God's [a]camp."
And he called the name of that place Mahanaim.[1]

3Then Jacob sent messengers before
him to Esau his brother [a]in the land of Seir,
[b]the country of Edom. 4And he commanded
them, saying, [a]"Speak thus to my lord Esau,
'Thus your servant Jacob says: "I have dwelt
with Laban and stayed there until now. 5[a]I
have oxen, donkeys, flocks, and male and
female servants; and I have sent to tell my
lord, that [b]I may find favor in your sight." ' "

6Then the messengers returned to Jacob, saying, "We came to your brother Esau,
and [a]he also is coming to meet you, and
four hundred men *are* with him." 7So Jacob
was greatly afraid and [a]distressed; and he
divided the people that *were* with him, and
the flocks and herds and camels, into two
companies. 8And he said, "If Esau comes
to the one company and attacks it, then the
other company which is left will escape."

9[a]Then Jacob said, [b]"O God of my father Abraham and God of my father Isaac,
the LORD [c]who said to me, 'Return to your
country and to your family, and I will deal
well with you': 10I am not worthy of the least
of all the [a]mercies and of all the truth which
You have shown Your servant; for I crossed
over this Jordan with [b]my staff, and now I
have become two companies. 11[a]Deliver me,
I pray, from the hand of my brother, from
the hand of Esau; for I fear him, lest he
come and attack me *and* [b]the mother with
the children. 12For [a]You said, 'I will surely
treat you well, and make your descendants
as the [b]sand of the sea, which cannot be
numbered for multitude.' "

13So he lodged there that same night,
and took what came to his hand as [a]a present for Esau his brother: 14two hundred
female goats and twenty male goats, two
hundred ewes and twenty rams, 15thirty
milk camels with their colts, forty cows and
ten bulls, twenty female donkeys and ten
foals. 16Then he delivered *them* to the hand
of his servants, every drove by itself, and
said to his servants, "Pass over before me,
and put some distance between successive
droves." 17And he commanded the first one,
saying, "When Esau my brother meets you
and asks you, saying, 'To whom do you belong, and where are you going? Whose *are*
these in front of you?' 18then you shall say,
'They *are* your servant Jacob's. It *is* a present sent to my lord Esau; and behold, he
also *is* behind us.' " 19So he commanded the
second, the third, and all who followed the
droves, saying, "In this manner you shall
speak to Esau when you find him; 20and
also say, 'Behold, your servant Jacob *is* behind us.' " For he said, "I will [a]appease him

---

31:47 [1] Literally, in Aramaic, *Heap of Witness* [2] Literally, in Hebrew, *Heap of Witness* 31:48 [a] Josh. 24:27 31:49 [a] Judg. 10:17; 11:29; 1 Sam. 7:5, 6 [1] Literally *Watch* 31:53 [a] Gen. 16:5 [b] Gen. 21:23 [c] Gen. 31:42 31:55 [a] Gen. 29:11, 13; 31:28, 43 [b] Gen. 28:1 [c] Gen. 18:33; 30:25; Num. 24:25 32:1 [a] Num. 22:31; 2 Kin. 6:16, 17; [Ps. 34:7; 91:1; Heb. 1:14] 32:2 [a] Josh. 5:14; Ps. 103:21; 148:2; Luke 2:13 [1] Literally *Double Camp* 32:3 [a] Gen. 14:6; 33:14, 16 [b] Gen. 25:30; 36:6–9; Deut. 2:5; Josh. 24:4 32:4 [a] Prov. 15:1 32:5 [a] Gen. 30:43 [b] Gen. 33:8, 15 32:6 [a] Gen. 33:1 32:7 [a] Gen. 32:11; 35:3 32:9 [a] [Ps. 50:15] [b] Gen. 28:13; 31:42 [c] Gen. 31:3, 13 32:10 [a] Gen. 24:27 [b] Job 8:7 32:11 [a] Ps. 59:1, 2 [b] Hos. 10:14 32:12 [a] Gen. 28:13–15 [b] Gen. 22:17 32:13 [a] Gen. 43:11 32:20 [a] [Prov. 21:14]

with the present that goes before me, and
afterward I will see his face; perhaps he
will accept me." 21So the present went on
over before him, but he himself lodged that
night in the camp.

Wrestling with God

22And he arose that night and took his
two wives, his two female servants, and his
eleven sons, [a]and crossed over the ford of
Jabbok. 23He took them, sent them over the
brook, and sent over what he had. 24Then
Jacob was left alone; and [a]a Man wrestled
with him until the breaking of day. 25Now
when He saw that He did not prevail against
him, He touched the socket of his hip; and
[a]the socket of Jacob's hip was out of joint as
He wrestled with him. 26And [a]He said, "Let
Me go, for the day breaks."

But he said, [b]"I will not let You go unless
You bless me!"

27So He said to him, "What *is* your
name?"

He said, "Jacob."

28And He said, [a]"Your name shall no longer be called Jacob, but Israel;[1] for you have
[b]struggled with God and [c]with men, and
have prevailed."

29Then Jacob asked, saying, "Tell *me*
Your name, I pray."

And He said, [a]"Why *is* it *that* you ask
about My name?" And He [b]blessed him
there.

30So Jacob called the name of the place
Peniel:[1] "For [a]I have seen God face to face,
and my life is preserved." 31Just as he
crossed over Penuel[1] the sun rose on him,
and he limped on his hip. 32Therefore to
this day the children of Israel do not eat
the muscle that shrank, which *is* on the
hip socket, because He touched the socket
of Jacob's hip in the muscle that shrank.

Jacob and Esau Meet

33 Now Jacob lifted his eyes and
looked, and there, [a]Esau was coming, and with him were four hundred men.
So he divided the children among Leah,
Rachel, and the two maidservants. 2And he
put the maidservants and their children in
front, Leah and her children behind, and
Rachel and Joseph last. 3Then he crossed
over before them and [a]bowed himself to
the ground seven times, until he came near
to his brother.

4[a]But Esau ran to meet him, and embraced him, [b]and fell on his neck and kissed
him, and they wept. 5And he lifted his eyes
and saw the women and children, and said,
"Who *are* these with you?"

So he said, "The children [a]whom God
has graciously given your servant." 6Then
the maidservants came near, they and
their children, and bowed down. 7And Leah
also came near with her children, and they
bowed down. Afterward Joseph and Rachel
came near, and they bowed down.

8Then Esau said, "What *do* you *mean by*
[a]all this company which I met?"

And he said, "*These are* [b]to find favor in
the sight of my lord."

9But Esau said, "I have enough, my
brother; keep what you have for yourself."

10And Jacob said, "No, please, if I have
now found favor in your sight, then receive
my present from my hand, inasmuch as I
[a]have seen your face as though I had seen
the face of God, and you were pleased
with me. 11Please, take [a]my blessing that
is brought to you, because God has dealt
[b]graciously with me, and because I have
enough." [c]So he urged him, and he took *it*.

12Then Esau said, "Let us take our journey; let us go, and I will go before you."

13But Jacob said to him, "My lord knows
that the children *are* weak, and the flocks
and herds which are nursing *are* with me.
And if the men should drive them hard one
day, all the flock will die. 14Please let my lord
go on ahead before his servant. I will lead
on slowly at a pace which the livestock that
go before me, and the children, are able to
endure, until I come to my lord [a]in Seir."

15And Esau said, "Now let me leave with
you *some* of the people who *are* with me."

But he said, "What need is there? [a]Let

32:22 [a] Num. 21:24; Deut. 3:16; Josh. 12:2 **32:24** [a] Josh. 5:13–15; Hos. 12:2–4 **32:25** [a] Matt. 26:41; 2 Cor. 12:7 **32:26** [a] Luke 24:28 [b] Hos. 12:4 **32:28** [a] Gen. 35:10; 1 Kin. 18:31; 2 Kin. 17:34 [b] Hos. 12:3, 4 [c] Gen. 25:31; 27:33 [1] Literally *Prince with God* **32:29** [a] Judg. 13:17, 18 [b] Gen. 35:9 **32:30** [a] Gen. 16:13; Ex. 24:10, 11; 33:20; Num. 12:8; Deut. 5:24; Judg. 6:22; Is. 6:5; [Matt. 5:8; 1 Cor. 13:12] [1] Literally *Face of God* **32:31** [1] Same as *Peniel*, verse 30 **33:1** [a] Gen. 32:6 **33:3** [a] Gen. 18:2; 42:6 **33:4** [a] Gen. 32:28 [b] Gen. 45:14, 15 **33:5** [a] Gen. 48:9; [Ps. 127:3]; Is. 8:18 **33:8** [a] Gen. 32:13–16 [b] Gen. 32:5 **33:10** [a] Gen. 43:3; 2 Sam. 3:13; 14:24, 28, 32 **33:11** [a] Judg. 1:15; 1 Sam. 25:27; 30:26 [b] Gen. 30:43; Ex. 33:19 [c] 2 Kin. 5:23 **33:14** [a] Gen. 32:3; 36:8 **33:15** [a] Gen. 34:11; 47:25; Ruth 2:13

me find favor in the sight of my lord." 16So
Esau returned that day on his way to Seir.
17And Jacob journeyed to [a]Succoth, built
himself a house, and made booths for his
livestock. Therefore the name of the place
is called Succoth.[1]

Jacob Comes to Canaan

18Then Jacob came safely to [a]the city of
[b]Shechem, which *is* in the land of Canaan,
when he came from Padan Aram; and he
pitched his tent before the city. 19And [a]he
bought the parcel of land, where he had
pitched his tent, from the children of Hamor, Shechem's father, for one hundred
pieces of money. 20Then he erected an altar
there and called it [a]El Elohe Israel.[1]

The Dinah Incident

34 Now [a]Dinah the daughter of Leah,
whom she had borne to Jacob, went
out to see the daughters of the land. 2And
when Shechem the son of Hamor the Hivite, prince of the country, saw her, he
[a]took her and lay with her, and violated
her. 3His soul was strongly attracted to Dinah the daughter of Jacob, and he loved
the young woman and spoke kindly to the
young woman. 4So Shechem [a]spoke to his
father Hamor, saying, "Get me this young
woman as a wife."

5And Jacob heard that he had defiled Dinah his daughter. Now his sons were with
his livestock in the field; so Jacob [a]held his
peace until they came. 6Then Hamor the father of Shechem went out to Jacob to speak
with him. 7And the sons of Jacob came in
from the field when they heard *it;* and the
men were grieved and very angry, because
he [a]had done a disgraceful thing in Israel by
lying with Jacob's daughter, [b]a thing which
ought not to be done. 8But Hamor spoke
with them, saying, "The soul of my son Shechem longs for your daughter. Please give
her to him as a wife. 9And make marriages
with us; give your daughters to us, and take
our daughters to yourselves. 10So you shall
dwell with us, and the land shall be before
you. Dwell and trade in it, and acquire possessions for yourselves in it."

11Then Shechem said to her father and
her brothers, "Let me find favor in your
eyes, and whatever you say to me I will give.
12Ask me ever so much [a]dowry and gift, and
I will give according to what you say to me;
but give me the young woman as a wife."

13But the sons of Jacob answered Shechem and Hamor his father, and spoke
[a]deceitfully, because he had defiled Dinah
their sister. 14And they said to them, "We
cannot do this thing, to give our sister to
one who is [a]uncircumcised, for [b]that *would*
be a reproach to us. 15But on this *condition*
we will consent to you: If you will become
as we *are,* if every male of you is circumcised, 16then we will give our daughters to
you, and we will take your daughters to us;
and we will dwell with you, and we will become one people. 17But if you will not heed
us and be circumcised, then we will take
our daughter and be gone."

18And their words pleased Hamor and
Shechem, Hamor's son. 19So the young
man did not delay to do the thing, because
he delighted in Jacob's daughter. He *was*
[a]more honorable than all the household
of his father.

20And Hamor and Shechem his son
came to the [a]gate of their city, and spoke
with the men of their city, saying: 21"These
men *are* at peace with us. Therefore let
them dwell in the land and trade in it. For
indeed the land *is* large enough for them.
Let us take their daughters to us as wives,
and let us give them our daughters. 22Only
on this *condition* will the men consent to
dwell with us, to be one people: if every
male among us is circumcised as they *are*
circumcised. 23*Will* not their livestock,
their property, and every animal of theirs
be ours? Only let us consent to them, and
they will dwell with us." 24And all who went
out of the gate of his city heeded Hamor
and Shechem his son; every male was circumcised, all who [a]went out of the gate of
his city.

33:17 [a] Josh. 13:27; Judg. 8:5; Ps. 60:6 [1] Literally *Booths* 33:18 [a] John 3:23 [b] Gen. 12:6; 35:4; Josh. 24:1; Judg. 9:1; Ps. 60:6 33:19 [a] Josh. 24:32; John 4:5 33:20 [a] Gen. 35:7 [1] Literally *God, the God of Israel* 34:1 [a] Gen. 30:21 34:2 [a] Gen. 20:2 34:4 [a] Judg. 14:2 34:5 [a] 2 Sam. 13:22 34:7 [a] Deut. 22:20–30; Josh. 7:15; Judg. 20:6 [b] Deut. 23:17; 2 Sam. 13:12 34:12 [a] Ex. 22:16, 17; Deut. 22:29 34:13 [a] Gen. 31:7; Ex. 8:29 34:14 [a] Ex. 12:48 [b] Josh. 5:2–9 34:19 [a] 1 Chr. 4:9 34:20 [a] Gen. 19:1; 23:10; Ruth 4:1, 11; 2 Sam. 15:2 34:24 [a] Gen. 23:10, 18

25Now it came to pass on the third day,
when they were in pain, that two of the
sons of Jacob, [a]Simeon and Levi, Dinah's
brothers, each took his sword and came
boldly upon the city and killed all the males.
26And they [a]killed Hamor and Shechem his
son with the edge of the sword, and took Dinah from Shechem's house, and went out.
27The sons of Jacob came upon the slain,
and plundered the city, because their sister
had been defiled. 28They took their sheep,
their oxen, and their donkeys, what *was* in
the city and what *was* in the field, 29and all
their wealth. All their little ones and their
wives they took captive; and they plundered
even all that *was* in the houses.
30Then Jacob said to Simeon and Levi,
[a]"You have [b]troubled me [c]by making me
obnoxious among the inhabitants of the
land, among the Canaanites and the Perizzites; [d]and since I *am* few in number, they
will gather themselves together against
me and kill me. I shall be destroyed, my
household and I."
31But they said, "Should he treat our sister like a harlot?"

Jacob's Return to Bethel

35 Then God said to Jacob, "Arise, go
up to [a]Bethel and dwell there; and
make an altar there to God, [b]who appeared
to you [c]when you fled from the face of Esau
your brother."
2And Jacob said to his [a]household and
to all who *were* with him, "Put away [b]the
foreign gods that *are* among you, [c]purify
yourselves, and change your garments.
3Then let us arise and go up to Bethel; and
I will make an altar there to God, [a]who answered me in the day of my distress [b]and
has been with me in the way which I have
gone." 4So they gave Jacob all the foreign
gods which *were* in their hands, and the
[a]earrings which *were* in their ears; and Jacob hid them under [b]the terebinth tree
which *was* by Shechem.
5And they journeyed, and [a]the terror
of God was upon the cities that *were* all
around them, and they did not pursue the
sons of Jacob. 6So Jacob came to [a]Luz (that
is, Bethel), which *is* in the land of Canaan,
he and all the people who *were* with him.
7And he [a]built an altar there and called the
place El Bethel,[1] because [b]there God appeared to him when he fled from the face
of his brother.
8Now [a]Deborah, Rebekah's nurse, died,
and she was buried below Bethel under the
terebinth tree. So the name of it was called
Allon Bachuth.[1]
9Then [a]God appeared to Jacob again,
when he came from Padan Aram, and
[b]blessed him. 10And God said to him, "Your
name *is* Jacob; [a]your name shall not be
called Jacob anymore, [b]but Israel shall be
your name." So He called his name Israel.
11Also God said to him: [a]"I *am* God Almighty.
[b]Be fruitful and multiply; [c]a nation and a
company of nations shall proceed from
you, and kings shall come from your body.
12The [a]land which I gave Abraham and Isaac
I give to you; and to your descendants after you I give this land." 13Then God [a]went
up from him in the place where He talked
with him. 14So Jacob [a]set up a pillar in the
place where He talked with him, a pillar of
stone; and he poured a drink offering on it,
and he poured oil on it. 15And Jacob called
the name of the place where God spoke
with him, [a]Bethel.

Death of Rachel

16Then they journeyed from Bethel. And
when there was but a little distance to go
to Ephrath, Rachel labored *in childbirth,*
and she had hard labor. 17Now it came to
pass, when she was in hard labor, that the
midwife said to her, "Do not fear; [a]you will
have this son also." 18And so it was, as her
soul was departing (for she died), that she
called his name Ben-Oni;[1] but his father
called him Benjamin.[2] 19So [a]Rachel died

34:25 [a] Gen. 29:33, 34; 42:24; 49:5–7 34:26 [a] Gen. 49:5, 6 34:30 [a] Gen. 49:6 [b] Josh. 7:25 [c] Ex. 5:21; 1 Sam. 13:4; 2 Sam. 10:6 [d] Gen. 46:26, 27; Deut. 4:27; 1 Chr. 16:19; Ps. 105:12 35:1 [a] Gen. 28:19; 31:13 [b] Gen. 28:13 [c] Gen. 27:43 35:2 [a] Gen. 18:19; Josh. 24:15 [b] Gen. 31:19, 30, 34; Josh. 24:2, 14, 23 [c] Ex. 19:10, 14; Lev. 13:6 35:3 [a] Gen. 32:7, 24; Ps. 107:6 [b] Gen. 28:15, 20; 31:3, 42 35:4 [a] Hos. 2:13 [b] Josh. 24:26; Judg. 9:6 35:5 [a] Ex. 15:16; 23:27; [Deut. 2:25; 11:25]; Josh. 2:9; 1 Sam. 14:15 35:6 [a] Gen. 28:19, 22; 48:3 35:7 [a] Gen. 33:20; 35:3; Eccl. 5:4 [b] Gen. 28:13 [1] Literally *God of the House of God* 35:8 [a] Gen. 24:59 [1] Literally *Terebinth of Weeping* 35:9 [a] Josh. 5:13; Dan. 10:5 [b] Gen. 32:29; Hos. 12:4 35:10 [a] Gen. 17:5 [b] Gen. 32:28 35:11 [a] Gen. 17:1; 28:3; 48:3, 4; Ex. 6:3 [b] Gen. 9:1, 7 [c] Gen. 17:5, 6, 16; 28:3; 48:4 35:12 [a] Gen. 12:7; 13:15; 26:3, 4; 28:13; 48:4; Ex. 32:13 35:13 [a] Gen. 17:22; 18:33 35:14 [a] Gen. 28:18, 19; 31:45 35:15 [a] Gen. 28:19 35:17 [a] Gen. 30:24; 1 Sam. 4:20 35:18 [1] Literally *Son of My Sorrow* [2] Literally *Son of the Right Hand* 35:19 [a] Gen. 48:7

and was buried on the way to [b]Ephrath (that
is, Bethlehem). 20And Jacob set a pillar on
her grave, which *is* the pillar of Rachel's
grave [a]to this day.

21Then Israel journeyed and pitched his
tent beyond [a]the tower of Eder. 22And it
happened, when Israel dwelt in that land,
that Reuben went and [a]lay with Bilhah
his father's concubine; and Israel heard
about it.

Jacob's Twelve Sons

Now the sons of Jacob were twelve: 23the
sons of Leah *were* [a]Reuben, Jacob's firstborn, and Simeon, Levi, Judah, Issachar,
and Zebulun; 24the sons of Rachel *were* Joseph and Benjamin; 25the sons of Bilhah,
Rachel's maidservant, *were* Dan and Naphtali; 26and the sons of Zilpah, Leah's maidservant, *were* Gad and Asher. These *were*
the sons of Jacob who were born to him in
Padan Aram.

Death of Isaac

27Then Jacob came to his father Isaac at
[a]Mamre, or [b]Kirjath Arba[1] (that *is,* Hebron),
where Abraham and Isaac had dwelt. 28Now
the days of Isaac were one hundred and
eighty years. 29So Isaac breathed his last
and died, and [a]was gathered to his people,
being old and full of days. And [b]his sons
Esau and Jacob buried him.

The Family of Esau
(1 Chr. 1:35–42)

36 Now this *is* the genealogy of Esau,
[a]who is Edom. 2[a]Esau took his wives
from the daughters of Canaan: Adah the
daughter of Elon the [b]Hittite; [c]Aholibamah
the daughter of Anah, the daughter of Zibeon the Hivite; 3and [a]Basemath, Ishmael's
daughter, sister of Nebajoth. 4Now [a]Adah
bore Eliphaz to Esau, and Basemath bore
Reuel. 5And Aholibamah bore Jeush, Jaalam, and Korah. These *were* the sons of Esau
who were born to him in the land of Canaan.

6Then Esau took his wives, his sons,
his daughters, and all the persons of his
household, his cattle and all his animals,
and all his goods which he had gained in
the land of Canaan, and went to a country
away from the presence of his brother Jacob. 7[a]For their possessions were too great
for them to dwell together, and [b]the land
where they were strangers could not support them because of their livestock. 8So
Esau dwelt in [a]Mount Seir. [b]Esau *is* Edom.

9And this *is* the genealogy of Esau the father of the Edomites in Mount Seir. 10These
were the names of Esau's sons: [a]Eliphaz the
son of Adah the wife of Esau, and Reuel the
son of Basemath the wife of Esau. 11And the
sons of Eliphaz were Teman, Omar, Zepho,[1]
Gatam, and Kenaz.

12Now Timna was the concubine of Eliphaz, Esau's son, and she bore [a]Amalek
to Eliphaz. These *were* the sons of Adah,
Esau's wife.

13These *were* the sons of Reuel: Nahath,
Zerah, Shammah, and Mizzah. These were
the sons of Basemath, Esau's wife.

14These were the sons of Aholibamah,
Esau's wife, the daughter of Anah, the
daughter of Zibeon. And she bore to Esau:
Jeush, Jaalam, and Korah.

The Chiefs of Edom

15These *were* the chiefs of the sons of
Esau. The sons of Eliphaz, the firstborn
son of Esau, were Chief Teman, Chief Omar,
Chief Zepho, Chief Kenaz, 16Chief Korah,[1]
Chief Gatam, *and* Chief Amalek. These *were*
the chiefs of Eliphaz in the land of Edom.
They *were* the sons of Adah.

17These *were* the sons of Reuel, Esau's
son: Chief Nahath, Chief Zerah, Chief Shammah, and Chief Mizzah. These *were* the
chiefs of Reuel in the land of Edom. These
were the sons of Basemath, Esau's wife.

18And these *were* the sons of Aholibamah, Esau's wife: Chief Jeush, Chief Jaalam, and Chief Korah. These *were* the chiefs
who descended from Aholibamah, Esau's
wife, the daughter of Anah. 19These *were*
the sons of Esau, who is Edom, and these
were their chiefs.

35:19 [b] Ruth 1:2; 4:11; Mic. 5:2; Matt. 2:6 35:20 [a] 1 Sam. 10:2 35:21 [a] Mic. 4:8 35:22 [a] Gen. 49:4; 1 Chr. 5:1 35:23 [a] Gen. 29:31–35; 30:18–20; 46:8; Ex. 1:1–4 35:27 [a] Gen. 13:18; 18:1; 23:19 [b] Josh. 14:15 [1] Literally *Town of Arba* 35:29 [a] Gen. 15:15; 25:8; 49:33 [b] Gen. 25:9; 49:31 36:1 [a] Gen. 25:30 36:2 [a] Gen. 26:34; 28:9 [b] 2 Kin. 7:6 [c] Gen. 36:25 36:3 [a] Gen. 28:9 36:4 [a] 1 Chr. 1:35 36:7 [a] Gen. 13:6, 11 [b] Gen. 17:8; 28:4; Heb. 11:9 36:8 [a] Gen. 32:3; Deut. 2:5; Josh. 24:4 [b] Gen. 36:1, 19 36:10 [a] 1 Chr. 1:35 36:11 [1] Spelled *Zephi* in 1 Chronicles 1:36 36:12 [a] Ex. 17:8–16; Num. 24:20; Deut. 25:17–19; 1 Sam. 15:2, 3 36:16 [1] Samaritan Pentateuch omits *Chief Korah.*

The Sons of Seir

20[a]These *were* the sons of Seir [b]the Horite who inhabited the land: Lotan, Shobal, Zibeon, Anah, 21Dishon, Ezer, and Dishan. These *were* the chiefs of the Horites, the sons of Seir, in the land of Edom.

22And the sons of Lotan were Hori and Hemam.[1] Lotan's sister *was* Timna.

23These *were* the sons of Shobal: Alvan,[1] Manahath, Ebal, Shepho,[2] and Onam.

24These *were* the sons of Zibeon: both Ajah and Anah. This *was the* Anah who found the water[1] in the wilderness as he pastured [a]the donkeys of his father Zibeon. 25These *were* the children of Anah: Dishon and Aholibamah the daughter of Anah.

26These *were* the sons of Dishon:[1] Hemdan,[2] Eshban, Ithran, and Cheran. 27These *were* the sons of Ezer: Bilhan, Zaavan, and Akan.[1] 28These *were* the sons of Dishan: [a]Uz and Aran.

29These *were* the chiefs of the Horites: Chief Lotan, Chief Shobal, Chief Zibeon, Chief Anah, 30Chief Dishon, Chief Ezer, and Chief Dishan. These *were* the chiefs of the Horites, according to their chiefs in the land of Seir.

The Kings of Edom

31[a]Now these *were* the kings who reigned in the land of Edom before any king reigned over the children of Israel: 32Bela the son of Beor reigned in Edom, and the name of his city *was* Dinhabah. 33And when Bela died, Jobab the son of Zerah of Bozrah reigned in his place. 34When Jobab died, Husham of the land of the Temanites reigned in his place. 35And when Husham died, Hadad the son of Bedad, who attacked Midian in the field of Moab, reigned in his place. And the name of his city *was* Avith. 36When Hadad died, Samlah of Masrekah reigned in his place. 37And when Samlah died, Saul of [a]Rehoboth-*by*-the-River reigned in his place. 38When Saul died, Baal-Hanan the son of Achbor reigned in his place. 39And when Baal-Hanan the son of Achbor died, Hadar[1] reigned in his place; and the name of his city *was* Pau.[2] His wife's name *was* Mehetabel, the daughter of Matred, the daughter of Mezahab.

The Chiefs of Esau

40And these *were* the names of the chiefs of Esau, according to their families and their places, by their names: Chief Timnah, Chief Alvah,[1] Chief Jetheth, 41Chief Aholibamah, Chief Elah, Chief Pinon, 42Chief Kenaz, Chief Teman, Chief Mibzar, 43Chief Magdiel, and Chief Iram. These *were* the chiefs of Edom, according to their dwelling places in the land of their possession. Esau *was* the father of the Edomites.

Joseph Dreams of Greatness

37 Now Jacob dwelt in the land [a]where his father was a stranger, in the land of Canaan. 2This *is* the history of Jacob.

Joseph, *being* seventeen years old, was feeding the flock with his brothers. And the lad *was* with the sons of Bilhah and the sons of Zilpah, his father's wives; and Joseph brought [a]a bad report of them to his father.

3Now Israel loved Joseph more than all his children, because he *was* [a]the son of his old age. Also he [b]made him a tunic of *many* colors. 4But when his brothers saw that their father loved him more than all his brothers, they [a]hated him and could not speak peaceably to him.

5Now Joseph had a dream, and he told *it* to his brothers; and they hated him even more. 6So he said to them, "Please hear this dream which I have dreamed: 7[a]There we were, binding sheaves in the field. Then behold, my sheaf arose and also stood upright; and indeed your sheaves stood all around and bowed down to my sheaf."

8And his brothers said to him, "Shall you indeed reign over us? Or shall you indeed have dominion over us?" So they hated him even more for his dreams and for his words.

36:20 [a] 1 Chr. 1:38–42 [b] Gen. 14:6; Deut. 2:12, 22 **36:22** [1] Spelled *Homam* in 1 Chronicles 1:39 **36:23** [1] Spelled *Alian* in 1 Chronicles 1:40 [2] Spelled *Shephi* in 1 Chronicles 1:40 **36:24** [a] Lev. 19:19 [1] Following Masoretic Text and Vulgate (*hot springs*); Septuagint reads *Jamin;* Targum reads *mighty men;* Talmud interprets as *mules.* **36:26** [1] Hebrew *Dishan* [2] Spelled *Hamran* in 1 Chronicles 1:41 **36:27** [1] Spelled *Jaakan* in 1 Chronicles 1:42 **36:28** [a] Job 1:1 **36:31** [a] Gen. 17:6, 16; 35:11; 1 Chr. 1:43 **36:37** [a] Gen. 10:11 **36:39** [1] Spelled *Hadad* in Samaritan Pentateuch, Syriac, and 1 Chronicles 1:50 [2] Spelled *Pai* in 1 Chronicles 1:50 **36:40** [1] Spelled *Aliah* in 1 Chronicles 1:51 **37:1** [a] Gen. 17:8; 23:4; 28:4; 36:7; Heb. 11:9 **37:2** [a] Gen. 35:25, 26; 1 Sam. 2:22–24 **37:3** [a] Gen. 44:20 [b] Gen. 37:23, 32; Judg. 5:30; 1 Sam. 2:19 **37:4** [a] Gen. 27:41; 49:23; 1 Sam. 17:28; John 15:18–20 **37:7** [a] Gen. 42:6, 9; 43:26; 44:14

9Then he dreamed still another dream
and told it to his brothers, and said, "Look,
I have dreamed another dream. And this
time, [a]the sun, the moon, and the eleven
stars bowed down to me."
10So he told *it* to his father and his
brothers; and his father rebuked him and
said to him, "What *is* this dream that you
have dreamed? Shall your mother and I
and [a]your brothers indeed come to bow
down to the earth before you?" 11And [a]his
brothers envied him, but his father [b]kept
the matter *in mind.*

Joseph Sold by His Brothers

12Then his brothers went to feed their father's flock in [a]Shechem. 13And Israel said
to Joseph, "Are not your brothers feeding
the flock in Shechem? Come, I will send you
to them."
So he said to him, "Here I am."
14Then he said to him, "Please go and see
if it is well with your brothers and well with
the flocks, and bring back word to me." So
he sent him out of the Valley of [a]Hebron,
and he went to Shechem.
15Now a certain man found him, and
there he was, wandering in the field. And
the man asked him, saying, "What are you
seeking?"
16So he said, "I am seeking my brothers.
[a]Please tell me where they are feeding *their
flocks.*"
17And the man said, "They have departed
from here, for I heard them say, 'Let us go to
Dothan.'" So Joseph went after his brothers
and found them in [a]Dothan.
18Now when they saw him afar off, even
before he came near them, [a]they conspired
against him to kill him. 19Then they said to
one another, "Look, this dreamer is coming! 20[a]Come therefore, let us now kill him
and cast him into some pit; and we shall
say, 'Some wild beast has devoured him.' We
shall see what will become of his dreams!"
21But [a]Reuben heard *it,* and he delivered
him out of their hands, and said, "Let us
not kill him." 22And Reuben said to them,
"Shed no blood, *but* cast him into this pit
which *is* in the wilderness, and do not lay a
hand on him"—that he might deliver him
out of their hands, and bring him back to
his father.
23So it came to pass, when Joseph had
come to his brothers, that they [a]stripped Joseph *of* his tunic, the tunic of *many* colors
that *was* on him. 24Then they took him and
cast him into a pit. And the pit *was* empty;
there was no water in it.
25[a]And they sat down to eat a meal. Then
they lifted their eyes and looked, and there
was a company of [b]Ishmaelites, coming
from Gilead with their camels, bearing
spices, [c]balm, and myrrh, on their way to
carry *them* down to Egypt. 26So Judah said
to his brothers, "What profit *is there* if we
kill our brother and [a]conceal his blood?
27Come and let us sell him to the Ishmaelites, and [a]let not our hand be upon him, for
he *is* [b]our brother *and* [c]our flesh." And his
brothers listened. 28Then [a]Midianite traders passed by; so *the brothers* pulled Joseph
up and lifted him out of the pit, [b]and sold
him to the Ishmaelites for [c]twenty *shekels*
of silver. And they took Joseph to Egypt.
29Then Reuben returned to the pit, and
indeed Joseph *was* not in the pit; and he
[a]tore his clothes. 30And he returned to his
brothers and said, "The lad [a]*is* no *more;* and
I, where shall I go?"
31So they took [a]Joseph's tunic, killed a
kid of the goats, and dipped the tunic in the
blood. 32Then they sent the tunic of *many*
colors, and they brought *it* to their father
and said, "We have found this. Do you know
whether it *is* your son's tunic or not?"
33And he recognized it and said, "*It is* my
son's tunic. A [a]wild beast has devoured him.
Without doubt Joseph is torn to pieces."
34Then Jacob [a]tore his clothes, put sackcloth on his waist, and [b]mourned for his
son many days. 35And all his sons and all
his daughters [a]arose to comfort him; but he
refused to be comforted, and he said, "For
[b]I shall go down into the grave to my son in
mourning." Thus his father wept for him.

37:9 [a] Gen. 46:29; 47:25 37:10 [a] Gen. 27:29 37:11 [a] Matt. 27:17, 18; Acts 7:9 [b] Dan. 7:28; Luke 2:19, 51 37:12 [a] Gen. 33:18–20
37:14 [a] Gen. 13:18; 23:2, 19; 35:27; Josh. 14:14, 15; Judg. 1:10 37:16 [a] Song 1:7 37:17 [a] 2 Kin. 6:13 37:18 [a] 1 Sam. 19:1; Ps. 31:13; 37:12,
32; Matt. 21:38; 26:3, 4; 27:1; Mark 14:1; John 11:53; Acts 23:12 37:20 [a] Gen. 37:22; Prov. 1:11 37:21 [a] Gen. 42:22 37:23 [a] Matt. 27:28
37:25 [a] Prov. 30:20 [b] Gen. 16:11, 12; 37:28, 36; 39:1 [c] Jer. 8:22 37:26 [a] Gen. 37:20 37:27 [a] 1 Sam. 18:17 [b] Gen. 42:21 [c] Gen. 29:14
37:28 [a] Gen. 37:25; Judg. 6:1–3; 8:22, 24 [b] Gen. 45:4, 5; Ps. 105:17; Acts 7:9 [c] Matt. 27:9 37:29 [a] Gen. 37:34; 44:13; Job 1:20
37:30 [a] Gen. 42:13, 36 37:31 [a] Gen. 37:3, 23 37:33 [a] Gen. 37:20 37:34 [a] Gen. 37:29; 2 Sam. 3:31 [b] Gen. 50:10
37:35 [a] 2 Sam. 12:17 [b] Gen. 25:8; 35:29; 42:38; 44:29, 31

36Now [a]the Midianites[1] had sold him in
Egypt to Potiphar, an officer of Pharaoh
and captain of the guard.

Judah and Tamar

38 It came to pass at that time that
Judah departed from his brothers,
and [a]visited a certain Adullamite whose
name *was* Hirah. 2And Judah [a]saw there
a daughter of a certain Canaanite whose
name *was* [b]Shua, and he married her and
went in to her. 3So she conceived and bore
a son, and he called his name [a]Er. 4She conceived again and bore a son, and she called
his name [a]Onan. 5And she conceived yet
again and bore a son, and called his name
[a]Shelah. He was at Chezib when she bore
him.

6Then Judah [a]took a wife for Er his firstborn, and her name *was* [b]Tamar. 7But [a]Er,
Judah's firstborn, was wicked in the sight
of the LORD, [b]and the LORD killed him.
8And Judah said to Onan, "Go in to [a]your
brother's wife and marry her, and raise up
an heir to your brother." 9But Onan knew
that the heir would not be [a]his; and it came
to pass, when he went in to his brother's
wife, that he emitted on the ground, lest
he should give an heir to his brother. 10And
the thing which he did displeased the LORD;
therefore He killed [a]him also.

11Then Judah said to Tamar his daughter-
in-law, [a]"Remain a widow in your father's
house till my son Shelah is grown." For he
said, "Lest he also die like his brothers."
And Tamar went and dwelt [b]in her father's
house.

12Now in the process of time the daughter of Shua, Judah's wife, died; and Judah
[a]was comforted, and went up to his sheepshearers at Timnah, he and his friend Hirah the Adullamite. 13And it was told Tamar,
saying, "Look, your father-in-law is going
up [a]to Timnah to shear his sheep." 14So she
took off her widow's garments, covered *her-*
self with a veil and wrapped herself, and
[a]sat in an open place which *was* on the way
to Timnah; for she saw [b]that Shelah was
grown, and she was not given to him as
a wife. 15When Judah saw her, he thought
she *was* a harlot, because she had covered
her face. 16Then he turned to her by the
way, and said, "Please let me come in to
you"; for he did not know that she *was* his
daughter-in-law.

So she said, "What will you give me, that
you may come in to me?"

17And he said, [a]"I will send a young goat
from the flock."

So she said, [b]"Will you give *me* a pledge
till you send *it?*"

18Then he said, "What pledge shall I give
you?"

So she said, [a]"Your signet and cord, and
your staff that *is* in your hand." Then he
gave *them* to her, and went in to her, and
she conceived by him. 19So she arose and
went away, and [a]laid aside her veil and put
on the garments of her widowhood.

20And Judah sent the young goat by the
hand of his friend the Adullamite, to receive *his* pledge from the woman's hand,
but he did not find her. 21Then he asked
the men of that place, saying, "Where is the
harlot who *was* openly by the roadside?"

And they said, "There was no harlot in
this *place.*"

22So he returned to Judah and said, "I
cannot find her. Also, the men of the place
said there was no harlot in this *place.*"

23Then Judah said, "Let her take *them* for
herself, lest we be shamed; for I sent this
young goat and you have not found her."

24And it came to pass, about three
months after, that Judah was told, saying,
"Tamar your daughter-in-law has [a]played
the harlot; furthermore she *is* with child
by harlotry."

So Judah said, "Bring her out [b]and let
her be burned!"

25When she *was* brought out, she sent
to her father-in-law, saying, "By the man to
whom these belong, I *am* with child." And
she said, [a]"Please determine whose these
are—the signet and cord, and staff."

26So Judah [a]acknowledged *them* and

37:36 [a] Gen. 39:1 [1] Masoretic Text reads *Medanites.* 38:1 [a] 2 Kin. 4:8 38:2 [a] Gen. 34:2 [b] 1 Chr. 2:3 38:3 [a] Gen. 46:12; Num. 26:19 38:4 [a] Gen. 46:12; Num. 26:19 38:5 [a] Num. 26:20 38:6 [a] Gen. 21:21 [b] Ruth 4:12 38:7 [a] Gen. 46:12; Num. 26:19 [b] 1 Chr. 2:3 38:8 [a] Deut. 25:5, 6; Matt. 22:24 38:9 [a] Deut. 25:6 38:10 [a] Gen. 46:12; Num. 26:19 38:11 [a] Ruth 1:12, 13 [b] Lev. 22:13 38:12 [a] 2 Sam. 13:39 38:13 [a] Josh. 15:10, 57; Judg. 14:1 38:14 [a] Prov. 7:12 [b] Gen. 38:11, 26 38:17 [a] Judg. 15:1; Ezek. 16:33 [b] Gen. 38:20 38:18 [a] Gen. 38:25; 41:42 38:19 [a] Gen. 38:14 38:24 [a] Judg. 19:2 [b] Lev. 20:14; 21:9; Deut. 22:21 38:25 [a] Gen. 37:32; 38:18 38:26 [a] Gen. 37:33

said, [b]"She has been more righteous than
I, because [c]I did not give her to Shelah my
son." And he [d]never knew her again.
27Now it came to pass, at the time for
giving birth, that behold, twins *were* in her
womb. 28And so it was, when she was giving
birth, that *the one* put out *his* hand; and the
midwife took a scarlet *thread* and bound
it on his hand, saying, "This one came out
first." 29Then it happened, as he drew back
his hand, that his brother came out unexpectedly; and she said, "How did you break
through? *This* breach *be* upon you!" Therefore his name was called [a]Perez.[1] 30After-
ward his brother came out who had the
scarlet *thread* on his hand. And his name
was called [a]Zerah.

Joseph a Slave in Egypt

39 Now Joseph had been taken [a]down
to Egypt. And [b]Potiphar, an officer of Pharaoh, captain of the guard, an
Egyptian, [c]bought him from the Ishmaelites who had taken him down there. 2[a]The
LORD was with Joseph, and he was a successful man; and he was in the house of
his master the Egyptian. 3And his master
saw that the LORD *was* with him and that
the LORD [a]made all he did to prosper in
his hand. 4So Joseph [a]found favor in his
sight, and served him. Then he made him
[b]overseer of his house, and all *that* he had
he put under his authority. 5So it was, from
the time *that* he had made him overseer
of his house and all that he had, that [a]the
LORD blessed the Egyptian's house for Joseph's sake; and the blessing of the LORD
was on all that he had in the house and in
the field. 6Thus he left all that he had in
Joseph's hand, and he did not know what
he had except for the bread which he ate.
Now Joseph [a]was handsome in form and
appearance.
7And it came to pass after these things
that his master's wife cast longing eyes on
Joseph, and she said, [a]"Lie with me."
8But he refused and said to his master's
wife, "Look, my master does not know what
is with me in the house, and he has committed all that he has to my hand. 9*There is* no
one greater in this house than I, nor has he
kept back anything from me but you, because you *are* his wife. [a]How then can I do
this great wickedness, and [b]sin against God?"

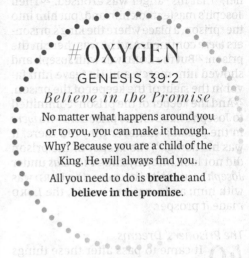

#OXYGEN

GENESIS 39:2

Believe in the Promise

No matter what happens around you
or to you, you can make it through.
Why? Because you are a child of the
King. He will always find you.
All you need to do is **breathe** and
believe in the promise.

10So it was, as she spoke to Joseph day
by day, that he [a]did not heed her, to lie with
her *or* to be with her.
11But it happened about this time, when
Joseph went into the house to do his work,
and none of the men of the house *was* inside, 12that she [a]caught him by his garment,
saying, "Lie with me." But he left his garment in her hand, and fled and ran outside. 13And so it was, when she saw that he
had left his garment in her hand and fled
outside, 14that she called to the men of her
house and spoke to them, saying, "See, he
has brought in to us a [a]Hebrew to mock us.
He came in to me to lie with me, and I cried
out with a loud voice. 15And it happened,
when he heard that I lifted my voice and
cried out, that he left his garment with me,
and fled and went outside."
16So she kept his garment with her until
his master came home. 17Then she [a]spoke
to him with words like these, saying, "The
Hebrew servant whom you brought to us

38:26 [b] 1 Sam. 24:17 [c] Gen. 38:14 [d] Job 34:31, 32 38:29 [a] Gen. 46:12; Num. 26:20; Ruth 4:12; 1 Chr. 2:4; Matt. 1:3 [1] Literally *Breach* or *Breakthrough* 38:30 [a] Gen. 46:12; 1 Chr. 2:4; Matt. 1:3 39:1 [a] Gen. 12:10; 43:15 [b] Gen. 37:36; Ps. 105:17 [c] Gen. 37:28; 45:4 39:2 [a] Gen. 26:24, 28; 28:15; 35:3; 39:3, 21, 23; 1 Sam. 16:18; 18:14, 28; Acts 7:9 39:3 [a] Ps. 1:3 39:4 [a] Gen. 18:3; 19:19; 39:21 [b] Gen. 24:2, 10; 39:8, 22; 41:40 39:5 [a] Gen. 18:26; 30:27; 2 Sam. 6:11 39:6 [a] Gen. 29:17; 1 Sam. 16:12 39:7 [a] 2 Sam. 13:11 39:9 [a] Lev. 20:10; Prov. 6:29, 32 [b] Gen. 20:6; 42:18; 2 Sam. 12:13; Ps. 51:4 39:10 [a] Prov. 1:10 39:12 [a] Prov. 7:13 39:14 [a] Gen. 14:13; 41:12 39:17 [a] Ex. 23:1; Ps. 120:3; Prov. 26:28

came in to me to mock me; 18so it happened,
as I lifted my voice and cried out, that he
left his garment with me and fled outside."
19So it was, when his master heard the
words which his wife spoke to him, saying,
"Your servant did to me after this manner," that his [a]anger was aroused. 20Then
Joseph's master took him and [a]put him into
the [b]prison, a place where the king's prisoners *were* confined. And he was there in the
prison. 21But the LORD was with Joseph and
showed him mercy, and He [a]gave him favor in the sight of the keeper of the prison.
22And the keeper of the prison [a]committed
to Joseph's hand all the prisoners who *were*
in the prison; whatever they did there, it
was his doing. 23The keeper of the prison
did not look into anything *that was* under
Joseph's authority,[1] because [a]the LORD was
with him; and whatever he did, the LORD
made *it* prosper.

The Prisoners' Dreams

40 It came to pass after these things
that the [a]butler and the baker of the
king of Egypt offended their lord, the king
of Egypt. 2And Pharaoh was [a]angry with
his two officers, the chief butler and the
chief baker. 3[a]So he put them in custody
in the house of the captain of the guard,
in the prison, the place where Joseph *was*
confined. 4And the captain of the guard
charged Joseph with them, and he served
them; so they were in custody for a while.
5Then the butler and the baker of the
king of Egypt, who *were* confined in the
prison, [a]had a dream, both of them, each
man's dream in one night *and* each man's
dream with its *own* interpretation. 6And Joseph came in to them in the morning and
looked at them, and saw that they *were* sad.
7So he asked Pharaoh's officers who *were*
with him in the custody of his lord's house,
saying, [a]"Why do you look *so* sad today?"
8And they said to him, [a]"We each have
had a dream, and *there is* no interpreter
of it."
So Joseph said to them, [b]"Do not interpretations belong to God? Tell *them* to me,
please."
9Then the chief butler told his dream
to Joseph, and said to him, "Behold, in my
dream a vine *was* before me, 10and in the
vine *were* three branches; it *was* as though
it budded, its blossoms shot forth, and its
clusters brought forth ripe grapes. 11Then
Pharaoh's cup *was* in my hand; and I took
the grapes and pressed them into Pharaoh's
cup, and placed the cup in Pharaoh's hand."
12And Joseph said to him, [a]"This *is* the
interpretation of it: The three branches [b]*are*
three days. 13Now within three days Pharaoh will [a]lift up your head and restore you
to your place, and you will put Pharaoh's
cup in his hand according to the former
manner, when you were his butler. 14But
[a]remember me when it is well with you, and
[b]please show kindness to me; make mention of me to Pharaoh, and get me out of
this house. 15For indeed I was [a]stolen away
from the land of the Hebrews; [b]and also I
have done nothing here that they should
put me into the dungeon."
16When the chief baker saw that the interpretation was good, he said to Joseph,
"I also *was* in my dream, and there *were*
three white baskets on my head. 17In the
uppermost basket *were* all kinds of baked
goods for Pharaoh, and the birds ate them
out of the basket on my head."
18So Joseph answered and said, [a]"This *is*
the interpretation of it: The three baskets
are three days. 19[a]Within three days Pharaoh will lift off your head from you and
[b]hang you on a tree; and the birds will eat
your flesh from you."
20Now it came to pass on the third day,
which was Pharaoh's [a]birthday, that he
[b]made a feast for all his servants; and he
[c]lifted up the head of the chief butler and
of the chief baker among his servants.
21Then he [a]restored the chief butler to his
butlership again, and [b]he placed the cup in
Pharaoh's hand. 22But he [a]hanged the chief

39:19 [a] Prov. 6:34, 35 **39:20** [a] Ps. 105:18; [1 Pet. 2:19] [b] Gen. 40:3, 15; 41:14 **39:21** [a] Gen. 39:2; Ex. 3:21; Ps. 105:19; [Prov. 16:7]; Dan. 1:9; Acts 7:9, 10 **39:22** [a] Gen. 39:4; 40:3, 4 **39:23** [a] Gen. 39:2, 3 [1] Literally *his hand* **40:1** [a] Gen. 40:11, 13; Neh. 1:11 **40:2** [a] Prov. 16:14 **40:3** [a] Gen. 39:1, 20, 23; 41:10 **40:5** [a] Gen. 37:5; 41:1 **40:7** [a] Neh. 2:2 **40:8** [a] Gen. 41:15 [b] [Gen. 41:16; Dan. 2:11, 20–22, 27, 28, 47] **40:12** [a] Gen. 40:18; 41:12, 25; Judg. 7:14; Dan. 2:36; 4:18, 19 [b] Gen. 40:18; 42:17 **40:13** [a] 2 Kin. 25:27; Ps. 3:3; Jer. 52:31 **40:14** [a] 1 Sam. 25:31; Luke 23:42 [b] Gen. 24:49; 47:29; Josh. 2:12; 1 Sam. 20:14, 15; 2 Sam. 9:1; 1 Kin. 2:7 **40:15** [a] Gen. 37:26–28 [b] Gen. 39:20 **40:18** [a] Gen. 40:12 **40:19** [a] Gen. 40:13 [b] Deut. 21:22 **40:20** [a] Matt. 14:6–10 [b] Mark 6:21 [c] Gen. 40:13, 19; 2 Kin. 25:27; Jer. 52:31; Matt. 25:19 **40:21** [a] Gen. 40:13 [b] Neh. 2:1 **40:22** [a] Gen. 40:19; Deut. 21:23; Esth. 7:10

baker, as Joseph had interpreted to them. 23 Yet the chief butler did not remember Joseph, but [a]forgot him.

Pharaoh's Dreams

41 Then it came to pass, at the end of two full years, that [a]Pharaoh had a dream; and behold, he stood by the river. 2 Suddenly there came up out of the river seven cows, fine looking and fat; and they fed in the meadow. 3 Then behold, seven other cows came up after them out of the river, ugly and gaunt, and stood by the *other* cows on the bank of the river. 4 And the ugly and gaunt cows ate up the seven fine looking and fat cows. So Pharaoh awoke. 5 He slept and dreamed a second time; and suddenly seven heads of grain came up on one stalk, plump and good. 6 Then behold, seven thin heads, blighted by the [a]east wind, sprang up after them. 7 And the seven thin heads devoured the seven plump and full heads. So Pharaoh awoke, and indeed, *it was* a dream. 8 Now it came to pass in the morning [a]that his spirit was troubled, and he sent and called for all [b]the magicians of Egypt and all its [c]wise men. And Pharaoh told them his dreams, but *there was* no one who could interpret them for Pharaoh.

9 Then the [a]chief butler spoke to Pharaoh, saying: "I remember my faults this day. 10 When Pharaoh was [a]angry with his servants, [b]and put me in custody in the house of the captain of the guard, *both* me and the chief baker, 11 [a]we each had a dream in one night, he and I. Each of us dreamed according to the interpretation of his *own* dream. 12 Now there *was* a young [a]Hebrew man with us there, a [b]servant of the captain of the guard. And we told him, and he [c]interpreted our dreams for us; to each man he interpreted according to his *own* dream. 13 And it came to pass, just [a]as he interpreted for us, so it happened. He restored me to my office, and he hanged him."

14 [a]Then Pharaoh sent and called Joseph, and they [b]brought him quickly [c]out of the dungeon; and he shaved, [d]changed his clothing, and came to Pharaoh. 15 And Pharaoh said to Joseph, "I have had a dream, and *there is* no one who can interpret it. [a]But I have heard it said of you *that* you can understand a dream, to interpret it."

16 So Joseph answered Pharaoh, saying, [a]"*It is* not in me; [b]God will give Pharaoh an answer of peace."

17 Then Pharaoh said to Joseph: "Behold, [a]in my dream I stood on the bank of the river. 18 Suddenly seven cows came up out of the river, fine looking and fat; and they fed in the meadow. 19 Then behold, seven other cows came up after them, poor and very ugly and gaunt, such ugliness as I have never seen in all the land of Egypt. 20 And the gaunt and ugly cows ate up the first seven, the fat cows. 21 When they had eaten them up, no one would have known that they had eaten them, for they *were* just as ugly as at the beginning. So I awoke. 22 Also I saw in my dream, and suddenly seven heads came up on one stalk, full and good. 23 Then behold, seven heads, withered, thin, *and* blighted by the east wind, sprang up after them. 24 And the thin heads devoured the seven good heads. So [a]I told *this* to the magicians, but *there was* no one who could explain *it* to me."

25 Then Joseph said to Pharaoh, "The dreams of Pharaoh *are* one; [a]God has shown Pharaoh what He *is* about to do: 26 The seven good cows *are* seven years, and the seven good heads *are* seven years; the dreams *are* one. 27 And the seven thin and ugly cows which came up after them *are* seven years, and the seven empty heads blighted by the east wind are [a]seven years of famine. 28 [a]This *is* the thing which I have spoken to Pharaoh. God has shown Pharaoh what He *is* about to do. 29 Indeed [a]seven years of great plenty will come throughout all the land of Egypt; 30 but after them seven years of famine will [a]arise, and all the plenty will be forgotten in the land of Egypt; and the famine [b]will deplete the land. 31 So the plenty will not be known in the land because of the famine following,

---

40:23 [a] Job 19:14; Ps. 31:12; Eccl. 9:15, 16; Is. 49:15; Amos 6:6 **41:1** [a] Gen. 40:5; Judg. 7:13 **41:6** [a] Ex. 10:13; Ezek. 17:10 **41:8** [a] Dan. 2:1, 3; 4:5, 19 [b] Ex. 7:11, 22; Is. 29:14; Dan. 1:20; 2:2; 4:7 [c] Matt. 2:1 **41:9** [a] Gen. 40:1, 14, 23 **41:10** [a] Gen. 40:2, 3 [b] Gen. 39:20 **41:11** [a] Gen. 40:5; Judg. 7:15 **41:12** [a] Gen. 39:14; 43:32 [b] Gen. 37:36 [c] Gen. 40:12 **41:13** [a] Gen. 40:21, 22 **41:14** [a] Ps. 105:20 [b] Dan. 2:25 [c] [1 Sam. 2:8] [d] 2 Kin. 25:27–29 **41:15** [a] Gen. 41:8, 12; Dan. 5:16 **41:16** [a] Dan. 2:30; Acts 3:12; [2 Cor. 3:5] [b] Gen. 40:8; 41:25, 28, 32; Deut. 29:29; Dan. 2:22, 28, 47 **41:17** [a] Gen. 41:1 **41:24** [a] Gen. 41:8; Ex. 7:11; Is. 8:19; Dan. 4:7 **41:25** [a] Gen. 41:28, 32; Dan. 2:28, 29, 45; Rev. 4:1 **41:27** [a] 2 Kin. 8:1 **41:28** [a] [Gen. 41:25, 32; Dan. 2:28] **41:29** [a] Gen. 41:47 **41:30** [a] Gen. 41:54, 56 [b] Gen. 47:13; Ps. 105:16

for it *will be* very severe. 32And the dream
was repeated to Pharaoh twice because the
[a]thing *is* established by God, and God will
shortly bring it to pass.

33"Now therefore, let Pharaoh select a
discerning and wise man, and set him over
the land of Egypt. 34Let Pharaoh do *this,* and
let him appoint officers over the land, [a]to
collect one-fifth *of the produce* of the land
of Egypt in the seven plentiful years. 35And
[a]let them gather all the food of those good
years that are coming, and store up grain
under the authority of Pharaoh, and let
them keep food in the cities. 36Then that
food shall be as a reserve for the land for
the seven years of famine which shall be in
the land of Egypt, that the land [a]may not
perish during the famine."

Joseph's Rise to Power

37So [a]the advice was good in the eyes of
Pharaoh and in the eyes of all his servants.
38And Pharaoh said to his servants, "Can
we find *such a one* as this, a man [a]in whom
is the Spirit of God?"

39Then Pharaoh said to Joseph, "Inasmuch as God has shown you all this, *there
is* no one as discerning and wise as you.
40[a]You shall be over my house, and all my
people shall be ruled according to your
word; only in regard to the throne will I
be greater than you." 41And Pharaoh said
to Joseph, "See, I have [a]set you over all the
land of Egypt."

42Then Pharaoh [a]took his signet ring
off his hand and put it on Joseph's hand;
and he [b]clothed him in garments of fine
linen [c]and put a gold chain around his neck.
43And he had him ride in the second [a]char-
iot which he had; [b]and they cried out before
him, "Bow the knee!" So he set him [c]over
all the land of Egypt. 44Pharaoh also said to
Joseph, "I *am* Pharaoh, and without your
consent no man may lift his hand or foot in
all the land of Egypt." 45And Pharaoh called
Joseph's name Zaphnath-Paaneah. And he
gave him as a wife [a]Asenath, the daughter
of Poti-Pherah priest of On. So Joseph went
out over *all* the land of Egypt.

46Joseph was thirty years old when he
[a]stood before Pharaoh king of Egypt. And
Joseph went out from the presence of Pharaoh, and went throughout all the land of
Egypt. 47Now in the seven plentiful years
the ground brought forth abundantly. 48So
he gathered up all the food of the seven
years which were in the land of Egypt, and
laid up the food in the cities; he laid up
in every city the food of the fields which
surrounded them. 49Joseph gathered very
much grain, [a]as the sand of the sea, until he
stopped counting, for *it was* immeasurable.

50[a]And to Joseph were born two sons before the years of famine came, whom Asenath, the daughter of Poti-Pherah priest of
On, bore to him. 51Joseph called the name
of the firstborn Manasseh:[1] "For God has
made me forget all my toil and all my [a]fa-
ther's house." 52And the name of the second
he called Ephraim:[1] "For God has caused me
to be [a]fruitful in the land of my affliction."

53Then the seven years of plenty which
were in the land of Egypt ended, 54[a]and
the seven years of famine began to come,
[b]as Joseph had said. The famine was in all
lands, but in all the land of Egypt there was
bread. 55So when all the land of Egypt was
famished, the people cried to Pharaoh for
bread. Then Pharaoh said to all the Egyptians, "Go to Joseph; [a]whatever he says to
you, do." 56The famine was over all the face
of the earth, and Joseph opened all the
storehouses[1] and [a]sold to the Egyptians.
And the famine became severe in the land
of Egypt. 57[a]So all countries came to Joseph
in Egypt to [b]buy *grain,* because the famine
was severe in all lands.

Joseph's Brothers Go to Egypt

42 When [a]Jacob saw that there was
grain in Egypt, Jacob said to his
sons, "Why do you look at one another?"
2And he said, "Indeed I have heard that
there is grain in Egypt; go down to that

41:32 [a] Gen. 41:25, 28; Num. 23:19; Is. 46:10, 11 41:34 [a] [Prov. 6:6–8] 41:35 [a] Gen. 41:48 41:36 [a] Gen. 47:15, 19 41:37 [a] Ps. 105:19; Acts 7:10 41:38 [a] Num. 27:18; [Job 32:8; Prov. 2:6]; Dan. 4:8, 9, 18; 5:11, 14; 6:3 41:40 [a] Ps. 105:21; Acts 7:10 41:41 [a] Gen. 42:6; Ps. 105:21; Dan. 6:3; Acts 7:10 41:42 [a] Esth. 3:10 [b] Esth. 8:2, 15 [c] Dan. 5:7, 16, 29 41:43 [a] Gen. 46:29 [b] Esth. 6:9 [c] Gen. 42:6 41:45 [a] Gen. 46:20 41:46 [a] 1 Sam. 16:21; 1 Kin. 12:6, 8; Dan. 1:19 41:49 [a] Gen. 22:17; Judg. 7:12; 1 Sam. 13:5 41:50 [a] Gen. 46:20; 48:5 41:51 [a] Ps. 45:10 [1] Literally *Making Forgetful* 41:52 [a] Gen. 17:6; 28:3; 49:22 [1] Literally *Fruitfulness* 41:54 [a] Ps. 105:16; Acts 7:11 [b] Gen. 41:30 41:55 [a] John 2:5 41:56 [a] Gen. 42:6 [1] Literally *all that was in them* 41:57 [a] Ezek. 29:12 [b] Gen. 27:28, 37; 42:3 42:1 [a] Acts 7:12

place and buy for us there, that we may
[a]live and not die."
3So Joseph's ten brothers went down
to buy grain in Egypt. 4But Jacob did not
send Joseph's brother Benjamin with his
brothers, for he said, [a]"Lest some calamity
befall him." 5And the sons of Israel went
to buy *grain* among those who journeyed,
for the famine was [a]in the land of Canaan.
6Now Joseph *was* governor [a]over the
land; and it was he who sold to all the
people of the land. And Joseph's brothers
came and [b]bowed down before him with
their faces to the earth. 7Joseph saw his
brothers and recognized them, but he acted
as [a]a stranger to them and spoke roughly
to them. Then he said to them, "Where do
you come from?"
And they said, "From the land of Canaan
to buy food."
8So Joseph recognized his brothers, but
they did not recognize him. 9Then Joseph
[a]remembered the dreams which he had
dreamed about them, and said to them,
"You *are* spies! You have come to see the
nakedness of the land!"
10And they said to him, "No, my lord, but
your servants have come to buy food. 11We
are all one man's sons; we *are* honest *men;*
your servants are not spies."
12But he said to them, "No, but you have
come to see the nakedness of the land."
13And they said, "Your servants *are*
twelve brothers, the sons of one man in the
land of Canaan; and in fact, the youngest *is*
with our father today, and one [a]*is* no more."
14But Joseph said to them, "It *is* as I spoke
to you, saying, 'You *are* spies!' 15In this *man-*
ner you shall be tested: [a]By the life of Pharaoh, you shall not leave this place unless
your youngest brother comes here. 16Send
one of you, and let him bring your brother;
and you shall be kept in prison, that your
words may be tested to see whether *there is*
any truth in you; or else, by the life of Pharaoh, surely you *are* spies!" 17So he put them
all together in prison [a]three days.
18Then Joseph said to them the third day,
"Do this and live, [a]*for* I fear God: 19If you
are honest *men,* let one of your brothers
be confined to your prison house; but
you, go and carry grain for the famine of
your houses. 20And [a]bring your youngest
brother to me; so your words will be veri-
fied, and you shall not die."
And they did so. 21Then they said to one
another, [a]"We *are* truly guilty concerning
our brother, for we saw the anguish of
his soul when he pleaded with us, and we
would not hear; [b]therefore this distress has
come upon us."
22And Reuben answered them, saying,
[a]"Did I not speak to you, saying, 'Do not
sin against the boy'; and you would not
listen? Therefore behold, his blood is now
[b]required of us." 23But they did not know
that Joseph understood *them,* for he spoke
to them through an interpreter. 24And he
turned himself away from them and [a]wept.
Then he returned to them again, and talked
with them. And he took [b]Simeon from them
and bound him before their eyes.

The Brothers Return to Canaan

25Then Joseph [a]gave a command to fill
their sacks with grain, to [b]restore every
man's money to his sack, and to give them
provisions for the journey. [c]Thus he did for
them. 26So they loaded their donkeys with
the grain and departed from there. 27But
as [a]one *of them* opened his sack to give his
donkey feed at the encampment, he saw his
money; and there it was, in the mouth of
his sack. 28So he said to his brothers, "My
money has been restored, and there it is,
in my sack!" Then their hearts failed *them*
and they were afraid, saying to one another,
"What *is* this *that* God has done to us?"
29Then they went to Jacob their father
in the land of Canaan and told him all that
had happened to them, saying: 30"The man
who is lord of the land [a]spoke roughly to
us, and took us for spies of the country.
31But we said to him, 'We *are* honest *men;*
we are not spies. 32We *are* twelve brothers,
sons of our father; one *is* no *more,* and the

42:2 [a] Gen. 43:8; Ps. 33:18, 19; Is. 38:1 **42:4** [a] Gen. 42:38 **42:5** [a] Gen. 12:10; 26:1; 41:57; Acts 7:11 **42:6** [a] Gen. 41:41, 55 [b] Gen. 37:7–10; 41:43; Is. 60:14 **42:7** [a] Gen. 45:1, 2 **42:9** [a] Gen. 37:5–9 **42:13** [a] Gen. 37:30; 42:32; 44:20; Lam. 5:7 **42:15** [a] 1 Sam. 1:26; 17:55 **42:17** [a] Gen. 40:4, 7, 12 **42:18** [a] Gen. 22:12; 39:9; Ex. 1:17; Lev. 25:43; Neh. 5:15; Prov. 1:7; 9:10 **42:20** [a] Gen. 42:34; 43:5; 44:23 **42:21** [a] Gen. 37:26–28; 44:16; 45:3; Job 36:8, 9; Hos. 5:15 [b] Prov. 21:13; Matt. 7:2 **42:22** [a] Gen. 37:21, 22, 29 [b] Gen. 9:5, 6; 1 Kin. 2:32; 2 Chr. 24:22; Ps. 9:12; Luke 11:50, 51 **42:24** [a] Gen. 43:30; 45:14, 15 [b] Gen. 34:25, 30; 43:14, 23 **42:25** [a] Gen. 44:1 [b] Gen. 43:12 [c] [Matt. 5:44; Rom. 12:17, 20, 21; 1 Pet. 3:9] **42:27** [a] Gen. 43:21, 22 **42:30** [a] Gen. 42:7

youngest *is* with our father this day in the land of Canaan.' 33Then the man, the lord of the country, said to us, [a]'By this I will know that you *are* honest *men:* Leave one of your brothers *here* with me, take *food for* the famine of your households, and be gone. 34And bring your [a]youngest brother to me; so I shall know that you *are* not spies, but *that* you *are* honest *men.* I will grant your brother to you, and you may [b]trade in the land.' "

35Then it happened as they emptied their sacks, that surprisingly [a]each man's bundle of money *was* in his sack; and when they and their father saw the bundles of money, they were afraid. 36And Jacob their father said to them, "You have [a]bereaved me: Joseph is no *more,* Simeon is no *more,* and you want to take [b]Benjamin. All these things are against me."

37Then Reuben spoke to his father, saying, "Kill my two sons if I do not bring him *back* to you; put him in my hands, and I will bring him back to you."

38But he said, "My son shall not go down with you, for [a]his brother is dead, and he is left alone. [b]If any calamity should befall him along the way in which you go, then you would [c]bring down my gray hair with sorrow to the grave."

Joseph's Brothers Return with Benjamin

43 Now the famine *was* [a]severe in the land. 2And it came to pass, when they had eaten up the grain which they had brought from Egypt, that their father said to them, "Go [a]back, buy us a little food."

3But Judah spoke to him, saying, "The man solemnly warned us, saying, 'You shall not see my face unless your [a]brother *is* with you.' 4If you send our brother with us, we will go down and buy you food. 5But if you will not send *him,* we will not go down; for the man said to us, 'You shall not see my face unless your brother *is* with you.' "

6And Israel said, "Why did you deal *so* wrongfully with me *as* to tell the man whether you had still *another* brother?"

7But they said, "The man asked us pointedly about ourselves and our family, saying, '*Is* your father still alive? Have you *another* brother?' And we told him according to these words. Could we possibly have known that he would say, 'Bring your brother down'?"

8Then Judah said to Israel his father, "Send the lad with me, and we will arise and go, that we may [a]live and not die, both we and you *and* also our little ones. 9I myself will be surety for him; from my hand you shall require him. [a]If I do not bring him *back* to you and set him before you, then let me bear the blame forever. 10For if we had not lingered, surely by now we would have returned this second time."

11And their father Israel said to them, "If *it must be* so, then do this: Take some of the best fruits of the land in your vessels and [a]carry down a present for the man—a little [b]balm and a little honey, spices and myrrh, pistachio nuts and almonds. 12Take double money in your hand, and take back in your hand the money [a]that was returned in the mouth of your sacks; perhaps it was an oversight. 13Take your brother also, and arise, go back to the man. 14And may God [a]Almighty [b]give you mercy before the man, that he may release your other brother and Benjamin. [c]If I am bereaved, I am bereaved!"

15So the men took that present and Benjamin, and they took double money in their hand, and arose and went [a]down to Egypt; and they stood before Joseph. 16When Joseph saw Benjamin with them, he said to the [a]steward of his house, "Take *these* men to my home, and slaughter an animal and make ready; for *these* men will dine with me at noon." 17Then the man did as Joseph ordered, and the man brought the men into Joseph's house.

18Now the men were [a]afraid because they were brought into Joseph's house; and they said, "*It is* because of the money, which was returned in our sacks the first time, that we are brought in, so that he may make a case

---

42:33 [a] Gen. 42:15, 19, 20 42:34 [a] Gen. 42:20; 43:3, 5 [b] Gen. 34:10 42:35 [a] Gen. 43:12, 15, 21 42:36 [a] Gen. 43:14 [b] Gen. 35:18; [Rom. 8:28, 31] 42:38 [a] Gen. 37:22; 42:13; 44:20, 28 [b] Gen. 42:4; 44:29 [c] Gen. 37:35; 44:31 43:1 [a] Gen. 41:54, 57; 42:5; 45:6, 11 43:2 [a] Gen. 42:2; 44:25 43:3 [a] Gen. 42:20; 43:5; 44:23 43:8 [a] Gen. 42:2; 47:19 43:9 [a] Gen. 42:37; 44:32; Philem. 18, 19 43:11 [a] Gen. 32:20; 33:10; 43:25, 26; [Prov. 18:16] [b] Gen. 37:25; Jer. 8:22; Ezek. 27:17 43:12 [a] Gen. 42:25, 35; 43:21, 22 43:14 [a] Gen. 17:1; 28:3; 35:11; 48:3 [b] Gen. 39:21; Ps. 106:46 [c] Gen. 42:36; Esth. 4:16 43:15 [a] Gen. 39:1; 46:3, 6 43:16 [a] Gen. 24:2; 39:4; 44:1 43:18 [a] Gen. 42:28

against us and seize us, to take us as slaves with our donkeys."

19When they drew near to the steward of Joseph's house, they talked with him at the door of the house, 20and said, "O sir, [a]we indeed came down the first time to buy food; 21but [a]it happened, when we came to the encampment, that we opened our sacks, and there, *each* man's money *was* in the mouth of his sack, our money in full weight; so we have brought it back in our hand. 22And we have brought down other money in our hands to buy food. We do not know who put our money in our sacks."

23But he said, "Peace *be* with you, do not be afraid. Your God and the God of your father has given you treasure in your sacks; I had your money." Then he brought [a]Simeon out to them.

24So the man brought the men into Joseph's house and [a]gave *them* water, and they washed their feet; and he gave their donkeys feed. 25Then they made the present ready for Joseph's coming at noon, for they heard that they would eat bread there.

26And when Joseph came home, they brought him the present which *was* in their hand into the house, and [a]bowed down before him to the earth. 27Then he asked them about *their* well-being, and said, "*Is* your father well, the old man [a]of whom you spoke? *Is* he still alive?"

28And they answered, "Your servant our father *is* in good health; he *is* still alive." [a]And they bowed their heads down and prostrated themselves.

29Then he lifted his eyes and saw his brother Benjamin, [a]his mother's son, and said, "*Is* this your younger brother [b]of whom you spoke to me?" And he said, "God be gracious to you, my son." 30Now [a]his heart yearned for his brother; so Joseph made haste and sought *somewhere* to weep. And he went into *his* chamber and [b]wept there. 31Then he washed his face and came out; and he restrained himself, and said, "Serve the [a]bread."

32So they set him a place by himself, and them by themselves, and the Egyptians who ate with him by themselves; because the Egyptians could not eat food with the [a]Hebrews, for that *is* [b]an abomination to the Egyptians. 33And they sat before him, the firstborn according to his [a]birthright and the youngest according to his youth; and the men looked in astonishment at one another. 34Then he took servings to them from before him, but Benjamin's serving was [a]five times as much as any of theirs. So they drank and were merry with him.

Joseph's Cup

44 And he commanded the [a]steward of his house, saying, [b]"Fill the men's sacks with food, as much as they can carry, and put each man's money in the mouth of his sack. 2Also put my cup, the silver cup, in the mouth of the sack of the youngest, and his grain money." So he did according to the word that Joseph had spoken. 3As soon as the morning dawned, the men were sent away, they and their donkeys. 4When they had gone out of the city, *and* were not *yet* far off, Joseph said to his steward, "Get up, follow the men; and when you overtake them, say to them, 'Why have you [a]repaid evil for good? 5*Is* not this *the one* from which my lord drinks, and with which he indeed practices divination? You have done evil in so doing.'"

6So he overtook them, and he spoke to them these same words. 7And they said to him, "Why does my lord say these words? Far be it from us that your servants should do such a thing. 8Look, we brought back to you from the land of Canaan [a]the money which we found in the mouth of our sacks. How then could we steal silver or gold from your lord's house? 9With whomever of your servants it is found, [a]let him die, and we also will be my lord's slaves."

10And he said, "Now also *let* it *be* according to your words; he with whom it is found shall be my slave, and you shall be blameless." 11Then each man speedily let down his sack to the ground, and each opened his sack. 12So he searched. He began with the oldest and left off with the youngest;

43:20 [a] Gen. 42:3, 10 **43:21** [a] Gen. 42:27, 35 **43:23** [a] Gen. 42:24 **43:24** [a] Gen. 18:4; 19:2; 24:32 **43:26** [a] Gen. 37:7, 10; 42:6; 44:14 **43:27** [a] Gen. 29:6; 42:11, 13; 43:7; 45:3; 2 Kin. 4:26 **43:28** [a] Gen. 37:7, 10 **43:29** [a] Gen. 35:17, 18 [b] Gen. 42:13 **43:30** [a] 1 Kin. 3:26 [b] Gen. 42:24; 45:2, 14, 15; 46:29 **43:31** [a] Gen. 43:25 **43:32** [a] Gen. 41:12; Ex. 1:15 [b] Gen. 46:34; Ex. 8:26 **43:33** [a] Gen. 27:36; 42:7; Deut. 21:16, 17 **43:34** [a] Gen. 35:24; 45:22 **44:1** [a] Gen. 43:16 [b] Gen. 42:25 **44:4** [a] 1 Sam. 25:21 **44:8** [a] Gen. 43:21 **44:9** [a] Gen. 31:32

and the cup was found in Benjamin's sack.
13Then they [a]tore their clothes, and each
man loaded his donkey and returned to
the city.
14So Judah and his brothers came to Joseph's house, and he *was* still there; and
they [a]fell before him on the ground. 15And
Joseph said to them, "What deed *is* this you
have done? Did you not know that such a
man as I can certainly practice divination?"
16Then Judah said, "What shall we say
to my lord? What shall we speak? Or how
shall we clear ourselves? God has [a]found
out the iniquity of your servants; here [b]we
are, my lord's slaves, both we and *he* also
with whom the cup was found."
17But he said, [a]"Far be it from me that I
should do so; the man in whose hand the
cup was found, he shall be my slave. And
as for you, go up in peace to your father."

Judah Intercedes for Benjamin

18Then Judah came near to him and said:
"O my lord, please let your servant speak a
word in my lord's hearing, and [a]do not let
your anger burn against your servant; for
you *are* even like Pharaoh. 19My lord asked
his servants, saying, 'Have you a father or
a brother?' 20And we said to my lord, 'We
have a father, an old man, and [a]a child of *his*
old age, *who is* young; his brother is [b]dead,
and he [c]alone is left of his mother's children, and his [d]father loves him.' 21Then you
said to your servants, [a]'Bring him down to
me, that I may set my eyes on him.' 22And
we said to my lord, 'The lad cannot leave
his father, for *if* he should leave his father,
his father would die.' 23But you said to your
servants, [a]'Unless your youngest brother
comes down with you, you shall see my
face no more.'
24"So it was, when we went up to your
servant my father, that we told him the
words of my lord. 25And [a]our father said,
'Go back *and* buy us a little food.' 26But we
said, 'We cannot go down; if our youngest
brother is with us, then we will go down; for
we may not see the man's face unless our
youngest brother *is* with us.' 27Then your
servant my father said to us, 'You know
that [a]my wife bore me two sons; 28and the
one went out from me, and I said, [a]"Surely
he is torn to pieces"; and I have not seen
him since. 29But if you [a]take this one also
from me, and calamity befalls him, you
shall bring down my gray hair with sorrow
to the grave.'
30"Now therefore, when I come to your
servant my father, and the lad *is* not with
us, since [a]his life is bound up in the lad's
life, 31it will happen, when he sees that the
lad *is* not *with us,* that he will die. So your
servants will bring down the gray hair of
your servant our father with sorrow to the
grave. 32For your servant became surety
for the lad to my father, saying, [a]'If I do
not bring him *back* to you, then I shall bear
the blame before my father forever.' 33Now
therefore, please [a]let your servant remain
instead of the lad as a slave to my lord, and
let the lad go up with his brothers. 34For
how shall I go up to my father if the lad *is*
not with me, lest perhaps I see the evil that
would come upon my father?"

Joseph Revealed to His Brothers

45 Then Joseph could not restrain himself before all those who stood by
him, and he cried out, "Make everyone
go out from me!" So no one stood with
him [a]while Joseph made himself known
to his brothers. 2And he [a]wept aloud, and
the Egyptians and the house of Pharaoh
heard *it.*
3Then Joseph said to his brothers, [a]"I *am*
Joseph; does my father still live?" But his
brothers could not answer him, for they
were dismayed in his presence. 4And Joseph said to his brothers, "Please come
near to me." So they came near. Then he
said: "I *am* Joseph your brother, [a]whom you
sold into Egypt. 5But now, do not therefore
be grieved or angry with yourselves because you sold me here; [a]for God sent me
before you to preserve life. 6For these two
years the [a]famine *has been* in the land, and

44:13 [a] Gen. 37:29, 34; Num. 14:6; 2 Sam. 1:11 44:14 [a] Gen. 37:7, 10 44:16 [a] [Num. 32:23] [b] Gen. 44:9 44:17 [a] Prov. 17:15
44:18 [a] Gen. 18:30, 32; Ex. 32:22 44:20 [a] Gen. 37:3; 43:8; 44:30 [b] Gen. 42:38 [c] Gen. 46:19 [d] Gen. 42:4 44:21 [a] Gen. 42:15, 20
44:23 [a] Gen. 43:3, 5 44:25 [a] Gen. 43:2 44:27 [a] Gen. 30:22–24; 35:16–18; 46:19 44:28 [a] Gen. 37:31–35
44:29 [a] Gen. 42:36, 38; 44:31 44:30 [a] [1 Sam. 18:1; 25:29] 44:32 [a] Gen. 43:9 44:33 [a] Ex. 32:32 45:1 [a] Acts 7:13
45:2 [a] Gen. 43:30; 46:29 45:3 [a] Gen. 43:27; Acts 7:13 45:4 [a] Gen. 37:28; 39:1; Ps. 105:17
45:5 [a] Gen. 45:7, 8; 50:20; Ps. 105:16, 17 45:6 [a] Gen. 43:1; 47:4, 13

there are still five years in which *there will*
be neither plowing nor harvesting. 7And
God [a]sent me before you to preserve a posterity for you in the earth, and to save your
lives by a great deliverance. 8So now *it was*
not you *who* sent me here, but [a]God; and
He has made me [b]a father to Pharaoh, and
lord of all his house, and a [c]ruler throughout all the land of Egypt.
9"Hurry and go up to my father, and say
to him, 'Thus says your son Joseph: "God
has made me lord of all Egypt; come down
to me, do not tarry. 10[a]You shall dwell in the
land of Goshen, and you shall be near to
me, you and your children, your children's
children, your flocks and your herds, and
all that you have. 11There I will [a]provide for
you, lest you and your household, and all
that you have, come to poverty; for *there*
are still five years of famine."'
12"And behold, your eyes and the eyes
of my brother Benjamin see that *it is* [a]my
mouth that speaks to you. 13So you shall tell
my father of all my glory in Egypt, and of
all that you have seen; and you shall hurry
and [a]bring my father down here."
14Then he fell on his brother Benjamin's neck and wept, and Benjamin wept
on his neck. 15Moreover he [a]kissed all his
brothers and wept over them, and after that
his brothers talked with him.
16Now the report of it was heard in Pharaoh's house, saying, "Joseph's brothers
have come." So it pleased Pharaoh and his
servants well. 17And Pharaoh said to Joseph, "Say to your brothers, 'Do this: Load

GENESIS 45:5

I AM JOSEPH

"But now, do not therefore be grieved or angry with yourselves because you sold me here; for God sent me before you to preserve life." Genesis 45:5

I am Joseph, the second youngest of twelve brothers. My father, Jacob, loved me most because I was born to him in his old age and was the son of his favorite wife. For this, I was despised by my brothers. Added to that, I told my brothers about two of my dreams in which they bowed before me. After hearing these dreams, they hated me even more and plotted my demise. Rather than have my blood on their hands, they sold me as a slave to a traveling group of Midianites. The Midianites in turn sold me to Potiphar, an officer of the pharaoh of Egypt.

There, though, I found favor in the eyes of the Lord. Although I was a slave, He gave me success in everything I did. Even when I was wrongly sent to prison when Potiphar's wife lied about me, the Lord gave me favor with the warden. Ultimately, the Lord gave me favor in the eyes of Pharaoh when the Lord allowed me to interpret his dreams. These dreams warned of a great famine coming upon Egypt. I told Pharaoh of a plan to avoid starvation, and he elevated me to second-in-command of Egypt.

During the famine, ten of my brothers came to Egypt for grain and were brought into my presence. They did not recognize me. I accused them of being spies and ordered them to bring my youngest brother, Benjamin, to Egypt. They complied, and then in front of all eleven of my brothers, I revealed who I was. Overcome with love and forgiveness, I told them to forgive themselves for selling me because God used it to save and bless both Egypt and the tribes of Israel.

†

Even though there are those who mean us harm, it is God's plan always to work for our good and for His glory. Sometimes He does that behind the scenes. God can use even the worst of situations to bless many, while we trust Him and forgive and pray for those who have done us wrong.

45:7 [a] Gen. 45:5; 50:20 45:8 [a] [Rom. 8:28] [b] Judg. 17:10; Is. 22:21 [c] Gen. 41:43; 42:6 45:10 [a] Gen. 46:28, 34; 47:1, 6; Ex. 9:26 45:11 [a] Gen. 47:12 45:12 [a] Gen. 42:23 45:13 [a] Gen. 46:6–28; Acts 7:14 45:15 [a] Gen. 48:10

your animals and depart; go to the land
of Canaan. 18Bring your father and your
households and come to me; I will give
you the best of the land of Egypt, and you
will eat [a]the fat of the land. 19Now you are
commanded—do this: Take carts out of the
land of Egypt for your little ones and your
wives; bring your father and come. 20Also
do not be concerned about your goods, for
the best of all the land of Egypt *is* yours.'"

21Then the sons of Israel did so; and Joseph gave them [a]carts, according to the
command of Pharaoh, and he gave them
provisions for the journey. 22He gave to
all of them, to each man, [a]changes of garments; but to Benjamin he gave three
hundred *pieces* of silver and [b]five changes
of garments. 23And he sent to his father
these *things:* ten donkeys loaded with the
good things of Egypt, and ten female donkeys loaded with grain, bread, and food for
his father for the journey. 24So he sent his
brothers away, and they departed; and he
said to them, "See that you do not become
troubled along the way."

25Then they went up out of Egypt, and
came to the land of Canaan to Jacob their
father. 26And they told him, saying, "Joseph
is still alive, and he *is* governor over all the
land of Egypt." [a]And Jacob's heart stood
still, because he did not believe them. 27But
when they told him all the words which Joseph had said to them, and when he saw
the carts which Joseph had sent to carry
him, the spirit [a]of Jacob their father revived. 28Then Israel said, "*It is* enough. Joseph my son *is* still alive. I will go and see
him before I die."

Jacob's Journey to Egypt
(Ex. 6:14–25)

46 So Israel took his journey with all
that he had, and came to [a]Beer-
sheba, and offered sacrifices [b]to the God of
his father Isaac. 2Then God spoke to Israel
[a]in the visions of the night, and said, "Jacob, Jacob!"

And he said, "Here I am."

3So He said, "I *am* God, [a]the God of your
father; do not fear to go down to Egypt, for
I will [b]make of you a great nation there. 4[a]I
will go down with you to Egypt, and I will
also surely [b]bring you up *again;* and [c]Jo-
seph will put his hand on your eyes."

5Then [a]Jacob arose from Beersheba; and
the sons of Israel carried their father Jacob, their little ones, and their wives, in
the carts [b]which Pharaoh had sent to carry
him. 6So they took their livestock and their
goods, which they had acquired in the land
of Canaan, and went to Egypt, [a]Jacob and
all his descendants with him. 7His sons
and his sons' sons, his daughters and his
sons' daughters, and all his descendants
he brought with him to Egypt.

8Now [a]these *were* the names of the children of Israel, Jacob and his sons, who went
to Egypt: [b]Reuben *was* Jacob's firstborn.
9The [a]sons of Reuben *were* Hanoch, Pallu,
Hezron, and Carmi. 10[a]The sons of Simeon
were Jemuel,[1] Jamin, Ohad, Jachin,[2] Zohar,[3]
and Shaul, the son of a Canaanite woman.
11The sons of [a]Levi *were* Gershon, Kohath,
and Merari. 12The sons of [a]Judah *were* [b]Er,
Onan, Shelah, Perez, and Zerah (but Er and
Onan died in the land of Canaan). [c]The sons
of Perez were Hezron and Hamul. 13The
sons of Issachar *were* Tola, Puvah,[1] Job,[2]
and Shimron. 14The [a]sons of Zebulun *were*
Sered, Elon, and Jahleel. 15These *were* the
[a]sons of Leah, whom she bore to Jacob in
Padan Aram, with his daughter Dinah. All
the persons, his sons and his daughters,
were thirty-three.

16The sons of Gad *were* Ziphion,[1] Haggi,
Shuni, Ezbon,[2] Eri, Arodi,[3] and Areli. 17[a]The
sons of Asher *were* Jimnah, Ishuah, Isui,
Beriah, and Serah, their sister. And the sons
of Beriah *were* Heber and Malchiel. 18[a]These
were the sons of Zilpah, [b]whom Laban gave

45:18 [a] Gen. 27:28; 47:6; Deut. 32:9–14 **45:21** [a] Gen. 45:19; 46:5 **45:22** [a] 2 Kin. 5:5 [b] Gen. 43:34 **45:26** [a] Job 29:24; Ps. 126:1; Luke 24:11, 41 **45:27** [a] Judg. 15:19; Is. 40:29 **46:1** [a] Gen. 21:31, 33; 26:32, 33; 28:10 [b] Gen. 26:24, 25; 28:13; 31:42; 32:9 **46:2** [a] Gen. 15:1; 22:11; 31:11; Num. 12:6; Job 33:14, 15 **46:3** [a] Gen. 17:1; 28:13 [b] Gen. 12:2; Ex. 1:9; 12:37; Deut. 26:5 **46:4** [a] Gen. 28:15; 31:3; 48:21; Ex. 3:12 [b] Gen. 15:16; 50:12, 24, 25; Ex. 3:8 [c] Gen. 50:1 **46:5** [a] Gen. 47:9; Acts 7:15 [b] Gen. 45:19–21 **46:6** [a] Deut. 26:5; Josh. 24:4; Ps. 105:23; Is. 52:4; Acts 7:15 **46:8** [a] Ex. 1:1–4 [b] Num. 26:4, 5; 1 Chr. 2:1 **46:9** [a] Ex. 6:14 **46:10** [a] Ex. 6:15; Num. 26:12 [1] Spelled *Nemuel* in 1 Chronicles 4:24 [2] Called *Jarib* in 1 Chronicles 4:24 [3] Called *Zerah* in 1 Chronicles 4:24 **46:11** [a] Ex. 6:16, 17; 1 Chr. 6:1, 16 **46:12** [a] Num. 26:19, 20; 1 Chr. 2:3; 4:21 [b] Gen. 38:3, 7, 10 [c] Gen. 38:29 **46:13** [1] Spelled *Puah* in 1 Chronicles 7:1 [2] Same as *Jashub* in Numbers 26:24 and 1 Chronicles 7:1 **46:14** [a] Num. 26:26 **46:15** [a] Gen. 35:23; 49:31 **46:16** [1] Spelled *Zephon* in Samaritan Pentateuch, Septuagint, and Numbers 26:15 [2] Called *Ozni* in Numbers 26:16 [3] Spelled *Arod* in Numbers 26:17 **46:17** [a] Num. 26:44–47; 1 Chr. 7:30 **46:18** [a] Gen. 30:10; 37:2 [b] Gen. 29:24

to Leah his daughter; and these she bore
to Jacob: sixteen persons.
19 The [a]sons of Rachel, [b]Jacob's wife, *were*
Joseph and Benjamin. 20 [a]And to Joseph
in the land of Egypt were born Manasseh
and Ephraim, whom Asenath, the daughter of Poti-Pherah priest of On, bore to him.
21 [a]The sons of Benjamin *were* Belah, Becher,
Ashbel, Gera, Naaman, [b]Ehi, Rosh, [c]Mup-
pim, Huppim,[1] and Ard. 22 These *were* the
sons of Rachel, who were born to Jacob:
fourteen persons in all.
23 The son of Dan *was* Hushim.[1] 24 [a]The
sons of Naphtali *were* Jahzeel,[1] Guni, Jezer, and Shillem.[2] 25 [a]These *were* the sons
of Bilhah, [b]whom Laban gave to Rachel
his daughter, and she bore these to Jacob:
seven persons in all.
26 [a]All the persons who went with Jacob
to Egypt, who came from his body, [b]besides
Jacob's sons' wives, *were* sixty-six persons
in all. 27 And the sons of Joseph who were
born to him in Egypt *were* two persons. [a]All
the persons of the house of Jacob who went
to Egypt were seventy.

Jacob Settles in Goshen

28 Then he sent Judah before him to Joseph, [a]to point out before him *the way* to Goshen. And they came [b]to the land of Goshen.
29 So Joseph made ready his [a]chariot and
went up to Goshen to meet his father Israel;
and he presented himself to him, and [b]fell on
his neck and wept on his neck a good while.
30 And Israel said to Joseph, [a]"Now let me
die, since I have seen your face, because
you *are* still alive."
31 Then Joseph said to his brothers and
to his father's household, [a]"I will go up and
tell Pharaoh, and say to him, 'My brothers
and those of my father's house, who *were*
in the land of Canaan, have come to me.
32 And the men *are* [a]shepherds, for their
occupation has been to feed livestock; and
they have brought their flocks, their herds,
and all that they have.' 33 So it shall be, when
Pharaoh calls you and says, [a]'What is your
occupation?' 34 that you shall say, 'Your servants' [a]occupation has been with livestock
[b]from our youth even till now, both we *and*
also our fathers,' that you may dwell in the
land of Goshen; for every shepherd *is* [c]an
abomination to the Egyptians."

47 Then Joseph [a]went and told Pharaoh, and said, "My father and my
brothers, their flocks and their herds and
all that they possess, have come from the
land of Canaan; and indeed they *are* in [b]the
land of Goshen." 2 And he took five men
from among his brothers and [a]presented
them to Pharaoh. 3 Then Pharaoh said to
his brothers, [a]"What *is* your occupation?"
And they said to Pharaoh, [b]"Your servants *are* shepherds, both we *and* also our
fathers." 4 And they said to Pharaoh, [a]"We
have come to dwell in the land, because
your servants have no pasture for their
flocks, [b]for the famine *is* severe in the land
of Canaan. Now therefore, please let your
servants [c]dwell in the land of Goshen."
5 Then Pharaoh spoke to Joseph, saying,
"Your father and your brothers have come
to you. 6 [a]The land of Egypt *is* before you.
Have your father and brothers dwell in the
best of the land; let them dwell [b]in the land
of Goshen. And if you know *any* competent
men among them, then make them chief
herdsmen over my livestock."
7 Then Joseph brought in his father Jacob and set him before Pharaoh; and Jacob
[a]blessed Pharaoh. 8 Pharaoh said to Jacob,
"How old *are* you?"
9 And Jacob said to Pharaoh, [a]"The days
of the years of my pilgrimage *are* [b]one hundred and thirty years; [c]few and evil have
been the days of the years of my life, and
[d]they have not attained to the days of the
years of the life of my fathers in the days of
their pilgrimage." 10 So Jacob [a]blessed Pharaoh, and went out from before Pharaoh.
11 And Joseph situated his father and his
brothers, and gave them a possession in

46:19 [a] Gen. 35:24 [b] Gen. 44:27 **46:20** [a] Gen. 41:45, 50–52; 48:1 **46:21** [a] 1 Chr. 7:6; 8:1 [b] Num. 26:38 [c] Num. 26:39; 1 Chr. 7:12 [1] Called *Hupham* in Numbers 26:39 **46:23** [1] Called *Shuham* in Numbers 26:42 **46:24** [a] Num. 26:48 [1] Spelled *Jahziel* in 1 Chronicles 7:13 [2] Spelled *Shallum* in 1 Chronicles 7:13 **46:25** [a] Gen. 30:5, 7 [b] Gen. 29:29 **46:26** [a] Ex. 1:5 [b] Gen. 35:11 **46:27** [a] Ex. 1:5; Deut. 10:22; Acts 7:14 **46:28** [a] Gen. 31:21 [b] Gen. 47:1 **46:29** [a] Gen. 41:43 [b] Gen. 45:14, 15 **46:30** [a] Luke 2:29, 30 **46:31** [a] Gen. 47:1 **46:32** [a] Gen. 47:3 **46:33** [a] Gen. 47:2, 3 **46:34** [a] Gen. 47:3 [b] Gen. 30:35; 34:5; 37:17 [c] Gen. 43:32; Ex. 8:26 **47:1** [a] Gen. 46:31 [b] Gen. 45:10; 46:28; 50:8 **47:2** [a] Acts 7:13 **47:3** [a] Gen. 46:33; Jon. 1:8 [b] Gen. 46:32, 34; Ex. 2:17, 19 **47:4** [a] Gen. 15:13; Deut. 26:5; Ps. 105:23 [b] Gen. 43:1; Acts 7:11 [c] Gen. 46:34 **47:6** [a] Gen. 20:15; 45:10, 18; 47:11 [b] Gen. 47:4 **47:7** [a] Gen. 47:10; 48:15, 20; 2 Sam. 14:22; 1 Kin. 8:66; Heb. 7:7 **47:9** [a] Ps. 39:12; [Heb. 11:9, 13] [b] Gen. 47:28 [c] [Job 14:1] [d] Gen. 5:5; 11:10, 11; 25:7, 8; 35:28 **47:10** [a] Gen. 47:7

the land of Egypt, in the best of the land, in the land of [a]Rameses, [b]as Pharaoh had commanded. 12Then Joseph provided [a]his father, his brothers, and all his father's household with bread, according to the number in *their* families.

Joseph Deals with the Famine

13Now *there was* no bread in all the land; for the famine *was* very severe, [a]so that the land of Egypt and the land of Canaan languished because of the famine. 14[a]And Joseph gathered up all the money that was found in the land of Egypt and in the land of Canaan, for the grain which they bought; and Joseph brought the money into Pharaoh's house.

15So when the money failed in the land of Egypt and in the land of Canaan, all the Egyptians came to Joseph and said, "Give us bread, for [a]why should we die in your presence? For the money has failed."

16Then Joseph said, "Give your livestock, and I will give you *bread* for your livestock, if the money is gone." 17So they brought their livestock to Joseph, and Joseph gave them bread *in exchange* for the horses, the flocks, the cattle of the herds, and for the donkeys. Thus he fed them with bread *in exchange* for all their livestock that year.

18When that year had ended, they came to him the next year and said to him, "We will not hide from my lord that our money is gone; my lord also has our herds of livestock. There is nothing left in the sight of my lord but our bodies and our lands. 19Why should we die before your eyes, both we and our land? Buy us and our land for bread, and we and our land will be servants of Pharaoh; give *us* seed, that we may [a]live and not die, that the land may not be desolate."

20Then Joseph [a]bought all the land of Egypt for Pharaoh; for every man of the Egyptians sold his field, because the famine was severe upon them. So the land became Pharaoh's. 21And as for the people, he moved them into the cities,[1] from *one* end of the borders of Egypt to the *other* end. 22[a]Only the land of the [b]priests he did not buy; for the priests had rations *allotted to them* by Pharaoh, and they ate their rations which Pharaoh gave them; therefore they did not sell their lands.

23Then Joseph said to the people, "Indeed I have bought you and your land this day for Pharaoh. Look, *here is* seed for you, and you shall sow the land. 24And it shall come to pass in the harvest that you shall give one-fifth to Pharaoh. Four-fifths shall be your own, as seed for the field and for your food, for those of your households and as food for your little ones."

25So they said, "You have saved [a]our lives; let us find favor in the sight of my lord, and we will be Pharaoh's servants." 26And Joseph made it a law over the land of Egypt to this day, *that* Pharaoh should have one-fifth, [a]except for the land of the priests only, *which* did not become Pharaoh's.

Joseph's Vow to Jacob

27So Israel [a]dwelt in the land of Egypt, in the country of Goshen; and they had possessions there and [b]grew and multiplied exceedingly. 28And Jacob lived in the land of Egypt seventeen years. So the length of Jacob's life was one hundred and forty-seven years. 29When the time [a]drew near that Israel must die, he called his son Joseph and said to him, "Now if I have found favor in your sight, please [b]put your hand under my thigh, and [c]deal kindly and truly with me. [d]Please do not bury me in Egypt, 30but [a]let me lie with my fathers; you shall carry me out of Egypt and [b]bury me in their burial place."

And he said, "I will do as you have said."

31Then he said, "Swear to me." And he swore to him. So [a]Israel bowed himself on the head of the bed.

Jacob Blesses Joseph's Sons
(Heb. 11:21)

48 Now it came to pass after these things that Joseph was told, "Indeed your father *is* sick"; and he took with him his two sons, [a]Manasseh and Ephraim. 2And Jacob

---

47:11 [a] Ex. 1:11; 12:37 [b] Gen. 47:6, 27 **47:12** [a] Gen. 45:11; 50:21 **47:13** [a] Gen. 41:30; Acts 7:11 **47:14** [a] Gen. 41:56; 42:6 **47:15** [a] Gen. 47:19 **47:19** [a] Gen. 43:8 **47:20** [a] Jer. 32:43 **47:21** [1] Following Masoretic Text and Targum; Samaritan Pentateuch, Septuagint, and Vulgate read *made the people virtual slaves.* **47:22** [a] Lev. 25:34; Ezra 7:24 [b] Gen. 41:45 **47:25** [a] Gen. 33:15 **47:26** [a] Gen. 47:22 **47:27** [a] Gen. 47:11 [b] Gen. 17:6; 26:4; 35:11; 46:3; Ex. 1:7; Deut. 26:5; Acts 7:17 **47:29** [a] Deut. 31:14; 1 Kin. 2:1 [b] Gen. 24:2–4 [c] Gen. 24:49; Josh. 2:14 [d] Gen. 50:25 **47:30** [a] 2 Sam. 19:37 [b] Gen. 49:29; 50:5–13; Heb. 11:21 **47:31** [a] Gen. 48:2; 1 Kin. 1:47; Heb. 11:21 **48:1** [a] Gen. 41:51, 56; 46:20; 50:23; Josh. 14:4

was told, "Look, your son Joseph is coming to you"; and Israel strengthened himself and sat up on the bed. 3Then Jacob said to Joseph: "God [a]Almighty appeared to me at [b]Luz in the land of Canaan and blessed me, 4and said to me, 'Behold, I will [a]make you fruitful and multiply you, and I will make of you a multitude of people, and [b]give this land to your descendants after you [c]*as* an everlasting possession.' 5And now your [a]two sons, Ephraim and Manasseh, who were born to you in the land of Egypt before I came to you in Egypt, *are* mine; as Reuben and Simeon, they shall be mine. 6Your offspring whom you beget after them shall be yours; they will be called by the name of their brothers in their inheritance. 7But as for me, when I came from Padan, [a]Rachel died beside me in the land of Canaan on the way, when *there was* but a little distance to go to Ephrath; and I buried her there on the way to Ephrath (that is, Bethlehem)."

8Then Israel saw Joseph's sons, and said, "Who *are* these?"

9Joseph said to his father, "They *are* my sons, whom God has given me in this *place.*"

And he said, "Please bring them to me, and [a]I will bless them." 10Now [a]the eyes of Israel were dim with age, *so that* he could not see. Then Joseph brought them near him, and he [b]kissed them and embraced them. 11And Israel said to Joseph, [a]"I had not thought to see your face; but in fact, God has also shown me your offspring!"

12So Joseph brought them from beside his knees, and he bowed down with his face to the earth. 13And Joseph took them both, Ephraim with his right hand toward Israel's left hand, and Manasseh with his left hand toward Israel's right hand, and brought *them* near him. 14Then Israel stretched out his right hand and [a]laid *it* on Ephraim's head, who *was* the younger, and his left hand on Manasseh's head, [b]guiding his hands knowingly, for Manasseh *was* the [c]firstborn. 15And [a]he blessed Joseph, and said:

"God, [b]before whom my fathers
Abraham and Isaac walked,
The God who has fed me all
my life long to this day,
16 The Angel [a]who has redeemed
me from all evil,
Bless the lads;
Let [b]my name be named upon
them,
And the name of my fathers
Abraham and Isaac;
And let them [c]grow into a multitude
in the midst of the earth."

17Now when Joseph saw that his father [a]laid his right hand on the head of Ephraim, it displeased him; so he took hold of his father's hand to remove it from Ephraim's head to Manasseh's head. 18And Joseph said to his father, "Not so, my father, for this *one is* the firstborn; put your right hand on his head."

19But his father refused and said, [a]"I know, my son, I know. He also shall become a people, and he also shall be great; but truly [b]his younger brother shall be greater than he, and his descendants shall become a multitude of nations."

20So he blessed them that day, saying, [a]"By you Israel will bless, saying, 'May God make you as Ephraim and as Manasseh!'" And thus he set Ephraim before Manasseh.

21Then Israel said to Joseph, "Behold, I am dying, but [a]God will be with you and bring you back to the land of your fathers. 22Moreover [a]I have given to you one portion above your brothers, which I took from the hand [b]of the Amorite with my sword and my bow."

Jacob's Last Words to His Sons

49 And Jacob called his sons and said, "Gather together, that I may [a]tell you what shall befall you [b]in the last days:

2 "Gather together and hear,
you sons of Jacob,
And listen to Israel your father.

48:3 [a] Gen. 43:14; 49:25 [b] Gen. 28:13, 19; 35:6, 9 48:4 [a] Gen. 46:3 [b] Gen. 35:12; Ex. 6:8 [c] Gen. 17:8 48:5 [a] Gen. 41:50; 46:20; 48:8; Josh. 13:7; 14:4 48:7 [a] Gen. 35:9, 16, 19, 20 48:9 [a] Gen. 27:4; 47:15 48:10 [a] Gen. 27:1; 1 Sam. 3:2 [b] Gen. 27:27; 45:15; 50:1 48:11 [a] Gen. 45:26 48:14 [a] Matt. 19:15; Mark 10:16 [b] Gen. 48:19 [c] Gen. 41:51, 52; Josh. 17:1 48:15 [a] Gen. 47:7, 10; 49:24; [Heb. 11:21] [b] Gen. 17:1; 24:40; 2 Kin. 20:3 48:16 [a] Gen. 22:11, 15–18; 28:13–15; 31:11; [Ps. 34:22; 121:7] [b] Amos 9:12; Acts 15:17 [c] Num. 26:34, 37 48:17 [a] Gen. 48:14 48:19 [a] Gen. 48:14 [b] Num. 1:33, 35; Deut. 33:17 48:20 [a] Ruth 4:11, 12 48:21 [a] Gen. 28:15; 46:4; 50:24 48:22 [a] Gen. 14:7; Josh. 24:32; John 4:5 [b] Gen. 34:28 49:1 [a] Deut. 33:1, 6–25; [Amos 3:7] [b] Num. 24:14; [Deut. 4:30]; Is. 2:2; 39:6; Jer. 23:20; Heb. 1:2

3 "Reuben, you are [a]my firstborn,
My might and the beginning
of my strength,
The excellency of dignity and
the excellency of power.
4 Unstable as water, you shall not excel,
Because you [a]went up to
your father's bed;
Then you defiled *it*—
He went up to my couch.

5 "Simeon and Levi *are* brothers;
Instruments of cruelty *are in*
their dwelling place.
6 [a]Let not my soul enter their council;
Let not my honor be united
[b]to their assembly;
[c]For in their anger they slew a man,
And in their self-will they
hamstrung an ox.
7 Cursed *be* their anger, for *it is* fierce;
And their wrath, for it is cruel!
[a]I will divide them in Jacob
And scatter them in Israel.

8 "Judah,[a] you *are he* whom your
brothers shall praise;
[b]Your hand *shall be* on the
neck of your enemies;
[c]Your father's children shall
bow down before you.
9 Judah *is* [a]a lion's whelp;
From the prey, my son,
you have gone up.
[b]He bows down, he lies down as a lion;
And as a lion, who shall rouse him?
10 [a]The scepter shall not
depart from Judah,
Nor [b]a lawgiver from between his feet,
[c]Until Shiloh comes;
[d]And to Him *shall be* the
obedience of the people.
11 Binding his donkey to the vine,
And his donkey's colt to
the choice vine,
He washed his garments in wine,
And his clothes in the blood of grapes.
12 His eyes *are* darker than wine,
And his teeth whiter than milk.

13 "Zebulun[a] shall dwell by the
haven of the sea;
He *shall become* a haven for ships,
And his border shall [b]adjoin Sidon.

14 "Issachar[a] is a strong donkey,
Lying down between two burdens;
15 He saw that rest *was* good,
And that the land *was* pleasant;
He bowed [a]his shoulder
to bear *a burden,*
And became a band of slaves.

16 "Dan[a] shall judge his people
As one of the tribes of Israel.
17 [a]Dan shall be a serpent by the way,
A viper by the path,
That bites the horse's heels
So that its rider shall fall backward.
18 [a]I have waited for your
salvation, O LORD!

19 "Gad,[a] a troop shall tramp upon him,
But he shall triumph at last.

20 "Bread from [a]Asher *shall be* rich,
And he shall yield royal dainties.

21 "Naphtali[a] *is* a deer let loose;
He uses beautiful words.

22 "Joseph *is* a fruitful bough,
A fruitful bough by a well;
His branches run over the wall.
23 The archers have [a]bitterly
grieved him,
Shot *at him* and hated him.
24 But his [a]bow remained in strength,
And the arms of his hands
were made strong
By the hands of [b]the Mighty
God of Jacob
[c](From there [d]*is* the Shepherd,
[e]the Stone of Israel),

49:3 [a] Gen. 29:32 49:4 [a] Gen. 35:22; Deut. 27:20; 1 Chr. 5:1 49:6 [a] Ps. 64:2; Prov. 1:15, 16 [b] Ps. 26:9; Eph. 5:11 [c] Gen. 34:26 49:7 [a] Num. 18:24; Josh. 19:1, 9; 21:1–42; 1 Chr. 4:24–27 49:8 [a] Deut. 33:7; Rev. 5:5 [b] Ps. 18:40 [c] Gen. 27:29; 1 Chr. 5:2 49:9 [a] Deut. 33:22; Ezek. 19:5–7; Mic. 5:8; [Rev. 5:5] [b] Num. 23:24; 24:9 49:10 [a] Num. 24:17; Jer. 30:21; Matt. 1:3; 2:6; Luke 3:33; Rev. 5:5 [b] Ps. 60:7 [c] Is. 11:1; [Matt. 21:9] [d] Deut. 18:15; Ps. 2:6–9; 72:8–11; Is. 42:1, 4; 49:6; 60:1–5; [Luke 2:30–32] 49:13 [a] Deut. 33:18, 19; Josh. 19:10, 11 [b] Gen. 10:19; Josh. 11:8 49:14 [a] 1 Chr. 12:32 49:15 [a] 1 Sam. 10:9 49:16 [a] Gen. 30:6; Deut. 33:22; Judg. 18:26, 27 49:17 [a] Judg. 18:27 49:18 [a] Ex. 15:2; Ps. 25:5; 40:1–3; 119:166, 174; Is. 25:9; Mic. 7:7 49:19 [a] Gen. 30:11; Deut. 33:20; 1 Chr. 5:18 49:20 [a] Deut. 33:24; Josh. 19:24–31 49:21 [a] Deut. 33:23 49:23 [a] Gen. 37:4, 24; Ps. 118:13 49:24 [a] Job 29:20; Ps. 37:15 [b] Ps. 132:2, 5; Is. 1:24; 49:26 [c] Gen. 45:11; 47:12 [d] [Ps. 23:1; 80:1] [e] [Ps. 118:22]; Is. 28:16; [1 Pet. 2:6–8]

25 [a]By the God of your father
who will help you,
[b]And by the Almighty [c]who
will bless you
With blessings of heaven above,
Blessings of the deep that lies beneath,
Blessings of the breasts
and of the womb.
26 The blessings of your father
Have excelled the blessings
of my ancestors,
[a]Up to the utmost bound of
the everlasting hills.
[b]They shall be on the head of Joseph,
And on the crown of the head of him
who was separate from his brothers.

27 "Benjamin is a [a]ravenous wolf;
In the morning he shall
devour the prey,
[b]And at night he shall divide the spoil."

28 All these *are* the twelve tribes of Israel,
and this *is* what their father spoke to them.
And he blessed them; he blessed each one
according to his own blessing.

Jacob's Death and Burial

29 Then he charged them and said to
them: "I [a]am to be gathered to my people; [b]bury me with my fathers [c]in the cave
that *is* in the field of Ephron the Hittite,
30 in the cave that *is* in the field of Machpelah, which *is* before Mamre in the land
of Canaan, [a]which Abraham bought with
the field of Ephron the Hittite as a possession for a burial place. 31 [a]There they buried Abraham and Sarah his wife, [b]there
they buried Isaac and Rebekah his wife,
and there I buried Leah. 32 The field and the
cave that *is* there *were* purchased from the
sons of Heth." 33 And when Jacob had finished commanding his sons, he drew his
feet up into the bed and breathed his last,
and was gathered to his people.

50 Then Joseph [a]fell on his father's face
and [b]wept over him, and kissed him.
2 And Joseph commanded his servants the
physicians to [a]embalm his father. So the physicians embalmed Israel. 3 Forty days were
required for him, for such are the days required for those who are embalmed; and the
Egyptians [a]mourned for him seventy days.
4 Now when the days of his mourning
were past, Joseph spoke to [a]the household
of Pharaoh, saying, "If now I have found favor in your eyes, please speak in the hearing of Pharaoh, saying, 5 [a]'My father made
me swear, saying, "Behold, I am dying; in
my grave [b]which I dug for myself in the
land of Canaan, there you shall bury me."
Now therefore, please let me go up and
bury my father, and I will come back.'"
6 And Pharaoh said, "Go up and bury
your father, as he made you swear."
7 So Joseph went up to bury his father;
and with him went up all the servants of
Pharaoh, the elders of his house, and all the
elders of the land of Egypt, 8 as well as all
the house of Joseph, his brothers, and his
father's house. Only their little ones, their
flocks, and their herds they left in the land
of Goshen. 9 And there went up with him
both chariots and horsemen, and it was a
very great gathering.
10 Then they came to the threshing floor
of Atad, which *is* beyond the Jordan, and
they [a]mourned there with a great and very
solemn lamentation. [b]He observed seven
days of mourning for his father. 11 And when
the inhabitants of the land, the Canaanites,
saw the mourning at the threshing floor
of Atad, they said, "This *is* a deep mourning of the Egyptians." Therefore its name
was called Abel Mizraim,[1] which *is* beyond
the Jordan.
12 So his sons did for him just as he had
commanded them. 13 For [a]his sons carried
him to the land of Canaan, and buried him
in the cave of the field of Machpelah, before
Mamre, which Abraham [b]bought with the
field from Ephron the Hittite as property
for a burial place. 14 And after he had buried his father, Joseph returned to Egypt, he
and his brothers and all who went up with
him to bury his father.

49:25 [a] Gen. 28:13; 32:9; 35:3; 43:23; 50:17 [b] Gen. 17:1; 35:11 [c] Deut. 33:13 **49:26** [a] Deut. 33:15; Hab. 3:6 [b] Deut. 33:16 **49:27** [a] Judg. 20:21, 25 [b] Num. 23:24; Esth. 8:11; Ezek. 39:10; Zech. 14:1 **49:29** [a] Gen. 15:15; 25:8; 35:29 [b] Gen. 47:30; 2 Sam. 19:37 [c] Gen. 23:16–20; 50:13 **49:30** [a] Gen. 23:3–20 **49:31** [a] Gen. 23:19, 20; 25:9 [b] Gen. 35:29; 50:13 **50:1** [a] Gen. 46:4, 29 [b] 2 Kin. 13:14 **50:2** [a] Gen. 50:26; 2 Chr. 16:14; Matt. 26:12; Mark 16:1; Luke 24:1; John 19:39, 40 **50:3** [a] Gen. 37:34; Num. 20:29; Deut. 34:8 **50:4** [a] Esth. 4:2 **50:5** [a] Gen. 47:29–31 [b] 2 Chr. 16:14; Is. 22:16; Matt. 27:60 **50:10** [a] Acts 8:2 [b] 1 Sam. 31:13; Job 2:13 **50:11** [1] Literally *Mourning of Egypt* **50:13** [a] Gen. 49:29–31; Acts 7:16 [b] Gen. 23:16–20

Joseph Reassures His Brothers

15When Joseph's brothers saw that their
father was dead, [a]they said, "Perhaps Joseph will hate us, and may actually repay
us for all the evil which we did to him." 16So
they sent *messengers* to Joseph, saying, "Before your father died he commanded, saying, 17'Thus you shall say to Joseph: "I beg
you, please forgive the trespass of your
brothers and their sin; [a]for they did evil
to you."' Now, please, forgive the trespass
of the servants of [b]the God of your father."
And Joseph wept when they spoke to him.
18Then his brothers also went and [a]fell
down before his face, and they said, "Behold, we *are* your servants."
19Joseph said to them, [a]"Do not be afraid,
[b]for *am* I in the place of God? 20[a]But as for
you, you meant evil against me; *but* [b]God
meant it for good, in order to bring it about
as *it is* this day, to save many people alive.
21Now therefore, do not be afraid; [a]I will
provide for you and your little ones." And
he comforted them and spoke kindly to
them.

Death of Joseph
(Heb. 11:22)

22So Joseph dwelt in Egypt, he and
his father's household. And Joseph lived
one hundred and ten years. 23Joseph saw
Ephraim's children [a]to the third *generation.* [b]The children of Machir, the son of
Manasseh, [c]were also brought up on Joseph's knees.
24And Joseph said to his brethren, "I
am dying; but [a]God will surely visit you,
and bring you out of this land to the land
[b]of which He swore to Abraham, to Isaac,
and to Jacob." 25Then [a]Joseph took an oath
from the children of Israel, saying, "God
will surely visit you, and [b]you shall carry
up my [c]bones from here." 26So Joseph died,
being one hundred and ten years old; and
they embalmed him, and he was put in a
coffin in Egypt.

50:15 [a] [Job 15:21] 50:17 [a] [Prov. 28:13] [b] Gen. 49:25 50:18 [a] Gen. 37:7–10; 41:43; 44:14 50:19 [a] Gen. 45:5 [b] Gen. 30:2; 2 Kin. 5:7 50:20 [a] Gen. 45:5, 7; Ps. 56:5 [b] [Acts 3:13–15] 50:21 [a] [Matt. 5:44] 50:23 [a] Gen. 48:1; Job 42:16 [b] Num. 26:29; 32:39 [c] Gen. 30:3 50:24 [a] Gen. 15:14; 46:4; 48:21; Ex. 3:16, 17; Josh. 3:17; Heb. 11:22 [b] Gen. 26:3; 35:12; 46:4; Ex. 6:8 50:25 [a] Gen. 47:29, 30; Ex. 13:19; Josh. 24:32; Acts 7:15, 16; Heb. 11:22 [b] Gen. 17:8; 28:13; 35:12; Deut. 1:8; 30:1–8 [c] Ex. 13:19

THE SECOND BOOK OF MOSES CALLED

EXODUS

OVERVIEW

Exodus, written by the prophet Moses, is the second book of the Pentateuch (the five books of the original Jewish scriptures). Exodus continues the story of the patriarch Jacob's family. Near the conclusion of Genesis, Joseph was ordained by God to be second-in-command of Egypt during a time of great famine. Jacob's entire family migrated to Egypt, where food was plentiful due to Joseph's wise leadership. Over the generations, Jacob's descendants (the Israelites) grew into a multitude and ended up being enslaved by the Egyptians (see Ex. 1:8–14).

The Latin word *exodus* means "to exit" or "to depart." The Book of Exodus details the Israelites' departure from Egypt, following their four-hundred-year captivity.

God demonstrated His concern for the Israelites as they cried out to Him regarding the promise He had made to Abraham, Isaac, and Jacob (see 2:23–25; cf. Gen. 12:1–3). God had promised to make them a great nation that would be greatly blessed. Yet, the Israelites had been in bondage to Egypt for many generations. In response to the people's cries, God set apart a deliverer named Moses to lead the Israelites out of bondage (see Ex. 3:7–10). In obedience to God, Moses appeared before the pharaoh of Egypt nine times, demanding that he free the Israelites. Each time, Pharaoh denied them freedom and God visited Egypt with a devastating plague (see 7:14—10:29). The tenth and final plague would bring death to the firstborn of Egyptians and Israelites (see 11:1—12:12). But God instructed the Israelites to paint the blood of a lamb on their doorposts. Because of the blood, the Lord passed over the Israelite homes, sparing them from death. At this point, Pharaoh proclaimed the Israelites a free people. Millions of Israelites followed Moses out of Egypt into the wilderness toward their Promised Land. God performed many miracles as He led the Israelites on their journey through the wilderness, including parting the Red Sea (see 14:21–31), providing food (see 16:1–12) and water (see 17:3–6), and giving improbable victories over fierce enemies (see 17:8–16).

Moses led the Israelites to Mount Sinai, where he sought God for guidance and direction. Here, God set forth His covenant with His people (see 19:1–6). In chapters 20–23, the law of God is outlined, with the Ten Commandments at its core (see 20:1–17). These laws established how God required the Israelites to interact with Him and one another.

Chapters 25–31 contain God's direction to Moses for the people to build a tabernacle of worship. This was a portable sanctuary in which God's glory dwelled with His people. God designated specific materials, furnishings, and craftsmen to fashion each aspect of the tabernacle (see 25:1–40; 31:1–11). The final chapters (32–40) describe a mixture of the rebelliousness and obedience of the Israelites and God's faithfulness in granting His continual presence and action on their behalf.

Redemption is the major theme of Exodus. God redeems the Israelites by delivering them from slavery in Egypt. When the Israelites rebelled, God chose to redeem them rather than separate Himself from them. He reestablished His covenant with them, solidifying Himself as their God and acknowledging them as His chosen people.

BREATHE IT IN

God originally sent the Israelites, His chosen people, to Egypt to escape a famine in their homeland of Canaan. When they arrived, they were prosperous for many generations. However, in time, their prosperity and numerical growth frightened the pharaoh. As a result, he ordered them to be enslaved. Finding themselves in bondage and their lives drastically altered, the Israelites turned to God for deliverance.

The Book of Exodus is a road map for deliverance from spiritual, physical, mental, emotional, or financial bondage. God hears the cries of His people and is concerned about them. He acts on their behalf.

This desire for freedom from bondage, though, requires calling upon God with the understanding that the journey to freedom may not be easy. Before God delivered the Israelites from Egypt, they experienced hardship. When God delivered them, their path through the wilderness offered many challenges and obstacles. The Israelites complained frequently and loudly about their experiences in the wilderness, and they were quite impatient throughout their journey toward the Promised Land. Despite their discontentment on their difficult journey from bondage to freedom, the Israelites learned much about God. They learned about the power of God as they witnessed the many miracles He performed. They learned the meaning of being in covenant relationship with God. They learned of God's expectations of them. They learned why and how to worship God. They learned that God forgives. They learned that God is always present.

Often, circumstances beyond our control lead us into bondage, such as the generational trauma associated with the slavery of African Americans. Other times, our own choices lead us there. Whatever type of bondage we experience, God can deliver us. As believers, we must be courageous enough to follow His lead. When we become discouraged, we must remember that God is always present and that He keeps His promises to His people. He has the power to deliver us. Ask Him. Believe He hears. Obey His leading. God will do the rest.

THE SECOND BOOK OF MOSES CALLED

EXODUS

Israel's Suffering in Egypt

1 Now [a]these *are* the names of the children of Israel who came to Egypt; each man and his household came with Jacob: 2Reuben, Simeon, Levi, and Judah; 3Issachar, Zebulun, and Benjamin; 4Dan, Naphtali, Gad, and Asher. 5All those who were descendants[1] of Jacob were [a]seventy[2] persons (for Joseph was in Egypt *already*). 6And [a]Joseph died, all his brothers, and all that generation. 7[a]But the children of Israel were fruitful and increased abundantly, multiplied and grew exceedingly mighty; and the land was filled with them.

8Now there arose a new king over Egypt, [a]who did not know Joseph. 9And he said to his people, "Look, the people of the children of Israel *are* more and [a]mightier than we; 10[a]come, let us [b]deal shrewdly with them, lest they multiply, and it happen, in the event of war, that they also join our enemies and fight against us, and *so* go up out of the land." 11Therefore they set taskmasters over them [a]to afflict them with their [b]burdens. And they built for Pharaoh [c]supply cities, Pithom [d]and Raamses. 12But the more they afflicted them, the more they multiplied and grew. And they were in dread of the children of Israel. 13So the Egyptians made the children of Israel [a]serve with rigor. 14And they [a]made their lives bitter with hard bondage—[b]in mortar, in brick, and in all manner of service in the field. All their service in which they made them serve *was* with rigor.

15Then the king of Egypt spoke to the [a]Hebrew midwives, of whom the name of one *was* Shiphrah and the name of the other Puah; 16and he said, "When you do the duties of a midwife for the Hebrew women, and see *them* on the birthstools, if it *is* a [a]son, then you shall kill him; but if it *is* a daughter, then she shall live." 17But the midwives [a]feared God, and did not do [b]as the king of Egypt commanded them, but saved the male children alive. 18So the king of Egypt called for the midwives and said to them, "Why have you done this thing, and saved the male children alive?"

19And [a]the midwives said to Pharaoh, "Because the Hebrew women *are* not like the Egyptian women; for they *are* lively and give birth before the midwives come to them."

20[a]Therefore God dealt well with the midwives, and the people multiplied and grew very mighty. 21And so it was, because the midwives feared God, [a]that He provided households for them.

22So Pharaoh commanded all his people, saying, [a]"Every son who is born[1] you shall cast into the river, and every daughter you shall save alive."

Moses Is Born
(Heb. 11:23)

2 And [a]a man of the house of Levi went and took *as wife* a daughter of Levi. 2So the woman conceived and bore a son. And [a]when she saw that he *was* a beautiful *child,*

1:1 [a] Gen. 46:8–27; Ex. 6:14–16 1:5 [a] Gen. 46:26, 27; [Deut. 10:22] [1] Literally *who came from the loins of* [2] Dead Sea Scrolls and Septuagint read *seventy-five* (compare Acts 7:14). 1:6 [a] Gen. 50:26; Acts 7:15 1:7 [a] Gen. 12:2; 28:3; 35:11; 46:3; 47:27; 48:4; Num. 22:3; Deut. 1:10, 11; 26:5; Ps. 105:24; Acts 7:17 1:8 [a] Acts 7:18, 19 1:9 [a] Gen. 26:16 1:10 [a] Ps. 83:3, 4 [b] Ps. 105:25; [Prov. 16:25]; Acts 7:19 1:11 [a] Gen. 15:13; Ex. 3:7; 5:6 [b] Ex. 1:14; 2:11; 5:4–9; 6:6 [c] 1 Kin. 9:19; 2 Chr. 8:4 [d] Gen. 47:11 1:13 [a] Gen. 15:13; Ex. 5:7–19 1:14 [a] Ex. 2:23; 6:9; Num. 20:15; [Acts 7:19, 34] [b] Ps. 81:6 1:15 [a] Ex. 2:6 1:16 [a] Matt. 2:16; Acts 7:19 1:17 [a] Ex. 1:21; Prov. 16:6 [b] Dan. 3:16, 18; Acts 4:18–20; 5:29 1:19 [a] Josh. 2:4; 2 Sam. 17:19, 20 1:20 [a] Gen. 15:1; Ruth 2:12; [Prov. 11:18]; Eccl. 8:12; [Is. 3:10]; Heb. 6:10 1:21 [a] 1 Sam. 2:35; 2 Sam. 7:11, 13, 27, 29; 1 Kin. 2:24; 11:38; [Ps. 127:1] 1:22 [a] Acts 7:19 [1] Samaritan Pentateuch, Septuagint, and Targum add *to the Hebrews.* 2:1 [a] Ex. 6:16–20; Num. 26:59; 1 Chr. 23:14 2:2 [a] Acts 7:20; Heb. 11:23

she hid him three months. 3But when she
could no longer hide him, she took an ark
of [a]bulrushes for him, daubed it with [b]as-
phalt and [c]pitch, put the child in it, and laid
it in the reeds [d]by the river's bank. 4[a]And
his sister stood afar off, to know what would
be done to him.

5Then the [a]daughter of Pharaoh came
down to bathe at the river. And her maidens walked along the riverside; and when
she saw the ark among the reeds, she sent
her maid to get it. 6And when she opened
it, she saw the child, and behold, the baby
wept. So she had compassion on him, and
said, "This is one of the Hebrews' children."

7Then his sister said to Pharaoh's daughter, "Shall I go and call a nurse for you from
the Hebrew women, that she may nurse the
child for you?"

8And Pharaoh's daughter said to her,
"Go." So the maiden went and called the
child's mother. 9Then Pharaoh's daughter said to her, "Take this child away and
nurse him for me, and I will give *you* your

RECONCILE HURT WITH HEALING

INHALE

I am nowhere near where I thought I would be in my career. I have done everything I know how to do. I have gotten a good education and gotten good experience, but there is still a racial barrier that I have not been able to break through. It seems like no matter how good my résumé is, I cannot get to that next level once they see the color of my skin. Where is the fairness in this? God made me with the skin I am in. I cannot change that, and I would not want to. But if God loves us as much as He loves people of other races, why does He allow racism to persist? How can I trust in God when I feel like He has let all of this happen and allows opportunities to pass me by?

EXHALE

Every one of us is wonderfully and fearfully made by God's own hand. Racism is a relatively new human invention (probably emerging in the 1500s), but people mistreating other people who are different from them goes all the way back to Cain killing his brother Abel because God accepted Abel's sacrifice and not Cain's. Of course, the whole New Testament speaks about the Jews being looked down upon by the Romans. God did not make one person or group of persons better than another; those institutions are man-made. He is not a respecter of persons. He makes no mistakes, and thus no corrections are needed. God knows exactly what He is doing.

Exodus 1:8–10 tells us, "Now there arose a new king over Egypt, who did not know Joseph. And he said to his people, 'Look, the people of the children of Israel are more and mightier than we; come, let us deal shrewdly with them, lest they multiply, and it happen, in the event of war, that they also join our enemies and fight against us, and so go up out of the land.'" We see here that the new king feared that these people, who had different ways from the Egyptians, would take control of Egypt. He feared that they would gain power, so he persecuted them. But in His own time, God delivered His people out of bondage.

God never promises that we will not face hardships, but He does call us to rely on Him in the midst of every hardship and stand fast to the gospel, no matter what. We have to trust that God will make a way out of no way and make a new path for us when the path that others take has been denied to us. Remember that the things you are facing are the ways of the world, built by human hands, which will all vanish. When we are oppressed and treated badly, we are not to respond the way the world responds, "for in Him we live and move and have our being" (Acts 17:28). We move and act according to His direction. No one can deny what God has in store for you. Be patient. Trust God and do what He says to do.

2:3 [a] Is. 18:2 [b] Gen. 14:10 [c] Gen. 6:14; Is. 34:9 [d] Is. 19:6 2:4 [a] Ex. 15:20; Num. 26:59 2:5 [a] Ex. 7:15; Acts 7:21

wages." So the woman took the child and nursed him. 10 And the child grew, and she brought him to Pharaoh's daughter, and he became [a]her son. So she called his name Moses,[1] saying, "Because I drew him out of the water."

#OXYGEN

EXODUS 2:7

Reconcile Hurt with Healing

Participate in healing by showing up and speaking up. Your words and actions matter. Offer healing to others through your presence and your voice.

Be bold, **breathe**, and **reconcile hurt with healing**.

Moses Flees to Midian

(Heb. 11:24, 25)

11 Now it came to pass in those days, [a]when Moses was grown, that he went out to his brethren and looked at their burdens. And he saw an Egyptian beating a Hebrew, one of his brethren. 12 So he looked this way and that way, and when he saw no one, he [a]killed the Egyptian and hid him in the sand. 13 And [a]when he went out the second day, behold, two Hebrew men [b]were fighting, and he said to the one who did the wrong, "Why are you striking your companion?"

14 Then he said, [a]"Who made you a prince and a judge over us? Do you intend to kill me as you killed the Egyptian?"

So Moses [b]feared and said, "Surely this thing is known!" 15 When Pharaoh heard of this matter, he sought to kill Moses. But [a]Moses fled from the face of Pharaoh and dwelt in the land of [b]Midian; and he sat down by [c]a well.

16 [a]Now the priest of Midian had seven daughters. [b]And they came and drew water, and they filled the [c]troughs to water their father's flock. 17 Then the [a]shepherds came and [b]drove them away; but Moses stood up and helped them, and [c]watered their flock.

18 When they came to [a]Reuel their father, [b]he said, "How *is it that* you have come so soon today?"

19 And they said, "An Egyptian delivered us from the hand of the shepherds, and he also drew enough water for us and watered the flock."

20 So he said to his daughters, "And where *is* he? Why *is* it *that* you have left the man? Call him, that he may [a]eat bread."

21 Then Moses was content to live with the man, and he gave [a]Zipporah his daughter to Moses. 22 And she bore *him* a son. He called his name [a]Gershom,[1] for he said, "I have been [b]a stranger in a foreign land."

23 Now it happened [a]in the process of time that the king of Egypt died. Then the children of Israel [b]groaned because of the bondage, and they cried out; and [c]their cry came up to God because of the bondage. 24 So God [a]heard their groaning, and God [b]remembered His [c]covenant with Abraham, with Isaac, and with Jacob. 25 And God [a]looked upon the children of Israel, and God [b]acknowledged *them.*

Moses at the Burning Bush

(Ex. 6:2—7:7; 11:1–4; 12:35, 36)

3 Now Moses was tending the flock of [a]Jethro his father-in-law, [b]the priest of Midian. And he led the flock to the back of the desert, and came to [c]Horeb, [d]the mountain of God. 2 And [a]the Angel of the LORD appeared to him in a flame of fire from the midst of a bush. So he looked, and behold, the bush was burning with fire, but the bush *was* not consumed. 3 Then Moses said, "I will now turn aside and see this [a]great sight, why the bush does not burn."

4 So when the LORD saw that he turned

2:10 [a] Acts 7:21 [1] Literally *Drawn Out* **2:11** [a] Acts 7:23, 24; Heb. 11:24–26 **2:12** [a] Acts 7:24, 25 **2:13** [a] Acts 7:26–28 [b] Prov. 25:8 **2:14** [a] Gen. 19:9; Acts 7:27, 28 [b] Judg. 6:27; Heb. 11:27 **2:15** [a] Acts 7:29; Heb. 11:27 [b] Ex. 3:1 [c] Gen. 24:11; 29:2; Ex. 15:27 **2:16** [a] Ex. 3:1; 4:18; 18:12 [b] Gen. 24:11, 13, 19; 29:6–10; 1 Sam. 9:11 [c] Gen. 30:38 **2:17** [a] Gen. 47:3; 1 Sam. 25:7 [b] Gen. 26:19–21 [c] Gen. 29:3, 10 **2:18** [a] Num. 10:29 [b] Ex. 3:1; 4:18 **2:20** [a] Gen. 31:54; 43:25 **2:21** [a] Ex. 4:25; 18:2 **2:22** [a] Ex. 4:20; 18:3, 4 [b] Gen. 23:4; Lev. 25:23; Acts 7:29; Heb. 11:13, 14 [1] Literally *Stranger There* **2:23** [a] Acts 7:34 [b] Deut. 26:7 [c] Ex. 3:7, 9; James 5:4 **2:24** [a] Ex. 6:5; Acts 7:34 [b] Gen. 15:13; 22:16–18; 26:2–5; 28:13–15; Ps. 105:8, 42 [c] Gen. 12:1–3; 15:14; 17:1–14 **2:25** [a] Ex. 4:31; Luke 1:25; Acts 7:34 [b] Ex. 3:7 **3:1** [a] Ex. 4:18 [b] Ex. 2:16 [c] Ex. 17:6; 1 Kin. 19:8 [d] Ex. 18:5 **3:2** [a] Deut. 33:16; Mark 12:26; Luke 20:37; Acts 7:30 **3:3** [a] Acts 7:31

aside to look, God called [a]to him from the midst of the bush and said, "Moses, Moses!"

And he said, "Here I am."

5 Then He said, "Do not draw near this place. [a]Take your sandals off your feet, for the place where you stand *is* holy ground." 6 Moreover He said, [a]"I *am* the God of your father—the God of Abraham, the God of Isaac, and the God of Jacob." And Moses hid his face, for [b]he was afraid to look upon God.

7 And the LORD said: [a]"I have surely seen the oppression of My people who *are* in Egypt, and have heard their cry [b]because of their taskmasters, [c]for I know their sorrows. 8 So [a]I have come down to [b]deliver them out of the hand of the Egyptians, and to bring them up from that land [c]to a good and large land, to a land [d]flowing with milk and honey, to the place of [e]the Canaanites and the Hittites and the Amorites and the Perizzites and the Hivites and the Jebusites. 9 Now therefore, behold, [a]the cry of the children of Israel has come to Me, and I have also seen the [b]oppression with which the Egyptians oppress them. 10 [a]Come now, therefore, and I will send you to Pharaoh that you may bring My people, the children of Israel, out of Egypt."

11 But Moses said to God, [a]"Who *am* I that I should go to Pharaoh, and that I should bring the children of Israel out of Egypt?"

12 So He said, [a]"I will certainly be with you. And this *shall be* a [b]sign to you that I have sent you: When you have brought the people out of Egypt, you shall serve God on this mountain."

13 Then Moses said to God, "Indeed, *when* I come to the children of Israel and say to them, 'The God of your fathers has sent me to you,' and they say to me, 'What *is* His name?' what shall I say to them?"

14 And God said to Moses, "I AM WHO I AM." And He said, "Thus you shall say to the children of Israel, [a]'I AM has sent me to you.'" 15 Moreover God said to Moses, "Thus you shall say to the children of Israel: 'The LORD God of your fathers, the God of Abraham, the God of Isaac, and the God of Jacob, has sent me to you. This *is* [a]My name forever, and this *is* My memorial to all generations.' 16 Go and [a]gather the elders of Israel together, and say to them, 'The LORD God of your fathers, the God of Abraham, of Isaac, and of Jacob, appeared to me, saying, [b]"I have surely visited you and *seen* what is done to you in Egypt; 17 and I have said [a]I will bring you up out of the affliction of Egypt to the land of the Canaanites and the Hittites and the Amorites and the Perizzites and the Hivites and the Jebusites, to a land flowing with milk and honey."' 18 Then [a]they will heed your voice; and [b]you shall come, you and the elders of Israel, to the king of Egypt; and you shall say to him, 'The LORD God of the Hebrews has [c]met with us; and now, please, let us go three days' journey into the wilderness, that we may sacrifice to the LORD our God.' 19 But I am sure that the king of Egypt [a]will not let you go, no, not even by a mighty hand. 20 So I will [a]stretch out My hand and strike Egypt with [b]all My wonders which I will do in its midst; and [c]after that he will let you go. 21 And [a]I will give this people favor in the sight of the Egyptians; and it shall be, when you go, that you shall not go empty-handed. 22 [a]But every woman shall ask of her neighbor, namely, of her who dwells near her house, [b]articles of silver, articles of gold, and clothing; and you shall put *them* on your sons and on your daughters. So [c]you shall plunder the Egyptians."

Miraculous Signs for Pharaoh

4 Then Moses answered and said, "But suppose they will not believe me or listen to my voice; suppose they say, 'The LORD has not appeared to you.'"

2 So the LORD said to him, "What *is* that in your hand?"

He said, "A rod."

3:4 [a] Ex. 4:5; Deut. 33:16 3:5 [a] Josh. 5:15; Acts 7:33 3:6 [a] Gen. 28:13; Ex. 3:16; 4:5; [Matt. 22:32; Mark 12:26, 27; Luke 20:37, 38]; Acts 7:32 [b] 1 Kin. 19:13 3:7 [a] Ex. 2:23–25; Neh. 9:9; Ps. 106:44 [b] Ex. 1:11 [c] Gen. 18:21; Ex. 2:25 3:8 [a] Gen. 15:13–16; 46:4; 50:24, 25 [b] Ex. 6:6–8; 12:51 [c] Num. 13:27; Deut. 1:25; 8:7–9; Josh. 3:17 [d] Ex. 3:17; 13:5; Jer. 11:5; Ezek. 20:6 [e] Gen. 15:19–21; Josh. 24:11 3:9 [a] Ex. 2:23 [b] Ex. 1:11, 13, 14 3:10 [a] Gen. 15:13, 14; Ex. 12:40, 41; [Mic. 6:4]; Acts 7:6, 7 3:11 [a] Ex. 4:10; 6:12; 1 Sam. 18:18 3:12 [a] Gen. 31:3; Ex. 4:12, 15; 33:14–16; Deut. 31:23; Josh. 1:5; Is. 43:2; Rom. 8:31 [b] Ex. 4:8; 19:3 3:14 [a] [Ex. 6:3; John 8:24, 28, 58; Heb. 13:8; Rev. 1:8; 4:8] 3:15 [a] Ps. 30:4; 97:12; 102:12; 135:13; [Hos. 12:5] 3:16 [a] Ex. 4:29 [b] Gen. 50:24; Ex. 2:25; 4:31; Ps. 33:18; Luke 1:68 3:17 [a] Gen. 15:13–21; 46:4; 50:24, 25 3:18 [a] Ex. 4:31 [b] Ex. 5:1, 3 [c] Num. 23:3, 4, 15, 16 3:19 [a] Ex. 5:2 3:20 [a] Ex. 6:6; 9:15 [b] Deut. 6:22; Neh. 9:10; Ps. 105:27; 135:9; Jer. 32:20; Acts 7:36 [c] Ex. 11:1; 12:31–37 3:21 [a] Ex. 11:3; 12:36; 1 Kin. 8:50; Ps. 105:37; 106:46; [Prov. 16:7] 3:22 [a] Ex. 11:2 [b] Ex. 33:6 [c] Job 27:17; Prov. 13:22; [Ezek. 39:10]

3And He said, "Cast it on the ground." So he cast it on the ground, and it became a serpent; and Moses fled from it. 4Then the LORD said to Moses, "Reach out your hand and take *it* by the tail" (and he reached out his hand and caught it, and it became a rod in his hand), 5"that they may [a]believe that the [b]LORD God of their fathers, the God of Abraham, the God of Isaac, and the God of Jacob, has appeared to you."

6Furthermore the LORD said to him, "Now put your hand in your bosom." And he put his hand in his bosom, and when he took it out, behold, his hand *was* leprous, [a]like snow. 7And He said, "Put your hand in your bosom again." So he put his hand in his bosom again, and drew it out of his bosom, and behold, [a]it was restored like his *other* flesh. 8"Then it will be, if they do not believe you, nor heed the message of the [a]first sign, that they may believe the message of the latter sign. 9And it shall be, if they do not believe even these two signs, or listen to your voice, that you shall take water from the river[1] and pour *it* on the dry *land.* [a]The water which you take from the river will become blood on the dry *land.*"

10Then Moses said to the LORD, "O my Lord, I *am* not eloquent, neither before nor since You have spoken to Your servant; but [a]I *am* slow of speech and slow of tongue."

11So the LORD said to him, [a]"Who has made man's mouth? Or who makes the mute, the deaf, the seeing, or the blind? *Have* not I, the LORD? 12Now therefore, go, and I will be [a]with your mouth and teach you what you shall say."

13But he said, "O my Lord, [a]please send by the hand of whomever *else* You may send."

14So [a]the anger of the LORD was kindled against Moses, and He said: "Is not Aaron the Levite your [b]brother? I know that he can speak well. And look, [c]he is also coming out to meet you. When he sees you, he will be glad in his heart. 15Now [a]you shall speak to him and [b]put the words in his mouth. And I will be with your mouth and with his mouth, and [c]I will teach you what you shall do. 16So he shall be your spokesman to the people. And he himself shall be as a mouth for you, and [a]you shall be to him as God. 17And you shall take this rod in your hand, with which you shall do the signs."

Moses Goes to Egypt

18So Moses went and returned to [a]Jethro his father-in-law, and said to him, "Please let me go and return to my brethren who *are* in Egypt, and see whether they are still alive."

And Jethro said to Moses, [b]"Go in peace."

19Now the LORD said to Moses in [a]Midian, "Go, return to [b]Egypt; for all the men who [c]sought your life are dead." 20Then Moses [a]took his wife and his sons and set them on a donkey, and he returned to the land of Egypt. And Moses took [b]the rod of God in his hand.

21And the LORD said to Moses, "When you go back to Egypt, see that you do all those [a]wonders before Pharaoh which I have put in your hand. But [b]I will harden his heart, so that he will not let the people go. 22Then you shall [a]say to Pharaoh, 'Thus says the LORD: [b]"Israel *is* My son, [c]My firstborn. 23So I say to you, let My son go that he may serve Me. But if you refuse to let him go, indeed [a]I will kill your son, your firstborn." ' "

24And it came to pass on the way, at the [a]encampment, that the LORD [b]met him and sought to [c]kill him. 25Then [a]Zipporah took [b]a sharp stone and cut off the foreskin of her son and cast *it* at *Moses'*[1] feet, and said, "Surely you *are* a husband of blood to me!" 26So He let him go. Then she said, "*You are* a husband of blood!"—because of the circumcision.

27And the LORD said to Aaron, "Go into the wilderness [a]to meet Moses." So he went and met him on [b]the mountain of God, and

---

4:5 [a] Ex. 4:31; 19:9 [b] Gen. 28:13; 48:15; Ex. 3:6, 15 4:6 [a] Num. 12:10; 2 Kin. 5:27 4:7 [a] Num. 12:13–15; Deut. 32:39 4:8 [a] Ex. 7:6–13 4:9 [a] Ex. 7:19, 20 [1] That is, the Nile 4:10 [a] Ex. 3:11; 4:1; 6:12; Jer. 1:6 4:11 [a] Ps. 94:9; 146:8; Matt. 11:5; Luke 1:20, 64 4:12 [a] Ex. 4:15, 16; Deut. 18:18; Is. 50:4; Jer. 1:9; [Matt. 10:19; Mark 13:11; Luke 12:11, 12; 21:14, 15] 4:13 [a] Jon. 1:3 4:14 [a] Num. 11:1, 33 [b] Num. 26:59 [c] Ex. 4:27; 1 Sam. 10:2, 3, 5 4:15 [a] Ex. 4:12, 30; 7:1, 2 [b] Num. 23:5, 12; Deut. 18:18; 2 Sam. 14:3, 19; Is. 51:16; 59:21; Jer. 1:9 [c] Deut. 5:31 4:16 [a] Ex. 7:1, 2 4:18 [a] Ex. 2:21; 3:1; 4:18 [b] Gen. 43:23; Judg. 18:6 4:19 [a] Ex. 3:1; 18:1 [b] Gen. 46:3, 6 [c] Ex. 2:15, 23; Matt. 2:20 4:20 [a] Ex. 18:2–5; Acts 7:29 [b] Ex. 4:17; 17:9; Num. 20:8, 9, 11 4:21 [a] Ex. 3:20; 11:9, 10 [b] Ex. 7:3, 13; 9:12, 35; 10:1, 20, 27; 14:4, 8; Deut. 2:30; Josh. 11:20; 1 Sam. 6:6; Is. 63:17; John 12:40; Rom. 9:18 4:22 [a] Ex. 5:1 [b] Is. 63:16; 64:8; Hos. 11:1; [Rom. 9:4; 2 Cor. 6:16, 18] [c] Jer. 31:9; [James 1:18] 4:23 [a] Ex. 11:5; 12:29; Ps. 105:36; 135:8; 136:10 4:24 [a] Gen. 42:27 [b] Ex. 3:18; 5:3; Num. 22:22 [c] Gen. 17:14 4:25 [a] Ex. 2:21; 18:2 [b] Gen. 17:14; Josh. 5:2, 3 [1] Literally *his* 4:27 [a] Ex. 4:14 [b] Ex. 3:1; 18:5; 24:13

kissed him. 28So Moses [a]told Aaron all the words of the LORD who had sent him, and all the [b]signs which He had commanded him. 29Then Moses and Aaron [a]went and gathered together all the elders of the children of Israel. 30[a]And Aaron spoke all the words which the LORD had spoken to Moses. Then he did the signs in the sight of the people. 31So the people [a]believed; and when they heard that the LORD had [b]visited the children of Israel and that He [c]had looked on their affliction, then [d]they bowed their heads and worshiped.

First Encounter with Pharaoh

5 Afterward Moses and Aaron went in and told Pharaoh, "Thus says the LORD God of Israel: 'Let My people go, that they may hold [a]a feast to Me in the wilderness.'"

2And Pharaoh said, [a]"Who *is* the LORD, that I should obey His voice to let Israel go? I do not know the LORD, [b]nor will I let Israel go."

3So they said, [a]"The God of the Hebrews has [b]met with us. Please, let us go three days' journey into the desert and sacrifice to the LORD our God, lest He fall upon us with [c]pestilence or with the sword."

4Then the king of Egypt said to them, "Moses and Aaron, why do you take the people from their work? Get *back* to your [a]labor." 5And Pharaoh said, "Look, the people of the land *are* [a]many now, and you make them rest from their labor!"

6So the same day Pharaoh commanded the [a]taskmasters of the people and their officers, saying, 7"You shall no longer give the people straw to make [a]brick as before. Let them go and gather straw for themselves. 8And you shall lay on them the quota of bricks which they made before. You shall not reduce it. For they are idle; therefore they cry out, saying, 'Let us go *and* sacrifice to our God.' 9Let more work be laid on the men, that they may labor in it, and let them not regard false words."

10And the taskmasters of the people and their officers went out and spoke to the people, saying, "Thus says Pharaoh: 'I will not give you straw. 11Go, get yourselves straw where you can find it; yet none of your work will be reduced.'" 12So the people were scattered abroad throughout all the land of Egypt to gather stubble instead of straw. 13And the taskmasters forced *them* to hurry, saying, "Fulfill your work, *your* daily quota, as when there was straw." 14Also the [a]officers of the children of Israel, whom Pharaoh's taskmasters had set over them, were [b]beaten *and* were asked, "Why have you not fulfilled your task in making brick both yesterday and today, as before?"

15Then the officers of the children of Israel came and cried out to Pharaoh, saying, "Why are you dealing thus with your servants? 16There is no straw given to your servants, and they say to us, 'Make brick!' And indeed your servants *are* beaten, but the fault *is* in your *own* people."

17But he said, "You *are* idle! Idle! Therefore you say, 'Let us go *and* sacrifice to the LORD.' 18Therefore go now *and* work; for no straw shall be given you, yet you shall deliver the quota of bricks." 19And the officers of the children of Israel saw *that* they *were* in trouble after it was said, "You shall not reduce *any* bricks from your daily quota."

20Then, as they came out from Pharaoh, they met Moses and Aaron who stood there to meet them. 21[a]And they said to them, "Let the LORD look on you and judge, because you have made us abhorrent in the sight of Pharaoh and in the sight of his servants, to put a sword in their hand to kill us."

Israel's Deliverance Assured

(Ex. 3:1—4:17)

22So Moses returned to the LORD and said, "Lord, why have You brought trouble on this people? Why *is* it You have sent me? 23For since I came to Pharaoh to speak in Your name, he has done evil to this people; neither have You delivered Your people at all."

6 Then the LORD said to Moses, "Now you shall see what I will do to Pharaoh. For [a]with a strong hand he will let them go, and with a strong hand [b]he will drive them out of his land."

2And God spoke to Moses and said to

4:28 [a] Ex. 4:15, 16 [b] Ex. 4:8, 9 4:29 [a] Ex. 3:16; 12:21 4:30 [a] Ex. 4:15, 16 4:31 [a] Ex. 3:18; 4:8, 9; 19:9 [b] Gen. 50:24; Ex. 3:16 [c] Ex. 2:25; 3:7 [d] Gen. 24:26; Ex. 12:27; 1 Chr. 29:20 5:1 [a] Ex. 3:18; 7:16; 10:9 5:2 [a] 2 Kin. 18:35; 2 Chr. 32:14; Job 21:15 [b] Ex. 3:19; 7:14 5:3 [a] Ex. 3:18; 7:16 [b] Ex. 4:24; Num. 23:3 [c] Ex. 9:15 5:4 [a] Ex. 1:11; 2:11; 6:6 5:5 [a] Ex. 1:7, 9 5:6 [a] Ex. 1:11; 3:7; 5:10, 13, 14 5:7 [a] Ex. 1:14 5:14 [a] Ex. 5:6 [b] Is. 10:24 5:21 [a] Ex. 6:9; 14:11; 15:24; 16:2 6:1 [a] Ex. 3:19 [b] Ex. 12:31, 33, 39

him: "I *am* the LORD. 3[a]I appeared to Abraham, to Isaac, and to Jacob, as [b]God Almighty, but *by* My name [c]LORD[1] I was not
known to them. 4[a]I have also established
My covenant with them, [b]to give them the
land of Canaan, the land of their pilgrimage, [c]in which they were strangers. 5And [a]I
have also heard the groaning of the children of Israel whom the Egyptians keep in
bondage, and I have remembered My covenant. 6Therefore say to the children of Israel: [a]'I *am* the LORD; [b]I will bring you out
from under the burdens of the Egyptians,
I will [c]rescue you from their bondage, and I
will redeem you with an outstretched arm
and with great judgments. 7I will [a]take you
as My people, and [b]I will be your God. Then
you shall know that I *am* the LORD your
God who brings you out [c]from under the
burdens of the Egyptians. 8And I will bring
you into the land which I [a]swore to give to
Abraham, Isaac, and Jacob; and I will give
it to you *as* a heritage: I *am* the LORD.'" 9So
Moses spoke thus to the children of Israel;
[a]but they did not heed Moses, because of
[b]anguish of spirit and cruel bondage.

10And the LORD spoke to Moses, saying,
11"Go in, tell Pharaoh king of Egypt to let
the children of Israel go out of his land."

12And Moses spoke before the LORD, saying, "The children of Israel have not heeded
me. How then shall Pharaoh heed me, for
[a]I *am* of uncircumcised lips?"

13Then the LORD spoke to Moses and
Aaron, and gave them a [a]command for the
children of Israel and for Pharaoh king of
Egypt, to bring the children of Israel out
of the land of Egypt.

The Family of Moses and Aaron
(Gen. 46:8–27)

14These *are* the heads of their fathers'
houses: [a]The sons of Reuben, the firstborn
of Israel, *were* Hanoch, Pallu, Hezron, and
Carmi. These are the families of Reuben.
15[a]And the sons of Simeon *were* Jemuel,[1]
Jamin, Ohad, Jachin, Zohar, and Shaul the
son of a Canaanite woman. These *are* the
families of Simeon. 16These *are* the names of
[a]the sons of Levi according to their generations: Gershon, Kohath, and Merari. And the
years of the life of Levi *were* one hundred
and thirty-seven. 17[a]The sons of Gershon
were Libni and Shimi according to their
families. 18And [a]the sons of Kohath *were*
Amram, Izhar, Hebron, and Uzziel. And the
years of the life of Kohath *were* one hundred
and thirty-three. 19[a]The sons of Merari *were*
Mahli and Mushi. These *are* the families of
Levi according to their generations.

20Now [a]Amram took for himself [b]Joche-
bed, his father's sister, as wife; and she bore
him [c]Aaron and Moses. And the years of
the life of Amram *were* one hundred and
thirty-seven. 21[a]The sons of Izhar *were* Korah, Nepheg, and Zichri. 22And [a]the sons of
Uzziel *were* Mishael, Elzaphan, and Zithri.
23Aaron took to himself Elisheba, daughter
of [a]Amminadab, sister of Nahshon, as wife;
and she bore him [b]Nadab, Abihu, [c]Eleazar,
and Ithamar. 24And [a]the sons of Korah *were*
Assir, Elkanah, and Abiasaph. These are the
families of the Korahites. 25Eleazar, Aaron's
son, took for himself one of the daughters of
Putiel as wife; and [a]she bore him Phinehas.
These *are* the heads of the fathers' houses
of the Levites according to their families.

26These *are the same* Aaron and Moses
to whom the LORD said, "Bring out the children of Israel from the land of Egypt according to their [a]armies." 27These *are* the
ones who spoke to Pharaoh king of Egypt,
[a]to bring out the children of Israel from
Egypt. These *are the same* Moses and Aaron.

Aaron Is Moses' Spokesman

28And it came to pass, on the day the
LORD spoke to Moses in the land of Egypt,
29that the LORD spoke to Moses, saying, "I
am the LORD. [a]Speak to Pharaoh king of
Egypt all that I say to you."

30But Moses said before the LORD,

6:3 [a] Gen. 17:1; 35:9; 48:3 [b] Gen. 28:3; 35:11 [c] Ex. 3:14, 15; 15:3; Ps. 68:4; 83:18; Is. 52:6; Jer. 16:21; Ezek. 37:6, 13; John 8:58 [1] Hebrew *YHWH*, traditionally *Jehovah* 6:4 [a] Gen. 12:7; 15:18; 17:4, 7, 8; 26:3; 28:4, 13 [b] Gen. 47:9; Lev. 25:23 [c] Gen. 28:4 6:5 [a] Ex. 2:24; [Job 34:28]; Acts 7:34 6:6 [a] Ex. 13:3, 14; 20:2; Deut. 6:12 [b] Ex. 3:17; 7:4; 12:51; 16:6; 18:1; Deut. 26:8; Ps. 136:11 [c] Ex. 15:13; Deut. 7:8; 1 Chr. 17:21; Neh. 1:10 6:7 [a] Ex. 19:5; Deut. 4:20; 7:6; 2 Sam. 7:24 [b] Gen. 17:7; Ex. 29:45, 46; Lev. 26:12, 13, 45; Deut. 29:13; Rev. 21:7 [c] Ex. 5:4, 5 6:8 [a] Gen. 15:18; 26:3; Num. 14:30; Neh. 9:15; Ezek. 20:5, 6 6:9 [a] Ex. 5:21 [b] Ex. 2:23; Num. 21:4 6:12 [a] Ex. 4:10; 6:30; Jer. 1:6 6:13 [a] Num. 27:19, 23; Deut. 31:14 6:14 [a] Gen. 46:9; Num. 26:5–11; 1 Chr. 5:3 6:15 [a] Gen. 46:10; Num. 26:12–14; 1 Chr. 4:24 [1] Spelled *Nemuel* in Numbers 26:12 6:16 [a] Gen. 46:11; Num. 3:17; 1 Chr. 6:16–30 6:17 [a] 1 Chr. 6:17 6:18 [a] 1 Chr. 6:2, 18 6:19 [a] 1 Chr. 6:19; 23:21 6:20 [a] Ex. 2:1, 2; Num. 3:19 [b] Num. 26:59 [c] Num. 26:59 6:21 [a] Num. 16:1; 1 Chr. 6:37, 38 6:22 [a] Lev. 10:4 6:23 [a] Ruth 4:19, 20; 1 Chr. 2:10; Matt. 1:4 [b] Lev. 10:1; Num. 3:2; 26:60 [c] Ex. 28:1 6:24 [a] Num. 26:11 6:25 [a] Num. 25:7, 11; Josh. 24:33 6:26 [a] Ex. 7:4; 12:17, 51; Num. 33:1 6:27 [a] Ex. 6:13; 32:7; 33:1; Ps. 77:20 6:29 [a] Ex. 6:11; 7:2

"Behold, [a]I *am* of uncircumcised lips, and
how shall Pharaoh heed me?"
7 So the LORD said to Moses: "See, I have
made you [a]*as* God to Pharaoh, and Aaron
your brother shall be [b]your prophet. 2You
[a]shall speak all that I command you. And
Aaron your brother shall tell Pharaoh to
send the children of Israel out of his land.
3And [a]I will harden Pharaoh's heart, and
[b]multiply My [c]signs and My wonders in the
land of Egypt. 4But [a]Pharaoh will not heed
you, so [b]that I may lay My hand on Egypt and
bring My armies *and* My people, the children of Israel, out of the land of Egypt [c]by
great judgments. 5And the Egyptians [a]shall
know that I *am* the LORD, when I [b]stretch out
My hand on Egypt and [c]bring out the children of Israel from among them."

6Then Moses and Aaron [a]did *so;* just
as the LORD commanded them, so they
did. 7And Moses *was* [a]eighty years old and
[b]Aaron eighty-three years old when they
spoke to Pharaoh.

Aaron's Miraculous Rod
(Ex. 4:1–5)

8Then the LORD spoke to Moses and
Aaron, saying, 9"When Pharaoh speaks
to you, saying, [a]'Show a miracle for yourselves,' then you shall say to Aaron, [b]'Take
your rod and cast *it* before Pharaoh, *and*
let it become a serpent.'" 10So Moses and
Aaron went in to Pharaoh, and they did so,
just [a]as the LORD commanded. And Aaron
cast down his rod before Pharaoh and before his servants, and it [b]became a serpent.

11But Pharaoh also [a]called the wise men
and [b]the sorcerers; so the magicians of
Egypt, they also [c]did in like manner with
their enchantments. 12For every man threw
down his rod, and they became serpents.
But Aaron's rod swallowed up their rods.
13And Pharaoh's heart grew hard, and he
did not heed them, as the LORD had said.

The First Plague: Waters Become Blood

14So the LORD said to Moses: [a]"Pharaoh's
heart *is* hard; he refuses to let the people go.
15Go to Pharaoh in the morning, when he
goes out to the [a]water, and you shall stand
by the river's bank to meet him; and [b]the rod
which was turned to a serpent you shall take
in your hand. 16And you shall say to him,
[a]'The LORD God of the Hebrews has sent me
to you, saying, "Let My people go, [b]that they
may serve Me in the wilderness"; but indeed,
until now you would not hear! 17Thus says
the LORD: "By this [a]you shall know that I *am*
the LORD. Behold, I will strike the waters
which *are* in the river with the rod that *is* in
my hand, and [b]they shall be turned [c]to blood.
18And the fish that *are* in the river shall die,
the river shall stink, and the Egyptians will
[a]loathe to drink the water of the river."'"

19Then the LORD spoke to Moses, "Say
to Aaron, 'Take your rod and [a]stretch out
your hand over the waters of Egypt, over
their streams, over their rivers, over their
ponds, and over all their pools of water,
that they may become blood. And there
shall be blood throughout all the land of
Egypt, both in *buckets of* wood and *pitchers*
of stone.'" 20And Moses and Aaron did so,
just as the LORD commanded. So he [a]lifted
up the rod and struck the waters that *were*
in the river, in the sight of Pharaoh and in
the sight of his servants. And all the [b]wa-
ters that *were* in the river were turned to
blood. 21The fish that *were* in the river died,
the river stank, and the Egyptians [a]could
not drink the water of the river. So there
was blood throughout all the land of Egypt.

22[a]Then the magicians of Egypt did
[b]so with their enchantments; and Pharaoh's heart grew hard, and he did not heed
them, [c]as the LORD had said. 23And Pharaoh
turned and went into his house. Neither
was his heart moved by this. 24So all the
Egyptians dug all around the river for water to drink, because they could not drink
the water of the river. 25And seven days
passed after the LORD had struck the river.

The Second Plague: Frogs

8 And the LORD spoke to Moses, "Go to
Pharaoh and say to him, 'Thus says the

6:30 [a] Ex. 4:10; 6:12; Jer. 1:6 **7:1** [a] Ex. 4:16; Jer. 1:10 [b] Ex. 4:15, 16 **7:2** [a] Ex. 4:15; Deut. 18:18 **7:3** [a] Ex. 4:21; 9:12 [b] Ex. 11:9; Acts 7:36 [c] Ex. 4:7; Deut. 4:34 **7:4** [a] Ex. 3:19, 20; 10:1; 11:9 [b] Ex. 9:14 [c] Ex. 6:6; 12:12 **7:5** [a] Ex. 7:17; 8:22; 14:4, 18; Ps. 9:16 [b] Ex. 9:15 [c] Ex. 3:20; 6:6; 12:51 **7:6** [a] Ex. 7:2 **7:7** [a] Deut. 29:5; 31:2; 34:7; Acts 7:23, 30 [b] Num. 33:39 **7:9** [a] Ex. 10:1; Is. 7:11; John 2:18; 6:30 [b] Ex. 4:2, 3, 17 **7:10** [a] Ex. 7:9 [b] Ex. 4:3 **7:11** [a] Gen. 41:8 [b] Dan. 2:2; 2 Tim. 3:8 [c] Ex. 7:22; 8:7, 18; 2 Tim. 3:9; Rev. 13:13, 14 **7:14** [a] Ex. 8:15; 10:1, 20, 27 **7:15** [a] Ex. 2:5; 8:20 [b] Ex. 4:2, 3; 7:10 **7:16** [a] Ex. 3:13, 18; 4:22 [b] Ex. 3:12, 18; 4:23; 5:1, 3; 8:1 **7:17** [a] Ex. 5:2; 7:5; 10:2; Ps. 9:16; Ezek. 25:17 [b] Ex. 4:9; 7:20 [c] Rev. 11:6; 16:4, 6 **7:18** [a] Ex. 7:24 **7:19** [a] Ex. 8:5, 6, 16; 9:22; 10:12, 21; 14:21, 26 **7:20** [a] Ex. 17:5 [b] Ps. 78:44; 105:29, 30 **7:21** [a] Ex. 7:18 **7:22** [a] Ex. 7:11 [b] Ex. 8:7 [c] Ex. 3:19; 7:3

LORD: "Let My people go, [a]that they may
serve Me. 2But if you [a]refuse to let *them* go,
behold, I will smite all your territory with
[b]frogs. 3So the river shall bring forth frogs
abundantly, which shall go up and come
into your house, into your [a]bedroom, on
your bed, into the houses of your servants,
on your people, into your ovens, and into
your kneading bowls. 4And the frogs shall
come up on you, on your people, and on
all your servants." ' "
5Then the LORD spoke to Moses, "Say to
Aaron, [a]'Stretch out your hand with your
rod over the streams, over the rivers, and
over the ponds, and cause frogs to come up
on the land of Egypt.' " 6So Aaron stretched
out his hand over the waters of Egypt, and
[a]the frogs came up and covered the land
of Egypt. 7[a]And the magicians did so with
their enchantments, and brought up frogs
on the land of Egypt.
8Then Pharaoh called for Moses and
Aaron, and said, [a]"Entreat the LORD that
He may take away the frogs from me and
from my people; and I will let the people
[b]go, that they may sacrifice to the LORD."
9And Moses said to Pharaoh, "Accept the
honor of saying when I shall intercede for
you, for your servants, and for your people, to destroy the frogs from you and your
houses, *that* they may remain in the river
only."
10So he said, "Tomorrow." And he said,
"*Let it be* according to your word, that you
may know that [a]*there is* no one like the
LORD our God. 11And the frogs shall depart
from you, from your houses, from your servants, and from your people. They shall remain in the river only."
12Then Moses and Aaron went out from
Pharaoh. And Moses [a]cried out to the LORD
concerning the frogs which He had brought
against Pharaoh. 13So the LORD did according to the word of Moses. And the frogs died
out of the houses, out of the courtyards,
and out of the fields. 14They gathered them
together in heaps, and the land stank. 15But
when Pharaoh saw that there was [a]relief,
[b]he hardened his heart and did not heed
them, as the LORD had said.

The Third Plague: Lice

16So the LORD said to Moses, "Say to
Aaron, 'Stretch out your rod, and strike the
dust of the land, so that it may become lice
throughout all the land of Egypt.' " 17And
they did so. For Aaron stretched out his
hand with his rod and struck the dust of
the earth, and [a]it became lice on man and
beast. All the dust of the land became lice
throughout all the land of Egypt.
18Now [a]the magicians so worked with
their enchantments to bring forth lice, but
they [b]could not. So there were lice on man
and beast. 19Then the magicians said to
Pharaoh, "This *is* [a]the finger of God." But
Pharaoh's [b]heart grew hard, and he did not
heed them, just as the LORD had said.

The Fourth Plague: Flies

20And the LORD said to Moses, [a]"Rise early
in the morning and stand before Pharaoh as
he comes out to the water. Then say to him,
'Thus says the LORD: [b]"Let My people go, that
they may serve Me. 21Or else, if you will not
let My people go, behold, I will send swarms
of flies on you and your servants, on your
people and into your houses. The houses of
the Egyptians shall be full of swarms *of flies,*
and also the ground on which they *stand.*
22And in that day [a]I will set apart the land of
[b]Goshen, in which My people dwell, that no
swarms *of flies* shall be there, in order that
you may [c]know that I *am* the LORD in the
midst of the [d]land. 23I will make a difference[1]
between My people and your people. Tomorrow this [a]sign shall be." ' " 24And the LORD
did so. [a]Thick swarms *of flies* came into the
house of Pharaoh, *into* his servants' houses,
and into all the land of Egypt. The land was
corrupted because of the swarms *of flies.*
25Then Pharaoh called for Moses and
Aaron, and said, "Go, sacrifice to your God
in the land."
26And Moses said, "It is not right to
do so, for we would be sacrificing [a]the

8:1 [a] Ex. 3:12, 18; 4:23; 5:1, 3 **8:2** [a] Ex. 7:14; 9:2 [b] Rev. 16:13 **8:3** [a] Ps. 105:30 **8:5** [a] Ex. 7:19 **8:6** [a] Ps. 78:45; 105:30 **8:7** [a] Ex. 7:11, 22 **8:8** [a] Ex. 8:28; 9:28; 10:17; Num. 21:7; 1 Kin. 13:6 [b] Ex. 10:8, 24 **8:10** [a] Ex. 9:14; 15:11; Deut. 4:35, 39; 33:26; 2 Sam. 7:22; 1 Chr. 17:20; Ps. 86:8; Is. 46:9; [Jer. 10:6, 7] **8:12** [a] Ex. 8:30; 9:33; 10:18; 32:11; [James 5:16–18] **8:15** [a] Eccl. 8:11 [b] Ex. 7:14, 22; 9:34; 1 Sam. 6:6 **8:17** [a] Ps. 105:31 **8:18** [a] Ex. 7:11, 12; 8:7 [b] Dan. 5:8; 2 Tim. 3:8, 9 **8:19** [a] Ex. 7:5; 10:7; 1 Sam. 6:3, 9; Ps. 8:3; Luke 11:20 [b] Ex. 8:15 **8:20** [a] Ex. 7:15; 9:13 [b] Ex. 3:18; 4:23; 5:1, 3; 8:1 **8:22** [a] Ex. 9:4, 6, 26; 10:23; 11:6, 7; 12:13 [b] Gen. 50:8 [c] Ex. 7:5, 17; 10:2; 14:4 [d] Ex. 9:29 **8:23** [a] Ex. 4:8 [1] Literally *set a ransom* (compare Exodus 9:4 and 11:7) **8:24** [a] Ps. 78:45; 105:31 **8:26** [a] Gen. 43:32; 46:34; [Deut. 7:25, 26; 12:31]

abomination of the Egyptians to the LORD
our God. If we sacrifice the abomination of
the Egyptians before their eyes, then will
they not stone us? 27 We will go [a]three days'
journey into the wilderness and sacrifice to
the LORD our God as [b]He will command us."
28 So Pharaoh said, "I will let you go, that
you may sacrifice to the LORD your God in
the wilderness; only you shall not go very
far away. [a]Intercede for me."
29 Then Moses said, "Indeed I am going
out from you, and I will entreat the LORD,
that the swarms *of flies* may depart tomorrow from Pharaoh, from his servants, and
from his people. But let Pharaoh not [a]deal
deceitfully anymore in not letting the people go to sacrifice to the LORD."
30 So Moses went out from Pharaoh and
[a]entreated the LORD. 31 And the LORD did according to the word of Moses; He removed
the swarms *of flies* from Pharaoh, from his
servants, and from his people. Not one remained. 32 But Pharaoh [a]hardened his heart
at this time also; neither would he let the
people go.

The Fifth Plague: Livestock Diseased

9 Then the LORD said to Moses, [a]"Go in
to Pharaoh and tell him, 'Thus says the
LORD God of the Hebrews: "Let My people go, that they may [b]serve Me. 2 For if you
[a]refuse to let *them* go, and still hold them,
3 behold, the [a]hand of the LORD will be on
your cattle in the field, on the horses, on
the donkeys, on the camels, on the oxen,
and on the sheep—a very severe pestilence.
4 And [a]the LORD will make a difference between the livestock of Israel and the livestock of Egypt. So nothing shall die of all
that belongs to the children of Israel." ' "
5 Then the LORD appointed a set time, saying, "Tomorrow the LORD will do this thing
in the land."
6 So the LORD did this thing on the next
day, and [a]all the livestock of Egypt died;
but of the livestock of the children of Israel, not one died. 7 Then Pharaoh sent, and
indeed, not even one of the livestock of
the Israelites was dead. But the [a]heart of
Pharaoh became hard, and he did not let
the people go.

The Sixth Plague: Boils
(Deut. 28:27)

8 So the LORD said to Moses and Aaron,
"Take for yourselves handfuls of ashes
from a furnace, and let Moses scatter it toward the heavens in the sight of Pharaoh.
9 And it will become fine dust in all the land
of Egypt, and it will cause [a]boils that break
out in sores on man and beast throughout all the land of Egypt." 10 Then they took
ashes from the furnace and stood before
Pharaoh, and Moses scattered *them* toward
heaven. And *they* caused [a]boils that break
out in sores on man and beast. 11 And the
[a]magicians could not stand before Moses
because of the [b]boils, for the boils were on
the magicians and on all the Egyptians.
12 But the LORD hardened the heart of Pharaoh; and he [a]did not heed them, just [b]as the
LORD had spoken to Moses.

The Seventh Plague: Hail

13 Then the LORD said to Moses, [a]"Rise
early in the morning and stand before
Pharaoh, and say to him, 'Thus says the
LORD God of the Hebrews: "Let My people go, that they may [b]serve Me, 14 for at
this time I will send all My plagues to your
very heart, and on your servants and on
your people, [a]that you may know that *there*
is none like Me in all the earth. 15 Now if I
had [a]stretched out My hand and struck you
and your people with [b]pestilence, then you
would have been cut off from the earth.
16 But indeed for [a]this *purpose* I have raised
you up, that I may [b]show My power *in* you,
and that My [c]name may be declared in all
the earth. 17 As yet you exalt yourself against
My people in that you will not let them go.
18 Behold, tomorrow about this time I will
cause very heavy hail to rain down, such
as has not been in Egypt since its founding
until now. 19 Therefore send now *and* gather
your livestock and all that you have in the

8:27 [a] Ex. 3:18; 5:3 [b] Ex. 3:12 **8:28** [a] Ex. 8:8, 15, 29, 32; 9:28; 1 Kin. 13:6 **8:29** [a] Ex. 8:8, 15 **8:30** [a] Ex. 8:12 **8:32** [a] Ex. 4:21; 8:8, 15; Ps. 52:2 **9:1** [a] Ex. 4:23; 8:1 [b] Ex. 7:16 **9:2** [a] Ex. 8:2 **9:3** [a] Ex. 7:4; 1 Sam. 5:6; Ps. 39:10; Acts 13:11 **9:4** [a] Ex. 8:22 **9:6** [a] Ex. 9:19, 20, 25; Ps. 78:48, 50 **9:7** [a] Ex. 7:14; 8:32 **9:9** [a] Deut. 28:27; Rev. 16:2 **9:10** [a] Deut. 28:27 **9:11** [a] [Ex. 8:18, 19; 2 Tim. 3:9] [b] Deut. 28:27; Job 2:7; Rev. 16:1, 2 **9:12** [a] Ex. 7:13 [b] Ex. 4:21 **9:13** [a] Ex. 8:20 [b] Ex. 9:1 **9:14** [a] Ex. 8:10; Deut. 3:24; 2 Sam. 7:22; 1 Chr. 17:20; Ps. 86:8; Is. 45:5–8; 46:9; Jer. 10:6, 7 **9:15** [a] Ex. 3:20; 7:5 [b] Ex. 5:3 **9:16** [a] Ex. 14:17; Prov. 16:4; [Rom. 9:17, 18; 1 Pet. 2:8, 9] [b] Ex. 7:4, 5; 10:1; 11:9; 14:17 [c] 1 Kin. 8:43

field, for the hail shall come down on every man and every animal which is found
in the field and is not brought home; and
they shall die."'"
20 He who [a]feared the word of the LORD
among the [b]servants of Pharaoh made
his servants and his livestock flee to the
houses. 21 But he who did not regard the
word of the LORD left his servants and his
livestock in the field.
22 Then the LORD said to Moses, "Stretch
out your hand toward heaven, that there
may be [a]hail in all the land of Egypt—on
man, on beast, and on every herb of the
field, throughout the land of Egypt." 23 And
Moses stretched out his rod toward heaven;
and [a]the LORD sent thunder and hail, and
fire darted to the ground. And the LORD
rained hail on the land of Egypt. 24 So there
was hail, and fire mingled with the hail, so
very heavy that there was none like it in all
the land of Egypt since it became a nation.
25 And the [a]hail struck throughout the whole
land of Egypt, all that *was* in the field, both
man and beast; and the hail struck every
herb of the field and broke every tree of the
field. 26 [a]Only in the land of Goshen, where
the children of Israel *were,* there was no hail.
27 And Pharaoh sent and [a]called for Moses and Aaron, and said to them, [b]"I have
sinned this time. [c]The LORD *is* righteous,
and my people and I *are* wicked. 28 [a]Entreat
the LORD, that there may be no *more* mighty
thundering and hail, for *it is* enough. I will
let you [b]go, and you shall stay no longer."
29 So Moses said to him, "As soon as I
have gone out of the city, I will [a]spread out
my hands to the LORD; the thunder will
cease, and there will be no more hail, that
you may know that the [b]earth *is* the LORD's.
30 But as for you and your servants, [a]I know
that you will not yet fear the LORD God."
31 Now the flax and the barley were
struck, [a]for the barley *was* in the head and
the flax *was* in bud. 32 But the wheat and
the spelt were not struck, for they *are* late
crops.
33 So Moses went out of the city from
Pharaoh and [a]spread out his hands to the
LORD; then the thunder and the hail ceased,
and the rain was not poured on the earth.
34 And when Pharaoh saw that the rain, the
hail, and the thunder had ceased, he sinned
yet more; and he hardened his heart, he
and his servants. 35 So [a]the heart of Pharaoh was hard; neither would he let the children of Israel go, as the LORD had spoken
by Moses.

The Eighth Plague: Locusts
(Joel 1:2–4)

10 Now the LORD said to Moses, "Go in
to Pharaoh; [a]for I have hardened his
heart and the hearts of his servants, [b]that I
may show these signs of Mine before him,
2 and that [a]you may tell in the hearing of
your son and your son's son the mighty
things I have done in Egypt, and My signs
which I have done among them, that you
may [b]know that I *am* the LORD."
3 So Moses and Aaron came in to Pharaoh and said to him, "Thus says the LORD
God of the Hebrews: 'How long will you
refuse to [a]humble yourself before Me? Let
My people go, that they may [b]serve Me. 4 Or
else, if you refuse to let My people go, behold, tomorrow I will bring [a]locusts into
your territory. 5 And they shall cover the
face of the earth, so that no one will be able
to see the earth; and [a]they shall eat the residue of what is left, which remains to you
from the hail, and they shall eat every tree
which grows up for you out of the field.
6 They shall [a]fill your houses, the houses of
all your servants, and the houses of all the
Egyptians—which neither your fathers nor
your fathers' fathers have seen, since the
day that they were on the earth to this day.'"
And he turned and went out from Pharaoh.
7 Then Pharaoh's [a]servants said to him,
"How long shall this man be [b]a snare to us?
Let the men go, that they may serve the
LORD their God. Do you not yet know that
Egypt is destroyed?"

9:20 [a] Ex. 1:17; 14:31; [Prov. 13:13] [b] Ex. 8:19; 10:7 **9:22** [a] Rev. 16:21 **9:23** [a] Gen. 19:24; Josh. 10:11; Ps. 18:13; 78:47; 105:32; 148:8; Is. 30:30; Ezek. 38:22; Rev. 8:7 **9:25** [a] Ex. 9:19; Ps. 78:47, 48; 105:32, 33 **9:26** [a] Ex. 8:22, 23; 9:4, 6; 10:23; 11:7; 12:13; Is. 32:18, 19 **9:27** [a] Ex. 8:8 [b] Ex. 9:34; 10:16, 17 [c] 2 Chr. 12:6; Ps. 129:4; 145:17; Lam. 1:18 **9:28** [a] Ex. 8:8, 28; 10:17; Acts 8:24 [b] Ex. 8:25; 10:8, 24 **9:29** [a] 1 Kin. 8:22, 38; Ps. 143:6; Is. 1:15 [b] Ex. 8:22; 19:5; 20:11; Ps. 24:1; 1 Cor. 10:26, 28 **9:30** [a] Ex. 8:29; [Is. 26:10] **9:31** [a] Ruth 1:22; 2:23 **9:33** [a] Ex. 8:12; 9:29 **9:35** [a] Ex. 4:21 **10:1** [a] Ex. 4:21; 7:14; 9:12; 10:27; 11:10; 14:4; Josh. 11:20; John 12:40; Rom. 9:18 [b] Ex. 7:4; 9:16 **10:2** [a] Ex. 12:26; 13:8, 14; Deut. 4:9; 6:7; 11:19; Ps. 44:1; 78:5; Joel 1:3 [b] Ex. 7:5, 17; 8:22 **10:3** [a] [1 Kin. 21:29; 2 Chr. 34:27]; Job 42:6; [James 4:10; 1 Pet. 5:6] [b] Ex. 4:23; 8:1; 9:1 **10:4** [a] Prov. 30:27; Rev. 9:3 **10:5** [a] Ex. 9:32; Joel 1:4; 2:25 **10:6** [a] Ex. 8:3, 21 **10:7** [a] Ex. 7:5; 8:19; 9:20; 12:33 [b] Ex. 23:33; Josh. 23:13; 1 Sam. 18:21; Eccl. 7:26; 1 Cor. 7:35

8So Moses and Aaron were brought
again to Pharaoh, and he said to them, "Go,
serve the LORD your God. Who *are* the ones
that are going?"
9And Moses said, "We will go with our
young and our old; with our sons and our
daughters, with our flocks and our herds
we will go, for [a]we must hold a feast to the
LORD."
10Then he said to them, "The LORD had
better be with you when I let you and your
little ones go! Beware, for evil is ahead of
you. 11Not so! Go now, you *who are* men,
and serve the LORD, for that is what you
desired." And they were driven [a]out from
Pharaoh's presence.
12Then the LORD said to Moses, [a]"Stretch
out your hand over the land of Egypt for
the locusts, that they may come upon the
land of Egypt, and [b]eat every herb of the
land—all that the hail has left." 13So Moses stretched out his rod over the land
of Egypt, and the LORD brought an east
wind on the land all that day and all *that*
night. When it was morning, the east
wind brought the locusts. 14And [a]the locusts went up over all the land of Egypt
and rested on all the territory of Egypt.
They were very severe; [b]previously there
had been no such locusts as they, nor shall
there be such after them. 15For they [a]cov-
ered the face of the whole earth, so that

EXODUS 10:3

I AM MOSES

So Moses and Aaron came in to Pharaoh and said to him, "Thus says the LORD God of the Hebrews: 'How long will you refuse to humble yourself before Me? Let My people go, that they may serve Me.'" Exodus 10:3

I am Moses. God first called me from within a miraculous burning bush. There, He told me that He had seen the misery of Israel caused by the slave drivers in Egypt. God had heard their cries, and the time had come for their rescue and freedom.

Then, Almighty God said He was sending me to bring His people out of Egypt. How could I, a man who came from the Hebrew slaves and who was also slow of speech and tongue, accomplish such a task? I knew I had no power to free the Israelites. But God said He would be with me.

So that I could tell God's people who had sent me to them, I asked God His name. He answered, "I AM WHO I AM." He is the one true God. God's mighty hand would work amazing wonders and compel Pharaoh to release the people of Israel. I asked God to send someone else. He would not and instead made my brother, Aaron, my mouthpiece to speak to the Israelites.

I went to Pharaoh again and again, telling him to free God's people. But he was hard-hearted and refused. With each refusal, God brought a plague upon Egypt. Pharaoh remained hard-hearted through nine devastating plagues. Then, the tenth plague brought death to all the firstborn of the land. Pharaoh's own son was struck down. But the firstborn of Israel were passed over by the destroyer—the angel of death—because God had told us to place a lamb's blood around our doors to protect us.

†

God did as He promised. He freed His people from bondage in Egypt and led them to the land flowing with milk and honey. But Moses did not enter with them because of his disobedience to God. It is a reminder that when God calls us, we need to obey and act no matter who we are and what God calls us to do. He will equip us for the task.

10:9 [a] Ex. 5:1; 7:16 10:11 [a] Ex. 10:28 10:12 [a] Ex. 7:19 [b] Ex. 10:5, 15 10:14 [a] Deut. 28:38; Ps. 78:46; 105:34 [b] Joel 1:4, 7; 2:1–11; Rev. 9:3 10:15 [a] Ex. 10:5

the land was darkened; and they [b]ate every herb of the land and all the fruit of the
trees which the hail had left. So there remained nothing green on the trees or on
the plants of the field throughout all the
land of Egypt.
16Then Pharaoh called [a]for Moses and
Aaron in haste, and said, [b]"I have sinned
against the LORD your God and against you.
17Now therefore, please forgive my sin only
this once, and [a]entreat the LORD your God,
that He may take away from me this death
only." 18So he [a]went out from Pharaoh and
entreated the LORD. 19And the LORD turned
a very strong west wind, which took the locusts away and blew them [a]into the Red Sea.
There remained not one locust in all the
territory of Egypt. 20But the LORD [a]hard-
ened Pharaoh's heart, and he did not let
the children of Israel go.

The Ninth Plague: Darkness

21Then the LORD said to Moses, [a]"Stretch
out your hand toward heaven, that there
may be darkness over the land of Egypt,
darkness *which* may even be felt." 22So Moses stretched out his hand toward heaven,
and there was [a]thick darkness in all the
land of Egypt [b]three days. 23They did not
see one another; nor did anyone rise from
his place for three days. [a]But all the children of Israel had light in their dwellings.
24Then Pharaoh called to Moses and
[a]said, "Go, serve the LORD; only let your
flocks and your herds be kept back. Let your
[b]little ones also go with you."
25But Moses said, "You must also give us
sacrifices and burnt offerings, that we may
sacrifice to the LORD our God. 26Our [a]live-
stock also shall go with us; not a hoof shall
be left behind. For we must take some of
them to serve the LORD our God, and even
we do not know with what we must serve
the LORD until we arrive there."
27But the LORD [a]hardened Pharaoh's
heart, and he would not let them go. 28Then
Pharaoh said to him, [a]"Get away from me!
Take heed to yourself and see my face no
more! For in the day you see my face you
shall die!"
29So Moses said, "You have spoken well.
[a]I will never see your face again."

Death of the Firstborn Announced
(Ex. 3:21, 22; 12:35, 36)

11 And the LORD said to Moses, "I will
bring one more plague on Pharaoh
and on Egypt. [a]Afterward he will let you
go from here. [b]When he lets *you* go, he will
surely drive you out of here altogether.
2Speak now in the hearing of the people,
and let every man ask from his neighbor
and every woman from her neighbor, [a]ar-
ticles of silver and articles of gold." 3[a]And
the LORD gave the people favor in the sight
of the Egyptians. Moreover the man [b]Mo-
ses *was* very great in the land of Egypt, in
the sight of Pharaoh's servants and in the
sight of the people.
4Then Moses said, "Thus says the LORD:
[a]'About midnight I will go out into the
midst of Egypt; 5and [a]all the firstborn in the
land of Egypt shall die, from the firstborn
of Pharaoh who sits on his throne, even to
the firstborn of the female servant who *is*
behind the handmill, and all the firstborn
of the animals. 6[a]Then there shall be a great
cry throughout all the land of Egypt, [b]such
as was not like it *before,* nor shall be like it
again. 7[a]But against none of the children of
Israel [b]shall a dog move its tongue, against
man or beast, that you may know that the
LORD does make a difference between the
Egyptians and Israel.' 8And [a]all these your
servants shall come down to me and bow
down to me, saying, 'Get out, and all the
people who follow you!' After that I will go
out." [b]Then he went out from Pharaoh in
great anger.
9But the LORD said to Moses, [a]"Pharaoh
will not heed you, so that [b]My wonders may
be multiplied in the land of Egypt." 10So Moses and Aaron did all these wonders before
Pharaoh; [a]and the LORD hardened Pharaoh's heart, and he did not let the children
of Israel go out of his land.

10:15 [b] Ps. 105:35 10:16 [a] Ex. 8:8 [b] Ex. 9:27 10:17 [a] Ex. 8:8, 28; 9:28; 1 Kin. 13:6 10:18 [a] Ex. 8:30 10:19 [a] Joel 2:20 10:20 [a] Ex. 4:21; 10:1; 11:10 10:21 [a] Ex. 9:22 10:22 [a] Ps. 105:28; Rev. 16:10 [b] Ex. 3:18 10:23 [a] Ex. 8:22, 23 10:24 [a] Ex. 8:8, 25; 10:8 [b] Ex. 10:10 10:26 [a] Ex. 10:9 10:27 [a] Ex. 4:21; 10:1, 20; 14:4, 8 10:28 [a] Ex. 10:11 10:29 [a] Ex. 11:8; Heb. 11:27 11:1 [a] Ex. 12:31, 33, 39 [b] Ex. 6:1; 12:39 11:2 [a] Ex. 3:22; 12:35, 36 11:3 [a] Ex. 3:21; 12:36; Ps. 106:46 [b] Deut. 34:10–12; 2 Sam. 7:9; Esth. 9:4 11:4 [a] Ex. 12:12, 23, 29 11:5 [a] Ex. 4:23; 12:12, 29; Ps. 78:51; 105:36; 135:8; 136:10; Amos 4:10 11:6 [a] Ex. 12:30; Amos 5:17 [b] Ex. 10:14 11:7 [a] Ex. 8:22 [b] Josh. 10:21 11:8 [a] Ex. 12:31–33 [b] Ex. 10:29; Heb. 11:27 11:9 [a] Ex. 3:19; 7:4; 10:1 [b] Ex. 7:3; 9:16 11:10 [a] Ex. 7:3; 9:12; 10:1, 20, 27; Josh. 11:20; Is. 63:17; John 12:40; Rom. 2:5

The Passover Instituted
(Num. 9:1–14; Deut. 16:1–8; Ezek. 45:21–25)

12 Now the LORD spoke to Moses and
Aaron in the land of Egypt, saying,
2[a]"This month *shall be* your beginning of
months; it *shall be* the first month of the
year to you. 3Speak to all the congregation of
Israel, saying: 'On the [a]tenth of this month
every man shall take for himself a lamb, according to the house of *his* father, a lamb for
a household. 4And if the household is too
small for the lamb, let him and his neighbor next to his house take *it* according to
the number of the persons; according to
each man's need you shall make your count
for the lamb. 5Your lamb shall be [a]without
blemish, a male of the first year. You may
take *it* from the sheep or from the goats.
6Now you shall keep it until the [a]fourteenth
day of the same month. Then the whole assembly of the congregation of Israel shall
kill it at twilight. 7And they shall take *some*
of the blood and put *it* on the two doorposts
and on the lintel of the houses where they
eat it. 8Then they shall eat the flesh on that
[a]night; [b]roasted in fire, with [c]unleavened
bread *and* with bitter *herbs* they shall eat
it. 9Do not eat it raw, nor boiled at all with
water, but [a]roasted in fire—its head with its
legs and its entrails. 10[a]You shall let none of
it remain until morning, and what remains
of it until morning you shall burn with fire.
11And thus you shall eat it: *with* a belt on
your waist, your sandals on your feet, and
your staff in your hand. So you shall eat it
in haste. [a]It *is* the LORD's Passover.

12'For I [a]will pass through the land of
Egypt on that night, and will strike all the
firstborn in the land of Egypt, both man
and beast; and [b]against all the gods of Egypt
I will execute judgment: [c]I *am* the LORD.
13Now the blood shall be a sign for you on
the houses where you *are*. And when I see
the blood, I will pass over you; and the
plague shall not be on you to destroy *you*
when I strike the land of Egypt.

14'So this day shall be to you [a]a memorial;
and you shall keep it as a [b]feast to the
LORD throughout your generations. You
shall keep it as a feast [c]by an everlasting
ordinance. 15[a]Seven days you shall eat unleavened bread. On the first day you shall
remove leaven from your houses. For whoever eats leavened bread from the first day
until the seventh day, [b]that person shall be
cut off from Israel. 16On the first day *there
shall be* [a]a holy convocation, and on the
seventh day there shall be a holy convocation for you. No manner of work shall
be done on them; but *that* which everyone
must eat—that only may be prepared by
you. 17So you shall observe *the Feast of* Unleavened Bread, for [a]on this same day I will
have brought your armies [b]out of the land
of Egypt. Therefore you shall observe this
day throughout your generations as an everlasting ordinance. 18[a]In the first *month*, on
the fourteenth day of the month at evening,
you shall eat unleavened bread, until the
twenty-first day of the month at evening.
19For [a]seven days no leaven shall be found
in your houses, since whoever eats what is
leavened, that same person shall be cut off
from the congregation of Israel, whether *he
is* a stranger or a native of the land. 20You
shall eat nothing leavened; in all your dwellings you shall eat unleavened bread.' "

21Then [a]Moses called for all the [b]elders
of Israel and said to them, [c]"Pick out and
take lambs for yourselves according to your
families, and kill the Passover *lamb*. 22[a]And
you shall take a bunch of hyssop, dip *it* in
the blood that *is* in the basin, and [b]strike
the lintel and the two doorposts with the
blood that *is* in the basin. And none of you
shall go out of the door of his house until
morning. 23[a]For the LORD will pass through
to strike the Egyptians; and when He sees
the [b]blood on the lintel and on the two doorposts, the LORD will pass over the door and
[c]not allow [d]the destroyer to come into your
houses to strike *you*. 24And you shall [a]ob-
serve this thing as an ordinance for you
and your sons forever. 25It will come to pass

12:2 [a] Ex. 13:4; 23:15; 34:18; Deut. 16:1 **12:3** [a] Josh. 4:19 **12:5** [a] Lev. 22:18–21; 23:12; Mal. 1:8, 14; [Heb. 9:14; 1 Pet. 1:19] **12:6** [a] Ex. 12:14, 17; Lev. 23:5; Num. 9:1–3, 11; 28:16; Deut. 16:1, 4, 6 **12:8** [a] Ex. 34:25; Num. 9:12 [b] Deut. 16:7 [c] Deut. 16:3, 4; 1 Cor. 5:8 **12:9** [a] Deut. 16:7 **12:10** [a] Ex. 16:19; 23:18; 34:25 **12:11** [a] Ex. 12:13, 21, 27, 43 **12:12** [a] Ex. 11:4, 5 [b] Num. 33:4 [c] Ex. 6:2 **12:14** [a] Ex. 13:9 [b] Lev. 23:4, 5; 2 Kin. 23:21 [c] Ex. 12:17, 24; 13:10 **12:15** [a] Ex. 13:6, 7; 23:15; 34:18; Lev. 23:6; Num. 28:17; Deut. 16:3, 8 [b] Gen. 17:14; Ex. 12:19; Num. 9:13 **12:16** [a] Lev. 23:2, 7, 8; Num. 28:18, 25 **12:17** [a] Ex. 12:14; 13:3, 10 [b] Num. 33:1 **12:18** [a] Ex. 12:2; Lev. 23:5–8; Num. 28:16–25 **12:19** [a] Ex. 12:15; 23:15; 34:18 **12:21** [a] [Heb. 11:28] [b] Ex. 3:16 [c] Ex. 12:3; Num. 9:4; Josh. 5:10; 2 Kin. 23:21; Ezra 6:20; Mark 14:12–16 **12:22** [a] Heb. 11:28 [b] Ex. 12:7 **12:23** [a] Ex. 11:4; 12:12, 13 [b] Ex. 24:8 [c] Ezek. 9:6; Rev. 7:3; 9:4 [d] 1 Cor. 10:10; Heb. 11:28 **12:24** [a] Ex. 12:14, 17; 13:5, 10

when you come to the land which the LORD
will give you, [a]just as He promised, that you
shall keep this service. 26 [a]And it shall be,
when your children say to you, 'What do
you mean by this service?' 27 that you shall
say, [a]'It *is* the Passover sacrifice of the LORD,
who passed over the houses of the children
of Israel in Egypt when He struck the Egyptians and delivered our households.'" So the
people [b]bowed their heads and worshiped.
28 Then the children of Israel went away and
[a]did *so;* just as the LORD had commanded
Moses and Aaron, so they did.

The Tenth Plague: Death of the Firstborn
(Ex. 11:1–10)

29 [a]And it came to pass at midnight that
[b]the LORD struck all the firstborn in the
land of Egypt, from the firstborn of Pharaoh who sat on his throne to the firstborn
of the captive who *was* in the dungeon, and
all the firstborn of [c]livestock. 30 So Pharaoh
rose in the night, he, all his servants, and
all the Egyptians; and there was a great cry
in Egypt, for *there was* not a house where
there was not one dead.

The Exodus

31 Then he [a]called for Moses and Aaron by
night, and said, "Rise, go out from among
my people, [b]both you and the children of
Israel. And go, serve the LORD as you have
[c]said. 32 [a]Also take your flocks and your
herds, as you have said, and be gone; and
bless me also."

33 [a]And the Egyptians [b]urged the people, that they might send them out of the
land in haste. For they said, "We *shall* all *be*
dead." 34 So the people took their dough before it was leavened, having their kneading
bowls bound up in their clothes on their
shoulders. 35 Now the children of Israel had
done according to the word of Moses, and
they had asked from the Egyptians [a]arti-
cles of silver, articles of gold, and clothing.
36 [a]And the LORD had given the people favor
in the sight of the Egyptians, so that they
granted them *what they requested.* Thus
[b]they plundered the Egyptians.

37 Then [a]the children of Israel journeyed
from [b]Rameses to Succoth, about [c]six hundred thousand men on foot, besides children. 38 A [a]mixed multitude went up with
them also, and flocks and herds—a great
deal of [b]livestock. 39 And they baked unleavened cakes of the dough which they
had brought out of Egypt; for it was not
leavened, because [a]they were driven out
of Egypt and could not wait, nor had they
prepared provisions for themselves.

40 Now the sojourn of the children of
Israel who lived in Egypt[1] *was* [a]four hundred and thirty years. 41 And it came to pass
at the end of the four hundred and thirty
years—on that very same day—it came to
pass that [a]all the armies of the LORD went
out from the land of Egypt. 42 It *is* [a]a night of
solemn observance to the LORD for bringing them out of the land of Egypt. This *is*
that night of the LORD, a solemn observance for all the children of Israel throughout their generations.

Passover Regulations
(Gen. 17:9–14; Ex. 12:1–13)

43 And the LORD said to Moses and Aaron,
"This *is* [a]the ordinance of the Passover: No
foreigner shall eat it. 44 But every man's servant who is bought for money, when you
have [a]circumcised him, then he may eat it.
45 [a]A sojourner and a hired servant shall not
eat it. 46 In one house it shall be eaten; you
shall not carry any of the flesh outside the
house, [a]nor shall you break one of its bones.
47 [a]All the congregation of Israel shall keep
it. 48 And [a]when a stranger dwells with you
and wants to keep the Passover to the LORD,
let all his males be circumcised, and then
let him come near and keep it; and he shall
be as a native of the land. For no uncircumcised person shall eat it. 49 [a]One law shall
be for the native-born and for the stranger
who dwells among you."

50 Thus all the children of Israel did; as

12:25 [a] Ex. 3:8, 17 12:26 [a] Ex. 10:2; 13:8, 14, 15; Deut. 32:7; Josh. 4:6; Ps. 78:6 12:27 [a] Ex. 12:11 [b] Ex. 4:31 12:28 [a] [Heb. 11:28] 12:29 [a] Ex. 11:4, 5 [b] Num. 8:17; 33:4; Ps. 135:8; 136:10 [c] Ex. 9:6 12:31 [a] Ex. 10:28, 29 [b] Ex. 8:25; 11:1 [c] Ex. 10:9 12:32 [a] Ex. 10:9, 26 12:33 [a] Ex. 10:7 [b] Ex. 11:8; Ps. 105:38 12:35 [a] Ex. 3:21, 22; 11:2, 3; Ps. 105:37 12:36 [a] Ex. 3:21 [b] Gen. 15:14 12:37 [a] Num. 33:3, 5 [b] Gen. 47:11; Ex. 1:11; Num. 33:3, 4 [c] Gen. 12:2; Ex. 38:26; Num. 1:46; 2:32; 11:21; 26:51 12:38 [a] Num. 11:4 [b] Ex. 17:3; Num. 20:19; 32:1; Deut. 3:19 12:39 [a] Ex. 6:1; 11:1; 12:31–33 12:40 [a] Gen. 15:13, 16; Acts 7:6; Gal. 3:17 [1] Samaritan Pentateuch and Septuagint read *Egypt and Canaan.* 12:41 [a] Ex. 3:8, 10; 6:6; 7:4 12:42 [a] Ex. 13:10; 34:18; Deut. 16:1, 6 12:43 [a] Ex. 12:11; Num. 9:14 12:44 [a] Gen. 17:12, 13; Lev. 22:11 12:45 [a] Lev. 22:10 12:46 [a] Num. 9:12; Ps. 34:20; [John 19:33, 36] 12:47 [a] Ex. 12:6; Num. 9:13, 14 12:48 [a] Num. 9:14 12:49 [a] Lev. 24:22; Num. 15:15, 16; [Gal. 3:28]

the LORD commanded Moses and Aaron,
so they did. 51[a]And it came to pass, on that
very same day, that the LORD brought the
children of Israel out of the land of Egypt
[b]according to their armies.

The Firstborn Consecrated

13 Then the LORD spoke to Moses, saying,
2[a]"Consecrate to Me all the firstborn,
whatever opens the womb among the
children of Israel, *both* of man and beast;
it is Mine."

The Feast of Unleavened Bread
(Ex. 12:14–20)

3And Moses said to the people: [a]"Remember
this day in which you went out of
Egypt, out of the house of bondage; for [b]by
strength of hand the LORD brought you out
of this *place.* [c]No leavened bread shall be
eaten. 4[a]On this day you are going out, in
the month Abib. 5And it shall be, when the
LORD [a]brings you into the [b]land of the Canaanites
and the Hittites and the Amorites
and the Hivites and the Jebusites, which He
[c]swore to your fathers to give you, a land
flowing with milk and honey, [d]that you shall
keep this service in this month. 6[a]Seven
days you shall eat unleavened bread, and
on the seventh day *there shall be* a feast to
the LORD. 7Unleavened bread shall be eaten
seven days. And [a]no leavened bread shall be
seen among you, nor shall leaven be seen
among you in all your quarters. 8And you
shall [a]tell your son in that day, saying, '*This
is done* because of what the LORD did for
me when I came up from Egypt.' 9It shall
be as [a]a sign to you on your hand and as
a memorial between your eyes, that the
LORD's law may be in your mouth; for with a
strong hand the LORD has brought you out
of Egypt. 10[a]You shall therefore keep this
ordinance in its season from year to year.

The Law of the Firstborn

11"And it shall be, when the LORD [a]brings
you into the land of the [b]Canaanites, as He
swore to you and your fathers, and gives
it to you, 12[a]that you shall set apart to the
LORD all that open the womb, that is, every
firstborn that comes from an animal which
you have; the males *shall be* the LORD's.
13But [a]every firstborn of a donkey you shall
redeem with a lamb; and if you will not redeem
it, then you shall break its neck. And
all the firstborn of man among your sons
[b]you shall redeem. 14[a]So it shall be, when
your son asks you in time to come, saying,
'What *is* this?' that you shall say to him,
[b]'By strength of hand the LORD brought
us out of Egypt, out of the house of bondage.
15And it came to pass, when Pharaoh
was stubborn about letting us go, that [a]the
LORD killed all the firstborn in the land of
Egypt, both the firstborn of man and the
firstborn of beast. Therefore I sacrifice to
the LORD all males that open the womb,
but all the firstborn of my sons I redeem.'
16It shall be as [a]a sign on your hand and as
frontlets between your eyes, for by strength
of hand the LORD brought us out of Egypt."

The Wilderness Way
(Ex. 40:34–38; Num. 9:15–23; 1 Kin. 8:10, 11)

17Then it came to pass, when Pharaoh
had let the people go, that God did not lead
them *by* way of the land of the Philistines,
although that *was* near; for God said, "Lest
perhaps the people [a]change their minds
when they see war, and [b]return to Egypt."
18So God [a]led the people around *by* way of
the wilderness of the Red Sea. And the children
of Israel went up in orderly ranks out
of the land of Egypt.

19And Moses took the [a]bones of [b]Joseph
with him, for he had placed the children of
Israel under solemn oath, saying, [c]"God will
surely visit you, and you shall carry up my
bones from here with you."[1]

20So [a]they took their journey from [b]Succoth
and camped in Etham at the edge of
the wilderness. 21And [a]the LORD went before
them by day in a pillar of cloud to lead
the way, and by night in a pillar of fire to

12:51 [a] Ex. 12:41; 20:2 [b] Ex. 6:26 **13:2** [a] Ex. 13:12, 13, 15; 22:29; Lev. 27:26; Num. 3:13; 8:16; 18:15; Deut. 15:19; Luke 2:23 **13:3** [a] Ex. 12:42; Deut. 16:3 [b] Ex. 3:20; 6:1 [c] Ex. 12:8, 19 **13:4** [a] Ex. 12:2; 23:15; 34:18; Deut. 16:1 **13:5** [a] Ex. 3:8, 17; Josh. 24:11 [b] Gen. 17:8; Deut. 30:5 [c] Ex. 6:8 [d] Ex. 12:25, 26 **13:6** [a] Ex. 12:15–20 **13:7** [a] Ex. 12:19 **13:8** [a] Ex. 10:2; 12:26; 13:14; Ps. 44:1 **13:9** [a] Ex. 12:14; 13:16; 31:13; Deut. 6:8; 11:18; Matt. 23:5 **13:10** [a] Ex. 12:14, 24 **13:11** [a] Ex. 13:5 [b] Num. 21:3 **13:12** [a] Ex. 13:1, 2; 22:29; 34:19; Lev. 27:26; Num. 18:15; Ezek. 44:30; Luke 2:23 **13:13** [a] Ex. 34:20; Num. 18:15 [b] Num. 3:46, 47; 18:15, 16 **13:14** [a] Ex. 10:2; 12:26, 27; 13:8; Deut. 6:20; Josh. 4:6, 21 [b] Ex. 13:3, 9 **13:15** [a] Ex. 12:29 **13:16** [a] Ex. 13:9; Deut. 6:8 **13:17** [a] Ex. 14:11; Num. 14:1–4 [b] Deut. 17:16 **13:18** [a] Ex. 14:2; Num. 33:6 **13:19** [a] Gen. 50:24, 25; Josh. 24:32 [b] Ex. 1:6; Deut. 33:13–17 [c] Ex. 4:31 [1] Genesis 50:25 **13:20** [a] Num. 33:6–8 [b] Ex. 12:37 **13:21** [a] Ex. 14:19, 24; 33:9, 10; Num. 9:15; 14:14; Deut. 1:33; Neh. 9:12; Ps. 78:14; 99:7; 105:39; [Is. 4:5]; 1 Cor. 10:1

give them light, so as to go by day and night.
22He did not take away the pillar of cloud
by day or the pillar of fire by night *from* before the people.

The Red Sea Crossing

14 Now the LORD spoke to Moses, saying: 2"Speak to the children of Israel,
[a]that they turn and camp before [b]Pi Hahiroth, between [c]Migdol and the sea, opposite Baal Zephon; you shall camp before
it by the sea. 3For Pharaoh will say of the
children of Israel, [a]'They *are* bewildered by
the land; the wilderness has closed them
in.' 4Then [a]I will harden Pharaoh's heart, so
that he will pursue them; and I [b]will gain
honor over Pharaoh and over all his army,
[c]that the Egyptians may know that I *am* the
LORD." And they did so.

5Now it was told the king of Egypt that
the people had fled, and [a]the heart of Pharaoh and his servants was turned against
the people; and they said, "Why have we
done this, that we have let Israel go from
serving us?" 6So he made ready his chariot and took his people with him. 7Also, he
took [a]six hundred choice chariots, and all
the chariots of Egypt with captains over
every one of them. 8And the LORD [a]hard-
ened the heart of Pharaoh king of Egypt,
and he pursued the children of Israel; and
[b]the children of Israel went out with boldness. 9So the [a]Egyptians pursued them,
all the horses *and* chariots of Pharaoh,
his horsemen and his army, and overtook
them camping by the sea beside Pi Hahiroth, before Baal Zephon.

10And when Pharaoh drew near, the children of Israel lifted their eyes, and behold,
the Egyptians marched after them. So they
were very afraid, and the children of Israel
[a]cried out to the LORD. 11[a]Then they said to
Moses, "Because *there were* no graves in
Egypt, have you taken us away to die in the
wilderness? Why have you so dealt with us,
to bring us up out of Egypt? 12[a]*Is* this not
the word that we told you in Egypt, saying,
'Let us alone that we may serve the Egyptians'? For *it would have been* better for us
to serve the Egyptians than that we should
die in the wilderness."

13And Moses said to the people, [a]"Do not
be afraid. [b]Stand still, and see the [c]salvation
of the LORD, which He will accomplish for
you today. For the Egyptians whom you see
today, you shall [d]see again no more forever.
14[a]The LORD will fight for you, and you shall
[b]hold your peace."

15And the LORD said to Moses, "Why do
you cry to Me? Tell the children of Israel
to go forward. 16But [a]lift up your rod, and
stretch out your hand over the sea and divide it. And the children of Israel shall go
on dry *ground* through the midst of the sea.
17And I indeed will [a]harden the hearts of the
Egyptians, and they shall follow them. So I
will [b]gain honor over Pharaoh and over all
his army, his chariots, and his horsemen.
18Then the Egyptians shall know that I *am*
the LORD, when I have gained honor for
Myself over Pharaoh, his chariots, and his
horsemen."

19And the Angel of God, [a]who went before the camp of Israel, moved and went
behind them; and the pillar of cloud went
from before them and stood behind them.
20So it came between the camp of the Egyptians and the camp of Israel. Thus it was a
cloud and darkness *to the one,* and it gave
light by night *to the other,* so that the one
did not come near the other all that night.

21Then Moses stretched out his hand
over the sea; and the LORD caused the sea
to go *back* by a strong east wind all that
night, and [a]made the sea into dry *land,* and
the waters were [b]divided. 22So [a]the children of Israel went into the midst of the
sea on the dry *ground,* and the waters *were*
[b]a wall to them on their right hand and on
their left. 23And the Egyptians pursued and
went after them into the midst of the sea,
all Pharaoh's horses, his chariots, and his
horsemen.

24Now it came to pass, in the morning

14:2 [a] Ex. 13:18 [b] Num. 33:7 [c] Jer. 44:1 **14:3** [a] Ps. 71:11 **14:4** [a] Ex. 4:21; 7:3; 14:17 [b] Ex. 9:16; 14:17, 18, 23; Rom. 9:17, 22, 23 [c] Ex. 7:5; 14:25 **14:5** [a] Ps. 105:25 **14:7** [a] Ex. 15:4 **14:8** [a] Ex. 14:4 [b] Ex. 6:1; 13:9; Num. 33:3; Acts 13:17 **14:9** [a] Ex. 15:9; Josh. 24:6 **14:10** [a] Josh. 24:7; Neh. 9:9; Ps. 34:17; 107:6 **14:11** [a] Ex. 5:21; 15:24; 16:2; 17:3; Num. 14:2, 3; 20:3; Ps. 106:7, 8 **14:12** [a] Ex. 5:21; 6:9 **14:13** [a] Gen. 15:1; 46:3; Ex. 20:20; 2 Chr. 20:15, 17; Is. 41:10, 13, 14 [b] Ps. 46:10, 11 [c] Ex. 14:30; 15:2 [d] Deut. 28:68 **14:14** [a] Ex. 14:25; 15:3; Deut. 1:30; 3:22; Josh. 10:14, 42; 23:2; 2 Chr. 20:29; Neh. 4:20; Is. 31:4 [b] [Is. 30:15] **14:16** [a] Ex. 4:17, 20; 7:19; 14:21, 26; 17:5, 6, 9; Num. 20:8, 9, 11; Is. 10:26 **14:17** [a] Ex. 14:8 [b] Ex. 14:4 **14:19** [a] Ex. 13:21, 22; [Is. 63:9] **14:21** [a] Ps. 66:6; 106:9; 136:13, 14 [b] Ex. 15:8; Josh. 3:16; 4:23; Neh. 9:11; Ps. 74:13; 78:13; 114:3, 5; Is. 63:12, 13 **14:22** [a] Ex. 15:19; Josh. 3:17; 4:22; Neh. 9:11; Ps. 66:6; 78:13; Is. 63:13; 1 Cor. 10:1; Heb. 11:29 [b] Ex. 14:29; 15:8; Hab. 3:10

[a]watch, that [b]the LORD looked down upon
the army of the Egyptians through the pillar
of fire and cloud, and He troubled the army
of the Egyptians. 25And He took off[1] their
chariot wheels, so that they drove them
with difficulty; and the Egyptians said, "Let
us flee from the face of Israel, for the LORD
[a]fights for them against the Egyptians."
26Then the LORD said to Moses, "Stretch
out your hand over the sea, that the waters may come back upon the Egyptians,
on their chariots, and on their horsemen."
27And Moses stretched out his hand over
the sea; and when the morning appeared,
the sea [a]returned to its full depth, while the
Egyptians were fleeing into it. So the LORD
[b]overthrew the Egyptians in the midst of
the sea. 28Then [a]the waters returned and
covered the chariots, the horsemen, *and*
all the army of Pharaoh that came into the
sea after them. Not so much as one of them
remained. 29But [a]the children of Israel had
walked on dry *land* in the midst of the sea,
and the waters *were* a wall to them on their
right hand and on their left.
30So the LORD [a]saved Israel that day out
of the hand of the Egyptians, and Israel
[b]saw the Egyptians dead on the seashore.
31Thus Israel saw the great work which the
LORD had done in Egypt; so the people
feared the LORD, and [a]believed the LORD
and His servant Moses.

The Song of Moses
(Ex. 14:13, 14; Ps. 78:12–14)

15 Then [a]Moses and the children of Israel sang this song to the LORD, and
spoke, saying:

"I will [b]sing to the LORD,
For He has triumphed gloriously!
The horse and its rider
He has thrown into the sea!
2 The LORD *is* my strength and [a]song,
And He has become my salvation;
He *is* my God, and [b]I will praise Him;
My [c]father's God, and I [d]will exalt Him.
3 The LORD *is* a man of [a]war;
The LORD *is* His [b]name.
4 [a]Pharaoh's chariots and his army
He has cast into the sea;
[b]His chosen captains also are
drowned in the Red Sea.
5 The depths have covered them;
[a]They sank to the bottom like a stone.
6 "Your [a]right hand, O LORD, has
become glorious in power;
Your right hand, O LORD, has
dashed the enemy in pieces.
7 And in the greatness of
Your [a]excellence
You have overthrown those
who rose against You;
You sent forth [b]Your wrath;
It [c]consumed them [d]like stubble.
8 And [a]with the blast of Your nostrils
The waters were gathered together;
[b]The floods stood upright like a heap;
The depths congealed in
the heart of the sea.
9 [a]The enemy said, 'I will pursue,
I will overtake,
I will [b]divide the spoil;
My desire shall be satisfied on them.
I will draw my sword,
My hand shall destroy them.'
10 You blew with Your wind,
The sea covered them;
They sank like lead in the
mighty waters.
11 "Who[a] *is* like You, O LORD,
among the gods?
Who *is* like You, [b]glorious in holiness,
Fearful in [c]praises, [d]doing wonders?
12 You stretched out Your right hand;
The earth swallowed them.
13 You in Your mercy have [a]led forth
The people whom You have redeemed;
You have guided *them* in Your strength
To [b]Your holy habitation.

14:24 [a] Judg. 7:19 [b] Ex. 13:21 **14:25** [a] Ex. 7:5; 14:4, 14, 18 [1] Samaritan Pentateuch, Septuagint, and Syriac read *bound*.
14:27 [a] Josh. 4:18 [b] Ex. 15:1, 7; Deut. 11:4; Neh. 9:11; Ps. 78:53; Heb. 11:29 **14:28** [a] Ps. 78:53; 106:11 **14:29** [a] Ex. 14:22; Ps. 66:6; 78:52, 53; Is. 11:15 **14:30** [a] Ex. 14:13; Ps. 106:8, 10; Is. 63:8, 11 [b] Ps. 58:10; 59:10 **14:31** [a] Ex. 4:31; 19:9; Ps. 106:12; John 2:11; 11:45 **15:1** [a] Ps. 106:12; Rev. 15:3 [b] Is. 12:1–6 **15:2** [a] Ps. 18:1, 2; Is. 12:2; Hab. 3:18, 19 [b] Gen. 28:21, 22 [c] Ex. 3:6, 15, 16 [d] 2 Sam. 22:47; Ps. 99:5; Is. 25:1
15:3 [a] Ex. 14:14; Rev. 19:11 [b] Ex. 3:15; 6:2, 3, 7, 8; Ps. 24:8; 83:18 **15:4** [a] Ex. 14:28 [b] Ex. 14:7 **15:5** [a] Ex. 15:10; Neh. 9:11 **15:6** [a] Ex. 3:20; Ps. 17:7; 118:15 **15:7** [a] Deut. 33:26 [b] Ps. 78:49, 50 [c] Ps. 59:13 [d] Deut. 4:24; Is. 5:24; Heb. 12:29 **15:8** [a] Ex. 14:21, 22, 29 [b] Ps. 78:13 **15:9** [a] Judg. 5:30 [b] Is. 53:12 **15:11** [a] Ex. 8:10; 9:14; Deut. 3:24; 2 Sam. 7:22; 1 Kin. 8:23; Ps. 71:19; 86:8; Mic. 7:18 [b] Ps. 68:35; Is. 6:3; Rev. 4:8 [c] 1 Chr. 16:25 [d] Ex. 3:20; Ps. 77:11, 14
15:13 [a] Neh. 9:12; [Ps. 77:20] [b] Ex. 15:17; Deut. 12:5; Ps. 78:54

14 "The [a]people will hear *and* be afraid;
[b]Sorrow will take hold of the
inhabitants of Philistia.
15 [a]Then [b]the chiefs of Edom
will be dismayed;
[c]The mighty men of Moab,
Trembling will take hold of them;
[d]All the inhabitants of Canaan
will [e]melt away.
16 [a]Fear and dread will fall on them;
By the greatness of Your arm
They will be [b]*as* still as a stone,
Till Your people pass over, O LORD,
Till the people pass over
[c]Whom You have purchased.
17 You will bring them in
and [a]plant them
In the [b]mountain of Your inheritance,
In the place, O LORD, *which*
You have made
For Your own dwelling,
The [c]sanctuary, O Lord, *which*
Your hands have established.

18 "The[a] LORD shall reign
forever and ever."

19For the [a]horses of Pharaoh went with
his chariots and his horsemen into the sea,
and [b]the LORD brought back the waters of
the sea upon them. But the children of Israel went on dry *land* in the midst of the
sea.

The Song of Miriam
(Num. 26:59)

20Then Miriam [a]the prophetess, [b]the sister of Aaron, [c]took the timbrel in her hand;
and all the women went out after her [d]with
timbrels and with dances. 21And Miriam
[a]answered them:

[b]"Sing to the LORD,
For He has triumphed gloriously!
The horse and its rider
He has thrown into the sea!"

Bitter Waters Made Sweet

22So Moses brought Israel from the Red
Sea; then they went out into the Wilderness of [a]Shur. And they went three days in
the wilderness and found no [b]water. 23Now
when they came to [a]Marah, they could not
drink the waters of Marah, for they *were* bitter. Therefore the name of it was called Marah.[1] 24And the people [a]complained against
Moses, saying, "What shall we drink?" 25So
he cried out to the LORD, and the LORD
showed him a tree. [a]When he cast *it* into
the waters, the waters were made sweet.

There He [b]made a statute and an ordinance for them, and there [c]He tested them,
26and said, [a]"If you diligently heed the voice
of the LORD your God and do what is right
in His sight, give ear to His commandments
and keep all His statutes, I will put none of
the [b]diseases on you which I have brought
on the Egyptians. For I *am* the LORD [c]who
heals you."

27[a]Then they came to Elim, where there
were twelve wells of water and seventy
palm trees; so they camped there by the
waters.

Bread from Heaven

16 And they [a]journeyed from Elim, and
all the congregation of the children
of Israel came to the Wilderness of Sin,
which is between Elim and [b]Sinai, on the fifteenth day of the second month after they
departed from the land of Egypt. 2Then
the whole congregation of the children
of Israel [a]complained against Moses and
Aaron in the wilderness. 3And the children
of Israel said to them, [a]"Oh, that we had
died by the hand of the LORD in the land
of Egypt, [b]when we sat by the pots of meat
and when we ate bread to the full! For you
have brought us out into this wilderness
to kill this whole assembly with hunger."

4Then the LORD said to Moses, "Behold,
I will rain [a]bread from heaven for you. And
the people shall go out and gather a certain

15:14 [a] Josh. 2:9 [b] Ps. 48:6 15:15 [a] Gen. 36:15, 40 [b] Deut. 2:4 [c] Num. 22:3, 4 [d] Josh. 5:1 [e] Josh. 2:9–11, 24 15:16 [a] Ex. 23:27; Deut. 2:25; Josh. 2:9 [b] 1 Sam. 25:37 [c] Ex. 15:13; Ps. 74:2; Is. 43:1; Jer. 31:11; [Titus 2:14]; 2 Pet. 2:1 15:17 [a] Ps. 44:2; 80:8, 15 [b] Ps. 2:6; 78:54, 68 [c] Ps. 68:16; 76:2; 132:13, 14 15:18 [a] 2 Sam. 7:16; Ps. 10:16; 29:10; Is. 57:15 15:19 [a] Ex. 14:23 [b] Ex. 14:28 15:20 [a] Judg. 4:4 [b] Ex. 2:4; Num. 26:59; 1 Chr. 6:3; Mic. 6:4 [c] 1 Sam. 18:6; 1 Chr. 15:16; Ps. 68:25; 81:2; 149:3; Jer. 31:4 [d] Judg. 11:34; 21:21; 2 Sam. 6:16; Ps. 30:11; 150:4 15:21 [a] 1 Sam. 18:7 [b] Ex. 15:1 15:22 [a] Gen. 16:7; 20:1; 25:18; Num. 33:8 [b] Ex. 17:1; Num. 20:2 15:23 [a] Num. 33:8; Ruth 1:20 [1] Literally *Bitter* 15:24 [a] Ex. 14:11; 16:2; Ps. 106:13 15:25 [a] 2 Kin. 2:21 [b] Josh. 24:25 [c] Ex. 16:4; Deut. 8:2, 16; Judg. 2:22; 3:1, 4; Ps. 66:10 15:26 [a] Ex. 19:5, 6; Deut. 7:12, 15 [b] Deut. 28:27, 58, 60 [c] Ex. 23:25; Deut. 32:39; Ps. 41:3, 4; 103:3; 147:3 15:27 [a] Num. 33:9 16:1 [a] Num. 33:10, 11; Ezek. 30:15 [b] Ex. 12:6, 51; 19:1 16:2 [a] Ex. 14:11; 15:24; Ps. 106:25; 1 Cor. 10:10 16:3 [a] Ex. 17:3; Num. 14:2, 3; 20:3; Lam. 4:9 [b] Num. 11:4, 5 16:4 [a] Neh. 9:15; Ps. 78:23–25; 105:40; [John 6:31–35]; 1 Cor. 10:3

RELEASE // RECONCILE HURT WITH HEALING

From Hurt to Healing

Exodus 15:23 // Now when they came to Marah, they could not drink the waters of Marah, for they were bitter. Therefore the name of it was called Marah.

Summary Message // As you observe and experience the disarray of our country and world, it may seem surreal, but it is all too real. However, do not be dismayed. Find refuge through prayer and God's Word during these times.

In Exodus 15, we read of the Israelites' praise after God miraculously delivered them from Egypt. This story reminds us that life can present juxtapositions. God delivered Israel from slavery. They were free. But they soon found themselves trapped again. This time between an insurmountable obstacle and a pursuing army. Freedom stood side by side with impending captivity. Until God intervened.

Practical Application // Once the Israelites crossed the Red Sea, they entered the wilderness, where there was no water, and the people complained. When they finally found water, it was bitter. Again, they began to cry and complain.

Things can often seem to get worse before they get better. This is why in those times we must put our trust in the same God who brought us through our own "Red Sea." He is our Deliverer. He will move us from hurt to healing. He will make bitter become better. Do not judge or grade your life by your pain. With faith in God, your gain will outweigh your pain. It is important to keep in mind these encouragements from Scripture:

- There may be bitter times in your life (see Ex. 15:23).
- If you complain about those moments, you may be premature in judging what God intends to do with those situations (see Ex. 15:24–25).
- If you stand on the promises of God and continue in His ways, God will preserve you, heal you, and bring you great comfort (see Ex. 15:26–27).

Many times, our healing begins with reflection. When we take time to consider how we got to where we are, it allows us to breathe. Also, reflecting helps us to put things into perspective. Although we may not have reached our goal, we will realize that progress has been made and we are in a better place than when we began. Suddenly, a spirit of gratitude will overshadow our present situation. Do you remember your Red Sea? Rejoice and breathe.

Fervent Prayer // God, help us accept the fact that life is not perfect and will have twists and turns. Although we may be hurting now, we realize that You have brought us through many things and even protected us from what could have destroyed us. For this, we are truly grateful. Please God, teach us to pause for a moment during troubled times, bask in Your presence, and allow the healing waters of Your Spirit to fill our souls. In You, we will find serenity and renewed strength to move further along in our purpose. Thank You, Father, in advance for turning our bitter into sweet. In Jesus' name we pray. Amen.

---

quota every day, that I may [b]test them,
whether they will [c]walk in My law or not.
5And it shall be on the sixth day that they
shall prepare what they bring in, and [a]it
shall be twice as much as they gather daily."
6Then Moses and Aaron said to all the
children of Israel, [a]"At evening you shall
know that the LORD has brought you out
of the land of Egypt. 7And in the morning
you shall see [a]the glory of the LORD; for He
[b]hears your complaints against the LORD.
But [c]what *are* we, that you complain against
us?" 8Also Moses said, "*This shall be seen*
when the LORD gives you meat to eat in the
evening, and in the morning bread to the
full; for the LORD hears your complaints
which you make against Him. And what
are we? Your complaints *are* not against
us but [a]against the LORD."
9Then Moses spoke to Aaron, "Say to
all the congregation of the children of
Israel, [a]'Come near before the LORD, for
He has heard your complaints.'" 10Now it
came to pass, as Aaron spoke to the whole

16:4 [b] Ex. 15:25; Deut. 8:2, 16 [c] Judg. 2:22 16:5 [a] Ex. 16:22, 29; Lev. 25:21 16:6 [a] Ex. 6:7 16:7 [a] Ex. 16:10, 12; Is. 35:2; 40:5; John 11:4, 40 [b] Num. 14:27; 17:5 [c] Num. 16:11 16:8 [a] 1 Sam. 8:7; Luke 10:16; [Rom. 13:2]; 1 Thess. 4:8 16:9 [a] Num. 16:16

congregation of the children of Israel, that
they looked toward the wilderness, and behold, the glory of the LORD [a]appeared in
the cloud.

11And the LORD spoke to Moses, saying, 12[a]"I have heard the complaints of the
children of Israel. Speak to them, saying,
[b]'At twilight you shall eat meat, and [c]in the
morning you shall be filled with bread. And
you shall know that I *am* the LORD your
God.'"

13So it was that [a]quail came up at evening
and covered the camp, and in the morning
[b]the dew lay all around the camp. 14And
when the layer of dew lifted, there, on the
surface of the wilderness, was [a]a small
round [b]substance, *as* fine as frost on the
ground. 15So when the children of Israel
saw *it,* they said to one another, "What is
it?" For they did not know what it *was.*

And Moses said to them, [a]"This *is* the
bread which the LORD has given you to
eat. 16This is the thing which the LORD has
commanded: 'Let every man gather it [a]ac-
cording to each one's need, one [b]omer for
each person, *according to the* number of
persons; let every man take for *those* who
are in his tent.'"

17Then the children of Israel did so and
gathered, some more, some less. 18So when
they measured *it* by omers, [a]he who gathered much had nothing left over, and he
who gathered little had no lack. Every man
had gathered according to each one's need.
19And Moses said, "Let no one [a]leave any of
it till morning." 20Notwithstanding they did
not heed Moses. But some of them left part
of it until morning, and it bred worms and
stank. And Moses was angry with them. 21So
they gathered it every morning, every man
according to his need. And when the sun
became hot, it melted.

22And so it was, on the sixth day, *that*
they gathered twice as much bread, two
omers for each one. And all the rulers of the
congregation came and told Moses. 23Then
he said to them, "This *is what* the LORD has
said: 'Tomorrow *is* [a]a Sabbath rest, a holy
Sabbath to the LORD. Bake what you will
bake *today,* and boil what you will boil; and
lay up for yourselves all that remains, to be
kept until morning.'" 24So they laid it up
till morning, as Moses commanded; and it
did not [a]stink, nor were there any worms in
it. 25Then Moses said, "Eat that today, for
today *is* a Sabbath to the LORD; today you
will not find it in the field. 26[a]Six days you
shall gather it, but on the seventh day, the
Sabbath, there will be none."

27Now it happened *that some* of the people went out on the seventh day to gather,
but they found none. 28And the LORD said
to Moses, "How long [a]do you refuse to keep
My commandments and My laws? 29See!
For the LORD has given you the Sabbath;
therefore He gives you on the sixth day
bread for two days. Let every man remain
in his place; let no man go out of his place
on the seventh day." 30So the people rested
on the seventh day.

31And the house of Israel called its name
Manna.[1] And [a]it *was* like white coriander
seed, and the taste of it *was* like wafers
made with honey.

32Then Moses said, "This *is* the thing
which the LORD has commanded: 'Fill an
omer with it, to be kept for your generations, that they may see the bread with
which I fed you in the wilderness, when
I brought you out of the land of Egypt.'"
33And Moses said to Aaron, [a]"Take a pot and
put an omer of manna in it, and lay it up
before the LORD, to be kept for your generations." 34As the LORD commanded Moses,
so Aaron laid it up [a]before the Testimony,
to be kept. 35And the children of Israel [a]ate
manna [b]forty years, [c]until they came to an
inhabited land; they ate manna until they
came to the border of the land of Canaan.
36Now an omer *is* one-tenth of an ephah.

Water from the Rock
(Num. 20:1–13)

17 Then [a]all the congregation of the children of Israel set out on their journey from the Wilderness of [b]Sin, according

---

16:10 [a] Ex. 13:21; 16:7; Num. 16:19; 1 Kin. 8:10 **16:12** [a] Ex. 16:8; Num. 14:27 [b] Ex. 16:6 [c] Ex. 16:7; 1 Kin. 20:28; Joel 3:17 **16:13** [a] Num. 11:31; Ps. 78:27–29; 105:40 [b] Num. 11:9 **16:14** [a] Ex. 16:31; Num. 11:7, 8; Deut. 8:3; Neh. 9:15; Ps. 78:24; 105:40 [b] Ps. 147:16 **16:15** [a] Ex. 16:4; Neh. 9:15; Ps. 78:24; [John 6:31, 49, 58]; 1 Cor. 10:3 **16:16** [a] Ex. 12:4 [b] Ex. 16:32, 36 **16:18** [a] 2 Cor. 8:15 **16:19** [a] Ex. 12:10; 16:23; 23:18 **16:23** [a] Gen. 2:3; Ex. 20:8–11; 23:12; 31:15; 35:2; Lev. 23:3; Neh. 9:13, 14 **16:24** [a] Ex. 16:20 **16:26** [a] Ex. 20:9, 10 **16:28** [a] 2 Kin. 17:14; Ps. 78:10; 106:13 **16:31** [a] Num. 11:7–9; Deut. 8:3, 16 [1] Literally *What?* (compare Exodus 16:15) **16:33** [a] Heb. 9:4; Rev. 2:17 **16:34** [a] Ex. 25:16, 21; 27:21; 40:20; Num. 17:10 **16:35** [a] Deut. 8:3, 16 [b] Num. 33:38; John 6:31, 49 [c] Josh. 5:12; Neh. 9:20, 21 **17:1** [a] Ex. 16:1 [b] Num. 33:11–15

to the commandment of the LORD, and
camped in Rephidim; but *there was* no water for the people to [c]drink. 2 [a]Therefore the
people contended with Moses, and said,
"Give us water, that we may drink."

So Moses said to them, "Why do you
contend with me? Why do you [b]tempt the
LORD?"

3 And the people thirsted there for water,
and the people [a]complained against Moses,
and said, "Why *is* it you have brought us up
out of Egypt, to kill us and our children and
our [b]livestock with thirst?"

4 So Moses [a]cried out to the LORD, saying,
"What shall I do with this people? They are
almost ready to [b]stone me!"

5 And the LORD said to Moses, [a]"Go on before the people, and take with you some of
the elders of Israel. Also take in your hand
your rod with which [b]you struck the river,
and go. 6 [a]Behold, I will stand before you
there on the rock in Horeb; and you shall
strike the rock, and water will come out of
it, that the people may drink."

And Moses did so in the sight of the elders of Israel. 7 So he called the name of
the place [a]Massah[1] and Meribah,[2] because
of the contention of the children of Israel,
and because they tempted the LORD, saying, "Is the LORD among us or not?"

Victory over the Amalekites
(Gen. 14:7; Num. 13:29; 14:25)

8 [a]Now Amalek came and fought with
Israel in Rephidim. 9 And Moses said to
Joshua, "Choose us some men and go out,
fight with Amalek. Tomorrow I will stand
on the top of the hill with [a]the rod of God in
my hand." 10 So Joshua did as Moses said to
him, and fought with Amalek. And Moses,
Aaron, and Hur went up to the top of the
hill. 11 And so it was, when Moses [a]held up
his hand, that Israel prevailed; and when
he let down his hand, Amalek prevailed.
12 But Moses' hands *became* heavy; so they
took a stone and put *it* under him, and he
sat on it. And Aaron and Hur supported his
hands, one on one side, and the other on
the other side; and his hands were steady
until the going down of the sun. 13 So Joshua
defeated Amalek and his people with the
edge of the sword.

14 Then the LORD said to Moses, [a]"Write
this *for* a memorial in the book and recount
it in the hearing of Joshua, that [b]I will utterly blot out the remembrance of Amalek
from under heaven." 15 And Moses built an
altar and called its name, The-LORD-Is-My-
Banner;[1] 16 for he said, "Because the LORD
has [a]sworn: the LORD *will have* war with
Amalek from generation to generation."

Jethro's Advice
(Deut. 1:9–18)

18 And [a]Jethro, the priest of Midian,
Moses' father-in-law, heard of all that
[b]God had done for Moses and for Israel His
people—that the LORD had brought Israel
out of Egypt. 2 Then Jethro, Moses' father-
in-law, took [a]Zipporah, Moses' wife, after
he had sent her back, 3 with her [a]two sons,
of whom the name of one *was* Gershom
(for he said, [b]"I have been a stranger in a
foreign land")[1] 4 and the name of the other
was Eliezer[1] (for *he said,* "The God of my father *was* my [a]help, and delivered me from
the sword of Pharaoh"); 5 and Jethro, Moses' father-in-law, came with his sons and
his wife to Moses in the wilderness, where
he was encamped at [a]the mountain of God.
6 Now he had said to Moses, "I, your father-
in-law Jethro, am coming to you with your
wife and her two sons with her."

7 So Moses [a]went out to meet his father-
in-law, bowed down, and [b]kissed him. And
they asked each other about *their* well-
being, and they went into the tent. 8 And
Moses told his father-in-law all that the
LORD had done to Pharaoh and to the Egyptians for Israel's sake, all the hardship that
had come upon them on the way, and *how*
the LORD had [a]delivered them. 9 Then Jethro rejoiced for all the [a]good which the LORD
had done for Israel, whom He had delivered

17:1 [c] Ex. 15:22; Num. 20:2 17:2 [a] Ex. 14:11; Num. 20:2, 3, 13 [b] [Deut. 6:16]; Ps. 78:18, 41; [Matt. 4:7]; 1 Cor. 10:9 17:3 [a] Ex. 16:2, 3 [b] Ex. 12:38 17:4 [a] Ex. 14:15 [b] John 8:59; 10:31 17:5 [a] Ezek. 2:6 [b] Num. 20:8 17:6 [a] Num. 20:10, 11; Deut. 8:15; Neh. 9:15; Ps. 78:15; 105:41; 114:8; [1 Cor. 10:4] 17:7 [a] Num. 20:13, 24; 27:14; Ps. 81:7 [1] Literally *Tempted* [2] Literally *Contention* 17:8 [a] Gen. 36:12; Num. 24:20; Deut. 25:17–19; 1 Sam. 15:2 17:9 [a] Ex. 4:20 17:11 [a] [James 5:16] 17:14 [a] Ex. 24:4; 34:27; Num. 33:2 [b] Deut. 25:19; 1 Sam. 15:3; 2 Sam. 1:1; 1 Chr. 4:43 17:15 [1] Hebrew *YHWH Nissi* 17:16 [a] Gen. 22:14–16 18:1 [a] Ex. 2:16, 18; 3:1 [b] [Ps. 106:2, 8] 18:2 [a] Ex. 2:21; 4:20–26 18:3 [a] Ex. 2:20; 4:20; Acts 7:29 [b] Ex. 2:22 [1] Compare Exodus 2:22 18:4 [a] Gen. 49:25 [1] Literally *My God Is Help* 18:5 [a] Ex. 3:1, 12; 4:27; 24:13 18:7 [a] Gen. 18:2 [b] Gen. 29:13; Ex. 4:27 18:8 [a] Ex. 15:6, 16; Ps. 81:7 18:9 [a] [Is. 63:7–14]

out of the hand of the Egyptians. 10And
Jethro said, [a]"Blessed *be* the LORD, who has
delivered you out of the hand of the Egyptians and out of the hand of Pharaoh, *and*
who has delivered the people from under
the hand of the Egyptians. 11Now I know
that the LORD *is* [a]greater than all the gods;
[b]for in the very thing in which they behaved
[c]proudly, *He was* above them." 12Then Jethro, Moses' father-in-law, took[1] a burnt [a]of-
fering and *other* sacrifices *to offer* to God.
And Aaron came with all the elders of Israel [b]to eat bread with Moses' father-in-law
before God.

13And so it was, on the next day, that Moses [a]sat to judge the people; and the people
stood before Moses from morning until
evening. 14So when Moses' father-in-law
saw all that he did for the people, he said,
"What *is* this thing that you are doing for
the people? Why do you alone sit, and all
the people stand before you from morning
until evening?"

15And Moses said to his father-in-law,
"Because [a]the people come to me to inquire
of God. 16When they have [a]a difficulty, they
come to me, and I judge between one and
another; and I make known the statutes of
God and His laws."

17So Moses' father-in-law said to him,
"The thing that you do *is* not good. 18Both
you and these people who *are* with you will
surely wear yourselves out. For this thing
is too much for you; [a]you are not able to
perform it by yourself. 19Listen now to my
voice; I will give you counsel, and God will
be with you: Stand [a]before God for the people, so that you may [b]bring the difficulties to God. 20And you shall [a]teach them
the statutes and the laws, and show them
the way in which they must walk and [b]the
work they must do. 21Moreover you shall
select from all the people [a]able men, such
as [b]fear God, [c]men of truth, [d]hating covetousness; and place *such* over them *to be*
rulers of thousands, rulers of hundreds,
rulers of fifties, and rulers of tens. 22And let
them judge the people at all times. [a]Then
it will be *that* every great matter they shall
bring to you, but every small matter they
themselves shall judge. So it will be easier for you, for [b]they will bear *the burden*
with you. 23If you do this thing, and God
so commands you, then you will be able to
endure, and all this people will also go to
their [a]place in peace."

24So Moses heeded the voice of his
father-in-law and did all that he had said.
25And [a]Moses chose able men out of all
Israel, and made them heads over the
people: rulers of thousands, rulers of hundreds, rulers of fifties, and rulers of tens.
26So they judged the people at all times;
the [a]hard cases they brought to Moses, but
they judged every small case themselves.

27Then Moses let his father-in-law depart, and [a]he went his way to his own land.

Israel at Mount Sinai

19 In the third month after the children
of Israel had gone out of the land of
Egypt, on the same day, [a]they came *to* the
Wilderness of Sinai. 2For they had departed
from [a]Rephidim, had come *to* the Wilderness of Sinai, and camped in the wilderness. So Israel camped there before [b]the
mountain.

3And [a]Moses went up to God, and the
LORD [b]called to him from the mountain,
saying, "Thus you shall say to the house
of Jacob, and tell the children of Israel:
4[a]'You have seen what I did to the Egyptians, and *how* [b]I bore you on eagles' wings
and brought you to Myself. 5Now [a]therefore,
if you will indeed obey My voice and [b]keep
My covenant, then [c]you shall be a special
treasure to Me above all people; for all the
earth *is* [d]Mine. 6And you shall be to Me a
[a]kingdom of priests and a [b]holy nation.'
These *are* the words which you shall speak
to the children of Israel."

7So Moses came and called for the [a]elders

18:10 [a] Gen. 14:20; 2 Sam. 18:28; 1 Kin. 8:56; Ps. 68:19, 20 18:11 [a] Ex. 12:12; 15:11; 2 Chr. 2:5; Ps. 95:3; 97:9; 135:5 [b] Ex. 1:10, 16, 22; 5:2, 7 [c] Luke 1:51 18:12 [a] Ex. 24:5 [b] Gen. 31:54; Deut. 12:7 [1] Following Masoretic Text and Septuagint; Syriac, Targum, and Vulgate read *offered.* 18:13 [a] Deut. 33:4, 5; Matt. 23:2 18:15 [a] Lev. 24:12; Num. 9:6, 8; 27:5; Deut. 17:8–13 18:16 [a] Ex. 24:14; Deut. 19:17 18:18 [a] Num. 11:14, 17; Deut. 1:12 18:19 [a] Ex. 4:16; 20:19 [b] Num. 9:8; 27:5 18:20 [a] Deut. 5:1 [b] Deut. 1:18 18:21 [a] Ex. 18:24, 25; Deut. 1:13, 15; 2 Chr. 19:5–10; Ps. 15:1–5; Acts 6:3 [b] Gen. 42:18; 2 Sam. 23:3 [c] Ezek. 18:8 [d] Deut. 16:19 18:22 [a] Lev. 24:11; Deut. 1:17 [b] Num. 11:17 18:23 [a] Ex. 16:29 18:25 [a] Ex. 18:21; Deut. 1:15 18:26 [a] Job 29:16 18:27 [a] Num. 10:29, 30 19:1 [a] Num. 33:15 19:2 [a] Ex. 17:1 [b] Ex. 3:1, 12; 18:5 19:3 [a] Acts 7:38 [b] Ex. 3:4 19:4 [a] Deut. 29:2 [b] Deut. 32:11; Is. 63:9; Rev. 12:14 19:5 [a] Ex. 15:26; 23:22 [b] Deut. 5:2; Ps. 78:10 [c] Deut. 4:20; 7:6; 14:2; 26:18; 1 Kin. 8:53; Ps. 135:4; Titus 2:14; 1 Pet. 2:9 [d] Ex. 9:29; Deut. 10:14; Job 41:11; Ps. 50:12; 1 Cor. 10:26 19:6 [a] Deut. 33:2–4; [1 Pet. 2:5, 9; Rev. 1:6; 5:10] [b] Deut. 7:6; 14:21; 26:19; Is. 62:12; [1 Cor. 3:17] 19:7 [a] Ex. 4:29, 30

of the people, and laid before them all these words which the LORD commanded him. 8Then [a]all the people answered together and said, "All that the LORD has spoken we will do." So Moses brought back the words of the people to the LORD. 9And the LORD said to Moses, "Behold, I come to you [a]in the thick cloud, [b]that the people may hear when I speak with you, and believe you forever."

So Moses told the words of the people to the LORD.

10Then the LORD said to Moses, "Go to the people and [a]consecrate them today and tomorrow, and let them wash their clothes. 11And let them be ready for the third day. For on the third day the LORD will come down upon Mount Sinai in the sight of all the people. 12You shall set bounds for the people all around, saying, 'Take heed to yourselves *that* you do *not* go up to the mountain or touch its base. [a]Whoever touches the mountain shall surely be put to death. 13Not a hand shall touch him, but he shall surely be stoned or shot *with an arrow;* whether man or beast, he shall not live.' When the trumpet sounds long, they shall come near the mountain."

14So Moses went down from the mountain to the people and sanctified the people, and they washed their clothes. 15And he said to the people, "Be ready for the third day; [a]do not come near *your* wives."

16Then it came to pass on the third day, in the morning, that there were [a]thunderings and lightnings, and a thick cloud on the mountain; and the sound of the trumpet was very loud, so that all the people who *were* in the camp [b]trembled. 17And [a]Moses brought the people out of the camp to meet with God, and they stood at the foot of the mountain. 18Now [a]Mount Sinai *was* completely in smoke, because the LORD descended upon [b]it in fire. [c]Its smoke ascended like the smoke of a furnace, and the [d]whole mountain[1] quaked greatly. 19And when the blast of the trumpet sounded long and became louder and louder, [a]Moses spoke, and [b]God answered him by voice. 20Then the LORD came down upon Mount Sinai, on the top of the mountain. And the LORD called Moses to the top of the mountain, and Moses went up.

21And the LORD said to Moses, "Go down and warn the people, lest they break through [a]to gaze at the LORD, and many of them perish. 22Also let the [a]priests who come near the LORD [b]consecrate themselves, lest the LORD [c]break out against them."

23But Moses said to the LORD, "The people cannot come up to Mount Sinai; for You warned us, saying, [a]'Set bounds around the mountain and consecrate it.'"

24Then the LORD said to him, "Away! Get down and then come up, you and Aaron with you. But do not let the priests and the people break through to come up to the LORD, lest He break out against them." 25So Moses went down to the people and spoke to them.

The Ten Commandments
(Deut. 5:1–22)

20 And God spoke [a]all these words, saying:

2 [a]"I *am* the LORD your God, who brought you out of the land of Egypt, [b]out of the house of bondage.

3 [a]"You shall have no other gods before Me.

4 [a]"You shall not make for yourself a carved image—any likeness *of anything* that *is* in heaven above, or that *is* in the earth beneath, or that *is* in the water under the earth; 5[a]you shall not bow down to them nor serve them. [b]For I, the LORD your God, *am* a jealous God, [c]visiting the iniquity of the fathers upon the children to the third and fourth *generations* of those who hate Me, 6but [a]showing mercy to thousands, to those who love Me and keep My commandments.

19:8 [a] Ex. 4:31; 24:3, 7; Deut. 5:27; 26:17 19:9 [a] Ex. 19:16; 20:21; 24:15; Deut. 4:11; Ps. 99:7; Matt. 17:5 [b] Deut. 4:12, 36; John 12:29, 30 19:10 [a] Lev. 11:44, 45; [Heb. 10:22] 19:12 [a] Ex. 34:3; Heb. 12:20 19:15 [a] [1 Cor. 7:5] 19:16 [a] Heb. 12:18, 19 [b] Heb. 12:21 19:17 [a] Deut. 4:10 19:18 [a] Deut. 4:11; Judg. 5:5; Ps. 104:32; 144:5 [b] Ex. 3:2; 24:17; Deut. 5:4; 2 Chr. 7:1–3; Heb. 12:18 [c] Gen. 15:17; 19:28; Rev. 15:8 [d] Ps. 68:8; 1 Kin. 19:12; Jer. 4:24; [Heb. 12:26] [1] Septuagint reads *all the people.* 19:19 [a] Heb. 12:21 [b] Neh. 9:13; Ps. 81:7 19:21 [a] 1 Sam. 6:19 19:22 [a] Ex. 19:24; 24:5 [b] Lev. 10:3; 21:6–8 [c] 2 Sam. 6:7, 8 19:23 [a] Ex. 19:12 20:1 [a] Deut. 5:22 20:2 [a] Hos. 13:4 [b] Ex. 13:3; Deut. 7:8 20:3 [a] Deut. 6:14; 2 Kin. 17:35; Jer. 25:6; 35:15 20:4 [a] Lev. 19:4; 26:1; Deut. 4:15–19; 27:15 20:5 [a] Is. 44:15, 19 [b] Ex. 34:14; Deut. 4:24; Josh. 24:19; Nah. 1:2 [c] Num. 14:18, 33; Deut. 5:9, 10; 1 Kin. 21:29; Ps. 79:8; Jer. 32:18 20:6 [a] Deut. 7:9; Rom. 11:28

7 [a]"You shall not take the name of the LORD
your God in vain, for the LORD [b]will
not hold *him* guiltless who takes His
name in vain.
8 [a]"Remember the Sabbath day, to keep it
holy. 9 [a]Six days you shall labor and do
all your work, 10 but the [a]seventh day *is*
the Sabbath of the LORD your God. *In*
it you shall do no work: you, nor your
son, nor your daughter, nor your male
servant, nor your female servant, nor
your cattle, [b]nor your stranger who
is within your gates. 11 For [a]*in* six days
the LORD made the heavens and the
earth, the sea, and all that *is* in them,
and rested the seventh day. Therefore
the LORD blessed the Sabbath day and
hallowed it.
12 [a]"Honor your father and your mother,
that your days may be [b]long upon the
land which the LORD your God is giving you.
13 [a]"You shall not murder.
14 [a]"You shall not commit [b]adultery.
15 [a]"You shall not steal.
16 [a]"You shall not bear false witness against
your neighbor.
17 [a]"You shall not covet your neighbor's
house; [b]you shall not covet your
neighbor's wife, nor his male servant,
nor his female servant, nor his ox, nor
his donkey, nor anything that *is* your
neighbor's."

The People Afraid of God's Presence

18 Now [a]all the people [b]witnessed the thunderings, the lightning flashes, the sound of
the trumpet, and the mountain [c]smoking;
and when the people saw *it,* they trembled
and stood afar off. 19 Then they said to Moses, [a]"You speak with us, and we will hear;
but [b]let not God speak with us, lest we die."
20 And Moses said to the people, [a]"Do
not fear; [b]for God has come to test you, and
[c]that His fear may be before you, so that you
may not sin." 21 So the people stood afar off,
but Moses drew near [a]the thick darkness
where God *was.*

The Law of the Altar

22 Then the LORD said to Moses, "Thus
you shall say to the children of Israel: 'You
have seen that I have talked with you [a]from
heaven. 23 You shall not make *anything to*
be [a]with Me—gods of silver or gods of gold
you shall not make for yourselves. 24 An
altar of [a]earth you shall make for Me, and
you shall sacrifice on it your burnt offerings and your peace offerings, [b]your sheep
and your oxen. In every [c]place where I record My name I will come to you, and I will
[d]bless you. 25 And [a]if you make Me an altar of
stone, you shall not build it of hewn stone;
for if you [b]use your tool on it, you have profaned it. 26 Nor shall you go up by steps to
My altar, that your [a]nakedness may not be
exposed on it.'

The Law Concerning Servants
(Deut. 15:12–18)

21 "Now these *are* the judgments which
you shall [a]set before them: 2 [a]If you
buy a Hebrew servant, he shall serve six
years; and in the seventh he shall go out
free and pay nothing. 3 If he comes in by
himself, he shall go out by himself; if he
comes in married, then his wife shall go out
with him. 4 If his master has given him a
wife, and she has borne him sons or daughters, the wife and her children shall be her
master's, and he shall go out by himself.
5 [a]But if the servant plainly says, 'I love my
master, my wife, and my children; I will not
go out free,' 6 then his master shall bring
him to the [a]judges. He shall also bring him
to the door, or to the doorpost, and his master shall pierce his ear with an awl; and he
shall serve him forever.
7 "And if a man [a]sells his daughter to be
a female slave, she shall not go out as the

20:7 [a] Lev. 19:12; Deut. 6:13; 10:20; [Matt. 5:33–37] [b] Mic. 6:11 **20:8** [a] Ex. 23:12; 31:13–16; Lev. 26:2; Deut. 5:12 **20:9** [a] Ex. 34:21; 35:2, 3; Lev. 23:3; Deut. 5:13; Luke 13:14 **20:10** [a] Gen. 2:2, 3 [b] Neh. 13:16–19 **20:11** [a] Gen. 2:2, 3; Ex. 31:17 **20:12** [a] Lev. 19:3; Deut. 27:16; Matt. 15:4; 19:19; Mark 7:10; 10:19; Luke 18:20; Eph. 6:2 [b] Deut. 5:16, 33; 6:2; 11:8, 9 **20:13** [a] [Matt. 5:21, 22]; 19:18; Mark 10:19; Luke 18:20; Rom. 13:9; [1 John 3:15] **20:14** [a] Matt. 5:27; Mark 10:19; Luke 18:20; Rom. 13:9; James 2:11 [b] Lev. 20:10; Deut. 5:18 **20:15** [a] Ex. 21:16; Lev. 19:11, 13; Matt. 19:18; Rom. 13:9 **20:16** [a] Ex. 23:1, 7; Deut. 5:20; Matt. 19:18 **20:17** [a] [Luke 12:15]; Rom. 7:7; 13:9; [Eph. 5:3, 5]; Heb. 13:5 [b] 2 Sam. 11:2; [Matt. 5:28] **20:18** [a] Heb. 12:18, 19 [b] Rev. 1:10, 12 [c] Ex. 19:16, 18 **20:19** [a] Gal. 3:19; Heb. 12:19 [b] Deut. 5:5, 23–27 **20:20** [a] Ex. 14:13; [Is. 41:10, 13] [b] Ex. 15:25; [Deut. 13:3] [c] Deut. 4:10; 6:24; Prov. 3:7; 16:6; Is. 8:13 **20:21** [a] Ex. 19:16; Deut. 5:22 **20:22** [a] Deut. 4:36; 5:24, 26; Neh. 9:13 **20:23** [a] Ex. 32:1, 2, 4; Deut. 29:17 **20:24** [a] Ex. 20:25; 27:1–8 [b] Ex. 24:5; Lev. 1:2 [c] Deut. 12:5; 16:6, 11; 1 Kin. 9:3; 2 Chr. 6:6 [d] Gen. 12:2 **20:25** [a] Deut. 27:5 [b] Josh. 8:30, 31 **20:26** [a] Ex. 28:42, 43 **21:1** [a] Ex. 24:3, 4; Deut. 4:14; 6:1 **21:2** [a] Lev. 25:39–43; Deut. 15:12–18; Jer. 34:14 **21:5** [a] Deut. 15:16, 17 **21:6** [a] Ex. 12:12; 22:8, 9 **21:7** [a] Neh. 5:5

male slaves do. 8If she does not please her
master, who has betrothed her to himself,
then he shall let her be redeemed. He shall
have no right to sell her to a foreign people, since he has dealt deceitfully with her.
9And if he has betrothed her to his son, he
shall deal with her according to the custom
of daughters. 10If he takes another *wife,* he
shall not diminish her food, her clothing,
[a]and her marriage rights. 11And if he does
not do these three for her, then she shall
go out free, without *paying* money.

The Law Concerning Violence

12[a]"He who strikes a man so that he dies
shall surely be put to death. 13However, [a]if
he did not lie in wait, but God [b]delivered
him into his hand, then [c]I will appoint for
you a place where he may flee.

14"But if a man acts with [a]premeditation
against his neighbor, to kill him by treachery, [b]you shall take him from My altar, that
he may die.

15"And he who strikes his father or his
mother shall surely be put to death.

16[a]"He who kidnaps a man and [b]sells him,
or if he is [c]found in his hand, shall surely
be put to death.

17"And [a]he who curses his father or his
mother shall surely be put to death.

18"If men contend with each other, and
one strikes the other with a stone or with *his*
fist, and he does not die but is confined to
his bed, 19if he rises again and walks about
outside [a]with his staff, then he who struck
him shall be acquitted. He shall only pay
for the loss of his time, and shall provide
for him to be thoroughly healed.

20"And if a man beats his male or female
servant with a rod, so that he dies under his
hand, he shall surely be punished. 21Not-
withstanding, if he remains alive a day or
two, he shall not be punished; for he *is* his
[a]property.

22"If men fight, and hurt a woman with
child, so that she gives birth prematurely,
yet no harm follows, he shall surely be punished accordingly as the woman's husband
imposes on him; and he shall [a]pay as the
judges *determine.* 23But if *any* harm follows, then you shall give life for life, 24[a]eye
for eye, tooth for tooth, hand for hand, foot
for foot, 25burn for burn, wound for wound,
stripe for stripe.

26"If a man strikes the eye of his male or
female servant, and destroys it, he shall let
him go free for the sake of his eye. 27And if
he knocks out the tooth of his male or female servant, he shall let him go free for
the sake of his tooth.

Animal Control Laws

28"If an ox gores a man or a woman to
death, then [a]the ox shall surely be stoned,
and its flesh shall not be eaten; but the
owner of the ox *shall be* acquitted. 29But
if the ox tended to thrust with its horn in
times past, and it has been made known to
his owner, and he has not kept it confined,
so that it has killed a man or a woman, the
ox shall be stoned and its owner also shall
be put to death. 30If there is imposed on
him a sum of money, then he shall pay [a]to
redeem his life, whatever is imposed on
him. 31Whether it has gored a son or gored
a daughter, according to this judgment it
shall be done to him. 32If the ox gores a
male or female servant, he shall give to
their master [a]thirty shekels of silver, and
the [b]ox shall be stoned.

33"And if a man opens a pit, or if a man
digs a pit and does not cover it, and an ox
or a donkey falls in it, 34the owner of the pit
shall make *it* good; he shall give money to
their owner, but the dead *animal* shall be his.

35"If one man's ox hurts another's, so
that it dies, then they shall sell the live
ox and divide the money from it; and the
dead *ox* they shall also divide. 36Or if it was
known that the ox tended to thrust in time
past, and its owner has not kept it confined,
he shall surely pay ox for ox, and the dead
animal shall be his own.

Responsibility for Property

22 "If a man steals an ox or a sheep,
and slaughters it or sells it, he shall
[a]restore five oxen for an ox and four sheep

21:10 [a] [1 Cor. 7:3, 5] 21:12 [a] Gen. 9:6; Lev. 24:17; Num. 35:30; [Matt. 26:52] 21:13 [a] Deut. 19:4, 5 [b] 1 Sam. 24:4, 10, 18 [c] Num. 35:11; Deut. 19:3; Josh. 20:2 21:14 [a] Deut. 19:11, 12; [Heb. 10:26] [b] 1 Kin. 2:28–34 21:16 [a] Deut. 24:7 [b] Gen. 37:28 [c] Ex. 22:4
21:17 [a] Lev. 20:9; Prov. 20:20; Matt. 15:4; Mark 7:10 21:19 [a] 2 Sam. 3:29 21:21 [a] Lev. 25:44–46 21:22 [a] Ex. 18:21, 22; 21:30; Deut. 22:18
21:24 [a] Lev. 24:20; Deut. 19:21; [Matt. 5:38–44; 1 Pet. 2:19–21] 21:28 [a] Gen. 9:5 21:30 [a] Ex. 21:22; Num. 35:31
21:32 [a] Zech. 11:12, 13; Matt. 26:15; 27:3, 9 [b] Ex. 21:28 22:1 [a] 2 Sam. 12:6; Prov. 6:31; Luke 19:8

for a sheep. 2If the thief is found [a]breaking in, and he is struck so that he dies, *there shall be* [b]no guilt for his bloodshed. 3If the sun has risen on him, *there shall be* guilt for his bloodshed. He should make full restitution; if he has nothing, then he shall be [a]sold for his theft. 4If the theft is certainly [a]found alive in his hand, whether it is an ox or donkey or sheep, he shall [b]restore double.

5"If a man causes a field or vineyard to be grazed, and lets loose his animal, and it feeds in another man's field, he shall make restitution from the best of his own field and the best of his own vineyard.

6"If fire breaks out and catches in thorns, so that stacked grain, standing grain, or the field is consumed, he who kindled the fire shall surely make restitution.

7"If a man [a]delivers to his neighbor money or articles to keep, and it is stolen out of the man's house, [b]if the thief is found, he shall pay double. 8If the thief is not found, then the master of the house shall be brought to the [a]judges *to see* whether he has put his hand into his neighbor's goods.

9"For any kind of trespass, *whether it concerns* an ox, a donkey, a sheep, or clothing, *or* for any kind of lost thing which *another* claims to be his, the [a]cause of both parties shall come before the judges; *and* whomever the judges condemn shall pay double to his neighbor. 10If a man delivers to his neighbor a donkey, an ox, a sheep, or any animal to keep, and it dies, is hurt, or driven away, no one seeing *it,* 11*then* an [a]oath of the LORD shall be between them both, that he has not put his hand into his neighbor's goods; and the owner of it shall accept *that,* and he shall not make *it* good. 12But [a]if, in fact, it is stolen from him, he shall make restitution to the owner of it. 13If it is [a]torn to pieces *by a beast, then* he shall bring it as evidence, *and* he shall not make good what was torn.

14"And if a man borrows *anything* from his neighbor, and it becomes injured or dies, the owner of it not *being* with it, he shall surely make *it* good. 15If its owner *was* with it, he shall not make *it* good; if it *was* hired, it came for its hire.

Moral and Ceremonial Principles

16[a]"If a man entices a virgin who is not betrothed, and lies with her, he shall surely pay the bride-price for her *to be* his wife. 17If her father utterly refuses to give her to him, he shall pay money according to the [a]bride-price of virgins.

18[a]"You shall not permit a sorceress to live.

19[a]"Whoever lies with an animal shall surely be put to death.

20[a]"He who sacrifices to *any* god, except to the LORD only, he shall be utterly destroyed.

21[a]"You shall neither mistreat a stranger nor oppress him, for you were strangers in the land of Egypt.

22[a]"You shall not afflict any widow or fatherless child. 23If you afflict them in any way, *and* they [a]cry at all to Me, I will surely [b]hear their cry; 24and My [a]wrath will become hot, and I will kill you with the sword; [b]your wives shall be widows, and your children fatherless.

25[a]"If you lend money to *any of* My people *who are* poor among you, you shall not be like a moneylender to him; you shall not charge him [b]interest. 26[a]If you ever take your neighbor's garment as a pledge, you shall return it to him before the sun goes down. 27For that *is* his only covering, it *is* his garment for his skin. What will he sleep in? And it will be that when he cries to Me, I will hear, for I *am* [a]gracious.

28[a]"You shall not revile God, nor curse a [b]ruler of your people.

29"You shall not delay *to offer* [a]the first of your ripe produce and your juices. [b]The firstborn of your sons you shall give to Me. 30[a]Likewise you shall do with your oxen

---

22:2 [a] Job 24:16; Matt. 6:19; 24:43; 1 Pet. 4:15 [b] Num. 35:27 **22:3** [a] Ex. 21:2; Matt. 18:25 **22:4** [a] Ex. 21:16 [b] Prov. 6:31 **22:7** [a] Lev. 6:1–7 [b] Ex. 22:4 **22:8** [a] Ex. 21:6, 22; 22:28; Deut. 17:8, 9; 19:17 **22:9** [a] Deut. 25:1; 2 Chr. 19:10 **22:11** [a] Heb. 6:16 **22:12** [a] Gen. 31:39 **22:13** [a] Gen. 31:39 **22:16** [a] Deut. 22:28, 29 **22:17** [a] Gen. 34:12; 1 Sam. 18:25 **22:18** [a] Lev. 19:31; 20:6, 27; Deut. 18:10, 11; 1 Sam. 28:3–10; Jer. 27:9, 10 **22:19** [a] Lev. 18:23; 20:15, 16; Deut. 27:21 **22:20** [a] Ex. 32:8; 34:15; Lev. 17:7; Num. 25:2; Deut. 17:2, 3, 5; 1 Kin. 18:40; 2 Kin. 10:25 **22:21** [a] Ex. 23:9; Deut. 10:19; Zech. 7:10 **22:22** [a] Deut. 24:17, 18; Prov. 23:10, 11; Jer. 7:6, 7; [James 1:27] **22:23** [a] [Luke 18:7] [b] Deut. 10:17, 18; Ps. 18:6 **22:24** [a] Ps. 69:24 [b] Ps. 109:9 **22:25** [a] Lev. 25:35–37 [b] Deut. 23:19, 20; Neh. 5:1–13; Ps. 15:5; Ezek. 18:8 **22:26** [a] Deut. 24:6, 10–13; Job 24:3; Prov. 20:16; Amos 2:8 **22:27** [a] Ex. 34:6, 7 **22:28** [a] Eccl. 10:20 [b] Acts 23:5 **22:29** [a] Ex. 23:16, 19; Deut. 26:2–11; Prov. 3:9 [b] Ex. 13:2, 12, 15 **22:30** [a] Deut. 15:19

and your sheep. It shall be with its mother
[b]seven days; on the eighth day you shall
give it to Me.
31"And you shall be [a]holy men to Me: [b]you
shall not eat meat torn *by beasts* in the field;
you shall throw it to the dogs.

Justice for All

23 "You [a]shall not circulate a false report. Do not put your hand with the
wicked to be an [b]unrighteous witness. 2[a]You
shall not follow a crowd to do evil; [b]nor shall
you testify in a dispute so as to turn aside
after many to pervert *justice.* 3You shall not
show partiality to a [a]poor man in his dispute.
4[a]"If you meet your enemy's ox or his
donkey going astray, you shall surely bring
it back to him again. 5[a]If you see the donkey
of one who hates you lying under its burden, and you would refrain from helping
it, you shall surely help him with it.
6[a]"You shall not pervert the judgment
of your poor in his dispute. 7[a]Keep yourself
far from a false matter; [b]do not kill the innocent and righteous. For [c]I will not justify
the wicked. 8And [a]you shall take no bribe,
for a bribe blinds the discerning and perverts the words of the righteous.
9"Also [a]you shall not oppress a stranger,
for you know the heart of a stranger, because you were strangers in the land of
Egypt.

The Law of Sabbaths

10[a]"Six years you shall sow your land and
gather in its produce, 11but the seventh *year*
you shall let it rest and lie fallow, that the
poor of your people may eat; and what they
leave, the beasts of the field may eat. In like
manner you shall do with your vineyard
and your olive grove. 12[a]Six days you shall
do your work, and on the seventh day you
shall rest, that your ox and your donkey
may rest, and the son of your female servant and the stranger may be refreshed.
13"And in all that I have said to you, [a]be
circumspect and [b]make no mention of the
name of other gods, nor let it be heard from
your mouth.

Three Annual Feasts
(Ex. 34:18–26; Deut. 16:1–17)

14[a]"Three times you shall keep a feast to
Me in the year: 15[a]You shall keep the Feast
of Unleavened Bread (you shall eat unleavened bread seven days, as I commanded
you, at the time appointed in the month of
Abib, for in it you came out of Egypt; [b]none
shall appear before Me empty); 16[a]and the
Feast of Harvest, the firstfruits of your labors which you have sown in the field; and
[b]the Feast of Ingathering at the end of the
year, when you have gathered in *the fruit*
of your labors from the field.
17[a]"Three times in the year all your males
shall appear before the Lord GOD.[1]
18[a]"You shall not offer the blood of My
sacrifice with leavened [b]bread; nor shall the
fat of My sacrifice remain until morning.
19[a]The first of the firstfruits of your land
you shall bring into the house of the LORD
your God. [b]You shall not boil a young goat
in its mother's milk.

The Angel and the Promises

20[a]"Behold, I send an Angel before you
to keep you in the way and to bring you into
the place which I have prepared. 21Beware
of Him and obey His voice; [a]do not provoke
Him, for He will [b]not pardon your transgressions; for [c]My name *is* in Him. 22But if
you indeed obey His voice and do all that
I speak, then [a]I will be an enemy to your
enemies and an adversary to your adversaries. 23[a]For My Angel will go before you
and [b]bring you in to the Amorites and the
Hittites and the Perizzites and the Canaanites and the Hivites and the Jebusites; and
I will cut them off. 24You shall not [a]bow
down to their gods, nor serve them, [b]nor

22:30 [b] Lev. 22:27 **22:31** [a] Ex. 19:6; Lev. 11:44; 19:2 [b] Lev. 7:24; 17:15; Ezek. 4:14 **23:1** [a] Ex. 20:16; Lev. 19:11; Deut. 5:20; Ps. 101:5; [Prov. 10:18] [b] Deut. 19:16–21; Ps. 35:11; [Prov. 19:5]; Acts 6:11 **23:2** [a] Gen. 7:1 [b] Lev. 19:15 **23:3** [a] Ex. 23:6; Lev. 19:15; Deut. 1:17; 16:19 **23:4** [a] [Rom. 12:20] **23:5** [a] Deut. 22:4 **23:6** [a] Eccl. 5:8 **23:7** [a] Ex. 20:16; Ps. 119:29; Eph. 4:25 [b] Matt. 27:4 [c] Ex. 34:7; Deut. 25:1; Rom. 1:18 **23:8** [a] Deut. 10:17; 16:19; Prov. 15:27; 17:8, 23; Is. 5:22, 23 **23:9** [a] Ex. 22:21; Lev. 19:33; Deut. 24:17; 27:19 **23:10** [a] Lev. 25:1–7 **23:12** [a] Luke 13:14 **23:13** [a] Deut. 4:9, 23; 1 Tim. 4:16 [b] Josh. 23:7; Ps. 16:4; Hos. 2:17 **23:14** [a] Ex. 23:17; 34:22–24; Deut. 16:16 **23:15** [a] Ex. 12:14–20; Lev. 23:6–8; Num. 28:16–25 [b] Ex. 22:29; 34:20 **23:16** [a] Ex. 34:22; Lev. 23:10; Num. 28:26 [b] Deut. 16:13 **23:17** [a] Ex. 23:14; 34:23; Deut. 16:16 [1] Hebrew *YHWH,* usually translated *LORD* **23:18** [a] Ex. 34:25; Lev. 2:11 [b] Ex. 12:10; Lev. 7:15; Deut. 16:4 **23:19** [a] Ex. 22:29; 34:26; Deut. 26:2, 10; Neh. 10:35; Prov. 3:9 [b] Deut. 14:21 **23:20** [a] Ex. 3:2; 13:15; 14:19; Josh. 5:14 **23:21** [a] Num. 14:11; Deut. 9:7; Ps. 78:40, 56 [b] Deut. 18:19; 1 John 5:16 [c] Is. 9:6; Jer. 23:6 **23:22** [a] Gen. 12:3; Num. 24:9; Deut. 30:7; Jer. 30:20 **23:23** [a] Ex. 23:20 [b] Josh. 24:8, 11 **23:24** [a] Ex. 20:5; 23:13, 33 [b] Deut. 12:30, 31

do according to their works; [c]but you shall
utterly overthrow them and completely
break down their *sacred* pillars.
25“So you shall [a]serve the LORD your
God, and [b]He will bless your bread and your
water. And [c]I will take sickness away from
the midst of you. 26[a]No one shall suffer miscarriage or be barren in your land; I will
[b]fulfill the number of your days.

#OXYGEN

EXODUS 23:25

Reconcile Hurt with Healing

As you hurt, open yourself fully to the presence of God and the possibilities in God. Your healing is connected to your worship. Therefore, worship God!

Continue to **breathe** and **reconcile hurt with healing.**

27“I will send [a]My fear before you, I will
[b]cause confusion among all the people to
whom you come, and will make all your
enemies turn *their* backs to you. 28And [a]I
will send hornets before you, which shall
drive out the Hivite, the Canaanite, and the
Hittite from before you. 29[a]I will not drive
them out from before you in one year, lest
the land become desolate and the beasts
of the field become too numerous for you.
30Little by little I will drive them out from
before you, until you have increased, and
you inherit the land. 31And [a]I will set your
bounds from the Red Sea to the sea, Philistia, and from the desert to the River.[1] For I
will [b]deliver the inhabitants of the land into
your hand, and you shall drive them out
before you. 32[a]You shall make no covenant
with them, nor with their gods. 33They shall
not dwell in your land, lest they make you
sin against Me. For *if* you serve their gods,
[a]it will surely be a snare to you.”

Israel Affirms the Covenant

24 Now He said to Moses, “Come up to
the LORD, you and Aaron, [a]Nadab
and Abihu, [b]and seventy of the elders of
Israel, and worship from afar. 2And Moses
alone shall come near the LORD, but they
shall not come near; nor shall the people
go up with him.”
3So Moses came and told the people all
the words of the LORD and all the judgments. And all the people answered with
one voice and said, [a]“All the words which
the LORD has said we will do.” 4And Moses
[a]wrote all the words of the LORD. And he
rose early in the morning, and built an altar
at the foot of the mountain, and twelve [b]pil-
lars according to the twelve tribes of Israel.
5Then he sent young men of the children
of Israel, who offered [a]burnt offerings and
sacrificed peace offerings of oxen to the
LORD. 6And Moses [a]took half the blood and
put *it* in basins, and half the blood he sprinkled on the altar. 7Then he [a]took the Book of
the Covenant and read in the hearing of the
people. And they said, “All that the LORD
has said we will do, and be obedient.” 8And
Moses took the blood, sprinkled *it* on the
people, and said, “This is [a]the blood of the
covenant which the LORD has made with
you according to all these words.”

On the Mountain with God

9Then Moses went up, also Aaron, Nadab, and Abihu, and seventy of the elders
of Israel, 10and they [a]saw the God of Israel.
And *there was* under His feet as it were a
paved work of [b]sapphire stone, and it was
like the [c]very heavens in *its* clarity. 11But on
the nobles of the children of Israel He [a]did
not lay His hand. So [b]they saw God, and they
[c]ate and drank.
12Then the LORD said to Moses, [a]“Come
up to Me on the mountain and be there;

23:24 [c] Ex. 34:13; Num. 33:52; Deut. 7:5; 12:3; 2 Kin. 18:4 **23:25** [a] Deut. 6:13; [Matt. 4:10] [b] Deut. 28:5 [c] Ex. 15:26; Deut. 7:15 **23:26** [a] Deut. 7:14; 28:4; Mal. 3:11 [b] 1 Chr. 23:1 **23:27** [a] Gen. 35:5; Ex. 15:16; Deut. 2:25; Josh. 2:9 [b] Deut. 7:23 **23:28** [a] Deut. 7:20; Josh. 24:12 **23:29** [a] Deut. 7:22 **23:31** [a] Gen. 15:18; Deut. 1:7, 8; 11:24; 1 Kin. 4:21, 24 [b] Josh. 21:44 [1] Hebrew *Nahar,* the Euphrates **23:32** [a] Ex. 34:12, 15; Deut. 7:2 **23:33** [a] Ex. 34:12; Deut. 12:30; Josh. 23:13; Judg. 2:3; 1 Sam. 18:21; Ps. 106:36 **24:1** [a] Ex. 6:23; 28:1; Lev. 10:1, 2 [b] Ex. 1:5; Num. 11:16 **24:3** [a] Ex. 19:8; 24:7; Deut. 5:27; [Gal. 3:19] **24:4** [a] Ex. 17:14; 34:27; Deut. 31:9 [b] Gen. 28:18 **24:5** [a] Ex. 18:12; 20:24 **24:6** [a] Ex. 29:16, 20; Heb. 9:18 **24:7** [a] Ex. 24:4; Heb. 9:19 **24:8** [a] Zech. 9:11; [Matt. 26:28; Mark 14:24; Luke 22:20; 1 Cor. 11:25; Heb. 9:19, 20; 13:20; 1 Pet. 1:2] **24:10** [a] Ex. 24:11; Num. 12:8; Is. 6:5; [John 1:18; 6:46]; 1 John 4:12 [b] Ezek. 1:26; Rev. 4:3 [c] Matt. 17:2 **24:11** [a] Ex. 19:21 [b] Gen. 32:30; Judg. 13:22 [c] 1 Cor. 10:18 **24:12** [a] Ex. 24:2, 15

and I will give you [b]tablets of stone, and
the law and commandments which I have
written, that you may teach them."
13So Moses arose with [a]his assistant
Joshua, and Moses went up to the mountain of God. 14And he said to the elders,
"Wait here for us until we come back to you.
Indeed, Aaron and [a]Hur *are* with you. If any
man has a difficulty, let him go to them."
15Then Moses went up into the mountain,
and [a]a cloud covered the mountain.
16Now [a]the glory of the LORD rested on
Mount Sinai, and the cloud covered it six
days. And on the seventh day He called to
Moses out of the midst of the cloud. 17The
sight of the glory of the LORD *was* like [a]a
consuming fire on the top of the mountain in the eyes of the children of Israel.
18So Moses went into the midst of the cloud
and went up into the mountain. And [a]Mo-
ses was on the mountain forty days and
forty nights.

Offerings for the Sanctuary
(Ex. 35:4–9)

25 Then the LORD spoke to Moses, saying: 2"Speak to the children of Israel, that they bring Me an offering. [a]From
everyone who gives it willingly with his
heart you shall take My offering. 3And this
is the offering which you shall take from
them: gold, silver, and bronze; 4blue, purple, and scarlet *thread,* fine linen, and goats'
hair; 5ram skins dyed red, badger skins, and
acacia wood; 6[a]oil for the light, and [b]spices
for the anointing oil and for the sweet incense; 7onyx stones, and stones to be set
in the [a]ephod and in the breastplate. 8And
let them make Me a [a]sanctuary, that [b]I may
dwell among them. 9According to all that I
show you, *that is,* the pattern of the tabernacle and the pattern of all its furnishings,
just so you shall make *it.*

The Ark of the Testimony
(Ex. 37:1–9)

10[a]"And they shall make an ark of acacia wood; two and a half cubits *shall be* its
length, a cubit and a half its width, and a
cubit and a half its height. 11And you shall
overlay it with pure gold, inside and out
you shall overlay it, and shall make on it
a molding of [a]gold all around. 12You shall
cast four rings of gold for it, and put *them*
in its four corners; two rings *shall be* on
one side, and two rings on the other side.
13And you shall make poles *of* acacia wood,
and overlay them with gold. 14You shall put
the poles into the rings on the sides of the
ark, that the ark may be carried by them.
15[a]The poles shall be in the rings of the ark;
they shall not be taken from it. 16And you
shall put into the ark [a]the Testimony which
I will give you.
17[a]"You shall make a mercy seat of pure
gold; two and a half cubits *shall be* its length
and a cubit and a half its width. 18And you
shall make two cherubim of gold; of hammered work you shall make them at the
two ends of the mercy seat. 19Make one
cherub at one end, and the other cherub
at the other end; you shall make the cherubim at the two ends of it *of one piece* with
the mercy seat. 20And [a]the cherubim shall
stretch out *their* wings above, covering the
mercy seat with their wings, and they shall
face one another; the faces of the cherubim *shall be* toward the mercy seat. 21[a]You
shall put the mercy seat on top of the ark,
and [b]in the ark you shall put the Testimony
that I will give you. 22And [a]there I will meet
with you, and I will speak with you from
above the mercy seat, from [b]between the
two cherubim which *are* on the ark of the
Testimony, about everything which I will
give you in commandment to the children
of Israel.

The Table for the Showbread
(Ex. 37:10–16)

23[a]"You shall also make a table of acacia wood; two cubits *shall be* its length,
a cubit its width, and a cubit and a half
its height. 24And you shall overlay it with
pure gold, and make a molding of gold all
around. 25You shall make for it a frame of

24:12 [b] Ex. 31:18; 32:15; Deut. 5:22 **24:13** [a] Ex. 32:17 **24:14** [a] Ex. 17:10, 12 **24:15** [a] Ex. 19:9; Matt. 17:5 **24:16** [a] Ex. 16:10; 33:18; Num. 14:10 **24:17** [a] Ex. 3:2; Deut. 4:26, 36; 9:3; Heb. 12:18, 29 **24:18** [a] Ex. 34:28; Deut. 9:9; 10:10 **25:2** [a] Ex. 35:4–9, 21; 1 Chr. 29:3, 5, 9; Ezra 2:68; Neh. 11:2; [2 Cor. 8:11–13; 9:7] **25:6** [a] Ex. 27:20 [b] Ex. 30:23 **25:7** [a] Ex. 28:4, 6–14 **25:8** [a] Ex. 36:1, 3, 4; Lev. 4:6; 10:4; 21:12; Heb. 9:1, 2 [b] Ex. 29:45; 1 Kin. 6:13; [2 Cor. 6:16; Heb. 3:6; Rev. 2:13] **25:10** [a] Ex. 37:1–9; Deut. 10:3; Heb. 9:4 **25:11** [a] Ex. 37:2; Heb. 9:4 **25:15** [a] Num. 4:6; 1 Kin. 8:8 **25:16** [a] Ex. 16:34; 31:18; Deut. 10:2; 31:26; 1 Kin. 8:9; Heb. 9:4 **25:17** [a] Ex. 37:6; Heb. 9:5 **25:20** [a] 1 Kin. 8:7; 1 Chr. 28:18; Heb. 9:5 **25:21** [a] Ex. 26:34; 40:20 [b] Ex. 25:16 **25:22** [a] Ex. 29:42, 43; 30:6, 36; Lev. 16:2; Num. 17:4 [b] Num. 7:89; 1 Sam. 4:4; 2 Sam. 6:2; 2 Kin. 19:15; Ps. 80:1; Is. 37:16 **25:23** [a] Ex. 37:10–16; 1 Kin. 7:48; 2 Chr. 4:8; Heb. 9:2

a handbreadth all around, and you shall
make a gold molding for the frame all
around. 26And you shall make for it four
rings of gold, and put the rings on the four
corners that *are* at its four legs. 27The rings
shall be close to the frame, as holders for
the poles to bear the table. 28And you shall
make the poles of acacia wood, and overlay them with gold, that the table may be
carried with them. 29You shall make [a]its
dishes, its pans, its pitchers, and its bowls
for pouring. You shall make them of pure
gold. 30And you shall set the [a]showbread
on the table before Me always.

The Gold Lampstand
(Ex. 37:17–24)

31[a]"You shall also make a lampstand
of pure gold; the lampstand shall be of
hammered work. Its shaft, its branches, its
bowls, its *ornamental* knobs, and flowers
shall be *of one piece.* 32And six branches
shall come out of its sides: three branches
of the lampstand out of one side, and three
branches of the lampstand out of the other
side. 33[a]Three bowls *shall be* made like almond *blossoms* on one branch, *with* an
ornamental knob and a flower, and three
bowls made like almond *blossoms* on the
other branch, *with* an *ornamental* knob
and a flower—and so for the six branches
that come out of the lampstand. 34[a]On the
lampstand itself four bowls *shall be* made
like almond *blossoms, each with* its *ornamental* knob and flower. 35And *there shall
be* a knob under the *first* two branches of
the same, a knob under the *second* two
branches of the same, and a knob under
the *third* two branches of the same, according to the six branches that extend
from the lampstand. 36Their knobs and
their branches *shall be of one piece;* all of
it *shall be* one hammered piece of pure
gold. 37You shall make seven lamps for
it, and [a]they shall arrange its lamps so
that they [b]give light in front of it. 38And
its wick-trimmers and their trays *shall be*
of pure gold. 39It shall be made of a talent
of pure gold, with all these utensils. 40And
[a]see to it that you make *them* according to
the pattern which was shown you on the
mountain.

The Tabernacle
(Ex. 36:8–38)

26 "Moreover [a]you shall make the tabernacle *with* ten curtains *of* fine
woven linen and blue, purple, and scarlet *thread;* with artistic designs of cherubim you shall weave them. 2The length of
each curtain *shall be* twenty-eight cubits,
and the width of each curtain four cubits.
And every one of the curtains shall have
the same measurements. 3Five curtains
shall be coupled to one another, and *the
other* five curtains *shall be* coupled to one
another. 4And you shall make loops of blue
yarn on the edge of the curtain on the selvedge of *one* set, and likewise you shall do
on the outer edge of *the other* curtain of the
second set. 5Fifty loops you shall make in
the one curtain, and fifty loops you shall
make on the edge of the curtain that *is* on
the end of the second set, that the loops
may be clasped to one another. 6And you
shall make fifty clasps of gold, and couple
the curtains together with the clasps, so
that it may be one tabernacle.

7[a]"You shall also make curtains of goats'
hair, to be a tent over the tabernacle. You
shall make eleven curtains. 8The length
of each curtain *shall be* thirty cubits, and
the width of each curtain four cubits; and
the eleven curtains shall all have the same
measurements. 9And you shall couple five
curtains by themselves and six curtains by
themselves, and you shall double over the
sixth curtain at the forefront of the tent.
10You shall make fifty loops on the edge
of the curtain that is outermost in *one* set,
and fifty loops on the edge of the curtain
of the second set. 11And you shall make fifty
bronze clasps, put the clasps into the loops,
and couple the tent together, that it may
be one. 12The remnant that remains of the
curtains of the tent, the half curtain that
remains, shall hang over the back of the
tabernacle. 13And a cubit on one side and a
cubit on the other side, of what remains of
the length of the curtains of the tent, shall

25:29 [a] Ex. 37:16; Num. 4:7 25:30 [a] Ex. 39:36; 40:23; Lev. 24:5–9 25:31 [a] Ex. 37:17–24; 1 Kin. 7:49; Zech. 4:2; Heb. 9:2; Rev. 1:12 25:33 [a] Ex. 37:19 25:34 [a] Ex. 37:20–22 25:37 [a] Ex. 27:21; 30:8; Lev. 24:3, 4; 2 Chr. 13:11 [b] Num. 8:2 25:40 [a] Ex. 25:9; 26:30; Num. 8:4; 1 Chr. 28:11, 19; Acts 7:44; [Heb. 8:5] 26:1 [a] Ex. 36:8–19 26:7 [a] Ex. 36:14

hang over the sides of the tabernacle, on
this side and on that side, to cover it.

14[a]"You shall also make a covering of ram
skins dyed red for the tent, and a covering
of badger skins above that.

15"And for the tabernacle you shall [a]make
the boards of acacia wood, standing upright. 16Ten cubits *shall be* the length of a
board, and a cubit and a half *shall be* the
width of each board. 17Two tenons *shall be*
in each board for binding one to another.
Thus you shall make for all the boards of
the tabernacle. 18And you shall make the
boards for the tabernacle, twenty boards
for the south side. 19You shall make forty
sockets of silver under the twenty boards:
two sockets under each of the boards for
its two tenons. 20And for the second side
of the tabernacle, the north side, *there shall*
be twenty boards 21and their forty sockets of silver: two sockets under each of the
boards. 22For the far side of the tabernacle,
westward, you shall make six boards. 23And
you shall also make two boards for the two
back corners of the tabernacle. 24They shall
be coupled together at the bottom and they
shall be coupled together at the top by one
ring. Thus it shall be for both of them. They
shall be for the two corners. 25So there
shall be eight boards with their sockets of
silver—sixteen sockets—two sockets under each of the boards.

26"And you shall make bars of acacia
wood: five for the boards on one side of
the tabernacle, 27five bars for the boards
on the other side of the tabernacle, and five
bars for the boards of the side of the tabernacle, for the far side westward. 28The [a]mid-
dle bar shall pass through the midst of the
boards from end to end. 29You shall overlay
the boards with gold, make their rings of
gold *as* holders for the bars, and overlay the
bars with gold. 30And you shall raise up the
tabernacle [a]according to its pattern which
you were shown on the mountain.

31[a]"You shall make a veil woven of blue,
purple, and scarlet *thread,* and fine woven
linen. It shall be woven with an artistic design of cherubim. 32You shall hang it upon
the four pillars of acacia *wood* overlaid with
gold. Their hooks *shall be* gold, upon four
sockets of silver. 33And you shall hang the
veil from the clasps. Then you shall bring
[a]the ark of the Testimony in there, behind
the veil. The veil shall be a divider for you
between [b]the holy *place* and the Most Holy.
34[a]You shall put the mercy seat upon the ark
of the Testimony in the Most Holy. 35[a]You
shall set the table outside the veil, and [b]the
lampstand across from the table on the side
of the tabernacle toward the south; and you
shall put the table on the north side.

36[a]"You shall make a screen for the door
of the tabernacle, *woven of* blue, purple,
and scarlet *thread,* and fine woven linen,
made by a weaver. 37And you shall make for
the screen [a]five pillars of acacia *wood,* and
overlay them with gold; their hooks *shall*
be gold, and you shall cast five sockets of
bronze for them.

The Altar of Burnt Offering
(Ex. 38:1–7)

27 "You shall make [a]an altar of acacia
wood, five cubits long and five cubits wide—the altar shall be square—and
its height *shall be* three cubits. 2You shall
make its horns on its four corners; its horns
shall be of one piece with it. And you shall
overlay it with bronze. 3Also you shall make
its pans to receive its ashes, and its shovels
and its basins and its forks and its firepans;
you shall make all its utensils of bronze.
4You shall make a grate for it, a network
of bronze; and on the network you shall
make four bronze rings at its four corners.
5You shall put it under the rim of the altar
beneath, that the network may be midway
up the altar. 6And you shall make poles for
the altar, poles of acacia wood, and overlay
them with bronze. 7The poles shall be put in
the rings, and the poles shall be on the two
sides of the altar to bear it. 8You shall make
it hollow with boards; [a]as it was shown you
on the mountain, so shall they make *it.*

The Court of the Tabernacle
(Ex. 38:9–20)

9[a]"You shall also make the court of the
tabernacle. For the south side *there shall*

26:14 [a] Ex. 35:7, 23; 36:19 26:15 [a] Ex. 36:20–34 26:28 [a] Ex. 36:33 26:30 [a] Ex. 25:9, 40; 27:8; 39:32; Num. 8:4; Acts 7:44; [Heb. 8:2, 5] 26:31 [a] Ex. 27:21; 36:35–38; Lev. 16:2; 2 Chr. 3:14; Matt. 27:51; Heb. 9:3; 10:20 26:33 [a] Ex. 25:10–16; 40:21 [b] Lev. 16:2; Heb. 9:2, 3 26:34 [a] Ex. 25:17–22; 40:20; Heb. 9:5 26:35 [a] Ex. 40:22; Heb. 9:2 [b] Ex. 40:24 26:36 [a] Ex. 36:37 26:37 [a] Ex. 36:38 27:1 [a] Ex. 38:1; Ezek. 43:13 27:8 [a] Ex. 25:40; 26:30; Acts 7:44; [Heb. 8:5] 27:9 [a] Ex. 38:9–20

be hangings for the court *made of* fine woven linen, one hundred cubits long for
one side. 10 And its twenty pillars and their
twenty sockets *shall be* bronze. The hooks
of the pillars and their bands *shall be* silver. 11 Likewise along the length of the north
side *there shall be* hangings one hundred
cubits long, with its twenty pillars and their
twenty sockets of bronze, and the hooks of
the pillars and their bands of silver.

12 "And along the width of the court on
the west side *shall be* hangings of fifty cubits, with their ten pillars and their ten
sockets. 13 The width of the court on the east
side *shall be* fifty cubits. 14 The hangings on
one side *of the gate shall be* fifteen cubits,
with their three pillars and their three sockets. 15 And on the other side *shall be* hangings of fifteen *cubits, with* their three pillars
and their three sockets.

16 "For the gate of the court *there shall
be* a screen twenty cubits long, *woven of*
blue, purple, and scarlet *thread,* and fine
woven linen, made by a weaver. It *shall
have* four pillars and four sockets. 17 All the
pillars around the court shall have bands
of silver; their [a]hooks *shall be* of silver and
their sockets of bronze. 18 The length of
the court *shall be* one hundred cubits, the
width fifty throughout, and the height five
cubits, *made of* fine woven linen, and its
sockets of bronze. 19 All the utensils of the
tabernacle for all its service, all its pegs,
and all the pegs of the court, *shall be* of
bronze.

The Care of the Lampstand
(Lev. 24:1–4)

20 "And [a]you shall command the children of Israel that they bring you pure oil
of pressed olives for the light, to cause the
lamp to burn continually. 21 In the tabernacle of meeting, [a]outside the veil which *is*
before the Testimony, [b]Aaron and his sons
shall tend it from evening until morning
before the LORD. [c]*It shall be* a statute forever to their generations on behalf of the
children of Israel.

Garments for the Priesthood
(Ex. 39:1–7)

28 "Now take [a]Aaron your brother, and
his sons with him, from among the
children of Israel, that he may minister to
Me as [b]priest, Aaron *and* Aaron's sons: [c]Na-
dab, Abihu, [d]Eleazar, and Ithamar. 2 And
[a]you shall make holy garments for Aaron
your brother, for glory and for beauty. 3 So
[a]you shall speak to all *who are* gifted artisans, [b]whom I have filled with the spirit
of wisdom, that they may make Aaron's
garments, to consecrate him, that he may
minister to Me as priest. 4 And these *are*
the garments which they shall make: [a]a
breastplate, [b]an ephod,[1] [c]a robe, [d]a skillfully
woven tunic, a turban, and [e]a sash. So they
shall make holy garments for Aaron your
brother and his sons, that he may minister
to Me as priest.

The Ephod

5 "They shall take the gold, blue, purple,
and scarlet *thread,* and the fine linen, 6 [a]and
they shall make the ephod of gold, blue,
purple, *and* scarlet *thread,* and fine woven
linen, artistically worked. 7 It shall have two
shoulder straps joined at its two edges, and
so it shall be joined together. 8 And the intricately woven band of the ephod, which *is* on
it, shall be of the same workmanship, *made
of* gold, blue, purple, and scarlet *thread,* and
fine woven linen.

9 "Then you shall take two onyx [a]stones
and engrave on them the names of the sons
of Israel: 10 six of their names on one stone
and six names on the other stone, in order of their [a]birth. 11 With the work of an
[a]engraver in stone, *like* the engravings of
a signet, you shall engrave the two stones
with the names of the sons of Israel. You
shall set them in settings of gold. 12 And you
shall put the two stones on the shoulders
of the ephod *as* memorial stones for the
sons of Israel. So [a]Aaron shall bear their
names before the LORD on his two shoulders [b]as a memorial. 13 You shall also make
settings of gold, 14 and you shall make two

27:17 [a] Ex. 38:19 **27:20** [a] Ex. 35:8, 28; Lev. 24:1–4 **27:21** [a] Ex. 26:31, 33 [b] Ex. 30:8; 1 Sam. 3:3; 2 Chr. 13:11 [c] Ex. 28:43; 29:9; Lev. 3:17; 16:34; Num. 18:23; 19:21; 1 Sam. 30:25 **28:1** [a] Num. 3:10; 18:7 [b] Ps. 99:6; Heb. 5:4 [c] Ex. 24:1, 9; Lev. 10:1 [d] Ex. 6:23; Lev. 10:6, 16 **28:2** [a] Ex. 29:5, 29; 31:10; 39:1–31; Lev. 8:7–9, 30 **28:3** [a] Ex. 31:6; 36:1 [b] Ex. 31:3; 35:30, 31; Is. 11:2; Eph. 1:17 **28:4** [a] Ex. 28:15 [b] Ex. 28:6 [c] Ex. 28:31 [d] Ex. 28:39 [e] Lev. 8:7 [1] That is, an ornamented vest **28:6** [a] Ex. 39:2–7; Lev. 8:7 **28:9** [a] Ex. 35:27 **28:10** [a] Gen. 29:31—30:24; 35:16–18 **28:11** [a] Ex. 35:35 **28:12** [a] Ex. 28:29, 30; 39:6, 7 [b] Lev. 24:7; Num. 31:54; Josh. 4:7; Zech. 6:14; 1 Cor. 11:24

chains of pure gold like braided cords, and
fasten the braided chains to the settings.

The Breastplate
(Ex. 39:8–21)

15[a]"You shall make the breastplate of
judgment. Artistically woven according to
the workmanship of the ephod you shall
make it: of gold, blue, purple, and scarlet *thread,* and fine woven linen, you shall
make it. 16It shall be doubled into a square:
a span *shall be* its length, and a span *shall
be* its width. 17[a]And you shall put settings
of stones in it, four rows of stones: *The first*
row *shall be* a sardius, a topaz, and an emerald; *this shall be* the first row; 18the second
row *shall be* a turquoise, a sapphire, and a
diamond; 19the third row, a jacinth, an agate, and an amethyst; 20and the fourth row,
a beryl, an onyx, and a jasper. They shall
be set in gold settings. 21And the stones
shall have the names of the sons of Israel,
twelve according to their names, *like* the
engravings of a signet, each one with its
own name; they shall be according to the
twelve tribes.

22"You shall make chains for the breastplate at the end, like braided cords of pure
gold. 23And you shall make two rings of
gold for the breastplate, and put the two
rings on the two ends of the breastplate.
24Then you shall put the two braided *chains*
of gold in the two rings which are on the
ends of the breastplate; 25and the *other* two
ends of the two braided *chains* you shall
fasten to the two settings, and put them
on the shoulder straps of the ephod in the
front.

26"You shall make two rings of gold, and
put them on the two ends of the breastplate, on the edge of it, which is on the inner side of the ephod. 27And two *other* rings
of gold you shall make, and put them on
the two shoulder straps, underneath the
ephod toward its front, right at the seam
above the intricately woven band of the
ephod. 28They shall bind the breastplate by
means of its rings to the rings of the ephod,
using a blue cord, so that it is above the intricately woven band of the ephod, and so
that the breastplate does not come loose
from the ephod.

29"So Aaron shall [a]bear the names of the
sons of Israel on the breastplate of judgment over his heart, when he goes into
the holy *place,* as a memorial before the
LORD continually. 30And [a]you shall put in
the breastplate of judgment the Urim and
the Thummim,[1] and they shall be over Aaron's heart when he goes in before the LORD.
So Aaron shall bear the judgment of the
children of Israel over his heart before the
LORD continually.

Other Priestly Garments
(Ex. 39:22–31)

31[a]"You shall make the robe of the ephod
all of blue. 32There shall be an opening for
his head in the middle of it; it shall have
a woven binding all around its opening,
like the opening in a coat of mail, so that
it does not tear. 33And upon its hem you
shall make pomegranates of blue, purple,
and scarlet, all around its hem, and bells of
gold between them all around: 34a golden
bell and a pomegranate, a golden bell and
a pomegranate, upon the hem of the robe
all around. 35And it shall be upon Aaron
when he ministers, and its sound will be
heard when he goes into the holy *place* before the LORD and when he comes out, that
he may not die.

36[a]"You shall also make a plate of pure
gold and engrave on it, *like* the engraving
of a signet:

HOLINESS TO THE LORD.

37And you shall put it on a blue cord, that
it may be on the turban; it shall be on the
front of the turban. 38So it shall be on Aaron's forehead, that Aaron may [a]bear the iniquity of the holy things which the children
of Israel hallow in all their holy gifts; and it
shall always be on his forehead, that they
may be [b]accepted before the LORD.

39"You shall [a]skillfully weave the tunic of
fine linen *thread,* you shall make the turban of fine linen, and you shall make the
sash of woven work.

28:15 [a] Ex. 39:8–21 28:17 [a] Ex. 39:10 28:29 [a] Ex. 28:12 28:30 [a] Lev. 8:8; Num. 27:21; Deut. 33:8; 1 Sam. 28:6; Ezra 2:63; Neh. 7:65
[1] Literally *the Lights and the Perfections* (compare Leviticus 8:8) 28:31 [a] Ex. 39:22–26 28:36 [a] Ex. 39:30, 31; Lev. 8:9; Zech. 14:20
28:38 [a] Ex. 28:43; Lev. 10:17; 22:9, 16; Num. 18:1; [Is. 53:11]; Ezek. 4:4–6; [John 1:29; Heb. 9:28; 1 Pet. 2:24]
[b] Lev. 1:4; 22:27; 23:11; Is. 56:7 28:39 [a] Ex. 35:35; 39:27–29

40[a]“For Aaron’s sons you shall make tunics, and you shall make sashes for them. And you shall make hats for them, for glory and [b]beauty. 41So you shall put them on Aaron your brother and on his sons with him. You shall [a]anoint them, [b]consecrate them, and sanctify them, that they may minister to Me as priests. 42And you shall make [a]for them linen trousers to cover their nakedness; they shall reach from the waist to the thighs. 43They shall be on Aaron and on his sons when they come into the tabernacle of meeting, or when they come near [a]the altar to minister in the holy *place,* that they [b]do not incur iniquity and die. [c]*It shall be* a statute forever to him and his descendants after him.

Aaron and His Sons Consecrated
(Lev. 8:1–36)

29 “And this is what you shall do to them to hallow them for ministering to Me as priests: [a]Take one young bull and two rams without blemish, 2and [a]unleavened bread, unleavened cakes mixed with oil, and unleavened wafers anointed with oil (you shall make them of wheat flour). 3You shall put them in one basket and bring them in the basket, with the bull and the two rams.

4“And Aaron and his sons you shall bring to the door of the tabernacle of meeting, [a]and you shall wash them with water. 5[a]Then you shall take the garments, put the tunic on Aaron, and the robe of the ephod, the ephod, and the breastplate, and gird him with [b]the intricately woven band of the ephod. 6[a]You shall put the turban on his head, and put the holy crown on the turban. 7And you shall take the anointing [a]oil, pour *it* on his head, and anoint him. 8Then [a]you shall bring his sons and put tunics on them. 9And you shall gird them with sashes, Aaron and his sons, and put the hats on them. [a]The priesthood shall be theirs for a perpetual statute. So you shall [b]consecrate Aaron and his sons.

10“You shall also have the bull brought before the tabernacle of meeting, and [a]Aaron and his sons shall put their hands on the head of the bull. 11Then you shall kill the bull before the LORD, *by* the door of the tabernacle of meeting. 12You shall take *some* of the blood of the bull and put *it* on [a]the horns of the altar with your finger, and [b]pour all the blood beside the base of the altar. 13And [a]you shall take all the fat that covers the entrails, the fatty lobe *attached* to the liver, and the two kidneys and the fat that *is* on them, and burn *them* on the altar. 14But [a]the flesh of the bull, with its skin and its offal, you shall burn with fire outside the camp. It *is* a sin offering.

15[a]“You shall also take one ram, and Aaron and his sons shall [b]put their hands on the head of the ram; 16and you shall kill the ram, and you shall take its blood and [a]sprinkle *it* all around on the altar. 17Then you shall cut the ram in pieces, wash its entrails and its legs, and put *them* with its pieces and with its head. 18And you shall burn the whole ram on the altar. It *is* a [a]burnt offering to the LORD; it *is* a sweet aroma, an offering made by fire to the LORD.

19[a]“You shall also take the other ram, and Aaron and his sons shall put their hands on the head of the ram. 20Then you shall kill the ram, and take some of its blood and put *it* on the tip of the right ear of Aaron and on the tip of the right ear of his sons, on the thumb of their right hand and on the big toe of their right foot, and sprinkle the blood all around on the altar. 21And you shall take some of the blood that is on the altar, and some of [a]the anointing oil, and sprinkle *it* on Aaron and on his garments, on his sons and on the garments of his sons with him; and [b]he and his garments shall be hallowed, and his sons and his sons’ garments with him.

22“Also you shall take the fat of the ram, the fat tail, the fat that covers the entrails, the fatty lobe *attached to* the liver, the two kidneys and the fat on them, the right thigh (for it *is* a ram of consecration), 23[a]one loaf of bread, one cake *made with* oil, and one

---

28:40 [a] Ex. 28:4; 39:27–29, 41; Ezek. 44:17, 18 [b] Ex. 28:2 **28:41** [a] Ex. 29:7–9; 30:30; 40:15; Lev. 10:7 [b] Ex. 29:9; Lev. 8; Heb. 7:28 **28:42** [a] Ex. 39:28; Lev. 6:10; 16:4; Ezek. 44:18 **28:43** [a] Ex. 20:26 [b] Lev. 5:1, 17; 20:19, 20; 22:9; Num. 9:13; 18:22 [c] Ex. 27:21; Lev. 17:7 **29:1** [a] Lev. 8; [Heb. 7:26–28] **29:2** [a] Lev. 2:4; 6:19–23 **29:4** [a] Ex. 40:12; Lev. 8:6; [Heb. 10:22] **29:5** [a] Ex. 28:2; Lev. 8:7 [b] Ex. 28:8 **29:6** [a] Ex. 28:36, 37; Lev. 8:9 **29:7** [a] Ex. 25:6; 30:25–31; Lev. 8:12; 10:7; 21:10; Num. 35:25; Ps. 133:2 **29:8** [a] Ex. 28:39, 40; Lev. 8:13 **29:9** [a] Ex. 40:15; Num. 3:10; 18:7; 25:13; Deut. 18:5 [b] Ex. 28:41; Lev. 8 **29:10** [a] Lev. 1:4; 8:14 **29:12** [a] Lev. 8:15 [b] Ex. 27:2; 30:2; Lev. 4:7 **29:13** [a] Lev. 1:8; 3:3, 4 **29:14** [a] Lev. 4:11, 12, 21; Heb. 13:11 **29:15** [a] Lev. 8:18 [b] Lev. 1:4–9 **29:16** [a] Ex. 24:6; Lev. 1:5, 11 **29:18** [a] Ex. 20:24 **29:19** [a] Lev. 8:22 **29:21** [a] Ex. 30:25, 31; Lev. 8:30 [b] Ex. 28:41; 29:1; [Heb. 9:22] **29:23** [a] Lev. 8:26

wafer from the basket of the unleavened bread that *is* before the LORD; 24and you shall put all these in the hands of Aaron and in the hands of his sons, and you shall [a]wave them *as* a wave offering before the LORD. 25[a]You shall receive them back from their hands and burn *them* on the altar as a burnt offering, as a sweet aroma before the LORD. It *is* an offering made by fire to the LORD.

26"Then you shall take [a]the breast of the ram of Aaron's consecration and wave it *as* a wave offering before the LORD; and it shall be your portion. 27And from the ram of the consecration you shall consecrate [a]the breast of the wave offering which is waved, and the thigh of the heave offering which is raised, of *that* which *is* for Aaron and of *that* which is for his sons. 28It shall be from the children of Israel *for* Aaron and his sons [a]by a statute forever. For it is a heave offering; [b]it shall be a heave offering from the children of Israel from the sacrifices of their peace offerings, *that is,* their heave offering to the LORD.

29"And the [a]holy garments of Aaron [b]shall be his sons' after him, [c]to be anointed in them and to be consecrated in them. 30[a]That son who becomes priest in his place shall put them on for [b]seven days, when he enters the tabernacle of meeting to minister in the holy *place.*

31"And you shall take the ram of the consecration and [a]boil its flesh in the holy place. 32Then Aaron and his sons shall eat the flesh of the ram, and the [a]bread that *is* in the basket, *by* the door of the tabernacle of meeting. 33[a]They shall eat those things with which the atonement was made, to consecrate *and* to sanctify them; [b]but an outsider shall not eat *them,* because they *are* holy. 34And if any of the flesh of the consecration offerings, or of the bread, remains until the morning, then [a]you shall burn the remainder with fire. It shall not be eaten, because it *is* holy.

35"Thus you shall do to Aaron and his sons, according to all that I have commanded you. [a]Seven days you shall consecrate them. 36And you [a]shall offer a bull every day *as* a sin offering for atonement. [b]You shall cleanse the altar when you make atonement for it, and you shall anoint it to sanctify it. 37Seven days you shall make atonement for the altar and sanctify it. And the altar shall be most holy. [a]Whatever touches the altar must be holy.[1]

The Daily Offerings
(Num. 28:1–8)

38"Now this *is* what you shall offer on the altar: [a]two lambs of the first year, [b]day by day continually. 39One lamb you shall offer [a]in the morning, and the other lamb you shall offer at twilight. 40With the one lamb shall be one-tenth *of an ephah* of flour mixed with one-fourth of a hin of pressed oil, and one-fourth of a hin of wine *as* a drink offering. 41And the other lamb you shall [a]offer at twilight; and you shall offer with it the grain offering and the drink offering, as in the morning, for a sweet aroma, an offering made by fire to the LORD. 42*This shall be* [a]a continual burnt offering throughout your generations *at* the door of the tabernacle of meeting before the LORD, [b]where I will meet you to speak with you. 43And there I will meet with the children of Israel, and *the tabernacle* [a]shall be sanctified by My glory. 44So I will consecrate the tabernacle of meeting and the altar. I will also [a]consecrate both Aaron and his sons to minister to Me as priests. 45[a]I will dwell among the children of Israel and will [b]be their God. 46And they shall know that [a]I *am* the LORD their God, who [b]brought them up out of the land of Egypt, that I may dwell among them. I *am* the LORD their God.

The Altar of Incense
(Ex. 37:25–28)

30 "You shall make [a]an altar to burn incense on; you shall make it of acacia wood. 2A cubit *shall be* its length and a cubit its width—it shall be square—and two

29:24 [a] Lev. 7:30; 10:14 29:25 [a] Lev. 8:28 29:26 [a] Lev. 7:31, 34; 8:29 29:27 [a] Lev. 7:31, 34; Num. 18:11, 18; Deut. 18:3 29:28 [a] Lev. 10:15 [b] Lev. 3:1; 7:34 29:29 [a] Ex. 28:2 [b] Num. 20:26, 28 [c] Ex. 28:41; 30:30; Num. 18:8 29:30 [a] Num. 20:28 [b] Lev. 8:35 29:31 [a] Lev. 8:31 29:32 [a] Matt. 12:4 29:33 [a] Lev. 10:14, 15, 17 [b] Ex. 12:43; Lev. 22:10 29:34 [a] Ex. 12:10; 23:18; 34:25; Lev. 7:18; 8:32 29:35 [a] Lev. 8:33–35 29:36 [a] Heb. 10:11 [b] Ex. 30:26–29; 40:10, 11 29:37 [a] Num. 4:15; Hag. 2:11–13; Matt. 23:19 [1] Compare Numbers 4:15 and Haggai 2:11–13 29:38 [a] Num. 28:3–31; 29:6–38; 1 Chr. 16:40; Ezra 3:3 [b] Dan. 12:11 29:39 [a] Ezek. 46:13–15 29:41 [a] 1 Kin. 18:29, 36; 2 Kin. 16:15; Ezra 9:4, 5; Ps. 141:2 29:42 [a] Ex. 30:8 [b] Ex. 25:22; 33:7, 9; Num. 17:4 29:43 [a] Ex. 40:34; 1 Kin. 8:11; 2 Chr. 5:14; Ezek. 43:5; Hag. 2:7, 9 29:44 [a] Lev. 21:15 29:45 [a] Ex. 25:8; Lev. 26:12; Num. 5:3; Deut. 12:11; Zech. 2:10; [John 14:17, 23; Rev. 21:3] [b] Gen. 17:8; Lev. 11:45 29:46 [a] Ex. 16:12; 20:2; Deut. 4:35 [b] Lev. 11:45 30:1 [a] Ex. 37:25–29

cubits *shall be* its height. Its horns *shall be*
of one piece with it. 3And you shall overlay
its top, its sides all around, and its horns
with pure gold; and you shall make for it a
molding of gold all around. 4Two gold rings
you shall make for it, under the molding
on both its sides. You shall place *them* on
its two sides, and they will be holders for
the poles with which to bear it. 5You shall
make the poles of acacia wood, and overlay
them with gold. 6And you shall put it before
the [a]veil that *is* before the ark of the Testimony, before the [b]mercy seat that *is* over
the Testimony, where I will meet with you.
7"Aaron shall burn on it [a]sweet incense
every morning; when [b]he tends the lamps,
he shall burn incense on it. 8And when
Aaron lights the lamps at twilight, he shall
burn incense on it, a perpetual incense before the LORD throughout your generations.
9You shall not offer [a]strange incense on it,
or a burnt offering, or a grain offering; nor
shall you pour a drink offering on it. 10And
[a]Aaron shall make atonement upon its
horns once a year with the blood of the sin
offering of atonement; once a year he shall
make atonement upon it throughout your
generations. It *is* most holy to the LORD."

The Ransom Money

11Then the LORD spoke to Moses, saying:
12[a]"When you take the census of the children
of Israel for their number, then every man
shall give [b]a ransom for himself to the LORD,
when you number them, that there may be
no [c]plague among them when *you* number
them. 13[a]This is what everyone among those
who are numbered shall give: half a shekel
according to the shekel of the sanctuary [b](a
shekel *is* twenty gerahs). [c]The half-shekel
shall be an offering to the LORD. 14Everyone
included among those who are numbered,
from twenty years old and above, shall give
an offering to the LORD. 15The [a]rich shall not
give more and the poor shall not give less
than half a shekel, when *you* give an offering
to the LORD, to make atonement for yourselves. 16And you shall take the atonement
money of the children of Israel, and [a]shall
appoint it for the service of the tabernacle
of meeting, that it may be [b]a memorial for
the children of Israel before the LORD, to
make atonement for yourselves."

The Bronze Laver

17Then the LORD spoke to Moses, saying:
18[a]"You shall also make a laver of bronze,
with its base also of bronze, for washing.
You shall [b]put it between the tabernacle of
meeting and the altar. And you shall put
water in it, 19for Aaron and his sons [a]shall
wash their hands and their feet in water
from it. 20When they go into the tabernacle
of meeting, or when they come near the altar to minister, to burn an offering made by
fire to the LORD, they shall wash with water,
lest they die. 21So they shall wash their hands
and their feet, lest they die. And [a]it shall be
a statute forever to them—to him and his
descendants throughout their generations."

The Holy Anointing Oil
(Ex. 37:29)

22Moreover the LORD spoke to Moses,
saying: 23"Also take for yourself [a]qual-
ity spices—five hundred *shekels* of liquid
[b]myrrh, half as much sweet-smelling cinnamon (two hundred and fifty *shekels*), two
hundred and fifty *shekels* of sweet-smelling
[c]cane, 24five hundred *shekels* of [a]cassia, according to the shekel of the sanctuary, and
a [b]hin of olive oil. 25And you shall make
from these a holy anointing oil, an ointment compounded according to the art of
the perfumer. It shall be [a]a holy anointing
oil. 26[a]With it you shall anoint the tabernacle of meeting and the ark of the Testimony; 27the table and all its utensils, the
lampstand and its utensils, and the altar
of incense; 28the altar of burnt offering
with all its utensils, and the laver and its
base. 29You shall consecrate them, that
they may be most holy; [a]whatever touches
them must be holy.[1] 30[a]And you shall anoint
Aaron and his sons, and consecrate them,
that *they* may minister to Me as priests.

30:6 [a] Ex. 26:31–35 [b] Ex. 25:21, 22 **30:7** [a] Ex. 30:34; 1 Sam. 2:28; 1 Chr. 23:13; Luke 1:9 [b] Ex. 27:20, 21 **30:9** [a] Lev. 10:1 **30:10** [a] Lev. 16:3–34 **30:12** [a] Ex. 38:25, 26; Num. 1:2; 26:2; 2 Sam. 24:2 [b] Num. 31:50; [Matt. 20:28; 1 Pet. 1:18, 19] [c] 2 Sam. 24:15 **30:13** [a] Matt. 17:24 [b] Lev. 27:25; Num. 3:47; Ezek. 45:12 [c] Ex. 38:26 **30:15** [a] Job 34:19; Prov. 22:2; [Eph. 6:9] **30:16** [a] Ex. 38:25–31 [b] Num. 16:40 **30:18** [a] Ex. 38:8; 1 Kin. 7:38 [b] Ex. 40:30 **30:19** [a] Ex. 40:31, 32; Ps. 26:6; Is. 52:11; John 13:8, 10; Heb. 10:22 **30:21** [a] Ex. 28:43 **30:23** [a] Song 4:14; Ezek. 27:22 [b] Ps. 45:8; Prov. 7:17 [c] Song 4:14; Jer. 6:20 **30:24** [a] Ps. 45:8 [b] Ex. 29:40 **30:25** [a] Ex. 37:29; 40:9; Lev. 8:10; Num. 35:25; Ps. 89:20; 133:2 **30:26** [a] Ex. 40:9; Lev. 8:10; Num. 7:1 **30:29** [a] Ex. 29:37; Num. 4:15; Hag. 2:11–13 [1] Compare Numbers 4:15 and Haggai 2:11–13 **30:30** [a] Ex. 29:7; Lev. 8:12

31"And you shall speak to the children of
Israel, saying: 'This shall be a holy anointing oil to Me throughout your generations.
32It shall not be poured on man's flesh; nor
shall you make *any other* like it, according
to its composition. [a]It *is* holy, *and* it shall
be holy to you. 33[a]Whoever compounds *any*
like it, or whoever puts *any* of it on an outsider, [b]shall be cut off from his people.'"

The Incense
(Ex. 37:29)

34And the LORD said to Moses: [a]"Take
sweet spices, stacte and onycha and gal-
banum, and pure frankincense with *these*
sweet spices; there shall be equal amounts
of each. 35You shall make of these an incense, a compound [a]according to the art of
the perfumer, salted, pure, *and* holy. 36And
you shall beat *some* of it very fine, and put
some of it before the Testimony in the tabernacle of meeting [a]where I will meet with
you. [b]It shall be most holy to you. 37But *as for*
the incense which you shall make, [a]you shall
not make any for yourselves, according to
its composition. It shall be to you holy for
the LORD. 38[a]Whoever makes *any* like it, to
smell it, he shall be cut off from his people."

Artisans for Building the Tabernacle
(Ex. 35:30—36:1)

31 Then the LORD spoke to Moses, saying: 2[a]"See, I have called by name
Bezalel the [b]son of Uri, the son of Hur, of
the tribe of Judah. 3And I have [a]filled him
with the Spirit of God, in wisdom, in understanding, in knowledge, and in all *manner
of* workmanship, 4to design artistic works,
to work in gold, in silver, in bronze, 5in cutting jewels for setting, in carving wood,
and to work in all *manner of* workmanship.
6"And I, indeed I, have appointed with
him [a]Aholiab the son of Ahisamach, of the
tribe of Dan; and I have put wisdom in the
hearts of all the [b]gifted artisans, that they
may make all that I have commanded you:
7[a]the tabernacle of meeting, [b]the ark of the
Testimony and [c]the mercy seat that *is* on
it, and all the furniture of the tabernacle—
8[a]the table and its utensils, [b]the pure *gold*
lampstand with all its utensils, the altar
of incense, 9[a]the altar of burnt offering
with all its utensils, and [b]the laver and its
base— 10[a]the garments of ministry,[1] the
holy garments for Aaron the priest and
the garments of his sons, to minister as
priests, 11[a]and the anointing oil and [b]sweet
incense for the holy *place.* According to all
that I have commanded you they shall do."

The Sabbath Law

12And the LORD spoke to Moses, saying,
13"Speak also to the children of Israel, saying: [a]'Surely My Sabbaths you shall keep, for
it *is* a sign between Me and you throughout
your generations, that *you* may know that
I *am* the LORD who [b]sanctifies you. 14[a]You
shall keep the Sabbath, therefore, for *it is*
holy to you. Everyone who profanes it shall
surely be put to death; for [b]whoever does
any work on it, that person shall be cut off
from among his people. 15Work shall be
done for [a]six days, but the [b]seventh *is* the
Sabbath of rest, holy to the LORD. Whoever
does *any* work on the Sabbath day, he shall
surely be put to death. 16Therefore the children of Israel shall keep the Sabbath, to
observe the Sabbath throughout their generations *as* a perpetual covenant. 17It *is* [a]a
sign between Me and the children of Israel
forever; for [b]*in* six days the LORD made the
heavens and the earth, and on the seventh
day He rested and was refreshed.'"
18And when He had made an end of
speaking with him on Mount Sinai, He gave
Moses [a]two tablets of the Testimony, tablets of stone, written with the finger of God.

The Gold Calf
(Deut. 9:6–29)

32 Now when the people saw that Moses [a]delayed coming down from the
mountain, the people [b]gathered together
to Aaron, and said to him, [c]"Come, make us

30:32 [a] Ex. 30:25, 37 30:33 [a] Ex. 30:38 [b] Gen. 17:14; Ex. 12:15; Lev. 7:20, 21 30:34 [a] Ex. 25:6; 37:29 30:35 [a] Ex. 30:25 30:36 [a] Ex. 29:42; Lev. 16:2 [b] [Ex. 29:37; 30:32]; Lev. 2:3 30:37 [a] Ex. 30:32 30:38 [a] Ex. 30:33 31:2 [a] Ex. 35:30—36:1 [b] 1 Chr. 2:20 31:3 [a] Ex. 28:3; 35:31; 1 Kin. 7:14; Eph. 1:17 31:6 [a] Ex. 35:34 [b] Ex. 28:3; 35:10, 35; 36:1 31:7 [a] Ex. 36:8 [b] Ex. 37:1–5 [c] Ex. 37:6–9 31:8 [a] Ex. 37:10–16 [b] Ex. 37:17–24; Lev. 24:4 31:9 [a] Ex. 38:1–7 [b] Ex. 38:8 31:10 [a] Ex. 39:1, 41 [1] Or *woven garments* 31:11 [a] Ex. 30:23–33 [b] Ex. 30:34–38 31:13 [a] Ex. 31:17; Lev. 19:3, 30; 26:2; Ezek. 20:12, 20 [b] Lev. 20:8 31:14 [a] Ex. 20:8; Deut. 5:12 [b] Ex. 31:15; 35:2; Num. 15:32–36; John 7:23 31:15 [a] Ex. 20:9–11; Lev. 23:3; Deut. 5:12–14 [b] Gen. 2:2; Ex. 16:23; 20:8; 35:2 31:17 [a] Ex. 31:13; Ezek. 20:12 [b] Gen. 1:31; 2:2, 3; Ex. 20:11 31:18 [a] [Ex. 24:12; 32:15, 16; Deut. 4:13; 5:22; 2 Cor. 3:3] 32:1 [a] Ex. 24:18; Deut. 9:9–12 [b] Ex. 17:1–3 [c] Acts 7:40

gods that shall [d]go before us; for *as for* this
Moses, the man who [e]brought us up out of
the land of Egypt, we do not know what has
become of him."
2And Aaron said to them, "Break off the
[a]golden earrings which *are* in the ears of
your wives, your sons, and your daughters,
and bring *them* to me." 3So all the people
broke off the golden earrings which *were*
in their ears, and brought *them* to Aaron.
4[a]And he received *the gold* from their hand,
and he fashioned it with an engraving tool,
and made a molded calf.

Then they said, "This *is* your god, O Israel, that [b]brought you out of the land of
Egypt!"
5So when Aaron saw *it,* he built an altar
before it. And Aaron made a [a]proclamation
and said, "Tomorrow *is* a feast to the LORD."
6Then they rose early on the next day, offered burnt offerings, and brought peace
offerings; and the people [a]sat down to eat
and drink, and rose up to play.
7And the LORD said to Moses, [a]"Go, get
down! For your people whom you brought
out of the land of Egypt [b]have corrupted
themselves. 8They have turned aside quickly
out of the way which [a]I commanded them.
They have made themselves a molded calf,
and worshiped it and sacrificed to it, and
said, [b]'This *is* your god, O Israel, that brought
you out of the land of Egypt!'" 9And the LORD
said to Moses, [a]"I have seen this people, and
indeed it *is* a stiff-necked people! 10Now
therefore, [a]let Me alone, that [b]My wrath may
burn hot against them and I may consume
them. And [c]I will make of you a great nation."
11[a]Then Moses pleaded with the LORD
his God, and said: "LORD, why does Your
wrath burn hot against Your people whom
You have brought out of the land of Egypt
with great power and with a mighty hand?
12[a]Why should the Egyptians speak, and
say, 'He brought them out to harm them,
to kill them in the mountains, and to consume them from the face of the earth'?
Turn from Your fierce wrath, and [b]relent
from this harm to Your people. 13Remember
Abraham, Isaac, and Israel, Your servants,
to whom You [a]swore by Your own self, and
said to them, [b]'I will multiply your descendants as the stars of heaven; and all this land
that I have spoken of I give to your descendants, and they shall inherit *it* forever.'"[1] 14So
the LORD [a]relented from the harm which He
said He would do to His people.
15And [a]Moses turned and went down
from the mountain, and the two tablets of
the Testimony *were* in his hand. The tablets
were written on both sides; on the one *side*
and on the other they were written. 16Now
the [a]tablets *were* the work of God, and the
writing *was* the writing of God engraved
on the tablets.
17And when Joshua heard the noise of
the people as they shouted, he said to Moses, "*There is* a noise of war in the camp."
18But he said:

"*It is* not the noise of the
 shout of victory,
Nor the noise of the cry of defeat,
But the sound of singing I hear."

19So it was, as soon as he came near the
camp, that [a]he saw the calf *and* the dancing.
So Moses' anger became hot, and he cast the
tablets out of his hands and broke them at
the foot of the mountain. 20[a]Then he took
the calf which they had made, burned *it* in
the fire, and ground *it* to powder; and he
scattered *it* on the water and made the children of Israel drink *it.* 21And Moses said to
Aaron, [a]"What did this people do to you that
you have brought *so* great a sin upon them?"
22So Aaron said, "Do not let the anger of
my lord become hot. [a]You know the people,
that they *are set* on evil. 23For they said to
me, 'Make us gods that shall go before us; *as
for* this Moses, the man who brought us out
of the land of Egypt, we do not know what
has become of him.' 24And I said to them,
'Whoever has any gold, let them break *it*
off.' So they gave *it* to me, and I cast it into
the fire, and this calf came out."
25Now when Moses saw that the people

32:1 [d] Ex. 13:21 [e] Ex. 32:8 **32:2** [a] Ex. 11:2; 35:22; Judg. 8:24–27 **32:4** [a] Ex. 20:3, 4, 23; Deut. 9:16; Judg. 17:3, 4; 1 Kin. 12:28; Neh. 9:18; Ps. 106:19; Acts 7:41 [b] Ex. 29:45, 46 **32:5** [a] Lev. 23:2, 4, 21, 37; 2 Kin. 10:20; 2 Chr. 30:5 **32:6** [a] Ex. 32:17–19; Num. 25:2; 1 Cor. 10:7 **32:7** [a] Deut. 9:8–21; Dan. 9:14 [b] Gen. 6:11, 12 **32:8** [a] Ex. 20:3, 4, 23; Deut. 32:17 [b] 1 Kin. 12:28 **32:9** [a] Ex. 33:3, 5; 34:9; Deut. 9:6; 2 Chr. 30:8; Is. 48:4; [Acts 7:51] **32:10** [a] Deut. 9:14, 19 [b] Ex. 22:24 [c] Num. 14:12 **32:11** [a] Deut. 9:18, 26–29 **32:12** [a] Num. 14:13–19; Deut. 9:28; Josh. 7:9 [b] Ex. 32:14 **32:13** [a] Gen. 22:16–18; [Heb. 6:13] [b] Gen. 12:7; 13:15; 15:7, 18; 22:17; 26:4; 35:11, 12; Ex. 13:5, 11; 33:1 [1] Genesis 13:15 and 22:17 **32:14** [a] 2 Sam. 24:16 **32:15** [a] Deut. 9:15 **32:16** [a] Ex. 31:18 **32:19** [a] Deut. 9:16, 17 **32:20** [a] Num. 5:17, 24; Deut. 9:21 **32:21** [a] Gen. 26:10 **32:22** [a] Ex. 14:11; Deut. 9:24

were [a]unrestrained (for Aaron [b]had not restrained them, to *their* shame among their enemies), 26then Moses stood in the entrance of the camp, and said, "Whoever *is* on the LORD's side—*come* to me!" And all the sons of Levi gathered themselves together to him. 27And he said to them, "Thus says the LORD God of Israel: 'Let every man put his sword on his side, and go in and out from entrance to entrance throughout the camp, and [a]let every man kill his brother, every man his companion, and every man his neighbor.'" 28So the sons of Levi did according to the word of Moses. And about three thousand men of the people fell that day. 29[a]Then Moses said, "Consecrate yourselves today to the LORD, that He may bestow on you a blessing this day, for every man has opposed his son and his brother."

30Now it came to pass on the next day that Moses said to the people, [a]"You have committed a great sin. So now I will go up to the LORD; [b]perhaps I can [c]make atonement for your sin." 31Then Moses [a]returned to the LORD and said, "Oh, these people have committed a great sin, and have [b]made for themselves a god of gold! 32Yet now, if You will forgive their sin—but if not, I pray, [a]blot me [b]out of Your book which You have written."

33And the LORD said to Moses, [a]"Whoever has sinned against Me, I will [b]blot him out of My book. 34Now therefore, go, lead the people to *the place* of which I have [a]spoken to you. [b]Behold, My Angel shall go before you. Nevertheless, [c]in the day when I [d]visit for punishment, I will visit punishment upon them for their sin."

35So the LORD plagued the people because of [a]what they did with the calf which Aaron made.

The Command to Leave Sinai

33 Then the LORD said to Moses, "Depart *and* go up from here, you [a]and the people whom you have brought out of the land of Egypt, to the land of which I swore to Abraham, Isaac, and Jacob, saying, [b]'To your descendants I will give it.' 2[a]And I will send *My* Angel before you, [b]and I will drive out the Canaanite and the Amorite and the Hittite and the Perizzite and the Hivite and the Jebusite. 3*Go up* [a]to a land flowing with milk and honey; for I will not go up in your midst, lest [b]I consume you on the way, for you *are* a [c]stiff-necked people."

4And when the people heard this bad news, [a]they mourned, [b]and no one put on his ornaments. 5For the LORD had said to Moses, "Say to the children of Israel, 'You *are* a stiff-necked people. I could come up into your midst in one moment and consume you. Now therefore, take off your ornaments, that I may [a]know what to do to you.'" 6So the children of Israel stripped themselves of their ornaments by Mount Horeb.

Moses Meets with the LORD

7Moses took his tent and pitched it outside the camp, far from the camp, and [a]called it the tabernacle of meeting. And it came to pass *that* everyone who [b]sought the LORD went out to the tabernacle of meeting which *was* outside the camp. 8So it was, whenever Moses went out to the tabernacle, *that* all the people rose, and each man stood [a]*at* his tent door and watched Moses until he had gone into the tabernacle. 9And it came to pass, when Moses entered the tabernacle, that the pillar of cloud descended and stood *at* the door of the tabernacle, and *the LORD* [a]talked with Moses. 10All the people saw the pillar of cloud standing *at* the tabernacle door, and all the people rose and [a]worshiped, each man *in* his tent door. 11So [a]the LORD spoke to Moses face to face, as a man speaks to his friend. And he would return to the camp, but [b]his servant Joshua the son of Nun, a young man, did not depart from the tabernacle.

The Promise of God's Presence

12Then Moses said to the LORD, "See, [a]You say to me, 'Bring up this people.' But

---

32:25 [a] Ex. 33:4, 5 [b] 2 Chr. 28:19 32:27 [a] Num. 25:5–13 32:29 [a] Ex. 28:41; 1 Sam. 15:18, 22; Prov. 21:3; Zech. 13:3
32:30 [a] 1 Sam. 12:20, 23 [b] 2 Sam. 16:12 [c] Num. 25:13 32:31 [a] Deut. 9:18 [b] Ex. 20:23 32:32 [a] Ps. 69:28; Is. 4:3; Mal. 3:16; Rom. 9:3
[b] Dan. 12:1; Phil. 4:3; Rev. 3:5; 21:27 32:33 [a] Lev. 23:30; [Ezek. 18:4; 33:2, 14, 15] [b] Ex. 17:14; Deut. 29:20; Ps. 9:5; Rev. 3:5; 21:27
32:34 [a] Ex. 3:17 [b] Ex. 23:20; Josh. 5:14 [c] Deut. 32:35; Rom. 2:5, 6 [d] Ps. 89:32 32:35 [a] Neh. 9:18 33:1 [a] Ex. 32:1, 7, 13; Josh. 3:17
[b] Gen. 12:7 33:2 [a] Ex. 32:34; Josh. 5:14 [b] Ex. 23:27–31; Josh. 24:11 33:3 [a] Ex. 3:8 [b] Num. 16:21, 45
[c] Ex. 32:9; 33:5 33:4 [a] Num. 14:1, 39 [b] Ezra 9:3; Esth. 4:1, 4; Ezek. 24:17, 23 33:5 [a] [Ps. 139:23]
33:7 [a] Ex. 29:42, 43 [b] Deut. 4:29 33:8 [a] Num. 16:27 33:9 [a] Ex. 25:22; 31:18; Ps. 99:7
33:10 [a] Ex. 4:31 33:11 [a] Num. 12:8; Deut. 34:10 [b] Ex. 24:13 33:12 [a] Ex. 3:10; 32:34

You have not let me know whom You will
send with me. Yet You have said, [b]'I know
you by name, and you have also found
grace in My sight.' 13Now therefore, I pray,
[a]if I have found grace in Your sight, [b]show
me now Your way, that I may know You and
that I may find grace in Your sight. And
consider that this nation *is* [c]Your people."
14And He said, [a]"My Presence will go *with
you,* and I will give you [b]rest."
15Then he said to Him, [a]"If Your Presence
does not go *with us,* do not bring us up from
here. 16For how then will it be known that
Your people and I have found grace in Your
sight, [a]except You go with us? So we [b]shall
be separate, Your people and I, from all the
people who *are* upon the face of the earth."
17So the LORD said to Moses, [a]"I will also
do this thing that you have spoken; for you
have found grace in My sight, and I know
you by name."
18And he said, "Please, show me [a]Your
glory."
19Then He said, "I will make all My [a]good-
ness pass before you, and I will proclaim
the name of the LORD before you. [b]I will be
gracious to whom I will be [c]gracious, and I
will have compassion on whom I will have
compassion." 20But He said, "You cannot
see My face; for [a]no man shall see Me, and
live." 21And the LORD said, "Here is a place
by Me, and you shall stand on the rock. 22So
it shall be, while My glory passes by, that I
will put you [a]in the cleft of the rock, and
will [b]cover you with My hand while I pass
by. 23Then I will take away My hand, and
you shall see My back; but My face shall
[a]not be seen."

Moses Makes New Tablets
(Deut. 10:1–5)

34 And the LORD said to Moses, [a]"Cut
two tablets of stone like the first
ones, and [b]I will write on *these* tablets the
words that were on the first tablets which
you broke. 2So be ready in the morning, and
come up in the morning to Mount Sinai, and
present yourself to Me there [a]on the top of
the mountain. 3And no man shall [a]come up
with you, and let no man be seen throughout all the mountain; let neither flocks nor
herds feed before that mountain."
4So he cut two tablets of stone like the
first *ones.* Then Moses rose early in the
morning and went up Mount Sinai, as the
LORD had commanded him; and he took
in his hand the two tablets of stone.
5Now the LORD descended in the [a]cloud
and stood with him there, and [b]proclaimed
the name of the LORD. 6And the LORD
passed before him and proclaimed, "The
LORD, the LORD [a]God, merciful and gracious, longsuffering, and abounding in
[b]goodness and [c]truth, 7[a]keeping mercy for
thousands, [b]forgiving iniquity and transgression and sin, [c]by no means clearing *the
guilty,* visiting the iniquity of the fathers
upon the children and the children's children to the third and the fourth generation."
8So Moses made haste and [a]bowed his
head toward the earth, and worshiped.
9Then he said, "If now I have found grace
in Your sight, O Lord, [a]let my Lord, I pray,
go among us, even though we *are* a [b]stiff-
necked people; and pardon our iniquity
and our sin, and take us as [c]Your inheritance."

The Covenant Renewed
(Ex. 23:14–19; Deut. 7:1–6; 16:1–17)

10And He said: "Behold, [a]I make a covenant. Before all your people I will [b]do mar-
vels such as have not been done in all the
earth, nor in any nation; and all the people
among whom you *are* shall see the work of
the LORD. For it *is* [c]an awesome thing that
I will do with you. 11[a]Observe what I command you this day. Behold, [b]I am driving
out from before you the Amorite and the
Canaanite and the Hittite and the Perizzite
and the Hivite and the Jebusite. 12[a]Take
heed to yourself, lest you make a covenant

33:12 [b] Ex. 33:17; John 10:14, 15; 2 Tim. 2:19 **33:13** [a] Ex. 34:9 [b] Ps. 25:4; 27:11; 86:11; 119:33 [c] Ex. 3:7, 10; 5:1; 32:12, 14; Deut. 9:26, 29 **33:14** [a] Ex. 3:12; Deut. 4:37; Is. 63:9 [b] Deut. 12:10; 25:19; Josh. 21:44; 22:4 **33:15** [a] Ex. 33:3 **33:16** [a] Num. 14:14 [b] Ex. 34:10; Deut. 4:7, 34 **33:17** [a] [James 5:16] **33:18** [a] Ex. 24:16, 17; [1 Tim. 6:16] **33:19** [a] Ex. 34:6, 7 [b] [Rom. 9:15, 16, 18] [c] [Rom. 4:4, 16] **33:20** [a] [Gen. 32:30] **33:22** [a] Song 2:14; Is. 2:21 [b] Ps. 91:1, 4; Is. 49:2; 51:16 **33:23** [a] Ex. 33:20; [John 1:18] **34:1** [a] [Ex. 24:12; 31:18; 32:15, 16, 19; Deut. 4:13] [b] Deut. 10:2, 4 **34:2** [a] Ex. 19:11, 18, 20 **34:3** [a] Ex. 19:12, 13; 24:9–11 **34:5** [a] Ex. 19:9 [b] Ex. 33:19 **34:6** [a] Num. 14:18; Deut. 4:31; Neh. 9:17; Joel 2:13 [b] Rom. 2:4 [c] Ps. 108:4 **34:7** [a] Ex. 20:6 [b] Ps. 103:3, 4; Dan. 9:9; Eph. 4:32; 1 John 1:9 [c] Josh. 24:19; Job 10:14; Mic. 6:11; Nah. 1:3 **34:8** [a] Ex. 4:31 **34:9** [a] Ex. 33:12–16 [b] Ex. 33:3 [c] Ps. 33:12; 94:14 **34:10** [a] Ex. 34:27, 28; Deut. 5:2 [b] Deut. 4:32; Ps. 77:14 [c] Ps. 145:6 **34:11** [a] Deut. 6:25 [b] Ex. 23:20–33; 33:2; Josh. 11:23 **34:12** [a] Ex. 23:32, 33

with the inhabitants of the land where you are going, lest it be a snare in your midst. 13But you shall [a]destroy their altars, break their *sacred* pillars, and [b]cut down their wooden images 14(for you shall worship [a]no other god, for the LORD, whose [b]name *is* Jealous, *is* a [c]jealous God), 15lest you make a covenant with the inhabitants of the land, and they [a]play the harlot with their gods and make sacrifice to their gods, and *one of them* [b]invites you and you [c]eat of his sacrifice, 16and you take of [a]his daughters for your sons, and his daughters [b]play the harlot with their gods and make your sons play the harlot with their gods.

17[a]"You shall make no molded gods for yourselves.

18"The Feast of [a]Unleavened Bread you shall keep. Seven days you shall eat unleavened bread, as I commanded you, in the appointed time of the month of Abib; for in the [b]month of Abib you came out from Egypt.

19[a]"All that open the womb *are* Mine, and every male firstborn among your livestock, *whether* ox or sheep. 20But [a]the firstborn of a donkey you shall redeem with a lamb. And if you will not redeem *him,* then you shall break his neck. All the firstborn of your sons you shall redeem.

"And none shall appear before Me [b]empty-handed.

21[a]"Six days you shall work, but on the seventh day you shall rest; in plowing time and in harvest you shall rest.

22"And you shall observe the Feast of Weeks, of the firstfruits of wheat harvest, and the Feast of Ingathering at the year's end.

23[a]"Three times in the year all your men shall appear before the Lord, the LORD God of Israel. 24For I will [a]cast out the nations before you and enlarge your borders; neither will any man covet your land when you go up to appear before the LORD your God three times in the year.

25"You shall not offer the blood of My sacrifice with leaven, [a]nor shall the sacrifice of the Feast of the Passover be left until morning.

26[a]"The first of the firstfruits of your land you shall bring to the house of the LORD your God. You shall not boil a young goat in its mother's milk."

27Then the LORD said to Moses, "Write [a]these words, for according to the tenor of these words I have made a covenant with you and with Israel." 28[a]So he was there with the LORD forty days and forty nights; he neither ate bread nor drank water. And [b]He wrote on the tablets the words of the covenant, the Ten Commandments.[1]

The Shining Face of Moses

29Now it was so, when Moses came down from Mount Sinai (and the [a]two tablets of the Testimony *were* in Moses' hand when he came down from the mountain), that Moses did not know that [b]the skin of his face shone while he talked with Him. 30So when Aaron and all the children of Israel saw Moses, behold, the skin of his face shone, and they were afraid to come near him. 31Then Moses called to them, and Aaron and all the rulers of the congregation returned to him; and Moses talked with them. 32Afterward all the children of Israel came near, [a]and he gave them as commandments all that the LORD had spoken with him on Mount Sinai. 33And when Moses had finished speaking with them, he put [a]a veil on his face. 34But [a]whenever Moses went in before the LORD to speak with Him, he would take the veil off until he came out; and he would come out and speak to the children of Israel whatever he had been commanded. 35And whenever the children of Israel saw the face of Moses, that the skin of Moses' face shone, then Moses would put the veil on his face again, until he went in to speak with Him.

Sabbath Regulations

35 Then Moses gathered all the congregation of the children of Israel together, and said to them, [a]"These *are* the

34:13 [a] Ex. 23:24; Deut. 12:3 [b] Deut. 16:21; Judg. 6:25, 26; 2 Kin. 18:4; 2 Chr. 34:3, 4 34:14 [a] [Ex. 20:3–5] [b] [Is. 9:6; 57:15] [c] [Ex. 20:5; Deut. 4:24] 34:15 [a] Judg. 2:17 [b] Num. 25:1, 2; Deut. 32:37, 38 [c] 1 Cor. 8:4, 7, 10 34:16 [a] Gen. 28:1; Deut. 7:3; Josh. 23:12, 13; 1 Kin. 11:2; Ezra 9:2; Neh. 13:25 [b] Num. 25:1, 2; 1 Kin. 11:4 34:17 [a] Ex. 20:4, 23; 32:8; Lev. 19:4; Deut. 5:8 34:18 [a] Ex. 12:15, 16 [b] Ex. 12:2; 13:4 34:19 [a] Ex. 13:2; 22:29 34:20 [a] Ex. 13:13 [b] Ex. 22:29; 23:15; Deut. 16:16 34:21 [a] Ex. 20:9; 23:12; 31:15; 35:2; Lev. 23:3; Deut. 5:13 34:23 [a] Ex. 23:14–17 34:24 [a] [Ex. 33:2]; Josh. 11:23; 1 Kin. 4:21; 2 Chr. 36:14–16; Ps. 78:55 34:25 [a] Ex. 12:10 34:26 [a] Ex. 23:19; Deut. 26:2 34:27 [a] Ex. 17:14; 24:4; Deut. 31:9 34:28 [a] Ex. 24:18 [b] Ex. 34:1, 4; Deut. 4:31; 10:2, 4 [1] Literally *Ten Words* 34:29 [a] Ex. 32:15 [b] Matt. 17:2; 2 Cor. 3:7 34:32 [a] Ex. 24:3 34:33 [a] [2 Cor. 3:13, 14] 34:34 [a] [2 Cor. 3:13–16] 35:1 [a] Ex. 34:32

words which the LORD has commanded *you*
to do: 2 Work shall be done for [a]six days,
but the seventh day shall be a holy day for
you, a Sabbath of rest to the LORD. Whoever
does any work on it shall be put to [b]death.
3 [a]You shall kindle no fire throughout your
dwellings on the Sabbath day."

Offerings for the Tabernacle
(Ex. 25:1–9; 39:32–43)

4 And Moses spoke to all the congregation of the children of Israel, saying, [a]"This
is the thing which the LORD commanded,
saying: 5 'Take from among you an offering
to the LORD. [a]Whoever *is* of a willing heart,
let him bring it as an offering to the LORD:
[b]gold, silver, and bronze; 6 [a]blue, purple,
and scarlet *thread,* fine linen, and [b]goats'
hair; 7 ram skins dyed red, badger skins, and
acacia wood; 8 oil for the light, [a]and spices
for the anointing oil and for the sweet incense; 9 onyx stones, and stones to be set in
the ephod and in the breastplate.

Articles of the Tabernacle

10 [a]'All *who are* gifted artisans among you
shall come and make all that the LORD has
commanded: 11 [a]the tabernacle, its tent, its
covering, its clasps, its boards, its bars, its
pillars, and its sockets; 12 [a]the ark and its
poles, *with* the mercy seat, and the veil
of the covering; 13 the [a]table and its poles,
all its utensils, [b]and the showbread; 14 also
[a]the lampstand for the light, its utensils, its
lamps, and the oil for the light; 15 [a]the incense altar, its poles, [b]the anointing oil, [c]the
sweet incense, and the screen for the door
at the entrance of the tabernacle; 16 [a]the altar of burnt offering with its bronze grating, its poles, all its utensils, *and* the laver
and its base; 17 [a]the hangings of the court, its
pillars, their sockets, and the screen for the
gate of the court; 18 the pegs of the tabernacle, the pegs of the court, and their cords;
19 [a]the garments of ministry,[1] for ministering in the holy *place*—the holy garments
for Aaron the priest and the garments of
his sons, to minister as priests.'"

The Tabernacle Offerings Presented

20 And all the congregation of the children of Israel departed from the presence
of Moses. 21 Then everyone came [a]whose
heart was stirred, and everyone whose
spirit was willing, *and* they [b]brought the
LORD's offering for the work of the tabernacle of meeting, for all its service, and for the
holy garments. 22 They came, both men and
women, as many as had a willing heart, *and*
brought [a]earrings and nose rings, rings and
necklaces, all [b]jewelry of gold, that is, every
man who *made* an offering of gold to the
LORD. 23 And [a]every man, with whom was
found blue, purple, and scarlet *thread,* fine
linen, and goats' *hair,* red skins of rams, and
badger skins, brought *them.* 24 Everyone
who offered an offering of silver or bronze
brought the LORD's offering. And everyone with whom was found acacia wood for
any work of the service, brought *it.* 25 All
the women *who were* [a]gifted artisans spun
yarn with their hands, and brought what
they had spun, of blue, purple, *and* scarlet, and fine linen. 26 And all the women
whose hearts stirred with wisdom spun
yarn of goats' *hair.* 27 [a]The rulers brought
onyx stones, and the stones to be set in the
ephod and in the breastplate, 28 and [a]spices
and oil for the light, for the anointing oil,
and for the sweet incense. 29 The children
of Israel brought a [a]freewill offering to the
LORD, all the men and women whose hearts
were willing to bring *material* for all kinds
of work which the LORD, by the hand of Moses, had commanded to be done.

The Artisans Called by God
(Ex. 31:1–11)

30 And Moses said to the children of Israel, "See, [a]the LORD has called by name
Bezalel the son of Uri, the son of Hur, of the
tribe of Judah; 31 and He has filled him with
the Spirit of God, in wisdom and understanding, in knowledge and all manner of
workmanship, 32 to design artistic works,
to work in gold and silver and bronze, 33 in
cutting jewels for setting, in carving wood,

35:2 [a] Ex. 20:9, 10; Lev. 23:3; Deut. 5:13 [b] Num. 15:32–36 35:3 [a] Ex. 12:16; 16:23 35:4 [a] Ex. 25:1, 2 35:5 [a] Ex. 25:2; 1 Chr. 29:14; Mark 12:41–44; 2 Cor. 8:10–12; 9:7 [b] Ex. 38:24 35:6 [a] Ex. 36:8 [b] Ex. 36:14 35:8 [a] Ex. 25:6; 30:23–25 35:10 [a] Ex. 31:2–6; 36:1, 2 35:11 [a] Ex. 26:1, 2; 36:14 35:12 [a] Ex. 25:10–22 35:13 [a] Ex. 25:23 [b] Ex. 25:30; Lev. 24:5, 6 35:14 [a] Ex. 25:31 35:15 [a] Ex. 30:1 [b] Ex. 30:25 [c] Ex. 30:34–38 35:16 [a] Ex. 27:1–8 35:17 [a] Ex. 27:9–18 35:19 [a] Ex. 31:10; 39:1, 41 [1] Or *woven garments* 35:21 [a] Ex. 25:2; 35:5, 22, 26, 29; 36:2 [b] Ex. 35:24 35:22 [a] Ex. 32:2, 3 [b] Ex. 11:2 35:23 [a] 1 Chr. 29:8 35:25 [a] Ex. 28:3; 31:6; 36:1 35:27 [a] 1 Chr. 29:6; Ezra 2:68 35:28 [a] Ex. 30:23 35:29 [a] Ex. 35:5, 21; 36:3; 1 Chr. 29:9 35:30 [a] Ex. 31:1–6

and to work in all manner of artistic workmanship.

34“And He has put in his heart the ability to teach, *in* him and [a]Aholiab the son of Ahisamach, of the tribe of Dan. 35He has [a]filled them with skill to do all manner of work of the engraver and the designer and the tapestry maker, in blue, purple, and scarlet *thread,* and fine linen, and of the weaver—those who do every work and those who design artistic works.

36 “And Bezalel and Aholiab, and every [a]gifted artisan in whom the LORD has put wisdom and understanding, to know how to do all manner of work for the service of the [b]sanctuary, shall do according to all that the LORD has commanded.”

The People Give More than Enough

2Then Moses called Bezalel and Aholiab, and every gifted artisan in whose heart the LORD had put wisdom, everyone [a]whose heart was stirred, to come and do the work. 3And they received from Moses all the [a]offering which the children of Israel [b]had brought for the work of the service of making the sanctuary. So they continued bringing to him freewill offerings every morning. 4Then all the craftsmen who were doing all the work of the sanctuary came, each from the work he was doing, 5and they spoke to Moses, saying, [a]“The people bring much more than enough for the service of the work which the LORD commanded *us* to do.”

6So Moses gave a commandment, and they caused it to be proclaimed throughout the camp, saying, “Let neither man nor woman do any more work for the offering of the sanctuary.” And the people were restrained from bringing, 7for the material they had was sufficient for all the work to be done—indeed too [a]much.

Building the Tabernacle
(Ex. 26:1–37)

8[a]Then all the gifted artisans among them who worked on the tabernacle made ten curtains woven of fine linen, and of blue, purple, and scarlet *thread; with* artistic designs of cherubim they made them. 9The length of each curtain *was* twenty-eight cubits, and the width of each curtain four cubits; the curtains *were* all the same size. 10And he coupled five curtains to one another, and *the other* five curtains he coupled to one another. 11He made loops of blue *yarn* on the edge of the curtain on the selvedge of one set; likewise he did on the outer edge of *the other* curtain of the second set. 12[a]Fifty loops he made on one curtain, and fifty loops he made on the edge of the curtain on the end of the second set; the loops held one *curtain* to another. 13And he made fifty clasps of gold, and coupled the curtains to one another with the clasps, that it might be one tabernacle.

14[a]He made curtains of goats' *hair* for the tent over the tabernacle; he made eleven curtains. 15The length of each curtain *was* thirty cubits, and the width of each curtain four cubits; the eleven curtains *were* the same size. 16He coupled five curtains by themselves and six curtains by themselves. 17And he made fifty loops on the edge of the curtain that is outermost in one set, and fifty loops he made on the edge of the curtain of the second set. 18He also made fifty bronze clasps to couple the tent together, that it might be one. 19[a]Then he made a covering for the tent of ram skins dyed red, and a covering of badger skins above *that.*

20For the tabernacle [a]he made boards of acacia wood, standing upright. 21The length of each board *was* ten cubits, and the width of each board a cubit and a half. 22Each board had two tenons [a]for binding one to another. Thus he made for all the boards of the tabernacle. 23And he made boards for the tabernacle, twenty boards for the south side. 24Forty sockets of silver he made to go under the twenty boards: two sockets under each of the boards for its two tenons. 25And for the other side of the tabernacle, the north side, he made twenty boards 26and their forty sockets of silver: two sockets under each of the boards. 27For the west side of the tabernacle he made six boards. 28He also made two boards for the

35:34 [a] Ex. 31:6 35:35 [a] Ex. 31:3, 6; 35:31; 1 Kin. 7:14; 2 Chr. 2:14; Is. 28:26 36:1 [a] Ex. 28:3; 31:6; 35:10, 35 [b] Ex. 25:8 36:2 [a] Ex. 35:21, 26; 1 Chr. 29:5, 9, 17 36:3 [a] Ex. 35:5 [b] Ex. 35:27 36:5 [a] 2 Chr. 24:14; 31:6–10; [2 Cor. 8:2, 3] 36:7 [a] 1 Kin. 8:64 36:8 [a] Ex. 26:1–14 36:12 [a] Ex. 26:5 36:14 [a] Ex. 26:7 36:19 [a] Ex. 26:14 36:20 [a] Ex. 26:15–29 36:22 [a] Ex. 26:17

two back corners of the tabernacle. 29And
they were coupled at the bottom and coupled together at the top by one ring. Thus
he made both of them for the two corners.
30So there were eight boards and their
sockets—sixteen sockets of silver—two
sockets under each of the boards.

31And he made [a]bars of acacia wood: five
for the boards on one side of the tabernacle, 32five bars for the boards on the other
side of the tabernacle, and five bars for the
boards of the tabernacle on the far side
westward. 33And he made the middle bar
to pass through the boards from one end
to the other. 34He overlaid the boards with
gold, made their rings of gold *to be* holders
for the bars, and overlaid the bars with gold.

35And he made [a]a veil of blue, purple,
and scarlet *thread,* and fine woven linen; it
was worked *with* an artistic design of cherubim. 36He made for it four pillars of acacia *wood,* and overlaid them with gold, with
their hooks of gold; and he cast four sockets of silver for them.

37He also made a [a]screen for the tabernacle door, of blue, purple, and scarlet *thread,* and fine woven linen, made by
a weaver, 38and its five pillars with their
hooks. And he overlaid their capitals and
their rings with gold, but their five sockets
were bronze.

Making the Ark of the Testimony
(Ex. 25:10–22)

37 Then [a]Bezalel made [b]the ark of acacia wood; two and a half cubits *was*
its length, a cubit and a half its width, and
a cubit and a half its height. 2He overlaid
it with pure gold inside and outside, and
made a molding of gold all around it. 3And
he cast for it four rings of gold *to be set* in
its four corners: two rings on one side, and
two rings on the other side of it. 4He made
poles of acacia wood, and overlaid them
with gold. 5And he put the poles into the
rings at the sides of the ark, to bear the ark.
6He also made the [a]mercy seat of pure gold;
two and a half cubits *was* its length and a
cubit and a half its width. 7He made two
cherubim of beaten gold; he made them
of one piece at the two ends of the mercy
seat: 8one cherub at one end on this side,
and the other cherub at the *other* end on
that side. He made the cherubim at the two
ends *of one piece* with the mercy seat. 9The
cherubim spread out *their* wings above, *and*
covered the [a]mercy seat with their wings.
They faced one another; the faces of the
cherubim were toward the mercy seat.

Making the Table for the Showbread
(Ex. 25:23–30)

10He made [a]the table of acacia wood; two
cubits *was* its length, a cubit its width, and
a cubit and a half its height. 11And he overlaid it with pure gold, and made a molding of gold all around it. 12Also he made a
frame of a handbreadth all around it, and
made a molding of gold for the frame all
around it. 13And he cast for it four rings
of gold, and put the rings on the four corners that *were* at its four legs. 14The rings
were close to the frame, as holders for the
poles to bear the table. 15And he made the
poles of acacia wood to bear the table, and
overlaid them with gold. 16He made of pure
gold the utensils which were on the table:
its [a]dishes, its cups, its bowls, and its pitchers for pouring.

Making the Gold Lampstand
(Ex. 25:31–40)

17He also made the [a]lampstand of pure
gold; of hammered work he made the
lampstand. Its shaft, its branches, its bowls,
its *ornamental* knobs, and its flowers were
of the same piece. 18And six branches came
out of its sides: three branches of the lampstand out of one side, and three branches of
the lampstand out of the other side. 19There
were three bowls made like almond *blossoms* on one branch, with an *ornamental*
knob and a flower, and three bowls made
like almond *blossoms* on the other branch,
with an *ornamental* knob and a flower—
and so for the six branches coming out of
the lampstand. 20And on the lampstand
itself *were* four bowls made like almond
blossoms, each with its *ornamental* knob
and flower. 21*There was* a knob under the
first two branches of the same, a knob under the *second* two branches of the same,

---

36:31 [a] Ex. 26:26–29 36:35 [a] Ex. 26:31–37 36:37 [a] Ex. 26:36 37:1 [a] Ex. 35:30; 36:1 [b] Ex. 25:10–20 37:6 [a] Ex. 25:17
37:9 [a] Ex. 25:20 37:10 [a] Ex. 25:23–29 37:16 [a] Ex. 25:29 37:17 [a] Ex. 25:31–39

and a knob under the *third* two branches of the same, according to the six branches extending from it. 22Their knobs and their branches were of one piece; all of it *was* one hammered piece of pure gold. 23And he made its seven lamps, its [a]wick-trimmers, and its trays of pure gold. 24Of a talent of pure gold he made it, with all its utensils.

Making the Altar of Incense
(Ex. 30:1–5)

25[a]He made the incense altar of acacia wood. Its length *was* a cubit and its width a cubit—*it was* square—and two cubits *was* its height. Its horns were *of one piece* with it. 26And he overlaid it with pure gold: its top, its sides all around, and its horns. He also made for it a molding of gold all around it. 27He made two rings of gold for it under its molding, by its two corners on both sides, as holders for the poles with which to bear it. 28And he [a]made the poles of acacia wood, and overlaid them with gold.

Making the Anointing Oil and the Incense
(Ex. 30:22–38)

29He also made [a]the holy anointing oil and the pure incense of sweet spices, according to the work of the perfumer.

Making the Altar of Burnt Offering
(Ex. 27:1–8)

38 He made [a]the altar of burnt offering of acacia wood; five cubits *was* its length and five cubits its width—*it was* square—and its height *was* three cubits. 2He made its horns on its four corners; the horns were *of one piece* with it. And he overlaid it with bronze. 3He made all the utensils for the altar: the pans, the shovels, the basins, the forks, and the firepans; all its utensils he made of bronze. 4And he made a grate of bronze network for the altar, under its rim, midway from the bottom. 5He cast four rings for the four corners of the bronze grating, *as* holders for the poles. 6And he made the poles of acacia wood, and overlaid them with bronze. 7Then he put the poles into the rings on the sides of the altar, with which to bear it. He made the altar hollow with boards.

Making the Bronze Laver

8He made [a]the laver of bronze and its base of bronze, from the bronze mirrors of the serving women who assembled at the door of the tabernacle of meeting.

Making the Court of the Tabernacle
(Ex. 27:9–19)

9Then he made [a]the court on the south side; the hangings of the court *were of* fine woven linen, one hundred cubits long. 10There *were* twenty pillars for them, with twenty bronze sockets. The hooks of the pillars and their bands *were* silver. 11On the north side *the hangings were* one hundred cubits *long,* with twenty pillars and their twenty bronze sockets. The hooks of the pillars and their bands *were* silver. 12And on the west side *there were* hangings of fifty cubits, with ten pillars and their ten sockets. The hooks of the pillars and their bands *were* silver. 13For the east side *the hangings were* fifty cubits. 14The hangings of one side *of the gate were* fifteen cubits *long, with* their three pillars and their three sockets, 15and the same for the other side of the court gate; on this side and that *were* hangings of fifteen cubits, *with* their three pillars and their three sockets. 16All the hangings of the court all around *were of* fine woven linen. 17The sockets for the pillars *were* bronze, the hooks of the pillars and their bands *were* silver, and the overlay of their capitals *was* silver; and all the pillars of the court had bands of silver. 18The screen for the gate of the court *was* woven of blue, purple, and scarlet *thread,* and of fine woven linen. The length *was* twenty cubits, and the height along its width *was* five cubits, corresponding to the hangings of the court. 19And *there were* four pillars *with* their four sockets of bronze; their hooks *were* silver, and the overlay of their capitals and their bands *was* silver. 20All the [a]pegs of the tabernacle, and of the court all around, *were* bronze.

Materials of the Tabernacle

21This is the inventory of the tabernacle, [a]the tabernacle of the Testimony, which was counted according to the commandment of

---

37:23 [a] Num. 4:9 37:25 [a] Ex. 30:1–5 37:28 [a] Ex. 30:5 37:29 [a] Ex. 30:23–25 38:1 [a] Ex. 27:1–8 38:8 [a] Ex. 30:18 38:9 [a] Ex. 27:9–19 38:20 [a] Ex. 27:19 38:21 [a] Num. 1:50, 53; 9:15; 10:11; 17:7, 8; 2 Chr. 24:6; Acts 7:44

Moses, for the service of the Levites, [b]by the
hand of [c]Ithamar, son of Aaron the priest.
22 [a]Bezalel the son of Uri, the son of Hur,
of the tribe of Judah, made all that the
LORD had commanded Moses. 23 And with
him *was* [a]Aholiab the son of Ahisamach, of
the tribe of Dan, an engraver and designer,
a weaver of blue, purple, and scarlet *thread,*
and of fine linen.
24 All the gold that was used in all the
work of the holy *place,* that is, the gold of
the [a]offering, was twenty-nine talents and
seven hundred and thirty shekels, according to [b]the shekel of the sanctuary. 25 And
the silver from those who were [a]numbered
of the congregation *was* one hundred talents and one thousand seven hundred and
seventy-five shekels, according to the shekel of the sanctuary: 26 [a]a bekah for each man
(*that is,* half a shekel, according to the shekel of the sanctuary), for everyone included
in the numbering from twenty years old
and above, for [b]six hundred and three thousand, five hundred and fifty *men.* 27 And
from the hundred talents of silver were
cast [a]the sockets of the sanctuary and the
bases of the veil: one hundred sockets
from the hundred talents, one talent for
each socket. 28 Then from the one thousand seven hundred and seventy-five *shekels* he made hooks for the pillars, overlaid
their capitals, and [a]made bands for them.
29 The offering of bronze *was* seventy talents and two thousand four hundred shekels. 30 And with it he made the sockets for
the door of the tabernacle of meeting, the
bronze altar, the bronze grating for it, and
all the utensils for the altar, 31 the sockets
for the court all around, the bases for the
court gate, all the pegs for the tabernacle,
and all the pegs for the court all around.

Making the Garments of the Priesthood
(Ex. 28:1–43)

39 Of the [a]blue, purple, and scarlet
thread they made [b]garments of
ministry,[1] for ministering in the holy *place,*
and made the holy garments for Aaron, [c]as
the LORD had commanded Moses.

Making the Ephod

2 [a]He made the [b]ephod of gold, blue, purple, and scarlet *thread,* and of fine woven
linen. 3 And they beat the gold into thin
sheets and cut *it into* threads, to work *it* in
with the blue, purple, and scarlet *thread,*
and the fine linen, *into* artistic designs.
4 They made shoulder straps for it to couple *it* together; it was coupled together at its
two edges. 5 And the intricately woven band
of his ephod that *was* on it *was* of the same
workmanship, *woven of* gold, blue, purple,
and scarlet *thread,* and *of* fine woven linen,
as the LORD had commanded Moses.
6 [a]And they set onyx stones, enclosed in
settings of gold; they were engraved, as signets are engraved, with the names of the
sons of Israel. 7 He put them on the shoulders of the ephod *as* [a]memorial stones for
the sons of Israel, as the LORD had commanded Moses.

Making the Breastplate

8 [a]And he made the breastplate, artistically woven like the workmanship of the
ephod, of gold, blue, purple, and scarlet
thread, and of fine woven linen. 9 They made
the breastplate square by doubling it; a span
was its length and a span its width when
doubled. 10 [a]And they set in it four rows of
stones: a row with a sardius, a topaz, and
an emerald was the first row; 11 the second
row, a turquoise, a sapphire, and a diamond;
12 the third row, a jacinth, an agate, and an
amethyst; 13 the fourth row, a beryl, an onyx,
and a jasper. *They were* enclosed in settings
of gold in their mountings. 14 *There were*
[a]twelve stones according to the names of
the sons of Israel: according to their names,
engraved like a signet, each one with its own
name according to the twelve tribes. 15 And
they made chains for the breastplate at the
ends, like braided cords of pure gold. 16 They
also made two settings of gold and two gold
rings, and put the two rings on the two ends
of the breastplate. 17 And they put the two
braided *chains* of gold in the two rings on
the ends of the breastplate. 18 The two ends
of the two braided *chains* they fastened in

38:21 [b] Num. 4:28, 33 [c] Ex. 28:1; Lev. 10:6, 16 38:22 [a] Ex. 31:2, 6; 1 Chr. 2:18–20 38:23 [a] Ex. 31:6; 36:1 38:24 [a] Ex. 35:5, 22 [b] Ex. 30:13, 24; Lev. 5:15; 27:3, 25; Num. 3:47; 18:16 38:25 [a] Ex. 30:11–16; Num. 1:2 38:26 [a] Ex. 30:13, 15 [b] Ex. 12:37; Num. 1:46; 26:51 38:27 [a] Ex. 26:19, 21, 25, 32 38:28 [a] Ex. 27:17 39:1 [a] Ex. 25:4; 35:23 [b] Ex. 31:10; 35:19 [c] Ex. 28:4 [1] Or *woven garments* 39:2 [a] Ex. 28:6–14 [b] Lev. 8:7 39:6 [a] Ex. 28:9–11 39:7 [a] Ex. 28:12, 29; Josh. 4:7 39:8 [a] Ex. 28:15–30 39:10 [a] Ex. 28:17 39:14 [a] Rev. 21:12

the two settings, and put them on the shoulder straps of the ephod in the front. 19And
they made two rings of gold and put *them*
on the two ends of the breastplate, on the
edge of it, which *was* on the inward side
of the ephod. 20They made two *other* gold
rings and put them on the two shoulder
straps, underneath the ephod toward its
front, right at the seam above the intricately
woven band of the ephod. 21And they bound
the breastplate by means of its rings to the
rings of the ephod with a blue cord, so that it
would be above the intricately woven band
of the ephod, and that the breastplate would
not come loose from the ephod, as the LORD
had commanded Moses.

Making the Other Priestly Garments

22[a]He made the [b]robe of the ephod of
woven work, all of blue. 23And *there was*
an opening in the middle of the robe, like
the opening in a coat of mail, *with* a woven
binding all around the opening, so that it
would not tear. 24They made on the hem
of the robe pomegranates of blue, purple,
and scarlet, and of fine woven *linen.* 25And
they made [a]bells of pure gold, and put the
bells between the pomegranates on the
hem of the robe all around between the
pomegranates: 26a bell and a pomegranate, a bell and a pomegranate, all around
the hem of the robe to minister in, as the
LORD had commanded Moses.

27[a]They made tunics, artistically woven of
fine linen, for Aaron and his sons, 28[a]a turban of fine linen, exquisite hats of fine linen,
[b]short trousers of fine woven linen, 29[a]and a
sash of fine woven linen with blue, purple,
and scarlet *thread,* made by a weaver, as the
LORD had commanded Moses.

30[a]Then they made the plate of the holy
crown of pure gold, and wrote on it an inscription *like* the engraving of a signet:

[b]HOLINESS TO THE LORD.

31And they tied to it a blue cord, to fasten *it*
above on the turban, as the LORD had commanded Moses.

The Work Completed
(Ex. 35:10–19)

32Thus all the work of the tabernacle of
the tent of meeting was [a]finished. And the
children of Israel did [b]according to all that
the LORD had commanded Moses; so they
did. 33And they brought the tabernacle to
Moses, the tent and all its furnishings: its
clasps, its boards, its bars, its pillars, and its
sockets; 34the covering of ram skins dyed
red, the covering of badger skins, and the
veil of the covering; 35the ark of the Testimony with its poles, and the mercy seat;
36the table, all its utensils, and the [a]show-
bread; 37the pure *gold* lampstand with its
lamps (the lamps set in order), all its utensils, and the oil for light; 38the gold altar,
the anointing oil, and the sweet incense;
the screen for the tabernacle door; 39the
bronze altar, its grate of bronze, its poles,
and all its utensils; the laver with its base;
40the hangings of the court, its pillars and
its sockets, the screen for the court gate,
its cords, and its pegs; all the utensils for
the service of the tabernacle, for the tent of
meeting; 41and the garments of ministry,[1]
to minister in the holy *place:* the holy garments for Aaron the priest, and his sons'
garments, to minister as priests.

42According to all that the LORD had
commanded Moses, so the children of Israel [a]did all the work. 43Then Moses looked
over all the work, and indeed they had done
it; as the LORD had commanded, just so
they had done it. And Moses [a]blessed them.

The Tabernacle Erected and Arranged

40 Then the LORD [a]spoke to Moses, saying: 2"On the first day of the [a]first
month you shall set up [b]the tabernacle of
the tent of meeting. 3[a]You shall put in it the
ark of the Testimony, and partition off the
ark with the veil. 4[a]You shall bring in the
table and [b]arrange the things that are to be
set in order on it; [c]and you shall bring in the
lampstand and light its lamps. 5[a]You shall
also set the altar of gold for the incense before the ark of the Testimony, and put up
the screen for the door of the tabernacle.

39:22 [a] Ex. 28:31–35 [b] Ex. 29:5; Lev. 8:7 39:25 [a] Ex. 28:33 39:27 [a] Ex. 28:39, 40 39:28 [a] Ex. 28:4, 39; Lev. 8:9; Ezek. 44:18 [b] Ex. 28:42; Lev. 6:10 39:29 [a] Ex. 28:39 39:30 [a] Ex. 28:36, 37 [b] Zech. 14:20 39:32 [a] Ex. 40:17 [b] Ex. 25:40; 39:42, 43 39:36 [a] Ex. 25:23–30 39:41 [1] Or *woven garments* 39:42 [a] Ex. 35:10 39:43 [a] Lev. 9:22, 23; Num. 6:23–26; Josh. 22:6; 2 Sam. 6:18; 1 Kin. 8:14; 2 Chr. 30:27 40:1 [a] Ex. 25:1—31:18 40:2 [a] Ex. 12:2; 13:4 [b] Ex. 26:1, 30; 40:17 40:3 [a] Ex. 26:33; 40:21; Lev. 16:2; Num. 4:5 40:4 [a] Ex. 26:35; 40:22 [b] Ex. 25:30; 40:23 [c] Ex. 40:24, 25 40:5 [a] Ex. 40:26

6Then you shall set the [a]altar of the burnt
offering before the door of the tabernacle
of the tent of meeting. 7And [a]you shall set
the laver between the tabernacle of meeting and the altar, and put water in it. 8You
shall set up the court all around, and hang
up the screen at the court gate.

9"And you shall take the anointing oil,
and [a]anoint the tabernacle and all that *is* in
it; and you shall hallow it and all its utensils, and it shall be holy. 10You shall [a]anoint
the altar of the burnt offering and all its
utensils, and consecrate the altar. [b]The altar
shall be most holy. 11And you shall anoint
the laver and its base, and consecrate it.

12[a]"Then you shall bring Aaron and his
sons to the door of the tabernacle of meeting and wash them with water. 13You shall
put the holy [a]garments on Aaron, [b]and
anoint him and consecrate him, that he
may minister to Me as priest. 14And you
shall bring his sons and clothe them with
tunics. 15You shall anoint them, as you
anointed their father, that they may minister to Me as priests; for their anointing
shall surely be [a]an everlasting priesthood
throughout their generations."

16Thus Moses did; according to all that
the LORD had commanded him, so he did.

17And it came to pass in the first month
of the second year, on the first *day* of the
month, *that* the [a]tabernacle was raised up.
18So Moses raised up the tabernacle, fastened its sockets, set up its boards, put in
its bars, and raised up its pillars. 19And he
spread out the tent over the tabernacle and
put the covering of the tent on top of it, as
the LORD had commanded Moses. 20He
took [a]the Testimony and put *it* into the ark,
inserted the poles through the rings of the
ark, and put the mercy seat on top of the
ark. 21And he brought the ark into the tabernacle, [a]hung up the veil of the covering, and
partitioned off the ark of the Testimony, as
the LORD had commanded Moses.

22[a]He put the table in the tabernacle of meeting, on the north side of the
tabernacle, outside the veil; 23[a]and he
set the bread in order upon it before the
LORD, as the LORD had commanded Moses. 24[a]He put the lampstand in the tabernacle of meeting, across from the table, on
the south side of the tabernacle; 25and [a]he
lit the lamps before the LORD, as the LORD
had commanded Moses. 26[a]He put the gold
altar in the tabernacle of meeting in front
of the veil; 27[a]and he burned sweet incense
on it, as the LORD had commanded Moses.
28[a]He hung up the screen *at* the door of the
tabernacle. 29[a]And he put the altar of burnt
offering *before* the door of the tabernacle
of the tent of meeting, and [b]offered upon
it the burnt offering and the grain offering, as the LORD had commanded Moses.
30[a]He set the laver between the tabernacle of meeting and the altar, and put water there for washing; 31and Moses, Aaron,
and his sons would [a]wash their hands and
their feet *with water* from it. 32Whenever
they went into the tabernacle of meeting,
and when they came near the altar, they
washed, [a]as the LORD had commanded
Moses. 33[a]And he raised up the court all
around the tabernacle and the altar, and
hung up the screen of the court gate. So
Moses [b]finished the work.

The Cloud and the Glory
(Ex. 13:21, 22; Num. 9:15–23)

34[a]Then the [b]cloud covered the tabernacle of meeting, and the [c]glory of the LORD
filled the tabernacle. 35And Moses [a]was
not able to enter the tabernacle of meeting, because the cloud rested above it, and
the glory of the LORD filled the tabernacle.
36[a]Whenever the cloud was taken up from
above the tabernacle, the children of Israel
would go onward in all their journeys. 37But
[a]if the cloud was not taken up, then they did
not journey till the day that it was taken up.
38For [a]the cloud of the LORD *was* above the
tabernacle by day, and fire was over it by
night, in the sight of all the house of Israel,
throughout all their journeys.

40:6 [a] Ex. 39:39 40:7 [a] Ex. 30:18; 40:30 40:9 [a] Ex. 30:26; Lev. 8:10 40:10 [a] Ex. 30:26–30 [b] Ex. 29:36, 37 40:12 [a] Ex. 29:4–9; Lev. 8:1–13 40:13 [a] Ex. 29:5; 39:1, 41 [b] [Ex. 28:41]; Lev. 8:12 40:15 [a] Ex. 29:9; Num. 25:13 40:17 [a] Ex. 40:2; Num. 7:1 40:20 [a] Ex. 25:16; Deut. 10:5; 1 Kin. 8:9; 2 Chr. 5:10; Heb. 9:4 40:21 [a] Ex. 26:33 40:22 [a] Ex. 26:35 40:23 [a] Ex. 40:4; Lev. 24:5, 6 40:24 [a] Ex. 26:35 40:25 [a] Ex. 25:37; 30:7, 8; 40:4; Lev. 24:3, 4 40:26 [a] Ex. 30:1, 6; 40:5 40:27 [a] Ex. 30:7 40:28 [a] Ex. 26:36; 40:5 40:29 [a] Ex. 40:6 [b] Ex. 29:38–42 40:30 [a] Ex. 30:18; 40:7 40:31 [a] Ex. 30:19, 20; John 13:8 40:32 [a] Ex. 30:19 40:33 [a] Ex. 27:9–18; 40:8 [b] [Heb. 3:2–5] 40:34 [a] Ex. 29:43; Lev. 16:2; Num. 9:15; 2 Chr. 5:13; Is. 6:4 [b] 1 Kin. 8:10, 11 [c] Lev. 9:6, 23 40:35 [a] [Lev. 16:2]; 1 Kin. 8:11; 2 Chr. 5:13, 14 40:36 [a] Ex. 13:21, 22; Num. 9:17; Neh. 9:19 40:37 [a] Num. 9:19–22 40:38 [a] Ex. 13:21; Num. 9:15; Ps. 78:14; Is. 4:5

THE THIRD BOOK OF MOSES CALLED

LEVITICUS

OVERVIEW

Written by the prophet Moses, Leviticus is the third book of the Pentateuch (the first five books of the Bible as a collective unit). Leviticus outlines the laws and regulations God established for the Israelites.

In the exodus, we follow the Israelites' journey from bondage in Egypt to freedom. Upon gaining their freedom, God established a covenant with His people at Mount Sinai and instructed them to build a tabernacle in which to worship Him. The details of how the Israelites were expected to interact with God and how they should live with one another are outlined in Leviticus.

Leviticus opens with God speaking to Moses and providing instructions for how the Israelites should make offerings to Him. In chapters 1–5, the burnt offering (see 1:3–17), grain offering (see 2:1–16), peace offering (see 3:1–17), sin offering (see 4:1–35), and trespass offering (see 5:1–13) are described. In chapters 6–7, the laws associated with each offering are explained, as well as the priests' role in receiving the offerings and presenting them to God. Chapters 8–10 then give specific instructions on the consecration of the priests (see 8:1–36), their ministry (see 9:1–24), and their conduct (see 10:8–20).

Chapters 11–16 address the importance of cleanliness and holiness in entering the presence of God. The call for the Israelites to set themselves apart from others and keep the laws of God, as well as the punishments for not doing so, are found in chapters 17–20. The last chapters of Leviticus address the personal responsibilities of the priests (21–22), holy observances (23), laws and blessings for the Promised Land (24–26), and the dedication of tithes to God (27).

Leviticus serves as a guidebook for how the Israelites were to live in relationship with God and others. The major themes are sacrifice and the holiness of God. By offering sacrifices to God and living as a holy people, the Israelites were able to commune with God. Leviticus defines holiness and explains the laws established to guide the Israelites as they strove to live in a manner acceptable to God.

BREATHE IT IN

God establishes covenants with His people to solidify His relationship with them. These covenants often express the responsibilities of God's people to obey the Lord, their God. In Leviticus, God outlined His covenant expectations for the Israelites as they reformed as a nation. He detailed the sacrifices to be made to Him, how He should be worshiped, the laws the Israelites were to obey, and His promises to them. Every group and individual in covenant with God must be willing to sacrifice their own desires to live according to His commandments.

All Christians—no matter their race, ethnicity, gender, or nationality—are in a covenant relationship with God. As believers, God requires us to acknowledge His holiness and to strive to be holy in our lives. A life of holiness is not easy, particularly in today's society. We are surrounded by unholy ideas and behaviors that are promoted and practiced daily. However, we must fight against being distracted and keep our eyes on the things of God. To practice holiness, we must focus on the Word of God that instructs us how to commune with Him and how to live with

others. When we fall short (and we will), we have the assurance of God's ever-present forgiveness because of the atonement Christ provided.

In our relationship with God we make commitments, or promises, to God, and through His Word we remember the promises He has made to us. Often, our commitments to God focus on completing certain tasks or responding to situations according to His will. These tasks may be as simple as increasing the amount of time we spend in prayer or as difficult as stopping a sinful and harmful habit. God's promise may be to bless us or to deliver us from a burdensome situation. No matter the circumstances, God keeps His promises to us when we turn our hearts toward Him.

When we make a commitment to God, we must honor it. We cannot take it lightly. Honoring our commitments to God is a form of sacrifice because we often are required to do things differently than we normally would. We may need to act or speak in a way that feels uncomfortable or unnatural, like loving those who hate us. We are predisposed to act according to our feelings and emotions. Many times, we must fight to do what God says to do instead of what we feel like doing or what feels right. Sacrifice is not easy. It is hard work. But God promises that if we trust and obey Him, He will breathe new life into us, allowing us to inhale and exhale freely. Stay the course and receive all that He has promised.

+

THE THIRD BOOK OF
MOSES CALLED

LEVITICUS

The Burnt Offering

1 Now the LORD [a]called to Moses, and
spoke to him [b]from the tabernacle of
meeting, saying, 2“Speak to the children
of Israel, and say to them: [a]‘When any
one of you brings an offering to the LORD,
you shall bring your offering of the livestock—of the herd and of the flock.
3‘If his offering *is* a burnt sacrifice of the
herd, let him offer a male [a]without blemish;
he shall offer it of his own free will at the
door of the tabernacle of meeting before
the LORD. 4[a]Then he shall put his hand on
the head of the burnt offering, and it will be
[b]accepted on his behalf [c]to make atonement
for him. 5He shall kill the [a]bull before the
LORD; [b]and the priests, Aaron’s sons, shall
bring the blood [c]and sprinkle the blood all
around on the altar that *is by* the door of
the tabernacle of meeting. 6And he shall
[a]skin the burnt offering and cut it into its
pieces. 7The sons of Aaron the priest shall
put [a]fire on the altar, and [b]lay the wood in
order on the fire. 8Then the priests, Aaron’s sons, shall lay the parts, the head, and
the fat in order on the wood that *is* on the
fire upon the altar; 9but he shall wash its
entrails and its legs with water. And the
priest shall burn all on the altar as a burnt
sacrifice, an offering made by fire, a [a]sweet
aroma to the LORD.
10‘If his offering *is* of the flocks—of the
sheep or of the goats—as a burnt sacrifice, he shall bring a male [a]without blemish. 11[a]He shall kill it on the north side of
the altar before the LORD; and the priests,
Aaron’s sons, shall sprinkle its blood all
around on the altar. 12And he shall cut it
into its pieces, with its head and its fat; and
the priest shall lay them in order on the
wood that *is* on the fire upon the altar; 13but
he shall wash the entrails and the legs with
water. Then the priest shall bring *it* all and
burn *it* on the altar; it *is* a burnt sacrifice,
an [a]offering made by fire, a sweet aroma
to the LORD.
14‘And if the burnt sacrifice of his offering to the LORD *is* of birds, then he shall
bring his offering of [a]turtledoves or young
pigeons. 15The priest shall bring it to the altar, wring off its head, and burn *it* on the altar; its blood shall be drained out at the side
of the altar. 16And he shall remove its crop
with its feathers and cast it [a]beside the altar on the east side, into the place for ashes.
17Then he shall split it at its wings, *but* [a]shall
not divide *it* completely; and the priest shall
burn it on the altar, on the wood that *is* on
the fire. [b]It *is* a burnt sacrifice, an offering
made by fire, a sweet aroma to the LORD.

The Grain Offering

2 ‘When anyone offers [a]a grain offering
to the LORD, his offering shall be *of* fine
flour. And he shall pour oil on it, and put
[b]frankincense on it. 2He shall bring it to
Aaron’s sons, the priests, one of whom shall
take from it his handful of fine flour and
oil with all the frankincense. And the priest
shall burn [a]*it as* a memorial on the altar, an
offering made by fire, a sweet aroma to the
LORD. 3[a]The rest of the grain offering *shall*

1:1 [a] Ex. 19:3; 25:22; Num. 7:89 [b] Ex. 40:34 1:2 [a] Lev. 22:18, 19 1:3 [a] Ex. 12:5; Lev. 22:20–24; Deut. 15:21; Eph. 5:27; Heb. 9:14; 1 Pet. 1:19 1:4 [a] Ex. 29:10, 15, 19; Lev. 3:2, 8, 13; 4:15 [b] [Rom. 12:1]; Phil. 4:18 [c] Lev. 4:20, 26, 31; 2 Chr. 29:23, 24 1:5 [a] Mic. 6:6 [b] 2 Chr. 35:11 [c] Lev. 1:11; 3:2, 8, 13; [Heb. 12:24; 1 Pet. 1:2] 1:6 [a] Lev. 7:8 1:7 [a] Lev. 6:8–13; Mal. 1:10 [b] Gen. 22:9 1:9 [a] Gen. 8:21; [Ezek. 20:28, 41; 2 Cor. 2:15] 1:10 [a] Ex. 12:5; Lev. 1:3; Ezek. 43:22; [1 Pet. 1:19] 1:11 [a] Ex. 24:6; 40:22; Lev. 1:5; Ezek. 8:5 1:13 [a] Num. 15:4–7; 28:12–14 1:14 [a] Gen. 15:9; Lev. 5:7, 11; 12:8; Luke 2:24 1:16 [a] Lev. 6:10 1:17 [a] Gen. 15:10; Lev. 5:8 [b] Lev. 1:9, 13 2:1 [a] Lev. 6:14; 9:17; Num. 15:4 [b] Lev. 5:11 2:2 [a] Lev. 2:9; 5:12; 6:15; 24:7; Acts 10:4 2:3 [a] Lev. 7:9

be Aaron's and his [b]sons'. [c]*It is* most holy
of the offerings to the LORD made by fire.
4'And if you bring as an offering a grain
offering baked in the oven, *it shall be* unleavened cakes of fine flour mixed with oil,
or unleavened wafers [a]anointed with oil.
5But if your offering *is* a grain offering *baked*
in a pan, *it shall be of* fine flour, unleavened,
mixed with oil. 6You shall break it in pieces
and pour oil on it; it *is* a grain offering.

7'If your offering *is* a grain offering *baked*
in a [a]covered pan, it shall be made *of* fine
flour with oil. 8You shall bring the grain
offering that is made of these things to
the LORD. And when it is presented to the
priest, he shall bring it to the altar. 9Then
the priest shall take from the grain offering [a]a memorial portion, and burn *it* on the
altar. *It is* an [b]offering made by fire, a sweet
aroma to the LORD. 10And [a]what is left of
the grain offering *shall be* Aaron's and his
sons'. *It is* most holy of the offerings to the
LORD made by fire.
11'No grain offering which you bring to
the LORD shall be made with [a]leaven, for
you shall burn no leaven nor any honey in
any offering to the LORD made by fire. 12[a]As
for the offering of the firstfruits, you shall
offer them to the LORD, but they shall not
be burned on the altar for a sweet aroma.
13And every offering of your grain offering [a]you shall season with salt; you shall
not allow [b]the salt of the covenant of your
God to be lacking from your grain offering.
[c]With all your offerings you shall offer salt.
14'If you offer a grain offering of your
firstfruits to the LORD, [a]you shall offer for
the grain offering of your firstfruits green
heads of grain roasted on the fire, grain
beaten from [b]full heads. 15And [a]you shall
put oil on it, and lay frankincense on it. It
is a grain offering. 16Then the priest shall

EXALT HIS GUIDING LIGHT

INHALE

I am not trying to be cocky, but I came from the projects, and that did not hold me back. I was raised by a single mom, but that only made me stronger. I was first in my family to get a college degree. I am getting paid way more than the friends I grew up with. Don't get me wrong; I believe in God. I am just saying that I cast my own light. Counting on others is not the way to go. I count on myself. So, why should I follow God? What can He do for me that I have not done for myself? Why should I follow His way when following my own way has gotten me out of darkness?

EXHALE

Getting things done can be quite admirable. But you are never doing anything purely on your own. God is in control of all things. There are things that He allows and things that He will not allow. If your security rests solely on your own shoulders, you are in trouble, even if you might not know it.

You see, we are all sinners—rebels against God—and because of that we deserve eternal separation from God. Delivering us from sin is the one task that is impossible for anyone other than God, the Father, through Jesus, the Son, to do.

In Leviticus 1:1–9, we read about the sacrifices required by the Lord. From this, we can understand what has to happen for sin to be forgiven—sin deserves death, and a death sacrifice must be paid. But then the sacrifice of Jesus accomplished what you could never do on your own. He died so we can live. There is no other way. This is something you cannot do; it is a gift from God. All you have to do is receive the free gift of salvation that He offers us through repentance of our sin and acceptance of Jesus as our Lord and Savior. It is the only way.

2:3 [b] Lev. 6:6; 10:12, 13 [c] Ex. 29:37; Num. 18:9 2:4 [a] Ex. 29:2 2:7 [a] Lev. 7:9 2:9 [a] Lev. 2:2, 16; 5:12; 6:15 [b] Ex. 29:18 2:10 [a] Lev. 2:3; 6:16 2:11 [a] Ex. 23:18; 34:25; Lev. 6:16, 17; [Matt. 16:12; Mark 8:15; Luke 12:1; 1 Cor. 5:8; Gal. 5:9] 2:12 [a] Ex. 22:29; 34:22; Lev. 23:10, 11, 17, 18 2:13 [a] [Mark 9:49, 50; Col. 4:6] [b] Num. 18:19; 2 Chr. 13:5 [c] Ezek. 43:24 2:14 [a] Lev. 23:10, 14 [b] 2 Kin. 4:42 2:15 [a] Lev. 2:1

burn [a]the memorial portion: *part* of its
beaten grain and *part* of its oil, with all the
frankincense, as an offering made by fire
to the LORD.

The Peace Offering

3 'When his offering *is* a [a]sacrifice of
a peace offering, if he offers *it* of the
herd, whether male or female, he shall offer
it [b]without blemish before the LORD. 2 And
[a]he shall lay his hand on the head of his
offering, and kill it *at* the door of the tabernacle of meeting; and Aaron's sons, the
priests, shall [b]sprinkle the blood all around
on the altar. 3 Then he shall offer from the
sacrifice of the peace offering an offering
made by fire to the LORD. [a]The fat that covers the entrails and all the fat that *is* on the
entrails, 4 the two kidneys and the fat that
is on them by the flanks, and the fatty lobe
attached to the liver above the kidneys, he
shall remove; 5 and Aaron's sons [a]shall burn
it on the altar upon the [b]burnt sacrifice,
which *is* on the wood that *is* on the fire, *as*
an [c]offering made by fire, a [d]sweet aroma
to the LORD.

6 'If his offering as a sacrifice of a peace
offering to the LORD *is* of the flock, *whether*
male or female, [a]he shall offer it without
blemish. 7 If he offers a [a]lamb as his offering, then he shall [b]offer it [c]before the LORD.
8 And he shall lay his hand on the head of
his offering, and kill it before the tabernacle of meeting; and Aaron's sons shall
sprinkle its blood all around on the altar.

9 'Then he shall offer from the sacrifice of
the peace offering, as an offering made by
fire to the LORD, its fat *and* the whole fat tail
which he shall remove close to the backbone. And the fat that covers the entrails
and all the fat that *is* on the entrails, 10 the
two kidneys and the fat that *is* on them by
the flanks, and the fatty lobe *attached* to
the liver above the kidneys, he shall remove; 11 and the priest shall burn *them* on
the altar *as* [a]food, an offering made by fire
to the LORD.

12 'And if his [a]offering *is* a goat, then [b]he
shall offer it before the LORD. 13 He shall
lay his hand on its head and kill it before
the tabernacle of meeting; and the sons of
Aaron shall sprinkle its blood all around
on the altar. 14 Then he shall offer from
his offering, as an offering made by fire to
the LORD. The fat that covers the entrails
and all the fat that *is* on the entrails, 15 the
two kidneys and the fat that *is* on them by
the flanks, and the fatty lobe *attached* to
the liver above the kidneys, he shall remove; 16 and the priest shall burn them on
the altar *as* food, an offering made by fire
for a sweet aroma; [a]all the fat *is* the LORD's.

17 '*This shall be* a [a]perpetual statute
throughout your generations in all your
dwellings: you shall eat neither fat nor
[b]blood.'"

The Sin Offering

4 Now the LORD spoke to Moses, saying,
2 "Speak to the children of Israel, saying:
[a]'If a person sins unintentionally against
any of the commandments of the LORD
in anything which ought not to be done,
and does any of them, 3 [a]if the anointed
priest sins, bringing guilt on the people,
then let him offer to the LORD for his sin
which he has sinned [b]a young bull without
blemish as a [c]sin offering. 4 He shall bring
the bull [a]to the door of the tabernacle of
meeting before the LORD, lay his hand on
the bull's head, and kill the bull before the
LORD. 5 Then the anointed priest [a]shall take
some of the bull's blood and bring it to the
tabernacle of meeting. 6 The priest shall dip
his finger in the blood and sprinkle some
of the blood seven times before the LORD,
in front of the [a]veil of the sanctuary. 7 And
the priest shall [a]put some of the blood on
the horns of the altar of sweet incense before the LORD, which is in the tabernacle of
meeting; and he shall pour [b]the remaining
blood of the bull at the base of the altar of
the burnt offering, which is at the door of
the tabernacle of meeting. 8 He shall take
from it all the fat of the bull as the sin offering. The fat that covers the entrails and

---

2:16 [a] Lev. 2:2 3:1 [a] Lev. 7:11, 29 [b] Lev. 1:3; 22:20–24 3:2 [a] Ex. 29:10, 11, 16, 20; Lev. 1:4, 5; 16:21 [b] Lev. 1:5 3:3 [a] Ex. 29:13, 22; Lev. 1:8; 3:16; 4:8, 9 3:5 [a] Ex. 29:13; Lev. 6:12; 7:28–34 [b] 2 Chr. 35:14 [c] Num. 28:3–10 [d] Num. 15:8–10 3:6 [a] Lev. 3:1; 22:20–24 3:7 [a] Num. 15:4, 5 [b] 1 Kin. 8:62 [c] Lev. 17:8, 9 3:11 [a] Lev. 21:6, 8, 17, 21, 22; 22:25; Num. 28:2; [Ezek. 44:7; Mal. 1:7, 12] 3:12 [a] Num. 15:6–11 [b] Lev. 3:1, 7 3:16 [a] Lev. 7:23–25; 1 Sam. 2:15; 2 Chr. 7:7 3:17 [a] Lev. 6:18; 7:36; 17:7; 23:14 [b] Gen. 9:4; Lev. 7:23, 26; 17:10, 14; 1 Sam. 14:33 4:2 [a] Lev. 5:15–18; Num. 15:22–30; 1 Sam. 14:27; Acts 3:17 4:3 [a] Ex. 40:15; Lev. 8:12 [b] Lev. 3:1; 9:2 [c] Lev. 9:7 4:4 [a] Lev. 1:3, 4; 4:15; Num. 8:12 4:5 [a] Lev. 16:14; Num. 19:4 4:6 [a] Ex. 40:21, 26 4:7 [a] Lev. 4:18, 25, 30, 34; 8:15; 9:9; 16:18 [b] Ex. 40:5, 6; Lev. 5:9

all the fat which *is* on the entrails, 9the two
kidneys and the fat that *is* on them by the
flanks, and the fatty lobe *attached* to the
liver above the kidneys, he shall remove,
10[a]as it was taken from the bull of the sacrifice of the peace offering; and the priest
shall burn them on the altar of the burnt
offering. 11[a]But the bull's hide and all its
flesh, with its head and legs, its entrails
and offal— 12the whole bull he shall carry
outside the camp to a clean place, [a]where
the ashes are poured out, and [b]burn it on
wood with fire; where the ashes are poured
out it shall be burned.

13'Now [a]if the whole congregation of Israel sins unintentionally, [b]and the thing
is hidden from the eyes of the assembly,
and they have done *something against*
any of the commandments of the LORD *in*
anything which should not be done, and
are guilty; 14when the sin which they have
committed becomes known, then the assembly shall offer a young bull for the sin,
and bring it before the tabernacle of meeting. 15And the elders of the congregation
[a]shall lay their hands on the head of the
bull before the LORD. Then the bull shall
be killed before the LORD. 16[a]The anointed
priest shall bring some of the bull's blood
to the tabernacle of meeting. 17Then the
priest shall dip his finger in the blood and
sprinkle *it* seven times before the LORD, in
front of the veil. 18And he shall put *some* of
the blood on the horns of the altar which *is*
before the LORD, which *is* in the tabernacle
of meeting; and he shall pour the remaining blood at the base of the altar of burnt
offering, which is at the door of the tabernacle of meeting. 19He shall take all the fat
from it and burn *it* on the altar. 20And he
shall do [a]with the bull as he did with the
bull as a sin offering; thus he shall do with
it. [b]So the priest shall make atonement for
them, and it shall be forgiven them. 21Then
he shall carry the bull outside the camp,
and burn it as he burned the first bull. It *is*
a sin offering for the assembly.

22'When a ruler has sinned, and [a]done
something unintentionally *against* any of
the commandments of the LORD his God
in anything which should not be done, and
is guilty, 23or [a]if his sin which he has committed comes to his knowledge, he shall
bring as his offering a kid of the goats, a
male without blemish. 24And [a]he shall lay
his hand on the head of the goat, and kill
it at the place where they kill the burnt offering before the LORD. It *is* a sin offering.
25[a]The priest shall take some of the blood
of the sin offering with his finger, put *it*
on the horns of the altar of burnt offering,
and pour its blood at the base of the altar
of burnt offering. 26And he shall burn all
its fat on the altar, like [a]the fat of the sacrifice of the peace offering. [b]So the priest
shall make atonement for him concerning
his sin, and it shall be forgiven him.

27[a]'If anyone of the common people sins
unintentionally by doing *something against*
any of the commandments of the LORD
in anything which ought not to be done,
and is guilty, 28or [a]if his sin which he has
committed comes to his knowledge, then
he shall bring as his offering a kid of the
goats, a female without blemish, for his sin
which he has committed. 29[a]And he shall
lay his hand on the head of the sin offering, and kill the sin offering at the place of
the burnt offering. 30Then the priest shall
take *some* of its blood with his finger, put
it on the horns of the altar of burnt offering, and pour all *the remaining* blood at the
base of the altar. 31[a]He shall remove all its
fat, [b]as fat is removed from the sacrifice
of the peace offering; and the priest shall
burn it on the altar for a [c]sweet aroma to
the LORD. [d]So the priest shall make atonement for him, and it shall be forgiven him.

32'If he brings a lamb as his sin offering,
[a]he shall bring a female without blemish.
33Then he shall [a]lay his hand on the head
of the sin offering, and kill it as a sin offering at the place where they kill the burnt
offering. 34The priest shall take *some* of the
blood of the sin offering with his finger, put
it on the horns of the altar of burnt offering, and pour all *the remaining* blood at the
base of the altar. 35He shall remove all its

4:10 [a] Lev. 3:3–5 4:11 [a] Ex. 29:14; Lev. 9:11; Num. 19:5 4:12 [a] Lev. 4:21; 6:10, 11; 16:27 [b] [Heb. 13:11, 12] 4:13 [a] Num. 15:24–26; Josh. 7:11 [b] Lev. 5:2–4, 17 4:15 [a] Lev. 1:3, 4 4:16 [a] Lev. 4:5; [Heb. 9:12–14] 4:20 [a] Lev. 4:3 [b] Lev. 1:4; Num. 15:25 4:22 [a] Lev. 4:2, 13, 27 4:23 [a] Lev. 4:14; 5:4 4:24 [a] Lev. 4:4; [Is. 53:6] 4:25 [a] Lev. 4:7, 18, 30, 34 4:26 [a] Lev. 3:3–5 [b] Lev. 4:20; Num. 15:28 4:27 [a] Lev. 4:2; Num. 15:27 4:28 [a] Lev. 4:23 4:29 [a] Lev. 1:4; 4:4, 24 4:31 [a] Lev. 3:14 [b] Lev. 3:3, 4 [c] Gen. 8:21; Ex. 29:18; Lev. 1:9, 13; 2:2, 9, 12 [d] Lev. 4:26 4:32 [a] Lev. 4:28 4:33 [a] Lev. 1:4; Num. 8:12

fat, as the fat of the lamb is removed from the sacrifice of the peace offering. Then the priest shall burn it on the altar, [a]according to the offerings made by fire to the LORD. [b]So the priest shall make atonement for his sin that he has committed, and it shall be forgiven him.

The Trespass Offering

5 'If a person sins in [a]hearing the utterance of an oath, and *is* a witness, whether he has seen or known *of the matter*—if he does not tell *it,* he [b]bears guilt.

2'Or [a]if a person touches any unclean thing, whether *it is* the carcass of an unclean beast, or the carcass of unclean livestock, or the carcass of unclean creeping things, and he is unaware of it, he also shall be unclean and [b]guilty. 3Or if he touches [a]human uncleanness—whatever uncleanness with which a man may be defiled, and he is unaware of it—when he realizes *it,* then he shall be guilty.

4'Or if a person swears, speaking thoughtlessly with *his* lips [a]to do evil or [b]to do good, whatever *it is* that a man may pronounce by an oath, and he is unaware of it—when he realizes *it,* then he shall be guilty in any of these *matters.*

5'And it shall be, when he is guilty in any of these *matters,* that he shall [a]confess that he has sinned in that *thing;* 6and he shall bring his trespass offering to the LORD for his sin which he has committed, a female from the flock, a lamb or a kid of the goats as a sin offering. So the priest shall make atonement for him concerning his sin.

7[a]'If he is not able to bring a lamb, then he shall bring to the LORD, for his trespass which he has committed, two [b]turtledoves or two young pigeons: one as a sin offering and the other as a burnt offering. 8And he shall bring them to the priest, who shall offer *that* which *is* for the sin offering first, and [a]wring off its head from its neck, but shall not divide *it* completely. 9Then he shall sprinkle *some* of the blood of the sin offering on the side of the altar, and the [a]rest of the blood shall be drained out at the base of the altar. It *is* a sin offering. 10And he shall offer the second *as* a burnt offering according to the [a]prescribed manner. So [b]the priest shall make atonement on his behalf for his sin which he has committed, and it shall be forgiven him.

11'But if he is [a]not able to bring two turtledoves or two young pigeons, then he who sinned shall bring for his offering one-tenth of an ephah of fine flour as a sin offering. [b]He shall put no oil on it, nor shall he put frankincense on it, for it *is* a sin offering. 12Then he shall bring it to the priest, and the priest shall take his handful of it [a]as a memorial portion, and burn *it* on the altar [b]according to the offerings made by fire to the LORD. It *is* a sin offering. 13[a]The priest shall make atonement for him, for his sin that he has committed in any of these matters; and it shall be forgiven him. [b]*The rest* shall be the priest's as a grain offering.' "

Offerings with Restitution

14Then the LORD spoke to Moses, saying: 15[a]"If a person commits a trespass, and sins unintentionally in regard to the holy things of the LORD, then [b]he shall bring to the LORD as his trespass offering a ram without blemish from the flocks, with your valuation in shekels of silver according to [c]the shekel of the sanctuary, as a trespass offering. 16And he shall make restitution for the harm that he has done in regard to the holy thing, [a]and shall add one-fifth to it and give it to the priest. [b]So the priest shall make atonement for him with the ram of the trespass offering, and it shall be forgiven him.

17"If a person sins, and commits any of these things which are forbidden to be done by the commandments of the LORD, [a]though he does not know *it,* yet he is [b]guilty and shall bear his iniquity. 18[a]And he shall bring to the priest a ram without blemish from the flock, with your valuation, as a trespass offering. So the priest shall make atonement for him regarding

4:35 [a] Lev. 3:5 [b] Lev. 4:26, 31 5:1 [a] Prov. 29:24; [Jer. 23:10] [b] Lev. 5:17; 7:18; 17:16; 19:8; 20:17; Num. 9:13 5:2 [a] Lev. 11:24, 28, 31, 39; Num. 19:11–16; Deut. 14:8 [b] Lev. 5:17 5:3 [a] Lev. 5:12, 13, 15 5:4 [a] 1 Sam. 25:22; Acts 23:12 [b] [Matt. 5:33–37]; Mark 6:23; [James 5:12] 5:5 [a] Lev. 16:21; 26:40; Num. 5:7; Ezra 10:11, 12; Ps. 32:5; Prov. 28:13 5:7 [a] Lev. 12:6, 8; 14:21 [b] Lev. 1:14 5:8 [a] Lev. 1:15–17 5:9 [a] Lev. 4:7, 18, 30, 34 5:10 [a] Lev. 1:14–17 [b] Lev. 4:20, 26; 5:13, 16 5:11 [a] Lev. 14:21–32 [b] Lev. 2:1, 2; 6:15; Num. 5:15 5:12 [a] Lev. 2:2 [b] Lev. 4:35 5:13 [a] Lev. 4:26 [b] Lev. 2:3; 6:17, 26 5:15 [a] Lev. 4:2; 22:14; Num. 5:5–8 [b] Ezra 10:19 [c] Ex. 30:13; Lev. 27:25 5:16 [a] Lev. 6:5; 22:14; 27:13, 15, 27, 31; Num. 5:7 [b] Lev. 4:26 5:17 [a] Lev. 4:2, 13, 22, 27 [b] Lev. 5:1, 2 5:18 [a] Lev. 5:15

his ignorance in which he erred and did
not know *it*, and it shall be forgiven him.
19It is a trespass offering; [a]he has certainly
trespassed against the LORD."

6 And the LORD spoke to Moses, saying: 2"If a person sins and [a]commits a
trespass against the LORD by [b]lying to his
neighbor about [c]what was delivered to him
for safekeeping, or about a pledge, or about
a robbery, or if he has [d]extorted from his
neighbor, 3or if he [a]has found what was lost
and lies concerning it, and [b]swears falsely—in any one of these things that a man
may do in which he sins: 4then it shall be,
because he has sinned and is guilty, that
he shall restore [a]what he has stolen, or the
thing which he has extorted, or what was
delivered to him for safekeeping, or the
lost thing which he found, 5or all that about
which he has sworn falsely. He shall [a]re-
store its full value, add one-fifth more to it,
and give it to whomever it belongs, on the
day of his trespass offering. 6And he shall
bring his trespass offering to the LORD, [a]a
ram without blemish from the flock, with
your valuation, as a trespass offering, to the
priest. 7[a]So the priest shall make atonement
for him before the LORD, and he shall be
forgiven for any one of these things that
he may have done in which he trespasses."

The Law of the Burnt Offering

8Then the LORD spoke to Moses, saying,
9"Command Aaron and his sons, saying,
'This *is* the [a]law of the burnt offering: The
burnt offering *shall be* on the hearth upon
the altar all night until morning, and the
fire of the altar shall be kept burning on it.
10[a]And the priest shall put on his linen garment, and his linen trousers he shall put on
his body, and take up the ashes of the burnt
offering which the fire has consumed on
the altar, and he shall put them [b]beside the
altar. 11Then [a]he shall take off his garments,
put on other garments, and carry the ashes
outside the camp [b]to a clean place. 12And
the fire on the altar shall be kept burning
on it; it shall not be put out. And the priest
shall burn wood on it every morning, and
lay the burnt offering in order on it; and
he shall burn on it [a]the fat of the peace offerings. 13A fire shall always be burning on
the [a]altar; it shall never go out.

The Law of the Grain Offering

14'This *is* the law of the grain offering:
The sons of Aaron shall offer it on the altar before the LORD. 15He shall take from
it his handful of the fine flour of the grain
offering, with its oil, and all the frankincense which *is* on the grain offering, and
shall burn *it* on the altar *for* a sweet aroma,
as a memorial to the LORD. 16And the remainder of it Aaron and his sons shall eat;
with unleavened bread it shall be eaten in
a holy place; in the court of the tabernacle of meeting they shall eat it. 17It shall
not be baked with leaven. I have given it *as*
their portion of My offerings made by fire;
it *is* most holy, like the sin offering and the
[a]trespass offering. 18[a]All the males among
the children of Aaron may eat it. [b]*It shall
be* a statute forever in your generations
concerning the offerings made by fire to
the LORD. [c]Everyone who touches them
must be holy.'"[1]

19And the LORD spoke to Moses, saying,
20[a]"This *is* the offering of Aaron and his
sons, which they shall offer to the LORD,
beginning on the day when he is anointed:
one-tenth of an [b]ephah of fine flour as a
daily grain offering, half of it in the morning and half of it at night. 21It shall be made
in a [a]pan with oil. *When it is* mixed, you
shall bring it in. The baked pieces of the
grain offering you shall offer *for* a sweet
aroma to the LORD. 22The priest from
among his sons, [a]who is anointed in his
place, shall offer it. *It is* a statute forever to
the LORD. [b]It shall be wholly burned. 23For
every grain offering for the priest shall be
wholly burned. It shall not be eaten."

The Law of the Sin Offering

24Also the LORD spoke to Moses, saying,
25"Speak to Aaron and to his sons, saying,

5:19 [a] Ezra 10:2 6:2 [a] Num. 5:6 [b] Lev. 19:11; Acts 5:4; Col. 3:9 [c] Ex. 22:7, 10 [d] Prov. 24:28 6:3 [a] Ex. 23:4; Deut. 22:1–4 [b] Ex. 22:11; Lev. 19:12; Jer. 7:9; Zech. 5:4 6:4 [a] Lev. 24:18, 21 6:5 [a] Lev. 5:16; Num. 5:7, 8; 2 Sam. 12:6 6:6 [a] Lev. 1:3; 5:15 6:7 [a] Lev. 4:26 6:9 [a] Ex. 29:38–42; Num. 28:3–10 6:10 [a] Ex. 28:39–43; Lev. 16:4; Ezek. 44:17, 18 [b] Lev. 1:16 6:11 [a] Ezek. 44:19 [b] Lev. 4:12 6:12 [a] Lev. 3:3, 5, 9, 14 6:13 [a] Lev. 1:7 6:17 [a] Lev. 7:7 6:18 [a] Lev. 6:29; 7:6; Num. 18:10; 1 Cor. 9:13 [b] Lev. 3:17 [c] Ex. 29:37; Lev. 22:3–7; Num. 4:15; Hag. 2:11–13 [1] Compare Numbers 4:15 and Haggai 2:11–13 6:20 [a] Ex. 29:2 [b] Ex. 16:36 6:21 [a] Lev. 2:5; 7:9 6:22 [a] Lev. 4:3 [b] Ex. 29:25

'This *is* the law of the sin offering: [a]In the
place where the burnt offering is killed,
the sin offering shall be killed before the
LORD. It *is* most holy. 26 [a]The priest who offers it for sin shall eat it. In a holy place it
shall be eaten, in the court of the tabernacle of meeting. 27 [a]Everyone who touches its
flesh must be holy.[1] And when its blood is
sprinkled on any garment, you shall wash
that on which it was sprinkled, in a holy
place. 28 But the earthen vessel in which it
is boiled [a]shall be broken. And if it is boiled
in a bronze pot, it shall be both scoured and
rinsed in water. 29 All the males among the
priests may eat it. It *is* most holy. 30 [a]But no
sin offering from which *any* of the blood is
brought into the tabernacle of meeting, to
make atonement in the holy [b]*place*,[1] shall
be [c]eaten. It shall be [d]burned in the fire.

The Law of the Trespass Offering

7 'Likewise [a]this *is* the law of the trespass
offering (it *is* most holy): 2 In the place
where they kill the burnt offering they shall
kill the trespass offering. And its blood he
shall sprinkle all around on the altar. 3 And
he shall offer from it all its fat. The fat tail
and the fat that covers the entrails, 4 the
two kidneys and the fat that *is* on them
by the flanks, and the fatty lobe *attached*
to the liver above the kidneys, he shall remove; 5 and the priest shall burn them on
the altar *as* an offering made by fire to the
LORD. It *is* a trespass offering. 6 [a]Every male
among the priests may eat it. It shall be
eaten in a holy place. [b]It *is* most holy. 7 [a]The
trespass offering *is* like the sin offering;
there is one law for them both: the priest
who makes atonement with it shall have *it*.
8 And the priest who offers anyone's burnt
offering, that priest shall have for himself
the skin of the burnt offering which he has
offered. 9 Also [a]every grain offering that is
baked in the oven and all that is prepared
in the covered pan, or in a pan, shall be
the priest's who offers it. 10 Every grain offering, *whether* mixed with oil or dry, shall
belong to all the sons of Aaron, to one *as
much* as the other.

The Law of Peace Offerings

11 [a]'This *is* the law of the sacrifice of peace
offerings which he shall offer to the LORD:
12 If he offers it for a thanksgiving, then he
shall offer, with the sacrifice of thanksgiving, unleavened cakes mixed with oil,
unleavened wafers [a]anointed with oil, or
cakes of blended flour mixed with oil. 13 Besides the cakes, *as* his offering he shall offer
[a]leavened bread with the sacrifice of thanksgiving of his peace offering. 14 And from it he
shall offer one cake from each offering *as* a
heave offering to the LORD. [a]It shall belong
to the priest who sprinkles the blood of the
peace offering.

15 [a]'The flesh of the sacrifice of his peace
offering for thanksgiving shall be eaten the
same day it is offered. He shall not leave any
of it until morning. 16 But [a]if the sacrifice of
his offering *is* a vow or a voluntary offering,
it shall be eaten the same day that he offers
his sacrifice; but on the next day the remainder of it also may be eaten; 17 the remainder
of the flesh of the sacrifice on the third day
must be burned with fire. 18 And if *any* of the
flesh of the sacrifice of his peace offering is
eaten at all on the third day, it shall not be
accepted, nor shall it be [a]imputed to him; it
shall be an [b]abomination *to* him who offers it,
and the person who eats of it shall bear guilt.

19 'The flesh that touches any unclean
thing shall not be eaten. It shall be burned
with fire. And as for the *clean* flesh, all who
are clean may eat of it. 20 But the person who
eats the flesh of the sacrifice of the peace
offering that *belongs* to the [a]LORD, [b]while
he is unclean, that person [c]shall be cut off
from his people. 21 Moreover the person who
touches any unclean thing, *such as* [a]human
uncleanness, *an* [b]unclean animal, or any
[c]abominable unclean thing,[1] and who eats
the flesh of the sacrifice of the peace offering that *belongs* to the LORD, that person
[d]shall be cut off from his people.' "

6:25 [a] Lev. 1:1, 3, 5, 11 **6:26** [a] [Lev. 10:17, 18]; Num. 18:9, 10; [Ezek. 44:28, 29] **6:27** [a] Ex. 29:37; Num. 4:15; Hag. 2:11–13 [1] Compare Numbers 4:15 and Haggai 2:11–13 **6:28** [a] Lev. 11:33; 15:12 **6:30** [a] Lev. 4:7, 11, 12, 18, 21; 10:18; 16:27; [Heb. 13:11, 12] [b] Ex. 26:33 [c] Lev. 6:16, 23, 26 [d] Lev. 16:27 [1] The Most Holy Place when capitalized **7:1** [a] Lev. 5:14—6:7 **7:6** [a] Lev. 6:16–18, 29; Num. 18:9 [b] Lev. 2:3 **7:7** [a] Lev. 6:24–30; 14:13 **7:9** [a] Lev. 2:3, 10; Num. 18:9; Ezek. 44:29 **7:11** [a] Lev. 3:1; 22:18, 21; Ezek. 45:15 **7:12** [a] Lev. 2:4; Num. 6:15 **7:13** [a] Lev. 2:12; 23:17, 18; Amos 4:5 **7:14** [a] Num. 18:8, 11, 19 **7:15** [a] Lev. 22:29, 30 **7:16** [a] Lev. 19:5–8 **7:18** [a] Num. 18:27 [b] Lev. 11:10, 11, 41; 19:7; [Prov. 15:8] **7:20** [a] [Heb. 2:17] [b] Lev. 5:3; 15:3; 22:3–7; Num. 19:13; [1 Cor. 11:28] [c] Gen. 17:14; Ex. 31:14 **7:21** [a] Lev. 5:2, 3, 5 [b] Lev. 11:24, 28 [c] Ezek. 4:14 [d] Lev. 7:20 [1] Following Masoretic Text, Septuagint, and Vulgate; Samaritan Pentateuch, Syriac, and Targum read *swarming thing* (compare 5:2).

Fat and Blood May Not Be Eaten

22And the LORD spoke to Moses, saying,
23"Speak to the children of Israel, saying:
[a]'You shall not eat any fat, of ox or sheep or
goat. 24And the fat of an animal that dies
naturally, and the fat of what is torn by wild
beasts, may be used in any other way; but
you shall by no means eat it. 25For whoever
eats the fat of the animal of which men offer an offering made by fire to the LORD,
the person who eats *it* shall be cut off from
his people. 26[a]Moreover you shall not eat
any blood in any of your dwellings, *whether*
of bird or beast. 27Whoever eats any blood,
that person shall be cut off from his people.'"

The Portion of Aaron and His Sons

28Then the LORD spoke to Moses, saying,
29"Speak to the children of Israel, saying:
[a]'He who offers the sacrifice of his peace offering to the LORD shall bring his offering
to the LORD from the sacrifice of his peace
offering. 30[a]His own hands shall bring the
offerings made by fire to the LORD. The
fat with the breast he shall bring, that the
[b]breast may be waved *as* a wave offering before the LORD. 31[a]And the priest shall burn
the fat on the altar, but the [b]breast shall
be Aaron's and his sons'. 32[a]Also the right
thigh you shall give to the priest *as* a heave
offering from the sacrifices of your peace
offerings. 33He among the sons of Aaron,
who offers the blood of the peace offering
and the fat, shall have the right thigh for
his part. 34For [a]the breast of the wave offering and the thigh of the heave offering
I have taken from the children of Israel,
from the sacrifices of their peace offerings,
and I have given them to Aaron the priest
and to his sons from the children of Israel
by a statute forever.'"

35This *is* the consecrated portion for
Aaron and his sons, from the offerings
made by fire to the LORD, on the day when
Moses presented them to minister to the
LORD as priests. 36The LORD commanded
this to be given to them by the children of
Israel, [a]on the day that He anointed them,
by a statute forever throughout their generations.

37This *is* the law [a]of the burnt offering,
[b]the grain offering, [c]the sin offering, [d]the
trespass offering, [e]the consecrations, and
[f]the sacrifice of the peace offering, 38which
the LORD commanded Moses on Mount Sinai, on the day when He commanded the
children of Israel [a]to offer their offerings to
the LORD in the Wilderness of Sinai.

Aaron and His Sons Consecrated
(Ex. 29:1–37)

8 And the LORD spoke to Moses, saying:
2[a]"Take Aaron and his sons with him,
and [b]the garments, [c]the anointing oil, a
[d]bull as the sin offering, two [e]rams, and a
basket of unleavened bread; 3and gather
all the congregation together at the door
of the tabernacle of meeting."

4So Moses did as the LORD commanded
him. And the congregation was gathered
together at the door of the tabernacle of
meeting. 5And Moses said to the congregation, "This *is* what the LORD commanded
to be done."

6Then Moses brought Aaron and his
sons and [a]washed them with water. 7And
he [a]put the tunic on him, girded him with
the sash, clothed him with the robe, and put
the ephod on him; and he girded him with
the intricately woven band of the ephod,
and with it tied *the ephod* on him. 8Then
he put the breastplate on him, and he [a]put
the Urim and the Thummim[1] in the breastplate. 9[a]And he put the turban on his head.
Also on the turban, on its front, he put the
golden plate, the holy crown, as the LORD
had commanded Moses.

10[a]Also Moses took the anointing oil,
and anointed the tabernacle and all that
was in it, and consecrated them. 11He sprinkled some of it on the altar seven times,
anointed the altar and all its utensils, and
the laver and its base, to consecrate them.

7:23 [a] Lev. 3:17; 17:10–15; Deut. 14:21; Ezek. 4:14; 44:31 7:26 [a] Gen. 9:4; Lev. 3:17; 17:10–16; 19:26; Deut. 12:23; 1 Sam. 14:33; Ezek. 33:25; Acts 15:20, 29 7:29 [a] Lev. 3:1; 22:21; Ezek. 45:15 7:30 [a] Lev. 3:3, 4, 9, 14 [b] Ex. 29:24, 27; Lev. 8:27; 9:21; Num. 6:20 7:31 [a] Lev. 3:5, 11, 16 [b] Num. 18:11; Deut. 18:3 7:32 [a] Ex. 29:27; Lev. 7:34; 9:21; Num. 6:20 7:34 [a] Ex. 29:28; Lev. 10:14, 15; Num. 18:18, 19; Deut. 18:3 7:36 [a] Ex. 40:13–15; Lev. 8:12, 30 7:37 [a] Lev. 6:9 [b] Lev. 6:14 [c] Lev. 6:25 [d] Lev. 7:1 [e] Ex. 29:1; Lev. 6:20 [f] Lev. 7:11 7:38 [a] Lev. 1:1, 2; Deut. 4:5 8:2 [a] Ex. 29:1–3 [b] Ex. 28:2, 4 [c] Ex. 30:24, 25 [d] Ex. 29:10 [e] Ex. 29:15, 19 8:6 [a] Ex. 30:20; Heb. 10:22 8:7 [a] Ex. 39:1–31 8:8 [a] Ex. 28:30; Num. 27:21; Deut. 33:8; 1 Sam. 28:6; Ezra 2:63; Neh. 7:65 [1] Literally *the Lights and the Perfections* (compare Exodus 28:30) 8:9 [a] Ex. 28:36, 37; 29:6 8:10 [a] Ex. 30:26–29; 40:10, 11; Lev. 8:2

12And he [a]poured some of the anointing
oil on Aaron's head and anointed him, to
consecrate him.
13[a]Then Moses brought Aaron's sons
and put tunics on them, girded them with
sashes, and put hats on them, as the LORD
had commanded Moses.
14[a]And he brought the bull for the sin offering. Then Aaron and his sons [b]laid their
hands on the head of the bull for the sin offering, 15and Moses killed *it*. [a]Then he took
the blood, and put *some* on the horns of the
altar all around with his finger, and purified the altar. And he poured the blood at
the base of the altar, and consecrated it, to
make atonement for it. 16[a]Then he took all
the fat that *was* on the entrails, the fatty
lobe *attached to* the liver, and the two kidneys with their fat, and Moses burned *them*
on the altar. 17But the bull, its hide, its flesh,
and its offal, he burned with fire outside
the camp, as the LORD [a]had commanded
Moses.
18[a]Then he brought the ram as the burnt
offering. And Aaron and his sons laid their
hands on the head of the ram, 19and Moses
killed *it*. Then he sprinkled the blood all
around on the altar. 20And he cut the ram
into pieces; and Moses [a]burned the head,
the pieces, and the fat. 21Then he washed
the entrails and the legs in water. And Moses burned the whole ram on the altar. It

LEVITICUS 8:12

I AM AARON

And he poured some of the anointing oil on Aaron's head and anointed him, to consecrate him. Leviticus 8:12

I am Aaron, the brother of Moses. God told me to meet my brother in the wilderness, so I obeyed, and there Moses told me everything the Lord had said to him. He was to be used by God to lead our people to freedom, and I was to speak to the people of Israel and to Pharaoh as Moses directed. Amazingly, God also performed miracles through me as I followed Moses' instructions.

After the Israelites were set free from bondage, the Lord told Moses to have me serve as the first high priest of Israel. At God's instruction, Moses provided me with sacred garments that gave me dignity and honor. Every time I entered God's holy place, I represented the whole nation of Israel, as symbolized by the twelve stones on the breastplate I wore over my heart. I was consecrated along with my sons, my descendants, and the descendants of Levi to serve as a holy priesthood forever.

But my story has some low points too. When Moses was called onto the mountain of God, his return seemed delayed, causing impatience and doubt to overtake the people. Thinking God had failed them, they determined to make a god of their own. I joined in their sin when I collected their gold and fashioned a golden calf for them to worship.

Later, my sister, Miriam, and I also sinned when we spoke against Moses because he married an Ethiopian woman. I sinned another time when water was severely lacking for the people. The Lord told Moses to speak to a rock and water would flow. But he and I were both angry. Instead of simply speaking, Moses struck the rock. God told us we would not be allowed to lead Israel into the Promised Land because we did not trust Him to show His holiness to His people.

†

God used Aaron, who had greatly sinned against Him, and made him the first high priest. No matter what sins we have committed, God can use each one of us if we are willing to surrender our will to His.

8:12 [a] Ex. 29:7; 30:30; Lev. 21:10, 12; Ps. 133:2 8:13 [a] Ex. 29:8, 9 8:14 [a] Ex. 29:10; Ps. 66:15; Ezek. 43:19 [b] Lev. 4:4 8:15 [a] Ex. 29:12, 36; Lev. 4:7; Ezek. 43:20, 26; [Heb. 9:22] 8:16 [a] Ex. 29:13; Lev. 4:8 8:17 [a] Ex. 29:14; Lev. 4:11, 12 8:18 [a] Ex. 29:15 8:20 [a] Lev. 1:8

was a burnt sacrifice for a sweet aroma, an offering made by fire to the LORD, [a]as the LORD had commanded Moses.

22And [a]he brought the second ram, the ram of consecration. Then Aaron and his sons laid their hands on the head of the ram, 23and Moses killed *it.* Also he took *some* of [a]its blood and put it on the tip of Aaron's right ear, on the thumb of his right hand, and on the big toe of his right foot. 24Then he brought Aaron's sons. And Moses put *some* of the [a]blood on the tips of their right ears, on the thumbs of their right hands, and on the big toes of their right feet. And Moses sprinkled the blood all around on the altar. 25[a]Then he took the fat and the fat tail, all the fat that *was* on the entrails, the fatty lobe *attached to* the liver, the two kidneys and their fat, and the right thigh; 26[a]and from the basket of unleavened bread that was before the LORD he took one unleavened cake, a cake of bread *anointed with* oil, and one wafer, and put *them* on the fat and on the right thigh; 27and he put all *these* [a]in Aaron's hands and in his sons' hands, and waved them *as* a wave offering before the LORD. 28[a]Then Moses took them from their hands and burned *them* on the altar, on the burnt offering. They *were* consecration offerings for a sweet aroma. That *was* an offering made by fire to the LORD. 29And [a]Moses took the [b]breast and waved it *as* a wave offering before the LORD. It was Moses' [c]part of the ram of consecration, as the LORD had commanded Moses.

30Then [a]Moses took some of the anointing oil and some of the blood which *was* on the altar, and sprinkled *it* on Aaron, on his garments, on his sons, and on the garments of his sons with him; and he consecrated Aaron, his garments, his sons, and the garments of his sons with him.

31And Moses said to Aaron and his sons, [a]"Boil the flesh *at* the door of the tabernacle of meeting, and eat it there with the bread that *is* in the basket of consecration offerings, as I commanded, saying, 'Aaron and his sons shall eat it.' 32[a]What remains of the flesh and of the bread you shall burn with fire. 33And you shall not go outside the door of the tabernacle of meeting *for* seven days, until the days of your consecration are ended. For [a]seven days he shall consecrate you. 34[a]As he has done this day, *so* the LORD has commanded to do, to make atonement for you. 35Therefore you shall stay *at* the door of the tabernacle of meeting day and night for seven days, and [a]keep the charge of the LORD, so that you may not die; for so I have been commanded." 36So Aaron and his sons did all the things that the LORD had commanded by the hand of Moses.

The Priestly Ministry Begins

9 It came to pass on the [a]eighth day that Moses called Aaron and his sons and the elders of Israel. 2And he said to Aaron, "Take for yourself a young [a]bull as a sin offering and a ram as a burnt offering, without blemish, and offer *them* before the LORD. 3And to the children of Israel you shall speak, saying, [a]'Take a kid of the goats as a sin offering, and a calf and a lamb, *both* of the first year, without blemish, as a burnt offering, 4also a bull and a ram as peace offerings, to sacrifice before the LORD, and [a]a grain offering mixed with oil; for [b]today the LORD will appear to you.' "

5So they brought what Moses commanded before the tabernacle of meeting. And all the congregation drew near and stood before the LORD. 6Then Moses said, "This *is* the thing which the LORD commanded you to do, and the glory of the LORD will appear to you." 7And Moses said to Aaron, "Go to the altar, [a]offer your sin offering and your burnt offering, and make atonement for yourself and for the people. [b]Offer the offering of the people, and make atonement for them, as the LORD commanded."

8Aaron therefore went to the altar and killed the calf of the sin offering, which *was* for himself. 9Then the sons of Aaron brought the blood to him. And he dipped

8:21 [a] Ex. 29:18 8:22 [a] Ex. 29:19, 31; Lev. 8:2 8:23 [a] Ex. 29:20, 21; Lev. 14:14 8:24 [a] [Heb. 9:13, 14, 18–23] 8:25 [a] Ex. 29:22 8:26 [a] Ex. 29:23 8:27 [a] Ex. 29:24; Lev. 7:30, 34 8:28 [a] Ex. 29:25 8:29 [a] Ps. 99:6 [b] Ex. 29:27 [c] Ex. 29:26 8:30 [a] Ex. 29:21; 30:30; Num. 3:3 8:31 [a] Ex. 29:31, 32 8:32 [a] Ex. 29:34 8:33 [a] Ex. 29:30, 35; Lev. 10:7; Ezek. 43:25, 26 8:34 [a] [Heb. 7:16] 8:35 [a] Num. 1:53; 3:7; 9:19; Deut. 11:1; 1 Kin. 2:3; Ezek. 48:11 9:1 [a] Ezek. 43:27 9:2 [a] Ex. 29:21; Lev. 4:1–12 9:3 [a] Lev. 4:23, 28; Ezra 6:17; 10:19 9:4 [a] Lev. 2:4 [b] Ex. 29:43; Lev. 9:6, 23 9:7 [a] Lev. 4:3; 1 Sam. 3:14; [Heb. 5:3–5; 7:27] [b] Lev. 4:16, 20; Heb. 5:1

his finger in the blood, put *it* on the horns of
the altar, and poured the blood at the base
of the altar. 10[a]But the fat, the kidneys, and
the fatty lobe from the liver of the sin offering he burned on the altar, as the LORD
had commanded Moses. 11[a]The flesh and the
hide he burned with fire outside the camp.
12And he killed the burnt offering; and
Aaron's sons presented to him the blood,
[a]which he sprinkled all around on the altar.
13[a]Then they presented the burnt offering
to him, with its pieces and head, and he
burned *them* on the altar. 14[a]And he washed
the entrails and the legs, and burned *them*
with the burnt offering on the altar.

15[a]Then he brought the people's offering, and took the goat, which *was* the sin
offering for the people, and killed it and
offered it for sin, like the first one. 16And
he brought the burnt offering and offered
it [a]according to the prescribed manner.
17Then he brought the grain offering, took
a handful of it, and burned *it* on the altar,
[a]besides the burnt sacrifice of the morning.
18He also killed the bull and the ram *as*
[a]sacrifices of peace offerings, which *were*
for the people. And Aaron's sons presented
to him the blood, which he sprinkled all
around on the altar, 19and the fat from the
bull and the ram—the fatty tail, what covers
the entrails and the kidneys, and the fatty
lobe *attached to* the liver; 20and they put the
fat on the breasts. [a]Then he burned the fat
on the altar; 21but the breasts and the right
thigh Aaron waved [a]*as* a wave offering before the LORD, as Moses had commanded.
22Then Aaron lifted his hand toward
the people, [a]blessed them, and came down
from offering the sin offering, the burnt
offering, and peace offerings. 23And Moses and Aaron went into the tabernacle of
meeting, and came out and blessed the
people. Then the glory of the LORD appeared to all the people, 24and [a]fire came
out from before the LORD and consumed
the burnt offering and the fat on the altar.
When all the people saw *it*, they [b]shouted
and fell on their [c]faces.

The Profane Fire of Nadab and Abihu

10 Then [a]Nadab and Abihu, the sons of
Aaron, [b]each took his censer and put
fire in it, put incense on it, and offered [c]pro-
fane fire before the LORD, which He had not
commanded them. 2So [a]fire went out from
the LORD and devoured them, and they died
before the LORD. 3And Moses said to Aaron,
"This is what the LORD spoke, saying:

'By those [a]who come near Me
I must be regarded as holy;
And before all the people
I must be glorified.'"

So Aaron held his peace.
4Then Moses called Mishael and Elzaphan, the sons of Uzziel the uncle of Aaron,
and said to them, "Come near, [a]carry your
brethren from before the sanctuary out of
the camp." 5So they went near and carried
them by their tunics out of the camp, as
Moses had said.

6And Moses said to Aaron, and to Eleazar and Ithamar, his sons, "Do not uncover
your heads nor tear your clothes, lest you
die, and [a]wrath come upon all the people.
But let your brethren, the whole house of
Israel, bewail the burning which the LORD
has kindled. 7[a]You shall not go out from
the door of the tabernacle of meeting, lest
you die, [b]for the anointing oil of the LORD
is upon you." And they did according to the
word of Moses.

Conduct Prescribed for Priests

8Then the LORD spoke to Aaron, saying:
9[a]"Do not drink wine or intoxicating drink,
you, nor your sons with you, when you go
into the tabernacle of meeting, lest you die.
It shall be a statute forever throughout your
generations, 10that you may [a]distinguish
between holy and unholy, and between unclean and clean, 11[a]and that you may teach
the children of Israel all the statutes which
the LORD has spoken to them by the hand
of Moses."
12And Moses spoke to Aaron, and to

9:10 [a] Ex. 23:18; Lev. 8:16 9:11 [a] Lev. 4:11, 12; 8:17 9:12 [a] Lev. 1:5; 8:19 9:13 [a] Lev. 8:20 9:14 [a] Lev. 8:21 9:15 [a] [Is. 53:10; Heb. 2:17; 5:3] 9:16 [a] Lev. 1:1–13 9:17 [a] Ex. 29:38, 39 9:18 [a] Lev. 3:1–11 9:20 [a] Lev. 3:5, 16 9:21 [a] Ex. 29:24, 26, 27; Lev. 7:30–34 9:22 [a] Num. 6:22–26; Deut. 21:5; Luke 24:50 9:24 [a] Gen. 4:4; Judg. 6:21; 2 Chr. 7:1; Ps. 20:3 [b] Ezra 3:11 [c] 1 Kin. 18:38, 39 10:1 [a] Ex. 24:1, 9; Num. 3:2–4; 1 Chr. 24:2 [b] Lev. 16:12 [c] Ex. 30:9; 1 Sam. 2:17 10:2 [a] Gen. 19:24; Num. 11:1; 16:35; Rev. 20:9 10:3 [a] Ex. 19:22; Lev. 21:6; Is. 52:11; Ezek. 20:41 10:4 [a] Acts 5:6, 10 10:6 [a] Num. 1:53; 16:22, 46; 18:5; Josh. 7:1; 22:18, 20; 2 Sam. 24:1 10:7 [a] Lev. 8:33; 21:12 [b] Lev. 8:30 10:9 [a] Gen. 9:21; [Prov. 20:1; 31:5]; Is. 28:7; Ezek. 44:21; Hos. 4:11; Luke 1:15; [Eph. 5:18]; 1 Tim. 3:3; Titus 1:7 10:10 [a] Lev. 11:47; 20:25; Ezek. 22:26; 44:23 10:11 [a] Deut. 24:8; Neh. 8:2, 8; Jer. 18:18; Mal. 2:7

Eleazar and Ithamar, his sons who were
left: [a]"Take the grain offering that remains
of the offerings made by fire to the LORD,
and eat it without leaven beside the altar;
[b]for it *is* most holy. 13You shall eat it in a
[a]holy place, because it *is* your due and your
sons' due, of the sacrifices made by fire to
the LORD; for [b]so I have been commanded.
14[a]The breast of the wave offering and the
thigh of the heave offering you shall eat
in a clean place, you, your sons, and your
[b]daughters with you; for *they are* your due
and your sons' [c]due, *which* are given from
the sacrifices of peace offerings of the children of Israel. 15[a]The thigh of the heave offering and the breast of the wave offering
they shall bring with the offerings of fat
made by fire, to offer *as* a wave offering
before the LORD. And it shall be yours and
your sons' with you, by a statute forever, as
the LORD has commanded."

16Then Moses made careful inquiry
about [a]the goat of the sin offering, and there
it was—burned up. And he was angry with
Eleazar and Ithamar, the sons of Aaron *who
were* left, saying, 17[a]"Why have you not eaten
the sin offering in a holy place, since it *is*
most holy, and *God* has given it to you to
bear [b]the guilt of the congregation, to make
atonement for them before the LORD? 18See!
[a]Its blood was not brought inside the holy
place;[1] indeed you should have eaten it in
a holy *place*, [b]as I commanded."

19And Aaron said to Moses, "Look, [a]this
day they have offered their sin offering and
their burnt offering before the LORD, and
such things have befallen me! *If* I had eaten
the sin offering today, [b]would it have been
accepted in the sight of the LORD?" 20So
when Moses heard *that*, he was content.

Foods Permitted and Forbidden
(Deut. 14:3–21)

11 Now the LORD spoke to Moses and
Aaron, saying to them, 2"Speak to
the children of Israel, saying, [a]'These *are*
the animals which you may eat among all
the animals that *are* on the earth: 3Among
the animals, whatever divides the hoof, having cloven hooves *and* chewing the cud—
that you may eat. 4Nevertheless these you
shall [a]not eat among those that chew the
cud or those that have cloven hooves: the
camel, because it chews the cud but does
not have cloven hooves, is unclean to you;
5the rock hyrax, because it chews the cud
but does not have cloven hooves, *is* unclean
to you; 6the hare, because it chews the cud
but does not have cloven hooves, *is* unclean
to you; 7and the swine, though it divides the
hoof, having cloven hooves, yet does not
chew the cud, [a]*is* unclean to you. 8Their flesh
you shall not eat, and their carcasses you
shall not touch. [a]They *are* unclean to you.

9[a]'These you may eat of all that *are* in
the water: whatever in the water has fins
and scales, whether in the seas or in the
rivers—that you may eat. 10But all in the
seas or in the rivers that do not have fins
and scales, all that move in the water or any
living thing which *is* in the water, they *are*
an [a]abomination to you. 11They shall be an
abomination to you; you shall not eat their
flesh, but you shall regard their carcasses
as an abomination. 12Whatever in the water does not have fins or scales—that *shall
be* an abomination to you.

13[a]'And these you shall regard as an
abomination among the birds; they shall
not be eaten, they *are* an abomination: the
eagle, the vulture, the buzzard, 14the kite,
and the falcon after its kind; 15every raven after its kind, 16the ostrich, the short-
eared owl, the sea gull, and the hawk after
its kind; 17the little owl, the fisher owl, and
the screech owl; 18the white owl, the jackdaw, and the carrion vulture; 19the stork,
the heron after its kind, the hoopoe, and
the bat.

20'All flying insects that creep on *all*
fours *shall be* an abomination to you. 21Yet
these you may eat of every flying insect
that creeps on *all* fours: those which have
jointed legs above their feet with which
to leap on the earth. 22These you may eat:
[a]the locust after its kind, the destroying

10:12 [a] Num. 18:9 [b] Lev. 21:22 10:13 [a] Num. 18:10 [b] Lev. 2:3; 6:16 10:14 [a] Ex. 29:24, 26, 27; Lev. 7:30–34; Num. 18:11 [b] Lev. 22:13 [c] Num. 18:10 10:15 [a] Lev. 7:29, 30, 34 10:16 [a] Lev. 9:3, 15 10:17 [a] Lev. 6:24–30 [b] Ex. 28:38; Lev. 22:16; Num. 18:1 10:18 [a] Lev. 6:30 [b] Lev. 6:26, 30 [1] The Most Holy Place when capitalized 10:19 [a] Lev. 9:8, 12 [b] [Is. 1:11–15]; Jer. 6:20; 14:12; Hos. 9:4; [Mal. 1:10, 13; 3:1–4] 11:2 [a] Deut. 14:4; Ezek. 4:14; Dan. 1:8; [Matt. 15:11]; Acts 10:12, 14; [Rom. 14:14; Heb. 9:10; 13:9] 11:4 [a] Acts 10:14 11:7 [a] Is. 65:4; 66:3, 17; Mark 5:1–17 11:8 [a] Is. 52:11; [Mark 7:2, 15, 18]; Acts 10:14, 15; 15:29 11:9 [a] Deut. 14:9 11:10 [a] Lev. 7:18, 21; Deut. 14:3 11:13 [a] Deut. 14:12–19; Is. 66:17 11:22 [a] Matt. 3:4; Mark 1:6

locust after its kind, the cricket after its
kind, and the grasshopper after its kind.
23But all *other* flying insects which have
four feet *shall be* an abomination to you.

Unclean Animals

24'By these you shall become unclean;
whoever touches the carcass of any of them
shall be unclean until evening; 25whoever
carries part of the carcass of any of them
[a]shall wash his clothes and be unclean until
evening: 26*The carcass* of any animal which
divides the foot, but is not cloven-hoofed
or does not chew the cud, *is* unclean to you.
Everyone who touches it shall be unclean.
27And whatever goes on its paws, among all
kinds of animals that go on *all* fours, those
are unclean to you. Whoever touches any
such carcass shall be unclean until evening. 28Whoever carries *any such* carcass
shall wash his clothes and be unclean until
evening. It *is* unclean to you.

29'These also *shall be* unclean to you
among the creeping things that creep on
the earth: the mole, [a]the mouse, and the
large lizard after its kind; 30the gecko, the
monitor lizard, the sand reptile, the sand
lizard, and the chameleon. 31These *are* unclean to you among all that creep. Whoever [a]touches them when they are dead
shall be unclean until evening. 32Anything
on which *any* of them falls, when they are
dead shall be unclean, whether *it is* any
item of wood or clothing or skin or sack,
whatever item *it is*, in which *any* work is
done, [a]it must be put in water. And it shall
be unclean until evening; then it shall be
clean. 33Any [a]earthen vessel into which *any*
of them falls [b]you shall break; and whatever
is in it shall be unclean: 34in such a vessel,
any edible food upon which water falls becomes unclean, and any drink that may be
drunk from it becomes unclean. 35And everything on which *a part* of *any such* carcass falls shall be unclean; *whether it is* an
oven or cooking stove, it shall be broken
down; *for* they *are* unclean, and shall be
unclean to you. 36Nevertheless a spring or
a cistern, *in which there is* plenty of water,
shall be clean, but whatever touches any
such carcass becomes unclean. 37And if a
part of *any such* carcass falls on any planting seed which is to be sown, it *remains*
clean. 38But if water is put on the seed, and
if *a part* of *any such* carcass falls on it, it *becomes* unclean to you.

39'And if any animal which you may eat
dies, he who touches its carcass shall be
[a]unclean until evening. 40[a]He who eats of
its carcass shall wash his clothes and be
unclean until evening. He also who carries its carcass shall wash his clothes and
be unclean until evening.

41'And every creeping thing that creeps
on the earth *shall be* an abomination. It
shall not be eaten. 42Whatever crawls on its
belly, whatever goes on *all* fours, or whatever has many feet among all creeping
things that creep on the earth—these you
shall not eat, for they *are* an abomination.
43[a]You shall not make yourselves abominable with any creeping thing that creeps;
nor shall you make yourselves unclean with
them, lest you be defiled by them. 44For I
am the LORD your [a]God. You shall therefore consecrate yourselves, and [b]you shall
be holy; for I *am* holy. Neither shall you
defile yourselves with any creeping thing
that creeps on the earth. 45[a]For I *am* the
LORD who brings you up out of the land of
Egypt, to be your God. [b]You shall therefore
be holy, for I *am* holy.

46'This *is* the law of the animals and the
birds and every living creature that moves
in the waters, and of every creature that
creeps on the earth, 47[a]to distinguish between the unclean and the clean, and between the animal that may be eaten and
the animal that may not be eaten.'"

The Ritual After Childbirth

(cf. Luke 2:22–24)

12 Then the LORD spoke to Moses, saying, 2"Speak to the children of Israel, saying: 'If a [a]woman has conceived,
and borne a male child, then [b]she shall be

11:25 [a] Lev. 14:8; 15:5; Num. 19:10, 21, 22; 31:24; Zech. 13:1; [Heb. 9:10; 10:22; Rev. 7:14] 11:29 [a] Is. 66:17 11:31 [a] Hag. 2:13
11:32 [a] Lev. 15:12 11:33 [a] Lev. 6:28 [b] Lev. 15:12; Ps. 2:9; Jer. 48:38; [2 Tim. 2:21]; Rev. 2:27 11:39 [a] Hag. 2:11–13 11:40 [a] Ex. 22:31;
Lev. 17:15; 22:8; Deut. 14:21; Ezek. 4:14; 44:31 11:43 [a] Lev. 20:25 11:44 [a] Ex. 6:7; Lev. 22:33; 25:38; 26:45 [b] Ex. 19:6; Lev. 19:2; 20:7, 26;
[Amos 3:3]; Matt. 5:48; 1 Thess. 4:7; 1 Pet. 1:15, 16; [Rev. 22:11, 14] 11:45 [a] Ex. 6:7; 20:2; Lev. 22:33; 25:38; 26:45;
Ps. 105:43–45; Hos. 11:1 [b] Lev. 11:44 11:47 [a] Lev. 10:10; Ezek. 44:23; Mal. 3:18
12:2 [a] Lev. 15:19; [Job 14:4; Ps. 51:5] [b] Ex. 22:30; Lev. 8:33; 13:4; Luke 2:22

unclean seven days; [c]as in the days of her
customary impurity she shall be unclean.
3And on the [a]eighth day the flesh of his
foreskin shall be circumcised. 4She shall
then continue in the blood of *her* purification thirty-three days. She shall not touch
any hallowed thing, nor come into the sanctuary until the days of her purification are
fulfilled.

5'But if she bears a female child, then she
shall be unclean two weeks, as in her customary impurity, and she shall continue in
the blood of *her* purification sixty-six days.

6[a]'When the days of her purification are
fulfilled, whether for a son or a daughter,
she shall bring to the priest a [b]lamb of the
first year as a burnt offering, and a young
pigeon or a turtledove as a [c]sin offering,
to the door of the tabernacle of meeting.
7Then he shall offer it before the LORD, and
make atonement for her. And she shall be
clean from the flow of her blood. This *is*
the law for her who has borne a male or
a female.

8[a]'And if she is not able to bring a lamb,
then she may bring two turtledoves or
two young pigeons—one as a burnt offering and the other as a sin offering. [b]So the
priest shall make atonement for her, and
she will be clean.' "

The Law Concerning Leprosy

13 And the LORD spoke to Moses and
Aaron, saying: 2"When a man has on
the skin of his body a swelling, [a]a scab, or a
bright spot, and it becomes on the skin of
his body *like* a leprous[1] sore, [b]then he shall
be brought to Aaron the priest or to one of
his sons the priests. 3The priest shall examine the sore on the skin of the body; and if
the hair on the sore has turned white, and
the sore appears *to be* deeper than the skin
of his body, it *is* a leprous sore. Then the
priest shall examine him, and pronounce
him unclean. 4But if the bright spot *is* white
on the skin of his body, and does not appear
to be deeper than the skin, and its hair has
not turned white, then the priest shall isolate *the one who has* the sore [a]seven days.
5And the priest shall examine him on the
seventh day; and indeed *if* the sore appears
to be as it was, *and* the sore has not spread
on the skin, then the priest shall isolate
him another seven days. 6Then the priest
shall examine him again on the seventh
day; and indeed *if* the sore has faded, *and*
the sore has not spread on the skin, then
the priest shall pronounce him clean; it *is*
only a scab, and he [a]shall wash his clothes
and be clean. 7But if the scab should at all
spread over the skin, after he has been seen
by the priest for his cleansing, he shall be
seen by the priest again. 8And *if* the priest
sees that the scab has indeed spread on the
skin, then the priest shall pronounce him
unclean. It *is* leprosy.

9"When the leprous sore is on a person, then he shall be brought to the priest.
10[a]And the priest shall examine *him;* and
indeed *if* the swelling on the skin *is* white,
and it has turned the hair white, and *there*
is a spot of raw flesh in the swelling, 11it *is*
an old leprosy on the skin of his body. The
priest shall pronounce him unclean, and
shall not isolate him, for he *is* unclean.

12"And if leprosy breaks out all over the
skin, and the leprosy covers all the skin of
the one who has the sore, from his head to
his foot, wherever the priest looks, 13then
the priest shall consider; and indeed *if* the
leprosy has covered all his body, he shall
pronounce *him* clean *who has* the sore.
It has all turned [a]white. He *is* clean. 14But
when raw flesh appears on him, he shall
be unclean. 15And the priest shall examine
the raw flesh and pronounce him to be unclean; *for* the raw flesh *is* unclean. It *is* leprosy. 16Or if the raw flesh changes and turns
white again, he shall come to the priest.
17And the priest shall examine him; and
indeed *if* the sore has turned white, then
the priest shall pronounce *him* clean *who*
has the sore. He *is* clean.

18"If the body develops a [a]boil in the
skin, and it is healed, 19and in the place of
the boil there comes a white swelling or
a bright spot, reddish-white, then it shall
be shown to the priest; 20and *if,* when the
priest sees it, it indeed appears deeper than
the skin, and its hair has turned white, the

12:2 [c] Lev. 18:19 **12:3** [a] Gen. 17:12; Luke 1:59; 2:21; John 7:22, 23; Gal. 5:3 **12:6** [a] Luke 2:22 [b] [John 1:29; 1 Pet. 1:18, 19] [c] Lev. 5:7 **12:8** [a] Lev. 5:7; Luke 2:22–24 [b] Lev. 4:26 **13:2** [a] Deut. 28:27; Is. 3:17 [b] Deut. 17:8, 9; 24:8; Mal. 2:7; Luke 17:14 [1] Hebrew *saraath,* disfiguring skin diseases, including leprosy, and so in verses 2–46 and 14:1–32 **13:4** [a] Lev. 14:8 **13:6** [a] Lev. 11:25; 14:8; [John 13:8, 10] **13:10** [a] Num. 12:10, 12; 2 Kin. 5:27; 2 Chr. 26:19, 20 **13:13** [a] Ex. 4:6 **13:18** [a] Ex. 9:9; 15:26

priest shall pronounce him unclean. It *is*
a leprous sore which has broken out of the
boil. 21But if the priest examines it, and indeed *there are* no white hairs in it, and it
is not deeper than the skin, but has faded,
then the priest shall isolate him seven days;
22and if it should at all spread over the skin,
then the priest shall pronounce him unclean. It *is* a leprous sore. 23But if the bright
spot stays in one place, *and* has not spread,
it *is* the scar of the boil; and the priest shall
pronounce him clean.

24"Or if the body receives a [a]burn on its
skin by fire, and the raw *flesh* of the burn becomes a bright spot, reddish-white or white,
25then the priest shall examine it; and indeed *if* the hair of the bright spot has turned
white, and it appears deeper than the skin, it
is leprosy broken out in the burn. Therefore
the priest shall pronounce him unclean. It
is a leprous sore. 26But if the priest examines it, and indeed *there are* no white hairs
in the bright spot, and it *is* not deeper than
the skin, but has faded, then the priest shall
isolate him seven days. 27And the priest
shall examine him on the seventh day. If
it has at all spread over the skin, then the
priest shall pronounce him unclean. It *is* a
leprous sore. 28But if the bright spot stays in
one place, *and* has not spread on the skin,
but has faded, it *is* a swelling from the burn.
The priest shall pronounce him clean, for
it *is* the scar from the burn.

29"If a man or woman has a sore on the
head or the beard, 30then the priest shall
examine the sore; and indeed if it appears
deeper than the skin, *and there is* in it thin
yellow hair, then the priest shall pronounce
him unclean. It *is* a scaly leprosy of the head
or beard. 31But if the priest examines the
scaly sore, and indeed it does not appear
deeper than the skin, and *there is* no black
hair in it, then the priest shall isolate *the one
who has* the scale seven days. 32And on the
seventh day the priest shall examine the
sore; and indeed *if* the scale has not spread,
and there is no yellow hair in it, and the scale
does not appear deeper than the skin, 33he
shall shave himself, but the scale he shall
not shave. And the priest shall isolate *the
one who has* the scale another seven days.
34On the seventh day the priest shall examine the scale; and indeed *if* the scale has not
spread over the skin, and does not appear
deeper than the skin, then the priest shall
pronounce him clean. He shall wash his
clothes and be clean. 35But if the scale should
at all spread over the skin after his cleansing, 36then the priest shall examine him; and
indeed *if* the scale has spread over the skin,
the priest need not seek for yellow hair. He
is unclean. 37But if the scale appears to be at
a standstill, and there is black hair grown up
in it, the scale has healed. He *is* clean, and
the priest shall pronounce him clean.

38"If a man or a woman has bright spots
on the skin of the body, *specifically* white
bright spots, 39then the priest shall look;
and indeed *if* the bright spots on the skin
of the body *are* dull white, it *is* a white spot
that grows on the skin. He *is* clean.

40"As for the man whose hair has fallen
from his head, he *is* bald, *but* he *is* clean.
41He whose hair has fallen from his forehead, he *is* bald on the forehead, *but* he *is*
clean. 42And if there is on the bald head or
bald [a]forehead a reddish-white sore, it *is*
leprosy breaking out on his bald head or
his bald forehead. 43Then the priest shall
examine it; and indeed *if* the swelling of
the sore *is* reddish-white on his bald head
or on his bald forehead, as the appearance
of leprosy on the skin of the body, 44he is
a leprous man. He *is* unclean. The priest
shall surely pronounce him unclean; his
sore *is* on his [a]head.

45"Now the leper on whom the sore
is, his clothes shall be torn and his head
[a]bare; and he shall [b]cover his mustache,
and cry, [c]'Unclean! Unclean!' 46He shall be
unclean. All the days he has the sore he
shall be unclean. He *is* unclean, and he shall
dwell alone; his dwelling *shall be* [a]outside
the camp.

The Law Concerning Leprous Garments

47"Also, if a garment has a leprous
plague[1] in it, *whether it is* a woolen garment or a linen garment, 48whether *it is* in
the warp or woof of linen or wool, whether

13:24 [a] Is. 3:24 13:42 [a] 2 Chr. 26:19 13:44 [a] Is. 1:5 13:45 [a] Lev. 10:6; 21:10 [b] Ezek. 24:17, 22; Mic. 3:7 [c] Is. 6:5; 64:6; Lam. 4:15; Luke 5:8 13:46 [a] Num. 5:1–4; 12:14; 2 Kin. 7:3; 15:5; 2 Chr. 26:21; Ps. 38:11; Luke 17:12
13:47 [1] A mold, fungus, or similar infestation, and so in verses 47–59

in leather or in anything made of leather, 49and if the plague is greenish or reddish in the garment or in the leather, whether in the warp or in the woof, or in anything made of leather, it *is* a leprous plague and shall be shown to the priest. 50The priest shall examine the plague and isolate *that which has* the plague seven days. 51And he shall examine the plague on the seventh day. If the plague has spread in the garment, either in the warp or in the woof, in the leather *or* in anything made of leather, the plague *is* [a]an active leprosy. It *is* unclean. 52He shall therefore burn that garment in which is the plague, whether warp or woof, in wool or in linen, or anything of leather, for it *is* an active leprosy; *the garment* shall be burned in the fire.

53"But if the priest examines *it*, and indeed the plague has not spread in the garment, either in the warp or in the woof, or in anything made of leather, 54then the priest shall command that they wash *the thing* in which *is* the plague; and he shall isolate it another seven days. 55Then the priest shall examine the plague after it has been washed; and indeed *if* the plague has not changed its color, though the plague has not spread, it *is* unclean, and you shall burn it in the fire; it continues eating away, *whether* the damage *is* outside or inside. 56If the priest examines *it*, and indeed the plague has faded after washing it, then he shall tear it out of the garment, whether out of the warp or out of the woof, or out of the leather. 57But if it appears again in the garment, either in the warp or in the woof, or in anything made of leather, it *is* a spreading *plague;* you shall burn with fire that in which is the plague. 58And if you wash the garment, either warp or woof, or whatever is made of leather, if the plague has disappeared from it, then it shall be washed a second time, and shall be clean.

59"This *is* the law of the leprous plague in a garment of wool or linen, either in the warp or woof, or in anything made of leather, to pronounce it clean or to pronounce it unclean."

The Ritual for Cleansing Healed Lepers
(cf. Matt. 8:1–4; Luke 5:12–14)

14 Then the LORD spoke to Moses, saying, 2"This shall be the law of the leper for the day of his cleansing: He [a]shall be brought to the priest. 3And the priest shall go out of the camp, and the priest shall examine *him;* and indeed, *if* the leprosy is healed in the leper, 4then the priest shall command to take for him who is to be cleansed two living *and* clean birds, [a]cedar wood, [b]scarlet, and [c]hyssop. 5And the priest shall command that one of the birds be killed in an earthen vessel over running water. 6As for the living bird, he shall take it, the cedar wood and the scarlet and the hyssop, and dip them and the living bird in the blood of the bird *that was* killed over the running water. 7And he shall [a]sprinkle it [b]seven times on him who is to be cleansed from the leprosy, and shall pronounce him clean, and shall let the living bird loose in the open field. 8He who is to be cleansed [a]shall wash his clothes, shave off all his hair, and [b]wash himself in water, that he may be clean. After that he shall come into the camp, and [c]shall stay outside his tent seven days. 9But on the [a]seventh day he shall shave all the hair off his head and his beard and his eyebrows—all his hair he shall shave off. He shall wash his clothes and wash his body in water, and he shall be clean.

10"And on the eighth day [a]he shall take two male lambs without blemish, one ewe lamb of the first year without blemish, three-tenths *of an ephah* of fine flour mixed with oil as [b]a grain offering, and one log of oil. 11Then the priest who makes *him* clean shall present the man who is to be made clean, and those things, before the LORD, *at* the door of the tabernacle of meeting. 12And the priest shall take one male lamb and [a]offer it as a trespass offering, and the log of oil, and [b]wave them *as* a wave offering before the LORD. 13Then he shall kill the lamb [a]in the place where he kills the sin offering and the burnt offering, in a holy place; for [b]as the sin offering *is* the priest's, so *is* the trespass offering. [c]It *is*

13:51 [a] Lev. 14:44 14:2 [a] Matt. 8:2, 4; Mark 1:40, 44; Luke 5:12, 14; 17:14 14:4 [a] Lev. 14:6, 49, 51, 52; Num. 19:6; Heb. 9:19 [b] Ex. 25:4 [c] Ex. 12:22; Ps. 51:7 14:7 [a] Num. 19:18, 19; [Heb. 9:13, 21; 12:24] [b] 2 Kin. 5:10, 14; Ps. 51:2 14:8 [a] Lev. 11:25; 13:6; Num. 8:7 [b] Lev. 11:25; [Eph. 5:26; Heb. 10:22; Rev. 1:5, 6] [c] Lev. 13:5; Num. 5:2, 3; 12:14, 15; 2 Chr. 26:21 14:9 [a] Num. 19:19 14:10 [a] Matt. 8:4; Mark 1:44; Luke 5:14 [b] Lev. 2:1; Num. 15:4 14:12 [a] Lev. 5:6, 18; 6:6; 14:19 [b] Ex. 29:22–24, 26 14:13 [a] Ex. 29:11; Lev. 1:5, 11; 4:4, 24 [b] Lev. 6:24–30; 7:7 [c] Lev. 2:3; 7:6; 21:22

most holy. 14The priest shall take *some* of
the blood of the trespass offering, and the
priest shall put *it* [a]on the tip of the right
ear of him who is to be cleansed, on the
thumb of his right hand, and on the big toe
of his right foot. 15And the priest shall take
some of the log of oil, and pour *it* into the
palm of his own left hand. 16Then the priest
shall dip his right finger in the oil that *is* in
his left hand, and shall [a]sprinkle some of
the oil with his finger seven times before
the LORD. 17And of the rest of the oil in his
hand, the priest shall put *some* on the tip of
the right ear of him who is to be cleansed,
on the thumb of his right hand, and on the
big toe of his right foot, on the blood of the
trespass offering. 18The rest of the oil that
is in the priest's hand he shall put on the
head of him who is to be cleansed. [a]So the
priest shall make atonement for him before the LORD.

19"Then the priest shall offer [a]the sin offering, and make atonement for him who
is to be cleansed from his uncleanness.
Afterward he shall kill the burnt offering.
20And the priest shall offer the burnt offering and the grain offering on the altar. So
the priest shall make atonement for him,
and he shall be [a]clean.

21"But [a]if he *is* poor and cannot afford
it, then he shall take one male lamb *as* a
trespass offering to be waved, to make
atonement for him, one-tenth *of an ephah*
of fine flour mixed with oil as a grain offering, a log of oil, 22[a]and two turtledoves
or two young pigeons, such as he is able to
afford: one shall be a sin offering and the
other a burnt offering. 23[a]He shall bring
them to the priest on the eighth day for his
cleansing, to the door of the tabernacle of
meeting, before the LORD. 24[a]And the priest
shall take the lamb of the trespass offering
and the log of oil, and the priest shall wave
them *as* a wave offering before the LORD.
25Then he shall kill the lamb of the trespass
offering, [a]and the priest shall take *some* of
the blood of the trespass offering and put
it on the tip of the right ear of him who is
to be cleansed, on the thumb of his right
hand, and on the big toe of his right foot.
26And the priest shall pour some of the oil
into the palm of his own left hand. 27Then
the priest shall sprinkle with his right finger *some* of the oil that *is* in his left hand
seven times before the LORD. 28And the
priest shall put *some* of the oil that *is* in his
hand on the tip of the right ear of him who
is to be cleansed, on the thumb of the right
hand, and on the big toe of his right foot,
on the place of the blood of the trespass
offering. 29The rest of the oil that *is* in the
priest's hand he shall put on the head of
him who is to be cleansed, to make atonement for him before the LORD. 30And he
shall offer one of [a]the turtledoves or young
pigeons, such as he can afford— 31such as
he is able to afford, the one *as* a sin offering and the other *as* a burnt offering, with
the grain offering. So the priest shall make
atonement for him who is to be cleansed
before the LORD. 32This *is* the law *for one*
who had a leprous sore, who cannot afford
[a]the usual cleansing."

The Law Concerning Leprous Houses

33And the LORD spoke to Moses and
Aaron, saying: 34[a]"When you have come
into the land of Canaan, which I give you as
a possession, and [b]I put the leprous plague[1]
in a house in the land of your possession,
35and he who owns the house comes and
tells the priest, saying, 'It seems to me that
there is [a]some plague in the house,' 36then
the priest shall command that they empty
the house, before the priest goes *into it* to
examine the plague, that all that *is* in the
house may not be made unclean; and afterward the priest shall go in to examine the
house. 37And he shall examine the plague;
and indeed *if* the plague *is* on the walls of
the house with ingrained streaks, greenish
or reddish, which appear to be deep in the
wall, 38then the priest shall go out of the
house, to the door of the house, and shut up
the house seven days. 39And the priest shall
come again on the seventh day and look;
and indeed *if* the plague has spread on the
walls of the house, 40then the priest shall
command that they take away the stones
in which *is* the plague, and they shall cast

14:14 [a] Ex. 29:20; Lev. 8:23, 24 14:16 [a] Lev. 4:6 14:18 [a] Lev. 4:26; 5:6; Num. 15:28; [Heb. 2:17] 14:19 [a] Lev. 5:1, 6; 12:7; [2 Cor. 5:21] 14:20 [a] Lev. 14:8, 9 14:21 [a] Lev. 5:7, 11; 12:8; 27:8 14:22 [a] Lev. 12:8; 15:14, 15 14:23 [a] Lev. 14:10, 11 14:24 [a] Lev. 14:12 14:25 [a] Lev. 14:14, 17 14:30 [a] Lev. 14:22; 15:14, 15 14:32 [a] Lev. 14:10 14:34 [a] Gen. 12:7; 13:17; 17:8; Num. 32:22; Deut. 7:1; 32:49 [b] [Prov. 3:33]

[1] Decomposition by mildew, mold, dry rot, etc., and so in verses 34–53 14:35 [a] [Ps. 91:9, 10; Prov. 3:33; Zech. 5:4]

them into an unclean place outside the
city. 41And he shall cause the house to be
scraped inside, all around, and the dust
that they scrape off they shall pour out in
an unclean place outside the city. 42Then
they shall take other stones and put *them*
in the place of *those* stones, and he shall
take other mortar and plaster the house.

43"Now if the plague comes back and
breaks out in the house, after he has taken
away the stones, after he has scraped the
house, and after it is plastered, 44then the
priest shall come and look; and indeed *if*
the plague has spread in the house, it *is* [a]an
active leprosy in the house. It *is* unclean.
45And he shall break down the house, its
stones, its timber, and all the plaster of the
house, and he shall carry *them* outside the
city to an unclean place. 46Moreover he who
goes into the house at all while it is shut up
shall be unclean [a]until evening. 47And he
who lies down in the house shall [a]wash his
clothes, and he who eats in the house shall
wash his clothes.

48"But if the priest comes in and examines *it,* and indeed the plague has not spread
in the house after the house was plastered,
then the priest shall pronounce the house
clean, because the plague is healed. 49And
[a]he shall take, to cleanse the house, two
birds, cedar wood, scarlet, and hyssop.
50Then he shall kill one of the birds in an
earthen vessel over running water; 51and he
shall take the cedar wood, the hyssop, the
scarlet, and the living bird, and dip them in
the blood of the slain bird and in the running water, and sprinkle the house seven
times. 52And he shall cleanse the house with
the blood of the bird and the running water
and the living bird, with the cedar wood, the
hyssop, and the scarlet. 53Then he shall let
the living bird loose outside the city in the
open field, and [a]make atonement for the
house, and it shall be clean.

54"This *is* the law for any [a]leprous sore
and scale, 55for the [a]leprosy of a garment
[b]and of a house, 56[a]for a swelling and a scab
and a bright spot, 57to [a]teach when *it is* unclean and when *it is* clean. This *is* the law
of leprosy."

The Law Concerning Bodily Discharges

15 And the LORD spoke to Moses and
Aaron, saying, 2"Speak to the children of Israel, and say to them: [a]'When any
man has a discharge from his body, his discharge *is* unclean. 3And this shall be his
uncleanness in regard to his discharge—
whether his body runs with his discharge,
or his body is stopped up by his discharge,
it *is* his uncleanness. 4Every bed is unclean
on which he who has the discharge lies,
and everything on which he sits shall be
unclean. 5And whoever [a]touches his bed
shall [b]wash his clothes and [c]bathe in water, and be unclean until evening. 6He who
sits on anything on which he who has the
[a]discharge sat shall wash his clothes and
bathe in water, and be unclean until evening. 7And he who touches the body of
him who has the discharge shall wash his
clothes and bathe in water, and be unclean
until evening. 8If he who has the discharge
[a]spits on him who is clean, then he shall
wash his clothes and bathe in water, and
be unclean until evening. 9Any saddle on
which he who has the discharge rides shall
be unclean. 10Whoever touches anything
that was under him shall be unclean until evening. He who carries *any of* those
things shall wash his clothes and bathe in
water, and be unclean until evening. 11And
whomever the one who has the discharge
touches, and has not rinsed his hands in
water, he shall wash his clothes and bathe
in water, and be unclean until evening.
12The [a]vessel of earth that he who has the
discharge touches shall be broken, and every vessel of wood shall be rinsed in water.

13'And when he who has a discharge is
cleansed of his discharge, then [a]he shall
count for himself seven days for his cleansing, wash his clothes, and bathe his body
in running water; then he shall be clean.
14On the eighth day he shall take for himself
[a]two turtledoves or two young pigeons, and
come before the LORD, to the door of the
tabernacle of meeting, and give them to the
priest. 15Then the priest shall offer them,
[a]the one *as* a sin offering and the other *as*
a burnt offering. [b]So the priest shall make

14:44 [a] Lev. 13:51; [Zech. 5:4] 14:46 [a] Lev. 11:24; 15:5 14:47 [a] Lev. 14:8 14:49 [a] Lev. 14:4 14:53 [a] Lev. 14:20 14:54 [a] Lev. 13:30; 26:21 14:55 [a] Lev. 13:47–52 [b] Lev. 14:34 14:56 [a] Lev. 13:2 14:57 [a] Lev. 11:47; 20:25; Deut. 24:8; Ezek. 44:23 15:2 [a] Lev. 22:4; Num. 5:2; 2 Sam. 3:29 15:5 [a] Lev. 5:2; 14:46 [b] Lev. 14:8, 47 [c] Lev. 11:25; 17:15 15:6 [a] Lev. 15:10; Deut. 23:10 15:8 [a] Num. 12:14 15:12 [a] Lev. 6:28; 11:32, 33 15:13 [a] Lev. 14:8; 15:28; Num. 19:11, 12 15:14 [a] Lev. 14:22, 23, 30, 31 15:15 [a] Lev. 14:30, 31 [b] Lev. 14:19, 31

atonement for him before the LORD because of his discharge.
16[a]'If any man has an emission of semen,
then he shall wash all his body in water,
and be unclean until evening. 17And any
garment and any leather on which there is
semen, it shall be washed with water, and
be unclean until evening. 18Also, when a
woman lies with a man, and *there is* an
emission of semen, they shall bathe in water, and [a]be unclean until evening.
19[a]'If a woman has a discharge, *and* the
discharge from her body is blood, she
shall be set apart seven days; and whoever
touches her shall be unclean until evening.
20Everything that she lies on during her
impurity shall be unclean; also everything
that she sits on shall be unclean. 21Whoever
touches her bed shall wash his clothes and
bathe in water, and be unclean until evening. 22And whoever touches anything that
she sat on shall wash his clothes and bathe
in water, and be unclean until evening. 23If
anything is on *her* bed or on anything on
which she sits, when he touches it, he shall
be unclean until evening. 24And [a]if any man
lies with her at all, so that her impurity is
on him, he shall be unclean seven days; and
every bed on which he lies shall be unclean.
25'If [a]a woman has a discharge of blood
for many days, other than at the time of her
customary impurity, or if it runs beyond
her *usual time of* impurity, all the days of
her unclean discharge shall be as the days
of her *customary* impurity. She *shall be* unclean. 26Every bed on which she lies all the
days of her discharge shall be to her as the
bed of her impurity; and whatever she sits
on shall be unclean, as the uncleanness
of her impurity. 27Whoever touches those
things shall be unclean; he shall wash his
clothes and bathe in water, and be unclean
until evening.
28'But [a]if she is cleansed of her discharge,
then she shall count for herself seven days,
and after that she shall be clean. 29And on
the eighth day she shall take for herself
two turtledoves or two young pigeons, and
bring them to the priest, to the door of the
tabernacle of meeting. 30Then the priest
shall offer the one *as* a sin offering and the
other *as* a [a]burnt offering, and the priest
shall make atonement for her before the
LORD for the discharge of her uncleanness.
31"Thus you shall [a]separate the children
of Israel from their uncleanness, lest they
die in their uncleanness when they [b]defile
My tabernacle that *is* among them. 32[a]This
is the law for one who has a discharge, [b]and
for him who emits semen and is unclean
thereby, 33[a]and for her who is indisposed
because of her *customary* impurity, and
for one who has a discharge, either man
[b]or woman, [c]and for him who lies with her
who is unclean.' "

The Day of Atonement

16 Now the LORD spoke to Moses after
[a]the death of the two sons of Aaron,
when they offered *profane fire* before the
LORD, and died; 2and the LORD said to Moses: "Tell Aaron your brother [a]not to come
at *just* any time into the Holy *Place* inside
the veil, before the mercy seat which *is* on
the ark, lest he die; for [b]I will appear in the
cloud above the mercy seat.
3"Thus Aaron shall [a]come into the Holy
Place: [b]with *the blood of* a young bull as a
sin offering, and *of* a ram as a burnt offering. 4He shall put the [a]holy linen tunic
and the linen trousers on his body; he shall
be girded with a linen sash, and with the
linen turban he shall be attired. These *are*
holy garments. Therefore [b]he shall wash
his body in water, and put them on. 5And
he shall take from [a]the congregation of the
children of Israel two kids of the goats as
a sin offering, and one ram as a burnt offering.
6"Aaron shall offer the bull as a sin offering, which *is* for himself, and [a]make atonement for himself and for his house. 7He
shall take the two goats and present them
before the LORD *at* the door of the tabernacle of meeting. 8Then Aaron shall cast
lots for the two goats: one lot for the LORD

15:16 [a] Lev. 22:4; Deut. 23:10, 11 15:18 [a] [Ex. 19:15; 1 Sam. 21:4; 1 Cor. 6:18] 15:19 [a] Lev. 12:2 15:24 [a] Lev. 18:19; 20:18 15:25 [a] Matt. 9:20; Mark 5:25; Luke 8:43 15:28 [a] Lev. 15:13–15 15:30 [a] Lev. 5:7 15:31 [a] Lev. 11:47; 14:57; 22:2; Deut. 24:8; Ezek. 44:23; [Heb. 12:15] [b] Lev. 20:3; Num. 5:3; 19:13, 20; Ezek. 5:11; 23:38; 36:17 15:32 [a] Lev. 15:2 [b] Lev. 15:16 15:33 [a] Lev. 15:19 [b] Lev. 15:25 [c] Lev. 15:24 16:1 [a] Lev. 10:1, 2; 2 Sam. 6:6–8 16:2 [a] Ex. 30:10; Lev. 16:34; 23:27; [Heb. 6:19; 9:7, 8, 12; 10:19] [b] Ex. 25:21, 22; 40:34; 1 Kin. 8:10–12 16:3 [a] Lev. 4:1–12; 16:6; [Heb. 9:7, 12, 24, 25] [b] Lev. 4:3 16:4 [a] Ex. 28:39, 42, 43; Lev. 6:10; Ezek. 44:17, 18 [b] Ex. 30:20; Lev. 8:6, 7 16:5 [a] Lev. 4:14; Num. 29:11; 2 Chr. 29:21; Ezra 6:17; Ezek. 45:22, 23 16:6 [a] Lev. 9:7; [Heb. 5:3; 7:27, 28; 9:7]

and the other lot for the scapegoat. 9And
Aaron shall bring the goat on which the
LORD's lot fell, and offer it *as* a sin offering. 10But the goat on which the lot fell to
be the scapegoat shall be presented alive
before the LORD, to make [a]atonement upon
it, *and* to let it go as the scapegoat into the
wilderness.
11"And Aaron shall bring the bull of the
sin offering, which is for [a]himself, and
make atonement for himself and for his
house, and shall kill the bull as the sin offering which *is* for himself. 12Then he shall
take [a]a censer full of burning coals of fire
from the altar before the LORD, with his
hands full of [b]sweet incense beaten fine,
and bring *it* inside the veil. 13[a]And he shall
put the incense on the fire before the LORD,
that the cloud of incense may cover the
[b]mercy seat that *is* on the Testimony, lest
he [c]die. 14[a]He shall take some of the blood
of the bull and [b]sprinkle *it* with his finger
on the mercy seat on the east *side;* and before the mercy seat he shall sprinkle some
of the blood with his finger seven times.
15[a]"Then he shall kill the goat of the sin
offering, which *is* for the people, bring its
blood [b]inside the veil, do with that blood
as he did with the blood of the bull, and
sprinkle it on the mercy seat and before
the mercy seat. 16So he shall [a]make atonement for the Holy *Place,* because of the
uncleanness of the children of Israel, and
because of their transgressions, for all their
sins; and so he shall do for the tabernacle
of meeting which remains among them
in the midst of their uncleanness. 17There
shall be [a]no man in the tabernacle of meeting when he goes in to make atonement in
the Holy *Place,* until he comes out, that he
may make atonement for himself, for his
household, and for all the assembly of Israel. 18And he shall go out to the altar that *is*
before the LORD, and make atonement for
[a]it, and shall take some of the blood of the
bull and some of the blood of the goat, and
put it on the horns of the altar all around.
19Then he shall sprinkle some of the blood
on it with his finger seven times, cleanse it,
and [a]consecrate it from the uncleanness of
the children of Israel.
20"And when he has made an end of
atoning for the Holy *Place,* the tabernacle
of meeting, and the altar, he shall bring the
live goat. 21Aaron shall lay both his hands
on the head of the live goat, [a]confess over
it all the iniquities of the children of Israel,
and all their transgressions, concerning all
their sins, [b]putting them on the head of the
goat, and shall send *it* away into the wilderness by the hand of a suitable man. 22The
goat shall [a]bear on itself all their iniquities
to an uninhabited land; and he shall [b]re-
lease the goat in the wilderness.
23"Then Aaron shall come into the tabernacle of meeting, [a]shall take off the linen
garments which he put on when he went
into the Holy *Place,* and shall leave them
there. 24And he shall wash his body with
water in a holy place, put on his garments,
come out and offer his burnt offering and
the burnt offering of the people, and make
atonement for himself and for the people.
25[a]The fat of the sin offering he shall burn
on the altar. 26And he who released the goat
as the scapegoat shall wash his clothes [a]and
bathe his body in water, and afterward he
may come into the camp. 27[a]The bull *for* the
sin offering and the goat *for* the sin offering, whose blood was brought in to make
atonement in the Holy *Place,* shall be carried outside the camp. And they shall burn
in the fire their skins, their flesh, and their
offal. 28Then he who burns them shall wash
his clothes and bathe his body in water,
and afterward he may come into the camp.
29"*This* shall be a statute forever for you:
[a]In the seventh month, on the tenth *day*
of the month, you shall afflict your souls,
and do no work at all, *whether* a native of
your own country or a stranger who dwells
among you. 30For on that day *the priest*
shall make atonement for you, to [a]cleanse
you, *that* you may be clean from all your
sins before the LORD. 31[a]It *is* a sabbath of
solemn rest for you, and you shall afflict

16:10 [a] [Is. 53:5, 6; Rom. 3:25; Heb. 7:27; 9:23, 24; 1 John 2:2] 16:11 [a] [Heb. 7:27; 9:7] 16:12 [a] Lev. 10:1; Num. 16:7, 18; Is. 6:6, 7; Rev. 8:5 [b] Ex. 30:34–38 16:13 [a] Ex. 30:7, 8; Num. 16:7, 18, 46 [b] Ex. 25:21 [c] Ex. 28:43; Lev. 22:9; Num. 4:15, 20 16:14 [a] Lev. 4:5; [Heb. 9:25; 10:4] [b] Lev. 4:6, 17 16:15 [a] [Heb. 2:17] [b] [Heb. 6:19; 7:27; 9:3, 7, 12] 16:16 [a] Ex. 29:36; 30:10; Ezek. 45:18; [Heb. 9:22–24] 16:17 [a] Ex. 34:3; Luke 1:10 16:18 [a] Ex. 29:36 16:19 [a] Lev. 16:14; Ezek. 43:20 16:21 [a] Lev. 5:5; 26:40 [b] [Is. 53:6] 16:22 [a] Lev. 8:14; [Is. 53:6, 11, 12; John 1:29; Heb. 9:28; 1 Pet. 2:24] [b] Lev. 14:7 16:23 [a] Lev. 6:11; 16:4; Ezek. 42:14; 44:19 16:25 [a] Lev. 1:8; 4:10 16:26 [a] Lev. 15:5 16:27 [a] Lev. 4:12, 21; 6:30; Heb. 13:11 16:29 [a] Ex. 30:10; Lev. 23:27–32; Num. 29:7 16:30 [a] Ps. 51:2; Jer. 33:8; [Eph. 5:26; Heb. 9:13, 14; 1 John 1:7, 9] 16:31 [a] Lev. 23:27, 32; Ezra 8:21; Is. 58:3, 5; Dan. 10:12

your souls. *It is* a statute forever. 32[a]And the priest, who is anointed and [b]consecrated to minister as priest in his father's place, shall make atonement, and put on the linen clothes, the holy garments; 33then he shall make atonement for the Holy Sanctuary,[1] and he shall make atonement for the tabernacle of meeting and for the altar, and he shall make atonement for the priests and for all the people of the assembly. 34[a]This shall be an everlasting statute for you, to make atonement for the children of Israel, for all their sins, [b]once a year." And he did as the LORD commanded Moses.

The Sanctity of Blood

17 And the LORD spoke to Moses, saying, 2"Speak to Aaron, to his sons, and to all the children of Israel, and say to them, 'This *is* the thing which the LORD has commanded, saying: 3"Whatever man of the house of Israel who [a]kills an ox or lamb or goat in the camp, or who kills *it* outside the camp, 4and does not bring it to the door of the tabernacle of meeting to offer an offering to the LORD before the tabernacle of the LORD, the guilt of bloodshed shall be [a]imputed to that man. He has shed blood; and that man shall be cut off from among his people, 5to the end that the children of Israel may bring their sacrifices [a]which they offer in the open field, that they may bring them to the LORD at the door of the tabernacle of meeting, to the priest, and offer them *as* peace offerings to the LORD. 6And the priest [a]shall sprinkle the blood on the altar of the LORD *at* the door of the tabernacle of meeting, and [b]burn the fat for a sweet aroma to the LORD. 7They shall no more offer their sacrifices [a]to demons, after whom they [b]have played the harlot. This shall be a statute forever for them throughout their generations."'

8"Also you shall say to them: 'Whatever man of the house of Israel, or of the strangers who dwell among you, [a]who offers a burnt offering or sacrifice, 9and does not [a]bring it to the door of the tabernacle of meeting, to offer it to the LORD, that man shall be cut off from among his people.

10[a]'And whatever man of the house of Israel, or of the strangers who dwell among you, who eats any blood, [b]I will set My face against that person who eats blood, and will cut him off from among his people. 11For the [a]life of the flesh *is* in the blood, and I have given it to you upon the altar [b]to make atonement for your souls; for [c]it *is* the blood *that* makes atonement for the soul.' 12Therefore I said to the children of Israel, 'No one among you shall eat blood, nor shall any stranger who dwells among you eat blood.'

13"Whatever man of the children of Israel, or of the strangers who dwell among you, who [a]hunts and catches any animal or bird that may be eaten, he shall [b]pour out its blood and [c]cover it with dust; 14[a]for *it is* the life of all flesh. Its blood sustains its life. Therefore I said to the children of Israel, 'You shall not eat the blood of any flesh, for the life of all flesh is its blood. Whoever eats it shall be cut off.'

15[a]"And every person who eats what died *naturally* or what was torn *by beasts, whether he is* a native of your own country or a stranger, [b]he shall both wash his clothes and [c]bathe in water, and be unclean until evening. Then he shall be clean. 16But if he does not wash *them* or bathe his body, then [a]he shall bear his guilt."

Laws of Sexual Morality

18 Then the LORD spoke to Moses, saying, 2"Speak to the children of Israel, and say to them: [a]'I am the LORD your God. 3[a]According to the doings of the land of Egypt, where you dwelt, you shall not do; and [b]according to the doings of the land of Canaan, where I am bringing you, you shall not do; nor shall you walk in their ordinances. 4[a]You shall observe My judgments and keep My ordinances, to walk in them: I *am* the LORD your God. 5You shall

---

16:32 [a] Lev. 4:3, 5, 16; 21:10 [b] Ex. 29:29, 30; Num. 20:26, 28 **16:33** [1] That is, *the Most Holy Place* **16:34** [a] Lev. 23:31; Num. 29:7 [b] Ex. 30:10; [Heb. 9:7, 25, 28] **17:3** [a] Deut. 12:5, 15, 21 **17:4** [a] Rom. 5:13 **17:5** [a] Gen. 21:33; 22:2; 31:54; Deut. 12:1–27; Ezek. 20:28 **17:6** [a] Lev. 3:2 [b] Ex. 29:13, 18; Num. 18:17 **17:7** [a] Ex. 22:20; 32:8; 34:15; Deut. 32:17; 2 Chr. 11:15; Ps. 106:37; 1 Cor. 10:20 [b] Ex. 34:15; Deut. 31:16; Ezek. 23:8 **17:8** [a] Lev. 1:2, 3; 18:26 **17:9** [a] Lev. 14:23 **17:10** [a] Gen. 9:4; Lev. 3:17; 7:26, 27; Deut. 12:16, 23–25; 15:23; 1 Sam. 14:33 [b] Lev. 20:3, 5, 6 **17:11** [a] Gen. 9:4; Lev. 17:14 [b] [Matt. 26:28; Rom. 3:25; Eph. 1:7; Col. 1:14, 20; 1 Pet. 1:2; 1 John 1:7] [c] [Heb. 9:22] **17:13** [a] Lev. 7:26 [b] Deut. 12:16, 24 [c] Ezek. 24:7 **17:14** [a] Gen. 9:4; Lev. 17:11; Deut. 12:23 **17:15** [a] Ex. 22:31; Lev. 7:24; 22:8; Deut. 14:21; Ezek. 4:14; 44:31 [b] Lev. 11:25 [c] Lev. 15:5 **17:16** [a] Lev. 5:1 **18:2** [a] Ex. 6:7; Lev. 11:44, 45; 19:3; Ezek. 20:5, 7, 19, 20 **18:3** [a] Josh. 24:14; Ezek. 20:7, 8 [b] Ex. 23:24; Lev. 18:24–30; 20:23; Deut. 12:30, 31 **18:4** [a] Ezek. 20:19

therefore keep My statutes and My judgments, which if a man does, he shall live
by them: I *am* the LORD.
6'None of you shall approach anyone
who is near of kin to him, to uncover his
nakedness: I *am* the LORD. 7The nakedness of your father or the nakedness of
your mother you shall not uncover. She *is*
your mother; you shall not uncover her nakedness. 8The nakedness of your [a]father's
wife you shall not uncover; it *is* your father's nakedness. 9[a]The nakedness of your
sister, the daughter of your father, or the
daughter of your mother, *whether* born at
home or elsewhere, their nakedness you
shall not uncover. 10The nakedness of your
son's daughter or your daughter's daughter, their nakedness you shall not uncover;
for theirs *is* your own nakedness. 11The
nakedness of your father's wife's daughter, begotten by your father—she *is* your
sister—you shall not uncover her nakedness. 12[a]You shall not uncover the nakedness of your father's sister; she *is* near of
kin to your father. 13You shall not uncover
the nakedness of your mother's sister, for
she *is* near of kin to your mother. 14[a]You
shall not uncover the nakedness of your
father's brother. You shall not approach his
wife; she *is* your aunt. 15You shall not uncover the nakedness of your daughter-in-
law—she *is* your son's wife—you shall not
uncover her nakedness. 16You shall not uncover the nakedness of your brother's wife;
it *is* your brother's nakedness. 17You shall
not uncover the nakedness of a woman
and her [a]daughter, nor shall you take her
son's daughter or her daughter's daughter, to uncover her nakedness. They *are*
near of kin to her. It *is* wickedness. 18Nor
shall you take a woman [a]as a rival to her
sister, to uncover her nakedness while the
other is alive.
19'Also you shall not approach a woman
to uncover her nakedness as [a]long as she
is in her [b]*customary* impurity. 20[a]Moreover
you shall not lie carnally with your [b]neigh-
bor's wife, to defile yourself with her. 21And
you shall not let any of your descendants
[a]pass through [b]*the fire* to [c]Molech, nor shall
you profane the name of your God: I *am* the
LORD. 22You shall not lie with [a]a male as
with a woman. It *is* an abomination. 23Nor
shall you mate with any [a]animal, to defile
yourself with it. Nor shall any woman stand
before an animal to mate with it. It *is* perversion.
24[a]'Do not defile yourselves with any of
these things; [b]for by all these the nations
are defiled, which I am casting out before
you. 25For [a]the land is defiled; therefore I
[b]visit the punishment of its iniquity upon
it, and the land [c]vomits out its inhabitants.
26[a]You shall therefore keep My statutes and
My judgments, and shall not commit *any* of
these abominations, *either* any of your own
nation or any stranger who dwells among
you 27(for all these abominations the men
of the land have done, who *were* before
you, and thus the land is defiled), 28lest [a]the
land vomit you out also when you defile
it, as it vomited out the nations that *were*
before you. 29For whoever commits any
of these abominations, the persons who
commit *them* shall be cut off from among
their people.
30'Therefore you shall keep My ordinance, so [a]that *you* do not commit *any* of
these abominable customs which were
committed before you, and that you do
not defile yourselves by them: [b]I *am* the
LORD your God.'"

Moral and Ceremonial Laws

19 And the LORD spoke to Moses, saying, 2"Speak to all the congregation
of the children of Israel, and say to them:
[a]'You shall be holy, for I the LORD your God
am holy.
3[a]'Every one of you shall revere his
mother and his father, and [b]keep My Sabbaths: I *am* the LORD your God.
4[a]'Do not turn to idols, [b]nor make for
yourselves molded gods: I *am* the LORD
your God.
5'And [a]if you offer a sacrifice of a peace

18:8 [a] Gen. 35:22 18:9 [a] Lev. 18:11; 20:17; Deut. 27:22 18:12 [a] Lev. 20:19 18:14 [a] Lev. 20:20 18:17 [a] Lev. 20:14 18:18 [a] 1 Sam. 1:6, 8
18:19 [a] Ezek. 18:6 [b] Lev. 15:24; 20:18 18:20 [a] [Prov. 6:25–33] [b] Ex. 20:14; Lev. 20:10; [Matt. 5:27, 28; 1 Cor. 6:9; Heb. 13:4]
18:21 [a] Lev. 20:2–5; Deut. 12:31 [b] 2 Kin. 16:3 [c] 1 Kin. 11:7, 33; Acts 7:43 18:22 [a] Lev. 20:13; Rom. 1:27 18:23 [a] Ex. 22:19; Lev. 20:15, 16;
Deut. 27:21 18:24 [a] Matt. 15:18–20; 1 Cor. 3:17 [b] Lev. 18:3; 20:23; Deut. 18:12 18:25 [a] Num. 35:33, 34; Ezek. 36:17 [b] Is. 26:21; Jer. 5:9
[c] Lev. 18:28; 20:22 18:26 [a] Lev. 18:5, 30 18:28 [a] Jer. 9:19 18:30 [a] Lev. 18:3; 22:9 [b] Lev. 18:2 19:2 [a] Ex. 19:6; Lev. 11:44; 20:7, 26;
[Eph. 1:4]; 1 Pet. 1:16 19:3 [a] Ex. 20:12; Deut. 5:16; Matt. 15:4; Eph. 6:2 [b] Ex. 16:23; 20:8; 31:13
19:4 [a] Ex. 20:4; Ps. 96:5; 115:4–7; 1 Cor. 10:14; [Col. 3:5] [b] Ex. 34:17 19:5 [a] Lev. 7:16

offering to the LORD, you shall offer it of
your own free will. 6It shall be eaten the
same day you offer *it,* and on the next day.
And if any remains until the third day, it
shall be burned in the fire. 7And if it is eaten
at all on the third day, it *is* an abomination.
It shall not be accepted. 8Therefore *everyone* who eats it shall bear his iniquity, because he has profaned the hallowed *offering*
of the LORD; and that person shall be cut
off from his people.

9[a]'When you reap the harvest of your
land, you shall not wholly reap the corners
of your field, nor shall you gather the gleanings of your harvest. 10And you shall not
glean your vineyard, nor shall you gather
every grape of your vineyard; you shall
leave them for the poor and the stranger:
I *am* the LORD your God.

11[a]'You shall not steal, nor deal falsely,
[b]nor lie to one another. 12And you shall not
[a]swear by My name falsely, [b]nor shall you
profane the name of your God: I *am* the
LORD.

13[a]'You shall not cheat your neighbor,
nor rob *him.* [b]The wages of him who is hired
shall not remain with you all night until
morning. 14You shall not curse the deaf,
[a]nor put a stumbling block before the blind,
but shall fear your God: I *am* the LORD.

15'You shall do no injustice in [a]judgment.
You shall not [b]be partial to the poor, nor
honor the person of the mighty. In righteousness you shall judge your neighbor.
16You shall not go about *as* a [a]talebearer
among your people; nor shall you [b]take a
stand against the life of your neighbor: I
am the LORD.

17[a]'You shall not hate your brother in
your heart. [b]You shall surely rebuke your
neighbor, and not bear sin because of him.
18[a]You shall not take vengeance, nor bear
any grudge against the children of your
people, [b]but you shall love your neighbor
as yourself: I *am* the LORD.

19'You shall keep My statutes. You shall
not let your livestock breed with another
kind. You shall not sow your field with
mixed seed. Nor shall a garment of mixed
linen and wool come upon you.

20'Whoever lies carnally with a woman
who *is* [a]betrothed to a man as a concubine,
and who has not at all been redeemed nor
given her freedom, for this there shall be
scourging; *but* they shall not be put to
death, because she was not free. 21And
he shall bring his trespass offering to the
LORD, to the door of the tabernacle of meeting, a ram as a trespass offering. 22The
priest shall make atonement for him with
the ram of the trespass offering before the
LORD for his sin which he has committed.
And the sin which he has committed shall
be forgiven him.

23'When you come into the land, and
have planted all kinds of trees for food,
then you shall count their fruit as uncircumcised. Three years it shall be as uncircumcised to you. *It* shall not be eaten. 24But
in the fourth year all its fruit shall be holy,
a praise to the LORD. 25And in the fifth year
you may eat its fruit, that it may yield to
you its increase: I *am* the LORD your God.

26'You shall not eat *anything* with the
blood, nor shall you practice divination or
soothsaying. 27You shall not shave around
the sides of your head, nor shall you disfigure the edges of your beard. 28You shall
not [a]make any cuttings in your flesh for
the dead, nor tattoo any marks on you: I
am the LORD.

29[a]'Do not prostitute your daughter, to
cause her to be a harlot, lest the land fall
into harlotry, and the land become full of
wickedness.

30'You shall keep My Sabbaths and [a]rev-
erence My sanctuary: I *am* the LORD.

31'Give no regard to mediums and familiar spirits; do not seek after [a]them, to be
defiled by them: I *am* the LORD your God.

32[a]'You shall rise before the gray headed
and honor the presence of an old man, and
[b]fear your God: I *am* the LORD.

33'And [a]if a stranger dwells with you
in your land, you shall not mistreat him.
34[a]The stranger who dwells among you

19:9 [a] Lev. 23:22; Deut. 24:19–22 19:11 [a] Ex. 20:15, 16 [b] Jer. 9:3–5; Eph. 4:25 19:12 [a] Ex. 20:7; Deut. 5:11; [Matt. 5:33–37; James 5:12] [b] Lev. 18:21 19:13 [a] Ex. 22:7–15, 21–27; Mark 10:19 [b] Deut. 24:15; Mal. 3:5; James 5:4 19:14 [a] Deut. 27:18 19:15 [a] Deut. 16:19 [b] Ex. 23:3, 6; Deut. 1:17; 10:17; Ps. 82:2 19:16 [a] Prov. 11:13; 18:8; 20:19 [b] Ex. 23:7; Deut. 27:25; 1 Kin. 21:7–19 19:17 [a] [1 John 2:9, 11; 3:15] [b] Matt. 18:15; [Luke 17:3]; Eph. 5:11 19:18 [a] [Deut. 32:35; 1 Sam. 24:12; Rom. 12:19; Heb. 10:30] [b] Matt. 5:43; 19:19; Mark 12:31; Luke 10:27; [Rom. 13:9; Gal. 5:14]; James 2:8 19:20 [a] Deut. 22:23–27 19:28 [a] 1 Kin. 18:28; Jer. 16:6 19:29 [a] Lev. 21:9; Deut. 22:21; 23:17, 18 19:30 [a] Lev. 26:2; Eccl. 5:1 19:31 [a] Lev. 20:6, 27; Deut. 18:11; 1 Sam. 28:3; Is. 8:19 19:32 [a] Prov. 23:22; Lam. 5:12; 1 Tim. 5:1 [b] Lev. 19:14 19:33 [a] Ex. 22:21; Deut. 24:17, 18 19:34 [a] Ex. 12:48

RELEASE // EXALT HIS GUIDING LIGHT

Love Our City

Leviticus 19:15 // "You shall do no injustice in judgment. You shall not be partial to the poor, nor honor the person of the mighty. In righteousness you shall judge your neighbor."

Summary Message // Our world is getting darker. What we see on the news and social media and what we experience can be troubling. But these are the times when we need to lean in and follow God's leading and be His light in our communities.

In the Book of Leviticus, we learn of times that were also dark. God, however, was calling His people to be different and stand out against that dark backdrop. He was calling them to be holy. Leviticus 19 lists several laws of holiness. Some laws were specifically for the Levites, but several are relevant for us today.

Practical Application // We have all felt unfairly judged by someone. Many of us have experienced discrimination of some kind. Our country has a dark history of not treating people fairly. Although we have made progress, there are still systems of injustice in place. Unfortunately, many people that have participated in these unjust practices have claimed to be Christians. This false representation of Christ has pushed many people away from His light. It has created a false narrative about what the Christian faith truly is.

It is time we change the story and let His light shine brightly. The Bible is full of passages about justice. The teachings of Jesus and justice are inseparable as He tells us to love our neighbors as we love ourselves. His words echo the heart of Leviticus 19:15, where we are told to treat our neighbors fairly and equally. One of the best ways to love our neighbors is to serve them. Find creative ways to let your light shine for Christ as you love those you come in contact with.

Who are our neighbors? Those we live around, work around, shop around, and play around. Often, though, these neighbors look very different from us. Gentrification, immigration, and economic shifts have caused many cities to see major demographic changes. Our communities have become increasingly diverse. Our neighbors often do not look like us, think like us, vote like us, or worship like us. This is when this verse from Leviticus can get a little more challenging, but it is also when God's light can shine the brightest. He can use you to love neighbors who are totally different from you, and that is when love really shines.

Fervent Prayer // Heavenly Father, thank You for Your love and Your light. Help us be a conduit of both to our neighbors. Give us new vision to see people through Your eyes. Give us grace to love people who are different from us. Empower us to change the narrative about Christians, the church, and Your holy name. Your Word says the world will know us by our love. Set up divine appointments for us to love our neighbors in new, faithful ways. Help us to treat them as we would prefer to be treated. Help us bring change in our communities. In Jesus' name we pray. Amen.

---

shall be to you as one born among you,
and [b]you shall love him as yourself; for you
were strangers in the land of Egypt: I *am*
the LORD your God.

35'You shall do no injustice in judgment, in measurement of length, weight,
or volume. 36You shall have [a]honest scales,
honest weights, an honest ephah, and an
honest hin: I *am* the LORD your God, who
brought you out of the land of Egypt.

37[a]'Therefore you shall observe all My
statutes and all My judgments, and perform them: I *am* the LORD.'"

Penalties for Breaking the Law

20 Then the LORD spoke to Moses, saying, 2[a]"Again, you shall say to the
children of Israel: [b]'Whoever of the children of Israel, or of the strangers who dwell
in Israel, who gives *any* of his descendants
to Molech, he shall surely be put to death.
The people of the land shall [c]stone him with
stones. 3[a]I will set My face against that man,
and will cut him off from his people, because
he has given *some* of his descendants to Molech, to defile My sanctuary and profane My
holy name. 4And if the people of the land

19:34 [b] Deut. 10:19 19:36 [a] Deut. 25:13–15; Prov. 20:10 19:37 [a] Lev. 18:4, 5; Deut. 4:5, 6; 5:1; 6:25 20:2 [a] Lev. 18:2 [b] Lev. 18:21; 2 Kin. 23:10; 2 Chr. 33:6; Jer. 7:31 [c] Deut. 17:2–5 20:3 [a] Lev. 17:10

should in any way hide their eyes from the
man, when he gives *some* of his descendants
to Molech, and they do not kill him, 5then I
will set My face against that man and against
his family; and I will cut him off from his
people, and all who prostitute themselves
with him to commit harlotry with Molech.
6'And [a]the person who turns to mediums
and familiar spirits, to prostitute himself
with them, I will set My face against that
person and cut him off from his people.
7[a]Consecrate yourselves therefore, and be
holy, for I *am* the LORD your God. 8And you
shall keep [a]My statutes, and perform them:
[b]I *am* the LORD who sanctifies you.
9'For [a]everyone who curses his father or
his mother shall surely be put to death. He
has cursed his father or his mother. [b]His
blood *shall be* upon him.
10[a]'The man who commits adultery with
another man's wife, *he* who commits adultery with his neighbor's wife, the adulterer
and the adulteress, shall surely be put to
death. 11The man who lies with his [a]father's
wife has uncovered his father's nakedness;
both of them shall surely be put to death.
Their blood *shall be* upon them. 12If a man
lies with his [a]daughter-in-law, both of them
shall surely be put to death. They have
committed perversion. Their blood *shall
be* upon them. 13[a]If a man lies with a male
as he lies with a woman, both of them have
committed an abomination. They shall
surely be put to death. Their blood *shall be*
upon them. 14If a man marries a woman
and her [a]mother, it *is* wickedness. They shall
be burned with fire, both he and they, that
there may be no wickedness among you.
15If a man mates with an [a]animal, he shall
surely be put to death, and you shall kill
the animal. 16If a woman approaches any
animal and mates with it, you shall kill the
woman and the animal. They shall surely
be put to death. Their blood *is* upon them.
17'If a man takes his [a]sister, his father's
daughter or his mother's daughter, and
sees her nakedness and she sees his nakedness, it *is* a wicked thing. And they shall be
cut off in the sight of their people. He has
uncovered his sister's nakedness. He shall
bear his guilt. 18[a]If a man lies with a woman
during her sickness and uncovers her nakedness, he has exposed her flow, and she
has uncovered the flow of her blood. Both
of them shall be cut off from their people.
19'You shall not uncover the nakedness
of your [a]mother's sister nor of your [b]father's
sister, for that would uncover his near of
kin. They shall bear their guilt. 20If a man
lies with his [a]uncle's wife, he has uncovered
his uncle's nakedness. They shall bear their
sin; they shall die childless. 21If a man takes
his [a]brother's wife, it *is* an unclean thing.
He has uncovered his brother's nakedness.
They shall be childless.
22'You shall therefore keep all My [a]stat-
utes and all My judgments, and perform
them, that the land where I am bringing you
to dwell [b]may not vomit you out. 23[a]And you
shall not walk in the statutes of the nation
which I am casting out before you; for they
commit all these things, and [b]therefore I
abhor them. 24But [a]I have said to you, "You
shall inherit their land, and I will give it to
you to possess, a land flowing with milk and
honey." I *am* the LORD your God, [b]who has
separated you from the peoples. 25[a]You shall
therefore distinguish between clean animals and unclean, between unclean birds
and clean, [b]and you shall not make yourselves abominable by beast or by bird, or by
any kind of living thing that creeps on the
ground, which I have separated from you as
unclean. 26And you shall be holy to Me, [a]for
I the LORD *am* holy, and have separated you
from the peoples, that you should be Mine.
27[a]'A man or a woman who is a medium,
or who has familiar spirits, shall surely be
put to death; they shall stone them with
stones. Their blood *shall be* upon them.'"

Regulations for Conduct of Priests
(cf. Ezek. 44:15–31)

21 And the LORD said to Moses, "Speak
to the priests, the sons of Aaron, and
say to them: [a]'None shall defile himself for

20:6 [a] Lev. 19:31; 1 Sam. 28:7–25 **20:7** [a] Lev. 19:2; Heb. 12:14 **20:8** [a] Lev. 19:19, 37 [b] Ex. 31:13; Deut. 14:2; Ezek. 37:28 **20:9** [a] Ex. 21:17; Deut. 27:16; Prov. 20:20; Matt. 15:4 [b] 2 Sam. 1:16 **20:10** [a] Ex. 20:14; Lev. 18:20; Deut. 5:18; 22:22; John 8:4, 5 **20:11** [a] Lev. 18:7, 8; Deut. 27:20 **20:12** [a] Lev. 18:15 **20:13** [a] Lev. 18:22; Deut. 23:17; Judg. 19:22 **20:14** [a] Lev. 18:17 **20:15** [a] Lev. 18:23; Deut. 27:21 **20:17** [a] Lev. 18:9; Deut. 27:22 **20:18** [a] Lev. 15:24; 18:19 **20:19** [a] Lev. 18:13 [b] Lev. 18:12 **20:20** [a] Lev. 18:14 **20:21** [a] Lev. 18:16; Matt. 14:3, 4 **20:22** [a] Lev. 18:26; 19:37 [b] Lev. 18:25, 28; 2 Chr. 36:14–16 **20:23** [a] Lev. 18:3, 24 [b] Deut. 9:5 **20:24** [a] Ex. 3:17; 6:8; 13:5; 33:1–3 [b] Ex. 19:5; 33:16; Lev. 20:26; Deut. 7:6; 14:2; 1 Kin. 8:53 **20:25** [a] Lev. 10:10; 11:1–47; Deut. 14:3–21 [b] Lev. 11:43 **20:26** [a] Lev. 19:2; 1 Pet. 1:16 **20:27** [a] Lev. 19:31; 1 Sam. 28:9 **21:1** [a] Lev. 19:28; Ezek. 44:25

the dead among his people, 2except for
his relatives who are nearest to him: his
mother, his father, his son, his daughter,
and his brother; 3also his virgin sister who
is near to him, who has had no husband,
for her he may defile himself. 4*Otherwise*
he shall not defile himself, *being* a chief
man among his people, to profane himself.

5[a]'They shall not make any bald *place*
on their heads, nor shall they shave the
edges of their beards nor make any cuttings in their flesh. 6They shall be [a]holy to
their God and not profane the name of their
God, for they offer the offerings of the LORD
made by fire, *and* the [b]bread of their God;
[c]therefore they shall be holy. 7[a]They shall
not take a wife *who is* a harlot or a defiled
woman, nor shall they take a woman [b]di-
vorced from her husband; for *the priest*[1] is
holy to his God. 8Therefore you shall consecrate him, for he offers the bread of your
God. He shall be holy to you, for [a]I the LORD,
who [b]sanctify you, *am* holy. 9The daughter of any priest, if she profanes herself by
playing the harlot, she profanes her father.
She shall be [a]burned with fire.

10'*He who is* the high priest among his
brethren, on whose head the anointing
oil was [a]poured and who is consecrated to
wear the garments, shall not [b]uncover his
head nor tear his clothes; 11nor shall he go
[a]near any dead body, nor defile himself for
his father or his mother; 12[a]nor shall he go
out of the sanctuary, nor profane the sanctuary of his God; for the [b]consecration of
the anointing oil of his God *is* upon him:
I *am* the LORD. 13And he shall take a wife
in her virginity. 14A widow or a divorced
woman or a defiled woman *or* a harlot—
these he shall not marry; but he shall take a
virgin of his own people as wife. 15Nor shall
he profane his posterity among his people,
for I the LORD sanctify him.'"

16And the LORD spoke to Moses, saying,
17"Speak to Aaron, saying: 'No man of your
descendants in *succeeding* generations, who
has *any* defect, may approach to offer the
bread of his God. 18For any man who has a
[a]defect shall not approach: a man blind or
lame, who has a marred *face* or any *limb* [b]too
long, 19a man who has a broken foot or broken hand, 20or is a hunchback or a dwarf, or
a man who has a defect in his eye, or eczema
or scab, or is a eunuch. 21No man of the descendants of Aaron the priest, who has a defect, shall come near to offer the offerings
made by fire to the LORD. He has a defect; he
shall not come near to offer the bread of his
God. 22He may eat the bread of his God, *both*
the most holy and the holy; 23only he shall
not go near the [a]veil or approach the altar,
because he has a defect, lest [b]he profane My
sanctuaries; for I the LORD sanctify them.'"

24And Moses told *it* to Aaron and his
sons, and to all the children of Israel.

22 Then the LORD spoke to Moses, saying, 2"Speak to Aaron and his sons,
that they [a]separate themselves from the
holy things of the children of Israel, and
that they [b]do not profane My holy name *by*
what they [c]dedicate to Me: I *am* the LORD.
3Say to them: 'Whoever of all your descendants throughout your generations, who
goes near the holy things which the children
of Israel dedicate to the LORD, [a]while he has
uncleanness upon him, that person shall be
cut off from My presence: I *am* the LORD.

4'Whatever man of the descendants of
Aaron, who *is* a [a]leper or has [b]a discharge,
shall not eat the holy offerings [c]until he
is clean. And [d]whoever touches anything
made unclean *by* a corpse, or [e]a man who
has had an emission of semen, 5or [a]who-
ever touches any creeping thing by which
he would be made unclean, or [b]any person
by whom he would become unclean, whatever his uncleanness may be— 6the person
who has touched any such thing shall be
unclean until evening, and shall not eat
the holy *offerings* unless he [a]washes his
body with water. 7And when the sun goes
down he shall be clean; and afterward he
may eat the holy *offerings*, because [a]it *is* his
food. 8[a]Whatever dies *naturally* or is torn
by beasts he shall not eat, to defile himself
with it: I *am* the LORD.

21:5 [a] Lev. 19:27; Deut. 14:1; Ezek. 44:20 21:6 [a] Ex. 22:31 [b] Lev. 3:11 [c] Is. 52:11 21:7 [a] Ezek. 44:22 [b] Deut. 24:1, 2 [1] Literally *he* 21:8 [a] Lev. 11:44, 45 [b] Lev. 8:12, 30 21:9 [a] Deut. 22:21 21:10 [a] Lev. 8:12 [b] Lev. 10:6, 7 21:11 [a] Num. 19:14 21:12 [a] Lev. 10:7 [b] Ex. 29:6, 7 21:18 [a] Lev. 22:19–25 [b] Lev. 22:23 21:23 [a] Lev. 16:2 [b] Lev. 21:12 22:2 [a] Num. 6:3 [b] Lev. 18:21 [c] Ex. 28:38; Lev. 16:19; 25:10; Num. 18:32; Deut. 15:19 22:3 [a] Lev. 7:20, 21; Num. 19:13 22:4 [a] Num. 5:2 [b] Lev. 15:2 [c] Lev. 14:2; 15:13 [d] Lev. 11:24–28, 39, 40; Num. 19:11 [e] Lev. 15:16, 17 22:5 [a] Lev. 11:23–28 [b] Lev. 15:7, 19 22:6 [a] Lev. 15:5 22:7 [a] Lev. 21:22; Num. 18:11, 13 22:8 [a] Ex. 22:31; Lev. 7:24; 11:39, 40; 17:15; Ezek. 44:31

9 'They shall therefore keep [a]My ordinance, [b]lest they bear sin for it and die thereby, if they profane it: I the LORD sanctify them.

10 [a]'No outsider shall eat the holy *offering;* one who dwells with the priest, or a hired servant, shall not eat the holy thing. 11 But if the priest [a]buys a person with his money, he may eat it; and one who is born in his house may eat his food. 12 If the priest's daughter is married to an outsider, she may not eat of the holy offerings. 13 But if the priest's daughter is a widow or divorced, and has no child, and has returned to her father's house as in her youth, she may eat her father's food; but no outsider shall eat it.

14 'And if a man eats the holy *offering* unintentionally, then he shall restore a holy *offering* to the priest, and add one-fifth to it. 15 They shall not profane the [a]holy *offerings* of the children of Israel, which they offer to the LORD, 16 or allow them to bear the guilt of trespass when they eat their holy *offerings;* for I the LORD sanctify them.' "

Offerings Accepted and Not Accepted

17 And the LORD spoke to Moses, saying, 18 "Speak to Aaron and his sons, and to all the children of Israel, and say to them: [a]'Whatever man of the house of Israel, or of the strangers in Israel, who offers his sacrifice for any of his vows or for any of his freewill offerings, which they offer to the LORD as a burnt offering— 19 [a]*you shall offer* of your own free will a male without blemish from the cattle, from the sheep, or from the goats. 20 [a]Whatever has a defect, you shall not offer, for it shall not be acceptable on your behalf. 21 And [a]whoever offers a sacrifice of a peace offering to the LORD, [b]to fulfill *his* vow, or a freewill offering from the cattle or the sheep, it must be perfect to be accepted; there shall be no defect in it. 22 [a]Those *that are* blind or broken or maimed, or have an ulcer or eczema or scabs, you shall not offer to the LORD, nor make [b]an offering by fire of them on the altar to the LORD. 23 Either a bull or a lamb that has any limb [a]too long or too short you may offer *as* a freewill offering, but for a vow it shall not be accepted.

24 'You shall not offer to the LORD what is bruised or crushed, or torn or cut; nor shall you make *any offering of them* in your land. 25 Nor [a]from a foreigner's hand shall you offer any of these as [b]the bread of your God, because their [c]corruption *is* in them, *and* defects *are* in them. They shall not be accepted on your behalf.' "

26 And the LORD spoke to Moses, saying: 27 [a]"When a bull or a sheep or a goat is born, it shall be seven days with its mother; and from the eighth day and thereafter it shall be accepted as an offering made by fire to the LORD. 28 *Whether it is* a cow or ewe, do not kill both her [a]and her young on the same day. 29 And when you [a]offer a sacrifice of thanksgiving to the LORD, offer *it* of your own free will. 30 On the same day it shall be eaten; you shall leave [a]none of it until morning: I *am* the LORD.

31 [a]"Therefore you shall keep My commandments, and perform them: I *am* the LORD. 32 [a]You shall not profane My holy name, but [b]I will be hallowed among the children of Israel. I *am* the LORD who [c]sanctifies you, 33 [a]who brought you out of the land of Egypt, to be your God: I *am* the LORD."

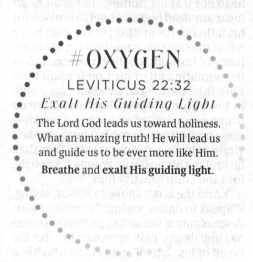

#OXYGEN

LEVITICUS 22:32

Exalt His Guiding Light

The Lord God leads us toward holiness. What an amazing truth! He will lead us and guide us to be ever more like Him.

Breathe and **exalt His guiding light**.

22:9 [a] Lev. 18:30 [b] Ex. 28:43; Lev. 22:16; Num. 18:22 22:10 [a] Ex. 29:33; Lev. 22:13; Num. 3:10 22:11 [a] Ex. 12:44 22:15 [a] Num. 18:32 22:18 [a] Lev. 1:2, 3, 10 22:19 [a] Lev. 1:3; Deut. 15:21 22:20 [a] Deut. 15:21; 17:1; Mal. 1:8, 14; [Eph. 5:27; Heb. 9:14; 1 Pet. 1:19] 22:21 [a] Lev. 3:1, 6 [b] Num. 15:3, 8; Ps. 61:8; 65:1; Eccl. 5:4, 5 22:22 [a] Lev. 22:20; Mal. 1:8 [b] Lev. 1:9, 13; 3:3, 5 22:23 [a] Lev. 21:18 22:25 [a] Num. 15:15, 16 [b] Lev. 21:6, 17 [c] Mal. 1:14 22:27 [a] Ex. 22:30 22:28 [a] Deut. 22:6, 7 22:29 [a] Lev. 7:12; Ps. 107:22; 116:17; Amos 4:5 22:30 [a] Lev. 7:15 22:31 [a] Lev. 19:37; Num. 15:40; Deut. 4:40 22:32 [a] Lev. 18:21 [b] Lev. 10:3; Matt. 6:9; Luke 11:2 [c] Lev. 20:8 22:33 [a] Lev. 19:36, 37; Num. 15:40; Deut. 4:40

Feasts of the LORD

23 And the LORD spoke to Moses, saying, 2"Speak to the children of Israel, and say to them: 'The feasts of the
LORD, which you shall proclaim *to be* [a]holy
convocations, these *are* My feasts.

The Sabbath

3[a]'Six days shall work be done, but the
seventh day *is* a Sabbath of solemn rest, a
holy convocation. You shall do no work *on*
it; it *is* the Sabbath of the LORD in all your
dwellings.

The Passover and Unleavened Bread
(Num. 28:16–25)

4[a]'These *are* the feasts of the LORD, holy
convocations which you shall proclaim
at their appointed times. 5[a]On the fourteenth *day* of the first month at twilight *is*
the LORD's Passover. 6And on the fifteenth
day of the same month *is* the Feast of Unleavened Bread to the LORD; seven days
you must eat unleavened bread. 7[a]On the
first day you shall have a holy convocation;
you shall do no customary work on it. 8But
you shall offer an offering made by fire to
the LORD for seven days. The seventh day
shall be a holy convocation; you shall do no
customary work *on it.*'"

The Feast of Firstfruits

9And the LORD spoke to Moses, saying,
10"Speak to the children of Israel, and say
to them: [a]'When you come into the land
which I give to you, and reap its harvest,
then you shall bring a sheaf of [b]the firstfruits of your harvest to the priest. 11He shall
[a]wave the sheaf before the LORD, to be accepted on your behalf; on the day after the
Sabbath the priest shall wave it. 12And you
shall offer on that day, when you wave the
sheaf, a male lamb of the first year, without
blemish, as a burnt offering to the LORD.
13Its grain offering *shall be* two-tenths *of*
an ephah of fine flour mixed with oil, an
offering made by fire to the LORD, for a
sweet aroma; and its drink offering *shall*
be of wine, one-fourth of a hin. 14You shall
eat neither bread nor parched grain nor
fresh grain until the same day that you have
brought an offering to your God; *it shall be*
a statute forever throughout your generations in all your dwellings.

The Feast of Weeks
(Ex. 34:22; Num. 28:26–31; Deut. 16:9, 10)

15'And you shall count for yourselves
from the day after the Sabbath, from the
day that you brought the sheaf of the wave
offering: seven Sabbaths shall be completed. 16Count [a]fifty days to the day after
the seventh Sabbath; then you shall offer
[b]a new grain offering to the LORD. 17You
shall bring from your dwellings two wave
loaves of two-tenths *of an ephah.* They shall
be of fine flour; they shall be baked with
leaven. *They are* [a]the firstfruits to the LORD.
18And you shall offer with the bread seven
lambs of the first year, without blemish,
one young bull, and two rams. They shall be
as a burnt offering to the LORD, with their
grain offering and their drink offerings, an
offering made by fire for a sweet aroma to
the LORD. 19Then you shall sacrifice [a]one
kid of the goats as a sin offering, and two
male lambs of the first year as a sacrifice
of a [b]peace offering. 20The priest shall wave
them with the bread of the firstfruits *as* a
wave offering before the LORD, with the
two lambs. [a]They shall be holy to the LORD
for the priest. 21And you shall proclaim on
the same day *that* it is a holy convocation
to you. You shall do no customary work
on it. It shall be a statute forever in all your
dwellings throughout your generations.
22[a]'When you reap the harvest of your
land, you shall not wholly reap the corners
of your field when you reap, nor shall you
gather any gleaning from your harvest. You
shall leave them for the poor and for the
stranger: I *am* the LORD your God.'"

The Feast of Trumpets
(Num. 29:1–6)

23Then the LORD spoke to Moses, saying,
24"Speak to the children of Israel, saying:
'In the [a]seventh month, on the first *day* of

23:2 [a] Ex. 12:16 23:3 [a] Ex. 20:9; 23:12; 31:15; Lev. 19:3; Deut. 5:13, 14; Luke 13:14 23:4 [a] Ex. 23:14–16; Lev. 23:2, 37 23:5 [a] Ex. 12:1–28; Num. 9:1–5; 28:16–25; Deut. 16:1–8; Josh. 5:10 23:7 [a] Ex. 12:16; Num. 28:18, 25 23:10 [a] Ex. 23:19; 34:26 [b] [Rom. 11:16]; James 1:18; Rev. 14:4 23:11 [a] Ex. 29:24 23:16 [a] Acts 2:1 [b] Num. 28:26 23:17 [a] Ex. 23:16, 19; Num. 15:17–21 23:19 [a] Lev. 4:23, 28; Num. 28:30; [2 Cor. 5:21] [b] Lev. 3:1 23:20 [a] Lev. 14:13; Num. 18:12; Deut. 18:4 23:22 [a] Lev. 19:9, 10; Deut. 24:19–22; Ruth 2:2, 15 23:24 [a] Num. 29:1

the month, you shall have a sabbath-*rest,*
[b]a memorial of blowing of trumpets, a holy
convocation. 25You shall do no customary
work *on it;* and you shall offer an offering
made by fire to the LORD.'"

The Day of Atonement
(Num. 29:7–11)

26And the LORD spoke to Moses, say-
ing: 27[a]"Also the tenth *day* of this seventh
month *shall be* the Day of Atonement. It
shall be a holy convocation for you; you
shall afflict your souls, and offer an offering
made by fire to the LORD. 28And you shall
do no work on that same day, for it *is* the
Day of Atonement, [a]to make atonement for
you before the LORD your God. 29For any
person who is not [a]afflicted *in soul* on that
same day [b]shall be cut off from his people.
30And any person who does any work on
that same day, [a]that person I will destroy
from among his people. 31You shall do no
manner of work; *it shall be* a statute forever throughout your generations in all
your dwellings. 32It *shall be* to you a sabbath of *solemn* rest, and you shall afflict
your souls; on the ninth *day* of the month
at evening, from evening to evening, you
shall celebrate your sabbath."

The Feast of Tabernacles
(Num. 29:12–40; Deut. 16:13–17)

33Then the LORD spoke to Moses, saying,
34"Speak to the children of Israel, saying:
[a]'The fifteenth day of this seventh month
shall be the Feast of Tabernacles *for* seven
days to the LORD. 35On the first day *there*
shall be a holy convocation. You shall do
no customary work *on it.* 36*For* seven days
you shall offer an [a]offering made by fire
to the LORD. [b]On the eighth day you shall
have a holy convocation, and you shall offer an offering made by fire to the LORD. It
is a [c]sacred assembly, *and* you shall do no
customary work *on it.*

37[a]'These *are* the feasts of the LORD which
you shall proclaim *to be* holy convocations,
to offer an offering made by fire to the
LORD, a burnt offering and a grain offering, a sacrifice and drink offerings, everything on its day— 38[a]besides the Sabbaths
of the LORD, besides your gifts, besides all
your vows, and besides all your freewill offerings which you give to the LORD.

39'Also on the fifteenth day of the seventh month, when you have [a]gathered in
the fruit of the land, you shall keep the feast
of the LORD *for* seven days; on the first day
there shall be a sabbath-*rest,* and on the
eighth day a sabbath-*rest.* 40And [a]you shall
take for yourselves on the first day the fruit
of beautiful trees, branches of palm trees,
the boughs of leafy trees, and willows of
the brook; [b]and you shall rejoice before
the LORD your God for seven days. 41[a]You
shall keep it as a feast to the LORD for seven
days in the year. *It shall be* a statute forever
in your generations. You shall celebrate it
in the seventh month. 42[a]You shall dwell
in booths for seven days. [b]All who are native Israelites shall dwell in booths, 43[a]that
your generations may [b]know that I made
the children of Israel dwell in booths when
[c]I brought them out of the land of Egypt: I
am the LORD your God.'"

44So Moses [a]declared to the children of
Israel the feasts of the LORD.

Care of the Tabernacle Lamps
(Ex. 27:20, 21)

24 Then the LORD spoke to Moses,
saying: 2[a]"Command the children
of Israel that they bring to you pure oil of
pressed olives for the light, to make the
lamps burn continually. 3Outside the veil
of the Testimony, in the tabernacle of meeting, Aaron shall be in charge of it from
evening until morning before the LORD
continually; *it shall be* a statute forever in
your generations. 4He shall be in charge
of the lamps on [a]the pure *gold* lampstand
before the LORD continually.

The Bread of the Tabernacle

5"And you shall take fine flour and bake
twelve [a]cakes with it. Two-tenths *of an*

23:24 [b] Lev. 25:9 23:27 [a] Lev. 16:1–34; 25:9; Num. 29:7 23:28 [a] Lev. 16:34 23:29 [a] Is. 22:12; Jer. 31:9; Ezek. 7:16 [b] Gen. 17:14; Lev. 13:46; Num. 5:2 23:30 [a] Lev. 20:3–6 23:34 [a] Ex. 23:16; Num. 29:12; Deut. 16:13–16; Ezra 3:4; Neh. 8:14; Zech. 14:16–19; John 7:2 23:36 [a] Num. 29:12–34 [b] Num. 29:35–38; Neh. 8:18; John 7:37 [c] Deut. 16:8; 2 Chr. 7:8 23:37 [a] Lev. 23:2, 4 23:38 [a] Num. 29:39 23:39 [a] Ex. 23:16; Deut. 16:13 23:40 [a] Neh. 8:15 [b] Deut. 12:7; 16:14, 15 23:41 [a] Num. 29:12; Neh. 8:18 23:42 [a] [Is. 4:6] [b] Neh. 8:14–16 23:43 [a] Ex. 13:14; Deut. 31:13; Ps. 78:5 [b] Ex. 10:2 [c] Lev. 22:33 23:44 [a] Lev. 23:2 24:2 [a] Ex. 27:20, 21 24:4 [a] Ex. 25:31; 31:8; 37:17 24:5 [a] Ex. 25:30; 39:36; 40:23

ephah shall be in each cake. 6You shall set
them in two rows, six in a row, [a]on the pure
gold table before the LORD. 7And you shall
put pure frankincense on *each* row, that it
may be on the bread for a [a]memorial, an
offering made by fire to the LORD. 8[a]Every
Sabbath he shall set it in order before the
LORD continually, *being taken* from the children of Israel by an everlasting covenant.
9And [a]it shall be for Aaron and his sons,
[b]and they shall eat it in a holy place; for it *is*
most holy to him from the offerings of the
LORD made by fire, by a perpetual statute."

The Penalty for Blasphemy

10Now the son of an Israelite woman,
whose father *was* an Egyptian, went out
among the children of Israel; and this Israelite *woman's* son and a man of Israel
fought each other in the camp. 11And the
Israelite woman's son [a]blasphemed the
name *of the LORD* and [b]cursed; and so they
[c]brought him to Moses. (His mother's name
was Shelomith the daughter of Dibri, of the
tribe of Dan.) 12Then they [a]put him in custody, [b]that the mind of the LORD might be
shown to them.

13And the LORD spoke to Moses, saying, 14"Take outside the camp him who
has cursed; then let all who heard *him* [a]lay
their hands on his head, and let all the congregation stone him.

15"Then you shall speak to the children
of Israel, saying: 'Whoever curses his God
[a]shall bear his sin. 16And whoever [a]blas-
phemes the name of the LORD shall surely
be put to death. All the congregation shall
certainly stone him, the stranger as well
as him who is born in the land. When he
blasphemes the name *of the LORD*, he shall
be put to death.

17[a]'Whoever kills any man shall surely
be put to death. 18[a]Whoever kills an animal shall make it good, animal for animal.

19'If a man causes disfigurement of his
neighbor, as [a]he has done, so shall it be
done to him— 20fracture for [a]fracture, [b]eye
for eye, tooth for tooth; as he has caused
disfigurement of a man, so shall it be done
to him. 21And whoever kills an animal shall
restore it; but whoever kills a man shall be
put to death. 22You shall have [a]the same
law for the stranger and for one from your
own country; for I *am* the LORD your God.'"

23Then Moses spoke to the children of
Israel; and they took outside the camp
him who had cursed, and stoned him with
stones. So the children of Israel did as the
LORD commanded Moses.

The Sabbath of the Seventh Year
(Deut. 15:1–11)

25 And the LORD spoke to Moses on
Mount [a]Sinai, saying, 2"Speak to the
children of Israel, and say to them: 'When
you come into the land which I give you,
then the land shall [a]keep a sabbath to the
LORD. 3Six years you shall sow your field,
and six years you shall prune your vineyard, and gather its fruit; 4but in the [a]sev-
enth year there shall be a sabbath of solemn
[b]rest for the land, a sabbath to the LORD.
You shall neither sow your field nor prune
your vineyard. 5[a]What grows of its own accord of your harvest you shall not reap, nor
gather the grapes of your untended vine,
for it is a year of rest for the land. 6And the
sabbath *produce* of the land shall be food
for you: for you, your male and female servants, your hired man, and the stranger
who dwells with you, 7for your livestock
and the beasts that *are* in your land—all
its produce shall be for food.

The Year of Jubilee

8'And you shall count seven sabbaths
of years for yourself, seven times seven
years; and the time of the seven sabbaths of
years shall be to you forty-nine years. 9Then
you shall cause the trumpet of the Jubilee
to sound on the tenth *day* of the seventh
month; [a]on the Day of Atonement you shall
make the trumpet to sound throughout all
your land. 10And you shall consecrate the
fiftieth year, and [a]proclaim liberty throughout *all* the land to all its inhabitants. It shall

24:6 [a] Ex. 25:23, 24; 1 Kin. 7:48; 2 Chr. 4:19; 13:11; Heb. 9:2 24:7 [a] Lev. 2:2, 9, 16 24:8 [a] Num. 4:7; 1 Chr. 9:32; 2 Chr. 2:4; Matt. 12:4, 5
24:9 [a] 1 Sam. 21:6; Matt. 12:4; Mark 2:26; Luke 6:4 [b] Ex. 29:33; Lev. 8:31 24:11 [a] Ex. 22:28 [b] Job 1:5, 11, 22; Is. 8:21 [c] Ex. 18:22, 26
24:12 [a] Num. 15:34 [b] Num. 27:5 24:14 [a] Deut. 13:9; 17:7 24:15 [a] Lev. 20:17; Num. 9:13 24:16 [a] Ex. 20:7; 1 Kin. 21:10, 13;
[Matt. 12:31; Mark 3:28, 29] 24:17 [a] Gen. 9:6; Ex. 21:12; Num. 35:30, 31; Deut. 19:11, 12; 27:24 24:18 [a] Lev. 24:21
24:19 [a] Ex. 21:24 24:20 [a] Ex. 21:23; Deut. 19:21 [b] [Matt. 5:38, 39] 24:22 [a] Ex. 12:49; Lev. 19:33–37; Num. 9:14; 15:15, 16, 29
25:1 [a] Lev. 26:46 25:2 [a] Lev. 26:34, 35 25:4 [a] Deut. 15:1; Neh. 10:31 [b] [Heb. 4:9] 25:5 [a] 2 Kin. 19:29
25:9 [a] Lev. 23:24, 27 25:10 [a] Is. 61:2; 63:4; Jer. 34:8, 15, 17; [Luke 4:19]

be a Jubilee for you; [b]and each of you shall
return to his possession, and each of you
shall return to his family. 11That fiftieth year
shall be a Jubilee to you; in it [a]you shall
neither sow nor reap what grows of its own
accord, nor gather *the grapes* of your untended vine. 12For it *is* the Jubilee; it shall
be holy to you; [a]you shall eat its produce
from the field.

13[a]'In this Year of Jubilee, each of you
shall return to his possession. 14And if
you sell anything to your neighbor or buy
from your neighbor's hand, you shall not
[a]oppress one another. 15[a]According to the
number of years after the Jubilee you shall
buy from your neighbor, and according to
the number of years of crops he shall sell to
you. 16According to the multitude of years
you shall increase its price, and according
to the fewer number of years you shall diminish its price; for he sells to you *according* to the number *of the years* of the crops.
17Therefore [a]you shall not oppress one another, [b]but you shall fear your God; for I *am*
the LORD your God.

Provisions for the Seventh Year

18[a]'So you shall observe My statutes and
keep My judgments, and perform them;
[b]and you will dwell in the land in safety.
19Then the land will yield its fruit, and [a]you
will eat your fill, and dwell there in safety.

20'And if you say, [a]"What shall we eat in
the seventh year, since [b]we shall not sow
nor gather in our produce?" 21Then I will
[a]command My blessing on you in the [b]sixth
year, and it will bring forth produce enough
for three years. 22[a]And you shall sow in the
eighth year, and eat [b]old produce until the
ninth year; until its produce comes in, you
shall eat *of* the old *harvest*.

Redemption of Property

23'The land shall not be sold permanently, for [a]the land *is* Mine; for you *are*
[b]strangers and sojourners with Me. 24And
in all the land of your possession you shall
grant redemption of the land.

25[a]'If one of your brethren becomes
poor, and has sold *some* of his possession,
and if [b]his redeeming relative comes to
redeem it, then he may redeem what his
brother sold. 26Or if the man has no one to
redeem it, but he himself becomes able to
redeem it, 27then [a]let him count the years
since its sale, and restore the remainder to
the man to whom he sold it, that he may
return to his possession. 28But if he is not
able to have *it* restored to himself, then
what was sold shall remain in the hand of
him who bought it until the Year of Jubilee;
[a]and in the Jubilee it shall be released, and
he shall return to his possession.

29'If a man sells a house in a walled city,
then he may redeem it within a whole year
after it is sold; *within* a full year he may redeem it. 30But if it is not redeemed within
the space of a full year, then the house in
the walled city shall belong permanently to
him who bought it, throughout his generations. It shall not be released in the Jubilee. 31However the houses of villages which
have no wall around them shall be counted
as the fields of the country. They may be
redeemed, and they shall be released in
the Jubilee. 32Nevertheless [a]the cities of
the Levites, *and* the houses in the cities of
their possession, the Levites may redeem at
any time. 33And if a man purchases a house
from the Levites, then the house that was
sold in the city of his possession shall be
released in the Jubilee; for the houses in
the cities of the Levites *are* their possession among the children of Israel. 34But
[a]the field of the common-land of their cities may not be [b]sold, for it *is* their perpetual possession.

Lending to the Poor

35'If one of your brethren becomes
poor, and falls into poverty among you,
then you shall [a]help him, like a stranger
or a sojourner, that he may live with you.
36[a]Take no usury or interest from him; but
[b]fear your God, that your brother may live
with you. 37You shall not lend him your

25:10 [b] Lev. 25:13, 28, 54; Num. 36:4 25:11 [a] Lev. 25:5 25:12 [a] Lev. 25:6, 7 25:13 [a] Lev. 25:10; 27:24; Num. 36:4 25:14 [a] Lev. 19:13 25:15 [a] Lev. 27:18, 23 25:17 [a] Lev. 25:14; Prov. 14:31; 22:22; Jer. 7:5, 6; 1 Thess. 4:6 [b] Lev. 19:14, 32; 25:43 25:18 [a] Lev. 19:37 [b] Lev. 26:5; Deut. 12:10; Ps. 4:8; Jer. 23:6 25:19 [a] Lev. 26:5; Ezek. 34:25 25:20 [a] Matt. 6:25, 31 [b] Lev. 25:4, 5 25:21 [a] Deut. 28:8 [b] Ex. 16:29 25:22 [a] 2 Kin. 19:29 [b] Lev. 26:10; Josh. 5:11 25:23 [a] Ex. 19:5; 2 Chr. 7:20 [b] Gen. 23:4; Ex. 6:4; 1 Chr. 29:15; Ps. 39:12; Heb. 11:13; 1 Pet. 2:11 25:25 [a] Ruth 2:20; 4:4, 6 [b] Num. 5:8; Ruth 3:2, 9, 12; [Job 19:25]; Jer. 32:7, 8 25:27 [a] Lev. 25:50–52 25:28 [a] Lev. 25:10, 13 25:32 [a] Num. 35:1–8; Josh. 21:2 25:34 [a] Num. 35:2–5 [b] Acts 4:36, 37 25:35 [a] Deut. 15:7–11; 24:14, 15; Luke 6:35; 1 John 3:17 25:36 [a] Ex. 22:25; Deut. 23:19, 20 [b] Neh. 5:9

money for usury, nor lend him your food
at a profit. 38[a]I *am* the LORD your God, who
brought you out of the land of Egypt, to give
you the land of Canaan *and* to be your God.

The Law Concerning Slavery

39'And if *one of* your brethren *who dwells*
by you becomes poor, and sells himself to
you, you shall not compel him to serve as a
slave. 40As a hired servant *and* a sojourner
he shall be with you, *and* shall serve you
until the Year of Jubilee. 41And *then* he shall
depart from you—he and his children [a]with
him—and shall return to his own family.
He shall return to the possession of his fathers. 42For they *are* [a]My servants, whom I
brought out of the land of Egypt; they shall
not be sold as slaves. 43[a]You shall not rule
over him [b]with rigor, but you [c]shall fear
your God. 44And as for your male and female slaves whom you may have—from
the nations that are around you, from
them you may buy male and female slaves.
45Moreover you may buy [a]the children of
the strangers who dwell among you, and
their families who are with you, which they
beget in your land; and they shall become
your property. 46And [a]you may take them
as an inheritance for your children after
you, to inherit *them as* a possession; they
shall be your permanent slaves. But regarding your brethren, the children of Israel, you shall not rule over one another
with rigor.

47'Now if a sojourner or stranger close to
you becomes rich, and *one of* your brethren *who dwells* by him becomes poor, and
sells himself to the stranger *or* sojourner
close to you, or to a member of the stranger's family, 48after he is sold he may be redeemed again. One of his brothers may
redeem him; 49or his uncle or his uncle's
son may redeem him; or *anyone* who is
near of kin to him in his family may redeem him; or if he is able he may redeem
himself. 50Thus he shall reckon with him
who bought him: The price of his release
shall be according to the number of years,
from the year that he was sold to him until
the Year of Jubilee; *it shall be* [a]according to
the time of a hired servant for him. 51If *there
are* still many years *remaining*, according
to them he shall repay the price of his redemption from the money with which he
was bought. 52And if there remain but a
few years until the Year of Jubilee, then
he shall reckon with him, *and* according
to his years he shall repay him the price of
his redemption. 53He shall be with him as a
yearly hired servant, and he shall not rule
with rigor over him in your sight. 54And if
he is not redeemed in these *years*, then he
shall be released in the Year of Jubilee—he
and his children with him. 55For the children of Israel *are* servants to Me; they *are*
My servants whom I brought out of the land
of Egypt: I *am* the LORD your God.

Promise of Blessing and Retribution
(Deut. 7:12–24; 28:1–68)

26 'You shall [a]not make idols for yourselves;
neither a carved image nor a *sacred* pillar shall you rear up for yourselves;
nor shall you set up an engraved stone
in your land, to bow down to it;
for I *am* the LORD your God.
2 [a]You shall keep My Sabbaths and reverence My sanctuary:
I *am* the LORD.

3 [a]'If you walk in My statutes and keep My
commandments, and perform them,
4 [a]then I will give you rain in its season,
[b]the land shall yield its produce, and
the trees of the field shall yield their
fruit.
5 [a]Your threshing shall last till the time of
vintage, and the vintage shall last till
the time of sowing;
you shall eat your bread to the full, and
[b]dwell in your land safely.
6 [a]I will give peace in the land, and [b]you
shall lie down, and none will make
you afraid;
I will rid the land of [c]evil beasts,
and [d]the sword will not go through your
land.

25:38 [a] Lev. 11:45; 22:32, 33 25:41 [a] Ex. 21:3 25:42 [a] Lev. 25:55; [Rom. 6:22; 1 Cor. 7:22, 23] 25:43 [a] Eph. 6:9; Col. 4:1 [b] Ex. 1:13, 14; Lev. 25:46, 53; Ezek. 34:4 [c] Ex. 1:17; Deut. 25:18; Mal. 3:5 25:45 [a] [Is. 56:3, 6, 7] 25:46 [a] Is. 14:2 25:50 [a] Job 7:1; Is. 16:14 26:1 [a] Ex. 20:4, 5; Deut. 4:15–18; 5:8 26:2 [a] Lev. 19:30 26:3 [a] Deut. 28:1–14 26:4 [a] Is. 30:23 [b] Ps. 67:6 26:5 [a] Deut. 11:15; Joel 2:19, 26; Amos 9:13 [b] Lev. 25:18, 19; Ezek. 34:25 26:6 [a] Is. 45:7 [b] Job 11:19; Ps. 4:8; Zeph. 3:13 [c] 2 Kin. 17:25; Hos. 2:18 [d] Ezek. 14:17

#OXYGEN

LEVITICUS 26:3-4

Exalt His Guiding Light

If we desire God's light to illuminate our paths, we must listen for His voice and obey His direction in our lives. He will faithfully lead us toward the fulfillment of His promises in our lives.

Breathe and **exalt His guiding light**.

7 You will chase your enemies, and they
shall fall by the sword before you.
8 [a]Five of you shall chase a hundred, and
a hundred of you shall put ten thousand to flight;
your enemies shall fall by the sword before you.
9 'For I will [a]look on you favorably and
[b]make you fruitful, multiply you and
confirm My [c]covenant with you.
10 You shall eat the [a]old harvest, and clear
out the old because of the new.
11 [a]I will set My tabernacle among you, and
My soul shall not abhor you.
12 [a]I will walk among you and be your God,
and you shall be My people.
13 I *am* the LORD your God, who brought
you out of the land of Egypt, that *you*
should not be their slaves;
I have broken the bands of your [a]yoke
and made you walk upright.

14 'But if you do not obey Me, and do not
observe all these commandments,
15 and if you despise My statutes, or if your
soul abhors My judgments, so that
you do not perform all My commandments, *but* break My covenant,
16 I also will do this to you:
I will even appoint terror over you,
[a]wasting disease and fever which
shall [b]consume the eyes and [c]cause
sorrow of heart.
And [d]you shall sow your seed in vain, for
your enemies shall eat it.
17 I will set [a]My face against you, and [b]you
shall be defeated by your enemies.
[c]Those who hate you shall reign over you,
and you shall [d]flee when no one pursues you.
18 'And after all this, if you do not obey Me,
then I will punish you [a]seven times
more for your sins.
19 I will [a]break the pride of your power;
I [b]will make your heavens like iron and
your earth like bronze.
20 And your [a]strength shall be spent in
vain;
for your [b]land shall not yield its produce,
nor shall the trees of the land yield
their fruit.

21 'Then, if you walk contrary to Me, and are
not willing to obey Me, I will bring on
you seven times more plagues, according to your sins.
22 [a]I will also send wild beasts among you,
which shall rob you of your children,
destroy your livestock, and make you
few in number;
and [b]your highways shall be desolate.

23 'And if [a]by these things you are not reformed by Me, but walk contrary
to Me,
24 [a]then I also will walk contrary to you, and
I will punish you yet seven times for
your sins.
25 And [a]I will bring a sword against you
that will execute the vengeance of the
covenant;
when you are gathered together within
your cities [b]I will send pestilence
among you;
and you shall be delivered into the hand
of the enemy.

26:8 [a] Deut. 32:30; Judg. 7:7–12 **26:9** [a] Ex. 2:25; 2 Kin. 13:23 [b] Gen. 17:6, 7; Ps. 107:38 [c] Gen. 17:1–7 **26:10** [a] Lev. 25:22 **26:11** [a] Ex. 25:8; 29:45, 46; Josh. 22:19; Ps. 76:2; Ezek. 37:26; Rev. 21:3 **26:12** [a] Deut. 23:14; [2 Cor. 6:16] **26:13** [a] Gen. 27:40 **26:16** [a] Deut. 28:22 [b] 1 Sam. 2:33 [c] Ezek. 24:23; 33:10 [d] Judg. 6:3–6; Job 31:8; Mic. 6:15 **26:17** [a] Ps. 34:16 [b] Deut. 28:25; 1 Sam. 4:10; 31:1 [c] Ps. 106:41 [d] Prov. 28:1 **26:18** [a] 1 Sam. 2:5 **26:19** [a] Is. 25:11 [b] Deut. 28:23 **26:20** [a] Ps. 127:1; Is. 17:10, 11; 49:4; Jer. 12:13 [b] Gen. 4:12; Deut. 11:17 **26:22** [a] Deut. 32:24; Ezek. 14:21 [b] Judg. 5:6; 2 Chr. 15:5; Zech. 7:14 **26:23** [a] Jer. 2:30; Amos 4:6–12 **26:24** [a] Lev. 26:28, 41; Ps. 18:26 **26:25** [a] Ezek. 5:17 [b] Num. 16:49; Deut. 28:21; 2 Sam. 24:15

26 [a]When I have cut off your supply of bread,
ten women shall bake your bread in one oven, and they shall bring back your bread by weight, [b]and you shall eat and not be satisfied.
27 'And after all this, if you do not obey Me,
but walk contrary to Me,
28 then I also will walk contrary to you in fury;
and I, even I, will chastise you seven times for your sins.
29 [a]You shall eat the flesh of your sons,
and you shall eat the flesh of your daughters.
30 [a]I will destroy your high places, cut down your incense altars, and cast your carcasses on the lifeless forms of your idols;
and My soul shall abhor you.
31 I will lay your [a]cities waste and [b]bring your sanctuaries to desolation, and I will not [c]smell the fragrance of your sweet aromas.
32 [a]I will bring the land to desolation, and your enemies who dwell in it shall be astonished at it.
33 [a]I will scatter you among the nations and draw out a sword after you;
your land shall be desolate and your cities waste.
34 [a]Then the land shall enjoy its sabbaths as long as it lies desolate and you *are* in your enemies' land;
then the land shall rest and enjoy its sabbaths.
35 As long as *it* lies desolate it shall rest—
for the time it did not rest on your [a]sabbaths when you dwelt in it.
36 'And as for those of you who are left, I will send [a]faintness into their hearts in the lands of their enemies;
the sound of a shaken leaf shall cause them to flee;
they shall flee as though fleeing from a sword, and they shall fall when no one pursues.
37 [a]They shall stumble over one another, as it were before a sword, when no one pursues;
and [b]you shall have no *power* to stand before your enemies.
38 You shall [a]perish among the nations,
and the land of your enemies shall eat you up.
39 And those of you who are left [a]shall waste away in their iniquity in your enemies' lands;
also in their [b]fathers' iniquities, which are with them, they shall waste away.
40 '*But* [a]if they confess their iniquity and the iniquity of their fathers, with their unfaithfulness in which they were unfaithful to Me, and that they also have walked contrary to Me,
41 and *that* I also have walked contrary to them and have brought them into the land of their enemies;
if their [a]uncircumcised hearts are [b]humbled, and they [c]accept their guilt—
42 then I will [a]remember My covenant with Jacob, and My covenant with Isaac and My covenant with Abraham I will remember;
I will [b]remember the land.
43 [a]The land also shall be left empty by them, and will enjoy its sabbaths while it lies desolate without them;
they will accept their guilt, because they [b]despised My judgments and because their soul abhorred My statutes.
44 Yet for all that, when they are in the land of their enemies, [a]I will not cast them away, nor shall I abhor them, to utterly destroy them and break My covenant with them;
for I *am* the LORD their God.

26:26 [a] Ps. 105:16; Is. 3:1; Ezek. 4:16, 17; 5:16 [b] Mic. 6:14; Hag. 1:6 **26:29** [a] Deut. 28:53; 2 Kin. 6:28, 29 **26:30** [a] 1 Kin. 13:2; 2 Chr. 34:3; Is. 27:9; Ezek. 6:3–6, 13 **26:31** [a] 2 Kin. 25:4, 10 [b] 2 Chr. 36:19; Ps. 74:7 [c] Is. 1:11–15 **26:32** [a] Jer. 9:11; 18:16 **26:33** [a] Deut. 4:27; Ps. 44:11; Ezek. 12:15; 20:23; 22:15; Zech. 7:14 **26:34** [a] Lev. 26:43; 2 Chr. 36:21 **26:35** [a] Lev. 25:2 **26:36** [a] Is. 30:17; Lam. 1:3, 6; 4:19; Ezek. 21:7, 12, 15 **26:37** [a] Judg. 7:22; 1 Sam. 14:15, 16; Is. 10:4 [b] Josh. 7:12, 13; Judg. 2:14 **26:38** [a] Deut. 4:26 **26:39** [a] Deut. 28:65; Ezek. 4:17; 33:10; Zech. 10:9 [b] Ex. 34:7 **26:40** [a] Num. 5:7; 1 Kin. 8:33, 34; Neh. 9:2; Luke 15:18; [1 John 1:9] **26:41** [a] Acts 7:51; Rom. 2:29 [b] 2 Chr. 12:6, 7, 12; 1 Pet. 5:5, 6 [c] Ps. 39:9; 51:3, 4; Dan. 9:7 **26:42** [a] Ex. 2:24; 6:5; Ps. 106:45; Ezek. 16:60 [b] Ps. 136:23 **26:43** [a] Lev. 26:34, 35 [b] Lev. 26:15 **26:44** [a] Deut. 4:31; 2 Kin. 13:23; Jer. 30:11; [Rom. 11:1–36]

45 But [a]for their sake I will remember the
covenant of their ancestors, [b]whom
I brought out of the land of Egypt [c]in
the sight of the nations, that I might
be their God:
I *am* the LORD.' "

46 [a]These *are* the statutes and judgments and laws which the LORD made between Himself and the children of Israel [b]on Mount Sinai by the hand of Moses.

Redeeming Persons and Property Dedicated to God

27 Now the LORD spoke to Moses, saying, 2 "Speak to the children of Israel, and say to them: [a]'When a man consecrates by a vow certain persons to the LORD, according to your valuation, 3 if your valuation is of a male from twenty years old up to sixty years old, then your valuation shall be fifty shekels of silver, [a]according to the shekel of the sanctuary. 4 If it *is* a female, then your valuation shall be thirty shekels; 5 and if from five years old up to twenty years old, then your valuation for a male shall be twenty shekels, and for a female ten shekels; 6 and if from a month old up to five years old, then your valuation for a male shall be five shekels of silver, and for a female your valuation shall be three shekels of silver; 7 and if from sixty years old and above, if *it is* a male, then your valuation shall be fifteen shekels, and for a female ten shekels.

8 'But if he is too poor to pay your valuation, then he shall present himself before the priest, and the priest shall set a value for [a]him; according to the ability of him who vowed, the priest shall value him.

9 'If *it is* an animal that men may bring as an offering to the LORD, all that *anyone* gives to the LORD shall be holy. 10 He shall not substitute it or exchange it, good for bad or bad for good; and if he at all exchanges animal for animal, then both it and the one exchanged for it shall be [a]holy. 11 If *it is* an unclean animal which they do not offer as a sacrifice to the LORD, then he shall present the animal before the priest; 12 and the priest shall set a value for it, whether it is good or bad; as you, the priest, value it, so it shall be. 13 [a]But if he *wants* at all *to* redeem it, then he must add one-fifth to your valuation.

14 'And when a man dedicates his house *to be* holy to the LORD, then the priest shall set a value for it, whether it is good or bad; as the priest values it, so it shall stand. 15 If he who dedicated it *wants to* redeem his house, then he must add one-fifth of the money of your valuation to it, and it shall be his.

16 'If a man dedicates to the LORD *part* of a field of his possession, then your valuation shall be according to the seed for it. A homer of barley seed *shall be valued* at fifty shekels of silver. 17 If he dedicates his field from the Year of Jubilee, according to your valuation it shall stand. 18 But if he dedicates his field after the Jubilee, then the priest shall [a]reckon to him the money due according to the years that remain till the Year of Jubilee, and it shall be deducted from your valuation. 19 And if he who dedicates the field ever wishes to redeem it, then he must add one-fifth of the money of your valuation to it, and it shall belong to him. 20 But if he does not want to redeem the field, or if he has sold the field to another man, it shall not be redeemed anymore; 21 but the field, [a]when it is released in the Jubilee, shall be holy to the LORD, as a [b]devoted field; it shall be [c]the possession of the priest.

22 'And if a man dedicates to the LORD a field which he has bought, which is not the field of [a]his possession, 23 then the priest shall reckon to him the worth of your valuation, up to the Year of Jubilee, and he shall give your valuation on that day *as* a holy *offering* to the LORD. 24 [a]In the Year of Jubilee the field shall return to him from whom it was bought, to the one who *owned* the land as a possession. 25 And all your valuations shall be according to the shekel of the sanctuary: [a]twenty gerahs to the shekel.

26:45 [a] [Rom. 11:28] [b] Lev. 22:33; 25:38 [c] Ps. 98:2; Ezek. 20:9, 14, 22 26:46 [a] Lev. 27:34; Deut. 6:1; 12:1; [John 1:17] [b] Lev. 25:1
27:2 [a] Lev. 7:16; Num. 6:2; Deut. 23:21–23; Judg. 11:30, 31, 39 27:3 [a] Ex. 30:13; Lev. 27:25; Num. 3:47; 18:16 27:8 [a] Lev. 5:11; 14:21–24
27:10 [a] Lev. 27:33 27:13 [a] Lev. 6:5; 22:14; 27:15, 19 27:18 [a] Lev. 25:15, 16, 28 27:21 [a] Lev. 25:10, 28, 31 [b] Lev. 27:28
[c] Num. 18:14; Ezek. 44:29 27:22 [a] Lev. 25:10, 25 27:24 [a] Lev. 25:10–13, 28
27:25 [a] Ex. 30:13; Lev. 27:3; Num. 3:47; 18:16; Ezek. 45:12

26 'But the [a]firstborn of the animals, which should be the LORD's firstborn, no man shall dedicate; whether *it is* an ox or sheep, it *is* the LORD's. 27 And if *it is* an unclean animal, then he shall redeem *it* according to your valuation, and [a]shall add one-fifth to it; or if it is not redeemed, then it shall be sold according to your valuation.

28 [a]'Nevertheless no devoted *offering* that a man may devote to the LORD of all that he has, *both* man and beast, or the field of his possession, shall be sold or redeemed; every devoted *offering is* most holy to the LORD. 29 [a]No person under the ban, who may become doomed to destruction among men, shall be redeemed, *but* shall surely be put to death. 30 And [a]all the tithe of the land, *whether* of the seed of the land *or* of the fruit of the tree, *is* the LORD's. It *is* holy to the LORD. 31 [a]If a man wants at all to redeem *any* of his tithes, he shall add one-fifth to it. 32 And concerning the tithe of the herd or the flock, of whatever [a]passes under the rod, the tenth one shall be holy to the LORD. 33 He shall not inquire whether it is good or bad, [a]nor shall he exchange it; and if he exchanges it at all, then both it and the one exchanged for it shall be holy; it shall not be redeemed.' "

34 [a]These *are* the commandments which the LORD commanded Moses for the children of Israel on Mount [b]Sinai.

27:26 [a] Ex. 13:2, 12; 22:30 27:27 [a] Lev. 27:11, 12 27:28 [a] Lev. 27:21; Num. 18:14; Josh. 6:17–19 27:29 [a] Num. 21:2 27:30 [a] Gen. 28:22; Num. 18:21, 24; 2 Chr. 31:5, 6, 12; Neh. 13:12; Mal. 3:8 27:31 [a] Lev. 27:13 27:32 [a] Jer. 33:13; Ezek. 20:37; Mic. 7:14 27:33 [a] Lev. 27:10 27:34 [a] Lev. 26:46; Deut. 4:5; Mal. 4:4 [b] Ex. 19:1–6, 25; [Heb. 12:18–29]

THE FOURTH BOOK OF MOSES CALLED

NUMBERS

OVERVIEW

The prophet Moses is the author of the Book of Numbers. It is the fourth book of the Pentateuch (the five books of the original Jewish scriptures). In this book, we continue to follow the Israelites' exodus from Egypt, picking up with their wilderness journey from Mount Sinai to the promised land of Canaan.

The title Numbers aligns with two censuses of the Israelites. The first was God's decree for Moses to count the Israelite families. God wanted to highlight the size and strength of the army in preparation for engaging in battle (chs. 1–2). Along with this, God commanded a count of the Levites (the descendants of Jacob's son Levi) and instructed them to encamp around the tabernacle to assist Moses and Aaron with their duties (chs. 3–4). The second census (ch. 26) took place roughly forty years later and was a count of the second generation of Israelites who would enter the Promised Land.

Numbers 7:1 records Moses setting up the tabernacle, alluding back to Exodus 40:17–33. At this time, the Levites received gifts from the Israelites to enable them to carry out their duties as the tabernacle was moved from place to place throughout the remainder of their journey (see Num. 7:2–88). Before continuing their wilderness journey, the Levites followed a prescribed cleansing (see 8:5–26) and the observance of Passover (see 9:1–14).

The Israelites then resumed their journey toward Canaan (see 9:15—10:10). God signaled their movement by a cloud over the tabernacle. When the cloud was present, they camped; when it was lifted, they journeyed (see 9:15–23).

On the journey to Canaan, the people of Israel angered God by complaining about His provision (see 11:1–35) and speaking against Moses (see 12:1–16). When they reached the outskirts of Canaan, Moses sent twelve men to spy out the land and its inhabitants. The spies returned to report fortified cities and people much larger and stronger than the Israelites. As a result, the Israelites refused to enter the land, claiming they would rather return to Egypt (see 14:1–4). In response to their rebelliousness, God declared they would remain in the wilderness for forty years. Only Joshua and Caleb, two spies who had brought back a good report, and the children of this rebellious generation would enter Canaan (see vv. 26–35).

Throughout their time in the wilderness, the Israelites continued to complain and rebel against God and His chosen leader, Moses (see 16:1–50). When the Israelites complained of no water, God instructed Moses to speak to a rock so that water would flow, as He had provided before (see 20:1–9; cf. Ex. 17:1–7). In anger, Moses struck the rock instead (see Num. 20:11). Because of Moses' disobedience, God did not allow Moses to lead the Israelites into Canaan (see 20:12).

Chapters 21–28 tell of the miraculous interventions of God as the first generation of Israelites gave way to the second. The next chapters outline new offerings to God and additional laws for the Israelites to follow (28–30). After a review of the Israelites' journey from Egypt (see 33:1–49), God gave His people instructions for inhabiting Canaan under Joshua's leadership (see 33:50—35:34).

The major theme of Numbers is faithfulness. It reinforces the foundational truth that God keeps His promises to His people. God promised Abraham that He would bless his descendants, the Israelites, and give them the land of Canaan. Several generations later, God remained faithful to His promise to prepare His people and lead them into the Promised Land.

BREATHE IT IN

After delivering the Israelites from bondage in Egypt and establishing His covenant with them, God led them toward Canaan, the land that He had promised to them. While thankful for their freedom at the beginning of the journey, the Israelites were not pleased with the path God set before them. As a result, they complained. They complained about God's provision. They complained about His chosen leader. They even questioned God's ability to protect them. Ultimately, their questions and complaints led to rebellion against God.

Like the Israelites, many of us, individually and collectively, have suffered great hardships. Our ancestors prayed for release from the bondage of slavery. Recent generations have prayed for deliverance from racism and inequality. The answers to our prayers have come in many forms: the abolishment of slavery, the passage of the Civil Rights and Voting Rights Acts, and other important milestones designed to level the playing field. We are grateful for God's mercy and grace in bringing us this far; however, we have not yet arrived at our destination. We cannot be ready for the road ahead without God's hand on us. God promises freedom for His people. Numbers demonstrates that God honors His promises. Despite the actions and sinfulness of the world, He remains faithful to His promises.

With God's hand guiding the way, we move forward, striving to make things better. But this does not mean we strike out on our own, complaining and rebelling against God. This was the attitude of the Israelites and the cause of God sentencing them to forty years in the wilderness. He punished them for their actions, but He did not go back on His word. Although He denied the privilege of entering the Promised Land to those who rebelled against His ways, He gave the land to their children.

Contrary to what some believe, following Christ and walking in His ways does not guarantee a life free of challenges, difficult situations, disappointment, and pain. There may be times in our lives when we have barely enough to make ends meet financially (sometimes, not even that). At other times, we may feel tired and overwhelmed from managing all our responsibilities at work, home, and church. The loss of loved ones leaves us sorrowful and aching. Yet, we find the strength to keep moving forward. These types of experiences do not mean God is not with us. God is faithful, and He never leaves or forsakes us.

Instead of feeling alone and abandoned or complaining and rebelling in moments when life is complicated, we need to remind ourselves of God's faithfulness and of all the wonderful things He has done in our lives. We need to remember the promises He made to us that have already come to pass and stand firmly in our faith that He will do exactly what He said He would do. We must learn to practice patience and be content in whatever situation we find ourselves in because God is there with us. He is leading us to the "land" that He promised us. If we remain on the path set before us and trust God, we will take possession of our promised land in due time.

†

THE FOURTH BOOK OF MOSES CALLED

NUMBERS

The First Census of Israel
(cf. 2 Sam. 24:1–9; 1 Chr. 21:1–6)

1 Now the LORD spoke to Moses [a]in the Wilderness of Sinai, [b]in the tabernacle of meeting, on the [c]first *day* of the second month, in the second year after they had come out of the land of Egypt, saying: 2 [a]"Take a census of all the congregation of the children of Israel, by their families, by their fathers' houses, according to the number of names, every male [b]individually, 3 from [a]twenty years old and above—all who *are able to* go to war in Israel. You and Aaron shall number them by their armies. 4 And with you there shall be a man from every tribe, each one the head of his father's house.

5 "These are the names of the men who shall stand with you: from Reuben, Elizur the son of Shedeur; 6 from Simeon, Shelumiel the son of Zurishaddai; 7 from Judah, Nahshon the son of Amminadab; 8 from Issachar, Nethanel the son of Zuar; 9 from Zebulun, Eliab the son of Helon; 10 from the sons of Joseph: from Ephraim, Elishama the son of Ammihud; from Manasseh, Gamaliel the son of Pedahzur; 11 from Benjamin, Abidan the son of Gideoni; 12 from Dan, Ahiezer the son of Ammishaddai; 13 from Asher, Pagiel the son of Ocran; 14 from Gad, Eliasaph the son of [a]Deuel;[1] 15 from Naphtali, Ahira the son of Enan." 16 [a]These *were* [b]chosen from the congregation, leaders of their fathers' tribes, [c]heads of the divisions in Israel.

17 Then Moses and Aaron took these men who had been mentioned [a]by name, 18 and they assembled all the congregation together on the first *day* of the second month; and they recited their [a]ancestry by families, by their fathers' houses, according to the number of names, from twenty years old and above, each one individually. 19 As the LORD commanded Moses, so he numbered them in the Wilderness of Sinai.

20 Now the [a]children of Reuben, Israel's oldest son, their genealogies by their families, by their fathers' house, according to the number of names, every male individually, from twenty years old and above, all who *were able to* go to war: 21 those who were numbered of the tribe of Reuben *were* forty-six thousand five hundred.

22 From the [a]children of Simeon, their genealogies by their families, by their fathers' house, of those who were numbered, according to the number of names, every male individually, from twenty years old and above, all who *were able to* go to war: 23 those who were numbered of the tribe of Simeon *were* fifty-nine thousand three hundred.

24 From the [a]children of Gad, their genealogies by their families, by their fathers' house, according to the number of names, from twenty years old and above, all who *were able to* go to war: 25 those who were numbered of the tribe of Gad *were* forty-five thousand six hundred and fifty.

26 From the [a]children of Judah, their genealogies by their families, by their fathers' house, according to the number of names, from twenty years old and above, all who *were able to* go to war: 27 those who

---

1:1 [a] Ex. 19:1; Num. 10:11, 12 [b] Ex. 25:22 [c] Ex. 40:2, 17; Num. 9:1; 10:11 1:2 [a] Ex. 30:12; Num. 26:2, 63, 64; 2 Sam. 24:2; 1 Chr. 21:2 [b] Ex. 30:12, 13; 38:26 1:3 [a] Ex. 30:14; 38:26 1:14 [a] Num. 7:42 [1] Spelled *Reuel* in 2:14 1:16 [a] Ex. 18:21; Num. 7:2; 1 Chr. 27:16–22 [b] Num. 16:2 [c] Ex. 18:21, 25; Jer. 5:5; Mic. 3:1, 9; 5:2 1:17 [a] Is. 43:1 1:18 [a] Ezra 2:59; Heb. 7:3 1:20 [a] Num. 2:10, 11; 26:5–11; 32:6, 15, 21, 29 1:22 [a] Num. 2:12, 13; 26:12–14 1:24 [a] Gen. 30:11; Num. 26:15–18; Josh. 4:12; Jer. 49:1 1:26 [a] Gen. 29:35; Num. 26:19–22; 2 Sam. 24:9; Ps. 78:68; Matt. 1:2

were numbered of the tribe of Judah *were*
[a]seventy-four thousand six hundred.
28From the [a]children of Issachar, their
genealogies by their families, by their fathers' house, according to the number of
names, from twenty years old and above,
all who *were able to* go to war: 29those who
were numbered of the tribe of Issachar
were fifty-four thousand four hundred.
30From the [a]children of Zebulun, their
genealogies by their families, by their fathers' house, according to the number of
names, from twenty years old and above,
all who *were able to* go to war: 31those who
were numbered of the tribe of Zebulun
were fifty-seven thousand four hundred.
32From the sons of Joseph, the [a]children
of Ephraim, their genealogies by their families, by their fathers' house, according to
the number of names, from twenty years
old and above, all who *were able to* go to
war: 33those who were numbered of the
tribe of Ephraim *were* forty thousand five
hundred.
34From the [a]children of Manasseh, their
genealogies by their families, by their fathers' house, according to the number of
names, from twenty years old and above,

ACT IN FAITH

INHALE

I am a person of faith. However, it is hard to show love and grace and to keep going when you see others physically assaulted, simply because of who they are. It is hard to stand for righteousness when wrong wins time and time again. I want to yell and scream. I want justice to be served. But it still feels so far away. Nonviolence doesn't seem to be enough. I do not understand the concept of turning the other cheek. If I defend myself or come to the defense of others, am I any less of a believer?

EXHALE

Let's be real. Our humanity can sometimes get the best of us. When we are wronged, we often want to react in anger and even seek revenge on our own because we are tired of seeing injustice run rampant around us. Turning the other cheek applies to our desire to avenge a wrongdoing or take revenge. Romans 12:19 says, "Beloved, do not avenge yourselves, but rather give place to wrath; for it is written, 'Vengeance is Mine, I will repay,' says the Lord." As followers of Christ, we will be persecuted, and we will suffer on His account.

But God does not ask Christians to be passive and never to defend themselves and others. But whatever actions we take should be biblically guided and directed through prayer.

The truth is that justice will be done. Second Chronicles 16:9 says that "the eyes of the LORD run to and fro throughout the whole earth, to show Himself strong on behalf of those whose heart is loyal to Him." God sees everything and holds everyone accountable. In Numbers 1:2, He instructed Moses to "take a census of all the congregation of the children of Israel, by their families, by their fathers' houses, according to the number of names, every male individually." Not one person escaped God's notice then, and not one person will now. God is aware of every person and what he or she does.

Also remember that God moves on His schedule, not ours. He never gets behind (though it may seem this way to us). God has a great deal of restraint, but do not confuse His patience and mercy with injustice. You can breathe easy that God will bring forth justice such as this world has never seen.

1:27 [a] 2 Chr. 17:14 1:28 [a] Num. 2:5, 6 1:30 [a] Num. 2:7, 8; 26:26, 27 1:32 [a] Gen. 48:1–22; Num. 26:28–37; Deut. 33:13–17; Jer. 7:15; Obad. 19 1:34 [a] Num. 2:20, 21; 26:28–34

all who *were able to* go to war: 35those who
were numbered of the tribe of Manasseh
were thirty-two thousand two hundred.
36From the [a]children of Benjamin, their
genealogies by their families, by their fathers' house, according to the number of
names, from twenty years old and above,
all who *were able to* go to war: 37those who
were numbered of the tribe of Benjamin
were thirty-five thousand four hundred.
38From the [a]children of Dan, their genealogies by their families, by their fathers'
house, according to the number of names,
from twenty years old and above, all who
were able to go to war: 39those who were
numbered of the tribe of Dan *were* sixty-
two thousand seven hundred.
40From the [a]children of Asher, their genealogies by their families, by their fathers'
house, according to the number of names,
from twenty years old and above, all who
were able to go to war: 41those who were
numbered of the tribe of Asher *were* forty-
one thousand five hundred.
42From the children of Naphtali, their
genealogies by their families, by their fathers' house, according to the number of
names, from twenty years old and above,
all who *were able to* go to war: 43those who
were numbered of the tribe of Naphtali
were fifty-three thousand four hundred.
44[a]These are the ones who were numbered, whom Moses and Aaron numbered,
with the leaders of Israel, twelve men, each
one representing his father's house. 45So all
who were numbered of the children of Israel, by their fathers' houses, from twenty
years old and above, all who *were able to* go
to war in Israel— 46all who were numbered
were [a]six hundred and three thousand five
hundred and fifty.
47But [a]the Levites were not numbered
among them by their fathers' tribe; 48for the
LORD had spoken to Moses, saying: 49[a]"Only
the tribe of Levi you shall not number, nor
take a census of them among the children
of Israel; 50[a]but you shall appoint the Levites over the tabernacle of the Testimony,
over all its furnishings, and over all things
that belong to it; they shall carry the tabernacle and all its furnishings; they shall attend to it [b]and camp around the tabernacle.
51[a]And when the tabernacle is to go forward,
the Levites shall take it down; and when the
tabernacle is to be set up, the Levites shall
set it [b]up. [c]The outsider who comes near
shall be put to death. 52The children of Israel shall pitch their tents, [a]everyone by his
own camp, everyone by his own standard,
according to their armies; 53[a]but the Levites shall camp around the tabernacle of
the Testimony, that there may be no [b]wrath
on the congregation of the children of Israel; and the Levites shall [c]keep charge of
the tabernacle of the Testimony."
54Thus the children of Israel did; according to all that the LORD commanded Moses, so they did.

The Tribes and Leaders by Armies

2 And the LORD spoke to Moses and
Aaron, saying: 2[a]"Everyone of the
children of Israel shall camp by his own
standard, beside the emblems of his father's house; they shall camp [b]some distance from the tabernacle of meeting. 3On
the [a]east side, toward the rising of the sun,
those of the standard of the forces with Judah shall camp according to their armies;
and [b]Nahshon the son of Amminadab *shall
be* the leader of the children of Judah."
4And his army was numbered at seventy-
four thousand six hundred.
5"Those who camp next to him *shall be*
the tribe of Issachar, and Nethanel the son
of Zuar *shall be* the leader of the children of
Issachar." 6And his army was numbered at
fifty-four thousand four hundred.
7"Then *comes* the tribe of Zebulun, and
Eliab the son of Helon *shall be* the leader
of the children of Zebulun." 8And his army
was numbered at fifty-seven thousand four
hundred. 9"All who were numbered according to their armies of the forces with Judah,
one hundred and eighty-six thousand four
hundred—[a]these shall break camp first.

1:36 [a] Gen. 49:27; Num. 26:38–41; 2 Chr. 17:17; Rev. 7:8 1:38 [a] Gen. 30:6; 46:23; Num. 2:25, 26; 26:42, 43 1:40 [a] Num. 2:27, 28; 26:44–47 1:44 [a] Num. 26:64 1:46 [a] Ex. 12:37; 38:26; Num. 2:32; 26:51, 63; Heb. 11:12; Rev. 7:4–8 1:47 [a] Num. 2:33; 3:14–22; 26:57–62; 1 Chr. 6:1–47; 21:6 1:49 [a] Num. 2:33; 26:62 1:50 [a] Ex. 38:21; Num. 3:7, 8; 4:15, 25–27, 33 [b] Num. 3:23, 29, 35, 38 1:51 [a] Num. 4:5–15; 10:17, 21 [b] Num. 10:21 [c] Num. 3:10, 38; 4:15, 19, 20; 18:22 1:52 [a] Num. 2:2, 34; 24:2 1:53 [a] Num. 1:50 [b] Lev. 10:6; Num. 8:19; 16:46; 18:5; 1 Sam. 6:19 [c] Num. 8:24; 18:2–4; 1 Chr. 23:32 2:2 [a] Num. 1:52; 24:2 [b] Josh. 3:4 2:3 [a] Num. 10:5 [b] Num. 1:7; 7:12; 10:14; Ruth 4:20; 1 Chr. 2:10; Matt. 1:4; Luke 3:32, 33 2:9 [a] Num. 10:14

10“On the [a]south side *shall be* the standard of the forces with Reuben according
to their armies, and the leader of the children of Reuben *shall be* Elizur the son of
Shedeur.” 11And his army was numbered at
forty-six thousand five hundred.
12“Those who camp next to him *shall be*
the tribe of Simeon, and the leader of the
children of Simeon *shall be* Shelumiel the
son of Zurishaddai.” 13And his army was
numbered at fifty-nine thousand three
hundred.
14“Then *comes* the tribe of Gad, and the
leader of the children of Gad *shall be* Eliasaph the son of Reuel.”[1] 15And his army was
numbered at forty-five thousand six hundred and fifty. 16“All who were numbered
according to their armies of the forces with
Reuben, one hundred and fifty-one thousand four hundred and fifty—[a]they shall
be the second to break camp.
17[a]“And the tabernacle of meeting shall
move out with the camp of the Levites [b]in
the middle of the camps; as they camp, so
they shall move out, everyone in his place,
by their standards.
18“On the west side *shall be* the standard
of the forces with Ephraim according to
their armies, and the leader of the children
of Ephraim *shall be* Elishama the son of
Ammihud.” 19And his army was numbered
at forty thousand five hundred.
20“Next to him *comes* the tribe of Manasseh, and the leader of the children of
Manasseh *shall be* Gamaliel the son of Pedahzur.” 21And his army was numbered at
thirty-two thousand two hundred.
22“Then *comes* the tribe of Benjamin,
and the leader of the children of Benjamin *shall be* Abidan the son of Gideoni.”
23And his army was numbered at thirty-
five thousand four hundred. 24“All who
were numbered according to their armies
of the forces with Ephraim, one hundred
and eight thousand one hundred—[a]they
shall be the third to break camp.
25“The standard of the forces with Dan
shall be on the north side according to
their armies, and the leader of the children of Dan *shall be* Ahiezer the son of
Ammishaddai.” 26And his army was numbered at sixty-two thousand seven hundred.
27“Those who camp next to him *shall
be* the tribe of Asher, and the leader of the
children of Asher *shall be* Pagiel the son of
Ocran.” 28And his army was numbered at
forty-one thousand five hundred.
29“Then *comes* the tribe of Naphtali, and
the leader of the children of Naphtali *shall
be* Ahira the son of Enan.” 30And his army
was numbered at fifty-three thousand four
hundred. 31“All who were numbered of the
forces with Dan, one hundred and fifty-
seven thousand six hundred—[a]they shall
break camp last, with their standards.”
32These *are* the ones who were numbered of the children of Israel by their fathers' houses. [a]All who were numbered
according to their armies of the forces
were six hundred and three thousand five
hundred and fifty. 33But [a]the Levites were
not numbered among the children of Israel, just as the LORD commanded Moses.
34Thus the children of Israel [a]did according to all that the LORD commanded Moses;
[b]so they camped by their standards and so
they broke camp, each one by his family,
according to their fathers' houses.

The Sons of Aaron
(Lev. 10:1–7)

3 Now these *are* the [a]records of Aaron
and Moses when the LORD spoke with
Moses on Mount Sinai. 2And these *are* the
names of the sons of Aaron: Nadab, the
[a]firstborn, and [b]Abihu, Eleazar, and Ithamar. 3These *are* the names of the sons
of Aaron, [a]the anointed priests, whom he
consecrated to minister as priests. 4[a]Na-
dab and Abihu had died before the LORD
when they offered profane fire before the
LORD in the Wilderness of Sinai; and they
had no children. So Eleazar and Ithamar
ministered as priests in the presence of
Aaron their father.

The Levites Serve in the Tabernacle

5And the LORD spoke to Moses, saying:
6[a]“Bring the tribe of Levi near, and present

2:10 [a] Num. 10:6 2:14 [1] Spelled *Deuel* in 1:14 and 7:42 2:16 [a] Num. 10:18 2:17 [a] Num. 10:17, 21 [b] Num. 1:53 2:24 [a] Num. 10:22
2:31 [a] Num. 10:25 2:32 [a] Ex. 38:26; Num. 1:46; 11:21 2:33 [a] Num. 1:47; 26:57–62 2:34 [a] Num. 1:54 [b] Num. 24:2, 5, 6
3:1 [a] Ex. 6:16–27 3:2 [a] Ex. 6:23 [b] Lev. 10:1, 2; Num. 26:60, 61; 1 Chr. 24:2 3:3 [a] Ex. 28:41; Lev. 8 3:4 [a] Lev. 10:1, 2;
Num. 26:61; 1 Chr. 24:2 3:6 [a] Num. 8:6–22; 18:1–7; Deut. 10:8; 33:8–11

them before Aaron the priest, that they may serve him. 7And they shall attend to his needs and the needs of the whole congregation before the tabernacle of meeting, to do [a]the work of the tabernacle. 8Also they shall attend to all the furnishings of the tabernacle of meeting, and to the needs of the children of Israel, to do the work of the tabernacle. 9And [a]you shall give the Levites to Aaron and his sons; they *are* given entirely to him[1] from among the children of Israel. 10So you shall appoint Aaron and his sons, [a]and they shall attend to their priesthood; [b]but the outsider who comes near shall be put to death."

11Then the LORD spoke to Moses, saying: 12"Now behold, [a]I Myself have taken the Levites from among the children of Israel instead of every firstborn who opens the womb among the children of Israel. Therefore the Levites shall be [b]Mine, 13because [a]all the firstborn *are* Mine. [b]On the day that I struck all the firstborn in the land of Egypt, I sanctified to Myself all the firstborn in Israel, both man and beast. They shall be Mine: I *am* the LORD."

Census of the Levites Commanded
(cf. Num. 1:47–54)

14Then the LORD spoke to Moses in the Wilderness of Sinai, saying: 15"Number the children of Levi by their fathers' houses, by their families; you shall number [a]every male from a month old and above."

16So Moses numbered them according to the word of the LORD, as he was commanded. 17[a]These were the sons of Levi by their names: Gershon, Kohath, and Merari. 18And these *are* the names of the sons of [a]Gershon by their families: [b]Libni and Shimei. 19And the sons of [a]Kohath by their families: [b]Amram, Izehar, Hebron, and Uzziel. 20[a]And the sons of Merari by their families: Mahli and Mushi. These *are* the families of the Levites by their fathers' houses.

21From Gershon *came* the family of the Libnites and the family of the Shimites; these *were* the families of the Gershonites. 22Those who were numbered, according to the number of all the males from a month old and above—of those who were numbered *there were* seven thousand five hundred. 23[a]The families of the Gershonites were to camp behind the tabernacle westward. 24And the leader of the father's house of the Gershonites *was* Eliasaph the son of Lael. 25[a]The duties of the children of Gershon in the tabernacle of meeting *included* [b]the tabernacle, [c]the tent with [d]its covering, [e]the screen for the door of the tabernacle of meeting, 26[a]the screen for the door of the court, [b]the hangings of the court which *are* around the tabernacle and the altar, and [c]their cords, according to all the work relating to them.

27[a]From Kohath *came* the family of the Amramites, the family of the Izharites, the family of the Hebronites, and the family of the Uzzielites; these *were* the families of the Kohathites. 28According to the number of all the males, from a month old and above, *there were* eight thousand six[1] hundred keeping charge of the sanctuary. 29[a]The families of the children of Kohath were to camp on the south side of the tabernacle. 30And the leader of the fathers' house of the families of the Kohathites *was* Elizaphan the son of [a]Uzziel. 31[a]Their duty *included* [b]the ark, [c]the table, [d]the lampstand, [e]the altars, the utensils of the sanctuary with which they ministered, [f]the screen, and all the work relating to them.

32And Eleazar the son of Aaron the priest *was to be* chief over the leaders of the Levites, *with* oversight of those who kept charge of the sanctuary.

33From Merari *came* the family of the Mahlites and the family of the Mushites; these *were* the families of Merari. 34And those who were numbered, according to the number of all the males from a month old and above, *were* six thousand two hundred. 35The leader of the fathers' house of the families of Merari *was* Zuriel the son of Abihail. [a]These *were* to camp on the

3:7 [a] Num. 1:50; 8:11, 15, 24, 26 3:9 [a] Num. 8:19; 18:6, 7 [1] Samaritan Pentateuch and Septuagint read *Me.* 3:10 [a] Ex. 29:9; Num. 18:7 [b] Num. 1:51; 3:38; 16:40 3:12 [a] Num. 3:41; 8:16; 18:6 [b] Ex. 13:2; Num. 3:45; 8:14 3:13 [a] Ex. 13:2; Lev. 27:26; Num. 8:16, 17; Neh. 10:36; Luke 2:23 [b] Ex. 13:12, 15; Num. 8:17 3:15 [a] Num. 3:39; 26:62 3:17 [a] Gen. 46:11; Ex. 6:16–22; Num. 26:57; 1 Chr. 6:1, 16; 23:6 3:18 [a] Num. 4:38–41 [b] Ex. 6:17 3:19 [a] Num. 4:34–37 [b] Ex. 6:18 3:20 [a] Ex. 6:19; Num. 4:42–45 3:23 [a] Num. 1:53 3:25 [a] Num. 4:24–26 [b] Ex. 25:9 [c] Ex. 26:1 [d] Ex. 26:7, 14 [e] Ex. 26:36 3:26 [a] Ex. 27:9, 12, 14, 15 [b] Ex. 27:16 [c] Ex. 35:18 3:27 [a] 1 Chr. 26:23 3:28 [1] Some manuscripts of the Septuagint read *three.* 3:29 [a] Ex. 6:18; Num. 1:53 3:30 [a] Lev. 10:4 3:31 [a] Num. 4:15 [b] Ex. 25:10 [c] Ex. 25:23 [d] Ex. 25:31 [e] Ex. 27:1; 30:1 [f] Ex. 26:31–33 3:35 [a] Num. 1:53; 2:25

north side of the tabernacle. 36 And [a]the appointed duty of the children of Merari *included* the boards of the tabernacle, its bars, its pillars, its sockets, its utensils, all the work relating to them, 37 and the pillars of the court all around, with their sockets, their pegs, and their cords.

38 [a]Moreover those who were to camp before the tabernacle on the east, before the tabernacle of meeting, *were* Moses, Aaron, and his sons, [b]keeping charge of the sanctuary, [c]to meet the needs of the children of Israel; but [d]the outsider who came near was to be put to death. 39 [a]All who were numbered of the Levites, whom Moses and Aaron numbered at the commandment of the LORD, by their families, all the males from a month old and above, *were* twenty-two thousand.

Levites Dedicated Instead of the Firstborn

40 Then the LORD said to Moses: [a]"Number all the firstborn males of the children of Israel from a month old and above, and take the number of their names. 41 [a]And you shall take the Levites for Me—I *am* the LORD—instead of all the firstborn among the children of Israel, and the livestock of the Levites instead of all the firstborn among the livestock of the children of Israel." 42 So Moses numbered all the firstborn among the children of Israel, as the LORD commanded him. 43 And all the firstborn males, according to the number of names from a month old and above, of those who were numbered of them, were twenty-two thousand two hundred and seventy-three.

44 Then the LORD spoke to Moses, saying: 45 [a]"Take the Levites instead of all the firstborn among the children of Israel, and the livestock of the Levites instead of their livestock. The Levites shall be Mine: I *am* the LORD. 46 And for [a]the redemption of the two hundred and seventy-three of the firstborn of the children of Israel, [b]who are more than the number of the Levites, 47 you shall take [a]five shekels for each one [b]individually; you shall take *them* in the currency of the shekel of the sanctuary, [c]the shekel of twenty gerahs. 48 And you shall give the money, with which the excess number of them is redeemed, to Aaron and his sons."

49 So Moses took the redemption money from those who were over and above those who were redeemed by the Levites. 50 From the firstborn of the children of Israel he took the money, [a]one thousand three hundred and sixty-five *shekels*, according to the shekel of the sanctuary. 51 And Moses [a]gave their redemption money to Aaron and his sons, according to the word of the LORD, as the LORD commanded Moses.

Duties of the Sons of Kohath

4 Then the LORD spoke to Moses and Aaron, saying: 2 "Take a census of the sons of [a]Kohath from among the children of Levi, by their families, by their fathers' house, 3 [a]from thirty years old and above, even to fifty years old, all who enter the service to do the work in the tabernacle of meeting.

4 [a]"This *is* the service of the sons of Kohath in the tabernacle of meeting, *relating to* [b]the most holy things: 5 When the camp prepares to journey, Aaron and his sons shall come, and they shall take down [a]the covering veil and cover the [b]ark of the Testimony with it. 6 Then they shall put on it a covering of badger skins, and spread over *that* a cloth entirely of [a]blue; and they shall insert [b]its poles.

7 "On the [a]table of showbread they shall spread a blue cloth, and put on it the dishes, the pans, the bowls, and the pitchers for pouring; and the [b]showbread[1] shall be on it. 8 They shall spread over them a scarlet cloth, and cover the same with a covering of badger skins; and they shall insert its poles. 9 And they shall take a blue cloth and cover the [a]lampstand of the light, [b]with its lamps, its wick-trimmers, its trays, and all its oil vessels, with which they service it. 10 Then they shall put it with all its utensils

---

3:36 [a] Num. 4:31, 32 3:38 [a] Num. 1:53 [b] Num. 18:5 [c] Num. 3:7, 8 [d] Num. 3:10 3:39 [a] Num. 3:43; 4:48; 26:62 3:40 [a] Num. 3:15 3:41 [a] Num. 3:12, 45 3:45 [a] Num. 3:12, 41 3:46 [a] Ex. 13:13, 15; Num. 18:15, 16 [b] Num. 3:39, 43 3:47 [a] Lev. 27:6; Num. 18:16 [b] Num. 1:2, 18, 20 [c] Ex. 30:13 3:50 [a] Num. 3:46, 47 3:51 [a] Num. 3:48 4:2 [a] Num. 3:27–32 4:3 [a] Num. 4:23, 30, 35; 8:24; 1 Chr. 23:3, 24, 27; Ezra 3:8 4:4 [a] Num. 4:15 [b] Num. 4:19 4:5 [a] Ex. 26:31; Heb. 9:3 [b] Ex. 25:10, 16 4:6 [a] Ex. 39:1 [b] Ex. 25:13; 1 Kin. 8:7, 8 4:7 [a] Ex. 25:23, 29, 30 [b] Lev. 24:5–9 [1] Literally *the continual bread* 4:9 [a] Ex. 25:31 [b] Ex. 25:37, 38

in a covering of badger skins, and put *it* on
a carrying beam.
11"Over [a]the golden altar they shall
spread a blue cloth, and cover it with a covering of badger skins; and they shall insert its poles. 12Then they shall take all the
[a]utensils of service with which they minister in the sanctuary, put *them* in a blue
cloth, cover them with a covering of badger skins, and put *them* on a carrying beam.
13Also they shall take away the ashes from
the altar, and spread a purple cloth over
it. 14They shall put on it all its implements
with which they minister there—the firepans, the forks, the shovels, the basins, and
all the utensils of the altar—and they shall
spread on it a covering of badger skins, and
insert its poles. 15And when Aaron and his
sons have finished covering the sanctuary and all the furnishings of the sanctuary, when the camp is set to go, then [a]the
sons of Kohath shall come to carry *them;*
[b]but they shall not touch any holy thing,
lest they die.
"[c]These *are* the things in the tabernacle of meeting which the sons of Kohath
are to carry.
16"The appointed duty of Eleazar the son
of Aaron the priest *is* [a]the oil for the light,
the [b]sweet incense, [c]the daily grain offering, the [d]anointing oil, the oversight of all
the tabernacle, of all that *is* in it, with the
sanctuary and its furnishings."
17Then the LORD spoke to Moses and
Aaron, saying: 18"Do not cut off the tribe of
the families of the Kohathites from among
the Levites; 19but do this in regard to them,
that they may live and not die when they
approach [a]the most holy things: Aaron
and his sons shall go in and appoint each
of them to his service and his task. 20[a]But
they shall not go in to watch while the holy
things are being covered, lest they die."

Duties of the Sons of Gershon

21Then the LORD spoke to Moses, saying:
22"Also take a census of the sons of [a]Ger-
shon, by their fathers' house, by their families. 23[a]From thirty years old and above,
even to fifty years old, you shall number
them, all who enter to perform the service,
to do the work in the tabernacle of meeting. 24This *is* the [a]service of the families
of the Gershonites, in serving and carrying: 25[a]They shall carry the [b]curtains of the
tabernacle and the tabernacle of meeting
with its covering, the covering of [c]badger
skins that *is* on it, the screen for the door
of the tabernacle of meeting, 26the screen
for the door of the gate of the court, the
hangings of the court which *are* around the
tabernacle and altar, and their cords, all the
furnishings for their service and all that is
made for these things: so shall they serve.
27"Aaron and his sons shall assign all the
service of the sons of the Gershonites, all
their tasks and all their service. And you
shall appoint to them all their tasks as their
duty. 28This *is* the service of the families of
the sons of Gershon in the tabernacle of
meeting. And their duties *shall be* [a]under
the authority[1] of Ithamar the son of Aaron
the priest.

Duties of the Sons of Merari

29"*As for* the sons of [a]Merari, you shall
number them by their families and by
their fathers' house. 30[a]From thirty years
old and above, even to fifty years old, you
shall number them, everyone who enters
the service to do the work of the tabernacle
of meeting. 31And [a]this *is* [b]what they must
carry as all their service for the tabernacle
of meeting: [c]the boards of the tabernacle,
its bars, its pillars, its sockets, 32and the
pillars around the court with their sockets,
pegs, and cords, with all their furnishings
and all their service; and you shall [a]assign
to each man by name the items he must
carry. 33This *is* the service of the families
of the sons of Merari, as all their service
for the tabernacle of meeting, under the
authority[1] of Ithamar the son of Aaron the
priest."

Census of the Levites

34[a]And Moses, Aaron, and the leaders
of the congregation numbered the sons

4:11 [a] Ex. 30:1–5 4:12 [a] Ex. 25:9; 1 Chr. 9:29 4:15 [a] Num. 7:9; 10:21; Deut. 31:9; Josh. 4:10; 2 Sam. 6:13; 1 Chr. 15:2, 15 [b] 2 Sam. 6:6, 7; 1 Chr. 13:9, 10 [c] Num. 3:31 4:16 [a] Ex. 25:6; Lev. 24:2 [b] Ex. 30:34 [c] Ex. 29:38 [d] Ex. 30:23–25 4:19 [a] Num. 4:4 4:20 [a] Ex. 19:21; 1 Sam. 6:19 4:22 [a] Num. 3:22 4:23 [a] Num. 4:3; 1 Chr. 23:3, 24, 27 4:24 [a] Num. 7:7 4:25 [a] Num. 3:25, 26 [b] Ex. 36:8 [c] Ex. 26:14 4:28 [a] Num. 4:33 [1] Literally *hand* 4:29 [a] Num. 3:33–37 4:30 [a] Num. 4:3; 8:24–26 4:31 [a] Num. 3:36, 37 [b] Num. 7:8 [c] Ex. 26:15 4:32 [a] Ex. 25:9; 38:21 4:33 [1] Literally *hand* 4:34 [a] Num. 4:2

RELEASE // ACT IN FAITH

Carrying Out Assignments

Numbers 4:15 // "And when Aaron and his sons have finished covering the sanctuary and all the furnishings of the sanctuary, when the camp is set to go, then the sons of Kohath shall come to carry them; but they shall not touch any holy thing, lest they die."

Summary Message // The message of the Book of Numbers is timeless. In it, we learn that God chose the Kohathites to carry out a holy task. This reminds us that God has given us assignments too. We need to act to bring our faith in God to life and fulfill the assignments He has given us. We will always reach a point of decision: Will we obey or disobey? Failure to follow God's assignments will always prove more costly than we imagined.

Numbers tells about Israel's wilderness experience beginning one year after their exodus from Egypt. Whenever the time came for them to journey onward, Moses gave the twelve tribes instructions concerning their positioning as they traveled through the wilderness. The tabernacle, however, was always to be positioned in the center of the camp.

Although our situation today is different from what the Israelites were facing in Numbers, their story serves as a good example of how God still gives assignments to carry out His divine plans and purposes. Sometimes, the tasks He assigns may not make sense to us (as Moses did not always understand the assignments he was given), but no matter, we are to obey the leading of our God.

Practical Application // Assignments are gifts from God that can come in large or small sizes. Our job is to receive these gifts, open them, and follow the instructions of their Giver. It is God's heart for His children to partner with Him. Many people, however, think God-given assignments are too difficult or even impossible. They are not. The Book of Numbers helps us understand that God often gives assignments that merely start us on the path to our destiny. As we obey, He slowly unfolds the bigger picture, making it easier for us to see. Therefore, saying yes to God's assignments allows His purpose to begin working in us. He will then bring that purpose to a conclusion as we follow His continued directions.

You have a God-given assignment. If you do not know what it is, go to God in prayer to discover it. What needs do you see around you? Look inside yourself. Are there matters you feel passionate about? What makes you angry? What excites you? The answers to these questions can help you discover the assignment God has for you.

Once you understand your assignment, wholeheartedly focus on completing it. Do not stop until you finish the task. Break out a pen and pad and start writing down ideas. Open a new screen on your computer and research those ideas. Then plan some time investigating opportunities. Ultimately, only you and God know what is required to get the job done. He will help you get it done right and on time.

Fervent Prayer // Heavenly Father, make our assignments known to us so that we may move forward by faith. Help us understand the importance of Your assignments and prepare ourselves for them. Give us confidence to fulfill them. Remind us to watch for Your directions, listen for Your voice, and diligently complete our assignments. We will be careful to give You all the glory along the way and when all is said and done. In Jesus' name we pray. Amen.

---

of the Kohathites by their families and by
their fathers' house, 35from thirty [a]years
old and above, even to fifty years old, everyone who entered the service for work in
the tabernacle of meeting; 36and those who
were numbered by their families were two
thousand seven hundred and fifty. 37These
were the ones who were numbered of the
families of the Kohathites, all who might
serve in the tabernacle of meeting, whom
Moses and Aaron numbered according
to the commandment of the LORD by the
hand of Moses.

38And those who were numbered of the
sons of Gershon, by their families and by
their fathers' house, 39from thirty years
old and above, even to fifty years old, everyone who entered the service for work in

4:35 [a] Num. 4:47

the tabernacle of meeting— 40those who
were numbered by their families, by their
fathers' house, were two thousand six hundred and thirty. 41[a]These *are* the ones who
were numbered of the families of the sons
of Gershon, of all who might serve in the
tabernacle of meeting, whom Moses and
Aaron numbered according to the commandment of the LORD.

42Those of the families of the sons of
Merari who were numbered, by their families, by their fathers' house, 43from thirty
years old and above, even to fifty years old,
everyone who entered the service for work
in the tabernacle of meeting— 44those who
were numbered by their families were three
thousand two hundred. 45These *are* the
ones who were numbered of the families
of the sons of Merari, whom Moses and
Aaron numbered [a]according to the word
of the LORD by the hand of Moses.

46All who were [a]numbered of the Levites,
whom Moses, Aaron, and the leaders of
Israel numbered, by their families and by
their fathers' houses, 47[a]from thirty years
old and above, even to fifty years old, everyone who came to do the work of service and the work of bearing burdens in
the tabernacle of meeting— 48those who
were numbered were eight thousand five
hundred and eighty.

49According to the commandment of
the LORD they were numbered by the hand
of Moses, [a]each according to his service and
according to his task; thus were they numbered by him, [b]as the LORD commanded
Moses.

Ceremonially Unclean Persons Isolated
(cf. Lev. 15:1–33)

5 And the LORD spoke to Moses, saying:
2"Command the children of Israel that
they put out of the camp every [a]leper, everyone who has a [b]discharge, and whoever becomes [c]defiled by a corpse. 3You
shall put out both male and female; you
shall put them outside the camp, that they
may not defile their camps [a]in the midst of
which I dwell." 4And the children of Israel
did so, and put them outside the camp; as
the LORD spoke to Moses, so the children
of Israel did.

Confession and Restitution
(Lev. 6:1–7)

5Then the LORD spoke to Moses, saying,
6"Speak to the children of Israel: [a]'When a
man or woman commits any sin that men
commit in unfaithfulness against the LORD,
and that person is guilty, 7[a]then he shall
confess the sin which he has committed.
He shall make restitution for his trespass
[b]in full, plus one-fifth of it, and give *it* to
the one he has wronged. 8But if the man
has no relative to whom restitution may be
made for the wrong, the restitution for the
wrong *must go* to the LORD for the priest,
in addition to [a]the ram of the atonement
with which atonement is made for him.
9Every [a]offering of all the holy things of
the children of Israel, which they bring to
the priest, shall be [b]his. 10And every man's
holy things shall be his; whatever any man
gives the priest shall be [a]his.'"

Concerning Unfaithful Wives

11And the LORD spoke to Moses, saying,
12"Speak to the children of Israel, and say
to them: 'If any man's wife goes astray and
behaves unfaithfully toward him, 13and a
man [a]lies with her carnally, and it is hidden from the eyes of her husband, and it
is concealed that she has defiled herself,
and *there was* no witness against her, nor
was she [b]caught— 14if the spirit of jealousy
comes upon him and he becomes [a]jealous
of his wife, who has defiled herself; or if the
spirit of jealousy comes upon him and he
becomes jealous of his wife, although she
has not defiled herself— 15then the man
shall bring his wife to the priest. He shall
[a]bring the offering required for her, one-
tenth of an ephah of barley meal; he shall
pour no oil on it and put no frankincense
on it, because it *is* a grain offering of jealousy, an offering for remembering, for
[b]bringing iniquity to remembrance.

16'And the priest shall bring her near, and

4:41 [a] Num. 4:22 4:45 [a] Num. 4:29 4:46 [a] Num. 3:39; 26:57–62; 1 Chr. 23:3–23 4:47 [a] Num. 4:3, 23, 30 4:49 [a] Num. 4:15, 24, 31 [b] Num. 4:1, 21 5:2 [a] Lev. 13:3, 8, 46; Num. 12:10, 14, 15 [b] Lev. 15:2 [c] Lev. 21:1; Num. 9:6, 10; 19:11, 13; 31:19 5:3 [a] Lev. 26:11, 12; Num. 35:34; [2 Cor. 6:16] 5:6 [a] Lev. 5:14—6:7 5:7 [a] Lev. 5:5; 26:40, 41; Josh. 7:19; Ps. 32:5; 1 John 1:9 [b] Lev. 6:4, 5 5:8 [a] Lev. 5:15; 6:6, 7; 7:7 5:9 [a] Ex. 29:28; Lev. 6:17, 18, 26; 7:6–14 [b] Lev. 7:32–34; 10:14, 15 5:10 [a] Lev. 10:13 5:13 [a] Lev. 18:20; 20:10 [b] John 8:4 5:14 [a] Prov. 6:34; Song 8:6 5:15 [a] Lev. 5:11 [b] 1 Kin. 17:18; Ezek. 29:16; Heb. 10:3

set her before the LORD. 17The priest shall
take holy water in an earthen vessel, and
take some of the dust that is on the floor
of the tabernacle and put *it* into the water.
18Then the priest shall stand the woman before the [a]LORD, uncover the woman's head,
and put the offering for remembering in
her hands, which *is* the grain offering of
jealousy. And the priest shall have in his
hand the bitter water that brings a curse.
19And the priest shall put her under oath,
and say to the woman, "If no man has lain
with you, and if you have not gone astray
to uncleanness *while* under your husband's
authority, be free from this bitter water
that brings a curse. 20But if you have gone
astray *while* under your husband's *authority,* and if you have defiled yourself and
some man other than your husband has
lain with you"— 21then the priest shall [a]put
the woman under the oath of the curse,
and he shall say to the woman—[b]"the LORD
make you a curse and an oath among your
people, when the LORD makes your thigh
rot and your belly swell; 22and may this
water that causes the curse [a]go into your
stomach, and make *your* belly swell and
your thigh rot."
[b]Then the woman shall say, "Amen, so
be it."
23'Then the priest shall write these
curses in a book, and he shall scrape *them*
off into the bitter water. 24And he shall
make the woman drink the bitter water that
brings a curse, and the water that brings
the curse shall enter her *to become* bitter.
25[a]Then the priest shall take the grain offering of jealousy from the woman's hand,
shall [b]wave the offering before the LORD,
and bring it to the altar; 26and the priest
shall take a handful of the offering, [a]as its
memorial portion, burn *it* on the altar, and
afterward make the woman drink the water.
27When he has made her drink the water,
then it shall be, if she has defiled herself
and behaved unfaithfully toward her husband, that the water that brings a [a]curse
will enter her *and become* bitter, and her
belly will swell, her thigh will rot, and the
woman [b]will become a curse among her
people. 28But if the woman has not defiled
herself, and is clean, then she shall be free
and may conceive children.
29'This *is* the law of jealousy, when a
wife, *while* under her husband's *authority,* [a]goes astray and defiles herself, 30or
when the spirit of jealousy comes upon a
man, and he becomes jealous of his wife;
then he shall stand the woman before the
LORD, and the priest shall execute all this
law upon her. 31Then the man shall be free
from iniquity, but that woman [a]shall bear
her guilt.' "

The Law of the Nazirite

6 Then the LORD spoke to Moses, saying,
2"Speak to the children of Israel, and
say to them: 'When either a man or woman
consecrates an offering to take the vow of a
Nazirite, [a]to separate himself to the LORD,
3[a]he shall separate himself from wine and
similar drink; he shall drink neither vinegar
made from wine nor vinegar made from
similar drink; neither shall he drink any
grape juice, nor eat fresh grapes or raisins.
4All the days of his separation he shall eat
nothing that is produced by the grapevine,
from seed to skin.
5'All the days of the vow of his separation no [a]razor shall come upon his head;
until the days are fulfilled for which he separated himself to the LORD, he shall be holy.
Then he shall let the locks of the hair of his
head grow. 6All the days that he separates
himself to the LORD [a]he shall not go near a
dead body. 7[a]He shall not make himself unclean even for his father or his mother, for
his brother or his sister, when they die, because his separation to God *is* on his head.
8[a]All the days of his separation he shall be
holy to the LORD.
9'And if anyone dies very suddenly beside him, and he defiles his consecrated
head, then he shall [a]shave his head on the
day of his cleansing; on the seventh day he
shall shave it. 10Then [a]on the eighth day he
shall bring two turtledoves or two young
pigeons to the priest, to the door of the

5:18 [a] Heb. 13:4 5:21 [a] Josh. 6:26; 1 Sam. 14:24; Neh. 10:29 [b] Jer. 29:22 5:22 [a] Ps. 109:18 [b] Deut. 27:15–26 5:25 [a] Lev. 8:27 [b] Lev. 2:2, 9 5:26 [a] Lev. 2:2, 9 5:27 [a] Deut. 28:37; Is. 65:15; Jer. 24:9; 29:18, 22; 42:18 [b] Num. 5:21 5:29 [a] Num. 5:19 5:31 [a] Lev. 20:17, 19, 20 6:2 [a] Lev. 27:2; Judg. 13:5; [Lam. 4:7; Amos 2:11, 12]; Acts 21:23; Rom. 1:1 6:3 [a] Lev. 10:9; Amos 2:12; Luke 1:15 6:5 [a] Judg. 13:5; 16:17; 1 Sam. 1:11 6:6 [a] Lev. 21:1–3, 11; Num. 19:11–22 6:7 [a] Lev. 21:1, 2, 11; Num. 9:6 6:8 [a] [2 Cor. 6:17, 18] 6:9 [a] Lev. 14:8, 9; Acts 18:18; 21:24 6:10 [a] Lev. 5:7; 14:22; 15:14, 29

tabernacle of meeting; 11and the priest shall offer one as a sin offering and *the* other as a burnt offering, and make atonement for him, because he sinned in regard to the corpse; and he shall sanctify his head that same day. 12He shall consecrate to the LORD the days of his separation, and bring a male lamb in its first year [a]as a trespass offering; but the former days shall be lost, because his separation was defiled.

13'Now this *is* the law of the Nazirite: [a]When the days of his separation are fulfilled, he shall be brought to the door of the tabernacle of meeting. 14And he shall present his offering to the LORD: one male lamb in its first year without blemish as a burnt offering, one ewe lamb in its first year without blemish [a]as a sin offering, one ram without blemish [b]as a peace offering, 15a basket of unleavened bread, [a]cakes of fine flour mixed with oil, unleavened wafers [b]anointed with oil, and their grain offering with their [c]drink offerings.

16'Then the priest shall bring *them* before the LORD and offer his sin offering and his burnt offering; 17and he shall offer the ram as a sacrifice of a peace offering to the LORD, with the basket of unleavened bread; the priest shall also offer its grain offering and its drink offering. 18[a]Then the Nazirite shall shave his consecrated head *at* the door of the tabernacle of meeting, and shall take the hair from his consecrated head and put *it* on the fire which is under the sacrifice of the peace offering.

19'And the priest shall take the [a]boiled shoulder of the ram, one [b]unleavened cake from the basket, and one unleavened wafer, and [c]put *them* upon the hands of the Nazirite after he has shaved his consecrated *hair,* 20and the priest shall wave them as a wave offering before the LORD; [a]they *are* holy for the priest, together with the breast of the wave offering and the thigh of the heave offering. After that the Nazirite may drink wine.'

21"This is the law of the Nazirite who vows to the LORD the offering for his separation, and besides that, whatever else his hand is able to provide; according to the vow which he takes, so he must do according to the law of his separation."

The Priestly Blessing

22And the LORD spoke to Moses, saying: 23"Speak to Aaron and his sons, saying, 'This is the way you shall bless the children of Israel. Say to them:

24"The LORD [a]bless you and [b]keep you;
25 The LORD [a]make His face
shine upon you,
And [b]be gracious to you;
26 [a]The LORD lift up His
countenance upon you,
And [b]give you peace."'

27[a]"So they shall put My name on the children of Israel, and [b]I will bless them."

Offerings of the Leaders

7 Now it came to pass, when Moses had finished [a]setting up the tabernacle, that he [b]anointed it and consecrated it and all its furnishings, and the altar and all its utensils; so he anointed them and consecrated them. 2Then [a]the leaders of Israel, the heads of their fathers' houses, who *were* the leaders of the tribes and over those who were numbered, made an offering. 3And they brought their offering before the LORD, six covered carts and twelve oxen, a cart for *every* two of the leaders, and for each one an ox; and they presented them before the tabernacle.

4Then the LORD spoke to Moses, saying, 5"Accept *these* from them, that they may be used in doing the work of the tabernacle of meeting; and you shall give them to the Levites, *to* every man according to his service." 6So Moses took the carts and the oxen, and gave them to the Levites. 7Two carts and four oxen [a]he gave to the sons of Gershon, according to their service; 8[a]and four carts and eight oxen he gave to the sons of Merari, according to their service, under the authority[1] of Ithamar the son of Aaron the priest. 9But to the sons of Kohath

6:12 [a] Lev. 5:6 6:13 [a] Acts 21:26 6:14 [a] Lev. 4:2, 27, 32 [b] Lev. 3:6 6:15 [a] Lev. 2:4 [b] Ex. 29:2 [c] Num. 15:5, 7, 10 6:18 [a] Num. 6:9; Acts 21:23, 24 6:19 [a] 1 Sam. 2:15 [b] Ex. 29:23, 24 [c] Lev. 7:30 6:20 [a] Ex. 29:27, 28 6:24 [a] Deut. 28:3–6 [b] Ps. 121:7; John 17:11 6:25 [a] Ps. 31:16; 67:1; 80:3, 7, 19; 119:135; Dan. 9:17 [b] Gen. 43:29; Ex. 33:19; Mal. 1:9 6:26 [a] Ps. 4:6; 89:15 [b] Lev. 26:6; Is. 26:3, 12; John 14:27; Phil. 4:7 6:27 [a] Deut. 28:10; 2 Sam. 7:23; 2 Chr. 7:14; Is. 43:7; Dan. 9:18, 19 [b] Ex. 20:24; Num. 23:20; Ps. 5:12; 67:7; 115:12, 13; Eph. 1:3 7:1 [a] Ex. 40:17–33 [b] Lev. 8:10, 11 7:2 [a] Num. 1:4 7:7 [a] Num. 4:24–28 7:8 [a] Num. 4:29–33 [1] Literally *hand*

he gave none, because theirs *was* [a]the service of the holy things, [b]*which* they carried
on their shoulders.

10Now the leaders offered [a]the dedication *offering* for the altar when it was
anointed; so the leaders offered their offering before the altar. 11For the LORD said
to Moses, "They shall offer their offering,
one leader each day, for the dedication of
the altar."

12And the one who offered his offering
on the first day *was* [a]Nahshon the son of
Amminadab, from the tribe of Judah. 13His
offering *was* one silver platter, the weight
of which *was* one hundred and thirty *shekels,* and one silver bowl of seventy shekels,
according to [a]the shekel of the sanctuary,
both of them full of fine flour mixed with
oil as a [b]grain offering; 14one gold pan of
ten *shekels,* full of [a]incense; 15[a]one young
bull, one ram, and one male lamb [b]in its
first year, as a burnt offering; 16one kid of
the goats as a [a]sin offering; 17and for [a]the
sacrifice of peace offerings: two oxen, five
rams, five male goats, and five male lambs
in their first year. This *was* the offering of
Nahshon the son of Amminadab.

18On the second day Nethanel the son
of Zuar, leader of Issachar, presented *an
offering.* 19*For* his offering he offered one
silver platter, the weight of which *was* one
hundred and thirty *shekels,* and one silver
bowl of seventy shekels, according to the
shekel of the sanctuary, both of them full
of fine flour mixed with oil as a grain offering; 20one gold pan of ten *shekels,* full of
incense; 21one young bull, one ram, and one
male lamb in its first year, as a burnt offering; 22one kid of the goats as a sin offering;
23and as the sacrifice of peace offerings:
two oxen, five rams, five male goats, and
five male lambs in their first year. This *was*
the offering of Nethanel the son of Zuar.

24On the third day Eliab the son of Helon, leader of the children of Zebulun, *presented an offering.* 25His offering *was* one
silver platter, the weight of which *was* one
hundred and thirty *shekels,* and one silver
bowl of seventy shekels, according to the
shekel of the sanctuary, both of them full
of fine flour mixed with oil as a grain offering; 26one gold pan of ten *shekels,* full
of incense; 27one young bull, one ram, and
one male lamb in its first year, as a burnt
offering; 28one kid of the goats as a sin offering; 29and for the sacrifice of peace offerings: two oxen, five rams, five male goats,
and five male lambs in their first year. This
was the offering of Eliab the son of Helon.

30On the fourth day [a]Elizur the son of
Shedeur, leader of the children of Reuben,
presented an offering. 31His offering *was* one
silver platter, the weight of which *was* one
hundred and thirty *shekels,* and one silver
bowl of seventy shekels, according to the
shekel of the sanctuary, both of them full
of fine flour mixed with oil as a grain offering; 32one gold pan of ten *shekels,* full of incense; 33one young bull, one ram, and one
male lamb in its first year, as a burnt offering; 34one kid of the goats as a sin offering;
35and as the sacrifice of peace offerings:
two oxen, five rams, five male goats, and
five male lambs in their first year. This *was*
the offering of Elizur the son of Shedeur.

36On the fifth day [a]Shelumiel the son of
Zurishaddai, leader of the children of Simeon, *presented an offering.* 37His offering
was one silver platter, the weight of which
was one hundred and thirty *shekels,* and
one silver bowl of seventy shekels, according to the shekel of the sanctuary, both of
them full of fine flour mixed with oil as a
grain offering; 38one gold pan of ten *shekels,* full of incense; 39one young bull, one
ram, and one male lamb in its first year,
as a burnt offering; 40one kid of the goats
as a sin offering; 41and as the sacrifice of
peace offerings: two oxen, five rams, five
male goats, and five male lambs in their
first year. This *was* the offering of Shelumiel the son of Zurishaddai.

42On the sixth day [a]Eliasaph the son of
Deuel,[1] leader of the children of Gad, *presented an offering.* 43His offering *was* one
silver platter, the weight of which *was* one
hundred and thirty *shekels,* and one silver bowl of seventy shekels, according to
the shekel of the sanctuary, both of them
full of fine flour mixed with oil as a grain

7:9 [a] Num. 4:15 [b] Num. 4:6–14 7:10 [a] Num. 7:1; Deut. 20:5; 1 Kin. 8:63; 2 Chr. 7:5, 9; Ezra 6:16; Neh. 12:27 7:12 [a] Num. 2:3 7:13 [a] Ex. 30:13 [b] Lev. 2:1 7:14 [a] Ex. 30:34, 35 7:15 [a] Lev. 1:2 [b] Ex. 12:5 7:16 [a] Lev. 4:23 7:17 [a] Lev. 3:1 7:30 [a] Num. 1:5; 2:10 7:36 [a] Num. 1:6; 2:12; 7:41 7:42 [a] Num. 1:14; 2:14; 10:20 [1] Spelled *Reuel* in 2:14

offering; 44one gold pan of ten *shekels,* full
of incense; 45one young bull, one ram, and
one male lamb in its first year, as [a]a burnt
offering; 46one kid of the goats as a sin offering; 47and as the sacrifice of peace offerings: two oxen, five rams, five male
goats, and five male lambs in their first
year. This *was* the offering of Eliasaph the
son of Deuel.
48On the seventh day [a]Elishama the
son of Ammihud, leader of the children
of Ephraim, *presented an offering.* 49His offering *was* one silver platter, the weight of
which *was* one hundred and thirty *shekels,*
and one silver bowl of seventy shekels, according to the shekel of the sanctuary, both
of them full of fine flour mixed with oil as a
grain offering; 50one gold pan of ten *shekels,* full of incense; 51one young bull, one
ram, and one male lamb in its first year,
as a burnt offering; 52one kid of the goats
as a sin offering; 53and as the sacrifice of
peace offerings: two oxen, five rams, five
male goats, and five male lambs in their
first year. This *was* the offering of Elishama the son of Ammihud.
54On the eighth day [a]Gamaliel the son
of Pedahzur, leader of the children of Manasseh, *presented an offering.* 55His offering
was one silver platter, the weight of which
was one hundred and thirty *shekels,* and
one silver bowl of seventy shekels, according to the shekel of the sanctuary, both of
them full of fine flour mixed with oil as a
grain offering; 56one gold pan of ten *shekels,* full of incense; 57one young bull, one
ram, and one male lamb in its first year,
as a burnt offering; 58one kid of the goats
as a sin offering; 59and as the sacrifice of
peace offerings: two oxen, five rams, five
male goats, and five male lambs in their
first year. This *was* the offering of Gamaliel the son of Pedahzur.
60On the ninth day [a]Abidan the son of
Gideoni, leader of the children of Benjamin, *presented an offering.* 61His offering
was one silver platter, the weight of which
was one hundred and thirty *shekels,* and
one silver bowl of seventy shekels, according to the shekel of the sanctuary, both of
them full of fine flour mixed with oil as a
grain offering; 62one gold pan of ten *shekels,* full of incense; 63one young bull, one
ram, and one male lamb in its first year,
as a burnt offering; 64one kid of the goats
as a sin offering; 65and as the sacrifice of
peace offerings: two oxen, five rams, five
male goats, and five male lambs in their
first year. This *was* the offering of Abidan
the son of Gideoni.
66On the tenth day [a]Ahiezer the son of
Ammishaddai, leader of the children of
Dan, *presented an offering.* 67His offering
was one silver platter, the weight of which
was one hundred and thirty *shekels,* and
one silver bowl of seventy shekels, according to the shekel of the sanctuary, both of
them full of fine flour mixed with oil as a
grain offering; 68one gold pan of ten *shekels,* full of incense; 69one young bull, one
ram, and one male lamb in its first year,
as a burnt offering; 70one kid of the goats
as a sin offering; 71and as the sacrifice of
peace offerings: two oxen, five rams, five
male goats, and five male lambs in their
first year. This *was* the offering of Ahiezer
the son of Ammishaddai.
72On the eleventh day [a]Pagiel the son of
Ocran, leader of the children of Asher, *presented an offering.* 73His offering *was* one
silver platter, the weight of which *was* one
hundred and thirty *shekels,* and one silver
bowl of seventy shekels, according to the
shekel of the sanctuary, both of them full
of fine flour mixed with oil as a grain offering; 74one gold pan of ten *shekels,* full
of incense; 75one young bull, one ram, and
one male lamb in its first year, as a burnt
offering; 76one kid of the goats as a sin offering; 77and as the sacrifice of peace offerings: two oxen, five rams, five male goats,
and five male lambs in their first year. This
was the offering of Pagiel the son of Ocran.
78On the twelfth day [a]Ahira the son of
Enan, leader of the children of Naphtali,
presented an offering. 79His offering *was*
one silver platter, the weight of which *was*
one hundred and thirty *shekels,* and one
silver bowl of seventy shekels, according to
the shekel of the sanctuary, both of them
full of fine flour mixed with oil as a grain
offering; 80one gold pan of ten *shekels,* full

7:45 [a] Ps. 40:6 7:48 [a] Num. 1:10; 2:18; 1 Chr. 7:26 7:54 [a] Num. 1:10; 2:20 7:60 [a] Num. 1:11; 2:22
7:66 [a] Num. 1:12; 2:25 7:72 [a] Num. 1:13; 2:27 7:78 [a] Num. 1:15; 2:29

of incense; 81one young bull, one ram, and
one male lamb in its first year, as a burnt
offering; 82one kid of the goats as a sin offering; 83and as the sacrifice of peace offerings: two oxen, five rams, five male goats,
and five male lambs in their first year. This
was the offering of Ahira the son of Enan.

84This *was* [a]the dedication *offering* for
the altar from the leaders of Israel, when it
was anointed: twelve silver platters, twelve
silver bowls, and twelve gold pans. 85Each
silver platter *weighed* one hundred and
thirty *shekels* and each bowl seventy *shekels.* All the silver of the vessels *weighed* two
thousand four hundred *shekels,* according
to the shekel of the sanctuary. 86The twelve
gold pans full of incense *weighed* ten *shekels* apiece, according to the shekel of the
sanctuary; all the gold of the pans *weighed*
one hundred and twenty *shekels.* 87All the
oxen for the burnt offering *were* twelve
young bulls, the rams twelve, the male
lambs in their first year twelve, with their
grain offering, and the kids of the goats as
a sin offering twelve. 88And all the oxen
for the sacrifice of peace offerings were
twenty-four bulls, the rams sixty, the male
goats sixty, and the lambs in their first year
sixty. This *was* the dedication *offering* for
the altar after it was [a]anointed.

89Now when Moses went into the tabernacle of meeting [a]to speak with Him, he
heard [b]the voice of One speaking to him
from above the mercy seat that *was* on the
ark of the Testimony, from [c]between the
two cherubim; thus He spoke to him.

Arrangement of the Lamps
(Ex. 25:31–40)

8 And the LORD spoke to Moses, saying: 2"Speak to Aaron, and say to him,
'When you [a]arrange the lamps, the seven
[b]lamps shall give light in front of the lampstand.'" 3And Aaron did so; he arranged the
lamps to face toward the front of the lampstand, as the LORD commanded Moses.
4[a]Now this workmanship of the lampstand
was hammered gold; from its shaft to its
flowers it *was* [b]hammered work. [c]According
to the pattern which the LORD had shown
Moses, so he made the lampstand.

Cleansing and Dedication of the Levites

5Then the LORD spoke to Moses, saying: 6"Take the Levites from among the
children of Israel and cleanse them *cer-
emonially.* 7Thus you shall do to them to
cleanse them: Sprinkle [a]water of purification on them, and [b]let them shave all their
body, and let them wash their clothes, and
so make themselves clean. 8Then let them
take a young bull with [a]its grain offering
of fine flour mixed with oil, and you shall
take another young bull as a sin offering.
9[a]And you shall bring the Levites before
the tabernacle of meeting, [b]and you shall
gather together the whole congregation of
the children of Israel. 10So you shall bring
the Levites before the LORD, and the children of Israel [a]shall lay their hands on the
Levites; 11and Aaron shall offer the Levites
before the LORD *like* a [a]wave offering from
the children of Israel, that they may perform the work of the LORD. 12[a]Then the Levites shall lay their hands on the heads of
the young bulls, and you shall offer one
as a sin offering and the other as a burnt
offering to the LORD, to make atonement
for the Levites.

13"And you shall stand the Levites before
Aaron and his sons, and then offer them
like a wave offering to the LORD. 14Thus you
shall [a]separate the Levites from among the
children of Israel, and the Levites shall be
[b]Mine. 15After that the Levites shall go in to
service the tabernacle of meeting. So you
shall cleanse them and [a]offer them *like* a
wave offering. 16For they *are* [a]wholly given
to Me from among the children of Israel; I
have taken them for Myself [b]instead of all
who open the womb, the firstborn of all the
children of Israel. 17[a]For all the firstborn
among the children of Israel *are* Mine, *both*
man and beast; on the day that I struck all
the firstborn in the land of Egypt I sanctified them to Myself. 18I have taken the
Levites instead of all the firstborn of the
children of Israel. 19And [a]I have given the

7:84 [a] Num. 7:10 7:88 [a] Num. 7:1, 10 7:89 [a] [Ex. 33:9, 11]; Num. 12:8 [b] Ex. 25:21, 22 [c] Ps. 80:1; 99:1 8:2 [a] Lev. 24:2–4 [b] Ex. 25:37; 40:25 8:4 [a] Ex. 25:31 [b] Ex. 25:18 [c] Ex. 25:40; Acts 7:44 8:7 [a] Num. 19:9, 13, 17, 20; Ps. 51:2, 7; [Heb. 9:13, 14] [b] Lev. 14:8, 9 8:8 [a] Lev. 2:1; Num. 15:8–10 8:9 [a] Ex. 29:4; 40:12 [b] Lev. 8:3 8:10 [a] Lev. 1:4 8:11 [a] Num. 18:6 8:12 [a] Ex. 29:10 8:14 [a] Num. 16:9 [b] Num. 3:12, 45; 16:9 8:15 [a] Num. 8:11, 13 8:16 [a] Num. 3:9 [b] Ex. 13:2; Num. 3:12, 45 8:17 [a] Ex. 12:2, 12, 13, 15; Num. 3:13; Luke 2:23 8:19 [a] Num. 3:9

Levites as a gift to Aaron and his sons from
among the children of Israel, to do the work
for the children of Israel in the tabernacle
of meeting, and to make atonement for the
children of Israel, [b]that there be no plague
among the children of Israel when the children of Israel come near the sanctuary."
20Thus Moses and Aaron and all the congregation of the children of Israel did to
the Levites; according to all that the LORD
commanded Moses concerning the Levites, so the children of Israel did to them.
21[a]And the Levites purified themselves and
washed their clothes; then Aaron presented
them *like* a wave offering before the LORD,
and Aaron made atonement for them to
cleanse them. 22[a]After that the Levites
went in to do their work in the tabernacle
of meeting before Aaron and his sons; [b]as
the LORD commanded Moses concerning
the Levites, so they did to them.
23Then the LORD spoke to Moses, say-
ing, 24"This *is* what *pertains* to the Levites:
[a]From twenty-five years old and above one
may enter to perform service in the work of
the tabernacle of meeting; 25and at the age
of fifty years they must cease performing
this work, and shall work no more. 26They
may minister with their brethren in the
tabernacle of meeting, [a]to attend to needs,
but they *themselves* shall do no work. Thus
you shall do to the Levites regarding their
duties."

The Second Passover
(Ex. 12:1–20)

9 Now the LORD spoke to Moses in the
Wilderness of Sinai, in the first month
of the second year after they had come out
of the land of Egypt, saying: 2"Let the children of Israel keep [a]the Passover at its appointed [b]time. 3On the fourteenth day of
this month, at twilight, you shall keep it
at its appointed time. According to all its
rites and ceremonies you shall keep it." 4So
Moses told the children of Israel that they
should keep the Passover. 5And [a]they kept
the Passover on the fourteenth day of the
first month, at twilight, in the Wilderness of
Sinai; according to all that the LORD commanded Moses, so the children of Israel
did.
6Now there were *certain* men who were
[a]defiled by a human corpse, so that they
could not keep the Passover on that day;
[b]and they came before Moses and Aaron
that day. 7And those men said to him, "We
became defiled by a human corpse. Why
are we kept from presenting the offering
of the LORD at its appointed time among
the children of Israel?"
8And Moses said to them, "Stand still,
that [a]I may hear what the LORD will command concerning you."
9Then the LORD spoke to Moses, saying,
10"Speak to the children of Israel, saying:
'If anyone of you or your posterity is unclean because of a corpse, or *is* far away
on a journey, he may still keep the LORD's
Passover. 11On [a]the fourteenth day of the
second month, at twilight, they may keep
it. They shall [b]eat it with unleavened bread
and bitter herbs. 12[a]They shall leave none
of it until morning, [b]nor break one of its
bones. [c]According to all the ordinances of
the Passover they shall keep it. 13But the
man who *is* clean and is not on a journey,
and ceases to keep the Passover, that same
person [a]shall be cut off from among his
people, because he [b]did not bring the offering of the LORD at its appointed time;
that man shall [c]bear his sin.
14'And if a stranger dwells among you,
and would keep the LORD's Passover, he
must do so according to the rite of the
Passover and according to its ceremony;
[a]you shall have one ordinance, both for
the stranger and the native of the land.'"

The Cloud and the Fire
(Ex. 13:21, 22; 40:34–38)

15Now [a]on the day that the tabernacle
was raised up, the cloud [b]covered the tabernacle, the tent of the Testimony; [c]from
evening until morning it was above the
tabernacle like the appearance of fire.
16So it was always: the cloud covered it *by
day,* and the appearance of fire by night.

8:19 [b] Num. 1:53; 16:46; 18:5; 2 Chr. 26:16 8:21 [a] Num. 8:7 8:22 [a] Num. 8:15 [b] Num. 8:5 8:24 [a] Num. 4:3; 1 Chr. 23:3, 24, 27
8:26 [a] Num. 1:53 9:2 [a] Ex. 12:1–16; Lev. 23:5; Num. 28:16; Deut. 16:1, 2 [b] 2 Chr. 30:1–15; Luke 22:7; [1 Cor. 5:7, 8] 9:5 [a] Josh. 5:10
9:6 [a] Num. 5:2; 19:11–22; John 18:28 [b] Ex. 18:15, 19, 26; Num. 27:2 9:8 [a] Ex. 18:22; Num. 27:5 9:11 [a] 2 Chr. 30:2, 15 [b] Ex. 12:8
9:12 [a] Ex. 12:10 [b] Ex. 12:46; [John 19:36] [c] Ex. 12:43 9:13 [a] Gen. 17:14; Ex. 12:15, 47 [b] Num. 9:7 [c] Num. 5:31 9:14 [a] Ex. 12:49;
Lev. 24:22; Num. 15:15, 16, 29 9:15 [a] Ex. 40:33, 34; Neh. 9:12, 19; Ps. 78:14 [b] Is. 4:5 [c] Ex. 13:21, 22; 40:38

17 Whenever the cloud [a]was taken up from
above the tabernacle, after that the children of Israel would journey; and in the
place where the cloud settled, there the
children of Israel would pitch their tents.
18 At the command of the LORD the children of Israel would journey, and at the
command of the LORD they would camp;
[a]as long as the cloud stayed above the tabernacle they remained encamped. 19 Even
when the cloud continued long, many days
above the tabernacle, the children of Israel
[a]kept the charge of the LORD and did not
journey. 20 So it was, when the cloud was
above the tabernacle a few days: according
to the command of the LORD they would
remain encamped, and according to the
command of the LORD they would journey. 21 So it was, when the cloud remained
only from evening until morning: when the
cloud was taken up in the morning, then
they would journey; whether by day or by
night, whenever the cloud was taken up,
they would journey. 22 *Whether it was* two
days, a month, or a year that the cloud remained above the tabernacle, the children
of Israel [a]would remain encamped and not
journey; but when it was taken up, they
would journey. 23 At the command of the
LORD they remained encamped, and at the
command of the LORD they journeyed; they
[a]kept the charge of the LORD, at the command of the LORD by the hand of Moses.

Two Silver Trumpets

10 And the LORD spoke to Moses, saying: 2 "Make two silver trumpets for
yourself; you shall make them of hammered work; you shall use them for [a]call-
ing the congregation and for directing the
movement of the camps. 3 When [a]they blow
both of them, all the congregation shall
gather before you at the door of the tabernacle of meeting. 4 But if they blow *only*
one, then the leaders, the [a]heads of the divisions of Israel, shall gather to you. 5 When
you sound the [a]advance, [b]the camps that
lie on the east side shall then begin their
journey. 6 When you sound the advance the
second time, then the camps that lie [a]on the
south side shall begin their journey; they
shall sound the call for them to begin their
journeys. 7 And when the assembly is to be
gathered together, [a]you shall blow, but not
[b]sound the advance. 8 [a]The sons of Aaron,
the priests, shall blow the trumpets; and
these shall be to you as an ordinance forever throughout your generations.

9 [a]"When you go to war in your land
against the enemy who [b]oppresses you,
then you shall sound an alarm with the
trumpets, and you will be [c]remembered
before the LORD your God, and you will be
saved from your enemies. 10 Also [a]in the day
of your gladness, in your appointed feasts,
and at the beginning of your months, you
shall blow the trumpets over your burnt
offerings and over the sacrifices of your
peace offerings; and they shall be [b]a memorial for you before your God: I *am* the
LORD your God."

Departure from Sinai

11 Now it came to pass on the twentieth
day of the second month, in the second
year, that the cloud [a]was taken up from
above the tabernacle of the Testimony.
12 And the children of Israel set out from
the [a]Wilderness of Sinai on [b]their journeys; then the cloud settled down in the

#OXYGEN

NUMBERS 9:19

Act in Faith

Sometimes in life we get impatient and move ahead of God instead of waiting on His timing.

God's delay is not a bad thing. His timing is always perfect.

Stand still, **breathe**, and **act in faith**.

9:17 [a] Ex. 40:36–38; Num. 10:11, 12, 33, 34; Ps. 80:1 9:18 [a] 1 Cor. 10:1 9:19 [a] Num. 1:53; 3:8 9:22 [a] Ex. 40:36, 37 9:23 [a] Num. 9:19 10:2 [a] Is. 1:13 10:3 [a] Jer. 4:5; Joel 2:15 10:4 [a] Ex. 18:21; Num. 1:16; 7:2 10:5 [a] Joel 2:1 [b] Num. 2:3 10:6 [a] Num. 2:10 10:7 [a] Num. 10:3 [b] Joel 2:1 10:8 [a] Num. 31:6; Josh. 6:4; 1 Chr. 15:24; 2 Chr. 13:12 10:9 [a] Num. 31:6; Josh. 6:5; 2 Chr. 13:14 [b] Judg. 2:18; 4:3; 6:9; 10:8, 12 [c] Gen. 8:1; Ps. 106:4 10:10 [a] Lev. 23:24; Num. 29:1; 1 Chr. 15:24; 2 Chr. 5:12; Ps. 81:3 [b] Lev. 23:24; Num. 10:9 10:11 [a] Num. 9:17 10:12 [a] Ex. 19:1; Num. 1:1; 9:5 [b] Ex. 40:36

[c]Wilderness of Paran. 13So they started out for the first time [a]according to the command of the LORD by the hand of Moses.

14The standard of the camp of the children of Judah [a]set out first according to their armies; over their army was [b]Nahshon the son of Amminadab. 15Over the army of the tribe of the children of Issachar *was* Nethanel the son of Zuar. 16And over the army of the tribe of the children of Zebulun *was* Eliab the son of Helon.

17Then [a]the tabernacle was taken down; and the sons of Gershon and the sons of Merari set out, [b]carrying the tabernacle.

18And [a]the standard of the camp of Reuben set out according to their armies; over their army *was* Elizur the son of Shedeur. 19Over the army of the tribe of the children of Simeon *was* Shelumiel the son of Zurishaddai. 20And over the army of the tribe of the children of Gad *was* Eliasaph the son of Deuel.

21Then the Kohathites set out, carrying the [a]holy things. (The tabernacle would be prepared for their arrival.)

22And [a]the standard of the camp of the children of Ephraim set out according to their armies; over their army *was* Elishama the son of Ammihud. 23Over the army of the tribe of the children of Manasseh *was* Gamaliel the son of Pedahzur. 24And over the army of the tribe of the children of Benjamin *was* Abidan the son of Gideoni.

25Then [a]the standard of the camp of the children of Dan (the rear guard of all the camps) set out according to their armies; over their army *was* Ahiezer the son of Ammishaddai. 26Over the army of the tribe of the children of Asher *was* Pagiel the son of Ocran. 27And over the army of the tribe of the children of Naphtali *was* Ahira the son of Enan.

28[a]Thus *was* the order of march of the children of Israel, according to their armies, when they began their journey.

29Now Moses said to [a]Hobab the son of [b]Reuel[1] the Midianite, Moses' father-in-law, "We are setting out for the place of which the LORD said, [c]'I will give it to you.' Come with us, and [d]we will treat you well; for [e]the LORD has promised good things to Israel."

30And he said to him, "I will not go, but I will depart to my *own* land and to my relatives."

31So *Moses* said, "Please do not leave, inasmuch as you know how we are to camp in the wilderness, and you can be our [a]eyes. 32And it shall be, if you go with us—indeed it shall be—that [a]whatever good the LORD will do to us, the same we will do to you."

33So they departed from [a]the mountain of the LORD on a journey of three days; and the ark of the covenant of the LORD [b]went before them for the three days' journey, to search out a resting place for them. 34And [a]the cloud of the LORD *was* above them by day when they went out from the camp.

35So it was, whenever the ark set out, that Moses said:

[a]"Rise up, O LORD!
Let Your enemies be scattered,
And let those who hate You
flee before You."

36And when it rested, he said:

"Return, O LORD,
To the many thousands of Israel."

The People Complain

11 Now [a]*when* the people complained, it displeased the LORD; [b]for the LORD heard *it,* and His anger was aroused. So the [c]fire of the LORD burned among them, and consumed *some* in the outskirts of the camp. 2Then the people [a]cried out to Moses, and when Moses [b]prayed to the LORD, the fire was quenched. 3So he called the name of the place Taberah,[1] because the fire of the LORD had burned among them.

4Now the [a]mixed multitude who were among them yielded to [b]intense craving; so the children of Israel also wept again and said: [c]"Who will give us meat to eat? 5[a]We remember the fish which we ate freely

10:12 [c] Gen. 21:21; Num. 12:16; Deut. 1:1 10:13 [a] Num. 10:5, 6 10:14 [a] Num. 2:3–9 [b] Num. 1:7 10:17 [a] Num. 1:51 [b] Num. 4:21–32; 7:7–9 10:18 [a] Num. 2:10–16 10:21 [a] Num. 4:4–20; 7:9 10:22 [a] Num. 2:18–24 10:25 [a] Num. 2:25–31; Josh. 6:9 10:28 [a] Num. 2:34 10:29 [a] Judg. 4:11 [b] Ex. 2:18; 3:1; 18:12 [c] Gen. 12:7; Ex. 6:4–8 [d] Judg. 1:16 [e] Gen. 32:12; Ex. 3:8 [1] Septuagint reads *Raguel* (compare Exodus 2:18). 10:31 [a] Job 29:15 10:32 [a] Ex. 18:9; Lev. 19:34; Judg. 1:16 10:33 [a] Ex. 3:1; Deut. 1:6 [b] Deut. 1:33; Josh. 3:3–6; Ezek. 20:6 10:34 [a] Ex. 13:21; Neh. 9:12, 19 10:35 [a] Ps. 68:1, 2; 132:8; Is. 17:12–14 11:1 [a] Num. 14:2; 16:11; 17:5; Deut. 9:22 [b] Ps. 78:21 [c] Lev. 10:2; 2 Kin. 1:12 11:2 [a] Num. 12:11, 13; 21:7 [b] [James 5:16] 11:3 [1] Literally *Burning* 11:4 [a] Ex. 12:38 [b] 1 Cor. 10:6 [c] [Ps. 78:18] 11:5 [a] Ex. 16:3

in Egypt, the cucumbers, the melons, the leeks, the onions, and the garlic; 6but now [a]our whole being *is* dried up; *there is* nothing at all except this manna *before* our eyes!"

7Now [a]the manna *was* like coriander seed, and its color like the color of bdellium. 8The people went about and gathered *it,* ground *it* on millstones or beat *it* in the mortar, cooked *it* in pans, and made cakes of it; and [a]its taste was like the taste of pastry prepared with oil. 9And [a]when the dew fell on the camp in the night, the manna fell on it.

10Then Moses heard the people weeping throughout their families, everyone at the door of his tent; and [a]the anger of the LORD was greatly aroused; Moses also was displeased. 11[a]So Moses said to the LORD, "Why have You afflicted Your servant? And why have I not found favor in Your sight, that You have laid the burden of all these people on me? 12Did I conceive all these people? Did I beget them, that You should say to me, [a]'Carry them in your bosom, as a [b]guardian carries a nursing child,' to the land which You [c]swore to their fathers? 13[a]Where am I to get meat to give to all these people? For they weep all over me, saying, 'Give us meat, that we may eat.' 14[a]I am not able to bear all these people alone, because the burden *is* too heavy for me. 15If You treat me like this, please kill me here and now—if I have found favor in Your sight—and [a]do not let me see my wretchedness!"

The Seventy Elders

16So the LORD said to Moses: "Gather to Me [a]seventy men of the elders of Israel, whom you know to be the elders of the people and [b]officers over them; bring them to the tabernacle of meeting, that they may stand there with you. 17Then I will come down and talk with you there. [a]I will take of the Spirit that *is* upon you and will put *the same* upon them; and they shall bear the burden of the people with you, that you may not bear *it* yourself alone. 18Then you shall say to the people, 'Consecrate yourselves for tomorrow, and you shall eat meat; for you have wept [a]in the hearing of the LORD, saying, "Who will give us meat to eat? For *it was* well with us in Egypt." Therefore the LORD will give you meat, and you shall eat. 19You shall eat, not one day, nor two days, nor five days, nor ten days, nor twenty days, 20[a]but *for* a whole month, until it comes out of your nostrils and becomes loathsome to you, because you have [b]despised the LORD who is among you, and have wept before Him, saying, [c]"Why did we ever come up out of Egypt?" ' "

21And Moses said, [a]"The people whom I *am* among *are* six hundred thousand men on foot; yet You have said, 'I will give them meat, that they may eat *for* a whole month.' 22[a]Shall flocks and herds be slaughtered for them, to provide enough for them? Or shall all the fish of the sea be gathered together for them, to provide enough for them?"

23And the LORD said to Moses, [a]"Has the LORD's arm been shortened? Now you shall see whether [b]what I say will happen to you or not."

24So Moses went out and told the people the words of the LORD, and he [a]gathered the seventy men of the elders of the people and placed them around the tabernacle. 25Then the LORD came down in the cloud, and spoke to him, and took of the Spirit that *was* upon him, and placed *the same* upon the seventy elders; and it happened, [a]when the Spirit rested upon them, that [b]they prophesied, although they never did *so* again.[1]

26But two men had remained in the camp: the name of one *was* Eldad, and the name of the other Medad. And the Spirit rested upon them. Now they *were* among those listed, but who [a]had not gone out to the tabernacle; yet they prophesied in the camp. 27And a young man ran and told Moses, and said, "Eldad and Medad are prophesying in the camp."

28So Joshua the son of Nun, Moses' assistant, *one* of his choice men, answered and said, "Moses my lord, [a]forbid them!"

11:6 [a] Num. 21:5 11:7 [a] Ex. 16:14, 31 11:8 [a] Ex. 16:31 11:9 [a] Ex. 16:13, 14 11:10 [a] Ps. 78:21 11:11 [a] Ex. 5:22; Deut. 1:12 11:12 [a] Is. 40:11 [b] Is. 49:23; 1 Thess. 2:7 [c] Gen. 26:3 11:13 [a] Matt. 15:33; Mark 8:4 11:14 [a] Ex. 18:18; Deut. 1:12 11:15 [a] Rev. 3:17 11:16 [a] Ex. 18:25; 24:1, 9 [b] Deut. 16:18 11:17 [a] 1 Sam. 10:6; 2 Kin. 2:15; [Joel 2:28] 11:18 [a] Ex. 16:7 11:20 [a] Ps. 78:29; 106:15 [b] 1 Sam. 10:19 [c] Num. 21:5 11:21 [a] Gen. 12:2; Ex. 12:37; Num. 1:46; 2:32 11:22 [a] 2 Kin. 7:2 11:23 [a] Is. 50:2; 59:1 [b] Num. 23:19 11:24 [a] Num. 11:16 11:25 [a] 2 Kin. 2:15 [b] 1 Sam. 10:5, 6, 10; Joel 2:28; Acts 2:17, 18; 1 Cor. 14:1 [1] Targum and Vulgate read *did not cease.* 11:26 [a] Jer. 36:5 11:28 [a] [Mark 9:38–40; Luke 9:49]

29 Then Moses said to him, "Are you zealous for my sake? [a]Oh, that all the LORD's people were prophets *and* that the LORD would put His Spirit upon them!" 30 And Moses returned to the camp, he and the elders of Israel.

The LORD Sends Quail

31 Now a [a]wind went out from the LORD, and it brought quail from the sea and left *them* fluttering near the camp, about a day's journey on this side and about a day's journey on the other side, all around the camp, and about two cubits above the surface of the ground. 32 And the people stayed up all that day, all night, and all the next day, and gathered the quail (he who gathered least gathered ten [a]homers); and they spread *them* out for themselves all around the camp. 33 But while the [a]meat *was* still between their teeth, before it was chewed, the wrath of the LORD was aroused against the people, and the LORD struck the people with a very great plague. 34 So he called the name of that place Kibroth Hattaavah,[1] because there they buried the people who had yielded to craving.

35 [a]From Kibroth Hattaavah the people moved to Hazeroth, and camped at Hazeroth.

Dissension of Aaron and Miriam

12 Then [a]Miriam and Aaron spoke [b]against Moses because of the Ethiopian woman whom he had married; for [c]he had married an Ethiopian woman. 2 So they said, "Has the LORD indeed spoken only through [a]Moses? [b]Has He not spoken through us also?" And the LORD [c]heard *it.* 3 (Now the man Moses *was* very humble, more than all men who *were* on the face of the earth.)

4 [a]Suddenly the LORD said to Moses, Aaron, and Miriam, "Come out, you three, to the tabernacle of meeting!" So the three came out. 5 [a]Then the LORD came down in the pillar of cloud and stood *in* the door of the tabernacle, and called Aaron and Miriam. And they both went forward. 6 Then He said,

"Hear now My words:
If there is a prophet among you,
I, the LORD, make Myself known
to him [a]in a vision;
I speak to him [b]in a dream.
7 Not so with [a]My servant Moses;
[b]He *is* faithful in all [c]My house.
8 I speak with him [a]face to face,
Even [b]plainly, and not in dark sayings;
And he sees [c]the form of the LORD.
Why then [d]were you not afraid
To speak against My servant Moses?"

9 So the anger of the LORD was aroused against them, and He departed. 10 And when the cloud departed from above the tabernacle, [a]suddenly Miriam *became* [b]leprous, as *white as* snow. Then Aaron turned toward Miriam, and there she was, a leper. 11 So Aaron said to Moses, "Oh, my lord! Please [a]do not lay *this* sin on us, in which we have done foolishly and in which we have sinned. 12 Please [a]do not let her be as one dead, whose flesh is half consumed when he comes out of his mother's womb!"

13 So Moses cried out to the LORD, saying, "Please [a]heal her, O God, I pray!"

14 Then the LORD said to Moses, "If her father had but [a]spit in her face, would she not be shamed seven days? Let her be [b]shut out of the camp seven days, and afterward she may be received *again.*" 15 [a]So Miriam was shut out of the camp seven days, and the people did not journey till Miriam was brought in *again.* 16 And afterward the people moved from [a]Hazeroth and camped in the Wilderness of Paran.

Spies Sent into Canaan
(Deut. 1:19–33)

13 And the LORD spoke to Moses, saying, 2 [a]"Send men to spy out the land of Canaan, which I am giving to the

11:29 [a] 1 Cor. 14:5 11:31 [a] Ex. 16:13; Ps. 78:26–28; 105:40 11:32 [a] Ex. 16:36; Ezek. 45:11 11:33 [a] Ps. 78:29–31; 106:15 11:34 [1] Literally *Graves of Craving* 11:35 [a] Num. 33:17 12:1 [a] Ex. 15:20, 21; Num. 20:1 [b] Num. 11:1 [c] Ex. 2:21 12:2 [a] Num. 16:3 [b] Ex. 15:20; Mic. 6:4 [c] Gen. 29:33; Num. 11:1; 2 Kin. 19:4; Is. 37:4; Ezek. 35:12, 13 12:4 [a] [Ps. 76:9] 12:5 [a] Ex. 19:9; 34:5; Num. 11:25; 16:19 12:6 [a] Gen. 46:2; 1 Sam. 3:15; Job 33:15; Ezek. 1:1; Dan. 8:2; Luke 1:11; Acts 10:11, 17; 22:17, 18 [b] Gen. 31:10; 1 Kin. 3:5, 15; Matt. 1:20 12:7 [a] Josh. 1:1; Ps. 105:26 [b] Heb. 3:2, 5 [c] 1 Tim. 1:12 12:8 [a] Ex. 33:11; Deut. 34:10; Hos. 12:13 [b] [1 Cor. 13:12] [c] Ex. 33:19–23 [d] 2 Pet. 2:10; Jude 8 12:10 [a] Deut. 24:9 [b] Ex. 4:6; 2 Kin. 5:27; 15:5; 2 Chr. 26:19, 20 12:11 [a] 2 Sam. 19:19; 24:10 12:12 [a] Ps. 88:4 12:13 [a] Ps. 103:3 12:14 [a] Deut. 25:9; Job 30:10; Is. 50:6 [b] Lev. 13:46; Num. 5:1–4 12:15 [a] Deut. 24:9; 2 Chr. 26:20, 21 12:16 [a] Num. 11:35; 33:17, 18 13:2 [a] Num. 32:8; Deut. 1:22; 9:23

children of Israel; from each tribe of their
fathers you shall send a man, every one a
leader among them."
3So Moses sent them [a]from the Wilderness of Paran according to the command of the LORD, all of them men who
were heads of the children of Israel. 4Now
these *were* their names: from the tribe of
Reuben, Shammua the son of Zaccur; 5from
the tribe of Simeon, Shaphat the son of
Hori; 6[a]from the tribe of Judah, [b]Caleb the
son of Jephunneh; 7from the tribe of Issachar, Igal the son of Joseph; 8from the
tribe of Ephraim, Hoshea[1] the son of Nun;
9from the tribe of Benjamin, Palti the son
of Raphu; 10from the tribe of Zebulun, Gad-
diel the son of Sodi; 11from the tribe of Joseph, *that is,* from the tribe of Manasseh,
Gaddi the son of Susi; 12from the tribe of
Dan, Ammiel the son of Gemalli; 13from
the tribe of Asher, Sethur the son of Michael; 14from the tribe of Naphtali, Nahbi
the son of Vophsi; 15from the tribe of Gad,
Geuel the son of Machi.
16These *are* the names of the men whom
Moses sent to spy out the land. And Moses
called [a]Hoshea[1] the son of Nun, Joshua.
17Then Moses sent them to spy out the
land of Canaan, and said to them, "Go up
this *way* into the South, and go up to [a]the
mountains, 18and see what the land is like:
whether the people who dwell in it *are*
strong or weak, few or many; 19whether the
land they dwell in *is* good or bad; whether
the cities they inhabit *are* like camps or
strongholds; 20whether the land *is* rich or
poor; and whether there are forests there or
not. [a]Be of good courage. And bring some

NUMBERS 12:1

I AM MIRIAM

Then Miriam and Aaron spoke against Moses because of the Ethiopian woman whom he had married; for he had married an Ethiopian woman. Numbers 12:1

I am Miriam, sister of Moses and Aaron. I am the first female prophet mentioned in the Bible. I led the women in worshiping God as we walked away from Egyptian captivity. My brothers and I were truly blessed and honored by the Lord. But I did not understand why Moses was the one people listened to or why he had been made our leader. Had I not also heard from God?

At one point, my brother Aaron and I spoke against Moses. We claimed it was because he married a foreigner—an Ethiopian woman. But God knew our true motivation. He commanded Moses, Aaron, and me to meet Him at the tabernacle of meeting. The Lord came down in a cloud, stood in the door of the tabernacle, and called Aaron and me to step forward. When we did, the Lord said prophets knew Him through visions and dreams, but to Moses, He spoke plainly and face to face. God asked why I was not afraid to speak against Moses when he had such a relationship with God. God was angry, and when His presence left, I was stricken with leprosy. But Moses begged God to heal me. After seven days, I was cleansed from the leprosy.

After Aaron and I suffered from the Lord's anger, the people understood that the consequences of speaking evil against those God called into authority would be swift and severe.

†

Miriam took her focus off her own gifts and assignments from God and, in selfishness and jealousy, spoke against another whom God had called. It was this attitude that resulted in God's anger and Miriam's penalty. We are responsible to submit to God's authority in our lives without questioning the authority He has given others.

13:3 [a] Num. 12:16; 32:8; Deut. 1:19; 9:23 13:6 [a] Num. 34:19 [b] Num. 14:6, 30; Josh. 14:6, 7; Judg. 1:12; 1 Chr. 4:15 13:8 [1] Septuagint and Vulgate read *Oshea.* 13:16 [a] Ex. 17:9; Deut. 32:44 [1] Septuagint and Vulgate read *Oshea.* 13:17 [a] Judg. 1:9 13:20 [a] Deut. 31:6, 7, 23

of the fruit of the land." Now the time *was*
the season of the first ripe grapes.
21So they went up and spied out the land
[a]from the Wilderness of Zin as far as [b]Re-
hob, near the entrance of [c]Hamath. 22And
they went up through the South and came
to [a]Hebron; Ahiman, Sheshai, and Talmai,
the descendants of [b]Anak, *were* there. (Now
Hebron was built seven years before Zoan
in Egypt.) 23[a]Then they came to the Valley of Eshcol, and there cut down a branch
with one cluster of grapes; they carried it
between two of them on a pole. *They* also
brought some of the pomegranates and
figs. 24The place was called the Valley of
Eshcol,[1] because of the cluster which the
men of Israel cut down there. 25And they
returned from spying out the land after
forty days.

26Now they departed and came back
to Moses and Aaron and all the congregation of the children of Israel in the Wilderness of Paran, at [a]Kadesh; they brought
back word to them and to all the congregation, and showed them the fruit of the
land. 27Then they told him, and said: "We
went to the land where you sent us. It truly
flows with [a]milk and honey, [b]and this *is* its
fruit. 28Nevertheless the [a]people who dwell
in the land *are* strong; the cities *are* fortified *and* very large; moreover we saw the
descendants of [b]Anak there. 29[a]The Amalekites dwell in the land of the South; the
Hittites, the Jebusites, and the Amorites
dwell in the mountains; and the Canaanites dwell by the sea and along the banks
of the Jordan."

30Then [a]Caleb quieted the people before Moses, and said, "Let us go up at once
and take possession, for we are well able
to overcome it."

31[a]But the men who had gone up with
him said, "We are not able to go up against
the people, for they *are* stronger than we."
32And they [a]gave the children of Israel a
bad report of the land which they had spied
out, saying, "The land through which we
have gone as spies *is* a land that devours its
inhabitants, and [b]all the people whom we
saw in it *are* men of *great* stature. 33There
we saw the giants[1] ([a]the descendants of
Anak came from the giants); and we were
[b]like grasshoppers in our own sight, and so
we were [c]in their sight."

Israel Refuses to Enter Canaan

14 So all the congregation lifted up
their voices and cried, and the peo-
ple [a]wept that night. 2[a]And all the children
of Israel complained against Moses and
Aaron, and the whole congregation said
to them, "If only we had died in the land
of Egypt! Or if only we had died in this
wilderness! 3Why has the LORD brought
us to this land to fall by the sword, that
our wives and [a]children should become
victims? Would it not be better for us to
return to Egypt?" 4So they said to one another, [a]"Let us select a leader and [b]return
to Egypt."

5Then Moses and Aaron fell on their
faces before all the assembly of the congregation of the children of Israel.

6But Joshua the son of Nun and Caleb
the son of Jephunneh, *who were* among
those who had spied out the land, tore
their clothes; 7and they spoke to all the
congregation of the children of Israel, saying: [a]"The land we passed through to spy
out *is* an exceedingly good land. 8If the
LORD [a]delights in us, then He will bring
us into this land and give it to us, [b]'a land
which flows with milk and honey.'[1] 9Only
[a]do not rebel against the LORD, [b]nor fear
the people of the land, for [c]they *are* our
bread; their protection has departed from
them, [d]and the LORD *is* with us. Do not fear
them."

10[a]And all the congregation said to stone
them with stones. Now [b]the glory of the
LORD appeared in the tabernacle of meeting before all the children of Israel.

13:21 [a] Num. 20:1; 27:14; 33:36; Josh. 15:1 [b] Josh. 19:28 [c] Num. 34:8; Josh. 13:5 13:22 [a] Josh. 15:13, 14; Judg. 1:10 [b] Josh. 11:21, 22 13:23 [a] Gen. 14:13; Num. 13:24; 32:9; Deut. 1:24, 25 13:24 [1] Literally *Cluster* 13:26 [a] Num. 20:1, 16; 32:8; 33:36; Deut. 1:19; Josh. 14:6 13:27 [a] Ex. 3:8, 17; 13:5; 33:3 [b] Deut. 1:25 13:28 [a] Deut. 1:28; 9:1, 2 [b] Josh. 11:21, 22 13:29 [a] Ex. 17:8; Judg. 6:3 13:30 [a] Num. 14:6, 24 13:31 [a] Num. 32:9; Deut. 1:28; 9:1–3; Josh. 14:8 13:32 [a] Num. 14:36, 37; Ps. 106:24 [b] Amos 2:9 13:33 [a] Deut. 1:28; 9:2; Josh. 11:21 [b] Is. 40:22 [c] 1 Sam. 17:42 [1] Hebrew *nephilim* 14:1 [a] Num. 11:4; Deut. 1:45 14:2 [a] Ex. 16:2; 17:3; Num. 16:41; Ps. 106:25; 1 Cor. 10:10 14:3 [a] Num. 14:31; Deut. 1:39 14:4 [a] Neh. 9:17 [b] Deut. 17:16; Acts 7:39 14:7 [a] Num. 13:27; Deut. 1:25 14:8 [a] Deut. 10:15; 2 Sam. 15:25, 26; 1 Kin. 10:9; Ps. 147:11 [b] Ex. 3:8; Num. 13:27 [1] Exodus 3:8 14:9 [a] Deut. 1:26; 9:7, 23, 24; 1 Sam. 15:23 [b] Deut. 7:18 [c] Num. 24:8 [d] Gen. 48:21; Ex. 33:16; Deut. 20:1, 3, 4; 31:6–8; Josh. 1:5; Judg. 1:22; 2 Chr. 13:12; Ps. 46:7, 11; Zech. 8:23; Matt. 28:20; Heb. 13:5 14:10 [a] Ex. 17:4 [b] Ex. 16:10; Lev. 9:23

Moses Intercedes for the People
11Then the LORD said to Moses: "How
long will these people [a]reject Me? And how
long will they not [b]believe Me, with all the
signs which I have performed among
them? 12I will strike them with the pestilence and disinherit them, and I will [a]make
of you a nation greater and mightier than
they."
13And [a]Moses said to the LORD: [b]"Then
the Egyptians will hear *it*, for by Your might
You brought these people up from among
them, 14and they will tell *it* to the inhabitants of this land. They have [a]heard that
You, LORD, *are* among these people; that
You, LORD, are seen face to face and Your
cloud stands above them, and You go before them in a pillar of cloud by day and
in a pillar of fire by night. 15Now *if* You kill
these people as one man, then the nations
which have heard of Your fame will speak,
saying, 16'Because the LORD was not [a]able
to bring this people to the land which He
swore to give them, therefore He killed
them in the wilderness.' 17And now, I pray,
let the power of my Lord be great, just as
You have spoken, saying, 18[a]'The LORD is
longsuffering and abundant in mercy, forgiving iniquity and transgression; but He
by no means clears *the guilty*, [b]visiting the
iniquity of the fathers on the children to
the third and fourth *generation*.'[1] 19[a]Pardon
the iniquity of this people, I pray, [b]accord-
ing to the greatness of Your mercy, just [c]as
You have forgiven this people, from Egypt
even until now."
20Then the LORD said: "I have pardoned,
[a]according to your word; 21but truly, as I
live, [a]all the earth shall be filled with the
glory of the LORD— 22[a]because all these
men who have seen My glory and the signs
which I did in Egypt and in the wilderness,
and have put Me to the test now [b]these ten
times, and have not heeded My voice, 23they
certainly shall not [a]see the land of which I
swore to their fathers, nor shall any of those
who rejected Me see it. 24But My servant
[a]Caleb, because he has a different spirit in
him and [b]has followed Me fully, I will bring
into the land where he went, and his descendants shall inherit it. 25Now the Amalekites and the Canaanites dwell in the
valley; tomorrow turn and [a]move out into
the wilderness by the Way of the Red Sea."

Death Sentence on the Rebels
26And the LORD spoke to Moses and
Aaron, saying, 27[a]"How long *shall I bear
with* this evil congregation who complain
against Me? [b]I have heard the complaints
which the children of Israel make against
Me. 28Say to them, [a]'As I live,' says the LORD,
'just as you have spoken in My hearing, so I
will do to you: 29The carcasses of you who
have complained against Me shall fall in
this wilderness, [a]all of you who were numbered, according to your entire number,
from twenty years old and above. 30[a]Except
for Caleb the son of Jephunneh and Joshua
the son of Nun, you shall by no means enter the land which I swore I would make
you dwell in. 31[a]But your little ones, whom
you said would be victims, I will bring in,
and they shall know the land which [b]you
have despised. 32But *as for* you, [a]your carcasses shall fall in this wilderness. 33And
your sons shall [a]be shepherds in the wilderness [b]forty years, and [c]bear the brunt
of your infidelity, until your carcasses are
consumed in the wilderness. 34[a]According
to the number of the days in which you
spied out the land, [b]forty days, for each day
you shall bear your guilt one year, *namely*
forty years, [c]and you shall know My rejection. 35[a]I the LORD have spoken this. I will
surely do so to all [b]this evil congregation
who are gathered together against Me. In
this wilderness they shall be consumed,
and there they shall die.'"
36Now the men whom Moses sent to spy
out the land, who returned and made all
the congregation complain against him by

14:11 [a] Ps. 95:8; Heb. 3:8 [b] Deut. 9:23; [John 12:37] 14:12 [a] Ex. 32:10 14:13 [a] Ps. 106:23 [b] Ex. 32:12; Deut. 9:26–28; 32:27 14:14 [a] Deut. 2:25 14:16 [a] Deut. 9:28 14:18 [a] Ex. 34:6, 7; Deut. 5:10; 7:9; Ps. 103:8; 145:8; Jon. 4:2 [b] Ex. 20:5; Deut. 5:9 [1] Exodus 34:6, 7 14:19 [a] Ex. 32:32; 34:9 [b] Ps. 51:1; 106:45 [c] Ps. 78:38 14:20 [a] 2 Sam. 12:13; Mic. 7:18–20; [1 John 5:14–16] 14:21 [a] Ps. 72:19; Is. 6:3; 66:18, 19; Hab. 2:14 14:22 [a] Deut. 1:35; 1 Cor. 10:5; Heb. 3:17 [b] Gen. 31:7 14:23 [a] Num. 26:65; 32:11; Heb. 3:18 14:24 [a] Josh. 14:6, 8, 9 [b] Num. 32:12 14:25 [a] Num. 21:4; Deut. 1:40 14:27 [a] Ex. 16:28 [b] Ex. 16:12 14:28 [a] Deut. 1:35; 2:14, 15; Heb. 3:16–19 14:29 [a] Num. 1:45, 46; 26:64; Josh. 5:6 14:30 [a] Num. 26:65; 32:12; Deut. 1:36–38; Josh. 14:6–15 14:31 [a] Num. 14:3; Deut. 1:39 [b] Ps. 106:24 14:32 [a] Num. 26:64, 65; 32:13; 1 Cor. 10:5 14:33 [a] Num. 32:13; Ps. 107:40 [b] Deut. 2:14 [c] Ezek. 23:35 14:34 [a] Num. 13:25 [b] Ps. 95:10; Ezek. 4:6 [c] 1 Kin. 8:56; [Heb. 4:1] 14:35 [a] Num. 23:19 [b] 1 Cor. 10:5

bringing a bad report of the land, [37]those very men who brought the evil report about the land, [a]died by the plague before the LORD. [38][a]But Joshua the son of Nun and Caleb the son of Jephunneh remained alive, of the men who went to spy out the land.

A Futile Invasion Attempt
(Deut. 1:41–45)

[39]Then Moses told these words to all the children of Israel, [a]and the people mourned greatly. [40]And they rose early in the morning and went up to the top of the mountain, saying, [a]"Here we are, and we will go up to the place which the LORD has promised, for we have sinned!"

[41]And Moses said, "Now why do you transgress the command of the LORD? For this will not succeed. [42][a]Do not go up, lest you be defeated by your enemies, for the LORD *is* not among you. [43]For the Amalekites and the Canaanites *are* there before you, and you shall fall by the sword; [a]because you have turned away from the LORD, the LORD will not be with you."

[44][a]But they presumed to go up to the mountaintop. Nevertheless, neither the ark of the covenant of the LORD nor Moses departed from the camp. [45]Then the Amalekites and the Canaanites who dwelt in that mountain came down and attacked them, and drove them back as far as [a]Hormah.

Laws of Grain and Drink Offerings

15 And the LORD spoke to Moses, saying, [2][a]"Speak to the children of Israel, and say to them: 'When you have come into the land you are to inhabit, which I am giving to you, [3]and you [a]make an offering by fire to the LORD, a burnt offering or a sacrifice, [b]to fulfill a vow or as a freewill offering or [c]in your appointed feasts, to make a [d]sweet aroma to the LORD, from the herd or the flock, [4]then [a]he who presents his offering to the LORD shall bring [b]a grain offering of one-tenth *of an ephah* of fine flour mixed [c]with one-fourth of a hin of oil; [5][a]and one-fourth of a hin of wine as a drink offering you shall prepare with the burnt offering or the sacrifice, for each [b]lamb. [6][a]Or for a ram you shall prepare as a grain offering two-tenths *of an ephah* of fine flour mixed with one-third of a hin of oil; [7]and as a drink offering you shall offer one-third of a hin of wine as a sweet aroma to the LORD. [8]And when you prepare a young bull as a burnt offering, or as a sacrifice to fulfill a vow, or as a [a]peace offering to the LORD, [9]then shall be offered [a]with the young bull a grain offering of three-tenths *of an ephah* of fine flour mixed with half a hin of oil; [10]and you shall bring as the drink offering half a hin of wine as an offering made by fire, a sweet aroma to the LORD.

[11][a]'Thus it shall be done for each young bull, for each ram, or for each lamb or young goat. [12]According to the number that you prepare, so you shall do with everyone according to their number. [13]All who are native-born shall do these things in this manner, in presenting an offering made by fire, a sweet aroma to the LORD. [14]And if a stranger dwells with you, or whoever *is* among you throughout your generations, and would present an offering made by fire, a sweet aroma to the LORD, just as you do, so shall he do. [15][a]One ordinance *shall be* for you of the assembly and for the stranger who dwells *with you,* an ordinance forever throughout your generations; as you are, so shall the stranger be before the LORD. [16]One law and one custom shall be for you and for the stranger who dwells with you.'"[1]

[17]Again the LORD spoke to Moses, saying, [18][a]"Speak to the children of Israel, and say to them: 'When you come into the land to which I bring you, [19]then it will be, when you eat of [a]the bread of the land, that you shall offer up a heave offering to the LORD. [20][a]You shall offer up a cake of the first of your ground meal *as* a heave offering; as [b]a heave offering of the threshing floor, so shall you offer it up. [21]Of the first of your ground meal you shall give to the LORD a heave offering throughout your generations.

14:37 [a] Num. 16:49; [1 Cor. 10:10]; Heb. 3:17, 18 14:38 [a] Josh. 14:6, 10 14:39 [a] Ex. 33:4 14:40 [a] Deut. 1:41–44 14:42 [a] Deut. 1:42; 31:17 14:43 [a] 2 Chr. 15:2 14:44 [a] Deut. 1:43 14:45 [a] Num. 21:3 15:2 [a] Lev. 23:10; Num. 15:18; Deut. 7:1 15:3 [a] Lev. 1:2, 3 [b] Lev. 7:16; 22:18, 21 [c] Lev. 23:2, 8, 12, 38; Num. 28:18, 19, 27; Deut. 16:10 [d] Gen. 8:21; Ex. 29:18; Lev. 1:9 15:4 [a] Lev. 2:1; 6:14 [b] Ex. 29:40; Lev. 23:13 [c] Lev. 14:10; Num. 28:5 15:5 [a] Num. 28:7, 14 [b] Lev. 1:10; 3:6; Num. 15:11; 28:4, 5 15:6 [a] Num. 28:12, 14 15:8 [a] Lev. 7:11 15:9 [a] Num. 28:12, 14 15:11 [a] Num. 28 15:15 [a] Ex. 12:49; Num. 9:14; 15:29 15:16 [1] Compare Exodus 12:49 15:18 [a] Num. 15:2; Deut. 26:1 15:19 [a] Josh. 5:11, 12 15:20 [a] Ex. 34:26; Lev. 23:10, 14, 17; Deut. 26:2, 10; Prov. 3:9, 10 [b] Lev. 2:14; 23:10, 16

Laws Concerning Unintentional Sin

22[a]'If you sin unintentionally, and do not observe all these commandments which the LORD has spoken to Moses— 23all that the LORD has commanded you by the hand of Moses, from the day the LORD gave commandment and onward throughout your generations— 24then it will be, [a]if it is unintentionally committed, without the knowledge of the congregation, that the whole congregation shall offer one young bull as a burnt offering, as a sweet aroma to the LORD, [b]with its grain offering and its drink offering, according to the ordinance, and [c]one kid of the goats as a sin offering. 25[a]So the priest shall make atonement for the whole congregation of the children of Israel, and it shall be forgiven them, for it was unintentional; they shall bring their offering, an offering made by fire to the LORD, and their sin offering before the LORD, for their unintended sin. 26It shall be forgiven the whole congregation of the children of Israel and the stranger who dwells among them, because all the people *did it* unintentionally.

27'And [a]if a person sins unintentionally, then he shall bring a female goat in its first year as a sin offering. 28[a]So the priest shall make atonement for the person who sins unintentionally, when he sins unintentionally before the LORD, to make atonement for him; and it shall be forgiven him. 29[a]You shall have one law for him who sins unintentionally, *for* him who is native-born among the children of Israel and for the stranger who dwells among them.

Law Concerning Presumptuous Sin

30[a]'But the person who does *anything* presumptuously, *whether he is* native-born or a stranger, that one brings reproach on the LORD, and he shall be cut off from among his people. 31Because he has [a]despised the word of the LORD, and has broken His commandment, that person shall be completely cut off; his guilt *shall be* upon him.'"

Penalty for Violating the Sabbath
(Ex. 31:12–17)

32Now while the children of Israel were in the wilderness, [a]they found a man gathering sticks on the Sabbath day. 33And those who found him gathering sticks brought him to Moses and Aaron, and to all the congregation. 34They put him [a]under guard, because it had not been explained what should be done to him.

35Then the LORD said to Moses, [a]"The man must surely be put to death; all the congregation shall [b]stone him with stones outside the camp." 36So, as the LORD commanded Moses, all the congregation brought him outside the camp and stoned him with stones, and he died.

Tassels on Garments

37Again the LORD spoke to Moses, saying, 38"Speak to the children of Israel: Tell [a]them to make tassels on the corners of their garments throughout their generations, and to put a blue thread in the tassels of the corners. 39And you shall have the tassel, that you may look upon it and [a]remember all the commandments of the LORD and do them, and that you [b]*may* not [c]follow the harlotry to which your own heart and your own eyes are inclined, 40and that you may remember and do all My commandments, and be [a]holy for your God. 41I *am* the LORD your God, who brought you out of the land of Egypt, to be your God: I *am* the LORD your God."

Rebellion Against Moses and Aaron

16 Now [a]Korah the son of Izhar, the son of Kohath, the son of Levi, with [b]Dathan and Abiram the sons of Eliab, and On the son of Peleth, sons of Reuben, took *men;* 2and they rose up before Moses with some of the children of Israel, two hundred and fifty leaders of the congregation, [a]representatives of the congregation, men of renown. 3[a]They gathered together against Moses and Aaron, and said to them, "*You take* too much upon yourselves, for [b]all the

---

15:22 [a] Lev. 4:2 15:24 [a] Lev. 4:13 [b] Num. 15:8–10 [c] Lev. 4:23 15:25 [a] Lev. 4:20; [Heb. 2:17] 15:27 [a] Lev. 4:27–31 15:28 [a] Lev. 4:35 15:29 [a] Num. 15:15 15:30 [a] Num. 14:40–44; Deut. 1:43; 17:12; Ps. 19:13; Heb. 10:26 15:31 [a] 2 Sam. 12:9; Prov. 13:13 15:32 [a] Ex. 31:14, 15; 35:2, 3 15:34 [a] Lev. 24:12 15:35 [a] Ex. 31:14, 15 [b] Lev. 24:14; Deut. 21:21; 1 Kin. 21:13; Acts 7:58 15:38 [a] Deut. 22:12; Matt. 23:5 15:39 [a] Ps. 103:18 [b] Deut. 29:19 [c] Ps. 73:27; 106:39; James 4:4 15:40 [a] [Lev. 11:44, 45; Rom. 12:1; Col. 1:22; 1 Pet. 1:15, 16] 16:1 [a] Ex. 6:21 [b] Num. 26:9; Deut. 11:6 16:2 [a] Num. 1:16; 26:9 16:3 [a] Num. 12:2; 14:2; Ps. 106:16 [b] Ex. 19:6

congregation *is* holy, every one of them,
[c]and the LORD *is* among them. Why then
do you exalt yourselves above the assembly of the LORD?"

4So when Moses heard *it,* he [a]fell on his
face; 5and he spoke to Korah and all his
company, saying, "Tomorrow morning the
LORD will show who *is* [a]His and *who is* [b]holy,
and will cause *him* to come near to Him.
That one whom He chooses He will cause
to [c]come near to Him. 6Do this: Take censers, Korah and all your company; 7put fire
in them and put incense in them before
the LORD tomorrow, and it shall be *that* the
man whom the LORD chooses *is* the holy
one. *You take* too much upon yourselves,
you sons of Levi!"

8Then Moses said to Korah, "Hear now,
you sons of Levi: 9*Is it* [a]a small thing to you
that the God of Israel has [b]separated you
from the congregation of Israel, to bring
you near to Himself, to do the work of the
tabernacle of the LORD, and to stand before the congregation to serve them; 10and
that He has brought you near *to Himself,*
you and all your brethren, the sons of Levi,
with you? And are you seeking the priesthood also? 11Therefore you and all your
company *are* gathered together against
the LORD. [a]And what *is* Aaron that you complain against him?"

12And Moses sent to call Dathan and Abiram the sons of Eliab, but they said, "We
will not come up! 13*Is it* a small thing that
you have brought us up out of [a]a land flowing with milk and honey, to kill us in the
wilderness, that you should [b]keep acting
like a prince over us? 14Moreover [a]you have
not brought us into [b]a land flowing with
milk and honey, nor given us inheritance
of fields and vineyards. Will you put out the
eyes of these men? We will not come up!"

15Then Moses was very angry, and said to
the LORD, [a]"Do not respect their offering.
[b]I have not taken one donkey from them,
nor have I hurt one of them."

16And Moses said to Korah, "Tomorrow, you and all your company be present
[a]before the LORD—you and they, as well as
Aaron. 17Let each take his censer and put
incense in it, and each of you bring his censer before the LORD, two hundred and fifty
censers; both you and Aaron, each *with* his
censer." 18So every man took his censer,
put fire in it, laid incense on it, and stood
at the door of the tabernacle of meeting
with Moses and Aaron. 19And Korah gathered all the congregation against them at
the door of the tabernacle of meeting. Then
[a]the glory of the LORD appeared to all the
congregation.

20And the LORD spoke to Moses and
Aaron, saying, 21[a]"Separate yourselves from
among this congregation, that I may [b]con-
sume them in a moment."

22Then they [a]fell on their faces, and said,
"O God, [b]the God of the spirits of all flesh,
shall one man sin, and You be angry with
all the [c]congregation?"

23So the LORD spoke to Moses, saying,
24"Speak to the congregation, saying, 'Get
away from the tents of Korah, Dathan, and
Abiram.'"

25Then Moses rose and went to Dathan
and Abiram, and the elders of Israel followed him. 26And he spoke to the congregation, saying, [a]"Depart now from the tents of
these wicked men! Touch nothing of theirs,
lest you be consumed in all their sins." 27So
they got away from around the tents of Korah, Dathan, and Abiram; and Dathan and
Abiram came out and stood at the door of
their tents, with their wives, their sons, and
their little [a]children.

28And Moses said: [a]"By this you shall
know that the LORD has sent me to do all
these works, for *I have* not *done them* [b]of my
own will. 29If these men die naturally like
all men, or if they are [a]visited by the common fate of all men, *then* the LORD has not
sent me. 30But if the LORD creates [a]a new
thing, and the earth opens its mouth and
swallows them up with all that belongs to
them, and they [b]go down alive into the pit,
then you will understand that these men
have rejected the LORD."

16:3 [c] Ex. 29:45 **16:4** [a] Num. 14:5; 20:6 **16:5** [a] [2 Tim. 2:19] [b] Lev. 21:6–8, 12 [c] Ezek. 40:46; 44:15, 16 **16:9** [a] 1 Sam. 18:23; Is. 7:13 [b] Num. 3:41, 45; 8:13–16; Deut. 10:8 **16:11** [a] Ex. 16:7, 8 **16:13** [a] Ex. 16:3; Num. 11:4–6 [b] Ex. 2:14; Acts 7:27, 35 **16:14** [a] Num. 14:1–4 [b] Ex. 3:8; Lev. 20:24 **16:15** [a] Gen. 4:4, 5 [b] 1 Sam. 12:3; Acts 20:33 **16:16** [a] 1 Sam. 12:3, 7 **16:19** [a] Ex. 16:7, 10; Lev. 9:6, 23; Num. 14:10 **16:21** [a] Gen. 19:17; Jer. 51:6 [b] Ex. 32:10; 33:5 **16:22** [a] Num. 14:5 [b] Num. 27:16; Job 12:10; Eccl. 12:7; Heb. 12:9 [c] Gen. 18:23–32; 20:4 **16:26** [a] Gen. 19:12, 14, 15, 17 **16:27** [a] Ex. 20:5; Num. 26:11 **16:28** [a] Ex. 3:12; John 5:36 [b] Num. 24:13; John 5:30 **16:29** [a] Ex. 20:5; Job 35:15; Is. 10:3 **16:30** [a] Job 31:3; Is. 28:21 [b] [Ps. 55:15]

31[a]Now it came to pass, as he finished speaking all these words, that the ground split apart under them, 32and the earth opened its mouth and swallowed them up, with their households and [a]all the men with Korah, with all *their* goods. 33So they and all those with them went down alive into the pit; the earth closed over them, and they perished from among the assembly. 34Then all Israel who *were* around them fled at their cry, for they said, "Lest the earth swallow us up *also!*"

35And [a]a fire came out from the LORD and consumed the two hundred and fifty men who were offering incense.

36Then the LORD spoke to Moses, saying: 37"Tell Eleazar, the son of Aaron the priest, to pick up the censers out of the blaze, for [a]they are holy, and scatter the fire some distance away. 38The censers of [a]these men who sinned against their own souls, let them be made into hammered plates as a covering for the altar. Because they presented them before the LORD, therefore they are holy; [b]and they shall be a sign to the children of Israel." 39So Eleazar the priest took the bronze censers, which those who were burned up had presented, and they were hammered out as a covering on the altar, 40*to be* a memorial to the children of Israel [a]that no outsider, who *is* not a descendant of Aaron, should come near to offer incense before the LORD, that he might not become like Korah and his companions, just as the LORD had said to him through Moses.

Complaints of the People

41On the next day [a]all the congregation of the children of Israel complained against Moses and Aaron, saying, "You have killed the people of the LORD." 42Now it happened, when the congregation had gathered against Moses and Aaron, that they turned toward the tabernacle of meeting; and suddenly [a]the cloud covered it, and the glory of the LORD appeared. 43Then Moses and Aaron came before the tabernacle of meeting.

44And the LORD spoke to Moses, saying, 45"Get away from among this congregation, that I may consume them in a moment."

And they fell on their faces.

46So Moses said to Aaron, "Take a censer and put fire in it from the altar, put incense *on it,* and take it quickly to the congregation and make atonement for them; [a]for wrath has gone out from the LORD. The plague has begun." 47Then Aaron took *it* as Moses commanded, and ran into the midst of the assembly; and already the plague had begun among the people. So he put in the incense and made atonement for the people. 48And he stood between the dead and the living; so [a]the plague was stopped. 49Now those who died in the plague were fourteen thousand seven hundred, besides those who died in the Korah incident. 50So Aaron returned to Moses at the door of the tabernacle of meeting, for the plague had stopped.

The Budding of Aaron's Rod

17 And the LORD spoke to Moses, saying: 2"Speak to the children of Israel, and get from them a rod from each father's house, all their leaders according to their fathers' houses—twelve rods. Write each man's name on his rod. 3And you shall write Aaron's name on the rod of Levi. For there shall be one rod for the head of *each* father's house. 4Then you shall place them in the tabernacle of meeting before [a]the Testimony, [b]where I meet with you. 5And it shall be *that* the rod of the man [a]whom I choose will blossom; thus I will rid Myself of the complaints of the children of Israel, [b]which they make against you."

6So Moses spoke to the children of Israel, and each of their leaders gave him a rod apiece, for each leader according to their fathers' houses, twelve rods; and the rod of Aaron *was* among their rods. 7And Moses placed the rods before the LORD in [a]the tabernacle of witness.

8Now it came to pass on the next day that Moses went into the tabernacle of witness, and behold, the [a]rod of Aaron, of the house

16:31 [a] Num. 26:10; Ps. 106:17 16:32 [a] Num. 26:11; 1 Chr. 6:22, 37 16:35 [a] Lev. 10:2; Num. 11:1–3; 26:10; Ps. 106:18 16:37 [a] Lev. 27:28 16:38 [a] Prov. 20:2; Hab. 2:10 [b] Num. 17:10; Ezek. 14:8 16:40 [a] Num. 3:10; 2 Chr. 26:18 16:41 [a] Num. 14:2; Ps. 106:25 16:42 [a] Ex. 40:34 16:46 [a] Lev. 10:6; Num. 18:5 16:48 [a] Num. 25:8; Ps. 106:30 17:4 [a] Ex. 25:16 [b] Ex. 25:22; 29:42, 43; 30:36; Num. 17:7 17:5 [a] Num. 16:5 [b] Num. 16:11 17:7 [a] Ex. 38:21; Num. 1:50, 51; 9:15; 18:2; Acts 7:44 17:8 [a] [Ezek. 17:24]; Heb. 9:4

of Levi, had sprouted and put forth buds,
had produced blossoms and yielded ripe
almonds. 9 Then Moses brought out all the
rods from before the LORD to all the children of Israel; and they looked, and each
man took his rod.
10 And the LORD said to Moses, "Bring
[a]Aaron's rod back before the Testimony, to
be kept [b]as a sign against the rebels, [c]that
you may put their complaints away from
Me, lest they die." 11 Thus did Moses; just as
the LORD had commanded him, so he did.
12 So the children of Israel spoke to Moses, saying, "Surely we die, we perish, we
all perish! 13 [a]Whoever even comes near the
tabernacle of the LORD must die. Shall we
all utterly die?"

Duties of Priests and Levites

18 Then the LORD said to Aaron: [a]"You
and your sons and your father's
house with you shall [b]bear the iniquity *related to* the sanctuary, and you and your
sons with you shall bear the iniquity *associated with* your priesthood. 2 Also bring
with you your brethren of the [a]tribe of Levi,
the tribe of your father, that they may be
[b]joined with you and serve you while you
and your sons *are* with you before the tabernacle of witness. 3 They shall attend to
your needs and [a]all the needs of the tabernacle; [b]but they shall not come near the
articles of the sanctuary and the altar, [c]lest
they die—they and you also. 4 They shall be
joined with you and attend to the needs of
the tabernacle of meeting, for all the work
of the tabernacle; [a]but an outsider shall
not come near you. 5 And you shall attend
to [a]the duties of the sanctuary and the duties of the altar, [b]that there *may* be no more
wrath on the children of Israel. 6 Behold, I
Myself have [a]taken your brethren the Levites from among the children of Israel;
[b]*they are* a gift to you, given by the LORD,
to do the work of the tabernacle of meeting. 7 Therefore [a]you and your sons with you
shall attend to your priesthood for everything at the altar and [b]behind the veil; and
you shall serve. I give your priesthood *to
you* as a [c]gift for service, but the outsider
who comes near shall be put to death."

Offerings for Support of the Priests

8 And the LORD spoke to Aaron: "Here,
[a]I Myself have also given you charge of My
heave offerings, all the holy gifts of the children of Israel; I have given them [b]as a portion to you and your sons, as an ordinance
forever. 9 This shall be yours of the most
holy things *reserved* from the fire: every
offering of theirs, every [a]grain offering and
every [b]sin offering and every [c]trespass offering which they render to Me, *shall be*
most holy for you and your sons. 10 [a]In a
most holy *place* you shall eat it; every male
shall eat it. It shall be holy to you.
11 "This also *is* yours: [a]the heave offering
of their gift, with all the wave offerings of
the children of Israel; I have given them to
you, and your sons and daughters with you,
as an ordinance forever. [b]Everyone who is
clean in your house may eat it.
12 [a]"All the best of the oil, all the best of
the new wine and the grain, [b]their firstfruits
which they offer to the LORD, I have given
them to you. 13 Whatever first ripe fruit is in
their land, [a]which they bring to the LORD,
shall be yours. Everyone who is clean in
your house may eat it.
14 [a]"Every devoted thing in Israel shall
be yours.
15 "Everything that first opens [a]the womb
of all flesh, which they bring to the LORD,
whether man or beast, shall be yours; nevertheless [b]the firstborn of man you shall
surely redeem, and the firstborn of unclean
animals you shall redeem. 16 And those redeemed of the devoted things you shall
redeem when one month old, [a]according
to your valuation, for five shekels of silver, according to the shekel of the sanctuary, which *is* [b]twenty gerahs. 17 [a]But the
firstborn of a cow, the firstborn of a sheep,
or the firstborn of a goat you shall not redeem; they *are* holy. [b]You shall sprinkle
their blood on the altar, and burn their

17:10 [a] Heb. 9:4 [b] Num. 16:38; Deut. 9:7, 24 [c] Num. 17:5 17:13 [a] Num. 1:51, 53; 18:4, 7 18:1 [a] Num. 17:13 [b] Ex. 28:38; Lev. 10:17; 22:16 18:2 [a] Gen. 29:34; Num. 1:47 [b] Num. 3:5–10 18:3 [a] Num. 3:25, 31, 36 [b] Num. 16:40 [c] Num. 4:15 18:4 [a] Num. 3:10 18:5 [a] Ex. 27:21; 30:7; Lev. 24:3 [b] Num. 8:19; 16:46 18:6 [a] Num. 3:12, 45 [b] Num. 3:9 18:7 [a] Num. 3:10; 18:5 [b] Heb. 9:3, 6 [c] Matt. 10:8; 1 Pet. 5:2, 3 18:8 [a] Lev. 6:16, 18; 7:28–34; Num. 5:9 [b] Ex. 29:29; 40:13, 15 18:9 [a] Lev. 2:2, 3; 10:12, 13 [b] Lev. 6:25, 26 [c] Lev. 7:7; Num. 5:8–10 18:10 [a] Lev. 6:16, 26 18:11 [a] Ex. 29:27, 28; Deut. 18:3–5 [b] Lev. 22:1–16 18:12 [a] Ex. 23:19; Neh. 10:35, 36 [b] Ex. 22:29; Lev. 23:20 18:13 [a] Ex. 22:29; 23:19; 34:26 18:14 [a] Lev. 27:1–33 18:15 [a] Ex. 13:2 [b] Ex. 13:12–15; Num. 3:46; Luke 2:22–24 18:16 [a] Lev. 27:6 [b] Ex. 30:13 18:17 [a] Deut. 15:19 [b] Lev. 3:2, 5

fat *as* an offering made by fire for a sweet aroma to the LORD. 18And their flesh shall be yours, just as the [a]wave breast and the right thigh are yours.

19"All the heave offerings of the holy things, which the children of Israel offer to the LORD, I have given to you and your sons and daughters with you as an ordinance forever; [a]it *is* a covenant of salt forever before the LORD with you and your descendants with you."

20Then the LORD said to Aaron: "You shall have [a]no inheritance in their land, nor shall you have any portion among them; [b]I *am* your portion and your inheritance among the children of Israel.

Tithes for Support of the Levites

21"Behold, [a]I have given the children of Levi all the tithes in Israel as an inheritance in return for the work which they perform, [b]the work of the tabernacle of meeting. 22[a]Hereafter the children of Israel shall not come near the tabernacle of meeting, [b]lest they bear sin and die. 23But the Levites shall perform the work of the tabernacle of meeting, and they shall bear their iniquity; *it shall be* a statute forever, throughout your generations, that among the children of Israel they shall have no inheritance. 24For the tithes of the children of Israel, which they offer up *as* a heave offering to the LORD, I have given to the Levites as an inheritance; therefore I have said to them, 'Among the children of Israel they shall have no inheritance.'"

The Tithe of the Levites

25Then the LORD spoke to Moses, saying, 26"Speak thus to the Levites, and say to them: 'When you take from the children of Israel the tithes which I have given you from them as your inheritance, then you shall offer up a heave offering of it to the LORD, [a]a tenth of the tithe. 27And your heave offering shall be reckoned to you as though *it were* the grain of the [a]threshing floor and as the fullness of the winepress. 28Thus you shall also offer a heave offering to the LORD from all your tithes which you receive from the children of Israel, and you shall give the LORD's heave offering from it to Aaron the priest. 29Of all your gifts you shall offer up every heave offering due to the LORD, from all the best of them, the consecrated part of them.' 30Therefore you shall say to them: 'When you have lifted up the best of it, then *the rest* shall be accounted to the Levites as the produce of the threshing floor and as the produce of the winepress. 31You may eat it in any place, you and your households, for it *is* [a]your reward for your work in the tabernacle of meeting. 32And you shall [a]bear no sin because of it, when you have lifted up the best of it. But you shall not [b]profane the holy gifts of the children of Israel, lest you die.'"

Laws of Purification

19 Now the LORD spoke to Moses and Aaron, saying, 2"This *is* the ordinance of the law which the LORD has commanded, saying: 'Speak to the children of Israel, that they bring you a red heifer without blemish, in which there *is* no [a]defect [b]*and* on which a yoke has never come. 3You shall give it to Eleazar the priest, that he may take it [a]outside the camp, and it shall be slaughtered before him; 4and Eleazar the priest shall take some of its blood with his finger, and [a]sprinkle some of its blood seven times directly in front of the tabernacle of meeting. 5Then the heifer shall be burned in his sight: [a]its hide, its flesh, its blood, and its offal shall be burned. 6And the priest shall take [a]cedar wood and [b]hyssop and scarlet, and cast *them* into the midst of the fire burning the heifer. 7[a]Then the priest shall wash his clothes, he shall bathe in water, and afterward he shall come into the camp; the priest shall be unclean until evening. 8And the one who burns it shall wash his clothes in water, bathe in water, and shall be unclean until evening. 9Then a man *who is* clean shall gather up [a]the ashes of the heifer, and store *them*

18:18 [a] Ex. 29:26–28; Lev. 7:31–36 18:19 [a] Lev. 2:13; 2 Chr. 13:5; [Mark 9:49, 50] 18:20 [a] Deut. 10:8, 9; 12:12; 14:27–29; 18:1, 2; Josh. 13:14, 33 [b] Ps. 16:5; Ezek. 44:28 18:21 [a] Lev. 27:30–33; Deut. 14:22–29; Neh. 10:37; 12:44; Mal. 3:8–10; [Heb. 7:4–10] [b] Num. 3:7, 8 18:22 [a] Num. 1:51 [b] Lev. 22:9 18:26 [a] Neh. 10:38 18:27 [a] Num. 15:20; [2 Cor. 8:12] 18:31 [a] [Matt. 10:10; Luke 10:7]; 1 Cor. 9:13; [1 Tim. 5:18] 18:32 [a] Lev. 19:8; 22:16; Ezek. 22:26 [b] Lev. 22:2, 15 19:2 [a] Lev. 22:20–25 [b] Deut. 21:3; 1 Sam. 6:7 19:3 [a] Lev. 4:12, 21; Num. 19:9; Heb. 13:11 19:4 [a] Lev. 4:6; Heb. 9:13 19:5 [a] Ex. 29:14; Lev. 4:11, 12; 9:11 19:6 [a] Lev. 14:4, 6, 49 [b] Ex. 12:22; 1 Kin. 4:33 19:7 [a] Lev. 11:25; 15:5; 16:26, 28 19:9 [a] [Heb. 9:13, 14]

outside the camp in a clean place; and they
shall be kept for the congregation of the
children of Israel [b]for the water of purification;[1] it *is* for purifying from sin. 10And
the one who gathers the ashes of the heifer
shall wash his clothes, and be unclean until
evening. It shall be a statute forever to the
children of Israel and to the stranger who
dwells among them.

11[a]'He who touches the dead body of anyone shall be unclean seven days. 12[a]He shall
purify himself with the water on the third
day and on the seventh day; *then* he will be
clean. But if he does not purify himself on
the third day and on the seventh day, he
will not be clean. 13Whoever touches the
body of anyone who has died, and [a]does
not purify himself, [b]defiles the tabernacle
of the LORD. That person shall be cut off
from Israel. He shall be unclean, because
[c]the water of purification was not sprinkled
on him; [d]his uncleanness *is* still on him.

14'This *is* the law when a man dies in a
tent: All who come into the tent and all
who *are* in the tent shall be unclean seven
days; 15and every [a]open vessel, which has
no cover fastened on it, *is* unclean. 16[a]Who-
ever in the open field touches one who is
slain by a sword or who has died, or a bone
of a man, or a grave, shall be unclean seven
days.

17'And for an unclean *person* they shall
take some of the [a]ashes of the heifer burnt
for purification from sin, and running water shall be put on them in a vessel. 18A
clean person shall take [a]hyssop and dip
it in the water, sprinkle *it* on the tent, on
all the vessels, on the persons who were
there, or on the one who touched a bone,
the slain, the dead, or a grave. 19The clean
person shall sprinkle the unclean on the
third day and on the seventh day; [a]and on
the seventh day he shall purify himself,
wash his clothes, and bathe in water; and
at evening he shall be clean.

20'But the man who is unclean and does
not purify himself, that person shall be cut
off from among the assembly, because he
has [a]defiled the sanctuary of the LORD. The
water of purification has not been sprinkled
on him; he *is* unclean. 21It shall be a perpetual statute for them. He who sprinkles the
water of purification shall wash his clothes;
and he who touches the water of purification shall be unclean until evening. 22[a]What-
ever the unclean *person* touches shall be
unclean; and [b]the person who touches *it*
shall be unclean until evening.'"

Moses' Error at Kadesh
(Ex. 17:1–7)

20 Then[a] the children of Israel, the
whole congregation, came into the
Wilderness of Zin in the first month, and
the people stayed in [b]Kadesh; and [c]Miriam
died there and was buried there.

2[a]Now there was no water for the congregation; [b]so they gathered together against
Moses and Aaron. 3And the people [a]con-
tended with Moses and spoke, saying: "If
only we had died [b]when our brethren died
before the LORD! 4[a]Why have you brought
up the assembly of the LORD into this wilderness, that we and our animals should
die here? 5And why have you made us
come up out of Egypt, to bring us to this
evil place? It *is* not a place of grain or figs
or vines or pomegranates; nor *is* there any
water to drink." 6So Moses and Aaron went
from the presence of the assembly to the
door of the tabernacle of meeting, and
[a]they fell on their faces. And [b]the glory of
the LORD appeared to them.

7Then the LORD spoke to Moses, saying, 8[a]"Take the rod; you and your brother
Aaron gather the congregation together.
Speak to the rock before their eyes, and it
will yield its water; thus [b]you shall bring water for them out of the rock, and give drink
to the congregation and their animals." 9So
Moses took the rod [a]from before the LORD
as He commanded him.

10And Moses and Aaron gathered the
assembly together before the rock; and he
said to them, [a]"Hear now, you rebels! Must
we bring water for you out of this rock?"

19:9 [b] Num. 19:13, 20, 21 [1] Literally *impurity* 19:11 [a] Lev. 21:1, 11; Num. 5:2; 6:6; 9:6, 10; 31:19; Lam. 4:14; Hag. 2:13 19:12 [a] Num. 19:19; 31:19 19:13 [a] Lev. 22:3–7 [b] Lev. 15:31 [c] Num. 8:7; 19:9 [d] Lev. 7:20; 22:3 19:15 [a] Lev. 11:32; Num. 31:20 19:16 [a] Num. 19:11; 31:19 19:17 [a] Num. 19:9 19:18 [a] Ps. 51:7 19:19 [a] Lev. 14:9 19:20 [a] Num. 19:13 19:22 [a] Hag. 2:11–13 [b] Lev. 15:5 20:1 [a] Num. 13:21; 33:36 [b] Num. 13:26 [c] Ex. 15:20; Num. 26:59 20:2 [a] Ex. 17:1 [b] Num. 16:19, 42 20:3 [a] Ex. 17:2; Num. 14:2 [b] Num. 11:1, 33; 14:37; 16:31–35, 49 20:4 [a] Ex. 17:3 20:6 [a] Num. 14:5; 16:4, 22, 45 [b] Num. 14:10 20:8 [a] Ex. 4:17, 20; 17:5, 6 [b] Neh. 9:15; Ps. 78:15, 16; 105:41; Is. 43:20; 48:21; [1 Cor. 10:4] 20:9 [a] Num. 17:10 20:10 [a] Ps. 106:33

11 Then Moses lifted his hand and struck the rock twice with his rod; [a]and water came out abundantly, and the congregation and their animals drank.

12 Then the LORD spoke to Moses and Aaron, "Because [a]you did not believe Me, to [b]hallow Me in the eyes of the children of Israel, therefore you shall not bring this assembly into the land which I have given them."

13 [a]This *was* the water of Meribah,[1] because the children of Israel contended with the LORD, and He was hallowed among them.

Passage Through Edom Refused

14 [a]Now Moses sent messengers from Kadesh to the king of [b]Edom. [c]"Thus says your brother Israel: 'You know all the hardship that has befallen us, 15 [a]how our fathers went down to Egypt, [b]and we dwelt in Egypt a long time, [c]and the Egyptians afflicted us and our fathers. 16 [a]When we cried out to the LORD, He heard our voice and [b]sent the Angel and brought us up out of Egypt; now here we are in Kadesh, a city on the edge of your border. 17 Please [a]let us pass through your country. We will not pass through fields or vineyards, nor will we drink water from wells; we will go along the King's Highway; we will not turn aside to the right hand or to the left until we have passed through your territory.'"

18 Then [a]Edom said to him, "You shall not pass through my *land,* lest I come out against you with the sword."

19 So the children of Israel said to him, "We will go by the Highway, and if I or my livestock drink any of your water, [a]then I will pay for it; let me only pass through on foot, nothing *more.*"

20 Then he said, [a]"You shall not pass through." So Edom came out against them with many men and with a strong hand. 21 Thus Edom [a]refused to give Israel passage through his territory; so Israel [b]turned away from him.

Death of Aaron

22 Now the children of Israel, the whole congregation, journeyed from [a]Kadesh [b]and came to Mount Hor. 23 And the LORD spoke to Moses and Aaron in Mount Hor by the border of the land of Edom, saying: 24 "Aaron shall be [a]gathered to his people, for he shall not enter the land which I have given to the children of Israel, because you rebelled against My word at the water of Meribah. 25 [a]Take Aaron and Eleazar his son, and bring them up to Mount Hor; 26 and strip Aaron of his garments and put them on Eleazar his son; for Aaron shall be gathered *to his people* and die there." 27 So Moses did just as the LORD commanded, and they went up to Mount Hor in the sight of all the congregation. 28 [a]Moses stripped Aaron of his garments and put them on Eleazar his son; and [b]Aaron died there on the top of the mountain. Then Moses and Eleazar came down from the mountain. 29 Now when all the congregation saw that Aaron was dead, all the house of Israel mourned for Aaron [a]thirty days.

Canaanites Defeated at Hormah

21 The [a]king of Arad, the Canaanite, who dwelt in the South, heard that Israel was coming on the road to Atharim. Then he fought against Israel and took *some* of them prisoners. 2 [a]So Israel made a vow to the LORD, and said, "If You will indeed deliver this people into my hand, then [b]I will utterly destroy their cities." 3 And the LORD listened to the voice of Israel and delivered up the Canaanites, and they utterly destroyed them and their cities. So the name of that place was called Hormah.[1]

The Bronze Serpent

4 Then they journeyed from Mount Hor by the Way of the Red Sea, to [a]go around the land of Edom; and the soul of the people became very discouraged on the way. 5 And the people [a]spoke against God and against Moses: "Why have you brought us

---

20:11 [a] Ex. 17:6; Deut. 8:15; Ps. 78:16; Is. 48:21; [1 Cor. 10:4] 20:12 [a] Num. 20:28; 27:14; Deut. 1:37; 3:26, 27; 34:5 [b] Lev. 10:3; Ezek. 20:41; 36:23; 1 Pet. 3:15 20:13 [a] Deut. 33:8; Ps. 106:32 [1] Literally *Contention* 20:14 [a] Judg. 11:16, 17 [b] Gen. 36:31–39 [c] Deut. 2:4; Obad. 10–12 20:15 [a] Gen. 46:6; Acts 7:15 [b] Ex. 12:40 [c] Ex. 1:11; Deut. 26:6; Acts 7:19 20:16 [a] Ex. 2:23; 3:7 [b] Ex. 3:2; 14:19 20:17 [a] Num. 21:22 20:18 [a] Num. 24:18; Ps. 137:7; Ezek. 25:12, 13; Obad. 10–15 20:19 [a] Deut. 2:6, 28 20:20 [a] Judg. 11:17 20:21 [a] Deut. 2:27, 30 [b] Deut. 2:8; Judg. 11:18 20:22 [a] Num. 33:37 [b] Num. 21:4 20:24 [a] Gen. 25:8; Deut. 32:50 20:25 [a] Num. 33:38; Deut. 32:50 20:28 [a] Ex. 29:29, 30; Deut. 10:6 [b] Num. 33:38 20:29 [a] Gen. 50:3, 10; Deut. 34:8 21:1 [a] Num. 33:40; Josh. 12:14; Judg. 1:16 21:2 [a] Gen. 28:20; Judg. 11:30 [b] Deut. 2:34 21:3 [1] Literally *Utter Destruction* 21:4 [a] Judg. 11:18 21:5 [a] Num. 20:4, 5

up out of Egypt to die in the wilderness?
For *there is* no food and no water, and our
soul loathes this worthless bread." 6So [a]the
LORD sent [b]fiery serpents among the people, and they bit the people; and many of
the people of Israel died.
7[a]Therefore the people came to Moses,
and said, "We have [b]sinned, for we have
spoken against the LORD and against you;
[c]pray to the LORD that He take away the
serpents from us." So Moses prayed for the
people.
8Then the LORD said to Moses, [a]"Make
a [b]fiery *serpent,* and set it on a pole; and it
shall be that everyone who is bitten, when
he looks at it, shall live." 9So [a]Moses made a
bronze serpent, and put it on a pole; and so
it was, if a serpent had bitten anyone, when
he looked at the bronze serpent, he lived.

From Mount Hor to Moab

10Now the children of Israel moved on
and [a]camped in Oboth. 11And they journeyed from Oboth and camped at Ije Abarim, in the wilderness which *is* east of
Moab, toward the sunrise. 12[a]From there
they moved and camped in the Valley of Zered. 13From there they moved and camped
on the other side of the Arnon, which *is* in
the wilderness that extends from the border of the Amorites; for [a]the Arnon *is* the
border of Moab, between Moab and the Amorites. 14Therefore it is said in the Book of
the Wars of the LORD:

"Waheb in Suphah,[1]
The brooks of the Arnon,
15 And the slope of the brooks
That reaches to the dwelling of [a]Ar,
And lies on the border of Moab."

16From there *they went* [a]to Beer, which
is the well where the LORD said to Moses,
"Gather the people together, and I will give
them water." 17[a]Then Israel sang this song:

"Spring up, O well!
All of you sing to it—
18 The well the leaders sank,
Dug by the nation's nobles,
By the [a]lawgiver, with their staves."

And from the wilderness *they went* to
Mattanah, 19from Mattanah to Nahaliel,
from Nahaliel to Bamoth, 20and from Bamoth, *in* the valley that *is* in the country
of Moab, to the top of Pisgah which looks
[a]down on the wasteland.[1]

King Sihon Defeated
(Deut. 2:26–37)

21Then [a]Israel sent messengers to Sihon
king of the Amorites, saying, 22[a]"Let me pass
through your land. We will not turn aside
into fields or vineyards; we will not drink
water from wells. We will go by the King's
Highway until we have passed through your
territory." 23[a]But Sihon would not allow Israel to pass through his territory. So Sihon
gathered all his people together and went
out against Israel in the wilderness, [b]and
he came to Jahaz and fought against Israel. 24Then [a]Israel defeated him with the
edge of the sword, and took possession of
his land from the Arnon to the Jabbok, as
far as the people of Ammon; for the border
of the people of Ammon *was* fortified. 25So
Israel took all these cities, and Israel [a]dwelt
in all the cities of the Amorites, in Heshbon and in all its villages. 26For Heshbon
was the city of Sihon king of the Amorites,
who had fought against the former king of
Moab, and had taken all his land from his
hand as far as the Arnon. 27Therefore those
who speak in proverbs say:

"Come to Heshbon, let it be built;
Let the city of Sihon be repaired.

28 "For [a]fire went out from Heshbon,
A flame from the city of Sihon;
It consumed [b]Ar of Moab,
The lords of the [c]heights of the Arnon.
29 Woe to you, [a]Moab!
You have perished, O people
of [b]Chemosh!

21:6 [a] 1 Cor. 10:9 [b] Deut. 8:15 **21:7** [a] Num. 11:2; Ps. 78:34; Is. 26:16; Hos. 5:15 [b] Lev. 26:40 [c] Ex. 8:8; 1 Sam. 12:19; 1 Kin. 13:6; Acts 8:24 **21:8** [a] [John 3:14, 15] [b] Is. 14:29; 30:6 **21:9** [a] 2 Kin. 18:4; John 3:14, 15 **21:10** [a] Num. 33:43, 44 **21:12** [a] Deut. 2:13 **21:13** [a] Num. 22:36; Judg. 11:18 **21:14** [1] Ancient unknown places; Vulgate reads *What He did in the Red Sea.* **21:15** [a] Num. 21:28; Deut. 2:9, 18, 29 **21:16** [a] Judg. 9:21 **21:17** [a] Ex. 15:1 **21:18** [a] Is. 33:22 **21:20** [a] Num. 23:28 [1] Hebrew *Jeshimon* **21:21** [a] Num. 32:33; Deut. 2:26–37; Judg. 11:19 **21:22** [a] Num. 20:16, 17 **21:23** [a] Deut. 29:7 [b] Deut. 2:32; Judg. 11:20 **21:24** [a] Deut. 2:33; Josh. 12:1; Neh. 9:22; Ps. 135:10; 136:19; Amos 2:9 **21:25** [a] Amos 2:10 **21:28** [a] Jer. 48:45, 46 [b] Deut. 2:9, 18; Is. 15:1 [c] Num. 22:41; 33:52 **21:29** [a] Jer. 48:46 [b] Judg. 11:24; 1 Kin. 11:33; 2 Kin. 23:13

He has given his [c]sons as fugitives,
And his [d]daughters into captivity,
To Sihon king of the Amorites.

30 "But we have shot at them;
Heshbon has perished
[a]as far as Dibon.
Then we laid waste as far as Nophah,
Which *reaches* to [b]Medeba."

31 Thus Israel dwelt in the land of the Amorites. 32 Then Moses sent to spy out [a]Jazer;
and they took its villages and drove out the
Amorites who *were* there.

King Og Defeated
(Deut. 3:1–22)

33 [a]And they turned and went up by the
way to [b]Bashan. So Og king of Bashan went
out against them, he and all his people, to
battle [c]at Edrei. 34 Then the LORD said to Moses, [a]"Do not fear him, for I have delivered
him into your hand, with all his people and
his land; and [b]you shall do to him as you did
to Sihon king of the Amorites, who dwelt
at Heshbon." 35 [a]So they defeated him, his
sons, and all his people, until there was no
survivor left him; and they took possession
of his land.

Balak Sends for Balaam

22 Then [a]the children of Israel moved,
and camped in the plains of Moab
on the side of the Jordan *across from* Jericho.
2 Now [a]Balak the son of Zippor saw all
that Israel had done to the Amorites. 3 And
[a]Moab was exceedingly afraid of the people because they *were* many, and Moab was
sick with dread because of the children of
Israel. 4 So Moab said to [a]the elders of Midian, "Now this company will lick up everything around us, as an ox licks up the grass
of the field." And Balak the son of Zippor
was king of the Moabites at that time. 5 Then
[a]he sent messengers to Balaam the son of
Beor at [b]Pethor, which *is* near the River[1]
in the land of the sons of his people,[2] to
call him, saying: "Look, a people has come
from Egypt. See, they cover the face of the
earth, and are settling next to me! 6 [a]There-
fore please come at once, [b]curse this people for me, for they *are* too mighty for me.
Perhaps I shall be able to defeat them and
drive them out of the land, for I know that
he whom you bless *is* blessed, and he whom
you curse is cursed."
7 So the elders of Moab and the elders of
Midian departed with [a]the diviner's fee in
their hand, and they came to Balaam and
spoke to him the words of Balak. 8 And he
said to them, [a]"Lodge here tonight, and I
will bring back word to you, as the LORD
speaks to me." So the princes of Moab
stayed with Balaam.
9 [a]Then God came to Balaam and said,
"Who *are* these men with you?"
10 So Balaam said to God, "Balak the son
of Zippor, king of Moab, has sent to me,
saying, 11 'Look, a people has come out of
Egypt, and they cover the face of the earth.
Come now, curse them for me; perhaps I
shall be able to overpower them and drive
them out.'"
12 And God said to Balaam, "You shall not
go with them; you shall not curse the people, for [a]they *are* blessed."
13 So Balaam rose in the morning and
said to the princes of Balak, "Go back to
your land, for the LORD has refused to give
me permission to go with you."
14 And the princes of Moab rose and went
to Balak, and said, "Balaam refuses to come
with us."
15 Then Balak again sent princes, more
numerous and more honorable than they.
16 And they came to Balaam and said to him,
"Thus says Balak the son of Zippor: 'Please
let nothing hinder you from coming to me;
17 for I will certainly [a]honor you greatly, and
I will do whatever you say to me. [b]Therefore
please come, curse this people for me.'"
18 Then Balaam answered and said to the
servants of Balak, [a]"Though Balak were to
give me his house full of silver and gold, [b]I
could not go beyond the word of the LORD

21:29 [c] Is. 15:2, 5 [d] Is. 16:2 **21:30** [a] Num. 32:3, 34; Jer. 48:18, 22 [b] Is. 15:2 **21:32** [a] Num. 32:1, 3, 35; Jer. 48:32 **21:33** [a] Deut. 29:7 [b] Deut. 3:1 [c] Josh. 13:12 **21:34** [a] Deut. 3:2 [b] Num. 21:24; Ps. 135:10; 136:20 **21:35** [a] Deut. 3:3, 4; 29:7; Josh. 13:12 **22:1** [a] Num. 33:48, 49 **22:2** [a] Josh. 24:9; Judg. 11:25; Mic. 6:5; Rev. 2:14 **22:3** [a] Ex. 15:15 **22:4** [a] Num. 25:15–18; 31:1–3; Josh. 13:21 **22:5** [a] Num. 31:8, 16; Deut. 23:4; Josh. 13:22; 24:9; Neh. 13:1, 2; Mic. 6:5; 2 Pet. 2:15; Jude 11; Rev. 2:14 [b] Deut. 23:4 [1] That is, the Euphrates [2] Or *the people of Amau* **22:6** [a] Num. 22:17; 23:7, 8 [b] Num. 22:12; 24:9 **22:7** [a] 1 Sam. 9:7, 8 **22:8** [a] Num. 22:19 **22:9** [a] Gen. 20:3 **22:12** [a] Num. 23:20; [Rom. 11:28] **22:17** [a] Num. 24:11 [b] Num. 22:6 **22:18** [a] Num. 22:38; 24:13 [b] 1 Kin. 22:14; 2 Chr. 18:13

my God, to do less or more. 19 Now therefore, please, you also [a]stay here tonight,
that I may know what more the LORD will
say to me."

20 [a]And God came to Balaam at night and
said to him, "If the men come to call you,
rise *and* go with them; but [b]only the word
which I speak to you—that you shall do."
21 So Balaam rose in the morning, saddled his
donkey, and went with the princes of Moab.

Balaam, the Donkey, and the Angel

22 Then God's anger was aroused because
he went, [a]and the Angel of the LORD took
His stand in the way as an adversary against
him. And he was riding on his donkey, and
his two servants *were* with him. 23 Now [a]the
donkey saw the Angel of the LORD standing in the way with His drawn sword in His
hand, and the donkey turned aside out of
the way and went into the field. So Balaam
struck the donkey to turn her back onto the
road. 24 Then the Angel of the LORD stood in
a narrow path between the vineyards, *with*
a wall on this side and a wall on that side.
25 And when the donkey saw the Angel of
the LORD, she pushed herself against the
wall and crushed Balaam's foot against the
wall; so he struck her again. 26 Then the Angel of the LORD went further, and stood in
a narrow place where there *was* no way to
turn either to the right hand or to the left.
27 And when the donkey saw the Angel of
the LORD, she lay down under Balaam; so
Balaam's anger was aroused, and he struck
the donkey with his staff.

28 Then the LORD [a]opened the mouth of
the donkey, and she said to Balaam, "What
have I done to you, that you have struck me
these three times?"

29 And Balaam said to the donkey, "Because you have abused me. I wish there
were a sword in my hand, [a]for now I would
kill you!"

30 [a]So the donkey said to Balaam, "*Am* I
not your donkey on which you have ridden,
ever since *I became* yours, to this day? Was
I ever disposed to do this to you?"

And he said, "No."

31 Then the LORD [a]opened Balaam's eyes,
and he saw the Angel of the LORD standing in the way with His drawn sword in His
hand; and he bowed his head and fell flat
on his face. 32 And the Angel of the LORD
said to him, "Why have you struck your
donkey these three times? Behold, I have
come out to stand against you, because
your way is [a]perverse before Me. 33 The donkey saw Me and turned aside from Me these
three times. If she had not turned aside
from Me, surely I would also have killed
you by now, and let her live."

34 And Balaam said to the Angel of the
LORD, [a]"I have sinned, for I did not know
You stood in the way against me. Now there-
fore, if it displeases You, I will turn back."

35 Then the Angel of the LORD said to Balaam, "Go with the men, [a]but only the word
that I speak to you, that you shall speak."
So Balaam went with the princes of Balak.

36 Now when Balak heard that Balaam
was coming, [a]he went out to meet him at
the city of Moab, [b]which *is* on the border
at the Arnon, the boundary of the territory. 37 Then Balak said to Balaam, "Did I
not earnestly send to you, calling for you?
Why did you not come to me? Am I not able
[a]to honor you?"

38 And Balaam said to Balak, "Look, I
have come to you! Now, have I any power
at all to say anything? [a]The word that God
puts in my mouth, that I must speak." 39 So
Balaam went with Balak, and they came to
Kirjath Huzoth. 40 Then Balak offered oxen
and sheep, and he sent *some* to Balaam and
to the princes who *were* with him.

Balaam's First Prophecy

41 So it was, the next day, that Balak took
Balaam and brought him up to the [a]high
places of Baal, that from there he might
observe the extent of the people.

23 Then Balaam said to Balak, [a]"Build
seven altars for me here, and prepare for me here seven bulls and seven
rams."

2 And Balak did just as Balaam had spoken, and Balak and Balaam [a]offered a bull

---

22:19 [a] Num. 22:8 22:20 [a] Num. 22:9 [b] Num. 22:35; 23:5, 12, 16, 26; 24:13 22:22 [a] Ex. 4:24 22:23 [a] Josh. 5:13; 2 Kin. 6:17; Dan. 10:7; Acts 22:9 22:28 [a] 2 Pet. 2:16 22:29 [a] [Prov. 12:10; Matt. 15:19] 22:30 [a] 2 Pet. 2:16 22:31 [a] Gen. 21:19; 2 Kin. 6:17; Luke 24:16, 31 22:32 [a] [2 Pet. 2:14, 15] 22:34 [a] 1 Sam. 15:24, 30; 26:21; 2 Sam. 12:13 22:35 [a] Num. 22:20 22:36 [a] Gen. 14:17 [b] Num. 21:13 22:37 [a] Num. 22:17; 24:11 22:38 [a] Num. 23:26; 24:13; 1 Kin. 22:14; 2 Chr. 18:13 22:41 [a] Num. 21:28; Deut. 12:2 23:1 [a] Num. 23:29 23:2 [a] Num. 23:14, 30

and a ram on *each* altar. 3Then Balaam said
to Balak, [a]"Stand by your burnt offering, and
I will go; perhaps the LORD will come [b]to
meet me, and whatever He shows me I will
tell you." So he went to a desolate height.
4[a]And God met Balaam, and he said to Him,
"I have prepared the seven altars, and I have
offered on *each* altar a bull and a ram."

5Then the LORD [a]put a word in Balaam's
mouth, and said, "Return to Balak, and thus
you shall speak." 6So he returned to him,
and there he was, standing by his burnt
offering, he and all the princes of Moab.

7And he [a]took up his oracle and said:

"Balak the king of Moab has
    brought me from Aram,
From the mountains of the east.
[b]'Come, curse Jacob for me,
And come, [c]denounce Israel!'

8 "How[a] shall I curse whom
    God has not cursed?
And how shall I denounce *whom*
    the LORD has not denounced?
9 For from the top of the rocks I see him,
And from the hills I behold him;
There! [a]A people dwelling alone,
[b]Not reckoning itself among
    the nations.

10 "Who[a] can count the dust[1] of Jacob,
Or number one-fourth of Israel?
Let me die [b]the death of the righteous,
And let my end be like his!"

11Then Balak said to Balaam, "What have
you done to me? [a]I took you to curse my
enemies, and look, you have blessed *them*
bountifully!"

12So he answered and said, [a]"Must I not
take heed to speak what the LORD has put
in my mouth?"

Balaam's Second Prophecy

13Then Balak said to him, "Please come
with me to another place from which you
may see them; you shall see only the outer
part of them, and shall not see them all;
curse them for me from there." 14So he
brought him to the field of Zophim, to the
top of Pisgah, [a]and built seven altars, and
offered a bull and a ram on *each* altar.

15And he said to Balak, "Stand here by
your burnt offering while I meet[1] *the LORD*
over there."

16Then the LORD met Balaam, and [a]put
a word in his mouth, and said, "Go back
to Balak, and thus you shall speak." 17So
he came to him, and there he was, standing by his burnt offering, and the princes
of Moab were with him. And Balak said to
him, "What has the LORD spoken?"

18Then he took up his oracle and said:

[a]"Rise up, Balak, and hear!
Listen to me, son of Zippor!

19 "God[a] *is* not a man, that He should lie,
Nor a son of man, that He
    should repent.
Has He [b]said, and will He not do?
Or has He spoken, and will
    He not make it good?
20 Behold, I have received *a*
    command to bless;
[a]He has blessed, and I cannot
    reverse it.

#OXYGEN

NUMBERS 23:19

Act in Faith

To rely on God truly, place confidence in Him. He is trustworthy. Your days still might not be easy. However, God wants you to have faith, especially when He calls you out of your comfort zone.

God is calling, so **breathe** and **act in faith.**

23:3 [a] Num. 23:15 [b] Num. 23:4, 16 23:4 [a] Num. 23:16 23:5 [a] Num. 22:20, 35, 38; 23:16; Deut. 18:18; Jer. 1:9 23:7 [a] Deut. 23:4; Job 27:1; 29:1; Ps. 78:2 [b] Num. 22:6, 11, 17 [c] 1 Sam. 17:10 23:8 [a] Num. 22:12 23:9 [a] Deut. 32:8; 33:28; Josh. 11:23 [b] Ex. 33:16; Ezra 9:2; [Eph. 2:14] 23:10 [a] Gen. 13:16; 22:17; 28:14; 2 Chr. 1:9 [b] Ps. 116:15 [1] Or *dust cloud* 23:11 [a] Num. 22:11 23:12 [a] Num. 22:38 23:14 [a] Num. 23:1, 2 23:15 [1] Following Masoretic Text, Targum, and Vulgate; Syriac reads *call;* Septuagint reads *go and ask God.* 23:16 [a] Num. 22:35; 23:5 23:18 [a] Judg. 3:20 23:19 [a] 1 Sam. 15:29; Mal. 3:6; James 1:17 [b] Num. 11:23; 1 Kin. 8:56 23:20 [a] Gen. 12:2; 22:17; Num. 22:12

21 "He[a] has not observed iniquity in Jacob,
Nor has He seen wickedness in Israel.
The LORD his God *is* with him,
[b]And the shout of a King
is among them.
22 [a]God brings them out of Egypt;
He has [b]strength like a wild ox.

23 "For *there is* no sorcery against Jacob,
Nor any divination against Israel.
It now must be said of Jacob
And of Israel, 'Oh, [a]what
God has done!'
24 Look, a people rises [a]like a lioness,
And lifts itself up like a lion;
[b]It shall not lie down until
it devours the prey,
And drinks the blood of the slain."

25Then Balak said to Balaam, "Neither
curse them at all, nor bless them at all!"
26So Balaam answered and said to Ba-
lak, "Did I not tell you, saying, [a]'All that the
LORD speaks, that I must do'?"

Balaam's Third Prophecy

27Then Balak said to Balaam, "Please
come, I will take you to another place; perhaps it will please God that you may curse
them for me from there." 28So Balak took
Balaam to the top of Peor, that [a]overlooks
the wasteland.[1] 29Then Balaam said to Balak, "Build for me here seven altars, and
prepare for me here seven bulls and seven
rams." 30And Balak did as Balaam had said,
and offered a bull and a ram on *every* altar.

24 Now when Balaam saw that it
pleased the LORD to bless Israel,
he did not go as at [a]other times, to seek to
use sorcery, but he set his face toward the
wilderness. 2And Balaam raised his eyes,
and saw Israel [a]encamped according to
their tribes; and [b]the Spirit of God came
upon him.
3[a]Then he took up his oracle and said:

"The utterance of Balaam
the son of Beor,
The utterance of the man
whose eyes are opened,
4 The utterance of him who
hears the words of God,
Who sees the vision of the Almighty,
Who [a]falls down, with eyes wide open:

5 "How lovely are your tents, O Jacob!
Your dwellings, O Israel!
6 Like valleys that stretch out,
Like gardens by the riverside,
[a]Like aloes [b]planted by the LORD,
Like cedars beside the waters.
7 He shall pour water from his buckets,
And his seed *shall be* [a]in many waters.

"His king shall be higher than [b]Agag,
And his [c]kingdom shall be exalted.

8 "God[a] brings him out of Egypt;
He has strength like a wild ox;
He shall [b]consume the
nations, his enemies;
He shall [c]break their bones
And [d]pierce *them* with his arrows.
9 'He[a] bows down, he lies
down as a lion;
And as a lion, who shall rouse him?'[1]

[b]"Blessed *is* he who blesses you,
And cursed *is* he who curses you."

10Then Balak's anger was aroused against
Balaam, and he [a]struck his hands together;
and Balak said to Balaam, [b]"I called you
to curse my enemies, and look, you have
bountifully blessed *them* these three times!
11Now therefore, flee to your place. [a]I said
I would greatly honor you, but in fact, the
LORD has kept you back from honor."
12So Balaam said to Balak, "Did I not also
speak to your messengers whom you sent
to me, saying, 13'If Balak were to give me
his house full of silver and gold, I could
not go beyond the word of the LORD, to
do good or bad of my own will. What the
LORD says, that I must speak'? 14And now,
indeed, I am going to my people. Come, [a]I

23:21 [a] Ps. 32:2; [Rom. 4:7, 8] [b] Ps. 89:15–18 **23:22** [a] Num. 24:8 [b] Deut. 33:17; Job 39:10 **23:23** [a] Ps. 31:19; 44:1 **23:24** [a] Gen. 49:9 [b] Gen. 49:27; Josh. 11:23 **23:26** [a] Num. 22:38 **23:28** [a] Num. 21:20 [1] Hebrew *Jeshimon* **24:1** [a] Num. 23:3, 15 **24:2** [a] Num. 2:2, 34 [b] Num. 11:25; 1 Sam. 10:10; 19:20, 23; 2 Chr. 15:1 **24:3** [a] Num. 23:7, 18 **24:4** [a] Ezek. 1:28 **24:6** [a] Ps. 1:3; Jer. 17:8 [b] Ps. 104:16 **24:7** [a] Jer. 51:13; Rev. 17:1, 15 [b] 1 Sam. 15:8, 9 [c] 2 Sam. 5:12; 1 Chr. 14:2 **24:8** [a] Num. 23:22 [b] Num. 14:9; 23:24 [c] Ps. 2:9; Jer. 50:17 [d] Ps. 45:5 **24:9** [a] Gen. 49:9; Num. 23:24 [b] Gen. 12:3; 27:29 [1] Genesis 49:9 **24:10** [a] Ezek. 21:14, 17 [b] Num. 23:11; Neh. 13:2 **24:11** [a] Num. 22:17, 37 **24:14** [a] [Mic. 6:5]

will advise you what this people will do to
your people in the [b]latter days."

Balaam's Fourth Prophecy

15So he took up his oracle and said:

"The utterance of Balaam
the son of Beor,
And the utterance of the man
whose eyes are opened;
16 The utterance of him who
hears the words of God,
And has the knowledge
of the Most High,
Who sees the vision of the Almighty,
Who falls down, with eyes
wide open:

17 "I[a] see Him, but not now;
I behold Him, but not near;
[b]A Star shall come out of Jacob;
[c]A Scepter shall rise out of Israel,
And batter the brow of Moab,
And destroy all the sons of tumult.[1]

18 "And [a]Edom shall be a possession;
Seir also, his enemies, shall
be a possession,
While Israel does valiantly.
19 [a]Out of Jacob One shall have dominion,
And destroy the remains of the city."

20Then he looked on Amalek, and he
took up his oracle and said:

"Amalek *was* first among the nations,
But *shall be* last until he perishes."

21Then he looked on the Kenites, and he
took up his oracle and said:

"Firm is your dwelling place,
And your nest is set in the rock;
22 Nevertheless Kain shall be burned.
How long until Asshur carries
you away captive?"

23Then he took up his oracle and said:

"Alas! Who shall live when
God does this?
24 But ships *shall come* from
the coasts of [a]Cyprus,[1]
And they shall afflict Asshur
and afflict [b]Eber,
And so shall *Amalek*,[2]
until he perishes."

25So Balaam rose and departed and [a]re-
turned to his place; Balak also went his way.

Israel's Harlotry in Moab

25 Now Israel remained in [a]Acacia
Grove,[1] and the [b]people began to
commit harlotry with the women of Moab.
2[a]They invited the people to [b]the sacrifices of their gods, and the people ate and
[c]bowed down to their gods. 3So Israel was
joined to Baal of Peor, and [a]the anger of the
LORD was aroused against Israel.

4Then the LORD said to Moses, [a]"Take
all the leaders of the people and hang the
offenders before the LORD, out in the sun,
[b]that the fierce anger of the LORD may turn
away from Israel."

5So Moses said to [a]the judges of Israel,
[b]"Every one of you kill his men who were
joined to Baal of Peor."

6And indeed, one of the children of Israel came and presented to his brethren
a Midianite woman in the sight of Moses
and in the sight of all the congregation of
the children of Israel, [a]who *were* weeping
at the door of the tabernacle of meeting.
7Now [a]when Phinehas [b]the son of Eleazar,
the son of Aaron the priest, saw *it,* he rose
from among the congregation and took a
javelin in his hand; 8and he went after the
man of Israel into the tent and thrust both
of them through, the man of Israel, and the
woman through her body. So [a]the plague
was [b]stopped among the children of Israel.
9And [a]those who died in the plague were
twenty-four thousand.

10Then the LORD spoke to Moses, saying:
11[a]"Phinehas the son of Eleazar, the son of
Aaron the priest, has turned back My wrath

24:14 [b] Gen. 49:1; Deut. 4:30; Dan. 2:28 **24:17** [a] Rev. 1:7; Matt. 1:2; Luke 3:34 [b] Matt. 2:2 [c] Gen. 49:10 [1] Hebrew *Sheth* (compare Jeremiah 48:45) **24:18** [a] 2 Sam. 8:14 **24:19** [a] Gen. 49:10; Amos 9:11, 12 **24:24** [a] Gen. 10:4; Ezek. 27:6; Dan. 11:30 [b] Gen. 10:21, 25 [1] Hebrew *Kittim* [2] Literally *he* or *that one* **24:25** [a] Num. 22:5; 31:8 **25:1** [a] Num. 33:49; Josh. 2:1 [b] Rev. 2:14 [1] Hebrew *Shittim* **25:2** [a] Josh. 22:17; Hos. 9:10 [b] Ex. 34:15; Deut. 32:38; 1 Cor. 10:20 [c] Ex. 20:5 **25:3** [a] Ps. 106:28, 29 **25:4** [a] Deut. 4:3 [b] Num. 25:11; Deut. 13:17 **25:5** [a] Ex. 18:21 [b] Deut. 13:6, 9 **25:6** [a] Joel 2:17 **25:7** [a] Ps. 106:30 [b] Ex. 6:25 **25:8** [a] Ps. 106:30 [b] Num. 16:46–48 **25:9** [a] Deut. 4:3 **25:11** [a] Ps. 106:30

from the children of Israel, because he was
zealous with My zeal among them, so that
I did not consume the children of Israel in
[b]My zeal. 12 Therefore say, [a]'Behold, I give to
him My [b]covenant of peace; 13 and it shall
be to him and [a]his descendants after him
a covenant of [b]an everlasting priesthood,
because he was [c]zealous for his God, and
[d]made atonement for the children of Israel.'"

14 Now the name of the Israelite who was
killed, who was killed with the Midianite
woman, *was* Zimri the son of Salu, a leader
of a father's house among the Simeonites.
15 And the name of the Midianite woman
who was killed *was* Cozbi the daughter of
[a]Zur; he *was* head of the people of a father's
house in Midian.

16 Then the LORD spoke to Moses, saying: 17 [a]"Harass the Midianites, and attack
them; 18 for they harassed you with their
[a]schemes by which they seduced you in the
matter of Peor and in the matter of Cozbi,
the daughter of a leader of Midian, their sister, who was killed in the day of the plague
because of Peor."

The Second Census of Israel

26 And it came to pass, after the
[a]plague, that the LORD spoke to
Moses and Eleazar the son of Aaron the
priest, saying: 2 [a]"Take a census of all the
congregation of the children of Israel [b]from
twenty years old and above, by their fathers' houses, all who are able to go to war
in Israel." 3 So Moses and Eleazar the priest
spoke with them [a]in the plains of Moab
by the Jordan, *across from* Jericho, saying:
4 "*Take a census of the people* from twenty
years old and above, just as the LORD [a]commanded Moses and the children of Israel
who came out of the land of Egypt."

5 [a]Reuben *was* the firstborn of Israel. The
children of Reuben *were: of* Hanoch, the
family of the Hanochites; *of* Pallu, the family of the Palluites; 6 *of* Hezron, the family
of the Hezronites; *of* Carmi, the family of
the Carmites. 7 These *are* the families of
the Reubenites: those who were numbered
of them were forty-three thousand seven
hundred and thirty. 8 And the son of Pallu
was Eliab. 9 The sons of Eliab *were* Nemuel,
Dathan, and Abiram. These *are* the Dathan
and Abiram, [a]representatives of the congregation, who contended against Moses
and Aaron in the company of Korah, when
they contended against the LORD; 10 [a]and
the earth opened its mouth and swallowed
them up together with Korah when that
company died, when the fire devoured two
hundred and fifty men; [b]and they became
a sign. 11 Nevertheless [a]the children of Korah did not die.

12 The sons of Simeon according to their
families *were: of* Nemuel,[1] the family of the
Nemuelites; *of* Jamin, the family of the Jaminites; *of* Jachin,[2] the family of the Jachinites; 13 *of* Zerah,[1] the family of the Zarhites; *of*
Shaul, the family of the Shaulites. 14 These
are the families of the Simeonites: twenty-two thousand two hundred.

15 The sons of Gad according to their
families *were: of* Zephon,[1] the family of
the Zephonites; *of* Haggi, the family of the
Haggites; *of* Shuni, the family of the Shunites; 16 *of* Ozni,[1] the family of the Oznites;
of Eri, the family of the Erites; 17 *of* Arod,[1] the
family of the Arodites; *of* Areli, the family
of the Arelites. 18 These *are* the families of
the sons of Gad according to those who
were numbered of them: forty thousand
five hundred.

19 [a]The sons of Judah *were* Er and Onan;
and Er and Onan died in the land of Canaan. 20 And [a]the sons of Judah according
to their families were: *of* Shelah, the family of the Shelanites; *of* Perez, the family
of the Parzites; *of* Zerah, the family of the
Zarhites. 21 And the sons of Perez were: *of*
Hezron, the family of the Hezronites; *of* Hamul, the family of the Hamulites. 22 These
are the families of Judah according to those
who were numbered of them: seventy-six
thousand five hundred.

25:11 [b] [Ex. 20:5]; Deut. 32:16, 21; 1 Kin. 14:22; Ps. 78:58; Ezek. 16:38 **25:12** [a] [Mal. 2:4, 5; 3:1] [b] Is. 54:10; Ezek. 34:25; 37:26; Mal. 2:5 **25:13** [a] 1 Chr. 6:4–15 [b] Ex. 40:15 [c] Acts 22:3; Rom. 10:2 [d] [Heb. 2:17] **25:15** [a] Num. 31:8; Josh. 13:21 **25:17** [a] Num. 31:1–3 **25:18** [a] Num. 31:16; Rev. 2:14 **26:1** [a] Num. 25:9 **26:2** [a] Ex. 30:12; 38:25, 26; Num. 1:2; 14:29 [b] Num. 1:3 **26:3** [a] Num. 22:1; 31:12; 33:48; 35:1 **26:4** [a] Num. 1:1 **26:5** [a] Gen. 46:8; Ex. 6:14; 1 Chr. 5:1–3 **26:9** [a] Num. 1:16; 16:1, 2 **26:10** [a] Num. 16:32–35 [b] Num. 16:38–40; 1 Cor. 10:6; 2 Pet. 2:6 **26:11** [a] Ex. 6:24; 1 Chr. 6:22, 23 **26:12** [1] Spelled *Jemuel* in Genesis 46:10 and Exodus 6:15 [2] Called *Jarib* in 1 Chronicles 4:24 **26:13** [1] Called *Zohar* in Genesis 46:10 **26:15** [1] Called *Ziphion* in Genesis 46:16 **26:16** [1] Called *Ezbon* in Genesis 46:16 **26:17** [1] Spelled *Arodi* in Samaritan Pentateuch, Syriac, and Genesis 46:16 **26:19** [a] Gen. 38:2; 46:12 **26:20** [a] 1 Chr. 2:3

23The sons of Issachar according to their
families *were: of* Tola, the family of the To-
laites; of Puah,[1] the family of the Punites;[2]
24of Jashub, the family of the Jashubites;
of Shimron, the family of the Shimronites.
25These *are* the families of Issachar according to those who were numbered of them:
sixty-four thousand three hundred.

26[a]The sons of Zebulun according to
their families *were:* of Sered, the family of
the Sardites; of Elon, the family of the Elon-
ites; of Jahleel, the family of the Jahleelites.
27These *are* the families of the Zebulunites
according to those who were numbered of
them: sixty thousand five hundred.

28[a]The sons of Joseph according to their
families, by Manasseh and Ephraim, *were:*
29The sons of [a]Manasseh: of [b]Machir, the
family of the Machirites; and Machir begot
Gilead; of Gilead, the family of the Gileadites.
30These *are* the sons of Gilead: *of* Jeezer,[1] the
family of the Jeezerites; of Helek, the family of the Helekites; 31*of* Asriel, the family
of the Asrielites; *of* Shechem, the family of
the Shechemites; 32*of* Shemida, the family
of the Shemidaites; *of* Hepher, the family of
the Hepherites. 33Now [a]Zelophehad the son
of Hepher had no sons, but daughters; and
the names of the daughters of Zelophehad
were Mahlah, Noah, Hoglah, Milcah, and Tirzah. 34These *are* the families of Manasseh;
and those who were numbered of them *were*
fifty-two thousand seven hundred.

35These *are* the sons of Ephraim according to their families: of Shuthelah,
the family of the Shuthalhites; of Becher,[1]
the family of the Bachrites; of Tahan, the
family of the Tahanites. 36And these *are*
the sons of Shuthelah: of Eran, the family
of the Eranites. 37These *are* the families of
the sons of Ephraim according to those
who were numbered of them: thirty-two
thousand five hundred.

These *are* the sons of Joseph according
to their families.

38[a]The sons of Benjamin according to
their families were: of Bela, the family of
the Belaites; of Ashbel, the family of the
Ashbelites; of [b]Ahiram, the family of the
Ahiramites; 39of [a]Shupham,[1] the family of
the Shuphamites; of Hupham,[2] the family
of the Huphamites. 40And the sons of Bela
were Ard[1] and Naaman: [a]*of Ard,* the family
of the Ardites; of Naaman, the family of the
Naamites. 41These *are* the sons of Benjamin
according to their families; and those who
were numbered of them *were* forty-five
thousand six hundred.

42These *are* the sons of Dan according
to their families: of Shuham,[1] the family of
the Shuhamites. These *are* the families of
Dan according to their families. 43All the
families of the Shuhamites, according to
those who were numbered of them, *were*
sixty-four thousand four hundred.

44[a]The sons of Asher according to their
families *were:* of Jimna, the family of the
Jimnites; of Jesui, the family of the Jesu-
ites; of Beriah, the family of the Beriites.
45Of the sons of Beriah: of Heber, the family of the Heberites; of Malchiel, the family
of the Malchielites. 46And the name of the
daughter of Asher *was* Serah. 47These *are*
the families of the sons of Asher according
to those who were numbered of them: fifty-
three thousand four hundred.

48[a]The sons of Naphtali according to
their families *were:* of Jahzeel,[1] the family of the Jahzeelites; of Guni, the family
of the Gunites; 49of Jezer, the family of the
Jezerites; of [a]Shillem, the family of the Shil-
lemites. 50These *are* the families of Naphtali according to their families; and those
who were numbered of them *were* forty-
five thousand four hundred.

51[a]These *are* those who were numbered
of the children of Israel: six hundred and
one thousand seven hundred and thirty.

52Then the LORD spoke to Moses, say-
ing: 53[a]"To these the land shall be [b]divided
as an inheritance, according to the number
of names. 54[a]To a large *tribe* you shall give
a larger inheritance, and to a small *tribe*
you shall give a smaller inheritance. Each

26:23 [1] Hebrew *Puvah* (compare Genesis 46:13 and 1 Chronicles 7:1); Samaritan Pentateuch, Septuagint, Syriac, and Vulgate read *Puah.* [2] Samaritan Pentateuch, Septuagint, Syriac, and Vulgate read *Puaites.* **26:26** [a] Gen. 46:14 **26:28** [a] Gen. 46:20; Deut. 33:16 **26:29** [a] Josh. 17:1 [b] 1 Chr. 7:14, 15 **26:30** [1] Called *Abiezer* in Joshua 17:2 **26:33** [a] Num. 27:1; 36:11 **26:35** [1] Called *Bered* in 1 Chronicles 7:20 **26:38** [a] Gen. 46:21; 1 Chr. 7:6 [b] Gen. 46:21; 1 Chr. 8:1, 2 **26:39** [a] 1 Chr. 7:12 [1] Masoretic Text reads *Shephupham,* spelled *Shephuphan* in 1 Chronicles 8:5. [2] Called *Huppim* in Genesis 46:21 **26:40** [a] 1 Chr. 8:3 [1] Called *Addar* in 1 Chronicles 8:3 **26:42** [1] Called *Hushim* in Genesis 46:23 **26:44** [a] Gen. 46:17; 1 Chr. 7:30 **26:48** [a] Gen. 46:24; 1 Chr. 7:13 [1] Spelled *Jahziel* in 1 Chronicles 7:13 **26:49** [a] 1 Chr. 7:13 **26:51** [a] Ex. 12:37; 38:26; Num. 1:46; 11:21 **26:53** [a] Josh. 11:23; 14:1 [b] Num. 33:54 **26:54** [a] Num. 33:54

shall be given its inheritance according to
those who were numbered of them. 55But
the land shall be [a]divided by lot; they shall
inherit according to the names of the tribes
of their fathers. 56According to the lot their
inheritance shall be divided between the
larger and the smaller."

57[a]And these *are* those who were numbered of the Levites according to their
families: of Gershon, the family of the
Gershonites; of Kohath, the family of the
Kohathites; of Merari, the family of the Me-
rarites. 58These *are* the families of the Levites: the family of the Libnites, the family
of the Hebronites, the family of the Mahlites,
the family of the Mushites, and the family of
the Korathites. And Kohath begot Amram.
59The name of Amram's wife *was* [a]Jochebed
the daughter of Levi, who was born to Levi
in Egypt; and to Amram she bore Aaron and
Moses and their sister Miriam. 60[a]To Aaron
were born Nadab and Abihu, Eleazar and
Ithamar. 61And [a]Nadab and Abihu died when
they offered profane fire before the LORD.

62[a]Now those who were numbered of them
were twenty-three thousand, every male
from a month old and above; [b]for they were
not numbered among the other children of
Israel, because there was [c]no inheritance
given to them among the children of Israel.

63These *are* those who were numbered by
Moses and Eleazar the priest, who numbered
the children of Israel [a]in the plains of Moab
by the Jordan, *across from* Jericho. 64[a]But
among these there was not a man of those
who were numbered by Moses and Aaron the
priest when they numbered the children of
Israel in the [b]Wilderness of Sinai. 65For the
LORD had said of them, "They [a]shall surely
die in the wilderness." So there was not left
a man of them, [b]except Caleb the son of Jephunneh and Joshua the son of Nun.

Inheritance Laws

27 Then came the daughters of [a]Zelo-
phehad the son of Hepher, the son
of Gilead, the son of Machir, the son of Manasseh, from the families of Manasseh the
son of Joseph; and these *were* the names
of his daughters: Mahlah, Noah, Hoglah,
Milcah, and Tirzah. 2And they stood before Moses, before Eleazar the priest, and
before the leaders and all the congregation, *by* the doorway of the tabernacle of
meeting, saying: 3"Our father [a]died in the
wilderness; but he was not in the company
of those who gathered together against the
LORD, [b]in company with Korah, but he died
in his own sin; and he had no sons. 4Why
should the name of our father be [a]removed
from among his family because he had no
son? [b]Give us a possession among our father's brothers."

5So Moses [a]brought their case before
the LORD.

6And the LORD spoke to Moses, saying:
7"The daughters of Zelophehad speak *what
is* right; [a]you shall surely give them a possession of inheritance among their father's
brothers, and cause the inheritance of their
father to pass to them. 8And you shall speak
to the children of Israel, saying: 'If a man
dies and has no son, then you shall cause
his inheritance to pass to his daughter. 9If
he has no daughter, then you shall give
his inheritance to his brothers. 10If he has
no brothers, then you shall give his inheritance to his father's brothers. 11And if his
father has no brothers, then you shall give
his inheritance to the relative closest to
him in his family, and he shall possess it.'"
And it shall be to the children of Israel [a]a
statute of judgment, just as the LORD commanded Moses.

Joshua the Next Leader of Israel
(Deut. 31:1–8)

12Now the LORD said to Moses: [a]"Go up
into this Mount Abarim, and see the land
which I have given to the children of Israel. 13And when you have seen it, you
also [a]shall be gathered to your people, as
Aaron your brother was gathered. 14For in
the Wilderness of Zin, during the strife of
the congregation, you [a]rebelled against My
command to hallow Me at the waters before

26:55 [a] Num. 33:54; 34:13; Josh. 11:23; 14:2 26:57 [a] Gen. 46:11; Ex. 6:16–19; Num. 3:15; 1 Chr. 6:1, 16 26:59 [a] Ex. 2:1, 2; 6:20 26:60 [a] Num. 3:2 26:61 [a] Lev. 10:1, 2; Num. 3:3, 4; 1 Chr. 24:2 26:62 [a] Num. 3:39 [b] Num. 1:49 [c] Num. 18:20, 23, 24 26:63 [a] Num. 26:3 26:64 [a] Num. 14:29–35; Deut. 2:14–16; Heb. 3:17 [b] Num. 1:1–46 26:65 [a] Num. 14:26–35; [1 Cor. 10:5, 6] [b] Num. 14:30 27:1 [a] Num. 26:33; 36:1, 11; Josh. 17:3 27:3 [a] Num. 14:35; 26:64, 65 [b] Num. 16:1, 2 27:4 [a] Deut. 25:6 [b] Josh. 17:4 27:5 [a] Ex. 18:13–26 27:7 [a] Num. 36:2; Josh. 17:4 27:11 [a] Num. 35:29 27:12 [a] Num. 33:47; Deut. 3:23–27; 32:48–52; 34:1–4 27:13 [a] Num. 20:12, 24, 28; 31:2; Deut. 10:6; 34:5, 6 27:14 [a] Num. 20:12, 24; Deut. 1:37; 32:51; Ps. 106:32, 33

their eyes." (These *are* the [b]waters of Meribah, at Kadesh in the Wilderness of Zin.)
15 Then Moses spoke to the LORD, saying:
16 "Let the LORD, [a]the God of the spirits of
all flesh, set a man over the congregation,
17 [a]who may go out before them and go in
before them, who may lead them out and
bring them in, that the congregation of the
LORD may not be [b]like sheep which have
no shepherd."
18 And the LORD said to Moses: "Take
Joshua the son of Nun with you, a man [a]in
whom *is* the Spirit, and [b]lay your hand on
him; 19 set him before Eleazar the priest and
before all the congregation, and [a]inaugu-
rate him in their sight. 20 And [a]you shall give
some of your authority to him, that all the
congregation of the children of Israel [b]may
be obedient. 21 [a]He shall stand before Eleazar
the priest, who shall inquire before the LORD
for him [b]by the judgment of the Urim. [c]At
his word they shall go out, and at his word
they shall come in, he and all the children
of Israel with him—all the congregation."
22 So Moses did as the LORD commanded
him. He took Joshua and set him before
Eleazar the priest and before all the congregation. 23 And he laid his hands on him
[a]and inaugurated him, just as the LORD
commanded by the hand of Moses.

Daily Offerings
(Ex. 29:38–46)

28 Now the LORD spoke to Moses, saying, 2 "Command the children of Israel, and say to them, 'My offering, [a]My food
for My offerings made by fire as a sweet
aroma to Me, you shall be careful to offer
to Me at their appointed time.'
3 "And you shall say to them, [a]'This *is* the
offering made by fire which you shall offer to the LORD: two male lambs in their
first year without blemish, day by day, as a
regular burnt offering. 4 The one lamb you
shall offer in the morning, the other lamb
you shall offer in the evening, 5 and [a]one-
tenth of an ephah of fine flour as a [b]grain
offering mixed with one-fourth of a hin of
pressed oil. 6 *It is* [a]a regular burnt offering
which was ordained at Mount Sinai for a
sweet aroma, an offering made by fire to
the LORD. 7 And its drink offering *shall be*
one-fourth of a hin for each lamb; [a]in a holy
place you shall pour out the drink to the
LORD as an offering. 8 The other lamb you
shall offer in the evening; as the morning
grain offering and its drink offering, you
shall offer *it* as an offering made by fire, a
sweet aroma to the LORD.

Sabbath Offerings

9 'And on the Sabbath day two lambs in
their first year, without blemish, and two-
tenths *of an ephah* of fine flour as a grain
offering, mixed with oil, with its drink offering— 10 *this is* [a]the burnt offering for
every Sabbath, besides the regular burnt
offering with its drink offering.

Monthly Offerings

11 [a]'At the beginnings of your months you
shall present a burnt offering to the LORD:
two young bulls, one ram, and seven lambs
in their first year, without blemish; 12 [a]three-
tenths *of an ephah* of fine flour as a grain
offering, mixed with oil, for each bull; two-
tenths *of an ephah* of fine flour as a grain
offering, mixed with oil, for the one ram;
13 and one-tenth *of an ephah* of fine flour,
mixed with oil, as a grain offering for each
lamb, as a burnt offering of sweet aroma, an
offering made by fire to the LORD. 14 Their
drink offering shall be half a hin of wine
for a bull, one-third of a hin for a ram, and
one-fourth of a hin for a lamb; this *is* the
burnt offering for each month throughout the months of the year. 15 Also [a]one kid
of the goats as a sin offering to the LORD
shall be offered, besides the regular burnt
offering and its drink offering.

Offerings at Passover
(Lev. 23:5–14)

16 [a]'On the fourteenth day of the first
month *is* the Passover of the LORD. 17 [a]And
on the fifteenth day of this month *is* the

27:14 [b] Ex. 17:7 27:16 [a] Num. 16:22; Heb. 12:9 27:17 [a] Deut. 31:2; 1 Sam. 8:20; 18:13; 2 Chr. 1:10 [b] 1 Kin. 22:17; Zech. 10:2; Matt. 9:36; Mark 6:34 27:18 [a] Gen. 41:38; Judg. 3:10; 1 Sam. 16:13, 18 [b] Deut. 34:9 27:19 [a] Deut. 3:28; 31:3, 7, 8, 23 27:20 [a] Num. 11:17 [b] Josh. 1:16–18 27:21 [a] Judg. 20:18, 23, 26; 1 Sam. 23:9; 30:7 [b] Ex. 28:30; 1 Sam. 28:6 [c] Josh. 9:14; 1 Sam. 22:10 27:23 [a] Deut. 3:28; 31:7, 8 28:2 [a] Lev. 3:11; 21:6, 8; [Mal. 1:7, 12] 28:3 [a] Ex. 29:38–42 28:5 [a] Ex. 16:36; Num. 15:4 [b] Lev. 2:1 28:6 [a] Ex. 29:42; Amos 5:25 28:7 [a] Ex. 29:42 28:10 [a] Ezek. 46:4 28:11 [a] Num. 10:10; 1 Sam. 20:5; 1 Chr. 23:31; 2 Chr. 2:4; Ezra 3:5; Neh. 10:33; Is. 1:13, 14; Ezek. 45:17; 46:6, 7; Hos. 2:11; Col. 2:16 28:12 [a] Num. 15:4–12 28:15 [a] Num. 15:24; 28:3, 22 28:16 [a] Ex. 12:1–20; Lev. 23:5–8; Num. 9:2–5; Deut. 16:1–8; Ezek. 45:21 28:17 [a] Lev. 23:6

feast; unleavened bread shall be eaten for seven days. 18On the [a]first day *you shall have* a holy convocation. You shall do no customary work. 19And you shall present an offering made by fire as a burnt offering to the LORD: two young bulls, one ram, and seven lambs in their first year. [a]Be sure they are without blemish. 20Their grain offering shall be of fine flour mixed with oil: three-tenths *of an ephah* you shall offer for a bull, and two-tenths for a ram; 21you shall offer one-tenth *of an ephah* for each of the seven lambs; 22also [a]one goat *as* a sin offering, to make atonement for you. 23You shall offer these besides the burnt offering of the morning, which *is* for a regular burnt offering. 24In this manner you shall offer the food of the offering made by fire daily for seven days, as a sweet aroma to the LORD; it shall be offered besides the regular burnt offering and its drink offering. 25And [a]on the seventh day you shall have a holy convocation. You shall do no customary work.

Offerings at the Feast of Weeks
(Lev. 23:15–22)

26'Also [a]on the day of the firstfruits, when you bring a new grain offering to the LORD at your *Feast of* Weeks, you shall have a holy convocation. You shall do no customary work. 27You shall present a burnt offering as a sweet aroma to the LORD: [a]two young bulls, one ram, and seven lambs in their first year, 28with their grain offering of fine flour mixed with oil: three-tenths *of an ephah* for each bull, two-tenths for the one ram, 29and one-tenth for each of the seven lambs; 30*also* one kid of the goats, to make atonement for you. 31[a]Be sure they are without blemish. You shall present *them* with their drink offerings, besides the regular burnt offering with its grain offering.

Offerings at the Feast of Trumpets
(Lev. 23:23–25)

29 'And in the seventh month, on the first *day* of the month, you shall have a holy convocation. You shall do no customary work. For you [a]it is a day of blowing the trumpets. 2You shall offer a burnt offering as a sweet aroma to the LORD: one young bull, one ram, *and* seven lambs in their first year, without blemish. 3Their grain offering *shall be* fine flour mixed with oil: three-tenths *of an ephah* for the bull, two-tenths for the ram, 4and one-tenth for each of the seven lambs; 5also one kid of the goats *as* a sin offering, to make atonement for you; 6besides [a]the burnt offering with its grain offering for the New Moon, [b]the regular burnt offering with its grain offering, and their drink offerings, [c]according to their ordinance, as a sweet aroma, an offering made by fire to the LORD.

Offerings on the Day of Atonement
(Lev. 23:26–32)

7[a]'On the tenth *day* of this seventh month you shall have a holy convocation. You shall [b]afflict your souls; you shall not do any work. 8You shall present a burnt offering to the LORD *as* a sweet aroma: one young bull, one ram, *and* seven lambs in their first year. [a]Be sure they are without blemish. 9Their grain offering *shall be of* fine flour mixed with oil: three-tenths *of an ephah* for the bull, two-tenths for the one ram, 10and one-tenth for each of the seven lambs; 11also one kid of the goats *as* a sin offering, besides [a]the sin offering for atonement, the regular burnt offering with its grain offering, and their drink offerings.

Offerings at the Feast of Tabernacles
(Lev. 23:33–44)

12[a]'On the fifteenth day of the seventh month you shall have a holy convocation. You shall do no customary work, and you shall keep a feast to the LORD seven days. 13[a]You shall present a burnt offering, an offering made by fire as a sweet aroma to the LORD: thirteen young bulls, two rams, *and* fourteen lambs in their first year. They shall be without blemish. 14Their grain offering *shall be of* fine flour mixed with oil: three-tenths *of an ephah* for each of the thirteen bulls, two-tenths for each of the two rams,

---

28:18 [a] Ex. 12:16; Lev. 23:7 28:19 [a] Lev. 22:20; Num. 28:31; 29:8; Deut. 15:21 28:22 [a] Num. 28:15 28:25 [a] Ex. 12:16; 13:6; Lev. 23:8 28:26 [a] Ex. 23:16; 34:22; Lev. 23:10–21; Deut. 16:9–12; Acts 2:1 28:27 [a] Lev. 23:18, 19 28:31 [a] Num. 28:3, 19 29:1 [a] Ex. 23:16; 34:22; Lev. 23:23–25 29:6 [a] Num. 28:11–15 [b] Num. 28:3 [c] Num. 15:11, 12 29:7 [a] Lev. 16:29–34; 23:26–32 [b] Ps. 35:13; Is. 58:5 29:8 [a] Num. 28:19 29:11 [a] Lev. 16:3, 5 29:12 [a] Lev. 23:33–35; Deut. 16:13–15; Ezek. 45:25 29:13 [a] Ezra 3:4

15and one-tenth for each of the fourteen
lambs; 16also one kid of the goats *as* a sin
offering, besides the regular burnt offering,
its grain offering, and its drink offering.
17'On the [a]second day *present* twelve
young bulls, two rams, fourteen lambs in
their first year without blemish, 18and their
grain offering and their drink offerings for
the bulls, for the rams, and for the lambs, by
their number, [a]according to the ordinance;
19also one kid of the goats *as* a sin offering,
besides the regular burnt offering with its
grain offering, and their drink offerings.
20'On the third day *present* eleven bulls,
two rams, fourteen lambs in their first year
without blemish, 21and their grain offering
and their drink offerings for the bulls, for
the rams, and for the lambs, by their number, [a]according to the ordinance; 22also one
goat *as* a sin offering, besides the regular
burnt offering, its grain offering, and its
drink offering.
23'On the fourth day *present* ten bulls,
two rams, *and* fourteen lambs in their first
year, without blemish, 24and their grain
offering and their drink offerings for the
bulls, for the rams, and for the lambs, by
their number, according to the ordinance;
25also one kid of the goats *as* a sin offering,
besides the regular burnt offering, its grain
offering, and its drink offering.
26'On the fifth day *present* nine bulls, two
rams, *and* fourteen lambs in their first year
without blemish, 27and their grain offering
and their drink offerings for the bulls, for
the rams, and for the lambs, by their number, according to the ordinance; 28also one
goat *as* a sin offering, besides the regular
burnt offering, its grain offering, and its
drink offering.
29'On the sixth day *present* eight bulls,
two rams, *and* fourteen lambs in their first
year without blemish, 30and their grain
offering and their drink offerings for the
bulls, for the rams, and for the lambs, by
their number, according to the ordinance;
31also one goat *as* a sin offering, besides the
regular burnt offering, its grain offering,
and its drink offering.
32'On the seventh day *present* seven
bulls, two rams, *and* fourteen lambs in their
first year without blemish, 33and their grain
offering and their drink offerings for the
bulls, for the rams, and for the lambs, by
their number, according to the ordinance;
34also one goat *as* a sin offering, besides the
regular burnt offering, its grain offering,
and its drink offering.
35'On the eighth day you shall have a [a]sa-
cred assembly. You shall do no customary
work. 36You shall present a burnt offering,
an offering made by fire as a sweet aroma
to the LORD: one bull, one ram, seven lambs
in their first year without blemish, 37and
their grain offering and their drink offerings for the bull, for the ram, and for the
lambs, by their number, according to the
ordinance; 38also one goat *as* a sin offering,
besides the regular burnt offering, its grain
offering, and its drink offering.
39'These you shall present to the LORD
at your [a]appointed feasts (besides your
[b]vowed offerings and your freewill offerings) as your burnt offerings and your grain
offerings, as your drink offerings and your
peace offerings.'"
40So Moses told the children of Israel
everything, just as the LORD commanded
Moses.

The Law Concerning Vows

30 Then Moses spoke to [a]the heads of
the tribes concerning the children
of Israel, saying, "This *is* the thing which the
LORD has commanded: 2[a]If a man makes a
vow to the LORD, or [b]swears an oath to bind
himself by some agreement, he shall not
break his word; he shall [c]do according to all
that proceeds out of his mouth.
3"Or if a woman makes a vow to the LORD,
and binds *herself* by some agreement while
in her father's house in her youth, 4and her
father hears her vow and the agreement by
which she has bound herself, and her father holds his peace, then all her vows shall
stand, and every agreement with which she
has bound herself shall stand. 5But if her father overrules her on the day that he hears,
then none of her vows nor her agreements
by which she has bound herself shall stand;

29:17 [a] Lev. 23:36 29:18 [a] Num. 15:12; 28:7, 14; 29:3, 4, 9, 10 29:21 [a] Num. 29:18 29:35 [a] Lev. 23:36 29:39 [a] Lev. 23:1–44; 1 Chr. 23:31; 2 Chr. 31:3; Ezra 3:5; Neh. 10:33; Is. 1:14 [b] Lev. 7:16; 22:18, 21, 23; 23:38 30:1 [a] Num. 1:4, 16; 7:2 30:2 [a] Lev. 27:2; Deut. 23:21–23; Judg. 11:30, 31, 35; Eccl. 5:4 [b] Lev. 5:4; Matt. 14:9; Acts 23:14 [c] Job 22:27; Ps. 22:25; 50:14; 66:13, 14; Nah. 1:15

and the LORD will release her, because her
father overruled her.

6"If indeed she takes a husband, while
bound by her vows or by a rash utterance
from her lips by which she bound herself,
7and her husband hears *it,* and makes no
response to her on the day that he hears,
then her vows shall stand, and her agreements by which she bound herself shall
stand. 8But if her husband [a]overrules her
on the day that he hears *it,* he shall make
void her vow which she took and what she
uttered with her lips, by which she bound
herself, and the LORD will release her.

9"Also any vow of a widow or a divorced
woman, by which she has bound herself,
shall stand against her.

10"If she vowed in her husband's house,
or bound herself by an agreement with an
oath, 11and her husband heard *it,* and made
no response to her *and* did not overrule
her, then all her vows shall stand, and every agreement by which she bound herself
shall stand. 12But if her husband truly made
them void on the day he heard *them,* then
whatever proceeded from her lips concerning her vows or concerning the agreement
binding her, it shall not stand; her husband
has made them void, and the LORD will release her. 13Every vow and every binding
oath to afflict her soul, her husband may
confirm it, or her husband may make it
void. 14Now if her husband makes no response whatever to her from day to day,
then he confirms all her vows or all the
agreements that bind her; he confirms
them, because he made no response to
her on the day that he heard *them.* 15But if
he does make them void after he has heard
them, then he shall bear her guilt."

16These *are* the statutes which the LORD
commanded Moses, between a man and his
wife, and between a father and his daughter
in her youth in her father's house.

Vengeance on the Midianites

31 And the LORD spoke to Moses, saying: 2[a]"Take vengeance on the Midianites for the children of Israel. Afterward
you shall [b]be gathered to your people."

3So Moses spoke to the people, saying,
"Arm some of yourselves for war, and let
them go against the Midianites to take vengeance for the LORD on [a]Midian. 4A thousand from each tribe of all the tribes of
Israel you shall send to the war."

5So there were recruited from the divisions of Israel one thousand from *each*
tribe, twelve thousand armed for war.
6Then Moses sent them to the war, one
thousand from *each* tribe; he sent them
to the war with Phinehas the son of Eleazar the priest, with the holy articles and
[a]the signal trumpets in his hand. 7And
they warred against the Midianites, just
as the LORD commanded Moses, and [a]they
killed all the [b]males. 8They killed the kings
of Midian with *the rest of* those who were
killed—[a]Evi, Rekem, [b]Zur, Hur, and Reba,
the five kings of Midian. [c]Balaam the son of
Beor they also killed with the sword.

9And the children of Israel took the
women of Midian captive, with their little ones, and took as spoil all their cattle,
all their flocks, and all their goods. 10They
also burned with fire all the cities where
they dwelt, and all their forts. 11And [a]they
took all the spoil and all the booty—of man
and beast.

Return from the War

12Then they brought the captives, the
booty, and the spoil to Moses, to Eleazar
the priest, and to the congregation of the
children of Israel, to the camp in the plains
of Moab by the Jordan, *across from* Jericho. 13And Moses, Eleazar the priest, and
all the leaders of the congregation, went
to meet them outside the camp. 14But Moses was angry with the officers of the army,
with the captains over thousands and captains over hundreds, who had come from
the battle.

15And Moses said to them: "Have you
kept [a]all the women alive? 16Look, [a]these
women caused the children of Israel,
through the [b]counsel of Balaam, to trespass against the LORD in the incident of
Peor, and [c]there was a plague among the
congregation of the LORD. 17Now therefore,

30:8 [a] [Gen. 3:16] 31:2 [a] Num. 25:17 [b] Num. 27:12, 13 31:3 [a] Josh. 13:21 31:6 [a] Num. 10:9 31:7 [a] Deut. 20:13; Judg. 21:11; 1 Sam. 27:9; 1 Kin. 11:15, 16 [b] Gen. 34:25 31:8 [a] Josh. 13:21 [b] Num. 25:15 [c] Num. 31:16; Josh. 13:22 31:11 [a] Deut. 20:14 31:15 [a] Deut. 20:14 31:16 [a] Num. 25:2 [b] Num. 24:14; 2 Pet. 2:15; Rev. 2:14 [c] Num. 25:9

[a]kill every male among the little ones, and
kill every woman who has known a man
intimately. 18But keep alive [a]for yourselves
all the young girls who have not known a
man intimately. 19And as for you, [a]remain
outside the camp seven days; whoever
has killed any person, and [b]whoever has
touched any slain, purify yourselves and
your captives on the third day and on the
seventh day. 20Purify every garment, everything made of leather, everything woven of
goats' *hair*, and everything made of wood."
21Then Eleazar the priest said to the men
of war who had gone to the battle, "This *is*
the ordinance of the law which the LORD
commanded Moses: 22Only the gold, the
silver, the bronze, the iron, the tin, and the
lead, 23everything that can endure fire, you
shall put through the fire, and it shall be
clean; and it shall be purified [a]with the
water of purification. But all that cannot
endure fire you shall put through water.
24[a]And you shall wash your clothes on the
seventh day and be clean, and afterward
you may come into the camp."

Division of the Plunder

25Now the LORD spoke to Moses, saying:
26"Count up the plunder that was taken—of
man and beast—you and Eleazar the priest
and the chief fathers of the congregation;
27and [a]divide the plunder into two parts,
between those who took part in the war,
who went out to battle, and all the congregation. 28And levy a tribute for the LORD
on the men of war who went out to battle: [a]one of every five hundred of the persons, the cattle, the donkeys, and the sheep;
29take *it* from their half, and [a]give *it* to Eleazar the priest as a heave offering to the
LORD. 30And from the children of Israel's
half you shall take [a]one of every fifty, drawn
from the persons, the cattle, the donkeys,
and the sheep, from all the livestock, and
give them to the Levites [b]who keep charge
of the tabernacle of the LORD." 31So Moses
and Eleazar the priest did as the LORD commanded Moses.
32The booty remaining from the plunder, which the men of war had taken, was
six hundred and seventy-five thousand
sheep, 33seventy-two thousand cattle,
34sixty-one thousand donkeys, 35and thirty-
two thousand persons in all, of women who
had not known a man intimately. 36And the
half, the portion for those who had gone
out to war, was in number three hundred
and thirty-seven thousand five hundred
sheep; 37and the LORD's tribute of the sheep
was six hundred and seventy-five. 38The
cattle *were* thirty-six thousand, of which
the LORD's tribute *was* seventy-two. 39The
donkeys *were* thirty thousand five hundred, of which the LORD's tribute *was* sixty-
one. 40The persons *were* sixteen thousand,
of which the LORD's tribute *was* thirty-two
persons. 41So Moses gave the tribute *which*
was the LORD's heave offering to Eleazar
the priest, [a]as the LORD commanded Moses.
42And from the children of Israel's half,
which Moses separated from the men who
fought— 43now the half belonging to the
congregation was three hundred and
thirty-seven thousand five hundred sheep,
44thirty-six thousand cattle, 45thirty thousand five hundred donkeys, 46and sixteen
thousand persons— 47and [a]from the children of Israel's half Moses took one of every fifty, drawn from man and beast, and
gave them to the Levites, who kept charge
of the tabernacle of the LORD, as the LORD
commanded Moses.
48Then the officers who *were* over thousands of the army, the captains of thousands and captains of hundreds, came
near to Moses; 49and they said to Moses,
"Your servants have taken a count of the
men of war who *are* under our command,
and not a man of us is missing. 50There-
fore we have brought an offering for the
LORD, what every man found of ornaments
of gold: armlets and bracelets and signet
rings and earrings and necklaces, [a]to make
atonement for ourselves before the LORD."
51So Moses and Eleazar the priest received
the gold from them, all the fashioned ornaments. 52And all the gold of the offering that they offered to the LORD, from the
captains of thousands and captains of hundreds, was sixteen thousand seven hundred

31:17 [a] Deut. 7:2; 20:16–18; Judg. 21:11 31:18 [a] Deut. 21:10–14 31:19 [a] Num. 5:2 [b] Num. 19:11–22 31:23 [a] Num. 19:9, 17
31:24 [a] Lev. 11:25 31:27 [a] Josh. 22:8; 1 Sam. 30:24 31:28 [a] Num. 31:30, 47 31:29 [a] Deut. 18:1–5 31:30 [a] Num. 31:42–47
[b] Num. 3:7, 8, 25, 31, 36; 18:3, 4 31:41 [a] Num. 5:9, 10; 18:8, 19 31:47 [a] Num. 31:30 31:50 [a] Ex. 30:12–16

and fifty shekels. 53[a](The men of war had
taken spoil, every man for himself.) 54And
Moses and Eleazar the priest received the
gold from the captains of thousands and
of hundreds, and brought it into the tabernacle of meeting [a]as a memorial for the
children of Israel before the LORD.

The Tribes Settling East of the Jordan
(Deut. 3:12–22)

32 Now the children of Reuben and
the children of Gad had a very great
multitude of livestock; and when they saw
the land of [a]Jazer and the land of [b]Gilead,
that indeed the region *was* a place for livestock, 2the children of Gad and the children
of Reuben came and spoke to Moses, to Eleazar the priest, and to the leaders of the
congregation, saying, 3"Ataroth, Dibon, Jazer, [a]Nimrah, [b]Heshbon, Elealeh, [c]Shebam,
Nebo, and [d]Beon, 4the country [a]which the
LORD defeated before the congregation
of Israel, *is* a land for livestock, and your
servants have livestock." 5Therefore they
said, "If we have found favor in your sight,
let this land be given to your servants as a
possession. Do not take us over the Jordan."

6And Moses said to the children of Gad
and to the children of Reuben: "Shall your
brethren go to war while you sit here? 7Now
why will you [a]discourage the heart of the
children of Israel from going over into the
land which the LORD has given them? 8Thus
your fathers did [a]when I sent them away
from Kadesh Barnea [b]to see the land. 9For
[a]when they went up to the Valley of Eshcol and saw the land, they discouraged the
heart of the children of Israel, so that they
did not go into the land which the LORD
had given them. 10[a]So the LORD's anger
was aroused on that day, and He swore an
oath, saying, 11'Surely none of the men who
came up from Egypt, [a]from twenty years
old and above, shall see the land of which
I swore to Abraham, Isaac, and Jacob, because [b]they have not wholly followed Me,
12except Caleb the son of Jephunneh, the
Kenizzite, and Joshua the son of Nun, [a]for
they have wholly followed the LORD.' 13So
the LORD's anger was aroused against Israel, and He made them [a]wander in the
wilderness forty years, until [b]all the generation that had done evil in the sight of
the LORD was gone. 14And look! You have
risen in your fathers' place, a brood of sinful men, to increase still more the [a]fierce
anger of the LORD against Israel. 15For if
you [a]turn away from following Him, He
will once again leave them in the wilderness, and you will destroy all these people."

16Then they came near to him and said:
"We will build sheepfolds here for our livestock, and cities for our little ones, 17but [a]we
ourselves will be armed, ready *to go* before
the children of Israel until we have brought
them to their place; and our little ones will
dwell in the fortified cities because of the
inhabitants of the land. 18[a]We will not return to our homes until every one of the
children of Israel has received his inheritance. 19For we will not inherit with them
on the other side of the Jordan and beyond,
[a]because our inheritance has fallen to us
on this eastern side of the Jordan."

20Then [a]Moses said to them: "If you do
this thing, if you arm yourselves before the
LORD for the war, 21and all your armed men
cross over the Jordan before the LORD until
He has driven out His enemies from before
Him, 22and [a]the land is subdued before the
LORD, then afterward [b]you may return and
be blameless before the LORD and before
Israel; and [c]this land shall be your possession before the LORD. 23But if you do not do
so, then take note, you have sinned against
the LORD; and be sure [a]your sin will find
you out. 24[a]Build cities for your little ones
and folds for your sheep, and do what has
proceeded out of your mouth."

25And the children of Gad and the children of Reuben spoke to Moses, saying:
"Your servants will do as my lord commands. 26[a]Our little ones, our wives, our
flocks, and all our livestock will be there in

31:53 [a] Num. 31:32; Deut. 20:14 **31:54** [a] Ex. 30:16 **32:1** [a] Num. 21:32; Josh. 13:25; 2 Sam. 24:5 [b] Deut. 3:13 **32:3** [a] Num. 32:36 [b] Josh. 13:17, 26 [c] Num. 32:38 [d] Num. 32:38 **32:4** [a] Num. 21:24, 34, 35 **32:7** [a] Num. 13:27—14:4 **32:8** [a] Num. 13:3, 26 [b] Deut. 1:19–25 **32:9** [a] Num. 13:24, 31; Deut. 1:24, 28 **32:10** [a] Num. 14:11; Deut. 1:34–36 **32:11** [a] Num. 14:28, 29; 26:63–65; Deut. 1:35 [b] Num. 14:24, 30 **32:12** [a] Num. 14:6–9, 24, 30; Deut. 1:36; Josh. 14:8, 9 **32:13** [a] Num. 14:33–35 [b] Num. 26:64, 65 **32:14** [a] Num. 11:1; Deut. 1:34 **32:15** [a] Deut. 30:17, 18; Josh. 22:16–18; 2 Chr. 7:19; 15:2 **32:17** [a] Josh. 4:12, 13 **32:18** [a] Josh. 22:1–4 **32:19** [a] Josh. 12:1; 13:8 **32:20** [a] Deut. 3:18; Josh. 1:14 **32:22** [a] Deut. 3:20; Josh. 11:23 [b] Josh. 22:4 [c] Deut. 3:12, 15, 16, 18; Josh. 1:15; 13:8, 32; 22:4, 9 **32:23** [a] Gen. 4:7; 44:16; Josh. 7:1–26; Is. 59:12; [Gal. 6:7] **32:24** [a] Num. 32:16 **32:26** [a] Josh. 1:14

the cities of Gilead; 27[a]but your servants will cross over, every man armed for war, before the LORD to battle, just as my lord says."

28So Moses gave command [a]concerning them to Eleazar the priest, to Joshua the son of Nun, and to the chief fathers of the tribes of the children of Israel. 29And Moses said to them: "If the children of Gad and the children of Reuben cross over the Jordan with you, every man armed for battle before the LORD, and the land is subdued before you, then you shall give them the land of Gilead as a possession. 30But if they do not cross over armed with you, they shall have possessions among you in the land of Canaan."

31Then the children of Gad and the children of Reuben answered, saying: "As the LORD has said to your servants, so we will do. 32We will cross over armed before the LORD into the land of Canaan, but the possession of our inheritance *shall remain* with us on this side of the Jordan."

33So [a]Moses gave to the children of Gad, to the children of Reuben, and to half the tribe of Manasseh the son of Joseph, [b]the kingdom of Sihon king of the Amorites and the kingdom of Og king of Bashan, the land with its cities within the borders, the cities of the surrounding country. 34And the children of Gad built [a]Dibon and Ataroth and [b]Aroer, 35Atroth and Shophan and [a]Jazer and Jogbehah, 36[a]Beth Nimrah and Beth Haran, [b]fortified cities, and folds for sheep. 37And the children of Reuben built [a]Heshbon and Elealeh and Kirjathaim, 38[a]Nebo and [b]Baal Meon [c](*their* names being changed) and Shibmah; and they gave *other* names to the cities which they built.

39And the children of [a]Machir the son of Manasseh went to Gilead and took it, and dispossessed the Amorites who *were* in it. 40So Moses [a]gave Gilead to Machir the son of Manasseh, and he dwelt in it. 41Also [a]Jair the son of Manasseh went and took its small towns, and called them [b]Havoth Jair.[1] 42Then Nobah went and took Kenath and its villages, and he called it Nobah, after his own name.

Israel's Journey from Egypt Reviewed

33 These *are* the journeys of the children of Israel, who went out of the land of Egypt by their armies under the [a]hand of Moses and Aaron. 2Now Moses wrote down the starting points of their journeys at the command of the LORD. And these *are* their journeys according to their starting points:

3They [a]departed from Rameses in [b]the first month, on the fifteenth day of the first month; on the day after the Passover the children of Israel went out [c]with boldness in the sight of all the Egyptians. 4For the Egyptians were burying all *their* firstborn, [a]whom the LORD had killed among them. Also [b]on their gods the LORD had executed judgments.

5[a]Then the children of Israel moved from Rameses and camped at Succoth. 6They departed from [a]Succoth and camped at Etham, which *is* on the edge of the wilderness. 7[a]They moved from Etham and turned back to Pi Hahiroth, which *is* east of Baal Zephon; and they camped near Migdol. 8They departed from before Hahiroth[1] and [a]passed through the midst of the sea into the wilderness, went three days' journey in the Wilderness of Etham, and camped at Marah. 9They moved from Marah and [a]came to Elim. At Elim *were* twelve springs of water and seventy palm trees; so they camped there.

10They moved from Elim and camped by the Red Sea. 11They moved from the Red Sea and camped in the [a]Wilderness of Sin. 12They journeyed from the Wilderness of Sin and camped at Dophkah. 13They departed from Dophkah and camped at Alush. 14They moved from Alush and camped at [a]Rephidim, where there was no water for the people to drink.

15They departed from Rephidim and camped in the [a]Wilderness of Sinai. 16They moved from the Wilderness of Sinai and

32:27 [a] Josh. 4:12 32:28 [a] Josh. 1:13 32:33 [a] Deut. 3:8–17; 29:8; Josh. 12:1–6; 13:8–31; 22:4 [b] Num. 21:24, 33, 35 32:34 [a] Num. 33:45, 46 [b] Deut. 2:36 32:35 [a] Num. 32:1, 3 32:36 [a] Num. 32:3 [b] Num. 32:24 32:37 [a] Num. 21:27 32:38 [a] Is. 46:1 [b] Ezek. 25:9 [c] Ex. 23:13; Josh. 23:7 32:39 [a] Gen. 50:23; Num. 27:1; 36:1 32:40 [a] Deut. 3:12, 13, 15; Josh. 13:31 32:41 [a] Deut. 3:14; Josh. 13:30 [b] Judg. 10:4; 1 Kin. 4:13 [1] Literally *Towns of Jair* 33:1 [a] Ps. 77:20 33:3 [a] Ex. 12:37 [b] Ex. 12:2; 13:4 [c] Ex. 14:8 33:4 [a] Ex. 12:29 [b] [Ex. 12:12; 18:11]; Is. 19:1 33:5 [a] Ex. 12:37 33:6 [a] Ex. 13:20 33:7 [a] Ex. 14:1, 2, 9 33:8 [a] Ex. 14:22; 15:22, 23
[1] Many Hebrew manuscripts, Samaritan Pentateuch, Syriac, Targum, and Vulgate read *from Pi Hahiroth* (compare verse 7).
33:9 [a] Ex. 15:27 33:11 [a] Ex. 16:1 33:14 [a] Ex. 17:1; 19:2 33:15 [a] Ex. 16:1; 19:1, 2

camped [a]at Kibroth Hattaavah. 17They
departed from Kibroth Hattaavah and
[a]camped at Hazeroth. 18They departed from
Hazeroth and camped at [a]Rithmah. 19They
departed from Rithmah and camped at
Rimmon Perez. 20They departed from Rimmon Perez and camped at Libnah. 21They
moved from Libnah and camped at Rissah.
22They journeyed from Rissah and camped
at Kehelathah. 23They went from Kehelathah and camped at Mount Shepher. 24They
moved from Mount Shepher and camped at
Haradah. 25They moved from Haradah and
camped at Makheloth. 26They moved from
Makheloth and camped at Tahath. 27They
departed from Tahath and camped at Terah. 28They moved from Terah and camped
at Mithkah. 29They went from Mithkah and
camped at Hashmonah. 30They departed
from Hashmonah and [a]camped at Moseroth. 31They departed from Moseroth and
camped at Bene Jaakan. 32They moved
from [a]Bene Jaakan and [b]camped at Hor
Hagidgad. 33They went from Hor Hagidgad
and camped at Jotbathah. 34They moved
from Jotbathah and camped at Abronah. 35They departed from Abronah [a]and
camped at Ezion Geber. 36They moved from
Ezion Geber and camped in the [a]Wilderness
of Zin, which *is* Kadesh. 37They moved from
[a]Kadesh and camped at Mount Hor, on the
boundary of the land of Edom.

38Then [a]Aaron the priest went up to
Mount Hor at the command of the LORD,
and died there in the fortieth year after the
children of Israel had come out of the land
of Egypt, on the first *day* of the fifth month.
39Aaron *was* one hundred and twenty-three
years old when he died on Mount Hor.

40Now [a]the king of Arad, the Canaanite,
who dwelt in the South in the land of Canaan, heard of the coming of the children
of Israel.

41So they departed from Mount Hor and
camped at Zalmonah. 42They departed
from Zalmonah and camped at Punon.
43They departed from Punon and [a]camped
at Oboth. 44[a]They departed from Oboth
and camped at Ije Abarim, at the border
of Moab. 45They departed from Ijim[1] and
camped [a]at Dibon Gad. 46They moved from
Dibon Gad and camped at [a]Almon Diblathaim. 47They moved from Almon Diblathaim [a]and camped in the mountains of
Abarim, before Nebo. 48They departed from
the mountains of Abarim and [a]camped in
the plains of Moab by the Jordan, *across
from* Jericho. 49They camped by the Jordan,
from Beth Jesimoth as far as the [a]Abel Acacia Grove[1] in the plains of Moab.

Instructions for the Conquest of Canaan

50Now the LORD spoke to Moses in the
plains of Moab by the Jordan, *across from*
Jericho, saying, 51"Speak to the children of
Israel, and say to them: [a]'When you have
crossed the Jordan into the land of Canaan,
52[a]then you shall drive out all the inhabitants of the land from before you, destroy
all their engraved stones, destroy all their
molded images, and demolish all their high
places; 53you shall dispossess *the inhabitants of* the land and dwell in it, for I have
given you the land to [a]possess. 54And [a]you
shall divide the land by lot as an inheritance among your families; to the larger
you shall give a larger inheritance, and to
the smaller you shall give a smaller inheritance; there everyone's *inheritance* shall be
whatever falls to him by lot. You shall inherit according to the tribes of your fathers.
55But if you do not drive out the inhabitants
of the land from before you, then it shall
be that those whom you let remain *shall be*
[a]irritants in your eyes and thorns in your
sides, and they shall harass you in the land
where you dwell. 56Moreover it shall be *that*
I will do to you as I thought to do to them.'"

The Appointed Boundaries of Canaan

34 Then the LORD spoke to Moses, saying, 2"Command the children of Israel, and say to them: 'When you come into
[a]the land of Canaan, this *is* the land that
shall fall to you as an inheritance—the
land of Canaan to its boundaries. 3[a]Your

33:16 [a] Num. 11:34 33:17 [a] Num. 11:35 33:18 [a] Num. 12:16 33:30 [a] Deut. 10:6 33:32 [a] Deut. 10:6 [b] Deut. 10:7 33:35 [a] Deut. 2:8; 1 Kin. 9:26; 22:48 33:36 [a] Num. 20:1; 27:14 33:37 [a] Num. 20:22, 23; 21:4 33:38 [a] Num. 20:25, 28; Deut. 10:6; 32:50 33:40 [a] Num. 21:1 33:43 [a] Num. 21:10 33:44 [a] Num. 21:11 33:45 [a] Num. 32:34 [1] Same as *Ije Abarim*, verse 44 33:46 [a] Jer. 48:22; Ezek. 6:14 33:47 [a] Num. 21:20; Deut. 32:49 33:48 [a] Num. 22:1; 31:12; 35:1 33:49 [a] Num. 25:1; Josh. 2:1 [1] Hebrew *Abel Shittim* 33:51 [a] Deut. 7:1, 2; 9:1; Josh. 3:17 33:52 [a] Ex. 23:24, 33; 34:13; Deut. 7:2, 5; 12:3; Judg. 2:2; Ps. 106:34–36 33:53 [a] Deut. 11:31; Josh. 21:43 33:54 [a] Num. 26:53–56 33:55 [a] Josh. 23:13; Judg. 2:3 34:2 [a] Gen. 17:8; Deut. 1:7, 8; Ps. 78:54, 55; 105:11 34:3 [a] Josh. 15:1–3; Ezek. 47:13, 19

southern border shall be from the Wilderness of Zin along the border of Edom; then your southern border shall extend eastward to the end of [b]the Salt Sea; 4your border shall turn from the southern side of [a]the Ascent of Akrabbim, continue to Zin, and be on the south of [b]Kadesh Barnea; then it shall go on to [c]Hazar Addar, and continue to Azmon; 5the border shall turn from Azmon [a]to the Brook of Egypt, and it shall end at the Sea.

6'As for the [a]western border, you shall have the Great Sea for a border; this shall be your western border.

7'And this shall be your northern border: From the Great Sea you shall mark out your *border* line to [a]Mount Hor; 8from Mount Hor you shall mark out *your border* [a]to the entrance of Hamath; then the direction of the border shall be toward [b]Zedad; 9the border shall proceed to Ziphron, and it shall end at [a]Hazar Enan. This shall be your northern border.

10'You shall mark out your eastern border from Hazar Enan to Shepham; 11the border shall go down from Shepham [a]to Riblah on the east side of Ain; the border shall go down and reach to the eastern side of the Sea [b]of Chinnereth; 12the border shall go down along the Jordan, and it shall end at [a]the Salt Sea. This shall be your land with its surrounding boundaries.'"

13Then Moses commanded the children of Israel, saying: [a]"This *is* the land which you shall inherit by lot, which the LORD has commanded to give to the nine tribes and to the half-tribe. 14[a]For the tribe of the children of Reuben according to the house of their fathers, and the tribe of the children of Gad according to the house of their fathers, have received *their inheritance;* and the half-tribe of Manasseh has received its inheritance. 15The two tribes and the half-tribe have received their inheritance on this side of the Jordan, *across from* Jericho eastward, toward the sunrise."

The Leaders Appointed to Divide the Land

16And the LORD spoke to Moses, saying, 17"These *are* the names of the men who shall divide the land among you as an inheritance: [a]Eleazar the priest and Joshua the son of Nun. 18And you shall take one [a]leader of every tribe to divide the land for the inheritance. 19These *are* the names of the men: from the tribe of Judah, Caleb the son of Jephunneh; 20from the tribe of the children of Simeon, Shemuel the son of Ammihud; 21from the tribe of Benjamin, Elidad the son of Chislon; 22a leader from the tribe of the children of Dan, Bukki the son of Jogli; 23from the sons of Joseph: a leader from the tribe of the children of Manasseh, Hanniel the son of Ephod, 24and a leader from the tribe of the children of Ephraim, Kemuel the son of Shiphtan; 25a leader from the tribe of the children of Zebulun, Elizaphan the son of Parnach; 26a leader from the tribe of the children of Issachar, Paltiel the son of Azzan; 27a leader from the tribe of the children of Asher, Ahihud the son of Shelomi; 28and a leader from the tribe of the children of Naphtali, Pedahel the son of Ammihud."

29These *are* the ones the LORD commanded to divide the inheritance among the children of Israel in the land of Canaan.

Cities for the Levites

35 And the LORD spoke to Moses in [a]the plains of Moab by the Jordan *across from* Jericho, saying: 2[a]"Command the children of Israel that they give the Levites cities to dwell in from the inheritance of their possession, and you shall *also* give the Levites [b]common-land around the cities. 3They shall have the cities to dwell in; and their common-land shall be for their cattle, for their herds, and for all their animals. 4The common-land of the cities which you will give the Levites *shall extend* from the wall of the city outward a thousand cubits all around. 5And you shall measure outside the city on the east side two thousand cubits, on the south side two thousand cubits, on the west side two thousand cubits, and on the north side two thousand cubits. The city *shall be* in the middle. This shall belong to them as common-land for the cities.

34:3 [b] Gen. 14:3; Josh. 15:2 34:4 [a] Josh. 15:3 [b] Num. 13:26; 32:8 [c] Josh. 15:3, 4 34:5 [a] Gen. 15:18; Josh. 15:4, 47; 1 Kin. 8:65; Is. 27:12 34:6 [a] Ex. 23:31; Josh. 15:12; Ezek. 47:20 34:7 [a] Num. 33:37 34:8 [a] Num. 13:21; Josh. 13:5; 2 Kin. 14:25 [b] Ezek. 47:15 34:9 [a] Ezek. 47:17 34:11 [a] 2 Kin. 23:33; Jer. 39:5, 6 [b] Deut. 3:17; Josh. 11:2; 12:3; 13:27; 19:35; Matt. 14:34; Luke 5:1 34:12 [a] Num. 34:3 34:13 [a] Gen. 15:18; Num. 26:52–56; Deut. 11:24; Josh. 14:1–5 34:14 [a] Num. 32:33 34:17 [a] Josh. 14:1, 2; 19:51 34:18 [a] Num. 1:4, 16 35:1 [a] Num. 33:50 35:2 [a] Josh. 14:3, 4; 21:2, 3; Ezek. 45:1; 48:10–20 [b] Lev. 25:32–34

6“Now among the cities which you will
give to the Levites *you shall appoint* [a]six
cities of refuge, to which a manslayer may
flee. And to these you shall add forty-two
cities. 7So all the cities you will give to the
Levites *shall be* [a]forty-eight; these *you shall
give* with their common-land. 8And the cities which you will give *shall be* [a]from the
possession of the children of Israel; [b]from
the larger *tribe* you shall give many, from
the smaller you shall give few. Each shall
give some of its cities to the Levites, in proportion to the inheritance that each receives.”

Cities of Refuge
(Deut. 19:1–13; Josh. 20:1–9)

9Then the LORD spoke to Moses, saying,
10“Speak to the children of Israel, and say
to them: [a]‘When you cross the Jordan into
the land of Canaan, 11then [a]you shall appoint cities to be cities of refuge for you,
that the manslayer who kills any person
accidentally may flee there. 12[a]They shall be
cities of refuge for you from the avenger,
that the manslayer may not die until he
stands before the congregation in judgment. 13And of the cities which you give,
you shall have [a]six cities of refuge. 14[a]You
shall appoint three cities on this side of
the Jordan, and three cities you shall appoint in the land of Canaan, *which* will be
cities of refuge. 15These six cities shall be
for refuge for the children of Israel, [a]for
the stranger, and for the sojourner among
them, that anyone who kills a person accidentally may flee there.

16[a]‘But if he strikes him with an iron implement, so that he dies, he *is* a murderer;
the murderer shall surely be put to death.
17And if he strikes him with a stone in the
hand, by which one could die, and he does
die, he *is* a murderer; the murderer shall
surely be put to death. 18Or *if* he strikes him
with a wooden hand weapon, by which one
could die, and he does die, he *is* a murderer;
the murderer shall surely be put to death.
19[a]The avenger of blood himself shall put
the murderer to death; when he meets him,
he shall put him to death. 20[a]If he pushes
him out of hatred or, [b]while lying in wait,
hurls something at him so that he dies, 21or
in enmity he strikes him with his hand so
that he dies, the one who struck *him* shall
surely be put to death. He *is* a murderer.
The avenger of blood shall put the murderer to death when he meets him.

22‘However, if he pushes him suddenly
[a]without enmity, or throws anything at him
without lying in wait, 23or uses a stone, by
which a man could die, throwing *it* at him
without seeing *him*, so that he dies, while
he was not his enemy or seeking his harm,
24then [a]the congregation shall judge between the manslayer and the avenger of
blood according to these judgments. 25So
the congregation shall deliver the manslayer from the hand of the avenger of
blood, and the congregation shall return
him to the city of refuge where he had fled,
and [a]he shall remain there until the death
of the high priest [b]who was anointed with
the holy oil. 26But if the manslayer at any
time goes outside the limits of the city of
refuge where he fled, 27and the avenger of
blood finds him outside the limits of his
city of refuge, and the avenger of blood
kills the manslayer, he shall not be guilty of
blood, 28because he should have remained
in his city of refuge until the death of the
high priest. But after the death of the high
priest the manslayer may return to the land
of his possession.

29‘And these *things* shall be [a]a statute of
judgment to you throughout your generations in all your dwellings. 30Whoever kills
a person, the murderer shall be put to death
on the [a]testimony of witnesses; but one
witness is not *sufficient* testimony against
a person for the death *penalty*. 31Moreover
you shall take no ransom for the life of a
murderer who *is* guilty of death, but he
shall surely be put to death. 32And you shall
take no ransom for him who has fled to his
city of refuge, that he may return to dwell
in the land before the death of the priest.

35:6 [a] Deut. 4:41; Josh. 20:2, 7, 8; 21:3, 13 35:7 [a] Josh. 21:41 35:8 [a] Josh. 21:3 [b] Num. 26:54; 33:54 35:10 [a] Deut. 19:2; Josh. 20:1–9
35:11 [a] Ex. 21:13; Num. 35:22–25; Deut. 19:1–13 35:12 [a] Deut. 19:6; Josh. 20:3, 5, 6 35:13 [a] Num. 35:6 35:14 [a] Deut. 4:41; Josh. 20:8
35:15 [a] Num. 15:16 35:16 [a] Ex. 21:12, 14; Lev. 24:17; Deut. 19:11, 12 35:19 [a] Num. 35:21, 24, 27; Deut. 19:6, 12
35:20 [a] Gen. 4:8; 2 Sam. 3:27; 20:10; 1 Kin. 2:31, 32 [b] Ex. 21:14; Deut. 19:11, 12 35:22 [a] Ex. 21:13
35:24 [a] Num. 35:12; Josh. 20:6 35:25 [a] Josh. 20:6 [b] Ex. 29:7; Lev. 4:3; 21:10 35:29 [a] Num. 27:11
35:30 [a] Deut. 17:6; 19:15; Matt. 18:16; John 7:51; 8:17, 18; 2 Cor. 13:1; Heb. 10:28

33 So you shall not pollute the land where
you *are;* for blood [a]defiles the land, and no
atonement can be made for the land, for
the blood that is shed on it, except [b]by the
blood of him who shed it. 34 Therefore [a]do
not defile the land which you inhabit, in
the midst of which I dwell; for [b]I the LORD
dwell among the children of Israel.'"

Marriage of Female Heirs

36 Now the chief fathers of the families of the [a]children of Gilead the
son of Machir, the son of Manasseh, of the
families of the sons of Joseph, came near
and [b]spoke before Moses and before the
leaders, the chief fathers of the children
of Israel. 2 And they said: [a]"The LORD commanded my lord *Moses* to give the land
as an inheritance by lot to the children of
Israel, and [b]my lord was commanded by
the LORD to give the inheritance of our
brother Zelophehad to his daughters. 3 Now
if they are married to any of the sons of the
other tribes of the children of Israel, then
their inheritance will be [a]taken from the
inheritance of our fathers, and it will be
added to the inheritance of the tribe into
which they marry; so it will be taken from
the lot of our inheritance. 4 And when [a]the
Jubilee of the children of Israel comes,
then their inheritance will be added to the
inheritance of the tribe into which they
marry; so their inheritance will be taken
away from the inheritance of the tribe of
our fathers."

5 Then Moses commanded the children
of Israel according to the word of the LORD,
saying: [a]"What the tribe of the sons of Joseph speaks is right. 6 This *is* what the LORD
commands concerning the daughters of
Zelophehad, saying, 'Let them marry whom
they think best, [a]but they may marry only
within the family of their father's tribe.'
7 So the inheritance of the children of Israel shall not change hands from tribe to
tribe, for every one of the children of Israel
shall [a]keep the inheritance of the tribe of
his fathers. 8 And [a]every daughter who possesses an inheritance in any tribe of the
children of Israel shall be the wife of one
of the family of her father's tribe, so that
the children of Israel each may possess the
inheritance of his fathers. 9 Thus no inheritance shall change hands from *one* tribe
to another, but every tribe of the children
of Israel shall keep its own inheritance."

10 Just as the LORD commanded Moses,
so did the daughters of Zelophehad; 11 [a]for
Mahlah, Tirzah, Hoglah, Milcah, and Noah,
the daughters of Zelophehad, were married
to the sons of their father's brothers. 12 They
were married into the families of the children of Manasseh the son of Joseph, and
their inheritance remained in the tribe of
their father's family.

13 These *are* the commandments and the
judgments which the LORD commanded
the children of Israel by the hand of Moses [a]in the plains of Moab by the Jordan,
across from Jericho.

35:33 [a] Deut. 21:7, 8; Ps. 106:38 [b] Gen. 9:6 35:34 [a] Lev. 18:24, 25; Deut. 21:23 [b] Ex. 29:45, 46 36:1 [a] Num. 26:29 [b] Num. 27:1–11
36:2 [a] Num. 26:55; 33:54; Josh. 17:4 [b] Num. 27:1, 5–7 36:3 [a] Num. 27:4 36:4 [a] Lev. 25:10 36:5 [a] Num. 27:7 36:6 [a] Num. 36:11, 12
36:7 [a] 1 Kin. 21:3 36:8 [a] 1 Chr. 23:22 36:11 [a] Num. 26:33; 27:1 36:13 [a] Num. 26:3; 33:50

THE FIFTH BOOK OF MOSES CALLED

DEUTERONOMY

OVERVIEW

Deuteronomy is the fifth and final book of the Pentateuch (the first five books of the Bible as a collective unit). Moses wrote the book around 1406 BC at the end of the Israelites' forty-year wilderness journey. The book details God's Law for the generation of Israelites who were allowed to enter the Promised Land.

The title of the book is derived from two Greek words: *deuter*, meaning "second," and *nomos*, meaning "law." This book records Moses sharing God's Law for a second time, which was the first hearing for this new generation of Israelites about to enter the Promised Land.

This book also describes Moses preparing this generation for entry into the Promised Land. God wanted the Israelites to continue honoring their covenant with Him once they entered Canaan. Deuteronomy provides the written account of the series of sermons Moses gave the Israelites, encouraging them not to repeat their parents' mistakes of failing to keep the Law and worshiping false gods.

In the first sermon, Moses reminded the Israelites of the events that took place in the wilderness, including the prior generation's refusal to enter the land when God instructed them to do so (see Deut. 1:19–46). He reminded them of God's power to defeat their enemies and His faithfulness to them despite their disobedience (see 2:1–25). Moses then acknowledged that he would not enter the land because of his disobedience (see 3:23–28) but instructed the Israelites to obey God and be on guard against idolatry (see 4:1–40).

Moses' second sermon shared God's Law with the new generation of Israelites. He outlined the Ten Commandments (see 5:1–22) and cautioned the people about disobedience in the new land (see 6:10–25). Moses detailed other fundamental aspects of the Law in chapters 8–11. He then covered specific regulations for living in covenant with God in chapters 12–26. These regulations addressed topics such as tithes, food, religious observances, property, leadership, and relationships.

In Moses' third and final sermon, he addressed blessings and curses and offered the fourth call for covenant renewal. He described how disobedience would bring curses upon the Israelites (see 27:11–26; 28:15–68) but how obedience would bring abundant blessing (see 28:1–14). In his final plea to the Israelites, Moses urged them to renew their covenant with God and accept the opportunity to choose life rather than death (chs. 29–30).

The remainder of the book deals with the transition of leadership of God's people. In preparation for his death, Moses identified Joshua, one of the two faithful spies, as the new leader of God's people (see 31:1–8). After giving his final blessing, Moses died, and the Israelites began to follow their new leader (chs. 33–34).

Deuteronomy serves to remind the Israelites of the journey that brought them to the Promised Land. The second reading of the Law reinforces God's holiness and faithfulness as well as the covenant He had made with them and their responsibilities as His chosen people. Through the retelling of their journey by Moses, God gave the Israelites the opportunity to reflect on mistakes that had been made and to renew the covenant before entering the land.

BREATHE IT IN

Before the Israelites entered the Promised Land, Moses told them to remember their journey from captivity to freedom. The Israelites had complained, disobeyed, and broken their covenant with God on numerous occasions. Yet, God redeemed them and remained true to His word.

Living in a society in which we can order an item today and have it arrive at our door tomorrow, we have come to expect immediacy. We forget that God is not on our schedules. We are on His schedule, taking the journey with Him. As He did with the Israelites, God sometimes must remind us of this. We are always eager to get to our "promised land" sooner rather than later, and any wait we might experience feels like far too long. We want everything to happen now, and that surely includes all that God has promised.

When God's timing differs from ours, many of us begin to doubt Him, just as the Israelites did. We wonder if He is going to do all that He has promised. In this state, we may try to "help" God by finding other avenues to get where we want to be. When we do this, though, we often also turn to false gods because we lack patience and faith. Those gods might be different ways to achieve what we want or the very things that we want. Sometimes, like Moses, we stand at the edge of our promised land, but we cannot enter because of our disobedience or lack of faith.

So, how should we, as children of the promise, live while we wait for God's timing? There are many lessons to learn while in the wilderness, such as patience and obedience. The Israelite nation had to wait on God as they passed through the wilderness, but they failed in both these areas and fell into sin over and over. If they wanted to emerge from the wilderness, however, they had no choice. The only path out was the one of obedience and patience. Through the cloud of His presence, God told them when to stay and when to move. This movement, however slow and tedious, was what brought them from Egypt, through the desert, and into the place they were promised.

Like the Israelites, we must keep moving forward, submitting to God's lead in whatever actions we take and not forgetting that movement is a process. Step by step, day by day, year by year, through small wins and big wins, and sometimes by roundabout, rocky paths, when we follow God's lead, the journey will always take us to the place He has prepared.

In the moments when it seems God is taking too long to get you to your promised land, go for a walk down memory lane. You may have forgotten just how far God has brought you and all that He has done for you. Think back over the last few years of your life. Remember the times when a situation seemed hopeless but God showed up and worked everything out. Think about the blessing you asked God for that appeared when you least expected it. Rejoice over all the times He delivered you, healed you, and comforted you.

Reflect also on your commitments to God. Do not focus only on His promises to you; consider carefully your promises to Him. Did you do all that was required of you? You will likely find that even when you did not do your part, God did His. Memories of all that God has done for you are evidence of His faithfulness in the past and evidence of His ability to lead you into your future.

THE FIFTH BOOK OF
MOSES CALLED

DEUTERONOMY

The Previous Command to Enter Canaan

1 These *are* the words which Moses spoke to all Israel [a]on this side of the Jordan in the wilderness, in the plain[1] opposite Suph,[2] between Paran, Tophel, Laban, Hazeroth, and Dizahab. 2 *It is* eleven days' *journey* from Horeb by way of Mount Seir [a]to Kadesh Barnea. 3 Now it came to pass [a]in the fortieth year, in the eleventh month, on the first *day* of the month, *that* Moses spoke to the children of Israel according to all that the LORD had given him as commandments to them, 4 [a]after he had killed Sihon king of the Amorites, who dwelt in Heshbon, and Og king of Bashan, who dwelt at Ashtaroth [b]in[1] Edrei.

5 On this side of the Jordan in the land of Moab, Moses began to explain this law, saying, 6 "The LORD our God spoke to us [a]in Horeb, saying: 'You have dwelt long [b]enough at this mountain. 7 Turn and take your journey, and go to the mountains of the Amorites, to all the neighboring *places* in the plain,[1] in the mountains and in the lowland, in the South and on the seacoast, to the land of the Canaanites and to Lebanon, as far as the great river, the River Euphrates. 8 See, I have set the land before you; go in and possess the land which the LORD swore to your fathers—to [a]Abraham, Isaac, and Jacob—to give to them and their descendants after them.'

Tribal Leaders Appointed
(Ex. 18:13–27)

9 "And [a]I spoke to you at that time, saying: 'I alone am not able to bear you. 10 The LORD your God has multiplied you, [a]and here you *are* today, as the stars of heaven in multitude. 11 [a]May the LORD God of your fathers make you a thousand times more numerous than you are, and bless you [b]as He has promised you! 12 [a]How can I alone bear your problems and your burdens and your complaints? 13 Choose wise, understanding, and knowledgeable men from among your tribes, and I will make them heads over you.' 14 And you answered me and said, 'The thing which you have told *us* to do *is* good.' 15 So I took [a]the heads of your tribes, wise and knowledgeable men, and made them heads over you, leaders of thousands, leaders of hundreds, leaders of fifties, leaders of tens, and officers for your tribes.

16 "Then I commanded your judges at that time, saying, 'Hear *the cases* between your brethren, and [a]judge righteously between a man and his [b]brother or the stranger who is with him. 17 [a]You shall not show partiality in judgment; you shall hear the small as well as the great; you shall not be afraid in any man's presence, for [b]the judgment *is* God's. The case that is too hard for you, [c]bring to me, and I will hear it.' 18 And I commanded you at that time all the things which you should do.

Israel's Refusal to Enter the Land
(Num. 13:1–33)

19 "So we departed from Horeb, [a]and went through all that great and terrible wilderness which you saw on the way to the mountains of the Amorites, as the LORD

1:1 [a] Deut. 4:44–46; Josh. 9:1, 10 [1] Hebrew *arabah* [2] One manuscript of the Septuagint, also Targum and Vulgate, read *Red Sea.* 1:2 [a] Num. 13:26; 32:8; Deut. 9:23 1:3 [a] Num. 33:38 1:4 [a] Num. 21:23, 24, 33–35; Deut. 2:26–35; Josh. 13:10; Neh. 9:22 [b] Josh. 13:12 [1] Septuagint, Syriac, and Vulgate read *and* (compare Joshua 12:4). 1:6 [a] Ex. 3:1, 12 [b] Ex. 19:1, 2 1:7 [1] Hebrew *arabah* 1:8 [a] Gen. 12:7; 15:5; 22:17; 26:3; 28:13; Ex. 33:1; Num. 14:23; 32:11 1:9 [a] Ex. 18:18, 24; Num. 11:14, 24 1:10 [a] Gen. 15:5; 22:17; Ex. 32:13; Deut. 7:7; 10:22; 26:5; 28:62 1:11 [a] 2 Sam. 24:3 [b] Gen. 15:5 1:12 [a] 1 Kin. 3:8, 9 1:15 [a] Ex. 18:25 1:16 [a] Deut. 16:18; John 7:24 [b] Lev. 24:22 1:17 [a] Lev. 19:15; Deut. 10:17; 16:19; 24:17; 1 Sam. 16:7; Prov. 24:23–26; Acts 10:34; James 2:1, 9 [b] 2 Chr. 19:6 [c] Ex. 18:22, 26 1:19 [a] Num. 10:12; Deut. 2:7; 8:15; 32:10; Jer. 2:6

our God had commanded us. Then [b]we came to Kadesh Barnea. 20And I said to you, 'You have come to the mountains of the Amorites, which the LORD our God is giving us. 21Look, the LORD your God has set the land before you; go up *and* possess *it*, as the LORD God of your fathers has spoken to you; [a]do not fear or be discouraged.'

22"And every one of you came near to me and said, 'Let us send men before us, and let them search out the land for us, and bring back word to us of the way by which we should go up, and of the cities into which we shall come.'

23"The plan pleased me well; so [a]I took twelve of your men, one man from *each* tribe. 24[a]And they departed and went up into the mountains, and came to the Valley of Eshcol, and spied it out. 25They also took *some* of the fruit of the land in their hands and brought *it* down to us; and they brought back word to us, saying, '*It is* a [a]good land which the LORD our God is giving us.'

26[a]"Nevertheless you would not go up, but rebelled against the command of the LORD your God; 27and you [a]complained in your tents, and said, 'Because the LORD [b]hates us, He has brought us out of the land of Egypt to deliver us into the hand of the Amorites, to destroy us. 28Where can we go up? Our brethren have discouraged our hearts, saying, [a]"The people *are* greater and taller than we; the cities *are* great and fortified up to heaven; moreover we have seen the sons of the [b]Anakim there." '

29"Then I said to you, 'Do not be terrified, [a]or afraid of them. 30[a]The LORD your God, who goes before you, He will fight for you, according to all He did for you in Egypt before your eyes, 31and in the wilderness where you saw how the LORD your God carried you, as a [a]man carries his son, in all the way that you went until you came to this place.' 32Yet, for all that, [a]you did not believe the LORD your God, 33[a]who went in the way before you [b]to search out a place for you to pitch your tents, to show you the way you should go, in the fire by night and in the cloud by day.

The Penalty for Israel's Rebellion
(Num. 14:20–45)

34"And the LORD heard the sound of your words, and was angry, [a]and took an oath, saying, 35[a]'Surely not one of these men of this evil generation shall see that good land of which I swore to give to your fathers, 36[a]except Caleb the son of Jephunneh; he shall see it, and to him and his children I am giving the land on which he walked, because [b]he wholly followed the LORD.' 37[a]The LORD was also angry with me for your sakes, saying, 'Even you shall not go in there. 38[a]Joshua the son of Nun, [b]who stands before you, he shall go in there. [c]Encourage him, for he shall cause Israel to inherit it.

39[a]'Moreover your little ones and your children, who [b]you say will be victims, who today [c]have no knowledge of good and evil, they shall go in there; to them I will give it, and they shall possess it. 40[a]But *as for* you, turn and take your journey into the wilderness by the Way of the Red Sea.'

41"Then you answered and said to me, [a]'We have sinned against the LORD; we will go up and fight, just as the LORD our God commanded us.' And when everyone of you had girded on his weapons of war, you were ready to go up into the mountain.

42"And the LORD said to me, 'Tell them, [a]"Do not go up nor fight, for I *am* not among you; lest you be defeated before your enemies." ' 43So I spoke to you; yet you would not listen, but [a]rebelled against the command of the LORD, and [b]presumptuously went up into the mountain. 44And the Amorites who dwelt in that mountain came out against you and chased you [a]as bees do, and drove you back from Seir to Hormah. 45Then you returned and wept before the LORD, but the LORD would not listen to your voice nor give ear to you.

1:19 [b] Num. 13:26 1:21 [a] Josh. 1:6, 9 1:23 [a] Num. 13:2, 3 1:24 [a] Num. 13:21–25 1:25 [a] Num. 13:27 1:26 [a] Num. 14:1–4; Ps. 106:24 1:27 [a] Ps. 106:25 [b] Deut. 9:28 1:28 [a] Num. 13:28, 31–33; Deut. 9:1, 2 [b] Num. 13:28 1:29 [a] Num. 14:9; Deut. 7:18 1:30 [a] Ex. 14:14; Deut. 3:22; 20:4; Neh. 4:20 1:31 [a] Deut. 32:10–12; Is. 46:3, 4; 63:9; Hos. 11:3 1:32 [a] Num. 14:11; 20:12; Ps. 106:24; Heb. 3:9, 10, 16–19; 4:1, 2; Jude 5 1:33 [a] Ex. 13:21; Num. 9:15–23; Neh. 9:12; Ps. 78:14 [b] Num. 10:33; Ezek. 20:6 1:34 [a] Deut. 2:14, 15 1:35 [a] Num. 14:22, 23; Ps. 95:10, 11 1:36 [a] Num. 14:24; [Josh. 14:9] [b] Num. 32:11, 12 1:37 [a] Num. 20:12; 27:14; Deut. 3:26; 4:21; 34:4; Ps. 106:32 1:38 [a] Num. 14:30 [b] Ex. 24:13; 33:11; 1 Sam. 16:22 [c] Num. 27:18, 19; Deut. 31:7, 23; Josh. 11:23 1:39 [a] Num. 14:31 [b] Num. 14:3 [c] Is. 7:15, 16 1:40 [a] Num. 14:25 1:41 [a] Num. 14:40 1:42 [a] Num. 14:41–43 1:43 [a] Num. 14:44 [b] Deut. 17:12, 13 1:44 [a] Num. 14:45; Ps. 118:12

RELEASE // TRUST IN HIS WORD

Ever-Increasing Faith

Deuteronomy 1:32–33 // "Yet, for all that, you did not believe the LORD your God, who went in the way before you to search out a place for you to pitch your tents, to show you the way you should go, in the fire by night and in the cloud by day."

Summary Message // In a world where the twenty-four-hour news cycle indoctrinates us with a sense of helplessness and despair, it is easy to doubt the promises we find in God's Word. The Bible was written thousands of years before the current events we see around us; however, its message is eternal. God's Word stands the test of the ages. We must trust that His Word is relevant for today. We must trust that His Word is truth. We must trust that His Word is living and active. Above all, we must trust that God cares for us. If we can come to a place of trust, it causes the world and all its distractions to grow dim as His Word becomes the light of our lives, as God designed it to be.

Practical Application // Have you ever read the Bible and thought, "That was then. This is now. This message is not for me"? It is easy to look at the extraordinary experiences of those in the past and be unable to relate to them. Most of the events in Scripture will not be repeated in our age. Seeing these stories as disconnected from our experience, then, is somewhat understandable. It is also easy to look to our past failures or disappointments or the failures of others and allow those experiences to overshadow any trust we may have had in God's Word.

These perspectives are understandable but still must be resisted. Instead, we must realize that God is not a human that He should lie or be untrustworthy. We must fight within our minds and hearts to cling to God's Word in absolute trust. Even so, trusting God is not something that happens overnight. It can take time for true faith to build. Faith is not something we have in ourselves; it is something that God gives us through His faithfulness. Every time God shows up and acts in our lives, we are able to trust Him a little more. The Israelites were faithless at times, and God had to teach them to trust Him. In Deuteronomy 1:32–33 we see that in the wilderness, they had no choice but to move when His cloud moved and to stay in the warmth of His fire by night. It was the only way for them to survive. They began to learn that God is trustworthy.

He continues to be who He says He is, and we begin to receive a stronger gift of faith. However, in the end, we must make the choice to give ourselves and all we trust in over to God. We have to make the choice to read the Bible and surround ourselves with encouraging teachings that bring inspiration and increase faith. As we do, we are to believe what God says about us. His truth overshadows anything else in our lives. So, we surrender all we are and all we have to Him and let His Word become the guide in our lives. Then our faith is perfected.

Fervent Prayer // Heavenly Father, we trust You with everything that is important to us: our careers, relationships, finances, hurts, pains, desires, and accomplishments. We realize You know what is best for us in all areas, and we trust Your Word as truth. We are thankful that You are alive and active in our lives. Our minds have been renewed, and we acknowledge You as first in all things. Thank You, Lord, for being with us in times of trouble and in moments of joy. We so appreciate all You have done in our lives and all You will continue to do. We are thankful and grateful that You are leading and guiding us into every possibility, and we are excited to see what will happen next. In Jesus' name we pray. Amen.

---

46 [a]"So you remained in Kadesh many days, according to the days that you spent *there.*

The Desert Years

2 "Then we turned and [a]journeyed into
the wilderness of the Way of the Red
Sea, [b]as the LORD spoke to me, and we
skirted Mount Seir for many days.
2"And the LORD spoke to me, saying:
3'You have skirted this mountain [a]long
enough; turn northward. 4And command
the people, saying, [a]"You *are about to* pass
through the territory of [b]your brethren,

1:46 [a] Num. 13:25; 20:1, 22; Deut. 2:7, 14 2:1 [a] Deut. 1:40 [b] Num. 14:25 2:3 [a] Deut. 2:7, 14
2:4 [a] Num. 20:14–21 [b] Deut. 23:7

the descendants of Esau, who live in Seir;
and they will be afraid of you. Therefore
watch yourselves carefully. 5Do not meddle with them, for I will not give you *any*
of their land, no, not so much as one foot-
step, [a]because I have given Mount Seir to
Esau *as* a possession. 6You shall buy food
from them with money, that you may eat;
and you shall also buy water from them
with money, that you may drink.
7"For the LORD your God has blessed you
in all the work of your hand. He knows your
trudging through this great wilderness.
[a]These forty years the LORD your God *has*
been with you; you have lacked nothing."'
8"And when we passed beyond our
brethren, the descendants of Esau who
dwell in Seir, away from the road of the
plain, away from [a]Elath and Ezion Geber,
we [b]turned and passed by way of the Wilderness of Moab. 9Then the LORD said to
me, 'Do not harass Moab, nor contend with
them in battle, for I will not give you *any* of
their land *as* a possession, because I have
given [a]Ar to [b]the descendants of Lot *as* a
possession.'"
10[a](The Emim had dwelt there in times
past, a people as great and numerous and
tall as [b]the Anakim. 11They were also regarded as giants,[1] like the Anakim, but the
Moabites call them Emim. 12[a]The Horites
formerly dwelt in Seir, but the descendants
of Esau dispossessed them and destroyed
them from before them, and dwelt in their
place, just as Israel did to the land of their
possession which the LORD gave them.)
13" 'Now rise and cross over [a]the Valley
of the Zered.' So we crossed over the Valley of the Zered. 14And the time we took
to come [a]from Kadesh Barnea until we
crossed over the Valley of the Zered *was*
thirty-eight years, [b]until all the generation
of the men of war was consumed from the
midst of the camp, [c]just as the LORD had
sworn to them. 15For indeed the hand of the
LORD was against them, to destroy them
from the midst of the camp until they were
consumed.
16"So it was, when all the men of war had
finally perished from among the people,
17that the LORD spoke to me, saying: 18'This
day you are to cross over at Ar, the boundary of Moab. 19And *when* you come near the
people of Ammon, do not harass them or
meddle with them, for I will not give you
any of the land of the people of Ammon
as a possession, because I have given it to
[a]the descendants of Lot *as* a possession.'"
20(That was also regarded as a land of giants;[1] giants formerly dwelt there. But the
Ammonites call them [a]Zamzummim, 21[a]a
people as great and numerous and tall as
the Anakim. But the LORD destroyed them
before them, and they dispossessed them
and dwelt in their place, 22just as He had
done for the descendants of Esau, [a]who
dwelt in Seir, when He destroyed [b]the Horites from before them. They dispossessed
them and dwelt in their place, even to this
day. 23And [a]the Avim, who dwelt in villages
as far as Gaza—[b]the Caphtorim, who came
from Caphtor, destroyed them and dwelt
in their place.)
24" 'Rise, take your journey, and [a]cross
over the River Arnon. Look, I have given
into your hand [b]Sihon the Amorite, king
of Heshbon, and his land. Begin to possess
it, and engage him in battle. 25[a]This day I
will begin to put the dread and fear of you
upon the nations under the whole heaven,
who shall hear the report of you, and shall
[b]tremble and be in anguish because of you.'

King Sihon Defeated
(Num. 21:21–32)

26"And I [a]sent messengers from the
Wilderness of Kedemoth to Sihon king
of Heshbon, [b]with words of peace, saying,
27[a]'Let me pass through your land; I will
keep strictly to the road, and I will turn neither to the right nor to the left. 28You shall
sell me food for money, that I may eat, and
give me water for money, that I may drink;
[a]only let me pass through on foot, 29[a]just
as the descendants of Esau who dwell in
Seir and the Moabites who dwell in Ar did

2:5 [a] Gen. 36:8; Josh. 24:4 2:7 [a] Deut. 8:2–4; [Matt. 6:8, 32] 2:8 [a] Judg. 11:18; 1 Kin. 9:26 [b] Num. 21:4 2:9 [a] Num. 21:15, 28; Deut. 2:18, 29 [b] Gen. 19:36–38 2:10 [a] Gen. 14:5 [b] Num. 13:22, 33; Deut. 9:2 2:11 [1] Hebrew *rephaim* 2:12 [a] Gen. 14:6; 36:20; Deut. 2:22 2:13 [a] Num. 21:12 2:14 [a] Num. 13:26 [b] Num. 14:33; 26:64; Deut. 1:34, 35 [c] Num. 14:35; Ezek. 20:15 2:19 [a] Gen. 19:38; Num. 21:24 2:20 [a] Gen. 14:5 [1] Hebrew *rephaim* 2:21 [a] Deut. 2:10 2:22 [a] Gen. 36:8; Deut. 2:5 [b] Gen. 14:6; 36:20–30 2:23 [a] Josh. 13:3 [b] Gen. 10:14; 1 Chr. 1:12; Jer. 47:4; Amos 9:7 2:24 [a] Num. 21:13, 14; Judg. 11:18 [b] Deut. 1:4 2:25 [a] Ex. 23:27; Deut. 11:25; Josh. 2:9 [b] Ex. 15:14–16 2:26 [a] Num. 21:21–32; Deut. 1:4; Judg. 11:19–21 [b] Deut. 20:10 2:27 [a] Num. 21:21, 22; Judg. 11:19 2:28 [a] Num. 20:19 2:29 [a] Num. 20:18; Deut. 23:3, 4; Judg. 11:17

for me, until I cross the Jordan to the land which the LORD our God is giving us.'

30 [a]"But Sihon king of Heshbon would not let us pass through, for [b]the LORD your God [c]hardened his spirit and made his heart obstinate, that He might deliver him into your hand, as *it is* this day.

31 "And the LORD said to me, 'See, I have begun to [a]give Sihon and his land over to you. Begin to possess *it*, that you may inherit his land.' 32 [a]Then Sihon and all his people came out against us to fight at Jahaz. 33 And [a]the LORD our God delivered him over to us; so [b]we defeated him, his sons, and all his people. 34 We took all his cities at that time, and we [a]utterly destroyed the men, women, and little ones of every city; we left none remaining. 35 We took only the livestock as plunder for ourselves, with the spoil of the cities which we took. 36 [a]From Aroer, which *is* on the bank of the River Arnon, and *from* [b]the city that *is* in the ravine, as far as Gilead, there was not one city too strong for us; [c]the LORD our God delivered all to us. 37 Only you did not go near the land of the people of Ammon—anywhere along the River [a]Jabbok, or to the cities of the mountains, or [b]wherever the LORD our God had forbidden us.

King Og Defeated
(Num. 21:33–35)

3 "Then we turned and went up the road to Bashan; and [a]Og king of Bashan came out against us, he and all his people, to battle [b]at Edrei. 2 And the LORD said to me, 'Do not fear him, for I have delivered him and all his people and his land into your hand; you shall do to him as you did to [a]Sihon king of the Amorites, who dwelt at Heshbon.'

3 "So the LORD our God also delivered into our hands Og king of Bashan, with all his people, and we attacked him until he had no survivors remaining. 4 And we took all his cities at that time; there was not a city which we did not take from them: sixty cities, [a]all the region of Argob, the kingdom of Og in Bashan. 5 All these cities *were* fortified with high walls, gates, and bars, besides a great many rural towns. 6 And we utterly destroyed them, as we did to Sihon king [a]of Heshbon, utterly destroying the men, women, and children of every city. 7 But all the livestock and the spoil of the cities we took as booty for ourselves.

8 "And at that time we took the [a]land from the hand of the two kings of the Amorites who *were* on this side of the Jordan, from the River Arnon to Mount [b]Hermon 9 (the Sidonians call [a]Hermon Sirion, and the Amorites call it Senir), 10 [a]all the cities of the plain, all Gilead, and [b]all Bashan, as far as Salcah and Edrei, cities of the kingdom of Og in Bashan.

11 [a]"For only Og king of Bashan remained of the remnant of [b]the giants.[1] Indeed his bedstead *was* an iron bedstead. (*Is* it not in [c]Rabbah of the people of Ammon?) Nine cubits *is* its length and four cubits its width, according to the standard cubit.

The Land East of the Jordan Divided
(Num. 32:25–41)

12 "And this [a]land, *which* we possessed at that time, [b]from Aroer, which *is* by the River Arnon, and half the mountains of Gilead and [c]its cities, I gave to the Reubenites and the Gadites. 13 [a]The rest of Gilead, and all Bashan, the kingdom of Og, I gave to half the tribe of Manasseh. (All the region of Argob, with all Bashan, was called the land of the giants.[1] 14 [a]Jair the son of Manasseh took all the region of Argob, [b]as far as the border of the Geshurites and the Maachathites, and [c]called Bashan after his own name, Havoth Jair,[1] to this day.)

15 "Also I gave [a]Gilead to Machir. 16 And to the Reubenites [a]and the Gadites I gave from Gilead as far as the River Arnon, the middle of the river as *the* border, as far as the River Jabbok, [b]the border of the people of Ammon; 17 the plain also, with the Jordan as *the* border, from Chinnereth [a]as

2:30 [a] Num. 21:23 [b] Josh. 11:20 [c] Ex. 4:21 2:31 [a] Deut. 1:3, 8 2:32 [a] Num. 21:23 2:33 [a] Ex. 23:31; Deut. 7:2 [b] Num. 21:24 2:34 [a] Lev. 27:28 2:36 [a] Deut. 3:12; 4:48; Josh. 13:9 [b] Josh. 13:9, 16 [c] Ps. 44:3 2:37 [a] Gen. 32:22; Num. 21:24; Deut. 3:16 [b] Deut. 2:5, 9, 19 3:1 [a] Num. 21:33–35; Deut. 29:7 [b] Deut. 1:4 3:2 [a] Num. 21:34; Josh. 13:21 3:4 [a] Deut. 3:13, 14 3:6 [a] Deut. 2:24, 34, 35 3:8 [a] Num. 32:33; Josh. 12:6; 13:8–12 [b] Deut. 4:48; 1 Chr. 5:23 3:9 [a] 1 Chr. 5:23 3:10 [a] Deut. 4:49 [b] Josh. 12:5; 13:11 3:11 [a] Amos 2:9 [b] Gen. 14:5; Deut. 2:11, 20 [c] 2 Sam. 12:26; Jer. 49:2; Ezek. 21:20 [1] Hebrew *rephaim* 3:12 [a] Num. 32:33; Josh. 12:6; 13:8–12 [b] Deut. 2:36; Josh. 12:2 [c] Num. 34:14 3:13 [a] Josh. 13:29–31; 17:1 [1] Hebrew *rephaim* 3:14 [a] 1 Chr. 2:22 [b] Josh. 13:13; 2 Sam. 3:3; 10:6 [c] Num. 32:41 [1] Literally *Towns of Jair* 3:15 [a] Num. 32:39, 40 3:16 [a] 2 Sam. 24:5 [b] Num. 21:24; Deut. 2:37; Josh. 12:2 3:17 [a] Num. 34:11, 12; Deut. 4:49; Josh. 12:3

far as the east side of the Sea of the Arabah
[b](the Salt Sea), below the slopes of Pisgah.
18 "Then I commanded you at that time,
saying: 'The LORD your God has given you
this land to possess. [a]All you men of valor
shall cross over armed before your brethren, the children of Israel. 19 But your wives,
your little ones, and your livestock (I know
that you have much livestock) shall stay in
your cities which I have given you, 20 until
the LORD has given [a]rest to your brethren as
to you, and they also possess the land which
the LORD your God is giving them beyond
the Jordan. Then each of you may [b]return
to his possession which I have given you.'
21 "And [a]I commanded Joshua at that
time, saying, 'Your eyes have seen all that
the LORD your God has done to these two
kings; so will the LORD do to all the kingdoms through which you pass. 22 You must
not fear them, for [a]the LORD your God Himself fights for you.'

Moses Forbidden to Enter the Land

23 "Then [a]I pleaded with the LORD at
that time, saying: 24 'O Lord GOD, You have
begun to show Your servant [a]Your greatness and Your mighty hand, for [b]what god
is there in heaven or on earth who can do
anything like Your works and Your mighty
deeds? 25 I pray, let me cross over and see
[a]the good land beyond the Jordan, those
pleasant mountains, and Lebanon.'
26 "But the LORD [a]was angry with me on
your account, and would not listen to me.
So the LORD said to me: 'Enough of that!
Speak no more to Me of this matter. 27 [a]Go
up to the top of Pisgah, and lift your eyes toward the west, the north, the south, and the
east; behold *it* with your eyes, for you shall
not cross over this Jordan. 28 But [a]command
Joshua, and encourage him and strengthen
him; for he shall go over before this people, and he shall cause them to inherit the
land which you will see.'
29 "So we stayed in [a]the valley opposite
Beth Peor.

Moses Commands Obedience

4 "Now, O Israel, listen to [a]the statutes
and the judgments which I teach you
to observe, that you may live, and go in and
possess the land which the LORD God of
your fathers is giving you. 2 [a]You shall not
add to the word which I command you, nor
take from it, that you may keep the commandments of the LORD your God which I
command you. 3 Your eyes have seen what
the LORD did at [a]Baal Peor; for the LORD
your God has destroyed from among you
all the men who followed Baal of Peor. 4 But
you who held fast to the LORD your God *are*
alive today, every one of you.
5 "Surely I have taught you statutes and
judgments, just as the LORD my God commanded me, that you should act according
to them in the land which you go to possess.
6 Therefore be careful to observe *them;* for
this *is* [a]your wisdom and your understanding in the sight of the peoples who will hear
all these statutes, and say, 'Surely this great
nation *is* a wise and understanding people.'
7 "For [a]what great nation *is there* that has
[b]God *so* near to it, as the LORD our God *is* to
us, for whatever *reason* we may call upon
Him? 8 And what great nation *is there* that
has *such* statutes and righteous judgments
as are in all this law which I set before you
this day? 9 Only take heed to yourself, and
diligently [a]keep yourself, lest you [b]forget
the things your eyes have seen, and lest
they depart from your heart all the days of
your life. And [c]teach them to your children
and your grandchildren, 10 *especially concerning* [a]the day you stood before the LORD
your God in Horeb, when the LORD said to
me, 'Gather the people to Me, and I will let
them hear My words, that they may learn to
fear Me all the days they live on the earth,
and *that* they may teach their children.'
11 "Then you came near and stood at the
foot of the mountain, and the mountain
burned with fire to the midst of heaven,
with darkness, cloud, and thick darkness.
12 [a]And the LORD spoke to you out of the

3:17 [b] Gen. 14:3; Josh. 3:16 3:18 [a] Num. 32:20; Josh. 4:12, 13 3:20 [a] Deut. 12:9, 10 [b] Josh. 22:4 3:21 [a] [Num. 27:22, 23]; Josh. 11:23 3:22 [a] Ex. 14:14; Deut. 1:30; 20:4; Neh. 4:20 3:23 [a] [2 Cor. 12:8, 9] 3:24 [a] Deut. 5:24; 11:2 [b] Ex. 8:10; 15:11; 2 Sam. 7:22; Ps. 71:19; 86:8 3:25 [a] Ex. 3:8; Deut. 4:22 3:26 [a] Num. 20:12; 27:14; Deut. 1:37; 31:2; 32:51, 52; 34:4 3:27 [a] Num. 23:14; 27:12 3:28 [a] Num. 27:18, 23; Deut. 31:3, 7, 8, 23 3:29 [a] Deut. 4:46; 34:6 4:1 [a] Lev. 19:37; 20:8; 22:31; Deut. 5:1; 8:1; Ezek. 20:11; [Rom. 10:5] 4:2 [a] Deut. 12:32; [Josh. 1:7]; Prov. 30:6; [Rev. 22:18, 19] 4:3 [a] Num. 25:1–9; Josh. 22:17; Ps. 106:28 4:6 [a] Deut. 30:19, 20; 32:46, 47; Job 28:28; Ps. 19:7; 111:10; Prov. 1:7; [2 Tim. 3:15] 4:7 [a] [Deut. 4:32–34; 2 Sam. 7:23] [b] [Ps. 46:1; Is. 55:6] 4:9 [a] Prov. 4:23 [b] Deut. 29:2–8 [c] Gen. 18:19; Deut. 4:10; 6:7, 20–25; Ps. 78:5, 6; Prov. 22:6; Eph. 6:4 4:10 [a] Ex. 19:9, 16, 17 4:12 [a] Deut. 5:4, 22

midst of the fire. You heard the sound of the words, but saw no form; [b]*you* only *heard* a voice. 13 [a]So He declared to you His covenant which He commanded you to perform, [b]the Ten Commandments; and [c]He wrote them on two tablets of stone. 14 And [a]the LORD commanded me at that time to teach you statutes and judgments, that you might observe them in the land which you cross over to possess.

Beware of Idolatry

15 [a]"Take careful heed to yourselves, for you saw no [b]form when the LORD spoke to you at Horeb out of the midst of the fire, 16 lest you [a]act corruptly and [b]make for yourselves a carved image in the form of any figure: [c]the likeness of male or female, 17 the likeness of any animal that *is* on the earth or the likeness of any winged bird that flies in the air, 18 the likeness of anything that creeps on the ground or the likeness of any fish that *is* in the water beneath the earth. 19 And *take heed,* lest you [a]lift your eyes to heaven, and *when* you see the sun, the moon, and the stars, [b]all the host of heaven, you feel driven to [c]worship them and serve them, which the LORD your God has given to all the peoples under the whole heaven as a heritage. 20 But the LORD has taken you and [a]brought you out of the iron furnace, out of Egypt, to be [b]His people, an inheritance, as you are this day. 21 Furthermore [a]the LORD was angry with me for your sakes, and swore that [b]I would not cross over the Jordan, and that I would not enter the good land which the LORD your God is giving you as an inheritance. 22 But [a]I must die in this land, [b]I must not cross over the Jordan; but you shall cross over and possess [c]that good land. 23 Take heed to yourselves, lest you forget the covenant of the LORD your God which He made with you, [a]and make for yourselves a carved image in the form of anything which the LORD your God has forbidden you. 24 For [a]the LORD your God *is* a consuming fire, [b]a jealous God.

25 "When you beget children and grandchildren and have grown old in the land, and act corruptly and make a carved image in the form of anything, and [a]do evil in the sight of the LORD your God to provoke Him to anger, 26 [a]I call heaven and earth to witness against you this day, that you will soon utterly perish from the land which you cross over the Jordan to possess; you will not prolong *your* days in it, but will be utterly destroyed. 27 And the LORD [a]will scatter you among the peoples, and you will be left few in number among the nations where the LORD will drive you. 28 And [a]there you will serve gods, the work of men's hands, wood and stone, [b]which neither see nor hear nor eat nor smell. 29 [a]But from there you will seek the LORD your God, and you will find *Him* if you seek Him with all your heart and with all your soul. 30 When you are in distress, and all these things come upon you in the [a]latter days, when you [b]turn to the LORD your God and obey His voice 31 (for the LORD your God *is* a merciful God), He will not forsake you nor [a]destroy you, nor forget the covenant of your fathers which He swore to them.

32 "For [a]ask now concerning the days that are past, which were before you, since the day that God created man on the earth, and *ask* [b]from one end of heaven to the other, whether *any* great *thing* like this has happened, or *anything* like it has been heard. 33 [a]Did *any* people *ever* hear the voice of God speaking out of the midst of the fire, as you have heard, and live? 34 Or did God *ever* try to go *and* take for Himself a nation from the midst of *another* nation, [a]by trials, [b]by signs, by wonders, by war, [c]by a mighty hand and [d]an outstretched arm, [e]and by great terrors, according to all that the LORD your God did for you in Egypt before your eyes? 35 To you it was shown, that you might know that the LORD Himself *is* God; [a]*there is* none other

---

4:12 [b] Ex. 19:17–19; 20:22; 1 Kin. 19:11–18 4:13 [a] Deut. 9:9, 11 [b] Ex. 34:28; Deut. 10:4 [c] Ex. 24:12 4:14 [a] Ex. 21:1 4:15 [a] Josh. 23:11 [b] Is. 40:18 4:16 [a] Ex. 32:7; Deut. 9:12; 31:29 [b] Ex. 20:4, 5 [c] Rom. 1:23 4:19 [a] Deut. 17:3; Job 31:26–28 [b] 2 Kin. 21:3 [c] [Rom. 1:25] 4:20 [a] 1 Kin. 8:51; Jer. 11:4 [b] Deut. 7:6; 27:9; [Titus 2:14] 4:21 [a] Num. 20:12; Deut. 1:37; 3:26 [b] Num. 27:13, 14 4:22 [a] 2 Pet. 1:13–15 [b] Deut. 3:27 [c] Deut. 3:25 4:23 [a] Ex. 20:4, 5; Deut. 4:16 4:24 [a] Ex. 24:17; Deut. 9:3; Is. 33:14; Heb. 12:29 [b] Ex. 20:5; 34:14 4:25 [a] 2 Kin. 17:17 4:26 [a] Deut. 30:18, 19; 2 Chr. 36:14–20; Is. 1:2; Mic. 6:2 4:27 [a] Lev. 26:33; Deut. 28:62; Neh. 1:8 4:28 [a] Deut. 28:64; 1 Sam. 26:19; Jer. 16:13 [b] Ps. 115:4–7; 135:15–17; Is. 44:9; 46:7 4:29 [a] [Lev. 26:39–45; Deut. 30:1–3; 2 Chr. 15:4; Neh. 1:9] 4:30 [a] Gen. 49:1; Deut. 31:29; Jer. 23:20; Hos. 3:5 [b] Joel 2:12; Heb. 1:2 4:31 [a] Lev. 26:44; Jer. 30:11 4:32 [a] Deut. 32:7; Job 8:8 [b] Deut. 28:64; Matt. 24:31 4:33 [a] Ex. 20:22; 24:11; Deut. 5:24–26 4:34 [a] Deut. 7:19 [b] Ex. 7:3 [c] Ex. 13:3 [d] Ex. 6:6 [e] Deut. 26:8 4:35 [a] Ex. 8:10; 9:14; [Deut. 4:39; 32:12, 39; 1 Sam. 2:2; Is. 43:10–12; 44:6–8; 45:5–7]; Mark 12:32

besides Him. 36[a]Out of heaven He let you
hear His voice, that He might instruct you;
on earth He showed you His great fire, and
you heard His words out of the midst of the
fire. 37And because [a]He loved your fathers,
therefore He chose their descendants after
them; and [b]He brought you out of Egypt
with His Presence, with His mighty power,
38[a]driving out from before you nations
greater and mightier than you, to bring
you in, to give you their land *as* an inheritance, as *it is* this day. 39Therefore know
this day, and consider *it* in your heart, that
[a]the LORD Himself *is* God in heaven above
and on the earth beneath; *there is* no other.
40[a]You shall therefore keep His statutes and
His commandments which I command you
today, that it may go well with you and with
your children after you, and that you may
prolong *your* days in the land which the
LORD your God is giving you for all time."

Cities of Refuge East of the Jordan

41Then Moses [a]set apart three cities on
this side of the Jordan, toward the rising of
the sun, 42[a]that the manslayer might flee
there, who kills his neighbor unintentionally, without having hated him in time past,
and that by fleeing to one of these cities he
might live: 43[a]Bezer in the wilderness on the
plateau for the Reubenites, Ramoth in Gilead for the Gadites, and Golan in Bashan
for the Manassites.

Introduction to God's Law

44Now this *is* the law which Moses set
before the children of Israel. 45These *are*
the testimonies, the statutes, and the judgments which Moses spoke to the children
of Israel after they came out of Egypt, 46on
this side of the Jordan, [a]in the valley opposite Beth Peor, in the land of Sihon king of
the Amorites, who dwelt at Heshbon, whom
Moses and the children of Israel [b]defeated
after they came out of Egypt. 47And they
took possession of his land and the land [a]of
Og king of Bashan, two kings of the Amorites, who *were* on this side of the Jordan,
toward the rising of the sun, 48[a]from Aroer,
which *is* on the bank of the River Arnon,
even to Mount Sion[1] (that is, [b]Hermon),
49and all the plain on the east side of the
Jordan as far as the Sea of the Arabah, below the [a]slopes of Pisgah.

The Ten Commandments Reviewed
(Ex. 20:1–17)

5 And Moses called all Israel, and said to
them: "Hear, O Israel, the statutes and
judgments which I speak in your hearing
today, that you may learn them and be careful to observe them. 2[a]The LORD our God
made a covenant with us in Horeb. 3The
LORD [a]did not make this covenant with our
fathers, but with us, those who *are* here
today, all of us who *are* alive. 4[a]The LORD
talked with you face to face on the mountain from the midst of the fire. 5[a]I stood
between the LORD and you at that time, to
declare to you the word of the LORD; for
[b]you were afraid because of the fire, and
you did not go up the mountain. *He* said:
6 [a]'I *am* the LORD your God who brought
you out of the land of Egypt, out of
the house of bondage.
7 [a]'You shall have no other gods before Me.
8 [a]'You shall not make for yourself a carved
image—any likeness *of anything* that
is in heaven above, or that *is* in the
earth beneath, or that *is* in the water
under the earth; 9you shall not [a]bow
down to them nor serve them. For I,
the LORD your God, *am* a jealous God,
visiting the iniquity of the fathers
upon the children to the third and
fourth *generations* of those who hate
Me, 10[a]but showing mercy to thousands, to those who love Me and keep
My commandments.
11 [a]'You shall not take the name of the LORD
your God in vain, for the LORD will
not hold *him* guiltless who takes His
name in vain.
12 [a]'Observe the Sabbath day, to keep it holy,
as the LORD your God commanded
you. 13[a]Six days you shall labor and

4:36 [a] Ex. 19:9, 19; 20:18, 22; Deut. 4:33; Neh. 9:13; Heb. 12:19, 25 4:37 [a] Deut. 7:7, 8; 10:15; 33:3 [b] Ex. 13:3, 9, 14 4:38 [a] Deut. 7:1 4:39 [a] Deut. 4:35; Josh. 2:11 4:40 [a] Lev. 22:31; Deut. 5:16; 32:46, 47 4:41 [a] Num. 35:6; Deut. 19:2–13; Josh. 20:7–9 4:42 [a] Deut. 19:4 4:43 [a] Josh. 20:8 4:46 [a] Deut. 3:29 [b] Num. 21:24; Deut. 1:4 4:47 [a] Num. 21:33–35 4:48 [a] Deut. 2:36; 3:12 [b] Deut. 3:9; Ps. 133:3 [1] Syriac reads *Sirion* (compare 3:9). 4:49 [a] Deut. 3:17 5:2 [a] Ex. 19:5; Deut. 4:23; Mal. 4:4 5:3 [a] Jer. 31:32; Matt. 13:17; Heb. 8:9 5:4 [a] Ex. 19:9 5:5 [a] Ex. 20:21; Gal. 3:19 [b] Ex. 19:16 5:6 [a] Ex. 20:2–17; Lev. 26:1; Deut. 6:4; Ps. 81:10 5:7 [a] Ex. 20:2, 3; 23:13; Hos. 13:4 5:8 [a] Ex. 20:4 5:9 [a] Ex. 34:7, 14–16; Num. 14:18; Deut. 7:10 5:10 [a] Num. 14:18; Deut. 7:9; Jer. 32:18; Dan. 9:4 5:11 [a] Ex. 20:7; Lev. 19:12; Deut. 6:13; 10:20; Matt. 5:33 5:12 [a] Ex. 20:8; Ezek. 20:12; Mark 2:27 5:13 [a] Ex. 23:12; 35:2

do all your work, 14but the seventh
day *is* the [a]Sabbath of the LORD your
God. *In it* you shall do no work: you,
nor your son, nor your daughter, nor
your male servant, nor your female
servant, nor your ox, nor your donkey, nor any of your cattle, nor your
stranger who *is* within your gates,
that your male servant and your
female servant may rest as well as
you. 15[a]And remember that you were
a slave in the land of Egypt, and the
LORD your God brought you out from
there [b]by a mighty hand and by an
outstretched arm; therefore the LORD
your God commanded you to keep
the Sabbath day.
16 [a]'Honor your father and your mother, as
the LORD your God has commanded
you, [b]that your days may be long, and
that it may be well with [c]you in the
land which the LORD your God is giving you.
17 [a]'You shall not murder.
18 [a]'You shall not commit adultery.
19 [a]'You shall not steal.
20 [a]'You shall not bear false witness against
your neighbor.
21 [a]'You shall not covet your neighbor's
wife; and you shall not desire your
neighbor's house, his field, his male
servant, his female servant, his ox,
his donkey, or anything that *is* your
neighbor's.'
22"These words the LORD spoke to all
your assembly, in the mountain from the
midst of the fire, the cloud, and the thick
darkness, with a loud voice; and He added
no more. And [a]He wrote them on two tablets of stone and gave them to me.

The People Afraid of God's Presence (Ex. 20:18–21)

23[a]"So it was, when you heard the voice
from the midst of the darkness, while the
mountain was burning with fire, that you
came near to me, all the heads of your
tribes and your elders. 24And you said:
'Surely the LORD our God has shown us
His glory and His greatness, and [a]we have
heard His voice from the midst of the fire.
We have seen this day that God speaks
with man; yet he [b]*still* lives. 25Now therefore, why should we die? For this great fire
will consume us; [a]if we hear the voice of
the LORD our God anymore, then we shall
die. 26[a]For who *is there* of all flesh who has
heard the voice of the living God speaking
from the midst of the fire, as we *have,* and
lived? 27You go near and hear all that the
LORD our God may say, and [a]tell us all that
the LORD our God says to you, and we will
hear and do *it.*'
28"Then the LORD heard the voice of
your words when you spoke to me, and the
LORD said to me: 'I have heard the voice of
the words of this people which they have
spoken to you. [a]They are right *in* all that
they have spoken. 29[a]Oh, that they had such
a heart in them that they would fear Me and
[b]always keep all My commandments, [c]that
it might be well with them and with their
children forever! 30Go and say to them, "Return to your tents." 31But as for you, stand
here by Me, [a]and I will speak to you all the
commandments, the statutes, and the judgments which you shall teach them, that
they may observe *them* in the land which
I am giving them to possess.'
32"Therefore you shall be careful to do as
the LORD your God has commanded you;
[a]you shall not turn aside to the right hand
or to the left. 33You shall walk in [a]all the
ways which the LORD your God has commanded you, that you may live [b]and *that
it may be* well with you, and *that* you may
prolong *your* days in the land which you
shall possess.

The Greatest Commandment

6 "Now this *is* [a]the commandment, *and
these are* the statutes and judgments
which the LORD your God has commanded
to teach you, that you may observe *them*
in the land which you are crossing over to
possess, 2[a]that you may fear the LORD your

5:14 [a] [Gen. 2:2]; Ex. 16:29; [Heb. 4:4] 5:15 [a] Deut. 15:15 [b] Deut. 4:34, 37 5:16 [a] Ex. 20:12; Lev. 19:3; Matt. 15:4; Eph. 6:2, 3; Col. 3:20 [b] Deut. 6:2 [c] Deut. 4:40 5:17 [a] Ex. 20:13; Matt. 5:21 5:18 [a] Ex. 20:14; Mark 10:19; Luke 18:20; [Rom. 13:9]; James 2:11 5:19 [a] Ex. 20:15; Lev. 19:11; [Rom. 13:9] 5:20 [a] Ex. 20:16; 23:1; Matt. 19:18 5:21 [a] Ex. 20:17; [Rom. 7:7; 13:9] 5:22 [a] Ex. 24:12; 31:18; Deut. 4:13 5:23 [a] Ex. 20:18, 19 5:24 [a] Ex. 19:19 [b] Deut. 4:33; Judg. 13:22 5:25 [a] Ex. 20:18, 19; Deut. 18:16 5:26 [a] Deut. 4:33 5:27 [a] Ex. 20:19; Heb. 12:19 5:28 [a] Deut. 18:17 5:29 [a] Deut. 32:29; Ps. 81:13; Is. 48:18 [b] Deut. 11:1 [c] Deut. 4:40 5:31 [a] [Gal. 3:19] 5:32 [a] Deut. 17:20; 28:14; Josh. 1:7; 23:6; Prov. 4:27 5:33 [a] Deut. 10:12; Ps. 119:3; Jer. 7:23; Luke 1:6 [b] Deut. 4:40; Eph. 6:3 6:1 [a] Deut. 12:1 6:2 [a] Ex. 20:20; Deut. 10:12, 13; [Ps. 111:10; 128:1; Eccl. 12:13]

God, to keep all His statutes and His commandments which I command you, you
and your son and your grandson, all the
days of your life, [b]and that your days may
be prolonged. 3Therefore hear, O Israel,
and be careful to observe *it,* that it may be
well with you, and that you may [a]multiply
greatly [b]as the LORD God of your fathers
has promised you—[c]'a land flowing with
milk and honey.'[1]

#OXYGEN

DEUTERONOMY 5:32–33

Trust in His Word

Reaching your blessings requires faith and action. Avoid sin, temptation, and distractions. Keep on the godly path. Stay focused through your victory. Walk into your purpose.

Breathe and **trust in His Word.**

4[a]"Hear, O Israel: The LORD our God, the
LORD *is* one![1] 5[a]You shall love the LORD your
God with all your heart, [b]with all your soul,
and with all your strength.

6"And [a]these words which I command
you today shall be in your heart. 7[a]You
shall teach them diligently to your children, and shall talk of them when you sit
in your house, when you walk by the way,
when you lie down, and when you rise up.
8[a]You shall bind them as a sign on your
hand, and they shall be as frontlets between
your eyes. 9[a]You shall write them on the
doorposts of your house and on your gates.

Caution Against Disobedience

10"So it shall be, when the LORD your
God brings you into the land of which He
swore to your fathers, to Abraham, Isaac,
and Jacob, to give you large and beautiful
cities [a]which you did not build, 11houses
full of all good things, which you did not
fill, hewn-out wells which you did not dig,
vineyards and olive trees which you did not
plant—[a]when you have eaten and are full—
12*then* beware, lest you forget the [a]LORD
who brought you out of the land of Egypt,
from the house of bondage. 13You shall
[a]fear the LORD your God and serve Him,
and [b]shall take oaths in His name. 14You
shall not go after other gods, [a]the gods of
the peoples who *are* all around you 15(for
[a]the LORD your God *is* a jealous God [b]among
you), lest the anger of the LORD your God be
aroused against you and destroy you from
the face of the earth.

16[a]"You shall not tempt the LORD your
God [b]as you tempted *Him* in Massah. 17You
shall [a]diligently keep the commandments
of the LORD your God, His testimonies, and
His statutes which He has commanded you.
18And you [a]shall do *what is* right and good
in the sight of the LORD, that it may be well
with you, and that you may go in and possess the good land of which the LORD swore
to your fathers, 19[a]to cast out all your enemies from before you, as the LORD has
spoken.

20[a]"When your son asks you in time to
come, saying, 'What *is the meaning of* the
testimonies, the statutes, and the judgments which the LORD our God has commanded you?' 21then you shall say to your
son: 'We were slaves of Pharaoh in Egypt,
and the LORD brought us out of Egypt [a]with
a mighty hand; 22and the LORD showed
signs and wonders before our eyes, great
and severe, against Egypt, Pharaoh, and all
his household. 23Then He brought us out
from there, that He might bring us in, to
give us the land of which He swore to our
fathers. 24And the LORD commanded us
to observe all these statutes, [a]to fear the
LORD our God, [b]for our good always, that
[c]He might preserve us alive, as *it is* this day.

6:2 [b] Deut. 4:40 6:3 [a] Deut. 7:13 [b] Gen. 22:17 [c] Ex. 3:8, 17 [1] Exodus 3:8 6:4 [a] Deut. 4:35; Mark 12:29; John 17:3; [1 Cor. 8:4, 6] [1] Or *The LORD is our God, the LORD alone* (that is, the only one) 6:5 [a] Matt. 22:37; Mark 12:30; Luke 10:27 [b] 2 Kin. 23:25 6:6 [a] Deut. 11:18–20; Ps. 119:11, 98 6:7 [a] Deut. 4:9; 11:19; [Eph. 6:4] 6:8 [a] Ex. 12:14; 13:9, 16; Deut. 11:18; Prov. 3:3; 6:21; 7:3 6:9 [a] Deut. 11:20; Is. 57:8 6:10 [a] Deut. 9:1; 19:1; Josh. 24:13; Ps. 105:44 6:11 [a] Deut. 8:10; 11:15; 14:29 6:12 [a] Deut. 8:11–18 6:13 [a] Deut. 13:4; Matt. 4:10; Luke 4:8 [b] Deut. 5:11; [Is. 45:23; Jer. 4:2] 6:14 [a] Deut. 13:7 6:15 [a] Ex. 20:5; Deut. 4:24 [b] Ex. 33:3 6:16 [a] Matt. 4:7; Luke 4:12 [b] [1 Cor. 10:9] 6:17 [a] Deut. 11:22; Ps. 119:4 6:18 [a] Ex. 15:26; Deut. 8:7–10 6:19 [a] Num. 33:52, 53 6:20 [a] Ex. 13:8, 14 6:21 [a] Ex. 13:3 6:24 [a] Deut. 6:2 [b] Deut. 10:12, 13; Job 35:7, 8; Jer. 32:39 [c] Deut. 4:1

25Then [a]it will be righteousness for us, if we
are careful to observe all these commandments before the LORD our God, as He has
commanded us.'

A Chosen People
(Ex. 34:10–16)

7 "When the LORD your God brings you
into the land which you go to [a]possess,
and has cast out many [b]nations before you,
[c]the Hittites and the Girgashites and the
Amorites and the Canaanites and the Perizzites and the Hivites and the Jebusites,
seven nations greater and mightier than
you, 2and when the LORD your God delivers
[a]them over to you, you shall conquer them
and utterly destroy them. [b]You shall make
no covenant with them nor show mercy
to them. 3[a]Nor shall you make marriages
with them. You shall not give your daughter to their son, nor take their daughter for
your son. 4For they will turn your sons away
from following Me, to serve other gods;
[a]so the anger of the LORD will be aroused
against you and destroy you suddenly. 5But
thus you shall deal with them: you shall
[a]destroy their altars, and break down their
sacred pillars, and cut down their wooden
images,[1] and burn their carved images with
fire.

6"For you *are* a holy people to the LORD
your God; [a]the LORD your God has chosen
you to be a people for Himself, a special
treasure above all the peoples on the face
of the earth. 7The LORD did not set His [a]love
on you nor choose you because you were
more in number than any other people,
for you were [b]the least of all peoples; 8but
[a]because the LORD loves you, and because
He would keep [b]the oath which He swore
to your fathers, [c]the LORD has brought you
out with a mighty hand, and redeemed you
from the house of bondage, from the hand
of Pharaoh king of Egypt.

9"Therefore know that the LORD your
God, He *is* God, [a]the faithful God [b]who keeps
covenant and mercy for a thousand generations with those who love Him and keep
His commandments; 10and He repays those
who hate Him to their face, to destroy them.
He will not be [a]slack with him who hates
Him; He will repay him to his face. 11There-
fore you shall keep the commandment, the
statutes, and the judgments which I command you today, to observe them.

Blessings of Obedience
(Lev. 26:1–13; Deut. 28:1–14)

12"Then it shall come to pass, because
you listen to these judgments, and keep
and do them, that the LORD your God will
keep with you the covenant and the mercy
which He swore to your fathers. 13And He
will [a]love you and bless you and multiply
you; [b]He will also bless the fruit of your
womb and the fruit of your land, your grain
and your new wine and your oil, the increase of your cattle and the offspring of
your flock, in the land of which He swore
to your fathers to give you. 14You shall be
blessed above all peoples; there shall not
be a male or female [a]barren among you or
among your livestock. 15And the LORD will
take away from you all sickness, and will afflict you with none of the [a]terrible diseases
of Egypt which you have known, but will
lay *them* on all those who hate you. 16Also
you shall destroy all the peoples whom
the LORD your God delivers over to you;
your eye shall have no pity on them; nor
shall you serve their gods, for that *will* [a]*be*
a snare to you.

17"If you should say in your heart, 'These
nations are greater than I; how can I dispossess them?'— 18you shall not be afraid
of them, *but* you shall [a]remember well what
the LORD your God did to Pharaoh and to
all Egypt: 19[a]the great trials which your eyes
saw, the signs and the wonders, the mighty
hand and the outstretched arm, by which
the LORD your God brought you out. So
shall the LORD your God do to all the peoples of whom you are afraid. 20[a]Moreover
the LORD your God will send the hornet
among them until those who are left, who
hide themselves from you, are destroyed.

6:25 [a] Deut. 24:13; [Rom. 10:3, 5] 7:1 [a] Deut. 6:10 [b] Gen. 15:19–21 [c] Ex. 33:2 7:2 [a] Num. 31:17; Deut. 20:16–18 [b] Ex. 23:32, 33; Josh. 2:14 7:3 [a] Ex. 34:15, 16; Josh. 23:12; 1 Kin. 11:2; Ezra 9:2 7:4 [a] Deut. 6:15 7:5 [a] Ex. 23:24; 34:13; Deut. 12:3 [1] Hebrew *Asherim,* Canaanite deities 7:6 [a] Ex. 19:5, 6; Amos 3:2; 1 Pet. 2:9 7:7 [a] Deut. 4:37 [b] Deut. 10:22 7:8 [a] Deut. 10:15 [b] Luke 1:55, 72, 73 [c] Ex. 13:3, 14 7:9 [a] 1 Cor. 1:9; 2 Thess. 3:3; 2 Tim. 2:13 [b] Ex. 20:6; Deut. 5:10; Neh. 1:5; Dan. 9:4 7:10 [a] [2 Pet. 3:9, 10] 7:13 [a] Ps. 146:8; Prov. 15:9; John 14:21 [b] Deut. 28:4 7:14 [a] Ex. 23:26 7:15 [a] Ex. 9:14; 15:26; Deut. 28:27, 60 7:16 [a] Ex. 23:33; Judg. 8:27; Ps. 106:36 7:18 [a] Ps. 105:5 7:19 [a] Deut. 4:34; 29:3 7:20 [a] Ex. 23:28; Josh. 24:12

21You shall not be terrified of them; for the
LORD your God, the great and awesome
God, *is* among you. 22And the LORD your
God will drive out those nations before you
[a]little by little; you will be unable to destroy
them at once, lest the beasts of the field
become *too* numerous for you. 23But the
LORD your God will deliver them over to
you, and will inflict defeat upon them until
they are destroyed. 24And [a]He will deliver
their kings into your hand, and you will destroy their name from under heaven; [b]no
one shall be able to stand against you until
you have destroyed them. 25You shall burn
the carved images of their gods with fire;
you shall not [a]covet the silver or gold *that*
is on them, nor take *it* for yourselves, lest
you be snared by it; for it *is* an abomination to the LORD your God. 26Nor shall you
bring an abomination into your house, lest
you be doomed to destruction like it. You
shall utterly detest it and utterly abhor it,
[a]for it *is* an accursed thing.

Remember the LORD Your God

8 "Every commandment which I command you today [a]you must be careful
to observe, that you may live and [b]multi-
ply, and go in and possess the land of which
the LORD swore to your fathers. 2And you
shall remember that the LORD your God
[a]led you all the way these forty years in the
wilderness, to humble you *and* [b]test you, [c]to
know what *was* in your heart, whether you
would keep His commandments or not. 3So
He humbled you, [a]allowed you to hunger,
and [b]fed you with manna which you did not
know nor did your fathers know, that He
might make you know that man shall [c]not
live by bread alone; but man lives by every
word that proceeds from the mouth of the
LORD. 4[a]Your garments did not wear out
on you, nor did your foot swell these forty
years. 5[a]You should know in your heart that
as a man chastens his son, *so* the LORD your
God chastens you.

6"Therefore you shall keep the commandments of the LORD your God, [a]to walk
in His ways and to fear Him. 7For the LORD
your God is bringing you into a good land,
[a]a land of brooks of water, of fountains and
springs, that flow out of valleys and hills;
8a land of wheat and barley, of vines and
fig trees and pomegranates, a land of olive
oil and honey; 9a land in which you will eat
bread without scarcity, in which you will
lack nothing; a land whose stones *are* iron
and out of whose hills you can dig copper.
10[a]When you have eaten and are full, then
you shall bless the LORD your God for the
good land which He has given you.

11"Beware that you do not forget the
LORD your God by not keeping His commandments, His judgments, and His
statutes which I command you today,
12[a]lest—*when* you have eaten and are full,
and have built beautiful houses and dwell
in them; 13and *when* your herds and your
flocks multiply, and your silver and your
gold are multiplied, and all that you have
is multiplied; 14[a]when your heart is lifted
up, and you [b]forget the LORD your God
who brought you out of the land of Egypt,
from the house of bondage; 15who [a]led you
through that great and terrible wilderness,
[b]*in which were* fiery serpents and scorpions and thirsty land where there was no
water; [c]who brought water for you out of
the flinty rock; 16who fed you in the wilderness with [a]manna, which your fathers
did not know, that He might humble you
and that He might test you, [b]to do you good
in the end— 17then you say in your heart,
'My power and the might of my hand have
gained me this wealth.'

18"And you shall remember the LORD
your God, [a]for *it is* He who gives you power
to get wealth, [b]that He may establish His
covenant which He swore to your fathers,
as *it is* this day. 19Then it shall be, if you by
any means forget the LORD your God, and
follow other gods, and serve them and worship them, [a]I testify against you this day
that you shall surely perish. 20As the nations which the LORD destroys before you,
[a]so you shall perish, because you would

7:22 [a] Ex. 23:29, 30 **7:24** [a] Josh. 10:24, 42; 12:1–24 [b] Josh. 23:9 **7:25** [a] Prov. 23:6 **7:26** [a] Deut. 13:17 **8:1** [a] Deut. 4:1; 6:24 [b] Deut. 30:16 **8:2** [a] Deut. 1:3; 2:7; 29:5; Ps. 136:16; Amos 2:10 [b] Ex. 16:4 [c] [John 2:25] **8:3** [a] Ex. 16:2, 3 [b] Ex. 16:12, 14, 35 [c] Matt. 4:4; Luke 4:4 **8:4** [a] Deut. 29:5; Neh. 9:21 **8:5** [a] 2 Sam. 7:14; Ps. 89:30–33; Prov. 3:11, 12; Heb. 12:5–11; Rev. 3:19 **8:6** [a] [Deut. 5:33] **8:7** [a] Deut. 11:9–12; Jer. 2:7 **8:10** [a] Deut. 6:11, 12 **8:12** [a] Deut. 28:47; Prov. 30:9; Hos. 13:6 **8:14** [a] 1 Cor. 4:7 [b] Deut. 8:11; Ps. 106:21 **8:15** [a] Is. 63:12–14 [b] Num. 21:6 [c] Ex. 17:6; Num. 20:11 **8:16** [a] Ex. 16:15 [b] Jer. 24:5, 6; [Heb. 12:11] **8:18** [a] Prov. 10:22; Hos. 2:8 [b] Deut. 7:8, 12 **8:19** [a] Deut. 4:26; 30:18 **8:20** [a] [Dan. 9:11, 12]

not be obedient to the voice of the LORD
your God.

Israel's Rebellions Reviewed
(Ex. 32:1–35)

9 “Hear, O Israel: You *are* to cross over the
Jordan today, and go in to dispossess
nations greater and mightier than yourself,
cities great and fortified up to heaven, 2 a
people great and tall, the [a]descendants of
the Anakim, whom you know, and *of whom*
you heard *it said,* ‘Who can stand before the
descendants of Anak?’ 3 Therefore understand today that the LORD your God *is* He
who [a]goes over before you *as* a [b]consuming
fire. [c]He will destroy them and bring them
down before you; [d]so you shall drive them
out and destroy them quickly, as the LORD
has said to you.

4[a]“Do not think in your heart, after the
LORD your God has cast them out before
you, saying, ‘Because of my righteousness
the LORD has brought me in to possess this
land’; but *it is* [b]because of the wickedness
of these nations *that* the LORD is driving
them out from before you. 5[a]*It is* not because of your righteousness or the uprightness of your heart *that* you go in to possess
their land, but because of the wickedness
of these nations *that* the LORD your God
drives them out from before you, and that
He may fulfill the [b]word which the LORD
swore to your fathers, to Abraham, Isaac,
and Jacob. 6 Therefore understand that the
LORD your God is not giving you this good
land to possess because of your righteousness, for you *are* a [a]stiff-necked people.

7“Remember! Do not forget how you
[a]provoked the LORD your God to wrath in
the wilderness. [b]From the day that you departed from the land of Egypt until you
came to this place, you have been rebellious against the LORD. 8 Also [a]in Horeb you
provoked the LORD to wrath, so that the
LORD was angry *enough* with you to have
destroyed you. 9[a]When I went up into the
mountain to receive the tablets of stone,
the tablets of the covenant which the LORD
made with you, then I stayed on the mountain forty days and [b]forty nights. I neither
ate bread nor drank water. 10[a]Then the
LORD delivered to me two tablets of stone
written with the finger of God, and on them
were all the words which the LORD had spoken to you on the mountain from the midst
of the fire [b]in the day of the assembly. 11 And
it came to pass, at the end of forty days and
forty nights, *that* the LORD gave me the two
tablets of stone, the tablets of the covenant.

12“Then the LORD said to me, [a]‘Arise, go
down quickly from here, for your people
whom you brought out of Egypt have acted
corruptly; they have [b]quickly turned aside
from the way which I commanded them;
they have made themselves a molded image.’

13“Furthermore [a]the LORD spoke to me,
saying, ‘I have seen this people, and indeed
[b]they are a stiff-necked people. 14[a]Let Me
alone, that I may destroy them and [b]blot
out their name from under heaven; [c]and
I will make of you a nation mightier and
greater than they.’

15[a]“So I turned and came down from the
mountain, and [b]the mountain burned with
fire; and the two tablets of the covenant
were in my two hands. 16 And [a]I looked,
and behold, you had sinned against the
LORD your God—had made for yourselves a
molded calf! You had turned aside quickly
from the way which the LORD had commanded you. 17 Then I took the two tablets
and threw them out of my two hands and
[a]broke them before your eyes. 18 And I [a]fell
down before the LORD, as at the first, forty
days and forty nights; I neither ate bread
nor drank water, because of all your sin
which you committed in doing wickedly
in the sight of the LORD, to provoke Him
to anger. 19[a]For I was afraid of the anger
and hot displeasure with which the LORD
was angry with you, to destroy you. [b]But
the LORD listened to me at that time also.
20 And the LORD was very angry with Aaron
and would have destroyed him; so I prayed
for Aaron also at the same time. 21 Then I

9:2 [a] Num. 13:22, 28, 33; Josh. 11:21, 22 9:3 [a] Deut. 1:33; 31:3; Josh. 3:11; 5:14; John 10:4 [b] Deut. 4:24; Heb. 12:29 [c] Deut. 7:24 [d] Ex. 23:31 9:4 [a] Deut. 8:17; [Rom. 11:6, 20; 1 Cor. 4:4, 7] [b] Gen. 15:16; Lev. 18:3, 24–30; Deut. 12:31; 18:9–14 9:5 [a] [Titus 3:5] [b] Gen. 50:24 9:6 [a] Ex. 34:9; Deut. 31:27 9:7 [a] Num. 14:22 [b] Ex. 14:11 9:8 [a] Ex. 32:1–8; Ps. 106:19 9:9 [a] Ex. 24:12, 15; Deut. 5:2–22 [b] Ex. 24:18 9:10 [a] Ex. 31:18; Deut. 4:13 [b] Ex. 19:17 9:12 [a] Ex. 32:7, 8 [b] Deut. 31:29 9:13 [a] Ex. 32:9 [b] Deut. 9:6 9:14 [a] Ex. 32:10 [b] Deut. 29:20 [c] Num. 14:12 9:15 [a] Ex. 32:15–19 [b] Ex. 19:18 9:16 [a] Ex. 32:19 9:17 [a] Ex. 32:19 9:18 [a] Ex. 34:28; Ps. 106:23 9:19 [a] Ex. 32:10, 11; Heb. 12:21 [b] Ex. 32:14

took your sin, the calf which you had made,
and burned it with fire and crushed it *and*
ground *it* very small, until it was as fine as
dust; and I [a]threw its dust into the brook
that descended from the mountain.
22"Also at [a]Taberah and [b]Massah and
[c]Kibroth Hattaavah you provoked the LORD
to wrath. 23Likewise, [a]when the LORD sent
you from Kadesh Barnea, saying, 'Go up
and possess the land which I have given
you,' then you rebelled against the commandment of the LORD your God, and [b]you
did not believe Him nor obey His voice.
24[a]You have been rebellious against the
LORD from the day that I knew you.
25[a]"Thus I prostrated myself before the
LORD; forty days and forty nights I kept
prostrating myself, because the LORD had
said He would destroy you. 26Therefore I
prayed to the LORD, and said: 'O Lord GOD,
do not destroy Your people and [a]Your inheritance whom You have redeemed
through Your greatness, whom You have
brought out of Egypt with a mighty hand.
27Remember Your servants, Abraham,
Isaac, and Jacob; do not look on the stubbornness of this people, or on their wickedness or their sin, 28lest the land from
which You brought us should say, "Because
the LORD was not able to bring them to the
land which He promised them, and because
He hated them, He has brought them out to
kill them in the wilderness." 29Yet they *are*
Your people and Your inheritance, whom
You brought out by Your mighty power and
by Your outstretched arm.'

The Second Pair of Tablets
(Ex. 34:1–9)

10 "At that time the LORD said to me, 'Hew
for yourself two tablets of stone like
the first, and come up to Me on the mountain
and make yourself an [a]ark of wood. 2And I
will write on the tablets the words that were
on the first tablets, which you broke; and
[a]you shall put them in the ark.'
3"So I made an ark of acacia wood,
hewed two tablets of stone like the first,
and went up the mountain, having the two
tablets in my hand. 4And He wrote on the
tablets according to the first writing, the
Ten Commandments, [a]which the LORD had
spoken to you in the mountain from the
midst of the fire in the day of the assembly; and the LORD gave them to me. 5Then
I turned and [a]came down from the mountain, and [b]put the tablets in the ark which
I had made; [c]and there they are, just as the
LORD commanded me."
6(Now the children of Israel journeyed
from the wells of Bene Jaakan to Mose-
rah, where Aaron [a]died, and where he was
buried; and Eleazar his son ministered as
priest in his stead. 7[a]From there they journeyed to Gudgodah, and from Gudgodah
to Jotbathah, a land of rivers of water. 8At
that time [a]the LORD separated the tribe of
Levi [b]to bear the ark of the covenant of the
LORD, [c]to stand before the LORD to minister
to Him and [d]to bless in His name, to this
day. 9[a]Therefore Levi has no portion nor
inheritance with his brethren; the LORD *is*
his inheritance, just as the LORD your God
promised him.)
10"As at the first time, [a]I stayed in the
mountain forty days and forty nights; [b]the
LORD also heard me at that time, *and* the
LORD chose not to destroy you. 11[a]Then
the LORD said to me, 'Arise, begin *your* journey before the people, that they may go in
and possess the land which I swore to their
fathers to give them.'

The Essence of the Law

12"And now, Israel, [a]what does the LORD
your God require of you, but to fear the
LORD your God, to walk in all His ways
and to [b]love Him, to serve the LORD your
God with all your heart and with all your
soul, 13*and* to keep the commandments of
the LORD and His statutes which I command you today [a]for your good? 14Indeed
heaven and the highest heavens belong to
the [a]LORD your God, *also* the earth with all
that *is* in it. 15The LORD delighted only in
your fathers, to love them; and He chose

9:21 [a] Ex. 32:20 9:22 [a] Num. 11:1, 3 [b] Ex. 17:7 [c] Num. 11:4, 34 9:23 [a] Num. 13:3 [b] Ps. 106:24, 25 9:24 [a] Deut. 9:7; 31:27 9:25 [a] Deut. 9:18 9:26 [a] Deut. 32:9 10:1 [a] Ex. 25:10 10:2 [a] Ex. 25:16, 21 10:4 [a] Ex. 20:1; 34:28 10:5 [a] Ex. 34:29 [b] Ex. 40:20 [c] 1 Kin. 8:9 10:6 [a] Num. 20:25–28; 33:38 10:7 [a] Num. 33:32–34 10:8 [a] Num. 3:6 [b] Num. 4:5, 15; 10:21 [c] Deut. 18:5 [d] Num. 6:23 10:9 [a] Num. 18:20, 24; Deut. 18:1, 2; Ezek. 44:28 10:10 [a] Ex. 34:28; Deut. 9:18 [b] Ex. 32:14 10:11 [a] Ex. 33:1 10:12 [a] Mic. 6:8 [b] Deut. 6:5; Matt. 22:37; 1 Tim. 1:5 10:13 [a] Deut. 6:24 10:14 [a] [Neh. 9:6; Ps. 68:33; 115:16]

their descendants after them, you above all peoples, as *it is* this day. 16 Therefore circumcise the foreskin of your [a]heart, and be [b]stiff-necked no longer. 17 For the LORD your God *is* [a]God of gods and [b]Lord of lords, the great God, [c]mighty and awesome, who [d]shows no partiality nor takes a bribe. 18 [a]He administers justice for the fatherless and the widow, and loves the stranger, giving him food and clothing. 19 Therefore love the stranger, for you were strangers in the land of Egypt. 20 [a]You shall fear the LORD your God; you shall serve Him, and to Him you shall hold fast, and take oaths in His name. 21 He *is* your praise, and He *is* your God, who has done for you these great and awesome things which your eyes have seen. 22 Your fathers went down to Egypt with seventy persons, and now the LORD your God has made you as the stars of heaven in multitude.

Love and Obedience Rewarded

11 "Therefore you shall love the LORD your God, and keep His charge, His statutes, His judgments, and His commandments always. 2 Know today that *I do* not *speak* with your children, who have not known and who have not seen the chastening of the LORD your God, His greatness and His mighty hand and His outstretched arm— 3 His signs and His acts which He did in the midst of Egypt, to Pharaoh king of Egypt, and to all his land; 4 what He did to the army of Egypt, to their horses and their chariots: [a]how He made the waters of the Red Sea overflow them as they pursued you, and *how* the LORD has destroyed them to this day; 5 what He did for you in the wilderness until you came to this place; 6 and [a]what He did to Dathan and Abiram the sons of Eliab, the son of Reuben: how the earth opened its mouth and swallowed them up, their households, their tents, and all the substance that *was* in their possession, in the midst of all Israel— 7 but your eyes have [a]seen every great act of the LORD which He did.

8 "Therefore you shall keep every commandment which I command you today, that you may [a]be strong, and go in and possess the land which you cross over to possess, 9 and [a]that you may prolong *your* days in the land [b]which the LORD swore to give your fathers, to them and their descendants, [c]'a land flowing with milk and honey.'[1] 10 For the land which you go to possess *is* not like the land of Egypt from which you have come, where you sowed your seed and watered *it* by foot, as a vegetable garden; 11 [a]but the land which you cross over to possess *is* a land of hills and valleys, which drinks water from the rain of heaven, 12 a land for which the LORD your God cares; [a]the eyes of the LORD your God *are* always on it, from the beginning of the year to the very end of the year.

13 'And it shall be that if you earnestly obey My commandments which I command you today, to love the LORD your God and serve Him with all your heart and with all your soul, 14 then [a]I[1] will give *you* the rain for your land in its season, [b]the early rain and the latter rain, that you may gather in your grain, your new wine, and your oil. 15 [a]And I will send grass in your fields for your livestock, that you may [b]eat and be filled.' 16 Take heed to yourselves, [a]lest your heart be deceived, and you turn aside and [b]serve other gods and worship them, 17 lest [a]the LORD's anger be aroused against you, and He [b]shut up the heavens so that there be no rain, and the land yield no produce, and [c]you perish quickly from the good land which the LORD is giving you.

18 "Therefore [a]you shall lay up these words of mine in your heart and in your [b]soul, and [c]bind them as a sign on your hand, and they shall be as frontlets between your eyes. 19 [a]You shall teach them to your children, speaking of them when you sit in your house, when you walk by the way, when you lie down, and when you rise up. 20 [a]And you shall write them on the doorposts of your house and on your

---

10:16 [a] Lev. 26:41; Deut. 30:6; Jer. 4:4; Rom. 2:28, 29 [b] Deut. 9:6, 13 10:17 [a] Deut. 4:35, 39; Is. 44:8; 46:9; Dan. 2:47; 1 Cor. 8:5, 6 [b] Rev. 19:16 [c] Deut. 7:21 [d] Acts 10:34 10:18 [a] Ex. 22:22–24; Ps. 68:5; 146:9 10:20 [a] Matt. 4:10 11:4 [a] Ex. 14:28; Ps. 106:11 11:6 [a] Num. 16:1–35; Ps. 106:16–18 11:7 [a] Deut. 10:21; 29:2 11:8 [a] Deut. 31:6, 7, 23; Josh. 1:6, 7 11:9 [a] Deut. 4:40; 5:16, 33; 6:2; Prov. 10:27 [b] Deut. 9:5 [c] Ex. 3:8 [1] Exodus 3:8 11:11 [a] Deut. 8:7 11:12 [a] 1 Kin. 9:3 11:14 [a] Lev. 26:4; Deut. 28:12 [b] Joel 2:23; James 5:7 [1] Following Masoretic Text and Targum; Samaritan Pentateuch, Septuagint, and Vulgate read *He*. 11:15 [a] Ps. 104:14 [b] Deut. 6:11; Joel 2:19 11:16 [a] Deut. 29:18; Job 31:27 [b] Deut. 8:19 11:17 [a] Deut. 6:15; 9:19 [b] Deut. 28:24; 1 Kin. 8:35; 2 Chr. 6:26; 7:13 [c] Deut. 4:26; 2 Chr. 36:14–20 11:18 [a] Deut. 6:6–9 [b] Ps. 119:2, 34 [c] Deut. 6:8 11:19 [a] Deut. 4:9, 10; 6:7; Prov. 22:6 11:20 [a] Deut. 6:9

gates, 21that [a]your days and the days of your
children may be multiplied in the land of
which the LORD swore to your fathers to
give them, like [b]the days of the heavens
above the earth.
22"For if [a]you carefully keep all these
commandments which I command you
to do—to love the LORD your God, to walk
in all His ways, and [b]to hold fast to Him—
23then the LORD will [a]drive out all these
nations from before you, and you will [b]dis-
possess greater and mightier nations than
yourselves. 24[a]Every place on which the sole
of your foot treads shall be yours: [b]from the
wilderness and Lebanon, from the river, the
River Euphrates, even to the Western Sea,[1]
shall be your territory. 25No man shall be
able to [a]stand against you; the LORD your
God will put the [b]dread of you and the fear
of you upon all the land where you tread,
just as He has said to you.
26[a]"Behold, I set before you today a
blessing and a curse: 27[a]the blessing, if you
obey the commandments of the LORD your
God which I command you today; 28and the
[a]curse, if you do not obey the commandments of the LORD your God, but turn aside
from the way which I command you today,
to go after other gods which you have not
known. 29Now it shall be, when the LORD
your God has brought you into the land
which you go to possess, that you shall put
the [a]blessing on Mount Gerizim and the
[b]curse on Mount Ebal. 30*Are* they not on

TRUST IN HIS WORD

INHALE

Name me a promise in Scripture, and I can share why it has not come true in my life. Yet, I am still holding on—trying to, anyway. But it's really hard to stand on His Word. It just feels like so much is closing in on me. Every time I read the Word and feel better, something else happens. It is always something. And when I say "something," I'm not talking about anything good. What am I supposed to do? How do I trust God when He's failed me time and time again? Does He really stand on what is in the Bible?

EXHALE

God has made it abundantly clear that His Word will never fail. That is so significant because God's Word represents His very nature and character. That is why it is so important that we trust in His Word.

God's promises are often without explanation and always without apology. You see, it is not that His promises are bad or untrue. It is so much bigger than that. The question is not *if* God will keep His promises, but *how*. We often simply cannot see or understand what God is up to in our lives. God's mission for our lives is to get us in on His plan and schedule, not for us to get Him in on ours. Deuteronomy 11:13–14 says, "And it shall be that if you earnestly obey My commandments which I command you today, to love the LORD your God and serve Him with all your heart and with all your soul, then I will give you the rain for your land in its season, the early rain and the latter rain, that you may gather in your grain, your new wine, and your oil." Notice the word "will." Not "might." Not "could." "Will." "I will give you the rain."

God wanted the Israelites not only to obey but to obey in confidence. He wants us to do the same. We can see His faithfulness to us, but even if we cannot, we can see it in others. God has never failed in anything. That should tell us everything we need to know about God and His promises. Remember what God has done for you and know He can do it again!

11:21 [a] Deut. 4:40 [b] Ps. 72:5; 89:29; Prov. 3:2; 4:10; 9:11 11:22 [a] Deut. 11:1 [b] Deut. 10:20 11:23 [a] Deut. 4:38 [b] Deut. 9:1 11:24 [a] Josh. 1:3; 14:9 [b] Gen. 15:18; Ex. 23:31; Deut. 1:7, 8 [1] That is, the Mediterranean 11:25 [a] Deut. 7:24 [b] Ex. 23:27; Deut. 2:25; Josh. 2:9–11 11:26 [a] Deut. 30:1, 15, 19 11:27 [a] Deut. 28:1–14 11:28 [a] Deut. 28:15–68 11:29 [a] Deut. 27:12, 13; Josh. 8:33 [b] Deut. 27:13–26

the other side of the Jordan, toward the setting sun, in the land of the Canaanites who
dwell in the plain opposite Gilgal, [a]beside
the terebinth trees of Moreh? 31For you will
cross over the Jordan and go in to possess
the land which the LORD your God is giving you, and you will possess it and dwell
in it. 32And you shall be careful to observe
all the statutes and judgments which I set
before you today.

A Prescribed Place of Worship

12 "These [a]*are* the statutes and judgments which you shall be careful to
observe in the land which the LORD God of
your fathers is giving you to possess, [b]all
the days that you live on the earth. 2[a]You
shall utterly destroy all the places where the
nations which you shall dispossess served
their gods, [b]on the high mountains and on
the hills and under every green tree. 3And
[a]you shall destroy their altars, break their
sacred pillars, and burn their wooden images with fire; you shall cut down the carved
images of their gods and destroy their
names from that place. 4You shall not [a]wor-
ship the LORD your God *with* such *things*.

5"But you shall seek the [a]place where
the LORD your God chooses, out of all your
tribes, to put His name for His [b]dwelling
place; and there you shall go. 6[a]There you
shall take your burnt offerings, your sacrifices, your tithes, the heave offerings of
your hand, your vowed offerings, your freewill offerings, and the [b]firstborn of your
herds and flocks. 7And [a]there you shall eat
before the LORD your God, and [b]you shall
rejoice in all to which you have put your
hand, you and your households, in which
the LORD your God has blessed you.

8"You shall not at all do as we are doing
here today—[a]every man doing whatever *is*
right in his own eyes— 9for as yet you have
not come to the [a]rest and the inheritance
which the LORD your God is giving you.
10But *when* you cross over the Jordan and
dwell in the land which the LORD your God
is giving you to inherit, and He gives you
[a]rest from all your enemies round about,
so that you dwell in safety, 11then there
will be the place where the LORD your God
chooses to make His name abide. There
you shall bring all that I command you:
your burnt offerings, your sacrifices, your
tithes, the heave offerings of your hand, and
all your choice offerings which you vow to
the LORD. 12And [a]you shall rejoice before the
LORD your God, you and your sons and your
daughters, your male and female servants,
and the [b]Levite who *is* within your gates,
since he has no portion nor inheritance
with you. 13Take heed to yourself that you do
not offer your burnt offerings in every place
that you see; 14but in the place which the
LORD chooses, in one of your tribes, there
you shall offer your burnt offerings, and
there you shall do all that I command you.

15"However, [a]you may slaughter and eat
meat within all your gates, whatever your
heart desires, according to the blessing of
the LORD your God which He has given you;
[b]the unclean and the clean may eat of it, [c]of
the gazelle and the deer alike. 16[a]Only you
shall not eat the blood; you shall pour it on
the earth like water. 17You may not eat within
your gates the tithe of your grain or your
new wine or your oil, of the firstborn of your
herd or your flock, of any of your offerings
which you vow, of your freewill offerings, or
of the heave offering of your hand. 18But you
must eat them before the LORD your God in
the place which the LORD your God chooses,
you and your son and your daughter, your
male servant and your female servant, and
the Levite who *is* within your gates; and you
shall rejoice before the LORD your God in all
to which you put your hands. 19Take heed to
yourself that you do not forsake the Levite
as long as you live in your land.

20"When the LORD your God [a]enlarges
your border as He has promised you, and
you say, 'Let me eat meat,' because you long
to eat meat, you may eat as much meat as
your heart desires. 21If the place where the
LORD your God chooses to put His name
is too far from [a]you, then you may slaughter from your herd and from your flock
which the LORD has given you, just as I have

11:30 [a] Gen. 12:6 12:1 [a] Deut. 6:1 [b] Deut. 4:9, 10; 1 Kin. 8:40 12:2 [a] Ex. 34:13 [b] 2 Kin. 16:4; 17:10, 11 12:3 [a] Num. 33:52; Deut. 7:5; Judg. 2:2 12:4 [a] Deut. 12:31 12:5 [a] Ex. 20:24 [b] Ex. 15:13; 1 Sam. 2:29 12:6 [a] Lev. 17:3, 4 [b] Deut. 14:23 12:7 [a] Deut. 14:26 [b] Deut. 12:12, 18 12:8 [a] Judg. 17:6; 21:25 12:9 [a] Deut. 3:20; 25:19; Ps. 95:11 12:10 [a] Josh. 11:23 12:12 [a] Deut. 12:18; 26:11 [b] Deut. 10:9; 14:29 12:15 [a] Deut. 12:21 [b] Deut. 12:22 [c] Deut. 14:5 12:16 [a] Gen. 9:4; Lev. 7:26; 17:10–12; 1 Sam. 14:33; Acts 15:20, 29 12:20 [a] Gen. 15:18; Ex. 34:24; Deut. 11:24; 19:8 12:21 [a] Deut. 14:24

commanded you, and you may eat within
your gates as much as your heart desires.
22Just as the gazelle and the deer are eaten,
so you may eat them; the unclean and the
clean alike may eat them. 23Only be sure that
you do not eat the blood, [a]for the blood *is* the
life; you may not eat the life with the meat.
24You shall not eat it; you shall pour it on the
earth like water. 25You shall not eat it, [a]that
it may go well with you and your children
after you, [b]when you do *what is* right in the
sight of the LORD. 26Only the [a]holy things
which you have, and your vowed offerings,
you shall take and go to the place which the
LORD chooses. 27And [a]you shall offer your
burnt offerings, the meat and the blood,
on the altar of the LORD your God; and the
blood of your sacrifices shall be poured out
on the altar of the LORD your God, and you
shall eat the meat. 28Observe and obey all
these words which I command you, [a]that it
may go well with you and your children after you forever, when you do *what is* good
and right in the sight of the LORD your God.

Beware of False Gods

29"When [a]the LORD your God cuts off
from before you the nations which you go
to dispossess, and you displace them and
dwell in their land, 30take heed to yourself
that you are not ensnared to follow them,
after they are destroyed from before you,
and that you do not inquire after their gods,
saying, 'How did these nations serve their
gods? I also will do likewise.' 31[a]You shall
not worship the LORD your God in that way;
for every abomination to the LORD which
He hates they have done to their gods; for
[b]they burn even their sons and daughters
in the fire to their gods.

32"Whatever I command you, be careful
to observe it; [a]you shall not add to it nor
take away from it.

Punishment of Apostates

13 "If there arises among you a prophet
or a [a]dreamer of dreams, [b]and he
gives you a sign or a wonder, 2and [a]the sign
or the wonder comes to pass, of which he
spoke to you, saying, 'Let us go after other
gods'—which you have not known—'and
let us serve them,' 3you shall not listen to
the words of that prophet or that dreamer
of dreams, for the LORD your God [a]is testing you to know whether you love the LORD
your God with all your heart and with all
your soul. 4You shall [a]walk after the LORD
your God and fear Him, and keep His commandments and obey His voice; you shall
serve Him and [b]hold fast to Him. 5But [a]that
prophet or that dreamer of dreams shall be
put to death, because he has spoken in order to turn *you* away from the LORD your
God, who brought you out of the land of
Egypt and redeemed you from the house
of bondage, to entice you from the way in
which the LORD your God commanded you
to walk. [b]So you shall put away the evil from
your midst.

6[a]"If your brother, the son of your
mother, your son or your daughter, [b]the
wife of your bosom, or your friend [c]who is
as your own soul, secretly entices you, saying, 'Let us go and serve other gods,' which
you have not known, neither you nor your
fathers, 7of the gods of the people which *are*
all around you, near to you or far off from
you, from *one* end of the earth to the *other*
end of the earth, 8you shall [a]not consent
to him or listen to him, nor shall your eye
pity him, nor shall you spare him or conceal him; 9but you shall surely kill him;
your hand shall be first against him to put
him to [a]death, and afterward the hand of all
the people. 10And you shall stone him with
stones until he dies, because he sought to
entice you away from the LORD your God,
who brought you out of the land of Egypt,
from the house of bondage. 11So all Israel
shall hear and [a]fear, and not again do such
wickedness as this among you.

12[a]"If you hear someone in one of your
cities, which the LORD your God gives you
to dwell in, saying, 13'Corrupt men have
gone out from among you and enticed
the inhabitants of their city, saying, "Let

12:23 [a] Gen. 9:4; Lev. 17:10–14; Deut. 12:16 12:25 [a] Deut. 4:40; 6:18; Is. 3:10 [b] Ex. 15:26; 1 Kin. 11:38 12:26 [a] Num. 5:9, 10; 18:19 12:27 [a] Lev. 1:5, 9, 13, 17 12:28 [a] Deut. 12:25 12:29 [a] Ex. 23:23; Deut. 19:1; Josh. 23:4 12:31 [a] Lev. 18:3, 26, 30; 20:1, 2 [b] Deut. 18:10; Ps. 106:37; Jer. 32:35 12:32 [a] Deut. 4:2; 13:18; Josh. 1:7; Prov. 30:6; Rev. 22:18, 19 13:1 [a] Num. 12:6; Jer. 23:28; Zech. 10:2 [b] Matt. 24:24; Mark 13:22; 2 Thess. 2:9 13:2 [a] Deut. 18:22 13:3 [a] Ex. 20:20; Deut. 8:2, 16 13:4 [a] Deut. 10:12, 20; 2 Kin. 23:3 [b] Deut. 30:20 13:5 [a] Deut. 18:20; Jer. 14:15 [b] Deut. 17:5, 7; 1 Cor. 5:13 13:6 [a] Deut. 17:2 [b] Gen. 16:5 [c] 1 Sam. 18:1, 3 13:8 [a] Deut. 7:16; Prov. 1:10 13:9 [a] Lev. 24:14; Deut. 17:7 13:11 [a] Deut. 17:13 13:12 [a] Judg. 20:1–48

us go and serve other gods"'—which you
have not known— 14 then you shall inquire,
search out, and ask diligently. And *if it is* indeed true *and* certain *that* such an abomination was committed among you, 15 you
shall surely strike the inhabitants of that
city with the edge of the sword, utterly destroying it, all that is in it and its livestock—
with the edge of the sword. 16 And you shall
gather all its plunder into the middle of the
street, and completely [a]burn with fire the
city and all its plunder, for the LORD your
God. It shall be [b]a heap forever; it shall not
be built again. 17 [a]So none of the accursed
things shall remain in your hand, that the
LORD may [b]turn from the fierceness of His
anger and show you mercy, have compassion on you and multiply you, just as He
swore to your fathers, 18 because you have
listened to the voice of the LORD your God,
[a]to keep all His commandments which I
command you today, to do *what is* right in
the eyes of the LORD your God.

Improper Mourning

14 "You *are* [a]the children of the LORD
your God; [b]you shall not cut yourselves nor shave the front of your head for
the dead. 2 [a]For you *are* a holy people to the
LORD your God, and the LORD has chosen
you to be a people for Himself, a special
treasure above all the peoples who *are* on
the face of the earth.

Clean and Unclean Meat
(Lev. 11:1–47)

3 [a]"You shall not eat any detestable thing.
4 [a]These *are* the animals which you may eat:
the ox, the sheep, the goat, 5 the deer, the gazelle, the roe deer, the wild goat, the mountain goat,[1] the antelope, and the mountain
sheep. 6 And you may eat every animal with
cloven hooves, having the hoof split into
two parts, *and that* chews the cud, among
the animals. 7 Nevertheless, of those that
chew the cud or have cloven hooves, you
shall not eat, *such as* these: the camel, the
hare, and the rock hyrax; for they chew the
cud but do not have cloven hooves; they *are*
unclean for you. 8 Also the swine is unclean
for you, because it has cloven hooves, yet
does not *chew* the cud; you shall not eat
their flesh [a]or touch their dead carcasses.

9 [a]"These you may eat of all that *are* in
the waters: you may eat all that have fins
and scales. 10 And whatever does not have
fins and scales you shall not eat; it *is* unclean for you.

11 "All clean birds you may eat. 12 [a]But
these you shall not eat: the eagle, the vulture, the buzzard, 13 the red kite, the falcon,
and the kite after their kinds; 14 every raven
after its kind; 15 the ostrich, the short-eared
owl, the sea gull, and the hawk after their
kinds; 16 the little owl, the screech owl, the
white owl, 17 the jackdaw, the carrion vulture, the fisher owl, 18 the stork, the heron
after its kind, and the hoopoe and the bat.

19 "Also [a]every creeping thing that flies is
unclean for you; [b]they shall not be eaten.

20 "You may eat all clean birds.

21 [a]"You shall not eat anything that dies
of itself; you may give it to the alien who *is*
within your gates, that he may eat it, or you
may sell it to a foreigner; [b]for you *are* a holy
people to the LORD your God.

"[c]You shall not boil a young goat in its
mother's milk.

Tithing Principles

22 [a]"You shall truly tithe all the increase
of your grain that the field produces year by
year. 23 [a]And you shall eat before the LORD
your God, in the place where He chooses
to make His name abide, the tithe of your
grain and your new wine and your oil, of
[b]the firstborn of your herds and your flocks,
that you may learn to fear the LORD your
God always. 24 But if the journey is too long
for you, so that you are not able to carry
the tithe, or [a]if the place where the LORD
your God chooses to put His name is too
far from you, when the LORD your God has
blessed you, 25 then you shall exchange *it*
for money, take the money in your hand,
and go to the place which the LORD your
God chooses. 26 And you shall spend that
money for whatever your heart desires: for

13:16 [a] Josh. 6:24 [b] Josh. 8:28; Is. 17:1; 25:2; Jer. 49:2 13:17 [a] Josh. 6:18 [b] Josh. 7:26 13:18 [a] Deut. 12:25, 28, 32 14:1 [a] [Rom. 8:16; Gal. 3:26] [b] Lev. 19:28; 21:1–5 14:2 [a] Lev. 20:26; Deut. 7:6; [Rom. 12:1] 14:3 [a] Ezek. 4:14 14:4 [a] Lev. 11:2–45 14:5 [1] Or *addax* 14:8 [a] Lev. 11:26, 27 14:9 [a] Lev. 11:9 14:12 [a] Lev. 11:13 14:19 [a] Lev. 11:20 [b] Lev. 11:23 14:21 [a] Lev. 17:15; 22:8; Ezek. 4:14; 44:31 [b] Deut. 14:2 [c] Ex. 23:19; 34:26 14:22 [a] Lev. 27:30; Deut. 12:6, 17; Neh. 10:37 14:23 [a] Deut. 12:5–7 [b] Deut. 15:19, 20 14:24 [a] Deut. 12:5, 21

oxen or sheep, for wine or similar drink,
for whatever your heart desires; you shall
eat there before the LORD your God, and
you shall [a]rejoice, you and your household.
27 You shall not forsake the [a]Levite who *is*
within your gates, for he has no part nor
inheritance with you.

28 [a]"At the end of *every* third year you
shall bring out the [b]tithe of your produce of
that year and store *it* up within your gates.
29 And the Levite, because he has no portion
nor inheritance with you, and the stranger
and the fatherless and the widow who *are*
within your gates, may come and eat and
be satisfied, that the LORD your God may
bless you in all the work of your hand which
you do.

Debts Canceled Every Seven Years
(Ex. 21:1–11; Lev. 25:1–7)

15 "At the end of [a]*every* seven years you
shall grant a release *of debts.* 2 And
this *is* the form of the release: Every creditor who has lent *anything* to his neighbor
shall release *it;* he shall not require *it* of
his neighbor or his brother, because it is
called the LORD's release. 3 Of a foreigner
you may require *it;* but you shall give up
your claim to what is owed by your brother,
4 except when there may be no poor among
you; for the LORD will greatly [a]bless you in
the land which the LORD your God is giving
you to possess *as* an inheritance— 5 only
if you carefully obey the voice of the LORD
your God, to observe with care all these
commandments which I command you today. 6 For the LORD your God will bless you
just as He promised you; [a]you shall lend to
many nations, but you shall not borrow;
you shall reign over many nations, but they
shall not reign over you.

Generosity to the Poor

7 "If there is among you a poor man of
your brethren, within any of the gates in
your land which the LORD your God is giving you, [a]you shall not harden your heart
nor shut your hand from your poor brother,
8 but [a]you shall open your hand wide to him
and willingly lend him sufficient for his
need, whatever he needs. 9 Beware lest there
be a wicked thought in your heart, saying,
'The seventh year, the year of release, is at
hand,' and your [a]eye be evil against your
poor brother and you give him nothing,
and [b]he cry out to the LORD against you,
and [c]it become sin among you. 10 You shall
surely give to him, and [a]your heart should
not be grieved when you give to him, because [b]for this thing the LORD your God
will bless you in all your works and in all
to which you put your hand. 11 For [a]the poor
will never cease from the land; therefore I
command you, saying, 'You shall open your
hand wide to your brother, to your poor and
your needy, in your land.'

The Law Concerning Bondservants

12 [a]"If your brother, a Hebrew man, or a
Hebrew woman, is [b]sold to you and serves
you six years, then in the seventh year you
shall let him go free from you. 13 And when
you send him away free from you, you shall
not let him go away empty-handed; 14 you
shall supply him liberally from your flock,
from your threshing floor, and from your
winepress. *From what* the LORD your God
has [a]blessed you with, you shall give to him.
15 [a]You shall remember that you were a slave
in the land of Egypt, and the LORD your
God redeemed you; therefore I command
you this thing today. 16 And [a]if it happens
that he says to you, 'I will not go away from
you,' because he loves you and your house,
since he prospers with you, 17 then you shall
take an awl and thrust *it* through his ear to
the door, and he shall be your servant forever. Also to your female servant you shall
do likewise. 18 It shall not seem hard to you
when you send him away free from you; for
he has been worth [a]a double hired servant
in serving you six years. Then the LORD
your God will bless you in all that you do.

The Law Concerning Firstborn Animals

19 [a]"All the firstborn males that come
from your herd and your flock you shall
sanctify to the LORD your God; you shall

14:26 [a] Deut. 12:7 14:27 [a] Deut. 12:12 14:28 [a] Deut. 26:12; Amos 4:4 [b] Num. 18:21–24 15:1 [a] Ex. 21:2; 23:10, 11; Lev. 25:4; Jer. 34:14 15:4 [a] Deut. 7:13 15:6 [a] Deut. 28:12, 44 15:7 [a] Ex. 23:6; Lev. 25:35–37; Deut. 24:12–14; [1 John 3:17] 15:8 [a] Matt. 5:42; Gal. 2:10 15:9 [a] Deut. 28:54, 56 [b] Ex. 22:23; Deut. 24:15; Job 34:28; Ps. 12:5; James 5:4 [c] [Matt. 25:41, 42] 15:10 [a] 2 Cor. 9:5, 7 [b] Deut. 14:29; Ps. 41:1; Prov. 22:9 15:11 [a] Matt. 26:11; Mark 14:7; John 12:8 15:12 [a] Ex. 21:2–6; Jer. 34:14 [b] Lev. 25:39–46 15:14 [a] Prov. 10:22 15:15 [a] Deut. 5:15 15:16 [a] Ex. 21:5, 6 15:18 [a] Is. 16:14 15:19 [a] Ex. 13:2, 12

do no work with the firstborn of your
herd, nor shear the firstborn of your flock.
20[a]You and your household shall eat *it* before the LORD your God year by year in the
place which the LORD chooses. 21[a]But if
there is a defect in it, *if it is* lame or blind
or has any serious defect, you shall not
sacrifice it to the LORD your God. 22You
may eat it within your gates; [a]the unclean
and the clean *person* alike *may eat it,* as *if
it were* a gazelle or a deer. 23Only you shall
not eat its blood; you shall pour it on the
ground like water.

The Passover Reviewed
(Ex. 12:1–20; 23:14–19; 34:18–26)

16 “Observe the [a]month of Abib, and
keep the Passover to the LORD your
God, for [b]in the month of Abib the LORD
your God brought you out of Egypt by
night. 2Therefore you shall sacrifice the
Passover to the LORD your God, from the
flock and [a]the herd, in the [b]place where the
LORD chooses to put His name. 3You shall
eat no leavened bread with it; [a]seven days
you shall eat unleavened bread with it, *that
is,* the bread of affliction (for you came out
of the land of Egypt in haste), that you may
[b]remember the day in which you came out
of the land of Egypt all the days of your
life. 4[a]And no leaven shall be seen among
you in all your territory for seven days, nor
shall *any* of the meat which you sacrifice
the first day at twilight remain overnight
until [b]morning.
5“You may not sacrifice the Passover
within any of your gates which the LORD
your God gives you; 6but at the place where
the LORD your God chooses to make His
name abide, there you shall sacrifice the
Passover [a]at twilight, at the going down of
the sun, at the time you came out of Egypt.
7And you shall roast and eat *it* [a]in the place
which the LORD your God chooses, and in
the morning you shall turn and go to your
tents. 8Six days you shall eat unleavened
bread, and [a]on the seventh day there *shall
be* a sacred assembly to the LORD your God.
You shall do no work *on it.*

The Feast of Weeks Reviewed
(Ex. 34:22; Lev. 23:15–21; Num. 28:26–31)

9“You shall count seven weeks for yourself; begin to count the seven weeks from
the time you begin *to put* the sickle to the
grain. 10Then you shall keep the [a]Feast of
Weeks to the LORD your God with the tribute of a freewill offering from your hand,
which you shall give [b]as the LORD your God
blesses you. 11[a]You shall rejoice before the
LORD your God, you and your son and your
daughter, your male servant and your female servant, the Levite who *is* within your
gates, the stranger and the fatherless and
the widow who *are* among you, at the place
where the LORD your God chooses to make
His name abide. 12[a]And you shall remember that you were a slave in Egypt, and you
shall be careful to observe these statutes.

The Feast of Tabernacles Reviewed
(Lev. 23:33–43; Num. 29:12–40)

13[a]“You shall observe the Feast of Tabernacles seven days, when you have gathered from your threshing floor and from
your winepress. 14And [a]you shall rejoice
in your feast, you and your son and your
daughter, your male servant and your female servant and the Levite, the stranger
and the fatherless and the widow, who *are*
within your gates. 15[a]Seven days you shall
keep a sacred feast to the LORD your God
in the place which the LORD chooses, because the LORD your God will bless you in
all your produce and in all the work of your
hands, so that you surely rejoice.
16[a]“Three times a year all your males
shall appear before the LORD your God in
the place which He chooses: at the Feast of
Unleavened Bread, at the Feast of Weeks,
and at the Feast of Tabernacles; and [b]they
shall not appear before the LORD empty-
handed. 17Every man *shall give* as he is able,
[a]according to the blessing of the LORD your
God which He has given you.

Justice Must Be Administered

18“You shall appoint [a]judges and officers
in all your gates, which the LORD your God

15:20 [a] Lev. 7:15–18; Deut. 12:5; 14:23 15:21 [a] Lev. 22:19–25; Deut. 17:1 15:22 [a] Deut. 12:15, 16, 22 16:1 [a] Ex. 12:2 [b] Ex. 13:4
16:2 [a] Num. 28:19 [b] Deut. 12:5, 26; 15:20 16:3 [a] Num. 29:12 [b] Ex. 13:3; Deut. 4:9 16:4 [a] Ex. 13:7 [b] Num. 9:12 16:6 [a] Ex. 12:7–10
16:7 [a] 2 Kin. 23:23 16:8 [a] Ex. 12:16; 13:6; Lev. 23:8, 36 16:10 [a] Ex. 34:22; Lev. 23:15, 16; Num. 28:26 [b] 1 Cor. 16:2 16:11 [a] Deut. 16:14
16:12 [a] Deut. 15:15 16:13 [a] Ex. 23:16 16:14 [a] Neh. 8:9 16:15 [a] Lev. 23:39–41 16:16 [a] Ex. 23:14–17; 34:22–24
[b] Ex. 23:15 16:17 [a] Lev. 14:30, 31; Deut. 16:10 16:18 [a] Ex. 23:1–8; Deut. 1:16, 17; John 7:24

gives you, according to your tribes, and
they shall judge the people with just judgment. 19[a]You shall not pervert justice; [b]you
shall not show partiality, [c]nor take a bribe,
for a bribe blinds the eyes of the wise and
twists the words of the righteous. 20You
shall follow what is altogether just, that
you may [a]live and inherit the land which
the LORD your God is giving you.

21[a]"You shall not plant for yourself any
tree, as a wooden image, near the altar
which you build for yourself to the LORD
your God. 22[a]You shall not set up a *sacred*
pillar, which the LORD your God hates.

17 "You [a]shall not sacrifice to the LORD
your God a bull or sheep which has
any blemish *or* defect, for that *is* an abomination to the LORD your God.

2[a]"If there is found among you, within
any of your gates which the LORD your God
gives you, a man or a woman who has been
wicked in the sight of the LORD your God,
[b]in transgressing His covenant, 3who has
gone and served other gods and worshiped
them, either [a]the sun or moon or any of
the host of heaven, [b]which I have not commanded, 4[a]and it is told you, and you hear
of it, then you shall inquire diligently. And
if *it is* indeed true *and* certain that such
an abomination has been committed in
Israel, 5then you shall bring out to your
gates that man or woman who has committed that wicked thing, and [a]shall stone
[b]to death that man or woman with stones.
6Whoever is deserving of death shall be put
to death on the testimony of two or three
[a]witnesses; he shall not be put to death on
the testimony of one witness. 7The hands
of the witnesses shall be the first against
him to put him to death, and afterward the
hands of all the people. So you shall put
away the evil from among [a]you.

8[a]"If a matter arises which is too hard for
you to judge, between degrees of guilt for
bloodshed, between one judgment or another, or between one punishment or another, matters of controversy within your
gates, then you shall arise and go up to the
[b]place which the LORD your God chooses.
9And [a]you shall come to the priests, the Levites, and [b]to the judge *there* in those days,
and inquire *of them;* [c]they shall pronounce
upon you the sentence of judgment. 10You
shall do according to the sentence which
they pronounce upon you in that place
which the LORD chooses. And you shall be
careful to do according to all that they order you. 11According to the sentence of the
law in which they instruct you, according
to the judgment which they tell you, you
shall do; you shall not turn aside *to* the
right hand or *to* the left from the sentence
which they pronounce upon you. 12Now
[a]the man who acts presumptuously and
will not heed the priest who stands to minister there before the LORD your God, or
the judge, that man shall die. So you shall
put away the evil from Israel. 13[a]And all the
people shall hear and fear, and no longer
act presumptuously.

Principles Governing Kings

14"When you come to the land which
the LORD your God is giving you, and possess it and dwell in it, and say, [a]'I will set
a king over me like all the nations that
are around me,' 15you shall surely set a
king over you [a]whom the LORD your God
chooses; *one* [b]from among your brethren
you shall set as king over you; you may
not set a foreigner over you, who *is* not
your brother. 16But he shall not multiply
[a]horses for himself, nor cause the people
[b]to return to Egypt to multiply horses, for
[c]the LORD has said to you, [d]'You shall not
return that way again.' 17Neither shall he
multiply wives for himself, lest his heart
turn away; nor shall he greatly multiply
silver and [a]gold for himself.

18"Also it shall be, when he sits on the
throne of his kingdom, that he shall write
for himself a copy of this law in a book,
from *the one* [a]before the priests, the Levites. 19And [a]it shall be with him, and he
shall read it all the days of his life, that he
may learn to fear the LORD his God and be

16:19 [a] Ex. 23:2, 6 [b] Deut. 1:17 [c] Ex. 23:8 16:20 [a] Ezek. 18:5–9 16:21 [a] Ex. 34:13 16:22 [a] Lev. 26:1 17:1 [a] Deut. 15:21; Mal. 1:8, 13 17:2 [a] Deut. 13:6 [b] Josh. 7:11 17:3 [a] Deut. 4:19 [b] Jer. 7:22 17:4 [a] Deut. 13:12, 14 17:5 [a] Lev. 24:14–16; Josh. 7:25 [b] Deut. 13:6–18 17:6 [a] Num. 35:30; Deut. 19:15; Matt. 18:16; John 8:17; 2 Cor. 13:1; 1 Tim. 5:19; Heb. 10:28 17:7 [a] Deut. 13:5; 19:19; 1 Cor. 5:13 17:8 [a] Deut. 1:17; 2 Chr. 19:10 [b] Deut. 12:5; 16:2 17:9 [a] Jer. 18:18 [b] Deut. 19:17–19 [c] Ezek. 44:24 17:12 [a] Num. 15:30; Deut. 1:43 17:13 [a] Deut. 13:11 17:14 [a] 1 Sam. 8:5, 19, 20; 10:19 17:15 [a] 1 Sam. 9:15, 16; 10:24; 16:12, 13; 1 Chr. 22:8–10; Hos. 8:4 [b] Jer. 30:21 17:16 [a] 1 Kin. 4:26; 10:26–29; Ps. 20:7 [b] Is. 31:1; Ezek. 17:15 [c] Ex. 13:17, 18; Hos. 11:5 [d] Deut. 28:68 17:17 [a] 1 Kin. 10:14 17:18 [a] Deut. 31:24–26 17:19 [a] Ps. 119:97, 98

careful to observe all the words of this law
and these statutes, 20that his heart may not
be lifted above his brethren, that he [a]may
not turn aside from the commandment *to*
the right hand or *to* the left, and that he may
prolong *his* days in his kingdom, he and his
children in the midst of Israel.

The Portion of the Priests and Levites

18 "The priests, the Levites—all the
tribe of Levi—shall have no part nor
[a]inheritance with Israel; they shall eat the
offerings of the LORD made by fire, and His
portion. 2Therefore they shall have no inheritance among their brethren; the LORD
is their inheritance, as He said to them.

3"And this shall be the priest's [a]due from
the people, from those who offer a sacrifice, whether *it is* bull or sheep: they shall
give to the priest the shoulder, the cheeks,
and the stomach. 4[a]The firstfruits of your
grain and your new wine and your oil, and
the first of the fleece of your sheep, you
shall give him. 5For [a]the LORD your God has
chosen him out of all your tribes [b]to stand
to minister in the name of the LORD, him
and his sons forever.

6"So if a Levite comes from any of your
gates, from where he [a]dwells among all Israel, and comes with all the desire of his
mind [b]to the place which the LORD chooses,
7then he may serve in the name of the LORD
his God [a]as all his brethren the Levites *do,*
who stand there before the LORD. 8They
shall have equal [a]portions to eat, besides
what comes from the sale of his inheritance.

Avoid Wicked Customs

9"When you come into the land which
the LORD your God is giving you, [a]you shall
not learn to follow the abominations of
those nations. 10There shall not be found
among you *anyone* who makes his son or
his daughter [a]pass through the fire, [b]*or one*
who practices witchcraft, *or* a soothsayer,
or one who interprets omens, or a sorcerer,
11[a]or one who conjures spells, or a medium,
or a spiritist, or [b]one who calls up the dead.
12For all who do these things *are* an abomination to the LORD, and [a]because of these
abominations the LORD your God drives
them out from before you. 13You shall be
blameless before the LORD your God. 14For
these nations which you will dispossess
listened to soothsayers and diviners; but
as for you, the LORD your God has not appointed such for you.

A New Prophet Like Moses

15[a]"The LORD your God will raise up for
you a Prophet like me from your midst,
from your brethren. Him you shall hear,
16according to all you desired of the LORD
your God in Horeb [a]in the day of the assembly, saying, [b]'Let me not hear again the
voice of the LORD my God, nor let me see
this great fire anymore, lest I die.'

17"And the LORD said to me: [a]'What they
have spoken is good. 18[a]I will raise up for
them a Prophet like you from among their
brethren, and [b]will put My words in His
mouth, [c]and He shall speak to them all that
I command Him. 19[a]And it shall be *that*
whoever will not hear My words, which
He speaks in My name, I will require *it* of
him. 20But [a]the prophet who presumes to
speak a word in My name, which I have
not commanded him to speak, or [b]who
speaks in the name of other gods, that
prophet shall die.' 21And if you say in your
heart, 'How shall we know the word which
the LORD has not spoken?'— 22[a]when a
prophet speaks in the name of the LORD,
[b]if the thing does not happen or come
to pass, that *is* the thing which the LORD
has not spoken; the prophet has spoken it
[c]presumptuously; you shall not be afraid
of him.

Three Cities of Refuge
(Num. 35:9–28; Josh. 20:1–9)

19 "When the LORD your God [a]has cut
off the nations whose land the LORD
your God is giving you, and you dispossess
them and dwell in their cities and in their

17:20 [a] Deut. 5:32; 1 Kin. 15:5 18:1 [a] Deut. 10:9; 1 Cor. 9:13 18:3 [a] Lev. 7:32–34; Num. 18:11, 12; 1 Sam. 2:13–16, 29 18:4 [a] Ex. 22:29 18:5 [a] Ex. 28:1 [b] Deut. 10:8 18:6 [a] Num. 35:2 [b] Deut. 12:5; 14:23 18:7 [a] Num. 1:50; 2 Chr. 31:2 18:8 [a] Lev. 27:30–33; Num. 18:21–24; 2 Chr. 31:4; Neh. 12:44 18:9 [a] Lev. 18:26, 27, 30; Deut. 12:29, 30; 20:16–18 18:10 [a] Lev. 18:21; Deut. 12:31 [b] Ex. 22:18; Lev. 19:26, 31; 20:6, 27; Is. 8:19 18:11 [a] Lev. 20:27 [b] 1 Sam. 28:7 18:12 [a] Lev. 18:24; Deut. 9:4 18:15 [a] Matt. 21:11; Luke 1:76; 2:25–34; 7:16; 24:19; Acts 3:22 18:16 [a] Deut. 5:23–27 [b] Ex. 20:18, 19; Heb. 12:19 18:17 [a] Deut. 5:28 18:18 [a] Deut. 34:10; John 1:45; Acts 3:22 [b] Num. 23:5; Is. 49:2; 51:16; John 17:8 [c] [John 4:25; 8:28] 18:19 [a] Acts 3:23; [Heb. 12:25] 18:20 [a] Deut. 13:5; Jer. 14:14, 15; Zech. 13:2–5 [b] Deut. 13:1–3; Jer. 2:8 18:22 [a] Jer. 28:9 [b] Deut. 13:2 [c] Deut. 18:20 19:1 [a] Deut. 12:29

houses, 2 [a]you shall separate three cities for
yourself in the midst of your land which
the LORD your God is giving you to possess. 3 You shall prepare roads for yourself,
and divide into three parts the territory
of your land which the LORD your God is
giving you to inherit, that any manslayer
may flee there.
4 "And [a]this *is* the case of the manslayer
who flees there, that he may live: Whoever kills his neighbor unintentionally, not
having hated him in time past— 5 as when
a man goes to the woods with his neighbor to cut timber, and his hand swings a
stroke with the ax to cut down the tree,
and the head slips from the handle and
strikes his neighbor so that he dies—he
shall flee to one of these cities and live;
6 [a]lest the avenger of blood, while his anger is hot, pursue the manslayer and overtake him, because the way is long, and kill
him, though he *was* not deserving of death,
since he had not hated the victim in time
past. 7 Therefore I command you, saying,
'You shall separate three cities for yourself.'
8 "Now if the LORD your God [a]enlarges
your territory, as He swore to [b]your fathers,
and gives you the land which He promised
to give to your fathers, 9 and if you keep
all these commandments and do them,
which I command you today, to love the
LORD your God and to walk always in His
ways, [a]then you shall add three more cities
for yourself besides these three, 10 [a]lest innocent blood be shed in the midst of your
land which the LORD your God is giving you
as an inheritance, and *thus* guilt of bloodshed be upon you.
11 "But [a]if anyone hates his neighbor,
lies in wait for him, rises against him and
strikes him mortally, so that he dies, and
he flees to one of these cities, 12 then the
elders of his city shall send and bring him
from there, and deliver him over to the
hand of the avenger of blood, that he may
die. 13 [a]Your eye shall not pity him, [b]but you
shall put away *the guilt of* innocent blood
from Israel, that it may go well with you.

Property Boundaries

14 [a]"You shall not remove your neighbor's
landmark, which the men of old have set,
in your inheritance which you will inherit
in the land that the LORD your God is giving you to possess.

The Law Concerning Witnesses

15 [a]"One witness shall not rise against a
man concerning any iniquity or any sin
that he commits; by the mouth of two or
three witnesses the matter shall be established. 16 If a false witness [a]rises against any
man to testify against him of wrongdoing,
17 then both men in the controversy shall
stand before the LORD, [a]before the priests
and the judges who serve in those days.
18 And the judges shall make careful inquiry,
and indeed, *if* the witness *is* a false witness,
who has testified falsely against his brother,
19 [a]then you shall do to him as he thought
to have done to his brother; so [b]you shall
put away the evil from among you. 20 [a]And
those who remain shall hear and fear, and
hereafter they shall not again commit such
evil among you. 21 [a]Your eye shall not pity:
[b]life *shall be* for life, eye for eye, tooth for
tooth, hand for hand, foot for foot.

Principles Governing Warfare

20 "When you go out to battle against
your enemies, and see [a]horses and
chariots *and* people more numerous than
you, do not be [b]afraid of them; for the LORD
your God *is* [c]with you, who brought you
up from the land of Egypt. 2 So it shall be,
when you are on the verge of battle, that the
priest shall approach and speak to the people. 3 And he shall say to them, 'Hear, O Israel: Today you are on the verge of battle
with your enemies. Do not let your heart
faint, do not be afraid, and do not tremble
or be terrified because of them; 4 for the
LORD your God *is* He who goes with you,
[a]to fight for you against your enemies, to
save you.'
5 "Then the officers shall speak to the
people, saying: 'What man *is there* who has

19:2 [a] Ex. 21:13; Num. 35:10–15; Deut. 4:41; Josh. 20:2 19:4 [a] Num. 35:9–34; Deut. 4:42 19:6 [a] Num. 35:12 19:8 [a] Deut. 12:20 [b] Gen. 15:18–21 19:9 [a] Josh. 20:7–9 19:10 [a] Num. 35:33; Deut. 21:1–9 19:11 [a] Num. 35:16, 24; Deut. 27:24; [1 John 3:15] 19:13 [a] Deut. 13:8 [b] Num. 35:33, 34; 1 Kin. 2:31 19:14 [a] Deut. 27:17; Job 24:2; Prov. 22:28; Hos. 5:10 19:15 [a] Num. 35:30; Deut. 17:6; Matt. 18:16; John 8:17; 2 Cor. 13:1; 1 Tim. 5:19; Heb. 10:28 19:16 [a] Ex. 23:1; Ps. 27:12; 35:11 19:17 [a] Deut. 17:8–11; 21:5 19:19 [a] Prov. 19:5; Dan. 6:24 [b] Deut. 13:5; 17:7; 21:21; 22:21 19:20 [a] Deut. 17:13; 21:21 19:21 [a] Deut. 19:13 [b] Ex. 21:23, 24; Lev. 24:20; Matt. 5:38, 39 20:1 [a] Ps. 20:7; Is. 31:1 [b] Deut. 7:18 [c] Num. 23:21; Deut. 5:6; 31:6, 8; 2 Chr. 13:12; 32:7, 8; Ps. 23:4; Is. 41:10 20:4 [a] Deut. 1:30; 3:22; Josh. 23:10

built a new house and has not [a]dedicated
it? Let him go and return to his house, lest
he die in the battle and another man dedicate it. 6Also what man *is there* who has
planted a vineyard and has not eaten of it?
Let him go and return to his house, lest he
die in the battle and another man eat of it.
7[a]And what man *is there* who is betrothed
to a woman and has not married her? Let
him go and return to his house, lest he die
in the battle and another man marry her.'
8"The officers shall speak further to the
people, and say, [a]'What man *is there who is*
fearful and fainthearted? Let him go and
return to his house, lest the heart of his
brethren faint[1] like his heart.' 9And so it
shall be, when the officers have finished
speaking to the people, that they shall make
captains of the armies to lead the people.
10"When you go near a city to fight
against it, [a]then proclaim an offer of peace
to it. 11And it shall be that if they accept your
offer of peace, and open to you, then all the
people *who are* found in it shall be placed
under tribute to you, and serve you. 12Now
if *the city* will not make peace with you, but
war against you, then you shall besiege it.
13And when the LORD your God delivers
it into your hands, [a]you shall strike every
male in it with the edge of the sword. 14But
the women, the little ones, [a]the livestock,
and all that is in the city, all its spoil, you
shall plunder for yourself; and [b]you shall
eat the enemies' plunder which the LORD
your God gives you. 15Thus you shall do to
all the cities *which are* very far from you,
which *are* not of the cities of these nations.
16"But [a]of the cities of these peoples
which the LORD your God gives you *as*
an inheritance, you shall let nothing that
breathes remain alive, 17but you shall utterly destroy them: the Hittite and the Amorite and the Canaanite and the Perizzite
and the Hivite and the Jebusite, just as the
LORD your God has commanded you, 18lest
[a]they teach you to do according to all their
abominations which they have done for
their gods, and you [b]sin against the LORD
your God.
19"When you besiege a city for a long
time, while making war against it to take
it, you shall not destroy its trees by wield-
ing an ax against them; if you can eat of
them, do not cut them down to use in the
siege, for the tree of the field *is* man's *food.*
20Only the trees which you know *are* not
trees for food you may destroy and cut
down, to build siegeworks against the city
that makes war with you, until it is subdued.

The Law Concerning Unsolved Murder

21 "If *anyone* is found slain, lying in
the field in the land which the LORD
your God is giving you to possess, *and* it is
not known who killed him, 2then your elders and your judges shall go out and measure *the distance* from the slain man to the
surrounding cities. 3And it shall be *that*
the elders of the city nearest to the slain
man will take a heifer which has not been
worked *and* which has not pulled with a
[a]yoke. 4The elders of that city shall bring
the heifer down to a valley with flowing
water, which is neither plowed nor sown,
and they shall break the heifer's neck there
in the valley. 5Then the priests, the sons of
Levi, shall come near, for [a]the LORD your
God has chosen them to minister to Him
and to bless in the name of the LORD; [b]by
their word every controversy and every
assault shall be *settled.* 6And all the elders
of that city nearest to the slain *man* [a]shall
wash their hands over the heifer whose
neck was broken in the valley. 7Then they
shall answer and say, 'Our hands have not
shed this blood, nor have our eyes seen *it.*
8Provide atonement, O LORD, for Your people Israel, whom You have redeemed, [a]and
do not lay innocent blood to the charge of
Your people Israel.' And atonement shall
be provided on their behalf for the blood.
9So [a]you shall put away the *guilt of* innocent
blood from among you when you do *what*
is right in the sight of the LORD.

Female Captives

10"When you go out to war against your
enemies, and the LORD your God delivers

20:5 [a] Neh. 12:27 20:7 [a] Deut. 24:5 20:8 [a] Judg. 7:3 [1] Following Masoretic Text and Targum; Samaritan Pentateuch, Septuagint, Syriac, and Vulgate read *lest he make his brother's heart faint.* 20:10 [a] 2 Sam. 10:19 20:13 [a] Num. 31:7 20:14 [a] Josh. 8:2 [b] 1 Sam. 14:30 20:16 [a] Ex. 23:31–33; Num. 21:2, 3; Deut. 7:1–5; Josh. 11:14 20:18 [a] Ex. 34:12–16; Deut. 7:4; 12:30; 18:9 [b] Ex. 23:33; 2 Kin. 21:3–15; Ps. 106:34–41 21:3 [a] Num. 19:2 21:5 [a] Deut. 10:8; 1 Chr. 23:13 [b] Deut. 17:8, 9 21:6 [a] Ps. 19:12; 26:6; Matt. 27:24 21:8 [a] Deut. 19:10, 13; Jon. 1:14 21:9 [a] Deut. 19:13

them into your hand, and you take them captive, 11and you see among the captives a beautiful woman, and desire her and would take her for your [a]wife, 12then you shall bring her home to your house, and she shall [a]shave her head and trim her nails. 13She shall put off the clothes of her captivity, remain in your house, and [a]mourn her father and her mother a full month; after that you may go in to her and be her husband, and she shall be your wife. 14And it shall be, if you have no delight in her, then you shall set her free, but you certainly shall not sell her for money; you shall not treat her brutally, because you have [a]humbled her.

Firstborn Inheritance Rights

15"If a man has two wives, one loved [a]and the other unloved, and they have borne him children, *both* the loved and the unloved, and *if* the firstborn son is of her who is unloved, 16then it shall be, [a]on the day he bequeaths his possessions to his sons, *that* he must not bestow firstborn status on the son of the loved wife in preference to the son of the unloved, the *true* firstborn. 17But he shall acknowledge the son of the unloved wife *as* the firstborn [a]by giving him a double portion of all that he has, for he [b]*is* the beginning of his strength; [c]the right of the firstborn *is* his.

The Rebellious Son

18"If a man has a stubborn and rebellious son who will not obey the voice of his father or the voice of his mother, and *who,* when they have chastened him, will not heed them, 19then his father and his mother shall take hold of him and bring him out to the elders of his city, to the gate of his city. 20And they shall say to the elders of his city, 'This son of ours is stubborn and rebellious; he will not obey our voice; he is a glutton and a drunkard.' 21Then all the men of his city shall stone him to death with stones; [a]so you shall put away the evil from among you, [b]and all Israel shall hear and fear.

Miscellaneous Laws

22"If a man has committed a sin [a]deserving of death, and he is put to death, and you hang him on a tree, 23[a]his body shall not remain overnight on the tree, but you shall surely bury him that day, so that [b]you do not defile the land which the LORD your God is giving you *as* an inheritance; for [c]he who is hanged *is* accursed of God.

22

"You [a]shall not see your brother's ox or his sheep going astray, and hide yourself from them; you shall certainly bring them back to your brother. 2And if your brother *is* not near you, or if you do not know him, then you shall bring it to your own house, and it shall remain with you until your brother seeks it; then you shall restore it to him. 3You shall do the same with his donkey, and so shall you do with his garment; with any lost thing of your brother's, which he has lost and you have found, you shall do likewise; you must not hide yourself.

4[a]"You shall not see your brother's donkey or his ox fall down along the road, and hide yourself from them; you shall surely help him lift *them* up again.

5"A woman shall not wear anything that pertains to a man, nor shall a man put on a woman's garment, for all who do so *are* an abomination to the LORD your God.

6"If a bird's nest happens to be before you along the way, in any tree or on the ground, with young ones or eggs, with the mother sitting on the young or on the eggs, [a]you shall not take the mother with the young; 7you shall surely let the mother go, and take the young for yourself, [a]that it may be well with you and *that* you may prolong *your* days.

8"When you build a new house, then you shall make a parapet for your roof, that you may not bring guilt of bloodshed on your household if anyone falls from it.

9[a]"You shall not sow your vineyard with different kinds of seed, lest the yield of the seed which you have sown and the fruit of your vineyard be defiled.

10[a]"You shall not plow with an ox and a donkey together.

21:11 [a] Num. 31:18 21:12 [a] Lev. 14:8, 9; Num. 6:9 21:13 [a] Ps. 45:10 21:14 [a] Gen. 34:2; Deut. 22:29; Judg. 19:24 21:15 [a] Gen. 29:33 21:16 [a] 1 Chr. 5:2; 26:10 21:17 [a] 2 Kin. 2:9 [b] Gen. 49:3 [c] Gen. 25:31, 33 21:21 [a] Deut. 13:5; 19:19, 20; 22:21, 24 [b] Deut. 13:11 21:22 [a] Deut. 22:26; Matt. 26:66; Mark 14:64; Acts 23:29 21:23 [a] Josh. 8:29; 10:26, 27; John 19:31 [b] Lev. 18:25; Num. 35:34 [c] Gal. 3:13 22:1 [a] Ex. 23:4 22:4 [a] Ex. 23:5 22:6 [a] Lev. 22:28 22:7 [a] Deut. 4:40 22:9 [a] Lev. 19:19 22:10 [a] [2 Cor. 6:14–16]

11[a]"You shall not wear a garment of different sorts, *such as* wool and linen mixed
together.
12"You shall make [a]tassels on the four
corners of the clothing with which you
cover *yourself.*

Laws of Sexual Morality

13"If any man takes a wife, and goes in
to her, and [a]detests her, 14and charges her
with shameful conduct, and brings a bad
name on her, and says, 'I took this woman,
and when I came to her I found she *was*
not a virgin,' 15then the father and mother
of the young woman shall take and bring
out *the evidence of* the young woman's virginity to the elders of the city at the gate.
16And the young woman's father shall say to
the elders, 'I gave my daughter to this man
as wife, and he detests her. 17Now he has
charged her with shameful conduct, saying,
"I found your daughter *was* not a virgin,"
and yet these *are the evidences of* my daughter's virginity.' And they shall spread the
cloth before the elders of the city. 18Then
the elders of that city shall take that man
and punish him; 19and they shall fine him
one hundred *shekels* of silver and give *them*
to the father of the young woman, because
he has brought a bad name on a virgin of
Israel. And she shall be his wife; he cannot
divorce her all his days.
20"But if the thing is true, *and evidences
of* virginity are not found for the young
woman, 21then they shall bring out the
young woman to the door of her father's
house, and the men of her city shall stone
her to death with [a]stones, because she has
[b]done a disgraceful thing in Israel, to play
the harlot in her father's house. [c]So you
shall put away the evil from among you.
22[a]"If a man is found lying with a woman
married to a husband, then both of them
shall die—the man that lay with the woman,
and the woman; so you shall put away the
evil from Israel.
23"If a young woman *who is* a virgin is
[a]betrothed to a husband, and a man finds
her in the city and lies with her, 24then you
shall bring them both out to the gate of that
city, and you shall stone them to death with
stones, the young woman because she did
not cry out in the city, and the man because
he [a]humbled his neighbor's wife; [b]so you
shall put away the evil from among you.
25"But if a man finds a betrothed young
woman in the countryside, and the man
forces her and lies with her, then only the
man who lay with her shall die. 26But you
shall do nothing to the young woman; *there
is* in the young woman no sin *deserving* of
death, for just as when a man rises against
his neighbor and kills him, even so *is* this
matter. 27For he found her in the countryside, *and* the betrothed young woman cried
out, but *there was* no one to save her.
28[a]"If a man finds a young woman *who
is* a virgin, who is not betrothed, and he
seizes her and lies with her, and they are
found out, 29then the man who lay with her
shall give to the young woman's father [a]fifty
shekels of silver, and she shall be his wife
[b]because he has humbled her; he shall not
be permitted to divorce her all his days.
30[a]"A man shall not take his father's wife,
nor [b]uncover his father's bed.

Those Excluded from the Congregation

23 "He who is emasculated by crushing or mutilation shall [a]not enter
the assembly of the LORD.
2"One of illegitimate birth shall not enter the assembly of the LORD; even to the
tenth generation none of his *descendants*
shall enter the assembly of the LORD.
3[a]"An Ammonite or Moabite shall not
enter the assembly of the LORD; even to
the tenth generation none of his *descendants* shall enter the assembly of the LORD
forever, 4[a]because they did not meet you
with bread and water on the road when
you came out of Egypt, and [b]because they
hired against you Balaam the son of Beor
from Pethor of Mesopotamia,[1] to curse you.
5Nevertheless the LORD your God would
not listen to Balaam, but the LORD your

22:11 [a] Lev. 19:19 22:12 [a] Num. 15:37–41; Matt. 23:5 22:13 [a] Deut. 21:15; 24:3 22:21 [a] Deut. 21:21 [b] Gen. 34:7; Judg. 20:5–10; 2 Sam. 13:12, 13 [c] Deut. 13:5 22:22 [a] Lev. 20:10; Num. 5:22–27; Ezek. 16:38; [Matt. 5:27, 28]; John 8:5; [1 Cor. 6:9; Heb. 13:4] 22:23 [a] Lev. 19:20–22; Matt. 1:18, 19 22:24 [a] Deut. 21:14 [b] Deut. 22:21, 22; 1 Cor. 5:2, 13 22:28 [a] Ex. 22:16, 17 22:29 [a] Ex. 22:16, 17 [b] Deut. 22:24 22:30 [a] Lev. 18:8; 20:11; Deut. 27:20; 1 Cor. 5:1 [b] Ruth 3:9; Ezek. 16:8 23:1 [a] Lev. 21:20; 22:24 23:3 [a] Neh. 13:1, 2 23:4 [a] Deut. 2:27–30 [b] Num. 22:5, 6; 23:7; Josh. 24:9; 2 Pet. 2:15; Jude 11 [1] Hebrew *Aram Naharaim*

God turned the curse into a blessing for
you, because the LORD your God [a]loves you.
6 [a]You shall not seek their peace nor their
prosperity all your days forever.
7 "You shall not abhor an Edomite, [a]for
he *is* your brother. You shall not abhor an
Egyptian, because [b]you were an alien in
his land. 8 The children of the third generation born to them may enter the assembly of the LORD.

Cleanliness of the Campsite

9 "When the army goes out against your
enemies, then keep yourself from every
wicked thing. 10 [a]If there is any man among
you who becomes unclean by some occurrence in the night, then he shall go outside the camp; he shall not come inside the
camp. 11 But it shall be, when evening comes,
that [a]he shall wash with water; and when
the sun sets, he may come into the camp.
12 "Also you shall have a place outside
the camp, where you may go out; 13 and
you shall have an implement among your
equipment, and when you sit down outside,
you shall dig with it and turn and cover
your refuse. 14 For the LORD your God [a]walks
in the midst of your camp, to deliver you
and give your enemies over to you; therefore your camp shall be holy, that He may
see no unclean thing among you, and turn
away from you.

Miscellaneous Laws

15 [a]"You shall not give back to his master
the slave who has escaped from his master to you. 16 He may dwell with you in your
midst, in the place which he chooses within
one of your gates, where it seems best to
him; [a]you shall not oppress him.
17 "There shall be no *ritual* harlot[1] [a]of the
daughters of Israel, or a [b]perverted[2] one of
the sons of Israel. 18 You shall not bring the
wages of a harlot or the price of a dog to the
house of the LORD your God for any vowed
offering, for both of these *are* an abomination to the LORD your God.
19 [a]"You shall not charge interest to your
brother—interest on money *or* food *or* anything that is lent out at interest. 20 [a]To a foreigner you may charge interest, but to your
brother you shall not charge interest, [b]that
the LORD your God may bless you in all to
which you set your hand in the land which
you are entering to possess.
21 [a]"When you make a vow to the LORD
your God, you shall not delay to pay it; for
the LORD your God will surely require it of
you, and it would be sin to you. 22 But if you
abstain from vowing, it shall not be sin to
you. 23 [a]That which has gone from your lips
you shall keep and perform, for you volun-
tarily vowed to the LORD your God what you
have promised with your mouth.
24 "When you come into your neighbor's
vineyard, you may eat your fill of grapes at
your pleasure, but you shall not put *any*
in your container. 25 When you come into
your neighbor's standing grain, [a]you may
pluck the heads with your hand, but you
shall not use a sickle on your neighbor's
standing grain.

Law Concerning Divorce

24 "When a [a]man takes a wife and marries her, and it happens that she
finds no favor in his eyes because he has
found some uncleanness in her, and he
writes her a [b]certificate of divorce, puts *it*
in her hand, and sends her out of his house,
2 when she has departed from his house, and
goes and becomes another man's *wife,* 3 *if*
the latter husband detests her and writes
her a certificate of divorce, puts *it* in her
hand, and sends her out of his house, or
if the latter husband dies who took her as
his wife, 4 [a]*then* her former husband who divorced her must not take her back to be his
wife after she has been defiled; for that *is* an
abomination before the LORD, and you shall
not bring sin on the land which the LORD
your God is giving you *as* an inheritance.

Miscellaneous Laws

5 [a]"When a man has taken a new wife,
he shall not go out to war or be charged

23:5 [a] Deut. 4:37 23:6 [a] Ezra 9:12 23:7 [a] Gen. 25:24–26; Deut. 2:4, 8; Amos 1:11; Obad. 10, 12 [b] Ex. 22:21; 23:9; Lev. 19:34; Deut. 10:19 23:10 [a] Lev. 15:16 23:11 [a] Lev. 15:5 23:14 [a] Lev. 26:12; Deut. 7:21 23:15 [a] 1 Sam. 30:15 23:16 [a] Ex. 22:21; Prov. 22:22 23:17 [a] Lev. 19:29; Deut. 22:21 [b] Gen. 19:5; 2 Kin. 23:7 [1] Hebrew *qedeshah,* feminine of *qadesh* (see next note) [2] Hebrew *qadesh,* that is, one practicing sodomy and prostitution in religious rituals 23:19 [a] Ex. 22:25; Lev. 25:35–37; Neh. 5:2–7; Ps. 15:5 23:20 [a] Deut. 15:3 [b] Deut. 15:10 23:21 [a] Num. 30:1, 2; Job 22:27; Ps. 61:8; Eccl. 5:4, 5; Matt. 5:33 23:23 [a] Num. 30:2; Ps. 66:13, 14 23:25 [a] Matt. 12:1; Mark 2:23; Luke 6:1 24:1 [a] [Matt. 5:31; 19:7; Mark 10:4] [b] [Jer. 3:8] 24:4 [a] [Jer. 3:1] 24:5 [a] Deut. 20:7

with any business; he shall be free at home
one year, and [b]bring happiness to his wife
whom he has taken.
6“No man shall take the lower or the upper millstone in pledge, for he takes *one's*
living in pledge.
7“If a man is [a]found kidnapping any of
his brethren of the children of Israel, and
mistreats him or sells him, then that kid-
napper shall die; [b]and you shall put away
the evil from among you.
8“Take heed in [a]an outbreak of leprosy,
that you carefully observe and do according to all that the priests, the Levites, shall
teach you; just as I commanded them, *so*
you shall be careful to do. 9[a]Remember
what the LORD your God did [b]to Miriam
on the way when you came out of Egypt!
10“When you [a]lend your brother anything, you shall not go into his house to get
his pledge. 11You shall stand outside, and
the man to whom you lend shall bring the
pledge out to you. 12And if the man *is* poor,
you shall not keep his pledge overnight.
13[a]You shall in any case return the pledge
to him again when the sun goes down, that
he may sleep in his own garment and [b]bless
you; and [c]it shall be righteousness to you
before the LORD your God.
14“You shall not [a]oppress a hired servant
who is poor and needy, *whether* one of your
brethren or one of the aliens who *is* in your
land within your gates. 15Each day [a]you shall
give *him* his wages, and not let the sun go
down on it, for he *is* poor and has set his
heart on it; [b]lest he cry out against you to
the LORD, and it be sin to you.
16[a]“Fathers shall not be put to death for
their children, nor shall children be put to
death for *their* fathers; a person shall be
put to death for his own sin.
17[a]“You shall not pervert justice due the
stranger or the fatherless, [b]nor take a widow's garment as a pledge. 18But [a]you shall
remember that you were a slave in Egypt,
and the LORD your God redeemed you from
there; therefore I command you to do this
thing.
19[a]“When you reap your harvest in your
field, and forget a sheaf in the field, you
shall not go back to get it; it shall be for the
stranger, the fatherless, and the widow, that
the LORD your God may [b]bless you in all
the work of your hands. 20When you beat
your olive trees, you shall not go over the
boughs again; it shall be for the stranger,
the fatherless, and the widow. 21When you
gather the grapes of your vineyard, you
shall not glean *it* afterward; it shall be for
the stranger, the fatherless, and the widow.
22And you shall remember that you were a
slave in the land of Egypt; therefore I command you to do this thing.

25 “If there is a [a]dispute between men,
and they come to court, that *the
judges* may judge them, and they [b]justify
the righteous and condemn the wicked,
2then it shall be, if the wicked man [a]de-
serves to be beaten, that the judge will
cause him to lie down [b]and be beaten in
his presence, according to his guilt, with a
certain number of blows. 3[a]Forty blows he
may give him *and* no more, lest he should
exceed this and beat him with many blows
above these, and your brother [b]be humiliated in your sight.
4[a]“You shall not muzzle an ox while it
treads out *the grain.*

Marriage Duty of the Surviving Brother

5[a]“If brothers dwell together, and one of
them dies and has no son, the widow of the
dead man shall not be *married* to a stranger
outside *the family;* her husband's brother
shall go in to her, take her as his wife, and
perform the duty of a husband's brother to
her. 6And it shall be *that* the firstborn son
which she bears [a]will succeed to the name
of his dead brother, that [b]his name may not
be blotted out of Israel. 7But if the man does
not want to take his brother's wife, then let
his brother's wife go up to the [a]gate to the
elders, and say, 'My husband's brother refuses to raise up a name to his brother in
Israel; he will not perform the duty of my
husband's brother.' 8Then the elders of his

24:5 [b] Prov. 5:18 24:7 [a] Ex. 21:16 [b] Deut. 19:19 24:8 [a] Lev. 13:2; 14:2 24:9 [a] [1 Cor. 10:6] [b] Num. 12:10 24:10 [a] Matt. 5:42 24:13 [a] Ex. 22:26; Ezek. 18:7 [b] Job 29:11; 2 Tim. 1:18 [c] Deut. 6:25; Ps. 106:31; Dan. 4:27 24:14 [a] Lev. 19:13; Deut. 15:7–18; [Prov. 14:31]; Amos 4:1; [Mal. 3:5; 1 Tim. 5:18] 24:15 [a] Lev. 19:13; Jer. 22:13 [b] Ex. 22:23; Deut. 15:9; Job 35:9; James 5:4 24:16 [a] 2 Kin. 14:6; 2 Chr. 25:4; Jer. 31:29, 30; Ezek. 18:20 24:17 [a] Ex. 23:6 [b] Ex. 22:26 24:18 [a] Deut. 24:22 24:19 [a] Lev. 19:9, 10 [b] Deut. 15:10; Ps. 41:1; Prov. 19:17 25:1 [a] Deut. 17:8–13; 19:17; Ezek. 44:24 [b] Prov. 17:15 25:2 [a] Prov. 19:29; Luke 12:48 [b] Matt. 10:17 25:3 [a] 2 Cor. 11:24 [b] Job 18:3 25:4 [a] [Prov. 12:10; 1 Cor. 9:9; 1 Tim. 5:18] 25:5 [a] Matt. 22:24; Mark 12:19; Luke 20:28 25:6 [a] Gen. 38:9 [b] Ruth 4:5, 10 25:7 [a] Ruth 4:1, 2

city shall call him and speak to him. But *if* he stands firm and says, [a]'I do not want to take her,' 9then his brother's wife shall come to him in the presence of the elders, [a]remove his sandal from his foot, spit in his face, and answer and say, 'So shall it be done to the man who will not [b]build up his brother's house.' 10And his name shall be called in Israel, 'The house of him who had his sandal removed.'

Miscellaneous Laws

11"If *two* men fight together, and the wife of one draws near to rescue her husband from the hand of the one attacking him, and puts out her hand and seizes him by the genitals, 12then you shall cut off her hand; [a]your eye shall not pity *her.*

13[a]"You shall not have in your bag differing weights, a heavy and a light. 14You shall not have in your house differing measures, a large and a small. 15You shall have a perfect and just weight, a perfect and just measure, [a]that your days may be lengthened in the land which the LORD your God is giving you. 16For [a]all who do such things, all who behave unrighteously, *are* an abomination to the LORD your God.

Destroy the Amalekites

17[a]"Remember what Amalek did to you on the way as you were coming out of Egypt, 18how he met you on the way and attacked your rear ranks, all the stragglers at your rear, when you *were* tired and weary; and he [a]did not fear God. 19Therefore it shall be, [a]when the LORD your God has given you rest from your enemies all around, in the land which the LORD your God is giving you to possess *as* an inheritance, *that* you will [b]blot out the remembrance of Amalek from under heaven. You shall not forget.

Offerings of Firstfruits and Tithes

26 "And it shall be, when you come into the land which the LORD your God is giving you *as* an inheritance, and you possess it and dwell in it, 2[a]that you shall take some of the first of all the produce of the ground, which you shall bring from your land that the LORD your God is giving you, and put *it* in a basket and [b]go to the place where the LORD your God chooses to make His name abide. 3And you shall go to the one who is priest in those days, and say to him, 'I declare today to the LORD your[1] God that I have come to the country which the LORD swore to our fathers to give us.'

4"Then the priest shall take the basket out of your hand and set it down before the altar of the LORD your God. 5And you shall answer and say before the LORD your God: 'My father *was* [a]a Syrian,[1] [b]about to perish, and [c]he went down to Egypt and dwelt there, [d]few in number; and there he became a nation, [e]great, mighty, and populous. 6But the [a]Egyptians mistreated us, afflicted us, and laid hard bondage on us. 7[a]Then we cried out to the LORD God of our fathers, and the LORD heard our voice and looked on our affliction and our labor and our oppression. 8So [a]the LORD brought us out of Egypt with a mighty hand and with an outstretched arm, [b]with great terror and with signs and wonders. 9He has brought us to this place and has given us this land, [a]"a land flowing with milk and honey";[1] 10and now, behold, I have brought the firstfruits of the land which you, O LORD, have given me.'

"Then you shall set it before the LORD your God, and worship before the LORD your God. 11So [a]you shall rejoice in every good *thing* which the LORD your God has given to you and your house, you and the Levite and the stranger who *is* among you.

12"When you have finished laying aside all the [a]tithe of your increase in the third year—[b]the year of tithing—and have given *it* to the Levite, the stranger, the fatherless, and the widow, so that they may eat within your gates and be filled, 13then you shall say before the LORD your God: 'I have removed the holy *tithe* from *my* house, and also have given them to the Levite, the stranger, the fatherless, and the widow, according to

---

25:8 [a] Ruth 4:6 25:9 [a] Ruth 4:7, 8 [b] Ruth 4:11 25:12 [a] Deut. 7:2; 19:13 25:13 [a] Lev. 19:35–37; Prov. 11:1; 20:23; Ezek. 45:10; Mic. 6:11 25:15 [a] Ex. 20:12 25:16 [a] Prov. 11:1; [1 Thess. 4:6] 25:17 [a] Ex. 17:8–16; 1 Sam. 15:1–3 25:18 [a] [Ps. 36:1]; Rom. 3:18 25:19 [a] 1 Sam. 15:3 [b] Ex. 17:14 26:2 [a] Ex. 22:29; 23:16, 19; Num. 18:13; Deut. 16:10; Prov. 3:9 [b] Deut. 12:5 26:3 [1] Septuagint reads *my.* 26:5 [a] Gen. 25:20; Hos. 12:12 [b] Gen. 43:1, 2; 45:7, 11 [c] Gen. 46:1, 6; Acts 7:15 [d] Gen. 46:27; Deut. 10:22 [e] Deut. 1:10 [1] Or *Aramean* 26:6 [a] Ex. 1:8–11, 14 26:7 [a] Ex. 2:23–25; 3:9; 4:31 26:8 [a] Ex. 12:37, 51; 13:3, 14, 16; Deut. 5:15 [b] Deut. 4:34; 34:11, 12 26:9 [a] Ex. 3:8, 17 [1] Exodus 3:8 26:11 [a] Deut. 12:7; 16:11; Eccl. 3:12, 13; 5:18–20 26:12 [a] Lev. 27:30; Num. 18:24 [b] Deut. 14:28, 29

all Your commandments which You have
commanded me; I have not transgressed
Your commandments, [a]nor have I forgotten *them.* 14 [a]I have not eaten any of it when
in mourning, nor have I removed *any* of
it for an unclean *use,* nor given *any* of it
for the dead. I have obeyed the voice of
the LORD my God, and have done according to all that You have commanded me.
15 [a]Look down from Your holy habitation,
from heaven, and bless Your people Israel
and the land which You have given us, just
as You swore to our fathers, [b]"a land flowing with milk and honey."'[1]

A Special People of God

16 "This day the LORD your God commands you to observe these statutes and
judgments; therefore you shall be careful to
observe them with all your heart and with all
your soul. 17 Today you have [a]proclaimed the
LORD to be your God, and that you will walk
in His ways and keep His statutes, His commandments, and His judgments, and that
you will [b]obey His voice. 18 Also today [a]the
LORD has proclaimed you to be His special
people, just as He promised you, that *you*
should keep all His commandments, 19 and
that He will set you [a]high above all nations
which He has made, in praise, in name, and
in honor, and that you may be [b]a holy people
to the LORD your God, just as He has spoken."

The Law Inscribed on Stones

27 Now Moses, with the elders of Israel, commanded the people, saying: "Keep all the commandments which
I command you today. 2 And it shall be, on
the day [a]when you cross over the Jordan to
the land which the LORD your God is giving
you, that [b]you shall set up for yourselves
large stones, and whitewash them with
lime. 3 You shall write on them all the words
of this law, when you have crossed over,
that you may enter the land which the LORD
your God is giving you, [a]'a land flowing with
milk and honey,'[1] just as the LORD God of
your fathers promised you. 4 Therefore it
shall be, when you have crossed over the
Jordan, *that* [a]on Mount Ebal you shall set
up these stones, which I command you today, and you shall whitewash them with
lime. 5 And there you shall build an altar
to the LORD your God, an altar of stones;
[a]you shall not use an iron *tool* on them.
6 You shall build with whole stones the altar of the LORD your God, and offer burnt
offerings on it to the LORD your God. 7 You
shall offer peace offerings, and shall eat
there, and [a]rejoice before the LORD your
God. 8 And you shall [a]write very plainly on
the stones all the words of this law."

9 Then Moses and the priests, the Levites,
spoke to all Israel, saying, "Take heed and
listen, O Israel: [a]This day you have become
the people of the LORD your God. 10 Therefore
you shall obey the voice of the LORD your
God, and observe His commandments and
His statutes which I command you today."

Curses Pronounced from Mount Ebal

11 And Moses commanded the people
on the same day, saying, 12 "These shall
stand [a]on Mount Gerizim to bless the people, when you have crossed over the Jordan: Simeon, Levi, Judah, Issachar, Joseph,
and Benjamin; 13 and [a]these shall stand on
Mount Ebal to curse: Reuben, Gad, Asher,
Zebulun, Dan, and Naphtali.

14 "And [a]the Levites shall speak with a
loud voice and say to all the men of Israel:
15 [a]'Cursed *is* the one who makes a carved
or molded image, an abomination to the
LORD, the work of the hands of the craftsman, and sets *it* up in secret.'

[b]"And all the people shall answer and
say, 'Amen!'

16 [a]'Cursed *is* the one who treats his father
or his mother with contempt.'

"And all the people shall say, 'Amen!'

17 [a]'Cursed *is* the one who moves his
neighbor's landmark.'

"And all the people shall say, 'Amen!'

18 [a]'Cursed *is* the one who makes the
blind to wander off the road.'

"And all the people shall say, 'Amen!'

26:13 [a] Ps. 119:141, 153, 176 **26:14** [a] Lev. 7:20; Jer. 16:7; Hos. 9:4 **26:15** [a] Ps. 80:14; Is. 63:15; Zech. 2:13 [b] Ex. 3:8 [1] Exodus 3:8 **26:17** [a] Ex. 20:19 [b] Deut. 15:5 **26:18** [a] Ex. 6:7; 19:5; Deut. 7:6; 14:2; 28:9; [Titus 2:14; 1 Pet. 2:9] **26:19** [a] Deut. 4:7, 8; 28:1 [b] Ex. 19:6; Deut. 7:6; 28:9; Is. 62:12; [1 Pet. 2:9] **27:2** [a] Josh. 4:1 [b] Josh. 8:32 **27:3** [a] Ex. 3:8 [1] Exodus 3:8 **27:4** [a] Deut. 11:29; Josh. 8:30, 31 **27:5** [a] Ex. 20:25; Josh. 8:31 **27:7** [a] Deut. 26:11 **27:8** [a] Josh. 8:32 **27:9** [a] Deut. 26:18 **27:12** [a] Deut. 11:29; Josh. 8:33; Judg. 9:7 **27:13** [a] Deut. 11:29; Josh. 8:33 **27:14** [a] Deut. 33:10; Josh. 8:33; Dan. 9:11 **27:15** [a] Ex. 20:4, 23; 34:17; Lev. 19:4; 26:1; Deut. 4:16, 23; Is. 44:9; Hos. 13:2 [b] Num. 5:22; Jer. 11:5; 1 Cor. 14:16 **27:16** [a] Ex. 20:12; Lev. 19:3; 20:9; Deut. 5:16; 21:18–21; Ezek. 22:7 **27:17** [a] Deut. 19:14; Prov. 22:28 **27:18** [a] Lev. 19:14

19[a]'Cursed *is* the one who perverts the
justice due the stranger, the fatherless, and
widow.'

"And all the people shall say, 'Amen!'

20[a]'Cursed *is* the one who lies with his
father's wife, because he has uncovered
his father's bed.'

"And all the people shall say, 'Amen!'

21[a]'Cursed *is* the one who lies with any
kind of animal.'

"And all the people shall say, 'Amen!'

22[a]'Cursed *is* the one who lies with his
sister, the daughter of his father or the
daughter of his mother.'

"And all the people shall say, 'Amen!'

23[a]'Cursed *is* the one who lies with his
mother-in-law.'

"And all the people shall say, 'Amen!'

24[a]'Cursed *is* the one who attacks his
neighbor secretly.'

"And all the people shall say, 'Amen!'

25[a]'Cursed *is* the one who takes a bribe
to slay an innocent person.'

"And all the people shall say, 'Amen!'

26[a]'Cursed *is* the one who does not confirm *all* the words of this law by observing them.'

"And all the people shall say, 'Amen!'"

Blessings on Obedience
(Lev. 26:1–13; Deut. 7:12–24)

28 "Now it shall come to pass, [a]if you
diligently obey the voice of the
LORD your God, to observe carefully all His
commandments which I command you today, that the LORD your God [b]will set you
high above all nations of the earth.
2And all
these blessings shall come upon you and
[a]overtake you, because you obey the voice
of the LORD your God:

3[a]"Blessed *shall* you *be* in the city, and
blessed *shall* you *be* [b]in the country.

4"Blessed *shall be* [a]the fruit of your body,
the produce of your ground and the increase of your herds, the increase of your
cattle and the offspring of your flocks.

5"Blessed *shall be* your basket and your
kneading bowl.

6[a]"Blessed *shall* you *be* when you come
in, and blessed *shall* you *be* when you go
out.

7"The LORD [a]will cause your enemies
who rise against you to be defeated before
your face; they shall come out against you
one way and flee before you seven ways.

8"The LORD will [a]command the blessing on you in your storehouses and in all
to which you [b]set your hand, and He will
bless you in the land which the LORD your
God is giving you.

9[a]"The LORD will establish you as a holy
people to Himself, just as He has sworn to
you, if you keep the commandments of
the LORD your God and walk in His ways.
10Then all peoples of the earth shall see that
you are [a]called by the name of the LORD,
and they shall be [b]afraid of you.
11And [a]the
LORD will grant you plenty of goods, in
the fruit of your body, in the increase of
your livestock, and in the produce of your
ground, in the land of which the LORD
swore to your fathers to give you.
12The
LORD will open to you His good treasure,
the heavens, [a]to give the rain to your land in
its season, and [b]to bless all the work of your
hand. [c]You shall lend to many nations, but
you shall not borrow.
13And the LORD will
make [a]you the head and not the tail; you
shall be above only, and not be beneath, if
you heed the commandments of the LORD
your God, which I command you today, and
are careful to observe *them*.
14[a]So you shall
not turn aside from any of the words which
I command you this day, *to* the right or the
left, to go after other gods to serve them.

Curses on Disobedience
(Lev. 26:14–46)

15"But it shall come to pass, [a]if you do not
obey the voice of the LORD your God, to observe carefully all His commandments and
His statutes which I command you today,
that all these curses will come upon you
and overtake you:

16"Cursed *shall* you *be* in the city, and
cursed *shall* you *be* in the country.

27:19 [a] Ex. 22:21, 22; 23:9; Lev. 19:33; Deut. 10:18; 24:17 **27:20** [a] Lev. 18:8; 20:11; Deut. 22:30; 1 Cor. 5:1 **27:21** [a] Ex. 22:19; Lev. 18:23; 20:15, 16 **27:22** [a] Lev. 18:9 **27:23** [a] Lev. 18:17; 20:14 **27:24** [a] Ex. 20:13; 21:12; Lev. 24:17; Num. 35:30, 31 **27:25** [a] Ex. 23:7; Ps. 15:5; Ezek. 22:12 **27:26** [a] Ps. 119:21; Jer. 11:3; Gal. 3:10 **28:1** [a] Ex. 15:26; Lev. 26:3–13; Deut. 7:12–26; 11:13 [b] Deut. 26:19; 1 Chr. 14:2 **28:2** [a] Deut. 28:15 **28:3** [a] Ps. 128:1, 4 [b] Gen. 39:5 **28:4** [a] Gen. 22:17 **28:6** [a] Ps. 121:8 **28:7** [a] Lev. 26:7, 8 **28:8** [a] Lev. 25:21 [b] Deut. 15:10 **28:9** [a] Ex. 19:5, 6 **28:10** [a] Num. 6:27; 2 Chr. 7:14; Is. 63:19; Dan. 9:18, 19 [b] Deut. 11:25 **28:11** [a] Deut. 30:9 **28:12** [a] Lev. 26:4; Deut. 11:14 [b] Deut. 14:29 [c] Deut. 15:6 **28:13** [a] [Is. 9:14, 15] **28:14** [a] Deut. 5:32; Josh. 1:7 **28:15** [a] Lev. 26:14–39; Josh. 23:15; Dan. 9:10–14; Mal. 2:2

LIFE SUPPORT

BE DEVOTED: BELIEVE GOD

"Now it shall come to pass, if you diligently obey the voice of the LORD your God, to observe carefully all His commandments which I command you today, that the LORD your God will set you high above all nations of the earth." Deuteronomy 28:1

LIFE: Be Devoted

When we are devoted to God, He does not expect us to be perfect; however, He does require that we have hearts aligned with His. Many distractions in our everyday lives try to throw us off our godly course. These distractions are designed by the Enemy to keep us from living according to God's plans.

When you are devoted to God, He blesses your life because He is faithful. He will not leave you to fight the Enemy alone. His desire is for you to live victoriously, so He will help you fight. God will always reward your diligence and your commitment to Him. He will always uphold His Word. There may be many things or people that you do not need in your life, but you will always need Jesus.

SUPPORT: Believe God

What a mandate! The Hebrew people were to demonstrate their allegiance to God by observing all that He had commanded. Each of the Ten Commandments and all the dozens and dozens of other commands mattered. Sure, it was much to obey. Sure, it was difficult. But God had been so good to His people, and if they only obeyed, He would continue to bless them abundantly. But despite God's goodness and promises, the people repeatedly turned their hearts from God, became disobedient, and worshiped other gods. They did not love Him.

The same is true today. We live in a corrupt time when many people mock God. At best, people give God lip service, if they acknowledge Him at all. But God has always called His people to be devoted to Him alone. This means we must lay down everything else, love God, and believe Him. God will faithfully honor His promise of an abundant and blessed life, both now and for eternity. If we will just believe Him, we can walk in newness of life.

SUPPORT EXAMPLE: Let the Holy Spirit be your guide.

17"Cursed *shall be* your basket and your kneading bowl.
18"Cursed *shall be* the fruit of your body and the produce of your land, the increase of your cattle and the offspring of your flocks.
19"Cursed *shall* you *be* when you come in, and cursed *shall* you *be* when you go out.
20"The LORD will send on you [a]cursing, [b]confusion, and [c]rebuke in all that you set your hand to do, until you are destroyed and until you perish quickly, because of the wickedness of your doings in which you have forsaken Me. 21The LORD will make the plague cling to you until He has consumed you from the land which you are going to possess. 22[a]The LORD will strike you with consumption, with fever, with inflammation, with severe burning fever, with the sword, with [b]scorching, and with mildew; they shall pursue you until you perish. 23And [a]your heavens which *are* over your head shall be bronze, and the earth which is under you *shall be* iron. 24The LORD will change the rain of your land to powder and dust; from the heaven it shall come down on you until you are destroyed.

28:20 [a] Mal. 2:2 [b] Is. 65:14 [c] Ps. 80:16; Is. 30:17 28:22 [a] Lev. 26:16 [b] Amos 4:9 28:23 [a] Lev. 26:19

25[a]"The LORD will cause you to be defeated before your enemies; you shall go
out one way against them and flee seven
ways before them; and you shall become
troublesome to all the kingdoms of the
earth. 26[a]Your carcasses shall be food for
all the birds of the air and the beasts of
the earth, and no one shall frighten *them*
away. 27The LORD will strike you with [a]the
boils of Egypt, with [b]tumors, with the scab,
and with the itch, from which you cannot
be healed. 28The LORD will strike you with
madness and blindness and [a]confusion of
heart. 29And you shall [a]grope at noonday, as
a blind man gropes in darkness; you shall
not prosper in your ways; you shall be only
oppressed and plundered continually, and
no one shall save *you.*

30[a]"You shall betroth a wife, but another
man shall lie with her; [b]you shall build a
house, but you shall not dwell in it; [c]you
shall plant a vineyard, but shall not gather
its grapes. 31Your ox *shall be* slaughtered before your eyes, but you shall not eat of it;
your donkey *shall be* violently taken away
from before you, and shall not be restored
to you; your sheep *shall be* given to your enemies, and you shall have no one to rescue
them. 32Your sons and your daughters *shall
be* given to [a]another people, and your eyes
shall look and [b]fail *with longing* for them all
day long; and *there shall be* no strength in
your [c]hand. 33A nation whom you have not
known shall eat [a]the fruit of your land and
the produce of your labor, and you shall be
only oppressed and crushed continually.
34So you shall be driven mad because of
the sight which your eyes see. 35The LORD
will strike you in the knees and on the legs
with severe boils which cannot be healed,
and from the sole of your foot to the top
of your head.

36"The LORD will [a]bring you and the
king whom you set over you to a nation
which neither you nor your fathers have
known, and [b]there you shall serve other
gods—wood and stone. 37And you shall become [a]an astonishment, a proverb, [b]and a
byword among all nations where the LORD
will drive you.

38[a]"You shall carry much seed out to the
field but gather little in, for [b]the locust shall
consume it. 39You shall plant vineyards and
tend *them,* but you shall neither drink *of* the
[a]wine nor gather the *grapes;* for the worms
shall eat them. 40You shall have olive trees
throughout all your territory, but you shall
not anoint *yourself* with the oil; for your olives shall drop off. 41You shall beget sons
and daughters, but they shall not be yours;
for [a]they shall go into captivity. 42Locusts
shall consume all your trees and the produce of your land.

43"The alien who *is* among you shall rise
higher and higher above you, and you shall
come down lower and lower. 44He shall lend
to you, but you shall not lend to him; he
shall be the head, and you shall be the tail.

45"Moreover all these curses shall come
upon you and pursue and overtake you,
until you are destroyed, because you did
not obey the voice of the LORD your God,
to keep His commandments and His statutes which He commanded you. 46And they
shall be upon [a]you for a sign and a wonder,
and on your descendants forever.

47[a]"Because you did not serve the LORD
your God with joy and gladness of heart,
[b]for the abundance of everything, 48there-
fore you shall serve your enemies, whom
the LORD will send against you, in [a]hun-
ger, in thirst, in nakedness, and in need
of everything; and He [b]will put a yoke of
iron on your neck until He has destroyed
you. 49[a]The LORD will bring a nation against
you from afar, from the end of the earth,
[b]*as swift* as the eagle flies, a nation whose
language you will not understand, 50a nation of fierce countenance, [a]which does
not respect the elderly nor show favor to
the young. 51And they shall eat the increase
of your livestock and the produce of your
land, until you are destroyed; they shall not
leave you grain or new wine or oil, *or* the
increase of your cattle or the offspring of
your flocks, until they have destroyed you.

28:25 [a] Deut. 32:30 28:26 [a] 1 Sam. 17:44; Ps. 79:2 28:27 [a] Ex. 15:26 [b] 1 Sam. 5:6 28:28 [a] Jer. 4:9 28:29 [a] Job 5:14 28:30 [a] 2 Sam. 12:11; Job 31:10; Jer. 8:10 [b] Amos 5:11; Zeph. 1:13 [c] Deut. 20:6; Job 31:8; Jer. 12:13; Mic. 6:15 28:32 [a] 2 Chr. 29:9 [b] Ps. 119:82 [c] Neh. 5:5 28:33 [a] Lev. 26:16; Jer. 5:15, 17 28:36 [a] 2 Kin. 17:4, 6; 24:12, 14; 25:7, 11; 2 Chr. 36:1–21; Jer. 39:1–9 [b] Deut. 4:28; Jer. 16:13 28:37 [a] 1 Kin. 9:7, 8; Jer. 24:9; 25:9 [b] Ps. 44:14 28:38 [a] Mic. 6:15; Hag. 1:6 [b] Ex. 10:4; Joel 1:4 28:39 [a] Zeph. 1:13 28:41 [a] Lam. 1:5 28:46 [a] Num. 26:10; Is. 8:18; Ezek. 14:8 28:47 [a] Deut. 12:7; Neh. 9:35–37 [b] Deut. 32:15 28:48 [a] Lam. 4:4–6 [b] Jer. 28:13, 14 28:49 [a] Is. 5:26–30; 7:18–20; Jer. 5:15 [b] Jer. 48:40; 49:22; Lam. 4:19; Hos. 8:1 28:50 [a] 2 Chr. 36:17

52“They shall [a]besiege you at all your
gates until your high and fortified walls,
in which you trust, come down throughout
all your land; and they shall besiege you
at all your gates throughout all your land
which the LORD your God has given you.
53[a]You shall eat the fruit of your own body,
the flesh of your sons and your daughters
whom the LORD your God has given you,
in the siege and desperate straits in which
your enemy shall distress you. 54The sensitive and very refined man among you [a]will
be hostile toward his brother, toward [b]the
wife of his bosom, and toward the rest of
his children whom he leaves behind, 55so
that he will not give any of them the flesh
of his children whom he will eat, because
he has nothing left in the siege and desperate straits in which your enemy shall
distress you at all your gates. 56The tender
and delicate woman among you, who would
not venture to set the sole of her foot on
the ground because of her delicateness and
sensitivity, will refuse[1] to the husband of
her bosom, and to her son and her daughter, 57her placenta which comes out [a]from
between her feet and her children whom
she bears; for she will eat them secretly for
lack of everything in the siege and desperate straits in which your enemy shall distress you at all your gates.

58“If you do not carefully observe all the
words of this law that are written in this
book, that you may fear [a]this glorious and
awesome name, THE LORD YOUR GOD,
59then the LORD will bring upon you and
your descendants [a]extraordinary plagues—
great and prolonged plagues—and serious
and prolonged sicknesses. 60Moreover He
will bring back on you all [a]the diseases of
Egypt, of which you were afraid, and they
shall cling to you. 61Also every sickness and
every plague, which *is* not written in this
Book of the Law, will the LORD bring upon
you until you are destroyed. 62You [a]shall
be left few in number, whereas you were
[b]as the stars of heaven in multitude, because you would not obey the voice of the
LORD your God. 63And it shall be, *that* just
as the LORD [a]rejoiced over you to do you
good and multiply you, so the LORD [b]will
rejoice over you to destroy you and bring
you to nothing; and you shall be [c]plucked
from off the land which you go to possess.

64“Then the LORD [a]will scatter you
among all peoples, from one end of the
earth to the other, and [b]there you shall
serve other gods, which neither you nor
your fathers have known—wood and stone.
65And [a]among those nations you shall find
no rest, nor shall the sole of your foot have
a resting place; [b]but there the LORD will
give you a trembling heart, failing eyes,
and [c]anguish of soul. 66Your life shall hang
in doubt before you; you shall fear day and
night, and have no assurance of life. 67[a]In
the morning you shall say, ‘Oh, that it were
evening!’ And at evening you shall say, ‘Oh,
that it were morning!’ because of the fear
which terrifies your heart, and [b]because of
the sight which your eyes see.

68“And the LORD [a]will take you back to
Egypt in ships, by the way of which I said
to you, [b]‘You shall never see it again.’ And
there you shall be offered for sale to your
enemies as male and female slaves, but no
one will buy *you.*”

The Covenant Renewed in Moab

29 These *are* the words of the covenant
which the LORD commanded Moses
to make with the children of Israel in the
land of Moab, besides the [a]covenant which
He made with them in Horeb.

2Now Moses called all Israel and said to
them: [a]“You have seen all that the LORD
did before your eyes in the land of Egypt,
to Pharaoh and to all his servants and to
all his land— 3[a]the great trials which your
eyes have seen, the signs, and those great
wonders. 4Yet [a]the LORD has not given you a
heart to perceive and eyes to see and ears to
hear, to this *very* day. 5[a]And I have led you
forty years in the wilderness. [b]Your clothes
have not worn out on you, and your sandals
have not worn out on your feet. 6[a]You have

28:52 [a] 2 Kin. 25:1, 2, 4 28:53 [a] Lev. 26:29; 2 Kin. 6:28, 29; Jer. 19:9; Lam. 2:20; 4:10 28:54 [a] Deut. 15:9 [b] Deut. 13:6
28:56 [1] Literally *her eye shall be evil toward* 28:57 [a] Gen. 49:10 28:58 [a] Ex. 6:3 28:59 [a] Dan. 9:12 28:60 [a] Deut. 7:15
28:62 [a] Deut. 4:27 [b] Deut. 10:22; Neh. 9:23 28:63 [a] Deut. 30:9; Jer. 32:41 [b] Prov. 1:26; [Is. 1:24] [c] Jer. 12:14; 45:4 28:64 [a] Lev. 26:33;
Deut. 4:27, 28; Neh. 1:8; Jer. 16:13; Amos 9:9 [b] Deut. 28:36 28:65 [a] Lam. 1:3; Amos 9:4 [b] Lev. 26:36 [c] Lev. 26:16 28:67 [a] Job 7:4
[b] Deut. 28:34 28:68 [a] Jer. 43:7; Hos. 8:13 [b] Deut. 17:16 29:1 [a] Lev. 26:46; Deut. 5:2, 3 29:2 [a] Ex. 19:4; Deut. 11:7
29:3 [a] Deut. 4:34; 7:19 29:4 [a] [Is. 6:9, 10; Ezek. 12:2]; Matt. 13:14; [Acts 28:26, 27]; Rom. 11:8; [Eph. 4:18]
29:5 [a] Deut. 1:3; 8:2 [b] Deut. 8:4 29:6 [a] Ex. 16:12; Deut. 8:3

not eaten bread, nor have you drunk wine or *similar* drink, that you may know that I *am* the LORD your God. 7And when you came to this place, [a]Sihon king of Heshbon and Og king of Bashan came out against us to battle, and we conquered them. 8We took their land and [a]gave it as an inheritance to the Reubenites, to the Gadites, and to half the tribe of Manasseh. 9Therefore [a]keep the words of this covenant, and do them, that you may [b]prosper in all that you do.

10"All of you stand today before the LORD your God: your leaders and your tribes and your elders and your officers, all the men of Israel, 11your little ones and your wives—also the stranger who *is* in your camp, from [a]the one who cuts your wood to the one who draws your water— 12that you may enter into covenant with the LORD your God, and [a]into His oath, which the LORD your God makes with you today, 13that He may [a]establish you today as a people for Himself, and *that* He may be God to you, [b]just as He has spoken to you, and [c]just as He has sworn to your fathers, to Abraham, Isaac, and Jacob.

14"I make this covenant and this oath, [a]not with you alone, 15but with *him* who stands here with us today before the LORD our God, [a]as well as with *him* who *is* not here with us today 16(for you know that we dwelt in the land of Egypt and that we came through the nations which you passed by, 17and you saw their abominations and their idols which *were* among them—wood and stone and silver and gold); 18so that there may not be among you man or woman or family or tribe, [a]whose heart turns away today from the LORD our God, to go *and* serve the gods of these nations, [b]and that there may not be among you a root bearing [c]bitterness or wormwood; 19and so it may not happen, when he hears the words of this curse, that he blesses himself in his heart, saying, 'I shall have peace, even though I follow the [a]dictates[1] of my heart'—[b]as though the drunkard could be included with the sober.

20[a]"The LORD would not spare him; for then [b]the anger of the LORD and [c]His jealousy would burn against that man, and every curse that is written in this book would settle on him, and the LORD [d]would blot out his name from under heaven. 21And the LORD [a]would separate him from all the tribes of Israel for adversity, according to all the curses of the covenant that are written in this Book of the [b]Law, 22so that the coming generation of your children who rise up after you, and the foreigner who comes from a far land, would say, when they [a]see the plagues of that land and the sicknesses which the LORD has laid on it:

23'The whole land *is* brimstone, [a]salt, and burning; it is not sown, nor does it bear, nor does any grass grow there, [b]like the overthrow of Sodom and Gomorrah, Admah, and Zeboiim, which the LORD overthrew in His anger and His wrath.' 24All nations would say, [a]'Why has the LORD done so to this land? What does the heat of this great anger mean?' 25Then *people* would say: 'Because they have forsaken the covenant of the LORD God of their fathers, which He made with them when He brought them out of the land of Egypt; 26for they went and served other gods and worshiped them, gods that they did not know and that He had not given to them. 27Then the anger of the LORD was aroused against this land, [a]to bring on it every curse that is written in this book. 28And the LORD [a]uprooted them from their land in anger, in wrath, and in great indignation, and cast them into another land, as *it is* this day.'

29"The secret *things belong* to the LORD our God, but those *things which are* revealed *belong* to us and to our children forever, that *we* may do all the words of this law.

The Blessing of Returning to God

30 "Now [a]it shall come to pass, when [b]all these things come upon you, the blessing and the [c]curse which I have set before you, and [d]you call *them* to mind

29:7 [a] Num. 21:23, 24; Deut. 2:26—3:3 29:8 [a] Num. 32:33; Deut. 3:12, 13 29:9 [a] Deut. 4:6; 1 Kin. 2:3 [b] Josh. 1:7 29:11 [a] Josh. 9:21, 23, 27 29:12 [a] Neh. 10:29 29:13 [a] Deut. 28:9 [b] Ex. 6:7 [c] Gen. 17:7, 8 29:14 [a] [Jer. 31:31; Heb. 8:7, 8] 29:15 [a] Acts 2:39 29:18 [a] Deut. 11:16 [b] Heb. 12:15 [c] Deut. 32:32; Acts 8:23 29:19 [a] Jer. 3:17; 7:24 [b] Is. 30:1 [1] Or *stubbornness* 29:20 [a] Ezek. 14:7 [b] Ps. 74:1 [c] Ps. 79:5; Ezek. 23:25 [d] Ex. 32:33; Deut. 9:14; 2 Kin. 14:27 29:21 [a] [Matt. 24:51] [b] Deut. 30:10 29:22 [a] Jer. 19:8; 49:17; 50:13 29:23 [a] Jer. 17:6; Zeph. 2:9 [b] Gen. 19:24, 25; Is. 1:9; Jer. 20:16; Hos. 11:8 29:24 [a] 1 Kin. 9:8; Jer. 22:8 29:27 [a] Dan. 9:11 29:28 [a] 1 Kin. 14:15; 2 Chr. 7:20; Ps. 52:5; Prov. 2:22 30:1 [a] Lev. 26:40 [b] Deut. 28:2 [c] Deut. 28:15–45 [d] Deut. 4:29, 30

among all the nations where the LORD
your God drives you, 2and you [a]return to
the LORD your God and obey His voice, according to all that I command you today,
you and your children, with all your heart
and with all your soul, 3[a]that the LORD your
God will bring you back from captivity, and
have compassion on you, and [b]gather you
again from all the nations where the LORD
your God has scattered you. 4[a]If *any* of you
are driven out to the farthest *parts* under
heaven, from there the LORD your God will
gather you, and from there He will bring
you. 5Then the LORD your God will bring
you to the land which your fathers possessed, and you shall possess it. He will
prosper you and multiply you more than
your fathers. 6And [a]the LORD your God will
circumcise your heart and the heart of your
descendants, to love the LORD your God
with all your heart and with all your soul,
that you may live.

7"Also the LORD your God will put all
these [a]curses on your enemies and on
those who hate you, who persecuted you.
8And you will [a]again obey the voice of the
LORD and do all His commandments which
I command you today. 9[a]The LORD your
God will make you abound in all the work of
your hand, in the fruit of your body, in the
increase of your livestock, and in the produce of your land for good. For the LORD
will again [b]rejoice over you for good as He
rejoiced over your fathers, 10if you obey the
voice of the LORD your God, to keep His
commandments and His statutes which
are written in this Book of the Law, *and* if
you turn to the LORD your God with all your
heart and with all your soul.

The Choice of Life or Death

11"For this commandment which I command you today [a]*is* not *too* mysterious for
you, nor *is* it far off. 12[a]It *is* not in heaven,
that you should say, 'Who will ascend into
heaven for us and bring it to us, that we
may hear it and do it?' 13Nor *is* it beyond
the sea, that you should say, 'Who will go
over the sea for us and bring it to us, that
we may hear it and do it?' 14But the word *is*
very near you, [a]in your mouth and in your
heart, that you may do it.

15"See, [a]I have set before you today life
and good, death and evil, 16in that I command you today to love the LORD your God,
to walk in His ways, and to keep His commandments, His statutes, and His judgments, that you may live and multiply; and
the LORD your God will bless you in the land
which you go to possess. 17But if your heart
turns away so that you do not hear, and
are drawn away, and worship other gods
and serve them, 18[a]I announce to you today that you shall surely perish; you shall
not prolong *your* days in the land which
you cross over the Jordan to go in and possess. 19[a]I call heaven and earth as witnesses
today against you, *that* [b]I have set before
you life and death, blessing and cursing;
therefore choose life, that both you and
your descendants may live; 20that you may
love the LORD your God, that you may obey
His voice, and that you may cling to Him,
for He *is* your [a]life and the length of your
days; and that you may dwell in the land
which the LORD swore to your fathers, to
Abraham, Isaac, and Jacob, to give them."

Joshua the New Leader of Israel
(Num. 27:12–23)

31 Then Moses went and spoke these
words to all Israel. 2And he said to
them: "I [a]*am* one hundred and twenty years
old today. I can no longer [b]go out and come
in. Also the LORD has said to me, [c]'You shall
not cross over this Jordan.' 3The LORD your
God [a]Himself crosses over before you; He
will destroy these nations from before you,
and you shall dispossess them. [b]Joshua
himself crosses over before you, just [c]as
the LORD has said. 4[a]And the LORD will do
to them [b]as He did to Sihon and Og, the
kings of the Amorites and their land, when
He destroyed them. 5[a]The LORD will give
them over to you, that you may do to them
according to every commandment which I

30:2 [a] Deut. 4:29, 30; Neh. 1:9; Is. 55:7; Lam. 3:40; Joel 2:12 30:3 [a] Ps. 106:45; Jer. 29:14; Lam. 3:22, 32 [b] Ps. 147:2; Jer. 32:37; Ezek. 34:13 30:4 [a] Deut. 28:64; Neh. 1:9; Is. 62:11 30:6 [a] Deut. 10:16; Jer. 32:39; Ezek. 11:19 30:7 [a] Is. 54:15–17; Jer. 30:16, 20 30:8 [a] Zeph. 3:20 30:9 [a] Deut. 28:11 [b] Deut. 28:63; Jer. 32:41 30:11 [a] Is. 45:19 30:12 [a] Prov. 30:4; Rom. 10:6–8 30:14 [a] Rom. 10:8 30:15 [a] Deut. 30:1, 19 30:18 [a] Deut. 4:26; 8:19 30:19 [a] Deut. 4:26 [b] Deut. 30:15 30:20 [a] Ps. 27:1; [John 11:25; 14:6; Col. 3:4] 31:2 [a] Ex. 7:7; Deut. 34:7 [b] Num. 27:17; 1 Kin. 3:7 [c] Num. 20:12 31:3 [a] Deut. 9:3; Josh. 11:23 [b] Num. 27:18 [c] Num. 27:21 31:4 [a] Deut. 3:21 [b] Num. 21:24, 33 31:5 [a] Deut. 7:2; 20:10–20

have commanded you. 6[a]Be strong and of good courage, [b]do not fear nor be afraid of them; for the LORD your God, [c]He *is* the One who goes with you. [d]He will not leave you nor forsake you."

#OXYGEN

DEUTERONOMY 31:6

Trust in His Word

God has a plan to get you through any crisis. It begins with knowing He is with you. Be strong and courageous. Do not fear. Do not waver. You are not alone. You can do it. You are going to make it.

Breathe and trust in His Word.

7Then Moses called Joshua and said to him in the sight of all Israel, [a]"Be strong and of good courage, for you must go with this people to the land which the LORD has sworn to their fathers to give them, and you shall cause them to inherit it. 8And the LORD, [a]He *is* the One who goes before you. [b]He will be with you, He will not leave you nor forsake you; do not fear nor be dismayed."

The Law to Be Read Every Seven Years

9So Moses wrote this law [a]and delivered it to the priests, the sons of Levi, [b]who bore the ark of the covenant of the LORD, and to all the elders of Israel. 10And Moses commanded them, saying: "At the end of *every* seven years, at the appointed time in the [a]year of release, [b]at the Feast of Tabernacles, 11when all Israel comes to [a]appear before the LORD your God in the [b]place which He chooses, [c]you shall read this law before all Israel in their hearing. 12[a]Gather the people together, men and women and little ones, and the stranger who *is* within your gates, that they may hear and that they may learn to fear the LORD your God and carefully observe all the words of this law, 13and *that* their children, [a]who have not known it, [b]may hear and learn to fear the LORD your God as long as you live in the land which you cross the Jordan to possess."

Prediction of Israel's Rebellion

14Then the LORD said to Moses, [a]"Behold, the days approach when you must die; call Joshua, and present yourselves in the tabernacle of meeting, that [b]I may inaugurate him."

So Moses and Joshua went and presented themselves in the tabernacle of meeting. 15Now [a]the LORD appeared at the tabernacle in a pillar of cloud, and the pillar of cloud stood above the door of the tabernacle.

16And the LORD said to Moses: "Behold, you will rest with your fathers; and this people will [a]rise and [b]play the harlot with the gods of the foreigners of the land, where they go *to be* among them, and they will [c]forsake Me and [d]break My covenant which I have made with them. 17Then My anger shall be [a]aroused against them in that day, and [b]I will forsake them, and I will [c]hide My face from them, and they shall be devoured. And many evils and troubles shall befall them, so that they will say in that day, [d]'Have not these evils come upon us because our God *is* [e]not among us?' 18And [a]I will surely hide My face in that day because of all the evil which they have done, in that they have turned to other gods.

19"Now therefore, write down this song for yourselves, and teach it to the children of Israel; put it in their mouths, that this song may be [a]a witness for Me against the children of Israel. 20When I have brought them to the land flowing with milk and honey, of which I swore to their fathers, and they have eaten and filled themselves [a]and grown fat, [b]then they will turn to other gods and serve them; and they will provoke

31:6 [a] Josh. 10:25; 1 Chr. 22:13 [b] Deut. 1:29 [c] Deut. 20:4 [d] Josh. 1:5; Heb. 13:5 31:7 [a] Num. 27:19; Deut. 31:23; Josh. 1:6 31:8 [a] Ex. 13:21 [b] Deut. 31:6; Josh. 1:5; 1 Chr. 28:20; Heb. 13:5 31:9 [a] Deut. 17:18; 31:25, 26 [b] Num. 4:5, 6, 15; Deut. 10:8; 31:25, 26; Josh. 3:3 31:10 [a] Deut. 15:1, 2 [b] Lev. 23:34; Deut. 16:13 31:11 [a] Deut. 16:16 [b] Deut. 12:5 [c] Josh. 8:34; 2 Kin. 23:2 31:12 [a] Deut. 4:10 31:13 [a] Deut. 11:2 [b] Ps. 78:6, 7 31:14 [a] Num. 27:13 [b] Num. 27:19; Deut. 3:28 31:15 [a] Ex. 33:9 31:16 [a] Deut. 29:22 [b] Ex. 34:15; Deut. 4:25–28; Judg. 2:11, 12, 17 [c] Deut. 32:15 [d] Judg. 2:20 31:17 [a] Judg. 2:14; 6:13 [b] 2 Chr. 15:2 [c] Deut. 32:20 [d] Judg. 6:13 [e] Num. 14:42 31:18 [a] Deut. 31:17; [Is. 1:15, 16] 31:19 [a] Deut. 31:22, 26 31:20 [a] Deut. 32:15–17 [b] Deut. 31:16

Me and break My covenant. 21Then it shall
be, [a]when many evils and troubles have
come upon them, that this song will testify against them as a witness; for it will
not be forgotten in the mouths of their descendants, for [b]I know the inclination [c]of
their behavior today, even before I have
brought them to the land of which I swore
to give them."

22Therefore Moses wrote this song the
same day, and taught it to the children of
Israel. 23[a]Then He inaugurated Joshua the
son of Nun, and said, [b]"Be strong and of
good courage; for you shall bring the children of Israel into the land of which I swore
to them, and I will be with you."

24So it was, when Moses had completed
writing the words of this law in a book,
when they were finished, 25that Moses commanded the Levites, who bore the ark of
the covenant of the LORD, saying: 26"Take
this Book of the Law, [a]and put it beside the
ark of the covenant of the LORD your God,
that it may be there [b]as a witness against
you; 27[a]for I know your rebellion and your
[b]stiff neck. *If* today, while I am yet alive with
you, you have been rebellious against the
LORD, then how much more after my death?
28Gather to me all the elders of your tribes,
and your officers, that I may speak these
words in their hearing [a]and call heaven and
earth to witness against them. 29For I know
that after my death you will [a]become utterly
corrupt, and turn aside from the way which
I have commanded you. And [b]evil will befall
you [c]in the latter days, because you will do
evil in the sight of the LORD, to provoke Him
to anger through the work of your hands."

The Song of Moses

30Then Moses spoke in the hearing of
all the assembly of Israel the words of this
song until they were ended:

32 "Give [a]ear, O heavens,
and I will speak;
And hear, O [b]earth, the
words of my mouth.

2 Let [a]my teaching drop as the rain,
My speech distill as the dew,
[b]As raindrops on the tender herb,
And as showers on the grass.

3 For I proclaim the [a]name of the LORD:
[b]Ascribe greatness to our God.

4 *He is* [a]the Rock, [b]His work *is* perfect;
For all His ways *are* justice,
[c]A God of truth and [d]without injustice;
Righteous and upright *is* He.

5 "They[a] have corrupted themselves;
They are not His children,
Because of their blemish:
A [b]perverse and crooked generation.

6 Do you thus [a]deal with the LORD,
O foolish and unwise people?
Is He not [b]your Father,
who [c]bought you?
Has He not [d]made you and
established you?

7 "Remember[a] the days of old,
Consider the years of
many generations.
[b]Ask your father, and he
will show you;
Your elders, and they will tell you:

8 When the Most High [a]divided their
inheritance to the nations,
When He [b]separated the
sons of Adam,
He set the boundaries of the peoples
According to the number of
the children of Israel.

9 For [a]the LORD's portion *is* His people;
Jacob *is* the place of His inheritance.

10 "He found him [a]in a desert land
And in the wasteland, a
howling wilderness;
He encircled him, He instructed him,
He [b]kept him as the apple of His eye.

11 [a]As an eagle stirs up its nest,
Hovers over its young,
Spreading out its wings,
taking them up,
Carrying them on its wings,

31:21 [a] Deut. 31:17 [b] Hos. 5:3 [c] Amos 5:25, 26 **31:23** [a] Num. 27:23; Deut. 31:14 [b] Deut. 31:7 **31:26** [a] 2 Kin. 22:8 [b] Deut. 31:19 **31:27** [a] Deut. 9:7, 24 [b] Ex. 32:9; Deut. 9:6, 13 **31:28** [a] Deut. 30:19 **31:29** [a] Deut. 32:5; Judg. 2:19; [Acts 20:29, 30] [b] Deut. 28:15 [c] Gen. 49:1; Deut. 4:30 **32:1** [a] Deut. 4:26; Ps. 50:4; Is. 1:2 [b] Jer. 6:19 **32:2** [a] Is. 55:10, 11 [b] Ps. 72:6 **32:3** [a] Deut. 28:58 [b] 1 Chr. 29:11 **32:4** [a] Deut. 32:15, 18, 30; Ps. 18:2 [b] 2 Sam. 22:31 [c] Deut. 7:9; Is. 65:16; Jer. 10:10 [d] Job 34:10 **32:5** [a] Deut. 4:25; 31:29 [b] Phil. 2:15 **32:6** [a] Ps. 116:12 [b] Ex. 4:22; Deut. 1:31; Is. 63:16 [c] Ps. 74:2 [d] Deut. 32:15 **32:7** [a] Ps. 44:1 [b] Ex. 12:26; 13:14; Ps. 78:5–8 **32:8** [a] Acts 17:26 [b] Gen. 11:8 **32:9** [a] Ex. 19:5 **32:10** [a] Jer. 2:6; Hos. 13:5 [b] Ps. 17:8; Prov. 7:2; Zech. 2:8 **32:11** [a] Is. 31:5

12 *So* the LORD alone led him,
And *there was* no foreign
god with him.

13 "He[a] made him ride in the
heights of the earth,
That he might eat the
produce of the fields;
He made him draw honey
from the rock,
And oil from the flinty rock;
14 Curds from the cattle, and
milk of the flock,
[a]With fat of lambs;
And rams of the breed of
Bashan, and goats,
With the choicest wheat;
And you drank wine, the
[b]blood of the grapes.

15 "But Jeshurun grew fat and kicked;
[a]You grew fat, you grew thick,
You are obese!
Then he [b]forsook God *who*
[c]made him,
And scornfully esteemed the
[d]Rock of his salvation.
16 [a]They provoked Him to jealousy
with foreign *gods;*
With abominations they
provoked Him to anger.
17 [a]They sacrificed to demons,
not to God,
To gods they did not know,
To new *gods,* new arrivals
That your fathers did not fear.
18 [a]Of the Rock *who* begot you,
you are unmindful,
And have [b]forgotten the God
who fathered you.

19 "And[a] when the LORD saw *it,*
He spurned *them,*
Because of the provocation of
His sons and His daughters.
20 And He said: 'I will hide My
face from them,
I will see what their end *will be,*
For they *are* a perverse generation,
[a]Children in whom *is* no faith.
21 [a]They have provoked Me to
jealousy by *what* is not God;
They have moved Me to anger
[b]by their foolish idols.
But [c]I will provoke them to jealousy
by *those who are* not a nation;
I will move them to anger
by a foolish nation.
22 For [a]a fire is kindled in My anger,
And shall burn to the lowest hell;
It shall consume the earth
with her increase,
And set on fire the foundations
of the mountains.

23 'I will [a]heap disasters on them;
[b]I will spend My arrows on them.
24 *They shall be* wasted with hunger,
Devoured by pestilence and
bitter destruction;
I will also send against them
the [a]teeth of beasts,
With the poison of serpents
of the dust.
25 The sword shall destroy outside;
There shall be terror within
For the young man and virgin,
The nursing child with the
man of gray hairs.
26 [a]I would have said, "I will
dash them in pieces,
I will make the memory of them
to cease from among men,"
27 Had I not feared the wrath
of the enemy,
Lest their adversaries should
misunderstand,
Lest they should say, [a]"Our
hand *is* high;
And it is not the LORD who
has done all this." '

28 "For they *are* a nation void
of counsel,
Nor *is there any* understanding
in them.
29 [a]Oh, that they were wise, *that*
they understood this,
That they would consider
their [b]latter end!

32:13 [a] Is. 58:14 32:14 [a] Ps. 81:16 [b] Gen. 49:11 32:15 [a] Deut. 31:20 [b] Is. 1:4 [c] Is. 51:13 [d] Ps. 95:1 32:16 [a] Ps. 78:58; 1 Cor. 10:22 32:17 [a] Rev. 9:20 32:18 [a] Is. 17:10 [b] Jer. 2:32 32:19 [a] Judg. 2:14 32:20 [a] Matt. 17:17 32:21 [a] Ps. 78:58 [b] Ps. 31:6 [c] Rom. 10:19 32:22 [a] Num. 16:33–35; Ps. 18:7, 8; Lam. 4:11 32:23 [a] Ex. 32:12; Deut. 29:21, 24 [b] Ps. 7:12, 13 32:24 [a] Lev. 26:22 32:26 [a] Ezek. 20:23 32:27 [a] Is. 10:12–15 32:29 [a] Ps. 81:13; [Luke 19:42] [b] Deut. 31:29

30 How could one chase a thousand,
And two put ten thousand to flight,
Unless their Rock [a]had sold them,
And the LORD had surrendered them?
31 For their rock *is* not like our Rock,
[a]Even our enemies themselves
being judges.
32 For [a]their vine *is* of the vine of Sodom
And of the fields of Gomorrah;
Their grapes *are* grapes of gall,
Their clusters *are* bitter.
33 Their wine *is* [a]the poison of serpents,
And the cruel [b]venom of cobras.

34 '*Is* this not [a]laid up in store with Me,
Sealed up among My treasures?
35 [a]Vengeance is Mine, and recompense;
Their foot shall slip in *due* time;
[b]For the day of their calamity *is* at hand,
And the things to come
hasten upon them.'

36 "For[a] the LORD will judge His people
[b]And have compassion on His servants,
When He sees that *their* power is gone,
And [c]*there is* no one *remaining*,
bond or free.
37 He will say: [a]'Where *are* their gods,
The rock in which they sought refuge?
38 Who ate the fat of their sacrifices,
And drank the wine of their
drink offering?
Let them rise and help you,
And be your refuge.

39 'Now see that [a]I, *even* I, *am* He,
And [b]*there is* no God besides Me;
[c]I kill and I make alive;
I wound and I heal;
Nor *is there any* who can
deliver from My hand.
40 For I raise My hand to heaven,
And say, "*As* I live forever,
41 [a]If I whet My glittering sword,
And My hand takes hold on judgment,
I will render vengeance
to My enemies,
And repay those who hate Me.
42 I will make My arrows
drunk with blood,
And My sword shall devour flesh,
With the blood of the slain
and the captives,
From the heads of the leaders
of the enemy."'

43 "Rejoice,[a] O Gentiles, *with* His people;[1]
For He will [b]avenge the blood
of His servants,
And render vengeance to
His adversaries;
He [c]will provide atonement for
His land *and* His people."

44 So Moses came with Joshua[1] the son of
Nun and spoke all the words of this song in
the hearing of the people. 45 Moses finished
speaking all these words to all Israel, 46 and
he said to them: [a]"Set your hearts on all
the words which I testify among you today,
which you shall command your [b]children
to be careful to observe—all the words of
this law. 47 For it *is* not a futile thing for you,
because it *is* your [a]life, and by this word you
shall prolong *your* days in the land which
you cross over the Jordan to possess."

Moses to Die on Mount Nebo

48 Then the LORD spoke to Moses that
very same day, saying: 49 [a]"Go up this mountain of the Abarim, Mount Nebo, which *is*
in the land of Moab, across from Jericho;
view the land of Canaan, which I give to the
children of Israel as a possession; 50 and die
on the mountain which you ascend, and
be gathered to your people, just as [a]Aaron
your brother died on Mount Hor and was
gathered to his people; 51 because [a]you trespassed against Me among the children of
Israel at the waters of Meribah Kadesh, in
the Wilderness of Zin, because you [b]did not
hallow Me in the midst of the children of
Israel. 52 [a]Yet you shall see the land before
you, though you shall not go there, into
the land which I am giving to the children
of Israel."

32:30 [a] Judg. 2:14; Ps. 44:12 32:31 [a] [1 Sam. 4:7, 8; Jer. 40:2, 3] 32:32 [a] Is. 1:8–10 32:33 [a] Ps. 58:4 [b] Rom. 3:13 32:34 [a] [Jer. 2:22] 32:35 [a] Ps. 94:1; Rom. 12:19; Heb. 10:30 [b] 2 Pet. 2:3 32:36 [a] Ps. 135:14; Heb. 10:30 [b] Ps. 106:45; Jer. 31:20 [c] 2 Kin. 14:26 32:37 [a] Judg. 10:14; Jer. 2:28 32:39 [a] Is. 41:4; 43:10 [b] Deut. 32:12; Is. 45:5 [c] 1 Sam. 2:6; Ps. 68:20 32:41 [a] Is. 1:24; 66:16; Jer. 50:28–32 32:43 [a] Rom. 15:10 [b] 2 Kin. 9:7; Rev. 6:10; 19:2 [c] Ps. 65:3; 79:9; 85:1 [1] A Dead Sea Scroll fragment adds *And let all the gods (angels) worship Him* (compare Septuagint and Hebrews 1:6). 32:44 [1] Hebrew *Hoshea* (compare Numbers 13:8, 16) 32:46 [a] Ezek. 40:4; 44:5 [b] Deut. 11:19 32:47 [a] Deut. 8:3; 30:15–20 32:49 [a] Num. 27:12–14; Deut. 3:27 32:50 [a] Num. 20:25, 28; 33:38 32:51 [a] Num. 20:11–13 [b] Lev. 10:3 32:52 [a] Num. 27:12; Deut. 34:1–5

Moses' Final Blessing on Israel

33 Now this *is* [a]the blessing with which
Moses [b]the man of God blessed the
children of Israel before his death. 2And
he said:

[a]"The LORD came from Sinai,
And dawned on them from [b]Seir;
He shone forth from [c]Mount Paran,
And He came with [d]ten
thousands of saints;
From His right hand
Came a fiery law for them.
3 Yes, [a]He loves the people;
[b]All His saints *are* in Your hand;
They [c]sit down at Your feet;
Everyone [d]receives Your words.
4 [a]Moses commanded a law for us,
[b]A heritage of the congregation
of Jacob.
5 And He was [a]King in [b]Jeshurun,
When the leaders of the
people were gathered,
All the tribes of Israel together.

6 "Let [a]Reuben live, and not die,
Nor let his men be few."

7And this he said of [a]Judah:

"Hear, LORD, the voice of Judah,
And bring him to his people;
[b]Let his hands be sufficient for him,
And may You be [c]a help
against his enemies."

8And of [a]Levi he said:

[b]"*Let* Your Thummim and Your
Urim *be* with Your holy one,
[c]Whom You tested at Massah,
And with whom You contended
at the waters of Meribah,
9 [a]Who says of his father and mother,
'I have not [b]seen them';
[c]Nor did he acknowledge his
brothers,
Or know his own children;
For [d]they have observed Your word
And kept Your covenant.
10 [a]They shall teach Jacob
Your judgments,
And Israel Your law.
They shall put incense before You,
[b]And a whole burnt sacrifice
on Your altar.
11 Bless his substance, LORD,
And [a]accept the work of his hands;
Strike the loins of those who
rise against him,
And of those who hate him,
that they rise not again."

12Of Benjamin he said:

"The beloved of the LORD shall
dwell in safety by Him,
Who shelters him all the day long;
And he shall dwell between
His shoulders."

13And of Joseph he said:

[a]"Blessed of the LORD *is* his land,
With the precious things of
heaven, with the [b]dew,
And the deep lying beneath,
14 With the precious fruits of the sun,
With the precious produce
of the months,
15 With the best things of [a]the
ancient mountains,
With the precious things [b]of
the everlasting hills,
16 With the precious things of the
earth and its fullness,
And the favor of [a]Him who
dwelt in the bush.
Let *the blessing* come [b][1]on
the head of Joseph,
And on the crown of the head
of him *who was* separate
from his brothers.'[1]
17 His glory *is like* a [a]firstborn bull,
And his horns *like* the [b]horns
of the wild ox;

33:1 [a] Gen. 49:28 [b] Ps. 90 33:2 [a] Ex. 19:18, 20; Ps. 68:8, 17; Hab. 3:3 [b] Deut. 2:1, 4 [c] Num. 10:12 [d] Dan. 7:10; Acts 7:53; Rev. 5:11 33:3 [a] Ps. 47:4; Hos. 11:1 [b] 1 Sam. 2:9 [c] [Luke 10:39] [d] Prov. 2:1 33:4 [a] Deut. 4:2; John 1:17; 7:19 [b] Ps. 119:111 33:5 [a] Ex. 15:18 [b] Deut. 32:15 33:6 [a] Gen. 49:3, 4 33:7 [a] Gen. 49:8–12 [b] Gen. 49:8 [c] Ps. 146:5 33:8 [a] Gen. 49:5 [b] Ex. 28:30; Lev. 8:8 [c] Num. 20:2–13; Deut. 6:2, 3, 16; Ps. 81:7 33:9 [a] [Num. 25:5–8; Matt. 10:37; 19:29] [b] [Gen. 29:32] [c] Ex. 32:26–28 [d] Mal. 2:5, 6 33:10 [a] Lev. 10:11; Deut. 31:9–13; Mal. 2:7 [b] Lev. 1:9; Ps. 51:19 33:11 [a] 2 Sam. 24:23; Ezek. 20:40 33:13 [a] Gen. 49:22–26 [b] Gen. 27:28 33:15 [a] Gen. 49:26 [b] Hab. 3:6 33:16 [a] Ex. 3:2–4; Acts 7:30–35 [b] Gen. 49:26 [1] Genesis 49:26 33:17 [a] 1 Chr. 5:1 [b] Num. 23:22

Together with them
[c]He shall push the peoples
To the ends of the earth;
[d]They *are* the ten thousands
of Ephraim,
And they *are* the thousands
of Manasseh."

18 And of Zebulun he said:

[a]"Rejoice, Zebulun, in your going out,
And Issachar in your tents!
19 They shall [a]call the peoples
to the mountain;
There [b]they shall offer sacrifices
of righteousness;
For they shall partake *of* the
abundance of the seas
And *of* treasures hidden in the sand."

20 And of Gad he said:

"Blessed *is* he who [a]enlarges Gad;
He dwells as a lion,
And tears the arm and the
crown of his head.
21 [a]He provided the first *part* for himself,
Because a lawgiver's portion
was reserved there.
[b]He came *with* the heads of the people;
He administered the
justice of the LORD,
And His judgments with Israel."

22 And of Dan he said:

"Dan *is* a lion's whelp;
[a]He shall leap from Bashan."

23 And of Naphtali he said:

"O Naphtali, [a]satisfied with favor,
And full of the blessing of the LORD,
[b]Possess the west and the south."

24 And of Asher he said:

[a]"Asher *is* most blessed of sons;
Let him be favored by his brothers,
And let him [b]dip his foot in oil.
25 Your sandals *shall be* [a]iron and bronze;
As your days, *so shall* your
strength *be*.

26 "*There is* [a]no one like the
God of [b]Jeshurun,
[c]*Who* rides the heavens to help you,
And in His excellency on the clouds.
27 The eternal God *is your* [a]refuge,
And underneath *are* the
everlasting arms;
[b]He will thrust out the enemy
from before you,
And will say, 'Destroy!'
28 Then [a]Israel shall dwell in safety,
[b]The fountain of Jacob [c]alone,
In a land of grain and new wine;
His [d]heavens shall also drop dew.
29 [a]Happy *are* you, O Israel!
[b]Who *is* like you, a people
saved by the LORD,
[c]The shield of your help
And the sword of your majesty!
Your enemies [d]shall submit to you,
And [e]you shall tread down
their high places."

Moses Dies on Mount Nebo

34 Then Moses went up from the plains
of Moab [a]to Mount Nebo, to the top
of Pisgah, which is across from Jericho.
And the LORD showed him all the land of
Gilead as far as Dan, 2 all Naphtali and the
land of Ephraim and Manasseh, all the
land of Judah as far as the Western Sea,[1]
3 the South, and the plain of the Valley of
Jericho, [a]the city of palm trees, as far as
Zoar. 4 Then the LORD said to him, [a]"This
is the land of which I swore to give Abraham, Isaac, and Jacob, saying, 'I will give
it to your descendants.' [b]I have caused you
to see *it* with your eyes, but you shall not
cross over there."
5 [a]So Moses the servant of the LORD died
there in the land of Moab, according to the
word of the LORD. 6 And He buried him in

33:17 [c] 1 Kin. 22:11; Ps. 44:5 [d] Gen. 48:19 33:18 [a] Gen. 49:13–15 33:19 [a] Ex. 15:17; Ps. 2:6; Is. 2:3 [b] Ps. 4:5; 51:19 33:20 [a] 1 Chr. 12:8 33:21 [a] Num. 32:16, 17 [b] Josh. 4:12 33:22 [a] Gen. 49:16, 17; Josh. 19:47 33:23 [a] Gen. 49:21 [b] Josh. 19:32 33:24 [a] Gen. 49:20 [b] Job 29:6 33:25 [a] Deut. 8:9 33:26 [a] Ex. 15:11; Deut. 4:35; Ps. 86:8; Jer. 10:6 [b] Deut. 32:15 [c] Deut. 10:14; Ps. 68:3, 33, 34; 104:3 33:27 [a] [Ps. 90:1; 91:2, 9] [b] Deut. 9:3–5 33:28 [a] Deut. 33:12; Jer. 23:6; 33:16 [b] Deut. 8:7, 8 [c] Num. 23:9 [d] Gen. 27:28 33:29 [a] Ps. 144:15 [b] Deut. 4:32–34; 2 Sam. 7:23 [c] Gen. 15:1; Ps. 115:9 [d] Ps. 18:44; 66:3 [e] Num. 33:52 34:1 [a] Num. 27:12; Deut. 32:49 34:2 [1] That is, the Mediterranean 34:3 [a] 2 Chr. 28:15 34:4 [a] Gen. 12:7 [b] Deut. 3:27 34:5 [a] Num. 20:12; Deut. 32:50; Josh. 1:1, 2

a valley in the land of Moab, opposite Beth
Peor; but [a]no one knows his grave to this
day. 7[a]Moses *was* one hundred and twenty
years old when he died. [b]His eyes were not
dim nor his natural vigor diminished. 8And
the children of Israel wept for Moses in the
plains of Moab [a]thirty days. So the days of
weeping *and* mourning for Moses ended.

9Now Joshua the son of Nun was full of
the [a]spirit of wisdom, for [b]Moses had laid
his hands on him; so the children of Israel
heeded him, and did as the LORD had commanded Moses.

10But since then there [a]has not arisen
in Israel a prophet like Moses, [b]whom the
LORD knew face to face, 11in all [a]the signs
and wonders which the LORD sent him to
do in the land of Egypt, before Pharaoh,
before all his servants, and in all his land,
12and by all that mighty power and all the
great terror which Moses performed in the
sight of all Israel.

34:6 [a] Jude 9 34:7 [a] Deut. 31:2 [b] Gen. 27:1; 48:10 34:8 [a] Gen. 50:3, 10 34:9 [a] Is. 11:2 [b] Num. 27:18, 23
34:10 [a] Deut. 18:15, 18 [b] Ex. 33:11; Num. 12:8; Deut. 5:4 34:11 [a] Deut. 7:19

THE BOOK OF

JOSHUA

OVERVIEW

Joshua, whom God chose to lead the Israelites into the Promised Land after the death of Moses, is believed to be the author of the Book of Joshua. Named for Joshua (a Hebrew name meaning "the Lord saves"), the book is a historical account of the Israelites taking possession of the land God had promised their ancestors. The book covers a period of twenty-five to thirty years as it details the battles the Israelites fought in the process of possessing the land.

The story begins when God instructed Joshua to lead His people into the land of Canaan. God promised Joshua that He would be with him, just as He had been with Moses (Josh. 1:1–9). Joshua then sent spies into the city of Jericho to assess the situation. Fearing capture, the spies turned to a resident named Rahab for help. Rahab hid the spies and helped them escape after asking them to promise that she and her family would be spared in Israel's victory (see 2:1–24).

Days after the spies returned, Joshua led the Israelites across the Jordan River that separated them from the land of promise. Similar to what He had done with the Red Sea, God stopped the waters of the Jordan River and the people crossed on dry ground (see 3:14–17; cf. Ex. 14).

Once the Israelites had crossed the Jordan, God led them into battle against Jericho. God instructed the army to march around the city walls for seven days. On the seventh day, He ordered the army to march around the city walls seven times and to blow trumpets. As God had promised, the walls of Jericho fell, and the city was defeated (see Josh. 6:1–21). True to the spies' word, Rahab and her family were spared, and because of her faith, she became part of God's people (see 6:22–25). Under Joshua's leadership and God's guidance and might, the Israelites continued to conquer the land (chs. 7–12).

With still much more land to conquer, God instructed Joshua to divide the remaining land as an inheritance among the tribes (chs. 13–19). He commanded the Israelites to identify cities of refuge (ch. 20) and cities of the Levites (ch. 21). Once the land had been conquered and divided, God's promise to the Israelites was fulfilled (see 21:43–45) and the tribes took possession of their respective lands (ch. 22).

Near the end of the book, Joshua reminded the Israelites of all God had done for them and the promises that He had kept, even as the great leader prepared for his death (see 23:1). He encouraged them to follow the laws and warned them against worshiping the false gods of their neighbors (see vv. 6–13). He cautioned them about the harm that would come if they turned away from the one true God (see vv. 14–16).

In chapter 24, Joshua gathered the people of Israel to affirm God's covenant with them. He outlined God's relationship with Abraham, Isaac, and Jacob and reminded the people of how God had led them from captivity to freedom, performing miracles along the way (see vv. 1–8). He recounted their military victories designed by God and supported by His power, which gave them possession of the land (see vv. 9–13). Joshua then instructed the Israelites, "Choose . . . this day whom you will serve" (v. 15), and they replied, "The Lord our God we will serve, and His voice we will obey!" (v. 24).

The theme of Joshua is God's faithfulness. God had promised He would lead the Israelites into the land He had given to Abraham. The Book of Joshua records the fulfillment of that promise. Despite the disobedience, rebelliousness, and doubt of the older generation of Israelites, God allowed the new generation to enter the land.

BREATHE IT IN

When God was ready for the Israelites to possess the Promised Land, He did not simply give them the land. He required something of them. They had to take action to access it. But God did not leave them to figure out the steps to take on their own. He guided them and empowered them to possess the land. Conquering the land did not come easy; they had to fight for it. They did not fight just one battle either, but several. But all along the way, God's presence and power were leading His people.

Like the Israelites' trek to the Promised Land, the journey of many marginalized people toward fair and just treatment has been long and filled with both victory and defeat. Many still have not arrived at their desired destination.

The Book of Joshua teaches that no matter how long the journey, God is always there with us. God led the Israelites out of bondage and tarried with them for forty years in the wilderness. He made a covenant with them that He honored even when they did not. He met their needs for food and shelter and protected them from their enemies. The journey was preparation for their eventual possession of the Promised Land—the land flowing with milk and honey.

God has not changed. He is faithful and will fulfill all the promises He has made. We must be committed to the journey, no matter how long it may take. Along the way, we will be called upon to develop and nurture our relationship with God. We will learn about His character, plans, and expectations for our lives. It is through the process that we learn the crucial lessons we need for when He fulfills His promises.

To take possession of our promises, we must begin with faith and be willing to do the work God has set aside for us. Before sending the Israelites into Canaan, God prepared them for the fight. He trained them for battle. He made sure they had an army, armor, and a battle plan. He even showed up to the battle. For the Israelites to be victorious, they had to trust God.

We, too, must trust God. We must also be willing to stand up and fight. But we must further recognize that we do not fight against people—our battle is not "against flesh and blood"; we fight against principalities and powers, the evil influences of this world (see Eph. 6:12). We have to prepare spiritually for a spiritual battle. We have to put on the armor of God (see 6:13–17). We have to believe we have the victory before the battle even begins. We have to be willing to persevere until God gives us that victory.

Though we may not be where we want to be as a people in this society, God has given us many victories along the way. If we continue to be obedient and trust in God rather than in this dying world, we can continue to be victorious in defeating our enemies. In the end, we will take possession of the land He has promised us.

THE BOOK OF

JOSHUA

God's Commission to Joshua

1 After the death of Moses the servant of
the LORD, it came to pass that the LORD
spoke to Joshua the son of Nun, Moses'
[a]assistant, saying: 2[a]“Moses My servant is
dead. Now therefore, arise, go over this Jordan, you and all this people, to the land
which I am giving to them—the children
of Israel. 3[a]Every place that the sole of your
foot will tread upon I have given you, as I
said to Moses. 4[a]From the wilderness and
this Lebanon as far as the great river, the
River Euphrates, all the land of the Hittites, and to the Great Sea toward the going down of the sun, shall be your territory.
5[a]No man shall *be able to* stand before you
all the days of your life; [b]as I was with Moses, *so* [c]I will be with you. [d]I will not leave
you nor forsake you. 6[a]Be strong and of
good courage, for to this people you shall
divide as an inheritance the land which I
swore to their fathers to give them. 7Only
be strong and very courageous, that you
may observe to do according to all the law
[a]which Moses My servant commanded you;
[b]do not turn from it to the right hand or to
the left, that you may prosper wherever you
go. 8[a]This Book of the Law shall not depart
from your mouth, but [b]you shall meditate
in it day and night, that you may observe
to do according to all that is written in it.
For then you will make your way prosperous, and then you will have good success.
9[a]Have I not commanded you? Be strong
and of good courage; [b]do not be afraid, nor
be dismayed, for the LORD your God *is* with
you wherever you go.”

The Order to Cross the Jordan

10Then Joshua commanded the officers of the people, saying, 11“Pass through
the camp and command the people, saying, ‘Prepare provisions for yourselves, for
[a]within three days you will cross over this
Jordan, to go in to possess the land which
the LORD your God is giving you to possess.’”
12And to the Reubenites, the Gadites, and
half the tribe of Manasseh Joshua spoke,
saying, 13“Remember [a]the word which Moses the servant of the LORD commanded
you, saying, ‘The LORD your God is giving
you rest and is giving you this land.’ 14Your
wives, your little ones, and your livestock
shall remain in the land which Moses gave
you on this side of the Jordan. But you shall
pass before your brethren armed, all your
mighty men of valor, and help them, 15un-
til the LORD has given your brethren rest,
as He *gave* you, and they also have taken
possession of the land which the LORD your
God is giving them. [a]Then you shall return
to the land of your possession and enjoy
it, which Moses the LORD's servant gave
you on this side of the Jordan toward the
sunrise.”
16So they answered Joshua, saying, “All
that you command us we will do, and wherever you send us we will go. 17Just as we
heeded Moses in all things, so we will heed
you. Only the LORD your God [a]be with you,
as He was with Moses. 18Whoever rebels
against your command and does not heed
your words, in all that you command him,
shall be put to death. Only be strong and
of good courage.”

1:1 [a] Ex. 24:13; Num. 13:16; 14:6, 29, 30, 37, 38; Deut. 1:38; Acts 7:45 1:2 [a] Num. 12:7; Deut. 34:5 1:3 [a] Deut. 11:24; Josh. 11:23
1:4 [a] Gen. 15:18; Ex. 23:31; Num. 34:3–12 1:5 [a] Deut. 7:24 [b] Ex. 3:12 [c] Deut. 31:8, 23 [d] Deut. 31:6, 7; Heb. 13:5 1:6 [a] Deut. 31:7, 23
1:7 [a] Num. 27:23; Deut. 31:7; Josh. 11:15 [b] Deut. 5:32 1:8 [a] Deut. 17:18, 19; 31:24, 26; Josh. 8:34 [b] Deut. 29:9; Ps. 1:1–3
1:9 [a] Deut. 31:7 [b] Ps. 27:1 1:11 [a] Deut. 9:1; Josh. 3:17 1:13 [a] Num. 32:20–28
1:15 [a] Josh. 22:1–4 1:17 [a] 1 Sam. 20:13; 1 Kin. 1:37

RELEASE // HOPE FOR TODAY

Trust the Process

Joshua 1:9 // "Have I not commanded you? Be strong and of good courage; do not be afraid, nor be dismayed, for the LORD your God is with you wherever you go."

Summary Message // Joshua was facing a travel-weary, murmuring megacongregation. The generation of Israelites who had fled bondage in Egypt were no longer living. Only Caleb and Joshua were left of those who saw the miracles of that time. Most of this younger generation had not seen the Nile River turn to blood or the locusts and frogs cover the land. Most had only heard about the darkened sun. Most only heard their elders speak of the night the firstborn of every living creature in Egypt died, except the Israelites, who had covered their doorposts with lamb's blood so that the Lord would pass over their homes.

As this generation stood facing the Promised Land, God spoke to Joshua and told him it was time for him to lead the nation of Israel into all that God had promised. For decades they had wandered, but now was their time. Joshua did not hesitate to grab on to God's command, and he led the people with strength and courage. The people likewise responded to God and to Joshua's leadership that had brought them to this place. They could see the fulfillment of God's promises. So, they blessed Joshua and committed to follow him as he urged them to be strong and of good courage.

Practical Application // The path to our individual promised land is littered with impossibilities, including fear, doubt, and unbelief. These can keep us going in circles and cause us to altogether miss God's plan and purpose for us. We all have our own plans and expectations of what our lives should be. But we must yield those plans and expectations to God's will for our lives. If we do not, then we are bound to face disappointment, anxiety, and anger when things don't turn out the way we want them to. Our core problem is that we are not in control.

Likewise, even expectations of God's highest and best for us, like freedom and justice, always seem out of reach. Repeated disappointment further diminishes our hopes. "Hope deferred makes the heart sick" (Prov. 13:12). Heart sickness can cause us to feel dry, withered, and trapped in despair.

The challenge is to attach ourselves stubbornly to a hope that refuses to be hardened by hatred, calloused by a prolonged hardship, or calcified by abuse or difficult circumstances. True hope in the God who always is at work cannot be destroyed by challenging moments or daily acts of microaggression. Faith is still the substance of our hope (see Heb. 11:1). Faith stands as a flickering candle, defying the winds of resistance that seek to hurl hope into the darkness.

Fervent Prayer // Sovereign God, You are amazing! You prepare our future in the reality of our present. You are our hope for today and every day. We trust that You will give us what we need when we need it. We ask that You strengthen our resolve with encouragement that undergirds our faith and keeps us hopeful until Your answer arrives. Putting our trust in You, we face forward, knowing that our yesterday cannot mess up our today or our tomorrow. Thank You that You are with us all the days of our lives. We have faith that You will be with us just as You were with Moses, Joshua, and all of Israel. In Jesus' name we pray. Amen.

Rahab Hides the Spies
(Heb. 11:31)

2 Now Joshua the son of Nun sent out
two men [a]from Acacia Grove[1] to spy
secretly, saying, "Go, view the land, especially Jericho."
So they went, and [b]came to the house of
a harlot named [c]Rahab, and lodged there.
2And [a]it was told the king of Jericho, saying,
"Behold, men have come here tonight
from the children of Israel to search out
the country."
3So the king of Jericho sent to Rahab, saying, "Bring out the men who have come to
you, who have entered your house, for they
have come to search out all the country."
4[a]Then the woman took the two men
and hid them. So she said, "Yes, the men

2:1 [a] Num. 25:1; Josh. 3:1 [b] Heb. 11:31; James 2:25 [c] Matt. 1:5 [1] Hebrew *Shittim* 2:2 [a] Josh. 2:22 2:4 [a] 2 Sam. 17:19, 20

came to me, but I did not know where they
were from. 5And it happened as the gate
was being shut, when it was dark, that the
men went out. Where the men went I do not
know; pursue them quickly, for you may
overtake them." 6(But [a]she had brought
them up to the roof and hidden them with
the stalks of flax, which she had laid in order on the roof.) 7Then the men pursued
them by the road to the Jordan, to the fords.
And as soon as those who pursued them
had gone out, they shut the gate.

8Now before they lay down, she came up
to them on the roof, 9and said to the men:
[a]"I know that the LORD has given you the
land, that [b]the terror of you has fallen on us,
and that all the inhabitants of the land [c]are
fainthearted because of you. 10For we have
heard how the LORD [a]dried up the water of
the Red Sea for you when you came out of
Egypt, and [b]what you did to the two kings
of the Amorites who *were* on the other side
of the Jordan, Sihon and Og, whom you [c]ut-
terly destroyed. 11And as soon as we [a]heard
these things, [b]our hearts melted; neither did
there remain any more courage in anyone
because of you, for [c]the LORD your God, He
is God in heaven above and on earth beneath. 12Now therefore, I beg you, [a]swear
to me by the LORD, since I have shown you
kindness, that you also will show kindness
to [b]my father's house, and [c]give me a true
token, 13and [a]spare my father, my mother,
my brothers, my sisters, and all that they
have, and deliver our lives from death."

14So the men answered her, "Our lives
for yours, if none of you tell this business
of ours. And it shall be, when the LORD has
given us the land, that [a]we will deal kindly
and truly with you."

15Then she [a]let them down by a rope
through the window, for her house *was* on
the city wall; she dwelt on the wall. 16And
she said to them, "Get to the mountain, lest
the pursuers meet you. Hide there three
days, until the pursuers have returned. Afterward you may go your way."

17So the men said to her: "We *will be*
[a]blameless of this oath of yours which you
have made us swear, 18[a]unless, *when* we
come into the land, you bind this line of
scarlet cord in the window through which
you let us down, [b]and unless you bring your
father, your mother, your brothers, and all
your father's household to your own home.
19So it shall be *that* whoever goes outside
the doors of your house into the street, his
blood *shall be* on his own head, and we *will
be* guiltless. And whoever is with you in the
house, [a]his blood *shall be* on our head if a
hand is laid on him. 20And if you tell this
business of ours, then we will be free from
your oath which you made us swear."

21Then she said, "According to your
words, so *be* it." And she sent them away,
and they departed. And she bound the scarlet cord in the window.

22They departed and went to the mountain, and stayed there three days until the
pursuers returned. The pursuers sought
them all along the way, but did not find
them. 23So the two men returned, descended from the mountain, and crossed
over; and they came to Joshua the son of
Nun, and told him all that had befallen
them. 24And they said to Joshua, "Truly
[a]the LORD has delivered all the land into
our hands, for indeed all the inhabitants of
the country are fainthearted because of us."

Israel Crosses the Jordan

3 Then Joshua rose early in the morning;
and they set out [a]from Acacia Grove[1]
and came to the Jordan, he and all the children of Israel, and lodged there before they
crossed over. 2So it was, [a]after three days,
that the officers went through the camp;
3and they commanded the people, saying,
[a]"When you see the ark of the covenant of
the LORD your God, [b]and the priests, the
Levites, bearing it, then you shall set out
from your place and go after it. 4[a]Yet there
shall be a space between you and it, about
two thousand cubits by measure. Do not
come near it, that you may know the way
by which you must go, for you have not
passed *this* way before."

5And Joshua said to the people,

2:6 [a] Ex. 1:17; 2 Sam. 17:19 2:9 [a] Deut. 1:8 [b] Gen. 35:5; Ex. 23:27; Deut. 2:25; 11:25; Josh. 9:9, 10 [c] Ex. 15:15; Josh. 5:1 2:10 [a] Ex. 14:21; Josh. 4:23 [b] Num. 21:21–35 [c] Deut. 20:17; Josh. 6:21 2:11 [a] Ex. 15:14, 15 [b] Josh. 5:1; 7:5; Ps. 22:14; Is. 13:7 [c] Deut. 4:39 2:12 [a] 1 Sam. 20:14, 15, 17 [b] 1 Tim. 5:8 [c] Ex. 12:13; Josh. 2:18 2:13 [a] Josh. 6:23–25 2:14 [a] Gen. 47:29; Judg. 1:24; [Matt. 5:7] 2:15 [a] Acts 9:25 2:17 [a] Ex. 20:7 2:18 [a] Josh. 2:12 [b] Josh. 6:23 2:19 [a] 1 Kin. 2:32; Matt. 27:25 2:24 [a] Ex. 23:31; Josh. 6:2; 21:44 3:1 [a] Josh. 2:1 [1] Hebrew *Shittim* 3:2 [a] Josh. 1:10, 11 3:3 [a] Num. 10:33 [b] Deut. 31:9, 25 3:4 [a] Ex. 19:12

[a]"Sanctify yourselves, for tomorrow the
LORD will do wonders among you." 6Then
Joshua spoke to the priests, saying, [a]"Take
up the ark of the covenant and cross over
before the people."

So they took up the ark of the covenant
and went before the people.

7And the LORD said to Joshua, "This day
I will begin to [a]exalt you in the sight of all
Israel, that they may know that, [b]as I was
with Moses, *so* I will be with you. 8You shall
command [a]the priests who bear the ark of
the covenant, saying, 'When you have come
to the edge of the water of the Jordan, [b]you
shall stand in the Jordan.'"

9So Joshua said to the children of Israel, "Come here, and hear the words of
the LORD your God." 10And Joshua said, "By
this you shall know that [a]the living God *is*
among you, and *that* He will without fail
[b]drive out from before you the [c]Canaan-
ites and the Hittites and the Hivites and
the Perizzites and the Girgashites and the
Amorites and the Jebusites: 11Behold, the
ark of the covenant of [a]the Lord of all
the earth is crossing over before you into
the Jordan. 12Now therefore, [a]take for yourselves twelve men from the tribes of Israel,
one man from every tribe. 13And it shall
come to pass, [a]as soon as the soles of the
feet of the priests who bear the ark of the
LORD, [b]the Lord of all the earth, shall rest
in the waters of the Jordan, *that* the waters
of the Jordan shall be cut off, the waters
that come down from upstream, and they
[c]shall stand as a heap."

JOSHUA 3:7

I AM JOSHUA

And the LORD said to Joshua, "This day I will begin to exalt you in the sight of all Israel, that they may know that, as I was with Moses, so I will be with you." Joshua 3:7

I am Joshua, son of Nun. I served Moses as his assistant and later as his general. I was one of the twelve spies Moses sent into the land of Canaan—the Promised Land God had given us. When we returned, Caleb and I were the only ones who gave a good report. The others told of the giants who inhabited the land, causing the people to be afraid. Caleb and I told them not to fear. The land was an exceedingly good land, and the Lord had promised it to us; therefore, He would deliver it to us. But fear had already gripped the people and they wanted to stone us. Because of their lack of trust in God, He declared that none of them would ever enter the Promised Land. An entire generation died in the wilderness within sight of the land God had promised. Caleb and I were the only ones from our generation allowed to enter the Promised Land.

I was later chosen to replace Moses as the people's leader. Before Moses died, he prayed for me, and God granted me great wisdom to lead. Moses encouraged me to be strong and courageous, promising that no one would be able to stand against me all the days of my life. As evidence that God was with me, just before entering into the battle of Jericho, I saw the Commander of the Lord's army standing next to me with His sword drawn. The Lord caused us to defeat Jericho along with all our enemies. Led forth by God, we took possession of the land that He had promised to us.

✝

Just as it was for Joshua, God will clear our path of all the obstacles before us if we believe Him and trust His promises to us. When we stand in the places God decrees, nothing will be able to stand against us all the days of our lives.

3:5 [a] Ex. 19:10, 14, 15; Lev. 20:7; Num. 11:18; Josh. 7:13; 1 Sam. 16:5; Job 1:5; Joel 2:16 3:6 [a] Num. 4:15 3:7 [a] Josh. 4:14; 1 Chr. 29:25; 2 Chr. 1:1 [b] Josh. 1:5, 9 3:8 [a] Josh. 3:3 [b] Josh. 3:17 3:10 [a] Deut. 5:26; Josh. 11:23; 1 Sam. 17:26; 2 Kin. 19:4; Hos. 1:10; Matt. 16:16; 1 Thess. 1:9 [b] Ex. 33:2; Deut. 7:1; 18:12; Ps. 44:2 [c] Acts 13:19 3:11 [a] Josh. 3:13; Job 41:11; Ps. 24:1; Mic. 4:13; Zech. 4:14; 6:5 3:12 [a] Josh. 4:2, 4 3:13 [a] Josh. 3:15, 16 [b] Josh. 3:11 [c] Ps. 78:13; 114:3

14So it was, when the people set out from
their camp to cross over the Jordan, with
the priests bearing the [a]ark of the covenant
before the people, 15and as those who bore
the ark came to the Jordan, and [a]the feet
of the priests who bore the ark dipped in
the edge of the water (for the [b]Jordan overflows all its banks [c]during the whole time
of harvest), 16that the waters which came
down from upstream stood *still, and* rose in
a heap very far away at Adam, the city that
is beside [a]Zaretan. So the waters that went
down [b]into the Sea of the Arabah, [c]the Salt
Sea, failed, *and* were cut off; and the people
crossed over opposite Jericho. 17Then the
priests who bore the ark of the covenant of
the LORD stood firm on dry ground in the
midst of the Jordan; [a]and all Israel crossed
over on dry ground, until all the people had
crossed completely over the Jordan.

The Memorial Stones

4 And it came to pass, when all the people
had completely crossed [a]over the Jordan, that the LORD spoke to Joshua, saying:
2[a]"Take for yourselves twelve men from the
people, one man from every tribe, 3and
command them, saying, 'Take for yourselves twelve stones from here, out of the
midst of the Jordan, from the place where
[a]the priests' feet stood firm. You shall carry
them over with you and leave them in [b]the
lodging place where you lodge tonight.'"
4Then Joshua called the twelve men
whom he had appointed from the children
of Israel, one man from every tribe; 5and
Joshua said to them: "Cross over before the
ark of the LORD your God into the midst of
the Jordan, and each one of you take up
a stone on his shoulder, according to the
number of the tribes of the children of Israel, 6that this may be [a]a sign among you
[b]when your children ask in time to come,
saying, 'What do these stones *mean* to you?'
7Then you shall answer them that [a]the waters of the Jordan were cut off before the
ark of the covenant of the LORD; when it
crossed over the Jordan, the waters of the
Jordan were cut off. And these stones shall
be for [b]a memorial to the children of Israel forever."
8And the children of Israel did so, just
as Joshua commanded, and took up twelve
stones from the midst of the Jordan, as the
LORD had spoken to Joshua, according to
the number of the tribes of the children of
Israel, and carried them over with them to
the place where they lodged, and laid them
down there. 9Then Joshua set up twelve
stones in the midst of the Jordan, in the
place where the feet of the priests who bore
the ark of the covenant stood; and they are
there to this day.
10So the priests who bore the ark stood in
the midst of the Jordan until everything was
finished that the LORD had commanded
Joshua to speak to the people, according
to all that Moses had commanded Joshua;
and the people hurried and crossed over.
11Then it came to pass, when all the people
had completely crossed over, that the [a]ark
of the LORD and the priests crossed over
in the presence of the people. 12And [a]the
men of Reuben, the men of Gad, and half
the tribe of Manasseh crossed over armed
before the children of Israel, as Moses had
spoken to them. 13About forty thousand
prepared for war crossed over before the
LORD for battle, to the plains of Jericho.
14On that day the LORD [a]exalted Joshua in
the sight of all Israel; and they feared him,
as they had feared Moses, all the days of
his life.
15Then the LORD spoke to Joshua, saying,
16"Command the priests who bear [a]the ark
of the Testimony to come up from the Jordan." 17Joshua therefore commanded the
priests, saying, "Come up from the Jordan."
18And it came to pass, when the priests who
bore the ark of the covenant of the LORD
had come from the midst of the Jordan,
and the soles of the priests' feet touched
the dry land, that the waters of the Jordan
returned to their place [a]and overflowed all
its banks as before.
19Now the people came up from the Jordan on the tenth *day* of the first month, and
they camped [a]in Gilgal on the east border of

3:14 [a] Ps. 132:8; Acts 7:44, 45 3:15 [a] Josh. 3:13 [b] 1 Chr. 12:15; Jer. 12:5; 49:19 [c] Josh. 4:18; 5:10, 12 3:16 [a] 1 Kin. 4:12; 7:46 [b] Deut. 3:17 [c] Gen. 14:3; Num. 34:3 3:17 [a] Gen. 50:24; Ex. 3:8; 6:1–8; 14:21, 22, 29; 33:1; Deut. 6:10; Heb. 11:29 4:1 [a] Deut. 27:2; Josh. 3:17 4:2 [a] Josh. 3:12 4:3 [a] Josh. 3:13 [b] Josh. 4:19, 20 4:6 [a] Deut. 27:2; Ps. 103:2 [b] Ex. 12:26; 13:14; Deut. 6:20 4:7 [a] Josh. 3:13, 16 [b] Ex. 12:14; Num. 16:40 4:11 [a] Josh. 3:11; 6:11 4:12 [a] Num. 32:17, 20, 27, 28; Josh. 1:14 4:14 [a] Josh. 3:7; 1 Chr. 29:25 4:16 [a] Ex. 25:16, 22 4:18 [a] Josh. 3:15; 1 Chr. 12:15 4:19 [a] Josh. 5:9

Jericho. 20 And [a]those twelve stones which
they took out of the Jordan, Joshua set up
in Gilgal. 21 Then he spoke to the children
of Israel, saying: [a]"When your children ask
their fathers in time to come, saying, 'What
are these stones?' 22 then you shall let your
children know, saying, [a]'Israel crossed over
this Jordan on [b]dry land'; 23 for the LORD
your God dried up the waters of the Jordan before you until you had crossed over,
as the LORD your God did to the Red Sea,
[a]which He dried up before us until we had
crossed over, 24 [a]that all the peoples of the
earth may know the hand of the LORD, that
it *is* [b]mighty, that you may [c]fear the LORD
your God forever."

#OXYGEN

JOSHUA 4:23–24

Hope for Today

When the transgenerational consequences of racial discrimination meet the mighty hand of God, all will know. Doors will swing wide open that no one can shut. The same God who brought our ancestors through will do the same for us.

So, just **breathe** and **hope for today.**

The Second Generation Circumcised

5 So it was, when all the kings of the Amorites who *were* on the west side of the
Jordan, and all the kings of the Canaanites
[a]who *were* by the sea, [b]heard that the LORD
had dried up the waters of the Jordan from
before the children of Israel until we[1] had
crossed over, that their heart melted; [c]and
there was no spirit in them any longer because of the children of Israel.
2 At that time the LORD said to Joshua,
"Make [a]flint knives for yourself, and circumcise the sons of Israel again the second
time." 3 So Joshua made flint knives for
himself, and circumcised the sons of Israel at the hill of the foreskins.[1] 4 And this *is*
the reason why Joshua circumcised them:
[a]All the people who came out of Egypt *who were* males, all the men of war, had died in
the wilderness on the way, after they had
come out of Egypt. 5 For all the people who
came out had been circumcised, but all the people born in the wilderness, on the way as they came out of Egypt, had not
been circumcised. 6 For the children of Is-
rael walked [a]forty years in the wilderness, till all the people *who were* men of war, who came out of Egypt, were consumed, because they did not obey the voice of the LORD—to whom the LORD swore that [b]He would not show them the land which the LORD had sworn to their fathers that He
would give us, [c]"a land flowing with milk
and honey."[1] 7 Then Joshua circumcised
[a]their sons *whom* He raised up in their place; for they were uncircumcised, because they had not been circumcised on the way.
8 So it was, when they had finished cir-
cumcising all the people, that they stayed
in their places in the camp [a]till they were
healed. 9 Then the LORD said to Joshua,
"This day I have rolled away [a]the reproach
of Egypt from you." Therefore the name of
the place is called [b]Gilgal[1] to this day.
10 Now the children of Israel camped in
Gilgal, and kept the Passover [a]on the fourteenth day of the month at twilight on the
plains of Jericho. 11 And they ate of the pro-
duce of the land on the day after the Passover, unleavened bread and parched grain,
on the very same day. 12 Then [a]the manna
ceased on the day after they had eaten the produce of the land; and the children of Israel no longer had manna, but they ate the food of the land of Canaan that year.

The Commander of the Army of the LORD

13 And it came to pass, when Joshua
was by Jericho, that he lifted his eyes and
looked, and behold, [a]a Man stood opposite

4:20 [a] Deut. 11:30; Josh. 4:3; 5:9, 10 4:21 [a] Josh. 4:6 4:22 [a] Ex. 12:26, 27; 13:8–14; Deut. 26:5–9 [b] Josh. 3:17 4:23 [a] Ex. 14:21 4:24 [a] 1 Kin. 8:42; 2 Kin. 19:19; Ps. 106:8 [b] Ex. 15:16; 1 Chr. 29:12; Ps. 89:13 [c] Ex. 14:31; Deut. 6:2; Ps. 76:7; Jer. 10:7 5:1 [a] Num. 13:29 [b] Ex. 15:14, 15 [c] Josh. 2:10, 11; 9:9; 1 Kin. 10:5 [1] Following Kethib; Qere, some Hebrew manuscripts and editions, Septuagint, Syriac, Targum, and Vulgate read *they.* 5:2 [a] Ex. 4:25 5:3 [1] Hebrew *Gibeath Haaraloth* 5:4 [a] Num. 14:29; 26:64, 65; Deut. 2:14–16 5:6 [a] Num. 14:33; Deut. 1:3; 29:5 [b] Num. 14:23, 29–35; 26:23–65; Heb. 3:11 [c] Ex. 3:8 [1] Exodus 3:8 5:7 [a] Num. 14:31; Deut. 1:39 5:8 [a] Gen. 34:25 5:9 [a] Gen. 34:14 [b] Josh. 4:19 [1] Literally *Rolling* 5:10 [a] Ex. 12:6; Num. 9:5 5:12 [a] Ex. 16:35 5:13 [a] Gen. 18:1, 2; 32:24, 30; Ex. 23:23; Num. 22:31; Zech. 1:8; Acts 1:10

him [b]with His sword drawn in His hand. And Joshua went to Him and said to Him, "*Are* You for us or for our adversaries?"

14So He said, "No, but *as* Commander of the army of the LORD I have now come."

And Joshua [a]fell on his face to the earth and [b]worshiped, and said to Him, "What does my Lord say to His servant?"

15Then the Commander of the LORD's army said to Joshua, [a]"Take your sandal off your foot, for the place where you stand *is* holy." And Joshua did so.

The Destruction of Jericho

6 Now [a]Jericho was securely shut up because of the children of Israel; none went out, and none came in. 2And the LORD said to Joshua: "See! [a]I have given Jericho into your hand, its [b]king, *and* the mighty men of valor. 3You shall march around the city, all *you* men of war; you shall go all around the city once. This you shall do six days. 4And seven priests shall bear seven [a]trumpets of rams' horns before the ark. But the seventh day you shall march around the city [b]seven times, and [c]the priests shall blow the trumpets. 5It shall come to pass, when they make a long *blast* with the ram's horn, *and* when you hear the sound of the trumpet, that all the people shall shout with a great shout; then the wall of the city will fall down flat. And the people shall go up every man straight before him."

6Then Joshua the son of Nun called the priests and said to them, "Take up the ark of the covenant, and let seven priests bear seven trumpets of rams' horns before the ark of the LORD." 7And he said to the people, "Proceed, and march around the city, and let him who is armed advance before the ark of the LORD."

8So it was, when Joshua had spoken to the people, that the seven priests bearing the seven trumpets of rams' horns before the LORD advanced and blew the trumpets, and the ark of the covenant of the LORD followed them. 9The armed men went before the priests who blew the trumpets, [a]and the rear guard came after the ark, while *the priests* continued blowing the trumpets. 10Now Joshua had commanded the people, saying, "You shall not shout or make any noise with your voice, nor shall a word proceed out of your mouth, until the day I say to you, 'Shout!' Then you shall shout." 11So he had [a]the ark of the LORD circle the city, going around *it* once. Then they came into the camp and lodged in the camp.

12And Joshua rose early in the morning, [a]and the priests took up the ark of the LORD. 13Then seven priests bearing seven trumpets of rams' horns before the ark of the LORD went on continually and blew with the trumpets. And the armed men went before them. But the rear guard came after the ark of the LORD, while *the priests* continued blowing the trumpets. 14And the second day they marched around the city once and returned to the camp. So they did six days.

15But it came to pass on the seventh day that they rose early, about the dawning of the day, and marched around the city seven times in the same manner. On that day only they marched around the city seven times. 16And the seventh time it happened, when the priests blew the trumpets, that Joshua said to the people: "Shout, for the LORD has given you the city! 17Now the city shall be [a]doomed by the LORD to destruction, it and all who *are* in it. Only [b]Rahab the harlot shall live, she and all who *are* with her in the house, because [c]she hid the messengers that we sent. 18And you, [a]by all means abstain from the accursed things, lest you become accursed when you take of the accursed things, and make the camp of Israel a curse, [b]and trouble it. 19But all the silver and gold, and vessels of bronze and iron, *are* consecrated to the LORD; they shall come into the treasury of the LORD."

20So the people shouted when *the priests* blew the trumpets. And it happened when the people heard the sound of the trumpet, and the people shouted with a great shout, that [a]the wall fell down flat. Then the people went up into the city, every man straight before him, and they took the city. 21And they [a]utterly destroyed all that *was* in the

5:13 [b] Num. 22:23; 1 Chr. 21:16 5:14 [a] Gen. 17:3; Num. 20:6 [b] Ex. 34:8 5:15 [a] Ex. 3:5; Acts 7:33 6:1 [a] Josh. 2:1 6:2 [a] Josh. 2:9, 24; 8:1 [b] Deut. 7:24 6:4 [a] Lev. 25:9; Judg. 7:16, 22 [b] 1 Kin. 18:43; 2 Kin. 4:35; 5:10 [c] Num. 10:8 6:9 [a] Num. 10:25 6:11 [a] Josh. 4:11 6:12 [a] Deut. 31:25 6:17 [a] Deut. 13:17; Josh. 7:1 [b] Josh. 2:1; Matt. 1:5 [c] Josh. 2:4, 6 6:18 [a] Deut. 7:26 [b] Josh. 7:1, 12, 25; 1 Kin. 18:17, 18; [Jon. 1:12] 6:20 [a] Heb. 11:30 6:21 [a] Deut. 7:2; 20:16, 17

city, both man and woman, young and old, ox and sheep and donkey, with the edge of the sword.

22 But Joshua had said to the two men who had spied out the country, "Go into the harlot's house, and from there bring out the woman and all that she has, [a]as you swore to her." 23 And the young men who had been spies went in and brought out Rahab, [a]her father, her mother, her brothers, and all that she had. So they brought out all her relatives and left them outside the camp of Israel. 24 But they burned the city and all that *was* in it with fire. Only the silver and gold, and the vessels of bronze and iron, they put into the treasury of the house of the LORD. 25 And Joshua spared Rahab the harlot, her father's household, and all that she had. So [a]she dwells in Israel to this day, because she hid the messengers whom Joshua sent to spy out Jericho.

26 Then Joshua charged *them* at that time, saying, [a]"Cursed *be* the man before the LORD who rises up and builds this city Jericho; he shall lay its foundation with his firstborn, and with his youngest he shall set up its gates."

27 So the LORD was with Joshua, and his fame spread throughout all the country.

Defeat at Ai

7 But the children of Israel committed a [a]trespass regarding the [b]accursed things, for [c]Achan the son of Carmi, the son of Zabdi,[1] the son of Zerah, of the tribe of Judah, took of the accursed things; so the anger of the LORD burned against the children of Israel.

2 Now Joshua sent men from Jericho to Ai, which *is* beside Beth Aven, on the east side of Bethel, and spoke to them, saying, "Go up and spy out the country." So the men went up and spied out Ai. 3 And they returned to Joshua and said to him, "Do not let all the people go up, but let about two or three thousand men go up and attack Ai. Do not weary all the people there, for *the people of Ai are* few." 4 So about three thousand men went up there from the people, [a]but they fled before the men of Ai. 5 And the men of Ai struck down about thirty-six men, for they chased them *from* before the gate as far as Shebarim, and struck them down on the descent; therefore [a]the hearts of the people melted and became like water.

6 Then Joshua [a]tore his clothes, and fell to the earth on his face before the ark of the LORD until evening, he and the elders of Israel; and they [b]put dust on their heads. 7 And Joshua said, "Alas, Lord GOD, [a]why have You brought this people over the Jordan at all—to deliver us into the hand of the Amorites, to destroy us? Oh, that we had been content, and dwelt on the other side of the Jordan! 8 O Lord, what shall I say when Israel turns its back before its enemies? 9 For the Canaanites and all the inhabitants of the land will hear *it,* and surround us, and [a]cut off our name from the earth. Then [b]what will You do for Your great name?"

The Sin of Achan

10 So the LORD said to Joshua: "Get up! Why do you lie thus on your face? 11 Israel has sinned, and they have also transgressed My covenant which I commanded them. [a]For they have even taken some of the accursed things, and have both stolen and [b]deceived; and they have also put *it* among their own stuff. 12 [a]Therefore the children of Israel could not stand before their enemies, *but* turned *their* backs before their enemies, because [b]they have become doomed to destruction. Neither will I be with you anymore, unless you destroy the accursed from among you. 13 Get up, [a]sanctify the people, and say, [b]'Sanctify yourselves for tomorrow, because thus says the LORD God of Israel: "*There is* an accursed thing in your midst, O Israel; you cannot stand before your enemies until you take away the accursed thing from among you." 14 In the morning therefore you shall be brought according to your tribes. And it shall be *that* the tribe which [a]the LORD takes shall come according to families; and the family which the LORD takes shall come by households; and the household which the LORD takes shall come man by man. 15 [a]Then it shall

6:22 [a] Josh. 2:12–19; Heb. 11:31 6:23 [a] Josh. 2:13 6:25 [a] [Matt. 1:5] 6:26 [a] 1 Kin. 16:34 7:1 [a] Josh. 7:20, 21 [b] Josh. 6:17–19 [c] Josh. 22:20 [1] Called *Zimri* in 1 Chronicles 2:6 7:4 [a] Lev. 26:17; Deut. 28:25 7:5 [a] Lev. 26:36; Josh. 2:9, 11 7:6 [a] Gen. 37:29, 34 [b] 1 Sam. 4:12 7:7 [a] Ex. 17:3; Num. 21:5 7:9 [a] Deut. 32:26 [b] Ex. 32:12; Num. 14:13 7:11 [a] Josh. 6:17–19 [b] Acts 5:1, 2 7:12 [a] Judg. 2:14 [b] Deut. 7:26; [Hag. 2:13, 14] 7:13 [a] Ex. 19:10 [b] Josh. 3:5 7:14 [a] [Prov. 16:33] 7:15 [a] 1 Sam. 14:38, 39

be *that* he who is taken with the accursed thing shall be burned with fire, he and all that he has, because he has [b]transgressed the covenant of the LORD, and because he [c]has done a disgraceful thing in Israel.' "

16So Joshua rose early in the morning and brought Israel by their tribes, and the tribe of Judah was taken. 17He brought the clan of Judah, and he took the family of the Zarhites; and he brought the family of the Zarhites man by man, and Zabdi was taken. 18Then he brought his household man by man, and Achan the son of Carmi, the son of Zabdi, the son of Zerah, of the tribe of Judah, [a]was taken.

19Now Joshua said to Achan, "My son, I beg you, [a]give glory to the LORD God of Israel, [b]and make confession to Him, and [c]tell me now what you have done; do not hide *it* from me."

20And Achan answered Joshua and said, "Indeed [a]I have sinned against the LORD God of Israel, and this is what I have done: 21When I saw among the spoils a beautiful Babylonian garment, two hundred shekels of silver, and a wedge of gold weighing fifty shekels, I coveted them and took them. And there they are, hidden in the earth in the midst of my tent, with the silver under it."

22So Joshua sent messengers, and they ran to the tent; and there it was, hidden in his tent, with the silver under it. 23And they took them from the midst of the tent, brought them to Joshua and to all the children of Israel, and laid them out before the LORD. 24Then Joshua, and all Israel with him, took Achan the son of Zerah, the silver, the garment, the wedge of gold, his sons, his daughters, his oxen, his donkeys, his sheep, his tent, and [a]all that he had, and they brought them to [b]the Valley of Achor. 25And Joshua said, [a]"Why have you troubled us? The LORD will trouble you this day." [b]So all Israel stoned him with stones; and they burned them with fire after they had stoned them with stones.

26Then they [a]raised over him a great heap of stones, still there to this day. So [b]the LORD turned from the fierceness of His anger. Therefore the name of that place has been called [c]the Valley of Achor[1] to this day.

The Fall of Ai

8 Now the LORD said to Joshua: [a]"Do not be afraid, nor be dismayed; take all the people of war with you, and arise, go up to Ai. See, [b]I have given into your hand the king of Ai, his people, his city, and his land. 2And you shall do to Ai and its king as you did to [a]Jericho and its king. Only [b]its spoil and its cattle you shall take as booty for yourselves. Lay an ambush for the city behind it."

3So Joshua arose, and all the people of war, to go up against Ai; and Joshua chose thirty thousand mighty men of valor and sent them away by night. 4And he commanded them, saying: "Behold, [a]you shall lie in ambush against the city, behind the city. Do not go very far from the city, but all of you be ready. 5Then I and all the people who *are* with me will approach the city; and it will come about, when they come out against us as at the first, that [a]we shall flee before them. 6For they will come out after us till we have drawn them from the city, for they will say, '*They are* fleeing before us as at the first.' Therefore we will flee before them. 7Then you shall rise from the ambush and seize the city, for the LORD your God will deliver it into your hand. 8And it will be, when you have taken the city, *that* you shall set the city on fire. According to the commandment of the LORD you shall do. [a]See, I have commanded you."

9Joshua therefore sent them out; and they went to lie in ambush, and stayed between Bethel and Ai, on the west side of Ai; but Joshua lodged that night among the people. 10Then Joshua rose up early in the morning and mustered the people, and went up, he and the elders of Israel, before the people to Ai. 11[a]And all the people of war who *were* with him went up and drew near; and they came before the city and camped on the north side of Ai. Now a valley *lay* between them and Ai. 12So he took about five thousand men and set them

7:15 [b] Josh. 7:11 [c] Gen. 34:7; Judg. 20:6 7:18 [a] 1 Sam. 14:42 7:19 [a] 1 Sam. 6:5; Jer. 13:16; John 9:24 [b] Num. 5:6, 7; 2 Chr. 30:22; Ezra 10:10, 11; Ps. 32:5; Prov. 28:13; Jer. 3:12, 13; Dan. 9:4 [c] 1 Sam. 14:43 7:20 [a] Num. 22:34; 1 Sam. 15:24 7:24 [a] Num. 16:32, 33; Dan. 6:24 [b] Josh. 7:26; 15:7 7:25 [a] Josh. 6:18; 1 Chr. 2:7; [Gal. 5:12] [b] Deut. 17:5 7:26 [a] Josh. 8:29; 2 Sam. 18:17; Lam. 3:53 [b] Deut. 13:17 [c] Josh. 7:24; Is. 65:10; Hos. 2:15 [1] Literally *Trouble* 8:1 [a] Deut. 1:21; 7:18; 31:8; Josh. 1:9; 10:8 [b] Josh. 6:2 8:2 [a] Josh. 6:21 [b] Deut. 20:14; Josh. 8:27 8:4 [a] Judg. 20:29 8:5 [a] Josh. 7:5; Judg. 20:32 8:8 [a] 2 Sam. 13:28 8:11 [a] Josh. 8:5

in ambush between Bethel and Ai, on the west side of the city. 13And when they had set the people, all the army that *was* on the north of the city, and its rear guard on the west of the city, Joshua went that night into the midst of the valley.

14Now it happened, when the king of Ai saw *it,* that the men of the city hurried and rose early and went out against Israel to battle, he and all his people, at an appointed place before the plain. But he [a]did not know that *there was* an ambush against him behind the city. 15And Joshua and all Israel [a]made as if they were beaten before them, and fled by the way of the wilderness. 16So all the people who *were* in Ai were called together to pursue them. And they pursued Joshua and were drawn away from the city. 17There was not a man left in Ai or Bethel who did not go out after Israel. So they left the city open and pursued Israel.

18Then the LORD said to Joshua, "Stretch out the spear that *is* in your hand toward Ai, for I will give it into your hand." And Joshua stretched out the spear that *was* in his hand toward the city. 19So *those in* ambush arose quickly out of their place; they ran as soon as he had stretched out his hand, and they entered the city and took it, and hurried to set the city on fire. 20And when the men of Ai looked behind them, they saw, and behold, the smoke of the city ascended to heaven. So they had no power to flee this way or that way, and the people who had fled to the wilderness turned back on the pursuers.

21Now when Joshua and all Israel saw that the ambush had taken the city and that the smoke of the city ascended, they turned back and struck down the men of Ai. 22Then the others came out of the city against them; so they were *caught* in the midst of Israel, some on this side and some on that side. And they struck them down, so that they [a]let none of them remain or escape. 23But the king of Ai they took alive, and brought him to Joshua.

24And it came to pass when Israel had made an end of slaying all the inhabitants of Ai in the field, in the wilderness where they pursued them, and when they all had fallen by the edge of the sword until they were consumed, that all the Israelites returned to Ai and struck it with the edge of the sword. 25So it was *that* all who fell that day, both men and women, *were* twelve thousand—all the people of Ai. 26For Joshua did not draw back his hand, with which he stretched out the spear, until he had [a]utterly destroyed all the inhabitants of Ai. 27[a]Only the livestock and the spoil of that city Israel took as booty for themselves, according to the word of the LORD which He had [b]commanded Joshua. 28So Joshua burned Ai and made it [a]a heap forever, a desolation to this day. 29[a]And the king of Ai he hanged on a tree until evening. [b]And as soon as the sun was down, Joshua commanded that they should take his corpse down from the tree, cast it at the entrance of the gate of the city, and [c]raise over it a great heap of stones *that remains* to this day.

Joshua Renews the Covenant
(cf. Deut. 27:4, 5)

30Now Joshua built an altar to the LORD God of Israel [a]in Mount Ebal, 31as Moses the servant of the LORD had commanded the children of Israel, as it is written in the Book of the Law of Moses: [a]"an altar of whole stones over which no man has wielded an iron *tool.*"[1] And [b]they offered on it burnt offerings to the LORD, and sacrificed peace offerings. 32And there, in the presence of the children of Israel, [a]he wrote on the stones a copy of the law of Moses, which he had written. 33Then all Israel, with their elders and officers and judges, stood on either side of the ark before the priests, the Levites, [a]who bore the ark of the covenant of the LORD, [b]the stranger as well as he who was born among them. Half of them *were* in front of Mount Gerizim and half of them in front of Mount Ebal, [c]as Moses the servant of the LORD had commanded before, that they should bless the people of Israel. 34And afterward [a]he read all the words of the law, [b]the blessings and the cursings, according to all that is written in the [c]Book

8:14 [a] Judg. 20:34; Eccl. 9:12 8:15 [a] Judg. 20:36 8:22 [a] Deut. 7:2 8:26 [a] Josh. 6:21 8:27 [a] Num. 31:22, 26 [b] Josh. 8:2 8:28 [a] Deut. 13:16 8:29 [a] Josh. 10:26 [b] Deut. 21:22, 23; Josh. 10:27 [c] Josh. 7:26; 10:27 8:30 [a] Deut. 27:4–8 8:31 [a] Ex. 20:25; Deut. 27:5, 6 [b] Ex. 20:24 [1] Deuteronomy 27:5, 6 8:32 [a] Deut. 27:2, 3, 8 8:33 [a] Deut. 31:9, 25 [b] Deut. 31:12 [c] Deut. 11:29; 27:12 8:34 [a] Deut. 31:11; Neh. 8:3 [b] Deut. 28:2, 15, 45; 29:20, 21; 30:19 [c] Josh. 1:8

of the Law. 35There was not a word of all that Moses had commanded which Joshua did not read before all the assembly of Israel, [a]with the women, the little ones, [b]and the strangers who were living among them.

The Treaty with the Gibeonites

9 And it came to pass when [a]all the kings who *were* on this side of the Jordan, in the hills and in the lowland and in all the coasts of [b]the Great Sea toward Lebanon—[c]the Hittite, the Amorite, the Canaanite, the Perizzite, the Hivite, and the Jebusite—heard *about it,* 2that they [a]gathered together to fight with Joshua and Israel with one accord.

3But when the inhabitants of [a]Gibeon [b]heard what Joshua had done to Jericho and Ai, 4they worked craftily, and went and pretended to be ambassadors. And they took old sacks on their donkeys, old wineskins torn and mended, 5old and patched sandals on their feet, and old garments on themselves; and all the bread of their provision was dry *and* moldy. 6And they went to Joshua, [a]to the camp at Gilgal, and said to him and to the men of Israel, "We have come from a far country; now therefore, make a covenant with us."

7Then the men of Israel said to the [a]Hivites, "Perhaps you dwell among us; so [b]how can we make a covenant with you?"

8But they said to Joshua, [a]"We *are* your servants."

And Joshua said to them, "Who *are* you, and where do you come from?"

9So they said to him: [a]"From a very far country your servants have come, because of the name of the LORD your God; for we have [b]heard of His fame, and all that He did in Egypt, 10and [a]all that He did to the two kings of the Amorites who *were* beyond the Jordan—to Sihon king of Heshbon, and Og king of Bashan, who was at Ashtaroth. 11Therefore our elders and all the inhabitants of our country spoke to us, saying, 'Take provisions with you for the journey, and go to meet them, and say to them, "We *are* your servants; now therefore, make a covenant with us." ' 12This bread of ours we took hot *for* our provision from our houses on the day we departed to come to you. But now look, it is dry and moldy. 13And these wineskins which we filled *were* new, and see, they are torn; and these our garments and our sandals have become old because of the very long journey."

14Then the men of Israel took some of their provisions; [a]but they did not ask counsel of the LORD. 15So Joshua [a]made peace with them, and made a covenant with them to let them live; and the rulers of the congregation swore to them.

16And it happened at the end of three days, after they had made a covenant with them, that they heard that they *were* their neighbors who dwelt near them. 17Then the children of Israel journeyed and came to their cities on the third day. Now their cities *were* [a]Gibeon, Chephirah, Beeroth, and Kirjath Jearim. 18But the children of Israel did not attack them, [a]because the rulers of the congregation had sworn to them by the LORD God of Israel. And all the congregation complained against the rulers.

19Then all the rulers said to all the congregation, "We have sworn to them by the LORD God of Israel; now therefore, we may not touch them. 20This we will do to them: We will let them live, lest [a]wrath be upon us because of the oath which we swore to them." 21And the rulers said to them, "Let them live, but let them be [a]woodcutters and water carriers for all the congregation, as the rulers had [b]promised them."

22Then Joshua called for them, and he spoke to them, saying, "Why have you deceived us, saying, [a]'We *are* very far from you,' when [b]you dwell near us? 23Now therefore, you *are* [a]cursed, and none of you shall be freed from being slaves—woodcutters and water carriers for the house of my God."

24So they answered Joshua and said, "Because your servants were clearly told that the LORD your God [a]commanded His servant Moses to give you all the land, and to destroy all the inhabitants of the land from before you; therefore [b]we were very

8:35 [a] Ex. 12:38; Deut. 31:12 [b] Josh. 8:33 9:1 [a] Num. 13:29; Josh. 3:10 [b] Num. 34:6 [c] Ex. 3:17; 23:23 9:2 [a] Josh. 10:5; Ps. 83:3, 5 9:3 [a] Josh. 9:17, 22; 10:2; 21:17; 2 Sam. 21:1, 2 [b] Josh. 6:27 9:6 [a] Josh. 5:10 9:7 [a] Josh. 9:1; 11:19 [b] Ex. 23:32; Deut. 7:2 9:8 [a] Deut. 20:11; 2 Kin. 10:5 9:9 [a] Deut. 20:15 [b] Ex. 15:14; Josh. 2:9, 10; 5:1 9:10 [a] Num. 21:24, 33 9:14 [a] Num. 27:21; Is. 30:1 9:15 [a] 2 Sam. 21:2 9:17 [a] Josh. 18:25 9:18 [a] Ps. 15:4 9:20 [a] 2 Sam. 21:1, 2, 6; Ezek. 17:13, 15 9:21 [a] Deut. 29:11 [b] Josh. 9:15 9:22 [a] Josh. 9:6, 9 [b] Josh. 9:16 9:23 [a] Gen. 9:25 9:24 [a] Ex. 23:31–33; Deut. 7:1, 2 [b] Ex. 15:14

much afraid for our lives because of you, and have done this thing. 25 And now, here we are, [a]in your hands; do with us as it seems good and right to do to us." 26 So he did to them, and delivered them out of the hand of the children of Israel, so that they did not kill them. 27 And that day Joshua made them [a]woodcutters and water carriers for the congregation and for the altar of the LORD, [b]in the place which He would choose, even to this day.

The Sun Stands Still

10 Now it came to pass when Adoni-Zedek king of Jerusalem [a]heard how Joshua had taken [b]Ai and had utterly destroyed it—[c]as he had done to Jericho and its king, so he had done to [d]Ai and its king—and [e]how the inhabitants of Gibeon had made peace with Israel and were among them, 2 that they [a]feared greatly, because Gibeon *was* a great city, like one of the royal cities, and because it *was* greater than Ai, and all its men *were* mighty. 3 Therefore Adoni-Zedek king of Jerusalem sent to Hoham king of Hebron, Piram king of Jarmuth, Japhia king of Lachish, and Debir king of Eglon, saying, 4 "Come up to me and help me, that we may attack Gibeon, for [a]it has made peace with Joshua and with the children of Israel." 5 Therefore the five kings of the [a]Amorites, the king of Jerusalem, the king of Hebron, the king of Jarmuth, the king of Lachish, *and* the king of Eglon, [b]gathered together and went up, they and all their armies, and camped before Gibeon and made war against it.

6 And the men of Gibeon sent to Joshua at the camp [a]at Gilgal, saying, "Do not forsake your servants; come up to us quickly, save us and help us, for all the kings of the Amorites who dwell in the mountains have gathered together against us."

7 So Joshua ascended from Gilgal, he and [a]all the people of war with him, and all the mighty men of valor. 8 And the LORD said to Joshua, [a]"Do not fear them, for I have delivered them into your hand; [b]not a man of them shall [c]stand before you." 9 Joshua therefore came upon them suddenly, having marched all night from Gilgal. 10 So the LORD [a]routed them before Israel, killed them with a great slaughter at Gibeon, chased them along the road that goes [b]to Beth Horon, and struck them down as far as [c]Azekah and Makkedah. 11 And it happened, as they fled before Israel *and* were on the descent of Beth Horon, [a]that the LORD cast down large hailstones from heaven on them as far as Azekah, and they died. *There were* more who died from the hailstones than the children of Israel killed with the sword.

12 Then Joshua spoke to the LORD in the day when the LORD delivered up the Amorites before the children of Israel, and he said in the sight of Israel:

[a]"Sun, stand still over Gibeon;
And Moon, in the Valley of [b]Aijalon."
13 So the sun stood still,
And the moon stopped,
Till the people had revenge
Upon their enemies.

[a]*Is* this not written in the Book of Jasher? So the sun stood still in the midst of heaven, and did not hasten to go *down* for about a whole day. 14 And there has been [a]no day like that, before it or after it, that the LORD heeded the voice of a man; for [b]the LORD fought for Israel.

15 [a]Then Joshua returned, and all Israel with him, to the camp at Gilgal.

The Amorite Kings Executed

16 But these five kings had fled and hidden themselves in a cave at Makkedah. 17 And it was told Joshua, saying, "The five kings have been found hidden in the cave at Makkedah."

18 So Joshua said, "Roll large stones against the mouth of the cave, and set men by it to guard them. 19 And do not stay *there* yourselves, *but* pursue your enemies, and attack their rear *guard*. Do not allow them to enter their cities, for the LORD your God has delivered them into your hand." 20 Then

9:25 [a] Gen. 16:6 9:27 [a] Josh. 9:21, 23 [b] Deut. 12:5 10:1 [a] Josh. 9:1 [b] Josh. 8:1 [c] Josh. 6:21 [d] Josh. 8:22, 26, 28 [e] Josh. 9:15 10:2 [a] Ex. 15:14–16; Deut. 11:25; 1 Chr. 14:17 10:4 [a] Josh. 9:15; 10:1 10:5 [a] Num. 13:29 [b] Josh. 9:2 10:6 [a] Josh. 5:10; 9:6 10:7 [a] Josh. 8:1 10:8 [a] Josh. 11:6; Judg. 4:14 [b] Josh. 1:5, 9 [c] Josh. 21:44 10:10 [a] Judg. 4:15; 1 Sam. 7:10, 12; Is. 28:21 [b] Josh. 16:3, 5 [c] Josh. 15:35 10:11 [a] Is. 30:30; Rev. 16:21 10:12 [a] Is. 28:21; Hab. 3:11 [b] Judg. 12:12 10:13 [a] 2 Sam. 1:18 10:14 [a] Is. 38:7, 8 [b] Ex. 14:14; Deut. 1:30; 20:4; Josh. 10:42; 23:3 10:15 [a] Josh. 10:43

it happened, while Joshua and the children
of Israel made an end of slaying them with
a very great slaughter, till they had finished,
that those who escaped entered fortified
cities. 21And all the people returned to the
camp, to Joshua at Makkedah, in peace.
[a]No one moved his tongue against any
of the children of Israel.
22Then Joshua said, "Open the mouth of
the cave, and bring out those five kings to
me from the cave." 23And they did so, and
brought out those five kings to him from
the cave: the king of Jerusalem, the king
of Hebron, the king of Jarmuth, the king
of Lachish, *and* the king of Eglon.
24So it was, when they brought out those
kings to Joshua, that Joshua called for all
the men of Israel, and said to the captains
of the men of war who went with him,
"Come near, put your feet on the necks of
these kings." And they drew near and [a]put
their feet on their necks. 25Then Joshua
said to them, [a]"Do not be afraid, nor be dismayed; be strong and of good courage, for
[b]thus the LORD will do to all your enemies
against whom you fight." 26And afterward
Joshua struck them and killed them, and
hanged them on five trees; and they [a]were
hanging on the trees until evening. 27So it
was at the time of the going down of the sun
that Joshua commanded, and they [a]took
them down from the trees, cast them into
the cave where they had been hidden, and
laid large stones against the cave's mouth,
which remain until this very day.

Conquest of the Southland

28On that day Joshua took Makkedah,
and struck it and its king with the edge of
the sword. He utterly [a]destroyed them[1]—all
the people who *were* in it. He let none remain. He also did to the king of Makkedah
[b]as he had done to the king of Jericho.
29Then Joshua passed from Makkedah,
and all Israel with him, to [a]Libnah; and they
fought against Libnah. 30And the LORD also
delivered it and its king into the hand of
Israel; he struck it and all the people who
were in it with the edge of the sword. He let
none remain in it, but did to its king as he
had done to the king of Jericho.
31Then Joshua passed from Libnah, and
all Israel with him, to Lachish; and they
encamped against it and fought against
it. 32And the LORD delivered Lachish into
the hand of Israel, who took it on the second day, and struck it and all the people
who *were* in it with the edge of the sword,
according to all that he had done to Libnah. 33Then Horam king of Gezer came up
to help Lachish; and Joshua struck him
and his people, until he left him none remaining.
34From Lachish Joshua passed to Eglon,
and all Israel with him; and they encamped
against it and fought against it. 35They took
it on that day and struck it with the edge of
the sword; all the people who *were* in it he
utterly destroyed that day, according to all
that he had done to Lachish.
36So Joshua went up from Eglon, and
all Israel with him, to [a]Hebron; and they
fought against it. 37And they took it and
struck it with the edge of the sword—its
king, all its cities, and all the people who
were in it; he left none remaining, according to all that he had done to Eglon, but
utterly destroyed it and all the people who
were in it.
38Then Joshua returned, and all Israel
with him, to [a]Debir; and they fought against
it. 39And he took it and its king and all its
cities; they struck them with the edge of the
sword and utterly destroyed all the people
who *were* in it. He left none remaining; as
he had done to Hebron, so he did to Debir
and its king, as he had done also to Libnah
and its king.
40So Joshua conquered all the land: the
[a]mountain country and the South[1] and the
lowland and the wilderness slopes, and
[b]all their kings; he left none remaining,
but [c]utterly destroyed all that breathed, as
the LORD God of Israel had commanded.
41And Joshua conquered them from [a]Ka-
desh Barnea as far as [b]Gaza, [c]and all the

10:21 [a] Ex. 11:7 10:24 [a] Ps. 107:40; Is. 26:5, 6; Mal. 4:3 10:25 [a] Deut. 31:6–8; Josh. 1:9 [b] Deut. 3:21; 7:19 10:26 [a] Josh. 8:29; 2 Sam. 21:9 10:27 [a] Deut. 21:22, 23; Josh. 8:29 10:28 [a] Deut. 7:2, 16 [b] Josh. 6:21 [1] Following Masoretic Text and most authorities; many Hebrew manuscripts, some manuscripts of the Septuagint, and some manuscripts of the Targum read *it.* 10:29 [a] Josh. 15:42; 21:13; 2 Kin. 8:22; 19:8 10:36 [a] Num. 13:22; Josh. 14:13–15; 15:13; Judg. 1:10, 20; 2 Sam. 5:1, 3, 5, 13; 2 Chr. 11:10 10:38 [a] Josh. 15:15; Judg. 1:11; 1 Chr. 6:58 10:40 [a] Deut. 1:7 [b] Deut. 7:24 [c] Deut. 20:16, 17 [1] Hebrew *Negev,* and so throughout this book 10:41 [a] Num. 13:26; Deut. 9:23 [b] Gen. 10:19; Josh. 11:22 [c] Josh. 11:16; 15:51

country of Goshen, even as far as Gibeon.
42 All these kings and their land Joshua took
at one time, [a]because the LORD God of Israel fought for Israel. 43 Then Joshua returned, and all Israel with him, to the camp
at Gilgal.

The Northern Conquest

11 And it came to pass, when Jabin king
of Hazor heard *these things,* that he
[a]sent to Jobab king of Madon, to the king
[b]of Shimron, to the king of Achshaph, 2 and
to the kings who *were* from the north, in
the mountains, in the plain south of [a]Chin-
neroth, in the lowland, and in the heights
[b]of Dor on the west, 3 to the Canaanites in
the east and in the west, the [a]Amorite, the
Hittite, the Perizzite, the Jebusite in the
mountains, [b]and the Hivite below [c]Her-
mon [d]in the land of Mizpah. 4 So they went
out, they and all their armies with them, *as*
many people [a]*as* the sand that *is* on the seashore in multitude, with very many horses
and chariots. 5 And when all these kings
had met together, they came and camped
together at the waters of Merom to fight
against Israel.
6 But the LORD said to Joshua, [a]"Do not
be afraid because of them, for tomorrow
about this time I will deliver all of them
slain before Israel. You shall [b]hamstring
their horses and burn their chariots with
fire." 7 So Joshua and all the people of war
with him came against them suddenly by
the waters of Merom, and they attacked
them. 8 And the LORD delivered them into
the hand of Israel, who defeated them and
chased them to Greater [a]Sidon, to the Brook
[b]Misrephoth,[1] and to the Valley of Mizpah
eastward; they attacked them until they

HOPE FOR TODAY

INHALE

Hope. Now, that's a joke. I have been hoping for things all my life. I was a D1 athlete, but I tore my ACL in my senior year and my chance to go pro went away. I have a job, but I don't like it. I would like to step out and open my own business. However, the banks aren't giving me loans. People with worse credit than mine get loans. If I would dare hope again, it would not be for equity and fairness. But I will not bother. More hope only leads to more disappointment. Why should I hope for anything today when God did not come through for me yesterday?

EXHALE

We can live without many things for a long time, but we cannot live without hope for long at all. Hope is what gets us up in the morning; it allows us to believe that today will be a good day. Hope is a real thing. For some people, it is all they have. Hope is what makes life exciting.

But hope is like a muscle. It has to be exercised, and it can take a long time to see any results. As believers, we have to have hope *and* faith working together. We do not have to understand *how* or *when* God works; we just need to know *that* He works. Most of us are looking at it the wrong way. We want proof of our hope and immediate payoff for it. That is not faith though. Instead, we need to maintain an eternal view even in a world that thinks differently. God sent His only Son to die for us, opening a way for hope and faith beyond this life, with all of its injustices and difficulties. We hold fast not to tomorrow's worldly hope but to God's eternal hope of glory!

Remember, the systems of the world were not fashioned by God, but He will have the final say in their outcomes. But it's even more than that. Joshua 10:42 reminds us that the Hebrews conquered the Promised Land because God fought for them. And He fights for us too. Keep the hope. God has things in store for your tomorrows that you cannot imagine, and He is working to bring it all to pass!

10:42 [a] Josh. 10:14 11:1 [a] Josh. 10:3 [b] Josh. 19:15 11:2 [a] Num. 34:11 [b] Josh. 17:11; Judg. 1:27; 1 Kin. 4:11 11:3 [a] Josh. 9:1 [b] Deut. 7:1; Judg. 3:3, 5; 1 Kin. 9:20 [c] Josh. 11:17; 13:5, 11 [d] Gen. 31:49 11:4 [a] Gen. 22:17; 32:12; Judg. 7:12; 1 Sam. 13:5 11:6 [a] Josh. 10:8 [b] 2 Sam. 8:4 11:8 [a] Gen. 49:13 [b] Josh. 13:6 [1] Hebrew *Misrephoth Maim*

left none of them remaining. 9So Joshua did to them as the LORD had told him: he hamstrung their horses and burned their chariots with fire.

10Joshua turned back at that time and took Hazor, and struck its king with the sword; for Hazor was formerly the head of all those kingdoms. 11And they struck all the people who *were* in it with the edge of the sword, [a]utterly destroying *them.* There was none left [b]breathing. Then he burned Hazor with fire.

12So all the cities of those kings, and all their kings, Joshua took and struck with the edge of the sword. He utterly destroyed them, [a]as Moses the servant of the LORD had commanded. 13But *as for* the cities that stood on their mounds,[1] Israel burned none of them, except Hazor only, *which* Joshua burned. 14And all the [a]spoil of these cities and the livestock, the children of Israel took as booty for themselves; but they struck every man with the edge of the sword until they had destroyed them, and they left none breathing. 15[a]As the LORD had commanded Moses His servant, so [b]Moses commanded Joshua, and [c]so Joshua did. He left nothing undone of all that the LORD had commanded Moses.

Summary of Joshua's Conquests

16Thus Joshua took all this land: [a]the mountain country, all the South, [b]all the land of Goshen, the lowland, and the Jordan plain[1]—the mountains of Israel and its lowlands, 17[a]from Mount Halak and the ascent to Seir, even as far as Baal Gad in the Valley of Lebanon below Mount Hermon. He captured [b]all their kings, and struck them down and killed them. 18Joshua made war a long time with all those kings. 19There was not a city that made peace with the children of Israel, except [a]the Hivites, the inhabitants of Gibeon. All *the others* they took in battle. 20For [a]it was of the LORD to harden their hearts, that they should come against Israel in battle, that He might utterly destroy them, *and* that they might receive no mercy, but that He might destroy them, [b]as the LORD had commanded Moses.

21And at that time Joshua came and cut off [a]the Anakim from the mountains: from Hebron, from Debir, from Anab, from all the mountains of Judah, and from all the mountains of Israel; Joshua utterly destroyed them with their cities. 22None of the Anakim were left in the land of the children of Israel; they remained only [a]in Gaza, in Gath, [b]and in Ashdod.

23So Joshua took the whole land, [a]according to all that the LORD had said to Moses; and Joshua gave it as an inheritance to Israel [b]according to their divisions by their tribes. Then the land [c]rested from war.

The Kings Conquered by Moses
(cf. Num. 21:21–35)

12 These *are* the kings of the land whom the children of Israel defeated, and whose land they possessed on the other side of the Jordan toward the rising of the sun, [a]from the River Arnon [b]to Mount Hermon, and all the eastern Jordan plain: 2*One king was* [a]Sihon king of the Amorites, who dwelt in Heshbon *and* ruled half of Gilead, from Aroer, which is on the bank of the River Arnon, from the middle of that river, even as far as the River Jabbok, *which is* the border of the Ammonites, 3and [a]the eastern Jordan plain from the Sea of Chinneroth as far as the Sea of the Arabah (the Salt Sea), [b]the road to Beth Jeshimoth, and southward below [c]the slopes of Pisgah. 4*The other king was* [a]Og king of Bashan and his territory, *who was* of [b]the remnant of the giants, [c]who dwelt at Ashtaroth and at Edrei, 5and reigned over [a]Mount Hermon, [b]over Salcah, over all Bashan, [c]as far as the border of the Geshurites and the Maachathites, and over half of Gilead *to* the border of Sihon king of Heshbon.

6[a]These Moses the servant of the LORD and the children of Israel had conquered; and [b]Moses the servant of the LORD had

---

11:11 [a] Deut. 20:16 [b] Josh. 10:40 11:12 [a] Num. 33:50–56; Deut. 7:2; 20:16 11:13 [1] Hebrew *tel,* a heap of successive city ruins 11:14 [a] Deut. 20:14–18 11:15 [a] Ex. 34:10–17 [b] Deut. 31:7, 8 [c] Josh. 1:7 11:16 [a] Josh. 12:8 [b] Josh. 10:40, 41 [1] Hebrew *arabah* 11:17 [a] Josh. 12:7 [b] Deut. 7:24 11:19 [a] Josh. 9:3–7 11:20 [a] Deut. 2:30 [b] Deut. 20:16, 17 11:21 [a] Num. 13:22, 33; Deut. 1:28; 9:2; Josh. 15:13, 14 11:22 [a] 1 Sam. 17:4 [b] Josh. 15:46; 1 Sam. 5:1; Is. 20:1 11:23 [a] Ex. 33:2; Num. 34:2–15 [b] Num. 26:53; Josh. 14; 15 [c] Deut. 12:9, 10; 25:19; [Heb. 4:8] 12:1 [a] Num. 21:24 [b] Deut. 3:8 12:2 [a] Num. 21:24; Deut. 2:24–27 12:3 [a] Deut. 3:17 [b] Josh. 13:20 [c] Deut. 3:17; 4:49 12:4 [a] Num. 21:33; Deut. 3:4, 10 [b] Deut. 3:11; Josh. 13:12 [c] Deut. 1:4 12:5 [a] Deut. 3:8 [b] Deut. 3:10; Josh. 13:11; 1 Chr. 5:11 [c] Deut. 3:14; 1 Sam. 27:8 12:6 [a] Num. 21:24, 35 [b] Num. 32:29–33; Deut. 3:12; Josh. 13:8

given it *as* a possession to the Reubenites,
the Gadites, and half the tribe of Manasseh.

The Kings Conquered by Joshua

7And these *are* the kings of the country
[a]which Joshua and the children of Israel
conquered on this side of the Jordan, on
the west, from Baal Gad in the Valley of Lebanon as far as Mount Halak and the ascent
to [b]Seir, which Joshua [c]gave to the tribes of
Israel *as* a possession according to their divisions, 8[a]in the mountain country, in the
lowlands, in the *Jordan* plain, in the slopes,
in the wilderness, and in the South—[b]the
Hittites, the Amorites, the Canaanites, the
Perizzites, the Hivites, and the Jebusites:
9[a]the king of Jericho, one; [b]the king of Ai,
which *is* beside Bethel, one; 10[a]the king of
Jerusalem, one; the king of Hebron, one;
11the king of Jarmuth, one; the king of Lachish, one; 12the king of Eglon, one; [a]the
king of Gezer, one; 13[a]the king of Debir, one;
the king of Geder, one; 14the king of Hormah, one; the king of Arad, one; 15[a]the king
of Libnah, one; the king of Adullam, one;
16[a]the king of Makkedah, one; [b]the king of
Bethel, one; 17the king of Tappuah, one; [a]the
king of Hepher, one; 18the king of Aphek,
one; the king of Lasharon, one; 19the king of
Madon, one; [a]the king of Hazor, one; 20the
king of [a]Shimron Meron, one; the king of
Achshaph, one; 21the king of Taanach, one;
the king of Megiddo, one; 22[a]the king of
Kedesh, one; the king of Jokneam in Carmel, one; 23the king of Dor in the [a]heights
of Dor, one; the king of [b]the people of Gilgal, one; 24the king of Tirzah, one—[a]all the
kings, thirty-one.

Remaining Land to Be Conquered

13 Now Joshua [a]was old, advanced in
years. And the LORD said to him:
"You are old, advanced in years, and there
remains very much land yet to be possessed. 2[a]This is the land that yet remains:
[b]all the territory of the Philistines and all
[c]*that of* the Geshurites, 3[a]from Sihor, which
is east of Egypt, as far as the border of Ekron
northward (*which* is counted as Canaanite); the [b]five lords of the Philistines—the
Gazites, the Ashdodites, the Ashkelonites,
the Gittites, and the Ekronites; also [c]the
Avites; 4from the south, all the land of the
Canaanites, and Mearah that belongs to the
Sidonians [a]as far as Aphek, to the border of
[b]the Amorites; 5the land of [a]the Gebalites,[1]
and all Lebanon, toward the sunrise, [b]from
Baal Gad below Mount Hermon as far as the
entrance to Hamath; 6all the inhabitants
of the mountains from Lebanon as far as
[a]the Brook Misrephoth,[1] *and* all the Sidonians—them [b]I will drive out from before
the children of Israel; only [c]divide it by lot
to Israel as an inheritance, as I have commanded you. 7Now therefore, divide this
land as an inheritance to the nine tribes
and half the tribe of Manasseh."

The Land Divided East of the Jordan

8With the other half-tribe the Reubenites and the Gadites received their inheritance, [a]which Moses had given them,
[b]beyond the Jordan eastward, as Moses the
servant of the LORD had given them: 9from
Aroer which *is* on the bank of the River Arnon, and the town that *is* in the midst of
the ravine, [a]and all the plain of Medeba as
far as Dibon; 10[a]all the cities of Sihon king
of the Amorites, who reigned in Heshbon,
as far as the border of the children of Ammon; 11[a]Gilead, and the border of the Geshurites and Maachathites, all Mount Hermon,
and all Bashan as far as Salcah; 12all the
kingdom of Og in Bashan, who reigned in
Ashtaroth and Edrei, who remained of [a]the
remnant of the giants; [b]for Moses had defeated and cast out these.
13Nevertheless the children of Israel [a]did
not drive out the Geshurites or the Maachathites, but the Geshurites and the Maachathites dwell among the Israelites until
this day.

12:7 [a] Josh. 11:17 [b] Gen. 14:6; 32:3; Deut. 2:1, 4 [c] Josh. 11:23 12:8 [a] Josh. 10:40; 11:16 [b] Ex. 3:8; 23:23; Josh. 9:1 12:9 [a] Josh. 6:2 [b] Josh. 8:29 12:10 [a] Josh. 10:23 12:12 [a] Josh. 10:33 12:13 [a] Josh. 10:38, 39 12:15 [a] Josh. 10:29, 30 12:16 [a] Josh. 10:28 [b] Josh. 8:17; Judg. 1:22 12:17 [a] 1 Kin. 4:10 12:19 [a] Josh. 11:10 12:20 [a] Josh. 11:1; 19:15 12:22 [a] Josh. 19:37; 20:7; 21:32 12:23 [a] Josh. 11:2 [b] Gen. 14:1, 2; Is. 9:1 12:24 [a] Deut. 7:24 13:1 [a] Josh. 14:10; 23:1, 2 13:2 [a] Judg. 3:1–3 [b] Joel 3:4 [c] Josh. 13:13; 2 Sam. 3:3 13:3 [a] 1 Chr. 13:5; Jer. 2:18 [b] Judg. 3:3 [c] Deut. 2:23 13:4 [a] Josh. 12:18; 19:30; 1 Sam. 4:1; 1 Kin. 20:26, 30 [b] Judg. 1:34 13:5 [a] 1 Kin. 5:18; Ezek. 27:9 [b] Josh. 12:7 [1] Or *Giblites* 13:6 [a] Josh. 11:8 [b] Josh. 23:13; Judg. 2:21, 23 [c] Josh. 14:1, 2 [1] Hebrew *Misrephoth Maim* 13:8 [a] Num. 32:33; Deut. 3:12, 13; Josh. 22:4 [b] Josh. 12:1–6 13:9 [a] Num. 21:30; Josh. 13:16 13:10 [a] Num. 21:24, 25 13:11 [a] Num. 32:1; Josh. 12:5 13:12 [a] Deut. 3:11; Josh. 12:4 [b] Num. 21:24, 34, 35 13:13 [a] Josh. 13:11

14[a]Only to the tribe of Levi he had given
no inheritance; the sacrifices of the LORD
God of Israel made by fire *are* their inheritance, [b]as He said to them.

The Land of Reuben

15[a]And Moses had given to the tribe of
the children of Reuben *an inheritance* according to their families. 16Their territory
was [a]from Aroer, which *is* on the bank of
the River Arnon, [b]and the city that *is* in the
midst of the ravine, [c]and all the plain by
Medeba; 17[a]Heshbon and all its cities that
are in the plain: Dibon, Bamoth Baal, Beth
Baal Meon, 18[a]Jahaza, Kedemoth, Mephaath, 19[a]Kirjathaim, [b]Sibmah, Zereth Sha-
har on the mountain of the valley, 20Beth
Peor, [a]the slopes of Pisgah, and Beth Jeshimoth— 21[a]all the cities of the plain and
all the kingdom of Sihon king of the Amorites, who reigned in Heshbon, [b]whom Moses had struck [c]with the princes of Midian:
Evi, Rekem, Zur, Hur, and Reba, who *were*
princes of Sihon dwelling in the country.
22The children of Israel also killed with the
sword [a]Balaam the son of Beor, the soothsayer, among those who were killed by
them. 23And the border of the children of
Reuben was the bank of the Jordan. This
was the inheritance of the children of Reuben according to their families, the cities
and their villages.

The Land of Gad

24[a]Moses also had given *an inheritance* to
the tribe of Gad, to the children of Gad according to their families. 25[a]Their territory
was Jazer, and all the cities of Gilead, [b]and
half the land of the Ammonites as far as
Aroer, which *is* before [c]Rabbah, 26and from
Heshbon to Ramath Mizpah and Betonim,
and from Mahanaim to the border of Debir,
27and in the valley [a]Beth Haram, Beth Nimrah, [b]Succoth, and Zaphon, the rest of the
kingdom of Sihon king of Heshbon, with
the Jordan as *its* border, as far as the edge
[c]of the Sea of Chinnereth, on the other side
of the Jordan eastward. 28This *is* the inheritance of the children of Gad according to
their families, the cities and their villages.

Half the Tribe of Manasseh (East)

29[a]Moses also had given *an inheritance*
to half the tribe of Manasseh; it was for
half the tribe of the children of Manasseh
according to their families: 30Their territory was from Mahanaim, all Bashan, all
the kingdom of Og king of Bashan, and [a]all
the towns of Jair which are in Bashan, sixty
cities; 31half of Gilead, and [a]Ashtaroth and
Edrei, cities of the kingdom of Og in Bashan, *were* for the [b]children of Machir the
son of Manasseh, for half of the children of
Machir according to their families.
32These *are the areas* which Moses had
distributed as an inheritance in the plains
of Moab on the other side of the Jordan,
by Jericho eastward. 33[a]But to the tribe of
Levi Moses had given no inheritance; the
LORD God of Israel *was* their inheritance,
[b]as He had said to them.

The Land Divided West of the Jordan

14 These *are the areas* which the children of Israel inherited in the land of
Canaan, [a]which Eleazar the priest, Joshua
the son of Nun, and the heads of the fathers of the tribes of the children of Israel distributed as an inheritance to them.
2Their inheritance *was* [a]by lot, as the LORD
had commanded by the hand of Moses, for
the nine tribes and the half-tribe. 3[a]For Moses had given the inheritance of the two
tribes and the half-tribe on the other side
of the Jordan; but to the Levites he had
given no inheritance among them. 4For
[a]the children of Joseph were two tribes:
Manasseh and Ephraim. And they gave no
part to the Levites in the land, except [b]cit-
ies to dwell *in,* with their common-lands
for their livestock and their property. 5[a]As
the LORD had commanded Moses, so the
children of Israel did; and they divided
the land.

13:14 [a] Num. 18:20, 23, 24; Deut. 18:1; Josh. 14:3, 4 [b] Josh. 13:33 13:15 [a] Num. 34:14; Josh. 13:15–23 13:16 [a] Josh. 12:2 [b] Num. 21:28 [c] Num. 21:30; Josh. 13:9 13:17 [a] Num. 21:28, 30 13:18 [a] Num. 21:23; Judg. 11:20; Is. 15:4; Jer. 48:34 13:19 [a] Num. 32:37; Jer. 48:1, 23; Ezek. 25:9 [b] Num. 32:38 13:20 [a] Deut. 3:17; Josh. 12:3 13:21 [a] Deut. 3:10 [b] Num. 21:24 [c] Num. 31:8 13:22 [a] Num. 22:5; 31:8 13:24 [a] Num. 34:14; 1 Chr. 5:11 13:25 [a] Num. 32:1, 35 [b] Judg. 11:13, 15 [c] Deut. 3:11; 2 Sam. 11:1; 12:26 13:27 [a] Num. 32:36 [b] Gen. 33:17; 1 Kin. 7:46 [c] Num. 34:11; Deut. 3:17 13:29 [a] Num. 34:14; 1 Chr. 5:23 13:30 [a] Num. 32:41; 1 Chr. 2:23 13:31 [a] Josh. 9:10; 12:4; 13:12; 1 Chr. 6:71 [b] Num. 32:39, 40; Josh. 17:1 13:33 [a] Deut. 18:1; Josh. 13:14; 18:7 [b] Num. 18:20; Deut. 10:9; 18:1, 2 14:1 [a] Num. 34:16–29 14:2 [a] Num. 26:55; 33:54; 34:13; Ps. 16:5 14:3 [a] Num. 32:33; Josh. 13:8, 32, 33 14:4 [a] Gen. 41:51; 46:20; 48:1, 5; Num. 26:28; 2 Chr. 30:1 [b] Num. 35:2–8; Josh. 21:1–42 14:5 [a] Num. 35:2; Josh. 21:2

Caleb Inherits Hebron

6 Then the children of Judah came to Joshua in Gilgal. And Caleb the son of Jephunneh the [a]Kenizzite said to him: "You know [b]the word which the LORD said to Moses the man of God concerning [c]you and me in Kadesh Barnea. 7 I *was* forty years old when Moses the servant of the LORD [a]sent me from Kadesh Barnea to spy out the land, and I brought back word to him as *it was* in my heart. 8 Nevertheless [a]my brethren who went up with me made the heart of the people melt, but I wholly [b]followed the LORD my God. 9 So Moses swore on that day, saying, [a]'Surely the land [b]where your foot has trodden shall be your inheritance and your children's forever, because you have wholly followed the LORD my God.' 10 And now, behold, the LORD has kept me [a]alive, [b]as He said, these forty-five years, ever since the LORD spoke this word to Moses while Israel wandered in the wilderness; and now, here I am this day, eighty-five years old. 11 [a]As yet I *am as* strong this day as on the day that Moses sent me; just as my strength *was* then, so now *is* my strength for war, both [b]for going out and for coming in. 12 Now therefore, give me this mountain of which the LORD spoke in that day; for you heard in that day how [a]the Anakim *were* there, and *that* the cities *were* great *and* fortified. [b]It may be that the LORD *will be* with me, and [c]I shall be able to drive them out as the LORD said."

13 And Joshua [a]blessed him, [b]and gave Hebron to Caleb the son of Jephunneh as an inheritance. 14 [a]Hebron therefore became the inheritance of Caleb the son of Jephunneh the Kenizzite to this day, because he [b]wholly followed the LORD God of Israel. 15 And [a]the name of Hebron formerly was Kirjath Arba (*Arba was* the greatest man among the Anakim).

[b]Then the land had rest from war.

The Land of Judah

15 So *this* was the lot of the tribe of the children of Judah according to their families:

[a]The border of Edom at the [b]Wilderness of Zin southward *was* the extreme southern boundary. 2 And their [a]southern border began at the shore of the Salt Sea, from the bay that faces southward. 3 Then it went out to the southern side of [a]the Ascent of Akrabbim, passed along to Zin, ascended on the south side of Kadesh Barnea, passed along to Hezron, went up to Adar, and went around to Karkaa. 4 *From there* it passed [a]toward Azmon and went out to the Brook of Egypt; and the border ended at the sea. This shall be your southern border.

5 The east border *was* the Salt Sea as far as the mouth of the Jordan.

And the [a]border on the northern quarter *began* at the bay of the sea at the mouth of the Jordan. 6 The border went up to [a]Beth Hoglah and passed north of Beth Arabah; and the border went up [b]to the stone of Bohan the son of Reuben. 7 Then the border went up toward [a]Debir from [b]the Valley of Achor, and it turned northward toward Gilgal, which *is* before the Ascent of Adummim, which *is* on the south side of the valley. The border continued toward the waters of En Shemesh and ended at [c]En Rogel. 8 And the border went up [a]by the Valley of the Son of Hinnom to the southern slope of the [b]Jebusite *city* (which *is* Jerusalem). The border went up to the top of the mountain that *lies* before the Valley of Hinnom westward, which *is* at the end of the Valley [c]of Rephaim[1] northward. 9 Then the border went around from the top of the hill to [a]the fountain of the water of Nephtoah, and extended to the cities of Mount Ephron. And the border went around [b]to Baalah (which *is* [c]Kirjath Jearim). 10 Then the border turned westward from Baalah to Mount Seir, passed along to the side of Mount Jearim on the north (which *is* Chesalon), went down to Beth Shemesh, and passed on to [a]Timnah. 11 And the border went out to the side of [a]Ekron northward. Then the border went around to Shicron, passed along to Mount Baalah, and extended to Jabneel; and the border ended at the sea.

14:6 [a] Num. 32:11, 12 [b] Num. 14:24, 30 [c] Num. 13:26 14:7 [a] Num. 13:6, 17; 14:6 14:8 [a] Num. 13:31, 32; Deut. 1:28 [b] Num. 14:24; Deut. 1:36 14:9 [a] Num. 14:23, 24 [b] Num. 13:22; Deut. 1:36 14:10 [a] Num. 14:24, 30, 38 [b] Josh. 5:6; Neh. 9:21 14:11 [a] Deut. 34:7 [b] Deut. 31:2 14:12 [a] Num. 13:28, 33 [b] Rom. 8:31 [c] Josh. 15:14; Judg. 1:20 14:13 [a] Josh. 22:6 [b] Josh. 10:37; 15:13 14:14 [a] Josh. 21:12 [b] Josh. 14:8, 9 14:15 [a] Gen. 23:2; Josh. 15:13 [b] Josh. 11:23 15:1 [a] Num. 34:3 [b] Num. 33:36 15:2 [a] Num. 34:3, 4 15:3 [a] Num. 34:4 15:4 [a] Num. 34:5 15:5 [a] Josh. 18:15–19 15:6 [a] Josh. 18:19, 21 [b] Josh. 18:17 15:7 [a] Josh. 13:26 [b] Josh. 7:26 [c] 2 Sam. 17:17; 1 Kin. 1:9 15:8 [a] Josh. 18:16; 2 Kin. 23:10; Jer. 19:2, 6 [b] Josh. 15:63; 18:28; Judg. 1:21; 19:10 [c] Josh. 18:16 [1] Literally *Giants* 15:9 [a] Josh. 18:15 [b] 1 Chr. 13:6 [c] Judg. 18:12 15:10 [a] Gen. 38:13; Judg. 14:1 15:11 [a] Josh. 19:43

12The west border *was* [a]the coastline of the Great Sea. This *is* the boundary of the children of Judah all around according to their families.

Caleb Occupies Hebron and Debir
(Judg. 1:11–15)

13[a]Now to Caleb the son of Jephunneh he gave a share among the children of [b]Judah, according to the commandment of the LORD to Joshua, *namely,* [c]Kirjath Arba, which *is* Hebron (*Arba was* the father of Anak). 14Caleb drove out [a]the three sons of Anak from there: [b]Sheshai, Ahiman, and Talmai, the children of Anak. 15Then [a]he went up from there to the inhabitants of Debir (formerly the name of Debir *was* Kirjath Sepher).

16[a]And Caleb said, "He who attacks Kirjath Sepher and takes it, to him I will give Achsah my daughter as wife." 17So [a]Othniel the [b]son of Kenaz, the brother of Caleb, took it; and he gave him [c]Achsah his daughter as wife. 18[a]Now it was so, when she came *to him,* that she persuaded him to ask her father for a field. So [b]she dismounted from *her* donkey, and Caleb said to her, "What do you wish?" 19She answered, "Give me a [a]blessing; since you have given me land in the South, give me also springs of water." So he gave her the upper springs and the lower springs.

The Cities of Judah

20This *was* the inheritance of the tribe of the children of Judah according to their families:

21The cities at the limits of the tribe of the children of Judah, toward the border of Edom in the South, were Kabzeel, [a]Eder, Jagur, 22Kinah, Dimonah, Adadah, 23Kedesh, Hazor, Ithnan, 24[a]Ziph, Telem, Bealoth, 25Hazor, Hadattah, Kerioth, Hezron (which *is* Hazor), 26Amam, Shema, Moladah, 27Hazar Gaddah, Heshmon, Beth Pelet, 28Hazar Shual, [a]Beersheba, Bizjothjah, 29Baalah, Ijim, Ezem, 30Eltolad, Chesil, [a]Hormah, 31[a]Ziklag, Madmannah, Sansannah, 32Lebaoth, Shilhim, Ain, and [a]Rimmon: all the cities *are* twenty-nine, with their villages.

33In the lowland: [a]Eshtaol, Zorah, Ashnah, 34Zanoah, En Gannim, Tappuah, Enam, 35Jarmuth, [a]Adullam, Socoh, Azekah, 36Sharaim, Adithaim, Gederah, and Gederothaim: fourteen cities with their villages; 37Zenan, Hadashah, Migdal Gad, 38Dilean, Mizpah, [a]Joktheel, 39[a]Lachish, Bozkath, [b]Eglon, 40Cabbon, Lahmas,[1] Kithlish, 41Gederoth, Beth Dagon, Naamah, and Makkedah: sixteen cities with their villages; 42[a]Libnah, Ether, Ashan, 43Jiphtah, Ashnah, Nezib, 44Keilah, Achzib, and Mareshah: nine cities with their villages; 45Ekron, with its towns and villages; 46from Ekron to the sea, all that *lay* near [a]Ashdod, with their villages; 47Ashdod with its towns and villages, Gaza with its towns and villages—as far as [a]the Brook of Egypt and [b]the Great Sea with *its* coastline.

48And in the mountain country: Shamir, Jattir, Sochoh, 49Dannah, Kirjath Sannah (which *is* Debir), 50Anab, Eshtemoh, Anim, 51[a]Goshen, Holon, and Giloh: eleven cities with their villages; 52Arab, Dumah, Eshean, 53Janum, Beth Tappuah, Aphekah, 54Humtah, [a]Kirjath Arba (which *is* Hebron), and Zior: nine cities with their villages; 55[a]Maon, Carmel, Ziph, Juttah, 56Jezreel, Jokdeam, Zanoah, 57Kain, Gibeah, and Timnah: ten cities with their villages; 58Halhul, Beth Zur, Gedor, 59Maarath, Beth Anoth, and Eltekon: six cities with their villages; 60[a]Kirjath Baal (which *is* Kirjath Jearim) and Rabbah: two cities with their villages.

61In the wilderness: Beth Arabah, Middin, Secacah, 62Nibshan, the City of Salt, and [a]En Gedi: six cities with their villages.

63As for the Jebusites, the inhabitants of Jerusalem, [a]the children of Judah could not drive them out; [b]but the Jebusites dwell with the children of Judah at Jerusalem to this day.

Ephraim and West Manasseh

16 The lot fell to the children of Joseph from the Jordan, by Jericho, to the waters of Jericho on the east, to the

15:12 [a] Num. 34:6, 7; Josh. 15:47 15:13 [a] Josh. 14:13 [b] Num. 13:6 [c] Josh. 14:15 15:14 [a] Judg. 1:10, 20 [b] Num. 13:22 15:15 [a] Josh. 10:38; Judg. 1:11 15:16 [a] Judg. 1:12 15:17 [a] Judg. 1:13; 3:9 [b] Num. 32:12; Josh. 14:6 [c] Judg. 1:12 15:18 [a] Judg. 1:14 [b] Gen. 24:64; 1 Sam. 25:23 15:19 [a] Gen. 33:11 15:21 [a] Gen. 35:21 15:24 [a] 1 Sam. 23:14 15:28 [a] Gen. 21:31; Josh. 19:2 15:30 [a] Josh. 19:4 15:31 [a] Josh. 19:5; 1 Sam. 27:6; 30:1 15:32 [a] Judg. 20:45, 47 15:33 [a] Judg. 13:25; 16:31 15:35 [a] 1 Sam. 22:1 15:38 [a] 2 Kin. 14:7 15:39 [a] 2 Kin. 14:19 [b] Josh. 10:3 15:40 [1] Or *Lahmam* 15:42 [a] Josh. 21:13 15:46 [a] Josh. 11:22 15:47 [a] Josh. 15:4 [b] Num. 34:6 15:51 [a] Josh. 10:41; 11:16 15:54 [a] Josh. 14:15 15:55 [a] 1 Sam. 23:24, 25 15:60 [a] Josh. 18:14; 1 Sam. 7:1, 2 15:62 [a] 1 Sam. 23:29; Ezek. 47:10 15:63 [a] Judg. 1:8, 21; 2 Sam. 5:6; 1 Chr. 11:4 [b] Judg. 1:21

[a]wilderness that goes up from Jericho
through the mountains to Bethel, 2then
went out from [a]Bethel to Luz,[1] passed along
to the border of the Archites at Ataroth,
3and went down westward to the boundary of the Japhletites, [a]as far as the boundary of Lower Beth Horon to [b]Gezer; and it
ended at the sea.
4[a]So the children of Joseph, Manasseh
and Ephraim, took their inheritance.

The Land of Ephraim

5[a]The border of the children of Ephraim,
according to their families, was *thus:* The
border of their inheritance on the east side
was [b]Ataroth Addar [c]as far as Upper Beth
Horon.
6And the border went out toward the sea
on the north side of [a]Michmethath; then
the border went around eastward to Taa-
nath Shiloh, and passed by it on the east of
Janohah. 7Then it went down from Janohah
to Ataroth and Naarah,[1] reached to Jericho,
and came out at the Jordan.
8The border went out from [a]Tappuah
westward to the [b]Brook Kanah, and it ended
at the sea. This *was* the inheritance of the
tribe of the children of Ephraim according
to their families. 9[a]The separate cities for
the children of Ephraim *were* among the
inheritance of the children of Manasseh,
all the cities with their villages.
10[a]And they did not drive out the Canaanites who dwelt in Gezer; but the Canaanites dwell among the Ephraimites to
this day and have become forced laborers.

The Other Half-Tribe of Manasseh (West)

17 There was also a lot for the tribe of
Manasseh, for he *was* the [a]firstborn
of Joseph: *namely* for [b]Machir the firstborn
of Manasseh, the father of Gilead, because
he was a man of war; therefore he was given
[c]Gilead and Bashan. 2And there was *a lot*
for [a]the rest of the children of Manasseh
according to their families: [b]for the children of Abiezer,[1] the children of Helek, [c]the
children of Asriel, the children of Shechem,
[d]the children of Hepher, and the children
of Shemida; these *were* the male children
of Manasseh the son of Joseph according
to their families.
3But [a]Zelophehad the son of Hepher, the
son of Gilead, the son of Machir, the son of
Manasseh, had no sons, but only daughters.
And these *are* the names of his daughters:
Mahlah, Noah, Hoglah, Milcah, and Tirzah.
4And they came near before [a]Eleazar the
priest, before Joshua the son of Nun, and
before the rulers, saying, [b]"The LORD commanded Moses to give us an inheritance
among our brothers." Therefore, according
to the commandment of the LORD, he gave
them an inheritance among their father's
brothers. 5Ten shares fell to [a]Manasseh, besides the land of Gilead and Bashan, which
were on the other side of the Jordan, 6be-
cause the daughters of Manasseh received
an inheritance among his sons; and the rest
of Manasseh's sons had the land of Gilead.
7And the territory of Manasseh was from
Asher to [a]Michmethath, that *lies* east of
Shechem; and the border went along south
to the inhabitants of En Tappuah. 8Manas-
seh had the land of Tappuah, but [a]Tappuah
on the border of Manasseh *belonged* to the
children of Ephraim. 9And the border descended to the Brook Kanah, southward
to the brook. [a]These cities of Ephraim *are*
among the cities of Manasseh. The border
of Manasseh *was* on the north side of the
brook; and it ended at the sea.
10Southward *it was* Ephraim's, northward *it was* Manasseh's, and the sea was
its border. Manasseh's territory was adjoining Asher on the north and Issachar on the
east. 11And in Issachar and in Asher, [a]Ma-
nasseh had [b]Beth Shean and its towns, Ibleam and its towns, the inhabitants of Dor
and its towns, the inhabitants of En Dor
and its towns, the inhabitants of Taanach
and its towns, and the inhabitants of Megiddo and its towns—three hilly regions.
12Yet [a]the children of Manasseh could not
drive out *the inhabitants of* those cities, but
the Canaanites were determined to dwell

16:1 [a] Josh. 8:15; 18:12 16:2 [a] Josh. 18:13; Judg. 1:26 [1] Septuagint reads *Bethel* (that is, Luz). 16:3 [a] Josh. 18:13; 1 Kin. 9:17; 2 Chr. 8:5 [b] Josh. 21:21; 1 Kin. 9:15; 1 Chr. 7:28 16:4 [a] Josh. 17:14 16:5 [a] Judg. 1:29; 1 Chr. 7:28, 29 [b] Josh. 18:13 [c] 2 Chr. 8:5 16:6 [a] Josh. 17:7 16:7 [1] Or *Naaran* (compare 1 Chronicles 7:28) 16:8 [a] Josh. 17:8 [b] Josh. 17:9 16:9 [a] Josh. 17:9 16:10 [a] Josh. 15:63; 17:12, 13; Judg. 1:29; 1 Kin. 9:16 17:1 [a] Gen. 41:51; 46:20; 48:18 [b] Gen. 50:23; Judg. 5:14 [c] Deut. 3:15 17:2 [a] Num. 26:29–33 [b] 1 Chr. 7:18 [c] Num. 26:31 [d] Num. 26:32 [1] Called *Jeezer* in Numbers 26:30 17:3 [a] Num. 26:33; 27:1; 36:2 17:4 [a] Josh. 14:1 [b] Num. 27:2–11 17:5 [a] Josh. 22:7 17:7 [a] Josh. 16:6 17:8 [a] Josh. 16:8 17:9 [a] Josh. 16:9 17:11 [a] 1 Chr. 7:29 [b] Judg. 1:27; 1 Sam. 31:10; 1 Kin. 4:12 17:12 [a] Judg. 1:19, 27, 28

in that land. 13 And it happened, when the
children of Israel grew strong, that they put
the Canaanites to [a]forced labor, but did not
utterly drive them out.

More Land for Ephraim and Manasseh

14 [a]Then the children of Joseph spoke to
Joshua, saying, "Why have you given us
only [b]one lot and one share to inherit, since
we *are* [c]a great people, inasmuch as the
LORD has blessed us until now?"
15 So Joshua answered them, "If you *are* a
great people, *then* go up to the forest *country* and clear a place for yourself there in
the land of the Perizzites and the giants,
since the mountains of Ephraim are too
confined for you."
16 But the children of Joseph said, "The
mountain country is not enough for us; and
all the Canaanites who dwell in the land of
the valley have [a]chariots of iron, *both those*
who *are* of Beth Shean and its towns and
those who *are* [b]of the Valley of Jezreel."
17 And Joshua spoke to the house of Joseph—to Ephraim and Manasseh—saying,
"You *are* a great people and have great
power; you shall not have *only* one lot, 18 but
the mountain country shall be yours. Although it *is* wooded, you shall cut it down,
and its farthest extent shall be yours; for
you shall drive out the Canaanites, [a]though
they have iron chariots *and* are strong."

The Remainder of the Land Divided

18 Now the whole congregation of the
children of Israel assembled to-
gether [a]at Shiloh, and [b]set up the tabernacle
of meeting there. And the land was subdued
before them. 2 But there remained among
the children of Israel seven tribes which
had not yet received their inheritance.
3 Then Joshua said to the children of
Israel: [a]"How long will you neglect to go
and possess the land which the LORD God
of your fathers has given you? 4 Pick out
from among you three men for *each* tribe,
and I will send them; they shall rise and
go through the land, survey it according
to their inheritance, and come *back* to
me. 5 And they shall divide it into seven
parts. [a]Judah shall remain in their territory on the south, and the [b]house of Joseph shall remain in their territory on the
north. 6 You shall therefore survey the land
in seven parts and bring *the survey* here to
me, [a]that I may cast lots for you here before
the LORD our God. 7 [a]But the Levites have no
part among you, for the priesthood of the
LORD *is* their inheritance. [b]And Gad, Reuben, and half the tribe of Manasseh have
received their inheritance beyond the Jordan on the east, which Moses the servant
of the LORD gave them."
8 Then the men arose to go away; and
Joshua charged those who went to survey the land, saying, "Go, walk [a]through
the land, survey it, and come back to me,
that I may cast lots for you here before the
LORD in Shiloh." 9 So the men went, passed
through the land, and wrote the survey in a
book in seven parts by cities; and they came
to Joshua at the camp in Shiloh. 10 Then
Joshua cast [a]lots for them in Shiloh before
the LORD, and there [b]Joshua divided the
land to the children of Israel according to
their divisions.

The Land of Benjamin

11 [a]Now the lot of the tribe of the children
of Benjamin came up according to their
families, and the territory of their lot came
out between the children of Judah and the
children of Joseph. 12 [a]Their border on the
north side began at the Jordan, and the
border went up to the side of Jericho on
the north, and went up through the mountains westward; it ended at the Wilderness
of Beth Aven. 13 The border went over from
there toward Luz, to the side of Luz [a](which
is Bethel) southward; and the border descended to Ataroth Addar, near the hill that
lies on the south side [b]of Lower Beth Horon.
14 Then the border extended around the
west side to the south, from the hill that
lies before Beth Horon southward; and it
ended at [a]Kirjath Baal (which *is* Kirjath Jearim), a city of the children of Judah. This
was the west side.

17:13 [a] Josh. 16:10 17:14 [a] Josh. 16:4 [b] Gen. 48:22 [c] Gen. 48:19; Num. 26:34, 37 17:16 [a] Josh. 17:18; Judg. 1:19; 4:3 [b] Josh. 19:18; 1 Kin. 4:12 17:18 [a] Deut. 20:1 18:1 [a] Josh. 19:51; 21:2; 22:9; Jer. 7:12 [b] Judg. 18:31; 1 Sam. 1:3, 24; 4:3, 4 18:3 [a] Judg. 18:9 18:5 [a] Josh. 15:1 [b] Josh. 16:1—17:18 18:6 [a] Josh. 14:2; 18:10 18:7 [a] Num. 18:7, 20; Josh. 13:33 [b] Josh. 13:8 18:8 [a] Gen. 13:17 18:10 [a] Acts 13:19 [b] Num. 34:16–29; Josh. 19:51 18:11 [a] Judg. 1:21 18:12 [a] Josh. 16:1 18:13 [a] Gen. 28:19; Josh. 16:2; Judg. 1:23 [b] Josh. 16:3 18:14 [a] Josh. 15:9

15The south side *began* at the end of
Kirjath Jearim, and the border extended
on the west and went out to [a]the spring of
the waters of Nephtoah. 16Then the border
came down to the end of the mountain that
lies before [a]the Valley of the Son of Hinnom,
which *is* in the Valley of the Rephaim[1] on
the north, descended to the Valley of Hinnom, to the side of the Jebusite *city* on the
south, and descended to [b]En Rogel. 17And
it went around from the north, went out to
En Shemesh, and extended toward Geliloth,
which is before the Ascent of Adummim,
and descended to [a]the stone of Bohan the
son of Reuben. 18Then it passed along toward the north side of Arabah,[1] and went
down to Arabah. 19And the border passed
along to the north side of Beth Hoglah;
then the border ended at the north bay at
the [a]Salt Sea, at the south end of the Jordan.
This *was* the southern boundary.

20The Jordan was its border on the east
side. This *was* the inheritance of the children of Benjamin, according to its boundaries all around, according to their families.

21Now the cities of the tribe of the children of Benjamin, according to their families, were Jericho, Beth Hoglah, Emek
Keziz, 22Beth Arabah, Zemaraim, Bethel,
23Avim, Parah, Ophrah, 24Chephar Haam-
moni, Ophni, and Gaba: twelve cities with
their villages; 25[a]Gibeon, [b]Ramah, Beeroth,
26Mizpah, Chephirah, Mozah, 27Rekem, Ir-
peel, Taralah, 28Zelah, Eleph, [a]Jebus (which
is Jerusalem), Gibeath, *and* Kirjath: fourteen cities with their villages. This was the
inheritance of the children of Benjamin
according to their families.

Simeon's Inheritance with Judah

19 The [a]second lot came out for Simeon, for the tribe of the children of
Simeon according to their families. [b]And
their inheritance was within the inheritance of the children of Judah. 2[a]They had
in their inheritance Beersheba (Sheba),
Moladah, 3Hazar Shual, Balah, Ezem, 4El-
tolad, Bethul, Hormah, 5Ziklag, Beth Marcaboth, Hazar Susah, 6Beth Lebaoth, and
Sharuhen: thirteen cities and their villages;
7Ain, Rimmon, Ether, and Ashan: four cities
and their villages; 8and all the villages that
were all around these cities as far as Baalath Beer, [a]Ramah of the South. This *was* the
inheritance of the tribe of the children of
Simeon according to their families.

9The inheritance of the children of Simeon *was included* in the share of the children of Judah, for the share of the children
of Judah was too much for them. [a]Therefore
the children of Simeon had *their* inheritance within the inheritance of that people.

The Land of Zebulun

10The third lot came out for the children
of Zebulun according to their families, and
the border of their inheritance was as far as
Sarid. 11[a]Their border went toward the west
and to Maralah, went to Dabbasheth, and
extended along the brook that is [b]east of
Jokneam. 12Then from Sarid it went eastward toward the sunrise along the border
of Chisloth Tabor, and went out toward
[a]Daberath, bypassing Japhia. 13And from
there it passed along on the east of [a]Gath
Hepher, toward Eth Kazin, and extended to
Rimmon, which borders on Neah. 14Then
the border went around it on the north side
of Hannathon, and it ended in the Valley of
Jiphthah El. 15Included were Kattath, Na-
hallal, Shimron, Idalah, and Bethlehem:
twelve cities with their villages. 16This *was*
the inheritance of the children of Zebulun
according to their families, these cities with
their villages.

The Land of Issachar

17The fourth lot came out to Issachar,
for the children of Issachar according to
their families. 18And their territory went to
Jezreel, and *included* Chesulloth, Shunem,
19Haphraim, Shion, Anaharath, 20Rabbith,
Kishion, Abez, 21Remeth, En Gannim, En
Haddah, and Beth Pazzez. 22And the border
reached to Tabor, Shahazimah, and [a]Beth
Shemesh; their border ended at the Jordan:
sixteen cities with their villages. 23This *was*
the inheritance of the tribe of the children
of Issachar according to their families, the
cities and their villages.

18:15 [a] Josh. 15:9 18:16 [a] Josh. 15:8 [b] Josh. 15:7 [1] Literally *Giants* 18:17 [a] Josh. 15:6 18:18 [1] Or *Beth Arabah* (compare 15:6 and 18:22) 18:19 [a] Josh. 15:2, 5 18:25 [a] Josh. 11:19; 21:17; 1 Kin. 3:4, 5 [b] Jer. 31:15 18:28 [a] Josh. 15:8, 63 19:1 [a] Judg. 1:3 [b] Josh. 19:9 19:2 [a] 1 Chr. 4:28 19:8 [a] 1 Sam. 30:27 19:9 [a] Josh. 19:1 19:11 [a] Gen. 49:13 [b] Josh. 12:22 19:12 [a] 1 Chr. 6:72 19:13 [a] 2 Kin. 14:25 19:22 [a] Josh. 15:10; Judg. 1:33

The Land of Asher

24[a]The fifth lot came out for the tribe of the children of Asher according to their families. 25And their territory included Helkath, Hali, Beten, Achshaph, 26Alammelech, Amad, and Mishal; it reached to [a]Mount Carmel westward, along *the Brook* Shihor Libnath. 27It turned toward the sunrise to Beth Dagon; and it reached to Zebulun and to the Valley of Jiphthah El, then northward beyond Beth Emek and Neiel, bypassing [a]Cabul *which was* on the left, 28including Ebron,[1] Rehob, Hammon, and Kanah, [a]as far as Greater Sidon. 29And the border turned to Ramah and to the fortified city of Tyre; then the border turned to Hosah, and ended at the sea by the region of [a]Achzib. 30Also Ummah, Aphek, and Rehob *were included:* twenty-two cities with their villages. 31This *was* the inheritance of the tribe of the children of Asher according to their families, these cities with their villages.

The Land of Naphtali

32[a]The sixth lot came out to the children of Naphtali, for the children of Naphtali according to their families. 33And their border began at Heleph, enclosing the territory from the terebinth tree in Zaanannim, Adami Nekeb, and Jabneel, as far as Lakkum; it ended at the Jordan. 34[a]From Heleph the border extended westward to Aznoth Tabor, and went out from there toward Hukkok; it adjoined Zebulun on the south side and Asher on the west side, and ended at Judah by the Jordan toward the sunrise. 35And the fortified cities *are* Ziddim, Zer, Hammath, Rakkath, Chinnereth, 36Adamah, Ramah, Hazor, 37[a]Kedesh, Edrei, En Hazor, 38Iron, Migdal El, Horem, Beth Anath, and Beth Shemesh: nineteen cities with their villages. 39This *was* the inheritance of the tribe of the children of Naphtali according to their families, the cities and their villages.

The Land of Dan

40[a]The seventh lot came out for the tribe of the children of Dan according to their families. 41And the territory of their inheritance was Zorah, [a]Eshtaol, Ir Shemesh, 42[a]Shaalabbin, [b]Aijalon, Jethlah, 43Elon, Timnah, [a]Ekron, 44Eltekeh, Gibbethon, Baalath, 45Jehud, Bene Berak, Gath Rimmon, 46Me Jarkon, and Rakkon, with the region near Joppa. 47And the [a]border of the children of Dan went beyond these, because the children of Dan went up to fight against Leshem and took it; and they struck it with the edge of the sword, took possession of it, and dwelt in it. They called Leshem, [b]Dan, after the name of Dan their father. 48This *is* the inheritance of the tribe of the children of Dan according to their families, these cities with their villages.

Joshua's Inheritance

49When they had made an end of dividing the land as an inheritance according to their borders, the children of Israel gave an inheritance among them to Joshua the son of Nun. 50According to the word of the LORD they gave him the city which he asked for, [a]Timnath [b]Serah in the mountains of Ephraim; and he built the city and dwelt in it.

51[a]These *were* the inheritances which Eleazar the priest, Joshua the son of Nun, and the heads of the fathers of the tribes of the children of Israel divided as an inheritance by lot [b]in Shiloh before the LORD, at the door of the tabernacle of meeting. So they made an end of dividing the country.

The Cities of Refuge
(Num. 35:9–28; Deut. 19:1–13)

20 The LORD also spoke to Joshua, saying, 2"Speak to the children of Israel, saying: [a]'Appoint for yourselves cities of refuge, of which I spoke to you through Moses, 3that the slayer who kills a person accidentally *or* unintentionally may flee there; and they shall be your refuge from the avenger of blood. 4And when he flees to one of those cities, and stands at the entrance of the gate of the city, and declares his case in the hearing of the elders of that

19:24 [a] Judg. 1:31, 32 19:26 [a] 1 Sam. 15:12; 1 Kin. 18:20; Is. 33:9; 35:2; Jer. 46:18 19:27 [a] 1 Kin. 9:13 19:28 [a] Gen. 10:19; Josh. 11:8; Judg. 1:31; Acts 27:3 [1] Following Masoretic Text, Targum, and Vulgate; a few Hebrew manuscripts read *Abdon* (compare 21:30 and 1 Chronicles 6:74). 19:29 [a] Judg. 1:31 19:32 [a] Josh. 19:32–39; Judg. 1:33 19:34 [a] Deut. 33:23 19:37 [a] Josh. 20:7 19:40 [a] Josh. 19:40–48; Judg. 1:34–36 19:41 [a] Josh. 15:33 19:42 [a] Judg. 1:35; 1 Kin. 4:9 [b] Josh. 10:12; 21:24 19:43 [a] Josh. 15:11; Judg. 1:18 19:47 [a] Judg. 18 [b] Judg. 18:29 19:50 [a] Josh. 24:30 [b] 1 Chr. 7:24 19:51 [a] Num. 34:17; Josh. 14:1 [b] Josh. 18:1, 10 20:2 [a] Ex. 21:13; Num. 35:6–34; Deut. 19:2, 9

city, they shall take him into the city as one
of them, and give him a place, that he may
dwell among them. 5[a]Then if the avenger of
blood pursues him, they shall not deliver
the slayer into his hand, because he struck
his neighbor unintentionally, but did not
hate him beforehand. 6And he shall dwell
in that city [a]until he stands before the congregation for judgment, *and* until the death
of the one who is high priest in those days.
Then the slayer may return and come to
his own city and his own house, to the city
from which he fled.'"

7So they appointed [a]Kedesh in Galilee, in
the mountains of Naphtali, [b]Shechem in the
mountains of Ephraim, and [c]Kirjath Arba
(which *is* Hebron) in [d]the mountains of Judah. 8And on the other side of the Jordan,
by Jericho eastward, they assigned [a]Bezer
in the wilderness on the plain, from the
tribe of Reuben, [b]Ramoth in Gilead, from
the tribe of Gad, and [c]Golan in Bashan, from
the tribe of Manasseh. 9[a]These were the
cities appointed for all the children of Israel and for the stranger who dwelt among
them, that whoever killed a person accidentally might flee there, and not die by
the hand of the avenger of blood [b]until he
stood before the congregation.

Cities of the Levites
(1 Chr. 6:54–81)

21 Then the heads of the fathers' *houses*
of the [a]Levites came near to [b]Eleazar
the priest, to Joshua the son of Nun, and to
the heads of the fathers' *houses* of the tribes
of the children of Israel. 2And they spoke
to them at [a]Shiloh in the land of Canaan,
saying, [b]"The LORD commanded through
Moses to give us cities to dwell in, with their
common-lands for our livestock." 3So the
children of Israel gave to the Levites from
their inheritance, at the commandment of
the LORD, these cities and their common-
lands:

4Now the lot came out for the families of
the Kohathites. And [a]the children of Aaron
the priest, *who were* of the Levites, [b]had
thirteen cities by lot from the tribe of Judah, from the tribe of Simeon, and from
the tribe of Benjamin. 5[a]The rest of the children of Kohath had ten cities by lot from
the families of the tribe of Ephraim, from
the tribe of Dan, and from the half-tribe
of Manasseh.

6And [a]the children of Gershon had thirteen cities by lot from the families of the
tribe of Issachar, from the tribe of Asher,
from the tribe of Naphtali, and from the
half-tribe of Manasseh in Bashan.

7[a]The children of Merari according to
their families had twelve cities from the
tribe of Reuben, from the tribe of Gad, and
from the tribe of Zebulun.

8[a]And the children of Israel gave these
cities with their common-lands by lot to
the Levites, [b]as the LORD had commanded
by the hand of Moses.

9So they gave from the tribe of the children of Judah and from the tribe of the
children of Simeon these cities which are
designated by name, 10which were for the
children of Aaron, one of the families of
the Kohathites, *who were* of the children
of Levi; for the lot was theirs first. 11[a]And
they gave them Kirjath Arba (*Arba was* the
father of [b]Anak), [c]which *is* Hebron, in the
mountains of Judah, with the common-
land surrounding it. 12But [a]the fields of the
city and its villages they gave to Caleb the
son of Jephunneh as his possession.

13Thus [a]to the children of Aaron the
priest they gave [b]Hebron with its common-
land (a city of refuge for the slayer), [c]Lib-
nah with its common-land, 14[a]Jattir with
its common-land, [b]Eshtemoa with its
common-land, 15[a]Holon with its common-
land, [b]Debir with its common-land, 16[a]Ain
with its common-land, [b]Juttah with its
common-land, and [c]Beth Shemesh with
its common-land: nine cities from those
two tribes; 17and from the tribe of Benjamin, [a]Gibeon with its common-land,
[b]Geba with its common-land, 18Anathoth
with its common-land, and [a]Almon with
its common-land: four cities. 19All the cities

20:5 [a] Num. 35:12 20:6 [a] Num. 35:12, 24, 25 20:7 [a] Josh. 21:32; 1 Chr. 6:76 [b] Josh. 21:21; 2 Chr. 10:1 [c] Josh. 14:15; 21:11, 13 [d] Luke 1:39 20:8 [a] Deut. 4:43; Josh. 21:36; 1 Chr. 6:78 [b] Josh. 21:38; 1 Kin. 22:3 [c] Josh. 21:27 20:9 [a] Num. 35:15 [b] Josh. 20:6 21:1 [a] Num. 35:1–8 [b] Num. 34:16–29; Josh. 14:1; 17:4 21:2 [a] Josh. 18:1 [b] Num. 35:2 21:4 [a] Josh. 21:8, 19 [b] Josh. 19:51 21:5 [a] Josh. 21:20 21:6 [a] Josh. 21:27 21:7 [a] Josh. 21:34 21:8 [a] Josh. 21:3 [b] Num. 35:2 21:11 [a] Josh. 20:7; 1 Chr. 6:55 [b] Josh. 14:15; 15:13, 14 [c] Josh. 20:7; Luke 1:39 21:12 [a] Josh. 14:14; 1 Chr. 6:56 21:13 [a] 1 Chr. 6:57 [b] Josh. 15:54; 20:2, 7 [c] Josh. 15:42; 2 Kin. 8:22 21:14 [a] Josh. 15:48 [b] Josh. 15:50 21:15 [a] 1 Chr. 6:58 [b] Josh. 15:49 21:16 [a] 1 Chr. 6:59 [b] Josh. 15:55 [c] Josh. 15:10 21:17 [a] Josh. 18:25 [b] Josh. 18:24 21:18 [a] 1 Chr. 6:60

of the children of Aaron, the priests, *were* thirteen cities with their common-lands.

20[a]And the families of the children of Kohath, the Levites, the rest of the children of Kohath, even they had the cities of their lot from the tribe of Ephraim. 21For they gave them [a]Shechem with its common-land in the mountains of Ephraim (a city of refuge for the slayer), [b]Gezer with its common-land, 22Kibzaim with its common-land, and Beth Horon with its common-land: four cities; 23and from the tribe of Dan, Eltekeh with its common-land, Gibbethon with its common-land, 24[a]Aijalon with its common-land, *and* Gath Rimmon with its common-land: four cities; 25and from the half-tribe of Manasseh, Tanach with its common-land and Gath Rimmon with its common-land: two cities. 26All the ten cities with their common-lands were for the rest of the families of the children of Kohath.

27[a]Also to the children of Gershon, of the families of the Levites, from the *other* half-tribe of Manasseh, *they gave* [b]Golan in Bashan with its common-land (a city of refuge for the slayer), and Be Eshterah with its common-land: two cities; 28and from the tribe of Issachar, Kishion with its common-land, Daberath with its common-land, 29Jarmuth with its common-land, *and* En Gannim with its common-land: four cities; 30and from the tribe of Asher, Mishal with its common-land, Abdon with its common-land, 31Helkath with its common-land, and Rehob with its common-land: four cities; 32and from the tribe of Naphtali, [a]Kedesh in Galilee with its common-land (a city of refuge for the slayer), Hammoth Dor with its common-land, and Kartan with its common-land: three cities. 33All the cities of the Gershonites according to their families *were* thirteen cities with their common-lands.

34[a]And to the families of the children of Merari, the rest of the Levites, from the tribe of Zebulun, Jokneam with its common-land, Kartah with its common-land, 35Dimnah with its common-land, *and* Nahalal with its common-land: four cities; 36and from the tribe of Reuben, [a]Bezer with its common-land, Jahaz with its common-land, 37Kedemoth with its common-land, and Mephaath with its common-land: four cities;[1] 38and from the tribe of Gad, [a]Ramoth in Gilead with its common-land (a city of refuge for the slayer), Mahanaim with its common-land, 39Heshbon with its common-land, *and* Jazer with its common-land: four cities in all. 40So all the cities for the children of Merari according to their families, the rest of the families of the Levites, were *by* their lot twelve cities.

41[a]All the cities of the Levites within the possession of the children of Israel *were* forty-eight cities with their common-lands. 42Every one of these cities had its common-land surrounding it; thus *were* all these cities.

The Promise Fulfilled

43So the LORD gave to Israel [a]all the land of which He had sworn to give to their fathers, and they [b]took possession of it and dwelt in it. 44[a]The LORD gave them [b]rest all around, according to all that He had sworn to their fathers. And [c]not a man of all their enemies stood against them; the LORD delivered all their enemies into their hand. 45[a]Not a word failed of any good thing which the LORD had spoken to the house of Israel. All came to pass.

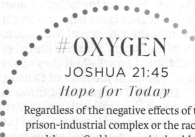

#OXYGEN

JOSHUA 21:45

Hope for Today

Regardless of the negative effects of the prison-industrial complex or the racial wealth gap, God has promised to bless all who walk in His ways and keep His commands. No matter what.

Trust the Promise Keeper, **breathe**, and **hope for today**.

21:20 [a] 1 Chr. 6:66 21:21 [a] Josh. 20:7 [b] Judg. 1:29 21:24 [a] Josh. 10:12 21:27 [a] Josh. 21:6; 1 Chr. 6:71 [b] Josh. 20:8 21:32 [a] Josh. 20:7 21:34 [a] Josh. 21:7; 1 Chr. 6:77–81 21:36 [a] Deut. 4:43; Josh. 20:8 21:37 [1] Following Septuagint and Vulgate (compare 1 Chronicles 6:78, 79); Masoretic Text, Bomberg, and Targum omit verses 36 and 37. 21:38 [a] Josh. 20:8 21:41 [a] Num. 35:7 21:43 [a] Gen. 12:7; 26:3, 4; 28:4, 13, 14 [b] Num. 33:53; Josh. 1:11 21:44 [a] Deut. 7:23, 24; Josh. 11:23; 22:4 [b] Josh. 1:13, 15; 11:23 [c] Deut. 7:24 21:45 [a] [Num. 23:19]; Josh. 23:14; 1 Kin. 8:56

Eastern Tribes Return to Their Lands

22 Then Joshua called the Reubenites,
the Gadites, and half the tribe of Manasseh, 2and said to them: "You have kept
[a]all that Moses the servant of the LORD commanded you, [b]and have obeyed my voice in
all that I commanded you. 3You have not
left your brethren these many days, up to
this day, but have kept the charge of the
commandment of the LORD your God. 4And
now the LORD your God has given [a]rest to
your brethren, as He promised them; now
therefore, return and go to your tents *and*
to the land of your possession, [b]which Moses the servant of the LORD gave you on the
other side of the Jordan. 5But [a]take careful
heed to do the commandment and the law
which Moses the servant of the LORD commanded you, [b]to love the LORD your God, to
walk in all His ways, to keep His commandments, to hold fast to Him, and to serve
Him with all your heart and with all your
soul." 6So Joshua [a]blessed them and sent
them away, and they went to their tents.

7Now to half the tribe of Manasseh Moses had given a possession in Bashan, [a]but
to the *other* half of it Joshua gave *a possession* among their brethren on this side of
the Jordan, westward. And indeed, when
Joshua sent them away to their tents, he
blessed them, 8and spoke to them, saying,
"Return with much riches to your tents,
with very much livestock, with silver, with
gold, with bronze, with iron, and with very
much clothing. [a]Divide the spoil of your
enemies with your brethren."

9So the children of Reuben, the children
of Gad, and half the tribe of Manasseh returned, and departed from the children
of Israel at Shiloh, which *is* in the land of
Canaan, to go to [a]the country of Gilead, to
the land of their possession, which they
had obtained according to the word of the
LORD by the hand of Moses.

An Altar by the Jordan

10And when they came to the region of
the Jordan which *is* in the land of Canaan,
the children of Reuben, the children of
Gad, and half the tribe of Manasseh built
an altar there by the Jordan—a great, impressive altar. 11Now the children of Israel
[a]heard *someone* say, "Behold, the children
of Reuben, the children of Gad, and half
the tribe of Manasseh have built an altar
on the frontier of the land of Canaan, in
the region of the Jordan—on the children
of Israel's side." 12And when the children of
Israel heard *of it,* [a]the whole congregation
of the children of Israel gathered together
at Shiloh to go to war against them.

13Then the children of Israel [a]sent [b]Phin-
ehas the son of Eleazar the priest to the children of Reuben, to the children of Gad, and
to half the tribe of Manasseh, into the land
of Gilead, 14and with him ten rulers, one ruler
each from the chief house of every tribe of
Israel; and [a]each one *was* the head of the
house of his father among the divisions[1] of
Israel. 15Then they came to the children of
Reuben, to the children of Gad, and to half
the tribe of Manasseh, to the land of Gilead,
and they spoke with them, saying, 16"Thus
says the whole congregation of the LORD:
'What [a]treachery *is* this that you have committed against the God of Israel, to turn away
this day from following the LORD, in that
you have built for yourselves an altar, [b]that
you might rebel this day against the LORD?
17*Is* the iniquity [a]of Peor not enough for us,
from which we are not cleansed till this day,
although there was a plague in the congregation of the LORD, 18but that you must
turn away this day from following the LORD?
And it shall be, if you rebel today against the
LORD, that tomorrow [a]He will be angry with
the whole congregation of Israel. 19Neverthe-
less, if the land of your possession *is* unclean,
then cross over to the land of the possession of the LORD, [a]where the LORD's tabernacle stands, and take possession among
us; but do not rebel against the LORD, nor
rebel against us, by building yourselves an
altar besides the altar of the LORD our God.
20[a]Did not Achan the son of Zerah commit a
trespass in the accursed thing, and wrath fell
on all the congregation of Israel? And that
man did not perish alone in his iniquity.'"

22:2 [a] Num. 32:20–22; Deut. 3:18 [b] Josh. 1:12–18 **22:4** [a] Josh. 21:44 [b] Num. 32:33 **22:5** [a] Deut. 6:6, 17; 11:22; Jer. 12:16 [b] Deut. 10:12; 11:13, 22 **22:6** [a] Gen. 47:7; Ex. 39:43; Josh. 14:13; 2 Sam. 6:18; Luke 24:50 **22:7** [a] Josh. 17:1–13 **22:8** [a] Num. 31:27; 1 Sam. 30:24 **22:9** [a] Num. 32:1, 26, 29 **22:11** [a] Deut. 13:12–18; Judg. 20:12, 13 **22:12** [a] Josh. 18:1; Judg. 20:1 **22:13** [a] Deut. 13:14; Judg. 20:12 [b] Ex. 6:25; Num. 25:7, 11–13 **22:14** [a] Num. 1:4 [1] Literally *thousands* **22:16** [a] Deut. 12:5–14 [b] Lev. 17:8, 9 **22:17** [a] Num. 25:1–9; Deut. 4:3 **22:18** [a] Num. 16:22 **22:19** [a] Josh. 18:1 **22:20** [a] Josh. 7:1–26

21 Then the children of Reuben, the children of Gad, and half the tribe of Manasseh
answered and said to the heads of the divisions[1] of Israel: 22 "The LORD [a]God of gods,
the LORD God of gods, He [b]knows, and let
Israel itself know—if *it is* in rebellion, or if
in treachery against the LORD, do not save
us this day. 23 If we have built ourselves an
altar to turn from following the LORD, or
if to offer on it burnt offerings or grain offerings, or if to offer peace offerings on it,
let the LORD Himself [a]require *an account.*
24 But in fact we have done it for fear, for a
reason, saying, 'In time to come your descendants may speak to our descendants,
saying, "What have you to do with the LORD
God of Israel? 25 For the LORD has made the
Jordan a border between you and us, *you*
children of Reuben and children of Gad.
You have no part in the LORD." So your descendants would make our descendants
cease fearing the LORD.' 26 Therefore we
said, 'Let us now prepare to build ourselves
an altar, not for burnt offering nor for sacrifice, 27 but *that* it *may be* [a]a witness between
you and us and our generations after us,
that we may [b]perform the service of the
LORD before Him with our burnt offerings,
with our sacrifices, and with our peace offerings; that your descendants may not say
to our descendants in time to come, "You
have no part in the LORD."' 28 Therefore we
said that it will be, when they say *this* to
us or to our generations in time to come,
that we may say, 'Here is the replica of the
altar of the LORD which our fathers made,
though not for burnt offerings nor for sacrifices; but it *is* a witness between you and
us.' 29 Far be it from us that we should rebel
against the LORD, and turn from following the LORD this day, [a]to build an altar for
burnt offerings, for grain offerings, or for
sacrifices, besides the altar of the LORD our
God which *is* before His tabernacle."

30 Now when Phinehas the priest and
the rulers of the congregation, the heads
of the divisions[1] of Israel who *were* with
him, heard the words that the children of
Reuben, the children of Gad, and the children of Manasseh spoke, it pleased them.
31 Then Phinehas the son of Eleazar the
priest said to the children of Reuben, the
children of Gad, and the children of Manasseh, "This day we perceive that the LORD *is*
[a]among us, because you have not committed this treachery against the LORD. Now
you have delivered the children of Israel
out of the hand of the LORD."

32 And Phinehas the son of Eleazar the
priest, and the rulers, returned from the
children of Reuben and the children of Gad,
from the land of Gilead to the land of Canaan, to the children of Israel, and brought
back word to them. 33 So the thing pleased
the children of Israel, and the children of
Israel [a]blessed God; they spoke no more
of going against them in battle, to destroy
the land where the children of Reuben and
Gad dwelt.

34 The children of Reuben and the children of Gad[1] called the altar, *Witness,* "For
it is a witness between us that the LORD
is God."

Joshua's Farewell Address

23 Now it came to pass, a long time after the LORD [a]had given rest to Israel from all their enemies round about,
that Joshua [b]was old, advanced in age. 2 And
Joshua [a]called for all Israel, for their elders,
for their heads, for their judges, and for
their officers, and said to them:

"I am old, advanced in age. 3 You have
seen all that the [a]LORD your God has done
to all these nations because of you, for the
[b]LORD your God *is* He who has fought for
you. 4 See, [a]I have divided to you by lot these
nations that remain, to be an inheritance
for your tribes, from the Jordan, with all
the nations that I have cut off, as far as the
Great Sea westward. 5 And the LORD your
God [a]will expel them from before you and
drive them out of your sight. So you shall
possess their land, [b]as the LORD your God
promised you. 6 [a]Therefore be very courageous to keep and to do all that is written

---

22:21 [1] Literally *thousands* 22:22 [a] Deut. 4:35; 10:17; Is. 44:8; 45:5; 46:9; [1 Cor. 8:5, 6] [b] [Job 10:7; 23:10; Jer. 12:3; 2 Cor. 11:11, 31]
22:23 [a] Deut. 18:19; 1 Sam. 20:16 22:27 [a] Gen. 31:48; Josh. 22:34; 24:27 [b] Deut. 12:5, 14 22:29 [a] Deut. 12:13, 14 22:30 [1] Literally *thousands* 22:31 [a] Ex. 25:8; Lev. 26:11, 12; 2 Chr. 15:2; Zech. 8:23 22:33 [a] 1 Chr. 29:20; Neh. 8:6; Dan. 2:19; Luke 2:28
22:34 [1] Septuagint adds *and half the tribe of Manasseh.* 23:1 [a] Josh. 21:44; 22:4 [b] Josh. 13:1; 24:29
23:2 [a] Deut. 31:28 23:3 [a] Ps. 44:3 [b] Ex. 14:14; Deut. 1:30; Josh. 10:14, 42 23:4 [a] Josh. 13:2, 6; 18:10
23:5 [a] Ex. 23:30; 33:2 [b] Num. 33:53 23:6 [a] Josh. 1:7

in the Book of the Law of Moses, [b]lest you
turn aside from it to the right hand or to
the left, 7*and* lest you [a]go among these nations, these who remain among you. You
shall not [b]make mention of the name of
their gods, nor cause *anyone* to [c]swear *by*
them; you shall not [d]serve them nor bow
down to them, 8but you shall [a]hold fast to
the LORD your God, as you have done to this
day. 9[a]For the LORD has driven out from
before you great and strong nations; but
as for you, no one has been able to stand
against you to this day. 10[a]One man of you
shall chase a thousand, for the LORD your
God *is* He who fights for you, [b]as He promised you. 11[a]Therefore take careful heed to
yourselves, that you love the LORD your
God. 12Or else, if indeed you do [a]go back,
and cling to the remnant of these nations—
these that remain among you—and [b]make
marriages with them, and go in to them
and they to you, 13know for certain that
[a]the LORD your God will no longer drive
out these nations from before you. [b]But
they shall be snares and traps to you, and
scourges on your sides and thorns in your
eyes, until you perish from this good land
which the LORD your God has given you.

14"Behold, this day [a]I *am* going the way of
all the earth. And you know in all your hearts
and in all your souls that [b]not one thing has
failed of all the good things which the LORD
your God spoke concerning you. All have
come to pass for you; not one word of them
has failed. 15[a]Therefore it shall come to pass,
that as all the good things have come upon
you which the LORD your God promised you,
so the LORD will bring upon you [b]all harmful things, until He has destroyed you from
this good land which the LORD your God has
given you. 16When you have transgressed the
covenant of the LORD your God, which He
commanded you, and have gone and served
other gods, and bowed down to them, then
the [a]anger of the LORD will burn against you,
and you shall perish quickly from the good
land which He has given you."

The Covenant at Shechem
(cf. Ex. 24:9–18)

24 Then Joshua gathered all the tribes
of Israel to [a]Shechem and [b]called
for the elders of Israel, for their heads, for
their judges, and for their officers; and they
[c]presented themselves before God. 2And
Joshua said to all the people, "Thus says
the LORD God of Israel: [a]'Your fathers, *in-*
cluding Terah, the father of Abraham and
the father of Nahor, dwelt on the other side
of the River[1] in old times; and [b]they served
other gods. 3[a]Then I took your father Abraham from the other side of the River, led
him throughout all the land of Canaan, and
multiplied his descendants and [b]gave him
Isaac. 4To Isaac I gave [a]Jacob and Esau. To
[b]Esau I gave the mountains of Seir to possess, [c]but Jacob and his children went down
to Egypt. 5[a]Also I sent Moses and Aaron,
and [b]I plagued Egypt, according to what
I did among them. Afterward I brought
you out.

6'Then I [a]brought your fathers out of
Egypt, and you came to the sea; and the
Egyptians pursued your fathers with chariots and horsemen to the Red Sea. 7So they
cried out to the LORD; and He put [a]darkness
between you and the Egyptians, brought
the sea upon them, and covered them. And
[b]your eyes saw what I did in Egypt. Then
you dwelt in the wilderness [c]a long time.
8And I brought you into the land of the
Amorites, who dwelt on the other side of
the Jordan, [a]and they fought with you. But
I gave them into your hand, that you might
possess their land, and I destroyed them
from before you. 9Then [a]Balak the son of
Zippor, king of Moab, arose to make war
against Israel, and [b]sent and called Balaam
the son of Beor to curse you. 10[a]But I would
not listen to Balaam; [b]therefore he continued to bless you. So I delivered you out of
his hand. 11Then [a]you went over the Jordan and came to Jericho. And [b]the men of
Jericho fought against you—*also* the Amorites, the Perizzites, the Canaanites, the

---

23:6 [b] Deut. 5:32 **23:7** [a] Ex. 23:33; Deut. 7:2, 3; [Prov. 4:14; Eph. 5:11] [b] Ex. 23:13; Ps. 16:4; Jer. 5:7; Hos. 2:17 [c] Deut. 6:13; 10:20 [d] Ex. 20:5 **23:8** [a] Deut. 10:20 **23:9** [a] Deut. 7:24; 11:23; Josh. 1:5 **23:10** [a] Lev. 26:8; Deut. 28:7; Is. 30:17 [b] Ex. 14:14 **23:11** [a] Josh. 22:5 **23:12** [a] [2 Pet. 2:20, 21] [b] Deut. 7:3, 4; Ezra 9:2; Neh. 13:25 **23:13** [a] Judg. 2:3 [b] Ex. 23:33; 34:12; Deut. 7:16 **23:14** [a] 1 Kin. 2:2 [b] Josh. 21:45; [Luke 21:33] **23:15** [a] Deut. 28:63 [b] Lev. 26:14–39; Deut. 28:15–68 **23:16** [a] Deut. 4:24–28 **24:1** [a] Gen. 35:4 [b] Josh. 23:2 [c] 1 Sam. 10:19 **24:2** [a] Gen. 11:7–32 [b] Josh. 24:14 [1] Hebrew *Nahar,* the Euphrates, and so in verses 3, 14, and 15 **24:3** [a] Gen. 12:1; Acts 7:2, 3 [b] Gen. 21:1–8; [Ps. 127:3] **24:4** [a] Gen. 25:24–26 [b] Gen. 36:8; Deut. 2:5 [c] Gen. 46:1, 3, 6 **24:5** [a] Ex. 3:10 [b] Ex. 7—10 **24:6** [a] Ex. 12:37, 51; 14:2–31 **24:7** [a] Ex. 14:20 [b] Deut. 4:34 [c] Josh. 5:6 **24:8** [a] Num. 21:21–35 **24:9** [a] Judg. 11:25 [b] Num. 22:2–14 **24:10** [a] Deut. 23:5 [b] Num. 23:11, 20; 24:10 **24:11** [a] Josh. 3:14, 17 [b] Josh. 6:1; 10:1

Hittites, the Girgashites, the Hivites, and
the Jebusites. But I delivered them into
your hand. 12[a]I sent the hornet before you
which drove them out from before you,
also the two kings of the Amorites, *but* [b]not
with your sword or with your bow. 13I have
given you a land for which you did not labor, and [a]cities which you did not build, and
you dwell in them; you eat of the vineyards
and olive groves which you did not plant.'

14[a]"Now therefore, fear the LORD, serve
Him in [b]sincerity and in truth, and [c]put
away the gods which your fathers served
on the other side of the River and [d]in Egypt.
Serve the LORD! 15And if it seems evil to you
to serve the LORD, [a]choose for yourselves
this day whom you will serve, whether [b]the
gods which your fathers served that *were*
on the other side of the River, or [c]the gods
of the Amorites, in whose land you dwell.
[d]But as for me and my house, we will serve
the LORD."

16So the people answered and said: "Far
be it from us that we should forsake the
LORD to serve other gods; 17for the LORD our
God *is* He who brought us and our fathers
up out of the land of Egypt, from the house
of bondage, who did those great signs in our
sight, and preserved us in all the way that
we went and among all the people through
whom we passed. 18And the LORD drove out
from before us all the people, including the
Amorites who dwelt in the land. [a]We also
will serve the LORD, for He *is* our God."

19But Joshua said to the people, [a]"You
cannot serve the LORD, for He *is* a [b]holy God.
He *is* [c]a jealous God; [d]He will not forgive
your transgressions nor your sins. 20[a]If you
forsake the LORD and serve foreign gods,
[b]then He will turn and do you harm and
consume you, after He has done you good."

21And the people said to Joshua, "No, but
we will serve the LORD!"

22So Joshua said to the people, "You *are*
witnesses against yourselves that [a]you have
chosen the LORD for yourselves, to serve
Him."

And they said, "*We are* witnesses!"

23"Now therefore," *he said*, [a]"put away the
foreign gods which *are* among you, and [b]in-
cline your heart to the LORD God of Israel."

24And the people [a]said to Joshua, "The
LORD our God we will serve, and His voice
we will obey!"

25So Joshua [a]made a covenant with the
people that day, and made for them a statute and an ordinance [b]in Shechem.

26Then Joshua [a]wrote these words in
the Book of the Law of God. And he took
[b]a large stone, and [c]set it up there [d]under
the oak that *was* by the sanctuary of the
LORD. 27And Joshua said to all the people,
"Behold, this stone shall be [a]a witness to us,
for [b]it has heard all the words of the LORD
which He spoke to us. It shall therefore be
a witness to you, lest you deny your God."
28So [a]Joshua let the people depart, each to
his own inheritance.

Death of Joshua and Eleazar

29[a]Now it came to pass after these things
that Joshua the son of Nun, the servant of
the LORD, died, *being* one hundred and ten
years old. 30And they buried him within the
border of his inheritance at [a]Timnath Serah, which *is* in the mountains of Ephraim,
on the north side of Mount Gaash.

31[a]Israel served the LORD all the days
of Joshua, and all the days of the elders
who outlived Joshua, who had [b]known all
the works of the LORD which He had done
for Israel.

32[a]The bones of Joseph, which the children of Israel had brought up out of Egypt,
they buried at Shechem, in the plot of
ground [b]which Jacob had bought from the
sons of Hamor the father of Shechem for
one hundred pieces of silver, and which had
become an inheritance of the children of
Joseph.

33And [a]Eleazar the son of Aaron died.
They buried him in a hill *belonging to* [b]Phin-
ehas his son, which was given to him in the
mountains of Ephraim.

24:12 [a] Ex. 23:28; Deut. 7:20 [b] Ps. 44:3 **24:13** [a] Deut. 6:10, 11 **24:14** [a] Deut. 10:12, 13; 1 Sam. 12:24 [b] 2 Cor. 1:12 [c] Josh. 24:2, 23; Ezek. 20:18 [d] Ezek. 20:7, 8 **24:15** [a] Ruth 1:15; 1 Kin. 18:21 [b] Josh. 24:2; Ezek. 20:39 [c] Ex. 23:24, 32 [d] Gen. 18:19; Ps. 101:2; [1 Tim. 3:4, 5] **24:18** [a] Ps. 116:16 **24:19** [a] Matt. 6:24 [b] Lev. 11:44, 45; 1 Sam. 6:20 [c] Ex. 20:5 [d] Ex. 23:21 **24:20** [a] 1 Chr. 28:9; Ezra 8:22; Is. 1:28; 63:10; 65:11, 12; Jer. 17:13 [b] Deut. 4:24–26; Josh. 23:15 **24:22** [a] Ps. 119:173 **24:23** [a] Gen. 35:2; Josh. 24:14; Judg. 10:15, 16; 1 Sam. 7:3 [b] 1 Kin. 8:57, 58; Ps. 119:36; 141:4 **24:24** [a] Ex. 19:8; 24:3, 7; Deut. 5:24–27 **24:25** [a] Ex. 15:25 [b] Josh. 24:1 **24:26** [a] Deut. 31:24 [b] Judg. 9:6 [c] Gen. 28:18 [d] Gen. 35:4 **24:27** [a] Gen. 31:48 [b] Deut. 32:1 **24:28** [a] Judg. 2:6, 7 **24:29** [a] Judg. 2:8 **24:30** [a] Josh. 19:50; Judg. 2:9 **24:31** [a] Judg. 2:7 [b] Deut. 11:2 **24:32** [a] Gen. 50:25; Ex. 13:19; Heb. 11:22 [b] Gen. 33:19; John 4:5 **24:33** [a] Ex. 28:1; Num. 20:28; Josh. 14:1 [b] Ex. 6:25

THE BOOK OF

JUDGES

OVERVIEW

Scholars attribute the authorship of this book to Samuel and believe the book was written around 1000 BC. Through the book's pages, we follow the Israelites' continuing story as they dwell in the Promised Land after Joshua's death until the time of Samuel, a period of roughly four hundred years. During this time, the Israelites were unfaithful to God and did not obey the Law. Their rebelliousness barred them from taking full possession of the land (see Judg. 1:27–36).

The Book of Judges introduces twelve leaders chosen by God to rule over the Israelites. Judges details the repeating cycle of Israel's disobedience, God's discipline, Israel's repentance, and God's provision of a judge to deliver and restore the people.

As the book opens, the Promised Land is inhabited by a new generation of Israelites who neither knew the Lord nor acknowledged what He had done for Israel (see 2:7–15). They had not witnessed God's miracles in the wilderness, and they had turned away from God and had begun worshiping the gods of the Canaanites (see vv. 16–23). This angered God, yet in His mercy and compassion, He raised judges to deliver His people. The people's hearts, however, were far from God, and they rebelled against Him and His ways once more (see 3:1–6).

The Israelites repeated this cycle of rebellion, oppression, distress, and deliverance for several generations. But each time other nations oppressed them, God demonstrated His faithfulness by sending yet another judge as a deliverer when His people cried out to Him. When the Israelites were oppressed by the Canaanites, God chose Deborah and Barak to deliver them (chs. 4–5). When they were oppressed by the Midianites, God used Gideon to deliver them (chs. 6–8). When the Philistines oppressed them, Samson served as God's deliverer (chs. 13–15).

The final chapters of Judges (17–21) detail the continued disobedience of the Israelites, including the accounts of Micah's idolatry (ch. 17) and the Levite's concubine (ch. 19). During the period described in the Book of Judges, the people's conduct is best summed up as this: "There was no king in Israel; everyone did what was right in his own eyes" (21:25).

The major theme of Judges is the price Israel paid each time they abandoned God and failed to obey Him. Their disobedience led to their downfall and caused their failure to possess all the land God had promised. Israel repeatedly rebelled against God, yet God was faithful to keep His covenant and love His people.

BREATHE IT IN

When the Israelites entered the Promised Land, they did not live in obedience to God according to the Law. They repeatedly allowed those around them to influence their behavior—they worshiped false gods and engaged in forbidden rituals. As a result, they did not possess all the land promised to them and experienced the pain of God's loving discipline. The failure of the Israelites to teach their children about their history and covenant with God caused troubling spiritual, political, social, and economic consequences.

Like the Israelites, many of us fail to teach our children about our history. They may gain some information from textbooks, but they have not heard our ancestors' stories. They have not learned about many of our real-life struggles for freedom, justice, and equality. They do not know how desperately those who came before them looked to God for guidance and deliverance. Their ancestors depended on God to direct their paths and deliver them from slavery to freedom and from social subjection to civil rights. We need to share these stories of sacrifice with our children so they understand their history and can more fully appreciate and enjoy their lives today.

Judges gives us many examples of just how committed God is to His people. The Israelites angered God by not obeying His instructions to take over the land and worship only Him. But when the Israelites' neighbors oppressed them, God sent judges to deliver His people and turn them back to Him. Though they failed Him repeatedly, He continued to redeem them.

How many times have we done everything God asked us to do in preparation to take possession of our own promised land? But when we entered the land, did we continue to honor our commitment to Him, or did we turn away from Him and go back to doing things our own way? Did we allow others to talk us into doing and saying things that we knew would not please God, or did we continue following His ways? Did we even remember to thank Him?

If we turn away from God and allow ourselves to be led astray by others, God will not be pleased. Our disobedience will have consequences. However, if we acknowledge our wrongdoing and repent, God will be faithful to forgive us and restore us as He forgave and restored the Israelites time and time again. But we cannot take God's forgiveness for granted. We are not to be like the Israelites and live in a cycle of oppression and deliverance.

As followers of Christ, we should aim to take possession of all the land God promised us. To possess the land in its entirety, we must be obedient to God and honor His covenant with us. We must follow His instructions and worship Him as the only true and living God. We cannot make people, belongings, and personal success our gods. We must resolve that we will place no other god before Him. Once we have taken these steps, we must teach our children our history with God for them to enter into covenant with Him and understand how to live in the land that they shall one day inherit.

THE BOOK OF

JUDGES

The Continuing Conquest of Canaan
(Josh. 15:13–19)

1 Now after the [a]death of Joshua it came
to pass that the children of Israel [b]asked
the LORD, saying, "Who shall be first to go
up for us against the [c]Canaanites to fight
against them?"

2And the LORD said, [a]"Judah shall go
up. Indeed I have delivered the land into
his hand."

3So Judah said to [a]Simeon his brother,
"Come up with me to my allotted territory,
that we may fight against the Canaanites;
and [b]I will likewise go with you to your allotted territory." And Simeon went with
him. 4Then Judah went up, and the LORD
delivered the Canaanites and the Perizzites into their hand; and they killed ten
thousand men at [a]Bezek. 5And they found
Adoni-Bezek in Bezek, and fought against
him; and they defeated the Canaanites and
the Perizzites. 6Then Adoni-Bezek fled, and
they pursued him and caught him and cut
off his thumbs and big toes. 7And Adoni-Bezek said, "Seventy kings with their thumbs
and big toes cut off used to gather *scraps*
under my table; [a]as I have done, so God has
repaid me." Then they brought him to Jerusalem, and there he died.

8Now [a]the children of Judah fought
against Jerusalem and took it; they struck
it with the edge of the sword and set the
city on fire. 9[a]And afterward the children
of Judah went down to fight against the
Canaanites who dwelt in the mountains,
in the South,[1] and in the lowland. 10Then
Judah went against the Canaanites who
dwelt in [a]Hebron. (Now the name of Hebron *was* formerly [b]Kirjath Arba.) And they
killed Sheshai, Ahiman, and Talmai.

11[a]From there they went against the
inhabitants of Debir. (The name of Debir
was formerly Kirjath Sepher.)

12[a]Then Caleb said, "Whoever attacks Kirjath Sepher and takes it, to him I will give
my daughter Achsah as wife." 13And Othniel
the son of Kenaz, [a]Caleb's younger brother,
took it; so he gave him his daughter Achsah as wife. 14[a]Now it happened, when she
came *to him,* that she urged him[1] to ask her
father for a field. And she dismounted from
her donkey, and Caleb said to her, "What do
you wish?" 15So she said to him, [a]"Give me a
blessing; since you have given me land in
the South, give me also springs of water."

And Caleb gave her the upper springs
and the lower springs.

16[a]Now the children of the Kenite, Moses' father-in-law, went up [b]from the City
of Palms with the children of Judah into
the Wilderness of Judah, which *lies* in the
South *near* [c]Arad; [d]and they went and dwelt
among the people. 17[a]And Judah went with
his brother Simeon, and they attacked the
Canaanites who inhabited Zephath, and utterly destroyed it. So the name of the city
was called [b]Hormah. 18Also Judah took
[a]Gaza with its territory, Ashkelon with its
territory, and Ekron with its territory. 19So
the LORD was with Judah. And they drove
out the mountaineers, but they could not
drive out the inhabitants of the lowland,

1:1 [a] Josh. 24:29 [b] Num. 27:21; Judg. 20:18 [c] Josh. 17:12, 13 1:2 [a] Gen. 49:8, 9; Rev. 5:5 1:3 [a] Josh. 19:1 [b] Judg. 1:17 1:4 [a] 1 Sam. 11:8 1:7 [a] Lev. 24:19; 1 Sam. 15:33; [James 2:13] 1:8 [a] Josh. 15:63; Judg. 1:21 1:9 [a] Josh. 10:36; 11:21; 15:13 [1] Hebrew *Negev,* and so throughout this book 1:10 [a] Josh. 15:13–19 [b] Josh. 14:15 1:11 [a] Josh. 15:15 1:12 [a] Josh. 15:16, 17 1:13 [a] Judg. 3:9 1:14 [a] Josh. 15:18, 19 [1] Septuagint and Vulgate read *he urged her.* 1:15 [a] Gen. 33:11 1:16 [a] Num. 10:29–32; Judg. 4:11, 17; 1 Sam. 15:6; 1 Chr. 2:55 [b] Deut. 34:3; Judg. 3:13 [c] Josh. 12:14 [d] 1 Sam. 15:6 1:17 [a] Judg. 1:3 [b] Num. 21:3; Josh. 19:4 1:18 [a] Josh. 11:22

because they had [a]chariots of iron. 20[a]And
they gave Hebron to Caleb, as Moses had
said. Then he expelled from there the
[b]three sons of Anak. 21[a]But the children of
Benjamin did not drive out the Jebusites
who inhabited Jerusalem; so the Jebusites
dwell with the children of Benjamin in Jerusalem to this day.

22And the house of Joseph also went
up against Bethel, [a]and the LORD *was* with
them. 23So the house of Joseph [a]sent men
to spy out Bethel. (The name of the city *was*
formerly [b]Luz.) 24And when the spies saw
a man coming out of the city, they said to
him, "Please show us the entrance to the
city, and [a]we will show you mercy." 25So he
showed them the entrance to the city, and
they struck the city with the edge of the
sword; but they let the man and all his family go. 26And the man went to the land of
the Hittites, built a city, and called its name
Luz, which *is* its name to this day.

Incomplete Conquest of the Land

27[a]However, Manasseh did not drive
out *the inhabitants of* Beth Shean and its
villages, or [b]Taanach and its villages, or
the inhabitants of [c]Dor and its villages, or
the inhabitants of Ibleam and its villages,
or the inhabitants of Megiddo and its villages; for the Canaanites were determined
to dwell in that land. 28And it came to pass,
when Israel was strong, that they put the
Canaanites under tribute, but did not completely drive them out.

29[a]Nor did Ephraim drive out the Canaanites who dwelt in Gezer; so the Canaanites dwelt in Gezer among them.

30Nor did [a]Zebulun drive out the inhabitants of Kitron or the inhabitants of Naha-
lol; so the Canaanites dwelt among them,
and were put under tribute.

31[a]Nor did Asher drive out the inhabitants of Acco or the inhabitants of Sidon,
or of Ahlab, Achzib, Helbah, Aphik, or Rehob. 32So the Asherites [a]dwelt among the
Canaanites, the inhabitants of the land; for
they did not drive them out.

33[a]Nor did Naphtali drive out the inhabitants of Beth Shemesh or the inhabitants
of Beth Anath; but they dwelt among the
Canaanites, the inhabitants of the land.
Nevertheless the inhabitants of Beth Shemesh and Beth Anath were put under tribute to them.

34And the Amorites forced the children
of Dan into the mountains, for they would
not allow them to come down to the valley; 35and the Amorites were determined
to dwell in Mount Heres, [a]in Aijalon, and
in Shaalbim;[1] yet when the strength of the
house of Joseph became greater, they were
put under tribute.

36Now the boundary of the Amorites *was*
[a]from the Ascent of Akrabbim, from Sela,
and upward.

Israel's Disobedience

2 Then the Angel of the LORD came up
from Gilgal to Bochim, and said: [a]"I
led you up from Egypt and [b]brought you to
the land of which I swore to your fathers;
and [c]I said, 'I will never break My covenant
with you. 2And [a]you shall make no covenant with the inhabitants of this land;
[b]you shall tear down their altars.' [c]But you
have not obeyed My voice. Why have you
done this? 3Therefore I also said, 'I will not
drive them out before you; but they shall be
[a]*thorns* in your side,[1] and [b]their gods shall
be a [c]snare to you.'" 4So it was, when the
Angel of the LORD spoke these words to
all the children of Israel, that the people
lifted up their voices and wept.

5Then they called the name of that place
Bochim;[1] and they sacrificed there to the
LORD. 6And when [a]Joshua had dismissed
the people, the children of Israel went each
to his own inheritance to possess the land.

Death of Joshua
(Josh. 24:29–31)

7[a]So the people served the LORD all the
days of Joshua, and all the days of the elders who outlived Joshua, who had seen all
the great works of the LORD which He had

1:19 [a] Josh. 17:16, 18; Judg. 4:3, 13 1:20 [a] Num. 14:24; Josh. 14:9, 14 [b] Josh. 15:14; Judg. 1:10 1:21 [a] Josh. 15:63; Judg. 1:8 1:22 [a] Judg. 1:19 1:23 [a] Josh. 2:1; 7:2 [b] Gen. 28:19 1:24 [a] Josh. 2:12, 14 1:27 [a] Josh. 17:11–13 [b] Josh. 21:25 [c] Josh. 17:11 1:29 [a] Josh. 16:10; 1 Kin. 9:16 1:30 [a] Josh. 19:10–16 1:31 [a] Josh. 19:24–31 1:32 [a] Ps. 106:34, 35 1:33 [a] Josh. 19:32–39 1:35 [a] Josh. 19:42 [1] Spelled *Shaalabbin* in Joshua 19:42 1:36 [a] Num. 34:4; Josh. 15:3 2:1 [a] Ex. 20:2; Judg. 6:8, 9 [b] Deut. 1:8 [c] Gen. 17:7, 8; Lev. 26:42, 44; Deut. 7:9; Ps. 89:34 2:2 [a] Ex. 23:32; Deut. 7:2 [b] Ex. 34:12, 13; Deut. 12:3 [c] Ps. 106:34 2:3 [a] Num. 33:55; Josh. 23:13 [b] Judg. 3:6 [c] Ex. 23:33; Deut. 7:16; Ps. 106:36 [1] Septuagint, Targum, and Vulgate read *enemies to you.* 2:5 [1] Literally *Weeping* 2:6 [a] Josh. 22:6; 24:28–31 2:7 [a] Josh. 24:31

done for Israel. 8Now [a]Joshua the son of Nun,
the servant of the LORD, died *when he was*
one hundred and ten years old. 9[a]And they
buried him within the border of his inheritance at [b]Timnath Heres, in the mountains
of Ephraim, on the north side of Mount Gaash. 10When all that generation had been
gathered to their fathers, another generation
arose after them who [a]did not know the LORD
nor the work which He had done for Israel.

Israel's Unfaithfulness

11Then the children of Israel did [a]evil
in the sight of the LORD, and served the
Baals; 12and they [a]forsook the LORD God of
their fathers, who had brought them out of
the land of Egypt; and they followed [b]other
gods from *among* the gods of the people
who *were* all around them, and they [c]bowed
down to them; and they provoked the LORD
to anger. 13They forsook the LORD [a]and
served Baal and the Ashtoreths.[1] 14[a]And
the anger of the LORD was hot against Israel. So He [b]delivered them into the hands
of plunderers who despoiled them; and
[c]He sold them into the hands of their enemies all around, so that they [d]could no longer stand before their enemies. 15Wherever
they went out, the hand of the LORD was
against them for calamity, as the LORD had
said, and as the LORD had [a]sworn to them.
And they were greatly distressed.

16Nevertheless, [a]the LORD raised up
judges who delivered them out of the hand
of those who plundered them. 17Yet they
would not listen to their judges, but they
[a]played the harlot with other gods, and
bowed down to them. They turned quickly
from the way in which their fathers walked,
in obeying the commandments of the
LORD; they did not do so. 18And when the
LORD raised up judges for them, [a]the LORD
was with the judge and delivered them out
of the hand of their enemies all the days of
the judge; [b]for the LORD was moved to pity
by their groaning because of those who oppressed them and harassed them. 19And it
came to pass, [a]when the judge was dead,
that they reverted and behaved more corruptly than their fathers, by following other
gods, to serve them and bow down to them.
They did not cease from their own doings
nor from their stubborn way.

20Then the anger of the LORD was hot
against Israel; and He said, "Because this
nation has [a]transgressed My covenant
which I commanded their fathers, and has
not heeded My voice, 21I also will no longer
drive out before them any of the nations
which Joshua [a]left when he died, 22so [a]that
through them I may [b]test Israel, whether
they will keep the ways of the LORD, to walk
in them as their fathers kept *them,* or not."
23Therefore the LORD left those nations,
without driving them out immediately; nor
did He deliver them into the hand of Joshua.

The Nations Remaining in the Land

3 Now these *are* [a]the nations which the
LORD left, that He might test Israel by
them, *that is,* all who had not known any of
the wars in Canaan 2(*this was* only so that the
generations of the children of Israel might
be taught to know war, at least those who
had not formerly known it), 3*namely,* [a]five
lords of the Philistines, all the Canaanites,
the Sidonians, and the Hivites who dwelt
in Mount Lebanon, from Mount Baal Hermon to the entrance of Hamath. 4And they
were *left, that He might* test Israel by them,
to know whether they would obey the commandments of the LORD, which He had commanded their fathers by the hand of Moses.

5[a]Thus the children of Israel dwelt
among the Canaanites, the Hittites, the
Amorites, the Perizzites, the Hivites, and
the Jebusites. 6And [a]they took their daughters to be their wives, and gave their daughters to their sons; and they served their
gods.

Othniel

7So the children of Israel did [a]evil in the
sight of the LORD. They [b]forgot the LORD
their God, and served the Baals and Ashe-
rahs.[1] 8Therefore the anger of the LORD was

2:8 [a] Josh. 24:29 **2:9** [a] Josh. 24:30 [b] Josh. 19:49, 50 **2:10** [a] Ex. 5:2; 1 Sam. 2:12; Gal. 4:8; [Titus 1:16] **2:11** [a] Judg. 3:7, 12; 4:1; 6:1 **2:12** [a] Deut. 31:16; Judg. 8:33; 10:6 [b] Deut. 6:14 [c] Ex. 20:5 **2:13** [a] Judg. 10:6; Ps. 106:36 [1] Canaanite goddesses **2:14** [a] Deut. 31:17; Judg. 3:8; Ps. 106:40–42 [b] 2 Kin. 17:20 [c] Is. 50:1 [d] Lev. 26:37; Josh. 7:12, 13 **2:15** [a] Lev. 26:14–26; Deut. 28:15–68 **2:16** [a] Judg. 3:9, 10, 15; Ps. 106:43–45 **2:17** [a] Ex. 34:15 **2:18** [a] Josh. 1:5 [b] Gen. 6:6 **2:19** [a] Judg. 3:12 **2:20** [a] [Josh. 23:16] **2:21** [a] Josh. 23:4, 5, 13 **2:22** [a] Judg. 3:1, 4 [b] Deut. 8:2, 16; 13:3 **3:1** [a] Judg. 1:1; 2:21, 22 **3:3** [a] Josh. 13:3 **3:5** [a] Ps. 106:35 **3:6** [a] Ex. 34:15, 16; Deut. 7:3, 4; Josh. 23:12 **3:7** [a] Judg. 2:11 [b] Deut. 32:18 [1] Name or symbol for Canaanite goddesses

hot against Israel, and He [a]sold them into
the hand of [b]Cushan-Rishathaim king of
Mesopotamia; and the children of Israel
served Cushan-Rishathaim eight years.
9When the children of Israel [a]cried out to
the LORD, the LORD [b]raised up a deliverer for
the children of Israel, who delivered them:
[c]Othniel the son of Kenaz, Caleb's younger
brother. 10[a]The Spirit of the LORD came
upon him, and he judged Israel. He went
out to war, and the LORD delivered Cushan-
Rishathaim king of Mesopotamia into his
hand; and his hand prevailed over Cushan-
Rishathaim. 11So the land had rest for forty
years. Then Othniel the son of Kenaz died.

Ehud

12[a]And the children of Israel again did
evil in the sight of the LORD. So the LORD
strengthened [b]Eglon king of Moab against
Israel, because they had done evil in the
sight of the LORD. 13Then he gathered to
himself the people of Ammon and [a]Am-
alek, went and defeated Israel, and took
possession of [b]the City of Palms. 14So the
children of Israel [a]served Eglon king of
Moab eighteen years.

15But when the children of Israel [a]cried
out to the LORD, the LORD raised up a deliverer for them: Ehud the son of Gera, the
Benjamite, a [b]left-handed man. By him the
children of Israel sent tribute to Eglon king
of Moab. 16Now Ehud made himself a dagger (it was double-edged and a cubit in
length) and fastened it under his clothes
on his right thigh. 17So he brought the tribute to Eglon king of Moab. (Now Eglon *was*
a very fat man.) 18And when he had finished
presenting the tribute, he sent away the
people who had carried the tribute. 19But
he himself turned back [a]from the stone images that *were* at Gilgal, and said, "I have a
secret message for you, O king."

He said, "Keep silence!" And all who attended him went out from him.

20So Ehud came to him (now he was sitting upstairs in his cool private chamber).
Then Ehud said, "I have a message from
God for you." So he arose from *his* seat.
21Then Ehud reached with his left hand,
took the dagger from his right thigh, and
thrust it into his belly. 22Even the hilt went
in after the blade, and the fat closed over
the blade, for he did not draw the dagger
out of his belly; and his entrails came out.
23Then Ehud went out through the porch
and shut the doors of the upper room behind him and locked them.

24When he had gone out, *Eglon's*[1] servants came to look, and *to their* surprise,
the doors of the upper room were locked.
So they said, "He is probably [a]attending to
his needs in the cool chamber." 25So they
waited till they were [a]embarrassed, and
still he had not opened the doors of the upper room. Therefore they took the key and
opened *them*. And there was their master,
fallen dead on the floor.

26But Ehud had escaped while they delayed, and passed beyond the stone images
and escaped to Seirah. 27And it happened,
when he arrived, that [a]he blew the trumpet in the [b]mountains of Ephraim, and the
children of Israel went down with him from
the mountains; and he led them. 28Then he
said to them, "Follow *me*, for [a]the LORD has
delivered your enemies the Moabites into
your hand." So they went down after him,
seized the [b]fords of the Jordan leading to
Moab, and did not allow anyone to cross
over. 29And at that time they killed about
ten thousand men of Moab, all stout men
of valor; not a man escaped. 30So Moab was
subdued that day under the hand of Israel.
And [a]the land had rest for eighty years.

Shamgar

31After him was [a]Shamgar the son of
Anath, who killed six hundred men of the
Philistines [b]with an ox goad; [c]and he also
delivered [d]Israel.

Deborah

4 When Ehud was dead, [a]the children of
Israel again did [b]evil in the sight of the
LORD. 2So the LORD [a]sold them into the
hand of Jabin king of Canaan, who reigned
in [b]Hazor. The commander of his army *was*

3:8 [a] Deut. 32:30; Judg. 2:14 [b] Hab. 3:7 3:9 [a] Judg. 3:15 [b] Judg. 2:16 [c] Judg. 1:13 3:10 [a] Num. 27:18; 1 Sam. 11:6; 2 Chr. 15:1
3:12 [a] Judg. 2:19 [b] 1 Sam. 12:9 3:13 [a] Judg. 5:14 [b] Deut. 34:3; Judg. 1:16; 2 Chr. 28:15 3:14 [a] Deut. 28:48 3:15 [a] Ps. 78:34
[b] Judg. 20:16 3:19 [a] Josh. 4:20 3:24 [a] 1 Sam. 24:3 [1] Literally *his* 3:25 [a] 2 Kin. 2:17; 8:11 3:27 [a] Judg. 6:34; 1 Sam. 13:3
[b] Josh. 17:15 3:28 [a] Judg. 7:9, 15; 1 Sam. 17:47 [b] Josh. 2:7; Judg. 12:5 3:30 [a] Judg. 3:11 3:31 [a] Judg. 5:6
[b] 1 Sam. 17:47 [c] Judg. 2:16 [d] 1 Sam. 4:1 4:1 [a] Judg. 2:19 [b] Judg. 2:11 4:2 [a] Judg. 2:14 [b] Josh. 11:1, 10

[c]Sisera, who dwelt in [d]Harosheth Hagoyim.
3And the children of Israel cried out to the
LORD; for Jabin had nine hundred [a]char-
iots of iron, and for twenty years [b]he had
harshly oppressed the children of Israel.
4Now Deborah, a prophetess, the wife of
Lapidoth, was judging Israel at that time.
5[a]And she would sit under the palm tree
of Deborah between Ramah and Bethel in
the mountains of Ephraim. And the children of Israel came up to her for judgment.
6Then she sent and called for [a]Barak the son
of Abinoam from [b]Kedesh in Naphtali, and
said to him, "Has not the LORD God of Israel
commanded, 'Go and deploy *troops* at Mount
[c]Tabor; take with you ten thousand men of
the sons of Naphtali and of the sons of Zebulun; 7and against you [a]I will deploy Sisera,
the commander of Jabin's army, with his
chariots and his multitude at the [b]River Kishon; and I will deliver him into your hand'?"
8And Barak said to her, "If you will go
with me, then I will go; but if you will not
go with me, I will not go!"
9So she said, "I will surely go with you;
nevertheless there will be no glory for you
in the journey you are taking, for the LORD
will [a]sell Sisera into the hand of a woman."
Then Deborah arose and went with Barak
to Kedesh. 10And Barak called [a]Zebulun and
Naphtali to Kedesh; he went up with ten
thousand men [b]under his command,[1] and
Deborah went up with him.
11Now Heber [a]the Kenite, of the children
of [b]Hobab the father-in-law of Moses, had
separated himself from the Kenites and
pitched his tent near the terebinth tree at
Zaanaim, [c]which *is* beside Kedesh.
12And they reported to Sisera that Barak
the son of Abinoam had gone up to Mount
Tabor. 13So Sisera gathered together all his
chariots, nine hundred chariots of iron,
and all the people who *were* with him, from
Harosheth Hagoyim to the River Kishon.
14Then Deborah said to Barak, "Up! For
this *is* the day in which the LORD has delivered Sisera into your hand. [a]Has not the
LORD gone out before you?" So Barak went
down from Mount Tabor with ten thousand
men following him. 15And the LORD routed
Sisera and all *his* chariots and all *his* army
with the edge of the sword before Barak;
and Sisera alighted from *his* chariot and
fled away on foot. 16But Barak pursued the
chariots and the army as far as Harosheth
Hagoyim, and all the army of Sisera fell by
the edge of the sword; not a man was [a]left.
17However, Sisera had fled away on foot
to the tent of [a]Jael, the wife of Heber the
Kenite; for *there was* peace between Jabin
king of Hazor and the house of Heber the
Kenite. 18And Jael went out to meet Sisera,
and said to him, "Turn aside, my lord, turn
aside to me; do not fear." And when he had
turned aside with her into the tent, she covered him with a blanket.
19Then he said to her, "Please give me a
little water to drink, for I am thirsty." So she
opened [a]a jug of milk, gave him a drink, and
covered him. 20And he said to her, "Stand at
the door of the tent, and if any man comes
and inquires of you, and says, 'Is there any
man here?' you shall say, 'No.'"
21Then Jael, Heber's wife, [a]took a tent peg
and took a hammer in her hand, and went
softly to him and drove the peg into his
temple, and it went down into the ground;
for he was fast asleep and weary. So he died.
22And then, as Barak pursued Sisera, Jael
came out to meet him, and said to him,
"Come, I will show you the man whom you
seek." And when he went into her *tent*, there
lay Sisera, dead with the peg in his temple.
23So on that day God subdued Jabin king
of Canaan in the presence of the children
of Israel. 24And the hand of the children of
Israel grew stronger and stronger against
Jabin king of Canaan, until they had destroyed Jabin king of Canaan.

The Song of Deborah

5 Then Deborah and Barak the son of
Abinoam [a]sang on that day, saying:

2 "When leaders [a]lead in Israel,
[b]When the people willingly
offer themselves,
Bless the LORD!

4:2 [c] 1 Sam. 12:9; Ps. 83:9 [d] Judg. 4:13, 16 4:3 [a] Deut. 20:1; Judg. 1:19 [b] Ps. 106:42 4:5 [a] Gen. 35:8 4:6 [a] Heb. 11:32 [b] Josh. 19:37; 21:32 [c] Judg. 8:18 4:7 [a] Ex. 14:4 [b] Judg. 5:21; 1 Kin. 18:40; Ps. 83:9, 10 4:9 [a] Judg. 2:14 4:10 [a] Judg. 5:18 [b] Ex. 11:8; 1 Kin. 20:10
[1] Literally *at his feet* 4:11 [a] Judg. 1:16 [b] Num. 10:29 [c] Judg. 4:6 4:14 [a] Deut. 9:3; 31:3; 2 Sam. 5:24; Ps. 68:7; Is. 52:12 4:16 [a] Ex. 14:28; Ps. 83:9 4:17 [a] Judg. 5:6 4:19 [a] Judg. 5:24–27 4:21 [a] Judg. 5:24–27
5:1 [a] Ex. 15:1; Judg. 4:4 5:2 [a] Ps. 18:47 [b] 2 Chr. 17:16

RELEASE // ELEVATE THE STANDS YOU TAKE

Faithfulness for the Fight

Judges 4:23 // So on that day God subdued Jabin king of Canaan in the presence of the children of Israel.

Summary Message // After the Israelites committed great evil, God sent the Canaanites to discipline them. When they cried out to God, He promised Deborah, judge over Israel, that He would go with His people into battle and they would defeat Sisera and his army. When she told the military commander, Barak, that the time had arrived to engage the enemy, he refused to lead the army without her. Deborah chided him because of his disobedience and fear. She agreed to go into battle, but she made it clear that Sisera would be delivered not into his hands but into the hands of a woman (see Judg. 4:9).

The war was short-lived. The Israelite army was victorious over the powerful troops of Canaan. The iron chariots and fierce warriors of Canaan were no match for the Israelites, who marched with God on their side. However, Sisera escaped and fled on foot to the tent of Jael, the wife of Heber. Jael carried out the execution of Sisera by hammering a peg through his head while he rested. Thus God ended twenty years of oppression under Jabin, king of Canaan, and the captain of his army, Sisera.

Practical Application // Deborah had heard from the Lord concerning the battle and Israel's victory, but Barak's refusal to lead the battle demonstrated that he did not believe that God would give him the battle alone. So, he became an accessory to the victory instead of the valiant victor. God used Deborah and Jael to bring about His will.

When God calls you to take a stand, do not let fear cause you to take a seat. Faith requires that you make the right choice between equivocating and elevating. What we hear from God may seem out of reach to us, but what God has promised often requires an inner work happening first. Just as Barak was called to believe God before he engaged in battle, we also must believe God's Word to us.

How often have we put our confidence in other people to do what God has spoken to us? If we will not follow through with the assignment, God will likely find someone who will. Let this cautionary tale encourage you. When the promise of God seems out of reach and you do not seem to have faith for the fight, elevate the stand you take to see it come to fruition. What if the outcome of a situation affecting others is based on your willingness to get involved? Will you elevate or equivocate?

Fervent Prayer // Father, we thank You that You have chosen us to be mighty and perform feats we may not feel equipped to carry out. Rather than shrink back in fear and faithlessness, we ask for Your strength to face the fight ahead of us. You have promised us victory if we would just go and be used mightily by You. Lord, we want to be strong in You and in the power of Your might. May we slay giants, pull down strongholds, and defeat the enemy of our souls wherever the battle may rage. We put our trust in You alone, not in our own might. Help us to be the warriors You have made us to be, as we know our help is in the name of the Lord. In Jesus' name we pray. Amen.

---

3 "Hear,[a] O kings! Give ear, O princes!
I, *even* [b]I, will sing to the LORD;
I will sing praise to the
LORD God of Israel.

4 "LORD, [a]when You went out from Seir,
When You marched from
[b]the field of Edom,
The earth trembled and the
heavens poured,
The clouds also poured water;
5 [a]The mountains gushed
before the LORD,
[b]This Sinai, before the LORD
God of Israel.

6 "In the days of [a]Shamgar, son of
Anath,
In the days of [b]Jael,
[c]The highways were deserted,

5:3 [a] Deut. 32:1, 3 [b] Ps. 27:6 5:4 [a] Deut. 33:2; Ps. 68:7 [b] Ps. 68:8 5:5 [a] Ps. 97:5 [b] Ex. 19:18
5:6 [a] Judg. 3:31 [b] Judg. 4:17 [c] Is. 33:8

And the travelers walked
along the byways.
7 Village life ceased, it ceased in Israel,
Until I, Deborah, arose,
Arose a mother in Israel.
8 They chose [a]new gods;
Then *there was* war in the gates;
Not a shield or spear was seen
among forty thousand in Israel.
9 My heart *is* with the rulers of Israel
Who offered themselves
willingly with the people.
Bless the LORD!

10 "Speak, you who ride on white [a]donkeys,
Who sit in judges' attire,
And who walk along the road.
11 Far from the noise of the archers,
among the watering places,
There they shall recount the
righteous acts of the LORD,
The righteous acts *for* His
villagers in Israel;
Then the people of the LORD
shall go down to the gates.

12 "Awake,[a] awake, Deborah!
Awake, awake, sing a song!
Arise, Barak, and lead your
captives away,
O son of Abinoam!

13 "Then the survivors came down,
the people against the nobles;
The LORD came down for me
against the mighty.
14 From Ephraim *were* those whose
roots were in [a]Amalek.
After you, Benjamin, with
your peoples,
From Machir rulers came down,
And from Zebulun those who
bear the recruiter's staff.
15 And the princes of Issachar[1]
were with Deborah;
As Issachar, so *was* Barak
Sent into the valley under
his command;[2]
Among the divisions of Reuben
There were great resolves of heart.
16 Why did you sit among the sheepfolds,
To hear the pipings for the flocks?
The divisions of Reuben have
great searchings of heart.
17 [a]Gilead stayed beyond the Jordan,
And why did Dan remain on ships?[1]
[b]Asher continued at the seashore,
And stayed by his inlets.
18 [a]Zebulun *is* a people *who* jeopardized
their lives to the point of death,
Naphtali also, on the heights
of the battlefield.

19 "The kings came *and* fought,
Then the kings of Canaan fought
In [a]Taanach, by the waters
of Megiddo;
They took no spoils of silver.
20 They fought from the heavens;
The stars from their courses
fought against Sisera.
21 [a]The torrent of Kishon
swept them away,
That ancient torrent, the
torrent of Kishon.
O my soul, march on in strength!
22 Then the horses' hooves pounded,
The galloping, galloping
of his steeds.
23 'Curse Meroz,' said the
angel[1] of the LORD,
'Curse its inhabitants bitterly,
Because they did not come to
the help of the LORD,
To the help of the LORD
against the mighty.'

24 "Most blessed among women is Jael,
The wife of Heber the Kenite;
[a]Blessed is she among women in tents.
25 He asked for water, she gave milk;
She brought out cream
in a lordly bowl.
26 She stretched her hand to the tent peg,
Her right hand to the
workmen's hammer;
She pounded Sisera, she
pierced his head,
She split and struck
through his temple.

5:8 [a] Deut. 32:17 5:10 [a] Judg. 10:4; 12:14 5:12 [a] Ps. 57:8 5:14 [a] Judg. 3:13 5:15 [1] Following Septuagint, Syriac, Targum, and Vulgate; Masoretic Text reads *And my princes in Issachar.* [2] Literally *at his feet* 5:17 [a] Josh. 22:9 [b] Josh. 19:29, 31 [1] Or *at ease* 5:18 [a] Judg. 4:6, 10 5:19 [a] Judg. 1:27 5:21 [a] Judg. 4:7 5:23 [1] Or *Angel* 5:24 [a] [Luke 1:28]

27 At her feet he sank, he fell, he lay still;
At her feet he sank, he fell;
Where he sank, there he fell [a]dead.

28 "The mother of Sisera looked
through the window,
And cried out through the lattice,
'Why is his chariot *so* long in coming?
Why tarries the clatter of his chariots?'
29 Her wisest ladies answered her,
Yes, she answered herself,
30 'Are they not finding and
dividing the spoil:
To every man a girl *or* two;
For Sisera, plunder of dyed garments,
Plunder of garments
embroidered and dyed,
Two pieces of dyed embroidery
for the neck of the looter?'

31 "Thus let all Your enemies
[a]perish, O LORD!
But *let* those who love Him
be [b]like the [c]sun
When it comes out in full [d]strength."

So the land had rest for forty years.

Midianites Oppress Israel

6 Then the children of Israel did [a]evil in
the sight of the LORD. So the LORD delivered them into the hand of [b]Midian for
seven years, 2and the hand of Midian prevailed against Israel. Because of the Midianites, the children of Israel made for
themselves the dens, [a]the caves, and the
strongholds which *are* in the mountains.
3So it was, whenever Israel had sown, Midianites would come up; also Amalekites
and the [a]people of the East would come up
against them. 4Then they would encamp
against them and [a]destroy the produce of
the earth as far as Gaza, and leave no sustenance for Israel, neither sheep nor ox
nor [b]donkey. 5For they would come up with
their livestock and their tents, coming in as
numerous as locusts; both they and their
camels were without number; and they
would enter the land to destroy it. 6So Israel was greatly impoverished because of
the Midianites, and the children of Israel
[a]cried out to the LORD.

7And it came to pass, when the children
of Israel cried out to the LORD because
of the Midianites, 8that the LORD sent a
prophet to the children of Israel, who said
to them, "Thus says the LORD God of Israel:
'I brought you up from Egypt and brought
you out of the [a]house of bondage; 9and I
delivered you out of the hand of the Egyptians and out of the hand of all who oppressed you, and [a]drove them out before
you and gave you their land. 10Also I said to
you, "I *am* the LORD your God; [a]do not fear
the gods of the Amorites, in whose land you
dwell." But you have not obeyed My [b]voice.'"

Gideon

11Now the Angel of the LORD came and
sat under the terebinth tree which *was*
in Ophrah, which *belonged* to Joash [a]the
Abiezrite, while his son [b]Gideon threshed
wheat in the winepress, in order to hide
it from the Midianites. 12And the [a]Angel
of the LORD appeared to him, and said to
him, "The LORD *is* [b]with you, you mighty
man of valor!"

13Gideon said to Him, "O my lord,[1] if the
LORD is with us, why then has all this happened to us? And [a]where *are* all His miracles [b]which our fathers told us about, saying,
'Did not the LORD bring us up from Egypt?'
But now the LORD has [c]forsaken us and delivered us into the hands of the Midianites."

14Then the LORD turned to him and said,
[a]"Go in this might of yours, and you shall
save Israel from the hand of the Midianites. [b]Have I not sent you?"

15So he said to Him, "O my Lord,[1] how
can I save Israel? Indeed [a]my clan *is* the
weakest in Manasseh, and I *am* the least
in my father's house."

16And the LORD said to him, [a]"Surely I
will be with you, and you shall defeat the
Midianites as one man."

17Then he said to Him, "If now I have

5:27 [a] Judg. 4:18–21 5:31 [a] Ps. 92:9 [b] 2 Sam. 23:4 [c] Ps. 37:6; 89:36, 37 [d] Ps. 19:5 6:1 [a] Judg. 2:11 [b] Num. 22:4; 31:1–3
6:2 [a] 1 Sam. 13:6; Heb. 11:38 6:3 [a] Judg. 7:12 6:4 [a] Lev. 26:16 [b] Deut. 28:31 6:6 [a] Ps. 50:15; Hos. 5:15 6:8 [a] Josh. 24:17
6:9 [a] Ps. 44:2, 3 6:10 [a] 2 Kin. 17:35, 37, 38; Jer. 10:2 [b] Judg. 2:1, 2 6:11 [a] Josh. 17:2; Judg. 6:15 [b] Judg. 7:1; Heb. 11:32
6:12 [a] Judg. 13:3; Luke 1:11, 28 [b] Josh. 1:5 6:13 [a] [Is. 59:1] [b] Josh. 4:6, 21; Ps. 44:1 [c] Deut. 31:17; 2 Chr. 15:2;
Ps. 44:9–16 [1] Hebrew *adoni,* used of man 6:14 [a] 1 Sam. 12:11 [b] Josh. 1:9 6:15 [a] 1 Sam. 9:21
[1] Hebrew *Adonai,* used of God 6:16 [a] Ex. 3:12; Josh. 1:5

found favor in Your sight, then [a]show me
a sign that it is You who talk with me. 18 [a]Do
not depart from here, I pray, until I come
to You and bring out my offering and set
it before You."

And He said, "I will wait until you come
back."

19 [a]So Gideon went in and prepared a
young goat, and unleavened bread from an
ephah of flour. The meat he put in a basket,
and he put the broth in a pot; and he brought
them out to Him under the terebinth tree
and presented *them.* 20 The Angel of God said
to him, "Take the meat and the unleavened
bread and [a]lay *them* on this rock, and [b]pour
out the broth." And he did so.

21 Then the Angel of the LORD put out
the end of the staff that *was* in His hand,
and touched the meat and the unleavened
bread; and [a]fire rose out of the rock and
consumed the meat and the unleavened
bread. And the Angel of the LORD departed
out of his sight.

22 Now Gideon [a]perceived that He *was* the
Angel of the LORD. So Gideon said, "Alas,
O Lord GOD! [b]For I have seen the Angel of
the LORD face to face."

23 Then the LORD said to him, [a]"Peace
be with you; do not fear, you shall not die."
24 So Gideon built an altar there to the LORD,
and called it The-LORD-*Is*-Peace.[1] To this
day it *is* still [a]in Ophrah of the Abiezrites.

JUDGES 6:13

I AM GIDEON

Gideon said to Him, "O my lord, if the LORD is with us, why then has all this happened to us? And where are all His miracles which our fathers told us about, saying, 'Did not the LORD bring us up from Egypt?' But now the LORD has forsaken us and delivered us into the hands of the Midianites." Judges 6:13

I am Gideon, son of Joash. One day, the Angel of the Lord appeared to me and told me that the Lord was with me and called me a mighty man of valor. I responded by asking why the Midianites were continuing to oppress my people if God was truly with us. The Lord told me He would use me to save the Israelites from the Midianites.

I was afraid because I was only one man and powerless to save my people. But I did as the Lord commanded and tore down the altar of Baal. The Midianites and Amalekites were angered and gathered to fight us. Then the Spirit of the Lord came upon me. When I blew the trumpet, the tribes of Israel came to defend us. We were a massive army, but the Lord said we were too many. With such a force of men, our success would be attributed to our great number of soldiers. To decrease our number, the Lord told me to send all who were afraid back home. He further reduced our ranks by sending home all who drank water from a stream in a certain way. After this, only three hundred Israelite warriors remained.

I gathered the three hundred and told them I would blow my trumpet and they were to blow their trumpets at the same moment. We were all to shout, "The sword of the LORD and of Gideon!" We did as the Lord directed. Amazingly, the Midianite soldiers drew their swords on each other and retreated. My men and I pursued them and defeated them.

†

During a time of oppression, God may prepare one or many to rise and vanquish an oppressor, but this can only be done with God's call and direction. We are not to act on our own or in our own way. Instead, we are to seek the Lord and His guidance.

6:17 [a] Judg. 6:36, 37; 2 Kin. 20:8; Ps. 86:17; Is. 7:11; 38:7, 8 6:18 [a] Gen. 18:3, 5 6:19 [a] Gen. 18:6–8 6:20 [a] Judg. 13:19 [b] 1 Kin. 18:33, 34 6:21 [a] Lev. 9:24 6:22 [a] Gen. 32:30; Ex. 33:20; Judg. 13:21, 22 [b] Gen. 16:13 6:23 [a] Dan. 10:19 6:24 [a] Judg. 8:32 [1] Hebrew *YHWH Shalom*

25Now it came to pass the same night
that the LORD said to him, "Take your father's young bull, the second bull of seven
years old, and [a]tear down the altar of [b]Baal
that your father has, and [c]cut down the
wooden image[1] that *is* beside it; 26and
build an altar to the LORD your God on
top of this rock in the proper arrangement,
and take the second bull and offer a burnt
sacrifice with the wood of the image which
you shall cut down." 27So Gideon took ten
men from among his servants and did as
the LORD had said to him. But because
he feared his father's household and the
men of the city too much to do *it* by day,
he did *it* by night.

Gideon Destroys the Altar of Baal

28And when the men of the city arose
early in the morning, there was the altar
of Baal, torn down; and the wooden image
that *was* beside it was cut down, and the
second bull was being offered on the altar
which had been built. 29So they said to one
another, "Who has done this thing?" And
when they had inquired and asked, they
said, "Gideon the son of Joash has done this
thing." 30Then the men of the city said to
Joash, "Bring out your son, that he may die,
because he has torn down the altar of Baal,
and because he has cut down the wooden
image that *was* beside it."

31But Joash said to all who stood against
him, "Would you plead for Baal? Would you
save him? Let the one who would plead for
him be put to death by morning! If he *is* a
god, let him plead for himself, because his
altar has been torn down!" 32Therefore on
that day he called him [a]Jerubbaal,[1] saying,
"Let Baal plead against him, because he
has torn down his altar."

33Then all [a]the Midianites and Amalekites, the people of the East, gathered
together; and they crossed over and encamped in [b]the Valley of Jezreel. 34But
[a]the Spirit of the LORD came upon Gideon; then he [b]blew the trumpet, and the
Abiezrites gathered behind him. 35And
he sent messengers throughout all Manasseh, who also gathered behind him.
He also sent messengers to [a]Asher, [b]Zeb-
ulun, and Naphtali; and they came up to
meet them.

The Sign of the Fleece

36So Gideon said to God, "If You will
save Israel by my hand as You have said—
37[a]look, I shall put a fleece of wool on the
threshing floor; if there is dew on the fleece
only, and *it is* dry on all the ground, then
I shall know that You will save Israel by
my hand, as You have said." 38And it was
so. When he rose early the next morning
and squeezed the fleece together, he wrung
the dew out of the fleece, a bowlful of water. 39Then Gideon said to God, [a]"Do not be
angry with me, but let me speak just once
more: Let me test, I pray, just once more
with the fleece; let it now be dry only on
the fleece, but on all the ground let there
be dew." 40And God did so that night. It was
dry on the fleece only, but there was dew
on all the ground.

Gideon's Valiant Three Hundred

7 Then [a]Jerubbaal (that *is*, Gideon) and
all the people who *were* with him rose
early and encamped beside the well of Ha-
rod, so that the camp of the Midianites was
on the north side of them by the hill of Moreh in the valley.

2And the LORD said to Gideon, "The people who *are* with you *are* too many for Me
to give the Midianites into their hands, lest
Israel [a]claim glory for itself against Me,
saying, 'My own hand has saved me.' 3Now
therefore, proclaim in the hearing of the
people, saying, [a]'Whoever *is* fearful and
afraid, let him turn and depart at once from
Mount Gilead.'" And twenty-two thousand
of the people returned, and ten thousand
remained.

4But the LORD said to Gideon, "The people *are* still *too* many; bring them down to
the water, and I will test them for you there.
Then it will be, *that* of whom I say to you,
'This one shall go with you,' the same shall
go with you; and of whomever I say to you,
'This one shall not go with you,' the same
shall not go." 5So he brought the people

6:25 [a] Judg. 2:2 [b] Judg. 3:7 [c] Ex. 34:13; Deut. 7:5 [1] Hebrew *Asherah*, a Canaanite goddess 6:32 [a] Judg. 7:1; 1 Sam. 12:11; 2 Sam. 11:21 [1] Literally *Let Baal Plead* 6:33 [a] Judg. 6:3 [b] Josh. 17:16; Hos. 1:5 6:34 [a] Judg. 3:10; 1 Chr. 12:18; 2 Chr. 24:20 [b] Num. 10:3; Judg. 3:27 6:35 [a] Judg. 5:17; 7:23 [b] Judg. 4:6, 10; 5:18 6:37 [a] [Ex. 4:3–7] 6:39 [a] Gen. 18:32 7:1 [a] Judg. 6:32 7:2 [a] Deut. 8:17; Is. 10:13 7:3 [a] Deut. 20:8

down to the water. And the LORD said to
Gideon, "Everyone who laps from the water with his tongue, as a dog laps, you shall
set apart by himself; likewise everyone who
gets down on his knees to drink." 6And the
number of those who lapped, *putting* their
hand to their mouth, was three hundred
men; but all the rest of the people got down
on their knees to drink water. 7Then the
LORD said to Gideon, [a]"By the three hundred men who lapped I will save you, and
deliver the Midianites into your hand. Let
all the *other* people go, every man to his
place." 8So the people took provisions and
their trumpets in their hands. And he sent
away all *the rest of* Israel, every man to his
tent, and retained those three hundred
men. Now the camp of Midian was below
him in the valley.

9It happened on the same [a]night that the
LORD said to him, "Arise, go down against
the camp, for I have delivered it into your
hand. 10But if you are afraid to go down, go
down to the camp with Purah your servant,
11and you shall [a]hear what they say; and afterward your hands shall be strengthened
to go down against the camp." Then he went
down with Purah his servant to the outpost
of the armed men who *were* in the camp.
12Now the Midianites and Amalekites, [a]all
the people of the East, were lying in the
valley [b]as numerous as locusts; and their
camels *were* without number, as the sand
by the seashore in multitude.

13And when Gideon had come, there was
a man telling a dream to his companion.
He said, "I have had a dream: *To my* surprise, a loaf of barley bread tumbled into
the camp of Midian; it came to a tent and
struck it so that it fell and overturned, and
the tent collapsed."

14Then his companion answered and
said, "This *is* nothing else but the sword
of Gideon the son of Joash, a man of Israel!
Into his hand [a]God has delivered Midian
and the whole camp."

15And so it was, when Gideon heard the
telling of the dream and its interpretation, that he worshiped. He returned to
the camp of Israel, and said, "Arise, for
the LORD has delivered the camp of Midian into your hand." 16Then he divided the
three hundred men *into* three companies,
and he put a trumpet into every man's
hand, with empty pitchers, and torches
inside the pitchers. 17And he said to them,
"Look at me and do likewise; watch, and
when I come to the edge of the camp you
shall do as I do: 18When I blow the trumpet, I and all who *are* with me, then you
also blow the trumpets on every side of
the whole camp, and say, '*The sword of* the
LORD and of Gideon!'"

19So Gideon and the hundred men who
were with him came to the outpost of the
camp at the beginning of the middle watch,
just as they had posted the watch; and they
blew the trumpets and broke the pitchers
that *were* in their hands. 20Then the three
companies blew the trumpets and broke
the pitchers—they held the torches in their
left hands and the trumpets in their right
hands for blowing—and they cried, "The
sword of the LORD and of Gideon!" 21And
[a]every man stood in his place all around
the camp; [b]and the whole army ran and
cried out and fled. 22When the three hundred [a]blew the trumpets, [b]the LORD set
[c]every man's sword against his companion throughout the whole camp; and the
army fled to Beth Acacia,[1] toward Zererah,
as far as the border of [d]Abel Meholah, by
Tabbath.

23And the men of Israel gathered together from [a]Naphtali, Asher, and all Manasseh, and pursued the Midianites.

24Then Gideon sent messengers
throughout all the [a]mountains of Ephraim,
saying, "Come down against the Midianites,
and seize from them the watering places as
far as Beth Barah and the Jordan." Then all
the men of Ephraim gathered together and
[b]seized the watering places as far as [c]Beth
Barah and the Jordan. 25And they captured
[a]two princes of the Midianites, [b]Oreb and
Zeeb. They killed Oreb at the rock of Oreb,
and Zeeb they killed at the winepress of
Zeeb. They pursued Midian and brought
the heads of Oreb and Zeeb to Gideon on
the [c]other side of the Jordan.

7:7 [a] 1 Sam. 14:6 7:9 [a] Gen. 46:2, 3; Judg. 6:25 7:11 [a] Gen. 24:14; 1 Sam. 14:9, 10 7:12 [a] Judg. 6:3, 33; 8:10 [b] Judg. 6:5
7:14 [a] Judg. 6:14, 16 7:21 [a] Ex. 14:13, 14; 2 Chr. 20:17 [b] 2 Kin. 7:7 7:22 [a] Josh. 6:4, 16, 20 [b] Ps. 83:9; Is. 9:4 [c] 1 Sam. 14:20;
2 Chr. 20:23 [d] 1 Kin. 4:12 [1] Hebrew *Beth Shittah* 7:23 [a] Judg. 6:35 7:24 [a] Judg. 3:27 [b] Judg. 3:28 [c] John 1:28
7:25 [a] Judg. 8:3 [b] Ps. 83:11; Is. 10:26 [c] Judg. 8:4

Gideon Subdues the Midianites

8 Now [a]the men of Ephraim said to him,
"Why have you done this to us by not
calling us when you went to fight with the
Midianites?" And they reprimanded him
sharply.
2So he said to them, "What have I done
now in comparison with you? *Is* not the
gleaning *of the grapes* of Ephraim better
than the vintage of [a]Abiezer? 3[a]God has delivered into your hands the princes of Midian, Oreb and Zeeb. And what was I able to
do in comparison with you?" Then their
[b]anger toward him subsided when he said
that.
4When Gideon came [a]to the Jordan, he
and [b]the three hundred men who *were* with
him crossed over, exhausted but still in
pursuit. 5Then he said to the men of [a]Suc-
coth, "Please give loaves of bread to the
people who follow me, for they are exhausted, and I am pursuing Zebah and Zalmunna, kings of Midian."
6And the leaders of Succoth said, [a]"*Are*
the hands of Zebah and Zalmunna now in
your hand, that [b]we should give bread to
your army?"
7So Gideon said, "For this cause, when
the LORD has delivered Zebah and Zalmunna into my hand, [a]then I will tear your
flesh with the thorns of the wilderness and
with briers!" 8Then he went up from there
[a]to Penuel and spoke to them in the same
way. And the men of Penuel answered him
as the men of Succoth had answered. 9So
he also spoke to the men of Penuel, saying,
"When I [a]come back in peace, [b]I will tear
down this tower!"
10Now Zebah and Zalmunna *were* at Kar-
kor, and their armies with them, about fifteen thousand, all who were left of [a]all the
army of the people of the East; for [b]one
hundred and twenty thousand men who
drew the sword had fallen. 11Then Gideon
went up by the road of those who dwell in
tents on the east of [a]Nobah and Jogbehah;
and he attacked the army while the camp
felt [b]secure. 12When Zebah and Zalmunna
fled, he pursued them; and he [a]took the two
kings of Midian, Zebah and Zalmunna, and
routed the whole army.
13Then Gideon the son of Joash returned
from battle, from the Ascent of Heres. 14And
he caught a young man of the men of Succoth and interrogated him; and he wrote
down for him the leaders of Succoth and
its elders, seventy-seven men. 15Then he
came to the men of Succoth and said, "Here
are Zebah and Zalmunna, about whom you
[a]ridiculed me, saying, '*Are* the hands of Zebah and Zalmunna now in your hand, that
we should give bread to your weary men?'"
16[a]And he took the elders of the city, and
thorns of the wilderness and briers, and
with them he taught the men of Succoth.
17[a]Then he tore down the tower of [b]Penuel
and killed the men of the city.
18And he said to Zebah and Zalmunna,
"What kind of men *were they* whom you
killed at [a]Tabor?"
So they answered, "As you *are,* so *were*
they; each one resembled the son of a king."
19Then he said, "They *were* my brothers,
the sons of my mother. *As* the LORD lives,
if you had let them live, I would not kill
you." 20And he said to Jether his firstborn,
"Rise, kill them!" But the youth would not
draw his sword; for he was afraid, because
he *was* still a youth.
21So Zebah and Zalmunna said, "Rise
yourself, and kill us; for as a man *is, so is*
his strength." So Gideon arose and [a]killed
Zebah and Zalmunna, and took the crescent
ornaments that *were* on their camels' necks.

Gideon's Ephod

22Then the men of Israel said to Gideon,
[a]"Rule over us, both you and your son, and
your grandson also; for you have [b]delivered
us from the hand of Midian."
23But Gideon said to them, "I will not
rule over you, nor shall my son rule over
you; [a]the LORD shall rule over you." 24Then
Gideon said to them, "I would like to make
a request of you, that each of you would
give me the earrings from his plunder." For
they had golden earrings, [a]because they
were Ishmaelites.

8:1 [a] Judg. 12:1; 2 Sam. 19:41 8:2 [a] Judg. 6:11 8:3 [a] Judg. 7:24, 25 [b] Prov. 15:1 8:4 [a] Judg. 7:25 [b] Judg. 7:6 8:5 [a] Gen. 33:17; Ps. 60:6 8:6 [a] 1 Kin. 20:11; Judg. 8:15 [b] 1 Sam. 25:11 8:7 [a] Judg. 8:16 8:8 [a] Gen. 32:30, 31; 1 Kin. 12:25 8:9 [a] 1 Kin. 22:27 [b] Judg. 8:17 8:10 [a] Judg. 7:12 [b] Judg. 6:5 8:11 [a] Num. 32:35, 42 [b] Judg. 18:27; [1 Thess. 5:3] 8:12 [a] Ps. 83:11 8:15 [a] Judg. 8:6 8:16 [a] Judg. 8:7 8:17 [a] Judg. 8:9 [b] 1 Kin. 12:25 8:18 [a] Judg. 4:6; Ps. 89:12 8:21 [a] Ps. 83:11 8:22 [a] [Judg. 9:8] [b] Judg. 3:9; 9:17 8:23 [a] 1 Sam. 8:7; 10:19; 12:12; Ps. 10:16 8:24 [a] Gen. 37:25, 28

25 So they answered, "We will gladly give
them." And they spread out a garment, and
each man threw into it the earrings from
his plunder. 26 Now the weight of the gold
earrings that he requested was one thousand seven hundred *shekels* of gold, besides the crescent ornaments, pendants,
and purple robes which *were* on the kings
of Midian, and besides the chains that *were*
around their camels' necks. 27 Then Gideon [a]made it into an ephod and set it up
in his city, [b]Ophrah. And all Israel [c]played
the harlot with it there. It became [d]a snare
to Gideon and to his house.

28 Thus Midian was subdued before the
children of Israel, so that they lifted their
heads no more. [a]And the country was quiet
for forty years in the days of Gideon.

Death of Gideon

29 Then [a]Jerubbaal the son of Joash went
and dwelt in his own house. 30 Gideon had
[a]seventy sons who were his own offspring,
for he had many wives. 31 [a]And his concubine who *was* in Shechem also bore him
a son, whose name he called Abimelech.
32 Now Gideon the son of Joash died [a]at a
good old age, and was buried in the tomb
of Joash his father, [b]in Ophrah of the Abiezrites.

33 So it was, [a]as soon as Gideon was dead,
that the children of Israel again [b]played the
harlot with the Baals, [c]and made Baal-Be-
rith their god. 34 Thus the children of Israel
[a]did not remember the LORD their God, who
had delivered them from the hands of all
their enemies on every side; 35 [a]nor did they
show kindness to the house of Jerubbaal
(Gideon) in accordance with the good he
had done for Israel.

Abimelech's Conspiracy

9 Then Abimelech the son of Jerubbaal
went to Shechem, to [a]his mother's
brothers, and spoke with them and with
all the family of the house of his mother's
father, saying, 2 "Please speak in the hearing
of all the men of Shechem: 'Which is better for you, that all [a]seventy of the sons of
Jerubbaal reign over you, or that one reign
over you?' Remember that I *am* your own
flesh and [b]bone."

3 And his mother's brothers spoke all
these words concerning him in the hearing of all the men of Shechem; and their
heart was inclined to follow Abimelech,
for they said, "He is our [a]brother." 4 So they
gave him seventy *shekels* of silver from the
temple of [a]Baal-Berith, with which Abimelech hired [b]worthless and reckless men;
and they followed him. 5 Then he went to
his father's house [a]at Ophrah and [b]killed
his brothers, the seventy sons of Jerubbaal, on one stone. But Jotham the youngest son of Jerubbaal was left, because he
hid himself. 6 And all the men of Shechem
gathered together, all of Beth Millo, and
they went and made Abimelech king beside the terebinth tree at the pillar that
was in Shechem.

The Parable of the Trees

7 Now when they told Jotham, he went
and stood on top of [a]Mount Gerizim, and
lifted his voice and cried out. And he said
to them:

"Listen to me, you men of Shechem,
That God may listen to you!
8 "The[a] trees once went forth to
anoint a king over them.
And they said to the olive tree,
[b]'Reign over us!'
9 But the olive tree said to them,
'Should I cease giving my oil,
[a]With which they honor God and men,
And go to sway over trees?'

10 "Then the trees said to the fig tree,
'You come *and* reign over us!'
11 But the fig tree said to them,
'Should I cease my sweetness
and my good fruit,
And go to sway over trees?'
12 "Then the trees said to the vine,
'You come *and* reign over us!'

8:27 [a] Judg. 17:5 [b] Judg. 6:11, 24 [c] [Ps. 106:39] [d] Deut. 7:16 8:28 [a] Judg. 5:31 8:29 [a] Judg. 6:32; 7:1 8:30 [a] Judg. 9:2, 5 8:31 [a] Judg. 9:1 8:32 [a] Gen. 25:8; Job 5:26 [b] Judg. 6:24; 8:27 8:33 [a] Judg. 2:19 [b] Judg. 2:17 [c] Judg. 9:4, 46 8:34 [a] Deut. 4:9; Judg. 3:7; Ps. 78:11, 42; 106:13, 21 8:35 [a] Judg. 9:16–18 9:1 [a] Judg. 8:31, 35 9:2 [a] Judg. 8:30; 9:5, 18 [b] Gen. 29:14 9:3 [a] Gen. 29:15 9:4 [a] Judg. 8:33 [b] Judg. 11:3; 2 Chr. 13:7; Acts 17:5 9:5 [a] Judg. 6:24 [b] Judg. 8:30; 9:2, 18; 2 Kin. 11:1, 2 9:7 [a] Deut. 11:29; 27:12; Josh. 8:33; John 4:20 9:8 [a] 2 Kin. 14:9 [b] Judg. 8:22, 23 9:9 [a] [John 5:23]

13 But the vine said to them,
'Should I cease my new wine,
[a]Which cheers *both* God and men,
And go to sway over trees?'

14 "Then all the trees said to the bramble,
'You come *and* reign over us!'
15 And the bramble said to the trees,
'If in truth you anoint me
as king over you,
Then come *and* take shelter
in my [a]shade;
But if not, [b]let fire come
out of the bramble
And devour the [c]cedars of Lebanon!'

16"Now therefore, if you have acted in
truth and sincerity in making Abimelech
king, and if you have dealt well with Jerubbaal and his house, and have done to him
[a]as he deserves— 17for my [a]father fought
for you, risked his life, and [b]delivered you
out of the hand of Midian; 18[a]but you have
risen up against my father's house this day,
and killed his seventy sons on one stone,
and made Abimelech, the son of his [b]fe-
male servant, king over the men of Shechem, because he is your brother— 19if
then you have acted in truth and sincerity
with Jerubbaal and with his house this day,
then [a]rejoice in Abimelech, and let him also
rejoice in you. 20But if not, [a]let fire come
from Abimelech and devour the men of
Shechem and Beth Millo; and let fire come
from the men of Shechem and from Beth
Millo and devour Abimelech!" 21And Jotham ran away and fled; and he went to
[a]Beer and dwelt there, for fear of Abimelech his brother.

Downfall of Abimelech

22After Abimelech had reigned over Israel three years, 23[a]God sent a [b]spirit of ill
will between Abimelech and the men of
Shechem; and the men of Shechem [c]dealt
treacherously with Abimelech, 24[a]that the
crime *done* to the seventy sons of Jerubbaal
might be settled and their [b]blood be laid on
Abimelech their brother, who killed them,
and on the men of Shechem, who aided
him in the killing of his brothers. 25And
the men of Shechem set men in ambush
against him on the tops of the mountains,
and they robbed all who passed by them
along that way; and it was told Abimelech.

26Now Gaal the son of Ebed came with
his brothers and went over to Shechem;
and the men of Shechem put their confidence in him. 27So they went out into
the fields, and gathered *grapes* from their
vineyards and trod *them,* and made merry.
And they went into [a]the house of their god,
and ate and drank, and cursed Abimelech.
28Then Gaal the son of Ebed said, [a]"Who *is*
Abimelech, and who *is* Shechem, that we
should serve him? *Is he* not the son of Jerubbaal, and *is not* Zebul his officer? Serve
the men of [b]Hamor the father of Shechem;
but why should we serve him? 29[a]If only
this people were under my authority![1] Then
I would remove Abimelech." So he[2] said
to Abimelech, "Increase your army and
come out!"

30When Zebul, the ruler of the city, heard
the words of Gaal the son of Ebed, his anger was aroused. 31And he sent messengers
to Abimelech secretly, saying, "Take note!
Gaal the son of Ebed and his brothers have
come to Shechem; and here they are, forti-
fying the city against you. 32Now therefore,
get up by night, you and the people who
are with you, and lie in wait in the field.
33And it shall be, as soon as the sun is up in
the morning, *that* you shall rise early and
rush upon the city; and *when* he and the
people who are with him come out against
you, you may then do to them as you find
opportunity."

34So Abimelech and all the people who
were with him rose by night, and lay in
wait against Shechem in four companies.
35When Gaal the son of Ebed went out and
stood in the entrance to the city gate, Abimelech and the people who *were* with him
rose from lying in wait. 36And when Gaal
saw the people, he said to Zebul, "Look,

9:13 [a] Ps. 104:15 9:15 [a] Is. 30:2; Dan. 4:12; Hos. 14:7 [b] Num. 21:28; Judg. 9:20; Ezek. 19:14 [c] 2 Kin. 14:9; Is. 2:13; Ezek. 31:3 9:16 [a] Judg. 8:35 9:17 [a] Judg. 7 [b] Judg. 8:22 9:18 [a] Judg. 8:30, 35; 9:2, 5, 6 [b] Judg. 8:31 9:19 [a] Is. 8:6; [Phil. 3:3] 9:20 [a] Judg. 9:15, 45, 56, 57 9:21 [a] Num. 21:16 9:23 [a] 1 Kin. 12:15; Is. 19:14 [b] 1 Sam. 16:14; 18:9, 10; 1 Kin. 22:22; 2 Chr. 18:22 [c] Is. 33:1 9:24 [a] 1 Kin. 2:32; Esth. 9:25; Matt. 23:35, 36 [b] Num. 35:33 9:27 [a] Judg. 9:4 9:28 [a] 1 Sam. 25:10; 1 Kin. 12:16 [b] Gen. 34:2, 6; Josh. 24:32 9:29 [a] 2 Sam. 15:4 [1] Literally *hand*
[2] Following Masoretic Text and Targum; Dead Sea Scrolls read *they;* Septuagint reads *I.*

people are coming down from the tops of
the mountains!"
But Zebul said to him, "You see the shadows of the mountains as *if they were* men."
37So Gaal spoke again and said, "See,
people are coming down from the center
of the land, and another company is coming from the Diviners'[1] Terebinth Tree."
38Then Zebul said to him, "Where indeed
is your mouth now, with which you [a]said,
'Who is Abimelech, that we should serve
him?' *Are* not these the people whom you
despised? Go out, if you will, and fight with
them now."
39So Gaal went out, leading the men
of Shechem, and fought with Abimelech.
40And Abimelech chased him, and he fled
from him; and many fell wounded, to the
very entrance of the gate. 41Then Abimelech dwelt at Arumah, and Zebul drove out
Gaal and his brothers, so that they would
not dwell in Shechem.
42And it came about on the next day
that the people went out into the field,
and they told Abimelech. 43So he took his
people, divided them into three companies, and lay in wait in the field. And he
looked, and there were the people, coming out of the city; and he rose against
them and attacked them. 44Then Abimelech and the company that *was* with him
rushed forward and stood at the entrance
of the gate of the city; and the *other* two
companies rushed upon all who *were* in
the fields and killed them. 45So Abimelech fought against the city all that day;
[a]he took the city and killed the people who
were in it; and he [b]demolished the city and
sowed it with salt.
46Now when all the men of the tower
of Shechem had heard *that,* they entered
the stronghold of the temple [a]of the god
Berith. 47And it was told Abimelech that
all the men of the tower of Shechem were
gathered together. 48Then Abimelech went
up to Mount [a]Zalmon, he and all the people
who *were* with him. And Abimelech took
an ax in his hand and cut down a bough
from the trees, and took it and laid *it* on
his shoulder; then he said to the people
who were with him, "What you have seen
me do, make haste *and* do as I *have done.*"
49So each of the people likewise cut down
his own bough and followed Abimelech,
put *them* against the stronghold, and set
the stronghold on fire above them, so that
all the people of the tower of Shechem died,
about a thousand men and women.
50Then Abimelech went to Thebez, and
he encamped against Thebez and took it.
51But there was a strong tower in the city,
and all the men and women—all the people of the city—fled there and shut themselves in; then they went up to the top of the
tower. 52So Abimelech came as far as the
tower and fought against it; and he drew
near the door of the tower to burn it with
fire. 53But a certain woman [a]dropped an
upper millstone on Abimelech's head and
crushed his skull. 54Then [a]he called quickly
to the young man, his armorbearer, and
said to him, "Draw your sword and kill me,
lest men say of me, 'A woman killed him.'"
So his young man thrust him through, and
he died. 55And when the men of Israel saw
that Abimelech was dead, they departed,
every man to his place.
56[a]Thus God repaid the wickedness of
Abimelech, which he had done to his father
by killing his seventy brothers. 57And all the
evil of the men of Shechem God returned
on their own heads, and on them came
[a]the curse of Jotham the son of Jerubbaal.

Tola

10 After Abimelech there [a]arose to save
Israel Tola the son of Puah, the son
of Dodo, a man of Issachar; and he dwelt
in Shamir in the mountains of Ephraim.
2He judged Israel twenty-three years; and
he died and was buried in Shamir.

Jair

3After him arose Jair, a Gileadite; and he
judged Israel twenty-two years. 4Now he
had thirty sons who [a]rode on thirty donkeys; they also had thirty towns, [b]which
are called "Havoth Jair"[1] to this day, which
are in the land of Gilead. 5And Jair died and
was buried in Camon.

9:37 [1] Hebrew *Meonenim* 9:38 [a] Judg. 9:28, 29 9:45 [a] Judg. 9:20 [b] Deut. 29:23; 2 Kin. 3:25 9:46 [a] Judg. 8:33 9:48 [a] Ps. 68:14 9:53 [a] 2 Sam. 11:21 9:54 [a] 1 Sam. 31:4 9:56 [a] Judg. 9:24; Job 31:3; Prov. 5:22 9:57 [a] Judg. 9:20 10:1 [a] Judg. 2:16 10:4 [a] Judg. 5:10; 12:14 [b] Deut. 3:14 [1] Literally *Towns of Jair* (compare Numbers 32:41 and Deuteronomy 3:14)

Israel Oppressed Again
6 Then [a]the children of Israel again did
evil in the sight of the LORD, and [b]served
the Baals and the Ashtoreths, [c]the gods of
Syria, the gods of [d]Sidon, the gods of Moab,
the gods of the people of Ammon, and the
gods of the Philistines; and they forsook
the LORD and did not serve Him. 7 So the
anger of the LORD was hot against Israel;
and He [a]sold them into the hands of the
[b]Philistines and into the hands of the people of [c]Ammon. 8 From that year they harassed and oppressed the children of Israel
for eighteen years—all the children of Israel who *were* on the other side of the Jordan in the [a]land of the Amorites, in Gilead.
9 Moreover the people of Ammon crossed
over the Jordan to fight against Judah also,
against Benjamin, and against the house
of Ephraim, so that Israel was severely distressed.
10 [a]And the children of Israel cried out to
the LORD, saying, "We have [b]sinned against
You, because we have both forsaken our
God and served the Baals!"
11 So the LORD said to the children of Israel, "*Did I* not *deliver you* [a]from the Egyptians and [b]from the Amorites and [c]from
the people of Ammon and [d]from the Philistines? 12 Also [a]the Sidonians [b]and Amalekites and Maonites[1] [c]oppressed you; and
you cried out to Me, and I delivered you
from their hand. 13 [a]Yet you have forsaken
Me and served other gods. Therefore I will
deliver you no more. 14 "Go and [a]cry out to
the gods which you have chosen; let them
deliver you in your time of distress."
15 And the children of Israel said to the
LORD, "We have sinned! [a]Do to us whatever seems best to You; only deliver us this
day, we pray." 16 [a]So they put away the foreign gods from among them and served
the LORD. And [b]His soul could no longer
endure the misery of Israel.
17 Then the people of Ammon gathered
together and encamped in Gilead. And the
children of Israel assembled together and
encamped in [a]Mizpah. 18 And the people,
the leaders of Gilead, said to one another,
"Who *is* the man who will begin the fight
against the people of Ammon? He shall [a]be
head over all the inhabitants of Gilead."

Jephthah
11 Now [a]Jephthah the Gileadite was [b]a
mighty man of valor, but he *was* the
son of a harlot; and Gilead begot Jephthah.
2 Gilead's wife bore sons; and when his wife's
sons grew up, they drove Jephthah out, and
said to him, "You shall have [a]no inheritance
in our father's house, for you *are* the son of
another woman." 3 Then Jephthah fled from
his brothers and dwelt in the land of [a]Tob;
and [b]worthless men banded together with
Jephthah and went out *raiding* with him.
4 It came to pass after a time that the
[a]people of Ammon made war against Israel.
5 And so it was, when the people of Ammon
made war against Israel, that the elders of
Gilead went to get Jephthah from the land
of Tob. 6 Then they said to Jephthah, "Come
and be our commander, that we may fight
against the people of Ammon."
7 So Jephthah said to the elders of Gilead,
[a]"Did you not hate me, and expel me from
my father's house? Why have you come to
me now when you are in distress?"
8 [a]And the elders of Gilead said to Jephthah, "That is why we have [b]turned again to
you now, that you may go with us and fight
against the people of Ammon, and be [c]our
head over all the inhabitants of Gilead."
9 So Jephthah said to the elders of Gilead,
"If you take me back home to fight against
the people of Ammon, and the LORD delivers them to me, shall I be your head?"
10 And the elders of Gilead said to Jephthah, [a]"The LORD will be a witness between
us, if we do not do according to your words."
11 Then Jephthah went with the elders of
Gilead, and the people made him [a]head
and commander over them; and Jephthah spoke all his words [b]before the LORD
in Mizpah.

10:6 [a] Judg. 2:11; 3:7; 6:1; 13:1 [b] Judg. 2:13 [c] Judg. 2:12 [d] 1 Kin. 11:33; Ps. 106:36 10:7 [a] Judg. 2:14; 4:2; 1 Sam. 12:9 [b] Judg. 13:1 [c] Judg. 3:13 10:8 [a] Num. 32:33 10:10 [a] Judg. 6:6; 1 Sam. 12:10 [b] Deut. 1:41 10:11 [a] Ex. 14:30 [b] Num. 21:21, 24, 25 [c] Judg. 3:12, 13 [d] Judg. 3:31 10:12 [a] Judg. 1:31; 5:19 [b] Judg. 6:3; 7:12 [c] Ps. 106:42, 43 [1] Some Septuagint manuscripts read *Midianites.* 10:13 [a] [Deut. 32:15; Judg. 2:12; Jer. 2:13] 10:14 [a] Deut. 32:37, 38 10:15 [a] 1 Sam. 3:18; 2 Sam. 15:26 10:16 [a] 2 Chr. 7:14; Jer. 18:7, 8 [b] Ps. 106:44, 45; Is. 63:9 10:17 [a] Gen. 31:49; Judg. 11:11, 29 10:18 [a] Judg. 11:8, 11 11:1 [a] Heb. 11:32 [b] Judg. 6:12; 2 Kin. 5:1 11:2 [a] Gen. 21:10; Deut. 23:2 11:3 [a] 2 Sam. 10:6, 8 [b] 1 Sam. 22:2 11:4 [a] Judg. 10:9, 17 11:7 [a] Gen. 26:27 11:8 [a] Judg. 10:18 [b] [Luke 17:4] [c] Judg. 10:18 11:10 [a] Gen. 31:49, 50; Jer. 29:23; 42:5 11:11 [a] Judg. 11:8 [b] Judg. 10:17; 20:1; 1 Sam. 10:17

12Now Jephthah sent messengers to
the king of the people of Ammon, saying,
[a]"What do you have against me, that you
have come to fight against me in my land?"
13And the king of the people of Ammon
answered the messengers of Jephthah,
[a]"Because Israel took away my land when
they came up out of Egypt, from [b]the Arnon as far as [c]the Jabbok, and to the Jordan. Now therefore, restore those *lands*
peaceably."
14So Jephthah again sent messengers
to the king of the people of Ammon, 15and
said to him, "Thus says Jephthah: [a]'Israel
did not take away the land of Moab, nor the
land of the people of Ammon; 16for when
Israel came up from Egypt, they walked
through the wilderness as far as the Red
Sea and [a]came to Kadesh. 17Then [a]Israel
sent messengers to the king of Edom,
saying, "Please let me pass through your
land." [b]But the king of Edom would not
heed. And in like manner they sent to the
[c]king of Moab, but he would not *consent.*
So Israel [d]remained in Kadesh. 18And they
[a]went along through the wilderness and
[b]bypassed the land of Edom and the land
of Moab, came to the east side of the land of
Moab, and encamped on the other side of
the Arnon. But they did not enter the border of Moab, for the Arnon *was* the border
of Moab. 19Then [a]Israel sent messengers to
Sihon king of the Amorites, king of Heshbon; and Israel said to him, "Please [b]let
us pass through your land into our place."
20[a]But Sihon did not trust Israel to pass
through his territory. So Sihon gathered
all his people together, encamped in Jahaz, and fought against Israel. 21And the
LORD God of Israel [a]delivered Sihon and
all his people into the hand of Israel, and
they [b]defeated them. Thus Israel gained
possession of all the land of the Amorites,
who inhabited that country. 22They took
possession of [a]all the territory of the Amorites, from the Arnon to the Jabbok and
from the wilderness to the Jordan.
23'And now the LORD God of Israel has
dispossessed the Amorites from before His
people Israel; should you then possess it?
24Will you not possess whatever [a]Chemosh
your god gives you to possess? So whatever [b]the LORD our God takes possession
of before us, we will possess. 25And now,
are you any better than [a]Balak the son of
Zippor, king of Moab? Did he ever strive
against Israel? Did he ever fight against
them? 26While Israel dwelt in [a]Heshbon and
its villages, in [b]Aroer and its villages, and
in all the cities along the banks of the Arnon, for three hundred years, why did you
not recover *them* within that time? 27There-
fore I have not sinned against you, but you
wronged me by fighting against me. May
the LORD, [a]the Judge, [b]render judgment this
day between the children of Israel and the
people of Ammon.'" 28However, the king
of the people of Ammon did not heed the
words which Jephthah sent him.

Jephthah's Vow and Victory

29Then [a]the Spirit of the LORD came
upon Jephthah, and he passed through Gilead and Manasseh, and passed through
Mizpah of Gilead; and from Mizpah of Gilead he advanced *toward* the people of Ammon. 30And Jephthah [a]made a vow to the
LORD, and said, "If You will indeed deliver
the people of Ammon into my hands, 31then
it will be that whatever comes out of the
doors of my house to meet me, when I return in peace from the people of Ammon,
[a]shall surely be the LORD's, [b]and I will offer
it up as a burnt offering."
32So Jephthah advanced toward the people of Ammon to fight against them, and
the LORD delivered them into his hands.
33And he defeated them from Aroer as far
as [a]Minnith—twenty cities—and to Abel
Keramim,[1] with a very great slaughter. Thus
the people of Ammon were subdued before
the children of Israel.

Jephthah's Daughter

34When Jephthah came to his house at
[a]Mizpah, there was [b]his daughter, coming

11:12 [a] 2 Sam. 16:10 **11:13** [a] Num. 21:24–26 [b] Josh. 13:9 [c] Gen. 32:22 **11:15** [a] Deut. 2:9, 19 **11:16** [a] Num. 13:26; 20:1 **11:17** [a] Num. 20:14 [b] Num. 20:14–21 [c] Josh. 24:9 [d] Num. 20:1 **11:18** [a] Deut. 2:9, 18, 19 [b] Num. 21:4 **11:19** [a] Num. 21:21; Deut. 2:26–36 [b] Num. 21:22; Deut. 2:27 **11:20** [a] Num. 21:23; Deut. 2:27 **11:21** [a] Josh. 24:8 [b] Num. 21:24, 25 **11:22** [a] Deut. 2:36, 37 **11:24** [a] Num. 21:29; 1 Kin. 11:7; Jer. 48:7 [b] [Deut. 9:4, 5; Josh. 3:10] **11:25** [a] Num. 22:2; Josh. 24:9; Mic. 6:5 **11:26** [a] Num. 21:25, 26 [b] Deut. 2:36 **11:27** [a] Gen. 18:25 [b] Gen. 16:5; 31:53; [1 Sam. 24:12, 15] **11:29** [a] Judg. 3:10 **11:30** [a] Gen. 28:20; Num. 30:2; 1 Sam. 1:11 **11:31** [a] Lev. 27:2, 3, 28; 1 Sam. 1:11 [b] Ps. 66:13 **11:33** [a] Ezek. 27:17 [1] Literally *Plain of Vineyards* **11:34** [a] Judg. 10:17; 11:11 [b] Ex. 15:20; 1 Sam. 18:6; Ps. 68:25; Jer. 31:4

out to meet him with timbrels and dancing; and she *was his* only child. Besides her
he had neither son nor daughter. 35And it
came to pass, when he saw her, that he [a]tore
his clothes, and said, "Alas, my daughter!
You have brought me very low! You are
among those who trouble me! For I [b]have
given my word to the LORD, and [c]I cannot
go back on it."

36So she said to him, "My father, *if* you
have given your word to the LORD, [a]do to
me according to what has gone out of your
mouth, because [b]the LORD has avenged
you of your enemies, the people of Ammon." 37Then she said to her father, "Let
this thing be done for me: let me alone for
two months, that I may go and wander on
the mountains and bewail my virginity, my
friends and I."

38So he said, "Go." And he sent her away
for two months; and she went with her
friends, and bewailed her virginity on the
mountains. 39And it was so at the end of
two months that she returned to her father,
and he [a]carried out his vow with her which
he had vowed. She knew no man.

And it became a custom in Israel 40*that*
the daughters of Israel went four days each
year to lament the daughter of Jephthah
the Gileadite.

Jephthah's Conflict with Ephraim

12 Then [a]the men of Ephraim gathered together, crossed over toward
Zaphon, and said to Jephthah, "Why did
you cross over to fight against the people
of Ammon, and did not call us to go with
you? We will burn your house down on you
with fire!"

2And Jephthah said to them, "My people and I were in a great struggle with the
people of Ammon; and when I called you,
you did not deliver me out of their hands.
3So when I saw that you would not deliver
me, I [a]took my life in my hands and crossed
over against the people of Ammon; and the
LORD delivered them into my hand. Why
then have you come up to me this day to
fight against me?" 4Now Jephthah gathered
together all the men of Gilead and fought
against Ephraim. And the men of Gilead
defeated Ephraim, because they said, "You
Gileadites [a]*are* fugitives of Ephraim among
the Ephraimites *and* among the Manassites." 5The Gileadites seized the [a]fords of
the Jordan before the Ephraimites *arrived.*
And when *any* Ephraimite who escaped
said, "Let me cross over," the men of Gilead would say to him, "*Are* you an Ephraimite?" If he said, "No," 6then they would
say to him, "Then say, [a]'Shibboleth'!" And
he would say, "Sibboleth," for he could not
pronounce *it* right. Then they would take
him and kill him at the fords of the Jordan.
There fell at that time forty-two thousand
Ephraimites.

7And Jephthah judged Israel six years.
Then Jephthah the Gileadite died and was
buried among the cities of Gilead.

Ibzan, Elon, and Abdon

8After him, Ibzan of Bethlehem judged
Israel. 9He had thirty sons. And he gave
away thirty daughters in marriage, and
brought in thirty daughters from elsewhere
for his sons. He judged Israel seven years.
10Then Ibzan died and was buried at Bethlehem.

11After him, Elon the Zebulunite judged
Israel. He judged Israel ten years. 12And
Elon the Zebulunite died and was buried
at Aijalon in the country of Zebulun.

13After him, Abdon the son of Hillel the
Pirathonite judged Israel. 14He had forty
sons and thirty grandsons, who [a]rode on
seventy young donkeys. He judged Israel
eight years. 15Then Abdon the son of Hillel the Pirathonite died and was buried in
Pirathon in the land of Ephraim, [a]in the
mountains of the Amalekites.

The Birth of Samson
(cf. Num. 6:1–21)

13 Again the children of Israel [a]did
evil in the sight of the LORD, and
the LORD delivered them [b]into the hand
of the Philistines for forty years.

2Now there was a certain man from [a]Zo-
rah, of the family of the Danites, whose
name *was* Manoah; and his wife *was* barren

11:35 [a] Gen. 37:29, 34 [b] Eccl. 5:2, 4, 5 [c] Num. 30:2 11:36 [a] Num. 30:2 [b] 2 Sam. 18:19, 31 11:39 [a] Judg. 11:31 12:1 [a] Judg. 8:1 12:3 [a] 1 Sam. 19:5; 28:21; Job 13:14 12:4 [a] 1 Sam. 25:10 12:5 [a] Josh. 22:11 12:6 [a] Ps. 69:2, 15 12:14 [a] Judg. 5:10; 10:4 12:15 [a] Judg. 3:13, 27; 5:14 13:1 [a] Judg. 2:11 [b] Judg. 10:7; 1 Sam. 12:9 13:2 [a] Josh. 19:41; Judg. 16:31

and had no children. 3And the [a]Angel of the LORD appeared to the woman and said to her, "Indeed now, you are barren and have borne no children, but you shall conceive and bear a son. 4Now therefore, please be careful [a]not to drink wine or *similar* drink, and not to eat anything unclean. 5For behold, you shall conceive and bear a son. And no [a]razor shall come upon his head, for the child shall be [b]a Nazirite to God from the womb; and he shall [c]begin to deliver Israel out of the hand of the Philistines."

6So the woman came and told her husband, saying, [a]"A Man of God came to me, and His [b]countenance *was* like the countenance of the Angel of God, very awesome; but I [c]did not ask Him where He *was* from, and He did not tell me His name. 7And He said to me, 'Behold, you shall conceive and bear a son. Now drink no wine or *similar* drink, nor eat anything unclean, for the child shall be a Nazirite to God from the womb to the day of his death.'"

8Then Manoah prayed to the LORD, and said, "O my Lord, please let the Man of God whom You sent come to us again and teach us what we shall do for the child who will be born."

9And God listened to the voice of Manoah, and the Angel of God came to the woman again as she was sitting in the field; but Manoah her husband *was* not with her. 10Then the woman ran in haste and told her husband, and said to him, "Look, the Man who came to me the *other* day has just now appeared to me!"

11So Manoah arose and followed his wife. When he came to the Man, he said to Him, "Are You the Man who spoke to this woman?"

And He said, "I *am*."

12Manoah said, "Now let Your words come *to pass!* What will be the boy's rule of life, and his work?"

13So the Angel of the LORD said to Manoah, "Of all that I said to the woman let her be careful. 14She may not eat anything that comes from the vine, [a]nor may she drink wine or *similar* drink, nor eat anything unclean. All that I commanded her let her observe."

15Then Manoah said to the Angel of the LORD, "Please [a]let us detain You, and we will prepare a young goat for You."

16And the Angel of the LORD said to Manoah, "Though you detain Me, I will not eat your food. But if you offer a burnt offering, you must offer it to the LORD." (For Manoah did not know He *was* the Angel of the LORD.)

17Then Manoah said to the Angel of the LORD, "What *is* Your name, that when Your words come *to pass* we may honor You?"

18And the Angel of the LORD said to him, [a]"Why do you ask My name, seeing it *is* wonderful?"

19So Manoah took the young goat with the grain offering, [a]and offered it upon the rock to the LORD. And He did a wondrous thing while Manoah and his wife looked on— 20it happened as the flame went up toward heaven from the altar—the Angel of the LORD ascended in the flame of the altar! When Manoah and his wife saw *this,* they [a]fell on their faces to the ground. 21When the Angel of the LORD appeared no more to Manoah and his wife, [a]then Manoah knew that He *was* the Angel of the LORD.

22And Manoah said to his wife, [a]"We shall surely die, because we have seen God!"

23But his wife said to him, "If the LORD had desired to kill us, He would not have accepted a burnt offering and a grain offering from our hands, nor would He have shown us all these *things,* nor would He have told us *such things* as these at this time."

24So the woman bore a son and called his name [a]Samson; and [b]the child grew, and the LORD blessed him. 25[a]And the Spirit of the LORD began to move upon him at Mahaneh Dan[1] [b]between Zorah and [c]Eshtaol.

Samson's Philistine Wife

14 Now Samson went down [a]to Timnah, and [b]saw a woman in Timnah of the daughters of the Philistines. 2So he went

---

13:3 [a] Judg. 6:12 13:4 [a] Num. 6:2, 3, 20; Judg. 13:4; Luke 1:15 13:5 [a] Num. 6:5; 1 Sam. 1:11 [b] Num. 6:2 [c] 1 Sam. 7:13; 2 Sam. 8:1; 1 Chr. 18:1 13:6 [a] Gen. 32:24–30 [b] Matt. 28:3; Luke 9:29; Acts 6:15 [c] Judg. 13:17, 18 13:14 [a] Num. 6:3, 4; Judg. 13:4 13:15 [a] Gen. 18:5; Judg. 6:18 13:18 [a] Gen. 32:29 13:19 [a] Judg. 6:19–21 13:20 [a] Lev. 9:24; 1 Chr. 21:16; Ezek. 1:28; Matt. 17:6 13:21 [a] Judg. 6:22 13:22 [a] Gen. 32:30; Ex. 33:20; Deut. 5:26; Judg. 6:22, 23 13:24 [a] Heb. 11:32 [b] 1 Sam. 3:19; Luke 1:80 13:25 [a] Judg. 3:10; 1 Sam. 11:6; Matt. 4:1 [b] Josh. 15:33; Judg. 18:11 [c] Judg. 16:31 [1] Literally *Camp of Dan* (compare 18:12)
14:1 [a] Gen. 38:13; Josh. 15:10, 57 [b] Gen. 34:2

up and told his father and mother, saying,
"I have seen a woman in Timnah of the
daughters of the Philistines; now therefore, [a]get her for me as a wife."
3Then his father and mother said to him,
"*Is there* no woman among the daughters
of [a]your brethren, or among all my people,
that you must go and get a wife from the
[b]uncircumcised Philistines?"
And Samson said to his father, "Get her
for me, for she pleases me well."
4But his father and mother did not know
that it was [a]of the LORD—that He was seeking an occasion to move against the Philistines. For at that time [b]the Philistines had
dominion over Israel.
5So Samson went down to Timnah with
his father and mother, and came to the
vineyards of Timnah.
Now *to his* surprise, a young lion *came*
roaring against him. 6And [a]the Spirit of the
LORD came mightily upon him, and he tore
the lion apart as one would have torn apart
a young goat, though *he had* nothing in his
hand. But he did not tell his father or his
mother what he had done.
7Then he went down and talked with the
woman; and she pleased Samson well. 8Af-
ter some time, when he returned to get
her, he turned aside to see the carcass of
the lion. And behold, a swarm of bees and
honey *were* in the carcass of the lion. 9He
took some of it in his hands and went along,
eating. When he came to his father and
mother, he gave *some* to them, and they
also ate. But he did not tell them that he
had taken the honey out of the [a]carcass
of the lion.
10So his father went down to the woman.
And Samson gave a feast there, for young
men used to do so. 11And it happened, when
they saw him, that they brought thirty companions to be with him.
12Then Samson said to them, "Let me
[a]pose a riddle to you. If you can correctly
solve and explain it to me [b]within the
seven days of the feast, then I will give you
thirty linen garments and thirty [c]changes
of clothing. 13But if you cannot explain *it*
to me, then you shall give me thirty linen
garments and thirty changes of clothing."
And they said to him, [a]"Pose your riddle,
that we may hear it."
14So he said to them:

"Out of the eater came
something to eat,
And out of the strong came
something sweet."

Now for three days they could not explain
the riddle.
15But it came to pass on the seventh[1] day
that they said to Samson's wife, [a]"Entice
your husband, that he may explain the riddle to us, [b]or else we will burn you and your
father's house with fire. Have you invited us
in order to take what is ours? *Is that* not *so?*"
16Then Samson's wife wept on him, and
said, [a]"You only hate me! You do not love
me! You have posed a riddle to the sons
of my people, but you have not explained
it to me."
And he said to her, "Look, I have not
explained *it* to my father or my mother;
so should I explain *it* to you?" 17Now she
had wept on him the seven days while
their feast lasted. And it happened on the
seventh day that he told her, because she
pressed him so much. Then she explained
the riddle to the sons of her people. 18So the
men of the city said to him on the seventh
day before the sun went down:

"What *is* sweeter than honey?
And what *is* stronger than a lion?"

And he said to them:

"If you had not plowed with my heifer,
You would not have solved my riddle!"

19Then [a]the Spirit of the LORD came
upon him mightily, and he went down to
Ashkelon and killed thirty of their men,
took their apparel, and gave the changes
of clothing to those who had explained the
riddle. So his anger was aroused, and he

14:2 [a] Gen. 21:21 14:3 [a] Gen. 24:3, 4 [b] Gen. 34:14; Ex. 34:16; Deut. 7:3 14:4 [a] Josh. 11:20; 1 Kin. 12:15; 2 Kin. 6:33; 2 Chr. 10:15 [b] Deut. 28:48; Judg. 13:1 14:6 [a] Judg. 3:10 14:9 [a] Lev. 11:27 14:12 [a] 1 Kin. 10:1; Ezek. 17:2 [b] Gen. 29:27 [c] Gen. 45:22; 2 Kin. 5:22 14:13 [a] Ezek. 17:2 14:15 [a] Judg. 16:5 [b] Judg. 15:6 [1] Following Masoretic Text, Targum, and Vulgate; Septuagint and Syriac read *fourth.* 14:16 [a] Judg. 16:15 14:19 [a] Judg. 3:10; 13:25

went back up to his father's house. 20 And
Samson's wife [a]was *given* to his companion, who had been [b]his best man.

Samson Defeats the Philistines

15 After a while, in the time of wheat
harvest, it happened that Samson
visited his wife with a [a]young goat. And
he said, "Let me go in to my wife, into *her*
room." But her father would not permit
him to go in.
2 Her father said, "I really thought that you
thoroughly [a]hated her; therefore I gave her
to your companion. *Is* not her younger sister better than she? Please, take her instead."
3 And Samson said to them, "This time
I shall be blameless regarding the Philistines if I harm them!" 4 Then Samson went
and caught three hundred foxes; and he
took torches, turned *the foxes* tail to tail,
and put a torch between each pair of tails.
5 When he had set the torches on fire, he let
the foxes go into the standing grain of the
Philistines, and burned up both the shocks
and the standing grain, as well as the vineyards *and* olive groves.
6 Then the Philistines said, "Who has
done this?"
And they answered, "Samson, the son-
in-law of the Timnite, because he has taken
his wife and given her to his companion."
[a]So the Philistines came up and burned her
and her father with fire.
7 Samson said to them, "Since you would
do a thing like this, I will surely take revenge on you, and after that I will cease."
8 So he attacked them hip and thigh with
a great slaughter; then he went down and
dwelt in the cleft of the rock of [a]Etam.
9 Now the Philistines went up, encamped
in Judah, and deployed themselves [a]against
Lehi. 10 And the men of Judah said, "Why
have you come up against us?"
So they answered, "We have come up
to arrest Samson, to do to him as he has
done to us."
11 Then three thousand men of Judah
went down to the cleft of the rock of Etam,
and said to Samson, "Do you not know that
the Philistines [a]rule over us? What *is* this
you have done to us?"
And he said to them, "As they did to me,
so I have done to them."
12 But they said to him, "We have come
down to arrest you, that we may deliver you
into the hand of the Philistines."
Then Samson said to them, "Swear to
me that you will not kill me yourselves."
13 So they spoke to him, saying, "No, but
we will tie you securely and deliver you into
their hand; but we will surely not kill you."
And they bound him with two [a]new ropes
and brought him up from the rock.
14 When he came to Lehi, the Philistines
came shouting against him. Then [a]the
Spirit of the LORD came mightily upon him;
and the ropes that *were* on his arms became like flax that is burned with fire, and
his bonds broke loose from his hands. 15 He
found a fresh jawbone of a donkey, reached
out his hand and took it, and [a]killed a thousand men with it. 16 Then Samson said:

"With the jawbone of a donkey,
Heaps upon heaps,
With the jawbone of a donkey
I have slain a thousand men!"

17 And so it was, when he had finished speaking, that he threw the jawbone from his
hand, and called that place Ramath Lehi.[1]
18 Then he became very thirsty; so he
cried out to the LORD and said, [a]"You have
given this great deliverance by the hand
of Your servant; and now shall I die of
thirst and fall into the hand of the uncircumcised?" 19 So God split the hollow place
that *is* in Lehi,[1] and water came out, and he
drank; and [a]his spirit returned, and he revived. Therefore he called its name En Hak-
kore,[2] which is in Lehi to this day. 20 And [a]he
judged Israel [b]twenty years [c]in the days of
the Philistines.

Samson and Delilah

16 Now Samson went to [a]Gaza and saw
a harlot there, and went in to her.
2 *When* the Gazites *were told,* "Samson has

14:20 [a] Judg. 15:2 [b] John 3:29 15:1 [a] Gen. 38:17 15:2 [a] Judg. 14:20 15:6 [a] Judg. 14:15 15:8 [a] 2 Chr. 11:6 15:9 [a] Judg. 15:19
15:11 [a] Lev. 26:25; Deut. 28:43; Judg. 13:1; 14:4; Ps. 106:40–42 15:13 [a] Judg. 16:11, 12 15:14 [a] Judg. 3:10; 14:6
15:15 [a] Lev. 26:8; Josh. 23:10; Judg. 3:31 15:17 [1] Literally *Jawbone Height* 15:18 [a] Ps. 3:7
15:19 [a] Gen. 45:27; Is. 40:29 [1] Literally *Jawbone* (compare verse 14) [2] Literally *Spring of the Caller*
15:20 [a] Judg. 10:2; 12:7–14 [b] Judg. 16:31 [c] Judg. 13:1 16:1 [a] Josh. 15:47

come here!" they [a]surrounded *the place* and lay in wait for him all night at the gate of the city. They were quiet all night, saying, "In the morning, when it is daylight, we will kill him." 3 And Samson lay *low* till midnight; then he arose at midnight, took hold of the doors of the gate of the city and the two gateposts, pulled them up, bar and all, put *them* on his shoulders, and carried them to the top of the hill that faces Hebron.

4 Afterward it happened that he loved a woman in the Valley of Sorek, whose name *was* Delilah. 5 And the [a]lords of the Philistines came up to her and said to her, [b]"Entice him, and find out where his great strength *lies,* and by what *means* we may overpower him, that we may bind him to afflict him; and every one of us will give you eleven hundred *pieces* of silver."

6 So Delilah said to Samson, "Please tell me where your great strength *lies,* and with what you may be bound to afflict you."

7 And Samson said to her, "If they bind me with seven fresh bowstrings, not yet dried, then I shall become weak, and be like any *other* man."

8 So the lords of the Philistines brought up to her seven fresh bowstrings, not yet dried, and she bound him with them. 9 Now *men were* lying in wait, staying with her in the room. And she said to him, "The Philistines *are* upon you, Samson!" But he broke the bowstrings as a strand of yarn breaks when it touches fire. So the secret of his strength was not known.

10 Then Delilah said to Samson, "Look, you have mocked me and told me lies. Now, please tell me what you may be bound with."

11 So he said to her, "If they bind me securely with [a]new ropes that have never been used, then I shall become weak, and be like any *other* man."

12 Therefore Delilah took new ropes and bound him with them, and said to him, "The Philistines *are* upon you, Samson!" And *men were* lying in wait, staying in the room. But he broke them off his arms like a thread.

13 Delilah said to Samson, "Until now you have mocked me and told me lies. Tell me what you may be bound with."

And he said to her, "If you weave the seven locks of my head into the web of the loom"—

14 So she wove *it* tightly with the batten of the loom, and said to him, "The Philistines *are* upon you, Samson!" But he awoke from his sleep, and pulled out the batten and the web from the loom.

15 Then she said to him, [a]"How can you say, 'I love you,' when your heart *is* not with me? You have mocked me these three times, and have not told me where your great strength *lies.*" 16 And it came to pass, when she pestered him daily with her words and pressed him, *so* that his soul was vexed to death, 17 that he [a]told her all his heart, and said to her, [b]"No razor has ever come upon my head, for I *have been* a Nazirite to God from my mother's womb. If I am shaven, then my strength will leave me, and I shall become weak, and be like any *other* man."

18 When Delilah saw that he had told her all his heart, she sent and called for the lords of the Philistines, saying, "Come up once more, for he has told me all his heart." So the lords of the Philistines came up to her and brought the money in their hand. 19 [a]Then she lulled him to sleep on her knees, and called for a man and had him shave off the seven locks of his head. Then she began to torment him,[1] and his strength left him. 20 And she said, "The Philistines *are* upon you, Samson!" So he awoke from his sleep, and said, "I will go out as before, at other times, and shake myself free!" But he did not know that the LORD [a]had departed from him.

21 Then the Philistines took him and put out his [a]eyes, and brought him down to Gaza. They bound him with bronze fetters, and he became a grinder in the prison. 22 However, the hair of his head began to grow again after it had been shaven.

Samson Dies with the Philistines

23 Now the lords of the Philistines gathered together to offer a great sacrifice to

---

16:2 [a] 1 Sam. 23:26; Ps. 118:10–12 16:5 [a] Josh. 13:3 [b] Judg. 14:15 16:11 [a] Judg. 15:13 16:15 [a] Judg. 14:16 16:17 [a] [Mic. 7:5] [b] Num. 6:5; Judg. 13:5 16:19 [a] Prov. 7:26, 27 [1] Following Masoretic Text, Targum, and Vulgate; Septuagint reads *he began to be weak.* 16:20 [a] Num. 14:9, 42, 43; [Josh. 7:12]; 1 Sam. 16:14; 18:12; 28:15, 16; 2 Chr. 15:2 16:21 [a] 2 Kin. 25:7

[a]Dagon their god, and to rejoice. And they said:

"Our god has delivered into
our hands
Samson our enemy!"

24When the people saw him, they [a]praised their god; for they said:

"Our god has delivered into
our hands our enemy,
The destroyer of our land,
And the one who multiplied
our dead."

25So it happened, when their hearts were [a]merry, that they said, "Call for Samson, that he may perform for us." So they called for Samson from the prison, and he performed for them. And they stationed him between the pillars. 26Then Samson said to the lad who held him by the hand, "Let me feel the pillars which support the temple, so that I can lean on them." 27Now the temple was full of men and women. All the lords of the Philistines *were* there—about three thousand men and women on the [a]roof watching while Samson performed.

28Then Samson called to the LORD, saying, "O Lord GOD, [a]remember me, I pray! Strengthen me, I pray, just this once, O God, that I may with one *blow* take vengeance on the Philistines for my two eyes!" 29And Samson took hold of the two middle pillars which supported the temple, and he braced himself against them, one on his right and the other on his left. 30Then Samson said, "Let me die with the Philistines!" And he pushed with *all his* might, and the temple fell on the lords and all the people who *were* in it. So the dead that he killed at his death were more than he had killed in his life.

31And his brothers and all his father's household came down and took him, and brought *him* up and [a]buried him between Zorah and Eshtaol in the tomb of his father Manoah. He had judged Israel [b]twenty years.

#OXYGEN

JUDGES 16:30

Elevate the Stands You Take

If you are going to do fantastically well in whatever you do, you must go up a level. Take your effort to a higher level in God. Your chains are broken. There is nothing to hold you back.

Go, **breathe**, and **elevate the stands you take.**

Micah's Idolatry

17 Now there was a man from the mountains of Ephraim, whose name *was* [a]Micah. 2And he said to his mother, "The eleven hundred *shekels* of silver that were taken from you, and on which you [a]put a curse, even saying it in my ears—here *is* the silver with me; I took it."

And his mother said, [b]"*May you be* blessed by the LORD, my son!" 3So when he had returned the eleven hundred *shekels* of silver to his mother, his mother said, "I had wholly dedicated the silver from my hand to the LORD for my son, to [a]make a carved image and a molded image; now therefore, I will return it to you." 4Thus he returned the silver to his mother. Then his mother [a]took two hundred *shekels* of silver and gave them to the silversmith, and he made it into a carved image and a molded image; and they were in the house of Micah.

5The man Micah had a [a]shrine, and made an [b]ephod and [c]household idols;[1] and he consecrated one of his sons, who became his priest. 6[a]In those days *there was* no king in Israel; [b]everyone did *what was* right in his own eyes.

7Now there was a young man from [a]Bethlehem in Judah, of the family of Judah; he *was* a Levite, and [b]was staying there. 8The man departed from the city of Bethlehem in Judah to stay wherever he could find *a*

16:23 [a] 1 Sam. 5:2 16:24 [a] Dan. 5:4 16:25 [a] Judg. 9:27 16:27 [a] Deut. 22:8 16:28 [a] Jer. 15:15 16:31 [a] Judg. 13:25 [b] Judg. 15:20
17:1 [a] Judg. 18:2 17:2 [a] Lev. 5:1 [b] Gen. 14:19 17:3 [a] Ex. 20:4, 23; 34:17; Lev. 19:4 17:4 [a] Is. 46:6 17:5 [a] Judg. 18:24 [b] Judg. 8:27; 18:14 [c] Gen. 31:19, 30; Hos. 3:4 [1] Hebrew *teraphim* 17:6 [a] Judg. 18:1; 19:1 [b] Deut. 12:8; Judg. 21:25 17:7 [a] Josh. 19:15; Judg. 19:1; Ruth 1:1, 2; Mic. 5:2; Matt. 2:1, 5, 6 [b] Deut. 18:6

place. Then he came to the mountains of Ephraim, to the house of Micah, as he journeyed. 9 And Micah said to him, "Where do you come from?"

So he said to him, "I *am* a Levite from Bethlehem in Judah, and I am on my way to find *a place* to stay."

10 Micah said to him, "Dwell with me, [a]and be a [b]father and a priest to me, and I will give you ten *shekels* of silver per year, a suit of clothes, and your sustenance." So the Levite went in. 11 Then the Levite was content to dwell with the man; and the young man became like one of his sons to him. 12 So Micah [a]consecrated the Levite, and the young man [b]became his priest, and lived in the house of Micah. 13 Then Micah said, "Now I know that the LORD will be good to me, since I have a Levite as [a]priest!"

The Danites Adopt Micah's Idolatry

18 In [a]those days *there was* no king in Israel. And in those days [b]the tribe of the Danites was seeking an inheritance for itself to dwell in; for until that day *their* inheritance among the tribes of Israel had not fallen to them. 2 So the children of Dan sent five men of their family from their territory, men of valor from [a]Zorah and Eshtaol, [b]to spy out the land and search it. They said to them, "Go, search the land." So they went to the mountains of Ephraim, to the [c]house of Micah, and lodged there. 3 While they *were* at the house of Micah, they recognized the voice of the young Levite. They turned aside and said to him, "Who brought you here? What are you doing in this *place?* What do you have here?"

4 He said to them, "Thus and so Micah did for me. He has [a]hired me, and I have become his priest."

5 So they said to him, "Please [a]inquire [b]of God, that we may know whether the journey on which we go will be prosperous."

6 And the priest said to them, [a]"Go in peace. The presence of the LORD *be* with you on your way."

7 So the five men departed and went to [a]Laish. They saw the people who *were* there, [b]how they dwelt safely, in the manner of the Sidonians, quiet and secure. *There were* no rulers in the land who might put *them* to shame for anything. They *were* far from the [c]Sidonians, and they had no ties with anyone.[1]

8 Then *the spies* came back to their brethren at [a]Zorah and Eshtaol, and their brethren said to them, "What *is* your *report?*"

9 So they said, [a]"Arise, let us go up against them. For we have seen the land, and indeed it *is* very good. *Would* you [b]*do* nothing? Do not hesitate to go, *and* enter to possess the land. 10 When you go, you will come to a [a]secure people and a large land. For God has given it into your hands, [b]a place where *there is* no lack of anything that *is* on the earth."

11 And six hundred men of the family of the Danites went from there, from Zorah and Eshtaol, armed with weapons of war. 12 Then they went up and encamped in [a]Kirjath Jearim in Judah. (Therefore they call that place [b]Mahaneh Dan[1] to this day. There *it is,* west of Kirjath Jearim.) 13 And they passed from there to the mountains of Ephraim, and came to [a]the house of Micah.

14 [a]Then the five men who had gone to spy out the country of Laish answered and said to their brethren, "Do you know that [b]there are in these houses an ephod, household idols, a carved image, and a molded image? Now therefore, consider what you should do." 15 So they turned aside there, and came to the house of the young Levite man—to the house of Micah—and greeted him. 16 The [a]six hundred men armed with their weapons of war, who *were* of the children of Dan, stood by the entrance of the gate. 17 Then [a]the five men who had gone to spy out the land went up. Entering there, they took [b]the carved image, the ephod, the household idols, and the molded image. The priest stood at the entrance of the gate with the six hundred men *who were* armed with weapons of war.

18 When these went into Micah's house

17:10 [a] Judg. 18:19 [b] Gen. 45:8; Job 29:16 17:12 [a] Judg. 17:5 [b] Judg. 18:30 17:13 [a] Judg. 18:4 18:1 [a] Judg. 17:6; 19:1; 21:25 [b] Josh. 19:40–48 18:2 [a] Judg. 13:25 [b] Num. 13:17; Josh. 2:1 [c] Judg. 17:1 18:4 [a] Judg. 17:10, 12 18:5 [a] 1 Kin. 22:5; [Is. 30:1]; Hos. 4:12 [b] Judg. 1:1; 17:5; 18:14 18:6 [a] 1 Kin. 22:6 18:7 [a] Josh. 19:47 [b] Judg. 18:27–29 [c] Judg. 10:12 [1] Following Masoretic Text, Targum, and Vulgate; Septuagint reads *with Syria.* 18:8 [a] Judg. 18:2 18:9 [a] Num. 13:30; Josh. 2:23, 24 [b] 1 Kin. 22:3 18:10 [a] Judg. 18:7, 27 [b] Deut. 8:9 18:12 [a] Josh. 15:60 [b] Judg. 13:25 [1] Literally *Camp of Dan* 18:13 [a] Judg. 18:2 18:14 [a] 1 Sam. 14:28 [b] Judg. 17:5 18:16 [a] Judg. 18:11 18:17 [a] Judg. 18:2, 14 [b] Judg. 17:4, 5

and took the carved image, the ephod, the household idols, and the molded image, the priest said to them, "What are you doing?"

19 And they said to him, "Be quiet, [a]put your hand over your mouth, and come with us; [b]be a father and a priest to us. *Is it* better for you to be a priest to the household of one man, or that you be a priest to a tribe and a family in Israel?" 20 So the priest's heart was glad; and he took the ephod, the household idols, and the carved image, and took his place among the people.

21 Then they turned and departed, and put the little ones, the livestock, and the goods in front of them. 22 When they were a good way from the house of Micah, the men who *were* in the houses near Micah's house gathered together and overtook the children of Dan. 23 And they called out to the children of Dan. So they turned around and said to Micah, [a]"What ails you, that you have gathered such a company?"

24 So he said, "You have [a]taken away my gods which I made, and the priest, and you have gone away. Now what more do I have? How can you say to me, 'What ails you?'"

25 And the children of Dan said to him, "Do not let your voice be heard among us, lest angry men fall upon you, and you lose your life, with the lives of your household!" 26 Then the children of Dan went their way. And when Micah saw that they *were* too strong for him, he turned and went back to his house.

Danites Settle in Laish

27 So they took *the things* Micah had made, and the priest who had belonged to him, and went to Laish, to a people quiet and secure; [a]and they struck them with the edge of the sword and burned the city with fire. 28 *There was* no deliverer, because it *was* [a]far from Sidon, and they had no ties with anyone. It was in the valley that belongs [b]to Beth Rehob. So they rebuilt the city and dwelt there. 29 And [a]they called the name of the city [b]Dan, after the name of Dan their father, who was born to Israel. However, the name of the city formerly *was* Laish.

30 Then the children of Dan set up for themselves the carved image; and Jonathan the son of Gershom, the son of Manasseh,[1] and his sons were priests to the tribe of Dan [a]until the day of the captivity of the land. 31 So they set up for themselves Micah's carved image which he made, [a]all the time that the house of God was in Shiloh.

The Levite's Concubine

19 And it came to pass in those days, [a]when *there was* no king in Israel, that there was a certain Levite staying in the remote mountains of Ephraim. He took for himself a concubine from [b]Bethlehem in Judah. 2 But his concubine played the harlot against him, and went away from him to her father's house at Bethlehem in Judah, and was there four whole months. 3 Then her husband arose and went after her, to [a]speak kindly to her *and* bring her back, having his servant and a couple of donkeys with him. So she brought him into her father's house; and when the father of the young woman saw him, he was glad to meet him. 4 Now his father-in-law, the young woman's father, detained him; and he stayed with him three days. So they ate and drank and lodged there.

5 Then it came to pass on the fourth day that they arose early in the morning, and he stood to depart; but the young woman's father said to his son-in-law, [a]"Refresh your heart with a morsel of bread, and afterward go your way."

6 So they sat down, and the two of them ate and drank together. Then the young woman's father said to the man, "Please be content to stay all night, and let your heart be merry." 7 And when the man stood to depart, his father-in-law urged him; so he lodged there again. 8 Then he arose early in the morning on the fifth day to depart, but the young woman's father said, "Please refresh your heart." So they delayed until afternoon; and both of them ate.

9 And when the man stood to depart—he and his concubine and his servant—his father-in-law, the young woman's father, said to him, "Look, the day is now drawing

---

18:19 [a] Job 21:5; 29:9; 40:4; Mic. 7:16 [b] Judg. 17:10 18:23 [a] 2 Kin. 6:28 18:24 [a] Gen. 31:30; Judg. 17:5 18:27 [a] Josh. 19:47 18:28 [a] Judg. 18:7 [b] Num. 13:21; 2 Sam. 10:6 18:29 [a] Josh. 19:47 [b] Judg. 20:1; 1 Kin. 12:29, 30; 15:20 18:30 [a] 2 Kin. 15:29 [1] Septuagint and Vulgate read *Moses.* 18:31 [a] Deut. 12:1–32; Josh. 18:1, 8; Judg. 19:18; 21:12 19:1 [a] Judg. 17:6; 18:1; 21:25 [b] Judg. 17:7; Ruth 1:1 19:3 [a] Gen. 34:3; 50:21 19:5 [a] Gen. 18:5; Judg. 19:8; Ps. 104:15

toward evening; please spend the night.
See, the day is coming to an end; lodge
here, that your heart may be merry. Tomorrow go your way early, so that you may
get home."
10 However, the man was not willing to
spend that night; so he rose and departed,
and came opposite [a]Jebus (that *is,* Jerusalem). With him were the two saddled donkeys; his concubine *was* also with him.
11 They *were* near Jebus, and the day was
far spent; and the servant said to his master, "Come, please, and let us turn aside into
this city [a]of the Jebusites and lodge in it."
12 But his master said to him, "We will
not turn aside here into a city of foreigners, who *are* not of the children of Israel;
we will go on [a]to Gibeah." 13 So he said to his
servant, "Come, let us draw near to one of
these places, and spend the night in Gibeah
or in [a]Ramah." 14 And they passed by and
went their way; and the sun went down on
them near Gibeah, which belongs to Benjamin. 15 They turned aside there to go in to
lodge in Gibeah. And when he went in, he
sat down in the open square of the city, for
no one would [a]take them into *his* house to
spend the night.
16 Just then an old man came in from
[a]his work in the field at evening, who also
was from the mountains of Ephraim; he
was staying in Gibeah, whereas the men of
the place *were* Benjamites. 17 And when he
raised his eyes, he saw the traveler in the
open square of the city; and the old man
said, "Where are you going, and where do
you come from?"
18 So he said to him, "We *are* passing from
Bethlehem in Judah toward the remote
mountains of Ephraim; I *am* from there.
I went to Bethlehem in Judah; *now* I am
going to [a]the house of the LORD. But there
is no one who will take me into his house,
19 although we have both straw and fodder
for our donkeys, and bread and wine for
myself, for your female servant, and for
the young man *who is* with your servant;
there is no lack of anything."
20 And the old man said, [a]"Peace *be* with
you! However, *let* all your needs *be* my responsibility; [b]only do not spend the night
in the open square." 21 [a]So he brought him
into his house, and gave fodder to the donkeys. [b]And they washed their feet, and ate
and drank.

Gibeah's Crime

22 As they were [a]enjoying themselves,
suddenly [b]certain men of the city, [c]per-
verted men,[1] surrounded the house *and*
beat on the door. They spoke to the master
of the house, the old man, saying, [d]"Bring
out the man who came to your house, that
we may know him *carnally!*"
23 But [a]the man, the master of the house,
went out to them and said to them, "No, my
brethren! I beg you, do not act *so* wickedly!
Seeing this man has come into my house,
[b]do not commit this outrage. 24 [a]Look, *here*
is my virgin daughter and *the man's*[1] concubine; let me bring them out now. [b]Humble
them, and do with them as you please; but
to this man do not do such a vile thing!"
25 But the men would not heed him. So the
man took his concubine and brought *her*
out to them. And they [a]knew her and abused
her all night until morning; and when the
day began to break, they let her go.
26 Then the woman came as the day was
dawning, and fell down at the door of the
man's house where her master *was,* till it
was light.
27 When her master arose in the morning, and opened the doors of the house
and went out to go his way, there was his
concubine, fallen *at* the door of the house
with her hands on the threshold. 28 And he
said to her, "Get up and let us be going." But
[a]there was no answer. So the man lifted her
onto the donkey; and the man got up and
went to his place.
29 When he entered his house he took a
knife, laid hold of his concubine, and [a]di-
vided her into twelve pieces, limb by limb,[1]
and sent her throughout all the territory
of Israel. 30 And so it was that all who saw

19:10 [a] Josh. 18:28; 1 Chr. 11:4, 5 19:11 [a] Josh. 15:8, 63; Judg. 1:21; 2 Sam. 5:6 19:12 [a] Josh. 18:28 19:13 [a] Josh. 18:25
19:15 [a] Matt. 25:43 19:16 [a] Ps. 104:23 19:18 [a] Josh. 18:1; Judg. 18:31; 20:18; 1 Sam. 1:3, 7 19:20 [a] Gen. 43:23; Judg. 6:23; 1 Sam. 25:6
[b] Gen. 19:2 19:21 [a] Gen. 24:32; 43:24 [b] Gen. 18:4; John 13:5 19:22 [a] Judg. 16:25; 19:6, 9 [b] Gen. 19:4, 5; Judg. 20:5; Hos. 9:9;
10:9 [c] Deut. 13:13; 1 Sam. 2:12; 1 Kin. 21:10; [2 Cor. 6:15] [d] Gen. 19:5; [Rom. 1:26, 27] [1] Literally *sons of Belial* 19:23 [a] Gen. 19:6, 7
[b] Gen. 34:7; Deut. 22:21; Judg. 20:6, 10; 2 Sam. 13:12 19:24 [a] Gen. 19:8 [b] Gen. 34:2; Deut. 21:14 [1] Literally *his*
19:25 [a] Gen. 4:1 19:28 [a] Judg. 20:5 19:29 [a] Judg. 20:6; 1 Sam. 11:7 [1] Literally *with her bones*

it said, "No such deed has been done or
seen from the day that the children of Israel came up from the land of Egypt until
this day. Consider it, [a]confer, and speak up!"

Israel's War with the Benjamites

20 So [a]all the children of Israel came
out, from [b]Dan to [c]Beersheba, as
well as from the land of Gilead, and the congregation gathered together as one man
before the LORD [d]at Mizpah. [2]And the leaders of all the people, all the tribes of Israel,
presented themselves in the assembly of
the people of God, four hundred thousand
foot soldiers [a]who drew the sword. [3](Now
the children of Benjamin heard that the
children of Israel had gone up to Mizpah.)
Then the children of Israel said, "Tell *us*,
how did this wicked deed happen?"
[4]So the Levite, the husband of the
woman who was murdered, answered and
said, "My concubine and [a]I went into Gibeah, which belongs to Benjamin, to spend
the night. [5][a]And the men of Gibeah rose
against me, and surrounded the house at
night because of me. They intended to kill
me, [b]but instead they ravished my concubine so that she died. [6]So [a]I took hold of my
concubine, cut her in pieces, and sent her
throughout all the territory of the inheritance of Israel, because they [b]committed
lewdness and outrage in Israel. [7]Look! All
of you *are* children of Israel; [a]give your advice and counsel here and now!"
[8]So all the people arose as one man, saying, "None *of us* will go to his tent, nor will
any turn back to his house; [9]but now this
is the thing which we will do to Gibeah: *We
will go up* [a]against it by lot. [10]We will take
ten men out of *every* hundred throughout
all the tribes of Israel, a hundred out of *every* thousand, and a thousand out of *every*
ten thousand, to make provisions for the
people, that when they come to Gibeah in
Benjamin, they may repay all the vileness
that they have done in Israel." [11]So all the
men of Israel were gathered against the
city, united together as one man.
[12][a]Then the tribes of Israel sent men
through all the tribe of Benjamin, saying,
"What *is* this wickedness that has occurred
among you? [13]Now therefore, deliver up the
men, [a]the perverted men[1] who *are* in Gibeah, that we may put them to death and [b]re-
move the evil from Israel!" But the children
of Benjamin would not listen to the voice
of their brethren, the children of Israel.
[14]Instead, the children of Benjamin gathered together from their cities to Gibeah,
to go to battle against the children of Israel. [15]And from their cities at that time [a]the
children of Benjamin numbered twenty-six
thousand men who drew the sword, besides
the inhabitants of Gibeah, who numbered
seven hundred select men. [16]Among all
this people *were* seven hundred select men
who were [a]left-handed; every one could
sling a stone at a hair's *breadth* and not
miss. [17]Now besides Benjamin, the men of
Israel numbered four hundred thousand
men who drew the sword; all of these *were*
men of war.
[18]Then the children of Israel arose and
[a]went up to the house of God[1] to [b]inquire
of God. They said, "Which of us shall go up
first to battle against the children of Benjamin?"
The LORD said, [c]"Judah first!"
[19]So the children of Israel rose in the
morning and encamped against Gibeah.
[20]And the men of Israel went out to battle against Benjamin, and the men of Israel put themselves in battle array to fight
against them at Gibeah. [21]Then [a]the children of Benjamin came out of Gibeah, and
on that day cut down to the ground twenty-
two thousand men of the Israelites. [22]And
the people, that is, the men of Israel, encouraged themselves and again formed
the battle line at the place where they had
put themselves in array on the first day.
[23][a]Then the children of Israel went up and
wept before the LORD until evening, and
asked counsel of the LORD, saying, "Shall I
again draw near for battle against the children of my brother Benjamin?"
And the LORD said, "Go up against him."
[24]So the children of Israel approached

19:30 [a] Judg. 20:7; Prov. 13:10 **20:1** [a] Josh. 22:12; Judg. 20:11; 21:5 [b] Judg. 18:29; 1 Sam. 3:20; 2 Sam. 3:10; 24:2 [c] Josh. 19:2 [d] Judg. 10:17; 1 Sam. 7:5 **20:2** [a] Judg. 8:10 **20:4** [a] Judg. 19:15 **20:5** [a] Judg. 19:22 [b] Judg. 19:25, 26 **20:6** [a] Judg. 19:29 [b] Josh. 7:15 **20:7** [a] Judg. 19:30 **20:9** [a] Judg. 1:3 **20:12** [a] Deut. 13:14; Josh. 22:13, 16 **20:13** [a] Deut. 13:13; Judg. 19:22 [b] Deut. 17:12; 1 Cor. 5:13 [1] Literally *sons of Belial* **20:15** [a] Num. 1:36, 37; 2:23; 26:41 **20:16** [a] Judg. 3:15; 1 Chr. 12:2 **20:18** [a] Judg. 20:23, 26 [b] Num. 27:21 [c] Judg. 1:1, 2 [1] Or *Bethel* **20:21** [a] [Gen. 49:27] **20:23** [a] Judg. 20:26, 27

the children of Benjamin on the second day. 25And [a]Benjamin went out against them from Gibeah on the second day, and cut down to the ground eighteen thousand more of the children of Israel; all these drew the sword.

26Then all the children of Israel, that is, all the people, [a]went up and came to the house of God[1] and wept. They sat there before the LORD and fasted that day until evening; and they offered burnt offerings and peace offerings before the LORD. 27So the children of Israel inquired of the LORD ([a]the ark of the covenant of God *was* there in those days, 28[a]and Phinehas the son of Eleazar, the son of Aaron, [b]stood before it in those days), saying, "Shall I yet again go out to battle against the children of my brother Benjamin, or shall I cease?"

And the LORD said, "Go up, for tomorrow I will deliver them into your hand."

29Then Israel [a]set men in ambush all around Gibeah. 30And the children of Israel went up against the children of Benjamin on the third day, and put themselves in battle array against Gibeah as at the other times. 31So the children of Benjamin went out against the people, *and* were drawn away from the city. They began to strike down *and* kill some of the people, as at the other times, in the highways [a](one of which goes up to Bethel and the other to Gibeah) and in the field, about thirty men of Israel. 32And the children of Benjamin said, "They *are* defeated before us, as at first."

But the children of Israel said, "Let us flee and draw them away from the city to the highways." 33So all the men of Israel rose from their place and put themselves in battle array at Baal Tamar. Then Israel's men in ambush burst forth from their position in the plain of Geba. 34And ten thousand select men from all Israel came against Gibeah, and the battle was fierce. [a]But *the Benjamites*[1] did not know that disaster *was* upon them. 35The LORD defeated Benjamin before Israel. And the children of Israel destroyed that day twenty-five thousand one hundred Benjamites; all these drew the sword.

36So the children of Benjamin saw that they were defeated. [a]The men of Israel had given ground to the Benjamites, because they relied on the men in ambush whom they had set against Gibeah. 37[a]And the men in ambush quickly rushed upon Gibeah; the men in ambush spread out and struck the whole city with the edge of the sword. 38Now the appointed signal between the men of Israel and the men in ambush was that they would make a great cloud of [a]smoke rise up from the city, 39whereupon the men of Israel would turn in battle. Now Benjamin had begun to strike *and* kill about thirty of the men of Israel. For they said, "Surely they are defeated before us, as *in* the first battle." 40But when the cloud began to rise from the city in a column of smoke, the Benjamites [a]looked behind them, and there was the whole city going up *in smoke* to heaven. 41And when the men of Israel turned back, the men of Benjamin panicked, for they saw that disaster had come upon them. 42Therefore they turned *their backs* before the men of Israel in the direction of the wilderness; but the battle overtook them, and whoever *came* out of the cities they destroyed in their midst. 43They surrounded the Benjamites, chased them, *and* easily trampled them down as far as the front of Gibeah toward the east. 44And eighteen thousand men of Benjamin fell; all these *were* men of valor. 45Then they[1] turned and fled toward the wilderness to the rock of [a]Rimmon; and they cut down five thousand of them on the highways. Then they pursued them relentlessly up to Gidom, and killed two thousand of them. 46So all who fell of Benjamin that day were twenty-five thousand men who drew the sword; all these *were* men of valor.

47[a]But six hundred men turned and fled toward the wilderness to the rock of Rimmon, and they stayed at the rock of Rimmon for four months. 48And the men of Israel turned back against the children of Benjamin, and struck them down with the edge of the sword—from *every* city, men and beasts, all who were found. They also set fire to all the cities they came to.

20:25 [a] Judg. 20:21 20:26 [a] Judg. 20:18, 23; 21:2 [1] Or *Bethel* 20:27 [a] Josh. 18:1; 1 Sam. 1:3; 3:3; 4:3, 4 20:28 [a] Num. 25:7, 13; Josh. 24:33 [b] Deut. 10:8; 18:5 20:29 [a] Josh. 8:4 20:31 [a] Judg. 21:19 20:34 [a] Josh. 8:14; Job 21:13; Is. 47:11 [1] Literally *they* 20:36 [a] Josh. 8:15 20:37 [a] Josh. 8:19 20:38 [a] Josh. 8:20 20:40 [a] Josh. 8:20 20:45 [a] Josh. 15:32; 1 Chr. 6:77; Zech. 14:10 [1] Septuagint reads *the rest.* 20:47 [a] Judg. 21:13

Wives Provided for the Benjamites

21 Now [a]the men of Israel had sworn
an oath at Mizpah, saying, "None of
us shall give his daughter to Benjamin as a
wife." 2Then the people came [a]to the house
of God,[1] and remained there before God till
evening. They lifted up their voices and
wept bitterly, 3and said, "O LORD God of
Israel, why has this come to pass in Israel,
that today there should be one tribe *missing* in Israel?"
4So it was, on the next morning, that the
people rose early and [a]built an altar there,
and offered burnt offerings and peace offerings. 5The children of Israel said, "Who
is there among all the tribes of Israel who
did not come up with the assembly to the
LORD?" [a]For they had made a great oath
concerning anyone who had not come up
to the LORD at Mizpah, saying, "He shall
surely be put to death." 6And the children of
Israel grieved for Benjamin their brother,
and said, "One tribe is cut off from Israel
today. 7What shall we do for wives for those
who remain, seeing we have sworn by the
LORD that we will not give them our daughters as wives?"
8And they said, "What one *is there* from
the tribes of Israel who did not come up to
Mizpah to the LORD?" And, in fact, no one
had come to the camp from [a]Jabesh Gilead to the assembly. 9For when the people
were counted, indeed, not one of the inhabitants of Jabesh Gilead *was* there. 10So the
congregation sent out there twelve thousand of their most valiant men, and commanded them, saying, [a]"Go and strike the
inhabitants of Jabesh Gilead with the edge
of the sword, including the women and
children. 11And this *is* the thing that you
shall do: [a]You shall utterly destroy every
male, and every woman who has known a
man intimately." 12So they found among the
inhabitants of Jabesh Gilead four hundred

ELEVATE THE STANDS YOU TAKE

INHALE

I am blessed! I made it out of poverty, and so I try to give back. But it is hard to speak to knuckle-headed kids who get paid big loot for doing the wrong things. They do not want to hear me telling them to go legit. How do I help them do what is right when their way is paying big dividends? How can I take a stand for justice when the streets have a louder voice?

EXHALE

It is good that you are grieved by this. We who have come to know God in a very personal way can take comfort in knowing that He wants to take on our cares and move on those we care about. As we think about your situation, remember that the world's ways are not God's ways, but they usually are so much more appealing, at least in the short-term and on the surface. Judges 21:25 tells us that Israel experienced generations of heartache and trouble for one simple reason: "Everyone did what was right in his own eyes." We know that following God's ways is best because being right with Him is worth far more than the thickest wad of cash, and the peace and assurance of living rightly is worth it all too. The challenge is helping someone else see that as clearly as we do.

One of the best ways you can help others is by praying for them. Pray that God opens their minds and hearts to His truth. This is where God can do His greatest work. Even when you feel God has sent you to tough places, decide that you will not turn back from the assignment. You see, God responds to our cries for help, and He will always give us direction. That means you also should continue to talk with them about the bigger picture of life and eternity they are missing. Do not just focus on what they might lose; help them see what God offers them. Using your faith to breathe life into others will certainly please God.

21:1 [a] Judg. 20:1 21:2 [a] Judg. 20:18, 26 [1] Or *Bethel* 21:4 [a] Deut. 12:5; 2 Sam. 24:25 21:5 [a] Judg. 20:1–3 21:8 [a] 1 Sam. 11:1; 31:11
21:10 [a] Num. 31:17; Judg. 5:23; 1 Sam. 11:7 21:11 [a] Num. 31:17; Deut. 20:13, 14

young virgins who had not known a man
intimately; and they brought them to the
camp at [a]Shiloh, which is in the land of
Canaan.
13Then the whole congregation sent
word to the children of Benjamin [a]who *were*
at the rock of Rimmon, and announced
peace to them. 14So Benjamin came back at
that time, and they gave them the women
whom they had saved alive of the women of
Jabesh Gilead; and yet they had not found
enough for them.
15And the people [a]grieved for Benjamin,
because the LORD had made a void in the
tribes of Israel.
16Then the elders of the congregation
said, "What shall we do for wives for those
who remain, since the women of Benjamin
have been destroyed?" 17And they said,
"*There must be* an inheritance for the survivors of Benjamin, that a tribe may not
be destroyed from Israel. 18However, we
cannot give them wives from our daughters, [a]for the children of Israel have sworn
an oath, saying, 'Cursed *be* the one who
gives a wife to Benjamin.'" 19Then they
said, "In fact, *there is* a yearly [a]feast of the
LORD in [b]Shiloh, which *is* north of Bethel,
on the east side of the [c]highway that goes
up from Bethel to Shechem, and south of
Lebonah."
20Therefore they instructed the children
of Benjamin, saying, "Go, lie in wait in the
vineyards, 21and watch; and just when the
daughters of Shiloh come out [a]to perform
their dances, then come out from the vineyards, and every man catch a wife for himself from the daughters of Shiloh; then go
to the land of Benjamin. 22Then it shall be,
when their fathers or their brothers come
to us to complain, that we will say to them,
'Be kind to them for our sakes, because we
did not take a wife for any of them in the
war; for *it is* not *as though* you have given
the *women* to them at this time, making
yourselves guilty of your oath.'"
23And the children of Benjamin did so;
they took enough wives for their number
from those who danced, whom they caught.
Then they went and returned to their inheritance, and they [a]rebuilt the cities and
dwelt in them. 24So the children of Israel
departed from there at that time, every
man to his tribe and family; they went out
from there, every man to his inheritance.
25[a]In those days *there was* no king in Israel; [b]everyone did *what was* right in his
own eyes.

21:12 [a] Josh. 18:1; Judg. 18:31 21:13 [a] Judg. 20:47 21:15 [a] Judg. 21:6 21:18 [a] Judg. 11:35; 21:1 21:19 [a] Lev. 23:2 [b] Deut. 12:5; Josh. 18:1; Judg. 18:31; 1 Sam. 1:3 [c] Judg. 20:31 21:21 [a] Ex. 15:20; Judg. 11:34; 1 Sam. 18:6 21:23 [a] Judg. 20:48 21:25 [a] Judg. 17:6; 18:1; 19:1 [b] Deut. 12:8; Judg. 17:6

THE BOOK OF

RUTH

OVERVIEW

Samuel is often suggested as the author of Ruth, based, in part, on when it was written, sometime between 1010 and 970 BC. Named for its main character, Ruth tells the story of a family's plight during the period of the judges (see 1:1). It is a story of the loving nature of God and the blessings He gives to those who honor their commitments.

During a famine in Bethlehem, Elimelech took his wife, Naomi, and their two sons to the foreign nation of Moab, where food was more plentiful (see 1:2). Elimelech died there, leaving Naomi a widow (see v. 3). The man's sons took wives in Moab, and Naomi was well cared for. However, after ten years, both sons also died (see vv. 4–5). Distraught and left with no one to care for her, Naomi decided to return to Bethlehem. She encouraged her daughters-in-law to return to their parents' homes (see vv. 6–13). One returned to her family, "but Ruth clung to" Naomi (v. 14), and the pair journeyed to Bethlehem (v. 19).

In Bethlehem, Ruth asked Naomi if she would allow her to glean in the fields of Boaz, a wealthy relative of Naomi's late husband (see 2:1–2). Naomi gave her permission, and while gleaning, Ruth drew the attention of Boaz. He had heard about the sacrifices Ruth had made for Naomi, so he showed her favor (see vv. 5–16). He told Ruth that God would repay her work and give her "a full reward" (v. 12). When she returned home, Ruth told Naomi of her encounter with Boaz (see vv. 19–21). Since he was a close relative of Naomi's husband, Boaz could marry the widowed Ruth and provide an heir in order to keep the property of Naomi's bereft family intact. (At this time in Near Eastern history, women could not own property.)

Naomi instructed Ruth to go to Boaz's threshing floor and lie down at his feet, which would be a signal that she was requesting that he marry her (see 3:1–5). Ruth followed her mother-in-law's instructions, and when Boaz fell asleep after eating and drinking, she uncovered his feet and lay down (see v. 7). When Boaz awakened, he called Ruth a "virtuous woman" (v. 11) but also recognized that she had one closer relative. If that relative did not choose to marry Ruth, Boaz would make her his wife (see vv. 12–13). Ruth reported this interaction to Naomi, who instructed her to wait until Boaz settled the matter.

Soon after, having gained the closer relative's permission in the presence of witnesses, Boaz married Ruth. The Lord blessed them with a son, Obed (see 4:1–17). Obed was the father of Jesse, who was the father of David (see v. 17), who later became king of Israel.

The Book of Ruth highlights the importance of relationships and reflects God's favor toward those who honor their commitments. Because Ruth was committed to her mother-in-law and did not want her to be left alone, she turned from her family and the place of her birth and traveled to a foreign land to live among strangers who worshiped a God she did not know. God so honored Ruth's service to Naomi that He placed her in a position for Boaz to notice her and show her favor. Ruth and Naomi initially only sought food when they returned to Bethlehem, but God had much more in store for them. God blessed Ruth's faithfulness with a husband and a son who became part of the lineage of King David and ultimately of Jesus.

BREATHE IT IN

The period of the judges ruling Israel was filled with turmoil, rebellion, and sin. Although the Book of Ruth records events that took place during this time, it tells a much different story from those throughout the Book of Judges. Ruth is an indication that even when the world around us is in chaos, if we remain faithful to God, we will find favor in His sight.

Like Naomi and Ruth, many of us have suffered loss. We have lost loved ones to natural causes and to senseless violence. We have lost leaders to assassins and neighbors to suicide. We have lost jobs and income, relationships and friends. We know loss and know it well. Yet, despite all our losses, we must remain faithful to God if we are to receive His rewards.

The Book of Ruth encourages those who have suffered loss to uplift and commit to one another. Ruth refused to leave her mother-in-law, Naomi, whose husband and sons had died. Ruth, too, had lost her husband and could have chosen to return to her own family. Instead, she remained with her mother-in-law to offer her support and assistance. Ruth's commitment to Naomi and her willingness to serve out of love and commitment, even in the face of her own loss, was pleasing to God.

Overcoming loss is difficult. We sometimes want to wallow in our sorrow, but we need to keep moving forward. When Naomi experienced loss, she picked up and returned to a familiar place. In her loss, Ruth focused on another's need rather than her own. Each was committed to making the best of a bad situation. As a result, they found great blessing.

Rarely do we consider the possibility that a loss may lead to blessing. We rarely consider that loss may have some positive outcome. What if the loss we suffered was God nudging us to do something we have never done before? Have we ever considered a loss as a signal for us to return to our "homeland," the place where we met God?

God wants us to go to Him, our source, in times of loss. He wants us to know that any loss we experience is part of His greater plan for our lives. It should never be that we focus so much on our losses and disappointments that we do not extend a hand to others who may be suffering. God will give us the strength to deal with our own situations and be there for others at the same time.

Our commitment pleases God, especially our commitment to Him. When our words and actions demonstrate our faithfulness to God and His Word, He will often use others to show us favor and deliver His blessings to us, just as He used Boaz in the lives of Ruth and Naomi.

While we may experience anguish and grief when we suffer loss, we should never become stagnant. We must keep moving forward to see what God has in store for us. The next time you experience loss, do not get stuck in the sadness. Take the time to grieve and then look ahead for the mighty blessing that God has prepared for you.

THE BOOK OF

RUTH

Elimelech's Family Goes to Moab

1 Now it came to pass, in the days when
[a]the judges ruled, that there was [b]a
famine in the land. And a certain man of
[c]Bethlehem, Judah, went to dwell in the
country of [d]Moab, he and his wife and his
two sons. 2 The name of the man *was* Elimelech, the name of his wife *was* Naomi, and
the names of his two sons *were* Mahlon
and Chilion—[a]Ephrathites of Bethlehem,
Judah. And they went [b]to the country of
Moab and remained there. 3 Then Elimelech, Naomi's husband, died; and she was
left, and her two sons. 4 Now they took wives
of the women of Moab: the name of the
one *was* Orpah, and the name of the other
Ruth. And they dwelt there about ten years.
5 Then both Mahlon and Chilion also died;
so the woman survived her two sons and
her husband.

Naomi Returns with Ruth

6 Then she arose with her daughters-in-
law that she might return from the country
of Moab, for she had heard in the country of
Moab that the LORD had [a]visited His people
by [b]giving them bread. 7 Therefore she went
out from the place where she was, and her
two daughters-in-law with her; and they
went on the way to return to the land of Judah. 8 And Naomi said to her two daughters-
in-law, [a]"Go, return each to her mother's
house. [b]The LORD deal kindly with you, as
you have dealt [c]with the dead and with me.
9 The LORD grant that you may find [a]rest,
each in the house of her husband."

So she kissed them, and they lifted up
their voices and wept. 10 And they said to
her, "Surely we will return with you to your
people."

11 But Naomi said, "Turn back, my daughters; why will you go with me? *Are* there
still sons in my womb, [a]that they may be
your husbands? 12 Turn back, my daughters,
go—for I am too old to have a husband. If
I should say I have hope, *if* I should have
a husband tonight and should also bear
sons, 13 would you wait for them till they
were grown? Would you restrain yourselves
from having husbands? No, my daughters;
for it grieves me very much for your sakes
that [a]the hand of the LORD has gone out
against me!"

14 Then they lifted up their voices
and wept again; and Orpah kissed her
mother-in-law, but Ruth [a]clung to her.

15 And she said, "Look, your sister-in-law
has gone back to [a]her people and to her
gods; [b]return after your sister-in-law."

16 But Ruth said:

[a]"Entreat me not to leave you,
Or to turn back from
following after you;
For wherever you go, I will go;
And wherever you lodge, I will lodge;
[b]Your people *shall be* my people,
And your God, my God.
17 Where you die, I will die,
And there will I be buried.
[a]The LORD do so to me, and more also,
If *anything but* death parts
you and me."

18 [a]When she saw that she was determined
to go with her, she stopped speaking to her.

1:1 [a] Judg. 2:16–18 [b] Gen. 12:10; 26:1; 2 Kin. 8:1 [c] Judg. 17:8; Mic. 5:2 [d] Gen. 19:37 1:2 [a] Gen. 35:19; 1 Sam. 1:1; 1 Kin. 11:26 [b] Judg. 3:30 1:6 [a] Ex. 3:16; 4:31; Jer. 29:10; Zeph. 2:7; Luke 1:68 [b] Ps. 132:15; Matt. 6:11 1:8 [a] Josh. 24:15 [b] 2 Tim. 1:16–18 [c] Ruth 2:20 1:9 [a] Ruth 3:1 1:11 [a] Gen. 38:11; Deut. 25:5 1:13 [a] Judg. 2:15; Job 19:21; Ps. 32:4; 38:2 1:14 [a] [Prov. 17:17] 1:15 [a] Judg. 11:24 [b] Josh. 1:15 1:16 [a] 2 Kin. 2:2, 4, 6 [b] Ruth 2:11, 12 1:17 [a] 1 Sam. 3:17; 2 Sam. 19:13; 2 Kin. 6:31 1:18 [a] Acts 21:14

19Now the two of them went until they
came to Bethlehem. And it happened, when
they had come to Bethlehem, that [a]all the
city was excited because of them; and the
women said, [b]"*Is* this Naomi?"
20But she said to them, "Do not call me
Naomi;[1] call me Mara,[2] for the Almighty
has dealt very bitterly with me. 21I went out
full, [a]and the LORD has brought me home
again empty. Why do you call me Naomi,
since the LORD has testified against me,
and the Almighty has afflicted me?"
22So Naomi returned, and Ruth the Moabitess her daughter-in-law with her, who
returned from the country of Moab. Now
they came to Bethlehem [a]at the beginning
of barley harvest.

Ruth Meets Boaz

2 There was a [a]relative of Naomi's husband, a man of great wealth, of the family of [b]Elimelech. His name *was* [c]Boaz. 2So
Ruth the Moabitess said to Naomi, "Please
let me go to the [a]field, and glean heads of
grain after *him* in whose sight I may find
favor."
And she said to her, "Go, my daughter."
3Then she left, and went and gleaned
in the field after the reapers. And she happened to come to the part of the field *belonging* to Boaz, who *was* of the family of
Elimelech.
4Now behold, Boaz came from [a]Bethle-
hem, and said to the reapers, [b]"The LORD
be with you!"

RUTH 1:16

I AM RUTH

But Ruth said: "Entreat me not to leave you, or to turn back from following after you; for wherever you go, I will go; and wherever you lodge, I will lodge; your people shall be my people, and your God, my God." Ruth 1:16

I am Ruth. Though I am a Moabite and my people do not worship God, I married a Hebrew man. After he died, I stayed with my mother-in-law, Naomi. I greatly respected her and her faith. When she left Moab to return to her home in Bethlehem, she told me to stay with my people. But I chose to follow her. I even chose to accept and follow her God.

When we arrived in Bethlehem, it was time for the barley harvest. I asked Naomi to allow me to glean leftover grain from the fields so we would have food to eat. With her approval, I entered a field belonging to Boaz, a relative of Naomi's late husband who was of high standing. Boaz came to the field and blessed all the workers. He saw me, and I found favor in his eyes. He even told his men to leave extra barley for me to pick up.

When Naomi found out I had worked for Boaz and what he had done, she praised God for His kindness. She hoped Boaz would be my kinsman-redeemer, a man who took on the duty and responsibility for any relative in need. But another man of the town was a closer relative than Boaz. In the public square, before all the elders, Boaz explained to him that Naomi's husband owned land in town that the man could claim, along with marrying me, the widow of Naomi's son. The man declined. So, Boaz bought the property himself, married me, and became kinsman-redeemer. I soon gave birth to a son and gave Naomi a new family to care for. My son's name was Obed, the grandfather of King David.

†

Sometimes life appears to offer only bitterness, but in God's timing, the greatest blessings can be ours if we surrender all to God.

1:19 [a] Matt. 21:10 [b] Is. 23:7; Lam. 2:15 1:20 [1] Literally *Pleasant* [2] Literally *Bitter* 1:21 [a] Job 1:21 1:22 [a] Ruth 2:23; 2 Sam. 21:9
2:1 [a] Ruth 3:2, 12 [b] Ruth 1:2 [c] Ruth 4:21 2:2 [a] Lev. 19:9, 10; 23:22; Deut. 24:19
2:4 [a] Ruth 1:1 [b] Ps. 129:7, 8; Luke 1:28; 2 Thess. 3:16

And they answered him, "The LORD
bless you!"
5Then Boaz said to his servant who was
in charge of the reapers, "Whose young
woman *is* this?"
6So the servant who was in charge of the
reapers answered and said, "It *is* the young
Moabite woman [a]who came back with Naomi from the country of Moab. 7And she
said, 'Please let me glean and gather after the reapers among the sheaves.' So she
came and has continued from morning
until now, though she rested a little in the
house."
8Then Boaz said to Ruth, "You will listen, my daughter, will you not? Do not go
to glean in another field, nor go from here,
but stay close by my young women. 9*Let*
your eyes *be* on the field which they reap,
and go after them. Have I not commanded
the young men not to touch you? And when
you are thirsty, go to the vessels and drink
from what the young men have drawn."
10So she [a]fell on her face, bowed down to
the ground, and said to him, "Why have I
found [b]favor in your eyes, that you should
take notice of me, since I *am* a foreigner?"
11And Boaz answered and said to her, "It
has been fully reported to me, [a]all that you
have done for your mother-in-law since the
death of your husband, and *how* you have
left your father and your mother and the
land of your birth, and have come to a people whom you did not know before. 12[a]The
LORD repay your work, and a full reward be
given you by the LORD God of Israel, [b]under
whose wings you have come for refuge."
13Then she said, [a]"Let me find favor in
your sight, my lord; for you have comforted
me, and have spoken kindly to your maidservant, [b]though I am not like one of your
maidservants."
14Now Boaz said to her at mealtime,
"Come here, and eat of the bread, and dip
your piece of bread in the vinegar." So
she sat beside the reapers, and he passed
parched *grain* to her; and she ate and [a]was
satisfied, and kept some back. 15And when
she rose up to glean, Boaz commanded his
young men, saying, "Let her glean even
among the sheaves, and do not reproach
her. 16Also let *grain* from the bundles fall
purposely for her; leave *it* that she may
glean, and do not rebuke her."

#OXYGEN
RUTH 2:12
Elevate the Stands You Take

If you want to live on the side of right, you must first decide to follow God. Live as God desires for you to live. Serve as God desires for you to serve. Love as God desires for you to love. When you stand for God, He will stand with you.

Breathe and elevate the stands you take.

17So she gleaned in the field until evening, and beat out what she had gleaned,
and it was about an ephah of [a]barley. 18Then
she took *it* up and went into the city, and
her mother-in-law saw what she had
gleaned. So she brought out and gave to
her [a]what she had kept back after she had
been satisfied.
19And her mother-in-law said to her,
"Where have you gleaned today? And where
did you work? Blessed be the one who [a]took
notice of you."
So she told her mother-in-law with
whom she had worked, and said, "The
man's name with whom I worked today
is Boaz."
20Then Naomi said to her daughter-in-law,
[a]"Blessed *be* he of the LORD, who [b]has not
forsaken His kindness to the living and the
dead!" And Naomi said to her, "This man *is* a
relation of ours, [c]one of our close relatives."
21Ruth the Moabitess said, "He also said
to me, 'You shall stay close by my young
men until they have finished all my harvest.'"
22And Naomi said to Ruth her daughter-
in-law, "*It is* good, my daughter, that you go

2:6 [a] Ruth 1:22 2:10 [a] 1 Sam. 25:23 [b] 1 Sam. 1:18 2:11 [a] Ruth 1:14–18 2:12 [a] 1 Sam. 24:19; Ps. 58:11 [b] Ruth 1:16; Ps. 17:8; 36:7; 57:1; 61:4; 63:7; 91:4 2:13 [a] Gen. 33:15; 1 Sam. 1:18 [b] 1 Sam. 25:41 2:14 [a] Ruth 2:18 2:17 [a] Ruth 1:22 2:18 [a] Ruth 2:14 2:19 [a] Ruth 2:10; [Ps. 41:1] 2:20 [a] Ruth 3:10; 2 Sam. 2:5 [b] Prov. 17:17 [c] Ruth 3:9; 4:4, 6

out with his young women, and that people
do not meet you in any other field." 23So
she stayed close by the young women of
Boaz, to glean until the end of barley harvest and wheat harvest; and she dwelt with
her mother-in-law.

Ruth's Redemption Assured

3 Then Naomi her mother-in-law said to
her, "My daughter, [a]shall I not seek [b]se-
curity for you, that it may be well with you?
2Now Boaz, [a]whose young women you were
with, *is he* not our relative? In fact, he is
winnowing barley tonight at the threshing
floor. 3Therefore wash yourself and [a]anoint
yourself, put on your *best* garment and go
down to the threshing floor; *but* do not
make yourself known to the man until he
has finished eating and drinking. 4Then it
shall be, when he lies down, that you shall
notice the place where he lies; and you shall
go in, uncover his feet, and lie down; and
he will tell you what you should do."

5And she said to her, "All that you say to
me I will do."

6So she went down to the threshing
floor and did according to all that her
mother-in-law instructed her. 7And after
Boaz had eaten and drunk, and [a]his heart
was cheerful, he went to lie down at the end
of the heap of grain; and she came softly,
uncovered his feet, and lay down.

8Now it happened at midnight that the
man was startled, and turned himself; and
there, a woman was lying at his feet. 9And
he said, "Who *are* you?"

So she answered, "I *am* Ruth, your maidservant. [a]Take your maidservant under
your wing,[1] for you are [b]a close relative."

10Then he said, [a]"Blessed *are* you of the
LORD, my daughter! For you have shown
more kindness at the end than [b]at the beginning, in that you did not go after young
men, whether poor or rich. 11And now, my
daughter, do not fear. I will do for you all
that you request, for all the people of my
town know that you *are* a [a]virtuous woman.
12Now it is true that I *am* a [a]close relative;
however, [b]there is a relative closer than
I. 13Stay this night, and in the morning it
shall be *that* if he will [a]perform the duty of
a close relative for you—good; let him do
it. But if he does not want to perform the
duty for you, then I will perform the duty
for you, [b]*as* the LORD lives! Lie down until
morning."

14So she lay at his feet until morning,
and she arose before one could recognize
another. Then he said, [a]"Do not let it be
known that the woman came to the threshing floor." 15Also he said, "Bring the shawl
that *is* on you and hold it." And when she
held it, he measured six *ephahs* of barley,
and laid *it* on her. Then she[1] went into the
city.

16When she came to her mother-in-law,
she said, "*Is* that you, my daughter?"

Then she told her all that the man had
done for her. 17And she said, "These six
ephahs of barley he gave me; for he said
to me, 'Do not go empty-handed to your
mother-in-law.'"

18Then she said, [a]"Sit still, my daughter,
until you know how the matter will turn
out; for the man will not rest until he has
concluded the matter this day."

Boaz Redeems Ruth

4 Now Boaz went up to the gate and sat
down there; and behold, [a]the close relative of whom Boaz had spoken came by.
So Boaz said, "Come aside, friend,[1] sit down
here." So he came aside and sat down. 2And
he took ten men of [a]the elders of the city,
and said, "Sit down here." So they sat down.
3Then he said to the close relative, "Naomi,
who has come back from the country of
Moab, sold the piece of land [a]which *belonged*
to our brother Elimelech. 4And I thought
to inform you, saying, [a]'Buy *it* back [b]in the
presence of the inhabitants and the elders
of my people. If you will redeem *it,* redeem
it; but if you[1] will not redeem *it, then* tell me,
that I may know; [c]for *there is* no one but
you to redeem *it,* and I *am* next after you.'"

And he said, "I will redeem *it.*"

3:1 [a] 1 Cor. 7:36; 1 Tim. 5:8 [b] Ruth 1:9 3:2 [a] Ruth 2:3, 8 3:3 [a] 2 Sam. 14:2 3:7 [a] Judg. 19:6, 9, 22; 2 Sam. 13:28; Esth. 1:10 3:9 [a] Ezek. 16:8 [b] Ruth 2:20; 3:12 [1] Or *Spread the corner of your garment over your maidservant* 3:10 [a] Ruth 2:20 [b] Ruth 1:8 3:11 [a] Prov. 12:4; 31:10–31 3:12 [a] Ruth 3:9 [b] Ruth 4:1 3:13 [a] Deut. 25:5–10; Ruth 4:5, 10; Matt. 22:24 [b] Judg. 8:19; Jer. 4:2; 12:16 3:14 [a] [Rom. 12:17; 14:16; 1 Cor. 10:32; 2 Cor. 8:21; 1 Thess. 5:22] 3:15 [1] Many Hebrew manuscripts, Syriac, and Vulgate read *she;* Masoretic Text, Septuagint, and Targum read *he.* 3:18 [a] [Ps. 37:3, 5] 4:1 [a] Ruth 3:12 [1] Hebrew *peloni almoni;* literally *so and so* 4:2 [a] 1 Kin. 21:8; Prov. 31:23 4:3 [a] Lev. 25:25 4:4 [a] Jer. 32:7, 8 [b] Gen. 23:18 [c] Lev. 25:25 [1] Following many Hebrew manuscripts, Septuagint, Syriac, Targum, and Vulgate; Masoretic Text reads *he.*

5Then Boaz said, "On the day you buy
the field from the hand of Naomi, you must
also buy *it* from Ruth the Moabitess, the
wife of the dead, [a]to perpetuate[1] the name
of the dead through his inheritance."
6[a]And the close relative said, "I cannot
redeem *it* for myself, lest I ruin my own inheritance. You redeem my right of redemption for yourself, for I cannot redeem *it*."
7[a]Now this *was the custom* in former
times in Israel concerning redeeming and
exchanging, to confirm anything: one man
took off his sandal and gave *it* to the other,
and this *was* a confirmation in Israel.
8Therefore the close relative said to
Boaz, "Buy *it* for yourself." So he took off
his sandal. 9And Boaz said to the elders
and all the people, "You *are* witnesses this
day that I have bought all that was Elimelech's, and all that *was* Chilion's and Mahlon's, from the hand of Naomi. 10Moreover,
Ruth the Moabitess, the widow of Mahlon,
I have acquired as my wife, to perpetuate
the name of the dead through his inheritance, [a]that the name of the dead may not
be cut off from among his brethren and
from his position at the gate.[1] You *are* witnesses this day."
11And all the people who *were* at the gate,
and the elders, said, "*We are* witnesses. [a]The
LORD make the woman who is coming to
your house like Rachel and Leah, the two
who [b]built the house of Israel; and may
you prosper in [c]Ephrathah and be famous
in [d]Bethlehem. 12May your house be like
the house of [a]Perez, [b]whom Tamar bore
to Judah, because of [c]the offspring which
the LORD will give you from this young
woman."

Descendants of Boaz and Ruth
(Matt. 1:2–6)

13So Boaz [a]took Ruth and she became his
wife; and when he went in to her, [b]the LORD
gave her conception, and she bore a son.
14Then [a]the women said to Naomi, "Blessed
be the LORD, who has not left you this day
without a close relative; and may his name
be famous in Israel! 15And may he be to
you a restorer of life and a nourisher of
your old age; for your daughter-in-law, who
loves you, who is [a]better to you than seven
sons, has borne him." 16Then Naomi took
the child and laid him on her bosom, and
became a nurse to him. 17[a]Also the neighbor
women gave him a name, saying, "There is
a son born to Naomi." And they called his
name Obed. He *is* the father of Jesse, the
father of David.
18[a]Now this *is* the genealogy of Perez:
[b]Perez begot Hezron; 19Hezron begot Ram,
and Ram begot Amminadab; 20Ammina-
dab begot [a]Nahshon, and Nahshon begot
[b]Salmon;[1] 21Salmon begot Boaz, and Boaz
begot Obed; 22Obed begot Jesse, and Jesse
begot [a]David.

4:5 [a] Gen. 38:8; Deut. 25:5, 6; Ruth 3:13; Matt. 22:24 [1] Literally *raise up* 4:6 [a] Ruth 3:12, 13; Job 19:14 4:7 [a] Deut. 25:7–10 4:10 [a] Deut. 25:6 [1] Probably his civic office 4:11 [a] Ps. 127:3; 128:3 [b] Gen. 29:25–30; Deut. 25:9 [c] Gen. 35:16–18 [d] 1 Sam. 16:4–13; Mic. 5:2; Matt. 2:1–8 4:12 [a] 1 Chr. 2:4; Matt. 1:3 [b] Gen. 38:6–29 [c] 1 Sam. 2:20 4:13 [a] Ruth 3:11 [b] Gen. 29:31; 33:5; Matt. 1:5 4:14 [a] Luke 1:58; [Rom. 12:15] 4:15 [a] 1 Sam. 1:8 4:17 [a] Luke 1:58 4:18 [a] 1 Chr. 2:4, 5; Matt. 1:1–7 [b] Num. 26:20, 21 4:20 [a] Num. 1:7 [b] Matt. 1:4 [1] Hebrew *Salmah* 4:22 [a] 1 Chr. 2:15; Matt. 1:6

THE FIRST BOOK OF

SAMUEL

OVERVIEW

The Book of 1 Samuel contains no reference to its author. It is believed that parts of it were written by the prophet Samuel and other parts were written after his death. The Book of 1 Samuel records about 115 years of Israel's history from the end of the period of the judges through the death of Saul, the nation's first king.

First Samuel begins with the birth of Samuel to Hannah, who had been barren. Hannah had begged for a child, promising God she would dedicate her child's life to the Lord's service if He would grant her request (see 1 Sam. 1:1–18). Hannah became pregnant and gave birth to a boy she named Samuel. Honoring her word, she gave Samuel to Israel's chief priest, Eli, to raise in service to God (see vv. 24–28).

Eli raised Samuel in the ways of the Lord, but Eli's own sons were far from them. They were corrupt, dishonored God, and disobeyed His laws (see 2:12–17). Because of this, God told Eli his sons would not be allowed to minister in His house. He would select a new priest from outside Eli's family instead (see vv. 27–36).

God began to speak to Samuel when he was a boy and raised him up as a prophet who delivered God's word to Israel (see 3:1—4:1). Samuel served as a prophet, priest, and judge and convinced the Israelites to stop worshiping other gods and remain true to their covenant with God.

The Israelites, however, were unhappy being ruled by judges. They demanded that Samuel appoint a king to govern them—they wanted to be like the nations around them (see 8:5). Samuel was not pleased. He took the matter to God, who gave him permission to grant their request; however, He instructed Samuel to warn the people about life under a king (see vv. 6–18). The people were undaunted and stood fast in their demand for a king.

Soon after, God chose Saul to serve as the first king of Israel. Samuel anointed Saul as king (chs. 9–10), and Saul began a reign that would last for forty years. Early on, Saul was victorious as a military leader, but he was also disobedient to God, leading to God rejecting him as king (chs. 13–15). God chose David as the new king (see 16:1–13) and withdrew His Spirit from Saul (see v. 14), but Saul continued to rule.

David, meanwhile, entered the service of Saul as a musician. Saul came to love David and made him the royal armor-bearer (see 16:19–23). David rose to fame when he defeated the Philistine giant Goliath (ch. 17). Soon, David, a skilled warrior, rose to military prominence. As a result, the Israelites adored him and he became more popular than King Saul. In response, Saul became jealous of David and sought to harm him (chs. 18–19). David fled from Saul, who was in constant pursuit of him (chs. 21–28). On two occasions, David spared Saul's life (chs. 24; 26). He also found refuge among the Philistines (see 27:1—28:2), who later rejected him (ch. 29). In the book's final chapter, Saul's sons were killed in a battle with the Philistines (see 31:2), and after his armor-bearer refused to kill him, Saul purposely fell upon a sword and died (see v. 4).

A continuation of the history of the Israelites, 1 Samuel chronicles the shift from leadership by judges to one of kings. While God was not in favor of this, He allowed it. With the new system of

governance in place, God still required obedience from His people and His chosen leaders. The events of 1 Samuel teach the importance of obeying God and the consequences of disobedience.

BREATHE IT IN

The Israelites asked Samuel to appoint a king to govern them so they could be like the nations around them. When God gave Samuel permission to appoint a king, He did so with a warning to the Israelites. Being led by a king like the nations around them would make them like those other nations in other ways too. They would lose their identity as the holy people of God. A king would rule according to his own plans and not according to God's will. Despite the warning, the people insisted upon a monarchy.

We are sometimes tempted to be like everybody else and assimilate into society at large. Our goal is simply to fit in. But fitting in has never been God's plan for His people. Just as Israel experienced calamity because of this desire to fit in, so can we. Instead, God desires to set us apart as a unique people. He warns us to be *in* the world but not *of* the world. He delights in the fact that we are fearfully and wonderfully made, both individually and as a people. We should cherish our God-given holy identity, not despise it.

As Christians, God has set us apart and placed before us the high calling of knowing and communing with Him. We must not seek to live like those who do not know Him, even if they prosper. Instead, our desire should be to live like our Savior, Jesus Christ. People will come and go. Places will change for better or worse. Material belongings will lose their luster and appeal. Only Christ is constant and everlasting. Seek first the kingdom of God and everything else will be added to your life.

Striving toward our high calling requires obedience to God. Have we obeyed all of God's commands? Did we forgive the person who wronged us? Did we ask for forgiveness when we offended our friend? Did we speak a kind word to or share our treasure with the homeless man we passed on the street? Did we follow God's instruction when making life-changing decisions?

When we are disobedient, we can suffer consequences as Saul did. Instead of waiting for Samuel to offer a sacrifice as instructed by God, Saul's arrogance led him to disobey God and dishonor His name. As a result, God rejected him and replaced him as king. When we obey God, peace and blessings follow. Our obedience demonstrates that we are trustworthy. It shows that we will not take God's blessings for granted but use them according to His purposes. It shows that we recognize God's sovereignty and our own lowly state. When we disobey, though, we communicate the opposite. And we position ourselves to be disciplined by our loving, holy, and righteous God.

Do not allow what is happening around you to take your focus from God. Allow God, not humanity, to govern your life. God's calling, His anointing, on your life does not exempt you from obedience; it expects it.

†

THE FIRST BOOK OF

SAMUEL

The Family of Elkanah

1 Now there was a certain man of Ramathaim Zophim, of the [a]mountains of Ephraim, and his name *was* [b]Elkanah the son of Jeroham, the son of Elihu,[1] the son of Tohu,[2] the son of Zuph, [c]an Ephraimite. 2 And he had [a]two wives: the name of one *was* Hannah, and the name of the other Peninnah. Peninnah had children, but Hannah had no children. 3 This man went up from his city [a]yearly [b]to worship and sacrifice to the LORD of hosts in [c]Shiloh. Also the two sons of Eli, Hophni and Phinehas, the priests of the LORD, *were* there. 4 And whenever the time came for Elkanah to make an [a]offering, he would give portions to Peninnah his wife and to all her sons and daughters. 5 But to Hannah he would give a double portion, for he loved Hannah, [a]although the LORD had closed her womb. 6 And her rival also [a]provoked her severely, to make her miserable, because the LORD had closed her womb. 7 So it was, year by year, when she went up to the house of the LORD, that she provoked her; therefore she wept and did not eat.

Hannah's Vow

8 Then Elkanah her husband said to her, "Hannah, why do you weep? Why do you not eat? And why is your heart grieved? *Am* I not [a]better to you than ten sons?"

9 So Hannah arose after they had finished eating and drinking in Shiloh. Now Eli the priest was sitting on the seat by the doorpost of [a]the tabernacle[1] of the LORD. 10 [a]And she *was* in bitterness of soul, and prayed to the LORD and wept in anguish.

11 Then she [a]made a vow and said, "O LORD of hosts, if You will indeed [b]look on the affliction of Your maidservant and [c]remember me, and not forget Your maidservant, but will give Your maidservant a male child, then I will give him to the LORD all the days of his life, and [d]no razor shall come upon his head."

12 And it happened, as she continued

#OXYGEN

1 SAMUEL 1:10

Believe in Prayer

Lemonade can be made by giving the lemons life gives you to God. Do not sit in bitterness. Rather, take those bitter lemons to God in prayer. He delights in making bitter, sweet.

Drink in His goodness, **breathe,** and **believe in prayer.**

praying before the LORD, that Eli watched her mouth. 13 Now Hannah spoke in her heart; only her lips moved, but her voice was not heard. Therefore Eli thought she was drunk. 14 So Eli said to her, "How long will you be drunk? Put your wine away from you!"

15 But Hannah answered and said, "No, my lord, I *am* a woman of sorrowful spirit. I have drunk neither wine nor intoxicating

---

1:1 [a] Josh. 17:17, 18; 24:33 [b] 1 Chr. 6:27, 33–38 [c] Ruth 1:2 [1] Spelled *Eliel* in 1 Chronicles 6:34 [2] Spelled *Toah* in 1 Chronicles 6:34
1:2 [a] Deut. 21:15–17 1:3 [a] Ex. 34:14, 23; Judg. 21:19; 1 Sam. 1:21; Luke 2:41 [b] Deut. 12:5–7; 16:16 [c] Josh. 18:1 1:4 [a] Deut. 12:17, 18
1:5 [a] Gen. 16:1; 30:1, 2 1:6 [a] Job 24:21 1:8 [a] Ruth 4:15 1:9 [a] 1 Sam. 3:3 [1] Hebrew *heykal,* palace or temple 1:10 [a] Job 7:11
1:11 [a] Gen. 28:20; Num. 30:6–11 [b] Ps. 25:18 [c] Gen. 8:1 [d] Num. 6:5; Judg. 13:5

drink, but have [a]poured out my soul before
the LORD. 16Do not consider your maidservant a [a]wicked woman,[1] for out of the
abundance of my complaint and grief I
have spoken until now."
17Then Eli answered and said, [a]"Go in
peace, and [b]the God of Israel grant your
petition which you have asked of Him."
18And she said, [a]"Let your maidservant
find favor in your sight." So the woman
[b]went her way and ate, and her face was
no longer *sad.*

Samuel Is Born and Dedicated

19Then they rose early in the morning
and worshiped before the LORD, and returned and came to their house at Ramah.
And Elkanah [a]knew Hannah his wife, and
the LORD [b]remembered her. 20So it came
to pass in the process of time that Hannah conceived and bore a son, and called
his name Samuel,[1] *saying,* "Because I have
asked for him from the LORD."
21Now the man Elkanah and all his house
[a]went up to offer to the LORD the yearly sacrifice and his vow. 22But Hannah did not go
up, for she said to her husband, "*Not* until
the child is weaned; then I will [a]take him,
that he may appear before the LORD and
[b]remain there [c]forever."
23So [a]Elkanah her husband said to her,
"Do what seems best to you; wait until you
have weaned him. Only let the LORD establish His[1] word." Then the woman stayed and
nursed her son until she had weaned him.
24Now when she had weaned him, she
[a]took him up with her, with three bulls,[1]
one ephah of flour, and a skin of wine, and
brought him to [b]the house of the LORD in
Shiloh. And the child *was* young. 25Then
they slaughtered a bull, and [a]brought the
child to Eli. 26And she said, "O my lord! [a]As
your soul lives, my lord, I *am* the woman
who stood by you here, praying to the
LORD. 27[a]For this child I prayed, and the
LORD has granted me my petition which I
asked of Him. 28Therefore I also have lent
him to the LORD; as long as he lives he shall
be lent to the LORD." So they [a]worshiped
the LORD there.

Hannah's Prayer
(cf. Luke 1:46–55)

2 And Hannah [a]prayed and said:

[b]"My heart rejoices in the LORD;
[c]My horn[1] is exalted in the LORD.
I smile at my enemies,
Because I [d]rejoice in Your salvation.

2 "No[a] one is holy like the LORD,
For *there is* [b]none besides You,
Nor *is there* any [c]rock like our God.

3 "Talk no more so very proudly;
[a]Let no arrogance come
from your mouth,
For the LORD *is* the God of [b]knowledge;
And by Him actions are weighed.

4 "The[a] bows of the mighty
men *are* broken,
And those who stumbled are
girded with strength.
5 *Those who were* full have hired
themselves out for bread,
And the hungry have ceased *to hunger.*
Even [a]the barren has borne seven,
And [b]she who has many children
has become feeble.

6 "The[a] LORD kills and makes alive;
He brings down to the grave
and brings up.
7 The LORD [a]makes poor
and makes rich;
[b]He brings low and lifts up.
8 [a]He raises the poor from the dust
And lifts the beggar from the ash heap,
[b]To set *them* among princes
And make them inherit
the throne of glory.

1:15 [a] Job 30:16; Ps. 42:4; 62:8; Lam. 2:19 1:16 [a] Deut. 13:13 [1] Literally *daughter of Belial* 1:17 [a] Judg. 18:6; 1 Sam. 25:35; 2 Kin. 5:19; Mark 5:34; Luke 7:50 [b] Ps. 20:3–5 1:18 [a] Gen. 33:15; Ruth 2:13 [b] Prov. 15:13; Eccl. 9:7; Rom. 15:13 1:19 [a] Gen. 4:1 [b] Gen. 21:1; 30:22 1:20 [1] Literally *Heard by God* 1:21 [a] Deut. 12:11; 1 Sam. 1:3 1:22 [a] Luke 2:22 [b] 1 Sam. 1:11, 28 [c] Ex. 21:6 1:23 [a] Num. 30:7, 10, 11 [1] Following Masoretic Text, Targum, and Vulgate; Dead Sea Scrolls, Septuagint, and Syriac read *your.* 1:24 [a] Num. 15:9, 10; Deut. 12:5, 6 [b] Josh. 18:1; 1 Sam. 4:3, 4 [1] Dead Sea Scrolls, Septuagint, and Syriac read *a three-year-old bull.* 1:25 [a] Luke 2:22 1:26 [a] 2 Kin. 2:2, 4, 6; 4:30 1:27 [a] [Matt. 7:7] 1:28 [a] Gen. 24:26, 52 2:1 [a] Phil. 4:6 [b] 1 Sam. 2:1–10; Ps. 97:11, 12; Luke 1:46–55 [c] Ps. 75:10; 89:17, 24; 92:10; 112:9 [d] Ps. 9:14; 13:5; 35:9; Is. 12:2, 3 [1] That is, strength 2:2 [a] Ex. 15:11; Ps. 86:8; Rev. 15:4 [b] Deut. 4:35 [c] Deut. 32:4, 30, 31; 2 Sam. 22:32; Ps. 18:2 2:3 [a] Ps. 94:4 [b] 1 Sam. 16:7 2:4 [a] Ps. 37:15; 46:9 2:5 [a] Ps. 113:9 [b] Is. 54:1; Jer. 15:9 2:6 [a] Deut. 32:39; 2 Kin. 5:7; Job 5:18; [Rev. 1:18] 2:7 [a] Deut. 8:17, 18; Job 1:21 [b] Job 5:11; Ps. 75:7; James 4:10 2:8 [a] Job 42:10–12; Ps. 75:7; 113:7; Luke 1:52 [b] Job 36:7; Ps. 113:8

[c]"For the pillars of the earth
are the LORD's,
And He has set the world upon them.
9 [a]He will guard the feet of His saints,
But the [b]wicked shall be
silent in darkness.

"For by strength no man shall prevail.
10 The adversaries of the LORD
shall be [a]broken in pieces;
[b]From heaven He will thunder
against them.
[c]The LORD will judge the
ends of the earth.

[d]"He will give [e]strength to His king,
And [f]exalt the horn of His anointed."

11Then Elkanah went to his house at Ramah.
But the child ministered to the LORD before Eli the priest.

The Wicked Sons of Eli

12Now the sons of Eli *were* [a]corrupt;[1]
[b]they did not know the LORD. 13And the
priests' custom with the people *was that*
when any man offered a sacrifice, the
priest's servant would come with a three-
pronged fleshhook in his hand while the
meat was boiling. 14Then he would thrust
it into the pan, or kettle, or caldron, or pot;
and the priest would take for himself all
that the fleshhook brought up. So they did
in [a]Shiloh to all the Israelites who came
there. 15Also, before they [a]burned the fat,
the priest's servant would come and say
to the man who sacrificed, "Give meat for
roasting to the priest, for he will not take
boiled meat from you, but raw."

16And *if* the man said to him, "They
should really burn the fat first; *then* you
may take *as much* as your heart desires," he
would then answer him, "*No,* but you must
give *it* now; and if not, I will take *it* by force."

17Therefore the sin of the young men
was very great [a]before the LORD, for men
[b]abhorred the offering of the LORD.

Samuel's Childhood Ministry

18[a]But Samuel ministered before the
LORD, *even as* a child, [b]wearing a linen
ephod. 19Moreover his mother used to make
him a little robe, and bring *it* to him year
by year when she [a]came up with her husband to offer the yearly sacrifice. 20And
Eli [a]would bless Elkanah and his wife, and
say, "The LORD give you descendants from
this woman for the loan that was [b]given
to the LORD." Then they would go to their
own home.

21And the LORD [a]visited Hannah, so that
she conceived and bore three sons and two
daughters. Meanwhile the child Samuel
[b]grew before the LORD.

Prophecy Against Eli's Household

22Now Eli was very old; and he heard
everything his sons did to all Israel,[1] and
how they lay with [a]the women who assembled at the door of the tabernacle of meeting. 23So he said to them, "Why do you do
such things? For I hear of your evil dealings
from all the people. 24No, my sons! For *it*
is not a good report that I hear. You make
the LORD's people transgress. 25If one man
sins against another, [a]God will judge him.
But if a man [b]sins against the LORD, who
will intercede for him?" Nevertheless they
did not heed the voice of their father, [c]be-
cause the LORD desired to kill them.

26And the child Samuel [a]grew in stature,
and [b]in favor both with the LORD and men.

27Then a [a]man of God came to Eli and
said to him, "Thus says the LORD: [b]'Did I not
clearly reveal Myself to the house of your
father when they were in Egypt in Pharaoh's
house? 28Did I not [a]choose him out of all
the tribes of Israel *to be* My priest, to offer
upon My altar, to burn incense, and to wear
an ephod before Me? And [b]did I not give to
the house of your father all the offerings of
the children of Israel made by fire? 29Why
do you [a]kick at My sacrifice and My offering which I have commanded *in My* [b]dwell-
ing place, and honor your sons more than

2:8 [c] Job 38:4–6; Ps. 75:3; 104:5 **2:9** [a] Ps. 37:23, 24; 91:11, 12; 94:18; 121:3; Prov. 3:26; [1 Pet. 1:5] [b] [Rom. 3:19] **2:10** [a] Ex. 15:6; Ps. 2:9 [b] 1 Sam. 7:10; 2 Sam. 22:14, 15; Ps. 18:13, 14 [c] Ps. 96:13; 98:9; [Matt. 25:31, 32] [d] [Matt. 28:18] [e] Ps. 21:1, 7 [f] Ps. 89:24 **2:12** [a] Deut. 13:13 [b] Judg. 2:10; [Rom. 1:28] [1] Literally *sons of Belial* **2:14** [a] 1 Sam. 1:3 **2:15** [a] Lev. 3:3–5, 16 **2:17** [a] Gen. 6:11 [b] [Mal. 2:7–9] **2:18** [a] 1 Sam. 2:11; 3:1 [b] Ex. 28:4 **2:19** [a] 1 Sam. 1:3, 21 **2:20** [a] Gen. 14:19 [b] 1 Sam. 1:11, 27, 28 **2:21** [a] Gen. 21:1 [b] Judg. 13:24; 1 Sam. 2:26; 3:19–21; Luke 1:80; 2:40 **2:22** [a] Ex. 38:8 [1] Following Masoretic Text, Targum, and Vulgate; Dead Sea Scrolls and Septuagint omit the rest of this verse. **2:25** [a] Deut. 1:17; 25:1, 2 [b] Num. 15:30 [c] Josh. 11:20 **2:26** [a] 1 Sam. 2:21 [b] Prov. 3:4 **2:27** [a] Deut. 33:1; Judg. 13:6; 1 Sam. 9:6; 1 Kin. 13:1 [b] Ex. 4:14–16; 12:1 **2:28** [a] Ex. 28:1, 4; Num. 16:5 [b] Lev. 2:3, 10; 6:16; 7:7, 8, 34, 35; Num. 5:9 **2:29** [a] Deut. 32:15 [b] Deut. 12:5; Ps. 26:8

[c]Me, to make yourselves fat with the best
of all the offerings of Israel My people?'
30 Therefore the LORD God of Israel says: [a]'I
said indeed *that* your house and the house
of your father would walk before Me forever.' But now the LORD says: [b]'Far be it
from Me; for those who honor Me I will
honor, and [c]those who despise Me shall be
lightly esteemed. 31 Behold, [a]the days are
coming that I will cut off your arm and the
arm of your father's house, so that there
will not be an old man in your house. 32 And
you will see an enemy *in My* dwelling place,
despite all the good which God does for Israel. And there shall not be [a]an old man in
your house forever. 33 But any of your men
whom I do not cut off from My altar shall
consume your eyes and grieve your heart.
And all the descendants of your house shall
die in the flower of their age. 34 Now this
shall be [a]a sign to you that will come upon
your two sons, on Hophni and Phinehas:
[b]in one day they shall die, both of them.
35 Then [a]I will raise up for Myself a faithful priest *who* shall do according to what
is in My heart and in My mind. [b]I will build
him a sure house, and he shall walk before
[c]My anointed forever. 36 [a]And it shall come
to pass that everyone who is left in your
house will come *and* bow down to him for
a piece of silver and a morsel of bread, and
say, "Please, put me in one of the priestly
positions, that I may eat a piece of bread." '"

Samuel's First Prophecy

3 Now [a]the boy Samuel ministered to the
LORD before Eli. And [b]the word of the
LORD was rare in those days; *there was* no
widespread revelation. 2 And it came to pass
at that time, while Eli *was* lying down in
his place, and when his eyes had begun to
grow [a]so dim that he could not see, 3 and
before [a]the lamp of God went out in the
tabernacle[1] of the LORD where the ark of
God *was,* and while Samuel was lying down,
4 that the LORD called Samuel. And he answered, "Here I am!" 5 So he ran to Eli and
said, "Here I am, for you called me."
And he said, "I did not call; lie down
again." And he went and lay down.
6 Then the LORD called yet again, "Samuel!"
So Samuel arose and went to Eli, and
said, "Here I am, for you called me." He
answered, "I did not call, my son; lie down
again." 7 (Now Samuel [a]did not yet know the
LORD, nor was the word of the LORD yet revealed to him.)
8 And the LORD called Samuel again the
third time. So he arose and went to Eli, and
said, "Here I am, for you did call me."
Then Eli perceived that the LORD had
called the boy. 9 Therefore Eli said to Samuel, "Go, lie down; and it shall be, if He calls
you, that you must say, [a]'Speak, LORD, for
Your servant hears.'" So Samuel went and
lay down in his place.
10 Now the LORD came and stood and
called as at other times, "Samuel! Samuel!"
And Samuel answered, "Speak, for Your
servant hears."
11 Then the LORD said to Samuel: "Behold,
I will do something in Israel [a]at which both
ears of everyone who hears it will tingle.
12 In that day I will perform against Eli [a]all
that I have spoken concerning his house,
from beginning to end. 13 [a]For I have told
him that I will [b]judge his house forever for
the iniquity which he knows, because [c]his
sons made themselves vile, and he [d]did not
restrain them. 14 And therefore I have sworn
to the house of Eli that the iniquity of Eli's
house [a]shall not be atoned for by sacrifice
or offering forever."
15 So Samuel lay down until morning,[1]
and opened the doors of the house of the
LORD. And Samuel was afraid to tell Eli the
vision. 16 Then Eli called Samuel and said,
"Samuel, my son!"
He answered, "Here I am."
17 And he said, "What *is* the word that
the LORD spoke to you? Please do not hide
it from me. [a]God do so to you, and more
also, if you hide anything from me of all the
things that He said to you." 18 Then Samuel
told him everything, and hid nothing from

2:29 [c] Matt. 10:37 **2:30** [a] Ex. 29:9; Num. 25:13 [b] Jer. 18:9, 10 [c] Ps. 91:14; Mal. 2:9–12 **2:31** [a] 1 Sam. 4:11–18; 22:18, 19; 1 Kin. 2:27, 35 **2:32** [a] Zech. 8:4 **2:34** [a] 1 Sam. 10:7–9; 1 Kin. 13:3 [b] 1 Sam. 4:11, 17 **2:35** [a] 1 Kin. 2:35; Ezek. 44:15; [Heb. 2:17; 7:26–28] [b] 2 Sam. 7:11, 27; 1 Kin. 11:38 [c] Ps. 18:50 **2:36** [a] 1 Kin. 2:27 **3:1** [a] 1 Sam. 2:11, 18 [b] Ps. 74:9; Ezek. 7:26; Amos 8:11, 12 **3:2** [a] Gen. 27:1; 48:10; 1 Sam. 4:15 **3:3** [a] Ex. 27:20, 21 [1] Hebrew *heykal,* palace or temple **3:7** [a] 1 Sam. 2:12; Acts 19:2; 1 Cor. 13:11 **3:9** [a] 1 Kin. 2:17 **3:11** [a] 2 Kin. 21:12; Jer. 19:3 **3:12** [a] 1 Sam. 2:27–36; Ezek. 12:25; Luke 21:33 **3:13** [a] 1 Sam. 2:29–31 [b] 1 Sam. 2:22; Ezek. 7:3; 18:30 [c] 1 Sam. 2:12, 17, 22 [d] 1 Sam. 2:23, 25 **3:14** [a] Num. 15:30, 31; Is. 22:14; Heb. 10:4, 26–31 **3:15** [1] Following Masoretic Text, Targum, and Vulgate; Septuagint adds *and he arose in the morning.* **3:17** [a] Ruth 1:17

him. And he said, [a]"It *is* the LORD. Let Him do what seems good to Him."

19So Samuel [a]grew, and [b]the LORD was with him [c]and let none of his words fall to the ground. 20And all Israel [a]from Dan to Beersheba knew that Samuel *had been* established as a prophet of the LORD. 21Then the LORD appeared again in Shiloh. For the LORD revealed Himself to Samuel in Shiloh by [a]the word of the LORD.

4 And the word of Samuel came to all Israel.[1]

The Ark of God Captured

Now Israel went out to battle against the Philistines, and encamped beside [a]Ebenezer; and the Philistines encamped in Aphek. 2Then the [a]Philistines put themselves in battle array against Israel. And when they joined battle, Israel was defeated by the Philistines, who killed about four thousand men of the army in the field. 3And when the people had come into the camp, the elders of Israel said, "Why has the LORD defeated us today before the Philistines? [a]Let us bring the ark of the covenant of the LORD from Shiloh to us, that when it comes among us it may save us from the hand of our enemies." 4So the people sent to Shiloh, that they might bring from there the ark of the covenant of the LORD of hosts, [a]who dwells *between* [b]the cherubim. And the [c]two sons of Eli, Hophni and Phinehas, *were* there with the ark of the covenant of God.

5And when the ark of the covenant of the LORD came into the camp, all Israel shouted so loudly that the earth shook. 6Now when the Philistines heard the noise of the shout, they said, "What *does* the sound of this great shout in the camp of the Hebrews *mean?*" Then they understood that the ark of the LORD had come into the camp. 7So the Philistines were afraid, for they said, "God has come into the camp!" And they said, [a]"Woe to us! For such a thing has never happened before. 8Woe to us! Who will deliver us from the hand of these mighty gods? These *are* the gods who struck the Egyptians with all the plagues in the wilderness. 9[a]Be strong and conduct yourselves like men, you Philistines, that you do not become servants of the Hebrews, [b]as they have been to you. Conduct yourselves like men, and fight!"

10So the Philistines fought, and [a]Israel was defeated, and every man fled to his tent. There was a very great slaughter, and there fell of Israel thirty thousand foot soldiers. 11Also [a]the ark of God was captured; and [b]the two sons of Eli, Hophni and Phinehas, died.

Death of Eli

12Then a man of Benjamin ran from the battle line the same day, and [a]came to Shiloh with his clothes torn and [b]dirt on his head. 13Now when he came, there was Eli, sitting on [a]a seat by the wayside watching,[1] for his heart trembled for the ark of God. And when the man came into the city and told *it,* all the city cried out. 14When Eli heard the noise of the outcry, he said, "What *does* the sound of this tumult *mean?*" And the man came quickly and told Eli. 15Eli was ninety-eight years old, and [a]his eyes were so dim that he could not see.

16Then the man said to Eli, "I *am* he who came from the battle. And I fled today from the battle line."

And he said, [a]"What happened, my son?"

17So the messenger answered and said, "Israel has fled before the Philistines, and there has been a great slaughter among the people. Also your two sons, Hophni and Phinehas, are dead; and the ark of God has been captured."

18Then it happened, when he made mention of the ark of God, that Eli fell off the seat backward by the side of the gate; and his neck was broken and he died, for the man was old and heavy. And he had judged Israel forty years.

3:18 [a] Gen. 24:50; Ex. 34:5–7; Lev. 10:3; Is. 39:8; Acts 5:39 3:19 [a] 1 Sam. 2:21 [b] Gen. 21:22; 28:15; 39:2, 21, 23 [c] 1 Sam. 9:6 3:20 [a] Judg. 20:1 3:21 [a] 1 Sam. 3:1, 4 4:1 [a] 1 Sam. 7:12 [1] Following Masoretic Text and Targum; Septuagint and Vulgate add *And it came to pass in those days that the Philistines gathered themselves together to fight;* Septuagint adds further *against Israel.* 4:2 [a] 1 Sam. 12:9 4:3 [a] Num. 10:35; Josh. 6:6–21 4:4 [a] Ex. 25:18–21; 1 Sam. 6:2; Ps. 80:1 [b] Num. 7:89 [c] 1 Sam. 2:12 4:7 [a] Ex. 15:14 4:9 [a] 1 Cor. 16:13 [b] Judg. 13:1; 1 Sam. 14:21 4:10 [a] Lev. 26:17; Deut. 28:15, 25; 1 Sam. 4:2; 2 Sam. 18:17; 19:8; 2 Kin. 14:12; 2 Chr. 25:22 4:11 [a] 1 Sam. 2:32; Ps. 78:60, 61 [b] 1 Sam. 2:34; Ps. 78:64 4:12 [a] 2 Sam. 1:2 [b] Josh. 7:6; 2 Sam. 13:19; 15:32; Neh. 9:1; Job 2:12 4:13 [a] 1 Sam. 1:9; 4:18 [1] Following Masoretic Text and Vulgate; Septuagint reads *beside the gate watching the road.* 4:15 [a] 1 Sam. 3:2; 1 Kin. 14:4 4:16 [a] 2 Sam. 1:4

Ichabod

19 Now his daughter-in-law, Phinehas' wife,
was with child, *due* to be delivered; and when
she heard the news that the ark of God was
captured, and that her father-in-law and her
husband were dead, she bowed herself and
gave birth, for her labor pains came upon
her. 20 And about the time of her death [a]the
women who stood by her said to her, "Do
not fear, for you have borne a son." But she
did not answer, nor did she regard *it.* 21 Then
she named the child [a]Ichabod,[1] saying, [b]"The
glory has departed from Israel!" because the
ark of God had been captured and because
of her father-in-law and her husband. 22 And
she said, "The glory has departed from Israel, for the ark of God has been captured."

The Philistines and the Ark

5 Then the Philistines took the ark of God
and brought it [a]from Ebenezer to Ashdod. 2 When the Philistines took the ark
of God, they brought it into the house of
[a]Dagon[1] and set it by Dagon. 3 And when
the people of Ashdod arose early in the
morning, there was Dagon, [a]fallen on its
face to the earth before the ark of the LORD.
So they took Dagon and [b]set it in its place
again. 4 And when they arose early the next
morning, there was Dagon, fallen on its
face to the ground before the ark of the
LORD. [a]The head of Dagon and both the
palms of its hands *were* broken off on the
threshold; only Dagon's *torso*[1] was left of it.
5 Therefore neither the priests of Dagon nor
any who come into Dagon's house [a]tread
on the threshold of Dagon in Ashdod to
this day.
6 But the [a]hand of the LORD was heavy
on the people of Ashdod, and He [b]ravaged
them and struck them with [c]tumors,[1] *both*
Ashdod and its [d]territory. 7 And when the
men of Ashdod saw how *it was,* they said,
"The ark of the [a]God of Israel must not remain with us, for His hand is harsh toward
us and Dagon our god." 8 Therefore they sent
and gathered to themselves all the [a]lords of
the Philistines, and said, "What shall we do
with the ark of the God of Israel?"
And they answered, "Let the ark of the
God of Israel be carried away to [b]Gath." So
they carried the ark of the God of Israel
away. 9 So it was, after they had carried it
away, that [a]the hand of the LORD was against
the city with a very great destruction; and
He struck the men of the city, both small
and great, and tumors broke out on them.
10 Therefore they sent the ark of God to
Ekron. So it was, as the ark of God came to
Ekron, that the Ekronites cried out, saying,
"They have brought the ark of the God of
Israel to us, to kill us and our people!" 11 So
they sent and gathered together all the lords
of the Philistines, and said, "Send away the
ark of the God of Israel, and let it go back to
its own place, so that it does not kill us and
our people." For there was a deadly destruction throughout all the city; the hand of God
was very heavy there. 12 And the men who
did not die were stricken with the tumors,
and the [a]cry of the city went up to heaven.

The Ark Returned to Israel

6 Now the ark of the LORD was in the
country of the Philistines seven
months. 2 And the Philistines [a]called for
the priests and the diviners, saying, "What
shall we do with the ark of the LORD? Tell us
how we should send it to its place."
3 So they said, "If you send away the ark
of the God of Israel, do not send it [a]empty;
but by all means return *it* to Him *with* [b]a
trespass offering. Then you will be healed,
and it will be known to you why His hand
is not removed from you."
4 Then they said, "What *is* the trespass
offering which we shall return to Him?"
They answered, [a]"Five golden tumors
and five golden rats, *according to* the number of the lords of the Philistines. For the
same plague *was* on all of you and on your
lords. 5 Therefore you shall make images of
your tumors and images of your rats that
[a]ravage the land, and you shall [b]give glory

4:20 [a] Gen. 35:16–19 4:21 [a] 1 Sam. 14:3 [b] Ps. 26:8; 78:61; [Jer. 2:11] [1] Literally *Inglorious* 5:1 [a] 1 Sam. 4:1; 7:12 5:2 [a] Judg. 16:23–30; 1 Chr. 10:8–10 [1] A Philistine idol 5:3 [a] Is. 19:1; 46:1, 2 [b] Is. 46:7 5:4 [a] Jer. 50:2; Ezek. 6:4, 6; Mic. 1:7 [1] Following Septuagint, Syriac, Targum, and Vulgate; Masoretic Text reads *Dagon.* 5:5 [a] Zeph. 1:9 5:6 [a] Ex. 9:3; Deut. 2:15; 1 Sam. 5:7; 7:13; Ps. 32:4; 145:20; 147:6 [b] 1 Sam. 6:5 [c] Deut. 28:27; Ps. 78:66 [d] Josh. 15:46, 47 [1] Probably bubonic plague. Septuagint and Vulgate add here *And in the midst of their land rats sprang up, and there was a great death panic in the city.* 5:7 [a] 1 Sam. 6:5 5:8 [a] 1 Sam. 6:4 [b] Josh. 11:22 5:9 [a] Deut. 2:15; 1 Sam. 5:11; 7:13; 12:15 5:12 [a] 1 Sam. 9:16; Jer. 14:2 6:2 [a] Gen. 41:8; Ex. 7:11; Is. 2:6; 47:13; Dan. 2:2; 5:7 6:3 [a] Ex. 23:15; Deut. 16:16 [b] Lev. 5:15, 16 6:4 [a] 1 Sam. 5:6, 9, 12; 6:17 6:5 [a] 1 Sam. 5:6 [b] Josh. 7:19; 1 Chr. 16:28, 29; Is. 42:12; Jer. 13:16; Mal. 2:2; Rev. 14:7

to the God of Israel; perhaps He will [c]lighten
His hand from you, from [d]your gods, and
from your land. 6Why then do you harden
your hearts [a]as the Egyptians and Pharaoh
hardened their hearts? When He did mighty
things among them, [b]did they not let the
people go, that they might depart? 7Now
therefore, make [a]a new cart, take two milk
cows [b]which have never been yoked, and
hitch the cows to the cart; and take their
calves home, away from them. 8Then take
the ark of the LORD and set it on the cart;
and put [a]the articles of gold which you are
returning to Him *as* a trespass offering in a
chest by its side. Then send it away, and let
it go. 9And watch: if it goes up the road to
its own territory, to [a]Beth Shemesh, *then* He
has done us this great evil. But if not, then
[b]we shall know that *it is* not His hand *that*
struck us—it happened to us by chance."
10Then the men did so; they took two
milk cows and hitched them to the cart,
and shut up their calves at home. 11And
they set the ark of the LORD on the cart,
and the chest with the gold rats and the
images of their tumors. 12Then the cows
headed straight for the road to Beth Shemesh, *and* went along the [a]highway, lowing
as they went, and did not turn aside to the
right hand or the left. And the lords of the
Philistines went after them to the border
of Beth Shemesh.
13Now *the people of* Beth Shemesh *were*
reaping their [a]wheat harvest in the valley;
and they lifted their eyes and saw the ark,
and rejoiced to see *it.* 14Then the cart came
into the field of Joshua of Beth Shemesh,
and stood there; a large stone *was* there. So
they split the wood of the cart and offered
the cows as a burnt offering to the LORD.
15The Levites took down the ark of the LORD
and the chest that *was* with it, in which *were*
the articles of gold, and put *them* on the
large stone. Then the men of Beth Shemesh
offered burnt offerings and made sacrifices
the same day to the LORD. 16So when [a]the
five lords of the Philistines had seen *it,* they
returned to Ekron the same day.
17[a]These *are* the golden tumors which
the Philistines returned *as* a trespass offering to the LORD: one for Ashdod, one
for Gaza, one for Ashkelon, one for [b]Gath,
one for Ekron; 18and the golden rats, *according to* the number of all the cities of the
Philistines *belonging* to the five lords, *both*
fortified cities and country villages, even
as far as the large *stone of* Abel on which
they set the ark of the LORD, *which stone
remains* to this day in the field of Joshua
of Beth Shemesh.
19Then [a]He struck the men of Beth Shemesh, because they had looked into the ark
of the LORD. He [b]struck fifty thousand and
seventy men[1] of the people, and the people
lamented because the LORD had struck the
people with a great slaughter.

The Ark at Kirjath Jearim

20And the men of Beth Shemesh said,
[a]"Who is able to stand before this holy LORD
God? And to whom shall it go up from us?"
21So they sent messengers to the inhabitants of [a]Kirjath Jearim, saying, "The Philistines have brought back the ark of the
LORD; come down *and* take it up with you."
7 Then the men of [a]Kirjath Jearim came
and took the ark of the LORD, and
brought it into the house of [b]Abinadab on
the hill, and [c]consecrated Eleazar his son
to keep the ark of the LORD.

Samuel Judges Israel

2So it was that the ark remained in Kirjath Jearim a long time; it was there twenty
years. And all the house of Israel lamented
after the LORD.
3Then Samuel spoke to all the house of
Israel, saying, "If you [a]return to the LORD
with all your hearts, *then* [b]put away the foreign gods and the [c]Ashtoreths[1] from among
you, and [d]prepare your hearts for the LORD,
and [e]serve Him only; and He will deliver you
from the hand of the Philistines." 4So the
children of Israel put away the [a]Baals and
the Ashtoreths,[1] and served the LORD only.
5And Samuel said, [a]"Gather all Israel to

6:5 [c] 1 Sam. 5:6, 11; Ps. 39:10 [d] 1 Sam. 5:3, 4, 7 6:6 [a] Ex. 7:13; 8:15; 9:34; 14:17 [b] Ex. 12:31 6:7 [a] 2 Sam. 6:3 [b] Num. 19:2; Deut. 21:3, 4 6:8 [a] 1 Sam. 6:4, 5 6:9 [a] Josh. 15:10; 21:16 [b] 1 Sam. 6:3 6:12 [a] Num. 20:19 6:13 [a] 1 Sam. 12:17 6:16 [a] Josh. 13:3; Judg. 3:3 6:17 [a] 1 Sam. 6:4 [b] 1 Sam. 5:8 6:19 [a] Ex. 19:21; Num. 4:5, 15, 16, 20 [b] 2 Sam. 6:7 [1] Or *He struck seventy men of the people and fifty oxen of a man* 6:20 [a] Lev. 11:44, 45; Ps. 24:3, 4; Mal. 3:2; Rev. 6:17 6:21 [a] Josh. 9:17; 15:9, 60; 18:14; Judg. 18:12; 1 Chr. 13:5, 6 7:1 [a] 1 Sam. 6:21; Ps. 132:6 [b] 2 Sam. 6:3, 4 [c] Lev. 21:8 7:3 [a] Deut. 30:2–10; 1 Kin. 8:48; Is. 55:7; Hos. 6:1; Joel 2:12–14 [b] Gen. 35:2; Josh. 24:14, 23; Judg. 10:16 [c] Judg. 2:13; 1 Sam. 31:10 [d] 2 Chr. 30:19; Job 11:13 [e] Deut. 6:13; 10:20; 13:4; Josh. 24:14; Matt. 4:10; Luke 4:8 [1] Canaanite goddesses 7:4 [a] Judg. 2:11; 10:16 [1] Canaanite goddesses 7:5 [a] Judg. 10:17; 20:1; 1 Sam. 10:17

Mizpah, and [b]I will pray to the LORD for
you." 6So they gathered together at Mizpah, [a]drew water, and poured *it* out before
the LORD. And they [b]fasted that day, and
said there, [c]"We have sinned against the
LORD." And Samuel judged the children of
Israel at Mizpah.
7Now when the Philistines heard that the
children of Israel had gathered together at
Mizpah, the lords of the Philistines went
up against Israel. And when the children
of Israel heard *of it,* they were afraid of the
Philistines. 8So the children of Israel said
to Samuel, [a]"Do not cease to cry out to the
LORD our God for us, that He may save us
from the hand of the Philistines."
9And Samuel took a [a]suckling lamb
and offered *it as* a whole burnt offering to

RELEASE // BELIEVE IN PRAYER

Simple, Yet Powerful

1 Samuel 7:7–8 // Now when the Philistines heard that the children of Israel had gathered together at Mizpah, the lords of the Philistines went up against Israel. And when the children of Israel heard of it, they were afraid of the Philistines. So the children of Israel said to Samuel, "Do not cease to cry out to the LORD our God for us, that He may save us from the hand of the Philistines."

Summary Message // While God can sometimes feel far away, He assures us through Scripture that He is always near. How? Through the simple yet powerful act of prayer.

Samuel's story reminds us that despite the circumstances and regardless of the odds, prayer can move God to intercede in our lives and make what seems impossible, possible. The question is, do we believe that to be true? If so, then our belief in prayer is the key to unlocking the power of God to effect change in us and in our world.

Practical Application // Have you ever felt like everything was stacked against you? That no matter how hard you tried, no matter what you did, the inevitable outcome was sure to be negative? Whatever the situation, moments like these can leave us feeling too hopeless to hope. Even more, faith can begin to feel like a fruitless exercise. Yet, throughout Scripture, God reminds us that He has provided a way to touch His heart and move Him to act on our behalf, no matter the odds: prayer.

In 1 Samuel 7, we learn the Israelites were confronting seemingly insurmountable odds. They faced an enemy that was determined to destroy them and steal everything they had (see vv. 6–7). However, the people of Israel did not initially rally the troops. Their first action was not to pick up their weapons and fight. Rather, they understood the assignment in that moment and urged Samuel to pray (see v. 8). Through Samuel's story, God reminds us of a few important truths:

- God hears and answers our prayers (see v. 9).
- God will exhibit His power in response to our prayers (see v. 10).
- With God, there is no enemy too great and no situation too insurmountable (see v. 11).

No matter the circumstance or situation, we serve a God who not only cares about our challenges but also wants to intervene on our behalf. The simple act of prayer (speaking to, spending time with, crying out to God) profoundly aligns us with what God already desires to do: love us! Our belief in prayer is simply our acknowledgment of God's love and power to effect change in us and in our world. The act of praying is our invitation for God to give us new life and new breath, to bring healing and wholeness, and even to work miracles wherever and whenever we need them most.

Fervent Prayer // Heavenly Father, the fact that You invite us to bring our cares and concerns, joys and hurts, and all that we experience to You daily astounds us. Thank You for loving us more than we could ever deserve. Thank You for wanting to be invited to go before us and do for us according to Your will. And thank You for the power that exists within the smallest of prayers—power to move You, to touch Your heart, to invite You to do what only You can do and bring healing and wholeness to a world in need. In Jesus' name we pray. Amen.

7:5[b] 1 Sam. 12:17–19 7:6 [a] 2 Sam. 14:14 [b] Judg. 20:26; Neh. 9:1, 2; Dan. 9:3–5; Joel 2:12 [c] Judg. 10:10; 1 Sam. 12:10; 1 Kin. 8:47; Ps. 106:6 7:8 [a] 1 Sam. 12:19–24; Is. 37:4 7:9 [a] Lev. 22:27

the LORD. Then [b]Samuel cried out to the
LORD for Israel, and the LORD answered
him. 10Now as Samuel was offering up the
burnt offering, the Philistines drew near to
battle against Israel. [a]But the LORD thundered with a loud thunder upon the Philistines that day, and so confused them that
they were overcome before Israel. 11And the
men of Israel went out of Mizpah and pursued the Philistines, and drove them back
as far as below Beth Car. 12Then Samuel
[a]took a stone and set *it* up between Mizpah
and Shen, and called its name Ebenezer,[1]
saying, "Thus far the LORD has helped us."

13[a]So the Philistines were subdued, and
they [b]did not come anymore into the territory of Israel. And the hand of the LORD
was against the Philistines all the days of
Samuel. 14Then the cities which the Philistines had taken from Israel were restored
to Israel, from Ekron to Gath; and Israel recovered its territory from the hands of the
Philistines. Also there was peace between
Israel and the Amorites.

15And Samuel [a]judged Israel all the days
of his life. 16He went from year to year on
a circuit to Bethel, Gilgal, and Mizpah, and
judged Israel in all those places. 17But [a]he
always returned to Ramah, for his home
was there. There he judged Israel, and there
he [b]built an altar to the LORD.

Israel Demands a King

8 Now it came to pass when Samuel was
[a]old that he [b]made his [c]sons judges over
Israel. 2The name of his firstborn was Joel,
and the name of his second, Abijah; *they
were* judges in Beersheba. 3But his sons [a]did
not walk in his ways; they turned aside [b]af-
ter dishonest gain, [c]took bribes, and perverted justice.

4Then all the elders of Israel gathered together and came to Samuel at Ramah, 5and
said to him, "Look, you are old, and your
sons do not walk in your ways. Now [a]make
us a king to judge us like all the nations."

6But the thing [a]displeased Samuel when
they said, "Give us a king to judge us." So
Samuel [b]prayed to the LORD. 7And the LORD
said to Samuel, "Heed the voice of the people in all that they say to you; for [a]they have
not rejected you, but [b]they have rejected
Me, that I should not reign over them. 8Ac-
cording to all the works which they have
done since the day that I brought them up
out of Egypt, even to this day—with which
they have forsaken Me and served other
gods—so they are doing to you also. 9Now
therefore, heed their voice. However, you
shall solemnly forewarn them, and [a]show
them the behavior of the king who will
reign over them."

10So Samuel told all the words of the
LORD to the people who asked him for a
king. 11And he said, [a]"This will be the behavior of the king who will reign over you:
He will take your [b]sons and appoint *them*
for his own [c]chariots and *to be* his horsemen, and *some* will run before his chariots. 12He will [a]appoint captains over his
thousands and captains over his fifties, *will
set some* to plow his ground and reap his
harvest, and *some* to make his weapons of
war and equipment for his chariots. 13He
will take your daughters *to be* perfumers,
cooks, and bakers. 14And [a]he will take the
best of your fields, your vineyards, and your
olive groves, and give *them* to his servants.
15He will take a tenth of your grain and your
vintage, and give it to his officers and servants. 16And he will take your male servants, your female servants, your finest
young men,[1] and your donkeys, and put
them to his work. 17He will take a tenth of
your sheep. And you will be his servants.
18And you will cry out in that day because
of your king whom you have chosen for
yourselves, and the LORD [a]will not hear
you in that day."

19Nevertheless the people [a]refused to
obey the voice of Samuel; and they said,
"No, but we will have a king over us, 20that
we also may be [a]like all the nations, and
that our king may judge us and go out before us and fight our battles."

21And Samuel heard all the words of the

7:9 [b] 1 Sam. 12:18; Ps. 99:6; Jer. 15:1 7:10 [a] Josh. 10:10; 2 Sam. 22:14, 15; Ps. 18:13, 14 7:12 [a] Gen. 28:18; 35:14; Josh. 4:9; 24:26 [1] Literally *Stone of Help* 7:13 [a] Judg. 13:1 [b] 1 Sam. 13:5 7:15 [a] 1 Sam. 12:11 7:17 [a] 1 Sam. 8:4 [b] Judg. 21:4 8:1 [a] 1 Sam. 12:2 [b] Deut. 16:18, 19; 2 Chr. 19:5 [c] Judg. 10:4 8:3 [a] Jer. 22:15–17 [b] Ex. 18:21 [c] Ex. 23:6–8; Deut. 16:19; 1 Sam. 12:3 8:5 [a] Deut. 17:14, 15; Hos. 13:10, 11; Acts 13:21 8:6 [a] 1 Sam. 12:17 [b] 1 Sam. 7:9 8:7 [a] Ex. 16:8 [b] 1 Sam. 10:19 8:9 [a] 1 Sam. 8:11–18 8:11 [a] Deut. 17:14–20 [b] 1 Sam. 14:52 [c] 2 Sam. 15:1 8:12 [a] 1 Sam. 22:7 8:14 [a] 1 Kin. 21:7; [Ezek. 46:18] 8:16 [1] Septuagint reads *cattle.* 8:18 [a] Prov. 1:25–28; Is. 1:15; Mic. 3:4 8:19 [a] Is. 66:4; Jer. 44:16 8:20 [a] 1 Sam. 8:5

1 SAMUEL 8:19

I AM SAMUEL

Nevertheless the people refused to obey the voice of Samuel; and they said, "No, but we will have a king over us." 1 Samuel 8:19

I am Samuel, a prophet of God and the last of the judges. One night, as a child, God called to me. I thought it was Eli, my teacher and the high priest. But after hearing the voice a few times and questioning Eli, he told me the Lord was speaking to me and that I should answer and listen. All the rest of my life, I heard from the Lord and told the people what God said.

The people trusted me and knew I was a prophet of God because everything I said came true. Yet, they still worshiped other gods even after I warned them not to. As a result, the Lord allowed them to be defeated by the Philistines, who took the ark of the covenant. When it was returned, the people asked me what had caused God's anger. I explained that God would deliver them from the Philistines if they would turn their hearts to the Lord and deny other gods. They obeyed and defeated the Philistines in battle.

Near the end of my life, the people came to me asking for a king to rule over them instead of continuing to be led by judges. They wanted to be like other nations. I asked the Lord, and He granted their request. God assured me their desire for a king was not a rejection of me or the judges; it was a rejection of Him as Lord. They did not trust God to care for them and preferred a mere man to rule them. Their denial of God's sovereignty resulted in over two hundred years of being ruled by human kings, most of whom brought evil and distress to the people.

†

Just because you get what you ask for does not make it God's highest and best for you. Unlike the people in Samuel's time, we can petition the Lord directly. However, we should not ask for what we want from God as much as what God wants for us.

people, and he repeated them in the hearing of the LORD. 22So the LORD said to Samuel, [a]"Heed their voice, and make them a
king."

And Samuel said to the men of Israel, "Every man go to his city."

Saul Chosen to Be King

9 There was a man of Benjamin whose
name *was* [a]Kish the son of Abiel, the
son of Zeror, the son of Bechorath, the son
of Aphiah, a Benjamite, a mighty man of
power. 2And he had a choice and handsome
son whose name *was* Saul. *There was* not a
more handsome person than he among the
children of Israel. [a]From his shoulders upward *he was* taller than any of the people.
3Now the donkeys of Kish, Saul's father,
were lost. And Kish said to his son Saul,
"Please take one of the servants with you,
and arise, go and look for the donkeys."
4So he passed through the mountains of
Ephraim and through the land of [a]Sha-
lisha, but they did not find *them.* Then
they passed through the land of Shaalim,
and *they were* not *there.* Then he passed
through the land of the Benjamites, but
they did not find *them.*
5When they had come to the land of
[a]Zuph, Saul said to his servant who *was*
with him, "Come, let [b]us return, lest my
father cease *caring* about the donkeys and
become worried about us."
6And he said to him, "Look now, *there is*
in this city [a]a man of God, and *he is* an honorable man; [b]all that he says surely comes

8:22 [a] 1 Sam. 8:7; Hos. 13:11 9:1 [a] 1 Sam. 14:51; 1 Chr. 8:33; 9:36–39 9:2 [a] 1 Sam. 10:23 9:4 [a] 2 Kin. 4:42
9:5 [a] 1 Sam. 1:1 [b] 1 Sam. 10:2 9:6 [a] Deut. 33:1; 1 Kin. 13:1; 2 Kin. 5:8 [b] 1 Sam. 3:19

to pass. So let us go there; perhaps he can
show us the way that we should go."
7Then Saul said to his servant, "But look,
if we go, [a]what shall we bring the man? For
the bread in our vessels is all gone, and
there is no present to bring to the man of
God. What do we have?"
8And the servant answered Saul again
and said, "Look, I have here at hand one-
fourth of a shekel of silver. I will give *that*
to the man of God, to tell us our way." 9(Formerly in Israel, when a man [a]went to inquire of God, he spoke thus: "Come, let us
go to the seer"; for *he who is* now *called* a
prophet was formerly called [b]a seer.)
10Then Saul said to his servant, "Well
said; come, let us go." So they went to the
city where the man of God *was.*
11As they went up the hill to the city,
[a]they met some young women going out
to draw water, and said to them, "Is the seer
here?"
12And they answered them and said,
"Yes, there he is, just ahead of you. Hurry
now; for today he came to this city, because
[a]there is a sacrifice of the people today [b]on
the high place. 13As soon as you come into
the city, you will surely find him before he
goes up to the high place to eat. For the people will not eat until he comes, because he
must bless the sacrifice; afterward those
who are invited will eat. Now therefore, go
up, for about this time you will find him."
14So they went up to the city. As they were
coming into the city, there was Samuel,
coming out toward them on his way up to
the high place.
15[a]Now the LORD had told Samuel in his
ear the day before Saul came, saying, 16"Tomorrow about this time [a]I will send you

BELIEVE IN PRAYER

INHALE

I am really trying to grow in my walk with God. I feel closer to Him than I have ever before. But just being honest, I think I ask for too much. My prayers seem all about my needs. I know He cares about my needs, but I want my prayers to be real. I just don't know how that looks. I pray when I need something. Also, I pray to thank God when He's answered. Is there something more? Is there anything else I need to be saying to God?

EXHALE

One of the most amazing things about our relationship with God is the fantastic line of communication we have with Him. The line is always open, and there are no busy signals. You see, we receive a great gift when we say yes to Jesus—we get complete access to God.

Now, it is true that some of us treat God like He's Santa. We recite long lists of what we want but mention very little of anything else. Our prayers can easily become all about us and not about anyone else or even Him. God wants to know our desires. He is a loving Father. But He is also the Most High God, the Creator and Sustainer of life. So, prayer is also designed to draw us to what He wants. God loves all people, so we should pray for others. God is glorious, so we should praise Him for who He is. And at the same time, you are right to thank Him for what He's already done.

But above all, we cannot forget that prayer is really just talking with God as we would talk with a friend. We can simply talk about how we feel and what we are thinking. We see this in 1 Samuel 9:15–16 in the way God and Samuel just talked: "Now the LORD had told Samuel in his ear the day before Saul came, saying, 'Tomorrow about this time I will send you a man from the land of Benjamin.'" This is a simple conversation. So, don't make prayer harder than it is. Talk with God. He's listening.

9:7 [a] Judg. 6:18; 13:17; 1 Kin. 14:3; 2 Kin. 4:42; 8:8 9:9 [a] Gen. 25:22 [b] 2 Sam. 24:11; 2 Kin. 17:13; 1 Chr. 26:28; 29:29; 2 Chr. 16:7, 10; Is. 30:10; Amos 7:12 9:11 [a] Gen. 24:11, 15; 29:8, 9; Ex. 2:16 9:12 [a] Gen. 31:54; 1 Sam. 16:2 [b] 1 Sam. 7:17; 10:5; 1 Kin. 3:2 9:15 [a] 1 Sam. 15:1 9:16 [a] Deut. 17:15

a man from the land of Benjamin, [b]and you shall anoint him commander over My people Israel, that he may save My people from the hand of the Philistines; for I have [c]looked upon My people, because their cry has come to Me."

17 So when Samuel saw Saul, the LORD said to him, [a]"There he is, the man of whom I spoke to you. This one shall reign over My people." 18 Then Saul drew near to Samuel in the gate, and said, "Please tell me, where *is* the seer's house?"

19 Samuel answered Saul and said, "I *am* the seer. Go up before me to the high place, for you shall eat with me today; and tomorrow I will let you go and will tell you all that *is* in your heart. 20 But as for [a]your donkeys that were lost three days ago, do not be anxious about them, for they have been found. And on whom [b]*is* all the desire of Israel? *Is it* not on you and on all your father's house?"

21 And Saul answered and said, [a]"*Am* I not a Benjamite, of the [b]smallest of the tribes of Israel, and [c]my family the least of all the families of the tribe[1] of Benjamin? Why then do you speak like this to me?"

22 Now Samuel took Saul and his servant and brought them into the hall, and had them sit in the place of honor among those who were invited; there *were* about thirty persons. 23 And Samuel said to the cook, "Bring the portion which I gave you, of which I said to you, 'Set it apart.'" 24 So the cook took up [a]the thigh with its upper part and set *it* before Saul. And *Samuel* said, "Here it is, what was kept back. *It* was set apart for you. Eat; for until this time it has been kept for you, since I said I invited the people." So Saul ate with Samuel that day.

25 When they had come down from the high place into the city, *Samuel* spoke with Saul on [a]the top of the house.[1] 26 They arose early; and it was about the dawning of the day that Samuel called to Saul on the top of the house, saying, "Get up, that I may send you on your way." And Saul arose, and both of them went outside, he and Samuel.

Saul Anointed King

27 As they were going down to the outskirts of the city, Samuel said to Saul, "Tell the servant to go on ahead of us." And he went on. "But you stand here awhile, that I may announce to you the word of God."

10 Then [a]Samuel took a flask of oil and poured *it* on his head, [b]and kissed him and said: "*Is it* not because [c]the LORD has anointed you commander over [d]His inheritance?[1] 2 When you have departed from me today, you will find two men by [a]Rachel's tomb in the territory of Benjamin [b]at Zelzah; and they will say to you, 'The donkeys which you went to look for have been found. And now your father has ceased caring about the donkeys and is worrying about [c]you, saying, "What shall I do about my son?"' 3 Then you shall go on forward from there and come to the terebinth tree of Tabor. There three men going up [a]to God at Bethel will meet you, one carrying three young goats, another carrying three loaves of bread, and another carrying a skin of wine. 4 And they will greet you and give you two *loaves* of bread, which you shall receive from their hands. 5 After that you shall come to the hill of God [a]where the Philistine garrison *is*. And it will happen, when you have come there to the city, that you will meet a group of prophets coming down [b]from the high place with a stringed instrument, a tambourine, a flute, and a harp before them; [c]and they will be prophesying. 6 Then [a]the Spirit of the LORD will come upon you, and [b]you will prophesy with them and be turned into another man. 7 And let it be, when these [a]signs come to you, *that* you do as the occasion demands; for [b]God *is* with you. 8 You shall go down before me [a]to Gilgal; and surely I will come

---

9:16 [b] 1 Sam. 10:1 [c] Ex. 2:23–25; 3:7, 9 **9:17** [a] 1 Sam. 16:12; Hos. 13:11 **9:20** [a] 1 Sam. 9:3 [b] 1 Sam. 8:5, 19; 12:13 **9:21** [a] 1 Sam. 15:17 [b] Judg. 20:46–48; Ps. 68:27 [c] Judg. 6:15 [1] Literally *tribes* **9:24** [a] Ex. 29:22, 27; Lev. 7:32, 33; Num. 18:18; Ezek. 24:4 **9:25** [a] Deut. 22:8; 2 Sam. 11:2; Luke 5:19; Acts 10:9 [1] Following Masoretic Text and Targum; Septuagint omits *He spoke with Saul on the top of the house;* Septuagint and Vulgate add *And he prepared a bed for Saul on the top of the house, and he slept.* **10:1** [a] Ex. 30:23–33; 1 Sam. 9:16; 16:13; 2 Kin. 9:3, 6 [b] Ps. 2:12 [c] 2 Sam. 5:2; Acts 13:21 [d] Ex. 34:9; Deut. 32:9; Ps. 78:71 [1] Following Masoretic Text, Targum, and Vulgate; Septuagint reads *His people Israel; and you shall rule the people of the Lord;* Septuagint and Vulgate add *And you shall deliver His people from the hands of their enemies all around them. And this shall be a sign to you, that God has anointed you to be a prince.* **10:2** [a] Gen. 35:16–20; 48:7 [b] Josh. 18:28 [c] 1 Sam. 9:3–5 **10:3** [a] Gen. 28:22; 35:1, 3, 7 **10:5** [a] 1 Sam. 13:2, 3 [b] 1 Sam. 19:12, 20; 2 Kin. 2:3, 5, 15 [c] Ex. 15:20, 21; 2 Kin. 3:15; 1 Chr. 25:1–6; 1 Cor. 14:1 **10:6** [a] Num. 11:25, 29; Judg. 14:6; 1 Sam. 16:13 [b] 1 Sam. 10:10; 19:23, 24 **10:7** [a] Ex. 4:8; Luke 2:12 [b] Josh. 1:5; Judg. 6:12; 1 Sam. 3:19; [Heb. 13:5] **10:8** [a] 1 Sam. 11:14, 15; 13:8

down to you to offer burnt offerings *and* make sacrifices of peace offerings. [b]Seven days you shall wait, till I come to you and show you what you should do."

9 So it was, when he had turned his back to go from Samuel, that God gave him another heart; and all those signs came to pass that day. 10 [a]When they came there to the hill, there was [b]a group of prophets to meet him; then the Spirit of God came upon him, and he prophesied among them. 11 And it happened, when all who knew him formerly saw that he indeed prophesied among the prophets, that the people said to one another, "What *is* this *that* has come upon the son of Kish? [a]*Is* Saul also among the prophets?" 12 Then a man from there answered and said, "But [a]who *is* their father?" Therefore it became a proverb: "*Is* Saul also among the prophets?" 13 And when he had finished prophesying, he went to the high place.

14 Then Saul's [a]uncle said to him and his servant, "Where did you go?"

So he said, "To look for the donkeys. When we saw that *they were* nowhere *to be found,* we went to Samuel."

15 And Saul's uncle said, "Tell me, please, what Samuel said to you."

16 So Saul said to his uncle, "He told us plainly that the donkeys had been [a]found." But about the matter of the kingdom, he did not tell him what Samuel had said.

Saul Proclaimed King

17 Then Samuel called the people together [a]to the LORD [b]at Mizpah, 18 and said to the children of Israel, [a]"Thus says the LORD God of Israel: 'I brought up Israel out of Egypt, and delivered you from the hand of the Egyptians *and* from the hand of all kingdoms and from those who oppressed you.' 19 [a]But you have today rejected your God, who Himself saved you from all your adversities and your tribulations; and you have said to Him, 'No, set a king over us!' Now therefore, present yourselves before the LORD by your tribes and by your clans."[1]

20 And when Samuel had [a]caused all the tribes of Israel to come near, the tribe of Benjamin was chosen. 21 When he had caused the tribe of Benjamin to come near by their families, the family of Matri was chosen. And Saul the son of Kish was chosen. But when they sought him, he could not be found. 22 Therefore they [a]inquired of the LORD further, "Has the man come here yet?"

And the LORD answered, "There he is, hidden among the equipment."

23 So they ran and brought him from there; and when he stood among the people, [a]he was taller than any of the people from his shoulders upward. 24 And Samuel said to all the people, "Do you see him [a]whom the LORD has chosen, that *there is* no one like him among all the people?"

So all the people shouted and said, [b]"Long live the king!"

25 Then Samuel explained to the people [a]the behavior of royalty, and wrote *it* in a book and laid *it* up before the LORD. And Samuel sent all the people away, every man to his house. 26 And Saul also went home [a]to Gibeah; and valiant *men* went with him, whose hearts God had touched. 27 [a]But some [b]rebels said, "How can this man save us?" So they despised him, [c]and brought him no presents. But he held his peace.

Saul Saves Jabesh Gilead

11 Then [a]Nahash the Ammonite came up and encamped against [b]Jabesh Gilead; and all the men of Jabesh said to Nahash, [c]"Make a covenant with us, and we will serve you."

2 And Nahash the Ammonite answered them, "On this *condition* I will make *a covenant* with you, that I may put out all your right eyes, and bring [a]reproach on all Israel."

3 Then the elders of Jabesh said to him, "Hold off for seven days, that we may send messengers to all the territory of Israel. And then, if *there is* no one to save us, we will come out to you."

10:8 [b] 1 Sam. 13:8–10 **10:10** [a] 1 Sam. 10:5 [b] 1 Sam. 19:20 **10:11** [a] 1 Sam. 19:24; Amos 7:14, 15; Matt. 13:54–57; John 7:15; Acts 4:13 **10:12** [a] John 5:30, 36 **10:14** [a] 1 Sam. 14:50 **10:16** [a] 1 Sam. 9:20 **10:17** [a] Judg. 20:1 [b] 1 Sam. 7:5, 6 **10:18** [a] Judg. 6:8, 9; 1 Sam. 8:8; 12:6, 8 **10:19** [a] 1 Sam. 8:7, 19; 12:12 [1] Literally *thousands* **10:20** [a] Acts 1:24, 26 **10:22** [a] 1 Sam. 23:2, 4, 10, 11 **10:23** [a] 1 Sam. 9:2 **10:24** [a] Deut. 17:15; 1 Sam. 9:16; 2 Sam. 21:6 [b] 1 Kin. 1:25, 39 **10:25** [a] Deut. 17:14–20; 1 Sam. 8:11–18 **10:26** [a] Judg. 20:14 **10:27** [a] 1 Sam. 11:12 [b] Deut. 13:13; 1 Sam. 25:17 [c] 2 Sam. 8:2; 1 Kin. 4:21; 10:25; 2 Chr. 17:5; Matt. 2:11 **11:1** [a] 1 Sam. 12:12 [b] Judg. 21:8; 1 Sam. 31:11 [c] Gen. 26:28; 1 Kin. 20:34; Job 41:4; Ezek. 17:13 **11:2** [a] Gen. 34:14; 1 Sam. 17:26; Ps. 44:13

[4]So the messengers came [a]to Gibeah of
Saul and told the news in the hearing of
the people. And [b]all the people lifted up
their voices and wept. [5]Now there was Saul,
coming behind the herd from the field; and
Saul said, "What *troubles* the people, that
they weep?" And they told him the words
of the men of Jabesh. [6][a]Then the Spirit of
God came upon Saul when he heard this
news, and his anger was greatly aroused.
[7]So he took a yoke of oxen and [a]cut them
in pieces, and sent *them* throughout all the
territory of Israel by the hands of messengers, saying, [b]"Whoever does not go out
with Saul and Samuel to battle, so it shall
be done to his oxen."

And the fear of the LORD fell on the people, and they came out with one consent.
[8]When he numbered them in [a]Bezek, the
children [b]of Israel were three hundred
thousand, and the men of Judah thirty
thousand. [9]And they said to the messengers who came, "Thus you shall say to the
men of Jabesh Gilead: 'Tomorrow, by *the
time* the sun is hot, you shall have help.'"
Then the messengers came and reported
it to the men of Jabesh, and they were glad.
[10]Therefore the men of Jabesh said, "Tomorrow we will come out to you, and you
may do with us whatever seems good to
you."

[11]So it was, on the next day, that [a]Saul
put the people [b]in three companies; and
they came into the midst of the camp in
the morning watch, and killed Ammonites
until the heat of the day. And it happened
that those who survived were scattered,
so that no two of them were left together.

[12]Then the people said to Samuel, [a]"Who
is he who said, 'Shall Saul reign over us?'
[b]Bring the men, that we may put them to
death."

[13]But Saul said, [a]"Not a man shall be put
to death this day, for today [b]the LORD has
accomplished salvation in Israel."

[14]Then Samuel said to the people, "Come,
let us go [a]to Gilgal and renew the kingdom
there." [15]So all the people went to Gilgal,
and there they made Saul king [a]before the
LORD in Gilgal. [b]There they made sacrifices of peace offerings before the LORD,
and there Saul and all the men of Israel
rejoiced greatly.

Samuel's Address at Saul's Coronation

12 Now Samuel said to all Israel: "Indeed I have heeded [a]your voice in all
that you said to me, and [b]have made a king
over you. [2]And now here is the king, [a]walk-
ing before you; [b]and I am old and grayheaded, and look, my sons *are* with you. I
have walked before you from my childhood
to this day. [3]Here I am. Witness against me
before the LORD and before [a]His anointed:
[b]Whose ox have I taken, or whose donkey
have I taken, or whom have I cheated?
Whom have I oppressed, or from whose
hand have I received *any* [c]bribe with which
to [d]blind my eyes? I will restore *it* to you."

[4]And they said, [a]"You have not cheated
us or oppressed us, nor have you taken anything from any man's hand."

[5]Then he said to them, "The LORD *is*
witness against you, and His anointed *is*
witness this day, [a]that you have not found
anything [b]in my hand."

And they answered, "*He is* witness."

[6]Then Samuel said to the people, [a]"*It is*
the LORD who raised up Moses and Aaron,
and who brought your fathers up from the
land of Egypt. [7]Now therefore, stand still,
that I may [a]reason with you before the
LORD concerning all the [b]righteous acts
of the LORD which He did to you and your
fathers: [8][a]When Jacob had gone into Egypt,[1]
and your fathers [b]cried out to the LORD,
then the LORD [c]sent Moses and Aaron,
who brought your fathers out of Egypt and
made them dwell in this place. [9]And when
they [a]forgot the LORD their God, He sold
them into the hand of [b]Sisera, commander
of the army of Hazor, into the hand of the

11:4 [a] 1 Sam. 10:26; 15:34; 2 Sam. 21:6 [b] Gen. 27:38; Judg. 2:4; 20:23, 26; 21:2; 1 Sam. 30:4 **11:6** [a] Judg. 3:10; 6:34; 11:29; 13:25; 14:6; 1 Sam. 10:10; 16:13 **11:7** [a] Judg. 19:29 [b] Judg. 21:5, 8, 10 **11:8** [a] Judg. 1:5 [b] 2 Sam. 24:9 **11:11** [a] 1 Sam. 31:11 [b] Judg. 7:16, 20 **11:12** [a] 1 Sam. 10:27 [b] Luke 19:27 **11:13** [a] 1 Sam. 10:27; 2 Sam. 19:22 [b] Ex. 14:13, 30; 1 Sam. 19:5 **11:14** [a] 1 Sam. 7:16; 10:8 **11:15** [a] 1 Sam. 10:17 [b] Josh. 8:31; 1 Sam. 10:8 **12:1** [a] 1 Sam. 8:5, 7, 9, 20, 22 [b] 1 Sam. 10:24; 11:14, 15 **12:2** [a] Num. 27:17; 1 Sam. 8:20 [b] 1 Sam. 8:1, 5 **12:3** [a] 1 Sam. 10:1; 24:6; 2 Sam. 1:14, 16 [b] Num. 16:15; Acts 20:33; 1 Thess. 2:5 [c] Ex. 23:8 [d] Deut. 16:19 **12:4** [a] Lev. 19:13 **12:5** [a] John 18:38; Acts 23:9; 24:20 [b] Ex. 22:4 **12:6** [a] Ex. 6:26; Mic. 6:4 **12:7** [a] Is. 1:18; Ezek. 20:35; Mic. 6:1–5 [b] Judg. 5:11; Ps. 103:6 **12:8** [a] Gen. 46:5, 6; Ps. 105:23 [b] Ex. 2:23–25 [c] Ex. 3:10; 4:14–16 [1] Following Masoretic Text, Targum, and Vulgate; Septuagint adds *and the Egyptians afflicted them.* **12:9** [a] Deut. 32:18; Judg. 3:7 [b] Judg. 4:2

[c]Philistines, and into the hand of the king
of [d]Moab; and they fought against them.
10Then they cried out to the LORD, and said,
[a]'We have sinned, because we have forsaken
the LORD [b]and served the Baals and Ashtoreths;[1] but now deliver us from the hand of
our enemies, and we will serve You.' 11And
the LORD sent Jerubbaal,[1] Bedan,[2] [a]Jeph-
thah, and [b]Samuel,[3] and delivered you out
of the hand of your enemies on every side;
and you dwelt in safety. 12And when you
saw that [a]Nahash king of the Ammonites
came against you, [b]you said to me, 'No, but
a king shall reign over us,' when [c]the LORD
your God *was* your king.
13"Now therefore, [a]here is the king
[b]whom you have chosen *and* whom you
have desired. And take note, [c]the LORD has
set a king over you. 14If you [a]fear the LORD
and serve Him and obey His voice, and do
not rebel against the commandment of
the LORD, then both you and the king who
reigns over you will continue following
the LORD your God. 15However, if you do
[a]not obey the voice of the LORD, but [b]rebel
against the commandment of the LORD,
then the hand of the LORD will be against
you, as *it was* against your fathers.

#OXYGEN

1 SAMUEL 12:15

Believe in Prayer

We need to be people of prayer. But prayer is not a one-way conversation. We speak, but so does God. And when He does, listen! Pay attention and let the Lord direct your path.

Walk with Him, **breathe**, and **believe in prayer**.

16"Now therefore, [a]stand and see this
great thing which the LORD will do before
your eyes: 17*Is* today not the [a]wheat harvest? [b]I will call to the LORD, and He will
send thunder and [c]rain, that you may perceive and see that [d]your wickedness *is* great,
which you have done in the sight of the
LORD, in asking a king for yourselves."
18So Samuel called to the LORD, and the
LORD sent thunder and rain that day; and
[a]all the people greatly feared the LORD and
Samuel.
19And all the people said to Samuel,
[a]"Pray for your servants to the LORD your
God, that we may not die; for we have added
to all our sins the evil of asking a king for
ourselves."
20Then Samuel said to the people, "Do
not fear. You have done all this wickedness; [a]yet do not turn aside from following the LORD, but serve the LORD with all
your heart. 21And [a]do not turn aside; [b]for
then you would go after empty things which
cannot profit or deliver, for they *are* nothing. 22For [a]the LORD will not forsake [b]His
people, [c]for His great name's sake, because
[d]it has pleased the LORD to make you His
people. 23Moreover, as for me, far be it from
me that I should sin against the LORD [a]in
ceasing to pray for you; but [b]I will teach you
the [c]good and the right way. 24[a]Only fear the
LORD, and serve Him in truth with all your
heart; for [b]consider what [c]great things He
has done for you. 25But if you still do wickedly, [a]you shall be swept away, [b]both you
and your king."

Saul's Unlawful Sacrifice

13 Saul reigned one year; and when he
had reigned two years over Israel,[1]
2Saul chose for himself three thousand
men of Israel. Two thousand were with
Saul in [a]Michmash and in the mountains
of Bethel, and a thousand were with [b]Jona-
than in [c]Gibeah of Benjamin. The rest of the
people he sent away, every man to his tent.

12:9 [c] Judg. 3:31; 10:7; 13:1 [d] Judg. 3:12–30 **12:10** [a] Judg. 10:10 [b] Judg. 2:13; 3:7 [1] Canaanite goddesses **12:11** [a] Judg. 11:1 [b] 1 Sam. 7:13 [1] Syriac reads *Deborah;* Targum reads *Gideon.* [2] Septuagint and Syriac read *Barak;* Targum reads *Simson.* [3] Syriac reads *Simson.* **12:12** [a] 1 Sam. 11:1, 2 [b] 1 Sam. 8:5, 19, 20 [c] Judg. 8:23; 1 Sam. 8:7; Ps. 59:13 **12:13** [a] 1 Sam. 10:24 [b] 1 Sam. 8:5; 12:17, 19 [c] Hos. 13:11 **12:14** [a] Josh. 24:14 **12:15** [a] Deut. 28:15 [b] Lev. 26:14, 15; Josh. 24:20; Is. 1:20 **12:16** [a] Ex. 14:13, 31 **12:17** [a] Gen. 30:14 [b] Josh. 10:12; 1 Sam. 7:9, 10; [James 5:16–18] [c] Ezra 10:9 [d] 1 Sam. 8:7 **12:18** [a] Ex. 14:31 **12:19** [a] Ex. 9:28; 1 Sam. 7:8; [James 5:15; 1 John 5:16] **12:20** [a] Deut. 11:16 **12:21** [a] 2 Chr. 25:15 [b] Is. 41:29; Jer. 16:19; Hab. 2:18; 1 Cor. 8:4 **12:22** [a] Deut. 31:6; 1 Kin. 6:13 [b] Is. 43:21 [c] Ex. 32:12; Num. 14:13; Josh. 7:9; Ps. 106:8; Jer. 14:21 [d] Deut. 7:6–11; 1 Pet. 2:9 **12:23** [a] Acts 12:5; Rom. 1:9; Col. 1:9; 2 Tim. 1:3 [b] Ps. 34:11; Prov. 4:11 [c] 1 Kin. 8:36 **12:24** [a] Eccl. 12:13 [b] Is. 5:12 [c] Deut. 10:21 **12:25** [a] Josh. 24:20 [b] Deut. 28:36 **13:1** [1] The Hebrew is difficult (compare 2 Samuel 5:4; 2 Kings 14:2; see also 2 Samuel 2:10; Acts 13:21). **13:2** [a] 1 Sam. 14:5, 31 [b] 1 Sam. 14:1 [c] 1 Sam. 10:26

3 And Jonathan attacked [a]the garrison of
the Philistines that *was* in [b]Geba, and the
Philistines heard *of it*. Then Saul blew the
trumpet throughout all the land, saying, "Let
the Hebrews hear!" 4 Now all Israel heard it
said *that* Saul had attacked a garrison of the
Philistines, and *that* Israel had also become
an abomination to the Philistines. And the
people were called together to Saul at Gilgal.
5 Then the Philistines gathered together
to fight with Israel, thirty[1] thousand chariots and six thousand horsemen, and people [a]as the sand which *is* on the seashore
in multitude. And they came up and encamped in Michmash, to the east of [b]Beth
Aven. 6 When the men of Israel saw that
they were in danger (for the people were
distressed), then the people [a]hid in caves,
in thickets, in rocks, in holes, and in pits.
7 And *some of* the Hebrews crossed over the
Jordan to the [a]land of Gad and Gilead.
As for Saul, he *was* still in Gilgal, and
all the people followed him trembling.
8 [a]Then he waited seven days, according
to the time set by Samuel. But Samuel did
not come to Gilgal; and the people were
scattered from him. 9 So Saul said, "Bring
a burnt offering and peace offerings here
to me." And he offered the burnt offering.
10 Now it happened, as soon as he had finished presenting the burnt offering, that
Samuel came; and Saul went out to meet
him, that he might greet him.
11 And Samuel said, "What have you
done?"
Saul said, "When I saw that the people
were scattered from me, and *that* you did
not come within the days appointed, and
that the Philistines gathered together at
Michmash, 12 then I said, 'The Philistines
will now come down on me at Gilgal, and
I have not made supplication to the LORD.'
Therefore I felt compelled, and offered a
burnt offering."
13 And Samuel said to Saul, [a]"You have
done foolishly. [b]You have not kept the commandment of the LORD your God, which
He commanded you. For now the LORD
would have established your kingdom over
Israel forever. 14 [a]But now your kingdom
shall not continue. [b]The LORD has sought
for Himself a man [c]after His own heart, and
the LORD has commanded him *to be* commander over His people, because you have
[d]not kept what the LORD commanded you."
15 Then Samuel arose and went up from
Gilgal to Gibeah of Benjamin.[1] And Saul
numbered the people present with him,
[a]about six hundred men.

No Weapons for the Army

16 Saul, Jonathan his son, and the people
present with them remained in Gibeah of
Benjamin. But the Philistines encamped
in Michmash. 17 Then raiders came out of
the camp of the Philistines in three companies. One company turned onto the road
to [a]Ophrah, to the land of Shual, 18 another
company turned to the road *to* [a]Beth Horon, and another company turned *to* the
road of the border that overlooks the Valley
of [b]Zeboim toward the wilderness.
19 Now [a]there was no blacksmith to be
found throughout all the land of Israel,
for the Philistines said, "Lest the Hebrews
make swords or spears." 20 But all the Israelites would go down to the Philistines to
sharpen each man's plowshare, his mat-
tock, his ax, and his sickle; 21 and the charge
for a sharpening was a pim[1] for the plowshares, the mattocks, the forks, and the
axes, and to set the points of the goads.
22 So it came about, on the day of battle, that
[a]there was neither sword nor spear found in
the hand of any of the people who *were* with
Saul and Jonathan. But they were found
with Saul and Jonathan his son.
23 [a]And the garrison of the Philistines
went out to the pass of Michmash.

Jonathan Defeats the Philistines

14 Now it happened one day that Jonathan the son of Saul said to the young
man who bore his armor, "Come, let us go
over to the Philistines' garrison that *is* on
the other side." But he did not tell his father.

13:3 [a] 1 Sam. 10:5 [b] 2 Sam. 5:25 13:5 [a] Judg. 7:12 [b] Josh. 7:2; 1 Sam. 14:23 [1] Following Masoretic Text, Septuagint, Targum, and Vulgate; Syriac and some manuscripts of the Septuagint read *three*. 13:6 [a] Judg. 6:2; 1 Sam. 14:11 13:7 [a] Num. 32:1–42 13:8 [a] 1 Sam. 10:8 13:13 [a] 2 Chr. 16:9 [b] 1 Sam. 15:11, 22, 28 13:14 [a] 1 Sam. 15:28; 31:6 [b] 1 Sam. 16:1 [c] Ps. 89:20; Acts 7:46; 13:22 [d] 1 Sam. 15:11, 19 13:15 [a] 1 Sam. 13:2, 6, 7; 14:2 [1] Following Masoretic Text and Targum; Septuagint and Vulgate add *And the rest of the people went up after Saul to meet the people who fought against them, going from Gilgal to Gibeah in the hill of Benjamin.* 13:17 [a] Josh. 18:23 13:18 [a] Josh. 16:3; 18:13, 14 [b] Gen. 14:2; Neh. 11:34 13:19 [a] Judg. 5:8; 2 Kin. 24:14; Jer. 24:1; 29:2 13:21 [1] About two-thirds shekel weight 13:22 [a] Judg. 5:8 13:23 [a] 1 Sam. 14:1, 4

2And Saul was sitting in the outskirts of [a]Gibeah under a pomegranate tree which *is* in Migron. The people who *were* with him *were* about six hundred men. 3[a]Ahijah the son of Ahitub, [b]Ichabod's brother, the son of Phinehas, the son of Eli, the LORD's priest in Shiloh, was [c]wearing an ephod. But the people did not know that Jonathan had gone.

4Between the passes, by which Jonathan sought to go over [a]to the Philistines' garrison, *there was* a sharp rock on one side and a sharp rock on the other side. And the name of one *was* Bozez, and the name of the other Seneh. 5The front of one faced northward opposite Michmash, and the other southward opposite Gibeah.

6Then Jonathan said to the young man who bore his armor, "Come, let us go over to the garrison of these [a]uncircumcised; it may be that the LORD will work for us. For nothing restrains the LORD [b]from saving by many or by few."

7So his armorbearer said to him, "Do all that is in your heart. Go then; here I am with you, according to your heart."

8Then Jonathan said, "Very well, let us cross over to *these* men, and we will show ourselves to them. 9If they say thus to us, 'Wait until we come to you,' then we will stand still in our place and not go up to them. 10But if they say thus, 'Come up to us,' then we will go up. For the LORD has delivered them into our hand, and [a]this *will be* a sign to us."

11So both of them showed themselves to the garrison of the Philistines. And the Philistines said, "Look, the Hebrews are coming out of the holes where they have [a]hidden." 12Then the men of the garrison called to Jonathan and his armorbearer, and said, "Come up to us, and we will show you something."

Jonathan said to his armorbearer, "Come up after me, for the LORD has delivered them into the hand of Israel." 13And Jonathan climbed up on his hands and knees with his armorbearer after him; and they [a]fell before Jonathan. And as he came after him, his armorbearer killed them. 14That first slaughter which Jonathan and his armorbearer made was about twenty men within about half an acre of land.[1]

15And [a]there was trembling in the camp, in the field, and among all the people. The garrison and [b]the raiders also trembled; and the earth quaked, so that it was [c]a very great trembling. 16Now the watchmen of Saul in Gibeah of Benjamin looked, and *there* was the multitude, melting away; and they [a]went here and there. 17Then Saul said to the people who *were* with him, "Now call the roll and see who has gone from us." And when they had called the roll, surprisingly, Jonathan and his armorbearer *were* not *there.* 18And Saul said to Ahijah, "Bring the ark[1] of God here" (for at that time the ark[2] of God was with the children of Israel). 19Now it happened, while Saul [a]talked to the priest, that the noise which *was* in the camp of the Philistines continued to increase; so Saul said to the priest, "Withdraw your hand." 20Then Saul and all the people who *were* with him assembled, and they went to the battle; and indeed [a]every man's sword was against his neighbor, *and there was* very great confusion. 21Moreover the Hebrews *who* were with the Philistines before that time, who went up with them into the camp *from the* surrounding *country,* they also joined the Israelites who *were* with Saul and Jonathan. 22Likewise all the men of Israel who [a]had hidden in the mountains of Ephraim, *when* they heard that the Philistines fled, they also followed hard after them in the battle. 23[a]So the LORD saved Israel that day, and the battle shifted [b]to Beth Aven.

Saul's Rash Oath

24And the men of Israel were distressed that day, for Saul had [a]placed the people under oath, saying, "Cursed *is* the man who eats *any* food until evening, before I have taken vengeance on my enemies." So none of the people tasted food. 25[a]Now all *the people* of the land came to a forest; and

14:2 [a] 1 Sam. 13:15, 16 14:3 [a] 1 Sam. 22:9, 11, 20 [b] 1 Sam. 4:21 [c] 1 Sam. 2:28 14:4 [a] 1 Sam. 13:23 14:6 [a] 1 Sam. 17:26, 36; Jer. 9:25, 26 [b] Judg. 7:4, 7; 1 Sam. 17:46, 47; 2 Chr. 14:11; [Ps. 115:3; 135:6; Zech. 4:6; Matt. 19:26; Rom. 8:31] 14:10 [a] Gen. 24:14; Judg. 6:36–40 14:11 [a] 1 Sam. 13:6; 14:22 14:13 [a] Lev. 26:8; Josh. 23:10 14:14 [1] Literally *half the area plowed by a yoke* (of oxen in a day) 14:15 [a] Deut. 28:7; 2 Kin. 7:6, 7; Job 18:11 [b] 1 Sam. 13:17 [c] Gen. 35:5 14:16 [a] 1 Sam. 14:20 14:18 [1] Following Masoretic Text, Targum, and Vulgate; Septuagint reads *ephod.* [2] Following Masoretic Text, Targum, and Vulgate; Septuagint reads *ephod.* 14:19 [a] Num. 27:21 14:20 [a] Judg. 7:22; 2 Chr. 20:23 14:22 [a] 1 Sam. 13:6 14:23 [a] Ex. 14:30; 2 Chr. 32:22; Hos. 1:7 [b] 1 Sam. 13:5 14:24 [a] Josh. 6:26 14:25 [a] Deut. 9:28; Matt. 3:5

there was [b]honey on the ground. 26And
when the people had come into the woods,
there was the honey, dripping; but no one
put his hand to his mouth, for the people feared the oath. 27But Jonathan had
not heard his father charge the people
with the oath; therefore he stretched out
the end of the rod that *was* in his hand
and dipped it in a honeycomb, and put his
hand to his mouth; and his countenance
brightened. 28Then one of the people said,
"Your father strictly charged the people
with an oath, saying, 'Cursed *is* the man
who eats food this day.'" And the people
were faint.

29But Jonathan said, "My father has
troubled the land. Look now, how my countenance has brightened because I tasted a
little of this honey. 30How much better if
the people had eaten freely today of the
spoil of their enemies which they found!
For now would there not have been a much
greater slaughter among the Philistines?"

31Now they had driven back the Philistines that day from Michmash to Aijalon.
So the people were very faint. 32And the
people rushed on the spoil, and took sheep,
oxen, and calves, and slaughtered *them* on
the ground; and the people ate *them* [a]with
the blood. 33Then they told Saul, saying,
"Look, the people are sinning against the
LORD by eating with the blood!"

So he said, "You have dealt treacherously; roll a large stone to me this day."
34Then Saul said, "Disperse yourselves
among the people, and say to them, 'Bring
me here every man's ox and every man's
sheep, slaughter *them* here, and eat; and do
not sin against the LORD by eating with the
blood.'" So every one of the people brought
his ox with him that night, and slaughtered
it there. 35Then Saul [a]built an altar to the
LORD. This was the first altar that he built
to the LORD.

36Now Saul said, "Let us go down after
the Philistines by night, and plunder them
until the morning light; and let us not leave
a man of them."

And they said, "Do whatever seems good
to you."

Then the priest said, "Let us draw near
to God here."

37So Saul [a]asked counsel of God, "Shall I
go down after the Philistines? Will You deliver them into the hand of Israel?" But [b]He
did not answer him that day. 38And Saul
said, [a]"Come over here, all you chiefs of the
people, and know and see what this sin was
today. 39For [a]*as* the LORD lives, who saves
Israel, though it be in Jonathan my son, he
shall surely die." But not a man among all
the people answered him. 40Then he said to
all Israel, "You be on one side, and my son
Jonathan and I will be on the other side."

And the people said to Saul, "Do what
seems good to you."

41Therefore Saul said to the LORD God
of Israel, [a]"Give a perfect *lot*."[1] [b]So Saul and
Jonathan were taken, but the people es-
caped. 42And Saul said, "Cast *lots* between
my son Jonathan and me." So Jonathan was
taken. 43Then Saul said to Jonathan, [a]"Tell
me what you have done."

And Jonathan told him, and said, [b]"I
only tasted a little honey with the end of
the rod that *was* in my hand. So now I must
die!"

44Saul answered, [a]"God do so and more
also; [b]for you shall surely die, Jonathan."

45But the people said to Saul, "Shall Jonathan die, who has accomplished this great
deliverance in Israel? Certainly not! [a]*As* the
LORD lives, not one hair of his head shall
fall to the ground, for he has worked [b]with
God this day." So the people rescued Jonathan, and he did not die.

46Then Saul returned from pursuing the
Philistines, and the Philistines went to their
own place.

Saul's Continuing Wars

47So Saul established his sovereignty
over Israel, and fought against all his enemies on every side, against Moab, against
the people of [a]Ammon, against Edom,
against the kings of [b]Zobah, and against

14:25 [b] Ex. 3:8; Num. 13:27; Matt. 3:4 14:32 [a] Gen. 9:4; Lev. 3:17; 17:10–14; 19:26; Deut. 12:16, 23, 24; Acts 15:20 14:35 [a] 1 Sam. 7:12, 17; 2 Sam. 24:25 14:37 [a] Judg. 20:18 [b] 1 Sam. 28:6 14:38 [a] Josh. 7:14; 1 Sam. 10:19 14:39 [a] 1 Sam. 14:24, 44; 2 Sam. 12:5 14:41 [a] Prov. 16:33; Acts 1:24–26 [b] Josh. 7:16; 1 Sam. 10:20, 21 [1] Following Masoretic Text and Targum; Septuagint and Vulgate read *Why do You not answer Your servant today? If the injustice is with me or Jonathan my son, O LORD God of Israel, give proof; and if You say it is with Your people Israel, give holiness.* 14:43 [a] Josh. 7:19 [b] 1 Sam. 14:27 14:44 [a] Ruth 1:17; 1 Sam. 25:22 [b] 1 Sam. 14:39 14:45 [a] 2 Sam. 14:11; 1 Kin. 1:52; Luke 21:18; Acts 27:34 [b] [2 Cor. 6:1; Phil. 2:12, 13] 14:47 [a] 1 Sam. 11:1–13 [b] 2 Sam. 10:6

the Philistines. Wherever he turned, he harassed *them.*[1] 48And he gathered an army and [a]attacked the Amalekites, and delivered Israel from the hands of those who plundered them.

49[a]The sons of Saul were Jonathan, Jishui,[1] and Malchishua. And the names of his two daughters *were these:* the name of the firstborn Merab, and the name of the younger [b]Michal. 50The name of Saul's wife *was* Ahinoam the daughter of Ahimaaz. And the name of the commander of his army *was* Abner the son of Ner, Saul's [a]uncle. 51[a]Kish *was* the father of Saul, and Ner the father of Abner *was* the son of Abiel.

52Now there was fierce war with the Philistines all the days of Saul. And when Saul saw any strong man or any valiant man, [a]he took him for himself.

Saul Spares King Agag

15 Samuel also said to Saul, [a]"The LORD sent me to anoint you king over His people, over Israel. Now therefore, heed the voice of the words of the LORD. 2Thus says the LORD of hosts: 'I will punish Amalek *for* what he did to Israel, [a]how he ambushed him on the way when he came up from Egypt. 3Now go and [a]attack Amalek, and [b]utterly destroy all that they have, and do not spare them. But kill both man and woman, infant and nursing child, ox and sheep, camel and donkey.' "

4So Saul gathered the people together and numbered them in Telaim, two hundred thousand foot soldiers and ten thousand men of Judah. 5And Saul came to a city of Amalek, and lay in wait in the valley.

6Then Saul said to [a]the Kenites, [b]"Go, depart, get down from among the Amalekites, lest I destroy you with them. For [c]you showed kindness to all the children of Israel when they came up out of Egypt." So the Kenites departed from among the Amalekites. 7[a]And Saul attacked the Amalekites, from [b]Havilah all the way to [c]Shur, which is east of Egypt. 8[a]He also took Agag king of the Amalekites alive, and [b]utterly destroyed all the people with the edge of the sword. 9But Saul and the people [a]spared Agag and the best of the sheep, the oxen, the fatlings, the lambs, and all *that was* good, and were unwilling to utterly destroy them. But everything despised and worthless, that they utterly destroyed.

Saul Rejected as King

10Now the word of the LORD came to Samuel, saying, 11[a]"I greatly regret that I have set up Saul *as* king, for he has [b]turned back from following Me, [c]and has not performed My commandments." And it [d]grieved Samuel, and he cried out to the LORD all night. 12So when Samuel rose early in the morning to meet Saul, it was told Samuel, saying, "Saul went to [a]Carmel, and indeed, he set up a monument for himself; and he has gone on around, passed by, and gone down to Gilgal." 13Then Samuel went to Saul, and Saul said to him, [a]"Blessed *are* you of the LORD! I have performed the commandment of the LORD."

14But Samuel said, "What then *is* this bleating of the sheep in my ears, and the lowing of the oxen which I hear?"

15And Saul said, "They have brought them from the Amalekites; [a]for the people spared the best of the sheep and the oxen, to sacrifice to the LORD your God; and the rest we have utterly destroyed."

16Then Samuel said to Saul, "Be quiet! And I will tell you what the LORD said to me last night."

And he said to him, "Speak on."

17So Samuel said, [a]"When you *were* little in your own eyes, *were* you not head of the tribes of Israel? And did not the LORD anoint you king over Israel? 18Now the LORD sent you on a mission, and said, 'Go, and utterly destroy the sinners, the Amalekites, and fight against them until they are consumed.' 19Why then did you not obey the voice of the LORD? Why did you swoop down on the spoil, and do evil in the sight of the LORD?"

14:47 [1] Septuagint and Vulgate read *prospered.* 14:48 [a] Ex. 17:16; 1 Sam. 15:3–7 14:49 [a] 1 Sam. 31:2; 1 Chr. 8:33 [b] 1 Sam. 18:17–20, 27; 19:12 [1] Called *Abinadab* in 1 Chronicles 8:33 and 9:39 14:50 [a] 1 Sam. 10:14 14:51 [a] 1 Sam. 9:1, 21 14:52 [a] 1 Sam. 8:11 15:1 [a] 1 Sam. 9:16; 10:1 15:2 [a] Ex. 17:8, 14; Num. 24:20; Deut. 25:17–19 15:3 [a] Deut. 25:19 [b] Lev. 27:28, 29; Num. 24:20; Deut. 20:16–18; Josh. 6:17–21 15:6 [a] Num. 24:21; Judg. 1:16; 4:11–22; 1 Chr. 2:55 [b] Gen. 18:25; 19:12, 14; Rev. 18:4 [c] Ex. 18:10, 19; Num. 10:29, 32 15:7 [a] 1 Sam. 14:48 [b] Gen. 2:11; 25:17, 18 [c] Gen. 16:7; Ex. 15:22; 1 Sam. 27:8 15:8 [a] 1 Sam. 15:32, 33 [b] 1 Sam. 27:8, 9 15:9 [a] 1 Sam. 15:3, 15, 19 15:11 [a] Gen. 6:6, 7; 1 Sam. 15:35; 2 Sam. 24:16 [b] Josh. 22:16; 1 Kin. 9:6 [c] 1 Sam. 13:13; 15:3, 9 [d] 1 Sam. 15:35; 16:1 15:12 [a] Josh. 15:55; 1 Sam. 25:2 15:13 [a] Gen. 14:19; Judg. 17:2; Ruth 3:10; 2 Sam. 2:5 15:15 [a] [Gen. 3:12, 13; Ex. 32:22, 23]; 1 Sam. 15:9, 21; [Prov. 28:13] 15:17 [a] 1 Sam. 9:21; 10:22

20And Saul said to Samuel, [a]"But I have
obeyed the voice of the LORD, and gone
on the mission on which the LORD sent
me, and brought back Agag king of Amalek; I have utterly destroyed the Amalekites. 21[a]But the people took of the plunder,
sheep and oxen, the best of the things
which should have been utterly destroyed,
to sacrifice to the LORD your God in Gilgal."
22So Samuel said:

[a]"Has the LORD *as great* delight in
burnt offerings and sacrifices,
As in obeying the voice of the LORD?
Behold, [b]to obey is better
than sacrifice,
And to heed than the fat of rams.
23 For rebellion *is as* the sin of witchcraft,
And stubbornness *is as*
iniquity and idolatry.
Because you have rejected
the word of the LORD,
[a]He also has rejected you
from *being* king."

24[a]Then Saul said to Samuel, "I have
sinned, for I have transgressed the commandment of the LORD and your words,
because I [b]feared the people and obeyed
their voice. 25Now therefore, please pardon my sin, and return with me, that I may
worship the LORD."
26But Samuel said to Saul, "I will not return with you, [a]for you have rejected the
word of the LORD, and the LORD has rejected you from being king over Israel."
27And as Samuel turned around to go
away, [a]*Saul* seized the edge of his robe,
and it tore. 28So Samuel said to him, [a]"The
LORD has torn the kingdom of Israel from
you today, and has given it to a neighbor of
yours, *who is* better than you. 29And also the
Strength of Israel [a]will not lie nor relent.
For He *is* not a man, that He should relent."
30Then he said, "I have sinned; *yet*
[a]honor me now, please, before the elders
of my people and before Israel, and return
with me, that I may worship the LORD your
God." 31So Samuel turned back after Saul,
and Saul worshiped the LORD.
32Then Samuel said, "Bring Agag king of
the Amalekites here to me." So Agag came
to him cautiously.
And Agag said, "Surely the bitterness of
death is past."
33But Samuel said, [a]"As your sword
has made women childless, so shall your
mother be childless among women." And
Samuel hacked Agag in pieces before the
LORD in Gilgal.
34Then Samuel went to [a]Ramah, and Saul
went up to his house at [b]Gibeah of Saul.
35And [a]Samuel went no more to see Saul
until the day of his death. Nevertheless
Samuel mourned for Saul, and the LORD
regretted that He had made Saul king over
Israel.

David Anointed King

16 Now the LORD said to Samuel, [a]"How
long will you mourn for Saul, seeing
I have rejected him from reigning over Israel? [b]Fill your horn with oil, and go; I am
sending you to [c]Jesse the Bethlehemite.
For [d]I have provided Myself a king among
his sons."
2And Samuel said, "How can I go? If Saul
hears *it,* he will kill me."
But the LORD said, "Take a heifer with
you, and say, [a]'I have come to sacrifice to
the LORD.' 3Then invite Jesse to the sacrifice, and I will show you what you shall
do; you shall anoint for Me the one I name
to you."
4So Samuel did what the LORD said, and
went to Bethlehem. And the elders of the
town [a]trembled at his coming, and said,
[b]"Do you come peaceably?"
5And he said, "Peaceably; I have come to
sacrifice to the LORD. [a]Sanctify yourselves,
and come with me to the sacrifice." Then
he consecrated Jesse and his sons, and invited them to the sacrifice.
6So it was, when they came, that he
looked at [a]Eliab and [b]said, "Surely the
LORD's anointed *is* before Him!"

15:20 [a] 1 Sam. 15:13; [Prov. 28:13] 15:21 [a] 1 Sam. 15:15 15:22 [a] Ps. 50:8, 9; 51:16, 17; [Prov. 21:3; Is. 1:11–17; Jer. 7:22, 23; Mic. 6:6–8; Heb. 10:4–10] [b] [Eccl. 5:1; Hos. 6:6; Matt. 5:24; 9:13; 12:7; Mark 12:33] 15:23 [a] 1 Sam. 13:14; 16:1 15:24 [a] Num. 22:34; Josh. 7:20; 1 Sam. 26:21; 2 Sam. 12:13; Ps. 51:4 [b] [Ex. 23:2; Prov. 29:25; Is. 51:12, 13] 15:26 [a] 1 Sam. 2:30 15:27 [a] 1 Kin. 11:30, 31 15:28 [a] 1 Sam. 28:17, 18; 1 Kin. 11:31 15:29 [a] Num. 23:19; Ezek. 24:14; 2 Tim. 2:13; Titus 1:2 15:30 [a] [John 5:44; 12:43] 15:33 [a] [Gen. 9:6]; Num. 14:45; Judg. 1:7; [Matt. 7:2] 15:34 [a] 1 Sam. 7:17 [b] 1 Sam. 11:4 15:35 [a] 1 Sam. 19:24 16:1 [a] 1 Sam. 15:23, 35 [b] 1 Sam. 9:16; 10:1; 2 Kin. 9:1 [c] Ruth 4:18–22 [d] Ps. 78:70, 71; Acts 13:22 16:2 [a] 1 Sam. 9:12 16:4 [a] 1 Sam. 21:1 [b] 1 Kin. 2:13; 2 Kin. 9:22 16:5 [a] Gen. 35:2; Ex. 19:10 16:6 [a] 1 Sam. 17:13, 28 [b] 1 Kin. 12:26

7But the LORD said to Samuel, [a]"Do not
look at his appearance or at his physical
stature, because I have refused him. [b]For
the LORD does not *see* as man sees;[1] for man
[c]looks at the outward appearance, but the
LORD looks at the [d]heart."
8So Jesse called Abinadab, and made
him pass before Samuel. And he said, "Neither has the LORD chosen this one." 9Then
Jesse made Shammah pass by. And he said,
"Neither has the LORD chosen this one."
10Thus Jesse made seven of his sons pass
before Samuel. And Samuel said to Jesse,
"The LORD has not chosen these." 11And
Samuel said to Jesse, "Are all the young
men here?" Then he said, "There remains
yet the youngest, and there he is, keeping
the [a]sheep."
And Samuel said to Jesse, "Send and
bring him. For we will not sit down[1] till he
comes here." 12So he sent and brought him
in. Now he *was* [a]ruddy, [b]with bright eyes,
and good-looking. [c]And the LORD said,
"Arise, anoint him; for this *is* the one!"
13Then Samuel took the horn of oil and
anointed him in the midst of his brothers;
and [a]the Spirit of the LORD came upon David from that day forward. So Samuel arose
and went to Ramah.

A Distressing Spirit Troubles Saul

14[a]But the Spirit of the LORD departed
from Saul, and [b]a distressing spirit from
the LORD troubled him. 15And Saul's servants said to him, "Surely, a distressing
spirit from God is troubling you. 16Let our
master now command your servants, *who
are* before you, to seek out a man *who is* a
skillful player on the harp. And it shall be
that he will [a]play it with his hand when the
distressing spirit from God is upon you,
and you shall be well."
17So Saul said to his servants, "Provide
me now a man who can play well, and bring
him to me."
18Then one of the servants answered and
said, "Look, I have seen a son of Jesse the
Bethlehemite, *who is* skillful in playing, a
mighty man of valor, a man of war, prudent in speech, and a handsome person;
and [a]the LORD *is* with him."
19Therefore Saul sent messengers to
Jesse, and said, "Send me your son David,
who *is* with the sheep." 20And Jesse [a]took
a donkey *loaded with* bread, a skin of wine,
and a young goat, and sent *them* by his
son David to Saul. 21So David came to Saul
and [a]stood before him. And he loved him
greatly, and he became his armorbearer.
22Then Saul sent to Jesse, saying, "Please
let David stand before me, for he has found
favor in my sight." 23And so it was, whenever the spirit from God was upon Saul, that
David would take a harp and play *it* with his
hand. Then Saul would become refreshed
and well, and the distressing spirit would
depart from him.

David and Goliath

17 Now the Philistines gathered their
armies together to battle, and were
gathered at [a]Sochoh, which *belongs* to Judah; they encamped between Sochoh and
Azekah, in Ephes Dammim. 2And Saul
and the men of Israel were gathered together, and they encamped in the Valley
of Elah, and drew up in battle array against
the Philistines. 3The Philistines stood on a
mountain on one side, and Israel stood on
a mountain on the other side, with a valley
between them.
4And a champion went out from the
camp of the Philistines, named [a]Goliath,
from [b]Gath, whose height *was* six cubits
and a span. 5*He had* a bronze helmet on
his head, and he *was* armed with a coat of
mail, and the weight of the coat *was* five
thousand shekels of bronze. 6And *he had*
bronze armor on his legs and a bronze javelin between his shoulders. 7Now the staff
of his spear *was* like a weaver's beam, and
his iron spearhead *weighed* six hundred
shekels; and a shield-bearer went before
him. 8Then he stood and cried out to the
armies of Israel, and said to them, "Why
have you come out to line up for battle?

16:7 [a] Ps. 147:10 [b] Is. 55:8, 9 [c] 2 Cor. 10:7 [d] 1 Kin. 8:39 [1] Septuagint reads *For God does not see as man sees;* Targum reads *It is not by the appearance of a man;* Vulgate reads *Nor do I judge according to the looks of a man.* 16:11 [a] 2 Sam. 7:8; Ps. 78:70–72 [1] Following Septuagint and Vulgate; Masoretic Text reads *turn around;* Targum and Syriac read *turn away.* 16:12 [a] 1 Sam. 17:42 [b] Gen. 39:6; Ex. 2:2; Acts 7:20 [c] 1 Sam. 9:17 16:13 [a] Num. 27:18; 1 Sam. 10:6, 9, 10 16:14 [a] Judg. 16:20; 1 Sam. 11:6; 18:12; 28:15 [b] Judg. 9:23; 1 Sam. 16:15, 16; 18:10; 19:9; 1 Kin. 22:19–22 16:16 [a] 1 Sam. 18:10; 19:9; 2 Kin. 3:15 16:18 [a] 1 Sam. 3:19; 18:12, 14 16:20 [a] 1 Sam. 10:4, 27; Prov. 18:16 16:21 [a] Gen. 41:46; Prov. 22:29 17:1 [a] Josh. 15:35; 2 Chr. 28:18 17:4 [a] 2 Sam. 21:19 [b] Josh. 11:21, 22

Am I not a Philistine, and you the [a]servants
of Saul? Choose a man for yourselves, and
let him come down to me. 9If he is able to
fight with me and kill me, then we will be
your servants. But if I prevail against him
and kill him, then you shall be our servants
and [a]serve us." 10And the Philistine said, "I
[a]defy the armies of Israel this day; give me
a man, that we may fight together." 11When
Saul and all Israel heard these words of the
Philistine, they were dismayed and greatly
afraid.

12Now David *was* [a]the son of that [b]Eph-
rathite of Bethlehem Judah, whose name
was Jesse, and who had [c]eight sons. And
the man was old, advanced *in years,* in the
days of Saul. 13The three oldest sons of Jesse
had gone to follow Saul to the battle. The
[a]names of his three sons who went to the
battle *were* Eliab the firstborn, next to him
Abinadab, and the third Shammah. 14David
was the youngest. And the three oldest followed Saul. 15But David occasionally went
and returned from Saul [a]to feed his father's
sheep at Bethlehem.

16And the Philistine drew near and presented himself forty days, morning and
evening.

17Then Jesse said to his son David, "Take
now for your brothers an ephah of this
dried *grain* and these ten loaves, and run
to your brothers at the camp. 18And carry
these ten cheeses to the captain of *their*
thousand, and [a]see how your brothers fare,
and bring back news of them." 19Now Saul
and they and all the men of Israel *were* in
the Valley of Elah, fighting with the Philistines.

20So David rose early in the morning,
left the sheep with a keeper, and took *the
things* and went as Jesse had commanded
him. And he came to the camp as the army
was going out to the fight and shouting
for the battle. 21For Israel and the Philistines had drawn up in battle array, army
against army. 22And David left his supplies
in the hand of the supply keeper, ran to the
army, and came and greeted his brothers.
23Then as he talked with them, there was
the champion, the Philistine of Gath, Goliath by name, coming up from the armies
of the Philistines; and he spoke [a]according
to the same words. So David heard *them.*
24And all the men of Israel, when they saw
the man, fled from him and were dreadfully
afraid. 25So the men of Israel said, "Have
you seen this man who has come up? Surely
he has come up to defy Israel; and it shall
be *that* the man who kills him the king will
enrich with great riches, [a]will give him his
daughter, and give his father's house ex-
emption *from taxes* in Israel."

26Then David spoke to the men who
stood by him, saying, "What shall be done
for the man who kills this Philistine and
takes away [a]the reproach from Israel? For
who *is* this [b]uncircumcised Philistine, that
he should [c]defy the armies of [d]the living
God?"

27And the people answered him in this
manner, saying, [a]"So shall it be done for
the man who kills him."

28Now Eliab his oldest brother heard
when he spoke to the men; and Eliab's [a]an-
ger was aroused against David, and he said,
"Why did you come down here? And with
whom have you left those few sheep in the
wilderness? I know your pride and the insolence of your heart, for you have come
down to see the battle."

29And David said, "What have I done
now? [a]*Is there* not a cause?" 30Then he
turned from him toward another and [a]said
the same thing; and these people answered
him as the first ones *did.*

31Now when the words which David
spoke were heard, they reported *them* to
Saul; and he sent for him. 32Then David said
to Saul, [a]"Let no man's heart fail because
of him; [b]your servant will go and fight with
this Philistine."

33And Saul said to David, [a]"You are not
able to go against this Philistine to fight
with him; for you *are* a youth, and he a man
of war from his youth."

34But David said to Saul, "Your servant
used to keep his father's sheep, and when a
[a]lion or a bear came and took a lamb out of

17:8 [a] 1 Sam. 8:17 17:9 [a] 1 Sam. 11:1 17:10 [a] 1 Sam. 17:26, 36, 45; 2 Sam. 21:21 17:12 [a] Ruth 4:22; 1 Sam. 16:1, 18; 17:58 [b] Gen. 35:19 [c] 1 Sam. 16:10, 11; 1 Chr. 2:13–15 17:13 [a] 1 Sam. 16:6, 8, 9; 1 Chr. 2:13 17:15 [a] 1 Sam. 16:11, 19; 2 Sam. 7:8 17:18 [a] Gen. 37:13, 14 17:23 [a] 1 Sam. 17:8–10 17:25 [a] Josh. 15:16 17:26 [a] 1 Sam. 11:2 [b] 1 Sam. 14:6; 17:36; Jer. 9:25, 26 [c] 1 Sam. 17:10 [d] Deut. 5:26; 2 Kin. 19:4; Jer. 10:10 17:27 [a] 1 Sam. 17:25 17:28 [a] Gen. 37:4, 8–36; [Prov. 18:19; Matt. 10:36] 17:29 [a] 1 Sam. 17:17 17:30 [a] 1 Sam. 17:26, 27 17:32 [a] Deut. 20:1–4 [b] 1 Sam. 16:18 17:33 [a] Num. 13:31; Deut. 9:2 17:34 [a] Judg. 14:5

the flock, [35]I went out after it and struck it, and delivered *the lamb* from its mouth; and when it arose against me, I caught *it* by its beard, and struck and killed it. [36]Your servant has killed both lion and bear; and this uncircumcised Philistine will be like one of them, seeing he has defied the armies of the living God." [37]Moreover David said, [a]"The LORD, who delivered me from the paw of the lion and from the paw of the bear, He will deliver me from the hand of this Philistine."

And Saul said to David, [b]"Go, and the LORD be with you!"

[38]So Saul clothed David with his armor, and he put a bronze helmet on his head; he also clothed him with a coat of mail. [39]David fastened his sword to his armor and tried to walk, for he had not tested *them.* And David said to Saul, "I cannot walk with these, for I have not tested *them.*" So David took them off.

[40]Then he took his staff in his hand; and he chose for himself five smooth stones from the brook, and put them in a shepherd's bag, in a pouch which he had, and his sling was in his hand. And he drew near to the Philistine. [41]So the Philistine came, and began drawing near to David, and the man who bore the shield *went* before him. [42]And when the Philistine looked about and saw David, he [a]disdained him; for he was *only* a youth, [b]ruddy and good-looking. [43]So the Philistine [a]said to David, "*Am* I a dog, that you come to me with sticks?" And the Philistine cursed David by his gods. [44]And the Philistine [a]said to David, "Come to me, and I will give your flesh to the birds of the air and the beasts of the field!"

[45]Then David said to the Philistine, "You come to me with a sword, with a spear, and with a javelin. [a]But I come to you in the name of the LORD of hosts, the God of the armies of Israel, whom you have [b]defied. [46]This day the LORD will deliver you into my hand, and I will strike you and take your head from you. And this day I will give [a]the carcasses of the camp of the Philistines to the birds of the air and the wild beasts of the earth, [b]that all the earth may know that there is a God in Israel. [47]Then all this assembly shall know that the LORD [a]does not save with sword and spear; for [b]the battle *is* the LORD's, and He will give you into our hands."

[48]So it was, when the Philistine arose and came and drew near to meet David, that David hurried and [a]ran toward the army to meet the Philistine. [49]Then David put his hand in his bag and took out a stone; and he slung *it* and struck the Philistine in his forehead, so that the stone sank into his forehead, and he fell on his face to the earth. [50]So David prevailed over the Philistine with a [a]sling and a stone, and struck the Philistine and killed him. But *there was* no sword in the hand of David. [51]Therefore David ran and stood over the Philistine, took his [a]sword and drew it out of its sheath and killed him, and cut off his head with it.

And when the Philistines saw that their champion was dead, [b]they fled. [52]Now the men of Israel and Judah arose and shouted, and pursued the Philistines as far as the entrance of the valley[1] and to the gates of Ekron. And the wounded of the Philistines fell along the road to [a]Shaaraim, even as far as Gath and Ekron. [53]Then the children of Israel returned from chasing the Philistines, and they plundered their tents. [54]And David took the head of the Philistine and brought it to Jerusalem, but he put his armor in his tent.

[55]When Saul saw David going out against the Philistine, he said to [a]Abner, the commander of the army, "Abner, [b]whose son *is* this youth?"

And Abner said, "As your soul lives, O king, I do not know."

[56]So the king said, "Inquire whose son this young man *is.*"

[57]Then, as David returned from the slaughter of the Philistine, Abner took him and brought him before Saul [a]with the head of the Philistine in his hand. [58]And Saul

17:37 [a] [2 Cor. 1:10; 2 Tim. 4:17, 18] [b] 1 Sam. 20:13; 1 Chr. 22:11, 16 17:42 [a] [Ps. 123:4; Prov. 16:18; 1 Cor. 1:27, 28] [b] 1 Sam. 16:12 17:43 [a] 1 Sam. 24:14; 2 Sam. 3:8; 9:8; 16:9; 2 Kin. 8:13 17:44 [a] 1 Sam. 17:46; 1 Kin. 20:10, 11 17:45 [a] 2 Sam. 22:33, 35; 2 Chr. 32:8; Ps. 124:8; [2 Cor. 10:4]; Heb. 11:33, 34 [b] 1 Sam. 17:10 17:46 [a] Deut. 28:26 [b] Josh. 4:24; 1 Kin. 8:43; 18:36; 2 Kin. 19:19; Is. 52:10 17:47 [a] 1 Sam. 14:6; 2 Chr. 14:11; 20:15; Ps. 44:6; Hos. 1:7; Zech. 4:6 [b] 2 Chr. 20:15 17:48 [a] Ps. 27:3 17:50 [a] Judg. 3:31; 15:15; 20:16 17:51 [a] 1 Sam. 21:9; 2 Sam. 23:21 [b] Heb. 11:34 17:52 [a] Josh. 15:36 [1] Following Masoretic Text, Syriac, Targum, and Vulgate; Septuagint reads *Gath.* 17:55 [a] 1 Sam. 14:50 [b] 1 Sam. 16:21, 22 17:57 [a] 1 Sam. 17:54

said to him, "Whose son *are* you, young
man?"
So David answered, [a]"*I am* the son of
your servant Jesse the Bethlehemite."

Saul Resents David

18 Now when he had finished speaking
to Saul, [a]the soul of Jonathan was
knit to the soul of David, [b]and Jonathan
loved him as his own soul. 2Saul took him
that day, [a]and would not let him go home
to his father's house anymore. 3Then Jonathan and David made a [a]covenant, because
he loved him as his own soul. 4And Jonathan took off the robe that *was* on him and
gave it to David, with his armor, even to his
sword and his bow and his belt.
5So David went out wherever Saul sent
him, *and* behaved wisely. And Saul set him
over the men of war, and he was accepted
in the sight of all the people and also in the
sight of Saul's servants. 6Now it had happened as they were coming *home,* when David was returning from the slaughter of the
Philistine, that [a]the women had come out
of all the cities of Israel, singing and dancing, to meet King Saul, with tambourines,
with joy, and with musical instruments. 7So
the women [a]sang as they danced, and said:

[b]"Saul has slain his thousands,
And David his ten thousands."

8Then Saul was very angry, and the saying
[a]displeased him; and he said, "They have
ascribed to David ten thousands, and to me
they have ascribed *only* thousands. Now
what more can he have but [b]the kingdom?"
9So Saul eyed David from that day forward.
10And it happened on the next day that
[a]the distressing spirit from God came upon
Saul, [b]and he prophesied inside the house.
So David [c]played *music* with his hand, as at
other times; [d]but *there was* a spear in Saul's
hand. 11And Saul [a]cast the spear, for he said,
"I will pin David to the wall!" But David escaped his presence twice.
12Now Saul was [a]afraid of David, because
[b]the LORD was with him, but had [c]departed
from Saul. 13Therefore Saul removed him
from his presence, and made him his captain over a thousand; and [a]he went out and
came in before the people. 14And David behaved wisely in all his ways, and [a]the LORD
was with him. 15Therefore, when Saul saw
that he behaved very wisely, he was afraid
of him. 16But [a]all Israel and Judah loved
David, because he went out and came in
before them.

David Marries Michal

17Then Saul said to David, "Here is my
older daughter Merab; [a]I will give her to
you as a wife. Only be valiant for me, and
fight [b]the LORD's battles." For Saul thought,
[c]"Let my hand not be against him, but let
the hand of the Philistines be against him."
18So David said to Saul, [a]"Who *am* I,
and what *is* my life *or* my father's family
in Israel, that I should be son-in-law to the
king?" 19But it happened at the time when
Merab, Saul's daughter, should have been
given to David, that she was given to [a]Adriel
the [b]Meholathite as a wife.
20[a]Now Michal, Saul's daughter, loved
David. And they told Saul, and the thing
pleased him. 21So Saul said, "I will give her
to him, that she may be a snare to him,
and that [a]the hand of the Philistines may
be against him." Therefore Saul said to David a second time, [b]"You shall be my son-
in-law today."
22And Saul commanded his servants,
"Communicate with David secretly, and
say, 'Look, the king has delight in you, and
all his servants love you. Now therefore,
become the king's son-in-law.'"
23So Saul's servants spoke those words
in the hearing of David. And David said,
"Does it seem to you *a* light *thing* to be a
king's son-in-law, seeing I *am* a poor and
lightly esteemed man?" 24And the servants
of Saul told him, saying, "In this manner
David spoke."
25Then Saul said, "Thus you shall say
to David: 'The king does not desire any

17:58 [a] 1 Sam. 17:12 **18:1** [a] Gen. 44:30 [b] Deut. 13:6; 1 Sam. 20:17; 2 Sam. 1:26 **18:2** [a] 1 Sam. 17:15 **18:3** [a] 1 Sam. 20:8–17 **18:6** [a] Ex. 15:20, 21; Judg. 11:34; Ps. 68:25; 149:3 **18:7** [a] Ex. 15:21 [b] 1 Sam. 21:11; 29:5 **18:8** [a] Eccl. 4:4 [b] 1 Sam. 15:28 **18:10** [a] 1 Sam. 16:14 [b] 1 Sam. 19:24; 1 Kin. 18:29; Acts 16:16 [c] 1 Sam. 16:23 [d] 1 Sam. 19:9, 10 **18:11** [a] 1 Sam. 19:10; 20:33 **18:12** [a] 1 Sam. 18:15, 29 [b] 1 Sam. 16:13, 18 [c] 1 Sam. 16:14; 28:15 **18:13** [a] Num. 27:17; 1 Sam. 18:16; 29:6; 2 Sam. 5:2 **18:14** [a] Gen. 39:2, 3, 23; Josh. 6:27; 1 Sam. 16:18 **18:16** [a] Num. 27:16, 17; 1 Sam. 18:5; 2 Sam. 5:2; 1 Kin. 3:7 **18:17** [a] 1 Sam. 14:49; 17:25 [b] Num. 32:20, 27, 29; 1 Sam. 25:28 [c] 1 Sam. 18:21, 25; 2 Sam. 12:9 **18:18** [a] 1 Sam. 9:21; 18:23; 2 Sam. 7:18 **18:19** [a] 2 Sam. 21:8 [b] Judg. 7:22; 2 Sam. 21:8; 1 Kin. 19:16 **18:20** [a] 1 Sam. 18:28 **18:21** [a] 1 Sam. 18:17 [b] 1 Sam. 18:26

[a]dowry but one hundred foreskins of the
Philistines, to take [b]vengeance on the king's
enemies.'" But Saul [c]thought to make David fall by the hand of the Philistines. [26]So
when his servants told David these words,
it pleased David well to become the king's
son-in-law. Now [a]the days had not expired;
[27]therefore David arose and went, he and
[a]his men, and killed two hundred men of
the Philistines. And [b]David brought their
foreskins, and they gave them in full count
to the king, that he might become the king's
son-in-law. Then Saul gave him Michal his
daughter as a wife.

[28]Thus Saul saw and knew that the LORD
was with David, and *that* Michal, Saul's
daughter, loved him; [29]and Saul was still
more afraid of David. So Saul became David's enemy continually. [30]Then the princes
of the Philistines [a]went out *to war.* And so
it was, whenever they went out, *that* David
[b]behaved more wisely than all the servants
of Saul, so that his name became highly
esteemed.

Saul Persecutes David

19 Now Saul spoke to Jonathan his son
and to all his servants, that they
should kill [a]David; but Jonathan, Saul's son,
[b]delighted greatly in David. [2]So Jonathan
told David, saying, "My father Saul seeks to
kill you. Therefore please be on your guard
until morning, and stay in a secret *place*
and hide. [3]And I will go out and stand beside my father in the field where you *are,*
and I will speak with my father about you.
Then what I observe, I will tell [a]you."

[4]Thus Jonathan [a]spoke well of David to
Saul his father, and said to him, "Let not
the king [b]sin against his servant, against
David, because he has not sinned against
you, and because his works *have been* very
good toward you. [5]For he took his [a]life in his
hands and [b]killed the Philistine, and [c]the
LORD brought about a great deliverance
for all Israel. You saw *it* and rejoiced. [d]Why
then will you [e]sin against innocent blood,
to kill David without a cause?"

[6]So Saul heeded the voice of Jonathan,
and Saul swore, "*As* the LORD lives, he shall
not be killed." [7]Then Jonathan called David,
and Jonathan told him all these things. So
Jonathan brought David to Saul, and he was
in his presence [a]as in times past.

[8]And there was war again; and David
went out and fought with the Philistines,
[a]and struck them with a mighty blow, and
they fled from him.

[9]Now [a]the distressing spirit from the
LORD came upon Saul as he sat in his house
with his spear in his hand. And David was
playing *music* with *his* hand. [10]Then Saul
sought to pin David to the wall with the
spear, but he slipped away from Saul's presence; and he drove the spear into the wall.
So David fled and escaped that night.

[11][a]Saul also sent messengers to David's
house to watch him and to kill him in the
morning. And Michal, David's wife, told
him, saying, "If you do not save your life
tonight, tomorrow you will be killed." [12]So
Michal [a]let David down through a window.
And he went and fled and escaped. [13]And
Michal took an image and laid *it* in the bed,
put a cover of goats' *hair* for his head, and
covered *it* with clothes. [14]So when Saul sent
messengers to take David, she said, "He
is sick."

[15]Then Saul sent the messengers *back* to
see David, saying, "Bring him up to me in
the bed, that I may kill him." [16]And when
the messengers had come in, there was
the image in the bed, with a cover of goats'
hair for his head. [17]Then Saul said to Michal, "Why have you deceived me like this,
and sent my enemy away, so that he has
escaped?"

And Michal answered Saul, "He said to
me, 'Let me go! [a]Why should I kill you?'"

[18]So David fled and escaped, and went to
[a]Samuel at [b]Ramah, and told him all that
Saul had done to him. And he and Samuel
went and stayed in Naioth. [19]Now it was
told Saul, saying, "Take note, David *is* at
Naioth in Ramah!" [20]Then [a]Saul sent messengers to take David. [b]And when they saw

---

18:25 [a] Gen. 34:12; Ex. 22:17 [b] 1 Sam. 14:24 [c] 1 Sam. 18:17 18:26 [a] 1 Sam. 18:21 18:27 [a] 1 Sam. 18:13 [b] 2 Sam. 3:14 18:30 [a] 2 Sam. 11:1 [b] 1 Sam. 18:5 19:1 [a] 1 Sam. 8:8, 9 [b] 1 Sam. 18:1 19:3 [a] 1 Sam. 20:8–13 19:4 [a] 1 Sam. 20:32; [Prov. 31:8, 9] [b] Gen. 42:22; [Prov. 17:13]; Jer. 18:20 19:5 [a] Judg. 9:17; 12:3 [b] 1 Sam. 17:49, 50 [c] 1 Sam. 11:13; 1 Chr. 11:14 [d] 1 Sam. 20:32 [e] [Deut. 19:10–13] 19:7 [a] 1 Sam. 16:21; 18:2, 10, 13 19:8 [a] 1 Sam. 18:27; 23:5 19:9 [a] 1 Sam. 16:14; 18:10, 11 19:11 [a] Judg. 16:2; Ps. 59:title 19:12 [a] Josh. 2:15; Acts 9:25; 2 Cor. 11:33 19:17 [a] 2 Sam. 2:22 19:18 [a] 1 Sam. 16:13 [b] 1 Sam. 7:17 19:20 [a] 1 Sam. 19:11, 14; John 7:32 [b] 1 Sam. 10:5, 6, 10; [1 Cor. 14:3, 24, 25]

the group of prophets prophesying, and
Samuel standing *as* leader over them, the
Spirit of God came upon the messengers of
Saul, and they also [c]prophesied. 21And when
Saul was told, he sent other messengers,
and they prophesied likewise. Then Saul
sent messengers again the third time, and
they prophesied also. 22Then he also went
to Ramah, and came to the great well that
is at Sechu. So he asked, and said, "Where
are Samuel and David?"

And *someone* said, "Indeed *they are* at
Naioth in Ramah." 23So he went there to
Naioth in Ramah. Then [a]the Spirit of God
was upon him also, and he went on and
prophesied until he came to Naioth in Ramah. 24[a]And he also stripped off his clothes
and prophesied before Samuel in like manner, and lay down [b]naked all that day and
all that night. Therefore they say, [c]"*Is* Saul
also among the prophets?"[1]

Jonathan's Loyalty to David

20 Then David fled from Naioth in
Ramah, and went and said to Jonathan, "What have I done? What *is* my iniquity, and what *is* my sin before your father,
that he seeks my life?"

2So Jonathan said to him, "By no means!
You shall not die! Indeed, my father will do
nothing either great or small without first
telling me. And why should my father hide
this thing from me? It *is* not *so!*"

3Then David took an oath again, and
said, "Your father certainly knows that I
have found favor in your eyes, and he has
said, 'Do not let Jonathan know this, lest
he be grieved.' But [a]truly, *as* the LORD lives
and *as* your soul lives, *there is* but a step between me and death."

4So Jonathan said to David, "Whatever
you yourself desire, I will do *it* for you."

5And David said to Jonathan, "Indeed
tomorrow *is* the [a]New Moon, and I should
not fail to sit with the king to eat. But let
me go, that I may [b]hide in the field until
the third *day* at evening. 6If your father
misses me at all, then say, 'David earnestly
asked *permission* of me that he might run
over [a]to Bethlehem, his city, for *there is* a
yearly sacrifice there for all the family.'
7[a]If he says thus: '*It is* well,' your servant
will be safe. But if he is very angry, be sure
that [b]evil is determined by him. 8Therefore
you shall [a]deal kindly with your servant,
for [b]you have brought your servant into
a covenant of the LORD with you. Nevertheless, [c]if there is iniquity in me, kill me
yourself, for why should you bring me to
your father?"

9But Jonathan said, "Far be it from you!
For if I knew certainly that evil was determined by my father to come upon you, then
would I not tell you?"

10Then David said to Jonathan, "Who
will tell me, or what *if* your father answers
you roughly?"

11And Jonathan said to David, "Come, let
us go out into the field." So both of them
went out into the field. 12Then Jonathan
said to David: "The LORD God of Israel *is*
witness! When I have sounded out my father sometime tomorrow, *or* the third *day,*
and indeed *there is* good toward David, and
I do not send to you and tell you, 13may [a]the
LORD do so and much more to Jonathan.
But if it pleases my father *to do* you evil,
then I will report it to you and send you
away, that you may go in safety. And [b]the
LORD be with you as He has [c]been with my
father. 14And you shall not only show me
the kindness of the LORD while I still live,
that I may not die; 15but [a]you shall not cut
off your kindness from my house forever,
no, not when the LORD has cut off every one
of the enemies of David from the face of the
earth." 16So Jonathan made *a covenant* with
the house of David, *saying,* [a]"Let the LORD
require *it* at the hand of David's enemies."

17Now Jonathan again caused David to
vow, because he loved him; [a]for he loved
him as he loved his own soul. 18Then Jonathan said to David, [a]"Tomorrow *is* the New
Moon; and you will be missed, because
your seat will be empty. 19And *when* you
have stayed three days, go down quickly
and come to [a]the place where you hid on
the day of the deed; and remain by the

19:20 [c] Num. 11:25; Joel 2:28 **19:23** [a] 1 Sam. 10:10 **19:24** [a] Is. 20:2 [b] Mic. 1:8 [c] 1 Sam. 10:10–12 [1] Compare 1 Samuel 10:12
20:3 [a] 1 Sam. 27:1; 2 Kin. 2:6 **20:5** [a] Num. 10:10; 28:11–15 [b] 1 Sam. 19:2, 3 **20:6** [a] 1 Sam. 16:4; 17:12; John 7:42 **20:7** [a] Deut. 1:23;
2 Sam. 17:4 [b] 1 Sam. 25:17; Esth. 7:7 **20:8** [a] Josh. 2:14 [b] 1 Sam. 18:3; 20:16; 23:18 [c] 2 Sam. 14:32 **20:13** [a] Ruth 1:17; 1 Sam. 3:17
[b] Josh. 1:5; 1 Sam. 17:37; 18:12; 1 Chr. 22:11, 16 [c] 1 Sam. 10:7 **20:15** [a] 1 Sam. 24:21; 2 Sam. 9:1, 3, 7; 21:7 **20:16** [a] Deut. 23:21;
1 Sam. 25:22; 31:2; 2 Sam. 4:7; 21:8 **20:17** [a] 1 Sam. 18:1 **20:18** [a] 1 Sam. 20:5, 24 **20:19** [a] 1 Sam. 19:2

stone Ezel. 20Then I will shoot three arrows to the side, as though I shot at a target; 21and there I will send a lad, *saying,* 'Go,
find the arrows.' If I expressly say to the lad,
'Look, the arrows *are* on this side of you;
get them and come'—then, [a]as the LORD
lives, *there is* safety for you and no harm.
22But if I say thus to the young man, 'Look,
the arrows *are* beyond you'—go your way,
for the LORD has sent you away. 23And as
for [a]the matter which you and I have spoken of, indeed the LORD *be* between you
and me forever."

24Then David hid in the field. And when
the New Moon had come, the king sat down
to eat the feast. 25Now the king sat on his
seat, as at other times, on a seat by the
wall. And Jonathan arose,[1] and Abner sat
by Saul's side, but David's place was empty.
26Nevertheless Saul did not say anything
that day, for he thought, "Something has
happened to him; he *is* unclean, surely he *is*
[a]unclean." 27And it happened the next day,
the second *day* of the month, that David's
place was empty. And Saul said to Jonathan
his son, "Why has the son of Jesse not come
to eat, either yesterday or today?"

28So Jonathan [a]answered Saul, "David
earnestly asked *permission* of me *to go* to
Bethlehem. 29And he said, 'Please let me
go, for our family has a sacrifice in the city,
and my brother has commanded me *to be
there.* And now, if I have found favor in your
eyes, please let me get away and see my
brothers.' Therefore he has not come to
the king's table."

30Then Saul's anger was aroused against
Jonathan, and he said to him, "You son of a
perverse, rebellious *woman!* Do I not know
that you have chosen the son of Jesse to
your own shame and to the shame of your
mother's nakedness? 31For as long as the
son of Jesse lives on the earth, you shall
not be established, nor your kingdom. Now
therefore, send and bring him to me, for he
shall surely die."

32And Jonathan answered Saul his father, and said to him, [a]"Why should he be
killed? What has he done?" 33Then Saul
[a]cast a spear at him to kill him, [b]by which
Jonathan knew that it was determined by
his father to kill David.

34So Jonathan arose from the table in
fierce anger, and ate no food the second
day of the month, for he was grieved for
David, because his father had treated him
shamefully.

35And so it was, in the morning, that Jonathan went out into the field at the time appointed with David, and a little lad *was* with
him. 36Then he said to his lad, "Now run,
find the arrows which I shoot." As the lad
ran, he shot an arrow beyond him. 37When
the lad had come to the place where the arrow was which Jonathan had shot, Jonathan
cried out after the lad and said, "*Is* not the
arrow beyond you?" 38And Jonathan cried
out after the lad, "Make haste, hurry, do not
delay!" So Jonathan's lad gathered up the
arrows and came back to his master. 39But
the lad did not know anything. Only Jonathan and David knew of the matter. 40Then
Jonathan gave his weapons to his lad, and
said to him, "Go, carry *them* to the city."

41As soon as the lad had gone, David
arose from *a place* toward the south, fell
on his face to the ground, and bowed down
three times. And they kissed one another;
and they wept together, but David more
so. 42Then Jonathan said to David, [a]"Go
in peace, since we have both sworn in the
name of the LORD, saying, 'May the LORD be
between you and me, and between your descendants and my descendants, forever.'"
So he arose and departed, and Jonathan
went into the city.

David and the Holy Bread

21 Now David came to Nob, to Ahimelech the priest. And [a]Ahimelech
was [b]afraid when he met David, and said
to him, "Why *are* you alone, and no one is
with you?"

2So David said to Ahimelech the priest,
"The king has ordered me on some business, and said to me, 'Do not let anyone
know anything about the business on which
I send you, or what I have commanded you.'
And I have directed *my* young men to such
and such a place. 3Now therefore, what have

20:21 [a] Jer. 4:2 20:23 [a] 1 Sam. 20:14, 15 20:25 [1] Following Masoretic Text, Syriac, Targum, and Vulgate; Septuagint reads *he sat across from Jonathan.* 20:26 [a] Lev. 7:20, 21; 15:5 20:28 [a] 1 Sam. 20:6 20:32 [a] Gen. 31:36; 1 Sam. 19:5; [Prov. 31:9]; Matt. 27:23; Luke 23:22 20:33 [a] 1 Sam. 18:11; 19:10 [b] 1 Sam. 20:7 20:42 [a] 1 Sam. 1:17 21:1 [a] 1 Sam. 14:3; Mark 2:26 [b] 1 Sam. 16:4

you on hand? Give *me* five *loaves of* bread
in my hand, or whatever can be found."
4 And the priest answered David and
said, "*There is* no common bread on hand;
but there is [a]holy bread, [b]if the young men
have at least kept themselves from women."
5 Then David answered the priest, and said
to him, "Truly, women *have been* kept from
us about three days since I came out. And
the [a]vessels of the young men are holy, and
the bread is in effect common, even though
it was consecrated [b]in the vessel this day."
6 So the priest [a]gave him holy *bread;* for
there was no bread there but the showbread [b]which had been taken from before
the LORD, in order to put hot bread *in its
place* on the day when it was taken away.
7 Now a certain man of the servants of
Saul *was* there that day, detained before the
LORD. And his name *was* [a]Doeg, an Edomite, the chief of the herdsmen who *belonged*
to Saul.
8 And David said to Ahimelech, "Is there
not here on hand a spear or a sword? For
I have brought neither my sword nor my
weapons with me, because the king's business required haste."
9 So the priest said, "The sword of Goliath the Philistine, whom you killed in
[a]the Valley of Elah, [b]there it is, wrapped in
a cloth behind the ephod. If you will take
that, take *it.* For *there is* no other except
that one here."
And David said, "*There is* none like it;
give it to me."

David Flees to Gath

10 Then David arose and fled that day
from before Saul, and went to Achish the
king of Gath. 11 And [a]the servants of Achish
said to him, "*Is* this not David the king of
the land? Did they not sing of him to one
another in dances, saying:

[b]'Saul has slain his thousands,
And David his ten thousands'?"[1]

12 Now David [a]took these words to heart,
and was very much afraid of Achish the
king of Gath. 13 So [a]he changed his behavior
before them, pretended madness in their
hands, scratched on the doors of the gate,
and let his saliva fall down on his beard.
14 Then Achish said to his servants, "Look,
you see the man is insane. Why have you
brought him to me? 15 Have I need of mad-
men, that you have brought this *fellow* to
play the madman in my presence? Shall
this *fellow* come into my house?"

David's Four Hundred Men
(1 Chr. 12:16–18)

22 David therefore departed from
there and [a]escaped [b]to the cave of
Adullam. So when his brothers and all his
father's house heard *it,* they went down
there to him. 2 [a]And everyone *who was* in
distress, everyone who *was* in debt, and
everyone *who was* discontented gathered
to him. So he became captain over them.
And there were about [b]four hundred men
with him.
3 Then David went from there to Mizpah
of [a]Moab; and he said to the king of Moab,
"Please let my father and mother come
here with you, till I know what God will do
for me." 4 So he brought them before the
king of Moab, and they dwelt with him all
the time that David was in the stronghold.
5 Now the prophet [a]Gad said to David,
"Do not stay in the stronghold; depart, and
go to the land of Judah." So David departed
and went into the forest of Hereth.

Saul Murders the Priests

6 When Saul heard that David and
the men who *were* with him had been
discovered—now Saul was staying in [a]Gib-
eah under a tamarisk tree in Ramah, with
his spear in his hand, and all his servants
standing about him— 7 then Saul said to
his servants who stood about him, "Hear
now, you Benjamites! Will the son of Jesse
[a]give every one of you fields and vineyards,
and make you all captains of thousands
and captains of hundreds? 8 All of you have
conspired against me, and *there is* no one
who reveals to me that [a]my son has made

21:4 [a] Ex. 25:30; Lev. 24:5–9; Matt. 12:4 [b] Ex. 19:15 **21:5** [a] Ex. 19:14, 15; 1 Thess. 4:4 [b] Lev. 8:26 **21:6** [a] Matt. 12:3, 4; Mark 2:25, 26; Luke 6:3, 4 [b] Lev. 24:8, 9 **21:7** [a] 1 Sam. 14:47; 22:9; Ps. 52:title **21:9** [a] 1 Sam. 17:2, 50 [b] 1 Sam. 31:10 **21:11** [a] Ps. 56:title [b] 1 Sam. 18:6–8; 29:5 [1] Compare 1 Samuel 18:7 **21:12** [a] Luke 2:19 **21:13** [a] Ps. 34:title **22:1** [a] Ps. 57:title; 142:title [b] Josh. 12:15; 15:35; 2 Sam. 23:13 **22:2** [a] Judg. 11:3 [b] 1 Sam. 25:13 **22:3** [a] 2 Sam. 8:2 **22:5** [a] 2 Sam. 24:11; 1 Chr. 21:9; 29:29; 2 Chr. 29:25 **22:6** [a] 1 Sam. 15:34 **22:7** [a] 1 Sam. 8:14 **22:8** [a] 1 Sam. 18:3; 20:16, 30

a covenant with the son of Jesse; and *there*
is not one of you who is sorry for me or
reveals to me that my son has stirred up
my servant against me, to lie in wait, as *it*
is this day."

9Then answered [a]Doeg the Edomite,
who was set over the servants of Saul, and
said, "I saw the son of Jesse going to Nob,
to [b]Ahimelech the son of [c]Ahitub. 10[a]And
he inquired of the LORD for him, [b]gave him
provisions, and gave him the sword of Goliath the Philistine."

11So the king sent to call Ahimelech the
priest, the son of Ahitub, and all his father's
house, the priests who *were* in Nob. And
they all came to the king. 12And Saul said,
"Hear now, son of Ahitub!"

He answered, "Here I am, my lord."

13Then Saul said to him, "Why have you
conspired against me, you and the son of
Jesse, in that you have given him bread
and a sword, and have inquired of God for
him, that he should rise against me, to lie
in wait, as it is this day?"

14So Ahimelech answered the king and
said, "And who among all your servants
is as [a]faithful as David, who is the king's
son-in-law, who goes at your bidding, and
is honorable in your house? 15Did I then
begin to inquire of God for him? Far be it
from me! Let not the king impute anything
to his servant, *or* to any in the house of my
father. For your servant knew nothing of all
this, little or much."

16And the king said, "You shall surely die,
Ahimelech, you and all [a]your father's house!"
17Then the king said to the guards who stood
about him, "Turn and kill the priests of the
LORD, because their hand also *is* with David, and because they knew when he fled
and did not tell it to me." But the servants of
the king [a]would not lift their hands to strike
the priests of the LORD. 18And the king said
to Doeg, "You turn and kill the priests!" So
Doeg the Edomite turned and struck the
priests, and [a]killed on that day eighty-five
men who wore a linen ephod. 19[a]Also Nob,
the city of the priests, he struck with the edge
of the sword, both men and women, children
and nursing infants, oxen and donkeys and
sheep—with the edge of the sword.

20[a]Now one of the sons of Ahimelech
the son of Ahitub, named Abiathar, [b]es-
caped and fled after David. 21And Abiathar
told David that Saul had killed the LORD's
priests. 22So David said to Abiathar, "I knew
that day, when Doeg the Edomite *was* there,
that he would surely tell Saul. I have caused
the death of all the persons of your father's
house. 23Stay with me; do not fear. [a]For he
who seeks my life seeks your life, but with
me you *shall be* safe."

David Saves the City of Keilah

23 Then they told David, saying, "Look,
the Philistines are fighting against
[a]Keilah, and they are robbing the threshing floors."

2Therefore David [a]inquired of the LORD,
saying, "Shall I go and attack these Philistines?"

And the LORD said to David, "Go and attack the Philistines, and save Keilah."

3But David's men said to him, "Look, we
are afraid here in Judah. How much more
then if we go to Keilah against the armies
of the Philistines?" 4Then David inquired
of the LORD once again.

And the LORD answered him and said,
"Arise, go down to Keilah. For I will deliver
the Philistines into your hand." 5And David and his men went to Keilah and [a]fought
with the Philistines, struck them with a
mighty blow, and took away their livestock.
So David saved the inhabitants of Keilah.

6Now it happened, when Abiathar the
son of Ahimelech [a]fled to David at Keilah,
that he went down *with* an ephod in his
hand.

7And Saul was told that David had gone
to Keilah. So Saul said, "God has delivered
him into my hand, for he has shut himself
in by entering a town that has gates and
bars." 8Then Saul called all the people together for war, to go down to Keilah to besiege David and his men.

9When David knew that Saul plotted evil
against him, [a]he said to Abiathar the priest,

22:9 [a] 1 Sam. 21:7; 22:22; Ps. 52:title [b] 1 Sam. 21:1 [c] 1 Sam. 14:3 22:10 [a] Num. 27:21; 1 Sam. 10:22 [b] 1 Sam. 21:6, 9
22:14 [a] 1 Sam. 19:4, 5; 20:32; 24:11 22:16 [a] Deut. 24:16 22:17 [a] Ex. 1:17 22:18 [a] 1 Sam. 2:31 22:19 [a] Josh. 21:1–45; 1 Sam. 22:9, 11
22:20 [a] 1 Sam. 23:6, 9; 30:7; 1 Kin. 2:26, 27 [b] 1 Sam. 2:33 22:23 [a] 1 Kin. 2:26 23:1 [a] Josh. 15:44; Neh. 3:17, 18
23:2 [a] 1 Sam. 22:10; 23:4, 6, 9; 28:6; 30:8; 2 Sam. 5:19, 23 23:5 [a] 1 Sam. 19:8; 2 Sam. 5:20
23:6 [a] 1 Sam. 22:20 23:9 [a] Num. 27:21; 1 Sam. 23:6; 30:7

"Bring the ephod here." [10]Then David said, "O LORD God of Israel, Your servant has certainly heard that Saul seeks to come to Keilah [a]to destroy the city for my sake. [11]Will the men of Keilah deliver me into his hand? Will Saul come down, as Your servant has heard? O LORD God of Israel, I pray, tell Your servant."

And the LORD said, "He will come down."

[12]Then David said, "Will the men of Keilah deliver me and my men into the hand of Saul?"

And the LORD said, "They will deliver *you*."

[13]So David and his men, [a]about six hundred, arose and departed from Keilah and went wherever they could go. Then it was told Saul that David had escaped from Keilah; so he halted the expedition.

David in Wilderness Strongholds

[14]And David stayed in strongholds in the wilderness, and remained in [a]the mountains in the Wilderness of [b]Ziph. Saul [c]sought him every day, but God did not deliver him into his hand. [15]So David saw that Saul had come out to seek his life. And David *was* in the Wilderness of Ziph in a forest.[1] [16]Then Jonathan, Saul's son, arose and went to David in the woods and strengthened his hand in God. [17]And he said to him, [a]"Do not fear, for the hand of Saul my father shall not find you. You shall be king over Israel, and I shall be next to you. [b]Even my father Saul knows that." [18]So the two of them [a]made a covenant before the LORD. And David stayed in the woods, and Jonathan went to his own house.

[19]Then the Ziphites [a]came up to Saul at Gibeah, saying, "Is David not hiding with us in strongholds in the woods, in the hill of Hachilah, which *is* on the south of Jeshimon? [20]Now therefore, O king, come down according to all the desire of your soul to come down; and [a]our part *shall be* to deliver him into the king's hand."

[21]And Saul said, "Blessed *are* you of the LORD, for you have compassion on me. [22]Please go and find out for sure, and see the place where his hideout is, *and* who has seen him there. For I am told he is very crafty. [23]See therefore, and take knowledge of all the lurking places where he hides; and come back to me with certainty, and I will go with you. And it shall be, if he is in the land, that I will search for him throughout all the clans[1] of Judah."

[24]So they arose and went to Ziph before Saul. But David and his men *were* in the Wilderness [a]of Maon, in the plain on the south of Jeshimon. [25]When Saul and his men went to seek *him,* they told David. Therefore he went down to the rock, and stayed in the Wilderness of Maon. And when Saul heard *that,* he pursued David in the Wilderness of Maon. [26]Then Saul went on one side of the mountain, and David and his men on the other side of the mountain. [a]So David made haste to get away from Saul, for Saul and his men [b]were encircling David and his men to take them.

[27][a]But a messenger came to Saul, saying, "Hurry and come, for the Philistines have invaded the land!" [28]Therefore Saul returned from pursuing David, and went against the Philistines; so they called that place the Rock of Escape.[1] [29]Then David went up from there and dwelt in strongholds at [a]En Gedi.

David Spares Saul

24 Now it happened, [a]when Saul had returned from following the Philistines, that it was told him, saying, "Take note! David *is* in the Wilderness of En Gedi." [2]Then Saul took three thousand chosen men from all Israel, and [a]went to seek David and his men on the Rocks of the Wild Goats. [3]So he came to the sheepfolds by the road, where there *was* a cave; and [a]Saul went in to [b]attend to his needs. ([c]David and his men were staying in the recesses of the cave.) [4][a]Then the men of David said to him, "This is the day of which the LORD said to you, 'Behold, I will deliver your enemy into your hand, that you may do to him as it seems good to you.'" And David arose and secretly cut off a corner of Saul's

---

23:10 [a] 1 Sam. 22:19 23:13 [a] 1 Sam. 22:2; 25:13 23:14 [a] Ps. 11:1 [b] Josh. 15:55; 2 Chr. 11:8 [c] Ps. 32:7; 54:3, 4 23:15 [1] Or *in Horesh* 23:17 [a] [Ps. 27:1–3; Heb. 13:6] [b] 1 Sam. 20:31; 24:20 23:18 [a] 1 Sam. 18:3; 20:12–17, 42; 2 Sam. 9:1; 21:7 23:19 [a] 1 Sam. 26:1; Ps. 54:title 23:20 [a] Ps. 54:3 23:23 [1] Literally *thousands* 23:24 [a] Josh. 15:55; 1 Sam. 25:2 23:26 [a] Ps. 31:22 [b] Ps. 17:9 23:27 [a] 2 Kin. 19:9 23:28 [1] Hebrew *Sela Hammahlekoth* 23:29 [a] Josh. 15:62; 2 Chr. 20:2 24:1 [a] 1 Sam. 23:19, 28, 29 24:2 [a] 1 Sam. 26:2; Ps. 38:12 24:3 [a] 1 Sam. 24:10 [b] Judg. 3:24 [c] Ps. 57:title; 142:title 24:4 [a] 1 Sam. 26:8–11

robe. 5Now it happened afterward that [a]David's heart troubled him because he had cut Saul's robe. 6And he said to his men, [a]"The LORD forbid that I should do this thing to my master, the LORD's anointed, to stretch out my hand against him, seeing he *is* the anointed of the LORD." 7So David [a]restrained his servants with *these* words, and did not allow them to rise against Saul. And Saul got up from the cave and went on *his* way.

8David also arose afterward, went out of the cave, and called out to Saul, saying, "My lord the king!" And when Saul looked behind him, David stooped with his face to the earth, and bowed down. 9And David said to Saul: [a]"Why do you listen to the words of men who say, 'Indeed David seeks your harm'? 10Look, this day your eyes have seen that the LORD delivered you today into my hand in the cave, and *someone* urged *me* to kill you. But *my eye* spared you, and I said, 'I will not stretch out my hand against my lord, for he *is* the LORD's anointed.' 11Moreover, my father, see! Yes, see the corner of your robe in my hand! For in that I cut off the corner of your robe, and did not kill you, know and see that *there is* [a]neither evil nor rebellion in my hand, and I have not sinned against you. Yet you [b]hunt my life to take it. 12[a]Let the LORD judge between you and me, and let the LORD avenge me on you. But my hand shall not be against you. 13As the proverb of the ancients says, [a]'Wickedness proceeds from the wicked.' But my hand shall not be against you. 14After whom has the king of Israel come out? Whom do you pursue? [a]A dead dog? [b]A flea? 15[a]Therefore let the LORD be judge, and judge between you and me, and [b]see and [c]plead my case, and deliver me out of your hand."

16So it was, when David had finished speaking these words to Saul, that Saul said, [a]"*Is* this your voice, my son David?" And Saul lifted up his voice and wept. 17[a]Then he said to David: "You *are* [b]more righteous than I; for [c]you have rewarded me with good, whereas I have rewarded you with evil. 18And you have shown this day how you have dealt well with me; for when [a]the LORD delivered me into your hand, you did not kill me. 19For if a man finds his enemy, will he let him get away safely? Therefore may the LORD reward you with good for what you have done to me this day. 20And now [a]I know indeed that you shall surely be king, and that the kingdom of Israel shall be established in your hand. 21[a]Therefore swear now to me by the LORD [b]that you will not cut off my descendants after me, and that you will not destroy my name from my father's house."

22So David swore to Saul. And Saul went home, but David and his men went up to [a]the stronghold.

Death of Samuel

25 Then [a]Samuel died; and the Israelites gathered together and [b]lamented for him, and buried him at his home in Ramah. And David arose and went down [c]to the Wilderness of Paran.[1]

David and the Wife of Nabal

2Now *there was* a man [a]in Maon whose business *was* in [b]Carmel, and the man *was* very rich. He had three thousand sheep and a thousand goats. And he was shearing his sheep in Carmel. 3The name of the man *was* Nabal, and the name of his wife Abigail. And *she was* a woman of good understanding and beautiful appearance; but the man *was* harsh and evil in *his* doings. He *was of the house of* [a]Caleb.

4When David heard in the wilderness that Nabal was [a]shearing his sheep, 5David sent ten young men; and David said to the young men, "Go up to Carmel, go to Nabal, and greet him in my name. 6And thus you shall say to him who lives *in prosperity:* [a]'Peace *be* to you, peace to your house, and peace to all that you have! 7Now I have heard that you have shearers. Your

---

24:5 [a] 2 Sam. 24:10 **24:6** [a] 1 Sam. 26:11 **24:7** [a] Ps. 7:4; [Matt. 5:44; Rom. 12:17, 19] **24:9** [a] Ps. 141:6; [Prov. 16:28; 17:9] **24:11** [a] Judg. 11:27; Ps. 7:3; 35:7 [b] 1 Sam. 26:20 **24:12** [a] Gen. 16:5; Judg. 11:27; 1 Sam. 26:10–23; Job 5:8 **24:13** [a] [Matt. 7:16–20] **24:14** [a] 1 Sam. 17:43; 2 Sam. 9:8 [b] 1 Sam. 26:20 **24:15** [a] 1 Sam. 24:12 [b] 2 Chr. 24:22 [c] Ps. 35:1; 43:1; 119:154; Mic. 7:9 **24:16** [a] 1 Sam. 26:17 **24:17** [a] 1 Sam. 26:21 [b] Gen. 38:26 [c] [Matt. 5:44] **24:18** [a] 1 Sam. 26:23 **24:20** [a] 1 Sam. 23:17 **24:21** [a] Gen. 21:23; 1 Sam. 20:14–17 [b] 2 Sam. 21:6–8 **24:22** [a] 1 Sam. 23:29 **25:1** [a] 1 Sam. 28:3 [b] Num. 20:29; Deut. 34:8 [c] Gen. 21:21; Num. 10:12; 13:3 [1] Following Masoretic Text, Syriac, Targum, and Vulgate; Septuagint reads *Maon.* **25:2** [a] 1 Sam. 23:24 [b] Josh. 15:55 **25:3** [a] Josh. 15:13; 1 Sam. 30:14 **25:4** [a] Gen. 38:13; 2 Sam. 13:23 **25:6** [a] Judg. 19:20; 1 Chr. 12:18; Ps. 122:7; Luke 10:5

shepherds were with us, and we did not
hurt them, [a]nor was there anything missing from them all the while they were in
Carmel. 8Ask your young men, and they
will tell you. Therefore let *my* young men
find favor in your eyes, for we come on [a]a
feast day. Please give whatever comes to
your hand to your servants and to your
son David.' "

9So when David's young men came, they
spoke to Nabal according to all these words
in the name of David, and waited.

10Then Nabal answered David's servants,
and said, [a]"Who *is* David, and who *is* the son
of Jesse? There are many servants nowa-
days who break away each one from his
master. 11[a]Shall I then take my bread and
my water and my meat that I have killed
for my shearers, and give *it* to men when I
do not know where they *are* from?"

12So David's young men turned on their
heels and went back; and they came and
told him all these words. 13Then David said
to his men, "Every man gird on his sword."
So every man girded on his sword, and David also girded on his sword. And about
four hundred men went with David, and
two hundred [a]stayed with the supplies.

14Now one of the young men told Abigail, Nabal's wife, saying, "Look, David sent
messengers from the wilderness to greet
our master; and he reviled them. 15But the
men *were* very good to us, and [a]we were not
hurt, nor did we miss anything as long as
we accompanied them, when we were in
the fields. 16They were [a]a wall to us both
by night and day, all the time we were with
them keeping the sheep. 17Now therefore,
know and consider what you will do, for
[a]harm is determined against our master
and against all his household. For he *is such*
a [b]scoundrel[1] that *one* cannot speak to him."

18Then Abigail made haste and [a]took
two hundred *loaves* of bread, two skins of
wine, five sheep already dressed, five seahs
of roasted *grain,* one hundred clusters of
raisins, and two hundred cakes of figs, and
loaded *them* on donkeys. 19And she said to
her servants, [a]"Go on before me; see, I am
coming after you." But she did not tell her
husband Nabal.

20So it was, *as* she rode on the donkey,
that she went down under cover of the hill;
and there were David and his men, coming down toward her, and she met them.
21Now David had said, "Surely in vain I have
protected all that this *fellow* has in the wilderness, so that nothing was missed of all
that *belongs* to him. And he has [a]repaid me
evil for good. 22[a]May God do so, and more
also, to the enemies of David, if I [b]leave [c]one
male of all who *belong* to him by morning light."

23Now when Abigail saw David, she [a]dis-
mounted quickly from the donkey, fell on
her face before David, and bowed down to
the ground. 24So she fell at his feet and said:
"On me, my lord, *on* me *let* this iniquity
be! And please let your maidservant speak
in your ears, and hear the words of your
maidservant. 25Please, let not my lord regard this scoundrel Nabal. For as his name
is, so *is* he: Nabal[1] *is* his name, and folly
is with him! But I, your maidservant, did
not see the young men of my lord whom
you sent. 26Now therefore, my lord, [a]*as* the
LORD lives and *as* your soul lives, since the
LORD has [b]held you back from coming to
bloodshed and from [c]avenging yourself
with your own hand, now then, [d]let your
enemies and those who seek harm for my
lord be as Nabal. 27And now [a]this present
which your maidservant has brought to my
lord, let it be given to the young men who
follow my lord. 28Please forgive the trespass of your maidservant. For [a]the LORD
will certainly make for my lord an enduring house, because my lord [b]fights the battles of the LORD, [c]and evil is not found in
you throughout your days. 29Yet a man has
risen to pursue you and seek your life, but
the life of my lord shall be [a]bound in the
bundle of the living with the LORD your
God; and the lives of your enemies He shall
[b]sling out, *as from* the pocket of a sling.
30And it shall come to pass, when the LORD

25:7 [a] 1 Sam. 25:15, 21 **25:8** [a] Neh. 8:10–12; Esth. 8:17; 9:19, 22 **25:10** [a] Judg. 9:28 **25:11** [a] Judg. 8:6, 15 **25:13** [a] 1 Sam. 30:24 **25:15** [a] 1 Sam. 25:7, 21 **25:16** [a] Ex. 14:22; Job 1:10 **25:17** [a] 1 Sam. 20:7 [b] Deut. 13:13; Judg. 19:22 [1] Literally *son of Belial* **25:18** [a] Gen. 32:13; [Prov. 18:16; 21:14] **25:19** [a] Gen. 32:16, 20 **25:21** [a] 1 Sam. 24:17; Ps. 109:5; [Prov. 17:13] **25:22** [a] Ruth 1:17; 1 Sam. 3:17; 20:13, 16 [b] 1 Sam. 25:34 [c] 1 Kin. 14:10; 21:21; 2 Kin. 9:8 **25:23** [a] Josh. 15:18; Judg. 1:14 **25:25** [1] Literally *Fool* **25:26** [a] 2 Kin. 2:2 [b] Gen. 20:6; 1 Sam. 25:33 [c] [Rom. 12:19] [d] 2 Sam. 18:32 **25:27** [a] Gen. 33:11; 1 Sam. 30:26; 2 Kin. 5:15 **25:28** [a] 2 Sam. 7:11–16, 27; 1 Kin. 9:5; 1 Chr. 17:10, 25 [b] 1 Sam. 18:17 [c] 1 Sam. 24:11; Ps. 7:3 **25:29** [a] [Ps. 66:9; Col. 3:3] [b] Jer. 10:18

has done for my lord according to all the
good that He has spoken concerning you,
and has appointed you [a]ruler over Israel,
31 that this will be no grief to you, nor offense of heart to my lord, either that you
have shed blood without cause, or that my
lord has avenged himself. But when the
LORD has dealt well with my lord, then remember your maidservant."

32 Then David said to Abigail: [a]"Blessed
is the LORD God of Israel, who sent you this
day to meet me! 33 And blessed *is* your advice and blessed *are* you, because you have
[a]kept me this day from coming to bloodshed and from avenging myself with my
own hand. 34 For indeed, *as* the LORD God
of Israel lives, who has [a]kept me back from
hurting you, unless you had hurried and
come to meet me, surely [b]by morning light
no males would have been left to Nabal!"
35 So David received from her hand what she
had brought him, and said to her, [a]"Go up
in peace to your house. See, I have heeded
your voice and [b]respected your person."

36 Now Abigail went to Nabal, and there
he was, [a]holding a feast in his house, like
the feast of a king. And Nabal's heart *was*
merry within him, for he *was* very drunk;
therefore she told him nothing, little or
much, until morning light. 37 So it was,
in the morning, when the wine had gone
from Nabal, and his wife had told him these
things, that his heart died within him, and
he became *like* a stone. 38 Then it happened,
after about ten days, that the LORD [a]struck
Nabal, and he died.

39 So when David heard that Nabal was
dead, he said, [a]"Blessed *be* the LORD, who
has [b]pleaded the cause of my reproach
from the hand of Nabal, and has [c]kept His
servant from evil! For the LORD has [d]re-
turned the wickedness of Nabal on his own
head."

And David sent and proposed to Abigail,
to take her as his wife. 40 When the servants
of David had come to Abigail at Carmel,
they spoke to her saying, "David sent us to
you, to ask you to become his wife."

41 Then she arose, bowed her face to the
earth, and said, "Here is your maidservant,
a servant to [a]wash the feet of the servants
of my lord." 42 So Abigail rose in haste and
rode on a donkey, attended by five of her
maidens; and she followed the messengers
of David, and became his wife. 43 David also
took Ahinoam [a]of Jezreel, [b]and so both of
them were his wives.

44 But Saul had given [a]Michal his daughter, David's wife, to Palti[1] the son of Laish,
who *was* from [b]Gallim.

David Spares Saul a Second Time

26 Now the Ziphites came to Saul at
Gibeah, saying, [a]"Is David not hiding in the hill of Hachilah, opposite Jeshimon?" 2 Then Saul arose and went down to
the Wilderness of Ziph, having [a]three thousand chosen men of Israel with him, to seek
David in the Wilderness of Ziph. 3 And Saul
encamped in the hill of Hachilah, which *is*
opposite Jeshimon, by the road. But David
stayed in the wilderness, and he saw that
Saul came after him into the wilderness.
4 David therefore sent out spies, and understood that Saul had indeed come.

5 So David arose and came to the place
where Saul had encamped. And David saw
the place where Saul lay, and [a]Abner the son
of Ner, the commander of his army. Now
Saul lay within the camp, with the people
encamped all around him. 6 Then David answered, and said to Ahimelech the Hittite
and to Abishai [a]the son of Zeruiah, brother
of [b]Joab, saying, "Who will [c]go down with
me to Saul in the camp?"

And [d]Abishai said, "I will go down with
you."

7 So David and Abishai came to the people by night; and there Saul lay sleeping
within the camp, with his spear stuck in
the ground by his head. And Abner and the
people lay all around him. 8 Then Abishai
said to David, [a]"God has delivered your enemy into your hand this day. Now therefore,
please, let me strike him at once with the

25:30 [a] 1 Sam. 13:14; 15:28 25:32 [a] Gen. 24:27; Ex. 18:10; 1 Kin. 1:48; Ps. 41:13; 72:18; 106:48; Luke 1:68 25:33 [a] 1 Sam. 25:26
25:34 [a] 1 Sam. 25:26 [b] 1 Sam. 25:22 25:35 [a] 1 Sam. 20:42; 2 Sam. 15:9; 2 Kin. 5:19; Luke 7:50; 8:48 [b] Gen. 19:21 25:36 [a] 2 Sam. 13:28; Prov. 20:1; Is. 5:11; Dan. 5:1; [Hos. 4:11] 25:38 [a] 1 Sam. 26:10; 2 Sam. 6:7; Ps. 104:29 25:39 [a] 1 Sam. 25:32 [b] 1 Sam. 24:15; Prov. 22:23 [c] 1 Sam. 25:26, 34 [d] 1 Kin. 2:44 25:41 [a] [Prov. 15:33]; Luke 7:38, 44 25:43 [a] Josh. 15:56 [b] 1 Sam. 27:3; 30:5
25:44 [a] 1 Sam. 18:20; 2 Sam. 3:14 [b] Is. 10:30 [1] Spelled *Paltiel* in 2 Samuel 3:15 26:1 [a] 1 Sam. 23:19; Ps. 54:title
26:2 [a] 1 Sam. 13:2; 24:2 26:5 [a] 1 Sam. 14:50, 51; 17:55 26:6 [a] 1 Chr. 2:16 [b] 2 Sam. 2:13 [c] Judg. 7:10, 11 [d] 2 Sam. 2:18, 24 26:8 [a] 1 Sam. 24:4

spear, right to the earth; and I will not *have*
to strike him a second time!"
9But David said to Abishai, "Do not destroy him; [a]for who can stretch out his hand
against the LORD's anointed, and be guiltless?" 10David said furthermore, "*As* the
LORD lives, [a]the LORD shall strike him, or
[b]his day shall come to die, or he shall [c]go
out to battle and perish. 11[a]The LORD forbid
that I should stretch out my hand against
the LORD's anointed. But please, take now
the spear and the jug of water that *are* by
his head, and let us go." 12So David took the
spear and the jug of water *by* Saul's head,
and they got away; and no man saw or
knew *it* or awoke. For they *were* all asleep,
because [a]a deep sleep from the LORD had
fallen on them.
13Now David went over to the other side,
and stood on the top of a hill afar off, a
great distance *being* between them. 14And
David called out to the people and to Abner the son of Ner, saying, "Do you not answer, Abner?"
Then Abner answered and said, "Who
are you, calling out to the king?"
15So David said to Abner, "*Are* you not
a man? And who *is* like you in Israel? Why
then have you not guarded your lord the
king? For one of the people came in to destroy your lord the king. 16This thing that
you have done *is* not good. *As* the LORD
lives, you deserve to die, because you
have not guarded your master, the LORD's
anointed. And now see where the king's
spear *is*, and the jug of water that *was* by
his head."
17Then Saul knew David's voice, and said,
[a]"*Is* that your voice, my son David?"
David said, "*It is* my voice, my lord,
O king." 18And he said, [a]"Why does my lord
thus pursue his servant? For what have I
done, or what evil *is* in my hand? 19Now
therefore, please, let my lord the king hear
the words of his servant: If the LORD has
[a]stirred you up against me, let Him accept an offering. But if *it is* the children of
men, *may* they *be* cursed before the LORD,
[b]for they have driven me out this day from
sharing in the [c]inheritance of the LORD,
saying, 'Go, serve other gods.' 20So now, do
not let my blood fall to the earth before the
face of the LORD. For the king of Israel has
come out to seek [a]a flea, as when one hunts
a partridge in the mountains."
21Then Saul said, [a]"I have sinned. Return,
my son David. For I will harm you no more,
because my life was precious in your eyes
this day. Indeed I have played the fool and
erred exceedingly."
22And David answered and said, "Here is
the king's spear. Let one of the young men
come over and get it. 23[a]May the LORD [b]re-
pay every man *for* his righteousness and
his faithfulness; for the LORD delivered you
into *my* hand today, but I would not stretch
out my hand against the LORD's anointed.
24And indeed, as your life was valued much
this day in my eyes, so let my life be valued
much in the eyes of the LORD, and let Him
deliver me out of all tribulation."
25Then Saul said to David, "*May* you *be*
blessed, my son David! You shall both do
great things and also still [a]prevail."
So David went on his way, and Saul returned to his place.

David Allied with the Philistines

27 And David said in his heart, "Now I
shall perish someday by the hand of
Saul. *There is* nothing better for me than
that I should speedily escape to the land
of the Philistines; and Saul will despair
of me, to seek me anymore in any part of
Israel. So I shall escape out of his hand."
2Then David arose [a]and went over with the
six hundred men who *were* with him [b]to
Achish the son of Maoch, king of Gath. 3So
David dwelt with Achish at Gath, he and
his men, each man with his household,
and David [a]with his two wives, Ahinoam
the Jezreelitess, and Abigail the Carmelitess, Nabal's widow. 4And it was told Saul
that David had fled to Gath; so he sought
him no more.
5Then David said to Achish, "If I have
now found favor in your eyes, let them give
me a place in some town in the country,

26:9 [a] 1 Sam. 24:6, 7; 2 Sam. 1:14, 16 26:10 [a] [Deut. 32:35]; 1 Sam. 25:26, 38; [Luke 18:7; Rom. 12:19; Heb. 10:30] [b] Gen. 47:29; Deut. 31:14; [Job 7:1; 14:5]; Ps. 37:13 [c] 1 Sam. 31:6 26:11 [a] 1 Sam. 24:6–12; [Rom. 12:17, 19] 26:12 [a] Gen. 2:21; 15:12; Is. 29:10 26:17 [a] 1 Sam. 24:16 26:18 [a] 1 Sam. 24:9, 11–14 26:19 [a] 2 Sam. 16:11; 24:1 [b] Deut. 4:27, 28 [c] 2 Sam. 14:16; 20:19 26:20 [a] 1 Sam. 24:14 26:21 [a] Ex. 9:27; 1 Sam. 15:24, 30; 24:17; 2 Sam. 12:13 26:23 [a] 1 Sam. 24:19; Ps. 7:8; 18:20; 62:12 [b] 2 Sam. 22:21 26:25 [a] Gen. 32:28; 1 Sam. 24:20 27:2 [a] 1 Sam. 25:13 [b] 1 Sam. 21:10; 1 Kin. 2:39 27:3 [a] 1 Sam. 25:42, 43

that I may dwell there. For why should your servant dwell in the royal city with you?" 6 So Achish gave him Ziklag that day. Therefore [a]Ziklag has belonged to the kings of Judah to this day. 7 Now the time that David [a]dwelt in the country of the Philistines was one full year and four months.

8 And David and his men went up and raided [a]the Geshurites, [b]the Girzites,[1] and the [c]Amalekites. For those *nations* were the inhabitants of the land from of old, [d]as you go to Shur, even as far as the land of Egypt. 9 Whenever David attacked the land, he left neither man nor woman alive, but took away the sheep, the oxen, the donkeys, the camels, and the apparel, and returned and came to Achish. 10 Then Achish would say, "Where have you made a raid today?" And David would say, "Against the southern *area* of Judah, or against the southern *area* of [a]the Jerahmeelites, or against the southern *area* of [b]the Kenites." 11 David would save neither man nor woman alive, to bring *news* to Gath, saying, "Lest they should inform on us, saying, 'Thus David did.'" And thus *was* his behavior all the time he dwelt in the country of the Philistines. 12 So Achish believed David, saying, "He has made his people Israel utterly abhor him; therefore he will be my servant forever."

28 Now [a]it happened in those days that the Philistines gathered their armies together for war, to fight with Israel. And Achish said to David, "You assuredly know that you will go out with me to battle, you and your men."

2 So David said to Achish, "Surely you know what your servant can do."

And Achish said to David, "Therefore I will make you one of my chief guardians forever."

Saul Consults a Medium
(cf. Deut. 18:9–14)

3 Now [a]Samuel had died, and all Israel had lamented for him and buried him in [b]Ramah, in his own city. And Saul had put [c]the mediums and the spiritists out of the land.

4 Then the Philistines gathered together, and came and encamped at [a]Shunem. So Saul gathered all Israel together, and they encamped at [b]Gilboa. 5 When Saul saw the army of the Philistines, he was [a]afraid, and his heart trembled greatly. 6 And when Saul inquired of the LORD, [a]the LORD did not answer him, either by [b]dreams or [c]by Urim or by the prophets.

7 Then Saul said to his servants, "Find me a woman who is a medium, [a]that I may go to her and inquire of her."

And his servants said to him, "In fact, *there is* a woman who is a medium at En Dor."

8 So Saul disguised himself and put on other clothes, and he went, and two men with him; and they came to the woman by night. And [a]he said, "Please conduct a séance for me, and bring up for me the one I shall name to you."

9 Then the woman said to him, "Look, you know what Saul has done, how he has [a]cut off the mediums and the spiritists from the land. Why then do you lay a snare for my life, to cause me to die?"

10 And Saul swore to her by the LORD, saying, "*As* the LORD lives, no punishment shall come upon you for this thing."

11 Then the woman said, "Whom shall I bring up for you?"

And he said, "Bring up Samuel for me."

12 When the woman saw Samuel, she cried out with a loud voice. And the woman spoke to Saul, saying, "Why have you deceived me? For you *are* Saul!"

13 And the king said to her, "Do not be afraid. What did you see?"

And the woman said to Saul, "I saw [a]a spirit[1] ascending out of the earth."

14 So he said to her, "What *is* his form?"

And she said, "An old man is coming up, and he *is* covered with [a]a mantle." And Saul perceived that it *was* Samuel, and he stooped with *his* face to the ground and bowed down.

27:6 [a] Josh. 15:31; 19:5; 1 Chr. 12:1; Neh. 11:28 **27:7** [a] 1 Sam. 29:3 **27:8** [a] Josh. 13:2, 13 [b] Josh. 16:10; Judg. 1:29 [c] Ex. 17:8, 16; 1 Sam. 15:7, 8 [d] Gen. 25:18; Ex. 15:22 [1] Or *Gezrites* **27:10** [a] 1 Chr. 2:9, 25 [b] Judg. 1:16 **28:1** [a] 1 Sam. 29:1, 2 **28:3** [a] 1 Sam. 25:1 [b] 1 Sam. 1:19 [c] Ex. 22:18; Lev. 19:31; 20:27; Deut. 18:10, 11; 1 Sam. 15:23; 28:9 **28:4** [a] Josh. 19:18; 1 Sam. 28:4; 1 Kin. 1:3; 2 Kin. 4:8 [b] 1 Sam. 31:1 **28:5** [a] Job 18:11; [Is. 57:20] **28:6** [a] 1 Sam. 14:37; Prov. 1:28; Lam. 2:9 [b] Num. 12:6; Joel 2:28 [c] Ex. 28:30; Num. 27:21; Deut. 33:8 **28:7** [a] 1 Chr. 10:13 **28:8** [a] Deut. 18:10, 11; 1 Chr. 10:13; Is. 8:19 **28:9** [a] 1 Sam. 28:3 **28:13** [a] Ex. 22:28; Ps. 138:1 [1] Hebrew *elohim* **28:14** [a] 1 Sam. 15:27; 2 Kin. 2:8, 13

15Now Samuel said to Saul, "Why have
you [a]disturbed me by bringing me up?"
And Saul answered, "I am deeply distressed;
for the Philistines make war against me, and [b]God has departed from
me and [c]does not answer me anymore, neither
by prophets nor by dreams. Therefore
I have called you, that you may reveal to
me what I should do."
16Then Samuel said: "So why do you ask
me, seeing the LORD has departed from
you and has become your enemy? 17And
the LORD has done for Himself[1] [a]as He
spoke by me. For the LORD has torn the
kingdom out of your hand and given it to
your neighbor, David. 18[a]Because you did
not obey the voice of the LORD nor execute
His fierce wrath upon [b]Amalek, therefore
the LORD has done this thing to you this
day. 19Moreover the LORD will also deliver
Israel with you into the hand of the Philistines.
And tomorrow you and your sons
will be with [a]me. The LORD will also deliver
the army of Israel into the hand of
the Philistines."
20Immediately Saul fell full length on
the ground, and was dreadfully afraid because
of the words of Samuel. And there
was no strength in him, for he had eaten
no food all day or all night.
21And the woman came to Saul and saw
that he was severely troubled, and said to
him, "Look, your maidservant has obeyed
your voice, and I have [a]put my life in my
hands and heeded the words which you
spoke to me. 22Now therefore, please, heed
also the voice of your maidservant, and let
me set a piece of bread before you; and eat,
that you may have strength when you go
on *your* way."
23But he refused and said, "I will not eat."
So his servants, together with the
woman, urged him; and he heeded their
voice. Then he arose from the ground and
sat on the bed. 24Now the woman had a fatted
calf in the house, and she hastened to
kill it. And she took flour and kneaded *it*,
and baked unleavened bread from it. 25So
she brought *it* before Saul and his servants,
and they ate. Then they rose and went away
that night.

The Philistines Reject David

29 Then [a]the Philistines gathered together
all their armies [b]at Aphek,
and the Israelites encamped by a fountain
which *is* in Jezreel. 2And the [a]lords of the
Philistines passed in review by hundreds
and by thousands, but [b]David and his men
passed in review at the rear with Achish.
3Then the princes of the Philistines said,
"What *are* these Hebrews *doing here?*"
And Achish said to the princes of the
Philistines, "*Is* this not David, the servant
of Saul king of Israel, who has been with
me [a]these days, or these years? And to this
day I have [b]found no fault in him since he
defected *to me.*"
4But the princes of the Philistines were
angry with him; so the princes of the Philistines
said to him, [a]"Make this fellow return,
that he may go back to the place which you
have appointed for him, and do not let him
go down with us to [b]battle, lest [c]in the battle
he become our adversary. For with what
could he reconcile himself to his master, if
not with the heads of these [d]men? 5*Is* this
not David, [a]of whom they sang to one another
in dances, saying:

[b]'Saul has slain his thousands,
And David his ten thousands'?"[1]

6Then Achish called David and said to
him, "Surely, *as* the LORD lives, you have
been upright, and [a]your going out and your
coming in with me in the army *is* good in
my sight. For to this day [b]I have not found
evil in you since the day of your coming
to me. Nevertheless the lords do not favor
you. 7Therefore return now, and go in
peace, that you may not displease the lords
of the Philistines."
8So David said to Achish, "But what
have I done? And to this day what have
you found in your servant as long as I have
been with you, that I may not go and fight
against the enemies of my lord the king?"

28:15 [a] Is. 14:9 [b] 1 Sam. 16:14; 18:12 [c] 1 Sam. 28:6 **28:17** [a] 1 Sam. 15:28 [1] Or *him*, that is, David **28:18** [a] 1 Sam. 13:9–13; 15:1–26; 1 Kin. 20:42; 1 Chr. 10:13; Jer. 48:10 [b] 1 Sam. 15:3–9 **28:19** [a] 1 Sam. 31:1–6; Job 3:17–19 **28:21** [a] Judg. 12:3; 1 Sam. 19:5; Job 13:14 **29:1** [a] 1 Sam. 28:1 [b] Josh. 12:18; 19:30; 1 Sam. 4:1; 1 Kin. 20:30 **29:2** [a] 1 Sam. 6:4; 7:7 [b] 1 Sam. 28:1, 2 **29:3** [a] 1 Sam. 27:7 [b] 1 Sam. 27:1–6; 1 Chr. 12:19, 20; Dan. 6:5 **29:4** [a] 1 Sam. 27:6 [b] 1 Sam. 14:21 [c] 1 Sam. 29:9 [d] 1 Chr. 12:19, 20 **29:5** [a] 1 Sam. 21:11 [b] 1 Sam. 18:7 [1] Compare 1 Samuel 18:7 **29:6** [a] 2 Sam. 3:25; 2 Kin. 19:27 [b] 1 Sam. 29:3

9Then Achish answered and said to David, "I know that you *are* as good in my
sight [a]as an angel of God; nevertheless [b]the
princes of the Philistines have said, 'He
shall not go up with us to the battle.' 10Now
therefore, rise early in the morning with
your master's servants [a]who have come
with you.[1] And as soon as you are up early
in the morning and have light, depart."
11So David and his men rose early to depart in the morning, to return to the land
of the Philistines. [a]And the Philistines went
up to Jezreel.

David's Conflict with the Amalekites

30 Now it happened, when David and
his men came to [a]Ziklag, on the
third day, that the [b]Amalekites had invaded
the South and Ziklag, attacked Ziklag and
burned it with fire, 2and had taken captive the [a]women and those who *were* there,
from small to great; they did not kill anyone, but carried *them* away and went their
way. 3So David and his men came to the
city, and there it was, burned with fire; and
their wives, their sons, and their daughters had been taken captive. 4Then David
and the people who *were* with him lifted
up their voices and wept, until they had
no more power to weep. 5And David's two
[a]wives, Ahinoam the Jezreelitess, and Abigail the widow of Nabal the Carmelite, had
been taken captive. 6Now David was greatly
distressed, for [a]the people spoke of stoning him, because the soul of all the people
was grieved, every man for his sons and his
daughters. [b]But David strengthened himself in the LORD his God.
7[a]Then David said to Abiathar the priest,
Ahimelech's son, "Please bring the ephod
here to me." And [b]Abiathar brought the
ephod to David. 8[a]So David inquired of the
LORD, saying, "Shall I pursue this troop?
Shall I overtake them?"
And He answered him, "Pursue, for you
shall surely overtake *them* and without fail
recover *all*."
9So David went, he and the six hundred
men who *were* with him, and came to the
Brook Besor, where those stayed who were
left behind. 10But David pursued, he and
four hundred men; [a]for two hundred stayed
behind, who were so weary that they could
not cross the Brook Besor.
11Then they found an Egyptian in the
field, and brought him to David; and they
gave him bread and he ate, and they let him
drink water. 12And they gave him a piece of
[a]a cake of figs and two clusters of raisins.
So [b]when he had eaten, his strength came
back to him; for he had eaten no bread
nor drunk water for three days and three
nights. 13Then David said to him, "To whom
do you *belong*, and where *are* you from?"
And he said, "I *am* a young man from
Egypt, servant of an Amalekite; and my
master left me behind, because three days
ago I fell sick. 14We made an invasion of
the southern *area* of [a]the Cherethites, in
the *territory* which *belongs* to Judah, and of
the southern *area* [b]of Caleb; and we burned
Ziklag with fire."
15And David said to him, "Can you take
me down to this troop?"
So he said, "Swear to me by God that you
will neither kill me nor deliver me into the
hands of my [a]master, and I will take you
down to this troop."
16And when he had brought him down,
there they were, spread out over all the land,
[a]eating and drinking and dancing, because
of all the great spoil which they had taken
from the land of the Philistines and from
the land of Judah. 17Then David attacked
them from twilight until the evening of the
next day. Not a man of them escaped, except four hundred young men who rode on
camels and fled. 18So David recovered all
that the Amalekites had carried away, and
David rescued his two wives. 19And nothing
of theirs was lacking, either small or great,
sons or daughters, spoil or anything which
they had taken from them; [a]David recovered all. 20Then David took all the flocks and
herds they had driven before those *other*
livestock, and said, "This *is* David's spoil."

29:9 [a] 2 Sam. 14:17, 20; 19:27 [b] 1 Sam. 29:4 29:10 [a] 1 Chr. 12:19, 22 [1] Following Masoretic Text, Targum, and Vulgate; Septuagint adds *and go to the place which I have selected for you there; and set no bothersome word in your heart, for you are good before me. And rise on your way.* 29:11 [a] 2 Sam. 4:4 30:1 [a] 1 Sam. 27:6 [b] 1 Sam. 15:7; 27:8 30:2 [a] 1 Sam. 27:2, 3 30:5 [a] 1 Sam. 25:42, 43 30:6 [a] Ex. 17:4; John 8:59 [b] 1 Sam. 23:16; Is. 25:4; Hab. 3:17–19 30:7 [a] 1 Sam. 23:2–9 [b] 1 Sam. 23:6 30:8 [a] 1 Sam. 23:2, 4; Ps. 50:15; 91:15 30:10 [a] 1 Sam. 30:9, 21 30:12 [a] 1 Sam. 25:18; 1 Kin. 20:7 [b] Judg. 15:19; 1 Sam. 14:27 30:14 [a] 2 Sam. 8:18; 1 Kin. 1:38, 44; Ezek. 25:16; Zeph. 2:5 [b] Josh. 14:13; 15:13 30:15 [a] Deut. 23:15 30:16 [a] 1 Thess. 5:3 30:19 [a] 1 Sam. 30:8

21 Now David came to the [a]two hundred
men who had been so weary that they could
not follow David, whom they also had made
to stay at the Brook Besor. So they went out
to meet David and to meet the people who
were with him. And when David came near
the people, he greeted them. 22 Then all the
wicked and [a]worthless men[1] of those who
went with David answered and said, "Because they did not go with us, we will not give
them *any* of the spoil that we have recovered,
except for every man's wife and children,
that they may lead *them* away and depart."

23 But David said, "My brethren, you shall
not do so with what the LORD has given us,
who has preserved us and delivered into
our hand the troop that came against us.
24 For who will heed you in this matter? But
[a]as his part *is* who goes down to the battle,
so *shall* his part *be* who stays by the supplies; they shall share alike." 25 So it was,
from that day forward; he made it a statute and an ordinance for Israel to this day.

26 Now when David came to Ziklag, he
sent *some* of the spoil to the elders of Judah, to his friends, saying, "Here is a present for you from the spoil of the enemies of
the LORD"— 27 to *those* who *were* in Bethel,
those who *were* in [a]Ramoth of the South,
those who *were* in [b]Jattir, 28 *those* who *were* in
[a]Aroer, *those* who *were* in [b]Siphmoth, *those*
who *were* in [c]Eshtemoa, 29 *those* who *were* in
Rachal, *those* who *were* in the cities of [a]the
Jerahmeelites, *those* who *were* in the cities
of the [b]Kenites, 30 *those* who *were* in [a]Hor-
mah, *those* who *were* in Chorashan,[1] *those*
who *were* in Athach, 31 *those* who *were* in [a]He-
bron, and to all the places where David himself and his men were accustomed to [b]rove.

The Tragic End of Saul and His Sons
(1 Chr. 10:1–14)

31 Now [a]the Philistines fought against
Israel; and the men of Israel fled
from before the Philistines, and fell slain
on Mount [b]Gilboa. 2 Then the Philistines
followed hard after Saul and his sons. And
the Philistines killed [a]Jonathan, Abinadab,
and Malchishua, Saul's sons. 3 [a]The battle
became fierce against Saul. The archers
hit him, and he was severely wounded by
the archers.

4 [a]Then Saul said to his armorbearer,
"Draw your sword, and thrust me through
with it, lest [b]these uncircumcised men come
and thrust me through and abuse me."

But his armorbearer would not, [c]for he
was greatly afraid. Therefore Saul took a
sword and [d]fell on it. 5 And when his armorbearer saw that Saul was dead, he also fell
on his sword, and died with him. 6 So Saul,
his three sons, his armorbearer, and all his
men died together that same day.

7 And when the men of Israel who *were*
on the other side of the valley, and *those*
who *were* on the other side of the Jordan,
saw that the men of Israel had fled and
that Saul and his sons were dead, they forsook the cities and fled; and the Philistines
came and dwelt in them. 8 So it happened
the next day, when the Philistines came to
strip the slain, that they found Saul and his
three sons fallen on Mount Gilboa. 9 And
they cut off his head and stripped off his
armor, and sent *word* throughout the land
of the Philistines, to [a]proclaim *it in* the temple of their idols and among the people.
10 [a]Then they put his armor in the temple
of the [b]Ashtoreths, and [c]they fastened his
body to the wall of [d]Beth Shan.[1]

11 [a]Now when the inhabitants of Jabesh
Gilead heard what the Philistines had done
to Saul, 12 [a]all the valiant men arose and
traveled all night, and took the body of
Saul and the bodies of his sons from the
wall of Beth Shan; and they came to Jabesh and [b]burned them there. 13 Then they
took their bones and [a]buried *them* under
the tamarisk tree at Jabesh, [b]and fasted
seven days.

30:21 [a] 1 Sam. 30:10 **30:22** [a] Deut. 13:13; Judg. 19:22 [1] Literally *men of Belial* **30:24** [a] Num. 31:27; Josh. 22:8 **30:27** [a] Josh. 19:8 [b] Josh. 15:48; 21:14 **30:28** [a] Josh. 13:16 [b] 1 Chr. 27:27 [c] Josh. 15:50 **30:29** [a] 1 Sam. 27:10 [b] Judg. 1:16; 1 Sam. 15:6; 27:10 **30:30** [a] Num. 14:45; 21:3; Josh. 12:14; 15:30; 19:4; Judg. 1:17 [1] Or *Borashan* **30:31** [a] Num. 13:22; Josh. 14:13–15; 21:11–13; 2 Sam. 2:1 [b] 1 Sam. 23:22 **31:1** [a] 1 Chr. 10:1–12 [b] 1 Sam. 28:4 **31:2** [a] 1 Sam. 14:49; 1 Chr. 8:33 **31:3** [a] 2 Sam. 1:6 **31:4** [a] Judg. 9:54; 1 Chr. 10:4 [b] Judg. 14:3; 1 Sam. 14:6; 17:26, 36 [c] 2 Sam. 1:14 [d] 2 Sam. 1:6, 10 **31:9** [a] Judg. 16:23, 24; 2 Sam. 1:20 **31:10** [a] 1 Sam. 21:9 [b] Judg. 2:13; 1 Sam. 7:3 [c] 2 Sam. 21:12 [d] Judg. 1:27 [1] Spelled *Beth Shean* in Joshua 17:11 and elsewhere **31:11** [a] 1 Sam. 11:1–13 **31:12** [a] 1 Sam. 11:1–11; 2 Sam. 2:4–7 [b] 2 Chr. 16:14; Jer. 34:5; Amos 6:10 **31:13** [a] 2 Sam. 2:4, 5; 21:12–14 [b] Gen. 50:10

THE SECOND BOOK OF

SAMUEL

OVERVIEW

The Book of 2 Samuel does not indicate an author. Some believe it may have been written by Nathan or Gad (see 1 Chr. 29:29). Second Samuel continues the account of Israel's monarchy where 1 Samuel left off and continues through the forty-year reign of King David from roughly 1010 to 970 BC.

First Samuel ends with the death of Saul and three of his four sons. When 2 Samuel begins, David has just learned of these deaths (see 2 Sam. 1:1–27). David's followers anoint him as king over Judah, the southern part of Israel (see 2:1–7), while Saul's followers establish Saul's only living son, Ishbosheth, as king over the remainder of the nation (see vv. 8–9). Ishbosheth reigned for two years before David defeated him (see v. 10).

After becoming king over all Israel, David defeated the Philistines (see 5:17–25). He then sought to bring the ark of the covenant to his newly established capital of Jerusalem as a sign that God reigned over His people. With the support and help of thousands of Israelites, David retrieved the ark of the covenant (see 6:1–5). Pleased with David's humility and his desire for His approval, God established a covenant with him, promising peace to Israel and declaring that David's kingdom would last forever (ch. 7).

David's reign, however, was far from perfect. When David saw Bathsheba, the wife of Uriah, one of his warriors, bathing, he sent for her and sinned against her, Uriah, and God. Bathsheba became pregnant, and David brought Uriah home from battle to try to cover up what he had done. When that failed, David sent Uriah back into the battle with a message for Joab, the commander, to send Uriah into the fiercest part of the battle and then to withdraw from him, knowing this would lead to Uriah's death. When news came that he had indeed died, David made Uriah's widow his wife (ch. 11).

Soon after, God sent the prophet Nathan to confront David about his sins (see 12:1–15). Because of what David had done, Nathan told him that God would "raise up adversity against" his house (v. 11). David repented for his sins, but his first child with Bathsheba died (see vv. 15–23). They had another son, Solomon, whom God loved (see vv. 24–25).

David also had another son named Absalom, who would fulfill God's promise of adversity and end up conspiring against his father. Winning the favor of the people, Absalom put an army together to overthrow David, and the people declared him king (see 15:1–12). David's army, however, easily defeated Absalom's army (see 18:6–8). Though David had given orders to spare his son's life, his men killed Absalom (see vv. 9–15). When David heard the news, he mourned deeply for his son (see vv. 32–33).

The remainder of 2 Samuel details the execution of Saul's descendants (ch. 21) and David's song of praise to God for delivering him from his enemies (ch. 22). In chapter 22, David named the warriors who helped him in battle. The book concludes with David conducting a census of Israel against the will of God. In response, God presented David with three options for punishment, and David chose a plague that killed seventy thousand people (see 24:1–17).

In 2 Samuel, we see that no person is perfect and God disciplines all who sin against Him. Even those whom God chooses to lead His people can fall prey to grievous sin and may suffer its consequences. Despite the suffering God brought to David and his family, He forgave David and, through Jesus, remained true to His promise that David's kingdom would last forever.

BREATHE IT IN

First Samuel 13:14 refers to David as "a man after [God's] own heart." Although David was not perfect and committed grievous sins, he lived up to this description because, overall, he desired to be faithful to God and was contrite when he sinned. David's heart, like God's, was for the people of Israel to come together as one nation and worship the Lord their God.

David was a man with a strong commitment to God, but even he sinned. Unlike many, however, he acknowledged his sin and prayed to God for forgiveness (see Ps. 51). God forgave David, but he and his family still experienced the devastating consequences of his behavior. David's family and the entire nation could not escape the turmoil and death that would come.

Some people do not realize that their thoughts and actions often affect their entire family. Our relationship with God is not just about us; it is also about those connected to us. How many times have we used inappropriate language in the presence of a young child, only to hear that child innocently repeat it later? Have we realized that we have likely repeated destructive or harmful behaviors learned from our parents? Do we have an ungodly habit, learned from another family member, that we have yet to conquer?

Recognizing that our relationship with God is not just about us but about our bloodline, and even our communities, should cause us to pause to reflect upon our family history. During this time of reflection, we should consider the positive and negative influences that have helped shape us. We should also think about how we want the future of our family to look. Then, we must decide if our present life will lead us to that future life we desire.

If your life does not reflect your desired future for your family, it might be time to make some changes and break some generational curses. Break the curse of addiction. Break the curse of divorce. Break the curse of poverty, and break the curse of sickness. Change your thoughts and behaviors so they align with God's Word and His will. Show God that you are committed to Him. Live in a way that is pleasing to God now to move toward God's favor in the lives of your children and the generations that follow.

†

THE SECOND BOOK OF

SAMUEL

The Report of Saul's Death

1 Now it came to pass after the [a]death of
Saul, when David had returned from
[b]the slaughter of the Amalekites, and David had stayed two days in Ziklag, 2 on the
third day, behold, it happened that [a]a man
came from Saul's camp [b]with his clothes
torn and dust on his head. So it was, when
he came to David, that he [c]fell to the ground
and prostrated himself.
3 And David said to him, "Where have
you come from?"
So he said to him, "I have escaped from
the camp of Israel."
4 Then David said to him, [a]"How did the
matter go? Please tell me."
And he answered, "The people have fled
from the battle, many of the people are
fallen and dead, and Saul and [b]Jonathan
his son are dead also."
5 So David said to the young man who
told him, "How do you know that Saul and
Jonathan his son are dead?"
6 Then the young man who told him
said, "As I happened by chance *to be* on
[a]Mount Gilboa, there was [b]Saul, leaning
on his spear; and indeed the chariots and
horsemen followed hard after him. 7 Now
when he looked behind him, he saw me
and called to me. And I answered, 'Here I
am.' 8 And he said to me, 'Who *are* you?' So
I answered him, 'I *am* an Amalekite.' 9 He
said to me again, 'Please stand over me
and kill me, for anguish has come upon
me, but my life still *remains* in me.' 10 So I
stood over him and [a]killed him, because
I was sure that he could not live after he
had fallen. And I took the crown that *was*
on his head and the bracelet that *was* on
his arm, and have brought them here to
my lord."
11 Therefore David took hold of his own
clothes and [a]tore them, and *so did* all
the men who *were* with him. 12 And they
[a]mourned and wept and [b]fasted until evening for Saul and for Jonathan his son, for
the [c]people of the LORD and for the house
of Israel, because they had fallen by the
sword.
13 Then David said to the young man who
told him, "Where *are* you from?"
And he answered, "I *am* the son of an
alien, an Amalekite."
14 So David said to him, "How [a]was it you
were not [b]afraid to [c]put forth your hand to
destroy the LORD's anointed?" 15 Then [a]Da-
vid called one of the young men and said,
"Go near, *and* execute him!" And he struck
him so that he died. 16 So David said to him,
[a]"Your blood *is* on your own head, for [b]your
own mouth has testified against you, saying, 'I have killed the LORD's anointed.'"

The Song of the Bow

17 Then David lamented with this lamentation over Saul and over Jonathan his
son, 18 [a]and he told *them* to teach the children of Judah *the Song of* the Bow; indeed
it is written [b]in the Book of Jasher:

19 "The beauty of Israel is slain
on your high places!
[a]How the mighty have fallen!
20 [a]Tell *it* not in Gath,
Proclaim *it* not in the streets
of [b]Ashkelon—

1:1 [a] 1 Sam. 31:6 [b] 1 Sam. 30:1, 17, 26 1:2 [a] 2 Sam. 4:10 [b] 1 Sam. 4:12 [c] 1 Sam. 25:23 1:4 [a] 1 Sam. 4:16; 31:3 [b] 1 Sam. 31:2
1:6 [a] 1 Sam. 31:1 [b] 1 Sam. 31:2–4 1:10 [a] Judg. 9:54; 2 Kin. 11:12 1:11 [a] 2 Sam. 3:31; 13:31 1:12 [a] 2 Sam. 3:31 [b] 1 Sam. 31:13 [c] 2 Sam. 6:21
1:14 [a] Num. 12:8 [b] 1 Sam. 31:4 [c] 1 Sam. 24:6; 26:9 1:15 [a] 2 Sam. 4:10, 12 1:16 [a] 1 Sam. 26:9; 2 Sam. 3:28; 1 Kin. 2:32–37 [b] 2 Sam. 1:10;
Luke 19:22 1:18 [a] 1 Sam. 31:3 [b] Josh. 10:13 1:19 [a] 2 Sam. 1:27 1:20 [a] 1 Sam. 27:2; 31:8–13; Mic. 1:10 [b] 1 Sam. 6:17; Jer. 25:20

Lest [c]the daughters of the
Philistines rejoice,
Lest the daughters of [d]the
uncircumcised triumph.

21 "O [a]mountains of Gilboa,
[b]*Let there be* no dew nor rain upon you,
Nor fields of offerings.
For the shield of the mighty
is cast away there!
The shield of Saul, not
[c]anointed with oil.
22 From the blood of the slain,
From the fat of the mighty,
[a]The bow of Jonathan did not turn back,
And the sword of Saul did
not return empty.

23 "Saul and Jonathan *were* beloved
and pleasant in their lives,
And in their [a]death they
were not divided;
They were swifter than eagles,
They were [b]stronger than lions.

24 "O daughters of Israel, weep over Saul,
Who clothed you in scarlet,
with luxury;
Who put ornaments of gold
on your apparel.

25 "How the mighty have fallen in
the midst of the battle!
Jonathan *was* slain in your high places.
26 I am distressed for you, my
brother Jonathan;
You have been very pleasant to me;
[a]Your love to me was wonderful,
Surpassing the love of women.

27 "How[a] the mighty have fallen,
And the weapons of war perished!"

David Anointed King of Judah

2 It happened after this that David [a]in-
quired of the LORD, saying, "Shall I go
up to any of the cities of Judah?"
And the LORD said to him, "Go up."
David said, "Where shall I go up?"
And He said, "To [b]Hebron."
2 So David went up there, and his [a]two
wives also, Ahinoam the Jezreelitess, and
Abigail the widow of Nabal the Carmelite.
3 And David brought up [a]the men who *were*
with him, every man with his household.
So they dwelt in the cities of Hebron.
4 [a]Then the men of Judah came, and
there they [b]anointed David king over the
house of Judah. And they told David, saying, [c]"The men of Jabesh Gilead *were the*
ones who buried Saul."
5 So David sent mes-
sengers to the men of Jabesh Gilead, and
said to them, [a]"You *are* blessed of the LORD,
for you have shown this kindness to your
lord, to Saul, and have buried him.
6 And
now may [a]the LORD show kindness and
truth to you. I also will repay you this kindness, because you have done this thing.
7 Now therefore, let your hands be strengthened, and be valiant; for your master Saul
is dead, and also the house of Judah has
anointed me king over them."

Ishbosheth Made King of Israel

8 But [a]Abner the son of Ner, commander
of Saul's army, took Ishbosheth[1] the son of
Saul and brought him over to [b]Mahanaim;
9 and he made him king over [a]Gilead, over
the [b]Ashurites, over [c]Jezreel, over Ephraim,
over Benjamin, and over all Israel.
10 Ish-
bosheth, Saul's son, *was* forty years old
when he began to reign over Israel, and
he reigned two years. Only the house of
Judah followed David.
11 And [a]the time that
David was king in Hebron over the house
of Judah was seven years and six months.

Israel and Judah at War

12 Now Abner the son of Ner, and the servants of Ishbosheth the son of Saul, went
out from Mahanaim to [a]Gibeon.
13 And [a]Joab
the son of Zeruiah, and the servants of David, went out and met them by [b]the pool of
Gibeon. So they sat down, one on one side
of the pool and the other on the other side
of the pool.
14 Then Abner said to Joab, "Let

1:20 [c] Ex. 15:20; Judg. 11:34; 1 Sam. 18:6 [d] 1 Sam. 31:4 **1:21** [a] 1 Sam. 31:1 [b] Ezek. 31:15 [c] 1 Sam. 10:1 **1:22** [a] Deut. 32:42; 1 Sam. 18:4 **1:23** [a] 1 Sam. 31:2–4 [b] Judg. 14:18 **1:26** [a] 1 Sam. 18:1–4; 19:2; 20:17 **1:27** [a] 2 Sam. 1:19, 25 **2:1** [a] Judg. 1:1; 1 Sam. 23:2, 4, 9; 30:7, 8 [b] 1 Sam. 30:31; 2 Sam. 2:11; 5:1–3; 1 Kin. 2:11 **2:2** [a] 1 Sam. 25:42, 43; 30:5 **2:3** [a] 1 Sam. 27:2, 3; 30:1; 1 Chr. 12:1 **2:4** [a] 1 Sam. 30:26; 2 Sam. 2:11; 5:5; 19:14, 41–43 [b] 1 Sam. 16:13; 2 Sam. 5:3 [c] 1 Sam. 31:11–13 **2:5** [a] Ruth 2:20; 3:10 **2:6** [a] Ex. 34:6; 2 Tim. 1:16, 18 **2:8** [a] 1 Sam. 14:50; 2 Sam. 3:6 [b] Gen. 32:2; Josh. 21:38; 2 Sam. 17:24 [1] Called *Esh-Baal* in 1 Chronicles 8:33 and 9:39 **2:9** [a] Josh. 22:9 [b] Judg. 1:32 [c] 1 Sam. 29:1 **2:11** [a] 2 Sam. 5:5; 1 Kin. 2:11 **2:12** [a] Josh. 10:2–12; 18:25 **2:13** [a] 1 Sam. 26:6; 2 Sam. 8:16; 1 Chr. 2:16; 11:6 [b] Jer. 41:12

RECONCILE WEAKNESSES WITH STRENGTH

INHALE

I have struggled with addiction since I was a teen. I have seen a licensed therapist. I have gotten church counseling. I have been to all the programs. I have quit more times than I can count, only to relapse and start the cycle again. If you look at me, you wouldn't know I am struggling. But I feel like I am going crazy trying to act like everything is fine when the wheels are falling off my life. I cannot drive anymore like this. I need the Lord to take the wheel and fix me. Should He? Can He? Will He?

EXHALE

Be encouraged and know this: God can take *anyone anywhere* and do *anything*! But when we surrender to Him—when we recognize our weaknesses and His strength—we put ourselves in His hands and can see Him do the most amazing things. Again, God can do anything He wants, with or without our help, but when we surrender to Him and stop fighting, we can best see and appreciate what He does.

So, you are onto something important when you mention giving God "the wheel." David did much the same thing in 2 Samuel 2:1, which says, "It happened after this that David inquired of the LORD, saying, 'Shall I go up to any of the cities of Judah?' And the LORD said to him, 'Go up.' David said, 'Where shall I go up?'" Now *that's* giving God the wheel! David positioned himself best to be used by God, and you will too.

One other thing to mention. There's no need to fake it in front of others. We all struggle. Few people who look like they are doing well actually are. So why fake it when they are probably faking it too? Why not be real and help each other? Remember that your purpose in life is not to please others. It's to please God. I was once told, "If you please God, it doesn't matter who you displease. But if you displease God, it doesn't matter who you please." Be real. Please God.

the young men now arise and compete before us."
And Joab said, "Let them arise."
15So they arose and went over by number, twelve from Benjamin, *followers* of
Ishbosheth the son of Saul, and twelve
from the servants of David. 16And each
one grasped his opponent by the head and
thrust his sword in his opponent's side; so
they fell down together. Therefore that
place was called the Field of Sharp Swords,[1]
which *is* in Gibeon. 17So there was a very
fierce battle that day, and Abner and the
men of Israel were beaten before the servants of David.
18Now the [a]three sons of Zeruiah were
there: Joab and Abishai and Asahel. And
Asahel *was* [b]*as* fleet of foot [c]as a wild gazelle. 19So Asahel pursued Abner, and in
going he did not turn to the right hand or
to the left from following Abner.
20Then Abner looked behind him and
said, "*Are* you Asahel?"
He answered, "I *am*."
21And Abner said to him, "Turn aside
to your right hand or to your left, and lay
hold on one of the young men and take
his armor for yourself." But Asahel would
not turn aside from following him. 22So
Abner said again to Asahel, "Turn aside
from following me. Why should I strike
you to the ground? How then could I face
your brother Joab?" 23However, he refused
to turn aside. Therefore Abner struck him
[a]in the stomach with the blunt end of the
spear, so that the spear came out of his
back; and he fell down there and died on
the spot. So it was *that* as many as came to

2:16 [1] Hebrew *Helkath Hazzurim* 2:18 [a] 1 Chr. 2:16 [b] 1 Chr. 12:8; Hab. 3:19 [c] Ps. 18:33 2:23 [a] 2 Sam. 3:27; 4:6; 20:10

the place where Asahel fell down and died,
stood [b]still.
24Joab and Abishai also pursued Abner.
And the sun was going down when they
came to the hill of Ammah, which *is* before
Giah by the road to the Wilderness of Gibeon. 25Now the children of Benjamin gathered together behind Abner and became a
unit, and took their stand on top of a hill.
26Then Abner called to Joab and said, "Shall
the sword devour forever? Do you not know
that it will be bitter in the latter end? How
long will it be then until you tell the people
to return from pursuing their brethren?"
27And Joab said, "*As* God lives, unless
[a]you had spoken, surely then by morning
all the people would have given up pursuing their brethren." 28So Joab blew a trumpet; and all the people stood still and did
not pursue Israel anymore, nor did they
fight anymore. 29Then Abner and his men
went on all that night through the plain,
crossed over the Jordan, and went through
all Bithron; and they came to Mahanaim.
30So Joab returned from pursuing Abner. And when he had gathered all the people together, there were missing of David's
servants nineteen men and Asahel. 31But
the servants of David had struck down, of
Benjamin and Abner's men, three hundred
and sixty men who died. 32Then they took
up Asahel and buried him in his father's
tomb, which *was in* [a]Bethlehem. And Joab
and his men went all night, and they came
to Hebron at daybreak.
3 Now there was a long [a]war between the
house of Saul and the house of David.
But David grew stronger and stronger, and
the house of Saul grew weaker and weaker.

Sons of David

2Sons were born [a]to David in Hebron:
His firstborn was Amnon [b]by Ahinoam
the Jezreelitess; 3his second, Chileab, by
Abigail the widow of Nabal the Carmelite;
the third, [a]Absalom the son of Maacah, the
daughter of Talmai, king [b]of Geshur; 4the
fourth, [a]Adonijah the son of Haggith;
the fifth, Shephatiah the son of Abital; 5and
the sixth, Ithream, by David's wife Eglah.
These were born to David in Hebron.

Abner Joins Forces with David

6Now it was so, while there was war between the house of Saul and the house of
David, that Abner was strengthening *his
hold* on the house of Saul.
7And Saul had a concubine, whose name
was [a]Rizpah, the daughter of Aiah. So *Ishbosheth* said to Abner, "Why have you [b]gone
in to my father's concubine?"
8Then Abner became very angry at the
words of Ishbosheth, and said, "*Am* I [a]a
dog's head that belongs to Judah? Today
I show loyalty to the house of Saul your
father, to his brothers, and to his friends,
and have not delivered you into the hand
of David; and you charge me today with a
fault concerning this woman? 9[a]May God
do so to Abner, and more also, if I do not do
for David [b]as the LORD has sworn to him—
10to transfer the kingdom from the house
of Saul, and set up the throne of David over
Israel and over Judah, [a]from Dan to Beersheba." 11And he could not answer Abner
another word, because he feared him.
12Then Abner sent messengers on his behalf to David, saying, "Whose *is* the land?"
saying *also,* "Make your covenant with me,
and indeed my hand *shall be* with you to
bring all Israel to you."
13And *David* said, "Good, I will make a
covenant with you. But one thing I require
of you: [a]you shall not see my face unless
you first bring [b]Michal, Saul's daughter,
when you come to see my face." 14So David
sent messengers to [a]Ishbosheth, Saul's son,
saying, "Give *me* my wife Michal, whom I
betrothed to myself [b]for a hundred foreskins of the Philistines." 15And Ishbosheth
sent and took her from *her* husband, from
Paltiel[1] the son of Laish. 16Then her husband went along with her to [a]Bahurim,
weeping behind her. So Abner said to him,
"Go, return!" And he returned.
17Now Abner had communicated with the
elders of Israel, saying, "In time past you
were seeking for David *to be* king over you.

2:23 [b] 2 Sam. 20:12 2:27 [a] 2 Sam. 2:14 2:32 [a] 1 Sam. 20:6 3:1 [a] 1 Kin. 14:30; [Ps. 46:9] 3:2 [a] 1 Chr. 3:1–4 [b] 1 Sam. 25:42, 43 3:3 [a] 2 Sam. 15:1–10 [b] Josh. 13:13; 1 Sam. 27:8; 2 Sam. 13:37; 14:32; 15:8 3:4 [a] 1 Kin. 1:5 3:7 [a] 2 Sam. 21:8–11 [b] 2 Sam. 16:21 3:8 [a] Deut. 23:18; 1 Sam. 24:14; 2 Sam. 9:8; 16:9 3:9 [a] Ruth 1:17; 1 Kin. 19:2 [b] 1 Sam. 15:28; 16:1, 12; 28:17; 1 Chr. 12:23 3:10 [a] Judg. 20:1; 1 Sam. 3:20; 2 Sam. 17:11; 1 Kin. 4:25 3:13 [a] Gen. 43:3 [b] 1 Sam. 18:20; 19:11; 25:44; 2 Sam. 6:16 3:14 [a] 2 Sam. 2:10 [b] 1 Sam. 18:25–27 3:15 [1] Spelled *Palti* in 1 Samuel 25:44 3:16 [a] 2 Sam. 16:5; 19:16

18Now then, do *it!* [a]For the LORD has spoken
of David, saying, 'By the hand of My servant
David, I[1] will save My people Israel from the
hand of the Philistines and the hand of all
their enemies.'" 19And Abner also spoke in
the hearing of [a]Benjamin. Then Abner also
went to speak in the hearing of David in Hebron all that seemed good to Israel and the
whole house of Benjamin.

20So Abner and twenty men with him
came to David at Hebron. And David made
a feast for Abner and the men who *were*
with him. 21Then Abner said to David, "I
will arise and go, and [a]gather all Israel to
my lord the king, that they may make a covenant with you, and that you may [b]reign
over all that your heart desires." So David
sent Abner away, and he went in peace.

Joab Murders Abner

22At that moment the servants of David
and Joab came from a raid and brought
much spoil with them. But Abner *was* not
with David in Hebron, for he had sent him
away, and he had gone in peace. 23When
Joab and all the troops that *were* with him
had come, they told Joab, saying, "Abner
the son of Ner came to the king, and he
sent him away, and he has gone in peace."
24Then Joab came to the king and said,
"What have you done? Look, Abner came
to you; why *is* it *that* you sent him away, and
he has already gone? 25Surely you realize
that Abner the son of Ner came to deceive
you, to know [a]your going out and your coming in, and to know all that you are doing."

26And when Joab had gone from David's
presence, he sent messengers after Abner,
who brought him back from the well of Si-
rah. But David did not know *it.* 27Now when
Abner had returned to Hebron, Joab [a]took
him aside in the gate to speak with him
privately, and there stabbed him [b]in the
stomach, so that he died for the blood of
[c]Asahel his brother.

28Afterward, when David heard *it,* he
said, "My kingdom and I *are* guiltless before the LORD forever of the blood of Abner the son of Ner. 29[a]Let it rest on the head
of Joab and on all his father's house; and
let there never fail to be in the house of
Joab one [b]who has a discharge or is a leper,
who leans on a staff or falls by the sword, or
who lacks bread." 30So Joab and Abishai his
brother killed Abner, because he had killed
their brother [a]Asahel at Gibeon in the battle.

David's Mourning for Abner

31Then David said to Joab and to all the
people who were with him, [a]"Tear your
clothes, [b]gird yourselves with sackcloth,
and mourn for Abner." And King David followed the coffin. 32So they buried Abner
in Hebron; and the king lifted up his voice
and wept at the grave of Abner, and all the
people wept. 33And the king sang *a lament*
over Abner and said:

"Should Abner die as a [a]fool dies?
34 Your hands were not bound
Nor your feet put into fetters;
As a man falls before wicked
men, *so* you fell."

Then all the people wept over him again.

35And when all the people came [a]to persuade David to eat food while it was still
day, David took an oath, saying, [b]"God do
so to me, and more also, if I taste bread
or anything else [c]till the sun goes down!"
36Now all the people took note *of it,* and it
pleased them, since whatever the king did
pleased all the people. 37For all the people
and all Israel understood that day that it
had not been the king's *intent* to kill Abner the son of Ner. 38Then the king said
to his servants, "Do you not know that a
prince and a great man has fallen this day
in Israel? 39And I *am* weak today, though
anointed king; and these men, the sons of
Zeruiah, [a]*are* too harsh for me. [b]The LORD
shall repay the evildoer according to his
wickedness."

Ishbosheth Is Murdered

4 When Saul's son[1] heard that Abner had
died in Hebron, [a]he lost heart, and all Israel was [b]troubled. 2Now Saul's son *had* two

3:18 [a] 2 Sam. 3:9 [1] Following many Hebrew manuscripts, Septuagint, Syriac, and Targum; Masoretic Text reads *he.*
3:19 [a] 1 Sam. 10:20, 21; 1 Chr. 12:29 3:21 [a] 2 Sam. 3:10, 12 [b] 1 Kin. 11:37 3:25 [a] Deut. 28:6; 1 Sam. 29:6; Is. 37:28 3:27 [a] 2 Sam. 20:9, 10; 1 Kin. 2:5 [b] 2 Sam. 4:6 [c] 2 Sam. 2:23 3:29 [a] Deut. 21:6–9; 1 Kin. 2:32, 33 [b] Lev. 15:2 3:30 [a] 2 Sam. 2:23 3:31 [a] Josh. 7:6; 2 Sam. 1:2, 11 [b] Gen. 37:34 3:33 [a] 2 Sam. 13:12, 13 3:35 [a] 2 Sam. 12:17; Jer. 16:7, 8 [b] Ruth 1:17 [c] Judg. 20:26; 2 Sam. 1:12
3:39 [a] 2 Sam. 19:5–7 [b] 1 Kin. 2:5, 6, 32–34; 2 Tim. 4:14 4:1 [a] Ezra 4:4; Is. 13:7 [b] Matt. 2:3 [1] That is, Ishbosheth

men *who were* captains of troops. The name
of one *was* Baanah and the name of the
other Rechab, the sons of Rimmon the Beerothite, of the children of Benjamin. (For
[a]Beeroth also was *part* of Benjamin, 3be-
cause the Beerothites fled to [a]Gittaim and
have been sojourners there until this day.)
4[a]Jonathan, Saul's son, had a son *who
was* lame in *his* feet. He was five years old
when the news about Saul and Jonathan
came [b]from Jezreel; and his nurse took him
up and fled. And it happened, as she made
haste to flee, that he fell and became lame.
His name *was* [c]Mephibosheth.[1]
5Then the sons of Rimmon the Beerothite, Rechab and Baanah, set out and
came at about the heat of the day to the
[a]house of Ishbosheth, who was lying on
his bed at noon. 6And they came there, all
the way into the house, *as though* to get
wheat, and they stabbed him [a]in the stomach. Then Rechab and Baanah his brother
escaped. 7For when they came into the
house, he was lying on his bed in his bedroom; then they struck him and killed him,
beheaded him and took his head, and were
all night escaping through the plain. 8And
they brought the head of Ishbosheth to David at Hebron, and said to the king, "Here
is the head of Ishbosheth, the son of Saul
your enemy, [a]who sought your life; and the
LORD has avenged my lord the king this day
of Saul and his descendants."
9But David answered Rechab and Baanah his brother, the sons of Rimmon the
Beerothite, and said to them, "As the LORD
lives, [a]who has redeemed my life from all
adversity, 10when [a]someone told me, saying, 'Look, Saul is dead,' thinking to have
brought good news, I arrested him and
had him executed in Ziklag—the one who
thought I would give him a reward for *his*
news. 11How much more, when wicked men
have killed a righteous person in his own
house on his bed? Therefore, shall I not
now [a]require his blood at your hand and
remove you from the earth?" 12So David
[a]commanded his young men, and they
executed them, cut off their hands and feet,
and hanged *them* by the pool in Hebron.
But they took the head of Ishbosheth and
buried *it* in the [b]tomb of Abner in Hebron.

David Reigns over All Israel
(1 Chr. 11:1–3)

5 Then all the tribes of Israel [a]came to
David at Hebron and spoke, saying,
"Indeed [b]we *are* your bone and your flesh.
2Also, in time past, when Saul was king over
us, [a]you were the one who led Israel out
and brought them in; and the LORD said
to you, [b]'You shall shepherd My people Israel, and be ruler over Israel.'" 3[a]Therefore
all the elders of Israel came to the king
at Hebron, [b]and King David made a covenant with them at Hebron [c]before the
LORD. And they anointed David king over
Israel. 4David *was* [a]thirty years old when
he began to reign, *and* [b]he reigned forty
years. 5In Hebron he reigned over Judah
[a]seven years and six months, and in Jerusalem he reigned thirty-three years over
all Israel and Judah.

The Conquest of Jerusalem
(1 Chr. 11:4–9; 14:1–7)

6[a]And the king and his men went to Jerusalem against [b]the Jebusites, the inhabitants of the land, who spoke to David,
saying, "You shall not come in here; but the
blind and the lame will repel you," thinking, "David cannot come in here." 7Never-
theless David took the stronghold of Zion
[a](that *is,* the City of David).
8Now David said on that day, "Whoever
climbs up by way of the water shaft and defeats the Jebusites (the lame and the blind,
who are hated by David's soul), [a]*he shall
be chief and captain.*"[1] Therefore they say,
"The blind and the lame shall not come
into the house."
9Then David dwelt in the stronghold,
and called it [a]the City of David. And David
built all around from the Millo[1] and inward.
10So David went on and became great, and
[a]the LORD God of hosts *was* with [b]him.

4:2 [a] Josh. 18:25 4:3 [a] Neh. 11:33 4:4 [a] 2 Sam. 9:3 [b] 1 Sam. 29:1, 11 [c] 2 Sam. 9:6 [1] Called *Merib-Baal* in 1 Chronicles 8:34 and 9:40 4:5 [a] 2 Sam. 2:8, 9 4:6 [a] 2 Sam. 2:23; 20:10 4:8 [a] 1 Sam. 19:2, 10, 11; 23:15; 25:29 4:9 [a] Gen. 48:16; 1 Kin. 1:29; Ps. 31:7 4:10 [a] 2 Sam. 1:2–16 4:11 [a] [Gen. 9:5, 6; Ps. 9:12] 4:12 [a] 2 Sam. 1:15 [b] 2 Sam. 3:32 5:1 [a] 1 Chr. 11:1–3 [b] Gen. 29:14; Judg. 9:2; 2 Sam. 19:12, 13 5:2 [a] 1 Sam. 18:5, 13, 16 [b] 1 Sam. 16:1 5:3 [a] 2 Sam. 3:17; 1 Chr. 11:3 [b] 2 Sam. 2:4; 3:21; 2 Kin. 11:17 [c] Judg. 11:11; 1 Sam. 23:18 5:4 [a] Gen. 41:46; Num. 4:3; Luke 3:23 [b] 1 Kin. 2:11; 1 Chr. 26:31; 29:27 5:5 [a] 2 Sam. 2:11; 1 Chr. 3:4; 29:27 5:6 [a] Judg. 1:21 [b] Josh. 15:63; Judg. 1:8; 19:11, 12 5:7 [a] 2 Sam. 6:12, 16; 1 Kin. 2:10; 8:1; 9:24 5:8 [a] 1 Chr. 11:6–9 [1] Compare 1 Chronicles 11:6 5:9 [a] 2 Sam. 5:7; 1 Kin. 9:15, 24 [1] Literally *The Landfill* 5:10 [a] 1 Sam. 17:45 [b] 1 Sam. 18:12, 28

11 Then [a]Hiram [b]king of Tyre sent messengers to David, and cedar trees, and carpenters and masons. And they built David
a house. 12 So David knew that the LORD had
established him as king over Israel, and
that He had [a]exalted His kingdom [b]for the
sake of His people Israel.

13 And [a]David took more concubines and
wives from Jerusalem, after he had come
from Hebron. Also more sons and daughters were born to David. 14 Now [a]these *are*
the names of those who were born to him
in Jerusalem: Shammua,[1] Shobab, Nathan,
[b]Solomon, 15 Ibhar, Elishua,[1] Nepheg, Japhia,
16 Elishama, Eliada, and Eliphelet.

The Philistines Defeated
(1 Chr. 14:8–17)

17 [a]Now when the Philistines heard that
they had anointed David king over Israel, all
the Philistines went up to search for David.
And David heard *of it* [b]and went down to the
stronghold. 18 The Philistines also went and
deployed themselves in [a]the Valley of Rephaim. 19 So David [a]inquired of the LORD, saying, "Shall I go up against the Philistines?
Will You deliver them into my hand?"

And the LORD said to David, "Go up, for
I will doubtless deliver the Philistines into
your hand."

20 So David went to [a]Baal Perazim, and
David defeated them there; and he said,
"The LORD has broken through my enemies before me, like a breakthrough of water." Therefore he called the name of that
place Baal Perazim.[1] 21 And they left their
images there, and David and his men [a]car-
ried them away.

22 [a]Then the Philistines went up once
again and deployed themselves in the
Valley of Rephaim. 23 Therefore [a]David inquired of the LORD, and He said, "You shall
not go up; circle around behind them, and
come upon them in front of the mulberry
trees. 24 And it shall be, when you [a]hear the
sound of marching in the tops of the mulberry trees, then you shall advance quickly.
For then [b]the LORD will go out before you
to strike the camp of the Philistines." 25 And
David did so, as the LORD commanded him;
and he drove back the Philistines from
[a]Geba[1] as far as [b]Gezer.

The Ark Brought to Jerusalem
(1 Chr. 13:1–14; 15:25—16:3)

6 Again David gathered all *the* choice
men of Israel, thirty thousand. 2 And
[a]David arose and went with all the people
who *were* with him from Baale Judah to
bring up from there the ark of God, whose
name is called by the Name,[1] the LORD of
Hosts, [b]who dwells *between* the cherubim.
3 So they set the ark of God on a new cart,
and brought it out of the house of Abinadab, which *was* on [a]the hill; and Uzzah and
Ahio, the sons of Abinadab, drove the new
cart.[1] 4 And they brought it out of [a]the house
of Abinadab, which *was* on the hill, accompanying the ark of God; and Ahio went before the ark. 5 Then David and all the house
of Israel [a]played *music* before the LORD
on all kinds of *instruments of* fir wood, on
harps, on stringed instruments, on tambourines, on sistrums, and on cymbals.

6 And when they came to [a]Nachon's
threshing floor, Uzzah put out *his* [b]*hand*
to the ark of God and took hold of it, for
the oxen stumbled. 7 Then the anger of the
LORD was aroused against Uzzah, and God
struck him there for *his* error; and he died
there by the ark of God. 8 And David became angry because of the LORD's outbreak
against Uzzah; and he called the name of
the place Perez Uzzah[1] to this day.

9 [a]David was afraid of the LORD that day;
and he said, "How can the ark of the LORD
come to me?" 10 So David would not move
the ark of the LORD with him into the [a]City
of David; but David took it aside into the
house of Obed-Edom the [b]Gittite. 11 [a]The
ark of the LORD remained in the house of
Obed-Edom the Gittite three months. And
the LORD [b]blessed Obed-Edom and all his
household.

5:11 [a] 1 Kin. 5:1–18 [b] 1 Chr. 14:1 5:12 [a] Num. 24:7 [b] Is. 45:4 5:13 [a] [Deut. 17:17]; 1 Chr. 3:9 5:14 [a] 1 Chr. 3:5–8 [b] 2 Sam. 12:24 [1] Spelled *Shimea* in 1 Chronicles 3:5 5:15 [1] Spelled *Elishama* in 1 Chronicles 3:6 5:17 [a] 1 Chr. 11:16 [b] 2 Sam. 23:14 5:18 [a] Gen. 14:5; Josh. 15:8; 1 Chr. 11:15; Is. 17:5 5:19 [a] 1 Sam. 23:2; 2 Sam. 2:1 5:20 [a] 1 Chr. 14:11; Is. 28:21 [1] Literally *Master of Breakthroughs* 5:21 [a] Deut. 7:5, 25 5:22 [a] 1 Chr. 14:13 5:23 [a] 2 Sam. 5:19 5:24 [a] 2 Kin. 7:6; 1 Chr. 14:15 [b] Judg. 4:14 5:25 [a] 1 Chr. 14:16 [b] Josh. 16:10 [1] Following Masoretic Text, Targum, and Vulgate; Septuagint reads *Gibeon.* 6:2 [a] 1 Chr. 13:5, 6 [b] Ex. 25:22; 1 Sam. 4:4; Ps. 80:1 [1] Septuagint, Targum, and Vulgate omit *by the Name;* many Hebrew manuscripts and Syriac read *there.* 6:3 [a] 1 Sam. 26:1 [1] Septuagint adds *with the ark.* 6:4 [a] 1 Sam. 7:1; 1 Chr. 13:7 6:5 [a] 1 Sam. 18:6, 7 6:6 [a] 1 Chr. 13:9 [b] Num. 4:15, 19, 20 6:8 [1] Literally *Outburst Against Uzzah* 6:9 [a] Deut. 9:19; Ps. 119:120; Luke 5:8 6:10 [a] 2 Sam. 5:7 [b] 1 Chr. 13:13; 26:4–8 6:11 [a] 1 Chr. 13:14 [b] Gen. 30:27; 39:5

12 Now it was told King David, saying,
"The LORD has blessed the house of Obed-
Edom and all that *belongs* to him, because
of the ark of God." [a]So David went and
brought up the ark of God from the house
of Obed-Edom to the City of David with
gladness. 13 And so it was, when [a]those bearing the ark of the LORD had gone six paces,
that he sacrificed [b]oxen and fatted sheep.
14 Then David [a]danced before the LORD
with all *his* might; and David *was* wearing [b]a linen ephod. 15 [a]So David and all the
house of Israel brought up the ark of the
LORD with shouting and with the sound of
the trumpet.

#OXYGEN
2 SAMUEL 6:14–15
Reconcile Weaknesses with Strength

Worship God and get stronger. Worship God and get bolder. Worship God and ignore the opinions and judgments of others. Worship through it all.

Breathe and **reconcile weaknesses with strength.**

16 Now as the ark of the LORD came into
the City of David, [a]Michal, Saul's daughter,
looked through a window and saw King David leaping and whirling before the LORD;
and she despised him in her heart. 17 So
[a]they brought the ark of the LORD, and set
it in [b]its place in the midst of the tabernacle
that David had erected for it. Then David
[c]offered burnt offerings and peace offerings before the LORD. 18 And when David
had finished offering burnt offerings and
peace offerings, [a]he blessed the people in
the name of the LORD of hosts. 19 [a]Then he
distributed among all the people, among
the whole multitude of Israel, both the
women and the men, to everyone a loaf
of bread, a piece *of meat,* and a cake of raisins. So all the people departed, everyone
to his house.

20 [a]Then David returned to bless his
household. And Michal the daughter of Saul
came out to meet David, and said, "How glorious was the king of Israel today, [b]uncover-
ing himself today in the eyes of the maids
of his servants, as one of the [c]base fellows
shamelessly uncovers himself!"

21 So David said to Michal, "*It was* before the LORD, [a]who chose me instead of
your father and all his house, to appoint me
ruler over the [b]people of the LORD, over Israel. Therefore I will play *music* before the
LORD. 22 And I will be even more undignified than this, and will be humble in my
own sight. But as for the maidservants of
whom you have spoken, by them I will be
held in honor."

23 Therefore Michal the daughter of Saul
had no children [a]to the day of her death.

God's Covenant with David
(1 Chr. 17:1–15)

7 Now it came to pass [a]when the king was
dwelling in his house, and the LORD
had given him rest from all his enemies
all around, 2 that the king said to Nathan
the prophet, "See now, I dwell in [a]a house
of cedar, [b]but the ark of God dwells inside
tent [c]curtains."

3 Then Nathan said to the king, "Go, do
all that *is* in your [a]heart, for the LORD *is*
with you."

4 But it happened that night that the
word of the LORD came to Nathan, saying,
5 "Go and tell My servant David, 'Thus says
the LORD: [a]"Would you build a house for Me
to dwell in? 6 For I have not dwelt in a house
[a]since the time that I brought the children
of Israel up from Egypt, even to this day,
but have moved about in [b]a tent and in a
tabernacle. 7 Wherever I have [a]moved about
with all the children of Israel, have I ever
spoken a word to anyone from the tribes of
Israel, whom I commanded [b]to shepherd
My people Israel, saying, 'Why have you not

6:12 [a] 1 Chr. 15:25—16:3 6:13 [a] Num. 4:15; Josh. 3:3; 1 Sam. 6:15; 2 Sam. 15:24; 1 Chr. 15:2, 15 [b] 1 Kin. 8:5 6:14 [a] Ps. 30:11; 149:3 [b] 1 Sam. 2:18, 28 6:15 [a] 1 Chr. 15:28 6:16 [a] 2 Sam. 3:14 6:17 [a] 1 Chr. 16:1 [b] 1 Chr. 15:1; 2 Chr. 1:4 [c] 1 Kin. 8:5, 62, 63 6:18 [a] 1 Kin. 8:14, 15, 55 6:19 [a] 1 Chr. 16:3 6:20 [a] Ps. 30:title [b] 2 Sam. 6:14, 16 [c] Judg. 9:4 6:21 [a] 1 Sam. 13:14; 15:28 [b] 2 Kin. 11:17 6:23 [a] 1 Sam. 15:35; Is. 22:14 7:1 [a] 1 Chr. 17:1–27 7:2 [a] 2 Sam. 5:11 [b] Acts 7:46 [c] Ex. 26:1 7:3 [a] 1 Kin. 8:17, 18; 1 Chr. 22:7 7:5 [a] 1 Kin. 5:3, 4; 8:19; 1 Chr. 22:8 7:6 [a] Josh. 18:1; 1 Kin. 8:16 [b] Ex. 40:18, 34 7:7 [a] Lev. 26:11, 12 [b] 2 Sam. 5:2; [Acts 20:28]

built Me a house of cedar?' " ' 8Now therefore, thus shall you say to My servant David, 'Thus says the LORD of hosts: [a]"I took
you from the sheepfold, from following the
sheep, to be ruler over My people, over Israel. 9And [a]I have been with you wherever
you have gone, [b]and have cut off all your
enemies from before you, and have made
you a great name, like the name of the great
men who *are* on the earth. 10Moreover I
will appoint a place for My people Israel,
and will [a]plant them, that they may dwell
in a place of their own and move no more;
[b]nor shall the sons of wickedness oppress
them anymore, as previously, 11[a]since the
time that I commanded judges *to be* over
My people Israel, and have caused you to
rest from all your enemies. Also the LORD
tells you [b]that He will make you a house.[1]
12[a]"When your days are fulfilled and you
[b]rest with your fathers, [c]I will set up your
seed after you, who will come from your
body, and I will establish his kingdom. 13[a]He
shall build a house for My name, and I will
[b]establish the throne of his kingdom forever. 14[a]I will be his Father, and he shall be
[b]My son. If he commits iniquity, I will chasten him with the rod of men and with the
blows of the sons of men. 15But My mercy
shall not depart from him, [a]as I took *it* from
Saul, whom I removed from before you.
16And [a]your house and your kingdom shall
be established forever before you.[1] Your
throne shall be established forever." ' "

17According to all these words and according to all this vision, so Nathan spoke
to David.

David's Thanksgiving to God
(1 Chr. 17:16–27)

18Then King David went in and sat before
the LORD; and he said: [a]"Who *am* I, O Lord
GOD? And what is my house, that You have
brought me this far? 19And yet this was a
small thing in Your sight, O Lord GOD; and
You have also spoken of Your servant's house
for a great while to come. [a]*Is* this the manner
of man, O Lord GOD? 20Now what more can
David say to You? For You, Lord GOD, [a]know
Your servant. 21For Your word's sake, and according to Your own heart, You have done
all these great things, to make Your servant
know *them.* 22Therefore [a]You are great,
O Lord GOD.[1] For [b]*there is* none like You, nor
is there any God besides You, according to
all that we have heard with our [c]ears. 23And
who *is* like Your people, like Israel, [a]the one
nation on the earth whom God went to redeem for Himself as a people, to make for
Himself a name—and to do for Yourself
great and awesome deeds for Your land—
before [b]Your people whom You redeemed for
Yourself from Egypt, the nations, and their
gods? 24For [a]You have made Your people Israel Your very own people forever; [b]and You,
LORD, have become their God.

25"Now, O LORD God, the word which You
have spoken concerning Your servant and
concerning his house, establish *it* forever
and do as You have said. 26So let Your name
be magnified forever, saying, 'The LORD
of hosts *is* the God over Israel.' And let the
house of Your servant David be established
before You. 27For You, O LORD of hosts, God
of Israel, have revealed *this* to Your servant,
saying, 'I will build you a house.' Therefore
Your servant has found it in his heart to
pray this prayer to You.

28"And now, O Lord GOD, You are God,
and [a]Your words are true, and You have
promised this goodness to Your servant.
29Now therefore, let it please You to bless
the house of Your servant, that it may continue before You forever; for You, O Lord
GOD, have spoken *it,* and with Your blessing let the house of Your servant be blessed
[a]forever."

David's Further Conquests
(1 Chr. 18:1–13)

8 After this it came to pass that David
attacked the Philistines and subdued
them. And David took Metheg Ammah
from the hand of the Philistines.

7:8 [a] 1 Sam. 16:11, 12; Ps. 78:70, 71 **7:9** [a] 1 Sam. 18:14; 2 Sam. 5:10 [b] 1 Sam. 31:6 **7:10** [a] Ex. 15:17; Ps. 44:2; 80:8; Jer. 24:6 [b] Ps. 89:22, 23; Is. 60:18 **7:11** [a] Judg. 2:14–16 [b] Ex. 1:21; 1 Sam. 25:28; 2 Sam. 7:27 [1] That is, a royal dynasty **7:12** [a] 1 Kin. 2:1 [b] Deut. 31:16; Acts 13:36 [c] 1 Kin. 8:20; Ps. 132:11; Matt. 1:6; Luke 3:31 **7:13** [a] 1 Kin. 5:5; 8:19; 2 Chr. 6:2 [b] 2 Sam. 7:16; [Is. 9:7; 49:8] **7:14** [a] [Heb. 1:5] [b] [Ps. 2:7; 89:26, 27, 30]; Matt. 3:17 **7:15** [a] 1 Sam. 15:23, 28; 16:14 **7:16** [a] 2 Sam. 7:13; Ps. 89:36, 37; Matt. 25:31; John 12:34 [1] Septuagint reads *Me.* **7:18** [a] Gen. 32:10; Ex. 3:11; 1 Sam. 18:18 **7:19** [a] [Is. 55:8, 9] **7:20** [a] [1 Sam. 16:7]; Ps. 139:1; John 21:17 **7:22** [a] Deut. 10:17; 1 Chr. 16:25; 2 Chr. 2:5; Ps. 86:10; Jer. 10:6 [b] Ex. 15:11; Deut. 3:24; 4:35; 32:39 [c] Ex. 10:2; Ps. 44:1 [1] Targum and Syriac read *O LORD God.* **7:23** [a] Ps. 147:20 [b] Deut. 9:26; 33:29 **7:24** [a] Gen. 17:7, 8; Ex. 6:7; [Deut. 26:18] [b] Ps. 48:14 **7:28** [a] Ex. 34:6; Josh. 21:45; John 17:17 **7:29** [a] 2 Sam. 22:51

RELEASE // RECONCILE WEAKNESSES WITH STRENGTH

Victory over Weaknesses

2 Samuel 7:18 //Then King David went in and sat before the LORD; and he said: "Who am I, O Lord GOD? And what is my house, that You have brought me this far?"

Summary Message // Although we all have experienced life differently, we all have had moments of strength and weakness. We all have sinned and fallen short of the glory of God (see Rom. 3:23). If we refuse to acknowledge these times of weakness in our past, we will not be able to apply their lessons to our future. But if we acknowledge our weaknesses and repent before God, those weak places can become our strengths. This is what God told Paul: "My grace is sufficient for you, for My strength is made perfect in weakness" (2 Cor. 12:9).

So it was with King David. His life contained weakness (see 2 Sam. 11) and strength (see 2 Sam. 9).

Practical Application //Our lives cannot be summed up by one anxious circumstance, one failed relationship, or one bad decision. We all have moments when our weaknesses show up, but those moments do not need to define us. People looking in on our lives today may think we are doing well and that life has always been good. But this is rarely, if ever, true. Success or position in one area does not mean we have mastered every other area of our lives. In fact, it is important to acknowledge and allow God to work on our weaknesses and character flaws as we move up the ladder of success. None of us has lived without troubles of our own interfering and interrupting our progress.

But we can overcome our weaknesses if we give them to God and allow Him to use those weaknesses to transform us. To do this, though, requires humility. We must first acknowledge where we are broken and lay that brokenness before the Lord so He can mend us and make us stronger. We see this in practice in David's life. God saw him in obscurity and chose to make him great. God knew David would show incredible weakness (as he did when he sinned against Bathsheba and Uriah the Hittite), but God still chose to use him. David also had incredible strengths. We know this because David is described as "a man after [God's] own heart" (1 Sam. 13:14). We can be sure God also knows our weaknesses and strengths.

When the prophet Nathan exposed David's sin to him, David accepted his guilt and said, "I have sinned against the LORD" (2 Sam. 12:13). And when, because of his sin, David's son died, David did not curse God; instead, he went into the house of the Lord and worshiped. That is the turning point. When we have sinned, how do we react? Do we humble ourselves before God, repent, and praise Him, or do we become arrogant, refuse to accept our guilt, and get angry with God?

In the end, David was overwhelmed by God's plan and love for him. He sat before the Lord and said: "Who am I, O Lord GOD? And what is my house, that You have brought me this far?" (7:18). He dropped any pride and fear, reconciled his weaknesses with strength, and honored God's instructions.

Fervent Prayer //God, we honor You as omniscient God. You created us and know every fiber of our being. We thank You for our strengths. We want You to work on our weaknesses. Today, we lay them at Your feet. We are so grateful that Your blessings and presence will be with us and our seed forever. In Jesus' name we pray. Amen.

2Then [a]he defeated Moab. Forcing them
down to the ground, he measured them off
with a line. With two lines he measured off
those to be put to death, and with one full
line those to be kept alive. So the Moabites
became David's [b]servants, *and* [c]brought
tribute.
3David also defeated Hadadezer the son
of Rehob, king of [a]Zobah, as he went to recover [b]his territory at the River Euphrates. 4David took from him one thousand
chariots, seven hundred[1] horsemen, and
twenty thousand foot soldiers. Also David
[a]hamstrung all the chariot *horses,* except

8:2 [a] Num. 24:17 [b] 2 Sam. 12:31 [c] 1 Sam. 10:27; 1 Kin. 4:21 8:3 [a] 1 Sam. 14:47; 2 Sam. 10:16, 19 [b] Gen. 15:18; 2 Sam. 10:15–19
8:4 [a] Josh. 11:6, 9 [1] Or *seven thousand* (compare 1 Chronicles 18:4)

that he spared *enough* of them for one hundred chariots.
5[a]When the Syrians of Damascus came
to help Hadadezer king of Zobah, David
killed twenty-two thousand of the Syrians.
6Then David put garrisons in Syria of Damascus; and the Syrians became David's
servants, *and* brought tribute. So [a]the LORD
preserved David wherever he went. 7And
David took [a]the shields of gold that had belonged to the servants of Hadadezer, and
brought them to Jerusalem. 8Also from
Betah[1] and from [a]Berothai, cities of Hadadezer, King David took a large amount
of bronze.
9When Toi[1] king of [a]Hamath heard that
David had defeated all the army of Hadadezer, 10then Toi sent Joram[1] his son to
King David, to greet him and bless him,
because he had fought against Hadadezer
and defeated him (for Hadadezer had been
at war with Toi); and *Joram* brought with
him articles of silver, articles of gold, and
articles of bronze. 11King David also [a]dedi-
cated these to the LORD, along with the silver and gold that he had dedicated from all
the nations which he had subdued— 12from
Syria,[1] from Moab, from the people of Ammon, from the [a]Philistines, from Amalek,
and from the spoil of Hadadezer the son
of Rehob, king of Zobah.
13And David made *himself* a [a]name when
he returned from killing [b]eighteen thousand Syrians[1] in [c]the Valley of Salt. 14He
also put garrisons in Edom; throughout all
Edom he put garrisons, and [a]all the Edomites became David's servants. And the LORD
preserved David wherever he went.

David's Administration
(1 Chr. 18:14–17)

15So David reigned over all Israel; and
David administered judgment and justice
to all his people. 16[a]Joab the son of Zeruiah
was over the army; [b]Jehoshaphat the son
of Ahilud *was* recorder; 17[a]Zadok the son of
Ahitub and Ahimelech the son of Abiathar
were the priests; Seraiah[1] *was* the scribe;
18[a]Benaiah the son of Jehoiada *was over*
both the [b]Cherethites and the Pelethites;
and David's sons were chief ministers.

David's Kindness to Mephibosheth

9 Now David said, "Is there still anyone
who is left of the house of Saul, that I
may [a]show him kindness for Jonathan's
sake?"
2And *there was* a servant of the house of
Saul whose name *was* [a]Ziba. So when they
had called him to David, the king said to
him, "*Are* you Ziba?"
He said, "At your service!"
3Then the king said, "*Is* there not still
someone of the house of Saul, to whom I
may show [a]the kindness of God?"
And Ziba said to the king, "There is still
a son of Jonathan *who is* [b]lame in *his* feet."
4So the king said to him, "Where *is* he?"
And Ziba said to the king, "Indeed he *is*
in the house of [a]Machir the son of Ammiel,
in Lo Debar."
5Then King David sent and brought him
out of the house of Machir the son of Ammiel, from Lo Debar.
6Now when [a]Mephibosheth the son of
Jonathan, the son of Saul, had come to David, he fell on his face and prostrated himself. Then David said, "Mephibosheth?"
And he answered, "Here is your servant!"
7So David said to him, "Do not fear, for I
will surely show you kindness for Jonathan
your father's sake, and will restore to you
all the land of Saul your grandfather; and
you shall eat bread at my table continually."
8Then he bowed himself, and said,
"What *is* your servant, that you should look
upon such [a]a dead dog as I?"
9And the king called to Ziba, Saul's servant, and said to him, [a]"I have given to your
master's son all that belonged to Saul and
to all his house. 10You therefore, and your
sons and your servants, shall work the land
for him, and you shall bring in *the harvest,*

8:5 [a] 1 Kin. 11:23–25 8:6 [a] 2 Sam. 7:9; 8:14 8:7 [a] 1 Kin. 10:16 8:8 [a] Ezek. 47:16 [1] Spelled *Tibhath* in 1 Chronicles 18:8
8:9 [a] 1 Kin. 8:65; 2 Kin. 14:28; 2 Chr. 8:4 [1] Spelled *Tou* in 1 Chronicles 18:9 8:10 [1] Spelled *Hadoram* in 1 Chronicles 18:10
8:11 [a] 1 Kin. 7:51 8:12 [a] 2 Sam. 5:17–25 [1] Septuagint, Syriac, and some Hebrew manuscripts read *Edom.* 8:13 [a] 2 Sam. 7:9
[b] 2 Kin. 14:7 [c] 1 Chr. 18:12; Ps. 60:title [1] Septuagint, Syriac, and some Hebrew manuscripts read *Edomites* (compare 1 Chronicles
18:12). 8:14 [a] Gen. 27:29, 37–40; Num. 24:18; 1 Kin. 11:15 8:16 [a] 2 Sam. 19:13; 20:23; 1 Chr. 11:6 [b] 1 Kin. 4:3 8:17 [a] 1 Chr. 6:4–8; 24:3
[1] Spelled *Shavsha* in 1 Chronicles 18:16 8:18 [a] 1 Kin. 1:8; 1 Chr. 18:17 [b] 1 Sam. 30:14; 1 Kin. 1:38 9:1 [a] 1 Sam. 18:3; 20:14–16; 2 Sam. 21:7;
[Prov. 27:10] 9:2 [a] 2 Sam. 16:1–4; 19:17, 29 9:3 [a] 1 Sam. 20:14 [b] 2 Sam. 4:4 9:4 [a] 2 Sam. 17:27–29
9:6 [a] 2 Sam. 16:4; 19:24–30 9:8 [a] 2 Sam. 16:9 9:9 [a] 2 Sam. 16:4; 19:29

that your master's son may have food to
eat. But Mephibosheth your master's son
[a]shall eat bread at my table always." Now
Ziba had [b]fifteen sons and twenty servants.
11 Then Ziba said to the king, "According
to all that my lord the king has commanded
his servant, so will your servant do."
"As for Mephibosheth," *said the king,* "he
shall eat at my table[1] like one of the king's
sons." 12 Mephibosheth had a young son
[a]whose name *was* Micha. And all who dwelt
in the house of Ziba *were* servants of Mephibosheth. 13 So Mephibosheth dwelt in
Jerusalem, [a]for he ate continually at the
king's table. And he [b]was lame in both his
feet.

The Ammonites and Syrians Defeated
(1 Chr. 19:1–19)

10 It happened after this that the [a]king
of the people of Ammon died, and
Hanun his son reigned in his place. 2 Then
David said, "I will show [a]kindness to Hanun
the son of [b]Nahash, as his father showed
kindness to me."
So David sent by the hand of his servants
to comfort him concerning his father. And
David's servants came into the land of the
people of Ammon. 3 And the princes of the
people of Ammon said to Hanun their lord,
"Do you think that David really honors your
father because he has sent comforters to
you? Has David not *rather* sent his servants
to you to search the city, to spy it out, and
to overthrow it?"
4 Therefore Hanun took David's servants,
shaved off half of their beards, cut off their
garments in the middle, [a]at their buttocks,
and sent them away. 5 When they told David, he sent to meet them, because the men
were greatly ashamed. And the king said,
"Wait at Jericho until your beards have
grown, and *then* return."
6 When the people of Ammon saw that
they [a]had made themselves repulsive to David, the people of Ammon sent and hired
[b]the Syrians of [c]Beth Rehob and the Syrians
of Zoba, twenty thousand foot soldiers; and
from the king of [d]Maacah one thousand
men, and from [e]Ish-Tob twelve thousand
men. 7 Now when David heard *of it,* he sent
Joab and all the army of [a]the mighty men.
8 Then the people of Ammon came out and
put themselves in battle array at the entrance of the gate. And [a]the Syrians of Zoba,
Beth Rehob, Ish-Tob, and Maacah *were* by
themselves in the field.
9 When Joab saw that the battle line was
against him before and behind, he chose
some of Israel's best and put *them* in battle
array against the Syrians. 10 And the rest of
the people he put under the command of
[a]Abishai his brother, that he might set *them*
in battle array against the people of Ammon. 11 Then he said, "If the Syrians are too
strong for me, then you shall help me; but
if the people of Ammon are too strong for
you, then I will come and help you. 12 [a]Be of
good courage, and let us [b]be strong for our
people and for the cities of our God. And
may [c]the LORD do *what is* good in His sight."
13 So Joab and the people who *were* with
him drew near for the battle against the
Syrians, and they fled before him. 14 When
the people of Ammon saw that the Syrians
were fleeing, they also fled before Abishai,
and entered the city. So Joab returned from
the people of Ammon and went to [a]Jeru-
salem.
15 When the Syrians saw that they had
been defeated by Israel, they gathered together. 16 Then Hadadezer[1] sent and brought
out the Syrians who *were* beyond the River,[2]
and they came to Helam. And Shobach the
commander of Hadadezer's army *went*
before them. 17 When it was told David, he
gathered all Israel, crossed over the Jordan, and came to Helam. And the Syrians
set themselves in battle array against David and fought with him. 18 Then the Syrians fled before Israel; and David killed
seven hundred charioteers and forty thousand [a]horsemen of the Syrians, and struck
Shobach the commander of their army,
who died there. 19 And when all the kings
who were servants to Hadadezer[1] saw that
they were defeated by Israel, they made
peace with Israel and [a]served them. So the

9:10 [a] 2 Sam. 9:7, 11, 13; 19:28 [b] 2 Sam. 19:17 9:11 [1] Septuagint reads *David's table.* 9:12 [a] 1 Chr. 8:34 9:13 [a] 2 Sam. 9:7, 10, 11; 1 Kin. 2:7; 2 Kin. 25:29 [b] 2 Sam. 9:3 10:1 [a] 2 Sam. 11:1; 1 Chr. 19:1 10:2 [a] 2 Sam. 9:1; 1 Kin. 2:7 [b] 1 Sam. 11:1 10:4 [a] Is. 20:4; 47:2 10:6 [a] Gen. 34:30; Ex. 5:21 [b] 2 Sam. 8:3, 5 [c] Judg. 18:28 [d] Deut. 3:14; Josh. 13:11, 13 [e] Judg. 11:3, 5 10:7 [a] 2 Sam. 23:8 10:8 [a] 2 Sam. 10:6 10:10 [a] 1 Sam. 26:6; 2 Sam. 3:30 10:12 [a] Deut. 31:6; Josh. 1:6, 7, 9; Neh. 4:14 [b] 1 Sam. 4:9; 1 Cor. 16:13 [c] 1 Sam. 3:18 10:14 [a] 2 Sam. 11:1 10:16 [1] Hebrew *Hadarezer* [2] That is, the Euphrates 10:18 [a] 1 Chr. 19:18 10:19 [a] 2 Sam. 8:6 [1] Hebrew *Hadarezer*

Syrians were afraid to help the people of
Ammon anymore.

David, Bathsheba, and Uriah

11 It happened in the spring of the year,
at the [a]time when kings go out *to battle,* that [b]David sent Joab and his servants
with him, and all Israel; and they destroyed
the people of Ammon and besieged [c]Rab-
bah. But David remained at Jerusalem.
2Then it happened one evening that David arose from his bed [a]and walked on the
roof of the king's house. And from the roof
he [b]saw a woman bathing, and the woman
was very beautiful to behold. 3So David
sent and inquired about the woman. And
someone said, "*Is* this not Bathsheba, the
daughter of Eliam, the wife [a]of Uriah the
[b]Hittite?" 4Then David sent messengers,
and took her; and she came to him, and [a]he
lay with her, for she was [b]cleansed from her
impurity; and she returned to her house.
5And the woman conceived; so she sent
and told David, and said, "I *am* with child."
6Then David sent to Joab, *saying,* "Send
me Uriah the Hittite." And Joab sent Uriah
to David. 7When Uriah had come to him,
David asked how Joab was doing, and how
the people were doing, and how the war
prospered. 8And David said to Uriah, "Go
down to your house and [a]wash your feet."
So Uriah departed from the king's house,
and a gift *of food* from the king followed
him. 9But Uriah slept at the [a]door of the
king's house with all the servants of his
lord, and did not go down to his house. 10So
when they told David, saying, "Uriah did
not go down to his house," David said to
Uriah, "Did you not come from a journey?
Why did you not go down to your house?"
11And Uriah said to David, [a]"The ark and
Israel and Judah are dwelling in tents, and
[b]my lord Joab and the servants of my lord
are encamped in the open fields. Shall I
then go to my house to eat and drink, and
to lie with my wife? *As* you live, and *as* your
soul lives, I will not do this thing."
12Then David said to Uriah, "Wait here
today also, and tomorrow I will let you depart." So Uriah remained in Jerusalem
that day and the next. 13Now when David
called him, he ate and drank before him;
and he made him [a]drunk. And at evening
he went out to lie on his bed [b]with the servants of his lord, but he did not go down
to his house.
14In the morning it happened that Da-
vid [a]wrote a letter to Joab and sent *it* by the
hand of Uriah. 15And he wrote in the letter,
saying, "Set Uriah in the forefront of the
hottest battle, and retreat from him, that
he may [a]be struck down and die." 16So it
was, while Joab besieged the city, that he
assigned Uriah to a place where he knew
there *were* valiant men. 17Then the men of
the city came out and fought with Joab.
And *some* of the people of the servants of
David fell; and Uriah the Hittite died also.
18Then Joab sent and told David all the
things concerning the war, 19and charged
the messenger, saying, "When you have
finished telling the matters of the war to
the king, 20if it happens that the king's
wrath rises, and he says to you: 'Why did
you approach so near to the city when you
fought? Did you not know that they would
shoot from the wall? 21Who struck [a]Abime-
lech the son of Jerubbesheth?[1] Was it not a
woman who cast a piece of a millstone on
him from the wall, so that he died in Thebez? Why did you go near the wall?'—then
you shall say, 'Your servant Uriah the Hittite is dead also.'"
22So the messenger went, and came and
told David all that Joab had sent by him.
23And the messenger said to David, "Surely
the men prevailed against us and came out
to us in the field; then we drove them back
as far as the entrance of the gate. 24The archers shot from the wall at your servants;
and *some* of the king's servants are dead,
and your servant Uriah the Hittite is dead
also."
25Then David said to the messenger,
"Thus you shall say to Joab: 'Do not let this
thing displease you, for the sword devours
one as well as another. Strengthen your attack against the city, and overthrow it.' So
encourage him."
26When the wife of Uriah heard that

11:1 [a] 1 Kin. 20:22–26 [b] 1 Chr. 20:1 [c] 2 Sam. 12:26; Jer. 49:2, 3; Amos 1:14 11:2 [a] Deut. 22:8; 1 Sam. 9:25; Matt. 24:17; Acts 10:9 [b] Gen. 34:2; [Ex. 20:17]; Job 31:1; [Matt. 5:28] 11:3 [a] 2 Sam. 23:39 [b] 1 Sam. 26:6 11:4 [a] [Lev. 20:10; Deut. 22:22]; Ps. 51:title; [James 1:14, 15] [b] Lev. 15:19, 28 11:8 [a] Gen. 18:4; 19:2 11:9 [a] 1 Kin. 14:27, 28 11:11 [a] 2 Sam. 7:2, 6 [b] 2 Sam. 20:6–22 11:13 [a] Gen. 19:33, 35 [b] 2 Sam. 11:9 11:14 [a] 1 Kin. 21:8, 9 11:15 [a] 2 Sam. 12:9 11:21 [a] Judg. 9:50–54 [1] Same as *Jerubbaal* (Gideon), Judges 6:32ff

Uriah her husband was dead, she mourned for her husband. 27 And when her mourning was over, David sent and brought her to his house, and she [a]became his wife and bore him a son. But the thing that David had done [b]displeased the LORD.

Nathan's Parable and David's Confession

12 Then the LORD sent Nathan to David. And [a]he came to him, and [b]said to him: "There were two men in one city, one rich and the other poor. 2 The rich *man* had exceedingly many flocks and herds. 3 But the poor *man* had nothing, except one little ewe lamb which he had bought and nourished; and it grew up together with him and with his children. It ate of his own food and drank from his own cup and lay in his bosom; and it was like a daughter to him. 4 And a traveler came to the rich man, who refused to take from his own flock and from his own herd to prepare one for the wayfaring man who had come to him; but he took the poor man's lamb and prepared it for the man who had come to him."

5 So David's anger was greatly aroused against the man, and he said to Nathan, "*As* the LORD lives, the man who has done this shall surely die! 6 And he shall restore [a]fourfold for the lamb, because he did this thing and because he had no pity."

7 Then Nathan said to David, "You *are* the man! Thus says the LORD God of Israel: 'I [a]anointed you king over Israel, and I delivered you from the hand of Saul. 8 I gave you your master's house and your master's wives into your keeping, and gave you the house of Israel and Judah. And if *that had been* too little, I also would have given you much more! 9 [a]Why have you [b]despised the commandment of the LORD, to do evil in His sight? [c]You have killed Uriah the Hittite with the sword; you have taken his wife *to be* your wife, and have killed him with the sword of the people of Ammon. 10 Now therefore, [a]the sword shall never depart from your house, because you have despised Me, and have taken the wife of Uriah the Hittite to be your wife.' 11 Thus says the LORD: 'Behold, I will raise up adversity against you from your own house; and I will [a]take your wives before your eyes and give *them* to your neighbor, and he shall lie with your wives in the sight of this sun. 12 For you did *it* secretly, [a]but I will do this thing before all Israel, before the sun.'"

13 [a]So David said to Nathan, [b]"I have sinned against the LORD."

And Nathan said to David, "The LORD also has [c]put away your sin; you shall not die. 14 However, because by this deed you have given great occasion to the enemies of the LORD [a]to blaspheme, the child also *who is* born to you shall surely die." 15 Then Nathan departed to his house.

The Death of David's Son

And the [a]LORD struck the child that Uriah's wife bore to David, and it became ill. 16 David therefore pleaded with God for the child, and David fasted and went in and [a]lay all night on the ground. 17 So the elders of his house arose *and went* to him, to raise him up from the ground. But he would not, nor did he eat food with them. 18 Then on the seventh day it came to pass that the child died. And the servants of David were afraid to tell him that the child was dead. For they said, "Indeed, while the child was alive, we spoke to him, and he would not heed our voice. How can we tell him that the child is dead? He may do some harm!"

19 When David saw that his servants were whispering, David perceived that the child was dead. Therefore David said to his servants, "Is the child dead?"

And they said, "He is dead."

20 So David arose from the ground, washed and [a]anointed himself, and changed his clothes; and he went into the house of the LORD and [b]worshiped. Then he went to his own house; and when he requested, they set food before him, and he ate. 21 Then his servants said to him, "What *is* this that you have done? You fasted and wept for the child *while he was* alive, but when the child died, you arose and ate food."

11:27 [a] 2 Sam. 12:9 [b] 1 Chr. 21:7; [Heb. 13:4] 12:1 [a] Ps. 51:title [b] 1 Kin. 20:35–41 12:6 [a] [Ex. 22:1]; Luke 19:8 12:7 [a] 1 Sam. 16:13; 2 Sam. 5:3 12:9 [a] 1 Sam. 15:19 [b] Num. 15:31 [c] 2 Sam. 11:14–17, 27 12:10 [a] 2 Sam. 13:28; 18:14; 1 Kin. 2:25; [Amos 7:9] 12:11 [a] Deut. 28:30; 2 Sam. 16:21, 22 12:12 [a] 2 Sam. 16:22 12:13 [a] 1 Sam. 15:24 [b] 2 Sam. 24:10; Job 7:20; Ps. 51; Luke 18:13 [c] 2 Sam. 24:10; Job 7:21; [Ps. 32:1–5; Prov. 28:13; Mic. 7:18]; Zech. 3:4 12:14 [a] Is. 52:5; [Ezek. 36:20, 23]; Rom. 2:24 12:15 [a] 1 Sam. 25:38 12:16 [a] 2 Sam. 13:31 12:20 [a] Ruth 3:3; Matt. 6:17 [b] Job 1:20

2 SAMUEL 12:13

I AM NATHAN

So David said to Nathan, "I have sinned against the LORD." And Nathan said to David, "The LORD also has put away your sin; you shall not die." 2 Samuel 12:13

I am Nathan, prophet, advisor, and friend of King David. I revealed to David the covenant God was making with him. Through me, God reminded David that He had taken him from being a simple shepherd to being the anointed king over God's people. God made him a great man among all the people of the earth and gave him rest from his enemies. God's covenant with him established a permanent place for Israel to live, free from oppression. God also promised that David's lineage and kingdom would be established forever. David was overwhelmed by God's promises but was grateful for God's covenant.

I was also the prophet who told David a parable about a rich man who took a poor man's only treasure. David had compassion for the poor man and condemned the rich man. He did not realize the parable was about him. David desired his neighbor's wife, Bathsheba. To gain her for himself, he had her husband, Uriah, sentenced to a sure death in battle. David thought his sin was secret, but nothing is hidden from God. When I revealed that he was thief, David was convicted and repented of his sin. David paid for this sin when God took away the first son he had with Bathsheba and in family strife that followed for many years.

I continued to advise David for the rest of his life. I intervened when David's son Adonijah tried to steal the throne as David was dying. David sent a priest and me to anoint Solomon as the next king of Israel. In obedience, we blew the shofar and shouted, "Long live King Solomon!"

God's promises never return void. David sinned greatly and paid for his sin, but God restored him. Israel also sinned greatly, but God fulfilled His promise and restored them to a permanent place to call their own. Our sins also have consequences, but as children of the promise, we trust God to fulfill all His promises. In the meantime, we praise Him and strive to live according to His decrees.

22And he said, "While the child was alive, I fasted and wept; [a]for I said, 'Who can tell *whether* the LORD[1] will be gracious to me, that the child may live?' 23But now he is dead; why should I fast? Can I bring him back again? I shall go [a]to him, but [b]he shall not return to me."

Solomon Is Born

24Then David comforted Bathsheba his wife, and went in to her and lay with her. So [a]she bore a son, and [b]he[1] called his name Solomon. Now the LORD loved him, 25and He sent *word* by the hand of Nathan the prophet: So he[1] called his name Jedidiah,[2] because of the LORD.

Rabbah Is Captured
(1 Chr. 20:1–3)

26Now [a]Joab fought against [b]Rabbah of the people of Ammon, and took the royal city. 27And Joab sent messengers to David, and said, "I have fought against Rabbah, and I have taken the city's water *supply.* 28Now therefore, gather the rest of the people together and encamp against the city and take it, lest I take the city and it be called after my name." 29So David gathered

12:22 [a] Is. 38:1–5; Joel 2:14; Jon. 3:9 [1] A few Hebrew manuscripts and Syriac read *God.* 12:23 [a] Gen. 37:35 [b] Job 7:8–10
12:24 [a] Matt. 1:6 [b] 1 Chr. 22:9 [1] Following Kethib, Septuagint, and Vulgate; Qere, a few Hebrew manuscripts, Syriac, and Targum read *she.* 12:25 [1] Qere, some Hebrew manuscripts, Syriac, and Targum read *she.*
[2] Literally *Beloved of the LORD* 12:26 [a] 1 Chr. 20:1 [b] Deut. 3:11; 2 Sam. 11:1

all the people together and went to Rabbah, fought against it, and took it. 30 [a]Then he took their king's crown from his head. Its weight *was* a talent of gold, with precious stones. And it was *set* on David's head. Also he brought out the spoil of the city in great abundance. 31 And he brought out the people who *were* in it, and put *them to work* with saws and iron picks and iron axes, and made them cross over to the brick works. So he did to all the cities of the people of Ammon. Then David and all the people returned to Jerusalem.

Amnon and Tamar

13 After this [a]Absalom the son of David had a lovely sister, whose name *was* [b]Tamar; and [c]Amnon the son of David loved her. 2 Amnon was so distressed over his sister Tamar that he became sick; for she *was* a virgin. And it was improper for Amnon to do anything to her. 3 But Amnon had a friend whose name *was* Jonadab [a]the son of Shimeah, David's brother. Now Jonadab *was* a very crafty man. 4 And he said to him, "Why *are* you, the king's son, becoming thinner day after day? Will you not tell me?"

Amnon said to him, "I love Tamar, my brother Absalom's sister."

5 So Jonadab said to him, "Lie down on your bed and pretend to be ill. And when your father comes to see you, say to him, 'Please let my sister Tamar come and give me food, and prepare the food in my sight, that I may see *it* and eat it from her hand.'" 6 Then Amnon lay down and pretended to be ill; and when the king came to see him, Amnon said to the king, "Please let Tamar my sister come and [a]make a couple of cakes for me in my sight, that I may eat from her hand."

7 And David sent home to Tamar, saying, "Now go to your brother Amnon's house, and prepare food for him." 8 So Tamar went to her brother Amnon's house; and he was lying down. Then she took flour and kneaded *it*, made cakes in his sight, and baked the cakes. 9 And she took the pan and placed *them* out before him, but he refused to eat. Then Amnon said, [a]"Have everyone go out from me." And they all went out from him. 10 Then Amnon said to Tamar, "Bring the food into the bedroom, that I may eat from your hand." And Tamar took the cakes which she had made, and brought *them* to Amnon her brother in the bedroom. 11 Now when she had brought *them* to him to eat, [a]he took hold of her and said to her, "Come, lie with me, my sister."

12 But she answered him, "No, my brother, do not force me, for [a]no such thing should be done in Israel. Do not do this [b]disgraceful thing! 13 And I, where could I take my shame? And as for you, you would be like one of the fools in Israel. Now therefore, please speak to the king; [a]for he will not withhold me from you." 14 However, he would not heed her voice; and being stronger than she, he [a]forced her and lay with her.

15 Then Amnon hated her exceedingly, so that the hatred with which he hated her *was* greater than the love with which he had loved her. And Amnon said to her, "Arise, be gone!"

16 So she said to him, "No, indeed! This evil of sending me away *is* worse than the other that you did to me."

But he would not listen to her. 17 Then he called his servant who attended him, and said, "Here! Put this *woman* out, away from me, and bolt the door behind her." 18 Now she had on [a]a robe of many colors, for the king's virgin daughters wore such apparel. And his servant put her out and bolted the door behind her.

19 Then Tamar put [a]ashes on her head, and tore her robe of many colors that *was* on her, and [b]laid her hand on her head and went away crying bitterly. 20 And Absalom her brother said to her, "Has Amnon your brother been with you? But now hold your peace, my sister. He *is* your brother; do not take this thing to heart." So Tamar remained desolate in her brother Absalom's house.

21 But when King David heard of all these things, he was very angry. 22 And Absalom spoke to his brother Amnon [a]neither good

12:30 [a] 1 Chr. 20:2 13:1 [a] 2 Sam. 3:2, 3; 1 Chr. 3:2 [b] 1 Chr. 3:9 [c] 2 Sam. 3:2 13:3 [a] 1 Sam. 16:9 13:6 [a] Gen. 18:6 13:9 [a] Gen. 45:1 13:11 [a] Gen. 39:12; [Deut. 27:22]; Ezek. 22:11 13:12 [a] [Lev. 18:9–11; 20:17] [b] Gen. 34:7; Judg. 19:23; 20:6 13:13 [a] Gen. 20:12 13:14 [a] Lev. 18:9; [Deut. 22:25; 27:22]; 2 Sam. 12:11 13:18 [a] Gen. 37:3; Judg. 5:30; Ps. 45:13, 14 13:19 [a] Josh. 7:6; 2 Sam. 1:2; Job 2:12; 42:6 [b] Jer. 2:37 13:22 [a] Gen. 24:50; 31:24

nor bad. For Absalom [b]hated Amnon, because he had forced his sister Tamar.

Absalom Murders Amnon

23And it came to pass, after two full years, that Absalom [a]had sheepshearers in Baal Hazor, which *is* near Ephraim; so Absalom invited all the king's sons. 24Then Absalom came to the king and said, "Kindly note, your servant has sheepshearers; please, let the king and his servants go with your servant."

25But the king said to Absalom, "No, my son, let us not all go now, lest we be a burden to you." Then he urged him, but he would not go; and he blessed him.

26Then Absalom said, "If not, please let my brother Amnon go with us."

And the king said to him, "Why should he go with you?" 27But Absalom urged him; so he let Amnon and all the king's sons go with him.

28Now Absalom had commanded his servants, saying, "Watch now, when Amnon's [a]heart is merry with wine, and when I say to you, 'Strike Amnon!' then kill him. Do not be afraid. Have I not commanded you? Be courageous and valiant." 29So the servants of Absalom [a]did to Amnon as Absalom had commanded. Then all the king's sons arose, and each one got on [b]his mule and fled.

30And it came to pass, while they were on the way, that news came to David, saying, "Absalom has killed all the king's sons, and not one of them is left!" 31So the king arose and [a]tore his garments and [b]lay on the ground, and all his servants stood by with their clothes torn. 32Then [a]Jonadab the son of Shimeah, David's brother, answered and said, "Let not my lord suppose they have killed all the young men, the king's sons, for only Amnon is dead. For by the command of Absalom this has been determined from the day that he forced his sister Tamar. 33Now therefore, [a]let not my lord the king take the thing to his heart, to think that all the king's sons are dead. For only Amnon is dead."

Absalom Flees to Geshur

34[a]Then Absalom fled. And the young man who was keeping watch lifted his eyes and looked, and there, many people were coming from the road on the hillside behind him.[1] 35And Jonadab said to the king, "Look, the king's sons are coming; as your servant said, so it is." 36So it was, as soon as he had finished speaking, that the king's sons indeed came, and they lifted up their voice and wept. Also the king and all his servants wept very bitterly.

37But Absalom fled and went to [a]Talmai the son of Ammihud, king of Geshur. And *David* mourned for his son every day. 38So Absalom fled and went to [a]Geshur, and was there three years. 39And King David[1] longed to go to[2] Absalom. For he had been [a]comforted concerning Amnon, because he was dead.

Absalom Returns to Jerusalem

14 So Joab the son of Zeruiah perceived that the king's heart *was* concerned [a]about Absalom. 2And Joab sent to [a]Tekoa and brought from there a wise woman, and said to her, "Please pretend to be a mourner, [b]and put on mourning apparel; do not anoint yourself with oil, but act like a woman who has been mourning a long time for the dead. 3Go to the king and speak to him in this manner." So Joab [a]put the words in her mouth.

4And when the woman of Tekoa spoke[1] to the king, she [a]fell on her face to the ground and prostrated herself, and said, [b]"Help, O king!"

5Then the king said to her, "What troubles you?"

And she answered, [a]"Indeed I *am* a widow, my husband is dead. 6Now your maidservant had two sons; and the two

---

13:22 [b] [Lev. 19:17, 18; 1 John 2:9, 11; 3:10, 12, 15] 13:23 [a] Gen. 38:12, 13; 1 Sam. 25:4 13:28 [a] Judg. 19:6, 9, 22; Ruth 3:7; 1 Sam. 25:36; Esth. 1:10 13:29 [a] 2 Sam. 12:10 [b] 2 Sam. 18:9; 1 Kin. 1:33, 38 13:31 [a] 2 Sam. 1:11 [b] 2 Sam. 12:16 13:32 [a] 2 Sam. 13:3–5 13:33 [a] 2 Sam. 19:19 13:34 [a] 2 Sam. 13:37, 38 [1] Septuagint adds *And the watchman went and told the king, and said, "I see men from the way of Horonaim, from the regions of the mountains."* 13:37 [a] 2 Sam. 3:3; 1 Chr. 3:2 13:38 [a] 2 Sam. 14:23, 32; 15:8 13:39 [a] Gen. 38:12; 2 Sam. 12:19, 23 [1] Following Masoretic Text, Syriac, and Vulgate; Septuagint reads *the spirit of the king;* Targum reads *the soul of King David.* [2] Following Masoretic Text and Targum; Septuagint and Vulgate read *ceased to pursue after.* 14:1 [a] 2 Sam. 13:39 14:2 [a] 2 Sam. 23:26; 2 Chr. 11:6; Amos 1:1 [b] Ruth 3:3 14:3 [a] Ex. 4:15; 2 Sam. 14:19 14:4 [a] 1 Sam. 20:41; 25:23; 2 Sam. 1:2 [b] 2 Kin. 6:26, 28 [1] Many Hebrew manuscripts, Septuagint, Syriac, and Vulgate read *came.* 14:5 [a] [Zech. 7:10]

fought with each other in the field, and
there was no one to part them, but the one
struck the other and killed him. 7And now
the whole family has risen up against your
maidservant, and they said, 'Deliver him
who struck his brother, that we may execute him [a]for the life of his brother whom
he killed; and we will destroy the heir also.'
So they would extinguish my ember that is
left, and leave to my husband *neither* name
nor remnant on the earth."

8Then the king said to the woman, "Go
to your house, and I will give orders concerning you."

9And the woman of Tekoa said to the
king, "My lord, O king, *let* [a]the iniquity *be*
on me and on my father's house, [b]and the
king and his throne *be* guiltless."

10So the king said, "Whoever says *anything* to you, bring him to me, and he shall
not touch you anymore."

11Then she said, "Please let the king remember the LORD your God, and do not
permit [a]the avenger of blood to destroy
anymore, lest they destroy my son."

And he said, [b]"*As* the LORD lives, not one
hair of your son shall fall to the ground."

12Therefore the woman said, "Please, let
your maidservant speak *another* word to
my lord the king."

And he said, "Say on."

13So the woman said: "Why then have
you schemed such a thing against [a]the people of God? For the king speaks this thing
as one who is guilty, *in that* the king does
not bring [b]his banished one home again.
14For we [a]will surely die and *become* like
water spilled on the ground, which cannot be gathered up again. Yet God does not
[b]take away a life; but He [c]devises means, so
that His banished ones are not expelled
from Him. 15Now therefore, I have come to
speak of this thing to my lord the king because the people have made me afraid. And
your maidservant said, 'I will now speak to
the king; it may be that the king will perform the request of his maidservant. 16For
the king will hear and deliver his maidservant from the hand of the man *who
would* destroy me and my son together
from the [a]inheritance of God.' 17Your maidservant said, 'The word of my lord the king
will now be comforting; for [a]as the angel
of God, so *is* my lord the king in [b]discern-
ing good and evil. And may the LORD your
God be with you.'"

18Then the king answered and said to
the woman, "Please do not hide from me
anything that I ask you."

And the woman said, "Please, let my lord
the king speak."

19So the king said, "*Is* the hand of Joab
with you in all this?" And the woman answered and said, "*As* you live, my lord the
king, no one can turn to the right hand or to
the left from anything that my lord the king
has spoken. For your servant Joab commanded me, and [a]he put all these words
in the mouth of your maidservant. 20To
bring about this change of affairs your servant Joab has done this thing; but my lord
is wise, [a]according to the wisdom of the
angel of God, to know everything that *is*
in the earth."

21And the king said to Joab, "All right, I
have granted this thing. Go therefore, bring
back the young man Absalom."

22Then Joab fell to the ground on his
face and bowed himself, and thanked the
king. And Joab said, "Today your servant
knows that I have found favor in your sight,
my lord, O king, in that the king has fulfilled
the request of his servant." 23So Joab arose
[a]and went to Geshur, and brought Absalom
to Jerusalem. 24And the king said, "Let him
return to his own house, but [a]do not let him
see my face." So Absalom returned to his
own house, but did not see the king's face.

David Forgives Absalom

25Now in all Israel there was no one who
was praised as much as Absalom for his good
looks. [a]From the sole of his foot to the crown
of his head there was no blemish in him.
26And when he cut the hair of his head—at
the end of every year he cut *it* because it was
heavy on him—when he cut it, he weighed
the hair of his head at two hundred shekels

14:7 [a] Num. 35:19; Deut. 19:12, 13 14:9 [a] Gen. 27:13; 43:9; 1 Sam. 25:24; Matt. 27:25 [b] 2 Sam. 3:28, 29; 1 Kin. 2:33 14:11 [a] Num. 35:19, 21; [Deut. 19:4–10] [b] 1 Sam. 14:45; 1 Kin. 1:52; Matt. 10:30; Acts 27:34 14:13 [a] Judg. 20:2 [b] 2 Sam. 13:37, 38 14:14 [a] Job 30:23; 34:15; [Heb. 9:27] [b] Job 34:19; Matt. 22:16; Acts 10:34; Rom. 2:11 [c] Num. 35:15 14:16 [a] Deut. 32:9; 1 Sam. 26:19; 2 Sam. 20:19 14:17 [a] 1 Sam. 29:9; 2 Sam. 19:27 [b] 1 Kin. 3:9 14:19 [a] 2 Sam. 14:3 14:20 [a] 2 Sam. 14:17; 19:27 14:23 [a] 2 Sam. 13:37, 38 14:24 [a] Gen. 43:3; 2 Sam. 3:13 14:25 [a] Deut. 28:35; Job 2:7; Is. 1:6

according to the king's standard. 27 [a]To Absalom were born three sons, and one daughter
whose name *was* Tamar. She was a woman
of beautiful appearance.
28 And Absalom dwelt two full years in
Jerusalem, [a]but did not see the king's face.
29 Therefore Absalom sent for Joab, to send
him to the king, but he would not come to
him. And when he sent again the second
time, he would not come. 30 So he said to his
servants, "See, Joab's field is near mine, and
he has barley there; go and set it on fire."
And Absalom's servants set the field on fire.
31 Then Joab arose and came to Absalom's house, and said to him, "Why have
your servants set my field on fire?"
32 And Absalom answered Joab, "Look,
I sent to you, saying, 'Come here, so that I
may send you to the king, to say, "Why have
I come from Geshur? *It would be* better for
me *to be* there still."' Now therefore, let me
see the king's face; but [a]if there is iniquity
in me, let him execute me."
33 So Joab went to the king and told him.
And when he had called for Absalom, he
came to the king and bowed himself on his
face to the ground before the king. Then
the king [a]kissed Absalom.

Absalom's Treason

15 After this [a]it happened that Absalom
[b]provided himself with chariots and
horses, and fifty men to run before him.
2 Now Absalom would rise early and stand
beside the way to the gate. *So* it was, whenever anyone who had a [a]lawsuit came to the
king for a decision, that Absalom would call
to him and say, "What city *are* you from?"
And he would say, "Your servant *is* from
such and such a tribe of Israel." 3 Then Absalom would say to him, "Look, your case
is good and right; but *there is* no deputy of
the king to hear you." 4 Moreover Absalom
would say, [a]"Oh, that I were made judge in
the land, and everyone who has any suit or
cause would come to me; then I would give
him justice." 5 And *so* it was, whenever anyone came near to bow down to him, that he
would put out his hand and take him and
[a]kiss him. 6 In this manner Absalom acted
toward all Israel who came to the king for
judgment. [a]So Absalom stole the hearts of
the men of Israel.
7 Now it came to pass [a]after forty[1] years
that Absalom said to the king, "Please, let
me go to [b]Hebron and pay the vow which I
made to the LORD. 8 [a]For your servant [b]took
a vow [c]while I dwelt at Geshur in Syria, saying, 'If the LORD indeed brings me back to
Jerusalem, then I will serve the LORD.'"
9 And the king said to him, "Go in peace."
So he arose and went to Hebron.
10 Then Absalom sent spies throughout
all the tribes of Israel, saying, "As soon as
you hear the sound of the trumpet, then
you shall say, 'Absalom [a]reigns in Hebron!'"
11 And with Absalom went two hundred men
[a]invited from Jerusalem, and they [b]went
along innocently and did not know anything. 12 Then Absalom sent for Ahithophel
the Gilonite, [a]David's counselor, from his
city—from [b]Giloh—while he offered sacrifices. And the conspiracy grew strong, for
the people with Absalom [c]continually increased in number.

David Escapes from Jerusalem

13 Now a messenger came to David, saying, [a]"The hearts of the men of Israel are
with Absalom."
14 So David said to all his servants who
were with him at Jerusalem, "Arise, and let
us [a]flee, or we shall not escape from Absalom. Make haste to depart, lest he overtake
us suddenly and bring disaster upon us, and
strike the city with the edge of the sword."
15 And the king's servants said to the
king, "We *are* your servants, *ready to do*
whatever my lord the king commands."
16 Then [a]the king went out with all his
household after him. But the king left [b]ten
women, concubines, to keep the house.
17 And the king went out with all the people after him, and stopped at the outskirts.
18 Then all his servants passed before him;
[a]and all the Cherethites, all the Pelethites,

14:27 [a] 2 Sam. 13:1; 18:18 14:28 [a] 2 Sam. 14:24 14:32 [a] 1 Sam. 20:8; [Prov. 28:13] 14:33 [a] Gen. 33:4; 45:15; Luke 15:20
15:1 [a] 2 Sam. 12:11 [b] 1 Kin. 1:5 15:2 [a] Deut. 19:17 15:4 [a] Judg. 9:29 15:5 [a] 2 Sam. 14:33; 20:9 15:6 [a] [Rom. 16:18]
15:7 [a] [Deut. 23:21] [b] 2 Sam. 3:2, 3 [1] Septuagint manuscripts, Syriac, and Josephus read *four.* 15:8 [a] 1 Sam. 16:2 [b] Gen. 28:20, 21
[c] 2 Sam. 13:38 15:10 [a] 1 Kin. 1:34; 2 Kin. 9:13 15:11 [a] 1 Sam. 16:3, 5 [b] Gen. 20:5 15:12 [a] 2 Sam. 16:15; 1 Chr. 27:33;
Ps. 41:9; 55:12–14 [b] Josh. 15:51 [c] Ps. 3:1 15:13 [a] Judg. 9:3; 2 Sam. 15:6 15:14 [a] 2 Sam. 12:11; Ps. 3:title
15:16 [a] Ps. 3:title [b] 2 Sam. 12:11; 16:21, 22 15:18 [a] 2 Sam. 8:18

and all the Gittites, [b]six hundred men who
had followed him from Gath, passed before the king.
19Then the king said to [a]Ittai the Gittite,
"Why are you also going with us? Return
and remain with the king. For you *are* a
foreigner and also an exile from your own
place. 20In fact, you came *only* yesterday.
Should I make you wander up and down
with us today, since I go [a]I know not where?
Return, and take your brethren back. Mercy
and truth *be* with you."
21But Ittai answered the king and said,
[a]"*As* the LORD lives, and *as* my lord the king
lives, surely in whatever place my lord the
king shall be, whether in death or life, even
there also your servant will be."
22So David said to Ittai, "Go, and cross
over." Then Ittai the Gittite and all his men
and all the little ones who *were* with him
crossed over. 23And all the country wept
with a loud voice, and all the people crossed
over. The king himself also crossed over the
Brook Kidron, and all the people crossed
over toward the way of the [a]wilderness.
24There was [a]Zadok also, and all the Levites with him, bearing the [b]ark of the covenant of God. And they set down the ark
of God, and [c]Abiathar went up until all the
people had finished crossing over from
the city. 25Then the king said to Zadok,
"Carry the ark of God back into the city.
If I find favor in the eyes of the LORD, He
[a]will bring me back and show me *both* it
and [b]His dwelling place. 26But if He says
thus: 'I have no [a]delight in you,' here I am,
[b]let Him do to me as seems good to Him."
27The king also said to Zadok the priest,
"*Are* you *not* a [a]seer? Return to the city in
peace, and [b]your two sons with you, Ahimaaz your son, and Jonathan the son of Abiathar. 28See, [a]I will wait in the plains of the
wilderness until word comes from you to
inform me." 29Therefore Zadok and Abiathar carried the ark of God back to Jerusalem. And they remained there.
30So David went up by the Ascent of the
Mount of Olives, and wept as he went up;
and he [a]had his head covered and went
[b]barefoot. And all the people who *were*
with him [c]covered their heads and went up,
[d]weeping as they went up. 31Then *someone*
told David, saying, [a]"Ahithophel *is* among
the conspirators with Absalom." And David said, "O LORD, I pray, [b]turn the counsel
of Ahithophel into foolishness!"
32Now it happened when David had
come to the top *of the mountain,* where he
worshiped God—there was Hushai the [a]Ar-
chite coming to meet him [b]with his robe
torn and dust on his head. 33David said
to him, "If you go on with me, then you
will become [a]a burden to me. 34But if you
return to the city, and say to Absalom, [a]'I
will be your servant, O king; *as* I *was* your
father's servant previously, so I *will* now
also *be* your servant,' then you may defeat
the counsel of Ahithophel for me. 35And
do you not *have* Zadok and Abiathar the
priests with you there? Therefore it will
be *that* whatever you hear from the king's
house, you shall tell to [a]Zadok and Abiathar
the priests. 36Indeed *they have* there [a]with
them their two sons, Ahimaaz, Zadok's *son,*
and Jonathan, Abiathar's *son;* and by them
you shall send me everything you hear."
37So Hushai, [a]David's friend, went into the
city. [b]And Absalom came into Jerusalem.

Mephibosheth's Servant

16 When[a] David was a little past the top
of the mountain, there was [b]Ziba the
servant of Mephibosheth, who met him
with a couple of saddled donkeys, and on
them two hundred *loaves* of bread, one
hundred clusters of raisins, one hundred
summer fruits, and a skin of wine. 2And
the king said to Ziba, "What do you mean
to do with these?"
So Ziba said, "The donkeys *are* for the
king's household to ride on, the bread and
summer fruit for the young men to eat, and
the wine for [a]those who are faint in the wilderness to drink."
3Then the king said, "And where *is* your
[a]master's son?"

15:18 [b] 1 Sam. 23:13; 25:13; 30:1, 9 15:19 [a] 2 Sam. 18:2 15:20 [a] 1 Sam. 23:13 15:21 [a] Ruth 1:16, 17; [Prov. 17:17] 15:23 [a] 2 Sam. 15:28; 16:2 15:24 [a] 2 Sam. 8:17 [b] Num. 4:15; 1 Sam. 4:4 [c] 1 Sam. 22:20 15:25 [a] [Ps. 43:3] [b] Ex. 15:13; Jer. 25:30 15:26 [a] Num. 14:8; 2 Sam. 22:20; 1 Kin. 10:9; 2 Chr. 9:8; Is. 62:4 [b] 1 Sam. 3:18 15:27 [a] 1 Sam. 9:6–9 [b] 2 Sam. 17:17–20 15:28 [a] Josh. 5:10; 2 Sam. 17:16 15:30 [a] 2 Sam. 19:4; Esth. 6:12; Ezek. 24:17, 23 [b] Is. 20:2–4 [c] Jer. 14:3, 4 [d] [Ps. 126:6] 15:31 [a] Ps. 3:1, 2; 55:12 [b] 2 Sam. 16:23; 17:14, 23 15:32 [a] Josh. 16:2 [b] 2 Sam. 1:2 15:33 [a] 2 Sam. 19:35 15:34 [a] 2 Sam. 16:19 15:35 [a] 2 Sam. 17:15, 16 15:36 [a] 2 Sam. 15:27 15:37 [a] 2 Sam. 16:16; 1 Chr. 27:33 [b] 2 Sam. 16:15 16:1 [a] 2 Sam. 15:30, 32 [b] 2 Sam. 9:2; 19:17, 29 16:2 [a] 2 Sam. 15:23; 17:29 16:3 [a] 2 Sam. 9:9, 10

[b]And Ziba said to the king, "Indeed he is staying in Jerusalem, for he said, 'Today the house of Israel will restore the kingdom of my father to me.'"

4So the king said to Ziba, "Here, all that *belongs* to Mephibosheth *is* yours."

And Ziba said, "I humbly bow before you, *that* I may find favor in your sight, my lord, O king!"

Shimei Curses David

5Now when King David came to [a]Bahurim, there was a man from the family of the house of Saul, whose name *was* [b]Shimei the son of Gera, coming from there. He came out, cursing continuously as he came. 6And he threw stones at David and at all the servants of King David. And all the people and all the mighty men *were* on his right hand and on his left. 7Also Shimei said thus when he cursed: "Come out! Come out! You bloodthirsty man, [a]you rogue! 8The LORD has [a]brought upon you all [b]the blood of the house of Saul, in whose place you have reigned; and the LORD has delivered the kingdom into the hand of Absalom your son. So now you *are caught* in your own evil, because you are a bloodthirsty man!"

9Then Abishai the son of Zeruiah said to the king, "Why should this [a]dead dog [b]curse my lord the king? Please, let me go over and take off his head!"

10But the king said, [a]"What have I to do with you, you sons of Zeruiah? So let him curse, because [b]the LORD has said to him, 'Curse David.' [c]Who then shall say, 'Why have you done so?'"

11And David said to Abishai and all his servants, "See how [a]my son who [b]came from my own body seeks my life. How much more now *may this* Benjamite? Let him alone, and let him curse; for so the LORD has ordered him. 12It may be that the LORD will look on my affliction,[1] and that the LORD will [a]repay me with [b]good for his cursing this day." 13And as David and his men went along the road, Shimei went along the hillside opposite him and cursed as he went, threw stones at him and kicked up dust. 14Now the king and all the people who *were* with him became weary; so they refreshed themselves there.

The Advice of Ahithophel

15Meanwhile [a]Absalom and all the people, the men of Israel, came to Jerusalem; and Ahithophel *was* with him. 16And so it was, when Hushai the Archite, [a]David's friend, came to Absalom, that [b]Hushai said to Absalom, "*Long* live the king! *Long* live the king!"

17So Absalom said to Hushai, "*Is* this your loyalty to your friend? [a]Why did you not go with your friend?"

18And Hushai said to Absalom, "No, but whom the LORD and this people and all the men of Israel choose, his I will be, and with him I will remain. 19Furthermore, [a]whom should I serve? *Should I* not *serve* in the presence of his son? As I have served in your father's presence, so will I be in your presence."

20Then Absalom said to [a]Ahithophel, "Give advice as to what we should do."

21And Ahithophel said to Absalom, "Go in to your father's [a]concubines, whom he has left to keep the house; and all Israel will hear that you [b]are abhorred by your father. Then [c]the hands of all who are with you will be strong." 22So they pitched a tent for Absalom on the top of the house, and Absalom went in to his father's concubines [a]in the sight of all Israel.

23Now the advice of Ahithophel, which he gave in those days, *was* as if one had inquired at the oracle of God. So *was* all the advice of Ahithophel [a]both with David and with Absalom.

17 Moreover Ahithophel said to Absalom, "Now let me choose twelve thousand men, and I will arise and pursue David tonight. 2I will come upon him while he *is* [a]weary and weak, and make him afraid. And all the people who *are* with him will flee, and I will [b]strike only the king. 3Then I will bring back all the people to you. When all

16:3 [b] 2 Sam. 19:27 16:5 [a] 2 Sam. 3:16 [b] 2 Sam. 19:21; 1 Kin. 2:8, 9, 44–46 16:7 [a] Deut. 13:13 16:8 [a] Judg. 9:24, 56, 57; 1 Kin. 2:32, 33 [b] 2 Sam. 1:16; 3:28, 29; 4:11, 12 16:9 [a] 1 Sam. 24:14; 2 Sam. 9:8 [b] Ex. 22:28 16:10 [a] 2 Sam. 3:39; 19:22; [1 Pet. 2:23] [b] 2 Kin. 18:25; [Lam. 3:38] [c] [Rom. 9:20] 16:11 [a] 2 Sam. 12:11 [b] Gen. 15:4 16:12 [a] Deut. 23:5; Neh. 13:2; Prov. 20:22 [b] Deut. 23:5; [Rom. 8:28; Heb. 12:10, 11] [1] Following Kethib, Septuagint, Syriac, and Vulgate; Qere reads *my eyes;* Targum reads *tears of my eyes.* 16:15 [a] 2 Sam. 15:12, 37 16:16 [a] 2 Sam. 15:37 [b] 2 Sam. 15:34 16:17 [a] 2 Sam. 19:25; [Prov. 17:17] 16:19 [a] 2 Sam. 15:34 16:20 [a] 2 Sam. 15:12 16:21 [a] 2 Sam. 15:16; 20:3 [b] Gen. 34:30; 1 Sam. 13:4 [c] 2 Sam. 2:7; Zech. 8:13 16:22 [a] 2 Sam. 12:11, 12 16:23 [a] 2 Sam. 15:12 17:2 [a] Deut. 25:18; 2 Sam. 16:14 [b] Zech. 13:7

return except the man whom you seek, all
the people will be at peace." 4And the saying pleased Absalom and all the [a]elders
of Israel.

The Advice of Hushai

5Then Absalom said, "Now call Hushai
the Archite also, and let us hear what he
[a]says too." 6And when Hushai came to
Absalom, Absalom spoke to him, saying,
"Ahithophel has spoken in this manner.
Shall we do as he says? If not, speak up."
7So Hushai said to Absalom: "The advice that Ahithophel has given *is* not good
at this time. 8For," said Hushai, "you know
your father and his men, that they *are*
mighty men, and they *are* enraged in their
minds, like [a]a bear robbed of her cubs in
the field; and your father *is* a man of war,
and will not camp with the people. 9Surely
by now he is hidden in some pit, or in some
other place. And it will be, when some of
them are overthrown at the first, that whoever hears *it* will say, 'There is a slaughter
among the people who follow Absalom.'
10And even he *who is* valiant, whose heart
is like the heart of a lion, will [a]melt completely. For all Israel knows that your father *is* a mighty man, and *those* who *are*
with him *are* valiant men. 11Therefore I advise that all Israel be fully gathered to you,
[a]from Dan to Beersheba, [b]like the sand that
is by the sea for multitude, and that you
go to battle in person. 12So we will come
upon him in some place where he may be
found, and we will fall on him as the dew
falls on the ground. And of him and all the
men who *are* with him there shall not be
left so much as one. 13Moreover, if he has
withdrawn into a city, then all Israel shall
bring ropes to that city; and we will [a]pull it
into the river, until there is not one small
stone found there."
14So Absalom and all the men of Israel
said, "The advice of Hushai the Archite *is*
better than the advice of Ahithophel." For
[a]the LORD had purposed to defeat the good
advice of Ahithophel, to the intent that the
LORD might bring disaster on Absalom.

Hushai Warns David to Escape

15[a]Then Hushai said to Zadok and Abiathar the priests, "Thus and so Ahithophel
advised Absalom and the elders of Israel,
and thus and so I have advised. 16Now
therefore, send quickly and tell David, saying, 'Do not spend this night [a]in the plains
of the wilderness, but speedily cross over,
lest the king and all the people who *are*
with him be swallowed up.'" 17[a]Now Jonathan and Ahimaaz [b]stayed at [c]En Rogel,
for they dared not be seen coming into the
city; so a female servant would come and
tell them, and they would go and tell King
David. 18Nevertheless a lad saw them, and
told Absalom. But both of them went away
quickly and came to a man's house [a]in Bahurim, who had a well in his court; and
they went down into it. 19[a]Then the woman
took and spread a covering over the well's
mouth, and spread ground grain on it; and
the thing was not known. 20And when Absalom's servants came to the woman at the
house, they said, "Where *are* Ahimaaz and
Jonathan?"
So [a]the woman said to them, "They have
gone over the water brook."
And when they had searched and could
not find *them*, they returned to Jerusalem.
21Now it came to pass, after they had departed, that they came up out of the well
and went and told King David, and said
to David, [a]"Arise and cross over the water
quickly. For thus has Ahithophel advised
against you." 22So David and all the people who *were* with him arose and crossed
over the Jordan. By morning light not one
of them was left who had not gone over
the Jordan.
23Now when Ahithophel saw that his advice was not followed, he saddled a donkey,
and arose and went home to [a]his house, to
his city. Then he put his [b]household in order, and [c]hanged himself, and died; and he
was buried in his father's tomb.
24Then David went to [a]Mahanaim. And
Absalom crossed over the Jordan, he and
all the men of Israel with him. 25And Absalom made [a]Amasa captain of the army

---

17:4 [a] 2 Sam. 5:3; 19:11 17:5 [a] 2 Sam. 15:32–34 17:8 [a] Hos. 13:8 17:10 [a] Josh. 2:11 17:11 [a] Judg. 20:1; 2 Sam. 3:10 [b] Gen. 22:17; Josh. 11:4; 1 Kin. 20:10 17:13 [a] Mic. 1:6 17:14 [a] 2 Sam. 15:31, 34 17:15 [a] 2 Sam. 15:35, 36 17:16 [a] 2 Sam. 15:28 17:17 [a] 2 Sam. 15:27, 36; 1 Kin. 1:42, 43 [b] Josh. 2:4–6 [c] Josh. 15:7; 18:16 17:18 [a] 2 Sam. 3:16; 16:5 17:19 [a] Josh. 2:4–6 17:20 [a] Ex. 1:19; [Lev. 19:11]; Josh. 2:3–5 17:21 [a] 2 Sam. 17:15, 16 17:23 [a] 2 Sam. 15:12 [b] 2 Kin. 20:1 [c] Matt. 27:5 17:24 [a] Gen. 32:2; Josh. 13:26; 2 Sam. 2:8; 19:32 17:25 [a] 2 Sam. 19:13; 20:9–12; 1 Kin. 2:5, 32

instead of Joab. This Amasa *was* the son of a man whose name *was* Jithra,[1] an Israelite,[2] who had gone in to [b]Abigail the daughter of Nahash, sister of Zeruiah, Joab's mother. 26So Israel and Absalom encamped in the land of Gilead.

27Now it happened, when David had come to Mahanaim, that [a]Shobi the son of Nahash from Rabbah of the people of Ammon, [b]Machir the son of Ammiel from Lo Debar, and [c]Barzillai the Gileadite from Rogelim, 28brought beds and basins, earthen vessels and wheat, barley and flour, parched *grain* and beans, lentils and parched *seeds*, 29honey and curds, sheep and cheese of the herd, for David and the people who *were* with him to eat. For they said, "The people are hungry and weary and thirsty [a]in the wilderness."

Absalom's Defeat and Death

18 And David numbered the people who *were* with him, and [a]set captains of thousands and captains of hundreds over them. 2Then David sent out one third of the people under the hand of Joab, [a]one third under the hand of Abishai the son of Zeruiah, Joab's brother, and one third under the hand of [b]Ittai the Gittite. And the king said to the people, "I also will surely go out with you myself."

3[a]But the people answered, "You shall not go out! For if we flee away, they will not care about us; nor if half of us die, will they care about us. But *you are* worth ten thousand of us now. For you are now more help to us in the city."

4Then the king said to them, "Whatever seems best to you I will do." So the king stood beside the gate, and all the people went out by hundreds and by thousands. 5Now the king had commanded Joab, Abishai, and Ittai, saying, "*Deal* gently for my sake with the young man Absalom." [a]And all the people heard when the king gave all the captains orders concerning Absalom.

6So the people went out into the field of battle against Israel. And the battle was in the [a]woods of Ephraim. 7The people of Israel were overthrown there before the servants of David, and a great slaughter of twenty thousand took place there that day. 8For the battle there was scattered over the face of the whole countryside, and the woods devoured more people that day than the sword devoured.

9Then Absalom met the servants of David. Absalom rode on a mule. The mule went under the thick boughs of a great terebinth tree, and [a]his head caught in the terebinth; so he was left hanging between heaven and earth. And the mule which *was* under him went on. 10Now a certain man saw *it* and told Joab, and said, "I just saw Absalom hanging in a terebinth tree!"

11So Joab said to the man who told him, "You just saw *him!* And why did you not strike him there to the ground? I would have given you ten *shekels* of silver and a belt."

12But the man said to Joab, "Though I were to receive a thousand *shekels* of silver in my hand, I would not raise my hand against the king's son. [a]For in our hearing the king commanded you and Abishai and Ittai, saying, 'Beware lest anyone *touch* the young man Absalom!'[1] 13Otherwise I would have dealt falsely against my own life. For there is nothing hidden from the king, and you yourself would have set yourself against *me*."

14Then Joab said, "I cannot linger with you." And he took three spears in his hand and thrust them through Absalom's heart, while he was *still* alive in the midst of the terebinth tree. 15And ten young men who bore Joab's armor surrounded Absalom, and struck and killed him.

16So Joab blew the trumpet, and the people returned from pursuing Israel. For Joab held back the people. 17And they took Absalom and cast him into a large pit in the woods, and [a]laid a very large heap of stones over him. Then all Israel [b]fled, everyone to his tent.

17:25 [b] 1 Chr. 2:16 [1] Spelled *Jether* in 1 Chronicles 2:17 and elsewhere [2] Following Masoretic Text, some manuscripts of the Septuagint, and Targum; some manuscripts of the Septuagint read *Ishmaelite* (compare 1 Chronicles 2:17); Vulgate reads *of Jezrael.* 17:27 [a] 1 Sam. 11:1; 2 Sam. 10:1; 12:29 [b] 2 Sam. 9:4 [c] 2 Sam. 19:31, 32; 1 Kin. 2:7 17:29 [a] 2 Sam. 16:2, 14 18:1 [a] Ex. 18:25; Num. 31:14; 1 Sam. 22:7 18:2 [a] Judg. 7:16; 1 Sam. 11:11 [b] 2 Sam. 15:19–22 18:3 [a] 2 Sam. 21:17 18:5 [a] 2 Sam. 18:12 18:6 [a] Josh. 17:15, 18; 2 Sam. 17:26 18:9 [a] 2 Sam. 14:26 18:12 [a] 2 Sam. 18:5 [1] The ancient versions read *'Protect the young man Absalom for me!'* 18:17 [a] Deut. 21:20, 21; Josh. 7:26; 8:29 [b] 2 Sam. 19:8; 20:1, 22

18Now Absalom in his lifetime had taken
and set up a pillar for himself, which *is* in
[a]the King's Valley. For he said, [b]"I have no
son to keep my name in remembrance." He
called the pillar after his own name. And to
this day it is called Absalom's Monument.

David Hears of Absalom's Death

19Then [a]Ahimaaz the son of Zadok said,
"Let me run now and take the news to the
king, how the LORD has avenged him of
his enemies."
20And Joab said to him, "You shall not
take the news this day, for you shall take the
news another day. But today you shall take
no news, because the king's son is dead."
21Then Joab said to the Cushite, "Go, tell the
king what you have seen." So the Cushite
bowed himself to Joab and ran.
22And Ahimaaz the son of Zadok said
again to Joab, "But whatever happens,
please let me also run after the Cushite."
So Joab said, "Why will you run, my son,
since you have no news ready?"
23"But whatever happens," *he said,* "let
me run."
So he said to him, "Run." Then Ahimaaz ran by way of the plain, and outran the
Cushite.
24Now David was sitting between the
[a]two gates. And the watchman went up to
the roof over the gate, to the wall, lifted his
eyes and looked, and there was a man, running alone. 25Then the watchman cried out
and told the king. And the king said, "If he
is alone, *there is* news in his mouth." And
he came rapidly and drew near.
26Then the watchman saw *another* man
running, and the watchman called to the
gatekeeper and said, "There is *another* man,
running alone!"
And the king said, "He also brings news."
27So the watchman said, "I think the running of the first is like the running of Ahimaaz the son of Zadok."
And the king said, "He *is* a good man,
and comes with [a]good news."
28So Ahimaaz called out and said to the
king, "All is well!" Then he bowed down with
his face to the earth before the king, and
said, [a]"Blessed *be* the LORD your God, who
has delivered up the men who raised their
hand against my lord the king!"
29The king said, "Is the young man Absalom safe?"
Ahimaaz answered, "When Joab sent the
king's servant and *me* your servant, I saw
a great tumult, but I did not know what *it
was about.*"
30And the king said, "Turn aside *and*
stand here." So he turned aside and stood
still.
31Just then the Cushite came, and the
Cushite said, "There is good news, my lord
the king! For the LORD has avenged you
this day of all those who rose against you."
32And the king said to the Cushite, "Is
the young man Absalom safe?"
So the Cushite answered, "May the enemies of my lord the king, and all who rise
against you to do harm, be like *that* young
man!"

David's Mourning for Absalom

33Then the king was deeply moved,
and went up to the chamber over the gate,
and wept. And as he went, he said thus:
[a]"O my son Absalom—my son, my son Absalom—if only I had died in your place!
O Absalom my son, [b]my son!"

19 And Joab was told, "Behold, the king
is weeping and [a]mourning for Absalom." 2So the victory that day was *turned*
into [a]mourning for all the people. For the
people heard it said that day, "The king is
grieved for his son." 3And the people stole
back [a]into the city that day, as people who
are ashamed steal away when they flee in
battle. 4But the king [a]covered his face, and
the king cried out with a loud voice, [b]"O my
son Absalom! O Absalom, my son, my son!"
5Then [a]Joab came into the house to
the king, and said, "Today you have disgraced all your servants who today have
saved your life, the lives of your sons and
daughters, the lives of your wives and the
lives of your concubines, 6in that you love
your enemies and hate your friends. For
you have declared today that you regard
neither princes nor servants; for today I

18:18 [a] Gen. 14:17 [b] 2 Sam. 14:27 18:19 [a] 2 Sam. 15:36; 17:17 18:24 [a] Judg. 5:11; 2 Sam. 13:34; 2 Kin. 9:17 18:27 [a] 1 Kin. 1:42 18:28 [a] 2 Sam. 16:12 18:33 [a] 2 Sam. 12:10 [b] 2 Sam. 19:4 19:1 [a] Jer. 14:2 19:2 [a] Esth. 4:3 19:3 [a] 2 Sam. 17:24, 27; 19:32 19:4 [a] 2 Sam. 15:30 [b] 2 Sam. 18:33 19:5 [a] 2 Sam. 18:14

perceive that if Absalom had lived and all
of us had died today, then it would have
pleased you well. 7 Now therefore, arise, go
out and speak comfort to your servants. For
I swear by the LORD, if you do not go out,
not one will stay with you this night. And
that will be worse for you than all the evil
that has befallen you from your youth until
now." 8 Then the king arose and sat in the
[a]gate. And they told all the people, saying,
"There is the king, sitting in the gate." So
all the people came before the king.
For everyone of Israel had [b]fled to his
tent.

David Returns to Jerusalem

9 Now all the people were in a dispute
throughout all the tribes of Israel, saying,
"The king saved us from the hand of our
[a]enemies, he delivered us from the hand
of the [b]Philistines, and now he has [c]fled
from the land because of Absalom. 10 But
Absalom, whom we anointed over us, has
died in battle. Now therefore, why do you
say nothing about bringing back the king?"
11 So King David sent to [a]Zadok and Abiathar the priests, saying, "Speak to the elders
of Judah, saying, 'Why are you the last to
bring the king back to his house, since the
words of all Israel have come to the king, to
his *very* house? 12 You *are* my brethren, you
are [a]my bone and my flesh. Why then are
you the last to bring back the king?' 13 [a]And
say to Amasa, '*Are* you not my bone and my
flesh? [b]God do so to me, and more also, if
you are not commander of the army before
me continually in place of Joab.'" 14 So he
swayed the hearts of all the men of Judah,
[a]just as *the heart of* one man, so that they
sent *this word* to the king: "Return, you and
all your servants!"
15 Then the king returned and came to
the Jordan. And Judah came to [a]Gilgal,
to go to meet the king, to escort the king
[b]across the Jordan. 16 And [a]Shimei the son
of Gera, a Benjamite, who *was* from Bahurim, hurried and came down with the men
of Judah to meet King David. 17 *There were* a
thousand men of [a]Benjamin with him, and
[b]Ziba the servant of the house of Saul, and
his fifteen sons and his twenty servants
with him; and they went over the Jordan
before the king. 18 Then a ferryboat went
across to carry over the king's household,
and to do what he thought good.

David's Mercy to Shimei

Now Shimei the son of Gera fell down before the king when he had crossed the Jordan. 19 Then he said to the king, [a]"Do not let
my lord impute iniquity to me, or remember what [b]wrong your servant did on the
day that my lord the king left Jerusalem,
that the king should [c]take *it* to heart. 20 For
I, your servant, know that I have sinned.
Therefore here I am, the first to come today of all [a]the house of Joseph to go down
to meet my lord the king."
21 But Abishai the son of Zeruiah answered and said, "Shall not Shimei be put
to death for this, [a]because he [b]cursed the
LORD's anointed?"
22 And David said, [a]"What have I to do
with you, you sons of Zeruiah, that you
should be adversaries to me today? [b]Shall
any man be put to death today in Israel?
For do I not know that today I *am* king
over Israel?" 23 Therefore [a]the king said to
Shimei, "You shall not die." And the king
swore to him.

David and Mephibosheth Meet

24 Now [a]Mephibosheth the son of Saul
came down to meet the king. And he had
not cared for his feet, nor trimmed his mustache, nor washed his clothes, from the day
the king departed until the day he returned
in peace. 25 So it was, when he had come to
Jerusalem to meet the king, that the king
said to him, [a]"Why did you not go with me,
Mephibosheth?"
26 And he answered, "My lord, O king,
my servant deceived me. For your servant
said, 'I will saddle a donkey for myself, that
I may ride on it and go to the king,' because
your servant *is* lame. 27 And [a]he has slan-
dered your servant to my lord the king, [b]but
my lord the king *is* like the angel of God.

19:8 [a] 2 Sam. 15:2; 18:24 [b] 2 Sam. 18:17 19:9 [a] 2 Sam. 8:1–14 [b] 2 Sam. 3:18 [c] 2 Sam. 15:14 19:11 [a] 2 Sam. 15:24 19:12 [a] 2 Sam. 5:1; 1 Chr. 11:1 19:13 [a] 2 Sam. 17:25; 1 Chr. 2:17 [b] Ruth 1:17 19:14 [a] Judg. 20:1 19:15 [a] Josh. 5:9; 1 Sam. 11:14, 15 [b] 2 Sam. 17:22 19:16 [a] 2 Sam. 16:5; 1 Kin. 2:8 19:17 [a] 2 Sam. 3:19; 1 Kin. 12:21 [b] 2 Sam. 9:2, 10; 16:1, 2 19:19 [a] 1 Sam. 22:15 [b] 2 Sam. 16:5, 6 [c] 2 Sam. 13:33 19:20 [a] Judg. 1:22; 1 Kin. 11:28 19:21 [a] [Ex. 22:28] [b] [1 Sam. 26:9] 19:22 [a] 2 Sam. 3:39; 16:10 [b] 1 Sam. 11:13 19:23 [a] 1 Kin. 2:8, 9, 37, 46 19:24 [a] 2 Sam. 9:6; 21:7 19:25 [a] 2 Sam. 16:17 19:27 [a] 2 Sam. 16:3, 4 [b] 2 Sam. 14:17, 20

Therefore do *what is* good in your eyes.
28For all my father's house were but dead
men before my lord the king. [a]Yet you set
your servant among those who eat at your
own table. Therefore what right have I still
to cry out anymore to the king?"
29So the king said to him, "Why do you
speak anymore of your matters? I have
said, 'You and Ziba divide the land.'"
30Then Mephibosheth said to the king,
"Rather, let him take it all, inasmuch as my
lord the king has come back in peace to his
own house."

David's Kindness to Barzillai

31And [a]Barzillai the Gileadite came down
from Rogelim and went across the Jordan
with the king, to escort him across the Jordan. 32Now Barzillai was a very aged man,
eighty years old. And [a]he had provided the
king with supplies while he stayed at Mahanaim, for he *was* a very rich man. 33And
the king said to Barzillai, "Come across with
me, and I will provide for you while you are
with me in Jerusalem."
34But Barzillai said to the king, "How
long have I to live, that I should go up with
the king to Jerusalem? 35I *am* today [a]eighty
years old. Can I discern between the good
and bad? Can your servant taste what I eat
or what I drink? Can I hear any longer the
voice of singing men and singing women?
Why then should your servant be a further
burden to my lord the king? 36Your servant will go a little way across the Jordan
with the king. And why should the king
repay me *with* such a reward? 37Please let
your servant turn back again, that I may
die in my own city, near the grave of my
father and mother. But here is your servant [a]Chimham; let him cross over with my
lord the king, and do for him what seems
good to you."
38And the king answered, "Chimham
shall cross over with me, and I will do for
him what seems good to you. Now whatever you request of me, I will do for you."
39Then all the people went over the Jordan.
And when the king had crossed over, the
king [a]kissed Barzillai and blessed him, and
he returned to his own place.

The Quarrel About the King

40Now the king went on to Gilgal, and
Chimham[1] went on with him. And all the
people of Judah escorted the king, and also
half the people of Israel. 41Just then all the
men of Israel came to the king, and said to
the king, "Why have our brethren, the men
of Judah, stolen you away and [a]brought the
king, his household, and all David's men
with him across the Jordan?"
42So all the men of Judah answered the
men of Israel, "Because the king *is* [a]a close
relative of ours. Why then are you angry
over this matter? Have we ever eaten at the
king's *expense?* Or has he given us any gift?"
43And the men of Israel answered the
men of Judah, and said, "We have [a]ten
shares in the king; therefore we also have
more *right* to David than you. Why then
do you despise us—were we not the first
to advise bringing back our king?"
Yet [b]the words of the men of Judah were
fiercer than the words of the men of Israel.

The Rebellion of Sheba

20 And there happened to be there a
rebel,[1] whose name *was* Sheba the
son of Bichri, a Benjamite. And he blew a
trumpet, and said:

[a]"We have no share in David,
Nor do we have inheritance
in the son of Jesse;
[b]Every man to his tents, O Israel!"

2So every man of Israel deserted David,
and followed Sheba the son of Bichri. But
the [a]men of Judah, from the Jordan as far
as Jerusalem, remained loyal to their king.
3Now David came to his house at Jerusalem. And the king took the ten women,
[a]his concubines whom he had left to keep
the house, and put them in seclusion and
supported them, but did not go in to them.
So they were shut up to the day of their
death, living in widowhood.

19:28 [a] 2 Sam. 9:7–13 19:31 [a] 2 Sam. 17:27–29; 1 Kin. 2:7 19:32 [a] 2 Sam. 17:27–29 19:35 [a] Ps. 90:10 19:37 [a] 2 Sam. 19:40; Jer. 41:17 19:39 [a] Gen. 31:55; Ruth 1:14; 2 Sam. 14:33 19:40 [1] Masoretic Text reads *Chimhan.* 19:41 [a] 2 Sam. 19:15 19:42 [a] 2 Sam. 19:12 19:43 [a] 1 Kin. 11:30, 31 [b] Judg. 8:1; 12:1 20:1 [a] 2 Sam. 19:43; 1 Kin. 12:16 [b] 1 Sam. 13:2; 2 Sam. 18:17; 2 Chr. 10:16 [1] Literally *man of Belial* 20:2 [a] 2 Sam. 19:14 20:3 [a] 2 Sam. 15:16; 16:21, 22

4And the king said to Amasa, [a]"Assemble the men of Judah for me within three
days, and be present here yourself." 5So
Amasa went to assemble *the men of* Judah.
But he delayed longer than the set time
which David had appointed him. 6And David said to [a]Abishai, "Now Sheba the son
of Bichri will do us more harm than Absalom. Take [b]your lord's servants and pursue
him, lest he find for himself fortified cities, and escape us." 7So Joab's men, with
the [a]Cherethites, the Pelethites, and [b]all the
mighty men, went out after him. And they
went out of Jerusalem to pursue Sheba the
son of Bichri. 8When they *were* at the large
stone which *is* in Gibeon, Amasa came before them. Now Joab was dressed in battle armor; on it was a belt *with* a sword
fastened in its sheath at his hips; and as
he was going forward, it fell out. 9Then
Joab said to Amasa, "*Are* you in health,
my brother?" [a]And Joab took Amasa by the
beard with his right hand to kiss him. 10But
Amasa did not notice the sword that *was*
in Joab's hand. And [a]he struck him with it
[b]in the stomach, and his entrails poured
out on the ground; and he did not *strike*
him again. Thus he died.

Then Joab and Abishai his brother pursued Sheba the son of Bichri. 11Meanwhile
one of Joab's men stood near Amasa, and
said, "Whoever favors Joab and whoever
is for David—follow Joab!" 12But Amasa
wallowed in *his* blood in the middle of the
highway. And when the man saw that all
the people stood still, he moved Amasa
from the highway to the field and threw a
garment over him, when he saw that everyone who came upon him halted. 13When
he was removed from the highway, all the
people went on after Joab to pursue Sheba
the son of Bichri.

14And he went through all the tribes
of Israel to [a]Abel and Beth Maachah and
all the Berites. So they were gathered together and also went after *Sheba*.[1] 15Then
they came and besieged him in Abel of Beth
Maachah; and they [a]cast up a siege mound
against the city, and it stood by the rampart.
And all the people who *were* with Joab bat-
tered the wall to throw it down.

16Then a wise woman cried out from the
city, "Hear, hear! Please say to Joab, 'Come
nearby, that I may speak with you.'" 17When
he had come near to her, the woman said,
"*Are* you Joab?"

He answered, "I *am*."

Then she said to him, "Hear the words
of your maidservant."

And he answered, "I am listening."

18So she spoke, saying, "They used to talk
in former times, saying, 'They shall surely
seek *guidance* at Abel,' and so they would
end *disputes*. 19I *am among the* peaceable
and faithful in Israel. You seek to destroy a
city and a mother in Israel. Why would you
swallow up [a]the inheritance of the LORD?"

20And Joab answered and said, "Far be
it, far be it from me, that I should swallow
up or destroy! 21That *is* not so. But a man
from the mountains of Ephraim, Sheba the
son of Bichri by name, has raised his hand
against the king, against David. Deliver him
only, and I will depart from the city."

So the woman said to Joab, "Watch, his
head will be thrown to you over the wall."
22Then the woman [a]in her wisdom went to
all the people. And they cut off the head of
Sheba the son of Bichri, and threw *it* out to
Joab. Then he blew a trumpet, and they withdrew from the city, every man to his tent.
So Joab returned to the king at Jerusalem.

David's Government Officers

23And [a]Joab *was* over all the army of
Israel; Benaiah the son of Jehoiada *was*
over the Cherethites and the Pelethites;
24Adoram *was* [a]in charge of revenue; [b]Je-
hoshaphat the son of Ahilud *was* recorder;
25Sheva *was* scribe; [a]Zadok and Abiathar
were the priests; 26[a]and Ira the Jairite was
a chief minister under David.

David Avenges the Gibeonites

21 Now there was a famine in the days of
David for three years, year after year;
and David [a]inquired of the LORD. And the
LORD answered, "*It is* because of Saul and

20:4 [a] 2 Sam. 17:25; 19:13 20:6 [a] 2 Sam. 21:17 [b] 2 Sam. 11:11; 1 Kin. 1:33 20:7 [a] 2 Sam. 8:18; 1 Kin. 1:38, 44 [b] 2 Sam. 15:18
20:9 [a] Matt. 26:49; Luke 22:47 20:10 [a] 2 Sam. 3:27; 1 Kin. 2:5 [b] 2 Sam. 2:23 20:14 [a] 1 Kin. 15:20; 2 Kin. 15:29; 2 Chr. 16:4
[1] Literally *him* 20:15 [a] 2 Kin. 19:32; Ezek. 4:2 20:19 [a] 1 Sam. 26:19; 2 Sam. 14:16; 21:3 20:22 [a] 2 Sam. 20:16; [Eccl. 9:13–16]
20:23 [a] 2 Sam. 8:16–18; 1 Kin. 4:3–6 20:24 [a] 1 Kin. 4:6 [b] 2 Sam. 8:16; 1 Kin. 4:3 20:25 [a] 2 Sam. 8:17;
1 Kin. 4:4 20:26 [a] 2 Sam. 8:18 21:1 [a] Num. 27:21; 2 Sam. 5:19

his bloodthirsty house, because he killed
the Gibeonites." 2So the king called the Gibeonites and spoke to them. Now the Gibeonites *were* not of the children of Israel,
but [a]of the remnant of the Amorites; the
children of Israel had sworn protection to
them, but Saul had sought to kill them [b]in
his zeal for the children of Israel and Judah.
3Therefore David said to the Gibeonites,
"What shall I do for you? And with what
shall I make atonement, that you may bless
[a]the inheritance of the LORD?"
4And the Gibeonites said to him, "We will
have no silver or gold from Saul or from
his house, nor shall you kill any man in
Israel for us."
So he said, "Whatever you say, I will do
for you."
5Then they answered the king, "As for
the man who consumed us and plotted
against us, *that* we should be destroyed
from remaining in any of the territories of
Israel, 6let seven men of his descendants
be delivered [a]to us, and we will hang them
before the LORD [b]in Gibeah of Saul, [c]*whom*
the LORD chose."
And the king said, "I will give *them.*"
7But the king spared [a]Mephibosheth the
son of Jonathan, the son of Saul, because of
[b]the LORD's oath that *was* between them, between David and Jonathan the son of Saul.
8So the king took Armoni and Mephibosheth, the two sons of [a]Rizpah the daughter
of Aiah, whom she bore to Saul, and the five
sons of Michal[1] the daughter of Saul, whom
she brought up for Adriel the son of Barzillai the Meholathite; 9and he delivered them
into the hands of the Gibeonites, and they
hanged them on the hill [a]before the LORD.
So they fell, *all* seven together, and were put
to death in the days of harvest, in the first
days, in the beginning of barley harvest.
10Now [a]Rizpah the daughter of Aiah took
sackcloth and spread it for herself on the
rock, [b]from the beginning of harvest until
the late rains poured on them from heaven.
And she did not allow the birds of the air to
rest on them by day nor the beasts of the
field by night.

#OXYGEN
2 SAMUEL 21:10
Reconcile Weaknesses with Strength

When powers outside of your control prevail, choose strength. When your voice is not valued, choose strength. Do what you can do and trust God to honor your strength.

Keep fighting, **breathe**, and **reconcile weaknesses with strength.**

11And David was told what Rizpah the
daughter of Aiah, the concubine of Saul,
had done. 12Then David went and took the
bones of Saul, and the bones of Jonathan
his son, from the men of [a]Jabesh Gilead
who had stolen them from the street of
Beth Shan,[1] where the [b]Philistines had hung
them up, after the Philistines had struck
down Saul in Gilboa. 13So he brought up
the bones of Saul and the bones of Jonathan his son from there; and they gathered
the bones of those who had been hanged.
14They buried the bones of Saul and Jonathan his son in the country of Benjamin
in [a]Zelah, in the tomb of Kish his father.
So they performed all that the king commanded. And after that [b]God heeded the
prayer for the land.

Philistine Giants Destroyed
(1 Chr. 20:4–8)

15When the Philistines were at war again
with Israel, David and his servants with
him went down and fought against the Philistines; and David grew faint. 16Then Ish-
bi-Benob, who *was* one of the sons of the
[a]giant, the weight of whose bronze spear
was three hundred *shekels,* who was bearing a new *sword,* thought he could kill David. 17But [a]Abishai the son of Zeruiah came
to his aid, and struck the Philistine and

21:2 [a] Josh. 9:3, 15–20 [b] [Ex. 34:11–16] **21:3** [a] 1 Sam. 26:19; 2 Sam. 20:19 **21:6** [a] Num. 25:4 [b] 1 Sam. 10:26 [c] 1 Sam. 10:24; [Hos. 13:11] **21:7** [a] 2 Sam. 4:4; 9:10 [b] 1 Sam. 18:3; 20:12–17; 23:18; 2 Sam. 9:1–7 **21:8** [a] 2 Sam. 3:7 [1] Or *Merab* (compare 1 Samuel 18:19 and 25:44; 2 Samuel 3:14 and 6:23) **21:9** [a] 2 Sam. 6:17 **21:10** [a] 2 Sam. 3:7; 21:8 [b] Deut. 21:23 **21:12** [a] 1 Sam. 31:11–13 [b] 1 Sam. 31:8 [1] Spelled *Beth Shean* in Joshua 17:11 and elsewhere **21:14** [a] Josh. 18:28 [b] Josh. 7:26; 2 Sam. 24:25 **21:16** [a] Num. 13:22, 28; Josh. 15:14; 2 Sam. 21:18–22 **21:17** [a] 2 Sam. 20:6–10

killed him. Then the men of David swore
to him, saying, [b]"You shall go out no more
with us to battle, lest you quench the [c]lamp
of Israel."

18 [a]Now it happened afterward that there
was again a battle with the Philistines at
Gob. Then [b]Sibbechai the Hushathite killed
Saph,[1] who *was* one of the sons of the giant. 19 Again there was war at Gob with the
Philistines, where [a]Elhanan the son of Jaare-Oregim[1] the Bethlehemite killed [b]*the
brother of* Goliath the Gittite, the shaft of
whose spear *was* like a weaver's beam.

20 Yet again [a]there was war at Gath, where
there was a man of *great* stature, who had
six fingers on each hand and six toes on
each foot, twenty-four in number; and he
also was born to the giant. 21 So when he
[a]defied Israel, Jonathan the son of Shimea,[1]
David's brother, killed him.

22 [a]These four were born to the giant in
Gath, and fell by the hand of David and by
the hand of his servants.

Praise for God's Deliverance
(Ps. 18:1–50)

22 Then David [a]spoke to the LORD the
words of this song, on the day when
the LORD had [b]delivered him from the hand
of all his enemies, and from the hand of
Saul. 2 And he [a]said:[1]

[b]"The LORD *is* my rock and my
[c]fortress and my deliverer;
3 The God of my strength, [a]in
whom I will trust;
My [b]shield and the [c]horn
of my salvation,
My [d]stronghold and my [e]refuge;
My Savior, You save me from violence.
4 I will call upon the LORD, *who
is worthy* to be praised;
So shall I be saved from my enemies.

5 "When the waves of death
surrounded me,
The floods of ungodliness
made me afraid.
6 The [a]sorrows of Sheol surrounded me;
The snares of death confronted me.
7 In my distress [a]I called upon the LORD,
And cried out to my God;
He [b]heard my voice from His temple,
And my cry *entered* His ears.

8 "Then [a]the earth shook and trembled;
[b]The foundations of heaven[1]
quaked and were shaken,
Because He was angry.
9 Smoke went up from His nostrils,
And devouring [a]fire from His mouth;
Coals were kindled by it.
10 He [a]bowed the heavens also,
and came down
With [b]darkness under His feet.
11 He rode upon a cherub, and flew;
And He was seen[1] [a]upon the
wings of the wind.
12 He made [a]darkness canopies
around Him,
Dark waters *and* thick
clouds of the skies.
13 From the brightness before Him
Coals of fire were kindled.

14 "The LORD [a]thundered from heaven,
And the Most High uttered
His voice.
15 He sent out [a]arrows and
scattered them;
Lightning bolts, and He
vanquished them.
16 Then the channels of the
sea [a]were seen,
The foundations of the world
were uncovered,
At the [b]rebuke of the LORD,
At the blast of the breath
of His nostrils.

17 "He[a] sent from above, He took me,
He drew me out of many waters.

21:17 [b] 2 Sam. 18:3 [c] 2 Sam. 22:29; 1 Kin. 11:36 **21:18** [a] 1 Chr. 20:4–8 [b] 1 Chr. 11:29; 27:11 [1] Spelled *Sippai* in 1 Chronicles 20:4 **21:19** [a] 2 Sam. 23:24 [b] 1 Sam. 17:4; 1 Chr. 20:5 [1] Spelled *Jair* in 1 Chronicles 20:5 **21:20** [a] 1 Chr. 20:6 **21:21** [a] 1 Sam. 17:10 [1] Spelled *Shammah* in 1 Samuel 16:9 and elsewhere **21:22** [a] 1 Chr. 20:8 **22:1** [a] Ex. 15:1; Deut. 31:30; Judg. 5:1 [b] Ps. 18:title; 34:19 **22:2** [a] Ps. 18 [b] Deut. 32:4; 1 Sam. 2:2 [c] Ps. 91:2 [1] Compare Psalm 18 **22:3** [a] Ps. 7:1; Heb. 2:13 [b] Gen. 15:1; Deut. 33:29; Ps. 84:11 [c] Luke 1:69 [d] Prov. 18:10 [e] Ps. 9:9; 46:1, 7, 11; Jer. 16:19 **22:6** [a] Ps. 116:3 **22:7** [a] Ps. 116:4; 120:1 [b] Ex. 3:7; Ps. 34:6, 15 **22:8** [a] Judg. 5:4; Ps. 77:18; 97:4 [b] Job 26:11 [1] Following Masoretic Text, Septuagint, and Targum; Syriac and Vulgate read *hills* (compare Psalm 18:7). **22:9** [a] Deut. 32:22; Ps. 97:3, 4; Heb. 12:29 **22:10** [a] Ex. 19:16–20; Is. 64:1 [b] Ex. 20:21 **22:11** [a] Ps. 104:3 [1] Following Masoretic Text and Septuagint; many Hebrew manuscripts, Syriac, and Vulgate read *He flew* (compare Psalm 18:10); Targum reads *He spoke with power.* **22:12** [a] Job 36:29; Ps. 97:2 **22:14** [a] 1 Sam. 2:10; Job 37:2–5; Ps. 29:3 **22:15** [a] Deut. 32:23; Josh. 10:10; 1 Sam. 7:10; Ps. 7:13 **22:16** [a] Nah. 1:4 [b] Ex. 15:8 **22:17** [a] Ps. 144:7; Is. 43:2

18 He delivered me from my
strong enemy,
From those who hated me;
For they were too strong for me.
19 They confronted me in the
day of my calamity,
But the LORD was my [a]support.
20 [a]He also brought me out
into a broad place;
He delivered me because
He [b]delighted in me.

21 "The[a] LORD rewarded me according
to my righteousness;
According to the [b]cleanness
of my hands
He has recompensed me.
22 For I have [a]kept the ways of the LORD,
And have not wickedly
departed from my God.
23 For all His [a]judgments *were* before me;
And *as for* His statutes, I did
not depart from them.
24 I was also [a]blameless before Him,
And I kept myself from my iniquity.
25 Therefore [a]the LORD has recompensed
me according to my righteousness,
According to my cleanness
in His eyes.[1]

26 "With [a]the merciful You will
show Yourself merciful;
With a blameless man You will
show Yourself blameless;
27 With the pure You will show
Yourself pure;
And [a]with the devious You will
show Yourself shrewd.
28 You will save the [a]humble people;
But Your eyes *are* on [b]the haughty,
that You may bring *them* down.

29 "For You *are* my [a]lamp, O LORD;
The LORD shall enlighten
my darkness.
30 For by You I can run against a troop;
By my God I can leap over a [a]wall.
31 *As for* God, [a]His way *is* perfect;
[b]The word of the LORD *is* proven;
He *is* a shield to all who trust in Him.

32 "For [a]who *is* God, except the LORD?
And who *is* a rock, except our God?
33 God *is* my [a]strength *and* power,[1]
And He [b]makes my[2] way [c]perfect.
34 He makes my[1] feet [a]like the *feet* of deer,
And [b]sets me on my high places.
35 He teaches my hands to make war,
So that my arms can bend
a bow of bronze.

36 "You have also given me the
shield of Your salvation;
Your gentleness has made me great.
37 You [a]enlarged my path under me;
So my feet did not slip.

38 "I have pursued my enemies
and destroyed them;
Neither did I turn back again
till they were destroyed.
39 And I have destroyed them
and wounded them,
So that they could not rise;
They have fallen [a]under my feet.
40 For You have [a]armed me with
strength for the battle;
You have subdued under me
[b]those who rose against me.
41 You have also given me the
[a]necks of my enemies,
So that I destroyed those who hated me.
42 They looked, but *there*
was none to save;
Even [a]to the LORD, but He
did not answer them.
43 Then I beat them as fine [a]as
the dust of the earth;
I trod them [b]like dirt in the streets,
And I spread them out.

22:19 [a] Is. 10:20 **22:20** [a] Ps. 31:8; 118:5 [b] 2 Sam. 15:26 **22:21** [a] 1 Sam. 26:23; [Ps. 7:8] [b] [Job 17:9]; Ps. 24:4 **22:22** [a] Gen. 18:19; 2 Chr. 34:33; Ps. 119:3 **22:23** [a] [Deut. 6:6–9; 7:12]; Ps. 119:30, 102 **22:24** [a] Gen. 6:9; 7:1; Job 1:1; [Eph. 1:4; Col. 1:21, 22] **22:25** [a] 2 Sam. 22:21 [1] Septuagint, Syriac, and Vulgate read *the cleanness of my hands in His sight* (compare Psalm 18:24); Targum reads *my cleanness before His word.* **22:26** [a] [Matt. 5:7] **22:27** [a] [Lev. 26:23, 24; Rom. 1:28] **22:28** [a] Ps. 72:12 [b] Job 40:11 **22:29** [a] Ps. 119:105; 132:17 **22:30** [a] 2 Sam. 5:6–8 **22:31** [a] [Deut. 32:4]; Dan. 4:37; [Matt. 5:48] [b] Ps. 12:6; [Prov. 30:5] **22:32** [a] Is. 45:5, 6 **22:33** [a] Ps. 27:1 [b] [Heb. 13:21] [c] Ps. 101:2, 6 [1] Dead Sea Scrolls, Septuagint, Syriac, and Vulgate read *It is God who arms me with strength* (compare Psalm 18:32); Targum reads *It is God who sustains me with strength.* [2] Following Qere, Septuagint, Syriac, Targum, and Vulgate (compare Psalm 18:32); Kethib reads *His.* **22:34** [a] 2 Sam. 2:18; Hab. 3:19 [b] Is. 33:16 [1] Following Qere, Septuagint, Syriac, Targum, and Vulgate (compare Psalm 18:33); Kethib reads *His.* **22:37** [a] 2 Sam. 22:20; Prov. 4:12 **22:39** [a] Mal. 4:3 **22:40** [a] [Ps. 18:32] [b] [Ps. 44:5] **22:41** [a] Gen. 49:8; Josh. 10:24 **22:42** [a] 1 Sam. 28:6; Prov. 1:28; Is. 1:15 **22:43** [a] 2 Kin. 13:7; Ps. 18:42 [b] Is. 10:6

44 "You[a] have also delivered me from
the strivings of my people;
You have kept me as the
[b]head of the nations.
[c]A people I have not known
shall serve me.
45 The foreigners submit to me;
As soon as they hear, they obey me.
46 The foreigners fade away,
And come frightened[1] [a]from
their hideouts.

47 "The LORD lives!
Blessed *be* my Rock!
Let God be exalted,
The [a]Rock of my salvation!
48 *It is* God who avenges me,
And [a]subdues the peoples under me;
49 He delivers me from my enemies.
You also lift me up above those
who rise against me;
You have delivered me from
the [a]violent man.
50 Therefore I will give thanks to You,
O LORD, among [a]the Gentiles,
And sing praises to Your [b]name.

51 "*He*[a] *is* the tower of salvation to His king,
And shows mercy to His [b]anointed,
To David and [c]his descendants
forevermore."

David's Last Words

23 Now these *are* the last words of
David.

Thus says David the son of Jesse;
Thus says [a]the man raised up on high,
[b]The anointed of the God of Jacob,
And the sweet psalmist of Israel:

2 "The[a] Spirit of the LORD spoke by me,
And His word *was* on my tongue.
3 The God of Israel said,
[a]The Rock of Israel spoke to me:
'He who rules over men *must be* just,
Ruling [b]in the fear of God.
4 And [a]*he shall be* like the light of the
morning *when* the sun rises,
A morning without clouds,
Like the tender grass *springing*
out of the earth,
By clear shining after rain.'

5 "Although my house *is* not so with God,
[a]Yet He has made with me an
everlasting covenant,
Ordered in all *things* and secure.
For *this is* all my salvation
and all *my* desire;
Will He not make *it* increase?
6 But *the sons* of rebellion *shall* all
be as thorns thrust away,
Because they cannot be
taken with hands.
7 But the man *who* touches them
Must be armed with iron and
the shaft of a spear,
And they shall be utterly burned
with fire in *their* place."

David's Mighty Men
(1 Chr. 11:10–47)

8These *are* the names of the mighty men
whom David had: Josheb-Basshebeth[1] the
Tachmonite, chief among the captains.[2]
He was called Adino the Eznite, because
he had killed eight hundred men at one
time. 9And after him *was* [a]Eleazar the son of
Dodo,[1] the Ahohite, *one* of the three mighty
men with David when they defied the Philistines *who* were gathered there for battle,
and the men of Israel had retreated. 10He
arose and attacked the Philistines until his
hand was [a]weary, and his hand stuck to the
sword. The LORD brought about a great victory that day; and the people returned after
him only to [b]plunder. 11And after him *was*
[a]Shammah the son of Agee the Hararite.
[b]The Philistines had gathered together into
a troop where there was a piece of ground
full of lentils. So the people fled from the
Philistines. 12But he stationed himself in
the middle of the field, defended it, and

22:44 [a] 2 Sam. 3:1 [b] Deut. 28:13 [c] [Is. 55:5] 22:46 [a] 1 Sam. 14:11; [Mic. 7:17] [1] Following Septuagint, Targum, and Vulgate (compare Psalm 18:45); Masoretic Text reads *gird themselves.* 22:47 [a] [2 Sam. 22:3]; Ps. 89:26 22:48 [a] 1 Sam. 24:12; Ps. 144:2 22:49 [a] Ps. 140:1, 4, 11 22:50 [a] 2 Sam. 8:1–14 [b] Ps. 57:7; Rom. 15:9 22:51 [a] Ps. 144:10 [b] Ps. 89:20 [c] 2 Sam. 7:12–16; Ps. 89:29 23:1 [a] 2 Sam. 7:8, 9; Ps. 78:70, 71 [b] 1 Sam. 16:12, 13; Ps. 89:20 23:2 [a] Matt. 22:43; [2 Pet. 1:21] 23:3 [a] [Deut. 32:4] [b] Ex. 18:21; [Is. 11:1–5] 23:4 [a] Ps. 89:36; Is. 60:1 23:5 [a] 2 Sam. 7:12; Ps. 89:29; Is. 55:3 23:8 [1] Literally *One Who Sits in the Seat* (compare 1 Chronicles 11:11) [2] Following Masoretic Text and Targum; Septuagint and Vulgate read *the three.* 23:9 [a] 1 Chr. 11:12; 27:4 [1] Spelled *Dodai* in 1 Chronicles 27:4 23:10 [a] Judg. 8:4 [b] 1 Sam. 30:24, 25 23:11 [a] 1 Chr. 11:27 [b] 1 Chr. 11:13, 14

killed the Philistines. So the LORD brought
about a great victory.
13Then [a]three of the thirty chief men
went down at harvest time and came to
David at [b]the cave of Adullam. And the
troop of Philistines encamped in [c]the Valley of Rephaim. 14David *was* then in [a]the
stronghold, and the garrison of the Philistines *was* then *in* Bethlehem. 15And David
said with longing, "Oh, that someone would
give me a drink of the water from the well
of Bethlehem, which *is* by the gate!" 16So
the three mighty men broke through the
camp of the Philistines, drew water from
the well of Bethlehem that *was* by the gate,
and took it and brought *it* to David. Nevertheless he would not drink it, but poured
it out to the LORD. 17And he said, "Far be it
from me, O LORD, that I should do this! Is
this not [a]the blood of the men who went in
jeopardy of their lives?" Therefore he would
not drink it.

These things were done by the three
mighty men.

18Now [a]Abishai the brother of Joab, the
son of Zeruiah, was chief of *another* three.[1]
He lifted his spear against three hundred
men, killed *them,* and won a name among
these three. 19Was he not the most honored
of three? Therefore he became their captain. However, he did not attain to the *first*
three.

20Benaiah *was* the son of Jehoiada, the
son of a valiant man from [a]Kabzeel, who
had done many deeds. [b]He had killed two
lion-like heroes of Moab. He also had gone
down and killed a lion in the midst of a pit
on a snowy day. 21And he killed an Egyptian, a spectacular man. The Egyptian *had* a
spear in his hand; so he went down to him
with a staff, wrested the spear out of the
Egyptian's hand, and killed him with his
own spear. 22These *things* Benaiah the son
of Jehoiada did, and won a name among
three mighty men. 23He was more honored than the thirty, but he did not attain
to the *first* three. And David appointed him
[a]over his guard.

24[a]Asahel the brother of Joab *was* one of
the thirty; Elhanan the son of Dodo of Bethlehem, 25[a]Shammah the Harodite, Elika the
Harodite, 26Helez the Paltite, Ira the son of
Ikkesh the Tekoite, 27Abiezer the Anathothite, Mebunnai the Hushathite, 28Zalmon the
Ahohite, Maharai the Netophathite, 29He-
leb the son of Baanah (the Netophathite),
Ittai the son of Ribai from Gibeah of the
children of Benjamin, 30Benaiah a Pirathonite, Hiddai from the brooks of [a]Ga-
ash, 31Abi-Albon the Arbathite, Azmaveth
the Barhumite, 32Eliahba the Shaalbonite
(of the sons of Jashen), Jonathan, 33[a]Sham-
mah the Hararite, Ahiam the son of Sharar
the Hararite, 34Eliphelet the son of Ahasbai,
the son of the Maachathite, Eliam the son
of [a]Ahithophel the Gilonite, 35Hezrai[1] the
Carmelite, Paarai the Arbite, 36Igal the son
of Nathan of [a]Zobah, Bani the Gadite, 37Ze-
lek the Ammonite, Naharai the Beerothite
(armorbearer of Joab the son of Zeruiah),
38[a]Ira the Ithrite, Gareb the Ithrite, 39*and*
[a]Uriah the Hittite: thirty-seven in all.

David's Census of Israel and Judah
(1 Chr. 21:1–6)

24 Again [a]the anger of the LORD was
aroused against Israel, and He
moved David against them to say, [b]"Go,
number Israel and Judah."

2So the king said to Joab the commander
of the army who *was* with him, "Now go
throughout all the tribes of Israel, [a]from
Dan to Beersheba, and count the people,
that [b]I may know the number of the people."

3And Joab said to the king, "Now may the
LORD your God [a]add to the people a hundred times more than there are, and may
the eyes of my lord the king see *it.* But why
does my lord the king desire this thing?"
4Nevertheless the king's word prevailed
against Joab and against the captains of
the army. Therefore Joab and the captains
of the army went out from the presence of
the king to count the people of Israel.

5And they crossed over the Jordan and

23:13 [a] 1 Chr. 11:15 [b] 1 Sam. 22:1 [c] 2 Sam. 5:18 23:14 [a] 1 Sam. 22:4, 5 23:17 [a] [Lev. 17:10] 23:18 [a] 2 Sam. 21:17; 1 Chr. 11:20 [1] Following Masoretic Text, Septuagint, and Vulgate; some Hebrew manuscripts and Syriac read *thirty;* Targum reads *the mighty men.* 23:20 [a] Josh. 15:21 [b] Ex. 15:15 23:23 [a] 2 Sam. 8:18; 20:23 23:24 [a] 2 Sam. 2:18; 1 Chr. 27:7 23:25 [a] 1 Chr. 11:27 23:30 [a] Judg. 2:9 23:33 [a] 2 Sam. 23:11 23:34 [a] 2 Sam. 15:12 23:35 [1] Spelled *Hezro* in 1 Chronicles 11:37 23:36 [a] 2 Sam. 8:3 23:38 [a] 1 Chr. 2:53 23:39 [a] 2 Sam. 11:3, 6 24:1 [a] 2 Sam. 21:1, 2 [b] Num. 26:2; 1 Chr. 27:23, 24 24:2 [a] Judg. 20:1; 2 Sam. 3:10 [b] [Jer. 17:5] 24:3 [a] Deut. 1:11

camped in [a]Aroer, on the right side of the
town which *is* in the midst of the ravine of
Gad, and toward [b]Jazer. 6Then they came
to Gilead and to the land of Tahtim Hod-
shi; they came to [a]Dan Jaan and around to
[b]Sidon; 7and they came to the stronghold of
[a]Tyre and to all the cities of the [b]Hivites and
the Canaanites. Then they went out to South
Judah *as far as* Beersheba. 8So when they
had gone through all the land, they came to
Jerusalem at the end of nine months and
twenty days. 9Then Joab gave the sum of the
number of the people to the king. [a]And there
were in Israel eight hundred thousand valiant men who drew the sword, and the men
of Judah were five hundred thousand men.

The Judgment on David's Sin
(1 Chr. 21:7–17)

10And [a]David's heart condemned him after he had numbered the people. So [b]David
said to the LORD, [c]"I have sinned greatly in
what I have done; but now, I pray, O LORD,
take away the iniquity of Your servant, for
I have [d]done very foolishly."

11Now when David arose in the morning,
the word of the LORD came to the prophet
[a]Gad, David's [b]seer, saying, 12"Go and tell David, 'Thus says the LORD: "I offer you three
things; choose one of them for yourself, that
I may do *it* to you." ' " 13So Gad came to David and told him; and he said to him, "Shall
[a]seven[1] years of famine come to you in your
land? Or shall you flee three months before
your enemies, while they pursue you? Or
shall there be three days' plague in your
land? Now consider and see what answer
I should take back to Him who sent me."

14And David said to Gad, "I am in great
distress. Please let us fall into the hand of
the LORD, [a]for His mercies *are* great; but
[b]do not let me fall into the hand of man."

15So [a]the LORD sent a plague upon Israel
from the morning till the appointed time.
From Dan to Beersheba seventy thousand
men of the people died. 16[a]And when the
angel[1] stretched out His hand over Jerusalem to destroy it, [b]the LORD relented from
the destruction, and said to the angel who
was destroying the people, "It is enough;
now restrain your hand." And the angel
of the LORD was by the threshing floor of
Araunah[2] the Jebusite.

17Then David spoke to the LORD when he
saw the angel who was striking the people,
and said, "Surely [a]I have sinned, and I have
done wickedly; but these sheep, what have
they done? Let Your hand, I pray, be against
me and against my father's house."

The Altar on the Threshing Floor
(1 Chr. 21:18–27)

18And Gad came that day to David and
said to him, [a]"Go up, erect an altar to the
LORD on the threshing floor of Araunah the
Jebusite." 19So David, according to the word
of Gad, went up as the LORD commanded.
20Now Araunah looked, and saw the king
and his servants coming toward him. So
Araunah went out and bowed before the
king with his face to the ground.

21Then Araunah said, "Why has my lord
the king come to his servant?"

[a]And David said, "To buy the threshing floor from you, to build an altar to the
LORD, that [b]the plague may be withdrawn
from the people."

22Now Araunah said to David, "Let my
lord the king take and offer up whatever
seems good to him. [a]Look, *here are* oxen
for burnt sacrifice, and threshing implements and the yokes of the oxen for wood.
23All these, O king, Araunah has given to
the king."

And Araunah said to the king, "May the
LORD your God [a]accept you."

24Then the king said to Araunah, "No, but
I will surely buy *it* from you for a price; nor
will I offer burnt offerings to the LORD my
God with that which costs me nothing." So
[a]David bought the threshing floor and the
oxen for fifty shekels of silver. 25And David
built there an altar to the LORD, and offered
burnt offerings and peace offerings. [a]So
the LORD heeded the prayers for the land,
and [b]the plague was withdrawn from Israel.

24:5 [a] Deut. 2:36; Josh. 13:9, 16 [b] Num. 32:1, 3 **24:6** [a] Josh. 19:47; Judg. 18:29 [b] Josh. 19:28; Judg. 18:28 **24:7** [a] Josh. 19:29 [b] Josh. 11:3; Judg. 3:3 **24:9** [a] 1 Chr. 21:5 **24:10** [a] 1 Sam. 24:5 [b] 2 Sam. 23:1 [c] 2 Sam. 12:13 [d] 1 Sam. 13:13; [2 Chr. 16:9] **24:11** [a] 1 Sam. 22:5 [b] 1 Sam. 9:9; 1 Chr. 29:29 **24:13** [a] Ezek. 14:21 [1] Following Masoretic Text, Syriac, Targum, and Vulgate; Septuagint reads *three* (compare 1 Chronicles 21:12). **24:14** [a] [Ps. 51:1; 103:8, 13, 14; 119:156; 130:4, 7] [b] [Is. 47:6; Zech. 1:15] **24:15** [a] 1 Chr. 21:14 **24:16** [a] Ex. 12:23; 2 Kin. 19:35; Acts 12:23 [b] Gen. 6:6; 1 Sam. 15:11 [1] Or *Angel* [2] Spelled *Ornan* in 1 Chronicles 21:15 **24:17** [a] 2 Sam. 7:8; 1 Chr. 21:17; Ps. 74:1 **24:18** [a] 1 Chr. 21:18 **24:21** [a] Gen. 23:8–16 [b] Num. 16:48, 50 **24:22** [a] 1 Sam. 6:14; 1 Kin. 19:21 **24:23** [a] [Ezek. 20:40, 41] **24:24** [a] 1 Chr. 21:24, 25 **24:25** [a] 2 Sam. 21:14 [b] 2 Sam. 24:21

THE FIRST BOOK OF THE

KINGS

OVERVIEW

Written around 560 BC, 1 Kings and 2 Kings were originally one book. This book was separated when the Bible was translated into Greek. Combined, these books cover over four hundred years of Israel's history. The author of 1 Kings is unknown, but it has been suggested that Ezra, Ezekiel, or Jeremiah may have written it.

First Kings details the death of King David, the reign of his son Solomon, and the division and decline of the kingdom of Israel after Solomon's death.

At the beginning of 1 Kings, David is near his death, and his son Adonijah has proclaimed himself king. David, however, instructed the prophet Nathan to anoint his other son, Solomon, as king. David also instructed Solomon to be obedient to God and His laws (see 1 Kin. 1:1—2:12). God then appeared to Solomon in a dream, offering to grant him one desire. Solomon asked God for wisdom to govern the people. His request pleased God, and God granted Solomon not only wealth but also long life (see 3:1–15). Solomon would become famous for his wisdom (see 3:28; 4:34) and affluence (see 10:21–23).

Solomon ruled successfully (chs. 4–10) until he married women from other nations who enticed him to worship other gods (see 11:1–8). Consequently, God told Solomon that his sin would divide the kingdom. God allowed Solomon's house to remain over Judah only in order to keep His covenant to David (see vv. 9–39).

When Solomon died, his son Rehoboam assumed the throne (see 11:43—12:1). Most of the Israelites rebelled against him, though, and crowned Jeroboam king over the northern tribes, which would be still known as Israel (see 12:16–19). Rehoboam continued to rule over the southern kingdom of Judah. Both kings, meanwhile, established idol worship in their kingdoms (chs. 12–16). Thus was the beginning of both Israel's and Judah's protracted slides deeper into idolatry and toward God's judgment.

Although 1 Kings focuses largely on the kingdom's leaders, it also includes God's prophets, beginning with Elijah (see 17:1). Most of Elijah's ministry focused on the northern kingdom during the reign of Ahab and his wife, Jezebel. The kings who had come before Ahab had continued to embed idolatry into Israel's culture, but he and Jezebel did so even more. In response, God instructed Elijah to proclaim a drought on the land, which continued for three years (see 17:1–7). Then, to prove to the people that God was the only true God, Elijah challenged the priests of the false god Baal to a contest on Mount Carmel. God's power easily prevailed when God sent fire from heaven, and the prophets of Baal were destroyed (see 18:20–40). Afterward, God brought the drought to an end (see vv. 41–46). In a fit of rage, Queen Jezebel vowed to have Elijah killed, so he fled for his life and hid in a cave. There, God spoke encouragement to him (see 19:9–18).

Despite Elijah's warnings, King Ahab continued his wickedness, which was encouraged by his wife (see 21:1–16). Elijah prophesied that dogs would lick the king's blood as punishment for his wickedness and that dogs would devour Jezebel (see vv. 17–24). The prophecy regarding Ahab was fulfilled when he died in battle (see 22:29–40). Jezebel lived for another ten years. She died by being thrown from a window, and as God had declared, dogs devoured her body

(see 2 Kin. 9:30–37). Her son Ahaziah succeeded Ahab and continued his father's wicked ways (see 1 Kin. 22:51–53).

First Kings highlights the dangers of worshiping false gods and God's mercy in giving His rebellious people many opportunities to repent. The idolatry that Solomon began continued well after his death, as God's people continued on a path of spiritual decline. God disciplined His people, but He also sent the prophet Elijah to warn them to turn from their wickedness and experience forgiveness and restoration. None, however, did. Instead, they continued to resist God's efforts and desire for reconciliation.

BREATHE IT IN

Before his death, David implored Solomon to "keep the charge of the LORD" (2:3). Solomon honored this charge and began his reign seeking to do what was right in the sight of God. Because of this, God offered Solomon a gift of his own choosing; Solomon requested wisdom. Pleased with the request, God granted Solomon wisdom, wealth, and long life, setting him aside from all other kings.

God has promised to give us the desires of our hearts when we delight in Him (see Ps. 37:4), but we must ensure we have the right desires in our hearts. Many of us are prone to ask God for wealth and personal possessions such as houses, cars, jobs, and money. We also make seemingly noble requests of God to benefit us as a people. These requests are often appeals to God to better our conditions by ending injustice, giving us equal opportunity, providing trustworthy leaders, and granting us worldly influence. These requests may rcflect our needs, and some may even bc selfless requests, but we do not have God's eternal vision to know if the fulfillment of these requests would be God's highest and best for us. This is why Solomon's request for God's wisdom was so wise in itself. What he asked for made him a just and honored authority that we still revere thousands of years later.

Proverbs 4:7 says, "Wisdom is the principal thing; therefore get wisdom." With God's wisdom come understanding, knowledge, and fear of the Lord that result in righteousness, justice, equity, and the right path. James 1:5 tells us, "If any of you lacks wisdom, let him ask of God, who gives to all liberally and without reproach, and it will be given to him." So, we can all have the same kind of wisdom that Solomon asked for and received. Solomon understood the importance of wisdom. He recognized the need to know right from wrong, good from bad, and knew how important it was for him to rule with God's view of each. He wanted to make decisions according to God's covenant and based on His desires for the people of Israel. We should not merely ask God for blessings, but we should also ask Him for wisdom and discernment so we can maintain, grow, and multiply those blessings and use them for God's glory.

Although Solomon began his journey as a king with good intentions and God blessed him abundantly, somewhere along the way, he allowed his weaknesses to steer him away from God and toward false gods. In this, we are reminded that it is not enough for us to start strong. We must be committed enough to run the race and finish strong too.

Life's race is given not to the swift but to those who endure. Prepare yourself for the journey. Ask God for wisdom to run the race He has put before you. His wisdom will keep you on the path of righteousness. It will strengthen you when you are tired, turn your confusion into clarity, bring your actions to faith, and release abundant blessings into your life. Run your race faithfully and discover God's best for your life.

†

THE FIRST BOOK OF THE

KINGS

Adonijah Presumes to Be King

1 Now King David was [a]old, advanced in
years; and they put covers on him, but he
could not get warm. 2 Therefore his servants
said to him, "Let a young woman, a virgin,
be sought for our lord the king, and let her
stand before the king, and let her care for
him; and let her lie in your bosom, that our
lord the king may be warm." 3 So they sought
for a lovely young woman throughout all
the territory of Israel, and found [a]Abishag
the [b]Shunammite, and brought her to the
king. 4 The young woman *was* very lovely;
and she cared for the king, and served him;
but the king did not know her.
5 Then [a]Adonijah the son of Haggith
exalted himself, saying, "I will be king";
and [b]he prepared for himself chariots and
horsemen, and fifty men to run before him.
6 (And his father had not rebuked him at any
time by saying, "Why have you done so?"
He *was* also very good-looking. [a]*His mother*
had borne him after Absalom.) 7 Then he
conferred with [a]Joab the son of Zeruiah
and with [b]Abiathar the priest, and [c]they
followed and helped Adonijah. 8 But [a]Za-
dok the priest, [b]Benaiah the son of Jehoiada, [c]Nathan the prophet, [d]Shimei, Rei, and
[e]the mighty men who *belonged* to David
were not with Adonijah.
9 And Adonijah sacrificed sheep and
oxen and fattened cattle by the stone of
Zoheleth, which *is* by [a]En Rogel; he also invited all his brothers, the king's sons, and
all the men of Judah, the king's servants.
10 But he did not invite Nathan the prophet,
Benaiah, the mighty men, or [a]Solomon his
brother.
11 So Nathan spoke to Bathsheba the
mother of Solomon, saying, "Have you not
heard that Adonijah the son of [a]Haggith
has become king, and David our lord does
not know *it?* 12 Come, please, let me now
give you advice, that you may save your
own life and the life of your son Solomon.
13 Go immediately to King David and say to
him, 'Did you not, my lord, O king, swear to
your maidservant, saying, [a]"Assuredly your
son Solomon shall reign after me, and he
shall sit on my throne"? Why then has Adonijah become king?' 14 Then, while you are
still talking there with the king, I also will
come in after you and confirm your words."
15 So Bathsheba went into the chamber
to the king. (Now the king was very old,
and Abishag the Shunammite was serving
the king.) 16 And Bathsheba bowed and did
homage to the king. Then the king said,
"What is your wish?"
17 Then she said to him, "My lord, [a]you
swore by the LORD your God to your maidservant, *saying,* 'Assuredly Solomon your
son shall reign after me, and he shall sit on
my throne.' 18 So now, look! Adonijah has
become king; and now, my lord the king,
you do not know about *it.* 19 [a]He has sacrificed oxen and fattened cattle and sheep in
abundance, and has invited all the sons of
the king, Abiathar the priest, and Joab the
commander of the army; but Solomon your
servant he has not invited. 20 And as for you,
my lord, O king, the eyes of all Israel *are*
on you, that you should tell them who will
sit on the throne of my lord the king after
him. 21 Otherwise it will happen, when my
lord the king [a]rests with his fathers, that

1:1 [a] 1 Chr. 23:1 1:3 [a] 1 Kin. 2:17 [b] Josh. 19:18; 1 Sam. 28:4 1:5 [a] 2 Sam. 3:4 [b] 2 Sam. 15:1 1:6 [a] 2 Sam. 3:3, 4; 1 Chr. 3:2 1:7 [a] 1 Chr. 11:6 [b] 2 Sam. 20:25 [c] 1 Kin. 2:22, 28 1:8 [a] 1 Kin. 2:35 [b] 1 Kin. 2:25; 2 Sam. 8:18 [c] 2 Sam. 12:1 [d] 1 Kin. 4:18 [e] 2 Sam. 23:8 1:9 [a] Josh. 15:7; 18:16; 2 Sam. 17:17 1:10 [a] 2 Sam. 12:24 1:11 [a] 2 Sam. 3:4 1:13 [a] 1 Kin. 1:30; 1 Chr. 22:9–13 1:17 [a] 1 Kin. 1:13, 30 1:19 [a] 1 Kin. 1:7–9, 25 1:21 [a] Deut. 31:16; 2 Sam. 7:12; 1 Kin. 2:10

I and my son Solomon will be counted as
offenders."
22And just then, while she was still
talking with the king, Nathan the prophet
also came in. 23So they told the king, saying,
"Here is Nathan the prophet." And when he
came in before the king, he bowed down
before the king with his face to the ground.
24And Nathan said, "My lord, O king, have
you said, 'Adonijah shall reign after me,
and he shall sit on my throne'? 25[a]For he
has gone down today, and has sacrificed
oxen and fattened cattle and sheep in abundance, and has invited all the king's sons,
and the commanders of the army, and Abiathar the priest; and look! They are eating and drinking before him; and they say,
[b]'*Long* live King Adonijah!' 26But he has not
invited me—me your servant—nor Zadok
the priest, nor Benaiah the son of Jehoiada, nor your servant Solomon. 27Has this
thing been done by my lord the king, and
you have not told your servant who should
sit on the throne of my lord the king after him?"

David Proclaims Solomon King
(1 Chr. 29:22–25)

28Then King David answered and said,
"Call Bathsheba to me." So she came into
the king's presence and stood before the
king. 29And the king took an oath and said,
[a]"*As* the LORD lives, who has redeemed my
life from every distress, 30[a]just as I swore
to you by the LORD God of Israel, saying,
'Assuredly Solomon your son shall be king

EXALT HIS AMAZING OMNIPRESENCE

INHALE

I am completely overwhelmed. In addition to figuring out my own life, so many others need me, my time, and my energy. But I cannot do it all. I cannot be everywhere at once. I cannot help my mom, my spouse, my kids, my employees, my church, and my neighbors all at the same time. Don't get me wrong: I want to. I care about all these people and want to do what I can to help. But I'm honestly reaching my breaking point. They all have real needs, but I do too. How can I be the answer to their problems when I need answers to my own?

EXHALE

Isn't it great to know that you aren't God! It is easy for us to get overwhelmed by the demands of life. You aren't alone in how you feel right now. But we also must realize that God never gets overwhelmed. He is as steady as steady can be. What is way too much for us is not even a slight problem for Him. Part of that is because He is omnipotent, or all-powerful. But it is also because He is omnipresent. That means He is not limited by location. God is everywhere at the same time. Right now, He's in California and He's in Connecticut. He's in Kenya and in Korea. And He's on earth and He's in the farthest corner of the universe.

I know our limited thinking makes this difficult to grasp. But that is an encouragement too! We cannot handle what is on God's plate, but He is more than capable of handling anything on our plates. So, while you cannot be there for everyone, God can. While you cannot be in two places at once, solving two problems at once, God can. While you can run out of energy or resources, God will not. Who can compare to the Almighty? *No* one!

First Kings 1:29 gives us some insight into how we can rest in God's ever-present care: "And the King took an oath and said, 'As the LORD lives, who has redeemed my life from every distress.'" Near the end of his life, King David knew that God had been there every minute of his life. This is the God we serve. Remember this the next time you have a lot going on.

1:25 [a] 1 Kin. 1:9, 19 [b] 1 Sam. 10:24 1:29 [a] 2 Sam. 4:9; 12:5 1:30 [a] 1 Kin. 1:13, 17

after me, and he shall sit on my throne in
my place,' so I certainly will do this day."
31 Then Bathsheba bowed with *her* face to
the earth, and paid homage to the king, and
said, [a]"Let my lord King David live forever!"
32 And King David said, "Call to me Zadok
the priest, Nathan the prophet, and Benaiah
the son of Jehoiada." So they came before
the king. 33 The king also said to them, [a]"Take
with you the servants of your lord, and have
Solomon my son ride on my own [b]mule, and
take him down to [c]Gihon. 34 There let Zadok
the priest and Nathan the prophet [a]anoint
him king over Israel; and [b]blow the horn,
and say, '*Long* live King Solomon!' 35 Then
you shall come up after him, and he shall
come and sit on my throne, and he shall be
king in my place. For I have appointed him
to be ruler over Israel and Judah."
36 Benaiah the son of Jehoiada answered
the king and said, [a]"Amen! May the LORD
God of my lord the king say so *too*. 37 [a]As the
LORD has been with my lord the king, even
so may He be with Solomon, and [b]make his
throne greater than the throne of my lord
King David."
38 So Zadok the priest, Nathan the
prophet, [a]Benaiah the son of Jehoiada,
the [b]Cherethites, and the Pelethites went
down and had Solomon ride on King David's mule, and took him to Gihon. 39 Then
Zadok the priest took a horn of [a]oil from
the tabernacle and [b]anointed Solomon.
And they blew the horn, [c]and all the people said, "*Long* live King Solomon!" 40 And
all the people went up after him; and the
people played the flutes and rejoiced with
great joy, so that the earth *seemed to* split
with their sound.
41 Now Adonijah and all the guests who
were with him heard *it* as they finished eating. And when Joab heard the sound of the
horn, he said, "Why *is* the city in such a
noisy uproar?" 42 While he was still speaking, there came [a]Jonathan, the son of Abiathar the priest. And Adonijah said to him,
"Come in, for [b]you *are* a prominent man,
and bring good news."
43 Then Jonathan answered and said to
Adonijah, "No! Our lord King David has
made Solomon king. 44 The king has sent
with him Zadok the priest, Nathan the
prophet, Benaiah the son of Jehoiada, the
Cherethites, and the Pelethites; and they
have made him ride on the king's mule.
45 So Zadok the priest and Nathan the
prophet have anointed him king at Gihon;
and they have gone up from there rejoicing, so that the city is in an uproar. This *is*
the noise that you have heard. 46 Also Solomon [a]sits on the throne of the kingdom.
47 And moreover the king's servants have
gone to bless our lord King David, saying,
[a]'May God make the name of Solomon better than your name, and may He make his
throne greater than your throne.' [b]Then
the king bowed himself on the bed. 48 Also
the king said thus, 'Blessed *be* the LORD
God of Israel, who has [a]given *one* to sit on
my throne this day, while my eyes see [b]*it!*'"
49 So all the guests who were with Adonijah were afraid, and arose, and each one
went his way.
50 Now Adonijah was afraid of Solomon;
so he arose, and went and [a]took hold of the
horns of the altar. 51 And it was told Solomon, saying, "Indeed Adonijah is afraid of
King Solomon; for look, he has taken hold
of the horns of the altar, saying, 'Let King
Solomon swear to me today that he will not
put his servant to death with the sword.'"
52 Then Solomon said, "If he proves himself a worthy man, [a]not one hair of him
shall fall to the earth; but if wickedness is
found in him, he shall die." 53 So King Solomon sent them to bring him down from
the altar. And he came and fell down before King Solomon; and Solomon said to
him, "Go to your house."

David's Instructions to Solomon

2 Now [a]the days of David drew near that
he should die, and he charged Sol-
omon his son, saying: 2 [a]"I go the way of all
the earth; [b]be strong, therefore, and prove
yourself a man. 3 And keep the charge of

1:31 [a] Neh. 2:3; Dan. 2:4; 3:9 1:33 [a] 2 Sam. 20:6 [b] Esth. 6:8 [c] 2 Chr. 32:30; 33:14 1:34 [a] 1 Sam. 10:1; 16:3, 12; 2 Sam. 2:4; 5:3; 1 Kin. 19:16; 2 Kin. 9:3; 11:12; 1 Chr. 29:22 [b] 2 Sam. 15:10; 2 Kin. 9:13; 11:14 1:36 [a] Jer. 28:6 1:37 [a] Josh. 1:5, 17; 1 Sam. 20:13 [b] 1 Kin. 1:47 1:38 [a] 2 Sam. 8:18; 23:20–23 [b] 2 Sam. 20:7; 1 Chr. 18:17 1:39 [a] Ex. 30:23, 25, 32; Ps. 89:20 [b] 1 Chr. 29:22 [c] 1 Sam. 10:24 1:42 [a] 2 Sam. 17:17, 20 [b] 2 Sam. 18:27 1:46 [a] 1 Kin. 2:12; 1 Chr. 29:23 1:47 [a] 1 Kin. 1:37 [b] Gen. 47:31 1:48 [a] 1 Kin. 3:6; [Ps. 132:11, 12] [b] 2 Sam. 7:12 1:50 [a] Ex. 27:2; 30:10; 1 Kin. 2:28 1:52 [a] 1 Sam. 14:45; 2 Sam. 14:11; Acts 27:34 2:1 [a] Gen. 47:29; Deut. 31:14 2:2 [a] Josh. 23:14 [b] Deut. 31:7, 23; 1 Chr. 22:13

the LORD your God: to walk in His ways, to keep His statutes, His commandments, His judgments, and His testimonies, as it is written in the Law of Moses, that you may [a]prosper in all that you do and wherever you turn; 4 that the LORD may [a]fulfill His word which He spoke concerning me, saying, [b]'If your sons take heed to their way, to [c]walk before Me in truth with all their heart and with all their soul,' He said, [d]'you shall not lack a man on the throne of Israel.'

5 "Moreover you know also what Joab the son of Zeruiah [a]did to me, *and* what he did to the two commanders of the armies of Israel, to [b]Abner the son of Ner and [c]Amasa the son of Jether, whom he killed. And he shed the blood of war in peacetime, and put the blood of war on his belt that *was* around his waist, and on his sandals that *were* on his feet. 6 Therefore do [a]according to your wisdom, and do not let his gray hair go down to the grave in peace.

7 "But show kindness to the sons of [a]Barzillai the Gileadite, and let them be among those who [b]eat at your table, for so [c]they came to me when I fled from Absalom your brother.

8 "And see, *you have* with you [a]Shimei the son of Gera, a Benjamite from Bahurim, who cursed me with a malicious curse in the day when I went to Mahanaim. But [b]he came down to meet me at the Jordan, and [c]I swore to him by the LORD, saying, 'I

1 KINGS 2:5

I AM JOAB

"Moreover you know also what Joab the son of Zeruiah did to me, and what he did to the two commanders of the armies of Israel, to Abner the son of Ner and Amasa the son of Jether, whom he killed. And he shed the blood of war in peacetime, and put the blood of war on his belt that was around his waist, and on his sandals that were on his feet." 1 Kings 2:5

I am Joab, a loyal warrior and nephew to King David. David knew that Abner, an Israelite military commander, had killed my brother, but he let Abner escape the consequences. So, I took it upon myself to kill Abner and avenge my brother's death. David grieved Abner's death and spoke a curse over my house.

Still, I was loyal to David and led his army in many successful battles. I helped David in his scheme to have Uriah the Hittite killed in battle.

However, I did not always agree with King David. Instead, I always did what I thought was best, like the time when Absalom, David's son, was disloyal and devious and rebelled against his father. David wanted to put down this revolt, but he did not want any harm to come to his son. I went against David's orders, though, and killed Absalom. Yet, my biggest mistake was backing Adonijah as David's successor instead of Solomon. When I heard that Solomon had been anointed king, I ran to the tabernacle for refuge and held on to the horns of the altar. As King David had advised, Solomon ordered me to be killed there for shedding the blood of many innocent people during a time of peace.

†

Joab was a mercenary. He did not obey God or the king unless it fit his self-interest. He lived by the sword, and he died by the sword with innocent blood on his hands. If God is not the one you serve, you are lost, and in the end, no good will come of your life.

2:3 [a] [Deut. 29:9; Josh. 1:7]; 1 Chr. 22:12, 13 2:4 [a] 2 Sam. 7:25 [b] [Ps. 132:12] [c] 2 Kin. 20:3 [d] 2 Sam. 7:12, 13; 1 Kin. 8:25 2:5 [a] 2 Sam. 3:39; 18:5, 12, 14 [b] 2 Sam. 3:27; 1 Kin. 2:32 [c] 2 Sam. 20:10 2:6 [a] 1 Kin. 2:9; Prov. 20:26 2:7 [a] 2 Sam. 19:31–39 [b] 2 Sam. 9:7, 10; 19:28 [c] 2 Sam. 17:17–29 2:8 [a] 2 Sam. 16:5–13 [b] 2 Sam. 19:18 [c] 2 Sam. 19:23

will not put you to death with the sword.'
9 Now therefore, [a]do not hold him guiltless,
for you *are* a wise man and know what you
ought to do to him; but [b]bring his gray hair
down to the grave with blood."

Death of David
(1 Chr. 3:4; 29:26–28)

10 So [a]David rested with his fathers, and
was buried in [b]the City of David. 11 The period that David [a]reigned over Israel *was*
forty years; seven years he reigned in Hebron, and in Jerusalem he reigned thirty-
three years. 12 [a]Then Solomon sat on the
throne of his father David; and his kingdom was [b]firmly established.

Solomon Executes Adonijah

13 Now Adonijah the son of Haggith came
to Bathsheba the mother of Solomon. So
she said, [a]"Do you come peaceably?"
And he said, "Peaceably." 14 Moreover he
said, "I have something *to say* to you."
And she said, "Say it."
15 Then he said, "You know that the kingdom was [a]mine, and all Israel had set their
expectations on me, that I should reign.
However, the kingdom has been turned
over, and has become my brother's; for [b]it
was his from the LORD. 16 Now I ask one petition of you; do not deny me."
And she said to him, "Say it."
17 Then he said, "Please speak to King Solomon, for he will not refuse you, that he
may give me [a]Abishag the Shunammite
as wife."
18 So Bathsheba said, "Very well, I will
speak for you to the king."
19 Bathsheba therefore went to King Solomon, to speak to him for Adonijah. And
the king rose up to meet her and [a]bowed
down to her, and sat down on his throne
and had a throne set for the king's mother;
[b]so she sat at his right hand. 20 Then she
said, "I desire one small petition of you;
do not refuse me."
And the king said to her, "Ask it, my
mother, for I will not refuse you."
21 So she said, "Let Abishag the Shunammite be given to Adonijah your brother as
wife."
22 And King Solomon answered and said
to his mother, "Now why do you ask Abishag the Shunammite for Adonijah? Ask
for him the kingdom also—for he *is* my
[a]older brother—for him, and for [b]Abiathar
the priest, and for Joab the son of Zeruiah."
23 Then King Solomon swore by the LORD,
saying, [a]"May God do so to me, and more
also, if Adonijah has not spoken this word
against his own life! 24 Now therefore, *as*
the LORD lives, who has confirmed me and
set me on the throne of David my father,
and who has established a house[1] for me,
as He [a]promised, Adonijah shall be put to
death today!"
25 So King Solomon sent by the hand of
[a]Benaiah the son of Jehoiada; and he struck
him down, and he died.

Abiathar Exiled, Joab Executed

26 And to Abiathar the priest the king
said, "Go to [a]Anathoth, to your own fields,
for you *are* deserving of death; but I will
not put you to death at this time, [b]because
you carried the ark of the Lord GOD before
my father David, and because you were afflicted every time my father was afflicted."
27 So Solomon removed Abiathar from being priest to the LORD, that he might [a]fulfill
the word of the LORD which He spoke concerning the house of Eli at Shiloh.
28 Then news came to Joab, for Joab [a]had
defected to Adonijah, though he had not
defected to Absalom. So Joab fled to the
tabernacle of the LORD, and [b]took hold of
the horns of the altar. 29 And King Solomon
was told, "Joab has fled to the tabernacle
of the LORD; there *he is,* by the altar." Then
Solomon sent Benaiah the son of Jehoiada,
saying, "Go, [a]strike him down." 30 So Benaiah went to the tabernacle of the LORD, and
said to him, "Thus says the king, [a]'Come
out!'"
And he said, "No, but I will die here." And
Benaiah brought back word to the king,
saying, "Thus said Joab, and thus he answered me."

2:9 [a] Ex. 20:7; Job 9:28 [b] Gen. 42:38; 44:31 2:10 [a] 1 Kin. 1:21; Acts 2:29; 13:36 [b] 2 Sam. 5:7; 1 Kin. 3:1 2:11 [a] 2 Sam. 5:4, 5; 1 Chr. 3:4; 29:26, 27 2:12 [a] 1 Kin. 1:46; 1 Chr. 29:23 [b] 1 Kin. 2:46; 2 Chr. 1:1 2:13 [a] 1 Sam. 16:4, 5 2:15 [a] 1 Kin. 1:11, 18 [b] 1 Chr. 22:9, 10; 28:5–7; [Dan. 2:21] 2:17 [a] 1 Kin. 1:3, 4 2:19 [a] [Ex. 20:12] [b] Ps. 45:9 2:22 [a] 1 Kin. 1:6; 2:15; 1 Chr. 3:2, 5 [b] 1 Kin. 1:7 2:23 [a] Ruth 1:17 2:24 [a] 2 Sam. 7:11, 13; 1 Chr. 22:10 [1] That is, a royal dynasty 2:25 [a] 2 Sam. 8:18; 1 Kin. 4:4 2:26 [a] Josh. 21:18; Jer. 1:1 [b] 1 Sam. 22:23; 23:6; 2 Sam. 15:14, 29 2:27 [a] 1 Sam. 2:31–35 2:28 [a] 1 Kin. 1:7 [b] 1 Kin. 1:50 2:29 [a] 1 Kin. 2:5, 6 2:30 [a] [Ex. 21:14]

31Then the king said to him, [a]"Do as he
has said, and strike him down and bury
him, [b]that you may take away from me and
from the house of my father the innocent
blood which Joab shed. 32So the LORD [a]will
return his blood on his head, because he
struck down two men more righteous [b]and
better than he, and killed them with the
sword—[c]Abner the son of Ner, the commander of the army of Israel, and [d]Amasa the son of Jether, the commander of
the army of Judah—though my father
David did not know *it.* 33Their blood shall
therefore return upon the head of Joab
and [a]upon the head of his descendants forever. [b]But upon David and his descendants,
upon his house and his throne, there shall
be peace forever from the LORD."
34So Benaiah the son of Jehoiada went
up and struck and killed him; and he was
buried in his own house in the wilderness.
35The king put Benaiah the son of Jehoiada
in his place over the army, and the king put
[a]Zadok the priest in the place of [b]Abiathar.

Shimei Executed

36Then the king sent and called for
[a]Shimei, and said to him, "Build yourself
a house in Jerusalem and dwell there, and
do not go out from there anywhere. 37For
it shall be, on the day you go out and cross
[a]the Brook Kidron, know for certain you
shall surely die; [b]your blood shall be on
your own head."
38And Shimei said to the king, "The saying *is* good. As my lord the king has said,
so your servant will do." So Shimei dwelt
in Jerusalem many days.
39Now it happened at the end of three
years, that two slaves of Shimei ran away to
[a]Achish the son of Maachah, king of Gath.
And they told Shimei, saying, "Look, your
slaves *are* in Gath!" 40So Shimei arose, saddled his donkey, and went to Achish at Gath
to seek his slaves. And Shimei went and
brought his slaves from Gath. 41And Solomon was told that Shimei had gone from
Jerusalem to Gath and had come back.
42Then the king sent and called for Shimei,
and said to him, "Did I not make you swear
by the LORD, and warn you, saying, 'Know
for certain that on the day you go out and
travel anywhere, you shall surely die'? And
you said to me, 'The word I have heard *is*
good.' 43Why then have you not kept the
oath of the LORD and the commandment
that I gave you?" 44The king said moreover to Shimei, "You know, as your heart
acknowledges, [a]all the wickedness that you
did to my father David; therefore the LORD
will [b]return your wickedness on your own
head. 45But King Solomon *shall be* blessed,
and [a]the throne of David shall be established before the LORD forever."
46So the king commanded Benaiah the
son of Jehoiada; and he went out and struck
him down, and he died. Thus the [a]kingdom
was established in the hand of Solomon.

Solomon Requests Wisdom
(2 Chr. 1:2–13)

3 Now [a]Solomon made a treaty with
Pharaoh king of Egypt, and married
Pharaoh's daughter; then he brought her
[b]to the City of David until he had finished
building his [c]own house, and [d]the house
of the LORD, and [e]the wall all around Jerusalem. 2[a]Meanwhile the people sacrificed
at the high places, because there was no
house built for the name of the LORD until
those days. 3And Solomon [a]loved the LORD,
[b]walking in the statutes of his father David, except that he sacrificed and burned
incense at the high places.
4Now [a]the king went to Gibeon to sacrifice there, [b]for that *was* the great high place:
Solomon offered a thousand burnt offerings on that altar. 5[a]At Gibeon the LORD appeared to Solomon [b]in a dream by night;
and God said, "Ask! What shall I give you?"
6[a]And Solomon said: "You have shown
great mercy to Your servant David my father, because he [b]walked before You in
truth, in righteousness, and in uprightness
of heart with You; You have continued this
great kindness for him, and You [c]have given

2:31 [a] [Ex. 21:14] [b] [Num. 35:33; Deut. 19:13; 21:8, 9] 2:32 [a] [Gen. 9:6]; Judg. 9:24, 57 [b] 2 Chr. 21:13, 14 [c] 2 Sam. 3:27 [d] 2 Sam. 20:9, 10 2:33 [a] 2 Sam. 3:29 [b] [Prov. 25:5] 2:35 [a] 1 Sam. 2:35; 1 Kin. 4:4; 1 Chr. 6:53; 24:3; 29:22 [b] 1 Kin. 2:27 2:36 [a] 2 Sam. 16:5–13; 1 Kin. 2:8 2:37 [a] 2 Sam. 15:23; 2 Kin. 23:6; John 18:1 [b] Lev. 20:9; Josh. 2:19; 2 Sam. 1:16; Ezek. 18:13 2:39 [a] 1 Sam. 27:2 2:44 [a] 2 Sam. 16:5–13 [b] 1 Sam. 25:39; 2 Kin. 11:1, 12–16; Ps. 7:16; Ezek. 17:19 2:45 [a] 2 Sam. 7:13; [Prov. 25:5] 2:46 [a] 1 Kin. 2:12; 2 Chr. 1:1 3:1 [a] 1 Kin. 7:8; 9:24 [b] 2 Sam. 5:7 [c] 1 Kin. 7:1 [d] 1 Kin. 6 [e] 1 Kin. 9:15, 19 3:2 [a] [Deut. 12:2–5, 13, 14]; 1 Kin. 11:7; 22:43 3:3 [a] [Rom. 8:28] [b] [1 Kin. 3:6, 14] 3:4 [a] 1 Kin. 9:2; 2 Chr. 1:3 [b] 1 Chr. 16:39; 21:29 3:5 [a] 1 Kin. 9:2; 11:9; 2 Chr. 1:7 [b] Num. 12:6; Matt. 1:20; 2:13 3:6 [a] 2 Chr. 1:8 [b] 1 Kin. 2:4; 9:4; 2 Kin. 20:3 [c] 2 Sam. 7:8–17; 1 Kin. 1:48

him a son to sit on his throne, as *it is* this day.
7Now, O LORD my God, You have made Your
servant king instead of my father David, but
I *am* a [a]little child; I do not know *how* [b]to
go out or come in. 8And Your servant *is* in
the midst of Your people whom You [a]have
chosen, a great people, [b]too numerous to
be numbered or counted. 9[a]Therefore give
to Your servant an understanding heart [b]to
judge Your people, that I may [c]discern between good and evil. For who is able to judge
this great people of Yours?"

10The speech pleased the Lord, that Solomon had asked this thing. 11Then God said
to him: "Because you have asked this thing,
and have [a]not asked long life for yourself,
nor have asked riches for yourself, nor have
asked the life of your enemies, but have
asked for yourself understanding to discern justice, 12[a]behold, I have done according to your words; [b]see, I have given you
a wise and understanding heart, so that
there has not been anyone like you before
you, nor shall any like you arise after you.
13And I have also [a]given you what you have
not asked: both [b]riches and honor, so that
there shall not be anyone like you among
the kings all your days. 14So [a]if you walk in
My ways, to keep My statutes and My commandments, [b]as your father David walked,
then I will [c]lengthen your days."

15Then Solomon [a]awoke; and indeed
it had been a dream. And he came to Jerusalem and stood before the ark of the
covenant of the LORD, offered up burnt offerings, offered peace offerings, and [b]made
a feast for all his servants.

Solomon's Wise Judgment

16Now two women *who were* harlots
came to the king, and [a]stood before him.
17And one woman said, "O my lord, this
woman and I dwell in the same house; and
I gave birth while she *was* in the house.
18Then it happened, the third day after
I had given birth, that this woman also
gave birth. And we *were* together; no one
was with us in the house, except the two
of us in the house. 19And this woman's
son died in the night, because she lay on
him. 20So she arose in the middle of the
night and took my son from my side, while
your maidservant slept, and laid him in
her bosom, and laid her dead child in my
bosom. 21And when I rose in the morning
to nurse my son, there he was, dead. But
when I had examined him in the morning, indeed, he was not my son whom I
had borne."

22Then the other woman said, "No! But
the living one *is* my son, and the dead one
is your son."

And the first woman said, "No! But the
dead one *is* your son, and the living one
is my son."

Thus they spoke before the king.

23And the king said, "The one says, 'This
is my son, who lives, and your son *is* the
dead one'; and the other says, 'No! But your
son *is* the dead one, and my son *is* the living one.'" 24Then the king said, "Bring me
a sword." So they brought a sword before
the king. 25And the king said, "Divide the
living child in two, and give half to one, and
half to the other."

26Then the woman whose son *was* living spoke to the king, for [a]she yearned
with compassion for her son; and she said,
"O my lord, give her the living child, and by
no means kill him!"

But the other said, "Let him be neither
mine nor yours, *but* divide *him*."

27So the king answered and said, "Give
the first woman the living child, and by no
means kill him; she *is* his mother."

28And all Israel heard of the judgment
which the king had rendered; and they
feared the king, for they saw that the [a]wisdom of God *was* in him to administer justice.

Solomon's Administration

4 So King Solomon was king over all
Israel. 2And these *were* his officials:
Azariah the son of Zadok, the priest; 3Elihoreph and Ahijah, the sons of Shisha,
scribes; [a]Jehoshaphat the son of Ahilud, the
recorder; 4[a]Benaiah the son of Jehoiada,

3:7 [a] 1 Chr. 22:5; Jer. 1:6, 7 [b] Num. 27:17; 2 Sam. 5:2 3:8 [a] [Ex. 19:6; Deut. 7:6] [b] Gen. 13:6; 15:5; 22:17 3:9 [a] 2 Chr. 1:10; [James 1:5] [b] Ps. 72:1, 2 [c] 2 Sam. 14:17; Is. 7:15; [Heb. 5:14] 3:11 [a] [James 4:3] 3:12 [a] [1 John 5:14, 15] [b] 1 Kin. 4:29–31; 5:12; 10:24; Eccl. 1:16 3:13 [a] [Matt. 6:33; Eph. 3:20] [b] 1 Kin. 4:21, 24; 10:23; 1 Chr. 29:12 3:14 [a] [1 Kin. 6:12] [b] 1 Kin. 15:5 [c] Ps. 91:16; Prov. 3:2 3:15 [a] Gen. 41:7 [b] Gen. 40:20; 1 Kin. 8:65; Esth. 1:3; Dan. 5:1; Mark 6:21 3:16 [a] Num. 27:2 3:26 [a] Gen. 43:30; Is. 49:15; Jer. 31:20; Hos. 11:8 3:28 [a] 1 Kin. 3:9, 11, 12; 2 Chr. 1:12; Dan. 1:17; [Col. 2:2, 3] 4:3 [a] 2 Sam. 8:16; 20:24 4:4 [a] 1 Kin. 2:35

over the army; Zadok and [b]Abiathar, the priests; 5Azariah the son of Nathan, over [a]the officers; Zabud the son of Nathan, [b]a priest *and* [c]the king's friend; 6Ahishar, over the household; and [a]Adoniram the son of Abda, over the labor force.

7And Solomon had twelve governors over all Israel, who provided food for the king and his household; each one made provision for one month of the year. 8These *are* their names: Ben-Hur,[1] in the mountains of Ephraim; 9Ben-Deker,[1] in Makaz, Shaalbim, Beth Shemesh, and Elon Beth Hanan; 10Ben-Hesed,[1] in Arubboth; to him *belonged* Sochoh and all the land of Hepher; 11Ben-Abinadab,[1] *in* all the regions of Dor; he had Taphath the daughter of Solomon as wife; 12Baana the son of Ahilud, *in* Taanach, Megiddo, and all Beth Shean, which *is* beside Zaretan below Jezreel, from Beth Shean to Abel Meholah, as far as the other side of Jokneam; 13Ben-Geber,[1] in Ramoth Gilead; to him *belonged* [a]the towns of Jair the son of Manasseh, in Gilead; to him *also belonged* [b]the region of Argob in Bashan—sixty large cities with walls and bronze gatebars; 14Ahinadab the son of Iddo, *in* Mahanaim; 15[a]Ahimaaz, in Naphtali; he also took Basemath the daughter of Solomon as wife; 16Baanah the son of [a]Hushai, in Asher and Aloth; 17Jehoshaphat the son of Paruah, in Issachar; 18[a]Shimei the son of Elah, in Benjamin; 19Geber the son of Uri, in the land of Gilead, *in* [a]the country of Sihon king of the Amorites, and of Og king of Bashan. *He was* the only governor who *was* in the land.

Prosperity and Wisdom of Solomon's Reign

20Judah and Israel *were* as numerous [a]as the sand by the sea in multitude, [b]eating and drinking and rejoicing. 21So [a]Solomon reigned over all kingdoms from [b]the River[1] *to* the land of the Philistines, as far as the border of Egypt. [c]*They* brought tribute and served Solomon all the days of his life.

22[a]Now Solomon's provision for one day was thirty kors of fine flour, sixty kors of meal, 23ten fatted oxen, twenty oxen from the pastures, and one hundred sheep, besides deer, gazelles, roebucks, and fatted fowl.

24For he had dominion over all *the region* on this side of the River[1] from Tiphsah even to Gaza, namely over [a]all the kings on this side of the River; and [b]he had peace on every side all around him. 25And Judah and Israel [a]dwelt safely, [b]each man under his vine and his fig tree, [c]from Dan as far as Beersheba, all the days of Solomon.

26[a]Solomon had forty[1] thousand stalls of [b]horses for his chariots, and twelve thousand horsemen. 27And [a]these governors, each man in his month, provided food for King Solomon and for all who came to King Solomon's table. There was no lack in their supply. 28They also brought barley and straw to the proper place, for the horses and steeds, each man according to his charge.

29And [a]God gave Solomon wisdom and exceedingly great understanding, and largeness of heart like the sand on the seashore. 30Thus Solomon's wisdom excelled the wisdom of all the men [a]of the East and all [b]the wisdom of Egypt. 31For he was [a]wiser than all men—[b]than Ethan the Ezrahite, [c]and Heman, Chalcol, and Darda, the sons of Mahol; and his fame was in all the surrounding nations. 32[a]He spoke three thousand proverbs, and his [b]songs were one thousand and five. 33Also he spoke of trees, from the cedar tree of Lebanon even to the hyssop that springs out of the wall; he spoke also of animals, of birds, of creeping things, and of fish. 34And men of all nations, from all the kings of the earth who had heard of his wisdom, [a]came to hear the wisdom of Solomon.

4:4 [b] 1 Kin. 2:27 4:5 [a] 1 Kin. 4:7 [b] 2 Sam. 8:18; 20:26 [c] 2 Sam. 15:37; 16:16; 1 Chr. 27:33 4:6 [a] 1 Kin. 5:14 4:8 [1] Literally *Son of Hur* 4:9 [1] Literally *Son of Deker* 4:10 [1] Literally *Son of Hesed* 4:11 [1] Literally *Son of Abinadab* 4:13 [a] Num. 32:41; 1 Chr. 2:22 [b] Deut. 3:4 [1] Literally *Son of Geber* 4:15 [a] 2 Sam. 15:27 4:16 [a] 2 Sam. 15:32; 1 Chr. 27:33 4:18 [a] 1 Kin. 1:8 4:19 [a] Deut. 3:8–10 4:20 [a] Gen. 22:17; 32:12; 1 Kin. 3:8; [Prov. 14:28] [b] Ps. 72:3, 7; Mic. 4:4 4:21 [a] Ex. 34:24; 2 Chr. 9:26; Ps. 72:8 [b] Gen. 15:18; Josh. 1:4 [c] Ps. 68:29 [1] That is, the Euphrates 4:22 [a] Neh. 5:18 4:24 [a] Ps. 72:11 [b] 1 Kin. 5:4; 1 Chr. 22:9 [1] That is, the Euphrates 4:25 [a] [Jer. 23:6] [b] [Mic. 4:4; Zech. 3:10] [c] Judg. 20:1 4:26 [a] 1 Kin. 10:26; 2 Chr. 1:14 [b] [Deut. 17:16] [1] Following Masoretic Text and most other authorities; some manuscripts of the Septuagint read *four* (compare 2 Chronicles 9:25). 4:27 [a] 1 Kin. 4:7 4:29 [a] 1 Kin. 3:12 4:30 [a] Gen. 25:6 [b] Is. 19:11, 12; Acts 7:22 4:31 [a] 1 Kin. 3:12 [b] 1 Chr. 15:19; Ps. 89:title [c] 1 Chr. 2:6; Ps. 88:title 4:32 [a] Prov. 1:1; 10:1; 25:1; Eccl. 12:9 [b] Song 1:1 4:34 [a] 1 Kin. 10:1; 2 Chr. 9:1, 23

Solomon Prepares to Build the Temple
(2 Chr. 2:1–18)

5 Now [a]Hiram king of Tyre sent his servants to Solomon, because he heard
that they had anointed him king in place of
his father, [b]for Hiram had always loved David. 2 Then [a]Solomon sent to Hiram, saying:

3 [a]You know how my father David could
not build a house for the name of the
LORD his God [b]because of the wars
which were fought against him on
every side, until the LORD put *his foes*[1]
under the soles of his feet.
4 But now the LORD my God has given
me [a]rest on every side; *there is* neither
adversary nor evil occurrence.
5 [a]And behold, I propose to build a
house for the name of the LORD my
God, [b]as the LORD spoke to my father
David, saying, "Your son, whom I will
set on your throne in your place, he
shall build the house for My name."
6 Now therefore, command that they cut
down [a]cedars for me from Lebanon;
and my servants will be with your
servants, and I will pay you wages for
your servants according to whatever
you say. For you know *there is* none
among us who has skill to cut timber
like the Sidonians.

7 So it was, when Hiram heard the words
of Solomon, that he rejoiced greatly and
said,

Blessed *be* the LORD this day, for He
has given David a wise son over this
great people!

8 Then Hiram sent to Solomon, saying:

I have considered *the message* which
you sent me, *and* I will do all you
desire concerning the cedar and
cypress logs.
9 My servants shall bring *them* down
[a]from Lebanon to the sea; I will float
them in rafts by sea to the place you
indicate to me, and will have them
broken apart there; then you can
take *them* away. And you shall fulfill
my desire [b]by giving food for my
household.

10 Then Hiram gave Solomon cedar and
cypress logs *according to* all his desire.
11 [a]And Solomon gave Hiram twenty thousand kors of wheat *as* food for his household, and twenty[1] kors of pressed oil. Thus
Solomon gave to Hiram year by year.
12 So the LORD gave Solomon wisdom, [a]as
He had promised him; and there was peace
between Hiram and Solomon, and the two
of them made a treaty together.
13 Then King Solomon raised up a labor
force out of all Israel; and the labor force
was thirty thousand men. 14 And he sent
them to Lebanon, ten thousand a month
in shifts: they were one month in Lebanon
and two months at home; [a]Adoniram *was*
in charge of the labor force. 15 [a]Solomon had
seventy thousand who carried burdens,
and eighty thousand who quarried *stone*
in the mountains, 16 besides three thousand three hundred[1] from the [a]chiefs of
Solomon's deputies, who supervised the
people who labored in the work. 17 And the
king commanded them to quarry large
stones, costly stones, *and* [a]hewn stones, to
lay the foundation of the temple.[1] 18 So Solomon's builders, Hiram's builders, and the
Gebalites quarried *them;* and they prepared
timber and stones to build the temple.

Solomon Builds the Temple
(2 Chr. 3:1–14)

6 And [a]it came to pass in the four hundred and eightieth[1] year after the children of Israel had come out of the land of
Egypt, in the fourth year of Solomon's reign
over Israel, in the month of Ziv, which *is* the
second month, [b]that he began to build the
house of the LORD. 2 Now [a]the house which
King Solomon built for the LORD, its length
was sixty cubits, its width twenty, and its

5:1 [a] 1 Kin. 5:10, 18; 2 Chr. 2:3 [b] 2 Sam. 5:11; 1 Chr. 14:1 5:2 [a] 2 Chr. 2:3 5:3 [a] 1 Chr. 28:2, 3 [b] 1 Chr. 22:8; 28:3 [1] Literally *them* 5:4 [a] 1 Kin. 4:24; 1 Chr. 22:9 5:5 [a] 2 Chr. 2:4 [b] 2 Sam. 7:12, 13; 1 Kin. 6:38; 1 Chr. 17:12; 22:10; 28:6; 2 Chr. 6:2 5:6 [a] 2 Chr. 2:8, 10 5:9 [a] Ezra 3:7 [b] Ezek. 27:17; Acts 12:20 5:11 [a] 2 Chr. 2:10 [1] Following Masoretic Text, Targum, and Vulgate; Septuagint and Syriac read *twenty thousand.* 5:12 [a] 1 Kin. 3:12 5:14 [a] 1 Kin. 12:18 5:15 [a] 1 Kin. 9:20–22; 2 Chr. 2:17, 18 5:16 [a] 1 Kin. 9:23 [1] Following Masoretic Text, Targum, and Vulgate; Septuagint reads *three thousand six hundred.* 5:17 [a] 1 Kin. 6:7; 1 Chr. 22:2 [1] Literally *house,* and so frequently throughout this book 6:1 [a] 2 Chr. 3:1, 2 [b] Acts 7:47 [1] Following Masoretic Text, Targum, and Vulgate; Septuagint reads *fortieth.* 6:2 [a] Ezek. 41:1

height thirty cubits. 3The vestibule in front of the sanctuary[1] of the house *was* twenty cubits long across the width of the house, *and* the width of *the vestibule*[2] *extended* ten cubits from the front of the house. 4And he made for the house [a]windows with beveled frames.

5Against the wall of the temple he built [a]chambers all around, *against* the walls of the temple, all around the sanctuary [b]and the inner sanctuary.[1] Thus he made side chambers all around it. 6The lowest chamber *was* five cubits wide, the middle *was* six cubits wide, and the third *was* seven cubits wide; for he made narrow ledges around the outside of the temple, so that *the support beams* would not be fastened into the walls of the temple. 7And [a]the temple, when it was being built, was built with stone finished at the quarry, so that no hammer or chisel *or* any iron tool was heard in the temple while it was being built. 8The doorway for the middle story[1] *was* on the right side of the temple. They went up by stairs to the middle *story,* and from the middle to the third.

9[a]So he built the temple and finished it, and he paneled the temple with beams and boards of cedar. 10And he built side chambers against the entire temple, each five cubits high; they were attached to the temple with cedar beams.

11Then the word of the LORD came to Solomon, saying: 12"*Concerning* this temple which you are building, [a]if you walk in My statutes, execute My judgments, keep all My commandments, and walk in them, then I will perform My word with you, [b]which I spoke to your father David. 13And [a]I will dwell among the children of Israel, and will not [b]forsake My people Israel."

14So Solomon built the temple and finished it. 15And he built the inside walls of the temple with cedar boards; from the floor of the temple to the ceiling he paneled the inside with wood; and he covered the floor of the temple with planks of cypress. 16Then he built the twenty-cubit room at the rear of the temple, from floor to ceiling, with cedar boards; he built *it* inside as the inner sanctuary, as the [a]Most Holy *Place.* 17And in front of it the temple sanctuary was forty cubits *long.* 18The inside of the temple was cedar, carved with ornamental buds and open flowers. All *was* cedar; there was no stone *to be* seen.

19And he prepared the inner sanctuary inside the temple, to set the ark of the covenant of the LORD there. 20The inner sanctuary *was* twenty cubits long, twenty cubits wide, and twenty cubits high. He overlaid it with pure gold, and overlaid the altar of cedar. 21So Solomon overlaid the inside of the temple with pure gold. He stretched gold chains across the front of the inner sanctuary, and overlaid it with gold. 22The whole temple he overlaid with gold, until he had finished all the temple; also he overlaid with gold [a]the entire altar that *was* by the inner sanctuary.

23Inside the inner sanctuary [a]he made two cherubim *of* olive wood, *each* ten cubits high. 24One wing of the cherub *was* five cubits, and the other wing of the cherub five cubits: ten cubits from the tip of one wing to the tip of the other. 25And the other cherub *was* ten cubits; both cherubim *were* of the same size and shape. 26The height of one cherub *was* ten cubits, and so *was* the other cherub. 27Then he set the cherubim inside the inner room;[1] and [a]they stretched out the wings of the cherubim so that the wing of the one touched *one* wall, and the wing of the other cherub touched the other wall. And their wings touched each other in the middle of the room. 28Also he overlaid the cherubim with gold.

29Then he carved all the walls of the temple all around, both the inner and outer *sanctuaries,* with carved [a]figures of cherubim, palm trees, and open flowers. 30And the floor of the temple he overlaid with gold, both the inner and outer *sanctuaries.*

31For the entrance of the inner sanctuary he made doors *of* olive wood; the lintel *and* doorposts *were* one-fifth *of the wall.* 32The two doors *were of* olive wood; and

---

6:3 [1] Hebrew *heykal;* here the main room of the temple, elsewhere called the holy place (compare Exodus 26:33 and Ezekiel 41:1) [2] Literally *it* 6:4 [a] Ezek. 40:16; 41:16 6:5 [a] Ezek. 41:6 [b] 1 Kin. 6:16, 19–21, 31 [1] Hebrew *debir;* here the inner room of the temple, elsewhere called the Most Holy Place (compare verse 16) 6:7 [a] Ex. 20:25; Deut. 27:5, 6 6:8 [1] Following Masoretic Text and Vulgate; Septuagint reads *upper story;* Targum reads *ground story.* 6:9 [a] 1 Kin. 6:14, 38 6:12 [a] 1 Kin. 2:4; 9:4 [b] [2 Sam. 7:13; 1 Chr. 22:10] 6:13 [a] Ex. 25:8; Lev. 26:11; [2 Cor. 6:16; Rev. 21:3] [b] [Deut. 31:6] 6:16 [a] Ex. 26:33; Lev. 16:2; 1 Kin. 8:6; 2 Chr. 3:8; Ezek. 45:3; Heb. 9:3 6:22 [a] Ex. 30:1, 3, 6 6:23 [a] Ex. 37:7–9; 2 Chr. 3:10–12 6:27 [a] Ex. 25:20; 37:9; 1 Kin. 8:7; 2 Chr. 5:8 [1] Literally *house* 6:29 [a] Ex. 36:8, 35

he carved on them figures of cherubim,
palm trees, and open flowers, and overlaid *them* with gold; and he spread gold on
the cherubim and on the palm trees. 33So
for the door of the sanctuary he also made
doorposts *of* olive wood, one-fourth *of the
wall.* 34And the two doors *were of* cypress
wood; [a]two panels *comprised* one folding
door, and two panels *comprised* the other
folding door. 35Then he carved cherubim,
palm trees, and open flowers *on them,* and
overlaid *them* with gold applied evenly on
the carved work.

36And he built the [a]inner court with
three rows of hewn stone and a row of cedar beams.

37[a]In the fourth year the foundation
of the house of the LORD was laid, in the
month of Ziv. 38And in the eleventh year,
in the month of Bul, which is the eighth
month, the house was finished in all its
details and according to all its plans. So he
was [a]seven years in building it.

Solomon's Other Buildings

7 But Solomon took [a]thirteen years to
build his own house; so he finished all
his house.

2He also built the [a]House of the Forest
of Lebanon; its length *was* one hundred
cubits, its width fifty cubits, and its height
thirty cubits, with four rows of cedar pillars, and cedar beams on the pillars. 3And
it was paneled with cedar above the beams
that *were* on forty-five pillars, fifteen *to*
a row. 4*There were* windows *with beveled
frames in* three rows, and window *was* opposite window *in* three tiers. 5And all the
doorways and doorposts *had* rectangular
frames; and window *was* opposite window
in three tiers.

6He also made the Hall of Pillars: its
length *was* fifty cubits, and its width thirty
cubits; and in front of them *was* a portico
with pillars, and a canopy *was* in front of
them.

7Then he made a hall for the throne, the
Hall of Judgment, where he might judge;
and *it was* paneled with cedar from floor
to ceiling.[1]

8And the house where he dwelt *had* another court inside the hall, of like workmanship. Solomon also made a house like
this hall for Pharaoh's daughter, [a]whom he
had taken *as wife.*

9All these *were of* costly stones cut to
size, trimmed with saws, inside and out,
from the foundation to the eaves, and also
on the outside to the great court. 10The
foundation *was of* costly stones, large
stones, some ten cubits and some eight
cubits. 11And above *were* costly stones,
hewn to size, and cedar wood. 12The great
court *was* enclosed with three rows of hewn
stones and a row of cedar beams. So were
the [a]inner court of the house of the LORD
[b]and the vestibule of the temple.

Hiram the Craftsman

13Now King Solomon sent and brought
Huram[1] from Tyre. 14[a]He *was* the son of a
widow from the tribe of Naphtali, and [b]his
father *was* a man of Tyre, a bronze worker;
[c]he was filled with wisdom and understanding and skill in working with all kinds of
bronze work. So he came to King Solomon
and did all his work.

The Bronze Pillars for the Temple
(2 Chr. 3:15–17)

15And he cast [a]two pillars of bronze,
each one eighteen cubits high, and a line
of twelve cubits measured the circumference of each. 16Then he made two capitals *of* cast bronze, to set on the tops of the
pillars. The height of one capital *was* five
cubits, and the height of the other capital *was* five cubits. 17*He made* a lattice network, with wreaths of chainwork, for the
capitals which *were* on top of the pillars:
seven chains for one capital and seven for
the other capital. 18So he made the pillars,
and two rows of pomegranates above the
network all around to cover the capitals
that *were* on top; and thus he did for the
other capital.

19The capitals which *were* on top of the
pillars in the hall *were* in the shape of lilies, four cubits. 20The capitals on the two
pillars also *had pomegranates* above, by the

6:34 [a] Ezek. 41:23–25 6:36 [a] 1 Kin. 7:12; Jer. 36:10 6:37 [a] 1 Kin. 6:1 6:38 [a] 2 Sam. 7:13; 1 Kin. 5:5; 6:1; 8:19 7:1 [a] 1 Kin. 3:1; 9:10; 2 Chr. 8:1 7:2 [a] 1 Kin. 10:17, 21; 2 Chr. 9:16 7:7 [1] Literally *floor,* that is, of the upper level 7:8 [a] 1 Kin. 3:1; 9:24; 11:1; 2 Chr. 8:11 7:12 [a] 1 Kin. 6:36 [b] John 10:23; Acts 3:11 7:13 [1] Hebrew *Hiram* (compare 2 Chronicles 2:13, 14) 7:14 [a] 2 Chr. 2:14 [b] 2 Chr. 4:16 [c] Ex. 31:3; 36:1 7:15 [a] 2 Kin. 25:17; 2 Chr. 3:15; 4:12; Jer. 52:21

convex surface which *was* next to the network; and there *were* [a]two hundred such
pomegranates in rows on each of the capitals all around.

21[a]Then he set up the pillars by the vestibule of the temple; he set up the pillar on
the right and called its name Jachin, and
he set up the pillar on the left and called its
name Boaz. 22The tops of the pillars were
in the shape of lilies. So the work of the pillars was finished.

The Sea and the Oxen

23And he made [a]the Sea of cast bronze,
ten cubits from one brim to the other; *it
was* completely round. Its height *was* five
cubits, and a line of thirty cubits measured
its circumference.

24Below its brim *were* ornamental buds
encircling it all around, ten to a cubit, [a]all
the way around the Sea. The ornamen-
tal buds *were* cast in two rows when it
was cast. 25It stood on [a]twelve oxen: three
looking toward the north, three looking
toward the west, three looking toward the
south, and three looking toward the east;
the Sea *was set* upon them, and all their
back parts *pointed* inward. 26It *was* a handbreadth thick; and its brim was shaped like
the brim of a cup, *like* a lily blossom. It contained two thousand[1] baths.

The Carts and the Lavers

27He also made ten carts of bronze; four
cubits *was* the length of each cart, four cubits its width, and three cubits its height.
28And this *was* the design of the carts: They
had panels, and the panels *were* between
frames; 29on the panels that *were* between
the frames *were* lions, oxen, and cherubim.
And on the frames *was* a pedestal on top.
Below the lions and oxen *were* wreaths of
plaited work. 30Every cart had four bronze
wheels and axles of bronze, and its four feet
had supports. Under the laver *were* supports of cast *bronze* beside each wreath.
31Its opening inside the crown at the top
was one cubit in diameter; and the opening *was* round, shaped *like* a pedestal, one
and a half cubits in outside diameter; and
also on the opening *were* engravings, but
the panels were square, not round. 32Under
the panels *were* the four wheels, and the axles of the wheels *were joined* to the cart. The
height of a wheel *was* one and a half cubits.
33The workmanship of the wheels *was* like
the workmanship of a chariot wheel; their
axle pins, their rims, their spokes, and their
hubs *were* all of cast *bronze*. 34And *there
were* four supports at the four corners of
each cart; its supports *were* part of the cart
itself. 35On the top of the cart, at the height
of half a cubit, *it was* perfectly round. And
on the top of the cart, its flanges and its
panels *were* of the same casting. 36On the
plates of its flanges and on its panels he
engraved cherubim, lions, and palm trees,
wherever there was a clear space on each,
with wreaths all around. 37Thus he made
the ten carts. All of them were of the same
mold, one measure, *and* one shape.

38Then [a]he made ten lavers of bronze;
each laver contained forty baths, *and* each
laver *was* four cubits. On each of the ten
carts *was* a laver. 39And he put five carts
on the right side of the house, and five on
the left side of the house. He set the Sea
on the right side of the house, toward the
southeast.

Furnishings of the Temple
(2 Chr. 4:11–18)

40[a]Huram[1] made the lavers and the shovels and the bowls. So Huram finished doing
all the work that he was to do for King Solomon *for* the house of the LORD: 41the two
pillars, the *two* bowl-shaped capitals that
were on top of the two pillars; the two [a]net-
works covering the two bowl-shaped capitals which *were* on top of the pillars; 42[a]four
hundred pomegranates for the two net-
works (two rows of pomegranates for each
network, to cover the two bowl-shaped capitals that *were* on top of the pillars); 43the
ten carts, and ten lavers on the carts; 44one
Sea, and twelve oxen under the Sea; 45[a]the
pots, the shovels, and the bowls.

All these articles which Huram[1] made
for King Solomon *for* the house of the
LORD *were of* burnished bronze. 46[a]In the

7:20 [a] 2 Chr. 3:16; 4:13; Jer. 52:23 7:21 [a] 2 Chr. 3:17 7:23 [a] 2 Kin. 25:13; 2 Chr. 4:2; Jer. 52:17 7:24 [a] 2 Chr. 4:3 7:25 [a] 2 Chr. 4:4, 5; Jer. 52:20 7:26 [1] Or *three thousand* (compare 2 Chronicles 4:5) 7:38 [a] Ex. 30:18; 2 Chr. 4:6 7:40 [a] 2 Chr. 4:11—5:1 [1] Hebrew *Hiram* (compare 2 Chronicles 2:13, 14) 7:41 [a] 1 Kin. 7:17, 18 7:42 [a] 1 Kin. 7:20 7:45 [a] Ex. 27:3; 2 Chr. 4:16 [1] Hebrew *Hiram* (compare 2 Chronicles 2:13, 14) 7:46 [a] 2 Chr. 4:17

plain of Jordan the king had them cast in
clay molds, between [b]Succoth and [c]Zare-
tan. 47And Solomon did not weigh all the
articles, because *there were* so many; the
weight of the bronze was not [a]determined.
48Thus Solomon had all the furnishings
made for the house of the LORD: [a]the altar
of gold, and [b]the table of gold on which *was*
[c]the showbread; 49the lampstands of pure
gold, five on the right *side* and five on the
left in front of the inner sanctuary, with
the flowers and the lamps and the wick-
trimmers of gold; 50the basins, the trimmers, the bowls, the ladles, and the censers
of pure gold; and the hinges of gold, *both*
for the doors of the inner room (the Most
Holy *Place*) *and* for the doors of the main
hall of the temple.
51So all the work that King Solomon had
done for the house of the LORD was finished; and Solomon brought in the things
[a]which his father David had dedicated: the
silver and the gold and the furnishings. He
put them in the treasuries of the house of
the LORD.

The Ark Brought into the Temple
(2 Chr. 5:2—6:2)

8 Now [a]Solomon assembled the elders
of Israel and all the heads of the tribes,
the chief fathers of the children of Israel,
to King Solomon in Jerusalem, [b]that they
might bring [c]up the ark of the covenant of
the LORD from the City of David, which *is*
Zion. 2Therefore all the men of Israel assembled with King Solomon at the [a]feast
in the month of Ethanim, which *is* the seventh month. 3So all the elders of Israel came,
[a]and the priests took up the ark. 4Then they
brought up the ark of the LORD, [a]the tabernacle of meeting, and all the holy furnishings that *were* in the tabernacle. The priests
and the Levites brought them up. 5Also King
Solomon, and all the congregation of Israel
who were assembled with him, *were* with
him before the ark, [a]sacrificing sheep and
oxen that could not be counted or numbered
for multitude. 6Then the priests [a]brought in
the ark of the covenant of the LORD to [b]its
place, into the inner sanctuary of the temple, to the Most Holy *Place*, [c]under the wings
of the cherubim. 7For the cherubim spread
their two wings over the place of the ark, and
the cherubim overshadowed the ark and its
poles. 8The poles [a]extended so that the ends
of the poles could be seen from the holy
place, in front of the inner sanctuary; but
they could not be seen from outside. And
they are there to this day. 9[a]Nothing *was* in
the ark [b]except the two tablets of stone which
Moses [c]put there at Horeb, [d]when the LORD
made *a covenant* with the children of Israel,
when they came out of the land of Egypt.
10And it came to pass, when the priests
came out of the holy *place*, that the cloud
[a]filled the house of the LORD, 11so that the
priests could not continue ministering
because of the cloud; for the [a]glory of the
LORD filled the house of the LORD.
12[a]Then Solomon spoke:

"The LORD said He would dwell
[b]in the dark cloud.
13 [a]I have surely built You an
exalted house,
[b]And a place for You to
dwell in forever."

Solomon's Speech at Completion of the Work
(2 Chr. 6:3–11)

14Then the king turned around and
[a]blessed the whole assembly of Israel,
while all the assembly of Israel was standing. 15And he said: [a]"Blessed *be* the LORD
God of Israel, who [b]spoke with His mouth
to my father David, and with His hand has
fulfilled *it*, saying, 16'Since the day that I
brought My people Israel out of Egypt, I
have chosen no city from any tribe of Israel
in which to build a house, that [a]My name
might be there; but I chose [b]David to be
over My people Israel.' 17Now [a]it was in the
heart of my father David to build a temple[1]

7:46 [b] Gen. 33:17; Josh. 13:27 [c] Josh. 3:16 7:47 [a] 1 Chr. 22:3, 14 7:48 [a] Ex. 37:25, 26; 2 Chr. 4:8 [b] Ex. 37:10, 11 [c] Lev. 24:5–8 7:51 [a] 2 Sam. 8:11; 1 Chr. 18:11; 2 Chr. 5:1 8:1 [a] Num. 1:4; 7:2; 2 Chr. 5:2–14 [b] 2 Sam. 6:12–17; 1 Chr. 15:25–29 [c] 2 Sam. 5:7; 6:12, 16 8:2 [a] Lev. 23:34; 1 Kin. 8:65; 2 Chr. 7:8–10 8:3 [a] Num. 4:15; 7:9; Deut. 31:9; Josh. 3:3, 6 8:4 [a] 1 Kin. 3:4; 2 Chr. 1:3 8:5 [a] 2 Sam. 6:13; 2 Chr. 1:6 8:6 [a] 2 Sam. 6:17 [b] Ex. 26:33, 34; 1 Kin. 6:19 [c] 1 Kin. 6:27 8:8 [a] Ex. 25:13–15; 37:4, 5 8:9 [a] Ex. 25:21; Deut. 10:2 [b] Ex. 25:16; Deut. 10:5; Heb. 9:4 [c] Ex. 24:7, 8; 40:20; Deut. 4:13 [d] Ex. 34:27, 28 8:10 [a] Ex. 40:34, 35; 2 Chr. 7:1, 2 8:11 [a] 2 Chr. 7:1, 2 8:12 [a] 2 Chr. 6:1 [b] Lev. 16:2; Ps. 18:11; 97:2 8:13 [a] 2 Sam. 7:13 [b] [Ex. 15:17]; Ps. 132:14 8:14 [a] 2 Sam. 6:18; 1 Kin. 8:55 8:15 [a] 1 Chr. 29:10, 20; Neh. 9:5; Luke 1:68 [b] 2 Sam. 7:2, 12, 13, 25; 1 Chr. 22:10 8:16 [a] Deut. 12:5; 1 Kin. 8:29 [b] 1 Sam. 16:1; 2 Sam. 7:8; 1 Chr. 28:4 8:17 [a] 2 Sam. 7:2, 3; 1 Chr. 17:1, 2 [1] Literally *house*, and so in verses 18–20

for the name of the LORD God of Israel.
18[a]But the LORD said to my father David,
'Whereas it was in your heart to build a
temple for My name, you did well that it
was in your heart. 19Nevertheless [a]you shall
not build the temple, but your son who will
come from your body, he shall build the
temple for My name.' 20So the LORD has
fulfilled His word which He spoke; and I
have filled the position of my father David,
and sit on the throne of Israel, [a]as the LORD
promised; and I have built a temple for the
name of the LORD God of Israel. 21And there
I have made a place for the ark, in which *is*
[a]the covenant of the LORD which He made
with our fathers, when He brought them
out of the land of Egypt."

Solomon's Prayer of Dedication
(2 Chr. 6:12–39)

22Then Solomon stood before [a]the altar
of the LORD in the presence of all the assembly of Israel, and [b]spread out his hands
toward heaven; 23and he said: "LORD God
of Israel, [a]*there is* no God in heaven above
or on earth below like You, [b]who keep *Your*
covenant and mercy with Your servants
who [c]walk before You with all their hearts.
24You have kept what You promised Your
servant David my father; You have both
spoken with Your mouth and fulfilled *it*
with Your hand, as *it is* this day. 25There-
fore, LORD God of Israel, now keep what
You promised Your servant David my father, saying, [a]'You shall not fail to have a
man sit before Me on the throne of Israel,
only if your sons take heed to their way, that
they walk before Me as you have walked before Me.' 26[a]And now I pray, O God of Israel,
let Your word come true, which You have
spoken to Your servant David my father.

27"But [a]will God indeed dwell on the
earth? Behold, heaven and the [b]heaven of
heavens cannot contain You. How much
less this temple which I have built! 28Yet
regard the prayer of Your servant and his
supplication, O LORD my God, and listen to
the cry and the prayer which Your servant is
praying before You today: 29that Your eyes
may be open toward this temple night and
day, toward the place of which You said,
[a]'My name shall be [b]there,' that You may
hear the prayer which Your servant makes
[c]toward this place. 30[a]And may You hear the
supplication of Your servant and of Your
people Israel, when they pray toward this
place. Hear in heaven Your dwelling place;
and when You hear, forgive.

31"When anyone sins against his neighbor, and is forced to take [a]an oath, and
comes *and* takes an oath before Your altar
in this temple, 32then hear in heaven, and
act, and judge Your servants, [a]condemning
the wicked, bringing his way on his head,
and justifying the righteous by giving him
according to his righteousness.

33[a]"When Your people Israel are defeated
before an enemy because they have sinned
against You, and [b]when they turn back to
You and confess Your name, and pray and
make supplication to You in this temple,
34then hear in heaven, and forgive the sin
of Your people Israel, and bring them back
to the land which You gave to their [a]fathers.

35[a]"When the heavens are shut up and
there is no rain because they have sinned
against You, when they pray toward this
place and confess Your name, and turn
from their sin because You afflict them,
36then hear in heaven, and forgive the sin of
Your servants, Your people Israel, that You
may [a]teach them [b]the good way in which
they should walk; and send rain on Your
land which You have given to Your people
as an inheritance.

37[a]"When there is famine in the land,
pestilence *or* blight *or* mildew, locusts *or*
grasshoppers; when their enemy besieges
them in the land of their cities; whatever plague or whatever sickness *there is;*
38whatever prayer, whatever supplication
is made by anyone, *or* by all Your people
Israel, when each one knows the plague of
his own heart, and spreads out his hands
toward this temple: 39then hear in heaven
Your dwelling place, and forgive, and act,

8:18 [a] 2 Chr. 6:8, 9 8:19 [a] 2 Sam. 7:5, 12, 13; 1 Kin. 5:3, 5; 6:38; 1 Chr. 17:11, 12; 22:8–10; 2 Chr. 6:2 8:20 [a] 1 Chr. 28:5, 6 8:21 [a] Deut. 31:26; 1 Kin. 8:9 8:22 [a] 1 Kin. 8:54; 2 Chr. 6:12 [b] Ex. 9:33; Ezra 9:5 8:23 [a] Ex. 15:11; 2 Sam. 7:22 [b] [Deut. 7:9; Neh. 1:5; Dan. 9:4] [c] [Gen. 17:1; 1 Kin. 3:6]; 2 Kin. 20:3 8:25 [a] 2 Sam. 7:12, 16; 1 Kin. 2:4; 9:5 8:26 [a] 2 Sam. 7:25 8:27 [a] [2 Chr. 2:6; Is. 66:1; Acts 7:49; 17:24] [b] 2 Cor. 12:2 8:29 [a] Deut. 12:11 [b] 1 Kin. 9:3; 2 Chr. 7:15 [c] Dan. 6:10 8:30 [a] Neh. 1:6 8:31 [a] Ex. 22:8–11 8:32 [a] Deut. 25:1 8:33 [a] Lev. 26:17; Deut. 28:25 [b] Lev. 26:39, 40 8:34 [a] [Lev. 26:40–42; Deut. 30:1–3] 8:35 [a] Lev. 26:19; Deut. 28:23 8:36 [a] Ps. 25:4; 27:11; 94:12 [b] 1 Sam. 12:23 8:37 [a] Lev. 26:16, 25, 26; Deut. 28:21, 22, 27, 38, 42, 52

and give to everyone according to all his
ways, whose heart You know (for You alone
[a]know the hearts of all the sons of men),
40 [a]that they may fear You all the days that
they live in the land which You gave to our
fathers.
41 "Moreover, concerning a foreigner,
who *is* not of Your people Israel, but has
come from a far country for Your name's
sake 42 (for they will hear of Your great
name and Your [a]strong hand and Your outstretched arm), when he comes and prays
toward this temple, 43 hear in heaven Your
dwelling place, and do according to all for
which the foreigner calls to You, [a]that all
peoples of the earth may know Your name
and [b]fear You, as *do* Your people Israel, and
that they may know that this temple which
I have built is called by Your name.
44 "When Your people go out to battle
against their enemy, wherever You send
them, and when they pray to the LORD toward the city which You have chosen and
the temple which I have built for Your
name, 45 then hear in heaven their prayer
and their supplication, and maintain their
cause.
46 "When they sin against You [a](for *there*
is no one who does not sin), and You become angry with them and deliver them
to the enemy, and they take them captive
[b]to the land of the enemy, far or near; 47 [a]*yet*
when they come to themselves in the land
where they were carried captive, and repent, and make supplication to You in the
land of those who took them captive, [b]say-
ing, 'We have sinned and done wrong, we
have committed wickedness'; 48 and *when*
they [a]return to You with all their heart and
with all their soul in the land of their enemies who led them away captive, and [b]pray
to You toward their land which You gave
to their fathers, the city which You have
chosen and the temple which I have built
for Your name: 49 then hear in heaven Your
dwelling place their prayer and their supplication, and maintain their cause, 50 and
forgive Your people who have sinned
against You, and all their transgressions
which they have transgressed against You;
and [a]grant them compassion before those
who took them captive, that they may have
compassion on them 51 (for [a]they *are* Your
people and Your inheritance, whom You
brought out of Egypt, [b]out of the iron furnace), 52 [a]that Your eyes may be open to the
supplication of Your servant and the supplication of Your people Israel, to listen to
them whenever they call to You. 53 For You
separated them from among all the peoples
of the earth *to be* Your inheritance, [a]as You
spoke by Your servant Moses, when You
brought our fathers out of Egypt, O Lord
GOD."

Solomon Blesses the Assembly
(2 Chr. 6:40–42)

54 [a]And so it was, when Solomon had finished praying all this prayer and supplication to the LORD, that he arose from before
the altar of the LORD, from kneeling on his
knees with his hands spread up to heaven.
55 Then he stood [a]and blessed all the assembly of Israel with a loud voice, saying:
56 "Blessed *be* the LORD, who has given [a]rest
to His people Israel, according to all that He
promised. [b]There has not failed one word of
all His good promise, which He promised
through His servant Moses. 57 May the LORD
our God be with us, as He was with our fathers. [a]May He not leave us nor forsake us,
58 that He may [a]incline our hearts to Himself, to walk in all His ways, and to keep His
commandments and His statutes and His
judgments, which He commanded our fathers. 59 And may these words of mine, with
which I have made supplication before the
LORD, be near the LORD our God day and
night, that He may maintain the cause of
His servant and the cause of His people
Israel, as each day may require, 60 [a]that all
the peoples of the earth may know that [b]the
LORD *is* God; *there is* no other. 61 Let your
[a]heart therefore be loyal to the LORD our

8:39 [a] [1 Sam. 16:7; 1 Chr. 28:9; Jer. 17:10]; Acts 1:24 8:40 [a] [Ps. 130:4] 8:42 [a] Ex. 13:3; Deut. 3:24 8:43 [a] [Ex. 9:16; 1 Sam. 17:46; 2 Kin. 19:19] [b] Ps. 102:15 8:46 [a] 2 Chr. 6:36; Ps. 130:3; Prov. 20:9; Eccl. 7:20; [Rom. 3:23; 1 John 1:8, 10] [b] Lev. 26:34, 44; Deut. 28:36, 64; 2 Kin. 17:6, 18; 25:21 8:47 [a] [Lev. 26:40–42]; Neh. 9:2 [b] Ezra 9:6, 7; Neh. 1:6; Ps. 106:6; Dan. 9:5 8:48 [a] Jer. 29:12–14 [b] Dan. 6:10; Jon. 2:4 8:50 [a] [2 Chr. 30:9]; Ezra 7:6; Ps. 106:46; Acts 7:10 8:51 [a] Ex. 32:11, 12; Deut. 9:26–29; Neh. 1:10; [Rom. 11:28, 29] [b] Deut. 4:20; Jer. 11:4 8:52 [a] 1 Kin. 8:29 8:53 [a] Ex. 19:5, 6 8:54 [a] 2 Chr. 7:1 8:55 [a] Num. 6:23–26; 2 Sam. 6:18; 1 Kin. 8:14 8:56 [a] 1 Chr. 22:18 [b] Deut. 12:10; Josh. 21:45; 23:14 8:57 [a] Deut. 31:6; Josh. 1:5; 1 Sam. 12:22; [Rom. 8:31–37]; Heb. 13:5 8:58 [a] Ps. 119:36; Jer. 31:33 8:60 [a] Josh. 4:24; 1 Sam. 17:46; 1 Kin. 8:43; 2 Kin. 19:19 [b] Deut. 4:35, 39; 1 Kin. 18:39; [Jer. 10:10–12] 8:61 [a] Deut. 18:13; 1 Kin. 11:4; 15:3, 14; 2 Kin. 20:3

God, to walk in His statutes and keep His
commandments, as at this day."

Solomon Dedicates the Temple
(2 Chr. 7:4–11)

62 Then [a]the king and all Israel with him
offered sacrifices before the LORD. 63 And
Solomon offered a sacrifice of peace offerings, which he offered to the LORD, twenty-
two thousand bulls and one hundred and
twenty thousand sheep. So the king and all
the children of Israel dedicated the house
of the LORD. 64 On [a]the same day the king
consecrated the middle of the court that
was in front of the house of the LORD; for
there he offered burnt offerings, grain offerings, and the fat of the peace offerings,
because the [b]bronze altar that *was* before
the LORD *was* too small to receive the burnt
offerings, the grain offerings, and the fat
of the peace offerings.

65 At that time Solomon held [a]a feast, and
all Israel with him, a great assembly from
[b]the entrance of Hamath to [c]the Brook of
Egypt, before the LORD our God, [d]seven
days and seven *more* days—fourteen days.
66 [a]On the eighth day he sent the people
away; and they blessed the king, and went
to their tents joyful and glad of heart for all
the good that the LORD had done for His
servant David, and for Israel His people.

God's Second Appearance to Solomon
(2 Chr. 7:12–22)

9 And [a]it came to pass, when Solomon
had finished building the house of the
LORD [b]and the king's house, and [c]all Solomon's desire which he wanted to do, 2 that
the LORD appeared to Solomon the second
time, [a]as He had appeared to him at Gibeon. 3 And the LORD said to him: [a]"I have
heard your prayer and your supplication
that you have made before Me; I have consecrated this house which you have built
[b]to put My name there forever, [c]and My
eyes and My heart will be there perpetually.
4 Now if you [a]walk before Me [b]as your father
David walked, in integrity of heart and in
uprightness, to do according to all that I
have commanded you, *and* if you [c]keep My
statutes and My judgments, 5 then I will establish the throne of your kingdom over
Israel forever, [a]as I promised David your
father, saying, 'You shall not fail to have a
man on the throne of Israel.' 6 [a]*But* if you
or your sons at all turn from following Me,
and do not keep My commandments *and*
My statutes which I have set before you, but
go and serve other gods and worship them,
7 [a]then I will cut off Israel from the land
which I have given them; and this house
which I have consecrated [b]for My name I
will cast out of My sight. [c]Israel will be a
proverb and a byword among all peoples.
8 And *as for* [a]this house, *which* is exalted, everyone who passes by it will be astonished
and will hiss, and say, [b]'Why has the LORD
done thus to this land and to this house?'
9 Then they will answer, 'Because they forsook the LORD their God, who brought their
fathers out of the land of Egypt, and have
embraced other gods, and worshiped them
and served them; therefore the LORD has
brought all this [a]calamity on them.'"

Solomon and Hiram Exchange Gifts

10 Now [a]it happened at the end of twenty
years, when Solomon had built the two
houses, the house of the LORD and the
king's house 11 [a](Hiram the king of Tyre had
supplied Solomon with cedar and cypress
and gold, as much as he desired), *that* King
Solomon then gave Hiram twenty cities in
the land of Galilee. 12 Then Hiram went from
Tyre to see the cities which Solomon had
given him, but they did not please him. 13 So
he said, "What *kind of* cities *are* these which
you have given me, my brother?" [a]And he
called them the land of Cabul,[1] as they are
to this day. 14 Then Hiram sent the king one
hundred and twenty talents of gold.

Solomon's Additional Achievements
(2 Chr. 8:3–16)

15 And this *is* the reason for [a]the labor
force which King Solomon raised: to build

8:62 [a] 2 Chr. 7:4–10 8:64 [a] 2 Chr. 7:7 [b] 2 Chr. 4:1 8:65 [a] Lev. 23:34; 1 Kin. 8:2 [b] Num. 34:8; Josh. 13:5; Judg. 3:3; 2 Kin. 14:25 [c] Gen. 15:18; Ex. 23:31; Num. 34:5 [d] 2 Chr. 7:8 8:66 [a] 2 Chr. 7:9 9:1 [a] 2 Chr. 7:11 [b] 1 Kin. 7:1 [c] 2 Chr. 8:6 9:2 [a] 1 Kin. 3:5; 11:9; 2 Chr. 1:7 9:3 [a] 2 Kin. 20:5; Ps. 10:17 [b] 1 Kin. 8:29 [c] Deut. 11:12 9:4 [a] Gen. 17:1 [b] 1 Kin. 11:4, 6; 15:5 [c] 1 Kin. 8:61 9:5 [a] 2 Sam. 7:12, 16; 1 Kin. 2:4; 6:12; 8:25; 1 Chr. 22:10; Matt. 1:6; 25:31 9:6 [a] 2 Sam. 7:14–16; 2 Chr. 7:19, 20; Ps. 89:30 9:7 [a] [Lev. 18:24–29]; Deut. 4:26; 2 Kin. 17:23; 25:21 [b] [Jer. 7:4–14] [c] Deut. 28:37; Ps. 44:14; Jer. 24:9 9:8 [a] 2 Chr. 7:21 [b] [Deut. 29:24–26]; Jer. 22:8, 9 9:9 [a] [Deut. 29:25–28] 9:10 [a] 1 Kin. 6:37, 38; 7:1; 2 Chr. 8:1 9:11 [a] 1 Kin. 5:1 9:13 [a] Josh. 19:27 [1] Literally *Good for Nothing* 9:15 [a] 1 Kin. 5:13

RELEASE // EXALT HIS AMAZING OMNIPRESENCE

God Sees You

1 Kings 9:3 // And the LORD said to him: "I have heard your prayer and your supplication that you have made before Me; I have consecrated this house which you have built to put My name there forever, and My eyes and My heart will be there perpetually."

Summary Message // God is everywhere and knows what is happening at every moment. We cannot hide from Him. He loves us and has many plans and blessings in store for our lives. But many of these things are conditional based on our response to Him.

In this passage, King Solomon had just completed building the temple. God appeared to him for a second time and told him His presence would always be within the temple. God also told Solomon He would establish Solomon's kingdom forever. This was great news! But there was a condition: Solomon and the people of God, including the future generations, were to follow God's commands and worship only Him. If they fell away, God assured Solomon that everything would be destroyed.

Practical Application // Our Creator has incredible plans for our lives. If we give our lives to Him, He promises that those plans will prosper us and not harm us. But if we want all that He has in store for us, we have to follow Him and die daily to ourselves, giving all that we have to Him. When we mess up (and we will), forgiveness is available through Jesus Christ. But often, there are still consequences of those sins. Certain things may be delayed in our lives or missed altogether. We live in a fallen world where other people's sins can also affect us. Even the sins of our family, our community, and our country can greatly affect our lives.

Israel sinned and fell away from God repeatedly. Namely, as a people, they worshiped false gods. Just as God had promised, disaster followed. Israel was invaded, many people were killed or captured, and Solomon's beautiful temple was destroyed. But even in the middle of that disaster, a remnant of people continued to worship God. His presence was with them even through destruction. In exile, their faith grew and more of the people repented and turned back to the one true God. Once again, God's presence was with them. He eventually rescued and restored them.

Maybe you have been slipping in some areas of your life and you think no one will notice. You think what you are doing is not hurting anyone. But God sees. He loves you and is there to forgive you. But in love, He might discipline you to draw you back to Him.

Fervent Prayer // Heavenly Father, thank You for Your presence that is in all places, at all times. You are with us as we are reading this Bible and pray this prayer. Forgive us for the areas we have failed in. Forgive those who have sinned against us and made our situation more difficult. Forgive those who have purposefully wronged us. Forgive us for when we have done the same. We want to walk in Your promises. Help us to be faithful to follow Your commands. We do not want to experience delay or denial due to our actions. We want to live out the plans You have for our lives. In Jesus' name we pray. Amen.

---

the house of the LORD, his own house, the
[b]Millo,[1] the wall of Jerusalem, [c]Hazor, [d]Me-
giddo, and [e]Gezer. 16(Pharaoh king of Egypt
had gone up and taken Gezer and burned
it with fire, [a]had killed the Canaanites who
dwelt in the city, and had given it *as* a dowry
to his daughter, Solomon's wife.) 17And
Solomon built Gezer, Lower [a]Beth Horon,
18[a]Baalath, and Tadmor in the wilderness,
in the land *of Judah,* 19all the storage cities
that Solomon had, cities for [a]his chariots
and cities for his [b]cavalry, and whatever
Solomon [c]desired to build in Jerusalem,
in Lebanon, and in all the land of his dominion.

20[a]All the people *who were* left of the
Amorites, Hittites, Perizzites, Hivites, and
Jebusites, who *were* not of the children of

9:15 [b] 2 Sam. 5:9; 1 Kin. 9:24 [c] Josh. 11:1; 19:36 [d] Josh. 17:11 [e] Josh. 16:10 [1] Literally *The Landfill* 9:16 [a] Josh. 16:10; Judg. 1:29 9:17 [a] Josh. 10:10; 16:3; 21:22; 2 Chr. 8:5 9:18 [a] Josh. 19:44; 2 Chr. 8:4 9:19 [a] 1 Kin. 10:26; 2 Chr. 1:14 [b] 1 Kin. 4:26 [c] 1 Kin. 9:1 9:20 [a] 2 Chr. 8:7

Israel— 21that is, their descendants [a]who
were left in the land after them, [b]whom the
children of Israel had not been able to destroy completely—[c]from these Solomon
raised [d]forced labor, as it is to this day. 22But
of the children of Israel Solomon [a]made no
forced laborers, because they *were* men of
war and his servants: his officers, his captains, commanders of his chariots, and his
cavalry.

23Others *were* chiefs of the officials who
were over Solomon's work: [a]five hundred
and fifty, who ruled over the people who
did the work.

24But [a]Pharaoh's daughter came up from
the City of David to [b]her house which *Sol-*
omon[1] had built for her. [c]Then he built the
Millo.

25[a]Now three times a year Solomon offered burnt offerings and peace offerings
on the altar which he had built for the
LORD, and he burned incense with them
on the altar that *was* before the LORD. So
he finished the temple.

26[a]King Solomon also built a fleet of
ships at [b]Ezion Geber, which *is* near Elath[1]
on the shore of the Red Sea, in the land
of Edom. 27[a]Then Hiram sent his servants
with the fleet, seamen who knew the sea, to
work with the servants of Solomon. 28And
they went to [a]Ophir, and acquired four hundred and twenty talents of gold from there,
and brought *it* to King Solomon.

The Queen of Sheba's Praise of Solomon
(2 Chr. 9:1–28)

10 Now when the [a]queen of Sheba
heard of the fame of Solomon concerning the name of the LORD, she came
[b]to test him with hard questions. 2She
came to Jerusalem with a very great retinue, with camels that bore spices, very
much gold, and precious stones; and when
she came to Solomon, she spoke with him
about all that was in her heart. 3So Solomon answered all her questions; there
was nothing so difficult for the king that he
could not explain *it* to her. 4And when the
queen of Sheba had seen all the wisdom of
Solomon, the house that he had built, 5the
food on his table, the seating of his servants, the service of his waiters and their
apparel, his cupbearers, [a]and his entryway by which he went up to the house of
the LORD, there was no more spirit in her.
6Then she said to the king: "It was a true
report which I heard in my own land about
your words and your wisdom. 7However I
did not believe the words until I came and
saw with my own eyes; and indeed the half
was not told me. Your wisdom and prosperity exceed the fame of which I heard.
8[a]Happy *are* your men and happy *are* these
your servants, who stand continually before you *and* hear your wisdom! 9[a]Blessed
be the LORD your God, who [b]delighted in
you, setting you on the throne of Israel!
Because the LORD has loved Israel forever,
therefore He made you king, [c]to do justice
and righteousness."

10Then she [a]gave the king one hundred
and twenty talents of gold, spices in great
quantity, and precious stones. There never
again came such abundance of spices as
the queen of Sheba gave to King Solomon.
11[a]Also, the ships of Hiram, which brought
gold from Ophir, brought great quantities
of almug[1] wood and precious stones from
Ophir. 12[a]And the king made steps of the
almug wood for the house of the LORD
and for the king's house, also harps and
stringed instruments for singers. There
never again came such [b]almug wood, nor
has the like been seen to this day.

13Now King Solomon gave the queen of
Sheba all she desired, whatever she asked,
besides what Solomon had given her according to the royal generosity. So she
turned and went to her own country, she
and her servants.

Solomon's Great Wealth

14The weight of gold that came to Solomon yearly was six hundred and sixty-
six talents of gold, 15besides *that* from the
[a]traveling merchants, from the income of

9:21 [a] Judg. 1:21–36; 3:1 [b] Josh. 15:63; 17:12, 13 [c] Judg. 1:28, 35 [d] Ezra 2:55, 58; Neh. 7:57 9:22 [a] [Lev. 25:39] 9:23 [a] 2 Chr. 8:10
9:24 [a] 1 Kin. 3:1 [b] 1 Kin. 7:8 [c] 2 Sam. 5:9; 1 Kin. 11:27; 2 Chr. 32:5 [1] Literally *he* (compare 2 Chronicles 8:11) 9:25 [a] Ex. 23:14–17; Deut. 16:16; 2 Chr. 8:12, 13 9:26 [a] 2 Chr. 8:17, 18 [b] Num. 33:35; Deut. 2:8; 1 Kin. 22:48 [1] Hebrew *Eloth* (compare 2 Kings 14:22)
9:27 [a] 1 Kin. 5:6, 9; 10:11 9:28 [a] Job 22:24 10:1 [a] 2 Chr. 9:1; Matt. 12:42; Luke 11:31 [b] Judg. 14:12; Ps. 49:4; Prov. 1:6 10:5 [a] 1 Chr. 26:16; 2 Chr. 9:4 10:8 [a] Prov. 8:34 10:9 [a] 1 Kin. 5:7 [b] 2 Sam. 22:20 [c] 2 Sam. 8:15; Ps. 72:2; [Prov. 8:15] 10:10 [a] Ps. 72:10, 15
10:11 [a] 1 Kin. 9:27, 28; Job 22:24 [1] Or *algum* (compare 2 Chronicles 9:10, 11)
10:12 [a] 2 Chr. 9:11 [b] 2 Chr. 9:10 10:15 [a] 2 Chr. 1:16

traders, [b]from all the kings of Arabia, and
from the governors of the country.
16And King Solomon made two hundred
large shields *of* hammered gold; six hundred *shekels* of gold went into each shield.
17He also *made* [a]three hundred shields *of*
hammered gold; three minas of gold went
into each shield. The king put them in the
[b]House of the Forest of Lebanon.
18[a]Moreover the king made a great
throne of ivory, and overlaid it with pure
gold. 19The throne had six steps, and the top
of the throne *was* round at the back; *there
were* armrests on either side of the place
of the seat, and two lions stood beside the
armrests. 20Twelve lions stood there, one
on each side of the six steps; nothing like
this had been made for any *other* kingdom.
21[a]All King Solomon's drinking vessels
were gold, and all the vessels of the House
of the Forest of Lebanon *were* pure gold.
Not *one was* silver, for this was accounted as
nothing in the days of Solomon. 22For the
king had [a]merchant ships[1] at sea with the
fleet of Hiram. Once every three years the
merchant [b]ships came bringing gold, silver,
ivory, apes, and monkeys.[2] 23So [a]King Solomon surpassed all the kings of the earth
in riches and wisdom.
24Now all the earth sought the presence
of Solomon to hear his wisdom, which God
had put in his heart. 25Each man brought
his present: articles of silver and gold, garments, armor, spices, horses, and mules, at
a set rate year by year.
26[a]And Solomon [b]gathered chariots and
horsemen; he had one thousand four hundred chariots and twelve thousand horsemen, whom he stationed[1] in the chariot
cities and with the king at Jerusalem. 27[a]The
king made silver *as common* in Jerusalem
as stones, and he made cedar trees as abundant as the sycamores which *are* in the lowland.
28[a]Also Solomon had horses imported
from Egypt and Keveh; the king's merchants bought them in Keveh at the *current*
price. 29Now a chariot that was imported
from Egypt cost six hundred *shekels* of silver, and a horse one hundred and fifty; [a]and
thus, through their agents,[1] they exported
them to all the kings of the Hittites and the
kings of Syria.

Solomon's Heart Turns from the LORD

11 But [a]King Solomon loved [b]many foreign women, as well as the daughter of
Pharaoh: women of the Moabites, Ammonites, Edomites, Sidonians, *and* Hittites—
2from the nations of whom the LORD had
said to the children of Israel, [a]"You shall
not intermarry with them, nor they with
you. Surely they will turn away your hearts
after their gods." Solomon clung to these
in love. 3And he had seven hundred wives,
princesses, and three hundred concubines;
and his wives turned away his heart. 4For
it was so, when Solomon was old, [a]that his
wives turned his heart after other gods;
and his [b]heart was not loyal to the LORD his
God, [c]as *was* the heart of his father David.
5For Solomon went after [a]Ashtoreth the
goddess of the Sidonians, and after [b]Mil-
com the abomination of the [c]Ammonites.
6Solomon did evil in the sight of the LORD,
and did not fully follow the LORD, as *did*
his father David. 7[a]Then Solomon built a
high place for [b]Chemosh the abomination

#OXYGEN
1 KINGS 11:4
Exalt His Amazing Omnipresence

Dedicate your work to God from a pure place. There is no need to seek the applause of people. The ever-present Holy Spirit will imprint His seal of approval on receiving hearts. Just do all for Him. **Breathe** and **exalt His amazing omnipresence.**

10:15 [b] 2 Chr. 9:24; Ps. 72:10 10:17 [a] 1 Kin. 14:26 [b] 1 Kin. 7:2 10:18 [a] 1 Kin. 10:22; 2 Chr. 9:17; Ps. 45:8 10:21 [a] 2 Chr. 9:20 10:22 [a] Gen. 10:4; 2 Chr. 20:36 [b] 1 Kin. 9:26–28; 22:48; Ps. 72:10 [1] Literally *ships of Tarshish,* deep-sea vessels [2] Or *peacocks* 10:23 [a] 1 Kin. 3:12, 13; 4:30; 2 Chr. 1:12 10:26 [a] 1 Kin. 4:26; 2 Chr. 1:14; 9:25 [b] [Deut. 17:16]; 1 Kin. 9:19 [1] Following Septuagint, Syriac, Targum, and Vulgate (compare 2 Chronicles 9:25); Masoretic Text reads *led.* 10:27 [a] [Deut. 17:17]; 2 Chr. 1:15–17 10:28 [a] [Deut. 17:16]; 2 Chr. 1:16; 9:28 10:29 [a] Josh. 1:4; 2 Kin. 7:6, 7 [1] Literally *by their hands* 11:1 [a] [Neh. 13:26] [b] [Deut. 17:17]; 1 Kin. 3:1 11:2 [a] Ex. 34:16; [Deut. 7:3, 4] 11:4 [a] [Deut. 17:17; Neh. 13:26] [b] 1 Kin. 8:61 [c] 1 Kin. 9:4 11:5 [a] Judg. 2:13; 1 Kin. 11:33 [b] [Lev. 20:2–5] [c] 2 Kin. 23:13 11:7 [a] Num. 33:52 [b] Num. 21:29; Judg. 11:24

of Moab, on [c]the hill that *is* east of Jerusalem, and for Molech the abomination of the
people of Ammon. 8And he did likewise for
all his foreign wives, who burned incense
and sacrificed to their gods.

9So the LORD became angry with Solomon, because his heart had turned from
the LORD God of Israel, [a]who had appeared
to him twice, 10and [a]had commanded him
concerning this thing, that he should not go
after other gods; but he did not keep what
the LORD had commanded. 11Therefore the
LORD said to Solomon, "Because you have
done this, and have not kept My covenant
and My statutes, which I have commanded
you, [a]I will surely tear the kingdom away
from you and give it to your [b]servant. 12Nev-
ertheless I will not do it in your days, for
the sake of your father David; I will tear it
out of the hand of your son. 13[a]However I
will not tear away the whole kingdom; I will
give [b]one tribe to your son [c]for the sake of
My servant David, and for the sake of Jerusalem [d]which I have chosen."

Adversaries of Solomon

14Now the LORD [a]raised up an adversary against Solomon, Hadad the Edomite; he *was* a descendant of the king in
Edom. 15[a]For it happened, when David was
in Edom, and Joab the commander of the
army had gone up to bury the slain, [b]after
he had killed every male in Edom 16(because for six months Joab remained there
with all Israel, until he had cut down every
male in Edom), 17that Hadad fled to go to
Egypt, he and certain Edomites of his father's servants with him. Hadad *was* still
a little child. 18Then they arose from Midian and came to Paran; and they took men
with them from Paran and came to Egypt,
to Pharaoh king of Egypt, who gave him a
house, apportioned food for him, and gave
him land. 19And Hadad found great favor in
the sight of Pharaoh, so that he gave him
as wife the sister of his own wife, that is,
the sister of Queen Tahpenes. 20Then the
sister of Tahpenes bore him Genubath his
son, whom Tahpenes weaned in Pharaoh's
house. And Genubath was in Pharaoh's
household among the sons of Pharaoh.

21[a]So when Hadad heard in Egypt that
David rested with his fathers, and that Joab
the commander of the army was dead, Hadad said to Pharaoh, "Let me depart, that I
may go to my own country."

22Then Pharaoh said to him, "But what
have you lacked with me, that suddenly you
seek to go to your own country?"

So he answered, "Nothing, but do let me
go anyway."

23And God raised up *another* adversary
against him, Rezon the son of Eliadah, who
had fled from his lord, [a]Hadadezer king of
Zobah. 24So he gathered men to him and
became captain over a band *of raiders,*
[a]when David killed those *of Zobah.* And they
went to Damascus and dwelt there, and
reigned in Damascus. 25He was an adversary of Israel all the days of Solomon (besides the trouble that Hadad *caused*); and
he abhorred Israel, and reigned over Syria.

Jeroboam's Rebellion

26Then Solomon's servant, [a]Jeroboam
the son of Nebat, an Ephraimite from
Zereda, whose mother's name *was* Zeruah,
a widow, [b]also [c]rebelled against the king.

27And this *is* what caused him to rebel
against the king: [a]Solomon had built the
Millo *and* repaired the damages to the City
of David his father. 28The man Jeroboam
was a mighty man of valor; and Solomon,
seeing that the young man was [a]industri-
ous, made him the officer over all the labor
force of the house of Joseph.

29Now it happened at that time, when
Jeroboam went out of Jerusalem, that the
prophet [a]Ahijah the Shilonite met him on
the way; and he had clothed himself with a
new garment, and the two *were* alone in the
field. 30Then Ahijah took hold of the new
garment that *was* on him, and [a]tore it *into*
twelve pieces. 31And he said to Jeroboam,
"Take for yourself ten pieces, for [a]thus says
the LORD, the God of Israel: 'Behold, I will
tear the kingdom out of the hand of Solomon and will give ten tribes to you 32(but

---

11:7 [c] 2 Kin. 23:13 11:9 [a] 1 Kin. 3:5; 9:2 11:10 [a] 1 Kin. 6:12; 9:6, 7 11:11 [a] 1 Kin. 11:31; 12:15, 16 [b] 1 Kin. 11:31, 37 11:13 [a] 2 Sam. 7:15; 1 Chr. 17:13; Ps. 89:33 [b] 1 Kin. 12:20 [c] 2 Sam. 7:15, 16 [d] Deut. 12:11; 1 Kin. 9:3; 14:21 11:14 [a] 1 Chr. 5:26 11:15 [a] 2 Sam. 8:14; 1 Chr. 18:12, 13 [b] Num. 24:18, 19; [Deut. 20:13] 11:21 [a] 1 Kin. 2:10, 34 11:23 [a] 2 Sam. 8:3; 10:16 11:24 [a] 2 Sam. 8:3; 10:8, 18 11:26 [a] 1 Kin. 12:2 [b] 1 Kin. 11:11; 2 Chr. 13:6 [c] 2 Sam. 20:21 11:27 [a] 1 Kin. 9:15, 24 11:28 [a] [Prov. 22:29] 11:29 [a] 1 Kin. 12:15; 14:2; 2 Chr. 9:29 11:30 [a] 1 Sam. 15:27, 28; 24:5 11:31 [a] 1 Kin. 11:11, 13

he shall have one tribe for the sake of My servant David, and for the sake of Jerusalem, the city which I have chosen out of all the tribes of Israel), 33[a]because they have[1] forsaken Me, and worshiped Ashtoreth the goddess of the Sidonians, Chemosh the god of the Moabites, and Milcom the god of the people of Ammon, and have not walked in My ways to do *what is* right in My eyes and *keep* My statutes and My judgments, as *did* his father David. 34However I will not take the whole kingdom out of his hand, because I have made him ruler all the days of his life for the sake of My servant David, whom I chose because he kept My commandments and My statutes. 35But [a]I will take the kingdom out of his son's hand and give it to you—ten tribes. 36And to his son I will give one tribe, that [a]My servant David may always have a lamp before Me in Jerusalem, the city which I have chosen for Myself, to put My name there. 37So I will take you, and you shall reign over all your heart desires, and you shall be king over Israel. 38Then it shall be, if you heed all that I command you, walk in My ways, and do *what is* right in My sight, to keep My statutes and My commandments, as My servant David did, then [a]I will be with you and [b]build for you an enduring house, as I built for David, and will give Israel to you. 39And I will afflict the descendants of David because of this, but not forever.' "

40Solomon therefore sought to kill Jeroboam. But Jeroboam arose and fled to Egypt, to [a]Shishak king of Egypt, and was in Egypt until the death of Solomon.

Death of Solomon
(2 Chr. 9:29–31)

41Now [a]the rest of the acts of Solomon, all that he did, and his wisdom, *are* they not written in the book of the acts of Solomon? 42[a]And the period that Solomon reigned in Jerusalem over all Israel *was* forty years. 43[a]Then Solomon rested with his fathers, and was buried in the City of David his father. And Rehoboam his son reigned in his [b]place.

The Revolt Against Rehoboam
(2 Chr. 10:1–19; 11:1–4)

12 And [a]Rehoboam went to [b]Shechem, for all Israel had gone to Shechem to make him king. 2So it happened, when [a]Jeroboam the son of Nebat heard *it* (he was still in [b]Egypt, for he had fled from the presence of King Solomon and had been dwelling in Egypt), 3that they sent and called him. Then Jeroboam and the whole assembly of Israel came and spoke to Rehoboam, saying, 4"Your father made our [a]yoke heavy; now therefore, lighten the burdensome service of your father, and his heavy yoke which he put on us, and we will serve you."

5So he said to them, "Depart *for* three days, then come back to me." And the people departed.

6Then King Rehoboam consulted the elders who stood before his father Solomon while he still lived, and he said, "How do you advise *me* to answer these people?"

7And they spoke to him, saying, [a]"If you will be a servant to these people today, and serve them, and answer them, and speak good words to them, then they will be your servants forever."

8But he rejected the advice which the elders had given him, and consulted the young men who had grown up with him, who stood before him. 9And he said to them, "What advice do you give? How should we answer this people who have spoken to me, saying, 'Lighten the yoke which your father put on us'?"

10Then the young men who had grown up with him spoke to him, saying, "Thus you should speak to this people who have spoken to you, saying, 'Your father made our yoke heavy, but you make *it* lighter on us'—thus you shall say to them: 'My little *finger* shall be thicker than my father's waist! 11And now, whereas my father put a heavy yoke on you, I will add to your yoke; my father chastised you with whips, but I will chastise you with scourges!' "[1]

12So Jeroboam and all the people came to Rehoboam the third day, as the king

---

11:33 [a] 1 Sam. 7:3; 1 Kin. 11:5–8 [1] Following Masoretic Text and Targum; Septuagint, Syriac, and Vulgate read *he has.* 11:35 [a] 1 Kin. 12:16, 17 11:36 [a] [1 Kin. 15:4; 2 Kin. 8:19] 11:38 [a] Deut. 31:8; Josh. 1:5 [b] 2 Sam. 7:11, 27 11:40 [a] 1 Kin. 11:17; 14:25; 2 Chr. 12:2–9 11:41 [a] 2 Chr. 9:29 11:42 [a] 2 Chr. 9:30 11:43 [a] 1 Kin. 2:10; 2 Chr. 9:31 [b] 1 Kin. 14:21; 2 Chr. 10:1 12:1 [a] 2 Chr. 10:1 [b] Judg. 9:6 12:2 [a] 1 Kin. 11:26 [b] 1 Kin. 11:40 12:4 [a] 1 Sam. 8:11–18; 1 Kin. 4:7; 5:13–15 12:7 [a] 2 Chr. 10:7; [Prov. 15:1] 12:11 [1] Literally *scorpions*

had directed, saying, "Come back to me the third day." 13 Then the king answered the people roughly, and rejected the advice which the elders had given him; 14 and he spoke to them according to the advice of the young men, saying, "My father made your yoke heavy, but I will add to your yoke; my father chastised you with whips, but I will chastise you with scourges!"[1] 15 So the king did not listen to the people; for [a]the turn *of events* was from the LORD, that He might fulfill His word, which the LORD had [b]spoken by Ahijah the Shilonite to Jeroboam the son of Nebat.

16 Now when all Israel saw that the king did not listen to them, the people answered the king, saying:

[a]"What share have we in David?
We have no inheritance in
the son of Jesse.
To your tents, O Israel!
Now, see to your own house, O David!"

So Israel departed to their tents. 17 But Rehoboam reigned over [a]the children of Israel who dwelt in the cities of Judah.

18 Then King Rehoboam [a]sent Adoram, who *was* in charge of the revenue; but all Israel stoned him with stones, and he died. Therefore King Rehoboam mounted his chariot in haste to flee to Jerusalem. 19 So [a]Israel has been in rebellion against the house of David to this day.

20 Now it came to pass when all Israel heard that Jeroboam had come back, they sent for him and called him to the congregation, and made him king over all [a]Israel. There was none who followed the house of David, but the tribe of Judah [b]only.

21 And when [a]Rehoboam came to Jerusalem, he assembled all the house of Judah with the tribe of [b]Benjamin, one hundred and eighty thousand chosen *men* who were warriors, to fight against the house of Israel, that he might restore the kingdom to Rehoboam the son of Solomon. 22 But [a]the word of God came to Shemaiah the man of God, saying, 23 "Speak to Rehoboam the son of Solomon, king of Judah, to all the house of Judah and Benjamin, and to the rest of the people, saying, 24 'Thus says the LORD: "You shall not go up nor fight against your brethren the children of Israel. Let every man return to his house, [a]for this thing is from Me." ' " Therefore they obeyed the word of the LORD, and turned back, according to the word of the LORD.

Jeroboam's Gold Calves

25 Then Jeroboam [a]built Shechem in the mountains of Ephraim, and dwelt there. Also he went out from there and built [b]Penuel. 26 And Jeroboam said in his heart, "Now the kingdom may return to the house of David: 27 If these people [a]go up to offer sacrifices in the house of the LORD at Jerusalem, then the heart of this people will turn back to their lord, Rehoboam king of Judah, and they will kill me and go back to Rehoboam king of Judah."

28 Therefore the king asked advice, [a]made two calves of gold, and said to the people, "It is too much for you to go up to Jerusalem. [b]Here are your gods, O Israel, which brought you up from the land of Egypt!" 29 And he set up one in [a]Bethel, and the other he put in [b]Dan. 30 Now this thing became [a]a sin, for the people went *to worship* before the one as far as Dan. 31 He made shrines[1] on the high places, [a]and made priests from every class of people, who were not of the sons of Levi.

32 Jeroboam ordained a feast on the fifteenth day of the eighth month, like [a]the feast that *was* in Judah, and offered sacrifices on the altar. So he did at Bethel, sacrificing to the calves that he had made. [b]And at Bethel he installed the priests of the high places which he had made. 33 So he made offerings on the altar which he had made at Bethel on the fifteenth day of the eighth month, in the month which he had [a]devised in his own heart. And he ordained a feast for the children of Israel, and offered sacrifices on the altar and [b]burned incense.

12:14 [1] Literally *scorpions* 12:15 [a] Deut. 2:30; Judg. 14:4; 1 Kin. 12:24; 2 Chr. 10:15 [b] 1 Kin. 11:11, 29, 31 12:16 [a] 2 Sam. 20:1 12:17 [a] 1 Kin. 11:13, 36; 2 Chr. 11:14–17 12:18 [a] 1 Kin. 4:6; 5:14 12:19 [a] 2 Kin. 17:21 12:20 [a] 2 Kin. 17:21 [b] 1 Kin. 11:13, 32, 36 12:21 [a] 2 Chr. 11:1–4 [b] 2 Sam. 19:17 12:22 [a] 2 Chr. 11:2; 12:5–7 12:24 [a] 1 Kin. 12:15 12:25 [a] Gen. 12:6; Judg. 9:45–49; 1 Kin. 12:1 [b] Gen. 32:30, 31; Judg. 8:8, 17 12:27 [a] [Deut. 12:5–7, 14] 12:28 [a] 2 Kin. 10:29; 17:16; [Hos. 8:4–7] [b] Ex. 32:4, 8 12:29 [a] Gen. 28:19 [b] Judg. 18:26–31 12:30 [a] 1 Kin. 13:34; 2 Kin. 17:21 12:31 [a] [Num. 3:10; 17:1–11]; Judg. 17:5; 1 Kin. 13:33; 2 Kin. 17:32; 2 Chr. 11:14, 15 [1] Literally *a house* 12:32 [a] Lev. 23:33, 34; Num. 29:12; 1 Kin. 8:2, 5 [b] Amos 7:10–13 12:33 [a] Num. 15:39 [b] 1 Kin. 13:1

The Message of the Man of God

13 And behold, [a]a man of God went
from Judah to Bethel by the word
of the LORD, [b]and Jeroboam stood by the
altar to burn incense. 2Then he cried out
against the altar by the word of the LORD,
and said, "O altar, altar! Thus says the LORD:
'Behold, a child, [a]Josiah by name, shall be
born to the house of David; and on you he
shall sacrifice the priests of the high places
who burn incense on you, and men's bones
shall be [b]burned on you.'" 3And he gave [a]a
sign the same day, saying, "This *is* the sign
which the LORD has spoken: Surely the altar
shall split apart, and the ashes on it shall
be poured out."

4So it came to pass when King Jeroboam
heard the saying of the man of God, who
cried out against the altar in Bethel, that
he stretched out his hand from the altar,
saying, "Arrest him!" Then his hand, which
he stretched out toward him, withered, so
that he could not pull it back to himself.
5The altar also was split apart, and the ashes
poured out from the altar, according to the
sign which the man of God had given by the
word of the LORD. 6Then the king answered
and said to the man of God, "Please [a]entreat
the favor of the LORD your God, and pray for
me, that my hand may be restored to me."

So the man of God entreated the LORD,
and the king's hand was restored to him,
and became as before. 7Then the king said
to the man of God, "Come home with me
and refresh yourself, and [a]I will give you
a reward."

8But the man of God said to the king,
[a]"If you were to give me half your house, I
would not go in with you; nor would I eat
bread nor drink water in this place. 9For
so it was commanded me by the word of
the LORD, saying, [a]'You shall not eat bread,
nor drink water, nor return by the same
way you came.'" 10So he went another way
and did not return by the way he came to
Bethel.

Death of the Man of God

11Now an [a]old prophet dwelt in Bethel,
and his sons came and told him all the
works that the man of God had done that
day in Bethel; they also told their father
the words which he had spoken to the king.
12And their father said to them, "Which way
did he go?" For his sons had seen[1] which
way the man of God went who came from
Judah. 13Then he said to his sons, "Saddle
the donkey for me." So they saddled the
donkey for him; and he rode on it, 14and
went after the man of God, and found him
sitting under an oak. Then he said to him,
"*Are* you the man of God who came from
Judah?"

And he said, "I *am.*"

15Then he said to him, "Come home with
me and eat bread."

16And he said, [a]"I cannot return with you
nor go in with you; neither can I eat bread
nor drink water with you in this place.
17For I have been told [a]by the word of the
LORD, 'You shall not eat bread nor drink
water there, nor return by going the way
you came.'"

18He said to him, "I too *am* a prophet
as you *are,* and an angel spoke to me by
the word of the LORD, saying, 'Bring him
back with you to your house, that he may
eat bread and drink water.'" (He was lying
to him.)

19So he went back with him, and ate
bread in his house, and drank water.

20Now it happened, as they sat at the
table, that the word of the LORD came to
the prophet who had brought him back;
21and he cried out to the man of God who
came from Judah, saying, "Thus says the
LORD: 'Because you have disobeyed the
word of the LORD, and have not kept the
commandment which the LORD your God
commanded you, 22but you came back,
ate bread, and drank water in the [a]place of
which *the LORD* said to you, "Eat no bread
and drink no water," your corpse shall not
come to the tomb of your fathers.'"

23So it was, after he had eaten bread
and after he had drunk, that he saddled
the donkey for him, the prophet whom he
had brought back. 24When he was gone, [a]a
lion met him on the road and killed him.
And his corpse was thrown on the road, and

13:1 [a] 2 Kin. 23:17 [b] 1 Kin. 12:32, 33 13:2 [a] 2 Kin. 23:15, 16 [b] [Lev. 26:30] 13:3 [a] Ex. 4:1–5; Judg. 6:17; Is. 7:14; 38:7; John 2:18; 1 Cor. 1:22 13:6 [a] Ex. 8:8; 9:28; 10:17; Num. 21:7; Jer. 37:3; Acts 8:24; [James 5:16] 13:7 [a] 1 Sam. 9:7; 2 Kin. 5:15 13:8 [a] Num. 22:18; 24:13; 1 Kin. 13:16, 17 13:9 [a] [1 Cor. 5:11] 13:11 [a] 1 Kin. 13:25 13:12 [1] Septuagint, Syriac, Targum, and Vulgate read *showed him.* 13:16 [a] 1 Kin. 13:8, 9 13:17 [a] 1 Kin. 20:35; 1 Thess. 4:15 13:22 [a] 1 Kin. 13:9 13:24 [a] 1 Kin. 20:36

the donkey stood by it. The lion also stood
by the corpse. 25 And there, men passed by
and saw the corpse thrown on the road,
and the lion standing by the corpse. Then
they went and told *it* in the city where the
old prophet dwelt.

26 Now when the prophet who had
brought him back from the way heard *it,*
he said, "It *is* the man of God who was disobedient to the word of the LORD. Therefore the LORD has delivered him to the lion,
which has torn him and killed him, according to the word of the LORD which He spoke
to him." 27 And he spoke to his sons, saying,
"Saddle the donkey for me." So they saddled
it. 28 Then he went and found his corpse
thrown on the road, and the donkey and
the lion standing by the corpse. The lion
had not eaten the corpse nor torn the donkey. 29 And the prophet took up the corpse
of the man of God, laid it on the donkey,
and brought it back. So the old prophet
came to the city to mourn, and to bury him.
30 Then he laid the corpse in his own tomb;
and they mourned over him, *saying,* [a]"Alas,
my brother!" 31 So it was, after he had buried him, that he spoke to his sons, saying,
"When I am dead, then bury me in the tomb
where the man of God *is* buried; [a]lay my
bones beside his bones. 32 [a]For the saying
which he cried out by the word of the LORD
against the altar in Bethel, and against all
the shrines[1] on the high places which *are*
in the cities of [b]Samaria, will surely come
to pass."

33 [a]After this event Jeroboam did not
turn from his evil way, but again he made
priests from every class of people for the
high places; whoever wished, he consecrated him, and he became *one* of the
priests of the high places. 34 [a]And this thing
was the sin of the house of Jeroboam, so
as [b]to exterminate and destroy *it* from the
face of the earth.

Judgment on the House of Jeroboam

14 At that time Abijah the son of Jeroboam became sick. 2 And Jeroboam
said to his wife, "Please arise, and disguise
yourself, that they may not recognize you
as the wife of Jeroboam, and go to Shiloh.
Indeed, Ahijah the prophet *is* there, who
told me that [a]*I would be* king over this people. 3 [a]Also take with you ten loaves, *some*
cakes, and a jar of honey, and go to him; he
will tell you what will become of the child."
4 And Jeroboam's wife did so; she arose [a]and
went to Shiloh, and came to the house of
Ahijah. But Ahijah could not see, for his
eyes were glazed by reason of his age.

5 Now the LORD had said to Ahijah, "Here
is the wife of Jeroboam, coming to ask you
something about her son, for he *is* sick.
Thus and thus you shall say to her; for it
will be, when she comes in, that she will
pretend *to be* another *woman.*"

6 And so it was, when Ahijah heard the
sound of her footsteps as she came through
the door, he said, "Come in, wife of Jeroboam. Why do you pretend *to be* another
person? For I *have been* sent to you *with*
bad *news.* 7 Go, tell Jeroboam, 'Thus says
the LORD God of Israel: [a]"Because I exalted
you from among the people, and made you
ruler over My people Israel, 8 and [a]tore the
kingdom away from the house of David,
and gave it to you; and *yet* you have not
been as My servant David, [b]who kept My
commandments and who followed Me with
all his heart, to do only *what was* right in
My eyes; 9 but you have done more evil
than all who were before you, [a]for you have
gone and made for yourself other gods and
molded images to provoke Me to anger, and
[b]have cast Me behind your back— 10 therefore behold! [a]I will bring disaster on the
house of Jeroboam, and [b]will cut off from
Jeroboam every male in Israel, [c]bond and
free; I will take away the remnant of the
house of Jeroboam, as one takes away refuse until it is all gone. 11 The dogs shall eat
[a]whoever belongs to Jeroboam and dies in
the city, and the birds of the air shall eat
whoever dies in the field; for the LORD has
spoken!"' 12 Arise therefore, go to your own
house. [a]When your feet enter the city, the
child shall die. 13 And all Israel shall mourn
for him and bury him, for he is the only one

13:30 [a] Jer. 22:18 13:31 [a] Ruth 1:17; 2 Kin. 23:17, 18 13:32 [a] 1 Kin. 13:2; 2 Kin. 23:16, 19 [b] 1 Kin. 16:24; John 4:5; Acts 8:14 [1] Literally *houses* 13:33 [a] 1 Kin. 12:31, 32; 2 Chr. 11:15; 13:9 13:34 [a] 1 Kin. 12:30; 2 Kin. 17:21 [b] [1 Kin. 14:10; 15:29, 30] 14:2 [a] 1 Kin. 11:29–31 14:3 [a] 1 Sam. 9:7, 8; 1 Kin. 13:7; 2 Kin. 4:42 14:4 [a] 1 Kin. 11:29 14:7 [a] 2 Sam. 12:7, 8; 1 Kin. 16:2 14:8 [a] 1 Kin. 11:31 [b] 1 Kin. 11:33, 38; 15:5 14:9 [a] 1 Kin. 12:28; 2 Chr. 11:15 [b] 2 Chr. 29:6; Neh. 9:26; Ps. 50:17 14:10 [a] 1 Kin. 15:29 [b] 1 Kin. 21:21; 2 Kin. 9:8 [c] Deut. 32:36; 2 Kin. 14:26 14:11 [a] 1 Kin. 16:4; 21:24 14:12 [a] 1 Kin. 14:17

of Jeroboam who shall come to the grave,
because in him [a]there is found something
good toward the LORD God of Israel in the
house of Jeroboam.
14[a]“Moreover the LORD will raise up
for Himself a king over Israel who shall
cut off the house of Jeroboam; this is the
day. What? Even now! 15For the LORD will
strike Israel, as a reed is shaken in the water. He will [a]uproot Israel from this [b]good
land which He gave to their fathers, and
will scatter them [c]beyond the River,[1] [d]be-
cause they have made their wooden images,[2] provoking the LORD to anger. 16And
He will give Israel up because of the sins
of Jeroboam, [a]who sinned and who made
Israel sin.”
17Then Jeroboam's wife arose and departed, and came to [a]Tirzah. [b]When she
came to the threshold of the house, the
child died. 18And they buried him; and all
Israel mourned for him, [a]according to the
word of the LORD which He spoke through
His servant Ahijah the prophet.

Death of Jeroboam

19Now the rest of the acts of Jeroboam,
how he [a]made war and how he reigned,
indeed they *are* written in the book of the
chronicles of the kings of Israel. 20The period that Jeroboam reigned *was* twenty-two
years. So he rested with his fathers. Then
[a]Nadab his son reigned in his place.

Rehoboam Reigns in Judah
(2 Chr. 11:5—12:16)

21And Rehoboam the son of Solomon
reigned in Judah. [a]Rehoboam *was* forty-
one years old when he became king. He
reigned seventeen years in Jerusalem,
the city [b]which the LORD had chosen out
of all the tribes of Israel, to put His name
there. [c]His mother's name *was* Naamah,
an Ammonitess. 22[a]Now Judah did evil in
the sight of the LORD, and they [b]provoked
Him to jealousy with their sins which they
committed, more than all that their fathers had done. 23For they also built for
themselves [a]high places, [b]*sacred* pillars,
and [c]wooden images on every high hill and
[d]under every green tree. 24[a]And there were
also perverted persons[1] in the land. They
did according to all the [b]abominations of
the nations which the LORD had cast out
before the children of [c]Israel.
25[a]It happened in the fifth year of King
Rehoboam *that* Shishak king of Egypt
came up against Jerusalem. 26[a]And he
took away the treasures of the house of
the LORD and the treasures of the king's
house; he took away everything. He also
took away all the gold shields [b]which Solomon had made. 27Then King Rehoboam
made bronze shields in their place, and
committed *them* to the hands of the captains of the guard, who guarded the doorway of the king's house. 28And whenever
the king entered the house of the LORD, the
guards carried them, then brought them
back into the guardroom.
29[a]Now the rest of the acts of Rehoboam,
and all that he did, *are* they not written in
the book of the chronicles of the kings of
Judah? 30And there was [a]war between Rehoboam and Jeroboam all *their* days. 31[a]So
Rehoboam rested with his fathers, and was
buried with his fathers in the City of David.
[b]His mother's name *was* Naamah, an Ammonitess. Then [c]Abijam[1] his son reigned
in his place.

Abijam Reigns in Judah
(2 Chr. 13:1—14:1)

15 [a]In the eighteenth year of King Jeroboam the son of Nebat, Abijam
became king over Judah. 2He reigned
three years in Jerusalem. [a]His mother's
name *was* [b]Maachah the granddaughter
of [c]Abishalom. 3And he walked in all the
sins of his father, which he had done before him; [a]his heart was not loyal to the
LORD his God, as was the heart of his father

14:13 [a] 2 Chr. 12:12; 19:3 14:14 [a] 1 Kin. 15:27–29 14:15 [a] Deut. 29:28; 2 Kin. 17:6; Ps. 52:5 [b] [Josh. 23:15, 16] [c] 2 Kin. 15:29 [d] [Ex. 34:13, 14; Deut. 12:3] [1] That is, the Euphrates [2] Hebrew *Asherim,* Canaanite deities 14:16 [a] 1 Kin. 12:30; 13:34; 15:30, 34; 16:2 14:17 [a] 1 Kin. 15:21, 33; 16:6, 8, 15, 23; Song 6:4 [b] 1 Kin. 14:12 14:18 [a] 1 Kin. 14:13 14:19 [a] 1 Kin. 14:30; 2 Chr. 13:2–20 14:20 [a] 1 Kin. 15:25 14:21 [a] 2 Chr. 12:13 [b] 1 Kin. 11:32, 36 [c] 1 Kin. 14:31 14:22 [a] 2 Chr. 12:1, 14 [b] Deut. 32:21; Ps. 78:58; 1 Cor. 10:22 14:23 [a] Deut. 12:2; Ezek. 16:24, 25 [b] [Deut. 16:22] [c] [2 Kin. 17:9, 10] [d] Is. 57:5; Jer. 2:20 14:24 [a] Gen. 19:5; Deut. 23:17; 1 Kin. 15:12; 22:46; 2 Kin. 23:7 [b] Deut. 20:18 [c] [Deut. 9:4, 5] [1] Hebrew *qadesh,* that is, one practicing sodomy and prostitution in religious rituals 14:25 [a] 1 Kin. 11:40; 2 Chr. 12:2 14:26 [a] 1 Kin. 15:18; 2 Chr. 12:9–11 [b] 1 Kin. 10:17 14:29 [a] 2 Chr. 12:15, 16 14:30 [a] 1 Kin. 12:21–24; 15:6 14:31 [a] 2 Chr. 12:16 [b] 1 Kin. 14:21 [c] 2 Chr. 12:16 [1] Spelled *Abijah* in 2 Chronicles 12:16ff 15:1 [a] 2 Chr. 13:1 15:2 [a] 2 Chr. 11:20–22 [b] 2 Chr. 13:2 [c] 2 Chr. 11:21 15:3 [a] 1 Kin. 11:4; Ps. 119:80

David. 4Nevertheless [a]for David's sake the
LORD his God gave him a lamp in Jerusalem, by setting up his son after him and
by establishing Jerusalem; 5because David [a]did *what was* right in the eyes of the
LORD, and had not turned aside from anything that He commanded him all the days
of his life, [b]except in the matter of Uriah
the Hittite. 6[a]And there was war between
Rehoboam[1] and Jeroboam all the days of
his life. 7[a]Now the rest of the acts of Abijam,
and all that he did, *are* they not written in
the book of the chronicles of the kings of
Judah? And there was war between Abijam
and Jeroboam.

8[a]So Abijam rested with his fathers, and
they buried him in the City of David. Then
Asa his son reigned in his place.

Asa Reigns in Judah
(2 Chr. 14:1—16:14)

9In the twentieth year of Jeroboam
king of Israel, Asa became king over Judah. 10And he reigned forty-one years in
Jerusalem. His grandmother's name *was*
Maachah the granddaughter of Abishalom.
11[a]Asa did *what was* right in the eyes of the
LORD, as *did* his father David. 12[a]And he banished the perverted persons[1] from the land,
and removed all the idols that his fathers
had made. 13Also he removed [a]Maachah his
grandmother from *being* queen mother, because she had made an obscene image of
Asherah.[1] And Asa cut down her obscene
image and [b]burned *it* by the Brook Kidron.
14[a]But the high places were not removed.
Nevertheless Asa's [b]heart was loyal to the
LORD all his days. 15He also brought into the
house of the LORD the things which his father [a]had dedicated, and the things which
he himself had dedicated: silver and gold
and utensils.

16Now there was war between Asa and
Baasha king of Israel all their days. 17And
[a]Baasha king of Israel came up against Judah, and built [b]Ramah, [c]that he might let
none go out or come in to Asa king of Judah. 18Then Asa took all the silver and gold
that was left in the treasuries of the house
of the LORD and the treasuries of the king's
house, and delivered them into the hand
of his servants. And King Asa sent them
to [a]Ben-Hadad the son of Tabrimmon, the
son of Hezion, king of Syria, who dwelt in
[b]Damascus, saying, 19"*Let there be* a treaty
between you and me, as there was between
my father and your father. See, I have sent
you a present of silver and gold. Come and
break your treaty with Baasha king of Israel, so that he will withdraw from me."

20So Ben-Hadad heeded King Asa, and
[a]sent the captains of his armies against
the cities of Israel. He attacked [b]Ijon, [c]Dan,
[d]Abel Beth Maachah, and all Chinneroth,
with all the land of Naphtali. 21Now it happened, when Baasha heard *it,* that he
stopped building Ramah, and remained
in [a]Tirzah.

22[a]Then King Asa made a proclamation
throughout all Judah; none *was* exempted.
And they took away the stones and timber of Ramah, which Baasha had used for
building; and with them King Asa built
[b]Geba of Benjamin, and [c]Mizpah.

23The rest of all the acts of Asa, all his
might, all that he did, and the cities which
he built, *are* they not written in the book of
the chronicles of the kings of Judah? But
[a]in the time of his old age he was diseased
in his feet. 24So Asa rested with his fathers,
and was buried with his fathers in the City
of David his father. [a]Then [b]Jehoshaphat his
son reigned in his place.

Nadab Reigns in Israel

25Now [a]Nadab the son of Jeroboam became king over Israel in the second year
of Asa king of Judah, and he reigned over
Israel two years. 26And he did evil in the
sight of the LORD, and walked in the way of
his father, and in [a]his sin by which he had
made Israel sin.

15:4 [a] 2 Sam. 21:17; 1 Kin. 11:32, 36; 2 Chr. 21:7 15:5 [a] 1 Kin. 9:4; 14:8; Luke 1:6 [b] 2 Sam. 11:3, 15–17; 12:9, 10 15:6 [a] 1 Kin. 14:30; 2 Chr. 12:15—13:20 [1] Following Masoretic Text, Septuagint, Targum, and Vulgate; some Hebrew manuscripts and Syriac read *Abijam.* 15:7 [a] 2 Chr. 13:2–22 15:8 [a] 2 Chr. 14:1 15:11 [a] 2 Chr. 14:2 15:12 [a] Deut. 23:17; 1 Kin. 14:24; 22:46 [1] Hebrew *qedeshim,* that is, those practicing sodomy and prostitution in religious rituals 15:13 [a] 2 Chr. 15:16–18 [b] Ex. 32:20 [1] A Canaanite goddess 15:14 [a] 1 Kin. 3:2; 22:43; 2 Kin. 12:3; 2 Chr. 15:17, 18 [b] [1 Sam. 16:7]; 1 Kin. 8:61; 15:3 15:15 [a] 1 Kin. 7:51 15:17 [a] 2 Chr. 16:1–6 [b] Josh. 18:25; 1 Kin. 15:21, 22 [c] 1 Kin. 12:26–29 15:18 [a] 2 Kin. 12:17, 18; 2 Chr. 16:2 [b] Gen. 14:15; 1 Kin. 11:23, 24 15:20 [a] 1 Kin. 20:1 [b] 2 Kin. 15:29 [c] Judg. 18:29; 1 Kin. 12:29 [d] 2 Sam. 20:14, 15 15:21 [a] 1 Kin. 14:17; 16:15–18 15:22 [a] 2 Chr. 16:6 [b] Josh. 21:17 [c] Josh. 18:26 15:23 [a] 2 Chr. 16:11–14 15:24 [a] 2 Chr. 17:1 [b] 1 Kin. 22:41–44; Matt. 1:8 15:25 [a] 1 Kin. 14:20 15:26 [a] 1 Kin. 12:28–33; 14:16

27[a]Then Baasha the son of Ahijah, of
the house of Issachar, conspired against
him. And Baasha killed him at [b]Gibbethon,
which *belonged* to the Philistines, while Nadab and all Israel laid siege to Gibbethon.
28Baasha killed him in the third year of Asa
king of Judah, and reigned in his place.
29And it was so, when he became king,
that he killed all the house of Jeroboam.
He did not leave to Jeroboam anyone that
breathed, until he had destroyed him, according to [a]the word of the LORD which He
had spoken by His servant Ahijah the Shilonite, 30[a]because of the sins of Jeroboam,
which he had sinned and by which he had
made Israel sin, because of his provocation
with which he had provoked the LORD God
of Israel to anger.

31Now the rest of the acts of Nadab, and
all that he did, *are* they not written in the
book of the chronicles of the kings of Israel? 32[a]And there was war between Asa and
Baasha king of Israel all their days.

Baasha Reigns in Israel

33In the third year of Asa king of Judah,
Baasha the son of Ahijah became king over
all Israel in Tirzah, and *reigned* twenty-four
years. 34He did evil in the sight of the LORD,
and walked in [a]the way of Jeroboam, and
in his sin by which he had made Israel sin.

16 Then the word of the LORD came to
[a]Jehu the son of [b]Hanani, against
[c]Baasha, saying: 2[a]"Inasmuch as I lifted you
out of the dust and made you ruler over
My people Israel, and [b]you have walked in
the way of Jeroboam, and have made My
people Israel sin, to provoke Me to anger
with their sins, 3surely I will [a]take away the
posterity of Baasha and the posterity of his
house, and I will make your house like [b]the
house of Jeroboam the son of Nebat. 4The
dogs shall eat [a]whoever belongs to Baasha
and dies in the city, and the birds of the air
shall eat whoever dies in the fields."

5Now the rest of the acts of Baasha, what
he did, and his might, [a]*are* they not written
in the book of the chronicles of the kings of
Israel? 6So Baasha rested with his fathers
and was buried in [a]Tirzah. Then Elah his
son reigned in his place.

7And also the word of the LORD came
by the prophet [a]Jehu the son of Hanani
against Baasha and his house, because of
all the evil that he did in the sight of the
LORD in provoking Him to anger with the
work of his hands, in being like the house
of Jeroboam, and because [b]he killed them.

Elah Reigns in Israel

8In the twenty-sixth year of Asa king of
Judah, Elah the son of Baasha became king
over Israel, *and reigned* two years in Tirzah. 9[a]Now his servant Zimri, commander
of half *his* chariots, conspired against him
as he was in Tirzah drinking himself drunk
in the house of Arza, [b]steward of *his* house
in Tirzah. 10And Zimri went in and struck
him and killed him in the twenty-seventh
year of Asa king of Judah, and reigned in
his place.

11Then it came to pass, when he began
to reign, as soon as he was seated on his
throne, *that* he killed all the household of
Baasha; he [a]did not leave him one male,
neither of his relatives nor of his friends.
12Thus Zimri destroyed all the household
of Baasha, [a]according to the word of the
LORD, which He spoke against Baasha by
Jehu the prophet, 13for all the sins of Baasha
and the sins of Elah his son, by which they
had sinned and by which they had made
Israel sin, in provoking the LORD God of
Israel to anger [a]with their idols.

14Now the rest of the acts of Elah, and all
that he did, *are* they not written in the book
of the chronicles of the kings of Israel?

Zimri Reigns in Israel

15In the twenty-seventh year of Asa
king of Judah, Zimri had reigned in Tirzah
seven days. And the people *were* encamped
[a]against Gibbethon, which *belonged* to the
Philistines. 16Now the people *who were*
encamped heard it said, "Zimri has conspired and also has killed the king." So all
Israel made Omri, the commander of the
army, king over Israel that day in the camp.

15:27 [a] 1 Kin. 14:14 [b] Josh. 19:44; 21:23; 1 Kin. 16:15 15:29 [a] 1 Kin. 14:10–14 15:30 [a] 1 Kin. 14:9, 16 15:32 [a] 1 Kin. 15:16 15:34 [a] 1 Kin. 13:33; 14:16 16:1 [a] 1 Kin. 16:7; 2 Chr. 19:2; 20:34 [b] 2 Chr. 16:7–10 [c] 1 Kin. 15:27 16:2 [a] 1 Sam. 2:8; 1 Kin. 14:7 [b] 1 Kin. 12:25–33; 15:34 16:3 [a] 1 Kin. 16:11; 21:21 [b] 1 Kin. 14:10; 15:29 16:4 [a] 1 Kin. 14:11; 21:24 16:5 [a] 2 Chr. 16:11 16:6 [a] 1 Kin. 14:17; 15:21 16:7 [a] 1 Kin. 16:1 [b] 1 Kin. 15:27, 29 16:9 [a] 2 Kin. 9:30–33 [b] Gen. 24:2; 39:4; 1 Kin. 18:3 16:11 [a] 1 Sam. 25:22 16:12 [a] 1 Kin. 16:3 16:13 [a] Deut. 32:21; 1 Sam. 12:21; [Is. 41:29; Jon. 2:8; 1 Cor. 8:4; 10:19] 16:15 [a] 1 Kin. 15:27

17 Then Omri and all Israel with him went up from Gibbethon, and they besieged Tirzah. 18 And it happened, when Zimri saw that the city was taken, that he went into the citadel of the king's house and burned the king's house down upon himself with fire, and died, 19 because of the sins which he had committed in doing evil in the sight of the LORD, [a]in walking in the [b]way of Jeroboam, and in his sin which he had committed to make Israel sin.

20 Now the rest of the acts of Zimri, and the treason he committed, *are* they not written in the book of the chronicles of the kings of Israel?

Omri Reigns in Israel

21 Then the people of Israel were divided into two parts: half of the people followed Tibni the son of Ginath, to make him king, and half followed Omri. 22 But the people who followed Omri prevailed over the people who followed Tibni the son of Ginath. So Tibni died and Omri reigned. 23 In the thirty-first year of Asa king of Judah, Omri became king over Israel, *and reigned* twelve years. Six years he reigned in [a]Tirzah. 24 And he bought the hill of Samaria from Shemer for two talents of silver; then he built on the hill, and called the name of the city which he built, [a]Samaria, after the name of Shemer, owner of the hill. 25 [a]Omri did evil in the eyes of the LORD, and did worse than all who *were* before him. 26 For he [a]walked in all the ways of Jeroboam the son of Nebat, and in his sin by which he had made Israel sin, provoking the LORD God of Israel to anger with their [b]idols.

27 Now the rest of the acts of Omri which he did, and the might that he showed, *are* they not written in the book of the chronicles of the kings of Israel?

28 So Omri rested with his fathers and was buried in Samaria. Then Ahab his son reigned in his place.

Ahab Reigns in Israel

29 In the thirty-eighth year of Asa king of Judah, Ahab the son of Omri became king over Israel; and Ahab the son of Omri reigned over Israel in Samaria twenty-two years. 30 Now Ahab the son of Omri did evil in the sight of the LORD, more than all who *were* before him. 31 And it came to pass, as though it had been a trivial thing for him to walk in the sins of Jeroboam the son of Nebat, [a]that he took as wife Jezebel the daughter of Ethbaal, king of the [b]Sidonians; [c]and he went and served Baal and worshiped him. 32 Then he set up an altar for Baal in [a]the temple of Baal, which he had built in Samaria. 33 [a]And Ahab made a wooden image.[1] Ahab [b]did more to provoke the LORD God of Israel to anger than all the kings of Israel who were before him. 34 In his days Hiel of Bethel built Jericho. He laid its foundation with Abiram his firstborn, and with his youngest *son* Segub he set up its gates, [a]according to the word of the LORD, which He had spoken through Joshua the son of Nun.[1]

Elijah Proclaims a Drought

17 And Elijah the Tishbite, of the [a]inhabitants of Gilead, said to Ahab, [b]"*As* the LORD God of Israel lives, [c]before whom I stand, [d]there shall not be dew nor rain [e]these years, except at my word."

2 Then the word of the LORD came to him, saying, 3 "Get away from here and turn eastward, and hide by the Brook Cherith, which flows into the Jordan. 4 And it will be *that* you shall drink from the brook, and I have commanded the [a]ravens to feed you there."

5 So he went and did according to the word of the LORD, for he went and stayed by the Brook Cherith, which flows into the Jordan. 6 The ravens brought him bread and meat in the morning, and bread and meat in the evening; and he drank from the brook. 7 And it happened after a while that the brook dried up, because there had been no rain in the land.

Elijah and the Widow

8 Then the word of the LORD came to him, saying, 9 "Arise, go to [a]Zarephath,

---

16:19 [a] 1 Kin. 15:26, 34 [b] 1 Kin. 12:25–33 16:23 [a] 1 Kin. 15:21; 2 Kin. 15:14 16:24 [a] 1 Kin. 13:32; 2 Kin. 17:24; John 4:4 16:25 [a] Mic. 6:16 16:26 [a] 1 Kin. 16:19 [b] 1 Kin. 16:13 16:31 [a] Deut. 7:3 [b] Judg. 18:7; 1 Kin. 11:1–5 [c] 1 Kin. 21:25, 26; 2 Kin. 10:18; 17:16 16:32 [a] 2 Kin. 10:21, 26, 27 16:33 [a] 2 Kin. 13:6 [b] 1 Kin. 14:9; 16:29, 30; 21:25 [1] Hebrew *Asherah,* a Canaanite goddess 16:34 [a] Josh. 6:26 [1] Compare Joshua 6:26 17:1 [a] Judg. 12:4 [b] 1 Kin. 18:10; 22:14; 2 Kin. 3:14; 5:20 [c] Deut. 10:8 [d] 1 Kin. 18:1; James 5:17 [e] Luke 4:25 17:4 [a] Job 38:41 17:9 [a] Obad. 20; Luke 4:25, 26

which *belongs* to [b]Sidon, and dwell there.
See, I have commanded a widow there to
provide for you." 10So he arose and went to
Zarephath. And when he came to the gate
of the city, indeed a widow *was* there gathering sticks. And he called to her and said,
"Please bring me a little water in a cup, that
I may drink." 11And as she was going to get
it, he called to her and said, "Please bring
me a morsel of bread in your hand."

12So she said, "As the LORD your God
lives, I do not have bread, only a handful
of flour in a bin, and a little oil in a jar; and
see, I *am* gathering a couple of sticks that I
may go in and prepare it for myself and my
son, that we may eat it, and [a]die."

13And Elijah said to her, "Do not fear;
go *and* do as you have said, but make me a
small cake from it first, and bring *it* to me;
and afterward make *some* for yourself and
your son. 14For thus says the LORD God of
Israel: 'The bin of flour shall not be used
up, nor shall the jar of oil run dry, until the
day the LORD sends rain on the earth.' "

15So she went away and did according to
the word of Elijah; and she and he and her
household ate for *many* days. 16The bin of
flour was not used up, nor did the jar of oil
run dry, according to the word of the LORD
which He spoke by Elijah.

Elijah Revives the Widow's Son

17Now it happened after these things *that*
the son of the woman who owned the house
became sick. And his sickness was so serious that there was no breath left in him.
18So she said to Elijah, [a]"What have I to do
with you, O man of God? Have you come to
me to bring my sin to remembrance, and
to kill my son?"

19And he said to her, "Give me your son."
So he took him out of her arms and carried
him to the upper room where he was staying, and laid him on his own bed. 20Then
he cried out to the LORD and said, "O LORD
my God, have You also brought tragedy on
the widow with whom I lodge, by killing her
son?" 21[a]And he stretched himself out on
the child three times, and cried out to the
LORD and said, "O LORD my God, I pray, let
this child's soul come back to him." 22Then
the LORD heard the voice of Elijah; and the
soul of the child came back to him, and he
[a]revived.

23And Elijah took the child and brought
him down from the upper room into the
house, and gave him to his mother. And
Elijah said, "See, your son lives!"

24Then the woman said to Elijah, "Now
by this [a]I know that you *are* a man of God,
and that the word of the LORD in your
mouth *is* the truth."

Elijah's Message to Ahab

18 And it came to pass *after* [a]many days
that the word of the LORD came to
Elijah, in the third year, saying, "Go, present yourself to Ahab, and [b]I will send rain
on the earth."

2So Elijah went to present himself to
Ahab; and *there was* a severe famine in
Samaria. 3And Ahab had called Obadiah,
who *was* in charge of *his* house. (Now Obadiah feared the LORD greatly. 4For so it was,
while Jezebel massacred the prophets of
the LORD, that Obadiah had taken one hundred prophets and hidden them, fifty to a
cave, and had fed them with bread and water.) 5And Ahab had said to Obadiah, "Go
into the land to all the springs of water and
to all the brooks; perhaps we may find grass
to keep the horses and mules alive, so that
we will not have to kill any livestock." 6So
they divided the land between them to explore it; Ahab went one way by himself,
and Obadiah went another way by himself.

7Now as Obadiah was on his way, suddenly Elijah met him; and he [a]recognized
him, and fell on his face, and said, "*Is* that
you, my lord Elijah?"

8And he answered him, "*It is* I. Go, tell
your master, 'Elijah *is here.*' "

9So he said, "How have I sinned, that
you are delivering your servant into the
hand of Ahab, to kill me? 10*As* the LORD
your God lives, there is no nation or kingdom where my master has not sent someone to hunt for you; and when they said,
'*He is* not *here,*' he took an oath from the
kingdom or nation that they could not
find you. 11And now you say, 'Go, tell your
master, "Elijah *is here*" '! 12And it shall

17:9 [b] 2 Sam. 24:6 17:12 [a] Deut. 28:23, 24 17:18 [a] Luke 5:8 17:21 [a] 2 Kin. 4:34, 35; Acts 20:10 17:22 [a] Luke 7:14, 15; Heb. 11:35 17:24 [a] John 2:11; 3:2; 16:30 18:1 [a] 1 Kin. 17:1; Luke 4:25; James 5:17 [b] Deut. 28:12 18:7 [a] 2 Kin. 1:6–8

come to pass, *as soon as* I am gone from
you, that [a]the Spirit of the LORD will carry
you to a place I do not know; so when I
go and tell Ahab, and he cannot find you,
he will kill me. But I your servant have
feared the LORD from my youth. 13Was it
not reported to my lord what I did when
Jezebel killed the prophets of the LORD,
how I hid one hundred men of the LORD's
prophets, fifty to a cave, and fed them with
bread and water? 14And now you say, 'Go,
tell your master, "Elijah *is here*."' He will
kill me!"

15Then Elijah said, "*As* the LORD of hosts
lives, before whom I stand, I will surely
present myself to him today."

16So Obadiah went to meet Ahab, and
told him; and Ahab went to meet Elijah.

17Then it happened, when Ahab saw Elijah, that Ahab said to him, [a]"*Is that* you,
O [b]troubler of Israel?"

18And he answered, "I have not troubled Israel, but you and your father's house
have, [a]in that you have forsaken the commandments of the LORD and have followed
the Baals. 19Now therefore, send *and* gather
all Israel to me on [a]Mount Carmel, the four
hundred and fifty prophets of Baal, [b]and
the four hundred prophets of Asherah,[1]
who eat at Jezebel's table."

Elijah's Mount Carmel Victory

20So Ahab sent for all the children of Israel, and [a]gathered the prophets together
on Mount Carmel. 21And Elijah came to all
the people, and said, [a]"How long will you
falter between two opinions? If the LORD *is*
God, follow Him; but if Baal, [b]follow him."
But the people answered him not a word.
22Then Elijah said to the people, [a]"I alone
am left a prophet of the LORD; [b]but Baal's
prophets *are* four hundred and fifty men.
23Therefore let them give us two bulls; and
let them choose one bull for themselves,
cut it in pieces, and lay *it* on the wood, but
put no fire *under it;* and I will prepare the
other bull, and lay *it* on the wood, but put
no fire *under it.* 24Then you call on the name
of your gods, and I will call on the name
of the LORD; and the God who [a]answers by
fire, He is God."

So all the people answered and said, "It
is well spoken."

25Now Elijah said to the prophets of Baal,
"Choose one bull for yourselves and prepare *it* first, for you *are* many; and call on
the name of your god, but put no fire *under it.*"

26So they took the bull which was given
them, and they prepared *it,* and called on
the name of Baal from morning even till
noon, saying, "O Baal, hear us!" But *there
was* [a]no voice; no one answered. Then
they leaped about the altar which they
had made.

27And so it was, at noon, that Elijah
mocked them and said, "Cry aloud, for he
is a god; either he is meditating, or he is
busy, or he is on a journey, *or* perhaps he
is sleeping and must be awakened." 28So
they cried aloud, and [a]cut themselves, as
was their custom, with knives and lances,
until the blood gushed out on them. 29And
when midday was past, [a]they prophesied
until the *time* of the offering of the *evening*
sacrifice. But *there was* [b]no voice; no one
answered, no one paid attention.

30Then Elijah said to all the people,
"Come near to me." So all the people came
near to him. [a]And he repaired the altar of
the LORD *that was* broken down. 31And Elijah took twelve stones, according to the
number of the tribes of the sons of Jacob,
to whom the word of the LORD had come,
saying, [a]"Israel shall be your name."[1] 32Then
with the stones he built an altar [a]in the
name of the LORD; and he made a trench
around the altar large enough to hold two
seahs of seed. 33And he [a]put the wood in order, cut the bull in pieces, and laid *it* on the
wood, and said, "Fill four waterpots with
water, and [b]pour *it* on the burnt sacrifice
and on the wood." 34Then he said, "Do *it*
a second time," and they did *it* a second
time; and he said, "Do *it* a third time," and
they did *it* a third time. 35So the water ran
all around the altar; and he also filled [a]the
trench with water.

18:12 [a] 2 Kin. 2:16; Ezek. 3:12, 14; Matt. 4:1; Acts 8:39 18:17 [a] 1 Kin. 21:20 [b] Josh. 7:25; Acts 16:20 18:18 [a] 1 Kin. 16:30–33; [2 Chr. 15:2] 18:19 [a] Josh. 19:26; 2 Kin. 2:25 [b] 1 Kin. 16:33 [1] A Canaanite goddess 18:20 [a] 1 Kin. 22:6 18:21 [a] 2 Kin. 17:41; [Matt. 6:24] [b] Josh. 24:15 18:22 [a] 1 Kin. 19:10, 14 [b] 1 Kin. 18:19 18:24 [a] 1 Kin. 18:38; 1 Chr. 21:26 18:26 [a] Ps. 115:5; Jer. 10:5; [1 Cor. 8:4] 18:28 [a] [Lev. 19:28; Deut. 14:1] 18:29 [a] Ex. 29:39, 41 [b] 1 Kin. 18:26 18:30 [a] 1 Kin. 19:10, 14; 2 Chr. 33:16 18:31 [a] Gen. 32:28; 35:10; 2 Kin. 17:34 [1] Genesis 32:28 18:32 [a] [Ex. 20:25; Col. 3:17] 18:33 [a] Gen. 22:9; Lev. 1:6–8 [b] Judg. 6:20 18:35 [a] 1 Kin. 18:32, 38

[36]And it came to pass, at *the time of* the
offering of the *evening* sacrifice, that Elijah the prophet came near and said, "LORD
[a]God of Abraham, Isaac, and Israel, [b]let it
be known this day that You *are* God in Israel and I *am* Your servant, and *that* [c]I have
done all these things at Your word. [37]Hear
me, O LORD, hear me, that this people may
know that You *are* the LORD God, and *that*
You have turned their hearts back *to You*
again."

#OXYGEN
1 KINGS 18:37
Exalt His Amazing Omnipresence

God's abundant blessings are found throughout the Bible and our lives. His greatest blessing to us, though, is Himself. God expects us to be an example to the next generation of always recognizing His presence. Teach them to recognize and enjoy His presence. Watch for His presence, **breathe,** and **exalt His amazing omnipresence.**

[38]Then [a]the fire of the LORD fell and consumed the burnt sacrifice, and the wood
and the stones and the dust, and it licked
up the water that *was* in the trench. [39]Now
when all the people saw *it,* they fell on their
faces; and they said, [a]"The LORD, He *is* God!
The LORD, He *is* God!"
[40]And Elijah said to them, [a]"Seize the
prophets of Baal! Do not let one of them
escape!" So they seized them; and Elijah
brought them down to the Brook [b]Kishon
and [c]executed them there.

The Drought Ends

[41]Then Elijah said to Ahab, "Go up, eat
and drink; for *there is* the sound of abundance of rain." [42]So Ahab went up to eat and
drink. And Elijah went up to the top of Carmel; [a]then he bowed down on the ground,
and put his face between his knees, [43]and
said to his servant, "Go up now, look toward the sea."
So he went up and looked, and said,
"*There is* nothing." And seven times he
said, "Go again."
[44]Then it came to pass the seventh *time,*
that he said, "There is a cloud, as small as
a man's hand, rising out of the sea!" So he
said, "Go up, say to Ahab, 'Prepare *your chariot,* and go down before the rain stops you.'"
[45]Now it happened in the meantime
that the sky became black with clouds and
wind, and there was a heavy rain. So Ahab
rode away and went to Jezreel. [46]Then the
[a]hand of the LORD came upon Elijah; and
he [b]girded up his loins and ran ahead of
Ahab to the entrance of Jezreel.

Elijah Escapes from Jezebel

19 And Ahab told Jezebel all that Elijah
had done, also how he had [a]executed
all the prophets with the sword. [2]Then Jezebel sent a messenger to Elijah, saying, [a]"So
let the gods do *to me,* and more also, if I
do not make your life as the life of one of
them by tomorrow about this time." [3]And
when he saw *that,* he arose and ran for his
life, and went to Beersheba, which *belongs*
to Judah, and left his servant there.
[4]But he himself went a day's journey into
the wilderness, and came and sat down
under a broom tree. And he [a]prayed that
he might die, and said, "It is enough! Now,
LORD, take my life, for I *am* no better than
my fathers!"
[5]Then as he lay and slept under a broom
tree, suddenly an angel[1] touched him,
and said to him, "Arise *and* eat." [6]Then he
looked, and there by his head *was* a cake
baked on coals, and a jar of water. So he ate
and drank, and lay down again. [7]And the
angel[1] of the LORD came back the second
time, and touched him, and said, "Arise
and eat, because the journey *is* too great
for you." [8]So he arose, and ate and drank;
and he went in the strength of that food
forty days and [a]forty nights as far as [b]Ho-
reb, the mountain of God.

18:36 [a] Gen. 28:13; Ex. 3:6; 4:5; [Matt. 22:32] [b] 1 Kin. 8:43; 2 Kin. 19:19 [c] Num. 16:28 **18:38** [a] Gen. 15:17; Lev. 9:24; 10:1, 2; Judg. 6:21; 2 Kin. 1:12; 1 Chr. 21:26; 2 Chr. 7:1; Job 1:16 **18:39** [a] 1 Kin. 18:21, 24 **18:40** [a] 2 Kin. 10:25 [b] Judg. 4:7; 5:21 [c] [Deut. 13:5; 18:20] **18:42** [a] James 5:17, 18 **18:46** [a] 2 Kin. 3:15; Is. 8:11; Ezek. 3:14 [b] 2 Kin. 4:29; 9:1; Jer. 1:17; 1 Pet. 1:13 **19:1** [a] 1 Kin. 18:40 **19:2** [a] Ruth 1:17; 1 Kin. 20:10; 2 Kin. 6:31 **19:4** [a] Num. 11:15; Jer. 20:14–18; Jon. 4:3, 8 **19:5** [1] Or *Angel* **19:7** [1] Or *Angel* **19:8** [a] Ex. 24:18; 34:28; Deut. 9:9–11, 18; Matt. 4:2 [b] Ex. 3:1; 4:27

9 And there he went into a cave, and
spent the night in that place; and behold,
the word of the LORD *came* to him, and He
said to him, "What are you doing here, Elijah?"
10 So he said, [a]"I have been very [b]zealous
for the LORD God of hosts; for the children
of Israel have forsaken Your covenant, torn
down Your altars, and [c]killed Your prophets
with the sword. [d]I alone am left; and they
seek to take my life."

God's Revelation to Elijah

11 Then He said, "Go out, and stand [a]on
the mountain before the LORD." And behold, the LORD [b]passed by, and [c]a great and
strong wind tore into the mountains and
broke the rocks in pieces before the LORD,
but the LORD *was* not in the wind; and after the wind an earthquake, *but* the LORD
was not in the earthquake; 12 and after the
earthquake a fire, *but* the LORD *was* not
in the fire; and after the fire a still small
voice.
13 So it was, when Elijah heard *it,* that [a]he
wrapped his face in his mantle and went
out and stood in the entrance of the cave.
[b]Suddenly a voice *came* to him, and said,
"What are you doing here, Elijah?"
14 [a]And he said, "I have been very zealous for the LORD God of hosts; because the
children of Israel have forsaken Your covenant, torn down Your altars, and killed
Your prophets with the sword. I alone am
left; and they seek to take my life."
15 Then the LORD said to him: "Go, return
on your way to the Wilderness of Damascus; [a]and when you arrive, anoint Hazael
as king over Syria. 16 Also you shall anoint
[a]Jehu the son of Nimshi *as* king over Israel.
And [b]Elisha the son of Shaphat of Abel Meholah you shall anoint *as* prophet in your
place. 17 [a]It shall be *that* whoever escapes
the sword of Hazael, Jehu will [b]kill; and
whoever escapes the sword of Jehu, [c]Eli-
sha will kill. 18 [a]Yet I have reserved seven
thousand in Israel, all whose knees have
not bowed to Baal, [b]and every mouth that
has not kissed him."

Elisha Follows Elijah

19 So he departed from there, and found
Elisha the son of Shaphat, who *was* plowing *with* twelve yoke *of oxen* before him,
and he was with the twelfth. Then Elijah
passed by him and threw his [a]mantle on
him. 20 And he left the oxen and ran after
Elijah, and said, [a]"Please let me kiss my
father and my mother, and *then* I will follow you."
And he said to him, "Go back again, for
what have I done to you?"
21 So *Elisha* turned back from him, and
took a yoke of oxen and slaughtered them
and [a]boiled their flesh, using the oxen's
equipment, and gave it to the people, and
they ate. Then he arose and followed Elijah, and became his servant.

Ahab Defeats the Syrians

20 Now [a]Ben-Hadad the king of Syria
gathered all his forces together;
thirty-two kings *were* with him, with horses
and chariots. And he went up and besieged
[b]Samaria, and made war against it. 2 Then
he sent messengers into the city to Ahab
king of Israel, and said to him, "Thus says
Ben-Hadad: 3 'Your silver and your gold *are*
mine; your loveliest wives and children
are mine.' "
4 And the king of Israel answered and
said, "My lord, O king, just as you say, I and
all that I have *are* yours."
5 Then the messengers came back and
said, "Thus speaks Ben-Hadad, saying,
'Indeed I have sent to you, saying, "You
shall deliver to me your silver and your
gold, your wives and your children"; 6 but
I will send my servants to you tomorrow
about this time, and they shall search your
house and the houses of your servants.
And it shall be, *that* whatever is pleasant
in your eyes, they will put *it* in their hands
and take *it.*' "
7 So the king of Israel called all the elders
of the land, and said, "Notice, please, and
see how this *man* seeks trouble, for he sent
to me for my wives, my children, my silver,
and my gold; and I did not deny him."

19:10 [a] Rom. 11:3 [b] Num. 25:11, 13; Ps. 69:9 [c] 1 Kin. 18:4 [d] 1 Kin. 18:22; Rom. 11:3 19:11 [a] Ex. 19:20; 24:12, 18 [b] Ex. 33:21, 22 [c] Ezek. 1:4; 37:7 19:13 [a] Ex. 3:6; Is. 6:2 [b] 1 Kin. 19:9 19:14 [a] 1 Kin. 19:10 19:15 [a] 2 Kin. 8:8–15 19:16 [a] 2 Kin. 9:1–10 [b] 1 Kin. 19:19–21; 2 Kin. 2:9–15 19:17 [a] 2 Kin. 8:12; 13:3, 22 [b] 2 Kin. 9:14—10:28 [c] [Hos. 6:5] 19:18 [a] Rom. 11:4 [b] Hos. 13:2 19:19 [a] 1 Sam. 28:14; 2 Kin. 2:8, 13, 14 19:20 [a] [Matt. 8:21, 22; Luke 9:61, 62]; Acts 20:37 19:21 [a] 2 Sam. 24:22 20:1 [a] 1 Kin. 15:18, 20; 2 Kin. 6:24 [b] 1 Kin. 16:24; 2 Kin. 6:24

8 And all the elders and all the people
said to him, "Do not listen or consent."
9 Therefore he said to the messengers
of Ben-Hadad, "Tell my lord the king, 'All
that you sent for to your servant the first
time I will do, but this thing I cannot do.'"
And the messengers departed and
brought back word to him.
10 Then Ben-Hadad sent to him and said,
[a]"The gods do so to me, and more also, if
enough dust is left of Samaria for a handful for each of the people who follow me."
11 So the king of Israel answered and said,
"Tell *him,* 'Let not the one who puts on *his*
armor [a]boast like the one who takes *it off.*'"
12 And it happened when *Ben-Hadad*
heard this message, as he and the kings
were [a]drinking at the command post, that
he said to his servants, "Get ready." And
they got ready to attack the city.
13 Suddenly a prophet approached Ahab
king of Israel, saying, "Thus says the LORD:
'Have you seen all this great multitude? Behold, [a]I will deliver it into your hand today,
and you shall know that I *am* the LORD.'"
14 So Ahab said, "By whom?"
And he said, "Thus says the LORD: 'By
the young leaders of the provinces.'"
Then he said, "Who will set the battle
in order?"
And he answered, "You."
15 Then he mustered the young leaders of
the provinces, and there were two hundred
and thirty-two; and after them he mustered
all the people, all the children of Israel—
seven thousand.
16 So they went out at noon. Meanwhile
Ben-Hadad and the thirty-two kings helping him were [a]getting drunk at the command post. 17 The young leaders of the
provinces went out first. And Ben-Hadad
sent out *a patrol,* and they told him, saying,
"Men are coming out of Samaria!" 18 So he
said, "If they have come out for peace, take
them alive; and if they have come out for
war, take them alive."
19 Then these young leaders of the provinces went out of the city with the army
which followed them. 20 And each one killed
his man; so the Syrians fled, and Israel
pursued them; and Ben-Hadad the king
of Syria escaped on a horse with the cavalry. 21 Then the king of Israel went out and
attacked the horses and chariots, and killed
the Syrians with a great slaughter.
22 And the prophet came to the king of Israel and said to him, "Go, strengthen yourself; take note, and see what you should do,
[a]for in the spring of the year the king of
Syria will come up against you."

The Syrians Again Defeated

23 Then the servants of the king of Syria
said to him, "Their gods *are* gods of the
hills. Therefore they were stronger than
we; but if we fight against them in the plain,
surely we will be stronger than they. 24 So do
this thing: Dismiss the kings, each from his
position, and put captains in their places;
25 and you shall muster an army like the
army that you have lost, horse for horse
and chariot for chariot. Then we will fight
against them in the plain; surely we will be
stronger than they."
And he listened to their voice and did so.
26 So it was, in the spring of the year, that
Ben-Hadad mustered the Syrians and went
up to [a]Aphek to fight against Israel. 27 And
the children of Israel were mustered and
given provisions, and they went against
them. Now the children of Israel encamped
before them like two little flocks of goats,
while the Syrians filled the [a]countryside.
28 Then a [a]man of God came and spoke
to the king of Israel, and said, "Thus says
the LORD: 'Because the Syrians have said,
"The LORD *is* God of the hills, but He *is* not
God of the valleys," therefore [b]I will deliver
all this great multitude into your hand, and
you shall know that I *am* the LORD.'" 29 And
they encamped opposite each other for
seven days. So it was that on the seventh
day the battle was joined; and the children
of Israel killed one hundred thousand foot
soldiers *of* the Syrians in one day. 30 But the
rest fled to Aphek, into the city; then a wall
fell on twenty-seven thousand of the men
who were left.
And Ben-Hadad fled and went into the
city, into an inner chamber.

20:10 [a] 1 Kin. 19:2; 2 Kin. 6:31 **20:11** [a] Prov. 27:1; [Eccl. 7:8] **20:12** [a] 1 Kin. 20:16 **20:13** [a] 1 Kin. 20:28 **20:16** [a] 1 Kin. 16:9; 20:12; [Prov. 20:1] **20:22** [a] 2 Sam. 11:1; 1 Kin. 20:26 **20:26** [a] Josh. 13:4; 2 Kin. 13:17 **20:27** [a] Judg. 6:3–5; 1 Sam. 13:5–8 **20:28** [a] 1 Kin. 17:18 [b] 1 Kin. 20:13

Ahab's Treaty with Ben-Hadad

31Then his servants said to him, "Look now, we have heard that the kings of the house of Israel *are* merciful kings. Please, let us [a]put sackcloth around our waists and ropes around our heads, and go out to the king of Israel; perhaps he will spare your life." 32So they wore sackcloth around their waists and *put* ropes around their heads, and came to the king of Israel and said, "Your servant Ben-Hadad says, 'Please let me live.'"

And he said, "*Is* he still alive? He *is* my brother."

33Now the men were watching closely to see whether *any sign of mercy would come* from him; and they quickly grasped *at this word* and said, "Your brother Ben-Hadad."

So he said, "Go, bring him." Then Ben-Hadad came out to him; and he had him come up into the chariot.

34So *Ben-Hadad* said to him, [a]"The cities which my father took from your father I will restore; and you may set up marketplaces for yourself in Damascus, as my father did in Samaria."

Then *Ahab said,* "I will send you away with this treaty." So he made a treaty with him and sent him away.

Ahab Condemned

35Now a certain man of [a]the sons of the prophets said to his neighbor [b]by the word of the LORD, "Strike me, please." And the man refused to strike him. 36Then he said to him, "Because you have not obeyed the voice of the LORD, surely, as soon as you depart from me, a lion shall kill you." And as soon as he left him, [a]a lion found him and killed him.

37And he found another man, and said, "Strike me, please." So the man struck him, inflicting a wound. 38Then the prophet departed and waited for the king by the road, and disguised himself with a bandage over his eyes. 39Now [a]as the king passed by, he cried out to the king and said, "Your servant went out into the midst of the battle; and there, a man came over and brought a man to me, and said, 'Guard this man; if by any means he is missing, [b]your life shall be for his life, or else you shall pay a talent of silver.' 40While your servant was busy here and there, he was gone."

Then the king of Israel said to him, "So *shall* your judgment *be;* you yourself have decided *it.*"

41And he hastened to take the bandage away from his eyes; and the king of Israel recognized him as one of the prophets. 42Then he said to him, "Thus says the LORD: [a]'Because you have let slip out of *your* hand a man whom I appointed to utter destruction, therefore your life shall go for his life, and your people for his people.'"

43So the king of Israel [a]went to his house sullen and displeased, and came to Samaria.

Naboth Is Murdered for His Vineyard

21 And it came to pass after these things *that* Naboth the Jezreelite had a vineyard which *was* in [a]Jezreel, next to the palace of Ahab king of Samaria. 2So Ahab spoke to Naboth, saying, "Give me your [a]vineyard, that I may have it for a vegetable garden, because it *is* near, next to my house; and for it I will give you a vineyard better than it. *Or,* if it seems good to you, I will give you its worth in money."

3But Naboth said to Ahab, "The LORD forbid [a]that I should give the inheritance of my fathers to you!"

4So Ahab went into his house sullen and displeased because of the word which Naboth the Jezreelite had spoken to him; for he had said, "I will not give you the inheritance of my fathers." And he lay down on his bed, and turned away his face, and would eat no food. 5But [a]Jezebel his wife came to him, and said to him, "Why is your spirit so sullen that you eat no food?"

6He said to her, "Because I spoke to Naboth the Jezreelite, and said to him, 'Give me your vineyard for money; or else, if it pleases you, I will give you *another* vineyard for it.' And he answered, 'I will not give you my vineyard.'"

7Then Jezebel his wife said to him, "You now exercise authority over Israel! Arise, eat food, and let your heart be cheerful; I

20:31 [a] Gen. 37:34; 2 Sam. 3:31 20:34 [a] 1 Kin. 15:20 20:35 [a] 2 Kin. 2:3, 5, 7, 15 [b] 1 Kin. 13:17, 18 20:36 [a] 1 Kin. 13:24 20:39 [a] 2 Sam. 12:1 [b] 2 Kin. 10:24 20:42 [a] 1 Kin. 22:31–37 20:43 [a] 1 Kin. 21:4 21:1 [a] Judg. 6:33; 1 Kin. 18:45, 46 21:2 [a] 1 Sam. 8:14 21:3 [a] [Lev. 25:23; Num. 36:7; Ezek. 46:18] 21:5 [a] 1 Kin. 19:1, 2

will give you the vineyard of Naboth the Jezreelite."

8And she wrote letters in Ahab's name, sealed *them* with his seal, and sent the letters to the elders and the nobles who *were* dwelling in the city with Naboth. 9She wrote in the letters, saying,

> Proclaim a fast, and seat Naboth with high honor among the people; 10and seat two men, scoundrels, before him to bear witness against him, saying, "You have [a]blasphemed God and the king." *Then* take him out, and [b]stone him, that he may die.

11So the men of his city, the elders and nobles who were inhabitants of his city, did as Jezebel had sent to them, as it *was* written in the letters which she had sent to them. 12[a]They proclaimed a fast, and seated Naboth with high honor among the people. 13And two men, scoundrels, came in and sat before him; and the scoundrels [a]witnessed against him, against Naboth, in the presence of the people, saying, "Naboth has blasphemed God and the king!" [b]Then they took him outside the city and stoned him with stones, so that he died. 14Then they sent to Jezebel, saying, "Naboth has been stoned and is dead."

15And it came to pass, when Jezebel heard that Naboth had been stoned and was dead, that Jezebel said to Ahab, "Arise, take possession of the vineyard of Naboth the Jezreelite, which he refused to give you for money; for Naboth is not alive, but dead." 16So it was, when Ahab heard that Naboth was dead, that Ahab got up and went down to take possession of the vineyard of Naboth the Jezreelite.

The LORD Condemns Ahab

17[a]Then the word of the LORD came to [b]Elijah the Tishbite, saying, 18"Arise, go down to meet Ahab king of Israel, [a]who *lives* in Samaria. There *he is,* in the vineyard of Naboth, where he has gone down to take possession of it. 19You shall speak to him, saying, 'Thus says the LORD: "Have you murdered and also taken possession?"' And you shall speak to him, saying, 'Thus says the LORD: [a]"In the place where dogs licked the blood of Naboth, dogs shall lick your blood, even yours."'"

20So Ahab said to Elijah, [a]"Have you found me, O my enemy?"

And he answered, "I have found *you,* because [b]you have sold yourself to do evil in the sight of the LORD: 21'Behold, [a]I will bring calamity on you. I will take away your [b]posterity, and will cut off from Ahab [c]every male in Israel, both [d]bond and free. 22I will make your house like the house of [a]Jeroboam the son of Nebat, and like the house of [b]Baasha the son of Ahijah, because of the provocation with which you have provoked *Me* to anger, and made Israel sin.' 23And [a]concerning Jezebel the LORD also spoke, saying, 'The dogs shall eat Jezebel by the wall[1] of Jezreel.' 24The dogs shall eat [a]whoever belongs to Ahab and dies in the city, and the birds of the air shall eat whoever dies in the field."

25But [a]there was no one like Ahab who sold himself to do wickedness in the sight of the LORD, [b]because Jezebel his wife stirred him up. 26And he behaved very abominably in following idols, according to all [a]*that* the Amorites had done, whom the LORD had cast out before the children of Israel.

27So it was, when Ahab heard those words, that he tore his clothes and [a]put sackcloth on his body, and fasted and lay in sackcloth, and went about mourning.

28And the word of the LORD came to Elijah the Tishbite, saying, 29"See how Ahab has humbled himself before Me? Because he [a]has humbled himself before Me, I will not bring the calamity in his days. [b]In the days of his son I will bring the calamity on his house."

Micaiah Warns Ahab
(2 Chr. 18:1–27)

22 Now three years passed without war between Syria and Israel. 2Then it came to pass, in the third year,

21:10 [a] [Ex. 22:28; Lev. 24:15, 16]; Acts 6:11 [b] [Lev. 24:14] 21:12 [a] Is. 58:4 21:13 [a] [Ex. 20:16; 23:1, 7] [b] 2 Kin. 9:26; 2 Chr. 24:21; Acts 7:58, 59; Heb. 11:37 21:17 [a] [Ps. 9:12] [b] 1 Kin. 19:1 21:18 [a] 1 Kin. 13:32; 2 Chr. 22:9 21:19 [a] 1 Kin. 22:38; 2 Kin. 9:26 21:20 [a] 1 Kin. 18:17 [b] 1 Kin. 21:25; 2 Kin. 17:17; [Rom. 7:14] 21:21 [a] 1 Kin. 14:10; 2 Kin. 9:8 [b] 2 Kin. 10:10 [c] 1 Sam. 25:22 [d] 1 Kin. 14:10 21:22 [a] 1 Kin. 15:29 [b] 1 Kin. 16:3, 11 21:23 [a] 2 Kin. 9:10, 30–37 [1] Following Masoretic Text and Septuagint; some Hebrew manuscripts, Syriac, Targum, and Vulgate read *plot of ground* (compare 2 Kings 9:36). 21:24 [a] 1 Kin. 14:11; 16:4 21:25 [a] 1 Kin. 16:30–33; 21:20 [b] 1 Kin. 16:31 21:26 [a] Gen. 15:16; [Lev. 18:25–30]; 2 Kin. 21:11 21:27 [a] Gen. 37:34; 2 Sam. 3:31; 2 Kin. 6:30 21:29 [a] [2 Kin. 22:19] [b] 2 Kin. 9:25; 10:11, 17

that [a]Jehoshaphat the king of Judah went
down to *visit* the king of Israel.
3 And the king of Israel said to his servants, "Do you know that [a]Ramoth in Gilead *is* ours, but we hesitate to take it out of
the hand of the king of Syria?" 4 So he said
to Jehoshaphat, "Will you go with me to
fight at Ramoth Gilead?"
Jehoshaphat said to the king of Israel,
[a]"I *am* as you *are,* my people as your people,
my horses as your horses." 5 Also Jehoshaphat said to the king of Israel, [a]"Please
inquire for the word of the LORD today."
6 Then the king of Israel [a]gathered the
prophets together, about four hundred
men, and said to them, "Shall I go against
Ramoth Gilead to fight, or shall I refrain?"
So they said, "Go up, for the Lord will deliver *it* into the hand of the king."
7 And [a]Jehoshaphat said, "*Is there* not
still a prophet of the LORD here, that we
may inquire of Him?"[1]
8 So the king of Israel said to Jehoshaphat, "*There is* still one man, Micaiah the
son of Imlah, by whom we may inquire
of the LORD; but I hate him, because he
does not prophesy good concerning me,
but evil."
And Jehoshaphat said, "Let not the king
say such things!"
9 Then the king of Israel called an officer and said, "Bring Micaiah the son of Imlah quickly!"
10 The king of Israel and Jehoshaphat the
king of Judah, having put on *their* robes,
sat each on his throne, at a threshing floor
at the entrance of the gate of Samaria; and
all the prophets prophesied before them.
11 Now Zedekiah the son of Chenaanah had
made [a]horns of iron for himself; and he
said, "Thus says the LORD: 'With these you
shall [b]gore the Syrians until they are destroyed.'" 12 And all the prophets prophesied so, saying, "Go up to Ramoth Gilead
and prosper, for the LORD will deliver *it*
into the king's hand."
13 Then the messenger who had gone to
call Micaiah spoke to him, saying, "Now
listen, the words of the prophets with one
accord encourage the king. Please, let your
word be like the word of one of them, and
speak encouragement."
14 And Micaiah said, "*As* the LORD lives,
[a]whatever the LORD says to me, that I will
speak."
15 Then he came to the king; and the king
said to him, "Micaiah, shall we go to war
against Ramoth Gilead, or shall we refrain?"
And he answered him, "Go and prosper,
for the LORD will deliver *it* into the hand
of the king!"
16 So the king said to him, "How many
times shall I make you swear that you tell
me nothing but the truth in the name of
the LORD?"
17 Then he said, "I saw all Israel [a]scattered
on the mountains, as sheep that have no
shepherd. And the LORD said, 'These have
no master. Let each return to his house in
peace.'"
18 And the king of Israel said to Jehoshaphat, "Did I not tell you he would not
prophesy good concerning me, but evil?"
19 Then *Micaiah* said, "Therefore hear the
word of the LORD: [a]I saw the LORD sitting
on His throne, [b]and all the host of heaven
standing by, on His right hand and on His
left. 20 And the LORD said, 'Who will persuade Ahab to go up, that he may fall at Ramoth Gilead?' So one spoke in this manner,
and another spoke in that manner. 21 Then
a spirit came forward and stood before the
LORD, and said, 'I will persuade him.' 22 The
LORD said to him, 'In what way?' So he said,
'I will go out and be a lying spirit in the
mouth of all his prophets.' And the LORD
said, [a]'You shall persuade *him,* and also prevail. Go out and do so.' 23 [a]Therefore look!
The LORD has put a lying spirit in the mouth
of all these prophets of yours, and the LORD
has declared disaster against you."
24 Now Zedekiah the son of Chenaanah
went near and [a]struck Micaiah on the cheek,
and said, [b]"Which way did the spirit from
the LORD go from me to speak to you?"
25 And Micaiah said, "Indeed, you shall
see on that day when you go into an [a]inner
chamber to hide!"

22:2 [a] 1 Kin. 15:24; 2 Chr. 18:2 **22:3** [a] Deut. 4:43; Josh. 21:38; 1 Kin. 4:13 **22:4** [a] 2 Kin. 3:7 **22:5** [a] 2 Kin. 3:11 **22:6** [a] 1 Kin. 18:19 **22:7** [a] 2 Kin. 3:11 [1] Or *him* **22:11** [a] Zech. 1:18–21 [b] Deut. 33:17 **22:14** [a] Num. 22:38; 24:13 **22:17** [a] Num. 27:17; 1 Kin. 22:34–36; 2 Chr. 18:16; Matt. 9:36; Mark 6:34 **22:19** [a] Is. 6:1; Ezek. 1:26–28; Dan. 7:9 [b] Job 1:6; 2:1; Ps. 103:20; Dan. 7:10; Zech. 1:10; [Matt. 18:10; Heb. 1:7, 14] **22:22** [a] Judg. 9:23; 1 Sam. 16:14; 18:10; 19:9; Job 12:16; [Ezek. 14:9; 2 Thess. 2:11] **22:23** [a] [Ezek. 14:9] **22:24** [a] Jer. 20:2 [b] 2 Chr. 18:23 **22:25** [a] 1 Kin. 20:30

26So the king of Israel said, "Take Micaiah, and return him to Amon the governor
of the city and to Joash the king's son; 27and
say, 'Thus says the king: "Put this *fellow* in
[a]prison, and feed him with bread of affliction and water of affliction, until I come
in peace." ' "
28But Micaiah said, "If you ever return
in peace, [a]the LORD has not spoken by me."
And he said, "Take heed, all you people!"

Ahab Dies in Battle
(2 Chr. 18:28–34)

29So the king of Israel and Jehoshaphat
the king of Judah went up to Ramoth Gilead. 30And the king of Israel said to Jehoshaphat, "I will disguise myself and go into
battle; but you put on your robes." So the
king of Israel [a]disguised himself and went
into battle.
31Now the [a]king of Syria had commanded
the thirty-two [b]captains of his chariots, saying, "Fight with no one small or great, but
only with the king of Israel." 32So it was,
when the captains of the chariots saw Jehoshaphat, that they said, "Surely it *is* the
king of Israel!" Therefore they turned
aside to fight against him, and Jehoshaphat [a]cried out. 33And it happened, when
the captains of the chariots saw that it *was*
not the king of Israel, that they turned back
from pursuing him. 34Now a *certain* man
drew a bow at random, and struck the king
of Israel between the joints of his armor. So
he said to the driver of his chariot, "Turn
around and take me out of the battle, for I
am wounded."
35The battle increased that day; and the
king was propped up in his chariot, facing
the Syrians, and died at evening. The blood
ran out from the wound onto the floor of
the chariot. 36Then, as the sun was going
down, a shout went throughout the army,
saying, "Every man to his city, and every
man to his own country!"
37So the king died, and was brought to
Samaria. And they buried the king in Samaria. 38Then *someone* washed the chariot
at a pool in Samaria, and the dogs licked
up his blood while the harlots bathed,[1] according [a]to the word of the LORD which He
had spoken.
39Now the rest of the acts of Ahab, and
all that he did, [a]the ivory house which he
built and all the cities that he built, *are* they
not written in the book of the chronicles of
the kings of Israel? 40So Ahab rested with
his fathers. Then [a]Ahaziah his son reigned
in his place.

Jehoshaphat Reigns in Judah
(2 Chr. 20:31—21:1)

41[a]Jehoshaphat the son of Asa had become king over Judah in the fourth year
of Ahab king of Israel. 42Jehoshaphat *was*
thirty-five years old when he became king,
and he reigned twenty-five years in Jerusalem. His mother's name *was* Azubah the
daughter of Shilhi. 43And [a]he walked in all
the ways of his father Asa. He did not turn
aside from them, doing *what was* right in
the eyes of the LORD. Nevertheless [b]the
high places were not taken away, *for* the
people offered sacrifices and burned incense on the high places. 44Also [a]Jehosh-
aphat made [b]peace with the king of Israel.
45Now the rest of the acts of Jehoshaphat, the might that he showed, and how he
made war, *are* they not written [a]in the book
of the chronicles of the kings of Judah?
46[a]And the rest of the perverted persons,[1]
who remained in the days of his father Asa,
he banished from the land. 47[a]*There was*
then no king in Edom, only a deputy of
the king.
48[a]Jehoshaphat [b]made merchant ships[1]
to go to [c]Ophir for gold; [d]but they never
sailed, for the ships were wrecked at [e]Ezion
Geber. 49Then Ahaziah the son of Ahab said
to Jehoshaphat, "Let my servants go with
your servants in the ships." But Jehoshaphat would not.
50And [a]Jehoshaphat rested with his fathers, and was buried with his fathers in
the City of David his father. Then Jehoram
his son reigned in his place.

22:27 [a] 2 Chr. 16:10; 18:25–27 **22:28** [a] Num. 16:29; Deut. 18:20–22 **22:30** [a] 2 Chr. 35:22 **22:31** [a] 1 Kin. 20:1 [b] 1 Kin. 20:24; 2 Chr. 18:30 **22:32** [a] 2 Chr. 18:31 **22:38** [a] 1 Kin. 21:19 [1] Syriac and Targum read *they washed his armor.* **22:39** [a] Ps. 45:8; Amos 3:15 **22:40** [a] 2 Kin. 1:2, 18 **22:41** [a] 2 Chr. 20:31 **22:43** [a] 2 Chr. 17:3; 20:32, 33 [b] 1 Kin. 14:23; 15:14; 2 Kin. 12:3 **22:44** [a] 2 Chr. 19:2 [b] 2 Chr. 18:1 **22:45** [a] 2 Chr. 20:34 **22:46** [a] Gen. 19:5; Deut. 23:17; 1 Kin. 14:24; 15:12; 2 Kin. 23:7; Jude 7 [1] Hebrew *qadesh,* that is, one practicing sodomy and prostitution in religious rituals **22:47** [a] 2 Sam. 8:14; 2 Kin. 3:9; 8:20 **22:48** [a] 2 Chr. 20:35–37 [b] 1 Kin. 10:22 [c] 1 Kin. 9:28 [d] 2 Chr. 20:37 [e] 1 Kin. 9:26 [1] Or *ships of Tarshish* **22:50** [a] 2 Chr. 21:1

Ahaziah Reigns in Israel
51[a]Ahaziah the son of Ahab became king
over Israel in Samaria in the seventeenth
year of Jehoshaphat king of Judah, and
reigned two years over Israel. 52He did evil
in the sight of the LORD, and [a]walked in
the way of his father and in the way of his
mother and in the way of Jeroboam the son
of Nebat, who had made Israel sin; 53for
[a]he served Baal and worshiped him, and
provoked the LORD God of Israel to anger,
[b]according to all that his father had done.

22:51 [a] 1 Kin. 22:40 22:52 [a] 1 Kin. 15:26; 21:25 22:53 [a] Judg. 2:11 [b] 1 Kin. 16:30–32

THE SECOND BOOK OF THE

KINGS

OVERVIEW

The author of 2 Kings is unknown, but it has been suggested that Ezra, Ezekiel, or Jeremiah may have written this book. Because 2 Kings was originally part of the same book as 1 Kings, its author would be the same as of that book.

The Book of 2 Kings continues to tell the history of the northern kingdom of Israel and the southern kingdom of Judah, highlighting their spiritual successes and failures. It also explains why God removed His protection from Israel and Judah, allowing them to be conquered by foreign powers.

Second Kings opens where 1 Kings ends. Ahab had died, and his son Ahaziah was the new ruler of Israel. As Elijah had prophesied, Ahaziah died and was succeeded by Jehoram (see 2 Kin. 1:1–18).

Elijah knew his days on earth were reaching an end, so he prepared Elisha to continue his prophetic ministry after his departure (see 2:1–8). Elisha requested that Elijah leave him a double portion of his spirit, which he received when he saw Elijah taken to heaven by a whirlwind without experiencing death (see vv. 9–11).

Like Elijah, Elisha became a well-known prophet and performed numerous miracles. He parted the Jordan River as Elijah had done (see 2:12–15; cf. 2:8), multiplied a widow's oil (see 4:1–7), raised a child from the dead (see 4:8–37), made poisonous food edible (see 4:38–41), cured a man of leprosy (see 5:8–14), and made an ax head float (see 6:1–7).

As 2 Kings continues the history of various kings who ruled Israel and Judah, most were wicked, such as Jehu (chs. 9–10) and Manasseh (see 21:1–18). A few of Judah's kings, however, were good, including Jehoash (ch. 12) and Josiah (see 22:1—23:25). The people experienced prosperity under the kings who followed God and suffered under those who did not.

Another of Judah's good kings was Hezekiah, who ruled for twenty-nine years. During his reign, Assyria destroyed the kingdom of Israel and threatened Judah (see 17:1–23; 18:9–16). However, God intervened. As the prophet Isaiah promised, God did not allow harm to come to Jerusalem, the capital of Judah. The Lord defended the city as the angel of the Lord killed the Assyrian army before they could enter Jerusalem (see 19:32–36).

But, like each of Judah's other periods of revival, this one, too, came to an end. Manasseh, the son of Hezekiah, angered God by rebuilding the pagan places of worship that Hezekiah had destroyed (see 21:1–18). Displeased by these actions, God said, "I will also remove Judah from My sight, as I have removed Israel" (23:27). Eventually, King Nebuchadnezzar of Babylon invaded Judah and destroyed the nation, sending most of the people into exile (see 24:10—25:30).

The theme of 2 Kings is God's faithfulness. God promised to bless those in covenant with Him. This book demonstrates how God deals with those who are faithful in contrast to those who are unfaithful. During the times that the kings of Judah led the people in righteousness and according to God's law, He blessed them. When the wicked kings reigned and went against God, He sent prophets to warn them of the consequences of their behavior. Then, when they

did not heed the warnings of the prophets, God brought His judgment on them, as a reminder that there are consequences to disobedience.

BREATHE IT IN

One of the foundational elements of God's covenant with His people is that they were to have no other gods before Him (see Ex. 20:3). But throughout His relationship with the Israelites, there were times when they turned away from God and worshiped idols. Idolatry was rampant in the Book of 2 Kings under evil rulers who disobeyed God. Consequently, God's judgment fell upon His rebellious people. But when faithful kings ruled, Judah flourished under God's blessings.

Being in covenant relationship with God requires that Christians recognize God's authority and depend on Him alone. We have all lived under many leaders, some good and some bad. We vote for political candidates because we expect certain things of them—namely, that the actions they take will enhance our lives and the lives of the people around us. However, we must realize that God's rule surpasses them all. Participating in the political system and exercising the right to vote is important and commendable. However, we should not make human leaders our gods and depend on them to give us what we need. Our covenant is with God, not with any human. Our foundational beliefs and our adherence to God's laws should not shift according to the beliefs and practices of those in power. We must remain true to God, His Word, and His ways.

Remaining focused on God is difficult when all those around us focus on other people and things. Many make gods of material possessions like homes and cars. Others make success their god, striving to make the most money and achieve positions of status and acclaim. Still others make fame their god, seeking notoriety and power. But our God is a jealous God and will not share our loyalty or worship. We provoke His anger and discipline when we give His rightful place away to the idols of life.

Second Kings provides many examples of God's anger and discipline in response to His people worshiping other gods. But His anger was also accompanied by His mercy and grace. God sent prophets to warn the people of what He would do if they did not stop their wicked ways. The prophets encouraged the people to set aside their idols and return to God, but they refused. It is never wise to ignore God's warnings. The accounts in 2 Kings should discourage us from idolatry, encourage us to repent, and strengthen our resolve to live only for the one true God. With so much confusion in the world, everyone is looking for something or someone to believe in. However, seeking fulfillment outside of God is a recipe for failure.

Declare the Lord as the only true and living God in all areas of your life. Have no other gods before Him and separate from those engaged in idolatry. Do not follow leaders who are unjust. Do not seek material possessions, fortune, and fame. Seek God. Honor your commitment to God and He will honor you. When the world around you turns away from Him to other gods, do not stray. Stand firm in your faith and declare the sovereignty of God.

†

THE SECOND BOOK OF THE

KINGS

God Judges Ahaziah

1 Moab [a]rebelled against Israel [b]after the
death of Ahab.
2 Now [a]Ahaziah fell through the lattice
of his upper room in Samaria, and was injured; so he sent messengers and said to
them, "Go, inquire of [b]Baal-Zebub, the god
of [c]Ekron, whether I shall recover from this
injury." 3 But the angel[1] of the LORD said to
Elijah the Tishbite, "Arise, go up to meet the
messengers of the king of Samaria, and say
to them, '*Is it* because *there is* no God in Israel *that* you are going to inquire of Baal-
Zebub, the god of Ekron?' 4 Now therefore,
thus says the LORD: 'You shall not come
down from the bed to which you have gone
up, but you shall surely die.'" So Elijah departed.
5 And when the messengers returned
to him, he said to them, "Why have you
come back?"
6 So they said to him, "A man came up to
meet us, and said to us, 'Go, return to the
king who sent you, and say to him, "Thus
says the LORD: '*Is it* because *there is* no God
in Israel *that* you are sending to inquire
of Baal-Zebub, the god of Ekron? Therefore you shall not come down from the bed
to which you have gone up, but you shall
surely die.'"'"
7 Then he said to them, "What kind of
man *was it* who came up to meet you and
told you these words?"
8 So they answered him, [a]"A hairy man
wearing a leather belt around his waist."
And he said, [b]"It *is* Elijah the Tishbite."
9 Then the king sent to him a captain of
fifty with his fifty men. So he went up to
him; and there he was, sitting on the top of
a hill. And he spoke to him: "Man of God,
the king has said, 'Come down!'"
10 So Elijah answered and said to the captain of fifty, "If I *am* a man of God, then [a]let
fire come down from heaven and consume
you and your fifty men." And fire came
down from heaven and consumed him and
his fifty. 11 Then he sent to him another captain of fifty with his fifty men.
And he answered and said to him: "Man
of God, thus has the king said, 'Come down
quickly!'"
12 So Elijah answered and said to them,
"If I *am* a man of God, let fire come down
from heaven and consume you and your
fifty men." And the fire of God came down
from heaven and consumed him and his
fifty.
13 Again, he sent a third captain of fifty
with his fifty men. And the third captain
of fifty went up, and came and fell on his
knees before Elijah, and pleaded with him,
and said to him: "Man of God, please let my
life and the life of these fifty servants of
yours [a]be precious in your sight. 14 Look, fire
has come down from heaven and burned
up the first two captains of fifties with their
fifties. But let my life now be precious in
your sight."
15 And the angel[1] of the LORD said to Elijah, "Go down with him; do not be afraid of
him." So he arose and went down with him
to the king. 16 Then he said to him, "Thus
says the LORD: 'Because you have sent messengers to inquire of Baal-Zebub, the god of
Ekron, *is it* because *there is* no God in Israel
to inquire of His word? Therefore you shall
not come down from the bed to which you
have gone up, but you shall surely die.'"

1:1 [a] 2 Sam. 8:2 [b] 2 Kin. 3:5 1:2 [a] 1 Kin. 22:40 [b] 2 Kin. 1:3, 6, 16; Matt. 10:25; Mark 3:22 [c] 1 Sam. 5:10 1:3 [1] Or *Angel* 1:8 [a] Zech. 13:4; Matt. 3:4; Mark 1:6 [b] 1 Kin. 18:7 1:10 [a] 1 Kin. 18:36–38; Luke 9:54 1:13 [a] 1 Sam. 26:21; Ps. 72:14 1:15 [1] Or *Angel*

#OXYGEN

2 KINGS 1:15

Act When He Calls

There are times when the blessings you are looking for are on the other side of the door. Stop looking at the door. Walk through it. See what awaits you on the other side. You have this.

Breathe and **act when He calls.**

17So *Ahaziah* died according to the word of the LORD which Elijah had spoken. Because he had no son, [a]Jehoram[1] became king in his place, in the second year of Jehoram the son of Jehoshaphat, king of Judah.

18Now the rest of the acts of Ahaziah which he did, *are* they not written in the book of the chronicles of the kings of Israel?

Elijah Ascends to Heaven

2 And it came to pass, when the LORD was about to [a]take up Elijah into heaven by a whirlwind, that Elijah went with [b]Elisha from Gilgal. 2Then Elijah said to Elisha, [a]"Stay here, please, for the LORD has sent me on to Bethel."

But Elisha said, "*As* the LORD lives, and [b]*as* your soul lives, I will not leave you!" So they went down to Bethel.

3Now [a]the sons of the prophets who *were* at Bethel came out to Elisha, and said to him, "Do you know that the LORD will take away your master from over you today?"

And he said, "Yes, I know; keep silent!"

4Then Elijah said to him, "Elisha, stay here, please, for the LORD has sent me on to Jericho."

But he said, "*As* the LORD lives, and *as* your soul lives, I will not leave you!" So they came to Jericho.

5Now the sons of the prophets who *were* at Jericho came to Elisha and said to him, "Do you know that the LORD will take away your master from over you today?"

So he answered, "Yes, I know; keep silent!"

6Then Elijah said to him, "Stay here, please, for the LORD has sent me on to the Jordan."

But he said, "*As* the LORD lives, and *as* your soul lives, I will not leave you!" So the two of them went on. 7And fifty men of the sons of the prophets went and stood facing *them* at a distance, while the two of them stood by the Jordan. 8Now Elijah took his mantle, rolled *it* up, and struck the water; and [a]it was divided this way and that, so that the two of them crossed over on dry [b]ground.

9And so it was, when they had crossed over, that Elijah said to Elisha, "Ask! What may I do for you, before I am taken away from you?"

Elisha said, "Please let a double portion of your spirit be upon me."

10So he said, "You have asked a hard thing. *Nevertheless,* if you see me *when I am* taken from you, it shall be so for you; but if not, it shall not be *so.*" 11Then it happened, as they continued on and talked, that suddenly [a]a chariot of fire *appeared* with horses of fire, and separated the two of them; and Elijah [b]went up by a whirlwind into heaven.

12And Elisha saw *it,* and he cried out, [a]"My father, my father, the chariot of Israel and its horsemen!" So he saw him no more. And he took hold of his own clothes and tore them into two pieces. 13He also took up the mantle of Elijah that had fallen from him, and went back and stood by the bank of the Jordan. 14Then he took the mantle of Elijah that had fallen from him, and struck the water, and said, "Where *is* the LORD God of Elijah?" And when he also had struck the water, [a]it was divided this way and that; and Elisha crossed over.

15Now when the sons of the prophets who *were* [a]from Jericho saw him, they said, "The spirit of Elijah rests on Elisha." And they came to meet him, and bowed to the ground before him. 16Then they said

1:17 [a] 1 Kin. 22:50; 2 Kin. 8:16; Matt. 1:8 [1] The son of Ahab king of Israel (compare 3:1) 2:1 [a] Gen. 5:24; [Heb. 11:5] [b] 1 Kin. 19:16–21 2:2 [a] Ruth 1:15, 16 [b] 1 Sam. 1:26; 2 Kin. 2:4, 6; 4:30 2:3 [a] 1 Kin. 20:35; 2 Kin. 2:5, 7, 15; 4:1, 38; 9:1 2:8 [a] Ex. 14:21, 22; Josh. 3:16; 2 Kin. 2:14 [b] Josh. 3:17 2:11 [a] 2 Kin. 6:17; Ps. 104:4 [b] Gen. 5:24; Heb. 11:5 2:12 [a] 2 Kin. 13:14 2:14 [a] 2 Kin. 2:8 2:15 [a] 2 Kin. 2:7

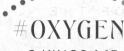

to him, "Look now, there are fifty strong
men with your servants. Please let them
go and search for your master, [a]lest perhaps the Spirit of the LORD has taken him
up and cast him upon some mountain or
into some valley."
And he said, "You shall not send anyone."
17But when they urged him till he was
[a]ashamed, he said, "Send *them!*" Therefore
they sent fifty men, and they searched for
three days but did not find him.
18And when
they came back to him, for he had stayed
in Jericho, he said to them, "Did I not say
to you, 'Do not go'?"

Elisha Performs Miracles

19Then the men of the city said to Elisha,
"Please notice, the situation of this city *is*
pleasant, as my lord sees; but the water *is*
bad, and the ground barren."
20And he said, "Bring me a new bowl,
and put salt in it." So they brought *it* to
him.
21Then he went out to the source of
the water, and [a]cast in the salt there, and
said, "Thus says the LORD: 'I have healed
this water; from it there shall be no more
death or barrenness.'"
22So the water re-
mains [a]healed to this day, according to the
word of Elisha which he spoke.
23Then he went up from there to Bethel;
and as he was going up the road, some
youths came from the city and mocked
him, and said to him, "Go up, you baldhead!
Go up, you baldhead!"
24So he turned around and looked at
them, and [a]pronounced a curse on them
in the name of the LORD. And two female
bears came out of the woods and mauled
forty-two of the youths.
25Then he went from there to [a]Mount Carmel, and from there he returned to Samaria.

2 KINGS 2:9

I AM ELIJAH

And so it was, when they had crossed over, that Elijah said to Elisha, "Ask! What may I do for you, before I am taken away from you?" Elisha said, "Please let a double portion of your spirit be upon me." 2 Kings 2:9

I am Elijah, prophet of God. I was the only prophet of the Lord left in Israel after Jezebel and Ahab killed all the others. Or so I thought. I ran far away, fearing that Jezebel and Ahab would kill me. But the Lord met with me and told me there were seven thousand people who had not bowed to Baal, and I was to return. I was to anoint a new king, and Elisha was to replace me as prophet. Elisha was plowing the fields when I found him. I draped my mantle on him as a sign of the Lord's prophetic call on his life. Afterward, Elisha never left my side. Wherever I went, he went. I stood one day with Elisha by the Jordan River, and the sons of the prophets were standing nearby. The swiftly flowing water barred our way, so I rolled up my mantle and struck the water. The current stopped and the waters parted. As we crossed the river on dry ground, I asked Elisha what I could do for him before I was taken away. He asked for a double portion of my spirit to be on him. I told him that if he saw me as I left the earth, a double portion would be granted to him. Then suddenly, a fiery chariot and horses appeared and I was carried into the heavens in a whirlwind. Elisha watched as I was taken away, as did the sons of the prophets who were standing nearby. They said, "The spirit of Elijah rests on Elisha." And they bowed down before Elisha.

There comes a time in our lives when we should focus on conferring our mantles on the next generation. It is our responsibility to train them, teach them about our history, and pass on the wisdom we have gained through our experiences. In this way, we have a part to play in whatever God calls them to do.

2:16 [a] 1 Kin. 18:12; Ezek. 8:3; Acts 8:39 2:17 [a] 2 Kin. 8:11 2:21 [a] Ex. 15:25, 26; 2 Kin. 4:41; 6:6; John 9:6
2:22 [a] Ezek. 47:8, 9 2:24 [a] Deut. 27:13–26 2:25 [a] 1 Kin. 18:19, 20; 2 Kin. 4:25

Moab Rebels Against Israel

3 Now [a]Jehoram the son of Ahab became king over Israel at Samaria in the eighteenth year of Jehoshaphat king of Judah, and reigned twelve years. 2 And he did evil in the sight of the LORD, but not like his father and mother; for he put away the *sacred* pillar of Baal [a]that his father had made. 3 Nevertheless he persisted in [a]the sins of Jeroboam the son of Nebat, who had made Israel sin; he did not depart from them.

4 Now Mesha king of Moab was a sheepbreeder, and he [a]regularly paid the king of Israel one hundred thousand [b]lambs and the wool of one hundred thousand rams. 5 But it happened, when [a]Ahab died, that the king of Moab rebelled against the king of Israel.

6 So King Jehoram went out of Samaria at that time and mustered all Israel. 7 Then he went and sent to Jehoshaphat king of Judah, saying, "The king of Moab has rebelled against me. Will you go with me to fight against Moab?"

And he said, "I will go up; [a]I *am* as you *are,* my people as your people, my horses as your horses." 8 Then he said, "Which way shall we go up?"

And he answered, "By way of the Wilderness of Edom."

9 So the king of Israel went with the king of Judah and the king of Edom, and they marched on that roundabout route seven days; and there was no water for the army, nor for the animals that followed them. 10 And the king of Israel said, "Alas! For the LORD has called these three kings together to deliver them into the hand of Moab."

11 But [a]Jehoshaphat said, "*Is there* no prophet of the LORD here, that we may inquire of the LORD by him?"

So one of the servants of the king of Israel answered and said, "Elisha the son of Shaphat *is* here, who [b]poured water on the hands of Elijah."

12 And Jehoshaphat said, "The word of the LORD is with him." So the king of Israel and Jehoshaphat and the king of Edom [a]went down to him.

13 Then Elisha said to the king of Israel, [a]"What have I to do with you? [b]Go to [c]the prophets of your father and the [d]prophets of your mother."

But the king of Israel said to him, "No, for the LORD has called these three kings *together* to deliver them into the hand of Moab."

14 And Elisha said, [a]"*As* the LORD of hosts lives, before whom I stand, surely were it not that I regard the presence of Jehoshaphat king of Judah, I would not look at you, nor see you. 15 But now bring me [a]a musician."

Then it happened, when the musician [b]played, that [c]the hand of the LORD came upon him. 16 And he said, "Thus says the LORD: [a]'Make this valley full of ditches.' 17 For thus says the LORD: 'You shall not see wind, nor shall you see rain; yet that valley shall be filled with water, so that you, your cattle, and your animals may drink.' 18 And this is a simple matter in the sight of the LORD; He will also deliver the Moabites into your hand. 19 Also you shall attack every fortified city and every choice city, and shall cut down every good tree, and stop up every spring of water, and ruin every good piece of land with stones."

20 Now it happened in the morning, when [a]the grain offering was offered, that suddenly water came by way of Edom, and the land was filled with water.

21 And when all the Moabites heard that the kings had come up to fight against them, all who were able to bear arms and older were gathered; and they stood at the border. 22 Then they rose up early in the morning, and the sun was shining on the water; and the Moabites saw the water on the other side *as* red as blood. 23 And they said, "This is blood; the kings have surely struck swords and have killed one another; now therefore, Moab, to the spoil!"

24 So when they came to the camp of Israel, Israel rose up and attacked the Moabites, so that they fled before them; and they entered *their* land, killing the Moabites. 25 Then they destroyed the cities, and each man threw a stone on every good piece of land and filled it; and they stopped up all the springs of water and cut down all the good trees. But they left the stones of

---

3:1 [a] 2 Kin. 1:17 3:2 [a] 1 Kin. 16:31, 32 3:3 [a] 1 Kin. 12:28–32 3:4 [a] 2 Sam. 8:2 [b] Is. 16:1, 2 3:5 [a] 2 Kin. 1:1 3:7 [a] 1 Kin. 22:4 3:11 [a] 1 Kin. 22:7 [b] 1 Kin. 19:21; [John 13:4, 5, 13, 14] 3:12 [a] 2 Kin. 2:25 3:13 [a] [Ezek. 14:3] [b] Judg. 10:14; Ruth 1:15 [c] 1 Kin. 22:6–11 [d] 1 Kin. 18:19 3:14 [a] 1 Kin. 17:1; 2 Kin. 5:16 3:15 [a] 1 Sam. 10:5 [b] 1 Sam. 16:16, 23; 1 Chr. 25:1 [c] Ezek. 1:3; 3:14, 22; 8:1 3:16 [a] Jer. 14:3 3:20 [a] Ex. 29:39, 40

[a]Kir Haraseth *intact.* However the slingers surrounded and attacked it.

26And when the king of Moab saw that the battle was too fierce for him, he took with him seven hundred men who drew swords, to break through to the king of Edom, but they could not. 27Then [a]he took his eldest son who would have reigned in his place, and offered him *as* a burnt offering upon the wall; and there was great indignation against Israel. [b]So they departed from him and returned to *their own* land.

Elisha and the Widow's Oil
(cf. 1 Kin. 17:14–16)

4 A certain woman of the wives of [a]the sons of the prophets cried out to Elisha, saying, "Your servant my husband is dead, and you know that your servant feared the LORD. And the creditor is coming [b]to take my two sons to be his slaves."

2So Elisha said to her, "What shall I do for you? Tell me, what do you have in the house?" And she said, "Your maidservant has nothing in the house but a jar of oil."

3Then he said, "Go, borrow vessels from everywhere, from all your neighbors—empty vessels; [a]do not gather just a few. 4And when you have come in, you shall shut the door behind you and your sons; then pour it into all those vessels, and set aside the full ones."

5So she went from him and shut the door behind her and her sons, who brought *the vessels* to her; and she poured *it* out. 6Now it came to pass, when the vessels were full, that she said to her son, "Bring me another vessel."

And he said to her, "*There is* not another vessel." So the oil ceased. 7Then she came and told the man of God. And he said, "Go, sell the oil and pay your debt; and you *and* your sons live on the rest."

Elisha Raises the Shunammite's Son
(cf. 1 Kin. 17:17–24)

8Now it happened one day that Elisha went to [a]Shunem, where there *was* a notable woman, and she persuaded him to eat some food. So it was, as often as he passed by, he would turn in there to eat some food. 9And she said to her husband, "Look now, I know that this *is* a holy man of God, who passes by us regularly. 10Please, let us make a small upper room on the wall; and let us put a bed for him there, and a table and a chair and a lampstand; so it will be, whenever he comes to us, he can turn in there."

11And it happened one day that he came there, and he turned in to the upper room and lay down there. 12Then he said to [a]Gehazi his servant, "Call this Shunammite woman." When he had called her, she stood before him. 13And he said to him, "Say now to her, 'Look, you have been concerned for us with all this care. What *can I* do for you? Do you want me to speak on your behalf to the king or to the commander of the army?'"

She answered, "I dwell among my own people."

14So he said, "What then *is* to be done for her?"

And Gehazi answered, "Actually, she has no son, and her husband is old."

15So he said, "Call her." When he had called her, she stood in the doorway. 16Then he said, "About this time next year you shall embrace a son."

And she said, "No, my lord. Man of God, [a]do not lie to your maidservant!"

17But the woman conceived, and bore a son when the appointed time had come, of which Elisha had told her.

18And the child grew. Now it happened one day that he went out to his father, to the reapers. 19And he said to his father, "My head, my head!"

So he said to a servant, "Carry him to his mother." 20When he had taken him and brought him to his mother, he sat on her knees till noon, and *then* died. 21And she went up and laid him on the bed of the man of God, shut *the door* upon him, and went out. 22Then she called to her husband, and said, "Please send me one of the young men and one of the donkeys, that I may run to the man of God and come back."

23So he said, "Why are you going to him today? *It is* neither the [a]New Moon nor the Sabbath."

3:25 [a] Is. 16:7, 11; Jer. 48:31, 36 3:27 [a] [Deut. 18:10; Amos 2:1; Mic. 6:7] [b] 2 Kin. 8:20 4:1 [a] 1 Kin. 20:35; 2 Kin. 2:3 [b] [Lev. 25:39–41, 48]; 1 Sam. 22:2; Neh. 5:2–5; Matt. 18:25 4:3 [a] 2 Kin. 3:16 4:8 [a] Josh. 19:18 4:12 [a] 2 Kin. 4:29–31; 5:20–27; 8:4, 5 4:16 [a] 2 Kin. 4:28 4:23 [a] Num. 10:10; 28:11; 1 Chr. 23:31

And she said, "*It is* well." 24Then she
saddled a donkey, and said to her servant,
"Drive, and go forward; do not slacken the
pace for me unless I tell you." 25And so she
departed, and went to the man of God [a]at
Mount Carmel.

So it was, when the man of God saw her
afar off, that he said to his servant Gehazi,
"Look, the Shunammite woman! 26Please
run now to meet her, and say to her, '*Is it*
well with you? *Is it* well with your husband?
Is it well with the child?'"

And she answered, "*It is* well." 27Now
when she came to the man of God at the
hill, she caught him by the feet, but Gehazi
came near to push her away. But the man
of God said, "Let her alone; for her soul *is*
in deep distress, and the LORD has hidden
it from me, and has not told me."

28So she said, "Did I ask a son of my lord?
[a]Did I not say, 'Do not deceive me'?"

29Then he said to Gehazi, [a]"Get yourself
ready, and take my staff in your hand, and
be on your way. If you meet anyone, [b]do
not greet him; and if anyone greets you,
do not answer him; but [c]lay my staff on the
face of the child."

30And the mother of the child said, [a]"As
the LORD lives, and *as* your soul lives, I will
not [b]leave you." So he arose and followed
her. 31Now Gehazi went on ahead of them,
and laid the staff on the face of the child;
but *there was* neither voice nor hearing.
Therefore he went back to meet him, and
told him, saying, "The child has [a]not awakened."

32When Elisha came into the house,
there was the child, lying dead on his bed.
33He [a]went in therefore, shut the door behind the two of them, [b]and prayed to the
LORD. 34And he went up and lay on the
child, and put his mouth on his mouth,
his eyes on his eyes, and his hands on his
hands; and [a]he stretched himself out on
the child, and the flesh of the child became
warm. 35He returned and walked back and
forth in the house, and again went up [a]and
stretched himself out on him; then [b]the
child sneezed seven times, and the child
opened his eyes. 36And he called Gehazi and
said, "Call this Shunammite woman." So he
called her. And when she came in to him,
he said, "Pick up your son." 37So she went
in, fell at his feet, and bowed to the ground;
then she [a]picked up her son and went out.

Elisha Purifies the Pot of Stew

38And Elisha returned to [a]Gilgal, and *there*
was a [b]famine in the land. Now the sons of
the prophets *were* [c]sitting before him; and
he said to his servant, "Put on the large pot,
and boil stew for the sons of the prophets."
39So one went out into the field to gather
herbs, and found a wild vine, and gathered
from it a lapful of wild gourds, and came and
sliced *them* into the pot of stew, though they
did not know *what they were.* 40Then they
served it to the men to eat. Now it happened,
as they were eating the stew, that they cried
out and said, "Man of God, *there is* [a]death in
the pot!" And they could not eat *it.*

41So he said, "Then bring some flour."
And [a]he put *it* into the pot, and said, "Serve
it to the people, that they may eat." And
there was nothing harmful in the pot.

Elisha Feeds One Hundred Men
(cf. Matt. 14:13–21; 15:32–39)

42Then a man came from [a]Baal Shalisha,
[b]and brought the man of God bread of the
firstfruits, twenty loaves of barley bread,
and newly ripened grain in his knapsack.
And he said, "Give *it* to the people, that they
may eat."

43But his servant said, [a]"What? Shall I set
this before one hundred men?"

He said again, "Give it to the people, that
they may eat; for thus says the LORD: [b]'They
shall eat and have *some* left over.'" 44So he
set *it* before them; and they ate [a]and had
some left over, according to the word of
the LORD.

Naaman's Leprosy Healed

5 Now [a]Naaman, commander of the army
of the king of Syria, was [b]a great and honorable man in the eyes of his master, because by him the LORD had given victory

---

4:25 [a] 2 Kin. 2:25 4:28 [a] 2 Kin. 4:16 4:29 [a] 1 Kin. 18:46; 2 Kin. 9:1 [b] Luke 10:4 [c] Ex. 7:19; 14:16; 2 Kin. 2:8, 14; Acts 19:12 4:30 [a] 2 Kin. 2:2 [b] 2 Kin. 2:4 4:31 [a] John 11:11 4:33 [a] 2 Kin. 4:4; [Matt. 6:6]; Luke 8:51 [b] 1 Kin. 17:20 4:34 [a] 1 Kin. 17:21–23; Acts 20:10 4:35 [a] 1 Kin. 17:21 [b] 2 Kin. 8:1, 5 4:37 [a] 1 Kin. 17:23; [Heb. 11:35] 4:38 [a] 2 Kin. 2:1 [b] 2 Kin. 8:1 [c] Luke 10:39; Acts 22:3 4:40 [a] Ex. 10:17 4:41 [a] Ex. 15:25; 2 Kin. 2:21 4:42 [a] 1 Sam. 9:4 [b] 1 Sam. 9:7; [1 Cor. 9:11; Gal. 6:6] 4:43 [a] Luke 9:13; John 6:9 [b] Luke 9:17; John 6:11 4:44 [a] Matt. 14:20; 15:37; John 6:13 5:1 [a] Luke 4:27 [b] Ex. 11:3

to Syria. He was also a mighty man of valor,
but a leper. 2And the Syrians had gone out
[a]on raids, and had brought back captive a
young girl from the land of Israel. She waited
on Naaman's wife. 3Then she said to her
mistress, "If only my master *were* with the
prophet who *is* in Samaria! For he would heal
him of his leprosy." 4And *Naaman* went in
and told his master, saying, "Thus and thus
said the girl who *is* from the land of Israel."
5Then the king of Syria said, "Go now,
and I will send a letter to the king of Israel."
So he departed and [a]took with him ten
talents of silver, six thousand *shekels* of
gold, and ten changes of clothing. 6Then
he brought the letter to the king of Israel,
which said,

> Now be advised, when this letter
> comes to you, that I have sent Naaman
> my servant to you, that you may heal
> him of his leprosy.

7And it happened, when the king of Israel
read the letter, that he tore his clothes and
said, "*Am* I [a]God, to kill and make alive, that
this man sends a man to me to heal him
of his leprosy? Therefore please consider,
and see how he seeks a quarrel with me."
8So it was, when Elisha the man of God
heard that the king of Israel had torn his
clothes, that he sent to the king, saying,
"Why have you torn your clothes? Please
let him come to me, and he shall know that
there is a prophet in Israel."
9Then Naaman went with his horses and
chariot, and he stood at the door of Elisha's house. 10And Elisha sent a messenger to him, saying, "Go and [a]wash in the
Jordan seven times, and your flesh shall
be restored to you, and *you shall* be clean."
11But Naaman became furious, and went
away and said, "Indeed, I said to myself,
'He will surely come out *to me,* and stand
and call on the name of the LORD his God,
and wave his hand over the place, and heal
the leprosy.' 12*Are* not the Abanah[1] and the
Pharpar, the rivers of Damascus, better
than all the waters of Israel? Could I not
wash in them and be clean?" So he turned
and went away in a rage. 13And his [a]ser-
vants came near and spoke to him, and
said, "My father, *if* the prophet had told
you *to do* something great, would you not
have done *it?* How much more then, when
he says to you, 'Wash, and be clean'?" 14So
he went down and dipped seven times in
the Jordan, according to the saying of the
man of God; and his [a]flesh was restored like
the flesh of a little child, and [b]he was clean.
15And he returned to the man of God, he
and all his aides, and came and stood before him; and he said, "Indeed, now I know
that *there is* [a]no God in all the earth, except
in Israel; now therefore, please take [b]a gift
from your servant."
16But he said, [a]"*As* the LORD lives, before
whom I stand, [b]I will receive nothing." And
he urged him to take *it,* but he refused.
17So Naaman said, "Then, if not, please
let your servant be given two mule-loads
of earth; for your servant will no longer
offer either burnt offering or sacrifice to
other gods, but to the LORD. 18Yet in this
thing may the LORD pardon your servant:
when my master goes into the temple of
Rimmon to worship there, and [a]he leans
on my hand, and I bow down in the temple of Rimmon—when I bow down in the
temple of Rimmon, may the LORD please
pardon your servant in this thing."
19Then he said to him, "Go in peace." So
he departed from him a short distance.

Gehazi's Greed

20But [a]Gehazi, the servant of Elisha the
man of God, said, "Look, my master has
spared Naaman this Syrian, while not receiving from his hands what he brought;
but *as* the LORD lives, I will run after him
and take something from him." 21So Gehazi
pursued Naaman. When Naaman saw *him*
running after him, he got down from the
chariot to meet him, and said, "*Is* all well?"
22And he said, "All *is* [a]well. My master
has sent me, saying, 'Indeed, just now two
young men of the sons of the prophets
have come to me from the mountains of
Ephraim. Please give them a talent of silver
and two changes of garments.'"

5:2 [a] 2 Kin. 6:23; 13:20 5:5 [a] 1 Sam. 9:8; 2 Kin. 8:8, 9 5:7 [a] [Gen. 30:2; Deut. 32:39; 1 Sam. 2:6] 5:10 [a] 2 Kin. 4:41; John 9:7 5:12 [1] Following Kethib, Septuagint, and Vulgate; Qere, Syriac, and Targum read *Amanah.* 5:13 [a] 1 Sam. 28:23 5:14 [a] 2 Kin. 5:10; Job 33:25 [b] Luke 4:27; 5:13 5:15 [a] Dan. 2:47; 3:29; 6:26, 27 [b] Gen. 33:11 5:16 [a] 2 Kin. 3:14 [b] Gen. 14:22, 23; 2 Kin. 5:20, 26; [Matt. 10:8]; Acts 8:18, 20 5:18 [a] 2 Kin. 7:2, 17 5:20 [a] 2 Kin. 4:12; 8:4, 5 5:22 [a] 2 Kin. 4:26

23 So Naaman said, "Please, take two talents." And he urged him, and bound two talents of silver in two bags, with two changes of garments, and handed *them* to two of his servants; and they carried *them* on ahead of him. 24 When he came to the citadel, he took *them* from their hand, and stored *them* away in the house; then he let the men go, and they departed. 25 Now he went in and stood before his master. Elisha said to him, "Where *did you go,* Gehazi?"

And he said, "Your servant did not go anywhere."

26 Then he said to him, "Did not my heart go *with you* when the man turned back from his chariot to meet you? *Is it* [a]time to receive money and to receive clothing, olive groves and vineyards, sheep and oxen, male and female servants? 27 Therefore the leprosy of Naaman [a]shall cling to you and your descendants forever." And he went out from his presence [b]leprous, *as white* as snow.

The Floating Ax Head

6 And [a]the sons of the prophets said to Elisha, "See now, the place where we dwell with you is too small for us. 2 Please, let us go to the Jordan, and let every man take a beam from there, and let us make there a place where we may dwell."

So he answered, "Go."

3 Then one said, [a]"Please consent to go with your servants."

And he answered, "I will go." 4 So he went with them. And when they came to the Jordan, they cut down trees. 5 But as one was cutting down a tree, the iron *ax head* fell into the water; and he cried out and said, "Alas, master! For it was [a]borrowed."

6 So the man of God said, "Where did it fall?" And he showed him the place. So [a]he cut off a stick, and threw *it* in there; and he made the iron float. 7 Therefore he said, "Pick *it* up for yourself." So he reached out his hand and took it.

The Blinded Syrians Captured

8 Now the [a]king of Syria was making war against Israel; and he consulted with his servants, saying, "My camp *will be* in such and such a place." 9 And the man of God sent to the king of Israel, saying, "Beware that you do not pass this place, for the Syrians are coming down there." 10 Then the king of Israel sent *someone* to the place of which the man of God had told him. Thus he warned him, and he was watchful there, not just once or twice.

11 Therefore the heart of the king of Syria was greatly troubled by this thing; and he called his servants and said to them, "Will you not show me which of us *is* for the king of Israel?"

12 And one of his servants said, "None, my lord, O king; but Elisha, the prophet who *is* in Israel, tells the king of Israel the words that you speak in your bedroom."

13 So he said, "Go and see where he *is,* that I may send and get him."

And it was told him, saying, "Surely *he is* in [a]Dothan."

14 Therefore he sent horses and chariots and a great army there, and they came by night and surrounded the city. 15 And when the servant of the man of God arose early and went out, there was an army, surrounding the city with horses and chariots. And his servant said to him, "Alas, my master! What shall we do?"

16 So he answered, [a]"Do not fear, for [b]those who *are* with us *are* more than those who *are* with them." 17 And Elisha prayed, and said, "LORD, I pray, open his eyes that he may see." Then the LORD [a]opened the eyes of the young man, and he saw. And behold, the mountain *was* full of [b]horses and chariots of fire all around Elisha. 18 So when *the Syrians* came down to him, Elisha prayed to the LORD, and said, "Strike this people, I pray, with blindness." And [a]He struck them with blindness according to the word of Elisha.

19 Now Elisha said to them, "This *is* not the way, nor *is* this the city. Follow me, and I will bring you to the man whom you seek." But he led them to Samaria.

20 So it was, when they had come to Samaria, that Elisha said, "LORD, open the eyes of these *men,* that they may see." And the LORD opened their eyes, and they saw; and there *they were,* inside Samaria!

5:26 [a] [Eccl. 3:1, 6] 5:27 [a] [1 Tim. 6:10] [b] Ex. 4:6; Num. 12:10; 2 Kin. 15:5 6:1 [a] 2 Kin. 4:38 6:3 [a] 2 Kin. 5:23 6:5 [a] [Ex. 22:14] 6:6 [a] Ex. 15:25; 2 Kin. 2:21; 4:41 6:8 [a] 2 Kin. 8:28, 29 6:13 [a] Gen. 37:17 6:16 [a] Ex. 14:13; 1 Kin. 17:13 [b] 2 Chr. 32:7; Ps. 55:18; [Rom. 8:31] 6:17 [a] Num. 22:31; Luke 24:31 [b] 2 Kin. 2:11; Ps. 34:7; 68:17; Zech. 1:8; 6:1–7 6:18 [a] Gen. 19:11; Acts 13:11

ACT WHEN HE CALLS

INHALE

I'm angry! Some friends and I were just out celebrating. We weren't speeding or anything, but then, from out of nowhere, we got pulled over. One minute we were having a good time, minding our own business. Then, the next minute, we were stretched out on the cold concrete along the side of the road. I have heard about "driving while Black," but nothing prepared me for that indignity. I'm embarrassed. I'm angry. I was made to feel less than human. All by those who are supposed to protect and serve. I want justice! I want them to feel what I felt. Is that wrong? I need to do something. What should that be?

EXHALE

What you describe is not easy to handle, to say the least. It is hard to be targeted for no apparent reason other than your appearance. It's understandable that you are angry and were made to feel the way you did. It's OK to want justice. But we need to go about that the right way.

Anger is a real emotion that shows up in moments like these, but we must bridle it and bring it under control. Why, you ask? Because anger is a path to destruction. And once we start down that road, it is difficult to turn around. Anger can cause us to say and do things that we will regret. We need Christlikeness to show up even in these moments—especially in these moments, actually. Moments of humiliation and hurt are not moments to be led by anger, even if it is justified. That anger will take us not toward justice but likely further from it. Instead, let Christ in you dominate these times and let your godly behavior convict that officer of wrongdoing.

The greatest witness for Christ will come in your most difficult experiences. If you allow Him to lead you in those moments, the greatness of Christ will prevail in and through you. And like Elisha prayed in 2 Kings 6:17, "LORD, I pray, open his eyes that he may see," ask that God would open the officer's eyes to see what is right. Act like Christ and pursue God's justice His way.

21Now when the king of Israel saw them,
he said to Elisha, "My [a]father, shall I kill
them? Shall I kill *them?*"
22But he answered, "You shall not kill
them. Would you kill those whom you have
taken captive with your sword and your
bow? [a]Set food and water before them, that
they may eat and drink and go to their master." 23Then he prepared a great feast for
them; and after they ate and drank, he sent
them away and they went to their master.
So [a]the bands of Syrian *raiders* came no
more into the land of Israel.

Syria Besieges Samaria in Famine

24And it happened after this that [a]Ben-
Hadad king of Syria gathered all his army,
and went up and besieged Samaria. 25And
there was a great [a]famine in Samaria; and
indeed they besieged it until a donkey's
head was *sold* for eighty *shekels* of silver,
and one-fourth of a kab of dove droppings
for five *shekels* of silver.
26Then, as the king of Israel was passing
by on the wall, a woman cried out to him,
saying, "Help, my lord, O king!"
27And he said, "If the LORD does not help
you, where can I find help for you? From
the threshing floor or from the winepress?"
28Then the king said to her, "What is troubling you?"

And she answered, "This woman said
to me, 'Give your son, that we may eat him
today, and we will eat my son tomorrow.'
29So [a]we boiled my son, and ate him. And I
said to her on the next day, 'Give your son,
that we may eat him'; but she has hidden
her son."

6:21 [a] 2 Kin. 2:12; 5:13; 8:9 6:22 [a] [Rom. 12:20] 6:23 [a] 2 Kin. 5:2; 6:8, 9 6:24 [a] 1 Kin. 20:1 6:25 [a] 2 Kin. 4:38; 8:1 6:29 [a] Lev. 26:27–29; Deut. 28:52–57; Lam. 4:10

30 Now it happened, when the king heard
the words of the woman, that he [a]tore his
clothes; and as he passed by on the wall,
the people looked, and there underneath
he had sackcloth on his body. 31 Then he
said, [a]"God do so to me and more also, if
the head of Elisha the son of Shaphat remains on him today!"

32 But Elisha was sitting in his house, and
[a]the elders were sitting with him. And *the*
king sent a man ahead of him, but before
the messenger came to him, he said to the
elders, [b]"Do you see how this son of [c]a murderer has sent someone to take away my
head? Look, when the messenger comes,
shut the door, and hold him fast at the door.
Is not the sound of his master's feet behind
him?" 33 And while he was still talking with
them, there was the messenger, coming
down to him; and then *the king* said, "Surely
this calamity *is* from the LORD; [a]why should
I wait for the LORD any longer?"

7 Then Elisha said, "Hear the word of the
LORD. Thus says the LORD: [a]'Tomorrow
about this time a seah of fine flour *shall be*
sold for a shekel, and two seahs of barley for
a shekel, at the gate of Samaria.'"

2 [a]So an officer on whose hand the king
leaned answered the man of God and said,
"Look, [b]*if* the LORD would make windows
in heaven, could this thing be?"

And he said, "In fact, you shall see *it* with
your eyes, but you shall not eat of it."

The Syrians Flee

3 Now there were four leprous men [a]at
the entrance of the gate; and they said to
one another, "Why are we sitting here until we die? 4 If we say, 'We will enter the city,'
the famine *is* in the city, and we shall die
there. And if we sit here, we die also. Now
therefore, come, let us surrender to the
[a]army of the Syrians. If they keep us alive,
we shall live; and if they kill us, we shall
only die." 5 And they rose at twilight to go to
the camp of the Syrians; and when they had
come to the outskirts of the Syrian camp,
to their surprise no one *was* there. 6 For the
Lord had caused the army of the Syrians [a]to
hear the noise of chariots and the noise of
horses—the noise of a great army; so they
said to one another, "Look, the king of Israel has hired against us [b]the kings of the
Hittites and the kings of the Egyptians to
attack us!" 7 Therefore they [a]arose and fled
at twilight, and left the camp intact—their
tents, their horses, and their donkeys—
and they fled for their lives. 8 And when
these lepers came to the outskirts of the
camp, they went into one tent and ate and
drank, and carried from it silver and gold
and clothing, and went and hid *them;* then
they came back and entered another tent,
and carried *some* from there *also,* and went
and hid *it.*

9 Then they said to one another, "We are
not doing right. This day *is* a day of good
news, and we remain silent. If we wait until morning light, some punishment will
come upon us. Now therefore, come, let
us go and tell the king's household." 10 So
they went and called to the gatekeepers of
the city, and told them, saying, "We went
to the Syrian camp, and surprisingly no
one *was* there, not a human sound—only
horses and donkeys tied, and the tents intact." 11 And the gatekeepers called out, and
they told *it* to the king's household inside.

12 So the king arose in the night and said to
his servants, "Let me now tell you what the
Syrians have done to us. They know that we
are [a]hungry; therefore they have gone out
of the camp to hide themselves in the field,
saying, 'When they come out of the city, we
shall catch them alive, and get into the city.'"

13 And one of his servants answered and
said, "Please, let several *men* take five of the
remaining horses which are left in the city.
Look, they *may either become* like all the multitude of Israel that are left in it; or indeed, *I*
say, they *may become* like all the multitude
of Israel left from those who are consumed;
so let us send them and see." 14 Therefore
they took two chariots with horses; and the
king sent them in the direction of the Syrian army, saying, "Go and see." 15 And they
went after them to the Jordan; and indeed
all the road *was* full of garments and weapons which the Syrians had thrown away in
their haste. So the messengers returned and

6:30 [a] 1 Kin. 21:27 6:31 [a] Ruth 1:17; 1 Kin. 19:2 6:32 [a] Ezek. 8:1; 14:1; 20:1 [b] Luke 13:32 [c] 1 Kin. 18:4, 13, 14; 21:10, 13 6:33 [a] Job 2:9
7:1 [a] 2 Kin. 7:18, 19 7:2 [a] 2 Kin. 5:18; 7:17, 19, 20 [b] Gen. 7:11; Mal. 3:10 7:3 [a] [Lev. 13:45, 46; Num. 5:2–4; 12:10–14] 7:4 [a] 2 Kin. 6:24
7:6 [a] 2 Sam. 5:24; 2 Kin. 19:7; Job 15:21 [b] 1 Kin. 10:29 7:7 [a] Ps. 48:4–6; [Prov. 28:1] 7:12 [a] 2 Kin. 6:24–29

told the king. 16Then the people went out
and plundered the tents of the Syrians. So
a seah of fine flour was *sold* for a shekel, and
two seahs of barley for a shekel, [a]according
to the word of the LORD.
17Now the king had appointed the officer
on whose hand he leaned to have charge
of the gate. But the people trampled him
in the gate, and he died, just [a]as the man
of God had said, who spoke when the king
came down to him. 18So it happened just
as the man of God had spoken to the king,
saying, [a]"Two seahs of barley for a shekel,
and a seah of fine flour for a shekel, shall
be *sold* tomorrow about this time in the
gate of Samaria."
19Then that officer had answered the
man of God, and said, "Now look, *if* the
LORD would make windows in heaven,
could such a thing be?"
And he had said, "In fact, you shall see *it*
with your eyes, but you shall not eat of it."
20And so it happened to him, for the people trampled him in the gate, and he died.

The King Restores the Shunammite's Land

8 Then Elisha spoke to the woman
[a]whose son he had restored to life, saying, "Arise and go, you and your household,
and stay wherever you can; for the LORD
[b]has called for a [c]famine, and furthermore,
it will come upon the land for seven years."
2So the woman arose and did according to
the saying of the man of God, and she went
with her household and dwelt in the land
of the Philistines seven years.
3It came to pass, at the end of seven
years, that the woman returned from the
land of the Philistines; and she went to
make an appeal to the king for her house
and for her land. 4Then the king talked with
[a]Gehazi, the servant of the man of God, saying, "Tell me, please, all the great things
Elisha has done." 5Now it happened, as he
was telling the king how he had restored
the dead to life, that there was the woman
whose son he had [a]restored to life, appealing to the king for her house and for her
land. And Gehazi said, "My lord, O king, this
is the woman, and this *is* her son whom Elisha restored to life." 6And when the king
asked the woman, she told him.
So the king appointed a certain officer
for her, saying, "Restore all that *was* hers,
and all the proceeds of the field from the
day that she left the land until now."

Death of Ben-Hadad

7Then Elisha went to Damascus, and
[a]Ben-Hadad king of Syria was sick; and it
was told him, saying, "The man of God has
come here." 8And the king said to [a]Hazael,
[b]"Take a present in your hand, and go to
meet the man of God, and [c]inquire of the
LORD by him, saying, 'Shall I recover from
this disease?' " 9So [a]Hazael went to meet
him and took a present with him, of every
good thing of Damascus, forty camel-loads;
and he came and stood before him, and
said, "Your son Ben-Hadad king of Syria
has sent me to you, saying, 'Shall I recover
from this disease?' "
10And Elisha said to him, "Go, say to him,
'You shall certainly recover.' However the
LORD has shown me that [a]he will really die."
11Then he set his countenance in a stare until he was ashamed; and the man of God
[a]wept. 12And Hazael said, "Why is my lord
weeping?"
He answered, "Because I know [a]the
evil that you will do to the children of Israel: Their strongholds you will set on fire,
and their young men you will kill with the
sword; and you [b]will dash their children,
and rip open their women with child."
13So Hazael said, "But what [a]*is* your servant—a dog, that he should do this gross
thing?"
And Elisha answered, [b]"The LORD has
shown me that you *will become* king over
Syria."
14Then he departed from Elisha, and
came to his master, who said to him, "What
did Elisha say to you?" And he answered,
"He told me you would surely recover."
15But it happened on the next day that he
took a thick cloth and dipped *it* in water,
and spread *it* over his face so that he died;
and Hazael reigned in his place.

7:16 [a] 2 Kin. 7:1 7:17 [a] 2 Kin. 6:32; 7:2 7:18 [a] 2 Kin. 7:1 8:1 [a] 2 Kin. 4:18, 31–35 [b] Ps. 105:16; Hag. 1:11 [c] 2 Sam. 21:1; 1 Kin. 18:2; 2 Kin. 4:38; 6:25 8:4 [a] 2 Kin. 4:12; 5:20–27 8:5 [a] 2 Kin. 4:35 8:7 [a] 2 Kin. 6:24 8:8 [a] 1 Kin. 19:15 [b] 1 Sam. 9:7; 1 Kin. 14:3; 2 Kin. 5:5 [c] 2 Kin. 1:2 8:9 [a] 1 Kin. 19:15 8:10 [a] 2 Kin. 8:15 8:11 [a] Luke 19:41 8:12 [a] 2 Kin. 10:32; 12:17; 13:3, 7; Amos 1:3, 4 [b] 2 Kin. 15:16; Hos. 13:16; Amos 1:13; Nah. 3:10 8:13 [a] 1 Sam. 17:43; 2 Sam. 9:8 [b] 1 Kin. 19:15

Jehoram Reigns in Judah
(2 Chr. 21:1–20)

16Now [a]in the fifth year of Joram the son
of Ahab, king of Israel, Jehoshaphat *having been* king of Judah, [b]Jehoram the son
of Jehoshaphat began to reign as king of
Judah. 17He was [a]thirty-two years old when
he became king, and he reigned eight years
in Jerusalem. 18And he walked in the way
of the kings of Israel, just as the house of
Ahab had done, for [a]the daughter of Ahab
was his wife; and he did evil in the sight of
the LORD. 19Yet the LORD would not destroy
Judah, for the sake of His servant David,
[a]as He promised him to give a lamp to him
and his sons forever.

20In his days [a]Edom revolted against
Judah's authority, [b]and made a king over
themselves. 21So Joram[1] went to Zair, and
all his chariots with him. Then he rose by
night and attacked the Edomites who had
surrounded him and the captains of the
chariots; and the troops fled to their tents.
22Thus Edom has been in revolt against Judah's authority to this day. [a]And Libnah revolted at that time.

23Now the rest of the acts of Joram, and
all that he did, *are* they not written in the
book of the chronicles of the kings of Judah? 24So Joram rested with his fathers,
and was buried with his fathers in the City
of David. Then [a]Ahaziah his son reigned
in his place.

Ahaziah Reigns in Judah
(2 Chr. 22:1–6)

25In the twelfth year of Joram the son
of Ahab, king of Israel, Ahaziah the son of
Jehoram, king of Judah, began to reign.
26Ahaziah *was* [a]twenty-two years old when
he became king, and he reigned one year
in Jerusalem. His mother's name *was* Athaliah the granddaughter of Omri, king of
Israel. 27[a]And he walked in the way of the
house of Ahab, and did evil in the sight of
the LORD, like the house of Ahab, for he
was the son-in-law of the house of Ahab.

28Now he went [a]with Joram the son of
Ahab to war against Hazael king of Syria at
[b]Ramoth Gilead; and the Syrians wounded
Joram. 29Then [a]King Joram went back to
Jezreel to recover from the wounds which
the Syrians had inflicted on him at Ramah, when he fought against Hazael king
of Syria. [b]And Ahaziah the son of Jehoram, king of Judah, went down to see Joram the son of Ahab in Jezreel, because
he was sick.

Jehu Anointed King of Israel

9 And Elisha the prophet called one of
[a]the sons of the prophets, and said to
him, [b]"Get yourself ready, take this flask of
oil in your hand, [c]and go to Ramoth Gilead.
2Now when you arrive at that place, look
there for Jehu the son of Jehoshaphat, the
son of Nimshi, and go in and make him
rise up from among [a]his associates, and
take him to an inner room. 3Then [a]take the
flask of oil, and pour *it* on his head, and say,
'Thus says the LORD: "I have anointed you
king over Israel." ' Then open the door and
flee, and do not delay."

4So the young man, the servant of the
prophet, went to Ramoth Gilead. 5And
when he arrived, there *were* the captains
of the army sitting; and he said, "I have a
message for you, Commander."

Jehu said, "For which *one* of us?"

And he said, "For you, Commander."
6Then he arose and went into the house.
And he poured the oil on his head, and said
to him, [a]"Thus says the LORD God of Israel:
'I have anointed you king over the people
of the LORD, over Israel. 7You shall strike
down the house of Ahab your master, that
I may [a]avenge the blood of My servants
the prophets, and the blood of all the servants of the LORD, [b]at the hand of Jezebel.
8For the whole house of Ahab shall perish;
and [a]I will cut off from Ahab all [b]the males
in Israel, both [c]bond and free. 9So I will
make the house of Ahab like the house of
[a]Jeroboam the son of Nebat, and like the
house of [b]Baasha the son of Ahijah. 10[a]The
dogs shall eat Jezebel on the plot *of ground*

8:16 [a] 2 Kin. 1:17; 3:1 [b] 2 Chr. 21:3 8:17 [a] 2 Chr. 21:5–10 8:18 [a] 2 Kin. 8:26, 27 8:19 [a] 2 Sam. 7:13; 1 Kin. 11:36; 15:4; 2 Chr. 21:7
8:20 [a] Gen. 27:40; 2 Chr. 21:8–10 [b] 1 Kin. 22:47 8:21 [1] Spelled *Jehoram* in verse 16 8:22 [a] Josh. 21:13; 2 Kin. 19:8;
2 Chr. 21:10 8:24 [a] 2 Chr. 22:1, 7 8:26 [a] 2 Chr. 22:2 8:27 [a] 2 Chr. 22:3, 4 8:28 [a] 2 Chr. 22:5 [b] 1 Kin. 22:3, 29
8:29 [a] 2 Kin. 9:15 [b] 2 Kin. 9:16; 2 Chr. 22:6, 7 9:1 [a] 1 Kin. 20:35 [b] 2 Kin. 4:29; Jer. 1:17 [c] 2 Kin. 8:28, 29
9:2 [a] 2 Kin. 9:5, 11 9:3 [a] 1 Kin. 19:16 9:6 [a] 1 Sam. 2:7, 8; 1 Kin. 19:16; 2 Kin. 9:3; 2 Chr. 22:7 9:7 [a] [Deut. 32:35, 41]
[b] 1 Kin. 18:4; 21:15 9:8 [a] 1 Kin. 14:10; 21:21; 2 Kin. 10:17 [b] 1 Sam. 25:22 [c] Deut. 32:36; 2 Kin. 14:26
9:9 [a] 1 Kin. 14:10; 15:29; 21:22 [b] 1 Kin. 16:3, 11 9:10 [a] 1 Kin. 21:23; 2 Kin. 9:35, 36

at Jezreel, and *there shall be* none to bury *her.*'" And he opened the door and fled.

11 Then Jehu came out to the servants of his master, and *one* said to him, "*Is* all well? Why did [a]this madman come to you?"

And he said to them, "You know the man and his babble."

12 And they said, "A lie! Tell us now."

So he said, "Thus and thus he spoke to me, saying, 'Thus says the LORD: "I have anointed you king over Israel."'"

13 Then each man hastened [a]to take his garment and put *it* under him on the top of the steps; and they blew trumpets, saying, "Jehu is king!"

Joram of Israel Killed

14 So Jehu the son of Jehoshaphat, the son of Nimshi, conspired against [a]Joram. (Now Joram had been defending Ramoth Gilead, he and all Israel, against Hazael king of Syria. 15 But [a]King Joram had returned to Jezreel to recover from the wounds which the Syrians had inflicted on him when he fought with Hazael king of Syria.) And Jehu said, "If you are so minded, let no one leave *or* escape from the city to go and tell *it* in Jezreel." 16 So Jehu rode in a chariot and went to Jezreel, for Joram was laid up there; [a]and Ahaziah king of Judah had come down to see Joram.

17 Now a watchman stood on the tower in Jezreel, and he saw the company of Jehu as he came, and said, "I see a company of men."

And Joram said, "Get a horseman and send him to meet them, and let him say, '*Is it* peace?'"

18 So the horseman went to meet him, and said, "Thus says the king: '*Is it* peace?'"

And Jehu said, "What have you to do with peace? Turn around and follow me."

So the watchman reported, saying, "The messenger went to them, but is not coming back."

19 Then he sent out a second horseman who came to them, and said, "Thus says the king: '*Is it* peace?'"

And Jehu answered, "What have you to do with peace? Turn around and follow me."

20 So the watchman reported, saying, "He went up to them and is not coming back; and the driving *is* like the driving of Jehu the son of Nimshi, for he drives furiously!"

21 Then Joram said, "Make ready." And his chariot was made ready. Then [a]Joram king of Israel and Ahaziah king of Judah went out, each in his chariot; and they went out to meet Jehu, and met him [b]on the property of Naboth the Jezreelite. 22 Now it happened, when Joram saw Jehu, that he said, "*Is it* peace, Jehu?"

So he answered, "What peace, as long as the harlotries of your mother Jezebel and her witchcraft *are so* many?"

23 Then Joram turned around and fled, and said to Ahaziah, "Treachery, Ahaziah!" 24 Now Jehu drew his bow with full strength and shot Jehoram between his arms; and the arrow came out at his heart, and he sank down in his chariot. 25 Then *Jehu* said to Bidkar his captain, "Pick *him* up, *and* throw him into the tract of the field of Naboth the Jezreelite; for remember, when you and I were riding together behind Ahab his father, that [a]the LORD laid this [b]burden upon him: 26 'Surely I saw yesterday the blood of Naboth and the blood of his sons,' says the LORD, [a]'and I will repay you in this plot,' says the LORD. Now therefore, take *and* throw him on the plot *of ground,* according to the word of the LORD."

Ahaziah of Judah Killed
(2 Chr. 22:7–9)

27 But when Ahaziah king of Judah saw *this,* he fled by the road to Beth Haggan.[1] So Jehu pursued him, and said, "Shoot him also in the chariot." *And they shot him* at the Ascent of Gur, which is by Ibleam. Then he fled to [a]Megiddo, and died there. 28 And his servants carried him in the chariot to Jerusalem, and buried him in his tomb with his fathers in the City of David. 29 In the eleventh year of Joram the son of Ahab, Ahaziah had become king over Judah.

Jezebel's Violent Death

30 Now when Jehu had come to Jezreel, Jezebel heard *of it;* [a]and she put paint on

---

9:11 [a] Jer. 29:26; Hos. 9:7; Mark 3:21; John 10:20; Acts 26:24; [1 Cor. 4:10] 9:13 [a] Matt. 21:7, 8; Mark 11:7, 8 9:14 [a] 2 Kin. 8:28 9:15 [a] 2 Kin. 8:29 9:16 [a] 2 Kin. 8:29 9:21 [a] 1 Kin. 19:17; 2 Chr. 22:7 [b] 1 Kin. 21:1–14 9:25 [a] 1 Kin. 21:19, 24–29 [b] Is. 13:1 9:26 [a] 1 Kin. 21:13, 19 9:27 [a] 2 Chr. 22:7, 9 [1] Literally *The Garden House* 9:30 [a] [Jer. 4:30]; Ezek. 23:40

her eyes and adorned her head, and looked
through a window. 31Then, as Jehu entered
at the gate, she said, [a]"*Is it* peace, Zimri,
murderer of your master?"
32And he looked up at the window, and
said, "Who *is* on my side? Who?" So two *or*
three eunuchs looked out at him. 33Then he
said, "Throw her down." So they threw her
down, and *some* of her blood spattered on
the wall and on the horses; and he trampled her underfoot. 34And when he had
gone in, he ate and drank. Then he said,
"Go now, see to this accursed *woman,* and
bury her, for [a]she was a king's daughter."
35So they went to bury her, but they found
no more of her than the skull and the feet
and the palms of *her* hands. 36Therefore
they came back and told him. And he said,
"This *is* the word of the LORD, which He
spoke by His servant Elijah the Tishbite,
saying, [a]'On the plot *of ground* at Jezreel
dogs shall eat the flesh of Jezebel;[1] 37and
the corpse of Jezebel shall be [a]as refuse on
the surface of the field, in the plot at Jezreel, so that they shall not say, "Here *lies*
Jezebel." ' "

Ahab's Seventy Sons Killed

10 Now Ahab had seventy sons in Samaria. And Jehu wrote and sent letters to Samaria, to the rulers of Jezreel,[1] to the elders, and to those who reared Ahab's *sons,* saying:

> 2 Now as soon as this letter comes to
> you, since your master's sons *are*
> with you, and you have chariots
> and horses, a fortified city also, and
> weapons, 3choose the best qualified
> of your master's sons, set *him* on his
> father's throne, and fight for your
> master's house.

4But they were exceedingly afraid, and
said, "Look, [a]two kings could not stand up
to him; how then can we stand?" 5And he
who *was* in charge of the house, and he
who *was* in charge of the city, the elders
also, and those who reared *the sons,* sent to
Jehu, saying, "We *are* your servants, we will
do all you tell us; but we will not make anyone king. Do *what is* good in your sight."
6Then he wrote a second letter to them,
saying:

> If you *are* for me and will obey my voice, take the heads of the men, your master's sons, and come to me at Jezreel by this time tomorrow.

Now the king's sons, seventy persons,
were with the great men of the city, *who*
were rearing them. 7So it was, when the letter came to them, that they took the king's
sons and [a]slaughtered seventy persons,
put their heads in baskets and sent *them*
to him at Jezreel.
8Then a messenger came and told him,
saying, "They have brought the heads of
the king's sons."

And he said, "Lay them in two heaps at the entrance of the gate until morning."

9So it was, in the morning, that he went
out and stood, and said to all the people,
"You *are* righteous. Indeed [a]I conspired
against my master and killed him; but who
killed all these? 10Know now that nothing
shall [a]fall to the earth of the word of the
LORD which the LORD spoke concerning
the house of Ahab; for the LORD has done
what He spoke [b]by His servant Elijah."
11So Jehu killed all who remained of the
house of Ahab in Jezreel, and all his great
men and his close acquaintances and his
priests, until he left him none remaining.

Ahaziah's Forty-two Brothers Killed

12And he arose and departed and went
to Samaria. On the way, at Beth Eked[1] of the
Shepherds, 13[a]Jehu met with the brothers
of Ahaziah king of Judah, and said, "Who
are you?"

So they answered, "We *are* the brothers of Ahaziah; we have come down to greet the sons of the king and the sons of the queen mother."

14And he said, "Take them alive!" So they
took them alive, and [a]killed them at the
well of Beth Eked, forty-two men; and he
left none of them.

9:31 [a] 1 Kin. 16:9–20; 2 Kin. 9:18–22 9:34 [a] [Ex. 22:28]; 1 Kin. 16:31 9:36 [a] 1 Kin. 21:23 [1] 1 Kings 21:23 9:37 [a] Ps. 83:10
10:1 [1] Following Masoretic Text, Syriac, and Targum; Septuagint reads *Samaria;* Vulgate reads *city.* 10:4 [a] 2 Kin. 9:24, 27
10:7 [a] Judg. 9:5; 1 Kin. 21:21; 2 Kin. 11:1 10:9 [a] 2 Kin. 9:14–24 10:10 [a] 1 Sam. 3:19; 1 Kin. 8:56; Jer. 44:28
[b] 1 Kin. 21:17–24, 29 10:12 [1] Or *The Shearing House* 10:13 [a] 2 Chr. 22:8 10:14 [a] 2 Chr. 22:8

The Rest of Ahab's Family Killed

15 Now when he departed from there, he
met [a]Jehonadab the son of [b]Rechab, *coming*
to meet him; and he greeted him and said
to him, "Is your heart right, as my heart *is*
toward your heart?"
And Jehonadab answered, "It is."
Jehu said, "If it is, [c]give *me* your hand."
So he gave *him* his hand, and he took him
up to him into the chariot. 16 Then he said,
"Come with me, and see my [a]zeal for the
LORD." So they had him ride in his chariot.
17 And when he came to Samaria, [a]he killed
all who remained to Ahab in Samaria, till
he had destroyed them, according to the
word of the LORD [b]which He spoke to Elijah.

Worshipers of Baal Killed

18 Then Jehu gathered all the people together, and said to them, [a]"Ahab served Baal
a little, Jehu will serve him much. 19 Now
therefore, call to me all the [a]prophets of Baal,
all his servants, and all his priests. Let no
one be missing, for I have a great sacrifice
for Baal. Whoever is missing shall not live."
But Jehu acted deceptively, with the intent
of destroying the worshipers of Baal. 20 And
Jehu said, "Proclaim a solemn assembly for
Baal." So they proclaimed *it.* 21 Then Jehu sent
throughout all Israel; and all the worshipers
of Baal came, so that there was not a man
left who did not come. So they came into
the temple[1] of Baal, and the [a]temple of Baal
was full from one end to the other. 22 And he
said to the one in charge of the wardrobe,
"Bring out vestments for all the worshipers
of Baal." So he brought out vestments for
them. 23 Then Jehu and Jehonadab the son
of Rechab went into the temple of Baal, and
said to the worshipers of Baal, "Search and
see that no servants of the LORD are here
with you, but only the worshipers of Baal."
24 So they went in to offer sacrifices and burnt
offerings. Now Jehu had appointed for himself eighty men on the outside, and had said,
"*If* any of the men whom I have brought into
your hands escapes, *whoever lets him escape,*
it shall be [a]his life for the life of the other."
25 Now it happened, as soon as he had
made an end of offering the burnt offering,
that Jehu said to the guard and to the captains, "Go in *and* kill them; let no one come
out!" And they killed them with the edge
of the sword; then the guards and the officers threw *them* out, and went into the inner room of the temple of Baal. 26 And they
brought the [a]*sacred* pillars out of the temple of Baal and burned them. 27 Then they
broke down the *sacred* pillar of Baal, and
tore down the temple of Baal and [a]made it
a refuse dump to this day. 28 Thus Jehu destroyed Baal from Israel.
29 However Jehu did not turn away from
the sins of Jeroboam the son of Nebat,
who had made Israel sin, *that is,* from [a]the
golden calves that *were* at Bethel and Dan.
30 And the LORD [a]said to Jehu, "Because you
have done well in doing *what is* right in My
sight, *and* have done to the house of Ahab
all that *was* in My heart, [b]your sons shall sit
on the throne of Israel to the fourth *generation.*" 31 But Jehu took no heed to walk in
the law of the LORD God of Israel with all
his heart; for he did not depart from [a]the
sins of Jeroboam, who had made Israel sin.

Death of Jehu

32 In those days the LORD began to cut
off *parts* of Israel; and [a]Hazael conquered
them in all the territory of Israel 33 from the
Jordan eastward: all the land of Gilead—
Gad, Reuben, and Manasseh—from [a]Aroer,
which *is* by the River Arnon, including [b]Gilead and Bashan.
34 Now the rest of the acts of Jehu, all that
he did, and all his might, *are* they not written in the book of the chronicles of the kings
of Israel? 35 So Jehu rested with his fathers,
and they buried him in Samaria. Then [a]Jehoahaz his son reigned in his place. 36 And
the period that Jehu reigned over Israel in
Samaria *was* twenty-eight years.

Athaliah Reigns in Judah
(2 Chr. 22:10–12)

11 When [a]Athaliah [b]the mother of Ahaziah saw that her son was [c]dead, she
arose and destroyed all the royal heirs. 2 But

10:15 [a] Jer. 35:6 [b] 1 Chr. 2:55 [c] Ezra 10:19; Ezek. 17:18 10:16 [a] 1 Kin. 19:10 10:17 [a] 2 Kin. 9:8; 2 Chr. 22:8 [b] 1 Kin. 21:21, 29
10:18 [a] 1 Kin. 16:31, 32 10:19 [a] 1 Kin. 18:19; 22:6 10:21 [a] 1 Kin. 16:32; 2 Kin. 11:18 [1] Literally *house,* and so elsewhere in this chapter
10:24 [a] 1 Kin. 20:39 10:26 [a] [Deut. 7:5, 25]; 1 Kin. 14:23; 2 Kin. 3:2 10:27 [a] Ezra 6:11; Dan. 2:5; 3:29 10:29 [a] 1 Kin. 12:28–30; 13:33, 34
10:30 [a] 2 Kin. 9:6, 7 [b] 2 Kin. 13:1, 10; 14:23; 15:8, 12 10:31 [a] 1 Kin. 14:16 10:32 [a] 1 Kin. 19:17; 2 Kin. 8:12; 13:22
10:33 [a] Deut. 2:36 [b] Amos 1:3–5 10:35 [a] 2 Kin. 13:1 11:1 [a] 2 Chr. 22:10 [b] 2 Kin. 8:26 [c] 2 Kin. 9:27

Jehosheba, the daughter of King Joram, sister of [a]Ahaziah, took Joash the son of Ahaziah, and stole him away from among the
king's sons *who were* being murdered; and
they hid him and his nurse in the bedroom,
from Athaliah, so that he was not killed. 3So
he was hidden with her in the house of the
LORD for six years, while Athaliah reigned
over the land.

Joash Crowned King of Judah
(2 Chr. 23:1–11)

4In [a]the seventh year Jehoiada sent and
brought the captains of hundreds—of the
bodyguards and the escorts—and brought
them into the house of the LORD to him.
And he made a covenant with them and
took an oath from them in the house of
the LORD, and showed them the king's
son. 5Then he commanded them, saying,
"This *is* what you shall do: One-third of you
who come on duty [a]on the Sabbath shall
be keeping watch over the king's house,
6one-third *shall be* at the gate of Sur, and
one-third at the gate behind the escorts.
You shall keep the watch of the house, lest
it be broken down. 7The two contingents of
you who go off duty on the Sabbath shall
keep the watch of the house of the LORD for
the king. 8But you shall surround the king
on all sides, every man with his weapons in
his hand; and whoever comes within range,
let him be put to death. You are to be with
the king as he goes out and as he comes in."

9[a]So the captains of the hundreds did
according to all that Jehoiada the priest
commanded. Each of them took his men
who were to be on duty on the Sabbath, with
those who were going off duty on the Sabbath, and came to Jehoiada the priest. 10And
the priest gave the captains of hundreds the
spears and shields which *had belonged* to
King David, [a]that were in the temple of the
LORD. 11Then the escorts stood, every man
with his weapons in his hand, all around the
king, from the right side of the temple to
the left side of the temple, by the altar and
the house. 12And he brought out the king's
son, put the crown on him, and *gave him*
the [a]Testimony;[1] they made him king and
anointed him, and they clapped their hands
and said, [b]"Long live the king!"

Death of Athaliah
(2 Chr. 23:12—24:1)

13[a]Now when Athaliah heard the noise of
the escorts *and* the people, she came to the
people *in* the temple of the LORD. 14When
she looked, there was the king standing by
[a]a pillar according to custom; and the leaders and the trumpeters were by the king.
All the people of the land were rejoicing
and blowing trumpets. So Athaliah tore her
clothes and cried out, "Treason! Treason!"

15And Jehoiada the priest commanded
the captains of the hundreds, the officers of
the army, and said to them, "Take her outside under guard, and slay with the sword
whoever follows her." For the priest had
said, "Do not let her be killed in the house
of the LORD." 16So they seized her; and she
went by way of the horses' entrance *into*
the king's house, and there she was killed.

17[a]Then Jehoiada [b]made a covenant between the LORD, the king, and the people,
that they should be the LORD's people,
and *also* [c]between the king and the people. 18And all the people of the land went to
the [a]temple of Baal, and tore it down. They
thoroughly [b]broke in pieces its altars and
images, and [c]killed Mattan the priest of Baal
before the altars. And [d]the priest appointed
officers over the house of the LORD. 19Then
he took the captains of hundreds, the bodyguards, the escorts, and all the people of
the land; and they brought the king down
from the house of the LORD, and went by
way of the gate of the escorts to the king's
house. Then he sat on the throne of the
kings. 20So all the people of the land rejoiced; and the city was quiet, for they had
slain Athaliah with the sword *in* the king's
house. 21Jehoash *was* [a]seven years old when
he became king.

Jehoash Repairs the Temple
(2 Chr. 24:1–14)

12 In the seventh year of Jehu, [a]Jeho-
ash[1] became king, and he reigned
forty years in Jerusalem. His mother's

11:2 [a] 2 Kin. 8:25 11:4 [a] 2 Kin. 12:2; 2 Chr. 23:1 11:5 [a] 1 Chr. 9:25 11:9 [a] 2 Chr. 23:8 11:10 [a] 2 Sam. 8:7; 1 Chr. 18:7 11:12 [a] Ex. 25:16; 31:18 [b] 1 Sam. 10:24 [1] That is, the Law (compare Exodus 25:16, 21 and Deuteronomy 31:9) 11:13 [a] 2 Kin. 8:26; 2 Chr. 23:12 11:14 [a] 2 Kin. 23:3; 2 Chr. 34:31 11:17 [a] 2 Chr. 23:16 [b] Josh. 24:24, 25; 2 Chr. 15:12–15 [c] 2 Sam. 5:3 11:18 [a] 2 Kin. 10:26, 27 [b] [Deut. 12:3] [c] 1 Kin. 18:40; 2 Kin. 10:11 [d] 2 Chr. 23:18 11:21 [a] 2 Chr. 24:1–14 12:1 [a] 2 Chr. 24:1 [1] Spelled *Joash* in 11:2ff

name *was* Zibiah of Beersheba. 2 Jehoash did *what was* right in the sight of the LORD all the days in which [a]Jehoiada the priest instructed him. 3 But [a]the high places were not taken away; the people still sacrificed and burned incense on the high places.

4 And Jehoash said to the priests, [a]"All the money of the dedicated gifts that are brought into the house of the LORD—each man's [b]census money, each man's [c]assessment money[1]—*and* all the money that a man [d]purposes in his heart to bring into the house of the LORD, 5 let the priests take *it* themselves, each from his constituency; and let them repair the damages of the temple, wherever any dilapidation is found."

6 Now it was so, by the twenty-third year of King Jehoash, [a]*that* the priests had not repaired the damages of the temple. 7 [a]So King Jehoash called Jehoiada the priest and the *other* priests, and said to them, "Why have you not repaired the damages of the temple? Now therefore, do not take *more* money from your constituency, but deliver it for repairing the damages of the temple." 8 And the priests agreed that they would neither receive *more* money from the people, nor repair the damages of the temple.

9 Then Jehoiada the priest took [a]a chest, bored a hole in its lid, and set it beside the altar, on the right side as one comes into the house of the LORD; and the priests who kept the door put [b]there all the money brought into the house of the LORD. 10 So it was, whenever they saw that *there was* much money in the chest, that the king's [a]scribe and the high priest came up and put it in bags, and counted the money that was found in the house of the LORD. 11 Then they gave the money, which had been apportioned, into the hands of those who did the work, who had the oversight of the house of the LORD; and they paid it out to the carpenters and builders who worked on the house of the LORD, 12 and to masons and stonecutters, and for buying timber and hewn stone, to [a]repair the damage of the house of the LORD, and for all that was paid out to repair the temple. 13 However [a]there were not made for the house of the LORD basins of silver, trimmers, sprinkling-bowls, trumpets, any articles of gold or articles of silver, from the money brought into the house of the LORD. 14 But they gave that to the workmen, and they repaired the house of the LORD with it. 15 Moreover [a]they did not require an account from the men into whose hand they delivered the money to be paid to workmen, for they dealt faithfully. 16 [a]The money from the trespass offerings and the money from the sin offerings was not brought into the house of the LORD. [b]It belonged to the priests.

Hazael Threatens Jerusalem

17 [a]Hazael king of Syria went up and fought against Gath, and took it; then [b]Hazael set his face to go up to Jerusalem. 18 And Jehoash king of Judah [a]took all the sacred things that his fathers, Jehoshaphat and Jehoram and Ahaziah, kings of Judah, had dedicated, and his own sacred things, and all the gold found in the treasuries of the house of the LORD and in the king's house, and sent *them* to Hazael king of Syria. Then he went away from Jerusalem.

Death of Joash
(2 Chr. 24:23–27)

19 Now the rest of the acts of Joash,[1] and all that he did, *are* they not written in the book of the chronicles of the kings of Judah?

20 And [a]his servants arose and formed a conspiracy, and killed Joash in the house of the Millo,[1] which goes down to Silla. 21 For Jozachar[1] the son of Shimeath and Jehozabad the son of Shomer,[2] his servants, struck him. So he died, and they buried him with his fathers in the City of David. Then [a]Amaziah his son reigned in his place.

Jehoahaz Reigns in Israel

13 In the twenty-third year of [a]Joash[1] the son of Ahaziah, king of Judah, [b]Jehoahaz the son of Jehu became king

---

12:2 [a] 2 Kin. 11:4 **12:3** [a] 1 Kin. 15:14; 22:43; 2 Kin. 14:4; 15:35 **12:4** [a] 2 Kin. 22:4 [b] Ex. 30:13–16 [c] Lev. 27:2–28 [d] Ex. 35:5; 1 Chr. 29:3–9 [1] Compare Leviticus 27:2ff **12:6** [a] 2 Chr. 24:5 **12:7** [a] 2 Chr. 24:6 **12:9** [a] 2 Chr. 23:1; 24:8 [b] Mark 12:41; Luke 21:1 **12:10** [a] 2 Sam. 8:17; 2 Kin. 19:2; 22:3, 4, 12 **12:12** [a] 2 Kin. 22:5, 6 **12:13** [a] 2 Chr. 24:14 **12:15** [a] 2 Kin. 22:7; [1 Cor. 4:2]; 2 Cor. 8:20 **12:16** [a] [Lev. 5:15, 18] [b] [Lev. 7:7; Num. 18:9] **12:17** [a] 2 Kin. 8:12 [b] 2 Chr. 24:23 **12:18** [a] 1 Kin. 15:18; 2 Kin. 16:8; 18:15, 16 **12:19** [1] Spelled *Jehoash* in 12:1ff **12:20** [a] 2 Kin. 14:5; 2 Chr. 24:25 [1] Literally *The Landfill* **12:21** [a] 2 Chr. 24:27 [1] Called *Zabad* in 2 Chronicles 24:26 [2] Called *Shimrith* in 2 Chronicles 24:26 **13:1** [a] 2 Kin. 12:1 [b] 2 Kin. 10:35 [1] Spelled *Jehoash* in 12:1ff

over Israel in Samaria, *and reigned* seventeen years. 2And he did evil in the sight of
the LORD, and followed the [a]sins of Jeroboam the son of Nebat, who had made Israel sin. He did not depart from them.
3Then [a]the anger of the LORD was
aroused against Israel, and He delivered
them into the hand of [b]Hazael king of
Syria, and into the hand of [c]Ben-Hadad
the son of Hazael, all *their* days. 4So Jehoahaz [a]pleaded with the LORD, and the LORD
listened to him; for [b]He saw the oppression of Israel, because the king of Syria oppressed them. 5[a]Then the LORD gave Israel
a deliverer, so that they escaped from under the hand of the Syrians; and the children of Israel dwelt in their tents as before.
6Nevertheless they did not depart from the
sins of the house of Jeroboam, who had
made Israel sin, *but* walked in them; [a]and
the wooden image[1] also remained in Samaria. 7For He left of the army of Jehoahaz only fifty horsemen, ten chariots, and
ten thousand foot soldiers; for the king of
Syria had destroyed them [a]and made them
[b]like the dust at threshing.
8Now the rest of the acts of Jehoahaz,
all that he did, and his might, *are* they not
written in the book of the chronicles of
the kings of Israel? 9So Jehoahaz rested
with his fathers, and they buried him in
Samaria. Then Joash his son reigned in
his place.

Jehoash Reigns in Israel

10In the thirty-seventh year of Joash
king of Judah, Jehoash[1] the son of Jehoahaz became king over Israel in Samaria,
and reigned sixteen years. 11And he did evil
in the sight of the LORD. He did not depart from all the sins of Jeroboam the son
of Nebat, who made Israel sin, *but* walked
in them.
12[a]Now the rest of the acts of Joash, [b]all
that he did, and [c]his might with which he
fought against Amaziah king of Judah, *are*
they not written in the book of the chronicles of the kings of Israel? 13So Joash [a]rested
with his fathers. Then Jeroboam sat on his
throne. And Joash was buried in Samaria
with the kings of Israel.

Death of Elisha

14Elisha had become sick with the illness
of which he would die. Then Joash the king
of Israel came down to him, and wept over
his face, and said, "O my father, my father,
[a]the chariots of Israel and their horsemen!"
15And Elisha said to him, "Take a bow and
some arrows." So he took himself a bow and
some arrows. 16Then he said to the king of
Israel, "Put your hand on the bow." So he put
his hand *on it,* and Elisha put his hands on
the king's hands. 17And he said, "Open the
east window"; and he opened *it.* Then Elisha said, "Shoot"; and he shot. And he said,
"The arrow of the LORD's deliverance and
the arrow of deliverance from Syria; for you
must strike the Syrians at [a]Aphek till you
have destroyed *them.*" 18Then he said, "Take
the arrows"; so he took *them.* And he said to
the king of Israel, "Strike the ground"; so he
struck three times, and stopped. 19And the
man of God was angry with him, and said,
"You should have struck five or six times;
then you would have struck Syria till you
had destroyed *it!* [a]But now you will strike
Syria *only* three times."
20Then Elisha died, and they buried
him. And the [a]*raiding* bands from Moab
invaded the land in the spring of the year.
21So it was, as they were burying a man, that
suddenly they spied a band *of raiders;* and
they put the man in the tomb of Elisha; and
when the man was let down and touched
the bones of Elisha, he revived and stood
on his feet.

Israel Recaptures Cities from Syria

22And [a]Hazael king of Syria oppressed
Israel all the days of Jehoahaz. 23But the
LORD was [a]gracious to them, had compassion on them, and [b]regarded them, [c]be-
cause of His covenant with Abraham, Isaac,
and Jacob, and would not yet destroy them
or cast them from His presence.
24Now Hazael king of Syria died. Then
Ben-Hadad his son reigned in his place.

13:2 [a] 1 Kin. 12:26–33 13:3 [a] Judg. 2:14 [b] 2 Kin. 8:12 [c] Amos 1:4 13:4 [a] [Ps. 78:34] [b] [Ex. 3:7, 9; Judg. 2:18]; 2 Kin. 14:26
13:5 [a] 2 Kin. 13:25; 14:25, 27; Neh. 9:27 13:6 [a] 1 Kin. 16:33 [1] Hebrew *Asherah,* a Canaanite goddess 13:7 [a] 2 Kin. 10:32 [b] [Amos 1:3]
13:10 [1] Spelled *Joash* in verse 9 13:12 [a] 2 Kin. 14:8–15 [b] 2 Kin. 13:14–19, 25 [c] 2 Kin. 14:9; 2 Chr. 25:17–25 13:13 [a] 2 Kin. 14:16
13:14 [a] 2 Kin. 2:12 13:17 [a] 1 Kin. 20:26 13:19 [a] 2 Kin. 13:25 13:20 [a] 2 Kin. 3:5; 24:2 13:22 [a] 2 Kin. 8:12, 13
13:23 [a] 2 Kin. 14:27 [b] [Ex. 2:24, 25] [c] Gen. 13:16, 17; 17:2–7; Ex. 32:13

25And Jehoash[1] the son of Jehoahaz recaptured from the hand of Ben-Hadad, the son
of Hazael, the cities which he had taken out
of the hand of Jehoahaz his father by war.
[a]Three times Joash defeated him and recaptured the cities of Israel.

Amaziah Reigns in Judah
(2 Chr. 25:1—26:2)

14 In [a]the second year of Joash the son
of Jehoahaz, king of Israel, [b]Amaziah
the son of Joash, king of Judah, became
king. 2He was twenty-five years old when he
became king, and he reigned twenty-nine
years in Jerusalem. His mother's name was
Jehoaddan of Jerusalem. 3And he did *what
was* right in the sight of the LORD, yet not
like his father David; he did everything [a]as
his father Joash had done. 4[a]However the
high places were not taken away, and the
people still sacrificed and burned incense
on the high places.
5Now it happened, as soon as the kingdom was established in his hand, that he
executed his servants [a]who had murdered
his father the king. 6But the children of the
murderers he did not execute, according
to what is written in the Book of the Law
of Moses, in which the LORD commanded,
saying, [a]"Fathers shall not be put to death
for their children, nor shall children be put
to death for their fathers; but a person shall
be put to death for his own sin."[1]
7[a]He killed ten thousand Edomites in
[b]the Valley of Salt, and took Sela by war,
[c]and called its name Joktheel to this day.
8[a]Then Amaziah sent messengers to Jehoash[1] the son of Jehoahaz, the son of Jehu,
king of Israel, saying, "Come, let us face one
another *in battle*." 9And Jehoash king of
Israel sent to Amaziah king of Judah, saying, [a]"The thistle that *was* in Lebanon sent
to the [b]cedar that *was* in Lebanon, saying,
'Give your daughter to my son as wife'; and
a wild beast that *was* in Lebanon passed by
and trampled the thistle. 10You have indeed
defeated Edom, and [a]your heart has lifted
you up. Glory *in that,* and stay at home; for
why should you meddle with trouble so that
you fall—you and Judah with you?"
11But Amaziah would not heed. Therefore Jehoash king of Israel went out; so
he and Amaziah king of Judah faced one
another at [a]Beth Shemesh, which *belongs*
to Judah. 12And Judah was defeated by Israel, and every man fled to his tent. 13Then
Jehoash king of Israel captured Amaziah
king of Judah, the son of Jehoash, the son
of Ahaziah, at Beth Shemesh; and he went
to Jerusalem, and broke down the wall of
Jerusalem from [a]the Gate of Ephraim to
[b]the Corner Gate—four hundred cubits.
14And he took all [a]the gold and silver, all
the articles that were found in the house
of the LORD and in the treasuries of the
king's house, and hostages, and returned
to Samaria.
15[a]Now the rest of the acts of Jehoash
which he did—his might, and how he
fought with Amaziah king of Judah—*are*
they not written in the book of the chronicles of the kings of Israel? 16So Jehoash
rested with his fathers, and was buried in
Samaria with the kings of Israel. Then Jeroboam his son reigned in his place.
17[a]Amaziah the son of Joash, king of Judah, lived fifteen years after the death of Jehoash the son of Jehoahaz, king of Israel.
18Now the rest of the acts of Amaziah, *are*
they not written in the book of the chronicles of the kings of Judah? 19And [a]they
formed a conspiracy against him in Jerusalem, and he fled to [b]Lachish; but they sent
after him to Lachish and killed him there.
20Then they brought him on horses, and he
was buried at Jerusalem with his fathers in
the City of David.
21And all the people of Judah took [a]Aza-
riah,[1] who *was* sixteen years old, and made
him king instead of his father Amaziah.
22He built [a]Elath and restored it to Judah,
after the king rested with his fathers.

Jeroboam II Reigns in Israel

23In the fifteenth year of Amaziah the
son of Joash, king of Judah, Jeroboam the

13:25 [a] 2 Kin. 13:18, 19 [1] Spelled *Joash* in verses 12–14, 25 14:1 [a] 2 Kin. 13:10 [b] 2 Chr. 25:1, 2 14:3 [a] 2 Kin. 12:2 14:4 [a] 2 Kin. 12:3 14:5 [a] 2 Kin. 12:20 14:6 [a] Deut. 24:16; [Jer. 31:30; Ezek. 18:4, 20] [1] Deuteronomy 24:16 14:7 [a] 2 Chr. 25:5–16 [b] 2 Sam. 8:13; 1 Chr. 18:12; Ps. 60:title [c] Josh. 15:38 14:8 [a] 2 Chr. 25:17, 18 [1] Spelled *Joash* in 13:12ff and 2 Chronicles 25:17ff 14:9 [a] Judg. 9:8–15 [b] 1 Kin. 4:33 14:10 [a] Deut. 8:14; 2 Chr. 32:25; [Ezek. 28:2, 5, 17; Hab. 2:4] 14:11 [a] Josh. 19:38; 21:16 14:13 [a] Neh. 8:16; 12:39 [b] Jer. 31:38; Zech. 14:10 14:14 [a] 1 Kin. 7:51; 2 Kin. 12:18; 16:8 14:15 [a] 2 Kin. 13:12, 13 14:17 [a] 2 Chr. 25:25–28 14:19 [a] 2 Chr. 25:27 [b] Josh. 10:31 14:21 [a] 2 Kin. 15:13; 2 Chr. 26:1 [1] Called *Uzziah* in 2 Chronicles 26:1ff, Isaiah 6:1, and elsewhere 14:22 [a] 1 Kin. 9:26; 2 Kin. 16:6; 2 Chr. 8:17

son of Joash, king of Israel, became king in Samaria, *and reigned* forty-one years. 24And he did evil in the sight of the LORD; he did not depart from all the [a]sins of Jeroboam the son of Nebat, who had made Israel sin. 25He [a]restored the territory of Israel [b]from the entrance of Hamath to [c]the Sea of the Arabah, according to the word of the LORD God of Israel, which He had spoken through His servant [d]Jonah the son of Amittai, the prophet who *was* from [e]Gath Hepher. 26For the LORD [a]saw *that* the affliction of Israel *was* very bitter; and whether bond or free, [b]there was no helper for Israel. 27[a]And the LORD did not say that He would blot out the name of Israel from under heaven; but He saved them by the hand of Jeroboam the son of Joash.

28Now the rest of the acts of Jeroboam, and all that he did—his might, how he made war, and how he recaptured for Israel, from [a]Damascus and Hamath, [b]*what had belonged* to Judah—*are* they not written in the book of the chronicles of the kings of Israel? 29So Jeroboam rested with his fathers, the kings of Israel. Then [a]Zechariah his son reigned in his place.

Azariah Reigns in Judah
(2 Chr. 26:3–23)

15 In the twenty-seventh year of Jeroboam king of Israel, [a]Azariah the son of Amaziah, king of Judah, [b]became king. 2He was sixteen years old when he became king, and he reigned fifty-two years in Jerusalem. His mother's name *was* Jecholiah of Jerusalem. 3And he did *what was* right in the sight of the LORD, according to all that his father Amaziah had done, 4[a]except that the high places were not removed; the people still sacrificed and burned incense on the high places. 5Then the LORD [a]struck the king, so that he was a leper until the day of his [b]death; so he [c]dwelt in an isolated house. And Jotham the king's son *was* over the *royal* house, judging the people of the land.

6Now the rest of the acts of Azariah, and all that he did, *are* they not written in the book of the chronicles of the kings of Judah? 7So Azariah rested with his fathers, and [a]they buried him with his fathers in the City of David. Then Jotham his son reigned in his place.

Zechariah Reigns in Israel

8In the thirty-eighth year of Azariah king of Judah, [a]Zechariah the son of Jeroboam reigned over Israel in Samaria six months. 9And he did evil in the sight of the LORD, [a]as his fathers had done; he did not depart from the sins of Jeroboam the son of Nebat, who had made Israel sin. 10Then Shallum the son of Jabesh conspired against him, and [a]struck and killed him in front of the people; and he reigned in his place.

11Now the rest of the acts of Zechariah, indeed they *are* written in the book of the chronicles of the kings of Israel.

12This *was* the word of the LORD which He spoke to Jehu, saying, [a]"Your sons shall sit on the throne of Israel to the fourth *generation.*"[1] And so it was.

Shallum Reigns in Israel

13Shallum the son of Jabesh became king in the thirty-ninth year of Uzziah[1] king of Judah; and he reigned a full month in Samaria. 14For Menahem the son of Gadi went up from [a]Tirzah, came to Samaria, and struck Shallum the son of Jabesh in Samaria and killed him; and he reigned in his place.

15Now the rest of the acts of Shallum, and the conspiracy which he led, indeed they *are* written in the book of the chronicles of the kings of Israel. 16Then from Tirzah, Menahem attacked [a]Tiphsah, all who *were* there, and its territory. Because they did not surrender, therefore he attacked *it.* All [b]the women there who were with child he ripped open.

Menahem Reigns in Israel

17In the thirty-ninth year of Azariah king of Judah, Menahem the son of Gadi

---

14:24 [a] 1 Kin. 12:26–33 14:25 [a] 2 Kin. 10:32; 13:5, 25 [b] Num. 13:21; 34:8; 1 Kin. 8:65 [c] Deut. 3:17 [d] Jon. 1:1; Matt. 12:39, 40 [e] Josh. 19:13
14:26 [a] Ex. 3:7; 2 Kin. 13:4; Ps. 106:44 [b] Deut. 32:36 14:27 [a] [2 Kin. 13:5, 23] 14:28 [a] 1 Kin. 11:24 [b] 2 Sam. 8:6; 1 Kin. 11:24; 2 Chr. 8:3
14:29 [a] 2 Kin. 15:8 15:1 [a] 2 Kin. 15:13, 30 [b] 2 Kin. 14:21; 2 Chr. 26:1, 3, 4 15:4 [a] 2 Kin. 12:3; 14:4; 15:35 15:5 [a] 2 Chr. 26:19–23;
Ps. 78:31 [b] Is. 6:1 [c] [Lev. 13:46]; Num. 12:14 15:7 [a] 2 Chr. 26:23 15:8 [a] 2 Kin. 14:29 15:9 [a] 2 Kin. 14:24
15:10 [a] Amos 7:9 15:12 [a] 2 Kin. 10:30 [1] 2 Kings 10:30 15:13 [1] Called *Azariah* in 14:21ff and 15:1ff
15:14 [a] 1 Kin. 14:17; Song 6:4 15:16 [a] 1 Kin. 4:24 [b] 2 Kin. 8:12; Hos. 13:16

became king over Israel, *and reigned* ten
years in Samaria. 18And he did evil in the
sight of the LORD; he did not depart all his
days from the sins of Jeroboam the son
of Nebat, who had made Israel sin. 19[a]Pul[1]
king of Assyria came against the land; and
Menahem gave Pul a thousand talents of
silver, that his hand might be with him to
[b]strengthen the kingdom under his control. 20And Menahem [a]exacted the money
from Israel, from all the very wealthy, from
each man fifty shekels of silver, to give to
the king of Assyria. So the king of Assyria
turned back, and did not stay there in the
land.
21Now the rest of the acts of Menahem,
and all that he did, *are* they not written in
the book of the chronicles of the kings of Israel? 22So Menahem rested with his fathers.
Then Pekahiah his son reigned in his place.

Pekahiah Reigns in Israel

23In the fiftieth year of Azariah king
of Judah, Pekahiah the son of Menahem
became king over Israel in Samaria, *and
reigned* two years. 24And he did evil in the
sight of the LORD; he did not depart from
the sins of Jeroboam the son of Nebat, who
had made Israel sin. 25Then Pekah the son
of Remaliah, an officer of his, conspired
against him and killed him in Samaria, in
the [a]citadel of the king's house, along with
Argob and Arieh; and with him were fifty
men of Gilead. He killed him and reigned
in his place.
26Now the rest of the acts of Pekahiah,
and all that he did, indeed they *are* written
in the book of the chronicles of the kings
of Israel.

Pekah Reigns in Israel

27In the fifty-second year of Azariah
king of Judah, [a]Pekah the son of Remaliah became king over Israel in Samaria,
and reigned twenty years. 28And he did evil
in the sight of the LORD; he did not depart
from the sins of Jeroboam the son of Nebat, who had made Israel sin. 29In the days
of Pekah king of Israel, Tiglath-Pileser king
of Assyria [a]came and took [b]Ijon, Abel Beth
Maachah, Janoah, Kedesh, Hazor, Gilead,
and Galilee, all the land of Naphtali; and
he [c]carried them captive to Assyria. 30Then
Hoshea the son of Elah led a conspiracy
against Pekah the son of Remaliah, and
struck and killed him; so he [a]reigned in
his place in the twentieth year of Jotham
the son of Uzziah.
31Now the rest of the acts of Pekah, and
all that he did, indeed they *are* written in
the book of the chronicles of the kings of
Israel.

Jotham Reigns in Judah
(2 Chr. 27:1–9)

32In the second year of Pekah the son of
Remaliah, king of Israel, [a]Jotham the son of
Uzziah, king of Judah, began to reign. 33He
was twenty-five years old when he became
king, and he reigned sixteen years in Jerusalem. His mother's name *was* Jerusha[1]
the daughter of Zadok. 34And he did *what
was* right in the sight of the LORD; he did
[a]according to all that his father Uzziah had
done. 35[a]However the high places were not
removed; the people still sacrificed and
burned incense on the high places. [b]He
built the Upper Gate of the house of the
LORD.
36Now the rest of the acts of Jotham,
and all that he did, *are* they not written
in the book of the chronicles of the kings
of Judah? 37In those days the LORD began
to send [a]Rezin king of Syria and [b]Pekah
the son of Remaliah against Judah. 38So
Jotham rested with his fathers, and was
buried with his fathers in the City of David his father. Then Ahaz his son reigned
in his place.

Ahaz Reigns in Judah
(2 Chr. 28:1–27)

16 In the seventeenth year of Pekah
the son of Remaliah, Ahaz the son
of Jotham, king of Judah, began to reign.
2Ahaz *was* twenty years old when he became king, and he reigned sixteen years
in Jerusalem; and he did not do *what was*
right in the sight of the LORD his God, as
his father David *had done.* 3But he walked

15:19 [a] 1 Chr. 5:26; Is. 66:19; Hos. 8:9 [b] 2 Kin. 14:5 [1] That is, Tiglath-Pileser III (compare verse 29) 15:20 [a] 2 Kin. 23:35
15:25 [a] 1 Kin. 16:18 15:27 [a] 2 Chr. 28:6; Is. 7:1 15:29 [a] 2 Kin. 16:7, 10; 1 Chr. 5:26 [b] 1 Kin. 15:20 [c] 2 Kin. 17:6 15:30 [a] 2 Kin. 17:1;
[Hos. 10:3, 7, 15] 15:32 [a] 2 Chr. 27:1 15:33 [1] Spelled *Jerushah* in 2 Chronicles 27:1 15:34 [a] 2 Kin. 15:3, 4; 2 Chr. 26:4, 5
15:35 [a] 2 Kin. 15:4 [b] 2 Chr. 23:20; 27:3 15:37 [a] 2 Kin. 16:5–9; Is. 7:1–17 [b] 2 Kin. 15:26, 27

in the way of the kings of Israel; indeed [a]he
made his son pass through the fire, according to the [b]abominations of the nations
whom the LORD had cast out from before
the children of Israel. 4And he sacrificed
and burned incense on the [a]high places,
[b]on the hills, and under every green tree.

5[a]Then Rezin king of Syria and Pekah
the son of Remaliah, king of Israel, came
up to Jerusalem to *make* war; and they besieged Ahaz but could not overcome *him.*
6At that time Rezin king of Syria [a]captured
Elath for Syria, and drove the men of Judah from Elath. Then the Edomites[1] went
to Elath, and dwell there to this day.

7So Ahaz sent messengers to [a]Tiglath-
Pileser king of Assyria, saying, "I *am* your
servant and your son. Come up and save
me from the hand of the king of Syria and
from the hand of the king of Israel, who rise
up against me." 8And Ahaz [a]took the silver
and gold that was found in the house of the
LORD, and in the treasuries of the king's
house, and sent *it as* a present to the king
of Assyria. 9So the king of Assyria heeded
him; for the king of Assyria went up against
[a]Damascus and [b]took it, carried *its people*
captive to [c]Kir, and killed Rezin.

10Now King Ahaz went to Damascus to
meet Tiglath-Pileser king of Assyria, and
saw an altar that *was* at Damascus; and
King Ahaz sent to Urijah the priest the design of the altar and its pattern, according
to all its workmanship. 11Then [a]Urijah the
priest built an altar according to all that
King Ahaz had sent from Damascus. So
Urijah the priest made *it* before King Ahaz
came back from Damascus. 12And when the
king came back from Damascus, the king
saw the altar; and [a]the king approached
the altar and made offerings on it. 13So he
burned his burnt offering and his grain
offering; and he poured his drink offering
and sprinkled the blood of his peace offerings on the altar. 14He also brought [a]the
bronze altar which *was* before the LORD,
from the front of the temple—from between the *new* altar and the house of the
LORD—and put it on the north side of the
new altar. 15Then King Ahaz commanded
Urijah the priest, saying, "On the great *new*
altar burn [a]the morning burnt offering, the
evening grain offering, the king's burnt sacrifice, and his grain offering, with the burnt
offering of all the people of the land, their
grain offering, and their drink offerings;
and sprinkle on it all the blood of the burnt
offering and all the blood of the sacrifice.
And the bronze altar shall be for me to inquire *by.*" 16Thus did Urijah the priest, according to all that King Ahaz commanded.

17[a]And King Ahaz cut off [b]the panels of
the carts, and removed the lavers from
them; and he took down [c]the Sea from the
bronze oxen that *were* under it, and put it
on a pavement of stones. 18Also he removed
the Sabbath pavilion which they had built
in the temple, and he removed the king's
outer entrance from the house of the LORD,
on account of the king of Assyria.

19Now the rest of the acts of Ahaz which
he did, *are* they not written in the book of
the chronicles of the kings of Judah? 20So
Ahaz rested with his fathers, and [a]was buried with his fathers in the City of David.
Then Hezekiah his son reigned in his place.

Hoshea Reigns in Israel

17 In the twelfth year of Ahaz king of Judah, [a]Hoshea the son of Elah became
king of Israel in Samaria, *and he reigned*
nine years. 2And he did evil in the sight of
the LORD, but not as the kings of Israel who
were before him. 3[a]Shalmaneser king of
Assyria came up against him; and Hoshea
[b]became his vassal, and paid him tribute
money. 4And the king of Assyria uncovered a conspiracy by Hoshea; for he had
sent messengers to So, king of Egypt, and
brought no tribute to the king of Assyria,
as *he had done* year by year. Therefore the
king of Assyria shut him up, and bound
him in prison.

Israel Carried Captive to Assyria
(2 Kin. 18:9–12)

5Now [a]the king of Assyria went throughout all the land, and went up to Samaria

16:3 [a] [Lev. 18:21]; 2 Kin. 17:17; 2 Chr. 28:3; Ps. 106:37, 38; Is. 1:1 [b] [Deut. 12:31]; 2 Kin. 21:2, 11 16:4 [a] 2 Kin. 15:34, 35 [b] [Deut. 12:2]; 1 Kin. 14:23 16:5 [a] 2 Kin. 15:37; Is. 7:1, 4 16:6 [a] 2 Kin. 14:22; 2 Chr. 26:2 [1] Some ancient authorities read *Syrians.* 16:7 [a] 2 Kin. 15:29; 1 Chr. 5:26; 2 Chr. 28:20 16:8 [a] 2 Kin. 12:17, 18; 2 Chr. 28:21 16:9 [a] 2 Kin. 14:28 [b] Amos 1:5 [c] Is. 22:6; Amos 9:7 16:11 [a] Is. 8:2 16:12 [a] 2 Chr. 26:16, 19 16:14 [a] Ex. 27:1, 2; 40:6, 29; 2 Chr. 4:1 16:15 [a] Ex. 29:39–41 16:17 [a] 2 Chr. 28:24 [b] 1 Kin. 7:27–29 [c] 1 Kin. 7:23–25 16:20 [a] 2 Chr. 28:27 17:1 [a] 2 Kin. 15:30 17:3 [a] 2 Kin. 18:9–12 [b] 2 Kin. 24:1 17:5 [a] 2 Kin. 18:9; Hos. 13:16

and besieged it for three years. 6[a]In the
ninth year of Hoshea, the king of Assyria
took Samaria and [b]carried Israel away to
Assyria, [c]and placed them in Halah and by
the Habor, the River of Gozan, and in the
cities of the Medes.

7For [a]so it was that the children of Israel
had sinned against the LORD their God,
who had brought them up out of the land
of Egypt, from under the hand of Pharaoh king of Egypt; and they had [b]feared
other gods, 8and [a]had walked in the statutes of the nations whom the LORD had
cast out from before the children of Israel,
and of the kings of Israel, which they had
made. 9Also the children of Israel secretly
did against the LORD their God things that
were not right, and they built for themselves high places in all their cities, [a]from
watchtower to fortified city. 10[a]They set up
for themselves *sacred* pillars and [b]wooden
images[1] [c]on every high hill and under every
green tree. 11There they burned incense on
all the high places, like the nations whom
the LORD had carried away before them;
and they did wicked things to provoke the
LORD to anger, 12for they served idols, [a]of
which the LORD had said to them, [b]"You
shall not do this thing."

13Yet the LORD testified against Israel
and against Judah, by all of His [a]prophets,
[b]every seer, saying, [c]"Turn from your evil
ways, and keep My commandments *and*
My statutes, according to all the law which I
commanded your fathers, and which I sent
to you by My servants the prophets." 14Nev-
ertheless they would not hear, but [a]stiff-
ened their necks, like the necks of their
fathers, who [b]did not believe in the LORD
their God. 15And they [a]rejected His statutes
[b]and His covenant that He had made with
their fathers, and His testimonies which He
had testified against them; they followed
[c]idols, [d]became idolaters, and *went* after the
nations who *were* all around them, *concerning* whom the LORD had charged them that
they should [e]not do like them. 16So they left
all the commandments of the LORD their
God, [a]made for themselves a molded image *and* two calves, [b]made a wooden image
and worshiped all the [c]host of heaven, [d]and
served Baal. 17[a]And they caused their sons
and daughters to pass through the fire,
[b]practiced witchcraft and soothsaying, and
[c]sold themselves to do evil in the sight of
the LORD, to provoke Him to anger. 18There-
fore the LORD was very angry with Israel,
and removed them from His sight; there
was none left [a]but the tribe of Judah alone.

19Also [a]Judah did not keep the commandments of the LORD their God, but
walked in the statutes of Israel which they
made. 20And the LORD rejected all the descendants of Israel, afflicted them, and [a]de-
livered them into the hand of plunderers,
until He had cast them from His [b]sight.
21For [a]He tore Israel from the house of David, and [b]they made Jeroboam the son of
Nebat king. Then Jeroboam drove Israel
from following the LORD, and made them
commit a great sin. 22For the children of
Israel walked in all the sins of Jeroboam
which he did; they did not depart from
them, 23until the LORD removed Israel out
of His sight, [a]as He had said by all His servants the prophets. [b]So Israel was carried
away from their own land to Assyria, *as it
is* to this day.

Assyria Resettles Samaria

24[a]Then the king of Assyria brought *people* from Babylon, Cuthah, [b]Ava, Hamath,
and from Sepharvaim, and placed *them* in
the cities of Samaria instead of the children
of Israel; and they took possession of Samaria and dwelt in its cities. 25And it was
so, at the beginning of their dwelling there,
that they did not fear the LORD; therefore
the LORD sent lions among them, which
killed *some* of them. 26So they spoke to the
king of Assyria, saying, "The nations whom
you have removed and placed in the cities

17:6 [a] 2 Kin. 18:10, 11; Is. 7:7–9; Hos. 1:4; 13:16; Amos 4:2 [b] Lev. 26:32, 33; [Deut. 28:36, 64; 29:27, 28] [c] 1 Chr. 5:26 17:7 [a] [Josh. 23:16] [b] Judg. 6:10 17:8 [a] [Lev. 18:3; Deut. 18:9]; 2 Kin. 16:3 17:9 [a] 2 Kin. 18:8 17:10 [a] 1 Kin. 14:23; Is. 57:5 [b] [Ex. 34:12–14; Deut. 16:21]; Mic. 5:14 [c] [Deut. 12:2]; 2 Kin. 16:4 [1] Hebrew *Asherim*, Canaanite deities 17:12 [a] [Ex. 20:3–5; Lev. 26:1; Deut. 5:7, 8] [b] [Deut. 4:19] 17:13 [a] Neh. 9:29, 30 [b] 1 Sam. 9:9 [c] [Jer. 18:11; 25:5; 35:15; Ezek. 18:31] 17:14 [a] Ex. 32:9; 33:3; Deut. 31:27; [Prov. 29:1; Acts 7:51] [b] Deut. 9:23; Ps. 78:22 17:15 [a] Jer. 44:3 [b] Ex. 24:6–8; Deut. 29:25 [c] Deut. 32:21; 1 Kin. 16:31; [1 Cor. 8:4] [d] 2 Chr. 13:7; Jer. 2:5; [Rom. 1:21–23] [e] [Deut. 12:30, 31] 17:16 [a] Ex. 32:8; 1 Kin. 12:28 [b] [1 Kin. 14:15] [c] [Deut. 4:19] [d] 1 Kin. 16:31; 22:53 17:17 [a] [Lev. 18:21]; 2 Kin. 16:3; Ezek. 23:37 [b] [Lev. 19:26; Deut. 18:10–12] [c] 1 Kin. 21:20 17:18 [a] 1 Kin. 11:13, 32 17:19 [a] Jer. 3:8 17:20 [a] Judg. 2:14; 2 Kin. 13:3; 15:29 [b] 2 Kin. 24:20 17:21 [a] 1 Kin. 11:11, 31 [b] 1 Kin. 12:20, 28 17:23 [a] 1 Kin. 14:16; Is. 8:4 [b] 2 Kin. 17:6 17:24 [a] Ezra 4:2, 10 [b] 2 Kin. 18:34

RELEASE // ACT WHEN HE CALLS

The Importance of Obedience

2 Kings 17:15 // And they rejected His statutes and His covenant that He had made with their fathers, and His testimonies which He had testified against them; they followed idols, became idolaters, and went after the nations who were all around them, concerning whom the LORD had charged them that they should not do like them.

Summary Message // It is often advantageous to know history because history can repeat itself. Nations that were once powerful, such as the Greek and Roman Empires, have disappeared in time. What destroyed these nations was disobedience to God's Word. It is prideful to do what God says not to do. When God's continuing warnings are ignored, His anger can be awakened. The consequences can be severe. By God's wrath, peoples and nations fall. Nations will continue to rise and fall until God's everlasting kingdom rules. Just as it is true of nations, individuals also fail because of their refusal to act when God calls for obedience to His will.

In the Book of 2 Kings, we follow the reigns of twelve kings of Israel. Sadly, we see Israel repeatedly rejecting God and going after false gods. They did not just deny God as an atheist does; they replaced Him. They followed worthless idols instead of the one true God. They refused to act when God continued to call for a change of heart. Second Kings 17 tells of the last king of Israel and serves as an epilogue reflecting all the disobedience that led to the tragedy of the northern kingdom's demise.

Practical Application // Obedience to God is one of the most common themes in the Bible. Disobedience is also everywhere we look around us today. It is evident in our homes, schools, governments, and even our churches. The great thing about being on this side of history is that we get to learn from others' mistakes, such as Israel's failure to repent. Obedience to God requires that we change our thinking and behavior from being worldly to becoming biblical. But changing our behavior requires an inner work of God. And the spiritual fitness of our hearts to prompt this work of God depends on our relationship with Him. What is your relationship with God like today? What would it take for you to have a heart that wants to do God's will?

Likewise, we must control our minds rather than letting them control us. Taking control of our minds leads to making the right choices that produce acts of obedience. One of the most important decisions we can make, then, is what and how we choose to think. What we think about is what we will move toward. We must keep our minds moving toward what God wants for our lives.

An accountability partner can help you greatly as you seek to obey and follow God with both your mind and heart. Ask God for a person who can help keep your heart and mind on track. A partner in faith is invaluable if you wish to recognize opportunities to obey and withstand the temptations of the world.

Fervent Prayer // Heavenly Father, help us avoid disobedience by failing to act when You call us to obey. Help us keep our minds and hearts focused on You rather than on earthly temptations or worthless idols. Send us accountability partners who will help us avoid temptation to disobey You. In Jesus' name we pray. Amen.

---

of Samaria do not know the rituals of the
God of the land; therefore He has sent lions
among them, and indeed, they are killing
them because they do not know the rituals
of the God of the land." 27Then the king of
Assyria commanded, saying, "Send there
one of the priests whom you brought from
there; let him go and dwell there, and let
him teach them the rituals of the God of
the land." 28Then one of the priests whom
they had carried away from Samaria came
and dwelt in Bethel, and taught them how
they should fear the LORD.

29However every nation continued to
make gods of its own, and put *them* [a]in
the shrines on the high places which the
Samaritans had made, *every* nation in
the cities where they dwelt. 30The men of
[a]Babylon made Succoth Benoth, the men
of Cuth made Nergal, the men of Hamath

17:29 [a] 1 Kin. 12:31; 13:32 17:30 [a] 2 Kin. 17:24

made Ashima, 31[a]and the Avites made
Nibhaz and Tartak; and the Sepharvites
[b]burned their children in fire to Adrammelech and Anammelech, the gods of Sepharvaim. 32So they feared the LORD, [a]and from
every class they appointed for themselves
priests of the high places, who sacrificed
for them in the shrines of the high places.
33[a]They feared the LORD, yet served their
own gods—according to the rituals of the
nations from among whom they were carried away.

34To this day they continue practicing
the former rituals; they do not fear the
LORD, nor do they follow their statutes or
their ordinances, or the law and commandment which the LORD had commanded
the children of Jacob, [a]whom He named
Israel, 35with whom the LORD had made a
covenant and charged them, saying: [a]"You
shall not fear other gods, nor [b]bow down
to them nor serve them nor sacrifice to
them; 36but the LORD, who [a]brought you
up from the land of Egypt with great power
and [b]an outstretched arm, [c]Him you shall
fear, Him you shall worship, and to Him
you shall offer sacrifice. 37And the statutes,
the ordinances, the law, and the commandment which He wrote for you, [a]you shall be
careful to observe forever; you shall not
fear other gods. 38And the covenant that
I have made with you, [a]you shall not forget, nor shall you fear other gods. 39But
the LORD your God you shall fear; and He
will deliver you from the hand of all your
enemies." 40However they did not obey,
but they followed their former rituals. 41[a]So
these nations feared the LORD, yet served
their carved images; also their children and
their children's children have continued
doing as their fathers did, even to this day.

Hezekiah Reigns in Judah
(2 Chr. 29:1, 2; 31:1)

18 Now it came to pass in the third year
of [a]Hoshea the son of Elah, king of Israel, *that* [b]Hezekiah the son of Ahaz, king of
Judah, began to reign. 2He was twenty-five
years old when he became king, and he
reigned twenty-nine years in Jerusalem.
His mother's name *was* [a]Abi[1] the daughter
of Zechariah. 3And he did *what was* right in
the sight of the LORD, according to all that
his father David had done.

4[a]He removed the high places and broke
the *sacred* pillars, cut down the wooden image[1] and broke in pieces the [b]bronze serpent that Moses had made; for until those
days the children of Israel burned incense
to it, and called it Nehushtan.[2] 5He [a]trusted
in the LORD God of Israel, [b]so that after him
was none like him among all the kings of
Judah, nor who were before him. 6For he
[a]held fast to the LORD; he did not depart
from following Him, but kept His commandments, which the LORD had commanded Moses. 7The LORD [a]was with him;
he [b]prospered wherever he went. And he
[c]rebelled against the king of Assyria and
did not serve him. 8[a]He subdued the Philistines, as far as Gaza and its territory, [b]from
watchtower to fortified city.

9Now [a]it came to pass in the fourth year
of King Hezekiah, which *was* the seventh
year of Hoshea the son of Elah, king of Israel, *that* Shalmaneser king of Assyria came
up against Samaria and besieged it. 10And
at the end of three years they took it. In the
sixth year of Hezekiah, that *is,* [a]the ninth
year of Hoshea king of Israel, Samaria was
taken. 11[a]Then the king of Assyria carried Israel away captive to Assyria, and put them
[b]in Halah and by the Habor, the River of
Gozan, and in the cities of the Medes, 12be-
cause they [a]did not obey the voice of the
LORD their God, but transgressed His covenant *and* all that Moses the servant of the
LORD had commanded; and they would
neither hear nor do *them.*

13And [a]in the fourteenth year of King
Hezekiah, Sennacherib king of Assyria
came up against all the fortified cities of
Judah and took them. 14Then Hezekiah king
of Judah sent to the king of Assyria at Lachish, saying, "I have done wrong; turn
away from me; whatever you impose on

17:31 [a] Ezra 4:9 [b] [Lev. 18:21; Deut. 12:31] 17:32 [a] 1 Kin. 12:31; 13:33 17:33 [a] Zeph. 1:5 17:34 [a] Gen. 32:28; 35:10 17:35 [a] Judg. 6:10 [b] [Ex. 20:5] 17:36 [a] Ex. 14:15–30 [b] Ex. 6:6; 9:15 [c] [Deut. 10:20] 17:37 [a] Deut. 5:32 17:38 [a] Deut. 4:23; 6:12 17:41 [a] 2 Kin. 17:32, 33 18:1 [a] 2 Kin. 17:1 [b] 2 Chr. 28:27; 29:1 18:2 [a] Is. 38:5 [1] Called *Abijah* in 2 Chronicles 29:1ff 18:4 [a] 2 Chr. 31:1 [b] Num. 21:5–9 [1] Hebrew *Asherah,* a Canaanite goddess [2] Literally *Bronze Thing* 18:5 [a] 2 Kin. 19:10; [Job 13:15; Ps. 13:5] [b] 2 Kin. 23:25 18:6 [a] Deut. 10:20; Josh. 23:8 18:7 [a] [2 Chr. 15:2] [b] Gen. 39:2, 3; 1 Sam. 18:5, 14; Ps. 60:12 [c] 2 Kin. 16:7 18:8 [a] 1 Chr. 4:41; 2 Chr. 28:18; Is. 14:29 [b] 2 Kin. 17:9 18:9 [a] 2 Kin. 17:3 18:10 [a] 2 Kin. 17:6 18:11 [a] 2 Kin. 17:6; Hos. 1:4; Amos 4:2 [b] 1 Chr. 5:26 18:12 [a] 2 Kin. 17:7–18 18:13 [a] 2 Chr. 32:1; Is. 36:1—39:8

me I will pay." And the king of Assyria as-
sessed Hezekiah king of Judah three hundred talents of silver and thirty talents of
gold. 15 So Hezekiah [a]gave *him* all the silver
that was found in the house of the LORD
and in the treasuries of the king's house.
16 At that time Hezekiah stripped *the gold*
from the doors of the temple of the LORD,
and *from* the pillars which Hezekiah king
of Judah had overlaid, and gave it to the
king of Assyria.

Sennacherib Boasts Against the LORD
(Is. 36:2–22; 2 Chr. 32:9–15)

17 Then the king of Assyria sent *the* Tar-
tan,[1] *the* Rabsaris,[2] *and the* Rabshakeh[3]
from Lachish, with a great army against Jerusalem, to King Hezekiah. And they went
up and came to Jerusalem. When they had
come up, they went and stood by the [a]aq-
ueduct from the upper pool, [b]which *was*
on the highway to the Fuller's Field. 18 And
when they had called to the king, [a]Eliakim
the son of Hilkiah, who *was* over the household, Shebna the scribe, and Joah the son
of Asaph, the recorder, came out to them.
19 Then *the* Rabshakeh said to them, "Say
now to Hezekiah, 'Thus says the great king,
the king of Assyria: [a]"What confidence *is*
this in which you trust? 20 You speak of *hav-*
ing plans and power for war; but *they are*
mere words. And in whom do you trust,
that you rebel against me? 21 [a]Now look! You
are trusting in the staff of this broken reed,
Egypt, on which if a man leans, it will go
into his hand and pierce it. So *is* Pharaoh
king of Egypt to all who trust in him. 22 But
if you say to me, 'We trust in the LORD our
God,' *is* it not He [a]whose high places and
whose altars Hezekiah has taken away, and
said to Judah and Jerusalem, 'You shall
worship before this altar in Jerusalem'?"'
23 Now therefore, I urge you, give a pledge
to my master the king of Assyria, and I will
give you two thousand horses—if you are
able on your part to put riders on them!
24 How then will you repel one captain of the
least of my master's servants, and put your
trust in Egypt for chariots and horsemen?
25 Have I now come up without the LORD
against this place to destroy it? The LORD
said to me, 'Go up against this land, and
destroy it.'"

26 [a]Then Eliakim the son of Hilkiah,
Shebna, and Joah said to *the* Rabshakeh,
"Please speak to your servants in [b]Aramaic,
for we understand *it;* and do not speak to
us in Hebrew[1] in the hearing of the people
who *are* on the wall."

27 But *the* Rabshakeh said to them, "Has
my master sent me to your master and to
you to speak these words, and not to the
men who sit on the wall, who will eat and
drink their own waste with you?"

28 Then *the* Rabshakeh stood and called
out with a loud voice in Hebrew, and spoke,
saying, "Hear the word of the great king,
the king of Assyria! 29 Thus says the king:
[a]'Do not let Hezekiah deceive you, for he
shall not be able to deliver you from his
hand; 30 nor let Hezekiah make you trust
in the LORD, saying, "The LORD will surely
deliver us; this city shall not be given into
the hand of the king of Assyria."' 31 Do not
listen to Hezekiah; for thus says the king
of Assyria: 'Make *peace* with me by a present and come out to me; and every one of
you eat from his own [a]vine and every one
from his own fig tree, and every one of you
drink the waters of his own cistern; 32 until I
come and take you away to a land like your
own land, [a]a land of grain and new wine, a
land of bread and vineyards, a land of olive groves and honey, that you may live and
not die. But do not listen to Hezekiah, lest
he persuade you, saying, "The LORD will
deliver us." 33 [a]Has any of the gods of the
nations at all delivered its land from the
hand of the king of Assyria? 34 Where *are*
the gods of [a]Hamath and Arpad? Where
are the gods of Sepharvaim and Hena and
[b]Ivah? Indeed, have they delivered Samaria
from my hand? 35 Who among all the gods
of the lands have delivered their countries
from my hand, [a]that the LORD should deliver Jerusalem from my hand?'"

36 But the people held their peace and
answered him not a word; for the king's

18:15 [a] 1 Kin. 15:18, 19; 2 Kin. 12:18; 16:8 18:17 [a] 2 Kin. 20:20 [b] Is. 7:3 [1] A title, probably *Commander in Chief* [2] A title, probably *Chief Officer* [3] A title, probably *Chief of Staff* or *Governor* 18:18 [a] 2 Kin. 19:2; Is. 22:20 18:19 [a] 2 Chr. 32:10; [Ps. 118:8, 9] 18:21 [a] Is. 30:2–7; Ezek. 29:6, 7 18:22 [a] 2 Kin. 18:4; 2 Chr. 31:1; 32:12 18:26 [a] Is. 36:11—39:8 [b] Ezra 4:7; Dan. 2:4 [1] Literally *Judean* 18:29 [a] 2 Chr. 32:15 18:31 [a] 1 Kin. 4:20, 25 18:32 [a] Deut. 8:7–9; 11:12 18:33 [a] 2 Kin. 19:12; Is. 10:10, 11 18:34 [a] 2 Kin. 19:13 [b] 2 Kin. 17:24 18:35 [a] Dan. 3:15

commandment was, "Do not answer him."
37 Then Eliakim the son of Hilkiah, who *was*
over the household, Shebna the scribe, and
Joah the son of Asaph, the recorder, came
to Hezekiah [a]with *their* clothes torn, and
told him the words of *the* Rabshakeh.

Isaiah Assures Deliverance
(Is. 37:1–7)

19 And [a]so it was, when King Hezekiah
heard *it,* that he tore his clothes, covered himself with [b]sackcloth, and went into
the house of the LORD. 2 Then he sent Eliakim, who *was* over the household, Shebna
the scribe, and the elders of the priests, covered with sackcloth, to Isaiah the prophet,
the son of Amoz. 3 And they said to him,
"Thus says Hezekiah: 'This day *is* a day of
trouble, and rebuke, and blasphemy; for
the children have come to birth, but *there*
is no strength to bring them forth. 4 [a]It may
be that the LORD your God will hear all the
words of *the* Rabshakeh, whom his master
the king of Assyria has sent to [b]reproach the
living God, and will [c]rebuke the words which
the LORD your God has heard. Therefore lift
up *your* prayer for the remnant that is left.'"
5 So the servants of King Hezekiah came
to Isaiah. 6 [a]And Isaiah said to them, "Thus
you shall say to your master, 'Thus says the
LORD: "Do not be [b]afraid of the words which
you have heard, with which the [c]servants
of the king of Assyria have blasphemed
Me. 7 Surely I will send [a]a spirit upon him,
and he shall hear a rumor and return to his
own land; and I will cause him to fall by the
sword in his own land."'"

Sennacherib's Threat and Hezekiah's Prayer
(Is. 37:8–20)

8 Then *the* Rabshakeh returned and
found the king of Assyria warring against
Libnah, for he heard that he had departed
[a]from Lachish. 9 And [a]the king heard concerning Tirhakah king of Ethiopia, "Look,
he has come out to make war with you."
So he again sent messengers to Hezekiah,
saying, 10 "Thus you shall speak to Hezekiah
king of Judah, saying: 'Do not let your God
[a]in whom you trust deceive you, saying, "Jerusalem shall not be given into the hand of
the king of Assyria." 11 Look! You have heard
what the kings of Assyria have done to all
lands by utterly destroying them; and shall
you be delivered? 12 [a]Have the gods of the

#OXYGEN
2 KINGS 19:6
Act When He Calls

God's plans are often much bigger than we can imagine. So be open. He wants our full cooperation without hesitation. Trust in God and His ability to enable you to hear His leading.

Just **breathe** and **act when He calls.**

nations delivered those whom my fathers
have destroyed, Gozan and Haran and Rezeph, and the people of [b]Eden who *were* in
Telassar? 13 [a]Where *is* the king of Hamath,
the king of Arpad, and the king of the city
of Sepharvaim, Hena, and Ivah?'"
14 [a]And Hezekiah received the letter from
the hand of the messengers, and read it;
and Hezekiah went up to the house of the
LORD, and spread it before the LORD. 15 Then
Hezekiah prayed before the LORD, and said:
"O LORD God of Israel, *the One* [a]who dwells
between the cherubim, [b]You are God, You
alone, of all the kingdoms of the earth.
You have made heaven and earth. 16 [a]In-
cline Your ear, O LORD, and hear; [b]open
Your eyes, O LORD, and see; and hear the
words of Sennacherib, [c]which he has sent
to reproach the living God. 17 Truly, LORD,
the kings of Assyria have laid waste the
nations and their lands, 18 and have cast
their gods into the fire; for they *were* [a]not
gods, but [b]the work of men's hands—wood
and stone. Therefore they destroyed them.
19 Now therefore, O LORD our God, I pray,

18:37 [a] Is. 33:7 19:1 [a] 2 Kin. 18:13; 2 Chr. 32:20–22; Is. 37:1 [b] Ps. 69:11 19:4 [a] 2 Sam. 16:12 [b] 2 Kin. 18:35 [c] Ps. 50:21 19:6 [a] Is. 37:6 [b] [Ps. 112:7] [c] 2 Kin. 18:17 19:7 [a] 2 Kin. 19:35–37; Jer. 51:1 19:8 [a] 2 Kin. 18:14, 17 19:9 [a] 1 Sam. 23:27; Is. 37:9 19:10 [a] 2 Kin. 18:5 19:12 [a] 2 Kin. 18:33, 34 [b] Ezek. 27:23 19:13 [a] 2 Kin. 18:34 19:14 [a] Is. 37:14 19:15 [a] Ex. 25:22; Ps. 80:1; Is. 37:16 [b] [Is. 44:6] 19:16 [a] Ps. 31:2; Is. 37:17 [b] 1 Kin. 8:29; 2 Chr. 6:40 [c] 2 Kin. 19:4 19:18 [a] [Is. 44:9–20; Jer. 10:3–5] [b] Ps. 115:4; Jer. 10:3; [Acts 17:29]

save us from his hand, [a]that all the kingdoms of the earth may [b]know that You *are*
the LORD God, You alone."

The Word of the LORD Concerning Sennacherib
(Is. 37:21–35)

20Then Isaiah the son of Amoz sent to
Hezekiah, saying, "Thus says the LORD God
of Israel: [a]'Because you have prayed to Me
against Sennacherib king of Assyria, [b]I have
heard.' 21This *is* the word which the LORD
has spoken concerning him:

'The virgin, [a]the daughter of Zion,
Has despised you, laughed
you to scorn;
The daughter of Jerusalem
[b]Has shaken *her* head
behind your back!

22 'Whom have you reproached
and blasphemed?
Against whom have you
raised *your* voice,
And lifted up your eyes on high?
Against [a]the Holy *One* of Israel.
23 [a]By your messengers you have
reproached the Lord,
And said: [b]"By the multitude
of my chariots
I have come up to the height
of the mountains,
To the limits of Lebanon;
I will cut down its tall cedars
And its choice cypress trees;
I will enter the extremity
of its borders,
To its fruitful forest.
24 I have dug and drunk strange water,
And with the soles of my
feet I have [a]dried up
All the brooks of defense."

25 'Did you not hear long ago
How [a]I made it,
From ancient times that I formed it?
Now I have brought it to pass,
That [b]you should be
For crushing fortified cities
into heaps of ruins.
26 Therefore their inhabitants
had little power;
They were dismayed and confounded;
They were *as* the grass of the field
And the green herb,
As [a]the grass on the housetops
And *grain* blighted before it is grown.

27 'But [a]I know your dwelling place,
Your going out and your coming in,
And your rage against Me.
28 Because your rage against
Me and your tumult
Have come up to My ears,
Therefore [a]I will put My
hook in your nose
And My bridle in your lips,
And I will turn you back
[b]By the way which you came.

29'This *shall be* a [a]sign to you:

'You shall eat this year such
as grows of itself,
And in the second year what
springs from the same;
Also in the third year sow and reap,
Plant vineyards and eat
the fruit of them.
30 [a]And the remnant who have
escaped of the house of Judah
Shall again take root downward,
And bear fruit upward.
31 For out of Jerusalem shall
go a remnant,
And those who escape
from Mount Zion.
[a]The zeal of the LORD of
hosts[1] will do this.'

32"Therefore thus says the LORD concerning the king of Assyria:

'He shall [a]not come into this city,
Nor shoot an arrow there,

19:19 [a] Ps. 83:18 [b] 1 Kin. 8:42, 43 19:20 [a] Is. 37:21 [b] 2 Kin. 20:5; Ps. 65:2 19:21 [a] Jer. 14:17; Lam. 2:13 [b] Ps. 22:7, 8 19:22 [a] Jer. 51:5 19:23 [a] 2 Kin. 18:17 [b] Ps. 20:7 19:24 [a] Is. 19:6 19:25 [a] [Is. 45:7] [b] Is. 10:5, 6 19:26 [a] Ps. 129:6 19:27 [a] Ps. 139:1–3; Is. 37:28 19:28 [a] Job 41:2; Ezek. 29:4; 38:4; Amos 4:2 [b] 2 Kin. 19:33, 36 19:29 [a] Ex. 3:12; 1 Sam. 2:34; 2 Kin. 20:8, 9; Is. 7:11–14; Luke 2:12 19:30 [a] 2 Kin. 19:4; 2 Chr. 32:22, 23 19:31 [a] 2 Kin. 25:26; Is. 9:7 [1] Following many Hebrew manuscripts and ancient versions (compare Isaiah 37:32); Masoretic Text omits *of hosts*. 19:32 [a] Is. 8:7–10

Nor come before it with shield,
Nor build a siege mound against it.
33 By the way that he came,
By the same shall he return;
And he shall not come into this city,'
Says the LORD.
34 'For [a]I will [b]defend this city, to save it
For My own sake and [c]for My
servant David's sake.'"

Sennacherib's Defeat and Death
(Is. 37:36–38; 2 Chr. 32:20–23)

35And [a]it came to pass on a certain night
that the angel[1] of the LORD went out, and
killed in the camp of the Assyrians one
hundred and eighty-five thousand; and
when *people* arose early in the morning,
there were the corpses—all dead. 36So Sennacherib king of Assyria departed and went
away, returned *home,* and remained at
[a]Nineveh. 37Now it came to pass, as he was
worshiping in the temple of Nisroch his
god, that his sons [a]Adrammelech and Sha-
rezer [b]struck him down with the sword; and
they escaped into the land of Ararat. Then
[c]Esarhaddon his son reigned in his place.

Hezekiah's Life Extended
(2 Chr. 32:24–26; Is. 38:1–8)

20 In [a]those days Hezekiah was sick
and near death. And Isaiah the
prophet, the son of Amoz, went to him
and said to him, "Thus says the LORD: 'Set
your house in order, for you shall die, and
not live.'"
2Then he turned his face toward the wall,
and prayed to the LORD, saying, 3[a]"Remember now, O LORD, I pray, how I have walked
before You in truth and with a loyal heart,
and have done *what was* good in Your
sight." And Hezekiah wept bitterly.
4And it happened, before Isaiah had
gone out into the middle court, that the
word of the LORD came to him, saying, 5"Return and tell Hezekiah [a]the leader of My
people, 'Thus says the LORD, the God of David your father: [b]"I have heard your prayer,
I have seen [c]your tears; surely I will heal
you. On the third day you shall go up to the
house of the LORD. 6And I will add to your
days fifteen years. I will deliver you and this
city from the hand of the king of Assyria;
and [a]I will defend this city for My own sake,
and for the sake of My servant David."'"
7Then [a]Isaiah said, "Take a lump of figs."
So they took and laid *it* on the boil, and he
recovered.
8And Hezekiah said to Isaiah, [a]"What
is the sign that the LORD will heal me, and
that I shall go up to the house of the LORD
the third day?"
9Then Isaiah said, [a]"This is the sign to
you from the LORD, that the LORD will do
the thing which He has spoken: *shall* the
shadow go forward ten degrees or go backward ten degrees?"
10And Hezekiah answered, "It is an easy
thing for the shadow to go down ten degrees; no, but let the shadow go backward
ten degrees."
11So Isaiah the prophet cried out to the
LORD, and [a]He brought the shadow ten degrees backward, by which it had gone down
on the sundial of Ahaz.

The Babylonian Envoys
(Is. 39:1–8)

12[a]At that time Berodach-Baladan[1] the
son of Baladan, king of Babylon, sent letters
and a present to Hezekiah, for he heard that
Hezekiah had been sick. 13And [a]Hezekiah
was attentive to them, and showed them all
the house of his treasures—the silver and
gold, the spices and precious ointment,
and all[1] his armory—all that was found
among his treasures. There was nothing
in his house or in all his dominion that
Hezekiah did not show them.
14Then Isaiah the prophet went to King
Hezekiah, and said to him, "What did these
men say, and from where did they come
to you?"
So Hezekiah said, "They came from a far
country, from Babylon."
15And he said, "What have they seen in
your house?"

19:34 [a] 2 Kin. 20:6; 2 Chr. 32:21 [b] Is. 31:5 [c] 1 Kin. 11:12, 13 19:35 [a] Ex. 12:29; Is. 10:12–19; 37:36; Hos. 1:7 [1] Or *Angel* 19:36 [a] Gen. 10:11 19:37 [a] 2 Kin. 17:31 [b] 2 Kin. 19:7; 2 Chr. 32:21 [c] Ezra 4:2 20:1 [a] 2 Kin. 18:13; 2 Chr. 32:24; Is. 38:1–22 20:3 [a] 2 Kin. 18:3–6; Neh. 13:22 20:5 [a] 1 Sam. 9:16; 10:1 [b] 2 Kin. 19:20; Ps. 65:2 [c] Ps. 39:12; 56:8 20:6 [a] 2 Kin. 19:34; 2 Chr. 32:21 20:7 [a] Is. 38:21 20:8 [a] Judg. 6:17, 37, 39; Is. 7:11, 14; 38:22 20:9 [a] Num. 23:19; Is. 38:7, 8 20:11 [a] Josh. 10:12–14; Is. 38:8 20:12 [a] 2 Kin. 8:8, 9; 2 Chr. 32:31; Is. 39:1–8 [1] Spelled *Merodach-Baladan* in Isaiah 39:1 20:13 [a] 2 Kin. 16:9; 2 Chr. 32:27, 31 [1] Following many Hebrew manuscripts, Syriac, and Targum; Masoretic Text omits *all*.

So Hezekiah answered, [a]"They have seen
all that *is* in my house; there is nothing
among my treasures that I have not shown
them."
16 Then Isaiah said to Hezekiah, "Hear the
word of the LORD: 17 'Behold, the days are
coming when all that *is* in your house, and
what your fathers have accumulated until
this day, [a]shall be carried to Babylon; nothing shall be left,' says the LORD. 18 'And [a]they
shall take away some of your sons who will
descend from you, whom you will beget;
[b]and they shall be [c]eunuchs in the palace
of the king of Babylon.' "
19 So Hezekiah said to Isaiah, [a]"The word
of the LORD which you have spoken *is*
good!" For he said, "Will there not be peace
and truth at least in my days?"

Death of Hezekiah
(2 Chr. 32:32, 33)

20 [a]Now the rest of the acts of Hezekiah—
all his might, and how he [b]made a [c]pool
and a tunnel and [d]brought water into the
city—*are* they not written in the book of
the chronicles of the kings of Judah? 21 So
[a]Hezekiah rested with his fathers. Then Manasseh his son reigned in his place.

Manasseh Reigns in Judah
(2 Chr. 33:1–20)

21 Manasseh [a]*was* twelve years old when
he became king, and he reigned fifty-
five years in Jerusalem. His mother's name
was Hephzibah. 2 And he did evil in the sight
of the LORD, [a]according to the abominations of the nations whom the LORD had
cast out before the children of Israel. 3 For
he rebuilt the high places [a]which Hezekiah
his father had destroyed; he raised up altars
for Baal, and made a wooden image,[1] [b]as
Ahab king of Israel had done; and he [c]wor-
shiped all the host of heaven[2] and served
them. 4 [a]He also built altars in the house
of the LORD, of which the LORD had said,
[b]"In Jerusalem I will put My name." 5 And
he built altars for all the host of heaven in
the [a]two courts of the house of the LORD.
6 [a]Also he made his son pass through the
fire, practiced [b]soothsaying, used witchcraft, and consulted spiritists and mediums. He did much evil in the sight of the
LORD, to provoke *Him* to anger. 7 He even
set a carved image of Asherah[1] that he had
made, in the house of which the LORD had
said to David and to Solomon his son, [a]"In
this house and in Jerusalem, which I have
chosen out of all the tribes of Israel, I will
put My name forever; 8 [a]and I will not make
the feet of Israel wander anymore from the
land which I gave their fathers—only if they
are careful to do according to all that I have
commanded them, and according to all the
law that My servant Moses commanded
them." 9 But they paid no attention, and Manasseh [a]seduced them to do more evil than
the nations whom the LORD had destroyed
before the children of Israel.
10 And the LORD spoke [a]by His servants
the prophets, saying, 11 [a]"Because Manasseh king of Judah has done these abominations ([b]he has acted more wickedly than
all the [c]Amorites who *were* before him, and
[d]has also made Judah sin with his idols),
12 therefore thus says the LORD God of Israel:
'Behold, *I* am bringing *such* calamity upon
Jerusalem and Judah, that whoever hears
of it, both [a]his ears will tingle. 13 And I will
stretch over Jerusalem [a]the measuring line
of Samaria and the plummet of the house of
Ahab; [b]I will wipe Jerusalem as *one* wipes a
dish, wiping *it* and turning *it* upside down.
14 So I will forsake the [a]remnant of My inheritance and deliver them into the hand of their
enemies; and they shall become victims of
plunder to all their enemies, 15 because they
have done evil in My sight, and have provoked Me to anger since the day their fathers came out of Egypt, even to this day.' "
16 [a]Moreover Manasseh shed very much
innocent blood, till he had filled Jerusalem from one end to another, besides his
sin by which he made Judah sin, in doing
evil in the sight of the LORD.

20:15 [a] 2 Kin. 20:13 **20:17** [a] 2 Kin. 24:13; 25:13–15; 2 Chr. 36:10; Jer. 27:21, 22; 52:17 **20:18** [a] 2 Kin. 24:12; 2 Chr. 33:11 [b] Dan. 1:3–7 [c] Dan. 1:11, 18 **20:19** [a] 1 Sam. 3:18 **20:20** [a] 2 Chr. 32:32 [b] Neh. 3:16 [c] 2 Kin. 18:17; Is. 7:3 [d] 2 Chr. 32:3, 30 **20:21** [a] 2 Kin. 16:20; 2 Chr. 32:33 **21:1** [a] 2 Chr. 33:1–9 **21:2** [a] 2 Kin. 16:3 **21:3** [a] 2 Kin. 18:4, 22 [b] 1 Kin. 16:31–33 [c] [Deut. 4:19; 17:2–5]; 2 Kin. 17:16; 23:5 [1] Hebrew *Asherah,* a Canaanite goddess [2] The gods of the Assyrians **21:4** [a] Jer. 7:30; 32:34 [b] 1 Kin. 11:13 **21:5** [a] 1 Kin. 6:36; 7:12; 2 Kin. 23:12 **21:6** [a] [Lev. 18:21; 20:2]; 2 Kin. 16:3; 17:17 [b] Lev. 19:26, 31; [Deut. 18:10–14]; 2 Kin. 17:17 **21:7** [a] 2 Sam. 7:13; 1 Kin. 8:29; 9:3; 2 Kin. 23:27; 2 Chr. 7:12, 16; Jer. 32:34 [1] A Canaanite goddess **21:8** [a] 2 Sam. 7:10; [2 Kin. 18:11, 12] **21:9** [a] [Prov. 29:12] **21:10** [a] 2 Kin. 17:13 **21:11** [a] 2 Kin. 23:26, 27; 24:3, 4 [b] 1 Kin. 21:26 [c] Gen. 15:16 [d] 2 Kin. 21:9 **21:12** [a] 1 Sam. 3:11; Jer. 19:3 **21:13** [a] Lam. 2:8; Amos 7:7, 8 [b] 2 Kin. 22:16–19; 25:4–11 **21:14** [a] Jer. 6:9 **21:16** [a] 2 Kin. 24:4

17Now [a]the rest of the acts of [b]Manas-
seh—all that he did, and the sin that he
committed—*are* they not written in the
book of the chronicles of the kings of Judah? 18So [a]Manasseh rested with his fathers,
and was buried in the garden of his own
house, in the garden of Uzza. Then his son
Amon reigned in his place.

Amon's Reign and Death
(2 Chr. 33:21–25)

19[a]Amon *was* twenty-two years old when
he became king, and he reigned two years
in Jerusalem. His mother's name *was* Me-
shullemeth the daughter of Haruz of Jot-
bah. 20And he did evil in the sight of the
LORD, [a]as his father Manasseh had done.
21So he walked in all the ways that his father
had walked; and he served the idols that his
father had served, and worshiped them.
22He [a]forsook the LORD God of his fathers,
and did not walk in the way of the LORD.

23[a]Then the servants of Amon [b]con-
spired against him, and killed the king
in his own house. 24But the people of the
land [a]executed all those who had conspired
against King Amon. Then the people of the
land made his son Josiah king in his place.

25Now the rest of the acts of Amon which
he did, *are* they not written in the book of the
chronicles of the kings of Judah? 26And he
was buried in his tomb in the garden of Uzza.
Then Josiah his son reigned in his place.

Josiah Reigns in Judah
(2 Chr. 34:1, 2)

22 Josiah [a]*was* eight years old when
he became king, and he reigned
thirty-one years in Jerusalem. His mother's
name *was* Jedidah the daughter of Adaiah
of [b]Bozkath. 2And he did *what was* right in
the sight of the LORD, and walked in all the
ways of his father David; he [a]did not turn
aside to the right hand or to the left.

Hilkiah Finds the Book of the Law
(2 Chr. 34:8–28)

3[a]Now it came to pass, in the eighteenth year of King Josiah, *that* the king
sent Shaphan the scribe, the son of Azaliah, the son of Meshullam, to the house
of the LORD, saying: 4"Go up to Hilkiah the
high priest, that he may count the money
which has been [a]brought into the house
of the LORD, which [b]the doorkeepers have
gathered from the people. 5And let them
[a]deliver it into the hand of those doing the
work, who are the overseers in the house of
the LORD; let them give it to those who *are*
in the house of the LORD doing the work,
to repair the damages of the house— 6to
carpenters and builders and masons—and
to buy timber and hewn stone to repair
the house. 7However [a]there need be no accounting made with them of the money delivered into their hand, because they deal
faithfully."

8Then Hilkiah the high priest said to
Shaphan the scribe, [a]"I have found the
Book of the Law in the house of the LORD."
And Hilkiah gave the book to Shaphan, and
he read it. 9So Shaphan the scribe went to
the king, bringing the king word, saying,
"Your servants have gathered the money
that was found in the house, and have delivered it into the hand of those who do the
work, who oversee the house of the LORD."
10Then Shaphan the scribe showed the king,
saying, "Hilkiah the priest has given me a
book." And Shaphan read it before the king.

11Now it happened, when the king heard
the words of the Book of the Law, that he
tore his clothes. 12Then the king commanded Hilkiah the priest, [a]Ahikam the
son of Shaphan, Achbor[1] the son of Michaiah, Shaphan the scribe, and Asaiah a
servant of the king, saying, 13"Go, inquire
of the LORD for me, for the people and for
all Judah, concerning the words of this
book that has been found; for great *is* [a]the
wrath of the LORD that is aroused against
us, because our fathers have not obeyed
the words of this book, to do according to
all that is written concerning us."

14So Hilkiah the priest, Ahikam, Achbor,
Shaphan, and Asaiah went to Huldah the
prophetess, the wife of Shallum the son of
[a]Tikvah, the son of Harhas, keeper of the

21:17 [a] 2 Chr. 33:11–19 [b] 2 Kin. 20:21 **21:18** [a] 2 Chr. 33:20 **21:19** [a] 2 Chr. 33:21–23 **21:20** [a] 2 Kin. 21:2–6, 11, 16 **21:22** [a] Judg. 2:12, 13; 1 Kin. 11:33; 1 Chr. 28:9 **21:23** [a] 1 Chr. 3:14; 2 Chr. 33:24, 25; Matt. 1:10 [b] 2 Kin. 12:20; 14:19 **21:24** [a] 2 Kin. 14:5 **22:1** [a] 1 Kin. 13:2; 2 Chr. 34:1 [b] Josh. 15:39 **22:2** [a] Deut. 5:32; Josh. 1:7 **22:3** [a] 2 Chr. 34:8 **22:4** [a] 2 Kin. 12:4 [b] 2 Kin. 12:9, 10 **22:5** [a] 2 Kin. 12:11–14 **22:7** [a] 2 Kin. 12:15; [1 Cor. 4:2] **22:8** [a] Deut. 31:24–26; 2 Chr. 34:14 **22:12** [a] 2 Kin. 25:22; Jer. 26:24 [1] *Abdon the son of Micah* in 2 Chronicles 34:20 **22:13** [a] [Deut. 29:23–28; 31:17, 18] **22:14** [a] 2 Chr. 34:22

wardrobe. (She dwelt in Jerusalem in the
Second Quarter.) And they spoke with her.
15Then she said to them, "Thus says the
LORD God of Israel, 'Tell the man who sent
you to Me, 16"Thus says the LORD: 'Behold,
[a]I will bring calamity on this place and on
its inhabitants—all the words of the book
which the king of Judah has read— 17[a]be-
cause they have forsaken Me and burned
incense to other gods, that they might
provoke Me to anger with all the works of
their hands. Therefore My wrath shall be
aroused against this place and shall not be
quenched.'"' 18But as for [a]the king of Judah,
who sent you to inquire of the LORD, in this
manner you shall speak to him, 'Thus says
the LORD God of Israel: "*Concerning* the
words which you have heard— 19because
your [a]heart was tender, and you [b]humbled
yourself before the LORD when you heard
what I spoke against this place and against
its inhabitants, that they would become
[c]a desolation and [d]a curse, and you tore
your clothes and wept before Me, I also
have heard *you*," says the LORD. 20"Surely,
therefore, I will gather you to your fathers,
and you [a]shall be gathered to your grave in
peace; and your eyes shall not see all the
calamity which I will bring on this place."'"
So they brought back word to the king.

Josiah Restores True Worship
(2 Chr. 34:29—35:19)

23 Now [a]the king sent them to gather
all the elders of Judah and Jerusalem to him. 2The king went up to the house
of the LORD with all the men of Judah, and
with him all the inhabitants of Jerusalem—
the priests and the prophets and all the
people, both small and great. And he [a]read
in their hearing all the words of the Book
of the Covenant [b]which had been found in
the house of the LORD.

3Then the king [a]stood by a pillar and
made a [b]covenant before the LORD, to
follow the LORD and to keep His commandments and His testimonies and His
statutes, with all *his* heart and all *his* soul,
to perform the words of this covenant that
were written in this book. And all the people took a stand for the covenant. 4And the
king commanded Hilkiah the high priest,
the [a]priests of the second order, and the
doorkeepers, to bring [b]out of the temple
of the LORD all the articles that were made
for Baal, for Asherah,[1] and for all the host of
heaven;[2] and he burned them outside Jerusalem in the fields of Kidron, and carried
their ashes to Bethel. 5Then he removed
the idolatrous priests whom the kings of
Judah had ordained to burn incense on
the high places in the cities of Judah and in
the places all around Jerusalem, and those
who burned incense to Baal, to the sun, to
the moon, to the constellations, and to [a]all
the host of heaven. 6And he brought out
the [a]wooden image[1] from the house of the
LORD, to the Brook Kidron outside Jerusalem, burned it at the Brook Kidron and
ground *it* to [b]ashes, and threw its ashes on
[c]the graves of the common people. 7Then
he tore down the *ritual* booths [a]of the perverted persons[1] that *were* in the house
of the LORD, [b]where the [c]women wove
hangings for the wooden image. 8And he
brought all the priests from the cities of
Judah, and defiled the high places where
the priests had burned incense, from [a]Geba
to Beersheba; also he broke down the high
places at the gates which *were* at the entrance of the Gate of Joshua the governor
of the city, which *were* to the left of the city
gate. 9[a]Nevertheless the priests of the high
places did not come up to the altar of the
LORD in Jerusalem, [b]but they ate unleavened bread among their brethren.

10And he defiled [a]Topheth, which *is* in
[b]the Valley of the Son[1] of Hinnom, [c]that no
man might make his son or his daughter
[d]pass through the fire to Molech. 11Then he
removed the horses that the kings of Judah
had dedicated to the sun, at the entrance to
the house of the LORD, by the chamber of
Nathan-Melech, the officer who *was* in the
court; and he burned the chariots of the sun
with fire. 12The altars that *were* [a]on the roof,

22:16 [a] Deut. 29:27; [Dan. 9:11–14] **22:17** [a] Deut. 29:25–27; 2 Kin. 21:22 **22:18** [a] 2 Chr. 34:26 **22:19** [a] 1 Sam. 24:5; [Ps. 51:17; Is. 57:15] [b] Ex. 10:3; 1 Kin. 21:29; [2 Chr. 7:14] [c] Lev. 26:31, 32 [d] Jer. 26:6; 44:22 **22:20** [a] 2 Kin. 23:30; [Ps. 37:37; Is. 57:1, 2] **23:1** [a] 2 Sam. 19:11; 2 Chr. 34:29, 30 **23:2** [a] Deut. 31:10–13 [b] 2 Kin. 22:8 **23:3** [a] 2 Kin. 11:14 [b] 2 Kin. 11:17 **23:4** [a] 2 Kin. 25:18; Jer. 52:24 [b] 2 Kin. 21:3–7 [1] A Canaanite goddess [2] The gods of the Assyrians **23:5** [a] 2 Kin. 21:3 **23:6** [a] 2 Kin. 21:7 [b] Ex. 32:20 [c] 2 Chr. 34:4 [1] Hebrew *Asherah,* a Canaanite goddess **23:7** [a] 1 Kin. 14:24; 15:12 [b] Ex. 35:25, 26; Ezek. 16:16 [c] Ex. 38:8 [1] Hebrew *qedeshim,* that is, those practicing sodomy and prostitution in religious rituals **23:8** [a] Josh. 21:17; 1 Kin. 15:22 **23:9** [a] [Ezek. 44:10–14] [b] 1 Sam. 2:36 **23:10** [a] Is. 30:33; Jer. 7:31, 32 [b] Josh. 15:8 [c] [Lev. 18:21; Deut. 18:10]; Ezek. 23:37–39 [d] 2 Kin. 21:6 [1] Kethib reads *Sons.* **23:12** [a] Jer. 19:13; Zeph. 1:5

the upper chamber of Ahaz, which the kings
of Judah had made, and the altars which
[b]Manasseh had made in the two courts of
the house of the LORD, the king broke down
and pulverized there, and threw their dust
into the Brook Kidron. 13 Then the king defiled the high places that *were* east of Jerusalem, which *were* on the south of the Mount
of Corruption, which [a]Solomon king of Israel had built for Ashtoreth the abomination
of the Sidonians, for Chemosh the abomination of the Moabites, and for Milcom the
abomination of the people of Ammon. 14 And
he [a]broke in pieces the *sacred* pillars and cut
down the wooden images, and filled their
places with the bones of men.

15 Moreover the altar that *was* at Bethel,
and the high place [a]which Jeroboam the
son of Nebat, who made Israel sin, had
made, both that altar and the high place he
broke down; and he burned the high place
and crushed *it* to powder, and burned the
wooden image. 16 As Josiah turned, he saw
the tombs that *were* there on the mountain. And he sent and took the bones out
of the tombs and burned *them* on the altar,
and defiled it according to the [a]word of the
LORD which the man of God proclaimed,
who proclaimed these words. 17 Then he
said, "What gravestone *is* this that I see?"

So the men of the city told him, "*It is* [a]the
tomb of the man of God who came from
Judah and proclaimed these things which
you have done against the altar of Bethel."

18 And he said, "Let him alone; let no
one move his bones." So they let his bones
alone, with the bones of [a]the prophet who
came from Samaria.

19 Now Josiah also took away all the
shrines of the high places that *were* [a]in
the cities of Samaria, which the kings of
Israel had made to provoke the LORD[1] to
anger; and he did to them according to all
the deeds he had done in Bethel. 20 [a]He [b]ex-
ecuted all the priests of the high places
who *were* there, on the altars, and [c]burned
men's bones on them; and he returned to
Jerusalem.

21 Then the king commanded all the people, saying, [a]"Keep the Passover to the LORD
your God, [b]as *it is* written in this Book of
the Covenant." 22 [a]Such a Passover surely
had never been held since the days of the
judges who judged Israel, nor in all the days
of the kings of Israel and the kings of Judah. 23 But in the eighteenth year of King Josiah this Passover was held before the LORD
in Jerusalem. 24 Moreover Josiah put away
those who consulted mediums and spiritists, the household gods and idols, all the
abominations that were seen in the land
of Judah and in Jerusalem, that he might
perform the words of [a]the law which were
written in the book [b]that Hilkiah the priest
found in the house of the LORD. 25 [a]Now before him there was no king like him, who
turned to the LORD with all his heart, with
all his soul, and with all his might, according to all the Law of Moses; nor after him
did *any* arise like him.

Impending Judgment on Judah

26 Nevertheless the LORD did not turn
from the fierceness of His great wrath, with
which His anger was aroused against Judah, [a]because of all the provocations with
which Manasseh had provoked Him. 27 And
the LORD said, "I will also remove Judah
from My sight, as [a]I have removed Israel,
and will cast off this city Jerusalem which
I have chosen, and the house of which I
said, [b]'My name shall be there.'"[1]

Josiah Dies in Battle
(2 Chr. 35:20—36:1)

28 Now the rest of the acts of Josiah, and
all that he did, *are* they not written in the
book of the chronicles of the kings of Judah? 29 [a]In his days Pharaoh Necho king of
Egypt went to the aid of the king of Assyria,
to the River Euphrates; and King Josiah
went against him. And *Pharaoh Necho* killed
him at [b]Megiddo when he [c]confronted him.
30 [a]Then his servants moved his body in a
chariot from Megiddo, brought him to Jerusalem, and buried him in his own tomb.

23:12 [b] 2 Kin. 21:5; 2 Chr. 33:5 **23:13** [a] 1 Kin. 11:5–7 **23:14** [a] [Ex. 23:24; Deut. 7:5–25] **23:15** [a] 1 Kin. 12:28–33 **23:16** [a] 1 Kin. 13:2 **23:17** [a] 1 Kin. 13:1, 30, 31 **23:18** [a] 1 Kin. 13:11, 31 **23:19** [a] 2 Chr. 34:6, 7 [1] Following Septuagint, Syriac, and Vulgate; Masoretic Text and Targum omit *the LORD*. **23:20** [a] 1 Kin. 13:2 [b] [Ex. 22:20]; 1 Kin. 18:40; 2 Kin. 10:25; 11:18 [c] 2 Chr. 34:5 **23:21** [a] Num. 9:5; Josh. 5:10; 2 Chr. 35:1 [b] Ex. 12:3; Lev. 23:5; Num. 9:2; Deut. 16:2–8 **23:22** [a] 2 Chr. 35:18, 19 **23:24** [a] [Lev. 19:31; 20:27]; Deut. 18:11 [b] 2 Kin. 22:8 **23:25** [a] 2 Kin. 18:5 **23:26** [a] 2 Kin. 21:11, 12; 24:3, 4; Jer. 15:4 **23:27** [a] 2 Kin. 17:18, 20; 18:11; 21:13 [b] 1 Kin. 8:29; 9:3; 2 Kin. 21:4, 7 [1] 1 Kings 8:29 **23:29** [a] 2 Chr. 35:20; Jer. 2:16; 46:2 [b] Judg. 5:19; Zech. 12:11 [c] 2 Kin. 14:8 **23:30** [a] 2 Chr. 35:24; 2 Kin. 22:20

And [b]the people of the land took Jehoahaz the son of Josiah, anointed him, and made him king in his father's place.

The Reign and Captivity of Jehoahaz
(2 Chr. 36:1–4)

31[a]Jehoahaz *was* twenty-three years old when he became king, and he reigned three months in Jerusalem. His mother's name *was* [b]Hamutal the daughter of Jeremiah of Libnah. 32And he did evil in the sight of the LORD, according to all that his fathers had done. 33Now Pharaoh Necho put him in prison [a]at Riblah in the land of Hamath, that he might not reign in Jerusalem; and he imposed on the land a tribute of one hundred talents of silver and a talent of gold. 34Then [a]Pharaoh Necho made Eliakim the son of Josiah king in place of his father Josiah, and [b]changed his name to [c]Jehoiakim. And *Pharaoh* took Jehoahaz [d]and went to Egypt, and he[1] died there.

Jehoiakim Reigns in Judah
(2 Chr. 36:5–8)

35So Jehoiakim gave [a]the silver and gold to Pharaoh; but he taxed the land to give money according to the command of Pharaoh; he exacted the silver and gold from the people of the land, from every one according to his assessment, to give *it* to Pharaoh Necho. 36[a]Jehoiakim *was* twenty-five years old when he became king, and he reigned eleven years in Jerusalem. His mother's name *was* Zebudah the daughter of Pedaiah of Rumah. 37And he did evil in the sight of the LORD, according to all that his fathers had done.

Judah Overrun by Enemies

24 In [a]his days Nebuchadnezzar king of [b]Babylon came up, and Jehoiakim became his vassal *for* three years. Then he turned and rebelled against him. 2[a]And the LORD sent against him *raiding* bands of Chaldeans, bands of Syrians, bands of Moabites, and bands of the people of Ammon; He sent them against Judah to destroy it, [b]according to the word of the LORD which He had spoken by His servants the prophets. 3Surely at the commandment of the LORD *this* came upon Judah, to remove *them* from His sight [a]because of the sins of Manasseh, according to all that he had done, 4[a]and also because of the innocent blood that he had shed; for he had filled Jerusalem with innocent blood, which the LORD would not pardon.

5Now the rest of the acts of Jehoiakim, and all that he did, *are* they not written in the book of the chronicles of the kings of Judah? 6[a]So Jehoiakim rested with his fathers. Then Jehoiachin his son reigned in his place.

7And [a]the king of Egypt did not come out of his land anymore, for [b]the king of Babylon had taken all that belonged to the king of Egypt from the Brook of Egypt to the River Euphrates.

The Reign and Captivity of Jehoiachin
(2 Chr. 36:9, 10)

8[a]Jehoiachin *was* eighteen years old when he became king, and he reigned in Jerusalem three months. His mother's name *was* Nehushta the daughter of Elnathan of Jerusalem. 9And he did evil in the sight of the LORD, according to all that his father had done.

10[a]At that time the servants of Nebuchadnezzar king of Babylon came up against Jerusalem, and the city was besieged. 11And Nebuchadnezzar king of Babylon came against the city, as his servants were besieging it. 12[a]Then Jehoiachin king of Judah, his mother, his servants, his princes, and his officers went out to the king of Babylon; and the king of Babylon, [b]in the eighth year of his reign, took him prisoner.

The Captivity of Jerusalem

13[a]And he carried out from there all the treasures of the house of the LORD and the treasures of the king's house, and he [b]cut in pieces all the articles of gold which Solomon king of Israel had made in the

---

23:30 [b] 2 Chr. 36:1–4 23:31 [a] 1 Chr. 3:15; Jer. 22:11 [b] 2 Kin. 24:18 23:33 [a] 2 Kin. 25:6; Jer. 52:27 23:34 [a] 2 Chr. 36:4 [b] 2 Kin. 24:17; Dan. 1:7 [c] Matt. 1:11 [d] Jer. 22:11, 12; Ezek. 19:3, 4 [1] That is, Jehoahaz 23:35 [a] 2 Kin. 23:33 23:36 [a] 2 Chr. 36:5; Jer. 22:18, 19; 26:1 24:1 [a] 2 Chr. 36:6; Jer. 25:1, 9; Dan. 1:1 [b] 2 Kin. 20:14 24:2 [a] Jer. 25:9; 32:28; 35:11; Ezek. 19:8 [b] 2 Kin. 20:17; 21:12–14; 23:27 24:3 [a] 2 Kin. 21:2, 11; 23:26 24:4 [a] 2 Kin. 21:16 24:6 [a] 2 Chr. 36:6, 8; Jer. 22:18, 19 24:7 [a] Jer. 37:5–7 [b] Jer. 46:2 24:8 [a] 1 Chr. 3:16; 2 Chr. 36:9 24:10 [a] Dan. 1:1 24:12 [a] Jer. 22:24–30; 24:1; 29:1, 2; Ezek. 17:12 [b] 2 Chr. 36:10 24:13 [a] 2 Kin. 20:17; Is. 39:6 [b] Dan. 5:2, 3

temple of the LORD, [c]as the LORD had said.
14 Also [a]he carried into captivity all Jerusalem: all the captains and all the mighty
men of valor, [b]ten thousand captives, and
[c]all the craftsmen and smiths. None remained except [d]the poorest people of the
land. 15 And [a]he carried Jehoiachin captive
to Babylon. The king's mother, the king's
wives, his officers, and the mighty of the
land he carried into captivity from Jerusalem to Babylon. 16 [a]All the valiant men,
seven thousand, and craftsmen and smiths,
one thousand, all *who were* strong *and* fit
for war, these the king of Babylon brought
captive to Babylon.

Zedekiah Reigns in Judah
(2 Chr. 36:11–14; Jer. 52:1–3)

17 Then [a]the king of Babylon made Mattaniah, [b]*Jehoiachin's*[1] uncle, king in his place,
and [c]changed his name to Zedekiah.

18 [a]Zedekiah *was* twenty-one years old
when he became king, and he reigned
eleven years in Jerusalem. His mother's
name *was* [b]Hamutal the daughter of Jeremiah of Libnah. 19 [a]He also did evil in the
sight of the LORD, according to all that Jehoiakim had done. 20 For because of the
anger of the LORD *this* happened in Jerusalem and Judah, that He finally cast them
out from His presence. [a]Then Zedekiah rebelled against the king of Babylon.

The Fall and Captivity of Judah
(2 Chr. 36:15–21; Jer. 52:4–30)

25 Now it came to pass [a]in the ninth
year of his reign, in the tenth
month, on the tenth *day* of the month, *that*
Nebuchadnezzar king of Babylon and all
his army came against Jerusalem and encamped against it; and they built a siege
wall against it all around. 2 So the city was
besieged until the eleventh year of King
Zedekiah. 3 By the ninth *day* of the [a]*fourth*
month the famine had become so severe
in the city that there was no food for the
people of the land.

4 Then [a]the city wall was broken through,
and all the men of war *fled* at night by way
of the gate between two walls, which was by
the king's garden, even though the Chaldeans *were* still encamped all around against
the city. And [b]*the king*[1] went by way of the
plain.[2] 5 But the army of the Chaldeans pursued the king, and they overtook him in
the plains of Jericho. All his army was scattered from him. 6 So they took the king and
brought him up to the king of Babylon [a]at
Riblah, and they pronounced judgment
on him. 7 Then they killed the sons of Zedekiah before his eyes, [a]put out the eyes of
Zedekiah, bound him with bronze fetters,
and took him to Babylon.

8 And in the fifth month, [a]on the seventh
day of the month (which *was* [b]the nineteenth year of King Nebuchadnezzar king
of Babylon), [c]Nebuzaradan the captain of
the guard, a servant of the king of Babylon,
came to Jerusalem. 9 [a]He burned the house
of the LORD [b]and the king's house; all the
houses of Jerusalem, that is, all the houses
of the great, [c]he burned with fire. 10 And all
the army of the Chaldeans who *were with*
the captain of the guard [a]broke down the
walls of Jerusalem all around.

11 Then Nebuzaradan the captain of the
guard carried away captive [a]the rest of the
people *who* remained in the city and the
defectors who had deserted to the king of
Babylon, with the rest of the multitude.
12 But the captain of the guard [a]left *some* of
the poor of the land as vinedressers and
farmers. 13 [a]The bronze [b]pillars that *were* in
the house of the LORD, and [c]the carts and
[d]the bronze Sea that *were* in the house of
the LORD, the Chaldeans broke in pieces,
and [e]carried their bronze to Babylon. 14 They
also took away [a]the pots, the shovels, the
trimmers, the spoons, and all the bronze
utensils with which the priests ministered.
15 The firepans and the basins, the things of
solid gold and solid silver, the captain of the
guard took away. 16 The two pillars, one Sea,
and the carts, which Solomon had made for

24:13 [c] Jer. 20:5 **24:14** [a] Is. 3:2, 3; Jer. 24:1 [b] 2 Kin. 24:16; Jer. 52:28 [c] 1 Sam. 13:19 [d] 2 Kin. 25:12 **24:15** [a] 2 Chr. 36:10; Esth. 2:6; Jer. 22:24–28; Ezek. 17:12 **24:16** [a] Jer. 52:28 **24:17** [a] Jer. 37:1 [b] 1 Chr. 3:15; 2 Chr. 36:10 [c] 2 Chr. 36:4 [1] Literally *his* **24:18** [a] 2 Chr. 36:11; Jer. 52:1 [b] 2 Kin. 23:31 **24:19** [a] 2 Chr. 36:12 **24:20** [a] 2 Chr. 36:13; Ezek. 17:15 **25:1** [a] 2 Chr. 36:17; Jer. 6:6; 34:2; Ezek. 4:2; 24:1, 2; Hab. 1:6 **25:3** [a] 2 Kin. 6:24, 25; Is. 3:1; Jer. 39:2; Lam. 4:9, 10 **25:4** [a] Jer. 39:2 [b] Jer. 39:4–7; Ezek. 12:12 [1] Literally *he* [2] Or *Arabah,* that is, the Jordan Valley **25:6** [a] 2 Kin. 23:33; Jer. 52:9 **25:7** [a] Jer. 39:7; Ezek. 17:16 **25:8** [a] Jer. 52:12 [b] 2 Kin. 24:12 [c] Jer. 39:9 **25:9** [a] 2 Kin. 25:13; 2 Chr. 36:19; Ps. 79:1; Jer. 7:14 [b] Jer. 39:8 [c] Jer. 17:27 **25:10** [a] 2 Kin. 14:13; Neh. 1:3 **25:11** [a] Is. 1:9; Jer. 5:19; 39:9 **25:12** [a] 2 Kin. 24:14; Jer. 39:10; 40:7; 52:16 **25:13** [a] Jer. 52:17 [b] 1 Kin. 7:15 [c] 1 Kin. 7:27 [d] 1 Kin. 7:23 [e] 2 Kin. 20:17; Jer. 27:19–22 **25:14** [a] Ex. 27:3; 1 Kin. 7:45

the house of the LORD, [a]the bronze of all these articles was beyond measure. 17 [a]The height of one pillar *was* eighteen cubits, and the capital on it *was* of bronze. The height of the capital was three cubits, and the network and pomegranates all around the capital were all of bronze. The second pillar was the same, with a network.

18 [a]And the captain of the guard took [b]Seraiah the chief priest, [c]Zephaniah the second priest, and the three doorkeepers. 19 He also took out of the city an officer who had charge of the men of war, [a]five men of the king's close associates who were found in the city, the chief recruiting officer of the army, who mustered the people of the land, and sixty men of the people of the land *who were* found in the city. 20 So Nebuzaradan, captain of the guard, took these and brought them to the king of Babylon at Riblah. 21 Then the king of Babylon struck them and put them to death at Riblah in the land of Hamath. [a]Thus Judah was carried away captive from its own land.

Gedaliah Made Governor of Judah
(Jer. 40:5—41:18)

22 Then he made Gedaliah the son of [a]Ahikam, the son of Shaphan, governor over [b]the people who remained in the land of Judah, whom Nebuchadnezzar king of Babylon had left. 23 Now when all the [a]captains of the armies, they and *their* men, heard that the king of Babylon had made Gedaliah governor, they came to Gedaliah at Mizpah—Ishmael the son of Nethaniah, Johanan the son of Careah, Seraiah the son of Tanhumeth the Netophathite, and Jaazaniah[1] the son of a Maachathite, they and their men. 24 And Gedaliah took an oath before them and their men, and said to them, "Do not be afraid of the servants of the Chaldeans. Dwell in the land and serve the king of Babylon, and it shall be well with you."

25 But [a]it happened in the seventh month that Ishmael the son of Nethaniah, the son of Elishama, of the royal family, came with ten men and struck and killed Gedaliah, the Jews, as well as the Chaldeans who were with him at Mizpah. 26 And all the people, small and great, and the captains of the armies, arose [a]and went to Egypt; for they were afraid of the Chaldeans.

Jehoiachin Released from Prison
(Jer. 52:31–34)

27 [a]Now it came to pass in the thirty-seventh year of the captivity of Jehoiachin king of Judah, in the twelfth month, on the twenty-seventh *day* of the month, *that* Evil-Merodach[1] king of Babylon, in the year that he began to reign, [b]released Jehoiachin king of Judah from prison. 28 He spoke kindly to him, and gave him a more prominent seat than those of the kings who *were* with him in Babylon. 29 So Jehoiachin changed from his prison garments, and he [a]ate bread regularly before the king all the days of his life. 30 And as for his provisions, *there was* a regular ration given him by the king, a portion for each day, all the days of his life.

25:16 [a] 1 Kin. 7:47 25:17 [a] 1 Kin. 7:15–22; Jer. 52:21 25:18 [a] Jer. 39:9–13; 52:12–16, 24 [b] 1 Chr. 6:14; Ezra 7:1 [c] Jer. 21:1; 29:25, 29 25:19 [a] Esth. 1:14; Jer. 52:25 25:21 [a] Lev. 26:33; Deut. 28:36, 64; 2 Kin. 23:27 25:22 [a] 2 Kin. 22:12 [b] Is. 1:9; Jer. 40:5 25:23 [a] Jer. 40:7–9 [1] Spelled *Jezaniah* in Jeremiah 40:8 25:25 [a] Jer. 41:1–3 25:26 [a] 2 Kin. 19:31; Jer. 43:4–7 25:27 [a] 2 Kin. 24:12, 15; Jer. 52:31–34 [b] Gen. 40:13, 20 [1] Literally *Man of Marduk* 25:29 [a] 2 Sam. 9:7

THE FIRST BOOK OF THE

CHRONICLES

OVERVIEW

Written after 450 BC, 1 Chronicles and 2 Chronicles were originally one book. The books were separated when the Bible was translated into Greek. The writer of 1 Chronicles is unknown, but scholars suggest that Ezra may have been its author.

First Chronicles describes the rule of David and Solomon, but unlike how it is presented in 2 Samuel and 1 Kings, the chronicler offers a more positive view, focusing on how God was always at work. Written to the returning exiles, 1 Chronicles was likely intended to encourage God's weary, unsettled people.

Opening with an extensive genealogy, 1 Chronicles outlines the lineage of David from Adam and the patriarchs (see 1:1–54) to David's throne (see 2:1—4:23). It also includes the genealogies of Israel before the exile (see 4:24—9:1), the story of the exiles returning to Jerusalem (see 9:2–34), and a brief summary of the reign of Saul (see 9:35—10:14).

The broader narrative of 1 Chronicles begins with David being anointed king and his army expanding (chs. 11–12). During David's righteous reign, he returned the ark of the covenant to Jerusalem and placed it in the tabernacle, reestablishing regular worship (chs. 13–16). He also developed plans for the temple and gave specific assignments to the people concerning their roles in the worship of God. But God would not allow David to build the temple. Instead, God entrusted this task to David's son Solomon (see 17:1–14).

Before he died, David anointed Solomon as king and instructed him to build the temple, giving him the plans that he had created (see 28:1–19). David then charged Solomon, "Be strong and of good courage . . . do not fear nor be dismayed, for the LORD God—my God—will be with you" (28:20). Informing the Israelites of the greatness of this task of building the temple, David encouraged the people to assist with the work (see 29:1–5). The leaders "offered willingly" (vv. 6, 9), and David "rejoiced greatly" (v. 9). The book ends with the death of David at the end of his forty-year reign as king of Israel (see 29:26–30).

First Chronicles is a reminder that God rewards obedience. David was a good king who upheld God's law; thus, the people of Israel experienced victory and blessings under his reign. David's commitment to bringing the people together to worship God brought peace and prosperity to the land. God was pleased with David and blessed him and his seed.

BREATHE IT IN

The Israelites who returned from exile in Babylon had little knowledge of the laws and ways of God. When they returned, they found it difficult to understand if and how God would fulfill His promises. First Chronicles was written to teach and encourage them of the importance of obeying God. It was to remind God's people of His commitment to them. David's relationship with God and the prosperity of the nation under his rule were retold as evidence of God's faithfulness in keeping His promises.

History is important. It is often said that if we do not know our history, we are doomed to repeat it. This is why it is important for us to teach our children our history—the good, the bad, and the ugly.

Our children need to know about the slave trade and the difficult journeys our ancestors endured traveling across the oceans from Africa to other parts of the world. They need to know the conditions of slavery and the widely held belief that our people were less than human and only as valuable as the hard labor they could perform. They should also be told about the slaves who resisted, ran, and worked for their freedom, often coming back to free others. They should know of those who risked being beaten or even killed to gain basic skills and abilities, such as reading. They should know of those who gave their lives for our freedom.

It is also necessary to teach our children about the Jim Crow era and the fight for our right to vote, to be educated, to eat in restaurants, and to sit where we choose in public places. They should be aware of lynching and the assassinations of many of our beloved leaders who worked hard and sacrificed so much for us. Just as important, it is necessary for them to know that progress has been made. Many throughout society have fought alongside us as we have watched the decline of these racist atrocities. Yet, the fight is not over. We each have a responsibility to do our part in making this nation a better place for all.

Not only must we teach the history of our people, but we must also teach the history of our families. We need to tell our children about their grandparents and great-grandparents, and great-great-grandparents. We must share with them the struggles of those who came before them and explain how our families became what they are today.

There is no need to be embarrassed if you or your people did not always follow God's plan. The moment you trusted in Christ, though, you entered into a relationship with Him and became one of His chosen people and an heir to His promises. God has a plan for each of us. Even if you are not living in God's ways now, it is never too late to turn back to Him and experience that plan. No matter the situation, God always provides an opportunity to repent, just as He did with the Israelites. Some of us may feel that we have drifted so far away from God or sinned so badly that there is no way that He will keep His promises to us. That will never be the case. God waits patiently for each one of us, but not passively. Just as God sent the prophets to draw His people back to Himself, God actively seeks to draw us back too.

The Book of 1 Chronicles serves as a reminder that God keeps His promises to His people. Do not be dismayed by your past mistakes or the context of your history. Instead, acknowledge your history and thank God for its lessons. Be reminded of God's faithfulness and never give up. You are a child of the King. Walk in His authority.

THE FIRST BOOK OF THE

CHRONICLES

The Family of Adam—Seth to Abraham
(Gen. 5:1–32; 10:1–32; 11:10–26; Luke 3:34–38)

1 Adam,[a] [b]Seth, Enosh, 2Cainan,[1] Mahalalel, Jared, 3Enoch, Methuselah, Lamech, 4[a]Noah,[1] Shem, Ham, and Japheth.

5[a]The sons of Japheth *were* Gomer, Magog, Madai, Javan, Tubal, Meshech, and Tiras. 6The sons of Gomer *were* Ashkenaz, Diphath,[1] and Togarmah. 7The sons of Javan *were* Elishah, Tarshishah,[1] Kittim, and Rodanim.[2]

8[a]The sons of Ham *were* Cush, Mizraim, Put, and Canaan. 9The sons of Cush *were* Seba, Havilah, Sabta,[1] Raama,[2] and Sabtecha. The sons of Raama *were* Sheba and Dedan. 10Cush [a]begot Nimrod; he began to be a mighty one on the earth. 11Mizraim begot Ludim, Anamim, Lehabim, Naphtuhim, 12Pathrusim, Casluhim (from whom came the Philistines and the [a]Caphtorim). 13[a]Canaan begot Sidon, his firstborn, and Heth; 14the Jebusite, the Amorite, and the Girgashite; 15the Hivite, the Arkite, and the Sinite; 16the Arvadite, the Zemarite, and the Hamathite.

17The sons of [a]Shem *were* Elam, Asshur, [b]Arphaxad, Lud, Aram, Uz, Hul, Gether, and Meshech.[1] 18Arphaxad begot Shelah, and Shelah begot Eber. 19To Eber were born two sons: the name of one *was* Peleg,[1] for in his days the earth was divided; and his brother's name *was* Joktan. 20[a]Joktan begot Almodad, Sheleph, Hazarmaveth, Jerah, 21Hadoram, Uzal, Diklah, 22Ebal,[1] Abimael, Sheba, 23Ophir, Havilah, and Jobab. All these *were* the sons of Joktan.

24[a]Shem, Arphaxad, Shelah, 25[a]Eber, Peleg, Reu, 26Serug, Nahor, Terah, 27and [a]Abram, who *is* Abraham. 28[a]The sons of Abraham *were* [b]Isaac and [c]Ishmael.

The Family of Ishmael
(Gen. 25:12–16)

29These *are* their genealogies: The [a]firstborn of Ishmael *was* Nebajoth; then Kedar, Adbeel, Mibsam, 30Mishma, Dumah, Massa, Hadad,[1] Tema, 31Jetur, Naphish, and Kedemah. These *were* the sons of Ishmael.

The Family of Keturah
(Gen. 25:1–4)

32Now [a]the sons born to Keturah, Abraham's concubine, *were* Zimran, Jokshan, Medan, Midian, Ishbak, and Shuah. The sons of Jokshan *were* Sheba and Dedan. 33The sons of Midian *were* Ephah, Epher, Hanoch, Abida, and Eldaah. All these were the children of Keturah.

The Family of Isaac
(Gen. 36:10–14)

34And [a]Abraham begot Isaac. [b]The sons of Isaac *were* Esau and Israel. 35The sons of [a]Esau *were* Eliphaz, Reuel, Jeush, Jaalam, and Korah. 36And the sons of Eliphaz *were* Teman, Omar, Zephi,[1] Gatam, *and* Kenaz; and *by* [a]Timna,[2] Amalek. 37The sons of Reuel *were* Nahath, Zerah, Shammah, and Mizzah.

1:1 [a] Gen. 1:27; 2:7; 5:1, 2, 5 [b] Gen. 4:25, 26; 5:3–9 1:2 [1] Hebrew *Qenan* 1:4 [a] Gen. 5:28—10:1 [1] Following Masoretic Text and Vulgate; Septuagint adds *the sons of Noah.* 1:5 [a] Gen. 10:2–4 1:6 [1] Spelled *Riphath* in Genesis 10:3 1:7 [1] Spelled *Tarshish* in Genesis 10:4 [2] Spelled *Dodanim* in Genesis 10:4 1:8 [a] Gen. 10:6 1:9 [1] Spelled *Sabtah* in Genesis 10:7 [2] Spelled *Raamah* in Genesis 10:7 1:10 [a] Gen. 10:8–10, 13 1:12 [a] Deut. 2:23 1:13 [a] Gen. 9:18, 25–27; 10:15 1:17 [a] Gen. 10:22–29; 11:10 [b] Luke 3:36 [1] Spelled *Mash* in Genesis 10:23 1:19 [1] Literally *Division* 1:20 [a] Gen. 10:26 1:22 [1] Spelled *Obal* in Genesis 10:28 1:24 [a] Gen. 11:10–26; Luke 3:34–36 1:25 [a] Gen. 11:15 1:27 [a] Gen. 17:5 1:28 [a] Gen. 21:2, 3 [b] Gen. 21:2 [c] Gen. 16:11, 15 1:29 [a] Gen. 25:13–16 1:30 [1] Spelled *Hadar* in Genesis 25:15 1:32 [a] Gen. 25:1–4 1:34 [a] Gen. 21:2 [b] Gen. 25:9, 25, 26, 29; 32:28 1:35 [a] Gen. 36:10–19 1:36 [a] Gen. 36:12 [1] Spelled *Zepho* in Genesis 36:11 [2] Compare Genesis 36:12

TRUST IN HIS WILL

INHALE

I just got another no. One more door slammed in my face. I know that working for "the man" will not build generational wealth. But every time I think God is providing a way that will lead me to realize my dreams, another door slams closed. I am not operating on my own here. I go to God for direction and study His Word to try to follow His plan for my life. I believe God wants me to take care of my family, so I believe the desires of my heart come from Him. Why aren't the dreams He placed within me being fulfilled? What am I doing wrong?

EXHALE

God can often seem to be a great enigma. How can we understand a mysterious God whose ways are so far above ours? At times, we just cannot seem to figure out what is going on in our lives. And that makes it even more difficult to know and trust God's will.

As for your question of what you might be doing wrong, let's eliminate that idea. Except for sin—rebelling against God and rejecting His will—the only wrong thing you could do here is give up on God. Following God's will always leads you somewhere. But there can be a great difference in what we see and what God sees, when we expect something and when God gives it, and what we define as a blessing and what God does. So, we must be careful not to let these differences discourage us from pursuing God's will. When specific opportunities do not come to pass, it doesn't mean that you missed the right one; rather, it means that God spared you from a different wrong one. This might sound strange, but every single open door and closed door in your life is a part of God's plan and will. God is not so much interested in giving you what you want as He is in growing you into the person He wants you to be.

First Chronicles 1 shows a lineage of God's people that we are tempted to read over. But when we stop and see each one for who he or she was—God's people who He had specific plans for—this reminds us that He has a plan for every single person on the face of the earth. Keep waiting. Keep watching. Keep trusting.

The Family of Seir
(Gen. 36:20–28)

38[a]The sons of Seir *were* Lotan, Shobal,
Zibeon, Anah, Dishon, Ezer, and Dishan.
39And the sons of Lotan *were* Hori and Homam; Lotan's sister *was* Timna. 40The sons
of Shobal *were* Alian,[1] Manahath, Ebal, Shephi,[2] and Onam. The sons of Zibeon *were*
Ajah and Anah. 41The son of Anah *was* [a]Di-
shon. The sons of Dishon *were* Hamran,[1]
Eshban, Ithran, and Cheran. 42The sons of
Ezer *were* Bilhan, Zaavan, *and* Jaakan.[1] The
sons of Dishan *were* Uz and Aran.

The Kings of Edom
(Gen. 36:31–43)

43Now these *were* the [a]kings who reigned
in the land of Edom before a king reigned
over the children of Israel: Bela the son of
Beor, and the name of his city was Dinhabah. 44And when Bela died, Jobab the son
of Zerah of Bozrah reigned in his place.
45When Jobab died, Husham of the land of
the Temanites reigned in his place. 46And
when Husham died, Hadad the son of Bedad, who attacked Midian in the field of
Moab, reigned in his place. The name of his
city *was* Avith. 47When Hadad died, Samlah
of Masrekah reigned in his place. 48[a]And
when Samlah died, Saul of Rehoboth-by-
the-River reigned in his place. 49When Saul
died, Baal-Hanan the son of Achbor reigned
in his place. 50And when Baal-Hanan died,
Hadad[1] reigned in his place; and the name
of his city was Pai.[2] His wife's name was
Mehetabel the daughter of Matred, the

1:38 [a] Gen. 36:20–28 1:40 [1] Spelled *Alvan* in Genesis 36:23 [2] Spelled *Shepho* in Genesis 36:23 1:41 [a] Gen. 36:25 [1] Spelled *Hemdan* in Genesis 36:26 1:42 [1] Spelled *Akan* in Genesis 36:27 1:43 [a] Gen. 36:31–43 1:48 [a] Gen. 36:37 1:50 [1] Spelled *Hadar* in Genesis 36:39 [2] Spelled *Pau* in Genesis 36:39

daughter of Mezahab. 51Hadad died also.
And the chiefs of Edom were Chief Timnah,
Chief Aliah,[1] Chief Jetheth, 52Chief Aho-
libamah, Chief Elah, Chief Pinon, 53Chief
Kenaz, Chief Teman, Chief Mibzar, 54Chief
Magdiel, and Chief Iram. These *were* the
chiefs of Edom.

The Family of Israel

(Gen. 35:23–26; 46:8–25)

2 These *were* the [a]sons of Israel: [b]Reuben,
Simeon, Levi, Judah, Issachar, Zebu-
lun, 2Dan, Joseph, Benjamin, Naphtali, Gad,
and Asher.

From Judah to David

(Ruth 4:18–22; Matt. 1:2–6; Luke 3:31–33)

3The sons of [a]Judah *were* Er, Onan, and
Shelah. *These* three were born to him by the
daughter of [b]Shua, the Canaanitess. [c]Er, the
firstborn of Judah, was wicked in the sight
of the LORD; so He killed him. 4And [a]Ta-
mar, his daughter-in-law, [b]bore him Perez
and Zerah. All the sons of Judah *were* five.

5The sons of [a]Perez *were* Hezron and
Hamul. 6The sons of Zerah *were* Zimri,
[a]Ethan, Heman, Calcol, and Dara—five of
them in all.

7The son of [a]Carmi *was* Achar,[1] the trou-
bler of Israel, who transgressed in the [b]ac-
cursed thing.

8The son of Ethan *was* Azariah.

9Also the sons of Hezron who were
born to him *were* Jerahmeel, Ram, and
Chelubai.[1] 10Ram [a]begot Amminadab, and
Amminadab begot Nahshon, [b]leader of the
children of Judah; 11Nahshon begot Salma,[1]
and Salma begot Boaz; 12Boaz begot Obed,
and Obed begot Jesse; 13[a]Jesse begot Eliab
his firstborn, Abinadab the second, Shimea[1]
the third, 14Nethanel the fourth, Raddai the
fifth, 15Ozem the sixth, *and* David the [a]sev-
enth.

16Now their sisters *were* Zeruiah and Abigail. [a]And the sons of Zeruiah *were* Abishai,
Joab, and Asahel—three. 17Abigail bore Amasa; and the father of Amasa *was* Jether the
Ishmaelite.[1]

The Family of Hezron

18Caleb the son of Hezron had children
by Azubah, *his* wife, and by Jerioth. Now
these were her sons: Jesher, Shobab, and
Ardon. 19When Azubah died, Caleb took
[a]Ephrath[1] as his wife, who bore him Hur.
20And Hur begot Uri, and Uri begot [a]Bez-
alel.

21Now afterward Hezron went in to the
daughter of [a]Machir the father of Gilead,
whom he married when he *was* sixty years
old; and she bore him Segub. 22Segub begot [a]Jair, who had twenty-three cities in the
land of Gilead. 23[a](Geshur and Syria took
from them the towns of Jair, with Kenath
and its towns—sixty towns.) All these *belonged to* the sons of Machir the father of
Gilead. 24After Hezron died in Caleb Ephrathah, Hezron's wife Abijah bore him [a]Ash-
hur the father of Tekoa.

The Family of Jerahmeel

25The sons of Jerahmeel, the firstborn
of Hezron, *were* Ram, the firstborn, and
Bunah, Oren, Ozem, *and* Ahijah. 26Jerah-
meel had another wife, whose name was
Atarah; she was the mother of Onam. 27The
sons of Ram, the firstborn of Jerahmeel,
were Maaz, Jamin, and Eker. 28The sons of
Onam were Shammai and Jada. The sons
of Shammai *were* Nadab and Abishur.

29And the name of the wife of Abishur
was Abihail, and she bore him Ahban and
Molid. 30The sons of Nadab *were* Seled and
Appaim; Seled died without children. 31The
son of Appaim *was* Ishi, the son of Ishi *was*
Sheshan, and [a]Sheshan's son *was* Ahlai.
32The sons of Jada, the brother of Shammai, *were* Jether and Jonathan; Jether died
without children. 33The sons of Jonathan
were Peleth and Zaza. These were the sons
of Jerahmeel.

34Now Sheshan had no sons, only daughters. And Sheshan had an Egyptian servant
whose name *was* Jarha. 35Sheshan gave his
daughter to Jarha his servant as wife, and
she bore him Attai. 36Attai begot Nathan,
and Nathan begot [a]Zabad; 37Zabad begot

1:51 [1] Spelled *Alvah* in Genesis 36:40 2:1 [a] Gen. 29:32–35; 35:23, 26; 46:8–27 [b] Gen. 29:32; 35:22 2:3 [a] Gen. 38:3–5; 46:12; Num. 26:19 [b] Gen. 38:2 [c] Gen. 38:7 2:4 [a] Gen. 38:6 [b] Matt. 1:3 2:5 [a] Gen. 46:12; Ruth 4:18 2:6 [a] 1 Kin. 4:31 2:7 [a] 1 Chr. 4:1 [b] Josh. 6:18 [1] Spelled *Achan* in Joshua 7:1 and elsewhere 2:9 [1] Spelled *Caleb* in 2:18, 42 2:10 [a] Ruth 4:19–22; Matt. 1:4 [b] Num. 1:7; 2:3 2:11 [1] Spelled *Salmon* in Ruth 4:21 and Luke 3:32 2:13 [a] 1 Sam. 16:6 [1] Spelled *Shammah* in 1 Samuel 16:9 and elsewhere 2:15 [a] 1 Sam. 16:10, 11; 17:12 2:16 [a] 2 Sam. 2:18 2:17 [1] Compare 2 Samuel 17:25 2:19 [a] 1 Chr. 2:50 [1] Spelled *Ephrathah* elsewhere 2:20 [a] Ex. 31:2; 38:22 2:21 [a] Num. 27:1; Judg. 5:14; 1 Chr. 7:14 2:22 [a] Judg. 10:3 2:23 [a] Num. 32:41; Deut. 3:14; Josh. 13:30 2:24 [a] 1 Chr. 4:5 2:31 [a] 1 Chr. 2:34, 35 2:36 [a] 1 Chr. 11:41

Ephlal, and Ephlal begot [a]Obed; 38Obed begot Jehu, and Jehu begot Azariah; 39Aza-
riah begot Helez, and Helez begot Eleasah;
40Eleasah begot Sismai, and Sismai begot
Shallum; 41Shallum begot Jekamiah, and
Jekamiah begot Elishama.

The Family of Caleb

42The descendants of Caleb the brother
of Jerahmeel *were* Mesha, his firstborn,
who was the father of Ziph, and the sons
of Mareshah the father of Hebron. 43The
sons of Hebron *were* Korah, Tappuah, Rekem, and Shema. 44Shema begot Raham
the father of Jorkoam, and Rekem begot
Shammai. 45And the son of Shammai *was*
Maon, and Maon *was* the father of Beth Zur.
46Ephah, Caleb's concubine, bore Haran,
Moza, and Gazez; and Haran begot Gazez.
47And the sons of Jahdai *were* Regem, Jotham, Geshan, Pelet, Ephah, and Shaaph.
48Maachah, Caleb's concubine, bore She-
ber and Tirhanah. 49She also bore Shaaph
the father of Madmannah, Sheva the father
of Machbenah and the father of Gibea. And
the daughter of Caleb *was* [a]Achsah.
50These were the descendants of Caleb:
The sons of [a]Hur, the firstborn of Ephrathah, *were* Shobal the father of [b]Kirjath Jearim, 51Salma the father of Bethlehem, *and*
Hareph the father of Beth Gader.
52And Shobal the father of Kirjath Jearim had descendants: Haroeh, *and* half of
the *families of* Manuhoth.[1] 53The families
of Kirjath Jearim *were* the Ithrites, the Pu-
thites, the Shumathites, and the Mishra-
ites. From these came the Zorathites and
the Eshtaolites.
54The sons of Salma *were* Bethlehem, the
Netophathites, Atroth Beth Joab, half of the
Manahethites, and the Zorites.
55And the families of the scribes who
dwelt at Jabez *were* the Tirathites, the
Shimeathites, *and* the Suchathites. These
were the [a]Kenites who came from Hammath, the father of the house of [b]Rechab.

The Family of David
(Matt. 1:6)

3 Now these were the sons of David who
were born to him in Hebron: The firstborn *was* [a]Amnon, by [b]Ahinoam the [c]Jez-
reelitess; the second, Daniel,[1] by [d]Abigail
the Carmelitess; 2the third, [a]Absalom the
son of Maacah, the daughter of Talmai, king
of Geshur; the fourth, [b]Adonijah the son of
Haggith; 3the fifth, Shephatiah, by Abital;
the sixth, Ithream, by his wife [a]Eglah.
4*These* six were born to him in Hebron. [a]There he reigned seven years and
six months, and [b]in Jerusalem he reigned
thirty-three years. 5[a]And these were born
to him in Jerusalem: Shimea,[1] Shobab, Nathan, and [b]Solomon—four by Bathshua[2]
the daughter of Ammiel.[3] 6Also *there* were
Ibhar, Elishama,[1] Eliphelet,[2] 7Nogah, Nepheg, Japhia, 8Elishama, Eliada,[1] and Eliphelet—[a]nine *in all.* 9*These were* all the sons of
David, besides the sons of the concubines,
and [a]Tamar their sister.

The Family of Solomon
(Matt. 1:7–11)

10Solomon's son *was* [a]Rehoboam; Abijah[1] *was* his son, Asa his son, Jehoshaphat
his son, 11Joram[1] his son, Ahaziah his son,
Joash[2] his son, 12Amaziah his son, Azariah[1] his son, Jotham his son, 13Ahaz his
son, Hezekiah his son, Manasseh his son,
14Amon his son, *and* Josiah his son. 15The
sons of Josiah *were* Johanan the firstborn,
the second Jehoiakim, the third Zedekiah,
and the fourth Shallum.[1] 16The sons of [a]Je-
hoiakim *were* Jeconiah his son *and* Zedekiah[1] his son.

The Family of Jeconiah

17And the sons of Jeconiah[1] *were* Assir,[2]
Shealtiel [a]his son, 18*and* Malchiram, Pedaiah, Shenazzar, Jecamiah, Hoshama, and
Nedabiah. 19The sons of Pedaiah *were* Zerubbabel and Shimei. The sons of Zerubbabel *were* Meshullam, Hananiah, Shelomith

---

2:37 [a] 2 Chr. 23:1 **2:49** [a] Josh. 15:17 **2:50** [a] 1 Chr. 4:4 [b] Josh. 9:17; 18:14 **2:52** [1] Same as *the Manahethites,* verse 54 **2:55** [a] Judg. 1:16 [b] 2 Kin. 10:15; Jer. 35:2 **3:1** [a] 2 Sam. 3:2–5 [b] 1 Sam. 25:43 [c] Josh. 15:56 [d] 1 Sam. 25:39–42 [1] Called *Chileab* in 2 Samuel 3:3 **3:2** [a] 2 Sam. 13:37; 15:1 [b] 1 Kin. 1:5 **3:3** [a] 2 Sam. 3:5 **3:4** [a] 2 Sam. 2:11 [b] 2 Sam. 5:5 **3:5** [a] 1 Chr. 14:4–7 [b] 2 Sam. 12:24, 25 [1] Spelled *Shammua* in 14:4 and 2 Samuel 5:14 [2] Spelled *Bathsheba* in 2 Samuel 11:3 [3] Called *Eliam* in 2 Samuel 11:3 **3:6** [1] Spelled *Elishua* in 14:5 and 2 Samuel 5:15 [2] Spelled *Elpelet* in 14:5 **3:8** [a] 2 Sam. 5:14–16 [1] Spelled *Beeliada* in 14:7 **3:9** [a] 2 Sam. 13:1 **3:10** [a] 1 Kin. 11:43; Matt. 1:7–10 [1] Spelled *Abijam* in 1 Kings 15:1 **3:11** [1] Spelled *Jehoram* in 2 Kings 1:17 and 8:16 [2] Spelled *Jehoash* in 2 Kings 12:1 **3:12** [1] Called *Uzziah* in Isaiah 6:1 **3:15** [1] Called *Jehoahaz* in 2 Kings 23:31 **3:16** [a] Matt. 1:11 [1] Compare 2 Kings 24:17 **3:17** [a] Matt. 1:12 [1] Also called *Coniah* in Jeremiah 22:24 and *Jehoiachin* in 2 Kings 24:8 [2] Or *Jeconiah the captive were*

their sister, 20and Hashubah, Ohel, Berechiah, Hasadiah, and Jushab-Hesed—five
in all.
21The sons of Hananiah *were* Pelatiah
and Jeshaiah, the sons of Rephaiah, the
sons of Arnan, the sons of Obadiah, and the
sons of Shechaniah. 22The son of Shechaniah was Shemaiah. The sons of Shemaiah *were* [a]Hattush, Igal, Bariah, Neariah,
and Shaphat—six *in all.* 23The sons of Neariah *were* Elioenai, Hezekiah, and Azrikam—three *in all.* 24The sons of Elioenai
were Hodaviah, Eliashib, Pelaiah, Akkub,
Johanan, Delaiah, and Anani—seven *in all.*

The Family of Judah

4 The sons of Judah *were* [a]Perez, Hezron, Carmi, Hur, and Shobal. 2And Reaiah the son of Shobal begot Jahath, and
Jahath begot Ahumai and Lahad. These
were the families of the Zorathites. 3These
were the sons of the father of Etam: Jezreel, Ishma, and Idbash; and the name of
their sister *was* Hazelelponi; 4and Penuel
was the father of Gedor, and Ezer *was the*
father of Hushah.
These *were* the sons of [a]Hur, the firstborn of Ephrathah the father of Bethlehem.
5And [a]Ashhur the father of Tekoa had
two wives, Helah and Naarah. 6Naarah bore
him Ahuzzam, Hepher, Temeni, and Haa-
hashtari. These *were* the sons of Naarah.
7The sons of Helah *were* Zereth, Zohar, and
Ethnan; 8and Koz begot Anub, Zobebah, and
the families of Aharhel the son of Harum.
9Now Jabez was [a]more honorable than
his brothers, and his mother called his
name Jabez,[1] saying, "Because I bore *him*
in pain." 10And Jabez called on the God of
Israel saying, "Oh, that You would bless
me indeed, and enlarge my territory, that
Your hand would be with me, and that You
would keep *me* from evil, that I may not
cause pain!" So God granted him what he
requested.
11Chelub the brother of [a]Shuhah begot
Mehir, who *was* the father of Eshton. 12And
Eshton begot Beth-Rapha, Paseah, and Te-
hinnah the father of Ir-Nahash. These *were*
the men of Rechah.

#OXYGEN

1 CHRONICLES 4:10

Trust in His Will

God will open doors and provide provisions for you to build and succeed in life. Trust God's process and how He provides. Align your heart, thoughts, and actions to His. Get sanctified.

Breathe and trust in His will.

13The sons of Kenaz *were* [a]Othniel and
Seraiah. The sons of Othniel *were* Hathath,[1]
14and Meonothai *who* begot Ophrah. Seraiah
begot Joab the father of [a]Ge Harashim,[1] for
they were craftsmen. 15The sons of [a]Caleb
the son of Jephunneh *were* Iru, Elah, and
Naam. The son of Elah *was* Kenaz. 16The
sons of Jehallelel *were* Ziph, Ziphah, Tiria,
and Asarel. 17The sons of Ezrah *were* Jether,
Mered, Epher, and Jalon. And *Mered's wife*[1]
bore Miriam, Shammai, and Ishbah the father of Eshtemoa. 18(His wife Jehudijah[1] bore
Jered the father of Gedor, Heber the father
of Sochoh, and Jekuthiel the father of Zanoah.) And these were the sons of Bithiah
the daughter of Pharaoh, whom Mered took.
19The sons of Hodiah's wife, the sister of
Naham, *were* the fathers of Keilah the Gar-
mite and of Eshtemoa the [a]Maachathite.
20And the sons of Shimon *were* Amnon,
Rinnah, Ben-Hanan, and Tilon. And the
sons of Ishi *were* Zoheth and Ben-Zoheth.
21The sons of [a]Shelah [b]the son of Judah
were Er the father of Lecah, Laadah the father of Mareshah, and the families of the
house of the linen workers of the house of
Ashbea; 22also Jokim, the men of Chozeba,
and Joash; Saraph, who ruled in Moab, and
Jashubi-Lehem. Now the records are ancient. 23These *were* the potters and those
who dwell at Netaim[1] and Gederah;[2] there
they dwelt with the king for his work.

3:22 [a] Ezra 8:2 4:1 [a] Gen. 38:29; 46:12 4:4 [a] Ex. 31:2; 1 Chr. 2:50 4:5 [a] 1 Chr. 2:24 4:9 [a] Gen. 34:19 [1] Literally *He Will Cause Pain* 4:11 [a] Job 8:1 4:13 [a] Josh. 15:17; Judg. 3:9, 11 [1] Septuagint and Vulgate add *and Meonothai.* 4:14 [a] Neh. 11:35 [1] Literally *Valley of Craftsmen* 4:15 [a] Josh. 14:6, 14; 15:13, 17; 1 Chr. 6:56 4:17 [1] Literally *she* 4:18 [1] Or *His Judean wife* 4:19 [a] 2 Kin. 25:23 4:21 [a] Gen. 38:11, 14 [b] Gen. 38:1–5; 46:12 4:23 [1] Literally *Plants* [2] Literally *Hedges*

The Family of Simeon
(Gen. 46:10)

24The [a]sons of Simeon *were* Nemuel, Jamin, Jarib,[1] Zerah,[2] *and* Shaul, 25Shallum his
son, Mibsam his son, and Mishma his son.
26And the sons of Mishma *were* Hamuel his
son, Zacchur his son, and Shimei his son.
27Shimei had sixteen sons and six daughters; but his brothers did not have many
children, [a]nor did any of their families multiply as much as the children of Judah.

28They dwelt at Beersheba, Moladah,
Hazar Shual, 29Bilhah, Ezem, Tolad, 30Be-
thuel, Hormah, Ziklag, 31Beth Marcaboth,
Hazar Susim, Beth Biri, and at Shaaraim.
These *were* their cities until the reign of
David. 32And their villages *were* Etam,
Ain, Rimmon, Tochen, and Ashan—five
cities— 33and all the villages that *were*
around these cities as far as Baal.[1] These
were their dwelling places, and they maintained their genealogy: 34Meshobab, Jam-
lech, and Joshah the son of Amaziah;
35Joel, and Jehu the son of Joshibiah, the
son of Seraiah, the son of Asiel; 36Elioenai,
Jaakobah, Jeshohaiah, Asaiah, Adiel, Je-
simiel, and Benaiah; 37Ziza the son of Shi-
phi, the son of Allon, the son of Jedaiah,
the son of Shimri, the son of Shemaiah—
38these mentioned by name *were* leaders
in their families, and their father's house
increased greatly.

39So they went to the entrance of Gedor,
as far as the east side of the valley, to seek
pasture for their flocks. 40And they found
rich, good pasture, and the land *was* broad,
quiet, and peaceful; for some Hamites formerly lived there.

41These recorded by name came in the
days of Hezekiah king of Judah; and they
[a]attacked their tents and the Meunites who
were found there, and [b]utterly destroyed
them, as it is to this day. So they dwelt in
their place, because *there was* pasture for
their flocks there. 42Now *some* of them, five
hundred men of the sons of Simeon, went
to Mount Seir, having as their captains Pelatiah, Neariah, Rephaiah, and Uzziel, the
sons of Ishi. 43And they defeated [a]the rest
of the Amalekites who had escaped. They
have dwelt there to this day.

The Family of Reuben
(Gen. 46:8, 9)

5 Now the sons of Reuben the firstborn
of Israel—[a]he *was* indeed the firstborn,
but because he [b]defiled his father's bed, [c]his
birthright was given to the sons of Joseph,
the son of Israel, so that the genealogy is
not listed according to the birthright; 2yet
[a]Judah prevailed over his brothers, and
from him *came* a [b]ruler, although the birthright was Joseph's— 3the sons of [a]Reuben
the firstborn of Israel were Hanoch, Pallu,
Hezron, and Carmi.

4The sons of Joel *were* Shemaiah his son,
Gog his son, Shimei his son, 5Micah his
son, Reaiah his son, Baal his son, 6and Be-
erah his son, whom Tiglath-Pileser[1] king
of Assyria [a]carried into captivity. He *was*
leader of the Reubenites. 7And his brethren by their families, [a]when the genealogy of their generations was registered:
the chief, Jeiel, and Zechariah, 8and Bela
the son of Azaz, the son of Shema, the son
of Joel, who dwelt in [a]Aroer, as far as Nebo
and Baal Meon. 9Eastward they settled as
far as the entrance of the wilderness this
side of the River Euphrates, because their
cattle had multiplied [a]in the land of Gilead.

10Now in the days of Saul they made war
[a]with the Hagrites, who fell by their hand;
and they dwelt in their tents throughout
the entire *area* east of Gilead.

The Family of Gad

11And the [a]children of Gad dwelt next
to them in the land of [b]Bashan as far as
[c]Salcah: 12Joel *was* the chief, Shapham the
next, then Jaanai and Shaphat in Bashan,
13and their brethren of their father's house:
Michael, Meshullam, Sheba, Jorai, Jachan,
Zia, and Eber—seven *in all.* 14These *were*
the children of Abihail the son of Huri, the
son of Jaroah, the son of Gilead, the son
of Michael, the son of Jeshishai, the son
of Jahdo, the son of Buz; 15Ahi the son of
Abdiel, the son of Guni, *was* chief of their

4:24 [a] Num. 26:12–14 [1] Called *Jachin* in Genesis 46:10 [2] Called *Zohar* in Genesis 46:10 4:27 [a] Num. 2:9 4:33 [1] Or *Baalath Beer* (compare Joshua 19:8) 4:41 [a] 2 Kin. 18:8 [b] 2 Kin. 19:11 4:43 [a] Ex. 17:14; 1 Sam. 15:8; 30:17 5:1 [a] Gen. 29:32; 49:3 [b] Gen. 35:22; 49:4 [c] Gen. 48:15, 22 5:2 [a] Gen. 49:8, 10; Ps. 60:7; 108:8 [b] Mic. 5:2; Matt. 2:6 5:3 [a] Gen. 46:9; Ex. 6:14; Num. 26:5 5:6 [a] 2 Kin. 18:11 [1] Hebrew *Tilgath-Pilneser* 5:7 [a] 1 Chr. 5:17 5:8 [a] Num. 32:34; Josh. 12:2; 13:15, 16 5:9 [a] Josh. 22:8, 9 5:10 [a] Gen. 25:12 5:11 [a] Num. 26:15–18 [b] Josh. 13:11, 24–28 [c] Deut. 3:10

father's house. 16And *the Gadites* dwelt in
Gilead, in Bashan and in its villages, and
in all the common-lands of [a]Sharon within
their borders. 17All these were registered by
genealogies in the days of [a]Jotham king of
Judah, and in the days of [b]Jeroboam king
of Israel.

18The sons of Reuben, the Gadites, and
half the tribe of Manasseh *had* forty-four
thousand seven hundred and sixty valiant
men, men able to bear shield and sword, to
shoot with the bow, and skillful in war, who
went to war. 19They made war with the Hagrites, [a]Jetur, Naphish, and Nodab. 20And
[a]they were helped against them, and the
Hagrites were delivered into their hand,
and all who *were* with them, for they [b]cried
out to God in the battle. He heeded their
prayer, because they [c]put their trust in Him.
21Then they took away their livestock—fifty
thousand of their camels, two hundred
and fifty thousand of their sheep, and two
thousand of their donkeys—also one hundred thousand of their men; 22for many
fell dead, because the war [a]*was* God's. And
they dwelt in their place until [b]the captivity.

The Family of Manasseh (East)

23So the children of the half-tribe of Manasseh dwelt in the land. Their *numbers* increased from Bashan to Baal Hermon, that
is, to [a]Senir, or Mount Hermon. 24These
were the heads of their fathers' houses:
Epher, Ishi, Eliel, Azriel, Jeremiah, Hodaviah, and Jahdiel. They were mighty men
of valor, famous men, *and* heads of their
fathers' houses.

25And they were unfaithful to the God of
their fathers, and [a]played the harlot after
the gods of the peoples of the land, whom
God had destroyed before them. 26So the
God of Israel stirred up the spirit of [a]Pul
king of Assyria, that is, [b]Tiglath-Pileser[1]
king of Assyria. He carried the Reubenites,
the Gadites, and the half-tribe of Manasseh
into captivity. He took them to [c]Halah, Habor, Hara, and the river of Gozan to this day.

The Family of Levi
(Gen. 46:11)

6 The sons of Levi *were* [a]Gershon, Kohath, and Merari. 2The sons of Kohath
were Amram, [a]Izhar, Hebron, and Uzziel.
3The children of Amram *were* Aaron, Moses, and Miriam. And the sons of Aaron
were [a]Nadab, Abihu, Eleazar, and Ithamar.
4Eleazar begot Phinehas, *and* Phinehas begot Abishua; 5Abishua begot Bukki, and
Bukki begot Uzzi; 6Uzzi begot Zerahiah,
and Zerahiah begot Meraioth; 7Meraioth
begot Amariah, and Amariah begot Ahitub;
8[a]Ahitub begot [b]Zadok, and Zadok begot
Ahimaaz; 9Ahimaaz begot Azariah, and Azariah begot Johanan; 10Johanan begot Azariah (it was he [a]who ministered as priest
in the [b]temple that Solomon built in Jerusalem); 11[a]Azariah begot [b]Amariah, and
Amariah begot Ahitub; 12Ahitub begot Zadok, and Zadok begot Shallum; 13Shallum
begot Hilkiah, and Hilkiah begot Azariah;
14Azariah begot [a]Seraiah, and Seraiah begot Jehozadak. 15Jehozadak went *into captivity* [a]when the LORD carried Judah and
Jerusalem into captivity by the hand of
Nebuchadnezzar.

16The sons of Levi *were* [a]Gershon,[1] Kohath, and Merari. 17These are the names
of the sons of Gershon: Libni and Shimei.
18The sons of Kohath *were* Amram, Izhar,
Hebron, and Uzziel. 19The sons of Merari
were Mahli and Mushi. Now these *are* the
families of the Levites according to their
fathers: 20Of Gershon *were* Libni his son,
Jahath his son, [a]Zimmah his son, 21Joah
his son, Iddo his son, Zerah his son, *and*
Jeatherai his son. 22The sons of Kohath
were Amminadab his son, [a]Korah his son,
Assir his son, 23Elkanah his son, Ebiasaph
his son, Assir his son, 24Tahath his son,
Uriel his son, Uzziah his son, and Shaul his
son. 25The sons of Elkanah *were* [a]Amasai
and Ahimoth. 26*As for* Elkanah,[1] the sons
of Elkanah *were* Zophai[2] his son, Nahath[3]
his son, 27Eliab[1] his son, Jeroham his son,
and Elkanah his son. 28The sons of Samuel

5:16 [a] 1 Chr. 27:29; Song 2:1; Is. 35:2; 65:10 5:17 [a] 2 Kin. 15:5, 32 [b] 2 Kin. 14:16, 28 5:19 [a] Gen. 25:15; 1 Chr. 1:31 5:20 [a] [1 Chr. 5:22] [b] 2 Chr. 14:11–13 [c] Ps. 9:10; 20:7, 8; 22:4, 5 5:22 [a] [Josh. 23:10; 2 Chr. 32:8; Rom. 8:31] [b] 2 Kin. 15:29; 17:6 5:23 [a] Deut. 3:9 5:25 [a] 2 Kin. 17:7 5:26 [a] 2 Kin. 15:19 [b] 2 Kin. 15:29 [c] 2 Kin. 17:6; 18:11 [1] Hebrew *Tilgath-Pilneser* 6:1 [a] Gen. 46:11; Ex. 6:16; Num. 26:57; 1 Chr. 23:6 6:2 [a] 1 Chr. 6:18, 22 6:3 [a] Lev. 10:1, 2 6:8 [a] 2 Sam. 8:17 [b] 2 Sam. 15:27 6:10 [a] 2 Chr. 26:17, 18 [b] 1 Kin. 6:1; 2 Chr. 3:1 6:11 [a] Ezra 7:3 [b] 2 Chr. 19:11 6:14 [a] 2 Kin. 25:18–21; Neh. 11:11 6:15 [a] 2 Kin. 25:21 6:16 [a] Gen. 46:11; Ex. 6:16 [1] Hebrew *Gershom* (alternate spelling of *Gershon,* as in verses 1, 17, 20, 43, 62, and 71) 6:20 [a] 1 Chr. 6:42 6:22 [a] Num. 16:1 6:25 [a] 1 Chr. 6:35, 36 6:26 [1] Compare verse 35 [2] Spelled *Zuph* in verse 35 and 1 Samuel 1:1 [3] Compare verse 34 6:27 [1] Compare verse 34

were Joel[1] the firstborn, and Abijah the
second.[2] 29The sons of Merari *were* Mahli,
Libni his son, Shimei his son, Uzzah his
son, 30Shimea his son, Haggiah his son,
and Asaiah his son.

Musicians in the House of the LORD

31Now these are [a]the men whom David
appointed over the service of song in the
house of the LORD, after the [b]ark came to
rest. 32They were ministering with music
before the dwelling place of the tabernacle of meeting, until Solomon had built the
house of the LORD in Jerusalem, and they
served in their office according to their
order.

33And these *are* the ones who ministered
with their sons: Of the sons of the [a]Kohath-
ites *were* Heman the singer, the son of Joel,
the son of Samuel, 34the son of Elkanah, the
son of Jeroham, the son of Eliel,[1] the son of
Toah,[2] 35the son of Zuph, the son of Elkanah, the son of Mahath, the son of Amasai,
36the son of Elkanah, the son of Joel, the
son of Azariah, the son of Zephaniah, 37the
son of Tahath, the son of Assir, the son of
[a]Ebiasaph, the son of Korah, 38the son of
Izhar, the son of Kohath, the son of Levi,
the son of Israel. 39And his brother [a]Asaph,
who stood at his right hand, *was* Asaph
the son of Berachiah, the son of Shimea,
40the son of Michael, the son of Baaseiah,
the son of Malchijah, 41the son of [a]Ethni,
the son of Zerah, the son of Adaiah, 42the
son of Ethan, the son of Zimmah, the son
of Shimei, 43the son of Jahath, the son of
Gershon, the son of Levi.

44Their brethren, the sons of Merari, on
the left hand, *were* Ethan the son of Kishi,
the son of Abdi, the son of Malluch, 45the
son of Hashabiah, the son of Amaziah, the
son of Hilkiah, 46the son of Amzi, the son
of Bani, the son of Shamer, 47the son of
Mahli, the son of Mushi, the son of Merari,
the son of Levi.

48And their brethren, the Levites, *were*
appointed to every [a]kind of service of the
tabernacle of the house of God.

The Family of Aaron

49[a]But Aaron and his sons offered sacrifices [b]on the altar of burnt offering and
[c]on the altar of incense, for all the work of
the Most Holy *Place,* and to make atonement for Israel, according to all that Moses the servant of God had commanded.
50Now these *are* the [a]sons of Aaron: Eleazar his son, Phinehas his son, Abishua his
son, 51Bukki his son, Uzzi his son, Zerahiah
his son, 52Meraioth his son, Amariah his
son, Ahitub his son, 53Zadok his son, *and*
Ahimaaz his son.

Dwelling Places of the Levites

(Josh. 21:1–42)

54[a]Now these *are* their dwelling places
throughout their settlements in their territory, for they were *given* by lot to the sons
of Aaron, of the family of the Kohathites:
55[a]They gave them Hebron in the land of Judah, with its surrounding common-lands.
56[a]But the fields of the city and its villages
they gave to Caleb the son of Jephunneh.
57And [a]to the sons of Aaron they gave *one
of* the cities of refuge, Hebron; also Libnah
with its common-lands, Jattir, Eshtemoa
with its common-lands, 58Hilen[1] with its
common-lands, Debir with its common-
lands, 59Ashan[1] with its common-lands,
and Beth Shemesh with its common-lands.
60And from the tribe of Benjamin: Geba
with its common-lands, Alemeth[1] with
its common-lands, and Anathoth with its
common-lands. All their cities among their
families *were* thirteen.

61[a]To the rest of the family of the tribe
of the Kohathites *they gave* [b]by lot ten cities from half the tribe of Manasseh. 62And
to the sons of Gershon, throughout their
families, *they gave* thirteen cities from the
tribe of Issachar, from the tribe of Asher,
from the tribe of Naphtali, and from the
tribe of Manasseh in Bashan. 63To the
sons of Merari, throughout their families,
they gave [a]twelve cities from the tribe of
Reuben, from the tribe of Gad, and from
the tribe of Zebulun. 64So the children of

6:28 [1] Following Septuagint, Syriac, and Arabic (compare verse 33 and 1 Samuel 8:2) [2] Hebrew *Vasheni* 6:31 [a] 1 Chr. 15:16–22, 27; 16:4–6 [b] 2 Sam. 6:17; 1 Kin. 8:4; 1 Chr. 15:25—16:1 6:33 [a] Num. 26:57 6:34 [1] Spelled *Elihu* in 1 Samuel 1:1 [2] Spelled *Tohu* in 1 Samuel 1:1 6:37 [a] Ex. 6:24 6:39 [a] 2 Chr. 5:12 6:41 [a] 1 Chr. 6:21 6:48 [a] 1 Chr. 9:14–34 6:49 [a] Ex. 28:1; [Num. 18:1–8] [b] Lev. 1:8, 9 [c] Ex. 30:7 6:50 [a] 1 Chr. 6:4–8; Ezra 7:5 6:54 [a] Josh. 21 6:55 [a] Josh. 14:13; 21:11, 12 6:56 [a] Josh. 14:13; 15:13 6:57 [a] Josh. 21:13, 19 6:58 [1] Spelled *Holon* in Joshua 21:15 6:59 [1] Spelled *Ain* in Joshua 21:16 6:60 [1] Spelled *Almon* in Joshua 21:18 6:61 [a] 1 Chr. 6:66–70 [b] Josh. 21:5 6:63 [a] Josh. 21:7, 34–40

Israel gave *these* cities with their common-
lands to the Levites. 65And they gave by
lot from the tribe of the children of Judah, from the tribe of the children of Simeon, and from the tribe of the children of
Benjamin these cities which are called by
their names.
66Now [a]some of the families of the sons
of Kohath *were given* cities as their territory
from the tribe of Ephraim. 67[a]And they gave
them *one of* the cities of refuge, Shechem
with its common-lands, in the mountains
of Ephraim, also Gezer with its common-
lands, 68[a]Jokmeam with its common-lands,
Beth Horon with its common-lands, 69Ai-
jalon with its common-lands, and Gath
Rimmon with its common-lands. 70And
from the half-tribe of Manasseh: Aner
with its common-lands and Bileam with
its common-lands, for the rest of the family of the sons of Kohath.
71From the family of the half-tribe of Manasseh the sons of Gershon *were given* Golan in Bashan with its common-lands and
Ashtaroth with its common-lands. 72And
from the tribe of Issachar: Kedesh with its
common-lands, Daberath with its common-
lands, 73Ramoth with its common-lands,
and Anem with its common-lands. 74And
from the tribe of Asher: Mashal with its
common-lands, Abdon with its common-
lands, 75Hukok with its common-lands,
and Rehob with its common-lands. 76And
from the tribe of Naphtali: Kedesh in Galilee with its common-lands, Hammon with
its common-lands, and Kirjathaim with its
common-lands.
77From the tribe of Zebulun the rest of
the children of Merari *were given* Rimmon[1]
with its common-lands and Tabor with its
common-lands. 78And on the other side of
the Jordan, across from Jericho, on the east
side of the Jordan, *they were given* from
the tribe of Reuben: Bezer in the wilderness with its common-lands, Jahzah with
its common-lands, 79Kedemoth with its
common-lands, and Mephaath with its
common-lands. 80And from the tribe of
Gad: Ramoth in Gilead with its common-
lands, Mahanaim with its common-lands,
81Heshbon with its common-lands, and Jazer with its common-lands.

The Family of Issachar
(Gen. 46:13)

7 The sons of Issachar *were* [a]Tola, Puah,[1]
Jashub, and Shimron—four *in all.* 2The
sons of Tola *were* Uzzi, Rephaiah, Jeriel,
Jahmai, Jibsam, and Shemuel, heads of
their father's house. *The sons* of Tola *were*
mighty men of valor in their generations;
[a]their number in the days of David *was*
twenty-two thousand six hundred. 3The
son of Uzzi *was* Izrahiah, and the sons of
Izrahiah *were* Michael, Obadiah, Joel, and
Ishiah. All five of them *were* chief men.
4And with them, by their generations,
according to their fathers' houses, *were*
thirty-six thousand troops ready for war;
for they had many wives and sons.
5Now their brethren among all the families of Issachar *were* mighty men of valor,
listed by their genealogies, eighty-seven
thousand in all.

The Family of Benjamin
(Gen. 46:21)

6*The sons* of [a]Benjamin *were* Bela, Becher, and Jediael—three *in all.* 7The sons
of Bela were Ezbon, Uzzi, Uzziel, Jerimoth,
and Iri—five *in all.* They *were* heads of *their*
fathers' houses, and they were listed by
their genealogies, twenty-two thousand
and thirty-four mighty men of valor.
8The sons of Becher *were* Zemirah, Joash,
Eliezer, Elioenai, Omri, Jerimoth, Abijah,
Anathoth, and Alemeth. All these *are* the
sons of Becher. 9And they were recorded by
genealogy according to their generations,
heads of their fathers' houses, twenty thousand two hundred mighty men of valor.
10The son of Jediael *was* Bilhan, and the sons
of Bilhan *were* Jeush, Benjamin, Ehud, Chenaanah, Zethan, Tharshish, and Ahishahar.
11All these sons of Jediael *were* heads
of their fathers' houses; *there were* seventeen thousand two hundred mighty men of
valor fit to go out for war *and* battle. 12Shup-
pim and Huppim[1] *were* the sons of Ir, *and*
Hushim *was* the son of Aher.

6:66 [a] 1 Chr. 6:61 6:67 [a] Josh. 21:21 6:68 [a] Josh. 21:22 6:77 [1] Hebrew *Rimmono,* alternate spelling of *Rimmon;* see 4:32
7:1 [a] Num. 26:23–25 [1] Spelled *Puvah* in Genesis 46:13 7:2 [a] 2 Sam. 24:1–9; 1 Chr. 27:1 7:6 [a] Gen. 46:21;
Num. 26:38–41; 1 Chr. 8:1 7:12 [1] Called *Hupham* in Numbers 26:39

The Family of Naphtali
(Gen. 46:24)

13The [a]sons of Naphtali *were* Jahziel,[1]
Guni, Jezer, and Shallum,[2] the sons of Bilhah.

The Family of Manasseh (West)

14The [a]descendants of Manasseh: his
Syrian concubine bore him [b]Machir the father of Gilead, the father of Asriel.[1] 15Machir
took as his wife *the sister* of Huppim and
Shuppim,[1] whose name *was* Maachah. The
name of *Gilead's* grandson[2] *was* [a]Zelophe-
had,[3] but Zelophehad begot only daughters. 16(Maachah the wife of Machir bore a
son, and she called his name Peresh. The
name of his brother *was* Sheresh, and his
sons *were* Ulam and Rakem. 17The son of
Ulam *was* [a]Bedan.) These *were* the descendants of Gilead the son of Machir, the son
of Manasseh.

18His sister Hammoleketh bore Ishhod,
Abiezer, and Mahlah.

19And the sons of Shemida were Ahian,
Shechem, Likhi, and Aniam.

The Family of Ephraim

20[a]The sons of Ephraim *were* Shuthelah,
Bered his son, Tahath his son, Eladah his
son, Tahath his son, 21Zabad his son, Shuthelah his son, and Ezer and Elead. The
men of Gath who were born in *that* land
killed *them* because they came down to take
away their cattle. 22Then Ephraim their father mourned many days, and his brethren
came to comfort him.

23And when he went in to his wife, she
conceived and bore a son; and he called his
name Beriah,[1] because tragedy had come
upon his house. 24Now his daughter *was*
Sheerah, who built Lower and Upper [a]Beth
Horon and Uzzen Sheerah; 25and Rephah
was his son, *as well* as Resheph, and Te-
lah his son, Tahan his son, 26Laadan his
son, Ammihud his son, [a]Elishama his son,
27Nun[1] his son, and [a]Joshua his son.

28Now their [a]possessions and dwelling
places *were* Bethel and its towns: to the east
Naaran, to the west Gezer and its towns,
and Shechem and its towns, as far as Ay-
yah[1] and its towns; 29and by the borders of
the children of [a]Manasseh *were* Beth Shean
and its towns, Taanach and its towns, [b]Me-
giddo and its towns, Dor and its towns. In
these dwelt the children of Joseph, the son
of Israel.

The Family of Asher
(Gen. 46:17)

30[a]The sons of Asher *were* Imnah, Ish-
vah, Ishvi, Beriah, and their sister Serah.
31The sons of Beriah *were* Heber and Malchiel, who was the father of Birzaith.[1] 32And
Heber begot Japhlet, Shomer,[1] Hotham,[2]
and their sister Shua. 33The sons of Japhlet
were Pasach, Bimhal, and Ashvath. These
were the children of Japhlet. 34The sons
of [a]Shemer *were* Ahi, Rohgah, Jehubbah,
and Aram. 35And the sons of his brother
Helem *were* Zophah, Imna, Shelesh, and
Amal. 36The sons of Zophah *were* Suah,
Harnepher, Shual, Beri, Imrah, 37Bezer,
Hod, Shamma, Shilshah, Jithran,[1] and Be-
era. 38The sons of Jether *were* Jephunneh,
Pispah, and Ara. 39The sons of Ulla *were*
Arah, Haniel, and Rizia.

40All these *were* the children of Asher,
heads of *their* fathers' houses, choice men,
mighty men of valor, chief leaders. And
they were recorded by genealogies among
the army fit for battle; their number *was*
twenty-six thousand.

The Family Tree of King Saul of Benjamin
(Gen. 46:21)

8 Now Benjamin begot [a]Bela his firstborn, Ashbel the second, Aharah[1] the
third, 2Nohah the fourth, and Rapha the
fifth. 3The sons of Bela *were* Addar,[1] Gera,
Abihud, 4Abishua, Naaman, Ahoah, 5Gera,
Shephuphan, and Huram.

6These *are* the sons of Ehud, who were
the heads of the fathers' *houses* of the
inhabitants of [a]Geba, and who forced them

7:13 [a] Num. 26:48–50 [1] Spelled *Jahzeel* in Genesis 46:24 [2] Spelled *Shillem* in Genesis 46:24 7:14 [a] Num. 26:29–34 [b] 1 Chr. 2:21 [1] The son of Gilead (compare Numbers 26:30, 31) 7:15 [a] Num. 26:30–33; 27:1 [1] Compare verse 12 [2] Literally *the second* [3] Compare Numbers 26:30–33 7:17 [a] 1 Sam. 12:11 7:20 [a] Num. 26:35–37 7:23 [1] Literally *In Tragedy* 7:24 [a] Josh. 16:3, 5; 2 Chr. 8:5 7:26 [a] Num. 10:22 7:27 [a] Ex. 17:9, 14; 24:13; 33:11 [1] Hebrew *Non* 7:28 [a] Josh. 16:1–10 [1] Many Hebrew manuscripts, Bomberg, Septuagint, Targum, and Vulgate read *Gazza.* 7:29 [a] Gen. 41:51; Josh. 17:7 [b] Josh. 17:11 7:30 [a] Gen. 46:17; Num. 26:44–47 7:31 [1] Or *Birzavith* or *Birzoth* 7:32 [1] Spelled *Shemer* in verse 34 [2] Spelled *Helem* in verse 35 7:34 [a] 1 Chr. 7:32 7:37 [1] Spelled *Jether* in verse 38 8:1 [a] Gen. 46:21; Num. 26:38; 1 Chr. 7:6 [1] Spelled *Ahiram* in Numbers 26:38 8:3 [1] Called *Ard* in Numbers 26:40 8:6 [a] 1 Chr. 6:60

to move to [b]Manahath: 7Naaman, Ahijah,
and Gera who forced them to move. He
begot Uzza and Ahihud.

8Also Shaharaim had children in the
country of Moab, after he had sent away
Hushim and Baara his wives. 9By Hodesh
his wife he begot Jobab, Zibia, Mesha, Malcam, 10Jeuz, Sachiah, and Mirmah. These
were his sons, heads of their fathers' *houses.*

11And by Hushim he begot Abitub and
Elpaal. 12The sons of Elpaal *were* Eber, Mi-
sham, and Shemed, who built Ono and Lod
with its towns; 13and Beriah and [a]Shema,
who *were* heads of their fathers' *houses* of
the inhabitants of Aijalon, who drove out
the inhabitants of Gath. 14Ahio, Shashak,
Jeremoth, 15Zebadiah, Arad, Eder, 16Mi-
chael, Ispah, and Joha *were* the sons of
Beriah. 17Zebadiah, Meshullam, Hizki, Heber, 18Ishmerai, Jizliah, and Jobab *were* the
sons of Elpaal. 19Jakim, Zichri, Zabdi, 20Eli-
enai, Zillethai, Eliel, 21Adaiah, Beraiah, and
Shimrath *were* the sons of Shimei. 22Ish-
pan, Eber, Eliel, 23Abdon, Zichri, Hanan,
24Hananiah, Elam, Antothijah, 25Iphde-
iah, and Penuel *were* the sons of Shashak.
26Shamsherai, Shehariah, Athaliah, 27Ja-
areshiah, Elijah, and Zichri *were* the sons
of Jeroham.

28These *were* heads of the fathers' *houses*
by their generations, chief men. These
dwelt in Jerusalem.

29Now the father of Gibeon, whose [a]wife's
name *was* Maacah, dwelt at Gibeon. 30And
his firstborn son *was* Abdon, then Zur, Kish,
Baal, Nadab, 31Gedor, Ahio, Zecher, 32and
Mikloth, *who* begot Shimeah.[1] They also
dwelt alongside their relatives in Jerusalem, with their brethren. 33[a]Ner[1] begot Kish,
Kish begot Saul, and Saul begot Jonathan,
Malchishua, Abinadab,[2] and Esh-Baal.[3]
34The son of Jonathan *was* Merib-Baal,[1]
and Merib-Baal begot [a]Micah. 35The sons
of Micah *were* Pithon, Melech, Tarea, and
Ahaz. 36And Ahaz begot Jehoaddah;[1] Jehoaddah begot Alemeth, Azmaveth, and
Zimri; and Zimri begot Moza. 37Moza begot
Binea, Raphah[1] his son, Eleasah his son,
and Azel his son.

38Azel had six sons whose names *were*
these: Azrikam, Bocheru, Ishmael, Sheariah, Obadiah, and Hanan. All these *were*
the sons of Azel. 39And the sons of Eshek
his brother *were* Ulam his firstborn, Jeush
the second, and Eliphelet the third.

40The sons of Ulam were mighty men of
valor—archers. *They* had many sons and
grandsons, one hundred and fifty *in all.*
These *were* all sons of Benjamin.

9 So [a]all Israel was recorded by genealogies, and indeed, they *were* inscribed
in the book of the kings of Israel. But Judah was carried away captive to Babylon
because of their unfaithfulness. 2[a]And the
first inhabitants who *dwelt* in their possessions in their cities *were* Israelites, priests,
Levites, and [b]the Nethinim.

Dwellers in Jerusalem

3Now in [a]Jerusalem the children of Judah dwelt, and some of the children of
Benjamin, and of the children of Ephraim
and Manasseh: 4Uthai the son of Ammihud, the son of Omri, the son of Imri, the
son of Bani, of the descendants of Perez,
the son of Judah. 5Of the Shilonites: Asaiah the firstborn and his sons. 6Of the sons
of Zerah: Jeuel, and their brethren—six
hundred and ninety. 7Of the sons of Benjamin: Sallu the son of Meshullam, the son
of Hodaviah, the son of Hassenuah; 8Ib-
neiah the son of Jeroham; Elah the son of
Uzzi, the son of Michri; Meshullam the son
of Shephatiah, the son of Reuel, the son of
Ibnijah; 9and their brethren, according to
their generations—nine hundred and fifty-
six. All these men *were* heads of a father's
house in their fathers' houses.

The Priests at Jerusalem

10[a]Of the priests: Jedaiah, Jehoiarib, and
Jachin; 11Azariah the son of Hilkiah, the
son of Meshullam, the son of Zadok, the
son of Meraioth, the son of Ahitub, the [a]of-
ficer over the house of God; 12Adaiah the
son of Jeroham, the son of Pashur, the son
of Malchijah; Maasai the son of Adiel, the
son of Jahzerah, the son of Meshullam, the
son of Meshillemith, the son of Immer;
13and their brethren, heads of their fathers'

8:6 [b] 1 Chr. 2:52 8:13 [a] 1 Chr. 8:21 8:29 [a] 1 Chr. 9:35–38 8:32 [1] Spelled *Shimeam* in 9:38 8:33 [a] 1 Sam. 14:51 [1] Also the son of Gibeon (compare 9:36, 39) [2] Called *Jishui* in 1 Samuel 14:49 [3] Called *Ishbosheth* in 2 Samuel 2:8 and elsewhere 8:34 [a] 2 Sam. 9:12 [1] Called *Mephibosheth* in 2 Samuel 4:4 8:36 [1] Spelled *Jarah* in 9:42 8:37 [1] Spelled *Rephaiah* in 9:43 9:1 [a] Ezra 2:59 9:2 [a] Ezra 2:70; Neh. 7:73 [b] Ezra 2:43; 8:20 9:3 [a] Neh. 11:1, 2 9:10 [a] Neh. 11:10–14 9:11 [a] 2 Chr. 31:13; Jer. 20:1

houses—one thousand seven hundred and
sixty. *They were* very able men for the work
of the service of the house of God.

The Levites at Jerusalem

14Of the Levites: Shemaiah the son of
Hasshub, the son of Azrikam, the son of
Hashabiah, of the sons of Merari; 15Bak-
bakkar, Heresh, Galal, and Mattaniah the
son of Micah, the son of [a]Zichri, the son
of Asaph; 16[a]Obadiah the son of [b]Shema-
iah, the son of Galal, the son of Jeduthun;
and Berechiah the son of Asa, the son of
Elkanah, who lived in the villages of the
Netophathites.

The Levite Gatekeepers

17And the gatekeepers *were* Shallum, Akkub, Talmon, Ahiman, and their brethren.
Shallum *was* the chief. 18Until then *they had
been* gatekeepers for the camps of the children of Levi at the King's Gate on the east.
19Shallum the son of Kore, the son of Ebiasaph, the son of Korah, and his brethren,
from his father's house, the Korahites, *were*
in charge of the work of the service, gatekeepers of the tabernacle. Their fathers had
been keepers of the entrance to the camp
of the LORD. 20And [a]Phinehas the son of
Eleazar had been the officer over them in
time past; the LORD *was* with him. 21[a]Zech-
ariah the son of Meshelemiah *was* keeper
of the door of the tabernacle of meeting.
22All those chosen as gatekeepers *were*
two hundred and twelve. [a]They were recorded by their genealogy, in their villages.
David and Samuel [b]the seer had appointed
them to their trusted office. 23So they and
their children *were* in charge of the gates of
the house of the LORD, the house of the tabernacle, by assignment. 24The gatekeepers
were assigned to the four directions: the
east, west, north, and south. 25And their
brethren in their villages *had* to come
with them from time to time [a]for seven
days. 26For in this trusted office *were* four
chief gatekeepers; they were Levites. And
they had charge over the chambers and
treasuries of the house of God. 27And they
lodged *all* around the house of God because
they *had* the [a]responsibility, and they *were*
in charge of opening *it* every morning.

Other Levite Responsibilities

28Now *some* of them were in charge of
the serving vessels, for they brought them
in and took them out by count. 29*Some* of
them *were* appointed over the furnishings
and over all the implements of the sanctuary, and over the [a]fine flour and the wine
and the oil and the incense and the spices.
30And *some* of the sons of the priests made
[a]the ointment of the spices.
31Mattithiah of the Levites, the firstborn
of Shallum the Korahite, had the trusted
office [a]over the things that were baked in
the pans. 32And some of their brethren of
the sons of the Kohathites [a]*were* in charge
of preparing the showbread for every Sabbath.
33These are [a]the singers, heads of the fathers' *houses* of the Levites, *who lodged* in
the chambers, *and were* free *from other duties;* for they were employed in *that* work
day and night. 34These heads of the fathers'
houses of the Levites *were* heads throughout
their generations. They dwelt at Jerusalem.

The Family of King Saul

35Jeiel the father of Gibeon, whose wife's
name *was* [a]Maacah, dwelt at Gibeon. 36His
firstborn son *was* Abdon, then Zur, Kish,
Baal, Ner, Nadab, 37Gedor, Ahio, Zechariah,[1]
and Mikloth. 38And Mikloth begot Shimeam.[1] They also dwelt alongside their relatives in Jerusalem, with their brethren.
39[a]Ner begot Kish, Kish begot Saul, and
Saul begot Jonathan, Malchishua, Abinadab, and Esh-Baal. 40The son of Jonathan
was Merib-Baal, and Merib-Baal begot Micah. 41The sons of Micah *were* Pithon, Melech, Tahrea,[1] [a]and Ahaz.[2] 42And Ahaz begot
Jarah;[1] Jarah begot Alemeth, Azmaveth,
and Zimri; and Zimri begot Moza; 43Moza
begot Binea, Rephaiah[1] his son, Eleasah his
son, and Azel his son.

9:15 [a] Neh. 11:17 9:16 [a] Neh. 11:17 [b] Neh. 11:17 9:20 [a] Num. 25:6–13; 31:6 9:21 [a] 1 Chr. 26:2, 14 9:22 [a] 1 Chr. 26:1, 2 [b] 1 Sam. 9:9 9:25 [a] 2 Kin. 11:4–7; 2 Chr. 23:8 9:27 [a] 1 Chr. 23:30–32 9:29 [a] 1 Chr. 23:29 9:30 [a] Ex. 30:22–25 9:31 [a] Lev. 2:5; 6:21 9:32 [a] Lev. 24:5–8 9:33 [a] 1 Chr. 6:31; 25:1 9:35 [a] 1 Chr. 8:29–32 9:37 [1] Called *Zecher* in 8:31 9:38 [1] Spelled *Shimeah* in 8:32 9:39 [a] 1 Chr. 8:33–38 9:41 [a] 1 Chr. 8:35 [1] Spelled *Tarea* in 8:35 [2] Following Arabic, Syriac, Targum, and Vulgate (compare 8:35); Masoretic Text and Septuagint omit *and Ahaz.* 9:42 [1] Spelled *Jehoaddah* in 8:36 9:43 [1] Spelled *Raphah* in 8:37

44And Azel had six sons whose names *were* these: Azrikam, Bocheru, Ishmael, Sheariah, Obadiah, and Hanan; these *were* the sons of Azel.

Tragic End of Saul and His Sons
(1 Sam. 31:1–13)

10 Now [a]the Philistines fought against Israel; and the men of Israel fled from before the Philistines, and fell slain on Mount Gilboa. 2Then the Philistines followed hard after Saul and his sons. And the Philistines killed Jonathan, Abinadab, and Malchishua, Saul's sons. 3The battle became fierce against Saul. The archers hit him, and he was wounded by the archers. 4Then Saul said to his armorbearer, "Draw your sword, and thrust me through with it, lest these uncircumcised men come and abuse me." But his armorbearer would not, for he was greatly afraid. Therefore Saul took a sword and fell on it. 5And when his armorbearer saw that Saul was dead, he also fell on his sword and died. 6So Saul and his three sons died, and all his house died together. 7And when all the men of Israel who *were* in the valley saw that they had fled and that Saul and his sons were dead, they forsook their cities and fled; then the Philistines came and dwelt in them.

8So it happened the next day, when the Philistines came to strip the slain, that they found Saul and his sons fallen on Mount Gilboa. 9And they stripped him and took his head and his armor, and sent word throughout the land of the Philistines to proclaim the news *in the temple* of their idols and among the people. 10[a]Then they put his armor in the temple of their gods, and fastened his head in the temple of Dagon.

11And when all Jabesh Gilead heard all that the Philistines had done to Saul, 12all the [a]valiant men arose and took the body of Saul and the bodies of his sons; and they brought them to [b]Jabesh, and buried their bones under the tamarisk tree at Jabesh, and fasted seven days.

13So Saul died for his unfaithfulness which he had committed against the LORD, [a]because he did not keep the word of the LORD, and also because [b]he consulted a medium for guidance. 14But *he* did not inquire of the LORD; therefore He killed him, and [a]turned the kingdom over to David the son of Jesse.

David Made King over All Israel
(2 Sam. 5:1–3)

11 Then [a]all Israel came together to David at Hebron, saying, "Indeed we *are* your bone and your flesh. 2Also, in time past, even when Saul was king, you *were* the one who led Israel out and brought them in; and the LORD your [a]God said to you, 'You shall [b]shepherd My people Israel, and be ruler over My people Israel.'" 3Therefore all the elders of Israel came to the king at Hebron, and David made a covenant with them at Hebron before the LORD. And [a]they anointed David king over Israel, according to the word of the LORD by [b]Samuel.

The City of David
(2 Sam. 5:6–10)

4And David and all Israel [a]went to Jerusalem, which is Jebus, [b]where the Jebusites *were,* the inhabitants of the land. 5But the inhabitants of Jebus said to David, "You shall not come in here!" Nevertheless David took the stronghold of Zion (that is, the City of David). 6Now David said, "Whoever attacks the Jebusites first shall be chief and captain." And Joab the son of Zeruiah went up first, and became chief. 7Then David dwelt in the stronghold; therefore they called it the City of David. 8And he built the city around it, from the Millo[1] to the surrounding area. Joab repaired the rest of the city. 9So David [a]went on and became great, and the LORD of hosts *was* with [b]him.

The Mighty Men of David
(2 Sam. 23:8–39)

10Now [a]these *were* the heads of the mighty men whom David had, who strengthened themselves with him in his kingdom, with all Israel, to make him king, according to [b]the word of the LORD concerning Israel.

10:1 [a] 1 Sam. 31:1, 2 10:10 [a] 1 Sam. 31:10 10:12 [a] 1 Sam. 14:52 [b] 2 Sam. 21:12 10:13 [a] 1 Sam. 13:13, 14; 15:22–26 [b] [Lev. 19:31; 20:6]; 1 Sam. 28:7 10:14 [a] 1 Sam. 15:28; 2 Sam. 3:9, 10; 5:3; 1 Chr. 12:23 11:1 [a] 2 Sam. 5:1 11:2 [a] 1 Sam. 16:1–3; Ps. 78:70–72 [b] 2 Sam. 7:7 11:3 [a] 2 Sam. 5:3 [b] 1 Sam. 16:1, 4, 12, 13 11:4 [a] 2 Sam. 5:6 [b] Josh. 15:8, 63; Judg. 1:21; 19:10, 11 11:8 [1] Literally *The Landfill* 11:9 [a] 2 Sam. 3:1 [b] 1 Sam. 16:18 11:10 [a] 2 Sam. 23:8 [b] 1 Sam. 16:1, 12

11And this *is* the number of the mighty
men whom David had: [a]Jashobeam the son
of a Hachmonite, [b]chief of the captains;[1] he
had lifted up his spear against three hundred, killed *by him* at one time.
12After him *was* Eleazar the son of [a]Dodo,
the Ahohite, who *was one* of the three
mighty men. 13He was with David at Pas-
dammim. Now there the Philistines were
gathered for battle, and there was a piece
of ground full of barley. So the people fled
from the Philistines. 14But they stationed
themselves in the middle of *that* field, defended it, and killed the Philistines. So the
LORD brought about a great victory.
15Now three of the thirty chief men [a]went
down to the rock to David, into the cave
of Adullam; and the army of the Philistines encamped [b]in the Valley of Rephaim.
16David *was* then in the stronghold, and
the garrison of the Philistines *was* then
in Bethlehem. 17And David said with longing, "Oh, that someone would give me a
drink of water from the well of Bethlehem,
which is by the gate!" 18So the three broke
through the camp of the Philistines, drew
water from the well of Bethlehem that *was*
by the gate, and took *it* and brought *it* to
David. Nevertheless David would not drink
it, but poured it out to the LORD. 19And he
said, "Far be it from me, O my God, that
I should do this! Shall I drink the blood
of these men *who have put* their lives *in
jeopardy?* For at the risk of their lives they
brought it." Therefore he would not drink
it. These things were done by the three
mighty men.
20[a]Abishai the brother of Joab was chief
of *another* three.[1] He had lifted up his spear
against three hundred *men,* killed *them,*
and won a name among *these* three. 21[a]Of
the three he was more honored than the
other two men. Therefore he became their
captain. However he did not attain to the
first three.
22Benaiah was the son of Jehoiada, the
son of a valiant man from Kabzeel, who
had done many deeds. [a]He had killed two
lion-like heroes of Moab. He also had gone
down and killed a lion in the midst of a pit
on a snowy day. 23And he killed an Egyptian, a man of *great* height, five cubits tall.
In the Egyptian's hand *there was* a spear
like a weaver's beam; and he went down to
him with a staff, wrested the spear out of
the Egyptian's hand, and killed him with his
own spear. 24These *things* Benaiah the son
of Jehoiada did, and won a name among
three mighty men. 25Indeed he was more
honored than the thirty, but he did not attain to the *first* three. And David appointed
him over his guard.
26Also the mighty warriors *were* [a]Asa-
hel the brother of Joab, Elhanan the son
of Dodo of Bethlehem, 27Shammoth the
Harorite,[1] [a]Helez the Pelonite,[2] 28[a]Ira the
son of Ikkesh the Tekoite, [b]Abiezer the Anathothite, 29Sibbechai the Hushathite, Ilai
the Ahohite, 30[a]Maharai the Netophathite,
Heled[1] the son of Baanah the Netophathite,
31Ithai[1] the son of Ribai of Gibeah, of the
sons of Benjamin, [a]Benaiah the Pirathonite, 32Hurai[1] of the brooks of Gaash, Abiel[2]
the Arbathite, 33Azmaveth the Baharum-
ite,[1] Eliahba the Shaalbonite, 34the sons of
Hashem the Gizonite, Jonathan the son
of Shageh the Hararite, 35Ahiam the son
of Sacar the Hararite, Eliphal the son of
Ur, 36Hepher the Mecherathite, Ahijah the
Pelonite, 37Hezro the Carmelite, Naarai the
son of Ezbai, 38Joel the brother of Nathan,
Mibhar the son of Hagri, 39Zelek the Ammonite, Naharai the Berothite[1] (the armorbearer of Joab the son of Zeruiah), 40Ira the
Ithrite, Gareb the Ithrite, 41[a]Uriah the Hittite, Zabad the son of Ahlai, 42Adina the son
of Shiza the Reubenite (a chief of the Reubenites) and thirty with him, 43Hanan the
son of Maachah, Joshaphat the Mithnite,
44Uzzia the Ashterathite, Shama and Jeiel
the sons of Hotham the Aroerite, 45Jediael
the son of Shimri, and Joha his brother,
the Tizite, 46Eliel the Mahavite, Jeribai and
Joshaviah the sons of Elnaam, Ithmah the
Moabite, 47Eliel, Obed, and Jaasiel the Me-
zobaite.

11:11 [a] 1 Chr. 27:2 [b] 1 Chr. 12:18 [1] Following Qere; Kethib, Septuagint, and Vulgate read *the thirty* (compare 2 Samuel 23:8). **11:12** [a] 1 Chr. 27:4 **11:15** [a] 2 Sam. 23:13 [b] 2 Sam. 5:18; 1 Chr. 14:9 **11:20** [a] 2 Sam. 23:18; 1 Chr. 18:12 [1] Following Masoretic Text, Septuagint, and Vulgate; Syriac reads *thirty*. **11:21** [a] 2 Sam. 23:19 **11:22** [a] 2 Sam. 23:20 **11:26** [a] 2 Sam. 23:24 **11:27** [a] 2 Sam. 23:26; 1 Chr. 27:10 [1] Spelled *Harodite* in 2 Samuel 23:25 [2] Called *Paltite* in 2 Samuel 23:26 **11:28** [a] 1 Chr. 27:9 [b] 1 Chr. 27:12 **11:30** [a] 1 Chr. 27:13 [1] Spelled *Heleb* in 2 Samuel 23:29 and *Heldai* in 1 Chronicles 27:15 **11:31** [a] 1 Chr. 27:14 [1] Spelled *Ittai* in 2 Samuel 23:29 **11:32** [1] Spelled *Hiddai* in 2 Samuel 23:30 [2] Spelled *Abi-Albon* in 2 Samuel 23:31 **11:33** [1] Spelled *Barhumite* in 2 Samuel 23:31 **11:39** [1] Spelled *Beerothite* in 2 Samuel 23:37 **11:41** [a] 2 Sam. 11

The Growth of David's Army
(1 Sam. 22:1, 2)

12 Now [a]these *were* the men who came
to David at [b]Ziklag while he was still
a fugitive from Saul the son of Kish; and
they *were* among the mighty men, helpers in the war, 2armed with bows, using
both the right hand and [a]the left in *hurling*
stones and *shooting* arrows with the bow.
They were of Benjamin, Saul's brethren.
3The chief *was* Ahiezer, then Joash, the
sons of Shemaah the Gibeathite; Jeziel and
Pelet the sons of Azmaveth; Berachah, and
Jehu the Anathothite; 4Ishmaiah the Gibeonite, a mighty man among the thirty, and
over the thirty; Jeremiah, Jahaziel, Johanan, and Jozabad the Gederathite; 5Eluzai,
Jerimoth, Bealiah, Shemariah, and Shephatiah the Haruphite; 6Elkanah, Jisshiah,
Azarel, Joezer, and Jashobeam, the Korahites; 7and Joelah and Zebadiah the sons of
Jeroham of Gedor.
8*Some* Gadites joined David at the
stronghold in the wilderness, mighty men
of valor, men trained for battle, who could
handle shield and spear, whose faces *were*
like the faces of lions, and *were* [a]as swift as
gazelles on the mountains: 9Ezer the first,
Obadiah the second, Eliab the third, 10Mish-
mannah the fourth, Jeremiah the fifth, 11At-
tai the sixth, Eliel the seventh, 12Johanan
the eighth, Elzabad the ninth, 13Jeremiah
the tenth, and Machbanai the eleventh.
14These *were* from the sons of Gad, captains
of the army; the least was over a hundred,
and the greatest was over a [a]thousand.
15These *are* the ones who crossed the Jordan in the first month, when it had overflowed all its [a]banks; and they put to flight
all *those* in the valleys, to the east and to
the west.
16Then some of the sons of Benjamin
and Judah came to David at the stronghold. 17And David went out to meet them,
and answered and said to them, "If you
have come peaceably to me to help me,
my heart will be united with you; but if to
betray me to my enemies, since *there is* no
wrong in my hands, may the God of our
fathers look and bring judgment." 18Then
the Spirit came upon [a]Amasai, chief of the
captains, *and he said:*

"*We are* yours, O David;
We *are* on your side, O son of Jesse!
Peace, peace to you,
And peace to your helpers!
For your God helps you."

So David received them, and made them
captains of the troop.
19And *some* from Manasseh defected to
David [a]when he was going with the Philistines to battle against Saul; but they did not
help them, for the lords of the Philistines
sent him away by agreement, saying, [b]"He
may defect to his master Saul *and endan-*
ger our heads." 20When he went to Ziklag,
those of Manasseh who defected to him
were Adnah, Jozabad, Jediael, Michael, Jozabad, Elihu, and Zillethai, captains of the
thousands who *were* from Manasseh. 21And
they helped David against [a]the bands *of*
raiders, for they *were* all mighty men of
valor, and they were captains in the army.
22For at *that* time they came to David day by
day to help him, until *it was* a great army,
[a]like the army of God.

David's Army at Hebron

23Now these *were* the numbers of the
divisions *that were* equipped for war, *and*
[a]came to David at [b]Hebron to [c]turn *over*
the kingdom of Saul to him, [d]according to
the word of the LORD: 24of the sons of Judah bearing shield and spear, six thousand
eight hundred armed for war; 25of the sons
of Simeon, mighty men of valor fit for war,
seven thousand one hundred; 26of the sons
of Levi four thousand six hundred; 27Jehoi-
ada, the leader of the Aaronites, and with
him three thousand seven hundred; 28[a]Za-
dok, a young man, a valiant warrior, and
from his father's house twenty-two captains; 29of the sons of Benjamin, relatives of
Saul, three thousand (until then [a]the greatest part of them had remained loyal to the
house of Saul); 30of the sons of Ephraim
twenty thousand eight hundred, mighty
men of valor, famous men throughout

12:1 [a] 1 Sam. 27:2 [b] 1 Sam. 27:6 12:2 [a] Judg. 3:15; 20:16 12:8 [a] 2 Sam. 2:18 12:14 [a] 1 Sam. 18:13 12:15 [a] Josh. 3:15; 4:18, 19
12:18 [a] 2 Sam. 17:25 12:19 [a] 1 Sam. 29:2 [b] 1 Sam. 29:4 12:21 [a] 1 Sam. 30:1, 9, 10 12:22 [a] Gen. 32:2; Josh. 5:13–15 12:23 [a] 2 Sam. 2:1–4
[b] 1 Chr. 11:1 [c] 1 Chr. 10:14 [d] 1 Sam. 16:1–4 12:28 [a] 2 Sam. 8:17; 1 Chr. 6:8, 53 12:29 [a] 2 Sam. 2:8, 9

their father's house; 31 of the half-tribe of Manasseh eighteen thousand, who were designated by name to come and make David king; 32 of the sons of Issachar [a]who had understanding of the times, to know what Israel ought to do, their chiefs were two hundred; and all their brethren were at their command; 33 of Zebulun there were fifty thousand who went out to battle, expert in war with all weapons of war, [a]stouthearted men who could keep ranks; 34 of Naphtali one thousand captains, and with them thirty-seven thousand with shield and spear; 35 of the Danites who could keep battle formation, twenty-eight thousand six hundred; 36 of Asher, those who could go out to war, able to keep battle formation, forty thousand; 37 of the Reubenites and the Gadites and the half-tribe of Manasseh, from the other side of the Jordan, one hundred and twenty thousand armed for battle with every *kind* of weapon of war.

38 All these men of war, who could keep ranks, came to Hebron with a loyal heart, to make David king over all Israel; and all the rest of Israel *were* of [a]one mind to make David king. 39 And they were there with David three days, eating and drinking, for their brethren had prepared for them. 40 Moreover those who were near to them, from as far away as Issachar and Zebulun and Naphtali, were bringing food on donkeys and camels, on mules and oxen—provisions of flour and cakes of figs and cakes of raisins, wine and oil and oxen and sheep abundantly, for *there was* joy in Israel.

The Ark Brought from Kirjath Jearim
(2 Sam. 6:1–11)

13 Then David consulted with the [a]captains of thousands and hundreds, *and* with every leader. 2 And David said to all the assembly of Israel, "If *it seems* good to you, and if it is of the LORD our God, let us send out to our brethren everywhere *who are* [a]left in all the land of Israel, and with them to the priests and Levites *who are* in their cities *and* their common-lands, that they may gather together to us; 3 and let us bring the ark of our God back to us, [a]for we have not inquired at it since the days of Saul." 4 Then all the assembly said that they would do so, for the thing was right in the eyes of all the people.

5 So [a]David gathered all Israel together, from [b]Shihor in Egypt to as far as the entrance of Hamath, to bring the ark of God [c]from Kirjath Jearim. 6 And David and all Israel went up to [a]Baalah,[1] to Kirjath Jearim, which belonged to Judah, to bring up from there the ark of God the LORD, [b]who dwells *between* the cherubim, where *His* name is proclaimed. 7 So they carried the ark of God [a]on a new cart [b]from the house of Abinadab, and Uzza and Ahio drove the cart. 8 Then [a]David and all Israel played *music* before God with all *their* might, with singing, on harps, on stringed instruments, on tambourines, on cymbals, and with trumpets.

9 And when they came to Chidon's[1] threshing floor, Uzza put out his hand to hold the ark, for the oxen stumbled. 10 Then the anger of the LORD was aroused against Uzza, and He struck him [a]because he put his hand to the ark; and he [b]died there before God. 11 And David became angry because of the LORD's outbreak against Uzza; therefore that place is called Perez Uzza[1] to this day. 12 David was afraid of God that day, saying, "How can I bring the ark of God to me?"

13 So David would not move the ark with him into the City of David, but took it aside into the house of Obed-Edom the Gittite. 14 [a]The ark of God remained with the family of Obed-Edom in his house three months. And the LORD blessed [b]the house of Obed-Edom and all that he had.

David Established at Jerusalem
(2 Sam. 5:11–16)

14 Now [a]Hiram king of Tyre sent messengers to David, and cedar trees, with masons and carpenters, to build him a house. 2 So David knew that the LORD had established him as king over Israel, for his kingdom was [a]highly exalted for the sake of His people Israel.

12:32 [a] Esth. 1:13 12:33 [a] Ps. 12:2; [James 1:8] 12:38 [a] 2 Chr. 30:12 13:1 [a] 1 Chr. 11:15; 12:34 13:2 [a] 1 Sam. 31:1; Is. 37:4 13:3 [a] 1 Sam. 7:1, 2 13:5 [a] 1 Sam. 7:5 [b] Josh. 13:3 [c] 1 Sam. 6:21; 7:1, 2 13:6 [a] Josh. 15:9, 60 [b] Ex. 25:22; 1 Sam. 4:4; 2 Kin. 19:15 [1] Called *Baale Judah* in 2 Samuel 6:2 13:7 [a] Num. 4:15; 1 Sam. 6:7 [b] 1 Sam. 7:1 13:8 [a] 2 Sam. 6:5 13:9 [1] Called *Nachon* in 2 Samuel 6:6 13:10 [a] [Num. 4:15]; 1 Chr. 15:13, 15 [b] Lev. 10:2 13:11 [1] Literally *Outburst Against Uzza* 13:14 [a] 2 Sam. 6:11 [b] [Gen. 30:27]; 1 Chr. 26:4–8 14:1 [a] 2 Sam. 5:11; 1 Kin. 5:1 14:2 [a] Num. 24:7

3Then David took more wives in Jerusalem, and David begot more sons and
daughters. 4And [a]these are the names of
his children whom he had in Jerusalem:
Shammua,[1] Shobab, Nathan, Solomon, 5Ib-
har, Elishua,[1] Elpelet,[2] 6Nogah, Nepheg, Japhia, 7Elishama, Beeliada,[1] and Eliphelet.

The Philistines Defeated
(2 Sam. 5:17–25)

8Now when the Philistines heard that
[a]David had been anointed king over all Israel, all the Philistines went up to search for
David. And David heard *of it* and went out
against them. 9Then the Philistines went
and made a raid [a]on the Valley of Rephaim.
10And David [a]inquired of God, saying, "Shall
I go up against the Philistines? Will You deliver them into my hand?"

The LORD said to him, "Go up, for I will
deliver them into your hand."
11So they went up to Baal Perazim, and
David defeated them there. Then David
said, "God has broken through my enemies by my hand like a breakthrough of
water." Therefore they called the name of
that place Baal Perazim.[1] 12And when they
left their gods there, David gave a commandment, and they were burned with fire.
13[a]Then the Philistines once again made
a raid on the valley. 14Therefore David inquired again of God, and God said to him,

1 CHRONICLES 14:2

I AM DAVID

So David knew that the LORD had established him as king over Israel, for his kingdom was highly exalted for the sake of His people Israel. 1 Chronicles 14:2

I am David, son of Jesse. When I was just a boy, God commanded the prophet Samuel to anoint me as the next king of Israel. After Samuel anointed me, King Saul brought me into the palace to play music to soothe his often-agitated mind. He also made me his armor-bearer. Even though I was young, I was strong in faith, and it enabled me to defeat the giant Goliath. As a result, I gained Saul's favor, and he promoted me to be a captain in his army. Soon after, I became a mighty warrior. My victories brought me favor with the people, but that enraged Saul. He pursued me relentlessly out of jealousy to take my life. But because God had anointed Saul as king, I still honored him.

After Saul's death, I became king. I certainly was not perfect. I saw my married neighbor, Bathsheba, and wanted her. I brought her to the palace and sinned against her, her husband, and God. When Bathsheba became pregnant, I sent her husband into the fiercest battlefield to die to cover my transgression. Once he was killed, I was free to marry Bathsheba.

But God, of course, saw my sins and sent a prophet to confront me. At once, I was convicted and earnestly repented before God. He was merciful and forgave me, although my sin was not without consequence. My young son, who was conceived in sin, paid the price with his life. Strife also plagued my family for the rest of my life.

Although God did not let me build the temple, I did have the honor of bringing the ark of the covenant to Jerusalem. There, it symbolized that God would dwell forever with His people. The greatest honor of my life is that I am a direct ancestor of Jesus Christ.

✝

Like David, none of us are perfect. But we are made perfect through faith in Jesus Christ. Like David, we can also remain steadfast in our love for God and follow after God's own heart. This is what each of us is called to.

14:4 [a] 1 Chr. 3:5–8 [1] Spelled *Shimea* in 3:5 14:5 [1] Spelled *Elishama* in 3:6 [2] Spelled *Eliphelet* in 3:6 14:7 [1] Spelled *Eliada* in 3:8
14:8 [a] 2 Sam. 5:17–21 14:9 [a] Josh. 17:15; 18:16; 1 Chr. 11:15; 14:13 14:10 [a] 1 Sam. 23:2, 4; 30:8; 2 Sam. 2:1; 5:19, 23; 21:1
14:11 [1] Literally *Master of Breakthroughs* 14:13 [a] 2 Sam. 5:22–25

"You shall not go up after them; circle around them, [a]and come upon them in front of the mulberry trees. 15And it shall be, when you hear a sound of marching in the tops of the mulberry trees, then you shall go out to battle, for God has gone out before you to strike the camp of the Philistines." 16So David did as God commanded him, and they drove back the army of the Philistines from Gibeon as far as Gezer. 17Then [a]the fame of David went out into all lands, and the LORD [b]brought the fear of him upon all nations.

The Ark Brought to Jerusalem
(2 Sam. 6:12–16)

15 *David* built houses for himself in the City of David; and he prepared a place for the ark of God, [a]and pitched a tent for it. 2Then David said, "No one may carry the [a]ark of God but the Levites, for [b]the LORD has chosen them to carry the ark of God and to minister before Him forever." 3And David [a]gathered all Israel together at Jerusalem, to bring up the ark of the LORD to its place, which he had prepared for it. 4Then David assembled the children of Aaron and the Levites: 5of the sons of Kohath, Uriel the chief, and one hundred and twenty of his brethren; 6of the sons of Merari, Asaiah the chief, and two hundred and twenty of his brethren; 7of the sons of Gershom, Joel the chief, and one hundred and thirty of his brethren; 8of the sons of [a]Elizaphan, Shemaiah the chief, and two hundred of his brethren; 9of the sons of [a]Hebron, Eliel the chief, and eighty of his brethren; 10of the sons of Uzziel, Amminadab the chief, and one hundred and twelve of his brethren.

11And David called for [a]Zadok and [b]Abiathar the priests, and for the Levites: for Uriel, Asaiah, Joel, Shemaiah, Eliel, and Amminadab. 12He said to them, "You *are* the heads of the fathers' *houses* of the Levites; sanctify yourselves, you and your brethren, that you may bring up the ark of the LORD God of Israel to *the place* I have prepared for it. 13For [a]because you *did* not *do it* the first *time,* [b]the LORD our God broke out against us, because we did not consult Him about the proper order."

14So the priests and the Levites sanctified themselves to bring up the ark of the LORD God of Israel. 15And the children of the Levites bore the ark of God on their shoulders, by its poles, as [a]Moses had commanded according to the word of the LORD.

16Then David spoke to the leaders of the Levites to appoint their brethren *to be* the singers accompanied by instruments of music, stringed instruments, harps, and cymbals, by raising the voice with resounding joy. 17So the Levites appointed [a]Heman the son of Joel; and of his brethren, [b]Asaph the son of Berechiah; and of their brethren, the sons of Merari, [c]Ethan the son of Kushaiah; 18and with them their brethren of the second *rank:* Zechariah, Ben,[1] Jaaziel, Shemiramoth, Jehiel, Unni, Eliab, Benaiah, Maaseiah, Mattithiah, Elipheleh, Mikneiah, Obed-Edom, and Jeiel, the gatekeepers; 19the singers, Heman, Asaph, and Ethan, *were* to sound the cymbals of bronze; 20Zechariah, Aziel, Shemiramoth, Jehiel, Unni, Eliab, Maaseiah, and Benaiah, with strings according to [a]Alamoth; 21Mattithiah, Elipheleh, Mikneiah, Obed-Edom, Jeiel, and Azaziah, to direct with harps on the [a]Sheminith; 22Chenaniah, leader of the Levites, was instructor *in charge of* the music, because he *was* skillful; 23Berechiah and Elkanah *were* doorkeepers for the ark; 24Shebaniah, Joshaphat, Nethanel, Amasai, Zechariah, Benaiah, and Eliezer, the priests, [a]were to blow the trumpets before the ark of God; and [b]Obed-Edom and Jehiah, doorkeepers for the ark.

25So [a]David, the elders of Israel, and the captains over thousands went to bring up the ark of the covenant of the LORD from the house of Obed-Edom with joy. 26And so it was, when God helped the Levites who bore the ark of the covenant of the LORD, that they offered seven bulls and seven rams. 27David was clothed with a robe

---

14:14 [a] 2 Sam. 5:23 14:17 [a] Josh. 6:27; 2 Chr. 26:8 [b] [Ex. 15:14–16; Deut. 2:25; 11:25]; 2 Chr. 20:29 15:1 [a] 1 Chr. 16:1 15:2 [a] [Num. 4:15]; 2 Sam. 6:1–11 [b] Num. 4:2–15; Deut. 10:8; 31:9 15:3 [a] Ex. 40:20, 21; 2 Sam. 6:12; 1 Kin. 8:1; 1 Chr. 13:5 15:8 [a] Ex. 6:22 15:9 [a] Ex. 6:18 15:11 [a] 2 Sam. 8:17; 15:24–29, 35, 36; 18:19, 22, 27; 19:11; 20:25; 1 Chr. 12:28 [b] 1 Sam. 22:20–23; 23:6; 30:7; 1 Kin. 2:22, 26, 27; Mark 2:6 15:13 [a] 2 Sam. 6:3 [b] 1 Chr. 13:7–11 15:15 [a] Ex. 25:14; Num. 4:15; 7:9 15:17 [a] 1 Chr. 6:33; 25:1 [b] 1 Chr. 6:39 [c] 1 Chr. 6:44
15:18 [1] Following Masoretic Text and Vulgate; Septuagint omits *Ben.* 15:20 [a] Ps. 46:title 15:21 [a] Ps. 6:title
15:24 [a] [Num. 10:8]; Ps. 81:3 [b] 1 Chr. 13:13, 14 15:25 [a] 2 Sam. 6:12, 13; 1 Kin. 8:1

of fine [a]linen, as were all the Levites who
bore the ark, the singers, and Chenaniah
the music master *with* the singers. David
also wore a linen ephod. 28 [a]Thus all Israel
brought up the ark of the covenant of the
LORD with shouting and with the sound of
the horn, with trumpets and with cymbals,
making music with stringed instruments
and harps.

29 And it happened, [a]*as* the ark of the
covenant of the LORD came to the City of
David, that Michal, Saul's daughter, looked
through a window and saw King David
whirling and playing music; and she despised him in her heart.

The Ark Placed in the Tabernacle
(2 Sam. 6:17–19)

16 So [a]they brought the ark of God, and
set it in the midst of the tabernacle
that David had erected for it. Then they
offered burnt offerings and peace offerings before God. 2 And when David had finished offering the burnt offerings and the
peace offerings, [a]he blessed the people in
the name of the LORD. 3 Then he distributed to everyone of Israel, both man and
woman, to everyone a loaf of bread, a piece
of meat, and a cake of raisins.

4 And he appointed some of the Levites
to minister before the ark of the LORD, to
[a]commemorate, to thank, and to praise the
LORD God of Israel: 5 Asaph the chief, and
next to him Zechariah, *then* [a]Jeiel, Shemiramoth, Jehiel, Mattithiah, Eliab, Benaiah,
and Obed-Edom: Jeiel with stringed instruments and harps, but Asaph made music
with cymbals; 6 Benaiah and Jahaziel the
priests regularly *blew* the trumpets before
the ark of the covenant of God.

David's Song of Thanksgiving
(Ps. 96:1–13; 105:1–15; 106:1, 47, 48)

7 On that day [a]David [b]first delivered *this
psalm* into the hand of Asaph and his brethren, to thank the LORD:

8 [a]Oh, give thanks to the LORD!
Call upon His name;
Make known His deeds
among the peoples!
9 Sing to Him, sing psalms to Him;
Talk of all His wondrous works!
10 Glory in His holy name;
Let the hearts of those rejoice
who seek the LORD!
11 Seek the LORD and His strength;
Seek His face evermore!
12 Remember His marvelous
works which He has done,
His wonders, and the judgments
of His mouth,
13 O seed of Israel His servant,
You children of Jacob,
His chosen ones!

14 He *is* the LORD our God;
His [a]judgments *are* in all the earth.
15 Remember His covenant forever,
The word which He commanded,
for a thousand generations,
16 *The* [a]*covenant which* He
made with Abraham,
And His oath to Isaac,
17 And [a]confirmed it to [b]Jacob
for a statute,
To Israel *for* an everlasting covenant,
18 Saying, "To you I will give
the land of Canaan
As the allotment of your inheritance,"
19 When you were [a]few in number,
Indeed very few, and strangers in it.

20 When they went from one
nation to another,
And from *one* kingdom to
another people,
21 He permitted no man to
do them wrong;
Yes, He [a]rebuked kings for
their sakes,
22 *Saying,* [a]"Do not touch My
anointed ones,
And do My prophets no harm."[1]

23 [a]Sing to the LORD, all the earth;
Proclaim the good news of His
salvation from day to day.

15:27 [a] 1 Sam. 2:18, 28 15:28 [a] Num. 23:21; Josh. 6:20; 1 Chr. 13:8; Zech. 4:7; 1 Thess. 4:16 15:29 [a] 1 Sam. 18:20, 27; 19:11–17; 2 Sam. 3:13, 14; 6:16, 20–23 16:1 [a] 2 Sam. 6:17; 1 Chr. 15:1 16:2 [a] 1 Kin. 8:14 16:4 [a] Ps. 38:title; 70:title 16:5 [a] 1 Chr. 15:18 16:7 [a] 2 Sam. 22:1; 23:1 [b] Ps. 105:1–15 16:8 [a] 1 Chr. 17:19, 20; Ps. 105:1–15 16:14 [a] Ps. 48:10; [Is. 26:9] 16:16 [a] Gen. 17:2; 26:3; 28:13; 35:11 16:17 [a] Gen. 35:11, 12 [b] Gen. 28:10–15 16:19 [a] Gen. 34:30; Deut. 7:7 16:21 [a] Gen. 12:17; 20:3; Ex. 7:15–18 16:22 [a] Gen. 20:7; Ps. 105:15

[1] Compare verses 8–22 with Psalm 105:1–15 16:23 [a] Ps. 96:1–13

24 Declare His glory among the nations,
His wonders among all peoples.

25 For the LORD *is* great and
greatly to be praised;
He *is* also to be feared above all gods.
26 For all the gods [a]of the
peoples *are* idols,
But the LORD made the heavens.
27 Honor and majesty *are* before Him;
Strength and gladness are
in His place.

28 Give to the LORD, O families
of the peoples,
Give to the LORD glory and strength.
29 Give to the LORD the glory
due His name;
Bring an offering, and
come before Him.
Oh, worship the LORD in the
beauty of holiness!
30 Tremble before Him, all the earth.
The world also is firmly established,
It shall not be moved.

31 Let the heavens rejoice, and
let the earth be glad;
And let them say among the
nations, "The LORD reigns."
32 Let the sea roar, and all its fullness;
Let the field rejoice, and all that *is* in it.
33 Then the [a]trees of the woods shall
rejoice before the LORD,
For He is [b]coming to judge the earth.[1]

34 [a]Oh, give thanks to the LORD,
for *He is* good!
For His mercy *endures* forever.[1]
35 [a]And say, "Save us, O God
of our salvation;
Gather us together, and deliver
us from the Gentiles,
To give thanks to Your holy name,
To triumph in Your praise."

36 [a]Blessed *be* the LORD God of Israel
From everlasting to everlasting![1]
And all [b]the people said, "Amen!" and
praised the LORD.

Regular Worship Maintained

37So he left [a]Asaph and his brothers
there before the ark of the covenant of
the LORD to minister before the ark regularly, as every day's work [b]required; 38and
[a]Obed-Edom with his sixty-eight brethren,
including Obed-Edom the son of Jeduthun,
and Hosah, *to be* gatekeepers; 39and Zadok
the priest and his brethren the priests, [a]be-
fore the tabernacle of the LORD [b]at the high
place that *was* at Gibeon, 40to offer burnt
offerings to the LORD on the altar of burnt
offering regularly [a]morning and evening,
and *to do* according to all that is written in
the Law of the LORD which He commanded
Israel; 41and with them Heman and Jeduthun and the rest who were chosen, who
were designated by name, to give thanks
to the LORD, [a]because His mercy *endures*
forever; 42and with them Heman and Jeduthun, to sound aloud with trumpets and
cymbals and the musical instruments of
God. Now the sons of Jeduthun *were* gatekeepers.
43[a]Then all the people departed, every
man to his house; and David returned to
bless his house.

God's Covenant with David
(2 Sam. 7:1–29)

17 Now [a]it came to pass, when David was
dwelling in his house, that David said
to Nathan the prophet, "See now, I dwell
in a house of cedar, but the ark of the covenant of the LORD *is* under tent curtains."
2Then Nathan said to David, "Do all that
is in your heart, for God *is* with you."
3But it happened that night that the
word of God came to Nathan, saying, 4"Go
and tell My servant David, 'Thus says the
LORD: "You shall [a]not build Me a house to
dwell in. 5For I have not dwelt in a house
since the time that I brought up Israel,
even to this day, but have gone from tent
to tent, and from *one* tabernacle *to another.*

16:26 [a] Lev. 19:4; [1 Cor. 8:5, 6] 16:33 [a] Is. 55:12, 13 [b] [Joel 3:1–14]; Zech. 14:1–14; [Matt. 25:31–46] [1] Compare verses 23–33 with Psalm 96:1–13 16:34 [a] 2 Chr. 5:13; 7:3; Ezra 3:11; Ps. 106:1; 107:1; 118:1; 136:1; Jer. 33:11 [1] Compare verse 34 with Psalm 106:1 16:35 [a] Ps. 106:47, 48 16:36 [a] 1 Kin. 8:15, 56; Ps. 72:18 [b] Deut. 27:15; Neh. 8:6 [1] Compare verses 35, 36 with Psalm 106:47, 48 16:37 [a] 1 Chr. 16:4, 5 [b] 2 Chr. 8:14; Ezra 3:4 16:38 [a] 1 Chr. 13:14 16:39 [a] 1 Chr. 21:29; 2 Chr. 1:3 [b] 1 Kin. 3:4 16:40 [a] [Ex. 29:38–42; Num. 28:3, 4] 16:41 [a] 1 Chr. 25:1–6; 2 Chr. 5:13; 7:3; Ezra 3:11; Jer. 33:11 16:43 [a] 2 Sam. 6:18–20 17:1 [a] 2 Sam. 7:1; 1 Chr. 14:1 17:4 [a] [1 Chr. 28:2, 3]

6Wherever I have moved about with all Israel, have I ever spoken a word to any of
the judges of Israel, whom I commanded
to shepherd My people, saying, 'Why have
you not built Me a house of cedar?'" ' 7Now
therefore, thus shall you say to My servant
David, 'Thus says the LORD of hosts: "I took
you [a]from the sheepfold, from following
the sheep, to be ruler over My people Israel. 8And I have been with you wherever
you have gone, and have cut off all your
enemies from before you, and have made
you a name like the name of the great men
who *are* on the earth. 9Moreover I will appoint a place for My people Israel, and will
[a]plant them, that they may dwell in a place
of their own and move no more; nor shall
the sons of wickedness oppress them anymore, as previously, 10since the time that I
commanded judges *to be* over My people
Israel. Also I will subdue all your enemies.
Furthermore I tell you that the LORD will
build you a house.[1] 11And it shall be, when
your days are [a]fulfilled, when you must go
to be with your fathers, that I will set up
your [b]seed after you, who will be of your
sons; and I will establish his kingdom. 12[a]He
shall build Me a house, and I will establish his throne forever. 13[a]I will be his Father, and he shall be My son; and I will not

RELEASE // TRUST IN HIS WILL

My Future in Him

1 Chronicles 17:8 // "And I have been with you wherever you have gone, and have cut off all your enemies from before you, and have made you a name like the name of the great men who are on the earth."

Summary Message // Faith in God includes trusting His will for our lives. In His will, we find the plans and provisions to fulfill every task He sets before us. Peace and rest abide in His will and provide a place of encouragement and motivation for our daily lives. We have the assurance that "all things work together for good to those who love God, to those who are the called according to His purpose" (Rom. 8:28). Therefore, we are to place our trust in God's ultimate goodness. In all situations, we should ask: "What is the will of the Lord for me here?" God has something for us in both the mountaintops and the valleys. We can be certain that the outcome will always ultimately be in our favor.

Practical Application // Take a moment to reflect on and assess where you are right now. Is there anything in your life that concerns you? Any anxious thoughts? Now, ask yourself: "What is the Lord's will for me here?" As you seek the Lord for the answer, allow yourself to trust that He will speak into the situation. Trust that His will for you is correct and true. Trust that His will is not beyond your capability. Trust that His will for you will result in every desire He placed within you being fulfilled. Believe this, receive it, and know it. God has a plan for your tomorrow, and He promises to direct your paths today. We can trust in this, in part, because of what we saw Him do yesterday. What He has done, He can do again. In light of that, what should you do next? Ask Him if you need to make any changes to any relationships. Set your finances before Him and ask Him if there are decisions that need to be reviewed. Is there anything that may need to be altered to come in line with His will for your life? In James 1:5 we are promised that if we need wisdom in a situation, we only need to ask God, and He will give it. God will make His will known to you. You only need to ask and seek.

Fervent Prayer // Heavenly Father, as Jesus has taught us to pray, we ask that Your kingdom come and Your will be done. Let this be our heart toward You today and every day. We wholly trust You and want to know Your will for our lives. We know whatever course You have us take will be perfect. We take our eyes off our current circumstances and trust completely in You. You are our heavenly Father, and we desire to be in Your perfect will. We are grateful for all You are doing and have done for us. We are thankful that You are always with us and will faithfully guide us all the days of our lives. In Jesus' name we pray. Amen.

17:7 [a] 1 Sam. 16:11–13 17:9 [a] [Deut. 30:1–9; Jer. 16:14–16; 23:5–8; 24:6; Ezek. 37:21–27]; Amos 9:14 17:10 [1] That is, a royal dynasty
17:11 [a] 1 Kin. 2:10; 1 Chr. 29:28 [b] 1 Kin. 5:5; 6:12; 8:19–21; [1 Chr. 22:9–13; 28:20]; Matt. 1:6; Luke 3:31 17:12 [a] 1 Kin. 6:38; 2 Chr. 6:2; [Ps. 89:20–37] 17:13 [a] 2 Sam. 7:14, 15; Matt. 3:17; Mark 1:11; Luke 3:22; 2 Cor. 6:18; Heb. 1:5

take My mercy away from him, [b]as I took
it from *him* who was before you. 14And [a]I
will establish him in My house and in My
kingdom forever; and his throne shall be
established forever." ' "
15According to all these words and according to all this vision, so Nathan spoke
to David.
16[a]Then King David went in and sat before the LORD; and he said: "Who *am* I,
O LORD God? And what is my house, that
You have brought me this far? 17And *yet*
this was a small thing in Your sight, O God;
and You have *also* spoken of Your servant's
house for a great while to come, and have
regarded me according to the rank of a
man of high degree, O LORD God. 18What
more can David *say* to You for the honor of
Your servant? For You know Your servant.
19O LORD, for Your servant's sake, and according to Your own heart, You have done
all this greatness, in making known all
these great things. 20O LORD, *there is* none
like You, nor *is there any* God besides You,
according to all that we have heard with
our ears. 21[a]And who *is* like Your people Israel, the one nation on the earth whom God
went to redeem for Himself *as* a people—to
make for Yourself a name by great and awesome deeds, by driving out nations from
before Your people whom You redeemed
from Egypt? 22For You have made Your people Israel Your very own people forever;
and You, LORD, have become their God.
23"And now, O LORD, the word which You
have spoken concerning Your servant and
concerning his house, *let it* be established
forever, and do as You have said. 24So let
it be established, that Your name may be
magnified forever, saying, 'The LORD of
hosts, the God of Israel, *is* Israel's God.' And
let the house of Your servant David be established before You. 25For You, O my God,
have revealed to Your servant that You will
build him a house. Therefore Your servant
has found it *in his heart* to pray before You.
26And now, LORD, You are God, and have
promised this goodness to Your servant.
27Now You have been pleased to bless the
house of Your servant, that it may continue
before You forever; for You have blessed
it, O LORD, and *it shall be* blessed forever."

David's Further Conquests
(2 Sam. 8:1–14)

18 After this [a]it came to pass that David attacked the Philistines, subdued
them, and took Gath and its towns from the
hand of the Philistines. 2Then he defeated
[a]Moab, and the Moabites became David's
[b]servants, *and* brought tribute.
3And [a]David defeated Hadadezer[1] king
of Zobah *as far as* Hamath, as he went to
establish his power by the River Euphrates. 4David took from him one thousand
chariots, seven thousand[1] horsemen, and
twenty thousand foot soldiers. Also David
hamstrung all the chariot *horses,* except
that he spared enough of them for one hundred chariots.
5When the [a]Syrians of Damascus came
to help Hadadezer king of Zobah, David
killed twenty-two thousand of the Syrians.
6Then David put *garrisons* in Syria of Damascus; and the Syrians became David's
servants, *and* brought tribute. So the LORD
preserved David wherever he went. 7And
David took the shields of gold that were
on the servants of Hadadezer, and brought
them to Jerusalem. 8Also from Tibhath[1]
and from Chun, cities of Hadadezer, David
brought a large amount of [a]bronze, with
which [b]Solomon made the bronze Sea, the
pillars, and the articles of bronze.
9Now when Tou[1] king of Hamath heard
that David had defeated all the army of
Hadadezer king of Zobah, 10he sent Hadoram[1] his son to King David, to greet him
and bless him, because he had fought
against Hadadezer and defeated him (for
Hadadezer had been at war with Tou); and
Hadoram brought with him all kinds of [a]ar-
ticles of gold, silver, and bronze. 11King David also dedicated these to the LORD, along
with the silver and gold that he had brought
from all *these* nations—from Edom, from
Moab, from the [a]people of Ammon, from
the [b]Philistines, and from [c]Amalek.

17:13 [b] [1 Sam. 15:23–28]; 1 Chr. 10:14 17:14 [a] Ps. 89:3, 4; Matt. 19:28; 25:31; [Luke 1:31–33] 17:16 [a] 2 Sam. 7:18 17:21 [a] [Deut. 4:6–8, 33–38]; Ps. 147:20 18:1 [a] 2 Sam. 8:1–18 18:2 [a] 2 Sam. 8:2; Zeph. 2:9 [b] Ps. 60:8 18:3 [a] 2 Sam. 8:3 [1] Hebrew *Hadarezer,* and so throughout chapters 18 and 19 18:4 [1] Or *seven hundred* (compare 2 Samuel 8:4) 18:5 [a] 2 Sam. 8:5, 6; 1 Kin. 11:23–25 18:8 [a] 2 Sam. 8:8 [b] 1 Kin. 7:15, 23; 2 Chr. 4:12, 15, 16 [1] Spelled *Betah* in 2 Samuel 8:8 18:9 [1] Spelled *Toi* in 2 Samuel 8:9, 10 18:10 [a] 2 Sam. 8:10–12 [1] Spelled *Joram* in 2 Samuel 8:10 18:11 [a] 2 Sam. 10:14 [b] 2 Sam. 5:17–25 [c] 2 Sam. 1:1

12Moreover [a]Abishai the son of Zeruiah
killed [b]eighteen thousand Edomites[1] in the
Valley of Salt. 13[a]He also put garrisons in
Edom, and all the Edomites became David's
servants. And the LORD preserved David
wherever he went.

David's Administration
(2 Sam. 8:15–18)

14So David reigned over all Israel, and
administered judgment and justice to all
his people. 15Joab the son of Zeruiah *was*
over the army; Jehoshaphat the son of Ahilud *was* recorder; 16Zadok the son of Ahitub
and Abimelech the son of Abiathar *were* the
priests; Shavsha[1] *was* the scribe; 17[a]Benaiah
the son of Jehoiada *was* over the Cherethites and the Pelethites; and David's sons
were chief ministers at the king's side.

The Ammonites and Syrians Defeated
(2 Sam. 10:1–19)

19 It[a] happened after this that Nahash
the king of the people of Ammon
died, and his son reigned in his place.
2Then David said, "I will show kindness
to Hanun the son of Nahash, because his
father showed kindness to me." So David
sent messengers to comfort him concerning his father. And David's servants came
to Hanun in the land of the people of Ammon to comfort him.

3And the princes of the people of Ammon said to Hanun, "Do you think that David really honors your father because he
has sent comforters to you? Did his servants not come to you to search and to
overthrow and to spy out the land?"

4Therefore Hanun took David's servants,
shaved them, and cut off their garments
in the middle, at their [a]buttocks, and sent
them away. 5Then *some* went and told David
about the men; and he sent to meet them,
because the men were greatly ashamed.
And the king said, "Wait at Jericho until
your beards have grown, and *then* return."

6When the people of Ammon saw that
they had made themselves repulsive to
David, Hanun and the people of Ammon
sent a thousand talents of silver to hire for
themselves chariots and horsemen from
Mesopotamia,[1] from Syrian Maacah, [a]and
from Zobah.[2] 7So they hired for themselves
thirty-two thousand chariots, with the king
of Maacah and his people, who came and
encamped before Medeba. Also the people
of Ammon gathered together from their
cities, and came to battle.

8Now when David heard *of it,* he sent
Joab and all the army of the mighty men.
9Then the people of Ammon came out
and put themselves in battle array before
the gate of the city, and the kings who had
come *were* by themselves in the field.

10When Joab saw that the battle line was
against him before and behind, he chose
some of Israel's best and put *them* in battle array against the Syrians. 11And the rest
of the people he put under the command
of Abishai his brother, and they set *themselves* in battle array against the people of
Ammon. 12Then he said, "If the Syrians are
too strong for me, then you shall help me;
but if the people of Ammon are too strong
for you, then I will help you. 13Be of good
courage, and let us be strong for our people
and for the cities of our God. And may the
LORD do *what is* good in His sight."

14So Joab and the people who *were* with
him drew near for the battle against the
Syrians, and they fled before him. 15When
the people of Ammon saw that the Syrians
were fleeing, they also fled before Abishai
his brother, and entered the city. So Joab
went to Jerusalem.

16Now when the Syrians saw that they
had been defeated by Israel, they sent messengers and brought the Syrians who were
beyond the River,[1] and Shophach[2] the commander of Hadadezer's army *went* before
them. 17When it was told David, he gathered all Israel, crossed over the Jordan and
came upon them, and set up in battle array
against them. So when David had set up in
battle array against the Syrians, they fought
with him. 18Then the Syrians fled before
Israel; and David killed seven thousand[1]
charioteers and forty thousand foot soldiers[2] of the Syrians, and killed Shophach
the commander of the army. 19And when

18:12 [a] 2 Sam. 23:18; 1 Chr. 2:16 [b] 2 Sam. 8:13 [1] Or *Syrians* (compare 2 Samuel 8:13) **18:13** [a] Gen. 27:29–40; Num. 24:18; 2 Sam. 8:14 **18:16** [1] Spelled *Seraiah* in 2 Samuel 8:17 **18:17** [a] 2 Sam. 8:18 **19:1** [a] 1 Sam. 11:1; 2 Sam. 10:1–19 **19:4** [a] Is. 20:4 **19:6** [a] 1 Chr. 18:5, 9 [1] Hebrew *Aram Naharaim* [2] Spelled *Zoba* in 2 Samuel 10:6 **19:16** [1] That is, the Euphrates [2] Spelled *Shobach* in 2 Samuel 10:16 **19:18** [1] Or *seven hundred* (compare 2 Samuel 10:18) [2] Or *horsemen* (compare 2 Samuel 10:18)

the servants of Hadadezer saw that they
were defeated by Israel, they made peace
with David and became his servants. So the
Syrians were not willing to help the people
of Ammon anymore.

Rabbah Is Conquered
(2 Sam. 11:1; 12:26–31)

20 It[a] happened in the spring of the
year, at the time kings go out *to bat-*
tle, that Joab led out the armed forces and
ravaged the country of the people of Ammon, and came and besieged Rabbah. But
[b]David stayed at Jerusalem. And [c]Joab defeated Rabbah and overthrew it. 2Then David [a]took their king's crown from his head,
and found it to weigh a talent of gold, and
there were precious stones in it. And it was
set on David's head. Also he brought out the
spoil of the city in great abundance. 3And
he brought out the people who *were* in it,
and put *them* to work[1] with saws, with iron
picks, and with axes. So David did to all the
cities of the people of Ammon. Then David
and all the people returned *to* Jerusalem.

Philistine Giants Destroyed
(2 Sam. 21:15–22)

4Now it happened afterward [a]that war
broke out at Gezer with the Philistines,
at which time [b]Sibbechai the Hushathite
killed Sippai,[1] *who was one* of the sons of
the giant. And they were subdued.
5Again there was war with the Philistines, and Elhanan the son of Jair[1] killed
Lahmi the brother of Goliath the Gittite,
the shaft of whose spear *was* like a weaver's [a]beam.
6Yet again [a]there was war at Gath, where
there was a man of *great* stature, with
twenty-four fingers and toes, six *on each*
hand and six *on each foot;* and he also was
born to the giant. 7So when he defied Israel, Jonathan the son of Shimea,[1] David's
brother, killed him.
8These were born to the giant in Gath,
and they fell by the hand of David and by
the hand of his servants.

The Census of Israel and Judah
(2 Sam. 24:1–25)

21 Now [a]Satan stood up against Israel,
and moved David to number Israel.
2So David said to Joab and to the leaders
of the people, "Go, number Israel from Beersheba to Dan, [a]and bring the number of
them to me that I may know *it.*"
3And Joab answered, "May the LORD
make His people a hundred times more
than they are. But, my lord the king, *are*
they not all my lord's servants? Why then
does my lord require this thing? Why
should he be a cause of guilt in Israel?"
4Nevertheless the king's word prevailed
against Joab. Therefore Joab departed and
went throughout all Israel and came to Jerusalem. 5Then Joab gave the sum of the
number of the people to David. All Israel
had one million one hundred thousand
men who drew the sword, and Judah *had*
four hundred and seventy thousand men
who drew the sword. 6[a]But he did not count
Levi and Benjamin among them, for the
king's word was abominable to Joab.
7And God was displeased with this thing;
therefore He struck Israel. 8So David said
to God, [a]"I have sinned greatly, because I
have done this thing; [b]but now, I pray, take
away the iniquity of Your servant, for I have
done very foolishly."
9Then the LORD spoke to Gad, David's
[a]seer, saying, 10"Go and tell David, [a]saying,
'Thus says the LORD: "I offer you three
things; choose one of them for yourself,
that I may do *it* to you." ' "
11So Gad came to David and said to him,
"Thus says the LORD: 'Choose for yourself,
12[a]either three[1] years of famine, or three
months to be defeated by your foes with the
sword of your enemies overtaking *you,* or
else for three days the sword of the LORD—
the plague in the land, with the angel[2] of the
LORD destroying throughout all the territory of Israel.' Now consider what answer
I should take back to Him who sent me."
13And David said to Gad, "I am in great
distress. Please let me fall into the hand of

20:1 [a] 2 Sam. 11:1 [b] 2 Sam. 11:2—12:25 [c] 2 Sam. 12:26 **20:2** [a] 2 Sam. 12:30, 31 **20:3** [1] Septuagint reads *cut them.* **20:4** [a] 2 Sam. 21:18 [b] 1 Chr. 11:29 [1] Spelled *Saph* in 2 Samuel 21:18 **20:5** [a] 1 Sam. 17:7; 1 Chr. 11:23 [1] Spelled *Jaare-Oregim* in 2 Samuel 21:19 **20:6** [a] 1 Sam. 5:8; 2 Sam. 21:20 **20:7** [1] Spelled *Shimeah* in 2 Samuel 21:21 and *Shammah* in 1 Samuel 16:9 **21:1** [a] 2 Sam. 24:1–25; Job 1:6 **21:2** [a] 1 Chr. 27:23, 24 **21:6** [a] 1 Chr. 27:24 **21:8** [a] 2 Sam. 24:10 [b] 2 Sam. 12:13 **21:9** [a] 1 Sam. 9:9; 2 Kin. 17:13; 1 Chr. 29:29; 2 Chr. 16:7, 10; Is. 30:9, 10; Amos 7:12, 13 **21:10** [a] 2 Sam. 24:12–14 **21:12** [a] 2 Sam. 24:13 [1] Or *seven* (compare 2 Samuel 24:13) [2] Or *Angel,* and so elsewhere in this chapter

the LORD, for His [a]mercies *are* very great;
but do not let me fall into the hand of man."
14So the LORD sent a [a]plague upon Israel,
and seventy thousand men of Israel fell.
15And God sent an [a]angel to Jerusalem to
destroy it. As he[1] was destroying, the LORD
looked and [b]relented of the disaster, and
said to the angel who was destroying, "It is
enough; now restrain your[2] hand." And the
angel of the LORD stood by the [c]threshing
floor of Ornan[3] the Jebusite.
16Then David lifted his eyes and [a]saw the
angel of the LORD standing between earth
and heaven, having in his hand a drawn
sword stretched out over Jerusalem. So
David and the elders, clothed in sackcloth,
fell on their faces. 17And David said to God,
"Was it not I who commanded the people to
be numbered? I am the one who has sinned
and done evil indeed; but these [a]sheep,
what have they done? Let Your hand, I pray,
O LORD my God, be against me and my father's house, but not against Your people
that they should be plagued."
18Therefore, the [a]angel of the LORD commanded Gad to say to David that David
should go and erect an altar to the LORD
on the threshing floor of Ornan the Jebusite. 19So David went up at the word of
Gad, which he had spoken in the name of
the LORD. 20Now Ornan turned and saw
the angel; and his four sons *who were* with
him hid themselves, but Ornan continued
threshing wheat. 21So David came to Ornan, and Ornan looked and saw David. And
he went out from the threshing floor, and
bowed before David with *his* face to the
ground. 22Then David said to Ornan, "Grant
me the place of *this* threshing floor, that I
may build an altar on it to the LORD. You
shall grant it to me at the full price, that the
plague may be withdrawn from the people."
23But Ornan said to David, "Take *it* to
yourself, and let my lord the king do *what
is* good in his eyes. Look, I *also* give *you* the
oxen for burnt offerings, the threshing implements for wood, and the wheat for the
grain offering; I give *it* all."
24Then King David said to Ornan, "No,
but I will surely buy *it* for the full price, for I
will not take what is yours for the LORD, nor
offer burnt offerings with *that which* costs
me nothing." 25So [a]David gave Ornan six
hundred shekels of gold by weight for the
place. 26And David built there an altar to
the LORD, and offered burnt offerings and
peace offerings, and called on the LORD;
and [a]He answered him from heaven by fire
on the altar of burnt offering.
27So the LORD commanded the angel,
and he returned his sword to its sheath.
28At that time, when David saw that the
LORD had answered him on the threshing
floor of Ornan the Jebusite, he sacrificed
there. 29[a]For the tabernacle of the LORD
and the altar of the burnt offering, which
Moses had made in the wilderness, *were* at
that time at the high place in [b]Gibeon. 30But
David could not go before it to inquire of
God, for he was afraid of the sword of the
angel of the LORD.

David Prepares to Build the Temple

22 Then David said, [a]"This *is* the house
of the LORD God, and this *is* the altar of burnt offering for Israel." 2So David
commanded to gather the [a]aliens who *were*
in the land of Israel; and he appointed masons to [b]cut hewn stones to build the house
of God. 3And David prepared iron in abundance for the nails of the doors of the gates
and for the joints, and bronze in abundance
[a]beyond measure, 4and cedar trees in abundance; for the [a]Sidonians and those from
Tyre brought much cedar wood to David.
5Now David said, [a]"Solomon my son *is*
young and inexperienced, and the house
to be built for the LORD *must be* exceedingly magnificent, famous and glorious
throughout all countries. I will now make
preparation for it." So David made abundant preparations before his death.
6Then he called for his son Solomon,
and charged him to build a house for the
LORD God of Israel. 7And David said to Solomon: "My son, as for me, [a]it was in my
mind to build a house [b]to the name of the
LORD my God; 8but the word of the LORD

21:13 [a] Ps. 51:1; 130:4, 7 21:14 [a] 1 Chr. 27:24 21:15 [a] 2 Sam. 24:16 [b] Gen. 6:6 [c] 2 Chr. 3:1 [1] Or *He* [2] Or *Your* [3] Spelled *Araunah* in 2 Samuel 24:16 21:16 [a] Josh. 5:13; 2 Chr. 3:1 21:17 [a] 2 Sam. 7:8; Ps. 74:1 21:18 [a] 1 Chr. 21:11, 12; 2 Chr. 3:1 21:25 [a] 2 Sam. 24:24 21:26 [a] Lev. 9:24; Judg. 6:21; 1 Kin. 18:36–38; 2 Chr. 3:1; 7:1 21:29 [a] 1 Kin. 3:4; 2 Chr. 1:3 [b] 1 Chr. 16:39 22:1 [a] Deut. 12:5; 2 Sam. 24:18; 1 Chr. 21:18, 19, 26, 28; 2 Chr. 3:1 22:2 [a] 1 Kin. 9:20, 21; 2 Chr. 2:17, 18 [b] 1 Kin. 5:17, 18 22:3 [a] 1 Kin. 7:47; 1 Chr. 22:14 22:4 [a] 1 Kin. 5:6–10 22:5 [a] 1 Kin. 3:7; 1 Chr. 29:1, 2 22:7 [a] 2 Sam. 7:1, 2; 1 Kin. 8:17; 1 Chr. 17:1; 28:2 [b] Deut. 12:5, 11

came to me, saying, [a]'You have shed much
blood and have made great wars; you shall
not build a house for My name, because
you have shed much blood on the earth
in My sight. 9 [a]Behold, a son shall be born
to you, who shall be a man of rest; and I
will give him [b]rest from all his enemies
all around. His name shall be Solomon,[1]
for I will give peace and quietness to Israel in his days. 10 [a]He shall build a house
for My name, and [b]he shall be My son, and
I *will be* his Father; and I will establish the
throne of his kingdom over Israel forever.'
11 Now, my son, may [a]the LORD be with you;
and may you prosper, and build the house
of the LORD your God, as He has said to
you. 12 Only may the LORD [a]give you wisdom and understanding, and give you
charge concerning Israel, that you may
keep the law of the LORD your God. 13 [a]Then
you will prosper, if you take care to fulfill
the statutes and judgments with which the
LORD charged Moses concerning Israel. [b]Be
strong and of good courage; do not fear
nor be dismayed. 14 Indeed I have taken
much trouble to prepare for the house of
the LORD one hundred thousand talents
of gold and one million talents of silver,
and bronze and iron [a]beyond measure, for
it is so abundant. I have prepared timber
and stone also, and you may add to them.
15 Moreover *there are* workmen with you in
abundance: woodsmen and stonecutters,
and all types of skillful men for every kind
of work. 16 Of gold and silver and bronze and
iron *there is* no limit. Arise and begin working, and [a]the LORD be with you."
17 David also commanded all the [a]leaders
of Israel to help Solomon his son, *saying,*
18 "*Is* not the LORD your God with you? [a]And
has He *not* given you rest on every side? For
He has given the inhabitants of the land
into my hand, and the land is subdued before the LORD and before His people. 19 Now
set your heart and your soul to seek the
LORD your God. Therefore arise and build
the sanctuary of the LORD God, to [a]bring
the ark of the covenant of the LORD and
the holy articles of God into the house that
is to be built [b]for the name of the LORD."

The Divisions of the Levites

23 So when David was old and full of
days, he made his son [a]Solomon
king over Israel.
2 And he gathered together all the leaders of Israel, with the priests and the Levites. 3 Now the Levites were numbered
from the age of [a]thirty years and above; and
the number of individual males was thirty-
eight thousand. 4 Of these, twenty-four
thousand *were* to [a]look after the work of the
house of the LORD, six thousand *were* [b]offi-
cers and judges, 5 four thousand *were* gatekeepers, and four thousand [a]praised the
LORD with *musical* instruments, [b]"which I
made," *said David,* "for giving praise."
6 Also [a]David separated them into divisions among the sons of Levi: Gershon,
Kohath, and Merari.
7 Of the [a]Gershonites: Laadan[1] and
Shimei. 8 The sons of Laadan: the first Jehiel, then Zetham and Joel—three *in all.*
9 The sons of Shimei: Shelomith, Haziel,
and Haran—three *in all.* These were the
heads of the fathers' *houses* of Laadan.
10 And the sons of Shimei: Jahath, Zina,[1]
Jeush, and Beriah. These *were* the four sons
of Shimei. 11 Jahath was the first and Zizah
the second. But Jeush and Beriah did not
have many sons; therefore they were assigned as one father's house.
12 [a]The sons of Kohath: Amram, Izhar,
Hebron, and Uzziel—four *in all.* 13 The sons
of [a]Amram: Aaron and Moses; and [b]Aaron
was set apart, he and his sons forever, that
he should sanctify the most holy things,
[c]to burn incense before the LORD, [d]to minister to Him, and [e]to give the blessing in
His name forever. 14 Now [a]the sons of Moses the man of God were reckoned to the
tribe of Levi. 15 [a]The sons of Moses *were* Gershon[1] and Eliezer. 16 Of the sons of Gershon,
[a]Shebuel[1] *was* the first. 17 Of the descendants

22:8 [a] 2 Sam. 7:5–13; 1 Kin. 5:3; 1 Chr. 28:3 **22:9** [a] 1 Chr. 28:5 [b] 1 Kin. 4:20, 25; 5:4 [1] Literally *Peaceful* **22:10** [a] 2 Sam. 7:13; 1 Kin. 5:5; 6:38; 1 Chr. 17:12, 13; 28:6; 2 Chr. 6:2 [b] Heb. 1:5 **22:11** [a] 1 Chr. 22:16 **22:12** [a] 1 Kin. 3:9–12; 2 Chr. 1:10 **22:13** [a] [Josh. 1:7, 8]; 1 Chr. 28:7 [b] [Deut. 31:7, 8; Josh. 1:6, 7, 9; 1 Chr. 28:20] **22:14** [a] 1 Chr. 22:3 **22:16** [a] 1 Chr. 22:11 **22:17** [a] 1 Chr. 28:1–6 **22:18** [a] Deut. 12:10; Josh. 22:4; 2 Sam. 7:1; [1 Kin. 5:4; 8:56] **22:19** [a] 1 Kin. 8:1–11; 2 Chr. 5:2–14 [b] 1 Kin. 5:3 **23:1** [a] 1 Kin. 1:33–40; 1 Chr. 28:4, 5 **23:3** [a] Num. 4:1–3 **23:4** [a] 2 Chr. 2:2, 18; Ezra 3:8, 9 [b] Deut. 16:18–20 **23:5** [a] 1 Chr. 15:16 [b] 2 Chr. 29:25–27 **23:6** [a] Ex. 6:16; Num. 26:57; 2 Chr. 8:14 **23:7** [a] 1 Chr. 26:21 [1] Spelled *Libni* in Exodus 6:17 **23:10** [1] Septuagint and Vulgate read *Zizah* (compare verse 11). **23:12** [a] Ex. 6:18 **23:13** [a] Ex. 6:20 [b] Ex. 28:1; Heb. 5:4 [c] Ex. 30:7; 1 Sam. 2:28 [d] [Deut. 21:5] [e] Num. 6:23 **23:14** [a] 1 Chr. 26:20–24 **23:15** [a] Ex. 18:3, 4 [1] Hebrew *Gershom* (compare 6:16) **23:16** [a] 1 Chr. 26:24 [1] Spelled *Shubael* in 24:20

of Eliezer, [a]Rehabiah was the first. And Eliezer had no other sons, but the sons of Rehabiah were very many. 18Of the sons of Izhar,
[a]Shelomith *was* the first. 19[a]Of the sons of
Hebron, Jeriah *was* the first, Amariah the
second, Jahaziel the third, and Jekameam
the fourth. 20Of the sons of Uzziel, Michah
was the first and Jesshiah the second.

21[a]The sons of Merari *were* Mahli and
Mushi. The sons of Mahli *were* Eleazar and
[b]Kish. 22And Eleazar died, and [a]had no sons,
but only daughters; and their brethren, the
sons of Kish, [b]took them *as wives.* 23[a]The
sons of Mushi *were* Mahli, Eder, and Jeremoth—three *in all.*

24These *were* the sons of [a]Levi by their
fathers' houses—the heads of the fathers'
houses as they were counted individually
by the number of their names, who did the
work for the service of the house of the
LORD, from the age of [b]twenty years and
above.

25For David said, "The LORD God of Israel [a]has given rest to His people, that they
may dwell in Jerusalem forever"; 26and also
to the Levites, "They shall no longer [a]carry
the tabernacle, or any of the articles for its
service." 27For by the [a]last words of David
the Levites *were* numbered from twenty
years old and above; 28because their duty
was to help the sons of Aaron in the service
of the house of the LORD, in the courts and
in the chambers, in the purifying of all holy
things and the work of the service of the
house of God, 29both with [a]the showbread
and [b]the fine flour for the grain offering,
with [c]the unleavened cakes and [d]*what is
baked in* the pan, with what is mixed and
with all kinds of [e]measures and sizes; 30to
stand every morning to thank and praise
the LORD, and likewise at evening; 31and
at every presentation of a burnt offering
to the LORD [a]on the Sabbaths and on the
New Moons and on the [b]set feasts, by number according to the ordinance governing
them, regularly before the LORD; 32and that
they should [a]attend to the [b]needs of the tabernacle of meeting, the needs of the holy
place, and the [c]needs of the sons of Aaron
their brethren in the work of the house of
the LORD.

The Divisions of the Priests

24 Now *these are* the divisions of the
sons of Aaron. [a]The sons of Aaron
were Nadab, Abihu, Eleazar, and Ithamar.
2And [a]Nadab and Abihu died before their
father, and had no children; therefore Eleazar and Ithamar ministered as priests.
3Then David with Zadok of the sons of Eleazar, and [a]Ahimelech of the sons of Ithamar,
divided them according to the schedule of
their service.

4There were more leaders found of the
sons of Eleazar than of the sons of Ithamar, and *thus* they were divided. Among
the sons of Eleazar *were* sixteen heads of
their fathers' houses, and eight heads of
their fathers' houses among the sons of
Ithamar. 5Thus they were divided by lot,
one group as another, for there were officials of the sanctuary and officials *of the
house* of God, from the sons of Eleazar and
from the sons of Ithamar. 6And the scribe,
Shemaiah the son of Nethanel, *one of* the
Levites, wrote them down before the king,
the leaders, Zadok the priest, Ahimelech
the son of Abiathar, and the heads of the
fathers' *houses* of the priests and Levites,
one father's house taken for Eleazar and
one for Ithamar.

7Now the first lot fell to Jehoiarib, the
second to Jedaiah, 8the third to Harim, the
fourth to Seorim, 9the fifth to Malchijah,
the sixth to Mijamin, 10the seventh to Hakkoz, the eighth to [a]Abijah, 11the ninth to
Jeshua, the tenth to Shecaniah, 12the eleventh to Eliashib, the twelfth to Jakim, 13the
thirteenth to Huppah, the fourteenth to
Jeshebeab, 14the fifteenth to Bilgah, the
sixteenth to Immer, 15the seventeenth to
Hezir, the eighteenth to Happizzez,[1] 16the
nineteenth to Pethahiah, the twentieth to
Jehezekel,[1] 17the twenty-first to Jachin, the
twenty-second to Gamul, 18the twenty-third
to Delaiah, the twenty-fourth to Maaziah.

23:17 [a] 1 Chr. 26:25 23:18 [a] 1 Chr. 24:22 23:19 [a] 1 Chr. 24:23 23:21 [a] 1 Chr. 24:26 [b] 1 Chr. 24:29 23:22 [a] 1 Chr. 24:28 [b] Num. 36:6 23:23 [a] 1 Chr. 24:30 23:24 [a] Num. 10:17, 21 [b] Num. 1:3; Ezra 3:8 23:25 [a] 1 Chr. 22:18 23:26 [a] Num. 4:5, 15; 7:9; Deut. 10:8 23:27 [a] 2 Sam. 23:1 23:29 [a] Ex. 25:30 [b] Lev. 6:20 [c] Lev. 2:1, 4 [d] Lev. 2:5, 7 [e] Lev. 19:35 23:31 [a] Num. 10:10 [b] Lev. 23:2–4 23:32 [a] 2 Chr. 13:10, 11 [b] [Num. 1:53]; 1 Chr. 9:27 [c] Num. 3:6–9, 38 24:1 [a] Lev. 10:1–6; Num. 26:60, 61; 1 Chr. 6:3 24:2 [a] Num. 3:1–4; 26:61 24:3 [a] 1 Chr. 18:16 24:10 [a] Neh. 12:4, 17; Luke 1:5 24:15 [1] Septuagint and Vulgate read *Aphses.*
24:16 [1] Masoretic Text reads *Jehezkel.*

19This *was* the schedule of their service [a]for coming into the house of the LORD according to their ordinance by the hand of Aaron their father, as the LORD God of Israel had commanded him.

Other Levites

20And the rest of the sons of Levi: of the sons of Amram, Shubael;[1] of the sons of Shubael, Jehdeiah. 21Concerning [a]Rehabiah, of the sons of Rehabiah, the first *was* Isshiah. 22Of the Izharites, Shelomoth;[1] of the sons of Shelomoth, Jahath. 23Of the sons *of [a]Hebron,[1]* Jeriah *was the first,[2]* Amariah the second, Jahaziel the third, *and* Jekameam the fourth. 24*Of* the sons of Uzziel, Michah; of the sons of Michah, Shamir. 25The brother of Michah, Isshiah; of the sons of Isshiah, Zechariah. 26[a]The sons of Merari *were* Mahli and Mushi; the son of Jaaziah, Beno. 27The sons of Merari by Jaaziah *were* Beno, Shoham, Zaccur, and Ibri. 28Of Mahli: Eleazar, [a]who had no sons. 29Of Kish: the son of Kish, Jerahmeel.

30Also [a]the sons of Mushi *were* Mahli, Eder, and Jerimoth. These *were* the sons of the Levites according to their fathers' houses.

31These also cast lots just as their brothers the sons of Aaron did, in the presence of King David, Zadok, Ahimelech, and the heads of the fathers' *houses* of the priests and Levites. The chief fathers *did* just as their younger brethren.

The Musicians

25 Moreover David and the captains of the army separated for the service *some* of the sons of [a]Asaph, of Heman, and of Jeduthun, who *should* prophesy with harps, stringed instruments, and cymbals. And the number of the skilled men performing their service was: 2Of the sons of Asaph: Zaccur, Joseph, Nethaniah, and Asharelah;[1] the sons of Asaph *were* under the direction of Asaph, who prophesied according to the order of the king. 3Of [a]Jeduthun, the sons of Jeduthun: Gedaliah, Zeri,[1] Jeshaiah, *Shimei*, Hashabiah, and Mattithiah, six,[2] under the direction of their father Jeduthun, who prophesied with a harp to give thanks and to praise the LORD. 4Of Heman, the sons of Heman: Bukkiah, Mattaniah, Uzziel,[1] Shebuel,[2] Jerimoth,[3] Hananiah, Hanani, Eliathah, Giddalti, Romamti-Ezer, Joshbekashah, Mallothi, Hothir, *and* Mahazioth. 5All these *were* the sons of Heman the king's seer in the words of God, to exalt his [a]horn.[1] For God gave Heman fourteen sons and three daughters.

6All these *were* under the direction of their father for the music *in* the house of the LORD, with cymbals, stringed instruments, and [a]harps, for the service of the house of God. Asaph, Jeduthun, and Heman *were* [b]under the authority of the king. 7So the [a]number of them, with their brethren who were instructed in the songs of the LORD, all who were skillful, *was* two hundred and eighty-eight.

8And they cast lots for their duty, the small as well as the great, [a]the teacher with the student.

9Now the first lot for Asaph came out for Joseph; the second for Gedaliah, him with his brethren and sons, twelve; 10the third for Zaccur, his sons and his brethren, twelve; 11the fourth for Jizri,[1] his sons and his brethren, twelve; 12the fifth for Nethaniah, his sons and his brethren, twelve; 13the sixth for Bukkiah, his sons and his brethren, twelve; 14the seventh for Jesharelah,[1] his sons and his brethren, twelve; 15the eighth for Jeshaiah, his sons and his brethren, twelve; 16the ninth for Mattaniah, his sons and his brethren, twelve; 17the tenth for Shimei, his sons and his brethren, twelve; 18the eleventh for Azarel,[1] his sons and his brethren, twelve; 19the twelfth for Hashabiah, his sons and his brethren, twelve; 20the thirteenth for Shubael,[1] his sons and his brethren, twelve;

24:19 [a] 1 Chr. 9:25 **24:20** [1] Spelled *Shebuel* in 23:16 **24:21** [a] 1 Chr. 23:17 **24:22** [1] Spelled *Shelomith* in 23:18 **24:23** [a] 1 Chr. 23:19; 26:31 [1] Supplied from 23:19 (following some Hebrew manuscripts and Septuagint manuscripts) [2] Supplied from 23:19 (following some Hebrew manuscripts and Septuagint manuscripts) **24:26** [a] Ex. 6:19; 1 Chr. 23:21 **24:28** [a] 1 Chr. 23:22 **24:30** [a] 1 Chr. 23:23
25:1 [a] 1 Chr. 6:30, 33, 39, 44; 2 Chr. 5:12 **25:2** [1] Spelled *Jesharelah* in verse 14 **25:3** [a] 1 Chr. 16:41, 42 [1] Spelled *Jizri* in verse 11 [2] *Shimei,* appearing in one Hebrew and several Septuagint manuscripts, completes the total of six sons (compare verse 17). **25:4** [1] Spelled *Azarel* in verse 18 [2] Spelled *Shubael* in verse 20 [3] Spelled *Jeremoth* in verse 22 **25:5** [a] 1 Chr. 16:42 [1] That is, to increase his power or influence **25:6** [a] 1 Chr. 15:16 [b] 1 Chr. 15:19; 25:2 **25:7** [a] 1 Chr. 23:5 **25:8** [a] 2 Chr. 23:13 **25:11** [1] Spelled *Zeri* in verse 3 **25:14** [1] Spelled *Asharelah* in verse 2 **25:18** [1] Spelled *Uzziel* in verse 4 **25:20** [1] Spelled *Shebuel* in verse 4

21the fourteenth for Mattithiah, his sons
and his brethren, twelve; 22the fifteenth
for Jeremoth,[1] his sons and his brethren,
twelve; 23the sixteenth for Hananiah, his
sons and his brethren, twelve; 24the seventeenth for Joshbekashah, his sons and
his brethren, twelve; 25the eighteenth for
Hanani, his sons and his brethren, twelve;
26the nineteenth for Mallothi, his sons and
his brethren, twelve; 27the twentieth for Eliathah, his sons and his brethren, twelve;
28the twenty-first for Hothir, his sons and
his brethren, twelve; 29the twenty-second
for Giddalti, his sons and his brethren,
twelve; 30the twenty-third for Mahazioth,
his sons and his brethren, twelve; 31the
twenty-fourth for Romamti-Ezer, his sons
and his brethren, twelve.

The Gatekeepers

26 Concerning the divisions of the
gatekeepers: of the Korahites, Meshelemiah the son of [a]Kore, of the sons of
Asaph. 2And the sons of Meshelemiah *were*
[a]Zechariah the firstborn, Jediael the second, Zebadiah the third, Jathniel the fourth,
3Elam the fifth, Jehohanan the sixth, Eliehoenai the seventh.
4Moreover the sons of [a]Obed-Edom *were*
Shemaiah the firstborn, Jehozabad the second, Joah the third, Sacar the fourth, Nethanel the fifth, 5Ammiel the sixth, Issachar
the seventh, Peulthai the eighth; for God
blessed him.
6Also to Shemaiah his son were sons
born who governed their fathers' houses,
because they *were* men of great ability. 7The
sons of Shemaiah *were* Othni, Rephael,
Obed, and Elzabad, whose brothers Elihu
and Semachiah *were* able men.
8All these *were* of the sons of Obed-
Edom, they and their sons and their brethren, [a]able men with strength for the work:
sixty-two of Obed-Edom.
9And Meshelemiah had sons and brethren, eighteen able men.
10Also [a]Hosah, of the children of Merari,
had sons: Shimri the first (for *though* he
was not the firstborn, his father made him
the first), 11Hilkiah the second, Tebaliah the
third, Zechariah the fourth; all the sons and
brethren of Hosah *were* thirteen.
12Among these *were* the divisions of the
gatekeepers, among the chief men, *hav-*
ing duties just like their brethren, to serve
in the house of the LORD. 13And they [a]cast
lots for each gate, the small as well as the
great, according to their father's house.
14The lot for the East *Gate* fell to Shelemiah.
Then they cast lots *for* his son Zechariah,
a wise counselor, and his lot came out for
the North Gate; 15to Obed-Edom the South
Gate, and to his sons the storehouse.[1] 16To
Shuppim and Hosah *the lot came out* for the
West Gate, with the Shallecheth Gate on the
[a]ascending highway—watchman opposite
watchman. 17On the east *were* six Levites,
on the north four each day, on the south
four each day, and for the storehouse[1] two
by two. 18As for the Parbar[1] on the west,
there were four on the highway *and* two at
the Parbar. 19These were the divisions of
the gatekeepers among the sons of Korah
and among the sons of Merari.

The Treasuries and Other Duties

20Of the Levites, Ahijah *was* [a]over the
treasuries of the house of God and over the
treasuries of the [b]dedicated things. 21The
sons of Laadan, the descendants of the Gershonites of Laadan, heads of their fathers'
houses, of Laadan the Gershonite: Jehieli.
22The sons of Jehieli, Zetham and Joel his
brother, *were* over the treasuries of the
house of the LORD. 23Of the [a]Amramites,
the Izharites, the Hebronites, and the Uzzielites: 24[a]Shebuel the son of Gershom, the
son of Moses, *was* overseer of the treasuries. 25And his brethren by Eliezer *were* Rehabiah his son, Jeshaiah his son, Joram his
son, Zichri his son, and [a]Shelomith his son.
26This Shelomith and his brethren
were over all the treasuries of the dedicated things [a]which King David and the
heads of fathers' *houses,* the captains over
thousands and hundreds, and the captains of the army, had dedicated. 27Some
of the spoils won in battles they dedicated

25:22 [1] Spelled *Jerimoth* in verse 4 26:1 [a] Ps. 42:title 26:2 [a] 1 Chr. 9:21 26:4 [a] 1 Chr. 15:18, 21 26:8 [a] 1 Chr. 9:13 26:10 [a] 1 Chr. 16:38 26:13 [a] 1 Chr. 24:5, 31; 25:8 26:15 [1] Hebrew *asuppim* 26:16 [a] 1 Kin. 10:5; 2 Chr. 9:4 26:17 [1] Hebrew *asuppim* 26:18 [1] Probably a court or colonnade extending west of the temple 26:20 [a] 1 Chr. 9:26 [b] 2 Sam. 8:11; 1 Chr. 26:22, 24, 26; 28:12; Ezra 2:69 26:23 [a] Ex. 6:18; Num. 3:19 26:24 [a] 1 Chr. 23:16 26:25 [a] 1 Chr. 23:18 26:26 [a] 2 Sam. 8:11

to maintain the house of the LORD. 28 And all that Samuel [a]the seer, Saul the son of Kish, Abner the son of Ner, and Joab the son of Zeruiah had dedicated, every dedicated *thing,* was under the hand of Shelomith and his brethren.

29 Of the Izharites, Chenaniah and his sons [a]*performed* duties as [b]officials and judges over Israel outside Jerusalem.

30 Of the Hebronites, [a]Hashabiah and his brethren, one thousand seven hundred able men, had the oversight of Israel on the west side of the Jordan for all the business of the LORD, and in the service of the king. 31 Among the Hebronites, [a]Jerijah *was* head of the Hebronites according to his genealogy of the fathers. In the fortieth year of the reign of David they were sought, and there were found among them capable men [b]at Jazer of Gilead. 32 And his brethren *were* two thousand seven hundred able men, heads of fathers' *houses,* whom King David made officials over the Reubenites, the Gadites, and the half-tribe of Manasseh, for every matter pertaining to God and the [a]affairs of the king.

The Military Divisions

27 And the children of Israel, according to their number, the heads of fathers' *houses,* the captains of thousands and hundreds and their officers, served the king in every matter of the *military* divisions. *These divisions* came in and went out month by month throughout all the months of the year, each division *having* twenty-four thousand.

2 Over the first division for the first month *was* [a]Jashobeam the son of Zabdiel, and in his division *were* twenty-four thousand; 3 *he was* of the children of Perez, and the chief of all the captains of the army for the first month. 4 Over the division of the second month *was* Dodai[1] an Ahohite, and of his division Mikloth also *was* the leader; in his division *were* twenty-four thousand. 5 The third captain of the army for the third month *was* [a]Benaiah, the son of Jehoiada the priest, who was chief; in his division *were* twenty-four thousand. 6 This was the Benaiah *who was* [a]mighty *among* the thirty, and was over the thirty; in his division *was* Ammizabad his son. 7 The fourth *captain* for the fourth month *was* [a]Asahel the brother of Joab, and Zebadiah his son after him; in his division *were* twenty-four thousand. 8 The fifth captain for the fifth month *was* Shamhuth[1] the Izrahite; in his division were twenty-four thousand. 9 The sixth *captain* for the sixth month *was* [a]Ira the son of Ikkesh the Tekoite; in his division *were* twenty-four thousand. 10 The seventh *captain* for the seventh month *was* [a]Helez the Pelonite, of the children of Ephraim; in his division *were* twenty-four thousand. 11 The eighth *captain* for the eighth month *was* [a]Sibbechai the Hushathite, of the Zarhites; in his division *were* twenty-four thousand. 12 The ninth *captain* for the ninth month *was* [a]Abiezer the Anathothite, of the Benjamites; in his division *were* twenty-four thousand. 13 The tenth *captain* for the tenth month *was* [a]Maharai the Netophathite, of the Zarhites; in his division *were* twenty-four thousand. 14 The eleventh *captain* for the eleventh month *was* [a]Benaiah the Pirathonite, of the children of Ephraim; in his division *were* twenty-four thousand. 15 The twelfth *captain* for the twelfth month *was* Heldai[1] the Netophathite, of Othniel; in his division *were* twenty-four thousand.

Leaders of Tribes

16 Furthermore, over the tribes of Israel: the officer over the Reubenites *was* Eliezer the son of Zichri; over the Simeonites, Shephatiah the son of Maachah; 17 *over* the Levites, [a]Hashabiah the son of Kemuel; over the Aaronites, Zadok; 18 *over* Judah, [a]Elihu, *one* of David's brothers; *over* Issachar, Omri the son of Michael; 19 *over* Zebulun, Ishmaiah the son of Obadiah; *over* Naphtali, Jerimoth the son of Azriel; 20 *over* the children of Ephraim, Hoshea the son of Azaziah; *over* the half-tribe of Manasseh, Joel the son of Pedaiah; 21 *over* the half-*tribe* of Manasseh in Gilead, Iddo the son of Zechariah; *over* Benjamin, Jaasiel the son of Abner; 22 *over* Dan, Azarel the son

---

26:28 [a] 1 Sam. 9:9 26:29 [a] Neh. 11:16 [b] 1 Chr. 23:4 26:30 [a] 1 Chr. 27:17 26:31 [a] 1 Chr. 23:19 [b] Josh. 21:39 26:32 [a] 2 Chr. 19:11
27:2 [a] 1 Chr. 11:11 27:4 [1] Hebrew *Dodai,* usually spelled *Dodo* (compare 2 Samuel 23:9) 27:5 [a] 1 Chr. 18:17 27:6 [a] 2 Sam. 23:20–23
27:7 [a] 2 Sam. 23:24; 1 Chr. 11:26 27:8 [1] Spelled *Shammoth* in 11:27 and *Shammah* in 2 Samuel 23:11 27:9 [a] 1 Chr. 11:28
27:10 [a] 1 Chr. 11:27 27:11 [a] 2 Sam. 21:18; 1 Chr. 11:29; 20:4 27:12 [a] 1 Chr. 11:28 27:13 [a] 2 Sam. 23:28; 1 Chr. 11:30 27:14 [a] 1 Chr. 11:31
27:15 [1] Spelled *Heled* in 11:30 and *Heleb* in 2 Samuel 23:29 27:17 [a] 1 Chr. 26:30 27:18 [a] 1 Sam. 16:6

of Jeroham. These *were* the leaders of the
tribes of Israel.
23But David did not take the number of
those twenty years old and under, because
[a]the LORD had said He would multiply Israel like the [b]stars of the heavens. 24Joab
the son of Zeruiah began a census, but he
did not finish, for [a]wrath came upon Israel
because of this census; nor was the number recorded in the account of the chronicles of King David.

Other State Officials

25And Azmaveth the son of Adiel *was*
over the king's treasuries; and Jehonathan
the son of Uzziah was over the storehouses
in the field, in the cities, in the villages, and
in the fortresses. 26Ezri the son of Chelub
was over those who did the work of the field
for tilling the ground. 27And Shimei the Ra-
mathite *was* over the vineyards, and Zabdi
the Shiphmite was over the produce of the
vineyards for the supply of wine. 28Baal-Ha-
nan the Gederite was over the olive trees
and the sycamore trees that *were* in the
lowlands, and Joash *was* over the store of
oil. 29And Shitrai the Sharonite *was* over
the herds that fed in Sharon, and Shaphat
the son of Adlai was over the herds *that*
were in the valleys. 30Obil the Ishmaelite
was over the camels, Jehdeiah the Meronothite *was* over the donkeys, 31and Jaziz the
[a]Hagrite *was* over the flocks. All these *were*
the officials over King David's property.
32Also Jehonathan, David's uncle, *was* a
counselor, a wise man, and a scribe; and Jehiel the son of Hachmoni *was* with the king's
sons. 33[a]Ahithophel *was* the king's counselor, and [b]Hushai the Archite *was* the king's
companion. 34After Ahithophel *was* Jehoiada the son of Benaiah, then [a]Abiathar. And
the general of the king's army *was* [b]Joab.

Solomon Instructed to Build the Temple

28 Now David assembled at Jerusalem
all [a]the leaders of Israel: the officers of the tribes and [b]the captains of the
divisions who served the king, the captains
over thousands and captains over hundreds, and [c]the stewards over all the substance and possessions of the king and of
his sons, with the officials, the valiant men,
and all [d]the mighty men of valor.
2Then King David rose to his feet and
said, "Hear me, my brethren and my people: [a]I *had* it in my heart to build a house of
rest for the ark of the covenant of the LORD,
and for [b]the footstool of our God, and had
made preparations to build it. 3But God
said to me, [a]'You shall not build a house for
My name, because you *have been* a man of
war and have shed [b]blood.' 4However the
LORD God of Israel [a]chose me above all
the house of my father to be king over Israel forever, for He has chosen [b]Judah *to be*
the ruler. And of the house of Judah, [c]the
house of my father, and [d]among the sons
of my father, He was pleased with me to
make *me* king over all Israel. 5[a]And of all
my sons (for the LORD has given me many
sons) [b]He has chosen my son Solomon to
sit on the throne of the kingdom of the
LORD over Israel. 6Now He said to me, 'It
is [a]your son Solomon *who* shall build My
house and My courts; for I have chosen
him *to be* My son, and I will be his Father.
7Moreover I will establish his kingdom forever, [a]if he is steadfast to observe My commandments and My judgments, as it is this
day.' 8Now therefore, in the sight of all Israel, the assembly of the LORD, and in the
hearing of our God, be careful to seek out
all the commandments of the LORD your
God, that you may possess this good land,
and leave *it* as an inheritance for your children after you forever.
9"As for you, my son Solomon, [a]know the
God of your father, and serve Him [b]with a
loyal heart and with a willing mind; for [c]the
LORD searches all hearts and understands
all the intent of the thoughts. [d]If you seek
Him, He will be found by you; but if you
forsake Him, He will [e]cast you off forever.
10Consider now, [a]for the LORD has chosen
you to build a house for the sanctuary; be
strong, and do it."

27:23 [a] [Deut. 6:3] [b] Gen. 15:5; 22:17; 26:4; Ex. 32:13; Deut. 1:10 **27:24** [a] 2 Sam. 24:12–15; 1 Chr. 21:1–7 **27:31** [a] 1 Chr. 5:10 **27:33** [a] 2 Sam. 15:12 [b] 2 Sam. 15:32–37 **27:34** [a] 1 Kin. 1:7 [b] 1 Chr. 11:6 **28:1** [a] 1 Chr. 27:16 [b] 1 Chr. 27:1, 2 [c] 1 Chr. 27:25 [d] 2 Sam. 23:8–39; 1 Chr. 11:10–47 **28:2** [a] 2 Sam. 7:2 [b] Ps. 99:5; 132:7; [Is. 66:1] **28:3** [a] 2 Sam. 7:5, 13; 1 Kin. 5:3 [b] [1 Chr. 17:4; 22:8] **28:4** [a] 1 Sam. 16:6–13 [b] Gen. 49:8–10; 1 Chr. 5:2; Ps. 60:7 [c] 1 Sam. 16:1 [d] 1 Sam. 13:14; 16:12, 13; Acts 13:22 **28:5** [a] 1 Chr. 3:1–9; 14:3–7; 23:1 [b] 1 Chr. 22:9; 29:1 **28:6** [a] 2 Sam. 7:13, 14; 1 Kin. 6:38; 1 Chr. 22:9, 10; 2 Chr. 1:9; 6:2 **28:7** [a] 1 Chr. 22:13 **28:9** [a] [1 Sam. 12:24]; Jer. 9:24; Hos. 4:1; [John 17:3] [b] 2 Kin. 20:3 [c] [1 Sam. 16:7; 1 Kin. 8:39; 1 Chr. 29:17]; Jer. 11:20; 17:10; 20:12; Rev. 2:23 [d] 2 Chr. 15:2; [Jer. 29:13] [e] Deut. 31:17 **28:10** [a] 1 Chr. 22:13; 28:6

11Then David gave his son Solomon [a]the
plans for the vestibule, its houses, its treasuries, its upper chambers, its inner chambers, and the place of the mercy seat; 12and
the [a]plans for all that he had by the Spirit,
of the courts of the house of the LORD, of
all the chambers all around, [b]of the treasuries of the house of God, and of the treasuries for the dedicated things; 13also for
the division of the priests and the [a]Levites,
for all the work of the service of the house
of the LORD, and for all the articles of service in the house of the LORD. 14*He gave* gold
by weight for *things* of gold, for all articles
used in every kind of service; also *silver* for
all articles of silver by weight, for all articles
used in every kind of service; 15the weight
for the [a]lampstands of gold, and their lamps
of gold, by weight for each lampstand and
its lamps; for the lampstands of silver by
weight, for the lampstand and its lamps, according to the use of each lampstand. 16And
by weight *he gave* gold for the tables of the
showbread, for each [a]table, and silver for the
tables of silver; 17also pure gold for the forks,
the basins, the pitchers of pure gold, and the
golden bowls—*he gave gold* by weight for
every bowl; and for the silver bowls, *silver*
by weight for every bowl; 18and refined gold
by weight for the [a]altar of incense, and for
the construction of the chariot, that is, the
gold [b]cherubim that spread *their wings* and
overshadowed the ark of the covenant of
the LORD. 19"All *this,*" *said David,* [a]"the LORD
made me understand in writing, by *His* hand
upon me, all the works of these plans."

20And David said to his son Solomon,
[a]"Be strong and of good courage, and do *it;*
do not fear nor be dismayed, for the LORD
God—my God—*will be* with you. [b]He will
not leave you nor forsake you, until you
have finished all the work for the service
of the house of the LORD. 21*Here are* [a]the
divisions of the priests and the Levites for
all the service of the house of God; and [b]ev-
ery willing craftsman *will be* with you for
all manner of workmanship, for every kind
of service; also the leaders and all the people *will be* completely at your command."

#OXYGEN

1 CHRONICLES 28:20

Trust in His Will

You are never alone, though it may seem so at times. Be encouraged. God will not only be with you but also see you through it. Keep your head up.

Breathe and **trust in His will.**

Offerings for Building the Temple

29 Furthermore King David said to all
the assembly: "My son Solomon,
whom alone God has [a]chosen, *is* [b]young and
inexperienced; and the work *is* great, because the temple[1] *is* not for man but for the
LORD God. 2Now for the house of my God I
have prepared with all my might: gold for
things to be made of gold, silver for *things*
of silver, bronze for *things of* bronze, iron
for *things of* iron, wood for *things of* wood,
[a]onyx stones, *stones* to be set, glistening
stones of various colors, all kinds of precious stones, and marble slabs in abundance. 3Moreover, because I have set my
affection on the house of my God, I have
given to the house of my God, over and
above all that I have prepared for the holy
house, my own special treasure of gold and
silver: 4three thousand talents of gold, of
the gold of [a]Ophir, and seven thousand talents of refined silver, to overlay the walls
of the houses; 5the gold for *things of* gold
and the silver for *things of* silver, and for
all kinds of work *to be done* by the hands of
craftsmen. Who *then* is [a]willing to consecrate himself this day to the LORD?"

6Then [a]the leaders of the fathers' *houses,*
leaders of the tribes of Israel, the captains of thousands and of hundreds, with
[b]the officers over the king's work, [c]offered

28:11 [a] 1 Kin. 6:3; 1 Chr. 28:19 28:12 [a] Ex. 25:40; Heb. 8:5 [b] 1 Chr. 26:20, 28 28:13 [a] 1 Chr. 23:6 28:15 [a] Ex. 25:31–39; 1 Kin. 7:49 28:16 [a] 1 Kin. 7:48 28:18 [a] Ex. 30:1–10 [b] Ex. 25:18–22; 1 Sam. 4:4; 1 Kin. 6:23 28:19 [a] Ex. 25:40; 1 Chr. 28:11, 12 28:20 [a] Deut. 31:6, 7; [Josh. 1:6–9]; 1 Chr. 22:13 [b] Josh. 1:5; Heb. 13:5 28:21 [a] 1 Chr. 24—26 [b] Ex. 35:25–35; 36:1, 2; 2 Chr. 2:13, 14 29:1 [a] 1 Chr. 28:5 [b] 1 Kin. 3:7; 1 Chr. 22:5; Prov. 4:3 [1] Literally *palace* 29:2 [a] Is. 54:11, 12; Rev. 21:18 29:4 [a] 1 Kin. 9:28 29:5 [a] 2 Chr. 29:31; [2 Cor. 8:5, 12] 29:6 [a] 1 Chr. 27:1; 28:1 [b] 1 Chr. 27:25–31 [c] Ex. 35:21–35

willingly. 7They gave for the work of the
house of God five thousand talents and ten
thousand darics of gold, ten thousand talents of silver, eighteen thousand talents of
bronze, and one hundred thousand talents
of iron. 8And whoever had *precious* stones
gave *them* to the treasury of the house of
the LORD, into the hand of [a]Jehiel[1] the Gershonite. 9Then the people rejoiced, for they
had offered willingly, because with a loyal
heart they had [a]offered willingly to the
LORD; and King David also rejoiced greatly.

David's Praise to God

10Therefore David blessed the LORD before all the assembly; and David said:

"Blessed are You, LORD God of Israel,
our Father, forever and ever.
11 [a]Yours, O LORD, *is* the greatness,
The power and the glory,
The victory and the majesty;
For all *that is* in heaven and
in earth *is Yours;*
Yours *is* the kingdom, O LORD,
And You are exalted as head over all.
12 [a]Both riches and honor *come* from You,
And You reign over all.
In Your hand *is* power and might;
In Your hand *it is* to make great
And to give strength to all.

13 "Now therefore, our God,
We thank You
And praise Your glorious name.
14 But who *am* I, and who *are* my people,
That we should be able to offer
so willingly as this?
For all things *come* from You,
And of Your own we have given You.
15 For [a]we *are* aliens and
pilgrims before You,
As *were* all our fathers;
[b]Our days on earth *are* as a shadow,
And without hope.

16"O LORD our God, all this abundance
that we have prepared to build You a house
for Your holy name is from Your hand, and
is all Your own. 17I know also, my God, that
You [a]test the heart and [b]have pleasure in
uprightness. As for me, in the uprightness
of my heart I have willingly offered all these
things; and now with joy I have seen Your
people, who are present here to offer willingly to You. 18O LORD God of Abraham,
Isaac, and Israel, our fathers, keep this forever in the intent of the thoughts of the
heart of Your people, and fix their heart
toward You. 19And [a]give my son Solomon
a loyal heart to keep Your commandments
and Your testimonies and Your statutes, to
do all *these things,* and to build the temple[1]
for which [b]I have made provision."

20Then David said to all the assembly,
"Now bless the LORD your God." So all the
assembly blessed the LORD God of their
fathers, and bowed their heads and prostrated themselves before the LORD and the
king.

Solomon Anointed King
(1 Kin. 1:38–40; 2:12)

21And they made sacrifices to the LORD
and offered burnt offerings to the LORD on
the next day: a thousand bulls, a thousand
rams, a thousand lambs, with their drink
offerings, and [a]sacrifices in abundance for
all Israel. 22So they ate and drank before the
LORD with great gladness on that day. And
they made Solomon the son of David king
the second time, and [a]anointed *him* before
the LORD *to be* the leader, and Zadok *to be*
priest. 23Then Solomon sat on the throne
of the LORD as king instead of David his father, and prospered; and all Israel obeyed
him. 24All the leaders and the mighty men,
and also all the sons of King David, [a]sub-
mitted themselves to King Solomon. 25So
the LORD exalted Solomon exceedingly in
the sight of all Israel, and [a]bestowed on him
such royal majesty as had not been on any
king before him in Israel.

The Close of David's Reign

26Thus David the son of Jesse reigned
over all Israel. 27[a]And the period that he
reigned over Israel *was* forty years; [b]seven

29:8 [a] 1 Chr. 23:8 [1] Possibly the same as *Jehieli* (compare 26:21, 22) **29:9** [a] Ex. 25:2; 1 Kin. 8:61; 2 Cor. 9:7 **29:11** [a] Matt. 6:13; 1 Tim. 1:17; Rev. 5:13 **29:12** [a] Rom. 11:36 **29:15** [a] Lev. 25:23; Ps. 39:12; Heb. 11:13, 14; 1 Pet. 2:11 [b] Job 14:2; Ps. 90:9 **29:17** [a] [1 Sam. 16:7; 1 Chr. 28:9] [b] Prov. 11:20 **29:19** [a] [1 Chr. 28:9]; Ps. 72:1 [b] 1 Chr. 29:1, 2 [1] Literally *palace* **29:21** [a] 1 Kin. 8:62, 63 **29:22** [a] 1 Kin. 1:32–35, 39; 1 Chr. 23:1 **29:24** [a] Eccl. 8:2 **29:25** [a] 1 Kin. 3:13; 2 Chr. 1:12; Eccl. 2:9 **29:27** [a] 2 Sam. 5:4; 1 Kin. 2:11 [b] 2 Sam. 5:5

years he reigned in Hebron, and thirty-
three *years* he reigned in Jerusalem. 28So
he [a]died in a good old age, [b]full of days and
riches and honor; and Solomon his son
reigned in his place. 29Now the acts of King
David, first and last, indeed they *are* written
in the book of Samuel the seer, in the book
of Nathan the prophet, and in the book of
Gad the seer, 30with all his reign and his
might, [a]and the events that happened to
him, to Israel, and to all the kingdoms of
the lands.

29:28 [a] Gen. 25:8 [b] 1 Chr. 23:1 29:30 [a] Dan. 2:21; 4:23, 25

THE SECOND BOOK OF THE

CHRONICLES

OVERVIEW

Written after 450 BC, 1 Chronicles and 2 Chronicles were originally one book. The books were separated when the Bible was translated into Greek. The author of 2 Chronicles is unknown, but scholars suggest that Ezra may have been the author of both books of Chronicles.

Second Chronicles retells the history of the southern kingdom of Judah, describing the reign of King Solomon and the building of the temple in Jerusalem. The temple was a significant aspect of the covenant between God and His chosen people, providing for their worship of Him.

The book opens on Solomon's reign, emphasizing that "God was with him and exalted him exceedingly" (1:1). God appeared to Solomon, inviting him to ask for whatever he wanted. Solomon requested "wisdom and knowledge" to rule the people well (vv. 7–10). In response to this humble request, God provided wisdom and knowledge, but He also promised to give Solomon riches, wealth, and honor (see vv. 11–12).

God next appointed Solomon to build a place of worship for Him. After selecting the builders and the materials, Solomon oversaw the building of the temple according to the plans of his father, David (chs. 3–4). When construction of the temple was complete, Solomon gathered the people to place the ark of the covenant in its new home (see 5:1–10). As the people praised and gave thanks, the "glory of the LORD filled the house of God" (v. 14).

In celebration of the completion of the temple, Solomon and the people offered sacrifices to God (see 7:4–7). God confirmed His covenant, saying, "If My people who are called by My name will humble themselves, and pray and seek My face, and turn from their wicked ways, then I will hear from heaven, and will forgive their sin and heal their land" (v. 14). But God further warned the people that turning from Him and worshiping other gods would bring evil upon them (see vv. 19–22). After the death of Solomon (see 9:29–31), the people's faithfulness declined under the rule of other kings, and evil would come upon them (see 10:1—28:27).

However, not all the kings were evil, a fact that 2 Chronicles emphasizes. During King Hezekiah's reign, "he did what was right in the sight of the LORD" (29:2). While on the throne, Hezekiah purified the temple, which had been defiled by ungodly kings before him, and restored rightful worship there. He also reorganized the priests and Levites and destroyed the idol images (see 29:3—31:21). Because of Hezekiah's faithfulness to God, Jerusalem was spared during Assyria's invasion (see 32:1–22).

At Hezekiah's death, his son Manasseh began to reign (see 32:32–33). During this time, Judah descended again into dishonoring the Lord (see 33:1–25). Although some reform later took place under the leadership of Josiah (see 34:1—35:27), Jerusalem was eventually destroyed, including the temple, and Judah was forced into exile by Nebuchadnezzar, king of Babylon (see 36:1–21). Cyrus, the king of Persia, would afterward overthrow Babylon, and we read at the end of 2 Chronicles of the exiles' return to Jerusalem and their rebuilding of the temple (see vv. 22–23).

Much of 2 Chronicles focuses on God's temple. When the people turned from God and worshiped idols, the temple was destroyed as a sign of God's displeasure with them. Although the

people of Judah often wavered in their commitment to the covenant, God was always willing to forgive and redeem them.

BREATHE IT IN

In 2 Chronicles, we read of Solomon's completion of God's temple. The temple represented God's presence among His people and was a powerful symbol of His covenant with them. But because the people of God rebelled, the temple was later destroyed.

African Americans have historically looked to the Black Church as their temple and the symbol of our relationship with God. During our time as slaves in this nation, we were rarely allowed to gather unless it was to worship the Lord. When we were freed, we established our own places of worship where we could commune with God and other believers.

Not only did the Black Church serve as a place of worship, but it also served as a place of refuge and support for our advancement as a people. We gathered in our churches to plan for our future. It was in our churches where we decided on our involvement in marches or sit-ins. It was in our churches where we collected money to send our children off to college, support worthy causes, and help fellow Christians in need. It was in our churches that we held Sunday school, learned to read, and participated in Bible studies to arm our families with the Word of God.

Perhaps it was not God's plan to have Black churches and White churches, but for many Black people now and in our past, the Black Church has been our refuge, as if God had covered this building with His wings. Under His wings we found refuge from the awful things that often awaited us outside. The church was, and is, a sanctuary wherein God nurtured us. It was the one place where we were equal, valued, and worthy because of Christ.

Going to church and worshiping together in God's house is always a joy for Christians, but our relationship with God is not confined to a physical building. God has declared that our bodies are also His temple (see 1 Cor. 6:19). This is true of all bodies regardless of their color. God took care in creating each one of us as a unique and valued individual, and in Christ He has placed the Holy Spirit within us. Our bodies belong to God. Therefore, we must treat them as the treasures they are.

Treating our bodies as temples requires that we refrain from physical temptation and sin. We should avoid situations we know may tempt us to disobey God. In addition, our temples should be kept physically, mentally, and spiritually healthy. We must allow only that which is good to enter our bodies, our minds, and our souls. We should eat properly, think positively, and commune with God on a regular basis. We should keep our bodies sacred and dedicated to God.

THE SECOND BOOK OF THE

CHRONICLES

Solomon Requests Wisdom
(1 Kin. 3:1–15)

1 Now [a]Solomon the son of David was
strengthened in his kingdom, and [b]the
LORD his God *was* with him and [c]exalted
him exceedingly.
2And Solomon spoke to all Israel, to [a]the
captains of thousands and of hundreds, to
the judges, and to every leader in all Israel,
the heads of the fathers' *houses.* 3Then Solomon, and all the assembly with him, went
to the high place that *was* at [a]Gibeon; for
the tabernacle of meeting with God was
there, which Moses the servant of the LORD
had [b]made in the wilderness. 4[a]But David
had brought up the ark of God from Kirjath
Jearim to *the place* David had prepared for
it, for he had pitched a tent for it at Jerusalem. 5Now [a]the bronze altar that [b]Bezalel
the son of Uri, the son of Hur, had made,
he put[1] before the tabernacle of the LORD;
Solomon and the assembly sought Him
there. 6And Solomon went up there to the
bronze altar before the LORD, which *was* at
the tabernacle of meeting, and [a]offered a
thousand burnt offerings on it.
7[a]On that night God appeared to Solomon,
and said to him, "Ask! What shall I give you?"
8And Solomon said to God: "You have
shown great [a]mercy to David my father,
and have made me [b]king in his place. 9Now,
O LORD God, let Your promise to David my
father be established, [a]for You have made
me king over a people like the [b]dust of the
earth in multitude. 10[a]Now give me wisdom and knowledge, that I may [b]go out and
come in before this people; for who can
judge this great people of Yours?"
11[a]Then God said to Solomon: "Because
this was in your heart, and you have not
asked riches or wealth or honor or the life
of your enemies, nor have you asked long
life—but have asked wisdom and knowledge for yourself, that you may judge My
people over whom I have made you king—
12wisdom and knowledge *are* granted to
you; and I will give you riches and wealth
and honor, such as [a]none of the kings have
had who *were* before you, nor shall any after you have the like."

Solomon's Military and Economic Power
(1 Kin. 10:26–29; 2 Chr. 9:25–28)

13So Solomon came to Jerusalem from
the high place that *was* at Gibeon, from before the tabernacle of meeting, and reigned
over Israel. 14[a]And Solomon gathered chariots and horsemen; he had one thousand
four hundred chariots and twelve thousand horsemen, whom he stationed in the
chariot cities and with the king in Jerusalem. 15[a]Also the king made silver and gold
as common in Jerusalem as stones, and
he made cedars as abundant as the sycamores which *are* in the lowland. 16[a]And
Solomon had horses imported from Egypt
and Keveh; the king's merchants bought
them in Keveh at the *current* price. 17They
also acquired and imported from Egypt a
chariot for six hundred *shekels* of silver,
and a horse for one hundred and fifty; thus,
through their agents,[1] they exported them

1:1 [a] 1 Kin. 2:46 [b] Gen. 39:2 [c] 1 Chr. 29:25 1:2 [a] 1 Chr. 27:1–34 1:3 [a] 1 Kin. 3:4; 1 Chr. 16:39; 21:29 [b] Ex. 25—27; 35:4—36:38
1:4 [a] Ex. 25:10–22; 2 Sam. 6:2–17; 1 Chr. 15:25—16:1 1:5 [a] Ex. 27:1, 2; 38:1, 2 [b] Ex. 31:2 [1] Some authorities read *it was there.*
1:6 [a] 1 Kin. 3:4 1:7 [a] 1 Kin. 3:5–14; 9:2 1:8 [a] Ps. 18:50 [b] 1 Chr. 28:5 1:9 [a] 2 Sam. 7:8–16; 1 Kin. 3:7, 8 [b] Gen. 13:16; Num. 23:10
1:10 [a] 1 Kin. 3:9 [b] Num. 27:17; Deut. 31:2 1:11 [a] 1 Kin. 3:11–13 1:12 [a] 1 Kin. 10:23; 1 Chr. 29:25; 2 Chr. 9:22; Eccl. 2:9
1:14 [a] 1 Kin. 10:26; 2 Chr. 9:25 1:15 [a] 1 Kin. 10:27; 2 Chr. 9:27; Job 22:24
1:16 [a] 1 Kin. 10:28; 22:36; 2 Chr. 9:28 1:17 [1] Literally *by their hands*

RELEASE // HOPE FOR PEACE

The Wisdom of Shalom

2 Chronicles 1:10 // "Now give me wisdom and knowledge, that I may go out and come in before this people; for who can judge this great people of Yours?"

Summary Message // Imagine God inviting you to ask Him for whatever you want and giving His assurance that your desire would be granted. This was God's offer to Solomon. In response, Solomon requested wisdom so he could properly lead God's people. He knew the authority of the king was vast and sweeping. He realized that a foolhardy monarch would soon invite trouble. Being more concerned about amassing power, wealth, or worldly pleasures had been the downfall of many nations' kings. Solomon knew his own shortcomings. He asked for the trait he knew would be of greatest value to him and the nation he was to rule.

The wisdom God granted Solomon would soon be revealed. Two women claimed the same child as their own. Knowing the real mother would be ever vigilant to protect her child, he offered to settle the dispute by cutting the child in two. The true mother, motivated by love for her child, agreed to allow the imposter mother to have the child, but Solomon gave the child to the true mother. This was justice arrived at by wisdom. Solomon was known far and wide as a very wise and effective ruler. Many came from foreign lands to seek out his wisdom. Solomon, whose name means "peace," enjoyed a peaceful reign over Israel.

Practical Application // How different might our world be if our leaders sought godly wisdom above all else? What could happen if wisdom—not power, wealth, or self-aggrandizement—became the virtue that world leaders, church leaders, corporate leaders, political leaders, judges, social media influencers, Hollywood celebrities, and every other person of influence sought? The possibility for peaceful outcomes should lead us to pray that our leaders will seek God and His wisdom and, moreover, that God would grant it.

Wise choices most often yield peaceful outcomes. When we walk in wisdom, we measure the consequences of our words before we speak. We consider the impact of our actions before making the first step. Wisdom cautions us to hold our tongues rather than utter a disparaging word or pass judgment over circumstances we do not fully understand. Wisdom leads us to pray rather than lash out in revenge or retaliation. Wisdom whispers "Fix your face" when we are confronted by the incredulous.

The Hebrew word for "peace" is *shalom*. Its meaning encompasses all blessings, both spiritual and temporal. If you have ever survived the absence of peace—an abusive relationship, an authoritarian employer, a vindictive neighbor—you know the value of *shalom*. We are doomed to a life lacking enjoyment when *shalom* is lacking.

Fervent Prayer // Lord, our earnest desire is to seek the things that are pleasing to You. We pray for guiding wisdom that will lead us to live in *shalom* within our world, no matter what others may choose. We pray to act justly within our circles of influence. We choose today to seek Your kingdom and Your righteousness, moving ahead in confidence that You will grant all other things that we need. In Jesus' name we pray. Amen.

---

to all the kings of the Hittites and the kings of Syria.

Solomon Prepares to Build the Temple
(1 Kin. 5:1–18)

2 Then Solomon [a]determined to build a temple for the name of the LORD, and
a royal house for himself. 2 [a]Solomon se-
lected seventy thousand men to bear burdens, eighty thousand to quarry *stone* in the
mountains, and three thousand six hundred to oversee them.
3 Then Solomon sent to Hiram[1] king of
Tyre, saying:

[a]As you have dealt with David my
father, and sent him cedars to build
himself a house to dwell in, *so deal
with me.* 4 Behold, [a]I am building a
temple for the name of the LORD my

2:1 [a] 1 Kin. 5:5 2:2 [a] 1 Kin. 5:15, 16; 2 Chr. 2:18 2:3 [a] 1 Chr. 14:1 [1] Hebrew *Huram* (compare 1 Kings 5:1) 2:4 [a] 2 Chr. 2:1

God, to dedicate *it* to Him, [b]to burn
before Him sweet incense, for [c]the
continual showbread, for [d]the burnt
offerings morning and evening, on
the [e]Sabbaths, on the New Moons, and
on the set feasts of the LORD our God.
This *is an ordinance* forever to Israel.

5 And the temple which I build *will be*
great, for [a]our God is greater than all
gods. 6 [a]But who is able to build Him a
temple, since heaven and the heaven
of heavens cannot contain Him? Who
am I then, that I should build Him a
temple, except to burn sacrifice before
Him?

7 Therefore send me at once a man
skillful to work in gold and silver,
in bronze and iron, in purple and
crimson and blue, who has skill to
engrave with the skillful men who
are with me in Judah and Jerusalem,
[a]whom David my father provided.
8 [a]Also send me cedar and cypress and
algum logs from Lebanon, for I know
that your servants have skill to cut
timber in Lebanon; and indeed my
servants *will be* with your servants, 9 to
prepare timber for me in abundance,
for the temple which I am about to
build *shall be* great and wonderful.
10 [a]And indeed I will give to your
servants, the woodsmen who cut
timber, twenty thousand kors of
ground wheat, twenty thousand kors
of barley, twenty thousand baths of
wine, and twenty thousand baths
of oil.

11 Then Hiram king of Tyre answered in
writing, which he sent to Solomon:

[a]Because the LORD loves His people,
He has made you king over them.

12 Hiram[1] also said:

[a]Blessed *be* the LORD God of Israel,
[b]who made heaven and earth, for
He has given King David a wise
son, endowed with prudence and
understanding, who will build a
temple for the LORD and a royal
house for himself!

13 And now I have sent a skillful man,
endowed with understanding, Huram[1]
my master[2] *craftsman* 14 [a](the son of a
woman of the daughters of Dan, and
his father was a man of Tyre), skilled
to work in gold and silver, bronze and
iron, stone and wood, purple and blue,
fine linen and crimson, and to make
any engraving and to accomplish any
plan which may be given to him, with
your skillful men and with the skillful
men of my lord David your father.

15 Now therefore, the wheat, the barley,
the oil, and the wine which [a]my lord
has spoken of, let him send to his
servants. 16 [a]And we will cut wood from
Lebanon, as much as you need; we will
bring it to you in rafts by sea to Joppa,
and you will carry it up to Jerusalem.

17 [a]Then Solomon numbered all the
aliens who *were* in the land of Israel, after
the census in which [b]David his father had
numbered them; and there were found to
be one hundred and fifty-three thousand
six hundred. 18 And he made [a]seventy thousand of them bearers of burdens, eighty
thousand stonecutters in the mountain,
and three thousand six hundred overseers
to make the people work.

Solomon Builds the Temple
(1 Kin. 6:1–22)

3 Now [a]Solomon began to build the house
of the LORD at [b]Jerusalem on Mount
Moriah, where *the LORD*[1] had appeared to
his father David, at the place that David
had prepared on the threshing floor of [c]Or-
nan[2] the Jebusite. 2 And he began to build

2:4 [b] Ex. 30:7 [c] Ex. 25:30; Lev. 24:8 [d] Ex. 29:38–42 [e] Num. 28:3, 9–11 2:5 [a] Ps. 135:5; [1 Cor. 8:5, 6] 2:6 [a] 1 Kin. 8:27; 2 Chr. 6:18; Is. 66:1 2:7 [a] 1 Chr. 22:15 2:8 [a] 1 Kin. 5:6 2:10 [a] 1 Kin. 5:11 2:11 [a] 1 Kin. 10:9; 2 Chr. 9:8 2:12 [a] 1 Kin. 5:7 [b] Gen. 1; 2; Acts 4:24; 14:15; Rev. 10:6 [1] Hebrew *Huram* (compare 1 Kings 5:1) 2:13 [1] Spelled *Hiram* in 1 Kings 7:13 [2] Literally *father* (compare 1 Kings 7:13, 14) 2:14 [a] 1 Kin. 7:13, 14 2:15 [a] 2 Chr. 2:10 2:16 [a] 1 Kin. 5:8, 9 2:17 [a] 1 Kin. 5:13; 2 Chr. 8:7, 8 [b] 1 Chr. 22:2 2:18 [a] 2 Chr. 2:2 3:1 [a] 1 Kin. 6:1 [b] Gen. 22:2–14 [c] 1 Chr. 21:18; 22:1 [1] Literally *He,* following Masoretic Text and Vulgate; Septuagint reads *the LORD;* Targum reads *the Angel of the LORD.* [2] Spelled *Araunah* in 2 Samuel 24:16ff

on the second *day* of the second month in
the fourth year of his reign.
3This is the foundation [a]which Solomon
laid for building the house of God: The
length *was* sixty cubits (by cubits according to the former measure) and the width
twenty cubits. 4And the [a]vestibule that *was*
in front *of the sanctuary*[1] was twenty cubits long across the width of the house,
and the height *was* one hundred and[2]
twenty. He overlaid the inside with pure
gold. 5[a]The larger room[1] he [b]paneled with
cypress which he overlaid with fine gold,
and he carved palm trees and chainwork
on it. 6And he decorated the house with
precious stones for beauty, and the gold
was gold from Parvaim. 7He also overlaid
the house—the beams and doorposts, its
walls and doors—with gold; and he carved
cherubim on the walls.

8And he made the [a]Most Holy Place. Its
length was according to the width of the
house, twenty cubits, and its width twenty
cubits. He overlaid it with six hundred talents of fine gold. 9The weight of the nails *was*
fifty shekels of gold; and he overlaid the upper [a]area with gold. 10[a]In the Most Holy Place
he made two cherubim, fashioned by carving, and overlaid them with gold. 11The wings
of the cherubim *were* twenty cubits in *overall*
length: one wing *of the one cherub was* five
cubits, touching the wall of the room, and
the other wing *was* five cubits, touching the
wing of the other cherub; 12*one* wing of the
other cherub *was* five cubits, touching the
wall of the room, and the other wing *also*
was five cubits, touching the wing of the
other cherub. 13The wings of these cherubim
spanned twenty cubits overall. They stood
on their feet, and they faced inward. 14And
he made the [a]veil of blue, purple, crimson,
and fine linen, and wove cherubim into it.

15Also he made in front of the temple[1]
[a]two pillars thirty-five[2] cubits high, and the
capital that *was* on the top of each of *them*
was five cubits. 16He made wreaths of chainwork, as in the inner sanctuary, and put *them*
on top of the pillars; and he made [a]one hundred pomegranates, and put *them* on the
wreaths of chainwork. 17Then he [a]set up the
pillars before the temple, one on the right
hand and the other on the left; he called the
name of the one on the right hand Jachin,
and the name of the one on the left Boaz.

Furnishings of the Temple
(1 Kin. 6:23–38; 7:13–51)

4 Moreover he made [a]a bronze altar:
twenty cubits was its length, twenty
cubits its width, and ten cubits its height.
2[a]Then he made the Sea of cast *bronze,*
ten cubits from one brim to the other; *it*
was completely round. Its height *was* five
cubits, and a line of thirty cubits measured
its circumference. 3[a]And under it *was* the
likeness of oxen encircling it all around,
ten to a cubit, all the way around the Sea.
The oxen *were* cast in two rows, when it
was cast. 4It stood on twelve [a]oxen: three
looking toward the north, three looking
toward the west, three looking toward the
south, and three looking toward the east;
the Sea *was set* upon them, and all their
back parts *pointed* inward. 5It *was* a handbreadth thick; and its brim was shaped like
the brim of a cup, *like* a lily blossom. It contained three thousand[1] baths.

6He also made [a]ten lavers, and put five
on the right side and five on the left, to
wash in them; such things as they offered
for the burnt offering they would wash in
them, but the Sea *was* for the [b]priests to
wash in. 7[a]And he made ten lampstands
of gold [b]according to their design, and set
them in the temple, five on the right side
and five on the left. 8[a]He also made ten tables, and placed *them* in the temple, five on
the right side and five on the left. And he
made one hundred [b]bowls of gold.

9Furthermore [a]he made the court of the
priests, and the [b]great court and doors for
the court; and he overlaid these doors with
bronze. 10[a]He set the Sea on the right side,
toward the southeast.

3:3 [a] 1 Kin. 6:2; 1 Chr. 28:11–19 3:4 [a] 1 Kin. 6:3; 1 Chr. 28:11 [1] The main room of the temple; elsewhere called the holy place (compare 1 Kings 6:3) [2] Following Masoretic Text, Septuagint, and Vulgate; Arabic, some manuscripts of the Septuagint, and Syriac omit *one hundred and.* 3:5 [a] 1 Kin. 6:17 [b] 1 Kin. 6:15; Jer. 22:14 [1] Literally *house* 3:8 [a] Ex. 26:33; 1 Kin. 6:16 3:9 [a] 1 Chr. 28:11 3:10 [a] Ex. 25:18–20; 1 Kin. 6:23–28 3:14 [a] Ex. 26:31; Matt. 27:51; Heb. 9:3 3:15 [a] 1 Kin. 7:15–20; Jer. 52:21 [1] Literally *house* [2] Or *eighteen* (compare 1 Kings 7:15; 2 Kings 25:17; and Jeremiah 52:21) 3:16 [a] 1 Kin. 7:20 3:17 [a] 1 Kin. 7:21 4:1 [a] Ex. 27:1, 2; 2 Kin. 16:14; Ezek. 43:13, 16 4:2 [a] Ex. 30:17–21; 1 Kin. 7:23–26 4:3 [a] 1 Kin. 7:24–26 4:4 [a] 1 Kin. 7:25 4:5 [1] Or *two thousand* (compare 1 Kings 7:26) 4:6 [a] 1 Kin. 7:38, 40 [b] Ex. 30:19–21 4:7 [a] 1 Kin. 7:49 [b] Ex. 25:31; 1 Chr. 28:12, 19 4:8 [a] 1 Kin. 7:48 [b] 1 Chr. 28:17 4:9 [a] 1 Kin. 6:36 [b] 2 Kin. 21:5 4:10 [a] 1 Kin. 7:39

11Then [a]Huram made the pots and the
shovels and the bowls. So Huram finished
doing the work that he was to do for King
Solomon for the house of God: 12the two
pillars and [a]the bowl-shaped capitals *that
were* on top of the two pillars; the two net-
works covering the two bowl-shaped capitals which *were* on top of the pillars; 13[a]four
hundred pomegranates for the two net-
works (two rows of pomegranates for each
network, to cover the two bowl-shaped
capitals that *were* on the pillars); 14he also
made [a]carts and the lavers on the carts;
15one Sea and twelve oxen under it; 16also
the pots, the shovels, the forks—and all
their articles [a]Huram his master[1] *craftsman* made of burnished bronze for King
Solomon for the house of the LORD.

17In the plain of Jordan the king had
them cast in clay molds, between Succoth
and Zeredah.[1] 18[a]And Solomon had all these
articles made in such great abundance that
the weight of the bronze was not determined.

19Thus [a]Solomon had all the furnishings made for the house of God: the altar
of gold and the tables on which *was* [b]the
showbread; 20the lampstands with their
lamps of pure gold, to burn [a]in the prescribed manner in front of the inner sanctuary, 21with [a]the flowers and the lamps and
the wick-trimmers of gold, of purest gold;
22the trimmers, the bowls, the ladles, and
the censers of pure gold. As for the entry of
the sanctuary, its inner doors to the Most
Holy *Place,* and the doors of the main hall
of the temple, *were* gold.

5 So [a]all the work that Solomon had done
for the house of the LORD was finished;
and Solomon brought in the things which
his father David had dedicated: the silver
and the gold and all the furnishings. And
he put *them* in the treasuries of the house
of God.

The Ark Brought into the Temple
(1 Kin. 8:1–13)

2[a]Now Solomon assembled the elders
of Israel and all the heads of the tribes, the
chief fathers of the children of Israel, in
Jerusalem, that they might bring the ark
of the covenant of the LORD up [b]from the
City of David, which *is* Zion. 3[a]Therefore
all the men of Israel assembled with the
king [b]at the feast, which *was* in the seventh
month. 4So all the elders of Israel came,
and the [a]Levites took up the ark. 5Then
they brought up the ark, the tabernacle
of meeting, and all the holy furnishings
that *were* in the tabernacle. The priests and
the Levites brought them up. 6Also King
Solomon, and all the congregation of Israel who were assembled with him before
the ark, were sacrificing sheep and oxen
that could not be counted or numbered
for multitude. 7Then the priests brought
in the ark of the covenant of the LORD to
its place, into the [a]inner sanctuary of the
temple,[1] to the Most Holy *Place,* under the
wings of the cherubim. 8For the cherubim
spread *their* wings over the place of the ark,
and the cherubim overshadowed the ark
and its poles. 9The poles extended so that
the ends of the [a]poles of the ark could be
seen from *the holy place,* in front of the inner sanctuary; but they could not be seen
from outside. And they are there to this
day. 10Nothing was in the ark except the
two tablets which Moses [a]put *there* at Horeb, when the LORD made *a covenant* with
the children of Israel, when they had come
out of Egypt.

11And it came to pass when the priests
came out of the *Most* Holy *Place* (for all the
priests who *were* present had sanctified
themselves, without keeping to their [a]di-
visions), 12[a]and the Levites *who were* the
singers, all those of Asaph and Heman
and Jeduthun, with their sons and their
brethren, stood at the east end of the altar, clothed in white linen, having cymbals, stringed instruments and harps, [b]and
with them one hundred and twenty priests
sounding with trumpets— 13indeed it came
to pass, when the trumpeters and singers
were as one, to make one sound to be heard
in praising and thanking the LORD, and
when they lifted up their voice with the

4:11 [a] 1 Kin. 7:40–51 4:12 [a] 1 Kin. 7:41 4:13 [a] 1 Kin. 7:20 4:14 [a] 1 Kin. 7:27, 43 4:16 [a] 1 Kin. 7:45; 2 Chr. 2:13 [1] Literally *father*
4:17 [1] Spelled *Zaretan* in 1 Kings 7:46 4:18 [a] 1 Kin. 7:47 4:19 [a] 1 Kin. 7:48–50 [b] Ex. 25:30 4:20 [a] Ex. 27:20, 21 4:21 [a] Ex. 25:31
5:1 [a] 1 Kin. 7:51 5:2 [a] 1 Kin. 8:1–9; Ps. 47:9 [b] 2 Sam. 6:12 5:3 [a] 1 Kin. 8:2 [b] Lev. 23:34; 2 Chr. 7:8–10 5:4 [a] 1 Chr. 15:2, 15
5:7 [a] 2 Chr. 4:20 [1] Literally *house* 5:9 [a] Ex. 25:13–15 5:10 [a] Ex. 25:16; Deut. 10:2, 5; 2 Chr. 6:11; Heb. 9:4
5:11 [a] 1 Chr. 24:1–5 5:12 [a] Ex. 32:26; 1 Chr. 25:1–7 [b] 1 Chr. 13:8; 15:16, 24

trumpets and cymbals and instruments
of music, and praised the LORD, *saying:*

[a]"*For He is* good,
For His mercy *endures* forever,"[1]

that the house, the house of the LORD, was
filled with a cloud, 14so that the priests
could not continue ministering because of
the cloud; [a]for the glory of the LORD filled
the house of God.

6 Then [a]Solomon spoke:

"The LORD said He would dwell
in the [b]dark cloud.
2 I have surely built You an
exalted house,
And [a]a place for You to
dwell in forever."

Solomon's Speech upon Completion of the Work
(1 Kin. 8:14–21)

3Then the king turned around and
[a]blessed the whole assembly of Israel,
while all the assembly of Israel was standing. 4And he said: "Blessed *be* the LORD God
of Israel, who has fulfilled with His hands
what He spoke with His mouth to my father David, [a]saying, 5'Since the day that I
brought My people out of the land of Egypt,
I have chosen no city from any tribe of Israel *in which* to build a house, that My name
might be there, nor did I choose any man
to be a ruler over My people Israel. 6[a]Yet
I have chosen Jerusalem, that My name
may be there, and I [b]have chosen David
to be over My people Israel.' 7Now [a]it was
in the heart of my father David to build a
temple[1] for the name of the LORD God of
Israel. 8But the LORD said to my father David, 'Whereas it was in your heart to build a
temple for My name, you did well in that it
was in your heart. 9Nevertheless you shall
not build the temple, but your son who will
come from your body, he shall build the
temple for My [a]name.' 10So the LORD has
fulfilled His word which He spoke, and I
have filled the position of my father David, and [a]sit on the throne of Israel, as the
LORD promised; and I have built the temple for the name of the LORD God of Israel.
11And there I have put the ark, [a]in which *is*
the covenant of the LORD which He made
with the children of Israel."

Solomon's Prayer of Dedication
(1 Kin. 8:22–53)

12[a]Then *Solomon*[1] stood before the altar
of the LORD in the presence of all the assembly of Israel, and spread out his hands
13(for Solomon had made a bronze platform
five cubits long, five cubits wide, and three
cubits high, and had set it in the midst of
the court; and he stood on it, knelt down on
his knees before all the assembly of Israel,
and spread out his hands toward heaven);
14and he said: "LORD God of Israel, [a]*there
is* no God in heaven or on earth like You,
who keep *Your* [b]covenant and mercy with
Your servants who walk before You with
all their hearts. 15[a]You have kept what You
promised Your servant David my father;
You have both spoken with Your mouth
and fulfilled *it* with Your hand, as *it is* this
day. 16Therefore, LORD God of Israel, now
keep what You promised Your servant David my father, saying, [a]'You shall not fail to
have a man sit before Me on the throne of
Israel, [b]only if your sons take heed to their
way, that they walk in My law as you have
walked before Me.' 17And now, O LORD God
of Israel, let Your word come true, which
You have spoken to Your servant David.

18"But will God indeed dwell with men on
the earth? [a]Behold, heaven and the heaven
of heavens cannot contain You. How much
less this temple[1] which I have built! 19Yet
regard the prayer of Your servant and his
supplication, O LORD my God, and listen to
the cry and the prayer which Your servant
is praying before You: 20that Your eyes may
be [a]open toward this temple day and night,
toward the place where *You* said *You would*
put Your name, that You may hear the
prayer which Your servant makes [b]toward

5:13 [a] 1 Chr. 16:34, 41; 2 Chr. 7:3; Ezra 3:11; Ps. 100:5; 106:1; 136; Jer. 33:11 [1] Compare Psalm 106:1 5:14 [a] Ex. 40:35; 1 Kin. 8:11; 2 Chr. 7:2; Ezek. 43:5 6:1 [a] Ex. 19:9; 20:21; 1 Kin. 8:12–21 [b] [Lev. 16:2]; Ps. 97:2 6:2 [a] 2 Sam. 7:13; 1 Chr. 17:12; 2 Chr. 7:12 6:3 [a] 2 Sam. 6:18 6:4 [a] 1 Chr. 17:5 6:6 [a] Deut. 12:5–7; 2 Chr. 12:13; Zech. 2:12 [b] 1 Sam. 16:7–13; 1 Chr. 28:4 6:7 [a] 2 Sam. 7:2; 1 Chr. 17:1; 28:2; Ps. 132:1–5 [1] Literally *house,* and so in verses 8–10 6:9 [a] 1 Chr. 28:3–6 6:10 [a] 1 Kin. 2:12; 10:9 6:11 [a] 2 Chr. 5:7–10 6:12 [a] 1 Kin. 8:22; 2 Chr. 7:7–9 [1] Literally *he* (compare 1 Kings 8:22) 6:14 [a] [Ex. 15:11; Deut. 4:39] [b] [Deut. 7:9] 6:15 [a] 1 Chr. 22:9, 10 6:16 [a] 2 Sam. 7:12, 16; 1 Kin. 2:4; 6:12; 2 Chr. 7:18 [b] Ps. 132:12 6:18 [a] [2 Chr. 2:6; Is. 66:1; Acts 7:49] [1] Literally *house* 6:20 [a] 2 Chr. 7:15 [b] Ps. 5:7; Dan. 6:10

HOPE FOR PEACE

INHALE

Another young life is gone. Senseless violence is all around me every day. I just do not understand how people can care so little about human life and the pain and anguish it causes. I have seen it and felt it for myself. I have had family and friends gone way too soon. And I have had enough of all this black-on-black crime. I have prayed. I have tried to be a peacemaker and make a difference. But nothing has changed. The fast life and the streets just keep winning. How about God? Will He ever do anything? Will He bring peace to our streets and neighborhoods?

EXHALE

Crime is hard for us to comprehend, let alone combat. But that doesn't mean we shouldn't try. I am glad you want to take a stand. From the world's perspective, crime exists because of injustices and inequalities. That might be true to a degree, but as people of faith, we know it is bigger than that. There's a deeper, truer reason for the crime on your streets and everywhere else.

The truth of the matter is that sin is at the root of all our crises. Why does crime exist? Because worship of God and obedience to Him do not always exist. People have rebelled against God and His ways, meaning they fail to see others as God's image bearers deserving of not just respect but love.

But this is where we can find great news for those of us who are overwhelmed by crime and long for peace. God cares and is at work to bring peace on our streets through the Prince of Peace, Jesus. When we live as Jesus lived and point others to Him, we bring that much more peace to our streets. Sometimes it is hard to tell a difference, but we just need to keep after it. One act of peace and one person coming to know the Prince of Peace at a time until He returns and brings about complete peace everywhere. God has promised this. When that feels too far off, read Solomon's speech in 2 Chronicles 6:3–10. God keeps all His promises. Keep believing. Keep working.

this place. 21And may You hear the supplications of Your servant and of Your people
Israel, when they pray toward this place.
Hear from heaven Your dwelling place, and
when You hear, [a]forgive.

22"If anyone sins against his neighbor,
and is forced to take an [a]oath, and comes
and takes an oath before Your altar in this
temple, 23then hear from heaven, and act,
and judge Your servants, bringing retribution on the wicked by bringing his way
on his own head, and justifying the righteous by giving him according to his [a]righ-
teousness.

24"Or if Your people Israel are defeated
before an [a]enemy because they have sinned
against You, and return and confess Your
name, and pray and make supplication before You in this temple, 25then hear from
heaven and forgive the sin of Your people
Israel, and bring them back to the land
which You gave to them and their fathers.

26"When the [a]heavens are shut up and
there is no rain because they have sinned
against You, when they pray toward this
place and confess Your name, and turn
from their sin because You afflict them,
27then hear *in* heaven, and forgive the sin
of Your servants, Your people Israel, that
You may teach them the good way in which
they should walk; and send rain on Your
land which You have given to Your people
as an inheritance.

28"When there [a]is famine in the land,
pestilence or blight or mildew, locusts or
grasshoppers; when their enemies besiege them in the land of their cities; whatever plague or whatever [b]sickness *there is;*
29whatever prayer, whatever supplication
is *made* by anyone, or by all Your people

6:21 [a] [Is. 43:25; 44:22; Mic. 7:18] 6:22 [a] Ex. 22:8–11 6:23 [a] [Job 34:11] 6:24 [a] 2 Kin. 21:14, 15 6:26 [a] Deut. 28:23, 24; 1 Kin. 17:1 6:28 [a] 2 Chr. 20:9 [b] [Mic. 6:13]

Israel, when each one knows his own burden and his own grief, and spreads out his
hands to this temple: 30then hear from
heaven Your dwelling place, and forgive,
and give to everyone according to all his
ways, whose heart You know (for You alone
[a]know the [b]hearts of the sons of men), 31that
they may fear You, to walk in Your ways as
long as they live in the land which You gave
to our fathers.

32"Moreover, concerning a foreigner,
[a]who is not of Your people Israel, but has
come from a far country for the sake of
Your great name and Your mighty hand
and Your outstretched arm, when they
come and pray in this temple; 33then hear
from heaven Your dwelling place, and do
according to all for which the foreigner
calls to You, that all peoples of the earth
may know Your name and fear You, as *do*
Your people Israel, and that they may know
that this temple which I have built is called
by Your name.

34"When Your people go out to battle
against their enemies, wherever You send
them, and when they pray to You toward
this city which You have chosen and the
temple which I have built for Your name,
35then hear from heaven their prayer and
their supplication, and maintain their
cause.

36"When they sin against You (for *there
is* [a]no one who does not sin), and You become angry with them and deliver them
to the enemy, and they take them [b]cap-
tive to a land far or near; 37*yet* when they
come to themselves in the land where
they were carried captive, and repent, and
make supplication to You in the land of
their captivity, saying, 'We have sinned,
we have done wrong, and have committed wickedness'; 38and *when* they return to
You with all their heart and with all their
soul in the land of their captivity, where
they have been carried captive, and pray
toward their land which You gave to their
fathers, the [a]city which You have chosen,
and toward the temple which I have built
for Your name: 39then hear from heaven
Your dwelling place their prayer and their
supplications, and maintain their cause,
and forgive Your people who have sinned
against You. 40Now, my God, I pray, let Your
eyes be [a]open and *let* Your ears *be* attentive
to the prayer *made* in this place.

41 "Now[a] therefore,
Arise, O LORD God, to Your
[b]resting place,
You and the ark of Your strength.
Let Your priests, O LORD God,
be clothed with salvation,
And let Your saints [c]rejoice
in goodness.

42"O LORD God, do not turn away
the face of Your Anointed;
[a]Remember the mercies of
Your servant David."[1]

Solomon Dedicates the Temple
(1 Kin. 8:62–66)

7 When [a]Solomon had finished praying,
[b]fire came down from heaven and consumed the burnt offering and the sacrifices; and [c]the glory of the LORD filled the
temple.[1] 2[a]And the priests could not enter
the house of the LORD, because the glory
of the LORD had filled the LORD's house.
3When all the children of Israel saw how the
fire came down, and the glory of the LORD
on the temple, they bowed their faces to the
ground on the pavement, and worshiped
and praised the LORD, *saying:*

[a]"For *He is* good,
[b]For His mercy *endures* forever."[1]

4[a]Then the king and all the people offered sacrifices before the LORD. 5King
Solomon offered a sacrifice of twenty-
two thousand bulls and one hundred and
twenty thousand sheep. So the king and
all the people dedicated the house of God.
6[a]And the priests attended to their services; the Levites also with instruments
of the music of the LORD, which King David had made to praise the LORD, saying,

6:30 [a] [1 Chr. 28:9; Prov. 21:2; 24:12] [b] [1 Sam. 16:7] 6:32 [a] John 12:20; Acts 8:27 6:36 [a] Prov. 20:9; Eccl. 7:20; [Rom. 3:9, 19; 5:12; Gal. 3:10]; James 3:2; 1 John 1:8 [b] Deut. 28:63–68 6:38 [a] Dan. 6:10 6:40 [a] 2 Chr. 6:20 6:41 [a] Ps. 132:8–10, 16 [b] 1 Chr. 28:2 [c] Neh. 9:25 6:42 [a] 2 Sam. 7:15; Ps. 89:49; 132:1, 8–10; Is. 55:3 [1] Compare Psalm 132:8–10 7:1 [a] 1 Kin. 8:54 [b] Lev. 9:24; Judg. 6:21; 1 Kin. 18:38; 1 Chr. 21:26 [c] 1 Kin. 8:10, 11 [1] Literally *house* 7:2 [a] 2 Chr. 5:14 7:3 [a] 2 Chr. 5:13; Ps. 106:1; 136:1 [b] 1 Chr. 16:41; 2 Chr. 20:21 [1] Compare Psalm 106:1 7:4 [a] 1 Kin. 8:62, 63 7:6 [a] 1 Chr. 15:16

"For His mercy *endures* forever,"[1] whenever
David offered praise by their ministry. [b]The
priests sounded trumpets opposite them,
while all Israel stood.

7Furthermore [a]Solomon consecrated
the middle of the court that *was* in front of
the house of the LORD; for there he offered
burnt offerings and the fat of the peace
offerings, because the bronze altar which
Solomon had made was not able to receive
the burnt offerings, the grain offerings,
and the fat.

8[a]At that time Solomon kept the feast
seven days, and all Israel with him, a very
great assembly [b]from the entrance of Hamath to [c]the Brook of Egypt.[1] 9And on the
eighth day they held a [a]sacred assembly, for
they observed the dedication of the altar
seven days, and the feast seven days. 10[a]On
the twenty-third day of the seventh month
he sent the people away to their tents, joyful and glad of heart for the good that the
LORD had done for David, for Solomon,
and for His people Israel. 11Thus [a]Solomon
finished the house of the LORD and the
king's house; and Solomon successfully
accomplished all that came into his heart
to make in the house of the LORD and in
his own house.

God's Second Appearance to Solomon
(1 Kin. 9:1–9)

12Then the LORD [a]appeared to Solomon
by night, and said to him: "I have heard
your prayer, [b]and have chosen this [c]place
for Myself as a house of sacrifice. 13[a]When
I shut up heaven and there is no rain, or
command the locusts to devour the land,
or send pestilence among My people, 14if
My people who are [a]called by My name will
[b]humble themselves, and pray and seek
My face, and turn from their wicked ways,
[c]then I will hear from heaven, and will forgive their sin and heal their land. 15Now [a]My
eyes will be open and My ears attentive to
prayer *made* in this place. 16For now [a]I have
chosen and sanctified this house, that My
name may be there forever; and My eyes
and My heart will be there perpetually. 17[a]As
for you, if you walk before Me as your father
David walked, and do according to all that I
have commanded you, and if you keep My
statutes and My judgments, 18then I will
establish the throne of your kingdom, as
I covenanted with David your father, saying, [a]'You shall not fail *to have* a man as
ruler in Israel.'

19[a]"But if you turn away and forsake My
statutes and My commandments which I
have set before you, and go and serve other
gods, and worship them, 20[a]then I will uproot them from My land which I have given
them; and this house which I have sanctified for My name I will cast out of My sight,
and will make it a proverb and a [b]byword
among all peoples.

21"And *as for* [a]this house, which is exalted, everyone who passes by it will be [b]as-
tonished and say, [c]'Why has the LORD done
thus to this land and this house?' 22Then
they will answer, 'Because they forsook the
LORD God of their fathers, who brought
them out of the land of Egypt, and embraced other gods, and worshiped them
and served them; therefore He has brought
all this calamity on them.'"

Solomon's Additional Achievements
(1 Kin. 9:10–28)

8 It [a]came to pass at the end of [b]twenty
years, when Solomon had built the
house of the LORD and his own house,
2that the cities which Hiram[1] had given
to Solomon, Solomon built them; and he
settled the children of Israel there. 3And
Solomon went to Hamath Zobah and seized
it. 4[a]He also built Tadmor in the wilderness,
and all the storage cities which he built in
[b]Hamath. 5He built Upper Beth Horon and
[a]Lower Beth Horon, fortified cities *with*
walls, gates, and bars, 6also Baalath and all
the storage cities that Solomon had, and
all the chariot cities and the cities of the
cavalry, and all that Solomon [a]desired to
build in Jerusalem, in Lebanon, and in all
the land of his dominion.

7:6 [b] 2 Chr. 5:12 [1] Compare Psalm 106:1 7:7 [a] 1 Kin. 8:64–66; 9:3 7:8 [a] 1 Kin. 8:65 [b] 1 Kin. 4:21, 24; 2 Kin. 14:25 [c] Josh. 13:3 [1] That is, the Shihor (compare 1 Chronicles 13:5) 7:9 [a] Lev. 23:36 7:10 [a] 1 Kin. 8:66 7:11 [a] 1 Kin. 9:1 7:12 [a] 1 Kin. 3:5; 11:9 [b] Deut. 12:5, 11 [c] 2 Chr. 6:20 7:13 [a] Deut. 28:23, 24; 1 Kin. 17:1; 2 Chr. 6:26–28 7:14 [a] Deut. 28:10; [Is. 43:7] [b] 2 Chr. 12:6, 7; [James 4:10] [c] 2 Chr. 6:27, 30 7:15 [a] 2 Chr. 6:20, 40 7:16 [a] 1 Kin. 9:3; 2 Chr. 6:6 7:17 [a] 1 Kin. 9:4 7:18 [a] 2 Sam. 7:12–16; 1 Kin. 2:4; 2 Chr. 6:16 7:19 [a] Lev. 26:14, 33; [Deut. 28:15, 36] 7:20 [a] Deut. 28:63–68; 2 Kin. 25:1–7 [b] Ps. 44:14 7:21 [a] 2 Kin. 25:9 [b] 2 Chr. 29:8 [c] [Deut. 29:24, 25; Jer. 22:8, 9] 8:1 [a] 1 Kin. 9:10–14 [b] 1 Kin. 6:38—7:1 8:2 [1] Hebrew *Huram* (compare 2 Chronicles 2:3) 8:4 [a] 1 Kin. 9:17, 18 [b] 1 Chr. 18:3, 9 8:5 [a] 1 Chr. 7:24 8:6 [a] 2 Chr. 7:11

7[a]All the people *who were* left of the Hittites, Amorites, Perizzites, Hivites, and Jebusites, who *were* not of Israel— 8that is,
their descendants who were left in the land
after them, whom the children of Israel did
not destroy—from these Solomon raised
forced labor, as it is to this day. 9But Solomon did not make the children of Israel
servants for his work. Some *were* men of
war, captains of his officers, captains of
his chariots, and his cavalry. 10And others *were* chiefs of the officials of King Solomon: [a]two hundred and fifty, who ruled
over the people.
11Now Solomon [a]brought the daughter of
Pharaoh up from the City of David to the
house he had built for her, for he said, "My
wife shall not dwell in the house of David
king of Israel, because *the places* to which
the ark of the LORD has come are holy."
12Then Solomon offered burnt offerings
to the LORD on the altar of the LORD which
he had built before the vestibule, 13accord-
ing to the [a]daily rate, offering according
to the commandment of Moses, for the
Sabbaths, the New Moons, and the [b]three
appointed yearly [c]feasts—the Feast of Unleavened Bread, the Feast of Weeks, and the
Feast of Tabernacles. 14And, according to
the order of David his father, he appointed
the [a]divisions of the priests for their service, [b]the Levites for their duties (to praise
and serve before the priests) as the duty of
each day required, and the [c]gatekeepers by
their divisions at each gate; for so David
the man of God had commanded. 15They
did not depart from the command of the
king to the priests and Levites concerning
any matter or concerning the [a]treasuries.
16Now all the work of Solomon was well-
ordered from[1] the day of the foundation of
the house of the LORD until it was finished.
So the house of the LORD was completed.
17Then Solomon went to [a]Ezion Geber
and Elath[1] on the seacoast, in the land of
Edom. 18[a]And Hiram sent him ships by the
hand of his servants, and servants who
knew the sea. They went with the servants
of Solomon to [b]Ophir, and acquired four
hundred and fifty talents of gold from
there, and brought it to King Solomon.

The Queen of Sheba's Praise of Solomon
(1 Kin. 10:1–13)

9 Now [a]when the queen of Sheba heard
of the fame of Solomon, she came to
Jerusalem to test Solomon with hard questions, *having* a very great retinue, camels
that bore spices, gold in abundance, and
precious stones; and when she came to
Solomon, she spoke with him about all that
was in her heart. 2So Solomon answered all
her questions; there was nothing so difficult for Solomon that he could not explain
it to her. 3And when the queen of Sheba had
seen the wisdom of Solomon, the house
that he had built, 4the food on his table,
the seating of his servants, the service of
his waiters and their apparel, his [a]cup-
bearers and their apparel, and his entryway by which he went up to the house of
the LORD, there was no more spirit in her.
5Then she said to the king: "*It was* a true
report which I heard in my own land about
your words and your wisdom. 6However I
did not believe their words until I came and
saw with my own eyes; and indeed the half
of the greatness of your wisdom was not
told me. You exceed the fame of which I
heard. 7Happy *are* your men and happy *are*
these your servants, who stand continually
before you and hear your wisdom! 8Blessed
be the LORD your God, who delighted in
you, setting you on His throne *to be* king
for the LORD your God! Because your God
has [a]loved Israel, to establish them forever,
therefore He made you king over them, to
do justice and righteousness."
9And she gave the king one hundred and
twenty talents of gold, spices in great abundance, and precious stones; there never
were any spices such as those the queen
of Sheba gave to King Solomon.
10Also, the servants of Hiram and the
servants of Solomon, [a]who brought gold
from Ophir, brought algum[1] wood and

8:7 [a] Gen. 15:18–21; 1 Kin. 9:20 8:10 [a] 1 Kin. 9:23 8:11 [a] 1 Kin. 3:1; 7:8; 9:24; 11:1 8:13 [a] Ex. 29:38–42; Num. 28:3, 9, 11, 26; 29:1 [b] Ex. 23:14–17; 34:22, 23; Deut. 16:16 [c] Lev. 23:1–44 8:14 [a] 1 Chr. 24:3 [b] 1 Chr. 25:1 [c] 1 Chr. 9:17; 26:1 8:15 [a] 1 Chr. 26:20–28 8:16 [1] Following Septuagint, Syriac, and Vulgate; Masoretic Text reads *as far as.* 8:17 [a] 1 Kin. 9:26; 2 Chr. 20:36 [1] Hebrew *Eloth* (compare 2 Kings 14:22) 8:18 [a] 1 Kin. 9:27; 2 Chr. 9:10, 13 [b] 1 Chr. 29:4 9:1 [a] 1 Kin. 10:1; Ps. 72:10; [Matt. 12:42; Luke 11:31] 9:4 [a] Neh. 1:11 9:8 [a] Deut. 7:8; 2 Chr. 2:11; [Ps. 44:3] 9:10 [a] 2 Chr. 8:18 [1] Or *almug* (compare 1 Kings 10:11, 12)

precious stones. 11 And the king made walk-
ways *of* the algum[1] wood for the house of
the LORD and for the king's house, also
harps and stringed instruments for singers; and there were none such *as these* seen
before in the land of Judah.
12 Now King Solomon gave to the queen
of Sheba all she desired, whatever she
asked, *much more* than she had brought
to the king. So she turned and went to her
own country, she and her servants.

Solomon's Great Wealth

(1 Kin. 10:14–29; 2 Chr. 1:14–17)

13[a] The weight of gold that came to Solomon yearly was six hundred and sixty-six
talents of gold, 14 besides *what* the traveling
merchants and traders brought. And all the
kings of Arabia and governors of the country brought gold and silver to Solomon.
15 And King Solomon made two hundred
large shields of hammered gold; six hundred *shekels* of hammered gold went into
each shield. 16 *He* also *made* three hundred
shields of hammered gold; three hundred
shekels[1] of gold went into each shield. The
king put them in the [a]House of the Forest
of Lebanon.
17 Moreover the king made a great throne
of ivory, and overlaid it with pure gold.
18 The throne *had* six steps, with a footstool of gold, *which were* fastened to the
throne; there were armrests on either side
of the place of the seat, and two lions stood
beside the armrests. 19 Twelve lions stood
there, one on each side of the six steps;
nothing like *this* had been made for any
other kingdom.
20 All King Solomon's drinking vessels
were gold, and all the vessels of the House
of the Forest of Lebanon *were* pure gold.
Not *one was* silver, for this was accounted

---

2 CHRONICLES 9:1

I AM THE QUEEN OF SHEBA

Now when the queen of Sheba heard of the fame of Solomon, she came to Jerusalem to test Solomon with hard questions, having a very great retinue, camels that bore spices, gold in abundance, and precious stones; and when she came to Solomon, she spoke with him about all that was in her heart. 2 Chronicles 9:1

I am the queen of Sheba. I had heard about this wise king named Solomon and the powerful God he served. If it were true that he had the wisdom of God, I wanted this wisdom for myself. I went to great lengths to find out whether the claims about him were valid. I packed up a huge caravan and made a grand entrance into his kingdom with the purpose of testing him. I did not come empty-handed. I brought him gifts of precious gems, gold, and spices from my faraway, eastern land. Solomon agreed to meet with me. I sat with him, asking very hard questions that burned in my heart. He answered each one. All that I had been told was true. Solomon's wisdom, the power of God in his life, and God's love for Israel took my breath away! It was clear that God had made Solomon as a channel of justice and righteousness. I was in awe and wondered if the gifts I brought him were meager at best. However, Solomon showered great gifts upon me as I left to return to my country.

†

In the days of the queen of Sheba, women, even queens, generally were not honored or respected for anything other than their beauty. However, this queen did not let anything stop her from chasing after wisdom. In reward, she received what she was seeking.

9:11 [1] Or *almug* (compare 1 Kings 10:11, 12) 9:13 [a] 1 Kin. 10:14–29 9:16 [a] 1 Kin. 7:2 [1] Or *three minas* (compare 1 Kings 10:17)

as nothing in the days of Solomon. 21For the king's ships went to [a]Tarshish with the servants of Hiram.[1] Once every three years the merchant ships[2] came, bringing gold, silver, ivory, apes, and monkeys.[3]

22So King Solomon surpassed all the kings of the earth in riches and wisdom. 23And all the kings of the earth sought the presence of Solomon to hear his wisdom, which God had put in his heart. 24Each man brought his present: articles of silver and gold, garments, [a]armor, spices, horses, and mules, at a set rate year by year.

25Solomon [a]had four thousand stalls for horses and chariots, and twelve thousand horsemen whom he stationed in the chariot cities and with the king at Jerusalem.

26[a]So he reigned over all the kings [b]from the River[1] to the land of the Philistines, as far as the border of Egypt. 27[a]The king made silver *as common* in Jerusalem as stones, and he made cedar trees [b]as abundant as the sycamores which *are* in the lowland. 28[a]And they brought horses to Solomon from Egypt and from all lands.

Death of Solomon
(1 Kin. 11:41–43)

29[a]Now the rest of the acts of Solomon, first and last, *are* they not written in the book of Nathan the prophet, in the prophecy of [b]Ahijah the Shilonite, and in the visions of [c]Iddo the seer concerning Jeroboam the son of Nebat? 30[a]Solomon reigned in Jerusalem over all Israel forty years. 31Then Solomon rested with his fathers, and was buried in the City of David his father. And Rehoboam his son reigned in his place.

The Revolt Against Rehoboam
(1 Kin. 12:1–19)

10 And [a]Rehoboam went to Shechem, for all Israel had gone to Shechem to make him king. 2So it happened, when Jeroboam the son of Nebat heard *it* (he was in Egypt, [a]where he had fled from the presence of King Solomon), that Jeroboam returned from Egypt. 3Then they sent for him and called him. And Jeroboam and all Israel came and spoke to Rehoboam, saying, 4"Your father made our yoke heavy; now therefore, lighten the burdensome service of your father and his heavy yoke which he put on us, and we will serve you."

5So he said to them, "Come back to me after three days." And the people departed.

6Then King Rehoboam consulted the elders who stood before his father Solomon while he still lived, saying, "How do you advise *me* to answer these people?"

7And they spoke to him, saying, "If you are kind to these people, and please them, and speak good words to them, they will be your servants forever."

8[a]But he rejected the advice which the elders had given him, and consulted the young men who had grown up with him, who stood before him. 9And he said to them, "What advice do you give? How should we answer this people who have spoken to me, saying, 'Lighten the yoke which your father put on us'?"

10Then the young men who had grown up with him spoke to him, saying, "Thus you should speak to the people who have spoken to you, saying, 'Your father made our yoke heavy, but you make *it* lighter on us'—thus you shall say to them: 'My little *finger* shall be thicker than my father's waist! 11And now, whereas my father put a heavy yoke on you, I will add to your yoke; my father chastised you with whips, but I *will chastise you* with scourges!'"[1]

12So [a]Jeroboam and all the people came to Rehoboam on the third day, as the king had directed, saying, "Come back to me the third day." 13Then the king answered them roughly. King Rehoboam rejected the advice of the elders, 14and he spoke to them according to the advice of the young men, saying, "My father[1] made your yoke heavy, but I will add to it; my father chastised you with whips, but I *will chastise you* with scourges!"[2] 15So the king did not listen to the people; [a]for the turn *of events* was

---

9:21 [a] 2 Chr. 20:36, 37; Ps. 72:10 [1] Hebrew *Huram* (compare 1 Kings 10:22) [2] Literally *ships of Tarshish* (deep-sea vessels) [3] Or *peacocks* 9:24 [a] 1 Kin. 20:11 9:25 [a] Deut. 17:16; 1 Kin. 4:26; 10:26; 2 Chr. 1:14; Is. 2:7 9:26 [a] 1 Kin. 4:21 [b] Gen. 15:18; Ps. 72:8 [1] That is, the Euphrates 9:27 [a] 1 Kin. 10:27 [b] 2 Chr. 1:15–17 9:28 [a] 1 Kin. 10:28; 2 Chr. 1:16 9:29 [a] 1 Kin. 11:41 [b] 1 Kin. 11:29 [c] 2 Chr. 12:15; 13:22 9:30 [a] 1 Kin. 4:21; 11:42, 43; 1 Chr. 29:28 10:1 [a] 1 Kin. 12:1–20 10:2 [a] 1 Kin. 11:40 10:8 [a] 1 Kin. 12:8–11 10:11 [1] Literally *scorpions* 10:12 [a] 1 Kin. 12:12–14 10:14 [1] Following many Hebrew manuscripts, Septuagint, Syriac, and Vulgate (compare verse 10 and 1 Kings 12:14); Masoretic Text reads *I*. [2] Literally *scorpions* 10:15 [a] Judg. 14:4; 1 Chr. 5:22; 2 Chr. 11:4; 22:7

from God, that the LORD might fulfill His
[b]word, which He had spoken by the hand
of Ahijah the Shilonite to Jeroboam the
son of Nebat.
16Now when all Israel *saw* that the king
did not listen to them, the people answered
the king, saying:

"What share have we in David?
We have no inheritance in
the son of Jesse.
Every man to your tents, O Israel!
Now see to your own house, O David!"

So all Israel departed to their tents. 17But
Rehoboam reigned over the children of Israel who dwelt in the cities of Judah.
18Then King Rehoboam sent Hadoram,
who *was* in charge of revenue; but the
children of Israel stoned him with stones,
and he died. Therefore King Rehoboam
mounted *his* chariot in haste to flee to Jerusalem. 19[a]So Israel has been in rebellion
against the house of David to this day.

11 Now [a]when Rehoboam came to Jerusalem, he assembled from the house
of Judah and Benjamin one hundred and
eighty thousand chosen *men* who were warriors, to fight against Israel, that he might
restore the kingdom to Rehoboam.
2But the word of the LORD came [a]to Shemaiah the man of God, saying, 3"Speak to
Rehoboam the son of Solomon, king of
Judah, and to all Israel in Judah and Benjamin, saying, 4'Thus says the LORD: "You
shall not go up or fight against your brethren! Let every man return to his house, for
this thing is from Me."'" Therefore they
obeyed the words of the LORD, and turned
back from attacking Jeroboam.

Rehoboam Fortifies the Cities

5So Rehoboam dwelt in Jerusalem, and
built cities for defense in Judah. 6And he
built Bethlehem, Etam, Tekoa, 7Beth Zur,
Sochoh, Adullam, 8Gath, Mareshah, Ziph,
9Adoraim, Lachish, Azekah, 10Zorah, Aijalon, and Hebron, which are in Judah and
Benjamin, fortified cities. 11And he fortified
the strongholds, and put captains in them,
and stores of food, oil, and wine. 12Also in
every city *he put* shields and spears, and
made them very strong, having Judah and
Benjamin on his side.

Priests and Levites Move to Judah
(1 Kin. 14:21–24)

13And from all their territories the priests
and the Levites who *were* in all Israel took
their stand with him. 14For the Levites left
[a]their common-lands and their possessions and came to Judah and Jerusalem,
for [b]Jeroboam and his sons had rejected
them from serving as priests to the LORD.
15[a]Then he appointed for himself priests for
the high places, for [b]the demons, and [c]the
calf idols which he had made. 16[a]And after
the Levites *left,*[1] those from all the tribes of
Israel, such as set their heart to seek the
LORD God of Israel, [b]came to Jerusalem to
sacrifice to the LORD God of their fathers.
17So they [a]strengthened the kingdom of Judah, and made Rehoboam the son of Solomon strong for three years, because they
walked in the way of David and Solomon
for three years.

The Family of Rehoboam

18Then Rehoboam took for himself
as wife Mahalath the daughter of Jerimoth the son of David, *and of* Abihail the
daughter of [a]Eliah the son of Jesse. 19And
she bore him children: Jeush, Shamariah,
and Zaham. 20After her he took [a]Maachah
the granddaughter[1] of [b]Absalom; and she
bore him [c]Abijah, Attai, Ziza, and Shelomith. 21Now Rehoboam loved Maachah the
granddaughter of Absalom more than all
his [a]wives and his concubines; for he took
eighteen wives and sixty concubines, and
begot twenty-eight sons and sixty daughters. 22And Rehoboam [a]appointed [b]Abijah
the son of Maachah as chief, *to be* leader
among his brothers; for he *intended* to
make him king. 23He dealt wisely, and dispersed some of his sons throughout all the
territories of Judah and Benjamin, to every
[a]fortified city; and he gave them provisions

10:15 [b] 1 Kin. 11:29–39 **10:19** [a] 1 Kin. 12:19 **11:1** [a] 1 Kin. 12:21–24 **11:2** [a] 1 Chr. 12:5; 2 Chr. 12:15 **11:14** [a] Num. 35:2–5 [b] 1 Kin. 12:28–33; 2 Chr. 13:9 **11:15** [a] 1 Kin. 12:31; 13:33; 14:9; [Hos. 13:2] [b] [Lev. 17:7; 1 Cor. 10:20] [c] 1 Kin. 12:28 **11:16** [a] 2 Chr. 14:7 [b] 2 Chr. 15:9, 10; 30:11, 18 [1] Literally *after them* **11:17** [a] 2 Chr. 12:1, 13 **11:18** [a] 1 Sam. 16:6 **11:20** [a] 2 Chr. 13:2 [b] 1 Kin. 15:2 [c] 1 Kin. 14:31 [1] Literally *daughter,* but in the broader sense of granddaughter (compare 2 Chronicles 13:2) **11:21** [a] Deut. 17:17 **11:22** [a] Deut. 21:15–17 [b] 2 Chr. 13:1 **11:23** [a] 2 Chr. 11:5

in abundance. He also sought many wives *for them.*

Egypt Attacks Judah

(1 Kin. 14:25–28)

12 Now [a]it came to pass, when Rehoboam had established the kingdom and had strengthened himself, that [b]he forsook the law of the LORD, and all Israel along with him. 2 [a]And it happened in the fifth year of King Rehoboam *that* Shishak king of Egypt came up against Jerusalem, because they had transgressed against the LORD, 3 with twelve hundred chariots, sixty thousand horsemen, and people without number who came with him out of Egypt—[a]the Lubim and the Sukkiim and the Ethiopians. 4 And he took the fortified cities of Judah and came to Jerusalem.

5 Then [a]Shemaiah the prophet came to Rehoboam and the leaders of Judah, who were gathered together in Jerusalem because of Shishak, and said to them, "Thus says the LORD: 'You have forsaken Me, and therefore I also have left you in the hand of Shishak.'"

6 So the leaders of Israel and the king [a]humbled themselves; and they said, [b]"The LORD *is* righteous."

7 Now when the LORD saw that they humbled themselves, [a]the word of the LORD came to Shemaiah, saying, "They have humbled themselves; *therefore* I will not destroy them, but I will grant them some deliverance. My wrath shall not be poured out on Jerusalem by the hand of Shishak. 8 Nevertheless [a]they will be his servants, that they may distinguish [b]My service from the service of the kingdoms of the nations."

9 [a]So Shishak king of Egypt came up against Jerusalem, and took away the treasures of the house of the LORD and the treasures of the king's house; he took everything. He also carried away the gold shields which Solomon had [b]made. 10 Then King Rehoboam made bronze shields in their place, and committed *them* [a]to the hands of the captains of the guard, who guarded the doorway of the king's house. 11 And whenever the king entered the house of the LORD, the guard would go and bring them out; then they would take them back into the guardroom. 12 When he humbled himself, the wrath of the LORD turned from him, so as not to destroy *him* completely; and things also went well in Judah.

The End of Rehoboam's Reign

(1 Kin. 14:21, 22, 29–31)

13 Thus King Rehoboam strengthened himself in Jerusalem and reigned. Now [a]Rehoboam *was* forty-one years old when he became king; and he reigned seventeen years in Jerusalem, [b]the city which the LORD had chosen out of all the tribes of Israel, to put His name there. His mother's name *was* Naamah, an [c]Ammonitess. 14 And he did evil, because he did not prepare his heart to seek the LORD.

15 The acts of Rehoboam, first and last, *are* they not written in the book of Shemaiah the prophet, [a]and of Iddo the seer concerning genealogies? [b]And *there were* wars between Rehoboam and Jeroboam all their days. 16 So Rehoboam rested with his fathers, and was buried in the City of David. Then [a]Abijah[1] his son reigned in his place.

Abijah Reigns in Judah

(1 Kin. 15:1–8)

13 In [a]the eighteenth year of King Jeroboam, Abijah became king over [b]Judah. 2 He reigned three years in Jerusalem. His mother's name *was* Michaiah[1] the daughter of Uriel of Gibeah.

And there was war between Abijah and Jeroboam. 3 Abijah set the battle in order with an army of valiant warriors, four hundred thousand choice men. Jeroboam also drew up in battle formation against him with eight hundred thousand choice men, mighty men of valor.

4 Then Abijah stood on Mount [a]Zemaraim, which *is* in the mountains of Ephraim, and said, "Hear me, Jeroboam and all Israel: 5 Should you not know that the LORD God of Israel [a]gave the dominion over Israel to David forever, to him

---

12:1 [a] 2 Chr. 11:17 [b] 1 Kin. 14:22–24 12:2 [a] 1 Kin. 11:40; 14:25 12:3 [a] 2 Chr. 16:8; Nah. 3:9 12:5 [a] 2 Chr. 11:2 12:6 [a] [James 4:10] [b] Ex. 9:27; [Dan. 9:14] 12:7 [a] 1 Kin. 21:28, 29 12:8 [a] Is. 26:13 [b] [Deut. 28:47, 48] 12:9 [a] 1 Kin. 14:25, 26 [b] 1 Kin. 10:16, 17; 2 Chr. 9:15, 16 12:10 [a] 1 Kin. 14:27 12:13 [a] 1 Kin. 14:21 [b] 2 Chr. 6:6 [c] 1 Kin. 11:1, 5 12:15 [a] 2 Chr. 9:29; 13:22 [b] 1 Kin. 14:30 12:16 [a] 2 Chr. 11:20–22 [1] Spelled *Abijam* in 1 Kings 14:31 13:1 [a] 1 Kin. 15:1 [b] 1 Kin. 12:17 13:2 [1] Spelled *Maachah* in 11:20, 21 and 1 Kings 15:2 13:4 [a] Josh. 18:22 13:5 [a] 2 Sam. 7:8–16

and his sons, [b]by a covenant of salt? 6Yet
Jeroboam the son of Nebat, the servant
of Solomon the son of David, rose up and
[a]rebelled against his lord. 7Then [a]worthless
rogues gathered to him, and strengthened
themselves against Rehoboam the son of
Solomon, when Rehoboam was [b]young and
inexperienced and could not withstand
them. 8And now you think to withstand
the kingdom of the LORD, which is in the
hand of the sons of David; and you *are* a
great multitude, and with you are the gold
calves which Jeroboam [a]made for you as
gods. 9[a]Have you not cast out the priests
of the LORD, the sons of Aaron, and the Levites, and made for yourselves priests, like
the peoples of *other* lands, [b]so that whoever comes to consecrate himself with a
young bull and seven rams may be a priest
of [c]*things that are* not gods? 10But as for us,
the LORD *is* our [a]God, and we have not forsaken Him; and the priests who minister
to the LORD *are* the sons of Aaron, and the
Levites *attend* to *their* duties. 11[a]And they
burn to the LORD every morning and every evening burnt sacrifices and sweet incense; *they* also *set* the [b]showbread *in order*
on the pure *gold* table, and the lampstand
of gold with its lamps [c]to burn every evening; for we keep the command of the LORD
our God, but you have forsaken Him. 12Now
look, God Himself is with us as *our* [a]head,
[b]and His priests with sounding trumpets to
sound the alarm against you. O children of
Israel, do not fight against the LORD God
of your fathers, for you shall not prosper!"
13But Jeroboam caused an ambush to
go around behind them; so they were in
front of Judah, and the ambush *was* behind
them. 14And when Judah looked around, to
their surprise the battle line *was* at both
front and rear; and they [a]cried out to the
LORD, and the priests sounded the trumpets. 15Then the men of Judah gave a shout;
and as the men of Judah shouted, it happened that God [a]struck Jeroboam and all
Israel before Abijah and Judah. 16And the
children of Israel fled before Judah, and
God delivered them into their hand. 17Then
Abijah and his people struck them with
a great slaughter; so five hundred thousand choice men of Israel fell slain. 18Thus
the children of Israel were subdued at that
time; and the children of Judah prevailed,
[a]because they relied on the LORD God of
their fathers.
19And Abijah pursued Jeroboam and
took cities from him: Bethel with its villages, Jeshanah with its villages, and
[a]Ephrain[1] with its villages. 20So Jeroboam
did not recover strength again in the days
of Abijah; and the LORD [a]struck him, and
[b]he died.
21But Abijah grew mighty, married fourteen wives, and begot twenty-two sons and
sixteen daughters. 22Now the rest of the
acts of Abijah, his ways, and his sayings *are*
written in [a]the annals of the prophet Iddo.
14 So Abijah rested with his fathers, and
they buried him in the City of David.
Then [a]Asa his son reigned in his place. In
his days the land was quiet for ten years.

Asa Reigns in Judah
(1 Kin. 15:9–15)

2Asa did *what was* good and right in the
eyes of the LORD his God, 3for he removed
the altars of the foreign *gods* and [a]the high
places, and [b]broke down the *sacred* pillars
[c]and cut down the wooden images. 4He
commanded Judah to [a]seek the LORD God
of their fathers, and to observe the law and
the commandment. 5He also removed the
high places and the incense altars from all
the cities of Judah, and the kingdom was
quiet under him. 6And he built fortified cities in Judah, for the land had rest; he had
no war in those years, because the LORD
had given him [a]rest. 7Therefore he said to
Judah, "Let us build these cities and make
walls around *them,* and towers, gates, and
bars, *while* the land *is* yet before us, because
we have sought the LORD our God; we have
sought *Him,* and He has given us rest on
every side." So they built and prospered.
8And Asa had an army of three hundred

13:5 [b] Lev. 2:13; Num. 18:19 13:6 [a] 1 Kin. 11:28; 12:20 13:7 [a] Judg. 9:4 [b] 2 Chr. 12:13 13:8 [a] 1 Kin. 12:28; 14:9; 2 Chr. 11:15; [Hos. 8:4–6] 13:9 [a] 2 Chr. 11:13–15 [b] Ex. 29:29–33 [c] Jer. 2:11; 5:7 13:10 [a] Josh. 24:15 13:11 [a] Ex. 29:38; 2 Chr. 2:4 [b] Ex. 25:30; Lev. 24:5–9 [c] Ex. 27:20, 21; Lev. 24:2, 3 13:12 [a] Josh. 5:13–15; [Heb. 2:10] [b] [Num. 10:8–10] 13:14 [a] Josh. 24:7; 2 Chr. 6:34, 35; 14:11 13:15 [a] 1 Kin. 14:14; 2 Chr. 14:12 13:18 [a] 1 Chr. 5:20; 2 Chr. 14:11; [Ps. 22:5] 13:19 [a] Josh. 15:9 [1] Or *Ephron* 13:20 [a] 1 Sam. 2:6; 25:38; Acts 12:23 [b] 1 Kin. 14:20 13:22 [a] 2 Chr. 9:29 14:1 [a] 1 Kin. 15:8 14:3 [a] 1 Kin. 15:14; 2 Chr. 15:17 [b] [Ex. 34:13] [c] 1 Kin. 11:7 14:4 [a] [2 Chr. 7:14] 14:6 [a] 2 Chr. 15:15

thousand from Judah who carried shields
and spears, and from Benjamin two hundred and eighty thousand men who carried shields and drew [a]bows; all these *were*
mighty men of [b]valor.
9 [a]Then Zerah the Ethiopian came out
against them with an army of a million men
and three hundred chariots, and he came
to [b]Mareshah. 10 So Asa went out against
him, and they set the troops in battle array in the Valley of Zephathah at Mareshah.
11 And Asa [a]cried out to the LORD his God,
and said, "LORD, *it is* [b]nothing for You to
help, whether with many or with those who
have no power; help us, O LORD our God,
for we rest on You, and [c]in Your name we go
against this multitude. O LORD, You *are* our
God; do not let man prevail against You!"
12 So the LORD [a]struck the Ethiopians before Asa and Judah, and the Ethiopians
fled. 13 And Asa and the people who *were*
with him pursued them to [a]Gerar. So the
Ethiopians were overthrown, and they
could not recover, for they were broken
before the LORD and His army. And they
carried away very much spoil. 14 Then they
defeated all the cities around Gerar, for [a]the
fear of the LORD came upon them; and they
plundered all the cities, for there was exceedingly much spoil in them. 15 They also
attacked the livestock enclosures, and carried off sheep and camels in abundance,
and returned to Jerusalem.

The Reforms of Asa

15 Now [a]the Spirit of God came upon Azariah the son of Oded. 2 And he went
out to meet Asa, and said to him: "Hear
me, Asa, and all Judah and Benjamin. [a]The
LORD *is* with you while you are with Him.
[b]If you seek Him, He will be found by you;
but [c]if you forsake Him, He will forsake you.
3 [a]For a long time Israel *has been* without the
true God, without a [b]teaching priest, and
without [c]law; 4 but [a]when in their trouble
they turned to the LORD God of Israel, and
sought Him, He was found by them. 5 And in
those times *there was* no peace to the one
who went out, nor to the one who came in,
but great turmoil *was* on all the inhabitants
of the lands. 6 [a]So nation was destroyed by
nation, and city by city, for God troubled
them with every adversity. 7 But you, be
strong and do not let your hands be weak,
for your work shall be rewarded!"
8 And when Asa heard these words and
the prophecy of Oded[1] the prophet, he took
courage, and removed the abominable
idols from all the land of Judah and Benjamin and from the cities [a]which he had
taken in the mountains of Ephraim; and
he restored the altar of the LORD that *was*
before the vestibule of the LORD. 9 Then
he gathered all Judah and Benjamin, and
[a]those who dwelt with them from Ephraim,
Manasseh, and Simeon, for they came over
to him in great numbers from Israel when
they saw that the LORD his God was with
him.
10 So they gathered together at Jerusalem in the third month, in the fifteenth
year of the reign of Asa. 11 [a]And they offered
to the LORD at that time seven hundred
bulls and seven thousand sheep from the
spoil they had brought. 12 Then they [a]en-
tered into a covenant to seek the LORD God
of their fathers with all their heart and with
all their soul; 13 [a]and whoever would not
seek the LORD God of Israel [b]was to be put
to death, whether small or great, whether
man or woman. 14 Then they took an oath
before the LORD with a loud voice, with
shouting and trumpets and rams' horns.
15 And all Judah rejoiced at the oath, for
they had sworn with all their heart and
[a]sought Him with all their soul; and He was
found by them, and the LORD gave them
[b]rest all around.
16 Also he removed [a]Maachah, the
mother of Asa the king, from *being* queen
mother, because she had made an obscene
image of Asherah;[1] and Asa cut down her
obscene image, then crushed and burned *it*
by the Brook Kidron. 17 But [a]the high places
were not removed from Israel. Nevertheless the heart of Asa was loyal all his days.

14:8 [a] 1 Chr. 12:2 [b] 2 Chr. 13:3 14:9 [a] 2 Chr. 12:2, 3; 16:8 [b] Josh. 15:44 14:11 [a] Ex. 14:10; 2 Chr. 13:14; [Ps. 22:5] [b] [1 Sam. 14:6] [c] 1 Sam. 17:45; [Prov. 18:10] 14:12 [a] 2 Chr. 13:15 14:13 [a] Gen. 10:19; 20:1 14:14 [a] Gen. 35:5; Deut. 11:25; Josh. 2:9; 2 Chr. 17:10 15:1 [a] Num. 24:2; Judg. 3:10; 2 Chr. 20:14; 24:20 15:2 [a] [James 4:8] [b] [1 Chr. 28:9]; 2 Chr. 14:4; 33:12, 13; [Jer. 29:13; Matt. 7:7] [c] 2 Chr. 24:20 15:3 [a] Hos. 3:4 [b] 2 Kin. 12:2 [c] Lev. 10:11; 2 Chr. 17:8, 9 15:4 [a] [Deut. 4:29] 15:6 [a] Matt. 24:7 15:8 [a] 2 Chr. 13:19 [1] Following Masoretic Text and Septuagint; Syriac and Vulgate read *Azariah the son of Oded* (compare verse 1). 15:9 [a] 2 Chr. 11:16 15:11 [a] 2 Chr. 14:13–15 15:12 [a] 2 Kin. 23:3; 2 Chr. 23:16; 34:31; Neh. 10:29 15:13 [a] Ex. 22:20 [b] Deut. 13:5–15 15:15 [a] 2 Chr. 15:2 [b] 2 Chr. 14:7 15:16 [a] 1 Kin. 15:2, 10, 13 [1] A Canaanite deity 15:17 [a] 1 Kin. 15:14; 2 Chr. 14:3, 5

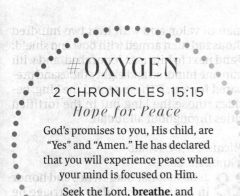

#OXYGEN
2 CHRONICLES 15:15
Hope for Peace
God's promises to you, His child, are
"Yes" and "Amen." He has declared
that you will experience peace when
your mind is focused on Him.
Seek the Lord, **breathe**, and
hope for peace.

18 He also brought into the house of God
the things that his father had dedicated and
that he himself had dedicated: silver and
gold and utensils. 19 And there was no war
until the thirty-fifth year of the reign of Asa.

Asa's Treaty with Syria
(1 Kin. 15:16–22)

16 In the thirty-sixth year of the reign
of Asa, [a]Baasha king of Israel came
up against Judah and built Ramah, [b]that
he might let none go out or come in to Asa
king of Judah. 2 Then Asa brought silver
and gold from the treasuries of the house
of the LORD and of the king's house, and
sent to Ben-Hadad king of Syria, who dwelt
in Damascus, saying, 3 "*Let there be* a treaty
between you and me, as there was between
my father and your father. See, I have sent
you silver and gold; come, break your treaty
with Baasha king of Israel, so that he will
withdraw from me."
4 So Ben-Hadad heeded King Asa, and
sent the captains of his armies against the
cities of Israel. They attacked Ijon, Dan,
Abel Maim, and all the storage cities of
Naphtali. 5 Now it happened, when Baasha
heard *it,* that he stopped building Ramah
and ceased his work. 6 Then King Asa took
all Judah, and they carried away the stones
and timber of Ramah, which Baasha had
used for building; and with them he built
Geba and Mizpah.

Hanani's Message to Asa

7 And at that time [a]Hanani the seer came
to Asa king of Judah, and said to him: [b]"Because you have relied on the king of Syria,
and have not relied on the LORD your God,
therefore the army of the king of Syria has
escaped from your hand. 8 Were [a]the Ethiopians and [b]the Lubim not a huge army with
very many chariots and horsemen? Yet, because you relied on the LORD, He delivered
them into your [c]hand. 9 [a]For the eyes of the
LORD run to and fro throughout the whole
earth, to show Himself strong on behalf of
those whose heart *is* loyal to Him. In this
[b]you have done foolishly; therefore from
now on [c]you shall have wars." 10 Then Asa
was angry with the seer, and [a]put him in
prison, for *he was* enraged at him because
of this. And Asa oppressed *some* of the people at that time.

Illness and Death of Asa
(1 Kin. 15:23, 24)

11 [a]Note that the acts of Asa, first and
last, are indeed written in the book of the
kings of Judah and Israel. 12 And in the
thirty-ninth year of his reign, Asa became
diseased in his feet, and his malady was
severe; yet in his disease he [a]did not seek
the LORD, but the physicians.
13 [a]So Asa rested with his fathers; he died
in the forty-first year of his reign. 14 They
buried him in his own tomb, which he had
made for himself in the City of David; and
they laid him in the bed which was filled
[a]with spices and various ingredients prepared in a mixture of ointments. They
made [b]a very great burning for him.

Jehoshaphat Reigns in Judah

17 Then [a]Jehoshaphat his son reigned
in his place, and strengthened himself against Israel. 2 And he placed troops
in all the fortified cities of Judah, and set
garrisons in the land of [a]Judah and in the
cities of Ephraim [b]which Asa his father had

16:1 [a] 1 Kin. 15:17–22 [b] 2 Chr. 15:9 16:7 [a] 1 Kin. 16:1; 2 Chr. 19:2 [b] 2 Chr. 32:8–10; Ps. 118:9; [Is. 31:1; Jer. 17:5] 16:8 [a] 2 Chr. 14:9 [b] 2 Chr. 12:3 [c] 2 Chr. 13:16, 18 16:9 [a] Job 34:21; [Prov. 5:21; 15:3; Jer. 16:17; 32:19]; Zech. 4:10 [b] 1 Sam. 13:13 [c] 1 Kin. 15:32 16:10 [a] 2 Chr. 18:26; Jer. 20:2; Matt. 14:3 16:11 [a] 1 Kin. 15:23, 24; 2 Chr. 14:2 16:12 [a] [Jer. 17:5] 16:13 [a] 1 Kin. 15:24 16:14 [a] Gen. 50:2; Mark 16:1; John 19:39, 40 [b] 2 Chr. 21:19; Jer. 34:5 17:1 [a] 1 Kin. 15:24; 2 Chr. 20:31 17:2 [a] 2 Chr. 11:5 [b] 2 Chr. 15:8

taken. 3Now the LORD was with Jehoshaphat, because he walked in the former
ways of his father David; he did not seek
the Baals, 4but sought the God[1] of his father,
and walked in His commandments and not
according to [a]the acts of Israel. 5Therefore
the LORD established the kingdom in his
hand; and all Judah [a]gave presents to Jehoshaphat, [b]and he had riches and honor
in abundance. 6And his heart took delight
in the ways of the LORD; moreover [a]he removed the high places and wooden images
from Judah.
7Also in the third year of his reign he
sent his leaders, Ben-Hail, Obadiah, Zechariah, Nethanel, and Michaiah, [a]to teach in
the cities of Judah. 8And with them *he sent*
Levites: Shemaiah, Nethaniah, Zebadiah,
Asahel, Shemiramoth, Jehonathan, Adonijah, Tobijah, and Tobadonijah—the Levites;
and with them Elishama and Jehoram, the
priests. 9[a]So they taught in Judah, and *had*
the Book of the Law of the LORD with them;
they went throughout all the cities of Judah and taught the people.
10And [a]the fear of the LORD fell on all the
kingdoms of the lands that *were* around Judah, so that they did not make war against
Jehoshaphat. 11Also *some* of the Philistines
[a]brought Jehoshaphat presents and silver
as tribute; and the Arabians brought him
flocks, seven thousand seven hundred
rams and seven thousand seven hundred
male goats.
12So Jehoshaphat became increasingly
powerful, and he built fortresses and storage cities in Judah. 13He had much property
in the cities of Judah; and the men of war,
mighty men of valor, *were* in Jerusalem.
14These *are* their numbers, according to
their fathers' houses. Of Judah, the captains
of thousands: Adnah the captain, and with
him three hundred thousand mighty men
of valor; 15and next to him *was* Jehohanan the captain, and with him two hundred
and eighty thousand; 16and next to him
was Amasiah the son of Zichri, [a]who willingly offered himself to the LORD, and with
him two hundred thousand mighty men
of valor. 17Of Benjamin: Eliada a mighty
man of valor, and with him two hundred
thousand men armed with bow and shield;
18and next to him *was* Jehozabad, and with
him one hundred and eighty thousand prepared for war. 19These served the king, besides [a]those the king put in the fortified
cities throughout all Judah.

Micaiah Warns Ahab
(1 Kin. 22:1–28)

18 Jehoshaphat [a]had riches and honor
in abundance; and by marriage he
[b]allied himself with [c]Ahab. 2[a]After some
years he went down to *visit* Ahab in Samaria; and Ahab killed sheep and oxen in
abundance for him and the people who
were with him, and persuaded him to go
up *with him* to Ramoth Gilead. 3So Ahab
king of Israel said to Jehoshaphat king of
Judah, "Will you go with me *against* Ramoth Gilead?"
And he answered him, "I *am* as you *are,*
and my people as your people; *we will be*
with you in the war."
4Also Jehoshaphat said to the king of
Israel, [a]"Please inquire for the word of the
LORD today."
5Then the king of Israel gathered the
prophets together, four hundred men, and
said to them, "Shall we go to war against
Ramoth Gilead, or shall I refrain?"
So they said, "Go up, for God will deliver
it into the king's hand."
6But Jehoshaphat said, "*Is there* not still
a prophet of the LORD here, that we may
inquire of [a]Him?"[1]
7So the king of Israel said to Jehoshaphat, "*There is* still one man by whom we
may inquire of the LORD; but I hate him,
because he never prophesies good concerning me, but always evil. He *is* Micaiah
the son of Imla."
And Jehoshaphat said, "Let not the king
say such things!"
8Then the king of Israel called one *of his*
officers and said, "Bring Micaiah the son of
Imla quickly!"
9The king of Israel and Jehoshaphat
king of Judah, clothed in *their* robes,
sat each on his throne; and they sat at a

17:4 [a] 1 Kin. 12:28 [1] Septuagint reads *LORD God.* 17:5 [a] 1 Sam. 10:27; 1 Kin. 10:25 [b] 2 Chr. 18:1 17:6 [a] 1 Kin. 22:43; 2 Chr. 15:17; 19:3; 20:33 17:7 [a] 2 Chr. 15:3; 35:3 17:9 [a] Deut. 6:4–9; 2 Chr. 35:3; Neh. 8:3, 7 17:10 [a] Gen. 35:5; 2 Chr. 14:14 17:11 [a] 2 Sam. 8:2; 2 Chr. 9:14; 26:8 17:16 [a] Judg. 5:2, 9; 1 Chr. 29:9 17:19 [a] 2 Chr. 17:2 18:1 [a] 2 Chr. 17:5 [b] 1 Kin. 22:44; 2 Kin. 8:18 [c] 1 Kin. 22:40 18:2 [a] [Ex. 23:2]; 1 Kin. 22:2 18:4 [a] 1 Sam. 23:2, 4, 9; 2 Sam. 2:1 18:6 [a] 2 Kin. 3:11 [1] Or *him*

threshing floor at the entrance of the gate
of Samaria; and all the prophets prophesied before them. 10 Now Zedekiah the son
of Chenaanah had made [a]horns of iron for
himself; and he said, "Thus says the LORD:
'With these you shall gore the Syrians until
they are destroyed.'"
11 And all the prophets prophesied so,
saying, "Go up to Ramoth Gilead and prosper, for the LORD will deliver *it* into the
king's hand."
12 Then the messenger who had gone to
call Micaiah spoke to him, saying, "Now listen, the words of the prophets with one accord encourage the king. Therefore please
let your word be like *the word of* one of
them, and speak encouragement."
13 And Micaiah said, "As the LORD lives,
[a]whatever my God says, that I will speak."
14 Then he came to the king; and the king
said to him, "Micaiah, shall we go to war
against Ramoth Gilead, or shall I refrain?"
And he said, "Go and prosper, and they
shall be delivered into your hand!"
15 So the king said to him, "How many
times shall I make you swear that you tell
me nothing but the truth in the name of
the LORD?"
16 Then he said, "I saw all Israel [a]scattered
on the mountains, as sheep that have no
[b]shepherd. And the LORD said, 'These have
no master. Let each return to his house in
peace.'"
17 And the king of Israel said to Jehoshaphat, "Did I not tell you he would not
prophesy good concerning me, but evil?"
18 Then *Micaiah* said, "Therefore hear the
word of the LORD: I saw the LORD sitting
on His [a]throne, and all the host of heaven
standing on His right hand and His left.
19 And the LORD said, 'Who will persuade
Ahab king of Israel to go up, that he may
fall at Ramoth Gilead?' So one spoke in this
manner, and another spoke in that manner.
20 Then a [a]spirit came forward and stood
before the LORD, and said, 'I will persuade
him.' The LORD said to him, 'In what way?'
21 So he said, 'I will go out and be a lying
spirit in the mouth of all his prophets.' And
the LORD said, 'You shall persuade *him* and
also prevail; go out and do so.' 22 Therefore
look! [a]The LORD has put a lying spirit in the
mouth of these prophets of yours, and the
LORD has declared disaster against you."
23 Then Zedekiah the son of Chenaanah
went near and [a]struck Micaiah on the
cheek, and said, "Which way did the spirit
from the LORD go from me to speak to
you?"
24 And Micaiah said, "Indeed you shall
see on that day when you go into an inner
chamber to hide!"
25 Then the king of Israel said, "Take Micaiah, and return him to Amon the governor of the city and to Joash the king's son;
26 and say, 'Thus says the king: [a]"Put this
fellow in prison, and feed him with bread
of affliction and water of affliction, until I
return in peace."'"
27 But Micaiah said, "If you ever return
in peace, the LORD has not spoken by [a]me."
And he said, "Take heed, all you people!"

Ahab Dies in Battle
(1 Kin. 22:29–40)

28 So the king of Israel and Jehoshaphat
the king of Judah went up to Ramoth Gilead. 29 And the king of Israel said to Jehoshaphat, "I will [a]disguise myself and go into
battle; but you put on your robes." So the
king of Israel disguised himself, and they
went into battle.
30 Now the king of Syria had commanded
the captains of the chariots who *were* with
him, saying, "Fight with no one small or
great, but only with the king of Israel."
31 So it was, when the captains of the
chariots saw Jehoshaphat, that they said,
"It *is* the king of Israel!" Therefore they surrounded him to attack; but Jehoshaphat
[a]cried out, and the LORD helped him, and
God diverted them from him. 32 For so it
was, when the captains of the chariots saw
that it was not the king of Israel, that they
turned back from pursuing him. 33 Now a
certain man drew a bow at random, and
struck the king of Israel between the joints
of his armor. So he said to the driver of his
chariot, "Turn around and take me out of
the battle, for I am wounded." 34 The battle

18:10 [a] Zech. 1:18–21 18:13 [a] Num. 22:18–20, 35; 23:12, 26; 1 Kin. 22:14 18:16 [a] [Jer. 23:1–8; 31:10] [b] Num. 27:17; 1 Kin. 22:17; [Ezek. 34:5–8]; Matt. 9:36; Mark 6:34 18:18 [a] Is. 6:1–5; Dan. 7:9, 10 18:20 [a] Job 1:6; 2 Thess. 2:9 18:22 [a] Job 12:16, 17; Is. 19:12–14; Ezek. 14:9 18:23 [a] Jer. 20:2; Mark 14:65; Acts 23:2 18:26 [a] 2 Chr. 16:10 18:27 [a] Deut. 18:22 18:29 [a] 2 Chr. 35:22 18:31 [a] 2 Chr. 13:14, 15

increased that day, and the king of Israel
propped *himself* up in *his* chariot facing the
Syrians until evening; and about the time
of sunset he died.

19 Then Jehoshaphat the king of Judah
returned safely to his house in Jerusalem. 2And Jehu the son of Hanani [a]the
seer went out to meet him, and said to King
Jehoshaphat, "Should you help the wicked
and [b]love those who hate the LORD? Therefore the [c]wrath of the LORD *is* upon you.
3Nevertheless [a]good things are found in
you, in that you have removed the wooden
images from the land, and have [b]prepared
your heart to seek God."

The Reforms of Jehoshaphat

4So Jehoshaphat dwelt at Jerusalem; and
he went out again among the people from
Beersheba to the mountains of Ephraim,
and brought them back to the LORD God of
their [a]fathers. 5Then he set [a]judges in the
land throughout all the fortified cities of
Judah, city by city, 6and said to the judges,
"Take heed to what you are doing, for [a]you
do not judge for man but for the LORD, [b]who
is with you in the judgment. 7Now therefore, let the fear of the LORD be upon you;
take care and do *it,* for [a]*there is* no iniquity
with the LORD our God, no [b]partiality, nor
taking of bribes."

8Moreover in Jerusalem, for the judgment of the LORD and for controversies, Jehoshaphat [a]appointed some of the Levites
and priests, and some of the chief fathers
of Israel, when they returned to Jerusalem.[1]
9And he commanded them, saying, "Thus
you shall act [a]in the fear of the LORD, faithfully and with a loyal heart: 10[a]Whatever
case comes to you from your brethren who
dwell in their cities, whether of bloodshed
or offenses against law or commandment,
against statutes or ordinances, you shall
warn them, lest they trespass against the
LORD and [b]wrath come upon [c]you and your
brethren. Do this, and you will not be guilty.
11And take notice: [a]Amariah the chief priest
is over you [b]in all matters of the LORD; and
Zebadiah the son of Ishmael, the ruler of
the house of Judah, for all the king's matters; also the Levites *will be* officials before
you. Behave courageously, and the LORD
will be [c]with the good."

Ammon, Moab, and Mount Seir Defeated

20 It happened after this *that* the
people of [a]Moab with the people
of [b]Ammon, and *others* with them besides
the [c]Ammonites,[1] came to battle against
Jehoshaphat. 2Then some came and told
Jehoshaphat, saying, "A great multitude
is coming against you from beyond the
sea, from Syria;[1] and they are [a]in Hazazon
Tamar" (which *is* [b]En Gedi). 3And Jehoshaphat feared, and set himself to [a]seek the
LORD, and [b]proclaimed a fast throughout
all Judah. 4So Judah gathered together to
ask [a]*help* from the LORD; and from all the
cities of Judah they came to seek the LORD.

5Then Jehoshaphat stood in the assembly of Judah and Jerusalem, in the house
of the LORD, before the new court, 6and
said: "O LORD God of our fathers, *are* You
not [a]God in heaven, and [b]do You *not* rule
over all the kingdoms of the nations, and
[c]in Your hand *is there not* power and might,
so that no one is able to withstand You? 7*Are*
You not [a]our God, *who* [b]drove out the inhabitants of this land before Your people Israel,
and gave it to the descendants of Abraham
[c]Your friend forever? 8And they dwell in it,
and have built You a sanctuary in it for Your
name, saying, 9[a]'If disaster comes upon
us—sword, judgment, pestilence, or famine—we will stand before this temple and
in Your presence (for Your [b]name *is* in this
temple), and cry out to You in our affliction, and You will hear and save.' 10And now,
here are the people of Ammon, Moab, and
Mount Seir—whom You [a]would not let Israel invade when they came out of the land
of Egypt, but [b]they turned from them and

19:2 [a] 1 Sam. 9:9; 1 Kin. 16:1; 2 Chr. 20:34 [b] Ps. 139:21 [c] 2 Chr. 32:25 19:3 [a] 2 Chr. 17:4, 6 [b] 2 Chr. 30:19 19:4 [a] 2 Chr. 15:8–13 19:5 [a] [Deut. 16:18–20] 19:6 [a] [Lev. 19:15; Deut. 1:17]; Ps. 58:1 [b] Ps. 82:1; [Eccl. 5:8] 19:7 [a] [Gen. 18:25; Deut. 32:4]; Rom. 9:17 [b] [Deut. 10:17, 18; Job 34:19]; Acts 10:34; Rom. 2:11; Gal. 2:6; [Eph. 6:9; Col. 3:25] 19:8 [a] Deut. 16:18; 2 Chr. 17:8 [1] Septuagint and Vulgate read *for the inhabitants of Jerusalem.* 19:9 [a] [2 Sam. 23:3] 19:10 [a] Deut. 17:8 [b] Num. 16:46 [c] [Ezek. 3:18] 19:11 [a] Ezra 7:3 [b] 1 Chr. 26:30 [c] [2 Chr. 15:2; 20:17] 20:1 [a] 1 Chr. 18:2 [b] 1 Chr. 19:15 [c] 2 Chr. 26:7 [1] Following Masoretic Text and Vulgate; Septuagint reads *Meunites* (compare 26:7). 20:2 [a] Gen. 14:7 [b] Josh. 15:62 [1] Following Masoretic Text, Septuagint, and Vulgate; some Hebrew manuscripts and Old Latin read *Edom.* 20:3 [a] 2 Chr. 19:3 [b] 1 Sam. 7:6; Ezra 8:21; Jer. 36:9; Jon. 3:5 20:4 [a] 2 Chr. 14:11 20:6 [a] Deut. 4:39; Josh. 2:11; [1 Kin. 8:23]; Matt. 6:9 [b] Ps. 22:28; 47:2, 8; Dan. 4:17, 25, 32 [c] 1 Chr. 29:12; 2 Chr. 25:8; Ps. 62:11; Matt. 6:13 20:7 [a] Gen. 13:14–17; 17:7; Ex. 6:7 [b] Ps. 44:2 [c] Is. 41:8; James 2:23 20:9 [a] 1 Kin. 8:33, 37; 2 Chr. 6:28–30 [b] 2 Chr. 6:20 20:10 [a] Deut. 2:4, 9, 19 [b] Num. 20:21

did not destroy them— 11 here they are, rewarding us [a]by coming to throw us out of
Your possession which You have given us
to inherit. 12 O our God, will You not [a]judge
them? For we have no power against this
great multitude that is coming against us;
nor do we know what to do, but [b]our eyes
are upon You."

13 Now all Judah, with their little ones,
their wives, and their children, stood before the LORD.

14 Then [a]the Spirit of the LORD came
upon Jahaziel the son of Zechariah, the
son of Benaiah, the son of Jeiel, the son of
Mattaniah, a Levite of the sons of Asaph,
in the midst of the assembly. 15 And he said,
"Listen, all you of Judah and you inhabitants of Jerusalem, and you, King Jehoshaphat! Thus says the LORD to you: [a]'Do not be
afraid nor dismayed because of this great
multitude, [b]for the battle *is* not yours, but
God's. 16 Tomorrow go down against them.
They will surely come up by the Ascent
of Ziz, and you will find them at the end
of the brook before the Wilderness of Je-
ruel. 17 [a]You will not *need* to fight in this
battle. Position yourselves, stand still and
see the salvation of the LORD, who is with
you, O Judah and Jerusalem!' Do not fear
or be dismayed; tomorrow go out against
them, [b]for the LORD *is* with you."

18 And Jehoshaphat [a]bowed his head with
his face to the ground, and all Judah and the
inhabitants of Jerusalem bowed before the
LORD, worshiping the LORD. 19 Then the Levites of the children of the Kohathites and
of the children of the Korahites stood up to
praise the LORD God of Israel with voices
loud and high.

20 So they rose early in the morning and
went out into the Wilderness of Tekoa; and
as they went out, Jehoshaphat stood and
said, "Hear me, O Judah and you inhabitants of Jerusalem: [a]Believe in the LORD
your God, and you shall be established; believe His prophets, and you shall prosper."
21 And when he had consulted with the people, he appointed those who should sing
to the LORD, [a]and who should praise the
beauty of holiness, as they went out before
the army and were saying:

[b]"Praise the LORD,
[c]For His mercy *endures* forever."[1]

22 Now when they began to sing and to
praise, [a]the LORD set ambushes against
the people of Ammon, Moab, and Mount
Seir, who had come against Judah; and they
were defeated. 23 For the people of Ammon
and Moab stood up against the inhabitants
of Mount Seir to utterly kill and destroy
them. And when they had made an end of
the inhabitants of Seir, [a]they helped to destroy one another.

24 So when Judah came to a place over-
looking the wilderness, they looked toward
the multitude; and there *were* their dead
bodies, fallen on the earth. No one had
escaped.

25 When Jehoshaphat and his people
came to take away their spoil, they found
among them an abundance of valuables
on the dead bodies,[1] and precious jewelry,
which they stripped off for themselves,
more than they could carry away; and they
were three days gathering the spoil because
there was so much. 26 And on the fourth day
they assembled in the Valley of Berachah,
for there they blessed the LORD; therefore

#OXYGEN

2 CHRONICLES 20:17

Hope for Peace

Do not be discouraged by what you see on the sociopolitical landscape. Rest assured, disorder, confusion, and unrest are not of God. His movement in the world is characterized by peace. Stand firm in the faith, **breathe**, and **hope for peace**.

20:11 [a] Ps. 83:1–18 **20:12** [a] Judg. 11:27; [1 Sam. 3:13] [b] Ps. 25:15; 121:1, 2; 123:1, 2; 141:8 **20:14** [a] Num. 11:25, 26; 24:2; 2 Chr. 15:1; 24:20 **20:15** [a] Ex. 14:13, 14; [Deut. 1:29, 30; 31:6, 8]; 2 Chr. 32:7 [b] 1 Sam. 17:47; Zech. 14:3 **20:17** [a] Ex. 14:13, 14 [b] Num. 14:9; [2 Chr. 15:2; 32:8] **20:18** [a] Ex. 4:31; 2 Chr. 7:3; 29:28 **20:20** [a] Is. 7:9 **20:21** [a] 1 Chr. 16:29; Ps. 29:2; 90:17; 96:9; 110:3 [b] 1 Chr. 16:34; Ps. 106:1; 136:1 [c] 1 Chr. 16:41; 2 Chr. 5:13 [1] Compare Psalm 106:1 **20:22** [a] Judg. 7:22; 1 Sam. 14:20 **20:23** [a] Judg. 7:22; 1 Sam. 14:20
20:25 [1] A few Hebrew manuscripts, Old Latin, and Vulgate read *garments;* Septuagint reads *armor.*

the name of that place was called The Valley of Berachah[1] until this day. [27]Then they returned, every man of Judah and Jerusalem, with Jehoshaphat in front of them, to go back to Jerusalem with joy, for the LORD had [a]made them rejoice over their enemies. [28]So they came to Jerusalem, with stringed instruments and harps and trumpets, to the house of the LORD. [29]And [a]the fear of God was on all the kingdoms of *those* countries when they heard that the LORD had fought against the enemies of Israel. [30]Then the realm of Jehoshaphat was quiet, for his [a]God gave him rest all around.

The End of Jehoshaphat's Reign
(1 Kin. 22:41–50)

[31][a]So Jehoshaphat was king over Judah. *He was* thirty-five years old when he became king, and he reigned twenty-five years in Jerusalem. His mother's name *was* Azubah the daughter of Shilhi. [32]And he walked in the way of his father [a]Asa, and did not turn aside from it, doing *what was* right in the sight of the LORD. [33]Nevertheless [a]the high places were not taken away, for as yet the people had not [b]directed their hearts to the God of their fathers.

[34]Now the rest of the acts of Jehoshaphat, first and last, indeed they *are* written in the book of Jehu the son of Hanani, [a]which *is* mentioned in the book of the kings of Israel.

[35]After this [a]Jehoshaphat king of Judah allied himself with Ahaziah king of Israel, [b]who acted very [c]wickedly. [36]And he allied himself with him [a]to make ships to go to Tarshish, and they made the ships in Ezion Geber. [37]But Eliezer the son of Dodavah of Mareshah prophesied against Jehoshaphat, saying, "Because you have allied yourself with Ahaziah, the LORD has destroyed your works." [a]Then the ships were wrecked, so that they were not able to go [b]to Tarshish.

Jehoram Reigns in Judah
(1 Kin. 22:50; 2 Kin. 8:16–24)

21 And [a]Jehoshaphat rested with his fathers, and was buried with his fathers in the City of David. Then Jehoram his son reigned in his place. [2]He had brothers, the sons of Jehoshaphat: Azariah, Jehiel, Zechariah, Azaryahu, Michael, and Shephatiah; all these *were* the sons of Jehoshaphat king of Israel. [3]Their father gave them great gifts of silver and gold and precious things, with fortified cities in Judah; but he gave the kingdom to Jehoram, because he *was* the firstborn.

[4]Now when Jehoram was established over the kingdom of his father, he strengthened himself and killed all his brothers with the sword, and also *others* of the princes of Israel.

[5][a]Jehoram *was* thirty-two years old when he became king, and he reigned eight years in Jerusalem. [6]And he walked in the way of the kings of Israel, just as the house of Ahab had done, for he had the daughter of [a]Ahab as a wife; and he did evil in the sight of the LORD. [7]Yet the LORD would not destroy the house of David, because of the [a]covenant that He had made with David, and since He had promised to give a lamp to him and to his [b]sons forever.

[8][a]In his days Edom revolted against Judah's authority, and made a king over themselves. [9]So Jehoram went out with his officers, and all his chariots with him. And he rose by night and attacked the Edomites who had surrounded him and the captains of the chariots. [10]Thus Edom has been in revolt against Judah's authority to this day. At that time Libnah revolted against his rule, because he had forsaken the LORD God of his fathers. [11]Moreover he made high places in the mountains of Judah, and caused the inhabitants of Jerusalem to [a]commit harlotry, and led Judah astray.

[12]And a letter came to him from Elijah the prophet, saying,

Thus says the LORD God of your father David:
Because you have not walked in the ways of Jehoshaphat your father, or in the ways of Asa king of Judah, [13]but have walked in the way of the kings of Israel, and have [a]made Judah and

20:26 [1] Literally *Blessing* 20:27 [a] Neh. 12:43 20:29 [a] 2 Chr. 14:14; 17:10 20:30 [a] 1 Kin. 22:41–43; 2 Chr. 14:6, 7; 15:15; Job 34:29 20:31 [a] [1 Kin. 22:41–43] 20:32 [a] 2 Chr. 14:2 20:33 [a] 2 Chr. 15:17; 17:6 [b] 2 Chr. 12:14; 19:3 20:34 [a] 1 Kin. 16:1, 7 20:35 [a] 2 Chr. 18:1 [b] 1 Kin. 22:48–53 [c] [2 Chr. 19:2] 20:36 [a] 1 Kin. 9:26; 10:22 20:37 [a] 1 Kin. 22:48 [b] 2 Chr. 9:21 21:1 [a] 1 Kin. 22:50 21:5 [a] 2 Kin. 8:17–22 21:6 [a] 2 Chr. 18:1 21:7 [a] 2 Sam. 7:8–17 [b] 1 Kin. 11:36; 2 Kin. 8:19; Ps. 132:11 21:8 [a] 2 Kin. 8:20; 14:7, 10; 2 Chr. 25:14, 19 21:11 [a] [Lev. 20:5] 21:13 [a] 2 Chr. 21:11

the inhabitants of Jerusalem to [b]play
the harlot like the [c]harlotry of the
house of Ahab, and also have [d]killed
your brothers, those of your father's
household, *who were* better than
yourself, 14behold, the LORD will strike
your people with a serious affliction—
your children, your wives, and all your
possessions; 15and you *will become*
very sick with a [a]disease of your
intestines, until your intestines come
out by reason of the sickness, day by
day.

16Moreover the [a]LORD [b]stirred up against
Jehoram the spirit of the Philistines and
the [c]Arabians who *were* near the Ethiopians. 17And they came up into Judah and
invaded it, and carried away all the possessions that were found in the king's house,
and also [a]his sons and his wives, so that
there was not a son left to him except Jehoahaz,[1] the youngest of his sons.
18After all this the LORD struck him [a]in
his intestines with an incurable disease.
19Then it happened in the course of time,
after the end of two years, that his intestines came out because of his sickness;
so he died in severe pain. And his people
made no burning for him, like [a]the burning for his fathers.
20He was thirty-two years old when he
became king. He reigned in Jerusalem
eight years and, to no one's sorrow, departed. However they buried him in the City
of David, but not in the tombs of the kings.

Ahaziah Reigns in Judah
(2 Kin. 8:25–29; 9:14–16, 27–29)

22 Then the inhabitants of Jerusalem
made [a]Ahaziah his youngest son
king in his place, for the raiders who came
with the [b]Arabians into the camp had killed
all the [c]older *sons.* So Ahaziah the son of Jehoram, king of Judah, reigned. 2Ahaziah
was forty-two[1] years old when he became
king, and he reigned one year in Jerusalem. His mother's name *was* [a]Athaliah the
granddaughter of Omri. 3He also walked
in the ways of the house of Ahab, for his
mother advised him to do wickedly. 4There-
fore he did evil in the sight of the LORD,
like the house of Ahab; for they were his
counselors after the death of his father,
to his destruction. 5He also followed their
advice, and went with Jehoram[1] the son of
Ahab king of Israel to war against Hazael
king of Syria at Ramoth Gilead; and the Syrians wounded Joram. 6[a]Then he returned to
Jezreel to recover from the wounds which
he had received at Ramah, when he fought
against Hazael king of Syria. And Azariah[1]
the son of Jehoram, king of Judah, went
down to see Jehoram the son of Ahab in
Jezreel, because he was sick.
7His going to Joram [a]was God's occasion for Ahaziah's downfall; for when he
arrived, [b]he went out with Jehoram against
Jehu the son of Nimshi, [c]whom the LORD
had anointed to cut off the house of Ahab.
8And it happened, when Jehu was [a]execut-
ing judgment on the house of Ahab, and
[b]found the princes of Judah and the sons
of Ahaziah's brothers who served Ahaziah,
that he killed them. 9[a]Then he searched for
Ahaziah; and they caught him (he was hiding in Samaria), and brought him to Jehu.
When they had killed him, they buried him,
"because," they said, "he is the son of [b]Je-
hoshaphat, who [c]sought the LORD with all
his heart."
So the house of Ahaziah had no one to
assume power over the kingdom.

Athaliah Reigns in Judah
(2 Kin. 11:1–3)

10[a]Now when Athaliah the mother of
Ahaziah saw that her son was dead, she
arose and destroyed all the royal heirs of
the house of Judah. 11But Jehoshabeath,[1]
the daughter of the king, took [a]Joash the
son of Ahaziah, and stole him away from
among the king's sons who were being
murdered, and put him and his nurse in a
bedroom. So Jehoshabeath, the daughter
of King Jehoram, the wife of Jehoiada the

21:13 [b] [Ex. 34:15]; Deut. 31:16 [c] 1 Kin. 16:31–33; 2 Kin. 9:22 [d] 1 Kin. 2:32; 2 Chr. 21:4 **21:15** [a] 2 Chr. 21:18, 19 **21:16** [a] 2 Chr. 33:11; [Jer. 51:11] [b] 1 Kin. 11:14, 23 [c] 2 Chr. 17:11 **21:17** [a] 2 Chr. 24:7 [1] Elsewhere called *Ahaziah* (compare 2 Chronicles 22:1) **21:18** [a] 2 Chr. 13:20; 21:15; Acts 12:23 **21:19** [a] 2 Chr. 16:14 **22:1** [a] 2 Chr. 21:17; 22:6 [b] 2 Chr. 21:16 [c] 2 Chr. 21:17 **22:2** [a] 2 Chr. 21:6 [1] Or *twenty-two* (compare 2 Kings 8:26) **22:5** [1] Also spelled *Joram* (compare verses 5 and 7; 2 Kings 8:28; and elsewhere) **22:6** [a] 2 Kin. 9:15 [1] Some Hebrew manuscripts, Septuagint, Syriac, Vulgate, and 2 Kings 8:29 read *Ahaziah.* **22:7** [a] Judg. 14:4; 1 Kin. 12:15; 2 Chr. 10:15 [b] 2 Kin. 9:21–24 [c] 2 Kin. 9:6, 7 **22:8** [a] 2 Kin. 9:22–24 [b] 2 Kin. 10:10–14; Hos. 1:4 **22:9** [a] [2 Kin. 9:27] [b] 1 Kin. 15:24 [c] 2 Chr. 17:4; 20:3, 4 **22:10** [a] 2 Kin. 11:1–3 **22:11** [a] 2 Kin. 12:18 [1] Spelled *Jehosheba* in 2 Kings 11:2

priest (for she was the sister of Ahaziah), hid him from Athaliah so that she did not kill him. 12 And he was hidden with them in the house of God for six years, while Athaliah reigned over the land.

Joash Crowned King of Judah
(2 Kin. 11:4–12)

23 In [a]the seventh year [b]Jehoiada strengthened himself, *and made a* covenant with the captains of hundreds: Azariah the son of Jeroham, Ishmael the son of Jehohanan, Azariah the son of [c]Obed, Maaseiah the son of Adaiah, and Elishaphat the son of Zichri. 2 And they went throughout Judah and gathered the Levites from all the cities of Judah, and the [a]chief fathers of Israel, and they came to Jerusalem.

3 Then all the assembly made a covenant with the king in the house of God. And he said to them, "Behold, the king's son shall reign, as the LORD has [a]said of the sons of David. 4 This *is* what you shall do: One-third of you [a]entering on the Sabbath, of the priests and the Levites, *shall be* keeping watch over the doors; 5 one-third *shall be* at the king's house; and one-third at the Gate of the Foundation. All the people *shall be* in the courts of the house of the LORD. 6 But let no one come into the house of the LORD except the priests and [a]those of the Levites who serve. They may go in, for they *are* holy; but all the people shall keep the watch of the LORD. 7 And the Levites shall surround the king on all sides, every man with his weapons in his hand; and whoever comes into the house, let him be put to death. You are to be with the king when he comes in and when he goes out."

8 So the Levites and all Judah did according to all that Jehoiada the priest commanded. And each man took his men who were to be on duty on the Sabbath, with those who were going *off duty* on the Sabbath; for Jehoiada the priest had not dismissed [a]the divisions. 9 And Jehoiada the priest gave to the captains of hundreds the spears and the large and small [a]shields which *had belonged* to King David, that *were* in the temple of God. 10 Then he set all the people, every man with his weapon in his hand, from the right side of the temple to the left side of the temple, along by the altar and by the temple, all around the king. 11 And they brought out the king's son, put the crown on him, [a]*gave him* the Testimony,[1] and made him king. Then Jehoiada and his sons anointed him, and said, "*Long* live the king!"

Death of Athaliah
(2 Kin. 11:13–20)

12 Now when [a]Athaliah heard the noise of the people running and praising the king, she came to the people *in* the temple of the LORD. 13 *When* she looked, there was the king standing by his pillar at the entrance; and the leaders and the trumpeters *were* by the king. All the people of the land were rejoicing and blowing trumpets, also the singers with musical instruments, and [a]those who led in praise. So Athaliah tore her clothes and said, [b]"Treason! Treason!"

14 And Jehoiada the priest brought out the captains of hundreds who were set over the army, and said to them, "Take her outside under guard, and slay with the sword whoever follows her." For the priest had said, "Do not kill her in the house of the LORD."

15 So they seized her; and she went by way of the entrance [a]of the Horse Gate *into* the king's house, and they killed her there.

16 Then Jehoiada made a [a]covenant between himself, the people, and the king, that they should be the LORD's people. 17 And all the people went to the temple[1] of Baal, and tore it down. They broke in pieces its altars and images, and [a]killed Mattan the priest of Baal before the altars. 18 Also Jehoiada appointed the oversight of the house of the LORD to the hand of the priests, the Levites, whom David had [a]assigned in the house of the LORD, to offer the burnt offerings of the LORD, as *it is* written in the [b]Law of Moses, with rejoicing and with singing, *as it was established* by David. 19 And he set the [a]gatekeepers at the gates of the house

---

23:1 [a] 2 Kin. 11:4 [b] 2 Kin. 12:2 [c] 1 Chr. 2:37, 38 23:2 [a] Ezra 1:5 23:3 [a] 2 Sam. 7:12; 1 Kin. 2:4; 9:5; 2 Chr. 6:16; 7:18; 21:7 23:4 [a] 1 Chr. 9:25 23:6 [a] 1 Chr. 23:28–32 23:8 [a] 1 Chr. 24:1–31 23:9 [a] 2 Sam. 8:7 23:11 [a] Deut. 17:18 [1] That is, the Law (compare Exodus 25:16, 21; 31:18) 23:12 [a] 2 Chr. 22:10 23:13 [a] 1 Chr. 25:6–8 [b] 2 Kin. 9:23 23:15 [a] Neh. 3:28; Jer. 31:40 23:16 [a] Josh. 24:24, 25; 2 Chr. 15:12–15 23:17 [a] Deut. 13:6–9; 1 Kin. 18:40 [1] Literally *house* 23:18 [a] 1 Chr. 23:6, 30, 31; 24:1 [b] Num. 28:2 23:19 [a] 1 Chr. 26:1–19

of the LORD, so that no one *who was* in any
way unclean should enter.
20[a]Then he took the captains of hundreds, the nobles, the governors of the
people, and all the people of the land, and
brought the king down from the house of
the LORD; and they went through the Upper Gate to the king's house, and set the
king on the throne of the kingdom. 21So
all the people of the land rejoiced; and the
city was quiet, for they had slain Athaliah
with the sword.

Joash Repairs the Temple
(2 Kin. 11:21—12:16)

24 Joash [a]*was* seven years old when he
became king, and he reigned forty
years in Jerusalem. His mother's name *was*
Zibiah of Beersheba. 2Joash [a]did *what was*
right in the sight of the LORD all the days
of Jehoiada the priest. 3And Jehoiada took
two wives for him, and he had sons and
daughters.
4Now it happened after this *that* Joash
set his heart on repairing the house of the
LORD. 5Then he gathered the priests and
the Levites, and said to them, "Go out to
the cities of Judah, and [a]gather from all
Israel money to repair the house of your
God from year to year, and see that you do
it quickly."
However the Levites did not do it
quickly. 6[a]So the king called Jehoiada the
chief *priest,* and said to him, "Why have
you not required the Levites to bring in
from Judah and from Jerusalem the collection, *according to the commandment* of
[b]Moses the servant of the LORD and of the
assembly of Israel, for the [c]tabernacle of
witness?" 7For [a]the sons of Athaliah, that
wicked woman, had broken into the house
of God, and had also presented all the [b]ded-
icated things of the house of the LORD to
the Baals.
8Then at the king's command [a]they
made a chest, and set it outside at the gate
of the house of the LORD. 9And they made a
proclamation throughout Judah and Jerusalem to bring to the LORD [a]the collection
that Moses the servant of God *had imposed*
on Israel in the wilderness. 10Then all the
leaders and all the people rejoiced, brought
their contributions, and put *them* into the
chest until all had given. 11So it was, at that
time, when the chest was brought to the
king's official by the hand of the Levites,
and [a]when they saw that *there was* much
money, that the king's scribe and the high
priest's officer came and emptied the chest,
and took it and returned it to its place. Thus
they did day by day, and gathered money
in abundance.
12The king and Jehoiada gave it to
those who did the work of the service of
the house of the LORD; and they hired masons and carpenters to [a]repair the house
of the LORD, and also those who worked in
iron and bronze to restore the house of the
LORD. 13So the workmen labored, and the
work was completed by them; they restored
the house of God to its original condition
and reinforced it. 14When they had finished,
they brought the rest of the money before
the king and Jehoiada; [a]they made from it
articles for the house of the LORD, articles
for serving and offering, spoons and vessels of gold and silver. And they offered
burnt offerings in the house of the LORD
continually all the days of Jehoiada.

Apostasy of Joash

15But Jehoiada grew old and was full of
days, and he died; *he was* one hundred and
thirty years old when he died. 16And they
buried him in the City of David among the
kings, because he had done good in Israel,
both toward God and His house.
17Now after the death of Jehoiada the
leaders of Judah came and bowed down
to the king. And the king listened to them.
18Therefore they left the house of the LORD
God of their fathers, and served [a]wooden
images and idols; and [b]wrath came upon
Judah and Jerusalem because of their trespass. 19Yet He [a]sent prophets to them, to
bring them back to the LORD; and they testified against them, but they would not listen.
20Then the Spirit of God came upon
[a]Zechariah the son of Jehoiada the priest,
who stood above the people, and said to

23:20 [a] 1 Kin. 9:22; 2 Kin. 11:19 24:1 [a] 2 Kin. 11:21; 12:1–15 24:2 [a] 2 Chr. 26:4, 5 24:5 [a] 2 Kin. 12:4 24:6 [a] 2 Kin. 12:7 [b] Ex. 30:12–16 [c] Num. 1:50; Acts 7:44 24:7 [a] 2 Chr. 21:17 [b] 2 Kin. 12:4 24:8 [a] 2 Kin. 12:9 24:9 [a] 2 Chr. 24:6 24:11 [a] 2 Kin. 12:10 24:12 [a] 2 Chr. 30:12 24:14 [a] 2 Kin. 12:13 24:18 [a] 1 Kin. 14:23 [b] [Ex. 34:12–14]; Judg. 5:8; 2 Chr. 19:2; 28:13; 29:8; 32:25 24:19 [a] 2 Kin. 17:13; 21:10–15; 2 Chr. 36:15, 16; Jer. 7:25, 26; 25:4 24:20 [a] Judg. 6:34; Matt. 23:35

them, "Thus says God: [b]'Why do you transgress the commandments of the LORD, so
that you cannot prosper? [c]Because you
have forsaken the LORD, He also has forsaken you.'" 21So they conspired against
him, and at the command of the king they
[a]stoned him with stones in the court of the
house of the LORD. 22Thus Joash the king
did not remember the kindness which Jehoiada his father had done to him, but
killed his son; and as he died, he said, "The
LORD look on *it*, and [a]repay!"

Death of Joash
(2 Kin. 12:19–21)

23So it happened in the spring of the year
that [a]the army of Syria came up against
him; and they came to Judah and Jerusalem, and destroyed all the leaders of the
people from among the people, and sent
all their spoil to the king of Damascus.
24For the army of the Syrians [a]came with a
small company of men; but the LORD [b]de-
livered a very great army into their hand,
because they had forsaken the LORD God
of their fathers. So they [c]executed judgment against Joash. 25And when they had
withdrawn from him (for they left him severely wounded), [a]his own servants conspired against him because of the blood of
the sons[1] of Jehoiada the priest, and killed
him on his bed. So he died. And they buried
him in the City of David, but they did not
bury him in the tombs of the kings.
26These are the ones who conspired
against him: Zabad[1] the son of Shimeath
the Ammonitess, and Jehozabad the son of
Shimrith[2] the Moabitess. 27Now *concerning*
his sons, and [a]the many oracles about him,
and the repairing of the house of God, indeed they *are* written in the annals of the
book of the kings. [b]Then Amaziah his son
reigned in his place.

Amaziah Reigns in Judah
(2 Kin. 14:1–6)

25 Amaziah [a]*was* twenty-five years
old *when* he became king, and he
reigned twenty-nine years in Jerusalem. His
mother's name *was* Jehoaddan of Jerusalem. 2And he did *what was* right in the sight
of the LORD, [a]but not with a loyal heart.
3[a]Now it happened, as soon as the kingdom was established for him, that he executed his servants who had murdered his
father the king. 4However he did not execute
their children, but *did* as *it is* written in the
Law in the Book of Moses, where the LORD
commanded, saying, [a]"The fathers shall not
be put to death for their children, nor shall
the children be put to death for their fathers;
but a person shall die for his own sin."[1]

The War Against Edom
(2 Kin. 14:7)

5Moreover Amaziah gathered Judah together and set over them captains of thousands and captains of hundreds, according
to *their* fathers' houses, throughout all
Judah and Benjamin; and he numbered
them [a]from twenty years old and above,
and found them to be three hundred thousand choice *men, able* to go to war, who
could handle spear and shield. 6He also
hired one hundred thousand mighty men
of valor from Israel for one hundred talents of silver. 7But a [a]man of God came to
him, saying, "O king, do not let the army
of Israel go with you, for the LORD *is* not
with Israel—*not with* any of the children of
Ephraim. 8But if you go, be gone! Be strong
in battle! *Even so,* God shall make you fall
before the enemy; for God has [a]power to
help and to overthrow."
9Then Amaziah said to the man of God,
"But what *shall we* do about the hundred
talents which I have given to the troops
of Israel?"
And the man of God answered, [a]"The
LORD is able to give you much more than
this." 10So Amaziah discharged the troops
that had come to him from Ephraim, to
go back home. Therefore their anger was
greatly aroused against Judah, and they
returned home in great anger.
11Then Amaziah strengthened himself,

24:20 [b] Num. 14:41; [Prov. 28:13] [c] [2 Chr. 15:2] **24:21** [a] [Neh. 9:26]; Matt. 23:35; Acts 7:58, 59 **24:22** [a] [Gen. 9:5] **24:23** [a] 2 Kin. 12:17; Is. 7:2 **24:24** [a] Lev. 26:8; [Deut. 32:30]; Is. 30:17 [b] Lev. 26:25; [Deut. 28:25] [c] 2 Chr. 22:8; Is. 10:5 **24:25** [a] 2 Kin. 12:20, 21; 2 Chr. 25:3 [1] Septuagint and Vulgate read *son* (compare verses 20–22). **24:26** [1] Or *Jozachar* (compare 2 Kings 12:21) [2] Or *Shomer* (compare 2 Kings 12:21) **24:27** [a] 2 Kin. 12:18 [b] 2 Kin. 12:21 **25:1** [a] 2 Kin. 14:1–6 **25:2** [a] 2 Kin. 14:4; 2 Chr. 25:14 **25:3** [a] 2 Kin. 14:5; 2 Chr. 24:25 **25:4** [a] Deut. 24:16; 2 Kin. 14:6; Jer. 31:30; [Ezek. 18:20] [1] Deuteronomy 24:16 **25:5** [a] Num. 1:3 **25:7** [a] 2 Chr. 11:2 **25:8** [a] 2 Chr. 14:11; 20:6 **25:9** [a] [Deut. 8:18]; Prov. 10:22

and leading his people, he went to [a]the Valley of Salt and killed ten thousand of the
people of Seir. 12Also the children of Judah
took captive ten thousand alive, brought
them to the top of the rock, and cast them
down from the top of the rock, so that they
all were dashed in pieces.

13But as for the soldiers of the army
which Amaziah had discharged, so that
they would not go with him to battle, they
raided the cities of Judah from Samaria to
Beth Horon, killed three thousand in them,
and took much spoil.

14Now it was so, after Amaziah came
from the slaughter of the Edomites, that
[a]he brought the gods of the people of Seir,
set them up *to be* [b]his gods, and bowed
down before them and burned incense to
them. 15Therefore the anger of the LORD
was aroused against Amaziah, and He sent
him a prophet who said to him, "Why have
you sought [a]the gods of the people, which
[b]could not rescue their own people from
your hand?"

16So it was, as he talked with him, that
the king said to him, "Have we made you
the king's counselor? Cease! Why should
you be killed?"

Then the prophet ceased, and said, "I
know that God has [a]determined to destroy
you, because you have done this and have
not heeded my advice."

Israel Defeats Judah
(2 Kin. 14:8–14)

17Now [a]Amaziah king of Judah asked advice and sent to Joash[1] the son of Jehoahaz, the son of Jehu, king of Israel, saying,
"Come, let us face one another *in battle.*"

18And Joash king of Israel sent to Amaziah king of Judah, saying, "The thistle that
was in Lebanon sent to the cedar that was
in Lebanon, saying, 'Give your daughter to
my son as wife'; and a wild beast that *was* in
Lebanon passed by and trampled the thistle. 19Indeed you say that you have defeated
the Edomites, and your heart is lifted up to
[a]boast. Stay at home now; why should you
meddle with trouble, that you should fall—
you and Judah with you?"

20But Amaziah would not heed, for [a]it
came from God, that He might give them
into the hand *of their enemies,* because they
[b]sought the gods of Edom. 21So Joash king
of Israel went out; and he and Amaziah
king of Judah faced one another at [a]Beth
Shemesh, which *belongs* to Judah. 22And
Judah was defeated by Israel, and every
man fled to his tent. 23Then Joash the king
of Israel captured Amaziah king of Judah,
the son of Joash, the son of [a]Jehoahaz, at
Beth Shemesh; and he brought him to Jerusalem, and broke down the wall of Jerusalem from the Gate of Ephraim to the Corner
Gate—four hundred cubits. 24And *he took*
all the gold and silver, all the articles that
were found in the house of God with [a]Obed-
Edom, the treasures of the king's house,
and hostages, and returned to Samaria.

Death of Amaziah
(2 Kin. 14:17–20)

25[a]Amaziah the son of Joash, king of Judah, lived fifteen years after the death of
Joash the son of Jehoahaz, king of Israel.
26Now the rest of the acts of Amaziah, from
first to last, indeed *are* they not written in
the book of the kings of Judah and Israel?
27After the time that Amaziah turned away
from following the LORD, they made a conspiracy against him in Jerusalem, and he
fled to Lachish; but they sent after him to
Lachish and killed him there. 28Then they
brought him on horses and buried him
with his fathers in the City of Judah.

Uzziah Reigns in Judah
(2 Kin. 14:21, 22; 15:1–3)

26 Now all the people of Judah took
Uzziah,[1] who *was* sixteen years old,
and made him king instead of his father
Amaziah. 2He built Elath[1] and restored it to
Judah, after the king rested with his fathers.

3Uzziah *was* sixteen years old when
he became king, and he reigned fifty-two
years in Jerusalem. His mother's name was
Jecholiah of Jerusalem. 4And he did *what*
was [a]right in the sight of the LORD, according to all that his father Amaziah had done.
5[a]He sought God in the days of Zechariah,

25:11 [a] 2 Kin. 14:7 25:14 [a] 2 Chr. 28:23 [b] [Ex. 20:3, 5] 25:15 [a] [Ps. 96:5] [b] 2 Chr. 25:11 25:16 [a] [1 Sam. 2:25] 25:17 [a] 2 Kin. 14:8–14 [1] Spelled *Jehoash* in 2 Kings 14:8ff 25:19 [a] 2 Chr. 26:16; 32:25; [Prov. 16:18] 25:20 [a] 1 Kin. 12:15; 2 Chr. 22:7 [b] 2 Chr. 25:14 25:21 [a] Josh. 19:38 25:23 [a] 2 Chr. 21:17; 22:1, 6 25:24 [a] 1 Chr. 26:15 25:25 [a] 2 Kin. 14:17–22 26:1 [1] Called *Azariah* in 2 Kings 14:21ff 26:2 [1] Hebrew *Eloth* 26:4 [a] 2 Chr. 24:2 26:5 [a] 2 Chr. 24:2

who [b]had understanding in the visions[1] of God; and as long as he sought the LORD, God made him [c]prosper.

6 Now he went out and [a]made war against the Philistines, and broke down the wall of Gath, the wall of Jabneh, and the wall of Ashdod; and he built cities *around* Ashdod and among the Philistines. 7 God helped him against [a]the Philistines, against the Arabians who lived in Gur Baal, and against the Meunites. 8 Also the Ammonites [a]brought tribute to Uzziah. His fame spread as far as the entrance of Egypt, for he became exceedingly strong.

9 And Uzziah built towers in Jerusalem at the [a]Corner Gate, at the Valley Gate, and at the corner buttress of the wall; then he fortified them. 10 Also he built towers in the desert. He dug many wells, for he had much livestock, both in the lowlands and in the plains; *he also had* farmers and vinedressers in the mountains and in Carmel, for he loved the soil.

11 Moreover Uzziah had an army of fighting men who went out to war by companies, according to the number on their roll as prepared by Jeiel the scribe and Maaseiah the officer, under the hand of Hananiah, *one* of the king's captains. 12 The total number of chief officers[1] of the mighty men of valor *was* two thousand six hundred. 13 And under their authority *was* an army of three hundred and seven thousand five hundred, that made war with mighty power, to help the king against the enemy. 14 Then Uzziah prepared for them, for the entire army, shields, spears, helmets, body armor, bows, and slings *to cast* stones. 15 And he made devices in Jerusalem, invented by [a]skillful men, to be on the towers and the corners, to shoot arrows and large stones. So his fame spread far and wide, for he was marvelously helped till he became strong.

The Penalty for Uzziah's Pride
(2 Kin. 15:4–7)

16 But [a]when he was strong his heart was [b]lifted up, to *his* destruction, for he transgressed against the LORD his God [c]by entering the temple of the LORD to burn incense on the altar of incense. 17 So [a]Azariah the priest went in after him, and with him were eighty priests of the LORD—valiant men. 18 And they withstood King Uzziah, and said to him, "*It* [a]*is* not for you, Uzziah, to burn incense to the LORD, but for the [b]priests, the sons of Aaron, who are consecrated to burn incense. Get out of the sanctuary, for you have trespassed! You *shall have* no honor from the LORD God."

19 Then Uzziah became furious; and he *had* a censer in his hand to burn incense. And while he was angry with the priests, [a]leprosy broke out on his forehead, before the priests in the house of the LORD, beside the incense altar. 20 And Azariah the chief priest and all the priests looked at him, and there, on his forehead, he *was* leprous; so they thrust him out of that place. Indeed he also [a]hurried to get out, because the LORD had struck him.

21 [a]King Uzziah was a leper until the day of his death. He dwelt in an [b]isolated house, because he was a leper; for he was cut off from the house of the LORD. Then Jotham his son *was* over the king's house, judging the people of the land.

22 Now the rest of the acts of Uzziah, from first to last, the prophet [a]Isaiah the son of Amoz wrote. 23 [a]So Uzziah rested with his fathers, and they buried him with his fathers in the field of burial which *belonged* to the kings, for they said, "He is a leper." Then Jotham his son reigned in his place.

Jotham Reigns in Judah
(2 Kin. 15:32–38)

27 Jotham [a]*was* twenty-five years old when he became king, and he reigned sixteen years in Jerusalem. His mother's name *was* Jerushah[1] the daughter of Zadok. 2 And he did *what was* right in the sight of the LORD, according to all that his father Uzziah had done (although he did not enter the temple of the LORD). But still [a]the people acted corruptly.

26:5 [b] Gen. 41:15; Dan. 1:17; 10:1 [c] [2 Chr. 15:2; 20:20; 31:21] [1] Several Hebrew manuscripts, Septuagint, Syriac, Targum, and Arabic read *fear.* 26:6 [a] Is. 14:29 26:7 [a] 2 Chr. 21:16 26:8 [a] 2 Sam. 8:2; 2 Chr. 17:11 26:9 [a] 2 Kin. 14:13; 2 Chr. 25:23; Neh. 3:13, 19, 32; Zech. 14:10 26:12 [1] Literally *chief fathers* 26:15 [a] Ex. 39:3, 8 26:16 [a] [Deut. 32:15] [b] Deut. 8:14; 2 Chr. 25:19 [c] 1 Kin. 13:1–4; 2 Kin. 16:12, 13 26:17 [a] 1 Chr. 6:10 26:18 [a] [Num. 3:10; 16:39, 40; 18:7] [b] Ex. 30:7, 8; Heb. 7:14 26:19 [a] Lev. 13:42; Num. 12:10; 2 Kin. 5:25–27 26:20 [a] Esth. 6:12 26:21 [a] 2 Kin. 15:5 [b] [Lev. 13:46; Num. 5:2] 26:22 [a] 2 Kin. 20:1; 2 Chr. 32:20, 32; Is. 1:1 26:23 [a] 2 Kin. 15:7; 2 Chr. 21:20; 28:27; Is. 6:1 27:1 [a] 2 Kin. 15:32–35 [1] Spelled *Jerusha* in 2 Kings 15:33 27:2 [a] 2 Kin. 15:35; Ezek. 20:44; 30:13

3 He built the Upper Gate of the house
of the LORD, and he built extensively on
the wall of [a]Ophel. 4 Moreover he built cities in the mountains of Judah, and in the
forests he built fortresses and towers. 5 He
also fought with the king of the [a]Ammon-
ites and defeated them. And the people of
Ammon gave him in that year one hundred talents of silver, ten thousand kors
of wheat, and ten thousand of barley. The
people of Ammon paid this to him in the
second and third years also. 6 So Jotham
became mighty, [a]because he prepared his
ways before the LORD his God.

7 Now the rest of the acts of Jotham, and all
his wars and his ways, indeed they *are* written in the book of the kings of Israel and Judah. 8 He was twenty-five years old when he
became king, and he reigned sixteen years
in Jerusalem. 9 [a]So Jotham rested with his fathers, and they buried him in the City of David. Then [b]Ahaz his son reigned in his place.

Ahaz Reigns in Judah
(2 Kin. 16:1–4)

28 Ahaz [a]*was* twenty years old when he
became king, and he reigned sixteen years in Jerusalem; and he did not do
what was right in the sight of the LORD, as
his father David *had done.* 2 For he walked
in the ways of the kings of Israel, and made
[a]molded images for [b]the Baals. 3 He burned
incense in [a]the Valley of the Son of Hinnom, and burned [b]his children in the [c]fire,
according to the abominations of the nations whom the LORD had [d]cast out before
the children of Israel. 4 And he sacrificed
and burned incense on the high places,
on the hills, and under every green tree.

Syria and Israel Defeat Judah
(2 Kin. 16:5, 6; Is. 7:1)

5 Therefore [a]the LORD his God delivered
him into the hand of the king of Syria. They
[b]defeated him, and carried away a great
multitude of them as captives, and brought
them to Damascus. Then he was also delivered into the hand of the king of Israel,
who defeated him with a great slaughter.
6 For [a]Pekah the son of Remaliah killed one
hundred and twenty thousand in Judah in
one day, all valiant men, [b]because they had
forsaken the LORD God of their fathers.
7 Zichri, a mighty man of Ephraim, killed
Maaseiah the king's son, Azrikam the officer over the house, and Elkanah *who was*
second to the king. 8 And the children of Israel carried away captive of their [a]brethren
two hundred thousand women, sons, and
daughters; and they also took away much
spoil from them, and brought the spoil to
Samaria.

Israel Returns the Captives

9 But a [a]prophet of the LORD was there,
whose name *was* Oded; and he went out
before the army that came to Samaria, and
said to them: "Look, [b]because the LORD God
of your fathers was angry with Judah, He
has delivered them into your hand; but you
have killed them in a rage *that* [c]reaches up
to heaven. 10 And now you propose to force
the children of Judah and Jerusalem to
be your [a]male and female slaves; *but are*
you not also guilty before the LORD your
God? 11 Now hear me, therefore, and return
the captives, whom you have taken captive
from your brethren, [a]for the fierce wrath of
the LORD *is* upon you."

12 Then some of the heads of the children
of Ephraim, Azariah the son of Johanan,
Berechiah the son of Meshillemoth, Jehiz-
kiah the son of Shallum, and Amasa the son
of Hadlai, stood up against those who came
from the war, 13 and said to them, "You shall
not bring the captives here, for we *already*
have offended the LORD. You intend to add
to our sins and to our guilt; for our guilt
is great, and *there is* fierce wrath against
Israel." 14 So the armed men left the captives and the spoil before the leaders and
all the assembly. 15 Then the men [a]who were
designated by name rose up and took the
captives, and from the spoil they clothed
all who were naked among them, dressed
them and gave them sandals, [b]gave them

27:3 [a] 2 Chr. 33:14; Neh. 3:26 **27:5** [a] 2 Chr. 26:8 **27:6** [a] 2 Chr. 26:5 **27:9** [a] 2 Kin. 15:38 [b] Is. 1:1; Hos. 1:1; Mic. 1:1 **28:1** [a] 2 Kin. 16:2–4 **28:2** [a] Ex. 34:17; Lev. 19:4 [b] Judg. 2:11 **28:3** [a] Josh. 15:8 [b] 2 Kin. 23:10 [c] [Lev. 18:21]; 2 Kin. 16:3; 2 Chr. 33:6 [d] [Lev. 18:24–30] **28:5** [a] [Is. 10:5] [b] 2 Kin. 16:5, 6; [2 Chr. 24:24]; Is. 7:1, 17 **28:6** [a] 2 Kin. 15:27 [b] [2 Chr. 29:8] **28:8** [a] Deut. 28:25, 41; 2 Chr. 11:4 **28:9** [a] 2 Chr. 25:15 [b] Ps. 69:26; [Is. 10:5; 47:6]; Ezek. 25:12, 15; 26:2; Obad. 10; [Zech. 1:15] [c] Ezra 9:6; Rev. 18:5 **28:10** [a] [Lev. 25:39, 42, 43, 46] **28:11** [a] Ps. 78:49; James 2:13 **28:15** [a] 2 Chr. 28:12 [b] [Prov. 25:21, 22; Luke 6:27; Rom. 12:20]

food and drink, and anointed them; and
they let all the feeble ones ride on donkeys.
So they brought them to their brethren at
Jericho, [c]the city of palm trees. Then they
returned to Samaria.

Assyria Refuses to Help Judah
(2 Kin. 16:7–9)

16[a]At the same time King Ahaz sent to the
kings[1] of Assyria to help him. 17For again
the [a]Edomites had come, attacked Judah,
and carried away captives. 18[a]The Philistines also had invaded the cities of the lowland and of the South of Judah, and had
taken Beth Shemesh, Aijalon, Gederoth,
Sochoh with its villages, Timnah with its
villages, and Gimzo with its villages; and
they dwelt there. 19For the LORD brought
Judah low because of Ahaz king of [a]Israel,
for he had [b]encouraged moral decline in
Judah and had been continually unfaithful
to the LORD. 20Also [a]Tiglath-Pileser[1] king of
Assyria came to him and distressed him,
and did not assist him. 21For Ahaz took part
of the treasures from the house of the LORD,
from the house of the king, and from the
leaders, and he gave *it* to the king of Assyria; but he did not help him.

Apostasy and Death of Ahaz
(2 Kin. 16:12–20)

22Now in the time of his distress King
Ahaz became increasingly unfaithful to the
LORD. This *is that* King Ahaz. 23For [a]he sacrificed to the gods of Damascus which had
defeated him, saying, "Because the gods of
the kings of Syria help them, I will sacrifice
to them [b]that they may help me." But they
were the ruin of him and of all Israel. 24So
Ahaz gathered the articles of the house of
God, cut in pieces the articles of the house
of God, [a]shut up the doors of the house of
the LORD, and made for himself altars in
every corner of Jerusalem. 25And in every
single city of Judah he made high places to
burn incense to other gods, and provoked
to anger the LORD God of his fathers.
26[a]Now the rest of his acts and all his
ways, from first to last, indeed they *are* written in the book of the kings of Judah and
Israel. 27So Ahaz rested with his fathers,
and they buried him in the city, in Jerusalem; but they [a]did not bring him into the
tombs of the kings of Israel. Then Hezekiah
his son reigned in his place.

Hezekiah Reigns in Judah
(2 Kin. 18:1–3)

29 Hezekiah [a]became king *when he*
was twenty-five years old, and he
reigned twenty-nine years in Jerusalem.
His mother's name *was* Abijah[1] the daughter of Zechariah. 2And he did *what was* right
in the sight of the LORD, according to all
that his father David had done.

Hezekiah Cleanses the Temple

3In the first year of his reign, in the first
month, he [a]opened the doors of the house
of the LORD and repaired them. 4Then he
brought in the priests and the Levites, and
gathered them in the East Square, 5and said
to them: "Hear me, Levites! Now sanctify
yourselves, [a]sanctify the house of the LORD
God of your fathers, and carry out the rubbish from the holy *place*. 6For our fathers
have trespassed and done evil in the eyes
of the LORD our God; they have forsaken
Him, have [a]turned their faces away from
the dwelling place of the LORD, and turned
their backs *on Him*. 7[a]They have also shut
up the doors of the vestibule, put out the
lamps, and have not burned incense or offered burnt offerings in the holy *place* to
the God of Israel. 8Therefore the [a]wrath of
the LORD fell upon Judah and Jerusalem,
and He has [b]given them up to trouble, to
desolation, and to [c]jeering, as you see with
your [d]eyes. 9For indeed, because of this [a]our
fathers have fallen by the sword; and our
sons, our daughters, and our wives *are* in
captivity.
10"Now *it is* in my heart to make [a]a covenant with the LORD God of Israel, that His
fierce wrath may turn away from us. 11My
sons, do not be negligent now, for the LORD

28:15 [c] Deut. 34:3; Judg. 1:16 28:16 [a] 2 Kin. 16:7 [1] Septuagint, Syriac, and Vulgate read *king* (compare verse 20). 28:17 [a] 2 Chr. 21:10; Obad. 10–14 28:18 [a] 2 Chr. 21:16, 17; Ezek. 16:27, 57 28:19 [a] 2 Kin. 16:2; 2 Chr. 21:2 [b] Ex. 32:25 28:20 [a] 2 Kin. 15:29; 16:7–9; 1 Chr. 5:26 [1] Hebrew *Tilgath-Pilneser* 28:23 [a] 2 Chr. 25:14 [b] Jer. 44:17, 18 28:24 [a] 2 Chr. 29:3, 7 28:26 [a] 2 Kin. 16:19, 20 28:27 [a] 2 Chr. 21:20; 24:25 29:1 [a] 2 Kin. 18:1; 2 Chr. 32:22, 33 [1] Spelled *Abi* in 2 Kings 18:2 29:3 [a] 2 Chr. 28:24; 29:7 29:5 [a] 1 Chr. 15:12; 2 Chr. 29:15, 34; 35:6 29:6 [a] [Is. 1:4]; Jer. 2:27; Ezek. 8:16 29:7 [a] 2 Chr. 28:24 29:8 [a] 2 Chr. 24:18 [b] 2 Chr. 28:5 [c] 1 Kin. 9:8; Jer. 18:16; 19:8; 25:9, 18; 29:18 [d] Deut. 28:32 29:9 [a] Deut. 28:25; 2 Chr. 28:5–8, 17 29:10 [a] 2 Chr. 15:12; 23:16

has [a]chosen you to stand before Him, to
serve Him, and that you should minister
to Him and burn incense."
12Then these Levites arose: [a]Mahath the
son of Amasai and Joel the son of Azariah,
of the sons of the [b]Kohathites; of the sons
of Merari, Kish the son of Abdi and Azariah
the son of Jehallelel; of the Gershonites,
Joah the son of Zimmah and Eden the son
of Joah; 13of the sons of Elizaphan, Shimri
and Jeiel; of the sons of Asaph, Zechariah
and Mattaniah; 14of the sons of Heman, Jehiel and Shimei; and of the sons of Jeduthun, Shemaiah and Uzziel.
15And they gathered their brethren,
[a]sanctified themselves, and went according to the commandment of the king, at the
words of the LORD, [b]to cleanse the house
of the LORD. 16Then the priests went into
the inner part of the house of the LORD to
cleanse *it,* and brought out all the debris
that they found in the temple of the LORD
to the court of the house of the LORD. And
the Levites took *it* out and carried *it* to the
Brook [a]Kidron.
17Now they began to sanctify on the first
day of the first month, and on the eighth
day of the month they came to the vestibule
of the LORD. So they sanctified the house
of the LORD in eight days, and on the sixteenth day of the first month they finished.
18Then they went in to King Hezekiah
and said, "We have cleansed all the house of
the LORD, the altar of burnt offerings with
all its articles, and the table of the showbread with all its articles. 19Moreover all the
articles which King Ahaz in his reign had
[a]cast aside in his transgression we have
prepared and sanctified; and there they
are, before the altar of the LORD."

Hezekiah Restores Temple Worship

20Then King Hezekiah rose early, gathered the rulers of the city, and went up to
the house of the LORD. 21And they brought
seven bulls, seven rams, seven lambs, and
seven male goats for a [a]sin offering for the
kingdom, for the sanctuary, and for Judah.
Then he commanded the priests, the sons
of Aaron, to offer *them* on the altar of the
LORD. 22So they killed the bulls, and the
priests received the blood and [a]sprinkled *it*
on the altar. Likewise they killed the rams
and sprinkled the blood on the altar. They
also killed the lambs and sprinkled the
blood on the altar. 23Then they brought
out the male goats *for* the sin offering before the king and the assembly, and they
laid their [a]hands on them. 24And the priests
killed them; and they presented their blood
on the altar as a sin offering [a]to make an
atonement for all Israel, for the king commanded *that* the burnt offering and the sin
offering *be made* for all Israel.
25[a]And he stationed the Levites in the
house of the LORD with cymbals, with
stringed instruments, and with harps, [b]ac-
cording to the commandment of David,
of [c]Gad the king's seer, and of Nathan the
prophet; [d]for thus *was* the commandment
of the LORD by His prophets. 26The Levites
stood with the instruments [a]of David, and
the priests with [b]the trumpets. 27Then Hezekiah commanded *them* to offer the burnt
offering on the altar. And when the burnt
offering began, [a]the song of the LORD *also*
began, with the trumpets and with the instruments of David king of Israel. 28So all
the assembly worshiped, the singers sang,
and the trumpeters sounded; all *this contin-*
ued until the burnt offering was finished.
29And when they had finished offering, [a]the
king and all who were present with him
bowed and worshiped. 30Moreover King
Hezekiah and the leaders commanded the
Levites to sing praise to the LORD with the
words of David and of Asaph the seer. So
they sang praises with gladness, and they
bowed their heads and worshiped.
31Then Hezekiah answered and said,
"Now *that* you have consecrated yourselves
to the LORD, come near, and bring sacrifices
and [a]thank offerings into the house of the
LORD." So the assembly brought in sacrifices and thank offerings, and as many as
were of a [b]willing heart *brought* burnt offerings. 32And the number of the burnt offerings which the assembly brought was

---

29:11 [a] Num. 3:6; 8:14; 18:2, 6; 2 Chr. 30:16, 17 **29:12** [a] 2 Chr. 31:13 [b] Num. 3:19, 20 **29:15** [a] 2 Chr. 29:5 [b] 1 Chr. 23:28 **29:16** [a] 2 Chr. 15:16; 30:14 **29:19** [a] 2 Chr. 28:24 **29:21** [a] Lev. 4:3–14 **29:22** [a] Lev. 8:14, 15, 19, 24; Heb. 9:21 **29:23** [a] Lev. 4:15, 24; 8:14 **29:24** [a] Lev. 14:20 **29:25** [a] 1 Chr. 16:4; 25:6 [b] 1 Chr. 23:5; 25:1; 2 Chr. 8:14 [c] 2 Sam. 24:11 [d] 2 Chr. 30:12 **29:26** [a] 1 Chr. 23:5; Amos 6:5 [b] Num. 10:8, 10; 1 Chr. 15:24; 16:6; 2 Chr. 5:12 **29:27** [a] 2 Chr. 23:18 **29:29** [a] 2 Chr. 20:18 **29:31** [a] Lev. 7:12 [b] Ex. 35:5, 22

seventy bulls, one hundred rams, *and* two hundred lambs; all these *were* for a burnt offering to the LORD. 33 The consecrated things *were* six hundred bulls and three thousand sheep. 34 But the priests were too few, so that they could not skin all the burnt offerings; therefore [a]their brethren the Levites helped them until the work was ended and until the *other* priests had sanctified themselves, [b]for the Levites were [c]more diligent in [d]sanctifying themselves than the priests. 35 Also the burnt offerings *were* in abundance, with [a]the fat of the peace offerings and *with* [b]the drink offerings for *every* burnt offering.

So the service of the house of the LORD was set in order. 36 Then Hezekiah and all the people rejoiced that God had prepared the people, since the events took place so suddenly.

Hezekiah Keeps the Passover

30 And Hezekiah sent to all Israel and Judah, and also wrote letters to Ephraim and Manasseh, that they should come to the house of the LORD at Jerusalem, to keep the Passover to the LORD God of Israel. 2 For the king and his leaders and all the assembly in Jerusalem had agreed to keep the Passover in the second [a]month. 3 For they could not keep it [a]at the regular time,[1] [b]because a sufficient number of priests had not consecrated themselves, nor had the people gathered together at Jerusalem. 4 And the matter pleased the king and all the assembly. 5 So they resolved to make a proclamation throughout all Israel, from Beersheba to Dan, that they should come to keep the Passover to the LORD God of Israel at Jerusalem, since they had not done *it* for a long *time* in the *prescribed* manner.

6 Then the [a]runners went throughout all Israel and Judah with the letters from the king and his leaders, and spoke according to the command of the king: "Children of Israel, [b]return to the LORD God of Abraham, Isaac, and Israel; then He will return to the remnant of you who have escaped from the hand of [c]the kings of [d]Assyria. 7 And do not be [a]like your fathers and your brethren, who trespassed against the LORD God of their fathers, so that He [b]gave them up to [c]desolation, as you see. 8 Now do not be [a]stiff-necked, as your fathers *were, but* yield yourselves to the LORD; and enter His sanctuary, which He has sanctified forever, and serve the LORD your God, [b]that the fierceness of His wrath may turn away from you. 9 For if you return to the LORD, your brethren and your children *will be treated* with [a]compassion by those who lead them captive, so that they may come back to this land; for the LORD your God *is* [b]gracious and merciful, and will not turn *His* face from you if you [c]return to Him."

10 So the runners passed from city to city through the country of Ephraim and Manasseh, as far as Zebulun; but [a]they laughed at them and mocked them. 11 Nevertheless [a]some from Asher, Manasseh, and Zebulun humbled themselves and came to Jerusalem. 12 Also [a]the hand of God was on Judah to give them singleness of heart to obey the command of the king and the leaders, [b]at the word of the LORD.

13 Now many people, a very great assembly, gathered at Jerusalem to keep the Feast of [a]Unleavened Bread in the second month. 14 They arose and took away the [a]altars that *were* in Jerusalem, and they took away all the incense altars and cast *them* into the Brook [b]Kidron. 15 Then they slaughtered the Passover *lambs* on the fourteenth *day* of the second month. The priests and the Levites were [a]ashamed, and sanctified themselves, and brought the burnt offerings to the house of the LORD. 16 They stood in their [a]place according to their custom, according to the Law of Moses the man of God; the priests sprinkled the blood *received* from the hand of the Levites. 17 For *there were* many in the assembly who had not sanctified themselves; [a]therefore the Levites had charge of the slaughter of the Passover *lambs* for everyone *who was* not clean, to sanctify *them* to the LORD. 18 For

---

29:34 [a] 2 Chr. 35:11 [b] 2 Chr. 30:3 [c] Ps. 7:10 [d] 2 Chr. 29:5 29:35 [a] Lev. 3:15, 16 [b] Num. 15:5–10 30:2 [a] Num. 9:10, 11; 2 Chr. 30:13, 15 30:3 [a] Ex. 12:6, 18 [b] 2 Chr. 29:17, 34 [1] That is, the first month (compare Leviticus 23:5); literally *at that time* 30:6 [a] Esth. 8:14; Job 9:25; Jer. 51:31 [b] [Jer. 4:1; Joel 2:13] [c] 2 Kin. 15:19, 29 [d] 2 Chr. 28:20 30:7 [a] Ezek. 20:18 [b] Is. 1:9 [c] 2 Chr. 29:8 30:8 [a] Ex. 32:9; Deut. 10:16; Acts 7:51 [b] 2 Chr. 29:10 30:9 [a] Ps. 106:46 [b] [Ex. 34:6; Mic. 7:18] [c] [Is. 55:7] 30:10 [a] 2 Chr. 36:16 30:11 [a] 2 Chr. 11:16; 30:18, 21 30:12 [a] [2 Cor. 3:5; Phil. 2:13; Heb. 13:20, 21] [b] 2 Chr. 29:25 30:13 [a] Lev. 23:6; Num. 9:11 30:14 [a] 2 Chr. 28:24 [b] 2 Chr. 29:16 30:15 [a] 2 Chr. 29:34 30:16 [a] 2 Chr. 35:10, 15 30:17 [a] 2 Chr. 29:34

a multitude of the people, [a]many from
Ephraim, Manasseh, Issachar, and Zebulun, had not cleansed themselves, [b]yet they
ate the Passover contrary to what was written. But Hezekiah prayed for them, saying,
"May the good LORD provide atonement for
everyone 19 *who* [a]prepares his heart to seek
God, the LORD God of his fathers, though
he is not *cleansed* according to the purification of the sanctuary." 20 And the LORD
listened to Hezekiah and healed the people.
21 So the children of Israel who were present at Jerusalem kept [a]the Feast of Unleavened Bread seven days with great gladness;
and the Levites and the priests praised the
LORD day by day, *singing* to the LORD, accompanied by loud instruments. 22 And Hezekiah
gave encouragement to all the Levites [a]who
taught the good knowledge of the LORD; and
they ate throughout the feast seven days, offering peace offerings and [b]making confession to the LORD God of their fathers.
23 Then the whole assembly agreed to
keep *the feast* [a]another seven days, and they
kept it *another* seven days with gladness.
24 For Hezekiah king of Judah [a]gave to the
assembly a thousand bulls and seven thousand sheep, and the leaders gave to the assembly a thousand bulls and ten thousand
sheep; and a great number of priests [b]sanc-
tified themselves. 25 The whole assembly of
Judah rejoiced, also the priests and Levites,
all the assembly that came from Israel, the
sojourners [a]who came from the land of Israel, and those who dwelt in Judah. 26 So
there was great joy in Jerusalem, for since
the time of [a]Solomon the son of David, king
of Israel, *there had* been nothing like this in
Jerusalem. 27 Then the priests, the Levites,
arose and [a]blessed the people, and their
voice was heard; and their prayer came
up to [b]His holy dwelling place, to heaven.

The Reforms of Hezekiah
(2 Kin. 18:4)

31 Now when all this was finished, all
Israel who were present went out to
the cities of Judah and [a]broke the *sacred*
pillars in pieces, cut down the wooden
images, and threw down the high places
and the altars—from all Judah, Benjamin,
Ephraim, and Manasseh—until they had
utterly destroyed them all. Then all the children of Israel returned to their own cities,
every man to his possession.
2 And Hezekiah appointed [a]the divisions
of the priests and the Levites according to
their divisions, each man according to his
service, the priests and Levites [b]for burnt
offerings and peace offerings, to serve, to
give thanks, and to praise in the gates of
the camp[1] of the LORD. 3 The king also *appointed* a portion of his [a]possessions for
the burnt offerings: for the morning and
evening burnt offerings, the burnt offerings for the Sabbaths and the New Moons
and the set feasts, as *it is* written in the [b]Law
of the LORD.
4 Moreover he commanded the people
who dwelt in Jerusalem to contribute [a]sup-
port for the priests and the Levites, that
they might devote themselves to [b]the Law
of the LORD.
5 As soon as the commandment was
circulated, the children of Israel brought
in abundance [a]the firstfruits of grain and
wine, oil and honey, and of all the produce
of the field; and they brought in abundantly
the [b]tithe of everything. 6 And the children
of Israel and Judah, who dwelt in the cities of Judah, brought the tithe of oxen and
sheep; also the [a]tithe of holy things which
were consecrated to the LORD their God
they laid in heaps.
7 In the third month they began laying
them in heaps, and they finished in the
seventh month. 8 And when Hezekiah and
the leaders came and saw the heaps, they
blessed the LORD and His people Israel.
9 Then Hezekiah questioned the priests and
the Levites concerning the heaps. 10 And Azariah the chief priest, from the [a]house of
Zadok, answered him and said, [b]"Since *the
people* began to bring the offerings into the
house of the LORD, we have had enough to
eat and have plenty left, for the LORD has

30:18 [a] 2 Chr. 30:1, 11, 25 [b] Ex. 12:43–49; [Num. 9:10] 30:19 [a] 2 Chr. 19:3 30:21 [a] Ex. 12:15; 13:6; 1 Kin. 8:65 30:22 [a] [Deut. 33:10]; 2 Chr. 17:9; 35:3 [b] Ezra 10:11 30:23 [a] 1 Kin. 8:65; 2 Chr. 35:17, 18 30:24 [a] 2 Chr. 35:7, 8 [b] 2 Chr. 29:34 30:25 [a] 2 Chr. 30:11, 18 30:26 [a] 2 Chr. 7:8–10 30:27 [a] Num. 6:23 [b] Deut. 26:15; Ps. 68:5 31:1 [a] 2 Kin. 18:4 31:2 [a] 1 Chr. 23:6; 24:1 [b] 1 Chr. 23:30, 31 [1] That is, the temple 31:3 [a] 2 Chr. 35:7 [b] Num. 28:1—29:40 31:4 [a] Num. 18:8; 2 Kin. 12:16; Neh. 13:10; Ezek. 44:29 [b] Mal. 2:7 31:5 [a] Ex. 22:29; Neh. 13:12 [b] [Lev. 27:30]; Deut. 14:28; 26:12, 13 31:6 [a] [Lev. 27:30]; Deut. 14:28 31:10 [a] 1 Chr. 6:8, 9 [b] [Mal. 3:10]

blessed His people; and what is left *is* this great [c]abundance."

11Now Hezekiah commanded *them* to prepare [a]rooms in the house of the LORD, and they prepared them. 12Then they faithfully brought in the offerings, the tithes, and the dedicated things; [a]Cononiah the Levite had charge of them, and Shimei his brother *was* the next. 13Jehiel, Azaziah, Nahath, Asahel, Jerimoth, Jozabad, Eliel, Ismachiah, Mahath, and Benaiah *were* overseers under the hand of Cononiah and Shimei his brother, at the commandment of Hezekiah the king and Azariah the [a]ruler of the house of God. 14Kore the son of Imnah the Levite, the keeper of the East Gate, *was* over the [a]freewill offerings to God, to distribute the offerings of the LORD and the most holy things. 15And under him *were* [a]Eden, Miniamin, Jeshua, Shemaiah, Amariah, and Shecaniah, *his* faithful assistants in [b]the cities of the priests, to distribute [c]allotments to their brethren by divisions, to the great as well as the small.

16Besides those males from three years old and up who were written in the genealogy, they distributed to everyone who entered the house of the LORD his daily portion for the work of his service, by his division, 17and to the priests who were written in the genealogy according to their father's house, and to the Levites [a]from twenty years old and up according to their work, by their divisions, 18and to all who were written in the genealogy—their little ones and their wives, their sons and daughters, the whole company of them—for in their faithfulness they sanctified themselves in holiness.

19Also for the sons of Aaron the priests, *who were* in [a]the fields of the common-lands of their cities, in every single city, *there were* men who were [b]designated by name to distribute portions to all the males among the priests and to all who were listed by genealogies among the Levites.

20Thus Hezekiah did throughout all Judah, and he [a]did what *was* good and right and true before the LORD his God. 21And in every work that he began in the service of the house of God, in the law and in the commandment, to seek his God, he did *it* with all his heart. So he [a]prospered.

Sennacherib Boasts Against the LORD
(2 Kin. 18:13—19:34; Is. 36:1–22)

32 After [a]these deeds of faithfulness, Sennacherib king of Assyria came and entered Judah; he encamped against the fortified cities, thinking to win them over to himself. 2And when Hezekiah saw that Sennacherib had come, and that his purpose was to make war against Jerusalem, 3he consulted with his leaders and commanders[1] to stop the water from the springs which *were* outside the city; and they helped him. 4Thus many people gathered together who stopped all the [a]springs and the brook that ran through the land, saying, "Why should the kings[1] of Assyria come and find much water?" 5And [a]he strengthened himself, [b]built up all the wall that was broken, raised *it* up to the towers, and *built* another wall outside; also he repaired the [c]Millo[1] *in* the City of David, and made weapons and shields in abundance. 6Then he set military captains over the people, gathered them together to him in the open square of the city gate, and [a]gave them encouragement, saying, 7[a]"Be strong and courageous; [b]do not be afraid nor dismayed before the king of Assyria, nor before all the multitude that *is* with him; for [c]*there are* more with us than with him. 8With him *is* an [a]arm of flesh; but [b]with us *is* the LORD our God, to help us and to fight our battles." And the people were strengthened by the words of Hezekiah king of Judah.

9[a]After this Sennacherib king of Assyria sent his servants to Jerusalem (but he and all the forces with him *laid siege* against Lachish), to Hezekiah king of Judah, and to all Judah who *were* in Jerusalem, saying, 10[a]"Thus says Sennacherib king of Assyria: 'In what do you trust, that you remain

31:10 [c] Ex. 36:5 31:11 [a] 1 Kin. 6:5–8 31:12 [a] 2 Chr. 35:9; Neh. 13:13 31:13 [a] 1 Chr. 9:11; Jer. 20:1 31:14 [a] Deut. 23:23; 2 Chr. 35:8 31:15 [a] 2 Chr. 29:12 [b] Josh. 21:1–3, 9 [c] 1 Chr. 9:26 31:17 [a] 1 Chr. 23:24, 27 31:19 [a] Lev. 25:34; Num. 35:1–4 [b] 2 Chr. 31:12–15 31:20 [a] 2 Kin. 20:3; 22:2 31:21 [a] 2 Chr. 26:5; 32:30; Ps. 1:3 32:1 [a] 2 Kin. 18:13—19:37; Is. 36:1—37:38 32:3 [1] Literally *mighty men* 32:4 [a] 2 Kin. 20:20 [1] Following Masoretic Text and Vulgate; Arabic, Septuagint, and Syriac read *king*. 32:5 [a] Is. 22:9, 10 [b] 2 Kin. 25:4; 2 Chr. 25:23 [c] 2 Sam. 5:9; 1 Kin. 9:15, 24; 11:27; 2 Kin. 12:20; 1 Chr. 11:8 [1] Literally *The Landfill* 32:6 [a] 2 Chr. 30:22; Is. 40:2 32:7 [a] [Deut. 31:6] [b] 2 Chr. 20:15 [c] 2 Kin. 6:16; [Rom. 8:31] 32:8 [a] [Jer. 17:5; 1 John 4:4] [b] Ex. 14:13; [1 Sam. 17:45–47]; 2 Chr. 13:12; 20:17; [Rom. 8:31] 32:9 [a] 2 Kin. 18:17 32:10 [a] 2 Kin. 18:19

under siege in Jerusalem? [11]Does not Hezekiah persuade you to give yourselves over
to die by famine and by thirst, saying, [a]"The
LORD our God will deliver us from the hand
of the king of Assyria"? [12][a]Has not the same
Hezekiah taken away His high places and
His altars, and commanded Judah and Jerusalem, saying, "You shall worship before
one altar and burn incense on [b]it"? [13]Do you
not know what I and my fathers have done
to all the peoples of *other* lands? [a]Were the
gods of the nations of those lands in any
way able to deliver their lands out of my
hand? [14]Who *was there* among all the gods
of those nations that my fathers utterly destroyed that could deliver his people from
my hand, that your God should be able to
deliver you from my [a]hand? [15]Now therefore, [a]do not let Hezekiah deceive you or
persuade you like this, and do not believe
him; for no god of any nation or kingdom
was able to deliver his people from my hand
or the hand of my fathers. How much less
will your God deliver you from my hand?' "

[16]Furthermore, his servants spoke
against the LORD God and against His servant Hezekiah.

[17]He also wrote letters to revile the LORD
God of Israel, and to speak against Him,
saying, [a]"As the gods of the nations of *other*
lands have not delivered their people from
my hand, so the God of Hezekiah will not
deliver His people from my [b]hand." [18][a]Then
they called out with a loud voice in Hebrew[1]
to the people of Jerusalem who *were* on
the wall, to frighten them and trouble
them, that they might take the city. [19]And
they spoke against the God of Jerusalem,
as against the gods of the people of the
earth—[a]the work of men's hands.

Sennacherib's Defeat and Death
(2 Kin. 19:35–37)

[20][a]Now because of this King Hezekiah
and [b]the prophet Isaiah, the son of Amoz,
prayed and cried out to heaven. [21][a]Then the
LORD sent an angel who cut down every
mighty man of valor, leader, and captain
in the camp of the king of Assyria. So he
returned [b]shamefaced to his own land. And
when he had gone into the temple of his
god, some of his own offspring struck him
down with the sword there.

[22]Thus the LORD saved Hezekiah and the
inhabitants of Jerusalem from the hand of
Sennacherib the king of Assyria, and from
the hand of all *others,* and guided them[1] on
every side. [23]And many brought gifts to the
LORD at Jerusalem, and [a]presents to Hezekiah king of Judah, so that he was [b]exalted
in the sight of all nations thereafter.

Hezekiah Humbles Himself
(2 Kin. 20:1–11; Is. 38:1–8)

[24][a]In those days Hezekiah was sick and
near death, and he prayed to the LORD; and
He spoke to him and gave him a sign. [25]But
Hezekiah [a]did not repay according to the
favor *shown* him, for [b]his heart was lifted
up; [c]therefore wrath was looming over him
and over Judah and Jerusalem. [26][a]Then
Hezekiah humbled himself for the pride of
his heart, he and the inhabitants of Jerusalem, so that the wrath of the LORD did not
come upon them [b]in the days of Hezekiah.

Hezekiah's Wealth and Honor
(2 Kin. 20:12–21; Is. 39:1–8)

[27]Hezekiah had very great riches and
honor. And he made himself treasuries
for silver, for gold, for precious stones, for
spices, for shields, and for all kinds of desirable items; [28]storehouses for the harvest of grain, wine, and oil; and stalls for
all kinds of livestock, and folds for flocks.[1]
[29]Moreover he provided cities for himself, and possessions of flocks and herds
in abundance; for [a]God had given him very
much property. [30][a]This same Hezekiah also
stopped the water outlet of Upper Gihon,
and brought the water by tunnel[1] to the
west side of the City of David. Hezekiah
[b]prospered in all his works.

[31]However, *regarding* the ambassadors

32:11 [a] 2 Kin. 18:30 **32:12** [a] 2 Kin. 18:22 [b] 2 Chr. 31:1, 2 **32:13** [a] 2 Kin. 18:33–35 **32:14** [a] [Is. 10:5–12] **32:15** [a] 2 Kin. 18:29 **32:17** [a] 2 Kin. 19:9; [1 Cor. 8:5, 6] [b] 2 Kin. 19:12; Dan. 3:15 **32:18** [a] 2 Kin. 18:28; Ps. 59:6 [1] Literally *Judean* **32:19** [a] 2 Kin. 19:18; [Ps. 96:5; 115:4–8] **32:20** [a] 2 Kin. 19:15 [b] 2 Kin. 19:2 **32:21** [a] 2 Kin. 19:35; Is. 10:12–19; Zech. 14:3 [b] Ps. 44:7 **32:22** [1] Septuagint reads *gave them rest;* Vulgate reads *gave them treasures.* **32:23** [a] 2 Sam. 8:10; 2 Chr. 17:5; 26:8; Ps. 45:12 [b] 2 Chr. 1:1 **32:24** [a] 2 Kin. 20:1–11; Is. 38:1–8 **32:25** [a] Ps. 116:12 [b] 2 Chr. 26:16; [Hab. 2:4] [c] 2 Chr. 24:18 **32:26** [a] Jer. 26:18, 19 [b] 2 Kin. 20:19 **32:28** [1] Following Septuagint and Vulgate; Arabic and Syriac omit *folds for flocks;* Masoretic Text reads *flocks for sheepfolds.* **32:29** [a] 1 Chr. 29:12 **32:30** [a] Is. 22:9–11 [b] 2 Chr. 31:21 [1] Literally *brought it straight* (compare 2 Kings 20:20)

of the princes of Babylon, whom they [a]sent
to him to inquire about the wonder that was
done in the land, God withdrew from him,
in order to [b]test him, that He might know
all *that was* in his heart.

Death of Hezekiah

32 Now the rest of the acts of Hezekiah,
and his goodness, indeed they *are* written
in [a]the vision of Isaiah the prophet, the
son of Amoz, *and* in the [b]book of the kings
of Judah and Israel. 33 [a]So Hezekiah rested
with his fathers, and they buried him in
the upper tombs of the sons of David; and
all Judah and the inhabitants of Jerusalem
[b]honored him at his death. Then Manasseh
his son reigned in his place.

Manasseh Reigns in Judah
(2 Kin. 21:1–9)

33 Manasseh [a]*was* twelve years old
when he became king, and he
reigned fifty-five years in Jerusalem. 2 But
he did evil in the sight of the LORD, according to the [a]abominations of the nations
whom the LORD had cast out before the
children of Israel. 3 For he rebuilt the high
places which Hezekiah his father had [a]bro-
ken down; he raised up altars for the Baals,
and [b]made wooden images; and he worshiped [c]all the host of heaven[1] and served
them. 4 He also built altars in the house of
the LORD, of which the LORD had said, [a]"In
Jerusalem shall My name be forever." 5 And
he built altars for all the host of heaven [a]in
the two courts of the house of the LORD.
6 [a]Also he caused his sons to pass through
the fire in the Valley of the Son of Hinnom;
he practiced [b]soothsaying, used witchcraft
and sorcery, and [c]consulted mediums and
spiritists. He did much evil in the sight of
the LORD, to provoke Him to anger. 7 [a]He
even set a carved image, the idol which he
had made, in the house of God, of which
God had said to David and to Solomon
his son, [b]"In this house and in Jerusalem,
which I have chosen out of all the tribes of
Israel, I will put My name forever; 8 [a]and
I will not again remove the foot of Israel
from the land which I have appointed for
your fathers—only if they are careful to do
all that I have commanded them, according to the whole law and the statutes and
the ordinances by the hand of Moses." 9 So
Manasseh seduced Judah and the inhabitants of Jerusalem to do more evil than
the nations whom the LORD had destroyed
before the children of Israel.

Manasseh Restored After Repentance

10 And the LORD spoke to Manasseh
and his people, but they would not listen.
11 [a]Therefore the LORD brought upon them
the captains of the army of the king of Assyria, who took Manasseh with hooks,[1]
[b]bound him with bronze *fetters,* and carried him off to Babylon. 12 Now when he
was in affliction, he implored the LORD
his God, and [a]humbled himself greatly before the God of his fathers, 13 and prayed to
Him; and He [a]received his entreaty, heard
his supplication, and brought him back to
Jerusalem into his kingdom. Then Manasseh [b]knew that the LORD *was* God.

14 After this he built a wall outside the
City of David on the west side of [a]Gihon,
in the valley, as far as the entrance of the
Fish Gate; and *it* [b]enclosed Ophel, and he
raised it to a very great height. Then he put
military captains in all the fortified cities
of Judah. 15 He took away [a]the foreign gods
and the idol from the house of the LORD,
and all the altars that he had built in the
mount of the house of the LORD and in Jerusalem; and he cast *them* out of the city.
16 He also repaired the altar of the LORD,
sacrificed peace offerings and [a]thank offerings on it, and commanded Judah to serve
the LORD God of Israel. 17 [a]Nevertheless the
people still sacrificed on the high places,
but only to the LORD their God.

Death of Manasseh
(2 Kin. 21:17, 18)

18 Now the rest of the acts of Manasseh,
his prayer to his God, and the words of [a]the

32:31 [a] 2 Kin. 20:12; Is. 39:1 [b] [Deut. 8:2, 16] 32:32 [a] Is. 36—39 [b] 2 Kin. 18—20 32:33 [a] 1 Kin. 1:21; 2 Kin. 20:21 [b] Ps. 112:6; Prov. 10:7 33:1 [a] 2 Kin. 21:1–9 33:2 [a] [Deut. 18:9–12]; 2 Chr. 28:3; [Jer. 15:4] 33:3 [a] 2 Kin. 18:4; 2 Chr. 30:14; 31:1 [b] Deut. 16:21; 2 Kin. 23:5, 6 [c] Deut. 17:3 [1] The gods of the Assyrians 33:4 [a] Deut. 12:11; 1 Kin. 8:29; 9:3; 2 Chr. 6:6; 7:16 33:5 [a] 2 Chr. 4:9 33:6 [a] [Lev. 18:21]; Deut. 18:10; 2 Kin. 23:10; 2 Chr. 28:3; Ezek. 23:37, 39 [b] Deut. 18:11; 2 Kin. 17:17 [c] [Lev. 19:31; 20:27]; 2 Kin. 21:6 33:7 [a] 2 Kin. 21:7; 2 Chr. 25:14 [b] Ps. 132:14 33:8 [a] 2 Sam. 7:10 33:11 [a] Deut. 28:36 [b] 2 Chr. 36:6; Job 36:8; Ps. 107:10, 11 [1] That is, nose hooks (compare 2 Kings 19:28) 33:12 [a] 2 Chr. 7:14; 32:26; [1 Pet. 5:6] 33:13 [a] 1 Chr. 5:20; Ezra 8:23 [b] 1 Kin. 20:13; Ps. 9:16; Dan. 4:25 33:14 [a] 1 Kin. 1:33 [b] 2 Chr. 27:3 33:15 [a] 2 Chr. 33:3, 5, 7 33:16 [a] Lev. 7:12 33:17 [a] 2 Chr. 32:12 33:18 [a] 1 Sam. 9:9

seers who spoke to him in the name of the
LORD God of Israel, indeed they *are written*
in the book[1] of the kings of Israel. 19Also
his prayer and *how God* received his entreaty, and all his sin and trespass, and the
sites where he built high places and set up
wooden images and carved images, before
he was humbled, indeed they *are* written
among the sayings of Hozai.[1] 20[a]So Manasseh rested with his fathers, and they buried
him in his own house. Then his son Amon
reigned in his place.

Amon's Reign and Death
(2 Kin. 21:19–26)

21[a]Amon *was* twenty-two years old when
he became king, and he reigned two years
in Jerusalem. 22But he did evil in the sight
of the LORD, as his father Manasseh had
done; for Amon sacrificed to all the carved
images which his father Manasseh had
made, and served them. 23And he did not
humble himself before the LORD, [a]as his father Manasseh had humbled himself; but
Amon trespassed more and more.
24[a]Then his servants conspired against
him, and [b]killed him in his own house.
25But the people of the land executed all
those who had conspired against King
Amon. Then the people of the land made
his son Josiah king in his place.

Josiah Reigns in Judah
(2 Kin. 22:1, 2)

34 Josiah [a]*was* eight years old when he
became king, and he reigned thirty-
one years in Jerusalem. 2And he did *what*
was right in the sight of the LORD, and
walked in the ways of his father David; *he* did
not turn aside to the right hand or to the left.
3For in the eighth year of his reign, while
he was still [a]young, he began to [b]seek the
God of his father David; and in the twelfth
year he began [c]to purge Judah and Jerusalem [d]of the high places, the wooden images, the carved images, and the molded
images. 4[a]They broke down the altars of the
Baals in his presence, and the incense altars which *were* above them he cut down;
and the wooden images, the carved images,
and the molded images he broke in pieces,
and made dust of them [b]and scattered *it*
on the graves of those who had sacrificed
to them. 5He also [a]burned the bones of the
priests on their [b]altars, and cleansed Judah and Jerusalem. 6And *so he did* in the
cities of Manasseh, Ephraim, and Simeon,
as far as Naphtali and all around, with axes.[1]
7When he had broken down the altars and
the wooden images, had [a]beaten the carved
images into powder, and cut down all the
incense altars throughout all the land of
Israel, he returned to Jerusalem.

Hilkiah Finds the Book of the Law
(2 Kin. 22:3–20)

8[a]In the eighteenth year of his reign,
when he had purged the land and the temple,[1] he sent [b]Shaphan the son of Azaliah,
Maaseiah the [c]governor of the city, and
Joah the son of Joahaz the recorder, to repair the house of the LORD his God. 9When
they came to Hilkiah the high priest, they
delivered [a]the money that was brought into
the house of God, which the Levites who
kept the doors had gathered from the hand
of Manasseh and Ephraim, from all the
[b]remnant of Israel, from all Judah and Benjamin, and *which* they had brought back to
Jerusalem. 10Then they put *it* in the hand
of the foremen who had the oversight of
the house of the LORD; and they gave it to
the workmen who worked in the house of
the LORD, to repair and restore the house.
11They gave *it* to the craftsmen and builders
to buy hewn stone and timber for beams,
and to floor the houses which the kings of
Judah had destroyed. 12And the men did
the work faithfully. Their overseers *were*
Jahath and Obadiah the Levites, of the sons
of Merari, and Zechariah and Meshullam,
of the sons of the Kohathites, to supervise.
Others of the Levites, all of whom were skillful with instruments of music, 13*were* [a]over
the burden bearers and *were* overseers of
all who did work in any kind of service.
[b]And *some* of the Levites *were* scribes, officers, and gatekeepers.

33:18 [1] Literally *words* 33:19 [1] Septuagint reads *the seers.* 33:20 [a] 1 Kin. 1:21; 2 Kin. 21:18 33:21 [a] 2 Kin. 21:19–24; 1 Chr. 3:14 33:23 [a] 2 Chr. 33:12, 19 33:24 [a] 2 Kin. 21:23, 24; 2 Chr. 24:25 [b] 2 Chr. 25:27 34:1 [a] 2 Kin. 22:1, 2; Jer. 1:2; 3:6 34:3 [a] Eccl. 12:1 [b] 2 Chr. 15:2; [Prov. 8:17] [c] 1 Kin. 13:2 [d] 2 Chr. 33:17–19, 22 34:4 [a] Lev. 26:30; 2 Kin. 23:4 [b] 2 Kin. 23:6 34:5 [a] 1 Kin. 13:2 [b] 2 Kin. 23:20 34:6 [1] Literally *swords* 34:7 [a] Deut. 9:21 34:8 [a] 2 Kin. 22:3–20 [b] 2 Kin. 25:22 [c] 2 Chr. 18:25 [1] Literally *house* 34:9 [a] 2 Kin. 12:4 [b] 2 Chr. 30:6 34:13 [a] 2 Chr. 8:10 [b] 1 Chr. 23:4, 5

14 Now when they brought out the money that was brought into the house of the LORD, Hilkiah the priest [a]found the Book of the Law of the LORD *given* by Moses. 15 Then Hilkiah answered and said to Shaphan the scribe, "I have found the Book of the Law in the house of the LORD." And Hilkiah gave the [a]book to Shaphan. 16 So Shaphan carried the book to the king, bringing the king word, saying, "All that was committed to your servants they are doing. 17 And they have gathered the money that was found in the house of the LORD, and have delivered it into the hand of the overseers and the workmen." 18 Then Shaphan the scribe told the king, saying, "Hilkiah the priest has given me a book." And Shaphan read it before the king.

19 Thus it happened, when the king heard the words of the Law, that he tore his clothes. 20 Then the king commanded Hilkiah, [a]Ahikam the son of Shaphan, Abdon[1] the son of Micah, Shaphan the scribe, and Asaiah a servant of the king, saying, 21 "Go, inquire of the LORD for me, and for those who are left in Israel and Judah, concerning the words of the book that is found; for great *is* the wrath of the LORD that is poured out on us, because our fathers have not [a]kept the word of the LORD, to do according to all that is written in this book."

22 So Hilkiah and those the king *had appointed* went to Huldah the prophetess, the wife of Shallum the son of Tokhath,[1] the son of Hasrah,[2] keeper of the wardrobe. (She dwelt in Jerusalem in the Second Quarter.) And they spoke to her to that *effect.*

23 Then she answered them, "Thus says the LORD God of Israel, 'Tell the man who sent you to Me, 24 "Thus says the LORD: 'Behold, I will [a]bring calamity on this place and on its inhabitants, all the curses that are written in the [b]book which they have read before the king of Judah, 25 because they have forsaken Me and burned incense to other gods, that they might provoke Me to anger with all the works of their hands. Therefore My wrath will be poured out on this place, and not be quenched.'" ' 26 But as for the king of Judah, who sent you to inquire of the LORD, in this manner you shall speak to him, 'Thus says the LORD God of Israel: "*Concerning* the words which you have heard— 27 because your heart was tender, and you humbled yourself before God when you heard His words against this place and against its inhabitants, and you humbled yourself before Me, and you tore your clothes and wept before Me, I also have heard *you,*" says the [a]LORD. 28 "Surely I will gather you to your fathers, and you shall be gathered to your grave in peace; and your eyes shall not see all the calamity which I will bring on this place and its inhabitants." ' " So they brought back word to the king.

Josiah Restores True Worship
(2 Kin. 23:1–20)

29 [a]Then the king sent and gathered all the elders of Judah and Jerusalem. 30 The king went up to the house of the LORD, with all the men of Judah and the inhabitants of Jerusalem—the priests and the Levites, and all the people, great and small. And he [a]read in their hearing all the words of the Book of the Covenant which had been found in the house of the LORD. 31 Then the king [a]stood in [b]his place and made a [c]covenant before the LORD, to follow the LORD, and to keep His commandments and His testimonies and His statutes with all his heart and all his soul, to perform the words of the covenant that were written in this book. 32 And he made all who were present in Jerusalem and Benjamin take a stand. So the inhabitants of Jerusalem did according to the covenant of God, the God of their fathers. 33 Thus Josiah removed all the [a]abominations from all the country that *belonged* to the children of Israel, and made all who were present in Israel diligently serve the LORD their God. [b]All his days they did not depart from following the LORD God of their fathers.

Josiah Keeps the Passover
(2 Kin. 23:21–23)

35 Now [a]Josiah kept a Passover to the LORD in Jerusalem, and they slaughtered the Passover *lambs* on the

34:14 [a] 2 Kin. 22:8 34:15 [a] Deut. 31:24, 26 34:20 [a] Jer. 26:24 [1] *Achbor the son of Michaiah* in 2 Kings 22:12 34:21 [a] 2 Kin. 17:15–19 34:22 [1] Spelled *Tikvah* in 2 Kings 22:14 [2] Spelled *Harhas* in 2 Kings 22:14 34:24 [a] 2 Chr. 36:14–20 [b] Deut. 28:15–68 34:27 [a] 2 Kin. 22:19; 2 Chr. 12:7; 30:6; 33:12, 13 34:29 [a] 2 Kin. 23:1–3 34:30 [a] Neh. 8:1–3 34:31 [a] 2 Chr. 6:13 [b] 2 Kin. 11:14; 23:3; 2 Chr. 30:16 [c] 2 Chr. 23:16; 29:10 34:33 [a] 1 Kin. 11:5; 2 Chr. 33:2 [b] Jer. 3:10 35:1 [a] 2 Kin. 23:21, 22

[b]fourteenth *day* of the first month. 2And
he set the priests in their [a]duties and [b]en-
couraged them for the service of the house
of the LORD. 3Then he said to the Levites
[a]who taught all Israel, who were holy to
the LORD: [b]"Put the holy ark [c]in the house
which Solomon the son of David, king of Israel, built. [d]*It shall* no longer *be* a burden on
your shoulders. Now serve the LORD your
God and His people Israel. 4Prepare *your-*
selves [a]according to your fathers' houses,
according to your divisions, following the
[b]written instruction of David king of Israel
and the [c]written instruction of Solomon his
son. 5And [a]stand in the holy *place* according to the divisions of the fathers' houses of
your brethren the *lay* people, and *according*
to the division of the father's house of the
Levites. 6So slaughter the Passover *offer-*
ings, [a]consecrate yourselves, and prepare
them for your brethren, that *they* may do
according to the word of the LORD by the
hand of Moses."

7Then Josiah [a]gave the *lay* people lambs
and young goats from the flock, all for Passover *offerings* for all who were present, to
the number of thirty thousand, as well as
three thousand cattle; these *were* from the
king's [b]possessions. 8And his [a]leaders gave
willingly to the people, to the priests, and
to the Levites. Hilkiah, Zechariah, and Jehiel, rulers of the house of God, gave to
the priests for the Passover *offerings* two
thousand six hundred *from the flock,* and
three hundred cattle. 9Also [a]Conaniah,
his brothers Shemaiah and Nethanel, and
Hashabiah and Jeiel and Jozabad, chief of
the Levites, gave to the Levites for Passover
offerings five thousand *from the flock* and
five hundred cattle.

10So the service was prepared, and the
priests [a]stood in their places, and the [b]Le-
vites in their divisions, according to the
king's command. 11And they slaughtered
the Passover *offerings;* and the priests
[a]sprinkled *the blood* with their hands, while
the Levites [b]skinned *the animals.* 12Then
they removed the burnt offerings that *they*
might give them to the divisions of the fathers' houses of the *lay* people, to offer to
the LORD, as *it is* written [a]in the Book of Moses. And so *they did* with the cattle. 13Also
they [a]roasted the Passover *offerings* with
fire according to the ordinance; but the
other holy *offerings* they [b]boiled in pots, in
caldrons, and in pans, and divided *them*
quickly among all the *lay* people. 14Then
afterward they prepared portions for themselves and for the priests, because the
priests, the sons of Aaron, *were busy* in offering burnt offerings and fat until night;
therefore the Levites prepared portions for
themselves and for the priests, the sons of
Aaron. 15And the singers, the sons of Asaph,
were in their places, according to the [a]com-
mand of David, Asaph, Heman, and Jeduthun the king's seer. Also the gatekeepers
[b]were at each gate; they did not have to
leave their position, because their brethren the Levites prepared portions for them.

16So all the service of the LORD was prepared the same day, to keep the Passover
and to offer burnt offerings on the altar of
the LORD, according to the command of
King Josiah. 17And the children of Israel
who were present kept the Passover at that
time, and the Feast of [a]Unleavened Bread
for seven days. 18[a]There had been no Passover kept in Israel like that since the days
of Samuel the prophet; and none of the
kings of Israel had kept such a Passover
as Josiah kept, with the priests and the Levites, all Judah and Israel who were present, and the inhabitants of Jerusalem. 19In
the eighteenth year of the reign of Josiah
this Passover was kept.

Josiah Dies in Battle
(2 Kin. 23:28–30)

20[a]After all this, when Josiah had prepared the temple, Necho king of Egypt
came up to fight against [b]Carchemish by
the Euphrates; and Josiah went out against
him. 21But he sent messengers to him, saying, "What have I to do with you, king of
Judah? *I have* not *come* against you this

35:1 [b] Ex. 12:6; Num. 9:3; Ezra 6:19 35:2 [a] 2 Chr. 23:18; Ezra 6:18 [b] 2 Chr. 29:5–15 35:3 [a] Deut. 33:10; 2 Chr. 17:8, 9; Neh. 8:7 [b] 2 Chr. 34:14 [c] Ex. 40:21; 2 Chr. 5:7 [d] 1 Chr. 23:26 35:4 [a] 1 Chr. 9:10–13 [b] 1 Chr. 23—26 [c] 2 Chr. 8:14 35:5 [a] Ps. 134:1 35:6 [a] 2 Chr. 29:5, 15 35:7 [a] 2 Chr. 30:24 [b] 2 Chr. 31:3 35:8 [a] Num. 7:2 35:9 [a] 2 Chr. 31:12 35:10 [a] Ezra 6:18; Heb. 9:6 [b] 2 Chr. 5:12; 7:6; 8:14, 15; 13:10; 29:25–34 35:11 [a] Ex. 12:22; 2 Chr. 29:22 [b] 2 Chr. 29:34 35:12 [a] Lev. 3:3; Ezra 6:18 35:13 [a] Ex. 12:8, 9; Deut. 16:7 [b] 1 Sam. 2:13–15 35:15 [a] 1 Chr. 25:1–6 [b] 1 Chr. 9:17, 18 35:17 [a] Ex. 12:15; 13:6; 2 Chr. 30:21 35:18 [a] 2 Kin. 23:22, 23 35:20 [a] 2 Kin. 23:29 [b] Is. 10:9; Jer. 46:2

day, but against the house with which
I have war; for God commanded me to
make haste. Refrain *from meddling with*
God, who *is* with me, lest He destroy you."
22 Nevertheless Josiah would not turn his
face from him, but [a]disguised himself so
that he might fight with him, and did not
heed the words of Necho from the mouth
of God. So he came to fight in the Valley
of Megiddo.
23 And the archers shot King Josiah; and
the king said to his servants, "Take me
away, for I am severely wounded." 24 [a]His
servants therefore took him out of that
chariot and put him in the second chariot
that he had, and they brought him to Jerusalem. So he died, and was buried in *one of*
the tombs of his fathers. And [b]all Judah and
Jerusalem mourned for Josiah.
25 Jeremiah also [a]lamented for [b]Josiah.
And to this day [c]all the singing men and
the singing women speak of Josiah in their
lamentations. [d]They made it a custom in
Israel; and indeed they *are* written in the
Laments.
26 Now the rest of the acts of Josiah and
his goodness, according to *what was* written in the Law of the LORD, 27 and his deeds
from first to last, indeed they *are* written in
the book of the kings of Israel and Judah.

The Reign and Captivity of Jehoahaz
(2 Kin. 23:31–33)

36 Then [a]the people of the land took
Jehoahaz the son of Josiah, and
made him king in his father's place in Jerusalem. 2 Jehoahaz[1] *was* twenty-three years
old when he became king, and he reigned
three months in Jerusalem. 3 Now the king
of Egypt deposed him at Jerusalem; and he
imposed on the land a tribute of one hundred talents of silver and a talent of gold.
4 Then the king of Egypt made *Jehoahaz's*[1]
brother Eliakim king over Judah and Jerusalem, and changed his name to Jehoiakim.
And Necho took Jehoahaz[2] his brother and
carried him off to Egypt.

The Reign and Captivity of Jehoiakim
(2 Kin. 23:34—24:7)

5 [a]Jehoiakim *was* twenty-five years old
when he became king, and he reigned
eleven years in Jerusalem. And he did [b]evil
in the sight of the LORD his God. 6 [a]Neb-
uchadnezzar king of Babylon came up
against him, and bound him in bronze
fetters to [b]carry him off to Babylon. 7 [a]Neb-
uchadnezzar also carried off *some* of the
articles from the house of the LORD to
Babylon, and put them in his temple at
Babylon. 8 Now the rest of the acts of Jehoiakim, the abominations which he did, and
what was found against him, indeed they
are written in the book of the kings of Israel and Judah. Then Jehoiachin his son
reigned in his place.

The Reign and Captivity of Jehoiachin
(2 Kin. 24:8–17)

9 [a]Jehoiachin *was* eight[1] years old when
he became king, and he reigned in Jerusalem three months and ten days. And he did
evil in the sight of the LORD. 10 At the turn of
the year [a]King Nebuchadnezzar summoned
him and took him to Babylon, [b]with the
costly articles from the house of the LORD,
and made [c]Zedekiah, *Jehoiakim's*[1] brother,
king over Judah and Jerusalem.

Zedekiah Reigns in Judah
(2 Kin. 24:18–20; Jer. 52:1–3)

11 [a]Zedekiah *was* twenty-one years old
when he became king, and he reigned
eleven years in Jerusalem. 12 He did evil
in the sight of the LORD his God, *and* [a]did
not humble himself before Jeremiah the
prophet, *who spoke* from the mouth of the
LORD. 13 And he also [a]rebelled against King
Nebuchadnezzar, who had made him swear
an oath by God; but he [b]stiffened his neck
and hardened his heart against turning to
the LORD God of Israel. 14 Moreover all the
leaders of the priests and the people transgressed more and more, *according* to all the
abominations of the nations, and defiled

35:22 [a] 1 Kin. 22:30; 2 Chr. 18:29 35:24 [a] 2 Kin. 23:30 [b] 1 Kin. 14:18; Zech. 12:11 35:25 [a] Lam. 4:20 [b] Jer. 22:10, 11 [c] Matt. 9:23 [d] Jer. 22:20 36:1 [a] 2 Kin. 23:30–34 36:2 [1] Masoretic Text reads *Joahaz.* 36:4 [1] Literally *his* [2] Masoretic Text reads *Joahaz.* 36:5 [a] 2 Kin. 23:36, 37; 1 Chr. 3:15 [b] [Jer. 22:13–19] 36:6 [a] 2 Kin. 24:1; Hab. 1:6 [b] [Deut. 29:22–29]; 2 Chr. 33:11; Jer. 36:30 36:7 [a] 2 Kin. 24:13; Dan. 1:1, 2 36:9 [a] 2 Kin. 24:8–17 [1] Some Hebrew manuscripts, Septuagint, Syriac, and 2 Kings 24:8 read *eighteen.* 36:10 [a] 2 Kin. 24:10–17 [b] Dan. 1:1, 2 [c] Jer. 37:1 [1] Literally *his* (compare 2 Kings 24:17) 36:11 [a] 2 Kin. 24:18–20; Jer. 52:1 36:12 [a] Jer. 21:3–7; 44:10 36:13 [a] Jer. 52:3; Ezek. 17:15 [b] 2 Kin. 17:14; [2 Chr. 30:8]

the house of the LORD which He had consecrated in Jerusalem.

The Fall of Jerusalem
(2 Kin. 25:1–21; Jer. 52:4–30)

15[a]And the LORD God of their fathers sent
warnings to them by His messengers, rising up early and sending *them,* because He
had compassion on His people and on His
dwelling place. 16But [a]they mocked the messengers of God, [b]despised His words, and
[c]scoffed at His prophets, until the [d]wrath
of the LORD arose against His people, till
there was no remedy.
17[a]Therefore He brought against them
the king of the Chaldeans, who [b]killed
their young men with the sword in the
house of their sanctuary, and had no compassion on young man or virgin, on the
aged or the weak; He gave *them* all into
his hand. 18[a]And all the articles from the
house of God, great and small, the treasures of the house of the LORD, and the
treasures of the king and of his leaders,
all *these* he took to Babylon. 19[a]Then they
burned the house of God, broke down the
wall of Jerusalem, burned all its palaces
with fire, and destroyed all its precious
possessions. 20And [a]those who escaped
from the sword he carried away to Babylon, [b]where they became servants to him
and his sons until the rule of the kingdom
of Persia, 21to fulfill the word of the LORD
by the mouth of [a]Jeremiah, until the land
[b]had enjoyed her Sabbaths. As long as she
lay desolate [c]she kept Sabbath, to fulfill
seventy years.

The Proclamation of Cyrus
(Ezra 1:1–4)

22[a]Now in the first year of Cyrus king of
Persia, that the word of the LORD by the
mouth of [b]Jeremiah might be fulfilled, the
LORD stirred up the spirit of [c]Cyrus king
of Persia, so that he made a proclamation
throughout all his kingdom, and also *put
it* in writing, saying,

23 [a]Thus says Cyrus king of Persia:
All the kingdoms of the earth the
LORD God of heaven has given me.
And He has commanded me to build
Him a house at Jerusalem which is in
Judah. Who *is* among you of all His
people? May the LORD his God *be* with
him, and let him go up!

36:15 [a] Jer. 7:13; 25:3, 4 36:16 [a] 2 Chr. 30:10; Jer. 5:12, 13 [b] [Prov. 1:24–32] [c] Jer. 38:6; Matt. 23:34 [d] 2 Chr. 34:25; Ps. 79:5
36:17 [a] Num. 33:56; Deut. 4:26; 28:49; 2 Kin. 25:1; Ezra 9:7; Is. 3:8 [b] Ps. 74:20 36:18 [a] 2 Kin. 25:13–15; 2 Chr. 36:7, 10
36:19 [a] 2 Kin. 25:9; Ps. 79:1, 7; Is. 1:7, 8; Jer. 52:13 36:20 [a] 2 Kin. 25:11; Jer. 5:19; Mic. 4:10 [b] Jer. 17:4; 27:7
36:21 [a] Jer. 25:9–12; 27:6–8; 29:10 [b] Lev. 26:34–43; Dan. 9:2 [c] Lev. 25:4, 5
36:22 [a] Ezra 1:1–3 [b] Jer. 29:10 [c] Is. 44:28; 45:1 36:23 [a] Ezra 1:2, 3

THE BOOK OF

EZRA

OVERVIEW

The Book of Ezra is believed to have been written after 458 BC by the priest Ezra while the Israelites were exiled in Babylon. It was set during the reign of King Artaxerxes I. In this book, we read of the exiled Israelites returning to Jerusalem.

When King Cyrus of Persia overthrew the Babylonians, who had exiled the Israelites for seventy years, he proclaimed that the Israelites could return to Jerusalem to rebuild their temple (see Ezra 1:1–6). He even returned to them the vessels that had been stolen from their temple by King Nebuchadnezzar (see vv. 7–11). Over forty-two thousand Israelites set out for their homeland (see 2:64).

Once they had returned and settled, the Israelites restored worship (see 3:1–7) and began rebuilding the temple that had been destroyed seventy years before (see vv. 8–13). When their neighboring enemies heard they were repairing the temple, they asked to help (see 4:1–2). Angered that Israel's leaders refused their request, the enemies set out to oppose their construction project instead. Eventually, Artaxerxes, the king of Persia, commanded that the Israelites stop construction on the temple (see vv. 6–23). The work on the temple ceased until King Darius succeeded Artaxerxes (see v. 24). Under his reign, the Israelites completed and dedicated the temple (see 5:1—6:18).

While Artaxerxes was still in power, he sent Ezra, a descendant of Aaron, to Jerusalem to teach the people the Law that God had given to Moses (see 7:1–10). A group of Israelites went with him on his journey (see 8:1–14).

After arriving in Jerusalem, Ezra learned that the people, the priests, and the Levites had not separated themselves from the other inhabitants of the land. Instead, they had gone against God's covenant, taking wives from among the neighboring tribes (see 9:1–2). This news greatly disturbed Ezra, and he went to God and recounted the many failures of the Israelites despite God's faithfulness (see vv. 3–15).

In response to Ezra's prayer, the people confessed their sins against God (see 10:1–2). Ezra instructed them to separate themselves from the people around them, even their foreign wives, which they promised to do (see vv. 3–5). Ezra also made a proclamation instructing all exiles to gather in Jerusalem. Those who did not come to the city within three days would lose their property and be expelled (see vv. 7–8). When the people arrived, Ezra told them that they must follow the God of their ancestors and do His will. The Israelites agreed and followed the priest's instruction (see vv. 10–17).

The Book of Ezra is further evidence of God's faithfulness to His people. As promised, God brought the Israelites out of captivity and rejoined them as a single nation. He called for Ezra to teach His Law to the people. This book reinforces the mandate for God's people to separate themselves from nonbelievers. When the Israelites acknowledged their sins, God forgave and restored them.

BREATHE IT IN

The Israelites lived in exile for many years due to their disobedience and rebelliousness. In time, however, God restored them by moving the heart of a pagan king to release them, allowing them to return to Jerusalem to rebuild the temple. The Book of Ezra exemplifies God's commitment to keeping His promises to His people. Although He may discipline His people, God will never go back on His word.

Knowing that God will always keep His promises gives us hope for the future. None of us are perfect; we all have sinned and fallen short of the glory of God (see Rom. 3:23). Yet, we serve a God who forgives. As with the Israelites, He may discipline us for our rebellious ways, but He always gives us an opportunity to repent of our sins.

Returning to God and repairing the temples of our hearts is a common cycle in the lives of Christians. No matter how far away we stray and no matter what we do wrong, God always allows us to come back to Him. It does not matter how long we have been away from Him. God is always ready to forgive us and receive us back into the fold. He will even remind us of His Word and the covenant He made with us. He will remind us of how He is there to restore us and how we can dedicate ourselves to His service once more.

Our times of straying from God are not the only times when we will likely experience difficulty, though. Even when we are doing our best to follow God, we will often face opposition. Just as the Israelites had their plans interrupted by their enemies when they were building the temple, our enemy, Satan, often interrupts us as we follow God. And like we discover in Ezra, sometimes Satan uses those who appear to be for us to work against us.

How many times has God revealed to us that the people we thought were with us were actually working against us? Unfortunately, there are people around us who may not have our best interests at heart. They offer their full support to us, and they encourage us in our presence, but in our absence, they tear us down. We must be careful who we allow in our close circle. We must not be fooled by those who speak one way in our ear and another way in the ears of others. Rely on the discernment God gives you to help you identify those who wish to deceive you and hinder your progress.

Life always presents us with challenges. There are times when challenges can lead us to question God's faithfulness and even turn us away from Him. But do not allow the Enemy to distract you or dissuade you through these challenges. If you ever find yourself walking on a path different from the one God placed you on, remember you can always get back on track. Acknowledge your sins. Ask God to restore you to your place in the kingdom. Call upon the Lord, your God, and He will lead you back to Him. He will receive you with open arms.

†

THE BOOK OF

EZRA

End of the Babylonian Captivity
(2 Chr. 36:22, 23)

1 Now in the first year of Cyrus king of
Persia, that the word of the LORD [a]by
the mouth of Jeremiah might be fulfilled,
the LORD stirred up the spirit of Cyrus king
of Persia, [b]so that he made a proclamation
throughout all his kingdom, and also *put
it* in writing, saying,

2 Thus says Cyrus king of Persia:
All the kingdoms of the earth the
LORD God of heaven has given me.
And He has [a]commanded me to build
Him a house at Jerusalem which *is* in
Judah. 3 Who *is* among you of all His
people? May his God be with him, and
let him go up to Jerusalem which *is*
in Judah, and build the house of the
LORD God of Israel [a](He *is* God), which
is in Jerusalem. 4 And whoever is left in
any place where he dwells, let the men
of his place help him with silver and
gold, with goods and livestock, besides
the freewill offerings for the house of
God which *is* in Jerusalem.

5 Then the heads of the fathers' *houses*
of Judah and Benjamin, and the priests
and the Levites, with all whose spirits [a]God
had moved, arose to go up and build the
house of the LORD which *is* in Jerusalem.
6 And all those who *were* around them encouraged them with articles of silver and
gold, with goods and livestock, and with
precious things, besides all *that* was [a]will-
ingly offered.
7 [a]King Cyrus also brought out the
articles of the house of the LORD, [b]which
Nebuchadnezzar had taken from Jerusalem and put in the temple of his gods;
8 and Cyrus king of Persia brought them
out by the hand of Mithredath the treasurer, and counted them out to [a]Sheshbaz-
zar the prince of Judah. 9 This *is* the number
of them: thirty gold platters, one thousand
silver platters, twenty-nine knives, 10 thirty
gold basins, four hundred and ten silver
basins of a similar *kind, and* one thousand
other articles. 11 All the articles of gold and
silver *were* five thousand four hundred.
All *these* Sheshbazzar took with the captives who were brought from Babylon to
Jerusalem.

The Captives Who Returned to Jerusalem
(Neh. 7:6–73)

2 Now[1] [a]these *are* the people of the province who came back from the captiv-
ity, of those who had been carried away,
[b]whom Nebuchadnezzar the king of Babylon had carried away to Babylon, and who
returned to Jerusalem and Judah, everyone
to his *own* city.
2 *Those* who came with Zerubbabel *were*
Jeshua, Nehemiah, Seraiah, Reelaiah, Mordecai, Bilshan, Mispar,[1] Bigvai, Rehum,[2]
and Baanah. The number of the men of
the people of Israel: 3 the people of Parosh,
two thousand one hundred and seventy-
two; 4 the people of Shephatiah, three hundred and seventy-two; 5 the people of Arah,
[a]seven hundred and seventy-five; 6 the
people of [a]Pahath-Moab, of the people of
Jeshua *and* Joab, two thousand eight hundred and twelve; 7 the people of Elam, one

---

1:1 [a] 2 Chr. 36:22, 23; Jer. 25:12; 29:10 [b] Ezra 5:13, 14; Is. 44:28—45:13 1:2 [a] Is. 44:28; 45:1, 13 1:3 [a] 1 Kin. 8:23; 18:39; Is. 37:16; Dan. 6:26 1:5 [a] [Phil. 2:13] 1:6 [a] Ezra 2:68 1:7 [a] Ezra 5:14; 6:5; Dan. 1:2; 5:2, 3 [b] 2 Kin. 24:13; 2 Chr. 36:7, 18 1:8 [a] Ezra 5:14, 16
2:1 [a] Neh. 7:6–73; Jer. 32:15; 50:5; Ezek. 14:22 [b] 2 Kin. 24:14–16; 25:11; 2 Chr. 36:20 [1] Compare this chapter with Nehemiah 7:6–73.
2:2 [1] Spelled *Mispereth* in Nehemiah 7:7 [2] Spelled *Nehum* in Nehemiah 7:7 2:5 [a] Neh. 7:10 2:6 [a] Neh. 7:11

thousand two hundred and fifty-four; 8the
people of Zattu, nine hundred and forty-
five; 9the people of Zaccai, seven hundred
and sixty; 10the people of Bani,[1] six hundred and forty-two; 11the people of Bebai,
six hundred and twenty-three; 12the people
of Azgad, one thousand two hundred and
twenty-two; 13the people of Adonikam, six
hundred and sixty-six; 14the people of Bigvai, two thousand and fifty-six; 15the people
of Adin, four hundred and fifty-four; 16the
people of Ater of Hezekiah, ninety-eight;
17the people of Bezai, three hundred and
twenty-three; 18the people of Jorah,[1] one
hundred and twelve; 19the people of Hashum, two hundred and twenty-three; 20the
people of Gibbar,[1] ninety-five; 21the people
of Bethlehem, one hundred and twenty-
three; 22the men of Netophah, fifty-six;
23the men of Anathoth, one hundred and
twenty-eight; 24the people of Azmaveth,[1]
forty-two; 25the people of Kirjath Arim,[1]
Chephirah, and Beeroth, seven hundred
and forty-three; 26the people of Ramah
and Geba, six hundred and twenty-one;
27the men of Michmas, one hundred and
twenty-two; 28the men of Bethel and Ai, two
hundred and twenty-three; 29the people of
Nebo, fifty-two; 30the people of Magbish,
one hundred and fifty-six; 31the people of
the other [a]Elam, one thousand two hundred and fifty-four; 32the people of Harim,
three hundred and twenty; 33the people
of Lod, Hadid, and Ono, seven hundred
and twenty-five; 34the people of Jericho,
three hundred and forty-five; 35the people of Senaah, three thousand six hundred
and thirty.

36The priests: the sons of [a]Jedaiah, of
the house of Jeshua, nine hundred and

E Z R A 1:2

I AM CYRUS

Thus says Cyrus king of Persia: All the kingdoms of the earth the LORD God of heaven has given me. And He has commanded me to build Him a house at Jerusalem which is in Judah. Ezra 1:2

I am King Cyrus of Persia. I easily captured Babylon about seventy years after the people of Israel were taken there as captives by King Nebuchadnezzar. During the first year of my reign in Babylon, the Spirit of God came upon me strongly and commanded me to allow the rebuilding of His temple in Jerusalem. My spirit was so stirred up that I issued a written proclamation, decreeing that Jerusalem and the temple would be restored. I added the God of Israel to the long list of other gods I was willing to follow.

The first thing I was compelled to do was return all the sacred articles Nebuchadnezzar had taken from the temple in Jerusalem. I also released the nation of Israel from their exile in Babylon, allowing them to return to their homeland. Forty-two thousand Israelites returned to Jerusalem and walked its streets for the first time in seventy years.

I was amazed to learn that my actions toward Israel had been predicted by Jeremiah the prophet nearly eighty years before I ended their captivity.

✝

King Cyrus of Persia was used by God even though he was not devoted to Him. We should not mistake being part of God's plan with true faith in God. After all, God used a talking donkey once. Not all who are used by God are saved, but all who are saved are used. We can only enter the kingdom of God through faith. We are to serve Him and Him alone.

2:10 [1] Spelled *Binnui* in Nehemiah 7:15 2:18 [1] Called *Hariph* in Nehemiah 7:24 2:20 [1] Called *Gibeon* in Nehemiah 7:25
2:24 [1] Called *Beth Azmaveth* in Nehemiah 7:28 2:25 [1] Called *Kirjath Jearim* in Nehemiah 7:29
2:31 [a] Ezra 2:7 2:36 [a] 1 Chr. 24:7–18

seventy-three; 37the sons of [a]Immer, one
thousand and fifty-two; 38the sons of [a]Pash-
hur, one thousand two hundred and forty-
seven; 39the sons of [a]Harim, one thousand
and seventeen.

40The Levites: the sons of Jeshua and
Kadmiel, of the sons of Hodaviah,[1] seventy-
four.

41The singers: the sons of Asaph, one
hundred and twenty-eight.

42The sons of the gatekeepers: the sons
of Shallum, the sons of Ater, the sons of Talmon, the sons of Akkub, the sons of Hatita,
and the sons of Shobai, one hundred and
thirty-nine *in* all.

43[a]The Nethinim: the sons of Ziha, the
sons of Hasupha, the sons of Tabbaoth, 44the
sons of Keros, the sons of Siaha,[1] the sons of
Padon, 45the sons of Lebanah, the sons of
Hagabah, the sons of Akkub, 46the sons
of Hagab, the sons of Shalmai, the sons
of Hanan, 47the sons of Giddel, the
sons of Gahar, the sons of Reaiah, 48the
sons of Rezin, the sons of Nekoda, the sons
of Gazzam, 49the sons of Uzza, the sons of
Paseah, the sons of Besai, 50the sons of As-
nah, the sons of Meunim, the sons of Nephusim,[1] 51the sons of Bakbuk, the sons of
Hakupha, the sons of Harhur, 52the sons
of Bazluth,[1] the sons of Mehida, the sons
of Harsha, 53the sons of Barkos, the sons of
Sisera, the sons of Tamah, 54the sons of
Neziah, and the sons of Hatipha.

55The sons of [a]Solomon's servants: the
sons of Sotai, the sons of [b]Sophereth, the
sons of Peruda,[1] 56the sons of Jaala, the sons
of Darkon, the sons of Giddel, 57the sons of
Shephatiah, the sons of Hattil, the sons of
Pochereth of Zebaim, and the sons of Ami.[1]
58All the [a]Nethinim and the children of [b]Sol-
omon's servants were three hundred and
ninety-two.

59And these *were* the ones who came
up from Tel Melah, Tel Harsha, Cherub,
Addan,[1] and Immer; but they could not
identify their father's house or their genealogy,[2] whether they *were* of Israel: 60the
sons of Delaiah, the sons of Tobiah, and
the sons of Nekoda, six hundred and fifty-
two; 61and of the sons of the priests: the
sons of [a]Habaiah, the sons of Koz,[1] and the
sons of [b]Barzillai, who took a wife of the
daughters of Barzillai the Gileadite, and
was called by their name. 62These sought
their listing *among* those who were registered by genealogy, but they were not
found; [a]therefore they *were excluded* from
the priesthood as defiled. 63And the governor[1] said to them that they [a]should not eat
of the most holy things till a priest could
consult with the [b]Urim and Thummim.

64[a]The whole assembly together *was*
forty-two thousand three hundred *and*
sixty, 65besides their male and female servants, of whom *there were* seven thousand
three hundred and thirty-seven; and they
had two hundred men and women singers.
66Their horses *were* seven hundred and
thirty-six, their mules two hundred and
forty-five, 67their camels four hundred and
thirty-five, and *their* donkeys six thousand
seven hundred and twenty.

68[a]*Some* of the heads of the fathers'
houses, when they came to the house of
the LORD which *is* in Jerusalem, offered
freely for the house of God, to erect it in
its place: 69According to their ability, they
gave to the [a]treasury for the work sixty-one
thousand gold drachmas, five thousand
minas of silver, and one hundred priestly
garments.

70[a]So the priests and the Levites, *some*
of the people, the singers, the gatekeepers,
and the Nethinim, dwelt in their cities, and
all Israel in their cities.

Worship Restored at Jerusalem

3 And when the [a]seventh month had
come, and the children of Israel *were*
in the cities, the people gathered together
as one man to Jerusalem. 2Then Jeshua
the son of [a]Jozadak[1] and his brethren the
priests, [b]and Zerubbabel the son of [c]She-
altiel and his brethren, arose and built the
altar of the God of Israel, to offer burnt
offerings on it, as *it is* [d]written in the Law

2:37 [a] 1 Chr. 24:14 2:38 [a] 1 Chr. 9:12 2:39 [a] 1 Chr. 24:8 2:40 [1] Spelled *Hodevah* in Nehemiah 7:43 2:43 [a] 1 Chr. 9:2; Ezra 7:7 2:44 [1] Spelled *Sia* in Nehemiah 7:47 2:50 [1] Spelled *Nephishesim* in Nehemiah 7:52 2:52 [1] Spelled *Bazlith* in Nehemiah 7:54 2:55 [a] 1 Kin. 9:21 [b] Neh. 7:57–60 [1] Spelled *Perida* in Nehemiah 7:57 2:57 [1] Spelled *Amon* in Nehemiah 7:59 2:58 [a] Josh. 9:21, 27; 1 Chr. 9:2 [b] 1 Kin. 9:21 2:59 [1] Spelled *Addon* in Nehemiah 7:61 [2] Literally *seed* 2:61 [a] Neh. 7:63 [b] 2 Sam. 17:27; 1 Kin. 2:7 [1] Or *Hakkoz* 2:62 [a] Num. 3:10 2:63 [a] Lev. 22:2, 10, 15, 16 [b] Ex. 28:30; Num. 27:21 [1] Hebrew *Tirshatha* 2:64 [a] Neh. 7:66; Is. 10:22 2:68 [a] Ezra 1:6; 3:5; Neh. 7:70 2:69 [a] 1 Chr. 26:20; Ezra 8:25–35 2:70 [a] Ezra 6:16, 17; Neh. 7:73 3:1 [a] Neh. 7:73; 8:1, 2 3:2 [a] 1 Chr. 6:14, 15; Ezra 4:3; Neh. 12:1, 8; Hag. 1:1; 2:2 [b] Ezra 2:2; 4:2, 3; 5:2 [c] 1 Chr. 3:17 [d] Deut. 12:5, 6 [1] Spelled *Jehozadak* in 1 Chronicles 6:14

of Moses the man of God. 3Though fear
had come upon them because of the people of those countries, they set the altar
on its bases; and they offered [a]burnt offerings on it to the LORD, *both* the morning and evening burnt offerings. 4[a]They
also kept the Feast of Tabernacles, [b]as *it is*
written, and [c]*offered* the daily burnt offerings in the number required by ordinance
for each day. 5Afterwards *they offered* the
[a]regular burnt offering, and *those* for New
Moons and for all the appointed feasts of
the LORD that were consecrated, and *those*
of everyone who willingly offered a freewill
offering to the LORD. 6From the first day
of the seventh month they began to offer
burnt offerings to the LORD, although the
foundation of the temple of the LORD had
not been laid. 7They also gave money to
the masons and the carpenters, and [a]food,
drink, and oil to the people of Sidon and
Tyre to bring cedar logs from Lebanon to
the sea, to [b]Joppa, [c]according to the permission which they had from Cyrus king
of Persia.

Restoration of the Temple Begins

8Now in the second month of the second
year of their coming to the house of God
at Jerusalem, [a]Zerubbabel the son of Shealtiel, Jeshua the son of Jozadak,[1] and the
rest of their brethren the priests and the
Levites, and all those who had come out
of the captivity to Jerusalem, began *work*
[b]and appointed the Levites from twenty
years old and above to oversee the work of
the house of the LORD. 9Then Jeshua *with*
his sons and brothers, Kadmiel *with* his
sons, and the sons of Judah,[1] arose as one
to oversee those working on the house of
God: the sons of Henadad *with* their sons
and their brethren the Levites.

10When the builders laid the foundation of the temple of the LORD, [a]the priests
stood[1] in their apparel with trumpets, and
the Levites, the sons of Asaph, with cymbals, to praise the LORD, according to the
[b]ordinance of David king of Israel. 11[a]And
they sang responsively, praising and giving thanks to the LORD:

[b]"For *He is* good,
[c]For His mercy *endures* forever
toward Israel."[1]

Then all the people shouted with a great
shout, when they praised the LORD, because the foundation of the house of the
LORD was laid.

12But many of the priests and Levites
and [a]heads of the fathers' *houses,* old men
who had seen the first temple, wept with
a loud voice when the foundation of this
temple was laid before their eyes. Yet many
shouted aloud for joy, 13so that the people
could not discern the noise of the shout
of joy from the noise of the weeping of the
people, for the people shouted with a loud
shout, and the sound was heard afar off.

Resistance to Rebuilding the Temple

4 Now when [a]the adversaries of Judah and
Benjamin heard that the descendants of
the captivity were building the temple of the
LORD God of Israel, 2they came to Zerubbabel and the heads of the fathers' *houses,* and
said to them, "Let us build with you, for we
seek your God as you *do;* and we have sacrificed to Him [a]since the days of Esarhaddon
king of Assyria, who brought us here." 3But
Zerubbabel and Jeshua and the rest of the
heads of the fathers' *houses* of Israel said to
them, [a]"You may do nothing with us to build
a house for our God; but we alone will build
to the LORD God of Israel, as [b]King Cyrus the
king of Persia has commanded us." 4Then
[a]the people of the land tried to discourage
the people of Judah. They troubled them
in building, 5and hired counselors against
them to frustrate their purpose all the days
of Cyrus king of Persia, even until the reign
of [a]Darius king of Persia.

Rebuilding of Jerusalem Opposed

6In the reign of Ahasuerus, in the beginning of his reign, they wrote an accusation

---

3:3 [a] Num. 28:3 3:4 [a] Lev. 23:33–43; Neh. 8:14–18; Zech. 14:16 [b] Ex. 23:16 [c] Num. 29:12, 13 3:5 [a] Ex. 29:38; Num. 28:3, 11, 19, 26; Ezra 1:4; 2:68; 7:15, 16; 8:28 3:7 [a] 1 Kin. 5:6, 9; 2 Chr. 2:10; Acts 12:20 [b] 2 Chr. 2:16; Acts 9:36 [c] Ezra 1:2; 6:3 3:8 [a] Ezra 3:2; 4:3 [b] 1 Chr. 23:4, 24 [1] Spelled *Jehozadak* in 1 Chronicles 6:14 3:9 [1] Or *Hodaviah* (compare 2:40) 3:10 [a] 1 Chr. 16:5, 6 [b] 1 Chr. 6:31; 16:4; 25:1 [1] Following Septuagint, Syriac, and Vulgate; Masoretic Text reads *they stationed the priests.* 3:11 [a] Ex. 15:21; 2 Chr. 7:3; Neh. 12:24 [b] 1 Chr. 16:34; Ps. 136:1 [c] 1 Chr. 16:41; Jer. 33:11 [1] Compare Psalm 136:1 3:12 [a] Ezra 2:68 4:1 [a] Ezra 4:7–9 4:2 [a] 2 Kin. 17:24; 19:37; Ezra 4:10 4:3 [a] Neh. 2:20 [b] Ezra 1:1–4 4:4 [a] Ezra 3:3 4:5 [a] Ezra 5:5; 6:1

against the inhabitants of Judah and Jerusalem.

7In the days of [a]Artaxerxes also, Bish-
lam, Mithredath, Tabel, and the rest of their
companions wrote to Artaxerxes king of
Persia; and the letter *was* written in [b]Ar-
amaic script, and translated into the Aramaic language. 8Rehum[1] the commander
and Shimshai the scribe wrote a letter
against Jerusalem to King Artaxerxes in
this fashion:

9 From[1] Rehum the commander,
Shimshai the scribe, and the rest of
their companions—*representatives*
of [a]the Dinaites, the Apharsathchites,
the Tarpelites, the people of Persia
and Erech and Babylon and Shushan,[2]
the Dehavites, the Elamites, 10[a]and the
rest of the nations whom the great
and noble Osnapper took captive and
settled in the cities of Samaria and the
remainder beyond the River[1]—[b]and so
forth.[2]

11(This *is* a copy of the letter that they
sent him.)

To King Artaxerxes from your
servants, the men *of the region* beyond
the River, and so forth:[1]

12 Let it be known to the king that the
Jews who came up from you have
come to us at Jerusalem, and are
building the [a]rebellious and evil
city, and are finishing *its* [b]walls and
repairing the foundations. 13Let it
now be known to the king that, if this
city is built and the walls completed,
they will not pay [a]tax, tribute, or
custom, and the king's treasury will
be diminished. 14Now because we
receive support from the palace, it
was not proper for us to see the king's
dishonor; therefore we have sent and
informed the king, 15that search may
be made in the book of the records of
your fathers. And you will find in the
book of the records and know that
this city *is* a rebellious city, harmful
to kings and provinces, and that they
have incited sedition within the city in
former times, for which cause this city
was destroyed.

16 We inform the king that if this city is
rebuilt and its walls are completed,
the result will be that you will have no
dominion beyond the River.

17The king sent an answer:

To Rehum the commander, *to*
Shimshai the scribe, *to* the rest of
their companions who dwell in
Samaria, and *to* the remainder
beyond the River:

Peace, and so forth.[1]

18 The letter which you sent to us has
been clearly read before me. 19And
I gave the command, and a search
has been made, and it was found
that this city in former times has
revolted against kings, and rebellion
and sedition have been fostered in it.
20There have also been mighty kings
over Jerusalem, who have [a]ruled over
all *the region* [b]beyond the River; and
tax, tribute, and custom were paid
to them. 21Now give the command to
make these men cease, that this city
may not be built until the command is
given by me.

22 Take heed now that you do not fail to
do this. Why should damage increase
to the hurt of the kings?

23Now when the copy of King Artaxerxes'
letter *was* read before Rehum, Shimshai the
scribe, and their companions, they went up
in haste to Jerusalem against the Jews, and
by force of arms made them cease. 24Thus
the work of the house of God which *is* at
Jerusalem ceased, and it was discontinued
until the second year of the reign of Darius
king of Persia.

4:7 [a] Ezra 7:1, 7, 21 [b] 2 Kin. 18:26 4:8 [1] The original language of Ezra 4:8 through 6:18 is Aramaic. 4:9 [a] 2 Kin. 17:30, 31 [1] Literally *Then* [2] Or *Susa* 4:10 [a] 2 Kin. 17:24; Ezra 4:1 [b] Ezra 4:11, 17; 7:12 [1] That is, the Euphrates [2] Literally *and now* 4:11 [1] Literally *and now* 4:12 [a] 2 Chr. 36:13 [b] Ezra 5:3, 9 4:13 [a] Ezra 4:20; 7:24 4:17 [1] Literally *and now* 4:20 [a] 1 Kin. 4:21; 1 Chr. 18:3; Ps. 72:8 [b] Gen. 15:18; Josh. 1:4

Restoration of the Temple Resumed
(Hab. 1:1; Zech. 1:1)

5 Then the prophet [a]Haggai and [b]Zechariah the son of Iddo, prophets, prophesied to the Jews who *were* in Judah and Jerusalem, in the name of the God of Israel, *who was* over them. 2So [a]Zerubbabel the son of Shealtiel and Jeshua the son of Jozadak[1] rose up and began to build the house of God which *is* in Jerusalem; and [b]the prophets of God *were* with them, helping them.

3At the same time [a]Tattenai the governor of *the region* beyond the River[1] and Shethar-Boznai and their companions came to them and spoke thus to them: [b]"Who has commanded you to build this temple and finish this wall?" 4[a]Then, accordingly, we told them the names of the men who were constructing this building. 5But [a]the eye of their God was upon the elders of the Jews, so that they could not make them cease till a report could go to Darius. Then a [b]written answer was returned concerning this *matter.* 6This is a copy of the letter that Tattenai sent:

The governor of *the region* beyond the River, and Shethar-Boznai, [a]and his companions, the Persians who *were in the region* beyond the River, to Darius the king.

7(They sent a letter to him, in which was written thus.)

To Darius the king:

All peace.

8 Let it be known to the king that we went into the province of Judea, to the temple of the great God, which is being built with heavy stones, and timber is being laid in the walls; and this work goes on diligently and prospers in their hands.

9 Then we asked those elders, *and* spoke thus to them: [a]"Who commanded you to build this temple and to finish these walls?" 10We also asked them their names to inform you, that we might write the names of the men who *were* chief among them.

11 And thus they returned us an answer, saying: "We are the servants of the God of heaven and earth, and we are rebuilding the temple that was built many years ago, which a great king of Israel built [a]and completed. 12But [a]because our fathers provoked the God of heaven to wrath, He gave them into the hand of [b]Nebuchadnezzar king of Babylon, the Chaldean, *who* destroyed this temple and [c]carried the people away to Babylon. 13However, in the first year of [a]Cyrus king of Babylon, King Cyrus issued a decree to build this house of God. 14Also, [a]the gold and silver articles of the house of God, which Nebuchadnezzar had taken from the temple that *was* in Jerusalem and carried into the temple of Babylon—those King Cyrus took from the temple of Babylon, and they were given to [b]one named Sheshbazzar, whom he had made governor. 15And he said to him, 'Take these articles; go, carry them to the temple *site* that *is* in Jerusalem, and let the house of God be rebuilt on its former site.' 16Then the same Sheshbazzar came *and* [a]laid the foundation of the house of God which *is* in Jerusalem; but from that time even until now it has been under construction, and [b]it is not finished."

17 Now therefore, if *it seems* good to the king, [a]let a search be made in the king's treasure house, which *is* there in Babylon, whether it is *so* that a decree was issued by King Cyrus to build this house of God at Jerusalem, and let the king send us his pleasure concerning this *matter.*

5:1 [a] Hag. 1:1 [b] Zech. 1:1 5:2 [a] Ezra 3:2; Hag. 1:12 [b] Ezra 6:14; Hag. 2:4 [1] Spelled *Jehozadak* in 1 Chronicles 6:14 5:3 [a] Ezra 5:6; 6:6 [b] Ezra 1:3; 5:9 [1] That is, the Euphrates 5:4 [a] Ezra 5:10 5:5 [a] 2 Chr. 16:9; Ezra 7:6, 28; Ps. 33:18 [b] Ezra 6:6 5:6 [a] Ezra 4:7–10 5:9 [a] Ezra 5:3, 4 5:11 [a] 1 Kin. 6:1, 38 5:12 [a] 2 Chr. 34:25; 36:16, 17 [b] 2 Kin. 24:2; 25:8–11; 2 Chr. 36:17; Jer. 52:12–15 [c] Jer. 13:19 5:13 [a] Ezra 1:1 5:14 [a] Ezra 1:7, 8; 6:5; Dan. 5:2 [b] Hag. 1:14; 2:2, 21 5:16 [a] Ezra 3:8–10; Hag. 2:18 [b] Ezra 6:15 5:17 [a] Ezra 6:1, 2

The Decree of Darius

6 Then King Darius issued a decree, [a]and
a search was made in the archives,[1]
where the treasures were stored in Babylon. 2 And at Achmetha,[1] in the palace
that *is* in the province of [a]Media, a scroll
was found, and in it a record *was* written
thus:

3 In the first year of King Cyrus, King
Cyrus issued a [a]decree *concerning*
the house of God at Jerusalem: "Let
the house be rebuilt, the place where
they offered sacrifices; and let the
foundations of it be firmly laid, its
height sixty cubits *and* its width sixty
cubits, 4 [a]*with* three rows of heavy
stones and one row of new timber. Let
the [b]expenses be paid from the king's
treasury. 5 Also let [a]the gold and silver
articles of the house of God, which
Nebuchadnezzar took from the temple
which *is* in Jerusalem and brought to
Babylon, be restored and taken back to
the temple which *is* in Jerusalem, *each*
to its place; and deposit *them* in the
house of God"—

6 [a]Now *therefore,* Tattenai, governor of
the region beyond the River, and
Shethar-Boznai, and your companions
the Persians who *are* beyond the River,
keep yourselves far from there. 7 Let
the work of this house of God alone;
let the governor of the Jews and the
elders of the Jews build this house of
God on its site.

8 Moreover I issue a decree *as to* what
you shall do for the elders of these
Jews, for the building of this house of
God: Let the cost be paid at the king's
expense from taxes *on the region*
beyond the River; this is to be given
immediately to these men, so that
they are not hindered. 9 And whatever
they need—young bulls, rams, and
lambs for the burnt offerings of the
God of heaven, wheat, salt, wine, and
oil, according to the request of the
priests who *are* in Jerusalem—let it
be given them day by day without
fail, 10 [a]that they may offer sacrifices
of sweet aroma to the God of heaven,
and pray for the life of the king and his
sons.

11 Also I issue a decree that whoever
alters this edict, let a timber be pulled
from his house and erected, and let
him be hanged on it; [a]and let his
house be made a refuse heap because
of this. 12 And may the God who causes
His [a]name to dwell there destroy any
king or people who put their hand
to alter it, or to destroy this house
of God which is in Jerusalem. I
Darius issue a decree; let it be done
diligently.

The Temple Completed and Dedicated

13 Then Tattenai, governor of *the region*
beyond the River, Shethar-Boznai, and their
companions diligently did according to
what King Darius had sent. 14 [a]So the elders of the Jews built, and they prospered
through the prophesying of Haggai the
prophet and Zechariah the son of Iddo. And
they built and finished *it,* according to the
commandment of the God of Israel, and
according to the command of [b]Cyrus, [c]Da-
rius, and [d]Artaxerxes king of Persia. 15 Now
the temple was finished on the third day of
the month of Adar, which was in the sixth
year of the reign of King Darius. 16 Then the
children of Israel, the priests and the Levites and the rest of the descendants of the
captivity, celebrated [a]the dedication of this
house of God with joy. 17 And they [a]offered
sacrifices at the dedication of this house of
God, one hundred bulls, two hundred rams,
four hundred lambs, and as a sin offering
for all Israel twelve male goats, according
to the number of the tribes of Israel. 18 They
assigned the priests to their [a]divisions and
the Levites to their [b]divisions, over the service of God in Jerusalem, [c]as it is written in
the Book of Moses.

6:1 [a] Ezra 5:17 [1] Literally *house of the scrolls* 6:2 [a] 2 Kin. 17:6 [1] Probably *Ecbatana,* the ancient capital of Media 6:3 [a] Ezra 1:1; 5:13
6:4 [a] 1 Kin. 6:36 [b] Ezra 3:7 6:5 [a] Ezra 1:7, 8; 5:14 6:6 [a] Ezra 5:3, 6 6:10 [a] Ezra 7:23; [Jer. 29:7; 1 Tim. 2:1, 2] 6:11 [a] Dan. 2:5; 3:29
6:12 [a] Deut. 12:5, 11; 1 Kin. 9:3 6:14 [a] Ezra 5:1, 2 [b] Ezra 1:1; 5:13; 6:3 [c] Ezra 4:24; 6:12 [d] Ezra 7:1, 11; Neh. 2:1
6:16 [a] 1 Kin. 8:63; 2 Chr. 7:5 6:17 [a] Ezra 8:35 6:18 [a] 1 Chr. 24:1; 2 Chr. 35:5
[b] 1 Chr. 23:6 [c] Num. 3:6; 8:9

The Passover Celebrated
(cf. Deut. 16:1–8)

19 And the descendants of the captivity kept the Passover [a]on the fourteenth *day* of the first month. 20 For the priests and the Levites had [a]purified themselves; all of them *were ritually* clean. And they [b]slaughtered the Passover *lambs* for all the descendants of the captivity, for their brethren the priests, and for themselves. 21 Then the children of Israel who had returned from the captivity ate together with all who had separated themselves from the [a]filth of the nations of the land in order to seek the LORD God of Israel. 22 And they kept the [a]Feast of Unleavened Bread seven days with joy; for the LORD made them joyful, and [b]turned the heart [c]of the king of Assyria toward them, to strengthen their hands in the work of the house of God, the God of Israel.

The Arrival of Ezra

7 Now after these things, in the reign of [a]Artaxerxes king of Persia, Ezra the [b]son of Seraiah, [c]the son of Azariah, the son of [d]Hilkiah, 2 the son of Shallum, the son of Zadok, the son of Ahitub, 3 the son of Amariah, the son of Azariah, the son of Meraioth, 4 the son of Zerahiah, the son of Uzzi, the son of Bukki, 5 the son of Abishua, the son of Phinehas, the son of Eleazar, the son of Aaron the chief priest— 6 this Ezra came up from Babylon; and he *was* [a]a skilled scribe in the Law of Moses, which the LORD God of Israel had given. The king granted him all his request, [b]according to the hand of the LORD his God upon him. 7 [a]*Some* of the children of Israel, the priests, [b]the Levites, the singers, the gatekeepers, and [c]the Nethinim came up to Jerusalem in the seventh year of King Artaxerxes. 8 And Ezra came to Jerusalem in the fifth month, which *was* in the seventh year of the king. 9 On the first *day* of the first month he began *his* journey from Babylon, and on the first *day* of the fifth month he came to Jerusalem, [a]according to the good hand of his God upon him. 10 For Ezra had prepared his heart to [a]seek the Law of the LORD, and to do *it,* and to [b]teach statutes and ordinances in Israel.

The Letter of Artaxerxes to Ezra

11 This *is* a copy of the letter that King Artaxerxes gave Ezra the priest, the scribe, expert in the words of the commandments of the LORD, and of His statutes to Israel:

12 Artaxerxes,[1] [a]king of kings,

To Ezra the priest, a scribe of the Law of the God of heaven:

Perfect *peace,* [b]and so forth.[2]

13 I issue a decree that all those of the people of Israel and the priests and Levites in my realm, who volunteer to go up to Jerusalem, may go with you. 14 And whereas you are being sent by the king and his [a]seven counselors to inquire concerning Judah and Jerusalem, with regard to the Law of your God which *is* in your hand; 15 and *whereas you are* to carry the silver and gold which the king and his counselors have freely offered to the God of Israel, [a]whose dwelling *is* in Jerusalem; 16 [a]and *whereas* all the silver and gold that you may find in all the province of Babylon, along with the freewill offering of the people and the priests, *are to be* [b]freely offered for the house of their God in Jerusalem— 17 now therefore, be careful to buy with this money bulls, rams, and lambs, with their [a]grain offerings and their drink offerings, and [b]offer them on the altar of the house of your God in Jerusalem.

18 And whatever seems good to you and your brethren to do with the rest of the silver and the gold, do it according to the will of your God. 19 Also the articles that are given to you for the

---

6:19 [a] Ex. 12:6 6:20 [a] 2 Chr. 29:34; 30:15 [b] 2 Chr. 35:11 6:21 [a] Ezra 9:11 6:22 [a] Ex. 12:15; 13:6, 7; 2 Chr. 30:21; 35:17 [b] Ezra 7:27; [Prov. 21:1] [c] 2 Kin. 23:29; 2 Chr. 33:11; Ezra 1:1; 6:1 7:1 [a] Neh. 2:1 [b] 1 Chr. 6:14 [c] Jer. 52:24 [d] 2 Chr. 35:8 7:6 [a] Ezra 7:11, 12, 21 [b] Ezra 7:9, 28; 8:22 7:7 [a] Ezra 8:1–14 [b] Ezra 8:15 [c] Ezra 2:43; 8:20 7:9 [a] Ezra 7:6; Neh. 2:8, 18 7:10 [a] Ps. 119:45 [b] Deut. 33:10; Ezra 7:6, 25; Neh. 8:1–8; [Mal. 2:7] 7:12 [a] Ezek. 26:7; Dan. 2:37 [b] Ezra 4:10 [1] The original language of Ezra 7:12–26 is Aramaic. [2] Literally *and now* 7:14 [a] Esth. 1:14 7:15 [a] 2 Chr. 6:2; Ezra 6:12; Ps. 135:21 7:16 [a] Ezra 8:25 [b] 1 Chr. 29:6, 9 7:17 [a] Num. 15:4–13 [b] Deut. 12:5–11

service of the house of your God,
deliver in full before the God of
Jerusalem. 20And whatever more
may be needed for the house of your
God, which you may have occasion
to provide, pay *for it* from the king's
treasury.

21 And I, *even* I, Artaxerxes the king,
issue a decree to all the treasurers
who *are in the region* beyond the
River, that whatever Ezra the priest,
the scribe of the Law of the God of
heaven, may require of you, let it be
done diligently, 22up to one hundred
talents of silver, one hundred kors of
wheat, one hundred baths of wine,
one hundred baths of oil, and salt
without prescribed limit. 23Whatever
is commanded by the God of heaven,
let it diligently be done for the house
of the God of heaven. For why should
there be wrath against the realm of
the king and his sons?

24 Also we inform you that it shall not
be lawful to impose tax, tribute, or
custom on any of the priests, Levites,
singers, gatekeepers, Nethinim, or
servants of this house of God. 25And
you, Ezra, according to your God-given
wisdom, [a]set magistrates and judges
who may judge all the people who *are
in the region* beyond the River, all such
as know the laws of your God; and
[b]teach those who do not know *them.*
26Whoever will not observe the law
of your God and the law of the king,
let judgment be executed speedily
on him, whether *it be* death, or
banishment, or confiscation of goods,
or imprisonment.

27[a]Blessed *be* the LORD God of our fathers, [b]who has put *such a thing* as this in
the king's heart, to beautify the house of
the LORD which *is* in Jerusalem, 28and [a]has
extended mercy to me before the king and
his counselors, and before all the king's
mighty princes.

So I was encouraged, as [b]the hand of the
LORD my God *was* upon me; and I gathered
leading men of Israel to go up with me.

Heads of Families Who Returned with Ezra

8 These *are* the heads of their fathers'
houses, and *this is* the genealogy of
those who went up with me from Babylon,
in the reign of King Artaxerxes: 2of the sons
of Phinehas, Gershom; of the sons of Ithamar, Daniel; of the sons of David, [a]Hat-
tush; 3of the sons of Shecaniah, of the sons
of [a]Parosh, Zechariah; and registered with
him *were* one hundred and fifty males; 4of
the sons of [a]Pahath-Moab, Eliehoenai the
son of Zerahiah, and with him two hundred
males; 5of the sons of Shechaniah,[1] Ben-Ja-
haziel, and with him three hundred males;
6of the sons of Adin, Ebed the son of Jonathan, and with him fifty males; 7of the sons
of Elam, Jeshaiah the son of Athaliah, and
with him seventy males; 8of the sons of
Shephatiah, Zebadiah the son of Michael,
and with him eighty males; 9of the sons of
Joab, Obadiah the son of Jehiel, and with
him two hundred and eighteen males; 10of
the sons of Shelomith,[1] Ben-Josiphiah, and
with him one hundred and sixty males; 11of
the sons of [a]Bebai, Zechariah the son of
Bebai, and with him twenty-eight males;
12of the sons of Azgad, Johanan the son of
Hakkatan, and with him one hundred and
ten males; 13of the last sons of Adonikam,
whose names *are* these—Eliphelet, Jeiel,
and Shemaiah—and with them sixty males;
14also of the sons of Bigvai, Uthai and Zab-
bud, and with them seventy males.

Servants for the Temple

15Now I gathered them by the river that
flows to Ahava, and we camped there three
days. And I looked among the people and
the priests, and found none of the [a]sons of
Levi there. 16Then I sent for Eliezer, Ariel,
Shemaiah, Elnathan, Jarib, Elnathan, Nathan, Zechariah, and [a]Meshullam, leaders; also for Joiarib and Elnathan, men of
understanding. 17And I gave them a command for Iddo the chief man at the place

7:25 [a] Ex. 18:21, 22; Deut. 16:18 [b] 2 Chr. 17:7; Ezra 7:10; [Mal. 2:7; Col. 1:28] 7:27 [a] 1 Chr. 29:10 [b] Ezra 6:22; [Prov. 21:1] 7:28 [a] Ezra 9:9 [b] Ezra 5:5; 7:6, 9; 8:18 8:2 [a] 1 Chr. 3:22; Ezra 2:68 8:3 [a] Ezra 2:3 8:4 [a] Ezra 10:30 8:5 [1] Following Masoretic Text and Vulgate; Septuagint reads *the sons of Zatho, Shechaniah.* 8:10 [1] Following Masoretic Text and Vulgate; Septuagint reads *the sons of Banni, Shelomith.* 8:11 [a] Ezra 10:28 8:15 [a] Ezra 7:7; 8:2 8:16 [a] Ezra 10:15

Casiphia, and I told them what they should
say to Iddo *and* his brethren[1] the Nethinim
at the place Casiphia—that they should
bring us servants for the house of our God.
18Then, by the good hand of our God upon
us, they [a]brought us a man of understanding, of the sons of Mahli the son of Levi,
the son of Israel, namely Sherebiah, with
his sons and brothers, eighteen men; 19and
[a]Hashabiah, and with him Jeshaiah of the
sons of Merari, his brothers and their sons,
twenty men; 20[a]also of the Nethinim, whom
David and the leaders had appointed for
the service of the Levites, two hundred and
twenty Nethinim. All of them were designated by name.

Fasting and Prayer for Protection

21Then I [a]proclaimed a fast there at the
river of Ahava, that we might [b]humble ourselves before our God, to seek from Him
the [c]right way for us and our little ones and
all our possessions. 22For [a]I was ashamed
to request of the king an escort of soldiers
and horsemen to help us against the enemy on the road, because we had spoken
to the king, saying, [b]"The hand of our God
is upon all those for [c]good who seek Him,
but His power and His wrath *are* [d]against
all those who [e]forsake Him." 23So we fasted
and entreated our God for this, and He [a]an-
swered our prayer.

Gifts for the Temple

24And I separated twelve of the leaders
of the priests—Sherebiah, Hashabiah, and
ten of their brethren with them— 25and
weighed out to them [a]the silver, the gold,
and the articles, the offering for the house
of our God which the king and his counselors and his princes, and all Israel *who were*
present, had offered. 26I weighed into their
hand six hundred and fifty talents of silver,
silver articles *weighing* one hundred talents, one hundred talents of gold, 27twenty
gold basins *worth* a thousand drachmas,
and two vessels of fine polished bronze,
precious as gold. 28And I said to them,
"You *are* [a]holy to the LORD; the articles
are [b]holy also; and the silver and the gold
are a freewill offering to the LORD God of
your fathers. 29Watch and keep *them* until
you weigh *them* before the leaders of the
priests and the Levites and [a]heads of the
fathers' *houses* of Israel in Jerusalem, *in*
the chambers of the house of the LORD."
30So the priests and the Levites received
the silver and the gold and the articles by
weight, to bring *them* to Jerusalem to the
house of our God.

The Return to Jerusalem

31Then we departed from the river of
Ahava on the twelfth *day* of the first month,
to go to Jerusalem. And [a]the hand of our
God was upon us, and He delivered us from
the hand of the enemy and from ambush
along the road. 32So we [a]came to Jerusalem, and stayed there three days.

33Now on the fourth day the silver and
the gold and the articles were [a]weighed in
the house of our God by the hand of Meremoth the son of Uriah the priest, and with
him *was* Eleazar the son of Phinehas; with
them *were* the Levites, [b]Jozabad the son
of Jeshua and Noadiah the son of Binnui,
34with the number *and* weight of everything. All the weight was written down at
that time.

35The children of those who had been
[a]carried away captive, who had come from
the captivity, [b]offered burnt offerings to
the God of Israel: twelve bulls for all Israel,
ninety-six rams, seventy-seven lambs, and
twelve male goats *as* a sin offering. All *this*
was a burnt offering to the LORD.

36And they delivered the king's [a]orders
to the king's satraps and the governors *in*
the region beyond the River. So they gave
support to the people and the house of God.

Intermarriage with Pagans

9 When these things were done, the leaders came to me, saying, "The people
of Israel and the priests and the Levites
have not [a]separated themselves from the

8:17 [1] Following Vulgate; Masoretic Text reads *to Iddo his brother;* Septuagint reads *to their brethren.* 8:18 [a] 2 Chr. 30:22; Neh. 8:7
8:19 [a] Neh. 12:24 8:20 [a] Ezra 2:43; 7:7 8:21 [a] 1 Sam. 7:6; 2 Chr. 20:3 [b] Lev. 16:29; 23:29; Is. 58:3, 5 [c] Ps. 5:8 8:22 [a] 1 Cor. 9:15
[b] Ezra 7:6, 9, 28 [c] [Ps. 33:18, 19; 34:15, 22; Rom. 8:28] [d] [Ps. 34:16] [e] [2 Chr. 15:2] 8:23 [a] [1 Chr. 5:20];
2 Chr. 33:13; Is. 19:22 8:25 [a] Ezra 7:15, 16 8:28 [a] Lev. 21:6–9; Deut. 33:8 [b] Lev. 22:2, 3; Num. 4:4, 15, 19, 20
8:29 [a] Ezra 4:3 8:31 [a] Ezra 7:6, 9, 28 8:32 [a] Neh. 2:11 8:33 [a] Ezra 8:26, 30 [b] Neh. 11:16
8:35 [a] Ezra 2:1 [b] Ezra 6:17 8:36 [a] Ezra 7:21–24 9:1 [a] Ezra 6:21; Neh. 9:2

peoples of the lands, [b]with respect to the abominations of the Canaanites, the Hittites, the Perizzites, the Jebusites, the Ammonites, the Moabites, the Egyptians, and the Amorites. 2For they have [a]taken some of their daughters *as wives* for themselves and their sons, so that the [b]holy seed is [c]mixed with the peoples of *those* lands. Indeed, the hand of the leaders and rulers has been foremost in this trespass." 3So when I heard this thing, [a]I tore my garment and my robe, and plucked out some of the hair of my head and beard, and sat down [b]astonished. 4Then everyone who [a]trembled at the words of the God of Israel assembled to me, because of the transgression of those who had been carried away captive, and I sat astonished until the [b]evening sacrifice.

5At the evening sacrifice I arose from my fasting; and having torn my garment and my robe, I fell on my knees and [a]spread out my hands to the LORD my God. 6And I said: "O my God, I am too [a]ashamed and humiliated to lift up my face to You, my God; for [b]our iniquities have risen higher than *our* heads, and our guilt has [c]grown up to the heavens. 7Since the days of our fathers to this day [a]we *have been* very guilty, and for our iniquities [b]we, our kings, *and* our priests have been delivered into the hand of the kings of the lands, to the [c]sword, to captivity, to plunder, and to [d]humiliation, as *it is* this day. 8And now for a little while grace has been *shown* from the LORD our God, to leave us a remnant to escape, and to give us a peg in His holy place, that our God may [a]enlighten our eyes and give us a measure of revival in our bondage. 9[a]For we *were* slaves. [b]Yet our God did not forsake us in our bondage; but [c]He extended mercy to us in the sight of the kings of Persia, to revive us, to repair the house of our God, to rebuild its ruins, and to give us [d]a wall in Judah and Jerusalem. 10And now, O our God, what shall we say after this? For we have forsaken Your commandments, 11which You commanded by Your servants the prophets, saying, 'The land which you are entering to possess is an unclean land, with the [a]uncleanness of the peoples of the lands, with their abominations which have filled it from one end to another with their impurity. 12Now therefore, [a]do not give your daughters as wives for their sons, nor take their daughters to your sons; and [b]never seek their peace or prosperity, that you may be strong and eat the good of the land, and [c]leave *it* as an inheritance to your children forever.' 13And after all that has come upon us for our evil deeds and for our great guilt, since You our God [a]have punished us less than our iniquities *deserve,* and have given us *such* deliverance as this, 14should we [a]again break Your commandments, and [b]join in marriage with the people *committing* these abominations? Would You not be [c]angry with us until You had consumed *us,* so that *there would be* no remnant or survivor? 15O LORD God of Israel, [a]You *are* righteous, for we are left as a remnant, as *it is* this day. [b]Here we *are* before You, [c]in our guilt, though no one can stand before You because of this!"

Confession of Improper Marriages

10 Now [a]while Ezra was praying, and while he was confessing, weeping, and bowing down [b]before the house of God, a very large assembly of men, women, and children gathered to him from Israel; for the people wept very [c]bitterly. 2And Shechaniah the son of Jehiel, *one* of the sons of Elam, spoke up and said to Ezra, "We have [a]trespassed against our God, and have taken pagan wives from the peoples of the land; yet now there is hope in Israel in spite of this. 3Now therefore, let us make [a]a covenant with our God to put away all these wives and those who have been born to them, according to the advice of my master and of those who [b]tremble at [c]the commandment of our God; and let it be done according to the [d]law. 4Arise, for *this* matter *is* your *responsibility.* We also *are* with you. [a]Be of good courage, and do *it.*"

5Then Ezra arose, and made the leaders

9:1 [b] Deut. 12:30, 31 9:2 [a] Ex. 34:16; [Deut. 7:3]; Ezra 10:2; Neh. 13:23 [b] Ex. 22:31; [Deut. 7:6] [c] [2 Cor. 6:14] 9:3 [a] Job 1:20 [b] Ps. 143:4 9:4 [a] Ezra 10:3; Is. 66:2 [b] Ex. 29:39 9:5 [a] Ex. 9:29 9:6 [a] Dan. 9:7, 8 [b] Ps. 38:4 [c] 2 Chr. 28:9; [Ezra 9:13, 15]; Rev. 18:5 9:7 [a] 2 Chr. 36:14–17; Ps. 106:6; Dan. 9:5, 6 [b] Deut. 28:36; Neh. 9:30 [c] Deut. 32:25 [d] Dan. 9:7, 8 9:8 [a] Ps. 34:5 9:9 [a] Neh. 9:36; Esth. 7:4 [b] Neh. 9:17; Ps. 136:23 [c] Ezra 7:28 [d] Is. 5:2 9:11 [a] Ezra 6:21 9:12 [a] [Ex. 23:32; 34:15, 16; Deut. 7:3, 4]; Ezra 9:2 [b] Deut. 23:6 [c] [Prov. 13:22; 20:7] 9:13 [a] [Ps. 103:10] 9:14 [a] [John 5:14; 2 Pet. 2:20] [b] Neh. 13:23 [c] Deut. 9:8 9:15 [a] Neh. 9:33; Dan. 9:14 [b] [Rom. 3:19] [c] 1 Cor. 15:17 10:1 [a] Dan. 9:4, 20 [b] 2 Chr. 20:9 [c] Neh. 8:1–9 10:2 [a] Ezra 10:10, 13, 14, 17, 18; Neh. 13:23–27 10:3 [a] 2 Chr. 34:31 [b] Ezra 9:4 [c] Deut. 7:2, 3 [d] Deut. 24:1, 2 10:4 [a] 1 Chr. 28:10

of the priests, the Levites, and all Israel [a]swear an oath that they would do according to this word. So they swore an oath. 6 Then Ezra rose up from before the house of God, and went into the chamber of Jehohanan the son of Eliashib; and *when* he came there, he [a]ate no bread and drank no water, for he mourned because of the guilt of those from the captivity.

7 And they issued a proclamation throughout Judah and Jerusalem to all the descendants of the captivity, that they must gather at Jerusalem, 8 and that whoever would not come within three days, according to the instructions of the leaders and elders, all his property would be confiscated, and he himself would be separated from the assembly of those from the captivity.

9 So all the men of Judah and Benjamin gathered at Jerusalem within three days. It *was* the ninth month, on the twentieth of the month; and [a]all the people sat in the open square of the house of God, trembling because of *this* matter and because of heavy rain. 10 Then Ezra the priest stood up and said to them, "You have transgressed and have taken pagan wives, adding to the guilt of Israel. 11 Now therefore, [a]make confession to the LORD God of your fathers, and do His will; [b]separate yourselves from the peoples of the land, and from the pagan wives."

12 Then all the assembly answered and said with a loud voice, "Yes! As you have said, so we must do. 13 But *there are* many people; *it is* the season for heavy rain, and we are not able to stand outside. Nor *is this* the work of one or two days, for *there are* many of us who have transgressed in this matter. 14 Please, let the leaders of our entire assembly stand; and let all those in our cities who have taken pagan wives come at appointed times, together with the elders and judges of their cities, until [a]the fierce wrath of our God is turned away from us in this matter." 15 Only Jonathan the son of Asahel and Jahaziah the son of Tikvah opposed this, and [a]Meshullam and Shabbethai the Levite gave them support.

16 Then the descendants of the captivity did so. And Ezra the priest, *with* certain [a]heads of the fathers' *households,* were set apart by the fathers' households, each of them by name; and they sat down on the first day of the tenth month to examine the matter. 17 By the first day of the first month they finished *questioning* all the men who had taken pagan wives.

Pagan Wives Put Away

18 And among the sons of the priests who had taken pagan wives *the following* were found of the sons of [a]Jeshua the son of Jozadak,[1] and his brothers: Maaseiah, Eliezer, Jarib, and Gedaliah. 19 And they [a]gave their promise that they would put away their wives; and *being* [b]guilty, *they presented* a ram of the flock as their [c]trespass offering.

20 Also of the sons of Immer: Hanani and Zebadiah; 21 of the sons of Harim: Maaseiah, Elijah, Shemaiah, Jehiel, and Uzziah; 22 of the sons of Pashhur: Elioenai, Maaseiah, Ishmael, Nethanel, Jozabad, and Elasah.

23 Also of the Levites: Jozabad, Shimei, Kelaiah (the same *is* Kelita), Pethahiah, Judah, and Eliezer.

24 Also of the singers: Eliashib; and of the gatekeepers: Shallum, Telem, and Uri.

25 And others of Israel: of the [a]sons of Parosh: Ramiah, Jeziah, Malchiah, Mijamin, Eleazar, Malchijah, and Benaiah; 26 of the sons of Elam: Mattaniah, Zechariah, Jehiel, Abdi, Jeremoth, and Eliah; 27 of the sons of Zattu: Elioenai, Eliashib, Mattaniah, Jeremoth, Zabad, and Aziza; 28 of the [a]sons of Bebai: Jehohanan, Hananiah, Zabbai, *and* Athlai; 29 of the sons of Bani: Meshullam, Malluch, Adaiah, Jashub, Sheal, *and* Ramoth;[1] 30 of the [a]sons of Pahath-Moab: Adna, Chelal, Benaiah, Maaseiah, Mattaniah, Bezalel, Binnui, and Manasseh; 31 *of* the sons of Harim: Eliezer, Ishijah, Malchijah, Shemaiah, Shimeon, 32 Benjamin, Malluch, *and* Shemariah; 33 of the sons of Hashum: Mattenai, Mattattah, Zabad, Eliphelet, Jeremai, Manasseh, *and* Shimei; 34 of the sons of Bani: Maadai, Amram, Uel, 35 Benaiah, Bedeiah, Cheluh,[1] 36 Vaniah,

---

10:5 [a] Ezra 10:12, 19; Neh. 5:12; 13:25 10:6 [a] Deut. 9:18 10:9 [a] 1 Sam. 12:18; Ezra 9:4; 10:3 10:11 [a] [Lev. 26:40–42]; Josh. 7:19; [Prov. 28:13] [b] Ezra 10:3 10:14 [a] 2 Kin. 23:26; 2 Chr. 28:11–13; 29:10; 30:8 10:15 [a] Ezra 8:16; Neh. 3:4 10:16 [a] Ezra 4:3 10:18 [a] Ezra 5:2; Hag. 1:1, 12; 2:4; Zech. 3:1; 6:11 [1] Spelled *Jehozadak* in 1 Chronicles 6:14 10:19 [a] 2 Kin. 10:15 [b] Lev. 6:4, 6 [c] Lev. 5:6, 15 10:25 [a] Ezra 2:3; 8:3; Neh. 7:8 10:28 [a] Ezra 8:11 10:29 [1] Or *Jeremoth* 10:30 [a] Ezra 8:4 10:35 [1] Or *Cheluhi,* or *Cheluhu*

Meremoth, Eliashib, 37Mattaniah, Mattenai, Jaasai,[1] 38Bani, Binnui, Shimei, 39Shel-
emiah, Nathan, Adaiah, 40Machnadebai,
Shashai, Sharai, 41Azarel, Shelemiah, Shemariah, 42Shallum, Amariah, *and* Joseph; 43of
the sons of Nebo: Jeiel, Mattithiah, Zabad,
Zebina, Jaddai,[1] Joel, *and* Benaiah.
44All these had taken pagan wives, and
some of them had wives *by whom* they had
children.

10:37 [1] Or *Jaasu* 10:43 [1] Or *Jaddu*

THE BOOK OF

NEHEMIAH

OVERVIEW

The Book of Nehemiah is believed to have been written by Nehemiah. However, because it was combined with the Book of Ezra at one time, there are those who believe it was written by Ezra instead. Written sometime between 430 BC and 420 BC, Nehemiah covers a thirteen-year span of Israel's return from exile (446–433 BC).

Nehemiah was an Israelite and cupbearer to the Persian king Artaxerxes. While in exile, Nehemiah learned from those who had returned to Jerusalem that the city was "in great distress" and that the walls of the city were "broken down, and its gates [were] burned with fire" (Neh. 1:3). This news saddened Nehemiah, and he fasted and prayed for his people (see vv. 5–11).

King Artaxerxes noticed Nehemiah's sadness and asked him what caused him to be in such a state. Nehemiah shared about the situation in Jerusalem and asked the king to allow him to go rebuild the walls. He also asked for lumber from the king's forest to repair the gates of the palace and the wall of the city. The king granted all of Nehemiah's requests and sent him to Jerusalem accompanied by army captains and horsemen (2:1–10).

As the Israelites repaired the walls, their enemies ridiculed them and threatened to attack them (see 4:1–14). In response to the threats, Nehemiah assigned half the people to work and the other half to stand guard (see vv. 15–18). The wall was completed in fifty-two days (see 6:15).

Nehemiah, who was appointed governor, then called all the people together as a congregation, and Ezra read the Law to the assembly (see 8:1–8). Upon hearing God's Word, the children of Israel fasted, confessed their sins, and worshiped God (see 9:1–3). After recounting the sins of their fathers and God's deliverance of them, the Israelites renewed their commitment to God's covenant with them (see vv. 4–38). They committed themselves to walk "in God's Law, which was given by Moses the servant of God, and to observe and do all the commandments of the LORD" (10:29).

Under Nehemiah's leadership, the people came together to dedicate the wall of Jerusalem (see 12:27). They loudly rejoiced and offered sacrifices to God (see v. 43).

As the governor, Nehemiah paid close attention to the actions of the Israelites to ensure that they kept the covenant with God. Because writings from Moses indicated that the Ammonites and the Moabites should not come into the congregation of God, Nehemiah separated them from the Israelites (see 13:1–3). Recognizing that the Levites had not received their portion, he gave them the tithe (see vv. 10–13). When he discovered Israelites working on the Sabbath, he chastised them and reestablished the Sabbath (see vv. 15–22).

The Book of Nehemiah demonstrates the importance of good leadership. Nehemiah was able to lead the Israelites back to God by reinforcing the tenets of God's covenant with them and correcting them when they were in error. God, in turn, renewed His covenant with them and blessed them for their obedience.

BREATHE IT IN

Nehemiah was saddened when he learned of the horrible conditions in Jerusalem. When he realized that work needed to be done there, he volunteered to go rebuild the walls and repair the gates. God gave Nehemiah favor with King Artaxerxes, and he returned to his homeland to lead the necessary repairs. Not only did Nehemiah restore the structure of the city, but he also reminded the Israelites of the Law of Moses and, along with Ezra, taught them how to honor God's covenant with them.

Just as Nehemiah faced a broken society, we face a society in which much work needs to be done. We often talk about how the world operates wrongly and how society has major issues that need to be addressed. Some of us complain about the problems in the educational system, inequality in the justice system, and corruption in the political system. Others complain that parents are not raising their children properly, health care is not available to all who need it, and employers are not treating employees fairly. Some even complain that the churches are not doing anything to make a difference in their communities and the world. While these complaints might be warranted, does complaining address the issues and solve the problems? If complaining is not accompanied by acting, it does not. Instead of complaining, we should seek to do something about the wrongs we see.

Taking the initiative to help improve a situation, however, is only the first step, and the next steps are not always easy. There will be those who mock us, and others will tell us that we are wasting our time. Find encouragement, though, that when the enemies of the Israelites mocked and threatened them, God did not allow it. When we do what God has called us to do, He will protect us and honor our efforts as long as we remain focused on completing the work He has given.

When we see issues in our society, in our communities, or in our jobs, we should be like Nehemiah and volunteer to work toward bringing about change. Each of us can contribute to making the world a better place. What is it that we are passionate about? If it is youth, then serve as a mentor. If it is homelessness, volunteer at a shelter. If it is hunger, feed families. Whatever it is, find a way to make a difference that will bring about change in the lives of others. Do not think that what we do will not matter. One person can make an enormous difference. Do not worry about the number of people's lives we might affect. We can make a difference one life at a time. As Christians, we have a privilege and responsibility to do good works here on earth. The ultimate calling of a Christian is to have the heart of a servant. Even Christ came to serve, not to be served (see Matt. 20:28). When we are meeting the needs of other people, God may use our service to soften hearts toward Him and lead others to salvation. Commit yourself to the service of others and of the world.

†

THE BOOK OF

NEHEMIAH

Nehemiah Prays for His People

1 The words of [a]Nehemiah the son of Hachaliah.

It came to pass in the month of Chislev, *in* the [b]twentieth year, as I was in [c]Shushan[1] the citadel, 2that [a]Hanani one of my brethren came with men from Judah; and I asked them concerning the Jews who had escaped, who had survived the captivity, and concerning Jerusalem. 3And they said to me, "The survivors who are left from the captivity in the [a]province *are* there in great distress and [b]reproach. [c]The wall of Jerusalem [d]*is* also broken down, and its gates are burned with fire."

4So it was, when I heard these words, that I sat down and wept, and mourned *for many* days; I was fasting and praying before the God of heaven.

5And I said: "I pray, [a]LORD God of heaven, O great and [b]awesome God, [c]*You* who keep *Your* covenant and mercy with those who love You[1] and observe Your[2] commandments, 6please let Your ear be attentive and [a]Your eyes open, that You may hear the prayer of Your servant which I pray before You now, day and night, for the children of Israel Your servants, and [b]confess the sins of the children of Israel which we have sinned against You. Both my father's house and I have sinned. 7[a]We have acted very corruptly against You, and have [b]not kept the commandments, the statutes, nor the ordinances which You commanded Your servant Moses. 8Remember, I pray, the word that You commanded Your servant Moses, saying, [a]'*If* you are unfaithful, I will scatter you among the nations;[1] 9[a]but *if* you return to Me, and keep My commandments and do them, [b]though some of you were cast out to the farthest part of the heavens, *yet* I will gather them from there, and bring them to the place which I have chosen as a dwelling for My name.'[1] 10[a]Now these *are* Your servants and Your people, whom You have redeemed by Your great power, and by Your strong hand. 11O Lord, I pray, please [a]let Your ear be attentive to the prayer of Your servant, and to the prayer of Your servants who [b]desire to fear Your name; and let Your servant prosper this day, I pray, and grant him mercy in the sight of this man."

For I was the king's [c]cupbearer.

#OXYGEN

NEHEMIAH 1:11

Exalt His Awesome Mercy

Abandonment and rejection are things of the past for the believer. God accepts you fully in Christ. But He also wants the best for you, even if you miss the mark. Rest in God's forgiveness that is without end.

Breathe and exalt His awesome mercy.

1:1 [a] Neh. 10:1 [b] Neh. 2:1 [c] Esth. 1:1, 2, 5; Dan. 8:2 [1] Or *Susa* 1:2 [a] Neh. 7:2 1:3 [a] Neh. 7:6 [b] Neh. 2:17 [c] Neh. 2:17 [d] 2 Kin. 25:10
1:5 [a] Dan. 9:4 [b] Neh. 4:14 [c] [Ex. 20:6; 34:6, 7]; Ps. 89:2, 3 [1] Literally *Him* [2] Literally *His* 1:6 [a] 1 Kin. 8:28, 29; 2 Chr. 6:40; Dan. 9:17, 18
[b] Ezra 10:1; Neh. 9:2; Dan. 9:20 1:7 [a] Ps. 106:6; Dan. 9:5 [b] Deut. 28:15 1:8 [a] Lev. 26:33; Deut. 4:25–27; 28:63–67
[1] Leviticus 26:33 1:9 [a] Lev. 26:39; [Deut. 4:29–31; 30:2–5] [b] Deut. 30:4 [1] Deuteronomy 30:2–5
1:10 [a] Ex. 32:11; Deut. 9:29; Dan. 9:15 1:11 [a] Neh. 1:6
[b] Is. 26:8; [Heb. 13:18] [c] Gen. 40:21; Neh. 2:1

Nehemiah Sent to Judah

2 And it came to pass in the month of Nisan, in the twentieth year of [a]King Artaxerxes, *when* wine *was* before him, that [b]I
took the wine and gave it to the king. Now
I had never been sad in his presence before. 2 Therefore the king said to me, "Why
is your face sad, since you *are* not sick? This
is nothing but [a]sorrow of heart."

So I became dreadfully afraid, 3 and said
to the king, [a]"May the king live forever! Why
should my face not be sad, when [b]the city,
the place of my fathers' tombs, *lies* waste,
and its gates are burned with [c]fire?"

4 Then the king said to me, "What do you
request?"

So I [a]prayed to the God of heaven. 5 And
I said to the king, "If it pleases the king,
and if your servant has found favor in your
sight, I ask that you send me to Judah, to
the city of my fathers' tombs, that I may
rebuild it."

6 Then the king said to me (the queen
also sitting beside him), "How long will your
journey be? And when will you return?" So
it pleased the king to send me; and I set
him [a]a time.

7 Furthermore I said to the king, "If it
pleases the king, let letters be given to me
for the [a]governors *of the region* beyond the
River,[1] that they must permit me to pass
through till I come to Judah, 8 and a letter to Asaph the keeper of the king's forest, that he must give me timber to make
beams for the gates of the citadel which
pertains [a]to the temple,[1] for the city wall,
and for the house that I will occupy." And
the king granted *them* to me [b]according to
the good hand of my God upon me.

9 Then I went to the governors *in the region* beyond the River, and gave them the
king's letters. Now the king had sent captains of the army and horsemen with me.
10 When [a]Sanballat the Horonite and Tobiah the Ammonite official[1] heard *of it,*
they were deeply disturbed that a man had
come to seek the well-being of the children of Israel.

Nehemiah Views the Wall of Jerusalem

11 So I [a]came to Jerusalem and was there
three days. 12 Then I arose in the night, I and
a few men with me; I told no one what my
God had put in my heart to do at Jerusalem;
nor was there any animal with me, except
the one on which I rode. 13 And I went out
by night [a]through the Valley Gate to the Serpent Well and the Refuse Gate, and viewed
the walls of Jerusalem which were [b]broken
down and its gates which were burned with
fire. 14 Then I went on to the [a]Fountain Gate
and to the [b]King's Pool, but *there was* no
room for the animal under me to pass. 15 So
I went up in the night by the [a]valley, and
viewed the wall; then I turned back and entered by the Valley Gate, and so returned.
16 And the officials did not know where I
had gone or what I had done; I had not yet
told the Jews, the priests, the nobles, the
officials, or the others who did the work.

17 Then I said to them, "You see the distress that we *are* in, how Jerusalem *lies*
waste, and its gates are burned with fire.
Come and let us build the wall of Jerusalem, that we may no longer be [a]a reproach."
18 And I told them of [a]the hand of my God
which had been good upon me, and also of
the king's words that he had spoken to me.

So they said, "Let us rise up and build."
Then they [b]set their hands to *this* good
work.

19 But when Sanballat the Horonite, Tobiah the Ammonite official, and Geshem
the Arab heard *of it,* they laughed at us and
despised us, and said, "What *is* this thing
that you are doing? [a]Will you rebel against
the king?"

20 So I answered them, and said to them,
"The God of heaven Himself will prosper
us; therefore we His servants will arise and
build, [a]but you have no heritage or right or
memorial in Jerusalem."

Rebuilding the Wall

3 Then [a]Eliashib the high priest rose up
with his brethren the priests [b]and built
the Sheep Gate; they consecrated it and

2:1 [a] Ezra 7:1 [b] Neh. 1:11 **2:2** [a] Prov. 15:13 **2:3** [a] 1 Kin. 1:31; Dan. 2:4; 5:10; 6:6, 21 [b] 2 Kin. 25:8–10; 2 Chr. 36:19; Jer. 52:12–14 [c] 2 Kin. 24:10; Neh. 1:3 **2:4** [a] Neh. 1:4 **2:6** [a] Neh. 5:14; 13:6 **2:7** [a] Ezra 7:21; 8:36 [1] That is, the Euphrates, and so elsewhere in this book **2:8** [a] Neh. 3:7 [b] Ezra 5:5; 7:6, 9, 28; Neh. 2:18 [1] Literally *house* **2:10** [a] Neh. 2:19; 4:1 [1] Literally *servant,* and so elsewhere in this book **2:11** [a] Ezra 8:32 **2:13** [a] 2 Chr. 26:9; Neh. 3:13 [b] Neh. 1:3; 2:17 **2:14** [a] Neh. 3:15 [b] 2 Kin. 20:20 **2:15** [a] 2 Sam. 15:23; Jer. 31:40 **2:17** [a] Neh. 1:3; Ps. 44:13; 79:4; Jer. 24:9; Ezek. 5:14, 15; 22:4 **2:18** [a] Neh. 2:8 [b] 2 Sam. 2:7 **2:19** [a] Neh. 6:6 **2:20** [a] Ezra 4:3; Neh. 6:16 **3:1** [a] Neh. 3:20; 12:10; 13:4, 7, 28 [b] John 5:2

hung its doors. They built [c]as far as the
Tower of the Hundred,[1] *and* consecrated it,
then as far as the Tower of [d]Hananel. 2Next
to *Eliashib*[1] [a]the men of Jericho built. And
next to them Zaccur the son of Imri built.
3Also the sons of Hassenaah built [a]the
Fish Gate; they laid its beams and [b]hung its
doors with its bolts and bars. 4And next to
them [a]Meremoth the son of Urijah, the son
of Koz,[1] made repairs. Next to them [b]Me-
shullam the son of Berechiah, the son of
Meshezabel, made repairs. Next to them Zadok the son of Baana made repairs. 5Next to
them the Tekoites made repairs; but their
nobles did not put their shoulders[1] to [a]the
work of their Lord.
6Moreover Jehoiada the son of Paseah
and Meshullam the son of Besodeiah repaired [a]the Old Gate; they laid its beams
and hung its doors, with its bolts and bars.
7And next to them Melatiah the Gibeonite,
Jadon the Meronothite, the [a]men of Gibeon
and Mizpah, repaired the [b]residence[1] of the
governor *of the region* beyond the River.
8Next to him Uzziel the son of Harhaiah,
one of the goldsmiths, made repairs. Also
next to him Hananiah, one[1] of the perfumers, made repairs; and they fortified Jerusalem as far as the [a]Broad Wall. 9And next
to them Rephaiah the son of Hur, leader
of half the district of Jerusalem, made repairs. 10Next to them Jedaiah the son of

NEHEMIAH 2:17

I AM NEHEMIAH

Then I said to them, "You see the distress that we are in, how Jerusalem lies waste, and its gates are burned with fire. Come and let us build the wall of Jerusalem, that we may no longer be a reproach." Nehemiah 2:17

I am Nehemiah, cupbearer for Artaxerxes, king of Persia. When I heard that the returned Babylonian exiles were in great distress and that the walls of Jerusalem were still in ruins, I mourned for Israel and the reproach this brought to God. I fasted and prayed before the Lord.

With the approval of King Artaxerxes and with the help of letters of passage he supplied, I went to Jerusalem to rebuild its walls. When I arrived, I solicited the help of all the Israelites. Working together, we would rebuild the walls around Jerusalem. Our enemies, however, mocked us as we undertook this great task. As they heard that our work neared completion, they were angry and planned to attack us. I told the people not to be afraid because the Lord would fight for us.

Not only did we have to contend with the enemies outside our gates, but there were also oppressors inside our gates. This angered me, and I rebuked the nobles and rulers, who repented and took an oath to restore the poor. Our enemies also tried to make me afraid through lies and false prophets. But I knew God was with me, so I was not afraid.

The wall around Jerusalem was completed in only fifty-two days. The exiled captives returned, numbering 42,360. Lest the people forget, Ezra read the Book of the Law of Moses to everyone. When they heard it, the people wept and repented, promising to live as God intended.

✝

Nehemiah's heart was stirred by the plight of his people, so he prayed, repented for himself and his people, and then asked God for help. God made Nehemiah the answer to his own prayer. Most importantly, Nehemiah did not just pray. He acted under the direction of the Lord, and he trusted that the Lord would see the work through to completion. We need to be people of prayer, but like Nehemiah, often God will use us as our own answer to those prayers. We pray, but we also act.

3:1 [c] Neh. 12:39 [d] Jer. 31:38; Zech. 14:10 [1] Hebrew *Hammeah,* also at 12:39 3:2 [a] Ezra 2:34; Neh. 7:36 [1] Literally *On his hand*
3:3 [a] 2 Chr. 33:14; Neh. 12:39; Zeph. 1:10 [b] Neh. 6:1; 7:1 3:4 [a] Ezra 8:33 [b] Ezra 10:15 [1] Or *Hakkoz* 3:5 [a] [Judg. 5:23] [1] Literally *necks*
3:6 [a] Neh. 12:39 3:7 [a] Neh. 7:25 [b] Ezra 8:36; Neh. 2:7–9 [1] Literally *throne* 3:8 [a] Neh. 12:38 [1] Literally *the son*

Harumaph made repairs in front of his house. And next to him Hattush the son of Hashabniah made repairs.

11Malchijah the son of Harim and Hashub the son of Pahath-Moab repaired another section, [a]as well as the Tower of the Ovens. 12And next to him was Shallum the son of Hallohesh, leader of half the district of Jerusalem; he and his daughters made repairs.

13Hanun and the inhabitants of Zanoah repaired [a]the Valley Gate. They built it, hung its doors with its bolts and bars, and *repaired* a thousand cubits of the wall as far as [b]the Refuse Gate.

14Malchijah the son of Rechab, leader of the district of [a]Beth Haccerem, repaired the Refuse Gate; he built it and hung its doors with its bolts and bars.

15Shallun the son of Col-Hozeh, leader of the district of Mizpah, repaired [a]the Fountain Gate; he built it, covered it, hung its doors with its bolts and bars, and repaired the wall of the Pool of [b]Shelah by the [c]King's Garden, as far as the stairs that go down from the City of David. 16After him Nehemiah the son of Azbuk, leader of half the district of Beth Zur, made repairs as far as *the place* in front of the tombs[1] of David, to the [a]man-made pool, and as far as the House of the Mighty.

17After him the Levites, *under* Rehum the son of Bani, made repairs. Next to him Hashabiah, leader of half the district of Keilah, made repairs for his district. 18After him their brethren, *under* Bavai[1] the son of Henadad, leader of the *other* half of the district of Keilah, made repairs. 19And next to him Ezer the son of Jeshua, the leader of Mizpah, repaired another section in front of the Ascent to the Armory at the [a]buttress. 20After him Baruch the son of Zabbai[1] carefully repaired the other section, from the buttress to the door of the house of Eliashib the high priest. 21After him Meremoth the son of Urijah, the son of Koz,[1] repaired another section, from the door of the house of Eliashib to the end of the house of Eliashib.

22And after him the priests, the men of the plain, made repairs. 23After him Benjamin and Hasshub made repairs opposite their house. After them Azariah the son of Maaseiah, the son of Ananiah, made repairs by his house. 24After him [a]Binnui the son of Henadad repaired another section, from the house of Azariah to [b]the buttress, even as far as the corner. 25Palal the son of Uzai *made repairs* opposite the buttress, and on the tower which projects from the king's upper house that *was* by the [a]court of the prison. After him Pedaiah the son of Parosh *made repairs.*

26Moreover [a]the Nethinim who dwelt in [b]Ophel *made repairs* as far as *the place* in front of [c]the Water Gate toward the east, and on the projecting tower. 27After them the Tekoites repaired another section, next to the great projecting tower, and as far as the wall of Ophel.

28Beyond the [a]Horse Gate the priests made repairs, each in front of his *own* house. 29After them Zadok the son of Immer made repairs in front of his *own* house. After him Shemaiah the son of Shechaniah, the keeper of the East Gate, made repairs. 30After him Hananiah the son of Shelemiah, and Hanun, the sixth son of Zalaph, repaired another section. After him Meshullam the son of Berechiah made repairs in front of his dwelling. 31After him Malchijah, one of the goldsmiths, made repairs as far as the house of the Nethinim and of the merchants, in front of the Miphkad[1] Gate, and as far as the upper room at the corner. 32And between the upper room at the corner, as far as the [a]Sheep Gate, the goldsmiths and the merchants made repairs.

The Wall Defended Against Enemies

4 But it so happened, [a]when Sanballat heard that we were rebuilding the wall, that he was furious and very indignant, and mocked the Jews. 2And he spoke before his brethren and the army of Samaria, and said, "What are these feeble Jews doing? Will they fortify themselves? Will they

3:11 [a] Neh. 12:38 3:13 [a] Neh. 2:13, 15 [b] Neh. 2:13 3:14 [a] Jer. 6:1 3:15 [a] Neh. 2:14 [b] Is. 8:6; John 9:7 [c] 2 Kin. 25:4
3:16 [a] 2 Kin. 20:20; Is. 7:3; 22:11 [1] Septuagint, Syriac, and Vulgate read *tomb.* 3:18 [1] Following Masoretic Text and Vulgate; some Hebrew manuscripts, Septuagint, and Syriac read *Binnui* (compare verse 24). 3:19 [a] 2 Chr. 26:9 3:20 [1] A few Hebrew manuscripts, Syriac, and Vulgate read *Zaccai.* 3:21 [1] Or *Hakkoz* 3:24 [a] Ezra 8:33 [b] Neh. 3:19 3:25 [a] Jer. 32:2; 33:1; 37:21
3:26 [a] Ezra 2:43; Neh. 11:21 [b] 2 Chr. 27:3 [c] Neh. 8:1, 3; 12:37 3:28 [a] 2 Kin. 11:16; 2 Chr. 23:15; Jer. 31:40
3:31 [1] Literally *Inspection* or *Recruiting* 3:32 [a] Neh. 3:1; 12:39 4:1 [a] Neh. 2:10, 19

offer sacrifices? Will they complete it in a
day? Will they revive the stones from the
heaps of rubbish—*stones* that are burned?"
3Now [a]Tobiah the Ammonite *was* beside
him, and he said, "Whatever they build, if
even a fox goes up *on it,* he will break down
their stone wall."
4[a]Hear, O our God, for we are despised;
[b]turn their reproach on their own heads,
and give them as plunder to a land of captivity! 5[a]Do not cover their iniquity, and do
not let their sin be blotted out from before
You; for they have provoked *You* to anger
before the builders.
6So we built the wall, and the entire wall
was joined together up to half its *height,* for
the people had a mind to work.
7Now it happened, [a]when Sanballat, Tobiah, [b]the Arabs, the Ammonites, and the
Ashdodites heard that the walls of Jerusalem were being restored and the gaps were
beginning to be closed, that they became
very angry, 8and all of them [a]conspired together to come *and* attack Jerusalem and
create confusion. 9Nevertheless [a]we made
our prayer to our God, and because of them
we set a watch against them day and night.
10Then Judah said, "The strength of the
laborers is failing, and *there is* so much rubbish that we are not able to build the wall."
11And our adversaries said, "They will
neither know nor see anything, till we come
into their midst and kill them and cause
the work to cease."
12So it was, when the Jews who dwelt
near them came, that they told us ten times,
"From whatever place you turn, *they will
be* upon us."
13Therefore I positioned *men* behind the
lower parts of the wall, at the openings; and
I set the people according to their families,
with their swords, their spears, and their
bows. 14And I looked, and arose and said to
the nobles, to the leaders, and to the rest of
the people, [a]"Do not be afraid of them. Remember the Lord, [b]great and awesome, and
[c]fight for your brethren, your sons, your
daughters, your wives, and your houses."
15And it happened, when our enemies
heard that it was known to us, and [a]*that* God
had brought their plot to nothing, that all
of us returned to the wall, everyone to his
work. 16So it was, from that time on, *that*
half of my servants worked at construction, while the other half held the spears,
the shields, the bows, and *wore* armor; and
the leaders *were* behind all the house of
Judah. 17Those who built on the wall, and
those who carried burdens, loaded themselves so that with one hand they worked
at construction, and with the other held a
weapon. 18Every one of the builders had
his sword girded at his side as he built. And
the one who sounded the trumpet *was* beside me.
19Then I said to the nobles, the rulers,
and the rest of the people, "The work *is*
great and extensive, and we are separated
far from one another on the wall. 20Wher-
ever you hear the sound of the trumpet,
rally to us there. [a]Our God will fight for us."
21So we labored in the work, and half of
the men[1] held the spears from daybreak
until the stars appeared. 22At the same
time I also said to the people, "Let each
man and his servant stay at night in Jerusalem, that they may be our guard by night
and a working party by day." 23So neither
I, my brethren, my servants, nor the men
of the guard who followed me took off our
clothes, *except* that everyone took them
off for washing.

Nehemiah Deals with Oppression

5 And there was a great [a]outcry of the
people and their wives against their
[b]Jewish brethren. 2For there were those
who said, "We, our sons, and our daughters *are* many; therefore let us get grain,
that we may eat and live."
3There were also *some* who said, "We
have mortgaged our lands and vineyards
and houses, that we might buy grain because of the famine."
4There were also those who said, "We
have borrowed money for the king's tax
on our lands and vineyards. 5Yet now [a]our
flesh *is* as the flesh of our brethren, our
children as their children; and indeed we
[b]are forcing our sons and our daughters to

4:3 [a] Neh. 2:10, 19 4:4 [a] Ps. 123:3, 4 [b] Ps. 79:12; Prov. 3:34 4:5 [a] Ps. 69:27, 28; 109:14, 15; Jer. 18:23 4:7 [a] Neh. 4:1 [b] Neh. 2:19
4:8 [a] Ps. 83:3–5 4:9 [a] [Ps. 50:15] 4:14 [a] [Num. 14:9]; Deut. 1:29 [b] [Deut. 10:17] [c] 2 Sam. 10:12 4:15 [a] Job 5:12 4:20 [a] Ex. 14:14, 25;
Deut. 1:30; 3:22; 20:4; Josh. 23:10; 2 Chr. 20:29 4:21 [1] Literally *them* 5:1 [a] Lev. 25:35–37; Neh. 5:7, 8
[b] Deut. 15:7 5:5 [a] Is. 58:7 [b] Ex. 21:7; [Lev. 25:39]

be slaves, and *some* of our daughters have been brought into slavery. *It is* not in our power *to redeem them,* for other men have our lands and vineyards."

6And I became very angry when I heard their outcry and these words. 7After serious thought, I rebuked the nobles and rulers, and said to them, [a]"Each of you is exacting usury from his brother." So I called a great assembly against them. 8And I said to them, "According to our ability we have [a]redeemed our Jewish brethren who were sold to the nations. Now indeed, will you even sell your brethren? Or should they be sold to us?"

Then they were silenced and found nothing *to say.* 9Then I said, "What you are doing *is* not good. Should you not walk [a]in the fear of our God [b]because of the reproach of the nations, our enemies? 10I also, *with* my brethren and my servants, am lending them money and grain. Please, let us stop this usury! 11Restore now to them, even this day, their lands, their vineyards, their olive groves, and their houses, also a hundredth of the money and the grain, the new wine and the oil, that you have charged them."

12So they said, "We will restore *it,* and will require nothing from them; we will do as you say."

Then I called the priests, [a]and required an oath from them that they would do according to this promise. 13Then [a]I shook out the fold of my garment[1] and said, "So may God shake out each man from his house, and from his property, who does not perform this promise. Even thus may he be shaken out and emptied."

And all the assembly said, "Amen!" and praised the LORD. [b]Then the people did according to this promise.

The Generosity of Nehemiah

14Moreover, from the time that I was appointed to be their governor in the land of Judah, from the twentieth year [a]until the thirty-second year of King Artaxerxes, twelve years, neither I nor my brothers [b]ate the governor's provisions. 15But the former governors who *were* before me laid burdens on the people, and took from them bread and wine, besides forty shekels of silver. Yes, even their servants bore rule over the people, but [a]I did not do so, because of the [b]fear of God. 16Indeed, I also continued the [a]work on this wall, and we[1] did not buy any land. All my servants *were* gathered there for the work.

17And [a]at my table *were* one hundred and fifty Jews and rulers, besides those who came to us from the nations around us. 18Now *that* [a]which was prepared daily *was* one ox *and* six choice sheep. Also fowl were prepared for me, and once every ten days an abundance of all kinds of wine. Yet in spite of this [b]I did not demand the governor's provisions, because the bondage was heavy on this people.

19[a]Remember me, my God, for good, *according to* all that I have done for this people.

Conspiracy Against Nehemiah

6 Now it happened [a]when Sanballat, Tobiah, Geshem the Arab, and the rest of our enemies heard that I had rebuilt the wall, and *that* there were no breaks left in it [b](though at that time I had not hung the doors in the gates), 2that Sanballat and Geshem [a]sent to me, saying, "Come, let us meet together among the villages in the plain of [b]Ono." But they [c]thought to do me harm.

3So I sent messengers to them, saying, "I *am* doing a great work, so that I cannot come down. Why should the work cease while I leave it and go down to you?"

4But they sent me this message four times, and I answered them in the same manner.

5Then Sanballat sent his servant to me as before, the fifth time, with an open letter in his hand. 6In it *was* written:

> It is reported among the nations, and Geshem[1] says, *that* you and the Jews plan to rebel; therefore, according to these rumors, you are rebuilding

---

5:7 [a] [Ex. 22:25; Lev. 25:36; Deut. 23:19, 20]; Ezek. 22:12 5:8 [a] Lev. 25:48 5:9 [a] Lev. 25:36 [b] 2 Sam. 12:14; Rom. 2:24; [1 Pet. 2:12] 5:12 [a] Ezra 10:5; Jer. 34:8, 9 5:13 [a] Matt. 10:14; Acts 13:51; 18:6 [b] 2 Kin. 23:3 [1] Literally *my lap* 5:14 [a] Neh. 2:1; 13:6 [b] [1 Cor. 9:4–15] 5:15 [a] 2 Cor. 11:9; 12:13 [b] Neh. 5:9 5:16 [a] Neh. 4:1; 6:1 [1] Following Masoretic Text; Septuagint, Syriac, and Vulgate read *I*. 5:17 [a] 2 Sam. 9:7; 1 Kin. 18:19 5:18 [a] 1 Kin. 4:22 [b] Neh. 5:14, 15 5:19 [a] 2 Kin. 20:3; Neh. 13:14, 22, 31 6:1 [a] Neh. 2:10, 19; 4:1, 7; 13:28 [b] Neh. 3:1, 3 6:2 [a] Prov. 26:24, 25 [b] 1 Chr. 8:12; Neh. 11:35 [c] Ps. 37:12, 32 6:6 [1] Hebrew *Gashmu* 6:6 [1] Hebrew *Gashmu*

the wall, [a]that you may be their
king. 7And you have also appointed
prophets to proclaim concerning
you at Jerusalem, saying, "*There is* a
king in Judah!" Now these matters
will be reported to the king. So come,
therefore, and let us consult together.

8Then I sent to him, saying, "No such
things as you say are being done, but you
invent them in your own heart."
9For they all *were trying to* make us
afraid, saying, "Their hands will be weakened in the work, and it will not be done."
Now therefore, *O God,* strengthen my
hands.
10Afterward I came to the house of Shemaiah the son of Delaiah, the son of Mehetabel, who *was* a secret informer; and he
said, "Let us meet together in the house of
God, within the temple, and let us close the
doors of the temple, for they are coming
to kill you; indeed, at night they will come
to kill you."
11And I said, "Should such a man as I flee?
And who *is there* such as I who would go into
the temple to save his life? I will not go in!"
12Then I perceived that God had not sent him
at all, but that [a]he pronounced *this* prophecy against me because Tobiah and Sanballat had hired him. 13For this reason he *was*
hired, that I should be afraid and act that way
and sin, so *that* they might have *cause* for an
evil report, that they might reproach me.
14[a]My God, remember Tobiah and Sanballat, according to these their works, and
the [b]prophetess Noadiah and the rest of the
prophets who would have made me afraid.

The Wall Completed

15So the wall was finished on the twenty-
fifth *day* of Elul, in fifty-two days. 16And it
happened, [a]when all our enemies heard *of
it,* and all the nations around us saw *these
things,* that they were very disheartened
in their own eyes; for [b]they perceived that
this work was done by our God.
17Also in those days the nobles of Judah sent many letters to Tobiah, and *the
letters of* Tobiah came to them. 18For many
in Judah were pledged to him, because he
was the [a]son-in-law of Shechaniah the son
of Arah, and his son Jehohanan had married the daughter of [b]Meshullam the son
of Berechiah. 19Also they reported his good
deeds before me, and reported my words
to him. Tobiah sent letters to frighten me.

7 Then it was, when the wall was built and
I had [a]hung the doors, when the gatekeepers, the singers, and the Levites had
been appointed, 2that I gave the charge
of Jerusalem to my brother [a]Hanani, and
Hananiah the leader [b]of the citadel, for he
was a faithful man and [c]feared God more
than many.
3And I said to them, "Do not let the gates
of Jerusalem be opened until the sun is hot;
and while they stand *guard,* let them shut
and bar the doors; and appoint guards from
among the inhabitants of Jerusalem, one
at his watch station and another in front
of his own house."

The Captives Who Returned to Jerusalem (Ezra 2:1–70)

4Now the city *was* large and spacious, but
the people in it *were* [a]few, and the houses
were not rebuilt. 5Then my God put it into
my heart to gather the nobles, the rulers,
and the people, that they might be registered by genealogy. And I found a register
of the genealogy of those who had come up
in the first *return,* and found written in it:

6 [a]These[1] *are* the people of the province
who came back from the captivity, of
those who had been carried away, whom
Nebuchadnezzar the king of Babylon
had carried away, and who returned to
Jerusalem and Judah, everyone to his
city.

7 Those who came with [a]Zerubbabel *were*
Jeshua, Nehemiah, Azariah, Raamiah,
Nahamani, Mordecai, Bilshan,
Mispereth,[1] Bigvai, Nehum, and Baanah.

The number of the men of the people of
Israel: 8the sons of Parosh, two thousand
one hundred and seventy-two;

6:6 [a] Neh. 2:19 6:12 [a] Ezek. 13:22 6:14 [a] Neh. 13:29 [b] Ezek. 13:17 6:16 [a] Neh. 2:10, 20; 4:1, 7; 6:1 [b] Ps. 126:2
6:18 [a] Neh. 13:4, 28 [b] Ezra 10:15; Neh. 3:4 7:1 [a] Neh. 6:1, 15 7:2 [a] Neh. 1:2 [b] Neh. 2:8; 10:23 [c] Ex. 18:21
7:4 [a] Deut. 4:27 7:6 [a] Ezra 2:1–70 [1] Compare verses 6–72 with Ezra 2:1–70
7:7 [a] Ezra 5:2; Neh. 12:1, 47; Matt. 1:12, 13 [1] Spelled *Mispar* in Ezra 2:2

9the sons of Shephatiah, three hundred and seventy-two;
10the sons of Arah, six hundred and fifty-two;
11the sons of Pahath-Moab, of the sons of Jeshua and Joab, two thousand eight hundred and eighteen;
12the sons of Elam, one thousand two hundred and fifty-four;
13the sons of Zattu, eight hundred and forty-five;
14the sons of Zaccai, seven hundred and sixty;
15the sons of Binnui,[1] six hundred and forty-eight;
16the sons of Bebai, six hundred and twenty-eight;
17the sons of Azgad, two thousand three hundred and twenty-two;
18the sons of Adonikam, six hundred and sixty-seven;
19the sons of Bigvai, two thousand and sixty-seven;
20the sons of Adin, six hundred and fifty-five;
21the sons of Ater of Hezekiah, ninety-eight;
22the sons of Hashum, three hundred and twenty-eight;
23the sons of Bezai, three hundred and twenty-four;
24the sons of Hariph,[1] one hundred and twelve;
25the sons of Gibeon,[1] ninety-five;
26the men of Bethlehem and Netophah, one hundred and eighty-eight;
27the men of Anathoth, one hundred and twenty-eight;
28the men of Beth Azmaveth,[1] forty-two;
29the men of Kirjath Jearim, Chephirah, and Beeroth, seven hundred and forty-three;
30the men of Ramah and Geba, six hundred and twenty-one;
31the men of Michmas, one hundred and twenty-two;
32the men of Bethel and Ai, one hundred and twenty-three;
33the men of the other Nebo, fifty-two;
34the sons of the other [a]Elam, one thousand two hundred and fifty-four;
35the sons of Harim, three hundred and twenty;
36the sons of Jericho, three hundred and forty-five;
37the sons of Lod, Hadid, and Ono, seven hundred and twenty-one;
38the sons of Senaah, three thousand nine hundred and thirty.

39 The priests: the sons of [a]Jedaiah, of the house of Jeshua, nine hundred and seventy-three;
40the sons of [a]Immer, one thousand and fifty-two;
41the sons of [a]Pashhur, one thousand two hundred and forty-seven;
42the sons of [a]Harim, one thousand and seventeen.

43 The Levites: the sons of Jeshua, of Kadmiel,
and of the sons of Hodevah,[1]
seventy-four.

44 The singers: the sons of Asaph, one hundred and forty-eight.

45 The gatekeepers: the sons of Shallum,
the sons of Ater,
the sons of Talmon,
the sons of Akkub,
the sons of Hatita,
the sons of Shobai, one hundred and thirty-eight.

46 The Nethinim: the sons of Ziha,
the sons of Hasupha,
the sons of Tabbaoth,
47the sons of Keros,
the sons of Sia,[1]
the sons of Padon,
48the sons of Lebana,[1]
the sons of Hagaba,[2]
the sons of Salmai,[3]
49the sons of Hanan,
the sons of Giddel,
the sons of Gahar,

7:15 [1] Spelled *Bani* in Ezra 2:10 7:24 [1] Called *Jorah* in Ezra 2:18 7:25 [1] Called *Gibbar* in Ezra 2:20 7:28 [1] Called *Azmaveth* in Ezra 2:24 7:34 [a] Neh. 7:12 7:39 [a] 1 Chr. 24:7 7:40 [a] 1 Chr. 9:12 7:41 [a] Ezra 2:38; 10:22 7:42 [a] 1 Chr. 24:8 7:43 [1] Spelled *Hodaviah* in Ezra 2:40 7:47 [1] Spelled *Siaha* in Ezra 2:44 7:48 [1] Masoretic Text reads *Lebanah.* [2] Masoretic Text reads *Hogabah.* [3] Or *Shalmai,* or *Shamlai*

50the sons of Reaiah,
the sons of Rezin,
the sons of Nekoda,
51the sons of Gazzam,
the sons of Uzza,
the sons of Paseah,
52the sons of Besai,
the sons of Meunim,
the sons of Nephishesim,[1]
53the sons of Bakbuk,
the sons of Hakupha,
the sons of Harhur,
54the sons of Bazlith,[1]
the sons of Mehida,
the sons of Harsha,
55the sons of Barkos,
the sons of Sisera,
the sons of Tamah,
56the sons of Neziah,
and the sons of Hatipha.

57 The sons of Solomon's servants: the
sons of Sotai,
the sons of Sophereth,
the sons of Perida,[1]
58the sons of Jaala,
the sons of Darkon,
the sons of Giddel,
59the sons of Shephatiah,
the sons of Hattil,
the sons of Pochereth of Zebaim,
and the sons of Amon.[1]
60All the Nethinim, and the sons
of Solomon's servants, *were* three
hundred and ninety-two.

61 And these *were* the ones who came up
from Tel Melah, Tel Harsha, Cherub,
Addon,[1] and Immer, but they could
not identify their father's house nor
their lineage, whether they *were* of
Israel: 62the sons of Delaiah,
the sons of Tobiah,
the sons of Nekoda, six hundred and
forty-two;
63and of the priests: the sons of Habaiah,
the sons of Koz,[1]
the sons of Barzillai, who took a wife of
the daughters of Barzillai the Gileadite,
and was called by their name.
64These sought their listing *among*
those who were registered by genealogy,
but it was not found; therefore they
were excluded from the priesthood
as defiled. 65And the governor[1] said to
them that they should not eat of the
most holy things till a priest could
consult with the Urim and Thummim.

66 Altogether the whole assembly *was*
forty-two thousand three hundred and
sixty, 67besides their male and female
servants, of whom *there were* seven
thousand three hundred and thirty-
seven; and they had two hundred and
forty-five men and women singers.
68Their horses were seven hundred and
thirty-six, their mules two hundred and
forty-five, 69*their* camels four hundred
and thirty-five, *and* donkeys six
thousand seven hundred and twenty.

70 And some of the heads of the fathers'
houses gave to the work. [a]The governor[1]
gave to the treasury one thousand
gold drachmas, fifty basins, and five
hundred and thirty priestly garments.
71Some of the heads of the fathers'
houses gave to the treasury of the work
[a]twenty thousand gold drachmas,
and two thousand two hundred silver
minas. 72And that which the rest of the
people gave *was* twenty thousand gold
drachmas, two thousand silver minas,
and sixty-seven priestly garments.

73So the priests, the Levites, the gatekeepers, the singers, *some* of the people, the
Nethinim, and all Israel dwelt in their cities.

Ezra Reads the Law

[a]When the seventh month came, the
children of Israel *were* in their cities.
8 Now all [a]the people gathered together
as one man in the open square that *was*
[b]in front of the Water Gate; and they told
Ezra the [c]scribe to bring the Book of the Law
of Moses, which the LORD had commanded
Israel. 2So Ezra the priest brought [a]the Law
before the assembly of men and women

7:52 [1] Spelled *Nephusim* in Ezra 2:50 7:54 [1] Spelled *Bazluth* in Ezra 2:52 7:57 [1] Spelled *Peruda* in Ezra 2:55 7:59 [1] Spelled *Ami* in Ezra 2:57 7:61 [1] Spelled *Addan* in Ezra 2:59 7:63 [1] Or *Hakkoz* 7:65 [1] Hebrew *Tirshatha* 7:70 [a] Neh. 8:9 [1] Hebrew *Tirshatha* 7:71 [a] Ezra 2:69 7:73 [a] Ezra 3:1 8:1 [a] Ezra 3:1 [b] Neh. 3:26 [c] Ezra 7:6 8:2 [a] [Deut. 31:11, 12]; Neh. 8:9

and all who *could* hear with understanding [b]on the first day of the seventh month.
3 Then he [a]read from it in the open square
that *was* in front of the Water Gate from
morning until midday, before the men and
women and those who could understand;
and the ears of all the people *were attentive* to the Book of the Law.
4 So Ezra the scribe stood on a platform
of wood which they had made for the purpose; and beside him, at his right hand,
stood Mattithiah, Shema, Anaiah, Urijah,
Hilkiah, and Maaseiah; and at his left hand
Pedaiah, Mishael, Malchijah, Hashum,
Hashbadana, Zechariah, *and* Meshullam.
5 And Ezra opened the book in the sight of
all the people, for he was *standing* above
all the people; and when he opened it, all
the people [a]stood up. 6 And Ezra blessed
the LORD, the great God.
Then all the people [a]answered, "Amen,
Amen!" while [b]lifting up their hands. And
they [c]bowed their heads and worshiped the
LORD with *their* faces to the ground.
7 Also Jeshua, Bani, Sherebiah, Jamin,
Akkub, Shabbethai, Hodijah, Maaseiah, Kelita, Azariah, Jozabad, Hanan, Pelaiah, and
the Levites, [a]helped the people to understand the Law; and the people [b]*stood* in
their place. 8 So they read distinctly from
the book, in the Law of God; and they gave
the sense, and helped *them* to understand
the reading.
9 [a]And Nehemiah, who *was* the governor,[1] Ezra the priest *and* scribe, and the
Levites who taught the people said to all
the people, [b]"This day *is* holy to the LORD
your God; [c]do not mourn nor weep." For
all the people wept, when they heard the
words of the Law.
10 Then he said to them, "Go your way, eat
the fat, drink the sweet, [a]and send portions
to those for whom nothing is prepared; for
this day *is* holy to our Lord. Do not sorrow,
for the joy of the LORD is your strength."
11 So the Levites quieted all the people,
saying, "Be still, for the day *is* holy; do not
be grieved." 12 And all the people went their
way to eat and drink, to [a]send portions and
rejoice greatly, because they [b]understood
the words that were declared to them.

The Feast of Tabernacles
(cf. Lev. 23:33–43)

13 Now on the second day the heads of the
fathers' *houses* of all the people, with the
priests and Levites, were gathered to Ezra
the scribe, in order to understand the words
of the Law. 14 And they found written in the
Law, which the LORD had commanded by
Moses, that the children of Israel should
dwell in [a]booths during the feast of the seventh month, 15 and [a]that they should announce and proclaim in all their cities and
[b]in Jerusalem, saying, "Go out to the mountain, and [c]bring olive branches, branches of
oil trees, myrtle branches, palm branches,
and branches of leafy trees, to make booths,
as *it is* written."
16 Then the people went out and brought
them and made themselves booths, each
one on the [a]roof of his house, or in their
courtyards or the courts of the house of
God, and in the open square of the [b]Water
Gate [c]and in the open square of the Gate of
Ephraim. 17 So the whole assembly of those
who had returned from the captivity made
booths and sat under the booths; for since
the days of Joshua the son of Nun until that
day the children of Israel had not done so.
And there was very [a]great gladness. 18 Also
[a]day by day, from the first day until the last
day, he read from the Book of the Law of
God. And they kept the feast [b]seven days;
and on the [c]eighth day *there was* a sacred assembly, according to the *prescribed* manner.

The People Confess Their Sins

9 Now on the twenty-fourth day of [a]this
month the children of Israel were assembled with fasting, in sackcloth, [b]and
with dust on their heads.[1] 2 Then [a]those
of Israelite lineage separated themselves
from all foreigners; and they stood and
[b]confessed their sins and the iniquities of
their fathers. 3 And they stood up in their

8:2 [b] Lev. 23:24; Num. 29:1–6 8:3 [a] Deut. 31:9–11; 2 Kin. 23:2 8:5 [a] Judg. 3:20; 1 Kin. 8:12–14 8:6 [a] Neh. 5:13; [1 Cor. 14:16] [b] Ps. 28:2; Lam. 3:41; 1 Tim. 2:8 [c] Ex. 4:31; 12:27; 2 Chr. 20:18 8:7 [a] Lev. 10:11; Deut. 33:10; 2 Chr. 17:7; [Mal. 2:7] [b] Neh. 9:3 8:9 [a] Ezra 2:63; Neh. 7:65, 70; 10:1 [b] Lev. 23:24; Num. 29:1 [c] Deut. 16:14; Eccl. 3:4 [1] Hebrew *Tirshatha* 8:10 [a] [Deut. 26:11–13]; Esth. 9:19, 22; Rev. 11:10 8:12 [a] Neh. 8:10 [b] Neh. 8:7, 8 8:14 [a] Lev. 23:34, 40, 42; Deut. 16:13 8:15 [a] Lev. 23:4 [b] Deut. 16:16 [c] Lev. 23:40 8:16 [a] Deut. 22:8 [b] Neh. 12:37 [c] 2 Kin. 14:13; Neh. 12:39 8:17 [a] 2 Chr. 30:21 8:18 [a] Deut. 31:11 [b] Lev. 23:36 [c] Num. 29:35 9:1 [a] Neh. 8:2 [b] Josh. 7:6; 1 Sam. 4:12; 2 Sam. 1:2; Job 2:12 [1] Literally *earth on them* 9:2 [a] Ezra 10:11; Neh. 13:3, 30 [b] Neh. 1:6

place and [a]read from the Book of the Law
of the LORD their God *for one*-fourth of the
day; and *for another* fourth they confessed
and worshiped the LORD their God.
4Then Jeshua, Bani, Kadmiel, Shebaniah, Bunni, Sherebiah, Bani, *and* Chenani
stood on the stairs of the Levites and cried
out with a loud voice to the LORD their God.
5And the Levites, Jeshua, Kadmiel, Bani,
Hashabniah, Sherebiah, Hodijah, Shebaniah, *and* Pethahiah, said:

"Stand up *and* bless the LORD your God
Forever and ever!

"Blessed be [a]Your glorious name,
Which is exalted above all
blessing and praise!
6 [a]You alone *are* the LORD;
[b]You have made heaven,
[c]The heaven of heavens,
with [d]all their host,
The earth and everything on it,
The seas and all that is in them,
And You [e]preserve them all.
The host of heaven worships You.

7 "You *are* the LORD God,
Who chose [a]Abram,
And brought him out of Ur
of the Chaldeans,
And gave him the name [b]Abraham;
8 You found his heart
[a]faithful before You,
And made a [b]covenant with him
To give the land of the Canaanites,
The Hittites, the Amorites,
The Perizzites, the Jebusites,
And the Girgashites—
To give *it* to his descendants.
You [c]have performed Your words,
For You *are* righteous.

9 "You[a] saw the affliction of
our fathers in Egypt,
And [b]heard their cry by the Red Sea.
10 You [a]showed signs and wonders
against Pharaoh,
Against all his servants,
And against all the people of his land.
For You knew that they [b]acted
proudly against them.
So You [c]made a name for
Yourself, as *it is* this day.
11 [a]And You divided the sea before them,
So that they went through the midst
of the sea on the dry land;
And their persecutors You
threw into the deep,
[b]As a stone into the mighty waters.
12 Moreover You [a]led them by
day with a cloudy pillar,
And by night with a pillar of fire,
To give them light on the road
Which they should travel.

13 "You[a] came down also on Mount Sinai,
And spoke with them from heaven,
And gave them [b]just ordinances
and true laws,
Good statutes and commandments.
14 You made known to them
Your [a]holy Sabbath,
And commanded them precepts,
statutes and laws,
By the hand of Moses Your servant.
15 You [a]gave them bread from
heaven for their hunger,
And [b]brought them water out of
the rock for their thirst,
And told them to [c]go in to
possess the land
Which You had sworn to give them.

16 "But[a] they and our fathers
acted proudly,
[b]Hardened their necks,
And did not heed Your
commandments.
17 They refused to obey,
And [a]they were not mindful
of Your wonders
That You did among them.
But they hardened their necks,
And in their rebellion[1]
They appointed [b]a leader

9:3 [a] Neh. 8:7, 8 9:5 [a] 1 Chr. 29:13 9:6 [a] Deut. 6:4; 2 Kin. 19:15, 19; [Ps. 86:10]; Is. 37:16, 20 [b] Gen. 1:1; Ex. 20:11; Rev. 14:7 [c] [Deut. 10:14]; 1 Kin. 8:27 [d] Gen. 2:1 [e] [Ps. 36:6] 9:7 [a] Gen. 11:31 [b] Gen. 17:5 9:8 [a] Gen. 15:6; 22:1–3; [James 2:21–23] [b] Gen. 15:18 [c] Josh. 23:14 9:9 [a] Ex. 2:25; 3:7 [b] Ex. 14:10 9:10 [a] Ex. 7—14 [b] Ex. 18:11 [c] Jer. 32:20 9:11 [a] Ex. 14:20–28 [b] Ex. 15:1, 5 9:12 [a] Ex. 13:21, 22 9:13 [a] Ex. 20:1–18 [b] [Rom. 7:12] 9:14 [a] Gen. 2:3; Ex. 16:23; 20:8; 23:12 9:15 [a] Ex. 16:14–17; John 6:31 [b] Ex. 17:6; Num. 20:8; [1 Cor. 10:4] [c] Deut. 1:8 9:16 [a] Ps. 106:6 [b] Deut. 1:26–33; 31:27; Neh. 9:29 9:17 [a] Ps. 78:11, 42–45 [b] Num. 14:4; Acts 7:39 [1] Following Masoretic Text and Vulgate; Septuagint reads *in Egypt*

To return to their bondage.
But You *are* God,
Ready to pardon,
[c]Gracious and merciful,
Slow to anger,
Abundant in kindness,
And did not forsake them.

18 "Even [a]when they made a molded
calf for themselves,
And said, 'This *is* your god
That brought you up out of Egypt,'
And worked great provocations,
19 Yet in Your [a]manifold mercies
You did not forsake them
in the wilderness.
The [b]pillar of the cloud did not
depart from them by day,
To lead them on the road;
Nor the pillar of fire by night,
To show them light,
And the way they should go.
20 You also gave Your [a]good
Spirit to instruct them,
And did not withhold Your
[b]manna from their mouth,
And gave them [c]water for
their thirst.
21 [a]Forty years You sustained
them in the wilderness;
They lacked nothing;
Their [b]clothes did not wear out[1]
And their feet did not swell.

22 "Moreover You gave them
kingdoms and nations,
And divided them into districts.[1]
So they took possession of
the land of [a]Sihon,
The land of[2] the king of Heshbon,
And the land of Og king of Bashan.
23 You also multiplied [a]their children
as the stars of heaven,
And brought them into the land
Which You had told their fathers
To go in and possess.
24 So [a]the people went in
And possessed the land;
[b]You subdued before them the
inhabitants of the land,
The Canaanites,
And gave them into their hands,
With their kings
And the people of the land,
That they might do with
them as they wished.
25 And they took strong cities
and a [a]rich land,
And possessed [b]houses
full of all goods,
Cisterns *already* dug,
vineyards, olive groves,
And fruit trees in abundance.
So they ate and were filled
and [c]grew fat,
And delighted themselves in
Your great [d]goodness.

26 "Nevertheless they [a]were disobedient
And rebelled against You,
[b]Cast Your law behind their backs
And killed Your [c]prophets, who
testified against them
To turn them to Yourself;
And they worked great provocations.
27 [a]Therefore You delivered them into
the hand of their enemies,
Who oppressed them;
And in the time of their trouble,
When they cried to You,
You [b]heard from heaven;
And according to Your
abundant mercies
[c]You gave them deliverers
who saved them
From the hand of their enemies.

28 "But after they had rest,
[a]They again did evil before You.
Therefore You left them in the
hand of their enemies,
So that they had dominion
over them;
Yet when they returned and
cried out to You,
You heard from heaven;

9:17 [c] Joel 2:13. 9:18 [a] Ex. 32:4–8, 31 9:19 [a] Ps. 106:45 [b] Ex. 13:20–22; 1 Cor. 10:1 9:20 [a] Num. 11:17 [b] Ex. 16:14–16 [c] Ex. 17:6
9:21 [a] Deut. 2:7 [b] Deut. 8:4; 29:5 [1] Compare Deuteronomy 29:5 9:22 [a] Num. 21:21–35 [1] Literally *corners* [2] Following Masoretic Text and Vulgate; Septuagint omits *The land of*. 9:23 [a] Gen. 15:5; 22:17; Heb. 11:12 9:24 [a] Josh. 1:2–4 [b] Josh. 18:1; [Ps. 44:2, 3] 9:25 [a] Num. 13:27 [b] Deut. 6:11; Josh. 24:13 [c] [Deut. 32:15] [d] Hos. 3:5
9:26 [a] Judg. 2:11 [b] 1 Kin. 14:9; Ps. 50:17 [c] 1 Kin. 18:4; 19:10; Matt. 23:37; Acts 7:52
9:27 [a] Judg. 2:14; Ps. 106:41 [b] Ps. 106:44 [c] Judg. 2:18 9:28 [a] Judg. 3:12

And [b]many times You delivered
them according to Your mercies,
29 And testified against them,
That You might bring them
back to Your law.
Yet they acted proudly,
And did not heed Your
commandments,
But sinned against Your judgments,
[a]'Which if a man does, he
shall live by them.'[1]
And they shrugged their shoulders,
Stiffened their necks,
And would not hear.
30 Yet for many years You had
patience with them,
And testified [a]against them by
Your Spirit [b]in Your prophets.
Yet they would not listen;
[c]Therefore You gave them into the
hand of the peoples of the lands.
31 Nevertheless in Your great mercy
[a]You did not utterly consume
them nor forsake them;
For You *are* God, gracious
and merciful.

32 "Now therefore, our God,
The great, the [a]mighty,
and awesome God,
Who keeps covenant and mercy:
Do not let all the trouble
seem small before You
That has come upon us,
Our kings and our princes,
Our priests and our prophets,
Our fathers and on all Your people,
[b]From the days of the kings of
Assyria until this day.
33 However [a]You *are* just in all
that has befallen us;
For You have dealt faithfully,
But [b]we have done wickedly.
34 Neither our kings nor our princes,
Our priests nor our fathers,
Have kept Your law,
Nor heeded Your commandments
and Your testimonies,
With which You testified against
them.
35 For they have [a]not served
You in their kingdom,
Or in the many good *things*
that You gave them,
Or in the large and rich land
which You set before them;
Nor did they turn from
their wicked works.

36 "Here [a]we *are,* servants today!
And the land that You gave
to our fathers,
To eat its fruit and its bounty,
Here we *are,* servants in it!
37 And [a]it yields much increase
to the kings
You have set over us,
Because of our sins;
Also they have [b]dominion over
our bodies and our cattle
At their pleasure;
And we *are* in great distress.

38 "And because of all this,
We [a]make a sure *covenant* and write *it;*
Our leaders, our Levites, *and*
our priests [b]seal *it.*"

The People Who Sealed the Covenant

10 Now those who placed *their* seal on
the document were:
Nehemiah the governor, [a]the son of Hac-
aliah, and Zedekiah, 2 [a]Seraiah, Azariah,
Jeremiah, 3 Pashhur, Amariah, Malchijah,
4 Hattush, Shebaniah, Malluch, 5 Harim,
Meremoth, Obadiah, 6 Daniel, Ginnethon,
Baruch, 7 Meshullam, Abijah, Mijamin, 8 Maaziah, Bilgai, *and* Shemaiah. These *were*
the priests.
9 The Levites: Jeshua the son of Azaniah,
Binnui of the sons of Henadad, *and* Kadmiel.
10 Their brethren: Shebaniah, Hodijah,
Kelita, Pelaiah, Hanan, 11 Micha, Rehob,
Hashabiah, 12 Zaccur, Sherebiah, Shebaniah, 13 Hodijah, Bani, *and* Beninu.
14 The leaders of the people: [a]Parosh, Pahath-Moab, Elam, Zattu, Bani, 15 Bunni, Azgad, Bebai, 16 Adonijah, Bigvai, Adin, 17 Ater,
Hezekiah, Azzur, 18 Hodijah, Hashum, Bezai,

9:28 [b] Ps. 106:43 9:29 [a] Lev. 18:5; Rom. 10:5; [Gal. 3:12] [1] Leviticus 18:5 9:30 [a] 2 Kin. 17:13–18; 2 Chr. 36:11–20; Jer. 7:25 [b] [Acts 7:51]; 1 Pet. 1:11 [c] Is. 5:5 9:31 [a] Jer. 4:27; [Rom. 11:2–5] 9:32 [a] [Ex. 34:6, 7] [b] 2 Kin. 15:19; 17:3–6; Ezra 4:2, 10 9:33 [a] Ps. 119:137; [Dan. 9:14] [b] Ps. 106:6; [Dan. 9:5, 6, 8] 9:35 [a] Deut. 28:47 9:36 [a] Deut. 28:48; Ezra 9:9 9:37 [a] Deut. 28:33, 51 [b] Deut. 28:48 9:38 [a] 2 Kin. 23:3; 2 Chr. 29:10; Ezra 10:3 [b] Neh. 10:1 10:1 [a] Neh. 1:1 10:2 [a] Neh. 12:1–21 10:14 [a] Ezra 2:3

19 Hariph, Anathoth, Nebai, 20 Magpiash, Meshullam, Hezir, 21 Meshezabel, Zadok, Jaddua, 22 Pelatiah, Hanan, Anaiah, 23 Hoshea, Hananiah, Hasshub, 24 Hallohesh, Pilha, Shobek, 25 Rehum, Hashabnah, Maaseiah, 26 Ahijah, Hanan, Anan, 27 Malluch, Harim, *and* Baanah.

The Covenant That Was Sealed

28 [a]Now the rest of the people—the priests, the Levites, the gatekeepers, the singers, the Nethinim, [b]and all those who had separated themselves from the peoples of the lands to the Law of God, their wives, their sons, and their daughters, everyone who had knowledge and understanding— 29 these joined with their brethren, their nobles, [a]and entered into a curse and an oath [b]to walk in God's Law, which was given by Moses the servant of God, and to observe and do all the commandments of the LORD our Lord, and His ordinances and His statutes: 30 We would not give [a]our daughters as wives to the peoples of the land, nor take their daughters for our sons; 31 [a]*if* the peoples of the land brought wares or any grain to sell on the Sabbath day, we would not buy it from them on the Sabbath, or on a holy day; and we would forego the [b]seventh year's *produce* and the [c]exacting of every debt.

32 Also we made ordinances for ourselves, to exact from ourselves yearly [a]one-third of a shekel for the service of the house of our God: 33 for [a]the showbread, for the regular grain offering, for the [b]regular burnt offering of the Sabbaths, the New Moons, and the set feasts; for the holy things, for the sin offerings to make atonement for Israel, and all the work of the house of our God. 34 We cast lots among the priests, the Levites, and the people, [a]for bringing the wood offering into the house of our God, according to our fathers' houses, at the appointed times year by year, to burn on the altar of the LORD our God [b]as *it is* written in the Law.

35 And *we made ordinances* [a]to bring the firstfruits of our ground and the firstfruits of all fruit of all trees, year by year, to the house of the LORD; 36 to bring the [a]firstborn of our sons and our cattle, as *it is* written in the Law, and the firstborn of our herds and our flocks, to the house of our God, to the priests who minister in the house of our God; 37 [a]to bring the firstfruits of our dough, our offerings, the fruit from all kinds of trees, *the* new wine and oil, to the priests, to the storerooms of the house of our God; and to bring [b]the tithes of our land to the Levites, for the Levites should receive the tithes in all our farming communities. 38 And the priest, the descendant of Aaron, shall be with the Levites [a]when the Levites receive tithes; and the Levites shall bring up a tenth of the tithes to the house of our God, to [b]the rooms of the storehouse.

39 For the children of Israel and the children of Levi [a]shall bring the offering of the grain, of the new wine and the oil, to the storerooms where the articles of the sanctuary *are, where* the priests who minister and the gatekeepers [b]and the singers *are;* and we will not [c]neglect the house of our God.

The People Dwelling in Jerusalem

11 Now the leaders of the people dwelt at Jerusalem; the rest of the people cast lots to bring one out of ten to dwell in Jerusalem, [a]the holy city, and nine-tenths *were to dwell* in *other* cities. 2 And the people blessed all the men who [a]willingly offered themselves to dwell at Jerusalem.

3 [a]These *are* the heads of the province who dwelt in Jerusalem. (But in the cities of Judah everyone dwelt in his own possession in their cities—Israelites, priests, Levites, [b]Nethinim, and [c]descendants of Solomon's servants.) 4 Also [a]in Jerusalem dwelt *some* of the children of Judah and of the children of Benjamin.

The children of Judah: Athaiah the son of Uzziah, the son of Zechariah, the son of

---

10:28 [a] Ezra 2:36–43 [b] Ezra 9:1; Neh. 13:3 10:29 [a] Deut. 29:12; Neh. 5:12; Ps. 119:106 [b] 2 Kin. 23:3; 2 Chr. 34:31 10:30 [a] Ex. 34:16; Deut. 7:3; [Ezra 9:12] 10:31 [a] Ex. 20:10; Lev. 23:3; Deut. 5:12 [b] Ex. 23:10, 11; Lev. 25:4; Jer. 34:14 [c] [Deut. 15:1, 2]; Neh. 5:12 10:32 [a] Ex. 30:11–16; 38:25, 26; 2 Chr. 24:6, 9; Matt. 17:24 10:33 [a] Lev. 24:5; 2 Chr. 2:4 [b] Num. 28; 29 10:34 [a] Neh. 13:31; [Is. 40:16] [b] Lev. 6:12 10:35 [a] Ex. 23:19; 34:26; Lev. 19:23; Num. 18:12; Deut. 26:1, 2 10:36 [a] Ex. 13:2, 12, 13; Lev. 27:26, 27; Num. 18:15, 16 10:37 [a] Lev. 23:17; Num. 15:19; 18:12; Deut. 18:4; 26:2 [b] Lev. 27:30; Num. 18:21; Mal. 3:10 10:38 [a] Num. 18:26 [b] 1 Chr. 9:26; 2 Chr. 31:11 10:39 [a] Deut. 12:6, 11; 2 Chr. 31:12; Neh. 13:12 [b] Neh. 13:10, 11 [c] [Heb. 10:25] 11:1 [a] Neh. 10:18; Matt. 4:5; 5:35; 27:53 11:2 [a] Judg. 5:9; 2 Chr. 17:16 11:3 [a] 1 Chr. 9:2, 3 [b] Ezra 2:43 [c] Ezra 2:55 11:4 [a] 1 Chr. 9:3

RELEASE // EXALT HIS AWESOME MERCY

Breaking the Patterns

Nehemiah 9:30–31 //"Yet for many years you had patience with them, and testified against them by Your Spirit in Your prophets. Yet they would not listen; therefore You gave them into the hand of the peoples of the lands. Nevertheless in Your great mercy You did not utterly consume them nor forsake them; for You are God, gracious and merciful."

Summary Message // Showing mercy is to give compassion or forgiveness to someone instead of extracting retaliation. We all appreciate mercy from others when we mess up. It is not always as easy for us to give it, though. This is especially true when others keep making the same mistakes.

Nehemiah 9 outlines some of Israel's history and how God had made a covenant with them, but they kept breaking it. The people of Israel would beg for mercy and God would give it. You would think they would have learned their lesson. But generation after generation kept messing up. Once they started feeling the consequences of their sin, they would run back to God. This chapter in Nehemiah is about God's people acknowledging their rebellious pattern, confessing their sins, worshiping God, and renewing a commitment to follow the covenant.

Practical Application // Many stories of the Bible can cause us to be frustrated with the people's repeated failures. We can put ourselves in their shoes and say things like, "If I would have seen the Red Sea split, I would never have complained and wanted to go back to Egypt." Or, "If I would have seen Jesus feed over five thousand people, I would not have been worried when four thousand needed to be fed soon after." We may not have been there to see those biblical miracles in person, but most of us have seen God work miracles in our lives or in the lives of people around us. He has come through for us in supernatural ways. Yet, when the next challenge comes along, we can quickly doubt God just like the Israelites in the Old Testament and the disciples in the New Testament. We are not that different, are we?

Thank God for His awesome mercy! Throughout the Bible, He was merciful in so many situations instead of giving people what they really deserved. Throughout our lives, He has been merciful to us too. Through all our drama, He pours out mercy on us instead of giving us what we really deserve. His mercy is a gift. We need to learn to *respect* it rather than *expect* it. It seems all too easy for us to take God's mercy for granted and continue in our sin patterns just as the Israelites did. Yes, God offers mercy, but there are still consequences for not following His plan for our lives. The Israelites lost everything multiple times because of their sinfulness. We need to learn from the sin patterns of the generations before us. With the help of Jesus, we can break those chains of addiction, abuse, anger, debt, poverty, and more. We can help our families walk in true freedom. As we create new family legacies and benefit from His awesome mercy, we can also learn to give more mercy to those who need it around us.

Fervent Prayer // Heavenly Father, thank You for Your awesome mercy. We acknowledge it as a gift. Forgive us for the times we have taken advantage of it. Give us the strength to break any sin patterns in our lives. We know we can find true freedom and victory with Your help. Give us the compassion to show mercy to those in our lives who need it. In Jesus' name we pray. Amen.

Amariah, the son of Shephatiah, the son of
Mahalalel, of the children of [b]Perez; 5and
Maaseiah the son of Baruch, the son of Col-
Hozeh, the son of Hazaiah, the son of Adaiah, the son of Joiarib, the son of Zechariah,
the son of Shiloni. 6All the sons of Perez
who dwelt at Jerusalem *were* four hundred
and sixty-eight valiant men.
7And these are the sons of Benjamin:
Sallu the son of Meshullam, the son of Joed,
the son of Pedaiah, the son of Kolaiah, the
son of Maaseiah, the son of Ithiel, the son of
Jeshaiah; 8and after him Gabbai *and* Sallai,
nine hundred and twenty-eight. 9Joel the
son of Zichri *was* their overseer, and Judah
the son of Senuah[1] *was* second over the city.
10[a]Of the priests: Jedaiah the son of Joiarib, and Jachin; 11Seraiah the son of Hilkiah,

11:4 [b] Gen. 38:29 11:9 [1] Or *Hassenuah* 11:10 [a] 1 Chr. 9:10

the son of Meshullam, the son of Zadok, the
son of Meraioth, the son of Ahitub, *was* the
leader of the house of God. 12Their brethren who did the work of the house *were*
eight hundred and twenty-two; and Adaiah the son of Jeroham, the son of Pela-
liah, the son of Amzi, the son of Zechariah,
the son of Pashhur, the son of Malchijah,
13and his brethren, heads of the fathers'
houses, were two hundred and forty-two;
and Amashai the son of Azarel, the son of
Ahzai, the son of Meshillemoth, the son of
Immer, 14and their brethren, mighty men of
valor, *were* one hundred and twenty-eight.
Their overseer *was* Zabdiel the son of *one
of* the great men.[1]

15Also of the Levites: Shemaiah the son
of Hasshub, the son of Azrikam, the son of
Hashabiah, the son of Bunni; 16[a]Shabbethai
and [b]Jozabad, of the heads of the Levites,
had the oversight of [c]the business outside
of the house of God; 17Mattaniah the son of
Micha,[1] the son of Zabdi, the son of Asaph,
the leader *who* began the thanksgiving with
prayer; Bakbukiah, the second among his
brethren; and Abda the son of Shammua,
the son of Galal, the son of Jeduthun. 18All
the Levites in [a]the holy city *were* two hundred and eighty-four.

19Moreover the gatekeepers, Akkub, Talmon, and their brethren who kept the gates,
were one hundred and seventy-two.

20And the rest of Israel, of the priests
and Levites, *were* in all the cities of Judah,
everyone in his inheritance. 21[a]But the
Nethinim dwelt in Ophel. And Ziha and
Gishpa *were* over the Nethinim.

22Also the overseer of the Levites at Jerusalem *was* Uzzi the son of Bani, the son
of Hashabiah, the son of Mattaniah, the son
of Micha, of the sons of Asaph, the singers in charge of the service of the house
of God. 23For [a]*it was* the king's command
concerning them that a certain portion
should be for the singers, a quota day by
day. 24Pethahiah the son of Meshezabel,
of the children of [a]Zerah the son of Judah,
was [b]the king's deputy[1] in all matters concerning the people.

The People Dwelling Outside Jerusalem

25And as for the villages with their fields,
some of the children of Judah dwelt in [a]Kir-
jath Arba and its villages, Dibon and its
villages, Jekabzeel and its villages; 26in
Jeshua, Moladah, Beth Pelet, 27Hazar Shual,
and Beersheba and its villages; 28in Ziklag
and Meconah and its villages; 29in En Rimmon, Zorah, Jarmuth, 30Zanoah, Adullam,
and their villages; in Lachish and its fields;
in Azekah and its villages. They dwelt from
Beersheba to the Valley of Hinnom.

31Also the children of Benjamin from
Geba *dwelt* in Michmash, Aija, and Bethel,
and their villages; 32in Anathoth, Nob, Ananiah; 33in Hazor, Ramah, Gittaim; 34in Hadid, Zeboim, Neballat; 35in Lod, Ono, *and*
[a]the Valley of Craftsmen. 36Some of the Judean divisions of Levites *were* in Benjamin.

The Priests and Levites
(cf. Ezra 2:36–40)

12 Now these *are* the [a]priests and the
Levites who came up with [b]Zerub-
babel the son of Shealtiel, and Jeshua: [c]Se-
raiah, Jeremiah, Ezra, 2Amariah, Malluch,
Hattush, 3Shechaniah, Rehum, Meremoth,
4Iddo, Ginnethoi,[1] [a]Abijah, 5Mijamin, Maadiah, Bilgah, 6Shemaiah, Joiarib, Jedaiah,
7Sallu, Amok, Hilkiah, *and* Jedaiah.

These *were* the heads of the priests and
their brethren in the days of [a]Jeshua.

8Moreover the Levites *were* Jeshua, Binnui, Kadmiel, Sherebiah, Judah, *and* Mattaniah [a]*who led* the thanksgiving *psalms,*
he and his brethren. 9Also Bakbukiah and
Unni, their brethren, *stood* across from
them in *their* duties.

10Jeshua begot Joiakim, Joiakim begot
Eliashib, Eliashib begot Joiada, 11Joiada begot Jonathan, and Jonathan begot Jaddua.

12Now in the days of Joiakim, the priests,
the [a]heads of the fathers' *houses were:* of
Seraiah, Meraiah; of Jeremiah, Hananiah;
13of Ezra, Meshullam; of Amariah, Jehoha-
nan; 14of Melichu,[1] Jonathan; of Shebaniah,[2]
Joseph; 15of Harim,[1] Adna; of Meraioth,[2]
Helkai; 16of Iddo, Zechariah; of Ginnethon,
Meshullam; 17of Abijah, Zichri; *the son* of

11:14 [1] Or *the son of Haggedolim* 11:16 [a] Ezra 10:15 [b] Ezra 8:33 [c] 1 Chr. 26:29 11:17 [1] Or *Michah* 11:18 [a] Neh. 11:1 11:21 [a] 2 Chr. 27:3; Neh. 3:26 11:23 [a] Ezra 6:8, 9; 7:20 11:24 [a] Gen. 38:30 [b] 1 Chr. 18:17 [1] Literally *at the king's hand* 11:25 [a] Josh. 14:15 11:35 [a] 1 Chr. 4:14 12:1 [a] Ezra 2:1, 2; 7:7 [b] Neh. 7:7; Matt. 1:12, 13 [c] Neh. 10:2–8 12:4 [a] Luke 1:5 [1] Or *Ginnethon* (compare verse 16) 12:7 [a] Ezra 3:2; Hag. 1:1; Zech. 3:1 12:8 [a] Neh. 11:17 12:12 [a] Neh. 7:70, 71; 8:13; 11:13 12:14 [1] Or *Malluch* (compare verse 2) [2] Or *Shechaniah* (compare verse 3) 12:15 [1] Or *Rehum* (compare verse 3) [2] Or *Meremoth* (compare verse 3)

Minjamin;[1] of Moadiah,[2] Piltai; 18of Bilgah,
Shammua; of Shemaiah, Jehonathan; 19of
Joiarib, Mattenai; of Jedaiah, Uzzi; 20of
Sallai,[1] Kallai; of Amok, Eber; 21of Hilkiah,
Hashabiah; *and* of Jedaiah, Nethanel.

22During the reign of Darius the Persian, a record *was also kept* of the Levites
and priests *who had been* [a]heads of their
fathers' *houses* in the days of Eliashib, Joiada, Johanan, and Jaddua. 23The sons of
Levi, the heads of the fathers' *houses* until
the days of Johanan the son of Eliashib,
were written in the book of the [a]chronicles.

24And the heads of the Levites *were*
Hashabiah, Sherebiah, and Jeshua the son
of Kadmiel, with their brothers across from
them, to [a]praise *and* give thanks, [b]group
alternating with group, [c]according to the
command of David the man of God. 25Mat-
taniah, Bakbukiah, Obadiah, Meshullam,
Talmon, and Akkub *were* gatekeepers keeping the watch at the storerooms of the
gates. 26These *lived* in the days of Joiakim
the son of Jeshua, the son of Jozadak,[1] and
in the days of Nehemiah [a]the governor, and
of Ezra the priest, [b]the scribe.

Nehemiah Dedicates the Wall

27Now at [a]the dedication of the wall of
Jerusalem they sought out the Levites in
all their places, to bring them to Jerusalem to celebrate the dedication with gladness, [b]both with thanksgivings and singing,
with cymbals and stringed instruments and
harps. 28And the sons of the singers gathered together from the countryside around
Jerusalem, from the [a]villages of the Netophathites, 29from the house of Gilgal, and
from the fields of Geba and Azmaveth; for
the singers had built themselves villages
all around Jerusalem. 30Then the priests
and Levites [a]purified themselves, and purified the people, the gates, and the wall.

31So I brought the leaders of Judah up on
the wall, and appointed two large thanksgiving choirs. [a]*One* went to the right hand
on the wall [b]toward the Refuse Gate. 32Af-
ter them went Hoshaiah and half of the
leaders of Judah, 33and Azariah, Ezra, Meshullam, 34Judah, Benjamin, Shemaiah,
Jeremiah, 35and some of the priests' sons
[a]with trumpets—Zechariah the son of
Jonathan, the son of Shemaiah, the son of
Mattaniah, the son of Michaiah, the son of
Zaccur, the son of Asaph, 36and his brethren, Shemaiah, Azarel, Milalai, Gilalai, Maai,
Nethanel, Judah, *and* Hanani, with [a]the musical [b]instruments of David the man of God.
And Ezra the scribe *went* before them. 37[a]By
the Fountain Gate, in front of them, they
went up [b]the stairs of the [c]City of David, on
the stairway of the wall, beyond the house
of David, as far as [d]the Water Gate eastward.

38[a]The other thanksgiving choir went the
opposite *way,* and I *was* behind them with
half of the people on the wall, going past
the [b]Tower of the Ovens as far as [c]the Broad
Wall, 39[a]and above the Gate of Ephraim,
above [b]the Old Gate, above [c]the Fish Gate,
[d]the Tower of Hananel, the Tower of the
Hundred, as far as [e]the Sheep Gate; and
they stopped by [f]the Gate of the Prison.

40So the two thanksgiving choirs stood
in the house of God, likewise I and the half
of the rulers with me; 41and the priests,
Eliakim, Maaseiah, Minjamin,[1] Michaiah,
Elioenai, Zechariah, *and* Hananiah, with
trumpets; 42also Maaseiah, Shemaiah, Eleazar, Uzzi, Jehohanan, Malchijah, Elam,
and Ezer. The singers sang loudly with Jez-
rahiah the director.

43Also that day they offered great sacrifices, and rejoiced, for God had made them
rejoice with great joy; the women and the
children also rejoiced, so that the joy of Jerusalem was heard [a]afar off.

Temple Responsibilities

44[a]And at the same time some were appointed over the rooms of the storehouse
for the offerings, the firstfruits, and the
[b]tithes, to gather into them from the fields
of the cities the portions specified by the
Law for the priests and Levites; for Judah rejoiced over the priests and Levites
who ministered. 45Both the singers and

12:17 [1] Or *Mijamin* (compare verse 5) [2] Or *Maadiah* (compare verse 5) **12:20** [1] Or *Sallu* (compare verse 7) **12:22** [a] 1 Chr. 24:6 **12:23** [a] 1 Chr. 9:14–22 **12:24** [a] Neh. 11:17 [b] Ezra 3:11 [c] 1 Chr. 23—26 **12:26** [a] Neh. 8:9 [b] Ezra 7:6, 11 [1] Spelled *Jehozadak* in 1 Chronicles 6:14 **12:27** [a] Deut. 20:5; Neh. 7:1; Ps. 30:title [b] 1 Chr. 25:6; 2 Chr. 5:13; 7:6 **12:28** [a] 1 Chr. 9:16 **12:30** [a] Ezra 6:20; Neh. 13:22, 30 **12:31** [a] Neh. 12:38 [b] Neh. 2:13; 3:13 **12:35** [a] Num. 10:2, 8 **12:36** [a] 1 Chr. 23:5 [b] 2 Chr. 29:26, 27 **12:37** [a] Neh. 2:14; 3:15 [b] Neh. 3:15 [c] 2 Sam. 5:7–9 [d] Neh. 3:26; 8:1, 3, 16 **12:38** [a] Neh. 12:31 [b] Neh. 3:11 [c] Neh. 3:8 **12:39** [a] 2 Kin. 14:13; Neh. 8:16 [b] Neh. 3:6 [c] Neh. 3:3 [d] Neh. 3:1 [e] Neh. 3:32 [f] Jer. 32:2 **12:41** [1] Or *Mijamin* (compare verse 5) **12:43** [a] Ezra 3:13 **12:44** [a] 2 Chr. 31:11, 12; Neh. 13:5, 12, 13 [b] Neh. 10:37–39

the gatekeepers kept the charge of their
God and the charge of the purification, [a]ac-
cording to the command of David *and* Solomon his son. 46For in the days of David
[a]and Asaph of old *there were* chiefs of the
singers, and songs of praise and thanksgiving to God. 47In the days of Zerubbabel and in the days of Nehemiah all Israel
gave the portions for the singers and the
gatekeepers, a portion for [a]each day. [b]They
also consecrated *holy things* for the Levites,
[c]and the Levites consecrated *them* for the
children of Aaron.

Principles of Separation
(Num. 22:1—24:25)

13 On that day [a]they read from the Book
of Moses in the hearing of the people, and in it was found written [b]that no
Ammonite or Moabite should ever come
into the assembly of God, 2because they had
not met the children of Israel with bread
and water, but [a]hired Balaam against them
to curse them. [b]However, our God turned
the curse into a blessing. 3So it was, when
they had heard the Law, [a]that they separated all the mixed multitude from Israel.

The Reforms of Nehemiah

4Now before this, [a]Eliashib the priest,
having authority over the storerooms of
the house of our God, *was* allied with [b]To-
biah. 5And he had prepared for him a large
room, [a]where previously they had stored
the grain offerings, the frankincense, the
articles, the tithes of grain, the new wine
and oil, [b]which were commanded *to be
given* to the Levites and singers and gatekeepers, and the offerings for the priests.
6But during all this I was not in Jerusalem,
[a]for in the thirty-second year of Artaxerxes
king of Babylon I had returned to the king.
Then after certain days I obtained leave
from the king, 7and I came to Jerusalem
and discovered the evil that Eliashib had
done for Tobiah, in [a]preparing a room for
him in the courts of the house of God. 8And
it grieved me bitterly; therefore I threw
all the household goods of Tobiah out of
the room. 9Then I commanded them to
[a]cleanse the rooms; and I brought back into
them the articles of the house of God, with
the grain offering and the frankincense.

10I also realized that the portions for the
Levites had [a]not been given *them;* for each
of the Levites and the singers who did the
work had gone back to [b]his field. 11So [a]I contended with the rulers, and said, [b]"Why is
the house of God forsaken?" And I gathered them together and set them in their
place. 12[a]Then all Judah brought the tithe
of the grain and the new wine and the oil to
the storehouse. 13[a]And I appointed as treasurers over the storehouse Shelemiah the
priest and Zadok the scribe, and of the Levites, Pedaiah; and next to them *was* Hanan
the son of Zaccur, the son of Mattaniah; for
they were considered [b]faithful, and their
task *was* to distribute to their brethren.

14[a]Remember me, O my God, concerning
this, and do not wipe out my good deeds
that I have done for the house of my God,
and for its services!

15In those days I saw *people* in Judah
treading winepresses [a]on the Sabbath, and
bringing in sheaves, and loading donkeys
with wine, grapes, figs, and all *kinds of* burdens, [b]which they brought into Jerusalem
on the Sabbath day. And I warned *them*
about the day on which they were selling

#OXYGEN
NEHEMIAH 13:2
Exalt His Awesome Mercy

You do not have to be perfect to accept God's perfect love. He cares for you always. He may discipline you, but He will never abandon you. Become stronger because of His mercy and grace.

Breathe and **exalt His awesome mercy.**

12:45 [a] 1 Chr. 25; 26 12:46 [a] 1 Chr. 25:1; 2 Chr. 29:30 12:47 [a] Neh. 11:23 [b] Num. 18:21, 24 [c] Num. 18:26 13:1 [a] [Deut. 31:11, 12]; 2 Kin. 23:2; Neh. 8:3, 8; 9:3; Is. 34:16 [b] Deut. 23:3, 4 13:2 [a] Num. 22:5; Josh. 24:9, 10 [b] Num. 23:1; 24:10; Deut. 23:5 13:3 [a] Neh. 9:2; 10:28 13:4 [a] Neh. 12:10 [b] Neh. 2:10; 4:3; 6:1 13:5 [a] Neh. 12:44 [b] Num. 18:21, 24 13:6 [a] Neh. 5:14–16 13:7 [a] Neh. 13:1, 5 13:9 [a] 2 Chr. 29:5, 15, 16 13:10 [a] Neh. 10:37; Mal. 3:8 [b] Num. 35:2 13:11 [a] Neh. 13:17, 25 [b] Neh. 10:39 13:12 [a] Neh. 10:38; 12:44 13:13 [a] 2 Chr. 31:12 [b] 1 Cor. 4:2 13:14 [a] Neh. 5:19; 13:22, 31 13:15 [a] [Ex. 20:10] [b] Neh. 10:31; [Jer. 17:21]

provisions. 16Men of Tyre dwelt there also, who brought in fish and all kinds of goods, and sold *them* on the Sabbath to the children of Judah, and in Jerusalem.

17Then I contended with the nobles of Judah, and said to them, "What evil thing *is* this that you do, by which you profane the Sabbath day? 18[a]Did not your fathers do thus, and did not our God bring all this disaster on us and on this city? Yet you bring added wrath on Israel by profaning the Sabbath."

19So it was, at the gates of Jerusalem, as it [a]began to be dark before the Sabbath, that I commanded the gates to be shut, and charged that they must not be opened till after the Sabbath. [b]Then I posted *some* of my servants at the gates, *so that* no burdens would be brought in on the Sabbath day. 20Now the merchants and sellers of all kinds of wares lodged outside Jerusalem once or twice.

21Then I warned them, and said to them, "Why do you spend the night around the wall? If you do *so* again, I will lay hands on you!" From that time on they came no *more* on the Sabbath. 22And I commanded the Levites that [a]they should cleanse themselves, and that they should go and guard the gates, to sanctify the Sabbath day.

Remember me, O my God, *concerning* this also, and spare me according to the greatness of Your mercy!

23In those days I also saw Jews *who* [a]had married women of [b]Ashdod, Ammon, *and* Moab. 24And half of their children spoke the language of Ashdod, and could not speak the language of Judah, but spoke according to the language of one or the other people.

25So I [a]contended with them and cursed them, struck some of them and pulled out their hair, and made them [b]swear by God, *saying,* "You shall not give your daughters as wives to their sons, nor take their daughters for your sons or yourselves. 26[a]Did not Solomon king of Israel sin by these things? Yet among many nations there was no king like him, [b]who was beloved of his God; and God made him king over all Israel. [c]Nevertheless pagan women caused even him to sin. 27Should we then hear of your doing all this great evil, [a]transgressing against our God by marrying pagan women?"

28And *one* of the sons [a]of Joiada, the son of Eliashib the high priest, *was* a son-in-law of [b]Sanballat the Horonite; therefore I drove him from me.

29[a]Remember them, O my God, because they have defiled the priesthood and [b]the covenant of the priesthood and the Levites.

30[a]Thus I cleansed them of everything pagan. I also [b]assigned duties to the priests and the Levites, each to his service, 31and *to bringing* [a]the wood offering and the firstfruits at appointed times.

[b]Remember me, O my God, for good!

13:18 [a] Ezra 9:13; [Jer. 17:21] 13:19 [a] Lev. 23:32 [b] Jer. 17:21, 22 13:22 [a] 1 Chr. 15:12; Neh. 12:30 13:23 [a] [Ex. 34:16; Deut. 7:3, 4]; Ezra 9:2; Neh. 10:30 [b] Neh. 4:7 13:25 [a] Prov. 28:4 [b] Ezra 10:5; Neh. 10:29, 30 13:26 [a] 1 Kin. 11:1, 2 [b] 2 Sam. 12:24, 25 [c] 1 Kin. 11:4–8 13:27 [a] [Ezra 10:2]; Neh. 13:23 13:28 [a] Neh. 12:10, 12 [b] Neh. 4:1, 7; 6:1, 2 13:29 [a] Neh. 6:14 [b] Mal. 2:4, 11, 12 13:30 [a] Neh. 10:30 [b] Neh. 12:1 13:31 [a] Neh. 10:34 [b] Neh. 13:14, 22

THE BOOK OF

ESTHER

OVERVIEW

The author of the Book of Esther is unknown, but many scholars attribute the writing to Mordecai, who was Esther's cousin. The two lived in Shushan (Susa) under the reign of King Ahasuerus of Persia, who reigned from 486 to 465 BC. Written around 475 BC, the account takes place after King Cyrus allowed the Jews to return to Jerusalem.

Esther opens with King Ahasuerus hosting a lavish feast in the palace (see 1:2–8). Ahasuerus commanded that Queen Vashti make an appearance so he could put her beauty on display before his guests (see vv. 10–11). When the queen refused, the king sought counsel from the wise men of the kingdom, who advised him to banish the queen. Ahasuerus consented, decreed that she was no longer queen, and sent her away (see vv. 19–22).

Sometime later, Ahasuerus's servants suggested that he choose a new wife from among the beautiful women in his kingdom (see 2:1–4). Esther was among the women taken to the palace to vie for the king's attention, but Mordecai instructed Esther to keep her nationality a secret (see vv. 5–10). Ahasuerus crowned Esther queen because he loved her "more than all the other women, and she obtained grace and favor in his sight" (v. 17).

Later, when Mordecai learned of a plot to kill the king, he shared the information with Esther. She then brought the matter to the king's attention, and the men who had made the plan were hanged (see 2:21–23).

About this same time, Haman, who was Ahasuerus's second-in-command, demanded that all citizens bow before him. Mordecai, however, refused because such an act was against the Law of Moses (see 3:1–4). Haman was thus consumed with anger toward Mordecai and asked the king's permission to kill all the Jews (see vv. 5–9). The king issued a decree "to destroy, to kill, and to annihilate all the Jews, both young and old, little children and women, in one day" (v. 13). Haman then had gallows built in anticipation of watching Mordecai die (see 5:9–14). Later, when King Ahasuerus learned about what Mordecai had done to save his life, he instructed Haman to publicly honor Mordecai (ch. 6). This only caused Haman's hatred for Mordecai to intensify.

Recognizing the peril he and his people were in, Mordecai sent Esther a written copy of the king's decree and implored her to speak to the king on behalf of her people (see 4:8). Tradition did not allow her to go the king unless he called for her, though. If Esther approached the king without being summoned, she risked death if he did not extend his golden scepter in welcome to her (4:11). Esther, however, decided that saving her people was worth the risk.

When she entered the king's court, he received her, and she was able to tell him of Haman's evil plan to destroy the Jews. The king had Haman hanged on the same gallows he had prepared for Mordecai (see 7:1–10). He gave the house of Haman to Esther (see 8:7) and allowed Mordecai to write a new decree in the king's name that allowed the Jews to defend themselves (see 8:9–14). The Jews celebrated their deliverance with the Feast of Purim (see 9:16–32), and the king "advanced" Mordecai (10:1–3).

The Book of Esther demonstrates God's power to bring life from sure death and foil even the evilest of plots against His people. God, who is all-knowing, had a plan already in place to pro-

tect the Jews from death. He placed Esther, one of His own, in the right place at the right time and gave her favor with the king. This favor ultimately led not only to the Jews' deliverance from death but also to their increased prosperity in a foreign land.

BREATHE IT IN

The Book of Esther is proof that God is always at work, even when it is behind the scenes and we might not see it. Although the name of God is not mentioned in this book, He is clearly at work throughout it. God arranged Esther's selection as the new queen of Persia so that she would be in a position to intercede for the Jews. He also placed Mordecai in the right place at the right time to overhear the plot against the king. God moved the king to allow Esther to approach him, and He further moved him to spare the Jews. Behind the scenes, God put all the pieces in place for His people's deliverance.

Can you imagine someone telling you they would kill your family if you refused to bow down to a powerful, evil politician? How would you respond? Would you bow down to save your family, or would you honor God by refusing? When Mordecai faced this situation, he stood fast in his commitment to God despite the threat of death. Instead of giving in, he sought intervention. As a result of his obedience and that of Queen Esther, God saved the Jews from death and Mordecai was promoted to a prominent position in the kingdom.

We often forget that nothing in our lives is coincidental. "All things work together for good to those who love God" (Rom. 8:28). Even so, life often does not make sense to us. Life can be challenging, and we might not understand why things happen the way they do. God's hand in our lives is not always recognized. There are times when we might question whether God is for us or against us. There are times we might wonder if He is even present at all. When going about our day-to-day activities and during trying situations, we might ask, "Why is this happening to me?" or "God, where are You?" But we can rest assured, knowing that God is always there. Even when we cannot feel His presence, He is orchestrating the events in our lives to fulfill His purposes.

As Christians, we cannot avoid hurt, pain, and the Enemy's attacks against us. This is part of life in a fallen world. But when we encounter these things, do we turn toward God, or do we turn away from Him? Do we trust God to fight our battles, or do we attempt to fight them in our own power? Even amid difficulties, trust that God has placed you exactly where you are. He always does. Do not see yourself as being in the wrong place at the wrong time. Although we may not see what God sees or know what God knows, we must believe with our hearts that He sees all things and knows what is best for us. Be patient and step out in faith as Esther did. Believe that everything will work out for your good, and watch the hand of God put all the pieces of the puzzle together for His glory.

†

THE BOOK OF

ESTHER

The King Dethrones Queen Vashti

1 Now it came to pass in the days of [a]Ahas-
uerus[1] (this *was* the Ahasuerus who
reigned [b]over one hundred and twenty-
seven provinces, [c]from India to Ethiopia),
2in those days when King Ahasuerus [a]sat
on the throne of his kingdom, which *was*
in [b]Shushan[1] the citadel, 3*that* in the third
year of his reign he [a]made a feast for all his
officials and servants—the powers of Persia and Media, the nobles, and the princes
of the provinces *being* before him— 4when
he showed the riches of his glorious kingdom and the splendor of his excellent majesty for many days, one hundred and eighty
days *in all.*

5And when these days were completed,
the king made a feast lasting seven days for
all the people who were present in Shushan
the citadel, from great to small, in the court
of the garden of the king's palace. 6*There
were* white and blue linen *curtains* fastened with cords of fine linen and purple
on silver rods and marble pillars; *and the*
[a]couches *were* of gold and silver on a *mosaic* pavement of alabaster, turquoise, and
white and black marble. 7And they served
drinks in golden vessels, each vessel being
different from the other, with royal wine in
abundance, [a]according to the generosity
of the king. 8In accordance with the law,
the drinking was not compulsory; for so
the king had ordered all the officers of his
household, that they should do according
to each man's pleasure.

9Queen Vashti also made a feast for the
women *in* the royal palace which *belonged*
to King Ahasuerus.

10On the seventh day, when the heart
of the king was merry with wine, he commanded Mehuman, Biztha, [a]Harbona, Big-
tha, Abagtha, Zethar, and Carcas, seven
eunuchs who served in the presence of
King Ahasuerus, 11to bring Queen Vashti
before the king, *wearing* her royal crown,
in order to show her beauty to the people
and the officials, for she *was* beautiful to
behold. 12But Queen Vashti refused to come
at the king's command *brought* by *his* eunuchs; therefore the king was furious, and
his anger burned within him.

13Then the king said to the [a]wise men
[b]who understood the times (for this *was*
the king's manner toward all who knew law
and justice, 14those closest to him *being* Car-
shena, Shethar, Admatha, Tarshish, Meres,
Marsena, and Memucan, the [a]seven princes
of Persia and Media, [b]who had access to the
king's presence, *and* who ranked highest in
the kingdom): 15"What *shall we* do to Queen
Vashti, according to law, because she did
not obey the command of King Ahasuerus
brought to her by the eunuchs?"

16And Memucan answered before the
king and the princes: "Queen Vashti has
not only wronged the king, but also all the
princes, and all the people who *are* in all
the provinces of King Ahasuerus. 17For the
queen's behavior will become known to all
women, so that they will [a]despise their husbands in their eyes, when they report, 'King
Ahasuerus commanded Queen Vashti to
be brought in before him, but she did not
come.' 18This very day the *noble* ladies of
Persia and Media will say to all the king's officials that they have heard of the behavior

---

1:1 [a] Ezra 4:6; Dan. 9:1 [b] Esth. 8:9 [c] Dan. 6:1 [1] Generally identified with Xerxes I (485–464 BC) 1:2 [a] 1 Kin. 1:46 [b] Neh. 1:1; Dan. 8:2 [1] Or *Susa,* and so throughout this book 1:3 [a] Gen. 40:20; Esth. 2:18 1:6 [a] Esth. 7:8; Ezek. 23:41; Amos 2:8; 6:4 1:7 [a] Esth. 2:18 1:10 [a] Esth. 7:9 1:13 [a] Jer. 10:7; Dan. 2:12; Matt. 2:1 [b] 1 Chr. 12:32 1:14 [a] Ezra 7:14 [b] 2 Kin. 25:19; [Matt. 18:10] 1:17 [a] [Eph. 5:33]

of the queen. Thus *there will be* excessive
contempt and wrath. 19If it pleases the king,
let a royal decree go out from him, and
let it be recorded in the laws of the Persians and the Medes, so that it will [a]not be
altered, that Vashti shall come no more
before King Ahasuerus; and let the king
give her royal position to another who is
better than she. 20When the king's decree
which he will make is proclaimed throughout all his empire (for it is great), all wives
will [a]honor their husbands, both great and
small."

21And the reply pleased the king and the
princes, and the king did according to the
word of Memucan. 22Then he sent letters to
all the king's provinces, [a]to each province in
its own script, and to every people in their
own language, that each man should [b]be
master in his own house, and speak in the
language of his own people.

Esther Becomes Queen

2 After these things, when the wrath of
King Ahasuerus subsided, he remembered Vashti, [a]what she had done, and what
had been decreed against her. 2Then the
king's servants who attended him said: "Let
beautiful young virgins be sought for the
king; 3and let the king appoint officers in
all the provinces of his kingdom, that they
may gather all the beautiful young virgins
to Shushan the citadel, into the women's
quarters, under the custody of Hegai[1] the
king's eunuch, custodian of the women.
And let beauty preparations be given *them.*
4Then let the young woman who pleases
the king be queen instead of Vashti."

This thing pleased the king, and he
did so.

5In Shushan the citadel there was a certain Jew whose name *was* Mordecai the son
of Jair, the son of Shimei, the son of [a]Kish,
a Benjamite. 6[a]*Kish*[1] had been carried away
from Jerusalem with the captives who had
been captured with Jeconiah[2] king of Judah, whom Nebuchadnezzar the king of
Babylon had carried away. 7And *Mordecai*
had brought up Hadassah, that *is,* Esther,
[a]his uncle's daughter, for she had neither
father nor mother. The young woman *was*
lovely and beautiful. When her father and
mother died, Mordecai took her as his own
daughter.

8So it was, when the king's command
and decree were heard, and when many
young women were [a]gathered at Shushan
the citadel, *under* the custody of Hegai, that
Esther also was taken to the king's palace,
into the care of Hegai the custodian of the
women. 9Now the young woman pleased
him, and she obtained his favor; so he
readily gave [a]beauty preparations to her,
besides her allowance. Then seven choice
maidservants were provided for her from
the king's palace, and he moved her and
her maidservants to the best *place* in the
house of the women.

10[a]Esther had not revealed her people or
family, for Mordecai had charged her not to
reveal *it.* 11And every day Mordecai paced
in front of the court of the women's quarters, to learn of Esther's welfare and what
was happening to her.

12Each young woman's turn came to go
in to King Ahasuerus after she had completed twelve months' preparation, according to the regulations for the women, for
thus were the days of their preparation apportioned: six months with oil of myrrh,
and six months with perfumes and preparations for beautifying women. 13Thus *prepared, each* young woman went to the king,
and she was given whatever she desired to
take with her from the women's quarters
to the king's palace. 14In the evening she
went, and in the morning she returned to
the second house of the women, to the custody of Shaashgaz, the king's eunuch who
kept the concubines. She would not go in
to the king again unless the king delighted
in her and called for her by name.

15Now when the turn came for Esther [a]the
daughter of Abihail the uncle of Mordecai,
who had taken her as his daughter, to go in
to the king, she requested nothing but what
Hegai the king's eunuch, the custodian of
the women, advised. And Esther [b]obtained
favor in the sight of all who saw her. 16So
Esther was taken to King Ahasuerus, into

1:19 [a] Esth. 8:8; Dan. 6:8 1:20 [a] [Eph. 5:33; Col. 3:18; 1 Pet. 3:1] 1:22 [a] Esth. 3:12; 8:9 [b] [Eph. 5:22–24; 1 Tim. 2:12] 2:1 [a] Esth. 1:19, 20
2:3 [1] Hebrew *Hege* 2:5 [a] 1 Sam. 9:1 2:6 [a] 2 Kin. 24:14, 15; 2 Chr. 36:10, 20; Jer. 24:1 [1] Literally *Who* [2] Same as *Jehoiachin,*
2 Kings 24:6 and elsewhere 2:7 [a] Esth. 2:15 2:8 [a] Esth. 2:3 2:9 [a] Esth. 2:3, 12 2:10 [a] Esth. 2:20
2:15 [a] Esth. 2:7; 9:29 [b] Esth. 5:2, 8

his royal palace, in the tenth month, which
is the month of Tebeth, in the seventh year
of his reign. 17The king loved Esther more
than all the *other* women, and she obtained
grace and favor in his sight more than all
the virgins; so he set the royal [a]crown upon
her head and made her queen instead of
Vashti. 18Then the king [a]made a great feast,
the Feast of Esther, for all his officials and
servants; and he proclaimed a holiday in
the provinces and gave gifts according to
the generosity of a king.

Mordecai Discovers a Plot

19When virgins were gathered together a
second time, Mordecai sat within the king's
gate. 20[a]*Now* Esther had not revealed her
family and her people, just as Mordecai had
charged her, for Esther obeyed the command of Mordecai as when she was brought
up by him.

21In those days, while Mordecai sat
within the king's gate, two of the king's eunuchs, Bigthan and Teresh, doorkeepers,
became furious and sought to lay hands on
King Ahasuerus. 22So the matter became
known to Mordecai, [a]who told Queen Esther, and Esther informed the king in Mordecai's name. 23And when an inquiry was
made into the matter, it was confirmed,
and both were hanged on a gallows; and it
was written in [a]the book of the chronicles
in the presence of the king.

Haman's Conspiracy Against the Jews

3 After these things King Ahasuerus promoted Haman, the son of Hammeda-
tha the [a]Agagite, and [b]advanced him and
set his seat above all the princes who *were*
with him. 2And all the king's servants who
were [a]within the king's gate bowed and
paid homage to Haman, for so the king had
commanded concerning him. But Mordecai [b]would not bow or pay homage. 3Then
the king's servants who *were* within the
king's gate said to Mordecai, "Why do you
transgress the [a]king's command?" 4Now it
happened, when they spoke to him daily
and he would not listen to them, that they
told *it* to Haman, to see whether Mordecai's words would stand; for *Mordecai* had
told them that he *was* a Jew. 5When Haman saw that Mordecai [a]did not bow or pay
him homage, Haman was [b]filled with wrath.
6But he disdained to lay hands on Mordecai alone, for they had told him of the people of Mordecai. Instead, Haman [a]sought
to destroy all the Jews who *were* throughout the whole kingdom of Ahasuerus—the
people of Mordecai.

7In the first month, which is the month
of Nisan, in the twelfth year of King Ahasuerus, [a]they cast Pur (that *is*, the lot), before Haman to determine the day and the
month,[1] until *it fell on the* twelfth *month*,[2]
which *is* the month of Adar.

8Then Haman said to King Ahasuerus,
"There is a certain people scattered and dispersed among the people in all the provinces of your kingdom; [a]their laws *are*
different from all *other* people's, and they
do not keep the king's laws. Therefore it *is*
not fitting for the king to let them remain.
9If it pleases the king, let *a decree* be written
that they be destroyed, and I will pay ten
thousand talents of silver into the hands
of those who do the work, to bring *it* into
the king's treasuries."

10So the king [a]took [b]his signet ring from
his hand and gave it to Haman, the son of
Hammedatha the Agagite, the [c]enemy of
the Jews. 11And the king said to Haman,
"The money and the people *are* given to
you, to do with them as seems good to you."

12[a]Then the king's scribes were called
on the thirteenth day of the first month,
and *a decree* was written according to all
that Haman commanded—to the king's
satraps, to the governors who *were* over
each province, to the officials of all people,
to every province [b]according to its script,
and to every people in their language. [c]In
the name of King Ahasuerus it was written, and sealed with the king's signet ring.
13And the letters were [a]sent by couriers into
all the king's provinces, to destroy, to kill,

2:17 [a] Esth. 1:11 2:18 [a] Esth. 1:3 2:20 [a] Esth. 2:10; [Prov. 22:6] 2:22 [a] Esth. 6:1, 2 2:23 [a] Esth. 6:1 3:1 [a] Num. 24:7; 1 Sam. 15:8 [b] Esth. 5:11 3:2 [a] Esth. 2:19, 21; 5:9 [b] Esth. 3:5; Ps. 15:4 3:3 [a] Esth. 3:2 3:5 [a] Esth. 3:2; 5:9 [b] Dan. 3:19 3:6 [a] Ps. 83:4; [Rev. 12:1–17] 3:7 [a] Esth. 9:24–26 [1] Septuagint adds *to destroy the people of Mordecai in one day;* Vulgate adds *the nation of the Jews should be destroyed.* [2] Following Masoretic Text and Vulgate; Septuagint reads *and the lot fell on the fourteenth of the month.*
3:8 [a] Ezra 4:12–15; Acts 16:20, 21 3:10 [a] Gen. 41:42 [b] Esth. 8:2, 8 [c] Esth. 7:6 3:12 [a] Esth. 8:9 [b] Esth. 1:22 [c] 1 Kin. 21:8; Esth. 8:8–10 3:13 [a] 2 Chr. 30:6; Esth. 8:10, 14

and to annihilate all the Jews, both young and old, little children and women, [b]in one day, on the thirteenth *day* of the twelfth month, which *is* the month of Adar, and [c]to plunder their possessions.[1] 14 [a]A copy of the document was to be issued as law in every province, being published for all people, that they should be ready for that day. 15 The couriers went out, hastened by the king's command; and the decree was proclaimed in Shushan the citadel. So the king and Haman sat down to drink, but [a]the city of Shushan was perplexed.

Esther Agrees to Help the Jews

4 When Mordecai learned all that had happened, he [a]tore his clothes and put on sackcloth [b]and ashes, and went out into the midst of the city. He [c]cried out with a loud and bitter cry. 2 He went as far as the front of the king's gate, for no one *might* enter the king's gate clothed with sackcloth. 3 And in every province where the king's command and decree arrived, *there was* great mourning among the Jews, with fasting, weeping, and wailing; and many lay in sackcloth and ashes.

4 So Esther's maids and eunuchs came and told her, and the queen was deeply distressed. Then she sent garments to clothe Mordecai and take his sackcloth away from him, but he would not accept *them.* 5 Then Esther called Hathach, *one* of the king's eunuchs whom he had appointed to attend her, and she gave him a command concerning Mordecai, to learn what and why this *was.* 6 So Hathach went out to Mordecai in the city square that *was* in front of the king's gate. 7 And Mordecai told him all that had happened to him, and [a]the sum of money that Haman had promised to pay into the king's treasuries to destroy the Jews. 8 He also gave him [a]a copy of the written decree for their destruction, which was given at Shushan, that he might show it to Esther and explain it to her, and that he might command her to go in to the king to make supplication to him and plead before him for her people.

9 So Hathach returned and told Esther the words of Mordecai.

10 Then Esther spoke to Hathach, and gave him a command for Mordecai: 11 "All the king's servants and the people of the king's provinces know that any man or woman who goes into [a]the inner court to the king, who has not been called, [b]*he has* but one law: put *all* to death, except the one [c]to whom the king holds out the golden scepter, that he may live. Yet I myself have not been [d]called to go in to the king these thirty days." 12 So they told Mordecai Esther's words.

13 And Mordecai told *them* to answer Esther: "Do not think in your heart that you will escape in the king's palace any more than all the other Jews. 14 For if you remain completely silent at this time, relief and deliverance will arise for the Jews from another place, but you and your father's house will perish. Yet who knows whether you have come to the kingdom for *such* a time as this?"

15 Then Esther told *them* to reply to Mordecai: 16 "Go, gather all the Jews who are present in Shushan, and fast for me; neither eat nor drink for [a]three days, night or day. My maids and I will fast likewise. And so I will go to the king, which *is* against the law; [b]and if I perish, I perish!"

17 So Mordecai went his way and did according to all that Esther commanded him.[1]

Esther's Banquet

5 Now it happened [a]on the third day that Esther put on *her* royal *robes* and stood in [b]the inner court of the king's palace, across from the king's house, while the king sat on his royal throne in the royal house, facing the entrance of the house.[1] 2 So it was, when the king saw Queen Esther standing in the court, *that* [a]she found favor in his sight, and [b]the king held out to Esther the golden scepter that *was* in his hand. Then Esther went near and touched the top of the scepter.

3 And the king said to her, "What do you wish, Queen Esther? What *is* your request?

3:13 [b] Esth. 8:12 [c] Esth. 8:11; 9:10 [1] Septuagint adds the text of the letter here. 3:14 [a] Esth. 8:13, 14 3:15 [a] Esth. 8:15; [Prov. 29:2]
4:1 [a] 2 Sam. 1:11; Esth. 3:8–10; Jon. 3:5, 6 [b] Josh. 7:6; Ezek. 27:30 [c] Gen. 27:34 4:7 [a] Esth. 3:9 4:8 [a] Esth. 3:14, 15 4:11 [a] Esth. 5:1; 6:4 [b] Dan. 2:9 [c] Esth. 5:2; 8:4 [d] Esth. 2:14 4:16 [a] Esth. 5:1 [b] Gen. 43:14 4:17 [1] Septuagint adds a prayer of Mordecai here.
5:1 [a] Esth. 4:16 [b] Esth. 4:11; 6:4 [1] Septuagint adds many extra details in verses 1 and 2.
5:2 [a] [Prov. 21:1] [b] Esth. 4:11; 8:4

[a]It shall be given to you—up to half the
kingdom!"
4 So Esther answered, "If it pleases the
king, let the king and Haman come today to
the banquet that I have prepared for him."
5 Then the king said, "Bring Haman
quickly, that he may do as Esther has said."
So the king and Haman went to the banquet that Esther had prepared.
6 At the banquet of wine [a]the king said
to Esther, [b]"What *is* your petition? It shall
be granted you. What *is* your request, up to
half the kingdom? It shall be done!"
7 Then Esther answered and said, "My
petition and request *is this:* 8 If I have
found favor in the sight of the king, and
if it pleases the king to grant my petition
and fulfill my request, then let the king and
Haman come to the [a]banquet which I will
prepare for them, and tomorrow I will do
as the king has said."

Haman's Plot Against Mordecai

9 So Haman went out that day [a]joyful and
with a glad heart; but when Haman saw
Mordecai in the king's gate, and [b]that he
did not stand or tremble before him, he
was filled with indignation against Mordecai. 10 Nevertheless Haman [a]restrained
himself and went home, and he sent and

ESTHER 4:14

I AM MORDECAI

"For if you remain completely silent at this time, relief and deliverance will arise for the Jews from another place, but you and your father's house will perish. Yet who knows whether you have come to the kingdom for such a time as this?" Esther 4:14

I am Mordecai. I raised my uncle's daughter, Hadassah, more commonly known by her Persian name, Esther. We were exiled Jews living in Persia under King Ahasuerus.

When King Ahasuerus sought to replace his queen, he summoned all available young women to his palace. Esther was included, so I warned her to keep her Israelite heritage a secret. Esther won favor with the king, and he made her his new queen.

A man named Haman held a high position in Persia. He loved the status and had men bow down to him, but I refused. This angered Haman, so he sought to destroy me and all the Jews. He told the king that the Jews did not obey Persian laws and urged the king to order the death of all the Jews in Persia. The king complied. Haman even built gallows specifically for me.

I was distraught over the king's decree. Esther inquired about my distress, so I told her about the decree. I told her to plead with the king for the lives of her people. Esther was afraid. Anyone who approached the king without being summoned could be killed. I helped Esther see that God could have ordained her position for this time—so she could save her people. Esther went to the king, and he gladly received her. She revealed Haman's evil plot. The furious king immediately ordered that Haman be killed on the very gallows he built for me. Then Esther and I issued an edict in the king's name that allowed the Jews to defend themselves against those who would soon attack them. My people defeated our enemies.

It was difficult for Mordecai to ask Esther to go to the king and risk her life. However, if he had held back, she may have missed the calling God had on her life. Integrity is when our words and deeds are in line with our beliefs. We should not hold back from speaking the truth in love, no matter the consequences.

5:3 [a] Esth. 7:2; Mark 6:23 5:6 [a] Esth. 7:2 [b] Esth. 9:12 5:8 [a] Esth. 6:14 5:9 [a] [Job 20:5; Luke 6:25] [b] Esth. 3:5 5:10 [a] 2 Sam. 13:22

EXALT HIS AWESOME MERCY

INHALE

Though I have known God for years, I have done a lot of wrong. A lot of very, very wrong. Basically, I have lived by the motto "If you ain't cheatin', then you ain't tryin'." I have used people and I have wronged people. Let's just say my life has followed the lists of what *not* to do in Scripture far more than what a Christian is to do. But I want to change all of that. I want to get serious with God. But it's hard to believe I deserve God's goodness when I have been anything but good myself. It's hard to even ask. Why should He forgive me? Why should He give me mercy and grace?

EXHALE

It might not feel like it, but you are off to a great start with getting serious with God. You've come to the right place (the Bible) and the right person (Jesus Christ). Jesus has been dealing with cases like yours since His earthly ministry. Meeting people where they are, taking them in, and then changing them to be who they were meant to be is His specialty. Jesus is the redeemer of not the spotless but the spotted.

The key here is to understand God's forgiveness. If you have never asked God to forgive you—if you've known about Jesus but have never placed your trust in Him—then all you need to do is that. Jesus came and died for people like you. No sin is too great and no sinner is too evil for God's forgiveness. You see, that's who our God is. He is the God who forgives.

Now, if you have trusted in Christ but have not been living like it, here's the amazing thing about God's forgiveness: it is unconditional and unchanging. All the sins you have done—and those you will do still—are forgiven. Jesus took them all! As Christians, we still need to repent of our sin. We need to turn away from it. But we do that not for forgiveness but because we are forgiven. We strive to live what is now true about us.

The two greatest and most difficult things to do are to give and forgive. Through the life and death of His Son, God has demonstrated the perfection of both these qualities. We would please Him and do ourselves a favor by forgiving ourselves and resting in His amazing grace (the unmerited favor of God). Esther 5 is a great example of the love of God. Go back and read this chapter and be amazed at His favor at work.

called for his friends and his wife Zeresh.
11Then Haman told them of his great riches,
[a]the multitude of his children, everything
in which the king had promoted him, and
how he had [b]advanced him above the officials and servants of the king.
12Moreover Haman said, "Besides, Queen
Esther invited no one but me to come in
with the king to the banquet that she prepared; and tomorrow I am again invited by
her, along with the king. 13Yet all this avails
me nothing, so long as I see Mordecai the
Jew sitting at the king's gate."
14Then his wife Zeresh and all his friends
said to him, "Let a [a]gallows be made, fifty
cubits high, and in the morning [b]suggest
to the king that Mordecai be hanged on it;
then go merrily with the king to the banquet."

And the thing pleased Haman; so he had [c]the gallows made.

The King Honors Mordecai

6 That night the king could not sleep.
So one was commanded to bring [a]the
book of the records of the chronicles; and
they were read before the king. 2And it was
found written that Mordecai had told of
Bigthana and Teresh, two of the king's eunuchs, the doorkeepers who had sought to

5:11 [a] Esth. 9:7–10 [b] Esth. 3:1 5:14 [a] Esth. 7:9 [b] Esth. 6:4 [c] Esth. 7:10 6:1 [a] Esth. 2:23; 10:2

lay hands on King Ahasuerus. 3Then the
king said, "What honor or dignity has been
bestowed on Mordecai for this?"

And the king's servants who attended
him said, "Nothing has been done for him."

4So the king said, "Who *is* in the court?"
Now Haman had *just* entered [a]the outer
court of the king's palace [b]to suggest that
the king hang Mordecai on the gallows that
he had prepared for him.

5The king's servants said to him, "Haman is there, standing in the court."

And the king said, "Let him come in."

6So Haman came in, and the king asked
him, "What shall be done for the man
whom the king delights to honor?"

Now Haman thought in his heart,
"Whom would the king delight to honor
more than [a]me?" 7And Haman answered
the king, "*For* the man whom the king delights to honor, 8let a royal robe be brought
which the king has worn, and [a]a horse on
which the king has ridden, which has a
royal crest placed on its head. 9Then let this
robe and horse be delivered to the hand of
one of the king's most noble princes, that
he may array the man whom the king delights to honor. Then parade him on horseback through the city square, [a]and proclaim
before him: 'Thus shall it be done to the
man whom the king delights to honor!'"

10Then the king said to Haman, "Hurry,
take the robe and the horse, as you have
suggested, and do so for Mordecai the Jew
who sits within the king's gate! Leave nothing undone of all that you have spoken."

11So Haman took the robe and the
horse, arrayed Mordecai and led him on
horseback through the city square, and
proclaimed before him, "Thus shall it be
done to the man whom the king delights
to honor!"

12Afterward Mordecai went back to the
king's gate. But Haman [a]hurried to his
house, mourning [b]and with his head covered. 13When Haman told his wife Zeresh
and all his friends everything that had happened to him, his wise men and his wife
Zeresh said to him, "If Mordecai, before
whom you have begun to fall, is of Jewish
descent, you will not prevail against [a]him
but will surely fall before him."

14While they *were* still talking with him,
the king's eunuchs came, and hastened to
bring Haman to [a]the banquet which Esther
had prepared.

Haman Hanged Instead of Mordecai

7 So the king and Haman went to dine
with Queen Esther. 2And on the second day, [a]at the banquet of wine, the king
again said to Esther, "What *is* your petition,
Queen Esther? It shall be granted you. And
what *is* your request, up to half the kingdom? It shall be done!"

3Then Queen Esther answered and said,
"If I have found favor in your sight, O king,
and if it pleases the king, let my life be given
me at my petition, and my people at my request. 4For we have been [a]sold, my people
and I, to be destroyed, to be killed, and to
be annihilated. Had we been sold as [b]male
and female slaves, I would have held my
tongue, although the enemy could never
compensate for the king's loss."

5So King Ahasuerus answered and said
to Queen Esther, "Who is he, and where is
he, who would dare presume in his heart
to do such a thing?"

6And Esther said, "The adversary and
[a]enemy *is* this wicked Haman!"

So Haman was terrified before the king
and queen.

7Then the king arose in his wrath from
the banquet of wine *and went* into the palace garden; but Haman stood before Queen
Esther, pleading for his life, for he saw that
evil was determined against him by the king.
8When the king returned from the palace
garden to the place of the banquet of wine,
Haman had fallen across [a]the couch where
Esther *was*. Then the king said, "Will he also
assault the queen while I *am* in the house?"

As the word left the king's mouth, they
[b]covered Haman's face. 9Now [a]Harbonah,
one of the eunuchs, said to the king, "Look!
[b]The gallows, fifty cubits high, which Haman made for Mordecai, who spoke [c]good
on the king's behalf, is standing at the
house of Haman."

6:4 [a] Esth. 5:1 [b] Esth. 5:14 6:6 [a] [Prov. 16:18; 18:12] 6:8 [a] 1 Kin. 1:33 6:9 [a] Gen. 41:43 6:12 [a] 2 Chr. 26:20 [b] 2 Sam. 15:30; Jer. 14:3, 4 6:13 [a] [Gen. 12:3]; Zech. 2:8 6:14 [a] Esth. 5:8 7:2 [a] Esth. 5:6 7:4 [a] Esth. 3:9; 4:7 [b] Deut. 28:68 7:6 [a] Esth. 3:10 7:8 [a] Esth. 1:6 [b] Job 9:24 7:9 [a] Esth. 1:10 [b] Esth. 5:14; [Ps. 7:16; Prov. 11:5, 6] [c] Esth. 6:2

Then the king said, "Hang him on it!"

10 So [a]they [b]hanged Haman on the gallows that he had prepared for Mordecai. Then the king's wrath subsided.

Esther Saves the Jews

8 On that day King Ahasuerus gave Queen Esther the house of Haman, the [a]enemy of the Jews. And Mordecai came before the king, for Esther had told [b]how he *was related* to her. 2 So the king took off [a]his signet ring, which he had taken from Haman, and gave it to Mordecai; and Esther appointed Mordecai over the house of Haman.

3 Now Esther spoke again to the king, fell down at his feet, and implored him with tears to counteract the evil of Haman the Agagite, and the scheme which he had devised against the Jews. 4 And [a]the king held out the golden scepter toward Esther. So Esther arose and stood before the king, 5 and said, "If it pleases the king, and if I have found favor in his sight and the thing *seems* right to the king and I am pleasing in his eyes, let it be written to revoke the [a]letters devised by Haman, the son of Hammedatha the Agagite, which he wrote to annihilate the Jews who *are* in all the king's provinces. 6 For how can I endure to see [a]the evil that will come to my people? Or how can I endure to see the destruction of my countrymen?"

7 Then King Ahasuerus said to Queen Esther and Mordecai the Jew, "Indeed, [a]I have given Esther the house of Haman, and they have hanged him on the gallows because he *tried to* lay his hand on the Jews. 8 You yourselves write *a decree* concerning the Jews, as you please, in the king's name, and seal *it* with the king's signet ring; for whatever is written in the king's name and sealed with the king's signet ring [a]no one can revoke."

9 [a]So the king's scribes were called at that time, in the third month, which *is* the month of Sivan, on the twenty-third *day;* and it was written, according to all that Mordecai commanded, to the Jews, the satraps, the governors, and the princes of the provinces [b]from India to Ethiopia, one hundred and twenty-seven provinces *in all,* to every province [c]in its own script, to every people in their own language, and to the Jews in their own script and language. 10 [a]And he wrote in the name of King Ahasuerus, sealed *it* with the king's signet ring, and sent letters by couriers on horseback, riding on royal horses bred from swift steeds.[1]

11 By these letters the king permitted the Jews who *were* in every city to [a]gather together and protect their lives—to [b]destroy, kill, and annihilate all the forces of any people or province that would assault them, *both* little children and women, and to plunder their possessions, 12 [a]on one day in all the provinces of King Ahasuerus, on the thirteenth *day* of the twelfth month, which *is* the month of Adar.[1] 13 [a]A copy of the document was to be issued as a decree in every province and published for all people, so that the Jews would be ready on that day to avenge themselves on their enemies. 14 The couriers who rode on royal horses went out, hastened and pressed on by the king's command. And the decree was issued in Shushan the citadel.

15 So Mordecai went out from the presence of the king in royal apparel of blue and white, with a great crown of gold and a garment of fine linen and purple; and [a]the city of Shushan rejoiced and was glad. 16 The Jews had [a]light and gladness, joy and honor. 17 And in every province and city, wherever the king's command and decree came, the Jews had joy and gladness, a feast [a]and a holiday. Then many of the people of the land [b]became Jews, because [c]fear of the Jews fell upon them.

The Jews Destroy Their Tormentors

9 Now [a]in the twelfth month, that *is,* the month of Adar, on the thirteenth day, [b]*the time* came for the king's command and his decree to be executed. On the day

---

7:10 [a] [Ps. 7:16; 94:23; Prov. 11:5, 6] [b] Ps. 37:35, 36; Dan. 6:24 **8:1** [a] Esth. 7:6 [b] Esth. 2:7, 15 **8:2** [a] Esth. 3:10 **8:4** [a] Esth. 4:11; 5:2 **8:5** [a] Esth. 3:13 **8:6** [a] Neh. 2:3; Esth. 7:4; 9:1 **8:7** [a] Esth. 8:1; Prov. 13:22 **8:8** [a] Esth. 1:19; Dan. 6:8, 12, 15 **8:9** [a] Esth. 3:12 [b] Esth. 1:1 [c] Esth. 1:22; 3:12 **8:10** [a] 1 Kin. 21:8; Esth. 3:12, 13 [1] Literally *sons of the swift horses* **8:11** [a] Esth. 9:2 [b] Esth. 9:10, 15, 16 **8:12** [a] Esth. 3:13; 9:1 [1] Septuagint adds the text of the letter here. **8:13** [a] Esth. 3:14, 15 **8:15** [a] Esth. 3:15; Prov. 29:2 **8:16** [a] Ps. 97:11; 112:4 **8:17** [a] 1 Sam. 25:8; Esth. 9:19 [b] Ps. 18:43 [c] Gen. 35:5; Ex. 15:16; Deut. 2:25; 11:25; 1 Chr. 14:17; Esth. 9:2 **9:1** [a] Esth. 8:12 [b] Esth. 3:13

that the enemies of the Jews had hoped to
overpower them, the opposite occurred,
in that the Jews themselves [c]overpowered
those who hated them. 2The Jews [a]gathered
together in their cities throughout all the
provinces of King Ahasuerus to lay hands
on those who [b]sought their harm. And no
one could withstand them, [c]because fear of
them fell upon all people. 3And all the officials of the provinces, the satraps, the governors, and all those doing the king's work,
helped the Jews, because the fear of Mordecai fell upon them. 4For Mordecai *was* great
in the king's palace, and his fame spread
throughout all the provinces; for this man
Mordecai [a]became increasingly prominent.
5Thus the Jews defeated all their enemies
with the stroke of the sword, with slaughter
and destruction, and did what they pleased
with those who hated them.
6And in [a]Shushan the citadel the Jews
killed and destroyed five hundred men.
7Also Parshandatha, Dalphon, Aspatha,
8Poratha, Adalia, Aridatha, 9Parmashta,
Arisai, Aridai, and Vajezatha— 10[a]the ten
sons of Haman the son of Hammedatha,
the enemy of the Jews—they killed; [b]but
they did not lay a hand on the plunder.
11On that day the number of those who
were killed in Shushan the citadel was
brought to the king. 12And the king said to
Queen Esther, "The Jews have killed and destroyed five hundred men in Shushan the
citadel, and the ten sons of Haman. What
have they done in the rest of the king's
provinces? Now [a]what *is* your petition? It
shall be granted to you. Or what *is* your further request? It shall be done."
13Then Esther said, "If it pleases the
king, let it be granted to the Jews who *are*
in Shushan to do again tomorrow [a]accord-
ing to today's decree, and let Haman's ten
sons [b]be hanged on the gallows."
14So the king commanded this to be
done; the decree was issued in Shushan,
and they hanged Haman's ten sons.
15And the Jews who *were* in Shushan
[a]gathered together again on the fourteenth
day of the month of Adar and killed three
hundred men at Shushan; [b]but they did not
lay a hand on the plunder.
16The remainder of the Jews in the king's
provinces [a]gathered together and protected
their lives, had rest from their enemies, and
killed seventy-five thousand of their enemies; [b]but they did not lay a hand on the
plunder. 17*This was* on the thirteenth day of
the month of Adar. And on the fourteenth
of *the month*[1] they rested and made it a day
of feasting and gladness.

The Feast of Purim

18But the Jews who *were* at Shushan assembled together [a]on the thirteenth *day,*
as well as on the fourteenth; and on the fifteenth of *the month*[1] they rested, and made
it a day of feasting and gladness. 19There-
fore the Jews of the villages who dwelt in
the unwalled towns celebrated the fourteenth day of the month of Adar [a]*with* gladness and feasting, [b]as a holiday, and for
[c]sending presents to one another.
20And Mordecai wrote these things
and sent letters to all the Jews, near and
far, who *were* in all the provinces of King
Ahasuerus, 21to establish among them that
they should celebrate yearly the fourteenth
and fifteenth days of the month of Adar,
22as the days on which the Jews had rest
from their enemies, as the month which
was turned from sorrow to joy for them,
and from mourning to a holiday; that they
should make them days of feasting and joy,
of [a]sending presents to one another and
gifts to the [b]poor. 23So the Jews accepted the
custom which they had begun, as Mordecai had written to them, 24because Haman,
the son of Hammedatha the Agagite, the
enemy of all the Jews, [a]had plotted against
the Jews to annihilate them, and had cast
Pur (that *is,* the lot), to consume them and
destroy them; 25but [a]when *Esther*[1] came before the king, he commanded by letter that
this[2] wicked plot which *Haman* had devised
against the Jews should [b]return on his own
head, and that he and his sons should be
hanged on the gallows.
26So they called these days Purim, after

9:1 [c] 2 Sam. 22:41 9:2 [a] Esth. 8:11; 9:15–18 [b] Ps. 71:13, 14 [c] Esth. 8:17 9:4 [a] 2 Sam. 3:1; 1 Chr. 11:9; [Prov. 4:18] 9:6 [a] Esth. 1:2; 3:15; 4:16 9:10 [a] Esth. 5:11; 9:7–10; Job 18:19; 27:13–15; Ps. 21:10 [b] Esth. 8:11 9:12 [a] Esth. 5:6; 7:2 9:13 [a] Esth. 8:11; 9:15 [b] 2 Sam. 21:6, 9 9:15 [a] Esth. 8:11; 9:2 [b] Esth. 9:10 9:16 [a] Esth. 9:2 [b] Esth. 8:11 9:17 [1] Literally *it* 9:18 [a] Esth. 9:11, 15 [1] Literally *it* 9:19 [a] Deut. 16:11, 14 [b] Esth. 8:16, 17 [c] Neh. 8:10, 12; Esth. 9:22 9:22 [a] Neh. 8:10; Esth. 9:19 [b] [Deut. 15:7–11]; Job 29:16 9:24 [a] Esth. 3:6, 7; 9:26 9:25 [a] Esth. 7:4–10; 8:3; 9:13, 14 [b] Esth. 7:10 [1] Literally *she* or *it* [2] Literally *his*

the name Pur. Therefore, because of all the
words of [a]this letter, what they had seen
concerning this matter, and what had happened to them, 27the Jews established and
imposed it upon themselves and their descendants and all who would [a]join them,
that without fail they should celebrate
these two days every year, according to the
written *instructions* and according to the
prescribed time, 28*that* these days *should*
be remembered and kept throughout every
generation, every family, every province,
and every city, that these days of Purim
should not fail *to be observed* among the
Jews, and *that* the memory of them should
not perish among their descendants.

29Then Queen Esther, [a]the daughter of
Abihail, with Mordecai the Jew, wrote with
full authority to confirm this [b]second letter
about Purim. 30And *Mordecai* sent letters
to all the Jews, to [a]the one hundred and
twenty-seven provinces of the kingdom of
Ahasuerus, *with* words of peace and truth,
31to confirm these days of Purim at their
appointed time, as Mordecai the Jew and
Queen Esther had prescribed for them, and
as they had decreed for themselves and
their descendants concerning matters of
their [a]fasting and lamenting. 32So the decree of Esther confirmed these matters of
Purim, and it was written in the book.

Mordecai's Advancement

10 And King Ahasuerus imposed tribute on the land and *on* [a]the islands of
the sea. 2Now all the acts of his power and
his might, and the account of the greatness
of Mordecai, [a]to which the king advanced
him, *are* they not written in the book of
the [b]chronicles of the kings of Media and
Persia? 3For Mordecai the Jew *was* [a]second
to King Ahasuerus, and was great among
the Jews and well received by the multitude of his brethren, [b]seeking the good of
his people and speaking peace to all his
countrymen.[1]

9:26 [a] Esth. 9:20 9:27 [a] Esth. 8:17; [Is. 56:3, 6]; Zech. 2:11 9:29 [a] Esth. 2:15 [b] Esth. 8:10; 9:20, 21 9:30 [a] Esth. 1:1 9:31 [a] Esth. 4:3, 16 10:1 [a] Gen. 10:5; Ps. 72:10; Is. 11:11; 24:15 10:2 [a] Esth. 8:15; 9:4 [b] Esth. 6:1 10:3 [a] Gen. 41:40, 43, 44; 2 Chr. 28:7 [b] Neh. 2:10; Ps. 122:8, 9 [1] Literally *seed*. Septuagint and Vulgate add a dream of Mordecai here; Vulgate adds six more chapters.

THE BOOK OF

JOB

OVERVIEW

The Book of Job was written by an unknown author, and the date of its writing is also undetermined. It is believed that Job lived before the time of Moses.

The Book of Job is the account of a faithful man who was "blameless and upright, and one who feared God" (Job 1:1). Job was a wealthy man with seven sons, three daughters, and great possessions, "the greatest of all the people of the East" (vv. 2–3).

In a conversation with Satan, God pointed to Job's staunch commitment to Him. Satan countered that the reason for that commitment was that God protected Job. Satan further claimed that if God removed that protection, Job would curse God (see 1:6–11). God allowed Satan to test Job's faithfulness by afflicting everything he had except for Job himself (see v. 12).

Satan stripped Job of everything, including his sons and daughters and livestock (see vv. 14–19). However, when Job received the reports of his losses, he did not curse God but instead "fell to the ground and worshiped" (v. 20).

In a second conversation, Satan told God that if Job suffered poor health, he would curse God (see 2:4–5). God then gave Satan permission to afflict Job but not to the point of taking his life (see v. 6). Satan struck Job with painful boils all over his body. Job's wife was horrified by all that had happened and told Job that he should "curse God and die" (vv. 7–9). But Job refused to speak against Almighty God (see v. 10).

Job 2:11–13 introduces Job's three friends—Eliphaz, Bildad, and Zophar—and chapters 3–31 detail Job's interactions with them. They each argued that Job experienced these trials because he had sinned against God and needed correction (see 5:6; 8:6). Such calamity had to be punishment from God. Job, however, maintained his righteousness, declaring himself clean before God (see 27:6). His only explanation was that God had made some sort of mistake or that there had been a misunderstanding. He longed to hear from God and be able to plead his case to Him.

At this point, a fourth person, Elihu, spoke up and chastised Job and his three friends for what they had each said (chs. 32–37). Chapters 38–41 then recount God's dialogue with Job. God questions Job about his knowledge of how He formed the world and how it operates. Job soon realized that he did not know enough to answer God, and he repented for attempting to understand the mind of God and questioning His actions (see 42:1–6).

God also rebuked Job's three friends for speaking against Him, and Job prayed for them. God accepted Job's prayers and returned to him more than he had lost. Job lived a long, full life and witnessed four generations of his family (see 42:7–17).

The Book of Job addresses human suffering. It teaches that even those who are righteous and trust God are not exempt from adversity and pain. We learn from Job's experiences that God knows best and that we are in no position to question why He allows suffering in our lives. Instead of questioning Him, we should remain committed to His promises and trust His wisdom.

BREATHE IT IN

Job was a man blessed by God. Because of Job's faithfulness, God looked upon him favorably. But for a reason we are not given, God allowed Satan to afflict Job and challenge his faith. Job's life fell apart. He lost his children, his possessions, and his health. Broken, distraught, and confused, Job tried to make sense of his suffering. He was sure he had done no wrong and did not deserve his suffering. His three friends were sure he must have done something wrong. They explored many possibilities, but none aligned with God's purpose.

Many Christians expect life to be smooth sailing once they accept Christ as their Savior. As a result, they are unprepared for, and resistant to, any semblance of suffering that might occur. Job, though, serves as an example that even those who are righteous can and will experience suffering. We must not only recognize this but also accept it. Instead of focusing our questions on why we suffer, we should consider how to respond when we do.

Although we may not know why we suffer, we should always remember that God is with us as we do. He is wise, powerful, and loving and can be trusted despite any painful circumstances we encounter. Our response to suffering should be accepting that God is in control. His ways are higher than our ways, and His thoughts are higher than our thoughts. Therefore, we will not understand the reasoning behind much of what we experience. We must simply trust that God will take care of us through it all and that our suffering has a purpose.

When it is difficult to understand the ways of God, like Job, we often seek answers from our friends, believing that they may have the answers we lack. But our friends are human just like we are. They cannot understand the mind of God any more than we can. It is good for our friends to be there for us as we suffer, and for us to be there for them when they suffer. However, we cannot depend on them for answers to our problems, nor should we attempt to offer answers to theirs. When Christians need answers, we must go to the source of all knowledge: God.

While God knows the answers to all our questions, He is not required to share any of His plans with us. This is where trust becomes necessary. We have to trust the wisdom and sovereignty of God. Through all the turmoil, chaos, and suffering that we experience, we must remember that God has everything under His control, whether we see it or not. He knows what is best for us.

Even knowing that God is good and in control, trusting Him in these times is still difficult. Suffering challenges our faithfulness perhaps like nothing else. Distress has a way of pushing out faithfulness. But God can use even this to grow us closer to Him. Not knowing what is happening to us and around us can teach us humility. We cannot know everything. And even if we did, we lack the power in ourselves to do what needs to be done. We are finite. God is infinite. In these times, God can use our suffering to draw us to a better understanding of who we are and who He is.

When things are not going well in your life, turn first to God. Seek God for direction. Bless Him in the midst of your trials. Do not waver in your faith but remain steadfast and immovable. God will reward faithfulness. He will bless us for standing strong despite what is happening around us.

†

THE BOOK OF

JOB

Job and His Family in Uz

1 There was a man [a]in the land of Uz,
whose name *was* [b]Job; and that man
was [c]blameless and upright, and one who
[d]feared God and shunned evil. 2And seven
sons and three daughters were born to him.
3Also, his possessions were seven thousand
sheep, three thousand camels, five hundred yoke of oxen, five hundred female
donkeys, and a very large household, so
that this man was the greatest of all the
people of the East.

4And his sons would go and feast *in their*
houses, each on his *appointed* day, and
would send and invite their three sisters
to eat and drink with them. 5So it was, when
the days of feasting had run their course,
that Job would send and sanctify them, and
he would rise early in the morning [a]and offer burnt offerings *according to* the number
of them all. For Job said, "It may be that my
sons have sinned and [b]cursed[1] God in their
hearts." Thus Job did regularly.

Satan Attacks Job's Character

6Now [a]there was a day when the sons of
God came to present themselves before the
LORD, and Satan[1] also came among them.
7And the LORD said to Satan, "From where
do you come?"

So Satan answered the LORD and said,
"From [a]going to and fro on the earth, and
from walking back and forth on it."

8Then the LORD said to Satan, "Have you
considered My servant Job, that *there is*
none like him on the earth, a blameless
and upright man, one who fears God and
shuns evil?"

9So Satan answered the LORD and said,
"Does Job fear God for nothing? 10[a]Have
You not made a hedge around him, around
his household, and around all that he has
on every side? [b]You have blessed the work
of his hands, and his possessions have increased in the land. 11[a]But now, stretch out
Your hand and touch all that he has, and he
will surely [b]curse You to Your face!"

12And the LORD said to Satan, "Behold,
all that he has *is* in your power; only do not
lay a hand on his *person*."

So Satan went out from the presence
of the LORD.

Job Loses His Property and Children

13Now there was a day [a]when his sons
and daughters *were* eating and drinking wine in their oldest brother's house;
14and a messenger came to Job and said,
"The oxen were plowing and the donkeys
feeding beside them, 15when the Sabeans[1]
raided *them* and took them away—indeed
they have killed the servants with the edge
of the sword; and I alone have escaped to
tell you!"

16While he *was* still speaking, another
also came and said, "The fire of God fell
from heaven and burned up the sheep and
the servants, and consumed them; and I
alone have escaped to tell you!"

17While he *was* still speaking, another
also came and said, "The Chaldeans formed
three bands, raided the camels and took
them away, yes, and killed the servants with
the edge of the sword; and I alone have escaped to tell you!"

18While he *was* still speaking, another

1:1 [a] 1 Chr. 1:17 [b] Ezek. 14:14, 20; James 5:11 [c] Gen. 6:9; 17:1; [Deut. 18:13] [d] [Prov. 16:6] 1:5 [a] Gen. 8:20; [Job 42:8] [b] 1 Kin. 21:10, 13 [1] Literally *blessed,* but used here in the evil sense, and so in verse 11 and 2:5, 9 1:6 [a] Job 2:1 [1] Literally *the Adversary,* and so throughout this book 1:7 [a] [1 Pet. 5:8] 1:10 [a] Job 29:2–6; Ps. 34:7; Is. 5:2 [b] [Ps. 128:1, 2; Prov. 10:22] 1:11 [a] Job 2:5; 19:21 [b] Is. 8:21; Mal. 3:13, 14 1:13 [a] [Eccl. 9:12] 1:15 [1] Literally *Sheba* (compare 6:19)

also came and said, [a]"Your sons and daughters *were* eating and drinking wine in their
oldest brother's house, 19and suddenly a
great wind came from across[1] the wilderness and struck the four corners of the
house, and it fell on the young people, and
they are dead; and I alone have escaped to
tell you!"
20Then Job arose, [a]tore his robe, and
shaved his head; and he [b]fell to the ground
and worshiped. 21And he said:

[a]"Naked I came from my
mother's womb,
And naked shall I return there.
The LORD [b]gave, and the
LORD has [c]taken away;
[d]Blessed be the name of the LORD."

22[a]In all this Job did not sin nor charge
God with wrong.

Satan Attacks Job's Health

2 Again [a]there was a day when the sons
of God came to present themselves before the LORD, and Satan came also among
them to present himself before the LORD.
2And the LORD said to Satan, "From where
do you come?"
[a]Satan answered the LORD and said,
"From going to and fro on the earth, and
from walking back and forth on it."
3Then the LORD said to Satan, "Have you
considered My servant Job, that *there is*
none like him on the earth, [a]a blameless
and upright man, one who fears God and
shuns evil? And still he [b]holds fast to his

JOB 1:21

I AM JOB

And he said: "Naked I came from my mother's womb, and naked shall I return there. The LORD gave, and the LORD has taken away; blessed be the name of the LORD." Job 1:21

I am Job. Unknown to me, God used me as a demonstration of faith to Satan. I was a man of great wealth and stature. Satan, however, told God my faithfulness was only because God had blessed and protected me. God gave Satan the authority to do what he wanted to me, though he could not harm me.

Satan took away my children and my possessions. When I stayed faithful to God through this painful loss, Satan argued with God that I did so only because I had my health. God let him take my good health, but he was not allowed to kill me. I lost everything on earth that brought me comfort and joy. I knew I had not done anything to displease God. It seemed as if God had made a mistake. My friends tried to tell me that I must have done something wrong, but their counsel was ungodly and they judged what they could not know.

I was confused. I had no peace, only turmoil. I was in misery and would have preferred to have never been born. In His own time, the Lord spoke to me from a whirlwind. He reminded me of His great power and holiness. I was overcome by His presence and repented of the way I had questioned His motives. God restored my health and my possessions, blessing me with twice as much as I had lost. He also gave me more children, and I lived a long and peaceful life.

†

We cannot understand why God has allowed so much evil to win in the world. But we do not need to know why. We only need to know and trust the Lord and make Him known to this dying world. This does not mean that we stand idly by, though. It means that our actions must be guided by His hand upon us.

1:18 [a] Job 1:4, 13 1:19 [1] Septuagint omits *across.* 1:20 [a] Gen. 37:29, 34; Josh. 7:6; Ezra 9:3 [b] [1 Pet. 5:6] 1:21 [a] [Ps. 49:17; Eccl. 5:15]; 1 Tim. 6:7 [b] Eccl. 5:19; [James 1:17] [c] Gen. 31:16; [1 Sam. 2:6] [d] Eph. 5:20; [1 Thess. 5:18] 1:22 [a] Job 2:10
2:1 [a] Job 1:6–8 2:2 [a] Job 1:7 2:3 [a] Job 1:1, 8 [b] Job 27:5, 6

integrity, although you incited Me against
him, [c]to destroy him without cause."
4So Satan answered the LORD and said,
"Skin for skin! Yes, all that a man has he will
give for his life. 5[a]But stretch out Your hand
now, and touch his [b]bone and his flesh, and
he will surely curse You to Your face!"
6[a]And the LORD said to Satan, "Behold,
he *is* in your hand, but spare his life."
7So Satan went out from the presence of
the LORD, and struck Job with painful boils
[a]from the sole of his foot to the crown of
his head. 8And he took for himself a potsherd with which to scrape himself [a]while
he sat in the midst of the ashes.
9Then his wife said to him, "Do you still
hold fast to your integrity? Curse God and
die!"
10But he said to her, "You speak as one
of the foolish women speaks. [a]Shall we indeed accept good from God, and shall we
not accept adversity?" [b]In all this Job did
not [c]sin with his lips.

#OXYGEN

JOB 2:9–10

Believe in the Father

Life is unpredictable. Its ever-changing nature can leave us feeling lost and confused. We must believe in God's ultimate goodness and hold fast to His unchanging hand.

Simply **breathe** and **believe in the Father**.

Job's Three Friends

11Now when Job's three friends heard of
all this adversity that had come upon him,
each one came from his own place—Eliphaz the [a]Temanite, Bildad the [b]Shuhite,
and Zophar the Naamathite. For they had
made an appointment together to come
[c]and mourn with him, and to comfort him.
12And when they raised their eyes from afar,
and did not recognize him, they lifted their
voices and wept; and each one tore his robe
and [a]sprinkled dust on his head toward
heaven. 13So they sat down with him on the
ground [a]seven days and seven nights, and
no one spoke a word to him, for they saw
that *his* grief was very great.

Job Deplores His Birth

3 After this Job opened his mouth and
cursed the day of his *birth.* 2And Job
spoke, and said:

3 "May[a] the day perish on
which I was born,
And the night *in which* it was said,
'A male child is conceived.'
4 May that day be darkness;
May God above not seek it,
Nor the light shine upon it.
5 May darkness and [a]the shadow
of death claim it;
May a cloud settle on it;
May the blackness of the day terrify it.
6 *As for* that night, may darkness seize it;
May it not rejoice[1] among
the days of the year,
May it not come into the
number of the months.
7 Oh, may that night be barren!
May no joyful shout come into it!
8 May those curse it who curse the day,
Those [a]who are ready to
arouse Leviathan.
9 May the stars of its morning be dark;
May it look for light, but *have* none,
And not see the dawning of the day;
10 Because it did not shut up the
doors of my *mother's* womb,
Nor hide sorrow from my eyes.

11 "Why[a] did I not die at birth?
Why did I *not* perish when I
came from the womb?
12 [a]Why did the knees receive me?
Or why the breasts, that
I should nurse?

2:3 [c] Job 9:17 2:5 [a] Job 1:11 [b] Job 19:20 2:6 [a] Job 1:12 2:7 [a] Is. 1:6 2:8 [a] Job 42:6; Jer. 6:26; Ezek. 27:30; Jon. 3:6; Matt. 11:21
2:10 [a] Job 1:21, 22; [Heb. 12:6; James 5:10, 11] [b] Job 1:22; [James 1:12] [c] Ps. 39:1 2:11 [a] Gen. 36:11; 1 Chr. 1:36; Job 6:19; Jer. 49:7; Obad.
9 [b] Gen. 25:2; 1 Chr. 1:32 [c] Job 42:11; Rom. 12:15 2:12 [a] Josh. 7:6; Neh. 9:1; Lam. 2:10; Ezek. 27:30 2:13 [a] Gen. 50:10; Ezek. 3:15
3:3 [a] Job 10:18, 19; Jer. 20:14–18 3:5 [a] Job 10:21, 22; Jer. 13:16; Amos 5:8 3:6 [1] Septuagint, Syriac, Targum,
and Vulgate read *be joined.* 3:8 [a] Jer. 9:17 3:11 [a] Job 10:18, 19 3:12 [a] Gen. 30:3

13 For now I would have lain
still and been quiet,
I would have been asleep;
Then I would have been at rest
14 With kings and counselors
of the earth,
Who [a]built ruins for themselves,
15 Or with princes who had gold,
Who filled their houses *with* silver;
16 Or *why* was I not hidden
[a]like a stillborn child,
Like infants who never saw light?
17 There the wicked cease *from* troubling,
And there the weary are at [a]rest.
18 *There* the prisoners rest together;
[a]They do not hear the voice
of the oppressor.
19 The small and great are there,
And the servant *is* free
from his master.

20 "Why[a] is light given to him
who is in misery,
And life to the [b]bitter of soul,
21 Who [a]long for death, but
it does not *come,*
And search for it more than
[b]hidden treasures;
22 Who rejoice exceedingly,
And are glad when they can
find the [a]grave?
23 *Why is light given* to a man
whose way is hidden,
[a]And whom God has hedged in?
24 For my sighing comes before I eat,[1]
And my groanings pour out like water.
25 For the thing I greatly [a]feared
has come upon me,
And what I dreaded has
happened to me.
26 I am not at ease, nor am I quiet;
I have no rest, for trouble comes."

Eliphaz: Job Has Sinned

4 Then Eliphaz the Temanite answered and said:

2 "*If* one attempts a word with you,
will you become weary?
But who can withhold himself
from speaking?
3 Surely you have instructed many,
And you [a]have strengthened
weak hands.
4 Your words have upheld him
who was stumbling,
And you [a]have strengthened
the feeble knees;
5 But now it comes upon you,
and you are weary;
It touches you, and you are troubled.
6 *Is* not [a]your reverence
[b]your confidence?
And the integrity of your
ways your hope?

7 "Remember now, [a]who *ever*
perished being innocent?
Or where were the upright *ever* cut off?
8 Even as I have seen,
[a]Those who plow iniquity
And sow trouble reap the same.
9 By the blast of God they perish,
And by the breath of His anger
they are consumed.
10 The roaring of the lion,
The voice of the fierce lion,
And [a]the teeth of the young
lions are broken.
11 [a]The old lion perishes for lack of prey,
And the cubs of the lioness
are scattered.

12 "Now a word was secretly
brought to me,
And my ear received a whisper of it.
13 [a]In disquieting thoughts from
the visions of the night,
When deep sleep falls on men,
14 Fear came upon me, and [a]trembling,
Which made all my bones shake.
15 Then a spirit passed before my face;
The hair on my body stood up.
16 It stood still,
But I could not discern its appearance.
A form *was* before my eyes;
There was silence;
Then I heard a voice *saying:*

3:14 [a] Job 15:28; Is. 58:12 3:16 [a] Ps. 58:8 3:17 [a] Job 17:16 3:18 [a] Job 39:7 3:20 [a] Jer. 20:18 [b] 2 Kin. 4:27 3:21 [a] Rev. 9:6 [b] Prov. 2:4 3:22 [a] Job 7:15, 16 3:23 [a] Job 19:8; Ps. 88:8; Lam. 3:7 3:24 [1] Literally *my bread* 3:25 [a] [Job 9:28; 30:15] 4:3 [a] Is. 35:3 4:4 [a] Is. 35:3 4:6 [a] Job 1:1 [b] Prov. 3:26 4:7 [a] [Job 8:20; 36:6, 7; Ps. 37:25] 4:8 [a] [Job 15:31, 35; Prov. 22:8; Hos. 10:13; Gal. 6:7] 4:10 [a] Job 5:15; Ps. 58:6 4:11 [a] Job 29:17; Ps. 34:10 4:13 [a] Job 33:15 4:14 [a] Hab. 3:16

17 'Can a mortal be more
righteous than God?
Can a man be more pure
than his Maker?
18 If He [a]puts no trust in His servants,
If He charges His angels with error,
19 How much more those who
dwell in houses of clay,
Whose foundation is in the dust,
Who are crushed before a moth?
20 [a]They are broken in pieces from
morning till evening;
They perish forever, with
no one regarding.
21 Does not their own
excellence go away?
They die, even without wisdom.'

Eliphaz: Job Is Chastened by God

5 "Call out now;
Is there anyone who will answer you?
And to which of the holy
ones will you turn?
2 For wrath kills a foolish man,
And envy slays a simple one.
3 [a]I have seen the foolish taking root,
But suddenly I cursed his
dwelling place.
4 His sons are [a]far from safety,
They are crushed in the gate,
And [b]*there is* no deliverer.
5 Because the hungry eat up his harvest,
Taking it even from the thorns,[1]
And a snare snatches their substance.[2]
6 For affliction does not come
from the dust,
Nor does trouble spring
from the ground;
7 Yet man is [a]born to trouble,
As the sparks fly upward.

8 "But as for me, I would seek God,
And to God I would commit
my cause—
9 Who does great things,
and unsearchable,
Marvelous things without number.
10 [a]He gives rain on the earth,
And sends waters on the fields.
11 [a]He sets on high those who are lowly,
And those who mourn are
lifted to safety.
12 [a]He frustrates the devices of the crafty,
So that their hands cannot
carry out their plans.
13 He catches the [a]wise in their
own craftiness,
And the counsel of the cunning
comes quickly upon them.
14 They meet with darkness
in the daytime,
And grope at noontime as in the night.
15 But [a]He saves the needy
from the sword,
From the mouth of the mighty,
And from their hand.
16 [a]So the poor have hope,
And injustice shuts her mouth.

17 "Behold,[a] happy *is* the man
whom God corrects;
Therefore do not despise the
chastening of the Almighty.
18 [a]For He bruises, but He binds up;
He wounds, but His hands
make whole.
19 [a]He shall deliver you in six troubles,
Yes, in seven [b]no evil shall touch you.
20 [a]In famine He shall redeem
you from death,
And in war from the power
of the sword.
21 [a]You shall be hidden from the
scourge of the tongue,
And you shall not be afraid of
destruction when it comes.
22 You shall laugh at destruction
and famine,
And [a]you shall not be afraid of
the [b]beasts of the earth.
23 [a]For you shall have a covenant
with the stones of the field,
And the beasts of the field shall
be at peace with you.
24 You shall know that your
tent *is* in peace;

4:18 [a] Job 15:15 4:20 [a] Ps. 90:5, 6 5:3 [a] [Ps. 37:35, 36]; Jer. 12:1–3 5:4 [a] Ps. 119:155 [b] Ps. 109:12 5:5 [1] Septuagint reads *They shall not be taken from evil men;* Vulgate reads *And the armed man shall take him by violence.* [2] Septuagint reads *The might shall draw them off;* Vulgate reads *And the thirsty shall drink up their riches.* 5:7 [a] Job 14:1 5:10 [a] [Job 36:27–29; 37:6–11; 38:26] 5:11 [a] Ps. 113:7 5:12 [a] Neh. 4:15 5:13 [a] [Job 37:24; 1 Cor. 3:19] 5:15 [a] Job 4:10, 11; Ps. 35:10 5:16 [a] 1 Sam. 2:8; Ps. 107:41, 42 5:17 [a] Ps. 94:12; [Prov. 3:11, 12; Heb. 12:5, 6; Rev. 3:19] 5:18 [a] [Deut. 32:39; 1 Sam. 2:6, 7]; Is. 30:26; Hos. 6:1 5:19 [a] Ps. 34:19; 91:3; [1 Cor. 10:13] [b] Ps. 91:10; [Prov. 24:16] 5:20 [a] Ps. 33:19, 20; 37:19 5:21 [a] Job 5:15; Ps. 31:20 5:22 [a] Ps. 91:13; Is. 11:9; 35:9; 65:25; Ezek. 34:25 [b] Hos. 2:18 5:23 [a] Ps. 91:12

You shall visit your dwelling
and find nothing amiss.
25 You shall also know that [a]your
descendants *shall be* many,
And your offspring [b]like the
grass of the earth.
26 [a]You shall come to the
grave at a full age,
As a sheaf of grain ripens
in its season.
27 Behold, this we have [a]searched out;
It *is* true.
Hear it, and know for yourself."

Job: My Complaint Is Just

6 Then Job answered and said:
2 "Oh, that my grief were fully weighed,
And my calamity laid with
it on the scales!
3 For then it would be heavier
than the sand of the sea—
Therefore my words have been rash.
4 [a]For the arrows of the Almighty
are within me;
My spirit drinks in their poison;
[b]The terrors of God are
arrayed [c]against me.
5 Does the [a]wild donkey bray
when it has grass,
Or does the ox low over its fodder?
6 Can flavorless food be
eaten without salt?
Or is there *any* taste in the
white of an egg?
7 My soul refuses to touch them;
They *are* as loathsome food to me.

8 "Oh, that I might have my request,
That God would grant *me* the
thing that I long for!
9 That it would please God
to crush me,
That He would loose His
hand and [a]cut me off!
10 Then I would still have comfort;
Though in anguish I would exult,
He will not spare;
For [a]I have not concealed the
words of [b]the Holy One.

11 "What strength do I have,
that I should hope?
And what *is* my end, that I
should prolong my life?
12 *Is* my strength the strength of stones?
Or is my flesh bronze?
13 *Is* my help not within me?
And is success driven from me?

14 "To[a] him who is afflicted, kindness
should be shown by his friend,
Even though he forsakes the
fear of the Almighty.
15 [a]My brothers have dealt
deceitfully like a brook,
[b]Like the streams of the
brooks that pass away,
16 Which are dark because of the ice,
And into which the snow vanishes.
17 When it is warm, they cease to flow;
When it is hot, they vanish
from their place.
18 The paths of their way turn aside,
They go nowhere and perish.
19 The caravans of [a]Tema look,
The travelers of [b]Sheba hope
for them.
20 They are [a]disappointed because
they were confident;
They come there and are confused.
21 For now [a]you are nothing,
You see terror and [b]are afraid.
22 Did I ever say, 'Bring *something* to me'?
Or, 'Offer a bribe for me
from your wealth'?
23 Or, 'Deliver me from the
enemy's hand'?
Or, 'Redeem me from the
hand of oppressors'?

24 "Teach me, and I will hold my tongue;
Cause me to understand
wherein I have erred.
25 How forceful are right words!
But what does your arguing prove?
26 Do you intend to rebuke *my* words,
And the speeches of a desperate
one, *which are* as wind?
27 Yes, you overwhelm the fatherless,
And you [a]undermine your friend.

5:25 [a] Ps. 112:2 [b] Ps. 72:16 5:26 [a] [Prov. 9:11; 10:27] 5:27 [a] Ps. 111:2 6:4 [a] Job 16:13; Ps. 38:2 [b] Ps. 88:15, 16 [c] Job 30:15 6:5 [a] Job 39:5–8 6:9 [a] Num. 11:15; 1 Kin. 19:4; Job 7:16; 9:21; 10:1 6:10 [a] Acts 20:20 [b] [Lev. 19:2; Is. 57:15] 6:14 [a] [Prov. 17:17] 6:15 [a] Ps. 38:11 [b] Jer. 15:18 6:19 [a] Gen. 25:15; Is. 21:14; Jer. 25:23 [b] 1 Kin. 10:1; Ps. 72:10; Ezek. 27:22, 23 6:20 [a] Jer. 14:3 6:21 [a] Job 13:4 [b] Ps. 38:11 6:27 [a] Ps. 57:6

28 Now therefore, be pleased
to look at me;
For I would never lie to your face.
29 [a]Yield now, let there be no injustice!
Yes, concede, my [b]righteousness
still stands!
30 Is there injustice on my tongue?
Cannot my taste discern the unsavory?

Job: My Suffering Is Comfortless

7 "*Is there* not [a]a time of hard
service for man on earth?
Are not his days also like the
days of a hired man?
2 Like a servant who earnestly
desires the shade,
And like a hired man who eagerly
looks for his wages,
3 So I have been allotted
[a]months of futility,
And wearisome nights have
been appointed to me.
4 [a]When I lie down, I say,
'When shall I arise,
And the night be ended?'
For I have had my fill of
tossing till dawn.
5 My flesh is [a]caked with
worms and dust,
My skin is cracked and
breaks out afresh.

6 "My[a] days are swifter than
a weaver's shuttle,
And are spent without hope.
7 Oh, remember that [a]my life
is a breath!
My eye will never again see good.
8 [a]The eye of him who sees me
will see me no *more;*
While your eyes *are* upon me,
I shall no longer *be.*
9 *As* the cloud disappears
and vanishes away,
So [a]he who goes down to the
grave does not come up.
10 He shall never return to his house,
[a]Nor shall his place know
him anymore.

11 "Therefore I will [a]not
restrain my mouth;
I will speak in the anguish
of my spirit;
I will [b]complain in the
bitterness of my soul.
12 *Am* I a sea, or a sea serpent,
That You set a guard over me?
13 [a]When I say, 'My bed will comfort me,
My couch will ease my complaint,'
14 Then You scare me with dreams
And terrify me with visions,
15 So that my soul chooses strangling
And death rather than my body.[1]
16 [a]I loathe *my life;*
I would not live forever.
[b]Let me alone,
For [c]my days *are but* a breath.

17 "What[a] *is* man, that You
should exalt him,
That You should set Your
heart on him,
18 That You should visit him
every morning,
And test him every moment?
19 How long?
Will You not look away from me,
And let me alone till I
swallow my saliva?
20 Have I sinned?
What have I done to You,
[a]O watcher of men?
Why [b]have You set me as Your target,
So that I am a burden to myself?[1]
21 Why then do You not pardon
my transgression,
And take away my iniquity?
For now I will lie down in the dust,
And You will seek me diligently,
But I *will* no longer *be.*"

Bildad: Job Should Repent

8 Then Bildad the Shuhite answered and
said:

2 "How long will you speak these *things,*
And the words of your mouth
be like a strong wind?

6:29 [a] Job 17:10 [b] Job 27:5, 6; 34:5 7:1 [a] [Job 14:5, 13, 14]; Ps. 39:4 7:3 [a] [Job 15:31] 7:4 [a] Deut. 28:67; Job 7:13, 14 7:5 [a] Is. 14:11 7:6 [a] Job 9:25; 16:22; 17:11; Is. 38:12; [James 4:14] 7:7 [a] Job 7:16; Ps. 78:39; 89:47 7:8 [a] Job 8:18; 20:9 7:9 [a] 2 Sam. 12:23 7:10 [a] Ps. 103:16 7:11 [a] Ps. 39:1, 9 [b] 1 Sam. 1:10 7:13 [a] Job 9:27 7:15 [1] Literally *my bones* 7:16 [a] Job 10:1 [b] Job 14:6 [c] Ps. 62:9 7:17 [a] Job 22:2; Ps. 8:4; 144:3; Heb. 2:6 7:20 [a] Ps. 36:6 [b] Ps. 21:12 [1] Following Masoretic Text, Targum, and Vulgate; Septuagint and Jewish tradition read *to You.*

3 [a]Does God subvert judgment?
Or does the Almighty pervert justice?
4 If [a]your sons have sinned against Him,
He has cast them away for
their transgression.
5 [a]If you would earnestly seek God
And make your supplication
to the Almighty,
6 If you *were* pure and upright,
Surely now He would awake for you,
And prosper your rightful
dwelling place.
7 Though your beginning was small,
Yet your latter end would
[a]increase abundantly.

8 "For[a] inquire, please, of the
former age,
And consider the things
discovered by their fathers;
9 For [a]we *were born* yesterday,
and know nothing,
Because our days on earth
are a shadow.
10 Will they not teach you and tell you,
And utter words from their heart?

11 "Can the papyrus grow up
without a marsh?
Can the reeds flourish without water?
12 [a]While it *is* yet green *and* not cut down,
It withers before any *other* plant.
13 So *are* the paths of all who [a]forget God;
And the hope of the [b]hypocrite
shall perish,
14 Whose confidence shall be cut off,
And whose trust *is* a spider's web.
15 [a]He leans on his house, but
it does not stand.
He holds it fast, but it does not endure.
16 He grows green in the sun,
And his branches spread
out in his garden.
17 His roots wrap around the rock heap,
And look for a place in the stones.
18 [a]If he is destroyed from his place,
Then *it* will deny him, *saying,*
'I have not seen you.'
19 "Behold, this is the joy of His way,
And [a]out of the earth others will grow.
20 Behold, [a]God will not cast
away the blameless,
Nor will He uphold the evildoers.
21 He will yet fill your mouth
with laughing,
And your lips with rejoicing.
22 Those who hate you will be
[a]clothed with shame,
And the dwelling place of the
wicked will come to nothing."[1]

Job: There Is No Mediator

9 Then Job answered and said:

2 "Truly I know *it is* so,
But how can a [a]man be
[b]righteous before God?
3 If one wished to contend with Him,
He could not answer Him one
time out of a thousand.
4 [a]*God is* wise in heart and
mighty in strength.
Who has hardened *himself* against
Him and prospered?
5 He removes the mountains,
and they do not know
When He overturns them
in His anger;
6 He [a]shakes the earth out of its place,
And its [b]pillars tremble;
7 He commands the sun, and
it does not rise;
He seals off the stars;
8 [a]He alone spreads out the heavens,
And treads on the waves of the sea;
9 [a]He made the Bear, Orion,
and the Pleiades,
And the chambers of the south;
10 [a]He does great things past finding out,
Yes, wonders without number.
11 [a]If He goes by me, I do not see *Him;*
If He moves past, I do not
perceive Him;
12 [a]If He takes away, who can hinder Him?
Who can say to Him, 'What
are You doing?'

8:3 [a] Gen. 18:25; [Deut. 32:4; 2 Chr. 19:7; Job 34:10, 12; 36:23; 37:23]; Rom. 3:5 8:4 [a] Job 1:5, 18, 19 8:5 [a] [Job 5:17–27; 11:13] 8:7 [a] Job 42:12 8:8 [a] Deut. 4:32; 32:7; Job 15:18; 20:4 8:9 [a] Gen. 47:9; [1 Chr. 29:15]; Job 7:6; [Ps. 39:5; 102:11; 144:4] 8:12 [a] Ps. 129:6 8:13 [a] Ps. 9:17 [b] Job 11:20; 18:14; 27:8; Ps. 112:10; [Prov. 10:28] 8:15 [a] Job 8:22; 27:18; Ps. 49:11 8:18 [a] Job 7:10 8:19 [a] Ps. 113:7 8:20 [a] Job 4:7 8:22 [a] Ps. 35:26; 109:29 [1] Literally *will not be* 9:2 [a] [Job 4:17; 15:14–16; Ps. 143:2; Rom. 3:20] [b] [Hab. 2:4; Rom. 1:17; Gal. 3:11; Heb. 10:38] 9:4 [a] Job 36:5 9:6 [a] Is. 2:19, 21; Hag. 2:6; Heb. 12:26 [b] Job 26:11 9:8 [a] Gen. 1:6; Job 37:18; Ps. 104:2, 3; Is. 40:22 9:9 [a] Gen. 1:16; Job 38:31; Amos 5:8 9:10 [a] Job 5:9 9:11 [a] [Job 23:8, 9; 35:14] 9:12 [a] [Is. 45:9; Dan. 4:35; Rom. 9:20]

RELEASE // BELIEVE IN THE FATHER

Our Sustaining Father

Job 8:8–10 // "For inquire, please, of the former age, and consider the things discovered by their fathers; for we were born yesterday, and know nothing, because our days on earth are a shadow. Will they not teach you and tell you, and utter words from their heart?"

Summary Message // Sometimes, life is hard. Sometimes, it feels all-consuming. And yet Scripture highlights that God, our heavenly Father, wants to sustain us, no matter the circumstance.

In Job 8, we are reminded that belief in God, our spiritual Father, can and will enable us to endure, even when all around us is falling apart. So, the question is, do we trust our Abba, Father? If so, then we can rest assured that nothing in this world can ever overcome us.

Practical Application // In the New Testament, Jesus made it clear that the lives of those who choose to serve Him would not be easy (see John 16:33). Sometimes we have to wonder if Jesus had a marketer who would occasionally pull Him aside and offer constructive critiques on His messaging. Promising a life of hardship alongside an invitation to "follow Me" does not feel like the best advertisement. However, the reality that Jesus invites us into is a belief in His Father that is so deep that it can sustain us through any trial or circumstance.

In Job 8, we find a man in the midst of a full life meltdown. He had lost his property, his family, and his health. To make matters worse, his friends berated him, and his wife encouraged him to "curse God and die" (Job 2:9). With friends and loved ones like his, Job certainly did not need any enemies! Through it all, Job maintained his belief in God, his heavenly Father. Why? Because Job understood a few key truths:

- The pain, suffering, and hardships we wrestle with each day are but momentary in the infinitude of God's kingdom.
- The knowledge we have of the people and circumstances we encounter daily is miniscule in comparison to God's omniscience.
- In all things, and in all ways, God is still with us and will never leave or forsake us.

Here is the truth: things will arise in our lives that challenge us and stretch us. Sometimes, they can even overwhelm us. However, God calls us to embrace our belief in Him, our Father, knowing His track record is never failing. We can be assured that no matter what we come up against, our God is right there in it with us. Our loving Father never leaves His children alone. We can breathe a little easier even when the walls feel like they are closing in.

Fervent Prayer // Heavenly Father, indeed, You are a good, good Father. Time and again, You have proven this to be true. When we were in pain, You were there. When we were struggling, You were there. When we were lost and afraid, You were there! Thank You for loving us so much that You draw close in our hour of need. Thank You for inviting us to bring our cares and worries and set them at Your feet. Thank You for sustaining us in all ways, every moment of every day. Keep us ever mindful of Your constant, loving presence in our lives. In Jesus' name we pray. Amen.

---

13 God will not withdraw His anger,
[a]The allies of the proud[1] lie
prostrate beneath Him.

14 "How then can I answer Him,
And choose my words *to*
reason with Him?
15 [a]For though I were righteous, I
could not answer Him;
I would beg mercy of my Judge.
16 If I called and He answered me,
I would not believe that He was
listening to my voice.
17 For He crushes me with
a tempest,
And multiplies my wounds
[a]without cause.
18 He will not allow me to
catch my breath,
But fills me with bitterness.

9:13 [a] Job 26:12 [1] Hebrew *rahab* 9:15 [a] Job 10:15; 23:1–7 9:17 [a] Job 2:3

19 If *it is a matter* of strength,
indeed *He is* strong;
And if of justice, who will
appoint my day *in court?*
20 Though I were righteous, my own
mouth would condemn me;
Though I *were* blameless, it
would prove me perverse.

21 "I am blameless, yet I do
not know myself;
I despise my life.
22 It *is* all one *thing;*
Therefore I say, [a]'He destroys the
blameless and the wicked.'
23 If the scourge slays suddenly,
He laughs at the plight of the innocent.
24 The earth is given into the
hand of the wicked.
He covers the faces of its judges.
If it is not *He,* who else could it be?

25 "Now [a]my days are swifter
than a runner;
They flee away, they see no good.
26 They pass by like swift ships,
[a]Like an eagle swooping on its prey.
27 [a]If I say, 'I will forget my complaint,
I will put off my sad face
and wear a smile,'
28 [a]I am afraid of all my sufferings;
I know that You [b]will not
hold me innocent.
29 *If* I am condemned,
Why then do I labor in vain?
30 [a]If I wash myself with snow water,
And cleanse my hands with soap,
31 Yet You will plunge me into the pit,
And my own clothes will abhor me.

32 "For [a]*He is* not a man, as I *am,*
That I may answer Him,
And that we should go to
court together.
33 [a]Nor is there any mediator between us,
Who may lay his hand on us both.
34 [a]Let Him take His rod away from me,
And do not let dread of
Him terrify me.
35 *Then* I would speak and not fear Him,
But it is not so with me.

Job: I Would Plead with God

10 "My [a]soul loathes my life;
I will give free course to
my complaint,
[b]I will speak in the bitterness
of my soul.
2 I will say to God, 'Do not condemn me;
Show me why You contend with me.
3 *Does it* seem good to You that
You should oppress,
That You should despise the
work of Your hands,
And smile on the counsel
of the wicked?
4 Do You have eyes of flesh?
Or [a]do You see as man sees?
5 *Are* Your days like the days
of a mortal man?
Are Your years like the days
of a mighty man,
6 That You should seek for my iniquity
And search out my sin,
7 Although You know that
I am not wicked,
And *there is* no one who can
deliver from Your hand?

8 'Your[a] hands have made me
and fashioned me,
An intricate unity;
Yet You would [b]destroy me.
9 Remember, I pray, [a]that You
have made me like clay.
And will You turn me into dust again?
10 [a]Did You not pour me out like milk,
And curdle me like cheese,
11 Clothe me with skin and flesh,
And knit me together with
bones and sinews?
12 You have granted me life and favor,
And Your care has preserved
my spirit.

13 'And these *things* You have
hidden in Your heart;
I know that this *was* with You:

9:22 [a] [Eccl. 9:2, 3]; Ezek. 21:3 9:25 [a] Job 7:6, 7 9:26 [a] Job 39:29; Hab. 1:8 9:27 [a] Job 7:13 9:28 [a] Ps. 119:120 [b] Ex. 20:7 9:30 [a] [Jer. 2:22] 9:32 [a] Eccl. 6:10; [Is. 45:9; Jer. 49:19; Rom. 9:20] 9:33 [a] [1 Sam. 2:25]; Job 9:19; Is. 1:18 9:34 [a] Job 13:20, 21; Ps. 39:10 10:1 [a] 1 Kin. 19:4; Job 7:16; Jon. 4:3 [b] Job 7:11 10:4 [a] [1 Sam. 16:7; Job 28:24; 34:21] 10:8 [a] Job 10:3; Ps. 119:73 [b] [Job 9:22] 10:9 [a] Gen. 2:7; Job 33:6 10:10 [a] [Ps. 139:14–16]

14 If I sin, then [a]You mark me,
And will not acquit me of my iniquity.
15 If I am wicked, [a]woe to me;
[b]Even *if* I am righteous, I
cannot lift up my head.
I am full of disgrace;
[c]See my misery!
16 If *my head* is exalted,
[a]You hunt me like a fierce lion,
And again You show Yourself
awesome against me.
17 You renew Your witnesses against me,
And increase Your indignation
toward me;
Changes and war are *ever* with me.

18 'Why[a] then have You brought
me out of the womb?
Oh, that I had perished and
no eye had seen me!
19 I would have been as though
I had not been.
I would have been carried from
the womb to the grave.
20 [a]Are not my days few?
Cease! [b]Leave me alone, that I
may take a little comfort,
21 Before I go *to the place from
which* I shall not return,
[a]To the land of darkness [b]and
the shadow of death,
22 A land as dark as darkness *itself,*
As the shadow of death,
without any order,
Where even the light *is* like
darkness.' "

Zophar Urges Job to Repent

11 Then Zophar the Naamathite answered and said:

2 "Should not the multitude of
words be answered?
And should a man full of
talk be vindicated?
3 Should your empty talk make
men hold their peace?
And when you mock, should
no one rebuke you?
4 For you have said,
[a]'My doctrine *is* pure,
And I am clean in your eyes.'
5 But oh, that God would speak,
And open His lips against you,
6 That He would show you the
secrets of wisdom!
For *they would* double *your* prudence.
Know therefore that [a]God
exacts from you
Less than your iniquity *deserves.*

7 "Can[a] you search out the
deep things of God?
Can you find out the limits
of the Almighty?
8 *They are* higher than
heaven—what can you do?
Deeper than Sheol—what
can you know?
9 Their measure *is* longer than the earth
And broader than the sea.

10 "If[a] He passes by, imprisons,
and gathers *to judgment,*
Then who can hinder Him?
11 For [a]He knows deceitful men;
He sees wickedness also.
Will He not then consider *it?*
12 For an [a]empty-headed
man will be wise,
When a wild donkey's colt
is born a man.

13 "If you would [a]prepare your heart,
And [b]stretch out your
hands toward Him;
14 If iniquity *were* in your hand,
and you put it far away,
And [a]would not let wickedness
dwell in your tents;
15 [a]Then surely you could lift up
your face without spot;
Yes, you could be steadfast,
and not fear;
16 Because you would [a]forget
your misery,
And remember *it* as waters
that have passed away,

10:14 [a] Job 7:20; Ps. 139:1 10:15 [a] Job 10:7; Is. 3:11 [b] [Job 9:12, 15] [c] Ps. 25:18 10:16 [a] Is. 38:13; Lam. 3:10; Hos. 13:7 10:18 [a] Job 3:11–13 10:20 [a] Ps. 39:5 [b] Job 7:16, 19 10:21 [a] Ps. 88:12 [b] Ps. 23:4 11:4 [a] Job 6:30 11:6 [a] [Ezra 9:13] 11:7 [a] Job 33:12, 13; 36:26; [Eccl. 3:11; Rom. 11:33] 11:10 [a] Job 9:12; [Rev. 3:7] 11:11 [a] [Ps. 10:14] 11:12 [a] [Ps. 39:5]; Rom. 1:22 11:13 [a] [1 Sam. 7:3] [b] Ps. 88:9 11:14 [a] Ps. 101:3 11:15 [a] Job 22:26; Ps. 119:6; [1 John 3:21] 11:16 [a] Is. 65:16

17 And *your* life [a]would be
brighter than noonday.
Though you were dark, you
would be like the morning.
18 And you would be secure,
because there is hope;
Yes, you would dig *around you,*
and [a]take your rest in safety.
19 You would also lie down, and no
one would make *you* afraid;
Yes, many would court your favor.
20 But [a]the eyes of the wicked will fail,
And they shall not escape,
And [b]their hope—loss of life!"

Job Answers His Critics

12 Then Job answered and said:

2 "No doubt you *are* the people,
And wisdom will die with you!
3 But I have understanding
as well as you;
I *am* not [a]inferior to you.
Indeed, who does not *know*
such things as these?

4 "I[a] am one mocked by his friends,
Who [b]called on God, and
He answered him,
The just and blameless
who is ridiculed.
5 A lamp[1] is despised in the thought
of one who is at ease;
It is made ready for [a]those
whose feet slip.
6 [a]The tents of robbers prosper,
And those who provoke
God are secure—
In what God provides by His hand.

7 "But now ask the beasts, and
they will teach you;
And the birds of the air, and
they will tell you;
8 Or speak to the earth, and
it will teach you;
And the fish of the sea will
explain to you.
9 Who among all these does not know
That the hand of the LORD
has done this,
10 [a]In whose hand *is* the life of
every living thing,
And the [b]breath of all mankind?
11 Does not the ear test words
And the mouth taste its food?
12 Wisdom *is* with aged men,
And with length of days,
understanding.

13 "With Him *are* [a]wisdom and strength,
He has counsel and understanding.
14 If [a]He breaks *a thing* down,
it cannot be rebuilt;
If He imprisons a man, there
can be no release.
15 If He [a]withholds the waters,
they dry up;
If He [b]sends them out, they
overwhelm the earth.
16 With Him *are* strength and prudence.
The deceived and the deceiver *are* His.
17 He leads counselors away plundered,
And makes fools of the judges.
18 He loosens the bonds of kings,
And binds their waist with a belt.
19 He leads princes[1] away plundered,
And overthrows the mighty.
20 [a]He deprives the trusted
ones of speech,
And takes away the discernment
of the elders.
21 [a]He pours contempt on princes,
And disarms the mighty.
22 He [a]uncovers deep things
out of darkness,
And brings the shadow
of death to light.
23 [a]He makes nations great,
and destroys them;
He enlarges nations, and guides them.
24 He takes away the understanding[1] of
the chiefs of the people of the earth,
And [a]makes them wander in
a pathless wilderness.
25 [a]They grope in the dark without light,
And He makes them [b]stagger
like a drunken *man.*

11:17 [a] Ps. 37:6; Prov. 4:18; Is. 58:8, 10 **11:18** [a] Lev. 26:5, 6; Ps. 3:5; Prov. 3:24 **11:20** [a] Lev. 26:16; Deut. 28:65; Job 17:5 [b] Job 18:14; [Prov. 11:7] **12:3** [a] Job 13:2 **12:4** [a] Job 21:3 [b] Ps. 91:15 **12:5** [a] Prov. 14:2 [1] Or *disaster* **12:6** [a] [Job 9:24; 21:6–16; Ps. 73:12; Jer. 12:1; Mal. 3:15] **12:10** [a] [Acts 17:28] [b] Job 27:3; 33:4 **12:13** [a] Job 9:4; 36:5 **12:14** [a] Job 11:10; Is. 25:2 **12:15** [a] Deut. 11:17; [1 Kin. 8:35, 36] [b] Gen. 7:11–24 **12:19** [1] Literally *priests,* but not in a technical sense **12:20** [a] Job 32:9 **12:21** [a] [Job 34:19]; Ps. 107:40; [Dan. 2:21] **12:22** [a] Dan. 2:22; [1 Cor. 4:5] **12:23** [a] Is. 9:3; 26:15 **12:24** [a] Ps. 107:4 [1] Literally *heart* **12:25** [a] Job 5:14; 15:30; 18:18 [b] Ps. 107:27

13 "Behold, my eye has seen all *this,*
My ear has heard and
understood it.
2 [a]What you know, I also know;
I *am* not inferior to you.
3 [a]But I would speak to the Almighty,
And I desire to reason with God.
4 But you forgers of lies,
[a]You *are* all worthless physicians.
5 Oh, that you would be silent,
And [a]it would be your wisdom!
6 Now hear my reasoning,
And heed the pleadings of my lips.
7 [a]Will you speak wickedly for God,
And talk deceitfully for Him?
8 Will you show partiality for Him?
Will you contend for God?
9 Will it be well when He
searches you out?
Or can you mock Him as
one mocks a man?
10 He will surely rebuke you
If you secretly show partiality.
11 Will not His excellence
make you afraid,
And the dread of Him fall upon you?
12 Your platitudes *are* proverbs
of ashes,
Your defenses are defenses
of clay.

13 "Hold your peace with me,
and let me speak,
Then let come on me what *may!*
14 Why [a]do I take my flesh in my teeth,
And put my life in my hands?
15 [a]Though He slay me, yet
will I trust Him.
[b]Even so, I will defend my
own ways before Him.
16 He also *shall* be my salvation,
For a [a]hypocrite could not
come before Him.
17 Listen carefully to my speech,
And to my declaration with your ears.
18 See now, I have prepared *my* case,
I know that I shall be [a]vindicated.
19 [a]Who *is* he *who* will contend with me?
If now I hold my tongue, I perish.

#OXYGEN

JOB 13:15

Believe in the Father

We all have issues, but those who are successful know how to manage their issues by giving them to God. Believe in God's ability to bring good from any and all situations. You can trust that He will bring brighter days to your future.

Breathe and believe in the Father.

Job's Despondent Prayer

20 "Only[a] two *things* do not do to me,
Then I will not hide myself from You:
21 [a]Withdraw Your hand far from me,
And let not the dread of
You make me afraid.
22 Then call, and I will [a]answer;
Or let me speak, then You
respond to me.
23 How many *are* my iniquities and sins?
Make me know my transgression
and my sin.
24 [a]Why do You hide Your face,
And [b]regard me as Your enemy?
25 [a]Will You frighten a leaf
driven to and fro?
And will You pursue dry stubble?
26 For You write bitter things against me,
And [a]make me inherit the
iniquities of my youth.
27 [a]You put my feet in the stocks,
And watch closely all my paths.
You set a limit[1] for the soles of my feet.

28 "*Man*[1] decays like a rotten thing,
Like a garment that is moth-eaten.

14 "Man *who is* born of woman
Is of few days and [a]full of trouble.
2 [a]He comes forth like a flower
and fades away;

13:2 [a] Job 12:3 13:3 [a] Job 23:3; 31:35 13:4 [a] Job 6:21; [Jer. 23:32] 13:5 [a] Job 13:13; 21:5; Prov. 17:28 13:7 [a] Job 27:4; 36:4 13:14 [a] Job 18:4 13:15 [a] Ps. 23:4; [Prov. 14:32] [b] Job 27:5 13:16 [a] Job 8:13 13:18 [a] [Rom. 8:34] 13:19 [a] Job 7:21; 10:8; Is. 50:8 13:20 [a] Job 9:34 13:21 [a] Job 9:34; Ps. 39:10 13:22 [a] Job 9:16; 14:15 13:24 [a] [Deut. 32:20]; Ps. 13:1 [b] Lam. 2:5 13:25 [a] Is. 42:3 13:26 [a] Job 20:11 13:27 [a] Job 33:11 [1] Literally *inscribe a print* 13:28 [1] Literally *He* 14:1 [a] Job 5:7; Eccl. 2:23 14:2 [a] Job 8:9; Ps. 90:5, 6, 9; 102:11; 103:15; 144:4; Is. 40:6; James 1:10, 11; 1 Pet. 1:24

He flees like a shadow and
does not continue.
3 And [a]do You open Your
eyes on such a one,
And [b]bring me[1] to judgment
with Yourself?
4 Who [a]can bring a clean *thing*
out of an unclean?
No one!
5 [a]Since his days *are* determined,
The number of his months *is* with You;
You have appointed his limits,
so that he cannot pass.
6 [a]Look away from him that he may rest,
Till [b]like a hired man he
finishes his day.

7 "For there is hope for a tree,
If it is cut down, that it
will sprout again,
And that its tender shoots
will not cease.
8 Though its root may grow
old in the earth,
And its stump may die in the ground,
9 *Yet* at the scent of water it will bud
And bring forth branches like a plant.
10 But man dies and is laid away;
Indeed he breathes his last
And where *is* [a]he?
11 *As* water disappears from the sea,
And a river becomes parched
and dries up,
12 So man lies down and does not rise.
[a]Till the heavens *are* no more,
They will not awake
Nor be roused from their sleep.

13 "Oh, that You would hide
me in the grave,
That You would conceal me
until Your wrath is past,
That You would appoint me a set
time, and remember me!
14 If a man dies, shall he live *again?*
All the days of my hard
service [a]I will wait,
Till my change comes.
15 [a]You shall call, and I will answer You;
You shall desire the work
of Your hands.
16 For now [a]You number my steps,
But do not watch over my sin.
17 [a]My transgression *is* sealed up in a bag,
And You cover[1] my iniquity.

18 "But *as* a mountain falls *and*
crumbles away,
And *as* a rock is moved from its place;
19 *As* water wears away stones,
And as torrents wash away
the soil of the earth;
So You destroy the hope of man.
20 You prevail forever against
him, and he passes on;
You change his countenance
and send him away.
21 His sons come to honor, and
[a]he does not know *it;*
They are brought low, and he
does not perceive *it.*
22 But his flesh will be in pain over it,
And his soul will mourn over it."

Eliphaz Accuses Job of Folly

15 Then [a]Eliphaz the Temanite answered and said:

2 "Should a wise man answer
with empty knowledge,
And fill himself with the east wind?
3 Should he reason with
unprofitable talk,
Or by speeches with which
he can do no good?
4 Yes, you cast off fear,
And restrain prayer before God.
5 For your iniquity teaches your mouth,
And you choose the tongue
of the crafty.
6 [a]Your own mouth condemns
you, and not I;
Yes, your own lips testify against you.

7 "*Are* you the first man *who* was born?
[a]Or were you made before the hills?

14:3 [a] Ps. 8:4; 144:3 [b] [Ps. 143:2] [1] Septuagint, Syriac, and Vulgate read *him.* 14:4 [a] [Job 15:14; 25:4; Ps. 51:2, 5, 10; John 3:6; Rom. 5:12; Eph. 2:3] 14:5 [a] Job 7:1; 21:21; Heb. 9:27 14:6 [a] Job 7:16, 19; Ps. 39:13 [b] Job 7:1 14:10 [a] Job 10:21, 22 14:12 [a] Ps. 102:25, 26; [Is. 51:6; 65:17; 66:22]; Acts 3:21; [2 Pet. 3:7, 10, 11; Rev. 20:11; 21:1] 14:14 [a] Job 13:15 14:15 [a] Job 13:22 14:16 [a] Job 10:6, 14; 13:27; 31:4; 34:21; Ps. 56:8; 139:1–3; Prov. 5:21; [Jer. 32:19] 14:17 [a] Deut. 32:32–34 [1] Literally *plaster over* 14:21 [a] Eccl. 9:5; Is. 63:16 15:1 [a] Job 4:1 15:6 [a] Job 9:20; [Luke 19:22] 15:7 [a] Job 38:4, 21; Ps. 90:2; Prov. 8:25

8 [a]Have you heard the counsel of God?
Do you limit wisdom to yourself?
9 [a]What do you know that
we do not know?
What do you understand
that *is* not in us?
10 [a]Both the gray-haired and the
aged *are* among us,
Much older than your father.
11 *Are* the consolations of God
too small for you,
And the word *spoken* gently[1] with you?
12 Why does your heart carry you away,
And what do your eyes wink at,
13 That you turn your spirit against God,
And let *such* words go out
of your mouth?

14 "What[a] *is* man, that he could be pure?
And *he who is* born of a woman,
that he could be righteous?
15 [a]If *God* puts no trust in His saints,
And the heavens are not
pure in His sight,
16 [a]How much less man, *who is*
abominable and filthy,
[b]Who drinks iniquity like water!

17 "I will tell you, hear me;
What I have seen I will declare,
18 What wise men have told,
Not hiding *anything received*
[a]from their fathers,
19 To whom alone the land was given,
And [a]no alien passed among them:
20 The wicked man writhes
with pain all *his* days,
[a]And the number of years is
hidden from the oppressor.
21 Dreadful sounds *are* in his ears;
[a]In prosperity the destroyer
comes upon him.
22 He does not believe that he will
[a]return from darkness,
For a sword is waiting for him.
23 He [a]wanders about for bread,
saying, 'Where *is it?*'
He knows [b]that a day of darkness
is ready at his hand.
24 Trouble and anguish make
him afraid;
They overpower him, like a
king ready for battle.
25 For he stretches out his
hand against God,
And acts defiantly against
the Almighty,
26 Running stubbornly against Him
With his strong, embossed shield.

27 "Though[a] he has covered his
face with his fatness,
And made *his* waist heavy with fat,
28 He dwells in desolate cities,
In houses which no one inhabits,
Which are destined to become ruins.
29 He will not be rich,
Nor will his wealth [a]continue,
Nor will his possessions
overspread the earth.
30 He will not depart from darkness;
The flame will dry out his
branches,
And [a]by the breath of His
mouth he will go away.
31 Let him not [a]trust in futile
things, deceiving himself,
For futility will be his reward.
32 It will be accomplished
[a]before his time,
And his branch will not be green.
33 He will shake off his unripe
grape like a vine,
And cast off his blossom
like an olive tree.
34 For the company of hypocrites
will be barren,
And fire will consume the
tents of bribery.
35 [a]They conceive trouble and
bring forth futility;
Their womb prepares deceit."

Job Reproaches His Pitiless Friends

16 Then Job answered and said:

2 "I have heard many such things;
[a]Miserable comforters *are* you all!

15:8 [a] Job 29:4; Rom. 11:34; [1 Cor. 2:11] 15:9 [a] Job 12:3; 13:2 15:10 [a] Job 8:8–10; 12:12; 32:6, 7 15:11 [1] Septuagint reads *a secret thing.* 15:14 [a] Job 14:4; Prov. 20:9; [Eccl. 7:20; 1 John 1:8, 10] 15:15 [a] Job 4:18; 25:5 15:16 [a] Job 4:19; Ps. 14:3; 53:3 [b] Job 34:7; Prov. 19:28 15:18 [a] Job 8:8; 20:4 15:19 [a] Joel 3:17 15:20 [a] Ps. 90:12 15:21 [a] Job 20:21; 1 Thess. 5:3 15:22 [a] Job 14:10–12 15:23 [a] Ps. 59:15; 109:10 [b] Job 18:12 15:27 [a] Ps. 17:10; 73:7; 119:70 15:29 [a] Job 20:28; 27:16, 17 15:30 [a] Job 4:9 15:31 [a] Job 35:13; Is. 59:4 15:32 [a] Job 22:16; Ps. 55:23; Eccl. 7:17 15:35 [a] Ps. 7:14; Is. 59:4; [Hos. 10:13] 16:2 [a] Job 13:4; 21:34

3 Shall words of wind have an end?
Or what provokes you
that you answer?
4 I also could speak as you *do,*
If your soul were in my soul's place.
I could heap up words against you,
And [a]shake my head at you;
5 *But* I would strengthen you
with my mouth,
And the comfort of my lips
would relieve *your grief.*

6 "Though I speak, my grief
is not relieved;
And *if* I remain silent, how am
I eased?
7 But now He has [a]worn me out;
You [b]have made desolate
all my company.
8 You have shriveled me up,
And it is a [a]witness *against me;*
My leanness rises up against me
And bears witness to my face.
9 [a]He tears *me* in His wrath,
and hates me;
He gnashes at me with His teeth;
[b]My adversary sharpens
His gaze on me.
10 They [a]gape at me with their mouth,
They [b]strike me reproachfully
on the cheek,
They gather together against me.
11 God [a]has delivered me to the ungodly,
And turned me over to the
hands of the wicked.
12 I was at ease, but He has
[a]shattered me;
He also has taken *me* by my neck,
and shaken me to pieces;
He has [b]set me up for His target,
13 His archers surround me.
He pierces my heart[1] and
does not pity;
He pours out my gall on the
ground.
14 He breaks me with wound
upon wound;
He runs at me like a warrior.[1]
15 "I have sewn sackcloth over my skin,
And [a]laid my head[1] in the dust.
16 My face is flushed from weeping,
And on my eyelids *is* the
shadow of death;
17 Although no violence *is* in my hands,
And my prayer *is* pure.

18 "O earth, do not cover my blood,
And [a]let my cry have no *resting* place!
19 Surely even now [a]my
witness *is* in heaven,
And my evidence *is* on high.
20 My friends scorn me;
My eyes pour out *tears* to God.
21 [a]Oh, that one might plead
for a man with God,
As a man *pleads* for his neighbor!
22 For when a few years are finished,
I shall [a]go the way of no return.

Job Prays for Relief

17 "My spirit is broken,
My days are extinguished,
[a]The grave *is ready* for me.
2 *Are* not mockers with me?
And does not my eye dwell
on their [a]provocation?

3 "Now put down a pledge for
me with Yourself.
Who *is* he *who* [a]will shake
hands with me?
4 For You have hidden their heart
from [a]understanding;
Therefore You will not exalt *them.*
5 He who speaks flattery to *his* friends,
Even the eyes of his children
will [a]fail.

6 "But He has made me [a]a
byword of the people,
And I have become one in
whose face men spit.
7 [a]My eye has also grown dim
because of sorrow,
And all my members *are* like
shadows.

16:4 [a] Ps. 22:7; 109:25; Lam. 2:15; Zeph. 2:15; Matt. 27:39 16:7 [a] Job 7:3 [b] Job 16:20; 19:13–15 16:8 [a] Job 10:17 16:9 [a] Job 10:16, 17; 19:11; Hos. 6:1 [b] Job 13:24; 33:10 16:10 [a] Ps. 22:13; 35:21 [b] Is. 50:6; Lam. 3:30; Mic. 5:1; Matt. 26:67; Mark 14:65; Luke 22:63; Acts 23:2 16:11 [a] Job 1:15, 17 16:12 [a] Job 9:17 [b] Job 7:20; Lam. 3:12 16:13 [1] Literally *kidneys* 16:14 [1] Vulgate reads *giant.* 16:15 [a] Job 30:19; Ps. 7:5 [1] Literally *horn* 16:18 [a] Job 27:9; [Ps. 66:18] 16:19 [a] Gen. 31:50; Rom. 1:9; Phil. 1:8; 1 Thess. 2:5 16:21 [a] Job 31:35; Eccl. 6:10; [Is. 45:9; Rom. 9:20] 16:22 [a] Job 10:21; Eccl. 12:5 17:1 [a] Ps. 88:3, 4 17:2 [a] 1 Sam. 1:6; Job 12:4; 17:6; 30:1, 9; 34:7 17:3 [a] Prov. 6:1; 17:18; 22:26 17:4 [a] Job 12:20; 32:9 17:5 [a] Job 11:20 17:6 [a] Job 30:9 17:7 [a] Ps. 6:7; 31:9

8 Upright *men* are astonished at this,
And the innocent stirs himself
up against the hypocrite.
9 Yet the righteous will hold to his [a]way,
And he who has [b]clean hands will
be stronger and stronger.

10 "But please, [a]come back
again, all of you,[1]
For I shall not find *one* wise
man among you.
11 [a]My days are past,
My purposes are broken off,
Even the thoughts of my heart.
12 They change the night into day;
'The light *is* near,' *they say,* in
the face of darkness.
13 If I wait *for* the grave *as* my house,
If I make my bed in the darkness,
14 If I say to corruption, 'You
are my father,'
And to the worm, 'You *are* my
mother and my sister,'
15 Where then *is* my [a]hope?
As for my hope, who can see it?
16 *Will* they go down [a]to the
gates of Sheol?
Shall *we have* [b]rest together
in the dust?"

Bildad: The Wicked Are Punished

18 Then [a]Bildad the Shuhite answered
and said:

2 "How long *till* you put an end to words?
Gain understanding, and
afterward we will speak.
3 Why are we counted [a]as beasts,
And regarded as stupid in your sight?
4 [a]You who tear yourself in anger,
Shall the earth be forsaken for you?
Or shall the rock be removed
from its place?

5 "The[a] light of the wicked
indeed goes out,
And the flame of his fire
does not shine.
6 The light is dark in his tent,
[a]And his lamp beside him is put out.
7 The steps of his strength
are shortened,
And [a]his own counsel casts
him down.
8 For [a]he is cast into a net
by his own feet,
And he walks into a snare.
9 The net takes *him* by the heel,
And [a]a snare lays hold of him.
10 A noose *is* hidden for him
on the ground,
And a trap for him in the road.
11 [a]Terrors frighten him on every side,
And drive him to his feet.
12 His strength is starved,
And [a]destruction *is* ready at his side.
13 It devours patches of his skin;
The firstborn of death
devours his limbs.
14 He is uprooted from [a]the
shelter of his tent,
And they parade him before
the king of terrors.
15 They dwell in his tent *who*
are none of his;
Brimstone is scattered on his
dwelling.
16 [a]His roots are dried out below,
And his branch withers above.
17 [a]The memory of him perishes
from the earth,
And he has no name among
the renowned.[1]
18 He is driven from light into
darkness,
And chased out of the world.
19 [a]He has neither son nor posterity
among his people,
Nor any remaining in his dwellings.
20 Those in the west are
astonished [a]at his day,
As those in the east are frightened.
21 Surely such *are* the dwellings
of the wicked,
And this *is* the place *of him who*
[a]does not know God."

17:9 [a] Prov. 4:18 [b] Ps. 24:4 17:10 [a] Job 6:29 [1] Following some Hebrew manuscripts, Septuagint, Syriac, and Vulgate; Masoretic Text and Targum read *all of them.* 17:11 [a] Job 7:6 17:15 [a] Job 7:6; 13:15; 14:19; 19:10 17:16 [a] Jon. 2:6 [b] Job 3:17–19; 21:33 18:1 [a] Job 8:1 18:3 [a] Ps. 73:22 18:4 [a] Job 13:14 18:5 [a] Job 21:17; Prov. 13:9; 20:20; 24:20 18:6 [a] Job 21:17; Ps. 18:28 18:7 [a] Job 5:12, 13; 15:6 18:8 [a] Job 22:10; Ps. 9:15; 35:8; Is. 24:17, 18 18:9 [a] Job 5:5 18:11 [a] Job 20:25; Jer. 6:25 18:12 [a] Job 15:23 18:14 [a] Job 11:20 18:16 [a] Job 29:19 18:17 [a] Job 24:20; [Ps. 34:16]; Prov. 10:7 [1] Literally *before the outside,* meaning distinguished, famous 18:19 [a] Job 27:14, 15; Is. 14:22 18:20 [a] Ps. 37:13; Jer. 50:27; Obad. 12 18:21 [a] Jer. 9:3; 1 Thess. 4:5

Job Trusts in His Redeemer

19 Then Job answered and said:
2 "How long will you torment my soul,
And break me in pieces with words?
3 These ten times you have
reproached me;
You are not ashamed *that*
you have wronged me.[1]
4 And if indeed I have erred,
My error remains with me.
5 If indeed you [a]exalt *yourselves*
against me,
And plead my disgrace against me,
6 Know then that [a]God has wronged me,
And has surrounded me with His net.

7 "If I cry out concerning wrong,
I am not heard.
If I cry aloud, *there is* no justice.
8 [a]He has fenced up my way, so
that I cannot pass;
And He has set darkness
in my paths.
9 [a]He has stripped me of my glory,
And taken the crown *from* my head.
10 He breaks me down on every side,
And I am gone;
My [a]hope He has uprooted like
a tree.
11 He has also kindled His
wrath against me,
And [a]He counts me as *one*
of His enemies.
12 His troops come together
And build up their road against me;
They encamp all around my tent.

13 "He[a] has removed my
brothers far from me,
And my acquaintances are
completely estranged from me.
14 My relatives have failed,
And my close friends have
forgotten me.
15 Those who dwell in my house,
and my maidservants,
Count me as a stranger;
I am an alien in their sight.
16 I call my servant, but he
gives no answer;
I beg him with my mouth.
17 My breath is offensive to my wife,
And I am repulsive to the
children of my own body.
18 Even [a]young children despise me;
I arise, and they speak against me.
19 [a]All my close friends abhor me,
And those whom I love have
turned against me.
20 [a]My bone clings to my skin
and to my flesh,
And I have escaped by the
skin of my teeth.

21 "Have pity on me, have pity on
me, O you my friends,
For the hand of God has struck me!
22 Why do you [a]persecute
me as God *does*,
And are not satisfied with my flesh?

23 "Oh, that my words were written!
Oh, that they were inscribed in a book!
24 That they were engraved on a rock
With an iron pen and lead, forever!
25 For I know *that* my Redeemer lives,
And He shall stand at last on the earth;
26 And after my skin is
destroyed, this *I know*,
That [a]in my flesh I shall see God,
27 Whom I shall see for myself,
And my eyes shall behold,
and not another.
How my heart yearns within me!
28 If you should say, 'How shall
we persecute him?'—
Since the root of the matter
is found in me,
29 Be afraid of the sword for yourselves;
For wrath *brings* the punishment
of the sword,
That you may know *there*
is a judgment."

Zophar's Sermon on the Wicked Man

20 Then [a]Zophar the Naamathite answered and said:

19:3 [1] A Jewish tradition reads *make yourselves strange to me.* 19:5 [a] Ps. 35:26; 38:16; 55:12, 13 19:6 [a] Job 16:11 19:8 [a] Job 3:23; Ps. 88:8; Lam. 3:7, 9 19:9 [a] Job 12:17, 19; Ps. 89:44 19:10 [a] Job 17:14–16 19:11 [a] Job 13:24; 33:10 19:13 [a] Job 16:20; Ps. 31:11; 38:11; 69:8; 88:8, 18 19:18 [a] 2 Kin. 2:23; Job 17:6 19:19 [a] Ps. 38:11; 55:12, 13 19:20 [a] Job 16:8; 33:21; Ps. 102:5; Lam. 4:8 19:22 [a] Job 13:24, 25; 16:11; 19:6; Ps. 69:26 19:26 [a] [Ps. 17:15]; Matt. 5:8; 1 Cor. 13:12; [1 John 3:2] 20:1 [a] Job 11:1

2 "Therefore my anxious thoughts
make me answer,
Because of the turmoil within me.
3 I have heard the rebuke
that reproaches me,
And the spirit of my understanding
causes me to answer.

4 "Do you *not* know this of [a]old,
Since man was placed on earth,
5 [a]That the triumphing of the
wicked is short,
And the joy of the hypocrite
is *but* for a [b]moment?
6 [a]Though his haughtiness mounts
up to the heavens,
And his head reaches to the clouds,
7 *Yet* he will perish forever
like his own refuse;
Those who have seen him
will say, 'Where is he?'
8 He will fly away [a]like a dream,
and not be found;
Yes, he [b]will be chased away
like a vision of the night.
9 The eye *that* saw him will
see him no more,
Nor will his place behold
him anymore.
10 His children will seek the
favor of the poor,
And his hands will restore his wealth.
11 His bones are full of [a]his
youthful vigor,
[b]But it will lie down with
him in the dust.

12 "Though evil is sweet in his mouth,
And he hides it under his tongue,
13 *Though* he spares it and
does not forsake it,
But still keeps it in his mouth,
14 *Yet* his food in his stomach
turns sour;
It becomes cobra venom within him.
15 He swallows down riches
And vomits them up again;
God casts them out of his belly.
16 He will suck the poison of cobras;
The viper's tongue will slay him.
17 He will not see [a]the streams,
The rivers flowing with
honey and cream.
18 He will restore that for
which he labored,
And will not swallow *it* down;
From the proceeds of business
He will get no enjoyment.
19 For he has oppressed *and*
forsaken the poor,
He has violently seized a house
which he did not build.

20 "Because[a] he knows no
quietness in his heart,[1]
He will not save anything he desires.
21 Nothing is left for him to eat;
Therefore his well-being will not last.
22 In his self-sufficiency he
will be in distress;
Every hand of misery will
come against him.
23 *When* he is about to fill his stomach,
God will cast on him the
fury of His wrath,
And will rain *it* on him
while he is eating.
24 [a]He will flee from the iron weapon;
A bronze bow will pierce
him through.
25 It is drawn, and comes out
of the body;
Yes, [a]the glittering *point*
comes out of his gall.
[b]Terrors *come* upon him;
26 Total darkness *is* reserved
for his treasures.
[a]An unfanned fire will consume him;
It shall go ill with him who
is left in his tent.
27 The heavens will reveal his iniquity,
And the earth will rise up against him.
28 The increase of his house
will depart,
And his goods will flow away in
the day of His [a]wrath.
29 [a]This *is* the portion from God
for a wicked man,
The heritage appointed
to him by God."

20:4 [a] Job 8:8; 15:10 20:5 [a] Ps. 37:35, 36 [b] [Job 8:13; 13:16; 15:34; 27:8] 20:6 [a] Is. 14:13, 14 20:8 [a] Ps. 73:20; 90:5 [b] Job 18:18; 27:21–23 20:11 [a] Job 13:26 [b] Job 21:26 20:17 [a] Ps. 36:8; Jer. 17:8 20:20 [a] Eccl. 5:13–15 [1] Literally *belly* 20:24 [a] Is. 24:18; Amos 5:19 20:25 [a] Job 16:13 [b] Job 18:11, 14 20:26 [a] Ps. 21:9 20:28 [a] Job 20:15; 21:30 20:29 [a] Job 27:13; 31:2, 3

Job's Discourse on the Wicked

21 Then Job answered and said:
2 "Listen carefully to my speech,
And let this be your consolation.
3 Bear with me that I may speak,
And after I have spoken,
keep [a]mocking.

4 "As for me, *is* my complaint
against man?
And if *it were,* why should
I not be impatient?
5 Look at me and be astonished;
[a]Put *your* hand over *your* mouth.
6 Even when I remember I am terrified,
And trembling takes hold
of my flesh.
7 [a]Why do the wicked live
and become old,
Yes, become mighty in power?
8 Their descendants are established
with them in their sight,
And their offspring before their eyes.
9 Their houses *are* safe from fear,
[a]Neither *is* the rod of God upon them.
10 Their bull breeds without failure;
Their cow calves [a]without
miscarriage.
11 They send forth their little
ones like a flock,
And their children dance.
12 They sing to the tambourine and harp,
And rejoice to the sound of the flute.
13 They [a]spend their days in wealth,
And in a moment go down
to the grave.[1]
14 [a]Yet they say to God, 'Depart from us,
For we do not desire the
knowledge of Your ways.
15 [a]Who *is* the Almighty, that we
should serve Him?
And [b]what profit do we have
if we pray to Him?'
16 Indeed their prosperity *is*
not in their hand;
[a]The counsel of the wicked
is far from me.

17 "How often is the lamp of
the wicked put out?
How often does their destruction
come upon them,
The sorrows *God* [a]distributes
in His anger?
18 [a]They are like straw before the wind,
And like chaff that a storm
carries away.
19 *They say,* 'God lays up one's[1]
iniquity [a]for his children';
Let Him recompense him,
that he may know *it.*
20 Let his eyes see his destruction,
And [a]let him drink of the
wrath of the Almighty.
21 For what does he care about
his household after him,
When the number of his
months is cut in half?

22 "Can[a] *anyone* teach God knowledge,
Since He judges those on high?
23 One dies in his full strength,
Being wholly at ease and secure;
24 His pails[1] are full of milk,
And the marrow of his bones
is moist.
25 Another man dies in the
bitterness of his soul,
Never having eaten with pleasure.
26 They [a]lie down alike in the dust,
And worms cover them.

27 "Look, I know your thoughts,
And the schemes *with which*
you would wrong me.
28 For you say,
'Where *is* the house of the prince?
And where *is* the tent,[1]
The dwelling place of the wicked?'
29 Have you not asked those
who travel the road?
And do you not know their signs?
30 [a]For the wicked are reserved
for the day of doom;
They shall be brought out
on the day of wrath.

21:3 [a] Job 16:10 21:5 [a] Judg. 18:19; Job 13:5; 29:9; 40:4 21:7 [a] Job 12:6; Ps. 17:10, 14; 73:3, 12; [Jer. 12:1]; Hab. 1:13, 16 21:9 [a] Ps. 73:5 21:10 [a] Ex. 23:26 21:13 [a] Job 21:23; 36:11 [1] Or *Sheol* 21:14 [a] Job 22:17 21:15 [a] Ex. 5:2; Job 22:17; 34:9 [b] Job 35:3; Mal. 3:14 21:16 [a] Job 22:18; Ps. 1:1; Prov. 1:10 21:17 [a] [Job 31:2, 3; Luke 12:46] 21:18 [a] Ps. 1:4; 35:5; Is. 17:13; Hos. 13:3 21:19 [a] [Ex. 20:5]; Jer. 31:29; Ezek. 18:2 [1] Literally *his* 21:20 [a] Ps. 75:8; Is. 51:17; Jer. 25:15; Rev. 14:10; 19:15 21:22 [a] Job 35:11; 36:22; [Is. 40:13; 45:9; Rom. 11:34; 1 Cor. 2:16] 21:24 [1] Septuagint and Vulgate read *bowels;* Syriac reads *sides;* Targum reads *breasts.* 21:26 [a] Job 3:13; 20:11; Eccl. 9:2 21:28 [1] Vulgate omits *the tent.* 21:30 [a] Job 20:29; [Prov. 16:4; 2 Pet. 2:9]

31 Who condemns his way to his face?
And who repays him *for*
what he has done?
32 Yet he shall be brought to the grave,
And a vigil kept over the tomb.
33 The clods of the valley shall
be sweet to him;
[a]Everyone shall follow him,
As countless *have gone* before him.
34 How then can you comfort
me with empty words,
Since falsehood remains
in your answers?"

Eliphaz Accuses Job of Wickedness

22 Then [a]Eliphaz the Temanite answered and said:

2 "Can[a] a man be profitable to God,
Though he who is wise may be
profitable to himself?
3 *Is it* any pleasure to the Almighty
that you are righteous?
Or *is it* gain *to Him* that you make
your ways blameless?

4 "Is it because of your fear of
Him that He corrects you,
And enters into judgment with you?
5 *Is* not your wickedness great,
And your iniquity without end?
6 For you have [a]taken pledges from
your brother for no reason,
And stripped the naked
of their clothing.
7 You have not given the
weary water to drink,
And you [a]have withheld bread
from the hungry.
8 But the mighty man
possessed the land,
And the honorable man dwelt in it.
9 You have sent widows away empty,
And the strength of the
fatherless was crushed.
10 Therefore snares *are* all around you,
And sudden fear troubles you,
11 Or darkness *so that* you cannot see;
And an abundance of
[a]water covers you.

12 "Is not God in the height of heaven?
And see the highest stars,
how lofty they are!
13 And you say, [a]'What does God know?
Can He judge through the
deep darkness?
14 [a]Thick clouds cover Him, so
that He cannot see,
And He walks above the
circle of heaven.'
15 Will you keep to the old way
Which wicked men have trod,
16 Who [a]were cut down before their time,
Whose foundations were
swept away by a flood?
17 [a]They said to God, 'Depart from us!
What can the Almighty do to them?'[1]
18 Yet He filled their houses
with good *things;*
But the counsel of the wicked
is far from me.

19 "The[a] righteous see *it* and are glad,
And the innocent laugh at them:
20 'Surely our adversaries[1] are cut down,
And the fire consumes their remnant.'

21 "Now acquaint yourself with
Him, and [a]be at peace;
Thereby good will come to you.
22 Receive, please, [a]instruction
from His mouth,
And [b]lay up His words in your heart.
23 If you return to the Almighty,
you will be built up;
You will remove iniquity
far from your tents.
24 Then you will [a]lay your gold in the dust,
And the *gold* of Ophir among
the stones of the brooks.
25 Yes, the Almighty will be your gold[1]
And your precious silver;
26 For then you will have your
[a]delight in the Almighty,
And lift up your face to God.

21:33 [a] Heb. 9:27 **22:1** [a] Job 4:1; 15:1; 42:9 **22:2** [a] Job 35:7; [Ps. 16:2; Luke 17:10] **22:6** [a] [Ex. 22:26, 27]; Deut. 24:6, 10, 17; Job 24:3, 9; Ezek. 18:16 **22:7** [a] Deut. 15:7; Job 31:17; Is. 58:7; Ezek. 18:7; Matt. 25:42 **22:11** [a] Job 38:34; Ps. 69:1, 2; 124:5; Lam. 3:54 **22:13** [a] Ps. 73:11 **22:14** [a] Ps. 139:11, 12 **22:16** [a] Job 14:19; 15:32; Ps. 90:5; Is. 28:2; Matt. 7:26, 27 **22:17** [a] Job 21:14, 15 [1] Septuagint and Syriac read *us.* **22:19** [a] Ps. 52:6; 58:10; 107:42 **22:20** [1] Septuagint reads *substance.* **22:21** [a] [Ps. 34:10]; Is. 27:5 **22:22** [a] Job 6:10; 23:12; Prov. 2:6 [b] [Ps. 119:11] **22:24** [a] 2 Chr. 1:15 **22:25** [1] The ancient versions suggest *defense;* Hebrew reads *gold* as in verse 24. **22:26** [a] Job 27:10; Ps. 37:4; Is. 58:14

27 [a]You will make your prayer to Him,
He will hear you,
And you will pay your vows.
28 You will also declare a thing,
And it will be established for you;
So light will shine on your ways.
29 When they cast *you* down, and you
say, 'Exaltation *will come!*'
Then [a]He will save the humble *person.*
30 He will *even* deliver one
who is not innocent;
Yes, he will be delivered by the
purity of your hands."

Job Proclaims God's Righteous Judgments

23 Then Job answered and said:
2 "Even today my [a]complaint is bitter;
My[1] hand is listless because
of my groaning.
3 [a]Oh, that I knew where I
might find Him,
That I might come to His seat!
4 I would present *my* case before Him,
And fill my mouth with arguments.
5 I would know the words *which*
He would answer me,
And understand what He
would say to me.
6 [a]Would He contend with me
in His great power?
No! But He would take *note* of me.
7 There the upright could
reason with Him,
And I would be delivered
forever from my Judge.

8 "Look,[a] I go forward, but He is not *there,*
And backward, but I cannot
perceive Him;
9 When He works on the left hand,
I cannot behold *Him;*
When He turns to the right
hand, I cannot see *Him.*
10 But [a]He knows the way that I take;
When [b]He has tested me, I shall
come forth as gold.
11 [a]My foot has held fast to His steps;
I have kept His way and
not turned aside.
12 I have not departed from the
[a]commandment of His lips;
[b]I have treasured the words
of His mouth
More than my necessary *food.*

13 "But He *is* unique, and who
can make Him change?
And *whatever* [a]His soul
desires, *that* He does.
14 For He performs *what is*
[a]appointed for me,
And many such *things are* with Him.
15 Therefore I am terrified
at His presence;
When I consider *this,* I
am afraid of Him.
16 For God [a]made my heart weak,
And the Almighty terrifies me;
17 Because I was not [a]cut off from
the presence of darkness,
And He did *not* hide deep
darkness from my face.

Job Complains of Violence on the Earth

24 "*Since* [a]times are not hidden
from the Almighty,
Why do those who know Him
see not His [b]days?

2 "*Some* remove [a]landmarks;
They seize flocks violently
and feed *on them;*
3 They drive away the donkey
of the fatherless;
They [a]take the widow's ox as a pledge.
4 They push the needy off the road;
All the [a]poor of the land
are forced to hide.
5 Indeed, *like* wild donkeys
in the desert,
They go out to their work,
searching for food.
The wilderness *yields* food for
them *and* for *their* children.

22:27 [a] Job 11:13; 33:26; [Is. 58:9–11] 22:29 [a] Job 5:11; [Matt. 23:12; James 4:6; 1 Pet. 5:5] 23:2 [a] Job 7:11 [1] Following Masoretic Text, Targum, and Vulgate; Septuagint and Syriac read *His.* 23:3 [a] Job 13:3, 18; 16:21; 31:35 23:6 [a] Is. 57:16 23:8 [a] Job 9:11; 35:14 23:10 [a] [Ps. 1:6; 139:1–3] [b] [Ps. 17:3; 66:10; James 1:12] 23:11 [a] Job 31:7; Ps. 17:5 23:12 [a] Job 6:10; 22:22 [b] Ps. 44:18 23:13 [a] [Ps. 115:3] 23:14 [a] [1 Thess. 3:2–4] 23:16 [a] Ps. 22:14 23:17 [a] Job 10:18, 19 24:1 [a] [Acts 1:7] [b] [Is. 2:12]; Jer. 46:10; [Obad. 15]; Zeph. 1:7 24:2 [a] [Deut. 19:14; 27:17]; Prov. 22:28; 23:10; Hos. 5:10 24:3 [a] [Deut. 24:6, 10, 12, 17]; Job 22:6, 9 24:4 [a] Job 29:16; Prov. 28:28

6 They gather their fodder in the field
And glean in the vineyard
of the wicked.
7 They [a]spend the night naked,
without clothing,
And have no covering in the cold.
8 They are wet with the showers
of the mountains,
And [a]huddle around the rock
for want of shelter.

9 "*Some* snatch the fatherless
from the breast,
And take a pledge from the poor.
10 They cause *the poor* to go
naked, without [a]clothing;
And they take away the sheaves
from the hungry.
11 They press out oil within their walls,
And tread winepresses,
yet suffer thirst.
12 The dying groan in the city,
And the souls of the wounded
cry out;
Yet God does not charge
them with wrong.

13 "There are those who rebel
against the light;
They do not know its ways
Nor abide in its paths.
14 [a]The murderer rises with the light;
He kills the poor and needy;
And in the night he is like a thief.
15 [a]The eye of the adulterer
waits for the twilight,
[b]Saying, 'No eye will see me';
And he disguises *his* face.
16 In the dark they break into houses
Which they marked for
themselves in the daytime;
[a]They do not know the light.
17 For the morning is the same to
them as the shadow of death;
If *someone* recognizes *them,*
They are in the terrors of
the shadow of death.

18 "They *should be* swift on the
face of the waters,
Their portion *should be*
cursed in the earth,
So that no *one would* turn into
the way of their vineyards.
19 As drought and heat consume
the snow waters,
So the grave[1] *consumes those*
who have sinned.
20 The womb *should* forget him,
The worm *should* feed sweetly on him;
[a]He *should* be remembered no more,
And wickedness *should* be
broken like a tree.
21 For he preys on the barren
who do not bear,
And does no good for the widow.

22 "But *God* draws the mighty
away with His power;
He rises up, but no *man* is sure of life.
23 He gives them security,
and they rely *on it;*
Yet [a]His eyes *are* on their ways.
24 They are exalted for a little while,
Then they are gone.
They are brought low;
They are taken out of the
way like all *others;*
They dry out like the heads of grain.

25 "Now if *it is* not *so,* who will
prove me a liar,
And make my speech worth
nothing?"

Bildad: How Can Man Be Righteous?

25 Then [a]Bildad the Shuhite answered
and said:

2 "Dominion and fear *belong* to Him;
He makes peace in His high places.
3 Is there any number to His armies?
Upon whom does [a]His light not rise?
4 [a]How then can man be
righteous before God?
Or how can he be [b]pure *who*
is born of a woman?
5 If even the moon does not shine,
And the stars are not pure
in His [a]sight,

24:7 [a] Ex. 22:26, 27; [Deut. 24:12, 13]; Job 22:6; [James 2:15, 16] 24:8 [a] Lam. 4:5 24:10 [a] Job 31:19 24:14 [a] Ps. 10:8 24:15 [a] Prov. 7:7–10 [b] Ps. 10:11 24:16 [a] [John 3:20] 24:19 [1] Or *Sheol* 24:20 [a] Job 18:17; Ps. 34:16; Prov. 10:7 24:23 [a] Ps. 11:4; [Prov. 15:3] 25:1 [a] Job 8:1; 18:1 25:3 [a] James 1:17 25:4 [a] Job 4:17; 15:14; Ps. 130:3; 143:2 [b] [Job 14:4] 25:5 [a] Job 15:15

6 How much less man, *who is* [a]a maggot,
And a son of man, *who is* a worm?"

Job: Man's Frailty and God's Majesty

26 But Job answered and said:

2 "How have you helped *him*
who is without power?
How have you saved the arm
that has no strength?
3 How have you counseled *one*
who has no wisdom?
And *how* have you declared
sound advice to many?
4 To whom have you uttered words?
And whose spirit came from you?

5 "The dead tremble,
Those under the waters and
those inhabiting them.
6 [a]Sheol *is* naked before Him,
And Destruction has no covering.
7 [a]He stretches out the north
over empty space;
He hangs the earth on nothing.
8 [a]He binds up the water in
His thick clouds,
Yet the clouds are not broken under it.
9 He covers the face of *His* throne,
And spreads His cloud over it.
10 [a]He drew a circular horizon on
the face of the waters,
At the boundary of light and
darkness.
11 The pillars of heaven tremble,
And are astonished at His rebuke.
12 [a]He stirs up the sea with His power,
And by His understanding He
breaks up the storm.
13 [a]By His Spirit He adorned
the heavens;
His hand pierced [b]the fleeing
serpent.
14 Indeed these *are* the mere
edges of His ways,
And how small a whisper
we hear of Him!
But the thunder of His power
who can understand?"

Job Maintains His Integrity

27 Moreover Job continued his discourse, and said:

2 "As God lives, [a]*who* has taken
away my justice,
And the Almighty, *who* has
made my soul bitter,
3 As long as my breath *is* in me,
And the breath of God in my nostrils,
4 My lips will not speak wickedness,
Nor my tongue utter deceit.
5 Far be it from me
That I should say you are right;
Till I die [a]I will not put away
my integrity from me.
6 My righteousness I [a]hold fast,
and will not let it go;
[b]My heart shall not reproach
me as long as I live.

7 "May my enemy be like the wicked,
And he who rises up against
me like the unrighteous.
8 [a]For what is the hope of the hypocrite,
Though he may gain *much,*
If God takes away his life?
9 [a]Will God hear his cry
When trouble comes upon him?
10 [a]Will he delight himself
in the Almighty?
Will he always call on God?

11 "I will teach you about the hand
of God;
What *is* with the Almighty
I will not conceal.
12 Surely all of you have seen *it;*
Why then do you behave with
complete nonsense?

13 "This[a] is the portion of a
wicked man with God,
And the heritage of oppressors,
received from the Almighty:
14 [a]If his children are multiplied,
it is for the sword;
And his offspring shall not be
satisfied with bread.

25:6 [a] Ps. 22:6 26:6 [a] [Ps. 139:8]; Prov. 15:11; [Heb. 4:13] 26:7 [a] Job 9:8; Ps. 24:2; 104:2 26:8 [a] Job 37:11; Prov. 30:4 26:10 [a] [Job 38:1–11]; Ps. 33:7; 104:9; Prov. 8:29; Jer. 5:22 26:12 [a] Ex. 14:21; Job 9:13; Is. 51:15; [Jer. 31:35] 26:13 [a] [Job 9:8]; Ps. 33:6 [b] Is. 27:1 27:2 [a] Job 34:5 27:5 [a] Job 2:9; 13:15 27:6 [a] Job 2:3; 33:9 [b] Acts 24:16 27:8 [a] Matt. 16:26; Luke 12:20 27:9 [a] Job 35:12, 13; Ps. 18:41; Prov. 1:28; 28:9; [Is. 1:15]; Jer. 14:12; Ezek. 8:18; [Mic. 3:4; John 9:31; James 4:3] 27:10 [a] Job 22:26, 27; [Ps. 37:4; Is. 58:14] 27:13 [a] Job 20:29 27:14 [a] Deut. 28:41; Esth. 9:10; Hos. 9:13

15 Those who survive him shall
be buried in death,
And [a]their[1] widows shall not weep,
16 Though he heaps up silver like dust,
And piles up clothing like clay—
17 He may pile *it* up, but [a]the
just will wear *it,*
And the innocent will divide the silver.
18 He builds his house like a moth,[1]
[a]Like a booth *which* a watchman makes.
19 The rich man will lie down,
But not be gathered *up;*[1]
He opens his eyes,
And he *is* [a]no more.
20 [a]Terrors overtake him like a flood;
A tempest steals him
away in the night.
21 The east wind carries him
away, and he is gone;
It sweeps him out of his place.
22 It hurls against him and
does not [a]spare;
He flees desperately from its power.
23 *Men* shall clap their hands at him,
And shall hiss him out
of his place.

Job's Discourse on Wisdom

28 "Surely there is a mine for silver,
And a place *where* gold is refined.
2 Iron is taken from the earth,
And copper *is* smelted *from* ore.
3 *Man* puts an end to darkness,
And searches every recess
For ore in the darkness and
the shadow of death.
4 He breaks open a shaft
away from people;
In places forgotten by feet
They hang far away from men;
They swing to and fro.
5 *As for* the earth, from it comes bread,
But underneath it is turned
up as by fire;
6 Its stones *are* the source of sapphires,
And it contains gold dust.
7 *That* path no bird knows,
Nor has the falcon's eye seen it.
8 The proud lions[1] have not trodden it,
Nor has the fierce lion passed over it.
9 He puts his hand on the flint;
He overturns the mountains
at the roots.
10 He cuts out channels in the rocks,
And his eye sees every precious thing.
11 He dams up the streams
from trickling;
What is hidden he brings forth to light.

12 "But[a] where can wisdom be found?
And where *is* the place of
understanding?
13 Man does not know its [a]value,
Nor is it found in the land of the living.
14 [a]The deep says, '*It is* not in me';
And the sea says, '*It is* not with me.'
15 It [a]cannot be purchased for gold,
Nor can silver be weighed *for* its price.
16 It cannot be valued in the
gold of Ophir,
In precious onyx or sapphire.
17 Neither [a]gold nor crystal can equal it,
Nor can it be exchanged for
jewelry of fine gold.
18 No mention shall be made
of coral or quartz,
For the price of wisdom
is above [a]rubies.
19 The topaz of Ethiopia cannot equal it,
Nor can it be valued in pure [a]gold.

20 "From[a] where then does wisdom come?
And where *is* the place of
understanding?
21 It is hidden from the eyes of all living,
And concealed from the
birds of the air.
22 [a]Destruction and Death say,
'We have heard a report about
it with our ears.'
23 God understands its way,
And He knows its place.
24 For He looks to the ends of the earth,
And [a]sees under the whole heavens,
25 [a]To establish a weight for the wind,
And apportion the waters by measure.

27:15 [a] Ps. 78:64 [1] Literally *his* 27:17 [a] Prov. 28:8; [Eccl. 2:26] 27:18 [a] Is. 1:8; Lam. 2:6 [1] Following Masoretic Text and Vulgate; Septuagint and Syriac read *spider* (compare 8:14); Targum reads *decay.* 27:19 [a] Job 7:8, 21; 20:7 [1] Following Masoretic Text and Targum; Septuagint and Syriac read *But shall not add* (that is, do it again); Vulgate reads *But take away nothing.* 27:20 [a] Job 18:11 27:22 [a] Jer. 13:14; Ezek. 5:11; 24:14 28:8 [1] Literally *sons of pride,* figurative of the great lions 28:12 [a] Eccl. 7:24 28:13 [a] Prov. 3:15 28:14 [a] Job 28:22 28:15 [a] Prov. 3:13–15; 8:10, 11, 19 28:17 [a] Prov. 8:10; 16:16 28:18 [a] Prov. 3:15; 8:11 28:19 [a] Prov. 8:19 28:20 [a] Job 28:12; [Ps. 111:10; Prov. 1:7; 9:10] 28:22 [a] Job 28:14 28:24 [a] [Ps. 11:4; 33:13, 14; 66:7; Prov. 15:3] 28:25 [a] Ps. 135:7

26 When He [a]made a law for the rain,
And a path for the thunderbolt,
27 Then He saw *wisdom*[1] and declared it;
He prepared it, indeed, He
searched it out.
28 And to man He said,
'Behold, [a]the fear of the
Lord, that *is* wisdom,
And to depart from evil *is*
understanding.'"

Job's Summary Defense

29 Job further continued his discourse, and said:

2 "Oh, that I were as *in* months [a]past,
As *in* the days *when* God
[b]watched over me;
3 [a]When His lamp shone upon my head,
And when by His light I walked
through darkness;
4 Just as I was in the days of my prime,
When [a]the friendly counsel of
God *was* over my tent;
5 When the Almighty *was* yet with me,
When my children *were* around me;
6 When [a]my steps were
bathed with cream,[1]
And [b]the rock poured out
rivers of oil for me!

7 "When I went out to the gate
by the city,
When I took my seat in
the open square,
8 The young men saw me and hid,
And the aged arose *and* stood;
9 The princes refrained from talking,
And [a]put *their* hand on their mouth;
10 The voice of nobles was hushed,
And their [a]tongue stuck to the
roof of their mouth.
11 When the ear heard, then
it blessed me,
And when the eye saw, then
it approved me;
12 Because [a]I delivered the
poor who cried out,
The fatherless and *the one*
who had no helper.
13 The blessing of a perishing
man came upon me,
And I caused the widow's
heart to sing for joy.
14 [a]I put on righteousness,
and it clothed me;
My justice *was* like a robe
and a turban.
15 I *was* [a]eyes to the blind,
And I *was* feet to the lame.
16 I *was* a father to the poor,
And [a]I searched out the case
that I did not know.
17 I broke [a]the fangs of the wicked,
And plucked the victim from his teeth.

18 "Then I said, [a]'I shall die in my nest,
And multiply *my* days as the sand.
19 [a]My root *is* spread out [b]to the waters,
And the dew lies all night
on my branch.
20 My glory *is* fresh within me,
And my [a]bow is renewed in my hand.'

21 "*Men* listened to me and waited,
And kept silence for my counsel.
22 After my words they did
not speak again,
And my speech settled
on them *as dew*.
23 They waited for me *as* for the rain,
And they opened their mouth
wide *as* for [a]the spring rain.
24 *If* I mocked at them, they
did not believe *it*,
And the light of my countenance
they did not cast down.
25 I chose the way for them,
and sat as chief;
So I dwelt as a king in the army,
As one *who* comforts mourners.

30 "But now they mock at me,
men younger than I,
Whose fathers I disdained to put
with the dogs of my flock.

28:26 [a] Job 37:3; 38:25 **28:27** [1] Literally *it* **28:28** [a] [Deut. 4:6; Ps. 111:10; Prov. 1:7; 9:10; Eccl. 12:13] **29:2** [a] Job 1:1–5 [b] Job 1:10 **29:3** [a] Job 18:6 **29:4** [a] Job 15:8; [Ps. 25:14; Prov. 3:32] **29:6** [a] Gen. 49:11; Deut. 32:14; Job 20:17 [b] Deut. 32:13; Ps. 81:16 [1] Masoretic Text reads *wrath;* ancient versions and some Hebrew manuscripts read *cream* (compare 20:17). **29:9** [a] Job 21:5 **29:10** [a] Ps. 137:6 **29:12** [a] Job 31:16–23; [Ps. 72:12; Prov. 21:13; 24:11] **29:14** [a] Deut. 24:13; Job 27:5, 6; Ps. 132:9; [Is. 59:17; 61:10; Eph. 6:14] **29:15** [a] Num. 10:31 **29:16** [a] Prov. 29:7 **29:17** [a] Ps. 58:6; Prov. 30:14 **29:18** [a] Ps. 30:6 **29:19** [a] Job 18:16 [b] Ps. 1:3; [Jer. 17:7, 8] **29:20** [a] Gen. 49:24; Ps. 18:34 **29:23** [a] [Zech. 10:1]

2 Indeed, what *profit* is the strength
of their hands to me?
Their vigor has perished.
3 *They are* gaunt from want and famine,
Fleeing late to the wilderness,
desolate and waste,
4 Who pluck mallow by the bushes,
And broom tree roots *for* their food.
5 They were driven out
from among *men,*
They shouted at them as *at* a thief.
6 *They had* to live in the
clefts of the valleys,
In caves of the earth and the rocks.
7 Among the bushes they brayed,
Under the nettles they nestled.
8 *They were* sons of fools,
Yes, sons of vile men;
They were scourged from the land.

9 "And[a] now I am their taunting song;
Yes, I am their byword.
10 They abhor me, they keep far from me;
They do not hesitate [a]to
spit in my face.
11 Because [a]He has loosed my[1]
bowstring and afflicted me,
They have cast off restraint
before me.
12 At *my* right *hand* the rabble arises;
They push away my feet,
And [a]they raise against me
their ways of destruction.
13 They break up my path,
They promote my calamity;
They have no helper.
14 They come as broad breakers;
Under the ruinous storm
they roll along.
15 Terrors are turned upon me;
They pursue my honor as the wind,
And my prosperity has
passed like a cloud.

16 "And[a] now my soul is [b]poured
out because of my *plight;*
The days of affliction take hold of me.
17 My bones are pierced in me at night,
And my gnawing pains take no rest.
18 By great force my garment
is disfigured;
It binds me about as the
collar of my coat.
19 He has cast me into the mire,
And I have become like
dust and ashes.

20 "I [a]cry out to You, but You
do not answer me;
I stand up, and You regard me.
21 *But* You have become cruel to me;
With the strength of Your
hand You [a]oppose me.
22 You lift me up to the wind and
cause me to ride *on it;*
You spoil my success.
23 For I know *that* You will
bring me *to* death,
And *to* the house [a]appointed
for all living.

24 "Surely He would not stretch
out *His* hand against
a heap of ruins,
If they cry out when He
destroys *it.*
25 [a]Have I not wept for him
who was in trouble?
Has *not* my soul grieved for the poor?
26 [a]But when I looked for good,
evil came *to me;*
And when I waited for light,
then came darkness.
27 My heart is in turmoil and
cannot rest;
Days of affliction confront me.
28 [a]I go about mourning, but
not in the sun;
I stand up in the assembly
and cry out for help.
29 [a]I am a brother of jackals,
And a companion of ostriches.
30 [a]My skin grows black and
falls from me;
[b]My bones burn with fever.
31 My harp is *turned* to mourning,
And my flute to the voice
of those who weep.

30:9 [a] Job 17:6; Ps. 69:12; Lam. 3:14, 63 30:10 [a] Num. 12:14; Deut. 25:9; Job 17:6; Is. 50:6; Matt. 26:67; 27:30 30:11 [a] Job 12:18
[1] Following Masoretic Text, Syriac, and Targum; Septuagint and Vulgate read *His.* 30:12 [a] Job 19:12 30:16 [a] Ps. 42:4 [b] Ps. 22:14; Is. 53:12 30:20 [a] Job 19:7 30:21 [a] Job 10:3; 16:9, 14; 19:6, 22 30:23 [a] [Heb. 9:27] 30:25 [a] Ps. 35:13, 14; Rom. 12:15 30:26 [a] Job 3:25, 26; Jer. 8:15 30:28 [a] Job 30:31; Ps. 38:6; 42:9; 43:2 30:29 [a] Ps. 44:19; 102:6; Mic. 1:8 30:30 [a] Ps. 119:83; Lam. 4:8; 5:10 [b] Ps. 102:3

31 "I have made a covenant
with my eyes;
Why then should I look upon
a [a]young woman?
2 For what *is* the [a]allotment
of God from above,
And the inheritance of the
Almighty from on high?
3 *Is* it not destruction for the wicked,
And disaster for the
workers of iniquity?
4 [a]Does He not see my ways,
And count all my steps?

5 "If I have walked with falsehood,
Or if my foot has hastened to deceit,
6 Let me be weighed on honest scales,
That God may know my [a]integrity.
7 If my step has turned from the way,
Or [a]my heart walked after my eyes,
Or if any spot adheres to my hands,
8 *Then* [a]let me sow, and another eat;
Yes, let my harvest be rooted out.

9 "If my heart has been enticed
by a woman,
Or *if* I have lurked at my
neighbor's door,
10 *Then* let my wife grind for [a]another,
And let others bow down over her.
11 For that *would be* wickedness;
Yes, [a]it *would be* iniquity
deserving of judgment.
12 For that *would be* a fire *that*
consumes to destruction,
And would root out all my increase.

13 "If I have [a]despised the cause of
my male or female servant
When they complained against me,
14 What then shall I do when
[a]God rises up?
When He punishes, how
shall I answer Him?
15 [a]Did not He who made me in
the womb make them?
Did not the same One fashion
us in the womb?

16 "If I have kept the poor
from *their* desire,
Or caused the eyes of the
widow to [a]fail,
17 Or eaten my morsel by myself,
So that the fatherless
could not eat of it
18 (But from my youth I reared
him as a father,
And from my mother's womb
I guided *the widow*[1]);
19 If I have seen anyone perish
for lack of clothing,
Or any poor *man* without covering;
20 If his heart[1] has not [a]blessed me,
And *if* he was *not* warmed with
the fleece of my sheep;
21 If I have raised my hand
[a]against the fatherless,
When I saw I had help in the gate;
22 *Then* let my arm fall from
my shoulder,
Let my arm be torn from the socket.
23 For [a]destruction *from* God
is a terror to me,
And because of His magnificence
I cannot endure.

24 "If[a] I have made gold my hope,
Or said to fine gold, '*You*
are my confidence';
25 [a]If I have rejoiced because
my wealth *was* great,
And because my hand
had gained much;
26 [a]If I have observed the sun[1]
when it shines,
Or the moon moving *in* brightness,
27 So that my heart has been
secretly enticed,
And my mouth has kissed my hand;
28 This also *would be* an iniquity
deserving of judgment,
For I would have denied
God *who is* above.

29 "If[a] I have rejoiced at the destruction
of him who hated me,

31:1 [a] [Matt. 5:28] 31:2 [a] Job 20:29 31:4 [a] [2 Chr. 16:9]; Job 24:23; 28:24; 34:21; 36:7; [Prov. 5:21; 15:3; Jer. 32:19] 31:6 [a] Job 23:10; 27:5, 6 31:7 [a] Num. 15:39; [Eccl. 11:9]; Ezek. 6:9; [Matt. 5:29] 31:8 [a] Lev. 26:16; Deut. 28:30, 38; Job 20:18; Mic. 6:15 31:10 [a] Deut. 28:30; 2 Sam. 12:11; Jer. 8:10 31:11 [a] Gen. 38:24; [Lev. 20:10; Deut. 22:22]; Job 31:28 31:13 [a] [Deut. 24:14, 15] 31:14 [a] [Ps. 44:21] 31:15 [a] Job 34:19; Prov. 14:31; 22:2; [Mal. 2:10] 31:16 [a] Job 29:12 31:18 [1] Literally *her* (compare verse 16) 31:20 [a] [Deut. 24:13] [1] Literally *loins* 31:21 [a] Job 22:9 31:23 [a] Is. 13:6 31:24 [a] [Matt. 6:19, 20; Mark 10:23–25] 31:25 [a] Job 1:3, 10; Ps. 62:10 31:26 [a] [Deut. 4:19; 17:3]; Ezek. 8:16 [1] Literally *light* 31:29 [a] [Prov. 17:5; 24:17]; Obad. 12

Or lifted myself up when
evil found him
30 [a](Indeed I have not allowed
my mouth to sin
By asking for a curse on his soul);
31 If the men of my tent have not said,
'Who is there that has not been
satisfied with his meat?'
32 [a](*But* no sojourner had to
lodge in the street,
For I have opened my doors
to the traveler[1]);
33 If I have covered my
transgressions [a]as Adam,
By hiding my iniquity in my bosom,
34 Because I feared the great [a]multitude,
And dreaded the contempt of families,
So that I kept silence
And did not go out of the door—
35 [a]Oh, that I had one to hear me!
Here is my mark.
Oh, [b]*that* the Almighty
would answer me,
That my Prosecutor had written a book!
36 Surely I would carry it on my shoulder,
And bind it on me *like* a crown;
37 I would declare to Him the
number of my steps;
Like a prince I would approach Him.

38 "If my land cries out against me,
And its furrows weep together;
39 If [a]I have eaten its fruit[1]
without money,
Or [b]caused its owners to
lose their lives;
40 *Then* let [a]thistles grow
instead of wheat,
And weeds instead of barley."

The words of Job are ended.

Elihu Contradicts Job's Friends

32 So these three men ceased answering Job, because he *was* [a]righteous
in his own eyes. 2Then the wrath of Elihu,
the son of Barachel the [a]Buzite, of the family of Ram, was aroused against Job; his
wrath was aroused because he [b]justified
himself rather than God. 3Also against his
three friends his wrath was aroused, because they had found no answer, and *yet*
had condemned Job.
4Now because they *were* years older than
he, Elihu had waited to speak to Job.[1] 5When
Elihu saw that *there was* no answer in the
mouth of these three men, his wrath was
aroused.
6So Elihu, the son of Barachel the Bu-
zite, answered and said:

"I *am* [a]young in years, and
you *are* very old;
Therefore I was afraid,
And dared not declare my
opinion to you.
7 I said, 'Age[1] should speak,
And multitude of years
should teach wisdom.'
8 But *there is* a spirit in man,
And [a]the breath of the Almighty
gives him understanding.
9 [a]Great men[1] are not *always* wise,
Nor do the aged *always*
understand justice.

10 "Therefore I say, 'Listen to me,
I also will declare my opinion.'
11 Indeed I waited for your words,
I listened to your reasonings, while
you searched out what to say.
12 I paid close attention to you;
And surely not one of you
convinced Job,
Or answered his words—
13 [a]Lest you say,
'We have found wisdom';
God will vanquish him, not man.
14 Now he has not directed *his*
words against me;
So I will not answer him
with your words.

15 "They are dismayed and
answer no more;
Words escape them.

31:30 [a] [Matt. 5:44] 31:32 [a] Gen. 19:2, 3 [1] Following Septuagint, Syriac, Targum, and Vulgate; Masoretic Text reads *road.* 31:33 [a] Gen. 3:10; [Prov. 28:13] 31:34 [a] Ex. 23:2 31:35 [a] Job 19:7; 30:20, 24, 28 [b] Job 13:22, 24; 33:10 31:39 [a] Job 24:6, 10–12; [James 5:4] [b] 1 Kin. 21:19 [1] Literally *its strength* 31:40 [a] Gen. 3:18 32:1 [a] Job 6:29; 31:6; 33:9 32:2 [a] Gen. 22:21 [b] Job 27:5, 6 32:4 [1] Vulgate reads *till Job had spoken.* 32:6 [a] Lev. 19:32 32:7 [1] Literally *Days,* that is, years 32:8 [a] 1 Kin. 3:12; 4:29; [Job 35:11; 38:36; Prov. 2:6; Eccl. 2:26; Dan. 1:17; 2:21; Matt. 11:25; James 1:5] 32:9 [a] [1 Cor. 1:26] [1] Or *Men of many years* 32:13 [a] [Jer. 9:23; 1 Cor. 1:29]

16 And I have waited, because
they did not speak,
Because they stood still *and*
answered no more.
17 I also will answer my part,
I too will declare my opinion.
18 For I am full of words;
The spirit within me compels me.
19 Indeed my belly *is* like wine
that has no vent;
It is ready to burst like new wineskins.
20 I will speak, that I may find relief;
I must open my lips and answer.
21 Let me not, I pray, show
partiality to anyone;
Nor let me flatter any man.
22 For I do not know how to flatter,
Else my Maker would soon
take me [a]away.

Elihu Contradicts Job

33 "But please, Job, hear my speech,
And listen to all my words.
2 Now, I open my mouth;
My tongue speaks in my mouth.
3 My words *come* from my
upright heart;
My lips utter pure knowledge.
4 [a]The Spirit of God has made me,
And the breath of the
Almighty gives me life.
5 If you can answer me,
Set *your words* in order before me;
Take your stand.
6 [a]Truly I *am* as your spokesman[1]
before God;
I also have been formed out of clay.
7 [a]Surely no fear of me will terrify you,
Nor will my hand be heavy on you.

8 "Surely you have spoken in my hearing,
And I have heard the sound
of *your* words, *saying,*
9 'I[a] *am* pure, without transgression;
I *am* innocent, and *there is*
no iniquity in me.
10 Yet He finds occasions against me,
[a]He counts me as His enemy;
11 [a]He puts my feet in the stocks,
He watches all my paths.'
12 "Look, *in* this you are not righteous.
I will answer you,
For God is greater than man.
13 Why do you [a]contend with Him?
For He does not give an accounting
of any of His words.
14 [a]For God may speak in one
way, or in another,
Yet man does not perceive it.
15 [a]In a dream, in a vision
of the night,
When deep sleep falls upon men,
While slumbering on their beds,
16 [a]Then He opens the ears of men,
And seals their instruction.
17 In order to turn man *from his* deed,
And conceal pride from man,
18 He keeps back his soul from the Pit,
And his life from perishing
by the sword.

19 "*Man* is also chastened with
pain on his [a]bed,
And with strong *pain* in
many of his bones,
20 [a]So that his life abhors [b]bread,
And his soul succulent food.
21 His flesh wastes away from sight,
And his bones stick out *which*
once were not seen.
22 Yes, his soul draws near the Pit,
And his life to the executioners.

23 "If there is a messenger for him,
A mediator, one among a thousand,
To show man His uprightness,
24 Then He is gracious to him,
and says,
'Deliver him from going
down to the Pit;
I have found a ransom';
25 His flesh shall be young like
a child's,
He shall return to the
days of his youth.
26 He shall pray to God, and He
will delight in him,
He shall see His face with joy,
For He restores to man
His righteousness.

32:22 [a] Job 27:8 33:4 [a] [Gen. 2:7]; Job 32:8 33:6 [a] Job 4:19 [1] Literally *as your mouth* 33:7 [a] Job 9:34 33:9 [a] Job 10:7 33:10 [a] Job 13:24; 16:9 33:11 [a] Job 13:27; 19:8 33:13 [a] Job 40:2; [Is. 45:9] 33:14 [a] Job 33:29; 40:5; Ps. 62:11 33:15 [a] [Num. 12:6] 33:16 [a] [Job 36:10, 15] 33:19 [a] Job 30:17 33:20 [a] Ps. 107:18 [b] Job 3:24; 6:7

27 Then he looks at men and [a]says,
'I have sinned, and perverted
what was right,
And it [b]did not profit me.'
28 He will [a]redeem his[1] soul from
going down to the Pit,
And his[2] life shall see the light.

29 "Behold, God works all these *things,*
Twice, *in fact,* three *times* with a man,
30 [a]To bring back his soul from the Pit,
That he may be enlightened
with the light of life.

31 "Give ear, Job, listen to me;
Hold your peace, and I will speak.
32 If you have anything to
say, answer me;
Speak, for I desire to justify you.
33 If not, [a]listen to me;
Hold your peace, and I will
teach you wisdom."

Elihu Proclaims God's Justice

34 Elihu further answered and said:
2 "Hear my words, you wise *men;*
Give ear to me, you who
have knowledge.
3 [a]For the ear tests words
As the palate tastes food.
4 Let us choose justice for ourselves;
Let us know among ourselves
what *is* good.

5 "For Job has said, [a]'I am righteous,
But [b]God has taken away my justice;
6 [a]Should I lie concerning my right?
My wound *is* incurable, *though I
am* without transgression.'
7 What man *is* like Job,
[a]*Who* drinks scorn like water,
8 Who goes in company with
the workers of iniquity,
And walks with wicked men?
9 For [a]he has said, 'It profits
a man nothing
That he should delight in God.'

10 "Therefore listen to me, you
men of understanding:
[a]Far be it from God *to do* wickedness,
And *from* the Almighty to
commit iniquity.
11 [a]For He repays man *according
to* his work,
And makes man to find a reward
according to *his* way.
12 Surely God will never do wickedly,
Nor will the Almighty [a]pervert justice.
13 Who gave Him charge over the earth?
Or who appointed *Him over*
the whole world?
14 If He should set His heart on it,
If He should [a]gather to Himself
His Spirit and His breath,
15 [a]All flesh would perish together,
And man would return to dust.

16 "If *you have* understanding, hear this;
Listen to the sound of my words:
17 [a]Should one who hates justice govern?
Will you [b]condemn *Him
who is* most just?
18 [a]*Is it fitting* to say to a king,
'*You are* worthless,'
And to nobles, '*You are* wicked'?
19 Yet He [a]is not partial to princes,
Nor does He regard the rich
more than the poor;
For [b]they *are* all the work of His hands.
20 In a moment they die, [a]in the
middle of the night;
The people are shaken and pass away;
The mighty are taken away
without a hand.

21 "For[a] His eyes *are* on the ways of man,
And He sees all his steps.
22 [a]There is no darkness nor
shadow of death
Where the workers of iniquity
may hide themselves.
23 For He need not further
consider a man,
That he should go before
God in judgment.

33:27 [a] [2 Sam. 12:13; Prov. 28:13; Luke 15:21; 1 John 1:9] [b] [Rom. 6:21] 33:28 [a] Is. 38:17 [1] Or *my* (Kethib) [2] Or *my* (Kethib) 33:30 [a] Ps. 56:13 33:33 [a] Ps. 34:11 34:3 [a] Job 6:30; 12:11 34:5 [a] Job 13:18; 33:9 [b] Job 27:2 34:6 [a] Job 6:4; 9:17 34:7 [a] Job 15:16 34:9 [a] Mal. 3:14 34:10 [a] [Gen. 18:25; Deut. 32:4; 2 Chr. 19:7]; Job 8:3; 36:23; Ps. 92:15; Rom. 9:14 34:11 [a] Job 34:25; Ps. 62:12; [Prov. 24:12; Jer. 32:19]; Ezek. 33:20; [Matt. 16:27]; Rom. 2:6; [2 Cor. 5:10; Rev. 22:12] 34:12 [a] Job 8:3 34:14 [a] Job 12:10; Ps. 104:29; [Eccl. 12:7] 34:15 [a] [Gen. 3:19]; Job 10:9; [Eccl. 12:7] 34:17 [a] 2 Sam. 23:3; Job 34:30 [b] Job 40:8 34:18 [a] Ex. 22:28 34:19 [a] [Deut. 10:17; Acts 10:34; Rom. 2:11, 12] [b] Job 31:15 34:20 [a] Ex. 12:29; Job 34:25; 36:20 34:21 [a] [2 Chr. 16:9]; Job 31:4; Ps. 34:15; [Prov. 5:21; 15:3; Jer. 16:17; 32:19] 34:22 [a] [Ps. 139:11, 12; Amos 9:2, 3]

24 [a]He breaks in pieces mighty
men without inquiry,
And sets others in their place.
25 Therefore He knows their works;
He overthrows *them* in the night,
And they are crushed.
26 He strikes them as wicked *men*
In the open sight of others,
27 Because they [a]turned back from Him,
And [b]would not consider
any of His ways,
28 So that they [a]caused the cry of
the poor to come to Him;
For He [b]hears the cry of the
afflicted.
29 When He gives quietness, who
then can make trouble?
And when He hides *His* face,
who then can see Him,
Whether *it is* against a nation
or a man alone?—
30 That the hypocrite should
not reign,
Lest the people be ensnared.

31 "For has *anyone* said to God,
'I have borne *chastening;*
I will offend no more;
32 Teach me *what* I do not see;
If I have done iniquity, I
will do no more'?
33 Should He repay *it* according
to your *terms,*
Just because you disavow it?
You must choose, and not I;
Therefore speak what you know.

34 "Men of understanding say to me,
Wise men who listen to me:
35 'Job[a] speaks without knowledge,
His words *are* without wisdom.'
36 Oh, that Job were tried
to the utmost,
Because *his* answers *are like*
those of wicked men!
37 For he adds [a]rebellion to his sin;
He claps *his hands* among us,
And multiplies his words
against God."

Elihu Condemns Self-Righteousness

35 Moreover Elihu answered and said:
2 "Do you think this is right?
Do you say,
'My righteousness is more than God's'?
3 For [a]you say,
'What advantage will it be to You?
What profit shall I have, more
than *if* I had sinned?'

4 "I will answer you,
And [a]your companions with you.
5 [a]Look to the heavens and see;
And behold the clouds—
They are higher than you.
6 If you sin, what do you
accomplish [a]against Him?
Or, *if* your transgressions are
multiplied, what do you do to Him?
7 [a]If you are righteous, what
do you give Him?
Or what does He receive
from your hand?
8 Your wickedness affects a
man such as you,
And your righteousness
a son of man.

9 "Because[a] of the multitude of
oppressions they cry out;
They cry out for help because
of the arm of the mighty.
10 But no one says, [a]'Where
is God my Maker,
[b]Who gives songs in the night,
11 Who [a]teaches us more than
the beasts of the earth,
And makes us wiser than
the birds of heaven?'
12 [a]There they cry out, but He
does not answer,
Because of the pride of evil men.
13 [a]Surely God will not listen
to empty *talk,*
Nor will the Almighty regard it.
14 [a]Although you say you do not see Him,
Yet justice *is* before Him, and
[b]you must wait for Him.

34:24 [a] Job 12:19; [Dan. 2:21] 34:27 [a] 1 Sam. 15:11 [b] Ps. 28:5; Is. 5:12 34:28 [a] Job 35:9; James 5:4 [b] [Ex. 22:23]; Job 22:27 34:35 [a] Job 35:16; 38:2 34:37 [a] Job 7:11; 10:1 35:3 [a] Job 21:15; 34:9 35:4 [a] Job 34:8 35:5 [a] Gen. 15:5; [Job 22:12; Ps. 8:3] 35:6 [a] Job 7:20; [Prov. 8:36; Jer. 7:19] 35:7 [a] Job 22:2; Ps. 16:2; Prov. 9:12; [Luke 17:10]; Rom. 11:35 35:9 [a] Job 34:28 35:10 [a] Is. 51:13 [b] Job 8:21; Ps. 42:8; 77:6; 149:5; Acts 16:25 35:11 [a] Job 36:22; Ps. 94:12; [Is. 48:17]; Jer. 32:33; [1 Cor. 2:13] 35:12 [a] Prov. 1:28 35:13 [a] Job 27:9; [Prov. 15:29; Is. 1:15]; Jer. 11:11; [Mic. 3:4] 35:14 [a] Job 9:11 [b] [Ps. 37:5, 6]

15 And now, because He has not
[a]punished in His anger,
Nor taken much notice of folly,
16 [a]Therefore Job opens his
mouth in vain;
He multiplies words without
knowledge."

Elihu Proclaims God's Goodness

36 Elihu also proceeded and said:

2 "Bear with me a little, and
I will show you
That *there are* yet words to
speak on God's behalf.
3 I will fetch my knowledge from afar;
I will ascribe righteousness
to my Maker.
4 For truly my words *are* not false;
One who is perfect in
knowledge *is* with you.

5 "Behold, God *is* mighty, but
despises *no one;*
[a]*He is* mighty in strength
of understanding.
6 He does not preserve the
life of the wicked,
But gives justice to the [a]oppressed.
7 [a]He does not withdraw His eyes
from the righteous;
But [b]*they are* on the throne with kings,
For He has seated them forever,
And they are exalted.
8 And [a]if *they are* bound in fetters,
Held in the cords of affliction,
9 Then He tells them their work
and their transgressions—
That they have acted defiantly.
10 [a]He also opens their ear to instruction,
And commands that they
turn from iniquity.
11 If they obey and serve *Him,*
They shall [a]spend their
days in prosperity,
And their years in pleasures.
12 But if they do not obey,
They shall perish by the sword,
And they shall die without
[a]knowledge.[1]
13 "But the hypocrites in heart
[a]store up wrath;
They do not cry for help
when He binds them.
14 [a]They die in youth,
And their life *ends* among the
perverted persons.[1]
15 He delivers the poor in their affliction,
And opens their ears in oppression.

16 "Indeed He would have brought
you out of dire distress,
[a]*Into* a broad place where
there is no restraint;
And [b]what is set on your table
would be full of [c]richness.
17 But you are filled with the
judgment due the [a]wicked;
Judgment and justice take
hold *of you.*
18 Because *there is* wrath, *beware* lest
He take you away with *one* blow;
For [a]a large ransom would
not help you avoid *it.*
19 [a]Will your riches,
Or all the mighty forces,
Keep you from distress?
20 Do not desire the night,
When people are cut off in
their place.
21 Take heed, [a]do not turn to iniquity,
For [b]you have chosen this
rather than affliction.

22 "Behold, God is exalted by His power;
Who teaches like Him?
23 [a]Who has assigned Him His way,
Or who has said, 'You have
done [b]wrong'?

Elihu Proclaims God's Majesty

24 "Remember to [a]magnify His work,
Of which men have sung.
25 Everyone has seen it;
Man looks on *it* from afar.

35:15 [a] Ps. 89:32 35:16 [a] Job 34:35; 38:2 36:5 [a] Job 12:13, 16; 37:23; [Ps. 99:2–5] 36:6 [a] Job 5:15 36:7 [a] [Ps. 33:18; 34:15] [b] Job 5:11; Ps. 113:8 36:8 [a] Ps. 107:10 36:10 [a] Job 33:16; 36:15 36:11 [a] Job 21:13; [Is. 1:19, 20] 36:12 [a] Job 4:21 [1] Masoretic Text reads *as one without knowledge.* 36:13 [a] [Rom. 2:5] 36:14 [a] Ps. 55:23 [1] Hebrew *qedeshim,* that is, those practicing sodomy and prostitution in religious rituals 36:16 [a] Ps. 18:19; 31:8; 118:5 [b] Ps. 23:5 [c] Ps. 36:8 36:17 [a] Job 22:5, 10, 11 36:18 [a] Ps. 49:7 36:19 [a] [Prov. 11:4] 36:21 [a] Job 36:10; [Ps. 31:6; 66:18] [b] Job 36:8, 15; [Heb. 11:25] 36:23 [a] Job 34:13; [Is. 40:13, 14] [b] [Deut. 32:4]; Job 8:3 36:24 [a] [Ps. 92:5; Rev. 15:3]

26 "Behold, God *is* great, and we
[a]do not know *Him;*
[b]Nor can the number of His
years *be* discovered.
27 For He [a]draws up drops of water,
Which distill as rain from the mist,
28 [a]Which the clouds drop down
And pour abundantly on man.
29 Indeed, can *anyone* understand
the spreading of clouds,
The thunder from His canopy?
30 Look, He [a]scatters His light upon it,
And covers the depths of the sea.
31 For [a]by these He judges the peoples;
He [b]gives food in abundance.
32 [a]He covers *His* hands with lightning,
And commands it to strike.
33 [a]His thunder declares it,
The cattle also, concerning
the rising *storm.*

37 "At this also my heart trembles,
And leaps from its place.
2 Hear attentively the thunder
of His voice,
And the rumbling *that* comes
from His mouth.
3 He sends it forth under
the whole heaven,
His lightning to the ends of the earth.
4 After it [a]a voice roars;
He thunders with His majestic voice,
And He does not restrain them
when His voice is heard.
5 God thunders marvelously
with His voice;
[a]He does great things which we
cannot comprehend.
6 For [a]He says to the snow,
'Fall *on* the earth';
Likewise to the gentle rain and the
heavy rain of His strength.
7 He seals the hand of every man,
[a]That [b]all men may know His work.
8 The beasts [a]go into dens,
And remain in their lairs.
9 From the chamber *of the south*
comes the whirlwind,
And cold from the scattering
winds *of the north.*
10 [a]By the breath of God ice is given,
And the broad waters are frozen.
11 Also with moisture He saturates
the thick clouds;
He scatters His bright clouds.
12 And they swirl about, being
turned by His guidance,
That they may [a]do whatever
He commands them
On the face of the whole earth.[1]
13 [a]He causes it to come,
Whether for correction,
Or [b]for His land,
Or [c]for mercy.

14 "Listen to this, O Job;
Stand still and [a]consider the
wondrous works of God.
15 Do you know when God
dispatches them,
And causes the light of His
cloud to shine?
16 [a]Do you know how the
clouds are balanced,
Those wondrous works of [b]Him
who is perfect in knowledge?
17 Why *are* your garments hot,
When He quiets the earth
by the south *wind?*
18 With Him, have you [a]spread
out the [b]skies,
Strong as a cast metal mirror?

19 "Teach us what we should say to Him,
For we can prepare nothing
because of the darkness.
20 Should He be told that I *wish to* speak?
If a man were to speak, surely
he would be swallowed up.
21 Even now *men* cannot look at the
light *when it is* bright in the skies,
When the wind has passed
and cleared them.
22 He comes from the north
as golden *splendor;*
With God *is* awesome majesty.

36:26 [a] Job 11:7–9; 37:23; [1 Cor. 13:12] [b] Job 10:5; [Ps. 90:2; 102:24, 27]; Heb. 1:12 36:27 [a] Job 5:10; 37:6, 11; 38:28; Ps. 147:8 36:28 [a] [Prov. 3:20] 36:30 [a] Job 37:3 36:31 [a] [Acts 14:17] [b] Gen. 9:3; Ps. 104:14, 15 36:32 [a] Ps. 147:8 36:33 [a] 1 Kin. 18:41; Job 37:2 37:4 [a] Ps. 29:3 37:5 [a] Job 5:9; 9:10; 36:26; Rev. 15:3 37:6 [a] Ps. 147:16, 17 37:7 [a] Ps. 109:27 [b] Ps. 19:3, 4 37:8 [a] Job 38:40; Ps. 104:21, 22 37:10 [a] Job 38:29, 30; Ps. 147:17, 18 37:12 [a] Job 36:32; Ps. 148:8 [1] Literally *the world of the earth* 37:13 [a] Ex. 9:18, 23; 1 Sam. 12:18, 19 [b] Job 38:26, 27 [c] 1 Kin. 18:41–46 37:14 [a] Ps. 111:2 37:16 [a] Job 36:29 [b] Job 36:4 37:18 [a] Gen. 1:6; [Is. 44:24] [b] Job 9:8; Ps. 104:2; [Is. 45:12; Jer. 10:12; Zech. 12:1]

23 *As for* the Almighty, [a]we
cannot find Him;
[b]*He is* excellent in power,
In judgment and abundant justice;
He does not oppress.
24 Therefore men [a]fear Him;
He shows no partiality to any
who are [b]wise of heart."

The LORD *Reveals His Omnipotence to Job*
(Gen. 1:1–10)

38 Then the LORD answered Job [a]out
of the whirlwind, and said:

2 "Who[a] *is* this who darkens counsel
By [b]words without knowledge?
3 [a]Now prepare yourself like a man;
I will question you, and you
shall answer Me.

4 "Where[a] were you when I laid the
foundations of the earth?
Tell *Me,* if you have understanding.
5 Who determined its measurements?
Surely you know!
Or who stretched the line upon it?
6 To what were its foundations
fastened?
Or who laid its cornerstone,
7 When the morning stars
sang together,
And all [a]the sons of God
shouted for joy?

8 "Or[a] *who* shut in the sea with doors,
When it burst forth *and*
issued from the womb;
9 When I made the clouds its garment,
And thick darkness its
swaddling band;
10 When [a]I fixed My limit for it,
And set bars and doors;
11 When I said,
'This far you may come,
but no farther,
And here your proud
waves [a]must stop!'

12 "Have you [a]commanded the morning
since your days *began,*
And caused the dawn to know its place,
13 That it might take hold of
the ends of the earth,
And [a]the wicked be shaken out of it?
14 It takes on form like clay *under* a seal,
And stands out like a garment.
15 From the wicked their
[a]light is withheld,
And [b]the upraised arm is broken.

16 "Have you [a]entered the
springs of the sea?
Or have you walked in search
of the depths?
17 Have [a]the gates of death
been revealed to you?
Or have you seen the doors of
the shadow of death?
18 Have you comprehended the
breadth of the earth?
Tell *Me,* if you know all this.

19 "Where *is* the way *to* the
dwelling of light?
And darkness, where *is* its place,
20 That you may take it to its territory,
That you may know the
paths *to* its home?
21 Do you know *it,* because
you were born then,
Or *because* the number of
your days *is* great?

22 "Have you entered [a]the
treasury of snow,
Or have you seen the treasury of hail,
23 [a]Which I have reserved for
the time of trouble,
For the day of battle and war?
24 By what way is light diffused,
Or the east wind scattered
over the earth?

25 "Who [a]has divided a channel for
the overflowing *water,*
Or a path for the thunderbolt,

37:23 [a] [Job 11:7, 8; Rom. 11:33, 34; 1 Tim. 6:16] [b] [Job 9:4; 36:5] 37:24 [a] [Matt. 10:28] [b] [Job 5:13; Matt. 11:25]; 1 Cor. 1:26
38:1 [a] Ex. 19:16; Job 40:6 38:2 [a] Job 34:35; 42:3 [b] 1 Tim. 1:7 38:3 [a] Job 40:7 38:4 [a] Job 15:7; Ps. 104:5
38:7 [a] Job 1:6 38:8 [a] Gen. 1:9; Ps. 33:7; 104:9; Prov. 8:29; [Jer. 5:22] 38:10 [a] Job 26:10
38:11 [a] [Ps. 89:9; 93:4] 38:12 [a] [Ps. 74:16; 148:5] 38:13 [a] Job 34:25; Ps. 104:35 38:15 [a] Job 18:5; [Prov. 13:9]
[b] [Num. 15:30]; Ps. 10:15; 37:17 38:16 [a] [Ps. 77:19]; Prov. 8:24 38:17 [a] Ps. 9:13 38:22 [a] Ps. 135:7
38:23 [a] Ex. 9:18; Josh. 10:11; Is. 30:30; Ezek. 13:11, 13; Rev. 16:21 38:25 [a] Job 28:26

26 To cause it to rain on a land
where there is no one,
A wilderness in which *there is* no man;
27 [a]To satisfy the desolate waste,
And cause to spring forth the
growth of tender grass?
28 [a]Has the rain a father?
Or who has begotten the drops of dew?
29 From whose womb comes the ice?
And the [a]frost of heaven,
who gives it birth?
30 The waters harden like stone,
And the surface of the deep is [a]frozen.

31 "Can you bind the cluster
of the [a]Pleiades,
Or loose the belt of Orion?
32 Can you bring out Mazzaroth[1]
in its season?
Or can you guide the Great
Bear with its cubs?
33 Do you know [a]the ordinances
of the heavens?
Can you set their dominion
over the earth?

34 "Can you lift up your voice
to the clouds,
That an abundance of water
may cover you?
35 Can you send out lightnings,
that they may go,
And say to you, 'Here we *are!*'?
36 [a]Who has put wisdom in the mind?[1]
Or who has given understanding
to the heart?
37 Who can number the
clouds by wisdom?
Or who can pour out the
bottles of heaven,
38 When the dust hardens in clumps,
And the clods cling together?

39 "Can[a] you hunt the prey for the lion,
Or satisfy the appetite of
the young lions,
40 When they crouch in *their* dens,
Or lurk in their lairs to lie in wait?
41 [a]Who provides food for the raven,
When its young ones cry to God,
And wander about for lack of food?

39 "Do you know the time when the
wild [a]mountain goats
bear young?
Or can you mark when [b]the
deer gives birth?
2 Can you number the months
that they fulfill?
Or do you know the time
when they bear young?
3 They bow down,
They bring forth their young,
They deliver their offspring.[1]
4 Their young ones are healthy,
They grow strong with grain;
They depart and do not
return to them.

5 "Who set the wild donkey free?
Who loosed the bonds of the onager,
6 [a]Whose home I have made
the wilderness,
And the barren land his dwelling?
7 He scorns the tumult of the city;
He does not heed the
shouts of the driver.
8 The range of the mountains
is his pasture,
And he searches after
[a]every green thing.

9 "Will the [a]wild ox be willing
to serve you?
Will he bed by your manger?
10 Can you bind the wild ox in
the furrow with ropes?
Or will he plow the valleys behind you?
11 Will you trust him because
his strength *is* great?
Or will you leave your labor to him?
12 Will you trust him to bring
home your grain,
And gather it to your threshing floor?

13 "The wings of the ostrich wave proudly,
But are her wings and pinions
like the kindly stork's?

38:27 [a] Ps. 104:13, 14; 107:35 **38:28** [a] Job 36:27, 28; [Ps. 147:8; Jer. 14:22] **38:29** [a] [Job 37:10]; Ps. 147:16, 17 **38:30** [a] [Job 37:10] **38:31** [a] Job 9:9; Amos 5:8 **38:32** [1] Literally *Constellations* **38:33** [a] [Ps. 148:6]; Jer. 31:35, 36 **38:36** [a] [Job 9:4; 32:8; Ps. 51:6; Eccl. 2:26; James 1:5] [1] Literally *inward parts* **38:39** [a] Ps. 104:21 **38:41** [a] Ps. 147:9; [Matt. 6:26; Luke 12:24] **39:1** [a] Deut. 14:5; 1 Sam. 24:2; Ps. 104:18 [b] Ps. 29:9 **39:3** [1] Literally *pangs,* figurative of offspring **39:6** [a] Job 24:5; Jer. 2:24; Hos. 8:9 **39:8** [a] Gen. 1:29 **39:9** [a] Num. 23:22; Deut. 33:17; Ps. 22:21; 29:6; 92:10; Is. 34:7

14 For she leaves her eggs on the ground,
And warms them in the dust;
15 She forgets that a foot
may crush them,
Or that a wild beast may break them.
16 She [a]treats her young harshly, as
though *they were* not hers;
Her labor is in vain, without concern,
17 Because God deprived her of wisdom,
And did not [a]endow her
with understanding.
18 When she lifts herself on high,
She scorns the horse and its rider.

19 "Have you given the horse strength?
Have you clothed his neck
with thunder?[1]
20 Can you frighten him like a locust?
His majestic snorting strikes terror.
21 He paws in the valley, and
rejoices in *his* strength;
[a]He gallops into the clash of arms.
22 He mocks at fear, and is
not frightened;
Nor does he turn back from the sword.
23 The quiver rattles against him,
The glittering spear and javelin.
24 He devours the distance with
fierceness and rage;
Nor does he come to a halt because
the trumpet *has* sounded.
25 At *the blast of* the trumpet
he says, 'Aha!'
He smells the battle from afar,
The thunder of captains and shouting.

26 "Does the hawk fly by your wisdom,
And spread its wings
toward the south?
27 Does the [a]eagle mount up
at your command,
And [b]make its nest on high?
28 On the rock it dwells and resides,
On the crag of the rock and
the stronghold.
29 From there it spies out the prey;
Its eyes observe from afar.
30 Its young ones suck up blood;
And [a]where the slain *are*, there it *is*."

40 Moreover the LORD [a]answered Job,
and said:

2 "Shall [a]the one who contends with
the Almighty correct *Him?*
He who [b]rebukes God, let
him answer it."

Job's Response to God

3 Then Job answered the LORD and said:

4 "Behold,[a] I am vile;
What shall I answer You?
[b]I lay my hand over my mouth.
5 Once I have spoken, but I
will not answer;
Yes, twice, but I will proceed
no further."

God's Challenge to Job

6 [a]Then the LORD answered Job out of
the whirlwind, and said:

7 "Now[a] prepare yourself like a man;
[b]I will question you, and you
shall answer Me:

8 "Would[a] you indeed annul
My judgment?
Would you condemn Me that
you may be justified?
9 Have you an arm like God?
Or can you thunder with
[a]a voice like His?
10 [a]Then adorn yourself *with*
majesty and splendor,
And array yourself with
glory and beauty.
11 Disperse the rage of your wrath;
Look on everyone *who is*
proud, and humble him.
12 Look on everyone *who is* [a]proud,
and bring him low;
Tread down the wicked in their place.
13 Hide them in the dust together,
Bind their faces in hidden *darkness*.
14 Then I will also confess to you
That your own right hand
can save you.

39:16 [a] Lam. 4:3 39:17 [a] Job 35:11 39:19 [1] Or *a mane* 39:21 [a] Jer. 8:6 39:27 [a] Prov. 30:18, 19 [b] Jer. 49:16; Obad. 4
39:30 [a] Matt. 24:28; Luke 17:37 40:1 [a] Job 38:1 40:2 [a] Job 9:3; 10:2; 33:13 [b] Job 13:3; 23:4 40:4 [a] Ezra 9:6; Job 42:6 [b] Job 29:9;
Ps. 39:9 40:6 [a] Job 38:1 40:7 [a] Job 38:3 [b] Job 42:4 40:8 [a] Job 16:11; 19:6; [Ps. 51:4; Rom. 3:4] 40:9 [a] Job 37:4;
[Ps. 29:3, 4] 40:10 [a] Ps. 93:1; 104:1 40:12 [a] 1 Sam. 2:7; [Is. 2:12; 13:11]; Dan. 4:37

15 "Look now at the behemoth,[1] which
I made *along* with you;
He eats grass like an ox.
16 See now, his strength *is* in his hips,
And his power *is* in his
stomach muscles.
17 He moves his tail like a cedar;
The sinews of his thighs
are tightly knit.
18 His bones *are like* beams of bronze,
His ribs like bars of iron.
19 He *is* the first of the [a]ways of God;
Only He who made him can
bring near His sword.
20 Surely the mountains
[a]yield food for him,
And all the beasts of the
field play there.
21 He lies under the lotus trees,
In a covert of reeds and marsh.
22 The lotus trees cover him
with their shade;
The willows by the brook
surround him.
23 Indeed the river may rage,
Yet he is not disturbed;
He is confident, though the Jordan
gushes into his mouth,
24 *Though* he takes it in his eyes,
Or one pierces *his* nose with a snare.

41

"Can you draw out [a]Leviathan[1]
with a hook,
Or *snare* his tongue with a
line *which* you lower?
2 Can you [a]put a reed through his nose,
Or pierce his jaw with a hook?
3 Will he make many
supplications to you?
Will he speak softly to you?
4 Will he make a covenant with you?
Will you take him as a servant forever?
5 Will you play with him as *with* a bird,
Or will you leash him for
your maidens?
6 Will *your* companions make
a banquet[1] of him?
Will they apportion him
among the merchants?
7 Can you fill his skin with harpoons,
Or his head with fishing spears?
8 Lay your hand on him;
Remember the battle—
Never do it again!
9 Indeed, *any* hope of
overcoming him is false;
Shall *one not* be overwhelmed
at the sight of him?
10 No one *is so* fierce that he
would dare stir him up.
Who then is able to stand against Me?
11 [a]Who has preceded Me, that
I should pay *him?*
[b]Everything under heaven is Mine.
12 "I will not conceal[1] his limbs,
His mighty power, or his
graceful proportions.
13 Who can remove his outer coat?
Who can approach *him* with
a double bridle?
14 Who can open the doors of his face,
With his terrible teeth all around?
15 *His* rows of scales are *his* pride,
Shut up tightly *as with* a seal;
16 One is so near another
That no air can come between them;
17 They are joined one to another,
They stick together and
cannot be parted.
18 His sneezings flash forth light,
And his eyes *are* like the
eyelids of the morning.
19 Out of his mouth go burning lights;
Sparks of fire shoot out.
20 Smoke goes out of his nostrils,
As *from* a boiling pot and
burning rushes.
21 His breath kindles coals,
And a flame goes out of his mouth.
22 Strength dwells in his neck,
And sorrow dances before him.
23 The folds of his flesh are
joined together;
They are firm on him and
cannot be moved.
24 His heart is as hard as stone,
Even as hard as the lower *millstone.*
25 When he raises himself up,
the mighty are afraid;

40:15 [1] A large animal, exact identity unknown 40:19 [a] Job 26:14 40:20 [a] Ps. 104:14 41:1 [a] Ps. 74:14; 104:26; Is. 27:1 [1] A large sea creature, exact identity unknown 41:2 [a] 2 Kin. 19:28; Is. 37:29 41:6 [1] Or *bargain over him* 41:11 [a] [Rom. 11:35] [b] Ex. 19:5; [Deut. 10:14; Job 9:5–10; 26:6–14]; Ps. 24:1; 50:12; 1 Cor. 10:26, 28 41:12 [1] Literally *keep silent about*

Because of his crashings they
are beside[1] themselves.
26 *Though* the sword reaches
him, it cannot avail;
Nor does spear, dart, or javelin.
27 He regards iron as straw,
And bronze as rotten wood.
28 The arrow cannot make him flee;
Slingstones become like
stubble to him.
29 Darts are regarded as straw;
He laughs at the threat of javelins.
30 His undersides *are* like
sharp potsherds;
He spreads pointed *marks* in the mire.
31 He makes the deep boil like a pot;
He makes the sea like a
pot of ointment.
32 He leaves a shining wake behind him;
One would think the deep
had white hair.
33 On earth there is nothing like him,
Which is made without fear.
34 He beholds every high *thing;*
He *is* king over all the
children of pride."

Job's Repentance and Restoration

42 Then Job answered the LORD and said:

2 "I know that You [a]can do everything,
And that no purpose *of Yours*
can be withheld from You.
3 *You asked,* [a]'Who *is* this who hides
counsel without knowledge?'
Therefore I have uttered what
I did not understand,
[b]Things too wonderful for me,
which I did not know.
4 Listen, please, and let me
speak;

BELIEVE IN THE FATHER

INHALE

I had been at my job longer than any of my coworkers—the only black in a white, corporate environment. I was productive. I did more because as a person of color I knew I had to. But when business got slow, I was the one they let go. How could the Lord, who led me to this job, allow them to fire me? How can I trust the Father when I cannot help but wonder if He is there? And if He is there and a loving God, then why doesn't He care?

EXHALE

Your questions are normal and to be expected. The racial injustice on your very doorstep is as real as it gets. The Black plight has been a weight that even the strongest of individuals have had a hard time carrying. So, to be hurt, confused, and even angry is understandable. But God is not the enemy of our situations. He is the One who walks with us through them.

We do not always know what God is doing and why He is doing it, but we always need to trust that He knows what He is doing and why He is doing it. Sometimes, God pulls us out of good places so He can put us in other better places. Your story has not completely been told. God is still telling it, and He will not leave you alone or abandon you in this moment. Instead, He will show up when and where you least expect Him. This was Job's story in the Bible. He struggled to understand what God was doing in his life. He had experienced unimaginable loss and sorrow. But then, in Job 42:2, Job said this about God: "I know that You can do everything, and that no purpose of Yours can be withheld from You."

Job was hurting and confused, but he held on to God. You can too. It is okay to question what God is doing in your life. However, be encouraged! For every question you have, God has an answer!

41:25 [1] Or *purify themselves* 42:2 [a] Gen. 18:14; [Matt. 19:26; Mark 10:27; 14:36; Luke 18:27]
42:3 [a] Job 38:2 [b] Ps. 40:5; 131:1; 139:6

You said, [a]'I will question you,
And you shall answer Me.'

5 "I have [a]heard of You by the hearing of the ear,
But now my eye sees You.
6 Therefore I [a]abhor *myself,*
And repent in dust and ashes."

7And so it was, after the LORD had spoken these words to Job, that the LORD
said to Eliphaz the Temanite, "My wrath is
aroused against you and your two friends,
for you have not spoken of Me *what is* right,
as My servant Job *has.* 8Now therefore, take
for yourselves [a]seven bulls and seven rams,
[b]go to My servant Job, and offer up for yourselves a burnt offering; and My servant Job
shall [c]pray for you. For I will accept him,
lest I deal with you *according to your* folly;
because you have not spoken of Me *what
is* right, as My servant Job *has.*"
9So Eliphaz the Temanite and Bildad the
Shuhite *and* Zophar the Naamathite went
and did as the LORD commanded them;
for the LORD had accepted Job. 10[a]And the
LORD restored Job's losses[1] when he prayed
for his friends. Indeed the LORD gave Job
[b]twice as much as he had before. 11Then [a]all
his brothers, all his sisters, and all those
who had been his acquaintances before,
came to him and ate food with him in his
house; and they consoled him and comforted him for all the adversity that the
LORD had brought upon him. Each one
gave him a piece of silver and each a ring
of gold.
12Now the LORD blessed [a]the latter *days*
of Job more than his beginning; for he had
[b]fourteen thousand sheep, six thousand
camels, one thousand yoke of oxen, and
one thousand female donkeys. 13[a]He also
had seven sons and three daughters. 14And
he called the name of the first Jemimah,
the name of the second Keziah, and the
name of the third Keren-Happuch. 15In all
the land were found no women *so* beautiful as the daughters of Job; and their father gave them an inheritance among their
brothers.
16After this Job [a]lived one hundred and
forty years, and saw his children and grandchildren *for* four generations. 17So Job died,
old and [a]full of days.

42:4 [a] Job 38:3; 40:7 42:5 [a] Job 26:14; [Rom. 10:17] 42:6 [a] Ezra 9:6; Job 40:4 42:8 [a] Num. 23:1 [b] [Matt. 5:24] [c] Gen. 20:17; [James 5:15, 16; 1 John 5:16] 42:10 [a] Deut. 30:3; Ps. 14:7; 85:1–3; 126:1 [b] Is. 40:2 [1] Literally *Job's captivity,* that is, what was captured from Job 42:11 [a] Job 19:13 42:12 [a] Job 1:10; 8:7; James 5:11 [b] Job 1:3 42:13 [a] Job 1:2 42:16 [a] Job 5:26; Prov. 3:16 42:17 [a] Gen. 15:15; 25:8; Job 5:26

THE BOOK OF

PSALMS

OVERVIEW

The Book of Psalms is a collection of songs written to and about the Lord by various people. David is noted as the author of seventy-three psalms. Twelve psalms are associated with Asaph, twelve with the sons of Korah, two with Solomon, one with Ethan, and one with Moses. As such, the Book of Psalms does not have a specific date of authorship; instead, it was written over a span of about one thousand years, from Moses' time, through the reign of David, to after the Babylonian captivity.

While many psalms do not provide the context of why they were written, several identify their setting. Psalm 3 was written about the time when David fled from his son Absalom. Psalm 56 is connected to the events in 1 Samuel 21:10–15, when the Philistines captured David. Psalm 59 is linked with 1 Samuel 19:11, when Saul sent men to kill David. Psalm 34 is associated with 1 Samuel 21:12—22:2 when David feigned insanity. And Psalm 51 was written after David was confronted about his sins against Bathsheba and Uriah as recorded in 2 Samuel 12.

The Book of Psalms is organized into five collections. Book One includes Psalms 1–41. Book Two includes Psalms 42–72, and Book Three includes Psalms 73–89. Psalms 90–106 are contained in Book Four, and Psalms 107–150 arc in Book Five. Each section opens with an introduction and concludes with a doxology.

The psalms became a part of Israel's worship practices in the temple, serving as the ancient hymnal of God's people. The poetry was often set to music, but not always. The psalms express the writers' emotions about God. Different types of psalms were written to communicate different feelings and thoughts regarding a psalmist's situation. Psalms of lament express the authors' crying out to God in difficult circumstances. Psalms of praise (also called hymns) proclaim admiration of God. Thanksgiving psalms reflect the authors' gratitude to God. Other types of psalms include pilgrim psalms, wisdom psalms, royal psalms, victory psalms, Law psalms, and songs of Zion.

The Book of Psalms shows the important role that God played in the lives of the Israelites and demonstrates just how much His people loved and valued Him. The psalms highlight God's greatness and His faithfulness to His people. The worship experiences presented in the Book of Psalms reveal that the authors were devoted to God, and their lives were changed because of their encounters with Him.

BREATHE IT IN

The Book of Psalms is about our relationship with God. It teaches us that we can approach God amid all we experience in life—the good, the bad, and the ugly. God hears us when we cry out in suffering, confess sin, and shout with joy and gladness. He is there to comfort and forgive us. He is there to celebrate our victories and encourage us to stand strong.

Psalms teaches us to communicate with God on a personal and intimate level. It shows us the value of sharing our frustrations and seeking God for understanding. This book invites us to

a place of safety when we have doubts and fears, of comfort when we are sad and distressed, and of rejoicing when we want to share victories with our Creator. Psalms takes us back to the source of our lives and connects our hearts to God's heart. We are in an age when people talk about how hard it is to open up and be vulnerable. In Psalms, we are led to a place of refuge where we can shout to the Lord with all that is in us and have no fear of rejection. God will always receive us and our praise.

The psalms also lead us to a place of worship in which we exalt and praise our God no matter what. All emotions deserve expression. The Book of Psalms is filled with God's children sharing their emotions with Him. God desires that we express our deepest, rawest emotions to Him. He is there to hear whatever we feel. When we bring painful thoughts and feelings to God, He will heal us and restore us. He can remove the pain and the shame that we might have been carrying around for years. He will teach us how to forgive those who have hurt us and how to move forward without the baggage from our past. If you are hurting, do as the psalmists did and share your thoughts with God. When you are in pain, write your feelings down and ask God to comfort you. At the same time, also share your joys with Him. When you are excited, shout to Him with a voice of triumph and let Him know just how thankful you are that He is your God. Thank Him for His many blessings. Rejoice in His presence and exalt His name. No matter the circumstances, share your emotions with God. That is the message of the Book of Psalms: God does not just welcome our sharing; He seeks it.

†

THE BOOK OF

PSALMS

BOOK ONE
PSALMS 1–41

Psalm 1
The Way of the Righteous and the End of the Ungodly

1 Blessed [a]*is* the man
Who walks not in the counsel
of the ungodly,
Nor stands in the path of sinners,
[b]Nor sits in the seat of the scornful;
2 But [a]his delight *is* in the
law of the LORD,
[b]And in His law he meditates
day and night.
3 He shall be like a tree
[a]Planted by the rivers of water,
That brings forth its
fruit in its season,
Whose leaf also shall not wither;
And whatever he does shall
[b]prosper.

4 The ungodly *are* not so,
But *are* [a]like the chaff which
the wind drives away.
5 Therefore the ungodly shall not
stand in the judgment,
Nor sinners in the congregation
of the righteous.

6 For [a]the LORD knows the
way of the righteous,
But the way of the ungodly
shall perish.

Psalm 2
The Messiah's Triumph and Kingdom (Acts 4:23–31)

1 Why [a]do the nations rage,
And the people plot a vain thing?
2 The kings of the earth set themselves,
And the [a]rulers take counsel together,
Against the LORD and against
His [b]Anointed, *saying,*
3 "Let [a]us break Their bonds in pieces
And cast away Their cords from us."

4 He who sits in the heavens [a]shall laugh;
The Lord shall hold them in derision.
5 Then He shall speak to
them in His wrath,
And distress them in His
deep displeasure:
6 "Yet I have set My King
On My holy hill of Zion."

7 "I will declare the decree:
The LORD has said to Me,
[a]'You *are* My Son,
Today I have begotten You.
8 Ask of Me, and I will give *You*
The nations *for* Your inheritance,
And the ends of the earth
for Your possession.
9 [a]You shall break[1] them
with a rod of iron;
You shall dash them to pieces
like a potter's vessel.'"

10 Now therefore, be wise, O kings;
Be instructed, you judges of the earth.

1:1 [a] Prov. 4:14 [b] Ps. 26:4, 5; Jer. 15:17 1:2 [a] Ps. 119:14, 16, 35 [b] [Josh. 1:8] 1:3 [a] [Ps. 92:12–14]; Jer. 17:8; Ezek. 19:10 [b] Gen. 39:2, 3, 23; Ps. 128:2 1:4 [a] Job 21:18; Ps. 35:5; Is. 17:13 1:6 [a] Ps. 37:18; [Nah. 1:7; John 10:14; 2 Tim. 2:19] 2:1 [a] Acts 4:25, 26 2:2 [a] [Matt. 12:14; 26:3, 4, 59–66; 27:1, 2; Mark 3:6; 11:18] [b] [John 1:41] 2:3 [a] Luke 19:14 2:4 [a] Ps. 37:13 2:7 [a] Matt. 3:17; Mark 1:1, 11; Luke 3:22; John 1:18; Acts 13:33; [Heb. 1:5; 5:5] 2:9 [a] Ps. 89:23; 110:5, 6; [Rev. 2:26, 27; 12:5; 19:15] [1] Following Masoretic Text and Targum; Septuagint, Syriac, and Vulgate read *rule* (compare Revelation 2:27).

11 Serve the LORD with fear,
And rejoice with trembling.
12 Kiss the Son,[1] lest He[2] be angry,
And you perish *in* the way,
When [a]His wrath is kindled
but a little.
[b]Blessed *are* all those who put
their trust in Him.

Psalm 3

The LORD Helps His Troubled People

A Psalm of David [a]when he fled from Absalom his son.

1 LORD, how they have increased
who trouble me!
Many *are* they who rise up
against me.
2 Many *are* they who say of me,
"*There is* no help for him
in God." *Selah*

3 But You, O LORD, *are* [a]a shield
for me,
My glory and [b]the One who
lifts up my head.
4 I cried to the LORD with
my voice,
And [a]He heard me from
His [b]holy hill. *Selah*

5 [a]I lay down and slept;
I awoke, for the LORD sustained me.
6 [a]I will not be afraid of ten
thousands of people
Who have set *themselves*
against me all around.

7 Arise, O LORD;
Save me, O my God!
[a]For You have struck all my
enemies on the cheekbone;
You have broken the teeth
of the ungodly.
8 [a]Salvation *belongs* to the LORD.
Your blessing *is* upon Your
people. *Selah*

Psalm 4

The Safety of the Faithful

To the Chief Musician. With stringed instruments. A Psalm of David.

1 Hear me when I call, O God
of my righteousness!
You have relieved me in *my* distress;
Have mercy on me, and
hear my prayer.

2 How long, O you sons of men,
Will you turn my glory to shame?
How long will you love worthlessness
And seek falsehood? *Selah*
3 But know that [a]the LORD has set apart[1]
for Himself him who is godly;
The LORD will hear when I call to Him.

4 [a]Be angry, and do not sin.
[b]Meditate within your heart on
your bed, and be still. *Selah*
5 Offer [a]the sacrifices of righteousness,
And [b]put your trust in the LORD.

6 *There are* many who say,
"Who will show us *any* good?"
[a]LORD, lift up the light of Your
countenance upon us.
7 You have put [a]gladness in my heart,
More than in the season that their
grain and wine increased.
8 [a]I will both lie down in
peace, and sleep;
[b]For You alone, O LORD, make
me dwell in safety.

Psalm 5

A Prayer for Guidance

To the Chief Musician. With flutes.[1] A Psalm of David.

1 Give [a]ear to my words, O LORD,
Consider my meditation.
2 Give heed to the voice of my cry,
My King and my God,
For to You I will pray.

2:12 [a] [Rev. 6:16, 17] [b] [Ps. 5:11; 34:22] [1] Septuagint and Vulgate read *Embrace discipline;* Targum reads *Receive instruction.* [2] Septuagint reads *the LORD.* **3:title** [a] 2 Sam. 15:13–17 **3:3** [a] Ps. 5:12; 28:7 [b] Ps. 9:13; 27:6 **3:4** [a] Ps. 4:3; 34:4 [b] Ps. 2:6; 15:1; 43:3 **3:5** [a] Lev. 26:6; Ps. 4:8; Prov. 3:24 **3:6** [a] Ps. 23:4; 27:3 **3:7** [a] Job 16:10 **3:8** [a] Ps. 28:8; 35:3; [Is. 43:11] **4:3** [a] [2 Tim. 2:19] [1] Many Hebrew manuscripts, Septuagint, Targum, and Vulgate read *made wonderful.* **4:4** [a] [Ps. 119:11; Eph. 4:26] [b] Ps. 77:6 **4:5** [a] Deut. 33:19; Ps. 51:19 [b] Ps. 37:3, 5; 62:8 **4:6** [a] Num. 6:26; Ps. 80:3, 7, 19 **4:7** [a] Ps. 97:11, 12; Is. 9:3; Acts 14:17 **4:8** [a] Job 11:19; Ps. 3:5 [b] [Lev. 25:18]; Deut. 12:10 **5:title** [1] Hebrew *nehiloth* **5:1** [a] Ps. 4:1

3 My voice You shall hear in
the morning, O LORD;
[a]In the morning I will direct
it to You,
And I will look up.

4 For You *are* not a God who takes
pleasure in wickedness,
Nor shall evil dwell with You.
5 The [a]boastful shall not
[b]stand in Your sight;
You hate all workers of iniquity.
6 You shall destroy those who
speak falsehood;
The LORD abhors the [a]bloodthirsty
and deceitful man.

7 But as for me, I will come
into Your house in the
multitude of Your mercy;
In fear of You I will worship
toward Your holy temple.
8 [a]Lead me, O LORD, in Your
righteousness because
of my enemies;
Make Your way straight
before my face.

9 For *there is* no faithfulness
in their mouth;
Their inward part *is* destruction;
[a]Their throat *is* an open tomb;
They flatter with their tongue.
10 Pronounce them guilty, O God!
Let them fall by their own
counsels;
Cast them out in the multitude
of their transgressions,
For they have rebelled
against You.

11 But let all those rejoice who
put their trust in You;
Let them ever shout for joy,
because You defend them;
Let those also who love Your
name
Be joyful in You.
12 For You, O LORD, will bless
the righteous;
With favor You will surround
him as *with* a shield.

Psalm 6

A Prayer of Faith in Time of Distress

To the Chief Musician. With stringed instruments. [a]On an eight-stringed harp.[1] A Psalm of David.

1 O LORD, [a]do not rebuke
me in Your anger,
Nor chasten me in Your
hot displeasure.
2 Have mercy on me, O LORD,
for I *am* weak;
O LORD, [a]heal me, for my
bones are troubled.
3 My soul also is greatly [a]troubled;
But You, O LORD—how long?

4 Return, O LORD, deliver me!
Oh, save me for Your mercies'
sake!
5 [a]For in death *there is* no
remembrance of You;
In the grave who will give
You thanks?

6 I am weary with my groaning;
All night I make my bed swim;
I drench my couch with my tears.
7 [a]My eye wastes away because
of grief;
It grows old because of
all my enemies.

8 [a]Depart from me, all you
workers of iniquity;
For the LORD has [b]heard the
voice of my weeping.
9 The LORD has heard my
supplication;
The LORD will receive my
prayer.
10 Let all my enemies be ashamed
and greatly troubled;
Let them turn back *and* be
ashamed suddenly.

5:3 [a] Ps. 55:17; 88:13 5:5 [a] [Hab. 1:13] [b] Ps. 1:5 5:6 [a] Ps. 55:23 5:8 [a] Ps. 25:4, 5; 27:11; 31:3 5:9 [a] Rom. 3:13 6:title [a] Ps. 12:title [1] Hebrew *Sheminith* 6:1 [a] Ps. 38:1; 118:18; [Jer. 10:24] 6:2 [a] Ps. 41:4; 147:3; [Hos. 6:1] 6:3 [a] Ps. 88:3; John 12:27 6:5 [a] Ps. 30:9; 88:10–12; 115:17; [Eccl. 9:10]; Is. 38:18 6:7 [a] Job 17:7; Ps. 31:9 6:8 [a] [Matt. 25:41] [b] Ps. 3:4; 28:6

Psalm 7

Prayer and Praise for Deliverance from Enemies

A [a]Meditation[1] of David, which he sang to the LORD [b]concerning the words of Cush, a Benjamite.

1 O LORD my God, in You I put my trust;
[a]Save me from all those
who persecute me;
And deliver me,
2 [a]Lest they tear me like a lion,
[b]Rending *me* in pieces, while
there is none to deliver.

3 O LORD my God, [a]if I have done this:
If there is [b]iniquity in my hands,
4 If I have repaid evil to him who
was at peace with me,
Or [a]have plundered my
enemy without cause,
5 Let the enemy pursue me
and overtake *me;*
Yes, let him trample my
life to the earth,
And lay my honor in the dust. *Selah*

6 Arise, O LORD, in Your anger;
[a]Lift Yourself up because of the
rage of my enemies;
[b]Rise up for me[1] *to* the judgment
You have commanded!
7 So the congregation of the
peoples shall surround You;
For their sakes, therefore,
return on high.
8 The LORD shall judge the peoples;
[a]Judge me, O LORD, [b]according
to my righteousness,
And according to my
integrity within me.

9 Oh, let the wickedness of the
wicked come to an end,
But establish the just;
[a]For the righteous God tests
the hearts and minds.
10 My defense *is* of God,
Who saves the [a]upright in heart.
11 God *is* a just judge,
And God is angry *with the*
wicked every day.
12 If he does not turn back,
He will [a]sharpen His sword;
He bends His bow and makes
it ready.
13 He also prepares for Himself
instruments of death;
He makes His arrows into fiery shafts.

14 [a]Behold, *the wicked* brings
forth iniquity;
Yes, he conceives trouble and
brings forth falsehood.
15 He made a pit and dug it out,
[a]And has fallen into the ditch
which he made.
16 [a]His trouble shall return
upon his own head,
And his violent dealing shall come
down on his own crown.

17 I will praise the LORD according
to His righteousness,
And will sing praise to the name
of the LORD Most High.

Psalm 8

The Glory of the LORD in Creation

To the Chief Musician. On the instrument of Gath.[1] A Psalm of David.

1 O LORD, our Lord,
How [a]excellent *is* Your name
in all the earth,
Who have [b]set Your glory
above the heavens!

2 [a]Out of the mouth of babes
and nursing infants
You have ordained strength,
Because of Your enemies,
That You may silence [b]the
enemy and the avenger.

3 When I [a]consider Your heavens,
the work of Your fingers,

7:title [a] Hab. 3:1 [b] 2 Sam. 16 [1] Hebrew *Shiggaion* 7:1 [a] Ps. 31:15 7:2 [a] Ps. 57:4; Is. 38:13 [b] Ps. 50:22 7:3 [a] 2 Sam. 16:7 [b] 1 Sam. 24:11 7:4 [a] 1 Sam. 24:7; 26:9 7:6 [a] Ps. 94:2 [b] Ps. 35:23; 44:23 [1] Following Masoretic Text, Targum, and Vulgate; Septuagint reads *O LORD my God.* 7:8 [a] Ps. 26:1; 35:24; 43:1 [b] Ps. 18:20; 35:24 7:9 [a] [1 Sam. 16:7] 7:10 [a] Ps. 97:10, 11; 125:4 7:12 [a] Deut. 32:41 7:14 [a] Job 15:35; Is. 59:4; [James 1:15] 7:15 [a] [Job 4:8]; Ps. 57:6 7:16 [a] Esth. 9:25; Ps. 140:9 8:title [1] Hebrew *Al Gittith* 8:1 [a] Ps. 148:13 [b] Ps. 113:4 8:2 [a] Matt. 21:16; [1 Cor. 1:27] [b] Ps. 44:16 8:3 [a] Ps. 111:2

The moon and the stars, which
You have ordained,
4 [a]What is man that You are
mindful of him,
And the son of man that
You [b]visit him?
5 For You have made him a little
lower than the angels,[1]
And You have crowned him
with glory and honor.

6 [a]You have made him to have
dominion over the works
of Your hands;
[b]You have put all *things* under his feet,
7 All sheep and oxen—
Even the beasts of the field,
8 The birds of the air,
And the fish of the sea
That pass through the
paths of the seas.

9 [a]O LORD, our Lord,
How excellent *is* Your name
in all the earth!

Psalm 9

Prayer and Thanksgiving for the LORD's Righteous Judgments

To the Chief Musician. To *the tune of* "Death of the Son."[1] A Psalm of David.

1 I will praise *You,* O LORD,
with my whole heart;
I will tell of all Your marvelous works.
2 I will be glad and [a]rejoice in You;
I will sing praise to Your
name, [b]O Most High.

3 When my enemies turn back,
They shall fall and perish
at Your presence.
4 For You have maintained my
right and my cause;
You sat on the throne judging
in righteousness.
5 You have rebuked the nations,
You have destroyed the wicked;
You have [a]blotted out their
name forever and ever.

6 O enemy, destructions are
finished forever!
And you have destroyed cities;
Even their memory has [a]perished.
7 [a]But the LORD shall endure forever;
He has prepared His throne
for judgment.
8 [a]He shall judge the world
in righteousness,
And He shall administer judgment
for the peoples in uprightness.

9 The LORD also will be a [a]refuge
for the oppressed,
A refuge in times of trouble.
10 And those who [a]know Your name
will put their trust in You;
For You, LORD, have not forsaken
those who seek You.

11 Sing praises to the LORD,
who dwells in Zion!
[a]Declare His deeds among the people.
12 [a]When He avenges blood, He
remembers them;
He does not forget the cry
of the humble.

13 Have mercy on me, O LORD!
Consider my trouble from
those who hate me,
You who lift me up from
the gates of death,
14 That I may tell of all Your praise
In the gates of the daughter of Zion.
I will [a]rejoice in Your salvation.

15 [a]The nations have sunk down in
the pit *which* they made;
In the net which they hid, their
own foot is caught.
16 The LORD is [a]known *by* the
judgment He executes;
The wicked is snared in the
work of his own hands.
[b]Meditation.[1] *Selah*

8:4 [a] Job 7:17, 18; [Heb. 2:6–8] [b] [Job 10:12] 8:5 [1] Hebrew *Elohim, God;* Septuagint, Syriac, Targum, and Jewish tradition translate as *angels.* 8:6 [a] [Gen. 1:26, 28] [b] [1 Cor. 15:27; Eph. 1:22; Heb. 2:8] 8:9 [a] Ps. 8:1 9:title [1] Hebrew *Muth Labben* 9:2 [a] Ps. 5:11; 104:34 [b] [Ps. 83:18; 92:1] 9:5 [a] Prov. 10:7 9:6 [a] [Ps. 34:16] 9:7 [a] Ps. 102:12, 26; Heb. 1:11 9:8 [a] [Ps. 96:13; 98:9; Acts 17:31] 9:9 [a] Ps. 32:7; 46:1; 91:2 9:10 [a] Ps. 91:14 9:11 [a] Ps. 66:16; 107:22 9:12 [a] [Gen. 9:5; Ps. 72:14] 9:14 [a] Ps. 13:5; 20:5; 35:9 9:15 [a] Ps. 7:15, 16 9:16 [a] Ex. 7:5 [b] Ps. 92:3 [1] Hebrew *Higgaion*

17 The wicked shall be turned
into hell,
And all the nations [a]that forget
God.
18 [a]For the needy shall not
always be forgotten;
[b]The expectation of the poor
shall *not* perish forever.

19 Arise, O LORD,
Do not let man prevail;
Let the nations be judged
in Your sight.
20 Put them in fear, O LORD,
That the nations may know
themselves *to be but*
men. *Selah*

Psalm 10

A Song of Confidence in God's Triumph over Evil

1 Why do You stand afar off,
O LORD?
Why do You hide in times
of trouble?
2 The wicked in *his* pride
persecutes the poor;
[a]Let them be caught in the plots
which they have devised.

3 For the wicked [a]boasts of
his heart's desire;
He [b]blesses the greedy *and*
renounces the LORD.
4 The wicked in his proud countenance
does not seek *God;*
God *is* in none of his [a]thoughts.

5 His ways are always prospering;
Your judgments *are* far
above, out of his sight;
As for all his enemies, he
sneers at them.
6 [a]He has said in his heart, "I
shall not be moved;
[b]I shall never be in adversity."
7 [a]His mouth is full of cursing and
[b]deceit and oppression;
Under his tongue *is* trouble
and iniquity.

8 He sits in the lurking places
of the villages;
In the secret places he
murders the innocent;
His eyes are secretly fixed
on the helpless.
9 He lies in wait secretly, as
a lion in his den;
He lies in wait to catch the poor;
He catches the poor when he
draws him into his net.
10 So he crouches, he lies low,
That the helpless may fall
by his strength.
11 He has said in his heart,
"God has forgotten;
He hides His face;
He will never see."

12 Arise, O LORD!
O God, [a]lift up Your hand!
Do not forget the [b]humble.
13 Why do the wicked renounce God?
He has said in his heart,
"You will not require *an account.*"

14 But You have [a]seen, for You
observe trouble and grief,
To repay *it* by Your hand.
The helpless [b]commits himself to You;
[c]You are the helper of the fatherless.
15 Break the arm of the wicked
and the evil *man;*
Seek out his wickedness
until You find none.

16 [a]The LORD *is* King forever and ever;
The nations have perished
out of His land.
17 LORD, You have heard the
desire of the humble;
You will prepare their heart;
You will cause Your ear to hear,
18 To do justice to the fatherless
and the oppressed,
That the man of the earth
may oppress no more.

9:17 [a] Job 8:13; Ps. 50:22 9:18 [a] Ps. 9:12; 12:5 [b] [Ps. 62:5; 71:5]; Prov. 23:18 10:2 [a] Ps. 7:16; 9:16 10:3 [a] Ps. 49:6; 94:3, 4 [b] Prov. 28:4 10:4 [a] Ps. 14:1; 36:1 10:6 [a] Ps. 49:11; [Eccl. 8:11] [b] Rev. 18:7 10:7 [a] [Rom. 3:14] [b] Ps. 55:10, 11 10:12 [a] Ps. 17:7; 94:2; Mic. 5:9 [b] Ps. 9:12 10:14 [a] [Ps. 11:4] [b] [2 Tim. 1:12] [c] Ps. 68:5; Hos. 14:3 10:16 [a] Ps. 29:10

Psalm 11

Faith in the LORD's Righteousness

To the Chief Musician. *A Psalm* of David.

1 In [a]the LORD I put my trust;
How can you say to my soul,
"Flee *as* a bird to your mountain"?
2 For look! [a]The wicked bend *their* bow,
They make ready their
arrow on the string,
That they may shoot secretly
at the upright in heart.
3 [a]If the foundations are destroyed,
What can the righteous do?

4 The LORD *is* in His holy temple,
The LORD's [a]throne *is* in heaven;
[b]His eyes behold,
His eyelids test the sons of men.
5 The LORD [a]tests the righteous,
But the wicked and the one who
loves violence His soul hates.
6 Upon the wicked He will rain coals;
Fire and brimstone and
a burning wind
[a]*Shall be* the portion of their cup.

7 For the LORD *is* righteous,
He [a]loves righteousness;
His countenance beholds the upright.[1]

Psalm 12

Man's Treachery and God's Constancy

To the Chief Musician. [a]On an eight-stringed harp.[1] A Psalm of David.

1 Help, LORD, for the godly man [a]ceases!
For the faithful disappear from
among the sons of men.
2 [a]They speak idly everyone
with his neighbor;
With flattering lips *and* a
double heart they speak.

3 May the LORD cut off all flattering lips,
And the tongue that speaks
proud things,
4 Who have said,
"With our tongue we will prevail;
Our lips *are* our own;
Who *is* lord over us?"

5 "For the oppression of the poor,
for the sighing of the needy,
Now I will arise," says the LORD;
"I will set *him* in the safety
for which he yearns."

6 The words of the LORD *are* [a]pure words,
Like silver tried in a furnace of earth,
Purified seven times.
7 You shall keep them, O LORD,
You shall preserve them from
this generation forever.

8 The wicked prowl on every side,
When vileness is exalted
among the sons of men.

Psalm 13

Trust in the Salvation of the LORD

To the Chief Musician. A Psalm of David.

1 How long, O LORD? Will You
forget me forever?
[a]How long will You hide
Your face from me?
2 How long shall I take
counsel in my soul,
Having sorrow in my heart daily?
How long will my enemy be
exalted over me?

3 Consider *and* hear me, O LORD my God;
[a]Enlighten my eyes,
[b]Lest I sleep the *sleep of* death;
4 Lest my enemy say,
"I have prevailed against him";
Lest those who trouble me
rejoice when I am moved.

5 But I have trusted in Your mercy;
My heart shall rejoice in Your salvation.
6 I will sing to the LORD,
Because He has dealt
bountifully with me.

11:1 [a] Ps. 56:11 11:2 [a] Ps. 64:3, 4 11:3 [a] Ps. 82:5; 87:1; 119:152 11:4 [a] Ps. 2:4; [Is. 66:1]; Matt. 5:34; 23:22; [Acts 7:49]; Rev. 4:2 [b] [Ps. 33:18; 34:15, 16] 11:5 [a] Gen. 22:1; [James 1:12] 11:6 [a] 1 Sam. 1:4; Ps. 75:8; Ezek. 38:22 11:7 [a] Ps. 33:5; 45:7 [1] Or *The upright beholds His countenance* 12:title [a] Ps. 6:title [1] Hebrew *Sheminith* 12:1 [a] [Is. 57:1]; Mic. 7:2 12:2 [a] Ps. 10:7; 41:6 12:6 [a] 2 Sam. 22:31; Ps. 18:30; 119:140; Prov. 30:5 13:1 [a] Job 13:24; Ps. 89:46 13:3 [a] 1 Sam. 14:29; Ezra 9:8; Job 33:30; Ps. 18:28 [b] Jer. 51:39

RECONCILE WRONGS WITH RIGHTS

INHALE

I have recently been made the community advocate for where I work. I put my name in for this position because I want to help make my community a better place. At the time, all my coworkers voted to support me in this role, but now they talk about me behind my back, want nothing to do with me, and aren't engaged in any of our community programs. I am frustrated because it seems that people of my own race are treating me worse than folks who have skin of a different color. Why did God let this go so wrong, when only by His grace did I get the position? How can I let go of the bitterness I feel and set my reputation right?

EXHALE

"Heavy is the head that wears the crown," said Shakespeare. Leading has never been easy, and it never will be. Leaders either inspire or expire. Leadership is difficult and takes courage, but it can be rewarding. Getting a position of leadership is only half the battle. Sometimes, those who you are going to lead are fully supportive up until the moment you become that leader, and then they only resist your leadership. While we need to make sure we lead in godly, honoring ways, sometimes the fault is not ours but those we lead. Sin makes everyone resist every sort of authority. You are feeling in a small way what God feels every day from eight billion people! He's right there with you. He knows what you are feeling, and He will give you the ability to let go of bitterness and guide your leadership.

As for your reputation, you keep following God and doing what you need to do, and that will all get sorted out on its own. Know that you aren't alone. King David was one of Israel's greatest leaders. Here is what he shared in Psalm 13:2: "How long shall I take counsel in my soul, having sorrow in my heart daily? How long will my enemy be exalted over me?" David was real with God about what he was feeling. He took it to God, but then he left it there. Notice how David wrapped up this psalm: "But I have trusted in Your mercy; my heart shall rejoice in Your salvation. I will sing to the LORD, because He has dealt bountifully with me" (vv. 5–6). Leaders cannot spend time concerned about their reputations. It's not about your reputation; it's about dedication.

God knows your heart. Keep focused on Him and stay faithful to Him no matter what. Do not be discouraged; just keep leading. Even if leading that group does not work out, your life will bear fruit.

Psalm 14

Folly of the Godless, and God's Final Triumph

(Ps. 53:1–6)

To the Chief Musician. *A Psalm* of David.

1 The [a]fool has said in his heart,
"*There is* no God."
They are corrupt,
They have done abominable
works,
There is none who does good.

2 [a]The LORD looks down from heaven
upon the children of men,
To see if there are any who
understand, who seek God.
3 [a]They have all turned aside,
They have together become corrupt;
There is none who does good,
No, not one.

4 Have all the workers of
iniquity no knowledge,
Who eat up my people *as*
they eat bread,
And [a]do not call on the LORD?
5 There they are in great fear,
For God *is* with the generation
of the righteous.

14:1 [a] Ps. 10:4; 53:1 14:2 [a] Ps. 33:13, 14; 102:19; Rom. 3:11 14:3 [a] Rom. 3:12 14:4 [a] Ps. 79:6; Is. 64:7; Jer. 10:25; Amos 8:4; Mic. 3:3

6 You shame the counsel of the poor,
But the LORD *is* his [a]refuge.

7 [a]Oh, that the salvation of Israel
would come out of Zion!
[b]When the LORD brings back the
captivity of His people,
Let Jacob rejoice *and* Israel be glad.

Psalm 15

The Character of Those Who May Dwell with the LORD

A Psalm of David.

1 LORD, [a]who may abide in
Your tabernacle?
Who may dwell in Your holy hill?

2 He who walks uprightly,
And works righteousness,
And speaks the [a]truth
in his heart;
3 He *who* [a]does not backbite
with his tongue,
Nor does evil to his neighbor,
[b]Nor does he take up a reproach
against his friend;
4 [a]In whose eyes a vile person
is despised,
But he honors those who
fear the LORD;
He *who* [b]swears to his own hurt
and does not change;
5 He *who* does not put out
his money at usury,
Nor does he take a bribe
against the innocent.

He who does these *things*
[a]shall never be moved.

Psalm 16

The Hope of the Faithful, and the Messiah's Victory

A [a]Michtam of David.

1 Preserve me, O God, for in
You I put my trust.

2 *O my soul,* you have said to the LORD,
"You *are* my Lord,
[a]My goodness is nothing
apart from You."
3 As for the saints who *are* on the earth,
"They are the excellent ones, in
[a]whom is all my delight."

4 Their sorrows shall be multiplied
who hasten *after* another *god;*
Their drink offerings of
[a]blood I will not offer,
[b]Nor take up their names on my lips.

5 O LORD, *You are* the portion of
my inheritance and my cup;
You maintain my lot.
6 The lines have fallen to me
in pleasant *places;*
Yes, I have a good inheritance.

7 I will bless the LORD who has
given me counsel;
My heart also instructs me
in the night seasons.
8 [a]I have set the LORD always
before me;
Because *He is* at my right hand
I shall not be moved.

9 Therefore my heart is glad,
and my glory rejoices;
My flesh also will rest in hope.
10 [a]For You will not leave my
soul in Sheol,
Nor will You allow Your Holy
One to see corruption.
11 You will show me the [a]path of life;
In Your presence *is* fullness of joy;
At Your right hand *are*
pleasures forevermore.

Psalm 17

Prayer with Confidence in Final Salvation

A Prayer of David.

1 Hear a just cause, O LORD,
Attend to my cry;

14:6 [a] Ps. 9:9; 40:17; 46:1; 142:5 14:7 [a] Ps. 53:6; [Rom. 11:25–27] [b] Deut. 30:3; Job 42:10 15:1 [a] Ps. 24:3–5 15:2 [a] Zech. 8:16; [Eph. 4:25] 15:3 [a] [Lev. 19:16–18] [b] Ex. 23:1 15:4 [a] Esth. 3:2 [b] Lev. 5:4 15:5 [a] 2 Pet. 1:10 16:title [a] Ps. 56—60 16:2 [a] Job 35:7 16:3 [a] Ps. 119:63 16:4 [a] Ps. 106:37, 38 [b] [Ex. 23:13]; Josh. 23:7 16:8 [a] [Acts 2:25–28] 16:10 [a] Ps. 49:15; 86:13; Acts 2:31, 32; Heb. 13:20 16:11 [a] Ps. 139:24; [Matt. 7:14]

Give ear to my prayer *which is*
not from deceitful lips.
2 Let my vindication come
from Your presence;
Let Your eyes look on the
things that are upright.

3 You have tested my heart;
You have visited *me* in the night;
[a]You have tried me and have
found nothing;
I have purposed that my mouth
shall not [b]transgress.
4 Concerning the works of men,
By the word of Your lips,
I have kept away from the
paths of the destroyer.
5 [a]Uphold my steps in Your paths,
That my footsteps may not slip.

6 [a]I have called upon You, for
You will hear me, O God;
Incline Your ear to me, *and*
hear my speech.
7 Show Your marvelous lovingkindness
by Your right hand,
O You who save those who trust *in You*
From those who rise up *against them.*
8 Keep me as the apple of Your eye;
Hide me under the shadow
of Your wings,
9 From the wicked who oppress me,
From my deadly enemies
who surround me.

10 They have closed up their [a]fat *hearts;*
With their mouths they
[b]speak proudly.
11 They have now surrounded
us in our steps;
They have set their eyes, crouching
down to the earth,
12 As a lion is eager to tear his prey,
And like a young lion lurking
in secret places.

13 Arise, O LORD,
Confront him, cast him down;
Deliver my life from the
wicked with Your sword,
14 With Your hand from men,
O LORD,
From men of the world *who have*
their portion in *this* life,
And whose belly You fill with
Your hidden treasure.
They are satisfied with children,
And leave the rest of their
possession for their babes.

15 As for me, [a]I will see Your
face in righteousness;
[b]I shall be satisfied when I
[c]awake in Your likeness.

Psalm 18

God the Sovereign Savior

(2 Sam. 22:1–51)

To the Chief Musician. A *Psalm* of David [a]the servant of the LORD, who spoke to the LORD the words of [b]this song on the day that the LORD delivered him from the hand of all his enemies and from the hand of Saul. And he said:

1 I [a]will love You, O LORD,
my strength.
2 The LORD is my rock and my
fortress and my deliverer;
My God, my strength, [a]in
whom I will trust;
My shield and the horn of my
salvation, my stronghold.
3 I will call upon the LORD, [a]*who*
is worthy to be praised;
So shall I be saved from
my enemies.

4 [a]The pangs of death surrounded me,
And the floods of ungodliness
made me afraid.
5 The sorrows of Sheol surrounded me;
The snares of death confronted me.
6 In my distress I called upon the LORD,
And cried out to my God;
He heard my voice from
His temple,
And my cry came before
Him, *even* to His ears.

17:3 [a] Job 23:10; Ps. 66:10; Zech. 13:9; [1 Pet. 1:7] [b] Ps. 39:1 17:5 [a] Job 23:11; Ps. 44:18; 119:133 17:6 [a] Ps. 86:7; 116:2 17:10 [a] Ezek. 16:49 [b] [1 Sam. 2:3] 17:15 [a] [1 John 3:2] [b] Ps. 4:6, 7; 16:11 [c] [Is. 26:19] 18:title [a] Ps. 36:title [b] 2 Sam. 22 18:1 [a] Ps. 144:1 18:2 [a] Heb. 2:13 18:3 [a] Ps. 76:4; Rev. 5:12 18:4 [a] Ps. 116:3

7 [a]Then the earth shook and trembled;
The foundations of the hills also
quaked and were shaken,
Because He was angry.
8 Smoke went up from His nostrils,
And devouring fire from His mouth;
Coals were kindled by it.
9 [a]He bowed the heavens also,
and came down
With darkness under His feet.
10 [a]And He rode upon a cherub, and flew;
[b]He flew upon the wings of the wind.
11 He made darkness His secret place;
[a]His canopy around Him
was dark waters
And thick clouds of the skies.
12 [a]From the brightness before Him,
His thick clouds passed with
hailstones and coals of fire.

13 The LORD thundered from heaven,
And the Most High uttered [a]His voice,
Hailstones and coals of fire.[1]
14 [a]He sent out His arrows and
scattered the foe,
Lightnings in abundance, and
He vanquished them.
15 Then the channels of the
sea were seen,
The foundations of the world
were uncovered
At Your rebuke, O LORD,
At the blast of the breath
of Your nostrils.

16 [a]He sent from above, He took me;
He drew me out of many waters.
17 He delivered me from my
strong enemy,
From those who hated me,
For they were too strong for me.
18 They confronted me in the
day of my calamity,
But the LORD was my support.
19 [a]He also brought me out
into a broad place;
He delivered me because
He delighted in me.

20 [a]The LORD rewarded me according
to my righteousness;
According to the cleanness
of my hands
He has recompensed me.
21 For I have kept the ways of the LORD,
And have not wickedly
departed from my God.
22 For all His judgments *were* before me,
And I did not put away His
statutes from me.
23 I was also blameless before Him,
And I kept myself from my iniquity.
24 [a]Therefore the LORD has recompensed
me according to my righteousness,
According to the cleanness of
my hands in His sight.

25 [a]With the merciful You will
show Yourself merciful;
With a blameless man You will
show Yourself blameless;
26 With the pure You will show
Yourself pure;
And [a]with the devious You will
show Yourself shrewd.
27 For You will save the humble people,
But will bring down [a]haughty looks.

28 [a]For You will light my lamp;
The LORD my God will
enlighten my darkness.
29 For by You I can run against a troop,
By my God I can leap over a wall.
30 *As for* God, [a]His way *is* perfect;
[b]The word of the LORD is proven;
He *is* a shield [c]to all who trust
in Him.

31 [a]For who *is* God, except the LORD?
And who *is* a rock, except our God?
32 *It is* God who [a]arms me with strength,
And makes my way perfect.
33 [a]He makes my feet like the *feet of* deer,
And [b]sets me on my high places.
34 [a]He teaches my hands to make war,
So that my arms can bend
a bow of bronze.

18:7 [a] Acts 4:31 18:9 [a] Ps. 144:5 18:10 [a] Ps. 80:1; 99:1 [b] [Ps. 104:3] 18:11 [a] Ps. 97:2 18:12 [a] Ps. 97:3; 140:10; Hab. 3:11 18:13 [a] [Ps. 29:3–9; 104:7] [1] Following Masoretic Text, Targum, and Vulgate; a few Hebrew manuscripts and Septuagint omit *Hailstones and coals of fire.* 18:14 [a] Josh. 10:10; Ps. 144:6; Is. 30:30; Hab. 3:11 18:16 [a] Ps. 144:7 18:19 [a] Ps. 4:1; 31:8; 118:5 18:20 [a] 1 Sam. 24:19; [Job 33:26]; Ps. 7:8 18:24 [a] 1 Sam. 26:23; Ps. 18:20 18:25 [a] [1 Kin. 8:32; Ps. 62:12]; Matt. 5:7 18:26 [a] [Lev. 26:23–28]; Prov. 3:34 18:27 [a] [Ps. 101:5]; Prov. 6:17 18:28 [a] 1 Kin. 15:4; Job 18:6; [Ps. 119:105] 18:30 [a] [Deut. 32:4]; Rev. 15:3 [b] Ps. 12:6; 119:140; [Prov. 30:5] [c] [Ps. 17:7] 18:31 [a] [Deut. 32:31, 39; 1 Sam. 2:2; Ps. 86:8–10; Is. 45:5] 18:32 [a] [Ps. 91:2] 18:33 [a] 2 Sam. 2:18; Hab. 3:19 [b] Deut. 32:13; 33:29 18:34 [a] Ps. 144:1

35 You have also given me the
shield of Your salvation;
Your right hand has held me up,
Your gentleness has made me great.
36 You enlarged my path under me,
[a]So my feet did not slip.

37 I have pursued my enemies
and overtaken them;
Neither did I turn back again
till they were destroyed.
38 I have wounded them,
So that they could not rise;
They have fallen under my feet.
39 For You have armed me with
strength for the battle;
You have subdued under me those
who rose up against me.
40 You have also given me the
necks of my enemies,
So that I destroyed those
who hated me.
41 They cried out, but *there*
was none to save;
[a]*Even* to the LORD, but He did
not answer them.
42 Then I beat them as fine as the
dust before the wind;
I [a]cast them out like dirt
in the streets.

43 You have delivered me from the
strivings of the people;
[a]You have made me the
head of the nations;
[b]A people I have not known
shall serve me.
44 As soon as they hear of
me they obey me;
The foreigners submit to me.
45 [a]The foreigners fade away,
And come frightened from
their hideouts.

46 The LORD lives!
Blessed *be* my Rock!
Let the God of my salvation be exalted.
47 *It is* God who avenges me,
[a]And subdues the peoples under me;
48 He delivers me from my enemies.
[a]You also lift me up above those
who rise against me;
You have delivered me from
the violent man.
49 [a]Therefore I will give thanks to You,
O LORD, among the Gentiles,
And sing praises to Your name.

50 [a]Great deliverance He gives to His king,
And shows mercy to His anointed,
To David and his descendants
forevermore.

Psalm 19

The Perfect Revelation of the LORD

To the Chief Musician. A Psalm of David.

1 The [a]heavens declare the glory of God;
And the [b]firmament shows
His handiwork.
2 Day unto day utters speech,
And night unto night
reveals knowledge.
3 *There is* no speech nor language
Where their voice is not heard.
4 [a]Their line[1] has gone out
through all the earth,
And their words to the
end of the world.

In them He has set a
tabernacle for the sun,
5 Which *is* like a bridegroom
coming out of his chamber,
[a]*And* rejoices like a strong
man to run its race.
6 Its rising *is* from one end of heaven,
And its circuit to the other end;
And there is nothing hidden
from its heat.

7 [a]The law of the LORD *is* perfect,
converting the soul;
The testimony of the LORD *is* sure,
making [b]wise the simple;
8 The statutes of the LORD *are*
right, rejoicing the heart;
The commandment of the LORD *is*
pure, enlightening the eyes;

18:36 [a] Ps. 66:9; Prov. 4:12 18:41 [a] Job 27:9; Prov. 1:28; Is. 1:15; Ezek. 8:18; Zech. 7:13 18:42 [a] Zech. 10:5 18:43 [a] 2 Sam. 8; Ps. 89:27 [b] Is. 52:15 18:45 [a] Mic. 7:17 18:47 [a] Ps. 47:3 18:48 [a] Ps. 27:6; 59:1 18:49 [a] 2 Sam. 22:50; Rom. 15:9 18:50 [a] 2 Sam. 7:12; Ps. 21:1; 144:10 19:1 [a] Is. 40:22; [Rom. 1:19, 20] [b] Gen. 1:6, 7 19:4 [a] Rom. 10:18 [1] Septuagint, Syriac, and Vulgate read *sound;* Targum reads *business.* 19:5 [a] Eccl. 1:5 19:7 [a] Ps. 111:7; [Rom. 7:12] [b] Ps. 119:130

9 The fear of the LORD *is* clean,
enduring forever;
The judgments of the LORD *are*
true *and* righteous altogether.
10 More to be desired *are they* than [a]gold,
Yea, than much fine gold;
Sweeter also than honey
and the honeycomb.
11 Moreover by them Your
servant is warned,
And in keeping them *there*
is great reward.

12 Who can understand *his* errors?
[a]Cleanse me from secret *faults.*
13 Keep back Your servant also
from [a]presumptuous *sins;*
Let them not have [b]dominion over me.
Then I shall be blameless,
And I shall be innocent of
great transgression.

14 [a]Let the words of my mouth and
the meditation of my heart
Be acceptable in Your sight,
O LORD, my strength and
my [b]Redeemer.

Psalm 20

The Assurance of God's Saving Work

To the Chief Musician. A Psalm of David.

1 May the LORD answer you
in the day of trouble;
May the name of the God of
Jacob defend you;
2 May He send you help from
the sanctuary,
And strengthen you out of Zion;
3 May He remember all your offerings,
And accept your burnt sacrifice. *Selah*

4 May He grant you according
to your heart's *desire,*
And [a]fulfill all your purpose.
5 We will rejoice in your salvation,
And in the name of our God we
will set up *our* banners!
May the LORD fulfill all your petitions.

6 Now I know that the LORD
saves His anointed;
He will answer him from
His holy heaven
With the saving strength
of His right hand.

7 Some *trust* in chariots, and
some in [a]horses;
But we will remember the name
of the LORD our God.
8 They have bowed down and fallen;
But we have risen and stand upright.

9 Save, LORD!
May the King answer us when we call.

Psalm 21

Joy in the Salvation of the LORD

To the Chief Musician. A Psalm of David.

1 The king shall have joy in
Your strength, O LORD;
And in Your salvation how
greatly shall he rejoice!
2 You have given him his heart's desire,
And have not withheld the
[a]request of his lips. *Selah*

3 For You meet him with the
blessings of goodness;
You set a crown of pure
gold upon his head.
4 [a]He asked life from You, *and*
You gave *it* to him—
Length of days forever and ever.
5 His glory *is* great in Your salvation;
Honor and majesty You have
placed upon him.
6 For You have made him
most blessed forever;
[a]You have made him exceedingly
glad with Your presence.
7 For the king trusts in the LORD,
And through the mercy of the Most
High he shall not be moved.

8 Your hand will find all Your
enemies;

19:10 [a] Ps. 119:72, 127; Prov. 8:10, 11, 19 19:12 [a] [Ps. 51:1, 2] 19:13 [a] Num. 15:30 [b] Ps. 119:133; [Rom. 6:12–14]
19:14 [a] Ps. 51:15 [b] Ps. 31:5; Is. 47:4 20:4 [a] Ps. 21:2 20:7 [a] Deut. 20:1; Ps. 33:16, 17; Prov. 21:31; Is. 31:1
21:2 [a] 2 Sam. 7:26–29 21:4 [a] Ps. 61:5, 6; 133:3 21:6 [a] Ps. 16:11; 45:7

Your right hand will find
those who hate You.
9 You shall make them as a fiery oven
in the time of Your anger;
The LORD shall swallow
them up in His wrath,
And the fire shall devour them.
10 Their offspring You shall
destroy from the earth,
And their descendants from
among the sons of men.
11 For they intended evil against You;
They devised a plot *which* they
are not able *to* [a]*perform.*
12 Therefore You will make
them turn their back;
You will make ready *Your arrows* on
Your string toward their faces.

13 Be exalted, O LORD, in
Your own strength!
We will sing and praise Your power.

Psalm 22

The Suffering, Praise, and Posterity of the Messiah

To the Chief Musician. Set to "The Deer of the Dawn."[1] A Psalm of David.

1 My [a]God, My God, why have
You forsaken Me?
Why are You so far from helping Me,
And from the words of My groaning?
2 O My God, I cry in the daytime,
but You do not hear;
And in the night season,
and am not silent.

3 But You *are* holy,
Enthroned in the [a]praises of Israel.
4 Our fathers trusted in You;
They trusted, and You delivered
them.
5 They cried to You, and were
delivered;
[a]They trusted in You, and
were not ashamed.

6 But I *am* [a]a worm, and no man;
[b]A reproach of men, and
despised by the people.
7 [a]All those who see Me ridicule Me;
They shoot out the lip, they
shake the head, *saying,*
8 "He[a] trusted[1] in the LORD, let
Him rescue Him;
[b]Let Him deliver Him, since
He delights in Him!"

9 [a]But You *are* He who took
Me out of the womb;
You made Me trust *while* on
My mother's breasts.
10 I was cast upon You from birth.
From My mother's womb
[a]You *have been* My God.
11 Be not far from Me,
For trouble *is* near;
For *there is* none to help.

12 [a]Many bulls have surrounded Me;
Strong *bulls* of [b]Bashan
have encircled Me.
13 [a]They gape at Me *with* their mouths,
Like a raging and roaring lion.

14 I am poured out like water,
[a]And all My bones are out of joint;
My heart is like wax;
It has melted within Me.
15 [a]My strength is dried up
like a potsherd,
And [b]My tongue clings to My jaws;
You have brought Me to
the dust of death.

16 For dogs have surrounded Me;
The congregation of the
wicked has enclosed Me.
[a]They pierced[1] My hands and My feet;
17 I can count all My bones.
[a]They look *and* stare at Me.
18 [a]They divide My garments
among them,
And for My clothing they
cast lots.

21:11 [a] Ps. 2:1–4 **22:title** [1] Hebrew *Aijeleth Hashahar* **22:1** [a] [Matt. 27:46; Mark 15:34] **22:3** [a] Deut. 10:21; Ps. 148:14 **22:5** [a] Is. 49:23 **22:6** [a] Job 25:6; Is. 41:14 [b] Ps. 109:25; [Is. 53:3]; Matt. 27:39–44 **22:7** [a] Matt. 27:39; Mark 15:29 **22:8** [a] Matt. 27:43; Luke 23:35 [b] Ps. 91:14 [1] Septuagint, Syriac, and Vulgate read *hoped;* Targum reads *praised.* **22:9** [a] [Ps. 71:5, 6] **22:10** [a] [Is. 46:3; 49:1]; Luke 1:35 **22:12** [a] Ps. 22:21; 68:30 [b] Deut. 32:14 **22:13** [a] Job 16:10; Ps. 35:21; Lam. 2:16; 3:46 **22:14** [a] Ps. 31:10; Dan. 5:6 **22:15** [a] Prov. 17:22 [b] John 19:28 **22:16** [a] Is. 53:7; Matt. 27:35; John 20:25 [1] Following some Hebrew manuscripts, Septuagint, Syriac, Vulgate; Masoretic Text reads *Like a lion.* **22:17** [a] Luke 23:27, 35 **22:18** [a] Matt. 27:35; Mark 15:24; Luke 23:34; John 19:24

19 But You, O LORD, do not
be far from Me;
O My Strength, hasten to help Me!
20 Deliver Me from the sword,
[a]My precious *life* from the
power of the dog.
21 [a]Save Me from the lion's mouth
And from the horns of the wild oxen!

[b]You have answered Me.

22 [a]I will declare Your name
to [b]My brethren;
In the midst of the assembly
I will praise You.
23 [a]You who fear the LORD, praise Him!
All you descendants of
Jacob, glorify Him,
And fear Him, all you
offspring of Israel!
24 For He has not despised nor abhorred
the affliction of the afflicted;
Nor has He hidden His face from Him;
But [a]when He cried to Him, He heard.

25 [a]My praise *shall be* of You in
the great assembly;
[b]I will pay My vows before
those who fear Him.
26 The poor shall eat and be satisfied;
Those who seek Him will
praise the LORD.
Let your heart live forever!

27 All the ends of the world
Shall remember and turn
to the LORD,
And all the families of the nations
Shall worship before You.[1]
28 [a]For the kingdom *is* the LORD's,
And He rules over the nations.

29 [a]All the prosperous of the earth
Shall eat and worship;
[b]All those who go down to the dust
Shall bow before Him,
Even he who cannot keep
himself alive.

30 A posterity shall serve Him.
It will be recounted of the Lord
to the *next* generation,
31 They will come and declare
His righteousness to a
people who will be born,
That He has done *this*.

Psalm 23

The LORD the Shepherd of His People

A Psalm of David.

1 The LORD *is* [a]my shepherd;
[b]I shall not want.
2 [a]He makes me to lie down
in green pastures;
[b]He leads me beside the still waters.
3 He restores my soul;
[a]He leads me in the paths
of righteousness
For His name's sake.

4 Yea, though I walk through the
valley of [a]the shadow of death,
[b]I will fear no evil;
[c]For You *are* with me;
Your rod and Your staff,
they comfort me.

5 You [a]prepare a table before me in
the presence of my enemies;
You [b]anoint my head with oil;
My cup runs over.
6 Surely goodness and mercy
shall follow me
All the days of my life;
And I will dwell[1] in the
house of the LORD
Forever.

Psalm 24

The King of Glory and His Kingdom

A Psalm of David.

1 The [a]earth *is* the LORD's,
and all its fullness,

22:20 [a] Ps. 35:17 **22:21** [a] 2 Tim. 4:17 [b] Is. 34:7 **22:22** [a] Matt. 4:23; Mark 1:21, 39; Heb. 2:12 [b] [Rom. 8:29] **22:23** [a] Ps. 135:19, 20 **22:24** [a] Ps. 31:22; Heb. 5:7 **22:25** [a] Ps. 35:18; 40:9, 10 [b] Ps. 61:8; Eccl. 5:4 **22:27** [1] Following Masoretic Text, Septuagint, and Targum; Arabic, Syriac, and Vulgate read *Him.* **22:28** [a] [Ps. 47:7]; Obad. 21; [Zech. 14:9]; Matt. 6:13 **22:29** [a] Ps. 17:10; 45:12; Hab. 1:16 [b] Ps. 28:1; [Is. 26:19] **23:1** [a] Ps. 78:52; 80:1; [Is. 40:11]; Ezek. 34:11, 12; [John 10:11; 1 Pet. 2:25; Rev. 7:16, 17] [b] [Ps. 34:9, 10; Phil. 4:19] **23:2** [a] Ps. 65:11–13; Ezek. 34:14 [b] [Rev. 7:17] **23:3** [a] Ps. 5:8; 31:3; Prov. 8:20 **23:4** [a] Job 3:5; 10:21, 22; 24:17; Ps. 44:19 [b] [Ps. 3:6; 27:1] [c] Ps. 16:8; [Is. 43:2] **23:5** [a] Ps. 104:15 [b] Ps. 92:10; Luke 7:46 **23:6** [1] Following Septuagint, Syriac, Targum, and Vulgate; Masoretic Text reads *return.* **24:1** [a] 1 Cor. 10:26, 28

The world and those who
dwell therein.
2 For He has [a]founded it upon the seas,
And established it upon the waters.

3 [a]Who may ascend into the
hill of the LORD?
Or who may stand in His holy place?
4 He who has [a]clean hands
and [b]a pure heart,
Who has not lifted up his
soul to an idol,
Nor [c]sworn deceitfully.
5 He shall receive blessing
from the LORD,
And righteousness from the
God of his salvation.
6 This *is* Jacob, the generation
of those who [a]seek Him,
Who seek Your face. *Selah*

7 [a]Lift up your heads, O you gates!
And be lifted up, you
everlasting doors!
[b]And the King of glory shall come in.
8 Who *is* this King of glory?
The LORD strong and mighty,
The LORD mighty in [a]battle.
9 Lift up your heads, O you gates!
Lift up, you everlasting doors!
And the King of glory shall come in.
10 Who is this King of glory?
The LORD of hosts,
He *is* the King of glory. *Selah*

Psalm 25

A Plea for Deliverance and Forgiveness

A *Psalm* of David.

1 To [a]You, O LORD, I lift up my soul.
2 O my God, I [a]trust in You;
Let me not be ashamed;
[b]Let not my enemies triumph over me.
3 Indeed, let no one who waits
on You be ashamed;
Let those be ashamed who deal
treacherously without cause.

4 [a]Show me Your ways, O LORD;
Teach me Your paths.
5 Lead me in Your truth and teach me,
For You *are* the God of my salvation;
On You I wait all the day.

6 Remember, O LORD, [a]Your tender
mercies and Your lovingkindnesses,
For they *are* from of old.
7 Do not remember [a]the sins of my
youth, nor my transgressions;
[b]According to Your mercy
remember me,
For Your goodness' sake, O LORD.

8 Good and upright *is* the LORD;
Therefore He teaches
sinners in the way.
9 The humble He guides in justice,
And the humble He teaches His way.
10 All the paths of the LORD
are mercy and truth,
To such as keep His covenant
and His testimonies.
11 [a]For Your name's sake, O LORD,
Pardon my iniquity, for it *is* great.

12 Who *is* the man that fears the LORD?
[a]Him shall He[1] teach in the
way He[2] chooses.
13 [a]He himself shall dwell in prosperity,
And [b]his descendants shall
inherit the earth.
14 [a]The secret of the LORD *is* with
those who fear Him,
And He will show them His
covenant.
15 [a]My eyes *are* ever toward the LORD,
For He shall pluck my feet
out of the net.

16 [a]Turn Yourself to me, and
have mercy on me,
For I *am* desolate and afflicted.
17 The troubles of my heart
have enlarged;
Bring me out of my distresses!
18 [a]Look on my affliction and my pain,
And forgive all my sins.

24:2 [a] Ps. 89:11 24:3 [a] Ps. 15:1–5 24:4 [a] [Job 17:9]; Ps. 26:6 [b] Ps. 51:10; 73:1; [Matt. 5:8] [c] Ps. 15:4 24:6 [a] Ps. 27:4, 8
24:7 [a] Ps. 118:20; Is. 26:2 [b] Ps. 29:2, 9; 97:6; Hag. 2:7; Acts 7:2; [1 Cor. 2:8] 24:8 [a] Rev. 19:13–16 25:1 [a] Ps. 86:4; 143:8 25:2 [a] Ps. 34:8
[b] Ps. 13:4; 41:11 25:4 [a] Ex. 33:13; Ps. 5:8; 27:11; 86:11; 119:27; 143:8 25:6 [a] Ps. 103:17; 106:1 25:7 [a] Job 13:26; [Jer. 3:25] [b] Ps. 51:1
25:11 [a] Ps. 31:3; 79:9; 109:21; 143:11 25:12 [a] [Ps. 25:8; 37:23] [1] Or *he* [2] Or *he* 25:13 [a] [Prov. 19:23] [b] Ps. 37:11; 69:36; Matt. 5:5
25:14 [a] [Prov. 3:32; John 7:17] 25:15 [a] [Ps. 123:2; 141:8] 25:16 [a] Ps. 69:16 25:18 [a] 2 Sam. 16:12; Ps. 31:7

19 Consider my enemies, for
they are many;
And they hate me with cruel hatred.
20 Keep my soul, and deliver me;
Let me not be ashamed, for
I put my trust in You.
21 Let integrity and uprightness
preserve me,
For I wait for You.

22 [a]Redeem Israel, O God,
Out of all their troubles!

Psalm 26

A Prayer for Divine Scrutiny and Redemption

A Psalm of David.

1 Vindicate [a]me, O LORD,
For I have [b]walked in my integrity.
[c]I have also trusted in the LORD;
I shall not slip.
2 [a]Examine me, O LORD, and prove me;
Try my mind and my heart.
3 For Your lovingkindness
is before my eyes,
And [a]I have walked in Your truth.
4 I have not [a]sat with idolatrous mortals,
Nor will I go in with hypocrites.
5 I have [a]hated the assembly of evildoers,
And will not sit with the wicked.

6 I will wash my hands in innocence;
So I will go about Your altar, O LORD,
7 That I may proclaim with the
voice of thanksgiving,
And tell of all Your wondrous works.
8 LORD, [a]I have loved the
habitation of Your house,
And the place where Your glory dwells.

9 [a]Do not gather my soul with sinners,
Nor my life with bloodthirsty men,
10 In whose hands *is* a sinister scheme,
And whose right hand is full of [a]bribes.

11 But as for me, I will walk
in my integrity;
Redeem me and be merciful to me.
12 [a]My foot stands in an even place;
In the congregations I will
bless the LORD.

Psalm 27

An Exuberant Declaration of Faith

A Psalm of David.

1 The LORD *is* my [a]light and
my salvation;
Whom shall I fear?
The [b]LORD *is* the strength
of my life;
Of whom shall I be afraid?
2 When the wicked came against me
To [a]eat up my flesh,
My enemies and foes,
They stumbled and fell.
3 [a]Though an army may
encamp against me,
My heart shall not fear;
Though war may rise against me,
In this I *will be* confident.

4 [a]One *thing* I have desired of the LORD,
That will I seek:
That I may [b]dwell in the
house of the LORD
All the days of my life,
To behold the beauty of the LORD,
And to inquire in His temple.
5 For [a]in the time of trouble
He shall hide me in His pavilion;
In the secret place of His
tabernacle
He shall hide me;
He shall [b]set me high upon a rock.

6 And now [a]my head shall be lifted up
above my enemies all around me;
Therefore I will offer sacrifices
of joy in His tabernacle;
I will sing, yes, I will sing
praises to the LORD.

7 Hear, O LORD, *when* I cry
with my voice!
Have mercy also upon me,
and answer me.

25:22 [a] [Ps. 130:8] 26:1 [a] Ps. 7:8 [b] 2 Kin. 20:3; [Prov. 20:7] [c] [Ps. 13:5; 28:7] 26:2 [a] Ps. 17:3; 139:23 26:3 [a] 2 Kin. 20:3; Ps. 86:11 26:4 [a] Ps. 1:1; Jer. 15:17 26:5 [a] Ps. 31:6; 139:21 26:8 [a] Ps. 27:4; 84:1–4, 10 26:9 [a] Ps. 28:3 26:10 [a] 1 Sam. 8:3 26:12 [a] Ps. 40:2 27:1 [a] Ps. 18:28; 84:11; [Is. 60:19, 20; Mic. 7:8] [b] Ex. 15:2; Ps. 62:7; 118:14; Is. 12:2; 33:2 27:2 [a] Ps. 14:4 27:3 [a] Ps. 3:6 27:4 [a] Ps. 26:8; 65:4 [b] Luke 2:37 27:5 [a] Ps. 31:20; 91:1 [b] Ps. 40:2 27:6 [a] Ps. 3:3

8 *When You said,* "Seek My face,"
My heart said to You, "Your
face, LORD, I will seek."
9 [a]Do not hide Your face from me;
Do not turn Your servant
away in anger;
You have been my help;
Do not leave me nor forsake me,
O God of my salvation.
10 [a]When my father and my
mother forsake me,
Then the LORD will take care
of me.

11 [a]Teach me Your way, O LORD,
And lead me in a smooth path,
because of my enemies.
12 Do not deliver me to the will
of my adversaries;
For [a]false witnesses have
risen against me,
And such as breathe out violence.
13 *I would have lost heart,*
unless I had believed
That I would see the
goodness of the LORD
[a]In the land of the living.

14 [a]Wait on the LORD;
Be of good courage,
And He shall strengthen your
heart;
Wait, I say, on the LORD!

Psalm 28

Rejoicing in Answered Prayer

A *Psalm* of David.

1 To You I will cry, O LORD my Rock:
[a]Do not be silent to me,
[b]Lest, if You *are* silent to me,
I become like those who
go down to the pit.
2 Hear the voice of my supplications
When I cry to You,
[a]When I lift up my hands [b]toward
Your holy sanctuary.
3 Do not take me away with the wicked
And with the workers of iniquity,
[a]Who speak peace to their neighbors,
But evil *is* in their hearts.
4 [a]Give them according to their deeds,
And according to the wickedness
of their endeavors;
Give them according to the
work of their hands;
Render to them what they deserve.
5 Because [a]they do not regard
the works of the LORD,
Nor the operation of His hands,
He shall destroy them
And not build them up.

6 Blessed *be* the LORD,
Because He has heard the voice
of my supplications!
7 The LORD *is* [a]my strength
and my shield;
My heart [b]trusted in Him,
and I am helped;
Therefore my heart greatly rejoices,
And with my song I will praise Him.

8 The LORD *is* their strength,[1]
And He *is* the [a]saving refuge
of His anointed.
9 Save Your people,
And bless [a]Your inheritance;
Shepherd them also,
[b]And bear them up forever.

Psalm 29

Praise to God in His Holiness and Majesty

A Psalm of David.

1 Give [a]unto the LORD, O you
mighty ones,
Give unto the LORD glory
and strength.
2 Give unto the LORD the glory
due to His name;
Worship the LORD in [a]the
beauty of holiness.

27:9 [a] Ps. 69:17; 143:7 27:10 [a] Is. 49:15 27:11 [a] Ps. 25:4; 86:11; 119:33 27:12 [a] Deut. 19:18; Ps. 35:11; Matt. 26:60; Mark 14:56; John 19:33 27:13 [a] Job 28:13; Ps. 52:5; 116:9; 142:5; Is. 38:11; Jer. 11:19; Ezek. 26:20 27:14 [a] Ps. 25:3; 37:34; 40:1; 62:5; 130:5; Prov. 20:22; Is. 25:9; [Hab. 2:3] 28:1 [a] Ps. 35:22; 39:12; 83:1 [b] Ps. 88:4; 143:7; Prov. 1:12 28:2 [a] Ps. 5:7 [b] Ps. 138:2 28:3 [a] Ps. 12:2; 55:21; 62:4; Jer. 9:8 28:4 [a] [Ps. 62:12]; 2 Tim. 4:14; [Rev. 18:6; 22:12] 28:5 [a] Is. 5:12 28:7 [a] Ps. 18:2; 59:17 [b] Ps. 13:5; 112:7 28:8 [a] Ps. 20:6 [1] Following Masoretic Text and Targum; Septuagint, Syriac, and Vulgate read *the strength of His people.* 28:9 [a] [Deut. 9:29; 32:9; 1 Kin. 8:51; Ps. 33:12]; 106:40 [b] Deut. 1:31; Is. 63:9 29:1 [a] 1 Chr. 16:28, 29 29:2 [a] 2 Chr. 20:21; Ps. 110:3

3 The voice of the LORD *is*
over the waters;
[a]The God of glory thunders;
The LORD *is* over many waters.
4 The voice of the LORD *is* powerful;
The voice of the LORD *is*
full of majesty.

5 The voice of the LORD
breaks [a]the cedars,
Yes, the LORD splinters the
cedars of Lebanon.
6 [a]He makes them also skip like a calf,
Lebanon and [b]Sirion like
a young wild ox.
7 The voice of the LORD divides
the flames of fire.

8 The voice of the LORD shakes
the wilderness;
The LORD shakes the
Wilderness of [a]Kadesh.
9 The voice of the LORD makes
the [a]deer give birth,
And strips the forests bare;
And in His temple everyone
says, "Glory!"

10 The [a]LORD sat *enthroned*
at the Flood,
And [b]the LORD sits as King forever.
11 [a]The LORD will give strength
to His people;
The LORD will bless His
people with peace.

Psalm 30

The Blessedness of Answered Prayer

A Psalm. A Song [a]at the dedication
of the house of David.

1 I will extol You, O LORD, for
You have [a]lifted me up,
And have not let my foes
[b]rejoice over me.
2 O LORD my God, I cried out to You,
And You [a]healed me.
3 O LORD, [a]You brought my soul
up from the grave;
You have kept me alive, that I
should not go down to the pit.[1]

4 [a]Sing praise to the LORD,
you saints of His,
And give thanks at the remembrance
of His holy name.[1]
5 For [a]His anger *is but for* a moment,
[b]His favor *is for* life;
Weeping may endure for a night,
But joy *comes* in the morning.

6 Now in my prosperity I said,
"I shall never be moved."
7 LORD, by Your favor You have made
my mountain stand strong;
[a]You hid Your face, *and* I was troubled.

8 I cried out to You, O LORD;
And to the LORD I made supplication:
9 "What profit *is there* in my blood,
When I go down to the pit?
[a]Will the dust praise You?
Will it declare Your truth?
10 Hear, O LORD, and have mercy on me;
LORD, be my helper!"

11 [a]You have turned for me my
mourning into dancing;
You have put off my sackcloth and
clothed me with gladness,
12 To the end that *my* glory may sing
praise to You and not be silent.
O LORD my God, I will give
thanks to You forever.

Psalm 31

The LORD a Fortress in Adversity

To the Chief Musician. A Psalm of David.

1 In [a]You, O LORD, I put my trust;
Let me never be ashamed;
Deliver me in Your righteousness.
2 [a]Bow down Your ear to me,
Deliver me speedily;

29:3 [a] [Job 37:4, 5]; Ps. 18:13; Acts 7:2 29:5 [a] Judg. 9:15; 1 Kin. 5:6; Ps. 104:16; Is. 2:13; 14:8 29:6 [a] Ps. 114:4 [b] Deut. 3:9
29:8 [a] Num. 13:26 29:9 [a] Job 39:1 29:10 [a] Gen. 6:17; Job 38:8, 25 [b] Ps. 10:16 29:11 [a] Ps. 28:8; 68:35; [Is. 40:29]
30:title [a] Deut. 20:5 30:1 [a] Ps. 28:9 [b] Ps. 25:2 30:2 [a] Ps. 6:2; 103:3; [Is. 53:5] 30:3 [a] Ps. 86:13 [1] Following Qere and Targum; Kethib, Septuagint, Syriac, and Vulgate read *from those who descend to the pit.* 30:4 [a] Ps. 97:12 [1] Or *His holiness*
30:5 [a] Ps. 103:9; Is. 26:20; 54:7, 8 [b] Ps. 63:3 30:7 [a] [Deut. 31:17; Ps. 104:29; 143:7] 30:9 [a] [Ps. 6:5]
30:11 [a] Eccl. 3:4; Is. 61:3; Jer. 31:4 31:1 [a] Ps. 22:5 31:2 [a] Ps. 17:6; 71:2; 86:1; 102:2

Be my rock of refuge,
A fortress of defense to save me.

3 [a]For You *are* my rock and my fortress;
Therefore, [b]for Your name's sake,
Lead me and guide me.
4 Pull me out of the net which they
have secretly laid for me,
For You *are* my strength.
5 [a]Into Your hand I commit my spirit;
You have redeemed me,
O LORD God of [b]truth.

6 I have hated those [a]who
regard useless idols;
But I trust in the LORD.
7 I will be glad and rejoice
in Your mercy,
For You have considered my trouble;
You have [a]known my soul
in adversities,
8 And have not [a]shut me up into
the hand of the enemy;
[b]You have set my feet in a wide place.

9 Have mercy on me, O LORD,
for I am in trouble;
[a]My eye wastes away with grief,
Yes, my soul and my body!
10 For my life is spent with grief,
And my years with sighing;
My strength fails because
of my iniquity,
And my bones waste away.
11 [a]I am a reproach among
all my enemies,
But [b]especially among my
neighbors,
And *am* repulsive to my
acquaintances;
[c]Those who see me outside
flee from me.
12 [a]I am forgotten like a dead
man, out of mind;
I am like a broken vessel.
13 [a]For I hear the slander of many;
[b]Fear *is* on every side;
While they [c]take counsel
together against me,
They scheme to take away my life.

14 But as for me, I trust in You, O LORD;
I say, "You *are* my God."
15 My times *are* in Your [a]hand;
Deliver me from the hand
of my enemies,
And from those who persecute me.
16 [a]Make Your face shine upon
Your servant;
Save me for Your mercies' sake.
17 [a]Do not let me be ashamed, O LORD,
for I have called upon You;
Let the wicked be ashamed;
[b]Let them be silent in the grave.
18 [a]Let the lying lips be put to silence,
Which [b]speak insolent things
proudly and contemptuously
against the righteous.

19 [a]Oh, how great *is* Your goodness,
Which You have laid up for
those who fear You,
Which You have prepared for
those who trust in You
In the presence of the sons of men!
20 [a]You shall hide them in the secret
place of Your presence
From the plots of man;
[b]You shall keep them secretly
in a pavilion
From the strife of tongues.

21 Blessed *be* the LORD,
For [a]He has shown me His marvelous
kindness in a strong city!
22 For I said in my haste,
"I am cut off from before Your eyes";
Nevertheless You heard the
voice of my supplications
When I cried out to You.

23 Oh, love the LORD, all you His
saints!
For the LORD preserves the faithful,
And fully repays the proud person.
24 [a]Be of good courage,
And He shall strengthen your heart,
All you who hope in the LORD.

31:3 [a] [Ps. 18:2] [b] Ps. 23:3; 25:11 31:5 [a] Luke 23:46 [b] [Deut. 32:4]; Ps. 71:22 31:6 [a] Jon. 2:8 31:7 [a] [John 10:27] 31:8 [a] [Deut. 32:30]; Ps. 37:33 [b] [Ps. 4:1; 18:19] 31:9 [a] Ps. 6:7 31:11 [a] [Is. 53:4] [b] Job 19:13; Ps. 38:11; 88:8, 18 [c] Ps. 64:8 31:12 [a] Ps. 88:4, 5 31:13 [a] Ps. 50:20; Jer. 20:10 [b] Lam. 2:22 [c] Ps. 62:4; Matt. 27:1 31:15 [a] [Job 14:5; 24:1] 31:16 [a] Ps. 4:6; 80:3 31:17 [a] Ps. 25:2, 20 [b] [1 Sam. 2:9]; Ps. 94:17; 115:17 31:18 [a] Ps. 109:2; 120:2 [b] [1 Sam. 2:3]; Ps. 94:4; [Jude 15] 31:19 [a] Ps. 145:7; [Rom. 2:4; 11:22] 31:20 [a] [Ps. 27:5; 32:7] [b] Job 5:21 31:21 [a] [Ps. 17:7] 31:24 [a] [Ps. 27:14]

Psalm 32

The Joy of Forgiveness

A Psalm of David. A Contemplation.[1]

1 Blessed *is he whose*
[a]transgression *is* forgiven,
Whose sin *is* covered.
2 Blessed *is* the man to whom the
LORD [a]does not impute iniquity,
And [b]in whose spirit *there is* no deceit.

3 When I kept silent, my bones grew old
Through my groaning all the day long.
4 For day and night Your [a]hand
was heavy upon me;
My vitality was turned into the
drought of summer. *Selah*
5 I acknowledged my sin to You,
And my iniquity I have not hidden.
[a]I said, "I will confess my
transgressions to the LORD,"
And You forgave the iniquity
of my sin. *Selah*

6 [a]For this cause everyone who is
godly shall [b]pray to You
In a time when You may be found;
Surely in a flood of great waters
They shall not come near him.
7 [a]You *are* my hiding place;
You shall preserve me from
trouble;
You shall surround me with
[b]songs of deliverance. *Selah*

8 I will instruct you and teach you
in the way you should go;
I will guide you with My eye.
9 Do not be like the [a]horse
or like the mule,
Which have no understanding,
Which must be harnessed
with bit and bridle,
Else they will not come near you.

10 [a]Many sorrows *shall be* to the wicked;
But [b]he who trusts in the LORD,
mercy shall surround him.
11 [a]Be glad in the LORD and
rejoice, you righteous;
And shout for joy, all *you*
upright in heart!

Psalm 33

The Sovereignty of the LORD in Creation and History

1 Rejoice [a]in the LORD, O you
righteous!
For praise from the upright
is beautiful.
2 Praise the LORD with the harp;
Make melody to Him with an
instrument of ten strings.
3 Sing to Him a new song;
Play skillfully with a shout of joy.

4 For the word of the LORD *is* right,
And all His work *is done* in truth.
5 He loves righteousness and justice;
The earth is full of the
goodness of the LORD.

6 [a]By the word of the LORD the
heavens were made,
And all the [b]host of them [c]by
the breath of His mouth.
7 [a]He gathers the waters of the
sea together as a heap;[1]
He lays up the deep in storehouses.

8 Let all the earth fear the LORD;
Let all the inhabitants of the
world stand in awe of Him.
9 For [a]He spoke, and it was *done;*
He commanded, and it stood fast.

10 [a]The LORD brings the counsel of
the nations to nothing;
He makes the plans of the
peoples of no effect.
11 [a]The counsel of the LORD
stands forever,
The plans of His heart to
all generations.

32:title [1] Hebrew *Maschil* 32:1 [a] [Ps. 85:2; 103:3]; Rom. 4:7, 8 32:2 [a] [2 Cor. 5:19] [b] John 1:47 32:4 [a] 1 Sam. 5:6; Ps. 38:2; 39:10 32:5 [a] 2 Sam. 12:13; Ps. 38:18; [Prov. 28:13; 1 John 1:9] 32:6 [a] [1 Tim. 1:16] [b] Ps. 69:13; Is. 55:6 32:7 [a] Ps. 9:9 [b] Ex. 15:1; Judg. 5:1; [Ps. 40:3] 32:9 [a] Prov. 26:3 32:10 [a] Ps. 16:4; [Prov. 13:21; Rom. 2:9] [b] [Ps. 5:11, 12]; Prov. 16:20 32:11 [a] Ps. 64:10; 68:3; 97:12 33:1 [a] Ps. 32:11; 97:12; Phil. 3:1; 4:4 33:6 [a] Gen. 1:6, 7; Ps. 148:5; [Heb. 11:3; 2 Pet. 3:5] [b] Gen. 2:1 [c] [Job 26:13] 33:7 [a] Gen. 1:9; Job 26:10; 38:8 [1] Septuagint, Targum, and Vulgate read *in a vessel.* 33:9 [a] Gen. 1:3; Ps. 148:5 33:10 [a] [Ps. 2:1–3]; Is. 8:10; 19:3 33:11 [a] [Job 23:13; Prov. 19:21]

RELEASE // RECONCILE WRONGS WITH RIGHTS

Let's Settle It

Psalm 33:5 // He loves righteousness and justice; the earth is full of the goodness of the LORD.

Summary Message // The world seems out of control. Spiritual principles are unpopular, and the world has discarded even the most common definition of what is right and wrong. Hate is rampant and played out every day in the news. So, what are we, as followers of Christ, to do? It is time for us to lead our communities, countries, and world in reconciliation. However, first we need to look deeply at the word *reconcile* to address the real issue. To reconcile means "to make good again" or, specifically, "to repair a relationship." Reconciliation applies not only to individuals but to societies too. As the sins of the world continue to take over, we only have one way to align all relationships, and that way is by seeking God, who can bring peace between people. Believers are to seek after that which is right, just, and peaceful according to the Word of God.

Practical Application // Psalm 33:5 lends depth to a New Testament truth found in Romans 12:18: "If it is possible, as much as depends on you, live peaceably with all men." The phrase "as much as depends on you" suggests that we should put forth extreme effort to get along with others no matter our differences. This is a personal call, and God will judge us for our actions, not the actions of others. So, the way we live and the way we respond to circumstances cannot be based upon the way others live or the way they respond to us. We cannot let the world be our model for how we should behave, but at all times we must be guided by the Holy Spirit and the Word of God, which tell the following:

- God's justice must reign (see Ps. 33:5).
- Darkened understanding seeks injustice (see Eph. 4:18).
- Believers should seek to do as God commands (see John 14:15).

Those of us who say we love Jesus must spread God's goodness and not evil. If we say we love God, we must choose to love everyone and everything He loves. We are to love even those people we find unlikable. We must seek to be reconciled with both God and others. Then, the Lord's goodness will be spread across the earth.

Fervent Prayer // Heavenly Father, breathe on us today and have mercy. Reveal by Your Spirit what is right and wrong. Give us pure and repentant hearts so we will turn from our wrongs and embrace what is right. Bless our nation with Your love. Help us to agree to disagree when needed and treat everyone with respect and dignity. Bless the peacemakers of this world and give us power over evil. In Jesus' name we pray. Amen.

---

12 Blessed *is* the nation whose
God *is* the LORD,
The people He has [a]chosen as
His own inheritance.

13 [a]The LORD looks from heaven;
He sees all the sons of men.
14 From the place of His
dwelling He looks
On all the inhabitants of the earth;
15 He fashions their hearts
individually;
[a]He considers all their works.

16 [a]No king *is* saved by the
multitude of an army;
A mighty man is not delivered
by great strength.
17 [a]A horse *is* a vain hope for safety;
Neither shall it deliver *any*
by its great strength.

18 [a]Behold, the eye of the LORD *is*
on those who fear Him,
On those who hope in His mercy,
19 To deliver their soul from death,
And [a]to keep them alive in famine.

33:12 [a] [Ex. 19:5; Deut. 7:6]; Ps. 28:9 33:13 [a] Job 28:24; [Ps. 14:2] 33:15 [a] [2 Chr. 16:9]; Job 34:21; [Jer. 32:19] 33:16 [a] Ps. 44:6; 60:11; [Jer. 9:23, 24] 33:17 [a] [Ps. 20:7; 147:10; Prov. 21:31] 33:18 [a] [Job 36:7]; Ps. 32:8; 34:15; [1 Pet. 3:12] 33:19 [a] Job 5:20; Ps. 37:19

20 Our soul waits for the LORD;
He *is* our help and our shield.
21 For our heart shall rejoice in Him,
Because we have trusted
in His holy name.
22 Let Your mercy, O LORD, be upon us,
Just as we hope in You.

Psalm 34

The Happiness of Those Who Trust in God

A Psalm of David [a]when he pretended madness before Abimelech, who drove him away, and he departed.

1 I will [a]bless the LORD at all times;
His praise *shall* continually
be in my mouth.
2 My soul shall make its
boast in the LORD;
The humble shall hear *of*
it and be glad.
3 Oh, magnify the LORD with me,
And let us exalt His name together.

4 I [a]sought the LORD, and He heard me,
And delivered me from all my fears.
5 They looked to Him and were radiant,
And their faces were not ashamed.
6 This poor man cried out, and
the LORD heard *him*,
And saved him out of all his troubles.
7 [a]The angel[1] of the LORD [b]encamps
all around those who fear Him,
And delivers them.

8 Oh, [a]taste and see that
the LORD *is* good;
[b]Blessed *is* the man *who* trusts
in Him!
9 Oh, fear the LORD, you His saints!
There is no want to those
who fear Him.
10 The young lions lack and
suffer hunger;
[a]But those who seek the LORD shall
not lack any good *thing*.

11 Come, you children, listen to me;
[a]I will teach you the fear of the LORD.
12 [a]Who *is* the man *who* desires life,
And loves *many* days, that
he may see good?
13 Keep your tongue from evil,
And your lips from speaking [a]deceit.
14 [a]Depart from evil and do good;
[b]Seek peace and pursue it.

15 [a]The eyes of the LORD *are*
on the righteous,
And His ears *are open* to their cry.
16 [a]The face of the LORD *is* against
those who do evil,
[b]To cut off the remembrance
of them from the earth.

17 *The righteous* cry out, and
[a]the LORD hears,
And delivers them out of
all their troubles.
18 [a]The LORD *is* near [b]to those who
have a broken heart,
And saves such as have
a contrite spirit.

19 [a]Many *are* the afflictions
of the righteous,
[b]But the LORD delivers him
out of them all.
20 He guards all his bones;
[a]Not one of them is broken.
21 [a]Evil shall slay the wicked,
And those who hate the righteous
shall be condemned.
22 The LORD [a]redeems the
soul of His servants,
And none of those who trust in
Him shall be condemned.

Psalm 35

The LORD the Avenger of His People

A Psalm of David.

1 Plead *my cause,* O LORD, with
those who strive with me;

34:title [a] 1 Sam. 21:10–15 34:1 [a] [Eph. 5:20; 1 Thess. 5:18] 34:4 [a] [2 Chr. 15:2; Ps. 9:10; Matt. 7:7; Luke 11:9] 34:7 [a] [Ps. 91:11]; Dan. 6:22 [b] 2 Kin. 6:17 [1] Or *Angel* 34:8 [a] Ps. 119:103; [Heb. 6:5]; 1 Pet. 2:3 [b] Ps. 2:12 34:10 [a] [Ps. 84:11] 34:11 [a] Ps. 32:8 34:12 [a] [1 Pet. 3:10–12] 34:13 [a] [Eph. 4:25] 34:14 [a] Ps. 37:27; Is. 1:16, 17 [b] [Rom. 14:19; Heb. 12:14] 34:15 [a] Job 36:7; [Ps. 33:18] 34:16 [a] Lev. 17:10; Jer. 44:11; Amos 9:4 [b] Job 18:17; Ps. 9:6; 109:15; [Prov. 10:7] 34:17 [a] Ps. 34:6; 145:19 34:18 [a] [Ps. 145:18] [b] Ps. 51:17; [Is. 57:15] 34:19 [a] Prov. 24:16 [b] Ps. 34:4, 6, 17 34:20 [a] John 19:33, 36 34:21 [a] Ps. 94:23; 140:11; Prov. 24:16 34:22 [a] 1 Kin. 1:29

Fight against those who
fight against me.
2 Take hold of shield and buckler,
And stand up for my help.
3 Also draw out the spear,
And stop those who pursue me.
Say to my soul,
"I *am* your salvation."

4 [a]Let those be put to shame and
brought to dishonor
Who seek after my life;
Let those be [b]turned back and
brought to confusion
Who plot my hurt.
5 [a]Let them be like chaff before the wind,
And let the angel[1] of the
LORD chase *them.*
6 Let their way be [a]dark and slippery,
And let the angel of the
LORD pursue them.
7 For without cause they have [a]hidden
their net for me *in* a pit,
Which they have dug without
cause for my life.
8 Let [a]destruction come upon
him unexpectedly,
And let his net that he has
hidden catch himself;
Into that very destruction let him fall.

9 And my soul shall be
joyful in the LORD;
It shall rejoice in His salvation.
10 [a]All my bones shall say,
"LORD, [b]who *is* like You,
Delivering the poor from him
who is too strong for him,
Yes, the poor and the needy from
him who plunders him?"

11 Fierce witnesses rise up;
They ask me *things* that I do not know.
12 [a]They reward me evil for good,
To the sorrow of my soul.
13 But as for me, [a]when they were sick,
My clothing *was* sackcloth;
I humbled myself with fasting;
And my prayer would return
to my own heart.
14 I paced about as though *he were*
my friend *or* brother;
I bowed down heavily, as one
who mourns *for his* mother.

15 But in my adversity they rejoiced
And gathered together;
Attackers gathered against me,
And I did not know *it;*
They tore *at me* and did not cease;
16 With ungodly mockers at feasts
They gnashed at me with their teeth.

17 Lord, how long will You [a]look on?
Rescue me from their destructions,
My precious *life* from the lions.
18 I will give You thanks in
the great assembly;
I will praise You among many
people.

19 [a]Let them not rejoice over me who
are wrongfully my enemies;
Nor let them wink with the eye
who hate me without a cause.
20 For they do not speak peace,
But they devise deceitful matters
Against *the* quiet ones in the land.
21 They also opened their mouth
wide against me,
And said, "Aha, aha!
Our eyes have seen *it.*"

22 *This* You have seen, O LORD;
Do not keep silence.
O Lord, do not be far from me.
23 Stir up Yourself, and awake
to my vindication,
To my cause, my God and my Lord.
24 Vindicate me, O LORD my God,
according to Your righteousness;
And let them not rejoice over me.
25 Let them not say in their hearts,
"Ah, so we would have it!"
Let them not say, "We have
swallowed him up."

26 Let them be ashamed and brought
to mutual confusion
Who rejoice at my hurt;

35:4 [a] Ps. 40:14, 15; 70:2, 3 [b] Ps. 129:5 35:5 [a] Job 21:18; Ps. 83:13; Is. 29:5 [1] Or *Angel* 35:6 [a] Ps. 73:18; Jer. 23:12 35:7 [a] Ps. 9:15
35:8 [a] [Ps. 55:23]; Is. 47:11; [1 Thess. 5:3] 35:10 [a] Ps. 51:8 [b] [Ex. 15:11]; Ps. 71:19; 86:8; [Mic. 7:18]
35:12 [a] Ps. 38:20; 109:5; Jer. 18:20; John 10:32 35:13 [a] Job 30:25 35:17 [a] Ps. 13:1; [Hab. 1:13]
35:19 [a] Ps. 69:4; 109:3; Lam. 3:52; [John 15:25]

Let them be [a]clothed with
shame and dishonor
Who exalt themselves against me.

27 [a]Let them shout for joy and be glad,
Who favor my righteous cause;
And let them say continually,
"Let the LORD be magnified,
Who has pleasure in the
prosperity of His servant."
28 And my tongue shall speak
of Your righteousness
And of Your praise all the day long.

Psalm 36

Man's Wickedness and God's Perfections

To the Chief Musician. *A Psalm* of David
the servant of the LORD.

1 An oracle within my heart concerning
the transgression of the wicked:
[a]*There is* no fear of God before his eyes.
2 For he flatters himself in his own eyes,
When he finds out his iniquity
and when he hates.
3 The words of his mouth *are*
wickedness and deceit;
[a]He has ceased to be wise
and to do good.
4 [a]He devises wickedness on his bed;
He sets himself [b]in a way
that is not good;
He does not abhor [c]evil.

5 Your mercy, O LORD, *is* in the heavens;
Your faithfulness *reaches*
to the clouds.
6 Your righteousness *is* like
the great mountains;
[a]Your judgments *are* a great deep;
O LORD, You preserve man and beast.

7 How precious *is* Your
lovingkindness, O God!
Therefore the children of men
[a]put their trust under the
shadow of Your wings.
8 [a]They are abundantly satisfied with
the fullness of Your house,
And You give them drink from
[b]the river of Your pleasures.
9 [a]For with You *is* the fountain of life;
[b]In Your light we see light.

10 Oh, continue Your lovingkindness
to those who know You,
And Your righteousness to
the upright in heart.
11 Let not the foot of pride
come against me,
And let not the hand of the
wicked drive me away.
12 There the workers of
iniquity have fallen;
They have been cast down
and are not able to rise.

Psalm 37

The Heritage of the Righteous and the Calamity of the Wicked

A Psalm of David.

1 Do[a] not fret because of evildoers,
Nor be envious of the
workers of iniquity.
2 For they shall soon be cut
down [a]like the grass,
And wither as the green herb.

3 Trust in the LORD, and do good;
Dwell in the land, and feed
on His faithfulness.
4 [a]Delight yourself also in the LORD,
And He shall give you the
desires of your [b]heart.

5 [a]Commit your way to the LORD,
Trust also in Him,
And He shall bring *it* to pass.
6 [a]He shall bring forth your
righteousness as the light,
And your justice as the noonday.

7 Rest in the LORD, [a]and wait
patiently for Him;

35:26 [a] Ps. 109:29 35:27 [a] Rom. 12:15 36:1 [a] Rom. 3:18 36:3 [a] Ps. 94:8; Jer. 4:22 36:4 [a] Prov. 4:16; [Mic. 2:1] [b] Is. 65:2 [c] [Ps. 52:3; Rom. 12:9] 36:6 [a] Job 11:8; Ps. 77:19; [Rom. 11:33] 36:7 [a] Ruth 2:12; Ps. 17:8; 57:1; 91:4 36:8 [a] Ps. 63:5; 65:4; Is. 25:6; Jer. 31:12–14 [b] Ps. 46:4; Rev. 22:1 36:9 [a] [Jer. 2:13; John 4:10, 14] [b] [1 Pet. 2:9] 37:1 [a] Ps. 73:3; [Prov. 23:17; 24:19] 37:2 [a] Job 14:2; Ps. 90:5, 6; 92:7; James 1:11 37:4 [a] Job 22:26; Ps. 94:19; Is. 58:14 [b] Ps. 21:2; 145:19; [Matt. 7:7, 8] 37:5 [a] [Ps. 55:22; Prov. 16:3; 1 Pet. 5:7] 37:6 [a] Job 11:17; [Is. 58:8, 10] 37:7 [a] Ps. 40:1; 62:5; [Lam. 3:26]

Do not fret because of him who
[b]prospers in his way,
Because of the man who brings
wicked schemes to pass.
8 [a]Cease from anger, and forsake wrath;
[b]Do not fret—*it* only *causes* harm.

9 For evildoers shall be cut off;
But those who wait on the LORD,
They shall [a]inherit the earth.
10 For [a]yet a little while and the
wicked *shall be* no *more;*
Indeed, [b]you will look
carefully for his place,
But it *shall be* no *more.*
11 [a]But the meek shall inherit the earth,
And shall delight themselves in
the abundance of peace.

12 The wicked plots against the just,
[a]And gnashes at him with his teeth.
13 [a]The Lord laughs at him,
For He sees that [b]his day is coming.
14 The wicked have drawn the sword
And have bent their bow,
To cast down the poor and needy,
To slay those who are of
upright conduct.
15 Their sword shall enter
their own heart,
And their bows shall be broken.

16 [a]A little that a righteous man has
Is better than the riches
of many wicked.
17 For the arms of the wicked
shall be broken,
But the LORD upholds the righteous.

18 The LORD knows the days
of the upright,
And their inheritance shall
be forever.
19 They shall not be ashamed
in the evil time,
And in the days of famine
they shall be satisfied.
20 But the wicked shall perish;
And the enemies of the LORD,
Like the splendor of the
meadows, shall vanish.
Into smoke they shall vanish away.

21 The wicked borrows and
does not repay,
But [a]the righteous shows
mercy and gives.
22 [a]For *those* blessed by Him
shall inherit the earth,
But *those* cursed by Him
shall be cut off.

23 [a]The steps of a *good* man are
ordered by the LORD,
And He delights in his way.
24 [a]Though he fall, he shall not
be utterly cast down;
For the LORD upholds *him*
with His hand.

25 I have been young, and *now* am old;
Yet I have not seen the
righteous forsaken,
Nor his descendants begging bread.
26 [a]*He is* ever merciful, and lends;
And his descendants *are* blessed.

27 Depart from evil, and do good;
And dwell forevermore.
28 For the LORD loves justice,
And does not forsake His saints;
They are preserved forever,
But the descendants of the
wicked shall be cut off.
29 [a]The righteous shall inherit the land,
And dwell in it forever.

30 [a]The mouth of the righteous
speaks wisdom,
And his tongue talks of justice.
31 The law of his God *is* in his heart;
None of his steps shall slide.

32 The wicked [a]watches the righteous,
And seeks to slay him.
33 The LORD [a]will not leave
him in his hand,
Nor condemn him when he is judged.

37:7 [b] [Ps. 73:3–12] 37:8 [a] [Eph. 4:26] [b] Ps. 73:3 37:9 [a] Ps. 25:13; Prov. 2:21; [Is. 57:13; 60:21; Matt. 5:5] 37:10 [a] [Heb. 10:37] [b] Job 7:10; Ps. 37:35, 36 37:11 [a] [Matt. 5:5] 37:12 [a] Ps. 35:16 37:13 [a] Ps. 2:4; 59:8 [b] 1 Sam. 26:10; Job 18:20 37:16 [a] Prov. 15:16; 16:8; [1 Tim. 6:6] 37:21 [a] Ps. 112:5, 9 37:22 [a] [Prov. 3:33] 37:23 [a] [1 Sam. 2:9]; Ps. 40:2; 66:9; 119:5 37:24 [a] Prov. 24:16 37:26 [a] [Deut. 15:8]; Ps. 37:21 37:29 [a] Ps. 37:9; Prov. 2:21 37:30 [a] [Matt. 12:35] 37:32 [a] Ps. 10:8; 17:11 37:33 [a] Ps. 31:8; [2 Pet. 2:9]

34 [a]Wait on the LORD,
And keep His way,
And He shall exalt you to
inherit the land;
When the wicked are cut
off, you shall see *it.*
35 I have seen the wicked in great power,
And spreading himself like
a native green tree.
36 Yet he passed away,[1] and
behold, he *was* no *more;*
Indeed I sought him, but he
could not be found.

37 Mark the blameless *man,* and
observe the upright;
For the future of *that* man *is* peace.
38 [a]But the transgressors shall
be destroyed together;
The future of the wicked
shall be cut off.

39 But the salvation of the righteous
is from the LORD;
He is their strength [a]in the
time of trouble.
40 And [a]the LORD shall help
them and deliver them;
He shall deliver them from
the wicked,
And save them,
[b]Because they trust in Him.

Psalm 38

Prayer in Time of Chastening

A Psalm of David. [a]To bring
to remembrance.

1 O LORD, do not [a]rebuke
me in Your wrath,
Nor chasten me in Your
hot displeasure!
2 For Your arrows pierce me deeply,
And Your hand presses me down.

3 *There is* no soundness in my flesh
Because of Your anger,
Nor *any* health in my bones
Because of my sin.
4 For my iniquities have
gone over my head;
Like a heavy burden they
are too heavy for me.
5 My wounds are foul *and* festering
Because of my foolishness.

6 I am troubled, I am bowed
down greatly;
I go mourning all the day long.
7 For my loins are full of inflammation,
And *there is* no soundness
in my flesh.
8 I am feeble and severely broken;
I groan because of the
turmoil of my heart.

9 Lord, all my desire *is* before You;
And my sighing is not
hidden from You.
10 My heart pants, my strength fails me;
As for the light of my eyes, it
also has gone from me.

11 My loved ones and my friends
[a]stand aloof from my plague,
And my relatives stand afar off.
12 Those also who seek my life
lay snares *for me;*
Those who seek my hurt
speak of destruction,
And plan deception all the day long.

13 But I, like a deaf *man,* do not hear;
And *I am* like a mute *who* does
not open his mouth.
14 Thus I am like a man who
does not hear,
And in whose mouth *is* no response.

15 For in You, O LORD, [a]I hope;
You will hear, O Lord my God.
16 For I said, "*Hear me,* lest
they rejoice over me,
Lest, when my foot slips, they
exalt *themselves* against me."

17 [a]For I *am* ready to fall,
And my sorrow *is* continually
before me.

37:34 [a] Ps. 27:14; 37:9 37:36 [1] Following Masoretic Text, Septuagint, and Targum; Syriac and Vulgate read *I passed by.*
37:38 [a] [Ps. 1:4–6; 37:20, 28] 37:39 [a] Ps. 9:9; 37:19 37:40 [a] Ps. 22:4; Is. 31:5; Dan. 3:17; 6:23 [b] 1 Chr. 5:20; Ps. 34:22
38:title [a] Ps. 70:title 38:1 [a] Ps. 6:1 38:11 [a] Ps. 31:11; 88:18 38:15 [a] [Ps. 39:7] 38:17 [a] Ps. 51:3

18 For I will [a]declare my iniquity;
I will be [b]in anguish over my sin.
19 But my enemies *are* vigorous,
and they are strong;
And those who hate me
wrongfully have multiplied.
20 Those also [a]who render evil
for good,
They are my adversaries, because
I follow *what is* good.

21 Do not forsake me, O LORD;
O my God, [a]be not far from me!
22 Make haste to help me,
O Lord, my salvation!

Psalm 39

Prayer for Wisdom and Forgiveness

To the Chief Musician. To Jeduthun.
A Psalm of David.

1 I said, "I will guard my ways,
Lest I sin with my [a]tongue;
I will restrain my mouth
with a muzzle,
While the wicked are before me."
2 [a]I was mute with silence,
I held my peace *even* from good;
And my sorrow was stirred up.
3 My heart was hot within me;
While I was musing, the fire burned.
Then I spoke with my tongue:

4 "LORD, [a]make me to know my end,
And what *is* the measure of my days,
That I may know how frail I *am.*
5 Indeed, You have made my
days *as* handbreadths,
And my age *is* as nothing before You;
Certainly every man at his best
state *is* but [a]vapor. *Selah*
6 Surely every man walks
about like a shadow;
Surely they busy themselves
in vain;
He heaps up *riches,*
And does not know who
will gather them.

7 "And now, Lord, what do I wait for?
My [a]hope *is* in You.
8 Deliver me from all my
transgressions;
Do not make me [a]the reproach
of the foolish.
9 [a]I was mute, I did not open my mouth,
Because it was [b]You who did *it.*
10 [a]Remove Your plague from me;
I am consumed by the
blow of Your hand.
11 When with rebukes You correct
man for iniquity,
You make his beauty [a]melt
away like a moth;
Surely every man *is* vapor. *Selah*

12 "Hear my prayer, O LORD,
And give ear to my cry;
Do not be silent at my tears;
For I *am* a stranger with You,
A sojourner, [a]as all my fathers *were.*
13 [a]Remove Your gaze from me,
that I may regain strength,
Before I go away and [b]am no more."

Psalm 40

Faith Persevering in Trial

(Ps. 70:1–5)

To the Chief Musician. A Psalm of David.

1 I [a]waited patiently for the LORD;
And He inclined to me,
And heard my cry.
2 He also brought me up out
of a horrible pit,
Out of [a]the miry clay,
And [b]set my feet upon a rock,
And established my steps.
3 [a]He has put a new song in my mouth—
Praise to our God;
Many will see *it* and fear,
And will trust in the LORD.

4 [a]Blessed *is* that man who makes
the LORD his trust,
And does not respect the proud,
nor such as turn aside to lies.

38:18 [a] Ps. 32:5 [b] [2 Cor. 7:9, 10] 38:20 [a] Ps. 35:12 38:21 [a] Ps. 22:19; 35:22 39:1 [a] Job 2:10; Ps. 34:13; [James 3:5–12] 39:2 [a] Ps. 38:13 39:4 [a] Ps. 90:12; 119:84 39:5 [a] Ps. 62:9; [Eccl. 6:12] 39:7 [a] Ps. 38:15 39:8 [a] Ps. 44:13; 79:4; 119:22 39:9 [a] Ps. 39:2 [b] 2 Sam. 16:10; Job 2:10 39:10 [a] Job 9:34; 13:21 39:11 [a] Job 13:28; [Ps. 90:7]; Is. 50:9 39:12 [a] Gen. 47:9; Lev. 25:23; 1 Chr. 29:15; Ps. 119:19; Heb. 11:13; 1 Pet. 2:11 39:13 [a] Job 7:19; 10:20, 21; 14:6; Ps. 102:24 [b] [Job 14:10] 40:1 [a] Ps. 25:5; 27:14; 37:7 40:2 [a] Ps. 69:2, 14; Jer. 38:6 [b] Ps. 27:5 40:3 [a] Ps. 32:7; 33:3 40:4 [a] Ps. 34:8; 84:12

5 [a]Many, O LORD my God, *are*
Your wonderful works
Which You have done;
[b]And Your thoughts toward us
Cannot be recounted to You in order;
If I would declare and speak *of them,*
They are more than can be numbered.

6 [a]Sacrifice and offering You
did not desire;
My ears You have opened.
Burnt offering and sin offering
You did not require.
7 Then I said, "Behold, I come;
In the scroll of the book *it*
is written of me.
8 [a]I delight to do Your will, O my God,
And Your law *is* [b]within my heart."

9 [a]I have proclaimed the good
news of righteousness
In the great assembly;
Indeed, [b]I do not restrain my lips,
O LORD, You Yourself know.
10 [a]I have not hidden Your
righteousness within my heart;
I have declared Your faithfulness
and Your salvation;
I have not concealed Your
lovingkindness and Your truth
From the great assembly.

11 Do not withhold Your tender
mercies from me, O LORD;
[a]Let Your lovingkindness and
Your truth continually
preserve me.
12 For innumerable evils have
surrounded me;
[a]My iniquities have overtaken me, so
that I am not able to look up;
They are more than the
hairs of my head;
Therefore my heart fails me.

13 [a]Be pleased, O LORD, to deliver me;
O LORD, make haste to help me!
14 [a]Let them be ashamed and brought
to mutual confusion
Who seek to destroy my life;
Let them be driven backward
and brought to dishonor
Who wish me evil.
15 Let them be [a]confounded
because of their shame,
Who say to me, "Aha, aha!"

16 [a]Let all those who seek You
rejoice and be glad in You;
Let such as love Your salvation
[b]say continually,
"The LORD be magnified!"
17 [a]But I *am* poor and needy;
[b]*Yet* the LORD thinks upon me.
You *are* my help and my
deliverer;
Do not delay, O my God.

Psalm 41

The Blessing and Suffering of the Godly

To the Chief Musician. A Psalm of David.

1 Blessed *is* he who considers
the poor;
The LORD will deliver him
in time of trouble.
2 The LORD will preserve him
and keep him alive,
And he will be blessed
on the earth;
[a]You will not deliver him to
the will of his enemies.
3 The LORD will strengthen him
on his bed of illness;
You will sustain him on his
sickbed.

4 I said, "LORD, be merciful
to me;
[a]Heal my soul, for I have
sinned against You."
5 My enemies speak evil of me:
"When will he die, and his
name perish?"
6 And if he comes to see *me,*
he speaks lies;

40:5 [a] Job 9:10 [b] Ps. 139:17; [Is. 55:8] 40:6 [a] [1 Sam. 15:22]; Ps. 51:16; Is. 1:11; [Jer. 6:20; 7:22, 23]; Amos 5:22; [Mic. 6:6–8; Heb. 10:5–9] 40:8 [a] [Matt. 26:39; John 4:34; 6:38]; Heb. 10:7 [b] [Ps. 37:31; Jer. 31:33; 2 Cor. 3:3] 40:9 [a] Ps. 22:22, 25 [b] Ps. 119:13 40:10 [a] Acts 20:20, 27 40:11 [a] Ps. 61:7; Prov. 20:28 40:12 [a] Ps. 38:4; 65:3 40:13 [a] Ps. 70:1 40:14 [a] Ps. 35:4, 26; 70:2; 71:13 40:15 [a] Ps. 73:19 40:16 [a] Ps. 70:4 [b] Ps. 35:27 40:17 [a] Ps. 70:5; 86:1; 109:22 [b] Ps. 40:5; 1 Pet. 5:7 41:2 [a] Ps. 27:12 41:4 [a] Ps. 6:2; 103:3; 147:3

#OXYGEN

PSALM 41:5-6

Reconcile Wrongs with Rights

When lies abound and your character is questioned, do not retaliate. Speak truth in power. Trust God for peace.

Inhale, exhale, **breathe**, and **reconcile wrongs with rights**.

His heart gathers iniquity to itself;
When he goes out, he tells *it*.

7 All who hate me whisper
together against me;
Against me they devise my hurt.
8 "An evil disease," *they say,*
"clings to him.
And *now* that he lies down, he
will rise up no more."
9 [a]Even my own familiar friend
in whom I trusted,
[b]Who ate my bread,
Has lifted up *his* heel against me.

10 But You, O LORD, be merciful
to me, and raise me up,
That I may repay them.
11 By this I know that You are
well pleased with me,
Because my enemy does not
triumph over me.
12 As for me, You uphold me
in my integrity,
And [a]set me before Your face forever.

13 [a]Blessed *be* the LORD God of Israel
From everlasting to everlasting!
Amen and Amen.

BOOK TWO

PSALMS 42–72

Psalm 42

Yearning for God in the Midst of Distresses

To the Chief Musician. A Contemplation[1] of the sons of Korah.

1 As the deer pants for the water brooks,
So pants my soul for You, O God.
2 [a]My soul thirsts for God, for
the [b]living God.
When shall I come and
appear before God?[1]
3 [a]My tears have been my
food day and night,
While they continually say to me,
[b]"Where *is* your God?"

4 When I remember these *things,*
[a]I pour out my soul within me.
For I used to go with the multitude;
[b]I went with them to the house of God,
With the voice of joy and praise,
With a multitude that kept
a pilgrim feast.

5 [a]Why are you cast down, O my soul?
And *why* are you disquieted
within me?
[b]Hope in God, for I shall yet praise Him
For the help of His countenance.[1]

6 O my God,[1] my soul is cast
down within me;
Therefore I will remember You
from the land of the Jordan,
And from the heights of Hermon,
From the Hill Mizar.
7 Deep calls unto deep at the
noise of Your waterfalls;
[a]All Your waves and billows
have gone over me.
8 The LORD will [a]command His
lovingkindness in the daytime,

41:9 [a] 2 Sam. 15:12; Job 19:13, 19 [b] Ps. 55:12 14, 20; Jer. 20:10; Obad. 7; [Mic. 7:5]; Matt. 26:14–16, 21–25, 47–50; John 13:18, 21–30; Acts 1:16, 17 **41:12** [a] [Job 36:7; Ps. 21:6; 34:15] **41:13** [a] Ps. 72:18, 19; 89:52; 106:48; 150:6 **42:title** [1] Hebrew *Maschil* **42:2** [a] Ps. 63:1; 84:2; 143:6; [Jer. 10:10] [b] Rom. 9:26; 1 Thess. 1:9 [1] Following Masoretic Text and Vulgate; some Hebrew manuscripts, Septuagint, Syriac, and Targum read *I see the face of God.* **42:3** [a] Ps. 80:5; 102:9 [b] Ps. 79:10; 115:2; Joel 2:17; Mic. 7:10 **42:4** [a] 1 Sam. 1:15; Job 30:16 [b] Ps. 55:14; 122:1; Is. 30:29 **42:5** [a] Ps. 42:11; 43:5 [b] Ps. 71:14; Lam. 3:24 [1] Following Masoretic Text and Targum; a few Hebrew manuscripts, Septuagint, Syriac, and Vulgate read *The help of my countenance, my God.* **42:6** [1] Following Masoretic Text and Targum; a few Hebrew manuscripts, Septuagint, Syriac, and Vulgate put *my God* at the end of verse 5. **42:7** [a] Ps. 69:1, 2; 88:7; Jon. 2:3 **42:8** [a] Deut. 28:8

And [b]in the night His song
shall be with me—
A prayer to the God of my life.

9 I will say to God my Rock,
[a]"Why have You forgotten me?
Why do I go mourning because of
the oppression of the enemy?"
10 *As* with a breaking of my bones,
My enemies reproach me,
[a]While they say to me all day long,
"Where *is* your God?"

11 [a]Why are you cast down, O my soul?
And why are you disquieted
within me?
Hope in God;
For I shall yet praise Him,
The help of my countenance
and my God.

Psalm 43

Prayer to God in Time of Trouble

1 Vindicate [a]me, O God,
And [b]plead my cause against
an ungodly nation;
Oh, deliver me from the
deceitful and unjust man!
2 For You *are* the God of my strength;
Why do You cast me off?
[a]Why do I go mourning because of
the oppression of the enemy?

3 [a]Oh, send out Your light and Your truth!
Let them lead me;
Let them bring me to [b]Your holy hill
And to Your tabernacle.
4 Then I will go to the altar of God,
To God my exceeding joy;
And on the harp I will praise You,
O God, my God.

5 [a]Why are you cast down, O my soul?
And why are you disquieted
within me?
Hope in God;
For I shall yet praise Him,
The help of my countenance
and my God.

Psalm 44

Redemption Remembered in Present Dishonor

To the Chief Musician. A [a]Contemplation[1] of the sons of Korah.

1 We have heard with our ears, O God,
[a]Our fathers have told us,
The deeds You did in their days,
In days of old:
2 [a]You drove out the nations
with Your hand,
But them You planted;
You afflicted the peoples,
and cast them out.
3 For [a]they did not gain possession
of the land by their own sword,
Nor did their own arm save them;
But it was Your right hand, Your arm,
and the light of Your countenance,
[b]Because You favored them.

4 [a]You are my King, O God;[1]
Command[2] victories for Jacob.
5 Through You [a]we will push
down our enemies;
Through Your name we will trample
those who rise up against us.
6 For [a]I will not trust in my bow,
Nor shall my sword save me.
7 But You have saved us
from our enemies,
And have put to shame
those who hated us.
8 [a]In God we boast all day long,
And praise Your name forever. *Selah*

9 But [a]You have cast *us* off
and put us to shame,
And You do not go out
with our armies.
10 You make us [a]turn back
from the enemy,

42:8 [b] Job 35:10; Ps. 149:5 **42:9** [a] Ps. 38:6 **42:10** [a] Ps. 42:3; Joel 2:17; Mic. 7:10 **42:11** [a] Ps. 43:5 **43:1** [a] [Ps. 26:1; 35:24] [b] 1 Sam. 24:15; Ps. 35:1 **43:2** [a] Ps. 42:9 **43:3** [a] [Ps. 40:11] [b] Ps. 3:4 **43:5** [a] Ps. 42:5, 11 **44:title** [a] Ps. 42:title [1] Hebrew *Maschil* **44:1** [a] [Ex. 12:26, 27; Deut. 6:20]; Judg. 6:13; Ps. 78:3 **44:2** [a] Ex. 15:17; 2 Sam. 7:10; Jer. 24:6; Amos 9:15 **44:3** [a] [Deut. 8:17, 18]; Josh. 24:12 [b] [Deut. 4:37; 7:7, 8] **44:4** [a] [Ps. 74:12] [1] Following Masoretic Text and Targum; Septuagint and Vulgate read *and my God.* [2] Following Masoretic Text and Targum; Septuagint, Syriac, and Vulgate read *Who commands.* **44:5** [a] Deut. 33:17; [Dan. 8:4] **44:6** [a] [1 Sam. 17:47]; Ps. 33:16; [Hos. 1:7] **44:8** [a] Ps. 34:2; [Jer. 9:24] **44:9** [a] Ps. 60:1 **44:10** [a] Lev. 26:17; Josh. 7:8, 12; Ps. 89:43

And those who hate us have
taken spoil for themselves.
11 [a]You have given us up like
sheep *intended* for food,
And have [b]scattered us
among the nations.
12 [a]You sell Your people for
next to nothing,
And are not enriched by selling them.

13 [a]You make us a reproach
to our neighbors,
A scorn and a derision to
those all around us.
14 [a]You make us a byword
among the nations,
[b]A shaking of the head
among the peoples.
15 My dishonor *is* continually before me,
And the shame of my face
has covered me,
16 Because of the voice of him who
reproaches and reviles,
[a]Because of the enemy and the avenger.

17 [a]All this has come upon us;
But we have not forgotten You,
Nor have we dealt falsely
with Your covenant.
18 Our heart has not turned back,
[a]Nor have our steps departed
from Your way;
19 But You have severely broken
us in [a]the place of jackals,
And covered us [b]with the
shadow of death.

20 If we had forgotten the
name of our God,
Or [a]stretched out our hands
to a foreign god,
21 [a]Would not God search this out?
For He knows the secrets
of the heart.
22 [a]Yet for Your sake we are
killed all day long;
We are accounted as sheep
for the slaughter.

23 [a]Awake! Why do You sleep, O Lord?
Arise! Do not cast *us* off forever.
24 [a]Why do You hide Your face,
And forget our affliction
and our oppression?
25 For [a]our soul is bowed
down to the dust;
Our body clings to the ground.
26 Arise for our help,
And redeem us for Your
mercies' sake.

Psalm 45

The Glories of the Messiah and His Bride

To the Chief Musician. [a]Set to "The Lilies."[1]
A Contemplation[2] of the sons of Korah.
A Song of Love.

1 My heart is overflowing
with a good theme;
I recite my composition
concerning the King;
My tongue *is* the pen of
a ready writer.

2 You are fairer than the sons
of men;
[a]Grace is poured upon Your lips;
Therefore God has blessed
You forever.
3 Gird Your [a]sword upon *Your*
thigh, [b]O Mighty One,
With Your [c]glory and Your majesty.
4 [a]And in Your majesty ride
prosperously because of truth,
humility, *and* righteousness;
And Your right hand shall teach
You awesome things.
5 Your arrows *are* sharp in the
heart of the King's enemies;
The peoples fall under You.

6 [a]Your throne, O God, *is*
forever and ever;
A [b]scepter of righteousness *is* the
scepter of Your kingdom.

44:11 [a] Ps. 44:22; Rom. 8:36 [b] Lev. 26:33; Deut. 4:27; 28:64; Ps. 106:27; Ezek. 20:23 **44:12** [a] Is. 52:3, 4; Jer. 15:13 **44:13** [a] Ps. 79:4; 80:6; Jer. 24:9 **44:14** [a] Deut. 28:37 [b] Job 16:4 **44:16** [a] Ps. 8:2 **44:17** [a] Dan. 9:13 **44:18** [a] Job 23:11 **44:19** [a] Is. 34:13 [b] [Ps. 23:4] **44:20** [a] [Deut. 6:14] **44:21** [a] Job 31:14; [Ps. 139:1, 2; Jer. 17:10] **44:22** [a] Rom. 8:36 **44:23** [a] Ps. 7:6 **44:24** [a] Job 13:24 **44:25** [a] Ps. 119:25 **45:title** [a] Ps. 69:title [1] Hebrew *Shoshannim* [2] Hebrew *Maschil* **45:2** [a] Luke 4:22 **45:3** [a] [Is. 49:2; Heb. 4:12]; Rev. 1:16 [b] [Is. 9:6] [c] Jude 25 **45:4** [a] Rev. 6:2 **45:6** [a] [Ps. 93:2]; Heb. 1:8, 9 [b] [Num. 24:17]

7 You love righteousness and
hate wickedness;
Therefore God, Your God,
has [a]anointed You
With the oil of [b]gladness more
than Your companions.
8 All Your garments *are* [a]*scented* with
myrrh and aloes *and* cassia,
Out of the ivory palaces, by which
they have made You glad.
9 [a]Kings' daughters *are* among
Your honorable women;
[b]At Your right hand stands the
queen in gold from Ophir.

10 Listen, O daughter,
Consider and incline your ear;
[a]Forget your own people also,
and your father's house;
11 So the King will greatly
desire your beauty;
[a]Because He *is* your Lord,
worship Him.
12 And the daughter of Tyre
will come with a gift;
[a]The rich among the people
will seek your favor.

13 The royal daughter *is* all glorious
within *the palace;*
Her clothing *is* woven with gold.
14 [a]She shall be brought to the King
in robes of many colors;
The virgins, her companions who
follow her, shall be brought
to You.
15 With gladness and rejoicing
they shall be brought;
They shall enter the King's
palace.

16 Instead of Your fathers
shall be Your sons,
[a]Whom You shall make princes
in all the earth.
17 [a]I will make Your name to be
remembered in all generations;
Therefore the people shall praise
You forever and ever.

Psalm 46

God the Refuge of His People and Conqueror of the Nations

To the Chief Musician. A *Psalm* of the sons of Korah. A Song [a]for Alamoth.

1 God *is* our [a]refuge and strength,
[b]A very present help in trouble.
2 Therefore we will not fear,
Even though the earth be removed,
And though the mountains be
carried into the midst of the sea;
3 [a]*Though* its waters roar
and be troubled,
Though the mountains shake
with its swelling. *Selah*

4 *There is* a [a]river whose streams shall
make glad the [b]city of God,
The holy *place* of the tabernacle
of the Most High.
5 God *is* [a]in the midst of her, she
shall not be moved;
God shall help her, just at
the break of dawn.
6 [a]The nations raged, the
kingdoms were moved;
He uttered His voice, the earth
melted.

7 The [a]LORD of hosts *is* with us;
The God of Jacob *is* our refuge. *Selah*

8 Come, behold the works of the LORD,
Who has made desolations
in the earth.
9 [a]He makes wars cease to the
end of the earth;
[b]He breaks the bow and cuts
the spear in two;
[c]He burns the chariot in the fire.

10 Be still, and know that I *am* God;
[a]I will be exalted among the
nations,
I will be exalted in the earth!

11 The LORD of hosts *is* with us;
The God of Jacob *is* our refuge. *Selah*

45:7 [a] Ps. 2:2 [b] Ps. 21:6; Heb. 1:8, 9 45:8 [a] Song 1:12, 13 45:9 [a] Song 6:8 [b] 1 Kin. 2:19 45:10 [a] Deut. 21:13; Ruth 1:16, 17 45:11 [a] Ps. 95:6; [Is. 54:5] 45:12 [a] Is. 49:23 45:14 [a] Song 1:4 45:16 [a] [1 Pet. 2:9; Rev. 1:6; 20:6] 45:17 [a] Mal. 1:11 46:title [a] 1 Chr. 15:20 46:1 [a] Ps. 62:7, 8 [b] [Deut. 4:7; Ps. 145:18] 46:3 [a] [Ps. 93:3, 4] 46:4 [a] [Ezek. 47:1–12] [b] Ps. 48:1, 8; Is. 60:14 46:5 [a] [Deut. 23:14; Is. 12:6]; Ezek. 43:7; Hos. 11:9; [Joel 2:27; Zeph. 3:15; Zech. 2:5, 10, 11; 8:3] 46:6 [a] Ps. 2:1, 2 46:7 [a] Num. 14:9; 2 Chr. 13:12 46:9 [a] Is. 2:4 [b] Ps. 76:3 [c] Ezek. 39:9 46:10 [a] [Is. 2:11, 17]

Psalm 47

Praise to God, the Ruler of the Earth

To the Chief Musician. A Psalm of the sons of Korah.

1 Oh, clap your hands, all you peoples!
Shout to God with the
voice of triumph!
2 For the LORD Most High *is* awesome;
He is a great [a]King over all the earth.
3 [a]He will subdue the peoples under us,
And the nations under our feet.
4 He will choose our [a]inheritance
for us,
The excellence of Jacob
whom He loves. *Selah*

5 [a]God has gone up with a shout,
The LORD with the sound of a trumpet.
6 Sing praises to God, sing praises!
Sing praises to our King, sing praises!
7 [a]For God *is* the King of all the earth;
[b]Sing praises with understanding.

8 [a]God reigns over the nations;
God [b]sits on His [c]holy throne.
9 The princes of the people
have gathered together,
[a]The people of the God of Abraham.
[b]For the shields of the earth
belong to God;
He is greatly exalted.

Psalm 48

The Glory of God in Zion

A Song. A Psalm of the sons of Korah.

1 Great *is* the LORD, and
greatly to be praised
In the [a]city of our God,
In His holy mountain.
2 [a]Beautiful in elevation,
The joy of the whole earth,
Is Mount Zion *on* the sides
of the north,
The city of the great King.
3 God *is* in her palaces;
He is known as her refuge.
4 For behold, [a]the kings assembled,
They passed by together.
5 They saw *it, and* so they marveled;
They were troubled, they
hastened away.
6 Fear [a]took hold of them there,
And pain, as of a woman in birth pangs,
7 *As when* You break the
[a]ships of Tarshish
With an east wind.

8 As we have heard,
So we have seen
In the city of the LORD of hosts,
In the city of our God:
God will [a]establish it forever. *Selah*

9 We have thought, O God, on
[a]Your lovingkindness,
In the midst of Your temple.
10 According to [a]Your name, O God,
So *is* Your praise to the
ends of the earth;
Your right hand is full of
righteousness.
11 Let Mount Zion rejoice,
Let the daughters of Judah be glad,
Because of Your judgments.

12 Walk about Zion,
And go all around her.
Count her towers;
13 Mark well her bulwarks;
Consider her palaces;
That you may [a]tell *it* to the
generation following.
14 For this *is* God,
Our God forever and ever;
[a]He will be our guide
Even to death.[1]

Psalm 49

The Confidence of the Foolish

To the Chief Musician. A Psalm of the sons of Korah.

1 Hear this, all peoples;
Give ear, all inhabitants of the world,

47:2 [a] Deut. 7:21; Neh. 1:5; Ps. 76:12 47:3 [a] Ps. 18:47 47:4 [a] [1 Pet. 1:4] 47:5 [a] Ps. 68:24, 25 47:7 [a] Zech. 14:9 [b] 1 Cor. 14:15 47:8 [a] 1 Chr. 16:31 [b] Ps. 97:2 [c] Ps. 48:1 47:9 [a] [Rom. 4:11, 12] [b] [Ps. 89:18] 48:1 [a] Ps. 46:4; 87:3; Matt. 5:35 48:2 [a] Ps. 50:2 48:4 [a] 2 Sam. 10:6, 14 48:6 [a] Ex. 15:15 48:7 [a] 1 Kin. 10:22; Ezek. 27:25 48:8 [a] [Ps. 87:5; Is. 2:2]; Mic. 4:1 48:9 [a] Ps. 26:3 48:10 [a] [Deut. 28:58]; Josh. 7:9; Mal. 1:11 48:13 [a] [Ps. 78:5–7] 48:14 [a] Is. 58:11 [1] Following Masoretic Text and Syriac; Septuagint and Vulgate read *Forever*.

2 Both low and high,
Rich and poor together.
3 My mouth shall speak wisdom,
And the meditation of my heart
shall give understanding.
4 I will incline my ear to a proverb;
I will disclose my dark
saying on the harp.

5 Why should I fear in the days of evil,
When the iniquity at my
heels surrounds me?
6 Those who [a]trust in their wealth
And boast in the multitude
of their riches,
7 None *of them* can by any means
redeem *his* brother,
Nor [a]give to God a ransom
for him—
8 For [a]the redemption of
their souls *is* costly,
And it shall cease forever—
9 That he should continue
to live eternally,
And [a]not see the Pit.

10 For he sees wise men die;
Likewise the fool and the
senseless person perish,
And leave their wealth to others.
11 Their inner thought *is that* their
houses *will last* forever,[1]
Their dwelling places to
all generations;
They [a]call *their* lands after
their own names.
12 Nevertheless man, *though* in
honor, does not remain;[1]
He is like the beasts *that* perish.

13 This is the way of those
who *are* [a]foolish,
And of their posterity who
approve their sayings. *Selah*
14 Like sheep they are laid in the grave;
Death shall feed on them;
[a]The upright shall have dominion
over them in the morning;
[b]And their beauty shall be consumed in
the grave, far from their dwelling.
15 But God [a]will redeem my soul
from the power of the grave,
For He shall [b]receive me. *Selah*

16 Do not be afraid when one
becomes rich,
When the glory of his
house is increased;
17 For when he dies he shall
carry nothing away;
His glory shall not descend after him.
18 Though while he lives [a]he
blesses himself
(For *men* will praise you when
you do well for yourself),
19 He shall go to the generation
of his fathers;
They shall never see [a]light.
20 A man *who is* in honor, yet
does not understand,
[a]Is like the beasts *that* perish.

Psalm 50

God the Righteous Judge

A Psalm of Asaph.

1 The [a]Mighty One, God the LORD,
Has spoken and called the earth
From the rising of the sun
to its going down.
2 Out of Zion, the perfection of beauty,
[a]God will shine forth.
3 Our God shall come, and
shall not keep silent;
[a]A fire shall devour before Him,
And it shall be very tempestuous
all around Him.

4 [a]He shall call to the heavens
from above,
And to the earth, that He
may judge His people:
5 "Gather [a]My saints together to Me,
[b]Those who have made a covenant
with Me by sacrifice."

49:6 [a] Job 31:24; Ps. 52:7; [Prov. 11:28; Mark 10:23, 24] 49:7 [a] Job 36:18, 19 49:8 [a] [Matt. 16:26] 49:9 [a] Ps. 89:48 49:11 [a] Gen. 4:17; Deut. 3:14 [1] Septuagint, Syriac, Targum, and Vulgate read *Their graves shall be their houses forever.* 49:12 [1] Following Masoretic Text and Targum; Septuagint, Syriac, and Vulgate read *understand* (compare verse 20). 49:13 [a] [Luke 12:20] 49:14 [a] Ps. 47:3; [Dan. 7:18; 1 Cor. 6:2; Rev. 2:26] [b] Job 4:21 49:15 [a] [Hos. 13:4]; Mark 16:6, 7; Acts 2:31, 32 [b] Ps. 73:24 49:18 [a] Deut. 29:19; Luke 12:19 49:19 [a] Job 33:30 49:20 [a] Eccl. 3:19 50:1 [a] Is. 9:6 50:2 [a] Deut. 33:2; Ps. 80:1 50:3 [a] Lev. 10:2; Num. 16:35; [Ps. 97:3] 50:4 [a] Deut. 4:26; 31:28; 32:1; Is. 1:2 50:5 [a] Deut. 33:3 [b] Ex. 24:7

6 Let the [a]heavens declare
His righteousness,
For [b]God Himself *is* Judge. *Selah*

7 "Hear, O My people, and I will speak,
O Israel, and I will testify against you;
[a]I *am* God, your God!
8 [a]I will not rebuke you [b]for
your sacrifices
Or your burnt offerings,
Which are continually before Me.
9 [a]I will not take a bull from your house,
Nor goats out of your folds.
10 For every beast of the forest *is* Mine,
And the cattle on a thousand hills.
11 I know all the birds of the mountains,
And the wild beasts of the
field *are* Mine.

12 "If I were hungry, I would not
tell you;
[a]For the world *is* Mine, and
all its fullness.
13 [a]Will I eat the flesh of bulls,
Or drink the blood of goats?
14 [a]Offer to God thanksgiving,
And [b]pay your vows to the Most High.
15 [a]Call upon Me in the day of trouble;
I will deliver you, and you
shall glorify Me."

16 But to the wicked God says:
"What *right* have you to
declare My statutes,
Or take My covenant in your mouth,
17 [a]Seeing you hate instruction
And cast My words behind you?
18 When you saw a thief, you
[a]consented[1] with him,
And have been a [b]partaker
with adulterers.
19 You give your mouth to evil,
And [a]your tongue frames deceit.
20 You sit *and* speak against
your brother;
You slander your own mother's son.
21 These *things* you have done,
and I kept silent;
[a]You thought that I was
altogether like you;
But I will rebuke you,
And [b]set *them* in order
before your eyes.

22 "Now consider this, you
who [a]forget God,
Lest I tear *you* in pieces,
And *there be* none to deliver:
23 Whoever offers praise glorifies Me;
And [a]to him who orders
his conduct *aright*
I will show the salvation
of God."

Psalm 51

A Prayer of Repentance

To the Chief Musician. A Psalm of David [a]when Nathan the prophet went to him, after he had gone in to Bathsheba.

1 Have mercy upon me, O God,
According to Your lovingkindness;
According to the multitude of
Your tender mercies,
[a]Blot out my transgressions.
2 [a]Wash me thoroughly from
my iniquity,
And cleanse me from my sin.

3 For I acknowledge my
transgressions,
And my sin *is* always before me.
4 [a]Against You, You only, have I sinned,
And done *this* evil [b]in Your sight—
[c]That You may be found just
when You speak,[1]
And blameless when You judge.

5 [a]Behold, I was brought forth
in iniquity,
And in sin my mother conceived me.
6 Behold, You desire truth in
the inward parts,
And in the hidden *part* You will
make me to know wisdom.

50:6 [a] [Ps. 97:6] [b] Ps. 75:7 50:7 [a] Ex. 20:2 50:8 [a] Jer. 7:22 [b] Is. 1:11; [Hos. 6:6] 50:9 [a] Ps. 69:31 50:12 [a] Ex. 19:5; [Deut. 10:14; Job 41:11]; 1 Cor. 10:26 50:13 [a] [Ps. 51:15–17] 50:14 [a] Hos. 14:2; Heb. 13:15 [b] Num. 30:2; Deut. 23:21 50:15 [a] Job 22:27; [Zech. 13:9] 50:17 [a] Neh. 9:26; Rom. 2:21 50:18 [a] [Rom. 1:32] [b] 1 Tim. 5:22 [1] Septuagint, Syriac, Targum, and Vulgate read *ran.* 50:19 [a] Ps. 52:2 50:21 [a] [Rom. 2:4] [b] [Ps. 90:8] 50:22 [a] [Job 8:13] 50:23 [a] Gal. 6:16 51:title [a] 2 Sam. 12:1 51:1 [a] [Is. 43:25; 44:22; Acts 3:19; Col. 2:14] 51:2 [a] Jer. 33:8; Ezek. 36:33; [Heb. 9:14; 1 John 1:7, 9] 51:4 [a] 2 Sam. 12:13 [b] [Luke 5:21] [c] Rom. 3:4 [1] Septuagint, Targum, and Vulgate read *in Your words.* 51:5 [a] [Job 14:4; Ps. 58:3; John 3:6; Rom. 5:12]

7 [a]Purge me with hyssop, and
I shall be clean;
Wash me, and I shall be
[b]whiter than snow.
8 Make me hear joy and gladness,
That the bones You have
broken [a]may rejoice.
9 Hide Your face from my sins,
And blot out all my iniquities.

10 [a]Create in me a clean heart, O God,
And renew a steadfast
spirit within me.
11 Do not cast me away from
Your presence,
And do not take Your [a]Holy
Spirit from me.

12 Restore to me the joy of
Your salvation,
And uphold me *by Your*
[a]generous Spirit.
13 *Then* I will teach transgressors
Your ways,
And sinners shall be converted
to You.

14 Deliver me from the guilt of
bloodshed, O God,
The God of my salvation,
And my tongue shall sing aloud
of Your righteousness.
15 O Lord, open my lips,
And my mouth shall show
forth Your praise.
16 For [a]You do not desire sacrifice,
or else I would give *it;*
You do not delight in burnt offering.
17 [a]The sacrifices of God *are*
a broken spirit,
A broken and a contrite heart—
These, O God, You will not despise.

18 Do good in Your good
pleasure to Zion;
Build the walls of Jerusalem.
19 Then You shall be pleased with [a]the
sacrifices of righteousness,
With burnt offering and
whole burnt offering;
Then they shall offer bulls
on Your altar.

Psalm 52

The End of the Wicked and the Peace of the Godly

To the Chief Musician. A Contemplation[1] of David [a]when Doeg the Edomite went and [b]told Saul, and said to him, "David has gone to the house of Ahimelech."

1 Why do you boast in evil,
O mighty man?
The goodness of God
endures continually.
2 Your tongue devises destruction,
Like a sharp razor, working
deceitfully.
3 You love evil more than good,
Lying rather than speaking
righteousness. *Selah*
4 You love all devouring words,
You deceitful tongue.

5 God shall likewise destroy
you forever;
He shall take you away, and pluck
you out of *your* dwelling place,
And uproot you from the
land of the living. *Selah*
6 The righteous also shall
see and fear,
And shall laugh at him, *saying,*
7 "Here is the man *who* did not
make God his strength,
But trusted in the abundance
of his riches,
And strengthened himself
in his wickedness."

8 But I *am* [a]like a green olive tree
in the house of God;
I trust in the mercy of God
forever and ever.
9 I will praise You forever,
Because You have done *it;*
And in the presence of Your saints
I will wait on Your name,
for *it is* good.

51:7 [a] Ex. 12:22; Lev. 14:4; Num. 19:18; Heb. 9:19 [b] [Is. 1:18] 51:8 [a] [Matt. 5:4] 51:10 [a] [Ezek. 18:31; Eph. 2:10] 51:11 [a] [Luke 11:13] 51:12 [a] [2 Cor. 3:17] 51:16 [a] [1 Sam. 15:22]; Ps. 50:8–14; [Mic. 6:6–8] 51:17 [a] Ps. 34:18; [Is. 57:15]; 66:2 51:19 [a] Ps. 4:5 52:title [a] 1 Sam. 22:9 [b] Ezek. 22:9 [1] Hebrew *Maschil* 52:8 [a] Jer. 11:16

Psalm 53

Folly of the Godless, and the Restoration of Israel
(Ps. 14:1–7)

To the Chief Musician. Set to "Mahalath." A Contemplation[1] of David.

1 The [a]fool has said in his heart,
"*There is* no God."
They are corrupt, and have done
abominable iniquity;
[b]*There is* none who does good.

2 God looks down from heaven
upon the children of men,
To see if there are *any* who
understand, who [a]seek God.
3 Every one of them has turned aside;
They have together become corrupt;
There is none who does good,
No, not one.

4 Have the workers of iniquity
[a]no knowledge,
Who eat up my people *as* they eat bread,
And do not call upon God?
5 [a]There they are in great fear
Where no fear was,
For God has scattered the bones of
him who encamps against you;
You have put *them* to shame,
Because God has despised them.

6 [a]Oh, that the salvation of Israel
would come out of Zion!
When God brings back the
captivity of His people,
Let Jacob rejoice *and* Israel be glad.

Psalm 54

Answered Prayer for Deliverance from Adversaries

To the Chief Musician. With stringed instruments.[1] A Contemplation[2] of David [a]when the Ziphites went and said to Saul, "Is David not hiding with us?"

1 Save me, O God, by Your name,
And vindicate me by Your strength.
2 Hear my prayer, O God;
Give ear to the words of my mouth.
3 For strangers have risen
up against me,
And oppressors have
sought after my life;
They have not set God
before them. *Selah*

4 Behold, God *is* my helper;
The Lord *is* with those who
uphold my life.
5 He will repay my enemies
for their evil.
Cut them off in Your truth.

6 I will freely sacrifice to You;
I will praise Your name,
O LORD, for *it is* good.
7 For He has delivered me
out of all trouble;
[a]And my eye has seen *its desire*
upon my enemies.

Psalm 55

Trust in God Concerning the Treachery of Friends

To the Chief Musician. With stringed instruments.[1] A Contemplation[2] of David.

1 Give ear to my prayer, O God,
And do not hide Yourself
from my supplication.
2 Attend to me, and hear me;
I [a]am restless in my complaint,
and moan noisily,
3 Because of the voice of the enemy,
Because of the oppression
of the wicked;
[a]For they bring down trouble upon me,
And in wrath they hate me.

4 [a]My heart is severely pained
within me,
And the terrors of death
have fallen upon me.
5 Fearfulness and trembling
have come upon me,
And horror has overwhelmed me.

53:title [1] Hebrew *Maschil* 53:1 [a] Ps. 10:4 [b] Rom. 3:10–12 53:2 [a] [2 Chr. 15:2] 53:4 [a] Jer. 4:22 53:5 [a] Lev. 26:17, 36; Prov. 28:1 53:6 [a] Ps. 14:7 54:title [a] 1 Sam. 23:19 [1] Hebrew *neginoth* [2] Hebrew *Maschil* 54:7 [a] Ps. 59:10 55:title [1] Hebrew *neginoth* [2] Hebrew *Maschil* 55:2 [a] Is. 38:14; 59:11; Ezek. 7:16 55:3 [a] 2 Sam. 16:7, 8 55:4 [a] Ps. 116:3

6 So I said, "Oh, that I had
wings like a dove!
I would fly away and be at rest.
7 Indeed, I would wander far off,
And remain in the wilderness. *Selah*
8 I would hasten my escape
From the windy storm *and* tempest."

9 Destroy, O Lord, *and* divide
their tongues,
For I have seen [a]violence
and strife in the city.
10 Day and night they go
around it on its walls;
[a]Iniquity and trouble *are* also
in the midst of it.
11 Destruction *is* in its midst;
[a]Oppression and deceit do not
depart from its streets.

12 [a]For *it is* not an enemy *who*
reproaches me;
Then I could bear *it*.
Nor *is it* one *who* hates me who has
[b]exalted *himself* against me;
Then I could hide from him.
13 But *it was* you, a man my equal,
[a]My companion and my acquaintance.
14 We took sweet counsel together,
And [a]walked to the house of
God in the throng.

15 Let death seize them;
Let them [a]go down alive into hell,
For wickedness *is* in their
dwellings *and* among them.

16 As for me, I will call upon God,
And the LORD shall save me.
17 [a]Evening and morning and at noon
I will pray, and cry aloud,
And He shall hear my voice.
18 He has redeemed my soul in peace
from the battle *that was* against me,
For [a]there were many against me.
19 God will hear, and afflict them,
[a]Even He who abides from
of old. *Selah*
Because they do not change,
Therefore they do not fear God.

20 He has [a]put forth his hands against
those who [b]were at peace with him;
He has broken his covenant.
21 [a]*The words* of his mouth were
smoother than butter,
But war *was* in his heart;
His words were softer than oil,
Yet they *were* drawn swords.

22 [a]Cast your burden on the LORD,
And [b]He shall sustain you;
He shall never permit the
righteous to be moved.

23 But You, O God, shall bring them
down to the pit of destruction;
[a]Bloodthirsty and deceitful men
[b]shall not live out half their days;
But I will trust in You.

Psalm 56

Prayer for Relief from Tormentors

To the Chief Musician. Set to "The Silent Dove in Distant Lands."[1] A Michtam of David when the [a]Philistines captured him in Gath.

1 Be [a]merciful to me, O God, for
man would swallow me up;
Fighting all day he oppresses me.
2 My enemies would [a]hound *me* all day,
For *there are* many who fight
against me, O Most High.

3 Whenever I am afraid,
I will trust in You.
4 In God (I will praise His word),
In God I have put my trust;
[a]I will not fear.
What can flesh do to me?

5 All day they twist my words;
All their thoughts *are*
against me for evil.
6 They gather together,
They hide, they mark my steps,
When they lie in wait for my life.

55:9 [a] Jer. 6:7 55:10 [a] Ps. 10:7 55:11 [a] Ps. 10:7 55:12 [a] Ps. 41:9 [b] Ps. 35:26; 38:16 55:13 [a] 2 Sam. 15:12 55:14 [a] Ps. 42:4 55:15 [a] Num. 16:30, 33 55:17 [a] Dan. 6:10; Luke 18:1; Acts 3:1; 10:3, 30 55:18 [a] 2 Chr. 32:7, 8 55:19 [a] [Deut. 33:27] 55:20 [a] Acts 12:1 [b] Ps. 7:4 55:21 [a] Ps. 28:3; 57:4; [Prov. 5:3, 4; 12:18] 55:22 [a] [Ps. 37:5; Matt. 6:25–34; Luke 12:22–31; 1 Pet. 5:7] [b] Ps. 37:24 55:23 [a] Ps. 5:6 [b] Prov. 10:27 56:title [a] 1 Sam. 21:11 [1] Hebrew *Jonath Elem Rechokim* 56:1 [a] Ps. 57:1 56:2 [a] Ps. 57:3 56:4 [a] Ps. 118:6; Is. 31:3; [Heb. 13:6]

7 Shall they escape by iniquity?
In anger cast down the peoples,
O God!

8 You number my wanderings;
Put my tears into Your bottle;
[a]*Are they* not in Your book?
9 When I cry out *to You,*
Then my enemies will turn back;
This I know, because [a]God *is* for me.
10 In God (I will praise *His* word),
In the LORD (I will praise *His* word),
11 In God I have put my trust;
I will not be afraid.
What can man do to me?

12 Vows *made* to You *are binding*
upon me, O God;
I will render praises to You,
13 [a]For You have delivered my
soul from death.
Have You not *kept* my feet
from falling,
That I may walk before God
In the [b]light of the living?

Psalm 57

Prayer for Safety from Enemies

(cf. Ps. 108:1–5)

To the Chief Musician. Set to "Do Not Destroy."[1] A Michtam of David [a]when he fled from Saul into the cave.

1 Be merciful to me, O God,
be merciful to me!
For my soul trusts in You;
[a]And in the shadow of Your wings
I will make my refuge,
[b]Until *these* calamities have passed by.

2 I will cry out to God Most High,
To God [a]who performs
all things for me.
3 [a]He shall send from heaven
and save me;
He reproaches the one who
would swallow me up. *Selah*
God [b]shall send forth His
mercy and His truth.

4 My soul *is* among lions;
I lie *among* the sons of men
Who are set on fire,
[a]Whose teeth *are* spears and arrows,
And their tongue a sharp sword.
5 [a]Be exalted, O God, above the heavens;
Let Your glory *be* above all the earth.

6 [a]They have prepared a net for
my steps;
My soul is bowed down;
They have dug a pit before me;
Into the midst of it they *themselves*
have fallen. *Selah*

7 [a]My heart is steadfast, O God,
my heart is steadfast;
I will sing and give praise.
8 Awake, [a]my glory!
Awake, lute and harp!
I will awaken the dawn.

9 [a]I will praise You, O Lord,
among the peoples;
I will sing to You among the nations.
10 [a]For Your mercy reaches
unto the heavens,
And Your truth unto the clouds.

11 [a]Be exalted, O God, above the heavens;
Let Your glory *be* above all the earth.

Psalm 58

The Just Judgment of the Wicked

To the Chief Musician. Set to "Do Not Destroy."[1] A Michtam of David.

1 Do you indeed speak righteousness,
you silent ones?
Do you judge uprightly,
you sons of men?
2 No, in heart you work wickedness;
You weigh out the violence of
your hands in the earth.

3 [a]The wicked are estranged
from the womb;
They go astray as soon as they
are born, speaking lies.

56:8 [a] [Mal. 3:16] 56:9 [a] [Ps. 118:6; Rom. 8:31] 56:13 [a] Ps. 116:8, 9 [b] Job 33:30 57:title [a] 1 Sam. 22:1 [1] Hebrew *Al Tashcheth* 57:1 [a] Ruth 2:12; Ps. 17:8; 63:7 [b] Is. 26:20 57:2 [a] [Ps. 138:8] 57:3 [a] Ps. 144:5, 7 [b] Ps. 43:3 57:4 [a] Prov. 30:14 57:5 [a] Ps. 108:5 57:6 [a] Ps. 9:15 57:7 [a] Ps. 108:1–5 57:8 [a] Ps. 16:9 57:9 [a] Ps. 108:3 57:10 [a] Ps. 103:11 57:11 [a] Ps. 57:5 58:title [1] Hebrew *Al Tashcheth* 58:3 [a] [Ps. 53:3; Is. 48:8]

4 [a]Their poison *is* like the
poison of a serpent;
They are like the deaf cobra
that stops its ear,
5 Which will not [a]heed the
voice of charmers,
Charming ever so skillfully.

6 [a]Break their teeth in their
mouth, O God!
Break out the fangs of the
young lions, O LORD!
7 [a]Let them flow away as waters
which run continually;
When he bends *his bow,*
Let his arrows be as if cut in pieces.
8 *Let them be* like a snail which
melts away as it goes,
[a]*Like* a stillborn child of a woman,
that they may not see the sun.

9 Before your [a]pots can feel
the burning thorns,
He shall take them away [b]as
with a whirlwind,
As in His living and burning wrath.
10 The righteous shall rejoice when
he sees the [a]vengeance;
[b]He shall wash his feet in the
blood of the wicked,
11 [a]So that men will say,
"Surely *there is* a reward
for the righteous;
Surely He is God who
[b]judges in the earth."

Psalm 59

The Assured Judgment of the Wicked

To the Chief Musician. Set to "Do Not Destroy."[1] A Michtam of David [a]when Saul sent men, and they watched the house in order to kill him.

1 Deliver me from my
enemies, O my God;
Defend me from those who
rise up against me.
2 Deliver me from the
workers of iniquity,
And save me from bloodthirsty men.

3 For look, they lie in wait for my life;
[a]The mighty gather against me,
Not *for* my transgression nor
for my sin, O LORD.
4 They run and prepare themselves
through no fault *of mine.*

[a]Awake to help me, and behold!
5 You therefore, O LORD God of
hosts, the God of Israel,
Awake to punish all the nations;
Do not be merciful to any
wicked transgressors. *Selah*

6 [a]At evening they return,
They growl like a dog,
And go all around the city.
7 Indeed, they belch with their mouth;
[a]Swords *are* in their lips;
For *they say,* [b]"Who hears?"

8 But [a]You, O LORD, shall laugh at them;
You shall have all the
nations in derision.
9 I will wait for You, O You his Strength;[1]
[a]For God *is* my defense.
10 My God of mercy[1] shall
[a]come to meet me;
God shall let [b]me see *my*
desire on my enemies.

11 Do not slay them, lest my
people forget;
Scatter them by Your power,
And bring them down,
O Lord our shield.
12 [a]*For* the sin of their mouth *and*
the words of their lips,
Let them even be taken in their pride,
And for the cursing and lying
which they speak.
13 [a]Consume *them* in wrath,
consume *them,*
That they *may* not *be;*

58:4 [a] Eccl. 10:11 58:5 [a] Jer. 8:17 58:6 [a] Job 4:10 58:7 [a] Josh. 2:11; 7:5; Ps. 112:10; Is. 13:7; Ezek. 21:7 58:8 [a] Job 3:16 58:9 [a] Ps. 118:12; Eccl. 7:6 [b] Job 27:21; Prov. 10:25 58:10 [a] [Deut. 32:43]; Jer. 11:20 [b] Ps. 68:23 58:11 [a] Ps. 92:15; Prov. 11:18; [2 Cor. 5:10] [b] Ps. 50:6; 75:7 59:title [a] 1 Sam. 19:11 [1] Hebrew *Al Tashcheth* 59:3 [a] Ps. 56:6 59:4 [a] Ps. 35:23 59:6 [a] Ps. 59:14 59:7 [a] Ps. 57:4; Prov. 12:18 [b] Job 22:13; Ps. 10:11 59:8 [a] Prov. 1:26 59:9 [a] [Ps. 62:2] [1] Following Masoretic Text and Syriac; some Hebrew manuscripts, Septuagint, Targum, and Vulgate read *my Strength.* 59:10 [a] Ps. 21:3 [b] Ps. 54:7 [1] Following Qere; some Hebrew manuscripts, Septuagint, and Vulgate read *My God, His mercy;* Kethib, some Hebrew manuscripts and Targum read *O God, my mercy;* Syriac reads *O God, Your mercy.* 59:12 [a] Prov. 12:13 59:13 [a] Ps. 104:35

And [b]let them know that
God rules in Jacob
To the ends of the earth. *Selah*

14 And [a]at evening they return,
They growl like a dog,
And go all around the city.
15 They [a]wander up and down for food,
And howl[1] if they are not satisfied.

16 But I will sing of Your power;
Yes, I will sing aloud of Your
mercy in the morning;
For You have been my defense
And refuge in the day of my trouble.
17 To You, [a]O my Strength, I
will sing praises;
For God *is* my defense,
My God of mercy.

Psalm 60

Urgent Prayer for the Restored Favor of God

(cf. Ps. 108:6–13)

To the Chief Musician. [a]Set to "Lily of the Testimony."[1] A Michtam of David. For teaching. [b]When he fought against Mesopotamia and Syria of Zobah, and Joab returned and killed twelve thousand Edomites in the Valley of Salt.

1 O God, [a]You have cast us off;
You have broken us down;
You have been displeased;
Oh, restore us again!
2 You have made the earth tremble;
You have broken it;
[a]Heal its breaches, for it is shaking.
3 [a]You have shown Your
people hard things;
[b]You have made us drink the
wine of confusion.

4 [a]You have given a banner to
those who fear You,
That it may be displayed
because of the truth. *Selah*

5 [a]That Your beloved may be delivered,
Save *with* Your right hand,
and hear me.

6 God has [a]spoken in His holiness:
"I will rejoice;
I will [b]divide [c]Shechem
And measure out [d]the
Valley of Succoth.
7 Gilead *is* Mine, and Manasseh *is* Mine;
[a]Ephraim also *is* the helmet
for My head;
[b]Judah *is* My lawgiver.
8 [a]Moab *is* My washpot;
[b]Over Edom I will cast My shoe;
[c]Philistia, shout in triumph
because of Me."

9 Who will bring me *to* the strong city?
Who will lead me to Edom?
10 *Is it* not You, O God, [a]*who* cast us off?
And You, O God, *who* did [b]not
go out with our armies?
11 Give us help from trouble,
[a]For the help of man *is* useless.
12 Through God [a]we will do valiantly,
For *it is* He *who* shall tread
down our enemies.[1]

Psalm 61

Assurance of God's Eternal Protection

To the Chief Musician. On a stringed instrument.[1] A *Psalm* of David.

1 Hear my cry, O God;
Attend to my prayer.
2 From the end of the earth
I will cry to You,
When my heart is overwhelmed;
Lead me to the rock that
is higher than I.

3 For You have been a shelter for me,
[a]A strong tower from the enemy.
4 I will abide in Your tabernacle forever;
[a]I will trust in the shelter
of Your wings. *Selah*

59:13 [b] Ps. 83:18 59:14 [a] Ps. 59:6 59:15 [a] Job 15:23 [1] Following Septuagint and Vulgate; Masoretic Text, Syriac, and Targum read *spend the night.* 59:17 [a] Ps. 18:1 60:title [a] Ps. 80 [b] 2 Sam. 8:3, 13; 1 Chr. 18:3 [1] Hebrew *Shushan Eduth* 60:1 [a] Ps. 44:9 60:2 [a] [2 Chr. 7:14]; Is. 30:26 60:3 [a] Ps. 71:20 [b] Is. 51:17, 22; Jer. 25:15 60:4 [a] Ps. 20:5; Is. 5:26; 11:12; 13:2 60:5 [a] Ps. 108:6–13 60:6 [a] Ps. 89:35 [b] Josh. 1:6 [c] Gen. 12:6 [d] Josh. 13:27 60:7 [a] Deut. 33:17 [b] [Gen. 49:10] 60:8 [a] 2 Sam. 8:2 [b] 2 Sam. 8:14; Ps. 108:9 [c] 2 Sam. 8:1 60:10 [a] Ps. 108:11 [b] Josh. 7:12 60:11 [a] Ps. 118:8; 146:3 60:12 [a] Num. 24:18 [1] Compare verses 5–12 with 108:6–13 61:title [1] Hebrew *neginah* 61:3 [a] Prov. 18:10 61:4 [a] Ps. 91:4

5 For You, O God, have heard my vows;
You have given *me* the heritage of
those who fear Your name.
6 You will prolong the king's life,
His years as many generations.
7 He shall abide before God forever.
Oh, prepare mercy [a]and truth,
which may preserve him!

8 So I will sing praise to Your
name forever,
That I may daily perform
my vows.

Psalm 62

A Calm Resolve to Wait
for the Salvation of God

To the Chief Musician. To [a]Jeduthun.
A Psalm of David.

1 Truly [a]my soul silently *waits* for God;
From Him *comes* my salvation.
2 He only *is* my rock and my salvation;
He is my defense;
I shall not be greatly [a]moved.

3 How long will you attack a man?
You shall be slain, all of you,
[a]Like a leaning wall and a
tottering fence.
4 They only consult to cast *him*
down from his high position;
They [a]delight in lies;
They bless with their mouth,
But they curse inwardly. *Selah*

5 My soul, wait silently for God alone,
For my expectation *is* from Him.
6 He only *is* my rock and my salvation;
He is my defense;
I shall not be moved.
7 [a]In God *is* my salvation and
my glory;
The rock of my strength,
And my refuge, *is* in God.

8 Trust in Him at all times, you people;
[a]Pour out your heart before Him;
God *is* a refuge for us. *Selah*

9 [a]Surely men of low degree *are*
a vapor,
Men of high degree *are* a lie;
If they are weighed on the scales,
They *are* altogether *lighter* than
vapor.
10 Do not trust in oppression,
Nor vainly hope in robbery;
[a]If riches increase,
Do not set *your* heart *on them.*

11 God has spoken once,
Twice I have heard this:
That power *belongs* to God.
12 Also to You, O Lord, *belongs*
mercy;
For [a]You render to each one
according to his work.

Psalm 63

Joy in the Fellowship of God

A Psalm of David [a]when he was
in the wilderness of Judah.

1 O God, You *are* my God;
Early will I seek You;
[a]My soul thirsts for You;
My flesh longs for You
In a dry and thirsty land
Where there is no water.
2 So I have looked for You
in the sanctuary,
To see [a]Your power and Your
glory.

3 [a]Because Your lovingkindness
is better than life,
My lips shall praise You.
4 Thus I will bless You while I live;
I will [a]lift up my hands in
Your name.
5 My soul shall be satisfied as
with marrow and fatness,
And my mouth shall praise
You with joyful lips.

6 When [a]I remember You on my bed,
I meditate on You in the *night*
watches.

61:7 [a] Ps. 40:11 62:title [a] 1 Chr. 25:1 62:1 [a] Ps. 33:20 62:2 [a] Ps. 55:22 62:3 [a] Is. 30:13 62:4 [a] Ps. 28:3 62:7 [a] [Jer. 3:23] 62:8 [a] 1 Sam. 1:15; Ps. 42:4; Lam. 2:19 62:9 [a] Job 7:16; Ps. 39:5; Is. 40:17 62:10 [a] Job 31:25; [Mark 10:24; Luke 12:15; 1 Tim. 6:10] 62:12 [a] [Matt. 16:27]; Rom. 2:6; 1 Cor. 3:8 63:title [a] 1 Sam. 22:5 63:1 [a] Ps. 42:2; [Matt. 5:6] 63:2 [a] Ps. 27:4 63:3 [a] Ps. 138:2 63:4 [a] Ps. 28:2; 143:6 63:6 [a] Ps. 42:8

7 Because You have been my help,
Therefore in the shadow of
Your wings I will rejoice.
8 My soul follows close behind You;
Your right hand upholds me.

9 But those *who* seek my
life, to destroy *it,*
Shall go into the lower
parts of the earth.
10 They shall fall by the sword;
They shall be a portion for jackals.

11 But the king shall rejoice in God;
[a]Everyone who swears by
Him shall glory;
But the mouth of those who
speak lies shall be stopped.

Psalm 64

Oppressed by the Wicked but Rejoicing in the LORD

To the Chief Musician. A Psalm of David.

1 Hear my voice, O God, in
my meditation;
Preserve my life from fear
of the enemy.
2 Hide me from the secret
plots of the wicked,
From the rebellion of the
workers of iniquity,
3 Who sharpen their tongue
like a sword,
[a]And bend *their bows to shoot*
their arrows—bitter words,
4 That they may shoot in secret
at the blameless;
Suddenly they shoot at him
and do not fear.

5 They encourage themselves
in an evil matter;
They talk of laying snares secretly;
[a]They say, "Who will see them?"
6 They devise iniquities:
"We have perfected a shrewd scheme."
Both the inward thought and
the heart of man are deep.

7 But God shall shoot at them
with an arrow;
Suddenly they shall be wounded.
8 So He will make them stumble
over their own tongue;
[a]All who see them shall flee away.
9 All men shall fear,
And shall [a]declare the work of God;
For they shall wisely
consider His doing.

10 [a]The righteous shall be glad in
the LORD, and trust in Him.
And all the upright in heart shall glory.

Psalm 65

Praise to God for His Salvation and Providence

To the Chief Musician. A Psalm of David.
A Song.

1 Praise is awaiting You, O God, in Zion;
And to You the vow shall
be performed.
2 O You who hear prayer,
[a]To You all flesh will come.
3 Iniquities prevail against me;
As for our transgressions,
You will [a]provide atonement for them.

4 [a]Blessed *is the man* You [b]choose,
And cause to approach *You,*
That he may dwell in Your courts.
[c]We shall be satisfied with the
goodness of Your house,
Of Your holy temple.

5 *By* awesome deeds in righteousness
You will answer us,
O God of our salvation,
You who are the confidence of
all the ends of the earth,
And of the far-off seas;
6 Who established the mountains
by His strength,
[a]*Being* clothed with power;
7 [a]You who still the noise of the seas,
The noise of their waves,
[b]And the tumult of the peoples.

63:11 [a] Deut. 6:13; [Is. 45:23; 65:16] 64:3 [a] Ps. 58:7 64:5 [a] Ps. 10:11; 59:7 64:8 [a] Ps. 31:11 64:9 [a] Jer. 50:28; 51:10 64:10 [a] Job 22:19; Ps. 32:11 65:2 [a] [Is. 66:23] 65:3 [a] Ps. 51:2; 79:9; Is. 6:7; [Heb. 9:14; 1 John 1:7, 9] 65:4 [a] Ps. 33:12 [b] Ps. 4:3 [c] Ps. 36:8 65:6 [a] Ps. 93:1 65:7 [a] Matt. 8:26 [b] Is. 17:12, 13

8 They also who dwell in the farthest
parts are afraid of Your signs;
You make the outgoings of the
morning and evening rejoice.

9 You visit the earth and [a]water it,
You greatly enrich it;
[b]The river of God is full of water;
You provide their grain,
For so You have prepared it.
10 You water its ridges abundantly,
You settle its furrows;
You make it soft with showers,
You bless its growth.

11 You crown the year with
Your goodness,
And Your paths drip *with* abundance.
12 They drop *on* the pastures
of the wilderness,
And the little hills rejoice
on every side.
13 The pastures are clothed with flocks;
[a]The valleys also are covered
with grain;
They shout for joy, they also sing.

Psalm 66

Praise to God for His Awesome Works

To the Chief Musician. A Song. A Psalm.

1 Make [a]a joyful shout to
God, all the earth!
2 Sing out the honor of His name;
Make His praise glorious.
3 Say to God,
"How [a]awesome are Your works!
[b]Through the greatness of Your power
Your enemies shall submit
themselves to You.
4 [a]All the earth shall worship You
And sing praises to You;
They shall sing praises *to*
Your name." *Selah*

5 Come and see the works of God;
He is awesome *in His* doing
toward the sons of men.
6 [a]He turned the sea into dry *land;*
[b]They went through the river on foot.
There we will rejoice in Him.
7 He rules by His power forever;
His eyes observe the nations;
Do not let the rebellious exalt
themselves. *Selah*

8 Oh, bless our God, you peoples!
And make the voice of His
praise to be heard,
9 Who keeps our soul among the living,
And does not allow our
feet to be moved.
10 For [a]You, O God, have tested us;
[b]You have refined us as silver
is refined.
11 [a]You brought us into the net;
You laid affliction on our backs.
12 [a]You have caused men to
ride over our heads;
[b]We went through fire and
through water;
But You brought us out to
rich *fulfillment.*

13 [a]I will go into Your house
with burnt offerings;
[b]I will pay You my vows,
14 Which my lips have uttered
And my mouth has spoken
when I was in trouble.
15 I will offer You burnt sacrifices
of fat animals,
With the sweet aroma of rams;
I will offer bulls with goats. *Selah*

16 Come *and* hear, all you who fear God,
And I will declare what He
has done for my soul.
17 I cried to Him with my mouth,
And He was extolled with my tongue.
18 [a]If I regard iniquity in my heart,
The Lord will not hear.
19 *But* certainly God [a]has heard *me;*
He has attended to the
voice of my prayer.

20 Blessed *be* God,
Who has not turned away my prayer,
Nor His mercy from me!

65:9 [a] [Deut. 11:12]; Jer. 5:24 [b] Ps. 46:4; 104:13; 147:8 65:13 [a] Is. 44:23; 55:12 66:1 [a] Ps. 100:1 66:3 [a] Ps. 65:5 [b] Ps. 18:44 66:4 [a] Ps. 117:1; Zech. 14:16 66:6 [a] Ex. 14:21 [b] Josh. 3:14–16 66:10 [a] Job 23:10; Ps. 17:3 [b] [Is. 48:10; Zech. 13:9; Mal. 3:3; 1 Pet. 1:7] 66:11 [a] Lam. 1:13; Ezek. 12:13 66:12 [a] Is. 51:23 [b] Is. 43:2 66:13 [a] Ps. 100:4; 116:14, 17–19 [b] [Eccl. 5:4] 66:18 [a] Job 27:9; [Prov. 15:29; 28:9]; Is. 1:15; [John 9:31; James 4:3] 66:19 [a] Ps. 116:1, 2

Psalm 67

An Invocation and a Doxology

To the Chief Musician. On stringed instruments.[1] A Psalm. A Song.

1 God be merciful to us and bless us,
And [a]cause His face to
shine upon us, *Selah*
2 That [a]Your way may be
known on earth,
[b]Your salvation among all nations.

3 Let the peoples praise You, O God;
Let all the peoples praise You.
4 Oh, let the nations be glad
and sing for joy!
For [a]You shall judge the
people righteously,
And govern the nations
on earth. *Selah*

5 Let the peoples praise You, O God;
Let all the peoples praise You.
6 [a]*Then* the earth shall yield her increase;
God, our own God, shall bless us.
7 God shall bless us,
And all the ends of the earth
shall fear Him.

Psalm 68

The Glory of God in His Goodness to Israel

To the Chief Musician. A Psalm of David. A Song.

1 Let [a]God arise,
Let His enemies be scattered;
Let those also who hate Him
flee before Him.
2 [a]As smoke is driven away,
So drive *them* away;
[b]As wax melts before the fire,
So let the wicked perish at
the presence of God.
3 But [a]let the righteous be glad;
Let them rejoice before God;
Yes, let them rejoice exceedingly.

4 Sing to God, sing praises to His name;
[a]Extol Him who rides on the clouds,[1]
[b]By His name YAH,
And rejoice before Him.

5 [a]A father of the fatherless, a
defender of widows,
Is God in His holy habitation.
6 [a]God sets the solitary in families;
[b]He brings out those who are
bound into prosperity;
But [c]the rebellious dwell in
a dry *land*.

7 O God, [a]when You went out
before Your people,
When You marched through
the wilderness, *Selah*
8 The earth shook;
The heavens also dropped *rain*
at the presence of God;
Sinai itself *was moved* at the presence
of God, the God of Israel.
9 [a]You, O God, sent a plentiful rain,
Whereby You confirmed
Your inheritance,
When it was weary.
10 Your congregation dwelt in it;
[a]You, O God, provided from Your
goodness for the poor.

11 The Lord gave the word;
Great *was* the company of
those who proclaimed *it*:
12 "Kings[a] of armies flee, they flee,
And she who remains at
home divides the spoil.
13 [a]Though you lie down among
the sheepfolds,
[b]*You will be* like the wings of a
dove covered with silver,
And her feathers with yellow gold."
14 [a]When the Almighty
scattered kings in it,
It was *white* as snow in Zalmon.

15 A mountain of God *is* the
mountain of Bashan;

67:title [1] Hebrew *neginoth* 67:1 [a] Num. 6:25 67:2 [a] Acts 18:25 [b] Is. 52:10; Titus 2:11 67:4 [a] [Ps. 96:10, 13; 98:9] 67:6 [a] Lev. 26:4; Ps. 85:12; [Ezek. 34:27]; Zech. 8:12 68:1 [a] Num. 10:35 68:2 [a] [Is. 9:18]; Hos. 13:3 [b] Ps. 97:5; Mic. 1:4 68:3 [a] Ps. 32:11 68:4 [a] Deut. 33:26 [b] [Ex. 6:3] [1] Masoretic Text reads *deserts;* Targum reads *heavens* (compare verse 34 and Isaiah 19:1). 68:5 [a] [Ps. 10:14, 18; 146:9] 68:6 [a] Ps. 107:4–7 [b] Acts 12:6–11 [c] Ps. 107:34 68:7 [a] Ex. 13:21; [Hab. 3:13] 68:9 [a] Lev. 26:4; Deut. 11:11; Job 5:10; Ezek. 34:26 68:10 [a] Deut. 26:5; Ps. 74:19 68:12 [a] Num. 31:8; Josh. 10:16; Judg. 5:19 68:13 [a] Ps. 81:6 [b] Ps. 105:37 68:14 [a] Josh. 10:10

A mountain *of many* peaks *is*
the mountain of Bashan.
16 Why do you fume with envy, you
mountains of *many* peaks?
[a]*This is* the mountain *which*
God desires to dwell in;
Yes, the LORD will dwell
in it forever.

17 [a]The chariots of God *are*
twenty thousand,
Even thousands of thousands;
The Lord is among them *as in*
Sinai, in the Holy *Place*.
18 [a]You have ascended on high,
[b]You have led captivity captive;
[c]You have received gifts
among men,
Even *from* [d]the rebellious,
[e]That the LORD God might
dwell *there*.

19 Blessed *be* the Lord,
Who daily loads us *with benefits*,
The God of our salvation! *Selah*
20 Our God *is* the God of salvation;
And [a]to GOD the Lord *belong*
escapes from death.

21 But [a]God will wound the
head of His enemies,
[b]The hairy scalp of the one who
still goes on in his trespasses.
22 The Lord said, "I will bring
[a]back from Bashan,
I will bring *them* back [b]from
the depths of the sea,
23 [a]That your foot may crush
them[1] in blood,
[b]And the tongues of your dogs
may have their portion
from *your* enemies."

24 They have seen Your
procession, O God,
The procession of my God, my
King, into the sanctuary.
25 [a]The singers went before, the players
on instruments *followed* after;
Among *them were* the maidens
playing timbrels.
26 Bless God in the congregations,
The Lord, from [a]the fountain
of Israel.
27 [a]There *is* little Benjamin, their leader,
The princes of Judah *and*
their company,
The princes of Zebulun *and*
the princes of Naphtali.

28 Your God has [a]commanded[1]
your strength;
Strengthen, O God, what You
have done for us.
29 Because of Your temple at Jerusalem,
[a]Kings will bring presents to You.
30 Rebuke the beasts of the reeds,
[a]The herd of bulls with the
calves of the peoples,
Till everyone [b]submits himself
with pieces of silver.
Scatter the peoples *who* delight in war.
31 [a]Envoys will come out of Egypt;
[b]Ethiopia will quickly [c]stretch
out her hands to God.

32 Sing to God, you [a]kingdoms
of the earth;
Oh, sing praises to the Lord, *Selah*
33 To Him [a]who rides on the heaven
of heavens, *which were*
of old!
Indeed, He sends out His
voice, a [b]mighty voice.
34 [a]Ascribe strength to God;
His excellence *is* over Israel,
And His strength *is* in the clouds.
35 O God, [a]*You are* more awesome
than Your holy places.
The God of Israel *is* He who
gives strength and power
to *His* people.

Blessed *be* God!

68:16 [a] [Deut. 12:5]; 1 Kin. 9:3 68:17 [a] Deut. 33:2; Dan. 7:10 68:18 [a] Mark 16:19; Acts 1:9; Eph. 4:8; Phil. 2:9; Col. 3:1; Heb. 1:3 [b] Judg. 5:12 [c] Acts 2:4, 33; 10:44–46; [1 Cor. 12:4–11; Eph. 4:7–12] [d] [1 Tim. 1:13] [e] Ps. 78:60 68:20 [a] [Deut. 32:39] 68:21 [a] Hab. 3:13 [b] Ps. 55:23 68:22 [a] Num. 21:33; Deut. 30:1–9; Amos 9:1–3 [b] Ex. 14:22 68:23 [a] Ps. 58:10 [b] 1 Kin. 21:19; Jer. 15:3 [1] Septuagint, Syriac, Targum, and Vulgate read *you may dip your foot.* 68:25 [a] 1 Chr. 13:8 68:26 [a] Deut. 33:28; Is. 48:1 68:27 [a] Judg. 5:14; 1 Sam. 9:21 68:28 [a] Ps. 42:8; Is. 26:12 [1] Septuagint, Syriac, Targum, and Vulgate read *Command, O God.* 68:29 [a] 1 Kin. 10:10, 25; 2 Chr. 32:23; Ps. 45:12; 72:10; Is. 18:7 68:30 [a] Ps. 22:12 [b] 2 Sam. 8:2 68:31 [a] Is. 19:19–23 [b] Is. 45:14; Zeph. 3:10 [c] Ps. 44:20 68:32 [a] [Ps. 67:3, 4] 68:33 [a] Deut. 33:26; Ps. 18:10 [b] Ps. 46:6; Is. 30:30 68:34 [a] Ps. 29:1 68:35 [a] Ps. 76:12

Psalm 69

An Urgent Plea for Help in Trouble

To the Chief Musician. Set to "The Lilies."[1]
A Psalm of David.

1 Save me, O God!
For [a]the waters have come
up to *my* neck.
2 [a]I sink in deep mire,
Where *there is* no standing;
I have come into deep waters,
Where the floods overflow me.
3 [a]I am weary with my crying;
My throat is dry;
[b]My eyes fail while I wait for my God.

4 Those who [a]hate me without a cause
Are more than the hairs of my head;
They are mighty who
would destroy me,
Being my enemies wrongfully;
Though I have stolen nothing,
I *still* must restore *it.*

5 O God, You know my foolishness;
And my sins are not hidden from You.
6 Let not those who wait for You,
O Lord GOD of hosts, be
ashamed because of me;
Let not those who seek You
be confounded because of
me, O God of Israel.
7 Because for Your sake I have
borne reproach;
Shame has covered my face.
8 [a]I have become a stranger
to my brothers,
And an alien to my mother's children;
9 [a]Because zeal for Your house
has eaten me up,
[b]And the reproaches of those who
reproach You have fallen on me.
10 When I wept *and chastened*
my soul with fasting,
That became my reproach.
11 I also made sackcloth my garment;
I became a byword to them.
12 Those who sit in the gate
speak against me,
And I *am* the song of the [a]drunkards.

13 But as for me, my prayer *is* to You,
O LORD, *in* the acceptable time;
O God, in the multitude of Your mercy,
Hear me in the truth of Your salvation.
14 Deliver me out of the mire,
And let me not sink;
Let me be delivered from
those who hate me,
And out of the deep waters.
15 Let not the floodwater overflow me,
Nor let the deep swallow me up;
And let not the pit shut
its mouth on me.

16 Hear me, O LORD, for Your
lovingkindness *is* good;
Turn to me according to the multitude
of Your tender mercies.
17 And do not hide Your face
from Your servant,
For I am in trouble;
Hear me speedily.
18 Draw near to my soul, *and* redeem it;
Deliver me because of my enemies.

19 You know [a]my reproach, my
shame, and my dishonor;
My adversaries *are* all before You.
20 Reproach has broken my heart,
And I am full of heaviness;
[a]I looked *for someone* to take
pity, but *there was* none;
And for [b]comforters, but I found none.
21 They also gave me gall for my food,
[a]And for my thirst they gave
me vinegar to drink.

22 [a]Let their table become a
snare before them,
And their well-being a trap.
23 [a]Let their eyes be darkened, so
that they do not see;
And make their loins
shake continually.
24 [a]Pour out Your indignation
upon them,
And let Your wrathful anger
take hold of them.
25 [a]Let their dwelling place be desolate;
Let no one live in their tents.

69:title [1] Hebrew *Shoshannim* 69:1 [a] Job 22:11; Jon. 2:5 69:2 [a] Ps. 40:2 69:3 [a] Ps. 6:6 [b] Deut. 28:32; Ps. 119:82, 123; Is. 38:14 69:4 [a] Ps. 35:19; John 15:25 69:8 [a] Is. 53:3; Mark 3:21; Luke 8:19; John 7:3–5 69:9 [a] John 2:17 [b] Rom. 15:3 69:12 [a] Job 30:9 69:19 [a] Ps. 22:6, 7; Heb. 12:2 69:20 [a] Is. 63:5 [b] Job 16:2 69:21 [a] Matt. 27:34, 48; Mark 15:23, 36; Luke 23:36; John 19:28–30 69:22 [a] Rom. 11:9, 10 69:23 [a] Is. 6:9, 10 69:24 [a] [Jer. 10:25; 1 Thess. 2:16] 69:25 [a] Matt. 23:38; Luke 13:35; Acts 1:20

26 For they persecute the *ones*
[a]You have struck,
And talk of the grief of those
You have wounded.
27 [a]Add iniquity to their iniquity,
[b]And let them not come into
Your righteousness.
28 Let them [a]be blotted out of
the book of the living,
[b]And not be written with the righteous.

29 But I *am* poor and sorrowful;
Let Your salvation, O God,
set me up on high.
30 [a]I will praise the name of
God with a song,
And will magnify Him
with thanksgiving.
31 [a]*This* also shall please the LORD
better than an ox *or* bull,
Which has horns and hooves.
32 [a]The humble shall see *this and* be glad;
And you who seek God, [b]your
hearts shall live.
33 For the LORD hears the poor,
And does not despise [a]His prisoners.

34 [a]Let heaven and earth praise Him,
The seas [b]and everything
that moves in them.
35 [a]For God will save Zion
And build the cities of Judah,
That they may dwell there
and possess it.
36 Also, [a]the descendants of His
servants shall inherit it,
And those who love His
name shall dwell in it.

Psalm 70

Prayer for Relief from Adversaries (Ps. 40:13–17)

To the Chief Musician. *A Psalm* of David.
[a]To bring to remembrance.

1 *Make haste,* [a]O God, to deliver me!
Make haste to help me, O LORD!
2 [a]Let them be ashamed and confounded
Who seek my life;
Let them be turned back[1]
and confused
Who desire my hurt.
3 [a]Let them be turned back
because of their shame,
Who say, "Aha, aha!"

4 Let all those who seek You
rejoice and be glad in You;
And let those who love Your
salvation say continually,
"Let God be magnified!"

5 [a]But I *am* poor and needy;
[b]Make haste to me, O God!
You *are* my help and my deliverer;
O LORD, do not delay.

Psalm 71

God the Rock of Salvation

1 In [a]You, O LORD, I put my trust;
Let me never be put to shame.
2 [a]Deliver me in Your righteousness,
and cause me to escape;
[b]Incline Your ear to me, and save me.
3 [a]Be my strong refuge,
To which I may resort continually;
You have given the
[b]commandment to save me,
For You *are* my rock and my fortress.

4 [a]Deliver me, O my God, out of
the hand of the wicked,
Out of the hand of the
unrighteous and cruel man.
5 For You are [a]my hope, O Lord GOD;
You are my trust from my youth.
6 [a]By You I have been upheld from birth;
You are He who took me out
of my mother's womb.
My praise *shall be* continually of You.

7 [a]I have become as a wonder to many,
But You *are* my strong refuge.

69:26 [a] [Is. 53:4; 1 Pet. 2:24] **69:27** [a] Neh. 4:5; [Rom. 1:28] [b] [Is. 26:10] **69:28** [a] [Ex. 32:32]; Phil. 4:3; [Rev. 3:5; 13:8] [b] Ezek. 13:9; Luke 10:20; Heb. 12:23 **69:30** [a] [Ps. 28:7] **69:31** [a] Ps. 50:13, 14, 23; 51:16 **69:32** [a] Ps. 34:2 [b] Ps. 22:26 **69:33** [a] [Ps. 68:6]; Eph. 3:1 **69:34** [a] Ps. 96:11; Is. 44:23; 49:13 [b] Is. 55:12 **69:35** [a] Ps. 51:18; Is. 44:26 **69:36** [a] Ps. 102:28 **70:title** [a] Ps. 38:title **70:1** [a] Ps. 40:13–17 **70:2** [a] Ps. 35:4, 26 [1] Following Masoretic Text, Septuagint, Targum, and Vulgate; some Hebrew manuscripts and Syriac read *be appalled* (compare 40:15). **70:3** [a] Ps. 40:15 **70:5** [a] Ps. 72:12, 13 [b] Ps. 141:1 **71:1** [a] Ps. 25:2, 3 **71:2** [a] Ps. 31:1 [b] Ps. 17:6 **71:3** [a] Ps. 31:2, 3 [b] Ps. 44:4 **71:4** [a] Ps. 140:1, 3 **71:5** [a] Jer. 14:8; 17:7, 13, 17; 50:7 **71:6** [a] Ps. 22:9, 10; Is. 46:3 **71:7** [a] Is. 8:18; Zech. 3:8; 1 Cor. 4:9

8 Let [a]my mouth be filled
with Your praise
And with Your glory all the day.

9 Do not cast me off in the
time of old age;
Do not forsake me when
my strength fails.
10 For my enemies speak against me;
And those who lie in wait for my
life [a]take counsel together,
11 Saying, "God has forsaken him;
Pursue and take him, for *there*
is none to deliver *him*."

12 [a]O God, do not be far from me;
O my God, [b]make haste to help me!
13 Let them be confounded
and consumed
Who are adversaries of my life;
Let them be covered *with*
reproach and dishonor
Who seek my hurt.

14 But I will hope continually,
And will praise You yet
more and more.
15 My mouth shall tell of Your
righteousness
And Your salvation all the day,
For I do not know *their* limits.
16 I will go in the strength
of the Lord GOD;
I will make mention of Your
righteousness, of Yours only.

17 O God, You have taught me
from my [a]youth;
And to this *day* I declare
Your wondrous works.
18 Now also [a]when *I am* old
and grayheaded,
O God, do not forsake me,
Until I declare Your strength
to *this* generation,
Your power to everyone
who is to come.

19 Also [a]Your righteousness,
O God, *is* very high,
You who have done great things;
[b]O God, who *is* like You?
20 [a]*You,* who have shown me great
and severe troubles,
[b]Shall revive me again,
And bring me up again from
the depths of the earth.
21 You shall increase my greatness,
And comfort me on every side.

22 Also [a]with the lute I will praise You—
And Your faithfulness, O my God!
To You I will sing with the harp,
O [b]Holy One of Israel.
23 My lips shall greatly rejoice
when I sing to You,
And [a]my soul, which You
have redeemed.
24 My tongue also shall talk of Your
righteousness all the day long;
For they are confounded,
For they are brought to shame
Who seek my hurt.

Psalm 72

Glory and Universality
of the Messiah's Reign

A Psalm [a]of Solomon.

1 Give the king Your judgments, O God,
And Your righteousness
to the king's Son.
2 [a]He will judge Your people
with righteousness,
And Your poor with justice.
3 [a]The mountains will bring
peace to the people,
And the little hills, by righteousness.
4 [a]He will bring justice to the
poor of the people;
He will save the children of the needy,
And will break in pieces the oppressor.

5 They shall fear You[1]
[a]As long as the sun and moon endure,
Throughout all generations.
6 [a]He shall come down like rain upon
the grass before mowing,
Like showers *that* water the earth.

71:8 [a] Ps. 35:28 **71:10** [a] 2 Sam. 17:1 **71:12** [a] Ps. 35:22 [b] Ps. 70:1 **71:17** [a] Deut. 4:5; 6:7 **71:18** [a] [Is. 46:4] **71:19** [a] Deut. 3:24; Ps. 57:10 [b] Ps. 35:10 **71:20** [a] Ps. 60:3 [b] Hos. 6:1, 2 **71:22** [a] Ps. 92:1–3 [b] 2 Kin. 19:22; Is. 1:4 **71:23** [a] Ps. 103:4 **72:title** [a] Ps. 127:title **72:2** [a] [Is. 9:7; 11:2–5; 32:1] **72:3** [a] Ps. 85:10 **72:4** [a] Is. 11:4 **72:5** [a] Ps. 72:7, 17; 89:36 [1] Following Masoretic Text and Targum; Septuagint and Vulgate read *They shall continue.* **72:6** [a] Deut. 32:2; 2 Sam. 23:4; Hos. 6:3

7 In His days the righteous
shall flourish,
[a]And abundance of peace,
Until the moon is no more.

8 [a]He shall have dominion
also from sea to sea,
And from the River to the
ends of the earth.
9 [a]Those who dwell in the wilderness
will bow before Him,
[b]And His enemies will lick the dust.
10 [a]The kings of Tarshish and of the isles
Will bring presents;
The kings of Sheba and Seba
Will offer gifts.
11 [a]Yes, all kings shall fall
down before Him;
All nations shall serve Him.

12 For He [a]will deliver the
needy when he cries,
The poor also, and *him*
who has no helper.
13 He will spare the poor and needy,
And will save the souls of the needy.
14 He will redeem their life from
oppression and violence;
And [a]precious shall be their
blood in His sight.

15 And He shall live;
And the gold of [a]Sheba will
be given to Him;
Prayer also will be made for
Him continually,
And daily He shall be praised.

16 There will be an abundance
of grain in the earth,
On the top of the mountains;
Its fruit shall wave like Lebanon;
[a]And *those* of the city shall flourish
like grass of the earth.

17 [a]His name shall endure forever;
His name shall continue
as long as the sun.
And [b]*men* shall be blessed in Him;
[c]All nations shall call Him blessed.

18 [a]Blessed *be* the LORD God,
the God of Israel,
[b]Who only does wondrous things!
19 And [a]blessed *be* His glorious
name forever!
[b]And let the whole earth be
filled *with* His glory.
Amen and Amen.

20 The prayers of David the son
of Jesse are ended.

BOOK THREE

PSALMS 73–89

Psalm 73

*The Tragedy of the Wicked,
and the Blessedness of Trust in God*

A Psalm of [a]Asaph.

1 Truly God *is* good to Israel,
To such as are pure in heart.
2 But as for me, my feet had
almost stumbled;
My steps had nearly [a]slipped.
3 [a]For I *was* envious of the boastful,
When I saw the prosperity
of the [b]wicked.

4 For *there are* no pangs in their death,
But their strength *is* firm.
5 [a]They *are* not in trouble *as other* men,
Nor are they plagued like *other* men.
6 Therefore pride serves as
their necklace;
Violence covers them [a]*like* a garment.
7 [a]Their eyes bulge[1] with abundance;
They have more than heart
could wish.
8 [a]They scoff and speak wickedly
concerning oppression;
They [b]speak loftily.

72:7 [a] Is. 2:4 72:8 [a] Ex. 23:31; [Is. 9:6; Zech. 9:10] 72:9 [a] Ps. 74:14; Is. 23:13 [b] Is. 49:23; Mic. 7:17 72:10 [a] 1 Kin. 10:2; 2 Chr. 9:21 72:11 [a] Is. 49:23 72:12 [a] Job 29:12 72:14 [a] 1 Sam. 26:21; [Ps. 116:15] 72:15 [a] Is. 60:6 72:16 [a] 1 Kin. 4:20 72:17 [a] [Ps. 89:36] [b] [Gen. 12:3] [c] Luke 1:48 72:18 [a] 1 Chr. 29:10 [b] Ex. 15:11; Job 5:9 72:19 [a] [Neh. 9:5] [b] Num. 14:21; Hab. 2:14 73:title [a] Ps. 50:title 73:2 [a] Job 12:5 73:3 [a] Ps. 37:1, 7; [Prov. 23:17] [b] Job 21:5–16; Jer. 12:1 73:5 [a] Job 21:9 73:6 [a] Ps. 109:18 73:7 [a] Job 15:27; Jer. 5:28 [1] Targum reads *face bulges;* Septuagint, Syriac, and Vulgate read *iniquity bulges*. 73:8 [a] Ps. 53:1 [b] 2 Pet. 2:18; Jude 16

9 They set their mouth
[a]against the heavens,
And their tongue walks
through the earth.

10 Therefore his people return here,
[a]And waters of a full *cup* are
drained by them.
11 And they say, [a]"How does God know?
And is there knowledge in
the Most High?"
12 Behold, these *are* the ungodly,
Who are always at ease;
They increase *in* riches.
13 Surely I have cleansed my
heart *in* [a]vain,
And washed my hands in innocence.
14 For all day long I have been plagued,
And chastened every morning.

15 If I had said, "I will speak thus,"
Behold, I would have been untrue to
the generation of Your children.
16 When I thought *how* to
understand this,
It *was* too painful for me—
17 Until I went into the sanctuary of God;
Then I understood their [a]end.

18 Surely [a]You set them in
slippery places;
You cast them down to destruction.
19 Oh, how they are *brought* to
desolation, as in a moment!
They are utterly consumed
with terrors.
20 As a dream when *one* awakes,
So, Lord, when You awake,
You shall despise their image.

21 Thus my heart was grieved,
And I was vexed in my mind.
22 [a]I *was* so foolish and ignorant;
I was *like* a beast before You.
23 Nevertheless I *am*
continually with You;
You hold *me* by my right hand.
24 [a]You will guide me with Your counsel,
And afterward receive me *to* glory.

25 [a]Whom have I in heaven *but You?*
And *there is* none upon earth
that I desire besides You.
26 [a]My flesh and my heart fail;
But God *is* the strength of my heart
and my [b]portion forever.

27 For indeed, [a]those who are far
from You shall perish;
You have destroyed all those who
desert You for harlotry.
28 But *it is* good for me to
[a]draw near to God;
I have put my trust in the Lord GOD,
That I may [b]declare all Your works.

Psalm 74

A Plea for Relief from Oppressors

A Contemplation[1] of Asaph.

1 O God, why have You cast
us off forever?
Why does Your anger smoke against
the sheep of Your pasture?
2 Remember Your congregation, *which*
You have purchased of old,
The tribe of Your inheritance,
which You have redeemed—
This Mount Zion where
You have dwelt.
3 Lift up Your feet to the
perpetual desolations.
The enemy has damaged
everything in the sanctuary.
4 [a]Your enemies roar in the midst
of Your meeting place;
[b]They set up their banners *for* signs.
5 They seem like men who lift up
Axes among the thick trees.
6 And now they break down its
carved work, all at once,
With axes and hammers.
7 They have set fire to Your
sanctuary;
They have defiled the dwelling place
of Your name to the ground.
8 [a]They said in their hearts,
"Let us destroy them altogether."

73:9 [a] Rev. 13:6 73:10 [a] [Ps. 75:8] 73:11 [a] Job 22:13 73:13 [a] Job 21:15; 35:3; Mal. 3:14 73:17 [a] [Ps. 37:38; 55:23] 73:18 [a] Ps. 35:6 73:22 [a] Ps. 92:6 73:24 [a] Ps. 32:8; 48:14; Is. 58:11 73:25 [a] [Phil. 3:8] 73:26 [a] Ps. 84:2 [b] Ps. 16:5 73:27 [a] [Ps. 119:155] 73:28 [a] [Heb. 10:22; James 4:8] [b] Ps. 116:10; 2 Cor. 4:13 74:title [1] Hebrew *Maschil* 74:4 [a] Lam. 2:7 [b] Num. 2:2 74:8 [a] Ps. 83:4

They have burned up all the meeting
places of God in the land.

9 We do not see our signs;
[a]*There is* no longer any prophet;
Nor *is there* any among us
who knows how long.
10 O God, how long will the
adversary reproach?
Will the enemy blaspheme
Your name forever?
11 [a]Why do You withdraw Your hand,
even Your right hand?
Take it out of Your bosom
and destroy *them.*
12 For [a]God *is* my King from of old,
Working salvation in the
midst of the earth.
13 [a]You divided the sea by Your strength;
You broke the heads of the sea
serpents in the waters.
14 You broke the heads of
Leviathan in pieces,
And gave him *as* food to the people
inhabiting the wilderness.
15 [a]You broke open the fountain
and the flood;
[b]You dried up mighty rivers.
16 The day *is* Yours, the night
also *is* [a]Yours;
[b]You have prepared the
light and the sun.
17 You have [a]set all the borders
of the earth;
[b]You have made summer and winter.

18 Remember this, *that* the enemy
has reproached, O LORD,
And *that* a foolish people has
blasphemed Your name.
19 Oh, do not deliver the life of Your
turtledove to the wild beast!
Do not forget the life of
Your poor forever.
20 [a]Have respect to the covenant;
For the dark places of the earth are
full of the haunts of cruelty.
21 Oh, do not let the oppressed
return ashamed!
Let the poor and needy
praise Your name.

22 Arise, O God, plead Your own cause;
Remember how the foolish man
reproaches You daily.
23 Do not forget the voice of
Your enemies;
The tumult of those who rise up
against You increases continually.

Psalm 75

Thanksgiving for God's Righteous Judgment

To the Chief Musician. Set to [a]"Do Not Destroy."[1] A Psalm of Asaph. A Song.

1 We give thanks to You, O God,
we give thanks!
For Your wondrous works declare
that Your name is near.

2 "When I choose the proper time,
I will judge uprightly.
3 The earth and all its inhabitants
are dissolved;
I set up its pillars firmly. *Selah*

4 "I said to the boastful, 'Do
not deal boastfully,'
And to the wicked, [a]'Do not
lift up the horn.
5 Do not lift up your horn on high;
Do *not* speak with a stiff neck.'"

6 For exaltation *comes* neither
from the east
Nor from the west nor from the south.
7 But [a]God *is* the Judge:
[b]He puts down one,
And exalts another.
8 For [a]in the hand of the
LORD *there is* a cup,
And the wine is red;
It is fully mixed, and He pours it out;
Surely its dregs shall all the
wicked of the earth
Drain *and* drink down.

74:9 [a] 1 Sam. 3:1; Lam. 2:9; Ezek. 7:26; Amos 8:11 **74:11** [a] Lam. 2:3 **74:12** [a] Ps. 44:4 **74:13** [a] Ex. 14:21 **74:15** [a] Ex. 17:5, 6; Num. 20:11; Ps. 105:41; Is. 48:21 [b] Ex. 14:21, 22; Josh. 2:10; 3:13 **74:16** [a] Job 38:12 [b] Gen. 1:14–18 **74:17** [a] Deut. 32:8; Acts 17:26 [b] Gen. 8:22 **74:20** [a] Gen. 17:7, 8; Lev. 26:44, 45 **75:title** [a] Ps. 57:title [1] Hebrew *Al Tashcheth* **75:4** [a] [1 Sam. 2:3]; Ps. 94:4 **75:7** [a] Ps. 50:6 [b] 1 Sam. 2:7; Ps. 147:6; Dan. 2:21 **75:8** [a] Job 21:20; Ps. 60:3; Jer. 25:15; Rev. 14:10; 16:19

9 But I will declare forever,
I will sing praises to the God of Jacob.

10 "All[a] the horns of the wicked
I will also cut off,
But [b]the horns of the righteous
shall be [c]exalted."

Psalm 76

The Majesty of God in Judgment

To the Chief Musician. On stringed instruments.[1] A Psalm of Asaph. A Song.

1 In [a]Judah God *is* known;
His name *is* great in Israel.
2 In Salem[1] also is His tabernacle,
And His dwelling place in Zion.
3 There He broke the arrows
of the bow,
The shield and sword of battle. *Selah*

4 You *are* more glorious and excellent
[a]*Than* the mountains of prey.
5 [a]The stouthearted were plundered;
[b]They have sunk into their sleep;
And none of the mighty men have
found the use of their hands.
6 [a]At Your rebuke, O God of Jacob,
Both the chariot and horse were
cast into a dead sleep.

7 You, Yourself, *are* to be feared;
And [a]who may stand in Your
presence
When once You are angry?
8 [a]You caused judgment to be
heard from heaven;
[b]The earth feared and was still,
9 When God [a]arose to judgment,
To deliver all the oppressed
of the earth. *Selah*

10 [a]Surely the wrath of man
shall praise You;
With the remainder of wrath
You shall gird Yourself.

11 [a]Make vows to the LORD your
God, and pay *them;*
[b]Let all who are around Him
bring presents to Him who
ought to be feared.
12 He shall cut off the spirit of princes;
[a]*He is* awesome to the
kings of the earth.

Psalm 77

The Consoling Memory of God's Redemptive Works

To the Chief Musician. [a]To Jeduthun. A Psalm of Asaph.

1 I cried out to God with my voice—
To God with my voice;
And He gave ear to me.
2 In the day of my trouble I
sought the Lord;
My hand was stretched out in
the night without ceasing;
My soul refused to be comforted.
3 I remembered God, and was troubled;
I complained, and my spirit
was overwhelmed. *Selah*

4 You hold my eyelids *open;*
I am so troubled that I cannot speak.
5 I have considered the days of old,
The years of ancient times.
6 I call to remembrance my
song in the night;
I meditate within my heart,
And my spirit makes diligent search.

7 Will the Lord cast off forever?
And will He be favorable no more?
8 Has His mercy ceased forever?
Has *His* [a]promise failed forevermore?
9 Has God forgotten to be gracious?
Has He in anger shut up His
tender mercies? *Selah*

10 And I said, "This *is* my anguish;
But I will remember the years of the
right hand of the Most High."
11 I will remember the works
of the LORD;
Surely I will remember Your
wonders of old.

75:10 [a] Ps. 101:8; Jer. 48:25 [b] Ps. 89:17; 148:14 [c] 1 Sam. 2:1 **76:title** [1] Hebrew *neginoth* **76:1** [a] Ps. 48:1, 3 **76:2** [1] That is, Jerusalem **76:4** [a] Ezek. 38:12 **76:5** [a] Is. 10:12; 46:12 [b] Ps. 13:3 **76:6** [a] Ex. 15:1–21; Ezek. 39:20; Nah. 2:13; Zech. 12:4 **76:7** [a] [Ezra 9:15; Nah. 1:6; Mal. 3:2; Rev. 6:17] **76:8** [a] Ex. 19:9 [b] 1 Chr. 16:30; 2 Chr. 20:29 **76:9** [a] [Ps. 9:7–9] **76:10** [a] Ex. 9:16; Rom. 9:17 **76:11** [a] [Eccl. 5:4–6] [b] 2 Chr. 32:22, 23 **76:12** [a] Ps. 68:35 **77:title** [a] Ps. 39:title **77:8** [a] [2 Pet. 3:8, 9]

12 I will also meditate on all Your work,
And talk of Your deeds.
13 Your way, O God, *is* in the [a]sanctuary;
Who *is* so great a God as *our* God?
14 You *are* the God who does wonders;
You have declared Your strength
among the peoples.
15 You have with *Your* arm
redeemed Your people,
The sons of Jacob and Joseph. *Selah*

16 The waters saw You, O God;
The waters saw You, they were [a]afraid;
The depths also trembled.
17 The clouds poured out water;
The skies sent out a sound;
Your arrows also flashed about.
18 The voice of Your thunder
was in the whirlwind;
The lightnings lit up the world;
The earth trembled and shook.
19 Your way *was* in the sea,
Your path in the great waters,
And Your footsteps were not known.
20 You led Your people like a flock
By the hand of Moses and Aaron.

Psalm 78

God's Kindness to Rebellious Israel

A [a]Contemplation[1] of Asaph.

1 Give ear, O my people, *to* my law;
Incline your ears to the
words of my mouth.
2 I will open my mouth in a [a]parable;
I will utter dark sayings of old,
3 Which we have heard and known,
And our fathers have told us.
4 [a]We will not hide *them* from
their children,
[b]Telling to the generation to come
the praises of the LORD,
And His strength and His wonderful
works that He has done.

5 For [a]He established a
testimony in Jacob,
And appointed a law in Israel,
Which He commanded our fathers,
That [b]they should make them
known to their children;
6 [a]That the generation to come
might know *them,*
The children *who* would be born,
That they may arise and declare
them to their children,
7 That they may set their hope in God,
And not forget the works of God,
But keep His commandments;
8 And [a]may not be like their fathers,
[b]A stubborn and rebellious generation,
A generation [c]*that* did not
set its heart aright,
And whose spirit was not
faithful to God.

9 The children of Ephraim, *being*
armed *and* carrying bows,
Turned back in the day of battle.
10 [a]They did not keep the
covenant of God;
They refused to walk in His law,
11 And [a]forgot His works
And His wonders that He
had shown them.

12 [a]Marvelous things He did in the
sight of their fathers,
In the land of Egypt, [b]*in*
the field of Zoan.
13 [a]He divided the sea and caused
them to pass through;
And [b]He made the waters
stand up like a heap.
14 [a]In the daytime also He led
them with the cloud,
And all the night with a light of fire.
15 [a]He split the rocks in the wilderness,
And gave *them* drink in
abundance like the depths.
16 He also brought [a]streams
out of the rock,
And caused waters to run
down like rivers.

17 But they sinned even
more against Him

77:13 [a] Ps. 73:17 77:16 [a] Ex. 14:21; Hab. 3:8, 10 78:title [a] Ps. 74:title [1] Hebrew *Maschil* 78:2 [a] Matt. 13:34, 35 78:4 [a] Ex. 12:26, 27; Deut. 4:9; 6:7; Job 15:18; Is. 38:19; Joel 1:3 [b] Ex. 13:8, 14 78:5 [a] Ps. 147:19 [b] Deut. 4:9; 11:19 78:6 [a] Ps. 102:18 78:8 [a] 2 Kin. 17:14; 2 Chr. 30:7; Ezek. 20:18 [b] Ex. 32:9; Deut. 9:7, 24; 31:27; Judg. 2:19; Is. 30:9 [c] Job 11:13; Ps. 78:37 78:10 [a] 2 Kin. 17:15 78:11 [a] Ps. 106:13 78:12 [a] Ex. 7—12 [b] Num. 13:22; Is. 19:11; 30:4; Ezek. 30:14 78:13 [a] Ex. 14:21 [b] Ex. 15:8 78:14 [a] Ex. 13:21 78:15 [a] Ex. 17:6; Num. 20:11; Is. 48:21; [1 Cor. 10:4] 78:16 [a] Num. 20:8, 10, 11

By [a]rebelling against the Most
High in the wilderness.
18 And [a]they tested God in their heart
By asking for the food of their fancy.
19 [a]Yes, they spoke against God:
They said, "Can God prepare a
table in the wilderness?
20 [a]Behold, He struck the rock,
So that the waters gushed out,
And the streams overflowed.
Can He give bread also?
Can He provide meat for His people?"

21 Therefore the LORD heard
this and [a]was furious;
So a fire was kindled against Jacob,
And anger also came up against Israel,
22 Because they [a]did not believe in God,
And did not trust in His salvation.
23 Yet He had commanded
the clouds above,
[a]And opened the doors of heaven,
24 [a]Had rained down manna
on them to eat,
And given them of the
bread of [b]heaven.
25 Men ate angels' food;
He sent them food to the full.
26 [a]He caused an east wind to
blow in the heavens;
And by His power He brought
in the south wind.
27 He also rained meat on
them like the dust,
Feathered fowl like the
sand of the seas;
28 And He let *them* fall in the
midst of their camp,
All around their dwellings.
29 [a]So they ate and were well filled,
For He gave them their own desire.
30 They were not deprived
of their craving;
But [a]while their food *was*
still in their mouths,
31 The wrath of God came against them,
And slew the stoutest of them,
And struck down the choice
men of Israel.

32 In spite of this [a]they still sinned,
And [b]did not believe in His
wondrous works.
33 [a]Therefore their days He
consumed in futility,
And their years in fear.

34 [a]When He slew them, then
they sought Him;
And they returned and sought
earnestly for God.
35 Then they remembered that
[a]God *was* their rock,
And the Most High God
[b]their Redeemer.
36 Nevertheless they [a]flattered
Him with their mouth,
And they lied to Him with
their tongue;
37 For their heart was not
steadfast with Him,
Nor were they faithful in His covenant.
38 [a]But He, *being* full of [b]compassion,
forgave *their* iniquity,
And did not destroy *them*.
Yes, many a time [c]He turned
His anger away,
And [d]did not stir up all His wrath;
39 For [a]He remembered [b]that
they *were but* flesh,
[c]A breath that passes away and
does not come again.

40 How often they [a]provoked
Him in the wilderness,
And grieved Him in the desert!
41 Yes, [a]again and again they
tempted God,
And limited the Holy One of Israel.
42 They did not remember His power:
The day when He redeemed
them from the enemy,
43 When He worked His signs in Egypt,
And His wonders in the field of Zoan;
44 [a]Turned their rivers into blood,

78:17 [a] Deut. 9:22; Is. 63:10; Heb. 3:16 78:18 [a] Ex. 16:2 78:19 [a] Ex. 16:3; Num. 11:4; 20:3; 21:5 78:20 [a] Num. 20:11 78:21 [a] Num. 11:1 78:22 [a] Deut. 1:32; 9:23; [Heb. 3:18] 78:23 [a] Gen. 7:11; [Mal. 3:10] 78:24 [a] Ex. 16:4 [b] John 6:31 78:26 [a] Num. 11:31 78:29 [a] Num. 11:19, 20 78:30 [a] Num. 11:33 78:32 [a] Num. 14:16, 17 [b] Num. 14:11; Ps. 78:11, 22 78:33 [a] Num. 14:29, 35 78:34 [a] Num. 21:7; [Hos. 5:15] 78:35 [a] [Deut. 32:4, 15] [b] [Ex. 15:13]; Deut. 7:8; Is. 41:14; 44:6; 63:9 78:36 [a] Ex. 24:7, 8; Ezek. 33:31 78:38 [a] [Num. 14:18–20] [b] Ex. 34:6 [c] [Is. 48:9] [d] 1 Kin. 21:29 78:39 [a] Job 10:9; Ps. 103:14–16 [b] John 3:6 [c] [Job 7:7, 16; James 4:14] 78:40 [a] Ps. 95:8–10; [Eph. 4:30]; Heb. 3:16 78:41 [a] Num. 14:22; Deut. 6:16 78:44 [a] Ex. 7:20

And their streams, that they
could not drink.
45 [a]He sent swarms of flies among
them, which devoured them,
And [b]frogs, which destroyed them.
46 He also gave their crops
to the caterpillar,
And their labor to the [a]locust.
47 [a]He destroyed their vines with hail,
And their sycamore trees with frost.
48 He also gave up their [a]cattle to the hail,
And their flocks to fiery lightning.
49 He cast on them the fierceness
of His anger,
Wrath, indignation, and trouble,
By sending angels of
destruction *among them.*
50 He made a path for His anger;
He did not spare their soul from death,
But gave their life over to the plague,
51 And destroyed all the
[a]firstborn in Egypt,
The first of *their* strength
in the tents of Ham.
52 But He [a]made His own people
go forth like sheep,
And guided them in the
wilderness like a flock;
53 And He [a]led them on safely, so
that they did not fear;
But the sea [b]overwhelmed
their enemies.
54 And He brought them to
His [a]holy border,
This mountain [b]*which* His right
hand had acquired.
55 [a]He also drove out the
nations before them,
[b]Allotted them an inheritance
by survey,
And made the tribes of Israel
dwell in their tents.

56 [a]Yet they tested and provoked
the Most High God,
And did not keep His testimonies,
57 But [a]turned back and acted
unfaithfully like their fathers;
They were turned aside
[b]like a deceitful bow.
58 [a]For they provoked Him to anger
with their [b]high places,
And moved Him to jealousy
with their carved images.
59 When God heard *this,* He was furious,
And greatly abhorred Israel,
60 [a]So that He forsook the
tabernacle of Shiloh,
The tent He had placed among men,
61 [a]And delivered His strength
into captivity,
And His glory into the enemy's hand.
62 [a]He also gave His people
over to the sword,
And was furious with His inheritance.
63 The fire consumed their young men,
And [a]their maidens were not
given in marriage.
64 [a]Their priests fell by the sword,
And [b]their widows made
no lamentation.

65 Then the Lord awoke as *from* sleep,
[a]Like a mighty man who shouts
because of wine.
66 And [a]He beat back His enemies;
He put them to a perpetual reproach.

67 Moreover He rejected the
tent of Joseph,
And did not choose the
tribe of Ephraim,
68 But chose the tribe of Judah,
Mount Zion [a]which He loved.
69 And He built His [a]sanctuary
like the heights,
Like the earth which He has
established forever.
70 [a]He also chose David His servant,
And took him from the sheepfolds;
71 From following [a]the ewes that
had young He brought him,
[b]To shepherd Jacob His people,
And Israel His inheritance.
72 So he shepherded them according
to the [a]integrity of his heart,

78:45 [a] Ex. 8:24 [b] Ex. 8:6 78:46 [a] Ex. 10:14 78:47 [a] Ex. 9:23–25 78:48 [a] Ex. 9:19 78:51 [a] Ex. 12:29, 30 78:52 [a] Ps. 77:20 78:53 [a] Ex. 14:19, 20 [b] Ex. 14:27, 28 78:54 [a] Ex. 15:17 [b] Ps. 44:3 78:55 [a] Josh. 11:16–23; Ps. 44:2 [b] Josh. 13:7; 19:51; 23:4 78:56 [a] Judg. 2:11–13 78:57 [a] Ezek. 20:27, 28 [b] Hos. 7:16 78:58 [a] Deut. 32:16, 21; Judg. 2:12; 1 Kin. 14:9; Is. 65:3 [b] Deut. 12:2 78:60 [a] 1 Sam. 4:11; Jer. 7:12–14; 26:6–9 78:61 [a] Judg. 18:30 78:62 [a] Judg. 20:21; 1 Sam. 4:10 78:63 [a] Jer. 7:34; 16:9; 25:10 78:64 [a] 1 Sam. 4:17; 22:18 [b] Job 27:15; Ezek. 24:23 78:65 [a] Is. 42:13 78:66 [a] 1 Sam. 5:6 78:68 [a] [Ps. 87:2] 78:69 [a] 1 Kin. 6:1–38 78:70 [a] 1 Sam. 16:11, 12; 2 Sam. 7:8 78:71 [a] 2 Sam. 7:8; [Is. 40:11] [b] 2 Sam. 5:2; 1 Chr. 11:2 78:72 [a] 1 Kin. 9:4

And guided them by the
skillfulness of his hands.

Psalm 79

A Dirge and a Prayer for Israel, Destroyed by Enemies

A Psalm of Asaph.

1 O God, the nations have come
into [a]Your inheritance;
Your holy temple they have defiled;
[b]They have laid Jerusalem in heaps.
2 [a]The dead bodies of Your servants
They have given *as* food for
the birds of the heavens,
The flesh of Your saints to the
beasts of the earth.
3 Their blood they have shed like
water all around Jerusalem,
And *there was* no one to bury *them.*
4 We have become a reproach
to our [a]neighbors,
A scorn and derision to those
who are around us.

5 [a]How long, LORD?
Will You be angry forever?
Will Your [b]jealousy burn like fire?
6 [a]Pour out Your wrath on the nations
that [b]do not know You,
And on the kingdoms that [c]do
not call on Your name.
7 For they have devoured Jacob,
And laid waste his dwelling place.

8 [a]Oh, do not remember former
iniquities against us!
Let Your tender mercies come
speedily to meet us,
For we have been brought very low.
9 Help us, O God of our salvation,
For the glory of Your name;
And deliver us, and provide
atonement for our sins,
[a]For Your name's sake!
10 [a]Why should the nations say,
"Where *is* their God?"
Let there be known among
the nations in our sight
The avenging of the blood of Your
servants *which has been* shed.

11 Let [a]the groaning of the prisoner
come before You;
According to the greatness
of Your power
Preserve those who are
appointed to die;
12 And return to our neighbors
[a]sevenfold into their bosom
[b]Their reproach with which they
have reproached You, O Lord.

13 So [a]we, Your people and
sheep of Your pasture,
Will give You thanks forever;
[b]We will show forth Your praise
to all generations.

Psalm 80

Prayer for Israel's Restoration

To the Chief Musician. [a]Set to "The Lilies."[1]
A Testimony[2] of Asaph. A Psalm.

1 Give ear, O Shepherd of Israel,
[a]You who lead Joseph [b]like a flock;
You who dwell *between* the
cherubim, [c]shine forth!
2 Before [a]Ephraim, Benjamin,
and Manasseh,
Stir up Your strength,
And come *and* save us!

3 [a]Restore us, O God;
[b]Cause Your face to shine,
And we shall be saved!

4 O LORD God of hosts,
[a]How long will You be angry
Against the prayer of Your people?
5 [a]You have fed them with
the bread of tears,
And given them tears to drink
in great measure.

79:1 [a] Ps. 74:2 [b] 2 Kin. 25:9, 10; 2 Chr. 36:17–19; Jer. 26:18; 52:12–14; Mic. 3:12 79:2 [a] Deut. 28:26; Jer. 7:33; 19:7; 34:20 79:4 [a] Ps. 44:13; [Dan. 9:16] 79:5 [a] Ps. 74:1, 9 [b] [Zeph. 3:8] 79:6 [a] Jer. 10:25; [Zeph. 3:8] [b] Is. 45:4, 5; 1 Thess. 4:5; [2 Thess. 1:8] [c] Ps. 53:4 79:8 [a] Is. 64:9 79:9 [a] Jer. 14:7, 21 79:10 [a] Ps. 42:10 79:11 [a] Ps. 102:20 79:12 [a] Gen. 4:15; Lev. 26:21; Prov. 6:31; Is. 30:26 [b] Ps. 74:10, 18, 22 79:13 [a] Ps. 74:1; 95:7 [b] Is. 43:21 80:title [a] Ps. 45:title [1] Hebrew *Shoshannim* [2] Hebrew *Eduth* 80:1 [a] [Ex. 25:20–22]; 1 Sam. 4:4; 2 Sam. 6:2 [b] Ps. 77:20 [c] Deut. 33:2 80:2 [a] Ps. 78:9, 67 80:3 [a] Lam. 5:21 [b] Num. 6:25; Ps. 4:6 80:4 [a] Ps. 79:5 80:5 [a] Ps. 42:3; Is. 30:20

6 You have made us a strife
to our neighbors,
And our enemies laugh
among themselves.

7 Restore us, O God of hosts;
Cause Your face to shine,
And we shall be saved!

8 You have brought [a]a vine out of Egypt;
[b]You have cast out the nations,
and planted it.
9 You prepared *room* for it,
And caused it to take deep root,
And it filled the land.
10 The hills were covered with its shadow,
And the mighty cedars
with its [a]boughs.
11 She sent out her boughs to the Sea,[1]
And her branches to the River.[2]

12 Why have You [a]broken
down her hedges,
So that all who pass by the
way pluck her *fruit?*
13 The boar out of the woods
uproots it,
And the wild beast of the
field devours it.

14 Return, we beseech You,
O God of hosts;
[a]Look down from heaven and see,
And visit this vine
15 And the vineyard which Your
right hand has planted,
And the branch *that* You made
strong [a]for Yourself.
16 *It is* burned with fire, *it is* cut down;
[a]They perish at the rebuke of
Your countenance.
17 [a]Let Your hand be upon the
man of Your right hand,
Upon the son of man *whom* You
made strong for Yourself.
18 Then we will not turn back
from You;
Revive us, and we will call
upon Your name.

19 Restore us, O LORD God of hosts;
Cause Your face to shine,
And we shall be saved!

Psalm 81

An Appeal for Israel's Repentance

To the Chief Musician. [a]On an instrument of Gath.[1] A *Psalm* of Asaph.

1 Sing aloud to God our strength;
Make a joyful shout to
the God of Jacob.
2 Raise a song and strike the timbrel,
The pleasant harp with the lute.

3 Blow the trumpet at the time
of the New Moon,
At the full moon, on our
solemn feast day.
4 For [a]this *is* a statute for Israel,
A law of the God of Jacob.
5 This He established in Joseph
as a testimony,
When He went throughout
the land of Egypt,
[a]*Where* I heard a language I
did not understand.

6 "I removed his shoulder
from the burden;
His hands were freed from the baskets.
7 [a]You called in trouble, and
I delivered you;
[b]I answered you in the secret
place of thunder;
I [c]tested you at the waters
of Meribah. *Selah*

8 "Hear,[a] O My people, and I
will admonish you!
O Israel, if you will listen to Me!
9 There shall be no [a]foreign
god among you;
Nor shall you worship any
foreign god.
10 [a]I *am* the LORD your God,
Who brought you out of
the land of Egypt;

80:8 [a] [Is. 5:1, 7]; Jer. 2:21; Ezek. 15:6; 17:6; 19:10 [b] Ps. 44:2; Acts 7:45 80:10 [a] Lev. 23:40 80:11 [1] That is, the Mediterranean [2] That is, the Euphrates 80:12 [a] Is. 5:5; Nah. 2:2 80:14 [a] Is. 63:15 80:15 [a] [Is. 49:5] 80:16 [a] [Ps. 39:11] 80:17 [a] Ps. 89:21 81:title [a] Ps. 8:title [1] Hebrew *Al Gittith* 81:4 [a] Lev. 23:24; Num. 10:10 81:5 [a] Deut. 28:49; Ps. 114:1; Jer. 5:15 81:7 [a] Ex. 2:23; 14:10; Ps. 50:15 [b] Ex. 19:19; 20:18 [c] Ex. 17:6, 7; Num. 20:13 81:8 [a] [Ps. 50:7] 81:9 [a] [Ex. 20:3; Deut. 5:7; 32:12]; Ps. 44:20; [Is. 43:12] 81:10 [a] Ex. 20:2; Deut. 5:6

[b]Open your mouth wide, and I will fill it.

11 "But My people would not
heed My voice,
And Israel would *have* [a]none of Me.
12 [a]So I gave them over to their
own stubborn heart,
To walk in their own counsels.

13 "Oh,[a] that My people would listen to Me,
That Israel would walk in My ways!
14 I would soon subdue their enemies,
And turn My hand against
their adversaries.
15 [a]The haters of the LORD would
pretend submission to Him,
But their fate would endure forever.
16 He would [a]have fed them also
with the finest of wheat;
And with honey [b]from the rock I
would have satisfied you."

Psalm 82

A Plea for Justice

A Psalm of Asaph.

1 God [a]stands in the congregation
of the mighty;
He judges among [b]the gods.[1]
2 How long will you judge unjustly,
And [a]show partiality to
the wicked? *Selah*
3 Defend the poor and fatherless;
Do justice to the afflicted and [a]needy.
4 Deliver the poor and needy;
Free *them* from the hand of the wicked.

5 They do not know, nor do
they understand;
They walk about in darkness;
All the [a]foundations of the
earth are unstable.

6 I said, [a]"You *are* gods,[1]
And all of you *are* children
of the Most High.
7 But you shall die like men,
And fall like one of the princes."
8 Arise, O God, judge the earth;
[a]For You shall inherit all nations.

Psalm 83

Prayer to Frustrate Conspiracy Against Israel

A Song. A Psalm of Asaph.

1 Do[a] not keep silent, O God!
Do not hold Your peace,
And do not be still, O God!
2 For behold, [a]Your enemies
make a tumult;
And those who hate You have
lifted up their head.
3 They have taken crafty counsel
against Your people,
And consulted together [a]against
Your sheltered ones.
4 They have said, "Come, and [a]let us
cut them off from *being* a nation,
That the name of Israel may be
remembered no more."

5 For they have consulted together
with one consent;
They form a confederacy against You:
6 [a]The tents of Edom and
the Ishmaelites;
Moab and the Hagrites;
7 Gebal, Ammon, and Amalek;
Philistia with the inhabitants of Tyre;
8 Assyria also has joined with them;
They have helped the
children of Lot. *Selah*

9 Deal with them as *with* [a]Midian,
As *with* [b]Sisera,
As *with* Jabin at the Brook Kishon,
10 Who perished at En Dor,
[a]*Who* became *as* refuse on the earth.
11 Make their nobles like
[a]Oreb and like Zeeb,
Yes, all their princes like
[b]Zebah and Zalmunna,

81:10 [b] Ps. 103:5 81:11 [a] Ex. 32:1; Deut. 32:15 81:12 [a] [Job 8:4; Acts 7:42; Rom. 1:24, 26] 81:13 [a] [Deut. 5:29; Is. 48:18] 81:15 [a] Rom. 1:30 81:16 [a] Deut. 32:14 [b] Job 29:6 82:1 [a] [2 Chr. 19:6; Eccl. 5:8] [b] Ps. 82:6 [1] Hebrew *elohim, mighty ones;* that is, the judges 82:2 [a] [Deut. 1:17]; Prov. 18:5 82:3 [a] [Deut. 24:17; Is. 11:4; Jer. 22:16] 82:5 [a] Ps. 11:3 82:6 [a] John 10:34 [1] Hebrew *elohim, mighty ones;* that is, the judges 82:8 [a] Ps. 2:8; [Rev. 11:15] 83:1 [a] Ps. 28:1 83:2 [a] Ps. 81:15; Is. 17:12; Acts 4:25 83:3 [a] [Ps. 27:5] 83:4 [a] Esth. 3:6, 9; Jer. 11:19; 31:36 83:6 [a] 2 Chr. 20:1, 10, 11 83:9 [a] Num. 31:7; Judg. 7:22 [b] Judg. 4:15–24; 5:20, 21 83:10 [a] Zeph. 1:17 83:11 [a] Judg. 7:25 [b] Judg. 8:12–21

12 Who said, "Let us take for ourselves
The pastures of God for a possession."

13 [a]O my God, make them like
the whirling dust,
[b]Like the chaff before the wind!
14 As the fire burns the woods,
And as the flame [a]sets the
mountains on fire,
15 So pursue them with Your tempest,
And frighten them with Your storm.
16 Fill their faces with shame,
That they may seek Your
name, O LORD.
17 Let them be confounded and
dismayed forever;
Yes, let them be put to
shame and perish,
18 [a]That they may know that You, whose
[b]name alone *is* the LORD,
Are [c]the Most High over all
the earth.

Psalm 84

The Blessedness of Dwelling in the House of God

To the Chief Musician. [a]On an instrument of Gath.[1] A Psalm of the sons of Korah.

1 How [a]lovely *is* Your tabernacle,
O LORD of hosts!
2 [a]My soul longs, yes, even faints
For the courts of the LORD;
My heart and my flesh cry
out for the living God.

3 Even the sparrow has found a home,
And the swallow a nest for herself,
Where she may lay her young—
Even Your altars, O LORD of hosts,
My King and my God.
4 Blessed *are* those who dwell
in Your [a]house;
They will still be praising You. *Selah*

5 Blessed *is* the man whose
strength *is* in You,
Whose heart *is* set on pilgrimage.
6 *As they* pass through the
Valley [a]of Baca,
They make it a spring;
The rain also covers it with pools.
7 They go [a]from strength to strength;
Each one [b]appears before God in Zion.[1]

8 O LORD God of hosts, hear
my prayer;
Give ear, O God of Jacob! *Selah*
9 [a]O God, behold our shield,
And look upon the face of
Your anointed.

10 For a day in Your courts *is*
better than a thousand.
I would rather be a doorkeeper
in the house of my God
Than dwell in the tents of wickedness.
11 For the LORD God *is* [a]a sun and [b]shield;
The LORD will give grace and glory;
[c]No good *thing* will He withhold
From those who walk uprightly.

12 O LORD of hosts,
[a]Blessed *is* the man who trusts in You!

Psalm 85

Prayer that the LORD Will Restore Favor to the Land

To the Chief Musician. A Psalm [a]of the sons of Korah.

1 LORD, You have been
favorable to Your land;
You have [a]brought back the
captivity of Jacob.
2 You have forgiven the iniquity
of Your people;
You have covered all their sin. *Selah*
3 You have taken away all
Your wrath;
You have turned from the
fierceness of Your anger.

4 [a]Restore us, O God of our salvation,
And cause Your anger
toward us to cease.

83:13 [a] Is. 17:13 [b] Job 21:18; Ps. 35:5; Is. 40:24; Jer. 13:24 83:14 [a] Ex. 19:18; Deut. 32:22 83:18 [a] Ps. 59:13 [b] Ex. 6:3 [c] [Ps. 92:8] 84:title [a] Ps. 8:title [1] Hebrew *Al Gittith* 84:1 [a] Ps. 27:4; 46:4, 5 84:2 [a] Ps. 42:1, 2 84:4 [a] [Ps. 65:4] 84:6 [a] 2 Sam. 5:22–25 84:7 [a] Prov. 4:18; Is. 40:31; John 1:16; 2 Cor. 3:18 [b] Ex. 34:23; Deut. 16:16 [1] Septuagint, Syriac, and Vulgate read *The God of gods shall be seen.* 84:9 [a] Gen. 15:1 84:11 [a] Is. 60:19, 20; Mal. 4:2; Rev. 21:23 [b] Gen. 15:1 [c] Ps. 34:9, 10 84:12 [a] [Ps. 2:12; 40:4] 85:title [a] Ps. 42:title 85:1 [a] Ezra 1:11—2:1; Ps. 14:7; Jer. 30:18; 31:23; Ezek. 39:25; Hos. 6:11; Joel 3:1 85:4 [a] Ps. 80:3, 7

5 [a]Will You be angry with us forever?
Will You prolong Your anger
to all generations?
6 Will You not [a]revive us again,
That Your people may rejoice in You?
7 Show us Your mercy, LORD,
And grant us Your salvation.

8 I will hear what God the
LORD will speak,
For He will speak peace
To His people and to His saints;
But let them not turn back to folly.
9 Surely [a]His salvation *is* near
to those who fear Him,
[b]That glory may dwell in our land.

10 Mercy and truth have met together;
[a]Righteousness and peace
have kissed.
11 Truth shall spring out of the earth,
And righteousness shall look
down from heaven.
12 [a]Yes, the LORD will give *what is* good;
And our land will yield its increase.
13 Righteousness will go before Him,
And shall make His footsteps
our pathway.

Psalm 86

Prayer for Mercy, with Meditation on the Excellencies of the LORD

A Prayer of David.

1 Bow down Your ear, O LORD,
hear me;
For I *am* poor and needy.
2 Preserve my life, for I *am* holy;
You are my God;
Save Your servant who trusts
in You!
3 Be merciful to me, O Lord,
For I cry to You all day long.
4 Rejoice the soul of Your servant,
[a]For to You, O Lord, I lift up my soul.
5 For [a]You, Lord, *are* good,
and ready to forgive,
And abundant in mercy to all
those who call upon You.
6 Give ear, O LORD, to my prayer;
And attend to the voice of
my supplications.
7 In the day of my trouble I
will call upon You,
For You will answer me.

8 [a]Among the gods *there is*
none like You, O Lord;
Nor *are there any works*
like Your works.
9 All nations whom You have made
Shall come and worship
before You, O Lord,
And shall glorify Your name.
10 For You *are* great, and [a]do
wondrous things;
[b]You alone *are* God.

11 [a]Teach me Your way, O LORD;
I will walk in Your truth;
Unite my heart to fear Your name.
12 I will praise You, O Lord my
God, with all my heart,
And I will glorify Your
name forevermore.
13 For great *is* Your mercy toward me,
And You have delivered my soul
from the depths of Sheol.

14 O God, the proud have
risen against me,
And a mob of violent *men*
have sought my life,
And have not set You before them.
15 But [a]You, O Lord, *are* a God full of
compassion, and gracious,
Longsuffering and abundant
in mercy and truth.

16 Oh, turn to me, and have
mercy on me!
Give Your strength to Your servant,
And save the son of Your
maidservant.
17 Show me a sign for good,
That those who hate me may
see *it* and be ashamed,
Because You, LORD, have helped
me and comforted me.

85:5 [a] Ps. 79:5 **85:6** [a] Hab. 3:2 **85:9** [a] Is. 46:13 [b] Hag. 2:7; Zech. 2:5; [John 1:14] **85:10** [a] Ps. 72:3; [Is. 32:17]; Luke 2:14 **85:12** [a] [Ps. 84:11; James 1:17] **86:4** [a] Ps. 25:1; 143:8 **86:5** [a] Ps. 130:7; 145:9; [Joel 2:13] **86:8** [a] [Ex. 15:11]; 2 Sam. 7:22; 1 Kin. 8:23; Ps. 89:6; Jer. 10:6 **86:10** [a] [Ex. 15:11] [b] Deut. 6:4; Is. 37:16; Mark 12:29; 1 Cor. 8:4 **86:11** [a] Ps. 27:11; 143:8 **86:15** [a] Ex. 34:6; [Ps. 86:5]

Psalm 87

The Glories of the City of God

A Psalm of the sons of Korah. A Song.

1 His foundation *is* in the
holy mountains.
2 [a]The LORD loves the gates of Zion
More than all the dwellings of Jacob.
3 [a]Glorious things are spoken of you,
O city of God! *Selah*

4 "I will make mention of Rahab and
Babylon to those who know Me;
Behold, O Philistia and
Tyre, with Ethiopia:
'This *one* was born there.'"

5 And of Zion it will be said,
"This *one* and that *one* were born in her;
And the Most High Himself
shall establish her."
6 The LORD will record,
When He [a]registers the peoples:
"This *one* was born there." *Selah*

7 Both the singers and the players
on instruments *say,*
"All my springs *are* in you."

Psalm 88

A Prayer for Help in Despondency

A Song. A Psalm of the sons of Korah. To the Chief Musician. Set to "Mahalath Leannoth." A Contemplation[1] of [a]Heman the Ezrahite.

1 O LORD, [a]God of my salvation,
I have cried out day and
night before You.
2 Let my prayer come before You;
Incline Your ear to my cry.

3 For my soul is full of troubles,
And my life [a]draws near to the grave.
4 I am counted with those who
[a]go down to the pit;
[b]I am like a man *who has* no strength,
5 Adrift among the dead,
Like the slain who lie in the grave,
Whom You remember no more,
And who are cut off from
Your hand.

6 You have laid me in the lowest pit,
In darkness, in the depths.
7 Your wrath lies heavy upon me,
And You have afflicted *me* with
all [a]Your waves. *Selah*
8 [a]You have put away my
acquaintances far from me;
You have made me an
abomination to them;
[b]*I am* shut up, and I cannot get out;
9 My eye wastes away because
of affliction.

[a]LORD, I have called daily upon You;
I have stretched out my hands to You.
10 Will You work wonders
for the dead?
Shall the dead arise *and*
praise You? *Selah*
11 Shall Your lovingkindness be
declared in the grave?
Or Your faithfulness in the
place of destruction?
12 Shall Your wonders be
known in the dark?
And Your righteousness in the
land of forgetfulness?

13 But to You I have cried out, O LORD,
And in the morning my prayer
comes before You.
14 LORD, why do You cast off my soul?
Why do You hide Your face from me?
15 I *have been* afflicted and ready
to die from *my* youth;
I suffer Your terrors;
I am distraught.
16 Your fierce wrath has gone over me;
Your terrors have cut me off.
17 They came around me all
day long like water;
They engulfed me altogether.
18 [a]Loved one and friend You
have put far from me,
And my acquaintances
into darkness.

87:2 [a] Ps. 78:67, 68 87:3 [a] Is. 60:1 87:6 [a] Is. 4:3 88:title [a] 1 Kin. 4:31; 1 Chr. 2:6 [1] Hebrew *Maschil* 88:1 [a] Ps. 27:9; [Luke 18:7] 88:3 [a] Ps. 107:18 88:4 [a] [Ps. 28:1] [b] Ps. 31:12 88:7 [a] Ps. 42:7 88:8 [a] Job 19:13, 19; Ps. 31:11; 142:4 [b] Lam. 3:7 88:9 [a] Ps. 86:3 88:18 [a] Job 19:13; Ps. 31:11; 38:11

Psalm 89

Remembering the Covenant with David, and Sorrow for Lost Blessings

A Contemplation[1] of [a]Ethan the Ezrahite.

1 I will sing of the mercies of
the LORD forever;
With my mouth will I make known
Your faithfulness to all
generations.
2 For I have said, "Mercy shall
be built up forever;
[a]Your faithfulness You shall
establish in the very heavens."

3 "I[a] have made a covenant
with My chosen,
I have [b]sworn to My servant David:
4 'Your seed I will establish forever,
And build up your throne [a]to
all generations.'" *Selah*

5 And [a]the heavens will praise
Your wonders, O LORD;
Your faithfulness also in the
assembly of the saints.
6 [a]For who in the heavens can be
compared to the LORD?
Who among the sons of the mighty
can be likened to the LORD?
7 [a]God is greatly to be feared in the
assembly of the saints,
And to be held in reverence by
all *those* around Him.
8 O LORD God of hosts,
Who *is* mighty like You, O LORD?
Your faithfulness also surrounds You.
9 [a]You rule the raging of the sea;
When its waves rise, You still them.
10 [a]You have broken Rahab in
pieces, as one who is slain;
You have scattered Your enemies
with Your mighty arm.

11 [a]The heavens *are* Yours, the
earth also *is* Yours;
The world and all its fullness,
You have founded them.
12 The north and the south, You
have created them;
[a]Tabor and [b]Hermon rejoice
in Your name.
13 You have a mighty arm;
Strong is Your hand, *and* high
is Your right hand.
14 Righteousness and justice *are* the
foundation of Your throne;
Mercy and truth go before Your face.
15 Blessed *are* the people who
know the [a]joyful sound!
They walk, O LORD, in the light
of Your countenance.
16 In Your name they rejoice all day long,
And in Your righteousness
they are exalted.
17 For You *are* the glory of their strength,
And in Your favor our horn is [a]exalted.
18 For our shield *belongs* to the LORD,
And our king to the Holy One
of Israel.

19 Then You spoke in a vision
to Your holy one,[1]
And said: "I have given help
to *one who is* mighty;
I have exalted one [a]chosen
from the people.
20 [a]I have found My servant David;
With My holy oil I have anointed him,
21 [a]With whom My hand shall
be established;
Also My arm shall strengthen him.
22 The enemy shall not outwit him,
Nor the son of wickedness afflict him.
23 I will beat down his foes
before his face,
And plague those who hate him.

24 "But My faithfulness and My
mercy *shall be* with him,
And in My name his horn
shall be exalted.
25 Also I will [a]set his hand over the sea,
And his right hand over the rivers.
26 He shall cry to Me, 'You *are* [a]my Father,
My God, and [b]the rock of my salvation.'

89:title [a] 1 Kin. 4:31 [1] Hebrew *Maschil* 89:2 [a] [Ps. 119:89, 90] 89:3 [a] 1 Kin. 8:16 [b] 2 Sam. 7:11; 1 Chr. 17:10–12 89:4 [a] [2 Sam. 7:13; Is. 9:7; Luke 1:33] 89:5 [a] [Ps. 19:1] 89:6 [a] Ps. 86:8; 113:5 89:7 [a] Ps. 76:7, 11 89:9 [a] Ps. 65:7; 93:3, 4; 107:29 89:10 [a] Ex. 14:26–28; Ps. 87:4; Is. 30:7; 51:9 89:11 [a] [Gen. 1:1; 1 Chr. 29:11] 89:12 [a] Josh. 19:22; Judg. 4:6; Jer. 46:18 [b] Deut. 3:8; Josh. 11:17; 12:1; Song 4:8 89:15 [a] Lev. 23:24; Num. 10:10; Ps. 98:6 89:17 [a] Ps. 75:10; 92:10; 132:17 89:19 [a] 1 Kin. 11:34 [1] Following many Hebrew manuscripts; Masoretic Text, Septuagint, Targum, and Vulgate read *holy ones.* 89:20 [a] 1 Sam. 13:14; 16:1–12; Acts 13:22 89:21 [a] Ps. 80:17 89:25 [a] Ps. 72:8 89:26 [a] 2 Sam. 7:14; [1 Chr. 22:10]; Jer. 3:19 [b] 2 Sam. 22:47

LIFE SUPPORT

BE RIGHTEOUS: PURSUE RIGHTEOUSNESS AND JUSTICE

Righteousness and justice are the foundation of Your throne;
mercy and truth go before Your face. Psalm 89:14

LIFE: Be Righteous

God always wants justice and righteousness for His people. He also requires us to be doers of justice and righteousness. Despite what the world may say, it is always right to do what is right and to treat others right. We are to treat others as God would treat them. He is not callous. God is compassionate. He is loving. He is helpful. The world says to put ourselves first and do what is best for us even at the expense of others. But God says to serve others in love first. We cannot treat others in an unjust way and expect our lives to please God.

To please God, we must first have faith and then demonstrate our faith through the way we live. We must be in right relationship with every person we meet. When we encounter people who are different from us or who act in ways that are strange to us, we should not judge them but be ready to accept their differences and love them. See the interaction as an opportunity to demonstrate the love of God.

Maybe you have been treated poorly or in an unjust way. Perhaps someone kicked you while you were down. It is best to let God deal with that person. You cannot let the wrongs of others change your heart. You have to remain in a pure place. Remember to treat others right at all times so you will remain in the will of God.

SUPPORT: Pursue Righteousness and Justice

What a directive! Pursuing righteousness and justice is a twofold instruction, yet it is like examining two sides of the same coin.

To pursue righteousness, we must understand that we cannot please God in our sinful state. We must move from attempting to excuse our actions to recognizing our need for the mercy of God. We need to look for Him to transform our minds and cleanse our hearts. We resolve to walk in the Spirit and surrender daily to the Lord. We seek God diligently, listen attentively for His voice, and allow Him to lead our steps.

We pursue justice when we first realize that no one is perfect. Yes, we hold people accountable, but with an attitude of grace because God has given His grace to us. Once grace is in place, we can pursue God's justice. This is not merely receiving justice from the courts, the police, or others in government. Instead, it is about ensuring we act justly toward others. This quest also requires that we act mercifully toward others, especially those who are defenseless, underprivileged, or oppressed. This pursuit requires daily help from God. We need Him to walk alongside us as we strive to bring His justice on behalf of those who have been subject to injustice.

SUPPORT EXAMPLE: Defend the fatherless through mentoring.

27 Also I will make him [a]*My* firstborn,
[b]The highest of the kings of the earth.
28 [a]My mercy I will keep for him
forever,
And My covenant shall stand
firm with him.
29 His seed also I will make
to endure forever,

89:27 [a] Ex. 4:22; Ps. 2:7; Jer. 31:9; [Col. 1:15, 18] [b] Num. 24:7; [Ps. 72:11]; Rev. 19:16 89:28 [a] Is. 55:3

[a]And his throne [b]as the days of heaven.

30 "If[a] his sons [b]forsake My law
And do not walk in My judgments,
31 If they break My statutes
And do not keep My commandments,
32 Then I will punish their
transgression with the rod,
And their iniquity with stripes.
33 [a]Nevertheless My lovingkindness I
will not utterly take from him,
Nor allow My faithfulness to fail.
34 My covenant I will not break,
Nor [a]alter the word that has
gone out of My lips.
35 Once I have sworn [a]by My holiness;
I will not lie to David:
36 [a]His seed shall endure forever,
And his throne [b]as the sun before Me;
37 It shall be established forever
like the moon,
Even *like* the faithful witness
in the sky." *Selah*

38 But You have [a]cast off and [b]abhorred,
You have been furious with
Your anointed.
39 You have renounced the
covenant of Your servant;
[a]You have profaned his crown *by*
casting it to the ground.
40 You have broken down all his
hedges;
You have brought his
strongholds to ruin.
41 All who pass by the way [a]plunder him;
He is a reproach to his neighbors.
42 You have exalted the right
hand of his adversaries;
You have made all his enemies rejoice.
43 You have also turned back
the edge of his sword,
And have not sustained
him in the battle.
44 You have made his glory cease,
And cast his throne down
to the ground.
45 The days of his youth You
have shortened;
You have covered him
with shame. *Selah*

46 How long, LORD?
Will You hide Yourself forever?
Will Your wrath burn like fire?
47 Remember how short my time [a]is;
For what [b]futility have You created
all the children of men?
48 What man can live and not
see [a]death?
Can he deliver his life from the
power of the grave? *Selah*

49 Lord, where *are* Your former
lovingkindnesses,
Which You [a]swore to David
[b]in Your truth?
50 Remember, Lord, the reproach
of Your servants—
[a]*How* I bear in my bosom
the reproach of all the
many peoples,
51 [a]With which Your enemies have
reproached, O LORD,
With which they have reproached
the footsteps of Your anointed.

52 [a]Blessed *be* the LORD forevermore!
Amen and Amen.

BOOK FOUR
PSALMS 90–106

Psalm 90

The Eternity of God, and Man's Frailty

A Prayer [a]of Moses the man of God.

1 Lord, [a]You have been our dwelling
place[1] in all generations.
2 [a]Before the mountains were
brought forth,
Or ever You had formed the
earth and the world,
Even from everlasting to
everlasting, You *are* God.

89:29 [a] [1 Kin. 2:4; Is. 9:7]; Jer. 33:17 [b] Deut. 11:21 89:30 [a] [2 Sam. 7:14] [b] Ps. 119:53 89:33 [a] 2 Sam. 7:14, 15 89:34 [a] [Num. 23:19]; Jer. 33:20–22 89:35 [a] [1 Sam. 15:29]; Amos 4:2; [Titus 1:2] 89:36 [a] [Luke 1:33] [b] Ps. 72:17 89:38 [a] [1 Chr. 28:9] [b] Deut. 32:19 89:39 [a] Ps. 74:7; Lam. 5:16 89:41 [a] Ps. 80:12 89:47 [a] Ps. 90:9 [b] Ps. 62:9 89:48 [a] [Eccl. 3:19] 89:49 [a] [2 Sam. 7:15]; Jer. 30:9; Ezek. 34:23 [b] Ps. 54:5 89:50 [a] Ps. 69:9, 19 89:51 [a] Ps. 74:10, 18, 22 89:52 [a] Ps. 41:13 90:title [a] Deut. 33:1 90:1 [a] [Deut. 33:27; Ezek. 11:16] [1] Septuagint, Targum, and Vulgate read *refuge*. 90:2 [a] Job 15:7; [Prov. 8:25, 26]

3 You turn man to destruction,
And say, [a]"Return, O children of men."
4 [a]For a thousand years in Your sight
Are like yesterday when it is past,
And *like* a watch in the night.
5 You carry them away *like* a flood;
[a]*They are* like a sleep.
In the morning [b]they are like
grass *which* grows up:
6 In the morning it flourishes
and grows up;
In the evening it is cut
down and withers.

7 For we have been consumed
by Your anger,
And by Your wrath we are terrified.
8 [a]You have set our iniquities before You,
Our [b]secret *sins* in the light
of Your countenance.
9 For all our days have passed
away in Your wrath;
We finish our years like a sigh.
10 The days of our lives *are* seventy years;
And if by reason of strength
they are eighty years,
Yet their boast *is* only
labor and sorrow;
For it is soon cut off, and we fly away.
11 Who knows the power of Your anger?
For as the fear of You, *so is* Your wrath.
12 [a]So teach *us* to number our days,
That we may gain a heart of wisdom.

13 Return, O LORD!
How long?
And [a]have compassion on
Your servants.
14 Oh, satisfy us early with Your mercy,
[a]That we may rejoice and be
glad all our days!
15 Make us glad according to the days
in which You have afflicted us,
The years *in which* we have seen evil.
16 Let [a]Your work appear to
Your servants,
And Your glory to their children.
17 [a]And let the beauty of the LORD
our God be upon us,
And [b]establish the work of
our hands for us;
Yes, establish the work of our hands.

Psalm 91

Safety of Abiding in the Presence of God

1 He [a]who dwells in the secret
place of the Most High
Shall abide [b]under the shadow
of the Almighty.
2 [a]I will say of the LORD, "*He is* my
refuge and my fortress;
My God, in Him I will trust."

3 Surely [a]He shall deliver you from
the snare of the fowler[1]
And from the perilous pestilence.
4 [a]He shall cover you with His feathers,
And under His wings you
shall take refuge;
His truth *shall be your*
shield and buckler.
5 [a]You shall not be afraid of
the terror by night,
Nor of the arrow *that* flies by day,
6 *Nor* of the pestilence *that*
walks in darkness,
Nor of the destruction *that*
lays waste at noonday.

7 A thousand may fall at your side,
And ten thousand at your right hand;
But it shall not come near you.
8 Only [a]with your eyes shall you look,
And see the reward of the wicked.

9 Because you have made the
LORD, *who is* [a]my refuge,
Even the Most High, [b]your
dwelling place,
10 [a]No evil shall befall you,
Nor shall any plague come
near your dwelling;
11 [a]For He shall give His angels
charge over you,
To keep you in all your ways.

90:3 [a] Gen. 3:19; Job 34:14, 15 90:4 [a] 2 Pet. 3:8 90:5 [a] Ps. 73:20 [b] Is. 40:6 90:8 [a] Ps. 50:21; [Jer. 16:17] [b] Ps. 19:12; [Eccl. 12:14] 90:12 [a] Deut. 32:29; Ps. 39:4 90:13 [a] Ex. 32:12; Deut. 32:36 90:14 [a] Ps. 85:6 90:16 [a] [Deut. 32:4]; Hab. 3:2 90:17 [a] Ps. 27:4 [b] Is. 26:12 91:1 [a] Ps. 27:5; 31:20; 32:7 [b] Ps. 17:8; Is. 25:4; 32:2 91:2 [a] Ps. 142:5 91:3 [a] Ps. 124:7; Prov. 6:5 [1] That is, one who catches birds in a trap or snare 91:4 [a] Ps. 17:8 91:5 [a] [Job 5:19; Ps. 112:7; Is. 43:2] 91:8 [a] Ps. 37:34; Mal. 1:5 91:9 [a] Ps. 91:2 [b] Ps. 90:1 91:10 [a] [Prov. 12:21] 91:11 [a] Ps. 34:7; Matt. 4:6; Luke 4:10; [Heb. 1:14]

#OXYGEN

PSALM 91:9-10

Reconcile Wrongs with Rights

You are blessed, and the Enemy cannot do anything about that truth. So, seek to know God and His ways and flee from sin. Seek forgiveness, **breathe**, and **reconcile wrongs with rights.**

12 In *their* hands they shall
bear you up,
[a]Lest you dash your foot
against a stone.
13 You shall tread upon the
lion and the cobra,
The young lion and the serpent
you shall trample underfoot.

14 "Because he has set his love upon
Me, therefore I will deliver him;
I will set him on high, because
he has [a]known My name.
15 He shall [a]call upon Me, and
I will answer him;
I *will be* [b]with him in trouble;
I will deliver him and honor him.
16 With long life I will satisfy him,
And show him My salvation."

Psalm 92

Praise to the LORD for His Love and Faithfulness

A Psalm. A Song for the Sabbath day.

1 *It is* [a]good to give thanks to the LORD,
And to sing praises to Your
name, O Most High;
2 To [a]declare Your lovingkindness
in the morning,
And Your faithfulness every night,
3 [a]On an instrument of ten strings,
On the lute,
And on the harp,
With harmonious sound.
4 For You, LORD, have made me
glad through Your work;
I will triumph in the works
of Your hands.

5 [a]O LORD, how great are Your works!
[b]Your thoughts are very deep.
6 [a]A senseless man does not know,
Nor does a fool understand this.
7 When [a]the wicked spring
up like grass,
And when all the workers
of iniquity flourish,
It is that they may be
destroyed forever.

8 [a]But You, LORD, *are* on
high forevermore.
9 For behold, Your enemies, O LORD,
For behold, Your enemies
shall perish;
All the workers of iniquity
shall [a]be scattered.

10 But [a]my horn You have
exalted like a wild ox;
I have been [b]anointed with fresh oil.
11 [a]My eye also has seen *my*
desire on my enemies;
My ears hear *my desire*
on the wicked
Who rise up against me.

12 [a]The righteous shall flourish
like a palm tree,
He shall grow like a cedar
in Lebanon.
13 Those who are planted in the
house of the LORD
Shall flourish in the courts
of our God.
14 They shall still bear fruit in old age;
They shall be fresh and flourishing,
15 To declare that the LORD is upright;
[a]*He is* my rock, and [b]*there is* no
unrighteousness in Him.

91:12 [a] Matt. 4:6; Luke 4:11 91:14 [a] [Ps. 9:10] 91:15 [a] Job 12:4; Ps. 50:15 [b] Is. 43:2 92:1 [a] Ps. 147:1 92:2 [a] Ps. 89:1 92:3 [a] 1 Chr. 23:5 92:5 [a] Ps. 40:5; [Rev. 15:3] [b] Ps. 139:17, 18; [Is. 28:29; Rom. 11:33, 34] 92:6 [a] Ps. 73:22 92:7 [a] Job 12:6; Ps. 37:1, 2; Jer. 12:1, 2; [Mal. 3:15] 92:8 [a] [Ps. 83:18] 92:9 [a] Ps. 68:1 92:10 [a] Ps. 89:17 [b] Ps. 23:5 92:11 [a] Ps. 54:7 92:12 [a] Num. 24:6; Ps. 52:8; Jer. 17:8; Hos. 14:5, 6 92:15 [a] [Deut. 32:4] [b] [Rom. 9:14]

Psalm 93

The Eternal Reign of the LORD

1 The [a]LORD reigns, He is
clothed with majesty;
The LORD is clothed,
[b]He has girded Himself with strength.
Surely the world is established,
so that it cannot be moved.
2 [a]Your throne *is* established from of old;
You *are* from everlasting.

3 The floods have lifted up, O LORD,
The floods have lifted up their voice;
The floods lift up their waves.
4 [a]The LORD on high *is* mightier
Than the noise of many waters,
Than the mighty waves of the sea.

5 Your testimonies are very sure;
Holiness adorns Your house,
O LORD, forever.

Psalm 94

God the Refuge of the Righteous

1 O LORD God, [a]to whom
vengeance belongs—
O God, to whom vengeance
belongs, shine forth!
2 Rise up, O [a]Judge of the earth;
Render punishment to the proud.
3 LORD, [a]how long will the wicked,
How long will the wicked triumph?

4 They [a]utter speech, *and*
speak insolent things;
All the workers of iniquity
boast in themselves.
5 They break in pieces Your
people, O LORD,
And afflict Your heritage.
6 They slay the widow and
the stranger,
And murder the fatherless.
7 [a]Yet they say, "The LORD
does not see,
Nor does the God of Jacob
understand."
8 Understand, you senseless
among the people;
And *you* fools, when will you be wise?
9 [a]He who planted the ear,
shall He not hear?
He who formed the eye,
shall He not see?
10 He who instructs the nations,
shall He not correct,
He who teaches man knowledge?
11 The LORD [a]knows the
thoughts of man,
That they *are* futile.

12 Blessed *is* the man whom
You [a]instruct, O LORD,
And teach out of Your law,
13 That You may give him rest
from the days of adversity,
Until the pit is dug for the wicked.
14 For the LORD will not cast
off His people,
Nor will He forsake His inheritance.
15 But judgment will return
to righteousness,
And all the upright in
heart will follow it.

16 Who will rise up for me
against the evildoers?
Who will stand up for me against
the workers of iniquity?
17 Unless the LORD *had been* my help,
My soul would soon have
settled in silence.
18 If I say, "My foot slips,"
Your mercy, O LORD, will
hold me up.
19 In the multitude of my
anxieties within me,
Your comforts delight my soul.

20 Shall [a]the throne of iniquity,
which devises evil by law,
Have fellowship with You?
21 They gather together against
the life of the righteous,
And condemn [a]innocent blood.
22 But the LORD has been my defense,
And my God the rock of my refuge.

93:1 [a] Ps. 96:10 [b] Ps. 65:6 93:2 [a] Ps. 45:6; [Lam. 5:19] 93:4 [a] Ps. 65:7 94:1 [a] Deut. 32:35; [Is. 35:4; Nah. 1:2; Rom. 12:19] 94:2 [a] [Gen. 18:25] 94:3 [a] [Job 20:5] 94:4 [a] Ps. 31:18; Jude 15 94:7 [a] Job 22:13; Ps. 10:11 94:9 [a] [Ex. 4:11; Prov. 20:12] 94:11 [a] Job 11:11; 1 Cor. 3:20 94:12 [a] [Deut. 8:5; Job 5:17; Ps. 119:71; Prov. 3:11, 12; Heb. 12:5, 6] 94:20 [a] Amos 6:3 94:21 [a] [Ex. 23:7]; Ps. 106:38; [Prov. 17:15]; Matt. 27:4

23 He has brought on them
their own iniquity,
And shall cut them off in
their own wickedness;
The LORD our God shall cut them off.

Psalm 95

A Call to Worship and Obedience

1 Oh come, let us sing to the LORD!
Let us shout joyfully to the
Rock of our salvation.
2 Let us come before His presence
with thanksgiving;
Let us shout joyfully to
Him with [a]psalms.
3 For [a]the LORD *is* the great God,
And the great King above all gods.
4 In His hand *are* the deep
places of the earth;
The heights of the hills *are* His also.
5 [a]The sea *is* His, for He made it;
And His hands formed the dry *land*.

6 Oh come, let us worship
and bow down;
Let [a]us kneel before the
LORD our Maker.
7 For He *is* our God,
And [a]we *are* the people of His pasture,
And the sheep of His hand.

[b]Today, if you will hear His voice:
8 "Do not harden your hearts,
as in the rebellion,[1]
[a]As *in* the day of trial[2] in the
wilderness,
9 When [a]your fathers tested Me;
They tried Me, though they
[b]saw My work.
10 For [a]forty years I was grieved
with *that* generation,
And said, 'It *is* a people who go
astray in their hearts,
And they do not know My ways.'
11 So [a]I swore in My wrath,
'They shall not enter My rest.'"

Psalm 96

A Song of Praise to God Coming in Judgment

(1 Chr. 16:23–33)

1 Oh, [a]sing to the LORD a new song!
Sing to the LORD, all the earth.
2 Sing to the LORD, bless His name;
Proclaim the good news of His
salvation from day to day.
3 Declare His glory among the nations,
His wonders among all peoples.

4 For [a]the LORD *is* great and
[b]greatly to be praised;
[c]He *is* to be feared above all gods.
5 For [a]all the gods of the
peoples *are* idols,
[b]But the LORD made the heavens.
6 Honor and majesty *are* before Him;
Strength and [a]beauty *are*
in His sanctuary.

7 [a]Give to the LORD, O families
of the peoples,
Give to the LORD glory and strength.
8 Give to the LORD the glory
due His name;
Bring an offering, and come
into His courts.
9 Oh, worship the LORD [a]in the
beauty of holiness!
Tremble before Him, all the earth.

10 Say among the nations,
[a]"The LORD reigns;
The world also is firmly established,
It shall not be moved;
[b]He shall judge the peoples righteously."

11 [a]Let the heavens rejoice, and
let the earth be glad;
[b]Let the sea roar, and all its fullness;
12 Let the field be joyful, and
all that *is* in it.
Then all the trees of the
woods will rejoice
13 before the LORD.

95:2 [a] Eph. 5:19; James 5:13 95:3 [a] [Ps. 96:4; 1 Cor. 8:5, 6] 95:5 [a] Gen. 1:9, 10; Jon. 1:9 95:6 [a] 2 Chr. 6:13; Dan. 6:10; [Phil. 2:10] 95:7 [a] Ps. 79:13 [b] Heb. 3:7–11, 15; 4:7 95:8 [a] Ex. 17:2–7; Num. 20:13 [1] Or *Meribah* [2] Or *Massah* 95:9 [a] Ps. 78:18; [1 Cor. 10:9] [b] Num. 14:22 95:10 [a] Acts 7:36; 13:18; Heb. 3:10, 17 95:11 [a] Num. 14:23, 28–30; Deut. 1:35; Heb. 4:3, 5 96:1 [a] 1 Chr. 16:23–33 96:4 [a] Ps. 145:3 [b] Ps. 18:3 [c] Ps. 95:3 96:5 [a] 1 Chr. 16:26; [Jer. 10:11] [b] Ps. 115:15; Is. 42:5 96:6 [a] Ps. 29:2 96:7 [a] 1 Chr. 16:28, 29; Ps. 29:1, 2 96:9 [a] 1 Chr. 16:29; 2 Chr. 20:21; Ps. 29:2 96:10 [a] Ps. 93:1; 97:1; [Rev. 11:15; 19:6] [b] Ps. 67:4 96:11 [a] Ps. 69:34; Is. 49:13 [b] Ps. 98:7

For He is coming, for He is
coming to judge the earth.
[a]He shall judge the world
with righteousness,
And the peoples with His truth.

Psalm 97

A Song of Praise to the Sovereign LORD

1 The LORD [a]reigns;
Let the earth rejoice;
Let the multitude of isles be glad!

2 [a]Clouds and darkness surround Him;
[b]Righteousness and justice *are* the
foundation of His throne.
3 [a]A fire goes before Him,
And burns up His enemies
round about.
4 [a]His lightnings light the world;
The earth sees and trembles.
5 [a]The mountains melt like wax at
the presence of the LORD,
At the presence of the Lord
of the whole earth.
6 [a]The heavens declare His
righteousness,
And all the peoples see
His glory.

7 [a]Let all be put to shame who
serve carved images,
Who boast of idols.
[b]Worship Him, all *you* gods.
8 Zion hears and is glad,
And the daughters of Judah rejoice
Because of Your judgments,
O LORD.
9 For You, LORD, *are* [a]most high
above all the earth;
[b]You are exalted far above all gods.

10 You who love the LORD, [a]hate evil!
[b]He preserves the souls of His saints;
[c]He delivers them out of the
hand of the wicked.
11 [a]Light is sown for the righteous,
And gladness for the upright
in heart.
12 [a]Rejoice in the LORD, you righteous,
[b]And give thanks at the remembrance
of His holy name.[1]

Psalm 98

A Song of Praise to the LORD for His Salvation and Judgment

A Psalm.

1 Oh, [a]sing to the LORD a new song!
For He has [b]done marvelous things;
His right hand and His holy arm
have gained Him the victory.
2 [a]The LORD has made known
His salvation;
[b]His righteousness He has revealed
in the sight of the nations.
3 He has remembered His
mercy and His faithfulness
to the house of Israel;
[a]All the ends of the earth have seen
the salvation of our God.

4 Shout joyfully to the LORD,
all the earth;
Break forth in song, rejoice,
and sing praises.
5 Sing to the LORD with the harp,
With the harp and the
sound of a psalm,
6 With trumpets and the
sound of a horn;
Shout joyfully before the
LORD, the King.

7 Let the sea roar, and all its fullness,
The world and those who dwell in it;
8 Let the rivers clap *their* hands;
Let the hills be joyful together
9 before the LORD,
[a]For He is coming to judge the earth.
With righteousness He shall
judge the world,
And the peoples with equity.

96:13 [a] [Rev. 19:11] 97:1 [a] [Ps. 96:10] 97:2 [a] Ex. 19:9; Deut. 4:11; 1 Kin. 8:12; Ps. 18:11 [b] [Ps. 89:14] 97:3 [a] Ps. 18:8; Dan. 7:10; Hab. 3:5 97:4 [a] Ex. 19:18 97:5 [a] Ps. 46:6; Amos 9:5; Mic. 1:4; Nah. 1:5 97:6 [a] Ps. 19:1 97:7 [a] [Ex. 20:4] [b] [Heb. 1:6] 97:9 [a] Ps. 83:18 [b] Ex. 18:11; Ps. 95:3; 96:4 97:10 [a] [Ps. 34:14; Prov. 8:13; Amos 5:15; Rom. 12:9] [b] Ps. 31:23; 145:20; Prov. 2:8 [c] Ps. 37:40; Jer. 15:21; Dan. 3:28 97:11 [a] Job 22:28; Ps. 112:4; Prov. 4:18 97:12 [a] Ps. 33:1 [b] Ps. 30:4 [1] Or *His holiness* 98:1 [a] Ps. 33:3; Is. 42:10 [b] Ex. 15:11; Ps. 77:14 98:2 [a] Is. 52:10; [Luke 1:77; 2:30, 31] [b] Is. 62:2; Rom. 3:25 98:3 [a] [Is. 49:6]; Luke 3:6; [Acts 13:47; 28:28] 98:9 [a] [Ps. 96:10, 13]

Psalm 99

Praise to the LORD for His Holiness

1 The LORD reigns;
Let the peoples tremble!
[a]He dwells *between* the cherubim;
Let the earth be moved!
2 The LORD *is* great in Zion,
And He *is* high above all the peoples.
3 Let them praise Your great
and awesome name—
He *is* holy.

4 The King's strength also loves justice;
You have established equity;
You have executed justice and
righteousness in Jacob.
5 Exalt the LORD our God,
And worship at His footstool—
He *is* holy.

6 Moses and Aaron were
among His priests,
And Samuel was among those
who [a]called upon His name;
They called upon the LORD,
and He answered them.
7 He spoke to them in the cloudy pillar;
They kept His testimonies and
the ordinance He gave them.

8 You answered them, O LORD our God;
You were to them God-Who-Forgives,
Though You took vengeance
on their deeds.
9 Exalt the LORD our God,
And worship at His holy hill;
For the LORD our God *is* holy.

Psalm 100

A Song of Praise for the LORD's Faithfulness to His People

[a]A Psalm of Thanksgiving.

1 Make [a]a joyful shout to the
LORD, all you lands!
2 Serve the LORD with gladness;
Come before His presence
with singing.
3 Know that the LORD, He *is* God;
[a]*It is* He *who* has made us,
and not we ourselves;[1]
[b]*We are* His people and the
sheep of His pasture.

4 [a]Enter into His gates with thanksgiving,
And into His courts with praise.
Be thankful to Him, *and*
bless His name.
5 For the LORD *is* good;
[a]His mercy *is* everlasting,
And His truth *endures* to
all generations.

Psalm 101

Promised Faithfulness to the LORD

A Psalm of David.

1 I will sing of mercy and justice;
To You, O LORD, I will sing praises.

2 I will behave wisely in a perfect way.
Oh, when will You come to me?
I will [a]walk within my house
with a perfect heart.

3 I will set nothing wicked
before my eyes;
[a]I hate the work of those [b]who fall away;
It shall not cling to me.
4 A perverse heart shall depart from me;
I will not [a]know wickedness.

5 Whoever secretly slanders his neighbor,
Him I will destroy;
[a]The one who has a haughty
look and a proud heart,
Him I will not endure.

6 My eyes *shall be* on the
faithful of the land,
That they may dwell with me;
He who walks in a perfect way,
He shall serve me.
7 He who works deceit shall not
dwell within my house;
He who tells lies shall not
continue in my presence.

99:1 [a] Ex. 25:22; 1 Sam. 4:4; Ps. 80:1 99:6 [a] 1 Sam. 7:9; 12:18 100:title [a] Ps. 145:title 100:1 [a] Ps. 95:1 100:3 [a] Job 10:3, 8; Ps. 119:73; 139:13, 14; [Eph. 2:10] [b] Ps. 95:7; [Is. 40:11]; Ezek. 34:30, 31 [1] Following Kethib, Septuagint, and Vulgate; Qere, many Hebrew manuscripts, and Targum read *we are His.* 100:4 [a] Ps. 66:13; 116:17–19 100:5 [a] Ps. 136:1 101:2 [a] 1 Kin. 11:4 101:3 [a] Ps. 97:10 [b] Josh. 23:6 101:4 [a] [Ps. 119:115] 101:5 [a] Prov. 6:17

8 [a]Early I will destroy all the
wicked of the land,
That I may cut off all the evildoers
[b]from the city of the LORD.

Psalm 102

The LORD's Eternal Love

A Prayer of the afflicted, [a]when he is overwhelmed and pours out his complaint before the LORD.

1 Hear my prayer, O LORD,
And let my cry come to You.
2 [a]Do not hide Your face from me
in the day of my trouble;
Incline Your ear to me;
In the day that I call, answer
me speedily.

3 For my days are [a]consumed like smoke,
And my bones are burned like a hearth.
4 My heart is stricken and
withered like grass,
So that I forget to eat my bread.
5 Because of the sound of my groaning
My bones cling to my skin.
6 I am like a pelican of the wilderness;
I am like an owl of the desert.
7 I lie awake,
And am like a sparrow alone
on the housetop.

8 My enemies reproach me all day long;
Those who deride me swear
an oath against me.
9 For I have eaten ashes like bread,
And mingled my drink with weeping,
10 Because of Your indignation
and Your wrath;
For You have lifted me up
and cast me away.
11 My days *are* like a shadow
that lengthens,
And I wither away like grass.

12 But You, O LORD, shall endure forever,
And the remembrance of Your
name to all generations.
13 You will arise *and* have mercy on Zion;
For the time to favor her,
Yes, the set time, has come.
14 For Your servants take
pleasure in her stones,
And show favor to her dust.
15 So the nations shall [a]fear the
name of the LORD,
And all the kings of the earth Your glory.
16 For the LORD shall build up Zion;
[a]He shall appear in His glory.
17 [a]He shall regard the prayer
of the destitute,
And shall not despise their prayer.

18 This will be [a]written for the
generation to come,
That [b]a people yet to be created
may praise the LORD.
19 For He [a]looked down from the
height of His sanctuary;
From heaven the LORD
viewed the earth,
20 [a]To hear the groaning of the prisoner,
To release those appointed
to death,
21 To [a]declare the name of
the LORD in Zion,
And His praise in Jerusalem,
22 [a]When the peoples are
gathered together,
And the kingdoms, to serve the LORD.

23 He weakened my strength in the way;
He [a]shortened my days.
24 [a]I said, "O my God,
Do not take me away in the
midst of my days;
[b]Your years *are* throughout
all generations.
25 [a]Of old You laid the foundation
of the earth,
And the heavens *are* the
work of Your hands.
26 [a]They will perish, but You will endure;
Yes, they will all grow old
like a garment;
Like a cloak You will change them,
And they will be changed.

101:8 [a] [Ps. 75:10]; Jer. 21:12 [b] Ps. 48:2, 8 102:title [a] Ps. 61:2 102:2 [a] Ps. 27:9; 69:17 102:3 [a] James 4:14 102:15 [a] 1 Kin. 8:43 102:16 [a] [Is. 60:1, 2] 102:17 [a] Neh. 1:6; Ps. 22:24 102:18 [a] Deut. 31:19; [Rom. 15:4; 1 Cor. 10:11] [b] Ps. 22:31 102:19 [a] Deut. 26:15; Ps. 14:2 102:20 [a] Ps. 79:11 102:21 [a] Ps. 22:22 102:22 [a] [Is. 2:2, 3; 49:22, 23; 60:3]; Zech. 8:20–23 102:23 [a] Job 21:21 102:24 [a] [Ps. 39:13]; Is. 38:10 [b] Job 36:26; [Ps. 90:2]; Hab. 1:12 102:25 [a] [Gen. 1:1; Neh. 9:6; Heb. 1:10–12] 102:26 [a] Is. 34:4; 51:6; Matt. 24:35; [2 Pet. 3:7, 10–12]; Rev. 20:11

27 But [a]You *are* the same,
And Your years will have no end.
28 [a]The children of Your servants
will continue,
And their descendants will be
established before You."

Psalm 103

Praise for the LORD's Mercies

A Psalm of David.

1 Bless [a]the LORD, O my soul;
And all that is within me,
bless His holy name!
2 Bless the LORD, O my soul,
And forget not all His benefits:
3 [a]Who forgives all your iniquities,
Who [b]heals all your diseases,
4 Who redeems your life
from destruction,
[a]Who crowns you with lovingkindness
and tender mercies,
5 Who satisfies your mouth
with good *things,*
So that [a]your youth is renewed
like the eagle's.

6 The LORD executes righteousness
And justice for all who are
oppressed.
7 [a]He made known His ways to Moses,
His acts to the children of Israel.
8 [a]The LORD *is* merciful and gracious,
Slow to anger, and
abounding in mercy.
9 [a]He will not always strive *with us,*
Nor will He keep *His anger* forever.
10 [a]He has not dealt with us
according to our sins,
Nor punished us according
to our iniquities.

11 For as the heavens are high
above the earth,
So great is His mercy toward
those who fear Him;
12 As far as the east is from the west,
So far has He [a]removed our
transgressions from us.
13 [a]As a father pities *his* children,
So the LORD pities those who fear Him.
14 For He knows our frame;
He remembers that we *are* dust.

15 *As for* man, [a]his days *are* like grass;
As a flower of the field, so he flourishes.
16 [a]For the wind passes over
it, and it is gone,
And [b]its place remembers it no more.[1]
17 But the mercy of the LORD *is* from
everlasting to everlasting
On those who fear Him,
And His righteousness to
children's children,
18 [a]To such as keep His covenant,
And to those who remember His
commandments to do them.

19 The LORD has established
His throne in heaven,
And [a]His kingdom rules over all.

20 [a]Bless the LORD, you His angels,
Who excel in strength,
who [b]do His word,
Heeding the voice of His word.
21 Bless the LORD, all *you* His hosts,
[a]*You* ministers of His, who
do His pleasure.
22 Bless the LORD, all His works,
In all places of His dominion.

Bless the LORD, O my soul!

Psalm 104

Praise to the Sovereign LORD for His Creation and Providence

(cf. Gen. 1:1–31)

1 Bless [a]the LORD, O my soul!

O LORD my God, You are very great:
You are clothed with honor
and majesty,

102:27 [a] [Is. 41:4; 43:10; Mal. 3:6; Heb. 13:8]; James 1:17 102:28 [a] Ps. 69:36 103:1 [a] Ps. 104:1, 35 103:3 [a] Ps. 130:8; Is. 33:24 [b] [Ex. 15:26]; Ps. 147:3; [Is. 53:5]; Jer. 17:14 103:4 [a] [Ps. 5:12] 103:5 [a] [Is. 40:31] 103:7 [a] Ex. 33:12–17; Ps. 147:19 103:8 [a] [Ex. 34:6, 7; Num. 14:18]; Deut. 5:10; Neh. 9:17; Ps. 86:15; Jer. 32:18; Jon. 4:2; James 5:11 103:9 [a] [Ps. 30:5; Is. 57:16]; Jer. 3:5; [Mic. 7:18] 103:10 [a] [Ezra 9:13; Lam. 3:22] 103:12 [a] [2 Sam. 12:13; Is. 38:17; 43:25; Zech. 3:9; Heb. 9:26] 103:13 [a] Mal. 3:17 103:15 [a] Is. 40:6–8; James 1:10, 11; 1 Pet. 1:24 103:16 [a] [Is. 40:7] [b] Job 7:10 [1] Compare Job 7:10 103:18 [a] [Deut. 7:9]; Ps. 25:10 103:19 [a] [Ps. 47:2; Dan. 4:17, 25] 103:20 [a] Ps. 148:2 [b] [Matt. 6:10] 103:21 [a] [Heb. 1:14] 104:1 [a] Ps. 103:1

2 Who cover *Yourself* with light
as *with* a garment,
Who stretch out the heavens
like a curtain.

3 [a]He lays the beams of His upper
chambers in the waters,
Who makes the clouds His chariot,
Who walks on the wings of the wind,
4 Who makes His angels spirits,
His ministers a flame of fire.

5 *You who* laid the foundations
of the earth,
So *that* it should not be moved forever,
6 You [a]covered it with the deep
as *with* a garment;
The waters stood above
the mountains.
7 At Your rebuke they fled;
At the voice of Your thunder
they hastened away.
8 They went up over the mountains;
They went down into the valleys,
To the place which You
founded for them.
9 You have [a]set a boundary that
they may not pass over,
[b]That they may not return
to cover the earth.

10 He sends the springs into the valleys;
They flow among the hills.
11 They give drink to every
beast of the field;
The wild donkeys quench their thirst.
12 By them the birds of the
heavens have their home;
They sing among the branches.
13 [a]He waters the hills from His
upper chambers;
The earth is satisfied with [b]the
fruit of Your works.

14 [a]He causes the grass to
grow for the cattle,
And vegetation for the service of man,
That he may bring forth
[b]food from the earth,
15 And [a]wine *that* makes glad
the heart of man,
Oil to make *his* face shine,
And bread *which* strengthens
man's heart.
16 The trees of the LORD are full *of sap,*
The cedars of Lebanon
which He planted,
17 Where the birds make their nests;
The stork has her home in the fir trees.
18 The high hills *are* for the wild goats;
The cliffs are a refuge for
the [a]rock badgers.[1]

19 [a]He appointed the moon for seasons;
The [b]sun knows its going down.
20 [a]You make darkness, and it is night,
In which all the beasts of the
forest creep about.
21 [a]The young lions roar after their prey,
And seek their food from God.
22 *When* the sun rises, they
gather together
And lie down in their dens.
23 Man goes out to [a]his work
And to his labor until the evening.

24 [a]O LORD, how manifold are Your works!
In wisdom You have made them all.
The earth is full of Your
[b]possessions—
25 This great and wide sea,
In which *are* innumerable
teeming things,
Living things both small and great.
26 There the ships sail about;
There is that [a]Leviathan
Which You have made to play there.

27 [a]These all wait for You,
That You may give *them* their
food in due season.
28 *What* You give them they gather in;
You open Your hand, they
are filled with good.
29 You hide Your face, they are
troubled;
[a]You take away their breath, they
die and return to their dust.

104:3 [a] [Amos 9:6] 104:6 [a] Gen. 1:6 104:9 [a] Job 26:10; Ps. 33:7; [Jer. 5:22] [b] Gen. 9:11–15 104:13 [a] Ps. 147:8 [b] Jer. 10:13 104:14 [a] Gen. 1:29 [b] Job 28:5 104:15 [a] Judg. 9:13; Ps. 23:5; Prov. 31:6; Eccl. 10:19 104:18 [a] Lev. 11:5 [1] Or *rock hyrax* (compare Leviticus 11:5) 104:19 [a] Gen. 1:14 [b] Job 38:12; Ps. 19:6 104:20 [a] [Ps. 74:16; Is. 45:7] 104:21 [a] Job 38:39 104:23 [a] Gen. 3:19 104:24 [a] Ps. 40:5; Prov. 3:19; [Jer. 10:12]; 51:15 [b] Ps. 65:9 104:26 [a] Job 41:1; Is. 27:1 104:27 [a] Job 36:31; Ps. 136:25 104:29 [a] Job 34:15; [Eccl. 12:7]

30 [a]You send forth Your Spirit,
they are created;
And You renew the face of the earth.

31 May the glory of the LORD
endure forever;
May the LORD [a]rejoice in His works.
32 He looks on the earth, and it [a]trembles;
[b]He touches the hills, and they smoke.

33 [a]I will sing to the LORD as long as I live;
I will sing praise to my God
while I have my being.
34 May my [a]meditation be sweet to Him;
I will be glad in the LORD.
35 May [a]sinners be consumed
from the earth,
And the wicked be no more.

Bless the LORD, O my soul!
Praise the LORD!

Psalm 105

The Eternal Faithfulness of the LORD
(Ex. 7:8—11:10; 1 Chr. 16:8–22)

1 Oh, [a]give thanks to the LORD!
Call upon His name;
[b]Make known His deeds
among the peoples!
2 Sing to Him, sing psalms to Him;
[a]Talk of all His wondrous works!
3 Glory in His holy name;
Let the hearts of those rejoice
who seek the LORD!
4 Seek the LORD and His strength;
[a]Seek His face evermore!
5 [a]Remember His marvelous
works which He has done,
His wonders, and the judgments
of His mouth,
6 O seed of Abraham His servant,
You children of Jacob,
His chosen ones!

7 He *is* the LORD our God;
[a]His judgments *are* in all the earth.
8 He [a]remembers His covenant forever,
The word *which* He commanded,
for a thousand generations,
9 [a]*The covenant* which He
made with Abraham,
And His oath to Isaac,
10 And confirmed it to Jacob
for a statute,
To Israel *as* an everlasting covenant,
11 Saying, [a]"To you I will give
the land of Canaan
As the allotment of your inheritance,"
12 [a]When they were few in number,
Indeed very few, [b]and strangers in it.

13 When they went from one
nation to another,
From *one* kingdom to another people,
14 [a]He permitted no one to
do them wrong;
Yes, [b]He rebuked kings for their sakes,
15 *Saying,* "Do not touch My
anointed ones,
And do My prophets no harm."

16 Moreover [a]He called for a
famine in the land;
He destroyed all the
[b]provision of bread.
17 [a]He sent a man before them—
Joseph—*who* [b]was sold as a slave.
18 [a]They hurt his feet with fetters,
He was laid in irons.
19 Until the time that his
word came to pass,
[a]The word of the LORD tested him.
20 [a]The king sent and released him,
The ruler of the people let him go free.
21 [a]He made him lord of his house,
And ruler of all his possessions,
22 To bind his princes at his pleasure,
And teach his elders wisdom.

23 [a]Israel also came into Egypt,
And Jacob dwelt [b]in the land of Ham.
24 [a]He increased His people greatly,
And made them stronger
than their enemies.

104:30 [a] Is. 32:15 104:31 [a] Gen. 1:31; Prov. 8:31 104:32 [a] Hab. 3:10 [b] Ex. 19:18; Ps. 144:5 104:33 [a] Ps. 63:4 104:34 [a] Ps. 19:14 104:35 [a] Ps. 37:38 105:1 [a] 1 Chr. 16:8–22, 34; Ps. 106:1; Is. 12:4 [b] Ps. 145:12 105:2 [a] Ps. 119:27 105:4 [a] Ps. 27:8 105:5 [a] Ps. 77:11 105:7 [a] [Is. 26:9] 105:8 [a] Luke 1:72 105:9 [a] Gen. 17:2; Luke 1:73; [Gal. 3:17]; Heb. 6:17 105:11 [a] Gen. 13:15; 15:18 105:12 [a] Gen. 34:30; [Deut. 7:7] [b] Gen. 23:4; Heb. 11:9 105:14 [a] Gen. 35:5 [b] Gen. 12:17 105:16 [a] Gen. 41:54 [b] Lev. 26:26; Is. 3:1; Ezek. 4:16 105:17 [a] [Gen. 45:5] [b] Gen. 37:28, 36; Acts 7:9 105:18 [a] Gen. 40:15 105:19 [a] Gen. 39:11–21; 41:25, 42, 43 105:20 [a] Gen. 41:14 105:21 [a] Gen. 41:40–44 105:23 [a] Gen. 46:6; Acts 7:15 [b] Ps. 78:51 105:24 [a] Ex. 1:7, 9

25 [a]He turned their heart to
hate His people,
To deal craftily with His servants.

26 [a]He sent Moses His servant,
And Aaron whom He had chosen.
27 They [a]performed His signs
among them,
And wonders in the land of Ham.
28 He sent darkness, and made *it* dark;
And they did not rebel
against His word.
29 [a]He turned their waters into blood,
And killed their fish.
30 [a]Their land abounded with frogs,
Even in the chambers of their kings.
31 [a]He spoke, and there came
swarms of flies,
And lice in all their territory.
32 [a]He gave them hail for rain,
And flaming fire in their land.
33 [a]He struck their vines also,
and their fig trees,
And splintered the trees
of their territory.
34 [a]He spoke, and locusts came,
Young locusts without number,
35 And ate up all the vegetation
in their land,
And devoured the fruit
of their ground.
36 [a]He also destroyed all the
firstborn in their land,
[b]The first of all their strength.

37 [a]He also brought them out
with silver and gold,
And *there was* none feeble
among His tribes.
38 [a]Egypt was glad when they departed,
For the fear of them had
fallen upon them.
39 [a]He spread a cloud for a covering,
And fire to give light in the night.
40 [a]*The people* asked, and He
brought quail,
And [b]satisfied them with
the bread of heaven.

41 [a]He opened the rock, and
water gushed out;
It ran in the dry places *like* a river.

42 For He remembered [a]His
holy promise,
And Abraham His servant.
43 He brought out His people with joy,
His chosen ones with gladness.
44 [a]He gave them the lands
of the Gentiles,
And they inherited the
labor of the nations,
45 [a]That they might observe His statutes
And keep His laws.

Praise the LORD!

Psalm 106

Joy in Forgiveness of Israel's Sins

1 Praise the LORD!

[a]Oh, give thanks to the LORD,
for *He is* good!
For His mercy *endures* forever.

2 Who can utter the mighty
acts of the LORD?
Who can declare all His praise?
3 Blessed *are* those who keep justice,
And he who [a]does[1] righteousness
at [b]all times!

4 [a]Remember me, O LORD, with the favor
You have toward Your people.
Oh, visit me with Your salvation,
5 That I may see the benefit
of Your chosen ones,
That I may rejoice in the
gladness of Your nation,
That I may glory with
Your inheritance.

6 [a]We have sinned with our fathers,
We have committed iniquity,
We have done wickedly.

105:25 [a] Ex. 1:8–10; 4:21 105:26 [a] Ex. 3:10; 4:12–15 105:27 [a] Ex. 7—12; Ps. 78:43 105:29 [a] Ex. 7:20, 21; Ps. 78:44 105:30 [a] Ex. 8:6 105:31 [a] Ex. 8:16, 17 105:32 [a] Ex. 9:23–25 105:33 [a] Ps. 78:47 105:34 [a] Ex. 10:4 105:36 [a] Ex. 12:29; 13:15; Ps. 135:8; 136:10 [b] Gen. 49:3 105:37 [a] Ex. 12:35, 36 105:38 [a] Ex. 12:33 105:39 [a] Ex. 13:21; Neh. 9:12; Ps. 78:14; Is. 4:5 105:40 [a] Ex. 16:12 [b] Ps. 78:24 105:41 [a] Ex. 17:6; Num. 20:11; Ps. 78:15; 114:8; Is. 48:21; [1 Cor. 10:4] 105:42 [a] Gen. 15:13, 14; Ps. 105:8 105:44 [a] Josh. 11:16–23; 13:7; Ps. 78:55 105:45 [a] [Deut. 4:1, 40] 106:1 [a] 1 Chr. 16:34, 41 106:3 [a] Ps. 15:2 [b] [Gal. 6:9] [1] Septuagint, Syriac, Targum, and Vulgate read *those who do.* 106:4 [a] Ps. 119:132 106:6 [a] 1 Kin. 8:47; [Ezra 9:7; Neh. 1:7; Jer. 3:25; Dan. 9:5]

7 Our fathers in Egypt did not
understand Your wonders;
They did not remember the
multitude of Your mercies,
[a]But rebelled by the sea—the Red Sea.

8 Nevertheless He saved them
for His name's sake,
[a]That He might make His
mighty power known.
9 [a]He rebuked the Red Sea
also, and it dried up;
So [b]He led them through the depths,
As through the wilderness.
10 He [a]saved them from the hand
of him who hated *them*,
And redeemed them from
the hand of the enemy.
11 [a]The waters covered their enemies;
There was not one of them left.
12 [a]Then they believed His words;
They sang His praise.

13 [a]They soon forgot His works;
They did not wait for His counsel,
14 [a]But lusted exceedingly in
the wilderness,
And tested God in the desert.
15 [a]And He gave them their request,
But [b]sent leanness into their soul.

16 When [a]they envied Moses in the camp,
And Aaron the saint of the LORD,
17 [a]The earth opened up and
swallowed Dathan,
And covered the faction of Abiram.
18 [a]A fire was kindled in their company;
The flame burned up the wicked.

19 [a]They made a calf in Horeb,
And worshiped the molded image.
20 Thus [a]they changed their glory
Into the image of an ox that eats grass.
21 They forgot God their Savior,
Who had done great things in Egypt,
22 Wondrous works in the land of Ham,
Awesome things by the Red Sea.

23 [a]Therefore He said that He
would destroy them,
Had not Moses His chosen one
[b]stood before Him in the breach,
To turn away His wrath, lest
He destroy *them*.

24 Then they despised [a]the pleasant land;
They [b]did not believe His word,
25 [a]But complained in their tents,
And did not heed the voice of the LORD.
26 [a]Therefore He raised His hand
in an oath against them,
[b]To overthrow them in the wilderness,
27 [a]To overthrow their descendants
among the nations,
And to scatter them in the lands.

28 [a]They joined themselves
also to Baal of Peor,
And ate sacrifices made to the dead.
29 Thus they provoked *Him* to
anger with their deeds,
And the plague broke out
among them.
30 [a]Then Phinehas stood up
and intervened,
And the plague was stopped.
31 And that was accounted to
him [a]for righteousness
To all generations forevermore.

32 [a]They angered *Him* also at
the waters of strife,[1]
[b]So that it went ill with Moses
on account of them;
33 [a]Because they rebelled
against His Spirit,
So that he spoke rashly with his lips.

34 [a]They did not destroy the peoples,
[b]Concerning whom the LORD
had commanded them,
35 [a]But they mingled with the Gentiles
And learned their works;
36 [a]They served their idols,
[b]Which became a snare to them.

106:7 [a] Ex. 14:11, 12 **106:8** [a] Ex. 9:16 **106:9** [a] Ex. 14:21; Ps. 18:15; Is. 51:10; Nah. 1:4 [b] Is. 63:11–13 **106:10** [a] Ex. 14:30 **106:11** [a] Ex. 14:27, 28; 15:5 **106:12** [a] Ex. 15:1–21 **106:13** [a] Ex. 15:24; 16:2; 17:2 **106:14** [a] Num. 11:4; 1 Cor. 10:6 **106:15** [a] Num. 11:31 [b] Is. 10:16 **106:16** [a] Num. 16:1–3 **106:17** [a] Num. 16:31, 32; Deut. 11:6 **106:18** [a] Num. 16:35, 46 **106:19** [a] Ex. 32:1–4; Deut. 9:8; Acts 7:41 **106:20** [a] Jer. 2:11; Rom. 1:23 **106:23** [a] Ex. 32:10; Deut. 9:19 [b] Ezek. 22:30 **106:24** [a] Deut. 8:7; Jer. 3:19; Ezek. 20:6 [b] Deut. 1:32; 9:23; [Heb. 3:18, 19] **106:25** [a] Num. 14:2, 27; Deut. 1:27 **106:26** [a] Ezek. 20:15, 16; [Heb. 3:11, 18] [b] Num. 14:28–30 **106:27** [a] Lev. 26:33; Ezek. 20:23 **106:28** [a] Num. 25:3; Deut. 4:3; Hos. 9:10 **106:30** [a] Num. 25:7, 8 **106:31** [a] Gen. 15:6; Num. 25:11–13 **106:32** [a] Num. 20:3–13; Ps. 81:7 [b] Deut. 1:37; 3:26 [1] Or *Meribah* **106:33** [a] Num. 20:3, 10 **106:34** [a] Judg. 1:21 [b] [Deut. 7:2, 16]; Judg. 2:2 **106:35** [a] Judg. 3:5, 6 **106:36** [a] Judg. 2:12 [b] Deut. 7:16

37 [a]They even sacrificed their sons
And their daughters to [b]demons,
38 And shed innocent blood,
The blood of their sons and daughters,
Whom they sacrificed to
the idols of Canaan;
And [a]the land was polluted with blood.
39 Thus they were [a]defiled by
their own works,
And [b]played the harlot by
their own deeds.

40 Therefore [a]the wrath of the LORD
was kindled against His people,
So that He abhorred [b]His
own inheritance.
41 And [a]He gave them into the
hand of the Gentiles,
And those who hated them
ruled over them.
42 Their enemies also oppressed them,
And they were brought into
subjection under their hand.
43 [a]Many times He delivered them;
But they rebelled in their counsel,
And were brought low for their iniquity.

44 Nevertheless He regarded
their affliction,
When [a]He heard their cry;
45 [a]And for their sake He
remembered His covenant,
And [b]relented [c]according to the
multitude of His mercies.
46 [a]He also made them to be pitied
By all those who carried
them away captive.

47 [a]Save us, O LORD our God,
And gather us from among the Gentiles,
To give thanks to Your holy name,
To triumph in Your praise.

48 [a]Blessed *be* the LORD God of Israel
From everlasting to everlasting!
And let all the people say, "Amen!"

Praise the LORD!

BOOK FIVE
PSALMS 107–150

Psalm 107

Thanksgiving to the LORD for His Great Works of Deliverance

1 Oh, [a]give thanks to the
LORD, for *He is* good!
For His mercy *endures* forever.
2 Let the redeemed of the LORD say *so,*
Whom He has redeemed from
the hand of the enemy,
3 And [a]gathered out of the lands,
From the east and from the west,
From the north and from the south.

4 They wandered in [a]the wilderness
in a desolate way;
They found no city to dwell in.
5 Hungry and thirsty,
Their soul fainted in them.
6 [a]Then they cried out to the
LORD in their trouble,
And He delivered them out
of their distresses.
7 And He led them forth
by the [a]right way,
That they might go to a city
for a dwelling place.
8 [a]Oh, that *men* would give thanks to
the LORD *for* His goodness,
And *for* His wonderful works
to the children of men!
9 For [a]He satisfies the longing soul,
And fills the hungry soul
with goodness.

10 Those who [a]sat in darkness and
in the shadow of death,
[b]Bound in affliction and irons—
11 Because they [a]rebelled against
the words of God,
And despised [b]the counsel
of the Most High,
12 Therefore He brought down
their heart with labor;

106:37 [a] [Deut. 12:31; 32:17, 18]; 2 Kin. 16:3; 17:17; Ezek. 16:20, 21; [1 Cor. 10:20] [b] [Lev. 17:7] 106:38 [a] [Num. 35:33; Is. 24:5; Jer. 3:1, 2] 106:39 [a] [Lev. 18:24]; Ezek. 20:18 [b] [Lev. 17:7; Num. 15:39]; Judg. 2:17; Hos. 4:12 106:40 [a] Judg. 2:14; Ps. 78:59 [b] [Deut. 9:29; 32:9] 106:41 [a] Judg. 2:14; [Neh. 9:27] 106:43 [a] Judg. 2:16; [Neh. 9:27] 106:44 [a] Judg. 3:9; 6:7; 10:10 106:45 [a] [Lev. 26:41, 42] [b] Judg. 2:18 [c] Ps. 69:16 106:46 [a] 1 Kin. 8:50; [2 Chr. 30:9]; Ezra 9:9; Neh. 1:11; Jer. 42:12 106:47 [a] 1 Chr. 16:35, 36 106:48 [a] Ps. 41:13 107:1 [a] 1 Chr. 16:34; Ps. 106:1; Jer. 33:11 107:3 [a] Is. 43:5, 6; Jer. 29:14; 31:8–10; [Ezek. 39:27, 28] 107:4 [a] Num. 14:33; 32:13; [Deut. 2:7; 32:10]; Josh. 5:6; 14:10 107:6 [a] Ps. 50:15; [Hos. 5:15] 107:7 [a] Ezra 8:21; Ps. 5:8; Jer. 31:9 107:8 [a] Ps. 107:15, 21 107:9 [a] [Ps. 34:10; Luke 1:53] 107:10 [a] [Is. 42:7; Mic. 7:8; Luke 1:79] [b] Job 36:8 107:11 [a] Lam. 3:42 [b] [Ps. 73:24]

They fell down, and *there*
was [a]none to help.
13 Then they cried out to the
LORD in their trouble,
And He saved them out of
their distresses.
14 [a]He brought them out of darkness
and the shadow of death,
And broke their chains in pieces.
15 Oh, that *men* would give thanks to
the LORD *for* His goodness,
And *for* His wonderful works
to the children of men!
16 For He has [a]broken the
gates of bronze,
And cut the bars of iron in two.

17 Fools, [a]because of their transgression,
And because of their iniquities,
were afflicted.
18 [a]Their soul abhorred all
manner of food,
And they [b]drew near to
the gates of death.
19 Then they cried out to the
LORD in their trouble,
And He saved them out of
their distresses.
20 [a]He sent His word and [b]healed them,
And [c]delivered *them* from
their destructions.
21 Oh, that *men* would give thanks to
the LORD *for* His goodness,
And *for* His wonderful works
to the children of men!
22 [a]Let them sacrifice the sacrifices
of thanksgiving,
And [b]declare His works with rejoicing.

23 Those who go down to the sea in ships,
Who do business on great waters,
24 They see the works of the LORD,
And His wonders in the deep.
25 For He commands and [a]raises
the stormy wind,
Which lifts up the waves of the sea.
26 They mount up to the heavens,
They go down again to the depths;
[a]Their soul melts because of trouble.
27 They reel to and fro, and stagger
like a drunken man,
And are at their wits' end.
28 Then they cry out to the
LORD in their trouble,
And He brings them out
of their distresses.
29 [a]He calms the storm,
So that its waves are still.
30 Then they are glad because
they are quiet;
So He guides them to their
desired haven.
31 [a]Oh, that *men* would give thanks to
the LORD *for* His goodness,
And *for* His wonderful works
to the children of men!
32 Let them exalt Him also [a]in the
assembly of the people,
And praise Him in the
company of the elders.

33 He [a]turns rivers into a wilderness,
And the watersprings into
dry ground;
34 A [a]fruitful land into barrenness,
For the wickedness of those
who dwell in it.
35 [a]He turns a wilderness into
pools of water,
And dry land into watersprings.
36 There He makes the hungry dwell,
That they may establish a city
for a dwelling place,
37 And sow fields and plant vineyards,
That they may yield a fruitful
harvest.
38 [a]He also blesses them, and
they multiply greatly;
And He does not let their
cattle [b]decrease.

39 When they are [a]diminished
and brought low
Through oppression,
affliction, and sorrow,
40 [a]He pours contempt on princes,
And causes them to wander in the
wilderness *where there is* no way;

107:12 [a] Ps. 22:11 107:14 [a] Ps. 68:6 107:16 [a] Is. 45:1, 2 107:17 [a] [Is. 65:6, 7; Jer. 30:14, 15]; Lam. 3:39; Ezek. 24:23 107:18 [a] Job 33:20 [b] Job 33:22 107:20 [a] Matt. 8:8 [b] 2 Kin. 20:5; Ps. 30:2 [c] Job 33:28, 30 107:22 [a] Lev. 7:12; Ps. 50:14; Heb. 13:15 [b] Ps. 9:11 107:25 [a] Jon. 1:4 107:26 [a] Ps. 22:14 107:29 [a] Ps. 89:9; Matt. 8:26; Luke 8:24 107:31 [a] Ps. 107:8, 15, 21 107:32 [a] Ps. 22:22, 25 107:33 [a] 1 Kin. 17:1, 7; Is. 50:2 107:34 [a] Gen. 13:10; Deut. 29:23 107:35 [a] Ps. 114:8; [Is. 41:17, 18] 107:38 [a] Gen. 12:2; 17:16, 20 [b] Ex. 1:7; [Deut. 7:14] 107:39 [a] 2 Kin. 10:32 107:40 [a] Job 12:21, 24

41 [a]Yet He sets the poor on high,
far from affliction,
And [b]makes *their* families like a flock.
42 [a]The righteous see *it* and rejoice,
And all [b]iniquity stops its mouth.

43 [a]Whoever *is* wise will observe
these *things*,
And they will understand the
lovingkindness of the LORD.

Psalm 108

Assurance of God's Victory over Enemies

(Ps. 57:7–11; 60:5–12)

A Song. A Psalm of David.

1 O [a]God, my heart is steadfast;
I will sing and give praise,
even with my glory.
2 [a]Awake, lute and harp!
I will awaken the dawn.
3 I will praise You, O LORD,
among the peoples,
And I will sing praises to You
among the nations.
4 For Your mercy *is* great
above the heavens,
And Your truth *reaches* to the clouds.

5 [a]Be exalted, O God, above the heavens,
And Your glory above all the earth;
6 [a]That Your beloved may be delivered,
Save *with* Your right hand,
and hear me.

7 God has spoken in His holiness:
"I will rejoice;
I will divide Shechem
And measure out the Valley of Succoth.
8 Gilead *is* Mine; Manasseh *is* Mine;
Ephraim also *is* the helmet
for My head;
[a]Judah *is* My lawgiver.
9 Moab *is* My washpot;
Over Edom I will cast My shoe;
Over Philistia I will triumph."

10 [a]Who will bring me *into* the strong city?
Who will lead me to Edom?
11 *Is it* not You, O God, *who* cast us off?
And *You,* O God, *who* did not
go out with our armies?
12 Give us help from trouble,
For the help of man is useless.
13 [a]Through God we will do valiantly,
For *it is* He *who* shall tread
down our enemies.[1]

Psalm 109

Plea for Judgment of False Accusers

To the Chief Musician. A Psalm of David.

1 Do[a] not keep silent,
O God of my praise!
2 For the mouth of the wicked and
the mouth of the deceitful
Have opened against me;
They have spoken against me
with a [a]lying tongue.
3 They have also surrounded me
with words of hatred,
And fought against me
[a]without a cause.
4 In return for my love they
are my accusers,
But I *give myself to* prayer.
5 Thus [a]they have rewarded
me evil for good,
And hatred for my love.

6 Set a wicked man over him,
And let [a]an accuser[1] stand
at his right hand.
7 When he is judged, let him
be found guilty,
And [a]let his prayer become sin.
8 Let his days be [a]few,
And [b]let another take his office.
9 [a]Let his children be fatherless,
And his wife a widow.
10 Let his children continually
be vagabonds, and beg;
Let them seek *their bread*[1] also
from their desolate places.

107:41 [a] 1 Sam. 2:8; [Ps. 113:7, 8] [b] Ps. 78:52 107:42 [a] Job 5:15, 16 [b] Job 5:16; Ps. 63:11; [Rom. 3:19] 107:43 [a] Ps. 64:9; Jer. 9:12; [Hos. 14:9] 108:1 [a] Ps. 57:7–11 108:2 [a] Ps. 57:8–11 108:5 [a] Ps. 57:5, 11 108:6 [a] Ps. 60:5–12 108:8 [a] [Gen. 49:10] 108:10 [a] Ps. 60:9 108:13 [a] Ps. 60:12 [1] Compare verses 6–13 with 60:5–12 109:1 [a] Ps. 83:1 109:2 [a] Ps. 27:12 109:3 [a] Ps. 35:7; 69:4; John 15:25 109:5 [a] Ps. 35:7, 12; 38:20; Prov. 17:13 109:6 [a] Zech. 3:1 [1] Hebrew *satan* 109:7 [a] [Prov. 28:9] 109:8 [a] [Ps. 55:23]; John 17:12 [b] Ps. 69:25; Acts 1:20 109:9 [a] Ex. 22:24 109:10 [1] Following Masoretic Text and Targum; Septuagint and Vulgate read *be cast out*.

11 [a]Let the creditor seize all that he has,
And let strangers plunder his labor.
12 Let there be none to extend
mercy to him,
Nor let there be any to favor
his fatherless children.
13 [a]Let his posterity be cut off,
And in the generation following let
their [b]name be blotted out.

14 [a]Let the iniquity of his fathers be
remembered before the LORD,
And let not the sin of his
mother [b]be blotted out.
15 Let them be continually
before the LORD,
That He may [a]cut off the memory
of them from the earth;
16 Because he did not remember
to show mercy,
But persecuted the poor
and needy man,
That he might even slay the
[a]broken in heart.
17 [a]As he loved cursing, so let
it come to him;
As he did not delight in blessing,
so let it be far from him.
18 As he clothed himself with
cursing as with his garment,
So let it [a]enter his body like water,
And like oil into his bones.
19 Let it be to him like the garment
which covers him,
And for a belt with which he
girds himself continually.
20 *Let* this *be* the LORD's reward
to my accusers,
And to those who speak evil
against my person.

21 But You, O GOD the Lord,
Deal with me for Your name's sake;
Because Your mercy *is* good, deliver me.
22 For I *am* poor and needy,
And my heart is wounded within me.
23 I am gone [a]like a shadow
when it lengthens;
I am shaken off like a locust.
24 My [a]knees are weak through fasting,
And my flesh is feeble from
lack of fatness.
25 I also have become [a]a
reproach to them;
When they look at me, [b]they
shake their heads.

26 Help me, O LORD my God!
Oh, save me according to Your mercy,
27 [a]That they may know that
this *is* Your hand—
That You, LORD, have done it!
28 [a]Let them curse, but You bless;
When they arise, let them be ashamed,
But let [b]Your servant rejoice.
29 [a]Let my accusers be clothed
with shame,
And let them cover themselves with
their own disgrace as with
a mantle.

30 I will greatly praise the LORD
with my mouth;
Yes, [a]I will praise Him among
the multitude.
31 For [a]He shall stand at the
right hand of the poor,
To save *him* from those
who condemn him.

Psalm 110

Announcement of the Messiah's Reign (Matt. 22:44; Acts 2:34, 35)

A Psalm of David.

1 The [a]LORD said to my Lord,
"Sit at My right hand,
Till I make Your enemies
Your [b]footstool."
2 The LORD shall send the rod of
Your strength [a]out of Zion.
[b]Rule in the midst of Your enemies!

3 [a]Your people *shall be* volunteers
In the day of Your power;

109:11 [a] Neh. 5:7; Job 5:5; 18:9 109:13 [a] Job 18:19; Ps. 37:28 [b] Prov. 10:7 109:14 [a] [Ex. 20:5; Num. 14:18]; Is. 65:6; [Jer. 32:18] [b] Neh. 4:5; Jer. 18:23 109:15 [a] Job 18:17; [Ps. 34:16] 109:16 [a] [Ps. 34:18] 109:17 [a] Prov. 14:14; [Matt. 7:2] 109:18 [a] Num. 5:22 109:23 [a] Ps. 102:11 109:24 [a] Heb. 12:12 109:25 [a] Ps. 22:7; Jer. 18:16; Lam. 2:15 [b] Matt. 27:39; Mark 15:29 109:27 [a] Job 37:7 109:28 [a] 2 Sam. 6:11, 12 [b] Is. 65:14 109:29 [a] Job 8:22; Ps. 35:26 109:30 [a] Ps. 35:18; 111:1 109:31 [a] [Ps. 16:8] 110:1 [a] Matt. 22:44; Mark 12:36; 16:19; Luke 20:42, 43; Acts 2:34, 35; Col. 3:1; Heb. 1:13 [b] [1 Cor. 15:25; Eph. 1:22] 110:2 [a] [Rom. 11:26, 27] [b] [Ps. 2:9; Dan. 7:13, 14] 110:3 [a] Judg. 5:2; Neh. 11:2

[b]In the beauties of holiness, from
the womb of the morning,
You have the dew of Your youth.
4 The LORD has sworn
And [a]will not relent,
"You *are* a [b]priest forever
According to the order of
[c]Melchizedek."

5 The Lord *is* [a]at Your right hand;
He shall execute kings [b]in
the day of His wrath.
6 He shall judge among the nations,
He shall fill *the places*
with dead bodies,
[a]He shall execute the heads
of many countries.
7 He shall drink of the brook
by the wayside;
[a]Therefore He shall lift up the head.

Psalm 111

Praise to God for His Faithfulness and Justice

1 Praise the LORD!

[a]I will praise the LORD with
my whole heart,
In the assembly of the upright
and *in* the congregation.

2 [a]The works of the LORD *are* great,
[b]Studied by all who have
pleasure in them.
3 His work *is* [a]honorable and glorious,
And His righteousness
endures forever.
4 He has made His wonderful
works to be remembered;
[a]The LORD *is* gracious and
full of compassion.
5 He has given food to those
who fear Him;
He will ever be mindful
of His covenant.
6 He has declared to His people
the power of His works,
In giving them the heritage
of the nations.

7 The works of His hands *are*
[a]verity and justice;
All His precepts *are* sure.
8 [a]They stand fast forever and ever,
And are [b]done in truth
and uprightness.
9 [a]He has sent redemption
to His people;
He has commanded His
covenant forever:
[b]Holy and awesome *is* His name.
10 [a]The fear of the LORD *is* the
beginning of wisdom;
A good understanding have all those
who do *His commandments*.
His praise endures forever.

Psalm 112

The Blessed State of the Righteous

1 Praise the LORD!

Blessed *is* the man *who* fears the LORD,
Who [a]delights greatly in His
commandments.

2 [a]His descendants will be
mighty on earth;
The generation of the upright
will be blessed.
3 [a]Wealth and riches *will be* in his house,
And his righteousness
endures forever.
4 [a]Unto the upright there arises
light in the darkness;
He is gracious, and full of
compassion, and righteous.
5 [a]A good man deals graciously
and lends;
He will guide his affairs
[b]with discretion.
6 Surely he will never be shaken;
[a]The righteous will be in
everlasting remembrance.

110:3 [b] 1 Chr. 16:29; Ps. 96:9 110:4 [a] [Num. 23:19] [b] [Zech. 6:13] [c] [Heb. 5:6, 10; 6:20] 110:5 [a] [Ps. 16:8] [b] Ps. 2:5, 12; [Rom. 2:5; Rev. 6:17] 110:6 [a] Ps. 68:21 110:7 [a] [Is. 53:12] 111:1 [a] Ps. 35:18 111:2 [a] Ps. 92:5 [b] Ps. 143:5 111:3 [a] Ps. 145:4, 5 111:4 [a] [Ps. 86:5] 111:7 [a] [Rev. 15:3] 111:8 [a] Is. 40:8; Matt. 5:18 [b] [Rev. 15:3] 111:9 [a] Luke 1:68 [b] Luke 1:49 111:10 [a] Job 28:28; [Prov. 1:7; 9:10]; Eccl. 12:13 112:1 [a] Ps. 128:1 112:2 [a] [Ps. 102:28] 112:3 [a] Prov. 3:16; 8:18; [Matt. 6:33] 112:4 [a] Job 11:17; Ps. 97:11 112:5 [a] Ps. 37:26; [Luke 6:35] [b] [Eph. 5:15; Col. 4:5] 112:6 [a] Prov. 10:7

7 [a]He will not be afraid of evil tidings;
His heart is steadfast,
trusting in the LORD.
8 His [a]heart *is* established;
[b]He will not be afraid,
Until he [c]sees *his desire*
upon his enemies.

9 He has dispersed abroad,
He has given to the poor;
His righteousness endures forever;
His horn will be exalted with honor.
10 The wicked will see *it* and be grieved;
He will gnash his teeth and melt away;
The desire of the wicked shall perish.

Psalm 113

The Majesty and Condescension of God

1 Praise the LORD!

[a]Praise, O servants of the LORD,
Praise the name of the LORD!
2 [a]Blessed be the name of the LORD
From this time forth and forevermore!
3 [a]From the rising of the sun
to its going down
The LORD's name *is* to be praised.

4 The LORD *is* [a]high above all nations,
[b]His glory above the heavens.
5 [a]Who *is* like the LORD our God,
Who dwells on high,
6 [a]Who humbles Himself to behold
The things that are in the
heavens and in the earth?

7 [a]He raises the poor out of the dust,
And lifts the [b]needy out
of the ash heap,
8 That He may [a]seat *him* with princes—
With the princes of His people.
9 [a]He grants the barren woman a home,
Like a joyful mother of children.

Praise the LORD!

Psalm 114

The Power of God in His Deliverance of Israel

(cf. Ex. 14:1–31)

1 When [a]Israel went out of Egypt,
The house of Jacob [b]from a
people of strange language,
2 [a]Judah became His sanctuary,
And Israel His dominion.

3 [a]The sea saw *it* and fled;
[b]Jordan turned back.
4 [a]The mountains skipped like rams,
The little hills like lambs.
5 [a]What ails you, O sea, that you fled?
O Jordan, *that* you turned back?
6 O mountains, *that* you
skipped like rams?
O little hills, like lambs?

7 Tremble, O earth, at the
presence of the Lord,
At the presence of the God of Jacob,
8 [a]Who turned the rock *into*
a pool of water,
The flint into a fountain
of waters.

Psalm 115

The Futility of Idols and the Trustworthiness of God

1 Not [a]unto us, O LORD, not unto us,
But to Your name give glory,
Because of Your mercy,
Because of Your truth.
2 Why should the Gentiles say,
[a]"So where *is* their God?"

3 [a]But our God *is* in heaven;
He does whatever He pleases.
4 [a]Their idols *are* silver and gold,
The work of men's hands.
5 They have mouths, but
they do not speak;
Eyes they have, but they do not see;

112:7 [a] [Prov. 1:33] 112:8 [a] Heb. 13:9 [b] [Ps. 27:1; 56:11]; Prov. 1:33; 3:24; [Is. 12:2] [c] Ps. 59:10 113:1 [a] Ps. 135:1 113:2 [a] [Dan. 2:20] 113:3 [a] Is. 59:19; Mal. 1:11 113:4 [a] Ps. 97:9; 99:2 [b] [Ps. 8:1] 113:5 [a] Ps. 89:6; [Is. 57:15] 113:6 [a] [Ps. 11:4; Is. 57:15] 113:7 [a] 1 Sam. 2:8; Ps. 107:41 [b] Ps. 72:12 113:8 [a] [Job 36:7] 113:9 [a] 1 Sam. 2:5; Is. 54:1 114:1 [a] Ex. 12:51; 13:3 [b] Ps. 81:5 114:2 [a] Ex. 6:7; 19:6; 25:8; 29:45, 46; Deut. 27:9 114:3 [a] Ex. 14:21; Ps. 77:16 [b] Josh. 3:13–16 114:4 [a] Ex. 19:18; Judg. 5:5; Ps. 29:6; Hab. 3:6 114:5 [a] Hab. 3:8 114:8 [a] Ex. 17:6; Num. 20:11; Ps. 107:35 115:1 [a] [Is. 48:11]; Ezek. 36:32 115:2 [a] Ps. 42:3, 10 115:3 [a] [1 Chr. 16:26] 115:4 [a] Deut. 4:28; 2 Kin. 19:18; Is. 37:19; 44:10, 20; Jer. 10:3

6 They have ears, but they do not hear;
Noses they have, but they do not smell;
7 They have hands, but they
do not handle;
Feet they have, but they do not walk;
Nor do they mutter through
their throat.
8 [a]Those who make them are like them;
So is everyone who trusts in them.

9 [a]O Israel, trust in the LORD;
[b]He *is* their help and their shield.
10 O house of Aaron, trust in the LORD;
He *is* their help and their shield.
11 You who fear the LORD,
trust in the LORD;
He *is* their help and their shield.

12 The LORD has been mindful of *us;*
He will bless us;
He will bless the house of Israel;
He will bless the house of Aaron.
13 [a]He will bless those who fear the LORD,
Both small and great.

14 May the LORD give you increase
more and more,
You and your children.
15 *May* you *be* [a]blessed by the LORD,
[b]Who made heaven and earth.

16 The heaven, *even* the heavens,
are the LORD's;
But the earth He has given to
the children of men.
17 [a]The dead do not praise the LORD,
Nor any who go down into silence.
18 [a]But we will bless the LORD
From this time forth and forevermore.

Praise the LORD!

Psalm 116

Thanksgiving for Deliverance from Death

1 I [a]love the LORD, because He has heard
My voice *and* my supplications.
2 Because He has inclined His ear to me,
Therefore I will call *upon*
Him as long as I live.

3 [a]The pains of death surrounded me,
And the pangs of Sheol laid hold of me;
I found trouble and sorrow.
4 Then I called upon the
name of the LORD:
"O LORD, I implore You,
deliver my soul!"

5 [a]Gracious *is* the LORD, and [b]righteous;
Yes, our God *is* merciful.
6 The LORD preserves the simple;
I was brought low, and He saved me.
7 Return to your [a]rest, O my soul,
For [b]the LORD has dealt
bountifully with you.

8 [a]For You have delivered my
soul from death,
My eyes from tears,
And my feet from falling.
9 I will walk before the LORD
[a]In the land of the living.
10 [a]I believed, therefore I spoke,
"I am greatly afflicted."
11 [a]I said in my haste,
[b]"All men *are* liars."

12 What shall I render to the LORD
For all His benefits toward me?
13 I will take up the cup of salvation,
And call upon the name of the LORD.
14 [a]I will pay my vows to the LORD
Now in the presence of all His people.

15 [a]Precious in the sight of the LORD
Is the death of His saints.

16 O LORD, truly [a]I *am* Your servant;
I *am* Your servant, [b]the son
of Your maidservant;
You have loosed my bonds.
17 I will offer to You [a]the sacrifice
of thanksgiving,
And will call upon the
name of the LORD.

115:8 [a] Ps. 135:18; Is. 44:9–11 115:9 [a] Ps. 118:2, 3 [b] Ps. 33:20 115:13 [a] Ps. 128:1, 4 115:15 [a] [Gen. 14:19] [b] Gen. 1:1; Acts 14:15; Rev. 14:7 115:17 [a] Ps. 6:5; 88:10–12; [Is. 38:18] 115:18 [a] Ps. 113:2; Dan. 2:20 116:1 [a] Ps. 18:1 116:3 [a] Ps. 18:4–6 116:5 [a] [Ps. 103:8] [b] [Ezra 9:15]; Neh. 9:8; [Ps. 119:137; 145:17; Jer. 12:1; Dan. 9:14] 116:7 [a] [Jer. 6:16; Matt. 11:29] [b] Ps. 13:6 116:8 [a] Ps. 56:13 116:9 [a] Ps. 27:13 116:10 [a] 2 Cor. 4:13 116:11 [a] Ps. 31:22 [b] Rom. 3:4 116:14 [a] Ps. 116:18 116:15 [a] Ps. 72:14; [Rev. 14:13] 116:16 [a] Ps. 119:125; 143:12 [b] Ps. 86:16 116:17 [a] Lev. 7:12; Ps. 50:14; 107:22

18 I will pay my vows to the LORD
Now in the presence of all His people,
19 In the [a]courts of the LORD's house,
In the midst of you, O Jerusalem.

Praise the LORD!

Psalm 117

Let All Peoples Praise the LORD

1 Praise [a]the LORD, all you Gentiles!
Laud Him, all you peoples!
2 For His merciful kindness
is great toward us,
And [a]the truth of the LORD
endures forever.

Praise the LORD!

Psalm 118

Praise to God for His Everlasting Mercy

1 Oh, [a]give thanks to the
LORD, for *He is* good!
[b]For His mercy *endures* forever.

2 [a]Let Israel now say,
"His mercy *endures* forever."
3 Let the house of Aaron now say,
"His mercy *endures* forever."
4 Let those who fear the LORD now say,
"His mercy *endures* forever."

5 [a]I called on the LORD in distress;
The LORD answered me *and*
[b]*set me* in a broad place.
6 [a]The LORD *is* on my side;
I will not fear.
What can man do to me?
7 [a]The LORD is for me among
those who help me;
Therefore [b]I shall see *my desire*
on those who hate me.
8 [a]*It is* better to trust in the LORD
Than to put confidence in man.
9 [a]*It is* better to trust in the LORD
Than to put confidence in princes.

10 All nations surrounded me,
But in the name of the LORD
I will destroy them.
11 They [a]surrounded me,
Yes, they surrounded me;
But in the name of the LORD
I will destroy them.
12 They surrounded me [a]like bees;
They were quenched [b]like
a fire of thorns;
For in the name of the LORD
I will destroy them.
13 You pushed me violently,
that I might fall,
But the LORD helped me.
14 [a]The LORD *is* my strength and song,
And He has become my salvation.[1]

15 The voice of rejoicing and salvation
Is in the tents of the righteous;
The right hand of the LORD
does valiantly.
16 [a]The right hand of the LORD is exalted;
The right hand of the LORD
does valiantly.
17 [a]I shall not die, but live,
And [b]declare the works of the LORD.
18 The LORD has [a]chastened me severely,
But He has not given me over to death.

19 [a]Open to me the gates of
righteousness;
I will go through them,
And I will praise the LORD.
20 [a]This is the gate of the LORD,
[b]Through which the righteous
shall enter.

21 I will praise You,
For You have [a]answered me,
And have become my salvation.

22 [a]The stone *which* the builders
rejected
Has become the chief cornerstone.

116:19 [a] Ps. 96:8 117:1 [a] Rom. 15:11 117:2 [a] [Ps. 100:5] 118:1 [a] 1 Chr. 16:8, 34; Jer. 33:11 [b] 2 Chr. 5:13; 7:3; Ezra 3:11; [Ps. 136:1–26] 118:2 [a] [Ps. 115:9] 118:5 [a] Ps. 120:1 [b] Ps. 18:19 118:6 [a] Ps. 27:1; 56:9; [Rom. 8:31; Heb. 13:6] 118:7 [a] Ps. 54:4 [b] Ps. 59:10 118:8 [a] 2 Chr. 32:7, 8; Ps. 40:4; Is. 31:1, 3; 57:13; Jer. 17:5 118:9 [a] Ps. 146:3 118:11 [a] Ps. 88:17 118:12 [a] Deut. 1:44 [b] Eccl. 7:6; Nah. 1:10 118:14 [a] Ex. 15:2; Is. 12:2 [1] Compare Exodus 15:2 118:16 [a] Ex. 15:6 118:17 [a] [Ps. 6:5]; Hab. 1:12 [b] Ps. 73:28 118:18 [a] Ps. 73:14; Jer. 31:18; [1 Cor. 11:32]; 2 Cor. 6:9 118:19 [a] Is. 26:2 118:20 [a] Ps. 24:7 [b] Is. 35:8; [Rev. 21:27; 22:14, 15] 118:21 [a] Ps. 116:1 118:22 [a] Matt. 21:42; Mark 12:10, 11; Luke 20:17; Acts 4:11; [Eph. 2:20; 1 Pet. 2:7, 8]

23 This was the LORD's doing;
It *is* marvelous in our eyes.
24 This *is* the day the LORD has made;
We will rejoice and be glad in it.

25 Save now, I pray, O LORD;
O LORD, I pray, send now
prosperity.
26 [a]Blessed *is* he who comes in
the name of the LORD!
We have blessed you from
the house of the LORD.
27 God *is* the LORD,
And He has given us [a]light;
Bind the sacrifice with cords
to the horns of the altar.
28 You *are* my God, and I will
praise You;
[a]*You are* my God, I will exalt You.

29 Oh, give thanks to the LORD,
for *He is* good!
For His mercy *endures* forever.

Psalm 119

Meditations on the Excellencies of the Word of God

א ALEPH

1 Blessed *are* the undefiled in the way,
[a]Who walk in the law of the LORD!
2 Blessed *are* those who keep
His testimonies,
Who seek Him with the [a]whole heart!
3 [a]They also do no iniquity;
They walk in His ways.
4 You have commanded *us*
To keep Your precepts diligently.
5 Oh, that my ways were directed
To keep Your statutes!
6 [a]Then I would not be ashamed,
When I look into all Your
commandments.
7 I will praise You with
uprightness of heart,
When I learn Your righteous
judgments.
8 I will keep Your statutes;
Oh, do not forsake me utterly!

ב BETH

9 How can a young man
cleanse his way?
By taking heed according
to Your word.
10 With my whole heart I
have [a]sought You;
Oh, let me not wander from
Your commandments!
11 [a]Your word I have hidden in my heart,
That I might not sin against You.
12 Blessed *are* You, O LORD!
Teach me Your statutes.
13 With my lips I have [a]declared
All the judgments of Your mouth.
14 I have rejoiced in the way of
Your testimonies,
As *much as* in all riches.
15 I will meditate on Your precepts,
And contemplate Your ways.
16 I will [a]delight myself in Your statutes;
I will not forget Your word.

ג GIMEL

17 [a]Deal bountifully with Your servant,
That I may live and keep Your word.
18 Open my eyes, that I may see
Wondrous things from Your law.
19 [a]I *am* a stranger in the earth;
Do not hide Your commandments
from me.
20 [a]My soul breaks with longing
For Your judgments at all times.
21 You rebuke the proud—the cursed,
Who stray from Your commandments.
22 [a]Remove from me reproach
and contempt,
For I have kept Your testimonies.
23 Princes also sit *and* speak against me,
But Your servant meditates
on Your statutes.
24 Your testimonies also *are* my delight
And my counselors.

ד DALETH

25 [a]My soul clings to the dust;
[b]Revive me according to Your word.
26 I have declared my ways, and
You answered me;
[a]Teach me Your statutes.

118:26 [a] Matt. 21:9; 23:39; Mark 11:9; Luke 13:35; 19:38 **118:27** [a] Esth. 8:16; [1 Pet. 2:9] **118:28** [a] Ex. 15:2; Is. 25:1 **119:1** [a] Ps. 128:1; [Ezek. 11:20; 18:17]; Mic. 4:2 **119:2** [a] Deut. 6:5; 10:12; 11:13; 13:3 **119:3** [a] [1 John 3:9; 5:18] **119:6** [a] Job 22:26 **119:10** [a] 2 Chr. 15:15 **119:11** [a] Ps. 37:31; Luke 2:19 **119:13** [a] Ps. 34:11 **119:16** [a] Ps. 1:2 **119:17** [a] Ps. 116:7 **119:19** [a] Gen. 47:9; Lev. 25:23; 1 Chr. 29:15; Ps. 39:12; Heb. 11:13 **119:20** [a] Ps. 42:1, 2; 63:1; 84:2 **119:22** [a] Ps. 39:8 **119:25** [a] Ps. 44:25 [b] Ps. 143:11 **119:26** [a] Ps. 25:4; 27:11; 86:11

27 Make me understand the
way of Your precepts;
So [a]shall I meditate on Your
wonderful works.
28 [a]My soul melts from heaviness;
Strengthen me according to Your word.
29 Remove from me the way of lying,
And grant me Your law graciously.
30 I have chosen the way of truth;
Your judgments I have laid *before me.*
31 I cling to Your testimonies;
O LORD, do not put me to shame!
32 I will run the course of Your
commandments,
For You shall [a]enlarge my heart.

ה HE

33 [a]Teach me, O LORD, the way
of Your statutes,
And I shall keep it *to* the end.
34 [a]Give me understanding, and
I shall keep Your law;
Indeed, I shall observe it
with *my* whole heart.
35 Make me walk in the path of
Your commandments,
For I delight in it.
36 Incline my heart to Your testimonies,
And not to [a]covetousness.
37 [a]Turn away my eyes from [b]looking
at worthless things,
And revive me in Your way.[1]
38 [a]Establish Your word to Your servant,
Who *is devoted* to fearing You.
39 Turn away my reproach which I dread,
For Your judgments *are* good.
40 Behold, I long for Your precepts;
Revive me in Your righteousness.

ו WAW

41 Let Your mercies come also
to me, O LORD—
Your salvation according to Your word.
42 So shall I have an answer for
him who reproaches me,
For I trust in Your word.
43 And take not the word of truth
utterly out of my mouth,
For I have hoped in Your ordinances.
44 So shall I keep Your law continually,
Forever and ever.
45 And I will walk at [a]liberty,
For I seek Your precepts.
46 [a]I will speak of Your testimonies
also before kings,
And will not be ashamed.
47 And I will delight myself in
Your commandments,
Which I love.
48 My hands also I will lift up to
Your commandments,
Which I love,
And I will meditate on Your statutes.

ז ZAYIN

49 Remember the word to Your servant,
Upon which You have
caused me to hope.
50 This *is* my [a]comfort in my affliction,
For Your word has given me life.
51 The proud have me in great derision,
Yet I do not turn aside from
Your law.
52 I remembered Your judgments
of old, O LORD,
And have comforted myself.
53 [a]Indignation has taken hold of me
Because of the wicked, who
forsake Your law.
54 Your statutes have been my songs
In the house of my pilgrimage.
55 [a]I remember Your name in
the night, O LORD,
And I keep Your law.
56 This has become mine,
Because I kept Your precepts.

ח HETH

57 [a]*You are* my portion, O LORD;
I have said that I would
keep Your words.
58 I entreated Your favor with
my whole heart;
Be merciful to me according
to Your word.
59 I [a]thought about my ways,
And turned my feet to
Your testimonies.

119:27 [a] Ps. 145:5, 6 119:28 [a] Ps. 107:26 119:32 [a] 1 Kin. 4:29; Is. 60:5; 2 Cor. 6:11, 13 119:33 [a] [Matt. 10:22; Rev. 2:26] 119:34 [a] [Prov. 2:6; James 1:5] 119:36 [a] Ezek. 33:31; [Mark 7:20–23]; Luke 12:15; [Heb. 13:5] 119:37 [a] Is. 33:15 [b] Prov. 23:5 [1] Following Masoretic Text, Septuagint, and Vulgate; Targum reads *Your words.* 119:38 [a] 2 Sam. 7:25 119:45 [a] Prov. 4:12 119:46 [a] Ps. 138:1; Matt. 10:18; Acts 26 119:50 [a] Job 6:10; [Rom. 15:4] 119:53 [a] Ex. 32:19; Ezra 9:3; Neh. 13:25 119:55 [a] Ps. 63:6 119:57 [a] Num. 18:20; Ps. 16:5; Jer. 10:16; Lam. 3:24 119:59 [a] Mark 14:72; Luke 15:17

60 I made haste, and did not delay
To keep Your commandments.
61 The cords of the wicked
have bound me,
But I have not forgotten Your law.
62 [a]At midnight I will rise to
give thanks to You,
Because of Your righteous judgments.
63 I *am* a companion of all who fear You,
And of those who keep Your precepts.
64 [a]The earth, O LORD, is full
of Your mercy;
Teach me Your statutes.

ט TETH

65 You have dealt well with Your servant,
O LORD, according to Your word.
66 Teach me good judgment
and [a]knowledge,
For I believe Your commandments.
67 Before I was [a]afflicted I went astray,
But now I keep Your word.
68 You *are* [a]good, and do good;
Teach me Your statutes.
69 The proud have [a]forged
a lie against me,
But I will keep Your precepts
with *my* whole heart.
70 [a]Their heart is as fat as grease,
But I delight in Your law.
71 *It is* good for me that I have
been afflicted,
That I may learn Your statutes.
72 [a]The law of Your mouth *is* better to me
Than thousands of *coins*
of gold and silver.

י YOD

73 [a]Your hands have made me
and fashioned me;
Give me understanding, that I may
learn Your commandments.
74 [a]Those who fear You will be
glad when they see me,
Because I have hoped in Your word.
75 I know, O LORD, [a]that Your
judgments *are* right,
And *that* in faithfulness You
have afflicted me.
76 Let, I pray, Your merciful kindness
be for my comfort,
According to Your word
to Your servant.
77 Let Your tender mercies come
to me, that I may live;
For Your law *is* my delight.
78 Let the proud [a]be ashamed,
For they treated me wrongfully
with falsehood;
But I will meditate on Your precepts.
79 Let those who fear You turn to me,
Those who know Your testimonies.
80 Let my heart be blameless
regarding Your statutes,
That I may not be ashamed.

כ KAPH

81 [a]My soul faints for Your salvation,
But I hope in Your word.
82 My eyes fail *from searching* Your word,
Saying, "When will You comfort me?"
83 For [a]I have become like a
wineskin in smoke,
Yet I do not forget Your statutes.
84 [a]How many *are* the days
of Your servant?
[b]When will You execute judgment
on those who persecute me?
85 [a]The proud have dug pits for me,
Which *is* not according to Your law.
86 All Your commandments *are* faithful;
They persecute me [a]wrongfully;
Help me!
87 They almost made an end
of me on earth,
But I did not forsake Your precepts.
88 Revive me according to
Your lovingkindness,
So that I may keep the
testimony of Your mouth.

ל LAMED

89 [a]Forever, O LORD,
Your word is settled in heaven.
90 Your faithfulness *endures*
to all generations;
You established the earth,
and it abides.

119:62 [a] Acts 16:25 **119:64** [a] Ps. 33:5 **119:66** [a] Phil. 1:9 **119:67** [a] Prov. 3:11; Jer. 31:18, 19; [Heb. 12:5–11] **119:68** [a] Ps. 106:1; 107:1; [Matt. 19:17] **119:69** [a] Job 13:4; Ps. 109:2 **119:70** [a] Deut. 32:15; Job 15:27; Ps. 17:10; Is. 6:10; Jer. 5:28; Acts 28:27 **119:72** [a] Ps. 19:10; Prov. 8:10, 11, 19 **119:73** [a] Job 10:8; 31:15; [Ps. 139:15, 16] **119:74** [a] Ps. 34:2 **119:75** [a] [Heb. 12:10] **119:78** [a] Ps. 25:3 **119:81** [a] Ps. 73:26; 84:2 **119:83** [a] Job 30:30 **119:84** [a] Ps. 39:4 [b] Rev. 6:10 **119:85** [a] Ps. 35:7; Prov. 16:27; Jer. 18:22 **119:86** [a] Ps. 35:19 **119:89** [a] Ps. 89:2; Is. 40:8; Matt. 24:35; [1 Pet. 1:25]

91 They continue this day according
to [a]Your ordinances,
For all *are* Your servants.
92 Unless Your law *had been* my delight,
I would then have perished
in my affliction.
93 I will never forget Your precepts,
For by them You have given me life.
94 I *am* Yours, save me;
For I have sought Your precepts.
95 The wicked wait for me to destroy me,
But I will consider Your testimonies.
96 [a]I have seen the consummation
of all perfection,
But Your commandment *is*
exceedingly broad.

מ MEM

97 Oh, how I love Your law!
[a]It *is* my meditation all the day.
98 You, through Your commandments,
make me [a]wiser than my enemies;
For they *are* ever with me.
99 I have more understanding
than all my teachers,
[a]For Your testimonies *are*
my meditation.
100 [a]I understand more than the ancients,
Because I keep Your precepts.
101 I have restrained my feet
from every evil way,
That I may keep Your word.
102 I have not departed from
Your judgments,
For You Yourself have taught me.
103 [a]How sweet are Your words to my taste,
Sweeter than honey to my mouth!
104 Through Your precepts I
get understanding;
Therefore I hate every false way.

נ NUN

105 [a]Your word *is* a lamp to my feet
And a light to my path.
106 [a]I have sworn and confirmed
That I will keep Your
righteous judgments.
107 I am afflicted very much;
Revive me, O LORD, according
to Your word.
108 Accept, I pray, [a]the freewill offerings
of my mouth, O LORD,
And teach me Your judgments.
109 [a]My life *is* continually in my hand,
Yet I do not forget Your law.
110 [a]The wicked have laid a snare for me,
Yet I have not strayed from
Your precepts.
111 [a]Your testimonies I have taken
as a heritage forever,
For they *are* the rejoicing
of my heart.
112 I have inclined my heart to
perform Your statutes
Forever, to the very end.

ס SAMEK

113 I hate the double-minded,
But I love Your law.
114 [a]You *are* my hiding place
and my shield;
I hope in Your word.
115 [a]Depart from me, you evildoers,
For I will keep the commandments
of my God!
116 Uphold me according to Your
word, that I may live;
And do not let me [a]be
ashamed of my hope.
117 Hold me up, and I shall be safe,
And I shall observe Your
statutes continually.
118 You reject all those who stray
from Your statutes,
For their deceit *is* falsehood.
119 You put away all the wicked
of the earth [a]*like* dross;
Therefore I love Your testimonies.
120 [a]My flesh trembles for fear of You,
And I am afraid of Your judgments.

ע AYIN

121 I have done justice and
righteousness;
Do not leave me to my oppressors.
122 Be [a]surety for Your servant for good;
Do not let the proud oppress me.
123 My eyes fail *from seeking*
Your salvation
And Your righteous word.

119:91 [a] Jer. 33:25 **119:96** [a] Matt. 5:18 **119:97** [a] Ps. 1:2 **119:98** [a] Deut. 4:6 **119:99** [a] [2 Tim. 3:15] **119:100** [a] [Job 32:7–9] **119:103** [a] Ps. 19:10; Prov. 8:11 **119:105** [a] Prov. 6:23 **119:106** [a] Neh. 10:29 **119:108** [a] Hos. 14:2; Heb. 13:15 **119:109** [a] Judg. 12:3; Job 13:14 **119:110** [a] Ps. 140:5 **119:111** [a] Deut. 33:4 **119:114** [a] [Ps. 32:7] **119:115** [a] Ps. 6:8; Matt. 7:23 **119:116** [a] Ps. 25:2; [Rom. 5:5; 9:33; 10:11; Phil. 1:20] **119:119** [a] Is. 1:22, 25; Ezek. 22:18, 19 **119:120** [a] Job 4:14; Hab. 3:16 **119:122** [a] Job 17:3; Heb. 7:22

124 Deal with Your servant
according to Your mercy,
And teach me Your statutes.
125 [a]I *am* Your servant;
Give me understanding,
That I may know Your testimonies.
126 *It is* time for *You* to act, O LORD,
For they have regarded
Your law as void.
127 [a]Therefore I love Your
commandments
More than gold, yes, than fine gold!
128 Therefore all *Your* precepts
concerning all *things*
I consider *to be* right;
I hate every false way.

פ PE

129 Your testimonies are wonderful;
Therefore my soul keeps them.
130 The entrance of Your
words gives light;
[a]It gives understanding to the [b]simple.
131 I opened my mouth and [a]panted,
For I longed for Your
commandments.
132 [a]Look upon me and be merciful to me,
[b]As Your custom *is* toward those
who love Your name.
133 [a]Direct my steps by Your word,
And [b]let no iniquity have
dominion over me.
134 [a]Redeem me from the
oppression of man,
That I may keep Your precepts.
135 [a]Make Your face shine upon
Your servant,
And teach me Your statutes.
136 [a]Rivers of water run down
from my eyes,
Because *men* do not keep Your law.

צ TSADDE

137 [a]Righteous *are* You, O LORD,
And upright *are* Your judgments.
138 [a]Your testimonies, *which* You
have commanded,
Are righteous and very faithful.
139 [a]My zeal has consumed me,
Because my enemies have
forgotten Your words.
140 [a]Your word *is* very pure;
Therefore Your servant loves it.
141 I *am* small and despised,
Yet I do not forget Your precepts.
142 Your righteousness *is* an
everlasting righteousness,
And Your law *is* [a]truth.
143 Trouble and anguish have
overtaken me,
Yet Your commandments
are my delights.
144 The righteousness of Your
testimonies *is* everlasting;
Give me understanding,
and I shall live.

ק QOPH

145 I cry out with *my* whole heart;
Hear me, O LORD!
I will keep Your statutes.
146 I cry out to You;
Save me, and I will keep
Your testimonies.
147 [a]I rise before the dawning
of the morning,
And cry for help;
I hope in Your word.
148 [a]My eyes are awake through
the *night* watches,
That I may meditate on Your word.
149 Hear my voice according to
Your lovingkindness;
O LORD, revive me according
to Your justice.
150 They draw near who follow
after wickedness;
They are far from Your law.
151 You *are* [a]near, O LORD,
And all Your commandments *are* truth.
152 Concerning Your testimonies,
I have known of old that You have
founded them [a]forever.

ר RESH

153 [a]Consider my affliction
and deliver me,
For I do not forget Your law.

119:125 [a] Ps. 116:16 119:127 [a] Ps. 19:10 119:130 [a] Prov. 6:23 [b] [Ps. 19:7]; Prov. 1:4 119:131 [a] Ps. 42:1 119:132 [a] Ps. 106:4 [b] Ps. 51:1; [2 Thess. 1:6] 119:133 [a] Ps. 17:5 [b] [Ps. 19:13; Rom. 6:12] 119:134 [a] Luke 1:74 119:135 [a] Num. 6:25; Ps. 4:6 119:136 [a] Jer. 9:1, 18; 14:17; Lam. 3:48; Ezek. 9:4 119:137 [a] Ezra 9:15; Neh. 9:33; Jer. 12:1; Lam. 1:18; Dan. 9:7, 14 119:138 [a] [Ps. 19:7–9] 119:139 [a] Ps. 69:9; John 2:17 119:140 [a] Ps. 12:6 119:142 [a] [Ps. 19:9; John 17:17] 119:147 [a] Ps. 5:3 119:148 [a] Ps. 63:1, 6 119:151 [a] [Ps. 145:18]; Is. 50:8 119:152 [a] Luke 21:33 119:153 [a] Lam. 5:1

154 [a]Plead my cause and redeem me;
Revive me according to Your word.
155 Salvation *is* far from the wicked,
For they do not seek Your statutes.
156 Great *are* Your tender
mercies, O LORD;
Revive me according to
Your judgments.
157 Many *are* my persecutors
and my enemies,
Yet I do not [a]turn from
Your testimonies.
158 I see the treacherous, and
[a]am disgusted,
Because they do not keep Your word.
159 Consider how I love Your precepts;
Revive me, O LORD, according
to Your lovingkindness.
160 The entirety of Your word *is* truth,
And every one of Your righteous
judgments *endures* forever.

ש SHIN

161 [a]Princes persecute me without a cause,
But my heart stands in
awe of Your word.
162 I rejoice at Your word
As one who finds great treasure.
163 I hate and abhor lying,
But I love Your law.
164 Seven times a day I praise You,
Because of Your righteous judgments.
165 [a]Great peace have those
who love Your law,
And nothing causes them to stumble.
166 [a]LORD, I hope for Your salvation,
And I do Your commandments.
167 My soul keeps Your testimonies,
And I love them exceedingly.
168 I keep Your precepts and
Your testimonies,
[a]For all my ways *are* before You.

ת TAU

169 Let my cry come before You, O LORD;
[a]Give me understanding
according to Your word.
170 Let my supplication come before You;
Deliver me according to Your word.
171 [a]My lips shall utter praise,
For You teach me Your statutes.
172 My tongue shall speak of Your word,
For all Your commandments
are righteousness.
173 Let Your hand become my help,
For [a]I have chosen Your precepts.
174 [a]I long for Your salvation, O LORD,
And [b]Your law *is* my delight.
175 Let my soul live, and it shall praise You;
And let Your judgments help me.
176 [a]I have gone astray like a lost sheep;
Seek Your servant,
For I do not forget Your
commandments.

Psalm 120

Plea for Relief from Bitter Foes

A Song of Ascents.

1 In [a]my distress I cried to the LORD,
And He heard me.
2 Deliver my soul, O LORD,
from lying lips
And from a deceitful tongue.

3 What shall be given to you,
Or what shall be done to you,
You false tongue?
4 Sharp arrows of the warrior,
With coals of the broom tree!

5 Woe is me, that I dwell in [a]Meshech,
[b]*That* I dwell among the tents of Kedar!
6 My soul has dwelt too long
With one who hates peace.
7 I *am for* peace;
But when I speak, they *are* for war.

Psalm 121

God the Help of Those Who Seek Him

A Song of Ascents.

1 I [a]will lift up my eyes to the hills—
From whence comes my help?
2 [a]My help *comes* from the LORD,
Who made heaven and earth.

119:154 [a] 1 Sam. 24:15; Mic. 7:9 119:157 [a] Ps. 44:18 119:158 [a] Ezek. 9:4 119:161 [a] 1 Sam. 24:11; 26:18 119:165 [a] Prov. 3:2; [Is. 26:3; 32:17] 119:166 [a] Gen. 49:18 119:168 [a] Job 24:23; Prov. 5:21 119:169 [a] Ps. 119:27, 144 119:171 [a] Ps. 119:7 119:173 [a] Josh. 24:22; Luke 10:42 119:174 [a] Ps. 119:166 [b] Ps. 119:16, 24 119:176 [a] [Is. 53:6]; Jer. 50:6; Matt. 18:12; Luke 15:4; [1 Pet. 2:25] 120:1 [a] Jon. 2:2 120:5 [a] Gen. 10:2; 1 Chr. 1:5; Ezek. 27:13; 38:2, 3; 39:1 [b] Gen. 25:13; Is. 21:16; 60:7; Jer. 2:10; 49:28; Ezek. 27:21 121:1 [a] [Jer. 3:23] 121:2 [a] [Ps. 124:8]

3 [a]He will not allow your
foot to be moved;
[b]He who keeps you will not slumber.
4 Behold, He who keeps Israel
Shall neither slumber nor sleep.

5 The LORD *is* your keeper;
The LORD *is* [a]your shade [b]at
your right hand.
6 [a]The sun shall not strike you by day,
Nor the moon by night.

7 The LORD shall preserve
you from all evil;
He shall [a]preserve your soul.
8 The LORD shall [a]preserve your
going out and your coming in
From this time forth, and
even forevermore.

Psalm 122

The Joy of Going to the House of the LORD

A Song of Ascents. Of David.

1 I was glad when they said to me,
[a]"Let us go into the house of the LORD."
2 Our feet have been standing
Within your gates, O Jerusalem!

3 Jerusalem is built
As a city that is [a]compact together,
4 [a]Where the tribes go up,
The tribes of the LORD,
To [b]the Testimony of Israel,
To give thanks to the
name of the LORD.
5 [a]For thrones are set there
for judgment,
The thrones of the house of David.

6 [a]Pray for the peace of Jerusalem:
"May they prosper who love you.
7 Peace be within your walls,
Prosperity within your palaces."
8 For the sake of my brethren
and companions,
I will now say, "Peace *be* within you."
9 Because of the house of
the LORD our God
I will [a]seek your good.

Psalm 123

Prayer for Relief from Contempt

A Song of Ascents.

1 Unto You [a]I lift up my eyes,
O You [b]who dwell in the heavens.
2 Behold, as the eyes of servants *look*
to the hand of their masters,
As the eyes of a maid to the
hand of her mistress,
[a]So our eyes *look* to the LORD
our God,
Until He has mercy on us.

3 Have mercy on us, O LORD,
have mercy on us!
For we are exceedingly filled
with contempt.
4 Our soul is exceedingly filled
With the scorn of those
who are at ease,
With the contempt of the proud.

Psalm 124

The LORD the Defense of His People

A Song of Ascents. Of David.

1 "If it had not been the LORD
who was on our [a]side,"
[b]Let Israel now say—
2 "If it had not been the LORD
who was on our side,
When men rose up against us,
3 Then they would have
[a]swallowed us alive,
When their wrath was
kindled against us;
4 Then the waters would have
overwhelmed us,
The stream would have
gone over our soul;
5 Then the swollen waters
Would have gone over our soul."

121:3 [a] 1 Sam. 2:9; Prov. 3:23, 26 [b] [Ps. 127:1; Prov. 24:12]; Is. 27:3 121:5 [a] Is. 25:4 [b] Ps. 16:8 121:6 [a] Ps. 91:5; Is. 49:10; Jon. 4:8; Rev. 7:16 121:7 [a] Ps. 41:2 121:8 [a] Deut. 28:6; [Prov. 2:8; 3:6] 122:1 [a] [Is. 2:3; Mic. 4:2]; Zech. 8:21 122:3 [a] 2 Sam. 5:9 122:4 [a] Ex. 23:17; Deut. 16:16 [b] Ex. 16:34 122:5 [a] Deut. 17:8; 2 Chr. 19:8 122:6 [a] Ps. 51:18 122:9 [a] Neh. 2:10; Esth. 10:3 123:1 [a] Ps. 121:1; 141:8 [b] Ps. 2:4; 11:4; 115:3 123:2 [a] Ps. 25:15 124:1 [a] Ps. 118:6; [Rom. 8:31] [b] Ps. 129:1 124:3 [a] Num. 16:30; Ps. 56:1, 2; 57:3; Prov. 1:12

6 Blessed *be* the LORD,
Who has not given us *as*
prey to their teeth.
7 [a]Our soul has escaped [b]as a bird
from the snare of the fowlers;[1]
The snare is broken, and
we have escaped.
8 [a]Our help *is* in the name of the LORD,
[b]Who made heaven and earth.

Psalm 125

The LORD the Strength of His People

A Song of Ascents.

1 Those who trust in the LORD
Are like Mount Zion,
Which cannot be moved,
but abides forever.
2 As the mountains surround
Jerusalem,
So the LORD surrounds His people
From this time forth and forever.

3 For [a]the scepter of wickedness
shall not rest
On the land allotted to the
righteous,
Lest the righteous reach out
their hands to iniquity.

4 Do good, O LORD, to *those
who are* good,
And to *those who are* upright
in their hearts.

5 As for such as turn aside to
their [a]crooked ways,
The LORD shall lead them away
With the workers of iniquity.

[b]Peace *be* upon Israel!

Psalm 126

A Joyful Return to Zion

A Song of Ascents.

1 When [a]the LORD brought back
the captivity of Zion,
[b]We were like those who
dream.
2 Then [a]our mouth was filled
with laughter,
And our tongue with singing.
Then they said among the nations,
"The LORD has done great
things for them."
3 The LORD has done great things for us,
And we are glad.

4 Bring back our captivity, O LORD,
As the streams in the South.

5 [a]Those who sow in tears
Shall reap in joy.
6 He who continually goes
forth weeping,
Bearing seed for sowing,
Shall doubtless come again
with [a]rejoicing,
Bringing his sheaves *with him.*

Psalm 127

*Laboring and Prospering
with the LORD*

A Song of Ascents. Of Solomon.

1 Unless the LORD builds
the house,
They labor in vain who build it;
Unless [a]the LORD guards the city,
The watchman stays awake in vain.
2 *It is* vain for you to rise up early,
To sit up late,
To [a]eat the bread of sorrows;
For so He gives His beloved sleep.

3 Behold, [a]children *are* a
heritage from the LORD,
[b]The fruit of the womb *is* a [c]reward.
4 Like arrows in the hand
of a warrior,
So *are* the children of one's youth.
5 [a]Happy *is* the man who has
his quiver full of them;
[b]They shall not be ashamed,
But shall speak with their
enemies in the gate.

124:7 [a] Ps. 91:3 [b] Prov. 6:5; Hos. 9:8 [1] That is, persons who catch birds in a trap or snare 124:8 [a] [Ps. 121:2] [b] Gen. 1:1; Ps. 134:3
125:3 [a] Prov. 22:8; Is. 14:5 125:5 [a] Prov. 2:15; Is. 59:8 [b] Ps. 128:6; [Gal. 6:16] 126:1 [a] Ps. 85:1; Jer. 29:14; Hos. 6:11; Joel 3:1 [b] Acts 12:9
126:2 [a] Job 8:21 126:5 [a] Is. 35:10; 51:11; 61:7; Jer. 31:9; [Gal. 6:9] 126:6 [a] Is. 61:3 127:1 [a] [Ps. 121:3–5] 127:2 [a] [Gen. 3:17, 19]
127:3 [a] [Gen. 33:5; Josh. 24:3, 4; Ps. 113:9] [b] Deut. 7:13; 28:4; Is. 13:18 [c] [Ps. 113:9] 127:5 [a] Ps. 128:2, 3 [b] Job 5:4; Prov. 27:11

Psalm 128

Blessings of Those Who Fear the LORD

A Song of Ascents.

1 Blessed [a]*is* every one who
fears the LORD,
Who walks in His ways.

2 [a]When you eat the labor
of your hands,
You *shall be* happy, and *it*
shall be [b]well with you.
3 Your wife *shall be* [a]like a fruitful vine
In the very heart of your house,
Your [b]children [c]like olive plants
All around your table.
4 Behold, thus shall the man be blessed
Who fears the LORD.

5 [a]The LORD bless you out of Zion,
And may you see the good
of Jerusalem
All the days of your life.
6 Yes, may you [a]see your
children's children.

[b]Peace *be* upon Israel!

Psalm 129

Song of Victory over Zion's Enemies

A Song of Ascents.

1 "Many a time they have [a]afflicted
me from [b]my youth,"
[c]Let Israel now say—
2 "Many a time they have afflicted
me from my youth;
Yet they have not prevailed
against me.
3 The plowers plowed on my back;
They made their furrows long."
4 The LORD *is* righteous;
He has cut in pieces the
cords of the wicked.

5 Let all those who hate Zion
Be put to shame and turned back.
6 Let them be as the [a]grass
on the housetops,
Which withers before it grows up,
7 With which the reaper does
not fill his hand,
Nor he who binds sheaves,
his arms.
8 Neither let those who
pass by them say,
[a]"The blessing of the LORD *be*
upon you;
We bless you in the name
of the LORD!"

Psalm 130

Waiting for the Redemption of the LORD

A Song of Ascents.

1 Out [a]of the depths I have
cried to You, O LORD;
2 Lord, hear my voice!
Let Your ears be attentive
To the voice of my supplications.

3 [a]If You, LORD, should mark
iniquities,
O Lord, who could [b]stand?
4 But *there is* [a]forgiveness
with You,
That [b]You may be feared.

5 [a]I wait for the LORD, my soul waits,
And [b]in His word I do hope.
6 [a]My soul *waits* for the Lord
More than those who watch
for the morning—
Yes, more than those who
watch for the morning.

7 [a]O Israel, hope in the LORD;
For [b]with the LORD *there*
is mercy,
And with Him *is* abundant
redemption.
8 And [a]He shall redeem Israel
From all his iniquities.

128:1 [a] Ps. 119:1 128:2 [a] Is. 3:10 [b] Deut. 4:40 128:3 [a] Ezek. 19:10 [b] Ps. 127:3–5 [c] Ps. 52:8; 144:12 128:5 [a] Ps. 134:3
128:6 [a] Gen. 48:11; 50:23; Job 42:16; Ps. 103:17; [Prov. 17:6] [b] Ps. 125:5 129:1 [a] [Jer. 1:19; 15:20]; Matt. 16:18; 2 Cor. 4:8, 9 [b] Ezek. 23:3;
Hos. 2:15 [c] Ps. 124:1 129:6 [a] Ps. 37:2 129:8 [a] Ruth 2:4 130:1 [a] Lam. 3:55 130:3 [a] [Ps. 143:2] [b] [Nah. 1:6; Mal. 3:2];
Rev. 6:17 130:4 [a] [Ex. 34:7; Neh. 9:17; Ps. 86:5; Is. 55:7; Dan. 9:9] [b] [1 Kin. 8:39, 40; Jer. 33:8, 9]
130:5 [a] [Ps. 27:14] [b] Ps. 119:81 130:6 [a] Ps. 119:147 130:7 [a] Ps. 131:3 [b] [Ps. 86:5, 15; Is. 55:7]
130:8 [a] [Ps. 103:3, 4]; Luke 1:68; Titus 2:14

Psalm 131

Simple Trust in the LORD

A Song of Ascents. Of David.

1 LORD, my heart is not haughty,
Nor my eyes lofty.
[a]Neither do I concern myself
with great matters,
Nor with things too profound for me.

2 Surely I have calmed and
quieted my soul,
[a]Like a weaned child with his mother;
Like a weaned child *is* my
soul within me.

3 [a]O Israel, hope in the LORD
From this time forth and forever.

Psalm 132

The Eternal Dwelling of God in Zion

A Song of Ascents.

1 LORD, remember David
And all his afflictions;
2 How he swore to the LORD,
[a]*And* vowed to [b]the Mighty
One of Jacob:
3 "Surely I will not go into the
chamber of my house,
Or go up to the comfort of my bed;
4 I will [a]not give sleep to my eyes
Or slumber to my eyelids,
5 Until I [a]find a place for the LORD,
A dwelling place for the
Mighty One of Jacob."

6 Behold, we heard of it [a]in Ephrathah;
[b]We found it [c]in the fields
of the woods.[1]
7 Let us go into His tabernacle;
[a]Let us worship at His footstool.
8 [a]Arise, O LORD, to Your resting place,
You and [b]the ark of Your strength.
9 Let Your priests [a]be clothed
with righteousness,
And let Your saints shout for joy.
10 For Your servant David's sake,
Do not turn away the face
of Your Anointed.

11 [a]The LORD has sworn *in* truth to David;
He will not turn from it:
"I will set upon your throne
[b]the fruit of your body.
12 If your sons will keep My covenant
And My testimony which
I shall teach them,
Their sons also shall sit upon
your throne forevermore."

13 [a]For the LORD has chosen Zion;
He has desired *it* for His
dwelling place:
14 "This[a] *is* My resting place forever;
Here I will dwell, for I have desired it.
15 [a]I will abundantly bless her provision;
I will satisfy her poor with bread.
16 [a]I will also clothe her priests
with salvation,
[b]And her saints shall shout
aloud for joy.
17 [a]There I will make the horn
of David grow;
[b]I will prepare a lamp for My Anointed.
18 His enemies I will [a]clothe with shame,
But upon Himself His crown
shall flourish."

Psalm 133

Blessed Unity of the People of God

A Song of Ascents. Of David.

1 Behold, how good and
how pleasant *it is*
For [a]brethren to dwell
together in unity!

2 *It is* like the precious oil
upon the head,
Running down on the beard,
The beard of Aaron,
Running down on the edge
of his garments.

131:1 [a] Jer. 45:5; [Rom. 12:16] **131:2** [a] [Matt. 18:3; 1 Cor. 14:20] **131:3** [a] [Ps. 130:7] **132:2** [a] Ps. 65:1 [b] Gen. 49:24; Is. 49:26; 60:16 **132:4** [a] Prov. 6:4 **132:5** [a] 1 Kin. 8:17; 1 Chr. 22:7; Ps. 26:8; Acts 7:46 **132:6** [a] 1 Sam. 17:12 [b] 1 Sam. 7:1 [c] 1 Chr. 13:5 [1] Hebrew *Jaar* **132:7** [a] Ps. 5:7; 99:5 **132:8** [a] Num. 10:35 [b] Ps. 78:61 **132:9** [a] Job 29:14 **132:11** [a] [Ps. 89:3, 4, 33; 110:4] [b] 2 Sam. 7:12; [1 Kin. 8:25; 2 Chr. 6:16; Luke 1:69; Acts 2:30] **132:13** [a] [Ps. 48:1, 2] **132:14** [a] Ps. 68:16; Matt. 23:21 **132:15** [a] Ps. 147:14 **132:16** [a] 2 Chr. 6:41; Ps. 132:9; 149:4 [b] 1 Sam. 4:5; Hos. 11:12 **132:17** [a] Ezek. 29:21; Luke 1:69 [b] 1 Kin. 11:36; 15:4; 2 Kin. 8:19; 2 Chr. 21:7; Ps. 18:28 **132:18** [a] Job 8:22; Ps. 35:26 **133:1** [a] Gen. 13:8; Heb. 13:1

3 *It is* like the dew of [a]Hermon,
Descending upon the
mountains of Zion;
For [b]there the LORD commanded
the blessing—
Life forevermore.

Psalm 134

Praising the LORD in His House at Night

A Song of Ascents.

1 Behold, bless the LORD,
All *you* servants of the LORD,
Who by night stand in the
house of the LORD!
2 [a]Lift up your hands *in* the sanctuary,
And bless the LORD.

3 The LORD who made heaven
and earth
Bless you from Zion!

Psalm 135

Praise to God in Creation and Redemption

1 Praise the LORD!

Praise the name of the LORD;
[a]Praise *Him,* O you servants
of the LORD!
2 [a]You who stand in the
house of the LORD,
In [b]the courts of the house of our God,
3 Praise the LORD, for [a]the LORD *is* good;
Sing praises to His name,
[b]for *it is* pleasant.
4 For [a]the LORD has chosen
Jacob for Himself,
Israel for His special treasure.

5 For I know that [a]the LORD *is* great,
And our Lord *is* above all gods.
6 [a]Whatever the LORD pleases He does,
In heaven and in earth,
In the seas and in all deep places.
7 [a]He causes the vapors to ascend
from the ends of the earth;
[b]He makes lightning for the rain;
He brings the wind out of
His [c]treasuries.

8 [a]He destroyed the firstborn
of Egypt,
Both of man and beast.
9 [a]He sent signs and wonders into
the midst of you, O Egypt,
[b]Upon Pharaoh and all his servants.
10 [a]He defeated many nations
And slew mighty kings—
11 Sihon king of the Amorites,
Og king of Bashan,
And [a]all the kingdoms of Canaan—
12 [a]And gave their land *as* a heritage,
A heritage to Israel His people.

13 [a]Your name, O LORD, *endures*
forever,
Your fame, O LORD, throughout
all generations.
14 [a]For the LORD will judge His people,
And He will have compassion
on His servants.

15 [a]The idols of the nations
are silver and gold,
The work of men's hands.
16 They have mouths, but
they do not speak;
Eyes they have, but they do not see;
17 They have ears, but they do not hear;
Nor is there *any* breath
in their mouths.
18 Those who make them are like them;
So is everyone who trusts in them.

19 [a]Bless the LORD, O house of Israel!
Bless the LORD, O house of Aaron!
20 Bless the LORD, O house of Levi!
You who fear the LORD,
bless the LORD!
21 Blessed be the LORD [a]out of Zion,
Who dwells in Jerusalem!

Praise the LORD!

133:3 [a] Deut. 4:48 [b] Lev. 25:21; Deut. 28:8; Ps. 42:8 134:2 [a] [1 Tim. 2:8] 135:1 [a] Ps. 113:1 135:2 [a] Luke 2:37 [b] Ps. 116:19 135:3 [a] [Ps. 119:68] [b] Ps. 147:1 135:4 [a] [Ex. 19:5]; Mal. 3:17; [Titus 2:14; 1 Pet. 2:9] 135:5 [a] Ps. 95:3; 97:9 135:6 [a] Ps. 115:3 135:7 [a] Jer. 10:13 [b] Job 28:25, 26; 38:24–28 [c] Jer. 51:16 135:8 [a] Ex. 12:12; Ps. 78:51 135:9 [a] Ex. 7:10; Deut. 6:22; Ps. 78:43 [b] Ps. 136:15 135:10 [a] Num. 21:24; Ps. 136:17 135:11 [a] Josh. 12:7–24 135:12 [a] Ps. 78:55; 136:21, 22 135:13 [a] [Ex. 3:15; Ps. 102:12] 135:14 [a] Deut. 32:36 135:15 [a] [Ps. 115:4–8] 135:19 [a] [Ps. 115:9] 135:21 [a] Ps. 134:3

Psalm 136

Thanksgiving to God for His Enduring Mercy

1 Oh, [a]give thanks to the
LORD, for *He is* good!
[b]For His mercy *endures* forever.
2 Oh, give thanks to [a]the God of gods!
For His mercy *endures* forever.
3 Oh, give thanks to the Lord of lords!
For His mercy *endures* forever:

4 To Him [a]who alone does
great wonders,
For His mercy *endures* forever;
5 [a]To Him who by wisdom
made the heavens,
For His mercy *endures* forever;
6 [a]To Him who laid out the earth
above the waters,
For His mercy *endures* forever;
7 [a]To Him who made great lights,
For His mercy *endures* forever—
8 [a]The sun to rule by day,
For His mercy *endures* forever;
9 The moon and stars to rule by night,
For His mercy *endures* forever.

10 [a]To Him who struck Egypt
in their firstborn,
For His mercy *endures* forever;
11 [a]And brought out Israel
from among them,
For His mercy *endures* forever;
12 [a]With a strong hand, and with
an outstretched arm,
For His mercy *endures* forever;
13 [a]To Him who divided the
Red Sea in two,
For His mercy *endures* forever;
14 And made Israel pass through
the midst of it,
For His mercy *endures* forever;
15 [a]But overthrew Pharaoh and
his army in the Red Sea,
For His mercy *endures* forever;
16 [a]To Him who led His people
through the wilderness,
For His mercy *endures* forever;
17 [a]To Him who struck down great kings,
For His mercy *endures* forever;
18 [a]And slew famous kings,
For His mercy *endures* forever—
19 [a]Sihon king of the Amorites,
For His mercy *endures* forever;
20 [a]And Og king of Bashan,
For His mercy *endures* forever—
21 [a]And gave their land as a heritage,
For His mercy *endures* forever;
22 A heritage to Israel His servant,
For His mercy *endures* forever.

23 Who [a]remembered us in
our lowly state,
For His mercy *endures* forever;
24 And [a]rescued us from our enemies,
For His mercy *endures* forever;
25 [a]Who gives food to all flesh,
For His mercy *endures* forever.

26 Oh, give thanks to the God of heaven!
For His mercy *endures* forever.

Psalm 137

Longing for Zion in a Foreign Land

1 By the rivers of Babylon,
There we sat down, yea, we wept
When we remembered Zion.
2 We hung our harps
Upon the willows in the midst of it.
3 For there those who carried us away
captive asked of us a song,
And those who [a]plundered
us *requested* mirth,
Saying, "Sing us *one* of the
songs of Zion!"

4 How shall we sing the LORD's song
In a foreign land?
5 If I forget you, O Jerusalem,
Let my right hand forget *its skill!*
6 If I do not remember you,
Let my [a]tongue cling to the
roof of my mouth—

136:1 [a] Ps. 106:1 [b] 1 Chr. 16:34; Jer. 33:11 136:2 [a] [Deut. 10:17] 136:4 [a] Deut. 6:22; Job 9:10; Ps. 72:18 136:5 [a] Gen. 1:1, 6–8; Prov. 3:19; Jer. 51:15 136:6 [a] Gen. 1:9; Ps. 24:2; [Is. 42:5]; Jer. 10:12 136:7 [a] Gen. 1:14–18 136:8 [a] Gen. 1:16 136:10 [a] Ex. 12:29; Ps. 135:8 136:11 [a] Ex. 12:51; 13:3, 16 136:12 [a] Ex. 6:6; Deut. 4:34; 5:15; 7:19; 9:29; 11:2; 2 Kin. 17:36; 2 Chr. 6:32; Jer. 32:17 136:13 [a] Ex. 14:21 136:15 [a] Ex. 14:27 136:16 [a] Ex. 13:18; 15:22; Deut. 8:15 136:17 [a] Ps. 135:10–12 136:18 [a] Deut. 29:7 136:19 [a] Num. 21:21 136:20 [a] Num. 21:33 136:21 [a] Josh. 12:1 136:23 [a] Gen. 8:1; Deut. 32:36; Ps. 113:7 136:24 [a] Ps. 44:7 136:25 [a] Ps. 104:27; 145:15 137:3 [a] Ps. 79:1 137:6 [a] Job 29:10; Ps. 22:15; Ezek. 3:26

If I do not exalt Jerusalem
Above my chief joy.

7 Remember, O LORD, against
[a]the sons of Edom
The day of Jerusalem,
Who said, "Raze *it,* raze *it,*
To its very foundation!"

8 O daughter of Babylon, [a]who
are to be destroyed,
Happy the one [b]who repays you
as you have served us!
9 Happy the one who takes and [a]dashes
Your little ones against the rock!

Psalm 138

The LORD's Goodness to the Faithful

A Psalm of David.

1 I will praise You with my whole heart;
[a]Before the gods I will sing
praises to You.
2 [a]I will worship [b]toward Your holy temple,
And praise Your name
For Your lovingkindness
and Your truth;
For You have [c]magnified Your
word above all Your name.
3 In the day when I cried out,
You answered me,
And made me bold *with*
strength in my soul.

4 [a]All the kings of the earth shall
praise You, O LORD,
When they hear the words
of Your mouth.
5 Yes, they shall sing of the
ways of the LORD,
For great *is* the glory of the LORD.
6 [a]Though the LORD *is* on high,
Yet [b]He regards the lowly;
But the proud He knows from afar.

7 [a]Though I walk in the midst of
trouble, You will revive me;
You will stretch out Your hand
Against the wrath of my enemies,
And Your right hand will save me.
8 [a]The LORD will perfect *that*
which concerns me;
Your mercy, O LORD, *endures* forever;
[b]Do not forsake the works
of Your hands.

Psalm 139

God's Perfect Knowledge of Man

For the Chief Musician. A Psalm of David.

1 O LORD, [a]You have searched
me and known *me.*
2 [a]You know my sitting down
and my rising up;
You [b]understand my thought afar off.
3 [a]You comprehend my path
and my lying down,
And are acquainted with all my ways.
4 For *there is* not a word on my tongue,
But behold, O LORD, [a]You
know it altogether.
5 You have hedged me
behind and before,
And laid Your hand upon me.
6 [a]*Such* knowledge *is* too
wonderful for me;
It is high, I cannot *attain* it.

7 [a]Where can I go from Your Spirit?
Or where can I flee from
Your presence?
8 [a]If I ascend into heaven,
You *are* there;
[b]If I make my bed in hell,
behold, You *are there.*
9 *If* I take the wings of the morning,
And dwell in the uttermost
parts of the sea,
10 Even there Your hand shall lead me,
And Your right hand shall hold me.
11 If I say, "Surely the darkness
shall fall[1] on me,"
Even the night shall be light
about me;

137:7 [a] Jer. 49:7–22; Lam. 4:21; Ezek. 25:12–14; 35:2; Amos 1:11; Obad. 10–14 137:8 [a] Is. 13:1–6; 47:1 [b] Jer. 50:15; Rev. 18:6 137:9 [a] 2 Kin. 8:12; Is. 13:16; Hos. 13:16; Nah. 3:10 138:1 [a] Ps. 119:46 138:2 [a] Ps. 28:2 [b] 1 Kin. 8:29 [c] Is. 42:21 138:4 [a] Ps. 102:15 138:6 [a] [Ps. 113:4–7] [b] Prov. 3:34; [Is. 57:15]; Luke 1:48; [James 4:6; 1 Pet. 5:5] 138:7 [a] [Ps. 23:3, 4] 138:8 [a] Ps. 57:2; [Phil. 1:6] [b] Job 10:3, 8 139:1 [a] Ps. 17:3; Jer. 12:3 139:2 [a] 2 Kin. 19:27 [b] Is. 66:18; Matt. 9:4 139:3 [a] Job 14:16; 31:4 139:4 [a] [Heb. 4:13] 139:6 [a] Job 42:3; Ps. 40:5 139:7 [a] [Jer. 23:24; Amos 9:2–4] 139:8 [a] [Amos 9:2–4] [b] [Job 26:6; Prov. 15:11] 139:11 [1] Vulgate and Symmachus read *cover.*

12 Indeed, [a]the darkness shall
not hide from You,
But the night shines as the day;
The darkness and the light
are both alike *to You.*

13 For You formed my inward parts;
You covered me in my mother's womb.
14 I will praise You, for I am fearfully
and wonderfully made;[1]
Marvelous are Your works,
And *that* my soul knows very well.
15 [a]My frame was not hidden from You,
When I was made in secret,
And skillfully wrought in the
lowest parts of the earth.
16 Your eyes saw my substance,
being yet unformed.
And in Your book they all were written,
The days fashioned for me,
When *as yet there were* none
of them.

17 [a]How precious also are Your
thoughts to me, O God!
How great is the sum of them!
18 *If* I should count them, they would be
more in number than the sand;
When I awake, I am still with You.

19 Oh, that You would [a]slay
the wicked, O God!
[b]Depart from me, therefore,
you bloodthirsty men.
20 For they [a]speak against You wickedly;
Your enemies take *Your name* in vain.[1]
21 [a]Do I not hate them, O LORD,
who hate You?
And do I not loathe those who
rise up against You?
22 I hate them with perfect hatred;
I count them my enemies.

23 [a]Search me, O God, and know
my heart;
Try me, and know my anxieties;
24 And see if *there is any*
wicked way in me,
And [a]lead me in the way everlasting.

Psalm 140

Prayer for Deliverance from Evil Men

To the Chief Musician. A Psalm of David.

1 Deliver me, O LORD, from
evil men;
Preserve me from violent men,
2 Who plan evil things in *their* hearts;
[a]They continually gather
together *for* war.
3 They sharpen their tongues
like a serpent;
The [a]poison of asps *is* under
their lips. *Selah*

4 [a]Keep me, O LORD, from the
hands of the wicked;
Preserve me from violent men,
Who have purposed to make
my steps stumble.
5 The proud have hidden a
[a]snare for me, and cords;
They have spread a net by the wayside;
They have set traps for me. *Selah*

6 I said to the LORD: "You *are*
my God;
Hear the voice of my
supplications, O LORD.
7 O GOD the Lord, the strength
of my salvation,
You have covered my head
in the day of battle.
8 Do not grant, O LORD, the
desires of the wicked;
Do not further his *wicked* scheme,
[a]*Lest* they be exalted. *Selah*

9 "*As for* the head of those
who surround me,
Let the evil of their lips cover them;
10 [a]Let burning coals fall upon them;
Let them be cast into the fire,
Into deep pits, that they
rise not up again.
11 Let not a slanderer be
established in the earth;
Let evil hunt the violent man
to overthrow *him.*"

139:12 [a] Job 26:6; 34:22; [Dan. 2:22; Heb. 4:13] 139:14 [1] Following Masoretic Text and Targum; Septuagint, Syriac, and Vulgate read *You are fearfully wonderful.* 139:15 [a] Job 10:8, 9; Eccl. 11:5 139:17 [a] [Ps. 40:5; Rom. 11:33] 139:19 [a] [Is. 11:4] [b] Ps. 119:115 139:20 [a] Jude 15 [1] Septuagint and Vulgate read *They take Your cities in vain.* 139:21 [a] 2 Chr. 19:2 139:23 [a] Job 31:6; Ps. 26:2 139:24 [a] Ps. 5:8; 143:10 140:2 [a] Ps. 56:6 140:3 [a] Ps. 58:4; Rom. 3:13; James 3:8 140:4 [a] Ps. 71:4 140:5 [a] Ps. 35:7; Jer. 18:22 140:8 [a] Deut. 32:27 140:10 [a] Ps. 11:6

12 I know that the LORD will [a]maintain
The cause of the afflicted,
And justice for the poor.
13 Surely the righteous shall give
thanks to Your name;
The upright shall dwell in
Your presence.

Psalm 141

Prayer for Safekeeping from Wickedness

A Psalm of David.

1 LORD, I cry out to You;
Make haste to me!
Give ear to my voice when
I cry out to You.
2 Let my prayer be set before
You [a]*as* incense,
[b]The lifting up of my hands *as*
[c]the evening sacrifice.

3 Set a guard, O LORD, over
my [a]mouth;
Keep watch over the door
of my lips.
4 Do not incline my heart
to any evil thing,
To practice wicked works
With men who work iniquity;
[a]And do not let me eat of
their delicacies.

5 [a]Let the righteous strike me;
It shall be a kindness.
And let him rebuke me;
It shall be as excellent oil;
Let my head not refuse it.

For still my prayer *is* against
the deeds of the wicked.
6 Their judges are overthrown
by the sides of the cliff,
And they hear my words,
for they are sweet.
7 Our bones are scattered at the
mouth of the grave,
As when one plows and
breaks up the earth.

8 But [a]my eyes *are* upon You,
O GOD the Lord;
In You I take refuge;
Do not leave my soul destitute.
9 Keep me from [a]the snares
they have laid for me,
And from the traps of the
workers of iniquity.
10 [a]Let the wicked fall into
their own nets,
While I escape safely.

Psalm 142

A Plea for Relief from Persecutors

A [a]Contemplation[1] of David. A Prayer [b]when he was in the cave.

1 I cry out to the LORD with my voice;
With my voice to the LORD I
make my supplication.
2 I pour out my complaint
before Him;
I declare before Him my trouble.

3 When my spirit was
[a]overwhelmed within me,
Then You knew my path.
In the way in which I walk
They have secretly [b]set
a snare for me.
4 Look on *my* right hand and see,
For *there is* no one who
acknowledges me;
Refuge has failed me;
No one cares for my soul.

5 I cried out to You, O LORD:
I said, "You *are* my refuge,
My portion in the land
of the living.
6 Attend to my cry,
For I am brought very low;
Deliver me from my persecutors,
For they are stronger than I.
7 Bring my soul out of prison,
That I may [a]praise Your name;
The righteous shall surround me,
For You shall deal bountifully
with me."

140:12 [a] 1 Kin. 8:45; Ps. 9:4 141:2 [a] [Ex. 30:8]; Luke 1:10; [Rev. 5:8; 8:3, 4] [b] Ps. 134:2; [1 Tim. 2:8] [c] Ex. 29:39, 41; 1 Kin. 18:29, 36; Dan. 9:21 141:3 [a] [Prov. 13:3; 21:23] 141:4 [a] Prov. 23:6 141:5 [a] [Prov. 9:8; Eccl. 7:5; Gal. 6:1] 141:8 [a] 2 Chr. 20:12; Ps. 25:15 141:9 [a] Ps. 119:110 141:10 [a] Ps. 35:8 142:title [a] Ps. 32:title [b] 1 Sam. 22:1; Ps. 57:title [1] Hebrew *Maschil* 142:3 [a] Ps. 77:3 [b] Ps. 141:9 142:7 [a] Ps. 34:1, 2

Psalm 143

An Earnest Appeal for Guidance and Deliverance

A Psalm of David.

1 Hear my prayer, O LORD,
Give ear to my supplications!
In Your faithfulness answer me,
And in Your righteousness.
2 Do not enter into judgment
with Your servant,
[a]For in Your sight no one
living is righteous.

3 For the enemy has
persecuted my soul;
He has crushed my life
to the ground;
He has made me dwell in darkness,
Like those who have long been dead.
4 [a]Therefore my spirit is
overwhelmed within me;
My heart within me is distressed.

5 [a]I remember the days of old;
I meditate on all Your works;
I muse on the work of Your hands.
6 I spread out my hands to You;
[a]My soul *longs* for You like a
thirsty land. *Selah*

7 Answer me speedily, O LORD;
My spirit fails!
Do not hide Your face from me,
[a]Lest I be like those who go
down into the pit.
8 Cause me to hear Your lovingkindness
[a]in the morning,
For in You do I trust;
[b]Cause me to know the way in
which I should walk,
For [c]I lift up my soul to You.

9 Deliver me, O LORD, from
my enemies;
In You I take shelter.[1]
10 [a]Teach me to do Your will,
For You *are* my God;
[b]Your Spirit *is* good.
Lead me in [c]the land of uprightness.

11 [a]Revive me, O LORD, for
Your name's sake!
For Your righteousness' sake
bring my soul out of trouble.
12 In Your mercy [a]cut off my enemies,
And destroy all those who
afflict my soul;
For I *am* Your servant.

Psalm 144

A Song to the LORD Who Preserves and Prospers His People

A Psalm of David.

1 Blessed *be* the LORD my Rock,
[a]Who trains my hands for war,
And my fingers for battle—
2 My lovingkindness and my fortress,
My high tower and my deliverer,
My shield and *the One* in
whom I take refuge,
Who subdues my people[1] under me.

3 [a]LORD, what *is* man, that You
take knowledge of him?
Or the son of man, that You
are mindful of him?
4 [a]Man is like a breath;
[b]His days *are* like a passing shadow.

5 [a]Bow down Your heavens,
O LORD, and come down;
[b]Touch the mountains, and
they shall smoke.
6 [a]Flash forth lightning and scatter them;
Shoot out Your arrows
and destroy them.
7 Stretch out Your hand from above;
Rescue me and deliver me
out of great waters,
From the hand of foreigners,
8 Whose mouth [a]speaks lying words,
And whose right hand *is* a
right hand of falsehood.

143:2 [a] [Ex. 34:7]; Job 4:17; 9:2; 25:4; Ps. 130:3; Eccl. 7:20; [Rom. 3:20–23; Gal. 2:16] 143:4 [a] Ps. 77:3 143:5 [a] Ps. 77:5, 10, 11 143:6 [a] Ps. 63:1 143:7 [a] Ps. 28:1 143:8 [a] Ps. 46:5 [b] Ps. 5:8 [c] Ps. 25:1 143:9 [1] Septuagint and Vulgate read *To You I flee.* 143:10 [a] Ps. 25:4, 5 [b] Neh. 9:20 [c] Is. 26:10 143:11 [a] Ps. 119:25 143:12 [a] Ps. 54:5 144:1 [a] 2 Sam. 22:35; Ps. 18:34 144:2 [1] Following Masoretic Text, Septuagint, and Vulgate; Syriac and Targum read *the peoples* (compare 18:47). 144:3 [a] Job 7:17; Ps. 8:4; Heb. 2:6 144:4 [a] Ps. 39:11 [b] Job 8:9; 14:2; Ps. 102:11 144:5 [a] Ps. 18:9; Is. 64:1 [b] Ps. 104:32 144:6 [a] Ps. 18:13, 14 144:8 [a] Ps. 12:2

9 I will [a]sing a new song to You, O God;
On a harp of ten strings I will
sing praises to You,
10 *The One* who gives salvation to kings,
[a]Who delivers David His servant
From the deadly sword.

11 Rescue me and deliver me from
the hand of foreigners,
Whose mouth speaks lying words,
And whose right hand *is* a right
hand of falsehood—
12 That our sons *may be* [a]as plants
grown up in their youth;
That our daughters *may be* as pillars,
Sculptured in palace style;
13 *That* our barns *may be* full,
Supplying all kinds of produce;
That our sheep may bring
forth thousands
And ten thousands in our fields;
14 *That* our oxen *may be* well laden;
That there be no breaking
in or going out;
That there be no outcry in our streets.
15 [a]Happy *are* the people who
are in such a state;
Happy *are* the people whose
God *is* the LORD!

Psalm 145

A Song of God's Majesty and Love

[a]A Praise of David.

1 I will extol You, my God, O King;
And I will bless Your name
forever and ever.
2 Every day I will bless You,
And I will praise Your name
forever and ever.
3 [a]Great *is* the LORD, and
greatly to be praised;
And [b]His greatness *is* unsearchable.

4 [a]One generation shall praise
Your works to another,
And shall declare Your mighty acts.
5 I[1] will meditate on the glorious
splendor of Your majesty,
And on Your wondrous works.[2]
6 *Men* shall speak of the might
of Your awesome acts,
And I will declare Your greatness.
7 They shall utter the memory
of Your great goodness,
And shall sing of Your righteousness.

8 [a]The LORD *is* gracious and
full of compassion,
Slow to anger and great in mercy.
9 [a]The LORD *is* good to all,
And His tender mercies *are*
over all His works.

10 [a]All Your works shall praise
You, O LORD,
And Your saints shall bless You.
11 They shall speak of the glory
of Your kingdom,
And talk of Your power,
12 To make known to the sons of
men His mighty acts,
And the glorious majesty
of His kingdom.
13 [a]Your kingdom *is* an
everlasting kingdom,
And Your dominion *endures*
throughout all generations.[1]

14 The LORD upholds all who fall,
And [a]raises up all *who*
are bowed down.
15 [a]The eyes of all look expectantly
to You,
And [b]You give them their
food in due season.
16 You open Your hand
[a]And satisfy the desire of
every living thing.

17 The LORD *is* righteous in all His ways,
Gracious in all His works.
18 [a]The LORD *is* near to all who
call upon Him,
To all who call upon Him [b]in truth.

144:9 [a] Ps. 33:2, 3; 40:3 144:10 [a] Ps. 18:50 144:12 [a] Ps. 128:3 144:15 [a] Deut. 33:29; [Ps. 33:12; Jer. 17:7] 145:title [a] Ps. 100:title 145:3 [a] [Ps. 147:5] [b] Job 5:9; 9:10; 11:7; Is. 40:28; [Rom. 11:33] 145:4 [a] Is. 38:19 145:5 [1] Following Masoretic Text and Targum; Dead Sea Scrolls, Septuagint, Syriac, and Vulgate read *They.* [2] Literally *on the words of Your wondrous works* 145:8 [a] [Ex. 34:6, 7; Num. 14:18]; Ps. 86:5, 15 145:9 [a] [Ps. 100:5]; Jer. 33:11; Nah. 1:7; [Matt. 19:17; Mark 10:18] 145:10 [a] Ps. 19:1 145:13 [a] Dan. 2:44; 4:3; [1 Tim. 1:17; 2 Pet. 1:11] [1] Following Masoretic Text and Targum; Dead Sea Scrolls, Septuagint, Syriac, and Vulgate add *The LORD is faithful in all His words, And holy in all His works.* 145:14 [a] Ps. 146:8 145:15 [a] Ps. 104:27 [b] Ps. 136:25 145:16 [a] Ps. 104:21, 28 145:18 [a] [Deut. 4:7] [b] [John 4:24]

19 He will fulfill the desire of
those who fear Him;
He also will hear their cry
and save them.
20 [a]The LORD preserves all who love Him,
But all the wicked He will destroy.
21 My mouth shall speak the
praise of the LORD,
And all flesh shall bless His holy name
Forever and ever.

Psalm 146

The Happiness of Those Whose Help Is the LORD

1 Praise the LORD!

[a]Praise the LORD, O my soul!
2 [a]While I live I will praise the LORD;
I will sing praises to my God
while I have my being.

3 [a]Do not put your trust in princes,
Nor in a son of man, in whom
there is no help.
4 [a]His spirit departs, he
returns to his earth;
In that very day [b]his plans perish.

5 [a]Happy *is he* who *has* the God
of Jacob for his help,
Whose hope *is* in the LORD his God,
6 [a]Who made heaven and earth,
The sea, and all that *is* in them;
Who keeps truth forever,
7 [a]Who executes justice for
the oppressed,
[b]Who gives food to the hungry.
[c]The LORD gives freedom
to the prisoners.

8 [a]The LORD opens *the eyes of* the blind;
[b]The LORD raises those who
are bowed down;
The LORD loves the righteous.
9 [a]The LORD watches over the strangers;
He relieves the fatherless and widow;
[b]But the way of the wicked He
turns upside down.

10 [a]The LORD shall reign forever—
Your God, O Zion, to all generations.

Praise the LORD!

Psalm 147

Praise to God for His Word and Providence

1 Praise the LORD!
For [a]*it is* good to sing
praises to our God;
[b]For *it is* pleasant, *and*
[c]praise is beautiful.

2 The LORD [a]builds up Jerusalem;
[b]He gathers together the
outcasts of Israel.
3 [a]He heals the brokenhearted
And binds up their wounds.
4 [a]He counts the number of the stars;
He calls them all by name.
5 [a]Great *is* our Lord, and [b]mighty in power;
[c]His understanding *is* infinite.
6 [a]The LORD lifts up the humble;
He casts the wicked down
to the ground.

7 Sing to the LORD with thanksgiving;
Sing praises on the harp to our God,
8 [a]Who covers the heavens with clouds,
Who prepares rain for the earth,
Who makes grass to grow
on the mountains.
9 [a]He gives to the beast its food,
And [b]to the young ravens that cry.

10 [a]He does not delight in the
strength of the horse;
He takes no pleasure in
the legs of a man.
11 The LORD takes pleasure in
those who fear Him,
In those who hope in His mercy.

145:20 [a] [Ps. 31:23] 146:1 [a] Ps. 103:1 146:2 [a] Ps. 104:33 146:3 [a] [Is. 2:22] 146:4 [a] [Eccl. 12:7] [b] [Ps. 33:10; 1 Cor. 2:6] 146:5 [a] Jer. 17:7 146:6 [a] Gen. 1:1; Ex. 20:11; Acts 4:24; Rev. 14:7 146:7 [a] Ps. 103:6 [b] Ps. 107:9 [c] Ps. 107:10; Is. 61:1 146:8 [a] Matt. 9:30; [John 9:7, 32, 33] [b] Luke 13:13 146:9 [a] Deut. 10:18; Ps. 68:5 [b] Ps. 147:6 146:10 [a] Ex. 15:18; Ps. 10:16; [Rev. 11:15] 147:1 [a] Ps. 92:1 [b] Ps. 135:3 [c] Ps. 33:1 147:2 [a] Ps. 102:16 [b] Deut. 30:3; Is. 11:12; 56:8; Ezek. 39:28 147:3 [a] [Ps. 51:17]; Is. 61:1; Luke 4:18 147:4 [a] Is. 40:26 147:5 [a] Ps. 48:1 [b] Nah. 1:3 [c] Is. 40:28 147:6 [a] Ps. 146:8, 9 147:8 [a] Job 38:26; Ps. 104:13 147:9 [a] Job 38:41 [b] [Matt. 6:26] 147:10 [a] Ps. 33:16, 17

12 Praise the LORD, O Jerusalem!
Praise your God, O Zion!
13 For He has strengthened the
bars of your gates;
He has blessed your
children within you.
14 [a]He makes peace *in* your
borders,
And [b]fills you with the finest wheat.

15 [a]He sends out His command
to the earth;
His word runs very swiftly.
16 [a]He gives snow like wool;
He scatters the frost like ashes;
17 He casts out His hail like morsels;
Who can stand before His cold?
18 [a]He sends out His word
and melts them;
He causes His wind to blow,
and the waters flow.

19 [a]He declares His word to Jacob,
[b]His statutes and His
judgments to Israel.
20 [a]He has not dealt thus with
any nation;
And *as for His* judgments, they
have not known them.

Praise the LORD!

Psalm 148

Praise to the LORD from Creation

1 Praise the LORD!

Praise the LORD from the
heavens;
Praise Him in the heights!
2 Praise Him, all His angels;
Praise Him, all His hosts!
3 Praise Him, sun and moon;
Praise Him, all you stars of light!
4 Praise Him, [a]you heavens
of heavens,
And [b]you waters above the
heavens!

5 Let them praise the name of the LORD,
For [a]He commanded and
they were created.
6 [a]He also established them
forever and ever;
He made a decree which
shall not pass away.

7 Praise the LORD from the earth,
[a]You great sea creatures
and all the depths;
8 Fire and hail, snow and clouds;
Stormy wind, fulfilling His word;
9 [a]Mountains and all hills;
Fruitful trees and all cedars;
10 Beasts and all cattle;
Creeping things and flying fowl;
11 Kings of the earth and all peoples;
Princes and all judges of the earth;
12 Both young men and maidens;
Old men and children.

13 Let them praise the name
of the LORD,
For His [a]name alone is exalted;
His glory *is* above the
earth and heaven.
14 And He [a]has exalted the
horn of His people,
The praise of [b]all His saints—
Of the children of Israel,
[c]A people near to Him.

Praise the LORD!

Psalm 149

Praise to God for His Salvation and Judgment

1 Praise the LORD!

[a]Sing to the LORD a new song,
And His praise in the
assembly of saints.

2 Let Israel rejoice in their Maker;
Let the children of Zion be
joyful in their [a]King.

147:14 [a] Is. 54:13; 60:17, 18 [b] Ps. 132:15 147:15 [a] [Ps. 107:20] 147:16 [a] Job 37:6 147:18 [a] Job 37:10 147:19 [a] Deut. 33:4; Ps. 103:7 [b] Mal. 4:4 147:20 [a] Deut. 4:32–34; [Rom. 3:1, 2] 148:4 [a] Deut. 10:14; 1 Kin. 8:27; [Neh. 9:6] [b] Gen. 1:7 148:5 [a] Gen. 1:1, 6 148:6 [a] Ps. 89:37; [Jer. 31:35, 36; 33:20, 25] 148:7 [a] Is. 43:20 148:9 [a] Is. 44:23; 49:13 148:13 [a] Ps. 8:1 148:14 [a] 1 Sam. 2:1; Ps. 75:10 [b] Ps. 149:9 [c] Lev. 10:3; Eph. 2:17 149:1 [a] Ps. 33:3 149:2 [a] Judg. 8:23; Zech. 9:9; Matt. 21:5

3 [a]Let them praise His name
with the dance;
Let them sing praises to Him
with the timbrel and harp.
4 For [a]the LORD takes pleasure
in His people;
[b]He will beautify the humble
with salvation.

5 Let the saints be joyful in glory;
Let them [a]sing aloud on their beds.
6 *Let* the high praises of God
be in their mouth,
And [a]a two-edged sword in
their hand,
7 To execute vengeance on
the nations,
And punishments on the peoples;
8 To bind their kings with chains,
And their nobles with fetters
of iron;
9 [a]To execute on them the
written judgment—
[b]This honor have all His saints.

Praise the LORD!

Psalm 150

Let All Things Praise the LORD

1 Praise[a] the LORD!

Praise God in His sanctuary;
Praise Him in His mighty firmament!

2 Praise Him for His mighty acts;
Praise Him according to His
excellent [a]greatness!

3 Praise Him with the sound
of the trumpet;
Praise Him with the lute and harp!
4 Praise Him with the
timbrel and dance;
Praise Him with stringed
instruments and flutes!
5 Praise Him with loud cymbals;
Praise Him with clashing cymbals!

6 Let everything that has breath
praise the LORD.

Praise the LORD!

149:3 [a] Ex. 15:20; Ps. 81:2 149:4 [a] Ps. 35:27 [b] Ps. 132:16; Is. 61:3 149:5 [a] Job 35:10 149:6 [a] Heb. 4:12; Rev. 1:16 149:9 [a] Deut. 7:1, 2; Ezek. 28:26 [b] Ps. 148:14; 1 Cor. 6:2 150:1 [a] Ps. 145:5, 6 150:2 [a] Deut. 3:24

THE BOOK OF

PROVERBS

OVERVIEW

The Book of Proverbs is a collection of practical guidelines—wisdom for everyday living. Solomon wrote most of the Book of Proverbs (1:1—22:15; 25:1—29:27) when he was at the height of his reign as king. Solomon was recognized by all as a man of great wisdom (see 1 Kin. 4:29–34). Approximately three thousand proverbs and over one thousand songs have been attributed to him. Solomon wrote more of the Old Testament than any other person besides Moses. In addition to Solomon's contribution to Proverbs, the author of Proverbs 30 was Agur, and the author of Proverbs 31 was Lemuel. This collection of wise counsel was gathered during the tenth century BC. The Book of Proverbs appeared in its final form between 729 and 686 BC.

The purpose of Proverbs is to provide a guide for living wisely. Above all, wise living requires being in right relationship with God. Proverbs gives invaluable insight into how knowledge about God results in godly decisions and translates into direction for everyday life.

With wisdom as its focus, Proverbs contrasts concepts such as good and evil, prosperity and poverty, fidelity and adultery, and truth and lies. We learn that wisdom comes only from God and is available to everyone. God rewards the wise for their righteousness, but the foolish suffer the consequences of their unwise actions.

Proverbs 1–9 deals with wisdom, and Proverbs 10–29 focuses on righteous living. The call for everyone to seek wisdom and understand its value is presented in Proverbs 1:20—2:22. Throughout Proverbs, many of life's issues are addressed and warnings are offered against immorality (see 5:1–23; 6:20—7:27), idleness (see 6:1–19), and infidelity (see 6:27–35). Proverbs warns the reader against choosing worldly riches over "a good name" (22:1) and being "envious of evil men" (24:1–2).

Proverbs 30:5 declares that "every word of God is pure; He is a shield to those who put their trust in Him." This proverb reminds readers that God's Word will not return void. It will accomplish whatever God designed it to accomplish.

Proverbs 31 is one of the more well-known passages in this book. It outlines the traits of a virtuous woman. The proverb declares that such a woman is trusted by her husband (see v. 11), helps the poor (see v. 20), speaks with wisdom and kindness (see v. 26), and fears the Lord (see v. 30).

The Book of Proverbs gives believers a plan for living a successful life, which is accomplished only by being led by wisdom through daily activities. The proverbs are easy to understand and can be applied to almost any situation. Acknowledging that people often struggle with good and evil, Proverbs gives a clear indication of the consequences involved with pursuing each choice. The writers of Proverbs advise rightly that we should seek wise counsel and remain teachable as we walk out our lives.

BREATHE IT IN

The Book of Proverbs is a practical book that teaches Christians how they should live and interact with others. It offers guidance on many facets of life, including parenting, conducting

business, maintaining relationships, and acting responsibly. Wisdom is the foundation of all proper living presented in Proverbs.

When we trust in Christ as our Savior, we have taken the first step on our lifelong journey of learning the ways of God and how He expects us to live as His ambassadors here on earth. This knowledge is not automatically planted and rooted in our lives. Instead, we must seek it, accept it, and apply it. While the Bible is filled with hundreds of stories and lessons to help us please God with our lives, Proverbs presents us with clear and simple instructions for how to do this. Early in Proverbs, Solomon writes, "A wise man will hear and increase learning" (1:5). This increase in learning comes from seeking wisdom, like that presented in Proverbs.

Those who have been walking with Christ for many years sometimes feel that they know everything they need to know about God. They can believe that their ability to quote Scripture or their demonstration of spiritual gifts supersedes their need to continuously seek wisdom. This could not be further from the truth. As Christians, we should be lifelong learners. The more we learn of Him, the more we should see we have yet to learn. We should continually seek to know more about God and improve our daily walk with Him.

Proverbs teaches us right from wrong and acknowledges the blessings and curses that result from the choices we make. It teaches us how to treat our spouses and raise our children. It teaches us how to conduct business and make important decisions. It even teaches us about the different types of people that we encounter in life and the best way to interact with them. In essence, as Christians, Proverbs helps us answer the question "What would Jesus do?"

Not only does Proverbs teach us, but it also warns us. It warns us against practicing deception. It warns us against committing adultery and against being greedy and covetous. It warns us about the destruction that awaits those who think and act wickedly instead of righteously.

When was the last time you evaluated your daily living? Have you sought to expand your knowledge? Do you seek the wisdom of God when making decisions and going about your daily routines? Are you following the free but priceless instruction that is available to us in Proverbs?

No matter how far along we are on our journey with Christ, we have so much further to go. Why not utilize this playbook that God left as a guide for us? Take time to reacquaint yourself with the Book of Proverbs. As you read it, you will be reminded of situations you handled well and others in which you might have lacked wisdom. The book contains so many jewels of wisdom that can change our perspective on life, direct our daily activities, and improve our relationships with others. Remember, "when wisdom enters your heart, and knowledge is pleasant to your soul, discretion will preserve you; understanding will keep you" (2:10–11).

THE BOOK OF

PROVERBS

The Beginning of Knowledge

1 The [a]proverbs of Solomon the son of David, king of Israel:

2 To know wisdom and instruction,
To perceive the words of understanding,
3 To receive the instruction of wisdom,
Justice, judgment, and equity;
4 To give prudence to the [a]simple,
To the young man knowledge and discretion—
5 [a]A wise *man* will hear and increase learning,
And a man of understanding will attain wise counsel,
6 To understand a proverb and an enigma,
The words of the wise and their [a]riddles.

7 [a]The fear of the LORD *is* the beginning of knowledge,
But fools despise wisdom and instruction.

Shun Evil Counsel

8 [a]My son, hear the instruction of your father,
And do not forsake the law of your mother;
9 For they *will be* a [a]graceful ornament on your head,
And chains about your neck.

10 My son, if sinners entice you,
[a]Do not consent.
11 If they say, "Come with us,
Let us [a]lie in wait to *shed* blood;
Let us lurk secretly for the innocent without cause;
12 Let us swallow them alive like Sheol,[1]
And whole, [a]like those who go down to the Pit;
13 We shall find all *kinds* of precious possessions,
We shall fill our houses with spoil;
14 Cast in your lot among us,
Let us all have one purse"—
15 My son, [a]do not walk in the way with them,
[b]Keep your foot from their path;
16 [a]For their feet run to evil,
And they make haste to shed blood.
17 Surely, in vain the net is spread
In the sight of any bird;
18 But they lie in wait for their *own* blood,
They lurk secretly for their *own* lives.
19 [a]So *are* the ways of everyone who is greedy for gain;
It takes away the life of its owners.

The Call of Wisdom

20 [a]Wisdom calls aloud outside;
She raises her voice in the open squares.
21 She cries out in the chief concourses,[1]
At the openings of the gates in the city
She speaks her words:
22 "How long, you simple ones, will you love simplicity?
For scorners delight in their scorning,
And fools hate knowledge.

1:1 [a] 1 Kin. 4:32; Prov. 10:1; 25:1; Eccl. 12:9 1:4 [a] Prov. 9:4 1:5 [a] Prov. 9:9 1:6 [a] Num. 12:8; Ps. 78:2; Dan. 8:23 1:7 [a] Job 28:28; Ps. 111:10; Prov. 9:10; 15:33; [Eccl. 12:13] 1:8 [a] Prov. 4:1 1:9 [a] Prov. 3:22 1:10 [a] Gen. 39:7–10; Deut. 13:8; Ps. 50:18; [Eph. 5:11] 1:11 [a] Prov. 12:6; Jer. 5:26 1:12 [a] Ps. 28:1 [1] Or *the grave* 1:15 [a] Ps. 1:1; Prov. 4:14 [b] Ps. 119:101 1:16 [a] Prov. 6:17, 18; [Is. 59:7]; Rom. 3:15 1:19 [a] Prov. 15:27; [1 Tim. 6:10] 1:20 [a] Prov. 8:1; 9:3; [John 7:37]
1:21 [1] Septuagint, Syriac, and Targum read *top of the walls;* Vulgate reads *the head of multitudes.*

23 Turn at my rebuke;
Surely [a]I will pour out my
spirit on you;
I will make my words known to you.
24 [a]Because I have called and you refused,
I have stretched out my hand
and no one regarded,
25 Because you [a]disdained
all my counsel,
And would have none of my rebuke,
26 [a]I also will laugh at your calamity;
I will mock when your terror comes,
27 When [a]your terror comes like a storm,
And your destruction comes
like a whirlwind,
When distress and anguish
come upon you.

28 "Then[a] they will call on me,
but I will not answer;
They will seek me diligently,
but they will not find me.
29 Because they [a]hated knowledge
And did not [b]choose the
fear of the LORD,
30 [a]They would have none of my counsel
And despised my every rebuke.
31 Therefore [a]they shall eat the
fruit of their own way,
And be filled to the full with
their own fancies.
32 For the turning away of the
simple will slay them,
And the complacency of fools
will destroy them;

PROVERBS 1:7

I AM SOLOMON

The fear of the LORD is the beginning of knowledge, but fools despise wisdom and instruction. Proverbs 1:7

I am Solomon, son of King David. I was favored by God and succeeded my father as king of Israel. As the kingdom passed to me, the Lord came to me in a dream. He asked me what He could give me. I knew ruling the people of Israel would require much wisdom, so I asked the Lord for an understanding heart and the ability to discern justice. God honored my request and granted me long life and riches also.

I was known throughout the nations as a wise king. God was with me, and there was peace and safety throughout Israel during my reign. I wrote many proverbs, longing to pass along the wisdom God had given me.

As the Lord had told my father, I built the temple of the Lord. When the temple was finished, the Lord appeared to me. He warned that if I or my sons turned from Him to worship other gods, He would cut our people off from the land He promised them.

As wise as I was, I still struggled with sin like all others. I was a lover of women from foreign lands. My involvement with them led me to compromise my faith. Bit by bit, compromise turned to acceptance, and I also began to worship their gods. Without the favor of the Lord upon me, our adversaries arose, and we were faced with wars again.

†

God bestowed upon Solomon every great gift a person could desire. Yet, Solomon allowed himself to be tempted and followed other gods. Be careful how closely you align yourself with those who allow causes or convictions to become idols, replacing God in their affections and focus. Our purpose as God's people is to bring the good news of Jesus Christ to all, not to adopt the ways of the world.

1:23 [a] Is. 32:15; Joel 2:28; [John 7:39] 1:24 [a] Is. 65:12; 66:4; Jer. 7:13; Zech. 7:11 1:25 [a] Ps. 107:11; Luke 7:30 1:26 [a] Ps. 2:4
1:27 [a] [Prov. 10:24, 25] 1:28 [a] 1 Sam. 8:18; Job 27:9; 35:12; Ps. 18:41; Is. 1:15; Jer. 11:11; 14:12; Ezek. 8:18; Mic. 3:4; Zech. 7:13; [James 4:3]
1:29 [a] Job 21:14; Prov. 1:22 [b] Ps. 119:173 1:30 [a] Ps. 81:11; Prov. 1:25 1:31 [a] Job 4:8; Prov. 5:22, 23; 22:8; Is. 3:11; Jer. 6:19

33 But whoever listens to me
will dwell [a]safely,
And [b]will be secure, without
fear of evil."

The Value of Wisdom

2 My son, if you receive my words,
And [a]treasure my commands
within you,
2 So that you incline your ear to wisdom,
And apply your heart to
understanding;
3 Yes, if you cry out for discernment,
And lift up your voice for
understanding,
4 [a]If you seek her as silver,
And search for her as *for*
hidden treasures;
5 [a]Then you will understand
the fear of the LORD,
And find the knowledge of God.
6 [a]For the LORD gives wisdom;
From His mouth *come* knowledge
and understanding;
7 He stores up sound wisdom
for the upright;
[a]*He is* a shield to those who
walk uprightly;
8 He guards the paths of justice,
And [a]preserves the way of His saints.
9 Then you will understand
righteousness and justice,
Equity *and* every good path.

10 When wisdom enters your heart,
And knowledge is pleasant
to your soul,
11 Discretion will preserve you;
[a]Understanding will keep you,
12 To deliver you from the way of evil,
From the man who speaks
perverse things,
13 From those who leave the
paths of uprightness
To [a]walk in the ways of darkness;
14 [a]Who rejoice in doing evil,
And delight in the perversity
of the wicked;
15 [a]Whose ways *are* crooked,
And *who are* devious in their paths;
16 To deliver you from [a]the
immoral woman,
[b]From the seductress *who*
flatters with her words,
17 Who forsakes the companion
of her youth,
And forgets the covenant of her God.
18 For [a]her house leads down to death,
And her paths to the dead;
19 None who go to her return,
Nor do they regain the paths of life—
20 So you may walk in the
way of goodness,
And keep *to* the paths of
righteousness.
21 For the upright will dwell in the [a]land,
And the blameless will remain in it;
22 But the wicked will be cut
off from the earth,
And the unfaithful will be
uprooted from it.

Guidance for the Young

3 My son, do not forget my law,
[a]But let your heart keep
my commands;
2 For length of days and long life
And [a]peace they will add to you.

3 Let not mercy and truth forsake you;
[a]Bind them around your neck,
[b]Write them on the tablet of your
heart,
4 [a]*And* so find favor and high esteem
In the sight of God and man.

5 [a]Trust in the LORD with all your heart,
[b]And lean not on your own
understanding;
6 [a]In all your ways acknowledge Him,
And He shall direct[1] your paths.

7 Do not be wise in your own [a]eyes;
Fear the LORD and depart from evil.
8 It will be health to your flesh,[1]
And [a]strength[2] to your bones.

1:33 [a] Prov. 3:24–26 [b] Ps. 112:7 2:1 [a] [Prov. 4:21] 2:4 [a] [Prov. 3:14] 2:5 [a] [James 1:5, 6] 2:6 [a] 1 Kin. 3:9, 12; [Job 32:8; James 1:5] 2:7 [a] [Ps. 84:11]; Prov. 30:5 2:8 [a] [1 Sam. 2:9]; Ps. 66:9 2:11 [a] Prov. 4:6; 6:22 2:13 [a] Ps. 82:5; Prov. 4:19; [John 3:19, 20] 2:14 [a] Prov. 10:23; Jer. 11:15; [Rom. 1:32] 2:15 [a] Ps. 125:5; [Prov. 21:8] 2:16 [a] Prov. 5:20; 6:24; 7:5 [b] Prov. 5:3 2:18 [a] Prov. 7:27 2:21 [a] Ps. 37:3 3:1 [a] Deut. 8:1 3:2 [a] Ps. 119:165; Prov. 4:10 3:3 [a] Ex. 13:9; Deut. 6:8; Prov. 6:21 [b] Prov. 7:3; Jer. 17:1; [2 Cor. 3:3] 3:4 [a] 1 Sam. 2:26; Luke 2:52; Rom. 14:18 3:5 [a] [Ps. 37:3, 5]; Prov. 22:19 [b] Prov. 23:4; [Jer. 9:23, 24] 3:6 [a] [1 Chr. 28:9]; Prov. 16:3; [Phil. 4:6; James 1:5] [1] Or *make smooth* or *straight* 3:7 [a] Rom. 12:16 3:8 [a] Job 21:24 [1] Literally *navel*, figurative of the body [2] Literally *drink* or *refreshment*

ELEVATE HOW YOU SERVE OTHERS

INHALE

I know that the Bible tells me that I am supposed to serve others, but honestly, I am just way too busy to do that. Every minute of every hour of every day is taken up with one thing or the other. Just to be transparent, even if I had time to serve in some way, I'm barely able to take care of my own family. It is not like I was born with my forty acres and a mule. How can I serve others when I have no time and I need help myself?

EXHALE

Time is the most precious gift God gives us. We must remember that every minute of every hour of every day is given to us by God. We aren't owed a single second even. Instead, God wants us to be good stewards of our time and all the rest of our resources. The first step, then, is to evaluate how you are using your time. Your calendar is full, but is it full of things that you need to be doing? Are there some things in your life—even good things—that perhaps you should stop doing to free up time to do better things, like serving?

But even if your calendar is completely full of the best things and there is still no room for service, remember that God is a miracle-working God. He can make a way when we see no way. Your heart is right in wanting to serve. God will honor that. And as you seek to serve others, God can also move others to serve you and your family. Take those steps of faith God puts before you and then watch what He does.

So, now is as good of a time as any to take your eyes off yourself primarily and place them on God and others. JOY stands for Jesus, Others, and Yourself. God works the most in our lives when we look at life in that order. Proverbs 3:5–7 says, "Trust in the LORD with all your heart, and lean not on your own understanding; in all your ways acknowledge Him, and He shall direct your paths." Now *that* is elevating your service.

9 [a]Honor the LORD with
your possessions,
And with the firstfruits of
all your increase;
10 [a]So your barns will be filled with plenty,
And your vats will overflow
with new wine.

11 [a]My son, do not despise the
chastening of the LORD,
Nor detest His correction;
12 For whom the LORD loves He corrects,
[a]Just as a father the son *in*
whom he delights.

13 [a]Happy *is* the man *who* finds wisdom,
And the man *who* gains
understanding;
14 [a]For her proceeds *are* better
than the profits of silver,
And her gain than fine gold.
15 She *is* more precious than rubies,
And [a]all the things you may desire
cannot compare with her.
16 [a]Length of days *is* in her right hand,
In her left hand riches and honor.
17 [a]Her ways *are* ways of pleasantness,
And all her paths *are* peace.
18 She *is* [a]a tree of life to those
who take hold of her,
And happy *are all* who retain her.

19 [a]The LORD by wisdom
founded the earth;
By understanding He
established the heavens;

3:9 [a] Ex. 22:29; Deut. 26:2; [Mal. 3:10] 3:10 [a] Deut. 28:8 3:11 [a] Job 5:17; Ps. 94:12; Heb. 12:5, 6; Rev. 3:19 3:12 [a] Deut. 8:5; Prov. 13:24 3:13 [a] Prov. 8:32, 34, 35 3:14 [a] Job 28:13 3:15 [a] Matt. 13:44 3:16 [a] Prov. 8:18; [1 Tim. 4:8] 3:17 [a] [Matt. 11:29] 3:18 [a] Gen. 2:9; Prov. 11:30; 13:12; 15:4; Rev. 2:7 3:19 [a] Ps. 104:24; Prov. 8:27

20 By His knowledge the depths
were [a]broken up,
And clouds drop down the dew.

21 My son, let them not depart
from your eyes—
Keep sound wisdom and discretion;
22 So they will be life to your soul
And grace to your neck.
23 [a]Then you will walk safely in your way,
And your foot will not stumble.
24 When you lie down, you
will not be afraid;
Yes, you will lie down and your
sleep will be sweet.
25 [a]Do not be afraid of sudden terror,
Nor of trouble from the
wicked when it comes;
26 For the LORD will be your confidence,
And will keep your foot
from being caught.

27 [a]Do not withhold good from
those to whom it is due,
When it is in the power of
your hand to do *so*.
28 [a]Do not say to your neighbor,
"Go, and come back,
And tomorrow I will give *it*,"
When you have it with you.
29 Do not devise evil against
your neighbor,
For he dwells by you for safety's sake.
30 [a]Do not strive with a man
without cause,
If he has done you no harm.

31 [a]Do not envy the oppressor,
And choose none of his ways;
32 For the perverse *person is* an
abomination to the LORD,
[a]But His secret counsel *is*
with the upright.
33 [a]The curse of the LORD *is* on
the house of the wicked,
But [b]He blesses the home of the just.
34 [a]Surely He scorns the scornful,
But gives grace to the humble.
35 The wise shall inherit glory,
But shame shall be the legacy of fools.

Security in Wisdom

4 Hear, [a]*my* children, the instruction
of a father,
And give attention to know
understanding;
2 For I give you good doctrine:
Do not forsake my law.
3 When I was my father's son,
[a]Tender and the only one in
the sight of my mother,
4 [a]He also taught me, and said to me:
"Let your heart retain my words;
[b]Keep my commands, and live.
5 [a]Get wisdom! Get understanding!
Do not forget, nor turn away from
the words of my mouth.
6 Do not forsake her, and she
will preserve you;
[a]Love her, and she will keep you.
7 [a]Wisdom *is* the principal thing;
Therefore get wisdom.
And in all your getting, get
understanding.
8 [a]Exalt her, and she will promote you;
She will bring you honor,
when you embrace her.
9 She will place on your head
[a]an ornament of grace;
A crown of glory she will
deliver to you."

10 Hear, my son, and receive
my sayings,
[a]And the years of your life
will be many.
11 I have [a]taught you in the
way of wisdom;
I have led you in right paths.
12 When you walk, [a]your steps
will not be hindered,
[b]And when you run, you
will not stumble.
13 Take firm hold of instruction,
do not let go;
Keep her, for she *is* your life.

3:20 [a] Gen. 7:11 3:23 [a] [Ps. 37:24; 91:11, 12]; Prov. 10:9 3:25 [a] Ps. 91:5; 1 Pet. 3:14 3:27 [a] Rom. 13:7; [Gal. 6:10] 3:28 [a] Lev. 19:13; Deut. 24:15 3:30 [a] Prov. 26:17; [Rom. 12:18] 3:31 [a] Ps. 37:1; Prov. 24:1 3:32 [a] Ps. 25:14 3:33 [a] Lev. 26:14, 16; Deut. 11:28; Zech. 5:3, 4; Mal. 2:2 [b] Job 8:6; Ps. 1:3 3:34 [a] James 4:6; 1 Pet. 5:5 4:1 [a] Ps. 34:11; Prov. 1:8 4:3 [a] 1 Chr. 29:1 4:4 [a] 1 Chr. 28:9; Eph. 6:4 [b] Prov. 7:2 4:5 [a] Prov. 2:2, 3 4:6 [a] 2 Thess. 2:10 4:7 [a] Prov. 3:13, 14; Matt. 13:44 4:8 [a] 1 Sam. 2:30 4:9 [a] Prov. 3:22 4:10 [a] Prov. 3:2 4:11 [a] 1 Sam. 12:23 4:12 [a] Job 18:7; Ps. 18:36 [b] [Ps. 91:11]; Prov. 3:23

14 [a]Do not enter the path of the wicked,
And do not walk in the way of evil.
15 Avoid it, do not travel on it;
Turn away from it and pass on.
16 [a]For they do not sleep unless
they have done evil;
And their sleep is taken away
unless they make *someone* fall.
17 For they eat the bread of wickedness,
And drink the wine of violence.

18 [a]But the path of the just [b]*is*
like the shining sun,[1]
That shines ever brighter
unto the perfect day.
19 [a]The way of the wicked *is* like darkness;
They do not know what
makes them stumble.

20 My son, give attention to my words;
Incline your ear to my sayings.
21 Do not let them depart
from your eyes;
Keep them in the midst of your heart;
22 For they *are* life to those
who find them,
And health to all their flesh.
23 Keep your heart with all diligence,
For out of it *spring* the issues of [a]life.
24 Put away from you a deceitful mouth,
And put perverse lips far from you.
25 Let your eyes look straight ahead,
And your eyelids look
right before you.
26 Ponder the path of your [a]feet,
And let all your ways be established.
27 Do not turn to the right or the left;
Remove your foot from evil.

The Peril of Adultery

5 My son, pay attention to my wisdom;
Lend your ear to my understanding,
2 That you may preserve discretion,
And your lips [a]may keep knowledge.
3 [a]For the lips of an immoral
woman drip honey,
And her mouth *is* [b]smoother than oil;
4 But in the end she is bitter
as wormwood,
Sharp as a two-edged sword.
5 Her feet go down to death,
[a]Her steps lay hold of hell.[1]
6 Lest you ponder *her* path of life—
Her ways are unstable;
You do not know *them.*

7 Therefore hear me now, *my* children,
And do not depart from the
words of my mouth.
8 Remove your way far from her,
And do not go near the
door of her house,
9 Lest you give your honor to others,
And your years to the cruel *one;*
10 Lest aliens be filled with your wealth,
And your labors *go* to the
house of a foreigner;
11 And you mourn at last,
When your flesh and your
body are consumed,
12 And say:
"How I have hated instruction,
And my heart despised correction!
13 I have not obeyed the voice
of my teachers,
Nor inclined my ear to those
who instructed me!
14 I was on the verge of total ruin,
In the midst of the assembly
and congregation."

15 Drink water from your own cistern,
And running water from
your own well.
16 Should your fountains be
dispersed abroad,
Streams of water in the streets?
17 Let them be only your own,
And not for strangers with you.
18 Let your fountain be blessed,
And rejoice with [a]the wife
of your youth.
19 [a]*As a* loving deer and a graceful doe,
Let her breasts satisfy you at all times;
And always be enraptured
with her love.
20 For why should you, my son, be
enraptured by [a]an immoral woman,
And be embraced in the
arms of a seductress?

4:14 [a] Ps. 1:1; Prov. 1:15 4:16 [a] Ps. 36:4; Mic. 2:1 4:18 [a] Is. 26:7; Matt. 5:14, 45; Phil. 2:15 [b] 2 Sam. 23:4 [1] Literally *light*
4:19 [a] 1 Sam. 2:9; [Job 18:5, 6]; Prov. 2:13; [Is. 59:9, 10; Jer. 23:12]; John 12:35 4:23 [a] [Matt. 12:34; 15:18, 19; Mark 7:21; Luke 6:45]
4:26 [a] Prov. 5:21; Heb. 12:13 5:2 [a] Mal. 2:7 5:3 [a] Prov. 2:16 [b] Ps. 55:21 5:5 [a] Prov. 7:27 [1] Or *Sheol*
5:18 [a] Deut. 24:5; Eccl. 9:9; Mal. 2:14 5:19 [a] Song 2:9 5:20 [a] Prov. 2:16

21 [a]For the ways of man *are* before
the eyes of the LORD,
And He ponders all his paths.
22 [a]His own iniquities entrap
the wicked *man,*
And he is caught in the cords of his sin.
23 [a]He shall die for lack of instruction,
And in the greatness of his
folly he shall go astray.

Dangerous Promises

6 My son, [a]if you become surety
for your friend,
If you have shaken hands in
pledge for a stranger,
2 You are snared by the words
of your mouth;
You are taken by the words
of your mouth.
3 So do this, my son, and
deliver yourself;
For you have come into the
hand of your friend:
Go and humble yourself;
Plead with your friend.
4 [a]Give no sleep to your eyes,
Nor slumber to your eyelids.
5 Deliver yourself like a gazelle
from the hand *of the hunter,*
And like a bird from the
hand of the fowler.[1]

The Folly of Indolence

6 [a]Go to the ant, you sluggard!
Consider her ways and be wise,
7 Which, having no captain,
Overseer or ruler,
8 Provides her supplies in the summer,
And gathers her food in the harvest.
9 [a]How long will you slumber,
O sluggard?
When will you rise from your sleep?
10 A little sleep, a little slumber,
A little folding of the hands to sleep—
11 [a]So shall your poverty come
on you like a prowler,
And your need like an armed man.

The Wicked Man

12 A worthless person, a wicked man,
Walks with a perverse mouth;
13 [a]He winks with his eyes,
He shuffles his feet,
He points with his fingers;
14 Perversity *is* in his heart,
[a]He devises evil continually,
[b]He sows discord.
15 Therefore his calamity shall
come [a]suddenly;
Suddenly he shall [b]be broken
[c]without remedy.

16 These six *things* the LORD hates,
Yes, seven *are* an abomination to Him:
17 [a]A proud look,
[b]A lying tongue,
[c]Hands that shed innocent blood,
18 [a]A heart that devises wicked plans,
[b]Feet that are swift in running to evil,
19 [a]A false witness *who* speaks lies,
And one who [b]sows discord
among brethren.

Beware of Adultery

20 [a]My son, keep your father's
command,
And do not forsake the law
of your mother.
21 [a]Bind them continually
upon your heart;
Tie them around your neck.
22 [a]When you roam, they[1] will lead you;
When you sleep, [b]they will keep you;
And *when* you awake, they
will speak with you.
23 [a]For the commandment *is* a lamp,
And the law a light;
Reproofs of instruction
are the way of life,
24 [a]To keep you from the evil woman,
From the flattering tongue
of a seductress.
25 [a]Do not lust after her beauty
in your heart,
Nor let her allure you with her eyelids.

5:21 [a] 2 Chr. 16:9; Job 31:4; 34:21; Prov. 15:3; Jer. 16:17; 32:19; Hos. 7:2; Heb. 4:13 5:22 [a] Num. 32:23; Ps. 9:5; Prov. 1:31; Is. 3:11 5:23 [a] Job 4:21 6:1 [a] Prov. 11:15 6:4 [a] Ps. 132:4 6:5 [1] That is, one who catches birds in a trap or snare 6:6 [a] Job 12:7 6:9 [a] Prov. 24:33, 34 6:11 [a] Prov. 10:4 6:13 [a] Job 15:12; Ps. 35:19; Prov. 10:10 6:14 [a] Prov. 3:29; Mic. 2:1 [b] Prov. 6:19 6:15 [a] Prov. 24:22; Is. 30:13; 1 Thess. 5:3 [b] Jer. 19:11 [c] 2 Chr. 36:16 6:17 [a] Ps. 101:5; Prov. 21:4 [b] Ps. 120:2; Prov. 12:22 [c] Deut. 19:10; Prov. 28:17; Is. 1:15 6:18 [a] Gen. 6:5; Ps. 36:4; Prov. 24:2; Jer. 18:18; Mark 14:1, 43–46 [b] 2 Kin. 5:20–27; Is. 59:7; Rom. 3:15 6:19 [a] Ps. 27:12; Prov. 19:5, 9; Matt. 26:59–66 [b] Prov. 6:14; 1 Cor. 1:11–13; [Jude 3, 4, 16–19] 6:20 [a] Eph. 6:1 6:21 [a] Prov. 3:3 6:22 [a] [Prov. 3:23] [b] Prov. 2:11 [1] Literally *it* 6:23 [a] Ps. 19:8; 2 Pet. 1:19 6:24 [a] Prov. 2:16 6:25 [a] Matt. 5:28

26 For [a]by means of a harlot
A man is reduced to a crust of bread;
[b]And an adulteress[1] will [c]prey
upon his precious life.
27 Can a man take fire to his bosom,
And his clothes not be burned?
28 Can one walk on hot coals,
And his feet not be seared?
29 So *is* he who goes in to his
neighbor's wife;
Whoever touches her shall
not be innocent.

30 *People* do not despise a thief
If he steals to satisfy himself
when he is starving.
31 Yet *when* he is found, [a]he must
restore sevenfold;
He may have to give up all the
substance of his house.
32 Whoever commits adultery with a
woman [a]lacks understanding;
He *who* does so destroys his
own soul.
33 Wounds and dishonor he will get,
And his reproach will not
be wiped away.
34 For [a]jealousy *is* a husband's fury;
Therefore he will not spare in
the day of vengeance.
35 He will accept no recompense,
Nor will he be appeased though
you give many gifts.

7 My son, keep my words,
And [a]treasure my commands
within you.
2 [a]Keep my commands and live,
[b]And my law as the apple of your eye.
3 [a]Bind them on your fingers;
Write them on the tablet
of your heart.
4 Say to wisdom, "You *are* my sister,"
And call understanding
your nearest kin,
5 [a]That they may keep you from
the immoral woman,
From the seductress *who*
flatters with her words.

The Crafty Harlot

6 For at the window of my house
I looked through my lattice,
7 And saw among the simple,
I perceived among the youths,
A young man [a]devoid of
understanding,
8 Passing along the street
near her corner;
And he took the path to her house
9 [a]In the twilight, in the evening,
In the black and dark night.

10 And there a woman met him,
With the attire of a harlot,
and a crafty heart.
11 [a]She *was* loud and rebellious,
[b]Her feet would not stay at home.
12 At times *she was* outside, at
times in the open square,
Lurking at every corner.
13 So she caught him and kissed him;
With an impudent face she said to him:
14 "*I have* peace offerings with me;
Today I have paid my vows.
15 So I came out to meet you,
Diligently to seek your face,
And I have found you.
16 I have spread my bed with tapestry,
Colored coverings of [a]Egyptian linen.
17 I have perfumed my bed
With myrrh, aloes, and cinnamon.
18 Come, let us take our fill of
love until morning;
Let us delight ourselves with love.
19 For my husband *is* not at home;
He has gone on a long journey;
20 He has taken a bag of money with him,
And will come home on
the appointed day."

21 With [a]her enticing speech she
caused him to yield,
[b]With her flattering lips
she seduced him.
22 Immediately he went after her, as
an ox goes to the slaughter,
Or as a fool to the correction
of the stocks,[1]

6:26 [a] Prov. 29:3 [b] Gen. 39:14 [c] Ezek. 13:18 [1] Literally *a man's wife,* that is, of another 6:31 [a] Ex. 22:1–4 6:32 [a] Prov. 7:7 6:34 [a] Prov. 27:4; Song 8:6 7:1 [a] Prov. 2:1 7:2 [a] Lev. 18:5; Prov. 4:4; [Is. 55:3] [b] Deut. 32:10; Ps. 17:8; Zech. 2:8 7:3 [a] Deut. 6:8; Prov. 6:21 7:5 [a] Prov. 2:16; 5:3 7:7 [a] [Prov. 6:32; 9:4, 16] 7:9 [a] Job 24:15 7:11 [a] Prov. 9:13; 1 Tim. 5:13 [b] Titus 2:5 7:16 [a] Is. 19:9; Ezek. 27:7 7:21 [a] Prov. 5:3 [b] Ps. 12:2 7:22 [1] Septuagint, Syriac, and Targum read *as a dog to bonds;* Vulgate reads *as a lamb . . . to bonds.*

23 Till an arrow struck his liver.
[a]As a bird hastens to the snare,
He did not know it *would cost* his life.

24 Now therefore, listen to
me, *my* children;
Pay attention to the words
of my mouth:
25 Do not let your heart turn
aside to her ways,
Do not stray into her paths;
26 For she has cast down many wounded,
And [a]all who were slain by
her were strong *men.*
27 [a]Her house *is* the way to hell,[1]
Descending to the chambers
of death.

The Excellence of Wisdom

8 Does not [a]wisdom cry out,
And understanding lift up her voice?
2 She takes her stand on the
top of the high hill,
Beside the way, where the paths meet.
3 She cries out by the gates, at
the entry of the city,
At the entrance of the doors:
4 "To you, O men, I call,
And my voice *is* to the sons of men.
5 O you simple ones,
understand prudence,
And you fools, be of an
understanding heart.
6 Listen, for I will speak of
[a]excellent things,
And from the opening of my
lips *will come* right things;
7 For my mouth will speak truth;
Wickedness *is* an abomination
to my lips.
8 All the words of my mouth
are with righteousness;
Nothing crooked or
perverse *is* in them.
9 They *are* all plain to him
who understands,
And right to those who
find knowledge.
10 Receive my instruction, and not silver,
And knowledge rather
than choice gold;
11 [a]For wisdom *is* better than rubies,
And all the things one may desire
cannot be compared with her.

12 "I, wisdom, dwell with prudence,
And find out knowledge
and discretion.
13 [a]The fear of the LORD *is* to hate evil;
[b]Pride and arrogance and the evil way
And [c]the perverse mouth I hate.
14 Counsel *is* mine, and sound wisdom;
I *am* understanding, [a]I have
strength.
15 [a]By me kings reign,
And rulers decree justice.
16 By me princes rule, and nobles,
All the judges of the earth.[1]
17 [a]I love those who love me,
And [b]those who seek me
diligently will find me.
18 [a]Riches and honor *are* with me,
Enduring riches and
righteousness.
19 My fruit *is* better than gold,
yes, than fine gold,
And my revenue than choice silver.
20 I traverse the way of righteousness,
In the midst of the paths of justice,
21 That I may cause those who
love me to inherit wealth,
That I may fill their treasuries.

22 "The[a] LORD possessed me at the
beginning of His way,
Before His works of old.
23 [a]I have been established
from everlasting,
From the beginning, before
there was ever an earth.
24 When *there were* no depths
I was brought forth,
When *there were* no fountains
abounding with water.
25 [a]Before the mountains were settled,
Before the hills, I was brought forth;

7:23 [a] Eccl. 9:12 **7:26** [a] Neh. 13:26 **7:27** [a] Prov. 2:18; 5:5; 9:18; [1 Cor. 6:9, 10; Rev. 22:15] [1] Or *Sheol* **8:1** [a] Prov. 1:20, 21; 9:3; [1 Cor. 1:24] **8:6** [a] Prov. 22:20 **8:11** [a] Job 28:15; Ps. 19:10; 119:127; Prov. 3:14, 15; 4:5, 7; 16:16 **8:13** [a] Prov. 3:7; 16:6 [b] 1 Sam. 2:3; [Prov. 16:17, 18; Is. 13:11] [c] Prov. 4:24 **8:14** [a] Eccl. 7:19; 9:16 **8:15** [a] 2 Chr. 1:10; Prov. 29:4; Dan. 2:21; [Matt. 28:18]; Rom. 13:1 **8:16** [1] Masoretic Text, Syriac, Targum, and Vulgate read *righteousness;* Septuagint, Bomberg, and some manuscripts and editions read *earth.* **8:17** [a] 1 Sam. 2:30; [Ps. 91:14]; Prov. 4:6; [John 14:21] [b] Prov. 2:4, 5; John 7:37; James 1:5 **8:18** [a] Prov. 3:16; [Matt. 6:33] **8:22** [a] Job 28:26–28; Ps. 104:24; Prov. 3:19; [John 1:1] **8:23** [a] [Ps. 2:6] **8:25** [a] Job 15:7, 8

26 While as yet He had not made
the earth or the fields,
Or the primal dust of the world.
27 When He prepared the
heavens, I *was* there,
When He drew a circle on
the face of the deep,
28 When He established the
clouds above,
When He strengthened the
fountains of the deep,
29 [a]When He assigned to the sea its limit,
So that the waters would not
transgress His command,
When [b]He marked out the
foundations of the earth,
30 [a]Then I was beside Him *as* a
master craftsman;[1]
[b]And I was daily *His* delight,
Rejoicing always before Him,
31 Rejoicing in His inhabited world,
And [a]my delight *was* with
the sons of men.

32 "Now therefore, listen to
me, *my* children,
For [a]blessed *are those who*
keep my ways.
33 Hear instruction and be wise,
And do not disdain *it.*
34 [a]Blessed is the man who listens to me,
Watching daily at my gates,
Waiting at the posts of my doors.
35 For whoever finds me finds life,
And [a]obtains favor from the LORD;
36 But he who sins against me
[a]wrongs his own soul;
All those who hate me love death."

The Way of Wisdom

9 Wisdom has [a]built her house,
She has hewn out her seven pillars;
2 [a]She has slaughtered her meat,
[b]She has mixed her wine,
She has also furnished her table.
3 She has sent out her maidens,
She cries out from the highest
places of the city,
4 "Whoever[a] *is* simple, let
him turn in here!"
As for him who lacks understanding,
she says to him,
5 "Come,[a] eat of my bread
And drink of the wine I have mixed.
6 Forsake foolishness and live,
And go in the way of understanding.

7 "He who corrects a scoffer gets
shame for himself,
And he who rebukes a wicked
man only harms himself.
8 [a]Do not correct a scoffer,
lest he hate you;
[b]Rebuke a wise *man,* and
he will love you.
9 Give *instruction* to a wise *man,*
and he will be still wiser;
Teach a just *man,* [a]and he will
increase in learning.

10 "The[a] fear of the LORD *is* the
beginning of wisdom,
And the knowledge of the Holy
One *is* understanding.
11 [a]For by me your days will be multiplied,
And years of life will be added to you.
12 [a]If you are wise, you are
wise for yourself,
And *if* you scoff, you will bear *it* alone."

The Way of Folly

13 [a]A foolish woman is clamorous;
She is simple, and knows nothing.
14 For she sits at the door of her house,
On a seat [a]*by* the highest
places of the city,
15 To call to those who pass by,
Who go straight on their way:
16 "Whoever[a] *is* simple, let
him turn in here";
And *as for* him who lacks
understanding, she says to him,
17 "Stolen[a] water is sweet,
And bread *eaten* in secret is pleasant."
18 But he does not know that
[a]the dead *are* there,

8:29 [a] Gen. 1:9, 10; Job 38:8–11; Ps. 33:7; 104:9; Jer. 5:22 [b] Job 28:4, 6; Ps. 104:5 8:30 [a] [John 1:1–3, 18] [b] [Matt. 3:17] [1] A Jewish tradition reads *one brought up.* 8:31 [a] Ps. 16:3; John 13:1 8:32 [a] Ps. 119:1, 2; 128:1; Prov. 29:18; Luke 11:28 8:34 [a] Prov. 3:13, 18 8:35 [a] Prov. 3:4; 12:2; [John 17:3] 8:36 [a] Prov. 20:2 9:1 [a] [Matt. 16:18; 1 Cor. 3:9, 10; Eph. 2:20–22; 1 Pet. 2:5] 9:2 [a] Matt. 22:4 [b] Prov. 23:30 9:4 [a] Ps. 19:7 9:5 [a] Song 5:1; Is. 55:1; [John 6:27] 9:8 [a] Prov. 15:12; Matt. 7:6 [b] Ps. 141:5; Prov. 10:8 9:9 [a] [Matt. 13:12] 9:10 [a] Job 28:28; Ps. 111:10; Prov. 1:7 9:11 [a] Prov. 3:2, 16 9:12 [a] Job 35:6, 7; Prov. 16:26 9:13 [a] Prov. 7:11 9:14 [a] Prov. 9:3 9:16 [a] Prov. 7:7, 8 9:17 [a] Prov. 20:17 9:18 [a] Prov. 2:18; 7:27

That her guests *are* in the
depths of hell.[1]

Wise Sayings of Solomon

10 The proverbs of [a]Solomon:

[b]A wise son makes a glad father,
But a foolish son *is* the
grief of his mother.

2 [a]Treasures of wickedness
profit nothing,
[b]But righteousness delivers
from death.
3 [a]The LORD will not allow the
righteous soul to famish,
But He casts away the desire
of the wicked.

4 [a]He who has a slack hand
becomes poor,
But [b]the hand of the
diligent makes rich.
5 He who gathers in [a]summer
is a wise son;
He who sleeps in harvest *is* [b]a
son who causes shame.

6 Blessings *are* on the head
of the righteous,
But violence covers the
mouth of the wicked.
7 [a]The memory of the
righteous *is* blessed,
But the name of the wicked will rot.

8 The wise in heart will
receive commands,
[a]But a prating fool will fall.

9 [a]He who walks with integrity
walks securely,
But he who perverts his ways
will become known.

10 He who winks with the eye
causes trouble,
But a prating fool will fall.

11 The mouth of the righteous
is a well of life,
But violence covers the
mouth of the wicked.

12 Hatred stirs up strife,
But [a]love covers all sins.

13 Wisdom is found on the lips of
him who has understanding,
But [a]a rod *is* for the back of him who
is devoid of understanding.

14 Wise *people* store up knowledge,
But [a]the mouth of the foolish
is near destruction.

15 The [a]rich man's wealth *is*
his strong city;
The destruction of the poor
is their poverty.

16 The labor of the righteous
leads to [a]life,
The wages of the wicked to sin.

17 He who keeps instruction
is in the way of life,
But he who refuses correction
goes astray.

18 Whoever [a]hides hatred *has*
lying lips,
And [b]whoever spreads
slander *is* a fool.

19 [a]In the multitude of words
sin is not lacking,
But [b]he who restrains his lips *is* wise.
20 The tongue of the righteous
is choice silver;
The heart of the wicked *is worth* little.
21 The lips of the righteous feed many,
But fools die for lack of wisdom.[1]

22 [a]The blessing of the LORD
makes *one* rich,
And He adds no sorrow with it.

9:18 [1] Or *Sheol* **10:1** [a] Prov. 1:1; 25:1 [b] Prov. 15:20; 17:21, 25; 19:13; 29:3, 15 **10:2** [a] Ps. 49:7; Prov. 11:4; 21:6; Ezek. 7:19; [Luke 12:19, 20] [b] Dan. 4:27 **10:3** [a] Ps. 34:9, 10; 37:25; Prov. 28:25; [Matt. 6:33] **10:4** [a] Prov. 19:15 [b] Prov. 12:24; 13:4; 21:5 **10:5** [a] Prov. 6:8 [b] Prov. 19:26 **10:7** [a] Ps. 112:6; Eccl. 8:10 **10:8** [a] Prov. 10:10 **10:9** [a] [Ps. 23:4; Prov. 3:23; 28:18; Is. 33:15, 16] **10:12** [a] Prov. 17:9; [1 Cor. 13:4–7; James 5:20]; 1 Pet. 4:8 **10:13** [a] Prov. 26:3 **10:14** [a] Prov. 18:7 **10:15** [a] Job 31:24; Ps. 52:7; Prov. 18:11; [1 Tim. 6:17] **10:16** [a] Prov. 6:23 **10:18** [a] Prov. 26:24 [b] Ps. 15:3; 101:5 **10:19** [a] Job 11:2; [Prov. 18:21]; Eccl. 5:3 [b] Prov. 17:27; [James 1:19; 3:2] **10:21** [1] Literally *heart* **10:22** [a] Gen. 24:35; 26:12; Deut. 8:18; Ps. 37:22; Prov. 8:21

23 [a]To do evil *is* like sport to a fool,
But a man of understanding
has wisdom.
24 [a]The fear of the wicked will
come upon him,
And [b]the desire of the righteous
will be granted.
25 When the whirlwind passes by,
[a]the wicked *is* no *more,*
But [b]the righteous *has* an
everlasting foundation.

26 As vinegar to the teeth and
smoke to the eyes,
So *is* the lazy *man* to those
who send him.

27 [a]The fear of the LORD prolongs days,
But [b]the years of the wicked
will be shortened.
28 The hope of the righteous
will be gladness,
But the [a]expectation of the
wicked will perish.
29 The way of the LORD *is* strength
for the upright,
But [a]destruction *will come* to
the workers of iniquity.

30 [a]The righteous will never be
removed,
But the wicked will not
inhabit the earth.
31 [a]The mouth of the righteous
brings forth wisdom,
But the perverse tongue
will be cut out.
32 The lips of the righteous know
what is acceptable,
But the mouth of the wicked
what is perverse.

11

[a]Dishonest scales *are* an
abomination to the LORD,
But a just weight *is* His delight.

2 When pride comes, then
comes [a]shame;
But with the humble *is* wisdom.

3 The integrity of the upright
will guide [a]them,
But the perversity of the
unfaithful will destroy them.

4 [a]Riches do not profit in
the day of wrath,
But [b]righteousness delivers
from death.
5 The righteousness of the blameless
will direct[1] his way aright,
But the wicked will fall by
his own [a]wickedness.
6 The righteousness of the
upright will deliver them,
But the unfaithful will be
caught by *their* lust.

7 When a wicked man dies, *his*
expectation will [a]perish,
And the hope of the unjust perishes.
8 [a]The righteous is delivered
from trouble,
And it comes to the wicked instead.
9 The hypocrite with *his* mouth
destroys his neighbor,
But through knowledge the
righteous will be delivered.
10 [a]When it goes well with the
righteous, the city rejoices;
And when the wicked perish,
there is jubilation.
11 By the blessing of the upright
the city is [a]exalted,
But it is overthrown by the
mouth of the wicked.

12 He who is devoid of wisdom
despises his neighbor,
But a man of understanding
holds his peace.

13 [a]A talebearer reveals secrets,
But he who is of a faithful
spirit [b]conceals a matter.

14 [a]Where *there is* no counsel,
the people fall;
But in the multitude of
counselors *there is* safety.

10:23 [a] Prov. 2:14; 15:21 **10:24** [a] Job 15:21; Prov. 1:27; Is. 66:4 [b] Ps. 145:19; Prov. 15:8; Matt. 5:6; [1 John 5:14, 15] **10:25** [a] Ps. 37:9, 10 [b] Ps. 15:5; Prov. 12:3; Matt. 7:24, 25 **10:27** [a] Prov. 9:11 [b] Job 15:32 **10:28** [a] Job 8:13 **10:29** [a] Ps. 1:6 **10:30** [a] Ps. 37:22; Prov. 2:21 **10:31** [a] Ps. 37:30; Prov. 10:13 **11:1** [a] Lev. 19:35, 36; Deut. 25:13–16; Prov. 20:10, 23; Mic. 6:11 **11:2** [a] Prov. 16:18; 18:12; 29:23 **11:3** [a] Prov. 13:6 **11:4** [a] Prov. 10:2; Ezek. 7:19; Zeph. 1:18 [b] Gen. 7:1 **11:5** [a] Prov. 5:22 [1] Or *make smooth* or *straight* **11:7** [a] Prov. 10:28 **11:8** [a] Prov. 21:18 **11:10** [a] Prov. 28:12 **11:11** [a] Prov. 14:34 **11:13** [a] Lev. 19:16; Prov. 20:19; 1 Tim. 5:13 [b] Prov. 19:11 **11:14** [a] 1 Kin. 12:1

15 He who is [a]surety for a
stranger will suffer,
But one who hates being
surety is secure.

16 A gracious woman retains honor,
But ruthless *men* retain riches.
17 [a]The merciful man does good
for his own soul,
But *he who is* cruel troubles
his own flesh.
18 The wicked *man* does
deceptive work,
But [a]he who sows righteousness
will have a sure reward.
19 As righteousness *leads* to [a]life,
So he who pursues evil *pursues*
it to his own [b]death.
20 Those who are of a perverse heart
are an abomination to the LORD,
But *the* blameless in their
ways *are* His delight.
21 [a]*Though they join* forces,[1] the wicked
will not go unpunished;
But [b]the posterity of the
righteous will be delivered.

22 *As* a ring of gold in a swine's snout,
So is a lovely woman who
lacks discretion.

23 The desire of the righteous
is only good,
But the expectation of the
wicked [a]*is* wrath.

24 There is *one* who [a]scatters,
yet increases more;
And there is *one* who withholds
more than is right,
But it *leads* to poverty.
25 [a]The generous soul will be made rich,
[b]And he who waters will also
be watered himself.
26 The people will curse [a]him
who withholds grain,
But [b]blessing *will be* on the
head of him who sells *it*.

27 He who earnestly seeks
good finds favor,
[a]But trouble will come to
him who seeks *evil*.

28 [a]He who trusts in his riches will fall,
But [b]the righteous will
flourish like foliage.

29 He who troubles his own house
[a]will inherit the wind,
And the fool *will be* [b]servant
to the wise of heart.

30 The fruit of the righteous
is a tree of life,
And [a]he who wins souls *is* wise.

31 [a]If the righteous will be
recompensed on the earth,
How much more the ungodly
and the sinner.

12 Whoever loves instruction
loves knowledge,
But he who hates correction *is* stupid.

2 A good *man* obtains favor
from the LORD,
But a man of wicked intentions
He will condemn.

3 A man is not established
by wickedness,
But the [a]root of the righteous
cannot be moved.

4 [a]An excellent[1] wife *is* the
crown of her husband,
But she who causes shame *is* [b]like
rottenness in his bones.

5 The thoughts of the
righteous *are* right,
But the counsels of the
wicked *are* deceitful.
6 [a]The words of the wicked *are*,
"Lie in wait for blood,"

11:15 [a] Prov. 6:1, 2 11:17 [a] [Matt. 5:7; 25:34–36] 11:18 [a] Hos. 10:12; [Gal. 6:8, 9]; James 3:18 11:19 [a] Prov. 10:16; 12:28 [b] Prov. 21:16; [Rom. 6:23; James 1:15] 11:21 [a] Prov. 16:5 [b] Ps. 112:2; Prov. 14:26 [1] Literally *hand to hand* 11:23 [a] Prov. 10:28; Rom. 2:8, 9 11:24 [a] Ps. 112:9; Prov. 13:7; 19:17 11:25 [a] Prov. 3:9, 10; [2 Cor. 9:6, 7] [b] [Matt. 5:7] 11:26 [a] Amos 8:5, 6 [b] Job 29:13 11:27 [a] Esth. 7:10; Ps. 7:15, 16; 57:6 11:28 [a] Job 31:24 [b] Ps. 1:3; Jer. 17:8 11:29 [a] Eccl. 5:16 [b] Prov. 14:19 11:30 [a] Prov. 14:25; [Dan. 12:3; 1 Cor. 9:19–22; James 5:20] 11:31 [a] Jer. 25:29 12:3 [a] [Prov. 10:25] 12:4 [a] Prov. 31:23; 1 Cor. 11:7 [b] Prov. 14:30; Hab. 3:16 [1] Literally *A wife of valor* 12:6 [a] Prov. 1:11, 18

[b]But the mouth of the upright
will deliver them.

7 [a]The wicked are overthrown
and *are* no more,
But the house of the
righteous will stand.

8 A man will be commended
according to his wisdom,
[a]But he who is of a perverse
heart will be despised.

9 [a]Better *is the one* who is slighted
but has a servant,
Than he who honors himself
but lacks bread.

10 [a]A righteous *man* regards the
life of his animal,
But the tender mercies of
the wicked *are* cruel.

11 [a]He who tills his land will be
satisfied with [b]bread,
But he who follows frivolity [c]*is*
devoid of understanding.[1]

12 The wicked covet the catch of evil *men,*
But the root of the righteous
yields *fruit.*
13 [a]The wicked is ensnared by the
transgression of *his* lips,
[b]But the righteous will come
through trouble.
14 [a]A man will be satisfied with good
by the fruit of *his* mouth,
[b]And the recompense of a man's
hands will be rendered to him.

15 [a]The way of a fool *is* right
in his own eyes,
But he who heeds counsel *is* wise.
16 [a]A fool's wrath is known at once,
But a prudent *man* covers shame.

17 [a]He *who* speaks truth declares
righteousness,
But a false witness, deceit.

18 [a]There is one who speaks like
the piercings of a sword,
But the tongue of the wise
promotes health.
19 The truthful lip shall be
established forever,
[a]But a lying tongue *is* but for a moment.
20 Deceit is in the heart of those
who devise evil,
But counselors of peace have joy.
21 [a]No grave trouble will overtake
the righteous,
But the wicked shall be filled with evil.
22 [a]Lying lips *are* an abomination
to the LORD,
But those who deal truthfully
are His delight.

23 [a]A prudent man conceals knowledge,
But the heart of fools
proclaims foolishness.

24 [a]The hand of the diligent will rule,
But the lazy *man* will be
put to forced labor.

25 [a]Anxiety in the heart of man
causes depression,
But [b]a good word makes it glad.

26 The righteous should choose
his friends carefully,
For the way of the wicked
leads them astray.

27 The lazy *man* does not roast
what he took in hunting,
But diligence *is* man's
precious possession.

28 In the way of righteousness *is* life,
And in *its* pathway *there is* no death.

13 A wise son *heeds* his father's
instruction,
[a]But a scoffer does not listen to rebuke.

2 [a]A man shall eat well by the
fruit of *his* mouth,

12:6 [b] Prov. 14:3 12:7 [a] Ps. 37:35–37; Prov. 11:21; Matt. 7:24–27 12:8 [a] 1 Sam. 25:17; Prov. 18:3 12:9 [a] Prov. 13:7 12:10 [a] Deut. 25:4 12:11 [a] Gen. 3:19 [b] Prov. 28:19 [c] Prov. 6:32 [1] Literally *heart* 12:13 [a] Prov. 18:7 [b] [2 Pet. 2:9] 12:14 [a] Prov. 13:2; 15:23; 18:20 [b] Job 34:11; Prov. 1:31; 24:12; [Is. 3:10, 11]; Hos. 4:9 12:15 [a] Prov. 3:7; Luke 18:11 12:16 [a] Prov. 11:13; 29:11 12:17 [a] Prov. 14:5 12:18 [a] Ps. 57:4; Prov. 4:22; 15:4 12:19 [a] [Ps. 52:4, 5]; Prov. 19:9 12:21 [a] Ps. 91:10; Prov. 1:33; 1 Pet. 3:13 12:22 [a] Prov. 6:17; 11:20; Rev. 22:15 12:23 [a] Prov. 13:16 12:24 [a] Prov. 10:4 12:25 [a] Prov. 15:13 [b] Is. 50:4 13:1 [a] Is. 28:14, 15 13:2 [a] Prov. 12:14

But the soul of the unfaithful
feeds on violence.
3 [a]He who guards his mouth
preserves his life,
But he who opens wide his lips
shall have destruction.

4 [a]The soul of a lazy *man* desires,
and *has* nothing;
But the soul of the diligent
shall be made rich.

5 A righteous *man* hates lying,
But a wicked *man* is loathsome
and comes to shame.
6 [a]Righteousness guards *him*
whose way is blameless,
But wickedness overthrows the sinner.

7 [a]There is one who makes himself
rich, yet *has* nothing;
And one who makes himself
poor, yet *has* great riches.

8 The ransom of a man's
life *is* his riches,
But the poor does not hear rebuke.

9 The light of the righteous rejoices,
[a]But the lamp of the wicked
will be put out.

10 By pride comes nothing but [a]strife,
But with the well-advised *is* wisdom.

11 [a]Wealth *gained by* dishonesty
will be diminished,
But he who gathers by
labor will increase.

12 Hope deferred makes the heart sick,
But [a]*when* the desire comes,
it is a tree of life.

13 He who [a]despises the word
will be destroyed,
But he who fears the commandment
will be rewarded.
14 [a]The law of the wise *is* a fountain of life,
To turn *one* away from [b]the
snares of death.

15 Good understanding gains [a]favor,
But the way of the unfaithful *is* hard.
16 [a]Every prudent *man* acts
with knowledge,
But a fool lays open *his* folly.

17 A wicked messenger falls into trouble,
But [a]a faithful ambassador
brings health.

18 Poverty and shame *will come* to
him who disdains correction,
But [a]he who regards a rebuke
will be honored.

19 A desire accomplished is
sweet to the soul,
But *it is* an abomination to
fools to depart from evil.

20 He who walks with wise
men will be wise,
But the companion of fools
will be destroyed.

21 [a]Evil pursues sinners,
But to the righteous, good
shall be repaid.

22 A good *man* leaves an inheritance
to his children's children,
But [a]the wealth of the sinner is
stored up for the righteous.

23 [a]Much food *is in* the fallow
ground of the poor,
And for lack of justice there is waste.[1]

24 [a]He who spares his rod hates his son,
But he who loves him disciplines
him promptly.

25 [a]The righteous eats to the
satisfying of his soul,
But the stomach of the wicked
shall be in want.

13:3 [a] Ps. 39:1; Prov. 21:23; [James 3:2] 13:4 [a] Prov. 10:4 13:6 [a] Prov. 11:3, 5, 6 13:7 [a] [Prov. 11:24; 12:9; Luke 12:20, 21] 13:9 [a] Job 18:5, 6; 21:17; Prov. 24:20 13:10 [a] Prov. 10:12 13:11 [a] Prov. 10:2; 20:21 13:12 [a] Prov. 13:19 13:13 [a] Num. 15:31; 2 Chr. 36:16; Is. 5:24 13:14 [a] Prov. 6:22; 10:11; 14:27 [b] 2 Sam. 22:6 13:15 [a] Ps. 111:10; Prov. 3:4 13:16 [a] Prov. 12:23 13:17 [a] Prov. 25:13 13:18 [a] Prov. 15:5, 31, 32 13:21 [a] Ps. 32:10; Is. 47:11 13:22 [a] Job 27:16, 17; Prov. 28:8; [Eccl. 2:26] 13:23 [a] Prov. 12:11 [1] Literally *what is swept away* 13:24 [a] Prov. 19:18 13:25 [a] Ps. 34:10; Prov. 10:3

14 The wise woman builds her house,
But the foolish pulls it down
with her hands.

2 He who walks in his uprightness
fears the LORD,
[a]But *he who is* perverse in his
ways despises Him.

3 In the mouth of a fool *is* a rod of pride,
[a]But the lips of the wise will
preserve them.

4 Where no oxen *are,* the
trough *is* clean;
But much increase *comes* by
the strength of an ox.

5 A [a]faithful witness does not lie,
But a false witness will utter [b]lies.

6 A scoffer seeks wisdom and
does not *find it,*
But [a]knowledge *is* easy to him
who understands.
7 Go from the presence of a foolish man,
When you do not perceive *in*
him the lips of [a]knowledge.
8 The wisdom of the prudent *is*
to understand his way,
But the folly of fools *is* deceit.

9 [a]Fools mock at sin,
But among the upright *there is* favor.

10 The heart knows its own bitterness,
And a stranger does not share its joy.

11 [a]The house of the wicked
will be overthrown,
But the tent of the upright
will flourish.

12 [a]There is a way *that seems*
right to a man,
But [b]its end *is* the way of [c]death.

13 Even in laughter the heart may sorrow,
And [a]the end of mirth *may be* grief.

14 The backslider in heart will be
[a]filled with his own ways,
But a good man *will be*
satisfied from [b]above.[1]

15 The simple believes every word,
But the prudent considers
well his steps.
16 [a]A wise *man* fears and
departs from evil,
But a fool rages and is self-confident.
17 A quick-tempered *man* acts foolishly,
And a man of wicked
intentions is hated.
18 The simple inherit folly,
But the prudent are crowned
with knowledge.
19 The evil will bow before the good,
And the wicked at the gates
of the righteous.

20 [a]The poor *man* is hated even
by his own neighbor,
But the rich *has* many [b]friends.
21 He who despises his neighbor sins;
[a]But he who has mercy on
the poor, happy *is* he.

22 Do they not go astray who devise evil?
But mercy and truth *belong* to
those who devise good.

23 In all labor there is profit,
But idle chatter[1] *leads* only to poverty.

24 The crown of the wise is their riches,
But the foolishness of fools *is* folly.

25 A true witness delivers [a]souls,
But a deceitful *witness* speaks lies.

26 In the fear of the LORD *there*
is strong confidence,
And His children will have
a place of refuge.
27 [a]The fear of the LORD *is* a
fountain of life,
To turn *one* away from the
snares of death.

14:2 [a] [Rom. 2:4] 14:3 [a] Prov. 12:6 14:5 [a] Rev. 1:5; 3:14 [b] Ex. 23:1; Deut. 19:16; Prov. 6:19; 12:17 14:6 [a] Prov. 8:9; 17:24
14:7 [a] Prov. 23:9 14:9 [a] Prov. 10:23 14:11 [a] Job 8:15 14:12 [a] Prov. 16:25 [b] Rom. 6:21 [c] Prov. 12:15 14:13 [a] Prov. 5:4; Eccl. 2:1, 2
14:14 [a] Prov. 1:31; 12:15 [b] Prov. 13:2; 18:20 [1] Literally *from above himself* 14:16 [a] Job 28:28; Ps. 34:14; Prov. 22:3
14:20 [a] Prov. 19:7 [b] Prov. 19:4 14:21 [a] Ps. 112:9; [Prov. 19:17] 14:23 [1] Literally *talk of the lips*
14:25 [a] [Ezek. 3:18–21] 14:27 [a] Prov. 13:14

28 In a multitude of people
is a king's honor,
But in the lack of people *is* the
downfall of a prince.

29 [a]*He who is* slow to wrath has
great understanding,
But *he who is* impulsive[1]
exalts folly.

30 A sound heart *is* life to the body,
But [a]envy *is* [b]rottenness
to the bones.

31 [a]He who oppresses the poor
reproaches [b]his Maker,
But he who honors Him has
mercy on the needy.

32 The wicked is banished in
his wickedness,
But [a]the righteous has a
refuge in his death.

33 Wisdom rests in the heart of him
who has understanding,
But [a]*what is* in the heart of
fools is made known.

34 Righteousness exalts a [a]nation,
But sin *is* a reproach to *any* people.

35 [a]The king's favor *is* toward
a wise servant,
But his wrath *is against* him
who causes shame.

15 A [a]soft answer turns away wrath,
But [b]a harsh word stirs up anger.

2 The tongue of the wise uses
knowledge rightly,
[a]But the mouth of fools pours
forth foolishness.

3 [a]The eyes of the LORD *are*
in every place,
Keeping watch on the evil
and the good.

4 A wholesome tongue *is* a tree of life,
But perverseness in it
breaks the spirit.

5 [a]A fool despises his father's instruction,
[b]But he who receives
correction is prudent.

6 *In* the house of the righteous
there is much treasure,
But in the revenue of the
wicked is trouble.

7 The lips of the wise disperse
knowledge,
But the heart of the fool *does* not *do* so.

8 [a]The sacrifice of the wicked *is* an
abomination to the LORD,
But the prayer of the upright
is His delight.

9 The way of the wicked *is* an
abomination to the LORD,
But He loves him who [a]follows
righteousness.

10 [a]Harsh discipline *is* for him
who forsakes the way,
And [b]he who hates correction will die.

11 [a]Hell[1] and Destruction[2] *are*
before the LORD;
So how much more [b]the hearts
of the sons of men.

12 [a]A scoffer does not love one
who corrects him,
Nor will he go to the wise.

13 [a]A merry heart makes a
cheerful countenance,
But [b]by sorrow of the heart
the spirit is broken.

14 The heart of him who has
understanding seeks knowledge,
But the mouth of fools feeds
on foolishness.

14:29 [a] Prov. 16:32; 19:11; Eccl. 7:9; James 1:19 [1] Literally *short of spirit* 14:30 [a] Ps. 112:10 [b] Prov. 12:4; Hab. 3:16 14:31 [a] Prov. 17:5; Matt. 25:40; 1 John 3:17 [b] [Job 31:15; Prov. 22:2] 14:32 [a] Gen. 49:18; Job 13:15; [Ps. 16:11; 73:24]; 2 Cor. 1:9; 5:8; [2 Tim. 4:18] 14:33 [a] Prov. 12:16 14:34 [a] Prov. 11:11 14:35 [a] Matt. 24:45–47 15:1 [a] Prov. 25:15 [b] 1 Sam. 25:10 15:2 [a] Prov. 12:23 15:3 [a] 2 Chr. 16:9; Job 34:21; Prov. 5:21; Jer. 16:17; 32:19; Zech. 4:10; Heb. 4:13 15:5 [a] Prov. 10:1 [b] Prov. 13:18 15:8 [a] Prov. 21:27; Eccl. 5:1; Is. 1:11; Jer. 6:20; Mic. 6:7 15:9 [a] Prov. 21:21 15:10 [a] 1 Kin. 22:8 [b] Prov. 5:12 15:11 [a] Job 26:6; Ps. 139:8 [b] 1 Sam. 16:7; 2 Chr. 6:30; Ps. 44:21; Acts 1:24 [1] Or *Sheol* [2] Hebrew *Abaddon* 15:12 [a] Prov. 13:1; Amos 5:10; 2 Tim. 4:3 15:13 [a] Prov. 12:25 [b] Prov. 17:22

15 All the days of the afflicted *are* evil,
[a]But he who is of a merry heart
has a continual feast.

16 [a]Better *is* a little with the
fear of the LORD,
Than great treasure with trouble.
17 [a]Better *is* a dinner of herbs[1] where love is,
Than a fatted calf with hatred.

18 [a]A wrathful man stirs up strife,
But *he who is* slow to anger
allays contention.

19 [a]The way of the lazy *man is*
like a hedge of thorns,
But the way of the upright *is* a highway.

20 [a]A wise son makes a father glad,
But a foolish man despises his mother.

21 [a]Folly *is* joy *to him who is*
destitute of discernment,
[b]But a man of understanding
walks uprightly.

22 [a]Without counsel, plans go awry,
But in the multitude of counselors
they are established.

23 A man has joy by the answer
of his mouth,
And [a]a word *spoken* in due
season, how good *it is!*

24 [a]The way of life *winds*
upward for the wise,
That he may [b]turn away
from hell[1] below.

25 [a]The LORD will destroy the
house of the proud,
But [b]He will establish the
boundary of the widow.

26 [a]The thoughts of the wicked *are* an
abomination to the LORD,
[b]But the words of the pure *are* pleasant.

27 [a]He who is greedy for gain
troubles his own house,
But he who hates bribes will live.

28 The heart of the righteous
[a]studies how to answer,
But the mouth of the wicked
pours forth evil.

29 [a]The LORD *is* far from the wicked,
But [b]He hears the prayer
of the righteous.

30 The light of the eyes rejoices
the heart,
And a good report makes
the bones healthy.[1]

31 The ear that hears the rebukes of life
Will abide among the wise.
32 He who disdains instruction
despises his own soul,
But he who heeds rebuke
gets understanding.
33 [a]The fear of the LORD *is* the
instruction of wisdom,
And [b]before honor *is* humility.

16

The [a]preparations of the heart
belong to man,
[b]But the answer of the tongue
is from the LORD.

2 All the ways of a man *are*
pure in his own [a]eyes,
But the LORD weighs the spirits.

3 [a]Commit your works to the LORD,
And your thoughts will be established.

4 The [a]LORD has made all for Himself,
[b]Yes, even the wicked for
the day of doom.

5 [a]Everyone proud in heart *is* an
abomination to the LORD;
Though they join forces,[1] none
will go unpunished.

15:15 [a] Prov. 17:22 15:16 [a] Ps. 37:16; Prov. 16:8; Eccl. 4:6; 1 Tim. 6:6 15:17 [a] Prov. 17:1 [1] Or *vegetables* 15:18 [a] Prov. 26:21 15:19 [a] Prov. 22:5 15:20 [a] Prov. 10:1 15:21 [a] Prov. 10:23 [b] Eph. 5:15 15:22 [a] Prov. 11:14 15:23 [a] Prov. 25:11; Is. 50:4 15:24 [a] Phil. 3:20; [Col. 3:1, 2] [b] Prov. 14:16 [1] Or *Sheol* 15:25 [a] Prov. 12:7; Is. 2:11 [b] Ps. 68:5, 6 15:26 [a] Prov. 6:16, 18 [b] Ps. 37:30 15:27 [a] Is. 5:8; [Jer. 17:11] 15:28 [a] 1 Pet. 3:15 15:29 [a] Ps. 10:1; 34:16 [b] Ps. 145:18; [James 5:16] 15:30 [1] Literally *fat* 15:33 [a] Prov. 1:7 [b] Prov. 18:12 16:1 [a] Jer. 10:23 [b] Matt. 10:19 16:2 [a] Prov. 21:2 16:3 [a] Ps. 37:5; Prov. 3:6; [1 Pet. 5:7] 16:4 [a] Is. 43:7; Rom. 11:36 [b] Job 21:30; [Rom. 9:22] 16:5 [a] Prov. 6:17; 8:13 [1] Literally *hand to hand*

6 [a]In mercy and truth
Atonement is provided for iniquity;
And [b]by the fear of the LORD
one departs from evil.

7 When a man's ways please the LORD,
He makes even his enemies
to be at peace with him.

8 [a]Better *is* a little with righteousness,
Than vast revenues without justice.

9 [a]A man's heart plans his way,
[b]But the LORD directs his steps.

10 Divination *is* on the lips of the king;
His mouth must not transgress
in judgment.
11 [a]Honest weights and scales
are the LORD's;
All the weights in the bag
are His work.
12 *It is* an abomination for kings
to commit wickedness,
For [a]a throne is established
by righteousness.
13 [a]Righteous lips *are* the delight of kings,
And they love him who
speaks *what is* right.
14 As messengers of death *is*
the king's wrath,
But a wise man will [a]appease it.
15 In the light of the king's face *is* life,
And his favor *is* like a [a]cloud
of the latter rain.

16 [a]How much better to get
wisdom than gold!
And to get understanding is to be
chosen rather than silver.

17 The highway of the upright
is to depart from evil;
He who keeps his way
preserves his soul.

18 Pride *goes* before destruction,
And a haughty spirit before a fall.
19 Better *to be* of a humble
spirit with the lowly,
Than to divide the spoil
with the proud.

20 He who heeds the word
wisely will find good,
And whoever [a]trusts in the
LORD, happy *is* he.

21 The wise in heart will be
called prudent,
And sweetness of the lips
increases learning.

22 Understanding *is* a wellspring
of life to him who has it.
But the correction of fools *is* folly.

23 The heart of the wise
teaches his mouth,
And adds learning to his lips.

24 Pleasant words *are like* a honeycomb,
Sweetness to the soul and
health to the bones.

25 There is a way *that seems*
right to a man,
But its end *is* the way of [a]death.

26 The person who labors,
labors for himself,
For his *hungry* mouth drives [a]him *on.*

27 An ungodly man digs up evil,
And *it is* on his lips like a burning [a]fire.
28 A perverse man sows strife,
And [a]a whisperer separates
the best of friends.
29 A violent man entices his neighbor,
And leads him in a way
that is not good.
30 He winks his eye to devise
perverse things;
He purses his lips *and*
brings about evil.

31 [a]The silver-haired head *is*
a crown of glory,
If it is found in the way of
righteousness.

16:6 [a] Dan. 4:27; Luke 11:41 [b] Prov. 8:13; 14:16 16:8 [a] Ps. 37:16; Prov. 15:16 16:9 [a] Prov. 19:21 [b] Ps. 37:23; Prov. 20:24; Jer. 10:23 16:11 [a] Lev. 19:36 16:12 [a] Prov. 25:5 16:13 [a] Prov. 14:35 16:14 [a] Prov. 25:15 16:15 [a] Zech. 10:1 16:16 [a] Prov. 8:10, 11, 19 16:20 [a] Ps. 34:8; Jer. 17:7 16:25 [a] Prov. 14:12 16:26 [a] [Eccl. 6:7; John 6:35] 16:27 [a] [James 3:6] 16:28 [a] Prov. 17:9 16:31 [a] Prov. 20:29

32 [a]*He who is* slow to anger *is*
better than the mighty,
And he who rules his spirit
than he who takes a city.

33 The lot is cast into the lap,
But its every decision *is*
from the LORD.

17

1 Better *is* [a]a dry morsel
with quietness,
Than a house full of
feasting[1] *with* strife.

2 A wise servant will rule over [a]a
son who causes shame,
And will share an inheritance
among the brothers.

3 The refining pot *is* for silver
and the furnace for gold,
[a]But the LORD tests the hearts.

4 An evildoer gives heed to false lips;
A liar listens eagerly to a
spiteful tongue.

5 [a]He who mocks the poor
reproaches his Maker;
[b]He who is glad at calamity will
not go unpunished.

6 [a]Children's children *are* the
crown of old men,
And the glory of children
is their father.

7 Excellent speech is not
becoming to a fool,
Much less lying lips to a prince.

8 A present *is* a precious stone in
the eyes of its possessor;
Wherever he turns, he prospers.

9 [a]He who covers a transgression
seeks love,
But [b]he who repeats a matter
separates friends.

10 [a]Rebuke is more effective
for a wise *man*
Than a hundred blows on a fool.

11 An evil *man* seeks only rebellion;
Therefore a cruel messenger
will be sent against him.

12 Let a man meet [a]a bear
robbed of her cubs,
Rather than a fool in his folly.

13 Whoever [a]rewards evil for good,
Evil will not depart from his house.

14 The beginning of strife *is*
like releasing water;
Therefore [a]stop contention
before a quarrel starts.

15 [a]He who justifies the wicked, and
he who condemns the just,
Both of them alike *are* an
abomination to the LORD.

16 Why *is there* in the hand of a fool
the purchase price of wisdom,
Since *he has* no heart *for it?*

17 [a]A friend loves at all times,
And a brother is born for adversity.

18 [a]A man devoid of understanding
shakes hands in a pledge,
And becomes surety for his friend.

19 He who loves transgression
loves strife,
And [a]he who exalts his gate
seeks destruction.

20 He who has a deceitful
heart finds no good,
And he who has [a]a perverse
tongue falls into evil.

21 He who begets a scoffer *does*
so to his sorrow,
And the father of a fool has no joy.

16:32 [a] Prov. 14:29; 19:11 17:1 [a] Prov. 15:17 [1] Or *sacrificial meals* 17:2 [a] Prov. 10:5 17:3 [a] 1 Chr. 29:17; Ps. 26:2; Prov. 15:11; Jer. 17:10; [Mal. 3:3] 17:5 [a] Prov. 14:31 [b] Job 31:29; Prov. 24:17; Obad. 12; 1 Cor. 13:6 17:6 [a] [Ps. 127:3; 128:3] 17:9 [a] [Prov. 10:12; 1 Cor. 13:5–7; James 5:20] [b] Prov. 16:28 17:10 [a] Prov. 10:17; [Mic. 7:9] 17:12 [a] 2 Sam. 17:8; Hos. 13:8 17:13 [a] Ps. 109:4, 5; Jer. 18:20; Rom. 12:17; 1 Thess. 5:15; [1 Pet. 3:9] 17:14 [a] [Prov. 20:3; 1 Thess. 4:11] 17:15 [a] Ex. 23:7; Prov. 24:24; Is. 5:23 17:17 [a] Ruth 1:16; Prov. 18:24 17:18 [a] Prov. 6:1 17:19 [a] Prov. 16:18 17:20 [a] James 3:8

22 A [a]merry heart does good,
like medicine,[1]
But a broken spirit dries the bones.

23 A wicked *man* accepts a bribe
behind the back[1]
To pervert the ways of justice.

24 [a]Wisdom *is* in the sight of him
who has understanding,
But the eyes of a fool *are* on
the ends of the earth.

25 A [a]foolish son *is* a grief to his father,
And bitterness to her who bore him.

26 Also, to punish the righteous
is not good,
Nor to strike princes for
their uprightness.

27 [a]He who has knowledge
spares his words,
And a man of understanding
is of a calm spirit.
28 [a]Even a fool is counted wise
when he holds his peace;
When he shuts his lips, *he is*
considered perceptive.

18

A man who isolates himself
seeks his own desire;
He rages against all wise judgment.

2 A fool has no delight in
understanding,
But in expressing his [a]own heart.

3 When the wicked comes,
contempt comes also;
And with dishonor *comes* reproach.

4 [a]The words of a man's mouth
are deep waters;
[b]The wellspring of wisdom
is a flowing brook.

5 *It is* not good to show partiality
to the wicked,
Or to overthrow the righteous
in [a]judgment.

6 A fool's lips enter into contention,
And his mouth calls for blows.
7 [a]A fool's mouth *is* his destruction,
And his lips *are* the snare
of his [b]soul.
8 [a]The words of a talebearer
are like tasty trifles,[1]
And they go down into
the inmost body.

9 He who is slothful in his work
Is a brother to him who is
a great destroyer.

10 The name of the LORD *is*
a strong [a]tower;
The righteous run to it and are safe.
11 The rich man's wealth *is*
his strong city,
And like a high wall in
his own esteem.

12 [a]Before destruction the heart
of a man is haughty,
And before honor *is* humility.

13 He who answers a matter
before he hears *it,*
It *is* folly and shame to him.

14 The spirit of a man will sustain
him in sickness,
But who can bear a broken spirit?

15 The heart of the prudent
acquires knowledge,
And the ear of the wise
seeks knowledge.

16 [a]A man's gift makes room for him,
And brings him before great men.

17 The first *one* to plead his
cause *seems* right,
Until his neighbor comes
and examines him.

17:22 [a] Prov. 12:25; 15:13, 15 [1] Or *makes medicine even better* 17:23 [1] Literally *from the bosom* 17:24 [a] Eccl. 2:14 17:25 [a] Prov. 10:1; 15:20; 19:13 17:27 [a] Prov. 10:19; James 1:19 17:28 [a] Job 13:5 18:2 [a] Eccl. 10:3 18:4 [a] Prov. 10:11 [b] [James 3:17] 18:5 [a] Lev. 19:15; Deut. 1:17; 16:19; Ps. 82:2; Prov. 17:15 18:7 [a] Ps. 64:8; 140:9; Prov. 10:14 [b] Eccl. 10:12 18:8 [a] Prov. 12:18 [1] A Jewish tradition reads *wounds.* 18:10 [a] 2 Sam. 22:2, 3, 33; Ps. 18:2; 61:3; 91:2; 144:2 18:12 [a] Prov. 15:33; 16:18 18:16 [a] Gen. 32:20, 21; 1 Sam. 25:27; Prov. 17:8; 21:14

18 Casting [a]lots causes
contentions to cease,
And keeps the mighty apart.

19 A brother offended *is harder to*
win than a strong city,
And contentions *are* like
the bars of a castle.

20 [a]A man's stomach shall be satisfied
from the fruit of his mouth;
From the produce of his lips
he shall be filled.

21 [a]Death and life *are* in the
power of the tongue,
And those who love it will eat its fruit.

22 [a]*He who* finds a wife finds a good *thing,*
And obtains favor from the LORD.

23 The poor *man* uses entreaties,
But the rich answers [a]roughly.

24 A man *who has* friends must
himself be friendly,[1]
[a]But there is a friend *who* sticks
closer than a brother.

19 Better [a]*is* the poor who walks
in his integrity
Than *one who is* perverse in
his lips, and is a fool.

2 Also it is not good *for* a soul *to*
be without knowledge,
And he sins who hastens with *his* feet.

3 The foolishness of a man twists his way,
And his heart frets against the LORD.

4 [a]Wealth makes many friends,
But the poor is separated
from his friend.

5 A [a]false witness will not go unpunished,
And *he who* speaks lies will not escape.

6 Many entreat the favor
of the nobility,
And every man *is* a friend to
one who gives gifts.

7 [a]All the brothers of the poor hate him;
How much more do his friends
go [b]far from him!
He may pursue *them with* words,
yet they abandon *him.*

8 He who gets wisdom loves
his own soul;
He who keeps understanding
[a]will find good.

9 A false witness will not go
unpunished,
And *he who* speaks lies shall perish.

10 Luxury is not fitting for a fool,
Much less [a]for a servant to
rule over princes.

11 [a]The discretion of a man makes
him slow to anger,
[b]And his glory *is* to overlook
a transgression.

12 [a]The king's wrath *is* like the
roaring of a lion,
But his favor *is* [b]like dew on the grass.

13 [a]A foolish son *is* the ruin of his father,
[b]And the contentions of a wife
are a continual dripping.

14 [a]Houses and riches *are* an
inheritance from fathers,
But [b]a prudent wife *is* from the LORD.

15 [a]Laziness casts *one* into a deep sleep,
And an idle person will [b]suffer hunger.

16 [a]He who keeps the commandment
keeps his soul,
But he who is careless[1] of
his ways will die.

18:18 [a] [Prov. 16:33] **18:20** [a] Prov. 12:14; 14:14 **18:21** [a] Prov. 12:13; 13:3; Matt. 12:37 **18:22** [a] Gen. 2:18; [Prov. 12:4; 19:14] **18:23** [a] James 2:3, 6 **18:24** [a] Prov. 17:17; [John 15:14, 15] [1] Following Greek manuscripts, Syriac, Targum, and Vulgate; Masoretic Text reads *may come to ruin.* **19:1** [a] Prov. 28:6 **19:4** [a] Prov. 14:20 **19:5** [a] Ex. 23:1; Deut. 19:16–19; Prov. 6:19; 21:28 **19:7** [a] Prov. 14:20 [b] Ps. 38:11 **19:8** [a] Prov. 16:20 **19:10** [a] Prov. 30:21, 22 **19:11** [a] James 1:19 [b] Prov. 16:32; [Matt. 5:44]; Eph. 4:32; Col. 3:13 **19:12** [a] Prov. 16:14 [b] Gen. 27:28; Deut. 33:28; Ps. 133:3; Hos. 14:5; Mic. 5:7 **19:13** [a] Prov. 10:1 [b] Prov. 21:9, 19 **19:14** [a] 2 Cor. 12:14 [b] Prov. 18:22 **19:15** [a] Prov. 6:9 [b] Prov. 10:4 **19:16** [a] Prov. 13:13; 16:17; Luke 10:28; 11:28
[1] Literally *despises,* figurative of recklessness or carelessness

17 [a]He who has pity on the poor
lends to the LORD,
And He will pay back what
he has given.

18 [a]Chasten your son while there is hope,
And do not set your heart
on his destruction.[1]

19 *A man of* great wrath will
suffer punishment;
For if you rescue *him,* you will
have to do it again.

20 Listen to counsel and
receive instruction,
That you may be wise [a]in
your latter days.

21 There are many plans in a man's heart,
[a]Nevertheless the LORD's
counsel—that will stand.

22 What is desired in a man is kindness,
And a poor man is better than a liar.

23 [a]The fear of the LORD *leads* to life,
And *he who has it* will abide
in satisfaction;
He will not be visited with evil.

24 [a]A lazy *man* buries his hand in the bowl,[1]
And will not so much as bring
it to his mouth again.

25 Strike a scoffer, and the simple
[a]will become wary;
[b]Rebuke one who has understanding,
and he will discern knowledge.

26 He who mistreats *his* father *and*
chases away *his* mother
Is [a]a son who causes shame
and brings reproach.

27 Cease listening to instruction, my son,
And you will stray from the
words of knowledge.

28 A disreputable witness
scorns justice,
And [a]the mouth of the wicked
devours iniquity.

29 Judgments are prepared
for scoffers,
[a]And beatings for the backs of fools.

20 Wine [a]*is* a mocker,
Strong drink *is* a brawler,
And whoever is led astray
by it is not wise.

2 The wrath[1] of a king *is* like
the roaring of a lion;
Whoever provokes him to anger
sins *against* his own life.

3 [a]*It is* honorable for a man
to stop striving,
Since any fool can start a quarrel.

4 [a]The lazy *man* will not plow
because of winter;
[b]He will beg during harvest
and *have* nothing.

5 Counsel in the heart of man
is like deep water,
But a man of understanding
will draw it out.

6 Most men will proclaim each
his own goodness,
But who can find a faithful man?

7 [a]The righteous *man* walks
in his integrity;
[b]His children *are* blessed after him.

8 A king who sits on the
throne of judgment
Scatters all evil with his eyes.

9 [a]Who can say, "I have made
my heart clean,
I am pure from my sin"?

19:17 [a] Deut. 15:7, 8; Job 23:12, 13; Prov. 28:27; Eccl. 11:1; Matt. 10:42; 25:40; [2 Cor. 9:6–8]; Heb. 6:10 19:18 [a] Prov. 13:24 [1] Literally *to put him to death;* a Jewish tradition reads *on his crying.* 19:20 [a] Ps. 37:37 19:21 [a] Ps. 33:10, 11; Prov. 16:9; Is. 46:10; Heb. 6:17 19:23 [a] Prov. 14:27; [1 Tim. 4:8] 19:24 [a] Prov. 15:19 [1] Septuagint and Syriac read *bosom;* Targum and Vulgate read *armpit.* 19:25 [a] Deut. 13:11 [b] Prov. 9:8 19:26 [a] Prov. 17:2 19:28 [a] Job 15:16 19:29 [a] Prov. 26:3 20:1 [a] Gen. 9:21; Prov. 23:29–35; Is. 28:7; Hos. 4:11 20:2 [1] Literally *fear* or *terror* which is produced by the king's wrath 20:3 [a] Prov. 17:14 20:4 [a] Prov. 10:4 [b] Prov. 19:15 20:7 [a] 2 Cor. 1:12 [b] Ps. 37:26 20:9 [a] [1 Kin. 8:46; 2 Chr. 6:36]; Job 9:30, 31; 14:4; [Ps. 51:5; Eccl. 7:20; Rom. 3:9; 1 John 1:8]

10 [a]Diverse weights *and* diverse measures,
They *are* both alike, an
abomination to the LORD.

11 Even a child is [a]known by his deeds,
Whether what he does *is*
pure and right.

12 [a]The hearing ear and the seeing eye,
The LORD has made them both.

13 [a]Do not love sleep, lest you
come to poverty;
Open your eyes, *and* you will
be satisfied with bread.

14 "*It is* good for nothing,"[1]
cries the buyer;
But when he has gone his
way, then he boasts.

15 There is gold and a
multitude of rubies,
But [a]the lips of knowledge
are a precious jewel.

16 [a]Take the garment of one who
is surety *for* a stranger,
And hold it as a pledge *when*
it is for a seductress.

17 [a]Bread gained by deceit *is*
sweet to a man,
But afterward his mouth will
be filled with gravel.

18 [a]Plans are established by counsel;
[b]By wise counsel wage war.

19 [a]He who goes about *as* a
talebearer reveals secrets;
Therefore do not associate with
one [b]who flatters with his lips.

20 [a]Whoever curses his father
or his mother,
[b]His lamp will be put out
in deep darkness.

21 [a]An inheritance gained hastily
at the beginning
[b]Will not be blessed at the end.

22 [a]Do not say, "I will recompense evil";
[b]Wait for the LORD, and He will save you.

23 Diverse weights *are* an
abomination to the LORD,
And dishonest scales *are* not good.

24 A man's steps *are* of the LORD;
How then can a man understand
his own way?

25 *It is* a snare for a man to devote
rashly *something as* holy,
And afterward to reconsider *his* vows.

26 [a]A wise king sifts out the wicked,
And brings the threshing
wheel over them.

27 [a]The spirit of a man *is* the
lamp of the LORD,
Searching all the inner
depths of his heart.[1]

28 [a]Mercy and truth preserve the king,
And by lovingkindness he
upholds his throne.

29 The glory of young men
is their strength,
And [a]the splendor of old men
is their gray head.

30 Blows that hurt cleanse away evil,
As *do* stripes the inner
depths of the heart.[1]

21

The king's heart *is* in the
hand of the LORD,
Like the rivers of water;
He turns it wherever He wishes.

2 [a]Every way of a man *is* right
in his own eyes,

20:10 [a] Deut. 25:13 **20:11** [a] Matt. 7:16 **20:12** [a] Ex. 4:11; Ps. 94:9 **20:13** [a] Rom. 12:11 **20:14** [1] Literally *evil, evil* **20:15** [a] [Job 28:12–19; Prov. 3:13–15] **20:16** [a] Prov. 22:26 **20:17** [a] Prov. 9:17 **20:18** [a] Prov. 24:6 [b] Luke 14:31 **20:19** [a] Prov. 11:13 [b] Rom. 16:18 **20:20** [a] Ex. 21:17; Lev. 20:9; Prov. 30:11; Matt. 15:4 [b] Job 18:5, 6; Prov. 24:20 **20:21** [a] Prov. 28:20 [b] Hab. 2:6 **20:22** [a] [Deut. 32:35]; Prov. 17:13; 24:29; [Rom. 12:17–19]; 1 Thess. 5:15; [1 Pet. 3:9] [b] 2 Sam. 16:12 **20:26** [a] Ps. 101:8 **20:27** [a] 1 Cor. 2:11 [1] Literally *the rooms of the belly* **20:28** [a] Ps. 101:1; Prov. 21:21 **20:29** [a] Prov. 16:31 **20:30** [1] Literally *the rooms of the belly* **21:2** [a] Prov. 16:2

[b]But the LORD weighs
the hearts.

3 [a]To do righteousness and justice
Is more acceptable to the
LORD than sacrifice.

4 [a]A haughty look, a proud heart,
And the plowing[1] of the wicked *are* sin.

5 [a]The plans of the diligent
lead surely to plenty,
But *those of* everyone *who is*
hasty, surely to poverty.

6 [a]Getting treasures by a lying tongue
Is the fleeting fantasy of
those who seek death.[1]

7 The violence of the wicked
will destroy them,[1]
Because they refuse to do justice.

8 The way of a guilty man *is* perverse;[1]
But *as for* the pure, his work *is* right.

9 Better to dwell in a corner
of a housetop,
Than in a house shared with
[a]a contentious woman.

10 [a]The soul of the wicked desires evil;
His neighbor finds no
favor in his eyes.

11 When the scoffer is punished,
the simple is made wise;
But when the [a]wise is instructed,
he receives knowledge.

12 The righteous *God* wisely considers
the house of the wicked,
Overthrowing the wicked
for *their* wickedness.

13 [a]Whoever shuts his ears to
the cry of the poor
Will also cry himself and not be heard.

14 A gift in secret pacifies anger,
And a bribe behind the
back,[1] strong wrath.

15 *It is* a joy for the just to do justice,
But destruction *will come* to
the workers of iniquity.

16 A man who wanders from the
way of understanding
Will rest in the assembly of the [a]dead.

17 He who loves pleasure *will*
be a poor man;
He who loves wine and oil
will not be rich.

18 The wicked *shall be* a ransom
for the righteous,
And the unfaithful for the upright.

19 Better to dwell in the wilderness,
Than with a contentious
and angry woman.

20 [a]*There is* desirable treasure,
And oil in the dwelling of the wise,
But a foolish man squanders it.

21 [a]He who follows righteousness
and mercy
Finds life, righteousness, and honor.

22 A [a]wise *man* scales the
city of the mighty,
And brings down the
trusted stronghold.

23 [a]Whoever guards his mouth
and tongue
Keeps his soul from troubles.

24 A proud *and* haughty
man—"Scoffer" *is* his name;
He acts with arrogant pride.

25 The [a]desire of the lazy *man* kills him,
For his hands refuse to labor.

21:2 [b] Prov. 24:12; Luke 16:15 **21:3** [a] 1 Sam. 15:22; Prov. 15:8; Is. 1:11, 16, 17; Hos. 6:6; [Mic. 6:7, 8] **21:4** [a] Prov. 6:17 [1] Or *lamp* **21:5** [a] Prov. 10:4 **21:6** [a] 2 Pet. 2:3 [1] Septuagint reads *Pursue vanity on the snares of death;* Vulgate reads *Is vain and foolish, and shall stumble on the snares of death;* Targum reads *They shall be destroyed, and they shall fall who seek death.* **21:7** [1] Literally *drag them away* **21:8** [1] Or *The way of a man is perverse and strange* **21:9** [a] Prov. 19:13 **21:10** [a] James 4:5 **21:11** [a] Prov. 19:25 **21:13** [a] [Matt. 7:2; 18:30–34]; James 2:13; 1 John 3:17 **21:14** [1] Literally *in the bosom* **21:16** [a] Ps. 49:14 **21:20** [a] Ps. 112:3; Prov. 8:21 **21:21** [a] Prov. 15:9; Matt. 5:6; [Rom. 2:7]; 1 Cor. 15:58 **21:22** [a] 2 Sam. 5:6–9; Prov. 24:5; Eccl. 7:19; 9:15, 16 **21:23** [a] Prov. 12:13; 13:3; 18:21; [James 3:2] **21:25** [a] Prov. 13:4

26 He covets greedily all day long,
But the righteous [a]gives
and does not spare.

27 [a]The sacrifice of the wicked
is an abomination;
How much more *when* he brings
it with wicked intent!

28 A false witness shall perish,
But the man who hears *him*
will speak endlessly.

29 A wicked man hardens his face,
But *as for* the upright, he
establishes[1] his way.

30 [a]*There is* no wisdom or
understanding
Or counsel against the LORD.

31 The horse *is* prepared for
the day of battle,
But [a]deliverance *is* of the LORD.

22 A [a]*good* name is to be chosen
rather than great riches,
Loving favor rather than
silver and gold.

2 The [a]rich and the poor have
this in common,
The [b]LORD *is* the maker of them all.

3 A prudent *man* foresees evil
and hides himself,
But the simple pass on
and are [a]punished.

4 By humility *and* the fear of the LORD
Are riches and honor and life.

5 Thorns *and* snares *are* in the
way of the perverse;
He who guards his soul will
be far from them.

6 [a]Train up a child in the
way he should go,
And when he is old he will
not depart from it.

7 The [a]rich rules over the poor,
And the borrower *is* servant
to the lender.

8 He who sows iniquity will
reap [a]sorrow,
And the rod of his anger will fail.

9 [a]He who has a generous eye
will be [b]blessed,
For he gives of his bread to the poor.

#OXYGEN

PROVERBS 22:9

Elevate How You Serve Others

If you desire to succeed in life, trust God, love people, and assist all in need. You will be rewarded when you share what God has given you.

Breathe and elevate how you serve others.

10 [a]Cast out the scoffer, and
contention will leave;
Yes, strife and reproach will cease.

11 [a]He who loves purity of heart
And has grace on his lips,
The king *will be* his friend.

12 The eyes of the LORD
preserve knowledge,
But He overthrows the words
of the faithless.

13 [a]The lazy *man* says, "*There
is* a lion outside!
I shall be slain in the streets!"

21:26 [a] [Prov. 22:9; Eph. 4:28] 21:27 [a] Prov. 15:8; Is. 66:3; Jer. 6:20; Amos 5:22 21:29 [1] Qere and Septuagint read *understands*. 21:30 [a] Is. 8:9, 10; [Jer. 9:23, 24]; Acts 5:39; 1 Cor. 3:19, 20 21:31 [a] Ps. 3:8; Jer. 3:23; [1 Cor. 15:57] 22:1 [a] [Prov. 10:7]; Eccl. 7:1 22:2 [a] Prov. 29:13 [b] Job 31:15; [Prov. 14:31] 22:3 [a] Prov. 27:12; Is. 26:20 22:6 [a] Eph. 6:4; 2 Tim. 3:15 22:7 [a] Prov. 18:23; James 2:6 22:8 [a] Job 4:8 22:9 [a] 2 Cor. 9:6 [b] [Prov. 19:17] 22:10 [a] Ps. 101:5 22:11 [a] Ps. 101:6 22:13 [a] Prov. 26:13

14 [a]The mouth of an immoral
woman *is* a deep pit;
[b]He who is abhorred by the
LORD will fall there.

15 Foolishness *is* bound up in
the heart of a child;
[a]The rod of correction will
drive it far from him.

16 He who oppresses the poor
to increase his *riches,*
And he who gives to the rich, *will*
surely *come* to poverty.

Sayings of the Wise

17 Incline your ear and hear
the words of the wise,
And apply your heart to
my knowledge;
18 For *it is* a pleasant thing if you
keep them within you;
Let them all be fixed upon your lips,
19 So that your trust may be in the LORD;
I have instructed you today, even you.
20 Have I not written to you
excellent things
Of counsels and knowledge,
21 [a]That I may make you know the
certainty of the words of truth,
[b]That you may answer words of truth
To those who send to you?

22 Do not rob the [a]poor
because he *is* poor,
Nor oppress the afflicted at the gate;
23 [a]For the LORD will plead their cause,
And plunder the soul of those
who plunder them.

24 Make no friendship with
an angry man,
And with a [a]furious man do not go,
25 Lest you learn his ways
And set a snare for your soul.

26 [a]Do not be one of those who
shakes hands in a pledge,
One of those who is surety for debts;
27 If you have nothing *with which* to pay,
Why should he take away your
bed from under you?

28 [a]Do not remove the ancient landmark
Which your fathers have set.

29 Do you see a man *who*
excels in his work?
He will stand before kings;
He will not stand before
unknown *men.*

23 When you sit down to
eat with a ruler,
Consider carefully what *is* before you;
2 And put a knife to your throat
If you *are* a man given to appetite.
3 Do not desire his delicacies,
For they *are* deceptive food.

4 [a]Do not overwork to be rich;
[b]Because of your own
understanding, cease!
5 Will you set your eyes on
that which is not?
For *riches* certainly make
themselves wings;
They fly away like an eagle
toward heaven.

6 Do not eat the bread of [a]a miser,[1]
Nor desire his delicacies;
7 For as he thinks in his heart, so *is* he.
"Eat and drink!" [a]he says to you,
But his heart is not with you.
8 The morsel you have eaten,
you will vomit up,
And waste your pleasant words.

9 [a]Do not speak in the hearing of a fool,
For he will despise the
wisdom of your words.

10 Do not remove the ancient landmark,
Nor enter the fields of the fatherless;
11 [a]For their Redeemer *is* mighty;
He will plead their cause against you.

12 Apply your heart to instruction,
And your ears to words of knowledge.

22:14 [a] Prov. 2:16; 5:3; 7:5 [b] Eccl. 7:26 22:15 [a] Prov. 13:24; 23:13, 14 22:21 [a] Luke 1:3, 4 [b] Prov. 25:13; 1 Pet. 3:15 22:22 [a] Ex. 23:6; Job 31:16–21; Zech. 7:10 22:23 [a] 1 Sam. 24:12; Ps. 12:5; 140:12 22:24 [a] Prov. 29:22 22:26 [a] Prov. 11:15 22:28 [a] Deut. 19:14; 27:17; Job 24:2; Prov. 23:10 23:4 [a] [Prov. 28:20; Matt. 6:19; 1 Tim. 6:9, 10; Heb. 13:5] [b] Rom. 12:16 23:6 [a] Deut. 15:9; Prov. 28:22
[1] Literally *one who has an evil eye* 23:7 [a] Prov. 12:2 23:9 [a] Prov. 9:8; Matt. 7:6 23:11 [a] Prov. 22:23

13 [a]Do not withhold correction
from a child,
For *if* you beat him with a
rod, he will not die.
14 You shall beat him with a rod,
And deliver his soul from hell.[1]

15 My son, if your heart is wise,
My heart will rejoice—indeed,
I myself;
16 Yes, my inmost being will rejoice
When your lips speak right things.

17 [a]Do not let your heart envy sinners,
But [b]*be zealous* for the fear of
the LORD all the day;
18 [a]For surely there is a hereafter,
And your hope will not be cut off.

19 Hear, my son, and be wise;
And guide your heart in the way.
20 [a]Do not mix with winebibbers,
Or with gluttonous eaters of meat;
21 For the drunkard and the glutton
will come to poverty,
And drowsiness will clothe
a man with rags.

22 [a]Listen to your father who begot you,
And do not despise your
mother when she is old.

23 [a]Buy the truth, and do not sell *it,*
Also wisdom and instruction
and understanding.

24 [a]The father of the righteous
will greatly rejoice,
And he who begets a wise *child*
will delight in him.
25 Let your father and your
mother be glad,
And let her who bore you rejoice.

26 My son, give me your heart,
And let your eyes observe my ways.
27 [a]For a harlot *is* a deep pit,
And a seductress *is* a narrow well.
28 [a]She also lies in wait as *for* a victim,
And increases the unfaithful
among men.

29 [a]Who has woe?
Who has sorrow?
Who has contentions?
Who has complaints?
Who has wounds without cause?
Who [b]has redness of eyes?
30 [a]Those who linger long at the wine,
Those who go in search
of [b]mixed wine.
31 Do not look on the wine when it is red,
When it sparkles in the cup,
When it swirls around smoothly;
32 At the last it bites like a serpent,
And stings like a viper.
33 Your eyes will see strange things,
And your heart will utter
perverse things.
34 Yes, you will be like one who lies
down in the midst of the sea,
Or like one who lies at the top
of the mast, *saying:*
35 "They[a] have struck me, *but*
I was not hurt;
They have beaten me, but
I did not feel *it.*
When shall [b]I awake, that I may
seek another *drink?*"

24 Do not be [a]envious of evil men,
Nor desire to be with them;
2 For their heart devises violence,
And their lips talk of troublemaking.

3 Through wisdom a house is built,
And by understanding it
is established;
4 By knowledge the rooms are filled
With all precious and pleasant riches.

5 [a]A wise man *is* strong,
Yes, a man of knowledge
increases strength;
6 [a]For by wise counsel you will
wage your own war,
And in a multitude of
counselors *there is* safety.

23:13 [a] Prov. 13:24 23:14 [1] Or *Sheol* 23:17 [a] Ps. 37:1; Prov. 24:1, 19 [b] Prov. 28:14 23:18 [a] [Ps. 37:37] 23:20 [a] Prov. 20:1; 23:29, 30; Is. 5:22; Matt. 24:49; [Luke 21:34]; Rom. 13:13; [Eph. 5:18] 23:22 [a] Prov. 1:8; Eph. 6:1 23:23 [a] Prov. 4:7; 18:15; [Matt. 13:44] 23:24 [a] Prov. 10:1 23:27 [a] Prov. 22:14 23:28 [a] Prov. 7:12; Eccl. 7:26 23:29 [a] Is. 5:11, 22 [b] Gen. 49:12 23:30 [a] 1 Sam. 25:36; Prov. 20:1; 21:17; Is. 5:11; 28:7; [Eph. 5:18] [b] Ps. 75:8 23:35 [a] Prov. 27:22; Jer. 5:3 [b] Eph. 4:19 24:1 [a] Ps. 1:1; 37:1; Prov. 23:17 24:5 [a] Prov. 21:22; Eccl. 9:16 24:6 [a] Luke 14:31

7 [a]Wisdom *is* too lofty for a fool;
He does not open his
mouth in the gate.

8 He who [a]plots to do evil
Will be called a schemer.
9 The devising of foolishness *is* sin,
And the scoffer *is* an
abomination to men.

10 *If* you [a]faint in the day of adversity,
Your strength *is* small.

11 [a]Deliver *those who* are drawn
toward death,
And hold back *those* stumbling
to the slaughter.
12 If you say, "Surely we did
not know this,"
Does not [a]He who weighs the
hearts consider *it?*
He who keeps your soul,
does He *not* know *it?*
And will He *not* render to *each*
man [b]according to his deeds?

13 My son, [a]eat honey because
it is good,
And the honeycomb *which*
is sweet to your taste;
14 [a]So *shall* the knowledge of
wisdom *be* to your soul;
If you have found *it,* there
is a prospect,
And your hope will not be cut off.

15 Do not lie in wait, O wicked
man, against the dwelling
of the righteous;
Do not plunder his resting place;
16 [a]For a righteous *man* may
fall seven times
And rise again,
[b]But the wicked shall fall by calamity.

17 [a]Do not rejoice when your enemy falls,
And do not let your heart be
glad when he stumbles;
18 Lest the LORD see *it,* and
it displease Him,
And He turn away His wrath
from him.

19 [a]Do not fret because of evildoers,
Nor be envious of the wicked;
20 For there will be no prospect
for the evil *man;*
The lamp of the wicked will
be put out.

21 My son, [a]fear the LORD and the king;
Do not associate with those
given to change;
22 For their calamity will rise suddenly,
And who knows the ruin
those two can bring?

Further Sayings of the Wise

23 These *things* also *belong* to the wise:

[a]*It is* not good to show
partiality in judgment.
24 [a]He who says to the wicked,
"You *are* righteous,"
Him the people will curse;
Nations will abhor him.
25 But those who rebuke *the*
wicked will have [a]delight,
And a good blessing will
come upon them.

26 He who gives a right answer
kisses the lips.

27 [a]Prepare your outside work,
Make it fit for yourself in the field;
And afterward build your house.

28 [a]Do not be a witness against your
neighbor without cause,
For would you deceive[1]
with your lips?
29 [a]Do not say, "I will do to him just
as he has done to me;
I will render to the man
according to his work."

24:7 [a] Ps. 10:5; Prov. 14:6 **24:8** [a] Prov. 6:14; 14:22; Rom. 1:30 **24:10** [a] Deut. 20:8; Job 4:5; Jer. 51:46; Heb. 12:3 **24:11** [a] Ps. 82:4; Is. 58:6, 7; 1 John 3:16 **24:12** [a] 1 Sam. 16:7; Prov. 21:2 [b] Job 34:11; Ps. 62:12; Rev. 2:23; 22:12 **24:13** [a] Ps. 19:10; 119:103; Prov. 25:16; Song 5:1 **24:14** [a] Ps. 19:10; 58:11; Prov. 23:18 **24:16** [a] Job 5:19; [Ps. 34:19; 37:24; Mic. 7:8] [b] Esth. 7:10; Amos 5:2 **24:17** [a] Job 31:29; Ps. 35:15, 19; [Prov. 17:5]; Obad. 12 **24:19** [a] Ps. 37:1 **24:21** [a] [Rom. 13:7; 1 Pet. 2:17] **24:23** [a] Lev. 19:15; Deut. 1:17; 16:19; [John 7:24] **24:24** [a] Prov. 17:15; Is. 5:23 **24:25** [a] Prov. 28:23 **24:27** [a] 1 Kin. 5:17; Prov. 27:23–27 **24:28** [a] Lev. 6:2, 3; 19:11; Eph. 4:25

[1] Septuagint and Vulgate read *Do not deceive.* **24:29** [a] [Prov. 20:22; Matt. 5:39–44; Rom. 12:17–19]

30 I went by the field of the lazy *man*,
And by the vineyard of the man
devoid of understanding;
31 And there it was, [a]all
overgrown with thorns;
Its surface was covered with nettles;
Its stone wall was broken down.
32 When I saw *it,* I considered *it* well;
I looked on *it and* received
instruction:
33 [a]A little sleep, a little slumber,
A little folding of the hands to rest;
34 [a]So shall your poverty come
like a prowler,
And your need like an armed man.

Further Wise Sayings of Solomon

25 These[a] also *are* proverbs of Solomon which the men of Hezekiah king of Judah copied:

2 [a]*It is* the glory of God to
conceal a matter,
But the glory of kings *is* to
search out a matter.

3 *As* the heavens for height and
the earth for depth,
So the heart of kings *is* unsearchable.

4 [a]Take away the dross from silver,
And it will go to the
silversmith *for* jewelry.
5 Take away the wicked from
before the king,
And his throne will be established
in [a]righteousness.

6 Do not exalt yourself in the
presence of the king,
And do not stand in the
place of the great;
7 [a]For *it is* better that he say to you,
"Come up here,"
Than that you should be put lower
in the presence of the prince,
Whom your eyes have seen.

8 [a]Do not go hastily to court;
For what will you do in the end,
When your neighbor has
put you to shame?
9 [a]Debate your case with your neighbor,
And do not disclose the
secret to another;
10 Lest he who hears *it* expose
your shame,
And your reputation be ruined.

11 A word fitly [a]spoken *is like*
apples of gold
In settings of silver.
12 *Like* an earring of gold and an
ornament of fine gold
Is a wise rebuker to an
obedient ear.

13 [a]Like the cold of snow in
time of harvest
Is a faithful messenger to
those who send him,
For he refreshes the soul
of his masters.

14 [a]Whoever falsely boasts of giving
Is like [b]clouds and wind
without rain.

15 [a]By long forbearance a
ruler is persuaded,
And a gentle tongue breaks a bone.

16 Have you found honey?
Eat only as much as you need,
Lest you be filled with it and vomit.

17 Seldom set foot in your
neighbor's house,
Lest he become weary of
you and hate you.

18 [a]A man who bears false witness
against his neighbor
Is like a club, a sword, and
a sharp arrow.

19 Confidence in an unfaithful
man in time of trouble
Is like a bad tooth and a
foot out of joint.

24:31 [a] Gen. 3:18 24:33 [a] Prov. 6:9, 10 24:34 [a] Prov. 6:9–11 25:1 [a] 1 Kin. 4:32 25:2 [a] Deut. 29:29; Rom. 11:33 25:4 [a] 2 Tim. 2:21 25:5 [a] Prov. 16:12; 20:8 25:7 [a] Luke 14:7–11 25:8 [a] Prov. 17:14; Matt. 5:25 25:9 [a] [Matt. 18:15] 25:11 [a] Prov. 15:23; Is. 50:4 25:13 [a] Prov. 13:17 25:14 [a] Prov. 20:6 [b] Jude 12 25:15 [a] Prov. 15:1 25:18 [a] Ps. 57:4; Prov. 12:18

20 *Like* one who takes away a
garment in cold weather,
And like vinegar on soda,
Is one who [a]sings songs
to a heavy heart.

21 [a]If your enemy is hungry,
give him bread to eat;
And if he is thirsty, give
him water to drink;
22 For *so* you will heap coals
of fire on his head,
[a]And the LORD will reward you.

23 The north wind brings forth rain,
And [a]a backbiting tongue an
angry countenance.

24 [a]*It is* better to dwell in a
corner of a housetop,
Than in a house shared with
a contentious woman.

25 *As* cold water to a weary soul,
So *is* [a]good news from
a far country.

26 A righteous *man* who falters
before the wicked
Is like a murky spring and
a polluted well.

27 *It is* not good to eat much honey;
So [a]to seek one's own glory
is not glory.

28 [a]Whoever *has* no rule over
his own spirit
Is like a city broken down,
without walls.

26

As snow in summer [a]and
rain in harvest,
So honor is not fitting for a fool.

2 Like a flitting sparrow, like
a flying swallow,
So [a]a curse without cause
shall not alight.

3 [a]A whip for the horse,
A bridle for the donkey,
And a rod for the fool's back.
4 Do not answer a fool
according to his folly,
Lest you also be like him.
5 [a]Answer a fool according to his folly,
Lest he be wise in his own eyes.
6 He who sends a message by
the hand of a fool
Cuts off *his own* feet *and*
drinks violence.
7 *Like* the legs of the lame
that hang limp
Is a proverb in the mouth of fools.
8 Like one who binds a stone in a sling
Is he who gives honor to a fool.
9 *Like* a thorn *that* goes into the
hand of a drunkard
Is a proverb in the mouth of fools.
10 The great *God* who formed everything
Gives the fool *his* hire and the
transgressor *his* wages.[1]
11 [a]As a dog returns to his own vomit,
[b]*So* a fool repeats his folly.
12 [a]Do you see a man wise
in his own eyes?
There is more hope for a
fool than for him.

13 The lazy *man* says, "*There*
is a lion in the road!
A fierce lion *is* in the streets!"
14 *As* a door turns on its hinges,
So *does* the lazy *man* on his bed.
15 The [a]lazy *man* buries his
hand in the bowl;[1]
It wearies him to bring it
back to his mouth.
16 The lazy *man is* wiser in his own eyes
Than seven men who can
answer sensibly.

17 He who passes by *and* meddles
in a quarrel not his own
Is like one who takes a dog by the ears.

18 Like a madman who throws
firebrands, arrows, and death,

25:20 [a] Dan. 6:18 25:21 [a] Ex. 23:4, 5; 2 Kin. 6:22; 2 Chr. 28:15; Matt. 5:44; Rom. 12:20 25:22 [a] 2 Sam. 16:12; [Matt. 6:4, 6] 25:23 [a] Ps. 101:5 25:24 [a] Prov. 19:13 25:25 [a] Prov. 15:30 25:27 [a] Prov. 27:2; [Luke 14:11] 25:28 [a] Prov. 16:32 26:1 [a] 1 Sam. 12:17 26:2 [a] Num. 23:8; Deut. 23:5; 2 Sam. 16:12 26:3 [a] Ps. 32:9; Prov. 19:29 26:5 [a] Matt. 16:1–4; Rom. 12:16 26:10 [1] The Hebrew is difficult; ancient and modern translators differ greatly. 26:11 [a] 2 Pet. 2:22 [b] Ex. 8:15 26:12 [a] Prov. 29:20; Luke 18:11, 12; [Rev. 3:17] 26:15 [a] Prov. 19:24 [1] Compare 19:24

19 *Is* the man *who* deceives his neighbor,
And says, [a]"I was only joking!"

20 Where *there is* no wood,
the fire goes out;
And where *there is* no
talebearer, strife ceases.
21 [a]*As* charcoal *is* to burning
coals, and wood to fire,
So *is* a contentious man
to kindle strife.
22 The words of a talebearer
are like tasty trifles,
And they go down into
the inmost body.

23 Fervent lips with a wicked heart
Are like earthenware covered
with silver dross.

24 He who hates, disguises
it with his lips,
And lays up deceit within himself;
25 [a]When he speaks kindly, do
not believe him,
For *there are* seven abominations
in his heart;
26 *Though his* hatred is covered by deceit,
His wickedness will be revealed
before the assembly.

27 [a]Whoever digs a pit will fall into it,
And he who rolls a stone will
have it roll back on him.

28 A lying tongue hates *those*
who are crushed by it,
And a flattering mouth works [a]ruin.

27

Do[a] not boast about tomorrow,
For you do not know what a
day may bring forth.

2 [a]Let another man praise you,
and not your own mouth;
A stranger, and not your own lips.

3 A stone *is* heavy and sand *is* weighty,
But a fool's wrath *is* heavier
than both of them.

4 Wrath *is* cruel and anger a torrent,
But [a]who *is* able to stand
before jealousy?

5 [a]Open rebuke *is* better
Than love carefully concealed.

6 Faithful *are* the wounds of a friend,
But the kisses of an enemy
are [a]deceitful.

7 A satisfied soul loathes
the honeycomb,
But to a hungry soul every
bitter thing *is* sweet.

8 Like a bird that wanders
from its nest
Is a man who wanders from his place.

9 Ointment and perfume
delight the heart,
And the sweetness of a man's friend
gives delight by hearty counsel.

10 Do not forsake your own friend
or your father's friend,
Nor go to your brother's house
in the day of your calamity;
[a]Better *is* a neighbor nearby
than a brother far away.

11 My son, be wise, and make
my heart glad,
[a]That I may answer him who
reproaches me.

12 A prudent *man* foresees evil
and hides himself;
The simple pass on *and*
are [a]punished.

13 Take the garment of him who
is surety for a stranger,
And hold it in pledge *when* he
is surety for a seductress.

14 He who blesses his friend with a loud
voice, rising early in the morning,
It will be counted a curse to him.

26:19 [a] Eph. 5:4 26:21 [a] Prov. 15:18 26:25 [a] Ps. 28:3; Prov. 26:23; Jer. 9:8 26:27 [a] Esth. 7:10; Ps. 7:15; Prov. 28:10; Eccl. 10:8
26:28 [a] Prov. 29:5 27:1 [a] Luke 12:19–21; James 4:13–16 27:2 [a] Prov. 25:27; 2 Cor. 10:12, 18; 12:11 27:4 [a] Prov. 6:34; 1 John 3:12
27:5 [a] [Prov. 28:23]; Gal. 2:14 27:6 [a] Matt. 26:49 27:10 [a] Prov. 17:17; 18:24 27:11 [a] Prov. 10:1; 23:15–26 27:12 [a] Prov. 22:3

15 A [a]continual dripping on
a very rainy day
And a contentious woman are alike;
16 Whoever restrains her
restrains the wind,
And grasps oil with his right hand.

17 *As* iron sharpens iron,
So a man sharpens the
countenance of his friend.

18 [a]Whoever keeps the fig tree
will eat its fruit;
So he who waits on his master
will be honored.

19 As in water face *reflects* face,
So a man's heart *reveals* the man.

20 [a]Hell[1] and Destruction[2] are never full;
So [b]the eyes of man are
never satisfied.

21 [a]The refining pot *is* for silver
and the furnace for gold,
And a man *is valued* by what
others say of him.

22 [a]Though you grind a fool in a
mortar with a pestle along
with crushed grain,
Yet his foolishness will not
depart from him.

23 Be diligent to know the
state of your [a]flocks,
And attend to your herds;
24 For riches *are* not forever,
Nor does a crown *endure*
to all generations.
25 [a]*When* the hay is removed, and the
tender grass shows itself,
And the herbs of the mountains
are gathered in,
26 The lambs *will provide* your clothing,
And the goats the price of a field;
27 *You shall have* enough goats'
milk for your food,
For the food of your household,
And the nourishment of
your maidservants.

28

The [a]wicked flee when
no one pursues,
But the righteous are bold as a lion.

2 Because of the transgression of a
land, many *are* its princes;
But by a man of understanding
and knowledge
Right will be prolonged.

3 [a]A poor man who oppresses the poor
Is like a driving rain which
leaves no food.

4 [a]Those who forsake the law
praise the wicked,
[b]But such as keep the law
contend with them.

5 [a]Evil men do not understand justice,
But [b]those who seek the
LORD understand all.

6 Better *is* the poor who walks
in his integrity
Than one perverse *in his* ways,
though he *be* rich.

7 Whoever keeps the law *is*
a discerning son,
But a companion of gluttons
shames his father.

8 One who increases his possessions
by usury and extortion
Gathers it for him who
will pity the poor.

9 One who turns away his ear
from hearing the law,
[a]Even his prayer *is* an abomination.

10 [a]Whoever causes the upright to
go astray in an evil way,
He himself will fall into his own pit;
[b]But the blameless will inherit good.

27:15 [a] Prov. 19:13 27:18 [a] 2 Kin. 18:31; Song 8:12; Is. 36:16; [1 Cor. 3:8; 9:7–13]; 2 Tim. 2:6 27:20 [a] Prov. 30:15, 16; Hab. 2:5 [b] Eccl. 1:8; 4:8 [1] Or *Sheol* [2] Hebrew *Abaddon* 27:21 [a] Prov. 17:3 27:22 [a] Prov. 23:35; 26:11; Jer. 5:3 27:23 [a] Prov. 24:27 27:25 [a] Ps. 104:14 28:1 [a] Lev. 26:17, 36; Ps. 53:5 28:3 [a] Matt. 18:28 28:4 [a] Ps. 49:18; Rom. 1:32 [b] 1 Kin. 18:18; Neh. 13:11, 15; Matt. 3:7; 14:4; Eph. 5:11 28:5 [a] Ps. 92:6; Is. 6:9; 44:18 [b] Ps. 119:100; Prov. 2:9; John 17:17; 1 Cor. 2:15; [1 John 2:20, 27] 28:9 [a] Ps. 66:18; 109:7; Prov. 15:8 28:10 [a] Ps. 7:15; Prov. 26:27 [b] [Matt. 6:33; Heb. 6:12; 1 Pet. 3:9]

11 The rich man *is* wise in his own eyes,
But the poor who has understanding
searches him out.

12 When the righteous rejoice,
there is great [a]glory;
But when the wicked arise,
men hide themselves.

13 [a]He who covers his sins
will not prosper,
But whoever confesses and
forsakes *them* will have mercy.

14 Happy *is* the man who is
always reverent,
But he who hardens his heart
will fall into calamity.

15 [a]*Like* a roaring lion and a charging bear
[b]*Is* a wicked ruler over poor people.

16 A ruler who lacks understanding
is a great [a]oppressor,
But he who hates covetousness
will prolong *his* days.

17 [a]A man burdened with bloodshed
will flee into a pit;
Let no one help him.

18 Whoever walks blamelessly
will be saved,
But *he who is* perverse *in his*
ways will suddenly fall.

19 [a]He who tills his land will
have plenty of bread,
But he who follows frivolity will
have poverty enough!

20 A faithful man will abound
with blessings,
[a]But he who hastens to be rich
will not go unpunished.

21 [a]To show partiality *is* not good,
[b]Because for a piece of bread
a man will transgress.

22 A man with an evil eye
hastens after riches,
And does not consider that
[a]poverty will come upon him.

23 [a]He who rebukes a man will find
more favor afterward
Than he who flatters with the tongue.

24 Whoever robs his father or his mother,
And says, "*It is* no transgression,"
The same [a]*is* companion to a destroyer.

25 [a]He who is of a proud heart
stirs up strife,
[b]But he who trusts in the LORD
will be prospered.

26 He who [a]trusts in his own
heart is a fool,
But whoever walks wisely
will be delivered.

27 [a]He who gives to the poor will not lack,
But he who hides his eyes
will have many curses.

28 When the wicked arise, [a]men
hide themselves;
But when they perish, the
righteous increase.

29 He[a] who is often rebuked, *and*
hardens *his* neck,
Will suddenly be destroyed,
and that without remedy.

2 When the righteous are in
authority, the [a]people rejoice;
But when a wicked *man* rules,
[b]the people groan.

3 Whoever loves wisdom makes
his father rejoice,
But a companion of harlots
wastes *his* wealth.

4 The king establishes the
land by justice,

28:12 [a] Prov. 11:10; 29:2 28:13 [a] Ps. 32:3–5; 1 John 1:8–10 28:15 [a] Prov. 19:12; 1 Pet. 5:8 [b] Ex. 1:14; Prov. 29:2; Matt. 2:16
28:16 [a] Eccl. 10:16; Is. 3:12 28:17 [a] Gen. 9:6 28:19 [a] Prov. 12:11; 20:13 28:20 [a] Prov. 13:11; 20:21; 23:4; 1 Tim. 6:9 28:21 [a] Prov. 18:5
[b] Ezek. 13:19 28:22 [a] Prov. 21:5 28:23 [a] Prov. 27:5, 6 28:24 [a] Prov. 18:9 28:25 [a] Prov. 13:10 [b] Prov. 29:25; 1 Tim. 6:6
28:26 [a] Prov. 3:5 28:27 [a] Deut. 15:7; Prov. 19:17; 22:9 28:28 [a] Job 24:4 29:1 [a] 2 Chr. 36:16; Prov. 6:15
29:2 [a] Esth. 8:15; Prov. 28:12 [b] Esth. 4:3

But he who receives bribes
overthrows it.

5 A man who [a]flatters his neighbor
Spreads a net for his feet.

6 By transgression an evil
man is snared,
But the righteous sings and rejoices.

7 The righteous [a]considers the
cause of the poor,
But the wicked does not
understand *such* knowledge.

8 Scoffers [a]set a city aflame,
But wise *men* turn away wrath.

9 *If* a wise man contends
with a foolish man,
[a]Whether *the fool* rages or
laughs, *there is* no peace.

10 [a]The bloodthirsty hate the blameless,
But the upright seek his well-being.[1]

11 A fool vents all his [a]feelings,[1]
But a wise *man* holds them back.

12 If a ruler pays attention to lies,
All his servants *become* wicked.

13 The poor *man* and the oppressor
have this in common:
[a]The LORD gives light to
the eyes of both.

14 The king who judges the
[a]poor with truth,
His throne will be established forever.

15 The rod and rebuke give [a]wisdom,
But a child left *to himself* brings
shame to his mother.

16 When the wicked are multiplied,
transgression increases;
But the righteous will see their [a]fall.

17 Correct your son, and he
will give you rest;
Yes, he will give delight
to your soul.

18 [a]Where *there is* no revelation,[1] the
people cast off restraint;
But [b]happy *is* he who keeps the law.

19 A servant will not be corrected
by mere words;
For though he understands,
he will not respond.

20 Do you see a man hasty
in his words?
[a]*There is* more hope for a
fool than for him.

21 He who pampers his servant
from childhood
Will have him as a son in the end.

22 [a]An angry man stirs up strife,
And a furious man abounds
in transgression.

23 [a]A man's pride will bring him low,
But the humble in spirit
will retain honor.

24 Whoever is a partner with a
thief hates his own life;
[a]He swears to tell the truth,[1]
but reveals nothing.

25 [a]The fear of man brings a snare,
But whoever trusts in the
LORD shall be safe.

26 [a]Many seek the ruler's favor,
But justice for man *comes*
from the LORD.

27 An unjust man *is* an abomination
to the righteous,
And *he who is* upright in the way *is*
an abomination to the wicked.

29:5 [a] Prov. 26:28 **29:7** [a] Job 29:16; Ps. 41:1; Prov. 31:8, 9 **29:8** [a] Prov. 11:11 **29:9** [a] Matt. 11:17 **29:10** [a] Gen. 4:5–8; 1 John 3:12 [1] Literally *soul* **29:11** [a] Prov. 14:33 [1] Literally *spirit* **29:13** [a] [Matt. 5:45] **29:14** [a] Ps. 72:4; Is. 11:4 **29:15** [a] Prov. 22:15 **29:16** [a] Ps. 37:34; Prov. 21:12 **29:18** [a] 1 Sam. 3:1; Ps. 74:9; Amos 8:11, 12 [b] Prov. 8:32; John 13:17 [1] Or *prophetic vision* **29:20** [a] Prov. 26:12 **29:22** [a] Prov. 26:21 **29:23** [a] Job 22:29; Prov. 15:33; 18:12; Is. 66:2; Dan. 4:30; Matt. 23:12; Luke 14:11; 18:14; Acts 12:23; [James 4:6–10; 1 Pet. 5:5, 6] **29:24** [a] Lev. 5:1 [1] Literally *hears the adjuration* **29:25** [a] Gen. 12:12; 20:2; Luke 12:4; John 12:42, 43 **29:26** [a] Ps. 20:9

The Wisdom of Agur

30 The words of Agur the son of Jakeh, *his* utterance. This man declared to Ithiel—to Ithiel and Ucal:

2 [a]Surely I *am* more stupid
than *any* man,
And do not have the
understanding of a man.
3 I neither learned wisdom
Nor have [a]knowledge of the Holy One.

4 [a]Who has ascended into
heaven, or descended?
[b]Who has gathered the
wind in His fists?
Who has bound the waters
in a garment?
Who has established all the
ends of the earth?
What *is* His name, and what
is His Son's name,
If you know?

5 [a]Every word of God *is* pure;
[b]He *is* a shield to those who
put their trust in Him.
6 [a]Do not add to His words,
Lest He rebuke you, and
you be found a liar.

7 Two *things* I request of You
(Deprive me not before I die):
8 Remove falsehood and
lies far from me;
Give me neither poverty nor riches—
[a]Feed me with the food allotted to me;
9 [a]Lest I be full and deny *You*,
And say, "Who *is* the LORD?"
Or lest I be poor and steal,
And profane the name of my God.

10 Do not malign a servant to his master,
Lest he curse you, and you
be found guilty.

11 *There is* a generation *that*
curses its [a]father,
And does not bless its mother.
12 *There is* a generation [a]*that is*
pure in its own eyes,
Yet is not washed from its filthiness.
13 *There is* a generation—oh, how
[a]lofty are their eyes!
And their eyelids are lifted up.
14 [a]*There is* a generation whose
teeth *are like* swords,
And whose fangs *are like* knives,
[b]To devour the poor from off the earth,
And the needy from *among* men.

15 The leech has two daughters—
Give *and* Give!

There are three *things that*
are never satisfied,
Four never say, "Enough!":
16 [a]The grave,[1]
The barren womb,
The earth *that* is not satisfied
with water—
And the fire never says, "Enough!"

17 [a]The eye *that* mocks *his* father,
And scorns obedience to *his* mother,
The ravens of the valley will
pick it out,
And the young eagles will eat it.

18 There are three *things which*
are too wonderful for me,
Yes, four *which* I do not understand:
19 The way of an eagle in the air,
The way of a serpent on a rock,
The way of a ship in the
midst of the sea,
And the way of a man with a virgin.

20 This *is* the way of an
adulterous woman:
She eats and wipes her mouth,
And says, "I have done
no wickedness."

21 For three *things* the earth is perturbed,
Yes, for four it cannot bear up:
22 [a]For a servant when he reigns,
A fool when he is filled with food,

30:2 [a] Ps. 73:22; Prov. 12:1 **30:3** [a] [Prov. 9:10] **30:4** [a] [Ps. 68:18; John 3:13] [b] Job 38:4; Ps. 104:3; Is. 40:12 **30:5** [a] Ps. 12:6; 19:8; 119:140 [b] Ps. 18:30; 84:11; 115:9–11 **30:6** [a] Deut. 4:2; 12:32; Rev. 22:18 **30:8** [a] Job 23:12; Matt. 6:11; [Phil. 4:19] **30:9** [a] Deut. 8:12–14; Neh. 9:25, 26; Hos. 13:6 **30:11** [a] Ex. 21:17; Prov. 20:20 **30:12** [a] [Prov. 16:2]; Is. 65:5; Luke 18:11; [Titus 1:15, 16] **30:13** [a] Ps. 131:1; Prov. 6:17; Is. 2:11; 5:15 **30:14** [a] Job 29:17; Ps. 52:2 [b] Ps. 14:4; Amos 8:4 **30:16** [a] Prov. 27:20; Hab. 2:5 [1] Or *Sheol* **30:17** [a] Gen. 9:22; Lev. 20:9; Prov. 20:20 **30:22** [a] Prov. 19:10; Eccl. 10:7

23 A hateful *woman* when she
is married,
And a maidservant who
succeeds her mistress.

24 There are four *things which*
are little on the earth,
But they *are* exceedingly wise:
25 [a]The ants *are* a people not strong,
Yet they prepare their food
in the summer;
26 [a]The rock badgers[1] are a feeble folk,
Yet they make their homes
in the crags;
27 The locusts have no king,
Yet they all advance in ranks;
28 The spider[1] skillfully grasps
with its hands,
And it is in kings' palaces.

29 There are three *things which*
are majestic in pace,
Yes, four *which* are stately in walk:
30 A lion, *which is* mighty among beasts
And does not turn away from any;
31 A greyhound,[1]
A male goat also,
And a king *whose* troops
are with him.[2]

32 If you have been foolish in
exalting yourself,
Or if you have devised evil, [a]*put
your* hand on *your* mouth.
33 For *as* the churning of milk
produces butter,
And wringing the nose
produces blood,
So the forcing of wrath
produces strife.

The Words of King Lemuel's Mother

31 The words of King Lemuel, the utterance which his mother taught him:

2 What, my son?
And what, son of my womb?
And what, [a]son of my vows?
3 [a]Do not give your strength to women,
Nor your ways [b]to that which
destroys kings.

4 [a]*It is* not for kings, O Lemuel,
It is not for kings to drink wine,
Nor for princes intoxicating drink;
5 [a]Lest they drink and forget the law,
And pervert the justice of
all the afflicted.
6 [a]Give strong drink to him
who is perishing,
And wine to those who
are bitter of heart.
7 Let him drink and forget his poverty,
And remember his misery no more.

8 [a]Open your mouth for the speechless,
In the cause of all *who are*
appointed to die.[1]
9 Open your mouth, [a]judge righteously,
And [b]plead the cause of the
poor and needy.

The Virtuous Wife

10 [a]Who[1] can find a virtuous[2] wife?
For her worth *is* far above rubies.
11 The heart of her husband
safely trusts her;
So he will have no lack of gain.
12 She does him good and not evil
All the days of her life.
13 She seeks wool and flax,
And willingly works with her hands.
14 She is like the merchant ships,
She brings her food from afar.
15 [a]She also rises while it is yet night,
And [b]provides food for her household,
And a portion for her maidservants.
16 She considers a field and buys it;
From her profits she plants
a vineyard.
17 She girds herself with strength,
And strengthens her arms.
18 She perceives that her
merchandise *is* good,
And her lamp does not
go out by night.

30:25 [a] Prov. 6:6 30:26 [a] Lev. 11:5; Ps. 104:18 [1] Or *hyraxes* 30:28 [1] Or *lizard* 30:31 [1] Exact identity unknown [2] A Jewish tradition reads *a king against whom there is no uprising.* 30:32 [a] Job 21:5; 40:4; Mic. 7:16 31:2 [a] Is. 49:15 31:3 [a] Prov. 5:9 [b] Deut. 17:17; 1 Kin. 11:1; Neh. 13:26; Prov. 7:26; Hos. 4:11 31:4 [a] Eccl. 10:17 31:5 [a] Hos. 4:11 31:6 [a] Ps. 104:15 31:8 [a] Job 29:15, 16; Ps. 82 [1] Literally *sons of passing away* 31:9 [a] Lev. 19:15; Deut. 1:16 [b] Job 29:12; Is. 1:17; Jer. 22:16 31:10 [a] Ruth 3:11; Prov. 12:4; 19:14 [1] Verses 10 through 31 are an alphabetic acrostic in Hebrew (compare Psalm 119). [2] Literally *a wife of valor,* in the sense of all forms of excellence 31:15 [a] Prov. 20:13; Rom. 12:11 [b] Luke 12:42

RELEASE // ELEVATE HOW YOU SERVE OTHERS

Service with Your Scepter

Proverbs 31:8–9 // Open your mouth for the speechless, in the cause of all who are appointed to die. Open your mouth, judge righteously, and plead the cause of the poor and needy.

Summary Message // Social injustice, although perhaps new to the current generation, is not new to the civil rights movement in the United States. But still we ask the same questions: "What is to be done about injustice? Who are the agents of change? Where do we go from here?" According to the wisdom in this proverb, change is made when each person commits to bringing an end to the injustice around him or her in every way possible.

In these verses, King Lemuel shared the wisdom he learned from his mother of taking up the causes of others and advocating for those who have no voice. His mother had admonished him to use his voice for those who cannot speak or who are not heard when they speak. She told him to advocate for those who are powerless, to speak truth to power, and to ensure that justice is served for the poor and downtrodden.

Practical Application // It is interesting that the Book of Proverbs that is filled with a father's impartation of wisdom to his son concludes with wisdom from a mother. Some scholars believe that Lemuel was a nickname for King Solomon and the wisdom of Proverbs 31 is that of his mother, Bathsheba. If this was the case, this wisdom shows the true content of Bathsheba's character. She was a woman of great virtue.

Whoever provided the wisdom of this chapter, she knew that kings could use their power to either subjugate or advocate. This mother, though, was not willing to leave that choice to chance. She instructed her son how to use the power rightly that he would one day wield. According to her wisdom, true kingship was found in advocacy and caring for others. Real royalty on the earth is best expressed in what we do for others, not in what they do for us.

The parable of the good Samaritan teaches us that helping those in need should not be based on proximity or station. No matter what our position, it is our honor and calling to help those in need. The Jews and Samaritans were traditionally enemies, with the Jews maintaining the bulk of power and influence in that day. This Samaritan, however, flipped those roles and became the surety for a Jewish man's well-being and put oversight of the stranger's recovery on his schedule. The Samaritan's risk made him reputable, and his good deed made his "neighbor" whole. With justice at the root of our advocacy, making alliances with others not like us, we will boldly answer the call to elevate our service to our neighbors in need.

Fervent Prayer // Lord, we thank You for wisdom that teaches us how to be an ally. You have given us all things pertaining to life and godliness. Now, we pray that You would teach us how to use them in service to others. Father, forgive our selfishness that impedes true allyship and remind us that the greatest among us is servant of all. Father, strengthen our hands as we work to dismantle systems of subjugation, social ills, and prejudice. We trust You to elevate our voices as we speak up for those with no voice. We trust You to amplify our advocacy so that those whose voices are ignored are heard and those in need are helped. Our help comes from You, so we ask Your strength to help us help others. In Jesus' name we pray. Amen.

19 She stretches out her hands
to the distaff,
And her hand holds the spindle.
20 [a]She extends her hand to the poor,
Yes, she reaches out her
hands to the needy.
21 She is not afraid of snow
for her household,
For all her household *is*
clothed with scarlet.
22 She makes tapestry for herself;
Her clothing *is* fine linen
and purple.
23 [a]Her husband is known in the gates,
When he sits among the
elders of the land.

31:20 [a] Deut. 15:11; Job 31:16–20; Prov. 22:9; Rom. 12:13; Eph. 4:28; Heb. 13:16   31:23 [a] Prov. 12:4

24 She makes linen garments
and sells *them,*
And supplies sashes for
the merchants.
25 Strength and honor *are* her clothing;
She shall rejoice in time to come.
26 She opens her mouth with wisdom,
And on her tongue *is* the
law of kindness.
27 She watches over the ways
of her household,
And does not eat the bread of idleness.
28 Her children rise up and
call her blessed;
Her husband *also,* and he praises her:
29 "Many daughters have done well,
But you excel them all."
30 Charm *is* deceitful and
beauty *is* passing,
But a woman *who* fears the
LORD, she shall be praised.
31 Give her of the fruit of her hands,
And let her own works praise
her in the gates.

THE BOOK OF

ECCLESIASTES

OVERVIEW

The Book of Ecclesiastes, one of the wisdom books of the Bible, does not identify an author, but scholars attribute its writing to Solomon because specific passages portray a background similar to his. The writer describes himself as "the Preacher, the son of David, king in Jerusalem" (Eccl. 1:1) and as a man who has "gained more wisdom than all who were before me" (v. 16). Since both passages describe Solomon, he was the likely author and penned this book sometime around 931 BC.

Ecclesiastes is Solomon's reflection on his experiences of life and the rewards that came with them. When looking back over his life, he recognized that seeking pleasure is not as rewarding as it seems. He concluded with the idea that a person's ultimate responsibility in life is to "fear God and keep His commandments" (12:13).

Solomon gives readers a very human view of life. He begins Ecclesiastes with the warning that "all is vanity" (1:2). He recounts his quest for "wisdom concerning all that is done under heaven" (v. 13) and realizes that "in much wisdom is much grief, and he who increases knowledge increases sorrow" (v. 18). He further outlines the relationship between vanity, pleasure, and hard work (see 2:1–23).

Chapter 3 is one of the most popular chapters in Ecclesiastes. It opens with the statement "To everything there is a season, a time for every purpose under heaven" (v. 1). The chapter goes on to outline various times for opposite actions in life, like "a time to be born, and a time to die; a time to plant, and a time to pluck what is planted" (v. 2). Solomon continues to explain that all times of life are determined by God, and all are judged by Him (see vv. 10–22).

Chapters 4–11 continue to warn against various types of vanity. Oppression and political success are mentioned in chapter 4, false worship is mentioned in chapter 5, and riches are mentioned in chapters 5 and 6. Chapter 7 discusses wickedness, and chapters 8–11 describe a person's inability to understand God, the uncertainties of life, and aging. In closing, chapter 12 encourages God's people to serve Him throughout their lives, beginning in their youth (see v. 1).

The Book of Ecclesiastes recounts Solomon's journey through life—all that he witnessed and came to understand as a wise man. But with all his wisdom, he still had to search for the meaning of life. He ultimately concluded that a well-lived life is one lived in God's presence and one that does not focus on vain pursuits. Despite all that Solomon encountered, he recognized that God was ever present in every situation and the ruler of all things.

BREATHE IT IN

The Book of Ecclesiastes details Solomon's search for the meaning of life. As he reflected on his life, he realized that much of what he had witnessed and many things he had done were all pursuits of vanity. As he analyzed his life to that point, he came to recognize that God's presence is the most important aspect of a person's existence and that God's deeds are eternal and beyond the understanding of humans.

It is human nature to ask questions, though. As Christians, we often want to know when, why, where, how, and what. *When* will I receive the blessings that God has promised? *Why* is there so much trouble in the world? *Where* would God have me to go? *How* will I get through this difficult time? *What* is my purpose in life?

As we go through different stages in life, the answers to these questions may differ. The when, why, where, how and what often change according to the situation at hand. Do you ever struggle to find the answers to questions about life? Have you discovered the true meaning of life? Do you know and understand the plans God has for you in this season?

Even if it might be difficult to see at times, every life has a purpose. When our purpose eludes us, we might take jobs that are unrelated to what it is. We can forge relationships with people who do not support our purpose. We might earn degrees in fields that do not help us to advance our purpose. Ultimately, when we do not know our purpose, we can easily find our lives unfulfilling and lacking meaning.

Do you know what God has called you to do? Have you done like Solomon and taken time to reflect on your life thus far? Periodic reflection is good. You do not have to wait until you are older to look back on your journey. This is something you should do often. Check to see if you are in the right career, surrounded by the right people, and headed in the right direction. If you have not consulted God about what you should be doing, where you should be going, and with whom you should be doing all this, you may not be living your life on purpose. You may merely be existing.

Christians discover the true meaning of life only when they live in the presence of God. Everything else is vanity. Christians should not live focused on money and success. Instead, a child of God should focus on the One who makes provisions for all creation. We may have periods of abundance and periods of lack. We will have both positive and negative experiences. Know, though, that God is there in the midst of them all, guiding us. Embrace His wisdom and obey His instruction. There are blessings that come with submission and obedience.

Ecclesiastes reminds us that there is a season and a time for everything. Do you know what season you are in? Is it time for you to plant or harvest? Is it time to tear down or build? Is it time to be silent or speak? Whatever season you are in, take the time to go through the process. You cannot rush God. Everything will happen how and when He intends. Our job is simple: watch and wait! Reflect on your past and prepare for the future He has in store for you.

THE BOOK OF

ECCLESIASTES

The Vanity of Life

1 The words of the Preacher, the son of
David, [a]king in Jerusalem.

2 "Vanity[a][1] of vanities," says the Preacher;
"Vanity of vanities, [b]all *is* vanity."

3 [a]What profit has a man
from all his labor
In which he toils under the sun?
4 *One* generation passes away, and
another generation comes;
[a]But the earth abides forever.
5 [a]The sun also rises, and the
sun goes down,
And hastens to the place
where it arose.
6 [a]The wind goes toward the south,
And turns around to the north;
The wind whirls about continually,
And comes again on its circuit.
7 [a]All the rivers run into the sea,
Yet the sea *is* not full;
To the place from which
the rivers come,
There they return again.
8 All things *are* full of labor;
Man cannot express *it*.
[a]The eye is not satisfied with seeing,
Nor the ear filled with hearing.

9 [a]That which has been *is* what will be,
That which *is* done is what
will be done,
And *there is* nothing new
under the sun.
10 Is there anything of which
it may be said,
"See, this *is* new"?
It has already been in ancient
times before us.
11 *There is* [a]no remembrance
of former *things*,
Nor will there be any
remembrance of *things*
that are to come
By *those* who will come after.

The Grief of Wisdom

12 I, the Preacher, was king over Israel in
Jerusalem. 13 And I set my heart to seek and
[a]search out by wisdom concerning all that
is done under heaven; [b]this burdensome
task God has given to the sons of man, by
which they may be exercised. 14 I have seen
all the works that are done under the sun;
and indeed, all *is* vanity and grasping for
the wind.

15 [a]*What is* crooked cannot
be made straight,
And what is lacking cannot
be numbered.

16 I communed with my heart, saying,
"Look, I have attained greatness, and have
gained [a]more wisdom than all who were before me in Jerusalem. My heart has understood great wisdom and knowledge." 17 [a]And
I set my heart to know wisdom and to know
madness and folly. I perceived that this also
is grasping for the wind.

18 For [a]in much wisdom *is* much grief,
And he who increases knowledge
increases sorrow.

1:1 [a] Prov. 1:1 1:2 [a] Ps. 39:5, 6; 62:9; 144:4; Eccl. 12:8 [b] [Rom. 8:20, 21] [1] Or *Absurdity, Frustration, Futility, Nonsense;* and so throughout this book 1:3 [a] Eccl. 2:22; 3:9 1:4 [a] Ps. 104:5; 119:90 1:5 [a] Ps. 19:4–6 1:6 [a] Eccl. 11:5; John 3:8 1:7 [a] [Ps. 104:8, 9; Jer. 5:22] 1:8 [a] Prov. 27:20; Eccl. 4:8 1:9 [a] Eccl. 3:15 1:11 [a] Eccl. 2:16 1:13 [a] [Eccl. 7:25; 8:16, 17] [b] Gen. 3:19; Eccl. 3:10 1:15 [a] Eccl. 7:13 1:16 [a] 1 Kin. 3:12, 13; Eccl. 2:9 1:17 [a] Eccl. 2:3, 12; 7:23, 25; [1 Thess. 5:21] 1:18 [a] Eccl. 12:12

LIFE SUPPORT

BE PERSISTENT: CHASE AFTER GOD

I have seen all the works that are done under the sun; and indeed, all is vanity and grasping for the wind. Ecclesiastes 1:14

LIFE: Be Persistent

In Mark 8:36, we read, "For what will it profit a man if he gains the whole world, and loses his own soul?" Jesus teaches here that we can have everything we want or think we need, but if we do not have God, none of it matters. Furthermore, there is a saying: "Without God we are nothing. With God we are everything." When we have God, we do not lack anything. So, everything we do and everything we have on this earth is excess. We do not need it. It is fleeting. As Ecclesiastes 1:14 says, pursuing the things of this world is like "grasping for the wind." The things of the earth are here today and gone tomorrow; none of it is eternal.

Our lives should be driven by the eternal. We should be chasing after the heart of God every day. Persistence matters in the kingdom of God. Like food and water are crucial for our bodies, our spiritual existence is tied to our hunger and thirst for Him. God will honor our persistence with Him. We see this clearly in two parables. Luke 11:5–8 tells the story of a neighbor who honored his friend's multiple late-night requests for food to feed his guests. It was because of the friend's persistence that the man arose from his sleep to give him all he needed. We see the same theme in the parable of the persistent widow in Luke 18:1–8. The woman sought justice against her adversary and asked a judge to intervene. He refused at first but then gave her what she asked because of her often-repeated requests. Jesus told this story to His disciples to encourage them to continue in prayer and not lose heart.

God wants us to have an abundant life. But He does not want His blessings to become more important to us than He is.

SUPPORT: Chase After God

What a challenge! To chase after God, we must have the right perspective. Often, we have it wrong by wanting God to do all the work of chasing after us, answering our prayers the way we want them answered, and being there instantly when we call on Him with no responsibility on our part to live as He decrees. Remember that we must seek Him, too, and not half-heartedly. We need to go after God with vigor and zeal. We must realize that when we chase after God, we will find everything we need in Him.

Chasing after God is making sure He is the center of our lives. He should be a part of all we do, all we seek to achieve, and all that we aim to be. In the morning, He should be on our minds. In the noon day, He should be in our hearts. Through the evening, He should encompass our souls. We are busy; however, nothing should happen in a believer's life without us taking time to realize how our heavenly Father is in every situation we experience. Only by chasing after God do we genuinely invite Him to flow in us and through us and truly position ourselves to breathe.

SUPPORT EXAMPLE: Start a daily devotional Bible study.

The Vanity of Pleasure
(cf. 1 Kin. 4:20–28)

2 I said [a]in my heart, "Come now, I will test you with [b]mirth; therefore enjoy
pleasure"; but surely, [c]this also *was* vanity. 2I said of laughter—"Madness!"; and
of mirth, "What does it accomplish?" 3[a]I
searched in my heart *how* to gratify my

2:1 [a] Luke 12:19 [b] Prov. 14:13; [Eccl. 7:4; 8:15] [c] Eccl. 1:2 2:3 [a] Eccl. 1:17

flesh with wine, while guiding my heart
with wisdom, and how to lay hold on folly,
till I might see what *was* [b]good for the sons
of men to do under heaven all the days of
their lives.
4 I made my works great, I built myself
[a]houses, and planted myself vineyards.
5 I
made myself gardens and orchards, and
I planted all *kinds* of fruit trees in them.
6 I made myself water pools from which
to water the growing trees of the grove.
7 I
acquired male and female servants, and
had servants born in my house. Yes, I had
greater possessions of herds and flocks
than all who were in Jerusalem before me.
8 [a]I also gathered for myself silver and gold
and the special treasures of kings and of
the provinces. I acquired male and female
singers, the delights of the sons of men, *and*
musical instruments[1] of all kinds.
9 [a]So I became great and excelled [b]more
than all who were before me in Jerusalem.
Also my wisdom remained with me.

10 Whatever my eyes desired I
did not keep from them.
I did not withhold my heart
from any pleasure,
For my heart rejoiced in all my labor;
And [a]this was my reward
from all my labor.
11 Then I looked on all the works
that my hands had done
And on the labor in which I had toiled;
And indeed all *was* [a]vanity and
grasping for the wind.
There was no profit under the sun.

The End of the Wise and the Fool

12 Then I turned myself to consider
wisdom [a]and madness and folly;
For what *can* the man *do* who
succeeds the king?—
Only what he has already [b]done.
13 Then I saw that wisdom [a]excels folly
As light excels darkness.
14 [a]The wise man's eyes *are* in his head,
But the fool walks in darkness.
Yet I myself perceived
That [b]the same event
happens to them all.

15 So I said in my heart,
"As it happens to the fool,
It also happens to me,
And why was I then more wise?"
Then I said in my heart,
"This also *is* vanity."
16 For *there is* [a]no more remembrance of
the wise than of the fool forever,
Since all that now *is* will be
forgotten in the days to come.
And how does a wise *man* die?
As the fool!

17 Therefore I hated life because the work
that was done under the sun *was* distressing to me, for all *is* vanity and grasping for
the wind.
18 Then I hated all my labor in which I
had toiled under the sun, because [a]I must
leave it to the man who will come after me.
19 And who knows whether he will be wise or
a fool? Yet he will rule over all my labor in
which I toiled and in which I have shown
myself wise under the sun. This also *is* vanity.
20 Therefore I turned my heart and despaired of all the labor in which I had toiled
under the sun.
21 For there is a man whose
labor *is* with wisdom, knowledge, and skill;
yet he must leave his heritage to a man who
has not labored for it. This also *is* vanity and
a great evil.
22 [a]For what has man for all his
labor, and for the striving of his heart with
which he has toiled under the sun?
23 For all
his days *are* [a]sorrowful, and his work burdensome; even in the night his heart takes
no rest. This also is vanity.
24 [a]Nothing *is* better for a man *than* that
he should eat and drink, and *that* his soul
should enjoy good in his labor. This also,
I saw, was from the hand of God.
25 For
who can eat, or who can have enjoyment,
more than I?[1]
26 For *God* gives [a]wisdom and
knowledge and joy to a man who *is* good
in His sight; but to the sinner He gives the
work of gathering and collecting, that [b]he
may give to *him who is* good before God.

2:3 [b] [Eccl. 3:12, 13; 5:18; 6:12] **2:4** [a] 1 Kin. 7:1–12 **2:8** [a] 1 Kin. 9:28; 10:10, 14, 21 [1] Exact meaning unknown **2:9** [a] Eccl. 1:16 [b] 2 Chr. 9:22 **2:10** [a] Eccl. 3:22; 5:18; 9:9 **2:11** [a] Eccl. 1:3, 14 **2:12** [a] Eccl. 1:17; 7:25 [b] Eccl. 1:9 **2:13** [a] Eccl. 7:11, 14, 19; 9:18; 10:10 **2:14** [a] Prov. 17:24; Eccl. 8:1 [b] Ps. 49:10; Eccl. 9:2, 3, 11 **2:16** [a] Eccl. 1:11; 4:16 **2:18** [a] Ps. 49:10 **2:22** [a] Eccl. 1:3; 3:9 **2:23** [a] Job 5:7; 14:1 **2:24** [a] Eccl. 3:12, 13, 22; Is. 56:12; Luke 12:19; 1 Cor. 15:32; [1 Tim. 6:17] **2:25** [1] Following Masoretic Text, Targum, and Vulgate; some Hebrew manuscripts, Septuagint, and Syriac read *without Him.* **2:26** [a] Job 32:8; Prov. 2:6; James 1:5 [b] Job 27:16, 17; Prov. 28:8

This also *is* vanity and grasping for the wind.

Everything Has Its Time

3 To everything *there is* a season,
A [a]time for every purpose
under heaven:

2 A time to be born,
And [a]a time to die;
A time to plant,
And a time to pluck *what is* planted;
3 A time to kill,
And a time to heal;
A time to break down,
And a time to build up;
4 A time to [a]weep,
And a time to laugh;
A time to mourn,
And a time to dance;
5 A time to cast away stones,
And a time to gather stones;
[a]A time to embrace,
And a time to refrain
from embracing;
6 A time to gain,
And a time to lose;
A time to keep,
And a time to throw away;
7 A time to tear,
And a time to sew;
[a]A time to keep silence,
And a time to [b]speak;
8 A time to love,
And a time to [a]hate;
A time of war,
And a time of peace.

The God-Given Task

9[a]What profit has the worker from that
in which he labors? 10[a]I have seen the God-
given task with which the sons of men are
to be occupied. 11He has made everything
beautiful in its time. Also He has put eternity in their hearts, except that [a]no one can
find out the work that God does from beginning to end.
12I know that nothing *is* [a]better for them
than to rejoice, and to do good in their lives,
13and also that [a]every man should eat and
drink and enjoy the good of all his labor—it
is the gift of God.

14 I know that whatever God does,
It shall be forever.
[a]Nothing can be added to it,
And nothing taken from it.
God does *it,* that men should
fear before Him.
15 [a]That which is has already been,
And what is to be has already been;
And God requires an account
of what is past.

Injustice Seems to Prevail

16Moreover [a]I saw under the sun:

In the place of judgment,
Wickedness *was* there;
And *in* the place of righteousness,
Iniquity *was* there.

17I said in my heart,

[a]"God shall judge the righteous
and the wicked,
For *there is* a time there for every
purpose and for every work."

18I said in my heart, "Concerning the condition of the sons of men, God tests them,
that they may see that they themselves
are *like* animals." 19[a]For what happens to
the sons of men also happens to animals;
one thing befalls them: as one dies, so dies
the other. Surely, they all have one breath;
man has no advantage over animals, for
all *is* vanity. 20All go to one place: [a]all are
from the dust, and all return to dust. 21[a]Who
knows the spirit of the sons of men, which
goes upward, and the spirit of the animal,
which goes down to the earth?[1] 22[a]So I perceived that nothing *is* better than that a
man should rejoice in his own works, for
[b]that *is* his heritage. [c]For who can bring him
to see what will happen after him?

3:1 [a] Eccl. 3:17; 8:6 3:2 [a] Job 14:5; Heb. 9:27 3:4 [a] Rom. 12:15 3:5 [a] Joel 2:16; 1 Cor. 7:5 3:7 [a] Amos 5:13 [b] Prov. 25:11 3:8 [a] Prov. 13:5; Luke 14:26 3:9 [a] Eccl. 1:3 3:10 [a] Eccl. 1:13 3:11 [a] Job 5:9; Eccl. 7:23; 8:17; Rom. 11:33 3:12 [a] Eccl. 2:3, 24 3:13 [a] Eccl. 2:24 3:14 [a] James 1:17 3:15 [a] Eccl. 1:9 3:16 [a] Eccl. 5:8 3:17 [a] Gen. 18:25; Ps. 96:13; Eccl. 11:9; [Matt. 16:27; Rom. 2:6–10; 2 Cor. 5:10; 2 Thess. 1:6–9] 3:19 [a] Ps. 49:12, 20; 73:22; [Eccl. 2:16] 3:20 [a] Gen. 3:19; Ps. 103:14 3:21 [a] Eccl. 12:7 [1] Septuagint, Syriac, Targum, and Vulgate read *Who knows whether the spirit . . . goes upward, and whether . . . goes downward to the earth?* 3:22 [a] Eccl. 2:24; 5:18 [b] Eccl. 2:10 [c] Eccl. 6:12; 8:7

4 Then I returned and considered all the [a]oppression that is done under the sun:

And look! The tears of the oppressed,
But they have no comforter—
On the side of their oppressors
there is power,
But they have no comforter.
2 [a]Therefore I praised the dead
who were already dead,
More than the living who are still alive.
3 [a]Yet, better than both *is he*
who has never existed,
Who has not seen the evil work
that is done under the sun.

The Vanity of Selfish Toil

4Again, I saw that for all toil and every
skillful work a man is envied by his neighbor. This also *is* vanity and grasping for
the wind.

5 [a]The fool folds his hands
And consumes his own flesh.
6 [a]Better a handful *with* quietness
Than both hands full, *together with*
toil and grasping for the wind.

7Then I returned, and I saw vanity under the sun:

8 There is one alone, without
companion:
He has neither son nor brother.
Yet *there is* no end to all his labors,
Nor is his [a]eye satisfied with riches.
But [b]*he never asks,*
"For whom do I toil and deprive
myself of [c]good?"
This also *is* vanity and a
grave misfortune.

The Value of a Friend

9 Two *are* better than one,
Because they have a good
reward for their labor.
10 For if they fall, one will lift
up his companion.
But woe to him *who is* alone
when he falls,
For *he has* no one to help him up.
11 Again, if two lie down together,
they will keep warm;
But how can one be warm *alone?*
12 Though one may be overpowered by
another, two can withstand him.
And a threefold cord is not
quickly broken.

#OXYGEN

ECCLESIASTES 4:12

Elevate How You Serve Others

Living alone is tough. Everyone needs a friend—someone to lean on. You can be that friend for others. Be a giver.

Breathe and elevate how you serve others.

Popularity Passes Away

13 Better a poor and wise youth
Than an old and foolish king who
will be admonished no more.
14 For he comes out of prison to be king,
Although he was born poor
in his kingdom.
15 I saw all the living who
walk under the sun;
They were with the second youth
who stands in his place.
16 *There was* no end of all the people
over whom he was made king;
Yet those who come afterward
will not rejoice in him.
Surely this also *is* vanity and
grasping for the wind.

Fear God, Keep Your Vows

5 Walk [a]prudently when you go to the
house of God; and draw near to hear
rather [b]than to give the sacrifice of fools,
for they do not know that they do evil.

4:1 [a] Job 35:9; Ps. 12:5; Eccl. 3:16; 5:8; Is. 5:7 4:2 [a] Job 3:17, 18 4:3 [a] Job 3:11–22; Eccl. 6:3; Luke 23:29 4:5 [a] Prov. 6:10; 24:33 4:6 [a] Prov. 15:16, 17; 16:8 4:8 [a] Prov. 27:20; Eccl. 5:10; [1 John 2:16] [b] Ps. 39:6 [c] Eccl. 2:18–21 5:1 [a] Ex. 3:5; Is. 1:12 [b] [1 Sam. 15:22]; Ps. 50:8; Prov. 15:8; 21:27; [Hos. 6:6]

2 Do not be [a]rash with your mouth,
And let not your heart utter
anything hastily before God.
For God *is* in heaven, and
you on earth;
Therefore let your words [b]be few.
3 For a dream comes through
much activity,
And [a]a fool's voice *is known*
by *his* many words.

4 [a]When you make a vow to God,
do not delay to [b]pay it;
For *He has* no pleasure in fools.
Pay what you have vowed—
5 [a]Better not to vow than to
vow and not pay.

6Do not let your [a]mouth cause your flesh
to sin, [b]nor say before the messenger *of*
God that it *was* an error. Why should God
be angry at your excuse[1] and destroy the
work of your hands? 7For in the multitude
of dreams and many words *there is* also
vanity. But [a]fear God.

The Vanity of Gain and Honor

8If you [a]see the oppression of the poor, and the violent perversion of justice and righteousness in a province, do not marvel at the matter; for [b]high official watches over high official, and higher officials are over them.

9Moreover the profit of the land is for all; *even* the king is served from the field.

10 He who loves silver will not
be satisfied with silver;
Nor he who loves abundance,
with increase.
This also *is* vanity.

11 When goods increase,
They increase who eat them;
So what profit have the owners
Except to see *them* with their eyes?

12 The sleep of a laboring man *is* sweet,
Whether he eats little or much;
But the abundance of the rich
will not permit him to sleep.

13 [a]There is a severe evil *which* I
have seen under the sun:
Riches kept for their owner to his hurt.
14 But those riches perish
through misfortune;
When he begets a son, *there*
is nothing in his hand.
15 [a]As he came from his mother's
womb, naked shall he return,
To go as he came;
And he shall take nothing
from his labor
Which he may carry away in his hand.

16 And this also *is* a severe evil—
Just exactly as he came, so shall he go.
And [a]what profit has he [b]who
has labored for the wind?
17 All his days [a]he also eats in darkness,
And *he has* much sorrow and
sickness and anger.

18Here is what I have seen: [a]*It is* good
and fitting *for one* to eat and drink, and to
enjoy the good of all his labor in which he
toils under the sun all the days of his life
which God gives him; [b]for it *is* his heritage.
19As for [a]every man to whom God has given
riches and wealth, and given him power to
eat of it, to receive his heritage and rejoice
in his labor—this *is* the [b]gift of God. 20For
he will not dwell unduly on the days of his
life, because God keeps *him* busy with the
joy of his heart.

6 There[a] is an evil which I have seen under the sun, and it *is* common among
men: 2A man to whom God has given riches
and wealth and honor, [a]so that he lacks
nothing for himself of all he desires; [b]yet
God does not give him power to eat of it,
but a foreigner consumes it. This *is* vanity,
and it *is* an evil affliction.

3If a man begets a hundred *children* and
lives many years, so that the days of his
years are many, but his soul is not satisfied with goodness, or [a]indeed he has no

5:2 [a] Prov. 20:25 [b] Prov. 10:19; Matt. 6:7 5:3 [a] Prov. 10:19 5:4 [a] Num. 30:2; Deut. 23:21–23; Ps. 50:14; 76:11 [b] Ps. 66:13, 14 5:5 [a] Prov. 20:25; Acts 5:4 5:6 [a] Prov. 6:2 [b] 1 Cor. 11:10 [1] Literally *voice* 5:7 [a] [Eccl. 12:13] 5:8 [a] Eccl. 3:16 [b] [Ps. 12:5; 58:11; 82:1] 5:13 [a] Eccl. 6:1, 2 5:15 [a] Job 1:21; Ps. 49:17; 1 Tim. 6:7 5:16 [a] Eccl. 1:3 [b] Prov. 11:29 5:17 [a] Ps. 127:2 5:18 [a] Eccl. 2:24; 3:12, 13; [1 Tim. 6:17] [b] Eccl. 2:10; 3:22 5:19 [a] [Eccl. 6:2] [b] Eccl. 2:24; 3:13 6:1 [a] Eccl. 5:13 6:2 [a] Job 21:10; Ps. 17:14; 73:7 [b] Luke 12:20 6:3 [a] 2 Kin. 9:35; Is. 14:19, 20; Jer. 22:19

burial, I say *that* [b]a stillborn child *is* better
than he— 4for it comes in vanity and departs in darkness, and its name is covered
with darkness. 5Though it has not seen the
sun or known *anything,* this has more rest
than that man, 6even if he lives a thousand
years twice—but has not seen goodness.
Do not all go to one [a]place?

7 [a]All the labor of man *is* for
his mouth,
And yet the soul is not satisfied.
8 For what more has the wise
man than the fool?
What does the poor man have,
Who knows *how* to walk
before the living?
9 Better *is* the [a]sight of the eyes than
the wandering of desire.
This also *is* vanity and
grasping for the wind.

10 Whatever one is, he has been
named [a]already,
For it is known that he *is* man;
[b]And he cannot contend with Him
who is mightier than he.
11 Since there are many things
that increase vanity,
How *is* man the better?

12For who knows what *is* good for man
in life, all the days of his vain life which he
passes like [a]a shadow? [b]Who can tell a man
what will happen after him under the sun?

The Value of Practical Wisdom

7 A [a]good name *is* better than
precious ointment,
And the day of death than
the day of one's [b]birth;
2 Better to go to the house of mourning
Than to go to the house of feasting,
For that *is* the end of all men;
And the living will take *it* to [a]heart.
3 Sorrow *is* better than laughter,
[a]For by a sad countenance the
heart is made better.
4 The heart of the wise *is* in the
house of mourning,
But the heart of fools *is* in
the house of mirth.

5 [a]*It is* better to hear the
rebuke of the wise
Than for a man to hear
the song of fools.
6 [a]For like the crackling of
thorns under a pot,
So *is* the laughter of the fool.
This also is vanity.
7 Surely oppression destroys
a wise *man's* reason,
[a]And a bribe debases the heart.

8 The end of a thing *is* better
than its beginning;
[a]The patient in spirit *is* better
than the proud in spirit.
9 [a]Do not hasten in your
spirit to be angry,
For anger rests in the bosom
of fools.
10 Do not say,
"Why were the former days
better than these?"
For you do not inquire wisely
concerning this.

11 Wisdom *is* good with an inheritance,
And profitable [a]to those
who see the sun.
12 For wisdom *is* a [a]defense *as*
money *is* a defense,
But the excellence of knowledge
is that wisdom gives [b]life
to those who have it.

13 Consider the work of God;
For [a]who can make straight what
He has made crooked?
14 [a]In the day of prosperity be joyful,
But in the day of adversity consider:
Surely God has appointed the
one as well as the other,
So that man can find out nothing
that will come after him.

15I have seen everything in my days of
vanity:

6:3 [b] Job 3:16; Ps. 58:8; Eccl. 4:3 6:6 [a] Eccl. 2:14, 15 6:7 [a] Prov. 16:26 6:9 [a] Eccl. 11:9 6:10 [a] Eccl. 1:9; 3:15 [b] Job 9:32; Is. 45:9; Jer. 49:19 6:12 [a] Ps. 102:11; James 4:14 [b] Ps. 39:6; Eccl. 3:22 7:1 [a] Prov. 22:1 [b] Eccl. 4:2 7:2 [a] [Ps. 90:12] 7:3 [a] [2 Cor. 7:10] 7:5 [a] Ps. 141:5; [Prov. 13:18; 15:31, 32] 7:6 [a] Eccl. 2:2 7:7 [a] Ex. 23:8; Deut. 16:19; [Prov. 17:8, 23] 7:8 [a] Prov. 14:29; Gal. 5:22; Eph. 4:2 7:9 [a] Prov. 14:17; James 1:19 7:11 [a] Eccl. 11:7 7:12 [a] Eccl. 9:18 [b] Prov. 3:18 7:13 [a] Job 12:14 7:14 [a] Deut. 28:47

[a]There is a just *man* who perishes
in his righteousness,
And there is a wicked *man* who
prolongs *life* in his wickedness.

16 [a]Do not be overly righteous,
[b]Nor be overly wise:
Why should you destroy yourself?
17 Do not be overly wicked,
Nor be foolish:
[a]Why should you die before your time?
18 *It is* good that you grasp this,
And also not remove your
hand from the other;
For he who [a]fears God will
escape them all.

19 [a]Wisdom strengthens the wise
More than ten rulers of the city.

20 [a]For *there is* not a just man on
earth who does good
And does not sin.

21 Also do not take to heart
everything people say,
Lest you hear your servant
cursing you.
22 For many times, also, your
own heart has known
That even you have cursed others.

23 All this I have proved by wisdom.
[a]I said, "I will be wise";
But it *was* far from me.
24 [a]As for that which is far off
and [b]exceedingly deep,
Who can find it out?
25 [a]I applied my heart to know,
To search and seek out wisdom
and the reason *of things*,
To know the wickedness of folly,
Even of foolishness *and* madness.
26 [a]And I find more bitter than death
The woman whose heart
is snares and nets,
Whose hands *are* fetters.
He who pleases God shall
escape from her,
But the sinner shall be trapped
by her.

27 "Here is what I have found,"
says [a]the Preacher,
"*Adding* one thing to the other
to find out the reason,
28 Which my soul still seeks
but I cannot find:
[a]One man among a thousand
I have found,
But a woman among all these
I have not found.
29 Truly, this only I have found:
[a]That God made man upright,
But [b]they have sought out
many schemes."

8 Who *is* like a wise *man?*
And who knows the
interpretation of a thing?
[a]A man's wisdom makes his face shine,
And [b]the sternness of his
face is changed.

Obey Authorities for God's Sake

2 I *say,* "Keep the king's commandment
[a]for the sake of your oath to God. 3 [a]Do not
be hasty to go from his presence. Do not
take your stand for an evil thing, for he does
whatever pleases him."

4 Where the word of a king
is, there is power;
And [a]who may say to him,
"What are you doing?"
5 He who keeps his command will
experience nothing harmful;
And a wise man's heart discerns
both time and judgment,
6 Because [a]for every matter there
is a time and judgment,
Though the misery of man
increases greatly.
7 [a]For he does not know
what will happen;
So who can tell him when it will occur?
8 [a]No one has power over the
spirit to retain the spirit,

7:15 [a] Eccl. 8:12–14 7:16 [a] Prov. 25:16; Phil. 3:6 [b] Rom. 12:3 7:17 [a] Job 15:32; Ps. 55:23 7:18 [a] Eccl. 3:14; 5:7; 8:12, 13 7:19 [a] Prov. 21:22; Eccl. 9:13–18 7:20 [a] 1 Kin. 8:46; 2 Chr. 6:36; Prov. 20:9; Rom. 3:23; 1 John 1:8 7:23 [a] Rom. 1:22 7:24 [a] Job 28:12; 1 Tim. 6:16 [b] Rom. 11:33 7:25 [a] Eccl. 1:17 7:26 [a] Prov. 5:3, 4 7:27 [a] Eccl. 1:1, 2 7:28 [a] Job 33:23 7:29 [a] Gen. 1:27 [b] Gen. 3:6, 7 8:1 [a] Prov. 4:8, 9; Acts 6:15 [b] Deut. 28:50 8:2 [a] Ex. 22:11; 2 Sam. 21:7; 1 Chr. 29:24; Ezek. 17:18; [Rom. 13:5] 8:3 [a] Eccl. 10:4 8:4 [a] 1 Sam. 13:11, 13; Job 34:18 8:6 [a] Eccl. 3:1, 17 8:7 [a] Prov. 24:22; Eccl. 6:12 8:8 [a] Ps. 49:6, 7; Job 14:5

And no one has power in
the day of death.
There is [b]no release from that war,
And wickedness will not deliver
those who are given to it.

9 All this I have seen, and applied my
heart to every work that is done under the
sun: *There is* a time in which one man rules
over another to his own hurt.

Death Comes to All

10 Then I saw the wicked buried, who had
come and gone from the place of holiness,
and they were [a]forgotten[1] in the city where
they had so done. This also *is* vanity. 11 [a]Be-
cause the sentence against an evil work is
not executed speedily, therefore the heart
of the sons of men is fully set in them to
do evil. 12 [a]Though a sinner does evil a hundred *times,* and his *days* are prolonged, yet
I surely know that [b]it will be well with those
who fear God, who fear before Him. 13 But
it will not be well with the wicked; nor will
he prolong *his* days, *which are* as a shadow,
because he does not fear before God.

14 There is a vanity which occurs on earth,
that there are just *men* to whom it [a]happens
according to the work of the wicked; again,
there are wicked *men* to whom it happens
according to the work of the [b]righteous. I
said that this also *is* vanity.

15 [a]So I commended enjoyment, because
a man has nothing better under the sun
than to eat, drink, and be merry; for this will
remain with him in his labor *all* the days of
his life which God gives him under the sun.

16 When I applied my heart to know wisdom and to see the business that is done on
earth, even though one sees no sleep day
or night, 17 then I saw all the work of God,
that [a]a man cannot find out the work that
is done under the sun. For though a man
labors to discover *it,* yet he will not find *it;*
moreover, though a wise *man* attempts to
know *it,* he will not be able to find *it.*

9 For I considered all this in my heart,
so that I could declare it all: [a]that the
righteous and the wise and their works *are*
in the hand of God. People know neither
love nor hatred *by* anything *they see* before
them. 2 [a]All things *come* alike to all:

One event *happens* to the
righteous and the wicked;
To the good,[1] the clean,
and the unclean;
To him who sacrifices and him
who does not sacrifice.
As is the good, so *is* the sinner;
He who takes an oath as *he*
who fears an oath.

3 This *is* an evil in all that is done under the
sun: that one thing *happens* to all. Truly the
hearts of the sons of men are full of evil;
madness *is* in their hearts while they live, and
after that *they go* to the dead. 4 But for him
who is joined to all the living there is hope,
for a living dog is better than a dead lion.

5 For the living know that they will die;
But [a]the dead know nothing,
And they have no more reward,
For [b]the memory of them is forgotten.
6 Also their love, their hatred, and
their envy have now perished;
Nevermore will they have a share
In anything done under the sun.

7 Go, [a]eat your bread with joy,
And drink your wine with
a merry heart;
For God has already accepted
your works.
8 Let your garments always be white,
And let your head lack no oil.

9 Live joyfully with the wife whom you
love all the days of your vain life which He
has given you under the sun, all your days
of vanity; [a]for that *is* your portion in life,
and in the labor which you perform under the sun.

10 [a]Whatever your hand finds to do, do *it*
with your [b]might; for *there is* no work or device or knowledge or wisdom in the grave
where you are going.

8:8 [b] Deut. 20:5–8 8:10 [a] Eccl. 2:16; 9:5 [1] Some Hebrew manuscripts, Septuagint, and Vulgate read *praised.* 8:11 [a] Ps. 10:6; 50:21; Is. 26:10 8:12 [a] Is. 65:20; [Rom. 2:5–7] [b] [Deut. 4:40; Ps. 37:11, 18, 19; Prov. 1:32, 33; Is. 3:10; Matt. 25:34, 41] 8:14 [a] Ps. 73:14 [b] Eccl. 2:14; 7:15; 9:1–3 8:15 [a] Eccl. 2:24 8:17 [a] Job 5:9; Ps. 73:16; Eccl. 3:11; Rom. 11:33 9:1 [a] Deut. 33:3; Job 12:10; Eccl. 8:14 9:2 [a] Gen. 3:17–19; Job 21:7; Ps. 73:3, 12, 13; Mal. 3:15 [1] Septuagint, Syriac, and Vulgate read *good and bad.* 9:5 [a] Job 14:21; Is. 63:16 [b] Job 7:8–10; Eccl. 1:11; 2:16; 8:10; Is. 26:14 9:7 [a] Eccl. 8:15 9:9 [a] Eccl. 2:10 9:10 [a] [Col. 3:17] [b] Rom. 12:11; Col. 3:23

11I returned [a]and saw under the sun that—

The race *is* not to the swift,
Nor the battle to the strong,
Nor bread to the wise,
Nor riches to men of understanding,
Nor favor to men of skill;
But time and [b]chance
happen to them all.
12 For [a]man also does not know his time:
Like fish taken in a cruel net,
Like birds caught in a snare,
So the sons of men *are*
[b]snared in an evil time,
When it falls suddenly upon them.

Wisdom Superior to Folly

13This wisdom I have also seen under the
sun, and it *seemed* great to me: 14[a]*There was*
a little city with few men in it; and a great
king came against it, besieged it, and built
great snares[1] around it. 15Now there was
found in it a poor wise man, and he by his
wisdom delivered the city. Yet no one remembered that same poor man.
16Then I said:

"Wisdom *is* better than [a]strength.
Nevertheless [b]the poor man's
wisdom *is* despised,
And his words are not heard.
17 Words of the wise, *spoken*
quietly, *should be* heard
Rather than the shout of
a ruler of fools.
18 Wisdom *is* better than weapons
of war;
But [a]one sinner destroys much good."

10 Dead flies putrefy[1] the perfumer's
ointment,
And cause it to give off a foul odor;
So does a little folly to one respected
for wisdom *and* honor.
2 A wise man's heart *is* at his right hand,
But a fool's heart at his left.
3 Even when a fool walks along the way,
He lacks wisdom,
[a]And he shows everyone
that he *is* a fool.
4 If the spirit of the ruler
rises against you,
[a]Do not leave your post;
For [b]conciliation pacifies
great offenses.

5 There is an evil I have seen
under the sun,
As an error proceeding from
the ruler:
6 [a]Folly is set in great dignity,
While the rich sit in a lowly place.
7 I have seen servants [a]on horses,
While princes walk on the
ground like servants.

8 [a]He who digs a pit will fall into it,
And whoever breaks through a wall
will be bitten by a serpent.
9 He who quarries stones may
be hurt by them,
And he who splits wood may
be endangered by it.
10 If the ax is dull,
And one does not sharpen
the edge,
Then he must use more strength;
But wisdom brings success.

11 A serpent may bite [a]when
it is not charmed;
The babbler is no different.
12 [a]The words of a wise man's
mouth *are* gracious,
But [b]the lips of a fool shall
swallow him up;
13 The words of his mouth begin
with foolishness,
And the end of his talk *is*
raving madness.
14 [a]A fool also multiplies words.
No man knows what is to be;
Who can tell him [b]what
will be after him?
15 The labor of fools wearies them,
For they do not even know
how to go to the city!

9:11 [a] Jer. 9:23; Amos 2:14, 15 [b] 1 Sam. 6:9 9:12 [a] Eccl. 8:7 [b] Prov. 29:6; Luke 12:20, 39; 17:26; 1 Thess. 5:3 9:14 [a] 2 Sam. 20:16–22 [1] Septuagint, Syriac, and Vulgate read *bulwarks.* 9:16 [a] Eccl. 7:12, 19 [b] Mark 6:2, 3 9:18 [a] Josh. 7:1–26; 2 Kin. 21:2–17
10:1 [1] Targum and Vulgate omit *putrefy.* 10:3 [a] Prov. 13:16; 18:2 10:4 [a] Eccl. 8:3 [b] 1 Sam. 25:24–33; Prov. 25:15 10:6 [a] Esth. 3:1 10:7 [a] Prov. 19:10; 30:22 10:8 [a] Ps. 7:15; Prov. 26:27 10:11 [a] Ps. 58:4, 5; Jer. 8:17 10:12 [a] Prov. 10:32; Luke 4:22 [b] Prov. 10:14; Eccl. 4:5 10:14 [a] [Prov. 15:2]; Eccl. 5:3 [b] Eccl. 3:22; 8:7

16 [a]Woe to you, O land, when
your king *is* a child,
And your princes feast
in the morning!
17 Blessed *are* you, O land, when your
king *is* the son of nobles,
And your [a]princes feast at
the proper time—
For strength and not for drunkenness!
18 Because of laziness the
building decays,
And [a]through idleness of
hands the house leaks.
19 A feast is made for laughter,
And [a]wine makes merry;
But money answers everything.

20 [a]Do not curse the king, even
in your thought;
Do not curse the rich, even
in your bedroom;
For a bird of the air may
carry your voice,
And a bird in flight may
tell the matter.

The Value of Diligence

11 Cast your bread [a]upon the waters,
[b]For you will find it after many days.
2 [a]Give a serving [b]to seven,
and also to eight,
[c]For you do not know what evil
will be on the earth.

3 If the clouds are full of rain,
They empty *themselves*
upon the earth;
And if a tree falls to the
south or the north,
In the place where the tree
falls, there it shall lie.
4 He who observes the wind will not sow,
And he who regards the
clouds will not reap.

5 As [a]you do not know what *is*
the way of the wind,[1]
[b]*Or* how the bones *grow* in the
womb of her who is with child,
So you do not know the works of
God who makes everything.
6 In the morning sow your seed,
And in the evening do not
withhold your hand;
For you do not know which
will prosper,
Either this or that,
Or whether both alike *will be* good.

7 Truly the light is sweet,
And *it is* pleasant for the eyes
[a]to behold the sun;
8 But if a man lives many years
And [a]rejoices in them all,
Yet let him [b]remember the
days of darkness,
For they will be many.
All that is coming *is* vanity.

Seek God in Early Life

9 Rejoice, O young man, in your youth,
And let your heart cheer you in
the days of your youth;
[a]Walk in the ways of your heart,
And in the sight of your eyes;
But know that for all these
[b]God will bring you into judgment.
10 Therefore remove sorrow
from your heart,
And [a]put away evil from your flesh,
[b]For childhood and youth *are* vanity.

12 Remember[a] now your Creator
in the days of your youth,
Before the difficult days come,
And the years draw near
[b]when you say,
"I have no pleasure in them":
2 While the sun and the light,
The moon and the stars,
Are not darkened,
And the clouds do not
return after the rain;
3 In the day when the keepers
of the house tremble,
And the strong men bow down;
When the grinders cease
because they are few,

10:16 [a] Is. 3:4, 5; 5:11 10:17 [a] Prov. 31:4; Is. 5:11 10:18 [a] Prov. 24:30–34 10:19 [a] Judg. 9:13; Ps. 104:15; Eccl. 2:3 10:20 [a] Ex. 22:28; Acts 23:5 11:1 [a] Is. 32:20 [b] [Deut. 15:10; Prov. 19:17; Matt. 10:42; 2 Cor. 9:8; Gal. 6:9, 10; Heb. 6:10] 11:2 [a] Ps. 112:9; Matt. 5:42; Luke 6:30; [1 Tim. 6:18, 19] [b] Mic. 5:5 [c] Eph. 5:16 11:5 [a] John 3:8 [b] Ps. 139:14 [1] Or *spirit* 11:7 [a] Eccl. 7:11 11:8 [a] Eccl. 9:7 [b] Eccl. 12:1 11:9 [a] Num. 15:39; Job 31:7; Eccl. 2:10 [b] Eccl. 3:17; 12:14; [Rom. 14:10] 11:10 [a] 2 Cor. 7:1; 2 Tim. 2:22 [b] Ps. 39:5 12:1 [a] 2 Chr. 34:3; Prov. 22:6; Lam. 3:27 [b] 2 Sam. 19:35

And those that look through
the windows grow dim;
4 When the doors are shut in the streets,
And the sound of grinding is low;
When one rises up at the
sound of a bird,
And all [a]the daughters of
music are brought low.
5 Also they are afraid of height,
And of terrors in the way;
When the almond tree blossoms,
The grasshopper is a burden,
And desire fails.
For man goes to [a]his eternal home,
And [b]the mourners go
about the streets.

6 *Remember your Creator* before
the silver cord is loosed,[1]
Or the golden bowl is broken,
Or the pitcher shattered
at the fountain,
Or the wheel broken at the well.
7 [a]Then the dust will return to
the earth as it was,
[b]And the spirit will return
to God [c]who gave it.

8 "Vanity[a] of vanities," says the Preacher,
"All *is* vanity."

The Whole Duty of Man

9 And moreover, because the Preacher
was wise, he still taught the people knowledge; yes, he pondered and sought out
and [a]set in order many proverbs. 10 The
Preacher sought to find acceptable words;
and *what was* written *was* upright—words
of truth. 11 The words of the wise are like
goads, and the words of scholars[1] are like
well-driven nails, given by one Shepherd.
12 And further, my son, be admonished by
these. Of making many books *there is* no
end, and [a]much study *is* wearisome to the
flesh.
13 Let us hear the conclusion of the whole
matter:

[a]Fear God and keep His
commandments,
For this is man's all.
14 For [a]God will bring every
work into judgment,
Including every secret thing,
Whether good or evil.

12:4 [a] 2 Sam. 19:35 12:5 [a] Job 17:13 [b] Gen. 50:10; Jer. 9:17 12:6 [1] Following Qere and Targum; Kethib reads *removed;* Septuagint and Vulgate read *broken.* 12:7 [a] Gen. 3:19; Job 34:15; Ps. 90:3 [b] Eccl. 3:21 [c] Num. 16:22; 27:16; Job 34:14; Is. 57:16; Zech. 12:1 12:8 [a] Ps. 62:9 12:9 [a] 1 Kin. 4:32 12:11 [1] Literally *masters of the assemblies* 12:12 [a] Eccl. 1:18 12:13 [a] [Deut. 6:2; 10:12]; Mic. 6:8 12:14 [a] Eccl. 11:9; Matt. 12:36; [Acts 17:30, 31; Rom. 2:16; 1 Cor. 4:5; 2 Cor. 5:10]

THE

SONG OF SOLOMON

OVERVIEW

The Song of Solomon is a wedding song that describes the love between a groom and his bride. Written by Solomon during his forty-year reign between 971 and 931 BC, this wisdom book does not contain a direct reference to God.

The title of the book in Hebrew is *Shir Hashirim*, which literally translates as "song of songs." As one of the more than one thousand songs written by Solomon, this one is considered his greatest. This book is read on Jewish feast days, along with the Books of Ruth, Esther, Ecclesiastes, and Lamentations.

Song of Solomon highlights the love and devotion between a husband and wife who are committed to each other. It expresses deep and intense emotions, highlighting the joy and excitement that come with finding true love. Many scholars describe the book as being analogous to the relationship between God and the Israelites, as well as Christ's relationship with the church.

The book is a poem divided into five sections. It opens with Solomon identifying himself as the author (see 1:1). The first section is composed of the Shulamite woman's expressions of desire for love (vv. 2–6). She then speaks directly to her suitor, and they engage in a teasing exchange (see vv. 7–11). The couple speaks of their admiration of each other (see 1:12—2:7). He speaks of her beauty, saying, "Behold, you are fair, my love!" (1:15). She responds with, "Behold, you are handsome, my beloved!" (1:16). The first section closes with the Shulamite describing her journey to be with her beloved. Having found him, she "held him and would not let him go" (3:4).

Section 2 of the Song of Solomon describes the couple's wedding. The groom praises his bride's beauty (see 4:1–15). He reveals that she has "ravished" his heart (v. 9) and declares her love is better than wine (see v. 10). The groom toasts his marriage, encouraging everyone to eat and drink (see 5:1).

In section 3, the bride tells of a dream in which her husband came to her door. He departed because of her slow response to him, so she went to find him (see 5:2–8). In her frustration, she sought help from others and gave a detailed description of her beloved (see 5:9—6:3).

Section 4 is an exchange of mutual admiration between the bride and groom. The groom describes her as "awesome" (6:4) and "perfect" (v. 9). She invites him to "lodge in the villages" (7:11), where she will give him her love (see v. 12).

The final section of Song of Solomon reveals the depth of the couple's commitment. The bride reflects upon the deepness of their love (see 8:6–7), and the groom longs for more. In the closing verse, the Shulamite bride exclaims, "Make haste, my beloved" (v. 14).

Song of Solomon depicts a couple mutually devoted to and respectful of each other. A poetic dialogue, it includes comments by friends who support the couple's relationship. The book expresses a level of intimacy that demonstrates the joy experienced in a loving and committed relationship. Its inclusion in the Bible is evidence of the importance of romance and marriage in the sight of God.

BREATHE IT IN

Song of Solomon is a biblical love story. It takes the reader on a relationship journey with a couple from the courtship stage through marriage. Through their poetic exchanges, the couple demonstrates the intensity of their love and commitment to each other.

We all desire love. While no love is comparable to the love of God, it is our privilege and responsibility as Christians to emulate the unconditional love of God in all our relationships, especially in marriage.

With a rising number of people who have never been married and an increasing divorce rate, many believe that romance is dead and that a good mate is hard to find. This could not be further from the truth. Instead of buying into these myths, ask yourself what love really means to you.

Is your definition of love in agreement with God's definition of love? Do you seek the intimate love described in Song of Solomon or the shallow, physical infatuation depicted in books and movies? Is your heart open to receive love, or has it been hardened by your past? These are questions everyone should ponder as they reflect on the romantic relationships they may have had, have, or desire.

When considering what love really means, remember that God's love is unconditional and permanent, and physical love is often conditional and temporary. True love requires a decision to commit oneself to another. Only this type of love withstands the test of time. It remains even if feelings and beauty fade.

If we desire to find love and marry one day, we should think about our readiness to give love to a spouse. Are we willing to consider someone else's thoughts and feelings when making decisions? Do we have a forgiving heart, or do we hold on to grudges? Is our view of marriage fiction or reality? Can we give as well as receive? How well do we compromise? Will we make a commitment and refuse to give up?

For those of us who have found true love, our romantic journey can be ongoing. Romance is about selflessness. When we enter a romantic relationship, we must be willing to put our partner's needs before our own. If it becomes necessary, we must be willing to deny our own wants in preference to our spouse's and give so he or she might receive. We must be willing to forgive large offenses and small grievances often and completely, as God has forgiven us.

If your romantic journey has led you to marriage, you have made a lifetime commitment. Take your marital vows seriously. God expects us to treat our spouses with kindness, demonstrate our love with actions, and express our feelings verbally. When was the last time you took your spouse on a date or gave him or her an unexpected gift? How often do you say "I love you" or "thank you" for the kindness shown to you? Do you compliment your spouse and express your appreciation? If not, find inspiration to do so in Song of Solomon. Communicating your love for each other helps the relationship grow deeper and increases your intimacy.

Song of Solomon is an example of a healthy romantic relationship. Solomon and his bride longed for each other's presence. They complimented each other often and expressed their desire to be together. The foundation of their love was mutual respect and appreciation.

Likewise, successful marriages require deep levels of commitment and intimacy. Always be open to learning and growing in your relationship. Create a safe space for the two of you to share your innermost thoughts, feelings, and secrets. Find joy in doing and saying the things that make your spouse happy. Celebrate your love and thank God for placing that special person in your life and making one out of two.

THE

SONG OF SOLOMON

1 The [a]song of songs, which *is* Solomon's.

The Banquet

The Shulamite[1]

2 Let him kiss me with the
kisses of his mouth—
[a]For your[2] love *is* better than wine.
3 Because of the fragrance of
your good ointments,
Your name *is* ointment poured forth;
Therefore the virgins love you.
4 [a]Draw me away!

The Daughters of Jerusalem

[b]We will run after you.[1]

The Shulamite

The king [c]has brought me
into his chambers.

The Daughters of Jerusalem

We will be glad and rejoice in you.[2]

We will remember your[3]
love more than wine.

The Shulamite

Rightly do they love you.[4]

5 I *am* dark, but lovely,
O daughters of Jerusalem,
Like the tents of Kedar,
Like the curtains of Solomon.
6 Do not look upon me,
because I *am* dark,
Because the sun has tanned me.
My mother's sons were angry with me;
They made me the keeper
of the vineyards,
But my own [a]vineyard I have not kept.

(To Her Beloved)

7 Tell me, O you whom I love,
Where you feed *your flock,*
Where you make *it* rest at noon.
For why should I be as one
who veils herself[1]
By the flocks of your companions?

The Beloved

8 If you do not know, [a]O fairest
among women,
Follow in the footsteps of the flock,
And feed your little goats
Beside the shepherds' tents.
9 I have compared you, [a]my love,
[b]To my filly among Pharaoh's chariots.
10 [a]Your cheeks are lovely
with ornaments,
Your neck with chains *of gold.*

The Daughters of Jerusalem

11 We will make you[1] ornaments of gold
With studs of silver.

The Shulamite

12 While the king *is* at his table,
My spikenard sends forth
its fragrance.
13 A bundle of myrrh *is* my
beloved to me,
That lies all night between my breasts.

1:1 [a] 1 Kin. 4:32 1:2 [a] Song 4:10 [1] A young woman from the town of Shulam or Shunem (compare 6:13). The speaker and audience are identified according to the number, gender, and person of the Hebrew words. Occasionally the identity is not certain. [2] Masculine singular, that is, the Beloved 1:4 [a] Hos. 11:4; John 6:44; 12:32 [b] Phil. 3:12–14 [c] Ps. 45:14, 15; John 14:2; Eph. 2:6 [1] Masculine singular, that is, the Beloved [2] Feminine singular, that is, the Shulamite [3] Masculine singular, that is, the Beloved [4] Masculine singular, that is, the Beloved 1:6 [a] Song 8:11, 12 1:7 [1] Septuagint, Syriac, and Vulgate read *wanders.* 1:8 [a] Song 5:9 1:9 [a] Song 2:2, 10, 13; 4:1, 7; John 15:14 [b] 2 Chr. 1:16 1:10 [a] Ezek. 16:11 1:11 [1] Feminine singular, that is, the Shulamite

14 My beloved *is* to me a cluster
of henna *blooms*
In the vineyards of En Gedi.

The Beloved

15 [a]Behold, you *are* fair, my love!
Behold, you *are* fair!
You *have* dove's eyes.

The Shulamite

16 Behold, you *are* [a]handsome,
my beloved!
Yes, pleasant!
Also our bed *is* green.
17 The beams of our houses
are cedar,
And our rafters of fir.

2 I *am* the rose of Sharon,
And the lily of the valleys.

The Beloved

2 Like a lily among thorns,
So is my love among the daughters.

The Shulamite

3 Like an apple tree among the
trees of the woods,
So *is* my beloved among the sons.
I sat down in his shade
with great delight,
And [a]his fruit *was* sweet
to my taste.

The Shulamite to the Daughters of Jerusalem

4 He brought me to the
banqueting house,
And his banner over me *was* love.
5 Sustain me with cakes of raisins,
Refresh me with apples,
For I *am* lovesick.

6 [a]His left hand *is* under my head,
And his right hand embraces me.
7 [a]I charge you, O daughters
of Jerusalem,
By the gazelles or by the
does of the field,
Do not stir up nor awaken love
Until it pleases.

The Beloved's Request

The Shulamite

8 The voice of my beloved!
Behold, he comes
Leaping upon the mountains,
Skipping upon the hills.
9 [a]My beloved is like a gazelle
or a young stag.
Behold, he stands behind our wall;
He is looking through the windows,
Gazing through the lattice.

10 My beloved spoke, and said to me:
"Rise up, my love, my fair one,
And come away.
11 For lo, the winter is past,
The rain is over *and* gone.
12 The flowers appear on the earth;
The time of singing has come,
And the voice of the turtledove
Is heard in our land.
13 The fig tree puts forth her green figs,
And the vines *with* the tender grapes
Give a *good* smell.
Rise up, my love, my fair one,
And come away!

14 "O my [a]dove, in the clefts of the rock,
In the secret *places* of the cliff,
Let me see your face,
[b]Let me hear your voice;
For your voice *is* sweet,
And your face *is* lovely."

Her Brothers

15 Catch us [a]the foxes,
The little foxes that spoil the vines,
For our vines *have* tender grapes.

The Shulamite

16 [a]My beloved *is* mine, and I *am* his.
He feeds *his flock* among the lilies.

(To Her Beloved)

17 [a]Until the day breaks
And the shadows flee away,
Turn, my beloved,
And be [b]like a gazelle
Or a young stag
Upon the mountains of Bether.[1]

1:15 [a] Song 4:1; 5:12 1:16 [a] Song 5:10–16 2:3 [a] Song 4:16; Rev. 22:1, 2 2:6 [a] Song 8:3 2:7 [a] Song 3:5; 8:4 2:9 [a] Prov. 6:5; Song 2:17 2:14 [a] Song 5:2 [b] Song 8:13 2:15 [a] Ps. 80:13; Ezek. 13:4; Luke 13:32 2:16 [a] Song 6:3 2:17 [a] Song 4:6 [b] Song 8:14 [1] Literally *Separation*

A Troubled Night
The Shulamite

3 By [a]night on my bed I sought
the one I love;
I sought him, but I did not find him.
2 "I will rise now," *I said,*
"And go about the city;
In the streets and in the squares
I will seek the one I love."
I sought him, but I did not find him.
3 [a]The watchmen who go about
the city found me;
I said,
"Have you seen the one I love?"

4 Scarcely had I passed by them,
When I found the one I love.
I held him and would not let him go,
Until I had brought him to the
[a]house of my mother,
And into the chamber of her
who conceived me.

5 [a]I charge you, O daughters
of Jerusalem,
By the gazelles or by the
does of the field,
Do not stir up nor awaken love
Until it pleases.

The Coming of Solomon
The Shulamite

6 [a]Who *is* this coming out
of the wilderness
Like pillars of smoke,
Perfumed with myrrh and
frankincense,
With all the merchant's
fragrant powders?
7 Behold, it *is* Solomon's couch,
With sixty valiant men around it,
Of the valiant of Israel.
8 They all hold swords,
Being expert in war.
Every man *has* his sword on his thigh
Because of fear in the night.

9 Of the wood of Lebanon
Solomon the King
Made himself a palanquin:[1]
10 He made its pillars *of* silver,
Its support *of* gold,
Its seat *of* purple,
Its interior paved *with* love
By the daughters of Jerusalem.
11 Go forth, O daughters of Zion,
And see King Solomon
with the crown
With which his mother crowned him
On the day of his wedding,
The day of the gladness of his heart.

The Bridegroom Praises the Bride
The Beloved

4 Behold, [a]you *are* fair, my love!
Behold, you *are* fair!
You *have* dove's eyes behind your veil.
Your hair *is* like a [b]flock of goats,
Going down from Mount Gilead.
2 [a]Your teeth *are* like a flock
of shorn *sheep*
Which have come up from
the washing,
Every one of which bears twins,
And none *is* barren among them.
3 Your lips *are* like a strand of scarlet,
And your mouth is lovely.
[a]Your temples behind your veil
Are like a piece of pomegranate.
4 [a]Your neck *is* like the tower of David,
Built [b]for an armory,
On which hang a thousand bucklers,
All shields of mighty men.
5 [a]Your two breasts *are* like two fawns,
Twins of a gazelle,
Which feed among the lilies.

6 [a]Until the day breaks
And the shadows flee away,
I will go my way to the
mountain of myrrh
And to the hill of frankincense.

7 [a]You *are* all fair, my love,
And *there is* no spot in you.
8 Come with me from
Lebanon, *my* spouse,
With me from Lebanon.
Look from the top of Amana,
From the top of Senir [a]and Hermon,

3:1 [a] Is. 26:9 3:3 [a] Song 5:7; Is. 21:6–8, 11, 12 3:4 [a] Song 8:2 3:5 [a] Song 2:7; 8:4 3:6 [a] Song 8:5 3:9 [1] A portable enclosed chair
4:1 [a] Song 1:15; 5:12 [b] Song 6:5 4:2 [a] Song 6:6 4:3 [a] Song 6:7 4:4 [a] Song 7:4 [b] Neh. 3:19 4:5 [a] Prov. 5:19; Song 7:3
4:6 [a] Song 2:17 4:7 [a] Song 1:15; Eph. 5:27 4:8 [a] Deut. 3:9; 1 Chr. 5:23; Ezek. 27:5

From the lions' dens,
From the mountains of the leopards.

9 You have ravished my heart,
My sister, *my* spouse;
You have ravished my heart
With one *look* of your eyes,
With one link of your necklace.
10 How fair is your love,
My sister, *my* spouse!
[a]How much better than
wine is your love,
And the scent of your perfumes
Than all spices!
11 Your lips, O *my* spouse,
Drip as the honeycomb;
[a]Honey and milk *are* under
your tongue;
And the fragrance of your garments
Is [b]like the fragrance of Lebanon.

12 A garden enclosed
Is my sister, *my* spouse,
A spring shut up,
A fountain sealed.
13 Your plants *are* an orchard
of pomegranates
With pleasant fruits,
Fragrant henna with spikenard,
14 Spikenard and saffron,
Calamus and cinnamon,
With all trees of frankincense,
Myrrh and aloes,
With all the chief spices—
15 A fountain of gardens,
A well of [a]living waters,
And streams from Lebanon.

The Shulamite

16 Awake, O north *wind,*
And come, O south!
Blow upon my garden,
That its spices may flow out.
[a]Let my beloved come
to his garden
And eat its pleasant [b]fruits.

SONG OF SOLOMON 4:7

I AM THE SHULAMITE WOMAN

You are all fair, my love, and there is no spot in you. Song of Solomon 4:7

I am the Shulamite woman whom Solomon loved. For me, Solomon wrote not just a song but the greatest of songs. His words are about the mysteries of intimate love. They reveal how pure and sacred love between a man and woman can be. The message is clear: marriage is a wonderful gift, not meant to be entered into casually.

The Song of Solomon tells the story of me, a poor girl from Kedar, when I was working in the vineyards with my brothers. King Solomon passed by, and my beauty stood out to him. He described me as a "lily among thorns." There was a sensuous element about our first attraction; however, we did not allow that to awaken. Such things had to wait until the day when a marriage covenant was forged between us. Our courtship was a delicate one, committed to growing our love like one grows a garden.

When our love grew to full bloom, we committed to marriage, entering into that God-ordained covenant. We never held back in our praises of one another. We continued to speak freely of our love, and we were confident in each other. There is great power in our love.

†

A marriage covenant is sacred and personal. No one besides God should be allowed to enter in or intrude into it. Never break the covenant with your spouse by sharing with others what you have been entrusted with in your marriage.

4:10 [a] Song 1:2, 4 4:11 [a] Prov. 24:13, 14; Song 5:1 [b] Gen. 27:27; Hos. 14:6, 7
4:15 [a] Zech. 14:8; John 4:10; 7:38 4:16 [a] Song 5:1 [b] Song 7:13

The Beloved

5 I [a]have come to my garden, my
[b]sister, *my* spouse;
I have gathered my myrrh
with my spice;
[c]I have eaten my honeycomb
with my honey;
I have drunk my wine with my milk.

(To His Friends)
Eat, O [d]friends!
Drink, yes, drink deeply,
O beloved ones!

The Shulamite's Troubled Evening

The Shulamite

2 I sleep, but my heart is awake;
It is the voice of my beloved!
[a]He knocks, *saying,*
"Open for me, my sister, my love,
My dove, my perfect one;
For my head is covered with dew,
My locks with the drops of the night."

3 I have taken off my robe;
How can I put it on *again?*
I have washed my feet;
How can I defile them?
4 My beloved put his hand
By the latch *of the door,*
And my heart yearned for him.
5 I arose to open for my beloved,
And my hands dripped *with* myrrh,
My fingers with liquid myrrh,
On the handles of the lock.

6 I opened for my beloved,
But my beloved had turned
away *and* was gone.
My heart leaped up when he spoke.
[a]I sought him, but I could
not find him;
I called him, but he gave
me no answer.
7 [a]The watchmen who went about
the city found me.
They struck me, they wounded me;
The keepers of the walls
Took my veil away from me.
8 I charge you, O daughters
of Jerusalem,
If you find my beloved,
That you tell him I *am* lovesick!

The Daughters of Jerusalem

9 What *is* your beloved
More than *another* beloved,
[a]O fairest among women?
What *is* your beloved
More than *another* beloved,
That you so charge us?

The Shulamite

10 My beloved *is* white and ruddy,
Chief among ten thousand.
11 His head *is like* the finest gold;
His locks *are* wavy,
And black as a raven.
12 [a]His eyes *are* like doves
By the rivers of waters,
Washed with milk,
And fitly set.
13 His cheeks *are* like a bed of spices,
Banks of scented herbs.
His lips *are* lilies,
Dripping liquid myrrh.

14 His hands *are* rods of gold
Set with beryl.
His body *is* carved ivory
Inlaid *with* sapphires.
15 His legs *are* pillars of marble
Set on bases of fine gold.
His countenance *is* like Lebanon,
Excellent as the cedars.
16 His mouth *is* most sweet,
Yes, he *is* altogether lovely.
This *is* my beloved,
And this *is* my friend,
O daughters of Jerusalem!

The Daughters of Jerusalem

6 Where has your beloved gone,
[a]O fairest among women?
Where has your beloved turned aside,
That we may seek him with you?

The Shulamite

2 My beloved has gone to his [a]garden,
To the beds of spices,
To feed *his flock* in the gardens,
And to gather lilies.

5:1 [a] Song 4:16 [b] Song 4:9 [c] Song 4:11 [d] Luke 15:7, 10; John 3:29 5:2 [a] Rev. 3:20 5:6 [a] Song 3:1 5:7 [a] Song 3:3 5:9 [a] Song 1:8; 6:1 5:12 [a] Song 1:15; 4:1 6:1 [a] Song 1:8; 5:9 6:2 [a] Song 4:16; 5:1

3 [a]I *am* my beloved's,
And my beloved *is* mine.
He feeds *his flock* among the lilies.

Praise of the Shulamite's Beauty

The Beloved

4 O my love, you *are as*
beautiful as Tirzah,
Lovely as Jerusalem,
Awesome as *an army* with banners!
5 Turn your eyes away from me,
For they have overcome me.
Your hair *is* [a]like a flock of goats
Going down from Gilead.
6 [a]Your teeth *are* like a flock
of sheep
Which have come up from
the washing;
Every one bears twins,
And none *is* barren among them.
7 [a]Like a piece of pomegranate
Are your temples behind
your veil.

8 There are sixty queens
And eighty concubines,
And [a]virgins without number.
9 My dove, my [a]perfect one,
Is the only one,
The only one of her mother,
The favorite of the one
who bore her.
The daughters saw her
And called her blessed,
The queens and the concubines,
And they praised her.

10 Who is she who looks forth
as the morning,
Fair as the moon,
Clear as the sun,
[a]Awesome as *an army* with
banners?

The Shulamite

11 I went down to the garden of nuts
To see the verdure of the valley,
[a]To see whether the vine had budded
And the pomegranates had
bloomed.
12 Before I was even aware,
My soul had made me
As the chariots of my noble people.[1]

The Beloved and His Friends

13 Return, return, O Shulamite;
Return, return, that we may
look upon you!

The Shulamite

What would you see in
the Shulamite—
As it were, the dance of
the two camps?[1]

Expressions of Praise

The Beloved

7 How beautiful are your feet
in sandals,
[a]O prince's daughter!
The curves of your thighs
are like jewels,
The work of the hands of a
skillful workman.
2 Your navel *is* a rounded goblet;
It lacks no blended beverage.
Your waist *is* a heap of wheat
Set about with lilies.
3 [a]Your two breasts *are* like two fawns,
Twins of a gazelle.
4 [a]Your neck *is* like an ivory tower,
Your eyes *like* the pools in Heshbon
By the gate of Bath Rabbim.
Your nose *is* like the tower
of Lebanon
Which looks toward Damascus.
5 Your head *crowns* you like
Mount Carmel,
And the hair of your head
is like purple;
A king *is* held captive by
your tresses.

6 How fair and how pleasant you are,
O love, with your delights!
7 This stature of yours is
like a palm tree,
And your breasts *like* its clusters.
8 I said, "I will go up to the palm tree,
I will take hold of its branches."

6:3 [a] Song 2:16; 7:10 6:5 [a] Song 4:1 6:6 [a] Song 4:2 6:7 [a] Song 4:3 6:8 [a] Song 1:3 6:9 [a] Song 2:14; 5:2 6:10 [a] Song 6:4 6:11 [a] Song 7:12 6:12 [1] Hebrew *Ammi Nadib* 6:13 [1] Hebrew *Mahanaim* 7:1 [a] Ps. 45:13 7:3 [a] Song 4:5 7:4 [a] Song 4:4

Let now your breasts be like
clusters of the vine,
The fragrance of your
breath like apples,
9 And the roof of your mouth
like the best wine.

The Shulamite
The wine goes *down* smoothly
for my beloved,
Moving gently the lips
of sleepers.[1]
10 [a]I *am* my beloved's,
And [b]his desire *is* toward me.

11 Come, my beloved,
Let us go forth to the field;
Let us lodge in the villages.
12 Let us get up early to the
vineyards;
Let us [a]see if the vine has budded,
Whether the grape blossoms
are open,
And the pomegranates are
in bloom.
There I will give you my love.
13 The [a]mandrakes give off
a fragrance,
And at our gates [b]*are* pleasant
fruits,
All manner, new and old,
Which I have laid up for
you, my beloved.

8 Oh, that you were like my brother,
Who nursed at my mother's
breasts!
If I should find you outside,
I would kiss you;
I would not be despised.
2 I would lead you *and* bring you
Into the [a]house of my mother,
She *who* used to instruct me.
I would cause you to drink
of [b]spiced wine,
Of the juice of my pomegranate.

(To the Daughters of Jerusalem)
3 [a]His left hand *is* under my head,
And his right hand embraces me.
4 [a]I charge you, O daughters
of Jerusalem,
Do not stir up nor awaken love
Until it pleases.

Love Renewed in Lebanon
A Relative
5 [a]Who *is* this coming up from
the wilderness,
Leaning upon her beloved?

I awakened you under the
apple tree.
There your mother brought
you forth;
There she *who* bore you
brought *you* forth.

The Shulamite to Her Beloved
6 [a]Set me as a seal upon your heart,
As a seal upon your arm;
For love *is as* strong as death,
[b]Jealousy *as* cruel as the grave;[1]
Its flames *are* flames of fire,
A most vehement flame.[2]

7 Many waters cannot quench love,
Nor can the floods drown it.
[a]If a man would give for love
All the wealth of his house,
It would be utterly despised.

The Shulamite's Brothers
8 [a]We have a little sister,
And she has no breasts.
What shall we do for our sister
In the day when she is
spoken for?
9 If she *is* a wall,
We will build upon her
A battlement of silver;
And if she *is* a door,
We will enclose her
With boards of cedar.

The Shulamite
10 I *am* a wall,
And my breasts like towers;
Then I became in his eyes
As one who found peace.

7:9 [1] Septuagint, Syriac, and Vulgate read *lips and teeth.* 7:10 [a] Song 2:16; 6:3 [b] Ps. 45:11 7:12 [a] Song 6:11 7:13 [a] Gen. 30:14 [b] Song 2:3; 4:13, 16; Matt. 13:52 8:2 [a] Song 3:4 [b] Prov. 9:2 8:3 [a] Song 2:6 8:4 [a] Song 2:7; 3:5 8:5 [a] Song 3:6 8:6 [a] Is. 49:16; Jer. 22:24; Hag. 2:23 [b] Prov. 6:34, 35 [1] Or *Sheol* [2] Literally *A flame of YAH* (a poetic form of *YHWH, the* LORD) 8:7 [a] Prov. 6:35 8:8 [a] Ezek. 23:33

11 Solomon had a vineyard
at Baal Hamon;
[a]He leased the vineyard to keepers;
Everyone was to bring for its fruit
A thousand silver *coins*.

(To Solomon)
12 My own vineyard *is* before me.
You, O Solomon, *may have* a thousand,
And those who tend its
fruit two hundred.

The Beloved
13 You who dwell in the gardens,
The companions listen
for your voice—
[a]Let me hear it!

The Shulamite
14 [a]Make haste, my beloved,
And [b]be like a gazelle
Or a young stag
On the mountains of spices.

8:11 [a] Matt. 21:33 8:13 [a] Song 2:14 8:14 [a] Rev. 22:17, 20 [b] Song 2:7, 9, 17

THE BOOK OF

ISAIAH

OVERVIEW

The Book of Isaiah, written sometime around 700–690 BC, bears the name of its author, the prophet Isaiah. The Hebrew translation of the name Isaiah means "Yahweh saves." This is the message that Isaiah preached to the southern kingdom of Judah.

Isaiah was the son of Amoz (Is. 1:1). He was married to "the prophetess" who was the mother of his two sons (8:3; see 7:3). When God spoke to Isaiah concerning His need to send someone to His people, Isaiah responded: "Here am I! Send me" (6:8).

Isaiah delivered God's prophetic message to the people of Judah and acted as an advisor to four kings: Uzziah, Jotham, Ahaz, and Hezekiah. During the time of Isaiah's ministry, God's people had turned away from Him. They allowed pagan worship within their nation while making token, hypocritical sacrifices to God. They also treated their neighbors unfairly. God chose Isaiah to call on the people to turn back to Him. The messages Isaiah delivered concerned judgment, salvation, and the coming of the Messiah.

The Book of Isaiah can be divided into three sections. In the first section, chapters 1–39, the prophet urges the people of Judah to turn away from their sinful ways and to worship the one true God. He warns of the judgment that would be brought upon Israel and other nations because of their sins (chs. 13–23). God's final judgment on the world is described in chapters 24–34. Restoration is promised to the Israelites in chapter 35. Isaiah prophesies that "they shall obtain joy and gladness, and sorrow and sighing shall flee away" (35:10). In chapters 36–39, the Israelites are directed to choose whom they will trust.

Section 2 (chs. 40–55) outlines God's promises to the Israelites while they were in Babylonian exile. Isaiah's messages assured God's people that He had not forgotten them. The section opens with the words "'Comfort, yes, comfort My people!' says your God" (40:1). God promised that He would "do a new thing" (43:19) and give the Israelites joy and peace (see 55:12).

Section 3 encompasses chapters 56–66. These chapters foreshadow Israel's return to Jerusalem. Isaiah describes God's plan for salvation and His judgment of the enemies of the Israelites.

Throughout the Book of Isaiah, the prophet speaks clearly and with assurance of the coming of the Messiah, Jesus Christ. In chapter 40, Jesus' coming is foretold (see vv. 3–5), and in 7:14 His virgin birth as a sign from God is declared. Jesus' sacrificial death is prophesied in 52:13—53:12, and His proclamation of the Good News appears in chapter 61. The Book of Isaiah is the Old Testament book that most clearly communicates such significant information about the Messiah and His sacrifice for the world.

The Book of Isaiah also contains God's judgments against the people who have turned their backs on Him. The text demonstrates that those who continually rebel against God will receive judgment. It also reinforces God's willingness to redeem His people and bless those who are obedient. The overall message is that only God can grant salvation; this He promised through His Son, Jesus.

BREATHE IT IN

The prophet Isaiah declared God's judgment upon His people for their sins. Two of those sins were treating people unjustly and offering hypocritical sacrifices to Him. God's judgment against these sins indicates His desire for Christians to treat others fairly and to offer pure sacrifices to Him.

Christians are often eager to please God in the early days after salvation. We spend much of our time communing with God by studying the Word, praying, and worshiping. We are excited about our new relationship and want to learn as much as we can about God. We want to please Him with our words and our deeds, so we go out of our way to show God and those around us the change that has taken place in our lives. We begin to act better, to treat others better, and to live better.

Unfortunately, after a while, the excitement of salvation can wear off and we can simply go through the motions. We go to church on Sundays, we tithe, we read the Bible, and we pray. But we do these things out of habit instead of hunger for God. When our walk with God becomes merely a routine, our determination to keep our eyes on Him, treat others better, and live better can begin to diminish. As a result, our eyes may stray to other "gods," and we end up slipping into our old behaviors. When this happens, our relationship with God becomes distant and strained.

God wants our relationship with Him to be intimate. He wants our sacrifices to Him to be pure, not robotic. God desires that we spend time with Him because we want a relationship with Him. He desires that we tithe with an open heart because we recognize that He is our source of everything. He desires that we treat others fairly and with respect because of the love in our hearts for Him. God wants us to do the right thing because it is what He has taught us to do.

Do you see anything in your life that signals an impurity in your sacrifices to God? Do you complain about tithing or dread going to church? Have you reduced the amount of time you spend praying and studying the Bible? Do you still worship God and thank Him for the many blessings in your life? Have your eyes strayed back toward the world and its ways?

What about your treatment of others? Is it fair? How do you interact with family, colleagues, and even strangers? Are you unkind? Disdainful? Are you mean or selfish? Do you act as if others are beneath you?

Isaiah's message is a call for Christians who have strayed like Israel to return to purity in our love for God and people. It is not too late to refocus our lives and rediscover the zeal we had when we first believed. God is our redeemer. When we make our desires known to Him, commit ourselves to spending more time nurturing our relationship with Him, and rediscover walking in right relationship with Him, the love of God will flow from our hearts, and we will treat those around us with kindness and fairness.

THE BOOK OF

ISAIAH

1 The [a]vision of Isaiah the son of Amoz, which he saw concerning Judah and Jerusalem in the [b]days of Uzziah, Jotham, Ahaz, *and* Hezekiah, kings of Judah.

The Wickedness of Judah

2 [a]Hear, O heavens, and give ear,
O earth!
For the LORD has spoken:
"I have nourished and
brought up children,
And they have rebelled against Me;
3 [a]The ox knows its owner
And the donkey its master's crib;
But Israel [b]does not know,
My people do not consider."

4 Alas, sinful nation,
A people laden with iniquity,
[a]A brood of evildoers,
Children who are corrupters!
They have forsaken the LORD,
They have provoked to anger
The Holy One of Israel,
They have turned away backward.

5 [a]Why should you be stricken again?
You will revolt more and more.
The whole head is sick,
And the whole heart faints.
6 From the sole of the foot
even to the head,
There is no soundness in it,
But wounds and bruises and
putrefying sores;
They have not been closed
or bound up,
Or soothed with ointment.

7 [a]Your country *is* desolate,
Your cities *are* burned with fire;
Strangers devour your land
in your presence;
And *it is* desolate, as overthrown
by strangers.
8 So the daughter of Zion is left
[a]as a booth in a vineyard,
As a hut in a garden of cucumbers,
[b]As a besieged city.
9 [a]Unless the LORD of hosts
Had left to us a very small remnant,
We would have become like [b]Sodom,
We would have been made
like Gomorrah.

10 Hear the word of the LORD,
You rulers [a]of Sodom;
Give ear to the law of our God,
You people of Gomorrah:
11 "To what purpose *is* the multitude
of your [a]sacrifices to Me?"
Says the LORD.
"I have had enough of burnt
offerings of rams
And the fat of fed cattle.
I do not delight in the blood of bulls,
Or of lambs or goats.

12 "When you come [a]to appear
before Me,
Who has required this
from your hand,
To trample My courts?
13 Bring no more [a]futile sacrifices;
Incense is an abomination to Me.
The New Moons, the Sabbaths, and
[b]the calling of assemblies—

1:1 [a] Num. 12:6 [b] 2 Chr. 26—32 1:2 [a] Jer. 2:12 1:3 [a] Jer. 8:7 [b] Jer. 9:3, 6 1:4 [a] Is. 57:3, 4; Matt. 3:7 1:5 [a] Jer. 5:3 1:7 [a] Deut. 28:51, 52; 2 Chr. 36:19 1:8 [a] Job 27:18 [b] Jer. 4:17 1:9 [a] 2 Kin. 25:11, 22; Lam. 3:22 [b] Gen. 19:24; Rom. 9:29 1:10 [a] Deut. 32:32 1:11 [a] [1 Sam. 15:22] 1:12 [a] Ex. 23:17 1:13 [a] Matt. 15:9 [b] Joel 1:14

I cannot endure iniquity and
the sacred meeting.
14 Your [a]New Moons and your
[b]appointed feasts
My soul hates;
They are a trouble to Me,
I am weary of bearing *them.*
15 [a]When you spread out your hands,
I will hide My eyes from you;
[b]Even though you make many prayers,
I will not hear.
Your hands are full of blood.

16 "Wash[a] yourselves, make
yourselves clean;
Put away the evil of your doings
from before My eyes.
[b]Cease to do evil,
17 Learn to do good;
Seek justice,
Rebuke the oppressor;[1]
Defend the fatherless,
Plead for the widow.

18 "Come now, and let us
[a]reason together,"
Says the LORD,
"Though your sins are like scarlet,
[b]They shall be as white as snow;
Though they are red like crimson,
They shall be as wool.
19 If you are willing and obedient,
You shall eat the good of the land;
20 But if you refuse and rebel,
You shall be devoured by
the sword";

ISAIAH 1:17

I AM ISAIAH

Learn to do good; seek justice, rebuke the oppressor; defend the fatherless, plead for the widow. Isaiah 1:17

I am Isaiah, a prophet of the Lord. I was called through a vision of God when He sent an angel to touch my mouth with a live coal. The Lord asked, "Who will go for Us?" and I answered, "Here am I! Send me." After that, the Lord began to speak through me to the people about the time in which we lived and the coming age. Many of my prophecies were warnings against sin, which has harmed the relationship between God and people since the time of Adam and Eve. We sin, God disciplines us, we repent, but then we sin again.

The Lord sent me to remind Judah and Israel of our rebellious history. Though we had sinned against Him and done evil in His eyes, God had shown His chosen people great favor. He told me to warn the people of the danger in trusting in human beings, and He directed me to remind them to put their trust in God. I was faithful to tell them to choose what is right and to seek justice. I rebuked the oppressors, but the people did not listen. They continued to exploit one another and to be overcome with drunkenness and arrogance. Confusion and conceit ruled over them.

Even still, I also encouraged the people. I told them about the hope we could have in the future and God's forgiveness. I told them that Babylon would fall and that God would punish the unrighteous. I assured them that, in the end, one from the house of David who would seek justice and the cause of righteousness would arise and sit on the throne forever.

†

Many of Isaiah's prophecies have been fulfilled in the life, death, and resurrection of Jesus Christ; however, many are still to be fulfilled. We have much to look forward to. We can be sure that the current times and circumstances are only temporary. We are just passing through on our pilgrimage to the time when the people of God will rule and reign with Jesus Christ.

1:14 [a] Num. 28:11 [b] Lam. 2:6 1:15 [a] Prov. 1:28 [b] Ps. 66:18; Is. 59:1–3; Mic. 3:4 1:16 [a] Jer. 4:14 [b] Rom. 12:9 1:17 [1] Some ancient versions read *the oppressed.* 1:18 [a] Is. 43:26; Mic. 6:2 [b] Ps. 51:7; [Is. 43:25]; Rev. 7:14

[a]For the mouth of the
LORD has spoken.

The Degenerate City

21 [a]How the faithful city has
become a harlot!
It was full of justice;
Righteousness lodged in it,
But now [b]murderers.
22 [a]Your silver has become dross,
Your wine mixed with water.
23 [a]Your princes *are* rebellious,
And [b]companions of thieves;
[c]Everyone loves bribes,
And follows after rewards.
They [d]do not defend the fatherless,
Nor does the cause of the widow
come before them.

24 Therefore the Lord says,
The LORD of hosts, the
Mighty One of Israel,
"Ah, [a]I will rid Myself of My adversaries,
And take vengeance on My enemies.
25 I will turn My hand against you,
And [a]thoroughly purge
away your dross,
And take away all your alloy.
26 I will restore your judges
[a]as at the first,
And your counselors as
at the beginning.
Afterward [b]you shall be called the city
of righteousness, the faithful city."

27 Zion shall be redeemed with justice,
And her penitents with righteousness.
28 The [a]destruction of transgressors
and of sinners *shall be* together,
And those who forsake the
LORD shall be consumed.
29 For they[1] shall be ashamed
of the terebinth trees
Which you have desired;
And you shall be embarrassed
because of the gardens
Which you have chosen.
30 For you shall be as a terebinth
whose leaf fades,
And as a garden that has
no water.
31 [a]The strong shall be as tinder,
And the work of it as a spark;
Both will burn together,
And no one shall [b]quench *them.*

The Future House of God
(Mic. 4:1–5)

2 The word that Isaiah the son of Amoz saw concerning Judah and Jerusalem.

2 Now [a]it shall come to pass
[b]in the latter days
[c]*That* the mountain of the
LORD's house
Shall be established on the
top of the mountains,
And shall be exalted above the hills;
And all nations shall flow to it.
3 Many people shall come and say,
[a]"Come, and let us go up to the
mountain of the LORD,
To the house of the God of Jacob;
He will teach us His ways,
And we shall walk in His paths."
[b]For out of Zion shall go forth the law,
And the word of the LORD
from Jerusalem.
4 He shall judge between the nations,
And rebuke many people;
They shall beat their swords
into plowshares,
And their spears into pruning
hooks;
Nation shall not lift up sword
against nation,
Neither shall they learn war
anymore.

The Day of the LORD

5 O house of Jacob, come
and let us [a]walk
In the light of the LORD.

6 For You have forsaken Your
people, the house of Jacob,
Because they are filled
[a]with eastern ways;

1:20 [a] Is. 40:5; 58:14; Mic. 4:4; [Titus 1:2] **1:21** [a] Is. 57:3–9; Jer. 2:20 [b] Mic. 3:1–3 **1:22** [a] Jer. 6:28 **1:23** [a] Hos. 9:15 [b] Prov. 29:24 [c] Jer. 22:17 [d] Is. 10:2; Jer. 5:28; Ezek. 22:7; Zech. 7:10 **1:24** [a] Deut. 28:63 **1:25** [a] Is. 48:10; Ezek. 22:19–22; Mal. 3:3 **1:26** [a] Jer. 33:7–11 [b] Is. 33:5; Zech. 8:3 **1:28** [a] Job 31:3; Ps. 9:5; [Is. 66:24; 2 Thess. 1:8, 9] **1:29** [1] Following Masoretic Text, Septuagint, and Vulgate; some Hebrew manuscripts and Targum read *you.* **1:31** [a] Ezek. 32:21 [b] Is. 66:24; Matt. 3:12; Mark 9:43 **2:2** [a] Mic. 4:1 [b] Gen. 49:1 [c] Ps. 68:15 **2:3** [a] Jer. 50:5; [Zech. 8:21–23; 14:16–21] [b] Luke 24:47 **2:5** [a] Eph. 5:8 **2:6** [a] Num. 23:7

They *are* [b]soothsayers like
the Philistines,
[c]And they are pleased with the
children of foreigners.
7 [a]Their land is also full of
silver and gold,
And there is no end to their
treasures;
Their land is also full of horses,
And there is no end to their chariots.
8 [a]Their land is also full of idols;
They worship the work of
their own hands,
That which their own
fingers have made.
9 People bow down,
And each man humbles himself;
Therefore do not forgive them.

10 [a]Enter into the rock, and
hide in the dust,
From the terror of the LORD
And the glory of His majesty.
11 The lofty looks of man
shall be [a]humbled,
The haughtiness of men
shall be bowed down,
And the LORD alone shall be
exalted [b]in that day.

12 For the day of the LORD of hosts
Shall come upon everything
proud and lofty,
Upon everything lifted up—
And it shall be brought low—
13 Upon all [a]the cedars of Lebanon
that are high and lifted up,
And upon all the oaks
of Bashan;
14 [a]Upon all the high mountains,
And upon all the hills
that are lifted up;
15 Upon every high tower,
And upon every fortified wall;
16 [a]Upon all the ships of Tarshish,
And upon all the beautiful sloops.
17 The loftiness of man shall
be bowed down,
And the haughtiness of men
shall be brought low;
The LORD alone will be
exalted in that day,
18 But the idols He shall utterly abolish.

19 They shall go into the
[a]holes of the rocks,
And into the caves of the earth,
[b]From the terror of the LORD
And the glory of His majesty,
When He arises [c]to shake
the earth mightily.

20 In that day a man will cast
away his idols of silver
And his idols of gold,
Which they made, *each* for
himself to worship,
To the moles and bats,
21 To go into the clefts of the rocks,
And into the crags of
the rugged rocks,
From the terror of the LORD
And the glory of His majesty,
When He arises to shake
the earth mightily.

22 [a]Sever yourselves from such a man,
Whose [b]breath *is* in his nostrils;
For of what account is he?

Judgment on Judah and Jerusalem

3 For behold, the Lord, the
LORD of hosts,
[a]Takes away from Jerusalem
and from Judah
[b]The stock and the store,
The whole supply of bread and
the whole supply of water;
2 [a]The mighty man and the
man of war,
The judge and the prophet,
And the diviner and the elder;
3 The captain of fifty and the
honorable man,
The counselor and the skillful
artisan,
And the expert enchanter.

4 "I will give [a]children *to be* their princes,
And babes shall rule over them.

2:6 [b] Deut. 18:14 [c] Ps. 106:35 2:7 [a] Deut. 17:16; Is. 30:16; 31:1; Mic. 5:10 2:8 [a] Is. 40:19, 20; Jer. 2:28 2:10 [a] Is. 2:19, 21; Rev. 6:15, 16 2:11 [a] Prov. 16:5; Is. 5:15 [b] Hos. 2:16 2:13 [a] Is. 14:8; Zech. 11:1, 2 2:14 [a] Is. 30:25 2:16 [a] 1 Kin. 10:22; Is. 23:1, 14; 60:9 2:19 [a] Hos. 10:8; [Rev. 9:6] [b] [2 Thess. 1:9] [c] Ps. 18:7; Is. 2:21; 13:13; 24:1, 19, 20; Hag. 2:6, 7; Heb. 12:26 2:22 [a] Ps. 146:3; Jer. 17:5 [b] Job 27:3 3:1 [a] 2 Kin. 25:3; Is. 5:13; Jer. 37:21 [b] Lev. 26:26 3:2 [a] 2 Kin. 24:14; Is. 9:14, 15; Ezek. 17:12, 13 3:4 [a] Eccl. 10:16

5 The people will be oppressed,
Every one by another and every
one by his neighbor;
The child will be insolent
toward the elder,
And the base toward the honorable."

6 When a man takes hold of his brother
In the house of his father, *saying,*
"You have clothing;
You be our ruler,
And *let* these ruins *be*
under your power,"[1]
7 In that day he will protest, saying,
"I cannot cure *your* ills,
For in my house *is* neither
food nor clothing;
Do not make me a ruler of the people."

8 For [a]Jerusalem stumbled,
And Judah is fallen,
Because their tongue and their doings
Are against the LORD,
To provoke the eyes of His glory.
9 The look on their countenance
witnesses against them,
And they declare their sin as [a]Sodom;
They do not hide *it*.
Woe to their soul!
For they have brought evil
upon themselves.

10 "Say to the righteous [a]that *it*
shall be well *with them,*
[b]For they shall eat the fruit
of their doings.
11 Woe to the wicked! [a]*It shall*
be ill *with him,*
For the reward of his hands
shall be given him.
12 *As for* My people, children
are their oppressors,
And women rule over them.
O My people! [a]Those who lead
you cause *you* to err,
And destroy the way of your paths."

Oppression and Luxury Condemned

13 The LORD stands up [a]to plead,
And stands to judge the people.
14 The LORD will enter into judgment
With the elders of His people
And His princes:
"For you have eaten up [a]the vineyard;
The plunder of the poor
is in your houses.
15 What do you mean by
[a]crushing My people
And grinding the faces of the poor?"
Says the Lord GOD of hosts.

16 Moreover the LORD says:

"Because the daughters of
Zion are haughty,
And walk with outstretched necks
And wanton eyes,
Walking and mincing *as* they go,
Making a jingling with their feet,
17 Therefore the Lord will
strike with [a]a scab
The crown of the head of the
daughters of Zion,
And the LORD will [b]uncover
their secret parts."

18 In that day the Lord will
take away the finery:
The jingling anklets, the scarves,
and the [a]crescents;
19 The pendants, the bracelets,
and the veils;
20 The headdresses, the leg ornaments,
and the headbands;
The perfume boxes, the charms,
21 and the rings;
The nose jewels,
22 the festal apparel, and the mantles;
The outer garments, the purses,
23 and the mirrors;
The fine linen, the turbans,
and the robes.

24 And so it shall be:

Instead of a sweet smell
there will be a stench;
Instead of a sash, a rope;
Instead of well-set hair,
[a]baldness;

3:6 [1] Literally *hand* 3:8 [a] 2 Chr. 36:16, 17; Mic. 3:12 3:9 [a] Gen. 13:13; Is. 1:10–15 3:10 [a] [Deut. 28:1–14; Eccl. 8:12; Is. 54:17] [b] Ps. 128:2 3:11 [a] [Ps. 11:6; Eccl. 8:12, 13] 3:12 [a] Is. 9:16 3:13 [a] Is. 66:16; Hos. 4:1; Mic. 6:2 3:14 [a] Matt. 21:33 3:15 [a] Mic. 3:2, 3 3:17 [a] Deut. 28:27 [b] Jer. 13:22 3:18 [a] Judg. 8:21, 26 3:24 [a] Is. 22:12; Ezek. 27:31; Amos 8:10

Instead of a rich robe, a
girding of sackcloth;
And branding instead of beauty.
25 Your men shall fall by the sword,
And your mighty in the war.

26 [a]Her gates shall lament and mourn,
And she *being* desolate [b]shall
sit on the ground.

4 And [a]in that day seven women shall
take hold of one man, saying,
"We will [b]eat our own food and
wear our own apparel;
Only let us be called by your name,
To take away [c]our reproach."

The Renewal of Zion

2 In that day [a]the Branch of the LORD
shall be beautiful and glorious;
And the fruit of the earth *shall*
be excellent and appealing
For those of Israel who have escaped.

3And it shall come to pass that *he who*
is left in Zion and remains in Jerusalem
[a]will be called holy—everyone who is [b]re-
corded among the living in Jerusalem.
4When [a]the Lord has washed away the
filth of the daughters of Zion, and purged
the blood of Jerusalem from her midst, by
the spirit of judgment and by the spirit of
burning, 5then the LORD will create above
every dwelling place of Mount Zion, and
above her assemblies, [a]a cloud and smoke
by day and [b]the shining of a flaming fire by
night. For over all the glory there *will be* a
covering. 6And there will be a tabernacle
for shade in the daytime from the heat, [a]for
a place of refuge, and for a shelter from
storm and rain.

God's Disappointing Vineyard

5 Now let me sing to my Well-beloved
A song of my Beloved
[a]regarding His vineyard:

My Well-beloved has a vineyard
On a very fruitful hill.
2 He dug it up and cleared out its stones,
And planted it with the choicest vine.
He built a tower in its midst,
And also made a winepress in it;
[a]So He expected *it* to bring
forth *good* grapes,
But it brought forth wild grapes.

3 "And now, O inhabitants of
Jerusalem and men of Judah,
[a]Judge, please, between Me
and My vineyard.
4 What more could have been
done to My vineyard
That I have not done in [a]it?
Why then, when I expected *it* to
bring forth *good* grapes,
Did it bring forth wild grapes?
5 And now, please let Me tell you
what I will do to My vineyard:
[a]I will take away its hedge,
and it shall be burned;
And break down its wall, and it
shall be trampled down.
6 I will lay it [a]waste;
It shall not be pruned or dug,
But there shall come up
briers and [b]thorns.
I will also command the clouds
That they rain no rain on it."

7 For the vineyard of the LORD of
hosts *is* the house of Israel,
And the men of Judah are
His pleasant plant.
He looked for justice, but
behold, oppression;
For righteousness, but
behold, a cry *for help*.

Impending Judgment on Excesses

8 Woe to those who join
[a]house to house;
They add field to field,
Till *there is* no place
Where they may dwell alone
in the midst of the land!
9 [a]In my hearing the LORD of hosts *said*,
"Truly, many houses shall be desolate,

3:26 [a] Jer. 14:2; Lam. 1:4 [b] Lam. 2:10 4:1 [a] Is. 2:11, 17 [b] 2 Thess. 3:12 [c] Luke 1:25 4:2 [a] Is. 12:1–6; [Jer. 23:5]; Zech. 3:8 4:3 [a] Is. 60:21 [b] Phil. 4:3 4:4 [a] Mal. 3:2, 3 4:5 [a] Ex. 13:21, 22; Num. 9:15–23 [b] Zech. 2:5 4:6 [a] Ps. 27:5; Is. 25:4 5:1 [a] Ps. 80:8; Jer. 2:21; Matt. 21:33; Mark 12:1; Luke 20:9 5:2 [a] Deut. 32:6 5:3 [a] [Rom. 3:4] 5:4 [a] 2 Chr. 36:15, 16; Jer. 2:5; 7:25, 26; Mic. 6:3; Matt. 23:37 5:5 [a] 2 Chr. 36:19; Ps. 80:12; 89:40, 41 5:6 [a] 2 Chr. 36:19–21 [b] Is. 7:19–25; Jer. 25:11 5:8 [a] Jer. 22:13–17; Mic. 2:2; Hab. 2:9–12 5:9 [a] Is. 22:14

Great and beautiful ones,
without inhabitant.
10 For ten acres of vineyard
shall yield one [a]bath,
And a homer of seed shall
yield one ephah."

11 [a]Woe to those who rise early
in the morning,
That they may follow
intoxicating drink;
Who continue until night, *till*
wine inflames them!
12 [a]The harp and the strings,
The tambourine and flute,
And wine are in their feasts;
But [b]they do not regard the
work of the LORD,
Nor consider the operation
of His hands.

13 [a]Therefore my people have
gone into captivity,
Because *they have* no [b]knowledge;
Their honorable men *are* famished,
And their multitude dried
up with thirst.
14 Therefore Sheol has enlarged itself
And opened its mouth
beyond measure;
Their glory and their multitude
and their pomp,
And he who is jubilant, shall
descend into it.
15 People shall be brought down,
[a]Each man shall be humbled,
And the eyes of the lofty
shall be humbled.
16 But the LORD of hosts shall be
[a]exalted in judgment,
And God who is holy shall be
hallowed in righteousness.
17 Then the lambs shall feed
in their pasture,
And in the waste places of [a]the
fat ones strangers shall eat.

18 Woe to those who draw iniquity
with cords of vanity,
And sin as if with a cart rope;
19 [a]That say, "Let Him make speed
and hasten His work,
That we may see *it;*
And let the counsel of the Holy One
of Israel draw near and come,
That we may know *it.*"

20 Woe to those who call evil
good, and good evil;
Who put darkness for light,
and light for darkness;
Who put bitter for sweet,
and sweet for bitter!

21 Woe to *those who are* [a]wise
in their own eyes,
And prudent in their own sight!

22 Woe to men mighty at drinking wine,
Woe to men valiant for mixing
intoxicating drink,
23 Who [a]justify the wicked for a bribe,
And take away justice from
the righteous man!

24 Therefore, [a]as the fire
devours the stubble,
And the flame consumes the chaff,
So [b]their root will be as rottenness,
And their blossom will
ascend like dust;
Because they have rejected the
law of the LORD of hosts,
And despised the word of the
Holy One of Israel.
25 [a]Therefore the anger of the LORD is
aroused against His people;
He has stretched out His
hand against them
And stricken them,
And [b]the hills trembled.
Their carcasses *were* as refuse
in the midst of the streets.

[c]For all this His anger is
not turned away,
But His hand *is* stretched out still.

26 [a]He will lift up a banner to
the nations from afar,

5:10 [a] Ezek. 45:11 5:11 [a] Prov. 23:29, 30; Eccl. 10:16, 17; Is. 5:22 5:12 [a] Amos 6:5 [b] Job 34:27; Ps. 28:5 5:13 [a] 2 Kin. 24:14–16 [b] Is. 1:3; 27:11; Hos. 4:6 5:15 [a] Is. 2:9, 11 5:16 [a] Is. 2:11 5:17 [a] Is. 10:16 5:19 [a] Jer. 17:15; Amos 5:18 5:21 [a] Prov. 3:7; Rom. 1:22; 12:16; [1 Cor. 3:18–20] 5:23 [a] Ex. 23:8; Prov. 17:15; Is. 1:23; Mic. 3:11; 7:3 5:24 [a] Ex. 15:7 [b] Job 18:16 5:25 [a] 2 Kin. 22:13, 17; Is. 66:15 [b] Ps. 18:7; Is. 64:3; Jer. 4:24; Nah. 1:5 [c] Is. 9:12, 17; Jer. 4:8; Dan. 9:16 5:26 [a] Is. 11:10, 12

And will [b]whistle to them from
[c]the end of the earth;
Surely [d]they shall come
with speed, swiftly.
27 No one will be weary or
stumble among them,
No one will slumber or sleep;
Nor [a]will the belt on their
loins be loosed,
Nor the strap of their
sandals be broken;
28 [a]Whose arrows *are* sharp,
And all their bows bent;
Their horses' hooves will
seem like flint,
And their wheels like
a whirlwind.
29 Their roaring *will be* like a lion,
They will roar like young lions;
Yes, they will roar
And lay hold of the prey;
They will carry *it* away safely,
And no one will deliver.
30 In that day they will roar
against them
Like the roaring of the sea.
And if *one* [a]looks to the land,
Behold, darkness *and* sorrow;
And the light is darkened
by the clouds.

Isaiah Called to Be a Prophet
(cf. Ezek. 1:4–28)

6 In the year that [a]King Uzziah died, I
[b]saw the Lord sitting on a throne, high
and lifted up, and the train of His *robe* filled
the temple. 2 Above it stood seraphim; each
one had six wings: with two he covered his
face, [a]with two he covered his feet, and with
two he flew. 3 And one cried to another and
said:

[a]"Holy, holy, holy *is* the LORD of hosts;
[b]The whole earth *is* full of His glory!"

4 And the posts of the door were shaken
by the voice of him who cried out, and the
house was filled with smoke.
5 So I said:

"Woe *is* me, for I am undone!
Because I *am* a man of [a]unclean lips,
And I dwell in the midst of a
people of unclean lips;
For my eyes have seen the King,
The LORD of hosts."

6 Then one of the seraphim flew to me,
having in his hand a live coal *which* he had
taken with the tongs from [a]the altar. 7 And
he [a]touched my mouth *with it,* and said:

"Behold, this has touched your lips;
Your iniquity is taken away,
And your sin purged."

8 Also I heard the voice of the Lord, saying:

"Whom shall I send,
And who will go for [a]Us?"

Then I said, "Here *am* I! Send me."
9 And He said, "Go, and [a]tell this people:

'Keep on hearing, but do
not understand;
Keep on seeing, but do not
perceive.'

10 "Make [a]the heart of this people dull,
And their ears heavy,
And shut their eyes;
[b]Lest they see with their eyes,
And hear with their ears,
And understand with their heart,
And return and be healed."

11 Then I said, "Lord, how long?"
And He answered:

[a]"Until the cities are laid waste
and without inhabitant,
The houses are without a man,
The land is utterly desolate,
12 [a]The LORD has removed
men far away,
And the forsaken places *are* many
in the midst of the land.

5:26 [b] Is. 7:18; Zech. 10:8 [c] Mal. 1:11 [d] Joel 2:7 5:27 [a] Dan. 5:6 5:28 [a] Jer. 5:16 5:30 [a] Is. 8:22; Jer. 4:23–28; Joel 2:10; Luke 21:25, 26 6:1 [a] 2 Kin. 15:7; 2 Chr. 26:23; Is. 1:1 [b] John 12:41; Rev. 4:2, 3; 20:11 6:2 [a] Ezek. 1:11 6:3 [a] Rev. 4:8 [b] Num. 14:21; Ps. 72:19 6:5 [a] Ex. 6:12, 30 6:6 [a] Rev. 8:3 6:7 [a] Jer. 1:9; Dan. 10:16 6:8 [a] Gen. 1:26 6:9 [a] Is. 43:8; Matt. 13:14; Mark 4:12; Luke 8:10; John 12:40; Acts 28:26; Rom. 11:8 6:10 [a] Ps. 119:70; Mark 6:1–6; Acts 7:51; Rom. 10:1–4 [b] Jer. 5:21 6:11 [a] Mic. 3:12 6:12 [a] 2 Kin. 25:21; Is. 5:9

13 But yet a tenth *will be* in it,
And will return and be for
consuming,
As a terebinth tree or as an oak,
Whose stump *remains*
when it is cut down.
So [a]the holy seed *shall be* its stump."

Isaiah Sent to King Ahaz
(2 Kin. 16:5; 2 Chr. 28:5–15)

7 Now it came to pass in the days of [a]Ahaz
the son of Jotham, the son of Uzziah,
king of Judah, *that* Rezin king of Syria and
Pekah the son of Remaliah, king of Israel,
went up to Jerusalem to *make* war against
[b]it, but could not prevail against it. 2And
it was told to the house of David, saying,
"Syria's forces are deployed in Ephraim."
So his heart and the heart of his people
were moved as the trees of the woods are
moved with the wind.
3Then the LORD said to Isaiah, "Go out
now to meet Ahaz, you and Shear-Jashub[1]
your son, at the end of the aqueduct from
the upper pool, on the highway to the Fuller's Field, 4and say to him: 'Take heed, and
be [a]quiet; do not fear or be fainthearted for
these two stubs of smoking firebrands, for
the fierce anger of Rezin and Syria, and the
son of Remaliah. 5Because Syria, Ephraim,
and the son of Remaliah have plotted evil
against you, saying, 6"Let us go up against
Judah and trouble it, and let us make a gap
in its wall for ourselves, and set a king over
them, the son of Tabel"— 7thus says the
Lord GOD:

[a]"It shall not stand,
Nor shall it come to pass.
8 [a]For the head of Syria *is* Damascus,
And the head of Damascus *is* Rezin.
Within sixty-five years
Ephraim will be broken,
So that it will not *be* a people.
9 The head of Ephraim *is* Samaria,
And the head of Samaria
is Remaliah's son.
[a]If you will not believe,
Surely you shall not be established." ' "

The Immanuel Prophecy

10Moreover the LORD spoke again to
Ahaz, saying, 11[a]"Ask a sign for yourself
from the LORD your God; ask it either in
the depth or in the height above."
12But Ahaz said, "I will not ask, nor will
I test the LORD!"
13Then he said, "Hear now, O house of
David! *Is it* a small thing for you to weary
men, but will you weary my God also?
14Therefore the Lord Himself will give you
a sign: [a]Behold, the virgin shall conceive
and bear [b]a Son, and shall call His name
[c]Immanuel.[1] 15Curds and honey He shall
eat, that He may know to refuse the evil
and choose the good. 16[a]For before the Child
shall know to refuse the evil and choose
the good, the land that you dread will be
forsaken by [b]both her kings. 17[a]The LORD
will bring the king of Assyria upon you
and your people and your father's house—
days that have not come since the day that
[b]Ephraim departed from Judah."

18 And it shall come to pass in that day
That the LORD [a]will whistle for the fly
That *is* in the farthest part of
the rivers of Egypt,
And for the bee that *is* in
the land of Assyria.
19 They will come, and all
of them will rest
In the desolate valleys and in
[a]the clefts of the rocks,
And on all thorns and in all pastures.

20 In the same day the Lord will
shave with a [a]hired [b]razor,
With those from beyond the River,[1]
with the king of Assyria,
The head and the hair of the legs,
And will also remove the beard.

21 It shall be in that day
That a man will keep alive a
young cow and two sheep;
22 So it shall be, from the abundance
of milk they give,
That he will eat curds;

6:13 [a] Deut. 7:6; Ezra 9:2 7:1 [a] 2 Chr. 28 [b] 2 Kin. 16:5, 9 7:3 [1] Literally *A Remnant Shall Return* 7:4 [a] Ex. 14:13; Is. 30:15; Lam. 3:26 7:7 [a] 2 Kin. 16:5; Is. 8:10; Acts 4:25, 26 7:8 [a] 2 Sam. 8:6; 2 Kin. 17:6 7:9 [a] 2 Chr. 20:20; Is. 5:24 7:11 [a] Matt. 12:38 7:14 [a] Matt. 1:23; Luke 1:31; John 1:45; Rev. 12:5 [b] [Is. 9:6] [c] Is. 8:8, 10 [1] Literally *God-With-Us* 7:16 [a] Is. 8:4 [b] 2 Kin. 15:30 7:17 [a] 2 Chr. 28:19, 20; Is. 8:7, 8; 10:5, 6 [b] 1 Kin. 12:16 7:18 [a] Is. 5:26 7:19 [a] Is. 2:19; Jer. 16:16 7:20 [a] Is. 10:5, 15 [b] 2 Kin. 16:7; 2 Chr. 28:20 [1] That is, the Euphrates

For curds and honey everyone will
eat who is left in the land.
23 It shall happen in that day,
That wherever there could
be a thousand vines
Worth a thousand *shekels* of silver,
[a]It will be for briers and thorns.
24 With arrows and bows *men*
will come there,
Because all the land will become
briers and thorns.

25 And to any hill which could
be dug with the hoe,
You will not go there for fear
of briers and thorns;
But it will become a range for oxen
And a place for sheep to roam.

Assyria Will Invade the Land

8 Moreover the LORD said to me, "Take
a large scroll, and [a]write on it with a
man's pen concerning Maher-Shalal-Hash-
Baz.[1] 2And I will take for Myself faithful
witnesses to record, [a]Uriah the priest and
Zechariah the son of Jeberechiah."
3Then I went to the prophetess, and she
conceived and bore a son. Then the LORD
said to me, "Call his name Maher-Shal-
al-Hash-Baz; 4[a]for before the child shall
have knowledge to cry 'My father' and 'My
mother,' [b]the riches of Damascus and the
spoil of Samaria will be taken away before
the king of Assyria."
5The LORD also spoke to me again, saying:

6 "Inasmuch as these people refused
The waters of [a]Shiloah that
flow softly,
And rejoice [b]in Rezin and
in Remaliah's son;
7 Now therefore, behold, the Lord
brings up over them
The waters of the River,[1]
strong and mighty—
The king of Assyria and all his glory;
He will go up over all his channels
And go over all his banks.
8 He will pass through Judah,
He will overflow and pass over,
[a]He will reach up to the neck;
And the stretching out
of his wings
Will fill the breadth of Your
land, O [b]Immanuel.[1]

9 "Be[a] shattered, O you peoples,
and be broken in pieces!
Give ear, all you from far
countries.
Gird yourselves, but be
broken in pieces;
Gird yourselves, but be
broken in pieces.
10 [a]Take counsel together, but it
will come to nothing;
Speak the word, [b]but it will
not stand,
[c]For God *is* with us."[1]

Fear God, Heed His Word

11For the LORD spoke thus to me with
a strong hand, and instructed me that I
should not walk in the way of this people,
saying:

12 "Do not say, 'A conspiracy,'
Concerning all that this people
call a conspiracy,
Nor be afraid of their threats,
nor be troubled.
13 The LORD of hosts, Him
you shall hallow;
Let Him *be* your fear,
And *let* Him *be* your dread.
14 [a]He will be as a sanctuary,
But [b]a stone of stumbling
and a rock of offense
To both the houses of Israel,
As a trap and a snare to the
inhabitants of Jerusalem.
15 And many among them
shall [a]stumble;
They shall fall and be broken,
Be snared and taken."

16 Bind up the testimony,
Seal the law among my disciples.

7:23 [a] Is. 5:6 8:1 [a] Is. 30:8; Hab. 2:2 [1] Literally *Speed the Spoil, Hasten the Booty* 8:2 [a] 2 Kin. 16:10 8:4 [a] 2 Kin. 17:6; Is. 7:16 [b] 2 Kin. 15:29 8:6 [a] John 9:7 [b] Is. 7:1, 2 8:7 [1] That is, the Euphrates 8:8 [a] Is. 30:28 [b] Is. 7:14; Matt. 1:23 [1] Literally *God-With-Us* 8:9 [a] Joel 3:9 8:10 [a] Is. 7:7; Acts 5:38 [b] Is. 7:14 [c] Rom. 8:31 [1] Hebrew *Immanuel* 8:14 [a] Is. 4:6; 25:4; Ezek. 11:16 [b] Luke 2:34; 20:17; Rom. 9:33; 1 Pet. 2:8 8:15 [a] Matt. 21:44

17 And I will wait on the LORD,
Who [a]hides His face from
the house of Jacob;
And I [b]will hope in Him.
18 [a]Here am I and the children whom
the LORD has given me!
We [b]are for signs and wonders in Israel
From the LORD of hosts,
Who dwells in Mount Zion.

19 And when they say to you, [a]"Seek those
who are mediums and wizards, [b]who whisper and mutter," should not a people seek
their God? *Should they* [c]*seek* the dead on behalf of the living? 20 [a]To the law and to the
testimony! If they do not speak according
to this word, *it is* because [b]*there is* no light
in them.

21 They will pass through it hard-pressed
and hungry; and it shall happen, when they
are hungry, that they will be enraged and
[a]curse their king and their God, and look
upward. 22 Then they will look to the earth,
and see trouble and darkness, gloom of anguish; and *they will be* driven into darkness.

The Government of the Promised Son (Is. 11:1–9)

9 Nevertheless [a]the gloom *will* not *be*
upon her who *is* distressed,
As when at [b]first He lightly esteemed
The land of Zebulun and
the land of Naphtali,
And [c]afterward more heavily
oppressed *her,*
By the way of the sea,
beyond the Jordan,
In Galilee of the Gentiles.
2 [a]The people who walked in darkness
Have seen a great light;
Those who dwelt in the land
of the shadow of death,
Upon them a light has shined.

3 You have multiplied the nation
And increased its joy;[1]
They rejoice before You
According to the joy of harvest,
As *men* rejoice [a]when they
divide the spoil.
4 For You have broken the
yoke of his burden
And the staff of his shoulder,
The rod of his oppressor,
As in the day of [a]Midian.
5 For every warrior's sandal
from the noisy battle,
And garments rolled in blood,
[a]Will be used for burning
and fuel of fire.

6 [a]For unto us a Child is born,
Unto us a [b]Son is given;
And [c]the government will be
upon His shoulder.
And His name will be called
[d]Wonderful, Counselor, [e]Mighty God,
Everlasting Father, [f]Prince of Peace.
7 Of the increase of *His*
government and peace
[a]*There will be* no end,
Upon the throne of David
and over His kingdom,
To order it and establish it with
judgment and justice
From that time forward, even forever.
The [b]zeal of the LORD of hosts
will perform this.

The Punishment of Samaria

8 The Lord sent a word against [a]Jacob,
And it has fallen on Israel.
9 All the people will know—
Ephraim and the inhabitant
of Samaria—
Who say in pride and
arrogance of heart:
10 "The bricks have fallen down,
But we will rebuild with hewn stones;
The sycamores are cut down,
But we will replace *them* with cedars."
11 Therefore the LORD shall set up
The adversaries of Rezin against him,
And spur his enemies on,
12 The Syrians before and the
Philistines behind;

8:17 [a] Deut. 31:17; Is. 54:8 [b] Hab. 2:3 8:18 [a] Heb. 2:13 [b] Ps. 71:7 8:19 [a] 1 Sam. 28:8 [b] Is. 29:4 [c] Ps. 106:28 8:20 [a] Is. 1:10; 8:16; Luke 16:29 [b] Is. 8:22; Mic. 3:6 8:21 [a] Rev. 16:11 9:1 [a] Is. 8:22 [b] 2 Kin. 15:29; 2 Chr. 16:4 [c] Matt. 4:13–16 9:2 [a] Matt. 4:16; Luke 1:79; 2 Cor. 4:6; Eph. 5:8 9:3 [a] Judg. 5:30 [1] Following Qere and Targum; Kethib and Vulgate read *not increased joy;* Septuagint reads *Most of the people You brought down in Your joy.* 9:4 [a] Judg. 7:22 9:5 [a] Is. 66:15 9:6 [a] [Is. 7:14; Luke 2:11]; John 1:45 [b] Luke 2:7; [John 3:16; 1 John 4:9] [c] [Matt. 28:18; 1 Cor. 15:25]; Rev. 12:5 [d] Judg. 13:18 [e] Titus 2:13 [f] Eph. 2:14 9:7 [a] Dan. 2:44; Matt. 1:1, 6; Luke 1:32, 33; John 7:42 [b] Is. 37:32 9:8 [a] Gen. 32:28

And they shall devour Israel
with an open mouth.

For all this His anger is
not turned away,
But His hand *is* stretched out still.

13 For the people do not turn to
Him who strikes them,
Nor do they seek the LORD of hosts.
14 Therefore the LORD will cut off
head and tail from Israel,
Palm branch and bulrush
[a]in one day.
15 The elder and honorable,
he *is* the head;
The prophet who teaches
lies, he *is* the tail.
16 For [a]the leaders of this people
cause *them* to err,
And *those who are* led by
them are destroyed.
17 Therefore the Lord [a]will have no
joy in their young men,
Nor have mercy on their
fatherless and widows;
For everyone *is* a hypocrite
and an evildoer,
And every mouth speaks folly.

[b]For all this His anger is
not turned away,
But His hand *is* stretched out still.

18 For wickedness [a]burns as the fire;
It shall devour the briers and thorns,
And kindle in the thickets
of the forest;
They shall mount up *like* rising smoke.
19 Through the wrath of the
LORD of hosts
[a]The land is burned up,
And the people shall be as
fuel for the fire;
[b]No man shall spare his brother.
20 And he shall snatch on the right hand
And be hungry;
He shall devour on the left hand
[a]And not be satisfied;
[b]Every man shall eat the
flesh of his own arm.
21 Manasseh *shall devour* Ephraim,
and Ephraim Manasseh;
Together they *shall be* [a]against Judah.

[b]For all this His anger is
not turned away,
But His hand *is* stretched out still.

10 "Woe to those who [a]decree
unrighteous decrees,
Who write misfortune,
Which they have prescribed
2 To rob the needy of justice,
And to take what is right from
the poor of My people,
That widows may be their prey,
And *that* they may rob the fatherless.
3 [a]What will you do in [b]the
day of punishment,
And in the desolation *which*
will come from [c]afar?
To whom will you flee for help?
And where will you leave your glory?
4 Without Me they shall bow down
among the [a]prisoners,
And they shall fall among
the slain."

[b]For all this His anger is
not turned away,
But His hand *is* stretched out still.

Arrogant Assyria Also Judged

5 "Woe to Assyria, [a]the rod of My anger
And the staff in whose hand
is My indignation.
6 I will send him against [a]an
ungodly nation,
And against the people of My wrath
I will [b]give him charge,
To seize the spoil, to take the prey,
And to tread them down like
the mire of the streets.
7 [a]Yet he does not mean so,
Nor does his heart think so;
But *it is* in his heart to destroy,
And cut off not a few nations.

9:14 [a] Rev. 18:8 9:16 [a] Is. 3:12; Mic. 3:1, 5, 9; Matt. 15:14 9:17 [a] Ps. 147:10 [b] Is. 5:25 9:18 [a] Ps. 83:14; [Is. 1:7; 10:17]; Nah. 1:10; Mal. 4:1
9:19 [a] Is. 8:22 [b] Mic. 7:2, 6 9:20 [a] Lev. 26:26 [b] Jer. 19:9 9:21 [a] 2 Chr. 28:6, 8; Is. 11:13 [b] Is. 9:12, 17 10:1 [a] Ps. 58:2
10:3 [a] Job 31:14 [b] Is. 13:6; Jer. 9:9; Hos. 9:7; Luke 19:44 [c] Is. 5:26 10:4 [a] Is. 24:22 [b] Is. 5:25 10:5 [a] Jer. 51:20
10:6 [a] Is. 9:17 [b] 2 Kin. 17:6; Jer. 34:22 10:7 [a] Gen. 50:20; Mic. 4:11, 12; Acts 2:23, 24

8 [a]For he says,
'*Are* not my princes altogether kings?
9 *Is* not [a]Calno [b]like Carchemish?
Is not Hamath like Arpad?
Is not Samaria [c]like Damascus?
10 As my hand has found the
kingdoms of the idols,
Whose carved images excelled those
of Jerusalem and Samaria,
11 As I have done to Samaria
and her idols,
Shall I not do also to Jerusalem
and her idols?'"

12Therefore it shall come to pass, when
the Lord has performed all His work [a]on
Mount Zion and on Jerusalem, *that He will*
say, [b]"I will punish the fruit of the arrogant
heart of the king of Assyria, and the glory
of his haughty looks."
13[a]For he says:

"By the strength of my hand
I have done *it,*
And by my wisdom, for I am prudent;
Also I have removed the
boundaries of the people,
And have robbed their treasuries;
So I have put down the inhabitants
like a valiant *man.*
14 [a]My hand has found like a nest
the riches of the people,
And as one gathers eggs *that are* left,
I have gathered all the earth;
And there was no one who
moved *his* wing,
Nor opened *his* mouth
with even a peep."

15 Shall [a]the ax boast itself against
him who chops with it?
Or shall the saw exalt itself against
him who saws with it?
As if a rod could wield *itself*
against those who lift it up,
Or as if a staff could lift up,
as if it were not wood!
16 Therefore the Lord, the Lord[1] of hosts,
Will send leanness among his fat ones;
And under his glory
He will kindle a burning
Like the burning of a fire.
17 So the Light of Israel will be for a fire,
And his Holy One for a flame;
[a]It will burn and devour
His thorns and his briers in one day.
18 And it will consume the glory of his
forest and of [a]his fruitful field,
Both soul and body;
And they will be as when a
sick man wastes away.
19 Then the rest of the trees of his forest
Will be so few in number
That a child may write them.

The Returning Remnant of Israel

20 And it shall come to pass in that day
That the remnant of Israel,
And such as have escaped of
the house of Jacob,
[a]Will never again depend on
him who defeated them,
But will depend on the LORD, the
Holy One of Israel, in truth.
21 The remnant will return, the
remnant of Jacob,
To the [a]Mighty God.
22 [a]For though your people, O Israel,
be as the sand of the sea,
[b]A remnant of them will return;
The destruction decreed shall
overflow with righteousness.
23 [a]For the Lord GOD of hosts
Will make a determined end
In the midst of all the land.

24Therefore thus says the Lord GOD of
hosts: "O My people, who dwell in Zion, [a]do
not be afraid of the Assyrian. He shall strike
you with a rod and lift up his staff against
you, in the manner of [b]Egypt. 25For yet a
very little while [a]and the indignation will
cease, as will My anger in their destruction." 26And the LORD of hosts will stir up [a]a
scourge for him like the slaughter of [b]Mid-
ian at the rock of Oreb; [c]*as* His rod was on
the sea, so will He lift it up in the manner
of Egypt.

10:8 [a] 2 Kin. 19:10 10:9 [a] Gen. 10:10; Amos 6:2 [b] 2 Chr. 35:20 [c] 2 Kin. 16:9 10:12 [a] 2 Kin. 19:31; Is. 28:21 [b] 2 Kin. 19:35; 2 Chr. 32:21; Jer. 50:18 10:13 [a] [2 Kin. 19:22–24]; Is. 37:24–27; Ezek. 28:4; Dan. 4:30 10:14 [a] Job 31:25 10:15 [a] Jer. 51:20 10:16 [1] Following Bomberg; Masoretic Text and Dead Sea Scrolls read *YHWH* (*the* LORD). 10:17 [a] Is. 9:18 10:18 [a] 2 Kin. 19:23 10:20 [a] 2 Kin. 16:7 10:21 [a] [Is. 9:6] 10:22 [a] Rom. 9:27, 28 [b] Is. 6:13 10:23 [a] Is. 28:22; Dan. 9:27; Rom. 9:28 10:24 [a] Is. 7:4; 12:2 [b] Ex. 14 10:25 [a] Is. 10:5; 26:20; Dan. 11:36 10:26 [a] 2 Kin. 19:35 [b] Judg. 7:25; Is. 9:4 [c] Ex. 14:26, 27

27 It shall come to pass in that day
That his burden will be taken
away from your shoulder,
And his yoke from your neck,
And the yoke will be destroyed
because of [a]the anointing oil.

28 He has come to Aiath,
He has passed Migron;
At Michmash he has attended
to his equipment.
29 They have gone along [a]the ridge,
They have taken up lodging at Geba.
Ramah is afraid,
[b]Gibeah of Saul has fled.
30 Lift up your voice,
O daughter [a]of Gallim!
Cause it to be heard as far as [b]Laish—
O poor Anathoth![1]
31 [a]Madmenah has fled,
The inhabitants of Gebim seek refuge.
32 As yet he will remain [a]at Nob
that day;
He will [b]shake his fist at the mount
of [c]the daughter of Zion,
The hill of Jerusalem.

33 Behold, the Lord,
The LORD of hosts,
Will lop off the bough with terror;
[a]Those of high stature *will*
be hewn down,
And the haughty will be humbled.
34 He will cut down the thickets
of the forest with iron,
And Lebanon will fall by
the Mighty One.

The Reign of Jesse's Offspring
(Is. 9:1–7)

11 There [a]shall come forth a Rod from
the stem of [b]Jesse,
And [c]a Branch shall grow
out of his roots.
2 [a]The Spirit of the LORD shall
rest upon Him,
The Spirit of wisdom and
understanding,
The Spirit of counsel and might,
The Spirit of knowledge and
of the fear of the LORD.

3 His delight *is* in the fear of the LORD,
And He shall not judge by
the sight of His eyes,
Nor decide by the hearing of His ears;
4 But [a]with righteousness He
shall judge the poor,
And decide with equity for
the meek of the earth;
He shall [b]strike the earth with
the rod of His mouth,
And with the breath of His lips
He shall slay the wicked.
5 Righteousness shall be the
belt of His loins,
And faithfulness the belt of His waist.

6 "The[a] wolf also shall dwell
with the lamb,
The leopard shall lie down
with the young goat,
The calf and the young lion
and the fatling together;
And a little child shall lead them.
7 The cow and the bear shall graze;
Their young ones shall lie
down together;
And the lion shall eat straw like the ox.
8 The nursing child shall play
by the cobra's hole,
And the weaned child shall put
his hand in the viper's den.
9 [a]They shall not hurt nor destroy
in all My holy mountain,
For [b]the earth shall be full of the
knowledge of the LORD
As the waters cover the sea.

10 "And[a] in that day [b]there shall
be a Root of Jesse,
Who shall stand as a [c]banner
to the people;
For the [d]Gentiles shall seek Him,
And His resting place
shall be glorious."

10:27 [a] Ps. 105:15; [1 John 2:20] 10:29 [a] 1 Sam. 13:23 [b] 1 Sam. 11:4 10:30 [a] 1 Sam. 25:44 [b] Judg. 18:7 [1] Following Masoretic Text, Targum, and Vulgate; Septuagint and Syriac read *Listen to her, O Anathoth.* 10:31 [a] Josh. 15:31 10:32 [a] 1 Sam. 21:1; Neh. 11:32 [b] Is. 13:2 [c] Is. 37:22 10:33 [a] Is. 37:24, 36–38; Ezek. 31:3; Amos 2:9 11:1 [a] [Zech. 6:12]; Rev. 5:5 [b] [Is. 9:7; 11:10]; Matt. 1:5; [Acts 13:23] [c] Is. 4:2 11:2 [a] [Is. 42:1; 48:16; 61:1; Matt. 3:16]; Mark 1:10; Luke 3:22; [John 1:32] 11:4 [a] Rev. 19:11 [b] Job 4:9; Is. 30:28, 33; Mal. 4:6; 2 Thess. 2:8 11:6 [a] Hos. 2:18 11:9 [a] Job 5:23; Is. 65:25; Ezek. 34:25; Hos. 2:18 [b] Ps. 98:2, 3; Is. 45:6; Hab. 2:14 11:10 [a] Is. 2:11 [b] Is. 11:1; Rom. 15:12 [c] Is. 27:12, 13 [d] Rom. 15:10

11 It shall come to pass in that day
That the LORD shall set His hand
again the second time
To recover the remnant of His
people who are left,
[a]From Assyria and Egypt,
From Pathros and Cush,
From Elam and Shinar,
From Hamath and the
islands of the sea.

12 He will set up a banner for
the nations,
And will assemble the
outcasts of Israel,
And gather together [a]the
dispersed of Judah
From the four corners of the earth.
13 Also [a]the envy of Ephraim
shall depart,
And the adversaries of Judah
shall be cut off;
Ephraim shall not envy Judah,
And Judah shall not harass
Ephraim.
14 But they shall fly down upon the
shoulder of the Philistines
toward the west;
Together they shall plunder
the people of the East;
[a]They shall lay their hand
on Edom and Moab;
And the people of Ammon
shall obey them.
15 The LORD [a]will utterly destroy[1] the
tongue of the Sea of Egypt;
With His mighty wind He will
shake His fist over the River,[2]
And strike it in the seven
streams,
And make *men* cross over
dry-shod.
16 [a]There will be a highway for the
remnant of His people
Who will be left from Assyria,
[b]As it was for Israel
In the day that he came up
from the land of Egypt.

A Hymn of Praise

12 And [a]in that day you will say:

"O LORD, I will praise You;
Though You were angry with me,
Your anger is turned away,
and You comfort me.
2 Behold, God *is* my salvation,
I will trust and not be afraid;
[a]'For [b]YAH, the LORD, *is* my
strength and song;
He also has become my salvation.'"[1]

3 Therefore with joy you will draw [a]water
From the wells of salvation.

4 And in that day you will say:

[a]"Praise the LORD, call upon His name;
[b]Declare His deeds among the peoples,
Make mention that His
[c]name is exalted.
5 [a]Sing to the LORD,
For He has done excellent things;
This *is* known in all the earth.
6 [a]Cry out and shout,
O inhabitant of Zion,
For great *is* [b]the Holy One of
Israel in your midst!"

Proclamation Against Babylon

13 The [a]burden against Babylon which
Isaiah the son of Amoz saw.

2 "Lift[a] up a banner [b]on the
high mountain,
Raise your voice to them;
[c]Wave your hand, that they may
enter the gates of the nobles.
3 I have commanded My
sanctified ones;
I have also called [a]My mighty
ones for My anger—
Those who [b]rejoice in My exaltation."

4 The [a]noise of a multitude
in the mountains,
Like that of many people!

11:11 [a] Is. 19:23–25; Hos. 11:11; Zech. 10:10 **11:12** [a] John 7:35 **11:13** [a] Is. 9:21; Jer. 3:18; Ezek. 37:16, 17, 22; Hos. 1:11 **11:14** [a] Is. 63:1; Dan. 11:41; Joel 3:19; Amos 9:12 **11:15** [a] Is. 50:2; 51:10, 11; Zech. 10:10, 11 [1] Following Masoretic Text and Vulgate; Septuagint, Syriac, and Targum read *dry up*. [2] That is, the Euphrates **11:16** [a] Is. 19:23 [b] Ex. 14:29 **12:1** [a] Is. 2:11 **12:2** [a] Ps. 83:18 [b] Ex. 15:2; Ps. 118:14 [1] Exodus 15:2 **12:3** [a] [John 4:10, 14; 7:37, 38] **12:4** [a] 1 Chr. 16:8; Ps. 105:1 [b] Ps. 145:4–6 [c] Ps. 34:3 **12:5** [a] Ex. 15:1; Ps. 98:1; Is. 24:14; 42:10, 11; 44:23 **12:6** [a] Is. 52:9; 54:1; Zeph. 3:14, 15 [b] Ps. 89:18 **13:1** [a] Jer. 50; 51; Matt. 1:11; Rev. 14:8 **13:2** [a] Is. 18:3 [b] Jer. 51:25 [c] Is. 10:32 **13:3** [a] Joel 3:11 [b] Ps. 149:2 **13:4** [a] Is. 17:12; Joel 3:14

ACT OUT OF SELFLESSNESS

INHALE

I try to live by the Golden Rule and do for others what I would like done for me. My problem is that because of this, those in a position of influence at my company see me as way too nice and soft and will not go to bat for me. They don't think I have what it takes to be promoted, lead people, and make bigger business decisions. So, why should I continue helping others when my kindness gets taken for weakness? I help others, so why isn't God prompting people at my company to help me?

EXHALE

Other people will always be our single greatest test, one we will continually need to pass. This test is anything but easy, but it is incredibly important because Jesus said that loving others is the second greatest command in the Bible after loving God (see Matt. 22:36–40). The answer, then, is not to stop being kind and loving to others. People mistook Jesus' love and kindness for weakness too. So, you're in good company!

If there is one thing for you to consider, though, it seems that you might be relying on people too much and not relying on God nearly enough. The greatest position of influence is to know that God can change the attitude, mindset, and even the thoughts of those around you. Maybe God wants to help you and you cannot see it because you're looking in the wrong direction. If only you would look to Him. God will never turn away from you, and He will never leave you because doing that would be totally opposite of His character.

Give God a chance to take care of your work situation by you focusing more on Him and less on yourself and others. In the day when you see the greatness of God, you will sound like Isaiah 12:2: "Behold, God is my salvation, I will trust and not be afraid; for YAH, the LORD, is my strength and song; He also has become my salvation." Help others as God is helping you, and leave the outcome to Him.

A tumultuous noise of the kingdoms
of nations gathered together!
The LORD of hosts musters
The army for battle.
5 They come from a far country,
From the end of heaven—
The [a]LORD and His weapons
of indignation,
To destroy the whole [b]land.

6 Wail, [a]for the day of the
LORD *is* at hand!
[b]It will come as destruction
from the Almighty.
7 Therefore all hands will
be limp,
Every man's heart will melt,
8 And they will be afraid.
[a]Pangs and sorrows will
take hold of *them;*
They will be in pain as a
woman in childbirth;
They will be amazed at one another;
Their faces *will be like* flames.

9 Behold, [a]the day of the LORD comes,
Cruel, with both wrath
and fierce anger,
To lay the land desolate;
And He will destroy [b]its
sinners from it.
10 For the stars of heaven and
their constellations
Will not give their light;
The sun will be [a]darkened
in its going forth,

13:5 [a] Is. 42:13 [b] Is. 24:1; 34:2 13:6 [a] Is. 2:12; Ezek. 30:3; Amos 5:18; Zeph. 1:7; Rev. 6:17 [b] Is. 10:25; Job 31:23; Joel 1:15 13:8 [a] Ps. 48:6 13:9 [a] Mal. 4:1 [b] Ps. 104:35; Prov. 2:22 13:10 [a] Is. 24:21–23; Ezek. 32:7; Joel 2:31; Matt. 24:29; Mark 13:24; Luke 21:25

And the moon will not cause
its light to shine.

11 "I will [a]punish the world for *its* evil,
And the wicked for their iniquity;
[b]I will halt the arrogance of the proud,
And will lay low the haughtiness
of the terrible.
12 I will make a mortal more
rare than fine gold,
A man more than the golden
wedge of Ophir.
13 [a]Therefore I will shake the heavens,
And the earth will move
out of her place,
In the wrath of the LORD of hosts
And in [b]the day of His fierce anger.
14 It shall be as the hunted gazelle,
And as a sheep that no man takes up;
[a]Every man will turn to his own
people,
And everyone will flee to his own land.
15 Everyone who is found will
be thrust through,
And everyone who is captured
will fall by the sword.
16 Their children also will be [a]dashed
to pieces before their eyes;
Their houses will be plundered
And their wives [b]ravished.

17 "Behold,[a] I will stir up the
Medes against them,
Who will not regard silver;
And *as for* gold, they will
not delight in it.
18 Also *their* bows will dash the
young men to pieces,
And they will have no pity on
the fruit of the womb;
Their eye will not spare children.
19 [a]And Babylon, the glory of kingdoms,
The beauty of the Chaldeans' pride,
Will be as when God overthrew
[b]Sodom and Gomorrah.
20 [a]It will never be inhabited,
Nor will it be settled from
generation to generation;
Nor will the Arabian pitch tents there,
Nor will the shepherds make
their sheepfolds there.
21 [a]But wild beasts of the
desert will lie there,
And their houses will be full of owls;
Ostriches will dwell there,
And wild goats will caper there.
22 The hyenas will howl in their citadels,
And jackals in their pleasant
palaces.
[a]Her time *is* near to come,
And her days will not be prolonged."

Mercy on Jacob

14 For the LORD [a]will have mercy on Jacob, and [b]will still choose Israel, and
settle them in their own land. [c]The strangers will be joined with them, and they will
cling to the house of Jacob. 2 Then people
will take them [a]and bring them to their
place, and the house of Israel will possess
them for servants and maids in the land
of the LORD; they will take them captive
whose captives they were, [b]and rule over
their oppressors.

Fall of the King of Babylon

3 It shall come to pass in the day the
LORD gives you rest from your sorrow, and
from your fear and the hard bondage in
which you were made to serve, 4 that you
[a]will take up this proverb against the king
of Babylon, and say:

"How the oppressor has ceased,
The [b]golden[1] city ceased!
5 The LORD has broken [a]the
staff of the wicked,
The scepter of the rulers;
6 He who struck the people in wrath
with a continual stroke,
He who ruled the nations in anger,
Is persecuted *and* no one hinders.
7 The whole earth is at rest *and* quiet;
They break forth into singing.
8 [a]Indeed the cypress trees
rejoice over you,
And the cedars of Lebanon,
Saying, 'Since you were cut down,

13:11 [a] Is. 26:21 [b] [Is. 2:17] 13:13 [a] Is. 34:4; 51:6; Hag. 2:6 [b] Ps. 110:5; Lam. 1:12 13:14 [a] Jer. 50:16; 51:9 13:16 [a] Ps. 137:8, 9; Is. 13:18; 14:21; Hos. 10:14; Nah. 3:10 [b] Zech. 14:2 13:17 [a] Is. 21:2; Jer. 51:11, 28; Dan. 5:28, 31 13:19 [a] Is. 14:4; Dan. 4:30; Rev. 18:11–16, 19, 21 [b] Gen. 19:24; Deut. 29:23; Jer. 50:40; Amos 4:11 13:20 [a] Jer. 50:3 13:21 [a] Is. 34:11–15; Zeph. 2:14; Rev. 18:2 13:22 [a] Jer. 51:33 14:1 [a] Ps. 102:13; Is. 49:13, 15; 54:7, 8 [b] Is. 41:8, 9; Zech. 1:17; 2:12 [c] Is. 60:4, 5, 10 14:2 [a] Is. 49:22; 60:9; 66:20 [b] Is. 60:14 14:4 [a] Is. 13:19; Hab. 2:6 [b] Rev. 18:16 [1] Or *insolent* 14:5 [a] Ps. 125:3 14:8 [a] Is. 55:12; Ezek. 31:16

No woodsman has come
up against us.'

9 "Hell[a] from beneath is
excited about you,
To meet *you* at your coming;
It stirs up the dead for you,
All the chief ones of the earth;
It has raised up from their thrones
All the kings of the nations.
10 They all shall [a]speak and say to you:
'Have you also become as weak as we?
Have you become like us?
11 Your pomp is brought down to Sheol,
And the sound of your
stringed instruments;
The maggot is spread under you,
And worms cover you.'

The Fall of Lucifer

12 "How[a] you are fallen from heaven,
O Lucifer,[1] son of the morning!
How you are cut down to the ground,
You who weakened the nations!
13 For you have said in your heart:
[a]'I will ascend into heaven,
[b]I will exalt my throne above
the stars of God;
I will also sit on the [c]mount
of the congregation
[d]On the farthest sides of the north;
14 I will ascend above the
heights of the clouds,
[a]I will be like the Most High.'
15 Yet you [a]shall be brought
down to Sheol,
To the lowest depths of the Pit.

16 "Those who see you will
gaze at you,
And consider you, *saying:*
'*Is* this the man who made
the earth tremble,
Who shook kingdoms,
17 Who made the world as
a wilderness
And destroyed its cities,
Who did not open the house
of his prisoners?'

18 "All the kings of the nations,
All of them, sleep in glory,
Everyone in his own house;
19 But you are cast out of your grave
Like an abominable branch,
Like the garment of those
who are slain,
Thrust through with a sword,
Who go down to the stones of the pit,
Like a corpse trodden underfoot.
20 You will not be joined with
them in burial,
Because you have destroyed your land
And slain your people.
[a]The brood of evildoers shall
never be named.
21 Prepare slaughter for his children
[a]Because of the iniquity
of their fathers,
Lest they rise up and possess the land,
And fill the face of the
world with cities."

Babylon Destroyed

22 "For I will rise up against them,"
says the LORD of hosts,
"And cut off from Babylon [a]the
name and [b]remnant,
[c]And offspring and posterity,"
says the LORD.
23 "I will also make it a possession
for the [a]porcupine,
And marshes of muddy water;
I will sweep it with the broom
of destruction," says
the LORD of hosts.

Assyria Destroyed

24 The LORD of hosts has sworn, saying,
"Surely, as I have thought, so
it shall come to pass,
And as I have purposed,
so it shall [a]stand:
25 That I will break the
[a]Assyrian in My land,
And on My mountains tread
him underfoot.
Then [b]his yoke shall be
removed from them,

14:9 [a] Ezek. 32:21 14:10 [a] Ezek. 32:21 14:12 [a] Is. 34:4; Luke 10:18; [Rev. 12:7–9] [1] Literally *Day Star* 14:13 [a] Ezek. 28:2; Matt. 11:23 [b] Dan. 8:10; 2 Thess. 2:4 [c] Ezek. 28:14 [d] Ps. 48:2 14:14 [a] Is. 47:8; 2 Thess. 2:4 14:15 [a] Ezek. 28:8; Matt. 11:23; Luke 10:15 14:20 [a] Job 18:19; Ps. 21:10; 109:13; Is. 1:4; 31:2 14:21 [a] Ex. 20:5; Lev. 26:39; Is. 13:16; Matt. 23:35 14:22 [a] Prov. 10:7; Is. 26:14; Jer. 51:62 [b] 1 Kin. 14:10 [c] Job 18:19; Is. 47:9 14:23 [a] Is. 34:11; Zeph. 2:14 14:24 [a] Is. 43:13 14:25 [a] Mic. 5:5, 6; Zeph. 2:13 [b] Is. 10:27; Nah. 1:13

And his burden removed
from their shoulders.
26 This *is* the [a]purpose that is purposed
against the whole earth,
And this *is* the hand that is stretched
out over all the nations.
27 For the LORD of hosts has [a]purposed,
And who will annul *it?*
His hand *is* stretched out,
And who will turn it back?"

Philistia Destroyed

28 This is the burden which came in the
year that [a]King Ahaz died.

29 "Do not rejoice, all you of Philistia,
[a]Because the rod that struck
you is broken;
For out of the serpent's roots
will come forth a viper,
[b]And its offspring *will be* a
fiery flying serpent.
30 The firstborn of the poor will feed,
And the needy will lie down in safety;
I will kill your roots with famine,
And it will slay your remnant.
31 Wail, O gate! Cry, O city!
All you of Philistia *are* dissolved;
For smoke will come from the north,
And no one *will be* alone in
his appointed times."

32 What will they answer the
messengers of the nation?
That [a]the LORD has founded Zion,
And [b]the poor of His people
shall take refuge in it.

Proclamation Against Moab

15 The [a]burden against Moab.

Because in the night [b]Ar of
[c]Moab is laid waste
And destroyed,
Because in the night Kir of
Moab is laid waste
And destroyed,
2 He has gone up to the
temple[1] and Dibon,
To the high places to weep.
Moab will wail over Nebo
and over Medeba;
[a]On all their heads *will be* baldness,
And every beard cut off.
3 In their streets they will clothe
themselves with sackcloth;
On the tops of their houses
And in their streets
Everyone will wail, [a]weeping bitterly.
4 Heshbon and Elealeh will cry out,
Their voice shall be heard
as far as [a]Jahaz;
Therefore the armed soldiers[1]
of Moab will cry out;
His life will be burdensome to him.

5 "My[a] heart will cry out for Moab;
His fugitives *shall flee* to Zoar,
Like a three-year-old heifer.[1]
For [b]by the Ascent of Luhith
They will go up with weeping;
For in the way of Horonaim
They will raise up a cry
of destruction,
6 For the waters [a]of Nimrim
will be desolate,
For the green grass has withered away;
The grass fails, there is nothing green.
7 Therefore the abundance
they have gained,
And what they have laid up,
They will carry away to the
Brook of the Willows.
8 For the cry has gone all around
the borders of Moab,
Its wailing to Eglaim
And its wailing to Beer Elim.
9 For the waters of Dimon[1]
will be full of blood;
Because I will bring more
upon Dimon,[2]
[a]Lions upon him who
escapes from Moab,
And on the remnant of the land."

14:26 [a] Is. 23:9; Zeph. 3:6, 8 14:27 [a] 2 Chr. 20:6; Job 9:12; 23:13; Ps. 33:11; Prov. 19:21; 21:30; Is. 43:13; Dan. 4:31, 35 14:28 [a] 2 Kin. 16:20; 2 Chr. 28:27 14:29 [a] 2 Chr. 26:6 [b] 2 Kin. 18:8 14:32 [a] Ps. 87:1, 5 [b] Zech. 11:11 15:1 [a] 2 Kin. 3:4 [b] Deut. 2:9; Num. 21:28 [c] Is. 15:1—16:14; Jer. 25:21; 48:1–47; Amos 2:1–3; Zeph. 2:8–11 15:2 [a] Lev. 21:5; Jer. 48:37 [1] Hebrew *bayith,* literally *house* 15:3 [a] Jer. 48:38 15:4 [a] Num. 21:28; 32:3; Jer. 48:34 [1] Following Masoretic Text, Targum, and Vulgate; Septuagint and Syriac read *loins.* 15:5 [a] Is. 16:11; Jer. 48:31 [b] Jer. 48:5 [1] Or *The Third Eglath,* an unknown city (compare Jeremiah 48:34) 15:6 [a] Num. 32:36 15:9 [a] 2 Kin. 17:25; Jer. 50:17 [1] Following Masoretic Text and Targum; Dead Sea Scrolls and Vulgate read *Dibon;* Septuagint reads *Rimon.* [2] Following Masoretic Text and Targum; Dead Sea Scrolls and Vulgate read *Dibon;* Septuagint reads *Rimon.*

Moab Destroyed

16 Send [a]the lamb to the ruler
of the land,
[b]From Sela to the wilderness,
To the mount of the daughter of Zion.
2 For it shall be as a [a]wandering
bird thrown out of the nest;
So shall be the daughters of Moab
at the fords of the [b]Arnon.

3 "Take counsel, execute judgment;
Make your shadow like the night
in the middle of the day;
Hide the outcasts,
Do not betray him who escapes.
4 Let My outcasts dwell with
you, O Moab;
Be a shelter to them from
the face of the spoiler.
For the extortioner is at an end,
Devastation ceases,
The oppressors are consumed
out of the land.
5 In mercy [a]the throne will
be established;
And One will sit on it in truth,
in the tabernacle of David,
[b]Judging and seeking justice and
hastening [c]righteousness."

6 We have heard of the [a]pride of Moab—
He is very proud—
Of his haughtiness and his
pride and his wrath;
[b]*But* his lies *shall* not *be* so.
7 Therefore Moab shall [a]wail for Moab;
Everyone shall wail.
For the foundations [b]of Kir
Hareseth you shall mourn;
Surely *they are* stricken.

8 For [a]the fields of Heshbon languish,
And [b]the vine of Sibmah;
The lords of the nations have
broken down its choice plants,
Which have reached to Jazer
And wandered through
the wilderness.
Her branches are stretched out,
They are gone over the [c]sea.
9 Therefore I will bewail the
vine of Sibmah,
With the weeping of Jazer;
I will drench you with my tears,
[a]O Heshbon and Elealeh;
For battle cries have fallen
Over your summer fruits
and your harvest.

10 [a]Gladness is taken away,
And joy from the plentiful field;
In the vineyards there
will be no singing,
Nor will there be shouting;
No treaders will tread out
wine in the presses;
I have made their shouting cease.
11 Therefore [a]my heart shall resound
like a harp for Moab,
And my inner being for Kir Heres.

12 And it shall come to pass,
When it is seen that Moab is
weary on [a]the high place,
That he will come to his
sanctuary to pray;
But he will not prevail.

13 This *is* the word which the LORD has
spoken concerning Moab since that time.
14 But now the LORD has spoken, saying,
"Within three years, [a]as the years of a hired
man, the glory of Moab will be despised
with all that great multitude, and the remnant *will be* very small *and* feeble."

Proclamation Against Syria and Israel

17 The [a]burden against Damascus.

"Behold, Damascus will cease
from *being* a city,
And it will be a ruinous heap.
2 The cities of [a]Aroer *are* forsaken;[1]
They will be for flocks
Which lie down, and [b]no one
will make *them* afraid.

16:1 [a] 2 Kin. 3:4; Ezra 7:17 [b] 2 Kin. 14:7; Is. 42:11 16:2 [a] Prov. 27:8 [b] Num. 21:13 16:5 [a] [Is. 9:6, 7; 32:1; 55:4; Dan. 7:14; Mic. 4:7; Luke 1:33; Rev. 11:15] [b] Ps. 72:2 [c] Is. 9:7 16:6 [a] Jer. 48:29; Amos 2:1; Obad. 3, 4; Zeph. 2:8, 10 [b] Is. 28:15 16:7 [a] Jer. 48:20 [b] 2 Kin. 3:25; Jer. 48:31 16:8 [a] Is. 24:7 [b] Is. 16:9 [c] Jer. 48:32 16:9 [a] Is. 15:4 16:10 [a] Is. 24:8; Jer. 48:33 16:11 [a] Is. 15:5; 63:15; Jer. 48:36; Hos. 11:8; Phil. 2:1 16:12 [a] Is. 15:2 16:14 [a] Job 7:1; 14:6; Is. 21:16 17:1 [a] Gen. 14:15; 15:2; 2 Kin. 16:9; Jer. 49:23; Amos 1:3–5; Zech. 9:1; Acts 9:2 17:2 [a] Num. 32:34 [b] Jer. 7:33 [1] Following Masoretic Text and Vulgate; Septuagint reads *It shall be forsaken forever;* Targum reads *Its cities shall be forsaken and desolate.*

3 [a]The fortress also will cease
from Ephraim,
The kingdom from Damascus,
And the remnant of Syria;
They will be as the glory of
the children of Israel,"
Says the LORD of hosts.

4 "In that day it shall come to pass
That the glory of Jacob will wane,
And [a]the fatness of his flesh grow lean.
5 [a]It shall be as when the harvester
gathers the grain,
And reaps the heads with his arm;
It shall be as he who gathers
heads of grain
In the Valley of Rephaim.
6 [a]Yet gleaning grapes will be left in it,
Like the shaking of an olive tree,
Two *or* three olives at the top
of the uppermost bough,
Four *or* five in its most
fruitful branches,"
Says the LORD God of Israel.

7 In that day a man will
[a]look to his Maker,
And his eyes will have respect
for the Holy One of Israel.
8 He will not look to the altars,
The work of his hands;
He will not respect what his
[a]fingers have made,
Nor the wooden images[1] nor
the incense altars.

9 In that day his strong cities will
be as a forsaken bough[1]
And an uppermost branch,[2]
Which they left because of
the children of Israel;
And there will be desolation.

10 Because you have forgotten [a]the
God of your salvation,
And have not been mindful of the
Rock of your stronghold,
Therefore you will plant
pleasant plants
And set out foreign seedlings;
11 In the day you will make
your plant to grow,
And in the morning you will
make your seed to flourish;
But the harvest *will be* a heap of ruins
In the day of grief and
desperate sorrow.

12 Woe to the multitude of many people
Who make a noise [a]like the
roar of the seas,
And to the rushing of nations
That make a rushing like the
rushing of mighty waters!
13 The nations will rush like the
rushing of many waters;
But *God* will [a]rebuke them and
they will flee far away,
And [b]be chased like the chaff of the
mountains before the wind,
Like a rolling thing before
the whirlwind.
14 Then behold, at eventide, trouble!
And before the morning,
he *is* no more.
This *is* the portion of those
who plunder us,
And the lot of those who rob us.

Proclamation Against Ethiopia

18 Woe [a]to the land shadowed
with buzzing wings,
Which *is* beyond the rivers
of Ethiopia,
2 Which sends ambassadors by sea,
Even in vessels of reed on
the waters, *saying,*
"Go, swift messengers, to a nation
tall and smooth *of skin,*
To a people terrible from their
beginning onward,
A nation powerful and treading down,
Whose land the rivers divide."

3 All inhabitants of the world and
dwellers on the earth:
[a]When he lifts up a banner on
the mountains, you see *it;*

17:3 [a] Is. 7:16; 8:4 17:4 [a] Is. 10:16 17:5 [a] Is. 17:11; Jer. 51:33; Joel 3:13; Matt. 13:30 17:6 [a] Deut. 4:27; Is. 24:13; Obad. 5 17:7 [a] Is. 10:20; Hos. 3:5; Mic. 7:7 17:8 [a] Is. 2:8; 31:7 [1] Hebrew *Asherim,* Canaanite deities 17:9 [1] Septuagint reads *Hivites;* Targum reads *laid waste;* Vulgate reads *as the plows.* [2] Septuagint reads *Amorites;* Targum reads *in ruins;* Vulgate reads *corn.* 17:10 [a] Ps. 68:19; Is. 51:13 17:12 [a] Is. 5:30; Jer. 6:23; Ezek. 43:2; Luke 21:25 17:13 [a] Ps. 9:5; Is. 41:11 [b] Ps. 83:13; Hos. 13:3 18:1 [a] 2 Kin. 19:9; Is. 20:4, 5; Ezek. 30:4, 5, 9; Zeph. 2:12; 3:10 18:3 [a] Is. 5:26

And when he blows a
trumpet, you hear *it.*
4 For so the LORD said to me,
"I will take My rest,
And I will look from My dwelling place
Like clear heat in sunshine,
Like a cloud of dew in the
heat of harvest."
5 For before the harvest, when
the bud is perfect
And the sour grape is
ripening in the flower,
He will both cut off the sprigs
with pruning hooks
And take away *and* cut
down the branches.
6 They will be left together for the
mountain birds of prey
And for the beasts of the earth;
The birds of prey will
summer on them,
And all the beasts of the earth
will winter on them.

7 In that time [a]a present will be
brought to the LORD of hosts
From[1] a people tall and smooth *of skin,*
And from a people terrible from
their beginning onward,
A nation powerful and treading down,
Whose land the rivers divide—
To the place of the name of
the LORD of hosts,
To Mount Zion.

Proclamation Against Egypt

19 The [a]burden against Egypt.

Behold, the LORD [b]rides
on a swift cloud,
And will come into Egypt;
[c]The idols of Egypt will totter
at His presence,
And the heart of Egypt will
melt in its midst.

2 "I will [a]set Egyptians against Egyptians;
Everyone will fight against his brother,
And everyone against his neighbor,
City against city, kingdom
against kingdom.
3 The spirit of Egypt will fail in its midst;
I will destroy their counsel,
And they will [a]consult the
idols and the charmers,
The mediums and the sorcerers.
4 And the Egyptians I will give
[a]Into the hand of a cruel master,
And a fierce king will rule over them,"
Says the Lord, the LORD of hosts.

5 [a]The waters will fail from the sea,
And the river will be wasted
and dried up.
6 The rivers will turn foul;
The brooks [a]of defense will be
emptied and dried up;
The reeds and rushes will wither.
7 The papyrus reeds by the River,[1]
by the mouth of the River,
And everything sown by the River,
Will wither, be driven away,
and be no more.
8 The fishermen also will mourn;
All those will lament who cast
hooks into the River,
And they will languish who
spread nets on the waters.
9 Moreover those who work in [a]fine flax
And those who weave fine
fabric will be ashamed;
10 And its foundations will be broken.
All who make wages *will be*
troubled of soul.

11 Surely the princes of [a]Zoan *are* fools;
Pharaoh's wise counselors
give foolish counsel.
[b]How do you say to Pharaoh, "I
am the son of the wise,
The son of ancient kings?"
12 [a]Where *are* they?
Where are your wise men?
Let them tell you now,
And let them know what the LORD of
hosts has [b]purposed against Egypt.

18:7 [a] Ps. 68:31; 72:10; Is. 16:1; Zeph. 3:10; Mal. 1:11; Acts 8:27–38 [1] Following Dead Sea Scrolls, Septuagint, and Vulgate; Masoretic Text omits *From;* Targum reads *To.* 19:1 [a] Jer. 9:25, 26; Ezek. 29:1—30:19; Joel 3:19 [b] Ps. 18:10; 104:3; Matt. 26:64; Rev. 1:7 [c] Ex. 12:12; Jer. 43:12 19:2 [a] Judg. 7:22; 1 Sam. 14:16, 20; 2 Chr. 20:23; Matt. 10:21, 36 19:3 [a] 1 Chr. 10:13; Is. 8:19; 47:12; Dan. 2:2 19:4 [a] Is. 20:4; Jer. 46:26; Ezek. 29:19 19:5 [a] Is. 50:2; Jer. 51:36; Ezek. 30:12 19:6 [a] 2 Kin. 19:24 19:7 [1] That is, the Nile 19:9 [a] 1 Kin. 10:28; Prov. 7:16; Ezek. 27:7 19:11 [a] Num. 13:22; Ps. 78:12, 43; Is. 30:4 [b] Gen. 41:38, 39; 1 Kin. 4:29, 30; Acts 7:22 19:12 [a] 1 Cor. 1:20 [b] Ps. 33:11

13 The princes of Zoan have
become fools;
[a]The princes of Noph[1] are deceived;
They have also deluded Egypt,
Those who are the mainstay
of its tribes.
14 The LORD has mingled [a]a
perverse spirit in her midst;
And they have caused Egypt
to err in all her work,
As a drunken man staggers
in his vomit.
15 Neither will there be *any*
work for Egypt,
Which [a]the head or tail,
Palm branch or bulrush,
may do.[1]

16In that day Egypt will [a]be like women,
and will be afraid and fear because of the
waving of the hand of the LORD of hosts,
[b]which He waves over it. 17And the land of
Judah will be a terror to Egypt; everyone
who makes mention of it will be afraid
in himself, because of the counsel of the
LORD of hosts which He has [a]determined
against it.

Egypt, Assyria, and Israel Blessed

18In that day five cities in the land of
Egypt will [a]speak the language of Canaan
and [b]swear by the LORD of hosts; one will
be called the City of Destruction.[1]
19In that day [a]there will be an altar
to the LORD in the midst of the land of
Egypt, and a pillar to the [b]LORD at its border. 20And [a]it will be for a sign and for a
witness to the LORD of hosts in the land
of Egypt; for they will cry to the LORD because of the oppressors, and He will send
them a [b]Savior and a Mighty One, and He
will deliver them. 21Then the LORD will
be known to Egypt, and the Egyptians
will [a]know the LORD in that day, and [b]will
make sacrifice and offering; yes, they will
make a vow to the LORD and perform *it.*
22And the LORD will strike Egypt, He will
strike and [a]heal *it;* they will return to the
LORD, and He will be entreated by them
and heal them.
23In that day [a]there will be a highway
from Egypt to Assyria, and the Assyrian
will come into Egypt and the Egyptian into
Assyria, and the Egyptians will [b]serve with
the Assyrians.
24In that day Israel will be one of three
with Egypt and Assyria—a blessing in the
midst of the land, 25whom the LORD of
hosts shall bless, saying, "Blessed *is* Egypt
My people, and Assyria [a]the work of My
hands, and Israel My inheritance."

The Sign Against Egypt and Ethiopia

20 In the year that [a]Tartan[1] came to
Ashdod, when Sargon the king of
Assyria sent him, and he fought against
Ashdod and took it, 2at the same time the
LORD spoke by Isaiah the son of Amoz, saying, "Go, and remove [a]the sackcloth from
your body, and take your sandals off your
feet." And he did so, [b]walking naked and
barefoot.
3Then the LORD said, "Just as My servant
Isaiah has walked naked and barefoot three
years [a]*for* a sign and a wonder against Egypt
and Ethiopia, 4so shall the [a]king of Assyria
lead away the Egyptians as prisoners and
the Ethiopians as captives, young and old,
naked and barefoot, [b]with their buttocks
uncovered, to the shame of Egypt. 5[a]Then
they shall be afraid and ashamed of Ethiopia their expectation and Egypt their glory.
6And the inhabitant of this territory will
say in that day, 'Surely such *is* our expectation, wherever we flee for [a]help to be delivered from the king of Assyria; and how
shall we escape?' "

The Fall of Babylon Proclaimed

21 The burden against the Wilderness
of the Sea.

As [a]whirlwinds in the South
pass through,

19:13 [a] Jer. 2:16; Ezek. 30:13 [1] That is, ancient Memphis 19:14 [a] 1 Kin. 22:22; Is. 29:10 19:15 [a] Is. 9:14–16 [1] Compare Isaiah 9:14–16 19:16 [a] Jer. 51:30; Nah. 3:13 [b] Is. 11:15 19:17 [a] Is. 14:24; Dan. 4:35 19:18 [a] Zeph. 3:9 [b] Is. 45:23 [1] Some Hebrew manuscripts, Arabic, Dead Sea Scrolls, Targum, and Vulgate read *Sun;* Septuagint reads *Asedek* (literally *Righteousness*). 19:19 [a] Gen. 28:18; Ex. 24:4; Josh. 22:10, 26, 27; Is. 56:7; 60:7 [b] Ps. 68:31 19:20 [a] Josh. 4:20; 22:27 [b] Is. 43:11 19:21 [a] [Is. 2:3, 4; 11:9] [b] Is. 56:7; 60:7; Zech. 14:16–18; Mal. 1:11 19:22 [a] Deut. 32:39; Is. 30:26; 57:18; [Heb. 12:11] 19:23 [a] Is. 11:16; 35:8; 49:11; 62:10 [b] Is. 27:13 19:25 [a] Deut. 14:2; Ps. 100:3; Is. 29:23; Hos. 2:23; [Eph. 2:10] 20:1 [a] 2 Kin. 18:17 [1] Or *the Commander in Chief* 20:2 [a] Zech. 13:4; Matt. 3:4 [b] 1 Sam. 19:24; Mic. 1:8 20:3 [a] Is. 8:18 20:4 [a] Is. 19:4 [b] 2 Sam. 10:4; Is. 3:17; Jer. 13:22; Mic. 1:11 20:5 [a] 2 Kin. 18:21; Is. 30:3–5; 31:1; Ezek. 29:6, 7 20:6 [a] Is. 30:5, 7 21:1 [a] Zech. 9:14

So it comes from the desert,
from a terrible land.
2 A distressing vision is declared to me;
[a]The treacherous dealer
deals treacherously,
And the plunderer plunders.
[b]Go up, O Elam!
Besiege, O Media!
All its sighing I have made to cease.

3 Therefore [a]my loins are
filled with pain;
[b]Pangs have taken hold of me, like
the pangs of a woman in labor.
I was distressed when *I* heard *it;*
I was dismayed when *I* saw *it.*
4 My heart wavered, fearfulness
frightened me;
[a]The night for which I longed He
turned into fear for me.
5 [a]Prepare the table,
Set a watchman in the tower,
Eat and drink.
Arise, you princes,
Anoint the shield!

6 For thus has the Lord said to me:
"Go, set a watchman,
Let him declare what he sees."
7 And he saw a chariot *with*
a pair of horsemen,
A chariot of donkeys, *and*
a chariot of camels,
And he listened earnestly
with great care.
8 Then he cried, "A lion,[1] my Lord!
I stand continually on the
[a]watchtower in the daytime;
I have sat at my post every night.
9 And look, here comes a chariot of
men *with* a pair of horsemen!"
Then he answered and said,
[a]"Babylon is fallen, is fallen!
And [b]all the carved images
of her gods
He has broken to the ground."

10 [a]Oh, my threshing and the
grain of my floor!
That which I have heard from
the LORD of hosts,
The God of Israel,
I have declared to you.

Proclamation Against Edom

11 [a]The burden against Dumah.

He calls to me out of [b]Seir,
"Watchman, what of the night?
Watchman, what of the night?"
12 The watchman said,
"The morning comes, and
also the night.
If you will inquire, inquire;
Return! Come back!"

Proclamation Against Arabia

13 [a]The burden against Arabia.

In the forest in Arabia you
will lodge,
O you traveling companies
[b]of Dedanites.
14 O inhabitants of the land of Tema,
Bring water to him who is thirsty;
With their bread they met
him who fled.
15 For they fled from the swords,
from the drawn sword,
From the bent bow, and from
the distress of war.

16 For thus the LORD has said to me:
"Within a year, [a]according to the year of a
hired man, all the glory of [b]Kedar will fail;
17 and the remainder of the number of archers, the mighty men of the people of Kedar, will be diminished; for the LORD God
of Israel has spoken *it.*"

Proclamation Against Jerusalem

22 The burden against the Valley of
Vision.

What ails you now, that you have
all gone up to the housetops,
2 You who are full of noise,
A tumultuous city, [a]a joyous city?

21:2 [a] Is. 33:1 [b] Is. 13:17; 22:6; Jer. 49:34 21:3 [a] Is. 15:5; 16:11 [b] Is. 13:8 21:4 [a] Deut. 28:67 21:5 [a] Jer. 51:39; Dan. 5:5 21:8 [a] Hab. 2:1 [1] Dead Sea Scrolls read *Then the observer cried.* 21:9 [a] Is. 13:19; 47:5, 9; 48:14; Jer. 51:8; Dan. 5:28, 31; Rev. 14:8; 18:2 [b] Is. 46:1; Jer. 50:2; 51:44 21:10 [a] Jer. 51:33; Mic. 4:13 21:11 [a] Gen. 25:14; 1 Chr. 1:30; Josh. 15:52 [b] Gen. 32:3; Jer. 49:7; Ezek. 35:2; Obad. 1 21:13 [a] Jer. 25:24; 49:28 [b] Gen. 10:7; 1 Chr. 1:9, 32; Jer. 25:23; Ezek. 27:15 21:16 [a] Is. 16:14 [b] Ps. 120:5; Song 1:5; Is. 42:11; 60:7; Ezek. 27:21 22:2 [a] Is. 32:13

Your slain *men are* not slain
with the sword,
Nor dead in battle.
3 All your rulers have fled together;
They are captured by the archers.
All who are found in you
are bound together;
They have fled from afar.
4 Therefore I said, "Look away
from me,
[a]I will weep bitterly;
Do not labor to comfort me
Because of the plundering of the
daughter of my people."
5 [a]For *it is* a day of trouble and
treading down and perplexity
[b]By the Lord GOD of hosts
In the Valley of Vision—
Breaking down the walls
And of crying to the mountain.
6 [a]Elam bore the quiver
With chariots of men *and* horsemen,
And [b]Kir uncovered the shield.
7 It shall come to pass *that*
your choicest valleys
Shall be full of chariots,
And the horsemen shall set
themselves in array at the gate.
8 [a]He removed the protection
of Judah.
You looked in that day to the armor
[b]of the House of the Forest;
9 [a]You also saw the damage
to the city of David,
That it was great;
And you gathered together the
waters of the lower pool.
10 You numbered the houses
of Jerusalem,
And the houses you broke down
To fortify the wall.
11 [a]You also made a reservoir
between the two walls
For the water of the old [b]pool.
But you did not look to its Maker,
Nor did you have respect for Him
who fashioned it long ago.
12 And in that day the Lord GOD
of hosts
[a]Called for weeping and for mourning,
[b]For baldness and for girding
with sackcloth.
13 But instead, joy and gladness,
Slaying oxen and killing sheep,
Eating meat and [a]drinking wine:
[b]"Let us eat and drink, for
tomorrow we die!"

14 [a]Then it was revealed in my hearing
by the LORD of hosts,
"Surely for this iniquity there [b]will
be no atonement for you,
Even to your death," says the
Lord GOD of hosts.

The Judgment on Shebna

15 Thus says the Lord GOD of hosts:

"Go, proceed to this steward,
To [a]Shebna, who *is* over
the house, *and say:*
16 'What have you here, and
whom have you here,
That you have hewn a sepulcher here,
As he [a]who hews himself a
sepulcher on high,
Who carves a tomb for
himself in a rock?
17 Indeed, the LORD will throw
you away violently,
O mighty man,
[a]And will surely seize you.
18 He will surely turn violently
and toss you like a ball
Into a large country;
There you shall die, and there
[a]your glorious chariots
Shall be the shame of your
master's house.
19 So I will drive you out of your office,
And from your position he
will pull you down.[1]

20 'Then it shall be in that day,
That I will call My servant
[a]Eliakim the son of Hilkiah;

22:4 [a] Jer. 4:19 22:5 [a] Is. 37:3 [b] Lam. 1:5; 2:2 22:6 [a] Jer. 49:35 [b] Is. 15:1 22:8 [a] 2 Kin. 18:15, 16 [b] 1 Kin. 7:2; 10:17 22:9 [a] 2 Kin. 20:20; 2 Chr. 32:4; Neh. 3:16 22:11 [a] Neh. 3:16 [b] 2 Kin. 20:20; 2 Chr. 32:3, 4 22:12 [a] Is. 32:11; Joel 1:13; 2:17 [b] Ezra 9:3; Is. 15:2; Mic. 1:16 22:13 [a] Is. 5:11, 22; 28:7, 8; Luke 17:26–29 [b] Is. 56:12; 1 Cor. 15:32 22:14 [a] Is. 5:9 [b] 1 Sam. 3:14; Ezek. 24:13 22:15 [a] 2 Kin. 18:37; Is. 36:3 22:16 [a] 2 Sam. 18:18; 2 Chr. 16:14; Matt. 27:60 22:17 [a] Esth. 7:8 22:18 [a] Is. 2:7 22:19 [1] Septuagint omits *he will pull you down;* Syriac, Targum, and Vulgate read *I will pull you down.* 22:20 [a] 2 Kin. 18:18; Is. 36:3, 22; 37:2

21 I will clothe him with your robe
And strengthen him with your belt;
I will commit your responsibility
into his hand.
He shall be a father to the
inhabitants of Jerusalem
And to the house of Judah.
22 The key of the house of David
I will lay on his [a]shoulder;
So he shall [b]open, and no
one shall shut;
And he shall shut, and no
one shall open.
23 I will fasten him *as* [a]a peg
in a secure place,
And he will become a glorious
throne to his father's house.

24'They will hang on him all the glory of
his father's house, the offspring and the
posterity, all vessels of small quantity, from
the cups to all the pitchers. 25In that day,'
says the LORD of hosts, 'the peg that is fastened in the secure place will be removed
and be cut down and fall, and the burden
that *was* on it will be cut off; for the LORD
has spoken.'"

Proclamation Against Tyre

23 The [a]burden against Tyre.

Wail, you ships of Tarshish!
For it is laid waste,
So that there is no house,
no harbor;
From the land of Cyprus[1] it
is revealed to them.

2 Be still, you inhabitants
of the coastland,
You merchants of Sidon,
Whom those who cross the
sea have filled.[1]
3 And on great waters the
grain of Shihor,
The harvest of the River,[1]
is her revenue;
And [a]she is a marketplace
for the nations.

4 Be ashamed, O Sidon;
For the sea has spoken,
The strength of the sea, saying,
"I do not labor, nor bring
forth children;
Neither do I rear young men,
Nor bring up virgins."
5 [a]When the report *reaches* Egypt,
They also will be in agony
at the report of Tyre.

6 Cross over to Tarshish;
Wail, you inhabitants of the coastland!
7 *Is* this your [a]joyous *city,*
Whose antiquity *is* from ancient days,
Whose feet carried her far off to dwell?
8 Who has taken this counsel against
Tyre, [a]the crowning *city,*
Whose merchants *are* princes,
Whose traders *are* the
honorable of the earth?
9 The LORD of hosts has [a]purposed it,
To bring to dishonor the
[b]pride of all glory,
To bring into contempt all the
honorable of the earth.

10 Overflow through your
land like the River,[1]
O daughter of Tarshish;
There is no more strength.
11 He stretched out His hand
over the sea,
He shook the kingdoms;
The LORD has given a commandment
[a]against Canaan
To destroy its strongholds.
12 And He said, "You will rejoice
no more,
O you oppressed virgin
daughter of Sidon.
Arise, [a]cross over to Cyprus;
There also you will have no rest."

13 Behold, the land of the [a]Chaldeans,
This people *which* was not;
Assyria founded it for [b]wild
beasts of the desert.
They set up its towers,

22:22 [a] Is. 9:6 [b] Job 12:14; Rev. 3:7 22:23 [a] Ezra 9:8; Zech. 10:4 23:1 [a] Jer. 25:22; 47:4; Ezek. 26—28; Amos 1:9; Zech. 9:2, 4 [1] Hebrew *Kittim,* western lands, especially Cyprus 23:2 [1] Following Masoretic Text and Vulgate; Septuagint and Targum read *Passing over the water;* Dead Sea Scrolls read *Your messengers passing over the sea.* 23:3 [a] Ezek. 27:3–23 [1] That is, the Nile 23:5 [a] Is. 19:16 23:7 [a] Is. 22:2; 32:13 23:8 [a] Ezek. 28:2, 12 23:9 [a] Is. 14:26 [b] Job 40:11, 12; Is. 13:11; 24:4; Dan. 4:37 23:10 [1] That is, the Nile 23:11 [a] Zech. 9:2–4 23:12 [a] Ezek. 26:13, 14; Rev. 18:22 23:13 [a] Is. 47:1 [b] Ps. 72:9

They raised up its palaces,
And brought it to ruin.

14 [a]Wail, you ships of Tarshish!
For your strength is laid waste.

15 Now it shall come to pass in that day that Tyre will be forgotten seventy years, according to the days of one king. At the end of seventy years it will happen to Tyre as *in* the song of the harlot:

16 "Take a harp, go about the city,
You forgotten harlot;
Make sweet melody, sing many songs,
That you may be remembered."

17 And it shall be, at the end of seventy years, that the LORD will deal with Tyre. She will return to her hire, and [a]commit fornication with all the kingdoms of the world on the face of the earth.
18 Her gain and her pay [a]will be set apart for the LORD; it will not be treasured nor laid up, for her gain will be for those who dwell before the LORD, to eat sufficiently, and for fine clothing.

Impending Judgment on the Earth

24 Behold, the LORD makes the earth
empty and makes it waste,
Distorts its surface
And scatters abroad its inhabitants.
2 And it shall be:
As with the people, so with the [a]priest;
As with the servant, so
with his master;
As with the maid, so with her mistress;
[b]As with the buyer, so with the seller;
As with the lender, so with
the borrower;
As with the creditor, so
with the debtor.
3 The land shall be entirely emptied
and utterly plundered,
For the LORD has spoken this word.

4 The earth mourns *and* fades away,
The world languishes *and* fades away;
The [a]haughty people of
the earth languish.
5 [a]The earth is also defiled
under its inhabitants,
Because they have
[b]transgressed the laws,
Changed the ordinance,
Broken the [c]everlasting covenant.
6 Therefore [a]the curse has
devoured the earth,
And those who dwell in it are desolate.
Therefore the inhabitants of
the earth are [b]burned,
And few men *are* left.

7 [a]The new wine fails, the
vine languishes,
All the merry-hearted sigh.
8 The mirth [a]of the tambourine ceases,
The noise of the jubilant ends,
The joy of the harp ceases.
9 They shall not drink wine with a song;
Strong drink is bitter to
those who drink it.
10 The city of confusion is broken down;
Every house is shut up, so
that none may go in.
11 *There is* a cry for wine in the streets,
All joy is darkened,
The mirth of the land is gone.
12 In the city desolation is left,
And the gate is stricken
with destruction.
13 When it shall be thus in the midst
of the land among the people,
[a]*It shall be* like the shaking
of an olive tree,
Like the gleaning of grapes
when the vintage is done.

14 They shall lift up their voice,
they shall sing;
For the majesty of the LORD
They shall cry aloud from the sea.
15 Therefore [a]glorify the LORD
in the dawning light,
[b]The name of the LORD God of Israel
in the coastlands of the sea.
16 From the ends of the earth
we have heard songs:
"Glory to the righteous!"
But I said, "I am ruined, ruined!

23:14 [a] Ezek. 27:25–30 23:17 [a] Rev. 17:2 23:18 [a] Ex. 28:36; Zech. 14:20, 21 24:2 [a] Hos. 4:9 [b] Ezek. 7:12, 13 24:4 [a] Is. 25:11 24:5 [a] Gen. 3:17; Num. 35:33; Is. 9:17; 10:6 [b] Is. 59:12 [c] 1 Chr. 16:14–19; Ps. 105:7–12 24:6 [a] Mal. 4:6 [b] Is. 9:19 24:7 [a] Is. 16:8–10; Joel 1:10, 12 24:8 [a] Is. 5:12, 14; Jer. 7:34; 16:9; 25:10; Ezek. 26:13; Hos. 2:11; Rev. 18:22 24:13 [a] [Is. 17:5, 6; 27:12] 24:15 [a] Is. 25:3 [b] Mal. 1:11

Woe to me!
[a]The treacherous dealers have
dealt treacherously,
Indeed, the treacherous dealers
have dealt very treacherously."

17 [a]Fear and the pit and the snare
Are upon you, O inhabitant
of the earth.
18 And it shall be
That he who flees from the
noise of the fear
Shall fall into the pit,
And he who comes up from
the midst of the pit
Shall be caught in the snare;
For [a]the windows from
on high are open,
And [b]the foundations of the
earth are shaken.

19 [a]The earth is violently broken,
The earth is split open,
The earth is shaken exceedingly.
20 The earth shall [a]reel to and
fro like a drunkard,
And shall totter like a hut;
Its transgression shall be heavy upon it,
And it will fall, and not rise again.

21 It shall come to pass in that day
That the LORD will punish on high
the host of exalted ones,
And on the earth [a]the
kings of the earth.
22 They will be gathered together,
As prisoners are gathered in the pit,
And will be shut up in the prison;
After many days they will be punished.
23 Then the [a]moon will be disgraced
And the sun ashamed;
For the LORD of hosts will [b]reign
On [c]Mount Zion and in Jerusalem
And before His elders, gloriously.

Praise to God

25 O LORD, You *are* my God.
[a]I will exalt You,
I will praise Your name,
[b]For You have done wonderful *things;*
[c]*Your* counsels of old *are*
faithfulness *and* truth.
2 For You have made [a]a city a ruin,
A fortified city a ruin,
A palace of foreigners to
be a city no more;
It will never be rebuilt.
3 Therefore the strong people
will [a]glorify You;
The city of the terrible
nations will fear You.
4 For You have been a
strength to the poor,
A strength to the needy in his distress,
[a]A refuge from the storm,
A shade from the heat;
For the blast of the terrible ones
is as a storm *against* the wall.
5 You will reduce the noise of aliens,
As heat in a dry place;
As heat in the shadow of a cloud,
The song of the terrible ones
will be diminished.

6 And in [a]this mountain
[b]The LORD of hosts will
make for [c]all people
A feast of choice pieces,
A feast of wines on the lees,
Of fat things full of marrow,
Of well-refined wines on the lees.
7 And He will destroy on this mountain
The surface of the covering
cast over all people,
And [a]the veil that is spread
over all nations.
8 He will [a]swallow up death forever,
And the Lord GOD will [b]wipe
away tears from all faces;
The rebuke of His people
He will take away from all the earth;
For the LORD has spoken.

9 And it will be said in that day:
"Behold, this *is* our God;
[a]We have waited for Him,
and He will save us.
This *is* the LORD;

24:16 [a] Is. 21:2; 33:1; Jer. 3:20; 5:11 24:17 [a] Jer. 48:43; Amos 5:19 24:18 [a] Gen. 7:11 [b] Ps. 18:7; 46:2; Is. 2:19, 21; 13:13 24:19 [a] Jer. 4:23 24:20 [a] Is. 19:14; 24:1; 28:7 24:21 [a] Ps. 76:12 24:23 [a] Is. 13:10; 60:19; Ezek. 32:7; Joel 2:31; 3:15 [b] Rev. 19:4, 6 [c] [Heb. 12:22] 25:1 [a] Ex. 15:2 [b] Ps. 98:1 [c] Num. 23:19 25:2 [a] Is. 21:9; 23:13; Jer. 51:37 25:3 [a] Is. 24:15; Rev. 11:13 25:4 [a] Is. 4:6 25:6 [a] [Is. 2:2–4; 56:7] [b] Prov. 9:2; Matt. 22:4 [c] [Dan. 7:14; Matt. 8:11] 25:7 [a] 2 Cor. 3:15; [Eph. 4:18] 25:8 [a] [Hos. 13:14; 1 Cor. 15:54; Rev. 20:14] [b] Is. 30:19; Rev. 7:17; 21:4 25:9 [a] Gen. 49:18; Is. 8:17; 26:8; [Titus 2:13]

We have waited for Him;
[b]We will be glad and rejoice
in His salvation."
10 For on this mountain the hand
of the LORD will rest,
And [a]Moab shall be trampled
down under Him,
As straw is trampled down
for the refuse heap.
11 And He will spread out His
hands in their midst
As a swimmer reaches out to swim,
And He will bring down their [a]pride
Together with the trickery
of their hands.
12 The [a]fortress of the high
fort of your walls
He will bring down, lay low,
And bring to the ground,
down to the dust.

A Song of Salvation

26 In [a]that day this song will be sung
in the land of Judah:

"We have a strong city;
[b]*God* will appoint salvation *for*
walls and bulwarks.
2 [a]Open the gates,
That the righteous nation which
keeps the truth may enter in.
3 You will keep *him* in perfect [a]peace,
Whose mind *is* stayed *on You,*
Because he trusts in You.
4 Trust in the LORD forever,
[a]For in YAH, the LORD, *is*
everlasting strength.[1]
5 For He brings down those
who dwell on high,
[a]The lofty city;
He lays it low,
He lays it low to the ground,
He brings it down to the dust.
6 The foot shall tread it down—
The feet of the poor
And the steps of the needy."

7 The way of the just *is* uprightness;
[a]O Most Upright,
You weigh the path of the just.
8 Yes, [a]in the way of Your judgments,
O LORD, we have [b]waited for You;
The desire of *our* soul *is* for Your name
And for the remembrance of You.
9 [a]With my soul I have desired
You in the night,
Yes, by my spirit within me
I will seek You early;
For when Your judgments
are in the earth,
The inhabitants of the world
will learn righteousness.

10 [a]Let grace be shown to the wicked,
Yet he will not learn righteousness;
In [b]the land of uprightness
he will deal unjustly,
And will not behold the
majesty of the LORD.
11 LORD, *when* Your hand is lifted
up, [a]they will not see.
But they will see and be ashamed
For *their* envy of people;
Yes, the fire of Your enemies
shall devour them.

12 LORD, You will establish peace for us,
For You have also done all
our works in us.
13 O LORD our God, [a]masters besides You
Have had dominion over us;
But by You only we make
mention of Your name.
14 *They are* dead, they will not live;
They are deceased, they will not rise.
Therefore You have punished
and destroyed them,
And made all their memory to [a]perish.
15 You have increased the
nation, O LORD,
You have [a]increased the nation;
You are glorified;
You have expanded all the
borders of the land.

16 LORD, [a]in trouble they
have visited You,

25:9 [b] Ps. 20:5 **25:10** [a] Is. 16:14; Jer. 48:1–47; Ezek. 25:8–11; Amos 2:1–3; Zeph. 2:9 **25:11** [a] Is. 24:4; 26:5 **25:12** [a] Is. 26:5
26:1 [a] Is. 2:11; 12:1 [b] Is. 60:18 **26:2** [a] Ps. 118:19, 20 **26:3** [a] Is. 57:19; [Phil. 4:6, 7] **26:4** [a] Is. 12:2; 45:17 [1] Or *Rock of Ages*
26:5 [a] Is. 25:11, 12 **26:7** [a] Ps. 37:23 **26:8** [a] Is. 64:5 [b] Is. 25:9; 33:2 **26:9** [a] Ps. 63:6; Song 3:1; Is. 50:10; Luke 6:12
26:10 [a] Eccl. 8:12; [Rom. 2:4] [b] Ps. 143:10 **26:11** [a] Job 34:27; Ps. 28:5; Is. 5:12 **26:13** [a] 2 Chr. 12:8
26:14 [a] Eccl. 9:5; Is. 14:22 **26:15** [a] Is. 9:3 **26:16** [a] Is. 37:3; Hos. 5:15

They poured out a prayer *when* Your
chastening *was* upon them.
17 As [a]a woman with child
Is in pain and cries out in her pangs,
When she draws near the
time of her delivery,
So have we been in Your sight, O LORD.
18 We have been with child, we
have been in pain;
We have, as it were, brought forth wind;
We have not accomplished any
deliverance in the earth,
Nor have [a]the inhabitants
of the world fallen.

19 [a]Your dead shall live;
Together with my dead body[1]
they shall arise.
[b]Awake and sing, you who dwell in dust;
For your dew *is like* the dew of herbs,
And the earth shall cast out the dead.

Take Refuge from the Coming Judgment

20 Come, my people, [a]enter
your chambers,
And shut your doors behind you;
Hide yourself, as it were,
[b]for a little moment,
Until the indignation is past.
21 For behold, the LORD [a]comes
out of His place
To punish the inhabitants of the
earth for their iniquity;
The earth will also disclose her blood,
And will no more cover her slain.

27

In that day the LORD with His
severe sword, great and strong,
Will punish Leviathan the
fleeing serpent,
[a]Leviathan that twisted serpent;
And He will slay [b]the reptile
that *is* in the sea.

The Restoration of Israel

2 In that day [a]sing to her,
[b]"A vineyard of red wine![1]
3 [a]I, the LORD, keep it,
I water it every moment;
Lest any hurt it,
I keep it night and day.
4 Fury *is* not in Me.
Who would set [a]briers *and* thorns
Against Me in battle?
I would go through them,
I would burn them together.
5 Or let him take hold [a]of My strength,
That he may [b]make peace with Me;
And he shall make peace with Me."

6 Those who come He shall cause
[a]to take root in Jacob;
Israel shall blossom and bud,
And fill the face of the world with fruit.

7 [a]Has He struck Israel as He struck
those who struck him?
Or has He been slain according
to the slaughter of those
who were slain by Him?
8 [a]In measure, by sending it away,
You contended with it.
[b]He removes *it* by His rough wind
In the day of the east wind.
9 Therefore by this the iniquity
of Jacob will be covered;
And this *is* all the fruit of
taking away his sin:
When he makes all the
stones of the altar
Like chalkstones that are
beaten to dust,
Wooden images[1] and incense
altars shall not stand.

10 Yet the fortified city *will be* [a]desolate,
The habitation forsaken and
left like a wilderness;
There the calf will feed, and
there it will lie down
And consume its branches.
11 When its boughs are withered,
they will be broken off;
The women come *and* set them on fire.

26:17 [a] Is. 13:8; [John 16:21] **26:18** [a] Ps. 17:14 **26:19** [a] Is. 25:8; [Ezek. 37:1–14] [b] [Dan. 12:2]; Hos. 13:14 [1] Following Masoretic Text and Vulgate; Syriac and Targum read *their dead bodies;* Septuagint reads *those in the tombs.* **26:20** [a] Ex. 12:22, 23; [Ps. 91:1, 4] [b] [Ps. 30:5; Is. 54:7, 8; 2 Cor. 4:17] **26:21** [a] Mic. 1:3; [Jude 14] **27:1** [a] Gen. 3:1; Ps. 74:13, 14; Rev. 12:9, 15 [b] Is. 51:9; Ezek. 29:3; 32:2 **27:2** [a] Is. 5:1 [b] Ps. 80:8; Is. 5:7; Jer. 2:21 [1] Following Masoretic Text (Kittel's *Biblia Hebraica*), Bomberg, and Vulgate; Masoretic Text (*Biblia Hebraica Stuttgartensia*), some Hebrew manuscripts, and Septuagint read *delight;* Targum reads *choice vineyard.* **27:3** [a] 1 Sam. 2:9; Ps. 121:4, 5; Is. 31:5; [John 10:28] **27:4** [a] 2 Sam. 23:6; Is. 9:18 **27:5** [a] Is. 25:4 [b] Job 22:21; Is. 26:3, 12; [Rom. 5:1; 2 Cor. 5:20] **27:6** [a] Is. 37:31; Hos. 14:5, 6 **27:7** [a] Is. 10:12, 17; 30:30–33 **27:8** [a] Job 23:6; Ps. 6:1; Jer. 10:24; 30:11; 46:28; [1 Cor. 10:13] [b] [Ps. 78:38] **27:9** [1] Hebrew *Asherim,* Canaanite deities **27:10** [a] Is. 5:6, 17; 32:14; Jer. 26:18

For [a]it *is* a people of no understanding;
Therefore He who made them will
[b]not have mercy on them,
And [c]He who formed them will
show them no favor.

12 And it shall come to pass in that day
That the LORD will thresh,
From the channel of the River[1]
to the Brook of Egypt;
And you will be [a]gathered one by one,
O you children of Israel.

13 [a]So it shall be in that day:
[b]The great trumpet will be blown;
They will come, who are about to
perish in the land of Assyria,
And they who are outcasts
in the land of [c]Egypt,
And shall [d]worship the LORD in
the holy mount at Jerusalem.

Woe to Ephraim and Jerusalem

28 Woe to the crown of pride, to
the drunkards of Ephraim,
Whose glorious beauty *is*
a fading flower
Which *is* at the head of the
verdant valleys,
To those who are overcome
with wine!
2 Behold, the Lord has a mighty
and strong one,
[a]Like a tempest of hail and
a destroying storm,
Like a flood of mighty
waters overflowing,
Who will bring *them* down to
the earth with *His* hand.
3 The crown of pride, the
drunkards of Ephraim,
Will be trampled underfoot;
4 And the glorious beauty
is a fading flower
Which *is* at the head of the
verdant valley,
Like the first fruit before the summer,
Which an observer sees;
He eats it up while it is
still in his hand.

5 In that day the LORD of hosts will be
For a crown of glory and a
diadem of beauty
To the remnant of His people,
6 For a spirit of justice to him
who sits in judgment,
And for strength to those who turn
back the battle at the gate.

7 But they also [a]have erred
through wine,
And through intoxicating
drink are out of the way;
[b]The priest and the prophet have
erred through intoxicating drink,
They are swallowed up by wine,
They are out of the way through
intoxicating drink;
They err in vision, they
stumble *in* judgment.
8 For all tables are full of vomit
and filth;
No place *is clean.*

9 "Whom[a] will he teach knowledge?
And whom will he make to
understand the message?
Those *just* weaned from milk?
Those *just* drawn from the breasts?
10 [a]For precept *must be* upon precept,
precept upon precept,
Line upon line, line upon line,
Here a little, there a little."

11 For with [a]stammering lips
and another tongue
He will speak to this people,
12 To whom He said, "This *is*
the [a]rest *with which*
You may cause the weary to rest,"
And, "This *is* the refreshing";
Yet they would not hear.
13 But the word of the LORD was to them,
"Precept upon precept,
precept upon precept,
Line upon line, line upon line,
Here a little, there a little,"
That they might go and fall
backward, and be broken
And snared and caught.

27:11 [a] Deut. 32:28; Is. 1:3 [b] Is. 9:17 [c] Deut. 32:18; Is. 43:1, 7; 44:2, 21, 24 **27:12** [a] [Is. 11:11; 56:8] [1] That is, the Euphrates **27:13** [a] Is. 2:11 [b] Lev. 25:9; 1 Chr. 15:24; Matt. 24:31; Rev. 11:15 [c] Is. 19:21, 22 [d] [Is. 2:3]; Zech. 14:16; [Heb. 12:22] **28:2** [a] Is. 30:30; Ezek. 13:11 **28:7** [a] Prov. 20:1; Is. 5:11, 22; Hos. 4:11 [b] Is. 56:10, 12 **28:9** [a] Jer. 6:10 **28:10** [a] [2 Chr. 36:15; Neh. 9:30; Jer. 25:3, 4; 35:15; 44:4] **28:11** [a] Is. 33:19; 1 Cor. 14:21 **28:12** [a] Is. 30:15; Jer. 6:16; [Matt. 11:28, 29]

14 Therefore hear the word of the
LORD, you scornful men,
Who rule this people who
are in Jerusalem,
15 Because you have said, "We have
made a covenant with death,
And with Sheol we are in agreement.
When the overflowing scourge
passes through,
It will not come to us,
[a]For we have made lies our refuge,
And under falsehood we have
hidden ourselves."

A Cornerstone in Zion

16 Therefore thus says the Lord GOD:

"Behold, I lay in Zion [a]a stone
for a foundation,
A tried stone, a precious cornerstone,
a sure foundation;
Whoever believes will not act
hastily.
17 Also I will make justice the
measuring line,
And righteousness the plummet;
The hail will sweep away
the refuge of lies,
And the waters will overflow
the hiding place.
18 Your covenant with death
will be annulled,
And your agreement with
Sheol will not stand;
When the overflowing scourge
passes through,
Then you will be trampled
down by it.
19 As often as it goes out it will
take you;
For morning by morning
it will pass over,
And by day and by night;
It will be a terror just to
understand the report."

20 For the bed is too short
to stretch out *on,*
And the covering so narrow that
one cannot wrap himself *in it.*

21 For the LORD will rise up as
at Mount [a]Perazim,
He will be angry as in the
Valley of [b]Gibeon—
That He may do His work,
[c]His awesome work,
And bring to pass His act,
His unusual act.
22 Now therefore, do not
be mockers,
Lest your bonds be made strong;
For I have heard from the
Lord GOD of hosts,
[a]A destruction determined even
upon the whole earth.

Listen to the Teaching of God

23 Give ear and hear my voice,
Listen and hear my speech.
24 Does the plowman keep
plowing all day to sow?
Does he keep turning his soil
and breaking the clods?
25 When he has leveled its surface,
Does he not sow the black cummin
And scatter the cummin,
Plant the wheat in rows,
The barley in the appointed place,
And the spelt in its place?
26 For He instructs him in
right judgment,
His God teaches him.

27 For the black cummin is
not threshed with a
threshing sledge,
Nor is a cartwheel rolled
over the cummin;
But the black cummin is
beaten out with a stick,
And the cummin with a rod.
28 Bread *flour* must be ground;
Therefore he does not
thresh it forever,
Break *it with* his cartwheel,
Or crush it *with* his horsemen.
29 This also comes from the
LORD of hosts,
[a]*Who* is wonderful in counsel
and excellent in guidance.

28:15 [a] Is. 9:15; Ezek. 13:22; Amos 2:4 28:16 [a] Gen. 49:24; Ps. 118:22; Is. 8:14, 15; Matt. 21:42; Mark 12:10; Luke 20:17; Acts 4:11; Rom. 9:33; 10:11; Eph. 2:20; 1 Pet. 2:6–8 28:21 [a] 2 Sam. 5:20; 1 Chr. 14:11 [b] Josh. 10:10, 12; 2 Sam. 5:25; 1 Chr. 14:16 [c] [Lam. 3:33; Luke 19:41–44] 28:22 [a] Is. 10:22; Dan. 9:27
28:29 [a] Ps. 92:5; Is. 9:6; Jer. 32:19

Woe to Jerusalem

29 "Woe [a]to Ariel,[1] to Ariel, the
city [b]*where* David dwelt!
Add year to year;
Let feasts come around.
2 Yet I will distress Ariel;
There shall be heaviness and sorrow,
And it shall be to Me as Ariel.
3 I will encamp against you all around,
I will lay siege against you
with a mound,
And I will raise siegeworks
against you.
4 You shall be brought down,
You shall speak out of the ground;
Your speech shall be low,
out of the dust;
Your voice shall be like a medium's,
[a]out of the ground;
And your speech shall whisper
out of the dust.

5 "Moreover the multitude of your [a]foes
Shall be like fine dust,
And the multitude of the terrible ones
Like [b]chaff that passes away;
Yes, it shall be [c]in an instant, suddenly.
6 [a]You will be punished by
the LORD of hosts
With thunder and [b]earthquake
and great noise,
With storm and tempest
And the flame of devouring fire.
7 [a]The multitude of all the nations
who fight against Ariel,
Even all who fight against
her and her fortress,
And distress her,
Shall be [b]as a dream of a night vision.
8 [a]It shall even be as when a
hungry man dreams,
And look—he eats;
But he awakes, and his
soul is still empty;
Or as when a thirsty man dreams,
And look—he drinks;
But he awakes, and indeed *he is* faint,
And his soul still craves:
So the multitude of all the
nations shall be,
Who fight against Mount Zion."

The Blindness of Disobedience

9 Pause and wonder!
Blind yourselves and be blind!
[a]They are drunk, [b]but not with wine;
They stagger, but not with
intoxicating drink.
10 For [a]the LORD has poured out on you
The spirit of deep sleep,
And has [b]closed your eyes,
namely, the prophets;
And He has covered your
heads, *namely,* [c]the seers.

11 The whole vision has become to you
like the words of a book [a]that is sealed,
which *men* deliver to one who is literate,
saying, "Read this, please."
[b]And he says, "I cannot, for it *is* sealed."
12 Then the book is delivered to one who
is illiterate, saying, "Read this, please."
And he says, "I am not literate."
13 Therefore the Lord said:

[a]"Inasmuch as these people draw
near with their mouths
And honor Me [b]with their lips,
But have removed their
hearts far from Me,
And their fear toward Me is taught
by the commandment of men,
14 [a]Therefore, behold, I will again
do a marvelous work
Among this people,
A marvelous work and a wonder;
[b]For the wisdom of their wise
men shall perish,
And the understanding of their
prudent *men* shall be hidden."

15 [a]Woe to those who seek deep to hide
their counsel far from the LORD,
And their works are in the dark;
[b]They say, "Who sees us?"
and, "Who knows us?"

29:1 [a] Ezek. 24:6, 9 [b] 2 Sam. 5:9 [1] That is, Jerusalem **29:4** [a] Is. 8:19 **29:5** [a] Is. 25:5 [b] Job 21:18; Is. 17:13 [c] Is. 30:13; 47:11; 1 Thess. 5:3 **29:6** [a] Is. 28:2; 30:30 [b] 1 Sam. 2:10; Zech. 14:4; Matt. 24:7; Mark 13:8; Luke 21:11; Rev. 16:18, 19 **29:7** [a] Is. 37:36; Mic. 4:11, 12; Zech. 12:9 [b] Job 20:8 **29:8** [a] Ps. 73:20 **29:9** [a] Is. 28:7, 8 [b] Is. 51:21 **29:10** [a] Ps. 69:23; Is. 6:9, 10; Mic. 3:6; Rom. 11:8 [b] Ps. 69:23; Is. 6:10 [c] 1 Sam. 9:9; Is. 44:18; Mic. 3:6; [2 Thess. 2:9–12] **29:11** [a] Is. 8:16 [b] Dan. 12:4, 9; [Matt. 13:11–16]; Rev. 5:1–5, 9 **29:13** [a] Ps. 78:36; Ezek. 33:31; Matt. 15:8, 9; Mark 7:6, 7 [b] Col. 2:22 **29:14** [a] Is. 6:9, 10; 28:21; Hab. 1:5 [b] Is. 44:25; Jer. 49:7; Obad. 8; 1 Cor. 1:19 **29:15** [a] Is. 30:1 [b] Ps. 10:11; 94:7; Is. 47:10; Ezek. 8:12; Mal. 2:17

16 Surely you have things turned around!
Shall the potter be esteemed
as the clay;
For shall the [a]thing made say
of him who made it,
"He did not make me"?
Or shall the thing formed say
of him who formed it,
"He has no understanding"?

Future Recovery of Wisdom

17 *Is* it not yet a very little while
Till [a]Lebanon shall be turned
into a fruitful field,
And the fruitful field be
esteemed as a forest?
18 [a]In that day the deaf shall hear
the words of the book,
And the eyes of the blind
shall see out of obscurity
and out of darkness.
19 [a]The humble also shall increase
their joy in the LORD,
And [b]the poor among
men shall rejoice
In the Holy One of Israel.
20 For the terrible one is
brought to nothing,
[a]The scornful one is consumed,
And all who [b]watch for
iniquity are cut off—
21 Who make a man an
offender by a word,
And [a]lay a snare for him who
reproves in the gate,
And turn aside the just
[b]by empty words.

22 Therefore thus says the LORD, [a]who
redeemed Abraham, concerning the house
of Jacob:

"Jacob shall not now be [b]ashamed,
Nor shall his face now grow pale;
23 But when he sees his children,
[a]The work of My hands, in his midst,
They will hallow My name,
And hallow the Holy One of Jacob,
And fear the God of Israel.
24 These also [a]who erred in spirit
will come to understanding,
And those who complained
will learn doctrine."

Futile Confidence in Egypt

30 "Woe to the rebellious children,"
says the LORD,
[a]"Who take counsel, but not of Me,
And who devise plans, but
not of My Spirit,
[b]That they may add sin to sin;
2 [a]Who walk to go down to Egypt,
And [b]have not asked My advice,
To strengthen themselves in
the strength of Pharaoh,
And to trust in the shadow of Egypt!
3 [a]Therefore the strength of Pharaoh
Shall be your shame,
And trust in the shadow of Egypt
Shall be *your* humiliation.
4 For his princes were at [a]Zoan,
And his ambassadors came to Hanes.
5 [a]They were all ashamed of a people
who could not benefit them,
Or be help or benefit,
But a shame and also a reproach."

6 [a]The burden against the beasts of the
South.

Through a land of trouble
and anguish,
From which *came* the lioness and lion,
[b]The viper and fiery flying serpent,
They will carry their riches on
the backs of young donkeys,
And their treasures on the
humps of camels,
To a people *who* shall not profit;
7 [a]For the Egyptians shall help in
vain and to no purpose.
Therefore I have called her
Rahab-Hem-Shebeth.[1]

A Rebellious People

8 Now go, [a]write it before
them on a tablet,
And note it on a scroll,

29:16 [a] Is. 45:9; Jer. 18:1–6; [Rom. 9:19–21] 29:17 [a] Is. 32:15 29:18 [a] Is. 35:5; Matt. 11:5; Mark 7:37 29:19 [a] [Ps. 25:9; 37:11; Is. 11:4; 61:1; Matt. 5:5; 11:29] [b] Is. 14:30; [Matt. 5:3; 11:5; James 2:5] 29:20 [a] Is. 28:14 [b] Is. 59:4; Mic. 2:1 29:21 [a] Amos 5:10, 12 [b] Prov. 28:21 29:22 [a] Josh. 24:3 [b] Is. 45:17 29:23 [a] [Is. 45:11; 49:20–26; Eph. 2:10] 29:24 [a] Is. 28:7 30:1 [a] Is. 29:15 [b] Deut. 29:19 30:2 [a] Is. 31:1; Jer. 43:7 [b] Num. 27:21; Josh. 9:14; 1 Kin. 22:7; Jer. 21:2; 42:2, 20 30:3 [a] Is. 20:5; Jer. 37:5, 7 30:4 [a] Is. 19:11 30:5 [a] Jer. 2:36 30:6 [a] Is. 57:9; Hos. 8:9; 12:1 [b] Deut. 8:15; Is. 14:29 30:7 [a] Jer. 37:7 [1] Literally *Rahab Sits Idle* 30:8 [a] Hab. 2:2

That it may be for time to come,
Forever and ever:
9 That [a]this *is* a rebellious people,
Lying children,
Children *who* will not hear
the law of the LORD;
10 [a]Who say to the seers, "Do not see,"
And to the prophets, "Do not
prophesy to us right things;
[b]Speak to us smooth things,
prophesy deceits.
11 Get out of the way,
Turn aside from the path,
Cause the Holy One of Israel
To cease from before us."

12Therefore thus says the Holy One of Israel:

"Because you [a]despise this word,
And trust in oppression
and perversity,
And rely on them,
13 Therefore this iniquity shall be to you
[a]Like a breach ready to fall,
A bulge in a high wall,
Whose breaking [b]comes
suddenly, in an instant.
14 And [a]He shall break it like the
breaking of the potter's vessel,
Which is broken in pieces;
He shall not spare.
So there shall not be found
among its fragments
A shard to take fire from the hearth,
Or to take water from the cistern."

15For thus says the Lord GOD, the Holy One of Israel:

[a]"In returning and rest you
shall be saved;
In quietness and confidence
shall be your strength."
[b]But you would not,
16 And you said, "No, for we
will flee on horses"—
Therefore you shall flee!
And, "We will ride on swift *horses*"—
Therefore those who pursue
you shall be swift!

17 [a]One thousand *shall flee* at
the threat of one,
At the threat of five you shall flee,
Till you are left as a pole on
top of a mountain
And as a banner on a hill.

God Will Be Gracious

18 Therefore the LORD will wait, that
He may be [a]gracious to you;
And therefore He will be exalted,
that He may have mercy on you.
For the LORD *is* a God of justice;
[b]Blessed *are* all those who
[c]wait for Him.

19 For the people [a]shall dwell
in Zion at Jerusalem;
You shall [b]weep no more.
He will be very gracious to you
at the sound of your cry;
When He hears it, He will [c]answer you.
20 And *though* the Lord gives you
[a]The bread of adversity and
the water of affliction,
Yet [b]your teachers will not be
moved into a corner anymore,
But your eyes shall see your teachers.
21 Your ears shall hear a word
behind you, saying,
"This *is* the way, walk in it,"
Whenever you [a]turn to the right hand
Or whenever you turn to the left.
22 [a]You will also defile the covering
of your images of silver,
And the ornament of your
molded images of gold.
You will throw them away
as an unclean thing;
[b]You will say to them, "Get away!"

23 [a]Then He will give the rain
for your seed
With which you sow the ground,

30:9 [a] Deut. 32:20; Is. 1:2, 4; 65:2 30:10 [a] Is. 5:20; Jer. 11:21; Amos 2:12; Mic. 2:6 [b] 1 Kin. 22:8, 13; Jer. 6:14; 23:17, 26; Ezek. 13:7; Mic. 2:11; Rom. 16:18; 2 Tim. 4:3, 4 30:12 [a] Lev. 26:43; Num. 15:31; Prov. 1:30; 13:13; Is. 5:24; Ezek. 20:13, 16, 24; Amos 2:4 30:13 [a] 1 Kin. 20:30; Ps. 62:3, 4; Is. 58:12 [b] Is. 29:5 30:14 [a] Ps. 2:9; Jer. 19:11 30:15 [a] Ps. 116:7; Is. 7:4; 28:12 [b] Matt. 23:37 30:17 [a] Lev. 26:36; Deut. 28:25; 32:30; Josh. 23:10; [Prov. 28:1] 30:18 [a] Is. 33:2 [b] Ps. 2:12; 34:8; Prov. 16:20; Jer. 17:7 [c] Is. 26:8 30:19 [a] Is. 65:9; [Ezek. 37:25, 28] [b] Is. 25:8 [c] Ps. 50:15; Is. 65:24; [Matt. 7:7–11] 30:20 [a] 1 Kin. 22:27; Ps. 127:2 [b] Ps. 74:9; Amos 8:11 30:21 [a] Josh. 1:7 30:22 [a] 2 Chr. 31:1; Is. 2:20; 31:7 [b] Hos. 14:8 30:23 [a] [Matt. 6:33]; 1 Tim. 6:8

And bread of the increase of the earth;
It will be fat and plentiful.
In that day your cattle will feed
In large pastures.
24 Likewise the oxen and the young
donkeys that work the ground
Will eat cured fodder,
Which has been winnowed
with the shovel and fan.
25 There will be [a]on every high mountain
And on every high hill
Rivers *and* streams of waters,
In the day of the [b]great slaughter,
When the towers fall.
26 Moreover [a]the light of the moon
will be as the light of the sun,
And the light of the sun
will be sevenfold,
As the light of seven days,
In the day that the LORD binds
up the bruise of His people
And heals the stroke of their wound.

Judgment on Assyria

27 Behold, the name of the LORD
comes from afar,
Burning *with* His anger,
And *His* burden *is* heavy;
His lips are full of indignation,
And His tongue like a devouring fire.
28 [a]His breath is like an
overflowing stream,
[b]Which reaches up to the neck,
To sift the nations with the
sieve of futility;
And *there shall be* [c]a bridle in
the jaws of the people,
Causing *them* to err.

29 You shall have a song
As in the night *when* a holy
festival is kept,
And gladness of heart as when
one goes with a flute,
To come into [a]the mountain
of the LORD,
To the Mighty One of Israel.
30 [a]The LORD will cause His glorious
voice to be heard,
And show the descent of His arm,
With the indignation of *His* anger
And the flame of a devouring fire,
With scattering, tempest,
[b]and hailstones.
31 For [a]through the voice of the LORD
Assyria will be beaten down,
As He strikes with the [b]rod.
32 And *in* every place where the
staff of punishment passes,
Which the LORD lays on him,
It will be with tambourines
and harps;
And in battles of [a]brandishing
He will fight with it.
33 [a]For Tophet *was* established of old,
Yes, for the king it is prepared.
He has made *it* deep and large;
Its pyre *is* fire with much wood;
The breath of the LORD, like a
stream of brimstone,
Kindles it.

The Folly of Not Trusting God

31 Woe to those [a]who go down to
Egypt for help,
And [b]rely on horses,
Who trust in chariots because
they are many,
And in horsemen because
they are very strong,
But who do not look to the
Holy One of Israel,
[c]Nor seek the LORD!
2 Yet He also *is* wise and
will bring disaster,
And [a]will not call back His words,
But will arise against the
house of evildoers,
And against the help of those
who work iniquity.
3 Now the Egyptians *are*
men, and not God;
And their horses are flesh,
and not spirit.
When the LORD stretches
out His hand,
Both he who helps will fall,
And he who is helped will
fall down;
They all will perish [a]together.

30:25 [a] Is. 2:14, 15 [b] Is. 2:10–21; 34:2 30:26 [a] [Is. 60:19, 20; Rev. 21:23; 22:5] 30:28 [a] Is. 11:4; 2 Thess. 2:8 [b] Is. 8:8 [c] 2 Kin. 19:28; Is. 37:29 30:29 [a] [Is. 2:3] 30:30 [a] Is. 29:6 [b] Is. 28:2 30:31 [a] Is. 14:25; 37:36 [b] Is. 10:5, 24 30:32 [a] Is. 11:15 30:33 [a] 2 Kin. 23:10; Jer. 7:31 31:1 [a] Is. 30:1, 2 [b] Deut. 17:16; Ps. 20:7; Is. 2:7; 30:16 [c] Is. 9:13; Dan. 9:13; Amos 5:4–8 31:2 [a] Num. 23:19; Jer. 44:29 31:3 [a] Is. 20:6

God Will Deliver Jerusalem

4 For thus the LORD has spoken to me:

[a]"As a lion roars,
And a young lion over his prey
(When a multitude of shepherds
is summoned against him,
He will not be afraid of their voice
Nor be disturbed by their noise),
So the LORD of hosts will come down
To fight for Mount Zion and
for its hill.
5 [a]Like birds flying about,
So will the LORD of hosts
defend Jerusalem.
Defending, He will also deliver *it;*
Passing over, He will preserve *it.*"

6 Return *to Him* against whom the children of Israel have [a]deeply revolted. 7 For
in that day every man shall [a]throw away his
idols of silver and his idols of gold—[b]sin,
which your own hands have made for yourselves.

8 "Then Assyria shall [a]fall by
a sword not of man,
And a sword not of mankind
shall [b]devour him.
But he shall flee from the sword,
And his young men shall
become forced labor.
9 [a]He shall cross over to his
stronghold for fear,
And his princes shall be
afraid of the banner,"
Says the LORD,
Whose fire *is* in Zion
And whose furnace *is* in Jerusalem.

A Reign of Righteousness

32 Behold, [a]a king will reign in
righteousness,
And princes will rule with justice.
2 A man will be as a hiding
place from the wind,
And [a]a cover from the tempest,
As rivers of water in a dry place,
As the shadow of a great
rock in a weary land.
3 [a]The eyes of those who see
will not be dim,
And the ears of those who
hear will listen.
4 Also the heart of the rash will
[a]understand knowledge,
And the tongue of the stammerers
will be ready to speak plainly.

5 The foolish person will no
longer be called generous,
Nor the miser said *to be* bountiful;
6 For the foolish person will
speak foolishness,
And his heart will work [a]iniquity:
To practice ungodliness,
To utter error against the LORD,
To keep the hungry unsatisfied,
And he will cause the drink
of the thirsty to fail.
7 Also the schemes of the
schemer *are* evil;
He devises wicked plans
To destroy the poor with [a]lying words,
Even when the needy speaks justice.
8 But a generous man devises
generous things,
And by generosity he shall stand.

Consequences of Complacency

9 Rise up, you women [a]who are at ease,
Hear my voice;
You complacent daughters,
Give ear to my speech.
10 In a year and *some* days
You will be troubled, you
complacent women;
For the vintage will fail,
The gathering will not come.
11 Tremble, you *women* who are at ease;
Be troubled, you complacent ones;
Strip yourselves, make
yourselves bare,
And gird *sackcloth* on *your* waists.

12 People shall mourn upon their breasts
For the pleasant fields, for
the fruitful vine.
13 [a]On the land of my people will
come up thorns *and* briers,

31:4 [a] Num. 24:9; Hos. 11:10; Amos 3:8 31:5 [a] Deut. 32:11; Ps. 91:4 31:6 [a] Hos. 9:9 31:7 [a] Is. 2:20; 30:22 [b] 1 Kin. 12:30 31:8 [a] 2 Kin. 19:35, 36 [b] Is. 37:36 31:9 [a] Is. 37:37 32:1 [a] Ps. 45:1 32:2 [a] Is. 4:6 32:3 [a] Is. 29:18; 35:5 32:4 [a] Is. 29:24 32:6 [a] Prov. 24:7–9 32:7 [a] Jer. 5:26–28; Mic. 7:3 32:9 [a] Is. 47:8; Amos 6:1; Zeph. 2:15 32:13 [a] Is. 7:23–25; Hos. 9:6

Yes, on all the happy homes
in [b]the joyous city;
14 [a]Because the palaces will be forsaken,
The bustling city will be deserted.
The forts and towers will
become lairs forever,
A joy of wild donkeys, a
pasture of flocks—
15 Until [a]the Spirit is poured
upon us from on high,
And [b]the wilderness becomes
a fruitful field,
And the fruitful field is
counted as a forest.

The Peace of God's Reign

16 Then justice will dwell in
the wilderness,
And righteousness remain
in the fruitful field.
17 [a]The work of righteousness will be peace,
And the effect of righteousness,
quietness and assurance forever.
18 My people will dwell in a
peaceful habitation,
In secure dwellings, and in
quiet [a]resting places,
19 [a]Though hail comes down
[b]on the forest,
And the city is brought low
in humiliation.

20 Blessed *are* you who sow
beside all waters,
Who send out freely the feet of
[a]the ox and the donkey.

A Prayer in Deep Distress

33 Woe to you [a]who plunder, though
you *have* not *been* plundered;
And you who deal treacherously,
though they have not dealt
treacherously with you!
[b]When you cease plundering,
You will be [c]plundered;
When you make an end of
dealing treacherously,
They will deal treacherously with you.

2 O LORD, be gracious to us;
[a]We have waited for You.
Be their[1] arm every morning,
Our salvation also in the
time of trouble.
3 At the noise of the tumult
the people [a]shall flee;
When You lift Yourself up, the
nations shall be scattered;
4 And Your plunder shall be gathered
Like the gathering of the caterpillar;
As the running to and fro of locusts,
He shall run upon them.

5 [a]The LORD is exalted, for
He dwells on high;
He has filled Zion with justice
and righteousness.
6 Wisdom and knowledge will be
the stability of your times,
And the strength of salvation;
The fear of the LORD *is* His treasure.

7 Surely their valiant ones
shall cry outside,
[a]The ambassadors of peace
shall weep bitterly.
8 [a]The highways lie waste,
The traveling man ceases.
[b]He has broken the covenant,
He has despised the cities,[1]
He regards no man.
9 [a]The earth mourns *and* languishes,
Lebanon is shamed *and* shriveled;
Sharon is like a wilderness,
And Bashan and Carmel
shake off *their fruits*.

Impending Judgment on Zion

10 "Now[a] I will rise," says the LORD;
"Now I will be exalted,
Now I will lift Myself up.
11 [a]You shall conceive chaff,
You shall bring forth stubble;
Your breath, *as* fire, shall
devour you.
12 And the people shall be *like*
the burnings of lime;

32:13 [b] Is. 22:2 32:14 [a] Is. 27:10 32:15 [a] [Is. 11:2]; Ezek. 39:29; [Joel 2:28] [b] Ps. 107:35; Is. 29:17 32:17 [a] Ps. 119:165; Is. 2:4; Rom. 14:17; James 3:18 32:18 [a] Is. 11:10; 14:3; 30:15; [Hos. 2:18–23; Zech. 2:5; 3:10] 32:19 [a] Is. 30:30 [b] Zech. 11:2 32:20 [a] [Eccl. 11:1]; Is. 30:23, 24 33:1 [a] Is. 21:2; Hab. 2:8 [b] Rev. 13:10 [c] Is. 10:12; 14:25; 31:8 33:2 [a] Is. 25:9; 26:8 [1] Septuagint omits *their;* Syriac, Targum, and Vulgate read *our*. 33:3 [a] Is. 17:13 33:5 [a] Ps. 97:9 33:7 [a] 2 Kin. 18:18, 37 33:8 [a] Judg. 5:6 [b] 2 Kin. 18:13–17 [1] Following Masoretic Text and Vulgate; Dead Sea Scrolls read *witnesses;* Septuagint omits *cities;* Targum reads *They have been removed from their cities.* 33:9 [a] Is. 24:4 33:10 [a] Ps. 12:5; Is. 2:19, 21 33:11 [a] [Ps. 7:14; Is. 26:18; 59:4; James 1:15]

[a]*Like* thorns cut up they shall
be burned in the fire.
13 Hear, [a]you *who are* afar off,
what I have done;
And you *who are* near,
acknowledge My might."
14 The sinners in Zion are afraid;
Fearfulness has seized the hypocrites:
"Who among us shall dwell
with the devouring [a]fire?
Who among us shall dwell with
everlasting burnings?"
15 He who [a]walks righteously
and speaks uprightly,
He who despises the gain
of oppressions,
Who gestures with his hands,
refusing bribes,
Who stops his ears from
hearing of bloodshed,
And [b]shuts his eyes from seeing evil:
16 He will dwell on high;
His place of defense *will be*
the fortress of rocks;
Bread will be given him,
His water *will be* sure.

The Land of the Majestic King

17 Your eyes will see the King
in His [a]beauty;
They will see the land that
is very far off.
18 Your heart will meditate on terror:
[a]"Where *is* the scribe?
Where *is* he who weighs?
Where *is* he who counts the towers?"
19 [a]You will not see a fierce people,
[b]A people of obscure speech,
beyond perception,
Of a stammering tongue *that*
you cannot understand.

20 [a]Look upon Zion, the city of
our appointed feasts;
Your eyes will see [b]Jerusalem,
a quiet home,
A tabernacle *that* will not
be taken down;
[c]Not one of [d]its stakes will
ever be removed,
Nor will any of its cords be broken.
21 But there the majestic
LORD *will be* for us
A place of broad rivers *and* streams,
In which no galley with oars will sail,
Nor majestic ships pass by
22 (For the LORD *is* our [a]Judge,
The LORD *is* our [b]Lawgiver,
[c]The LORD *is* our King;
He will save us);
23 Your tackle is loosed,
They could not strengthen
their mast,
They could not spread the sail.

Then the prey of great
plunder is divided;
The lame take the prey.
24 And the inhabitant will not
say, "I am sick";
[a]The people who dwell in it *will*
be forgiven *their* iniquity.

Judgment on the Nations

34 Come [a]near, you nations, to hear;
And heed, you people!
[b]Let the earth hear, and all that is in it,
The world and all things that
come forth from it.
2 For the indignation of the LORD
is against all nations,
And *His* fury against all their armies;
He has utterly destroyed them,
He has given them over
to the [a]slaughter.
3 Also their slain shall be thrown out;
[a]Their stench shall rise
from their corpses,
And the mountains shall be
melted with their blood.
4 [a]All the host of heaven
shall be dissolved,
And the heavens shall be
rolled up like a scroll;
[b]All their host shall fall down
As the leaf falls from the vine,
And as [c]*fruit* falling from a fig tree.

33:12 [a] Is. 9:18 33:13 [a] Ps. 48:10; Is. 49:1 33:14 [a] Is. 30:27, 30; Heb. 12:29 33:15 [a] Ps. 15:2; 24:3, 4; Is. 58:6–11 [b] Ps. 119:37 33:17 [a] Ps. 27:4 33:18 [a] 1 Cor. 1:20 33:19 [a] 2 Kin. 19:32 [b] Deut. 28:49, 50; Is. 28:11; Jer. 5:15 33:20 [a] Ps. 48:12 [b] Ps. 46:5; 125:1; Is. 32:18 [c] Is. 37:33 [d] Is. 54:2 33:22 [a] [Acts 10:42] [b] Is. 1:10; 51:4, 7; James 4:12 [c] Ps. 89:18; Is. 25:9; 35:4; Zech. 9:9 33:24 [a] Is. 40:2; Jer. 50:20; Mic. 7:18, 19; 1 John 1:7–9 34:1 [a] Ps. 49:1; Is. 41:1; 43:9 [b] Deut. 32:1; Is. 1:2 34:2 [a] Is. 13:5 34:3 [a] Joel 2:20; Amos 4:10 34:4 [a] Ps. 102:26; Is. 13:13; Ezek. 32:7, 8; Joel 2:31; Matt. 24:29; 2 Pet. 3:10 [b] Is. 14:12 [c] Rev. 6:12–14

5 "For [a]My sword shall be
bathed in heaven;
Indeed it [b]shall come down on Edom,
And on the people of My
curse, for judgment.
6 The [a]sword of the LORD is
filled with blood,
It is made overflowing with fatness,
With the blood of lambs and goats,
With the fat of the kidneys of rams.
For [b]the LORD has a
sacrifice in Bozrah,
And a great slaughter in
the land of Edom.
7 The wild oxen shall come
down with them,
And the young bulls with
the mighty bulls;
Their land shall be soaked with blood,
And their dust saturated with fatness."

8 For *it is* the day of the
LORD's [a]vengeance,
The year of recompense for
the cause of Zion.
9 [a]Its streams shall be turned into pitch,
And its dust into brimstone;
Its land shall become burning pitch.
10 It shall not be quenched night or day;
[a]Its smoke shall ascend forever.
[b]From generation to generation
it shall lie waste;
No one shall pass through
it forever and ever.
11 [a]But the pelican and the
porcupine shall possess it,
Also the owl and the raven
shall dwell in it.
And [b]He shall stretch out over it
The line of confusion and the
stones of emptiness.
12 They shall call its nobles
to the kingdom,
But none *shall be* there, and all
its princes shall be nothing.

13 And [a]thorns shall come
up in its palaces,
Nettles and brambles in its fortresses;
[b]It shall be a habitation of jackals,
A courtyard for ostriches.
14 The wild beasts of the desert shall
also meet with the jackals,
And the wild goat shall bleat
to its companion;
Also the night creature shall rest there,
And find for herself a place of rest.
15 There the arrow snake shall
make her nest and lay *eggs*
And hatch, and gather *them*
under her shadow;
There also shall the hawks
be gathered,
Every one with her mate.

16 "Search from [a]the book of
the LORD, and read:
Not one of these shall fail;
Not one shall lack her mate.
For My mouth has commanded it,
and His Spirit has gathered them.
17 He has cast the lot for them,
And His hand has divided it among
them with a measuring line.
They shall possess it forever;
From generation to generation
they shall dwell in it."

The Future Glory of Zion

35 The [a]wilderness and the wasteland
shall be glad for them,
And the [b]desert shall rejoice
and blossom as the rose;
2 [a]It shall blossom abundantly
and rejoice,
Even with joy and singing.
The glory of Lebanon shall
be given to it,
The excellence of Carmel and Sharon.
They shall see the [b]glory of the LORD,
The excellency of our God.

3 [a]Strengthen the weak hands,
And make firm the feeble knees.
4 Say to those *who are* fearful-hearted,
"Be strong, do not fear!
Behold, your God will come
with [a]vengeance,

34:5 [a] Deut. 32:41, 42; Jer. 46:10; Ezek. 21:3–5 [b] Is. 63:1; Jer. 49:7, 8, 20; Ezek. 25:12–14; 35:1–15; Amos 1:11, 12; Obad. 1–14; Mal. 1:4
34:6 [a] Is. 66:16 [b] Zeph. 1:7 34:8 [a] Is. 63:4 34:9 [a] Deut. 29:23; Ps. 11:6; Is. 30:33 34:10 [a] Rev. 14:11; 18:18; 19:3 [b] Is. 13:20–22; 24:1; 34:10–15; Mal. 1:3, 4 34:11 [a] Is. 14:23; Zeph. 2:14; Rev. 18:2 [b] 2 Kin. 21:13; Lam. 2:8 34:13 [a] Is. 32:13; Hos. 9:6 [b] Is. 13:21
34:16 [a] [Mal. 3:16] 35:1 [a] Is. 32:15; 55:12 [b] Is. 41:19; 51:3 35:2 [a] Is. 32:15 [b] Is. 40:5
35:3 [a] Job 4:3, 4; Heb. 12:12 35:4 [a] Is. 34:8

With the recompense of God;
He will come and [b]save you."

5 Then the [a]eyes of the blind
shall be opened,
And [b]the ears of the deaf
shall be unstopped.
6 Then the [a]lame shall leap like a deer,
And the [b]tongue of the dumb sing.
For [c]waters shall burst forth
in the wilderness,
And streams in the desert.
7 The parched ground shall
become a pool,
And the thirsty land springs of water;
In [a]the habitation of jackals,
where each lay,
There shall be grass with
reeds and rushes.

8 A [a]highway shall be there, and a road,
And it shall be called the
Highway of Holiness.
[b]The unclean shall not pass over it,
But it *shall be* for others.
Whoever walks the road,
although a fool,
Shall not go astray.
9 [a]No lion shall be there,
Nor shall *any* ravenous
beast go up on it;
It shall not be found there.
But the redeemed shall walk *there,*
10 And the [a]ransomed of the
LORD shall return,
And come to Zion with singing,
With everlasting joy on their heads.
They shall obtain joy and gladness,
And [b]sorrow and sighing
shall flee away.

Sennacherib Boasts Against the LORD
(2 Kin. 18:13–37; 2 Chr. 32:1–19)

36 Now [a]it came to pass in the fourteenth year of King Hezekiah *that*
Sennacherib king of Assyria came up
against all the fortified cities of Judah and
took them. 2Then the king of Assyria sent
the Rabshakeh[1] with a great army from
Lachish to King Hezekiah at Jerusalem.
And he stood by the aqueduct from the
upper pool, on the highway to the Fuller's
Field. 3And [a]Eliakim the son of Hilkiah,
who was over the household, [b]Shebna the
scribe, and Joah the son of Asaph, the recorder, came out to him.
4[a]Then *the* Rabshakeh said to them, "Say
now to Hezekiah, 'Thus says the great king,
the king of Assyria: "What confidence is
this in which you trust? 5I say you speak of
having plans and power for war; but *they
are* mere words. Now in whom do you trust,
that you rebel against me? 6Look! You are
trusting in the [a]staff of this broken reed,
Egypt, on which if a man leans, it will go
into his hand and pierce it. So *is* Pharaoh
king of Egypt to all who [b]trust in him.
7"But if you say to me, 'We trust in the
LORD our God,' *is it* not He whose high
places and whose altars Hezekiah has taken
away, and said to Judah and Jerusalem,
'You shall worship before this altar'?"' 8Now
therefore, I urge you, give a pledge to my
master the king of Assyria, and I will give
you two thousand horses—if you are able
on your part to put riders on them! 9How
then will you repel one captain of the least
of my master's servants, and put your trust
in Egypt for chariots and horsemen? 10Have
I now come up without the LORD against
this land to destroy it? The LORD said to me,
'Go up against this land, and destroy it.'"
11Then Eliakim, Shebna, and Joah said
to *the* Rabshakeh, "Please speak to your
servants in Aramaic, for we understand *it;*
and do not speak to us in Hebrew[1] in the
hearing of the people who *are* on the wall."
12But *the* Rabshakeh said, "Has my master sent me to your master and to you to
speak these words, and not to the men who
sit on the wall, who will eat and drink their
own waste with you?"
13Then *the* Rabshakeh stood and called
out with a loud voice in Hebrew, and said,
"Hear the words of the great king, the king
of Assyria! 14Thus says the king: 'Do not
let Hezekiah deceive you, for he will not
be able to deliver you; 15nor let Hezekiah

35:4 [b] Ps. 145:19; Is. 33:22 35:5 [a] Is. 29:18; Matt. 9:27; John 9:6, 7 [b] [Matt. 11:5] 35:6 [a] Matt. 11:5; 15:30; John 5:8, 9; Acts 8:7 [b] Is. 32:4; Matt. 9:32; 12:22 [c] Is. 41:18; [John 7:38] 35:7 [a] Is. 34:13 35:8 [a] Is. 19:23 [b] Is. 52:1; Joel 3:17; [Matt. 7:13, 14]; 1 Pet. 1:15, 16; Rev. 21:27 35:9 [a] Lev. 26:6; [Is. 11:7, 9]; Ezek. 34:25 35:10 [a] Is. 51:11 [b] Is. 25:8; 30:19; 65:19; [Rev. 7:17; 21:4] 36:1 [a] 2 Kin. 18:13, 17; 2 Chr. 32:1 36:2 [1] A title, probably *Chief of Staff* or *Governor* 36:3 [a] Is. 22:20 [b] Is. 22:15 36:4 [a] 2 Kin. 18:19 36:6 [a] Ezek. 29:6 [b] Ps. 146:3; Is. 30:3, 5, 7 36:11 [1] Literally *Judean*

make you trust in the LORD, saying, "The LORD will surely deliver us; this city will not be given into the hand of the king of Assyria."' 16 Do not listen to Hezekiah; for thus says the king of Assyria: 'Make *peace* with me *by a* present and come out to me; [a]and every one of you eat from his own vine and every one from his own fig tree, and every one of you drink the waters of his own cistern; 17 until I come and take you away to a land like your own land, a land of grain and new wine, a land of bread and vineyards. 18 *Beware* lest Hezekiah persuade you, saying, "The LORD will deliver us." Has any one of the [a]gods of the nations delivered its land from the hand of the king of Assyria? 19 Where *are* the gods of Hamath and Arpad? Where *are* the gods of Sepharvaim? Indeed, have they delivered [a]Samaria from my hand? 20 Who among all the gods of these lands have delivered their countries from my hand, that the LORD should deliver Jerusalem from my hand?'"

21 But they held their peace and answered him not a word; for the king's commandment was, "Do not answer him." 22 Then Eliakim the son of Hilkiah, who *was* over the household, Shebna the scribe, and Joah the son of Asaph, the recorder, came to Hezekiah with *their* clothes torn, and told him the words of *the* Rabshakeh.

Isaiah Assures Deliverance
(2 Kin. 19:1–7)

37 And [a]so it was, when King Hezekiah heard *it,* that he tore his clothes, covered himself with sackcloth, and went into the house of the LORD. 2 Then he sent Eliakim, who *was* over the household, Shebna the scribe, and the elders of the priests, covered with sackcloth, to Isaiah the prophet, the son of Amoz. 3 And they said to him, "Thus says Hezekiah: 'This day *is* a day of [a]trouble and rebuke and blasphemy; for the children have come to birth, but *there is* no strength to bring them forth. 4 It may be that the LORD your God will hear the words of *the* Rabshakeh, whom his master the king of Assyria has sent to [a]reproach the living God, and will rebuke the words which the LORD your God has heard. Therefore lift up *your* prayer for the remnant that is left.'"

5 So the servants of King Hezekiah came to Isaiah. 6 And Isaiah said to them, "Thus you shall say to your master, 'Thus says the LORD: "Do not be afraid of the words which you have heard, with which the servants of the king of Assyria have blasphemed Me. 7 Surely I will send a spirit upon him, and he shall hear a rumor and return to his own land; and I will cause him to fall by the sword in his own land."'"

Sennacherib's Threat and Hezekiah's Prayer
(2 Kin. 19:8–19)

8 Then *the* Rabshakeh returned, and found the king of Assyria warring against Libnah, for he heard that he had departed from Lachish. 9 And the king heard concerning Tirhakah king of Ethiopia, "He has come out to make war with you." So when he heard *it,* he sent messengers to Hezekiah, saying, 10 "Thus you shall speak to Hezekiah king of Judah, saying: 'Do not let your God in whom you trust deceive you, saying, "Jerusalem shall not be given into the hand of the king of Assyria." 11 Look! You have heard what the kings of Assyria have done to all lands by utterly destroying them; and shall you be delivered? 12 Have the [a]gods of the nations delivered those whom my fathers have destroyed, Gozan and Haran and Rezeph, and the people of Eden who *were* in Telassar? 13 Where *is* the king of [a]Hamath, the king of Arpad, and the king of the city of Sepharvaim, Hena, and Ivah?'"

14 And Hezekiah received the letter from the hand of the messengers, and read it; and Hezekiah went up to the house of the LORD, and spread it before the LORD. 15 Then Hezekiah prayed to the LORD, saying: 16 "O LORD of hosts, God of Israel, *the One* who dwells *between* the cherubim, You *are* God, You [a]alone, of all the kingdoms of the earth. You have made heaven and earth. 17 [a]Incline Your ear, O LORD, and hear; open Your eyes, O LORD, and see; and [b]hear all

---

36:16 [a] 1 Kin. 4:25; Mic. 4:4; Zech. 3:10 36:18 [a] 2 Kin. 19:12; Is. 37:12 36:19 [a] 2 Kin. 17:6 37:1 [a] 2 Kin. 19:1–37; Is. 37:1–38 37:3 [a] Is. 22:5; 26:16; 33:2 37:4 [a] Is. 36:15, 18, 20 37:12 [a] Is. 36:18, 19 37:13 [a] Is. 49:23 37:16 [a] Is. 43:10, 11 37:17 [a] 2 Chr. 6:40; Ps. 17:6; Dan. 9:18 [b] Ps. 74:22

the words of Sennacherib, which he has
sent to reproach the living God. 18Truly,
LORD, the kings of Assyria have laid waste
all the nations and their [a]lands, 19and have
cast their gods into the fire; for they *were*
[a]not gods, but the work of men's hands—
wood and stone. Therefore they destroyed
them. 20Now therefore, O LORD our God,
[a]save us from his hand, that all the kingdoms of the earth may [b]know that You *are*
the LORD, You alone."

The Word of the LORD Concerning Sennacherib
(2 Kin. 19:20–34)

21Then Isaiah the son of Amoz sent to
Hezekiah, saying, "Thus says the LORD God
of Israel, 'Because you have prayed to Me
against Sennacherib king of Assyria, 22this
is the word which the LORD has spoken concerning him:

"The virgin, the daughter of Zion,
Has despised you, laughed
you to scorn;
The daughter of Jerusalem
Has shaken *her* head
behind your back!

23 "Whom have you reproached
and blasphemed?
Against whom have you
raised *your* voice,
And lifted up your eyes on high?
Against the Holy One of Israel.
24 By your servants you have
reproached the Lord,
And said, 'By the multitude
of my chariots
I have come up to the height
of the mountains,
To the limits of Lebanon;
I will cut down its tall cedars
And its choice cypress trees;
I will enter its farthest height,
To its fruitful forest.
25 I have dug and drunk water,
And with the soles of my
feet I have dried up
All the brooks of defense.'

26 "Did you not hear [a]long ago
How I made it,
From ancient times that I formed it?
Now I have brought it to pass,
That you should be
For crushing fortified cities
into heaps of ruins.
27 Therefore their inhabitants
had little power;
They were dismayed and
confounded;
They were *as* the grass of the field
And the green herb,
As the grass on the housetops
And *grain* blighted before it is grown.

28 "But I know your dwelling place,
Your going out and your coming in,
And your rage against Me.
29 Because your rage against
Me and your tumult
Have come up to My ears,
Therefore [a]I will put My
hook in your nose
And My bridle in your lips,
And I will [b]turn you back
By the way which you came."'

30 "This *shall be* a sign to you:

You shall eat this year such
as grows of itself,
And the second year what
springs from the same;
Also in the third year sow and reap,
Plant vineyards and eat
the fruit of them.
31 And the remnant who have
escaped of the house of Judah
Shall again take root downward,
And bear fruit upward.
32 For out of Jerusalem shall
go a remnant,
And those who escape
from Mount Zion.
The [a]zeal of the LORD of
hosts will do this.

33 "Therefore thus says the LORD concerning the king of Assyria:

37:18 [a] 2 Kin. 15:29; 16:9; 17:6, 24; 1 Chr. 5:26 37:19 [a] Is. 40:19, 20 37:20 [a] Is. 33:22 [b] Ps. 83:18 37:26 [a] Is. 25:1; 40:21; 45:21
37:29 [a] 2 Kin. 19:35–37; 2 Chr. 32:21; Is. 30:28; Ezek. 38:4 [b] Ezek. 38:4; 39:2
37:32 [a] 2 Kin. 19:31; Is. 9:7; 59:17; Joel 2:18; Zech. 1:14

'He shall not come into this city,
Nor shoot an arrow there,
Nor come before it with shield,
Nor build a siege mound against it.
34 By the way that he came,
By the same shall he return;
And he shall not come into this city,'
Says the LORD.
35 'For I will [a]defend this city, to save it
For My own sake and for My
servant [b]David's sake.'"

Sennacherib's Defeat and Death
(2 Kin. 19:35–37)

36 Then the [a]angel[1] of the LORD went out,
and killed in the camp of the Assyrians
one hundred and eighty-five thousand;
and when *people* arose early in the morning, there were the corpses—all dead. 37 So
Sennacherib king of Assyria departed and
went away, returned *home,* and remained
at Nineveh. 38 Now it came to pass, as he
was worshiping in the house of Nisroch his
god, that his sons Adrammelech and Sha-
rezer struck him down with the sword; and
they escaped into the land of Ararat. Then
[a]Esarhaddon his son reigned in his place.

Hezekiah's Life Extended
(2 Kin. 20:1–11; 2 Chr. 32:24–26)

38 In [a]those days Hezekiah was sick and
near death. And Isaiah the prophet,
the son of Amoz, went to him and said to
him, "Thus says the LORD: [b]'Set your house
in order, for you shall die and not live.'"
2 Then Hezekiah turned his face toward
the wall, and prayed to the LORD, 3 and said,
[a]"Remember now, O LORD, I pray, how I
have walked before You in truth and with
a loyal heart, and have done *what is* good
in Your [b]sight." And Hezekiah wept bitterly.
4 And the word of the LORD came to Isaiah, saying, 5 "Go and tell Hezekiah, 'Thus
says the LORD, the God of David your father:
"I have heard your prayer, I have seen your
tears; surely I will add to your days fifteen
years. 6 I will deliver you and this city from
the hand of the king of Assyria, and [a]I will
defend this city."' 7 And this *is* [a]the sign to
you from the LORD, that the LORD will do
this thing which He has spoken: 8 Behold, I
will bring the shadow on the sundial, which
has gone down with the sun on the sundial
of Ahaz, ten degrees backward." So the sun
returned ten degrees on the dial by which
it had gone down.
9 This is the writing of Hezekiah king of
Judah, when he had been sick and had recovered from his sickness:

10 I said,
"In the prime of my life
I shall go to the gates of Sheol;
I am deprived of the remainder
of my years."
11 I said,
"I shall not see YAH,
The LORD[1] [a]in the land of the living;
I shall observe man no more among
the inhabitants of the world.[2]
12 [a]My life span is gone,
Taken from me like a shepherd's tent;
I have cut off my life like a weaver.
He cuts me off from the loom;
From day until night You
make an end of me.
13 I have considered until morning—
Like a lion,
So He breaks all my bones;
From day until night You
make an end of me.
14 Like a crane *or* a swallow,
so I chattered;
[a]I mourned like a dove;
My eyes fail *from looking* upward.
O LORD,[1] I am oppressed;
Undertake for me!

15 "What shall I say?
He has both spoken to me,[1]
And He Himself has done *it.*
I shall walk carefully all my years
[a]In the bitterness of my soul.
16 O Lord, by these *things men* live;
And in all these *things is*
the life of my spirit;

37:35 [a] 2 Kin. 20:6; Is. 31:5; 38:6 [b] 1 Kin. 11:13 37:36 [a] 2 Kin. 19:35; Is. 10:12, 33, 34 [1] Or *Angel* 37:38 [a] Ezra 4:2 38:1 [a] 2 Kin. 20:1–6, 9–11; 2 Chr. 32:24; Is. 38:1–8 [b] 2 Sam. 17:23 38:3 [a] Neh. 13:14 [b] 2 Kin. 18:5, 6; Ps. 26:3 38:6 [a] 2 Kin. 19:35–37; 2 Chr. 32:21; Is. 31:5; 37:35 38:7 [a] Judg. 6:17, 21, 36–40; 2 Kin. 20:8; Is. 7:11 38:11 [a] Ps. 27:13; 116:9 [1] Hebrew *YAH, YAH* [2] Following some Hebrew manuscripts; Masoretic Text and Vulgate read *rest;* Septuagint omits *among the inhabitants of the world;* Targum reads *land.* 38:12 [a] Job 7:6 38:14 [a] Is. 59:11; Ezek. 7:16; Nah. 2:7 [1] Following Bomberg; Masoretic Text and Dead Sea Scrolls read *Lord.* 38:15 [a] Job 7:11; 10:1; Is. 38:17 [1] Following Masoretic Text and Vulgate; Dead Sea Scrolls and Targum read *And shall I say to Him;* Septuagint omits first half of this verse.

So You will restore me
and make me live.
17 Indeed *it was* for *my own* peace
That I had great bitterness;
But You have lovingly *delivered* my
soul from the pit of corruption,
For You have cast all my sins
behind Your back.
18 For [a]Sheol cannot thank You,
Death cannot praise You;
Those who go down to the pit
cannot hope for Your truth.
19 The living, the living man,
he shall praise You,
As I *do* this day;
[a]The father shall make known
Your truth to the children.

20 "The LORD *was ready* to save me;
Therefore we will sing my songs
with stringed instruments
All the days of our life, in the
house of the LORD."

21 Now [a]Isaiah had said, "Let them take a
lump of figs, and apply *it* as a poultice on
the boil, and he shall recover."
22 And [a]Hezekiah had said, "What *is* the
sign that I shall go up to the house of the
LORD?"

The Babylonian Envoys
(2 Kin. 20:12–19)

39 At [a]that time Merodach-Baladan[1]
the son of Baladan, king of Babylon, sent letters and a present to Hezekiah, for he heard that he had been sick
and had recovered. 2 [a]And Hezekiah was
pleased with them, and showed them the
house of his treasures—the silver and gold,
the spices and precious ointment, and all
his armory—all that was found among his
treasures. There was nothing in his house
or in all his dominion that Hezekiah did
not show them.
3 Then Isaiah the prophet went to King
Hezekiah, and said to him, "What did these
men say, and from where did they come
to you?"
So Hezekiah said, "They came to me
from a [a]far country, from Babylon."
4 And he said, "What have they seen in
your house?"
So Hezekiah answered, "They have seen
all that *is* in my house; there is nothing
among my treasures that I have not shown
them."
5 Then Isaiah said to Hezekiah, "Hear
the word of the LORD of hosts: 6 'Behold,
the days are coming [a]when all that *is* in
your house, and what your fathers have
accumulated until this day, shall be carried to Babylon; nothing shall be left,' says
the LORD. 7 'And they shall take away *some*
of your [a]sons who will descend from you,
whom you will beget; and they shall be eunuchs in the palace of the king of Babylon.'"
8 So Hezekiah said to Isaiah, [a]"The word
of the LORD which you have spoken *is*
good!" For he said, "At least there will be
peace and truth in my days."

God's People Are Comforted
(cf. Luke 3:4–6)

40 "Comfort, yes, comfort
My people!"
Says your God.
2 "Speak comfort to Jerusalem,
and cry out to her,
That her warfare is ended,
That her iniquity is pardoned;
[a]For she has received from
the LORD's hand
Double for all her sins."

3 [a]The voice of one crying
in the wilderness:
[b]"Prepare the way of the LORD;
[c]Make straight in the desert[1]
A highway for our God.
4 Every valley shall be exalted
And every mountain and
hill brought low;
[a]The crooked places shall
be made straight
And the rough places smooth;
5 The [a]glory of the LORD
shall be revealed,

38:18 [a] Ps. 6:5; 30:9; 88:11; 115:17; [Eccl. 9:10] 38:19 [a] Deut. 4:9; 6:7; Ps. 78:3, 4 38:21 [a] 2 Kin. 20:7 38:22 [a] 2 Kin. 20:8 39:1 [a] 2 Kin. 20:12–19; 2 Chr. 32:31; Is. 39:1–8 [1] Spelled *Berodach-Baladan* in 2 Kings 20:12 39:2 [a] 2 Chr. 32:25, 31; Job 31:25 39:3 [a] Deut. 28:49; Jer. 5:15 39:6 [a] 2 Kin. 24:13; 25:13–15; Jer. 20:5 39:7 [a] Dan. 1:1–7 39:8 [a] 1 Sam. 3:18 40:2 [a] Is. 61:7 40:3 [a] Matt. 3:3; Mark 1:3; Luke 3:4–6; John 1:23 [b] [Mal. 3:1; 4:5, 6] [c] Ps. 68:4 [1] Following Masoretic Text, Targum, and Vulgate; Septuagint omits *in the desert.* 40:4 [a] Is. 45:2 40:5 [a] Is. 35:2

And all flesh shall see *it* together;
For the mouth of the LORD
has spoken."

6 The voice said, "Cry out!"
And he[1] said, "What shall I cry?"

[a]"All flesh *is* grass,
And all its loveliness *is* like
the flower of the field.
7 The grass withers, the flower fades,
Because the breath of the
LORD blows upon it;
Surely the people *are* grass.
8 The grass withers, the flower fades,
But [a]the word of our God
stands forever."

9 O Zion,
You who bring good tidings,
Get up into the high mountain;
O Jerusalem,
You who bring good tidings,
Lift up your voice with strength,
Lift *it* up, be not afraid;
Say to the cities of Judah,
"Behold your God!"

10 Behold, the Lord GOD shall
come with a strong *hand,*
And [a]His arm shall rule for Him;
Behold, [b]His reward *is* with Him,
And His work before Him.
11 He will [a]feed His flock like a shepherd;
He will gather the lambs with His arm,
And carry *them* in His bosom,
And gently lead those who
are with young.

12 [a]Who has measured the waters[1]
in the hollow of His hand,
Measured heaven with a span
And calculated the dust of the
earth in a measure?
Weighed the mountains in scales
And the hills in a balance?
13 [a]Who has directed the
Spirit of the LORD,
Or *as* His counselor has taught Him?
14 With whom did He take counsel,
and *who* instructed Him,
And [a]taught Him in the
path of justice?
Who taught Him knowledge,
And showed Him the way
of understanding?

15 Behold, the nations *are* as
a drop in a bucket,
And are counted as the small
dust on the scales;
Look, He lifts up the isles
as a very little thing.
16 And Lebanon *is* not sufficient
to burn,
Nor its beasts sufficient for
a burnt offering.
17 All nations before Him
are as [a]nothing,
And [b]they are counted by Him less
than nothing and worthless.

18 To whom then will you [a]liken God?
Or what likeness will you
compare to Him?
19 [a]The workman molds an image,
The goldsmith overspreads
it with gold,
And the silversmith casts
silver chains.
20 Whoever *is* too impoverished
for *such* a contribution
Chooses a tree *that* will not rot;
He seeks for himself a
skillful workman
[a]To prepare a carved image
that will not totter.

21 [a]Have you not known?
Have you not heard?
Has it not been told you
from the beginning?
Have you not understood from
the foundations of the earth?
22 *It is* He who sits above the
circle of the earth,

40:6 [a] Job 14:2; James 1:10; 1 Pet. 1:24, 25 [1] Following Masoretic Text and Targum; Dead Sea Scrolls, Septuagint, and Vulgate read *I.* 40:8 [a] [John 12:34] 40:10 [a] Is. 59:16, 18 [b] Is. 62:11; Rev. 22:12 40:11 [a] Jer. 31:10; [Ezek. 34:23, 31]; Mic. 5:4; [John 10:11, 14–16; Heb. 13:20; 1 Pet. 2:25] 40:12 [a] Prov. 30:4 [1] Following Masoretic Text, Septuagint, and Vulgate; Dead Sea Scrolls read *waters of the sea;* Targum reads *waters of the world.* 40:13 [a] Job 21:22; Rom. 11:34; [1 Cor. 2:16] 40:14 [a] Job 36:22, 23 40:17 [a] Dan. 4:35 [b] Ps. 62:9 40:18 [a] Ex. 8:10; 15:11; 1 Sam. 2:2; Is. 46:5; [Mic. 7:18]; Acts 17:29 40:19 [a] Ps. 115:4–8; Is. 41:7; 44:10; Hab. 2:18, 19 40:20 [a] 1 Sam. 5:3, 4; Is. 41:7; 46:7; Jer. 10:3 40:21 [a] Ps. 19:1; Is. 37:26; Acts 14:17; Rom. 1:19

And its inhabitants *are*
like grasshoppers,
Who [a]stretches out the
heavens like a curtain,
And spreads them out like
a [b]tent to dwell in.
23 He brings the [a]princes to nothing;
He makes the judges of
the earth useless.

24 Scarcely shall they be planted,
Scarcely shall they be sown,
Scarcely shall their stock
take root in the earth,
When He will also blow on them,
And they will wither,
And the whirlwind will take
them away like stubble.

25 "To[a] whom then will you liken Me,
Or *to whom* shall I be equal?"
says the Holy One.
26 Lift up your eyes on high,
And see who has created these *things*,
Who brings out their host by number;
[a]He calls them all by name,
By the greatness of His might
And the strength of *His* power;
Not one is missing.

27 [a]Why do you say, O Jacob,
And speak, O Israel:
"My way is hidden from the LORD,
And my just claim is passed
over by my God"?
28 Have you not known?
Have you not heard?
The everlasting God, the LORD,
The Creator of the ends of the earth,
Neither faints nor is weary.
[a]His understanding is unsearchable.
29 He gives power to the weak,
And to *those who have* no might
He increases strength.
30 Even the youths shall faint
and be weary,
And the young men shall utterly fall,
31 But those who [a]wait on the LORD
[b]Shall renew *their* strength;
They shall mount up with
wings like eagles,
They shall run and not be weary,
They shall walk and not faint.

Israel Assured of God's Help

41 "Keep [a]silence before Me,
O coastlands,
And let the people renew
their strength!
Let them come near, then
let them speak;
Let us [b]come near together
for judgment.

2 "Who raised up one [a]from the east?
Who in righteousness called
him to His feet?
Who [b]gave the nations before him,
And made *him* rule over kings?
Who gave *them* as the
dust *to* his sword,
As driven stubble to his bow?
3 Who pursued them, *and* passed safely
By the way *that* he had not
gone with his feet?
4 [a]Who has performed and done *it*,
Calling the generations
from the beginning?
'I, the LORD, am [b]the first;
And with the last I *am* [c]He.'"

5 The coastlands saw *it* and feared,
The ends of the earth were afraid;
They drew near and came.
6 [a]Everyone helped his neighbor,
And said to his brother,
"Be of good courage!"
7 [a]So the craftsman encouraged
the [b]goldsmith;
He who smooths *with* the hammer
inspired him who strikes
the anvil,
Saying, "It *is* ready for the soldering";
Then he fastened it with pegs,
[c]*That* it might not totter.

8 "But you, Israel, *are* My servant,
Jacob whom I have [a]chosen,

40:22 [a] Job 9:8; Ps. 104:2; Is. 42:5; 44:24; Jer. 10:12 [b] Job 36:29; Ps. 19:4 40:23 [a] Job 12:21; Ps. 107:40; Is. 34:12; [1 Cor. 1:26–29] 40:25 [a] [Deut. 4:15]; Is. 40:18; [John 14:9; Col. 1:15] 40:26 [a] Ps. 147:4 40:27 [a] Is. 54:7, 8 40:28 [a] Ps. 147:5; Eccl. 11:5; Rom. 11:33 40:31 [a] Is. 30:15; 49:23 [b] [Job 17:9]; Ps. 103:5; [2 Cor. 4:8–10, 16] 41:1 [a] Hab. 2:20; Zech. 2:13 [b] Is. 1:18 41:2 [a] Is. 46:11 [b] Gen. 14:14; Is. 45:1, 13 41:4 [a] Is. 41:26 [b] Rev. 1:8, 17; 22:13 [c] Is. 43:10; 44:6 41:6 [a] Is. 40:19 41:7 [a] Is. 44:13 [b] Is. 40:19 [c] Is. 40:20 41:8 [a] Deut. 7:6; 10:15; Ps. 135:4; [Is. 43:1]

#OXYGEN

ISAIAH 41:6

Act out of Selflessness

You need to take care of yourself. However, do not think only in terms of "me, myself, and I." In the kingdom, we are commissioned to be other-centered, not self-centered. Think instead in terms of "if you are okay, then I am okay."

Breathe and **act out of selflessness.**

The descendants of
Abraham My [b]friend.
9 *You* whom I have taken from
the ends of the earth,
And called from its farthest regions,
And said to you,
'You *are* My servant,
I have chosen you and have
not cast you away:
10 [a]Fear not, [b]for I *am* with you;
Be not dismayed, for I *am* your God.
I will strengthen you,
Yes, I will help you,
I will uphold you with My
righteous right hand.'

11 "Behold, all those who were
incensed against you
Shall be [a]ashamed and disgraced;
They shall be as nothing,
And those who strive with
you shall perish.
12 You shall seek them and
not find them—
Those who contended with you.
Those who war against you
Shall be as nothing,
As a nonexistent thing.
13 For I, the LORD your God, will
hold your right hand,
Saying to you, 'Fear not,
I will help you.'

14 "Fear not, you [a]worm Jacob,
You men of Israel!
I will help you," says the LORD
And your Redeemer, the
Holy One of Israel.
15 "Behold, [a]I will make you into a new
threshing sledge with sharp teeth;
You shall thresh the mountains
and beat *them* small,
And make the hills like chaff.
16 You shall [a]winnow them, the
wind shall carry them away,
And the whirlwind shall scatter them;
You shall rejoice in the LORD,
And [b]glory in the Holy One of Israel.

17 "The poor and needy seek
water, but *there is* none,
Their tongues fail for thirst.
I, the LORD, will hear them;
I, the God of Israel, will
not [a]forsake them.
18 I will open [a]rivers in desolate heights,
And fountains in the midst
of the valleys;
I will make the [b]wilderness
a pool of water,
And the dry land springs of water.
19 I will plant in the wilderness the
cedar and the acacia tree,
The myrtle and the oil tree;
I will set in the [a]desert the
cypress tree *and* the pine
And the box tree together,
20 [a]That they may see and know,
And consider and
understand together,
That the hand of the LORD
has done this,
And the Holy One of Israel
has created it.

The Futility of Idols

21 "Present your case," says the LORD.
"Bring forth your strong *reasons*,"
says the [a]King of Jacob.
22 "Let[a] them bring forth and show
us what will happen;
Let them show the [b]former
things, what they *were*,

41:8 [b] 2 Chr. 20:7; James 2:23 41:10 [a] Is. 41:13, 14; 43:5 [b] [Deut. 31:6] 41:11 [a] Ex. 23:22; Is. 45:24; 60:12; Zech. 12:3 41:14 [a] Job 25:6; Ps. 22:6 41:15 [a] Mic. 4:13; Hab. 3:12; [2 Cor. 10:4] 41:16 [a] Jer. 51:2 [b] Is. 45:25 41:17 [a] Ps. 94:14; Rom. 11:2 41:18 [a] Is. 35:6, 7; 43:19; 44:3 [b] Ps. 107:35 41:19 [a] Is. 35:1 41:20 [a] Job 12:9; Is. 66:14 41:21 [a] Is. 43:15 41:22 [a] Is. 45:21 [b] Is. 43:9

That we may consider them,
And know the latter end of them;
Or declare to us things to come.
23 [a]Show the things that are
to come hereafter,
That we may know that you *are* gods;
Yes, [b]do good or do evil,
That we may be dismayed
and see *it* together.
24 Indeed [a]you *are* nothing,
And your work *is* nothing;
He who chooses you *is* an
abomination.

25 "I have raised up one from the north,
And he shall come;
From the rising of the sun [a]he
shall call on My name;
[b]And he shall come against
princes as *though* mortar,
As the potter treads clay.
26 [a]Who has declared from the
beginning, that we may know?
And former times, that we may
say, '*He is* righteous'?
Surely *there is* no one who shows,
Surely *there is* no one who declares,
Surely *there is* no one who
hears your words.
27 [a]The first time [b]*I said* to Zion,
'Look, there they are!'
And I will give to Jerusalem one
who brings good tidings.
28 [a]For I looked, and *there was* no man;
I looked among them, but
there was no counselor,
Who, when I asked of them,
could answer a word.
29 [a]Indeed they *are* all worthless;[1]
Their works *are* nothing;
Their molded images *are*
wind and confusion.

The Servant of the LORD

42 "Behold! [a]My Servant
whom I uphold,
My Elect One *in whom* My
soul [b]delights!
[c]I have put My Spirit upon Him;
He will bring forth justice
to the Gentiles.
2 He will not cry out, nor raise *His voice,*
Nor cause His voice to be
heard in the street.
3 A bruised reed He will not break,
And smoking flax He will
not quench;
He will bring forth justice for truth.
4 He will not fail nor be discouraged,
Till He has established
justice in the earth;
[a]And the coastlands shall
wait for His law."

5 Thus says God the LORD,
[a]Who created the heavens and
stretched them out,
Who spread forth the earth and
that which comes from it,
[b]Who gives breath to the people on it,
And spirit to those who walk on it:
6 "I,[a] the LORD, have called You
in righteousness,
And will hold Your hand;
I will keep You [b]and give You as
a covenant to the people,
As [c]a light to the Gentiles,
7 [a]To open blind eyes,
To [b]bring out prisoners
from the prison,
Those who sit in [c]darkness
from the prison house.
8 I *am* the LORD, that *is* My name;
And My [a]glory I will not
give to another,
Nor My praise to carved images.
9 Behold, the former things
have come to pass,
And new things I declare;
Before they spring forth I
tell you of them."

Praise to the LORD

10 [a]Sing to the LORD a new song,
And His praise from the
ends of the earth,

41:23 [a] Is. 42:9; 44:7, 8; 45:3; [John 13:19] [b] Jer. 10:5 **41:24** [a] Ps. 115:8; Is. 44:9; [Rom. 3:10–20; 1 Cor. 8:4] **41:25** [a] Ezra 1:2 [b] Is. 41:2; Jer. 50:3 **41:26** [a] Is. 43:9 **41:27** [a] Is. 41:4 [b] Is. 40:9; Nah. 1:15 **41:28** [a] Is. 63:5 **41:29** [a] Is. 41:24 [1] Following Masoretic Text and Vulgate; Dead Sea Scrolls, Syriac, and Targum read *nothing;* Septuagint omits the first line. **42:1** [a] Is. 43:10; 49:3, 6; Matt. 12:18; [Phil. 2:7] [b] Matt. 3:17; 17:5; Mark 1:11; Luke 3:22; Eph. 1:6 [c] [Is. 11:2]; Matt. 3:16; [Luke 4:18, 19, 21]; John 3:34 **42:4** [a] [Gen. 49:10] **42:5** [a] Is. 44:24; Zech. 12:1 [b] Job 12:10; 33:4; Is. 57:16; Dan. 5:23; Acts 17:25 **42:6** [a] Is. 43:1 [b] Is. 49:8 [c] Is. 49:6; Luke 2:32; [Acts 10:45; 13:47; Gal. 3:14] **42:7** [a] Is. 35:5 [b] Is. 61:1; Luke 4:18; [2 Tim. 2:26; Heb. 2:14] [c] Is. 9:2 **42:8** [a] Ex. 20:3–5; Is. 48:11 **42:10** [a] Ps. 33:3; 40:3; 98:1

RELEASE // ACT OUT OF SELFLESSNESS

Develop a Servant's Heart

Isaiah 42:2–3 //"He will not cry out, nor raise His voice, nor cause His voice to be heard in the street. A bruised reed He will not break, and smoking flax He will not quench; He will bring forth justice for truth."

Summary Message //Isaiah 42 is the first of four "Servant Songs" in the Book of Isaiah in which God the Father refers to a righteous servant. When Isaiah wrote these songs, the Israelites were in serious trouble because they had turned away from God. Captivity loomed over their future. God then told His people the kind of servant He chooses and in whom He delights: a selfless servant who will bring justice to the nations.

In this Servant Song, God let the Israelites know that what they truly needed was a godly, righteous, truthful, just, selfless helper. They needed a God-approved servant who would not act in a loud, contentious, intimidating, ostentatious, or boastful way. Instead, God wanted to send a servant who would behave with great humility and meekness. God said He would provide such a servant to hold their hands and lead them out of their plight by opening the eyes of those blinded to Him and releasing those in captivity.

Practical Application //Our time is much like the days of Isaiah. God has always provided servants who act out of selflessness to help His people, and He is still blessing us with selfless servants today. When we look at *selfless*, it tells us all we need to know about God-chosen servants. If we flip *selfless* around, it becomes "less self." So, in practicing this trait, we determine to think less often of ourselves and think more often of everyone else.

With all the divisiveness in the world today, selflessness is an essential trait that can unify, motivate, and lead us to be world changers. When we act out of selflessness, we seek to serve others. One selfless act can have a ripple effect on others, creating strong communities of godly servants who create a better environment for all. Selflessness is a quality that pleases God.

Some people are naturally more selfless, while others must learn to be this way. Thankfully, God knows that either way, developing the habit of selflessness is a daily process. How can we become less selfish and more selfless in our daily lives? We can start by doing acts of selflessness and kindness like volunteering. We can talk less about ourselves and listen more to the heart of others. We can serve others who have been marginalized or ignored and let them know how much they matter. By willing ourselves to do more selfless acts, we can actually become more generous, compassionate, kind, thoughtful, and humble. Even if it does not come naturally, with practice we can become the servants, in both thoughts and deeds, that God has called us to be.

Fervent Prayer //Heavenly Father, open our eyes to the needs of others. Help us be considerate to others to decrease conflict and increase unity in our community. Help us show humility to represent Your heart to others. Give us a spirit of selflessness so that we can be servants who will bring You glory. In Jesus' name we pray. Amen.

---

[b]You who go down to the sea,
and all that is in it,
You coastlands and you
inhabitants of them!
11 Let the wilderness and its
cities lift up *their voice,*
The villages *that* Kedar
inhabits.
Let the inhabitants of Sela sing,
Let them shout from the top
of the mountains.
12 Let them give glory to the LORD,
And declare His praise in
the coastlands.
13 The LORD shall go forth
like a mighty man;
He shall stir up *His* zeal
like a man of war.
He shall cry out, [a]yes, shout aloud;
He shall prevail against His enemies.

Promise of the LORD's Help

14 "I have held My peace a long time,
I have been still and restrained Myself.

42:10 [b] Ps. 107:23 42:13 [a] Is. 31:4

Now I will cry like a woman in labor,
I will pant and gasp at once.
15 I will lay waste the
mountains and hills,
And dry up all their vegetation;
I will make the rivers coastlands,
And I will dry up the pools.
16 I will bring the blind by a way
they did not know;
I will lead them in paths
they have not known.
I will make darkness light
before them,
And crooked places straight.
These things I will do for them,
And not forsake them.
17 They shall be [a]turned back,
They shall be greatly ashamed,
Who trust in carved images,
Who say to the molded images,
'You *are* our gods.'

18 "Hear, you deaf;
And look, you blind, that you may see.
19 [a]Who *is* blind but My servant,
Or deaf as My messenger
whom I send?
Who *is* blind as *he who is* perfect,
And blind as the LORD's servant?
20 Seeing many things, [a]but
you do not observe;
Opening the ears, but he
does not hear."

Israel's Obstinate Disobedience

21 The LORD is well pleased for
His righteousness' sake;
He will exalt the law and
make *it* honorable.
22 But this *is* a people robbed
and plundered;
All of them are snared in holes,
And they are hidden in prison houses;
They are for prey, and no one delivers;
For plunder, and no one
says, "Restore!"

23 Who among you will give ear to this?
Who will listen and hear for
the time to come?
24 Who gave Jacob for plunder,
and Israel to the robbers?
Was it not the LORD,
He against whom we have sinned?
[a]For they would not walk in His ways,
Nor were they obedient to His law.
25 Therefore He has poured on
him the fury of His anger
And the strength of battle;
[a]It has set him on fire all around,
[b]Yet he did not know;
And it burned him,
Yet he did not take *it* to [c]heart.

The Redeemer of Israel

43 But now, thus says the LORD, who
created you, O Jacob,
And He who formed you, O Israel:
"Fear not, [a]for I have redeemed you;
[b]I have called *you* by your name;
You *are* Mine.
2 [a]When you pass through the
waters, [b]I *will be* with you;
And through the rivers, they
shall not overflow you.
When you [c]walk through the fire,
you shall not be burned,
Nor shall the flame scorch you.
3 For I *am* the LORD your God,
The Holy One of Israel, your Savior;
[a]I gave Egypt for your ransom,
Ethiopia and Seba in your place.
4 Since you were precious in My sight,
You have been honored,
And I have [a]loved you;
Therefore I will give men for you,
And people for your life.
5 [a]Fear not, for I *am* with you;
I will bring your descendants
from the east,
And [b]gather you from the west;
6 I will say to the [a]north, 'Give
them up!'
And to the south, 'Do not
keep them back!'
Bring My sons from afar,
And My daughters from the
ends of the earth—
7 Everyone who is [a]called by My name,
Whom [b]I have created for My glory;

42:17 [a] Ps. 97:7; Is. 1:29; 44:11; 45:16 42:19 [a] Is. 43:8; Ezek. 12:2; [John 9:39, 41] 42:20 [a] Rom. 2:21 42:24 [a] Is. 65:2 42:25 [a] 2 Kin. 25:9 [b] Is. 1:3; 5:13; Hos. 7:9 [c] Is. 29:13 43:1 [a] Is. 43:5; 44:6 [b] Is. 42:6; 45:4 43:2 [a] [Ps. 66:12; 91:3] [b] [Deut. 31:6]; Jer. 30:11 [c] Dan. 3:25 43:3 [a] [Prov. 11:8; 21:18] 43:4 [a] Is. 63:9 43:5 [a] Is. 41:10; 44:2; Jer. 30:10; 46:27, 28 [b] Is. 54:7 43:6 [a] Is. 49:12 43:7 [a] Is. 63:19; James 2:7 [b] Ps. 100:3; Is. 29:23; [John 3:2, 3; 2 Cor. 5:17; Eph. 2:10]

I have formed him, yes, I
have made him."

8 [a]Bring out the blind people
who have eyes,
And the [b]deaf who have ears.
9 Let all the nations be
gathered together,
And let the people be assembled.
[a]Who among them can declare this,
And show us former things?
Let them bring out their witnesses,
that they may be justified;
Or let them hear and say, "*It is* truth."
10 "You[a] *are* My witnesses," says the LORD,
[b]"And My servant whom I have chosen,
That you may know and [c]believe Me,
And understand that I *am* He.
Before Me there was no God formed,
Nor shall there be after Me.
11 I, *even* I, [a]*am* the LORD,
And besides Me *there is* no savior.
12 I have declared and saved,
I have proclaimed,
And *there was* no [a]foreign
god among you;
[b]Therefore you *are* My witnesses,"
Says the LORD, "that I *am* God.
13 [a]Indeed before the day *was,* I *am* He;
And *there is* no one who can
deliver out of My hand;
I work, and who will [b]reverse it?"

14 Thus says the LORD, your Redeemer,
The Holy One of Israel:
"For your sake I will send
to Babylon,
And bring them all down
as fugitives—
The Chaldeans, who rejoice
in their ships.
15 I *am* the LORD, your Holy One,
The Creator of Israel, your [a]King."

16 Thus says the LORD, who
[a]makes a way in the sea
And a [b]path through the
mighty waters,
17 Who [a]brings forth the
chariot and horse,
The army and the power
(They shall lie down together,
they shall not rise;
They are extinguished, they are
quenched like a wick):
18 "Do[a] not remember the former things,
Nor consider the things of old.
19 Behold, I will do a [a]new thing,
Now it shall spring forth;
Shall you not know it?
[b]I will even make a road
in the wilderness
And rivers in the desert.
20 The beast of the field will honor Me,
The jackals and the ostriches,
Because [a]I give waters in
the wilderness
And rivers in the desert,
To give drink to My people, My chosen.
21 [a]This people I have formed for Myself;
They shall declare My [b]praise.

Pleading with Unfaithful Israel

22 "But you have not called
upon Me, O Jacob;
And you [a]have been weary
of Me, O Israel.
23 [a]You have not brought Me the sheep
for your burnt offerings,
Nor have you honored Me
with your sacrifices.
I have not caused you to serve
with grain offerings,
Nor wearied you with incense.
24 You have bought Me no sweet
cane with money,
Nor have you satisfied Me with
the fat of your sacrifices;
But you have burdened
Me with your sins,
You have [a]wearied Me with
your iniquities.

25 "I, *even* I, *am* He who [a]blots out your
transgressions [b]for My own sake;
[c]And I will not remember your sins.

43:8 [a] Is. 6:9; 42:19; Ezek. 12:2 [b] Is. 29:18 43:9 [a] Is. 41:21, 22, 26 43:10 [a] Is. 44:8 [b] Is. 55:4 [c] Is. 41:4; 44:6 43:11 [a] Is. 45:21; Hos. 13:4 43:12 [a] Deut. 32:16; Ps. 81:9 [b] Is. 44:8 43:13 [a] Ps. 90:2; Is. 48:16 [b] Job 9:12; Is. 14:27 43:15 [a] Is. 41:20, 21 43:16 [a] Ex. 14:16, 21, 22; Ps. 77:19; Is. 51:10 [b] Josh. 3:13 43:17 [a] Ex. 14:4–9, 25 43:18 [a] Jer. 16:14 43:19 [a] Is. 42:9; 48:6; [2 Cor. 5:17; Rev. 21:5] [b] Ex. 17:6; Num. 20:11; Deut. 8:15; Ps. 78:16; Is. 35:1, 6 43:20 [a] Is. 48:21 43:21 [a] Ps. 102:18; Is. 42:12; [Luke 1:74, 75; Eph. 1:5, 6; 1 Pet. 2:9] [b] Jer. 13:11 43:22 [a] Mic. 6:3; Mal. 1:13; 3:14 43:23 [a] Amos 5:25 43:24 [a] Ps. 95:10; Is. 1:14; 7:13; Ezek. 6:9; Mal. 2:17 43:25 [a] Is. 44:22; Jer. 50:20; [Acts 3:19] [b] Ezek. 36:22 [c] Is. 1:18; Jer. 31:34

26 Put Me in remembrance;
Let us contend together;
State your *case,* that you
may be acquitted.
27 Your first father sinned,
And your mediators have
transgressed against Me.
28 Therefore I will profane the
princes of the sanctuary;
[a]I will give Jacob to the curse,
And Israel to reproaches.

God's Blessing on Israel

44 "Yet hear now, O Jacob My servant,
And Israel whom I have chosen.
2 Thus says the LORD who made you
And formed you from the
womb, *who* will help you:
'Fear not, O Jacob My servant;
And you, Jeshurun, whom
I have chosen.
3 For I will pour water on
him who is thirsty,
And floods on the dry ground;
I will pour My Spirit on
your descendants,
And My blessing on your offspring;
4 They will spring up among the grass
Like willows by the watercourses.'
5 One will say, 'I *am* the LORD's';
Another will call *himself* by
the name of Jacob;
Another will write *with* his
hand, 'The LORD's,'
And name *himself* by the
name of Israel.

There Is No Other God

6 "Thus says the LORD, the King of Israel,
And his Redeemer, the LORD of hosts:
[a]'I *am* the First and I *am* the Last;
Besides Me *there is* no God.
7 And [a]who can proclaim as I do?
Then let him declare it and
set it in order for Me,
Since I appointed the ancient
people.
And the things that are
coming and shall come,
Let them show these to them.
8 Do not fear, nor be afraid;
[a]Have I not told you from that
time, and declared *it?*
[b]You *are* My witnesses.
Is there a God besides Me?
Indeed [c]*there is* no other Rock;
I know not *one.*'"

Idolatry Is Foolishness

9 [a]Those who make an image,
all of them *are* useless,
And their precious things
shall not profit;
They *are* their own witnesses;
[b]They neither see nor know, that
they may be ashamed.
10 Who would form a god or
mold an image
[a]*That* profits him nothing?
11 Surely all his companions
would be [a]ashamed;
And the workmen, they *are* mere men.
Let them all be gathered together,
Let them stand up;
Yet they shall fear,
They shall be ashamed together.

12 [a]The blacksmith with the tongs
works one in the coals,
Fashions it with hammers,
And works it with the
strength of his arms.
Even so, he is hungry, and
his strength fails;
He drinks no water and is faint.

13 The craftsman stretches out *his* rule,
He marks one out with chalk;
He fashions it with a plane,
He marks it out with the compass,
And makes it like the figure
of a man,
According to the beauty of a man,
that it may remain in the house.
14 He cuts down cedars for himself,
And takes the cypress and the oak;
He secures *it* for himself among
the trees of the forest.
He plants a pine, and the
rain nourishes *it.*

43:28 [a] Ps. 79:4; Jer. 24:9; Dan. 9:11; Zech. 8:13 44:6 [a] Is. 41:4; [Rev. 1:8, 17; 22:13] 44:7 [a] Is. 41:4, 22, 26 44:8 [a] Is. 41:22 [b] Is. 43:10, 12 [c] Deut. 4:35; 32:39; 1 Sam. 2:2; 2 Sam. 22:32; Is. 45:5; Joel 2:27 44:9 [a] Is. 41:24 [b] Ps. 115:4 44:10 [a] Is. 41:29; Jer. 10:5; Hab. 2:18; Acts 19:26 44:11 [a] Ps. 97:7; Is. 1:29; 42:17 44:12 [a] Is. 40:19; Jer. 10:3–5

15 Then it shall be for a man to burn,
For he will take some of it
and warm himself;
Yes, he kindles *it* and bakes bread;
Indeed he makes a god
and worships *it;*
He makes it a carved image,
and falls down to it.
16 He burns half of it in the fire;
With this half he eats meat;
He roasts a roast, and is satisfied.
He even warms *himself* and says,
"Ah! I am warm,
I have seen the fire."
17 And the rest of it he makes into a god,
His carved image.
He falls down before it and worships *it,*
Prays to it and says,
"Deliver me, for you *are* my god!"

18 [a]They do not know nor understand;
For [b]He has shut their eyes, so
that they cannot see,
And their hearts, so that they
cannot [c]understand.
19 And no one [a]considers in his heart,
Nor *is there* knowledge nor
understanding to say,
"I have burned half of it in the fire,
Yes, I have also baked
bread on its coals;
I have roasted meat and eaten *it;*
And shall I make the rest of
it an abomination?
Shall I fall down before a
block of wood?"
20 He feeds on ashes;
[a]A deceived heart has
turned him aside;
And he cannot deliver his soul,
Nor say, "*Is there* not a [b]lie
in my right hand?"

Israel Is Not Forgotten

21 "Remember these, O Jacob,
And Israel, for you *are* My servant;
I have formed you, you *are* My servant;
O Israel, you will not be
[a]forgotten by Me!
22 [a]I have blotted out, like a thick
cloud, your transgressions,
And like a cloud, your sins.
Return to Me, for [b]I have
redeemed you."

23 [a]Sing, O heavens, for the
LORD has done *it!*
Shout, you lower parts of the earth;
Break forth into singing,
you mountains,
O forest, and every tree in it!
For the LORD has redeemed Jacob,
And [b]glorified Himself in Israel.

Judah Will Be Restored

24 Thus says the LORD, [a]your Redeemer,
And [b]He who formed you
from the womb:
"I *am* the LORD, who makes
all *things,*
[c]Who stretches out the
heavens all alone,
Who spreads abroad the
earth by Myself;
25 Who [a]frustrates the signs
[b]of the babblers,
And drives diviners mad;
Who turns wise men backward,
[c]And makes their knowledge
foolishness;
26 [a]Who confirms the word
of His servant,
And performs the counsel
of His messengers;
Who says to Jerusalem, 'You
shall be inhabited,'
To the cities of Judah, 'You
shall be built,'
And I will raise up her waste places;
27 [a]Who says to the deep, 'Be dry!
And I will dry up your rivers';
28 Who says of [a]Cyrus, '*He*
is My shepherd,
And he shall perform all My pleasure,
Saying to Jerusalem, [b]"You
shall be built,"
And to the temple, "Your
foundation shall be laid."'

44:18 [a] Is. 45:20 [b] [Ps. 81:12]; Is. 6:9, 10; 29:10; 2 Thess. 2:11 [c] Jer. 10:14 **44:19** [a] Is. 46:8 **44:20** [a] Job 15:31; Hos. 4:12; Rom. 1:21, 22; 2 Thess. 2:11; 2 Tim. 3:13 [b] Is. 57:11; 59:3, 4, 13; Rom. 1:25 **44:21** [a] Is. 49:15 **44:22** [a] Is. 43:25 [b] Is. 43:1; 1 Cor. 6:20; [1 Pet. 1:18, 19] **44:23** [a] Ps. 69:34; Is. 42:10; 49:13; Jer. 51:48; Rev. 18:20 [b] Is. 49:3; 60:21 **44:24** [a] Is. 43:14 [b] Is. 43:1 [c] Job 9:8 **44:25** [a] Is. 47:13 [b] Jer. 50:36 [c] 2 Sam. 15:31; Job 5:12–14; Ps. 33:10; Is. 29:14; Jer. 51:57; 1 Cor. 1:20, 27 **44:26** [a] Zech. 1:6; Matt. 5:18 **44:27** [a] Jer. 50:38; 51:36 **44:28** [a] 2 Chr. 36:22; Ezra 1:1; Is. 45:13 [b] Ezra 6:7

Cyrus, God's Instrument

45 "Thus says the LORD to His anointed,
To [a]Cyrus, whose [b]right
hand I have held—
[c]To subdue nations before him
And [d]loose the armor of kings,
To open before him the double doors,
So that the gates will not be shut:
2 'I will go before you
[a]And make the crooked places[1] straight;
[b]I will break in pieces the
gates of bronze
And cut the bars of iron.
3 I will give you the treasures
of darkness
And hidden riches of secret places,
[a]That you may know that I, the LORD,
Who [b]call *you* by your name,
Am the God of Israel.
4 For [a]Jacob My servant's sake,
And Israel My elect,
I have even called you by your name;
I have named you, though you
have not known Me.
5 I [a]*am* the LORD, and [b]*there is* no other;
There is no God besides Me.
[c]I will gird you, though you
have not known Me,
6 [a]That they may [b]know from the
rising of the sun to its setting
That *there is* none besides Me.
I *am* the LORD, and *there is* no other;
7 I form the light and create darkness,
I make peace and [a]create calamity;
I, the LORD, do all these *things*.'

8 "Rain[a] down, you heavens, from above,
And let the skies pour down
righteousness;
Let the earth open, let them
bring forth salvation,
And let righteousness
spring up together.
I, the LORD, have created it.

9 "Woe to him who strives
with [a]his Maker!
Let the potsherd *strive* with the
potsherds of the earth!
[b]Shall the clay say to him who forms
it, 'What are you making?'
Or shall your handiwork *say*,
'He has no hands'?
10 Woe to him who says to *his* father,
'What are you begetting?'
Or to the woman, 'What have
you brought forth?'"

11 Thus says the LORD,
The Holy One of Israel,
and his Maker:
[a]"Ask Me of things to come
concerning [b]My sons;
And concerning [c]the work of My
hands, you command Me.
12 [a]I have made the earth,
And [b]created man on it.
I—My hands—stretched
out the heavens,
And [c]all their host I have commanded.
13 [a]I have raised him up in righteousness,
And I will direct all his ways;
He shall [b]build My city
And let My exiles go free,
[c]Not for price nor reward,"
Says the LORD of hosts.

The LORD, the Only Savior

14 Thus says the LORD:

[a]"The labor of Egypt and
merchandise of Cush
And of the Sabeans, men of stature,
Shall come over to you, and
they shall be yours;
They shall walk behind you,
They shall come over [b]in chains;
And they shall bow down to you.
They will make supplication to you,
saying, [c]'Surely God *is* in you,
And *there is* no other;
[d]*There is* no other God.'"

15 Truly You *are* God, [a]who hide Yourself,
O God of Israel, the Savior!

45:1 [a] Is. 44:28 [b] Ps. 73:23; Is. 41:13 [c] Dan. 5:30 [d] Job 12:21; Is. 45:5 45:2 [a] Is. 40:4 [b] Ps. 107:16 [1] Dead Sea Scrolls and Septuagint read *mountains;* Targum reads *I will trample down the walls;* Vulgate reads *I will humble the great ones of the earth.* 45:3 [a] Is. 41:23 [b] Ex. 33:12 45:4 [a] Is. 44:1 45:5 [a] Deut. 4:35; 32:39; Is. 44:8 [b] Is. 45:14, 18 [c] Ps. 18:32 45:6 [a] Ps. 102:15; Is. 37:20; Mal. 1:11 [b] [Is. 11:9; 52:10] 45:7 [a] Is. 31:2; 47:11; Amos 3:6 45:8 [a] Ps. 85:11 45:9 [a] Is. 64:8 [b] Jer. 18:6; Rom. 9:20, 21 45:11 [a] Is. 8:19 [b] Jer. 31:9 [c] Is. 29:23; 60:21; 64:8 45:12 [a] Is. 42:5; Jer. 27:5 [b] Gen. 1:26 [c] Gen. 2:1; Neh. 9:6 45:13 [a] Is. 41:2 [b] 2 Chr. 36:22; Is. 44:28 [c] [Rom. 3:24] 45:14 [a] Ps. 68:31; 72:10, 11; Is. 14:1; 49:23; 60:9, 10, 14, 16; Zech. 8:22, 23 [b] Ps. 149:8 [c] Jer. 16:19; Zech. 8:20–23; 1 Cor. 14:25 [d] Is. 45:5 45:15 [a] Ps. 44:24; Is. 57:17

16 They shall be [a]ashamed
And also disgraced, all of them;
They shall go in confusion together,
Who are makers of idols.
17 [a]*But* Israel shall be saved by the LORD
With an [b]everlasting salvation;
You shall not be ashamed or [c]disgraced
Forever and ever.

18 For thus says the LORD,
[a]Who created the heavens,
Who is God,
Who formed the earth and made it,
Who has established it,
Who did not create it in vain,
Who formed it to be [b]inhabited:
[c]"I *am* the LORD, and *there is* no other.
19 I have not spoken in [a]secret,
In a dark place of the earth;
I did not say to the seed of Jacob,
'Seek Me in vain';
[b]I, the LORD, speak righteousness,
I declare things that are right.

20 "Assemble yourselves and come;
Draw near together,
You *who have* escaped
from the nations.
[a]They have no knowledge,
Who carry the wood of
their carved image,
And pray to a god *that* cannot save.
21 Tell and bring forth *your case;*
Yes, let them take counsel together.
[a]Who has declared this
from ancient time?
Who has told it from that time?
Have not I, the LORD?
[b]And *there is* no other God besides Me,
A just God and a Savior;
There is none besides Me.

22 "Look to Me, and be saved,
[a]All you ends of the earth!
For I *am* God, and *there is* no other.
23 [a]I have sworn by Myself;
The word has gone out of My
mouth *in* righteousness,
And shall not return,
That to Me every [b]knee shall bow,
[c]Every tongue shall take an oath.
24 He shall say,
'Surely in the LORD I have
[a]righteousness and strength.
To Him *men* shall come,
And [b]all shall be ashamed
Who are incensed against Him.
25 [a]In the LORD all the
descendants of Israel
Shall be justified, and [b]shall glory.' "

Dead Idols and the Living God

46 Bel [a]bows down, Nebo stoops;
Their idols were on the beasts
and on the cattle.
Your carriages *were* heavily loaded,
[b]A burden to the weary *beast.*
2 They stoop, they bow down together;
They could not deliver the burden,
[a]But have themselves gone
into captivity.

3 "Listen to Me, O house of Jacob,
And all the remnant of the
house of Israel,
[a]Who have been upheld
by Me from birth,
Who have been carried
from the womb:
4 Even to *your* old age, [a]I *am* He,
And *even* to gray hairs [b]I will carry *you!*
I have made, and I will bear;
Even I will carry, and will deliver *you.*

5 "To[a] whom will you liken Me,
and make *Me* equal
And compare Me, that we
should be alike?
6 [a]They lavish gold out of the bag,
And weigh silver on the scales;
They hire a [b]goldsmith, and
he makes it a god;
They prostrate themselves,
yes, they worship.
7 [a]They bear it on the shoulder,
they carry it

45:16 [a] Is. 44:11 45:17 [a] Is. 26:4; [Rom. 11:26] [b] Is. 51:6 [c] Is. 29:22 45:18 [a] Is. 42:5 [b] Gen. 1:26; Ps. 115:16; Acts 17:26 [c] Is. 45:5 45:19 [a] Deut. 30:11 [b] Ps. 19:8; Is. 45:23; 63:1 45:20 [a] Is. 44:9; 46:7; Jer. 10:5 45:21 [a] Is. 41:22; 43:9 [b] Is. 44:8 45:22 [a] Ps. 22:27; 65:5 45:23 [a] Gen. 22:16; Is. 62:8; [Heb. 6:13] [b] Rom. 14:11; [Phil. 2:10] [c] Deut. 6:13; Ps. 63:11; Is. 19:18; 65:16 45:24 [a] Is. 54:17; [Jer. 23:5; 1 Cor. 1:30] [b] Is. 41:11 45:25 [a] Is. 45:17 [b] 1 Cor. 1:31 46:1 [a] Is. 21:9; Jer. 50:2 [b] Jer. 10:5 46:2 [a] Judg. 18:17, 18, 24; 2 Sam. 5:21; Jer. 48:7; Hos. 10:5, 6 46:3 [a] Deut. 32:11; Ps. 71:6; Is. 63:9 46:4 [a] Mal. 3:6 [b] Ps. 48:14 46:5 [a] Is. 40:18, 25 46:6 [a] Is. 40:19; 41:6; Jer. 10:4 [b] Is. 44:12 46:7 [a] Is. 45:20; 46:1; Jer. 10:5

And set it in its place, and it stands;
From its place it shall not move.
Though [b]*one* cries out to it,
yet it cannot answer
Nor save him out of his trouble.

8 "Remember this, and show
yourselves men;
[a]Recall to mind, O you transgressors.
9 [a]Remember the former things of old,
For I *am* God, and [b]*there is* no other;
I am God, and *there is* none like Me,
10 [a]Declaring the end from the beginning,
And from ancient times *things*
that are not *yet* done,
Saying, [b]'My counsel shall stand,
And I will do all My pleasure,'
11 Calling a bird of prey [a]from the east,
The man [b]who executes My
counsel, from a far country.
Indeed [c]I have spoken *it;*
I will also bring it to pass.
I have purposed *it;*
I will also do it.

12 "Listen to Me, you [a]stubborn-hearted,
[b]Who *are* far from righteousness:
13 [a]I bring My righteousness near,
it shall not be far off;
My salvation [b]shall not linger.
And I will place [c]salvation in Zion,
For Israel My glory.

The Humiliation of Babylon

47 "Come [a]down and [b]sit in the dust,
O virgin daughter of [c]Babylon;
Sit on the ground without a throne,
O daughter of the Chaldeans!
For you shall no more be called
Tender and delicate.
2 [a]Take the millstones and grind meal.
Remove your veil,
Take off the skirt,
Uncover the thigh,
Pass through the rivers.
3 [a]Your nakedness shall be uncovered,
Yes, your shame will be seen;
[b]I will take vengeance,
And I will not arbitrate with a man."

4 *As for* [a]our Redeemer, the LORD
of hosts *is* His name,
The Holy One of Israel.

5 "Sit in [a]silence, and go into darkness,
O daughter of the Chaldeans;
[b]For you shall no longer be called
The Lady of Kingdoms.
6 [a]I was angry with My people;
[b]I have profaned My inheritance,
And given them into your hand.
You showed them no mercy;
[c]On the elderly you laid your
yoke very heavily.
7 And you said, 'I shall be
[a]a lady forever,'
So that you did not [b]take
these *things* to heart,
[c]Nor remember the latter end of them.

8 "Therefore hear this now, *you*
who are given to pleasures,
Who dwell securely,
Who say in your heart, 'I *am,* and
there is no one else besides me;
I shall not sit *as* a widow,
Nor shall I know the loss of children';
9 But these two *things* shall come to you
[a]In a moment, in one day:
The loss of children, and
widowhood.
They shall come upon you
in their fullness
Because of the multitude
of your sorceries,
For the great abundance of
your enchantments.

10 "For you have trusted in
your wickedness;
You have said, 'No one [a]sees me';
Your wisdom and your knowledge
have warped you;
And you have said in your heart,
'I *am,* and *there is* no one
else besides me.'

46:7 [b] Is. 45:20 **46:8** [a] Is. 44:19 **46:9** [a] Deut. 32:7; Is. 42:9; 65:17 [b] Is. 45:5, 21 **46:10** [a] Is. 45:21; 48:3 [b] Ps. 33:11; Prov. 19:21; 21:30; Is. 14:24; 25:1; Acts 5:39; Heb. 6:17 **46:11** [a] Is. 41:2, 25 [b] Is. 44:28 [c] Num. 23:19 **46:12** [a] Ps. 76:5; Is. 48:4; Zech. 7:11, 12; Mal. 3:13 [b] [Rom. 10:3] **46:13** [a] [Rom. 1:17] [b] Hab. 2:3 [c] Is. 62:11; Joel 3:17; [1 Pet. 2:6] **47:1** [a] Jer. 48:18 [b] Is. 3:26 [c] Is. 14:18–23; Jer. 25:12; 50:1—51:64 **47:2** [a] Ex. 11:5; Jer. 25:10 **47:3** [a] Is. 3:17; 20:4 [b] [Rom. 12:19] **47:4** [a] Jer. 50:34 **47:5** [a] 1 Sam. 2:9 [b] Is. 13:19; [Dan. 2:37]; Rev. 17:18 **47:6** [a] 2 Sam. 24:14 [b] Is. 43:28 [c] Deut. 28:49, 50 **47:7** [a] Rev. 18:7 [b] Is. 42:25; 46:8 [c] Deut. 32:29; Jer. 5:31; Ezek. 7:2, 3 **47:9** [a] Ps. 73:19; 1 Thess. 5:3; Rev. 18:8 **47:10** [a] Is. 29:15; Ezek. 8:12; 9:9

11 Therefore evil shall come upon you;
You shall not know from
where it arises.
And trouble shall fall upon you;
You will not be able to put it off.
And [a]desolation shall come
upon you [b]suddenly,
Which you shall not know.

12 "Stand now with your enchantments
And the multitude of your sorceries,
In which you have labored
from your youth—
Perhaps you will be able to profit,
Perhaps you will prevail.
13 [a]You are wearied in the multitude
of your counsels;
Let now [b]the astrologers,
the stargazers,
And the monthly prognosticators
Stand up and save you
From what shall come upon you.
14 Behold, they shall be [a]as stubble,
The fire shall [b]burn them;
They shall not deliver themselves
From the power of the flame;
It shall not *be* a coal to be warmed by,
Nor a fire to sit before!
15 Thus shall they be to you
With whom you have labored,
[a]Your merchants from your youth;
They shall wander each
one to his quarter.
No one shall save you.

Israel Refined for God's Glory

48 "Hear this, O house of Jacob,
Who are called by the
name of Israel,
And have come forth from the
wellsprings of Judah;
Who swear by the name of the LORD,
And make mention of
the God of Israel,
But [a]not in truth or in righteousness;
2 For they call themselves
[a]after the holy city,
And [b]lean on the God of Israel;
The LORD of hosts *is* His name:

3 "I have [a]declared the former
things from the beginning;
They went forth from My mouth,
and I caused them to hear it.
Suddenly I did *them,* [b]and
they came to pass.
4 Because I knew that you
were obstinate,
And [a]your neck *was* an iron sinew,
And your brow bronze,
5 Even from the beginning I
have declared *it* to you;
Before it came to pass I
proclaimed *it* to you,
Lest you should say, 'My
idol has done them,
And my carved image and
my molded image
Have commanded them.'

6 "You have heard;
See all this.
And will you not declare *it?*
I have made you hear new
things from this time,
Even hidden things, and you
did not know them.
7 They are created now and not
from the beginning;
And before this day you
have not heard them,
Lest you should say, 'Of
course I knew them.'
8 Surely you did not hear,
Surely you did not know;
Surely from long ago your
ear was not opened.
For I knew that you would deal
very treacherously,
And were called [a]a transgressor
from the womb.

9 "For[a] My name's sake [b]I will
defer My anger,
And *for* My praise I will
restrain it from you,
So that I do not cut you off.
10 Behold, [a]I have refined you,
but not as silver;

47:11 [a] Is. 13:6; Jer. 51:8, 43; Luke 17:27; 1 Thess. 5:3 [b] Is. 29:5 47:13 [a] Is. 57:10 [b] Is. 8:19; 44:25; 47:9; Dan. 2:2, 10 47:14 [a] Is. 5:24; Nah. 1:10; Mal. 4:1 [b] [Is. 10:17]; Jer. 51:58 47:15 [a] Rev. 18:11 48:1 [a] Is. 58:2; Jer. 4:2; 5:2 48:2 [a] Is. 52:1; 64:10 [b] Is. 10:20; Jer. 7:4; 21:2; Mic. 3:11; Rom. 2:17 48:3 [a] Is. 44:7, 8; 46:10 [b] Josh. 21:45; Is. 42:9 48:4 [a] Ex. 32:9; Deut. 31:27; Ezek. 2:4; 3:7 48:8 [a] Deut. 9:7, 24; Ps. 58:3; Is. 46:3, 8 48:9 [a] Ps. 79:9; 106:8; Is. 43:25; Ezek. 20:9, 14, 22, 44 [b] [Neh. 9:30, 31]; Ps. 78:38; Is. 30:18; 65:8 48:10 [a] Ps. 66:10; Jer. 9:7

I have tested you in the
[b]furnace of affliction.
11 For My own sake, for My
own sake, I will do *it;*
For [a]how should *My name*
be profaned?
And [b]I will not give My
glory to another.

God's Ancient Plan to Redeem Israel

12 "Listen to Me, O Jacob,
And Israel, My called:
I *am* He, [a]I *am* the [b]First,
I *am* also the Last.
13 Indeed [a]My hand has laid the
foundation of the earth,
And My right hand has stretched
out the heavens;
When [b]I call to them,
They stand up together.

14 "All of you, assemble
yourselves, and hear!
Who among them has
declared these *things?*
[a]The LORD loves him;
[b]He shall do His pleasure on Babylon,
And His arm *shall be against*
the Chaldeans.
15 I, *even* I, have spoken;
Yes, [a]I have called him,
I have brought him, and his
way will prosper.

16 "Come near to Me, hear this:
[a]I have not spoken in secret
from the beginning;
From the time that it was, I *was* there.
And now [b]the Lord GOD
and His Spirit
Have[1] sent Me."

17 Thus says [a]the LORD, your Redeemer,
The Holy One of Israel:
"I *am* the LORD your God,
Who teaches you to profit,
[b]Who leads you by the way
you should go.
18 [a]Oh, that you had heeded My
commandments!
[b]Then your peace would have
been like a river,
And your righteousness like
the waves of the sea.
19 [a]Your descendants also would
have been like the sand,
And the offspring of your body
like the grains of sand;
His name would not have been cut off
Nor destroyed from before Me."

20 [a]Go forth from Babylon!
Flee from the Chaldeans!
With a voice of singing,
Declare, proclaim this,
Utter it to the end of the earth;
Say, "The LORD has [b]redeemed
His servant Jacob!"
21 And they [a]did not thirst
When He led them through the deserts;
He [b]caused the waters to flow
from the rock for them;
He also split the rock, and the
waters gushed out.

22 "*There*[a] *is* no peace," says the
LORD, "for the wicked."

The Servant, the Light to the Gentiles

49 "Listen, [a]O coastlands, to Me,
And take heed, you
peoples from afar!
[b]The LORD has called Me
from the womb;
From the matrix of My mother He
has made mention of My name.
2 And He has made [a]My mouth
like a sharp sword;
[b]In the shadow of His hand
He has hidden Me,
And made Me [c]a polished shaft;
In His quiver He has hidden Me."

3 "And He said to me,
[a]'You *are* My servant, O Israel,
[b]In whom I will be glorified.'

48:10 [b] Deut. 4:20; 1 Kin. 8:51; Jer. 11:4 **48:11** [a] Lev. 22:2, 32; Deut. 32:26, 27; Ezek. 20:9 [b] Is. 42:8 **48:12** [a] Deut. 32:39 [b] Is. 44:6; [Rev. 22:13] **48:13** [a] Ex. 20:11; Ps. 102:25; Is. 42:5; 45:12, 18; Heb. 1:10–12 [b] Is. 40:26 **48:14** [a] Is. 45:1 [b] Is. 44:28; 47:1–15 **48:15** [a] Is. 45:1, 2 **48:16** [a] Is. 45:19 [b] Is. 61:1; Zech. 2:8, 9, 11 [1] The Hebrew verb is singular. **48:17** [a] Is. 43:14 [b] Ps. 32:8; Is. 49:9, 10 **48:18** [a] Deut. 5:29; Ps. 81:13 [b] Deut. 28:1–14; Ps. 119:165; Is. 32:16–18; 66:12 **48:19** [a] Gen. 22:17; Is. 10:22; 44:3, 4; 54:3; Jer. 33:22; Hos. 1:10 **48:20** [a] Jer. 50:8; 51:6, 45; Zech. 2:6, 7; Rev. 18:4 [b] [Ex. 19:4–6] **48:21** [a] [Is. 41:17, 18] [b] Ex. 17:6; Ps. 105:41 **48:22** [a] [Is. 57:21] **49:1** [a] Is. 41:1 [b] Jer. 1:5; Matt. 1:20; Luke 1:35; John 1:14; 10:36 **49:2** [a] Is. 11:4; Hos. 6:5; [Heb. 4:12]; Rev. 1:16; 2:12 [b] Is. 51:16 [c] Ps. 45:5 **49:3** [a] [Is. 41:8; 42:1; Zech. 3:8] [b] Is. 44:23; Matt. 12:18; [John 13:31, 32; 14:13; 15:8; 17:4; Eph. 1:6]

4 [a]Then I said, 'I have labored in vain,
I have spent my strength for
nothing and in vain;
Yet surely my just reward
is with the LORD,
And my work with my God.' "

5 "And now the LORD says,
Who formed Me from the
womb *to be* His Servant,
To bring Jacob back to Him,
So that Israel [a]is gathered to Him[1]
(For I shall be glorious in
the eyes of the LORD,
And My God shall be My strength),
6 Indeed He says,
'It is too small a thing that You
should be My Servant
To raise up the tribes of Jacob,
And to restore the preserved
ones of Israel;
I will also give You as a [a]light
to the Gentiles,
That You should be My salvation
to the ends of the earth.' "

7 Thus says the LORD,
The Redeemer of Israel, their Holy One,
[a]To Him whom man despises,
To Him whom the nation abhors,
To the Servant of rulers:
[b]"Kings shall see and arise,
Princes also shall worship,
Because of the LORD who is faithful,
The Holy One of Israel;
And He has chosen You."

8 Thus says the LORD:

"In an [a]acceptable time I
have heard You,
And in the day of salvation
I have helped You;
I will preserve You [b]and give You
As a covenant to the people,
To restore the earth,
To cause them to inherit the
desolate heritages;
9 That You may say [a]to the
prisoners, 'Go forth,'
To those who *are* in darkness,
'Show yourselves.'

"They shall feed along the roads,
And their pastures *shall be* on
all desolate heights.
10 They shall neither [a]hunger nor thirst,
[b]Neither heat nor sun shall
strike them;
For He who has mercy on
them [c]will lead them,
Even by the springs of water
He will guide them.
11 [a]I will make each of My
mountains a road,
And My highways shall be elevated.
12 Surely [a]these shall come from afar;
Look! Those from the
north and the west,
And these from the land of Sinim."

13 [a]Sing, O heavens!
Be joyful, O earth!
And break out in singing,
O mountains!
For the LORD has comforted
His people,
And will have mercy on His afflicted.

God Will Remember Zion

14 [a]But Zion said, "The LORD
has forsaken me,
And my Lord has forgotten me."

15 "Can[a] a woman forget her nursing child,
And not have compassion on
the son of her womb?
Surely they may forget,
[b]Yet I will not forget you.
16 See, [a]I have inscribed you on
the palms *of My hands;*
Your walls *are* continually before Me.
17 Your sons[1] shall make haste;
Your destroyers and those
who laid you waste
Shall go away from you.

49:4 [a] [Ezek. 3:19] 49:5 [a] Matt. 23:37; [Rom. 11:25–29] [1] Qere, Dead Sea Scrolls, and Septuagint read *is gathered to Him;* Kethib reads *is not gathered.* 49:6 [a] Is. 42:6; 51:4; [Luke 2:32]; Acts 13:47; [Gal. 3:14] 49:7 [a] [Ps. 22:6; Is. 53:3; Matt. 26:67; 27:41]; Mark 15:29; Luke 23:35 [b] [Is. 52:15] 49:8 [a] Ps. 69:13; 2 Cor. 6:2 [b] Is. 42:6 49:9 [a] Is. 61:1; Zech. 9:12; Luke 4:18 49:10 [a] Is. 33:16; 48:21; Rev. 7:16 [b] Ps. 121:6 [c] Ps. 23:2; Is. 40:11; 48:17 49:11 [a] Is. 40:4 49:12 [a] Is. 43:5, 6 49:13 [a] Is. 44:23 49:14 [a] Is. 40:27 49:15 [a] Ps. 103:13; Mal. 3:17 [b] Rom. 11:29 49:16 [a] Ex. 13:9; Song 8:6; Hag. 2:23 49:17 [1] Dead Sea Scrolls, Septuagint, Targum, and Vulgate read *builders.*

18 [a]Lift up your eyes, look around and see;
All these gather together
and come to you.
As I live," says the LORD,
"You shall surely clothe yourselves
with them all [b]as an ornament,
And bind them *on you* as a bride *does.*

19 "For your waste and desolate places,
And the land of your destruction,
[a]Will even now be too small
for the inhabitants;
And those who swallowed
you up will be far away.
20 [a]The children you will have,
[b]After you have lost the others,
Will say again in your ears,
'The place *is* too small for me;
Give me a place where I may dwell.'
21 Then you will say in your heart,
'Who has begotten these for me,
Since I have lost my children
and am desolate,
A captive, and wandering
to and fro?
And who has brought these up?
There I was, left alone;
But these, where *were* they?'"

22 [a]Thus says the Lord GOD:

"Behold, I will lift My hand in
an oath to the nations,
And set up My standard
for the peoples;
They shall bring your sons
in *their* arms,
And your daughters shall be
carried on *their* shoulders;
23 [a]Kings shall be your foster fathers,
And their queens your
nursing mothers;
They shall bow down to you with
their faces to the earth,
And [b]lick up the dust of your feet.
Then you will know that
I *am* the LORD,
[c]For they shall not be ashamed
who wait for Me."

24 [a]Shall the prey be taken
from the mighty,
Or the captives of the
righteous[1] be delivered?

25 But thus says the LORD:

"Even the captives of the mighty
shall be taken away,
And the prey of the terrible
be delivered;
For I will contend with him
who contends with you,
And I will save your children.
26 I will [a]feed those who oppress
you with their own flesh,
And they shall be drunk with their
own [b]blood as with sweet wine.
All flesh [c]shall know
That I, the LORD, *am* your Savior,
And your Redeemer, the
Mighty One of Jacob."

The Servant, Israel's Hope

50 Thus says the LORD:

"Where *is* [a]the certificate of
your mother's divorce,
Whom I have put away?
Or which of My [b]creditors *is it*
to whom I have sold you?
For your iniquities [c]you have
sold yourselves,
And for your transgressions your
mother has been put away.
2 Why, when I came, *was there* no man?
Why, when I called, *was there*
none to answer?
Is My hand shortened at all
that it cannot redeem?
Or have I no power to deliver?
Indeed with My [a]rebuke
I dry up the sea,
I make the rivers a wilderness;
Their fish stink because
there is no water,
And die of thirst.
3 [a]I clothe the heavens with blackness,
[b]And I make sackcloth their covering."

49:18 [a] Is. 60:4; John 4:35 [b] Prov. 17:6 49:19 [a] Is. 54:1, 2; Zech. 10:10 49:20 [a] Is. 60:4 [b] [Matt. 3:9; Rom. 11:11] 49:22 [a] Is. 60:4 49:23 [a] Ps. 72:11; Is. 52:15 [b] Ps. 72:9; Mic. 7:17 [c] Ps. 34:22; [Rom. 5:5] 49:24 [a] Matt. 12:29; Luke 11:21, 22 [1] Following Masoretic Text and Targum; Dead Sea Scrolls, Syriac, and Vulgate read *the mighty;* Septuagint reads *unjustly.* 49:26 [a] Is. 9:20 [b] Rev. 14:20 [c] Ps. 9:16; Is. 60:16 50:1 [a] Deut. 24:1; Jer. 3:8 [b] Deut. 32:30; 2 Kin. 4:1; Neh. 5:5 [c] Is. 52:3 50:2 [a] Ps. 106:9; Nah. 1:4 50:3 [a] Ex. 10:21 [b] Is. 13:10; Rev. 6:12

4 "The[a] Lord GOD has given Me
The tongue of the learned,
That I should know how
to speak
A word in season to *him*
who is [b]weary.
He awakens Me morning
by morning,
He awakens My ear
To hear as the learned.
5 The Lord GOD [a]has opened My ear;
And I was not [b]rebellious,
Nor did I turn away.
6 [a]I gave My back to those who struck *Me,*
And [b]My cheeks to those who
plucked out the beard;
I did not hide My face from
shame and [c]spitting.

7 "For the Lord GOD will help Me;
Therefore I will not be disgraced;
Therefore [a]I have set My
face like a flint,
And I know that I will not be
ashamed.
8 [a]*He is* near who justifies Me;
Who will contend with Me?
Let us stand together.
Who *is* My adversary?
Let him come near Me.
9 Surely the Lord GOD will help Me;
Who *is* he *who* will condemn Me?
[a]Indeed they will all grow
old like a garment;
[b]The moth will eat them up.

10 "Who among you fears the LORD?
Who obeys the voice of His Servant?
Who [a]walks in darkness
And has no light?
[b]Let him trust in the name of the LORD
And rely upon his God.
11 Look, all you who kindle a fire,
Who encircle *yourselves* with sparks:
Walk in the light of your fire and in
the sparks you have kindled—
[a]This you shall have from My hand:
You shall lie down [b]in torment.

The LORD Comforts Zion
(cf. Gen. 12:1–3)

51 "Listen to Me, [a]you who follow
after righteousness,
You who seek the LORD:
Look to the rock *from which*
you were hewn,
And to the hole of the pit *from*
which you were dug.
2 [a]Look to Abraham your father,
And to Sarah *who* bore you;
[b]For I called him alone,
And [c]blessed him and increased him."

3 For the LORD will [a]comfort Zion,
He will comfort all her waste places;
He will make her wilderness like Eden,
And her desert [b]like the
garden of the LORD;
Joy and gladness will be found in it,
Thanksgiving and the voice of melody.

4 "Listen to Me, My people;
And give ear to Me, O My nation:
[a]For law will proceed from Me,
And I will make My justice rest
[b]As a light of the peoples.
5 [a]My righteousness *is* near,
My salvation has gone forth,
[b]And My arms will judge the peoples;
[c]The coastlands will wait upon Me,
And [d]on My arm they will trust.
6 [a]Lift up your eyes to the heavens,
And look on the earth beneath.
For [b]the heavens will vanish
away like smoke,
[c]The earth will grow old like a garment,
And those who dwell in it will
die in like manner;
But My salvation will be [d]forever,
And My righteousness will
not be abolished.

7 "Listen to Me, you who know
righteousness,
You people [a]in whose heart *is* My law:
[b]Do not fear the reproach of men,
Nor be afraid of their insults.

50:4 [a] Ex. 4:11 [b] Matt. 11:28 50:5 [a] Ps. 40:6; Is. 35:5 [b] Matt. 26:39; Mark 14:36; Luke 22:42; John 8:29; 14:31; 15:10; Acts 26:19; [Phil. 2:8; Heb. 5:8; 10:7] 50:6 [a] Matt. 27:26; John 18:22 [b] Matt. 26:67; 27:30; Mark 14:65; 15:19 [c] Lam. 3:30 50:7 [a] Ezek. 3:8, 9; Luke 9:51 50:8 [a] Acts 2:24; [Rom. 8:32–34] 50:9 [a] Job 13:28; Ps. 102:26; Heb. 1:11 [b] Is. 51:6, 8 50:10 [a] Ps. 23:4 [b] 2 Chr. 20:20 50:11 [a] [John 9:39] [b] Ps. 16:4 51:1 [a] [Rom. 9:30–32] 51:2 [a] Rom. 4:1–3; Heb. 11:11 [b] Gen. 12:1 [c] Gen. 24:35; Deut. 1:10; Ezek. 33:24 51:3 [a] Is. 40:1; 52:9; Ps. 102:13 [b] Gen. 13:10; Joel 2:3 51:4 [a] Is. 2:3 [b] Is. 42:6 51:5 [a] Is. 46:13 [b] Ps. 67:4 [c] Is. 60:9 [d] [Rom. 1:16] 51:6 [a] Is. 40:26 [b] Ps. 102:25, 26; Is. 13:13; 34:4; Matt. 24:35; Heb. 1:10–12; 2 Pet. 3:10 [c] Is. 24:19, 20; 50:9; Heb. 1:10–12 [d] Is. 45:17 51:7 [a] Ps. 37:31; Jer. 31:33; [Heb. 10:16] [b] Is. 25:8; 54:4; [Matt. 5:11, 12; 10:28; Acts 5:41]

8 For [a]the moth will eat them
up like a garment,
And the worm will eat them like wool;
But My righteousness will be forever,
And My salvation from
generation to generation."

9 [a]Awake, awake, [b]put on strength,
O arm of the LORD!
Awake [c]as in the ancient days,
In the generations of old.
[d]*Are* You not *the arm* that
cut [e]Rahab apart,
And wounded the [f]serpent?
10 *Are* You not *the One* who
[a]dried up the sea,
The waters of the great deep;
That made the depths of the sea
a road
For the redeemed to cross over?
11 So [a]the ransomed of the
LORD shall return,
And come to Zion with singing,
With everlasting joy on their heads.
They shall obtain joy and gladness;
Sorrow and sighing shall flee away.

12 "I, *even* I, *am* He [a]who comforts you.
Who *are* you that you should be afraid
[b]Of a man *who* will die,
And of the son of a man *who*
will be made [c]like grass?
13 And [a]you forget the LORD your Maker,
[b]Who stretched out the heavens
And laid the foundations of the earth;
You have feared continually every day
Because of the fury of the oppressor,
When *he has* prepared to destroy.
[c]And where *is* the fury of
the oppressor?
14 The captive exile hastens,
that he may be loosed,
[a]That he should not die in the pit,
And that his bread should not fail.
15 But I *am* the LORD your God,
Who [a]divided the sea whose
waves roared—
The LORD of hosts *is* His name.
16 And [a]I have put My words
in your mouth;
[b]I have covered you with the
shadow of My hand,
[c]That I may plant the heavens,
Lay the foundations of the earth,
And say to Zion, 'You *are* My people.'"

God's Fury Removed

17 [a]Awake, awake!
Stand up, O Jerusalem,
You who [b]have drunk at the
hand of the LORD
The cup of His fury;
You have drunk the dregs of
the cup of trembling,
And drained *it* out.
18 *There is* no one to guide her
Among all the sons she
has brought forth;
Nor *is there any* who takes
her by the hand
Among all the sons she
has brought up.
19 [a]These two *things* have come to you;
Who will be sorry for you?—
Desolation and destruction,
famine and sword—
[b]By whom will I comfort you?
20 [a]Your sons have fainted,
They lie at the head of all the streets,
Like an antelope in a net;
They are full of the fury of the LORD,
The rebuke of your God.

21 Therefore please hear
this, you afflicted,
And drunk [a]but not with wine.
22 Thus says your Lord,
The LORD and your God,
Who [a]pleads the cause of His people:
"See, I have taken out of your hand
The cup of trembling,
The dregs of the cup of My fury;
You shall no longer drink it.
23 [a]But I will put it into the hand
of those who afflict you,
Who have said to you,[1]
'Lie down, that we may walk over you.'

51:8 [a] Is. 50:9 51:9 [a] Ps. 44:23 [b] Ps. 93:1 [c] Ps. 44:1 [d] Job 26:12; Ps. 89:10; Is. 30:7 [e] Ps. 87:4 [f] Ps. 74:13; Is. 27:1 51:10 [a] Ex. 14:21; Is. 63:11–13 51:11 [a] Is. 35:10; Jer. 31:11, 12 51:12 [a] 2 Cor. 1:3 [b] Ps. 118:6; Is. 2:22 [c] Is. 40:6, 7; James 1:10; 1 Pet. 1:24 51:13 [a] Deut. 6:12; 8:11; Is. 17:10; Jer. 2:32 [b] Ps. 104:2 [c] Job 20:7 51:14 [a] Zech. 9:11 51:15 [a] Job 26:12 51:16 [a] Deut. 18:18; Is. 59:21; John 3:34 [b] Ex. 33:22; Is. 49:2 [c] Is. 65:17 51:17 [a] Is. 52:1 [b] Job 21:20; Is. 29:9; Jer. 25:15; Rev. 14:10; 16:19 51:19 [a] Is. 47:9 [b] Amos 7:2 51:20 [a] Lam. 2:11 51:21 [a] Lam. 3:15 51:22 [a] Is. 3:12, 13; 49:25; Jer. 50:34 51:23 [a] Is. 14:2; Jer. 25:17, 26–28; Zech. 12:2 [1] Literally *your soul*

And you have laid your body
like the ground,
And as the street, for those
who walk over."

God Redeems Jerusalem

52 Awake, awake!
Put on your strength, O Zion;
Put on your beautiful garments,
O Jerusalem, the holy city!
For the uncircumcised
[a]and the unclean
Shall no longer come to you.
2 [a]Shake yourself from the dust, arise;
Sit down, O Jerusalem!
[b]Loose yourself from the
bonds of your neck,
O captive daughter of Zion!

3 For thus says the LORD:

[a]"You have sold yourselves for nothing,
And you shall be redeemed
[b]without money."

4 For thus says the Lord GOD:

"My people went down at first
Into [a]Egypt to dwell there;
Then the Assyrian oppressed
them without cause.
5 Now therefore, what have I
here," says the LORD,
"That My people are taken
away for nothing?
Those who rule over them
Make them wail,"[1] says the LORD,
"And My name *is* [a]blasphemed
continually every day.
6 Therefore My people shall
know My name;
Therefore *they shall know* in that day
That I *am* He who speaks:
'Behold, *it is* I.'"

7 [a]How beautiful upon the mountains
Are the feet of him who
brings good news,
Who proclaims peace,
Who brings glad tidings
of good *things*,
Who proclaims salvation,
Who says to Zion,
[b]"Your God reigns!"
8 Your watchmen shall lift
up *their* voices,
With their voices they shall
sing together;
For they shall see eye to eye
When the LORD brings back Zion.
9 Break forth into joy, sing together,
You waste places of Jerusalem!
For the LORD has comforted His people,
He has redeemed Jerusalem.
10 [a]The LORD has made bare His holy arm
In the eyes of [b]all the nations;
And all the ends of the earth shall see
The salvation of our God.

11 [a]Depart! Depart! Go out from there,
Touch no unclean *thing*;
Go out from the midst of her,
[b]Be clean,
You who bear the vessels of the LORD.
12 For [a]you shall not go out with haste,
Nor go by flight;
[b]For the LORD will go before you,
[c]And the God of Israel *will*
be your rear guard.

The Sin-Bearing Servant

13 Behold, [a]My Servant shall
deal prudently;
[b]He shall be exalted and extolled
and be very high.
14 Just as many were astonished at you,
So His [a]visage was marred
more than any man,
And His form more than
the sons of men;
15 [a]So shall He sprinkle[1] many nations.
Kings shall shut their mouths at Him;
For [b]what had not been told
them they shall see,
And what they had not heard
they shall consider.

52:1 [a] Neh. 11:1; Is. 48:2; 64:10; Zech. 14:20, 21; Matt. 4:5; [Rev. 21:2–27] 52:2 [a] Is. 3:26 [b] Is. 9:4; 10:27; 14:25; Zech. 2:7 52:3 [a] Ps. 44:12; Jer. 15:13 [b] Is. 45:13 52:4 [a] Gen. 46:6 52:5 [a] Ezek. 36:20, 23; Rom. 2:24
[1] Dead Sea Scrolls read *Mock;* Septuagint reads *Marvel and wail;* Targum reads *Boast themselves;* Vulgate reads *Treat them unjustly.* 52:7 [a] Is. 40:9; 61:1; Nah. 1:15; Rom. 10:15; Eph. 6:15 [b] Ps. 93:1; Is. 24:23 52:10 [a] Ps. 98:1–3 [b] Luke 3:6 52:11 [a] Is. 48:20; Jer. 50:8; Zech. 2:6, 7; 2 Cor. 6:17 [b] Lev. 22:2; [Is. 1:16] 52:12 [a] Ex. 12:11, 33; Deut. 16:3 [b] Mic. 2:13 [c] Ex. 14:19, 20; Is. 58:8 52:13 [a] Is. 42:1 [b] Is. 57:15; Phil. 2:9 52:14 [a] Ps. 22:6, 7; Matt. 26:67; 27:30; John 19:3 52:15 [a] Num. 19:18–21; Ezek. 36:25 [b] Rom. 15:21; [Eph. 3:5, 9]; 1 Pet. 1:2 [1] Or *startle*

53 Who [a]has believed our report?
And to whom has the arm of
the LORD been revealed?
2 For He shall grow up before
Him as a tender plant,
And as a root out of dry ground.
He has no form or comeliness;
And when we see Him,
There is no beauty that we
should desire Him.
3 [a]He is despised and rejected by men,
A Man of sorrows and
[b]acquainted with grief.
And we hid, as it were, *our*
faces from Him;
He was despised, and [c]we
did not esteem Him.

4 Surely [a]He has borne our griefs
And carried our sorrows;
Yet we esteemed Him stricken,
Smitten by God, and afflicted.
5 But He *was* [a]wounded for
our transgressions,
He was bruised for our iniquities;
The chastisement for our
peace *was* upon Him,
And by His [b]stripes we are healed.
6 All we like sheep have gone astray;
We have turned, every one,
to his own way;
And the LORD has laid on Him
the iniquity of us all.

7 He was oppressed and
He was afflicted,
Yet [a]He opened not His mouth;
[b]He was led as a lamb to the slaughter,
And as a sheep before its
shearers is silent,
So He opened not His mouth.
8 He was [a]taken from prison
and from judgment,
And who will declare His generation?
For [b]He was cut off from the
land of the living;
For the transgressions of My
people He was stricken.
9 [a]And they[1] made His grave
with the wicked—
But with the rich at His death,
Because He had done no violence,
Nor *was any* [b]deceit in His mouth.

10 Yet it pleased the LORD to bruise Him;
He has put *Him* to grief.
When You make His soul
[a]an offering for sin,
He shall see *His* seed, He
shall prolong *His* days,
And the pleasure of the LORD
shall prosper in His hand.
11 He shall see the labor of His
soul,[1] *and* be satisfied.
By His knowledge [a]My righteous
[b]Servant shall [c]justify many,
For He shall bear their iniquities.
12 [a]Therefore I will divide Him a
portion with the great,
[b]And He shall divide the spoil
with the strong,
Because He [c]poured out His
soul unto death,
And He was [d]numbered with
the transgressors,
And He bore the sin of many,
And [e]made intercession for
the transgressors.

A Perpetual Covenant of Peace

54 "Sing, O [a]barren,
You *who* have not borne!
Break forth into singing,
and cry aloud,
You *who* have not labored
with child!
For more *are* the children
of the desolate
Than the children of the married
woman," says the LORD.
2 "Enlarge[a] the place of your tent,
And let them stretch out the
curtains of your dwellings;
Do not spare;
Lengthen your cords,
And strengthen your stakes.

53:1 [a] John 12:38; Rom. 10:16 53:3 [a] Ps. 22:6; [Is. 49:7; Matt. 27:30, 31; Luke 18:31–33; 23:18] [b] [Heb. 4:15] [c] [John 1:10, 11] 53:4 [a] [Matt. 8:17; Heb. 9:28; 1 Pet. 2:24] 53:5 [a] [Is. 53:10; Rom. 4:25; 1 Cor. 15:3, 4] [b] [1 Pet. 2:24, 25] 53:7 [a] Matt. 26:63; 27:12–14; Mark 14:61; 15:5; Luke 23:9; John 19:9 [b] Acts 8:32, 33; Rev. 5:6 53:8 [a] Matt. 27:11–26; Luke 23:1–25 [b] [Dan. 9:26] 53:9 [a] Matt. 27:57–60; Luke 23:33 [b] 1 Pet. 2:22; 1 John 3:5 [1] Literally *he* or *He* 53:10 [a] John 1:29; Acts 2:24; [2 Cor. 5:21] 53:11 [a] [1 John 2:1] [b] Is. 42:1 [c] [Acts 13:38, 39; Rom. 5:15–18] [1] Following Masoretic Text, Targum, and Vulgate; Dead Sea Scrolls and Septuagint read *From the labor of His soul He shall see light.* 53:12 [a] Ps. 2:8 [b] Col. 2:15 [c] Is. 50:6; [Rom. 3:25] [d] Matt. 27:38; Mark 15:28; Luke 22:37; 2 Cor. 5:21 [e] Luke 23:34 54:1 [a] Gal. 4:27 54:2 [a] Is. 49:19, 20

3 For you shall expand to the
right and to the left,
And your descendants will
[a]inherit the nations,
And make the desolate
cities inhabited.

4 "Do[a] not fear, for you will
not be ashamed;
Neither be disgraced, for you
will not be put to shame;
For you will forget the
shame of your youth,
And will not remember the reproach
of your widowhood anymore.
5 [a]For your Maker *is* your husband,
The LORD of hosts *is* His name;
And your Redeemer *is* the
Holy One of Israel;
He is called [b]the God of
the whole earth.
6 For the LORD [a]has called you
Like a woman forsaken and
grieved in spirit,
Like a youthful wife when
you were refused,"
Says your God.
7 "For[a] a mere moment I
have forsaken you,
But with great mercies [b]I
will gather you.
8 With a little wrath I hid My face
from you for a moment;
[a]But with everlasting kindness I
will have mercy on you,"
Says the LORD, your Redeemer.

9 "For this *is* like the waters
of [a]Noah to Me;
For as I have sworn
That the waters of Noah would
no longer cover the earth,
So have I sworn
That I would not be angry with
[b]you, nor rebuke you.
10 For [a]the mountains shall depart
And the hills be removed,
[b]But My kindness shall not
depart from you,
Nor shall My covenant of
peace be removed,"
Says the LORD, who has mercy on you.

11 "O you afflicted one,
Tossed with tempest, *and*
not comforted,
Behold, I will lay your stones
with [a]colorful gems,
And lay your foundations
with sapphires.
12 I will make your pinnacles of rubies,
Your gates of crystal,
And all your walls of precious stones.
13 All your children *shall be*
[a]taught by the LORD,
And [b]great *shall be* the peace
of your children.
14 In righteousness you shall
be established;
You shall be far from oppression,
for you shall not fear;
And from terror, for it shall
not come near you.
15 Indeed they shall surely assemble,
but not because of Me.
Whoever assembles against you
shall [a]fall for your sake.

16 "Behold, I have created the blacksmith
Who blows the coals in the fire,
Who brings forth an
instrument for his work;
And I have created the
spoiler to destroy.
17 No weapon formed against
you shall [a]prosper,
And every tongue *which* rises
against you in judgment
You shall condemn.
This *is* the heritage of the
servants of the LORD,
[b]And their righteousness *is* from Me,"
Says the LORD.

An Invitation to Abundant Life

55 "Ho! [a]Everyone who thirsts,
Come to the waters;
And you who have no money,

54:3 [a] Is. 14:2; 49:22, 23; 60:9 54:4 [a] Is. 41:10 54:5 [a] Jer. 3:14; Hos. 2:19 [b] Zech. 14:9; Rom. 3:29 54:6 [a] Is. 62:4 54:7 [a] Ps. 30:5; Is. 26:20; 60:10; 2 Cor. 4:17 [b] [Is. 43:5; 56:8] 54:8 [a] Is. 55:3; Jer. 31:3 54:9 [a] Gen. 8:21; 9:11; [2 Pet. 3:6, 7] [b] Is. 12:1; Ezek. 39:29 54:10 [a] Ps. 46:2; Is. 51:6; Matt. 5:18 [b] 2 Sam. 23:5; Ps. 89:33, 34; Is. 55:3; 59:21; 61:8 54:11 [a] 1 Chr. 29:2; Job 28:16; Rev. 21:18, 19 54:13 [a] Jer. 31:34; [John 6:45; 1 Cor. 2:10]; 1 Thess. 4:9; [1 John 2:20] [b] Ps. 119:165 54:15 [a] Is. 41:11–16 54:17 [a] Is. 17:12–14; 29:8 [b] Is. 45:24, 25; 54:14 55:1 [a] [Matt. 5:6; John 4:14; 7:37; Rev. 21:6; 22:17]

[b]Come, buy and eat.
Yes, come, buy wine and milk
Without money and without price.
2 Why do you spend money
for *what is* not bread,
And your wages for *what*
does not satisfy?
Listen carefully to Me, and
eat *what is* good,
And let your soul delight
itself in abundance.
3 Incline your ear, and [a]come
to Me.
Hear, and your soul shall live;
[b]And I will make an everlasting
covenant with you—
The [c]sure mercies of David.
4 Indeed I have given him *as* [a]a
witness to the people,
[b]A leader and commander
for the people.
5 [a]Surely you shall call a nation
you do not know,
[b]And nations *who* do not know
you shall run to you,
Because of the LORD your God,
And the Holy One of Israel;
[c]For He has glorified you."

6 [a]Seek the LORD while He
may be [b]found,
Call upon Him while He is near.
7 [a]Let the wicked forsake his way,
And the unrighteous man
[b]his thoughts;
Let him return to the LORD,
[c]And He will have mercy on him;
And to our God,
For He will abundantly pardon.

8 "For[a] My thoughts *are* not
your thoughts,
Nor *are* your ways My ways,"
says the LORD.
9 "For[a] *as* the heavens are
higher than the earth,
So are My ways higher than your ways,
And My thoughts than your thoughts.
10 "For [a]as the rain comes down,
and the snow from heaven,
And do not return there,
But water the earth,
And make it bring forth and bud,
That it may give seed to the sower
And bread to the eater,
11 [a]So shall My word be that goes
forth from My mouth;
It shall not return to Me void,
But it shall accomplish what I please,
And it shall [b]prosper *in the
thing* for which I sent it.

12 "For[a] you shall go out with joy,
And be led out with peace;
The mountains and the hills
Shall [b]break forth into
singing before you,
And [c]all the trees of the field
shall clap *their* hands.
13 [a]Instead of [b]the thorn shall
come up the cypress tree,
And instead of the brier shall
come up the myrtle tree;
And it shall be to the
LORD [c]for a name,
For an everlasting sign *that*
shall not be cut off."

Salvation for the Gentiles

56 Thus says the LORD:
"Keep justice, and do righteousness,
[a]For My salvation *is* about to come,
And My righteousness to be revealed.
2 Blessed *is* the man *who* does this,
And the son of man *who*
lays hold on it;
[a]Who keeps from defiling the Sabbath,
And keeps his hand from
doing any evil."

3 Do not let [a]the son of the foreigner
Who has joined himself to the LORD
Speak, saying,
"The LORD has utterly separated
me from His people";

55:1 [b] [Matt. 13:44; Rev. 3:18] 55:3 [a] Matt. 11:28 [b] Is. 54:8; 61:8; Jer. 32:40 [c] 2 Sam. 7:8; Ps. 89:28; [Acts 13:34] 55:4 [a] [John 18:37; Rev. 1:5] [b] [Jer. 30:9; Ezek. 34:23; Dan. 9:25] 55:5 [a] Is. 52:15; Eph. 2:11, 12 [b] Is. 60:5 [c] Is. 60:9 55:6 [a] Matt. 5:25; 25:11; John 7:34; 8:21; 2 Cor. 6:2; [Heb. 3:13] [b] Ps. 32:6; Is. 49:8 55:7 [a] Is. 1:16 [b] Is. 59:7; Zech. 8:17 [c] Ps. 130:7; Jer. 3:12 55:8 [a] 2 Sam. 7:19 55:9 [a] Ps. 103:11 55:10 [a] Deut. 32:2 55:11 [a] Is. 45:23; Matt. 24:35 [b] Is. 46:9–11 55:12 [a] Is. 35:10 [b] Ps. 98:8 [c] 1 Chr. 16:33 55:13 [a] Is. 41:19 [b] Mic. 7:4 [c] Jer. 13:11 56:1 [a] Is. 46:13; Matt. 3:2; 4:17; Rom. 13:11, 12 56:2 [a] Ex. 20:8–11; 31:13–17; Is. 58:13; Jer. 17:21, 22; Ezek. 20:12, 20 56:3 [a] Is. 14:1; [Eph. 2:12–19]

RELEASE // TRUST IN HIS WAYS

His Ways Are Higher

Isaiah 55:9 // "For as the heavens are higher than the earth, so are My ways higher than your ways, and My thoughts than your thoughts."

Summary Message // This verse in Isaiah reminds us that God does things that are beyond human thought or ability. The distance between heaven and earth is so great, it is immeasurable—there is no comparison. The functioning of all existence from the beginning through eternity is in God's hands, while we cannot even see beyond the limitations of time and space.

That is why it is not up to us to figure out what God is doing. It is only for us to trust in who He is and the character of His holiness expressed to us through His goodness and love. His ways are pure, just, loving, and always in our best interest and the best interest of others, even when we cannot comprehend the outcome. Trusting in God's ways requires faith. It takes faith to put aside our needs and desires and to accept His way of doing things. It requires us to move from the place of reacting to the place of trusting and believing. A walk of faith requires that we invite and accept God's thoughts and ways in our lives.

Practical Application // As believers, our desire should be to live in a way that pleases God and to adopt His way of doing things in all areas of life. But often when life deviates from the path we have set for ourselves, we immediately jump in to try to steer it back onto that original path. And, if we are honest with ourselves, we get disgruntled with God because He allowed our life to get off track. We just cannot seem to let go of the reins.

The lack of peace and joy we feel in these off-track times is a sign that we have not given control to God in particular areas of our lives. We must ask ourselves: "Am I going to demand my own way or yield to God's?" The answer to this question will then unlock clarity about our faith walk. God's way will always be pure, just, and loving. Our way will more often than not be selfish, focused on benefiting only ourselves. To walk in His higher ways, we must set our ideas aside and do the following:

- Strive to renew our minds.
- Seek God while He may be found.
- Set aside the things that hinder us from following God.
- Make the kingdom of God a priority.

Fervent Prayer // Heavenly Father, we truly want to follow You and live according to Your ways. Help us seek You before we react to events in life. Help us show others the love, patience, and faithfulness You show us every day. We want to live in ways that honor You. Take control of our lives and renew our minds. Teach us to walk in ways that lift Your name and draw others to the love available to them through Christ. It is in His name we pray. Amen.

Nor let the [b]eunuch say,
"Here I am, a dry tree."
4 For thus says the LORD:
"To the eunuchs who keep
My Sabbaths,
And choose what pleases Me,
And hold fast My covenant,
5 Even to them I will give in [a]My house
And within My walls a
place [b]and a name
Better than that of sons
and daughters;
I will give them[1] an everlasting
name
That shall not be cut off.

6 "Also the sons of the foreigner
Who join themselves to the
LORD, to serve Him,
And to love the name of the
LORD, to be His servants—
Everyone who keeps from
defiling the Sabbath,
And holds fast My covenant—
7 Even them I will [a]bring to
My holy mountain,
And make them joyful in
My [b]house of prayer.
[c]Their burnt offerings and
their sacrifices
Will be [d]accepted on My altar;

56:3 [b] Deut. 23:1; Jer. 38:7; Acts 8:27 56:5 [a] 1 Tim. 3:15 [b] [1 John 3:1, 2] [1] Literally *him* 56:7 [a] [Is. 2:2, 3; 60:11; Mic. 4:1, 2] [b] Matt. 21:13; Mark 11:17; Luke 19:46 [c] [Rom. 12:1; Heb. 13:15; 1 Pet. 2:5] [d] Is. 60:7

For [e]My house shall be called a
house of prayer [f]for all nations."
8 The Lord GOD, [a]who gathers the
outcasts of Israel, says,
[b]"Yet I will gather to him
Others besides those who
are gathered to him."

Israel's Irresponsible Leaders

9 [a]All you beasts of the field,
come to devour,
All you beasts in the forest.
10 His watchmen *are* [a]blind,
They are all ignorant;
[b]They *are* all dumb dogs,
They cannot bark;
Sleeping, lying down,
loving to slumber.
11 Yes, *they are* [a]greedy dogs
Which [b]never have enough.
And they *are* shepherds
Who cannot understand;
They all look to their own way,
Every one for his own gain,
From his *own* territory.
12 "Come," *one says,* "I will
bring wine,
And we will fill ourselves with
intoxicating [a]drink;
[b]Tomorrow will be [c]as today,
And much more abundant."

Israel's Futile Idolatry

57 The righteous perishes,
And no man takes *it* to heart;
[a]Merciful men *are* taken away,
[b]While no one considers
That the righteous is taken
away from evil.
2 He shall enter into peace;
They shall rest in [a]their beds,
Each one walking *in* his
uprightness.

3 "But come here,
[a]You sons of the sorceress,
You offspring of the adulterer
and the harlot!
4 Whom do you ridicule?
Against whom do you make
a wide mouth
And stick out the tongue?
Are you not children of transgression,
Offspring of falsehood,
5 Inflaming yourselves with gods
[a]under every green tree,
[b]Slaying the children in the valleys,
Under the clefts of the rocks?
6 Among the smooth [a]*stones*
of the stream
Is your portion;
They, they, *are* your lot!
Even to them you have poured
a drink offering,
You have offered a grain offering.
Should I receive comfort in [b]these?

7 "On[a] a lofty and high mountain
You have set [b]your bed;
Even there you went up
To offer sacrifice.
8 Also behind the doors and their posts
You have set up your remembrance;
For you have uncovered yourself
to those other than Me,
And have gone up to them;
You have enlarged your bed
And made *a covenant* with them;
[a]You have loved their bed,
Where you saw *their* nudity.[1]
9 [a]You went to the king with ointment,
And increased your perfumes;
You sent your [b]messengers far off,
And *even* descended to Sheol.
10 You are wearied in the
length of your way;
[a]*Yet* you did not say, 'There is
no hope.'
You have found the life of your hand;
Therefore you were not grieved.

11 "And [a]of whom have you been
afraid, or feared,
That you have lied
And not remembered Me,
Nor taken *it* to your heart?

56:7 [e] Matt. 21:13 [f] [Mal. 1:11] 56:8 [a] Ps. 147:2; Is. 11:12; 27:12; 54:7 [b] Is. 60:3–11; 66:18–21; [John 10:16] 56:9 [a] Jer. 12:9 56:10 [a] Matt. 15:14 [b] Phil. 3:2 56:11 [a] Is. 28:7; Ezek. 13:19; [Mic. 3:5, 11] [b] Ezek. 34:2–10 56:12 [a] Is. 28:7 [b] Ps. 10:6; Prov. 23:35; Is. 22:13; Luke 12:19; 1 Cor. 15:32 [c] 2 Pet. 3:4 57:1 [a] Ps. 12:1 [b] 1 Kin. 14:13 57:2 [a] 2 Chr. 16:14 57:3 [a] Is. 1:4; Matt. 16:4 57:5 [a] 2 Kin. 16:4 [b] 2 Kin. 23:10; Ps. 106:37, 38; Jer. 7:31; Ezek. 16:20 57:6 [a] Jer. 3:9; Hab. 2:19 [b] Jer. 5:9, 29; 9:9 57:7 [a] Jer. 3:6; Ezek. 16:16 [b] Ezek. 23:41 57:8 [a] Ezek. 16:26 [1] Literally *hand,* a euphemism 57:9 [a] Hos. 7:11 [b] Ezek. 23:16, 40 57:10 [a] Jer. 2:25; 18:12 57:11 [a] Prov. 29:25; Is. 51:12, 13

Is it not because [b]I have held
My peace from of old
That you do not fear Me?
12 I will declare your righteousness
And your works,
For they will not profit you.
13 When you cry out,
Let your collection *of idols* deliver you.
But the wind will carry them all away,
A breath will take *them.*
But he who puts his trust in Me
shall possess the land,
And shall inherit My holy mountain."

Healing for the Backslider

14 And one shall say,
[a]"Heap it up! Heap it up!
Prepare the way,
Take the stumbling block out
of the way of My people."

15 For thus says the High and Lofty One
Who inhabits eternity,
[a]whose name *is* Holy:
[b]"I dwell in the high and holy *place,*
[c]With him *who* has a contrite
and humble spirit,
[d]To revive the spirit of the humble,
And to revive the heart of
the contrite ones.
16 [a]For I will not contend forever,
Nor will I always be angry;
For the spirit would fail before Me,
And the souls [b]*which* I have made.
17 For the iniquity of [a]his
covetousness
I was angry and struck him;
[b]I hid and was angry,
[c]And he went on backsliding
in the way of his heart.
18 I have seen his ways, and
[a]will heal him;
I will also lead him,
And restore comforts to him
And to [b]his mourners.

19 "I create [a]the fruit of the lips:
Peace, peace [b]to *him who is* far
off and to *him who is* near,"
Says the LORD,
"And I will heal him."
20 [a]But the wicked *are* like
the troubled sea,
When it cannot rest,
Whose waters cast up mire and dirt.

21 "*There*[a] *is* no peace,"
Says my God, "for the wicked."

Fasting that Pleases God

58 "Cry aloud, spare not;
Lift up your voice like a trumpet;
[a]Tell My people their transgression,
And the house of Jacob their sins.
2 Yet they seek Me daily,
And delight to know My ways,
As a nation that did righteousness,
And did not forsake the
ordinance of their God.
They ask of Me the
ordinances of justice;
They take delight in approaching God.
3 'Why[a] have we fasted,' *they say,*
'and You have not seen?
Why have we [b]afflicted our souls,
and You take no notice?'

"In fact, in the day of your fast
you find pleasure,
And exploit all your laborers.
4 [a]Indeed you fast for strife and debate,
And to strike with the fist
of wickedness.
You will not fast as *you do* this day,
To make your voice heard on high.
5 Is [a]it a fast that I have chosen,
[b]A day for a man to afflict his soul?
Is it to bow down his head
like a bulrush,
And [c]to spread out sackcloth
and ashes?
Would you call this a fast,
And an acceptable day
to the LORD?

6 "*Is* this not the fast that I have chosen:
To [a]loose the bonds of wickedness,
[b]To undo the heavy burdens,

57:11 [b] Ps. 50:21; Eccl. 8:11; Is. 42:14 57:14 [a] Is. 40:3; 62:10; Jer. 18:15 57:15 [a] Job 6:10; Luke 1:49 [b] Ps. 68:35; Zech. 2:13 [c] Ps. 34:18; 51:17; Is. 66:2 [d] Ps. 147:3; Is. 61:1–3 57:16 [a] Ps. 85:5; 103:9; [Mic. 7:18] [b] Num. 16:22; Job 34:14; Heb. 12:9 57:17 [a] Is. 2:7; 56:11; Jer. 6:13 [b] Is. 8:17; 45:15; 59:2 [c] Is. 9:13 57:18 [a] Jer. 3:22 [b] Is. 61:2 57:19 [a] Is. 6:7; 51:16; 59:21; Heb. 13:15 [b] Acts 2:39; Eph. 2:17 57:20 [a] Job 15:20; Prov. 4:16; Jude 13 57:21 [a] Is. 48:22 58:1 [a] Mic. 3:8 58:3 [a] Mal. 3:13–18; Luke 18:12 [b] Lev. 16:29; 23:27 58:4 [a] 1 Kin. 21:9 58:5 [a] Zech. 7:5 [b] Lev. 16:29 [c] Esth. 4:3; Job 2:8; Dan. 9:3 58:6 [a] Luke 4:18, 19 [b] Neh. 5:10–12

[c]To let the oppressed go free,
And that you break every yoke?
7 *Is it* not [a]to share your bread
with the hungry,
And that you bring to your house
the poor who are cast out;
[b]When you see the naked,
that you cover him,
And not hide yourself from
[c]your own flesh?

#OXYGEN

ISAIAH 58:7

Act out of Selflessness

What a blessing to have enough to eat. Never look down your nose at the beggar on the street. Instead, have compassion toward those who are less fortunate than you. Be thankful for God's grace; the situation could be reversed.

Breathe and **act out of selflessness.**

8 [a]Then your light shall break
forth like the morning,
Your healing shall spring
forth speedily,
And your righteousness
shall go before you;
[b]The glory of the LORD shall
be your rear guard.
9 Then you shall call, and the
LORD will answer;
You shall cry, and He will
say, 'Here I *am.*'

"If you take away the yoke
from your midst,
The pointing of the finger, and
[a]speaking wickedness,
10 *If* you extend your soul to the hungry
And satisfy the afflicted soul,
Then your light shall dawn
in the darkness,
And your darkness shall
be as the noonday.
11 The LORD will guide you continually,
And satisfy your soul in drought,
And strengthen your bones;
You shall be like a watered garden,
And like a spring of water,
whose waters do not fail.
12 Those from among you
[a]Shall build the old waste places;
You shall raise up the foundations
of many generations;
And you shall be called the
Repairer of the Breach,
The Restorer of Streets to Dwell In.

13 "If [a]you turn away your foot
from the Sabbath,
From doing your pleasure
on My holy day,
And call the Sabbath a delight,
The holy *day* of the LORD honorable,
And shall honor Him, not
doing your own ways,
Nor finding your own pleasure,
Nor speaking *your own* words,
14 [a]Then you shall delight
yourself in the LORD;
And I will cause you to [b]ride on
the high hills of the earth,
And feed you with the heritage
of Jacob your father.
[c]The mouth of the LORD has spoken."

Separated from God

59 Behold, the LORD's hand
is not [a]shortened,
That it cannot save;
Nor His ear heavy,
That it cannot hear.
2 But your iniquities have separated
you from your God;
And your sins have hidden
His face from you,
So that He will [a]not hear.
3 For [a]your hands are defiled with blood,
And your fingers with iniquity;
Your lips have spoken lies,
Your tongue has muttered
perversity.

58:6 [c] Jer. 34:9 58:7 [a] Ezek. 18:7; Matt. 25:35 [b] Job 31:19–22; James 2:14–17 [c] Gen. 29:14; Neh. 5:5 58:8 [a] Job 11:17 [b] Ex. 14:19; Is. 52:12 58:9 [a] Ps. 12:2; Is. 59:13 58:12 [a] Is. 61:4 58:13 [a] Ex. 31:16, 17; 35:2, 3; Is. 56:2, 4, 6; Jer. 17:21–27 58:14 [a] Job 22:26; Is. 61:10 [b] Deut. 32:13; 33:29; Is. 33:16; Hab. 3:19 [c] Is. 1:20; 40:5; Mic. 4:4 59:1 [a] Num. 11:23; Is. 50:2; Jer. 32:17 59:2 [a] Is. 1:15 59:3 [a] Is. 1:15, 21; Jer. 2:30, 34; Ezek. 7:23; Hos. 4:2

4 No one calls for justice,
Nor does *any* plead for truth.
They trust in [a]empty words
and speak lies;
[b]They conceive evil and
bring forth iniquity.
5 They hatch vipers' eggs and
weave the spider's web;
He who eats of their eggs dies,
And *from* that which is crushed
a viper breaks out.

6 [a]Their webs will not become garments,
Nor will they cover themselves
with their works;
Their works *are* works of iniquity,
And the act of violence *is*
in their hands.
7 [a]Their feet run to evil,
And they make haste to shed
[b]innocent blood;
[c]Their thoughts *are* thoughts
of iniquity;
Wasting and [d]destruction
are in their paths.
8 The way of [a]peace they
have not known,
And *there is* no justice in their ways;
[b]They have made themselves
crooked paths;
Whoever takes that way shall
not know peace.

Sin Confessed

9 Therefore justice is far from us,
Nor does righteousness overtake us;
[a]We look for light, but
there is darkness!
For brightness, *but* we
walk in blackness!
10 [a]We grope for the wall like the blind,
And we grope as if *we had* no eyes;
We stumble at noonday as at twilight;
We are as dead *men* in desolate places.
11 We all growl like bears,
And [a]moan sadly like doves;
We look for justice, but *there is* none;
For salvation, *but* it is far from us.
12 For our [a]transgressions are
multiplied before You,
And our sins testify against us;
For our transgressions *are* with us,
And *as for* our iniquities,
we know them:
13 In transgressing and lying
against the LORD,
And departing from our God,
Speaking oppression and revolt,
Conceiving and uttering [a]from the
heart words of falsehood.
14 Justice is turned back,
And righteousness stands afar off;
For truth is fallen in the street,
And equity cannot enter.
15 So truth fails,
And he *who* departs from evil
makes himself a [a]prey.

The Redeemer of Zion

Then the LORD saw *it,* and
it displeased Him
That *there was* no justice.
16 [a]He saw that *there was* no man,
And [b]wondered that *there*
was no intercessor;
[c]Therefore His own arm brought
salvation for Him;
And His own righteousness,
it sustained Him.
17 [a]For He put on righteousness
as a breastplate,
And a helmet of salvation
on His head;
He put on the garments of
vengeance for clothing,
And was clad with zeal as a cloak.
18 [a]According to *their* deeds,
accordingly He will repay,
Fury to His adversaries,
Recompense to His enemies;
The coastlands He will fully repay.
19 [a]So shall they fear
The name of the LORD from
the west,
And His glory from the
rising of the sun;
When the enemy comes
in [b]like a flood,
The Spirit of the LORD will lift
up a standard against him.

59:4 [a] Is. 30:12; Jer. 7:4 [b] Job 15:35; Ps. 7:14; Is. 33:11 59:6 [a] Job 8:14 59:7 [a] Prov. 1:16; Rom. 3:15 [b] Prov. 6:17 [c] Is. 55:7 [d] Rom. 3:16, 17 59:8 [a] Is. 57:20, 21 [b] Ps. 125:5; Prov. 2:15 59:9 [a] Jer. 8:15 59:10 [a] Deut. 28:29; Job 5:14; Amos 8:9 59:11 [a] Is. 38:14; Ezek. 7:16 59:12 [a] Is. 24:5; 58:1 59:13 [a] Matt. 12:34 59:15 [a] Is. 5:23; 10:2; 29:21; 32:7 59:16 [a] Is. 41:28; 63:5; 64:7; Ezek. 22:30 [b] Mark 6:6 [c] Ps. 98:1; Is. 63:5 59:17 [a] Eph. 6:14, 17; 1 Thess. 5:8 59:18 [a] Is. 63:6; Rom. 2:6 59:19 [a] Ps. 113:3; Mal. 1:11 [b] Rev. 12:15

20 "The[a] Redeemer will come to Zion,
And to those who turn from
transgression in Jacob,"
Says the LORD.

21 "As[a] for Me," says the LORD, "this *is* My
covenant with them: My Spirit who *is* upon
you, and My words which I have put in your
mouth, shall not depart from your mouth,
nor from the mouth of your descendants,
nor from the mouth of your descendants'
descendants," says the LORD, "from this
time and forevermore."

The Gentiles Bless Zion

60 Arise, [a]shine;
For your light has come!
And [b]the glory of the LORD
is risen upon you.
2 For behold, the darkness
shall cover the earth,
And deep darkness the people;
But the LORD will arise over you,
And His glory will be seen upon you.
3 The [a]Gentiles shall come to your light,
And kings to the brightness
of your rising.

4 "Lift[a] up your eyes all around, and see:
They all gather together,
[b]they come to you;
Your sons shall come from afar,
And your daughters shall be
nursed at *your* side.
5 Then you shall see and
become radiant,
And your heart shall swell with joy;
Because [a]the abundance of the
sea shall be turned to you,
The wealth of the Gentiles
shall come to you.
6 The multitude of camels
shall cover your *land,*
The dromedaries of Midian
and [a]Ephah;
All those from [b]Sheba shall come;
They shall bring [c]gold and incense,
And they shall proclaim the
praises of the LORD.
7 All the flocks of [a]Kedar shall be
gathered together to you,
The rams of Nebaioth shall
minister to you;
They shall ascend with
[b]acceptance on My altar,
And [c]I will glorify the
house of My glory.

8 "Who *are* these *who* fly like a cloud,
And like doves to their roosts?
9 [a]Surely the coastlands shall wait for Me;
And the ships of Tarshish
will come first,
[b]To bring your sons from afar,
[c]Their silver and their gold with them,
To the name of the LORD your God,
And to the Holy One of Israel,
[d]Because He has glorified you.

10 "The[a] sons of foreigners shall
build up your walls,
[b]And their kings shall minister to you;
For [c]in My wrath I struck you,
[d]But in My favor I have had
mercy on you.
11 Therefore your gates [a]shall
be open continually;
They shall not be shut day or night,
That *men* may bring to you the
wealth of the Gentiles,
And their kings in procession.
12 [a]For the nation and kingdom which
will not serve you shall perish,
And *those* nations shall
be utterly ruined.

13 "The[a] glory of Lebanon
shall come to you,
The cypress, the pine, and
the box tree together,
To beautify the place of My sanctuary;
And I will make [b]the place
of My feet glorious.
14 Also the sons of those who afflicted you
Shall come [a]bowing to you,
And all those who despised
you shall [b]fall prostrate at
the soles of your feet;

59:20 [a] Rom. 11:26 59:21 [a] [Heb. 8:10; 10:16] 60:1 [a] Eph. 5:14 [b] Mal. 4:2 60:3 [a] Is. 49:6, 23; Rev. 21:24 60:4 [a] Is. 49:18 [b] Is. 49:20–22 60:5 [a] [Rom. 11:25–27] 60:6 [a] Gen. 25:4 [b] Gen. 25:3; Ps. 72:10 [c] Is. 61:6; Matt. 2:11 60:7 [a] Gen. 25:13 [b] Is. 56:7 [c] Is. 60:13; Hag. 2:7, 9 60:9 [a] Ps. 72:10 [b] [Gal. 4:26] [c] Jer. 3:17 [d] Is. 55:5 60:10 [a] Is. 14:1, 2; 61:5; Zech. 6:15 [b] Is. 49:23; Rev. 21:24 [c] Is. 57:17 [d] Is. 54:7, 8 60:11 [a] Is. 26:2; 60:18; 62:10; Rev. 21:25, 26 60:12 [a] Is. 14:2; Zech. 14:17; Matt. 21:44 60:13 [a] Is. 35:2 [b] 1 Chr. 28:2; Ps. 132:7 60:14 [a] Is. 45:14 [b] Is. 49:23; Rev. 3:9

And they shall call you The
City of the LORD,
[c]Zion of the Holy One of Israel.

15 "Whereas you have been
forsaken and hated,
So that no one went through *you,*
I will make you an eternal excellence,
A joy of many generations.
16 You shall drink the milk of the Gentiles,
[a]And milk the breast of kings;
You shall know that [b]I, the
LORD, *am* your Savior
And your Redeemer, the
Mighty One of Jacob.

17 "Instead of bronze I will bring gold,
Instead of iron I will bring silver,
Instead of wood, bronze,
And instead of stones, iron.
I will also make your officers peace,
And your magistrates righteousness.
18 Violence shall no longer be
heard in your land,
Neither wasting nor destruction
within your borders;
But you shall call [a]your walls Salvation,
And your gates Praise.

God the Glory of His People

19 "The [a]sun shall no longer be
your light by day,
Nor for brightness shall the
moon give light to you;
But the LORD will be to you
an everlasting light,
And [b]your God your glory.
20 [a]Your sun shall no longer go down,
Nor shall your moon withdraw itself;
For the LORD will be your
everlasting light,
And the days of your mourning
shall be ended.
21 [a]Also your people *shall* all *be* righteous;
[b]They shall inherit the land forever,
[c]The branch of My planting,
[d]The work of My hands,
That I may be glorified.
22 [a]A little one shall become a thousand,
And a small one a strong nation.
I, the LORD, will hasten it in its time."

The Good News of Salvation

61 "The [a]Spirit of the Lord
GOD *is* upon Me,
Because the LORD [b]has anointed Me
To preach good tidings to the poor;
He has sent Me [c]to heal the
brokenhearted,
To proclaim [d]liberty to the captives,
And the opening of the prison
to *those who are* bound;
2 [a]To proclaim the acceptable
year of the LORD,
And [b]the day of vengeance of our God;
[c]To comfort all who mourn,
3 To console those who mourn in Zion,
[a]To give them beauty for ashes,
The oil of joy for mourning,
The garment of praise for the
spirit of heaviness;
That they may be called trees
of righteousness,
[b]The planting of the LORD, [c]that
He may be glorified."

4 And they shall [a]rebuild the old ruins,
They shall raise up the
former desolations,
And they shall repair the ruined cities,
The desolations of many generations.
5 [a]Strangers shall stand and
feed your flocks,
And the sons of the foreigner
Shall be your plowmen and
your vinedressers.
6 [a]But you shall be named the
priests of the LORD,
They shall call you the
servants of our God.
[b]You shall eat the riches of the Gentiles,
And in their glory you shall boast.
7 [a]Instead of your shame *you*
shall have double *honor,*
And *instead of* confusion they
shall rejoice in their portion.

60:14 [c] [Heb. 12:22; Rev. 14:1] 60:16 [a] Is. 49:23 [b] Is. 43:3 60:18 [a] Is. 26:1 60:19 [a] Rev. 21:23; 22:5 [b] Is. 41:16; 45:25; Zech. 2:5 60:20 [a] Amos 8:9 60:21 [a] Is. 52:1; Rev. 21:27 [b] Ps. 37:11; Matt. 5:5 [c] Is. 61:3; [Matt. 15:13; John 15:2] [d] Is. 29:23; [Eph. 2:10] 60:22 [a] Matt. 13:31, 32 61:1 [a] Is. 11:2; Matt. 3:17; Luke 4:18, 19; John 1:32; 3:34 [b] Ps. 45:7; Matt. 11:5; Luke 7:22 [c] Ps. 147:3 [d] Is. 42:7; [Acts 10:43] 61:2 [a] Lev. 25:9 [b] Is. 34:8; Mal. 4:1, 3; [2 Thess. 1:7] [c] Is. 57:18; Jer. 31:13; Matt. 5:4 61:3 [a] Ps. 30:11 [b] Is. 60:21; [Jer. 17:7, 8] [c] [John 15:8] 61:4 [a] Is. 49:8; 58:12; Ezek. 36:33; Amos 9:14 61:5 [a] [Eph. 2:12] 61:6 [a] Ex. 19:6 [b] Is. 60:5, 11 61:7 [a] Is. 40:2; Zech. 9:12

Therefore in their land they
shall possess double;
Everlasting joy shall be theirs.

8 "For [a]I, the LORD, love justice;
[b]I hate robbery for burnt offering;
I will direct their work in truth,
[c]And will make with them an
everlasting covenant.
9 Their descendants shall be
known among the Gentiles,
And their offspring among the people.
All who see them shall
acknowledge them,
[a]That they *are* the posterity *whom*
the LORD has blessed."

10 [a]I will greatly rejoice in the LORD,
My soul shall be joyful in my God;
For [b]He has clothed me with the
garments of salvation,
He has covered me with the
robe of righteousness,
[c]As a bridegroom decks *himself*
with ornaments,
And as a bride adorns *herself*
with her jewels.
11 For as the earth brings forth its bud,
As the garden causes the things that
are sown in it to spring forth,
So the Lord GOD will cause
[a]righteousness and [b]praise to
spring forth before all the nations.

Assurance of Zion's Salvation

62 For Zion's sake I will not
hold My peace,
And for Jerusalem's sake
I will not rest,
Until her righteousness goes
forth as brightness,
And her salvation as a
lamp *that* burns.
2 [a]The Gentiles shall see your
righteousness,
And all [b]kings your glory.
[c]You shall be called by a new name,
Which the mouth of the
LORD will name.
3 You shall also be [a]a crown of glory
In the hand of the LORD,
And a royal diadem
In the hand of your God.
4 [a]You shall no longer be
termed [b]Forsaken,
Nor shall your land any more
be termed [c]Desolate;
But you shall be called Hephzibah,[1]
and your land Beulah;[2]
For the LORD delights in you,
And your land shall be married.
5 For *as* a young man marries a virgin,
So shall your sons marry you;
And *as* the bridegroom
rejoices over the bride,
[a]*So* shall your God rejoice over you.

6 [a]I have set watchmen on your
walls, O Jerusalem;
They shall never hold their
peace day or night.
You who make mention of the
LORD, do not keep silent,
7 And give Him no rest till
He establishes
And till He makes Jerusalem
[a]a praise in the earth.

8 The LORD has sworn by His right hand
And by the arm of His strength:
"Surely I will no longer [a]give your grain
As food for your enemies;
And the sons of the foreigner shall
not drink your new wine,
For which you have labored.
9 But those who have gathered
it shall eat it,
And praise the LORD;
Those who have brought it together
shall drink it [a]in My holy courts."

10 Go through,
Go through the gates!
[a]Prepare the way for the people;
Build up,
Build up the highway!
Take out the stones,
[b]Lift up a banner for the peoples!

61:8 [a] Ps. 11:7 [b] Is. 1:11, 13 [c] Gen. 17:7; Ps. 105:10; Is. 55:3; Jer. 32:40 61:9 [a] Is. 65:23 61:10 [a] Hab. 3:18 [b] Ps. 132:9, 16 [c] Is. 49:18; Rev. 21:2 61:11 [a] Ps. 72:3; 85:11 [b] Is. 60:18; 62:7 62:2 [a] Is. 60:3 [b] Ps. 102:15, 16; 138:4, 5; 148:11, 13 [c] Is. 62:4, 12; 65:15 62:3 [a] Is. 28:5; Zech. 9:16; 1 Thess. 2:19 62:4 [a] Hos. 1:10; 1 Pet. 2:10 [b] Is. 49:14; 54:6, 7 [c] Is. 54:1 [1] Literally *My Delight Is in Her* [2] Literally *Married* 62:5 [a] Is. 65:19 62:6 [a] Is. 52:8; Jer. 6:17; Ezek. 3:17; 33:7 62:7 [a] Is. 60:18; 61:11; Jer. 33:9; Zeph. 3:19, 20 62:8 [a] Lev. 26:16; Deut. 28:31, 33; Judg. 6:3–6; Is. 1:7; Jer. 5:17 62:9 [a] Deut. 12:12; 14:23, 26 62:10 [a] Is. 40:3; 57:14 [b] Is. 11:12

11 Indeed the LORD has proclaimed
To the end of the world:
[a]"Say to the daughter of Zion,
'Surely your salvation is coming;
Behold, His [b]reward *is* with Him,
And His work before Him.'"
12 And they shall call them
The Holy People,
The Redeemed of the LORD;
And you shall be called Sought Out,
A City Not Forsaken.

The LORD in Judgment and Salvation

63 Who *is* this who comes
from Edom,
With dyed garments from Bozrah,
This *One who is* glorious
in His apparel,
Traveling in the greatness
of His strength?—

"I who speak in righteousness,
mighty to save."

2 Why [a]*is* Your apparel red,
And Your garments like one who
treads in the winepress?

3 "I have [a]trodden the winepress alone,
And from the peoples no
one *was* with Me.
For I have trodden them in My anger,
And trampled them in My fury;
Their blood is sprinkled
upon My garments,
And I have stained all My robes.
4 For the [a]day of vengeance
is in My heart,
And the year of My
redeemed has come.
5 [a]I looked, but [b]*there was* no
one to help,
And I wondered
That *there was* no one to uphold;
Therefore My own [c]arm brought
salvation for Me;
And My own fury, it sustained Me.
6 I have trodden down the
peoples in My anger,
Made them drunk in My fury,
And brought down their
strength to the earth."

God's Mercy Remembered

7 I will mention the lovingkindnesses
of the LORD
And the praises of the LORD,
According to all that the LORD
has bestowed on us,
And the great goodness toward
the house of Israel,
Which He has bestowed on them
according to His mercies,
According to the multitude of
His lovingkindnesses.
8 For He said, "Surely they
are My people,
Children *who* will not lie."
So He became their Savior.
9 [a]In all their affliction He was afflicted,
[b]And the Angel of His
Presence saved them;
[c]In His love and in His pity
He redeemed them;
And [d]He bore them and
carried them
All the days of old.
10 But they [a]rebelled and [b]grieved
His Holy Spirit;
[c]So He turned Himself against
them as an enemy,
And He fought against them.

11 Then he [a]remembered
the days of old,
Moses *and* his people, *saying:*
"Where *is* He who [b]brought
them up out of the sea
With the shepherd of His flock?
[c]Where *is* He who put His Holy
Spirit within them,
12 Who led *them* by the right
hand of Moses,
[a]With His glorious arm,
[b]Dividing the water before them
To make for Himself an
everlasting name,
13 [a]Who led them through the deep,
As a horse in the wilderness,
That they might not stumble?"

62:11 [a] Zech. 9:9; Matt. 21:5; John 12:15 [b] Is. 40:10; [Rev. 22:12] 63:2 [a] [Rev. 19:13, 15] 63:3 [a] Lam. 1:15; Rev. 14:19, 20; 19:15 63:4 [a] Is. 34:8; 35:4; 61:2; Jer. 51:6 63:5 [a] Is. 41:28; 59:16 [b] [John 16:32] [c] Ps. 98:1; Is. 59:16 63:9 [a] Judg. 10:16 [b] Ex. 14:19 [c] Deut. 7:7 [d] Ex. 19:4 63:10 [a] Ex. 15:24 [b] Num. 14:11; Ps. 78:40; Acts 7:51; 1 Cor. 10:1–11 [c] Ex. 23:21; Ps. 106:40 63:11 [a] Ps. 106:44, 45 [b] Ex. 14:30 [c] Num. 11:17, 25, 29; Hag. 2:5 63:12 [a] Ex. 15:6 [b] Ex. 14:21, 22; Josh. 3:16; Is. 11:15; 51:10 63:13 [a] Ps. 106:9

14 As a beast goes down into the valley,
And the Spirit of the LORD
causes him to rest,
So You lead Your people,
[a]To make Yourself a glorious name.

A Prayer of Penitence

15 [a]Look down from heaven,
And see [b]from Your habitation,
holy and glorious.
Where *are* Your zeal and
Your strength,
The yearning [c]of Your heart and
Your mercies toward me?
Are they restrained?
16 [a]Doubtless You *are* our Father,
Though Abraham [b]was ignorant of us,
And Israel does not acknowledge us.
You, O LORD, *are* our Father;
Our Redeemer from Everlasting
is Your name.
17 O LORD, why have You [a]made
us stray from Your ways,
And hardened our heart
from Your fear?
Return for Your servants' sake,
The tribes of Your inheritance.
18 [a]Your holy people have possessed
it but a little while;
[b]Our adversaries have trodden
down Your sanctuary.
19 We have become *like* those of old,
over whom You never ruled,
Those who were never called
by Your name.

64 Oh, that You would rend
the heavens!
That You would come down!
That the mountains might
shake at Your [a]presence—
2 As fire burns brushwood,
As fire causes water to boil—
To make Your name known
to Your adversaries,
That the nations may tremble
at Your presence!
3 When [a]You did awesome things
for which we did not look,
You came down,
The mountains shook at
Your presence.
4 For since the beginning of the world
[a]*Men* have not heard nor
perceived by the ear,
Nor has the eye seen any
God besides You,
Who acts for the one who
waits for Him.
5 You meet him who rejoices
and does righteousness,
Who remembers You in Your ways.
You are indeed angry, for
we have sinned—
[a]In these ways we continue;
And we need to be saved.

6 But we are all like an unclean *thing,*
And all [a]our righteousnesses
are like filthy rags;
We all [b]fade as a leaf,
And our iniquities, like the wind,
Have taken us away.
7 And *there is* no one who
calls on Your name,
Who stirs himself up to
take hold of You;
For You have hidden Your
face from us,
And have consumed us because
of our iniquities.

8 But now, O LORD,
You *are* our Father;
We *are* the clay, and You our [a]potter;
And all we *are* the work of Your hand.
9 Do not be furious, O LORD,
Nor remember iniquity forever;
Indeed, please look—we
all *are* Your people!
10 Your holy cities are a wilderness,
Zion is a wilderness,
Jerusalem a desolation.
11 Our holy and beautiful temple,
Where our fathers praised You,
Is burned up with fire;
And all [a]our pleasant things
are laid waste.
12 [a]Will You restrain Yourself because
of these *things,* O LORD?

63:14 [a] 2 Sam. 7:23 63:15 [a] Deut. 26:15; Ps. 80:14 [b] Ps. 33:14 [c] Jer. 31:20; Hos. 11:8 63:16 [a] Deut. 32:6 [b] Job 14:21 63:17 [a] Is. 6:9, 10; John 12:40 63:18 [a] Deut. 7:6 [b] Ps. 74:3–7; Is. 64:11 64:1 [a] Ex. 19:18; Ps. 18:9; 144:5; Mic. 1:3, 4; [Hab. 3:13] 64:3 [a] Ex. 34:10 64:4 [a] Ps. 31:19 64:5 [a] Mal. 3:6 64:6 [a] [Phil. 3:9] [b] Ps. 90:5, 6; Is. 1:30 64:8 [a] Is. 29:16; 45:9; Jer. 18:6; [Rom. 9:20, 21] 64:11 [a] Ezek. 24:21 64:12 [a] Is. 42:14

[b]Will You hold Your peace, and
afflict us very severely?

The Righteousness of God's Judgment

65 "I was [a]sought by *those who*
did not ask *for Me;*
I was found by *those who*
did not seek Me.
I said, 'Here I am, here I am,'
To a nation *that* [b]was not
called by My name.
2 [a]I have stretched out My hands all
day long to a [b]rebellious people,
Who [c]walk in a way *that is* not good,
According to their own thoughts;
3 A people [a]who provoke Me to
anger continually to My face;
[b]Who sacrifice in gardens,
And burn incense on altars of brick;
4 [a]Who sit among the graves,
And spend the night in the tombs;
[b]Who eat swine's flesh,
And the broth of abominable
things is *in* their vessels;
5 [a]Who say, 'Keep to yourself,
Do not come near me,
For I am holier than you!'
These *are* smoke in My nostrils,
A fire that burns all the day.

6 "Behold, [a]*it is* written before Me:
[b]I will not keep silence,
[c]but will repay—
Even repay into their bosom—
7 Your iniquities and [a]the iniquities
of your fathers together,"
Says the LORD,
[b]"Who have burned incense
on the mountains
[c]And blasphemed Me on the hills;
Therefore I will measure their
former work into their bosom."

8 Thus says the LORD:

"As the new wine is found
in the cluster,
And *one* says, 'Do not destroy it,
For [a]a blessing *is* in it,'
So will I do for My servants' sake,
That I may not destroy them [b]all.
9 I will bring forth descendants
from Jacob,
And from Judah an heir
of My mountains;
My [a]elect shall inherit it,
And My servants shall dwell there.
10 [a]Sharon shall be a fold of flocks,
And [b]the Valley of Achor a place
for herds to lie down,
For My people who have [c]sought Me.

11 "But you *are* those who
forsake the LORD,
Who forget [a]My holy mountain,
Who prepare [b]a table for Gad,[1]
And who furnish a drink
offering for Meni.[2]
12 Therefore I will number
you for the sword,
And you shall all bow down
to the slaughter;
[a]Because, when I called, you
did not answer;
When I spoke, you did not hear,
But did evil before My eyes,
And chose *that* in which
I do not delight."

13 Therefore thus says the Lord GOD:

"Behold, My servants shall eat,
But you shall be hungry;
Behold, My servants shall drink,
But you shall be thirsty;
Behold, My servants shall rejoice,
But you shall be ashamed;
14 Behold, My servants shall
sing for joy of heart,
But you shall cry for sorrow of heart,
And [a]wail for grief of spirit.
15 You shall leave your name [a]as
a curse to [b]My chosen;
For the Lord GOD will slay you,
And [c]call His servants by
another name;

64:12 [b] Ps. 83:1 65:1 [a] Rom. 9:24; 10:20 [b] Is. 63:19 65:2 [a] Rom. 10:21 [b] Is. 1:2, 23 [c] Is. 42:24 65:3 [a] Deut. 32:21 [b] Is. 1:29 65:4 [a] Deut. 18:11 [b] Lev. 11:7; Is. 66:17 65:5 [a] Matt. 9:11; Luke 7:39; 18:9–12 65:6 [a] Deut. 32:34 [b] Ps. 50:3 [c] Ps. 79:12 65:7 [a] Ex. 20:5 [b] Ezek. 18:6 [c] Is. 57:7; Ezek. 20:27, 28 65:8 [a] Joel 2:14 [b] Is. 1:9; Amos 9:8, 9 65:9 [a] Matt. 24:22 65:10 [a] Is. 33:9 [b] Josh. 7:24; Hos. 2:15 [c] Is. 55:6 65:11 [a] Is. 56:7 [b] Ezek. 23:41; [1 Cor. 10:21] [1] Literally *Troop* or *Fortune,* a pagan deity [2] Literally *Number* or *Destiny,* a pagan deity 65:12 [a] 2 Chr. 36:15, 16; Prov. 1:24; Is. 41:28; 50:2; 66:4; Jer. 7:13 65:14 [a] Matt. 8:12; Luke 13:28 65:15 [a] Jer. 29:22; Zech. 8:13 [b] Is. 65:9, 22 [c] [Acts 11:26]

16 [a]So that he who blesses
himself in the earth
Shall bless himself in the God of truth;
And [b]he who swears in the earth
Shall swear by the God of truth;
Because the former troubles
are forgotten,
And because they are hidden
from My eyes.

The Glorious New Creation

17 "For behold, I create [a]new
heavens and a new earth;
And the former shall not be
remembered or come to mind.
18 But be glad and rejoice forever
in what I create;
For behold, I create Jerusalem
as a rejoicing,
And her people a joy.
19 [a]I will rejoice in Jerusalem,
And joy in My people;
The [b]voice of weeping shall no
longer be heard in her,
Nor the voice of crying.

20 "No more shall an infant from
there *live but a few* days,
Nor an old man who has not
fulfilled his days;
For the child shall die one
hundred years old,
[a]But the sinner *being* one hundred
years old shall be accursed.
21 [a]They shall build houses
and inhabit *them;*
They shall plant vineyards
and eat their fruit.
22 They shall not build and
another inhabit;
They shall not plant and [a]another eat;
For [b]as the days of a tree, *so shall*
be the days of My people,
And [c]My elect shall long enjoy
the work of their hands.
23 They shall not labor in vain,
[a]Nor bring forth children
for trouble;
For [b]they *shall be* the descendants
of the blessed of the LORD,
And their offspring with them.

24 "It shall come to pass
That [a]before they call, I will answer;
And while they are still
speaking, I will [b]hear.
25 The [a]wolf and the lamb
shall feed together,
The lion shall eat straw like the ox,
[b]And dust *shall be* the serpent's food.
They shall not hurt nor destroy
in all My holy mountain,"
Says the LORD.

True Worship and False

66 Thus says the LORD:
[a]"Heaven *is* My throne,
And earth *is* My footstool.
Where *is* the house that
you will build Me?
And where *is* the place of My rest?
2 For all those *things* My hand has made,
And all those *things* exist,"
Says the LORD.
[a]"But on this *one* will I look:
[b]On *him who is* poor and of
a contrite spirit,
And who trembles at My word.

3 "He[a] who kills a bull *is as*
if he slays a man;
He who sacrifices a lamb, *as if*
he [b]breaks a dog's neck;
He who offers a grain offering,
as if he offers swine's blood;
He who burns incense, *as if*
he blesses an idol.
Just as they have chosen
their own ways,
And their soul delights in
their abominations,
4 So will I choose their delusions,
And bring their fears on them;
[a]Because, when I called,
no one answered,

65:16 [a] Ps. 72:17; Jer. 4:2 [b] Deut. 6:13; Zeph. 1:5 65:17 [a] Is. 51:16; 66:22; [2 Pet. 3:13]; Rev. 21:1 65:19 [a] Is. 62:4, 5 [b] Is. 35:10; 51:11; Rev. 7:17; 21:4 65:20 [a] Eccl. 8:12, 13; Is. 3:11; 22:14 65:21 [a] Ezek. 28:26; 45:4; Hos. 11:11; Amos 9:14 65:22 [a] Is. 62:8, 9 [b] Ps. 92:12 [c] Is. 65:9, 15 65:23 [a] Hos. 9:12 [b] Is. 61:9; [Jer. 32:38, 39; Acts 2:39] 65:24 [a] Ps. 91:15; Is. 58:9 [b] Is. 30:19; Dan. 9:20–23 65:25 [a] Is. 11:6–9 [b] Gen. 3:14; Mic. 7:17 66:1 [a] 1 Kin. 8:27; 2 Chr. 6:18; Ps. 11:4; Matt. 5:34; Acts 17:24 66:2 [a] Ps. 34:18; [Is. 57:15; 61:1; Matt. 5:3, 4; Luke 18:13, 14] [b] Ps. 34:18; 51:17 66:3 [a] [Is. 1:10–17; 58:1–7; Mic. 6:7, 8] [b] Deut. 23:18 66:4 [a] Prov. 1:24; Is. 65:12; Jer. 7:13

When I spoke they did not hear;
But they did evil before My eyes,
And chose *that* in which
I do not delight."

The LORD Vindicates Zion

5 Hear the word of the LORD,
You who tremble at His word:
"Your brethren who [a]hated you,
Who cast you out for My
name's sake, said,
[b]'Let the LORD be glorified,
That [c]we may see your joy.'
But they shall be ashamed."

6 The sound of noise from the city!
A voice from the temple!
The voice of the LORD,
Who fully repays His enemies!

7 "Before she was in labor, she gave
birth;
Before her pain came,
She delivered a male child.
8 Who has heard such a thing?
Who has seen such things?
Shall the earth be made to
give birth in one day?
Or shall a nation be born at once?
For as soon as Zion was in labor,
She gave birth to her children.
9 Shall I bring to the time of birth, and
not cause delivery?" says the LORD.
"Shall I who cause delivery shut up
the womb?" says your God.
10 "Rejoice with Jerusalem,
And be glad with her, all
you who love her;
Rejoice for joy with her, all
you who mourn for her;
11 That you may feed and be satisfied
With the consolation of her bosom,
That you may drink deeply
and be delighted
With the abundance of her glory."

12 For thus says the LORD:

"Behold, [a]I will extend peace
to her like a river,
And the glory of the Gentiles
like a flowing stream.
Then you shall [b]feed;
On *her* sides shall you be [c]carried,
And be dandled on *her* knees.
13 As one whom his mother comforts,
So I will [a]comfort you;
And you shall be comforted
in Jerusalem."

The Reign and Indignation of God

14 When you see *this,* your
heart shall rejoice,
And [a]your bones shall
flourish like grass;
The hand of the LORD shall be
known to His servants,
And *His* indignation to His enemies.
15 [a]For behold, the LORD will
come with fire
And with His chariots,
like a whirlwind,
To render His anger with fury,
And His rebuke with flames of fire.
16 For by fire and by [a]His sword
The LORD will judge all flesh;
And the slain of the LORD
shall be [b]many.

17 "Those[a] who sanctify themselves
and purify themselves,
To go to the gardens
After an *idol* in the midst,
Eating swine's flesh and the
abomination and the mouse,
Shall be consumed together,"
says the LORD.

18 "For I *know* their works and their
[a]thoughts. It shall be that I will [b]gather all
nations and tongues; and they shall come
and see My glory. 19 [a]I will set a sign among
them; and those among them who escape
I will send to the nations: *to* Tarshish and
Pul[1] and Lud, who draw the bow, and Tubal
and Javan, *to* the coastlands afar off who
have not heard My fame nor seen My glory.
[b]And they shall declare My glory among the
Gentiles. 20 Then they shall [a]bring all your
brethren [b]for an offering to the LORD out of

66:5 [a] Ps. 38:20; Is. 60:15; [Luke 6:22, 23] [b] Is. 5:19 [c] [2 Thess. 1:10; Titus 2:13] 66:12 [a] Is. 48:18; 60:5 [b] Is. 60:16 [c] Is. 49:22; 60:4 66:13 [a] Is. 51:3; [2 Cor. 1:3, 4] 66:14 [a] Ezek. 37:1 66:15 [a] Is. 9:5; [2 Thess. 1:8] 66:16 [a] Is. 27:1 [b] Is. 34:6 66:17 [a] Is. 65:3–8 66:18 [a] Is. 59:7 [b] Is. 45:22–25; Jer. 3:17 66:19 [a] Luke 2:34 [b] Mal. 1:11 [1] Following Masoretic Text and Targum; Septuagint reads *Put* (compare Jeremiah 46:9). 66:20 [a] Is. 49:22 [b] Is. 18:7; [Rom. 15:16]

all nations, on horses and in chariots and
in litters, on mules and on camels, to My
holy mountain Jerusalem," says the LORD,
"as the children of Israel bring an offering in a clean vessel into the house of the
LORD. 21And I will also take some of them
for [a]priests *and* Levites," says the LORD.

22 "For as [a]the new heavens
and the new earth
Which I will make shall remain
before Me," says the LORD,
"So shall your descendants and
your name remain.

23 And [a]it shall come to pass
That from one New Moon
to another,
And from one Sabbath to another,
[b]All flesh shall come to worship
before Me," says the LORD.

24 "And they shall go forth and look
Upon the corpses of the men
Who have transgressed against Me.
For their [a]worm does not die,
And their fire is not quenched.
They shall be an abhorrence
to all flesh."

66:21 [a] Ex. 19:6; Is. 61:6; 1 Pet. 2:9; Rev. 1:6 66:22 [a] Is. 65:17; Heb. 12:26, 27; 2 Pet. 3:13; Rev. 21:1 66:23 [a] Zech. 14:16 [b] Zech. 14:17–21 66:24 [a] Is. 14:11; Mark 9:44, 46, 48

THE BOOK OF

JEREMIAH

OVERVIEW

The Book of Jeremiah is named after its author, the prophet Jeremiah. It proclaims God's judgment against the Israelites but also offers hope for redemption. Jeremiah, whose name means "Yahweh exalts," was one of the major prophets of the Old Testament.

Jeremiah, who was born into the priestly family of Hilkiah, began his ministry in 626 BC and ended around 586 BC. God called Jeremiah to be a prophet during the thirteenth year of King Josiah's reign (see Jer. 1:2). Jeremiah served through the reigns of Jehoiakim and Zedekiah until Judah was carried into captivity. Most of his ministry occurred in Jerusalem with Baruch, a scribe and devoted friend, recording his prophecies (see 36:4). Ezekiel, Zephaniah, and Habakkuk were his contemporaries.

God called Jeremiah to speak to the nation of Judah about the judgment they would suffer due to their disobedience. The people were afraid of being conquered by other nations, yet they continued to disobey the Lord's commandments. Jeremiah lamented over Judah's sins and God's planned judgment. He has often been called "the weeping prophet" because of how he often tearfully implored God on behalf of the people.

The Book of Jeremiah opens with God's calling of Jeremiah to speak for Him as a prophet. He told Jeremiah, "Before I formed you in the womb I knew you; before you were born I sanctified you; I ordained you a prophet to the nations" (1:5). He charged Jeremiah, "Speak to them all that I command you" (1:17).

Jeremiah delivered God's message of Judah's guilt and punishment (chs. 2–6) and declared the judgment to be visited upon them for practicing false religion (chs. 7–10). In chapters 26–29, he foretold of the Babylonian exile, and he shared God's plan for restoration in chapters 30–33.

The people often resisted Jeremiah's prophecies. King Jehoiakim destroyed Jeremiah's scroll that spoke of the adversity God had planned for his kingdom. He then placed Jeremiah in prison, where he remained until Jerusalem fell into the hands of the Babylonians (chs. 36–38). The Babylonian king, Nebuchadnezzar, set him free (ch. 39).

After the fall of Jerusalem, God brought judgment against many peoples, including Egypt (ch. 46), Damascus (ch. 49), and Babylon (chs. 50–51). Chapter 52 summarizes the events that led up to Nebuchadnezzar's capture of Israel.

Jeremiah was faithful to God and showed compassion for His people. God used Jeremiah to reveal the new covenant He would make with His people (see 31:31). This new covenant was to be written on the hearts of people and fulfilled through the birth and death of the Messiah (see 31:33–34). Through the new covenant, every believer would have a personal relationship with God.

The Book of Jeremiah announced God's judgment on the Israelites and the many nations that rose against them. God gave the people numerous opportunities to turn away from their wickedness and toward Him, but they refused. His judgment became inevitable. However, He still offered a plan of redemption by promising His Son, Jesus.

BREATHE IT IN

The prophet Jeremiah delivered God's message of judgment and redemption to the Israelites. He was often disappointed because the people rejected the prophecies that God instructed him to deliver. He was even thrown into prison because he prophesied of the captivity of Israel. When Jeremiah was in prison, the Lord spoke to him, saying, "Call to Me, and I will answer you, and show you great and mighty things, which you do not know" (33:3).

Christians can learn lessons about the power of prayer from this book. Just as God invited Jeremiah to "call to" Him, we can be certain He offers the same to us. God wants us to call to Him in prayer. He longs to hear from us. Prayer is an important part of every Christian's relationship with God. It is not reserved for pastors, teachers, prophets, and other leaders within the church. We all are to pray as a way to draw closer to God, hear from Him, and share our thoughts, feelings, needs, desires, joys, disappointments, and whatever else we might experience. God desires to hear our innermost thoughts. He wants to hear from us in difficult times of trial and in pleasant times when life goes according to plan. It is during the peaceful times that our prayers can most easily focus on Him and not our desires. When we are at peace, we should fill our prayer time with praise, worship, and thanksgiving for all that God has done.

Never forget that prayer is two-way communication. We often get everything off our chests in prayer without taking the time to hear from God. We cannot forget that God also told Jeremiah, "I will answer you" (33:3). God speaks to His children in many ways. We must take the time to determine how God communicates with us. It may be different from how He communicates with others. Whatever the method He uses, God will answer us, just as He promised. That answer may not take the form we anticipate or come when we desire, but He will respond. We may not understand the reasons behind His answer, but we can trust that whatever God decrees is His best for us.

We also must remember that God is omniscient. He can answer all our questions from His infinite knowledge. Just as God promised Jeremiah, He will "show you great and mighty things, which you do not know" (33:3). He knows the end of all things from their beginning, while we see merely one small moment in time. When we ask God to guide us, He directs our paths according to His plan for our lives.

Never underestimate the power of prayer. Remember that God wants us to come to Him so that He can answer us and share His wisdom. Do not be afraid to share everything with God. Pour out your heart to Him. Lay everything at the altar.

Increase the amount of time you spend in prayer. Listen for God's response. If you take that first step of calling out to Him, prayer will become an important part of an intimate and fulfilling relationship with God. Do it today. He waits to hear your voice!

†

THE BOOK OF

JEREMIAH

1 The words of Jeremiah the son of Hilkiah, of the priests who *were* [a]in Anathoth in the land of Benjamin, 2to whom
the word of the LORD came in the days of
[a]Josiah the son of Amon, king of Judah, [b]in
the thirteenth year of his reign. 3It came
also in the days of [a]Jehoiakim the son of
Josiah, king of Judah, [b]until the end of the
eleventh year of Zedekiah the son of Josiah,
king of Judah, [c]until the carrying away of
Jerusalem captive [d]in the fifth month.

The Prophet Is Called

4Then the word of the LORD came to me,
saying:

5 "Before I [a]formed you in the
womb [b]I knew you;
Before you were born I [c]sanctified you;
I ordained you a prophet
to the nations."

6Then said I:

[a]"Ah, Lord GOD!
Behold, I cannot speak,
for I *am* a youth."

7But the LORD said to me:

"Do not say, 'I *am* a youth,'
For you shall go to all to
whom I send you,
And [a]whatever I command
you, you shall speak.
8 [a]Do not be afraid of their faces,
For [b]I *am* with you to deliver
you," says the LORD.

9Then the LORD put forth His hand and
[a]touched my mouth, and the LORD said
to me:

"Behold, I have [b]put My words
in your mouth.
10 [a]See, I have this day set you over the
nations and over the kingdoms,
To [b]root out and to pull down,
To destroy and to throw down,
To build and to plant."

11Moreover the word of the LORD came
to me, saying, "Jeremiah, what do you see?"
And I said, "I see a branch of an almond
tree."
12Then the LORD said to me, "You have
seen well, for I am ready to perform My
word."
13And the word of the LORD came to me
the second time, saying, "What do you see?"
And I said, "I see [a]a boiling pot, and it is
facing away from the north."
14Then the LORD said to me:

"Out of the [a]north calamity
shall break forth
On all the inhabitants of the land.
15 For behold, I am [a]calling
All the families of the kingdoms
of the north," says the LORD;
"They shall come and [b]each
one set his throne

1:1 [a] Josh. 21:18; 1 Kin. 2:26; 1 Chr. 6:60; Is. 10:30; Jer. 29:27 1:2 [a] 1 Kin. 13:2; 2 Kin. 21:24; 2 Chr. 34:1; Jer. 3:6; 36:2 [b] Jer. 25:3
1:3 [a] 2 Kin. 23:34; 1 Chr. 3:15; 2 Chr. 36:5–8; Jer. 25:1 [b] 2 Kin. 24:17; 1 Chr. 3:15; 2 Chr. 36:11–13; Jer. 39:2 [c] Jer. 52:12 [d] 2 Kin. 25:8
1:5 [a] Is. 49:1, 5 [b] Ex. 33:12 [c] [Luke 1:15]; Gal. 1:15 1:6 [a] Ex. 4:10; 6:12, 30 1:7 [a] Num. 22:20, 38; Jer. 1:17; Matt. 28:20 1:8 [a] Ezek. 2:6;
3:9 [b] Ex. 3:12; Deut. 31:6; Josh. 1:5; Jer. 15:20; Heb. 13:6 1:9 [a] Is. 6:7; Mark 7:33–35 [b] Ex. 4:11–16; Deut. 18:18; Is. 51:16
1:10 [a] 1 Kin. 19:17 [b] Jer. 18:7–10; Ezek. 22:18; [2 Cor. 10:4, 5] 1:13 [a] Ezek. 11:3; 24:3
1:14 [a] Jer. 6:1 1:15 [a] Jer. 6:22; 25:9 [b] Is. 22:7; Jer. 39:3

At the entrance of the
gates of Jerusalem,
Against all its walls all around,
And against all the cities of Judah.
16 I will utter My judgments
Against them concerning
all their wickedness,
Because [a]they have forsaken Me,
Burned [b]incense to other gods,
And worshiped the works
of their own [c]hands.

17 "Therefore [a]prepare yourself and arise,
And speak to them all that
I command you.
[b]Do not be dismayed before
their faces,
Lest I dismay you before them.
18 For behold, I have made you this day
[a]A fortified city and an iron pillar,
And bronze walls against
the whole land—
Against the kings of Judah,
Against its princes,
Against its priests,
And against the people of the land.
19 They will fight against you,
But they shall not prevail
against you.
For I *am* with you," says the
LORD, "to deliver you."

God's Case Against Israel

2 Moreover the word of the LORD came to
me, saying, 2"Go and cry in the hearing
of Jerusalem, saying, 'Thus says the LORD:

"I remember you,
The kindness of your [a]youth,
The love of your betrothal,
[b]When you went after Me
in the wilderness,
In a land not sown.
3 [a]Israel *was* holiness to the LORD,
[b]The firstfruits of His increase.
[c]All that devour him will offend;
Disaster will [d]come upon
them," says the LORD.'"

4Hear the word of the LORD, O house of
Jacob and all the families of the house of
Israel. 5Thus says the LORD:

[a]"What injustice have your
fathers found in Me,
That they have gone far from Me,
[b]Have followed idols,
And have become idolaters?
6 Neither did they say,
'Where *is* the LORD,
Who [a]brought us up out of
the land of Egypt,
Who led us through [b]the
wilderness,
Through a land of deserts and pits,
Through a land of drought and
the shadow of death,
Through a land that no one crossed
And where no one dwelt?'
7 I brought you into [a]a
bountiful country,
To eat its fruit and its goodness.
But when you entered, you
[b]defiled My land
And made My heritage
an abomination.
8 The priests did not say,
'Where *is* the LORD?'
And those who handle the
[a]law did not know Me;
The rulers also transgressed
against Me;
[b]The prophets prophesied by Baal,
And walked after *things*
that do not profit.

9 "Therefore [a]I will yet bring charges
against you," says the LORD,
"And against your children's
children I will bring charges.
10 For pass beyond the coasts
of Cyprus[1] and see,
Send to Kedar[2] and consider diligently,
And see if there has been
such *a* [a]*thing*.
11 [a]Has a nation changed *its* gods,
Which *are* [b]not gods?

1:16 [a] Deut. 28:20; Jer. 17:13 [b] Is. 65:3, 4; Jer. 7:9 [c] Is. 37:19; Jer. 2:28 1:17 [a] 1 Kin. 18:46; 2 Kin. 4:29; Job 38:3; Luke 12:35; [1 Pet. 1:13] [b] Ezek. 2:6 1:18 [a] Is. 50:7; Jer. 6:27; 15:20 2:2 [a] Ezek. 16:8; Hos. 2:15 [b] Deut. 2:7; Jer. 2:6 2:3 [a] [Ex. 19:5, 6; Deut. 7:6; 14:2] [b] James 1:18; Rev. 14:4 [c] Jer. 12:14 [d] Gen. 12:3; Is. 41:11; Jer. 30:15, 16; 50:7 2:5 [a] Is. 5:4; Mic. 6:3 [b] 2 Kin. 17:15; Jer. 8:19; [Jon. 2:8]; Rom. 1:21 2:6 [a] Ex. 20:2; Is. 63:11 [b] Deut. 8:15; 32:10 2:7 [a] Num. 13:27 [b] Num. 35:33; Is. 24:5; Hos. 4:3 2:8 [a] Rom. 2:20 [b] Jer. 23:13 2:9 [a] Jer. 2:35; Ezek. 20:35, 36; Mic. 6:2 2:10 [a] Jer. 18:13 [1] Hebrew *Kittim*, western lands, especially Cyprus [2] In the northern Arabian desert, representative of the eastern cultures 2:11 [a] Mic. 4:5 [b] Ps. 115:4; Is. 37:19

[c]But My people have
changed their Glory
For *what* does not profit.
12 Be astonished, O heavens, at this,
And be horribly afraid;
Be very desolate," says the LORD.
13 "For My people have
committed two evils:
They have forsaken Me, the
[a]fountain of living waters,
And hewn themselves
cisterns—broken cisterns
that can hold no water.

14 "*Is* Israel [a]a servant?
Is he a homeborn *slave?*
Why is he plundered?
15 [a]The young lions roared at
him, *and* growled;
They made his land waste;
His cities are burned,
without inhabitant.
16 Also the people of Noph[1]
and [a]Tahpanhes
Have broken the crown of your head.
17 [a]Have you not brought this on yourself,
In that you have forsaken
the LORD your God
When [b]He led you in the way?
18 And now why take [a]the road to Egypt,
To drink the waters of [b]Sihor?
Or why take the road to [c]Assyria,
To drink the waters of the River?[1]
19 Your own wickedness will [a]correct you,
And your backslidings will rebuke you.
Know therefore and see that *it*
is an evil and bitter *thing*
That you have forsaken the
LORD your God,
And the fear of Me *is* not in you,"
Says the Lord GOD of hosts.

20 "For of old I have [a]broken your
yoke *and* burst your bonds;
And [b]you said, 'I will not transgress,'
When [c]on every high hill and
under every green tree
You lay down, [d]playing the harlot.
21 Yet I had [a]planted you a noble
vine, a seed of highest quality.
How then have you turned before Me
Into [b]the degenerate plant
of an alien vine?
22 For though you wash yourself
with lye, and use much soap,
Yet your iniquity is [a]marked before
Me," says the Lord GOD.

23 "How[a] can you say, 'I am not polluted,
I have not gone after the Baals'?
See your way in the valley;
Know what you have done:
You are a swift dromedary
breaking loose in her ways,
24 A wild donkey used to the wilderness,
That sniffs at the wind in her desire;
In her time of mating, who
can turn her away?
All those who seek her will
not weary themselves;
In her month they will find her.
25 Withhold your foot from
being unshod, and your
throat from thirst.
But you said, [a]'There is no hope.
No! For I have loved [b]aliens,
and after them I will go.'

26 "As the thief is ashamed
when he is found out,
So is the house of Israel ashamed;
They and their kings and their
princes, and their priests
and their [a]prophets,
27 Saying to a tree, 'You *are* my father,'
And to a [a]stone, 'You gave
birth to me.'
For they have turned *their* back
to Me, and not *their* face.
But in the time of their [b]trouble
They will say, 'Arise and save us.'
28 But [a]where *are* your gods that you
have made for yourselves?
Let them arise,
If they [b]can save you in the
time of your trouble;

2:11 [c] Ps. 106:20; Rom. 1:23 2:13 [a] Ps. 36:9; Jer. 17:13; [John 4:14] 2:14 [a] [Ex. 4:22] 2:15 [a] Is. 1:7; Jer. 50:17 2:16 [a] 2 Kin. 23:29–37; Jer. 43:7–9 [1] That is, Memphis in ancient Egypt 2:17 [a] Jer. 4:18 [b] Deut. 32:10 2:18 [a] Is. 30:1–3 [b] Josh. 13:3 [c] Hos. 5:13 [1] That is, the Euphrates 2:19 [a] Is. 3:9; Jer. 4:18; Hos. 5:5 2:20 [a] Lev. 26:13 [b] Ex. 19:8; Josh. 24:18; Judg. 10:16; 1 Sam. 12:10 [c] Deut. 12:2; Is. 57:5, 7; Jer. 3:6 [d] Ex. 34:15 2:21 [a] Ex. 15:17; Ps. 44:2; 80:8; Is. 5:2 [b] Deut. 32:32; Is. 5:4 2:22 [a] Job 14:16, 17; Jer. 17:1, 2; Hos. 13:12 2:23 [a] Prov. 30:12 2:25 [a] Is. 57:10; Jer. 18:12 [b] Jer. 3:13 2:26 [a] Is. 28:7; Jer. 5:31 2:27 [a] Jer. 3:9 [b] Judg. 10:10; Is. 26:16; Hos. 5:15 2:28 [a] Deut. 32:37; Judg. 10:14 [b] Is. 45:20

For [c]*according to* the number
of your cities
Are your gods, O Judah.

29 "Why will you plead with Me?
You all have transgressed against
Me," says the LORD.
30 "In vain I have [a]chastened
your children;
They [b]received no correction.
Your sword has [c]devoured
your prophets
Like a destroying lion.

31 "O generation, see the
word of the LORD!
Have I been a wilderness to Israel,
Or a land of darkness?
Why do My people say, 'We are lords;
[a]We will come no more to You'?
32 Can a virgin forget her ornaments,
Or a bride her attire?
Yet My people [a]have forgotten
Me days without number.

33 "Why do you beautify your
way to seek love?
Therefore you have also taught
The wicked women your ways.
34 Also on your skirts is found
[a]The blood of the lives of
the poor innocents.
I have not found it by secret search,
But plainly on all these things.
35 [a]Yet you say, 'Because I am innocent,
Surely His anger shall turn from me.'
Behold, [b]I will plead My
case against you,
[c]Because you say, 'I have not sinned.'
36 [a]Why do you gad about so much
to change your way?
Also [b]you shall be ashamed of Egypt
[c]as you were ashamed of Assyria.
37 Indeed you will go forth from him
With your hands on [a]your head;
For the LORD has rejected
your trusted allies,
And you will [b]not prosper by them.

Israel Is Shameless

3 "They say, 'If a man divorces his wife,
And she goes from him
And becomes another man's,
[a]May he return to her again?'
Would not that [b]land be
greatly polluted?
But you have [c]played the harlot
with many lovers;
[d]Yet return to Me," says the LORD.

2 "Lift up your eyes to [a]the
desolate heights and see:
Where have you not lain *with men?*
[b]By the road you have sat for them
Like an Arabian in the wilderness;
[c]And you have polluted the land
With your harlotries and
your wickedness.
3 Therefore the [a]showers
have been withheld,
And there has been no latter rain.
You have had a [b]harlot's forehead;
You refuse to be ashamed.
4 Will you not from this time cry to Me,
'My Father, You *are* [a]the
guide of [b]my youth?
5 [a]Will He remain angry forever?
Will He keep it to the end?'
Behold, you have spoken
and done evil things,
As you were able."

A Call to Repentance

6 The LORD said also to me in the days
of Josiah the king: "Have you seen what
[a]backsliding Israel has done? She has [b]gone
up on every high mountain and under every green tree, and there played the harlot.
7 [a]And I said, after she had done all these
things, 'Return to Me.' But she did not return. And her treacherous [b]sister Judah saw
it. 8 Then I saw that [a]for all the causes for
which backsliding Israel had committed
adultery, I had [b]put her away and given her
a certificate of divorce; [c]yet her treacherous sister Judah did not fear, but went and
played the harlot also. 9 So it came to pass,

2:28 [c] 2 Kin. 17:30, 31; Jer. 11:13 **2:30** [a] Is. 9:13 [b] Is. 1:5; Jer. 5:3; 7:28 [c] Neh. 9:26; Jer. 26:20–24; Acts 7:52; 1 Thess. 2:15 **2:31** [a] Deut. 32:15; Jer. 2:20, 25 **2:32** [a] Ps. 106:21; Is. 17:10; Jer. 3:21; 13:25; Hos. 8:14 **2:34** [a] 2 Kin. 21:16; 24:4; Ps. 106:38; Jer. 7:6; 19:4 **2:35** [a] Jer. 2:23, 29; Mal. 2:17; 3:8 [b] Jer. 2:9 [c] [Prov. 28:13; 1 John 1:8, 10] **2:36** [a] Jer. 31:22; Hos. 5:13; 12:1 [b] Is. 30:3 [c] 2 Chr. 28:16 **2:37** [a] 2 Sam. 13:19; Jer. 14:3, 4 [b] Jer. 37:7–10 **3:1** [a] Deut. 24:1–4 [b] Jer. 2:7 [c] Jer. 2:20; Ezek. 16:26 [d] Jer. 4:1; [Zech. 1:3] **3:2** [a] Deut. 12:2; Jer. 2:20; 3:21; 7:29 [b] Prov. 23:28 [c] Jer. 2:7 **3:3** [a] Lev. 26:19; Jer. 14:3–6 [b] Zeph. 3:5 **3:4** [a] Ps. 71:17; Prov. 2:17 [b] Jer. 2:2; Hos. 2:15 **3:5** [a] Ps. 103:9; [Is. 57:16]; Jer. 3:12 **3:6** [a] Jer. 7:24 [b] Jer. 2:20 **3:7** [a] 2 Kin. 17:13 [b] Jer. 3:11; Ezek. 16:47, 48 **3:8** [a] Ezek. 23:9 [b] 2 Kin. 17:6; Is. 50:1 [c] Ezek. 23:11

through her casual harlotry, that she [a]de-
filed the land and committed adultery with
[b]stones and trees. 10 And yet for all this her
treacherous sister Judah has not turned to
Me [a]with her whole heart, but in pretense,"
says the LORD.

11 Then the LORD said to me, [a]"Backsliding Israel has shown herself more righteous than treacherous Judah. 12 Go and
proclaim these words toward [a]the north,
and say:

'Return, backsliding Israel,'
says the LORD;
'I will not cause My anger
to fall on you.
For I *am* [b]merciful,' says the LORD;
'I will not remain angry forever.
13 [a]Only acknowledge your iniquity,
That you have transgressed
against the LORD your God,
And have [b]scattered your charms
To [c]alien deities [d]under
every green tree,
And you have not obeyed My
voice,' says the LORD.

14 "Return, O backsliding children," says
the LORD; [a]"for I am married to you. I will
take you, [b]one from a city and two from a
family, and I will bring you to [c]Zion. 15 And
I will give you [a]shepherds according to My
heart, who will [b]feed you with knowledge
and understanding.

16 "Then it shall come to pass, when you
are multiplied and [a]increased in the land in
those days," says the LORD, "that they will
say no more, 'The ark of the covenant of
the LORD.' [b]It shall not come to mind, nor
shall they remember it, nor shall they visit
it, nor shall it be made anymore.

17 "At that time Jerusalem shall be called
The Throne of the LORD, and all the nations shall be gathered to it, [a]to the name
of the LORD, to Jerusalem. No more shall
they [b]follow the dictates of their evil hearts.

18 "In those days [a]the house of Judah
shall walk with the house of Israel, and they
shall come together out of the land of [b]the
north to [c]the land that I have given as an
inheritance to your fathers.

19 "But I said:

'How can I put you among the children
And give you [a]a pleasant land,
A beautiful heritage of the
hosts of nations?'

"And I said:

'You shall call Me, [b]"My Father,"
And not turn away from Me.'
20 Surely, *as* a wife treacherously
departs from her husband,
So [a]have you dealt
treacherously with Me,
O house of Israel," says the LORD.

21 A voice was heard on [a]the
desolate heights,
Weeping *and* supplications of
the children of Israel.
For they have perverted their way;
They have forgotten the
LORD their God.

22 "Return, you backsliding children,
And I will [a]heal your backslidings."

"Indeed we do come to You,
For You are the LORD our God.
23 [a]Truly, in vain *is salvation*
hoped for from the hills,
And from the multitude of mountains;
[b]Truly, in the LORD our God
Is the salvation of Israel.
24 [a]For shame has devoured
The labor of our fathers
from our youth—
Their flocks and their herds,
Their sons and their daughters.
25 We lie down in our shame,
And our reproach covers us.
[a]For we have sinned against
the LORD our God,
We and our fathers,

3:9 [a] Jer. 2:7 [b] Is. 57:6; Jer. 2:27 3:10 [a] Jer. 12:2; Hos. 7:14 3:11 [a] Ezek. 16:51, 52 3:12 [a] 2 Kin. 17:6 [b] Ps. 86:15; Jer. 12:15; 31:20; 33:26
3:13 [a] Lev. 26:40; Deut. 30:1, 2; [Prov. 28:13; 1 John 1:9] [b] Ezek. 16:15 [c] Jer. 2:25 [d] Deut. 12:2 3:14 [a] Jer. 31:32; Hos. 2:19, 20 [b] Jer. 31:6
[c] [Rom. 11:5] 3:15 [a] Jer. 23:4; 31:10; [Ezek. 34:23]; Eph. 4:11 [b] Acts 20:28 3:16 [a] Is. 49:19; Jer. 23:3 [b] Is. 65:17 3:17 [a] Is. 60:9
[b] Deut. 29:19; Jer. 7:24 3:18 [a] Is. 11:13; Jer. 50:4; Ezek. 37:16–22; Hos. 1:11 [b] Jer. 31:8 [c] Amos 9:15 3:19 [a] Ps. 106:24
[b] Is. 63:16; Jer. 3:4 3:20 [a] Is. 48:8 3:21 [a] Is. 15:2 3:22 [a] Jer. 30:17; 33:6; Hos. 6:1; 14:4 3:23 [a] Ps. 121:1, 2
[b] Ps. 3:8; Prov. 21:31; Jer. 17:14; 31:7; Jon. 2:9 3:24 [a] Jer. 11:13; 14:20; Hos. 9:10 3:25 [a] Ezra 9:6, 7

From our youth even to this day,
And [b]have not obeyed the voice
of the LORD our God."

4 "If you will return, O Israel,"
says the LORD,
[a]"Return to Me;
And if you will put away your
abominations out of My sight,
Then you shall not be moved.
2 [a]And you shall swear, 'The LORD lives,'
[b]In truth, in judgment, and
in righteousness;
[c]The nations shall bless
themselves in Him,
And in Him they shall [d]glory."

3 For thus says the LORD to the men of
Judah and Jerusalem:

[a]"Break up your fallow ground,
And [b]do not sow among thorns.
4 [a]Circumcise yourselves to the LORD,
And take away the foreskins
of your hearts,
You men of Judah and
inhabitants of Jerusalem,
Lest My fury come forth like fire,
And burn so that no one can quench *it*,
Because of the evil of your doings."

An Imminent Invasion

5 Declare in Judah and proclaim in Jerusalem, and say:

[a]"Blow the trumpet in the land;
Cry, 'Gather together,'
And say, [b]'Assemble yourselves,
And let us go into the fortified cities.'
6 Set up the standard toward Zion.
Take refuge! Do not delay!
For I will bring disaster
from the [a]north,
And great destruction."

7 [a]The lion has come up from his thicket,
And [b]the destroyer of
nations is on his way.
He has gone forth from his place
[c]To make your land desolate.
Your cities will be laid waste,
Without inhabitant.
8 For this, [a]clothe yourself
with sackcloth,
Lament and wail.
For the fierce anger of the LORD
Has not turned back from us.

9 "And it shall come to pass in
that day," says the LORD,
"*That* the heart of the king shall perish,
And the heart of the princes;
The priests shall be astonished,
And the prophets shall wonder."

10 Then I said, "Ah, Lord GOD!
[a]Surely You have greatly deceived
this people and Jerusalem,
[b]Saying, 'You shall have peace,'
Whereas the sword reaches
to the heart."

11 At that time it will be said
To this people and to Jerusalem,
[a]"A dry wind of the desolate heights
blows in the wilderness
Toward the daughter of My people—
Not to fan or to cleanse—
12 A wind too strong for these
will come for Me;
Now [a]I will also speak judgment
against them."

13 "Behold, he shall come up like clouds,
And [a]his chariots like a whirlwind.
[b]His horses are swifter than eagles.
Woe to us, for we are plundered!"

14 O Jerusalem, [a]wash your heart
from wickedness,
That you may be saved.
How long shall your evil thoughts
lodge within you?
15 For a voice declares [a]from Dan
And proclaims affliction
from Mount Ephraim:

3:25 [b] Jer. 22:21 4:1 [a] Jer. 3:1, 22; 15:19; Joel 2:12 4:2 [a] Deut. 10:20; Is. 45:23; 65:16; Jer. 12:16 [b] Is. 48:1; Zech. 8:8 [c] [Gen. 22:18]; Ps. 72:18; Is. 65:16; Jer. 3:17; [Gal. 3:8] [d] Is. 45:25; Jer. 9:24; 1 Cor. 1:31; 2 Cor. 10:17 4:3 [a] Hos. 10:12 [b] Matt. 13:7 4:4 [a] Deut. 10:16; 30:6; Jer. 9:25, 26; [Rom. 2:28, 29; Col. 2:11] 4:5 [a] Jer. 6:1; Hos. 8:1 [b] Josh. 10:20; Jer. 8:14 4:6 [a] Jer. 1:13–15; 6:1, 22; 50:17 4:7 [a] 2 Kin. 24:1; Dan. 7:4 [b] Jer. 25:9; Ezek. 26:7–10 [c] Is. 1:7; 6:11; Jer. 2:15 4:8 [a] Is. 22:12; Jer. 6:26 4:10 [a] 2 Kin. 25:10–12; Ezek. 14:9; 2 Thess. 2:11 [b] Jer. 5:12; 14:13 4:11 [a] Jer. 51:1; Ezek. 17:10; Hos. 13:15 4:12 [a] Jer. 1:16 4:13 [a] Is. 5:28 [b] Deut. 28:49; Lam. 4:19; Hos. 8:1; Hab. 1:8 4:14 [a] Prov. 1:22; Is. 1:16; Jer. 13:27; James 4:8 4:15 [a] Jer. 8:16; 50:17

16 "Make mention to the nations,
Yes, proclaim against Jerusalem,
That watchers come from
a [a]far country
And raise their voice against
the cities of Judah.
17 [a]Like keepers of a field they are
against her all around,
Because she has been rebellious
against Me," says the LORD.
18 "Your[a] ways and your doings
Have procured these *things* for you.
This *is* your wickedness,
Because it is bitter,
Because it reaches to your heart."

Sorrow for the Doomed Nation

19 O my [a]soul, my soul!
I am pained in my very heart!
My heart makes a noise in me;
I cannot hold my peace,
Because you have heard, O my soul,
The sound of the trumpet,
The alarm of war.
20 [a]Destruction upon destruction is cried,
For the whole land is plundered.
Suddenly [b]my tents are plundered,
And my curtains in a moment.
21 How long will I see the standard,
And hear the sound of the trumpet?

22 "For My people *are* foolish,
They have not known Me.
They *are* silly children,
And they have no understanding.
[a]They *are* wise to do evil,
But to do good they have
no knowledge."

23 [a]I beheld the earth, and indeed *it*
was [b]without form, and void;
And the heavens, they *had* no light.
24 [a]I beheld the mountains, and
indeed they trembled,
And all the hills moved back and forth.
25 I beheld, and indeed *there*
was no man,
And [a]all the birds of the
heavens had fled.
26 I beheld, and indeed the fruitful
land *was* a [a]wilderness,
And all its cities were broken down
At the presence of the LORD,
By His fierce anger.

27 For thus says the LORD:

"The whole land shall be desolate;
[a]Yet I will not make a full end.
28 For this [a]shall the earth mourn,
And [b]the heavens above be black,
Because I have spoken.
I have [c]purposed and [d]will not relent,
Nor will I turn back from it.
29 The whole city shall flee
from the noise of the
horsemen and bowmen.
They shall go into thickets and
climb up on the rocks.
Every city *shall be* forsaken,
And not a man shall dwell in it.

30 "And *when* you *are* plundered,
What will you do?
Though you clothe yourself
with crimson,
Though you adorn *yourself*
with ornaments of gold,
[a]Though you enlarge your
eyes with paint,
In vain you will make yourself fair;
[b]*Your* lovers will despise you;
They will seek your life.

31 "For I have heard a voice as
of a woman in labor,
The anguish as of her who
brings forth her first child,
The voice of the daughter of
Zion bewailing herself;
She [a]spreads her hands, *saying,*
'Woe *is* me now, for my soul is weary
Because of murderers!'

The Justice of God's Judgment

5 "Run to and fro through the
streets of Jerusalem;
See now and know;

4:16 [a] Is. 39:3; Jer. 5:15 4:17 [a] 2 Kin. 25:1, 4 4:18 [a] Ps. 107:17; Is. 50:1; Jer. 2:17, 19 4:19 [a] 2 Kin. 25:11; 2 Chr. 36:20; Is. 15:5; 16:11; 21:3; 22:4; Jer. 9:1, 10; 20:9 4:20 [a] Ps. 42:7; Ezek. 7:26 [b] Jer. 10:20 4:22 [a] Jer. 9:3; 13:23; Rom. 16:19; 1 Cor. 14:20 4:23 [a] Is. 24:19 [b] Gen. 1:2 4:24 [a] Is. 5:25; Jer. 10:10; Ezek. 38:20 4:25 [a] Jer. 9:10; 12:4; Zeph. 1:3 4:26 [a] Jer. 9:10 4:27 [a] Jer. 5:10, 18; 30:11; 46:28 4:28 [a] Jer. 12:4, 11; 14:2; Hos. 4:3 [b] Is. 5:30; 50:3; Joel 2:30, 31 [c] Is. 46:10, 11; [Dan. 4:35] [d] [Num. 23:19]; Jer. 7:16; 23:30; 30:24 4:30 [a] 2 Kin. 9:30; Ezek. 23:40 [b] Jer. 22:20, 22; Lam. 1:2, 19; Ezek. 23:9, 10, 22 4:31 [a] Is. 1:15; Lam. 1:17

And seek in her open places
[a]If you can find a man,
[b]If there is *anyone* who
executes judgment,
Who seeks the truth,
[c]And I will pardon her.
2 [a]Though they say, 'As [b]the LORD lives,'
Surely they [c]swear falsely."

3 O LORD, *are* not [a]Your
eyes on the truth?
You have [b]stricken them,
But they have not grieved;
You have consumed them,
But [c]they have refused to
receive correction.
They have made their faces
harder than rock;
They have refused to return.

4 Therefore I said, "Surely
these *are* poor.
They are foolish;
For [a]they do not know the
way of the LORD,
The judgment of their God.
5 I will go to the great men
and speak to them,
For [a]they have known the
way of the LORD,
The judgment of their God."

But these have altogether
[b]broken the yoke
And burst the bonds.
6 Therefore [a]a lion from the
forest shall slay them,
[b]A wolf of the deserts shall
destroy them;
[c]A leopard will watch over their cities.
Everyone who goes out from
there shall be torn in pieces,
Because their transgressions
are many;
Their backslidings have increased.

7 "How shall I pardon you for this?
Your children have forsaken Me
And [a]sworn by *those* [b]*that are* not gods.
[c]When I had fed them to the full,
Then they committed adultery
And assembled themselves by
troops in the harlots' houses.
8 [a]They were *like* well-fed lusty stallions;
Every one neighed after
his neighbor's wife.
9 Shall I not punish *them* for these
things?" says the LORD.
"And shall I not [a]avenge Myself
on such a nation as this?

10 "Go up on her walls and destroy,
But do not make a [a]complete end.
Take away her branches,
For they *are* not the LORD's.
11 For [a]the house of Israel and
the house of Judah
Have dealt very treacherously
with Me," says the LORD.

12 [a]They have lied about the LORD,
And said, [b]"*It is* not He.
[c]Neither will evil come upon us,
Nor shall we see sword or famine.
13 And the prophets become wind,
For the word *is* not in them.
Thus shall it be done to them."

14 Therefore thus says the LORD God of
hosts:

"Because you speak this word,
[a]Behold, I will make My words
in your mouth fire,
And this people wood,
And it shall devour them.
15 Behold, I will bring a [a]nation
against you [b]from afar,
O house of Israel," says the LORD.
"It *is* a mighty nation,
It *is* an ancient nation,
A nation whose language
you do not know,
Nor can you understand what they say.
16 Their quiver *is* like an open tomb;
They *are* all mighty men.

5:1 [a] Ezek. 22:30 [b] Gen. 18:23–32 [c] Gen. 18:26 5:2 [a] Is. 48:1; Titus 1:16 [b] Jer. 4:2 [c] Jer. 7:9 5:3 [a] 2 Kin. 25:1; [2 Chr. 16:9; Jer. 16:17] [b] Is. 1:5; 9:13; Jer. 2:30 [c] Is. 9:13; Jer. 7:28; Zeph. 3:2 5:4 [a] Is. 27:11; Jer. 8:7; Hos. 4:6 5:5 [a] Mic. 3:1 [b] Ex. 32:25; Ps. 2:3; Jer. 2:20 5:6 [a] Jer. 4:7 [b] Ps. 104:20; Ezek. 22:27; Hab. 1:8; Zeph. 3:3 [c] Hos. 13:7 5:7 [a] Josh. 23:7; Jer. 12:16; Zeph. 1:5 [b] Deut. 32:21; Jer. 2:11; Gal. 4:8 [c] Deut. 32:15 5:8 [a] Jer. 13:27; 29:23; Ezek. 22:11 5:9 [a] Jer. 9:9 5:10 [a] Jer. 4:27 5:11 [a] Jer. 3:6, 7, 20 5:12 [a] 2 Chr. 36:16; Jer. 4:10 [b] Is. 28:15; 47:8; Jer. 23:17 [c] Jer. 14:13 5:14 [a] Is. 24:6; Jer. 1:9; 23:29; Hos. 6:5; Zech. 1:6 5:15 [a] Deut. 28:49; Is. 5:26; Jer. 1:15; 6:22 [b] Is. 39:3; Jer. 4:16

17 And they shall eat up your
[a]harvest and your bread,
Which your sons and
daughters should eat.
They shall eat up your flocks
and your herds;
They shall eat up your vines
and your fig trees;
They shall destroy your fortified cities,
In which you trust, with the sword.

18 "Nevertheless in those days," says the
LORD, "I [a]will not make a complete end of
you. 19 And it will be when you say, [a]'Why
does the LORD our God do all these *things*
to us?' then you shall answer them, 'Just as
you have [b]forsaken Me and served foreign
gods in your land, so [c]you shall serve aliens
in a land *that is* not yours.'

20 "Declare this in the house of Jacob
And proclaim it in Judah, saying,
21 'Hear this now, O [a]foolish people,
Without understanding,
Who have eyes and see not,
And who have ears and hear not:
22 [a]Do you not fear Me?' says the LORD.
'Will you not tremble at My presence,
Who have placed the sand as
the [b]bound of the sea,
By a perpetual decree, that it
cannot pass beyond it?
And though its waves toss
to and fro,
Yet they cannot prevail;
Though they roar, yet they
cannot pass over it.
23 But this people has a defiant
and rebellious heart;
They have revolted and departed.
24 They do not say in their heart,
"Let us now fear the LORD our God,
[a]Who gives rain, both the [b]former
and the latter, in its season.
[c]He reserves for us the appointed
weeks of the harvest."
25 [a]Your iniquities have turned
these *things* away,
And your sins have withheld
good from you.

26 'For among My people are
found wicked *men;*
They [a]lie in wait as one
who sets snares;
They set a trap;
They catch men.
27 As a cage is full of birds,
So their houses *are* full of deceit.
Therefore they have become
great and grown rich.
28 They have grown [a]fat, they
are sleek;
Yes, they surpass the deeds
of the wicked;
They do not plead [b]the cause,
The cause of the fatherless;
[c]Yet they prosper,
And the right of the needy
they do not defend.
29 [a]Shall I not punish *them* for these
things?' says the LORD.
'Shall I not avenge Myself on
such a nation as this?'

30 "An astonishing and [a]horrible thing
Has been committed in the land:
31 The prophets prophesy [a]falsely,
And the priests rule by
their *own* power;
And My people [b]love *to have it* so.
But what will you do in the end?

Impending Destruction from the North

6 "O you children of Benjamin,
Gather yourselves to flee from
the midst of Jerusalem!
Blow the trumpet in Tekoa,
And set up a signal-fire in
[a]Beth Haccerem;
[b]For disaster appears out of the north,
And great destruction.
2 I have likened the daughter of Zion
To a lovely and delicate woman.
3 The [a]shepherds with their
flocks shall come to her.

5:17 [a] Lev. 26:16; Deut. 28:31, 33; Jer. 8:16; 50:7, 17 5:18 [a] Jer. 30:11; Amos 9:8 5:19 [a] Deut. 29:24–29; 1 Kin. 9:8, 9; Jer. 13:22; 16:10–13 [b] Jer. 1:16; 2:13 [c] Deut. 28:48; Jer. 16:13 5:21 [a] Is. 6:9; Jer. 6:10; Ezek. 12:2; Matt. 13:14; John 12:40; Acts 28:26; Rom. 11:8 5:22 [a] Deut. 28:58; Ps. 119:120; Jer. 2:19; 10:7; [Rev. 15:4] [b] Job 26:10 5:24 [a] Ps. 147:8; Jer. 14:22; [Matt. 5:45]; Acts 14:17 [b] Deut. 11:14; Joel 2:23; James 5:7 [c] [Gen. 8:22] 5:25 [a] Jer. 3:3 5:26 [a] Ps. 10:9; Prov. 1:11; Jer. 18:22; Hab. 1:15 5:28 [a] Deut. 32:15 [b] Is. 1:23; Jer. 7:6; 22:3; Zech. 7:10 [c] Job 12:6; Ps. 73:12 5:29 [a] Jer. 5:9; Mal. 3:5 5:30 [a] Jer. 23:14; Hos. 6:10; 2 Tim. 4:3 5:31 [a] Jer. 14:14; Ezek. 13:6 [b] Mic. 2:11 6:1 [a] Neh. 3:14 [b] Jer. 4:6 6:3 [a] 2 Kin. 25:1–4; Jer. 4:17; 12:10

They shall pitch *their* tents
against her all around.
Each one shall pasture in
his own place."

4 "Prepare[a] war against her;
Arise, and let us go up [b]at noon.
Woe to us, for the day goes away,
For the shadows of the evening
are lengthening.
5 Arise, and let us go by night,
And let us destroy her palaces."

6 For thus has the LORD of hosts said:

"Cut down trees,
And build a mound against Jerusalem.
This *is* the city to be punished.
She *is* full of oppression in her midst.
7 [a]As a fountain wells up with water,
So she wells up with her wickedness.
[b]Violence and plundering
are heard in her.
Before Me continually *are*
grief and wounds.
8 Be instructed, O Jerusalem,
Lest [a]My soul depart from you;
Lest I make you desolate,
A land not inhabited."

9 Thus says the LORD of hosts:

"They shall thoroughly glean as a
vine the remnant of Israel;
As a grape-gatherer, put your hand
back into the branches."

10 To whom shall I speak
and give warning,
That they may hear?
Indeed their [a]ear *is* uncircumcised,
And they cannot give heed.
Behold, [b]the word of the LORD
is a reproach to them;
They have no delight in it.
11 Therefore I am full of the
fury of the LORD.
[a]I am weary of holding *it* in.
"I will pour it out [b]on the
children outside,
And on the assembly of
young men together;
For even the husband shall
be taken with the wife,
The aged with *him who is* full of days.
12 And [a]their houses shall be
turned over to others,
Fields and wives together;
For I will stretch out My hand
Against the inhabitants of the
land," says the LORD.
13 "Because from the least of them
even to the greatest of them,
Everyone *is* given to [a]covetousness;
And from the prophet
even to the [b]priest,
Everyone deals falsely.
14 They have also [a]healed the hurt
of My people slightly,
[b]Saying, 'Peace, peace!'
When *there is* no peace.
15 Were they [a]ashamed when they
had committed abomination?
No! They were not at all ashamed;
Nor did they know how to blush.
Therefore they shall fall
among those who fall;
At the time I punish them,
They shall be cast down,"
says the LORD.

16 Thus says the LORD:

"Stand in the ways and see,
And ask for the [a]old paths,
where the good way *is*,
And walk in it;
Then you will find [b]rest
for your souls.
But they said, 'We will not walk *in it*.'
17 Also, I set [a]watchmen over you, *saying*,
[b]'Listen to the sound of the trumpet!'
But they said, 'We will not listen.'
18 Therefore hear, you nations,
And know, O congregation,
what *is* among them.
19 [a]Hear, O earth!
Behold, I will certainly bring
[b]calamity on this people—
[c]The fruit of their thoughts,

6:4 [a] Jer. 51:27; Joel 3:9 [b] Jer. 15:8; Zeph. 2:4 6:7 [a] Is. 57:20 [b] Ps. 55:9 6:8 [a] Ezek. 23:18; Hos. 9:12 6:10 [a] Ex. 6:12; Jer. 5:21; 7:26; [Acts 7:51] [b] Jer. 8:9; 20:8 6:11 [a] Jer. 20:9 [b] Jer. 9:21 6:12 [a] Deut. 28:30; Jer. 8:10; 38:22 6:13 [a] Is. 56:11; Jer. 8:10; 22:17 [b] Jer. 5:31; 23:11; Mic. 3:5, 11 6:14 [a] Jer. 8:11–15; Ezek. 13:10 [b] Jer. 4:10; 23:17 6:15 [a] Jer. 3:3; 8:12 6:16 [a] Is. 8:20; Jer. 18:15; Mal. 4:4; Luke 16:29 [b] Matt. 11:29 6:17 [a] Is. 21:11; 58:1; Jer. 25:4; Ezek. 3:17; Hab. 2:1 [b] Deut. 4:1 6:19 [a] Is. 1:2 [b] Jer. 19:3, 15 [c] Prov. 1:31

Because they have not
heeded My words
Nor My law, but rejected it.
20 [a]For what purpose to Me
Comes frankincense [b]from Sheba,
And [c]sweet cane from a far country?
[d]Your burnt offerings *are*
not acceptable,
Nor your sacrifices sweet to Me."

21 Therefore thus says the LORD:

"Behold, I will lay stumbling
blocks before this people,
And the fathers and the sons
together shall fall on them.
The neighbor and his
friend shall perish."

22 Thus says the LORD:

"Behold, a people comes from
the [a]north country,
And a great nation will be raised from
the farthest parts of the earth.
23 They will lay hold on bow and spear;
They *are* cruel and have no mercy;
Their voice [a]roars like the sea;
And they ride on horses,
As men of war set in array against
you, O daughter of Zion."

24 We have heard the report of it;
Our hands grow feeble.
[a]Anguish has taken hold of us,
Pain as of a woman in labor.
25 Do not go out into the field,
Nor walk by the way.
Because of the sword
of the enemy,
Fear *is* on every side.
26 O daughter of my people,
[a]Dress in sackcloth
[b]And roll about in ashes!
[c]Make mourning *as for* an only
son, most bitter lamentation;
For the plunderer will suddenly
come upon us.

27 "I have set you *as* an assayer *and* [a]a
fortress among My people,
That you may know and test their way.
28 [a]They *are* all stubborn rebels,
[b]walking as slanderers.
They are [c]bronze and iron,
They *are* all corrupters;
29 The bellows blow fiercely,
The lead is consumed by the fire;
The smelter refines in vain,
For the wicked are not drawn off.
30 *People* will call them [a]rejected silver,
Because the LORD has rejected them."

Trusting in Lying Words
(cf. Jer. 26:4–6)

7 The word that came to Jeremiah from
the LORD, saying, 2 [a]"Stand in the gate
of the LORD's house, and proclaim there
this word, and say, 'Hear the word of the
LORD, all *you of* Judah who enter in at these
gates to worship the LORD!'" 3 Thus says the
LORD of hosts, the God of Israel: [a]"Amend
your ways and your doings, and I will cause
you to dwell in this place. 4 [a]Do not trust in
these lying words, saying, 'The temple of
the LORD, the temple of the LORD, the temple of the LORD *are* these.'
5 "For if you thoroughly amend your ways
and your doings, if you thoroughly [a]execute
judgment between a man and his neighbor,
6 *if* you do not oppress the stranger, the fatherless, and the widow, and do not shed
innocent blood in this place, [a]or walk after
other gods to your hurt, 7 [a]then I will cause
you to dwell in this place, in [b]the land that
I gave to your fathers forever and ever.
8 "Behold, you trust in [a]lying words that
cannot profit. 9 [a]Will you steal, murder,
commit adultery, swear falsely, burn incense to Baal, and [b]walk after other gods
whom you do not know, 10 [a]and *then* come
and stand before Me in this house [b]which
is called by My name, and say, 'We are delivered to do all these abominations'? 11 Has
[a]this house, which is called by My name,
become a [b]den of thieves in your eyes? Behold, I, even I, have seen *it*," says the LORD.

6:20 [a] Ps. 40:6; 50:7–9; Is. 1:11; 66:3; Amos 5:21; Mic. 6:6, 7 [b] Is. 60:6 [c] Is. 43:24 [d] Jer. 7:21–23 6:22 [a] Jer. 1:15; 10:22; 50:41–43 6:23 [a] Is. 5:30 6:24 [a] Jer. 4:31; 13:21; 49:24 6:26 [a] Jer. 4:8 [b] Jer. 25:34; Mic. 1:10 [c] Amos 8:10; [Zech. 12:10] 6:27 [a] Jer. 1:18 6:28 [a] Jer. 5:23 [b] Jer. 9:4 [c] Ezek. 22:18 6:30 [a] Is. 1:22; Jer. 7:29 7:2 [a] Jer. 17:19; 26:2 7:3 [a] Jer. 4:1; 18:11; 26:13 7:4 [a] Jer. 7:8; Mic. 3:11 7:5 [a] 1 Kin. 6:12; Jer. 21:12; 22:3 7:6 [a] Deut. 6:14, 15; Jer. 13:10 7:7 [a] Deut. 4:40 [b] Jer. 3:18 7:8 [a] Jer. 5:31; 14:13, 14 7:9 [a] 1 Kin. 18:21; Hos. 4:1, 2; Zeph. 1:5 [b] Ex. 20:3; Jer. 7:6; 19:4 7:10 [a] Ezek. 23:39 [b] Jer. 7:11, 14; 32:34; 34:15 7:11 [a] Is. 56:7 [b] Matt. 21:13; Mark 11:17; Luke 19:46

12“But go now to [a]My place which *was* in
Shiloh, [b]where I set My name at the first,
and see [c]what I did to it because of the wickedness of My people Israel. 13And now, because you have done all these works,” says
the LORD, “and I spoke to you, [a]rising up
early and speaking, but you did not hear,
and I [b]called you, but you did not answer,
14therefore I will do to the house which is
called by My name, in which you trust, and
to this place which I gave to you and your
fathers, as I have done to [a]Shiloh. 15And I
will cast you out of My sight, [a]as I have cast
out all your brethren—[b]the whole posterity of Ephraim.

16“Therefore [a]do not pray for this people, nor lift up a cry or prayer for them, nor
make intercession to Me; [b]for I will not hear
you. 17Do you not see what they do in the
cities of Judah and in the streets of Jerusalem? 18[a]The children gather wood, the fathers kindle the fire, and the women knead
dough, to make cakes for the queen of
heaven; and *they* [b]pour out drink offerings
to other gods, that they may provoke Me to
anger. 19[a]Do they provoke Me to anger?” says
the LORD. “*Do they* not *provoke* themselves,
to the shame of their own faces?”

20Therefore thus says the Lord GOD: “Behold, My anger and My fury will be poured
out on this place—on man and on beast,
on the trees of the field and on the fruit
of the ground. And it will burn and not be
quenched.”

21Thus says the LORD of hosts, the God of
Israel: [a]“Add your burnt offerings to your
sacrifices and eat meat. 22[a]For I did not
speak to your fathers, or command them in
the day that I brought them out of the land
of Egypt, concerning burnt offerings or
sacrifices. 23But this is what I commanded
them, saying, [a]‘Obey My voice, and [b]I will
be your God, and you shall be My people.
And walk in all the ways that I have commanded you, that it may be well with you.’
24[a]Yet they did not obey or incline their ear,
but [b]followed the counsels *and* the dictates
of their evil hearts, and [c]went backward
and not forward. 25Since the day that your
fathers came out of the land of Egypt until this day, I have even [a]sent to you all My
servants the prophets, daily rising up early
and sending *them.* 26[a]Yet they did not obey
Me or incline their ear, but [b]stiffened their
neck. [c]They did worse than their fathers.

27“Therefore [a]you shall speak all these
words to them, but they will not obey you.
You shall also call to them, but they will
not answer you.

Judgment on Obscene Religion

28“So you shall say to them, ‘This *is* a
nation that does not obey the voice of
the LORD their God [a]nor receive correction. [b]Truth has perished and has been
cut off from their mouth. 29[a]Cut off your
hair and cast *it* away, and take up a lamentation on the desolate heights; for the
LORD has rejected and forsaken the generation of His wrath.’ 30For the children of
Judah have done evil in My sight,” says the
LORD. [a]“They have set their abominations
in the house which is called by My name,
to pollute it. 31And they have built the [a]high
places of Tophet, which *is* in the Valley of
the Son of Hinnom, to [b]burn their sons and
their daughters in the fire, [c]which I did not
command, nor did it come into My heart.

32“Therefore behold, [a]the days are coming,” says the LORD, “when it will no more
be called Tophet, or the Valley of the Son
of Hinnom, but the Valley of Slaughter;
[b]for they will bury in Tophet until there is
no room. 33The [a]corpses of this people will
be food for the birds of the heaven and for
the beasts of the earth. And no one will
frighten *them away.* 34Then I will cause to
[a]cease from the cities of Judah and from
the streets of Jerusalem the voice of mirth
and the voice of gladness, the voice of the
bridegroom and the voice of the bride. For
[b]the land shall be desolate.

7:12 [a] Josh. 18:1; Judg. 18:31 [b] Deut. 12:11 [c] 1 Sam. 4:10; Ps. 78:60; Jer. 26:6 **7:13** [a] 2 Chr. 36:15; Jer. 11:7 [b] Prov. 1:24; Is. 65:12; 66:4 **7:14** [a] 1 Sam. 4:10, 11; Ps. 78:60; Jer. 26:6, 9 **7:15** [a] 2 Kin. 17:23 [b] Ps. 78:67; Hos. 7:13; 9:13; 12:1 **7:16** [a] Ex. 32:10; Deut. 9:14; Jer. 11:14 [b] Jer. 15:1 **7:18** [a] Jer. 44:17 [b] Jer. 19:13 **7:19** [a] Deut. 32:16, 21 **7:21** [a] Is. 1:11; Jer. 6:20; Hos. 8:13; Amos 5:21, 22 **7:22** [a] 1 Sam. 15:22; Ps. 51:16; [Hos. 6:6] **7:23** [a] Ex. 15:26; 16:32; Deut. 6:3 [b] [Ex. 19:5, 6]; Lev. 26:12; [Jer. 11:4; 13:11] **7:24** [a] Ps. 81:11; Jer. 11:8 [b] Deut. 29:19; Jer. 9:14 [c] Jer. 32:33 **7:25** [a] 2 Chr. 36:15; Jer. 25:4; 29:19; Mark 12:1–10; Luke 11:47–49 **7:26** [a] Jer. 11:8 [b] Neh. 9:17 [c] Jer. 16:12; Matt. 23:32 **7:27** [a] Jer. 1:7; 26:2; 37:14, 15; 43:1–4; Ezek. 2:7 **7:28** [a] Jer. 5:3 [b] Jer. 9:3 **7:29** [a] Job 1:20; Is. 15:2; Jer. 48:37; Mic. 1:16 **7:30** [a] 2 Kin. 21:4; 2 Chr. 33:3–5, 7; Jer. 32:34, 35; Ezek. 7:20; Dan. 9:27; 11:31 **7:31** [a] 2 Kin. 23:10; Jer. 19:5; 32:35 [b] Lev. 18:21; 2 Kin. 17:17; Ps. 106:38 [c] Deut. 17:3 **7:32** [a] Jer. 19:6 [b] 2 Kin. 23:10; Jer. 19:11 **7:33** [a] Jer. 9:22; 19:11; Ezek. 6:5 **7:34** [a] Is. 24:7, 8; Jer. 16:9; 25:10; Ezek. 26:13; Hos. 2:11; Rev. 18:23 [b] Lev. 26:33; Is. 1:7; Jer. 4:27

8 "At that time," says the LORD, "they
shall bring out the bones of the kings
of Judah, and the bones of its princes, and
the bones of the priests, and the bones of
the prophets, and the bones of the inhabitants of Jerusalem, out of their graves.
2They shall spread them before the sun
and the moon and all the host of heaven,
which they have loved and which they have
served and after which they have walked,
which they have sought and [a]which they
have worshiped. They shall not be gathered [b]nor buried; they shall be like refuse
on the face of the earth. 3Then [a]death shall
be chosen rather than life by all the residue
of those who remain of this evil family, who
remain in all the places where I have driven
them," says the LORD of hosts.

The Peril of False Teaching

4"Moreover you shall say to them, 'Thus
says the LORD:

"Will they fall and not rise?
Will one turn away and not return?
5 Why has this people [a]slidden back,
Jerusalem, in a perpetual backsliding?
[b]They hold fast to deceit,
[c]They refuse to return.
6 [a]I listened and heard,
But they do not speak aright.
[b]No man repented of his wickedness,
Saying, 'What have I done?'
Everyone turned to his own course,
As the horse rushes into the battle.

7 "Even [a]the stork in the heavens
Knows her appointed times;
And the turtledove, the swift,
and the swallow
Observe the time of their coming.
But [b]My people do not know the
judgment of the LORD.

8 "How can you say, 'We *are* wise,
[a]And the law of the LORD *is* with us'?
Look, the false pen of the scribe
certainly works falsehood.
9 [a]The wise men are ashamed,
They are dismayed and taken.
Behold, they have rejected
the word of the LORD;
So [b]what wisdom do they have?
10 Therefore [a]I will give their
wives to others,
And their fields to those who
will inherit *them;*
Because from the least
even to the greatest
Everyone is given to [b]covetousness;
From the prophet even to the priest
Everyone deals falsely.
11 For they have [a]healed the hurt of the
daughter of My people slightly,
Saying, [b]'Peace, peace!'
When *there is* no peace.
12 Were they [a]ashamed when they
had committed abomination?
No! They were not at all ashamed,
Nor did they know how to blush.
Therefore they shall fall
among those who fall;
In the time of their punishment
They shall be cast down,"
says the LORD.

13 "I will surely consume them,"
says the LORD.
"No grapes *shall be* [a]on the vine,
Nor figs on the [b]fig tree,
And the leaf shall fade;
And *the things* I have given them
shall [c]pass away from them."'"

14 "Why do we sit still?
[a]Assemble yourselves,
And let us enter the fortified cities,
And let us be silent there.
For the LORD our God has
put us to silence
And given us [b]water of gall to drink,
Because we have sinned
against the LORD.

15 "*We* [a]looked for peace, but
no good *came;*

8:2 [a] 2 Kin. 23:5; Jer. 19:13; Ezek. 8:16; Zeph. 1:5; Acts 7:42 [b] Jer. 22:19 8:3 [a] Job 3:21, 22; 7:15, 16; Jon. 4:3; Rev. 9:6 8:5 [a] Jer. 7:24 [b] Jer. 9:6 [c] Jer. 5:3 8:6 [a] Ps. 14:2; [Is. 30:18; Mal. 3:16; 2 Pet. 3:9] [b] Ezek. 22:30; Mic. 7:2; Rev. 9:20 8:7 [a] Prov. 6:6–8; Song 2:12; Is. 1:3; Matt. 16:2, 3 [b] Jer. 5:4; 9:3 8:8 [a] Rom. 2:17 8:9 [a] Is. 19:11; Jer. 6:15; [1 Cor. 1:27] [b] Is. 44:25; Jer. 4:22 8:10 [a] Deut. 28:30; Amos 5:11; Zeph. 1:13 [b] Is. 56:11; 57:17; Jer. 6:13 8:11 [a] Jer. 6:14 [b] Ezek. 13:10 8:12 [a] Ps. 52:1, 7; Is. 3:9; Jer. 3:3; 6:15; Zeph. 3:5 8:13 [a] Jer. 5:17; 7:20; Joel 1:17 [b] Matt. 21:19; Luke 13:6 [c] Deut. 28:39, 40 8:14 [a] Jer. 4:5 [b] Deut. 29:18; Ps. 69:21; Jer. 9:15; Lam. 3:19; Matt. 27:34 8:15 [a] Jer. 14:19

And for a time of health, and
there was trouble!
16 The snorting of His horses
was heard from [a]Dan.
The whole land trembled at the sound
of the neighing of His [b]strong ones;
For they have come and devoured
the land and all that is in it,
The city and those who dwell in it."

17 "For behold, I will send
serpents among you,
Vipers which cannot be [a]charmed,
And they shall bite you,"
says the LORD.

The Prophet Mourns for the People

18 I would comfort myself in sorrow;
My heart *is* faint in me.
19 Listen! The voice,
The cry of the daughter of my people
From [a]a far country:
"*Is* not the LORD in Zion?
Is not her King in her?"

"Why have they provoked Me to anger
With their carved images—
With foreign idols?"

20 "The harvest is past,
The summer is ended,
And we are not saved!"

21 [a]For the hurt of the daughter
of my people I am hurt.
I am [b]mourning;
Astonishment has taken hold of me.
22 *Is there* no [a]balm in Gilead,
Is there no physician there?
Why then is there no recovery
For the health of the daughter
of my people?

9 Oh, [a]that my head were waters,
And my eyes a fountain of tears,
That I might weep day and night
For the slain of the daughter
of my people!
2 Oh, that I had in the wilderness
A lodging place for travelers;
That I might leave my people,
And go from them!
For [a]they *are* all adulterers,
An assembly of treacherous men.

3 "And *like* their bow [a]they have
bent their tongues *for* lies.
They are not valiant for the
truth on the earth.
For they proceed from [b]evil to evil,
And they [c]do not know
Me," says the LORD.
4 "Everyone[a] take heed to his neighbor,
And do not trust any brother;
For every brother will utterly supplant,
And every neighbor will
[b]walk with slanderers.
5 Everyone will [a]deceive his neighbor,
And will not speak the truth;
They have taught their
tongue to speak lies;
They weary themselves to
commit iniquity.
6 Your dwelling place *is* in
the midst of deceit;
Through deceit they refuse to
know Me," says the LORD.

7 Therefore thus says the LORD of hosts:
"Behold, [a]I will refine them
and try them;
[b]For how shall I deal with the
daughter of My people?
8 Their tongue *is* an arrow shot out;
It speaks [a]deceit;
One speaks [b]peaceably to his
neighbor with his mouth,
But in his heart he lies in wait.
9 [a]"Shall I not punish them for these
things?" says the LORD.
"Shall I not avenge Myself on
such a nation as this?"

10 I will take up a weeping and
wailing for the mountains,
And [a]for the dwelling places of the
wilderness a lamentation,

8:16 [a] Judg. 18:29; Jer. 4:15 [b] Jer. 47:3 8:17 [a] Ps. 58:4, 5 8:19 [a] Is. 39:3; Jer. 5:15 8:21 [a] Jer. 9:1 [b] Jer. 14:2; Joel 2:6; Nah. 2:10 8:22 [a] Gen. 37:25; Jer. 46:11 9:1 [a] Is. 22:4; Jer. 10:19; Lam. 2:18 9:2 [a] Jer. 5:7, 8; 23:10; Hos. 4:2 9:3 [a] Ps. 64:3; Is. 59:4; Jer. 9:8; Hos. 4:1, 2 [b] Jer. 4:22; 13:23 [c] Judg. 2:10; 1 Sam. 2:12; Jer. 4:22; Hos. 4:1; 1 Cor. 15:34 9:4 [a] Ps. 12:2; Prov. 26:24, 25; Jer. 9:8; Mic. 7:5, 6 [b] Ps. 15:3; Prov. 10:18; Jer. 6:28 9:5 [a] Ps. 36:3, 4; Is. 59:4 9:7 [a] Is. 1:25; Jer. 6:27; Mal. 3:3 [b] Hos. 11:8 9:8 [a] Ps. 12:2 [b] Ps. 55:21 9:9 [a] Is. 1:24; Jer. 5:9, 29 9:10 [a] Jer. 4:26; Hos. 4:3

Because they are burned up,
So that no one can pass through;
Nor can *men* hear the
voice of the cattle.
[b]Both the birds of the heavens
and the beasts have fled;
They are gone.

11 "I will make Jerusalem [a]a heap
of ruins, [b]a den of jackals.
I will make the cities of Judah
desolate, without an inhabitant."

12[a]Who *is* the wise man who may understand this? And *who is he* to whom the
mouth of the LORD has spoken, that he
may declare it? Why does the land perish
and burn up like a wilderness, so that no
one can pass through?
13And the LORD said, "Because they have
forsaken My law which I set before them,
and have [a]not obeyed My voice, nor walked
according to it, 14but they have [a]walked according to the dictates of their own hearts
and after the Baals, [b]which their fathers
taught them," 15therefore thus says the
LORD of hosts, the God of Israel: "Behold,
I will [a]feed them, this people, [b]with wormwood, and give them water of gall to drink.
16I will [a]scatter them also among the Gentiles, whom neither they nor their fathers
have known. [b]And I will send a sword after
them until I have consumed them."

The People Mourn in Judgment

17Thus says the LORD of hosts:

"Consider and call for [a]the
mourning women,
That they may come;
And send for skillful *wailing* women,
That they may come.
18 Let them make haste
And take up a wailing for us,
That [a]our eyes may run with tears,
And our eyelids gush with water.
19 For a voice of wailing is
heard from Zion:
'How we are plundered!
We are greatly ashamed,
Because we have forsaken the land,
Because we have been cast
out of [a]our dwellings.'"
20 Yet hear the word of the
LORD, O women,
And let your ear receive the
word of His mouth;
Teach your daughters wailing,
And everyone her neighbor
a lamentation.
21 For death has come through
our windows,
Has entered our palaces,
To kill off [a]the children—*no
longer to be* outside!
And the young men—*no
longer* on the streets!
22Speak, "Thus says the LORD:

'Even the carcasses of men shall fall
[a]as refuse on the open field,
Like cuttings after the harvester,
And no one shall gather *them.*'"

23Thus says the LORD:

[a]"Let not the wise *man* glory
in his wisdom,
Let not the mighty *man*
glory in his [b]might,
Nor let the rich *man* glory
in his riches;
24 But [a]let him who glories glory in this,
That he understands and knows Me,
That I *am* the LORD, exercising
lovingkindness, judgment, and
righteousness in the earth.
[b]For in these I delight," says the LORD.

25"Behold, the days are coming," says
the LORD, "that [a]I will punish all *who are*
circumcised with the uncircumcised—
26Egypt, Judah, Edom, the people of Ammon, Moab, and all *who are* in the [a]farthest

---

9:10 [b] Jer. 4:25; Hos. 4:3 9:11 [a] Is. 25:2; Jer. 19:3, 8; 26:9 [b] Is. 13:22; 34:13 9:12 [a] Ps. 107:43; Is. 42:23; Hos. 14:9 9:13 [a] Jer. 3:25; 7:24 9:14 [a] Jer. 7:24; 11:8; Rom. 1:21–24 [b] Gal. 1:14; 1 Pet. 1:18 9:15 [a] Ps. 80:5 [b] Deut. 29:18; Jer. 8:14; 23:15; Lam. 3:15 9:16 [a] Lev. 26:33; Deut. 28:64; Jer. 15:2–4 [b] Lev. 26:33; Jer. 44:27; Ezek. 5:2 9:17 [a] 2 Chr. 35:25; Job 3:8; Eccl. 12:5; Amos 5:16; Matt. 9:23 9:18 [a] Is. 22:4; Jer. 9:1; 14:17 9:19 [a] Lev. 18:28 9:21 [a] 2 Chr. 36:17; Jer. 6:11; 18:21; Ezek. 9:5, 6 9:22 [a] Ps. 83:10; Is. 5:25; Jer. 8:1, 2 9:23 [a] [Eccl. 9:11; Is. 47:10]; Ezek. 28:3–7 [b] Ps. 33:16–18 9:24 [a] Ps. 20:7; 44:8; Is. 41:16; Jer. 4:2; 1 Cor. 1:31; 2 Cor. 10:17; [Gal. 6:14] [b] Is. 61:8; Mic. 7:18 9:25 [a] [Jer. 4:4; Rom. 2:28, 29] 9:26 [a] Jer. 25:23

corners, who dwell in the wilderness. For all *these* nations *are* uncircumcised, and all the house of Israel *are* [b]uncircumcised in the heart."

Idols and the True God

10 Hear the word which the LORD speaks to you, O house of Israel.
2Thus says the LORD:

[a]"Do not learn the way of the Gentiles;
Do not be dismayed at the
signs of heaven,
For the Gentiles are dismayed at them.
3 For the customs of the
peoples *are* futile;
For [a]*one* cuts a tree from the forest,
The work of the hands of the
workman, with the ax.
4 They decorate it with silver and gold;
They [a]fasten it with nails
and hammers
So that it will not topple.
5 They *are* upright, like a palm tree,
And [a]they cannot speak;
They must be [b]carried,
Because they cannot go *by themselves.*
Do not be afraid of them,
For [c]they cannot do evil,
Nor can they do any good."

6 Inasmuch as *there is* none
[a]like You, O LORD
(You *are* great, and Your name
is great in might),
7 [a]Who would not fear You,
O King of the nations?
For this is Your rightful due.
For [b]among all the wise
men of the nations,
And in all their kingdoms,
There is none like You.
8 But they are altogether
[a]dull-hearted and foolish;
A wooden idol *is* a worthless doctrine.
9 Silver is beaten into plates;
It is brought from Tarshish,
And [a]gold from Uphaz,
The work of the craftsman
And of the hands of the metalsmith;
Blue and purple *are* their clothing;
They *are* all [b]the work of skillful *men.*
10 But the LORD *is* the true God;
He *is* [a]the living God and the
[b]everlasting King.
At His wrath the earth will tremble,
And the nations will not be able
to endure His indignation.

11Thus you shall say to them: [a]"The gods
that have not made the heavens and the
earth [b]shall perish from the earth and from
under these heavens."

12 He [a]has made the earth by His power,
He has [b]established the
world by His wisdom,
And [c]has stretched out the
heavens at His discretion.
13 [a]When He utters His voice,
There is a multitude of waters
in the heavens:
[b]"And He causes the vapors to ascend
from the ends of the earth.
He makes lightning for the rain,
He brings the wind out of
His treasuries."[1]

14 [a]Everyone is [b]dull-hearted,
without knowledge;
[c]Every metalsmith is put to
shame by an image;
[d]For his molded image *is* falsehood,
And *there is* no breath in them.
15 They *are* futile, a work of errors;
In the time of their punishment
they shall perish.
16 [a]The Portion of Jacob *is* not like them,
For He *is* the Maker of all *things,*
And [b]Israel *is* the tribe of
His inheritance;
[c]The LORD of hosts *is* His name.

The Coming Captivity of Judah

17 [a]Gather up your wares from the land,
O inhabitant of the fortress!

9:26 [b] Lev. 26:41; Jer. 4:4; 6:10; Ezek. 44:7; [Rom. 2:28] 10:2 [a] [Lev. 18:3; 20:23; Deut. 12:30] 10:3 [a] Is. 40:19; 45:20 10:4 [a] Is. 41:7 10:5 [a] Ps. 115:5; Is. 46:7; Jer. 10:5; 1 Cor. 12:2 [b] Ps. 115:7; Is. 46:1, 7 [c] Is. 41:23, 24 10:6 [a] Ex. 15:11; Deut. 33:26; Ps. 86:8, 10; Is. 46:5–9; Jer. 10:16 10:7 [a] Jer. 5:22; Rev. 15:4 [b] Ps. 89:6 10:8 [a] Ps. 115:8; Hab. 2:18 10:9 [a] Dan. 10:5 [b] Ps. 115:4 10:10 [a] 1 Tim. 6:17 [b] Ps. 10:16 10:11 [a] Ps. 96:5 [b] Is. 2:18; Zeph. 2:11 10:12 [a] Gen. 1:1, 6, 7; Jer. 51:15 [b] Ps. 93:1 [c] Job 9:8; Ps. 104:2; Is. 40:22 10:13 [a] Job 38:34 [b] Ps. 135:7 [1] Psalm 135:7 10:14 [a] Jer. 51:17 [b] Prov. 30:2 [c] Is. 42:17; 44:11 [d] Hab. 2:18 10:16 [a] Ps. 16:5; Jer. 51:19; Lam. 3:24 [b] Deut. 32:9; Ps. 74:2 [c] Is. 47:4 10:17 [a] Jer. 6:1

18For thus says the LORD:

"Behold, I will [a]throw out at this time
The inhabitants of the land,
And will distress them,
[b]That they may find *it so.*"

19 [a]Woe is me for my hurt!
My wound is severe.
But I say, [b]"Truly this *is* an infirmity,
And [c]I must bear it."
20 [a]My tent is plundered,
And all my cords are broken;
My children have gone from me,
And they *are* [b]no more.
There is no one to pitch
my tent anymore,
Or set up my curtains.

21 For the shepherds have
become dull-hearted,
And have not sought the LORD;
Therefore they shall not prosper,
And all their flocks shall
be [a]scattered.
22 Behold, the noise of the
report has come,
And a great commotion out
of the [a]north country,
To make the cities of Judah
desolate, a [b]den of jackals.

23 O LORD, I know the [a]way of
man *is* not in himself;
It is not in man who walks to
direct his own steps.
24 O LORD, [a]correct me, but
with justice;
Not in Your anger, lest You
bring me to nothing.
25 [a]Pour out Your fury on the Gentiles,
[b]who do not know You,
And on the families who do
not call on Your name;
For they have eaten up Jacob,
[c]Devoured him and consumed him,
And made his dwelling
place desolate.

The Broken Covenant

11 The word that came to Jeremiah from
the LORD, saying, 2"Hear the words of
this covenant, and speak to the men of Judah and to the inhabitants of Jerusalem;
3and say to them, 'Thus says the LORD God
of Israel: [a]"Cursed *is* the man who does not
obey the words of this covenant 4which
I commanded your fathers in the day I
brought them out of the land of Egypt,
[a]from the iron furnace, saying, [b]'Obey My
voice, and do according to all that I command you; so shall you be My people, and
I will be your God,' 5that I may establish the
[a]oath which I have sworn to your fathers,
to give them [b]'a land flowing with milk and
honey,'[1] as *it is* this day."'"
And I answered and said, "So be it,
LORD."
6Then the LORD said to me, "Proclaim
all these words in the cities of Judah and
in the streets of Jerusalem, saying: 'Hear
the words of this covenant [a]and do them.
7For I earnestly exhorted your fathers in
the day I brought them up out of the land
of Egypt, until this day, [a]rising early and
exhorting, saying, "Obey My voice." 8[a]Yet
they did not obey or incline their ear, but
[b]everyone followed the dictates of his evil
heart; therefore I will bring upon them all
the words of this covenant, which I commanded *them* to do, but *which* they have
not done.'"
9And the LORD said to me, [a]"A conspiracy has been found among the men of
Judah and among the inhabitants of Jerusalem. 10They have turned back to [a]the
iniquities of their forefathers who refused
to hear My words, and they have gone after other gods to serve them; the house of
Israel and the house of Judah have broken My covenant which I made with their
fathers."
11Therefore thus says the LORD: "Behold, I will surely bring calamity on them
which they will not be able to escape; and
[a]though they cry out to Me, I will not listen to them. 12Then the cities of Judah and

---

10:18 [a] 1 Sam. 25:29; 2 Chr. 36:20 [b] Ezek. 6:10 **10:19** [a] Jer. 8:21 [b] Ps. 77:10 [c] Mic. 7:9 **10:20** [a] Jer. 4:20; Lam. 2:4 [b] Jer. 31:15; Lam. 1:5 **10:21** [a] Jer. 23:2 **10:22** [a] Jer. 5:15 [b] Jer. 9:11 **10:23** [a] Prov. 16:1; 20:24 **10:24** [a] Ps. 6:1; 38:1; Jer. 30:11 **10:25** [a] Ps. 79:6, 7; Zeph. 3:8 [b] Job 18:21; 1 Thess. 4:5; [2 Thess. 1:8] [c] Jer. 8:16 **11:3** [a] Deut. 27:26; [Jer. 17:5]; Gal. 3:10 **11:4** [a] Deut. 4:20; 1 Kin. 8:51 [b] Lev. 26:3; Deut. 11:27; Jer. 7:23 **11:5** [a] Ex. 13:5; Deut. 7:12; Ps. 105:9; Jer. 32:22 [b] Ex. 3:8 [1] Exodus 3:8 **11:6** [a] Deut. 17:19; [Rom. 2:13]; James 1:22 **11:7** [a] Jer. 35:15 **11:8** [a] Jer. 7:26 [b] Jer. 13:10 **11:9** [a] Ezek. 22:25; Hos. 6:9 **11:10** [a] 1 Sam. 15:11; Jer. 3:10, 11; Ezek. 20:18 **11:11** [a] Ps. 18:41; Prov. 1:28; Is. 1:15; Jer. 14:12; Ezek. 8:18; Mic. 3:4; Zech. 7:13

the inhabitants of Jerusalem will go and
[a]cry out to the gods to whom they offer incense, but they will not save them at all in
the time of their trouble. 13For *according to*
the number of your [a]cities were your gods,
O Judah; and *according to* the number of
the streets of Jerusalem you have set up altars to *that* shameful thing, altars to burn
incense to Baal.

14"So [a]do not pray for this people, or lift
up a cry or prayer for them; for I will not
hear *them* in the time that they cry out to
Me because of their trouble.

15 "What[a] has My beloved to
do in My house,
Having [b]done lewd deeds with many?
And [c]the holy flesh has
passed from you.
When you do evil, then you [d]rejoice.
16 The LORD called your name,
[a]Green Olive Tree, Lovely
and of Good Fruit.
With the noise of a great tumult
He has kindled fire on it,
And its branches are broken.

17"For the LORD of hosts, [a]who planted
you, has pronounced doom against you
for the evil of the house of Israel and of
the house of Judah, which they have done
against themselves to provoke Me to anger
in offering incense to Baal."

Jeremiah's Life Threatened

18Now the LORD gave me knowledge *of it,*
and I know *it;* for You showed me their doings. 19But I *was* like a docile lamb brought
to the slaughter; and I did not know that
they had devised schemes against me, *saying,* "Let us destroy the tree with its fruit,
[a]and let us cut him off from [b]the land of
the living, that his name may be remembered no more."

20 But, O LORD of hosts,
You who judge righteously,
[a]Testing the mind and the heart,
Let me see Your [b]vengeance on them,
For to You I have revealed my cause.

21"Therefore thus says the LORD concerning the men of [a]Anathoth who seek
your life, saying, [b]'Do not prophesy in
the name of the LORD, lest you die by our
hand'— 22therefore thus says the LORD
of hosts: 'Behold, I will punish them. The
young men shall die by the sword, their
sons and their daughters shall [a]die by famine; 23and there shall be no remnant of
them, for I will bring catastrophe on the
men of Anathoth, *even* [a]the year of their
punishment.'"

Jeremiah's Question

12 Righteous [a]*are* You, O LORD,
when I plead with You;
Yet let me talk with You about
Your judgments.
[b]Why does the way of the
wicked prosper?
Why are those happy who
deal so treacherously?
2 You have planted them, yes,
they have taken root;
They grow, yes, they bear fruit.
[a]You *are* near in their mouth
But far from their mind.

3 But You, O LORD, [a]know me;
You have seen me,
And You have [b]tested my
heart toward You.
Pull them out like sheep
for the slaughter,
And prepare them for [c]the
day of slaughter.
4 How long will [a]the land mourn,
And the herbs of every field
wither?
[b]The beasts and birds are
consumed,
[c]For the wickedness of those
who dwell there,
Because they said, "He will
not see our final end."

11:12 [a] Deut. 32:37; Jer. 44:17 **11:13** [a] 2 Kin. 23:13; Jer. 2:28 **11:14** [a] Ex. 32:10; Jer. 7:16; 14:11; [1 John 5:16] **11:15** [a] Ps. 50:16 [b] Ezek. 16:25 [c] [Titus 1:15] [d] Prov. 2:14 **11:16** [a] Ps. 52:8; [Rom. 11:17] **11:17** [a] Is. 5:2; Jer. 2:21; 12:2 **11:19** [a] Ps. 83:4; Jer. 18:18 [b] Ps. 27:13 **11:20** [a] 1 Sam. 16:7; 1 Chr. 28:9; Ps. 7:9 [b] Jer. 15:15 **11:21** [a] Jer. 1:1; 12:5, 6 [b] Is. 30:10; Amos 2:12; Mic. 2:6 **11:22** [a] Jer. 9:21 **11:23** [a] Jer. 23:12; Hos. 9:7; Mic. 7:4 **12:1** [a] Ezra 9:15; Ps. 51:4; Jer. 11:20 [b] Job 12:6; Jer. 5:27, 28; Hab. 1:4; Mal. 3:15 **12:2** [a] Is. 29:13; Ezek. 33:31; Matt. 15:8; Mark 7:6 **12:3** [a] Ps. 17:3 [b] Ps. 7:9; 11:5; Jer. 11:20 [c] Jer. 17:18; 50:27; James 5:5 **12:4** [a] Jer. 23:10; Hos. 4:3 [b] Jer. 9:10; Hos. 4:3; Hab. 3:17 [c] Ps. 107:34

TRUST IN HIS WAYS

INHALE

All my life, I have tried to trust in God. I have taken every big decision to Him in prayer. I have sought biblical wisdom from others before I have taken any action. I have leaned on the Holy Spirit to guide me. But it was all for naught. It seems that every single major decision in my life has been the wrong one. I chose the wrong college, the wrong degree path, and the wrong company to work for, and I even married the wrong person. What am I missing here? Why trust God when this is where it has gotten me? How can I have faith in God to help me get my life together when He led me to this messed-up state?

EXHALE

Every step that you've taken in your life has been guided by God. So, to say that you chose the wrong school, career, place of work, and spouse makes God either absent, unwise, or inept in your life. And we *know* that cannot be the case, right? God is with you. He is wise. And He is all-powerful and good. So first, fight to recognize that you are right where you need to be. But then also recognize that your journey isn't done. The same God who led you to "the Red Sea" will lead you through it.

But while you shared about what feels to be some big and important "losses" in your life, I am sure there are wins that you have overlooked too. Our tendency is only to point out the things that didn't work out. But when we have the proper perspective, we will also see there are a number of times God provided and delivered. He always does. Don't just look at the "debits" in your account; look at the "deposits" as well.

It is hard to keep faith when your world seems to be falling apart, but that's why it's called faith. What you are going through is difficult, for sure, but fight to trust God that He has you in the place He wants you to be in for a reason. But you are not alone. Jeremiah pleaded much like you do. Jeremiah 12:1 says, "Righteous are You, O LORD, when I plead with You; yet let me talk with You about Your judgments. Why does the way of the wicked prosper?" See, there are Bible characters who had these similar challenges. But God never closed His ears to their needs, and in some fashion or way, He always delivered.

The LORD Answers Jeremiah

5 "If you have run with the footmen,
and they have wearied you,
Then how can you contend
with horses?
And *if* in the land of peace,
In which you trusted, *they wearied you,*
Then how will you do in [a]the
floodplain[1] of the Jordan?
6 For even [a]your brothers, the
house of your father,
Even they have dealt
treacherously with you;
Yes, they have called a
multitude after you.
[b]Do not believe them,
Even though they speak
smooth words to you.

7 "I have forsaken My house, I
have left My heritage;
I have given the dearly beloved
of My soul into the hand
of her enemies.
8 My heritage is to Me like a
lion in the forest;
It cries out against Me;
Therefore I have [a]hated it.
9 My heritage *is* to Me *like* a
speckled vulture;
The vultures all around
are against her.

12:5 [a] Josh. 3:15; 1 Chr. 12:15 [1] Or *thicket* 12:6 [a] Gen. 37:4–11; Job 6:15; Ps. 69:8; Jer. 9:4, 5 [b] Ps. 12:2; Prov. 26:25 12:8 [a] Hos. 9:15; Amos 6:8

Come, assemble all the
beasts of the field,
[a]Bring them to devour!

10 "Many [a]rulers[1] have destroyed
[b]My vineyard,
They have [c]trodden My
portion underfoot;
They have made My pleasant
portion a desolate wilderness.
11 They have made it [a]desolate;
Desolate, it mourns to Me;
The whole land is made desolate,
Because [b]no one takes *it*
to heart.
12 The plunderers have come
On all the desolate heights
in the wilderness,
For the sword of the LORD
shall devour
From *one* end of the land to
the *other* end of the land;
No flesh shall have peace.
13 [a]They have sown wheat but
reaped thorns;
They have put themselves to
pain *but* do not profit.
But be ashamed of your
harvest
Because of the fierce anger
of the LORD."

14 Thus says the LORD: "Against all My
evil neighbors who [a]touch the inheritance
which I have caused My people Israel to
inherit—behold, I will [b]pluck them out of
their land and pluck out the house of Judah from among them.
15 [a]Then it shall be,
after I have plucked them out, that I will
return and have compassion on them [b]and
bring them back, everyone to his heritage
and everyone to his land.
16 And it shall be,
if they will learn carefully the ways of My
people, [a]to swear by My name, 'As the LORD
lives,' as they taught My people to swear
by Baal, then they shall be [b]established in
the midst of My people.
17 But if they do not
[a]obey, I will utterly pluck up and destroy
that nation," says the LORD.

Symbol of the Linen Sash

13 Thus the LORD said to me: "Go and
get yourself a linen sash, and put it
around your waist, but do not put it in water."
2 So I got a sash according to the word
of the LORD, and put *it* around my waist.
3 And the word of the LORD came to me
the second time, saying,
4 "Take the sash
that you acquired, which *is* around your
waist, and arise, go to the Euphrates,[1] and
hide it there in a hole in the rock."
5 So I
went and hid it by the Euphrates, as the
LORD commanded me.
6 Now it came to pass after many days
that the LORD said to me, "Arise, go to the
Euphrates, and take from there the sash
which I commanded you to hide there."
7 Then I went to the Euphrates and dug, and
I took the sash from the place where I had
hidden it; and there was the sash, ruined.
It was profitable for nothing.
8 Then the word of the LORD came to
me, saying,
9 "Thus says the LORD: 'In this
manner [a]I will ruin the pride of Judah
and the great [b]pride of Jerusalem.
10 This
evil people, who [a]refuse to hear My words,
who [b]follow the dictates of their hearts, and
walk after other gods to serve them and
worship them, shall be just like this sash
which is profitable for nothing.
11 For as the
sash clings to the waist of a man, so I have
caused the whole house of Israel and the
whole house of Judah to cling to Me,' says
the LORD, 'that [a]they may become My people, [b]for renown, for praise, and for [c]glory;
but they would [d]not hear.'

Symbol of the Wine Bottles

12 "Therefore you shall speak to them this
word: 'Thus says the LORD God of Israel:
"Every bottle shall be filled with wine."'
"And they will say to you, 'Do we not certainly know that every bottle will be filled
with wine?'
13 "Then you shall say to them, 'Thus says
the LORD: "Behold, I will fill all the inhabitants of this land—even the kings who sit
on David's throne, the priests, the prophets, and all the inhabitants of Jerusalem—

12:9 [a] Lev. 26:22 12:10 [a] Jer. 6:3; 23:1 [b] Ps. 80:8–16; Is. 5:1–7 [c] Is. 63:18 [1] Literally *shepherds* or *pastors* 12:11 [a] Jer. 10:22; 22:6 [b] Is. 42:25 12:13 [a] Lev. 26:16; Deut. 28:38; Mic. 6:15; Hag. 1:6 12:14 [a] Jer. 2:3; 50:11, 12; Zech. 2:8 [b] Deut. 30:3; Ps. 106:47; Is. 11:11–16; Jer. 32:37 12:15 [a] Jer. 31:20; Lam. 3:32; Ezek. 28:25 [b] Amos 9:14 12:16 [a] [Jer. 4:2]; Zeph. 1:5 [b] [Eph. 2:20, 21; 1 Pet. 2:5] 12:17 [a] Ps. 2:8–12; Is. 60:12 13:4 [1] Hebrew *Perath* 13:9 [a] Lev. 26:19 [b] [Is. 2:10–17; 23:9]; Zeph. 3:11 13:10 [a] Jer. 16:12 [b] Jer. 7:24; 16:12 13:11 [a] [Ex. 19:5, 6; Deut. 32:10, 11] [b] Jer. 33:9 [c] Is. 43:21 [d] Ps. 81:11; Jer. 7:13, 24, 26

[a]with drunkenness! 14 And [a]I will dash them
one against another, even the fathers and
the sons together," says the LORD. "I will
not pity nor spare nor have mercy, but will
destroy them." ' "

Pride Precedes Captivity

15 Hear and give ear:
Do not be proud,
For the LORD has spoken.
16 [a]Give glory to the LORD your God
Before He causes [b]darkness,
And before your feet stumble
On the dark mountains,
And while you are [c]looking for light,
He turns it into [d]the shadow of death
And makes *it* dense darkness.
17 But if you will not hear it,
My soul will [a]weep in secret
for *your* pride;
My eyes will weep bitterly
And run down with tears,
Because the LORD's flock has
been taken captive.

18 Say to [a]the king and to the
queen mother,
"Humble yourselves;
Sit down,
For your rule shall collapse,
the crown of your glory."
19 The cities of the South
shall be shut up,
And no one shall open *them;*
Judah shall be carried away
captive, all of it;
It shall be wholly carried away captive.

20 Lift up your eyes and see
Those who come from the [a]north.
Where *is* the flock *that*
was given to you,
Your beautiful sheep?
21 What will you say when
He punishes you?
For you have taught them
To be chieftains, to be head over you.
Will not [a]pangs seize you,
Like a woman in labor?
22 And if you say in your heart,
[a]"Why have these things
come upon me?"
For the greatness of your iniquity
[b]Your skirts have been uncovered,
Your heels made bare.
23 Can the Ethiopian change his skin
or the leopard its spots?
Then may you also do good who
are accustomed to do evil.

24 "Therefore I will [a]scatter
them [b]like stubble
That passes away by the wind
of the wilderness.
25 [a]This is your lot,
The portion of your measures
from Me," says the LORD,
"Because you have forgotten Me
And trusted in [b]falsehood.
26 Therefore [a]I will uncover your
skirts over your face,
That your shame may appear.
27 I have seen your adulteries
And your *lustful* [a]neighings,
The lewdness of your harlotry,
Your abominations [b]on the
hills in the fields.
Woe to you, O Jerusalem!
Will you still not be made clean?"

Sword, Famine, and Pestilence

14 The word of the LORD that came to Jeremiah concerning the droughts.

2 "Judah mourns,
And [a]her gates languish;
They [b]mourn for the land,
And [c]the cry of Jerusalem has gone up.
3 Their nobles have sent
their lads for water;
They went to the cisterns
and found no water.
They returned with their
vessels empty;
They were [a]ashamed and confounded
[b]And covered their heads.

13:13 [a] Ps. 60:3; 75:8; Is. 51:17; 63:6; Jer. 25:27; 51:7, 57 13:14 [a] 2 Chr. 36:17; Ps. 2:9; Is. 9:20, 21; Jer. 19:9–11 13:16 [a] Josh. 7:19; Ps. 96:8; Mal. 2:2 [b] Is. 5:30; 8:22; Amos 8:9 [c] Is. 59:9 [d] Ps. 44:19; Jer. 2:6 13:17 [a] Ps. 119:136; Jer. 9:1; 14:17; Luke 19:41, 42 13:18 [a] 2 Kin. 24:12; Jer. 22:26 13:20 [a] Jer. 10:22; 46:20 13:21 [a] Jer. 6:24 13:22 [a] Jer. 16:10 [b] Is. 47:2; Ezek. 16:37; Nah. 3:5 13:24 [a] Lev. 26:33; Jer. 9:16; Ezek. 5:2, 12 [b] Ps. 1:4; Hos. 13:3 13:25 [a] Job 20:29; Ps. 11:6; Matt. 24:51 [b] Jer. 10:14 13:26 [a] Lam. 1:8; Ezek. 16:37; Hos. 2:10 13:27 [a] Jer. 5:7, 8 [b] Is. 65:7; Jer. 2:20; Ezek. 6:13 14:2 [a] 2 Kin. 25:3; Is. 3:26 [b] Jer. 8:21 [c] 1 Sam. 5:12; Jer. 11:11; 46:12; Zech. 7:13 14:3 [a] Job 6:20; Ps. 40:14 [b] 2 Sam. 15:30

4 Because the ground is parched,
For there was [a]no rain in the land,
The plowmen were ashamed;
They covered their heads.
5 Yes, the deer also gave
birth in the field,
But left because there was no grass.
6 And [a]the wild donkeys stood
in the desolate heights;
They sniffed at the wind like jackals;
Their eyes failed because
there was no grass."

7 O LORD, though our iniquities
testify against us,
Do it [a]for Your name's sake;
For our backslidings are many,
We have sinned against You.
8 [a]O the Hope of Israel, his Savior
in time of trouble,
Why should You be like a
stranger in the land,
And like a traveler *who* turns
aside to tarry for a night?
9 Why should You be like a
man astonished,
Like a mighty one [a]*who* cannot save?
Yet You, O LORD, [b]*are* in our midst,
And we are called by Your name;
Do not leave us!

10Thus says the LORD to this people:

[a]"Thus they have loved to wander;
They have not restrained their feet.
Therefore the LORD does
not accept them;
[b]He will remember their iniquity now,
And punish their sins."

11Then the LORD said to me, [a]"Do not
pray for this people, for *their* good. 12[a]When
they fast, I will not hear their cry; and
[b]when they offer burnt offering and grain
offering, I will not accept them. But [c]I will
consume them by the sword, by the famine, and by the pestilence."
13[a]Then I said, "Ah, Lord GOD! Behold,
the prophets say to them, 'You shall not see
the sword, nor shall you have famine, but I
will give you assured [b]peace in this place.'"
14And the LORD said to me, [a]"The prophets prophesy lies in My name. [b]I have not
sent them, commanded them, nor spoken to them; they prophesy to you a false
vision, divination, a worthless thing, and
the [c]deceit of their heart. 15Therefore thus
says the LORD concerning the prophets
who prophesy in My name, whom I did
not send, [a]and who say, 'Sword and famine shall not be in this land'—'By sword
and famine those prophets shall be consumed! 16And the people to whom they
prophesy shall be cast out in the streets
of Jerusalem because of the famine and
the sword; [a]they will have no one to bury
them—them nor their wives, their sons
nor their daughters—for I will pour their
wickedness on them.'
17"Therefore you shall say this word to
them:

[a]'Let my eyes flow with tears
night and day,
And let them not cease;
[b]For the virgin daughter of my people
Has been broken with a mighty
stroke, with a very severe blow.
18 If I go out to [a]the field,
Then behold, those slain
with the sword!
And if I enter the city,
Then behold, those sick from famine!
Yes, both prophet and [b]priest
go about in a land they
do not know.'"

The People Plead for Mercy

19 [a]Have You utterly rejected Judah?
Has Your soul loathed Zion?
Why have You stricken us so that
[b]*there is* no healing for us?
[c]We looked for peace, but
there was no good;
And for the time of healing,
and there was trouble.

14:4 [a] Jer. 3:3; Ezek. 22:24 **14:6** [a] Job 39:5, 6; Jer. 2:24 **14:7** [a] Ps. 25:11; Jer. 14:21 **14:8** [a] Jer. 17:13 **14:9** [a] Is. 59:1 [b] Ex. 29:45; Lev. 26:11; Ps. 46:5; Jer. 8:19 **14:10** [a] Jer. 2:23–25 [b] [Jer. 44:21–23]; Hos. 8:13 **14:11** [a] Ex. 32:10; Jer. 7:16; 11:14 **14:12** [a] Prov. 1:28; [Is. 1:15; 58:3–6]; Ezek. 8:18; Mic. 3:4; Zech. 7:13 [b] Jer. 6:20 [c] Jer. 9:16 **14:13** [a] Jer. 4:10 [b] Jer. 8:11; 23:17 **14:14** [a] Jer. 27:10 [b] Jer. 29:8, 9 [c] Jer. 23:16; Ezek. 12:24 **14:15** [a] Jer. 5:12; Ezek. 14:10 **14:16** [a] Ps. 79:2, 3; Jer. 7:32; 15:2, 3 **14:17** [a] Jer. 9:1; 13:17; Lam. 1:16 [b] Is. 37:22; Jer. 8:21; Lam. 1:15; 2:13 **14:18** [a] Jer. 6:25; Lam. 1:20; Ezek. 7:15 [b] Jer. 23:11 **14:19** [a] Jer. 6:30; 7:29; 12:7; Lam. 5:22 [b] Jer. 15:18 [c] Job 30:26; Jer. 8:15; 1 Thess. 5:3

20 We acknowledge, O LORD,
our wickedness
And the iniquity of our [a]fathers,
For [b]we have sinned against You.
21 Do not abhor *us*, for Your name's sake;
Do not disgrace the throne
of Your glory.
[a]Remember, do not break
Your covenant with us.
22 [a]Are there any among [b]the idols of
the nations that can cause [c]rain?
Or can the heavens give showers?
[d]*Are* You not He, O LORD our God?
Therefore we will wait for You,
Since You have made all these.

The LORD Will Not Relent

15 Then the LORD said to me, [a]"*Even* if
[b]Moses and [c]Samuel stood before Me,
My mind *would* not *be* favorable toward this
people. Cast *them* out of My sight, and let
them go forth. 2And it shall be, if they say to
you, 'Where should we go?' then you shall
tell them, 'Thus says the LORD:

[a]"Such as *are* for death, to death;
And such as *are* for the
sword, to the sword;
And such as *are* for the
famine, to the famine;
And such as *are* for the [b]captivity,
to the captivity."'

3"And I will [a]appoint over them four
forms *of destruction*," says the LORD: "the
sword to slay, the dogs to drag, [b]the birds of
the heavens and the beasts of the earth to
devour and destroy. 4I will hand them over
to [a]trouble, to all kingdoms of the earth,
because of [b]Manasseh the son of Hezekiah,
king of Judah, for what he did in Jerusalem.

5 "For who will have pity on
you, O Jerusalem?
Or who will bemoan you?
Or who will turn aside to ask
how you are doing?
6 [a]You have forsaken Me," says the LORD,
"You have [b]gone backward.
Therefore I will stretch out My hand
against you and destroy you;
[c]I am weary of relenting!
7 And I will winnow them
with a winnowing fan in
the gates of the land;
I will [a]bereave *them* of children;
I will destroy My people,
Since they [b]do not return
from their ways.
8 Their widows will be increased to Me
more than the sand of the seas;
I will bring against them,
Against the mother of the young men,
A plunderer at noonday;
I will cause anguish and terror
to fall on them [a]suddenly.

9 "She[a] languishes who has
borne seven;
She has breathed her last;
[b]Her sun has gone down
While *it was* yet day;
She has been ashamed
and confounded.
And the remnant of them I
will deliver to the sword
Before their enemies," says the LORD.

Jeremiah's Dejection

10 [a]Woe is me, my mother,
That you have borne me,
A man of strife and a man of
contention to the whole earth!
I have neither lent for interest,
Nor have men lent to me
for interest.
Every one of them curses me.

11The LORD said:

"Surely it will be well with
your remnant;
Surely I will cause [a]the enemy
to intercede with you
In the time of adversity and
in the time of affliction.
12 Can anyone break iron,
The northern iron and the bronze?

14:20 [a] Neh. 9:2; Ps. 32:5; Jer. 3:25 [b] Ps. 106:6; Jer. 8:14; 14:7; Dan. 9:8 14:21 [a] Ps. 106:45 14:22 [a] Zech. 10:1 [b] Deut. 32:21 [c] 1 Kin. 17:1; Jer. 5:24 [d] Ps. 135:7 15:1 [a] Ps. 99:6; Ezek. 14:14 [b] Ex. 32:11–14; Num. 14:13–20; Ps. 99:6 [c] 1 Sam. 7:9 15:2 [a] Jer. 43:11; Ezek. 5:2, 12; Zech. 11:9; [Rev. 13:10] [b] Jer. 9:16; 16:13 15:3 [a] Lev. 26:16, 21, 25; Jer. 12:3; Ezek. 14:21 [b] Jer. 7:33 15:4 [a] Deut. 28:25 [b] 2 Kin. 24:3, 4 15:6 [a] Jer. 2:13 [b] Is. 1:4; Jer. 7:24 [c] Jer. 20:16; Zech. 8:14 15:7 [a] Jer. 18:21; Hos. 9:12–16 [b] Is. 9:13; Jer. 5:3; Amos 4:10, 11 15:8 [a] Is. 29:5 15:9 [a] 1 Sam. 2:5; Is. 47:9 [b] Jer. 6:4; Amos 8:9 15:10 [a] Job 3:1; Jer. 20:14 15:11 [a] Jer. 40:4, 5

13 Your wealth and your treasures
I will give as [a]plunder without price,
Because of all your sins,
Throughout your territories.
14 And I will make *you* cross over
with[1] your enemies
[a]Into a land *which* you do not know;
For a [b]fire is kindled in My anger,
Which shall burn upon you."

15 O LORD, [a]You know;
Remember me and visit me,
And [b]take vengeance for me
on my persecutors.
In Your enduring patience,
do not take me away.
Know that [c]for Your sake I
have suffered rebuke.
16 Your words were found,
and I [a]ate them,
And [b]Your word was to me the joy
and rejoicing of my heart;
For I am called by Your name,
O LORD God of hosts.
17 [a]I did not sit in the assembly
of the mockers,
Nor did I rejoice;
I sat alone because of Your hand,
For You have filled me
with indignation.
18 Why is my [a]pain perpetual
And my wound incurable,
Which refuses to be healed?
Will You surely be to me [b]like
an unreliable stream,
As waters *that* fail?

The LORD Reassures Jeremiah

19 Therefore thus says the LORD:

[a]"If you return,
Then I will bring you back;
You shall [b]stand before Me;
If you [c]take out the precious
from the vile,
You shall be as My mouth.
Let them return to you,
But you must not return to them.
20 And I will make you to this people
a fortified bronze [a]wall;
And they will fight against you,
But [b]they shall not prevail against you;
For I *am* with you to save you
And deliver you," says the LORD.
21 "I will deliver you from the
hand of the wicked,
And I will redeem you from
the grip of the terrible."

Jeremiah's Lifestyle and Message

16 The word of the LORD also came to
me, saying, 2 "You shall not take a
wife, nor shall you have sons or daughters
in this place." 3 For thus says the LORD concerning the sons and daughters who are
born in this place, and concerning their
mothers who bore them and their fathers
who begot them in this land: 4 "They shall
die [a]gruesome deaths; they shall not be
[b]lamented nor shall they be [c]buried, *but*
they shall be [d]like refuse on the face of the
earth. They shall be consumed by the sword
and by famine, and their [e]corpses shall be
meat for the birds of heaven and for the
beasts of the earth."
5 For thus says the LORD: [a]"Do not enter
the house of mourning, nor go to lament
or bemoan them; for I have taken away My
peace from this people," says the LORD,
"lovingkindness and mercies. 6 Both the
great and the small shall die in this land.
They shall not be buried; [a]neither shall
men lament for them, [b]cut themselves, nor
[c]make themselves bald for them. 7 Nor shall
men break *bread* in mourning for them, to
comfort them for the dead; nor shall *men*
give them the cup of consolation to [a]drink
for their father or their mother. 8 Also you
shall not go into the house of feasting to
sit with them, to eat and drink."
9 For thus says the LORD of hosts, the
God of Israel: "Behold, [a]I will cause to cease
from this place, before your eyes and in
your days, the voice of mirth and the voice
of gladness, the voice of the bridegroom
and the voice of the bride.

15:13 [a] Ps. 44:12; Is. 52:3 15:14 [a] Deut. 28:36, 64; Jer. 16:13 [b] Deut. 32:22; Ps. 21:9; Jer. 17:4 [1] Following Masoretic Text and Vulgate; Septuagint, Syriac, and Targum read *cause you to serve* (compare 17:4). 15:15 [a] Jer. 12:3 [b] Jer. 20:12 [c] Ps. 69:7–9; Jer. 20:8 15:16 [a] Ezek. 3:1, 3; Rev. 10:9 [b] [Job 23:12; Ps. 119:72] 15:17 [a] Ps. 26:4, 5 15:18 [a] Job 34:6; Jer. 10:19; 30:15; Mic. 1:9 [b] Job 6:15 15:19 [a] Jer. 4:1; Zech. 3:7 [b] 1 Kin. 17:1; Jer. 15:1 [c] Jer. 6:29; Ezek. 22:26; 44:23 15:20 [a] Jer. 1:18; 6:27; Ezek. 3:9 [b] Ps. 46:7; Is. 41:10; Jer. 1:8, 19; 20:11; 37:21; 38:13; 39:11, 12 16:4 [a] Jer. 15:2 [b] Jer. 22:18; 25:33 [c] Jer. 14:16; 19:11 [d] Ps. 83:10; Jer. 8:2; 9:22 [e] Ps. 79:2; Is. 18:6; Jer. 7:33; 34:20 16:5 [a] Ezek. 24:17, 22, 23 16:6 [a] Jer. 22:18 [b] Lev. 19:28; Deut. 14:1; Jer. 41:5; 47:5 [c] Is. 22:12; Jer. 7:29 16:7 [a] Prov. 31:6 16:9 [a] Is. 24:7, 8; Jer. 7:34; 25:10; Ezek. 26:13; Hos. 2:11; Rev. 18:23

10"And it shall be, when you show this
people all these words, and they say to you,
[a]'Why has the LORD pronounced all this
great disaster against us? Or what *is* our iniquity? Or what *is* our sin that we have committed against the LORD our God?'
11then
you shall say to them, [a]'Because your fathers have forsaken Me,' says the LORD;
'they have walked after other gods and have
served them and worshiped them, and have
forsaken Me and not kept My law.
12And you
have done [a]worse than your fathers, for behold, [b]each one follows the dictates of his
own evil heart, so that no one listens to Me.
13[a]Therefore I will cast you out of this land
[b]into a land that you do not know, neither
you nor your fathers; and there you shall
serve other gods day and night, where I will
not show you favor.'

God Will Restore Israel
(cf. Jer. 23:7, 8)

14"Therefore behold, the [a]days are coming," says the LORD, "that it shall no more
be said, 'The LORD lives who brought up
the children of Israel from the land of
Egypt,'
15but, 'The LORD lives who brought
up the children of Israel from the land of
the [a]north and from all the lands where He
had driven them.' For [b]I will bring them
back into their land which I gave to their
fathers.

16"Behold, I will send for many
[a]fishermen," says the LORD, "and they shall
fish them; and afterward I will send for
many hunters, and they shall hunt them
from every mountain and every hill, and
out of the holes of the rocks.
17For My [a]eyes
are on all their ways; they are not hidden
from My face, nor is their iniquity hidden
from My eyes.
18And first I will repay [a]dou-
ble for their iniquity and their sin, because
[b]they have defiled My land; they have filled
My inheritance with the carcasses of their
detestable and abominable idols."

19 O LORD, [a]my strength and my fortress,
[b]My refuge in the day of affliction,
The Gentiles shall come to You
From the ends of the earth and say,
"Surely our fathers have inherited lies,
Worthlessness and
[c]unprofitable *things*."
20 Will a man make gods for himself,
[a]Which *are* not gods?

21 "Therefore behold, I will this
once cause them to know,
I will cause them to know
My hand and My might;
And they shall know that [a]My
name *is* the LORD.

Judah's Sin and Punishment

17 "The sin of Judah *is* [a]written
with a [b]pen of iron;
With the point of a diamond
it is [c]engraved
On the tablet of their heart,
And on the horns of your altars,
2 While their children remember
Their altars and their [a]wooden
images[1]
By the green trees on the high hills.
3 O My mountain in the field,
I will give as plunder your
wealth, all your treasures,
And your high places of sin
within all your borders.
4 And you, even yourself,
Shall let go of your heritage
which I gave you;
And I will cause you to
serve your enemies
In [a]the land which you do not know;
For [b]you have kindled a fire in My
anger *which* shall burn forever."

5Thus says the LORD:

[a]"Cursed *is* the man who trusts in man
And makes [b]flesh his strength,
Whose heart departs from the LORD.
6 For he shall be [a]like a shrub
in the desert,
And [b]shall not see when good comes,

16:10 [a] Deut. 29:24; 1 Kin. 9:8; Jer. 5:19 **16:11** [a] Deut. 29:25; 1 Kin. 9:9; 2 Chr. 7:22; Neh. 9:26–29; Jer. 22:9 **16:12** [a] Jer. 7:26 [b] Jer. 3:17; 18:12 **16:13** [a] Deut. 4:26; 28:36, 63 [b] Jer. 15:14 **16:14** [a] Is. 43:18; Jer. 23:7, 8; [Ezek. 37:21–25] **16:15** [a] Jer. 3:18 [b] Jer. 24:6; 30:3; 32:37 **16:16** [a] Amos 4:2; Hab. 1:15 **16:17** [a] 2 Chr. 16:9; Job 34:21; Ps. 90:8; Prov. 5:21; Jer. 23:24; 32:19; Zech. 4:10; [Luke 12:2; 1 Cor. 4:5]; Heb. 4:13 **16:18** [a] Is. 40:2; Jer. 17:18; Rev. 18:6 [b] [Ezek. 43:7] **16:19** [a] Ps. 18:1, 2; Is. 25:4 [b] Jer. 17:17 [c] Is. 44:10 **16:20** [a] Ps. 115:4–8; Is. 37:19; Jer. 2:11; 5:7; Hos. 8:4–6; Gal. 4:8 **16:21** [a] Ex. 15:3; Ps. 83:18; Is. 43:3; Jer. 33:2; Amos 5:8 **17:1** [a] Jer. 2:22 [b] Job 19:24 [c] Prov. 3:3; 7:3; Is. 49:16; 2 Cor. 3:3 **17:2** [a] Judg. 3:7 [1] Hebrew *Asherim,* Canaanite deities **17:4** [a] Jer. 16:13 [b] Is. 5:25; Jer. 15:14 **17:5** [a] Ps. 146:3; Is. 30:1, 2; 31:1 [b] Is. 31:3 **17:6** [a] Jer. 48:6 [b] Job 20:17

But shall inhabit the parched
places in the wilderness,
[c]*In* a salt land *which is* not inhabited.

7 "Blessed[a] *is* the man who
trusts in the LORD,
And whose hope is the LORD.
8 For he shall be [a]like a tree
planted by the waters,
Which spreads out its
roots by the river,
And will not fear[1] when heat comes;
But its leaf will be green,
And will not be anxious in
the year of drought,
Nor will cease from yielding fruit.

#OXYGEN

JEREMIAH 17:7-8

Trust in His Ways

Life's journey is filled with constant crossroads. Make wise choices at each. Walk with God. Remember, He will carry you in tough times. Choose His blessed path.

Breathe and **trust in His ways.**

9 "The [a]heart *is* deceitful above all *things,*
And desperately wicked;
Who can know it?
10 I, the LORD, [a]search the heart,
I test the mind,
[b]Even to give every man
according to his ways,
According to the fruit of his doings.

11 "*As* a partridge that broods
but does not hatch,
So is he who gets riches,
but not by right;
It [a]will leave him in the
midst of his days,
And at his end he will be [b]a fool."

12 A glorious high throne
from the beginning
Is the place of our sanctuary.
13 O LORD, [a]the hope of Israel,
[b]All who forsake You shall be ashamed.

"Those who depart from Me
Shall be [c]written in the earth,
Because they have forsaken the LORD,
The [d]fountain of living waters."

Jeremiah Prays for Deliverance

14 Heal me, O LORD, and I
shall be healed;
Save me, and I shall be saved,
For [a]You *are* my praise.
15 Indeed they say to me,
[a]"Where *is* the word of the LORD?
Let it come now!"
16 As for me, [a]I have not hurried
away from *being* a shepherd
who follows You,
Nor have I desired the woeful day;
You know what came out of my lips;
It was right there before You.
17 Do not be a terror to me;
[a]You *are* my hope in the day of doom.
18 [a]Let them be ashamed who
persecute me,
But [b]do not let me be put to shame;
Let them be dismayed,
But do not let me be dismayed.
Bring on them the day of doom,
And [c]destroy them with
double destruction!

Hallow the Sabbath Day

19Thus the LORD said to me: "Go and
stand in the gate of the children of the
people, by which the kings of Judah
come in and by which they go out, and
in all the gates of Jerusalem; 20and say to
them, [a]'Hear the word of the LORD, you
kings of Judah, and all Judah, and all the

17:6 [c] Deut. 29:23; Job 39:6 17:7 [a] Ps. 2:12; 34:8; 125:1; 146:5; Prov. 16:20; [Is. 30:18]; Jer. 39:18 17:8 [a] Job 8:16; [Ps. 1:3; Ezek. 31:3–9] [1] Qere and Targum read *see.* 17:9 [a] [Eccl. 9:3]; Matt. 15:19; [Mark 7:21, 22] 17:10 [a] 1 Sam. 16:7; 1 Chr. 28:9; Ps. 7:9; 139:23, 24; Prov. 17:3; Jer. 11:20; 20:12; Rom. 8:27; Rev. 2:23 [b] Ps. 62:12; Jer. 32:19; Rom. 2:6 17:11 [a] Ps. 55:23 [b] Luke 12:20 17:13 [a] Jer. 14:8 [b] [Ps. 73:27; Is. 1:28] [c] Luke 10:20 [d] Jer. 2:13 17:14 [a] Deut. 10:21; Ps. 109:1 17:15 [a] Is. 5:19; Ezek. 12:22; 2 Pet. 3:4 17:16 [a] Jer. 1:4–12 17:17 [a] Jer. 16:19; Nah. 1:7 17:18 [a] Ps. 35:4; 70:2; Jer. 15:10; 18:18 [b] Ps. 25:2 [c] Jer. 11:20 17:20 [a] Ps. 49:1, 2; Jer. 19:3, 4

inhabitants of Jerusalem, who enter by
these gates. 21Thus says the LORD: [a]"Take
heed to yourselves, and bear no burden on
the Sabbath day, nor bring *it* in by the gates
of Jerusalem; 22nor carry a burden out of
your houses on the Sabbath day, nor do
any work, but hallow the Sabbath day, as I
[a]commanded your fathers. 23[a]But they did
not obey nor incline their ear, but made
their neck stiff, that they might not hear
nor receive instruction.

24"And it shall be, [a]if you heed Me carefully,"
says the LORD, "to bring no burden
through the gates of this city on the [b]Sabbath
day, but hallow the Sabbath day, to
do no work in it, 25[a]then shall enter the
gates of this city kings and princes sitting
on the throne of David, riding in chariots
and on horses, they and their princes, accompanied
by the men of Judah and the
inhabitants of Jerusalem; and this city shall
remain forever. 26And they shall come from
the cities of Judah and from [a]the places
around Jerusalem, from the land of Benjamin
and from [b]the lowland, from the
mountains and from [c]the South, bringing
burnt offerings and sacrifices, grain offerings
and incense, bringing [d]sacrifices of
praise to the house of the LORD.

27"But if you will not heed Me to hallow
the Sabbath day, such as not carrying
a burden when entering the gates of Jerusalem
on the Sabbath day, then [a]I will kindle
a fire in its gates, [b]and it shall devour
the palaces of Jerusalem, and it shall not
be [c]quenched." ' "

The Potter and the Clay

18 The word which came to Jeremiah
from the LORD, saying: 2"Arise and
go down to the potter's house, and there I
will cause you to hear My words." 3Then I
went down to the potter's house, and there
he was, making something at the wheel.
4And the vessel that he made of clay was
marred in the hand of the potter; so he
made it again into another vessel, as it
seemed good to the potter to make.

5Then the word of the LORD came to me,
saying: 6"O house of Israel, [a]can I not do
with you as this potter?" says the LORD.
"Look, [b]as the clay *is* in the potter's hand,
so *are* you in My hand, O house of Israel!
7The instant I speak concerning a nation
and concerning a kingdom, to [a]pluck up, to
pull down, and to destroy *it,* 8[a]if that nation
against whom I have spoken turns from
its evil, [b]I will relent of the disaster that I
thought to bring upon it. 9And the instant
I speak concerning a nation and concerning
a kingdom, to build and to plant *it,* 10if it
does evil in My sight so that it does not obey
My voice, then I will relent concerning the
good with which I said I would benefit it.

11"Now therefore, speak to the men of
Judah and to the inhabitants of Jerusalem,
saying, 'Thus says the LORD: "Behold, I am
fashioning a disaster and devising a plan
against you. [a]Return now every one from
his evil way, and make your ways and your
doings [b]good." ' "

God's Warning Rejected

12And they said, [a]"That is hopeless! So
we will walk according to our own plans,
and we will every one obey the [b]dictates of
his evil heart."

13Therefore thus says the LORD:

[a]"Ask now among the Gentiles,
Who has heard such things?
The virgin of Israel has done
[b]a very horrible thing.
14 Will *a man* leave the snow
water of Lebanon,
Which comes from the
rock of the field?
Will the cold flowing waters be
forsaken for strange waters?

15 "Because My people have
forgotten [a]Me,
They have burned incense
to worthless idols.
And they have caused themselves
to stumble in their ways,

17:21 [a] Num. 15:32; Neh. 13:19; [John 5:9–12, 17; 7:22–24] **17:22** [a] Ex. 20:8; 31:13; Ezek. 20:12 **17:23** [a] Jer. 7:24, 26 **17:24** [a] Jer. 11:4; 26:3 [b] Ex. 16:23–30; 20:8–10; Num. 15:32–36; Deut. 5:12–14; Neh. 13:15; [Is. 58:13] **17:25** [a] Jer. 22:4 **17:26** [a] Jer. 33:13 [b] Zech. 7:7 [c] Judg. 1:9 [d] Ps. 107:22; 116:17; Jer. 33:11 **17:27** [a] Jer. 21:14; Lam. 4:11; Amos 1:4, 7, 10, 12 [b] 2 Kin. 25:9; 2 Chr. 36:19; Jer. 39:8; 52:13; Amos 2:5 [c] Jer. 7:20; Ezek. 20:47 **18:6** [a] Is. 45:9; Rom. 9:20, 21 [b] Is. 64:8 **18:7** [a] Jer. 1:10 **18:8** [a] Jer. 7:3–7; 12:16; [Ezek. 18:21; 33:11] [b] [Ps. 106:45]; Jer. 26:3; [Hos. 11:8; Joel 2:13]; Jon. 3:10 **18:11** [a] 2 Kin. 17:13; Is. 1:16–19; Jer. 4:1; Acts 26:20 [b] Jer. 7:3–7 **18:12** [a] Is. 57:10; Jer. 2:25 [b] Jer. 3:17; 23:17 **18:13** [a] Is. 66:8; Jer. 2:10, 11; 1 Cor. 5:1 [b] Jer. 5:30; Hos. 6:10 **18:15** [a] Jer. 2:13, 32

From the [b]ancient paths,
To walk in pathways and
not on a highway,
16 To make their land [a]desolate
and a perpetual [b]hissing;
Everyone who passes by it
will be astonished
And shake his head.
17 [a]I will scatter them [b]as with an
east wind before the enemy;
[c]I will show them[1] the back
and not the face
In the day of their calamity."

Jeremiah Persecuted

18 Then they said, [a]"Come and let us devise plans against Jeremiah; [b]for the law
shall not perish from the priest, nor counsel from the wise, nor the word from the
prophet. Come and let us attack him with
the tongue, and let us not give heed to any
of his words."

19 Give heed to me, O LORD,
And listen to the voice of those
who contend with me!
20 [a]Shall evil be repaid for good?
For they have [b]dug a pit for my life.
Remember that I [c]stood before You
To speak good for them,
To turn away Your wrath from them.
21 Therefore [a]deliver up their
children to the famine,
And pour out their *blood*
By the force of the sword;
Let their wives *become* widows
And [b]bereaved of their children.
Let their men be put to death,
Their young men *be* slain
By the sword in battle.
22 Let a cry be heard from their houses,
When You bring a troop
suddenly upon them;
For they have dug a pit to take me,
And hidden snares for my feet.
23 Yet, LORD, You know all their
counsel
Which is against me, to slay *me*.
[a]Provide no atonement
for their iniquity,
Nor blot out their sin from Your sight;
But let them be overthrown
before You.
Deal *thus* with them
In the time of Your [b]anger.

The Sign of the Broken Flask

19 Thus says the LORD: "Go and get a
potter's earthen flask, and *take* some
of the elders of the people and some of the
elders of the priests. 2 And go out to [a]the
Valley of the Son of Hinnom, which *is* by the
entry of the Potsherd Gate; and proclaim
there the words that I will tell you, 3 [a]and
say, 'Hear the word of the LORD, O kings of
Judah and inhabitants of Jerusalem. Thus
says the LORD of hosts, the God of Israel:
"Behold, I will bring such a catastrophe
on this place, that whoever hears of it, his
ears will [b]tingle.
4 "Because they [a]have forsaken Me and
made this an alien place, because they
have burned incense in it to other gods
whom neither they, their fathers, nor the
kings of Judah have known, and have filled
this place with [b]the blood of the innocents
5 [a](they have also built the high places of
Baal, to burn their sons with fire *for* burnt
offerings to Baal, [b]which I did not command or speak, nor did it come into My
mind), 6 therefore behold, the days are coming," says the LORD, "that this place shall no
more be called Tophet or [a]the Valley of the
Son of Hinnom, but the Valley of Slaughter. 7 And I will make void the counsel of
Judah and Jerusalem in this place, [a]and I
will cause them to fall by the sword before
their enemies and by the hands of those
who seek their lives; their [b]corpses I will
give as meat for the birds of the heaven and
for the beasts of the earth. 8 I will make this
city [a]desolate and a hissing; everyone who
passes by it will be astonished and hiss because of all its plagues. 9 And I will cause
them to eat the [a]flesh of their sons and the
flesh of their daughters, and everyone shall

18:15 [b] Jer. 6:16 18:16 [a] Jer. 19:8 [b] 1 Kin. 9:8; Lam. 2:15; Mic. 6:16 18:17 [a] Jer. 13:24 [b] Ps. 48:7 [c] Jer. 2:27 [1] Following Septuagint, Syriac, Targum, and Vulgate; Masoretic Text reads *look them in.* 18:18 [a] Jer. 11:19 [b] Lev. 10:11; Mal. 2:7; [John 7:48] 18:20 [a] Ps. 109:4 [b] Ps. 35:7; 57:6; Jer. 5:26 [c] Jer. 14:7—15:1 18:21 [a] Ps. 109:9–20; Jer. 11:22; 14:16 [b] Jer. 15:7, 8; Ezek. 22:25 18:23 [a] Neh. 4:5; Ps. 35:14; 109:14; Is. 2:9; Jer. 11:20 [b] Jer. 7:20 19:2 [a] Josh. 15:8; 2 Kin. 23:10; Jer. 7:31; 32:35 19:3 [a] Jer. 17:20 [b] 1 Sam. 3:11; 2 Kin. 21:12 19:4 [a] Deut. 28:20; Is. 65:11; Jer. 2:13, 17, 19; 15:6; 17:13 [b] 2 Kin. 21:12; Jer. 2:34; 7:6 19:5 [a] Num. 22:41; Jer. 7:31; 32:35 [b] Lev. 18:21; 2 Kin. 17:17; Ps. 106:37, 38 19:6 [a] Josh. 15:8; Jer. 7:32 19:7 [a] Lev. 26:17; Deut. 28:25; Jer. 15:2, 9 [b] Ps. 79:2; Jer. 7:33; 16:4; 34:20 19:8 [a] Jer. 18:16; 49:13; 50:13 19:9 [a] Lev. 26:29; Deut. 28:53, 55; Is. 9:20; Lam. 4:10; Ezek. 5:10

eat the flesh of his friend in the siege and in the desperation with which their enemies and those who seek their lives shall drive them to despair."'

10 [a]"Then you shall break the flask in the sight of the men who go with you, 11 and say to them, 'Thus says the LORD of hosts: [a]"Even so I will break this people and this city, as *one* breaks a potter's vessel, which cannot be made whole again; and they shall [b]bury *them* in Tophet till *there is* no place to bury. 12 Thus I will do to this place," says the LORD, "and to its inhabitants, and make this city like Tophet. 13 And the houses of Jerusalem and the houses of the kings of Judah shall be defiled [a]like the place of Tophet, because of all the houses on whose [b]roofs they have burned incense to all the host of heaven, and [c]poured out drink offerings to other gods."'"

14 Then Jeremiah came from Tophet, where the LORD had sent him to prophesy; and he stood in [a]the court of the LORD's house and said to all the people, 15 "Thus says the LORD of hosts, the God of Israel: 'Behold, I will bring on this city and on all her towns all the doom that I have pronounced against it, because [a]they have stiffened their necks that they might not hear My words.'"

The Word of God to Pashhur

20 Now [a]Pashhur the son of [b]Immer, the priest who *was* also chief governor in the house of the LORD, heard that Jeremiah prophesied these things. 2 Then Pashhur struck Jeremiah the prophet, and put him in the stocks that *were* in the high [a]gate of Benjamin, which *was* by the house of the LORD.

3 And it happened on the next day that Pashhur brought Jeremiah out of the stocks. Then Jeremiah said to him, "The LORD has not called your name Pashhur, but Magor-Missabib.[1] 4 For thus says the LORD: 'Behold, I will make you a terror to yourself and to all your friends; and they shall fall by the sword of their enemies, and your eyes shall see *it*. I will [a]give all Judah into the hand of the king of Babylon, and he shall carry them captive to Babylon and slay them with the sword. 5 Moreover I [a]will deliver all the wealth of this city, all its produce, and all its precious things; all the treasures of the kings of Judah I will give into the hand of their enemies, who will plunder them, seize them, and [b]carry them to Babylon. 6 And you, Pashhur, and all who dwell in your house, shall go into captivity. You shall go to Babylon, and there you shall die, and be buried there, you and all your friends, to whom you have [a]prophesied lies.'"

Jeremiah's Unpopular Ministry

7 O LORD, You induced me,
 and I was persuaded;
[a]You are stronger than I,
 and have prevailed.
[b]I am in derision daily;
Everyone mocks me.
8 For when I spoke, I cried out;
[a]I shouted, "Violence and plunder!"
Because the word of the
 LORD was made to me
A reproach and a derision daily.
9 Then I said, "I will not make
 mention of Him,
Nor speak anymore in His name."
But *His word* was in my heart
 like a [a]burning fire
Shut up in my bones;
I was weary of holding *it* back,
And [b]I could not.
10 [a]For I heard many mocking:
"Fear on every side!"
"Report," *they say,* "and
 we will report it!"
[b]All my acquaintances watched
 for my stumbling, *saying,*
"Perhaps he can be induced;
Then we will prevail against him,
And we will take our revenge on him."

11 But the LORD *is* [a]with me as a
 mighty, awesome One.

19:10 [a] Jer. 51:63, 64 19:11 [a] Ps. 2:9; Is. 30:14; Jer. 13:14; Lam. 4:2; Rev. 2:27 [b] Jer. 7:32 19:13 [a] 2 Kin. 23:10; Ps. 74:7; 79:1; Jer. 52:13; Ezek. 7:21, 22 [b] 2 Kin. 23:12; Jer. 32:29; Zeph. 1:5 [c] Jer. 7:18; Ezek. 20:28 19:14 [a] 2 Chr. 20:5; Jer. 26:2–8 19:15 [a] Neh. 9:17, 29; Jer. 7:26; 17:23 20:1 [a] Ezra 2:37, 38 [b] 1 Chr. 24:14 20:2 [a] Jer. 37:13; Zech. 14:10 20:3 [1] Literally *Fear on Every Side* 20:4 [a] Jer. 21:4–10 20:5 [a] 2 Kin. 20:17; 2 Chr. 36:10; Jer. 3:24; 27:21, 22 [b] Is. 39:6 20:6 [a] Jer. 14:13–15; Lam. 2:14 20:7 [a] Jer. 1:6, 7 [b] Job 12:4; Lam. 3:14 20:8 [a] Jer. 6:7 20:9 [a] Job 32:18–20; Ps. 39:3; Jer. 4:19; 23:9; [Ezek. 3:14]; Acts 4:20 [b] Job 32:18; Jer. 6:11; Acts 18:5 20:10 [a] Ps. 31:13 [b] Job 19:19; Ps. 41:9; 55:13, 14; Luke 11:53, 54 20:11 [a] Jer. 1:18, 19

Therefore my persecutors will
stumble, and will not [b]prevail.
They will be greatly ashamed,
for they will not prosper.
Their [c]everlasting confusion
will never be forgotten.
12 But, O LORD of hosts,
You who [a]test the righteous,
And see the mind and heart,
[b]Let me see Your vengeance on them;
For I have pleaded my
cause before You.

13 Sing to the LORD! Praise the LORD!
For [a]He has delivered the
life of the poor
From the hand of evildoers.

14 [a]Cursed *be* the day in which I was born!
Let the day not be blessed in
which my mother bore me!
15 Let the man *be* cursed
Who brought news to my
father, saying,
"A male child has been born to you!"
Making him very glad.
16 And let that man be like the cities
Which the LORD [a]overthrew,
and did not relent;
Let him [b]hear the cry in the morning
And the shouting at noon,
17 [a]Because he did not kill me
from the womb,
That my mother might have
been my grave,
And her womb always
enlarged *with me.*
18 [a]Why did I come forth from the
womb to [b]see labor and sorrow,
That my days should be
consumed with shame?

Jerusalem's Doom Is Sealed

21 The word which came to Jeremiah
from the LORD when [a]King Zedekiah
sent to him [b]Pashhur the son of Melchiah,
and [c]Zephaniah the son of Maaseiah, the
priest, saying, 2 [a]"Please inquire of the LORD
for us, for Nebuchadnezzar[1] king of Babylon
makes war against us. Perhaps the LORD will
deal with us according to all His wonderful
works, that *the king* may go away from us."
3 Then Jeremiah said to them, "Thus you
shall say to Zedekiah, 4 'Thus says the LORD
God of Israel: "Behold, I will turn back the
weapons of war that *are* in your hands, with
which you fight against the king of Babylon
and the Chaldeans[1] who besiege you outside
the walls; and [a]I will assemble them in the
midst of this city. 5 I [a]Myself will fight against
you with an [b]outstretched hand and with a
strong arm, even in anger and fury and great
wrath. 6 I will strike the inhabitants of this
city, both man and beast; they shall die of a
great pestilence. 7 And afterward," says the
LORD, [a]"I will deliver Zedekiah king of Judah, his servants and the people, and such
as are left in this city from the pestilence and
the sword and the famine, into the hand of
Nebuchadnezzar king of Babylon, into the
hand of their enemies, and into the hand of
those who seek their life; and he shall strike
them with the edge of the sword. [b]He shall
not spare them, or have pity or mercy."'
8 "Now you shall say to this people, 'Thus
says the LORD: "Behold, [a]I set before you
the way of life and the way of death. 9 He
who [a]remains in this city shall die by the
sword, by famine, and by pestilence; but he
who goes out and defects to the Chaldeans
who besiege you, he shall [b]live, and his life
shall be as a prize to him. 10 For I have [a]set
My face against this city for adversity and
not for good," says the LORD. [b]"It shall be
given into the hand of the king of Babylon,
and he shall [c]burn it with fire."'

Message to the House of David

11 "And concerning the house of the king
of Judah, *say,* 'Hear the word of the LORD,
12 O house of David! Thus says the LORD:

[a]"Execute judgment [b]in the morning;
And deliver *him who is* plundered

20:11 [b] Jer. 15:20; 17:18 [c] Jer. 23:40 **20:12** [a] Ps. 7:9; 11:5; 17:3; 139:23; [Jer. 11:20; 17:10] [b] Ps. 54:7; 59:10; Jer. 15:15 **20:13** [a] Ps. 35:9, 10; 109:30, 31 **20:14** [a] Job 3:3; Jer. 15:10 **20:16** [a] Gen. 19:25 [b] Jer. 18:22 **20:17** [a] Job 3:10, 11 **20:18** [a] Job 3:20; Jer. 15:10 [b] Lam. 3:1
21:1 [a] 2 Kin. 24:17, 18; Jer. 32:1–3; 37:1; 52:1–3 [b] 1 Chr. 9:12; Jer. 38:1 [c] 2 Kin. 25:18; Jer. 29:25; 37:3 **21:2** [a] Ex. 9:28; 1 Sam. 9:9; Jer. 37:3, 7; Ezek. 14:7; 20:1–3 [1] Hebrew *Nebuchadrezzar,* and so elsewhere **21:4** [a] Is. 13:4; Jer. 39:3; Lam. 2:5, 7; Zech. 14:2 [1] Or *Babylonians*
21:5 [a] Jer. 32:24; 33:5; Is. 63:10 [b] Ex. 6:6; Deut. 4:34; Jer. 6:12 **21:7** [a] 2 Kin. 25:5–7, 18–21; Jer. 37:17; 39:5; 52:9 [b] Deut. 28:50; 2 Chr. 36:17; Jer. 13:14; Ezek. 7:9; Hab. 1:6–10 **21:8** [a] Deut. 30:15, 19; Is. 1:19, 20 **21:9** [a] Jer. 38:2 [b] Jer. 39:18
21:10 [a] Lev. 17:10; Jer. 44:11, 27; Amos 9:4 [b] Jer. 38:3 [c] 2 Kin. 25:9; 2 Chr. 36:19; Jer. 34:2, 22; 37:10
21:12 [a] Ps. 72:1; Is. 1:17; Jer. 22:3; Zech. 7:9 [b] Ps. 101:8; Zeph. 3:5

Out of the hand of the oppressor,
Lest My fury go forth like fire
And burn so that no one can
quench *it,*
Because of the evil of your doings.

13 "Behold, [a]I *am* against you,
O inhabitant of the valley,
And rock of the plain," says
the LORD,
"Who say, [b]'Who shall come
down against us?
Or who shall enter our dwellings?'
14 But I will punish you according
to the [a]fruit of your doings,"
says the LORD;
"I will kindle a fire in its forest,
And [b]it shall devour all
things around it." ' "

22 Thus says the LORD: "Go down to
the house of the king of Judah, and
there speak this word, 2and say, [a]'Hear the
word of the LORD, O king of Judah, you who
sit on the throne of David, you and your
servants and your people who enter these
gates! 3Thus says the LORD: [a]"Execute judgment and righteousness, and deliver the
plundered out of the hand of the oppressor. Do no wrong and do no violence to the
stranger, the [b]fatherless, or the widow, nor
shed innocent blood in this place. 4For if
you indeed do this thing, [a]then shall enter
the gates of this house, riding on horses
and in chariots, accompanied by servants
and people, kings who sit on the throne of
David. 5But if you will not hear these words,
[a]I swear by Myself," says the LORD, "that
this house shall become a desolation." ' "

6For thus says the LORD to the house of
the king of Judah:

"You *are* [a]Gilead to Me,
The head of Lebanon;
Yet I surely will make you a wilderness,
Cities *which* are not inhabited.
7 I will prepare destroyers against you,
Everyone with his weapons;
They shall cut down [a]your
choice cedars
[b]And cast *them* into the fire.

8And many nations will pass by this city;
and everyone will say to his neighbor, [a]'Why
has the LORD done so to this great city?'
9Then they will answer, [a]'Because they have
forsaken the covenant of the LORD their
God, and worshiped other gods and served
them.' "

10 Weep not for [a]the dead,
nor bemoan him;
Weep bitterly for him [b]who
goes away,
For he shall return no more,
Nor see his native country.

Message to the Sons of Josiah

11For thus says the LORD concerning
[a]Shallum[1] the son of Josiah, king of Judah,
who reigned instead of Josiah his father,
[b]who went from this place: "He shall not
return here anymore, 12but he shall die in
the place where they have led him captive,
and shall see this land no more.

13 "Woe[a] to him who builds his
house by unrighteousness
And his chambers by injustice,
[b]*Who* uses his neighbor's
service without wages
And gives him nothing for his work,
14 Who says, 'I will build myself a wide
house with spacious chambers,
And cut out windows for it,
Paneling *it* with cedar
And painting *it* with vermilion.'

15 "Shall you reign because you
enclose *yourself* in cedar?
Did not your father eat and drink,
And do justice and righteousness?
Then [a]*it was* well with him.
16 He judged the cause of the
poor and needy;
Then *it was* well.

21:13 [a] [Jer. 23:30–32; Ezek. 13:8] [b] 2 Sam. 5:6, 7; Jer. 49:4; Lam. 4:12; Obad. 3, 4 21:14 [a] Prov. 1:31; Is. 3:10, 11; Jer. 17:10; 32:19 [b] 2 Chr. 36:19; Is. 10:16, 18; Jer. 11:16; 17:27; 52:13; Ezek. 20:47, 48 22:2 [a] Jer. 17:20 22:3 [a] Is. 58:6; Jer. 21:12; [Mic. 6:8]; Zech. 7:9; 8:16; Matt. 23:23 [b] Jer. 7:6; Zech. 7:10 22:4 [a] Jer. 17:25 22:5 [a] Matt. 23:38; Heb. 6:13, 17 22:6 [a] Gen. 37:25; Num. 32:1; Song 4:1 22:7 [a] Is. 37:24 [b] Jer. 21:14 22:8 [a] Deut. 29:24–26; 1 Kin. 9:8, 9; 2 Chr. 7:20–22; Jer. 16:10 22:9 [a] 2 Kin. 22:17; 2 Chr. 34:25; Jer. 11:3 22:10 [a] 2 Kin. 22:20 [b] Jer. 14:17; 22:11; Lam. 3:48 22:11 [a] 1 Chr. 3:15 [b] 2 Kin. 23:34; 2 Chr. 36:4; Ezek. 19:4 [1] Also called *Jehoahaz* 22:13 [a] 2 Kin. 23:35; Jer. 17:11; Ezek. 22:13 [b] Lev. 19:13; Deut. 24:14, 15; Mic. 3:10; Hab. 2:9; James 5:4 22:15 [a] 2 Kin. 23:25; Ps. 128:2; Is. 3:10; Jer. 7:23; 42:6

Was not this knowing Me?"
says the LORD.
17 "Yet[a] your eyes and your heart *are* for
nothing but your covetousness,
For shedding innocent blood,
And practicing oppression
and violence."

18Therefore thus says the LORD concerning Jehoiakim the son of Josiah, king of
Judah:

[a]"They shall not lament for him,
Saying, [b]'Alas, my brother!'
or 'Alas, my sister!'
"They shall not lament for him,
Saying, 'Alas, master!' or
'Alas, his glory!'
19 [a]He shall be buried with the
burial of a donkey,
Dragged and cast out beyond
the gates of Jerusalem.

20"Go up to Lebanon, and cry out,
And lift up your voice in Bashan;
Cry from Abarim,
For all your lovers are destroyed.
21 I spoke to you in your prosperity,
But you said, 'I will not hear.'
[a]This *has been* your manner
from your youth,
That you did not obey My voice.
22 The wind shall eat up all [a]your rulers,
And your lovers shall go into
captivity;
Surely then you will be
ashamed and humiliated
For all your wickedness.
23 O inhabitant of Lebanon,
Making your nest in the cedars,
How gracious will you be when
pangs come upon you,
Like [a]the pain of a woman in labor?

Message to Coniah

24"*As* I live," says the LORD, [a]"though Coniah[1] the son of Jehoiakim, king of Judah,
[b]were the signet on My right hand, yet I
would pluck you off; 25[a]and I will give you
into the hand of those who seek your life,
and into the hand *of those* whose face you
fear—the hand of Nebuchadnezzar king
of Babylon and the hand of the Chaldeans.
26[a]So I will cast you out, and your mother
who bore you, into another country where
you were not born; and there you shall die.
27But to the land to which they desire to return, there they shall not return.

28"Is this man Coniah a despised,
broken idol—
[a]A vessel in which *is* no
pleasure?
Why are they cast out, he
and his descendants,
And cast into a land which
they do not know?
29 [a]O earth, earth, earth,
Hear the word of the LORD!
30 Thus says the LORD:
'Write this man down as
[a]childless,
A man *who* shall not
prosper in his days;
For [b]none of his descendants
shall prosper,
Sitting on the throne of David,
And ruling anymore in Judah.'"

The Branch of Righteousness

23 "Woe [a]to the shepherds who destroy and scatter the sheep of My
pasture!" says the LORD. 2Therefore thus
says the LORD God of Israel against the
shepherds who feed My people: "You have
scattered My flock, driven them away, and
not attended to them. [a]Behold, I will attend to you for the evil of your doings,"
says the LORD. 3"But [a]I will gather the remnant of My flock out of all countries where
I have driven them, and bring them back to
their folds; and they shall be fruitful and increase. 4I will set up [a]shepherds over them
who will feed them; and they shall fear no
more, nor be dismayed, nor shall they be
lacking," says the LORD.

22:17 [a] Jer. 6:13; 8:10; Ezek. 19:6; [Luke 12:15–20] 22:18 [a] Jer. 16:4, 6 [b] 1 Kin. 13:30 22:19 [a] 1 Kin. 21:23, 24; 2 Chr. 36:6; Jer. 36:30; Dan. 1:2 22:21 [a] Jer. 3:24, 25; 32:30 22:22 [a] Jer. 23:1 22:23 [a] Jer. 6:24 22:24 [a] 2 Kin. 24:6, 8; 1 Chr. 3:16; 2 Chr. 36:9; Jer. 37:1 [b] Song 8:6; Is. 49:16; Hag. 2:23 [1] Also called *Jeconiah* and *Jehoiachin* 22:25 [a] 2 Kin. 24:15, 16; Jer. 34:20 22:26 [a] 2 Kin. 24:15; Jer. 10:18; 16:13 22:28 [a] Ps. 31:12; Jer. 48:38; Hos. 8:8 22:29 [a] Deut. 32:1; Is. 1:2; 34:1; Mic. 1:2 22:30 [a] 1 Chr. 3:16, 17; Matt. 1:12 [b] Ps. 94:20; Jer. 36:30 23:1 [a] Is. 56:9–12; Jer. 10:21 23:2 [a] Ex. 32:34 23:3 [a] Is. 11:11, 12, 16; Jer. 32:37 23:4 [a] Jer. 3:15; [Ezek. 34:23]

5 "Behold, [a]*the* days are coming,"
says the LORD,
"That I will raise to David a
Branch of righteousness;
A King shall reign and prosper,
[b]And execute judgment and
righteousness in the earth.
6 [a]In His days Judah will be saved,
And Israel [b]will dwell safely;
Now [c]this *is* His name by
which He will be called:

THE LORD OUR RIGHTEOUSNESS.[1]

7"Therefore, behold, [a]*the* days are coming," says the LORD, "that they shall no longer say, 'As the LORD lives who brought
up the children of Israel from the land of
Egypt,' 8but, 'As the LORD lives who brought
up and led the descendants of the house
of Israel from the north country [a]and from
all the countries where I had driven them.'
And they shall dwell in their own [b]land."

False Prophets and Empty Oracles

9 My heart within me is broken
Because of the prophets;
[a]All my bones shake.
I am like a drunken man,
And like a man whom wine
has overcome,
Because of the LORD,
And because of His holy words.
10 For [a]the land is full of adulterers;
For [b]because of a curse
the land mourns.
[c]The pleasant places of the
wilderness are dried up.
Their course of life is evil,
And their might *is* not right.

11 "For [a]both prophet and
priest are profane;
Yes, [b]in My house I have found their
wickedness," says the LORD.
12 "Therefore[a] their way shall be to them
Like slippery *ways;*
In the darkness they shall be driven on
And fall in them;
For I [b]will bring disaster on them,
The year of their punishment,"
says the LORD.
13 "And I have seen folly in the
prophets of Samaria:
[a]They prophesied by Baal
And [b]caused My people Israel to err.
14 Also I have seen a horrible thing
in the prophets of Jerusalem:
[a]They commit adultery and walk in lies;
They also [b]strengthen the
hands of evildoers,
So that no one turns back
from his wickedness.
All of them are like [c]Sodom to Me,
And her inhabitants like Gomorrah.

15"Therefore thus says the LORD of hosts
concerning the prophets:

'Behold, I will feed them
with [a]wormwood,
And make them drink the water of gall;
For from the prophets of Jerusalem
Profaneness has gone out
into all the land.'"

16Thus says the LORD of hosts:

"Do not listen to the words of the
prophets who prophesy to you.
They make you worthless;
[a]They speak a vision of their own heart,
Not from the mouth of the LORD.
17 They continually say to those
who despise Me,
'The LORD has said, [a]"You
shall have peace"';
And *to* everyone who [b]walks
according to the dictates of
his own heart, they say,
[c]'No evil shall come upon you.'"

18 For [a]who has stood in the
counsel of the LORD,

23:5 [a] Is. 4:2; 11:1; 40:10, 11; Jer. 33:14; [Dan. 9:24; Zech. 6:12]; Matt. 1:1, 6; Luke 3:31; [John 1:45; 7:42] [b] Ps. 72:2; Is. 9:7; 32:1, 18; [Dan. 9:24] **23:6** [a] Deut. 33:28; Jer. 30:10; Zech. 14:11 [b] Jer. 32:37 [c] Is. 45:24; Jer. 33:16; [Dan. 9:24; Rom. 3:22; 1 Cor. 1:30] [1] Hebrew *YHWH Tsidkenu* **23:7** [a] Is. 43:18, 19; Jer. 16:14 **23:8** [a] Is. 43:5, 6; Ezek. 34:13; Amos 9:14, 15 [b] Gen. 12:7; Jer. 16:14, 15; 31:8 **23:9** [a] Jer. 8:18; Hab. 3:16 **23:10** [a] Jer. 9:2 [b] Hos. 4:2; Mal. 3:5 [c] Ps. 107:34; Jer. 9:10 **23:11** [a] Jer. 6:13; Zeph. 3:4 [b] Jer. 7:30; 32:34; Ezek. 8:11; 23:39 **23:12** [a] Ps. 35:6; [Prov. 4:19]; Jer. 13:16 [b] Jer. 11:23 **23:13** [a] 1 Kin. 18:18–21; Jer. 2:8 [b] Is. 9:16 **23:14** [a] Jer. 29:23 [b] Jer. 23:22; Ezek. 13:22, 23 [c] Gen. 18:20; Deut. 32:32; Is. 1:9, 10 **23:15** [a] Deut. 29:18; Jer. 9:15 **23:16** [a] Jer. 14:14; Ezek. 13:3, 6 **23:17** [a] Jer. 8:11; Ezek. 13:10; Zech. 10:2 [b] Deut. 29:19; Jer. 3:17 [c] Jer. 5:12; Amos 9:10; Mic. 3:11 **23:18** [a] Job 15:8, 9; [Jer. 23:22; 1 Cor. 2:16]

And has perceived and
heard His word?
Who has marked His word
and heard *it?*
19 Behold, a [a]whirlwind of the LORD
has gone forth in fury—
A violent whirlwind!
It will fall violently on the
head of the wicked.
20 The [a]anger of the LORD
will not turn back
Until He has executed and performed
the thoughts of His heart.
[b]In the latter days you will
understand it perfectly.

21 "I[a] have not sent these
prophets, yet they ran.
I have not spoken to them,
yet they prophesied.
22 But if they had stood in My counsel,
And had caused My people
to hear My words,
Then they would have [a]turned
them from their evil way
And from the evil of their doings.

23 "*Am* I a God near at hand,"
says the LORD,
"And not a God afar off?
24 Can anyone [a]hide himself
in secret places,
So I shall not see him?" says the LORD;
[b]"Do I not fill heaven and
earth?" says the LORD.

25"I have heard what the prophets have
said who prophesy lies in My name, saying,
'I have dreamed, I have dreamed!' 26How
long will *this* be in the heart of the prophets
who prophesy lies? Indeed *they are* prophets of the deceit of their own heart, 27who
try to make My people forget My name
by their dreams which everyone tells his
neighbor, [a]as their fathers forgot My name
for Baal.

28"The prophet who has a dream,
let him tell a dream;
And he who has My word, let him
speak My word faithfully.
What *is* the chaff to the
wheat?" says the LORD.
29"*Is* not My word like a [a]fire?"
says the LORD,
"And like a hammer *that* breaks
the rock in pieces?

30"Therefore behold, [a]I *am* against the
prophets," says the LORD, "who steal My
words every one from his neighbor. 31Be-
hold, I *am* [a]against the prophets," says the
LORD, "who use their tongues and say, 'He
says.' 32Behold, I *am* against those who
prophesy false dreams," says the LORD,
"and tell them, and cause My people to err
by their [a]lies and by [b]their recklessness. Yet
I did not send them or command them;
therefore they shall not [c]profit this people
at all," says the LORD.

33"So when these people or the prophet
or the priest ask you, saying, 'What is [a]the
oracle of the LORD?' you shall then say
to them, 'What oracle?'[1] I will even forsake you," says the LORD. 34"And *as for* the
prophet and the priest and the people who
say, 'The oracle of the LORD!' I will even
punish that man and his house. 35Thus
every one of you shall say to his neighbor, and every one to his brother, 'What
has the LORD answered?' and, 'What has
the LORD spoken?' 36And the oracle of the
LORD you shall mention no more. For every
man's word will be his oracle, for you have
[a]perverted the words of the living God, the
LORD of hosts, our God. 37Thus you shall
say to the prophet, 'What has the LORD answered you?' and, 'What has the LORD spoken?' 38But since you say, 'The oracle of
the LORD!' therefore thus says the LORD:
'Because you say this word, "The oracle
of the LORD!" and I have sent to you, saying, "Do not say, 'The oracle of the LORD!'"
39therefore behold, I, even I, [a]will utterly
forget you and forsake you, and the city
that I gave you and your fathers, and *will
cast you* out of My presence. 40And I will
bring [a]an everlasting reproach upon you,

23:19 [a] Jer. 25:32; 30:23; Amos 1:14 23:20 [a] 2 Kin. 23:26, 27; Jer. 30:24 [b] Gen. 49:1 23:21 [a] Jer. 14:14; 23:32; 27:15 23:22 [a] Jer. 25:5 23:24 [a] [Ps. 139:7]; Amos 9:2, 3 [b] [1 Kin. 8:27]; Ps. 139:7 23:27 [a] Judg. 3:7 23:29 [a] Jer. 5:14 23:30 [a] Deut. 18:20; Ps. 34:16; Jer. 14:14, 15; Ezek. 13:8, 9 23:31 [a] Ezek. 13:9 23:32 [a] Jer. 20:6; 27:10; Lam. 2:14; 3:37 [b] Zeph. 3:4 [c] Jer. 7:8; Lam. 2:14 23:33 [a] Is. 13:1; Nah. 1:1; Hab. 1:1; Zech. 9:1; Mal. 1:1 [1] Septuagint, Targum, and Vulgate read '*You are the burden.*' 23:36 [a] Deut. 4:2 23:39 [a] Hos. 4:6 23:40 [a] Jer. 20:11; Ezek. 5:14, 15

and a perpetual [b]shame, which shall not be forgotten.' "

The Sign of Two Baskets of Figs

24 The [a]LORD showed me, and there were two baskets of figs set before the temple of the LORD, after Nebuchadnezzar [b]king of Babylon had carried away captive [c]Jeconiah the son of Jehoiakim, king of Judah, and the princes of Judah with the craftsmen and smiths, from Jerusalem, and had brought them to Babylon. 2One basket *had* very good figs, like the figs *that are* first ripe; and the other basket *had* very bad figs which could not be eaten, they were so [a]bad. 3Then the LORD said to me, "What do you see, Jeremiah?"

And I said, "Figs, the good figs, very good; and the bad, very bad, which cannot be eaten, they are so bad."

4Again the word of the LORD came to me, saying, 5"Thus says the LORD, the God of Israel: 'Like these good figs, so will I acknowledge those who are carried away captive from Judah, whom I have sent out of this place for *their own* good, into the land of the Chaldeans. 6For I will set My eyes on them for good, and [a]I will bring them back to this land; [b]I will build them and not pull *them* down, and I will plant them and not pluck *them* up. 7Then I will give them [a]a heart to know Me, that I *am* the LORD; and they shall be [b]My people, and I will be their God, for they shall return to Me [c]with their whole heart.

8'And as the bad [a]figs which cannot be eaten, they are so bad'—surely thus says the LORD—'so will I give up Zedekiah the king of Judah, his princes, the [b]residue of Jerusalem who remain in this land, and [c]those who dwell in the land of Egypt. 9I will deliver them to [a]trouble into all the kingdoms of the earth, for *their* harm, [b]*to be* a reproach and a byword, a taunt and a curse, in all places where I shall drive them. 10And I will send the sword, the famine, and the pestilence among them, till they are consumed from the land that I gave to them and their fathers.' "

Seventy Years of Desolation

25 The word that came to Jeremiah concerning all the people of Judah, [a]in the fourth year of [b]Jehoiakim the son of Josiah, king of Judah (which *was* the first year of Nebuchadnezzar king of Babylon), 2which Jeremiah the prophet spoke to all the people of Judah and to all the inhabitants of Jerusalem, saying: 3[a]"From the thirteenth year of Josiah the son of Amon, king of Judah, even to this day, this *is* the twenty-third year in which the word of the LORD has come to me; and I have spoken to you, rising early and speaking, [b]but you have not listened. 4And the LORD has sent to you all His servants the prophets, [a]rising early and sending *them,* but you have not listened nor inclined your ear to hear. 5They said, [a]'Repent now everyone of his evil way and his evil doings, and dwell in the land that the LORD has given to you and your fathers forever and ever. 6Do not go after other gods to serve them and worship them, and do not provoke Me to anger with the works of your hands; and I will not harm you.' 7Yet you have not listened to Me," says the LORD, "that you might [a]provoke Me to anger with the works of your hands to your own hurt.

8"Therefore thus says the LORD of hosts: 'Because you have not heard My words, 9behold, I will send and take [a]all the families of the north,' says the LORD, 'and Nebuchadnezzar the king of Babylon, [b]My servant, and will bring them against this land, against its inhabitants, and against these nations all around, and will utterly destroy them, and [c]make them an astonishment, a hissing, and perpetual desolations. 10Moreover I will take from them the [a]voice of mirth and the voice of gladness, the voice of the bridegroom and the voice of the bride, [b]the sound of the millstones and the light of the lamp. 11And this whole land shall be a desolation *and* an astonishment, and these nations shall serve the king of Babylon seventy [a]years.

23:40 [b] Mic. 3:5–7 **24:1** [a] Amos 7:1, 4; 8:1 [b] 2 Kin. 24:12–16; 2 Chr. 36:10 [c] Jer. 22:24–28; 29:2 **24:2** [a] Is. 5:4, 7; Jer. 29:17 **24:6** [a] Jer. 12:15; 29:10; Ezek. 11:17 [b] Jer. 32:41; 33:7; 42:10 **24:7** [a] [Deut. 30:6; Jer. 32:39; Ezek. 11:19; 36:26, 27] [b] Is. 51:16; Jer. 30:22; 31:33; 32:38; Ezek. 14:11; Zech. 8:8; [Heb. 8:10] [c] 1 Sam. 7:3; Ps. 119:2; Jer. 29:13 **24:8** [a] Jer. 29:17 [b] Jer. 39:9 [c] Jer. 44:1, 26–30 **24:9** [a] Deut. 28:25, 37; 1 Kin. 9:7; 2 Chr. 7:20; Jer. 15:4; 29:18; 34:17 [b] Ps. 44:13, 14 **25:1** [a] Jer. 36:1 [b] 2 Kin. 24:1, 2; 2 Chr. 36:4–6; Dan. 1:1, 2 **25:3** [a] Jer. 1:2 [b] Jer. 7:13; 11:7, 8, 10 **25:4** [a] Jer. 7:13, 25 **25:5** [a] 2 Kin. 17:13; [Is. 55:6, 7]; Jer. 18:11; Ezek. 18:30; [Jon. 3:8–10] **25:7** [a] Deut. 32:21; Jer. 7:19; 32:30 **25:9** [a] Jer. 1:15 [b] Is. 45:1; Jer. 27:6 [c] Jer. 18:16 **25:10** [a] Is. 24:7–11; Jer. 7:34; 16:9; Ezek. 26:13; Hos. 2:11; Rev. 18:23 [b] Eccl. 12:4; Is. 47:2 **25:11** [a] 2 Chr. 36:21; Jer. 29:10; Dan. 9:2; Zech. 7:5

12 'Then it will come to pass, [a]when seventy years are completed, *that* I will punish the king of Babylon and that nation, the
land of the Chaldeans, for their iniquity,'
says the LORD; [b]'and I will make it a perpetual desolation. 13 So I will bring on that
land all My words which I have pronounced
against it, all that is written in this book,
which Jeremiah has prophesied concerning all the nations. 14 [a](For many nations
[b]and great kings shall [c]be served by them
also; [d]and I will repay them according to
their deeds and according to the works of
their own hands.)' "

Judgment on the Nations

15 For thus says the LORD God of Israel to
me: "Take this [a]wine cup of fury from My
hand, and cause all the nations, to whom I
send you, to drink it. 16 And [a]they will drink
and stagger and go mad because of the
sword that I will send among them."

17 Then I took the cup from the LORD's
hand, and made all the nations drink, to
whom the LORD had sent me: 18 Jerusalem
and the cities of Judah, its kings and its
princes, to make them [a]a desolation, an astonishment, a hissing, and [b]a curse, as *it is*
this day; 19 Pharaoh king of Egypt, his servants, his princes, and all his people; 20 all
the mixed multitude, all the kings of [a]the
land of Uz, all the kings of the land of the
[b]Philistines (namely, Ashkelon, Gaza, Ekron, and [c]the remnant of Ashdod); 21 [a]Edom,
Moab, and the people of Ammon; 22 all the
kings of [a]Tyre, all the kings of Sidon, and
the kings of the coastlands which *are* across
the [b]sea; 23 [a]Dedan, Tema, Buz, and all *who
are* in the farthest corners; 24 all the kings
of Arabia and all the kings of the [a]mixed
multitude who dwell in the desert; 25 all the
kings of Zimri, all the kings of [a]Elam, and all
the kings of the [b]Medes; 26 [a]all the kings of
the north, far and near, one with another;
and all the kingdoms of the world which
are on the face of the earth. Also the king
of Sheshach[1] shall drink after them.

27 "Therefore you shall say to them, 'Thus
says the LORD of hosts, the God of Israel:
[a]"Drink, [b]be drunk, and vomit! Fall and rise
no more, because of the sword which I will
send among you." ' 28 And it shall be, if they
refuse to take the cup from your hand to
drink, then you shall say to them, 'Thus
says the LORD of hosts: "You shall certainly
drink! 29 For behold, [a]I begin to bring calamity on the city [b]which is called by My name,
and should you be utterly unpunished? You
shall not be unpunished, for [c]I will call for
a sword on all the inhabitants of the earth,"
says the LORD of hosts.'

30 "Therefore prophesy against them all
these words, and say to them:

'The LORD will [a]roar from on high,
And utter His voice from
[b]His holy habitation;
He will roar mightily against
[c]His fold.
He will give [d]a shout, as those
who tread *the grapes,*
Against all the inhabitants
of the earth.
31 A noise will come to the
ends of the earth—
For the LORD has [a]a controversy
with the nations;
[b]He will plead His case with all flesh.
He will give those *who are* wicked
to the sword,' says the LORD."

32 Thus says the LORD of hosts:

"Behold, disaster shall go forth
From nation to nation,
And [a]a great whirlwind
shall be raised up
From the farthest parts of the earth.

33 [a]And at that day the slain of the LORD
shall be from *one* end of the earth even to
the *other* end of the earth. They shall not
be [b]lamented, [c]or gathered, or buried; they
shall become refuse on the ground.

25:12 [a] 2 Chr. 36:21, 22; Ezra 1:1; Jer. 29:10; Dan. 9:2 [b] Is. 13:20; Jer. 50:3 **25:14** [a] Jer. 50:9; 51:27, 28 [b] Jer. 51:27 [c] Jer. 27:7 [d] Jer. 50:29; 51:6, 24 **25:15** [a] Job 21:20; Ps. 75:8; Is. 51:17; Rev. 14:10 **25:16** [a] Jer. 51:7; Ezek. 23:34; Nah. 3:11 **25:18** [a] Jer. 25:9, 11 [b] Jer. 24:9 **25:20** [a] Job 1:1; Lam. 4:21 [b] Jer. 47:1–7; Ezek. 25:16, 17 [c] Is. 20:1 **25:21** [a] Jer. 49:7 **25:22** [a] Jer. 47:4; Zech. 9:2–4 [b] Jer. 49:23 **25:23** [a] Is. 21:13; Jer. 49:7, 8 **25:24** [a] Jer. 25:20; 50:37; Ezek. 30:5 **25:25** [a] Gen. 10:22; Is. 11:11; Jer. 49:34 [b] Is. 13:17; Jer. 51:11, 28 **25:26** [a] Jer. 50:9 [1] A code word for Babylon (compare 51:41) **25:27** [a] Jer. 25:16; Hab. 2:16 [b] Is. 63:6 **25:29** [a] [Prov. 11:31]; Is. 10:12; Jer. 13:13; Ezek. 9:6; [Luke 23:31; 1 Pet. 4:17] [b] Dan. 9:18 [c] Ezek. 38:21 **25:30** [a] Is. 42:13; Joel 3:16; Amos 1:2 [b] Ps. 11:4 [c] 1 Kin. 9:3; Ps. 132:14 [d] Is. 16:9; Jer. 48:33 **25:31** [a] Hos. 4:1; Mic. 6:2 [b] Is. 66:16; Joel 3:2 **25:32** [a] Jer. 23:19; 30:23 **25:33** [a] Is. 34:2, 3; 66:16 [b] Jer. 16:4, 6; Ezek. 39:4, 17 [c] Ps. 79:3; Jer. 8:2; Rev. 11:9

34 "Wail,[a] shepherds, and cry!
Roll about *in the ashes,*
You leaders of the flock!
For the days of your slaughter and
your dispersions are fulfilled;
You shall fall like a precious vessel.
35 And the shepherds will
have no way to flee,
Nor the leaders of the flock
to escape.
36 A voice of the cry of the shepherds,
And a wailing of the leaders to
the flock *will be heard.*
For the LORD has plundered
their pasture,
37 And the peaceful dwellings
are cut down
Because of the fierce anger
of the LORD.
38 He has left His lair like the lion;
For their land is desolate
Because of the fierceness
of the Oppressor,
And because of His fierce
anger."

Jeremiah Saved from Death
(cf. Jer. 7:1–15)

26 In the beginning of the reign of Jehoiakim the son of Josiah, king of
Judah, this word came from the LORD, saying, 2"Thus says the LORD: 'Stand in [a]the
court of the LORD's house, and speak to all
the cities of Judah, which come to worship
in the LORD's house, [b]all the words that I
command you to speak to them. [c]Do not
diminish a word. 3[a]Perhaps everyone will
listen and turn from his evil way, that I may
[b]relent concerning the calamity which I
purpose to bring on them because of the
evil of their doings.' 4And you shall say to
them, 'Thus says the LORD: [a]"If you will
not listen to Me, to walk in My law which
I have set before you, 5to heed the words
of My servants the prophets [a]whom I sent
to you, both rising up early and sending
them (but you have not heeded), 6then I
will make this house like [a]Shiloh, and will
make this city [b]a curse to all the nations of
the earth."'"

7So the priests and the prophets and all
the people heard Jeremiah speaking these
words in the house of the LORD. 8Now it
happened, when Jeremiah had made an
end of speaking all that the LORD had commanded *him* to speak to all the people, that
the priests and the prophets and all the
people seized him, saying, "You will surely
die! 9Why have you prophesied in the name
of the LORD, saying, 'This house shall be
like Shiloh, and this city shall be [a]desolate,
without an inhabitant'?" And all the people were gathered against Jeremiah in the
house of the LORD.

10When the princes of Judah heard these
things, they came up from the king's house
to the house of the LORD and sat down in
the entry of the New Gate of the LORD's
house. 11And the priests and the prophets
spoke to the princes and all the people, saying, "This man deserves to [a]die! For he has
prophesied against this city, as you have
heard with your ears."

12Then Jeremiah spoke to all the princes
and all the people, saying: "The LORD sent
me to prophesy against this house and
against this city with all the words that you
have heard. 13Now therefore, [a]amend your
ways and your doings, and obey the voice
of the LORD your God; then the LORD will
relent concerning the doom that He has
pronounced against you. 14As for me, here
[a]I am, in your hand; do with me as seems
good and proper to you. 15But know for certain that if you put me to death, you will
surely bring innocent blood on yourselves,
on this city, and on its inhabitants; for truly
the LORD has sent me to you to speak all
these words in your hearing."

16So the princes and all the people said
to the priests and the prophets, "This man
does not deserve to die. For he has spoken
to us in the name of the LORD our God."

17[a]Then certain of the elders of the land
rose up and spoke to all the assembly of
the people, saying: 18[a]"Micah of Moresheth prophesied in the days of Hezekiah
king of Judah, and spoke to all the people
of Judah, saying, 'Thus says the LORD of
hosts:

25:34 [a] Jer. 4:8; 6:26; Ezek. 27:30 26:2 [a] 2 Chr. 24:20, 21; Jer. 19:14 [b] Deut. 4:2; Jer. 43:1; Ezek. 3:10; Matt. 28:20; [Rev. 22:19] [c] Acts 20:27 26:3 [a] Is. 1:16–19; Jer. 36:3–7 [b] Jer. 18:8; Jon. 3:9 26:4 [a] Lev. 26:14, 15; Deut. 28:15; 1 Kin. 9:6; Is. 1:20; Jer. 17:27; 22:5 26:5 [a] Jer. 25:4; 29:19 26:6 [a] 1 Sam. 4:10, 11; Ps. 78:60; Jer. 7:12, 14 [b] 2 Kin. 22:19; Is. 65:15; Jer. 24:9 26:9 [a] Jer. 9:11 26:11 [a] Jer. 38:4 26:13 [a] Jer. 7:3; [Joel 2:13]; Jon. 3:8 26:14 [a] Jer. 38:5 26:17 [a] Acts 5:34 26:18 [a] Mic. 1:1

[b]"Zion shall be plowed *like* a field,
Jerusalem shall become
[c]heaps of ruins,
And the mountain of the temple[1]
Like the bare hills of the forest."'[2]

19 Did Hezekiah king of Judah and all Judah
ever put him to death? [a]Did he not fear the
LORD and [b]seek the LORD's favor? And the
LORD [c]relented concerning the doom which
He had pronounced against them. [d]But we
are doing great evil against ourselves."
20 Now there was also a man who prophesied in the name of the LORD, Urijah the
son of Shemaiah of Kirjath Jearim, who
prophesied against this city and against
this land according to all the words of Jeremiah. 21 And when Jehoiakim the king,
with all his mighty men and all the princes,
heard his words, the king sought to put him
to death; but when Urijah heard *it,* he was
afraid and fled, and went to Egypt. 22 Then
Jehoiakim the king sent men to Egypt: Elnathan the son of Achbor, and *other* men
who went with him to Egypt. 23 And they
brought Urijah from Egypt and brought
him to Jehoiakim the king, who killed him
with the sword and cast his dead body into
the graves of the common people.
24 Nevertheless [a]the hand of Ahikam the
son of Shaphan was with Jeremiah, so that
they should not give him into the hand of
the people to put him to death.

Symbol of the Bonds and Yokes

27 In the beginning of the reign of Jehoiakim[1] the son of Josiah, [a]king of
Judah, this word came to Jeremiah from
the LORD, saying,[2] 2 "Thus says the LORD
to me: 'Make for yourselves bonds and
yokes, [a]and put them on your neck, 3 and
send them to the king of Edom, the king of
Moab, the king of the Ammonites, the king
of Tyre, and the king of Sidon, by the hand
of the messengers who come to Jerusalem
to Zedekiah king of Judah. 4 And command
them to say to their masters, "Thus says the
LORD of hosts, the God of Israel—thus you
shall say to your masters: 5 [a]'I have made
the earth, the man and the beast that *are*
on the ground, by My great power and by
My outstretched arm, and [b]have given it to
whom it seemed proper to Me. 6 [a]And now
I have given all these lands into the hand
of Nebuchadnezzar the king of Babylon,
[b]My servant; and [c]the beasts of the field I
have also given him to serve him. 7 [a]So all
nations shall serve him and his son and his
son's son, [b]until the time of his land comes;
[c]and then many nations and great kings
shall make him serve them. 8 And it shall be,
that the nation and kingdom which will not
serve Nebuchadnezzar the king of Babylon,
and which will not put its neck under the
yoke of the king of Babylon, that nation I
will punish,' says the LORD, 'with the sword,
the famine, and the pestilence, until I have
consumed them by his hand. 9 Therefore do
not listen to your prophets, your diviners,
your dreamers, your soothsayers, or your
sorcerers, who speak to you, saying, "You
shall not serve the king of Babylon." 10 For
they prophesy a [a]lie to you, to remove you
far from your land; and I will drive you out,
and you will perish. 11 But the nations that
bring their necks under the yoke of the king
of Babylon and serve him, I will let them remain in their own land,' says the LORD, 'and
they shall till it and dwell in it.'"'"
12 I also spoke to [a]Zedekiah king of Judah
according to all these words, saying, "Bring
your necks under the yoke of the king of
Babylon, and serve him and his people,
and live! 13 [a]Why will you die, you and your
people, by the sword, by the famine, and
by the pestilence, as the LORD has spoken
against the nation that will not serve the
king of Babylon? 14 Therefore [a]do not listen
to the words of the prophets who speak to
you, saying, 'You shall not serve the king
of Babylon,' for they prophesy [b]a lie to you;
15 for I have [a]not sent them," says the LORD,
"yet they prophesy a lie in My name, that I
may drive you out, and that you may perish, you and the prophets who prophesy
to you."

26:18 [b] Mic. 3:12 [c] Neh. 4:2; Ps. 79:1; Jer. 9:11 [1] Literally *house* [2] Compare Micah 3:12 **26:19** [a] 2 Chr. 32:26; Is. 37:1, 4, 15–20 [b] 2 Kin. 20:1–19 [c] Ex. 32:14; 2 Sam. 24:16; Jer. 18:8 [d] [Acts 5:39] **26:24** [a] 2 Kin. 22:12–14; Jer. 39:14; 40:5–7 **27:1** [a] Jer. 27:3, 12, 20; 28:1 [1] Following Masoretic Text, Targum, and Vulgate; some Hebrew manuscripts, Arabic, and Syriac read *Zedekiah* (compare 27:3, 12; 28:1). [2] Septuagint omits verse 1. **27:2** [a] Jer. 28:10, 12; Ezek. 4:1; 12:3; 24:3 **27:5** [a] Ps. 115:15; 146:6; Is. 45:12 [b] Deut. 9:29; Ps. 115:16; Jer. 32:17; Dan. 4:17, 25, 32 **27:6** [a] Jer. 28:14 [b] Jer. 25:9; 43:10; Ezek. 29:18, 20 [c] Jer. 28:14; Dan. 2:38 **27:7** [a] 2 Chr. 36:20 [b] Jer. 25:12; 50:27; [Dan. 5:26]; Zech. 2:8, 9 [c] Jer. 25:14 **27:10** [a] Jer. 23:16, 32; 28:15 **27:12** [a] Jer. 28:1; 38:17 **27:13** [a] [Prov. 8:36]; Jer. 27:8; 38:23; [Ezek. 18:31] **27:14** [a] Jer. 23:16 [b] Jer. 14:14; 23:21; 29:8, 9; Ezek. 13:22 **27:15** [a] Jer. 23:21; 29:9

16Also I spoke to the priests and to all
this people, saying, "Thus says the LORD:
'Do not listen to the words of your prophets who prophesy to you, saying, "Behold,
[a]the vessels of the LORD's house will now
shortly be brought back from Babylon"; for
they prophesy a lie to you. 17Do not listen to
them; serve the king of Babylon, and live!
Why should this city be laid waste? 18But if
they *are* prophets, and if the word of the
LORD is with them, let them now make intercession to the LORD of hosts, that the
vessels which are left in the house of the
LORD, *in* the house of the king of Judah,
and at Jerusalem, do not go to Babylon.'
19"For thus says the LORD of hosts [a]con-
cerning the pillars, concerning the Sea,
concerning the carts, and concerning the
remainder of the vessels that remain in
this city, 20which Nebuchadnezzar king of
Babylon did not take, when he carried away
[a]captive Jeconiah the son of Jehoiakim, king
of Judah, from Jerusalem to Babylon, and
all the nobles of Judah and Jerusalem—
21yes, thus says the LORD of hosts, the God of
Israel, concerning the [a]vessels that remain
in the house of the LORD, and in the house of
the king of Judah and of Jerusalem: 22'They
shall be [a]carried to Babylon, and there they
shall be until the day that I [b]visit them,' says
the LORD. 'Then [c]I will bring them up and
restore them to this place.'"

Hananiah's Falsehood and Doom

28 And [a]it happened in the same year,
at the beginning of the reign of Zedekiah king of Judah, in the [b]fourth year *and*
in the fifth month, *that* Hananiah the son
of [c]Azur the prophet, who *was* from Gibeon, spoke to me in the house of the LORD
in the presence of the priests and of all the
people, saying, 2"Thus speaks the LORD
of hosts, the God of Israel, saying: 'I have
broken [a]the yoke of the king of Babylon.
3[a]Within two full years I will bring back
to this place all the vessels of the LORD's
house, that Nebuchadnezzar king of Babylon [b]took away from this place and carried
to Babylon. 4And I will bring back to this
place Jeconiah the son of Jehoiakim, king
of Judah, with all the captives of Judah who
went to Babylon,' says the LORD, 'for I will
break the yoke of the king of Babylon.'"
5Then the prophet Jeremiah spoke to the
prophet Hananiah in the presence of the
priests and in the presence of all the people
who stood in the house of the LORD, 6and
the prophet Jeremiah said, [a]"Amen! The
LORD do so; the LORD perform your words
which you have prophesied, to bring back
the vessels of the LORD's house and all who
were carried away captive, from Babylon
to this place. 7Nevertheless hear now this
word that I speak in your hearing and in
the hearing of all the people: 8The prophets
who have been before me and before you of
old prophesied against many countries and
great kingdoms—of war and disaster and
pestilence. 9As for [a]the prophet who prophesies of [b]peace, when the word of the prophet
comes to pass, the prophet will be known *as*
one whom the LORD has truly sent."
10Then Hananiah the prophet took the
[a]yoke off the prophet Jeremiah's neck and
broke it. 11And Hananiah spoke in the presence of all the people, saying, "Thus says
the LORD: 'Even so I will break the yoke of
Nebuchadnezzar king of Babylon [a]from
the neck of all nations within the space of
two full years.'" And the prophet Jeremiah
went his way.
12Now the word of the LORD came to
Jeremiah, after Hananiah the prophet
had broken the yoke from the neck of the
prophet Jeremiah, saying, 13"Go and tell
Hananiah, saying, 'Thus says the LORD:
"You have broken the yokes of wood, but
you have made in their place yokes of iron."
14For thus says the LORD of hosts, the God
of Israel: [a]"I have put a yoke of iron on the
neck of all these nations, that they may
serve Nebuchadnezzar king of Babylon;
and they shall serve him. [b]I have given him
the beasts of the field also."'"
15Then the prophet Jeremiah said to
Hananiah the prophet, "Hear now, Hananiah, the LORD has not sent you, but
[a]you make this people trust in a [b]lie.

27:16 [a] 2 Kin. 24:13; 2 Chr. 36:7, 10; Jer. 28:3; Dan. 1:2 27:19 [a] 1 Kin. 7:15; 2 Kin. 25:13–17; Jer. 52:17, 20, 21 27:20 [a] 2 Kin. 24:14, 15; 2 Chr. 36:10, 18; Jer. 24:1 27:21 [a] Jer. 20:5 27:22 [a] 2 Kin. 25:13; 2 Chr. 36:18 [b] 2 Chr. 36:21; Jer. 29:10; 32:5 [c] Ezra 1:7; 7:19 28:1 [a] Jer. 27:1 [b] Jer. 51:59 [c] Ezek. 11:1 28:2 [a] Jer. 27:12 28:3 [a] Jer. 27:16 [b] 2 Kin. 24:13; Dan. 1:2 28:6 [a] 1 Kin. 1:36; Ps. 41:13; Jer. 11:5 28:9 [a] Deut. 18:22 [b] Jer. 23:17; Ezek. 13:10, 16 28:10 [a] Jer. 27:2 28:11 [a] Jer. 27:7 28:14 [a] Deut. 28:48; Jer. 27:7, 8 [b] Jer. 27:6

16Therefore thus says the LORD: 'Behold,
I will cast you from the face of the earth.
This year you shall [a]die, because you have
taught [b]rebellion against the LORD.' "
17So Hananiah the prophet died the
same year in the seventh month.

Jeremiah's Letter to the Captives

29 Now these *are* the words of the letter that Jeremiah the prophet sent
from Jerusalem to the remainder of the
elders who were [a]carried away captive—to
the priests, the prophets, and all the people
whom Nebuchadnezzar had carried away
captive from Jerusalem to Babylon. 2(This
happened after [a]Jeconiah the king, the
[b]queen mother, the eunuchs, the princes
of Judah and Jerusalem, the craftsmen,
and the smiths had departed from Jerusalem.) 3*The letter was sent* by the hand of
Elasah the son of [a]Shaphan, and Gemariah
the son of Hilkiah, whom Zedekiah king of
Judah sent to Babylon, to Nebuchadnezzar
king of Babylon, saying,

4 Thus says the LORD of hosts, the God
of Israel, to all who were carried away
captive, whom I have caused to be
carried away from Jerusalem to
Babylon:

5 Build houses and dwell *in them;* plant
gardens and eat their fruit. 6Take
wives and beget sons and daughters;
and take wives for your sons and give
your daughters to husbands, so that
they may bear sons and daughters—
that you may be increased there, and
not diminished. 7And seek the peace
of the city where I have caused you to
be carried away captive, [a]and pray to
the LORD for it; for in its peace you will
have peace. 8For thus says the LORD
of hosts, the God of Israel: Do not let
your prophets and your diviners who
are in your midst [a]deceive you, nor
listen to your dreams which you cause
to be dreamed. 9For they prophesy
[a]falsely to you in My name; I have not
sent them, says the LORD.

10 For thus says the LORD: After [a]seventy
years are completed at Babylon, I will
visit you and perform My good word
toward you, and cause you to [b]return
to this place. 11For I know the thoughts
that I think toward you, says the LORD,
thoughts of peace and not of evil, to
give you a future and a hope. 12Then
you will [a]call upon Me and go and pray
to Me, and I will [b]listen to you. 13And
[a]you will seek Me and find *Me,* when
you search for Me [b]with all your heart.
14[a]I will be found by you, says the LORD,
and I will bring you back from your
captivity; [b]I will gather you from all the
nations and from all the places where
I have driven you, says the LORD, and I
will bring you to the place from which
I cause you to be carried away captive.

#OXYGEN

JEREMIAH 29:11

Trust in His Ways

When you are going through the fire,
know that God has a plan. He is refining
you. Believe the pain you feel is gain
because He is the potter and you are
the clay. It is all working together.

Breathe and trust in His ways.

15 Because you have said, "The LORD
has raised up prophets for us in
Babylon"— 16[a]therefore thus says the
LORD concerning the king who sits on
the throne of David, concerning all
the people who dwell in this city, and
concerning your brethren who have

28:15 [a] Jer. 20:6; 29:31; Lam. 2:14; Ezek. 13:22; Zech. 13:3 [b] Jer. 27:10; 29:9 **28:16** [a] Jer. 20:6 [b] Deut. 13:5; Jer. 29:32 **29:1** [a] Jer. 27:20 **29:2** [a] 2 Kin. 24:12–16; 2 Chr. 36:9, 10; Jer. 22:24–28 [b] 2 Kin. 24:12, 15; Jer. 13:18 **29:3** [a] 2 Chr. 34:8 **29:7** [a] Ezra 6:10; Neh. 1:4–11; Dan. 9:16; 1 Tim. 2:2 **29:8** [a] Jer. 14:14; 23:21; 27:14, 15; Eph. 5:6 **29:9** [a] Jer. 28:15; 37:19 **29:10** [a] 2 Chr. 36:21–23; Ezra 1:1–4; Jer. 25:12; 27:22; Dan. 9:2; Zech. 7:5 [b] [Jer. 24:6, 7]; Zeph. 2:7 **29:12** [a] Ps. 50:15; Jer. 33:3; Dan. 9:3 [b] Ps. 145:19 **29:13** [a] Lev. 26:39–42; Deut. 30:1–3 [b] 1 Chr. 22:19; 2 Chr. 22:9; Jer. 24:7 **29:14** [a] [Deut. 4:7]; Ps. 32:6; 46:1; [Is. 55:6, 7]; Jer. 24:7 [b] Is. 43:5, 6; Jer. 23:8; 32:37 **29:16** [a] Jer. 38:2, 3, 17–23

not gone out with you into captivity—
17thus says the LORD of hosts: Behold,
I will send on them the sword, the
famine, and the pestilence, and will
make them like [a]rotten figs that
cannot be eaten, they are so bad. 18And
I will pursue them with the sword,
with famine, and with pestilence; and
I [a]will deliver them to trouble among
all the kingdoms of the earth—to be
[b]a curse, an astonishment, a hissing,
and a reproach among all the nations
where I have driven them, 19because
they have not heeded My words, says
the LORD, which [a]I sent to them by My
servants the prophets, rising up early
and sending *them;* neither would you
heed, says the LORD. 20Therefore hear
the word of the LORD, all you of the
captivity, whom I have sent from
Jerusalem to Babylon.

21 Thus says the LORD of hosts, the God
of Israel, concerning Ahab the son of
Kolaiah, and Zedekiah the son of
Maaseiah, who prophesy a [a]lie to you
in My name: Behold, I will deliver them
into the hand of Nebuchadnezzar king
of Babylon, and he shall slay them
before your eyes. 22[a]And because of
them a curse shall be taken up by all
the captivity of Judah who *are* in
Babylon, saying, "The LORD make you
like Zedekiah and Ahab, [b]whom the
king of Babylon roasted in the fire";
23because [a]they have done disgraceful
things in Israel, have committed
adultery with their neighbors' wives,
and have spoken lying words in My
name, which I have not commanded
them. Indeed I [b]know, and *am* a
witness, says the LORD.

24 You shall also speak to Shemaiah the
Nehelamite, saying, 25Thus speaks the
LORD of hosts, the God of Israel,
saying: You have sent letters in your
name to all the people who *are* at
Jerusalem, [a]to Zephaniah the son of
Maaseiah the priest, and to all the
priests, saying, 26"The LORD has made
you priest instead of Jehoiada the
priest, so that there should be [a]officers
in the house of the LORD over every
man *who* is [b]demented and considers
himself a prophet, that you should
[c]put him in prison and in the stocks.
27Now therefore, why have you not
rebuked Jeremiah of Anathoth who
makes himself a prophet to you? 28For
he has sent to us *in* Babylon, saying,
'This *captivity is* long; build houses and
dwell *in them,* and plant gardens and
eat their fruit.'"

29Now Zephaniah the priest read this letter in the hearing of Jeremiah the prophet.
30Then the word of the LORD came to Jeremiah, saying: 31Send to all those in captivity, saying, Thus says the LORD concerning
Shemaiah the Nehelamite: Because Shemaiah has prophesied to you, [a]and I have not
sent him, and he has caused you to trust
in a [b]lie— 32therefore thus says the LORD:
Behold, I will punish Shemaiah the Nehelamite and his family: he shall not have anyone to dwell among this people, nor shall
he see the good that I will do for My people, says the LORD, [a]because he has taught
rebellion against the LORD.

Restoration of Israel and Judah

30 The word that came to Jeremiah
from the LORD, saying, 2"Thus
speaks the LORD God of Israel, saying:
'Write in a book for yourself all the words
that I have spoken to you. 3For behold, the
days are coming,' says the LORD, 'that [a]I will
bring back from captivity My people Israel and Judah,' says the LORD. [b]'And I will
cause them to return to the land that I gave
to their fathers, and they shall possess it.'"
4Now these *are* the words that the LORD
spoke concerning Israel and Judah.
5"For thus says the LORD:

'We have heard a voice of trembling,
Of fear, and not of peace.

29:17 [a] Jer. 24:3, 8–10 29:18 [a] Deut. 28:25; 2 Chr. 29:8; Jer. 15:4; 24:9; 34:17; Ezek. 12:15 [b] Jer. 26:6; 42:18 29:19 [a] Jer. 25:4; 26:5; 35:15 29:21 [a] Jer. 14:14, 15; Lam. 2:14; 2 Pet. 2:1 29:22 [a] Gen. 48:20; Is. 65:15 [b] Dan. 3:6, 21 29:23 [a] Jer. 23:14 [b] [Prov. 5:21; Jer. 16:17]; Mal. 3:5; [Heb. 4:13] 29:25 [a] 2 Kin. 25:18; Jer. 21:1 29:26 [a] Jer. 20:1 [b] 2 Kin. 9:11; Hos. 9:7; Mark 3:21; John 10:20; Acts 26:24; [2 Cor. 5:13] [c] Jer. 20:1, 2; Acts 16:24 29:31 [a] Jer. 28:15 [b] Ezek. 13:8–16, 22, 23 29:32 [a] Jer. 28:16 30:3 [a] Ps. 53:6; Jer. 29:14; 30:18; 32:44; Ezek. 39:25; Amos 9:14; Zeph. 3:20 [b] Jer. 16:15; Ezek. 20:42; 36:24

6 Ask now, and see,
Whether a man is ever in
labor with child?
So why do I see every man *with*
his hands on his loins
[a]Like a woman in labor,
And all faces turned pale?
7 [a]Alas! For that day *is* great,
[b]So that none *is* like it;
And it *is* the time of Jacob's trouble,
But he shall be saved out of it.

8 'For it shall come to pass in that day,'
Says the LORD of hosts,
'*That* I will break his yoke
from your neck,
And will burst your bonds;
Foreigners shall no more
enslave them.
9 But they shall serve the
LORD their God,
And [a]David their king,
Whom I will [b]raise up for them.

10 'Therefore [a]do not fear, O My
servant Jacob,' says the LORD,
'Nor be dismayed, O Israel;
For behold, I will save you from afar,
And your seed [b]from the
land of their captivity.
Jacob shall return, have
rest and be quiet,
And no one shall make *him* afraid.
11 For I *am* with [a]you,' says the
LORD, 'to save you;
[b]Though I make a full end of all nations
where I have scattered you,
[c]Yet I will not make a
complete end of you.
But I will correct you [d]in justice,
And will not let you go
altogether unpunished.'

12"For thus says the LORD:

[a]'Your affliction *is* incurable,
Your wound *is* severe.
13 *There is* no one to plead your cause,
That you may be bound up;
[a]You have no healing medicines.
14 [a]All your lovers have forgotten you;
They do not seek you;
For I have wounded you with
the wound [b]of an enemy,
With the chastisement [c]of a cruel one,
For the multitude of your iniquities,
[d]*Because* your sins have increased.
15 Why [a]do you cry about your affliction?
Your sorrow *is* incurable.
Because of the multitude
of your iniquities,
Because your sins have increased,
I have done these things to you.

16 'Therefore all those who devour
you [a]shall be devoured;
And all your adversaries, every one
of them, shall go into [b]captivity;
Those who plunder you shall
become [c]plunder,
And all who prey upon you
I will make a [d]prey.
17 [a]For I will restore health to you
And heal you of your wounds,'
says the LORD,
'Because they called you
an outcast *saying:*
"This *is* Zion;
No one seeks her." '

18"Thus says the LORD:

'Behold, I will bring back the
captivity of Jacob's tents,
And [a]have mercy on his
dwelling places;
The city shall be built upon
its own mound,
And the palace shall remain
according to its own plan.
19 Then [a]out of them shall
proceed thanksgiving
And the voice of those
who make merry;
[b]I will multiply them, and they
shall not diminish;

30:6 [a] Jer. 4:31; 6:24 30:7 [a] [Is. 2:12]; Hos. 1:11; Joel 2:11; Amos 5:18; Zeph. 1:14 [b] Lam. 1:12; Dan. 9:12; 12:1 30:9 [a] Is. 55:3; Ezek. 34:23; 37:24; Hos. 3:5 [b] [Luke 1:69; Acts 2:30; 13:23] 30:10 [a] Is. 41:13; 43:5; 44:2; Jer. 46:27, 28 [b] Jer. 3:18 30:11 [a] [Is. 43:2–5] [b] Amos 9:8 [c] Jer. 4:27; 46:27, 28 [d] Ps. 6:1; Is. 27:8; Jer. 10:24; 46:28 30:12 [a] 2 Chr. 36:16; Jer. 15:18 30:13 [a] Jer. 8:22 30:14 [a] Jer. 22:20, 22; Lam. 1:2 [b] Job 13:24; 16:9; 19:11 [c] Job 30:21 [d] Jer. 5:6 30:15 [a] Jer. 15:18 30:16 [a] Ex. 23:22; Is. 41:11; Jer. 10:25 [b] Is. 14:2; Joel 3:8 [c] Is. 33:1; Ezek. 39:10 [d] Jer. 2:3 30:17 [a] Ex. 15:26; Ps. 107:20; Is. 30:26; Jer. 33:6 30:18 [a] Ps. 102:13 30:19 [a] Ps. 126:1, 2; Is. 51:11; Jer. 31:4; Zeph. 3:14 [b] Is. 49:19–21; Jer. 23:3; 33:22; Zech. 10:8

I will also glorify them, and
they shall not be small.
20 Their children also shall be [a]as before,
And their congregation shall
be established before Me;
And I will punish all who
oppress them.
21 Their nobles shall be from
among them,
[a]And their governor shall
come from their midst;
Then I will [b]cause him to draw near,
And he shall approach Me;
For who *is* this who pledged his heart
to approach Me?' says the LORD.
22 'You shall be [a]My people,
And I will be your God.'"

23 Behold, the [a]whirlwind of the LORD
Goes forth with fury,
A continuing whirlwind;
It will fall violently on the
head of the wicked.
24 The fierce anger of the LORD will
not return until He has done it,
And until He has performed
the intents of His heart.

[a]In the latter days you will consider it.

The Remnant of Israel Saved

31 "At [a]the same time," says the LORD,
[b]"I will be the God of all the families
of Israel, and they shall be My people."
2 Thus says the LORD:

"The people who survived the sword
Found grace in the wilderness—
Israel, when [a]I went to give him rest."

3 The LORD has appeared of
old to me, *saying:*
"Yes, [a]I have loved you with
[b]an everlasting love;
Therefore with lovingkindness
I have [c]drawn you.
4 Again [a]I will build you, and
you shall be rebuilt,
O virgin of Israel!
You shall again be adorned
with your [b]tambourines,
And shall go forth in the dances
of those who rejoice.
5 [a]You shall yet plant vines on the
mountains of Samaria;
The planters shall plant and eat
them as ordinary food.
6 For there shall be a day
When the watchmen will cry
on Mount Ephraim,
[a]'Arise, and let us go up *to* Zion,
To the LORD our God.'"

7 For thus says the LORD:

[a]"Sing with gladness for Jacob,
And shout among the chief
of the nations;
Proclaim, give praise, and say,
'O LORD, save Your people,
The remnant of Israel!'
8 Behold, I will bring them [a]from
the north country,
And [b]gather them from the
ends of the earth,
Among them the blind and the lame,
The woman with child
And the one who labors
with child, together;
A great throng shall return there.
9 [a]They shall come with weeping,
And with supplications I
will lead them.
I will cause them to walk [b]by
the rivers of waters,
In a straight way in which
they shall not stumble;
For I am a Father to Israel,
And Ephraim *is* My [c]firstborn.

10 "Hear the word of the LORD,
O nations,
And declare *it* in the isles
afar off, and say,
'He who scattered Israel
[a]will gather him,

30:20 [a] Is. 1:26 30:21 [a] Gen. 49:10 [b] Num. 16:5; Ps. 65:4 30:22 [a] Ex. 6:7; Jer. 32:38; Ezek. 36:28; Hos. 2:23; Zech. 13:9 30:23 [a] Jer. 23:19, 20; 25:32 30:24 [a] Gen. 49:1 31:1 [a] Jer. 30:24 [b] Jer. 30:22 31:2 [a] Ex. 33:14; Num. 10:33; Deut. 1:33; Josh. 1:13; Ps. 95:11; Is. 63:14 31:3 [a] Deut. 4:37; 7:8; Mal. 1:2 [b] Is. 43:4; Rom. 11:28 [c] Hos. 11:4 31:4 [a] Jer. 33:7 [b] Ex. 15:20; Judg. 11:34; Ps. 149:3 31:5 [a] Ps. 107:37; Is. 65:21; Ezek. 28:26; Amos 9:14 31:6 [a] [Is. 2:3; Jer. 31:12; 50:4, 5; Mic. 4:2] 31:7 [a] Is. 12:5, 6 31:8 [a] Jer. 3:12, 18; 23:8 [b] Deut. 30:4; Is. 43:6; Ezek. 20:34, 41; 34:13 31:9 [a] [Ps. 126:5; Jer. 50:4] [b] Is. 35:8; 43:19; 49:10, 11 [c] Ex. 4:22 31:10 [a] Is. 40:11; Ezek. 34:12–14

And keep him as a shepherd
does his flock.'
11 For [a]the LORD has redeemed Jacob,
And ransomed him [b]from the
hand of one stronger than he.
12 Therefore they shall come and
sing in [a]the height of Zion,
Streaming to [b]the goodness
of the LORD—
For wheat and new wine and oil,
For the young of the flock and the herd;
Their souls shall be like a
[c]well-watered garden,
[d]And they shall sorrow no more at all.

13 "Then shall the virgin rejoice
in the dance,
And the young men and
the old, together;
For I will turn their mourning to joy,
Will comfort them,
And make them rejoice
rather than sorrow.
14 I will satiate the soul of the
priests with abundance,
And My people shall be satisfied with
My goodness, says the LORD."

Mercy on Ephraim

15 Thus says the LORD:

[a]"A voice was heard in [b]Ramah,
Lamentation *and* bitter [c]weeping,
Rachel weeping for her children,
Refusing to be comforted
for her children,
Because [d]they *are* no more."

16 Thus says the LORD:

"Refrain your voice from [a]weeping,
And your eyes from tears;
For your work shall be
rewarded, says the LORD,
And they shall come back from
the land of the enemy.
17 There is [a]hope in your future,
says the LORD,
That *your* children shall come
back to their own border.

18 "I have surely heard Ephraim
bemoaning himself:
'You have [a]chastised me,
and I was chastised,
Like an untrained bull;
[b]Restore me, and I will return,
For You *are* the LORD my God.
19 Surely, [a]after my turning,
I repented;
And after I was instructed, I
struck myself on the thigh;
I was [b]ashamed, yes, even humiliated,
Because I bore the reproach
of my youth.'
20 *Is* Ephraim My dear son?
Is he a pleasant child?
For though I spoke against him,
I earnestly remember him still;
[a]Therefore My heart yearns for him;
[b]I will surely have mercy on
him, says the LORD.

21 "Set up signposts,
Make landmarks;
[a]Set your heart toward the highway,
The way in *which* you went.
Turn back, O virgin of Israel,
Turn back to these your cities.
22 How long will you [a]gad about,
O you [b]backsliding daughter?
For the LORD has created a
new thing in the earth—
A woman shall encompass a man."

Future Prosperity of Judah

23 Thus says the LORD of hosts, the God
of Israel: "They shall again use this speech
in the land of Judah and in its cities, when I
bring back their captivity: [a]'The LORD bless
you, O home of justice, *and* [b]mountain of
holiness!' 24 And there shall dwell in Judah
itself, and [a]in all its cities together, farmers and those going out with flocks. 25 For
I have satiated the weary soul, and I have
replenished every sorrowful soul."

31:11 [a] Is. 44:23; 48:20; Jer. 15:21; 50:19 [b] Is. 49:24 31:12 [a] Ezek. 17:23 [b] Hos. 3:5 [c] Is. 58:11 [d] Is. 35:10; 65:19; [John 16:22; Rev. 21:4] 31:15 [a] Matt. 2:17, 18 [b] Josh. 18:25; Judg. 4:5; Is. 10:29; Jer. 40:1 [c] Gen. 37:35 [d] Jer. 10:20 31:16 [a] [Is. 25:8; 30:19] 31:17 [a] Jer. 29:11 31:18 [a] Job 5:17; Ps. 94:12 [b] Ps. 80:3, 7, 19; Jer. 17:4; Lam. 5:21; [Acts 3:26] 31:19 [a] Deut. 30:2 [b] Ezek. 36:31; [Zech. 12:10] 31:20 [a] Gen. 43:30; Deut. 32:36; Judg. 10:16; Is. 63:15; Hos. 11:8 [b] Is. 57:18; Jer. 3:12; 12:15; [Hos. 14:4]; Mic. 7:18 31:21 [a] Jer. 50:5 31:22 [a] Jer. 2:18, 23, 36 [b] Jer. 3:6, 8, 11, 12, 14, 22 31:23 [a] Ps. 122:5–8; Is. 1:26 [b] [Zech. 8:3] 31:24 [a] Jer. 33:12

26 After this I awoke and looked around,
and my sleep was [a]sweet to me.
27 "Behold, the days are coming, says the
LORD, that [a]I will sow the house of Israel and
the house of Judah with the seed of man
and the seed of beast. 28 And it shall come
to pass, *that* as I have [a]watched over them
[b]to pluck up, to break down, to throw down,
to destroy, and to afflict, so I will watch over
them [c]to build and to plant, says the LORD.
29 [a]In those days they shall say no more:

'The fathers have eaten sour grapes,
And the children's teeth
are set on edge.'

30 [a]But every one shall die for his own iniquity; every man who eats the sour grapes,
his teeth shall be set on edge.

A New Covenant

31 "Behold, the [a]days are coming, says the
LORD, when I will make a new covenant
with the house of Israel and with the house
of Judah— 32 not according to the covenant that I made with their fathers in the
day *that* [a]I took them by the hand to lead
them out of the land of Egypt, My covenant
which they broke, though I was a husband
to them,[1] says the LORD. 33 [a]But this *is* the
covenant that I will make with the house
of Israel after those days, says the LORD: [b]I
will put My law in their minds, and write
it on their hearts; [c]and I will be their God,
and they shall be My people. 34 No more
shall every man teach his neighbor, and
every man his brother, saying, 'Know the
LORD,' for [a]they all shall know Me, from the
least of them to the greatest of them, says
the LORD. For [b]I will forgive their iniquity,
and their sin I will remember no more."

35 Thus says the LORD,
[a]Who gives the sun for a light by day,
The ordinances of the moon and
the stars for a light by night,
Who disturbs [b]the sea,
And its waves roar
[c](The LORD of hosts *is* His name):

36 "If [a]those ordinances depart
From before Me, says the LORD,
Then the seed of Israel shall also cease
From being a nation before
Me forever."

37 Thus says the LORD:

[a]"If heaven above can be measured,
And the foundations of the earth
searched out beneath,
I will also [b]cast off all the seed of Israel
For all that they have done,
says the LORD.

38 "Behold, the days are coming, says the
LORD, that the city shall be built for the
LORD [a]from the Tower of Hananel to the
Corner Gate. 39 [a]The surveyor's line shall
again extend straight forward over the
hill Gareb; then it shall turn toward Goath.
40 And the whole valley of the dead bodies
and of the ashes, and all the fields as far
as the Brook Kidron, [a]to the corner of the
Horse Gate toward the east, [b]*shall be* holy
to the LORD. It shall not be plucked up or
thrown down anymore forever."

Jeremiah Buys a Field

32 The word that came to Jeremiah
from the LORD [a]in the tenth year
of Zedekiah king of Judah, which was the
eighteenth year of Nebuchadnezzar. 2 For
then the king of Babylon's army besieged
Jerusalem, and Jeremiah the prophet was
shut up [a]in the court of the prison, which
was in the king of Judah's house. 3 For Zedekiah king of Judah had shut him up, saying, "Why do you [a]prophesy and say, 'Thus
says the LORD: [b]"Behold, I will give this
city into the hand of the king of Babylon,
and he shall take it; 4 and Zedekiah king of

31:26 [a] Prov. 3:24 31:27 [a] Ezek. 36:9–11; Hos. 2:23 31:28 [a] Jer. 44:27; Dan. 9:14 [b] Jer. 1:10; 18:7 [c] Jer. 24:6 31:29 [a] Lam. 5:7; Ezek. 18:2, 3 31:30 [a] Deut. 24:16; 2 Chr. 25:4; Is. 3:11; [Ezek. 18:4, 20; Gal. 6:5, 7] 31:31 [a] Jer. 32:40; 33:14; Ezek. 37:26; Heb. 8:8–12; 10:16, 17 31:32 [a] Deut. 1:31; Is. 63:12 [1] Following Masoretic Text, Targum, and Vulgate; Septuagint and Syriac read *and I turned away from them.* 31:33 [a] Jer. 32:40; Heb. 10:16 [b] Ps. 40:8; [Ezek. 11:19; 36:26, 27; 2 Cor. 3:3] [c] Jer. 24:7; 30:22; 32:38 31:34 [a] Is. 11:9; 54:13; Jer. 24:7; Hab. 2:14; [John 6:45; 1 Cor. 2:10; 1 John 2:20] [b] Jer. 33:8; 50:20; Mic. 7:18; [Acts 10:43; 13:39; Rom. 11:27] 31:35 [a] Gen. 1:14–18; Deut. 4:19; Ps. 72:5, 17; 89:2, 36; 119:91 [b] Is. 51:15 [c] Jer. 10:16 31:36 [a] Ps. 148:6; Is. 54:9, 10; Jer. 33:20 31:37 [a] Is. 40:12; Jer. 33:22 [b] Jer. 33:24–26; [Rom. 11:2–5, 26, 27] 31:38 [a] Neh. 3:1; 12:39; Zech. 14:10 31:39 [a] Ezek. 40:8; Zech. 2:1, 2 31:40 [a] 2 Kin. 11:16; 2 Chr. 23:15; Neh. 3:28 [b] [Joel 3:17]; Zech. 14:20 32:1 [a] 2 Kin. 25:1, 2; Jer. 39:1, 2 32:2 [a] Neh. 3:25; Jer. 33:1; 37:21; 39:14 32:3 [a] Jer. 26:8, 9 [b] Jer. 21:3–7; 34:2

Judah [a]shall not escape from the hand of
the Chaldeans, but shall surely be delivered into the hand of the king of Babylon,
and shall speak with him face to face,[1] and
see him [b]eye to eye; 5then he shall [a]lead
Zedekiah to Babylon, and there he shall be
[b]until I visit him," says the LORD; [c]"though
you fight with the Chaldeans, you shall not
succeed"'?"
6And Jeremiah said, "The word of the
LORD came to me, saying, 7'Behold, Hanamel the son of Shallum your uncle will
come to you, saying, "Buy my field which
is in Anathoth, for the [a]right of redemption *is* yours to buy *it*."' 8Then Hanamel
my uncle's son came to me in the court
of the prison according to the word of the
LORD, and said to me, 'Please buy my field
that *is* in Anathoth, which *is* in the country of Benjamin; for the right of inheritance *is* yours, and the redemption yours;
buy *it* for yourself.' Then I knew that this
was the word of the LORD. 9So I bought the
field from Hanamel, the son of my uncle
who *was* in Anathoth, and [a]weighed *out*
to him the money—seventeen shekels of
silver. 10And I signed the deed and sealed
it, took witnesses, and weighed the money
on the scales. 11So I took the purchase deed,
both that which was sealed *according* to the
law and custom, and that which was open;
12and I gave the purchase deed to [a]Baruch
the son of Neriah, son of Mahseiah, in the
presence of Hanamel my uncle's *son*, and in
the presence of the [b]witnesses who signed
the purchase deed, before all the Jews who
sat in the court of the prison.
13"Then I charged [a]Baruch before them,
saying, 14'Thus says the LORD of hosts, the
God of Israel: "Take these deeds, both this
purchase deed which is sealed and this
deed which is open, and put them in an
earthen vessel, that they may last many
days." 15For thus says the LORD of hosts,
the God of Israel: "Houses and fields and
vineyards shall be [a]possessed again in this
land."'

Jeremiah Prays for Understanding

16"Now when I had delivered the purchase deed to Baruch the son of Neriah,
I prayed to the LORD, saying: 17'Ah, Lord
GOD! Behold, [a]You have made the heavens and the earth by Your great power and
outstretched arm. [b]There is nothing too
hard for You. 18*You* show [a]lovingkindness
to thousands, and repay the iniquity of the
fathers into the bosom of their children
after them—the Great, [b]the Mighty God,
whose name *is* [c]the LORD of hosts. 19*You*
are [a]great in counsel and mighty in work,
for Your [b]eyes *are* open to all the ways of
the sons of men, [c]to give everyone according to his ways and according to the fruit of
his doings. 20You have set signs and wonders in the land of Egypt, to this day, and
in Israel and among *other* men; and You
have made Yourself [a]a name, as it is this
day. 21You [a]have brought Your people Israel out of the land of Egypt with signs and
wonders, with a strong hand and an outstretched arm, and with great terror; 22You
have given them this land, of which You
swore to their fathers to give them—[a]"a
land flowing with milk and honey."[1] 23And
they came in and took possession of it, but
[a]they have not obeyed Your voice or walked
in Your law. They have done nothing of all
that You commanded them to do; therefore You have caused all this calamity to
come upon them.
24'Look, the siege mounds! They have
come to the city to take it; and the city has
been given into the hand of the Chaldeans who fight against it, because of [a]the
sword and famine and pestilence. What
You have spoken has happened; there You
see *it*! 25And You have said to me, O Lord
GOD, "Buy the field for money, and take
witnesses"!—yet the city has been given
into the hand of the Chaldeans.'"

God's Assurance of the People's Return

26Then the word of the LORD came to
Jeremiah, saying, 27"Behold, I *am* the LORD,

32:4 [a] 2 Kin. 25:4–7; Jer. 34:3; 38:18, 23; 39:5; 52:9 [b] Jer. 39:5 [1] Literally *mouth to mouth* **32:5** [a] Jer. 27:22; 39:7; Ezek. 12:12, 13 [b] Jer. 27:22 [c] Jer. 21:4; 33:5 **32:7** [a] Lev. 25:24, 25, 32; Ruth 4:4 **32:9** [a] Gen. 23:16; Zech. 11:12 **32:12** [a] Jer. 36:4 [b] Is. 8:2 **32:13** [a] Jer. 36:4 **32:15** [a] Ezra 2:1; [Jer. 31:5, 12, 14]; Amos 9:14, 15; Zech. 3:10 **32:17** [a] 2 Kin. 19:15; Ps. 102:25; Is. 40:26–29; Jer. 27:5 [b] Gen. 18:14; Jer. 32:27; Zech. 8:6; Matt. 19:26; Mark 10:27; Luke 18:27 **32:18** [a] Ex. 20:6; 34:7; Deut. 5:9, 10 [b] Ps. 50:1; [Is. 9:6]; Jer. 20:11 [c] Jer. 10:16 **32:19** [a] Is. 28:29 [b] Job 34:21; Ps. 33:13; Prov. 5:21; Jer. 16:17 [c] Ps. 62:12; Jer. 17:10; [Matt. 16:27; John 5:29] **32:20** [a] Ex. 9:16; 1 Chr. 17:21; Is. 63:12; Jer. 13:11; Dan. 9:15 **32:21** [a] Ex. 6:6; 2 Sam. 7:23; 1 Chr. 17:21; Ps. 136:11, 12 **32:22** [a] Ex. 3:8, 17; Deut. 1:8; Ps. 105:9–11; Jer. 11:5 [1] Exodus 3:8 **32:23** [a] [Neh. 9:26]; Jer. 11:8; [Dan. 9:10–14] **32:24** [a] Jer. 14:12; Ezek. 14:21

the [a]God of all flesh. Is there anything too
hard for Me? 28Therefore thus says the
LORD: 'Behold, I will give this city into the
hand of the Chaldeans, into the hand of
Nebuchadnezzar king of Babylon, and he
shall take it. 29And the Chaldeans who fight
against this city shall come and [a]set fire to
this city and burn it, with the houses [b]on
whose roofs they have offered incense to
Baal and poured out drink offerings to other
gods, to provoke Me to anger; 30because the
children of Israel and the children of Judah
[a]have done only evil before Me from their
youth. For the children of Israel have provoked Me only to anger with the work of
their hands,' says the LORD. 31'For this city
has been to Me *a provocation of* My anger
and My fury from the day that they built it,
even to this day; [a]so I will remove it from
before My face 32because of all the evil of the
children of Israel and the children of Judah,
which they have done to provoke Me to anger—[a]they, their kings, their princes, their
priests, [b]their prophets, the men of Judah,
and the inhabitants of Jerusalem. 33And
they have turned to Me the [a]back, and not
the face; though I taught them, [b]rising up
early and teaching *them,* yet they have not
listened to receive instruction. 34But they
[a]set their abominations in the house which
is called by My name, to defile it. 35And they
built the high places of Baal which *are* in the
Valley of the Son of Hinnom, to [a]cause their
sons and their daughters to pass through
the fire to [b]Molech, [c]which I did not command them, nor did it come into My mind
that they should do this abomination, to
cause Judah to sin.'

36"Now therefore, thus says the LORD,
the God of Israel, concerning this city of
which you say, 'It shall be delivered into the
hand of the king of Babylon by the sword,
by the famine, and by the pestilence: 37Be-
hold, I will [a]gather them out of all countries
where I have driven them in My anger, in
My fury, and in great wrath; I will bring
them back to this place, and I will cause
them [b]to dwell safely. 38They shall be [a]My
people, and I will be their God; 39then I will
[a]give them one heart and one way, that they
may fear Me forever, for the good of them
and their children after them. 40And [a]I will
make an everlasting covenant with them,
that I will not turn away from doing them
good; but [b]I will put My fear in their hearts
so that they will not depart from Me. 41Yes,
[a]I will rejoice over them to do them good,
and [b]I will assuredly plant them in this
land, with all My heart and with all My soul.'

42"For thus says the LORD: [a]'Just as I have
brought all this great calamity on this people, so I will bring on them all the good that
I have promised them. 43And fields will be
bought in this land [a]of which you say, "*It is*
desolate, without man or beast; it has been
given into the hand of the Chaldeans." 44Men
will buy fields for money, sign deeds and
seal *them,* and take witnesses, in [a]the land
of Benjamin, in the places around Jerusalem, in the cities of Judah, in the cities of the
mountains, in the cities of the lowland, and
in the cities of the South; for [b]I will cause
their captives to return,' says the LORD."

Excellence of the Restored Nation

33 Moreover the word of the LORD
came to Jeremiah a second time,
while he was still [a]shut up in the court of
the prison, saying, 2"Thus says the LORD
[a]who made it, the LORD who formed it to
establish it [b](the LORD *is* His name): 3[a]'Call
to Me, and I will answer you, and show you
great and mighty things, which you do not
know.'

4"For thus says the LORD, the God of Israel, concerning the houses of this city and
the houses of the kings of Judah, which
have been pulled down *to fortify*[1] against
[a]the siege mounds and the sword: 5'They
come to fight with the Chaldeans, but *only*
to [a]fill their places[1] with the dead bodies
of men whom I will slay in My anger and

32:27 [a] [Num. 16:22] 32:29 [a] 2 Chr. 36:19; Jer. 21:10; 37:8, 10; 52:13 [b] Jer. 19:13 32:30 [a] Deut. 9:7–12; Is. 63:10; Jer. 2:7; 3:25; 7:22–26; Ezek. 20:28 32:31 [a] 2 Kin. 23:27; 24:3; Jer. 27:10 32:32 [a] Ezra 9:7; Is. 1:4, 6; Dan. 9:8 [b] Jer. 23:14 32:33 [a] Jer. 2:27; 7:24 [b] Jer. 7:13 32:34 [a] 2 Kin. 21:1–7; Jer. 7:10–12, 30; 23:11; Ezek. 8:5, 6 32:35 [a] 2 Chr. 28:2, 3; 33:6; Jer. 7:31; 19:5 [b] Lev. 18:21; 1 Kin. 11:33; 2 Kin. 23:10; Acts 7:43 [c] Jer. 7:31 32:37 [a] Deut. 30:3; Jer. 23:3; 29:14; 31:10; 50:19; Ezek. 37:21 [b] Jer. 33:16 32:38 [a] [Jer. 24:7; 30:22; 31:33] 32:39 [a] [Jer. 24:7; Ezek. 11:19] 32:40 [a] Is. 55:3; Jer. 31:31; Ezek. 37:26 [b] Deut. 31:6, 8; [Ezek. 39:29; Jer. 31:33] 32:41 [a] Deut. 30:9; Is. 62:5; 65:19; Zeph. 3:17 [b] Jer. 24:6; 31:28; Amos 9:15 32:42 [a] Jer. 31:28; Zech. 8:14, 15 32:43 [a] Jer. 33:10 32:44 [a] Jer. 17:26 [b] Jer. 33:7, 11 33:1 [a] Jer. 32:2, 3 33:2 [a] Is. 37:26 [b] Ex. 15:3; [Jer. 10:16]; Amos 5:8; 9:6 33:3 [a] Ps. 91:15; [Is. 55:6, 7]; Jer. 29:12 33:4 [a] Is. 22:10; Jer. 32:24; Ezek. 4:2; 21:22; Hab. 1:10 [1] Compare Isaiah 22:10 33:5 [a] 2 Kin. 23:14; Jer. 21:4–7; 32:5 [1] Compare 2 Kings 23:14

My fury, all for whose wickedness I have
hidden My face from this city. 6 Behold, [a]I
will bring it health and healing; I will heal
them and reveal to them the abundance
of peace and truth. 7 And [a]I will cause the
captives of Judah and the captives of Israel
to return, and will rebuild those places [b]as
at the first. 8 I will [a]cleanse them from all
their iniquity by which they have sinned
against Me, and I will pardon all their iniquities by which they have sinned and by
which they have transgressed against Me.
9 [a]Then it shall be to Me a name of joy, a
praise, and an honor before all nations of
the earth, who shall hear all the good that
I do to them; they shall [b]fear and tremble
for all the goodness and all the prosperity
that I provide for it.'

10 "Thus says the LORD: 'Again there shall
be heard in this place—[a]of which you say,
"It *is* desolate, without man and without
beast"—in the cities of Judah, in the streets
of Jerusalem that are desolate, without
man and without inhabitant and without
beast, 11 the [a]voice of joy and the voice of
gladness, the voice of the bridegroom and
the voice of the bride, the voice of those
who will say:

[b]"Praise the LORD of hosts,
For the LORD *is* good,
For His mercy *endures* forever"—

and of those *who will* bring [c]the sacrifice
of praise into the house of the LORD. For I
will cause the captives of the land to return
as at the first,' says the LORD.

12 "Thus says the LORD of hosts: [a]'In this
place which is desolate, without man and
without beast, and in all its cities, there
shall again be a dwelling place of shepherds causing *their* flocks to lie down. 13 [a]In
the cities of the mountains, in the cities of
the lowland, in the cities of the South, in
the land of Benjamin, in the places around
Jerusalem, and in the cities of Judah, the
flocks shall again [b]pass under the hands
of him who counts *them,*' says the LORD.

14 [a]'Behold, the days are coming,' says the
LORD, 'that [b]I will perform that good thing
which I have promised to the house of Israel and to the house of Judah:

15 'In those days and at that time
I will cause to grow up to David
A [a]Branch of righteousness;
He shall execute judgment and
righteousness in the earth.
16 In those days Judah will be saved,
And Jerusalem will dwell safely.
And this *is the name* by which
she will be called:

THE LORD OUR RIGHTEOUSNESS.'[1]

17 "For thus says the LORD: 'David shall
never [a]lack a man to sit on the throne of the
house of Israel; 18 nor shall the [a]priests, the
Levites, lack a man to [b]offer burnt offerings
before Me, to kindle grain offerings, and to
sacrifice continually.' "

The Permanence of God's Covenant

19 And the word of the LORD came to Jeremiah, saying, 20 "Thus says the LORD: 'If
you can break My covenant with the day
and My covenant with the night, so that
there will not be day and night in their season, 21 then [a]My covenant may also be broken with David My servant, so that he shall
not have a son to reign on his throne, and
with the Levites, the priests, My ministers.
22 As [a]the host of heaven cannot be numbered, nor the sand of the sea measured,
so will I [b]multiply the descendants of David My servant and the [c]Levites who minister to Me.' "

23 Moreover the word of the LORD came
to Jeremiah, saying, 24 "Have you not considered what these people have spoken,
saying, 'The two families which the LORD
has chosen, He has also cast them off'?

33:6 [a] Jer. 30:17; Hos. 6:1 33:7 [a] Ps. 85:1; Jer. 30:3; 32:44; Amos 9:14 [b] Is. 1:26; Jer. 24:6; 30:20; 31:4, 28; 42:10; Amos 9:14, 15 33:8 [a] Ps. 51:2; Is. 44:22; Jer. 50:20; Ezek. 36:25, 33; Mic. 7:18, 19; Zech. 13:1; [Heb. 9:11–14] 33:9 [a] Is. 62:7; Jer. 13:11 [b] Is. 60:5 33:10 [a] Jer. 32:43 33:11 [a] Jer. 7:34; 16:9; 25:10; Rev. 18:23 [b] 1 Chr. 16:8; 2 Chr. 5:13; Ezra 3:11; Ps. 136:1; Is. 12:4 [c] Lev. 7:12; Ps. 107:22; 116:17; Heb. 13:15 33:12 [a] Is. 65:10; [Jer. 31:24; 50:19; Ezek. 34:12–15; Zeph. 2:6, 7] 33:13 [a] Jer. 17:26; 32:44 [b] Lev. 27:32; [Luke 15:4] 33:14 [a] Jer. 23:5; 31:27, 31 [b] Is. 32:1; Jer. 29:10; 32:42; Ezek. 34:23–25; Hag. 2:6–9 33:15 [a] Is. 4:2; 11:1; Jer. 23:5; Zech. 3:8; 6:12, 13 33:16 [1] Compare 23:5, 6 33:17 [a] 2 Sam. 7:16; 1 Kin. 2:4; Ps. 89:29; [Luke 1:32] 33:18 [a] Num. 3:5–10; Deut. 18:1; 24:8; Josh. 3:3; Ezek. 44:15 [b] [Rom. 12:1; 15:16; 1 Pet. 2:5, 9; Rev. 1:6] 33:21 [a] 2 Sam. 23:5; 2 Chr. 7:18; 21:7; Ps. 89:34 33:22 [a] Gen. 15:5; 22:17; Jer. 31:37 [b] Jer. 30:19; Ezek. 36:10, 11 [c] Is. 66:21; Jer. 33:18

Thus they have [a]despised My people, as
if they should no more be a nation before
them.
25“Thus says the LORD: ‘If [a]My covenant
is not with day and night, *and if* I have not
[b]appointed the ordinances of heaven and
earth, 26[a]then I will [b]cast away the descendants of Jacob and David My servant, *so*
that I will not take *any* of his descendants
to be rulers over the descendants of Abraham, Isaac, and Jacob. For I will cause their
captives to return, and will have mercy on
them.’ ”

Zedekiah Warned by God

34 The word which came to Jeremiah
from the LORD, [a]when Nebuchadnezzar king of Babylon and all his army,
[b]all the kingdoms of the earth under his
dominion, and all the people, fought
against Jerusalem and all its cities, saying, 2“Thus says the LORD, the God of Israel: ‘Go and [a]speak to Zedekiah king of
Judah and tell him, “Thus says the LORD:
‘Behold, [b]I will give this city into the hand
of the king of Babylon, and he shall burn
it with fire. 3And [a]you shall not escape
from his hand, but shall surely be taken
and delivered into his hand; your eyes
shall see the eyes of the king of Babylon,
he shall speak with you [b]face to face,[1] and
you shall go to Babylon.’ ” ’ 4Yet hear the
word of the LORD, O Zedekiah king of Judah! Thus says the LORD concerning you:
‘You shall not die by the sword. 5You shall
die in peace; as in [a]the ceremonies of your
fathers, the former kings who were before you, [b]so they shall burn *incense* for
you and [c]lament for you, *saying,* “Alas,
lord!” For I have pronounced the word,
says the LORD.’ ”
6Then Jeremiah the prophet spoke all
these words to Zedekiah king of Judah in
Jerusalem, 7when the king of Babylon’s
army fought against Jerusalem and all
the cities of Judah that were left, against
Lachish and Azekah; for *only* [a]these fortified cities remained of the cities of Judah.

Treacherous Treatment of Slaves

8*This is* the word that came to Jeremiah
from the LORD, after King Zedekiah had
made a covenant with all the people who
were at Jerusalem to proclaim [a]liberty to
them: 9[a]that every man should set free his
male and female slave—a Hebrew man or
woman—[b]that no one should keep a Jewish brother in bondage. 10Now when all the
princes and all the people, who had entered
into the covenant, heard that everyone
should set free his male and female slaves,
that no one should keep them in bondage
anymore, they obeyed and let *them* go. 11But
afterward they changed their minds and
made the male and female slaves return,
whom they had set free, and brought them
into subjection as male and female slaves.
12Therefore the word of the LORD came
to Jeremiah from the LORD, saying, 13“Thus
says the LORD, the God of Israel: ‘I made a
[a]covenant with your fathers in the day that
I brought them out of the land of Egypt,
out of the house of bondage, saying, 14“At
the end of [a]seven years let every man set
free his Hebrew brother, who has been sold
to him; and when he has served you six
years, you shall let him go free from you.”
But your fathers did not obey Me nor incline their ear. 15Then you recently turned
and did what was right in My sight—every
man proclaiming liberty to his neighbor;
and you [a]made a covenant before Me [b]in
the house which is called by My name.
16Then you turned around and [a]profaned
My name, and every one of you brought
back his male and female slaves, whom
you had set at liberty, at their pleasure, and
brought them back into subjection, to be
your male and female slaves.’
17“Therefore thus says the LORD: ‘You
have not obeyed Me in proclaiming liberty,
every one to his brother and every one to
his neighbor. [a]Behold, I proclaim liberty
to you,’ says the LORD—[b]‘to the sword, to
pestilence, and to famine! And I will deliver you to [c]trouble among all the kingdoms of the earth. 18And I will give the men

33:24 [a] Neh. 4:2–4; Esth. 3:6–8; Ps. 44:13, 14; 83:4; Ezek. 36:2 33:25 [a] Gen. 8:22; Jer. 33:20 [b] Ps. 74:16; 104:19 33:26 [a] Jer. 31:37 [b] Rom. 11:1, 2 34:1 [a] 2 Kin. 25:1; Jer. 32:1, 2; 39:1; 52:4 [b] Jer. 1:15; 25:9; Dan. 2:37, 38 34:2 [a] 2 Chr. 36:11, 12; Jer. 22:1, 2; 37:1, 2 [b] 2 Kin. 25:9; Jer. 21:10; 32:3, 28 34:3 [a] 2 Kin. 25:4, 5; Jer. 21:7; 52:7–11 [b] 2 Kin. 25:6, 7; Jer. 32:4; 39:5, 6 [1] Literally *mouth to mouth* 34:5 [a] 2 Chr. 16:14; 21:19 [b] Dan. 2:46 [c] Jer. 22:18 34:7 [a] 2 Kin. 18:13; 19:8; 2 Chr. 11:5, 9 34:8 [a] Ex. 21:2; Lev. 25:10; Neh. 5:1–13; Is. 58:6; Jer. 34:14, 17 34:9 [a] Neh. 5:11 [b] Lev. 25:39–46 34:13 [a] Ex. 24:3, 7, 8; Deut. 5:2, 3, 27; Jer. 31:32 34:14 [a] Ex. 21:2; 23:10; Deut. 15:12; 1 Kin. 9:22 34:15 [a] 2 Kin. 23:3; Neh. 10:29 [b] Jer. 7:10 34:16 [a] Ex. 20:7; Lev. 19:12 34:17 [a] Lev. 26:34, 35; Esth. 7:10; Dan. 6:24; [Matt. 7:2; Gal. 6:7]; James 2:13 [b] Jer. 32:24, 36 [c] Deut. 28:25, 64; Jer. 29:18

who have transgressed My covenant, who
have not performed the words of the covenant which they made before Me, when
[a]they cut the calf in two and passed between the parts of it— 19the princes of Judah, the princes of Jerusalem, the eunuchs,
the priests, and all the people of the land
who passed between the parts of the calf—
20I will [a]give them into the hand of their
enemies and into the hand of those who
seek their life. Their [b]dead bodies shall be
for meat for the birds of the heaven and the
beasts of the earth. 21And I will give Zedekiah king of Judah and his princes into
the hand of their enemies, into the hand
of those who seek their life, and into the
hand of the king of Babylon's army [a]which
has gone back from you. 22[a]Behold, I will
command,' says the LORD, 'and cause them
to return to this city. They will fight against
it [b]and take it and burn it with fire; and [c]I
will make the cities of Judah a desolation
without inhabitant.' "

The Obedient Rechabites

35 The word which came to Jeremiah
from the LORD in the days of Jehoiakim the son of Josiah, king of Judah, saying, 2"Go to the house of the [a]Rechabites,
speak to them, and bring them into the
house of the LORD, into one of [b]the chambers, and give them wine to drink."

3Then I took Jaazaniah the son of Jeremiah, the son of Habazziniah, his brothers
and all his sons, and the whole house of
the Rechabites, 4and I brought them into
the house of the LORD, into the chamber
of the sons of Hanan the son of Igdaliah,
a man of God, which *was* by the chamber
of the princes, above the chamber of Maaseiah the son of Shallum, [a]the keeper of
the door. 5Then I set before the sons of the
house of the Rechabites bowls full of wine,
and cups; and I said to them, "Drink wine."

6But they said, "We will drink no wine,
for [a]Jonadab the son of Rechab, our father,
commanded us, saying, 'You shall drink [b]no
wine, you nor your sons, forever. 7You shall
not build a house, sow seed, plant a vineyard, nor have *any of these;* but all your days
you shall dwell in tents, [a]that you may live
many days in the land where you are sojourners.' 8Thus we have [a]obeyed the voice
of Jonadab the son of Rechab, our father,
in all that he charged us, to drink no wine
all our days, we, our wives, our sons, or our
daughters, 9nor to build ourselves houses
to dwell in; nor do we have vineyard, field,
or seed. 10But we have dwelt in tents, and
have obeyed and done according to all that
Jonadab our father commanded us. 11But it
came to pass, when Nebuchadnezzar king
of Babylon came up into the land, that we
said, 'Come, let us [a]go to Jerusalem for fear
of the army of the Chaldeans and for fear
of the army of the Syrians.' So we dwell at
Jerusalem."

12Then came the word of the LORD to
Jeremiah, saying, 13"Thus says the LORD
of hosts, the God of Israel: 'Go and tell the
men of Judah and the inhabitants of Jerusalem, "Will you not [a]receive instruction
to obey My words?" says the LORD. 14"The
words of Jonadab the son of Rechab, which
he commanded his sons, not to drink wine,
are performed; for to this day they drink
none, and obey their father's commandment. [a]But although I have spoken to you,
[b]rising early and speaking, you did not obey
Me. 15I have also sent to you all My [a]servants
the prophets, rising up early and sending
them, saying, [b]'Turn now everyone from his
evil way, amend your doings, and do not go
after other gods to serve them; then you
will [c]dwell in the land which I have given
you and your fathers.' But you have not
inclined your ear, nor obeyed Me. 16Surely
the sons of Jonadab the son of Rechab have
performed the commandment of their [a]fa-
ther, which he commanded them, but this
people has not obeyed Me." '

17"Therefore thus says the LORD God
of hosts, the God of Israel: 'Behold, I will
bring on Judah and on all the inhabitants
of Jerusalem all the doom that I have pronounced against them; [a]because I have

---

34:18 [a] Gen. 15:10, 17 34:20 [a] 2 Kin. 25:19–21; Jer. 22:25 [b] Deut. 28:26; 1 Sam. 17:44, 46; 1 Kin. 14:11; 16:4; Ps. 79:2; Jer. 7:33; 16:4; 19:7 34:21 [a] Jer. 37:5–11; 39:4–7 34:22 [a] Jer. 37:8, 10 [b] Jer. 38:3; 39:1, 2, 8; 52:7, 13 [c] Jer. 9:11; 44:2, 6 35:2 [a] 2 Sam. 4:2; 2 Kin. 10:15; 1 Chr. 2:55 [b] 1 Kin. 6:5, 8; 1 Chr. 9:26, 33 35:4 [a] 2 Kin. 12:9; 25:18; 1 Chr. 9:18, 19 35:6 [a] 2 Kin. 10:15, 23 [b] Lev. 10:9; Num. 6:2–4; Judg. 13:7, 14; Prov. 31:4; Ezek. 44:21; Luke 1:15 35:7 [a] Ex. 20:12; Eph. 6:2, 3 35:8 [a] [Prov. 1:8, 9; 4:1, 2, 10; 6:20; Eph. 6:1; Col. 3:20] 35:11 [a] Jer. 4:5–7; 8:14 35:13 [a] [Is. 28:9–12]; Jer. 6:10; 17:23; 32:33 35:14 [a] 2 Chr. 36:15 [b] Jer. 7:13; 25:3 35:15 [a] Jer. 26:4, 5; 29:19 [b] [Is. 1:16, 17]; Jer. 18:11; 25:5, 6; [Ezek. 18:30–32]; Acts 26:20 [c] Jer. 7:7; 25:5, 6 35:16 [a] [Heb. 12:9] 35:17 [a] Prov. 1:24; Is. 65:12; 66:4; Jer. 7:13

spoken to them but they have not heard,
and I have called to them but they have
not answered.' "

18 And Jeremiah said to the house of the
Rechabites, "Thus says the LORD of hosts,
the God of Israel: 'Because you have obeyed
the commandment of Jonadab your father,
and kept all his precepts and done according to all that he commanded you, 19 therefore thus says the LORD of hosts, the God of
Israel: "Jonadab the son of Rechab shall not
lack a man to [a]stand before Me forever." ' "

The Scroll Read in the Temple

36 Now it came to pass in the [a]fourth
year of Jehoiakim the son of Josiah,
king of Judah, *that* this word came to Jeremiah from the LORD, saying: 2 "Take a [a]scroll
of a book and [b]write on it all the words that
I have spoken to you against Israel, against
Judah, and against [c]all the nations, from the
day I spoke to you, from the days of [d]Josiah
even to this day. 3 It [a]may be that the house
of Judah will hear all the adversities which
I purpose to bring upon them, that everyone may [b]turn from his evil way, that I may
forgive their iniquity and their sin."

4 Then Jeremiah [a]called Baruch the son
of Neriah; and [b]Baruch wrote on a scroll of a
book, at the instruction of Jeremiah,[1] all the
words of the LORD which He had spoken to
him. 5 And Jeremiah commanded Baruch,
saying, "I *am* confined, I cannot go into the
house of the LORD. 6 You go, therefore, and
read from the scroll which you have written
at my instruction,[1] the words of the LORD,
in the hearing of the people in the LORD's
house on [a]the day of fasting. And you shall
also read them in the hearing of all Judah
who come from their cities. 7 It may be that
they will present their supplication before
the LORD, and everyone will turn from his
evil way. For great *is* the anger and the fury
that the LORD has pronounced against this
people." 8 And Baruch the son of Neriah did
according to all that Jeremiah the prophet
commanded him, reading from the book
the words of the LORD in the LORD's house.

9 Now it came to pass in the fifth year
of Jehoiakim the son of Josiah, king of
Judah, in the ninth month, *that* they proclaimed a fast before the LORD to all the
people in Jerusalem, and to all the people
who came from the cities of Judah to Jerusalem. 10 Then Baruch read from the book
the words of Jeremiah in the house of the
LORD, in the chamber of Gemariah the son
of Shaphan the scribe, in the upper court
at the [a]entry of the New Gate of the LORD's
house, in the hearing of all the people.

The Scroll Read in the Palace

11 When Michaiah the son of Gemariah,
the son of Shaphan, heard all the words of
the LORD from the book, 12 he then went
down to the king's house, into the scribe's
chamber; and there all the princes were sitting—[a]Elishama the scribe, Delaiah the son
of Shemaiah, [b]Elnathan the son of Achbor,
Gemariah the son of Shaphan, Zedekiah the
son of Hananiah, and all the princes. 13 Then
Michaiah declared to them all the words
that he had heard when Baruch read the
book in the hearing of the people. 14 Therefore all the princes sent Jehudi the son of
Nethaniah, the son of Shelemiah, the son
of Cushi, to Baruch, saying, "Take in your
hand the scroll from which you have read
in the hearing of the people, and come." So
Baruch the son of Neriah took the scroll in
his hand and came to them. 15 And they said
to him, "Sit down now, and read it in our
hearing." So Baruch read *it* in their hearing.

16 Now it happened, when they had heard
all the words, that they looked in fear from
one to another, and said to Baruch, "We
will surely tell the king of all these words."
17 And they asked Baruch, saying, "Tell us
now, how did you write all these words—at
his instruction?"[1]

18 So Baruch answered them, "He proclaimed with his mouth all these words to
me, and I wrote *them* with ink in the book."

19 Then the princes said to Baruch, "Go
and hide, you and Jeremiah; and let no one
know where you are."

The King Destroys Jeremiah's Scroll

20 And they went to the king, into the
court; but they stored the scroll in the

35:19 [a] [Ex. 20:12]; Jer. 15:19; [Luke 21:36; Eph. 6:2, 3] 36:1 [a] 2 Kin. 24:1; 2 Chr. 36:5–7; Jer. 25:1, 3; 45:1; Dan. 1:1 36:2 [a] Is. 8:1; Ezek. 2:9; Zech. 5:1 [b] Jer. 30:2; Hab. 2:2 [c] Jer. 25:15 [d] Jer. 25:3 36:3 [a] Jer. 26:3; Ezek. 12:3 [b] [Deut. 30:2, 8; 1 Sam. 7:3]; Is. 55:7; Jer. 18:8; Jon. 3:8 36:4 [a] Jer. 32:12 [b] Jer. 45:1 [1] Literally *from Jeremiah's mouth* 36:6 [a] Lev. 16:29; 23:27–32; Acts 27:9 [1] Literally *from my mouth* 36:10 [a] Jer. 26:10 36:12 [a] Jer. 41:1 [b] Jer. 26:22 36:17 [1] Literally *with his mouth*

chamber of Elishama the scribe, and told
all the words in the hearing of the king. 21 So
the king sent Jehudi to bring the scroll, and
he took it from Elishama the scribe's chamber. And Jehudi read it in the hearing of the
king and in the hearing of all the princes
who stood beside the king. 22 Now the king
was sitting in [a]the winter house in the ninth
month, with *a fire* burning on the hearth
before him. 23 And it happened, when Jehudi had read three or four columns, *that
the king* cut it with the scribe's knife and
cast *it* into the fire that *was* on the hearth,
until all the scroll was consumed in the fire
that *was* on the hearth. 24 Yet they were [a]not
afraid, nor did they [b]tear their garments,
the king nor any of his servants who heard
all these words. 25 Nevertheless Elnathan,
Delaiah, and Gemariah implored the king
not to burn the scroll; but he would not listen to them. 26 And the king commanded
Jerahmeel the king's[1] son, Seraiah the son
of Azriel, and Shelemiah the son of Abdeel,
to seize Baruch the scribe and Jeremiah the
prophet, but the LORD hid them.

Jeremiah Rewrites the Scroll

27 Now after the king had burned the
scroll with the words which Baruch had
written at the instruction of Jeremiah,[1] the
word of the LORD came to Jeremiah, saying:
28 "Take yet another scroll, and write on it
all the former words that were in the first
scroll which Jehoiakim the king of Judah
has burned. 29 And you shall say to Jehoiakim king of Judah, 'Thus says the LORD:
"You have burned this scroll, saying, [a]'Why
have you written in it that the king of Babylon will certainly come and destroy this
land, and cause man and beast to [b]cease
from here?'" 30 Therefore thus says the
LORD concerning Jehoiakim king of Judah: [a]"He shall have no one to sit on the
throne of David, and his dead body shall
be [b]cast out to the heat of the day and the
frost of the night. 31 I will punish him, his
family, and his servants for their iniquity;
and I will bring on them, on the inhabitants
of Jerusalem, and on the men of Judah all
the doom that I have pronounced against
them; but they did not heed."'"

32 Then Jeremiah took another scroll and
gave it to Baruch the scribe, the son of Neriah, who wrote on it at the instruction of
Jeremiah[1] all the words of the book which
Jehoiakim king of Judah had burned in
the fire. And besides, there were added to
them many similar words.

Zedekiah's Vain Hope
(2 Kin. 24:17; 2 Chr. 36:10)

37 Now King [a]Zedekiah the son of Josiah reigned instead of Coniah the
son of Jehoiakim, whom Nebuchadnezzar
king of Babylon made king in the land of
Judah. 2 [a]But neither he nor his servants
nor the people of the land gave heed to the
words of the LORD which He spoke by the
prophet Jeremiah.

3 And Zedekiah the king sent Jehucal the
son of Shelemiah, and [a]Zephaniah the son
of Maaseiah, the priest, to the prophet Jeremiah, saying, [b]"Pray now to the LORD our
God for us." 4 Now Jeremiah was coming
and going among the people, for they had
not *yet* put him in prison. 5 Then [a]Pharaoh's
army came up from Egypt; and when the
Chaldeans who were besieging Jerusalem
heard news of them, they departed from
Jerusalem.

6 Then the word of the LORD came to the
prophet Jeremiah, saying, 7 "Thus says the
LORD, the God of Israel, 'Thus you shall say
to the king of Judah, [a]who sent you to Me
to inquire of Me: "Behold, Pharaoh's army
which has come up to help you will return
to Egypt, to their own land. 8 [a]And the Chaldeans shall come back and fight against
this city, and take it and burn it with fire."'
9 Thus says the LORD: 'Do not deceive yourselves, saying, "The Chaldeans will surely
depart from us," for they will not depart.
10 [a]For though you had defeated the whole
army of the Chaldeans who fight against
you, and there remained *only* wounded
men among them, they would rise up,

36:22 [a] Judg. 3:20; Amos 3:15 36:24 [a] [Ps. 36:1]; Jer. 36:16 [b] Gen. 37:29, 34; 2 Sam. 1:11; 1 Kin. 21:27; 2 Kin. 19:1, 2; 22:11; Is. 36:22; 37:1; Jon. 3:6 36:26 [1] Hebrew *Hammelech* 36:27 [1] Literally *from Jeremiah's mouth* 36:29 [a] Jer. 32:3 [b] Jer. 25:9–11; 26:9 36:30 [a] Jer. 22:30 [b] Jer. 22:19 36:32 [1] Literally *from Jeremiah's mouth* 37:1 [a] 2 Kin. 24:17; 1 Chr. 3:15; 2 Chr. 36:10; Jer. 22:24 37:2 [a] 2 Kin. 24:19, 20; 2 Chr. 36:12–16; [Prov. 29:12] 37:3 [a] Jer. 21:1, 2; 29:25; 52:24 [b] 1 Kin. 13:6; Jer. 42:2; Acts 8:24 37:5 [a] 2 Kin. 24:7; Jer. 37:7; Ezek. 17:15 37:7 [a] Is. 36:6; Jer. 21:2; Ezek. 17:17 37:8 [a] 2 Chr. 36:19; Jer. 34:22 37:10 [a] Lev. 26:36–38; Is. 30:17; Jer. 21:4, 5

every man in his tent, and burn the city
with fire.'"

Jeremiah Imprisoned

11 And it happened, when the army of
the Chaldeans left *the siege* of Jerusalem
for fear of Pharaoh's army, 12 that Jeremiah
went out of Jerusalem to go into the land
of Benjamin to claim his property there
among the people. 13 And when he was in
the Gate of Benjamin, a captain of the guard
was there whose name *was* Irijah the son
of Shelemiah, the son of Hananiah; and he
seized Jeremiah the prophet, saying, "You
are defecting to the Chaldeans!"
14 Then Jeremiah said, "False! I am not
defecting to the Chaldeans." But he did not
listen to him.
So Irijah seized Jeremiah and brought
him to the princes. 15 Therefore the princes
were angry with Jeremiah, and they struck
him [a]and put him in prison in the [b]house
of Jonathan the scribe. For they had made
that the prison.
16 When Jeremiah entered [a]the dungeon
and the cells, and Jeremiah had remained
there many days, 17 then Zedekiah the king
sent and took him *out*. The king asked him
secretly in his house, and said, "Is there *any*
word from the LORD?"
And Jeremiah said, "There is." Then he
said, "You shall be [a]delivered into the hand
of the king of Babylon!"
18 Moreover Jeremiah said to King Zedekiah, "What offense have I committed
against you, against your servants, or
against this people, that you have put me
in prison? 19 Where now *are* your prophets
who prophesied to you, saying, 'The king
of Babylon will not come against you or
against this land'? 20 Therefore please hear
now, O my lord the king. Please, let my petition be accepted before you, and do not
make me return to the house of Jonathan
the scribe, lest I die there."
21 Then Zedekiah the king commanded
that they should commit Jeremiah [a]to the
court of the prison, and that they should
give him daily a piece of bread from the
bakers' street, [b]until all the bread in the city
was gone. Thus Jeremiah remained in the
court of the prison.

Jeremiah in the Dungeon

38 Now Shephatiah the son of Mattan,
Gedaliah the son of Pashhur, [a]Jucal[1]
the son of Shelemiah, and [b]Pashhur the
son of Malchiah [c]heard the words that Jeremiah had spoken to all the people, saying,
2 "Thus says the LORD: [a]'He who remains in
this city shall die by the sword, by famine,
and by pestilence; but he who goes over to
the Chaldeans shall live; his life shall be as
a prize to him, and he shall live.'[1] 3 Thus says
the LORD: [a]'This city shall surely be [b]given
into the hand of the king of Babylon's army,
which shall take it.'"
4 Therefore the princes said to the king,
"Please, [a]let this man be put to death, for
thus he weakens the hands of the men of
war who remain in this city, and the hands
of all the people, by speaking such words to
them. For this man does not seek the welfare of this people, but their harm."
5 Then Zedekiah the king said, "Look, he
is in your hand. For the king can *do* nothing
against you." 6 [a]So they took Jeremiah and
cast him into the dungeon of Malchiah the
king's[1] son, which *was* in the court of the
prison, and they let Jeremiah down with
ropes. And in the dungeon *there was* no water, but mire. So Jeremiah sank in the mire.
7 [a]Now Ebed-Melech the Ethiopian, one of
the eunuchs, who was in the king's house,
heard that they had put Jeremiah in the
dungeon. When the king was sitting at the
Gate of Benjamin, 8 Ebed-Melech went out
of the king's house and spoke to the king,
saying: 9 "My lord the king, these men have
done evil in all that they have done to Jeremiah the prophet, whom they have cast into
the dungeon, and he is likely to die from
hunger in the place where he is. For *there is*
[a]no more bread in the city." 10 Then the king
commanded Ebed-Melech the Ethiopian,
saying, "Take from here thirty men with
you, and lift Jeremiah the prophet out of the
dungeon before he dies." 11 So Ebed-Melech

37:15 [a] Jer. 20:2; [Matt. 21:35] [b] Gen. 39:20; 2 Chr. 16:10; 18:26; Jer. 38:26; Acts 5:18 37:16 [a] Jer. 38:6 37:17 [a] 2 Kin. 25:4–7; Jer. 21:7; Ezek. 12:12, 13; 17:19–21 37:21 [a] Jer. 32:2; 38:13, 28 [b] 2 Kin. 25:3; Jer. 38:9; 52:6 38:1 [a] Jer. 37:3 [b] Jer. 21:1 [c] Jer. 21:8 [1] Same as *Jehucal* (compare 37:3) 38:2 [a] Jer. 21:9 [1] Compare 21:9 38:3 [a] Jer. 21:10; 32:3 [b] Jer. 34:2 38:4 [a] Jer. 26:11 38:6 [a] Jer. 37:21; Lam. 3:55 [1] Hebrew *Hammelech* 38:7 [a] Jer. 39:16 38:9 [a] Jer. 37:21

took the men with him and went into the house of the king under the treasury, and took from there old clothes and old rags, and let them down by ropes into the dungeon to Jeremiah. 12Then Ebed-Melech the Ethiopian said to Jeremiah, "Please put these old clothes and rags under your armpits, under the ropes." And Jeremiah did so. 13So they pulled Jeremiah up with ropes and lifted him out of the dungeon. And Jeremiah remained [a]in the court of the prison.

Zedekiah's Fears and Jeremiah's Advice

14Then Zedekiah the king sent and had Jeremiah the prophet brought to him at the third entrance of the house of the LORD. And the king said to Jeremiah, "I will [a]ask you something. Hide nothing from me."

15Jeremiah said to Zedekiah, "If I declare *it* to you, will you not surely put me to death? And if I give you advice, you will not listen to me."

16So Zedekiah the king swore secretly to Jeremiah, saying, "As the LORD lives, [a]who made our very souls, I will not put you to death, nor will I give you into the hand of these men who seek your life."

17Then Jeremiah said to Zedekiah, "Thus says the LORD, the God of hosts, the God of Israel: 'If you surely [a]surrender [b]to the king of Babylon's princes, then your soul shall live; this city shall not be burned with fire, and you and your house shall live. 18But if you do not surrender to the king of Babylon's princes, then this city shall be given into the hand of the Chaldeans; they shall burn it with fire, and [a]you shall not escape from their hand.' "

19And Zedekiah the king said to Jeremiah, "I am afraid of the Jews who have [a]defected to the Chaldeans, lest they deliver me into their hand, and they [b]abuse me."

20But Jeremiah said, "They shall not deliver *you.* Please, obey the voice of the LORD which I speak to you. So it shall be [a]well with you, and your soul shall live. 21But if you refuse to surrender, this *is* the word that the LORD has shown me: 22'Now behold, all the [a]women who are left in the king of Judah's house *shall be* surrendered to the king of Babylon's princes, and those *women* shall say:

"Your close friends have set upon you
And prevailed against you;
Your feet have sunk in the mire,
And they have turned away again."

23'So they shall surrender all your wives and [a]children to the Chaldeans. [b]You shall not escape from their hand, but shall be taken by the hand of the king of Babylon. And you shall cause this city to be burned with fire.' "

24Then Zedekiah said to Jeremiah, "Let no one know of these words, and you shall not die. 25But if the princes hear that I have talked with you, and they come to you and say to you, 'Declare to us now what you have said to the king, and also what the king said to you; do not hide *it* from us, and we will not put you to death,' 26then you shall say to them, [a]'I presented my request before the king, that he would not make me return [b]to Jonathan's house to die there.' "

27Then all the princes came to Jeremiah and asked him. And he told them according to all these words that the king had commanded. So they stopped speaking with him, for the conversation had not been heard. 28Now [a]Jeremiah remained in the court of the prison until the day that Jerusalem was taken. And he was *there* when Jerusalem was taken.

The Fall of Jerusalem

(2 Kin. 25:1–12; Jer. 52:4–16)

39 In the [a]ninth year of Zedekiah king of Judah, in the tenth month, Nebuchadnezzar king of Babylon and all his army came against Jerusalem, and besieged it. 2In the [a]eleventh year of Zedekiah, in the fourth month, on the ninth *day* of the month, the city was penetrated.

3[a]Then all the princes of the king of Babylon came in and sat in the Middle Gate: Nergal-Sharezer, Samgar-Nebo, Sarsechim, Rabsaris,[1] Nergal-Sarezer, Rabmag,[2]

38:13 [a] Neh. 3:25; Jer. 37:21; Acts 23:35; 24:27; 28:16, 30 38:14 [a] Jer. 21:1, 2; 37:17 38:16 [a] Num. 16:22; Is. 57:16; Zech. 12:1; [Acts 17:25, 28] 38:17 [a] 2 Kin. 24:12 [b] Jer. 39:3 38:18 [a] Jer. 32:4; 34:3 38:19 [a] Jer. 39:9 [b] 1 Sam. 31:4 38:20 [a] Jer. 40:9 38:22 [a] Jer. 8:10 38:23 [a] Jer. 39:6; 41:10 [b] Jer. 39:5 38:26 [a] Jer. 37:20 [b] Jer. 37:15 38:28 [a] [Ps. 23:4]; Jer. 37:21; 39:14 39:1 [a] 2 Kin. 25:1–12; Jer. 52:4; Ezek. 24:1, 2 39:2 [a] Jer. 1:3 39:3 [a] Jer. 1:15; 38:17 [1] A title, probably *Chief Officer;* also verse 13
[2] A title, probably *Troop Commander;* also verse 13

with the rest of the princes of the king of Babylon.

4 [a]So it was, when Zedekiah the king of Judah and all the men of war saw them, that they fled and went out of the city by night, by way of the king's garden, by the gate between the two walls. And he went out by way of the plain.[1] 5 But the Chaldean army pursued them and [a]overtook Zedekiah in the plains of Jericho. And when they had captured him, they brought him up to Nebuchadnezzar king of Babylon, to [b]Riblah in the land of Hamath, where he pronounced judgment on him. 6 Then the king of Babylon killed the sons of Zedekiah before his [a]eyes in Riblah; the king of Babylon also killed all the [b]nobles of Judah. 7 Moreover [a]he put out Zedekiah's eyes, and bound him with bronze fetters to carry him off to Babylon. 8 [a]And the Chaldeans burned the king's house and the houses of the people with [b]fire, and broke down the [c]walls of Jerusalem. 9 [a]Then Nebuzaradan the captain of the guard carried away captive to Babylon the remnant of the people who remained in the city and those who [b]defected to him, with the rest of the people who remained. 10 But Nebuzaradan the captain of the guard left in the land of Judah the [a]poor people, who had nothing, and gave them vineyards and fields at the same time.

Jeremiah Goes Free

11 Now Nebuchadnezzar king of Babylon gave charge concerning Jeremiah to Nebuzaradan the captain of the guard, saying, 12 "Take him and look after him, and do him no [a]harm; but do to him just as he says to you." 13 So Nebuzaradan the captain of the guard sent Nebushasban, Rabsaris, Nergal-Sharezer, Rabmag, and all the king of Babylon's chief officers; 14 then they sent *someone* [a]to take Jeremiah from the court of the prison, and committed him [b]to Gedaliah the son of [c]Ahikam, the son of Shaphan, that he should take him home. So he dwelt among the people.

15 Meanwhile the word of the LORD had come to Jeremiah while he was shut up in the court of the prison, saying, 16 "Go and speak to [a]Ebed-Melech the Ethiopian, saying, 'Thus says the LORD of hosts, the God of Israel: "Behold, [b]I will bring My words upon this city for adversity and not for good, and they shall be *performed* in that day before you. 17 But I will deliver you in that day," says the LORD, "and you shall not be given into the hand of the men of whom you *are* afraid. 18 For I will surely deliver you, and you shall not fall by the sword; but [a]your life shall be as a prize to you, [b]because you have put your trust in Me," says the LORD.'"

Jeremiah with Gedaliah the Governor
(2 Kin. 25:22–26)

40 The word that came to Jeremiah from the LORD [a]after Nebuzaradan the captain of the guard had let him go from Ramah, when he had taken him bound in chains among all who were carried away captive from Jerusalem and Judah, who were carried away captive to Babylon.

2 And the captain of the guard took Jeremiah and [a]said to him: "The LORD your God has pronounced this doom on this place. 3 Now the LORD has brought *it,* and has done just as He said. [a]Because you *people* have sinned against the LORD, and not obeyed His voice, therefore this thing has come upon you. 4 And now look, I free you this day from the chains that *were* on your hand. [a]If it seems good to you to come with me to Babylon, come, and I will look after you. But if it seems wrong for you to come with me to Babylon, remain here. See, [b]all the land *is* before you; wherever it seems good and convenient for you to go, go there."

5 Now while Jeremiah had not yet gone back, *Nebuzaradan said,* "Go back to [a]Gedaliah the son of Ahikam, the son of Shaphan, [b]whom the king of Babylon has made governor over the cities of Judah, and dwell with him among the people. Or go wherever

39:4 [a] 2 Kin. 25:4; Is. 30:16; Jer. 52:7; Amos 2:14 [1] Or *the Arabah,* that is, the Jordan Valley 39:5 [a] Jer. 21:7; 32:4; 38:18, 23 [b] 2 Kin. 23:33; Jer. 52:9, 26, 27 39:6 [a] Deut. 28:34 [b] Jer. 34:19–21 39:7 [a] 2 Kin. 25:7; Jer. 52:11; Ezek. 12:13 39:8 [a] 2 Kin. 25:9; Jer. 38:18; 52:13 [b] Jer. 21:10 [c] 2 Kin. 25:10; Neh. 1:3; Jer. 52:14 39:9 [a] 2 Kin. 25:8, 11, 12, 20 [b] Jer. 38:19 39:10 [a] Jer. 40:7 39:12 [a] Jer. 1:18, 19; 15:20, 21 39:14 [a] Jer. 38:28 [b] Jer. 40:5 [c] 2 Kin. 22:12, 14; 2 Chr. 34:20; Jer. 26:24 39:16 [a] Jer. 38:7, 12 [b] Jer. 21:10; [Dan. 9:12; Zech. 1:6] 39:18 [a] Jer. 21:9; 45:5 [b] 1 Chr. 5:20; Ps. 37:40; [Jer. 17:7, 8] 40:1 [a] Jer. 39:9, 11 40:2 [a] Jer. 50:7 40:3 [a] Deut. 29:24, 25; Jer. 50:7; Dan. 9:11; [Rom. 2:5] 40:4 [a] Jer. 39:12 [b] Gen. 20:15 40:5 [a] Jer. 39:14 [b] 2 Kin. 25:22; Jer. 41:10

it seems convenient for you to go." So the
captain of the guard gave him rations and
a gift and let him go. [6][a]Then Jeremiah went
to Gedaliah the son of Ahikam, to [b]Mizpah,
and dwelt with him among the people who
were left in the land.
[7][a]And when all the captains of the
armies who *were* in the fields, they and
their men, heard that the king of Babylon
had made Gedaliah the son of Ahikam governor in the land, and had committed to
him men, women, children, and [b]the poorest of the land who had not been carried
away captive to Babylon, [8]then they came
to Gedaliah at Mizpah—[a]Ishmael the son
of Nethaniah, [b]Johanan and Jonathan the
sons of Kareah, Seraiah the son of Tanhumeth, the sons of Ephai the Netophathite,
and [c]Jezaniah[1] the son of a [d]Maachathite,
they and their men. [9]And Gedaliah the son
of Ahikam, the son of Shaphan, took an
oath before them and their men, saying,
"Do not be afraid to serve the Chaldeans.
Dwell in the land and serve the king of Babylon, and it shall be [a]well with you. [10]As for
me, I will indeed dwell at Mizpah and serve
the Chaldeans who come to us. But you,
gather wine and summer fruit and oil, put
them in your vessels, and dwell in your cities that you have taken." [11]Likewise, when
all the Jews who *were* in Moab, among the
Ammonites, in Edom, and who *were* in all
the countries, heard that the king of Babylon had left a remnant of Judah, and that
he had set over them Gedaliah the son of
Ahikam, the son of Shaphan, [12]then all the
Jews [a]returned out of all places where they
had been driven, and came to the land of

JEREMIAH 39:17

I AM EBED-MELECH

"But I will deliver you in that day," says the LORD, "and you shall not be given into the hand of the men of whom you are afraid." Jeremiah 39:17

I am Ebed-Melech, an Ethiopian and servant of King Zedekiah. During my day, it was quite fashionable for kings to have Ethiopian slaves watch over their harems; however, we were forced to be eunuchs, so the women were unquestionably safe from our attentions. I was a faithful servant of the king and had found favor in his sight. I loved God and His people, including the prophet Jeremiah.

Fearing the words that Jeremiah had spoken over Jerusalem, noblemen of the realm threw Jeremiah into a dungeon filled with deep mud. He had no food or water, and Jeremiah would surely have died had I not intervened. When I heard of Jeremiah's fate in this vile and decaying dungeon, I determined to use my influence with the king to rescue him. The people of the kingdom all knew Jeremiah was a true prophet, but I was the only one who came to his defense. I made the case for Jeremiah to the king, telling him that Jeremiah was an innocent man who had been treated cruelly and without justice. The king ordered me to take some men to rescue Jeremiah.

It took a lot of courage for me, a foreigner in this land, to approach the king against those in power. Although Zedekiah listened to my plea, he did not listen to the word of the Lord. Jeremiah spoke God's truth regarding His will for Israel, yet Zedekiah would not listen. As a result, he and all those in Jerusalem were carried away to Babylon or killed. When the Babylonians descended upon Israel, the Lord was merciful and spared my life along with the life of His servant Jeremiah.

†

Even when the odds are against us and our voice is the only one being raised, we must stand up and speak out against injustice. To be silent is to be complicit in wrongdoing.

40:6 [a] Jer. 39:14 [b] Judg. 20:1; 1 Sam. 7:5; 2 Chr. 16:6 40:7 [a] 2 Kin. 25:23, 24 [b] Jer. 39:10 40:8 [a] Jer. 41:1–10 [b] Jer. 41:11; 43:2 [c] Jer. 42:1 [d] Deut. 3:14; Josh. 12:5; 2 Sam. 10:6 [1] Spelled *Jaazaniah* in 2 Kings 25:23 40:9 [a] Jer. 27:11; 38:17–20 40:12 [a] Jer. 43:5

Judah, to Gedaliah at Mizpah, and gathered wine and summer fruit in abundance.
13 Moreover Johanan the son of Kareah
and all the captains of the forces that *were*
in the fields came to Gedaliah at Mizpah,
14 and said to him, "Do you certainly know
that [a]Baalis the king of the Ammonites has
sent Ishmael the son of Nethaniah to murder you?" But Gedaliah the son of Ahikam
did not believe them.
15 Then Johanan the son of Kareah spoke
secretly to Gedaliah in Mizpah, saying, "Let
me go, please, and I will kill Ishmael the
son of Nethaniah, and no one will know
it. Why should he murder you, so that all
the Jews who are gathered to you would
be scattered, and the [a]remnant in Judah
perish?"
16 But Gedaliah the son of Ahikam said
to Johanan the son of Kareah, "You shall
not do this thing, for you speak falsely concerning Ishmael."

Insurrection Against Gedaliah

41 Now it came to pass in the seventh
month [a]*that* Ishmael the son of Nethaniah, the son of Elishama, of the royal
family and of the officers of the king, came
with ten men to Gedaliah the son of Ahikam, at [b]Mizpah. And there they ate bread
together in Mizpah. 2 Then Ishmael the son
of Nethaniah, and the ten men who were
with him, arose and [a]struck Gedaliah the
son of [b]Ahikam, the son of Shaphan, with
the sword, and killed him whom the king of
Babylon had made [c]governor over the land.
3 Ishmael also struck down all the Jews who
were with him, *that is,* with Gedaliah at Mizpah, and the Chaldeans who were found
there, the men of war.
4 And it happened, on the second day after he had killed Gedaliah, when as yet no
one knew *it,* 5 that certain men came from
Shechem, from Shiloh, and from Samaria,
eighty men [a]with their beards shaved and
their clothes torn, having cut themselves,
with offerings and incense in their hand,
to bring *them* to [b]the house of the LORD.
6 Now Ishmael the son of Nethaniah went
out from Mizpah to meet them, weeping as
he went along; and it happened as he met
them that he said to them, "Come to Gedaliah the son of Ahikam!" 7 So it was, when
they came into the midst of the city, that
Ishmael the son of Nethaniah [a]killed them
and cast them into the midst of a pit, he
and the men who were with him. 8 But ten
men were found among them who said to
Ishmael, "Do not kill us, for we have treasures of wheat, barley, oil, and honey in the
field." So he desisted and did not kill them
among their brethren. 9 Now the pit into
which Ishmael had cast all the dead bodies
of the men whom he had slain, because of
Gedaliah, *was* [a]the same one Asa the king
had made for fear of Baasha king of Israel.
Ishmael the son of Nethaniah filled it with
the slain. 10 Then Ishmael carried away captive all the [a]rest of the people who *were* in
Mizpah, [b]the king's daughters and all the
people who remained in Mizpah, [c]whom
Nebuzaradan the captain of the guard had
committed to Gedaliah the son of Ahikam.
And Ishmael the son of Nethaniah carried
them away captive and departed to go over
to [d]the Ammonites.
11 But when [a]Johanan the son of Kareah
and all the captains of the forces that *were*
with him heard of all the evil that Ishmael
the son of Nethaniah had done, 12 they took
all the men and went to fight with Ishmael
the son of Nethaniah; and they found him
by [a]the great pool that *is* in Gibeon. 13 So it
was, when all the people who *were* with Ishmael saw Johanan the son of Kareah, and
all the captains of the forces who *were* with
him, that they were glad. 14 Then all the people whom Ishmael had carried away captive from Mizpah turned around and came
back, and went to Johanan the son of Kareah. 15 But Ishmael the son of Nethaniah
escaped from Johanan with eight men and
went to the Ammonites.
16 Then Johanan the son of Kareah, and
all the captains of the forces that were with
him, took from Mizpah all the [a]rest of the
people whom he had recovered from Ishmael the son of Nethaniah after he had
murdered Gedaliah the son of Ahikam—
the mighty men of war and the women

40:14 [a] Jer. 41:10 40:15 [a] Jer. 42:2 41:1 [a] 2 Kin. 25:25 [b] Jer. 40:6, 10 41:2 [a] 2 Sam. 3:27; 20:9, 10; 2 Kin. 25:25; Ps. 41:9; 109:5; John 13:18 [b] Jer. 26:24 [c] Jer. 40:5 41:5 [a] Lev. 19:27, 28; Deut. 14:1; Is. 15:2 [b] 1 Sam. 1:7; 2 Kin. 25:9; Neh. 10:34, 35 41:7 [a] Ps. 55:23; Is. 59:7; Ezek. 22:27; 33:24, 26 41:9 [a] 1 Kin. 15:22; 2 Chr. 16:6 41:10 [a] Jer. 40:11, 12 [b] Jer. 43:6 [c] Jer. 40:7 [d] Jer. 40:14 41:11 [a] Jer. 40:7, 8, 13–16 41:12 [a] 2 Sam. 2:13 41:16 [a] Jer. 40:11, 12; 43:4–7

and the children and the eunuchs, whom
he had brought back from Gibeon. 17And
they departed and dwelt in the habitation
of [a]Chimham, which is near Bethlehem, as
they went on their way to [b]Egypt, 18because
of the Chaldeans; for they were afraid of
them, because Ishmael the son of Nethaniah had murdered Gedaliah the son of
Ahikam, [a]whom the king of Babylon had
made governor in the land.

The Flight to Egypt Forbidden

42 Now all the captains of the forces,
[a]Johanan the son of Kareah, Jezaniah the son of Hoshaiah, and all the people, from the least to the greatest, came
near 2and said to Jeremiah the prophet,
[a]"Please, let our petition be acceptable to
you, and [b]pray for us to the LORD your God,
for all this remnant (since we are left *but* [c]a
few of many, as you can see), 3that the LORD
your God may show us [a]the way in which we
should walk and the thing we should do."
4Then Jeremiah the prophet said to
them, "I have heard. Indeed, I will pray
to the LORD your God according to your
words, and it shall be, *that* [a]whatever the
LORD answers you, I will declare *it* to you.
I will [b]keep nothing back from you."
5So they said to Jeremiah, [a]"Let the LORD
be a true and faithful witness between us,
if we do not do according to everything
which the LORD your God sends us by you.
6Whether *it is* pleasing or displeasing, we
will [a]obey the voice of the LORD our God
to whom we send you, [b]that it may be well
with us when we obey the voice of the LORD
our God."
7And it happened after ten days that the
word of the LORD came to Jeremiah. 8Then
he called Johanan the son of Kareah, all
the captains of the forces which *were* with
him, and all the people from the least even
to the greatest, 9and said to them, "Thus
says the LORD, the God of Israel, to whom
you sent me to present your petition before Him: 10'If you will still remain in this
land, then [a]I will build you and not pull *you*
down, and I will plant you and not pluck
you up. For I [b]relent concerning the disaster that I have brought upon you. 11Do not
be afraid of the king of Babylon, of whom
you are afraid; do not be afraid of him,'
says the LORD, [a]'for I *am* with you, to save
you and deliver you from his hand. 12And
[a]I will show you mercy, that he may have
mercy on you and cause you to return to
your own land.'
13"But if [a]you say, 'We will not dwell in
this land,' disobeying the voice of the LORD
your God, 14saying, 'No, but we will go to
the land of [a]Egypt where we shall see no
war, nor hear the sound of the trumpet,
nor be hungry for bread, and there we will
dwell'— 15Then hear now the word of the
LORD, O remnant of Judah! Thus says the
LORD of hosts, the God of Israel: 'If you
[a]wholly set [b]your faces to enter Egypt, and
go to dwell there, 16then it shall be *that* the
[a]sword which you feared shall overtake you
there in the land of Egypt; the famine of
which you were afraid shall follow close after you there *in* Egypt; and there you shall
die. 17So shall it be with all the men who set
their faces to go to Egypt to dwell there.
They shall die by the sword, by famine, and
by pestilence. And [a]none of them shall remain or escape from the disaster that I will
bring upon them.'
18"For thus says the LORD of hosts, the
God of Israel: 'As My anger and My fury
have been [a]poured out on the inhabitants
of Jerusalem, so will My fury be poured out
on you when you enter Egypt. And [b]you
shall be an oath, an astonishment, a curse,
and a reproach; and you shall see this place
no more.'
19"The LORD has said concerning you,
O remnant of Judah, [a]'Do not go to Egypt!'
Know certainly that I have admonished you
this day. 20For you were hypocrites in your
hearts when you sent me to the LORD your
God, saying, 'Pray for us to the LORD our God,
and according to all that the LORD your God

41:17 [a] 2 Sam. 19:37, 38 [b] Jer. 43:7 **41:18** [a] Jer. 40:5 **42:1** [a] Jer. 40:8, 13; 41:11 **42:2** [a] Jer. 15:11 [b] Ex. 8:28; 1 Sam. 7:8; 12:19; 1 Kin. 13:6; Is. 37:4; Jer. 37:3; Acts 8:24; [James 5:16] [c] Lev. 26:22; Deut. 28:62; Is. 1:9; Lam. 1:1 **42:3** [a] Ezra 8:21 **42:4** [a] 1 Kin. 22:14; Jer. 23:28 [b] 1 Sam. 3:17, 18; Ps. 40:10; Acts 20:20 **42:5** [a] Gen. 31:50; Judg. 11:10; Jer. 43:2; Mic. 1:2; Mal. 2:14; 3:5 **42:6** [a] Ex. 24:7; Deut. 5:27; Josh. 24:24 [b] Deut. 5:29, 33; 6:3; Jer. 7:23 **42:10** [a] Jer. 24:6; 31:28; 33:7; Ezek. 36:36 [b] Deut. 32:36; [Jer. 18:8] **42:11** [a] Num. 14:9; 2 Chr. 32:7, 8; Is. 8:9, 10; 43:2, 5; Jer. 1:19; 15:20; Rom. 8:31 **42:12** [a] Neh. 1:11; Ps. 106:46; Prov. 16:7 **42:13** [a] Jer. 44:16 **42:14** [a] Is. 31:1; Jer. 41:17; 43:7 **42:15** [a] Deut. 17:16; Jer. 44:12–14 [b] Luke 9:51 **42:16** [a] Jer. 44:13, 27; Ezek. 11:8; Amos 9:1–4 **42:17** [a] Jer. 44:14, 28 **42:18** [a] 2 Chr. 36:16–19; Jer. 7:20 [b] Deut. 29:21; Is. 65:15; Jer. 18:16; 24:9; 26:6; 29:18, 22; 44:12 **42:19** [a] Deut. 17:16; Is. 30:1–7

says, so declare to us and we will do *it.*' 21And
I have this day declared *it* to you, but you
have [a]not obeyed the voice of the LORD your
God, or anything which He has sent you by
me. 22Now therefore, know certainly that
you [a]shall die by the sword, by famine, and
by pestilence in the place where you desire
to go to dwell."

Jeremiah Taken to Egypt

43 Now it happened, when Jeremiah
had stopped speaking to all the people all the [a]words of the LORD their God, for
which the LORD their God had sent him to
them, all these words, 2[a]that Azariah the
son of Hoshaiah, Johanan the son of Kareah, and all the proud men spoke, saying
to Jeremiah, "You speak falsely! The LORD
our God has not sent you to say, 'Do not
go to Egypt to dwell there.' 3But [a]Baruch
the son of Neriah has set you against us,
to deliver us into the hand of the Chaldeans, that they may put us to death or carry
us away captive to Babylon." 4So Johanan
the son of Kareah, all the captains of the
forces, and all the people would [a]not obey
the voice of the LORD, to remain in the land
of Judah. 5But Johanan the son of Kareah
and all the captains of the forces took [a]all
the remnant of Judah who had returned
to dwell in the land of Judah, from all nations where they had been driven— 6men,
women, children, [a]the king's daughters,
[b]and every person whom Nebuzaradan the
captain of the guard had left with Gedaliah
the son of Ahikam, the son of Shaphan,
and Jeremiah the prophet and Baruch the
son of Neriah. 7[a]So they went to the land of
Egypt, for they did not obey the voice of the
LORD. And they went as far as [b]Tahpanhes.

8Then the [a]word of the LORD came to
Jeremiah in Tahpanhes, saying, 9"Take
large stones in your hand, and hide them
in the sight of the men of Judah, in the clay
in the brick courtyard which *is* at the entrance to Pharaoh's house in Tahpanhes;
10and say to them, 'Thus says the LORD of
hosts, the God of Israel: "Behold, I will send
and bring Nebuchadnezzar the king of Babylon, [a]My servant, and will set his throne
above these stones that I have hidden. And
he will spread his royal pavilion over them.
11[a]When he comes, he shall strike the land of
Egypt *and deliver* to death [b]*those appointed*
for death, and to captivity *those appointed*
for captivity, and to the sword *those ap-*
pointed for the sword. 12I[1] will kindle a fire
in the houses of [a]the gods of Egypt, and he
shall burn them and carry them away captive. And he shall array himself with the
land of Egypt, as a shepherd puts on his
garment, and he shall go out from there in
peace. 13He shall also break the *sacred* pillars of Beth Shemesh[1] that *are* in the land
of Egypt; and the houses of the gods of the
Egyptians he shall burn with fire."'"

Israelites Will Be Punished in Egypt

44 The word that came to Jeremiah
concerning all the Jews who dwell
in the land of Egypt, who dwell at [a]Migdol,
at [b]Tahpanhes, at [c]Noph,[1] and in the country
of [d]Pathros, saying, 2"Thus says the LORD
of hosts, the God of Israel: 'You have seen
all the calamity that I have brought on Jerusalem and on all the cities of Judah; and
behold, this day they *are* [a]a desolation, and
no one dwells in them, 3because of their
wickedness which they have committed
to provoke Me to anger, in that they went
[a]to burn incense *and* to [b]serve other gods
whom they did not know, they nor you nor
your fathers. 4However [a]I have sent to you
all My servants the prophets, rising early
and sending *them,* saying, "Oh, do not do
this abominable thing that I hate!" 5But
they did not listen or incline their ear to
turn from their wickedness, to burn no incense to other gods. 6So My fury and My
anger were poured out and kindled in the
cities of Judah and in the streets of Jerusalem; and they are wasted *and* desolate,
as it is this day.'

7"Now therefore, thus says the LORD, the
God of hosts, the God of Israel: 'Why do you
commit *this* great evil [a]against yourselves,

42:21 [a] Is. 30:1–7 42:22 [a] Jer. 42:17; Ezek. 6:11 43:1 [a] Jer. 42:9–18 43:2 [a] Jer. 42:1 43:3 [a] Jer. 36:4; 45:1 43:4 [a] 2 Kin. 25:26 43:5 [a] Jer. 40:11, 12 43:6 [a] Jer. 41:10 [b] Jer. 39:10; 40:7 43:7 [a] Jer. 42:19 [b] Jer. 2:16; 44:1 43:8 [a] Jer. 44:1–30 43:10 [a] Jer. 25:9; 27:6; Ezek. 29:18, 20 43:11 [a] Is. 19:1–25; Jer. 25:15–19; 44:13; 46:1, 2, 13–26; Ezek. 29:19, 20 [b] Jer. 15:2; Zech. 11:9 43:12 [a] Ex. 12:12; Is. 19:1; Jer. 46:25; Ezek. 30:13 [1] Following Masoretic Text and Targum; Septuagint, Syriac, and Vulgate read *He.* 43:13 [1] Literally *House of the Sun,* ancient On; later called Heliopolis 44:1 [a] Ex. 14:2; Jer. 46:14 [b] Jer. 43:7; Ezek. 30:18 [c] Is. 19:13; Jer. 2:16; 46:14; Ezek. 30:13, 16; Hos. 9:6 [d] Is. 11:11; Ezek. 29:14; 30:14 [1] That is, ancient Memphis 44:2 [a] Is. 6:11; Jer. 4:7; 9:11; 34:22; Mic. 3:12 44:3 [a] Jer. 19:4 [b] Deut. 13:6; 32:17 44:4 [a] 2 Chr. 36:15; Jer. 7:25; 25:4; 26:5; 29:19; Zech. 7:7 44:7 [a] Num. 16:38; Jer. 7:19; [Ezek. 33:11]; Hab. 2:10

to cut off from you man and woman, child and infant, out of Judah, leaving none to remain, 8in that you [a]provoke Me to wrath with the works of your hands, burning incense to other gods in the land of Egypt where you have gone to dwell, that you may cut yourselves off and be [b]a curse and a reproach among all the nations of the earth? 9Have you forgotten the wickedness of your fathers, the wickedness of the kings of Judah, the wickedness of their wives, your own wickedness, and the wickedness of your wives, which they committed in the land of Judah and in the streets of Jerusalem? 10They have not been [a]humbled, to this day, nor have they [b]feared; they have not walked in My law or in My statutes that I set before you and your fathers.'

11"Therefore thus says the LORD of hosts, the God of Israel: 'Behold, [a]I will set My face against you for catastrophe and for cutting off all Judah. 12And I will take the remnant of Judah who have set their faces to go into the land of Egypt to dwell there, and [a]they shall all be consumed *and* fall in the land of Egypt. They shall be consumed by the sword *and* by famine. They shall die, from the least to the greatest, by the sword and by famine; and [b]they shall be an oath, an astonishment, a curse and a reproach! 13[a]For I will punish those who dwell in the land of Egypt, as I have punished Jerusalem, by the sword, by famine, and by pestilence, 14so that none of the remnant of Judah who have gone into the land of Egypt to dwell there shall escape or survive, lest they return to the land of Judah, to which they [a]desire to return and dwell. For [b]none shall return except those who escape.' "

15Then all the men who knew that their wives had burned incense to other gods, with all the women who stood by, a great multitude, and all the people who dwelt in the land of Egypt, in Pathros, answered Jeremiah, saying: 16"*As for* the word that you have spoken to us in the name of the LORD, [a]we will not listen to you! 17But we will certainly do [a]whatever has gone out of our own mouth, to burn incense to the [b]queen of heaven and pour out drink offerings to her, as we have done, we and our fathers, our kings and our princes, in the cities of Judah and in the streets of Jerusalem. For *then* we had plenty of food, were well-off, and saw no trouble. 18But since we stopped burning incense to the queen of heaven and pouring out drink offerings to her, we have lacked everything and have been consumed by the sword and by famine."

19*The women also said,* [a]"And when we burned incense to the queen of heaven and poured out drink offerings to her, did we make cakes for her, to worship her, and pour out drink offerings to her without our husbands' *permission?*"

20Then Jeremiah spoke to all the people—the men, the women, and all the people who had given him *that* answer—saying: 21"The incense that you burned in the cities of Judah and in the streets of Jerusalem, you and your fathers, your kings and your princes, and the people of the land, did not the LORD remember them, and did it *not* come into His mind? 22So the LORD could no longer bear *it,* because of the evil of your doings *and* because of the abominations which you committed. Therefore your land is a desolation, an astonishment, a curse, and without an inhabitant, [a]as *it is* this day. 23Because you have burned incense and because you have sinned against the LORD, and have not obeyed the voice of the LORD or walked in His law, in His statutes or in His testimonies, [a]therefore this calamity has happened to you, as *at* this day."

24Moreover Jeremiah said to all the people and to all the women, "Hear the word of the LORD, all Judah who *are* in the land of Egypt! 25Thus says the LORD of hosts, the God of Israel, saying: 'You and your wives have spoken with your mouths and fulfilled with your hands, saying, "We will surely keep our vows that we have made, to burn incense to the queen of heaven and pour out drink offerings to her." You will surely keep your vows and perform your vows!' 26Therefore hear the word of the LORD, all

---

44:8 [a] 2 Kin. 17:15–17; Jer. 25:6, 7; 44:3; 1 Cor. 10:21, 22 [b] 1 Kin. 9:7, 8; 2 Chr. 7:20; Jer. 42:18 44:10 [a] 2 Chr. 36:12; Jer. 6:15; 8:12; Dan. 5:22 [b] [Prov. 28:14] 44:11 [a] Lev. 17:10; 20:5, 6; Jer. 21:10; Amos 9:4 44:12 [a] Jer. 42:15–17, 22 [b] Is. 65:15; Jer. 42:18 44:13 [a] Jer. 43:11 44:14 [a] Jer. 22:26, 27 [b] [Is. 4:2; 10:20]; Jer. 44:28; [Rom. 9:27] 44:16 [a] Jer. 6:16 44:17 [a] Num. 30:12; Deut. 23:23; Judg. 11:36 [b] 2 Kin. 17:16; Jer. 7:18 44:19 [a] Jer. 7:18 44:22 [a] Jer. 25:11, 18, 38 44:23 [a] 1 Kin. 9:9; Neh. 13:18; Jer. 44:2; Dan. 9:11, 12

Judah who dwell in the land of Egypt: 'Behold, [a]I have sworn by My [b]great name,' says
the LORD, 'that [c]My name shall no more be
named in the mouth of any man of Judah
in all the land of Egypt, saying, "The Lord
GOD lives." 27 Behold, I will watch over them
for adversity and not for good. And all the
men of Judah who *are* in the land of Egypt
[a]shall be consumed by the sword and by
famine, until there is an end to them. 28 Yet
[a]a small number who escape the sword
shall return from the land of Egypt to the
land of Judah; and all the remnant of Judah, who have gone to the land of Egypt to
dwell there, shall know whose words will
stand, Mine or theirs. 29 And this *shall be* a
sign to you,' says the LORD, 'that I will punish you in this place, that you may know
that My words will surely [a]stand against
you for adversity.'

30 "Thus says the LORD: 'Behold, [a]I will
give Pharaoh Hophra king of Egypt into
the hand of his enemies and into the hand
of those who seek his life, as I gave [b]Zede-
kiah king of Judah into the hand of Nebuchadnezzar king of Babylon, his enemy
who sought his life.' "

Assurance to Baruch

45 The [a]word that Jeremiah the prophet
spoke to [b]Baruch the son of Neriah, when he had written these words in
a book at the instruction of Jeremiah,[1] in
the [c]fourth year of Jehoiakim the son of Josiah, king of Judah, saying, 2 "Thus says the
LORD, the God of Israel, to you, O Baruch:
3 'You said, "Woe is me now! For the LORD
has added grief to my sorrow. I [a]fainted in
my sighing, and I find no rest." '

4 "Thus you shall say to him, 'Thus says
the LORD: "Behold, [a]what I have built I will
break down, and what I have planted I will
pluck up, that is, this whole land. 5 And do
you seek great things for yourself? Do not
seek *them;* for behold, [a]I will bring adversity on all flesh," says the LORD. "But I will
give your [b]life to you as a prize in all places,
wherever you go." ' "

Judgment on Egypt

46 The word of the LORD which came to
Jeremiah the prophet against [a]the
nations. 2 Against [a]Egypt.

[b]Concerning the army of Pharaoh Necho,
king of Egypt, which was by the River Euphrates in Carchemish, and which Nebuchadnezzar king of Babylon [c]defeated in
the [d]fourth year of Jehoiakim the son of
Josiah, king of Judah:

3 "Order the buckler and shield,
And draw near to battle!
4 Harness the horses,
And mount up, you horsemen!
Stand forth with *your* helmets,
Polish the spears,
[a]Put on the armor!
5 Why have I seen them dismayed
and turned back?
Their mighty ones are beaten down;
They have speedily fled,
And did not look back,
For [a]fear *was* all around,"
says the LORD.
6 "Do not let the swift flee away,
Nor the mighty man escape;
They will [a]stumble and fall
Toward the north, by the
River Euphrates.

7 "Who *is* this coming up [a]like a flood,
Whose waters move like the rivers?
8 Egypt rises up like a flood,
And *its* waters move like the rivers;
And he says, 'I will go up
and cover the earth,
I will destroy the city and
its inhabitants.'
9 Come up, O horses, and
rage, O chariots!
And let the mighty men come forth:
The Ethiopians and the Libyans
who handle the shield,
And the Lydians [a]who handle
and bend the bow.
10 For this *is* [a]the day of the
Lord GOD of hosts,

44:26 [a] Gen. 22:16; Deut. 32:40, 41; Jer. 22:5; Amos 6:8; Heb. 6:13 [b] Jer. 10:6 [c] Neh. 9:5; Ps. 50:16; Ezek. 20:39 **44:27** [a] Jer. 1:10; 31:28; Ezek. 7:6 **44:28** [a] Is. 10:19; 27:12, 13 **44:29** [a] [Ps. 33:11] **44:30** [a] Jer. 46:25, 26; Ezek. 29:3; 30:21 [b] 2 Kin. 25:4–7; Jer. 39:5 **45:1** [a] Jer. 36:1, 4, 32 [b] Jer. 32:12, 16; 43:3 [c] Jer. 25:1; 36:1; 46:2 [1] Literally *from Jeremiah's mouth* **45:3** [a] Ps. 6:6; 69:3; [2 Cor. 4:1, 16; Gal. 6:9] **45:4** [a] Is. 5:5; Jer. 1:10; 11:17; 18:7–10; 31:28 **45:5** [a] Jer. 25:17–26 [b] Jer. 21:9; 38:2; 39:18 **46:1** [a] Jer. 25:15 **46:2** [a] Jer. 25:17–19; Ezek. 29:2—32:32 [b] 2 Kin. 23:33–35 [c] 2 Kin. 23:29; 24:7; 2 Chr. 35:20 [d] Jer. 45:1 **46:4** [a] Is. 21:5; Jer. 51:11, 12; Joel 3:9; Nah. 2:1; 3:14 **46:5** [a] Jer. 49:29 **46:6** [a] Jer. 46:12, 16; Dan. 11:19 **46:7** [a] Is. 8:7, 8; Jer. 47:2; Dan. 11:22 **46:9** [a] Is. 66:19 **46:10** [a] Is. 13:6; Joel 1:15

A day of vengeance,
That He may avenge Himself
on His adversaries.
[b]The sword shall devour;
It shall be satiated and made
drunk with their blood;
For the Lord GOD of hosts
[c]has a sacrifice
In the north country by the
River Euphrates.

11 "Go[a] up to Gilead and take balm,
[b]O virgin, the daughter of Egypt;
In vain you will use many
medicines;
[c]You shall not be cured.
12 The nations have heard
of your [a]shame,
And your cry has filled the land;
For the mighty man has stumbled
against the mighty;
They both have fallen together."

Babylonia Will Strike Egypt

13 The word that the LORD spoke to Jeremiah the prophet, how Nebuchadnezzar king of Babylon would come *and* [a]strike the land of Egypt.

14 "Declare in Egypt, and
proclaim in [a]Migdol;
Proclaim in Noph[1] and in
[b]Tahpanhes;
Say, 'Stand fast and prepare
yourselves,
For the sword devours all around you.'
15 Why are your valiant *men* swept away?
They did not stand
Because the LORD drove them away.
16 He made many fall;
Yes, [a]one fell upon another.
And they said, 'Arise!
[b]Let us go back to our own people
And to the land of our nativity
From the oppressing sword.'
17 They cried there,
'Pharaoh, king of Egypt, *is but* a noise.
He has passed by the appointed time!'
18 "*As* I live," says the King,
[a]Whose name *is* the LORD of hosts,
"Surely as Tabor *is* among
the mountains
And as Carmel by the sea,
so he shall come.
19 O [a]you daughter dwelling in Egypt,
Prepare yourself [b]to go into captivity!
For Noph[1] shall be waste and
desolate, without inhabitant.

20 "Egypt *is* a very pretty [a]heifer,
But destruction comes, it
comes [b]from the north.
21 Also her mercenaries are in
her midst like fat bulls,
For they also are turned back,
They have fled away together.
They did not stand,
For [a]the day of their calamity
had come upon them,
The time of their punishment.
22 [a]Her noise shall go like a serpent,
For they shall march with an army
And come against her with axes,
Like those who chop wood.

23 "They shall [a]cut down her
forest," says the LORD,
"Though it cannot be searched,
Because they *are* innumerable,
And more numerous than
[b]grasshoppers.
24 The daughter of Egypt
shall be ashamed;
She shall be delivered into the hand
Of [a]the people of the north."

25 The LORD of hosts, the God of Israel,
says: "Behold, I will bring punishment on
Amon[1] of [a]No,[2] and Pharaoh and Egypt,
[b]with their gods and their kings—Pharaoh
and those who [c]trust in him. 26 [a]And I will
deliver them into the hand of those who
seek their lives, into the hand of Nebuchadnezzar king of Babylon and the hand of his
servants. [b]Afterward it shall be inhabited as
in the days of old," says the LORD.

46:10 [b] Deut. 32:42; Is. 31:8; Jer. 12:12 [c] Is. 34:6; Zeph. 1:7; Ezek. 39:17 **46:11** [a] Jer. 8:22 [b] Is. 47:1; Jer. 31:4, 21 [c] Ezek. 30:21 **46:12** [a] Jer. 2:36; Nah. 3:8–10 **46:13** [a] Is. 19:1; Jer. 43:10, 11; Ezek. 29:1–21 **46:14** [a] Jer. 44:1 [b] Ezek. 30:18 [1] That is, ancient Memphis **46:16** [a] Lev. 26:36, 37; Jer. 46:6 [b] Jer. 51:9 **46:18** [a] Is. 47:4; Jer. 48:15; Mal. 1:14 **46:19** [a] Jer. 48:18 [b] Is. 20:4 [1] That is, ancient Memphis **46:20** [a] Hos. 10:11 [b] Jer. 1:14 **46:21** [a] [Ps. 37:13]; Jer. 50:27 **46:22** [a] [Is. 29:4] **46:23** [a] Is. 10:34 [b] Judg. 6:5; 7:12; Joel 2:25 **46:24** [a] Jer. 1:15 **46:25** [a] Ezek. 30:14–16; Nah. 3:8 [b] Ex. 12:12; Jer. 43:12, 13; Ezek. 30:13; Zeph. 2:11 [c] Is. 30:1–5; 31:1–3 [1] A sun god [2] That is, ancient Thebes **46:26** [a] Jer. 44:30; Ezek. 32:11 [b] Ezek. 29:8–14

God Will Preserve Israel
(cf. Jer. 30:10, 11)

27 "But[a] do not fear, O My servant Jacob,
And do not be dismayed, O Israel!
For behold, I will [b]save you from afar,
And your offspring from the
land of their captivity;
Jacob shall return, have
rest and be at ease;
No one shall make *him* afraid.
28 Do not fear, O Jacob My
servant," says the LORD,
"For I *am* with you;
For I will make a complete
end of all the nations
To which I have driven you,
But I will not make [a]a
complete end of you.
I will rightly [b]correct you,
For I will not leave you
wholly unpunished."

Judgment on Philistia

47 The word of the LORD that came to Jeremiah the prophet [a]against the Philistines, [b]before Pharaoh attacked Gaza.
2 Thus says the LORD:

"Behold, [a]waters rise [b]out of the north,
And shall be an overflowing flood;
They shall overflow the land
and all that is in it,
The city and those who dwell within;
Then the men shall cry,
And all the inhabitants of
the land shall wail.
3 At the [a]noise of the stamping
hooves of his strong horses,
At the rushing of his chariots,
At the rumbling of his wheels,
The fathers will not look back
for *their* children,
Lacking courage,
4 Because of the day that comes to
plunder all the [a]Philistines,
To cut off from [b]Tyre and Sidon
every helper who remains;
For the LORD shall plunder
the Philistines,
[c]The remnant of the country
of [d]Caphtor.
5 [a]Baldness has come upon Gaza,
[b]Ashkelon is cut off
With the remnant of their valley.
How long will you cut yourself?

6 "O you [a]sword of the LORD,
How long until you are quiet?
Put yourself up into your scabbard,
Rest and be still!
7 How can it be quiet,
Seeing the LORD has [a]given it
a charge
Against Ashkelon and
against the seashore?
There He has [b]appointed it."

Judgment on Moab

48 Against [a]Moab.
Thus says the LORD of hosts, the God of Israel:

"Woe to [b]Nebo!
For it is plundered,
[c]Kirjathaim is shamed *and* taken;
The high stronghold[1] is shamed
and dismayed—
2 [a]No more praise of Moab.
In [b]Heshbon they have devised
evil against her:
'Come, and let us cut her
off as a nation.'
You also shall be cut down,
O [c]Madmen![1]
The sword shall pursue you;
3 A voice of crying *shall be*
from [a]Horonaim:
'Plundering and great destruction!'

4 "Moab is destroyed;
Her little ones have caused
a cry to be heard;[1]
5 [a]For in the Ascent of Luhith they
ascend with continual weeping;

46:27 [a] Is. 41:13, 14; 43:5; 44:2; Jer. 30:10, 11 [b] Is. 11:11; Jer. 23:3, 4; Mic. 7:12 46:28 [a] Jer. 10:24; Amos 9:8, 9 [b] Jer. 30:11 47:1 [a] Is. 14:29–31; Ezek. 25:15–17; Zeph. 2:4, 5; Zech. 9:6 [b] Amos 1:6 47:2 [a] Is. 8:7, 8; Jer. 46:7, 8 [b] Jer. 1:14 47:3 [a] Judg. 5:22; Jer. 8:16; Nah. 3:2 47:4 [a] Is. 14:29–31 [b] Is. 23:1–18; Jer. 25:22; Ezek. 26:1–21; 28:20–24; Amos 1:9, 10; Zech. 9:2–4 [c] Ezek. 25:16; Amos 1:8 [d] Gen. 10:14; Deut. 2:23; Amos 9:7 47:5 [a] Jer. 48:37; Mic. 1:16; Zeph. 2:4 [b] Judg. 1:18; Jer. 25:20; Amos 1:7, 8; Zech. 9:5 47:6 [a] Deut. 32:41; Judg. 7:20; Jer. 12:12; Ezek. 21:3–5 47:7 [a] Is. 10:6; Ezek. 14:17 [b] Mic. 6:9 48:1 [a] Is. 15:1—16:14; 25:10; Ezek. 25:8–11; Amos 2:1–3; Zeph. 2:8–11 [b] Is. 15:2 [c] Num. 32:37; Jer. 48:23; Ezek. 25:9 [1] Hebrew *Misgab* 48:2 [a] Is. 16:14 [b] Is. 15:4; Jer. 49:3 [c] Is. 10:31 [1] A city of Moab 48:3 [a] Is. 15:5; Jer. 48:5, 34 48:4 [1] Following Masoretic Text, Targum, and Vulgate; Septuagint reads *Proclaim it in Zoar*. 48:5 [a] Is. 15:5

For in the descent of Horonaim
the enemies have heard
a cry of destruction.

6 "Flee, save your lives!
And be like the [a]juniper[1]
in the wilderness.
7 For because you have trusted in
your works and your [a]treasures,
You also shall be taken.
And [b]Chemosh shall go
forth into captivity,
His [c]priests and his princes
together.
8 And [a]the plunderer shall come
against every city;
No one shall escape.
The valley also shall perish,
And the plain shall be destroyed,
As the LORD has spoken.

9 "Give[a] wings to Moab,
That she may flee and get away;
For her cities shall be desolate,
Without any to dwell in them.
10 [a]Cursed *is* he who does the work
of the LORD deceitfully,
And cursed *is* he who keeps back
his sword from blood.

11 "Moab has been at ease from
his[1] youth;
He [a]has settled on his dregs,
And has not been emptied
from vessel to vessel,
Nor has he gone into captivity.
Therefore his taste remained in him,
And his scent has not changed.

12 "Therefore behold, the days are
coming," says the LORD,
"That I shall send him wine-workers
Who will tip him over
And empty his vessels
And break the bottles.
13 Moab shall be ashamed of [a]Chemosh,
As the house of Israel [b]was ashamed
of [c]Bethel, their confidence.
14 "How can you say, [a]'We *are* mighty
And strong men for the war'?
15 Moab is plundered and gone
up *from* her cities;
Her chosen young men
have [a]gone down to the
slaughter," says [b]the King,
Whose name *is* the LORD of hosts.

16 "The calamity of Moab *is*
near at hand,
And his affliction comes quickly.
17 Bemoan him, all you who
are around him;
And all you who know his name,
Say, [a]'How the strong staff is broken,
The beautiful rod!'

18 "O [a]daughter inhabiting [b]Dibon,
Come down from *your* glory,
And sit in thirst;
For the plunderer of Moab
has come against you,
He has destroyed your strongholds.
19 O inhabitant of [a]Aroer,
[b]Stand by the way and watch;
Ask him who flees
And her who escapes;
Say, 'What has happened?'
20 Moab is shamed, for he
is broken down.
[a]Wail and cry!
Tell it in [b]Arnon, that Moab
is plundered.

21 "And judgment has come on
the plain country:
On Holon and Jahzah and Mephaath,
22 On Dibon and Nebo and
Beth Diblathaim,
23 On Kirjathaim and Beth
Gamul and Beth Meon,
24 On [a]Kerioth and Bozrah,
On all the cities of the land of Moab,
Far or near.
25 [a]The horn of Moab is cut off,
And his [b]arm is broken,"
says the LORD.

48:6 [a] Jer. 17:6 [1] Or *Aroer,* a city of Moab 48:7 [a] Ps. 52:7; Is. 59:4; Jer. 9:23; [1 Tim. 6:17] [b] Num. 21:29; Judg. 11:24; Jer. 48:13 [c] Jer. 49:3 48:8 [a] Jer. 6:26 48:9 [a] Ps. 55:6 48:10 [a] Judg. 5:23; 1 Sam. 15:3, 9; 1 Kin. 20:42 48:11 [a] Zeph. 1:12 [1] The Hebrew uses masculine and feminine pronouns interchangeably in this chapter. 48:13 [a] 1 Kin. 11:7 [b] Hos. 10:6 [c] 1 Kin. 12:29; 13:32–34; Hos. 8:5, 6 48:14 [a] Is. 16:6 48:15 [a] [Is. 40:30, 31]; Jer. 50:27 [b] Jer. 46:18; 51:57; Mal. 1:14 48:17 [a] Is. 9:4; 14:4, 5 48:18 [a] Is. 47:1 [b] Num. 21:30; Josh. 13:9, 17; Is. 15:2; Jer. 48:22 48:19 [a] Deut. 2:36; Josh. 12:2; Is. 17:2 [b] 1 Sam. 4:13, 14, 16 48:20 [a] Is. 16:7 [b] Num. 21:13 48:24 [a] Jer. 48:41; Amos 2:2 48:25 [a] Ps. 75:10; Zech. 1:19–21 [b] Ezek. 30:21

26 "Make[a] him drunk,
Because he exalted *himself*
against the LORD.
Moab shall wallow in his vomit,
And he shall also be in derision.
27 For [a]was not Israel a derision to you?
[b]Was he found among thieves?
For whenever you speak of him,
You shake *your head in* [c]scorn.
28 You who dwell in Moab,
Leave the cities and [a]dwell in the rock,
And be like [b]the dove *which*
makes her nest
In the sides of the cave's mouth.

29 "We have heard the [a]pride of Moab
(He *is* exceedingly proud),
Of his loftiness and
arrogance and [b]pride,
And of the haughtiness of his heart."

30 "I know his wrath," says the LORD,
"But it *is* not right;
[a]His lies have made nothing right.
31 Therefore [a]I will wail for Moab,
And I will cry out for all Moab;
I[1] will mourn for the men
of Kir Heres.
32 [a]O vine of Sibmah! I will weep for
you with the weeping of [b]Jazer.
Your plants have gone over the sea,
They reach to the sea of Jazer.
The plunderer has fallen on your
summer fruit and your vintage.
33 [a]Joy and gladness are taken
From the plentiful field
And from the land of Moab;
I have caused wine to fail
from the winepresses;
No one will tread with
joyous shouting—
Not joyous shouting!

34 "From[a] the cry of Heshbon to
[b]Elealeh and to Jahaz
They have uttered their voice,
[c]From Zoar to Horonaim,
Like a three-year-old heifer;[1]
For the waters of Nimrim
also shall be desolate.

35 "Moreover," says the LORD,
"I will cause to cease in Moab
[a]The one who offers *sacrifices*
in the high places
And burns incense to his gods.
36 Therefore [a]My heart shall wail
like flutes for Moab,
And like flutes My heart shall wail
For the men of Kir Heres.
Therefore [b]the riches they have
acquired have perished.

37 "For [a]every head *shall be* bald,
and every beard clipped;
On all the hands *shall be* cuts, and
[b]on the loins sackcloth—
38 A general lamentation
On all the [a]housetops of Moab,
And in its streets;
For I have [b]broken Moab like
a vessel in which *is* no
pleasure," says the LORD.
39 "They shall wail:
'How she is broken down!
How Moab has turned her
back with shame!'
So Moab shall be a derision
And a dismay to all those
about her."

40 For thus says the LORD:

"Behold, [a]one shall fly like an eagle,
And [b]spread his wings over Moab.
41 Kerioth is taken,
And the strongholds are
surprised;
[a]The mighty men's hearts in
Moab on that day shall be
Like the heart of a woman
in birth pangs.
42 And Moab shall be destroyed
[a]as a people,
Because he exalted *himself*
against the LORD.

48:26 [a] Jer. 25:15 48:27 [a] Zeph. 2:8 [b] Jer. 2:26 [c] Lam. 2:15; [Mic. 7:8–10] 48:28 [a] Ps. 55:6, 7 [b] Song 2:14 48:29 [a] Is. 16:6; Zeph. 2:8, 10 [b] Jer. 49:16 48:30 [a] Is. 16:6; Jer. 50:36 48:31 [a] Is. 15:5; 16:7, 11 [1] Following Dead Sea Scrolls, Septuagint, and Vulgate; Masoretic Text reads *He.* 48:32 [a] Is. 16:8, 9 [b] Num. 21:32; Is. 16:10 48:33 [a] Is. 16:10; Jer. 25:10; Joel 1:12 48:34 [a] Is. 15:4–6 [b] Num. 32:3, 37 [c] Is. 15:5, 6 [1] Or *The Third Eglath,* an unknown city (compare Isaiah 15:5) 48:35 [a] Is. 15:2; 16:12 48:36 [a] Is. 15:5; 16:11 [b] Is. 15:7 48:37 [a] Is. 15:2, 3; Jer. 16:6; 41:5; 47:5 [b] Gen. 37:34; Is. 15:3; 20:2 48:38 [a] Is. 15:3 [b] Jer. 22:28 48:40 [a] Deut. 28:49; Jer. 49:22; Hos. 8:1; Hab. 1:8 [b] Is. 8:8 48:41 [a] Is. 13:8; 21:3; Jer. 30:6; Mic. 4:9, 10 48:42 [a] Ps. 83:4; Jer. 48:2

43 [a]Fear and the pit and the snare
shall be upon you,
O inhabitant of Moab," says the LORD.
44 "He who flees from the fear
shall fall into the pit,
And he who gets out of the pit
shall be caught in the [a]snare.
For upon Moab, upon it [b]I will bring
The year of their punishment,"
says the LORD.

45 "Those who fled stood under
the shadow of Heshbon
Because of exhaustion.
But [a]a fire shall come out of Heshbon,
A flame from the midst of [b]Sihon,
And [c]shall devour the brow of Moab,
The crown of the head of
the sons of tumult.
46 [a]Woe to you, O Moab!
The people of Chemosh perish;
For your sons have been taken captive,
And your daughters captive.

47 "Yet I will bring back the
captives of Moab
[a]In the latter days," says the LORD.

Thus far *is* the judgment of Moab.

Judgment on Ammon

49 Against the [a]Ammonites.
Thus says the LORD:

"Has Israel no sons?
Has he no heir?
Why *then* does Milcom[1] inherit [b]Gad,
And his people dwell in its cities?
2 [a]Therefore behold, the days are
coming," says the LORD,
"That I will cause to be heard
an alarm of war
In [b]Rabbah of the Ammonites;
It shall be a desolate mound,
And her villages shall be
burned with fire.
Then Israel shall take possession of
his inheritance," says the LORD.

3 "Wail, O [a]Heshbon, for Ai is plundered!
Cry, you daughters of Rabbah,
[b]Gird yourselves with sackcloth!
Lament and run to and
fro by the walls;
For Milcom shall go into captivity
With his [c]priests and his
princes together.
4 Why [a]do you boast in the valleys,
Your flowing valley,
O [b]backsliding daughter?
Who trusted in her [c]treasures, [d]*saying,*
'Who will come against me?'
5 Behold, I will bring fear upon you,"
Says the Lord GOD of hosts,
"From all those who are around you;
You shall be driven out,
everyone headlong,
And no one will gather those
who wander off.
6 But [a]afterward I will bring back
The captives of the people of
Ammon," says the LORD.

Judgment on Edom

7 [a]Against Edom.
Thus says the LORD of hosts:

[b]"*Is* wisdom no more in Teman?
[c]Has counsel perished
from the prudent?
Has their wisdom [d]vanished?
8 Flee, turn back, dwell in the depths,
O inhabitants of [a]Dedan!
For I will bring the calamity
of Esau upon him,
The time *that* I will punish him.
9 [a]If grape-gatherers came to you,
Would they not leave *some*
gleaning grapes?
If thieves by night,
Would they not destroy until
they have enough?
10 [a]But I have made Esau bare;
I have uncovered his secret places,[1]
And he shall not be able
to hide himself.
His descendants are plundered,

48:43 [a] Is. 24:17, 18; Lam. 3:47 48:44 [a] 1 Kin. 19:17; Is. 24:18; Amos 5:19 [b] Jer. 11:23 48:45 [a] Num. 21:28, 29 [b] Num. 21:21, 26; Ps. 135:11 [c] Num. 24:17 48:46 [a] Num. 21:29 48:47 [a] Jer. 49:6, 39 49:1 [a] Deut. 23:3, 4; 2 Chr. 20:1; Jer. 25:21; Ezek. 21:28–32; 25:1–7 [b] Amos 1:13–15; Zeph. 2:8–11 [1] Hebrew *Malcam,* literally *their king,* a god of the Ammonites; also called *Molech* (compare verse 3) 49:2 [a] Amos 1:13–15 [b] Ezek. 25:5 49:3 [a] Jer. 48:2 [b] Is. 32:11; Jer. 48:37 [c] Jer. 48:7 49:4 [a] Jer. 9:23 [b] Jer. 3:14 [c] Jer. 48:7 [d] Jer. 21:13 49:6 [a] Jer. 48:47 49:7 [a] Gen. 25:30; 32:3; Is. 34:5, 6; Jer. 25:21; Ezek. 25:12–14; 35:1–15; Joel 3:19; Amos 1:11, 12; Obad. 1–9, 15, 16 [b] Gen. 36:11; Job 2:11 [c] Is. 19:11 [d] Jer. 8:9 49:8 [a] Is. 21:13; Jer. 25:23 49:9 [a] Obad. 5, 6 49:10 [a] Obad. 5, 6; Mal. 1:3 [1] Compare Obadiah 5, 6

His brethren and his neighbors,
And [b]he *is* no more.
11 Leave your fatherless children,
I will preserve *them* alive;
And let your widows trust in Me."

12For thus says the LORD: "Behold, [a]those
whose judgment *was* not to drink of the
cup have assuredly drunk. And *are* you the
one who will altogether go unpunished?
You shall not go unpunished, but you shall
surely drink *of it.* 13For [a]I have sworn by
Myself," says the LORD, "that [b]Bozrah shall
become a desolation, a reproach, a waste,
and a curse. And all its cities shall be perpetual wastes."

14 [a]I have heard a message
from the LORD,
And an ambassador has been
sent to the nations:
"Gather together, come against her,
And rise up to battle!

15 "For indeed, I will make you
small among nations,
Despised among men.
16 Your fierceness has deceived you,
The [a]pride of your heart,
O you who dwell in the
clefts of the rock,
Who hold the height of the hill!
[b]Though you make your [c]nest
as high as the eagle,
[d]I will bring you down from
there," says the LORD.[1]

17 "Edom also shall be an
astonishment;
[a]Everyone who goes by it
will be astonished
And will hiss at all its plagues.
18 [a]As in the overthrow of Sodom
and Gomorrah
And their neighbors," says the LORD,
"No one shall remain there,
Nor shall a son of man
dwell in it.

19 "Behold,[a] he shall come up like a lion
from [b]the floodplain[1] of the Jordan
Against the dwelling place
of the strong;
But I will suddenly make him
run away from her.
And who *is* a chosen *man that*
I may appoint over her?
For [c]who *is* like Me?
Who will arraign Me?
And [d]who *is* that shepherd
Who will withstand Me?"

20 [a]Therefore hear the counsel
of the LORD that He has
taken against Edom,
And His purposes that He
has proposed against the
inhabitants of Teman:
Surely the least of the flock
shall draw them out;
Surely He shall make their dwelling
places desolate with them.
21 [a]The earth shakes at the
noise of their fall;
At the cry its noise is heard
at the Red Sea.
22 Behold, [a]He shall come up
and fly like the eagle,
And spread His wings over Bozrah;
The heart of the mighty men of
Edom in that day shall be
Like the heart of a woman
in birth pangs.

Judgment on Damascus

23[a]Against Damascus.

[b]"Hamath and Arpad are shamed,
For they have heard bad news.
They are fainthearted;
[c]*There is* trouble on the sea;
It cannot be quiet.
24 Damascus has grown feeble;
She turns to flee,
And fear has seized *her*.
[a]Anguish and sorrows have taken
her like a woman in labor.

49:10 [b] Is. 17:14 49:12 [a] Jer. 25:29; Obad. 16 49:13 [a] Gen. 22:16; Is. 45:23; Jer. 44:26; Amos 6:8 [b] Gen. 36:33; 1 Chr. 1:44; Is. 34:6; 63:1; Amos 1:12 49:14 [a] Obad. 1–4 49:16 [a] Jer. 48:29 [b] Obad. 3, 4 [c] Job 39:27; Is. 14:13–15 [d] Amos 9:2 [1] Compare Obadiah 3, 4 49:17 [a] Jer. 18:16; 49:13; 50:13; Ezek. 35:7 49:18 [a] Gen. 19:24, 25; Deut. 29:23; Jer. 50:40; Amos 4:11; Zeph. 2:9 49:19 [a] Jer. 50:44 [b] Josh. 3:15; Jer. 12:5 [c] Ex. 15:11; Is. 46:9 [d] Job 41:10 [1] Or *thicket* 49:20 [a] Is. 14:24, 27; Jer. 50:45 49:21 [a] Jer. 50:46; Ezek. 26:15, 18 49:22 [a] Jer. 48:40, 41 49:23 [a] Is. 17:1–3; Amos 1:3, 5; Zech. 9:1, 2 [b] Jer. 39:5; Zech. 9:2 [c] [Is. 57:20] 49:24 [a] Is. 13:8; Jer. 4:31; 6:24; 48:21

25 Why is [a]the city of praise not
deserted, the city of My joy?
26 [a]Therefore her young men
shall fall in her streets,
And all the men of war shall be cut off
in that day," says the LORD of hosts.
27 "I[a] will kindle a fire in the
wall of Damascus,
And it shall consume the
palaces of Ben-Hadad."[1]

Judgment on Kedar and Hazor

28 [a]Against Kedar and against the kingdoms of Hazor, which Nebuchadnezzar
king of Babylon shall strike.
Thus says the LORD:

"Arise, go up to Kedar,
And devastate [b]the men of the East!
29 Their [a]tents and their flocks
they shall take away.
They shall take for themselves
their curtains,
All their vessels and their camels;
And they shall cry out to them,
[b]'Fear *is* on every side!'

30 "Flee, get far away! Dwell in the depths,
O inhabitants of Hazor!"
says the LORD.
"For Nebuchadnezzar king of Babylon
has taken counsel against you,
And has conceived a plan against you.

31 "Arise, go up to [a]the wealthy nation
that dwells securely," says
the LORD,
"Which has neither gates nor bars,
[b]Dwelling alone.
32 Their camels shall be for booty,
And the multitude of their
cattle for plunder.
I will [a]scatter to all winds those
in the farthest corners,
And I will bring their calamity from
all its sides," says the LORD.
33 "Hazor [a]shall be a dwelling for
jackals, a desolation forever;
No one shall reside there,
Nor son of man dwell in it."

Judgment on Elam

34 The word of the LORD that came to Jeremiah the prophet against [a]Elam, in the
[b]beginning of the reign of Zedekiah king
of Judah, saying, 35 "Thus says the LORD
of hosts:

'Behold, I will break [a]the bow of Elam,
The foremost of their might.
36 Against Elam I will bring
the four winds
From the four quarters of heaven,
And scatter them toward
all those winds;
There shall be no nations where the
outcasts of Elam will not go.
37 For I will cause Elam to be dismayed
before their enemies
And before those who seek their life.
[a]I will bring disaster upon them,
My fierce anger,' says the LORD;
'And I will send the sword after them
Until I have consumed them.
38 I will [a]set My throne in Elam,
And will destroy from there the king
and the princes,' says the LORD.

39 'But it shall come to pass
[a]in the latter days:
I will bring back the captives
of Elam,' says the LORD."

Judgment on Babylon and Babylonia

50 The word that the LORD spoke
[a]against Babylon *and* against the
land of the Chaldeans by Jeremiah the
prophet.

2 "Declare among the nations,
Proclaim, and set up a standard;
Proclaim—do not conceal *it*—
Say, 'Babylon is [a]taken, [b]Bel is shamed.
Merodach[1] is broken in pieces;
[c]Her idols are humiliated,
Her images are broken in pieces.'

49:25 [a] Jer. 33:9 **49:26** [a] Jer. 50:30; Amos 4:10 **49:27** [a] Amos 1:4 [1] Compare Amos 1:4 **49:28** [a] Gen. 25:13; Ps. 120:5; Is. 21:16, 17; Jer. 2:10; Ezek. 27:21 [b] Judg. 6:3; Job 1:3 **49:29** [a] Ps. 120:5 [b] Jer. 46:5 **49:31** [a] Ezek. 38:11 [b] Num. 23:9; Deut. 33:28; Mic. 7:16 **49:32** [a] Ezek. 5:10 **49:33** [a] Jer. 9:11; 10:22; Zeph. 2:9, 12–15; Mal. 1:3 **49:34** [a] Gen. 10:22; Jer. 25:25; Ezek. 32:24; Dan. 8:2 [b] 2 Kin. 24:17, 18; Jer. 28:1 **49:35** [a] Ps. 46:9; Is. 22:6 **49:37** [a] Jer. 9:16 **49:38** [a] Jer. 43:10 **49:39** [a] Jer. 48:47 **50:1** [a] Gen. 10:10; 11:9; 2 Kin. 17:24; Is. 13:1; 47:1; Dan. 1:1; Rev. 14:8 **50:2** [a] Is. 21:9 [b] Is. 46:1; Jer. 51:44 [c] Jer. 43:12, 13 [1] A Babylonian god; sometimes spelled *Marduk*

3 [a]For out of the north [b]a nation
comes up against her,
Which shall make her land desolate,
And no one shall dwell therein.
They shall move, they shall depart,
Both man and beast.

4 "In those days and in that
time," says the LORD,
"The children of Israel shall come,
[a]They and the children of
Judah together;
[b]With continual weeping
they shall come,
[c]And seek the LORD their God.
5 They shall ask the way to Zion,
With their faces toward it, *saying*,
'Come and let us join
ourselves to the LORD
In [a]a perpetual covenant
That will not be forgotten.'

6 "My people have been [a]lost sheep.
Their shepherds have led
them [b]astray;
They have turned them away
on [c]the mountains.
They have gone from mountain to hill;
They have forgotten their
resting place.
7 All who found them have
[a]devoured them;
And [b]their adversaries said,
[c]'We have not offended,
Because they have sinned against the
LORD, [d]the habitation of justice,
The LORD, [e]the hope of their fathers.'
8 "Move[a] from the midst of Babylon,
Go out of the land of the Chaldeans;
And be like the rams before the flocks.
9 [a]For behold, I will raise and cause
to come up against Babylon
An assembly of great nations
from the north country,
And they shall array
themselves against her;
From there she shall be captured.
Their arrows *shall be* like *those*
of an expert warrior;[1]
[b]None shall return in vain.
10 And Chaldea shall become plunder;
[a]All who plunder her shall be
satisfied," says the LORD.

11 "Because[a] you were glad,
because you rejoiced,
You destroyers of My heritage,
Because you have grown fat [b]like
a heifer threshing grain,
And you bellow like bulls,
12 Your mother shall be deeply ashamed;
She who bore you shall be ashamed.
Behold, the least of the nations
shall be a [a]wilderness,
A dry land and a desert.
13 Because of the wrath of the LORD
She shall not be inhabited,
[a]But she shall be wholly desolate.
[b]Everyone who goes by Babylon
shall be horrified
And hiss at all her plagues.

14 "Put[a] yourselves in array against
Babylon all around,
All you who bend the bow;
Shoot at her, spare no arrows,
For she has sinned against the LORD.
15 Shout against her all around;
She has [a]given her hand,
Her foundations have fallen,
[b]Her walls are thrown down;
For [c]it *is* the vengeance of the LORD.
Take vengeance on her.
As she has done, so do to her.
16 Cut off the sower from Babylon,
And him who handles the
sickle at harvest time.
For fear of the oppressing sword
[a]Everyone shall turn to his
own people,
And everyone shall flee
to his own land.

17 "Israel *is* like [a]scattered sheep;
[b]The lions have driven *him* away.

50:3 [a] Jer. 51:48; Dan. 5:30, 31 [b] Is. 13:17, 18, 20 50:4 [a] Ezra 2:1; Is. 11:12, 13; Jer. 3:18; 31:31; 33:7; Hos. 1:11 [b] Ezra 3:12, 13; [Ps. 126:5]; Jer. 31:9; [Zech. 12:10] [c] Hos. 3:5 50:5 [a] Jer. 31:31 50:6 [a] Is. 53:6; [Ezek. 34:15, 16]; Matt. 9:36; 10:6; 1 Pet. 2:25 [b] Jer. 23:1; Ezek. 34:2 [c] [Jer. 2:20; 3:6, 23] 50:7 [a] Ps. 79:7 [b] Jer. 40:2, 3; Zech. 11:5 [c] Jer. 2:3; Dan. 9:16 [d] [Ps. 90:1; 91:1] [e] Ps. 22:4; Jer. 14:8; 17:13 50:8 [a] Is. 48:20; Jer. 51:6, 45; Zech. 2:6, 7; [Rev. 18:4] 50:9 [a] Jer. 15:14; 51:27 [b] 2 Sam. 1:22 [1] Following some Hebrew manuscripts, Septuagint, and Syriac; Masoretic Text, Targum, and Vulgate read *a warrior who makes childless.* 50:10 [a] [Rev. 17:16] 50:11 [a] Is. 47:6 [b] Hos. 10:11 50:12 [a] Jer. 51:43 50:13 [a] Jer. 25:12 [b] Jer. 49:17 50:14 [a] Jer. 51:2 50:15 [a] 1 Chr. 29:24; 2 Chr. 30:8; Lam. 5:6; Ezek. 17:18 [b] Jer. 51:58 [c] Jer. 51:6, 11 50:16 [a] Is. 13:14; Jer. 51:9 50:17 [a] 2 Kin. 24:10, 14 [b] Jer. 2:15

First [c]the king of Assyria
devoured him;
Now at last this [d]Nebuchadnezzar king
of Babylon has broken his bones."

18 Therefore thus says the LORD of hosts,
the God of Israel:

"Behold, I will punish the king
of Babylon and his land,
As I have punished the
king of [a]Assyria.
19 [a]But I will bring back Israel
to his home,
And he shall feed on Carmel
and Bashan;
His soul shall be satisfied on
Mount Ephraim and Gilead.
20 In those days and in that
time," says the LORD,
[a]"The iniquity of Israel shall be
sought, but *there shall be* none;
And the sins of Judah, but
they shall not be found;
For I will pardon those
[b]whom I preserve.

21 "Go up against the land of
Merathaim, against it,
And against the inhabitants of [a]Pekod.
Waste and utterly destroy
them," says the LORD,
"And do [b]according to all that I
have commanded you.
22 [a]A sound of battle *is* in the land,
And of great destruction.
23 How [a]the hammer of the whole earth
has been cut apart and broken!
How Babylon has become a
desolation among the nations!
24 I have laid a snare for you;
You have indeed been
[a]trapped, O Babylon,
And you were not aware;
You have been found and also caught,
Because you have [b]contended
against the LORD.
25 The LORD has opened His armory,
And has brought out [a]the
weapons of His indignation;
For this *is* the work of the
Lord GOD of hosts
In the land of the Chaldeans.
26 Come against her from the
farthest border;
Open her storehouses;
Cast her up as heaps of ruins,
And destroy her utterly;
Let nothing of her be left.
27 Slay all her [a]bulls,
Let them go down to the
slaughter.
Woe to them!
For their day has come, the time
of [b]their punishment.
28 The voice of those who flee and
escape from the land of Babylon
[a]Declares in Zion the vengeance
of the LORD our God,
The vengeance of His temple.

29 "Call together the archers
against Babylon.
All you who bend the bow, encamp
against it all around;
Let none of them escape.[1]
[a]Repay her according to her work;
According to all she has
done, do to her;
[b]For she has been proud
against the LORD,
Against the Holy One of Israel.
30 [a]Therefore her young men
shall fall in the streets,
And all her men of war shall be cut
off in that day," says the LORD.
31 "Behold, I *am* against you,
O most haughty one!" says
the Lord GOD of hosts;
"For your day has come,
The time *that* I will punish you.[1]
32 The most [a]proud shall
stumble and fall,
And no one will raise him up;
[b]I will kindle a fire in his cities,
And it will devour all around him."

50:17 [c] 2 Kin. 15:29; 17:6; 18:9–13 [d] 2 Kin. 24:10–14; 25:1–7 50:18 [a] Is. 10:12; Ezek. 31:3, 11, 12; Nah. 3:7, 18, 19 50:19 [a] Is. 65:10; Jer. 33:12; Ezek. 34:13 50:20 [a] Num. 23:21; Is. 43:25; [Jer. 31:34; Mic. 7:19] [b] Is. 1:9 50:21 [a] Ezek. 23:23 [b] 2 Sam. 16:11; 2 Kin. 18:25; 2 Chr. 36:23; Is. 10:6; 44:28; 48:14 50:22 [a] Jer. 51:54 50:23 [a] Is. 14:6; Jer. 51:20–24 50:24 [a] Jer. 51:8, 31; Dan. 5:30 [b] [Is. 45:9] 50:25 [a] Is. 13:5 50:27 [a] Ps. 22:12; Is. 34:7; Jer. 46:21 [b] Ps. 37:13; Jer. 48:44; Ezek. 7:7 50:28 [a] Ps. 149:6–9; Jer. 51:10 50:29 [a] Ps. 137:8; Jer. 51:56; [2 Thess. 1:6]; Rev. 18:6 [b] [Is. 47:10] [1] Qere, some Hebrew manuscripts, Septuagint, and Targum add *to her*. 50:30 [a] Is. 13:18; Jer. 49:26; 51:4 50:31 [1] Following Masoretic Text and Targum; Septuagint and Vulgate read *The time of your punishment.* 50:32 [a] Is. 26:5; Mal. 4:1 [b] Jer. 21:14

33 Thus says the LORD of hosts:

"The children of Israel *were* oppressed,
Along with the children of Judah;
All who took them captive
have held them fast;
They have refused to let them go.
34 [a]Their Redeemer *is* strong;
[b]The LORD of hosts *is* His name.
He will thoroughly plead their [c]case,
That He may give rest to the land,
And disquiet the inhabitants
of Babylon.

35 "A sword *is* against the
Chaldeans," says the LORD,
"Against the inhabitants
of Babylon,
And [a]against her princes
and [b]her wise men.
36 A sword *is* [a]against the soothsayers,
and they will be fools.
A sword *is* against her mighty men,
and they will be dismayed.
37 A sword *is* against their horses,
Against their chariots,
And against all [a]the mixed peoples
who *are* in her midst;
And [b]they will become like women.
A sword *is* against her treasures,
and they will be robbed.
38 [a]A drought[1] *is* against her waters,
and they will be dried up.
For it *is* the land of carved images,
And they are insane with
their idols.

39 "Therefore[a] the wild desert beasts
shall dwell *there* with the jackals,
And the ostriches shall dwell in it.
[b]It shall be inhabited no more forever,
Nor shall it be dwelt in from
generation to generation.
40 [a]As God overthrew Sodom
and Gomorrah
And their neighbors," says the LORD,
"*So* no one shall reside there,
Nor son of man [b]dwell in it.

41 "Behold,[a] a people shall come
from the north,
And a great nation and many kings
Shall be raised up from the
ends of the earth.
42 [a]They shall hold the bow and the lance;
[b]They *are* cruel and shall
not show mercy.
[c]Their voice shall roar like the sea;
They shall ride on horses,
Set in array, like a man for the battle,
Against you, O daughter of Babylon.

43 "The king of Babylon has [a]heard
the report about them,
And his hands grow feeble;
Anguish has taken hold of him,
Pangs as of a woman in [b]childbirth.

44 "Behold,[a] he shall come up like a lion
from the floodplain[1]
of the Jordan
Against the dwelling place
of the strong;
But I will make them suddenly
run away from her.
And who *is* a chosen *man that*
I may appoint over her?
For who *is* like Me?
Who will arraign Me?
And [b]who *is* that shepherd
Who will withstand Me?"

45 Therefore hear [a]the counsel
of the LORD that He has
taken against Babylon,
And His [b]purposes that He
has proposed against the
land of the Chaldeans:
[c]Surely the least of the flock
shall draw them out;
Surely He will make their dwelling
place desolate with them.
46 [a]At the noise of the taking
of Babylon
The earth trembles,
And the cry is heard among
the nations.

50:34 [a] Prov. 23:11; Is. 43:14; Jer. 15:21; 31:11; Rev. 18:8 [b] Is. 47:4 [c] Jer. 51:36; Mic. 7:9 50:35 [a] Dan. 5:30 [b] Is. 47:13; Jer. 51:57 50:36 [a] Is. 44:25; Jer. 48:30 50:37 [a] Jer. 25:20; Ezek. 30:5 [b] Jer. 51:30; Nah. 3:13 50:38 [a] Is. 44:27; Jer. 51:36; Rev. 16:12 [1] Following Masoretic Text, Targum, and Vulgate; Syriac reads *sword;* Septuagint omits *A drought is.* 50:39 [a] Is. 13:21, 22; 34:14; Jer. 51:37; Rev. 18:2 [b] Is. 13:20; Jer. 25:12 50:40 [a] Gen. 19:24, 25; Is. 13:19; Jer. 49:18; [Luke 17:28–30]; 2 Pet. 2:6; Jude 7 [b] Is. 13:20 50:41 [a] Is. 13:2–5; Jer. 6:22; 25:14; 51:27 50:42 [a] Jer. 6:23 [b] Is. 13:18 [c] Is. 5:30 50:43 [a] Jer. 51:31 [b] Jer. 6:24 50:44 [a] Jer. 49:19–21 [b] Job 41:10; Jer. 49:19 [1] Or *thicket* 50:45 [a] [Ps. 33:11; Is. 14:24]; Jer. 51:10, 11 [b] Jer. 51:29 [c] Jer. 49:19, 20 50:46 [a] Rev. 18:9

The Utter Destruction of Babylon

51 Thus says the LORD:
"Behold, I will raise up
against [a]Babylon,
Against those who dwell
in Leb Kamai,[1]
[b]A destroying wind.
2 And I will send [a]winnowers
to Babylon,
Who shall winnow her and
empty her land.
[b]For in the day of doom
They shall be against her all around.
3 Against *her* [a]let the archer
bend his bow,
And lift himself up against
her in his armor.
Do not spare her young men;
[b]Utterly destroy all her army.
4 Thus the slain shall fall in the
land of the Chaldeans,
[a]And *those* thrust through
in her streets.
5 For Israel is [a]not forsaken, nor Judah,
By his God, the LORD of hosts,
Though their land was filled with sin
against the Holy One of Israel."

6 [a]Flee from the midst of Babylon,
And every one save his life!
Do not be cut off in her iniquity,
For [b]this *is* the time of the
LORD's vengeance;
[c]He shall recompense her.
7 [a]Babylon *was* a golden cup
in the LORD's hand,
That made all the earth drunk.
[b]The nations drank her wine;
Therefore the nations [c]are deranged.
8 Babylon has suddenly [a]fallen
and been destroyed.
[b]Wail for her!
[c]Take balm for her pain;
Perhaps she may be healed.

9 We would have healed Babylon,
But she is not healed.
Forsake her, and [a]let us go
everyone to his own country;
[b]For her judgment reaches to heaven
and is lifted up to the skies.
10 The LORD has [a]revealed
our righteousness.
Come and let us [b]declare in Zion
the work of the LORD our God.

11 [a]Make the arrows bright!
Gather the shields!
[b]The LORD has raised up the spirit
of the kings of the Medes.
[c]For His plan *is* against
Babylon to destroy it,
Because it *is* [d]the vengeance
of the LORD,
The vengeance for His temple.
12 [a]Set up the standard on the
walls of Babylon;
Make the guard strong,
Set up the watchmen,
Prepare the ambushes.
For the LORD has both
devised and done
What He spoke against the
inhabitants of Babylon.
13 [a]O you who dwell by many waters,
Abundant in treasures,
Your end has come,
The measure of your covetousness.
14 [a]The LORD of hosts has
sworn by Himself:
"Surely I will fill you with
men, [b]as with locusts,
And they shall lift [c]up a
shout against you."

15 [a]He has made the earth by His power;
He has established the world
by His wisdom,
And [b]stretched out the heaven
by His understanding.
16 When He utters *His* voice—
There is a multitude of waters
in the heavens:
[a]"He causes the vapors to ascend
from the ends of the earth;

51:1 [a] Is. 47:1; Jer. 50:1 [b] 2 Kin. 19:7; Jer. 4:11; Hos. 13:15 [1] A code word for Chaldea (Babylonia); may be translated *The Midst of Those Who Rise Up Against Me* 51:2 [a] Is. 41:16; Jer. 15:7; Matt. 3:12 [b] Jer. 50:14 51:3 [a] Jer. 50:14, 29 [b] Jer. 50:21 51:4 [a] Jer. 49:26; 50:30, 37 51:5 [a] [Is. 54:7, 8; Jer. 33:24–26; 46:28] 51:6 [a] Jer. 50:8; Rev. 18:4 [b] Jer. 50:15 [c] Jer. 25:14 51:7 [a] Jer. 25:15; Hab. 2:16; Rev. 17:4 [b] Rev. 14:8 [c] Jer. 25:16 51:8 [a] Is. 21:9; Jer. 50:2; Rev. 14:8; 18:2 [b] [Is. 48:20]; Rev. 18:9, 11, 19 [c] Jer. 46:11 51:9 [a] Is. 13:14; Jer. 46:16; 50:16 [b] Ezra 9:6; Rev. 18:5 51:10 [a] Ps. 37:6; Mic. 7:9 [b] [Is. 40:2]; Jer. 50:28 51:11 [a] Jer. 46:4, 9; Joel 3:9, 10 [b] Is. 13:17 [c] Jer. 50:45 [d] Jer. 50:28 51:12 [a] Nah. 2:1; 3:14 51:13 [a] Rev. 17:1, 15 51:14 [a] Jer. 49:13; Amos 6:8 [b] Jer. 51:27; Nah. 3:15 [c] Jer. 50:15 51:15 [a] Gen. 1:1, 6; Jer. 10:12–16 [b] Job 9:8; Ps. 104:2; Is. 40:22 51:16 [a] Ps. 135:7; Jer. 10:13

He makes lightnings for the rain;
He brings the wind out of
His treasuries."[1]

17 [a]Everyone is dull-hearted,
without knowledge;
Every metalsmith is put to shame
by the carved image;
[b]For his molded image
is falsehood,
And *there is* no breath in them.
18 They *are* futile, a work of errors;
In the time of their punishment
they shall perish.
19 The Portion of Jacob *is*
not like them,
For He *is* the Maker of all things;
And *Israel is* the tribe of
His inheritance.
The LORD of hosts *is* His name.

20 "You[a] *are* My battle-ax *and*
weapons of war:
For with you I will break the
nation in pieces;
With you I will destroy kingdoms;
21 With you I will break in pieces
the horse and its rider;
With you I will break in pieces
the chariot and its rider;
22 With you also I will break in
pieces man and woman;
With you I will break in
pieces [a]old and young;
With you I will break in pieces the
young man and the maiden;
23 With you also I will break in pieces
the shepherd and his flock;
With you I will break in pieces the
farmer and his yoke of oxen;
And with you I will break in
pieces governors and rulers.

24 "And[a] I will repay Babylon
And all the inhabitants of Chaldea
For all the evil they have done
In Zion in your sight," says the LORD.

25 "Behold, I *am* against you,
[a]O destroying mountain,
Who destroys all the earth,"
says the LORD.
"And I will stretch out My
hand against you,
Roll you down from the rocks,
[b]And make you a burnt mountain.
26 They shall not take from you
a stone for a corner
Nor a stone for a foundation,
[a]But you shall be desolate
forever," says the LORD.

27 [a]Set up a banner in the land,
Blow the trumpet among the nations!
[b]Prepare the nations against her,
Call [c]the kingdoms together
against her:
Ararat, Minni, and Ashkenaz.
Appoint a general against her;
Cause the horses to come up
like the bristling locusts.
28 Prepare against her the nations,
With the kings of the Medes,
Its governors and all its rulers,
All the land of his dominion.
29 And the land will tremble
and sorrow;
For every [a]purpose of the LORD shall
be performed against Babylon,
[b]To make the land of Babylon a
desolation without inhabitant.
30 The mighty men of Babylon
have ceased fighting,
They have remained in
their strongholds;
Their might has failed,
[a]They became *like* women;
They have burned her dwelling places,
[b]The bars of her *gate* are broken.
31 [a]One runner will run to meet another,
And one messenger to meet another,
To show the king of Babylon that
his city is taken on *all* sides;
32 [a]The passages are blocked,
The reeds they have burned
with fire,
And the men of war are terrified.

33 For thus says the LORD of hosts, the God of Israel:

51:16 [1] Psalm 135:7 51:17 [a] [Is. 44:18–20]; Jer. 10:14 [b] Jer. 50:2 51:20 [a] Is. 10:5, 15; Jer. 50:23 51:22 [a] 2 Chr. 36:17; Is. 13:15, 16 51:24 [a] Jer. 50:15, 29 51:25 [a] Is. 13:2; Zech. 4:7 [b] Rev. 8:8 51:26 [a] Jer. 50:26, 40 51:27 [a] Is. 13:2; Jer. 50:2; 51:12 [b] Jer. 25:14 [c] Jer. 50:41, 42 51:29 [a] Jer. 50:45 [b] Is. 13:19, 20; 47:11; Jer. 50:13; 51:26, 43 51:30 [a] Is. 19:16; Jer. 48:41 [b] Is. 45:1, 2; Lam. 2:9; Amos 1:5; Nah. 3:13 51:31 [a] Jer. 50:24 51:32 [a] Jer. 50:38

"The daughter of Babylon *is*
[a]like a threshing floor
When [b]*it is* time to thresh her;
Yet a little while
[c]And the time of her harvest
will come."

34 "Nebuchadnezzar the king of Babylon
Has [a]devoured me, he has
crushed me;
He has made me an [b]empty vessel,
He has swallowed me up
like a monster;
He has filled his stomach
with my delicacies,
He has spit me out.
35 Let the violence *done* to me and
my flesh *be* upon Babylon,"
The inhabitant of Zion will say;
"And my blood be upon the
inhabitants of Chaldea!"
Jerusalem will say.

36 Therefore thus says the LORD:

"Behold, [a]I will plead your case
and take vengeance for you.
[b]I will dry up her sea and
make her springs dry.
37 [a]Babylon shall become a heap,
A dwelling place for jackals,
[b]An astonishment and a hissing,
Without an inhabitant.
38 They shall roar together like lions,
They shall growl like lions' whelps.
39 In their excitement I will
prepare their feasts;
[a]I will make them drunk,
That they may rejoice,
And sleep a perpetual sleep
And not awake," says the LORD.
40 "I will bring them down
Like lambs to the slaughter,
Like rams with male goats.

41 "Oh, how [a]Sheshach[1] is taken!
Oh, how [b]the praise of the
whole earth is seized!
How Babylon has become
desolate among the nations!
42 [a]The sea has come up over Babylon;
She is covered with the
multitude of its waves.
43 [a]Her cities are a desolation,
A dry land and a wilderness,
A land where [b]no one dwells,
Through which no son of man passes.
44 I will punish [a]Bel in Babylon,
And I will bring out of his mouth
what he has swallowed;
And the nations shall not
stream to him anymore.
Yes, [b]the wall of Babylon shall fall.

45 "My[a] people, go out of the midst of her!
And let everyone deliver himself
from the fierce anger of the LORD.
46 And lest your heart faint,
And you fear [a]for the rumor that
will be heard in the land
(A rumor will come *one* year,
And after that, in *another* year
A rumor *will come,*
And violence in the land,
Ruler against ruler),
47 Therefore behold, the days
are coming
That I will bring judgment on the
carved images of Babylon;
Her whole land shall be ashamed,
And all her slain shall fall in her midst.
48 Then [a]the heavens and the earth
and all that *is* in them
Shall sing joyously over Babylon;
[b]For the plunderers shall come to her
from the north," says the LORD.

49 As Babylon *has caused* the
slain of Israel to fall,
So at Babylon the slain of all
the earth shall fall.
50 [a]You who have escaped the sword,
Get away! Do not stand still!
[b]Remember the LORD afar off,
And let Jerusalem come
to your mind.

51:33 [a] Is. 21:10; Dan. 2:35; Amos 1:3; Mic. 4:13 [b] Is. 41:15; Hab. 3:12 [c] Is. 17:5; Hos. 6:11; Joel 3:13; Rev. 14:15 51:34 [a] Jer. 50:17 [b] Is. 24:1–3 51:36 [a] [Ps. 140:12]; Jer. 50:34 [b] Jer. 50:38 51:37 [a] Is. 13:22; Jer. 50:39; [Rev. 18:2] [b] Jer. 25:9, 11 51:39 [a] Jer. 51:57 51:41 [a] Jer. 25:26 [b] Is. 13:19; Jer. 49:25; [Dan. 4:30] [1] A code word for Babylon (compare Jeremiah 25:26) 51:42 [a] Is. 8:7, 8; Jer. 51:55; Dan. 9:26 51:43 [a] Jer. 50:39, 40 [b] Is. 13:20 51:44 [a] Jer. 50:2; Is. 46:1 [b] Jer. 50:15 51:45 [a] Is. 48:20; [Jer. 50:8, 28; 51:6; Rev. 18:4] 51:46 [a] 2 Kin. 19:7; Is. 13:3–5 51:48 [a] Is. 44:23; 48:20; 49:13; Rev. 18:20 [b] Jer. 50:3, 41 51:50 [a] Jer. 44:28 [b] [Deut. 4:29–31]; Ezek. 6:9

51 [a]We are ashamed because we
have heard reproach.
Shame has covered our faces,
For strangers [b]have come into the
sanctuaries of the LORD's house.

52 "Therefore behold, the days are
coming," says the LORD,
"That I will bring judgment
on her carved images,
And throughout all her land
the wounded shall groan.
53 [a]Though Babylon were to
mount up to heaven,
And though she were to fortify
the height of her strength,
Yet from Me plunderers would
come to her," says the LORD.

54 [a]The sound of a cry *comes*
from Babylon,
And great destruction from the
land of the Chaldeans,
55 Because the LORD is
plundering Babylon
And silencing her loud voice,
Though her waves roar
like great waters,
And the noise of their voice is uttered,
56 Because the plunderer comes
against her, against Babylon,
And her mighty men are taken.
Every one of their bows is broken;
[a]For the LORD *is* the God
of recompense,
He will surely repay.

57 "And I will make drunk
Her princes and [a]wise men,
Her governors, her deputies,
and her mighty men.
And they shall sleep a perpetual sleep
And not awake," says [b]the King,
Whose name *is* the LORD of hosts.

58 Thus says the LORD of hosts:

"The broad walls of Babylon
shall be utterly [a]broken,
And her high gates shall be
burned with fire;
[b]The people will labor in vain,
And the nations, because of the fire;
And they shall be weary."

Jeremiah's Command to Seraiah

59 The word which Jeremiah the prophet
commanded Seraiah the son of [a]Neriah, the
son of Mahseiah, when he went with Zedekiah the king of Judah to Babylon in the
fourth year of his reign. And Seraiah *was*
the quartermaster. 60 So Jeremiah [a]wrote in
a book all the evil that would come upon
Babylon, all these words that are written
against Babylon. 61 And Jeremiah said to
Seraiah, "When you arrive in Babylon and
see it, and read all these words, 62 then you
shall say, 'O LORD, You have spoken against
this place to cut it off, so that [a]none shall
remain in it, neither man nor beast, but it
shall be desolate forever.' 63 Now it shall be,
when you have finished reading this book,
[a]*that* you shall tie a stone to it and throw
it out into the Euphrates. 64 Then you shall
say, 'Thus Babylon shall sink and not rise
from the catastrophe that I will bring upon
her. And they shall be weary.'"
Thus far *are* the words of Jeremiah.

The Fall of Jerusalem Reviewed
(2 Kin. 24:18—25:26; 2 Chr. 36:11–20; Jer. 39:1–10)

52 Zedekiah *was* [a]twenty-one years
old when he became king, and he
reigned eleven years in Jerusalem. His
mother's name *was* Hamutal the daughter of Jeremiah of [b]Libnah. 2 He also did
evil in the sight of the LORD, according to
all that Jehoiakim had done. 3 For because
of the anger of the LORD *this* happened in
Jerusalem and Judah, till He finally cast
them out from His presence. Then Zedekiah [a]rebelled against the king of Babylon.
4 Now it came to pass in the [a]ninth year
of his reign, in the tenth month, on the
tenth *day* of the month, *that* Nebuchadnezzar king of Babylon and all his army
came against Jerusalem and encamped

51:51 [a] Ps. 44:15; 79:4 [b] Ps. 74:3–8; Jer. 52:13; Lam. 1:10 51:53 [a] Gen. 11:4; Job 20:6; [Ps. 139:8–10; Is. 14:12–14]; Jer. 49:16; Amos 9:2; Obad. 4 51:54 [a] Jer. 50:22 51:56 [a] Ps. 94:1; Jer. 50:29 51:57 [a] Jer. 50:35 [b] Jer. 46:18; 48:15 51:58 [a] Jer. 50:15 [b] Hab. 2:13 51:59 [a] Jer. 32:12 51:60 [a] Is. 30:8; Jer. 36:2 51:62 [a] Is. 13:20; 14:22, 23; Jer. 50:3, 39 51:63 [a] Jer. 19:10, 11; Rev. 18:21 52:1 [a] 2 Kin. 24:18; 2 Chr. 36:11 [b] Josh. 10:29; 2 Kin. 8:22; Is. 37:8 52:3 [a] 2 Chr. 36:13 52:4 [a] 2 Kin. 25:1; Jer. 39:1; Ezek. 24:1, 2; Zech. 8:19

against it; and *they* built a siege wall against it all around. 5So the city was besieged until the eleventh year of King Zedekiah. 6By the fourth month, on the ninth day of the month, the famine had become so severe in the city that there was no food for the people of the land. 7Then the city *wall* was broken through, and all the men of war fled and went out of the city at night by way of the gate between the two walls, which *was* by the king's garden, even though the Chaldeans *were* near the city all around. And they went by way of the plain.[1]

8But the army of the Chaldeans pursued the king, and they overtook Zedekiah in the plains of Jericho. All his army was scattered from him. 9[a]So they took the king and brought him up to the king of Babylon at Riblah in the land of Hamath, and he pronounced judgment on him. 10[a]Then the king of Babylon killed the sons of Zedekiah before his eyes. And he killed all the princes of Judah in Riblah. 11He also [a]put out the eyes of Zedekiah; and the king of Babylon bound him in bronze fetters, took him to Babylon, and put him in prison till the day of his death.

The Temple and City Plundered and Burned

12[a]Now in the fifth month, on the tenth *day* of the month ([b]which *was* the nineteenth year of King Nebuchadnezzar king of Babylon), [c]Nebuzaradan, the captain of the guard, *who* served the king of Babylon, came to Jerusalem. 13He burned the house of the LORD and the king's house; all the houses of Jerusalem, that is, all the houses of the great, he burned with fire. 14And all the army of the Chaldeans who *were* with the captain of the guard broke down all the walls of Jerusalem all around. 15[a]Then Nebuzaradan the captain of the guard carried away captive *some* of the poor people, the rest of the people who remained in the city, the defectors who had deserted to the king of Babylon, and the rest of the craftsmen. 16But Nebuzaradan the captain of the guard left *some* of the poor of the land as vinedressers and farmers.

17[a]The [b]bronze pillars that *were* in the house of the LORD, and the carts and the bronze Sea that *were* in the house of the LORD, the Chaldeans broke in pieces, and carried all their bronze to Babylon. 18They also took away [a]the pots, the shovels, the trimmers, the bowls, the spoons, and all the bronze utensils with which the *priests* ministered. 19The basins, the firepans, the bowls, the pots, the lampstands, the spoons, and the cups, whatever *was* solid gold and whatever *was* solid silver, the captain of the guard took away. 20The two pillars, one Sea, the twelve bronze bulls which *were* under *it, and* the carts, which King Solomon had made for the house of the LORD—[a]the bronze of all these articles was beyond measure. 21Now *concerning* the [a]pillars: the height of one pillar *was* eighteen cubits, a measuring line of twelve cubits could measure its circumference, and its thickness *was* four fingers; *it was* hollow. 22A capital of bronze *was* on it; and the height of one capital *was* five cubits, with a network and pomegranates all around the capital, all of bronze. The second pillar, with pomegranates was the same. 23There were ninety-six pomegranates on the sides; [a]all the pomegranates, all around on the network, *were* one hundred.

The People Taken Captive to Babylonia

24[a]The captain of the guard took Seraiah the chief priest, [b]Zephaniah the second priest, and the three doorkeepers. 25He also took out of the city an officer who had charge of the men of war, seven men of the king's close associates who were found in the city, the principal scribe of the army who mustered the people of the land, and sixty men of the people of the land who were found in the midst of the city. 26And Nebuzaradan the captain of the guard took these and brought them to the king of Babylon at Riblah. 27Then the king of Babylon struck them and put them to death at Riblah in the land of Hamath. Thus Judah was carried away captive from its own land.

28[a]These *are* the people whom Nebuchadnezzar carried away captive: [b]in the

52:7 [1] Or *the Arabah,* that is, the Jordan Valley 52:9 [a] 2 Kin. 25:6; Jer. 32:4; 39:5 52:10 [a] Ezek. 12:13 52:11 [a] Ezek. 12:13 52:12 [a] 2 Kin. 25:8–21 [b] Jer. 52:29 [c] Jer. 39:9 52:15 [a] Jer. 39:9 52:17 [a] Jer. 27:19 [b] 1 Kin. 7:15, 23, 27, 50 52:18 [a] Ex. 27:3; 1 Kin. 7:40, 45; 2 Kin. 25:14 52:20 [a] 1 Kin. 7:47; 2 Kin. 25:16 52:21 [a] 1 Kin. 7:15; 2 Kin. 25:17; 2 Chr. 3:15 52:23 [a] 1 Kin. 7:20 52:24 [a] 2 Kin. 25:18; 1 Chr. 6:14; Ezra 7:1 [b] Jer. 21:1; 29:25 52:28 [a] 2 Kin. 24:2 [b] 2 Kin. 24:12

seventh year, [c]three thousand and twenty-
three Jews; 29[a]in the eighteenth year of
Nebuchadnezzar he carried away captive
from Jerusalem eight hundred and thirty-
two persons; 30in the twenty-third year of
Nebuchadnezzar, Nebuzaradan the captain of the guard carried away captive of
the Jews seven hundred and forty-five persons. All the persons *were* four thousand
six hundred.

Jehoiachin Released from Prison
(2 Kin. 25:27–30)

31[a]Now it came to pass in the thirty-
seventh year of the captivity of Jehoiachin
king of Judah, in the twelfth month, on the
twenty-fifth *day* of the month, *that* Evil-Merodach[1] king of Babylon, in the *first* year
of his reign, [b]lifted up the head of Jehoiachin king of Judah and brought him out of
prison. 32And he spoke kindly to him and
gave him a more prominent seat than those
of the kings who *were* with him in Babylon.
33So Jehoiachin changed from his prison
garments, [a]and he ate bread regularly before the *king* all the days of his life. 34And
as for his provisions, there was a regular
ration given him by the king of Babylon,
a portion for each day until the day of his
death, all the days of his life.

52:28 [c] 2 Kin. 24:14 52:29 [a] 2 Kin. 25:11; Jer. 39:9 52:31 [a] 2 Kin. 25:27–30 [b] Gen. 40:13, 20; Ps. 3:3; 27:6
[1] Or *Awil-Marduk* 52:33 [a] 2 Sam. 9:7, 13; 1 Kin. 2:7

THE BOOK OF

LAMENTATIONS

OVERVIEW

The Book of Lamentations is believed to have been authored by the prophet Jeremiah in 586 BC, at the end of his forty-year ministry. Lamentations describes the fall of Jerusalem at the hands of the Babylonians. As the title suggests, the book is an expression of Jeremiah's grief and sorrow over the destruction of Jerusalem and the capture of the people of Judah.

Lamentations consists of five poetic chapters. The book opens with Jeremiah recognizing "how lonely sits the city that was full of people!" (1:1). What follows is a description of the sadness in the city, comparing it to a widow left alone (see v. 2). Jeremiah explains, "Judah has gone into captivity, under affliction and hard servitude" (v. 3). The numerous sufferings of the Israelites were "because of the multitude of her transgressions" (v. 5). Jeremiah went on to acknowledge that the suffering existed because "Jerusalem . . . sinned gravely" (v. 8).

Chapter 2 describes God's anger toward Jerusalem. "The Lord was like an enemy" (2:5). He "spurned the king and the priest" (v. 6) and "abandoned His sanctuary" (v. 7). Tearful and with a "troubled" heart (v. 11), Jeremiah was distraught about children fainting from hunger and women eating their children (see vv. 19–20). He was troubled that God had "slaughtered and not pitied" (v. 21) the people of Judah. Yet, he understood that God had promised punishment if His people continued to dishonor His covenant with Him, which they did.

Despite the evidence of God's anger, Jeremiah encouraged the people. He described his own afflictions (see 3:1–21) and acknowledged that he was still hopeful because God's "compassions fail not. They are new every morning" (vv. 22–23). He encouraged the Israelites to "turn back to the LORD" (v. 40).

In chapter 4, Jeremiah revealed the conditions in Jerusalem during the Babylonian takeover and reiterated the cause. He then encouraged the people by promising that God's wrath would end one day, and He would "no longer send [them] into captivity" (v. 22). Chapter 5 is Jeremiah's prayer to God for redemption.

The Book of Lamentations examines the cause of Jerusalem's destruction, indicating that God's wrath was brought forth because of the people's disobedience. Jeremiah was heartbroken by the events that led to the capture and was devastated by the great losses. The temple and the throne were destroyed, and the people suffered immensely.

The destruction of Jerusalem is a reminder that God is faithful to His promises, even when He promises judgment. The Israelites were given many opportunities to turn back to God, but they refused, and God judged them harshly. However, as Jeremiah promised, the judgment came to an end and God restored His chosen people.

BREATHE IT IN

The prophet Jeremiah witnessed his prophecies come to pass when God delivered judgment on Judah. Although Jeremiah understood that the people were solely responsible for their demise,

he still lamented over the destruction of Jerusalem and prayed that God would restore His people one day.

The Old Testament has numerous stories of God sending judgment upon the Israelites because of their refusal to abide by the covenant He established with them. The Book of Lamentations gives an account of just how devastating and harsh God's righteous judgment can be. The Bible, however, also warns Christians about disobeying God and engaging in activities that are not pleasing in His sight.

Christians have varying responses to witnessing God's judgment in individual lives and society. Some have the attitude of "I told you so," "You should have known better," or "It is your fault." These people recognize that judgment comes as the result of some action taken, so they blame those under judgment for their suffering. While rebellion is the reason for God's judgment, this response is not proper for Christians when others are experiencing difficult situations. Instead, compassion is the appropriate attitude to display. Jeremiah exhibited such compassion in Lamentations. He recognized that Judah's actions prompted God's judgment, but instead of delighting in God's judgment of them, he expressed sorrow. He hated seeing them go through very trying situations. He offered them hope, and he prayed to God on their behalf, asking for restoration.

We should never find joy in the suffering of others. As Christians, we should show compassion and offer our support even when others suffer the repercussions of their choices. We must never forget that we have also sinned and fallen short of God's expectations of us. While we cannot keep God from delivering judgment, we can pray for others and encourage them to seek redemption.

When we evaluate our attitude toward others, particularly those experiencing difficulties, can we honestly say that we have compassion? Colossians 3:12 charges us to clothe ourselves with "tender mercies, kindness, humility, meekness, longsuffering." We should not reserve our compassion for Christians alone but have compassion for everyone we encounter—friends and loved ones, as well as strangers and enemies.

Compassion is about caring for one another. This may not always be easy, but it is our responsibility as Christians to demonstrate God's love for people through our interactions with them. Take the time to show people that you value them. Offer to assist them when needed. Compassion is not about grand gestures; it is about the little things that make a difference in someone's life.

Take time to pay attention to those around you. Greet them with a smile. If you notice someone in need, lend a helping hand. Be sure your compassionate acts are genuine and that you seek nothing in return. Remember, one day you may be the person who needs a smile from a stranger or a kind word from a friend. Pay it forward. Treat others the way you want to be treated. God loves us all, so we should love one another.

THE BOOK OF

LAMENTATIONS

Jerusalem in Affliction

1 How lonely sits the city
That was full of people!
[a]*How* like a widow is she,
Who *was* great among the nations!
The [b]princess among the provinces
Has become a slave!

2 She [a]weeps bitterly in the [b]night,
Her tears *are* on her cheeks;
Among all her lovers
She has none to comfort *her.*
All her friends have dealt
treacherously with her;
They have become her enemies.

3 [a]Judah has gone into captivity,
Under affliction and hard
servitude;
[b]She dwells among the nations,
She finds no [c]rest;
All her persecutors overtake
her in dire straits.

4 The roads to Zion mourn
Because no one comes
to the set feasts.
All her gates are [a]desolate;
Her priests sigh,
Her virgins are afflicted,
And she *is* in bitterness.

5 Her adversaries [a]have
become the master,
Her enemies prosper;
For the LORD has afflicted her
[b]Because of the multitude of
her transgressions.
Her [c]children have gone into
captivity before the enemy.

6 And from the daughter of Zion
All her splendor has departed.
Her princes have become
like deer
That find no pasture,
That flee without strength
Before the pursuer.

7 In the days of her affliction
and roaming,
Jerusalem [a]remembers all
her pleasant things
That she had in the days of old.
When her people fell into the
hand of the enemy,
With no one to help her,
The adversaries saw her
And mocked at her downfall.[1]

8 [a]Jerusalem has sinned gravely,
Therefore she has become vile.[1]
All who honored her despise her
Because [b]they have seen
her nakedness;
Yes, she sighs and turns away.

9 Her uncleanness *is* in her skirts;
She [a]did not consider her destiny;
Therefore her collapse was awesome;
She had no comforter.
"O LORD, behold my affliction,
For *the* enemy is exalted!"

10 The adversary has spread his hand
Over all her pleasant things;

1:1 [a] Is. 47:7–9 [b] 1 Kin. 4:21; Ezra 4:20; Jer. 31:7 1:2 [a] Jer. 13:17 [b] Job 7:3 1:3 [a] Jer. 52:27 [b] Lam. 2:9 [c] Deut. 28:65 1:4 [a] Is. 27:10 1:5 [a] Deut. 28:43 [b] Jer. 30:14, 15; Dan. 9:7, 16 [c] Jer. 52:28 1:7 [a] Ps. 137:1 [1] Vulgate reads *her Sabbaths.* 1:8 [a] [1 Kin. 8:46] [b] Jer. 13:22; Ezek. 16:37; Hos. 2:10 [1] Septuagint and Vulgate read *moved* or *removed.* 1:9 [a] Deut. 32:29; Is. 47:7; Jer. 5:31

For she has seen [a]the nations
enter her sanctuary,
Those whom You commanded
[b]Not to enter Your assembly.

11 All her people sigh,
[a]They seek bread;
They have given their valuables
for food to restore life.
"See, O LORD, and consider,
For I am scorned."

12 "*Is it* nothing to you, all
you who pass by?
Behold and see
[a]If there is any sorrow like my sorrow,
Which has been brought on me,
Which the LORD has inflicted
In the day of His fierce anger.

13 "From above He has sent
fire into my bones,
And it overpowered them;
He has [a]spread a net for my feet
And turned me back;
He has made me desolate
And faint all the day.

14 "The[a] yoke of my transgressions
was bound;[1]
They were woven together
by His hands,
And thrust upon my neck.
He made my strength fail;
The Lord delivered me into the
hands of *those whom* I am
not able to withstand.

15 "The Lord has trampled underfoot
all my mighty *men* in my midst;
He has called an assembly against me
To crush my young men;
[a]The Lord trampled *as* in a winepress
The virgin daughter of Judah.

16 "For these *things* I weep;
My eye, [a]my eye overflows with water;
Because the comforter, who
should restore my life,
Is far from me.
My children are desolate
Because the enemy prevailed."

17 [a]Zion spreads out her hands,
But no one comforts her;
The LORD has commanded
concerning Jacob
That those [b]around him
become his adversaries;
Jerusalem has become an
unclean thing among them.

18 "The LORD is [a]righteous,
For I [b]rebelled against His
commandment.
Hear now, all peoples,
And behold my sorrow;
My virgins and my young men
Have gone into captivity.

19 "I called for my lovers,
But they deceived me;
My priests and my elders
Breathed their last in the city,
While they sought food
To restore their life.

20 "See, O LORD, that I *am* in distress;
My [a]soul is troubled;
My heart is overturned within me,
For I have been very rebellious.
[b]Outside the sword bereaves,
At home *it is* like death.

21 "They have heard that I sigh,
But no one comforts me.
All my enemies have heard
of my trouble;
They are [a]glad that You have done *it*.
Bring on [b]the day You
have announced,
That they may become like me.

22 "Let[a] all their wickedness
come before You,
And do to them as You
have done to me
For all my transgressions;

1:10 [a] Ps. 74:4–8; Is. 64:10, 11; Jer. 51:51 [b] Deut. 23:3; Neh. 13:1 1:11 [a] Jer. 38:9; 52:6 1:12 [a] Dan. 9:12 1:13 [a] Ezek. 12:13; 17:20 1:14 [a] Deut. 28:48 [1] Following Masoretic Text and Targum; Septuagint, Syriac, and Vulgate read *watched over.* 1:15 [a] Is. 63:3; [Rev. 14:19] 1:16 [a] Ps. 69:20; Eccl. 4:1; Jer. 13:17; Lam. 2:18 1:17 [a] [Is. 1:15]; Jer. 4:31 [b] 2 Kin. 24:2–4; Jer. 12:9 1:18 [a] Neh. 9:33; Ps. 119:75; Dan. 9:7, 14 [b] 1 Sam. 12:14, 15; Jer. 4:17 1:20 [a] Job 30:27; Is. 16:11; Jer. 4:19; Lam. 2:11; Hos. 11:8 [b] Deut. 32:25; Ezek. 7:15 1:21 [a] Ps. 35:15; Jer. 48:27; 50:11; Lam. 2:15; Obad. 12 [b] Is. 13; [Jer. 46] 1:22 [a] Neh. 4:4, 5; Ps. 109:15; 137:7, 8; Jer. 30:16

For my sighs *are* many,
And my heart *is* faint."

God's Anger with Jerusalem

2 How the Lord has covered
the daughter of Zion
With a [a]cloud in His anger!
[b]He cast down from heaven to the earth
[c]The beauty of Israel,
And did not remember [d]His footstool
In the day of His anger.

2 The Lord has swallowed up
and has [a]not pitied
All the dwelling places of Jacob.
He has thrown down in His wrath
The strongholds of the
daughter of Judah;
He has brought *them* down
to the ground;
[b]He has profaned the kingdom
and its princes.

3 He has cut off in fierce anger
Every horn of Israel;
[a]He has drawn back His right hand
From before the enemy.
[b]He has blazed against Jacob
like a flaming fire
Devouring all around.

4 [a]Standing like an enemy, He
has bent His bow;
With His right hand, like an adversary,
He has slain [b]all *who were*
pleasing to His eye;
On the tent of the daughter of Zion,
He has poured out His fury like fire.

5 [a]The Lord was like an enemy.
He has swallowed up Israel,
He has swallowed up all her palaces;
[b]He has destroyed her strongholds,
And has increased mourning
and lamentation
In the daughter of Judah.

6 He has done violence [a]to
His tabernacle,
[b]*As if it were* a garden;
He has destroyed His place
of assembly;
The LORD has caused
The appointed feasts and Sabbaths
to be forgotten in Zion.
In His burning indignation He has
[c]spurned the king and the priest.

7 The Lord has spurned His altar,
He has [a]abandoned His sanctuary;
He has given up the walls
of her palaces
Into the hand of the enemy.
[b]They have made a noise in
the house of the LORD
As on the day of a set feast.

8 The LORD has purposed to destroy
The [a]wall of the daughter of Zion.
[b]He has stretched out a line;
He has not withdrawn His
hand from destroying;
Therefore He has caused the
rampart and wall to lament;
They languished together.

9 Her gates have sunk into the
ground;
He has destroyed and
[a]broken her bars.
[b]Her king and her princes *are*
among the nations;
[c]The Law *is* no *more*,
And her [d]prophets find no
vision from the LORD.

10 The elders of the daughter of Zion
[a]Sit on the ground *and* keep silence;
They [b]throw dust on their heads
And [c]gird themselves with sackcloth.
The virgins of Jerusalem
Bow their heads to the ground.

11 [a]My eyes fail with tears,
My heart is troubled;
[b]My bile is poured on the ground
Because of the destruction of
the daughter of my people,

2:1 [a] [Lam. 3:44] [b] Matt. 11:23 [c] 2 Sam. 1:19 [d] 1 Chr. 28:2; Ps. 99:5; Ezek. 43:7 2:2 [a] Ps. 21:9; Lam. 3:43 [b] Ps. 89:39, 40; Is. 43:28 2:3 [a] Ps. 74:11; Jer. 21:4, 5 [b] Ps. 89:46 2:4 [a] Is. 63:10 [b] Ezek. 24:25 2:5 [a] Jer. 30:14 [b] 2 Kin. 25:9; Jer. 52:13; Lam. 2:2 2:6 [a] Ps. 80:12; 89:40; Is. 5:5; Jer. 7:14 [b] Is. 1:8; Jer. 52:13 [c] Is. 43:28 2:7 [a] Ezek. 24:21 [b] Ps. 74:3–8 2:8 [a] Jer. 52:14 [b] [2 Kin. 21:13; Is. 34:11; Amos 7:7–9] 2:9 [a] Jer. 51:30 [b] Deut. 28:36; 2 Kin. 24:15; 25:7; Lam. 1:3; 4:20 [c] 2 Chr. 15:3 [d] Ps. 74:9; Mic. 3:6 2:10 [a] Job 2:13; Is. 3:26 [b] Job 2:12; Ezek. 27:30 [c] Is. 15:3; Jon. 3:6–8 2:11 [a] Ps. 6:7; Lam. 3:48 [b] Job 16:13; Ps. 22:14

LIFE SUPPORT

BE CARING: HAVE A HEART FOR OTHERS

My eyes fail with tears, my heart is troubled; my bile is poured on the ground because of the destruction of the daughter of my people, because the children and the infants faint in the streets of the city. Lamentations 2:11

LIFE: Be Caring

We read in Lamentations that the prophet Jeremiah was so distraught over the misery of his people that he made himself sick. He loved his people, and he cared deeply about what happened to them.

Throughout the New Testament, we also read how caring Jesus was. Jesus was moved by compassion for people who needed a miracle. He often stopped to meet the needs of those who needed His touch because He cared. Every day, God wants us to demonstrate care and concern for others. It costs absolutely nothing for us to be compassionate and kindhearted people.

Care begins with what is on the inside—what is in your heart. Jesus was caring because that was what was in His heart. He wants us to have the same love and kindness filling our own hearts. The Spirit of God must first condition our hearts so we can care and, in turn, for our actions to be caring. This is the nature and the character God wants us to have. He is kind to us; we should be kind to others.

SUPPORT: Have a Heart for Others

What a purpose! Having a heart for others means we need to love and care for them. But it is not easy to love those who have harsh and callous dispositions or who are condescending and heartless. We must consider this issue from a spiritual standpoint to learn how our love and care might prevail.

As Christians, God wants us to love others as He loves us. He has called us to love unconditionally and care for others and empathize with everyone. This is how God loves us. As such, love is the mark of authentic Christianity. It indicates that we follow Jesus. Those who reach out in love to all do so from a healthy spiritual life. When we feel a burden for someone, we should pray. When we feel a calling to help someone, we should act. Ask God to use you to help others. When we are a conduit for His love and compassion, the world is a better place and we all will be able to breathe.

SUPPORT EXAMPLE: Sit with a friend who is going through a hard time and listen without judgment or offering advice.

Because [c]the children and the infants
Faint in the streets of the city.

12 They say to their mothers,
"Where *is* grain and wine?"
As they swoon like the wounded
In the streets of the city,
As their life is poured out
In their mothers' bosom.

13 How shall I [a]console you?
To what shall I liken you,
O daughter of Jerusalem?
What shall I compare with you,
that I may comfort you,
O virgin daughter of Zion?
For your ruin *is* spread wide
as the sea;
Who can heal you?

2:11 [c] Lam. 4:4 2:13 [a] Lam. 1:12; Dan. 9:12

14 Your [a]prophets have seen for you
False and deceptive visions;
They have not [b]uncovered
your iniquity,
To bring back your captives,
But have envisioned for you false
[c]prophecies and delusions.

15 All who pass by [a]clap *their*
hands at you;
They hiss [b]and shake their heads
At the daughter of Jerusalem:
"*Is* this the city that is called
[c]'The perfection of beauty,
The joy of the whole earth'?"

16 [a]All your enemies have opened
their mouth against you;
They hiss and gnash *their* teeth.
They say, [b]"We have swallowed *her* up!
Surely this *is* the [c]day we
have waited for;
We have found *it*, [d]we have seen *it!*"

17 The LORD has done what
He [a]purposed;
He has fulfilled His word
Which He commanded in days
of old.
He has thrown down and
has not pitied,
And He has caused an enemy
to [b]rejoice over you;
He has exalted the horn of
your adversaries.

18 Their heart cried out to the Lord,
"O wall of the daughter of Zion,
[a]Let tears run down like a
river day and night;
Give yourself no relief;
Give your eyes no rest.

19 "Arise, [a]cry out in the night,
At the beginning of the watches;
[b]Pour out your heart like water
before the face of the Lord.
Lift your hands toward Him
For the life of your young children,
Who faint from hunger [c]at the
head of every street."

20 "See, O LORD, and consider!
To whom have You done this?
[a]Should the women eat their
offspring,
The children they have cuddled?[1]
Should the priest and prophet
be slain
In the sanctuary of the Lord?

21 "Young[a] and old lie
On the ground in the streets;
My virgins and my young men
Have fallen by the [b]sword;
You have slain *them* in the
day of Your anger,
You have slaughtered *and*
not pitied.

22 "You have invited as to a feast day
[a]The terrors that surround me.
In the day of the LORD's anger
There was no refugee or survivor.
[b]Those whom I have borne
and brought up
My enemies have [c]destroyed."

The Prophet's Anguish and Hope

3 I *am* the man *who* has seen affliction
by the rod of His wrath.
2 He has led me and made *me* walk
In darkness and not *in* light.
3 Surely He has turned His
hand against me
Time and time again
throughout the day.

4 He has aged [a]my flesh and
my skin,
And [b]broken my bones.
5 He has besieged me
And surrounded *me* with
bitterness and woe.
6 [a]He has set me in dark places
Like the dead of long ago.

2:14 [a] Jer. 2:8; 23:25–29; 29:8, 9; 37:19; Ezek. 13:2 [b] Is. 58:1; Ezek. 23:36; Mic. 3:8 [c] Jer. 23:33–36; Ezek. 22:25, 28 2:15 [a] 1 Kin. 9:8; Job 27:23; Jer. 18:16; Ezek. 25:6; Nah. 3:19 [b] 2 Kin. 19:21; Ps. 44:14 [c] [Ps. 48:2; 50:2]; Ezek. 16:14 2:16 [a] Job 16:9, 10; Ps. 22:13; Lam. 3:46 [b] Ps. 56:2; 124:3; Jer. 51:34 [c] Lam. 1:21; [Obad. 12–15] [d] Ps. 35:21 2:17 [a] Lev. 26:16 [b] Ps. 38:16 2:18 [a] Jer. 14:17; Lam. 1:16 2:19 [a] Ps. 119:147 [b] 1 Sam. 1:15; Ps. 42:4; 62:8 [c] Is. 51:20 2:20 [a] Lev. 26:29; Deut. 28:53; Jer. 19:9; Lam. 4:10; Ezek. 5:10 [1] Vulgate reads *a span long.* 2:21 [a] 2 Chr. 36:17; Jer. 6:11 [b] Jer. 18:21 2:22 [a] Ps. 31:13; Is. 24:17; Jer. 6:25 [b] Hos. 9:12 [c] Jer. 16:2–4; 44:7 3:4 [a] Job 16:8 [b] Ps. 51:8; Is. 38:13 3:6 [a] [Ps. 88:5, 6; 143:3]

7 [a]He has hedged me in so that
I cannot get out;
He has made my chain heavy.
8 Even [a]when I cry and shout,
He shuts out my prayer.
9 He has blocked my ways
with hewn stone;
He has made my paths crooked.

10 [a]He *has been* to me a bear lying in wait,
Like a lion in ambush.
11 He has turned aside my ways
and [a]torn me in pieces;
He has made me desolate.
12 He has bent His bow
And [a]set me up as a target
for the arrow.

13 He has caused [a]the arrows
of His quiver
To pierce my loins.[1]
14 I have become the [a]ridicule
of all my people—
[b]Their taunting song all the day.
15 [a]He has filled me with bitterness,
He has made me drink wormwood.

16 He has also broken my
teeth [a]with gravel,
And covered me with ashes.
17 You have moved my soul
far from peace;
I have forgotten prosperity.
18 [a]And I said, "My strength and
my hope
Have perished from the LORD."

19 Remember my affliction and
roaming,
[a]The wormwood and the gall.
20 My soul still remembers
And sinks within me.
21 This I recall to my mind,
Therefore I have [a]hope.

22 [a]*Through* the LORD's mercies
we are not consumed,
Because His compassions [b]fail not.
23 *They are* new [a]every morning;
Great *is* Your faithfulness.
24 "The LORD *is* my [a]portion,"
says my soul,
"Therefore I [b]hope in Him!"

25 The LORD *is* good to those
who [a]wait for Him,
To the soul *who* seeks Him.
26 *It is* good that *one* should
[a]hope [b]and wait quietly
For the salvation of the LORD.
27 [a]*It is* good for a man to bear
The yoke in his youth.

28 [a]Let him sit alone and keep silent,
Because *God* has laid *it* on him;
29 [a]Let him put his mouth in the dust—
There may yet be hope.
30 [a]Let him give *his* cheek to the
one who strikes him,
And be full of reproach.

31 [a]For the Lord will not cast off
forever.
32 Though He causes grief,
Yet He will show compassion
According to the multitude
of His mercies.
33 For [a]He does not afflict willingly,
Nor grieve the children of men.

34 To crush under one's feet
All the prisoners of the earth,
35 To turn aside the justice *due*
a man
Before the face of the Most High,
36 Or subvert a man in his cause—
[a]The Lord does not approve.

37 Who *is* he [a]*who* speaks and
it comes to pass,
When the Lord has not
commanded *it?*
38 *Is it* not from the mouth
of the Most High
That [a]woe and well-being
proceed?

3:7 [a] Job 3:23; 19:8; Hos. 2:6 **3:8** [a] Job 30:20; Ps. 22:2 **3:10** [a] Is. 38:13 **3:11** [a] Job 16:12, 13; Jer. 15:3; Hos. 6:1 **3:12** [a] Job 7:20; 16:12; Ps. 38:2 **3:13** [a] Job 6:4 [1] Literally *kidneys* **3:14** [a] Ps. 22:6, 7; 123:4; Jer. 20:7 [b] Job 30:9; Ps. 69:12; Lam. 3:63 **3:15** [a] Jer. 9:15 **3:16** [a] [Prov. 20:17] **3:18** [a] Ps. 31:22 **3:19** [a] Jer. 9:15; Lam. 3:5, 15 **3:21** [a] Ps. 130:7 **3:22** [a] [Mal. 3:6] [b] Ps. 78:38; [Jer. 3:12; 30:11] **3:23** [a] Is. 33:2; Zeph. 3:5 **3:24** [a] Ps. 16:5; 73:26; 119:57; Jer. 10:16 [b] Jer. 17:17; Mic. 7:7 **3:25** [a] Ps. 130:6; Is. 30:18 **3:26** [a] [Rom. 4:16–18] [b] Ex. 14:13; Ps. 37:7; Is. 7:4 **3:27** [a] Ps. 94:12 **3:28** [a] Jer. 15:17 **3:29** [a] Job 42:6 **3:30** [a] Job 16:10; Is. 50:6; [Matt. 5:39; 26:67]; Mark 14:65; Luke 22:63 **3:31** [a] Ps. 77:7; 94:14; [Is. 54:7–10] **3:33** [a] [Ps. 119:67, 71, 75; Is. 28:21; Ezek. 33:11; Heb. 12:10] **3:36** [a] [Jer. 22:3; Hab. 1:13] **3:37** [a] [Ps. 33:9–11] **3:38** [a] Job 2:10; [Is. 45:7]; Jer. 32:42; Amos 3:6; [James 3:10, 11]

39 [a]Why should a living man complain,
[b]A man for the punishment of his sins?

40 Let us search out and
examine our ways,
And turn back to the LORD;
41 [a]Let us lift our hearts and hands
To God in heaven.
42 [a]We have transgressed and rebelled;
You have not pardoned.

43 You have covered *Yourself* with anger
And pursued us;
You have slain *and* not pitied.
44 You have covered Yourself
with a cloud,
That prayer should not pass through.
45 You have made us an
[a]offscouring and refuse
In the midst of the peoples.

46 [a]All our enemies
Have opened their mouths against us.
47 [a]Fear and a snare have come upon us,
[b]Desolation and destruction.
48 [a]My eyes overflow with rivers of water
For the destruction of the
daughter of my people.

49 [a]My eyes flow and do not cease,
Without interruption,
50 Till the LORD from heaven
[a]Looks down and sees.
51 My eyes bring suffering to my soul
Because of all the daughters
of my city.

52 My enemies [a]without cause
Hunted me down like a bird.
53 They silenced[1] my life [a]in the pit
And [b]threw stones at me.
54 [a]The waters flowed over my head;
[b]I said, "I am cut off!"

55 [a]I called on Your name, O LORD,
From the lowest [b]pit.
56 [a]You have heard my voice:
"Do not hide Your ear
From my sighing, from
my cry for help."
57 You [a]drew near on the day
I called on You,
And said, [b]"Do not fear!"

58 O Lord, You have [a]pleaded
the case for my soul;
[b]You have redeemed my life.
59 O LORD, You have seen *how*
I am wronged;
[a]Judge my case.
60 You have seen all their vengeance,
All their [a]schemes against me.

61 You have heard their reproach, O LORD,
All their schemes against me,
62 The lips of my enemies
And their whispering against
me all the day.
63 Look at their [a]sitting down
and their rising up;
I *am* their taunting song.

64 [a]Repay them, O LORD,
According to the work of their hands.
65 Give them a veiled[1] heart;
Your curse *be* upon them!
66 In Your anger,
Pursue and destroy them
[a]From under the heavens of the [b]LORD.

The Degradation of Zion

4 How the gold has become dim!
How changed the fine gold!
The stones of the sanctuary
are scattered
At the head of every street.

2 The precious sons of Zion,
Valuable as fine gold,
How they are regarded [a]as clay pots,
The work of the hands of the potter!

3 Even the jackals present their breasts
To nurse their young;
But the daughter of my people *is* cruel,
[a]Like ostriches in the wilderness.

3:39 [a] Prov. 19:3 [b] Jer. 30:15; Mic. 7:9; [Heb. 12:5, 6] 3:41 [a] Ps. 86:4 3:42 [a] Neh. 9:26; Jer. 14:20; Dan. 9:5 3:45 [a] 1 Cor. 4:13 3:46 [a] Job 30:9, 10; Ps. 22:6–8; Lam. 2:16 3:47 [a] Is. 24:17, 18; Jer. 48:43, 44 [b] Is. 51:19 3:48 [a] Jer. 4:19; 14:17; Lam. 2:11 3:49 [a] Ps. 77:2; Jer. 14:17 3:50 [a] Ps. 80:14; Is. 63:15; Lam. 5:1 3:52 [a] Ps. 35:7, 19 3:53 [a] Jer. 37:16 [b] Dan. 6:17 [1] Septuagint reads *put to death.* 3:54 [a] Ps. 69:2; Jon. 2:3–5 [b] Is. 38:10 3:55 [a] Ps. 130:1; Jon. 2:2 [b] Jer. 38:6–13 3:56 [a] Ps. 3:4 3:57 [a] James 4:8 [b] Is. 41:10, 14; Dan. 10:12 3:58 [a] Ps. 35:1; Jer. 51:36 [b] Ps. 71:23 3:59 [a] Ps. 9:4 3:60 [a] Jer. 11:19 3:63 [a] Ps. 139:2 3:64 [a] Ps. 28:4; Jer. 11:20; 2 Tim. 4:14 3:65 [1] A Jewish tradition reads *sorrow of.* 3:66 [a] Deut. 25:19; Jer. 10:11 [b] Ps. 8:3 4:2 [a] Is. 30:14; Jer. 19:11; [2 Cor. 4:7] 4:3 [a] Job 39:14–17

4 The tongue of the infant clings
To the roof of its mouth for thirst;
[a]The young children ask for bread,
But no one breaks *it* for them.

5 Those who ate delicacies
Are desolate in the streets;
Those who were brought up in scarlet
[a]Embrace ash heaps.

6 The punishment of the iniquity of
the daughter of my people
Is greater than the punishment
of the [a]sin of Sodom,
Which was [b]overthrown in a moment,
With no hand to help her!

7 Her Nazirites[1] were brighter than snow
And whiter than milk;
They were more ruddy in
body than rubies,
Like sapphire in their appearance.

8 *Now* their appearance is
blacker than soot;
They go unrecognized in the streets;
[a]Their skin clings to their bones,
It has become as dry as wood.

9 *Those* slain by the sword are better off
Than *those* who die of hunger;
For these [a]pine away,
Stricken *for lack* of the
fruits of the [b]field.

10 The hands of the [a]compassionate
women
Have cooked their [b]own children;
They became [c]food for them
In the destruction of the
daughter of my people.

11 The LORD has fulfilled His fury,
[a]He has poured out His fierce anger.
[b]He kindled a fire in Zion,
And it has devoured its foundations.

12 The kings of the earth,
And all inhabitants of the world,
Would not have believed
That the adversary and the enemy
Could [a]enter the gates of Jerusalem—

13 [a]Because of the sins of her prophets
And the iniquities of her priests,
[b]Who shed in her midst
The blood of the just.

14 They wandered blind in the streets;
[a]They have defiled themselves
with blood,
[b]So that no one would touch
their garments.

15 They cried out to them,
"Go away, [a]unclean!
Go away, go away,
Do not touch us!"
When they fled and wandered,
Those among the nations said,
"They shall no longer dwell *here.*"

16 The face[1] of the LORD scattered them;
He no longer regards them.
[a]*The people* do not respect the priests
Nor show favor to the elders.

17 Still [a]our eyes failed us,
Watching vainly for our help;
In our watching we watched
For a nation *that* could not save *us.*

18 [a]They tracked our steps
So that we could not walk
in our streets.
[b]Our end was near;
Our days were over,
For our end had come.

19 Our pursuers were [a]swifter
Than the eagles of the heavens.
They pursued us on the mountains
And lay in wait for us in
the wilderness.

20 The [a]breath of our nostrils, the
anointed of the LORD,
[b]Was caught in their pits,

4:4 [a] Ps. 22:15 4:5 [a] Job 24:8 4:6 [a] Ezek. 16:48 [b] Gen. 19:25; Jer. 20:16 4:7 [1] Or *nobles* 4:8 [a] Job 19:20; Ps. 102:5 4:9 [a] Lev. 26:39; Ezek. 24:23 [b] Jer. 16:4 4:10 [a] Lev. 26:29; Deut. 28:57; 2 Kin. 6:29; Jer. 19:9; Lam. 2:20; Ezek. 5:10 [b] Is. 49:15 [c] Deut. 28:57 4:11 [a] Jer. 7:20; Lam. 2:17; Ezek. 22:31 [b] Deut. 32:22; Jer. 21:14 4:12 [a] Jer. 21:13 4:13 [a] Jer. 5:31; Ezek. 22:26, 28; Zeph. 3:4 [b] Jer. 2:30; 26:8, 9; Matt. 23:31 4:14 [a] Jer. 2:34 [b] Num. 19:16 4:15 [a] Lev. 13:45, 46 4:16 [a] Lam. 5:12 [1] Targum reads *anger.* 4:17 [a] 2 Kin. 24:7 4:18 [a] 2 Kin. 25:4 [b] Ezek. 7:2, 3, 6; Amos 8:2 4:19 [a] Deut. 28:49 4:20 [a] Gen. 2:7 [b] Jer. 52:9; Ezek. 12:13

Of whom we said, "Under his shadow
We shall live among the nations."

21 Rejoice and be glad,
O daughter of [a]Edom,
You who dwell in the land of Uz!
[b]The cup shall also pass over to you
And you shall become drunk
and make yourself naked.

22 [a]*The punishment of* your iniquity
is accomplished,
O daughter of Zion;
He will no longer send
you into captivity.
[b]He will punish your iniquity,
O daughter of Edom;
He will uncover your sins!

Prayer for Restoration

5 Remember, [a]O LORD, what
has come upon us;
Look, and behold [b]our reproach!
2 [a]Our inheritance has been
turned over to aliens,
And our houses to foreigners.
3 We have become orphans
and waifs,
Our mothers *are* like [a]widows.

4 We pay for the water we drink,
And our wood comes at a price.
5 [a]*They* pursue at our heels;[1]
We labor *and* have no rest.
6 [a]We have given our hand
[b]*to* the Egyptians
And the [c]Assyrians, to be
satisfied with bread.

7 [a]Our fathers sinned *and are* no more,
But we bear their iniquities.
8 Servants rule over us;
There is none to deliver *us*
from their hand.
9 We get our bread *at the*
risk of our lives,
Because of the sword in
the wilderness.

10 Our skin is hot as an oven,
Because of the fever of famine.
11 They [a]ravished the women in Zion,
The maidens in the cities of Judah.
12 Princes were hung up by their hands,
And elders were not respected.
13 Young men [a]ground at the millstones;
Boys staggered under *loads of* wood.
14 The elders have ceased
gathering at the gate,
And the young men from their [a]music.

15 The joy of our heart has ceased;
Our dance has turned into [a]mourning.
16 [a]The crown has fallen *from* our head.
Woe to us, for we have sinned!
17 Because of this our heart is faint;
[a]Because of these *things*
our eyes grow dim;
18 Because of Mount Zion
which is [a]desolate,
With foxes walking about on it.

19 You, O LORD, [a]remain forever;
[b]Your throne from generation
to generation.
20 [a]Why do You forget us forever,
And forsake us for so long a time?
21 [a]Turn us back to You, O LORD,
and we will be restored;
Renew our days as of old,
22 Unless You have utterly rejected us,
And are very angry with us!

4:21 [a] Ps. 83:3–6 [b] Jer. 25:15; Obad. 10 4:22 [a] [Is. 40:2; Jer. 33:7, 8] [b] Ps. 137:7 5:1 [a] Ps. 89:50 [b] Ps. 79:4; Lam. 2:15 5:2 [a] Ps. 79:1 5:3 [a] Ex. 22:24; Jer. 15:8; 18:21 5:5 [a] Deut. 28:48; Jer. 28:14 [1] Literally *necks* 5:6 [a] Gen. 24:2 [b] Hos. 9:3; 12:1 [c] Jer. 2:18; Hos. 5:13 5:7 [a] Jer. 31:29 5:11 [a] Is. 13:16; Zech. 14:2 5:13 [a] Judg. 16:21 5:14 [a] Is. 24:8; Jer. 7:34 5:15 [a] Jer. 25:10; Amos 8:10 5:16 [a] Job 19:9; Ps. 89:39; Jer. 13:18 5:17 [a] Ps. 6:7 5:18 [a] Is. 27:10 5:19 [a] Ps. 9:7; Hab. 1:12 [b] Ps. 45:6 5:20 [a] Ps. 13:1; 44:24 5:21 [a] Ps. 80:3, 7, 19; Jer. 31:18

THE BOOK OF

EZEKIEL

OVERVIEW

The Book of Ezekiel was written by the prophet Ezekiel, a descendant of the priestly family of Zadok. God called Ezekiel to prophesy to those who had been carried into Babylonian captivity. Ezekiel was one of the major prophets of the Old Testament, and his ministry was filled with visions and acts that represented God's messages to His people.

Ezekiel was carried into Babylonian captivity in 597 BC, during the reign of King Jehoiachin of Judah. His ministry began in 593 BC and lasted twenty-two years. The Book of Ezekiel can be divided into three sections: God's judgment of the Israelites (chs. 1–24), God's judgment of other nations (chs. 25–32), and God's salvation for His people (chs. 33–48).

God called Ezekiel to be a prophet in a vision in which He displayed His glory (ch. 1). He said to him, "Son of man, I am sending you to the children of Israel, to a rebellious nation that has rebelled against Me" (2:3). God charged Ezekiel, "Do not be afraid of them nor be afraid of their words" (v. 6). God set Ezekiel as "a watchman for the house of Israel" (3:17).

Ezekiel prophesied God's judgment on the Israelites due to their sins. He spoke of the siege of Jerusalem and the sword coming against it (chs. 4–5). God gave him a vision of the judgment that would take place at the temple because of "the great abominations that the house of Israel" committed there (8:6). As a result, "the glory of the LORD departed from the threshold of the temple" (10:18).

Ezekiel warned against false prophets (ch. 13), idolatrous elders (ch. 14), and the judgment that would come upon God's people (chs. 15–24). Despite the impending judgment, God promised to "be a little sanctuary for them" (11:16). Not only did Ezekiel prophesy judgment against the Israelites, but he also prophesied judgment against other nations (chs. 25–32).

In the last section of Ezekiel, the prophet gave the Israelites hope, telling them that God takes "no pleasure" in His judgment of the wicked (33:11). He prefers that they turn from their wicked ways. Ezekiel reminded the people of the cause of Judah's ruin (see vv. 23–29). In chapter 36, God promised to renew Israel and cleanse it from its iniquities (see vv. 16–38).

One of the most popular of Ezekiel's visions is the valley of dry bones in chapter 37. In the vision, God commanded Ezekiel to prophesy to the bones. When he did, flesh came upon the bones. The vision was a representation of the Israelites who, though spiritually dead, would be brought to life again by the word of God.

The last chapters of Ezekiel (40–48) contain a vision of the restoration of God's kingdom. In chapters 40–42, God promises the city and the temple would be rebuilt. "The glory of the LORD [would fill] the temple" (43:5), and worship would be restored (chs. 44–46).

The Book of Ezekiel describes God's judgment on the Israelites and His plan to redeem them. It outlines the offenses that caused God to bring judgment upon His people, but it also gave them hope for a future in which they would be reconnected to Him.

BREATHE IT IN

The prophet Ezekiel did not begin his ministry until five years after the Babylonians had taken the people of Judah into captivity. The people were lost, confused, and questioning God. Many of them complained about the judgment, and others believed that God had forsaken them forever. Ezekiel's messages about the Israelites causing their own destruction were not well received. However, Ezekiel did not just prophesy doom and gloom; he also spoke of God's deliverance. He promised that God would be a "sanctuary" (11:16), even in the midst of His judgment against them.

The sanctuary has always been an important place for Christians. It is a place precious to our hearts where we can worship and commune with God. A sanctuary offers refuge and protects us from the dangers around us. When God's temple was destroyed and His Spirit departed, He offered Himself as the sanctuary for the Israelites. When Jesus died on the cross and rose from the dead, He opened the door for sanctuaries to be built in the hearts of believers, giving direct access to Him.

Many Christians do not take advantage of their direct access to God. They think only of the church building when they hear the word "sanctuary." While it is good and right for us to come together and worship God collectively, each of us should develop our own personal relationship with Him. We must learn to enter the sanctuary of our hearts to worship and commune with God. It is there, in that place, where we will find peace and healing. It is there where our broken hearts are mended and our thoughts are redirected. It is there where we experience the glory of God.

Having a sanctuary in our hearts gives us the privilege of communing with God anytime and anywhere. We do not have to wait for the doors of the church to open; we are free to worship God whenever and however we choose. The more time we spend with God, the stronger our relationship grows.

If you have not done so, ask God to create in you a clean heart. Invite Him into the holy place He has created in your heart, and He will meet you there. When He enters in, worship Him in spirit and in truth.

Always thank God for His favor over your life and show appreciation for His faithfulness. Acknowledge His grace and mercy, and rest in His forgiveness of your sins. Confess your love and adoration for Him. Submit your will to Him and commit to honoring His Word. Tell Him about the joys and the disappointments of your day. Share with Him what is on your mind and in your heart. Ask Him for guidance when you have difficult decisions or confusing choices to make.

Every day is a day to commune with God. When you wake up in the morning, enter in. As you go about your daily routine, take time to enter your sanctuary. When you lie down at night, enter in. God is there waiting. All you have to do is enter in.

†

THE BOOK OF

EZEKIEL

Ezekiel's Vision of God

1 Now it came to pass in the thirtieth year,
in the fourth *month,* on the fifth *day* of
the month, as I *was* among the captives by
[a]the River Chebar, *that* [b]the heavens were
opened and I saw [c]visions[1] of God. 2On the
fifth *day* of the month, which *was* in the
fifth year of King Jehoiachin's captivity,
3the word of the LORD came expressly to
Ezekiel the priest, the son of Buzi, in the
land of the Chaldeans[1] by the River Chebar; and [a]the hand of the LORD was upon
him there.

4Then I looked, and behold, [a]a whirlwind was coming [b]out of the north, a great
cloud with raging fire engulfing itself; and
brightness *was* all around it and radiating
out of its midst like the color of amber, out
of the midst of the fire. 5[a]Also from within
it *came* the likeness of four living creatures. And [b]this *was* their appearance: they
had [c]the likeness of a man. 6Each one had
four faces, and each one had four wings.
7Their legs *were* straight, and the soles of
their feet *were* like the soles of calves' feet.
They sparkled [a]like the color of burnished
bronze. 8[a]The hands of a man *were* under
their wings on their four sides; and each of
the four had faces and wings. 9Their wings
touched one another. *The creatures* did not
turn when they went, but each one went
straight [a]forward.

10As for [a]the likeness of their faces, *each*
[b]had the face of a man; each of the four
had [c]the face of a lion on the right side,
[d]each of the four had the face of an ox on
the left side, [e]and each of the four had the
face of an eagle. 11Thus *were* their faces.
Their wings stretched upward; two *wings*
of each one touched one another, and [a]two
covered their bodies. 12And [a]each one went
straight forward; they went wherever the
spirit wanted to go, and they did not turn
when they went.

13As for the likeness of the living creatures, their appearance *was* like burning coals of fire, [a]like the appearance of
torches going back and forth among the
living creatures. The fire was bright, and
out of the fire went lightning. 14And the
living creatures ran back and forth, [a]in appearance like a flash of lightning.

15Now as I looked at the living creatures,
behold, [a]a wheel *was* on the earth beside
each living creature with its four faces.
16[a]The appearance of the wheels and their
workings *was* [b]like the color of beryl, and
all four had the same likeness. The appearance of their workings *was,* as it were, a
wheel in the middle of a wheel. 17When they
moved, they went toward any one of four
directions; they did not turn aside when
they went. 18As for their rims, they were so
high they were awesome; and their rims
were [a]full of eyes, all around the four of
them. 19[a]When the living creatures went,
the wheels went beside them; and when
the living creatures were lifted up from the
earth, the wheels were lifted up. 20Wherever
the spirit wanted to go, they went, *because*
there the spirit went; and the wheels were
lifted together with them, [a]for the spirit

1:1 [a] Ezek. 3:15, 23; 10:15 [b] Matt. 3:16; Mark 1:10; Luke 3:21; Acts 7:56; 10:11; Rev. 4:1; 19:11 [c] Ex. 24:10; Num. 12:6; Is. 1:1; 6:1; Ezek. 8:3; Dan. 8:1, 2 [1] Following Masoretic Text, Septuagint, and Vulgate; Syriac and Targum read *a vision.* 1:3 [a] 1 Kin. 18:46; 2 Kin. 3:15; Ezek. 3:14, 22 [1] Or *Babylonians,* and so elsewhere in this book 1:4 [a] Is. 21:1; Jer. 23:19; 25:32; Ezek. 13:11, 13 [b] Jer. 1:14 1:5 [a] Ezek. 10:15, 17, 20; Rev. 4:6–8 [b] Ezek. 10:8 [c] Ezek. 10:14 1:7 [a] Dan. 10:6; Rev. 1:15 1:8 [a] Ezek. 10:8, 21 1:9 [a] Ezek. 1:12; 10:20–22 1:10 [a] Ezek. 10:14; Rev. 4:7 [b] Num. 2:10 [c] Num. 2:3 [d] Num. 2:18 [e] Num. 2:25 1:11 [a] Is. 6:2; Ezek. 1:23 1:12 [a] Ezek. 10:11, 22 1:13 [a] Ps. 104:4; Rev. 4:5 1:14 [a] Zech. 4:10; [Matt. 24:27; Luke 17:24] 1:15 [a] Ezek. 10:9 1:16 [a] Ezek. 10:9, 10 [b] Dan. 10:6 1:18 [a] Ezek. 10:12; [Zech. 4:10]; Rev. 4:6, 8 1:19 [a] Ezek. 10:16, 17 1:20 [a] Ezek. 10:17

of the living creatures[1] *was* in the wheels.
21 When those went, *these* went; when those
stood, *these* stood; and when those were
lifted up from the earth, the wheels were
lifted up together with them, for the spirit
of the living creatures[1] *was* in the wheels.
22 [a]The likeness of the firmament above
the heads of the living creatures[1] *was* like
the color of an awesome [b]crystal, stretched
out [c]over their heads. 23 And under the firmament their wings *spread out* straight,
one toward another. Each one had two
which covered one side, and each one had
two which covered the other side of the
body. 24 [a]When they went, I heard the noise
of their wings, [b]like the noise of many waters, like [c]the voice of the Almighty, a tumult like the noise of an army; and when
they stood still, they let down their wings.
25 A voice came from above the firmament
that *was* over their heads; whenever they
stood, they let down their wings.
26 [a]And above the firmament over their
heads *was* the likeness of a throne, [b]in
appearance like a sapphire stone; on the
likeness of the throne *was* a likeness with
the appearance of a man high above [c]it.
27 Also from the appearance of His waist
and upward [a]I saw, as it were, the color
of amber with the appearance of fire all
around within it; and from the appearance
of His waist and downward I saw, as it were,
the appearance of fire with brightness all
around. 28 [a]Like the appearance of a rainbow in a cloud on a rainy day, so *was* the
appearance of the brightness all around it.
[b]This *was* the appearance of the likeness of
the glory of the LORD.

Ezekiel Sent to Rebellious Israel

So when I saw *it*, [c]I fell on my face, and
I heard a voice of One speaking.
2 And He said to me, "Son of man, [a]stand
on your feet, and I will speak to you."
2 Then [a]the Spirit entered me when He
spoke to me, and set me on my feet; and I
heard Him who spoke to me. 3 And He said
to me: "Son of man, I am sending you to
the children of Israel, to a rebellious nation that has [a]rebelled against Me; [b]they
and their fathers have transgressed against
Me to this very day. 4 [a]For *they are* impudent
and stubborn children. I am sending you to
them, and you shall say to them, 'Thus says
the Lord GOD.' 5 [a]As for them, whether they
hear or whether they refuse—for they *are* a
[b]rebellious house—yet they [c]will know that
a prophet has been among them.
6 "And you, son of man, [a]do not be afraid
of them nor be afraid of their words, though
[b]briers and thorns *are* with you and you
dwell among scorpions; [c]do not be afraid
of their words or dismayed by their looks,
[d]though they *are* a rebellious house. 7 [a]You
shall speak My words to them, whether they
hear or whether they refuse, for they *are* rebellious. 8 But you, son of man, hear what
I say to you. Do not be rebellious like that
rebellious house; open your mouth and
[a]eat what I give you."
9 Now when I looked, there was [a]a hand
stretched out to me; and behold, [b]a scroll
of a book *was* in it. 10 Then He spread it before me; and *there was* writing on the inside and on the outside, and written on it
were lamentations and mourning and woe.
3 Moreover He said to me, "Son of man,
eat what you find; [a]eat this scroll, and
go, speak to the house of Israel." 2 So I
opened my mouth, and He caused me to
eat that scroll.
3 And He said to me, "Son of man, feed
your belly, and fill your stomach with this
scroll that I give you." So I [a]ate, and it was
in my mouth [b]like honey in sweetness.
4 Then He said to me: "Son of man, go
to the house of Israel and speak with My
words to them. 5 For you *are* not sent to a
people of unfamiliar speech and of hard
language, *but* to the house of Israel, 6 not
to many people of unfamiliar speech and
of hard language, whose words you cannot

1:20 [1] Literally *living creature;* Septuagint and Vulgate read *spirit of life;* Targum reads *creatures.* **1:21** [1] Literally *living creature;* Septuagint and Vulgate read *spirit of life;* Targum reads *creatures.* **1:22** [a] Ezek. 10:1 [b] Rev. 4:6 [c] Ezek. 10:1 [1] Following Septuagint, Targum, and Vulgate; Masoretic Text reads *living creature.* **1:24** [a] Ezek. 3:13; 10:5 [b] Ezek. 43:2; Dan. 10:6; Rev. 1:15 [c] Job 37:4, 5; Ps. 29:3, 4; 68:33 **1:26** [a] Ezek. 10:1 [b] Ex. 24:10, 16; Ezek. 8:4; 11:22, 23; 43:4, 5 [c] Ezek. 8:2 **1:27** [a] Ezek. 8:2 **1:28** [a] [Gen. 9:13]; Rev. 4:3; 10:1 [b] Ezek. 3:23; 8:4 [c] Gen. 17:3; Ezek. 3:23; Dan. 8:17; Acts 9:4; Rev. 1:17 **2:1** [a] Dan. 10:11; Acts 9:6 **2:2** [a] Ezek. 3:24; Dan. 8:18 **2:3** [a] Ezek. 5:6; 20:8, 13, 18 [b] 1 Sam. 8:7, 8; Jer. 3:25; Ezek. 20:18, 21, 30 **2:4** [a] Ps. 95:8; Is. 48:4; Jer. 5:3; 6:15; Ezek. 3:7 **2:5** [a] Is. 6:9, 10; Ezek. 3:11, 26, 27; [Matt. 10:12–15; Acts 13:46] [b] Ezek. 3:26 [c] Ezek. 33:33; [Luke 10:10, 11; John 15:22] **2:6** [a] Is. 51:12; Jer. 1:8, 17; Ezek. 3:9; Luke 12:4 [b] [2 Sam. 23:6, 7; Is. 9:18]; Jer. 6:28; Ezek. 28:24; Mic. 7:4 [c] Ezek. 3:9; [1 Pet. 3:14] [d] Ezek. 3:9, 26, 27 **2:7** [a] Jer. 1:7, 17; [Ezek. 3:10, 17] **2:8** [a] Ezek. 3:1–3; Rev. 10:9 **2:9** [a] Jer. 1:9; [Ezek. 8:3] [b] Jer. 36:2; Ezek. 3:1; Rev. 5:1–5; 10:8–11 **3:1** [a] Ezek. 2:8, 9 **3:3** [a] Jer. 15:16; Rev. 10:9 [b] Ps. 19:10; 119:103

understand. Surely, [a]had I sent you to them,
they would have listened to you. 7But the
house of Israel will not listen to you, [a]be-
cause they will not listen to Me; [b]for all the
house of Israel *are* impudent and hard-
hearted. 8Behold, I have made your face
strong against their faces, and your forehead strong against their foreheads. 9[a]Like
adamant stone, harder than flint, I have
made your forehead; [b]do not be afraid
of them, nor be dismayed at their looks,
though they *are* a rebellious house."

10Moreover He said to me: "Son of man,
receive into your heart all My words that I
speak to you, and hear with your ears. 11And
go, get to the captives, to the children of
your people, and speak to them and tell
them, [a]'Thus says the Lord GOD,' whether
they hear, or whether they refuse."

12Then [a]the Spirit lifted me up, and I
heard behind me a great thunderous voice:
"Blessed *is* the [b]glory of the LORD from His
place!" 13*I* also *heard* the [a]noise of the wings
of the living creatures that touched one another, and the noise of the wheels beside
them, and a great thunderous noise. 14So
the Spirit lifted me up and took me away,
and I went in bitterness, in the heat of my
spirit; but [a]the hand of the LORD was strong
upon me. 15Then I came to the captives at
Tel Abib, who dwelt by the River Chebar;
and [a]I sat where they sat, and remained
there astonished among them seven days.

Ezekiel Is a Watchman

16Now it [a]came to pass at the end of
seven days that the word of the LORD came
to me, saying, 17[a]"Son of man, I have made
you [b]a watchman for the house of Israel;
therefore hear a word from My mouth, and
give them [c]warning from Me: 18When I say
to the wicked, 'You shall surely die,' and you
give him no warning, nor speak to warn the
wicked from his wicked way, to save his life,
that same wicked *man* [a]shall die in his iniquity; but his blood I will require at your
hand. 19Yet, if you warn the wicked, and he
does not turn from his wickedness, nor
from his wicked way, he shall die in his iniquity; [a]but you have delivered your soul.

20"Again, when a [a]righteous *man* turns
from his righteousness and commits iniquity, and I lay a stumbling block before
him, he shall die; because you did not give
him warning, he shall die in his sin, and his
righteousness which he has done shall not
be remembered; but his blood I will require
at your hand. 21Nevertheless if you warn the
righteous *man* that the righteous should
not sin, and he does not sin, he shall surely
live because he took warning; also you will
have delivered your soul."

22[a]Then the hand of the LORD was upon
me there, and He said to me, "Arise, go out
[b]into the plain, and there I shall talk with
you."

23So I arose and went out into the plain,
and behold, [a]the glory of the LORD stood
there, like the glory which I [b]saw by the
River Chebar; [c]and I fell on my face. 24Then
[a]the Spirit entered me and set me on my
feet, and spoke with me and said to me: "Go,
shut yourself inside your house. 25And you,
O son of man, surely [a]they will put ropes
on you and bind you with them, so that
you cannot go out among them. 26[a]I will
make your tongue cling to the roof of your
mouth, so that you shall be mute and [b]not
be one to rebuke them, [c]for they *are* a rebellious house. 27[a]But when I speak with you,
I will open your mouth, and you shall say
to them, [b]'Thus says the Lord GOD.' He who
hears, let him hear; and he who refuses, let
him refuse; for they *are* a rebellious house.

The Siege of Jerusalem Portrayed

4 "You also, son of man, take a clay tablet and lay it before you, and portray
on it a city, Jerusalem. 2[a]Lay siege against
it, build a [b]siege wall against it, and heap
up a mound against it; set camps against
it also, and place battering rams against it
all around. 3Moreover take for yourself an
iron plate, and set it *as* an iron wall between
you and the city. Set your face against it,
and it shall be [a]besieged, and you shall lay

3:6 [a] Jon. 3:5–10; Matt. 11:21 3:7 [a] John 15:20, 21 [b] Ezek. 2:4 3:9 [a] Is. 50:7; Jer. 1:18; Mic. 3:8 [b] Jer. 1:8, 17; Ezek. 2:6
3:11 [a] Ezek. 2:5, 7 3:12 [a] 1 Kin. 18:12; Ezek. 8:3; Acts 8:39 [b] Ezek. 1:28; 8:4 3:13 [a] Ezek. 1:24; 10:5 3:14 [a] 2 Kin. 3:15; Ezek. 1:3; 8:1
3:15 [a] Job 2:13; Ps. 137:1 3:16 [a] Jer. 42:7 3:17 [a] Ezek. 33:7–9 [b] Is. 52:8; 56:10; Jer. 6:17 [c] [Lev. 19:17; Prov. 14:25]; Is. 58:1
3:18 [a] Ezek. 33:6; [John 8:21, 24] 3:19 [a] Is. 49:4, 5; Ezek. 14:14, 20; Acts 18:6; 20:26; 1 Tim. 4:16 3:20 [a] Ps. 125:5; Ezek. 18:24; 33:18;
Zeph. 1:6 3:22 [a] Ezek. 1:3 [b] Ezek. 8:4 3:23 [a] Ezek. 1:28; Acts 7:55 [b] Ezek. 1:1 [c] Ezek. 1:28 3:24 [a] Ezek. 2:2 3:25 [a] Ezek. 4:8
3:26 [a] Ezek. 24:27; Luke 1:20, 22 [b] Hos. 4:17; Amos 8:11 [c] Ezek. 2:5–7 3:27 [a] Ex. 4:11, 12; Ezek. 24:27; 33:22
[b] Ezek. 3:11 4:2 [a] Jer. 6:6; Ezek. 21:22 [b] 2 Kin. 25:1 4:3 [a] Jer. 39:1, 2; Ezek. 5:2

siege against it. [b]This *will be* a sign to the
house of Israel.
4“Lie also on your left side, and lay the
iniquity of the house of Israel upon it. *According* to the number of the days that you
lie on it, you shall bear their iniquity. 5For I
have laid on you the years of their iniquity,
according to the number of the days, three
hundred and ninety days; [a]so you shall bear
the iniquity of the house of Israel. 6And
when you have completed them, lie again
on your right side; then you shall bear the
iniquity of the house of Judah forty days. I
have laid on you a day for each year.
7“Therefore you shall set your face toward the siege of Jerusalem; your arm
shall be uncovered, and you shall prophesy against it. 8[a]And surely I will restrain
you so that you cannot turn from one side
to another till you have ended the days of
your siege.
9“Also take for yourself wheat, barley,
beans, lentils, millet, and spelt; put them
into one vessel, and make bread of them
for yourself. *During* the number of days
that you lie on your side, three hundred
and ninety days, you shall eat it. 10And
your food which you eat *shall be* by weight,
twenty shekels a day; from time to time you
shall eat it. 11You shall also drink water by
measure, one-sixth of a hin; from time to
time you shall drink. 12And you shall eat it
as barley cakes; and bake it using fuel of
human waste in their sight.”
13Then the LORD said, “So [a]shall the children of Israel eat their defiled bread among
the Gentiles, where I will drive them.”
14So I said, [a]“Ah, Lord GOD! Indeed I have
never defiled myself from my youth till
now; I have never eaten [b]what died of itself
or was torn by beasts, nor has [c]abominable
flesh ever come into my mouth.”
15Then He said to me, “See, I am giving
you cow dung instead of human waste, and
you shall prepare your bread over it.”
16Moreover He said to me, “Son of man,
surely I will cut off the [a]supply of bread in
Jerusalem; they shall [b]eat bread by weight
and with anxiety, and shall [c]drink water by
measure and with dread, 17that they may
lack bread and water, and be dismayed with
one another, and [a]waste away because of
their iniquity.

A Sword Against Jerusalem

5 “And you, son of man, take a sharp
sword, take it as a barber’s razor, [a]and
pass *it* over your head and your beard; then
take scales to weigh and divide the *hair*.
2[a]You shall burn with fire one-third in the
midst of [b]the city, when [c]the days of the
siege are finished; then you shall take one-
third and strike around *it* with the sword,
and one-third you shall scatter in the wind:
I will draw out a sword after [d]them. 3[a]You
shall also take a small number of them and
bind them in the edge of your *garment*.
4Then take some of them again and [a]throw
them into the midst of the fire, and burn
them in the fire. From there a fire will go
out into all the house of Israel.
5“Thus says the Lord GOD: ‘This *is* Jerusalem; I have set her in the midst of the
nations and the countries all around her.
6She has rebelled against My judgments
by doing wickedness more than the nations, and against My statutes more than
the countries that *are* all around her; for
they have refused My judgments, and they
have not walked in My statutes.’ 7There-
fore thus says the Lord GOD: ‘Because you
have multiplied *disobedience* more than
the nations that *are* all around you, have
not walked in My statutes [a]nor kept My
judgments, nor even done[1] according to
the judgments of the nations that *are* all
around you’— 8therefore thus says the
Lord GOD: ‘Indeed I, even I, *am* against
you and will execute judgments in your
midst in the sight of the nations. 9[a]And I
will do among you what I have never done,
and the like of which I will never do again,
because of all your abominations. 10There-
fore fathers [a]shall eat *their* sons in your
midst, and sons shall eat their fathers; and
I will execute judgments among you, and

4:3 [b] Ezek. 12:6, 11; 24:24, 27 4:5 [a] Num. 14:34 4:8 [a] Ezek. 3:25 4:13 [a] Dan. 1:8; Hos. 9:3 4:14 [a] Acts 10:14 [b] Ex. 22:31; Lev. 17:15; 22:8; Ezek. 44:31 [c] Deut. 14:3; Is. 65:4; 66:17 4:16 [a] Lev. 26:26; Ps. 105:16; Is. 3:1; Ezek. 5:16; 14:13 [b] Ezek. 4:10, 11; 12:19 [c] Ezek. 4:11 4:17 [a] Lev. 26:39; Ezek. 24:23 5:1 [a] Lev. 21:5; Is. 7:20; Ezek. 44:20 5:2 [a] Ezek. 5:12 [b] Ezek. 4:1 [c] Ezek. 4:8, 9 [d] Lev. 26:25; Lam. 1:20 5:3 [a] Jer. 40:6; 52:16 5:4 [a] Jer. 41:1, 2; 44:14 5:7 [a] 2 Kin. 21:9–11; 2 Chr. 33:9; Jer. 2:10, 11; Ezek. 16:47 [1] Following Masoretic Text, Septuagint, Targum, and Vulgate; many Hebrew manuscripts and Syriac read *but have done* (compare 11:12). 5:9 [a] Lam. 4:6; Dan. 9:12; [Amos 3:2]; Matt. 24:21 5:10 [a] Lev. 26:29; Deut. 28:53; 2 Kin. 6:29; Jer. 19:9; Lam. 2:20; 4:10

all of you who remain I will [b]scatter to all
the winds.
11"Therefore, *as* I live,' says the Lord GOD,
'surely, because you have [a]defiled My sanctuary with all your [b]detestable things and
with all your abominations, therefore I
will also diminish *you;* [c]My eye will not
spare, nor will I have any pity. 12[a]One-third
of you shall die of the pestilence, and be
consumed with famine in your midst; and
one-third shall fall by the sword all around
you; and [b]I will scatter another third to all
the winds, and I will draw out a sword after [c]them.
13'Thus shall My anger [a]be spent, and I
will [b]cause My fury to rest upon them, [c]and I
will be avenged; [d]and they shall know that I,
the LORD, have spoken *it* in My zeal, when I
have spent My fury upon them. 14Moreover
[a]I will make you a waste and a reproach
among the nations that *are* all around you,
in the sight of all who pass by.
15'So it[1] shall be a [a]reproach, a taunt, a
[b]lesson, and an astonishment to the nations that *are* all around you, when I execute judgments among you in anger and
in fury and in [c]furious rebukes. I, the LORD,
have spoken. 16When I [a]send against them
the terrible arrows of famine which shall
be for destruction, which I will send to destroy you, I will increase the famine upon
you and cut off your [b]supply of bread. 17So
I will send against you famine and [a]wild
beasts, and they will bereave you. [b]Pesti-
lence and blood shall pass through you,
and I will bring the sword against you. I,
the LORD, have spoken.'"

Judgment on Idolatrous Israel

6 Now the word of the LORD came to me,
saying: 2"Son of man, [a]set your face toward the [b]mountains of Israel, and prophesy against them, 3and say, 'O mountains of
Israel, hear the word of the Lord GOD! Thus
says the Lord GOD to the mountains, to
the hills, to the ravines, and to the valleys:
"Indeed I, *even* I, will bring a sword against
you, and [a]I will destroy your high places.
4Then your altars shall be desolate, your
incense altars shall be broken, and [a]I will
cast down your slain *men* before your idols.
5And I will lay the corpses of the children of
Israel before their idols, and I will scatter
your bones all around your altars. 6In all
your dwelling places the cities shall be laid
waste, and the high places shall be desolate,
so that your altars may be laid waste and
made desolate, your idols may be broken
and made to cease, your incense altars may
be cut down, and your works may be abolished. 7The slain shall fall in your midst,
and [a]you shall know that I *am* the LORD.
8[a]"Yet I will leave a remnant, so that
you may have *some* who escape the sword
among the nations, when you are [b]scattered
through the countries. 9Then those of you
who escape will [a]remember Me among the
nations where they are carried captive, because [b]I was crushed by their adulterous
heart which has departed from Me, and
[c]by their eyes which play the harlot after
their idols; [d]they will loathe themselves for
the evils which they committed in all their
abominations. 10And they shall know that
I *am* the LORD; I have not said in vain that
I would bring this calamity upon them."
11"Thus says the Lord GOD: [a]"Pound your
fists and stamp your feet, and say, 'Alas,
for all the evil abominations of the house
of Israel! [b]For they shall fall by the sword,
by famine, and by pestilence. 12He who is
far off shall die by the pestilence, he who
is near shall fall by the sword, and he who
remains and is besieged shall die by the
famine. [a]Thus will I spend My fury upon
them. 13Then you shall know that I *am* the
LORD, when their slain are among their
idols all around their altars, [a]on every high
hill, [b]on all the mountaintops, [c]under every green tree, and under every thick oak,
wherever they offered sweet incense to
all their idols. 14So I will [a]stretch out My

5:10 [b] Lev. 26:33; Deut. 28:64; Ps. 44:11; Ezek. 5:2, 12; 6:8; 12:14; Amos 9:9; Zech. 2:6; 7:14 5:11 [a] 2 Chr. 36:14; [Jer. 7:9–11]; Ezek. 8:5, 6, 16 [b] Ezek. 11:21 [c] Ezek. 7:4, 9; 8:18; 9:10 5:12 [a] Jer. 15:2; 21:9; Ezek. 6:12 [b] Jer. 9:16; [Ezek. 6:8] [c] Jer. 43:10, 11; 44:27; Ezek. 5:2; 12:14 5:13 [a] Lam. 4:11; Ezek. 6:12; 7:8 [b] Ezek. 21:17 [c] [Deut. 32:36]; Is. 1:24 [d] Is. 59:17; Ezek. 36:6; 38:19 5:14 [a] Lev. 26:31; Neh. 2:17 5:15 [a] Deut. 28:37; 1 Kin. 9:7; Ps. 79:4; Jer. 24:9; Lam. 2:15 [b] [Is. 26:9]; Jer. 22:8, 9; 1 Cor. 10:11 [c] Is. 66:15, 16; Ezek. 5:8; 25:17
[1] Septuagint, Syriac, Targum, and Vulgate read *you*. 5:16 [a] Deut. 32:23 [b] Lev. 26:26; Ezek. 4:16; 14:13 5:17 [a] Lev. 26:22; Deut. 32:24; Ezek. 14:21; 33:27; 34:25; Rev. 6:8 [b] Ezek. 38:22 6:2 [a] Ezek. 20:46; 21:2; 25:2 [b] Ezek. 36:1 6:3 [a] Lev. 26:30 6:4 [a] Lev. 26:30 6:7 [a] Ezek. 7:4, 9 6:8 [a] Jer. 44:28; Ezek. 5:2, 12; 12:16; 14:22 [b] Ezek. 5:12 6:9 [a] [Deut. 4:29]; Ps. 137; Jer. 51:50 [b] Ps. 78:40; Is. 7:13; 43:24; Hos. 11:8 [c] Num. 15:39; Ezek. 20:7, 24 [d] Lev. 26:39; Job 42:6; Ezek. 20:43; 36:31 6:11 [a] Ezek. 21:14 [b] Ezek. 5:12 6:12 [a] Lam. 4:11, 22; Ezek. 5:13 6:13 [a] Jer. 2:20; 3:6 [b] 1 Kin. 14:23; 2 Kin. 16:4; Ezek. 20:28; Hos. 4:13 [c] Is. 57:5 6:14 [a] Is. 5:25; Ezek. 14:13; 20:33, 34

hand against them and make the land desolate, yes, more desolate than the wilderness toward [b]Diblah, in all their dwelling places. Then they shall know that I *am* the LORD.' " ' "

Judgment on Israel Is Near

7 Moreover the word of the LORD came to me, saying, 2"And you, son of man, thus says the Lord GOD to the land of Israel:

[a]'An end! The end has come upon
the four corners of the land.
3 Now the end *has come* upon you,
And I will send My anger against you;
I will judge you [a]according
to your ways,
And I will repay you for all
your abominations.
4 [a]My eye will not spare you,
Nor will I have pity;
But I will repay your ways,
And your abominations will
be in your midst;
[b]Then you shall know that
I *am* the LORD!'

5"Thus says the Lord GOD:

'A disaster, a singular [a]disaster;
Behold, it has come!
6 An end has come,
The end has come;
It has dawned for you;
Behold, it has come!
7 [a]Doom has come to you, you
who dwell in the land;
[b]The time has come,
A day of trouble *is* near,
And not of rejoicing in the mountains.
8 Now upon you I will soon
[a]pour out My fury,
And spend My anger upon you;
I will judge you according
to your ways,
And I will repay you for all
your abominations.
9 'My eye will not spare,
Nor will I have pity;
I will repay you according
to your ways,
And your abominations will
be in your midst.
Then you shall know that I *am*
the LORD who strikes.

10 'Behold, the day!
Behold, it has come!
[a]Doom has gone out;
The rod has blossomed,
Pride has budded.
11 [a]Violence has risen up into
a rod of wickedness;
None of them *shall remain,*
None of their multitude,
None of them;
[b]Nor *shall there be* wailing for them.
12 The time has come,
The day draws near.

'Let not the buyer [a]rejoice,
Nor the seller [b]mourn,
For wrath *is* on their whole multitude.
13 For the seller shall not return
to what has been sold,
Though he may still be alive;
For the vision concerns the
whole multitude,
And it shall not turn back;
No one will strengthen himself
Who lives in iniquity.

14 'They have blown the trumpet
and made everyone ready,
But no one goes to battle;
For My wrath *is* on all their multitude.
15 [a]The sword *is* outside,
And the pestilence and famine within.
Whoever *is* in the field
Will die by the sword;
And whoever *is* in the city,
Famine and pestilence
will devour him.

16 'Those who [a]survive will escape
and be on the mountains
Like doves of the valleys,
All of them mourning,
Each for his iniquity.

6:14 [b] Num. 33:46 7:2 [a] Ezek. 7:3, 5, 6; 11:13; Amos 8:2, 10; [Matt. 24:6, 13, 14] 7:3 [a] [Rom. 2:6] 7:4 [a] Ezek. 5:11 [b] Ezek. 12:20 7:5 [a] 2 Kin. 21:12, 13; Nah. 1:9 7:7 [a] Ezek. 7:10 [b] Zeph. 1:14, 15 7:8 [a] Ezek. 20:8, 21 7:10 [a] Ezek. 7:7 7:11 [a] Jer. 6:7 [b] Jer. 16:5, 6; Ezek. 24:16, 22 7:12 [a] Prov. 20:14; 1 Cor. 7:30 [b] Is. 24:2 7:15 [a] Deut. 32:25; Jer. 14:18; Lam. 1:20; Ezek. 5:12 7:16 [a] Ezra 9:15; Is. 37:31; Ezek. 6:8; 14:22

17 Every [a]hand will be feeble,
And every knee will be *as*
weak *as* water.
18 They will also [a]be girded
with sackcloth;
Horror will cover them;
Shame *will be* on every face,
Baldness on all their heads.

19 'They will throw their silver
into the streets,
And their gold will be like refuse;
Their [a]silver and their gold will
not be able to deliver them
In the day of the wrath of the LORD;
They will not satisfy their souls,
Nor fill their stomachs,
Because it became their
stumbling block of iniquity.

20 'As for the beauty of his ornaments,
He set it in majesty;
[a]But they made from it
The images of their abominations—
Their detestable things;
Therefore I have made it
Like refuse to them.
21 I will give it as [a]plunder
Into the hands of strangers,
And to the wicked of the earth as spoil;
And they shall defile it.
22 I will turn My face from them,
And they will defile My secret place;
For robbers shall enter it and defile it.

23 'Make a chain,
For [a]the land is filled with
crimes of blood,
And the city is full of violence.
24 Therefore I will bring the
[a]worst of the Gentiles,
And they will possess their houses;
I will cause the pomp of
the strong to cease,
And their holy places shall be [b]defiled.
25 Destruction comes;
They will seek peace, but
there shall be none.
26 [a]Disaster will come upon disaster,
And rumor will be upon rumor.
[b]Then they will seek a vision
from a prophet;
But the law will perish from the priest,
And counsel from the elders.

27 'The king will mourn,
The prince will be clothed
with desolation,
And the hands of the common
people will tremble.
I will do to them according
to their way,
And according to what they
deserve I will judge them;
Then they shall know that
I *am* the LORD!' "

Abominations in the Temple

8 And it came to pass in the sixth year,
in the sixth *month,* on the fifth *day* of
the month, as I sat in my house with [a]the
elders of Judah sitting before me, that [b]the
hand of the Lord GOD fell upon me there.
2 [a]Then I looked, and there was a likeness,
like the appearance of fire—from the appearance of His waist and downward, fire;
and from His waist and upward, like the
appearance of brightness, [b]like the color
of amber. 3 He [a]stretched out the form of
a hand, and took me by a lock of my hair;
and [b]the Spirit lifted me up between earth
and heaven, and [c]brought me in visions of
God to Jerusalem, to the door of the north
gate of the inner *court,* [d]where the seat of
the image of jealousy *was,* which [e]provokes
to jealousy. 4 And behold, the [a]glory of the
God of Israel *was* there, like the vision that
I [b]saw in the plain.
5 Then He said to me, "Son of man, lift
your eyes now toward the north." So I lifted
my eyes toward the north, and there, north
of the altar gate, was this image of jealousy
in the entrance.
6 Furthermore He said to me, "Son of
man, do you see what they are doing, the
great [a]abominations that the house of
Israel commits here, to make Me go far
away from My sanctuary? Now turn again,

7:17 [a] Is. 13:7; Jer. 6:24; Ezek. 21:7; Heb. 12:12 7:18 [a] Is. 3:24; 15:2, 3; Jer. 48:37; Ezek. 27:31; Amos 8:10 7:19 [a] Prov. 11:4; Jer. 15:13; Zeph. 1:18 7:20 [a] Jer. 7:30 7:21 [a] 2 Kin. 24:13; Jer. 20:5 7:23 [a] 2 Kin. 21:16 7:24 [a] Ezek. 21:31; 28:7 [b] 2 Chr. 7:20; Ezek. 24:21 7:26 [a] Deut. 32:23; Is. 47:11; Jer. 4:20 [b] Ps. 74:9; Lam. 2:9; Ezek. 20:1, 3; Mic. 3:6 8:1 [a] Ezek. 14:1; 20:1; 33:31 [b] Ezek. 1:3; 3:22 8:2 [a] Ezek. 1:26, 27 [b] Ezek. 1:4, 27 8:3 [a] Dan. 5:5 [b] Ezek. 3:14; Acts 8:39 [c] Ezek. 11:1, 24; 40:2 [d] Jer. 7:30; 32:34; Ezek. 5:11 [e] Ex. 20:4; Deut. 32:16, 21 8:4 [a] Ezek. 3:12; 9:3 [b] Ezek. 1:28; 3:22, 23 8:6 [a] 2 Kin. 23:4, 5; Ezek. 5:11; 8:9, 17

HOPE FOR THE SALVATION OF THE LOST

INHALE

My best friends are not believers. I have tried everything to tell them and show them who God is and why they need Him in their lives. For me, following God isn't about what He can do for me. He has already done enough by sending His Son to die for my sins. But that doesn't seem to be enough for my friends. What can I do to help them see the greatness of God and their need to trust in Jesus for their salvation?

EXHALE

A heart for God always leads to a heart for others. I'm glad to see that you have a heart for both. The real secret to winning people to Christ is really no secret at all. It's never about what we can do. It's about what God has done and will do.

Your friends may not have trusted in Christ, but they are being exposed to Christ because you are being faithful to do what you are supposed to do. We simply show and tell the gospel. The saving part is in the hands of God alone. Leading people to trust in Christ is not our responsibility. Our responsibility is to get them to the point where they can. The rest is between them and God.

While it can be discouraging to see your friends not make commitments for Christ because you care about them, never lose hope. It could be that you aren't the one to see your friends come to a saving relationship with Jesus. It may happen in some other place at some other time through some other relationship. Our greatest contribution to seeing our friends come to Christ is our loving them, serving them, and living the faith out before them.

You may never grasp how God is working out His salvation plan in the life of a friend, but you can certainly believe He is working it out. Ezekiel 8:1 uses the phrase "and it came to pass." Keep that phrase in mind the next time frustration creeps in your mind in concern for your friends' salvation. God will bring His will to pass.

you will see greater abominations." 7So
He brought me to the door of the court;
and when I looked, there was a hole in the
wall. 8Then He said to me, "Son of man, dig
into the wall"; and when I dug into the wall,
there was a door.
9And He said to me, "Go in, and see the
wicked abominations which they are doing
there." 10So I went in and saw, and there—
every [a]sort of [b]creeping thing, abominable beasts, and all the idols of the house
of Israel, portrayed all around on the
walls. 11And there stood before them [a]sev-
enty men of the elders of the house of Israel, and in their midst stood Jaazaniah
the son of Shaphan. Each man had a censer in his hand, and a thick cloud of incense went up. 12Then He said to me, "Son
of man, have you seen what the elders of
the house of Israel do in the dark, every
man in the room of his idols? For they say,
[a]'The LORD does not see us, the LORD has
forsaken the land.'"
13And He said to me, "Turn again, *and*
you will see greater abominations that they
are doing." 14So He brought me to the door
of the north gate of the LORD's house; and
to my dismay, women were sitting there
weeping for Tammuz.
15Then He said to me, "Have you seen
this, O son of man? Turn again, you will
see greater abominations than these." 16So
He brought me into the inner court of the
LORD's house; and there, at the door of the
temple of the LORD, [a]between the porch
and the altar, [b]*were* about twenty-five men

8:10 [a] Ex. 20:4; Deut. 4:16–18 [b] Rom. 1:23 8:11 [a] Num. 11:16, 25; Luke 10:1
8:12 [a] Ps. 14:1; Is. 29:15; Ezek. 9:9 8:16 [a] Joel 2:17 [b] Ezek. 11:1

[c]with their backs toward the temple of the
LORD and their faces toward the east, and
they were worshiping [d]the sun toward the
east.
17And He said to me, "Have you seen *this,*
O son of man? Is it a trivial thing to the
house of Judah to commit the abominations which they commit here? For they
have [a]filled the land with violence; then
they have returned to provoke Me to anger. Indeed they put the branch to their
nose. 18[a]Therefore I also will act in fury.
My [b]eye will not spare nor will I have pity;
and though they [c]cry in My ears with a loud
voice, I will not hear them."

The Wicked Are Slain

9 Then He called out in my hearing with
a loud voice, saying, "Let those who
have charge over the city draw near, each
with a deadly weapon in his hand." 2And
suddenly six men came from the direction of the upper gate, which faces north,
each with his battle-ax in his hand. [a]One
man among them *was* clothed with linen
and had a writer's inkhorn at his side. They
went in and stood beside the bronze altar.
3Now [a]the glory of the God of Israel had
gone up from the cherub, where it had
been, to the threshold of the temple.[1] And
He called to the man clothed with linen,
who *had* the writer's inkhorn at his side;
4and the LORD said to him, "Go through
the midst of the city, through the midst of
Jerusalem, and put [a]a mark on the foreheads of the men [b]who sigh and cry over all
the abominations that are done within it."
5To the others He said in my hearing,
"Go after him through the city and [a]kill; [b]do
not let your eye spare, nor have any pity.
6[a]Utterly slay old *and* young men, maidens
and little children and women; but [b]do not
come near anyone on whom *is* the mark;
and [c]begin at My sanctuary." [d]So they began
with the elders who *were* before the temple.
7Then He said to them, "Defile the temple,
and fill the courts with the slain. Go out!"
And they went out and killed in the city.
8So it was, that while they were killing
them, I was left *alone;* and I [a]fell on my face
and cried out, and said, [b]"Ah, Lord GOD!
Will You destroy all the remnant of Israel
in pouring out Your fury on Jerusalem?"
9Then He said to me, "The iniquity of the
house of Israel and Judah *is* exceedingly
great, and [a]the land is full of bloodshed,
and the city full of perversity; for they say,
[b]'The LORD has forsaken the land, and [c]the
LORD does not see!' 10And as for Me also,
My [a]eye will neither spare, nor will I have
pity, *but* [b]I will recompense their deeds on
their own head."
11Just then, the man clothed with linen,
who *had* the inkhorn at his side, reported
back and said, "I have done as You commanded me."

The Glory Departs from the Temple

10 And I looked, and there in the [a]fir-
mament that was above the head of
the cherubim, there appeared something
like a sapphire stone, having the appearance of the likeness of a throne. 2[a]Then
He spoke to the man clothed with linen,
and said, "Go in among the wheels, under
the cherub, fill your hands with [b]coals of
fire from among the cherubim, and [c]scat-
ter *them* over the city." And he went in as
I watched.
3Now the cherubim were standing on
the south side of the temple[1] when the
man went in, and the [a]cloud filled the inner
court. 4[a]Then the glory of the LORD went
up from the cherub, *and paused* over the
threshold of the temple; and [b]the house
was filled with the cloud, and the court was
full of the brightness of the LORD's [c]glory.
5And the [a]sound of the wings of the cherubim was heard *even* in the outer court, like
[b]the voice of Almighty God when He speaks.
6Then it happened, when He commanded the man clothed in linen, saying,

---

8:16 [c] 2 Chr. 29:6; Jer. 2:27; 32:33; Ezek. 23:39 [d] Deut. 4:19; 2 Kin. 23:5, 11; Job 31:26; Jer. 44:17 8:17 [a] Ezek. 9:9; Amos 3:10; Mic. 2:2 8:18 [a] Ezek. 5:13; 16:42; 24:13 [b] Ezek. 5:11; 7:4, 9; 9:5, 10 [c] Prov. 1:28; Is. 1:15; Jer. 11:11; 14:12; Mic. 3:4; Zech. 7:13 9:2 [a] Lev. 16:4; Ezek. 10:2; Rev. 15:6 9:3 [a] Ezek. 3:23; 8:4; 10:4, 18; 11:22, 23 [1] Literally *house* 9:4 [a] Ex. 12:7, 13; Ezek. 9:6; [2 Cor. 1:22; 2 Tim. 2:19]; Rev. 7:2, 3; 9:4; 14:1 [b] Ps. 119:53, 136; Jer. 13:17; Ezek. 6:11; 21:6; 2 Cor. 12:21; 2 Pet. 2:8 9:5 [a] Ezek. 7:9 [b] Ezek. 5:11 9:6 [a] 2 Chr. 36:17 [b] Ex. 12:23; Rev. 9:4 [c] Jer. 25:29; Amos 3:2; [Luke 12:42; 1 Pet. 4:17] [d] Ezek. 8:11, 12, 16 9:8 [a] Num. 14:5; 16:4, 22, 45; Josh. 7:6 [b] Ezek. 11:13; Amos 7:2–6 9:9 [a] 2 Kin. 21:16; Jer. 2:34; Ezek. 8:17 [b] Job 22:13; Ezek. 8:12 [c] Ps. 10:11; Is. 29:15 9:10 [a] Is. 65:6; Ezek. 5:11; 7:4; 8:18 [b] Ezek. 11:21; Hos. 9:7 10:1 [a] Ezek. 1:22, 26 10:2 [a] Ezek. 9:2, 3; Dan. 10:5 [b] Ps. 18:10–13; Is. 6:6; Ezek. 1:13 [c] Rev. 8:5 10:3 [a] 1 Kin. 8:10, 11 [1] Literally *house,* also in verses 4 and 18 10:4 [a] Ezek. 1:28 [b] 1 Kin. 8:10; Ezek. 43:5 [c] Ezek. 11:22, 23 10:5 [a] [Job 40:9]; Ezek. 1:24; [Rev. 10:3] [b] [Ps. 29:3]

"Take fire from among the wheels, from
among the cherubim," that he went in and
stood beside the wheels. 7And the cherub
stretched out his hand from among the
cherubim to the fire that *was* among the
cherubim, and took *some of it* and put *it*
into the hands of the *man* clothed with
linen, who took *it* and went out. 8[a]The cherubim appeared to have the form of a man's
hand under their wings.

9[a]And when I looked, there were four
wheels by the cherubim, one wheel by one
cherub and another wheel by each other
cherub; the wheels appeared *to have* the
color of a [b]beryl stone. 10*As for* their appearance, all four looked alike—as it were,
a wheel in the middle of a wheel. 11[a]When
they went, they went toward *any of* their
four directions; they did not turn aside
when they went, but followed in the direction the head was facing. They did not turn
aside when they went. 12And their whole
body, with their back, their hands, their
wings, and the wheels that the four had,
were [a]full of eyes all around. 13As for the
wheels, they were called in my hearing,
"Wheel."

14[a]Each one had four faces: the first face
was the face of a cherub, the second face
the face of a man, the third the face of a
lion, and the fourth the face of an eagle.
15And the cherubim were lifted up. This
was [a]the living creature I saw by the River
Chebar. 16[a]When the cherubim went, the
wheels went beside them; and when the
cherubim lifted their wings to mount up
from the earth, the same wheels also did
not turn from beside them. 17[a]When *the
cherubim*[1] stood still, *the wheels* stood still,
and when *one*[2] was lifted up, *the other*[3] lifted
itself up, for the spirit of the living creature
was in them.

18Then [a]the glory of the LORD [b]departed
from the threshold of the temple and stood
over the cherubim. 19And [a]the cherubim
lifted their wings and mounted up from the
earth in my sight. When they went out, the
wheels *were* beside them; and they stood
at the door of the [b]east gate of the LORD's
house, and the glory of the God of Israel
was above them.

20[a]This *is* the living creature I saw under
the God of Israel [b]by the River Chebar, and I
knew they *were* cherubim. 21[a]Each one had
four faces and each one four wings, and the
likeness of the hands of a man *was* under
their wings. 22And [a]the likeness of their
faces *was* the same *as* the faces which I
had seen by the River Chebar, their appearance and their persons. [b]They each went
straight forward.

Judgment on Wicked Counselors

11 Then [a]the Spirit lifted me up and
brought me to [b]the East Gate of the
LORD's house, which faces eastward; and
there [c]at the door of the gate were twenty-
five men, among whom I saw Jaazaniah the
son of Azzur, and Pelatiah the son of Benaiah, princes of the people. 2And He said to
me: "Son of man, these *are* the men who
devise iniquity and give wicked counsel
in this city, 3who say, '*The time is* not [a]near
to build houses; [b]this *city is* the caldron,
and we *are* the meat.' 4Therefore prophesy against them, prophesy, O son of man!"

5Then [a]the Spirit of the LORD fell upon
me, and said to me, "Speak! 'Thus says the
LORD: "Thus you have said, O house of
Israel; for [b]I know the things that come
into your mind. 6[a]You have multiplied
your slain in this city, and you have filled
its streets with the slain." 7Therefore thus
says the Lord GOD: [a]"Your slain whom you
have laid in its midst, they *are* the meat,
and this *city is* the caldron; [b]but I shall
bring you out of the midst of it. 8You have
[a]feared the sword; and I will bring a sword
upon you," says the Lord GOD. 9"And I will
bring you out of its midst, and deliver you
into the hands of strangers, and [a]execute
judgments on you. 10[a]You shall fall by the
sword. I will judge you at [b]the border of
Israel. [c]Then you shall know that I *am* the
LORD. 11[a]This *city* shall not be your caldron,
nor shall you be the meat in its midst. I will

10:8 [a] Ezek. 1:8; 10:21 10:9 [a] Ezek. 1:15 [b] Ezek. 1:16 10:11 [a] Ezek. 1:17 10:12 [a] Rev. 4:6, 8 10:14 [a] 1 Kin. 7:29, 36; Ezek. 1:6, 10, 11; Rev. 4:7 10:15 [a] Ezek. 1:3, 5 10:16 [a] Ezek. 1:19 10:17 [a] Ezek. 1:12, 20, 21 [1] Literally *they* [2] Literally *they* [3] Literally *they* 10:18 [a] Ezek. 10:4 [b] Hos. 9:12 10:19 [a] Ezek. 11:22 [b] Ezek. 11:1 10:20 [a] Ezek. 1:22 [b] Ezek. 1:1 10:21 [a] Ezek. 1:6, 8; 10:14; 41:18, 19 10:22 [a] Ezek. 1:10 [b] Ezek. 1:9, 12 11:1 [a] Ezek. 3:12, 14 [b] Ezek. 10:19 [c] Ezek. 8:16 11:3 [a] Ezek. 12:22, 27; 2 Pet. 3:4 [b] Jer. 1:13; Ezek. 11:7, 11; 24:3, 6 11:5 [a] Ezek. 2:2; 3:24 [b] [Jer. 16:17; 17:10] 11:6 [a] Is. 1:15; Ezek. 7:23; 22:2–6, 9, 12, 27 11:7 [a] Ezek. 24:3, 6; Mic. 3:2, 3 [b] 2 Kin. 25:18–22; Jer. 52:24–27; Ezek. 11:9 11:8 [a] Jer. 42:16 11:9 [a] Ezek. 5:8 11:10 [a] 2 Kin. 25:19–21; Jer. 39:6; 52:10 [b] 1 Kin. 8:65; 2 Kin. 14:25 [c] Ps. 9:16; Ezek. 6:7; 13:9, 14, 21, 23 11:11 [a] Ezek. 11:3, 7

judge you at the border of Israel. 12And you
shall know that I *am* the LORD; for you have
not walked in My statutes nor executed My
judgments, but [a]have done according to
the customs of the Gentiles which *are* all
around you."'"
13Now it happened, while I was prophesying, that [a]Pelatiah the son of Benaiah
died. Then [b]I fell on my face and cried with
a loud voice, and said, "Ah, Lord GOD! Will
You make a complete end of the remnant
of Israel?"

God Will Restore Israel

14Again the word of the LORD came to
me, saying, 15"Son of man, your brethren,
your relatives, your countrymen, and all
the house of Israel in its entirety, *are* those
about whom the inhabitants of Jerusalem
have said, 'Get far away from the LORD; this
land has been given to us as a possession.'
16Therefore say, 'Thus says the Lord GOD:
"Although I have cast them far off among
the Gentiles, and although I have scattered
them among the countries, [a]yet I shall be
a little sanctuary for them in the countries
where they have gone."' 17Therefore say,
'Thus says the Lord GOD: [a]"I will gather you
from the peoples, assemble you from the
countries where you have been scattered,
and I will give you the land of Israel."' 18And
they will go there, and they will take away
all its [a]detestable things and all its abominations from there. 19Then [a]I will give them
one heart, and I will put [b]a new spirit within
them,[1] and take [c]the stony heart out of their
flesh, and give them a heart of flesh, 20[a]that
they may walk in My statutes and keep My
judgments and do them; [b]and they shall
be My people, and I will be their God. 21But
as for those whose hearts follow the desire
for their detestable things and their abominations, [a]I will recompense their deeds on
their own heads," says the Lord GOD.
22So the cherubim [a]lifted up their wings,
with the wheels beside them, and the glory
of the God of Israel *was* high above them.
23And [a]the glory of the LORD went up
from the midst of the city and stood [b]on
the mountain, [c]which *is* on the east side
of the city.
24Then [a]the Spirit took me up and
brought me in a vision by the Spirit of God
into Chaldea,[1] to those in captivity. And the
vision that I had seen went up from me.
25So I spoke to those in captivity of all the
things the LORD had shown me.

Judah's Captivity Portrayed

12 Now the word of the LORD came to
me, saying: 2"Son of man, you dwell
in the midst of [a]a rebellious house, which
[b]has eyes to see but does not see, and ears
to hear but does not hear; [c]for they *are* a
rebellious house.
3"Therefore, son of man, prepare your
belongings for captivity, and go into captivity by day in their sight. You shall go from
your place into captivity to another place
in their sight. It may be that they will consider, though they *are* a rebellious house.
4By day you shall bring out your belongings
in their sight, as though going into captivity; and at evening you shall go in their
sight, like those who go into captivity. 5Dig
through the wall in their sight, and carry
your belongings out through it. 6In their
sight you shall bear *them* on *your* shoulders *and* carry *them* out at twilight; you
shall cover your face, so that you cannot
see the ground, [a]for I have made you a sign
to the house of Israel."
7So I did as I was commanded. I brought
out my belongings by day, as though going
into captivity, and at evening I dug through
the wall with my hand. I brought *them* out
at twilight, *and* I bore *them* on *my* shoulder in their sight.
8And in the morning the word of the
LORD came to me, saying, 9"Son of man,
has not the house of Israel, [a]the rebellious
house, said to you, [b]'What are you doing?'
10Say to them, 'Thus says the Lord GOD:
"This [a]burden *concerns* the prince in Jerusalem and all the house of Israel who are
among them."' 11Say, [a]'I *am* a sign to you.

11:12 [a] Lev. 18:3, 24; Deut. 12:30, 31; Ezek. 8:10, 14, 16 11:13 [a] Acts 5:5 [b] Ezek. 9:8 11:16 [a] Ps. 90:1; 91:9; Is. 8:14; Jer. 29:7, 11 11:17 [a] Is. 11:11–16; Jer. 3:12, 18; 24:5; Ezek. 20:41, 42; 28:5 11:18 [a] Ezek. 37:23 11:19 [a] Jer. 32:39; Ezek. 36:26; Zeph. 3:9 [b] Ps. 51:10; [Jer. 31:33]; Ezek. 18:31 [c] Zech. 7:12; [Rom. 2:4, 5] [1] Literally *you* 11:20 [a] Ps. 105:45 [b] Jer. 24:7; Ezek. 14:11; 36:28; 37:27 11:21 [a] Ezek. 9:10 11:22 [a] Ezek. 1:19 11:23 [a] Ezek. 8:4; 9:3 [b] Zech. 14:4 [c] Ezek. 43:2 11:24 [a] Ezek. 8:3; 2 Cor. 12:2–4 [1] Or *Babylon,* and so elsewhere in this book 12:2 [a] Is. 1:23; Ezek. 2:3, 6–8 [b] Is. 6:9; 42:20; Jer. 5:21; Matt. 13:13, 14; Mark 4:12; 8:18; [Luke 8:10; John 9:39–41; 12:40]; Acts 28:26; Rom. 11:8 [c] Ezek. 2:5 12:6 [a] Is. 8:18; Ezek. 4:3; 24:24 12:9 [a] Ezek. 2:5 [b] Ezek. 17:12; 24:19 12:10 [a] Mal. 1:1 12:11 [a] Ezek. 12:6

As I have done, so shall it be done to them;
[b]they shall be carried away into captivity.'
12And [a]the prince who *is* among them shall
bear *his belongings* on *his* shoulder at twilight and go out. They shall dig through the
wall to carry *them* out through it. He shall
cover his face, so that he cannot see the
ground with *his* eyes. 13I will also spread My
[a]net over him, and he shall be caught in My
snare. [b]I will bring him to Babylon, *to* the
land of the Chaldeans; yet he shall not see
it, though he shall die there. 14[a]I will scatter to every wind all who *are* around him
to help him, and all his troops; and [b]I will
draw out the sword after them.

15[a]"Then they shall know that I *am* the
LORD, when I scatter them among the nations and disperse them throughout the
countries. 16[a]But I will spare a few of their
men from the sword, from famine, and
from pestilence, that they may declare all
their abominations among the Gentiles
wherever they go. Then they shall know
that I *am* the LORD."

Judgment Not Postponed

17Moreover the word of the LORD came
to me, saying, 18"Son of man, [a]eat your
bread with quaking, and drink your water with trembling and anxiety. 19And say
to the people of the land, 'Thus says the
Lord GOD to the inhabitants of Jerusalem
and to the land of Israel: "They shall eat
their bread with anxiety, and drink their
water with dread, so that her land may [a]be
emptied of all who are in it, [b]because of
the violence of all those who dwell in it.
20Then the cities that are inhabited shall
be laid waste, and the land shall become
desolate; and you shall know that I *am*
the LORD." ' "

21And the word of the LORD came to me,
saying, 22"Son of man, what *is* this proverb
that you *people* have about the land of Israel, which says, [a]'The days are prolonged,
and every vision fails'? 23Tell them therefore, 'Thus says the Lord GOD: "I will lay this
proverb to rest, and they shall no more use
it as a proverb in Israel." ' But say to them,
'[a]"The days are at hand, and the fulfillment
of every vision. 24For [a]no more shall there
be any [b]false vision or flattering divination within the house of Israel. 25For I *am*
the LORD. I speak, and [a]the word which I
speak will come to pass; it will no more be
postponed; for in your days, O rebellious
house, I will say the word and [b]perform it,"
says the Lord GOD.' "

26Again the word of the LORD came to
me, saying, 27[a]"Son of man, look, the house
of Israel is saying, 'The vision that he sees
is [b]for many days *from now,* and he prophesies of times far off.' 28[a]Therefore say to
them, 'Thus says the Lord GOD: "None of
My words will be postponed any more, but
the word which I speak [b]will be done," says
the Lord GOD.' "

Woe to Foolish Prophets

13 And the word of the LORD came to
me, saying, 2"Son of man, prophesy
[a]against the prophets of Israel who prophesy, and say to [b]those who prophesy out
of their own [c]heart, 'Hear the word of the
LORD!' "

3Thus says the Lord GOD: "Woe to the
foolish prophets, who follow their own
spirit and have seen nothing! 4O Israel,
your prophets are [a]like foxes in the deserts.
5You [a]have not gone up into the gaps to
build a wall for the house of Israel to stand
in battle on the day of the LORD. 6[a]They
have envisioned futility and false divination, saying, 'Thus says the LORD!' But the
LORD has [b]not sent them; yet they hope
that the word may be confirmed. 7Have
you not seen a futile vision, and have you
not spoken false divination? You say, 'The
LORD says,' but I have not spoken."

8Therefore thus says the Lord GOD: "Because you have spoken nonsense and envisioned lies, therefore I *am* indeed against
you," says the Lord GOD. 9"My hand will be
[a]against the prophets who envision futility
and who [b]divine lies; they shall not be in the
assembly of My people, [c]nor be written in

12:11 [b] 2 Kin. 25:4, 5, 7 **12:12** [a] 2 Kin. 25:4; Jer. 39:4; 52:7; Ezek. 12:6 **12:13** [a] Job 19:6; Jer. 52:9; Lam. 1:13; Ezek. 17:20 [b] 2 Kin. 25:7; Jer. 52:11; Ezek. 17:16 **12:14** [a] 2 Kin. 25:4; Ezek. 5:10 [b] Ezek. 5:2, 12 **12:15** [a] [Ps. 9:16]; Ezek. 6:7, 14; 12:16, 20 **12:16** [a] 2 Kin. 25:11, 22; Ezek. 6:8–10 **12:18** [a] Lam. 5:9; Ezek. 4:16 **12:19** [a] Jer. 10:22; Ezek. 6:6, 7, 14; Mic. 7:13; Zech. 7:14 [b] Ps. 107:34 **12:22** [a] Jer. 5:12; Ezek. 11:3; 12:27; Amos 6:3; 2 Pet. 3:4 **12:23** [a] Ps. 37:13; Joel 2:1; Zeph. 1:14 **12:24** [a] Jer. 14:13–16; Ezek. 13:6; Zech. 13:2–4 [b] Lam. 2:14 **12:25** [a] [Is. 55:11]; Dan. 9:12; [Luke 21:33] [b] Num. 23:19; [Is. 14:24] **12:27** [a] Ezek. 12:22 [b] Dan. 10:14 **12:28** [a] Ezek. 12:23, 25 [b] Jer. 4:7 **13:2** [a] Is. 28:7; Jer. 23:1–40; Lam. 2:14; Ezek. 22:25–28 [b] Ezek. 13:17 [c] Jer. 14:14; 23:16, 26 **13:4** [a] Song 2:15 **13:5** [a] Ps. 106:23; [Jer. 23:22]; Ezek. 22:30 **13:6** [a] Jer. 29:8; Ezek. 22:28 [b] Jer. 27:8–15 **13:9** [a] Jer. 23:30 [b] Jer. 20:3–6 [c] Ezra 2:59, 62; Neh. 7:5; [Ps. 69:28]

the record of the house of Israel, [d]nor shall
they enter into the land of Israel. [e]Then you
shall know that I *am* the Lord GOD.
10“Because, indeed, because they have
seduced My people, saying, [a]‘Peace!’ when
there is no peace—and one builds a wall,
and they [b]plaster it with untempered *mortar*— 11say to those who plaster *it* with untempered *mortar,* that it will fall. [a]There
will be flooding rain, and you, O great hailstones, shall fall; and a stormy wind shall
tear *it* down. 12Surely, when the wall has
fallen, will it not be said to you, ‘Where *is*
the mortar with which you plastered *it?*’”
13Therefore thus says the Lord GOD: “I
will cause a stormy wind to break forth in
My fury; and there shall be a flooding rain
in My anger, and great hailstones in fury
to consume *it.* 14So I will break down the
wall you have plastered with untempered
mortar, and bring it down to the ground,
so that its foundation will be uncovered;
it will fall, and you shall be consumed in
the midst of it. [a]Then you shall know that
I *am* the LORD.
15“Thus will I accomplish My wrath on
the wall and on those who have plastered
it with untempered *mortar;* and I will say
to you, ‘The wall *is* no *more,* nor those who
plastered it, 16*that is,* the prophets of Israel
who prophesy concerning Jerusalem, and
who [a]see visions of peace for her when *there
is* no peace,’” says the Lord GOD.
17“Likewise, son of man, [a]set your face
against the daughters of your people, [b]who
prophesy out of their own heart; prophesy
against them, 18and say, ‘Thus says the Lord
GOD: “Woe to the *women* who sew *magic*
charms on their sleeves[1] and make veils
for the heads of people of every height to
hunt souls! Will you [a]hunt the souls of My
people, and keep yourselves alive? 19And
will you profane Me among My people
[a]for handfuls of barley and for pieces of
bread, killing people who should not die,
and keeping people alive who should not
live, by your lying to My people who listen to lies?”
20‘Therefore thus says the Lord GOD:
“Behold, I *am* against your *magic* charms
by which you hunt souls there like birds. I
will tear them from your arms, and let the
souls go, the souls you hunt like birds. 21I
will also tear off your veils and deliver My
people out of your hand, and they shall no
longer be as prey in your hand. [a]Then you
shall know that I *am* the LORD.
22“Because with [a]lies you have made the
heart of the righteous sad, whom I have not
made sad; and you have [b]strengthened the
hands of the wicked, so that he does not
turn from his wicked way to save his life.
23Therefore [a]you shall no longer envision
futility nor practice divination; for I will deliver My people out of your hand, and you
shall know that I *am* the LORD.”’”

Idolatry Will Be Punished

14 Now [a]some of the elders of Israel
came to me and sat before me. 2And
the word of the LORD came to me, saying,
3“Son of man, these men have set up their
idols in their hearts, and put before them
[a]that which causes them to stumble into
iniquity. [b]Should I let Myself be inquired
of at all by them?
4“Therefore speak to them, and say to
them, ‘Thus says the Lord GOD: “Everyone of the house of Israel who sets up his
idols in his heart, and puts before him what
causes him to stumble into iniquity, and
then comes to the prophet, I the LORD will
answer him who comes, according to the
multitude of his idols, 5that I may seize the
house of Israel by their heart, because they
are all estranged from Me by their idols.”’
6“Therefore say to the house of Israel,
‘Thus says the Lord GOD: “Repent, turn
away from your idols, and [a]turn your faces
away from all your abominations. 7For anyone of the house of Israel, or of the strangers who dwell in Israel, who separates
himself from Me and sets up his idols in
his heart and puts before him what causes
him to stumble into iniquity, then comes
to a prophet to inquire of him concerning

13:9 [d] Jer. 20:3–6 [e] Ezek. 11:10, 12 13:10 [a] Jer. 6:14; 8:11 [b] Ezek. 22:28 13:11 [a] Ezek. 38:22 13:14 [a] Ezek. 13:9, 21, 23; 14:8 13:16 [a] Jer. 6:14; 8:11; 28:9; Ezek. 13:10 13:17 [a] Ezek. 20:46; 21:2 [b] Ezek. 13:2; Rev. 2:20 13:18 [a] [2 Pet. 2:14] [1] Literally *over all the joints of My hands;* Vulgate reads *under every elbow;* Septuagint and Targum read *on all elbows of the hands.*
13:19 [a] 1 Sam. 2:15–17; Prov. 28:21; Mic. 3:5; Rom. 16:18; 1 Pet. 5:2 13:21 [a] Ezek. 13:9 13:22 [a] Jer. 28:15 [b] Jer. 23:14 13:23 [a] Ezek. 12:24; 13:6; Mic. 3:5, 6; Zech. 13:3 14:1 [a] 2 Kin. 6:32; Ezek. 8:1; 20:1; 33:31 14:3 [a] Ezek. 7:19; Zeph. 1:3 [b] 2 Kin. 3:13; Is. 1:15; Jer. 11:11; Ezek. 20:3, 31 14:6 [a] 1 Sam. 7:3; Neh. 1:9; Is. 2:20; 30:22; 55:6, 7; Ezek. 18:30

Me, I the LORD will answer him by Myself.
8 [a]I will set My face against that man and
make him a [b]sign and a proverb, and I will
cut him off from the midst of My people.
[c]Then you shall know that I *am* the LORD.
9 "And if the prophet is induced to speak
anything, I the LORD [a]have induced that
prophet, and I will stretch out My hand
against him and destroy him from among
My people Israel. 10 And they shall bear their
iniquity; the punishment of the prophet
shall be the same as the punishment of
the one who inquired, 11 that the house of
Israel may [a]no longer stray from Me, nor be
profaned anymore with all their transgressions, [b]but that they may be My people and
I may be their God," says the Lord GOD.'"

Judgment on Persistent Unfaithfulness

12 The word of the LORD came again to
me, saying: 13 "Son of man, when a land sins
against Me by persistent unfaithfulness, I
will stretch out My hand against it; I will
cut off its [a]supply of bread, send famine
on it, and cut off man and beast from it.
14 [a]Even *if* these three men, Noah, Daniel,
and Job, were in it, they would deliver *only*
themselves [b]by their righteousness," says
the Lord GOD.
15 "If I cause [a]wild beasts to pass through
the land, and they empty it, and make it so
desolate that no man may pass through
because of the beasts, 16 *even* [a]*though* these
three men *were* in it, *as* I live," says the Lord
GOD, "they would deliver neither sons nor
daughters; only they would be delivered,
and the land would be [b]desolate.
17 "Or *if* [a]I bring a sword on that land, and
say, 'Sword, go through the land,' and I [b]cut
off man and beast from it, 18 even [a]*though*
these three men *were* in it, *as* I live," says
the Lord GOD, "they would deliver neither
sons nor daughters, but only they themselves would be delivered.
19 "Or *if* I send [a]a pestilence into that
land and [b]pour out My fury on it in blood,
and cut off from it man and beast, 20 even
[a]*though* Noah, Daniel, and Job *were* in it, *as*
I live," says the Lord GOD, "they would deliver neither son nor daughter; they would
deliver *only* themselves by their righteousness."
21 For thus says the Lord GOD: "How
much more it shall be when [a]I send My
four severe judgments on Jerusalem—the
sword and famine and wild beasts and pestilence—to cut off man and beast from it?
22 [a]Yet behold, there shall be left in it a remnant who will be [b]brought out, *both* sons
and daughters; surely they will come out to
you, and [c]you will see their ways and their
doings. Then you will be comforted concerning the disaster that I have brought
upon Jerusalem, all that I have brought
upon it. 23 And they will comfort you, when
you see their ways and their doings; and
you shall know that I have done nothing
[a]without cause that I have done in it," says
the Lord GOD.

The Outcast Vine

15 Then the word of the LORD came
to me, saying: 2 "Son of man, how is
the wood of the vine *better* than any other
wood, the vine branch which is among the
trees of the forest? 3 Is wood taken from it
to make any object? Or can *men* make a peg
from it to hang any vessel on? 4 Instead,
[a]it is thrown into the fire for fuel; the fire
devours both ends of it, and its middle is
burned. Is it useful for *any* work? 5 Indeed,
when it was whole, no object could be made
from it. How much less will it be useful for
any work when the fire has devoured it,
and it is burned?
6 "Therefore thus says the Lord GOD:
'Like the wood of the vine among the trees
of the forest, which I have given to the fire
for fuel, so I will give up the inhabitants of
Jerusalem; 7 and [a]I will set My face against
them. [b]They will go out from *one* fire, but
another fire shall devour them. [c]Then you
shall know that I *am* the LORD, when I set
My face against them. 8 Thus I will make the
land desolate, because they have persisted
in unfaithfulness,' says the Lord GOD."

14:8 [a] Lev. 17:10; 20:3, 5, 6; Jer. 44:11; Ezek. 15:7 [b] Num. 26:10; Deut. 28:37; Ezek. 5:15 [c] Ezek. 6:7; 13:14 14:9 [a] 1 Kin. 22:23; Job 12:16; Is. 66:4; Jer. 4:10; 2 Thess. 2:11 14:11 [a] Ps. 119:67, 71; Jer. 31:18, 19; [Heb. 12:11]; 2 Pet. 2:15 [b] Ezek. 11:20; 37:27 14:13 [a] Lev. 26:26; 2 Kin. 25:3; Is. 3:1; Jer. 52:6; Ezek. 4:16; 5:16 14:14 [a] Jer. 15:1 [b] [Prov. 11:4] 14:15 [a] Lev. 26:22; Num. 21:6; Ezek. 5:17; 14:21 14:16 [a] Ezek. 14:14, 18, 20 [b] Ezek. 15:8; 33:28, 29 14:17 [a] Lev. 26:25; Ezek. 5:12; 21:3, 4; 29:8; 38:21 [b] Ezek. 25:13; Zeph. 1:3 14:18 [a] Ezek. 14:14 14:19 [a] 2 Sam. 24:15; Ezek. 38:22 [b] Ezek. 7:8 14:20 [a] Ezek. 14:14 14:21 [a] Ezek. 5:17; 33:27; Amos 4:6–10; Rev. 6:8 14:22 [a] 2 Kin. 25:11, 12; Ezra 2:1; Ezek. 12:16; 36:20 [b] Ezek. 6:8 [c] Ezek. 20:43 14:23 [a] Jer. 22:8, 9 15:4 [a] [John 15:6] 15:7 [a] Lev. 26:17; [Ps. 34:16]; Jer. 21:10; Ezek. 14:8 [b] Is. 24:18 [c] Ezek. 7:4

God's Love for Jerusalem

16 Again the word of the LORD came to me, saying, 2"Son of man, [a]cause Jerusalem to know her abominations, 3and say, 'Thus says the Lord GOD to Jerusalem: "Your birth [a]and your nativity *are* from the land of Canaan; [b]your father *was* an Amorite and your mother a Hittite. 4*As for* your nativity, [a]on the day you were born your navel cord was not cut, nor were you washed in water to cleanse *you;* you were not rubbed with salt nor wrapped in swaddling cloths. 5No eye pitied you, to do any of these things for you, to have compassion on you; but you were thrown out into the open field, when you yourself were loathed on the day you were born.

6"And when I passed by you and saw you struggling in your own blood, I said to you in your blood, 'Live!' Yes, I said to you in your blood, 'Live!' 7[a]I made you thrive like a plant in the field; and you grew, matured, and became very beautiful. *Your* breasts were formed, your hair grew, but you *were* naked and bare.

8"When I passed by you again and looked upon you, indeed your time *was* the time of love; [a]so I spread My wing over you and covered your nakedness. Yes, I [b]swore an oath to you and entered into a [c]covenant with you, and [d]you became Mine," says the Lord GOD.

9"Then I washed you in water; yes, I thoroughly washed off your blood, and I anointed you with oil. 10I clothed you in embroidered cloth and gave you sandals of badger skin; I clothed you with fine linen and covered you with silk. 11I adorned you with ornaments, [a]put bracelets on your wrists, [b]and a chain on your neck. 12And I put a jewel in your nose, earrings in your ears, and a beautiful crown on your head. 13Thus you were adorned with gold and silver, and your clothing *was of* fine linen, silk, and embroidered cloth. [a]You ate *pastry of* fine flour, honey, and oil. You were exceedingly [b]beautiful, and succeeded to royalty. 14[a]Your fame went out among the nations because of your beauty, for it *was* perfect through My splendor which I had bestowed on you," says the Lord GOD.

Jerusalem's Harlotry

15[a]"But you trusted in your own beauty, [b]played the harlot because of your fame, and poured out your harlotry on everyone passing by who *would have* it. 16[a]You took some of your garments and adorned multicolored high places for yourself, and played the harlot on them. *Such* things should not happen, nor be. 17You have also taken your beautiful jewelry from My gold and My silver, which I had given you, and made for yourself male images and played the harlot with them. 18You took your embroidered garments and covered them, and you set My oil and My incense before them. 19Also [a]My food which I gave you—the pastry of fine flour, oil, and honey *which* I fed you—you set it before them as sweet incense; and *so* it was," says the Lord GOD.

20[a]"Moreover you took your sons and your daughters, whom you bore to Me, and these you sacrificed to them to be devoured. *Were* your *acts* of harlotry a small matter, 21that you have slain My children and offered them up to them by causing them to pass through *the* [a]*fire?* 22And in all your abominations and acts of harlotry you did not remember the days of your [a]youth, [b]when you were naked and bare, struggling in your blood.

23"Then it was so, after all your wickedness—'Woe, woe to you!' says the Lord GOD— 24*that* [a]you also built for yourself a shrine, and [b]made a high place for yourself in every street. 25You built your high places [a]at the head of every road, and made your beauty to be abhorred. You offered yourself to everyone who passed by, and multiplied your acts of harlotry. 26You also committed harlotry with [a]the Egyptians, your very fleshly neighbors, and increased your acts of harlotry to [b]provoke Me to anger.

27"Behold, therefore, I stretched out My

16:2 [a] Is. 58:1; Ezek. 20:4; 22:2 **16:3** [a] Ezek. 21:30 [b] Gen. 15:16; Deut. 7:1; Josh. 24:15; Ezek. 16:45 **16:4** [a] Hos. 2:3 **16:7** [a] Ex. 1:7; Deut. 1:10 **16:8** [a] Ruth 3:9; Jer. 2:2 [b] Gen. 22:16–18 [c] Ex. 24:6–8 [d] [Ex. 19:5]; Jer. 2:2; Ezek. 20:5; [Hos. 2:19, 20] **16:11** [a] Gen. 24:22, 47; Is. 3:19; Ezek. 23:42 [b] Gen. 41:42; Prov. 1:9 **16:13** [a] Deut. 32:13, 14 [b] Ps. 48:2 **16:14** [a] Ps. 50:2; Lam. 2:15 **16:15** [a] Deut. 32:15; Jer. 7:4; Mic. 3:11 [b] Is. 1:21; 57:8; Jer. 2:20; 3:2, 6, 20; Ezek. 23:11–20; Hos. 1:2 **16:16** [a] 2 Kin. 23:7; Ezek. 7:20; Hos. 2:8 **16:19** [a] Hos. 2:8 **16:20** [a] 2 Kin. 16:3; Ps. 106:37; Is. 57:5; Jer. 7:31; Ezek. 20:26 **16:21** [a] 2 Kin. 17:17; Jer. 19:5; Ezek. 20:31; 23:37 **16:22** [a] Jer. 2:2; Hos. 11:1 [b] Ezek. 16:4–6 **16:24** [a] Jer. 11:13; Ezek. 16:31, 39; 20:28, 29 [b] Ps. 78:58; Is. 57:7; Jer. 2:20; 3:2 **16:25** [a] Prov. 9:14 **16:26** [a] Ezek. 16:26; 20:7, 8 [b] Deut. 31:20

hand against you, diminished your allotment, and gave you up to the will of those
who hate you, [a]the daughters of the Philistines, who were ashamed of your lewd behavior. 28You also played the harlot with
the [a]Assyrians, because you were insatia-
ble; indeed you played the harlot with them
and still were not satisfied. 29Moreover you
multiplied your acts of harlotry as far as
the land of the trader, [a]Chaldea; and even
then you were not satisfied.
30"How degenerate is your heart!" says
the LORD GOD, "seeing you do all these
things, the deeds of a brazen harlot.

Jerusalem's Adultery

31[a]"You erected your shrine at the head
of every road, and built your high place in
every street. Yet you were not like a harlot,
because you scorned [b]payment. 32*You are*
an adulterous wife, *who* takes strangers instead of her husband. 33Men make payment
to all harlots, but [a]you made your payments
to all your lovers, and hired them to come
to you from all around for your harlotry.
34You are the opposite of *other* women in
your harlotry, because no one solicited you
to be a harlot. In that you gave payment but
no payment was given you, therefore you
are the opposite."

Jerusalem's Lovers Will Abuse Her

35'Now then, O harlot, hear the word of
the LORD! 36Thus says the Lord GOD: "Because your filthiness was poured out and
your nakedness uncovered in your harlotry
with your lovers, and with all your abominable idols, and because of [a]the blood of
your children which you gave to them,
37surely, therefore, [a]I will gather all your
lovers with whom you took pleasure, all
those you loved, *and* all those you hated; I
will gather them from all around against
you and will uncover your nakedness to
them, that they may see all your nakedness. 38And I will judge you as [a]women who
break wedlock or [b]shed blood are judged; I
will bring blood upon you in fury and jealousy. 39I will also give you into their hand,
and they shall throw down your shrines
and break down [a]your high places. [b]They
shall also strip you of your clothes, take
your beautiful jewelry, and leave you naked and bare.
40[a]"They shall also bring up an assembly
against you, [b]and they shall stone you with
stones and thrust you through with their
swords. 41They shall [a]burn your houses with
fire, and [b]execute judgments on you in the
sight of many women; and I will make you
[c]cease playing the harlot, and you shall no
longer hire lovers. 42So [a]I will lay to rest My
fury toward you, and My jealousy shall depart from you. I will be quiet, and be angry
no more. 43Because [a]you did not remember the days of your youth, but agitated Me[1]
with all these *things,* surely [b]I will also recompense your deeds on *your own* head,"
says the Lord GOD. "And you shall not commit lewdness in addition to all your abominations.

More Wicked than Samaria and Sodom

44"Indeed everyone who quotes proverbs will use *this* proverb against you: 'Like
mother, like daughter!' 45You *are* your
mother's daughter, loathing husband and
children; and you *are* the [a]sister of your
sisters, who loathed their husbands and
children; [b]your mother *was* a Hittite and
your father an Amorite.
46"Your elder sister *is* Samaria, who
dwells with her daughters to the north of
you; and [a]your younger sister, who dwells to
the south of you, *is* Sodom and her daughters. 47You did not walk in their ways nor
act according to their abominations; but,
as *if that were* too little, [a]you became more
corrupt than they in all your ways.
48"As I live," says the Lord GOD, "neither
[a]your sister Sodom nor her daughters have
done as you and your daughters have done.
49Look, this was the iniquity of your sister
Sodom: She and her daughter had pride,

16:27 [a] 2 Chr. 28:18; Is. 9:12; Ezek. 16:57 **16:28** [a] 2 Kin. 16:7, 10–18; 2 Chr. 28:16, 20–23; Jer. 2:18, 36; Ezek. 23:12; Hos. 10:6 **16:29** [a] Ezek. 23:14–17 **16:31** [a] Ezek. 16:24, 39 [b] Is. 52:3 **16:33** [a] Is. 30:6; 57:9; Ezek. 16:41; Hos. 8:9, 10 **16:36** [a] Jer. 2:34; Ezek. 16:20 **16:37** [a] Jer. 13:22, 26; Lam. 1:8; Ezek. 23:9, 10, 22, 29; Hos. 2:10; 8:10; Nah. 3:5 **16:38** [a] Lev. 20:10; Deut. 22:22; Ezek. 23:45 [b] Gen. 9:6; Ex. 21:12; Ezek. 16:20, 36 **16:39** [a] Ezek. 16:24, 31 [b] Ezek. 23:26; Hos. 2:3 **16:40** [a] Ezek. 23:45–47; Hab. 1:6–10 [b] John 8:5, 7 **16:41** [a] Deut. 13:16; 2 Kin. 25:9; Jer. 39:8; 52:13 [b] Ezek. 5:8; 23:10, 48 [c] Ezek. 23:27 **16:42** [a] 2 Sam. 24:25; Ezek. 5:13; 21:17; Zech. 6:8 **16:43** [a] Ps. 78:42; Ezek. 16:22 [b] Ezek. 9:10; 11:21; 22:31 [1] Following Septuagint, Syriac, Targum, and Vulgate; Masoretic Text reads *were agitated with Me.* **16:45** [a] Ezek. 23:2–4 [b] Ezek. 16:3 **16:46** [a] Deut. 32:32; Is. 1:10 **16:47** [a] 2 Kin. 21:9; Ezek. 5:6, 7 **16:48** [a] Is. 3:9; Lam. 4:6; Matt. 10:15; 11:24; Rev. 11:8

RELEASE // HOPE FOR THE SALVATION OF THE LOST

Salvation Is Our Hope

Ezekiel 16:49 //"Look, this was the iniquity of your sister Sodom: She and her daughter had pride, fullness of food, and abundance of idleness; neither did she strengthen the hand of the poor and needy."

Summary Message //Ezekiel, whose name means "God will strengthen," was tasked with delivering a series of hard messages to a rebellious people. Jerusalem had descended to a new level of ungodliness. Ezekiel measured the wickedness of Jerusalem against the state of Sodom and claimed Jerusalem had sunk to even deeper levels of evil. He then referred to Jerusalem as sister to Sodom and Samaria. All of them had exhibited reprehensible levels of rebellion against God, as if it were a family trait.

As Ezekiel delivered stern messages to a people ensnared by unrighteousness, false prophets were telling the people what they wanted to hear. Yet the prophet remained steadfast in addressing prideful, greedy, gluttonous, lazy people who had no concern for the less fortunate. Despite his pronouncements upon their wretched condition, Ezekiel's message ended with a note of hope for their salvation. God would establish an unbreakable covenant with them and supply a way of atonement for their sin. He offered hope for their salvation, even as they were unfaithful to God.

Practical Application //Before the Global Positioning System (GPS) was invented, figuring out how to navigate a route that would lead to your destination required relying on maps, kind strangers, and even old-fashioned instinct. Getting lost could get really complicated.

It is the same when it comes to salvation. When we live safely under the protection of God's GPS (Grace Positioning System), we may look back with horror at how we lived during the days when we tried navigating our own way. But as we enjoy the sure and certain direction of God's GPS, many people remain lost, hopelessly wandering through life. These people are spiritually lost, mired in the jungle of wickedness, or moving speedily along the superhighway of greed that leads to destruction. They are seeking a better way to live with peace and purpose but have no guidance to reach this destination.

The Book of Ezekiel starts with a message of God's judgment and then takes us on a journey from condemnation to redemption. It gives us a road map and a message of hope for us who had no hope. It shows us that dry bones can live because God can fill us with breath, and we will come to life. No matter what we have done or how deep we are in sin, every one of us can be fully restored because God's grace is available to anyone who desires to receive it.

Fervent Prayer //Abba, continue to show us that we do not have to live as lost people. You have given Your Son as humanity's hope for salvation. Thank You that no matter how wretched our condition, You are willing to receive us and restore us when we come to You in repentance. Draw us ever closer to You. In Jesus' name we pray. Amen.

---

[a]fullness of food, and abundance of idleness; neither did she strengthen the hand
of the poor and needy. 50And they were
haughty and [a]committed abomination before Me; therefore [b]I took them away as I
saw *fit*.[1]
51"Samaria did not commit [a]half of your
sins; but you have multiplied your abominations more than they, and [b]have justified your sisters by all the abominations
which you have done. 52You who judged
your sisters, bear your own shame also,
because the sins which you committed
were more abominable than theirs; they
are more righteous than you. Yes, be disgraced also, and bear your own shame, because you justified your sisters.
53[a]"When I bring back their captives, the
captives of Sodom and her daughters, and
the captives of Samaria and her daughters,

16:49 [a] Gen. 13:10; Is. 22:13; Amos 6:4–6 16:50 [a] Gen. 13:13; 18:20; 19:5 [b] Gen. 19:24 [1] Vulgate reads *you saw;* Septuagint reads *he saw;* Targum reads *as was revealed to Me.* 16:51 [a] Ezek. 23:11 [b] Jer. 3:8–11; Matt. 12:41 16:53 [a] Is. 1:9; [Ezek. 16:60]

then *I will also bring back* [b]the captives of
your captivity among them, 54that you may
bear your own shame and be disgraced by
all that you did when [a]you comforted them.
55When your sisters, Sodom and her daughters, return to their former state, and Samaria and her daughters return to their
former state, then you and your daughters will return to your former state. 56For
your sister Sodom was not a byword in your
mouth in the days of your pride, 57before
your wickedness was uncovered. It was like
the time of the [a]reproach of the daughters
of Syria[1] and all *those* around her, and of
[b]the daughters of the Philistines, who despise you everywhere. 58[a]You have paid
for your lewdness and your abominations," says the LORD. 59For thus says the
Lord GOD: "I will deal with you as you have
done, who [a]despised [b]the oath by breaking
the covenant.

An Everlasting Covenant

60"Nevertheless I will [a]remember My
covenant with you in the days of your
youth, and I will establish [b]an everlasting
covenant with you. 61Then [a]you will remember your ways and be ashamed, when you
receive your older and your younger sisters; for I will give them to you for [b]daugh-
ters, [c]but not because of My covenant with
you. 62[a]And I will establish My covenant
with you. Then you shall know that I *am*
the LORD, 63that you may [a]remember and
be ashamed, [b]and never open your mouth
anymore because of your shame, when I
provide you an atonement for all you have
done," says the Lord GOD.' "

The Eagles and the Vine

17 And the word of the LORD came to
me, saying, 2"Son of man, pose a riddle, and speak a [a]parable to the house of
Israel, 3and say, 'Thus says the Lord GOD:

[a]"A great eagle with large wings
and long pinions,
Full of feathers of various colors,
Came to Lebanon
And [b]took from the cedar
the highest branch.
4 He cropped off its topmost
young twig
And carried it to a land of trade;
He set it in a city of merchants.
5 Then he took some of the
seed of the land
And planted it in [a]a fertile field;
He placed *it* by abundant waters
And set it [b]like a willow tree.
6 And it grew and became a
spreading vine [a]of low stature;
Its branches turned toward him,
But its roots were under it.
So it became a vine,
Brought forth branches,
And put forth shoots.

7 "But there was another[1] great
eagle with large wings
and many feathers;
And behold, [a]this vine bent
its roots toward him,
And stretched its branches
toward him,
From the garden terrace where
it had been planted,
That he might water it.
8 It was planted in good soil
by many waters,
To bring forth branches, bear fruit,
And become a majestic vine." '

9"Say, 'Thus says the Lord GOD:

"Will it thrive?
[a]Will he not pull up its roots,
Cut off its fruit,
And leave it to wither?
All of its spring leaves will wither,
And no great power or many
people
Will be needed to pluck
it up by its roots.
10 Behold, *it is* planted,
Will it thrive?

16:53 [b] Jer. 20:16 16:54 [a] Ezek. 14:22 16:57 [a] 2 Kin. 16:5; 2 Chr. 28:18; Is. 7:1; Ezek. 5:14, 15; 22:4 [b] Ezek. 16:27 [1] Following Masoretic Text, Septuagint, Targum, and Vulgate; many Hebrew manuscripts and Syriac read *Edom*. 16:58 [a] Ezek. 23:49 16:59 [a] Ezek. 17:13 [b] Deut. 29:12 16:60 [a] Lev. 26:42–45; Ps. 106:45 [b] Is. 55:3; Jer. 32:40; 50:5; Ezek. 37:26 16:61 [a] Jer. 50:4, 5; Ezek. 20:43; 36:31 [b] Is. 54:1; 60:4; [Gal. 4:26] [c] Jer. 31:31 16:62 [a] Hos. 2:19, 20 16:63 [a] Ezek. 36:31, 32; Dan. 9:7, 8 [b] Ps. 39:9; [Rom. 3:19] 17:2 [a] Ezek. 20:49; 24:3 17:3 [a] Jer. 48:40; Ezek. 17:12; Hos. 8:1 [b] 2 Kin. 24:12 17:5 [a] Deut. 8:7–9 [b] Is. 44:4 17:6 [a] Ezek. 17:14 17:7 [a] Ezek. 17:15 [1] Following Septuagint, Syriac, and Vulgate; Masoretic Text and Targum read *one*. 17:9 [a] 2 Kin. 25:7

[a]Will it not utterly wither when
the east wind touches it?
It will wither in the garden
terrace where it grew."'"

11Moreover the word of the LORD came
to me, saying, 12"Say now to [a]the rebellious
house: 'Do you not know what these *things*
mean?' Tell *them,* 'Indeed [b]the king of Babylon went to Jerusalem and took its king
and princes, and led them with him to Babylon. 13[a]And he took the king's offspring,
made a covenant with him, [b]and put him
under oath. He also took away the mighty
of the land, 14that the kingdom might be
[a]brought low and not lift itself up, *but* that
by keeping his covenant it might stand.
15But [a]he rebelled against him by sending
his ambassadors to Egypt, [b]that they might
give him horses and many people. [c]Will
he prosper? Will he who does such *things*
escape? Can he break a covenant and still
be delivered?

16'*As* I live,' says the Lord GOD, 'surely
[a]in the place *where* the king *dwells* who
made him king, whose oath he despised
and whose covenant he broke—with him in
the midst of Babylon he shall die. 17[a]Nor will
Pharaoh with *his* mighty army and great
company do anything in the war, [b]when
they heap up a siege mound and build a
wall to cut off many persons. 18Since he despised the oath by breaking the covenant,
and in fact [a]gave his hand and still did all
these *things,* he shall not escape.'"

19Therefore thus says the Lord GOD: "*As* I
live, surely My oath which he despised, and
My covenant which he broke, I will recompense on his own head. 20I will [a]spread My
net over him, and he shall be taken in My
snare. I will bring him to Babylon and [b]try
him there for the treason which he committed against Me. 21[a]All his fugitives[1] with
all his troops shall fall by the sword, and
those who remain shall be [b]scattered to
every wind; and you shall know that I, the
LORD, have spoken."

Israel Exalted at Last
(cf. Ezek. 31:1–9)

22Thus says the Lord GOD: "I will take
also *one* of the highest [a]branches of the
high cedar and set *it* out. I will crop off from
the topmost of its young twigs [b]a tender
one, and will [c]plant *it* on a high and prominent mountain. 23[a]On the mountain height
of Israel I will plant it; and it will bring forth
boughs, and bear fruit, and be a majestic
cedar. [b]Under it will dwell birds of every
sort; in the shadow of its branches they
will dwell. 24And all the trees of the field
shall know that I, the LORD, [a]have brought
down the high tree and exalted the low tree,
dried up the green tree and made the dry
tree flourish; [b]I, the LORD, have spoken and
have done *it.*"

A False Proverb Refuted

18 The word of the LORD came to me
again, saying, 2"What do you mean
when you use this proverb concerning the
land of Israel, saying:

'The [a]fathers have eaten sour grapes,
And the children's teeth
are set on edge'?

3"*As* I live," says the Lord GOD, "you shall
no longer use this proverb in Israel.

4 "Behold, all souls are [a]Mine;
The soul of the father
As well as the soul of the son is Mine;
[b]The soul who sins shall die.
5 But if a man is just
And does what is lawful and right;
6 [a]If he has not eaten on the mountains,
Nor lifted up his eyes to the idols
of the house of Israel,
Nor [b]defiled his neighbor's wife,
Nor approached [c]a woman
during her impurity;
7 If he has not [a]oppressed anyone,
But has restored to the
debtor his [b]pledge;

17:10 [a] Ezek. 19:12; Hos. 13:15 17:12 [a] Ezek. 2:3–5; 12:9 [b] 2 Kin. 24:11–16; Ezek. 1:2; 17:3 17:13 [a] 2 Kin. 24:17; Jer. 37:1; Ezek. 17:5 [b] 2 Chr. 36:13 17:14 [a] Ezek. 29:14 17:15 [a] 2 Kin. 24:20; 2 Chr. 36:13; Jer. 52:3; Ezek. 17:7 [b] Deut. 17:16; Is. 31:1, 3; 36:6, 9 [c] Ezek. 17:9 17:16 [a] Jer. 52:11; Ezek. 12:13 17:17 [a] Jer. 37:7; Ezek. 29:6 [b] Jer. 52:4; Ezek. 4:2 17:18 [a] 1 Chr. 29:24; Lam. 5:6 17:20 [a] Ezek. 12:13 [b] Jer. 2:35; Ezek. 20:36 17:21 [a] Ezek. 12:14 [b] Ezek. 12:15; 22:15 [1] Following Masoretic Text and Vulgate; many Hebrew manuscripts and Syriac read *choice men;* Targum reads *mighty men;* Septuagint omits *All his fugitives.* 17:22 [a] [Is. 11:1; Jer. 23:5; Zech. 3:8] [b] Is. 53:2 [c] [Ps. 2:6] 17:23 [a] [Is. 2:2, 3]; Ezek. 20:40; [Mic. 4:1] [b] Ezek. 31:6; Dan. 4:12 17:24 [a] Ezek. 37:3; Amos 9:11; Luke 1:52; [Rom. 11:23, 24] [b] Ezek. 22:14 18:2 [a] Jer. 31:29; Lam. 5:7 18:4 [a] Num. 16:22; 27:16; Is. 42:5; 57:16 [b] Ezek. 18:20; [Rom. 6:23] 18:6 [a] Ezek. 22:9 [b] Lev. 18:20; 20:10 [c] Lev. 18:19; 20:18 18:7 [a] Ex. 22:21; Lev. 19:15; 25:14 [b] Ex. 22:26; Deut. 24:12

Has robbed no one by violence,
But has [c]given his bread to the hungry
And covered the naked with [d]clothing;
8 If he has not exacted [a]usury
Nor taken any increase,
But has withdrawn his
hand from iniquity
And [b]executed true judgment
between man and man;
9 *If* he has walked in My statutes
And kept My judgments faithfully—
He *is* just;
He shall surely [a]live!"
Says the Lord GOD.

10 "If he begets a son *who is* a robber
Or [a]a shedder of blood,
Who does any of these *things*
11 And does none of those *duties,*
But has eaten on the mountains
Or defiled his neighbor's wife;
12 If he has oppressed the
poor and needy,
Robbed by violence,
Not restored the pledge,
Lifted his eyes to the idols,
Or [a]committed abomination;
13 If he has exacted usury
Or taken increase—
Shall he then live?
He shall not live!
If he has done any of these
abominations,
He shall surely die;
[a]His blood shall be upon him.

14 "*If,* however, he begets a son
Who sees all the sins which
his father has done,
And considers but does
not do likewise;
15 [a]*Who* has not eaten on the mountains,
Nor lifted his eyes to the idols
of the house of Israel,
Nor defiled his neighbor's wife;
16 Has not oppressed anyone,
Nor withheld a pledge,
Nor robbed by violence,
But has given his bread to the hungry
And covered the naked with clothing;
17 *Who* has withdrawn his
hand from the poor[1]
And not received usury or increase,
But has executed My judgments
And walked in My statutes—
He shall not die for the
iniquity of his father;
He shall surely live!

18 "*As for* his father,
Because he cruelly oppressed,
Robbed his brother by violence,
And did what *is* not good
among his people,
Behold, [a]he shall die for his iniquity.

Turn and Live

19"Yet you say, 'Why [a]should the son not
bear the guilt of the father?' Because the
son has done what is lawful and right, and
has kept all My statutes and observed them,
he shall surely live. 20[a]The soul who sins
shall die. [b]The son shall not bear the guilt
of the father, nor the father bear the guilt
of the son. [c]The righteousness of the righteous shall be upon himself, [d]and the wickedness of the wicked shall be upon himself.
21"But [a]if a wicked man turns from all
his sins which he has committed, keeps all
My statutes, and does what is lawful and
right, he shall surely live; he shall not die.
22[a]None of the transgressions which he has
committed shall be remembered against
him; because of the righteousness which
he has done, he shall [b]live. 23[a]Do I have any
pleasure at all that the wicked should die?"
says the Lord GOD, "*and* not that he should
turn from his ways and live?
24"But [a]when a righteous man turns
away from his righteousness and commits iniquity, and does according to all the
abominations that the wicked *man* does,
shall he live? [b]All the righteousness which
he has done shall not be remembered;

18:7 [c] Deut. 15:7, 11; Ezek. 18:16; [Matt. 25:35–40]; Luke 3:11 [d] Is. 58:7 18:8 [a] Ex. 22:25; Lev. 25:36; Deut. 23:19; Neh. 5:7; Ps. 15:5 [b] Deut. 1:16; Zech. 8:16 18:9 [a] Ezek. 20:11; Amos 5:4; [Hab. 2:4; Rom. 1:17] 18:10 [a] Gen. 9:6; Ex. 21:12; Num. 35:31 18:12 [a] 2 Kin. 21:11; Ezek. 8:6, 17 18:13 [a] Lev. 20:9, 11–13, 16, 27; Ezek. 3:18; Acts 18:6 18:15 [a] Ezek. 18:6 18:17 [1] Following Masoretic Text, Targum, and Vulgate; Septuagint reads *iniquity* (compare verse 8). 18:18 [a] Ezek. 3:18 18:19 [a] Ex. 20:5; Deut. 5:9; 2 Kin. 23:26; 24:3, 4 18:20 [a] 2 Kin. 14:6; 22:18–20; Ezek. 18:4 [b] Deut. 24:16; 2 Kin. 14:6; 2 Chr. 25:4; Jer. 31:29, 30 [c] 1 Kin. 8:32; Is. 3:10, 11; [Matt. 16:27] [d] Rom. 2:6–9 18:21 [a] Ezek. 18:27; 33:12, 19 18:22 [a] Is. 43:25; Jer. 50:20; Ezek. 18:24; 33:16; Mic. 7:19 [b] [Ps. 18:20–24] 18:23 [a] Lam. 3:33; [Ezek. 18:32; 33:11; 1 Tim. 2:4; 2 Pet. 3:9] 18:24 [a] 1 Sam. 15:11; 2 Chr. 24:2, 17–22; Ezek. 3:20; 18:26; 33:18 [b] [2 Pet. 2:20]

because of the unfaithfulness of which he
is guilty and the sin which he has committed, because of them he shall die.
25"Yet you say, [a]'The way of the Lord is
not fair.' Hear now, O house of Israel, is it
not My way which is fair, and your ways
which are not fair? 26[a]When a righteous
man turns away from his righteousness,
commits iniquity, and dies in it, it is because of the iniquity which he has done
that he dies. 27Again, [a]when a wicked *man*
turns away from the wickedness which he
committed, and does what is lawful and
right, he preserves himself alive. 28Because
he [a]considers and turns away from all the
transgressions which he committed, he
shall surely live; he shall not die. 29[a]Yet the
house of Israel says, 'The way of the Lord
is not fair.' O house of Israel, is it not My
ways which are fair, and your ways which
are not fair?
30[a]"Therefore I will judge you, O house
of Israel, every one according to his ways,"
says the Lord GOD. [b]"Repent, and turn from
all your transgressions, so that iniquity will
not be your ruin. 31[a]Cast away from you all
the transgressions which you have committed, and get yourselves a [b]new heart and a
new spirit. For why should you die, O house
of Israel? 32For [a]I have no pleasure in the
death of one who dies," says the Lord GOD.
"Therefore turn and [b]live!"

Israel Degraded

19 "Moreover [a]take up a lamentation
for the princes of Israel, 2and say:

'What *is* your mother? A lioness:
She lay down among the lions;
Among the young lions she
nourished her cubs.
3 She brought up one of her
cubs,
And [a]he became a young lion;
He learned to catch prey,
And he devoured men.
4 The nations also heard of him;
He was trapped in their pit,

#OXYGEN

EZEKIEL 18:31–32

Hope for the Salvation of the Lost

God's unconditional love for the entire world challenges us as believers to have renewed hearts and spirits and to model His love. This unconditional love in action will create social justice and authentic community.

Love everyone, **breathe**, and
**hope for the salvation
of the lost.**

And they brought him with
chains to the land of [a]Egypt.

5 'When she saw that she waited,
that her hope was lost,
She took [a]another of her cubs
and made him a young lion.
6 [a]He roved among the lions,
And [b]became a young lion;
He learned to catch prey;
He devoured men.
7 He knew their desolate places,[1]
And laid waste their cities;
The land with its fullness
was desolated
By the noise of his roaring.
8 [a]Then the nations set against him
from the provinces on every side,
And spread their net over him;
[b]He was trapped in their pit.
9 [a]They put him in a cage with chains,
And brought him to the
king of Babylon;
They brought him in nets,
That his voice should no longer be
heard on [b]the mountains of Israel.

10 'Your mother *was* [a]like a vine
in your bloodline,[1]
Planted by the waters,

18:25 [a] Ezek. 18:29; 33:17, 20; Mal. 2:17; 3:13–15 18:26 [a] Ezek. 18:24 18:27 [a] Ezek. 18:21 18:28 [a] Ezek. 18:14 18:29 [a] Ezek. 18:25
18:30 [a] Ezek. 7:3; 33:20 [b] Matt. 3:2; Rev. 2:5 18:31 [a] Is. 1:16; 55:7; Eph. 4:22, 23 [b] Ps. 51:10; Jer. 32:39; Ezek. 11:19; 36:26
18:32 [a] Lam. 3:33; Ezek. 33:11; [2 Pet. 3:9] [b] [Prov. 4:2, 5, 6] 19:1 [a] Ezek. 26:17; 27:2 19:3 [a] Ezek. 19:2; 2 Kin. 23:31, 32
19:4 [a] 2 Kin. 23:33, 34; 2 Chr. 36:4 19:5 [a] 2 Kin. 23:34 19:6 [a] 2 Kin. 24:8, 9 [b] Ezek. 19:3 19:7 [1] Septuagint reads *He stood in insolence;* Targum reads *He destroyed its palaces;* Vulgate reads *He learned to make widows.* 19:8 [a] 2 Kin. 24:2, 11 [b] Ezek. 19:4
19:9 [a] 2 Chr. 36:6; Jer. 22:18 [b] Ezek. 6:2 19:10 [a] Ezek. 17:6 [1] Literally *blood,* following Masoretic Text, Syriac, and Vulgate; Septuagint reads *like a flower on a pomegranate tree;* Targum reads *in your likeness.*

[b]Fruitful and full of branches
Because of many waters.
11 She had strong branches for
scepters of rulers.
[a]She towered in stature above
the thick branches,
And was seen in her height
amid the dense foliage.
12 But she was [a]plucked up in fury,
She was cast down to the ground,
And the [b]east wind dried her
fruit.
Her strong branches were
broken and withered;
The fire consumed them.
13 And now she *is* planted in
the wilderness,
In a dry and thirsty land.
14 [a]Fire has come out from a
rod of her branches
And devoured her fruit,
So that she has no strong branch—
a scepter for ruling.'"

[b]This *is* a lamentation, and has become
a lamentation.

The Rebellions of Israel

20 It came to pass in the seventh year,
in the fifth *month,* on the tenth *day*
of the month, *that* [a]certain of the elders of
Israel came to inquire of the LORD, and
sat before me. 2Then the word of the LORD
came to me, saying, 3"Son of man, speak
to the elders of Israel, and say to them,
'Thus says the Lord GOD: "Have you come
to inquire of Me? *As* I live," says the Lord
GOD, [a]"I will not be inquired of by you." '
4Will you judge them, son of man, will you
judge *them?* Then [a]make known to them the
abominations of their fathers.
5"Say to them, 'Thus says the Lord
GOD: "On the day when [a]I chose Israel and
raised My hand in an oath to the descendants of the house of Jacob, and made Myself [b]known to them in the land of Egypt, I
raised My hand in an oath to them, saying,
[c]'I *am* the LORD your God.' 6On that day I
raised My hand in an oath to them, [a]to bring
them out of the land of Egypt into a land
that I had searched out for them, [b]'flowing
with milk and honey,'[1] [c]the glory of all lands.
7Then I said to them, 'Each of you, [a]throw
away [b]the abominations which are before
his eyes, and do not defile yourselves with
[c]the idols of Egypt. I *am* the LORD your
God.' 8But they rebelled against Me and
would not obey Me. They did not all cast
away the abominations which were before
their eyes, nor did they forsake the idols of
Egypt. Then I said, 'I will [a]pour out My fury
on them and fulfill My anger against them
in the midst of the land of Egypt.' 9[a]But I
acted for My name's sake, that it should
not be profaned before the Gentiles among
whom they *were,* in whose sight I had made
Myself [b]known to them, to bring them out
of the land of Egypt.
10"Therefore I [a]made them go out of the
land of Egypt and brought them into the
wilderness. 11[a]And I gave them My statutes
and showed them My judgments, [b]'which, *if*
a man does, he shall live by them.'[1] 12More-
over I also gave them My [a]Sabbaths, to be
a sign between them and Me, that they
might know that I *am* the LORD who sanctifies them. 13Yet the house of Israel [a]re-
belled against Me in the wilderness; they
did not walk in My statutes; they [b]despised
My judgments, [c]'which, *if* a man does, he
shall live by them';[1] and they greatly [d]de-
filed My Sabbaths. Then I said I would pour
out My fury on them in the [e]wilderness, to
consume them. 14[a]But I acted for My name's
sake, that it should not be profaned before
the Gentiles, in whose sight I had brought
them out. 15So [a]I also raised My hand in
an oath to them in the wilderness, that I
would not bring them into the land which
I had given *them,* [b]'flowing with milk and
honey,'[1] [c]the glory of all lands, 16[a]because
they despised My judgments and did not
walk in My statutes, but profaned My Sabbaths; for [b]their heart went after their idols.

19:10 [b] Deut. 8:7–9 **19:11** [a] Ezek. 31:3; Dan. 4:11 **19:12** [a] Jer. 31:27, 28 [b] Ezek. 17:10; Hos. 13:5 **19:14** [a] Judg. 9:15; 2 Kin. 24:20; Ezek. 17:18 [b] Lam. 2:5 **20:1** [a] Ezek. 8:1, 11, 12; 14:1 **20:3** [a] Ezek. 7:26; 14:3 **20:4** [a] Ezek. 16:2; 22:2; Matt. 23:32 **20:5** [a] Ex. 6:6–8; Deut. 7:6 [b] Ex. 3:8; 4:31; Deut. 4:34 [c] Ex. 20:2 **20:6** [a] Ex. 3:8, 17; Deut. 8:7–9; Jer. 32:22 [b] Ex. 3:8 [c] Ex. 3:8, 17; 13:5; 33:3; Ps. 48:2; Jer. 11:5; 32:22; Ezek. 20:15; Dan. 8:9; Zech. 7:14 [1] Exodus 3:8 **20:7** [a] Ezek. 18:31 [b] 2 Chr. 15:8 [c] Lev. 18:3; Deut. 29:16; Josh. 24:14 **20:8** [a] Ezek. 7:8 **20:9** [a] Num. 14:13 [b] Josh. 2:10; 9:9, 10 **20:10** [a] Ex. 13:18 **20:11** [a] Deut. 4:8; Neh. 9:13; Ps. 147:19 [b] Lev. 18:5; Ezek. 20:13; Rom. 10:5; [Gal. 3:12] [1] Leviticus 18:5 **20:12** [a] Ex. 20:8; Deut. 5:12; Neh. 9:14 **20:13** [a] Num. 14:22; Ps. 78:40; Ezek. 20:8 [b] Prov. 1:25 [c] Lev. 18:5 [d] Ex. 16:27 [e] Num. 14:29; Ps. 106:23 [1] Leviticus 18:5 **20:14** [a] Ezek. 20:9, 20 **20:15** [a] Num. 14:28; Ps. 95:11; 106:26 [b] Ex. 3:8 [c] Ezek. 20:6 [1] Exodus 3:8 **20:16** [a] Ezek. 20:13, 24 [b] Num. 15:39; Ps. 78:37; Amos 5:25; Acts 7:42

17[a]Nevertheless My eye spared them from
destruction. I did not make an end of them
in the wilderness.

18"But I said to their children in the wilderness, 'Do not walk in the statutes of your
fathers, nor observe their judgments, nor
defile yourselves with their idols. 19I *am* the
LORD your God: [a]Walk in My statutes, keep
My judgments, and do them; 20[a]hallow My
Sabbaths, and they will be a sign between
Me and you, that you may know that I *am*
the LORD your God.'

21"Notwithstanding, [a]the children rebelled against Me; they did not walk in My
statutes, and were not careful to observe
My judgments, [b]'which, *if* a man does, he
shall live by them';[1] but they profaned My
Sabbaths. Then I said I would pour out My
fury on them and fulfill My anger against
them in the wilderness. 22Nevertheless I
withdrew My hand and acted for My name's
sake, that it should not be profaned in the
sight of the Gentiles, in whose sight I had
brought them out. 23Also I raised My hand
in an oath to those in the wilderness, that
[a]I would scatter them among the Gentiles
and disperse them throughout the countries, 24[a]because they had not executed My
judgments, but had despised My statutes,
profaned My Sabbaths, and [b]their eyes were
fixed on their fathers' idols.

25"Therefore [a]I also gave them up to statutes *that were* not good, and judgments
by which they could not live; 26and I pronounced them unclean because of their
ritual gifts, in that they caused all their
firstborn to pass [a]through *the fire,* that I
might make them desolate and that they
[b]might know that I am the LORD."'

27"Therefore, son of man, speak to the
house of Israel, and say to them, 'Thus says
the Lord GOD: "In this too your fathers have
[a]blasphemed Me, by being unfaithful to
Me. 28When I brought them into the land
concerning which I had raised My hand
in an oath to give them, and [a]they saw all
the high hills and all the thick trees, there
they offered their sacrifices and provoked
Me with their offerings. There they also
sent up their [b]sweet aroma and poured
out their drink offerings. 29Then I said
to them, 'What *is* this high place to which
you go?' So its name is called Bamah[1] to
this day."' 30Therefore say to the house of
Israel, 'Thus says the Lord GOD: "Are you
defiling yourselves in the manner of your
[a]fathers, and committing harlotry according to their [b]abominations? 31For when you
offer [a]your gifts and make your sons pass
through the fire, you defile yourselves with
all your idols, even to this day. So shall I
be inquired of by you, O house of Israel?
As I live," says the Lord GOD, "I will [b]not
be inquired of by you. 32[a]What you have in
your mind shall never be, when you say, 'We
will be like the Gentiles, like the families in
other countries, serving wood and stone.'

God Will Restore Israel

33"*As* I live," says the Lord GOD, "surely
with a mighty hand, [a]with an outstretched
arm, and with fury poured out, I will rule
over you. 34I will bring you out from the
peoples and gather you out of the countries where you are scattered, with a mighty
hand, with an outstretched arm, and with
fury poured out. 35And I will bring you into
the wilderness of the peoples, and there [a]I
will plead My case with you face to face.
36[a]Just as I pleaded My case with your fathers in the wilderness of the land of Egypt,
so I will plead My case with you," says the
Lord GOD.

37"I will make you [a]pass under the rod,
and I will bring you into the bond of the
[b]covenant; 38[a]I will purge the rebels from
among you, and those who transgress
against Me; I will bring them out of the
country where they dwell, but [b]they shall
not enter the land of Israel. Then you will
know that I *am* the LORD.

39"As for you, O house of Israel," thus
says the Lord GOD: [a]"Go, serve every one
of you his idols—and hereafter—if you will
not obey Me; [b]but profane My holy name
no more with your gifts and your idols.

20:17 [a] [Ps. 78:38] **20:19** [a] Deut. 5:32 **20:20** [a] Is. 58:13, 14; Jer. 17:22 **20:21** [a] Num. 25:1; Deut. 9:23 [b] Lev. 18:5 [1] Leviticus 18:5 **20:23** [a] Lev. 26:33; Deut. 28:64; Ps. 106:27; Jer. 15:4 **20:24** [a] Ezek. 20:13, 16 [b] Ezek. 6:9 **20:25** [a] Ps. 81:12; Rom. 1:24; 2 Thess. 2:11 **20:26** [a] 2 Kin. 17:17; 2 Chr. 28:3; Jer. 32:35; Ezek. 16:20 [b] Ezek. 6:7; 20:12, 20 **20:27** [a] Num. 15:30; Is. 65:7; Rom. 2:24 **20:28** [a] 1 Kin. 14:23; Ps. 78:58; Is. 57:5–7; Jer. 3:6; Ezek. 6:13 [b] Ezek. 16:19 **20:29** [1] Literally *High Place* **20:30** [a] Judg. 2:19 [b] Jer. 7:26; 16:12 **20:31** [a] Ps. 106:37–39; Jer. 7:31; Ezek. 16:20; 20:26 [b] Ezek. 20:3 **20:32** [a] Ezek. 11:5 **20:33** [a] Jer. 21:5 **20:35** [a] Jer. 2:9, 35; Ezek. 17:20 **20:36** [a] Num. 14:21–23, 28 **20:37** [a] Lev. 27:32; Jer. 33:13 [b] Ps. 89:30–34; Ezek. 16:60, 62 **20:38** [a] Ezek. 34:17; Amos 9:9, 10; Zech. 13:8, 9; [Mal. 3:3; 4:1–3; Matt. 25:32] [b] Jer. 44:14 **20:39** [a] Judg. 10:14; Ps. 81:12; Amos 4:4 [b] Is. 1:13–15; Ezek. 23:38

40For [a]on My holy mountain, on the mountain height of Israel," says the Lord GOD,
"there [b]all the house of Israel, all of them
in the land, shall serve Me; there [c]I will accept them, and there I will require your
offerings and the firstfruits of your sacrifices, together with all your holy things. 41I
will accept you as a [a]sweet aroma when I
bring you out from the peoples and gather
you out of the countries where you have
been scattered; and I will be hallowed in
you before the Gentiles. 42[a]Then you shall
know that I *am* the LORD, [b]when I bring
you into the land of Israel, into the country *for* which I raised My hand in an oath to
give to your fathers. 43And [a]there you shall
remember your ways and all your doings
with which you were defiled; and [b]you shall
loathe yourselves in your own sight because of all the evils that you have committed. 44[a]Then you shall know that I *am* the
LORD, when I have dealt with you [b]for My
name's sake, not according to your wicked
ways nor according to your corrupt doings,
O house of Israel," says the Lord GOD.'"

Fire in the Forest

45Furthermore the word of the LORD
came to me, saying, 46[a]"Son of man, set
your face toward the south; preach against
the south and prophesy against the forest land, the South,[1] 47and say to the forest
of the South, 'Hear the word of the LORD!
Thus says the Lord GOD: "Behold, [a]I will
kindle a fire in you, and it shall devour [b]ev-
ery green tree and every dry tree in you; the
blazing flame shall not be quenched, and
all faces [c]from the south to the north shall
be scorched by it. 48All flesh shall see that
I, the LORD, have kindled it; it shall not be
quenched."'"

49Then I said, "Ah, Lord GOD! They say of
me, 'Does he not speak [a]parables?'"

Babylon, the Sword of God

21 And the word of the LORD came to
me, saying, 2[a]"Son of man, set your
face toward Jerusalem, [b]preach against the
holy places, and prophesy against the land
of Israel; 3and say to the land of Israel, 'Thus
says the LORD: "Behold, I *am* [a]against you,
and I will draw My sword out of its sheath
and cut off both [b]righteous and wicked from
you. 4Because I will cut off both righteous
and wicked from you, therefore My sword
shall go out of its sheath against all flesh
[a]from south *to* north, 5that all flesh may
know that I, the LORD, have drawn My sword
out of its sheath; it [a]shall not return anymore."' 6[a]Sigh therefore, son of man, with
a breaking heart, and sigh with bitterness
before their eyes. 7And it shall be when they
say to you, 'Why are you sighing?' that you
shall answer, 'Because of the news; when
it comes, every heart will melt, [a]all hands
will be feeble, every spirit will faint, and all
knees will be weak *as* water. Behold, it is
coming and shall be brought to pass,' says
the Lord GOD."

8Again the word of the LORD came to
me, saying, 9"Son of man, prophesy and
say, 'Thus says the LORD!' Say:

[a]'A sword, a sword is sharpened
And also polished!
10 Sharpened to make a
dreadful slaughter,
Polished to flash like lightning!
Should we then make mirth?
It despises the scepter
of My son,
As it does all wood.
11 And He has given it to be
polished,
That it may be handled;
This sword is sharpened,
and it is polished
To be given into the hand
of [a]the slayer.'

12 "Cry and wail, son of man;
For it will be against My people,
Against all the princes of Israel.
Terrors including the sword
will be against My people;
Therefore [a]strike *your* thigh.

20:40 [a] Is. 2:2, 3; Ezek. 17:23; Mic. 4:1 [b] Ezek. 37:22 [c] Is. 56:7; 60:7; Ezek. 43:27; Zech. 8:20–22; Mal. 3:4; [Rom. 12:1] 20:41 [a] Eph. 5:2; Phil. 4:18 20:42 [a] Ezek. 36:23; 38:23 [b] Ezek. 11:17; 34:13; 36:24 20:43 [a] Ezek. 16:61 [b] Lev. 26:39; Ezek. 6:9; Hos. 5:15 20:44 [a] Ezek. 24:24 [b] Ezek. 36:22 20:46 [a] Ezek. 21:2; Amos 7:16 [1] Hebrew *Negev* 20:47 [a] Is. 9:18, 19; Jer. 21:14 [b] Luke 23:31 [c] Ezek. 21:4 20:49 [a] Ezek. 12:9; 17:2; Matt. 13:13; John 16:25 21:2 [a] Ezek. 20:46 [b] Amos 7:16 21:3 [a] Jer. 21:13; Ezek. 5:8; Nah. 2:13; 3:5 [b] Job 9:22 21:4 [a] Jer. 12:12; Ezek. 20:47 21:5 [a] [Is. 45:23; 55:11] 21:6 [a] Is. 22:4; Jer. 4:19; Luke 19:41 21:7 [a] Ezek. 7:17 21:9 [a] Deut. 32:41; Ezek. 5:1; 21:15, 28 21:11 [a] Ezek. 21:19 21:12 [a] Jer. 31:19

13 "Because *it is* [a]a testing,
And what if *the sword* despises
even the scepter?
[b]*The scepter* shall be no *more,*"
says the Lord GOD.

14 "You therefore, son of man, prophesy,
And [a]strike *your* hands together.
The third time let the sword
do double *damage.*
It *is* the sword *that* slays,
The sword that slays the great *men,*
That enters their [b]private chambers.
15 I have set the point of the sword
against all their gates,
That the heart may melt and
many may stumble.
Ah! [a]*It is* made bright;
It is grasped for slaughter:

16 "Swords[a] at the ready!
Thrust right!
Set your blade!
Thrust left—
Wherever your edge is ordered!

17 "I also will [a]beat My fists together,
And [b]I will cause My fury to rest;
I, the LORD, have spoken."

18The word of the LORD came to me
again, saying: 19"And son of man, appoint
for yourself two ways for the sword of the
king of Babylon to go; both of them shall
go from the same land. Make a sign; put
it at the head of the road to the city. 20Ap-
point a road for the sword to go to [a]Rab-
bah of the Ammonites, and to Judah, into
fortified Jerusalem. 21For the king of Babylon stands at the parting of the road, at the
fork of the two roads, to use divination: he
shakes the arrows, he consults the images,
he looks at the liver. 22In his right hand is
the divination for Jerusalem: to set up battering rams, to call for a slaughter, to [a]lift
the voice with shouting, [b]to set battering
rams against the gates, to heap up a *siege*
mound, and to build a wall. 23And it will be
to them like a false divination in the eyes
of those who [a]have sworn oaths with them;
but he will bring their iniquity to remembrance, that they may be taken.
24"Therefore thus says the Lord GOD:
'Because you have made your iniquity to
be remembered, in that your transgressions are uncovered, so that in all your doings your sins appear—because you have
come to remembrance, you shall be taken
in hand.
25'Now to you, O [a]profane, wicked prince
of Israel, [b]whose day has come, whose iniquity *shall* end, 26thus says the Lord GOD:

"Remove the turban, and
take off the crown;
Nothing *shall remain* the same.
[a]Exalt the humble, and
humble the exalted.
27 Overthrown, overthrown,
I will make it overthrown!
[a]It shall be no *longer,*
Until He comes whose right it is,
And I will give it *to* [b]*Him.*"'

A Sword Against the Ammonites

28"And you, son of man, prophesy and
say, 'Thus says the Lord GOD [a]concerning
the Ammonites and concerning their reproach,' and say:

'A sword, a sword *is* drawn,
Polished for slaughter,
For consuming, for flashing—
29 While they [a]see false visions for you,
While they divine a lie to you,
To bring you on the necks of
the wicked, the slain
[b]Whose day has come,
Whose iniquity *shall* end.

30 'Return[a] *it* to its sheath.
[b]I will judge you
In the place where you were created,
[c]In the land of your nativity.
31 I will [a]pour out My indignation on you;

21:13 [a] Job 9:23; 2 Cor. 8:2 [b] Ezek. 21:27 21:14 [a] Num. 24:10; Ezek. 6:11 [b] 1 Kin. 20:30 21:15 [a] Ezek. 21:10, 28 21:16 [a] Ezek. 14:17 21:17 [a] Ezek. 22:13 [b] Ezek. 5:13; 16:42; 24:13 21:20 [a] Deut. 3:11; Jer. 49:2; Ezek. 25:5; Amos 1:14 21:22 [a] Jer. 51:14 [b] Ezek. 4:2 21:23 [a] Ezek. 17:16, 18 21:25 [a] 2 Chr. 36:13; Jer. 52:2; Ezek. 12:10; 17:19 [b] Ezek. 21:29 21:26 [a] Luke 1:52 21:27 [a] Gen. 49:10; [Luke 1:32, 33; John 1:49] [b] Ps. 2:6; 72:7, 10; [Jer. 23:5, 6; Ezek. 34:24; 37:24] 21:28 [a] Jer. 25:21; 49:1–6; Ezek. 25:1–7; Amos 1:13; Zeph. 2:8–11 21:29 [a] Jer. 27:9; Ezek. 12:24; 13:6–9; 22:28 [b] Job 18:20; Ps. 37:17; Is. 10:3; Ezek. 7:2, 3, 7 21:30 [a] Jer. 47:6, 7 [b] Gen. 15:14 [c] Ezek. 16:3 21:31 [a] Ezek. 7:8

I will [b]blow against you with
the fire of My wrath,
And deliver you into the
hands of brutal men *who*
are skillful to [c]destroy.
32 You shall be fuel for the fire;
Your blood shall be in the
midst of the land.
[a]You shall not be remembered,
For I the LORD have spoken.'"

Sins of Jerusalem

22 Moreover the word of the LORD
came to me, saying, 2"Now, son of
man, [a]will you judge, will you judge [b]the
bloody city? Yes, show her all her abominations! 3Then say, 'Thus says the Lord GOD:
"The city sheds [a]blood in her own midst,
that her time may come; and she makes
idols within herself to defile herself. 4You
have become guilty by the blood which you
have [a]shed, and have defiled yourself with
the idols which you have made. You have
caused your days to draw near, and have
come to *the end of* your years; [b]therefore I
have made you a reproach to the nations,
and a mockery to all countries. 5*Those* near
and *those* far from you will mock you as in-
famous *and* full of tumult.

6"Look, [a]the princes of Israel: each one
has used his power to shed blood in you.
7In you they have [a]made light of father and
mother; in your midst they have [b]oppressed
the stranger; in you they have mistreated
the fatherless and the widow. 8You have
despised My holy things and [a]profaned My
Sabbaths. 9In you are [a]men who slander
to cause bloodshed; [b]in you are those who
eat on the mountains; in your midst they
commit lewdness. 10In you men [a]uncover
their fathers' nakedness; in you they vio-
late women who are [b]set apart during their
impurity. 11One commits abomination [a]with
his neighbor's wife; [b]another lewdly defiles
his daughter-in-law; and another in you vi-
olates his sister, his father's [c]daughter. 12In
you [a]they take bribes to shed blood; [b]you
take usury and increase; you have made
profit from your neighbors by extortion,
and [c]have forgotten Me," says the Lord GOD.

13"Behold, therefore, I [a]beat My fists at
the dishonest profit which you have made,
and at the bloodshed which has been in
your midst. 14[a]Can your heart endure, or
can your hands remain strong, in the days
when I shall deal with you? [b]I, the LORD,
have spoken, and will do *it.* 15[a]I will scatter you among the nations, disperse you
throughout the countries, and [b]remove
your filthiness completely from you. 16You
shall defile yourself in the sight of the nations; then [a]you shall know that I *am* the
LORD."'"

Israel in the Furnace

17The word of the LORD came to me, saying, 18"Son of man, [a]the house of Israel has
become dross to Me; they *are* all bronze,
tin, iron, and lead, in the midst of a [b]fur-
nace; they have become dross from silver.
19Therefore thus says the Lord GOD: 'Because you have all become dross, therefore
behold, I will gather you into the midst of
Jerusalem. 20*As men* gather silver, bronze,
iron, lead, and tin into the midst of a furnace, to blow fire on it, to [a]melt *it;* so I will
gather *you* in My anger and in My fury, and
I will leave *you there* and melt you. 21Yes, I
will gather you and blow on you with the
fire of My wrath, and you shall be melted in
its midst. 22As silver is melted in the midst
of a furnace, so shall you be melted in its
midst; then you shall know that I, the LORD,
have [a]poured out My fury on you.'"

Israel's Wicked Leaders

23And the word of the LORD came to me,
saying, 24"Son of man, say to her: 'You *are*
a land that is [a]not cleansed[1] or rained on
in the day of indignation.' 25[a]The conspiracy of her prophets[1] in her midst is like a
roaring lion tearing the prey; they [b]have

21:31 [b] Ps. 18:15; Is. 30:33; Ezek. 22:20, 21; Hag. 1:9 [c] Jer. 6:22, 23; 51:20, 21; Hab. 1:6–10 21:32 [a] Ezek. 25:10 22:2 [a] Ezek. 20:4 [b] Nah. 3:1 22:3 [a] Ezek. 24:6, 7 22:4 [a] 2 Kin. 21:16; Ezek. 24:7, 8 [b] Deut. 28:37; 1 Kin. 9:7; Ezek. 5:14; Dan. 9:16 22:6 [a] Is. 1:23; Ezek. 22:27; Mic. 3:1–3; Zeph. 3:3 22:7 [a] Ex. 20:12; Lev. 20:9; Deut. 5:16; 27:16 [b] Ex. 22:22; Jer. 5:28; Ezek. 22:25; Mal. 3:5 22:8 [a] Lev. 19:30 22:9 [a] Lev. 19:16; Jer. 9:4 [b] Ezek. 18:6, 11 22:10 [a] Lev. 18:7, 8 [b] Lev. 18:19; 20:18; Ezek. 18:6 22:11 [a] Lev. 18:20; Jer. 5:8; Ezek. 18:11 [b] Lev. 18:15 [c] Lev. 18:9 22:12 [a] Ex. 23:8; Deut. 16:19; 27:25; Mic. 7:2, 3 [b] Ex. 22:25 [c] Deut. 32:18; Ps. 106:21; Jer. 3:21; Ezek. 23:35 22:13 [a] Ezek. 21:17 22:14 [a] Ezek. 21:7 [b] Ezek. 17:24 22:15 [a] Deut. 4:27; Neh. 1:8; Ezek. 20:23; Zech. 7:14 [b] Ezek. 23:27, 48 22:16 [a] Ps. 9:16 22:18 [a] Ps. 119:119; Is. 1:22; Jer. 6:28; Lam. 4:1 [b] Prov. 17:3; Is. 48:10 22:20 [a] Is. 1:25; Jer. 9:7 22:22 [a] Ezek. 20:8, 33; Hos. 5:10 22:24 [a] Is. 9:13; Jer. 2:30; Ezek. 24:13; Zeph. 3:2 [1] Following Masoretic Text, Syriac, and Vulgate; Septuagint reads *showered upon.* 22:25 [a] Jer. 11:9; Hos. 6:9 [b] Matt. 23:14 [1] Following Masoretic Text and Vulgate; Septuagint reads *princes;* Targum reads *scribes.*

devoured people; [c]they have taken treasure and precious things; they have made
many widows in her midst. 26[a]Her priests
have violated My law and [b]profaned My
holy things; they have not [c]distinguished
between the holy and unholy, nor have they
made known *the difference* between the unclean and the clean; and they have hidden
their eyes from My Sabbaths, so that I am
profaned among them. 27Her [a]princes in
her midst *are* like wolves tearing the prey,
to shed blood, to destroy people, and to get
dishonest gain. 28[a]Her prophets plastered
them with untempered *mortar,* [b]seeing
false visions, and divining [c]lies for them,
saying, 'Thus says the Lord GOD,' when
the LORD had not spoken. 29The people of
the land have used oppressions, committed robbery, and mistreated the poor and
needy; and they wrongfully [a]oppress the
stranger. 30[a]So I sought for a man among
them who would [b]make a wall, and [c]stand
in the gap before Me on behalf of the land,
that I should not destroy it; but I found no
one. 31Therefore I have [a]poured out My indignation on them; I have consumed them
with the fire of My wrath; and I have recompensed [b]their deeds on their own heads,"
says the Lord GOD.

Two Harlot Sisters

23 The word of the LORD came again to me, saying:

2 "Son of man, there were [a]two women,
The daughters of one mother.
3 [a]They committed harlotry in Egypt,
They committed harlotry
in [b]their youth;
Their breasts were there embraced,
Their virgin bosom was there pressed.
4 Their names: Oholah[1] the elder
and Oholibah[2] [a]her sister;
[b]They were Mine,
And they bore sons and daughters.
As for their names,
Samaria *is* Oholah, and
Jerusalem *is* Oholibah.

The Older Sister, Samaria

5 "Oholah played the harlot even
though she was Mine;
And she lusted for her lovers, the
neighboring [a]Assyrians,
6 *Who were* clothed in purple,
Captains and rulers,
All of them desirable young men,
Horsemen riding on horses.
7 Thus she committed her
harlotry with them,
All of them choice men of Assyria;
And with all for whom she lusted,
With all their idols, she defiled
herself.
8 She has never given up her
harlotry *brought* [a]from Egypt,
For in her youth they had lain
with her,
Pressed her virgin bosom,
And poured out their
immorality upon her.

9 "Therefore I have delivered her
Into the hand of her lovers,
Into the hand of the [a]Assyrians,
For whom she lusted.
10 They uncovered her nakedness,
Took away her sons and daughters,
And slew her with the sword;
She became a byword among women,
For they had executed
judgment on her.

The Younger Sister, Jerusalem

11"Now [a]although her sister Oholibah saw
this, [b]she became more corrupt in her lust
than she, and in her harlotry more corrupt
than her sister's harlotry.

12 "She lusted for the neighboring
[a]Assyrians,
[b]Captains and rulers,
Clothed most gorgeously,
Horsemen riding on horses,
All of them desirable young men.
13 Then I saw that she was defiled;
Both *took* the same way.

22:25 [c] Mic. 3:11; Zeph. 3:3, 4 **22:26** [a] Jer. 32:32; Lam. 4:3; Mal. 2:8 [b] 1 Sam. 2:29 [c] Lev. 10:10 **22:27** [a] Is. 1:23; Ezek. 22:6; Mic. 3:1–3, 9–11; Zeph. 3:3 **22:28** [a] Ezek. 13:10 [b] Ezek. 13:6, 7 [c] Jer. 23:25–32; Ezek. 21:29 **22:29** [a] Ex. 23:9; Lev. 19:33 **22:30** [a] Is. 59:16; 63:5; Jer. 5:1 [b] Ezek. 13:5 [c] Ps. 106:23; Jer. 15:1 **22:31** [a] Ezek. 22:22 [b] Ezek. 9:10; [Rom. 2:8, 9] **23:2** [a] Jer. 3:7, 8; Ezek. 16:44–46 **23:3** [a] Lev. 17:7; Josh. 24:14; Jer. 3:9 [b] Ezek. 16:22 **23:4** [a] Jer. 3:6, 7 [b] Ezek. 16:8, 20 [1] Literally *Her Own Tabernacle* [2] Literally *My Tabernacle Is in Her* **23:5** [a] 2 Kin. 15:19; 16:7; 17:3; Ezek. 16:28; Hos. 5:13; 8:9, 10 **23:8** [a] Ex. 32:4; 1 Kin. 12:28; 2 Kin. 10:29; 17:16; Ezek. 23:3, 19 **23:9** [a] 2 Kin. 17:3 **23:11** [a] Jer. 3:8 [b] Jer. 3:8–11; Ezek. 16:51, 52 **23:12** [a] 2 Kin. 16:7, 8; Ezek. 16:28 [b] Ezek. 23:6, 23

14 But she increased her harlotry;
She looked at men portrayed
on the wall,
Images of [a]Chaldeans
portrayed in vermilion,
15 Girded with belts around their waists,
Flowing turbans on their heads,
All of them looking like captains,
In the manner of the
Babylonians of Chaldea,
The land of their nativity.
16 [a]As soon as her eyes saw them,
She lusted for them
And sent [b]messengers to
them in Chaldea.

17 "Then the Babylonians came to
her, into the bed of love,
And they defiled her with
their immorality;
So she was defiled by them, [a]and
alienated herself from them.
18 She revealed her harlotry and
uncovered her nakedness.
Then [a]I [b]alienated Myself from her,
As I had alienated Myself
from her sister.

19 "Yet she multiplied her harlotry
In calling to remembrance
the days of her youth,
[a]When she had played the harlot
in the land of Egypt.
20 For she lusted for her paramours,
Whose flesh *is like* the
flesh of donkeys,
And whose issue *is like* the
issue of horses.
21 Thus you called to remembrance
the lewdness of your youth,
When the [a]Egyptians
pressed your bosom
Because of your youthful breasts.

Judgment on Jerusalem

22 "Therefore, Oholibah, thus says the Lord GOD:

[a]'Behold, I will stir up your
lovers against you,
From whom you have
alienated yourself,
And I will bring them against
you from every side:
23 The Babylonians,
All the Chaldeans,
[a]Pekod, Shoa, Koa,
[b]All the Assyrians with them,
All of them desirable young men,
Governors and rulers,
Captains and men of renown,
All of them riding on horses.
24 And they shall come against you
With chariots, wagons,
and war-horses,
With a horde of people.
They shall array against you
Buckler, shield, and helmet all around.

'I will delegate judgment to them,
And they shall judge you according
to their judgments.
25 I will set My [a]jealousy against you,
And they shall deal furiously with you;
They shall remove your
nose and your ears,
And your remnant shall
fall by the sword;
They shall take your sons
and your daughters,
And your remnant shall be
devoured by fire.
26 [a]They shall also strip you
of your clothes
And take away your beautiful jewelry.

27 'Thus [a]I will make you cease your
lewdness and your [b]harlotry
Brought from the land of Egypt,
So that you will not lift
your eyes to them,
Nor remember Egypt anymore.'

28 "For thus says the Lord GOD: 'Surely I
will deliver you into the hand of [a]those you
hate, into the hand *of those* [b]from whom
you alienated yourself. 29 [a]They will deal
hatefully with you, take away all you have
worked for, and [b]leave you naked and bare.
The nakedness of your harlotry shall be

23:14 [a] Jer. 50:2; Ezek. 8:10; 16:29 23:16 [a] 2 Kin. 24:1 [b] Is. 57:9 23:17 [a] Ezek. 23:22, 28 23:18 [a] Jer. 6:8 [b] Ps. 78:59; 106:40; Jer. 12:8 23:19 [a] Lev. 18:3; Ezek. 23:2 23:21 [a] Ezek. 16:26 23:22 [a] Ezek. 16:37–41; 23:28 23:23 [a] Jer. 50:21 [b] Ezek. 23:12 23:25 [a] Ex. 34:14; Ezek. 5:13; 8:17, 18; Zeph. 1:18 23:26 [a] Is. 3:18–23; Ezek. 16:39 23:27 [a] Ezek. 16:41; 22:15 [b] Ezek. 23:3, 19 23:28 [a] Jer. 21:7–10; Ezek. 16:37–41 [b] Ezek. 23:17 23:29 [a] Deut. 28:48; Ezek. 23:25, 26, 45–47 [b] Ezek. 16:39

uncovered, both your lewdness and your
harlotry. 30 I will do these *things* to you because you have [a]gone as a harlot after the
Gentiles, because you have become defiled
by their idols. 31 You have walked in the way
of your sister; therefore I will put her [a]cup
in your hand.'
32 "Thus says the Lord GOD:

'You shall drink of your sister's cup,
The deep and wide one;
[a]You shall be laughed to scorn
And held in derision;
It contains much.
33 You will be filled with
drunkenness and sorrow,
The cup of horror and desolation,
The cup of your sister Samaria.
34 You shall [a]drink and drain it,
You shall break its shards,
And tear at your own breasts;
For I have spoken,'
Says the Lord GOD.

35 "Therefore thus says the Lord GOD:

'Because you [a]have forgotten Me
and [b]cast Me behind your back,
Therefore you shall bear the *penalty*
Of your lewdness and your harlotry.'"

Both Sisters Judged

36 The LORD also said to me: "Son of
man, will you [a]judge Oholah and Oholibah? Then [b]declare to them their abominations. 37 For they have committed adultery,
and [a]blood *is* on their hands. They have
committed adultery with their idols, and
even *sacrificed* their sons [b]whom they bore
to Me, passing them through *the fire,* to
devour *them.* 38 Moreover they have done
this to Me: They have [a]defiled My sanctuary on the same day and [b]profaned My
Sabbaths. 39 For after they had slain their
children for their idols, on the same day
they came into My sanctuary to profane
it; and indeed [a]thus they have done in the
midst of My house.

40 "Furthermore you sent for men to
come from afar, [a]to whom a messenger
was sent; and there they came. And you
[b]washed yourself for them, [c]painted your
eyes, and adorned yourself with ornaments. 41 You sat on a stately [a]couch, with a
table prepared before it, [b]on which you had
set My incense and My oil. 42 The sound of a
carefree multitude *was* with her, and Sabeans *were* brought from the wilderness with
men of the common sort, who put bracelets on their wrists and beautiful crowns
on their heads. 43 Then I said concerning
her who had grown old in adulteries, 'Will
they commit harlotry with her now, and
she *with them?*' 44 Yet they went in to her, as
men go in to a woman who plays the harlot;
thus they went in to Oholah and Oholibah,
the lewd women. 45 But righteous men will
[a]judge them after the manner of adulteresses, and after the manner of women who
shed blood, because they *are* adulteresses,
and [b]blood *is* on their hands.
46 "For thus says the Lord GOD: [a]'Bring
up an assembly against them, give them
up to trouble and plunder. 47 [a]The assembly
shall stone them with stones and execute
them with their swords; [b]they shall slay
their sons and their daughters, and burn
their houses with fire. 48 Thus [a]I will cause
lewdness to cease from the land, [b]that all
women may be taught not to practice your
lewdness. 49 They shall repay you for your
lewdness, and you shall [a]pay for your idolatrous sins. [b]Then you shall know that I *am*
the Lord GOD.'"

Symbol of the Cooking Pot
(cf. Jer. 1:13–19)

24 Again, in the ninth year, in the
tenth month, on the tenth *day* of
the month, the word of the LORD came to
me, saying, 2 "Son of man, write down the
name of the day, this very day—the king
of Babylon started his siege against Jerusalem [a]this very day. 3 [a]And utter a parable
to the rebellious house, and say to them,
'Thus says the Lord GOD:

23:30 [a] Ezek. 6:9 23:31 [a] 2 Kin. 21:13; Jer. 7:14, 15; 25:15; Ezek. 23:33 23:32 [a] Ezek. 22:4, 5 23:34 [a] Ps. 75:8; Is. 51:17 23:35 [a] Is. 17:10; Jer. 3:21; Ezek. 22:12; Hos. 8:14; 13:6 [b] 1 Kin. 14:9; Jer. 2:27; 32:33; Neh. 9:26 23:36 [a] Jer. 1:10; Ezek. 20:4; 22:2 [b] Is. 58:1; Ezek. 16:2; Mic. 3:8 23:37 [a] Ezek. 16:38 [b] Ezek. 16:20, 21, 36, 45; 20:26, 31 23:38 [a] 2 Kin. 21:4, 7; Ezek. 5:11; 7:20 [b] Ezek. 22:8 23:39 [a] 2 Kin. 21:2–8 23:40 [a] Is. 57:9 [b] Ruth 3:3 [c] 2 Kin. 9:30; Jer. 4:30 23:41 [a] Esth. 1:6; Is. 57:7; Amos 2:8; 6:4 [b] Prov. 7:17; Ezek. 16:18, 19; Hos. 2:8 23:45 [a] Ezek. 16:38 [b] Ezek. 23:37 23:46 [a] Ezek. 16:40 23:47 [a] Lev. 20:10; Ezek. 16:40 [b] 2 Chr. 36:17, 19; Ezek. 24:21 23:48 [a] Ezek. 22:15 [b] Deut. 13:11; Ezek. 22:15; 2 Pet. 2:6 23:49 [a] Is. 59:18; Ezek. 23:35 [b] Ezek. 20:38, 42, 44; 25:5 24:2 [a] 2 Kin. 25:1; Jer. 39:1; 52:4 24:3 [a] Ezek. 17:12

[b]"Put on a pot, set *it* on,
And also pour water into it.
4 Gather pieces *of meat* in it,
Every good piece,
The thigh and the shoulder.
Fill *it* with choice cuts;
5 Take the choice of the flock.
Also pile *fuel* bones under it,
Make it boil well,
And let the cuts simmer in it."

6'Therefore thus says the Lord GOD:

"Woe to [a]the bloody city,
To the pot whose scum *is* in it,
And whose scum is not gone
from it!
Bring it out piece by piece,
On which no [b]lot has fallen.
7 For her blood is in her midst;
She set it on top of a rock;
[a]She did not pour it on the ground,
To cover it with dust.
8 That it may raise up fury
and take vengeance,
[a]I have set her blood on top of a rock,
That it may not be covered."

9'Therefore thus says the Lord GOD:

[a]"Woe to the bloody city!
I too will make the pyre great.
10 Heap on the wood,
Kindle the fire;
Cook the meat well,
Mix in the spices,
And let the cuts be burned up.

11 "Then set the pot empty on the coals,
That it may become hot and
its bronze may burn,
That [a]its filthiness may be melted in it,
That its scum may be consumed.
12 She has grown weary with lies,
And her great scum has
not gone from her.
Let her scum *be* in the fire!
13 In your [a]filthiness *is* lewdness.
Because I have cleansed you,
and you were not cleansed,
You will [b]not be cleansed of
your filthiness anymore,
[c]Till I have caused My fury
to rest upon you.
14 [a]I, the LORD, have spoken *it;*
[b]It shall come to pass, and I will do *it;*
I will not hold back,
[c]Nor will I spare,
Nor will I relent;
According to your ways
And according to your deeds
They[1] will judge you,"
Says the Lord GOD.'"

The Prophet's Wife Dies

15 Also the word of the LORD came to
me, saying, 16 "Son of man, behold, I take
away from you the desire of your eyes with
one stroke; yet you shall [a]neither mourn
nor weep, nor shall your tears run down.
17 Sigh in silence, [a]make no mourning for
the dead; [b]bind your turban on your head,
and [c]put your sandals on your feet; [d]do not
cover *your* lips, and do not eat man's bread
of sorrow."
18 So I spoke to the people in the morning, and at evening my wife died; and the
next morning I did as I was commanded.
19 And the people said to me, [a]"Will you
not tell us what these *things signify* to us,
that you behave so?"
20 Then I answered them, "The word of
the LORD came to me, saying, 21 'Speak to the
house of Israel, "Thus says the Lord GOD:
'Behold, [a]I will profane My sanctuary, your
arrogant boast, the desire of your eyes, the
delight of your soul; [b]and your sons and
daughters whom you left behind shall fall
by the sword. 22 And you shall do as I have
done; [a]you shall not cover *your* lips nor eat
man's bread *of sorrow.* 23 Your turbans shall
be on your heads and your sandals on your
feet; [a]you shall neither mourn nor weep, but
[b]you shall pine away in your iniquities and
mourn with one another. 24 Thus [a]Ezekiel is
a sign to you; according to all that he has

24:3 [b] Jer. 1:13; Ezek. 11:3 **24:6** [a] 2 Kin. 24:3, 4; Ezek. 22:2, 3, 27; Mic. 7:2; Nah. 3:1 [b] 2 Sam. 8:2; Joel 3:3; Obad. 11; Nah. 3:10 **24:7** [a] Lev. 17:13; Deut. 12:16 **24:8** [a] [Matt. 7:2] **24:9** [a] Ezek. 24:6; Nah. 3:1; Hab. 2:12 **24:11** [a] Ezek. 22:15 **24:13** [a] Ezek. 23:36–48 [b] Jer. 6:28–30; Ezek. 22:24 [c] Ezek. 5:13; 8:18; 16:42 **24:14** [a] [1 Sam. 15:29] [b] Num. 23:19; Ps. 33:9; Is. 55:11 [c] Ezek. 5:11
[1] Septuagint, Syriac, Targum, and Vulgate read *I.* **24:16** [a] Jer. 16:5 **24:17** [a] Jer. 16:5 [b] Lev. 10:6; 21:10 [c] 2 Sam. 15:30 [d] Mic. 3:7 **24:19** [a] Ezek. 12:9; 37:18 **24:21** [a] Jer. 7:14; Lam. 2:7; Ezek. 7:20, 24 [b] Jer. 6:11; 16:3, 4; Ezek. 23:25, 47 **24:22** [a] Jer. 16:6, 7 **24:23** [a] Job 27:15; Ps. 78:64 [b] Lev. 26:39; Ezek. 33:10 **24:24** [a] Is. 20:3; Ezek. 4:3; 12:6, 11; Luke 11:29, 30

done you shall do; [b]and when this comes, [c]you shall know that I *am* the Lord GOD.' "

25 'And you, son of man—*will it* not *be* in the day when I take from them [a]their stronghold, their joy and their glory, the desire of their eyes, and that on which they set their minds, their sons and their daughters: 26 *that* on that day [a]one who escapes will come to you to let *you* hear *it* with *your* ears? 27 [a]On that day your mouth will be opened to him who has escaped; you shall speak and no longer be mute. Thus you will be a sign to them, and they shall know that I *am* the LORD.' "

Proclamation Against Ammon

25 The word of the LORD came to me, saying, 2 "Son of man, [a]set your face [b]against the Ammonites, and prophesy against them. 3 Say to the Ammonites, 'Hear the word of the Lord GOD! Thus says the Lord GOD: [a]"Because you said, 'Aha!' against My sanctuary when it was profaned, and against the land of Israel when it was desolate, and against the house of Judah when they went into captivity, 4 indeed, therefore, I will deliver you as a possession to the men of the East, and they shall set their encampments among you and make their dwellings among you; they shall eat your fruit, and they shall drink your milk. 5 And I will make [a]Rabbah [b]a stable for camels and Ammon a resting place for flocks. [c]Then you shall know that I *am* the LORD."

6 'For thus says the Lord GOD: "Because you [a]clapped *your* hands, stamped your feet, and [b]rejoiced in heart with all your disdain for the land of Israel, 7 indeed, therefore, I will [a]stretch out My hand against you, and give you as plunder to the nations; I will cut you off from the peoples, and I will cause you to perish from the countries; I will destroy you, and you shall know that I *am* the LORD."

Proclamation Against Moab

8 'Thus says the Lord GOD: "Because [a]Moab and [b]Seir say, 'Look! The house of Judah *is* like all the nations,' 9 therefore, behold, I will clear the territory of Moab of cities, of the cities on its frontier, the glory of the country, Beth Jeshimoth, Baal Meon, and [a]Kirjathaim. 10 [a]To the men of the East I will give it as a possession, together with the Ammonites, that the Ammonites [b]may not be remembered among the nations. 11 And I will execute judgments upon Moab, and they shall know that I *am* the LORD."

Proclamation Against Edom

12 'Thus says the Lord GOD: [a]"Because of what Edom did against the house of Judah by taking vengeance, and has greatly offended by avenging itself on them," 13 therefore thus says the Lord GOD: "I will also stretch out My hand against Edom, cut off man and beast from it, and make it desolate from Teman; Dedan shall fall by the sword. 14 [a]I will lay My vengeance on Edom by the hand of My people Israel, that they may do in Edom according to My anger and according to My fury; and they shall know My vengeance," says the Lord GOD.

Proclamation Against Philistia

15 'Thus says the Lord GOD: [a]"Because [b]the Philistines dealt vengefully and took vengeance with a spiteful heart, to destroy because of the old hatred," 16 therefore thus says the Lord GOD: [a]"I will stretch out My hand against the Philistines, and I will cut off the [b]Cherethites [c]and destroy the remnant of the seacoast. 17 I will [a]execute great vengeance on them with furious rebukes; [b]and they shall know that I *am* the LORD, when I lay My vengeance upon them." ' "

Proclamation Against Tyre

26 And it came to pass in the eleventh year, on the first *day* of the month, *that* the word of the LORD came to me, saying, 2 "Son of man, [a]because Tyre has said against Jerusalem, [b]'Aha! She is broken who *was* the gateway of the peoples; now she is turned over to me; I shall be filled; she is laid waste.'

24:24 [b] Jer. 17:15; John 13:19; 14:29 [c] Ezek. 6:7; 25:5 **24:25** [a] Ps. 48:2; 50:2; Ezek. 24:21 **24:26** [a] Ezek. 33:21 **24:27** [a] Ezek. 3:26; 33:22 **25:2** [a] Ezek. 35:2 [b] Jer. 49:1; Ezek. 21:28; Amos 1:13–15; Zeph. 2:9 **25:3** [a] Ps. 70:2, 3; [Prov. 17:5]; Ezek. 26:2 **25:5** [a] Deut. 3:11; 2 Sam. 12:26; Jer. 49:2; Ezek. 21:20 [b] Is. 17:2 [c] Ezek. 24:24 **25:6** [a] Job 27:23; Lam. 2:15; Nah. 3:19; Zeph. 2:15 [b] Ezek. 36:5 **25:7** [a] Ezek. 35:3 **25:8** [a] Is. 15:6; Jer. 48:1; Amos 2:1, 2 [b] Ezek. 35:2, 5 **25:9** [a] Num. 32:3, 38; Josh. 13:17; 1 Chr. 5:8; Jer. 48:23 **25:10** [a] Ezek. 25:4 [b] Ezek. 21:32 **25:12** [a] 2 Chr. 28:17; Ps. 137:7; Jer. 49:7, 8; Amos 1:11; Obad. 10–14 **25:14** [a] Is. 11:14 **25:15** [a] Jer. 25:20; Amos 1—6 [b] 2 Chr. 28:18 **25:16** [a] Zeph. 2:4 [b] 1 Sam. 30:14 [c] Jer. 47:4 **25:17** [a] Ezek. 5:15 [b] Ps. 9:16 **26:2** [a] 2 Sam. 5:11; Is. 23:1; Jer. 25:22; Amos 1:9; Zech. 9:2 [b] Ezek. 25:3

3"Therefore thus says the Lord GOD:
'Behold, I *am* against you, O Tyre, and will
cause many nations to come up against
you, as the sea causes its waves to come
up. 4And they shall destroy the walls of
Tyre and break down her towers; I will also
scrape her dust from her, and [a]make her
like the top of a rock. 5It shall be *a place for*
spreading nets [a]in the midst of the sea, for
I have spoken,' says the Lord GOD; 'it shall
become plunder for the nations. 6Also her
daughter *villages* which *are* in the fields
shall be slain by the sword. [a]Then they shall
know that I am the LORD.'

7"For thus says the Lord GOD: 'Behold,
I will bring against Tyre from the north
[a]Nebuchadnezzar[1] king of Babylon, [b]king
of kings, with horses, with chariots, and
with horsemen, and an army with many
people. 8He will slay with the sword your
daughter *villages* in the fields; he will [a]heap
up a siege mound against you, build a wall
against you, and raise a defense against
you. 9He will direct his battering rams
against your walls, and with his axes he
will break down your towers. 10Because of
the abundance of his horses, their dust
will cover you; your walls will shake at the
noise of the horsemen, the wagons, and the
chariots, when he enters your gates, as men
enter a city that has been breached. 11With
the hooves of his [a]horses he will trample all
your streets; he will slay your people by the
sword, and your strong pillars will fall to
the ground. 12They will plunder your riches
and pillage your merchandise; they will
break down your walls and destroy your
pleasant houses; they will lay your stones,
your timber, and your soil in the [a]midst of
the water. 13[a]I will put an end to the sound
of [b]your songs, and the sound of your harps
shall be heard no more. 14[a]I will make you
like the top of a rock; you shall be *a place
for* spreading nets, and you shall never be
rebuilt, for I the LORD have spoken,' says
the Lord GOD.

15"Thus says the Lord GOD to Tyre: 'Will
the coastlands not [a]shake at the sound of
your fall, when the wounded cry, when
slaughter is made in the midst of you?
16Then all the [a]princes of the sea will [b]come
down from their thrones, lay aside their
robes, and take off their embroidered garments; they will clothe themselves with
trembling; [c]they will sit on the ground,
[d]tremble *every* moment, and [e]be astonished
at you. 17And they will take up a [a]lamenta-
tion for you, and say to you:

"How you have perished,
O one inhabited by seafaring men,
O renowned city,
Who was [b]strong at sea,
She and her inhabitants,
Who caused their terror *to be*
on all her inhabitants!
18 Now [a]the coastlands tremble
on the day of your fall;
Yes, the coastlands by the sea are
troubled at your departure."'

19"For thus says the Lord GOD: 'When I
make you a desolate city, like cities that are
not inhabited, when I bring the deep upon
you, and great waters cover you, 20then I
will bring you down [a]with those who descend into the Pit, to the people of old, and
I will make you dwell in the lowest part of
the earth, in places desolate from antiquity,
with those who go down to the Pit, so that
you may never be inhabited; and I shall establish glory [b]in the land of the living. 21[a]I
will make you a terror, and you *shall be* no
more; [b]though you are sought for, you will
never be found again,' says the Lord GOD."

Lamentation for Tyre

27 The word of the LORD came again to
me, saying, 2"Now, son of man, [a]take
up a lamentation for Tyre, 3and say to Tyre,
[a]'You who are situated at the entrance of
the sea, [b]merchant of the peoples on many
coastlands, thus says the Lord GOD:

"O Tyre, you have said,
[c]'I *am* perfect in beauty.'

26:4 [a] Ezek. 26:14 26:5 [a] Ezek. 27:32 26:6 [a] Ezek. 25:5 26:7 [a] Jer. 27:3–6; Ezek. 29:18 [b] Ezra 7:12; Is. 10:8; Jer. 52:32; Dan. 2:37, 47 [1] Hebrew *Nebuchadrezzar,* and so elsewhere in this book 26:8 [a] Jer. 52:4; Ezek. 21:22 26:11 [a] Hab. 1:8 26:12 [a] Ezek. 27:27, 32 26:13 [a] Is. 14:11; 24:8; Jer. 7:34; 25:10; Amos 6:5 [b] Is. 23:16; Ezek. 28:13; Rev. 18:22 26:14 [a] Ezek. 26:4, 5 26:15 [a] Jer. 49:21; Ezek. 27:28 26:16 [a] Is. 23:8 [b] Jon. 3:6 [c] Job 2:13 [d] Ezek. 32:10; Hos. 11:10 [e] Ezek. 27:35 26:17 [a] Ezek. 27:2–36; Rev. 18:9 [b] Josh. 19:29; Is. 23:4 26:18 [a] Ezek. 26:15 26:20 [a] Ezek. 32:18 [b] Ezek. 32:23 26:21 [a] Ezek. 27:36; 28:19 [b] Ps. 37:10, 36; Ezek. 28:19 27:2 [a] Ezek. 26:17 27:3 [a] Ezek. 26:17; 28:2 [b] Is. 23:3 [c] Ezek. 28:12

4 Your borders *are* in the
midst of the seas.
Your builders have perfected
your beauty.
5 They made all *your* planks of
fir trees from [a]Senir;
They took a cedar from Lebanon
to make you a mast.
6 *Of* [a]oaks from Bashan they
made your oars;
The company of Ashurites
have inlaid your planks
With ivory from [b]the coasts
of Cyprus.[1]
7 Fine embroidered linen from Egypt
was what you spread for your sail;
Blue and purple from the coasts of
Elishah was what covered you.

8 "Inhabitants of Sidon and Arvad
were your oarsmen;
Your wise men, O Tyre, were in you;
They became your pilots.
9 Elders of [a]Gebal and its wise men
Were in you to caulk your seams;
All the ships of the sea
And their oarsmen were in you
To market your merchandise.

10 "Those from Persia, Lydia,[1] and Libya[2]
Were in your army as men of war;
They hung shield and helmet in you;
They gave splendor to you.
11 Men of Arvad with your army *were*
on your walls *all* around,
And the men of Gammad
were in your towers;
They hung their shields on
your walls *all* around;
They made [a]your beauty perfect.

12 [a]"Tarshish *was* your merchant because of your many luxury goods. They
gave you silver, iron, tin, and lead for your
goods. 13 [a]Javan, Tubal, and Meshech *were*
your traders. They bartered [b]human lives
and vessels of bronze for your merchandise. 14 Those from the house of [a]Togarmah
traded for your wares with horses, steeds,
and mules. 15 The men of [a]Dedan *were* your
traders; many isles *were* the market of your
hand. They brought you ivory tusks and
ebony as payment. 16 Syria *was* your merchant because of the abundance of goods
you made. They gave you for your wares
emeralds, purple, embroidery, fine linen,
corals, and rubies. 17 Judah and the land
of Israel *were* your traders. They traded
for your merchandise wheat of [a]Minnith,
millet, honey, oil, and [b]balm. 18 Damascus
was your merchant because of the abundance of goods you made, because of your
many luxury items, with the wine of Hel-
bon and with white wool. 19 Dan and Javan
paid for your wares, traversing back and
forth. Wrought iron, cassia, and cane were
among your merchandise. 20 [a]Dedan *was*
your merchant in saddlecloths for riding.
21 Arabia and all the princes of [a]Kedar *were*
your regular merchants. They traded with
you in lambs, rams, and goats. 22 The merchants of [a]Sheba and Raamah *were* your
merchants. They traded for your wares
the choicest spices, all kinds of precious
stones, and gold. 23 [a]Haran, Canneh, Eden,
the merchants of [b]Sheba, Assyria, *and* Chil-
mad *were* your merchants. 24 These *were*
your merchants in choice items—in purple clothes, in embroidered garments, in
chests of multicolored apparel, in sturdy
woven cords, which were in your marketplace.

25 "The [a]ships of Tarshish were
carriers of your merchandise.
You were filled and very glorious
[b]in the midst of the seas.
26 Your oarsmen brought you
into many waters,
But [a]the east wind broke you
in the midst of the seas.

27 "Your [a]riches, wares, and merchandise,
Your mariners and pilots,
Your caulkers and merchandisers,
All your men of war who *are* in you,

27:5 [a] Deut. 3:9; 1 Chr. 5:23; Song 4:8 27:6 [a] Is. 2:12, 13; Zech. 11:2 [b] Gen. 10:4; Is. 23:1, 12; Jer. 2:10 [1] Hebrew *Kittim,* western lands, especially Cyprus 27:9 [a] Josh. 13:5; 1 Kin. 5:18; Ps. 83:7 27:10 [1] Hebrew *Lud* [2] Hebrew *Put* 27:11 [a] Ezek. 27:3 27:12 [a] Gen. 10:4; 2 Chr. 20:36; Ezek. 38:13 27:13 [a] Gen. 10:2; Is. 66:19; Ezek. 27:19 [b] Joel 3:3–6; Rev. 18:13 27:14 [a] Gen. 10:3; Ezek. 38:6 27:15 [a] Gen. 10:7; Is. 21:13 27:17 [a] Judg. 11:33; 1 Kin. 5:9, 11; Ezra 3:7; Acts 12:20 [b] Jer. 8:22 27:20 [a] Gen. 25:3 27:21 [a] Gen. 25:13; Is. 60:7; Jer. 49:28 27:22 [a] Gen. 10:7; 1 Kin. 10:1, 2; Ps. 72:10; Is. 60:6; Ezek. 38:13 27:23 [a] Gen. 11:31; 2 Kin. 19:12; Is. 37:12 [b] Gen. 25:3 27:25 [a] Ps. 48:7; Is. 2:16 [b] Ezek. 27:4 27:26 [a] Ps. 48:7; Jer. 18:17; Acts 27:14 27:27 [a] [Prov. 11:4]

And the entire company
which *is* in your midst,
Will fall into the midst of the seas
on the day of your ruin.
28 The [a]common-land will shake at the
sound of the cry of your pilots.

29 "All [a]who handle the oar,
The mariners,
All the pilots of the sea
Will come down from their ships
and stand on the shore.
30 They will make their voice
heard because of you;
They will cry bitterly and [a]cast
dust on their heads;
They [b]will roll about in ashes;
31 They will [a]shave themselves
completely bald because
of you,
Gird themselves with sackcloth,
And weep for you
With bitterness of heart
and bitter wailing.
32 In their wailing for you
They will [a]take up a lamentation,
And lament for you:
[b]'What *city is* like Tyre,
Destroyed in the midst of the sea?

33 'When[a] your wares went out by sea,
You satisfied many people;
You enriched the kings of the earth
With your many luxury goods
and your merchandise.
34 But [a]you are broken by the seas
in the depths of the waters;
[b]Your merchandise and the entire
company will fall in your midst.
35 [a]All the inhabitants of the isles
will be astonished at you;
Their kings will be greatly afraid,
And *their* countenance
will be troubled.
36 The merchants among the
peoples [a]will hiss at you;
[b]You will become a horror, and
be no [c]more forever.'"'"

Proclamation Against the King of Tyre

28 The word of the LORD came to me
again, saying, 2"Son of man, say to
the prince of Tyre, 'Thus says the Lord GOD:

"Because your heart *is* [a]lifted up,
And [b]you say, 'I *am* a god,
I sit *in* the seat of gods,
[c]In the midst of the seas,'
[d]Yet you *are* a man, and not a god,
Though you set your heart
as the heart of a god
3 (Behold, [a]you *are* wiser than Daniel!
There is no secret that can
be hidden from you!
4 With your wisdom and
your understanding
You have gained [a]riches for yourself,
And gathered gold and silver
into your treasuries;
5 [a]By your great wisdom in trade you
have increased your riches,
And your heart is lifted up
because of your riches),"

6'Therefore thus says the Lord GOD:

"Because you have set your heart
as the heart of a god,
7 Behold, therefore, I will bring
[a]strangers against you,
[b]The most terrible of the nations;
And they shall draw their swords
against the beauty of your wisdom,
And defile your splendor.
8 They shall throw you down
into the [a]Pit,
And you shall die the
death of the slain
In the midst of the seas.

9 "Will you still [a]say before
him who slays you,
'I *am* a god'?
But you *shall be* a man, and not a god,
In the hand of him who slays you.
10 You shall die the death of
[a]the uncircumcised

27:28 [a] Ezek. 26:15 27:29 [a] Rev. 18:17 27:30 [a] 1 Sam. 4:12; 2 Sam. 1:2; Job 2:12; Lam. 2:10; Rev. 18:19 [b] Esth. 4:1, 3; Jer. 6:26; Jon. 3:6 27:31 [a] Is. 15:2; Jer. 16:6; Ezek. 29:18 27:32 [a] Ezek. 26:17 [b] Ezek. 26:4, 5; Rev. 18:18 27:33 [a] Rev. 18:19 27:34 [a] Ezek. 26:19 [b] Ezek. 27:27 27:35 [a] Is. 23:6; Ezek. 26:15, 16 27:36 [a] Jer. 18:16; Zeph. 2:15 [b] Ezek. 26:2 [c] Ps. 37:10, 36; Ezek. 28:19 28:2 [a] Jer. 49:16; Ezek. 31:10 [b] Is. 14:14; 47:8; Ezek. 28:9; 2 Thess. 2:4 [c] Ezek. 27:3, 4 [d] Is. 31:3; Ezek. 28:9 28:3 [a] Ezek. 14:14; Dan. 1:20; 2:20–23, 28; 5:11, 12; Zech. 9:3 28:4 [a] Ezek. 27:33; Zech. 9:1–3 28:5 [a] Ps. 62:10; Zech. 9:3 28:7 [a] Ezek. 26:7 [b] Ezek. 7:24; 21:31; 30:11; Hab. 1:6–8 28:8 [a] Is. 14:15 28:9 [a] Ezek. 28:2 28:10 [a] 1 Sam. 17:26, 36; Ezek. 31:18; 32:19, 21, 25, 27

By the hand of aliens;
For I have spoken," says
the Lord GOD.'"

Lamentation for the King of Tyre

11Moreover the word of the LORD came
to me, saying, 12"Son of man, [a]take up a
lamentation for the king of Tyre, and say
to him, 'Thus says the Lord GOD:

[b]"You *were* the seal of perfection,
Full of wisdom and perfect in beauty.
13 You were in [a]Eden, the garden of God;
Every precious stone *was*
your covering:
The sardius, topaz, and diamond,
Beryl, onyx, and jasper,
Sapphire, turquoise, and
emerald with gold.
The workmanship of [b]your
timbrels and pipes
Was prepared for you on the
day you were created.

14 "You *were* the anointed
[a]cherub who covers;
I established you;
You were on [b]the holy
mountain of God;
You walked back and forth in
the midst of fiery stones.
15 You *were* perfect in your ways from
the day you were created,
Till [a]iniquity was found in you.

16 "By the abundance of your trading
You became filled with
violence within,
And you sinned;
Therefore I cast you as a profane thing
Out of the mountain of God;
And I destroyed you,
[a]O covering cherub,
From the midst of the fiery stones.

17 "Your [a]heart was lifted up
because of your beauty;
You corrupted your wisdom for
the sake of your splendor;
I cast you to the ground,
I laid you before kings,
That they might gaze at you.

18 "You defiled your sanctuaries
By the multitude of your iniquities,
By the iniquity of your trading;
Therefore I brought fire
from your midst;
It devoured you,
And I turned you to ashes
upon the earth
In the sight of all who saw you.
19 All who knew you among the
peoples are astonished at you;
[a]You have become a horror,
And *shall be* no [b]more forever."'"

Proclamation Against Sidon

20Then the word of the LORD came to
me, saying, 21"Son of man, [a]set your face
[b]toward Sidon, and prophesy against her,
22and say, 'Thus says the Lord GOD:

[a]"Behold, I *am* against you, O Sidon;
I will be glorified in your midst;
And [b]they shall know that
I *am* the LORD,
When I execute judgments in her
and am [c]hallowed in her.
23 [a]For I will send pestilence upon her,
And blood in her streets;
The wounded shall be
judged in her midst
By the sword against her on every side;
Then they shall know that
I *am* the LORD.

24"And there shall no longer be a prick-
ing brier or [a]a painful thorn for the house
of Israel from among all *who are* around
them, who [b]despise them. Then they shall
know that I *am* the Lord GOD."

Israel's Future Blessing

25'Thus says the Lord GOD: "When I
have [a]gathered the house of Israel from
the peoples among whom they are scattered, and am [b]hallowed in them in the

28:12 [a] Ezek. 27:2 [b] Ezek. 27:3; 28:3 28:13 [a] Gen. 2:8; Is. 51:3; Ezek. 31:8, 9; 36:35 [b] Ezek. 26:13 28:14 [a] Ex. 25:20; Ezek. 28:16 [b] Is. 14:13; Ezek. 20:40 28:15 [a] [Is. 14:12] 28:16 [a] Ezek. 28:14 28:17 [a] Ezek. 28:2, 5 28:19 [a] Ezek. 26:21 [b] Ezek. 27:36 28:21 [a] Ezek. 6:2; 25:2; 29:2 [b] Gen. 10:15, 19; Is. 23:2, 4, 12; Ezek. 27:8; 32:30 28:22 [a] Ex. 14:4, 17; Ezek. 39:13 [b] Ps. 9:16 [c] Ezek. 28:25 28:23 [a] Ezek. 38:22 28:24 [a] Num. 33:55; Josh. 23:13; Is. 55:13; Ezek. 2:6 [b] Ezek. 16:57; 25:6, 7 28:25 [a] Ps. 106:47; Is. 11:12, 13; Jer. 32:37; Ezek. 11:17; 20:41; 34:13; 37:21 [b] Ezek. 28:22

sight of the Gentiles, then they will dwell
in their own land which I gave to My servant Jacob.
26And they will [a]dwell safely
there, [b]build houses, and [c]plant vineyards;
yes, they will dwell securely, when I execute
judgments on all those around them who
despise them. Then they shall know that I
am the LORD their God."'"

Proclamation Against Egypt

29 In the tenth year, in the tenth *month,*
on the twelfth *day* of the month, the
word of the LORD came to me, saying,
2"Son
of man, [a]set your face against Pharaoh king
of Egypt, and prophesy against him, and
[b]against all Egypt.
3Speak, and say, 'Thus
says the Lord GOD:

[a]"Behold, I *am* against you,
O Pharaoh king of Egypt,
O great [b]monster who lies in
the midst of his rivers,
[c]Who has said, 'My River[1] *is* my own;
I have made *it* for myself.'
4 But [a]I will put hooks in your jaws,
And cause the fish of your rivers
to stick to your scales;
I will bring you up out of the
midst of your rivers,
And all the fish in your rivers
will stick to your scales.
5 I will leave you in the wilderness,
You and all the fish of your rivers;
You shall fall on the open [a]field;
[b]You shall not be picked
up or gathered.[1]
[c]I have given you as food
To the beasts of the field
And to the birds of the heavens.

6 "Then all the inhabitants of Egypt
Shall know that I *am* the LORD,
Because they have been a [a]staff of
reed to the house of Israel.
7 [a]When they took hold of
you with the hand,
You broke and tore all their shoulders;[1]
When they leaned on you,
You broke and made all
their backs quiver."

8'Therefore thus says the Lord GOD:
"Surely I will bring [a]a sword upon you and
cut off from you man and beast.
9And the
land of Egypt shall become [a]desolate and
waste; then they will know that I *am* the
LORD, because he said, 'The River *is* mine,
and I have made *it.*'
10Indeed, therefore,
I *am* against you and against your rivers,
[a]and I will make the land of Egypt utterly
waste and desolate, [b]from Migdol[1] *to* Syene, as far as the border of Ethiopia.
11[a]Nei-
ther foot of man shall pass through it nor
foot of beast pass through it, and it shall be
uninhabited forty years.
12[a]I will make the
land of Egypt desolate in the midst of the
countries *that are* desolate; and among the
cities *that are* laid waste, her cities shall be
desolate forty years; and I will [b]scatter the
Egyptians among the nations and disperse
them throughout the countries."

13'Yet, thus says the Lord GOD: "At the
[a]end of forty years I will gather the Egyptians from the peoples among whom they
were scattered.
14I will bring back the cap-
tives of Egypt and cause them to return to
the land of Pathros, to the land of their origin, and there they shall be a [a]lowly kingdom.
15It shall be the lowliest of kingdoms;
it shall never again exalt itself above the
nations, for I will diminish them so that
they will not rule over the nations anymore.
16No longer shall it be [a]the confidence of
the house of Israel, but will remind them
of *their* iniquity when they turned to follow them. Then they shall know that I *am*
the Lord GOD."'"

Babylonia Will Plunder Egypt

17And it came to pass in the twenty-
seventh year, in the first *month,* on the first
day of the month, *that* the word of the LORD
came to me, saying,
18"Son of man, [a]Neb-
uchadnezzar king of Babylon caused his

28:26 [a] Jer. 23:6; Ezek. 36:28 [b] Is. 65:21; Jer. 32:15, 43, 44; Amos 9:13, 14 [c] Jer. 31:5; Amos 9:14 **29:2** [a] Ezek. 28:21 [b] Is. 19:1; Jer. 25:19; 46:2, 25; Ezek. 30:1—32:32; Joel 3:19 **29:3** [a] Jer. 44:30; Ezek. 28:22; 29:10 [b] Ps. 74:13, 14; Is. 37:1; 51:9; Ezek. 32:2 [c] Ezek. 28:2 [1] That is, the Nile **29:4** [a] 2 Kin. 19:28; Is. 37:29; Ezek. 38:4 **29:5** [a] Ezek. 32:4–6 [b] Jer. 8:2; 16:4; 25:33 [c] Jer. 7:33; 34:20; Ezek. 39:4 [1] Following Masoretic Text, Septuagint, and Vulgate; some Hebrew manuscripts and Targum read *buried.* **29:6** [a] 2 Kin. 18:21; Is. 36:6; Ezek. 17:15 **29:7** [a] Jer. 37:5, 7, 11; Ezek. 17:17 [1] Following Masoretic Text and Vulgate; Septuagint and Syriac read *hand.* **29:8** [a] Jer. 46:13; Ezek. 14:17; 32:11–13 **29:9** [a] Ezek. 30:7, 8 **29:10** [a] Ezek. 30:12 [b] Ezek. 30:6 [1] Or *tower* **29:11** [a] Jer. 43:11, 12; 46:19; Ezek. 32:13 **29:12** [a] Jer. 25:15–19; 27:6–11; Ezek. 30:7, 26 [b] Jer. 46:19; Ezek. 30:23, 26 **29:13** [a] Is. 19:23; Jer. 46:26 **29:14** [a] Ezek. 17:6, 14 **29:16** [a] Is. 30:2, 3; 36:4, 6; Lam. 4:17; Ezek. 17:15; 29:6 **29:18** [a] Jer. 25:9; 27:6; Ezek. 26:7–12

army to labor strenuously against Tyre;
every head *was* made [b]bald, and every
shoulder rubbed raw; yet neither he nor
his army received wages from Tyre, for the
labor which they expended on it. 19 Therefore thus says the Lord GOD: 'Surely I will
give the land of Egypt to [a]Nebuchadnez-
zar king of Babylon; he shall take away her
wealth, carry off her spoil, and remove her
pillage; and that will be the wages for his
army. 20 I have given him the land of Egypt
for his labor, because they [a]worked for Me,'
says the Lord GOD.

21 "In that day [a]I will cause the horn of the
house of Israel to spring forth, and I will
[b]open your mouth to speak in their midst.
Then they shall know that I *am* the LORD.'"

Egypt and Her Allies Will Fall

30 The word of the LORD came to me
again, saying, 2 "Son of man, prophesy and say, 'Thus says the Lord GOD:

[a]"Wail, 'Woe to the day!'
3 For [a]the day *is* near,
Even the day of the LORD *is* near;
It will be a day of clouds, the
time of the Gentiles.
4 The sword shall come upon Egypt,
And great anguish shall be in Ethiopia,
When the slain fall in Egypt,
And they [a]take away her wealth,
And [b]her foundations are
broken down.

5 "Ethiopia, Libya,[1] Lydia,[2] [a]all the mingled people, Chub, and the men of the lands
who are allied, shall fall with them by the
sword."

6 'Thus says the LORD:

"Those who uphold Egypt shall fall,
And the pride of her power
shall come down.
[a]From Migdol *to* Syene
Those within her shall fall
by the sword,"
Says the Lord GOD.

7 "They[a] shall be desolate in the midst
of the desolate countries,
And her cities shall be in the midst
of the cities *that are* laid waste.
8 Then they will know that
I *am* the LORD,
When I have set a fire in Egypt
And all her helpers are destroyed.
9 On that day [a]messengers shall
go forth from Me in ships
To make the careless
Ethiopians afraid,
And great anguish shall
come upon them,
As on the day of Egypt;
For indeed it is coming!"

10 "Thus says the Lord GOD:

[a]"I will also make a multitude
of Egypt to cease
By the hand of Nebuchadnezzar
king of Babylon.
11 He and his people with him, [a]the
most terrible of the nations,
Shall be brought to destroy the land;
They shall draw their swords
against Egypt,
And fill the land with the slain.
12 [a]I will make the rivers dry,
And [b]sell the land into the
hand of the wicked;
I will make the land waste,
and all that is in it,
By the hand of aliens.
I, the LORD, have spoken."

13 'Thus says the Lord GOD:

"I will also [a]destroy the idols,
And cause the images to
cease from Noph;[1]
[b]There shall no longer be princes
from the land of Egypt;
[c]I will put fear in the land of Egypt.
14 I will make [a]Pathros desolate,
Set fire to [b]Zoan,
[c]And execute judgments in No.[1]

29:18 [b] Jer. 48:37; Ezek. 27:31 29:19 [a] Jer. 43:10–13; Ezek. 30:10 29:20 [a] Is. 10:6, 7; 45:1–3; Jer. 25:9 29:21 [a] 1 Sam. 2:10; Ps. 92:10; 132:17 [b] Ezek. 24:27; Amos 3:7, 8; [Luke 21:15] 30:2 [a] Is. 13:6; 15:2; Ezek. 21:12; Joel 1:5, 11, 13 30:3 [a] Ezek. 7:7, 12; Joel 2:1; Obad. 15; Zeph. 1:7 30:4 [a] Ezek. 29:19 [b] Jer. 50:15 30:5 [a] Jer. 25:20, 24 [1] Hebrew *Put* [2] Hebrew *Lud* 30:6 [a] Ezek. 29:10 30:7 [a] Jer. 25:18–26; Ezek. 29:12 30:9 [a] Is. 18:1, 2 30:10 [a] Ezek. 29:19 30:11 [a] Ezek. 28:7; 31:12 30:12 [a] Is. 19:5, 6 [b] Is. 19:4 30:13 [a] Is. 19:1; Jer. 43:12; 46:25; Zech. 13:2 [b] Zech. 10:11 [c] Is. 19:16 [1] That is, ancient Memphis 30:14 [a] Is. 11:11; Jer. 44:1, 15; Ezek. 29:14 [b] Ps. 78:12, 43; Is. 19:11, 13 [c] Jer. 46:25; Ezek. 30:15, 16; Nah. 3:8–10 [1] That is, ancient Thebes

15 I will pour My fury on Sin,[1]
the strength of Egypt;
[a]I will cut off the multitude of No,
16 And [a]set a fire in Egypt;
Sin shall have great pain,
No shall be split open,
And Noph *shall be in* distress daily.
17 The young men of Aven[1] and Pi
Beseth shall fall by the sword,
And these *cities* shall go into captivity.
18 [a]At Tehaphnehes[1] the day shall
also be darkened,[2]
When I break the yokes of Egypt there.
And her arrogant strength
shall cease in her;
As for her, a cloud shall cover her,
And her daughters shall
go into captivity.
19 Thus I will [a]execute
judgments on Egypt,
Then they shall know that
I *am* the LORD."'"

Proclamation Against Pharaoh

20 And it came to pass in the eleventh
year, in the first *month,* on the seventh *day*
of the month, *that* the word of the LORD
came to me, saying, 21 "Son of man, I have
[a]broken the arm of Pharaoh king of Egypt;
and see, [b]it has not been bandaged for healing, nor a splint put on to bind it, to make
it strong enough to hold a sword. 22 Therefore thus says the Lord GOD: 'Surely I *am*
[a]against Pharaoh king of Egypt, and will
[b]break his arms, both the strong one and
the one that was broken; and I will make
the sword fall out of his hand. 23 [a]I will scatter the Egyptians among the nations, and
disperse them throughout the countries.
24 I will strengthen the arms of the king of
Babylon and put My sword in his hand;
but I will break Pharaoh's arms, and he
will groan before him with the groanings
of a mortally wounded *man.* 25 Thus I will
strengthen the arms of the king of Babylon,
but the arms of Pharaoh shall fall down;
[a]they shall know that I *am* the LORD, when
I put My sword into the hand of the king
of Babylon and he stretches it out against
the land of Egypt. 26 [a]I will scatter the Egyptians among the nations and disperse them
throughout the countries. Then they shall
know that I *am* the LORD.'"

Egypt Cut Down Like a Great Tree
(cf. Ezek. 17:22–24)

31 Now it came to pass in the [a]eleventh
year, in the third *month,* on the first
day of the month, *that* the word of the LORD
came to me, saying, 2 "Son of man, say to
Pharaoh king of Egypt and to his multitude:

[a]'Whom are you like in your greatness?
3 [a]Indeed Assyria *was* a
cedar in Lebanon,
With fine branches that
shaded the forest,
And of high stature;
And its top was among
the thick boughs.
4 [a]The waters made it grow;
Underground waters gave it height,
With their rivers running around
the place where it was planted,
And sent out rivulets to all
the trees of the field.

5 'Therefore [a]its height was exalted
above all the trees of the field;
Its boughs were multiplied,
And its branches became long
because of the abundance of water,
As it sent them out.
6 All the [a]birds of the heavens made
their nests in its boughs;
Under its branches all the beasts of
the field brought forth their young;
And in its shadow all great
nations made their home.

7 'Thus it was beautiful in greatness
and in the length of its branches,
Because its roots reached
to abundant waters.
8 The cedars in the [a]garden of
God could not hide it;

30:15 [a] Jer. 46:25 [1] That is, ancient Pelusium 30:16 [a] Ezek. 30:8 30:17 [1] That is, ancient On (Heliopolis) 30:18 [a] Jer. 2:16 [1] Spelled *Tahpanhes* in Jeremiah 43:7 and elsewhere [2] Following many Hebrew manuscripts, Bomberg, Septuagint, Syriac, Targum, and Vulgate; Masoretic Text reads *refrained.* 30:19 [a] [Ps. 9:16]; Ezek. 5:8; 25:11 30:21 [a] Jer. 48:25 [b] Jer. 46:11 30:22 [a] Jer. 46:25; Ezek. 29:3 [b] Ps. 37:17 30:23 [a] Ezek. 29:12; 30:17, 18, 26 30:25 [a] Ps. 9:16 30:26 [a] Ezek. 29:12 31:1 [a] Jer. 52:5, 6; Ezek. 30:20; 32:1 31:2 [a] Ezek. 31:18 31:3 [a] Is. 10:33, 34; Ezek. 17:3, 4, 22; 31:16; Dan. 4:10, 20–23 31:4 [a] Jer. 51:36; Ezek. 29:3–9 31:5 [a] Dan. 4:11 31:6 [a] Ezek. 17:23; 31:13; Dan. 4:12, 21; Matt. 13:32 31:8 [a] Gen. 2:8, 9; 13:10; Is. 51:3; Ezek. 28:13; 31:16, 18

The fir trees were not like its boughs,
And the chestnut[1] trees were
not like its branches;
No tree in the garden of God
was like it in beauty.
9 I made it beautiful with a
multitude of branches,
So that all the trees of Eden envied it,
That *were* in the garden of God.'

10 "Therefore thus says the Lord GOD: 'Because you have increased in height, and it
set its top among the thick boughs, and [a]its
heart was lifted up in its height, 11 therefore
I will deliver it into the hand of the [a]mighty
one of the nations, and he shall surely deal
with it; I have driven it out for its wickedness. 12 And aliens, [a]the most terrible of
the nations, have cut it down and left it; its
branches have fallen [b]on the mountains
and in all the valleys; its boughs lie [c]bro-
ken by all the rivers of the land; and all the
peoples of the earth have gone from under
its shadow and left it.

13 'On [a]its ruin will remain all the
birds of the heavens,
And all the beasts of the field
will come to its branches—

14 So that no trees by the waters may ever
again exalt themselves for their height, nor
set their tops among the thick boughs, that
no tree which drinks water may ever be
high enough to reach up to them.

'For [a]they have all been
delivered to death,
[b]To the depths of the earth,
Among the children of men
who go down to the Pit.'

15 "Thus says the Lord GOD: 'In the
day when it [a]went down to hell, I caused
mourning. I covered the deep because of
it. I restrained its rivers, and the great waters were held back. I caused Lebanon to
mourn for it, and all the trees of the field
wilted because of it. 16 I made the nations
[a]shake at the sound of its fall, when I [b]cast
it down to hell together with those who
descend into the Pit; and [c]all the trees of
Eden, the choice and best of Lebanon, all
that drink water, [d]were comforted in the
depths of the earth. 17 They also went down
to hell with it, with those slain by the sword;
and *those who were* its *strong* arm [a]dwelt in
its shadows among the nations.

18 [a]'To which of the trees in Eden will you
then be likened in glory and greatness? Yet
you shall be brought down with the trees of
Eden to the depths of the earth; [b]you shall
lie in the midst of the uncircumcised, with
those slain by the sword. This *is* Pharaoh
and all his multitude,' says the Lord GOD."

Lamentation for Pharaoh and Egypt

32

And it came to pass in the twelfth
year, in the [a]twelfth *month,* on the
first *day* of the month, *that* the word of the
LORD came to me, saying, 2 "Son of man,
[a]take up a lamentation for Pharaoh king
of Egypt, and say to him:

[b]'You are like a young lion
among the nations,
And [c]you *are* like a monster
in the seas,
[d]Bursting forth in your rivers,
Troubling the waters with your feet,
And [e]fouling their rivers.

3 'Thus says the Lord GOD:

"I will therefore [a]spread My net
over you with a company
of many people,
And they will draw you up in My net.
4 Then [a]I will leave you on the land;
I will cast you out on the open fields,
[b]And cause to settle on you all
the birds of the heavens.
And with you I will fill the
beasts of the whole earth.
5 I will lay your flesh [a]on the mountains,
And fill the valleys with your carcass.

31:8 [1] Hebrew *armon* 31:10 [a] 2 Chr. 32:25; Is. 10:12; 14:13, 14; Ezek. 28:17; Dan. 5:20 31:11 [a] Ezek. 30:10; Dan. 5:18, 19
31:12 [a] Ezek. 28:7; 30:11; 32:12 [b] Ezek. 32:5; 35:8 [c] Ezek. 30:24, 25 31:13 [a] Is. 18:6; Ezek. 32:4 31:14 [a] Ps. 82:7 [b] Ezek. 32:18
31:15 [a] Ezek. 32:22, 23 31:16 [a] Ezek. 26:15; Hag. 2:7 [b] Is. 14:15; Ezek. 32:18 [c] Is. 14:8; Hab. 2:17 [d] Ezek. 32:31 31:17 [a] Lam. 4:20
31:18 [a] Ezek. 32:19 [b] Jer. 9:25, 26; Ezek. 28:10; 32:19, 21 32:1 [a] Ezek. 31:1; 33:21 32:2 [a] Ezek. 27:2 [b] Jer. 4:7; Ezek. 19:2–6;
Nah. 2:11–13 [c] Is. 27:1; Ezek. 29:3 [d] Jer. 46:7, 8 [e] Ezek. 34:18 32:3 [a] Ezek. 12:13; 17:20
32:4 [a] Ezek. 29:5 [b] Is. 18:6; Ezek. 31:13 32:5 [a] Ezek. 31:12

6 "I will also water the land with
the flow of your blood,
Even to the mountains;
And the riverbeds will be full of you.
7 When *I* put out your light,
[a]I will cover the heavens, and
make its stars dark;
I will cover the sun with a cloud,
And the moon shall not give her light.
8 All the bright lights of the heavens
I will make dark over you,
And bring darkness upon your land,"
Says the Lord GOD.

9'I will also trouble the hearts of many
peoples, when I bring your destruction
among the nations, into the countries
which you have not known. 10Yes, I will
make many peoples astonished at you,
and their kings shall be horribly afraid
of you when I brandish My sword before
them; and [a]they shall tremble *every* moment, every man for his own life, in the
day of your fall.
11[a]'For thus says the Lord GOD: "The
sword of the king of Babylon shall come
upon you. 12By the swords of the mighty
warriors, all of them [a]the most terrible of
the nations, I will cause your multitude
to fall.

[b]"They shall plunder the pomp of Egypt,
And all its multitude shall
be destroyed.
13 Also I will destroy all its animals
From beside its great waters;
[a]The foot of man shall muddy
them no more,
Nor shall the hooves of
animals muddy them.
14 Then I will make their waters clear,
And make their rivers run like oil,"
Says the Lord GOD.

15 "When I make the land of
Egypt desolate,
And the country is destitute
of all that once filled it,
When I strike all who dwell in it,
[a]Then they shall know that
I *am* the LORD.

16 "This *is* the [a]lamentation
With which they shall lament her;
The daughters of the nations
shall lament her;
They shall lament for her, for Egypt,
And for all her multitude,"
Says the Lord GOD.'"

Egypt and Others Consigned to the Pit

17It came to pass also in the twelfth year,
on the fifteenth *day* of the month, [a]*that*
the word of the LORD came to me, saying:

18 "Son of man, wail over the
multitude of Egypt,
And [a]cast them down to the
depths of the earth,
Her and the daughters of
the famous nations,
With those who go down to the Pit:
19 'Whom [a]do you surpass in beauty?
[b]Go down, be placed with
the uncircumcised.'

20 "They shall fall in the midst of
those slain by the sword;
She is delivered to the sword,
[a]Drawing her and all her multitudes.
21 [a]The strong among the mighty
Shall speak to him out of
the midst of hell
With those who help him:
'They have [b]gone down,
They lie with the uncircumcised,
slain by the sword.'

22 "Assyria[a] *is* there, and all her company,
With their graves all around her,
All of them slain, fallen by the sword.
23 [a]Her graves are set in the
recesses of the Pit,
And her company is all
around her grave,
All of them slain, fallen by the sword,
Who [b]caused terror in the
land of the living.

32:7 [a] Is. 13:10; Joel 2:31; 3:15; Amos 8:9; Matt. 24:29; Mark 13:24; Luke 21:25; Rev. 6:12, 13; 8:12 **32:10** [a] Ezek. 26:16 **32:11** [a] Jer. 46:26; Ezek. 30:4 **32:12** [a] Ezek. 28:7; 30:11; 31:12 [b] Ezek. 29:19 **32:13** [a] Ezek. 29:11 **32:15** [a] Ex. 7:5; 14:4, 18; Ps. 9:16; Ezek. 6:7 **32:16** [a] 2 Sam. 1:17; 2 Chr. 35:25; Jer. 9:17; Ezek. 26:17 **32:17** [a] Ezek. 32:1; 33:21 **32:18** [a] Ezek. 26:20; 31:14 **32:19** [a] Jer. 9:25, 26; Ezek. 31:2, 18 [b] Ezek. 28:10 **32:20** [a] Ps. 28:3 **32:21** [a] Is. 1:31; 14:9, 10; Ezek. 32:27 [b] Ezek. 32:19, 25 **32:22** [a] Ezek. 31:3, 16 **32:23** [a] Is. 14:15 [b] Ezek. 32:24–27, 32

24 "There *is* [a]Elam and all her multitude,
All around her grave,
All of them slain, fallen by the sword,
Who have [b]gone down uncircumcised
to the lower parts of the earth,
[c]Who caused their terror in
the land of the living;
Now they bear their shame with
those who go down to the Pit.
25 They have set her [a]bed in the
midst of the slain,
With all her multitude,
With her graves all around it,
All of them uncircumcised,
slain by the sword;
Though their terror was caused
In the land of the living,
Yet they bear their shame
With those who go down to the Pit;
It was put in the midst of the slain.

26 "There *are* [a]Meshech and Tubal
and all their multitudes,
With all their graves around it,
All of them [b]uncircumcised,
slain by the sword,
Though they caused their terror
in the land of the living.
27 [a]They do not lie with the mighty
Who are fallen of the uncircumcised,
Who have gone down to hell
with their weapons of war;
They have laid their swords
under their heads,
But their iniquities will be
on their bones,
Because of the terror of the mighty
in the land of the living.
28 Yes, you shall be broken in the
midst of the uncircumcised,
And lie with *those* slain by
the sword.

29 "There *is* [a]Edom,
Her kings and all her princes,
Who despite their might
Are laid beside *those* slain
by the sword;
They shall lie with the uncircumcised,
And with those who go
down to the Pit.
30 [a]There *are* the princes of the north,
All of them, and all the [b]Sidonians,
Who have gone down with the slain
In shame at the terror which
they caused by their might;
They lie uncircumcised with
those slain by the sword,
And bear their shame with those
who go down to the Pit.

31 "Pharaoh will see them
And be [a]comforted over
all his multitude,
Pharaoh and all his army,
Slain by the sword,"
Says the Lord GOD.

32 "For I have caused My terror in
the land of the living;
And he shall be placed in the
midst of the uncircumcised
With *those* slain by the sword,
Pharaoh and all his multitude,"
Says the Lord GOD.

The Watchman and His Message

33 Again the word of the LORD came
to me, saying, 2 "Son of man, speak
to [a]the children of your people, and say to
them: [b]'When I bring the sword upon a land,
and the people of the land take a man from
their territory and make him their [c]watch-
man, 3 when he sees the sword coming upon
the land, if he blows the trumpet and warns
the people, 4 then whoever hears the sound
of the trumpet and does [a]not take warning,
if the sword comes and takes him away, [b]his
blood shall be on his *own* head. 5 He heard
the sound of the trumpet, but did not take
warning; his blood shall be upon himself.
But he who takes warning will save his life.
6 But if the watchman sees the sword coming
and does not blow the trumpet, and the people are not warned, and the sword comes
and takes *any* person from among them,
[a]he is taken away in his iniquity; but his
blood I will require at the watchman's hand.'

32:24 [a] Gen. 10:22; 14:1; Is. 11:11; Jer. 25:25; 49:34–39 [b] Ezek. 32:21 [c] Ezek. 32:23 32:25 [a] Ps. 139:8 32:26 [a] Gen. 10:2; Ezek. 27:13; 38:2, 3; 39:1 [b] Ezek. 32:19 32:27 [a] Is. 14:18, 19 32:29 [a] Is. 9:5, 6; 34:5, 6; Jer. 49:7–22; Ezek. 25:12–14 32:30 [a] Jer. 1:15; 25:26; Ezek. 38:6, 15; 39:2 [b] Jer. 25:22; Ezek. 28:21–23 32:31 [a] Ezek. 14:22; 31:16 33:2 [a] Ezek. 3:11 [b] Ezek. 14:17 [c] 2 Sam. 18:24, 25; 2 Kin. 9:17; Hos. 9:8 33:4 [a] 2 Chr. 25:16; Jer. 6:17; Zech. 1:4 [b] Ezek. 18:13; 35:9; [Acts 18:6] 33:6 [a] Ezek. 33:8

7[a]"So you, son of man: I have made you
a watchman for the house of Israel; therefore you shall hear a word from My mouth
and warn them for Me. 8When I say to the
wicked, 'O wicked *man*, you shall surely die!'
and you do not speak to warn the wicked
from his way, that wicked *man* shall die in
his iniquity; but his blood I will require at
your hand. 9Nevertheless if you warn the
wicked to turn from his way, and he does
not turn from his way, he shall die in his
iniquity; but you have delivered your soul.
10"Therefore you, O son of man, say to
the house of Israel: 'Thus you say, "If our
transgressions and our sins *lie* upon us,
and we [a]pine away in them, [b]how can we
then live?"' 11Say to them: 'As I live,' says
the Lord GOD, [a]'I have no pleasure in the
death of the wicked, but that the wicked
[b]turn from his way and live. Turn, turn from
your evil ways! For [c]why should you die,
O house of Israel?'

The Fairness of God's Judgment

12"Therefore you, O son of man, say to
the children of your people: 'The [a]righteousness of the righteous man shall not
deliver him in the day of his transgression;
as for the wickedness of the wicked, [b]he
shall not fall because of it in the day that
he turns from his wickedness; nor shall the
righteous be able to live because of *his righteousness* in the day that he sins.' 13When I
say to the righteous *that* he shall surely live,
[a]but he trusts in his own righteousness and
commits iniquity, none of his righteous

EZEKIEL 33:8

I AM EZEKIEL

"When I say to the wicked, 'O wicked man, you shall surely die!' and you do not speak to warn the wicked from his way, that wicked man shall die in his iniquity; but his blood I will require at your hand." Ezekiel 33:8

I am Ezekiel, a prophet of the Lord, held captive with my people in Babylon. The people of Israel had rebelled against God, so He sent me to speak His words to them. He told me to speak truth fearlessly to them whether they listened to me or not. As a watchman for the house of Israel, I was to hear from the Lord and inform the people. If I did not, their blood would be on my hands. However, if I warned them and they did not listen, their deaths would be by their own hands. If the righteous listened, they would be delivered by my obedience to God's word.

I faithfully delivered the word of the Lord to the people of Israel, but they were continuously rebellious and refused to listen. Therefore, the Lord brought judgment upon them, leaving only a remnant who would return from Babylonian captivity to rebuild their land. The Lord promised to restore Israel and that the people would be His people and He would be their God.

The Lord brought me in the Spirit to a valley full of dry bones. He asked me, "Son of man, can these bones live?" He had me prophesy to the bones that they would live again. Flesh and sinew grew upon them, and they rose from death to life. Just as those bones came to life before my eyes, the dry bones of Israel would surely live again.

†

Just as He revived the dry bones in the valley, God can breathe life into the most lost, the most wicked, the most hateful people. We are His watchmen, and we are to speak the life into others that was spoken into us when our bones were as dry as those in Ezekiel's vision. If we speak life and they refuse to listen, then their fate is their own. But if we fail to speak, we will be held accountable for their blood.

33:7 [a] Is. 62:6; Ezek. 3:17–21 33:10 [a] Lev. 26:39; Ezek. 24:23 [b] Is. 49:14; Ezek. 37:11 33:11 [a] [2 Sam. 14:14; Lam. 3:33]; Ezek. 18:23, 32; Hos. 11:8; [2 Pet. 3:9] [b] Ezek. 18:21, 30; [Hos. 14:1, 4; Acts 3:19] [c] [Is. 55:6, 7]; Jer. 3:22; Ezek. 18:30, 31; Hos. 14:1; [Acts 3:19] 33:12 [a] Ezek. 3:20; 18:24, 26 [b] [2 Chr. 7:14]; Ezek. 18:21; 33:19 33:13 [a] Ezek. 3:20; 18:24

works shall be remembered; but because
of the iniquity that he has committed, he
shall die. 14Again, [a]when I say to the wicked,
'You shall surely die,' if he turns from his
sin and does what is lawful and right, 15*if*
the wicked [a]restores the pledge, [b]gives back
what he has stolen, and walks in [c]the statutes of life without committing iniquity, he
shall surely live; he shall not die. 16[a]None
of his sins which he has committed shall
be remembered against him; he has done
what is lawful and right; he shall surely live.
17[a]"Yet the children of your people say,
'The way of the Lord is not fair.' But it is
their way which is not fair! 18[a]When the
righteous turns from his righteousness and
commits iniquity, he shall die because of it.
19But when the wicked turns from his wickedness and does what is lawful and right,
he shall live because of it. 20Yet you say,
[a]'The way of the Lord is not fair.' O house
of Israel, I will judge every one of you according to his own ways."

The Fall of Jerusalem

21And it came to pass in the twelfth year
[a]of our captivity, in the tenth *month,* on the
fifth *day* of the month, [b]*that* one who had
escaped from Jerusalem came to me and
said, [c]"The city has been captured!"
22Now [a]the hand of the LORD had been
upon me the evening before the man came
who had escaped. And He had [b]opened
my mouth; so when he came to me in the
morning, my mouth was opened, and I was
no longer mute.

The Cause of Judah's Ruin

23Then the word of the LORD came to
me, saying: 24"Son of man, [a]they who inhabit those [b]ruins in the land of Israel are
saying, [c]'Abraham was only one, and he
inherited the land. [d]But we *are* many; the
land has been given to us as a [e]possession.'
25"Therefore say to them, 'Thus says the
Lord GOD: [a]"You eat *meat* with blood, you
[b]lift up your eyes toward your idols, and
[c]shed blood. Should you then possess the
[d]land? 26You rely on your sword, you commit abominations, and you [a]defile one another's wives. Should you then possess the
land?"'
27"Say thus to them, 'Thus says the Lord
GOD: "*As* I live, surely [a]those who *are* in the
ruins shall fall by the sword, and the one
who *is* in the open field [b]I will give to the
beasts to be devoured, and those who *are*
in the strongholds and [c]caves shall die of
the pestilence. 28[a]For I will make the land
most desolate, her [b]arrogant strength shall
cease, and [c]the mountains of Israel shall be
so desolate that no one will pass through.
29Then they shall know that I *am* the LORD,
when I have made the land most desolate
because of all their abominations which
they have committed."'

Hearing and Not Doing

30"As for you, son of man, the children
of your people are talking about you beside
the walls and in the doors of the houses;
and they [a]speak to one another, everyone
saying to his brother, 'Please come and
hear what the word is that comes from
the LORD.' 31So [a]they come to you as people do, they [b]sit before you *as* My people,
and they [c]hear your words, but they do not
do them; [d]for with their mouth they show
much love, *but* [e]their hearts pursue their
own gain. 32Indeed you *are* to them as a
very lovely song of one who has a pleasant
voice and can play well on an instrument;
for they hear your words, but they do [a]not
do them. 33[a]And when this comes to pass—
surely it will come—then [b]they will know
that a prophet has been among them."

Irresponsible Shepherds

34 And the word of the LORD came to
me, saying, 2"Son of man, prophesy
against the shepherds of Israel, prophesy
and say to them, 'Thus says the Lord GOD
to the shepherds: [a]"Woe to the shepherds
of Israel who feed themselves! Should not

33:14 [a] [Is. 55:7]; Jer. 18:7, 8; Ezek. 3:18, 19; 18:27; Hos. 14:1, 4 33:15 [a] Ezek. 18:7 [b] Ex. 22:1–4; Lev. 6:2, 4, 5; Num. 5:6, 7; Luke 19:8 [c] Lev. 18:5; Ps. 119:59; 143:8; Ezek. 20:11, 13, 21 33:16 [a] [Is. 1:18; 43:25]; Ezek. 18:22 33:17 [a] Ezek. 18:25, 29 33:18 [a] Ezek. 18:26 33:20 [a] Ezek. 18:25, 29 33:21 [a] Ezek. 1:2 [b] Ezek. 24:26 [c] 2 Kin. 25:4 33:22 [a] Ezek. 1:3; 8:1; 37:1 [b] Ezek. 24:27 33:24 [a] Ezek. 34:2 [b] Ezek. 36:4 [c] Is. 51:2; [Acts 7:5; Rom. 4:12] [d] Mic. 3:11; [Matt. 3:9; John 8:39] [e] Ezek. 11:15 33:25 [a] Gen. 9:4; Lev. 3:17; 7:26; 17:10–14; 19:26; Deut. 12:16, 23; 15:23 [b] Ezek. 18:6 [c] Ezek. 22:6, 9 [d] Deut. 29:28 33:26 [a] Ezek. 18:6; 22:11 33:27 [a] Ezek. 33:24 [b] Ezek. 39:4 [c] Judg. 6:2; 1 Sam. 13:6; Is. 2:19 33:28 [a] Jer. 44:2, 6, 22; Ezek. 36:34, 35 [b] Ezek. 7:24; 24:21 [c] Ezek. 6:2, 3, 6 33:30 [a] Is. 29:13; Ezek. 14:3; 20:3, 31 33:31 [a] Ezek. 14:1 [b] Ezek. 8:1 [c] Is. 58:2 [d] Ps. 78:36, 37; Is. 29:13; Jer. 12:2; 1 John 3:18 [e] [Matt. 13:22] 33:32 [a] [Matt. 7:21–28; James 1:22–25] 33:33 [a] 1 Sam. 3:20 [b] Ezek. 2:5 34:2 [a] Jer. 23:1; Ezek. 22:25; Mic. 3:1–3, 11; Zech. 11:17

the shepherds feed the flocks? 3[a]You eat
the fat and clothe yourselves with the wool;
you [b]slaughter the fatlings, *but* you do not
feed the flock. 4[a]The weak you have not
strengthened, nor have you healed those
who were sick, nor bound up the broken,
nor brought back what was driven away, nor
[b]sought what was lost; but with [c]force and
cruelty you have ruled them. 5[a]So they were
[b]scattered because *there was* no shepherd;
[c]and they became food for all the beasts
of the field when they were scattered. 6My
sheep [a]wandered through all the mountains, and on every high hill; yes, My flock
was scattered over the whole face of the
earth, and no one was seeking or searching *for them*."

7"Therefore, you shepherds, hear the
word of the LORD: 8"*As* I live," says the
Lord GOD, "surely because My flock became a prey, and My flock [a]became food
for every beast of the field, because *there
was* no shepherd, nor did My shepherds
search for My flock, [b]but the shepherds fed
themselves and did not feed My flock"—
9therefore, O shepherds, hear the word of
the LORD! 10Thus says the Lord GOD: "Behold, I *am* [a]against the shepherds, and [b]I
will require My flock at their hand; I will
cause them to cease feeding the sheep,
and the shepherds shall [c]feed themselves
no more; for I will [d]deliver My flock from
their mouths, that they may no longer be
food for them."

God, the True Shepherd

11"For thus says the Lord GOD: "Indeed I
Myself will search for My sheep and seek
them out. 12As a [a]shepherd seeks out his
flock on the day he is among his scattered
sheep, so will I seek out My sheep and deliver them from all the places where they
were scattered on [b]a cloudy and dark day.
13And [a]I will bring them out from the peoples and gather them from the countries,
and will bring them to their own land; I will
feed them on the mountains of Israel, in
the valleys and in all the inhabited places
of the country. 14[a]I will feed them in good
pasture, and their fold shall be on the high
mountains of Israel. [b]There they shall lie
down in a good fold and feed in rich pasture on the mountains of Israel. 15I will feed
My flock, and I will make them lie down,"
says the Lord GOD. 16[a]"I will seek what was
lost and bring back what was driven away,
bind up the broken and strengthen what
was sick; but I will destroy [b]the fat and the
strong, and feed them [c]in judgment."

> #OXYGEN
> EZEKIEL 34:11-12
> ***Hope for the Salvation of the Lost***
>
> God has always had a plan to save the lost. He calls us to be on mission with Him. People need to know that God has not forgotten about them. Keep sharing the Good News! Preach, **breathe**, and **hope for the salvation of the lost.**

17"And *as for* you, O My flock, thus says
the Lord GOD: [a]"Behold, I shall judge between sheep and sheep, between rams
and goats. 18*Is it* too little for you to have
eaten up the good pasture, that you must
tread down with your feet the residue of
your pasture—and to have drunk of the
clear waters, that you must foul the residue with your feet? 19And *as for* My flock,
they eat what you have trampled with your
feet, and they drink what you have fouled
with your feet."

20"Therefore thus says the Lord GOD to
them: [a]"Behold, I Myself will judge between
the fat and the lean sheep. 21Because you
have pushed with side and shoulder, butted
all the weak ones with your horns, and scattered them abroad, 22therefore I will save

34:3 [a] Is. 56:11; Zech. 11:16 [b] Ezek. 33:25, 26; Mic. 3:1–3; Zech. 11:5 34:4 [a] Zech. 11:16 [b] Matt. 9:36; 10:16; 18:12, 13; Luke 15:4 [c] [1 Pet. 5:3] 34:5 [a] Ezek. 33:21 [b] Num. 27:17; 1 Kin. 22:17; Jer. 10:21; Matt. 9:36; Mark 6:34 [c] Is. 56:9; Jer. 12:9 34:6 [a] Jer. 40:11, 12; 50:6; Ezek. 7:16; 1 Pet. 2:25 34:8 [a] Ezek. 34:5, 6 [b] Ezek. 34:2, 10 34:10 [a] Jer. 21:13; 52:24–27; Ezek. 5:8; 13:8; Zech. 10:3 [b] Ezek. 3:18; Heb. 13:17 [c] Ezek. 34:2, 8 [d] Ps. 72:12–14; Ezek. 13:23 34:12 [a] Jer. 31:10 [b] Jer. 13:16; Ezek. 30:3; Joel 2:2 34:13 [a] Is. 65:9, 10; Jer. 23:3; Ezek. 11:17; 20:41; 28:25; 36:24; 37:21, 22 34:14 [a] Ps. 23:2; Jer. 3:15; [John 10:9] [b] Jer. 33:12 34:16 [a] Is. 40:11; Mic. 4:6; [Matt. 18:11; Mark 2:17; Luke 5:32] [b] Is. 10:16; Amos 4:1 [c] Jer. 10:24 34:17 [a] Ezek. 20:37; Mal. 4:1; [Matt. 25:32] 34:20 [a] Ezek. 34:17

My flock, and they shall no longer be a prey;
and I will judge between sheep and sheep.
23I will establish one [a]shepherd over them,
and he shall feed them—[b]My servant David.
He shall feed them and be their shepherd.
24And [a]I, the LORD, will be their God, and
My servant David [b]a prince among them;
I, the LORD, have spoken.
25[a]"I will make a covenant of peace with
them, and [b]cause wild beasts to cease from
the land; and they [c]will dwell safely in the
wilderness and sleep in the woods. 26I will
make them and the places all around [a]My
hill [b]a blessing; and I will [c]cause showers to
come down in their season; there shall be
[d]showers of blessing. 27Then [a]the trees of
the field shall yield their fruit, and the earth
shall yield her increase. They shall be safe
in their land; and they shall know that I *am*
the LORD, when I have [b]broken the bands
of their yoke and delivered them from the
hand of those who [c]enslaved them. 28And
they shall no longer be a prey for the nations, nor shall beasts of the land devour
them; but [a]they shall dwell safely, and no
one shall make *them* afraid. 29I will raise
up for them a [a]garden of renown, and they
shall [b]no longer be consumed with hunger
in the land, [c]nor bear the shame of the Gentiles anymore. 30Thus they shall know that
[a]I, the LORD their God, *am* with them, and
they, the house of Israel, *are* [b]My people,"
says the Lord GOD.'
31"You are My [a]flock, the flock of My pasture; you *are* men, *and* I *am* your God," says
the Lord GOD.

Judgment on Mount Seir

35 Moreover the word of the LORD
came to me, saying, 2"Son of man,
set your face against [a]Mount Seir and
[b]prophesy against it, 3and say to it, 'Thus
says the Lord GOD:

"Behold, O Mount Seir, I
am against you;
[a]I will stretch out My hand against you,
And make you most desolate;
4 I shall lay your cities waste,
And you shall be desolate.
Then you shall know that
I *am* the LORD.

5[a]"Because you have had an ancient hatred, and have shed *the blood of* the children of Israel by the power of the sword at
the time of their calamity, [b]when their iniquity *came to an* end, 6therefore, *as* I live,"
says the Lord GOD, "I will prepare you for
[a]blood, and blood shall pursue you; [b]since
you have not hated blood, therefore blood
shall pursue you. 7Thus I will make Mount
Seir most desolate, and cut off from it the
[a]one who leaves and the one who returns.
8And I will fill its mountains with the slain;
on your hills and in your valleys and in all
your ravines those who are slain by the
sword shall fall. 9[a]I will make you perpetually desolate, and your cities shall be uninhabited; [b]then you shall know that I *am*
the LORD.
10"Because you have said, 'These two
nations and these two countries shall be
mine, and we will [a]possess them,' although
[b]the LORD was there, 11therefore, *as* I live,"
says the Lord GOD, "I will do [a]according
to your anger and according to the envy
which you showed in your hatred against
them; and I will make Myself known among
them when I judge you. 12[a]Then you shall
know that I *am* the LORD. I have [b]heard all
your [c]blasphemies which you have spoken
against the mountains of Israel, saying,
'They are desolate; they are given to us to
consume.' 13Thus [a]with your mouth you
have boasted against Me and multiplied
your [b]words against Me; I have heard *them*."
14'Thus says the Lord GOD: [a]"The whole
earth will rejoice when I make you desolate.
15[a]As you rejoiced because the inheritance
of the house of Israel was desolate, [b]so I will
do to you; you shall be desolate, O Mount

34:23 [a] [Is. 40:11; Jer. 23:4, 5]; Hos. 1:11; [John 10:11; Heb. 13:20; 1 Pet. 2:25; 5:4] [b] Jer. 30:9; Ezek. 37:24; Hos. 3:5 34:24 [a] Ex. 29:45; Ezek. 37:25 [b] Is. 55:3; Jer. 30:9; Ezek. 37:24, 25; Hos. 3:5 34:25 [a] Ezek. 37:26 [b] Lev. 26:6; Job 5:22, 23; Is. 11:6–9; Hos. 2:18 [c] Jer. 23:6 34:26 [a] Is. 56:7 [b] Gen. 12:2; Is. 19:24; Zech. 8:13 [c] Lev. 26:4 [d] Ps. 68:9 34:27 [a] Lev. 26:4; Ps. 85:12; Is. 4:2 [b] Lev. 26:13; Is. 52:2, 3; Jer. 2:20 [c] Jer. 25:14 34:28 [a] Jer. 30:10; Ezek. 39:26 34:29 [a] [Is. 11:1] [b] Ezek. 36:29 [c] Ezek. 36:3, 6, 15 34:30 [a] Ezek. 34:24 [b] Ps. 46:7, 11; Ezek. 14:11; 36:28 34:31 [a] Ps. 100:3; Jer. 23:1; [John 10:11] 35:2 [a] Gen. 36:8; Deut. 2:5; Jer. 25:21; 49:7–22; Ezek. 25:12–14; Joel 3:19; Amos 1:11, 12; Obad. 1–9, 15, 16 [b] Amos 1:11 35:3 [a] Ezek. 6:14 35:5 [a] Ezek. 25:12 [b] Ps. 137:7; Dan. 9:24; Amos 1:11; Obad. 10 35:6 [a] Is. 63:1–6; Ezek. 16:38; 32:6 [b] Ps. 109:17 35:7 [a] Judg. 5:6 35:9 [a] Jer. 49:13; Ezek. 25:13 [b] Ezek. 36:11 35:10 [a] Ps. 83:4–12; Ezek. 36:2, 5 [b] [Ps. 48:1–3; 132:13, 14]; Is. 12:6; Ezek. 48:35; Zeph. 3:15 35:11 [a] [Matt. 7:2; James 2:13] 35:12 [a] Ps. 9:16 [b] Zeph. 2:8 [c] Is. 52:5 35:13 [a] [1 Sam. 2:3] [b] Ezek. 36:3 35:14 [a] Is. 65:13, 14 35:15 [a] Obad. 12, 15 [b] Jer. 50:11; Lam. 4:21

Seir, as well as all of Edom—all of it! Then
they shall know that I *am* the LORD."'

Blessing on Israel

36 "And you, son of man, prophesy to
the [a]mountains of Israel, and say,
'O mountains of Israel, hear the word of the
LORD! 2Thus says the Lord GOD: "Because
[a]the enemy has said of you, 'Aha! [b]The ancient heights [c]have become our possession,'"' 3therefore prophesy, and say, 'Thus
says the Lord GOD: "Because they made
you desolate and swallowed you up on every side, so that you became the possession of the rest of the nations, [a]and you are
taken up by the lips of [b]talkers and slan-
dered by the people"— 4therefore, O mountains of Israel, hear the word of the Lord
GOD! Thus says the Lord GOD to the mountains, the hills, the rivers, the valleys, the
desolate wastes, and the cities that have
been forsaken, which [a]became plunder
and [b]mockery to the rest of the nations all
around— 5therefore thus says the Lord
GOD: [a]"Surely I have spoken in My burning jealousy against the rest of the nations
and against all Edom, [b]who gave My land
to themselves as a possession, with whole-
hearted joy *and* spiteful minds, in order to
plunder its open country."'

6"Therefore prophesy concerning the
land of Israel, and say to the mountains, the
hills, the rivers, and the valleys, 'Thus says
the Lord GOD: "Behold, I have spoken in
My jealousy and My fury, because you have
[a]borne the shame of the nations." 7There-
fore thus says the Lord GOD: "I have [a]raised
My hand in an oath that surely the nations
that *are* around you shall [b]bear their own
shame. 8But you, O mountains of Israel,
you shall shoot forth your branches and
yield your fruit to My people Israel, for they
are about to come. 9For indeed I *am* for you,
and I will turn to you, and you shall be tilled
and sown. 10I will multiply men upon you,
all the house of Israel, all of it; and the cities
shall be inhabited and [a]the ruins rebuilt. 11[a]I
will multiply upon you man and beast; and
they shall increase and bear young; I will
make you inhabited as in former times, and
do [b]better *for you* than at your beginnings.
[c]Then you shall know that I *am* the LORD.
12Yes, I will cause men to walk on you, My
people Israel; [a]they shall take possession of
you, and you shall be their inheritance; no
more shall you [b]bereave them *of children*."

13"Thus says the Lord GOD: "Because they
say to you, [a]'You devour men and bereave
your nation *of children*,' 14therefore you
shall devour men no more, nor bereave
your nation anymore," says the Lord GOD.
15[a]"Nor will I let you hear the taunts of the
nations anymore, nor bear the reproach of
the peoples anymore, nor shall you cause
your nation to stumble anymore," says the
Lord GOD.'"

The Renewal of Israel

16Moreover the word of the LORD came
to me, saying: 17"Son of man, when the
house of Israel dwelt in their own land,
[a]they defiled it by their own ways and
deeds; to Me their way was like [b]the uncleanness of a woman in her customary
impurity. 18Therefore I poured out My fury
on them [a]for the blood they had shed on the
land, and for their idols *with which* they had
defiled it. 19So I [a]scattered them among the
nations, and they were dispersed throughout the countries; I judged them [b]accord-
ing to their ways and their deeds. 20When
they came to the nations, wherever they
went, they [a]profaned My holy name—when
they said of them, 'These *are* the people of
the LORD, *and* yet they have gone out of
His land.' 21But I had concern [a]for My holy
name, which the house of Israel had profaned among the nations wherever they
went.

22"Therefore say to the house of Israel,
'Thus says the Lord GOD: "I do not do *this*
for your sake, O house of Israel, [a]but for
My holy name's sake, which you have profaned among the nations wherever you
went. 23And I will sanctify My great name,
which has been profaned among the

36:1 [a] Ezek. 6:2, 3 36:2 [a] Jer. 33:24; Ezek. 25:3; 26:2 [b] Deut. 32:13; Ps. 78:69; Is. 58:14; Hab. 3:19 [c] Ezek. 35:10 36:3 [a] Deut. 28:37; 1 Kin. 9:7; Lam. 2:15; Dan. 9:16 [b] Ps. 44:13, 14; Jer. 18:16; Ezek. 35:13 36:4 [a] Ezek. 34:8, 28 [b] Ps. 79:4; Jer. 48:27 36:5 [a] Deut. 4:24; Ezek. 38:19 [b] Ezek. 35:10, 12 36:6 [a] Ps. 74:10; 123:3, 4; Ezek. 34:29 36:7 [a] Ezek. 20:5 [b] Jer. 25:9, 15, 29 36:10 [a] Is. 58:12; 61:4; Amos 9:14 36:11 [a] Jer. 31:27; 33:12 [b] Job 42:12; Is. 51:3 [c] Ezek. 35:9; 37:6, 13 36:12 [a] Obad. 17 [b] Jer. 15:7; Ezek. 22:12, 27 36:13 [a] Num. 13:32 36:15 [a] Is. 60:14; Ezek. 34:29 36:17 [a] Lev. 18:25, 27, 28; Jer. 2:7 [b] Lev. 15:19 36:18 [a] Ezek. 16:36, 38; 23:37 36:19 [a] Deut. 28:64; Ezek. 5:12; 22:15; Amos 9:9 [b] Ezek. 7:3; 18:30; 39:24; [Rom. 2:6] 36:20 [a] Is. 52:5; Ezek. 12:16; Rom. 2:24 36:21 [a] Ezek. 20:9, 14 36:22 [a] Ps. 106:8; Ezek. 20:44

nations, which you have profaned in their
midst; and the nations shall know that I
am the LORD," says the Lord GOD, "when
I am [a]hallowed in you before their eyes.
24For [a]I will take you from among the nations, gather you out of all countries, and
bring you into your own land. 25[a]Then I
will sprinkle clean water on you, and you
shall be clean; I will cleanse you [b]from all
your filthiness and from all your idols. 26I
will give you a [a]new heart and put a new
spirit within you; I will take the heart of
stone out of your flesh and give you a heart
of flesh. 27I will put My [a]Spirit within you
and cause you to walk in My statutes, and
you will keep My judgments and do *them.*
28[a]Then you shall dwell in the land that I
gave to your fathers; [b]you shall be My people, and I will be your God. 29I will [a]deliver
you from all your uncleannesses. [b]I will call
for the grain and multiply it, and [c]bring no
famine upon you. 30[a]And I will multiply
the fruit of your trees and the increase of
your fields, so that you need never again
bear the reproach of famine among the nations. 31Then [a]you will remember your evil
ways and your deeds that *were* not good;
and you [b]will loathe yourselves in your own
sight, for your iniquities and your abominations. 32[a]Not for your sake do I do *this,*"
says the Lord GOD, "let it be known to you.
Be ashamed and confounded for your own
ways, O house of Israel!"

33"Thus says the Lord GOD: "On the day
that I cleanse you from all your iniquities,
I will also enable *you* to dwell in the cities,
[a]and the ruins shall be rebuilt. 34The desolate land shall be tilled instead of lying
desolate in the sight of all who pass by. 35So
they will say, 'This land that was desolate
has become like the garden of [a]Eden; and
the wasted, desolate, and ruined cities *are*
now fortified *and* inhabited.' 36Then the
nations which are left all around you shall
know that I, the LORD, have rebuilt the ruined places *and* planted what was desolate.
[a]I, the LORD, have spoken *it,* and I will do *it.*"

37"Thus says the Lord GOD: [a]"I will also
let the house of Israel inquire of Me to do
this for them: I will [b]increase their men like
a flock. 38Like a flock *offered as* holy *sacri-*
fices, like the flock at Jerusalem on its feast
days, so shall the ruined cities be filled with
flocks of men. Then they shall know that I
am the LORD." ' "

The Dry Bones Live

37 The [a]hand of the LORD came upon
me and brought me out [b]in the Spirit
of the LORD, and set me down in the midst
of the valley; and it *was* full of bones. 2Then
He caused me to pass by them all around,
and behold, *there were* very many in the
open valley; and indeed *they were* very dry.
3And He said to me, "Son of man, can these
bones live?"

So I answered, "O Lord GOD, [a]You know."

4Again He said to me, "Prophesy to these
bones, and say to them, 'O dry bones, hear
the word of the LORD! 5Thus says the Lord
GOD to these bones: "Surely I will [a]cause
breath to enter into you, and you shall
live. 6I will put sinews on you and bring
flesh upon you, cover you with skin and
put breath in you; and you shall live. [a]Then
you shall know that I *am* the LORD." ' "

7So I prophesied as I was commanded;
and as I prophesied, there was a noise, and
suddenly a rattling; and the bones came together, bone to bone. 8Indeed, as I looked,
the sinews and the flesh came upon them,
and the skin covered them over; but *there*
was no breath in them.

9Also He said to me, "Prophesy to the
breath, prophesy, son of man, and say to
the breath, 'Thus says the Lord GOD: [a]"Come
from the four winds, O breath, and breathe
on these slain, that they may live." ' " 10So
I prophesied as He commanded me, [a]and
breath came into them, and they lived, and
stood upon their feet, an exceedingly great
army.

11Then He said to me, "Son of man, these
bones are the [a]whole house of Israel. They

36:23 [a] Is. 5:16; Ezek. 20:41; 28:22 **36:24** [a] Is. 43:5, 6; Ezek. 34:13; 37:21 **36:25** [a] Num. 19:17–19; Ps. 51:7; Is. 52:15; Heb. 9:13, 19; 10:22 [b] Jer. 33:8 **36:26** [a] Ps. 51:10; Jer. 32:39; Ezek. 11:19; [John 3:3] **36:27** [a] Is. 44:3; 59:21; Ezek. 11:19; 37:14; [Joel 2:28, 29] **36:28** [a] Ezek. 28:25; 37:25 [b] Jer. 30:22; Ezek. 11:20; 37:27 **36:29** [a] Zech. 13:1; [Matt. 1:21; Rom. 11:26] [b] Ps. 105:16 [c] Ezek. 34:27, 29; Hos. 2:21–23 **36:30** [a] Lev. 26:4; Ezek. 34:27 **36:31** [a] Ezek. 16:61, 63 [b] Lev. 26:39; Ezek. 6:9; 20:43 **36:32** [a] Deut. 9:5 **36:33** [a] Ezek. 36:10 **36:35** [a] Is. 51:3; Ezek. 28:13; Joel 2:3 **36:36** [a] Ezek. 17:24; 22:14; 37:14; Hos. 14:4–9 **36:37** [a] Ezek. 14:3; 20:3, 31 [b] Ezek. 36:10 **37:1** [a] Ezek. 1:3 [b] Ezek. 3:14; 8:3; 11:24; Acts 8:39 **37:3** [a] [Deut. 32:39; 1 Sam. 2:6; John 5:21; Rom. 4:17; 2 Cor. 1:9] **37:5** [a] Gen. 2:7; Ps. 104:29, 30; Ezek. 37:9, 10, 14 **37:6** [a] Is. 49:23; Ezek. 6:7; 35:12; Joel 2:27; 3:17 **37:9** [a] [Ps. 104:30] **37:10** [a] Rev. 11:11 **37:11** [a] Jer. 33:24; Ezek. 36:10

indeed say, [b]'Our bones are dry, our hope is
lost, and we ourselves are cut off!' 12There-
fore prophesy and say to them, 'Thus says
the Lord GOD: "Behold, [a]O My people, I will
open your graves and cause you to come up
from your graves, and [b]bring you into the
land of Israel. 13Then you shall know that
I *am* the LORD, when I have opened your
graves, O My people, and brought you up
from your graves. 14I [a]will put My Spirit in
you, and you shall live, and I will place you
in your own land. Then you shall know that
I, the LORD, have spoken *it* and performed
it," says the LORD.'"

One Kingdom, One King

15Again the word of the LORD came to
me, saying, 16"As for you, son of man, [a]take
a stick for yourself and write on it: 'For Judah and for [b]the children of Israel, his companions.' Then take another stick and write
on it, 'For Joseph, the stick of Ephraim, and
for all the house of Israel, his companions.'
17Then [a]join them one to another for yourself into one stick, and they will become
one in your hand.

18"And when the children of your people
speak to you, saying, [a]'Will you not show us
what you *mean* by these?'— 19[a]say to them,
'Thus says the Lord GOD: "Surely I will take
[b]the stick of Joseph, which *is* in the hand
of Ephraim, and the tribes of Israel, his
companions; and I will join them with it,
with the stick of Judah, and make them one
stick, and they will be one in My hand."'
20And the sticks on which you write will be
in your hand [a]before their eyes.

21"Then say to them, 'Thus says the Lord
GOD: "Surely [a]I will take the children of
Israel from among the nations, wherever
they have gone, and will gather them from
every side and bring them into their own
land; 22and [a]I will make them one nation in
the land, on the mountains of Israel; and
[b]one king shall be king over them all; they
shall no longer be two nations, nor shall
they ever be divided into two kingdoms
again. 23[a]They shall not defile themselves
anymore with their idols, nor with their
detestable things, nor with any of their
transgressions; but [b]I will deliver them
from all their dwelling places in which
they have sinned, and will cleanse them.
Then they shall be My people, and I will
be their God.

24[a]"David My servant *shall be* king over
them, and [b]they shall all have one shepherd; [c]they shall also walk in My judgments
and observe My statutes, and do them.
25[a]Then they shall dwell in the land that I
have given to Jacob My servant, where your
fathers dwelt; and they shall dwell there,
they, their children, and their children's
children, [b]forever; and [c]My servant David
shall be their prince forever. 26Moreover I
will make [a]a covenant of peace with them,
and it shall be an everlasting covenant with
them; I will establish them and [b]multiply
them, and I will set My [c]sanctuary in their
midst forevermore. 27[a]My tabernacle also
shall be with them; indeed I will be [b]their
God, and they shall be My people. 28[a]The
nations also will know that I, the LORD,
[b]sanctify Israel, when My sanctuary is in
their midst forevermore."'"

Gog and Allies Attack Israel

38 Now the word of the LORD came to
me, saying, 2[a]"Son of man, [b]set your
face against [c]Gog, of the land of [d]Magog, the
prince of Rosh,[1] [e]Meshech, and Tubal, and
prophesy against him, 3and say, 'Thus says
the Lord GOD: "Behold, I *am* against you,
O Gog, the prince of Rosh, Meshech, and
Tubal. 4[a]I will turn you around, put hooks
into your jaws, and [b]lead you out, with
all your army, horses, and horsemen, [c]all
splendidly clothed, a great company *with*
bucklers and shields, all of them handling
swords. 5Persia, Ethiopia,[1] and Libya[2] are
with them, all of them *with* shield and helmet; 6[a]Gomer and all its troops; the house

37:11 [b] Ps. 141:7; Is. 49:14 37:12 [a] Deut. 32:39; 1 Sam. 2:6; Is. 26:19; 66:14; [Dan. 12:2]; Hos. 13:14 [b] Ezek. 36:24 37:14 [a] Is. 32:15; Ezek. 36:27; [Joel 2:28, 29]; Zech. 12:10 37:16 [a] Num. 17:2, 3 [b] 2 Chr. 11:12, 13, 16; 15:9; 30:11, 18 37:17 [a] Is. 11:13; Jer. 50:4; Ezek. 37:22–24; Hos. 1:11; Zeph. 3:9 37:18 [a] Ezek. 12:9; 24:19 37:19 [a] Zech. 10:6 [b] Ezek. 37:16, 17 37:20 [a] Ezek. 12:3 37:21 [a] Is. 43:5, 6; Jer. 32:37; Ezek. 36:24; Amos 9:14, 15 37:22 [a] Is. 11:13; Jer. 3:18; Hos. 1:11 [b] Ezek. 34:23; John 10:16 37:23 [a] Ezek. 36:25 [b] Ezek. 36:28, 29 37:24 [a] Is. 40:11; [Jer. 23:5; 30:9]; Ezek. 34:23, 24; Hos. 3:5; [Luke 1:32] [b] [John 10:16] [c] Ezek. 36:27 37:25 [a] Ezek. 36:28 [b] Is. 60:21; Joel 3:20; Amos 9:15 [c] Ps. 89:3, 4; John 12:34 37:26 [a] Ps. 89:3; Is. 55:3; [Jer. 32:40] [b] Jer. 30:19; Ezek. 36:10 [c] [2 Cor. 6:16] 37:27 [a] Lev. 26:11; [John 1:14]; Rev. 21:3 [b] Ezek. 11:20 37:28 [a] Ezek. 36:23 [b] Ex. 31:13; Ezek. 20:12 38:2 [a] Ezek. 39:1 [b] Ezek. 35:2, 3 [c] Ezek. 38:1—39:24; Rev. 20:8 [d] Gen. 10:2; Ezek. 39:6; Rev. 20:8 [e] Ezek. 32:26 [1] Targum, Vulgate, and Aquila read *chief prince of* (also verse 3). 38:4 [a] 2 Kin. 19:28; Ezek. 29:4 [b] Is. 43:17 [c] Ezek. 23:12 38:5 [1] Hebrew *Cush* [2] Hebrew *Put* 38:6 [a] Gen. 10:2

of [b]Togarmah *from* the far north and all its
troops—many people *are* with you.
7 [a]"Prepare yourself and be ready, you
and all your companies that are gathered
about you; and be a guard for them. 8 [a]Af-
ter many days [b]you will be visited. In the
latter years you will come into the land of
those brought back from the sword [c]*and*
gathered from many people on [d]the mountains of Israel, which had long been desolate; they were brought out of the nations,
and now all of them [e]dwell safely. 9 You will
ascend, coming [a]like a storm, covering the
[b]land like a cloud, you and all your troops
and many peoples with you."
10 "Thus says the Lord GOD: "On that day
it shall come to pass *that* thoughts will arise
in your mind, and you will make an evil
plan: 11 You will say, 'I will go up against a
land of [a]unwalled villages; I will [b]go to a
peaceful people, [c]who dwell safely, all of
them dwelling without walls, and having
neither bars nor gates'— 12 to take plunder
and to take booty, to stretch out your hand
against the waste places *that are again* inhabited, [a]and against a people gathered
from the nations, who have acquired livestock and goods, who dwell in the midst of
the land. 13 [a]Sheba, [b]Dedan, the merchants
[c]of Tarshish, and all [d]their young lions will
say to you, 'Have you come to take plunder?
Have you gathered your army to take booty,
to carry away silver and gold, to take away
livestock and goods, to take great plunder?'"'
14 "Therefore, son of man, prophesy and
say to Gog, 'Thus says the Lord GOD: [a]"On
that day when My people Israel [b]dwell
safely, will you not know *it?* 15 [a]Then you will
come from your place out of the far north,
you and many peoples with you, all of them
riding on horses, a great company and a
mighty army. 16 You will come up against
My people Israel like a cloud, to cover the
land. It will be in the latter days that I will
bring you against My land, so that the nations may [a]know Me, when I am [b]hallowed
in you, O Gog, before their eyes." 17 Thus
says the Lord GOD: "Are *you* he of whom I
have spoken in former days by My servants
the prophets of Israel, who prophesied for
years in those days that I would bring you
against them?

Judgment on Gog

18 "And it will come to pass at the same
time, when Gog comes against the land of
Israel," says the Lord GOD, "*that* My fury
will show in My face. 19 For [a]in My jealousy
[b]*and* in the fire of My wrath I have spoken: [c]'Surely in that day there shall be a
great earthquake in the land of Israel, 20 so
that [a]the fish of the sea, the birds of the
heavens, the beasts of the field, all creeping things that creep on the earth, and all
men who *are* on the face of the earth shall
shake at My presence. [b]The mountains shall
be thrown down, the steep places shall fall,
and every wall shall fall to the ground.' 21 I
will [a]call for [b]a sword against Gog throughout all My mountains," says the Lord GOD.
[c]"Every man's sword will be against his
brother. 22 And I will [a]bring him to judgment with [b]pestilence and bloodshed; [c]I will
rain down on him, on his troops, and on the
many peoples who *are* with him, flooding
rain, [d]great hailstones, fire, and brimstone.
23 Thus I will magnify Myself and [a]sanctify
Myself, [b]and I will be known in the eyes of
many nations. Then they shall know that I
am the LORD."'

Gog's Armies Destroyed

39 "And [a]you, son of man, prophesy
against Gog, and say, 'Thus says the
Lord GOD: "Behold, I *am* against you, O Gog,
the prince of Rosh,[1] Meshech, and Tubal;
2 and I will [a]turn you around and lead you
on, [b]bringing you up from the far north,
and bring you against the mountains of Israel. 3 Then I will knock the bow out of your
left hand, and cause the arrows to fall out
of your right hand. 4 [a]You shall fall upon
the mountains of Israel, you and all your

38:6 [b] Gen. 10:3; Ezek. 27:14 38:7 [a] Is. 8:9, 10; Jer. 46:3, 4 38:8 [a] Deut. 4:30; Is. 24:22 [b] Is. 29:6 [c] Ezek. 34:13 [d] Ezek. 36:1, 4 [e] Jer. 23:6; Ezek. 34:25; 39:26 38:9 [a] Is. 28:2 [b] Jer. 4:13 38:11 [a] Zech. 2:4 [b] Jer. 49:31 [c] Ezek. 38:8 38:12 [a] Ezek. 38:8 38:13 [a] Ezek. 27:22 [b] Ezek. 27:15, 20 [c] Ezek. 27:12 [d] Ezek. 19:3, 5 38:14 [a] Is. 4:1 [b] Jer. 23:6; Ezek. 38:8, 11; [Zech. 2:5, 8] 38:15 [a] Ezek. 39:2 38:16 [a] Ezek. 35:11 [b] Is. 5:16; 8:13; 29:23; Ezek. 28:22 38:19 [a] Deut. 32:21, 22; Ps. 18:7, 8; Ezek. 36:5, 6; [Nah. 1:2]; Heb. 12:29 [b] Ps. 89:46 [c] Joel 3:16; Hag. 2:6, 7; Rev. 16:18 38:20 [a] Hos. 4:3 [b] Jer. 4:24; Nah. 1:5, 6 38:21 [a] Ps. 105:16 [b] Ezek. 14:17 [c] Judg. 7:22; 1 Sam. 14:20; 2 Chr. 20:23; Hag. 2:22 38:22 [a] Is. 66:16; Jer. 25:31 [b] Ezek. 5:17 [c] Ps. 11:6; Is. 30:30; Ezek. 13:11 [d] Rev. 16:21 38:23 [a] Ezek. 36:23 [b] Ps. 9:16; Ezek. 37:28; 38:16 39:1 [a] Ezek. 38:2, 3 [1] Targum, Vulgate and Aquila read *chief prince of.* 39:2 [a] Ezek. 38:8 [b] Ezek. 38:15 39:4 [a] Ezek. 38:4, 21

troops and the peoples who *are* with you;
[b]I will give you to birds of prey of every
sort and *to* the beasts of the field to be devoured. 5You shall fall on the open field; for
I have spoken," says the Lord GOD. 6[a]"And I
will send fire on Magog and on those who
live in security in [b]the coastlands. Then
they shall know that I *am* the LORD. 7[a]So
I will make My holy name known in the
midst of My people Israel, and I will not
let them [b]profane My holy name anymore.
[c]Then the nations shall know that *I am* the
LORD, the Holy One in Israel. 8[a]Surely it
is coming, and it shall be done," says the
Lord GOD. "This *is* the day [b]of which I have
spoken.
9"Then those who dwell in the cities of
Israel will go out and set on fire and burn
the weapons, both the shields and bucklers, the bows and arrows, the javelins and
spears; and they will make fires with them
for seven years. 10They will not take wood
from the field nor cut down *any* from the
forests, because they will make fires with
the weapons; [a]and they will plunder those
who plundered them, and pillage those
who pillaged them," says the Lord GOD.

The Burial of Gog

11"It will come to pass in that day *that* I
will give Gog a burial place there in Israel,
the valley of those who pass by east of the
sea; and it will obstruct travelers, because
there they will bury Gog and all his multitude. Therefore they will call *it* the Valley of
Hamon Gog.[1] 12For seven months the house
of Israel will be burying them, [a]in order to
cleanse the land. 13Indeed all the people
of the land will be burying, and they will
gain [a]renown for it on the day that [b]I am
glorified," says the Lord GOD. 14"They will
set apart men regularly employed, with
the help of a search party,[1] to pass through
the land and bury those bodies remaining
on the ground, in order [a]to cleanse it. At
the end of seven months they will make a
search. 15The search party will pass through
the land; and *when anyone* sees a man's
bone, he shall set up a marker by it, till the
buriers have buried it in the Valley of Hamon Gog. 16*The* name of *the* city *will* also
be Hamonah. Thus they shall [a]cleanse the
land."'

A Triumphant Festival

17"And as for you, son of man, thus says
the Lord GOD, [a]'Speak to every sort of bird
and to every beast of the field:

[b]"Assemble yourselves and come;
Gather together from all sides
to My [c]sacrificial meal
Which I am sacrificing for you,
A great sacrificial meal [d]on the
mountains of Israel,
That you may eat flesh
and drink blood.
18 [a]You shall eat the flesh of the mighty,
Drink the blood of the
princes of the earth,
Of rams and lambs,
Of goats and bulls,
All of them [b]fatlings of Bashan.
19 You shall eat fat till you are full,
And drink blood till you are drunk,
At My sacrificial meal
Which I am sacrificing for you.
20 [a]You shall be filled at My table
With horses and riders,
[b]With mighty men
And with all the men of war,"
says the Lord GOD.

Israel Restored to the Land

21[a]"I will set My glory among the nations; all the nations shall see My judgment
which I have executed, and [b]My hand which
I have laid on them. 22[a]So the house of Israel shall know that I *am* the LORD their
God from that day forward. 23[a]The Gentiles shall know that the house of Israel
went into captivity for their iniquity; because they were unfaithful to Me, therefore [b]I hid My face from them. I [c]gave them
into the hand of their enemies, and they
all fell by the sword. 24[a]According to their

39:4 [b] Ezek. 33:27 39:6 [a] Ezek. 38:22; Amos 1:4, 7, 10; Nah. 1:6 [b] Ps. 72:10; Is. 66:19; Jer. 25:22 39:7 [a] Ezek. 39:25 [b] Lev. 18:21; Ezek. 36:23 [c] Ezek. 38:16 39:8 [a] Rev. 16:17; 21:6 [b] Ezek. 38:17 39:10 [a] Is. 14:2; 33:1; Mic. 5:8; Hab. 2:8 39:11 [1] Literally *The Multitude of Gog* 39:12 [a] Deut. 21:23; Ezek. 39:14, 16 39:13 [a] Jer. 33:9; Zeph. 3:19, 20 [b] Ezek. 28:22 39:14 [a] Ezek. 39:12 [1] Literally *those who pass through* 39:16 [a] Ezek. 39:12 39:17 [a] Is. 56:9; [Jer. 12:9]; Ezek. 39:4; Rev. 19:17, 18 [b] Is. 18:6 [c] Is. 34:6, 7; Jer. 46:10; Zeph. 1:7 [d] Ezek. 39:4 39:18 [a] Ezek. 29:5; Rev. 19:18 [b] Deut. 32:14; Ps. 22:12 39:20 [a] Ps. 76:5, 6; Ezek. 38:4; Hag. 2:22 [b] Rev. 19:18 39:21 [a] Ex. 9:16; Is. 37:20; Ezek. 36:23; 38:23 [b] Ex. 7:4 39:22 [a] Ex. 39:7, 28 39:23 [a] Jer. 22:8, 9; 44:22; Ezek. 36:18–20, 23 [b] Deut. 31:17; Is. 1:15; 59:2; Ezek. 39:29 [c] Lev. 26:25 39:24 [a] 2 Kin. 17:7; Jer. 2:17, 19; 4:18; Ezek. 36:19

uncleanness and according to their transgressions I have dealt with them, and hidden My face from them."'
25"Therefore thus says the Lord GOD:
[a]'Now I will bring back the captives of Jacob, and have mercy on the [b]whole house
of Israel; and I will be jealous for My holy
name— 26[a]after they have borne their
shame, and all their unfaithfulness in
which they were unfaithful to Me, when
they [b]dwelt safely in their *own* land and
no one made *them* afraid. 27[a]When I have
brought them back from the peoples and
gathered them out of their enemies' lands,
and I [b]am hallowed in them in the sight
of many nations, 28[a]then they shall know
that I *am* the LORD their God, who sent
them into captivity among the nations,
but also brought them back to their land,
and left none of them captive any longer.
29[a]And I will not hide My face from them
anymore; for I shall have [b]poured out My
Spirit on the house of Israel,' says the
Lord GOD."

A New City, a New Temple

40 In the twenty-fifth year of our captivity, at the beginning of the year,
on the tenth *day* of the month, in the fourteenth year after [a]the city was captured, on
the very same day [b]the hand of the LORD
was upon me; and He took me there. 2[a]In
the visions of God He took me into the land
of Israel and [b]set me on a very high mountain; on it toward the south *was* something
like the structure of a city. 3He took me
there, and behold, *there was* a man whose
appearance *was* [a]like the appearance of
bronze. [b]He had a line of flax [c]and a measuring rod in his hand, and he stood in the
gateway.
4And the man said to me, [a]"Son of man,
look with your eyes and hear with your ears,
and fix your mind on everything I show
you; for you *were* brought here so that I
might show *them* to you. [b]Declare to the
house of Israel everything you see." 5Now
there was [a]a wall all around the outside of
the temple.[1] In the man's hand was a measuring rod six cubits *long, each being a* cubit and a handbreadth; and he measured
the width of the wall structure, one rod;
and the height, one rod.

The Eastern Gateway of the Temple

6Then he went to the gateway which
faced [a]east; and he went up its stairs and
measured the threshold of the gateway,
which was one rod wide, and the other
threshold *was* one rod wide. 7Each gate
chamber *was* one rod long and one rod
wide; between the gate chambers *was a*
space of five cubits; and the threshold of
the gateway by the vestibule of the inside
gate *was* one rod. 8He also measured the
vestibule of the inside gate, one rod. 9Then
he measured the vestibule of the gateway,
eight cubits; and the gateposts, two cubits.
The vestibule of the gate *was* on the inside.
10In the eastern gateway *were* three gate
chambers on one side and three on the
other; the three *were* all the same size; also
the gateposts were of the same size on this
side and that side.
11He measured the width of the entrance
to the gateway, ten cubits; *and* the length
of the gate, thirteen cubits. 12*There was* a
space in front of the gate chambers, one
cubit *on this side* and one cubit on that side;
the gate chambers *were* six cubits on this
side and six cubits on that side. 13Then he
measured the gateway from the roof of *one*
gate chamber to the roof of the other; the
width *was* twenty-five cubits, as door faces
door. 14He measured the gateposts, sixty
cubits high, and the court all around the
gateway *extended* to the gatepost. 15*From*
the front of the entrance gate to the front
of the vestibule of the inner gate *was* fifty
cubits. 16*There were* [a]beveled window *frames*
in the gate chambers and in their intervening archways on the inside of the gateway
all around, and likewise in the vestibules.
There were windows all around on the inside. And on each gatepost *were* [b]palm
trees.

39:25 [a] Is. 27:12, 13; Jer. 30:3, 18; Ezek. 34:13; 36:24 [b] Jer. 31:1; Ezek. 20:40; Hos. 1:11 39:26 [a] Dan. 9:16 [b] Lev. 26:5, 6 39:27 [a] Ezek. 28:25, 26 [b] Ezek. 36:23, 24; 38:16 39:28 [a] Ezek. 34:30 39:29 [a] Is. 54:8, 9 [b] Is. 32:15; Ezek. 36:27; 37:14; [Joel 2:28; Zech. 12:10]; Acts 2:17 40:1 [a] 2 Kin. 25:1–4; Jer. 39:2, 3; 52:4–7; Ezek. 33:21 [b] Ezek. 1:3; 3:14, 22; 37:1 40:2 [a] Ezek. 1:1; 3:14; 8:3; 37:1; Dan. 7:1, 7 [b] [Is. 2:2, 3]; Ezek. 17:23; 20:40; 37:22; [Mic. 4:1]; Rev. 21:10 40:3 [a] Ezek. 1:7; Dan. 10:6; Rev. 1:15 [b] Ezek. 47:3; Zech. 2:1, 2 [c] Rev. 11:1; 21:15 40:4 [a] Ezek. 44:5 [b] Ezek. 43:10 40:5 [a] [Is. 26:1]; Ezek. 42:20 [1] Literally *house,* and so elsewhere in this book 40:6 [a] Ezek. 43:1 40:16 [a] 1 Kin. 6:4; Ezek. 41:16, 26 [b] 1 Kin. 6:29, 32, 35; 2 Chr. 3:5; Ezek. 40:22, 26, 31, 34, 37; 41:18–20, 25, 26

The Outer Court

17 Then he brought me into [a]the outer
court; and *there were* [b]chambers and a
pavement made all around the court;
[c]thirty chambers faced the pavement. 18 The
pavement was by the side of the gateways,
corresponding to the length of the gateways; *this was* the lower pavement. 19 Then
he measured the width from the front of
the lower gateway to the front of the inner
court exterior, one hundred cubits toward
the east and the north.

The Northern Gateway

20 On the outer court was also a gateway
facing north, and he measured its length
and its width. 21 Its gate chambers, three on
this side and three on that side, its gateposts and its archways, had the same measurements as the first gate; its length *was*
fifty cubits and its width twenty-five cubits. 22 Its windows and those of its archways, and also its palm trees, *had* the same
measurements as the gateway facing east;
it was ascended by seven steps, and its archway *was* in front of it. 23 A gate of the inner
court was opposite the northern gateway,
just as the eastern *gateway;* and he measured from gateway to gateway, one hundred cubits.

The Southern Gateway

24 After that he brought me toward the
south, and there a gateway was facing
south; and he measured its gateposts and
archways according to these same measurements. 25 *There were* windows in it
and in its archways all around like those
windows; its length *was* fifty cubits and
its width twenty-five cubits. 26 Seven steps
led up to it, and its archway *was* in front
of them; and it had palm trees on its gateposts, one on this side and one on that side.
27 *There was* also a gateway on the inner
court, facing south; and he measured from
gateway to gateway toward the south, one
hundred cubits.

Gateways of the Inner Court

28 Then he brought me to the inner
court through the southern gateway; he
measured the southern gateway according to these same measurements. 29 Also
its gate chambers, its gateposts, and its
archways *were* according to these same
measurements; *there were* windows in it
and in its archways all around; *it was* fifty
cubits long and twenty-five cubits wide.
30 *There were* archways all around, [a]twenty-
five cubits long and five cubits wide. 31 Its
archways faced the outer court, palm trees
were on its gateposts, and going up to it
were eight steps.

32 And he brought me into the inner
court facing east; he measured the gateway
according to these same measurements.
33 Also its gate chambers, its gateposts, and
its archways *were* according to these same
measurements; and *there were* windows in
it and in its archways all around; *it was* fifty
cubits long and twenty-five cubits wide.
34 Its archways faced the outer court, and
palm trees *were* on its gateposts on this
side and on that side; and going up to it
were eight steps.

35 Then he brought me to the north gateway and measured *it* according to these
same measurements— 36 also its gate
chambers, its gateposts, and its archways.
It had windows all around; its length *was*
fifty cubits and its width twenty-five cubits. 37 Its gateposts faced the outer court,
palm trees *were* on its gateposts on this
side and on that side, and going up to it
were eight steps.

Where Sacrifices Were Prepared

38 *There was* a chamber and its entrance
by the gateposts of the gateway, where they
[a]washed the burnt offering. 39 In the vestibule of the gateway *were* two tables on this
side and two tables on that side, on which
to slay the burnt offering, [a]the sin offering,
and [b]the trespass offering. 40 At the outer
side of the *vestibule,* as one goes up to the
entrance of the northern gateway, *were* two
tables; and on the other side of the vestibule of the gateway *were* two tables. 41 Four
tables *were* on this side and four tables on
that side, by the side of the gateway, eight
tables on which they slaughtered *the sacrifices.* 42 *There were* also four tables of hewn

---

stone for the burnt offering, one cubit and
a half long, one cubit and a half wide, and
one cubit high; on these they laid the instruments with which they slaughtered the
burnt offering and the sacrifice. 43 Inside
were hooks, a handbreadth wide, fastened
all around; and the flesh of the sacrifices
was on the tables.

Chambers for Singers and Priests

44 Outside the inner gate *were* the chambers for [a]the singers in the inner court,
one facing south at the side of the northern gateway, and the other facing north at
the side of the southern[1] gateway. 45 Then
he said to me, "This chamber which faces
south *is* for [a]the priests who have charge
of the temple. 46 The chamber which faces
north *is* for the priests [a]who have charge
of the altar; these *are* the sons of [b]Zadok,
from the sons of Levi, who come near the
LORD to minister to Him."

Dimensions of the Inner
Court and Vestibule
(cf. 1 Kin. 7:14–22)

47 And he measured the court, one hundred cubits long and one hundred cubits
wide, foursquare. The altar *was* in front of
the temple. 48 Then he brought me to the
[a]vestibule of the temple and measured the
doorposts of the vestibule, five cubits on
this side and five cubits on that side; and
the width of the gateway was three cubits
on this side and three cubits on that side.
49 [a]The length of the vestibule *was* twenty
cubits, and the width eleven cubits; and by
the steps which led up to it *there were* [b]pil-
lars by the doorposts, one on this side and
another on that side.

Dimensions of the Sanctuary

41 Then he [a]brought me into the sanctuary[1] and measured the doorposts,
six cubits wide on one side and six cubits
wide on the other side—the width of the
tabernacle. 2 The width of the entryway
was ten cubits, and the side walls of the
entrance *were* five cubits on this side and
five cubits on the other side; and he measured its length, forty cubits, and its width,
twenty cubits.

3 Also he went inside and measured the
doorposts, two cubits; and the entrance, six
cubits *high;* and the width of the entrance,
seven cubits. 4 [a]He measured the length,
twenty cubits; and the width, twenty cubits, beyond the sanctuary; and he said to
me, "This *is* the Most Holy *Place.*"

The Side Chambers on the Wall

5 Next, he measured the wall of the
temple, six cubits. The width of each side
chamber all around the temple *was* four
cubits on every side. 6 [a]The side chambers
were in three stories, one above the other,
thirty chambers in each story; they rested
on ledges which *were* for the side chambers all around, that they might be supported, but [b]not fastened to the wall of
the temple. 7 As one went up from story to
story, the side chambers [a]became wider all
around, because their supporting ledges in
the wall of the temple ascended like steps;
therefore the width of the structure increased as one went up *from* the lowest
story to the highest by way of the middle
one. 8 I also saw an elevation all around
the temple; it was the foundation of the
side chambers, [a]a full rod, *that is,* six cubits *high.* 9 The thickness of the outer wall
of the side chambers *was* five cubits, and
so also the remaining terrace by the place
of the side chambers of the temple. 10 And
between *it and* the *wall* chambers was a
width of twenty cubits all around the temple on every side. 11 The doors of the side
chambers opened on the terrace, one door
toward the north and another toward the
south; and the width of the terrace *was* five
cubits all around.

The Building at the Western End

12 The building that faced the separating
courtyard at its western end *was* seventy
cubits wide; the wall of the building *was*
five cubits thick all around, and its length
ninety cubits.

40:44 [a] 1 Chr. 6:31, 32; 16:41–43; 25:1–7 [1] Following Septuagint; Masoretic Text and Vulgate read *eastern.* 40:45 [a] Lev. 8:35; Num. 3:27, 28, 32, 38; 18:5; 1 Chr. 9:23; 2 Chr. 13:11; Ps. 134:1 40:46 [a] Lev. 6:12, 13; Num. 18:5; Ezek. 44:15 [b] 1 Kin. 2:35; Ezek. 43:19; 44:15, 16 40:48 [a] 1 Kin. 6:3; 2 Chr. 3:4 40:49 [a] 1 Kin. 6:3 [b] 1 Kin. 7:15–22; 2 Chr. 3:17; Jer. 52:17–23; [Rev. 3:12] 41:1 [a] Ezek. 40:2, 3, 17 [1] Hebrew *heykal,* here the main room of the temple, sometimes called the *holy place* (compare Exodus 26:33) 41:4 [a] 1 Kin. 6:20; 2 Chr. 3:8 41:6 [a] 1 Kin. 6:5–10 [b] 1 Kin. 6:6, 10 41:7 [a] 1 Kin. 6:8 41:8 [a] Ezek. 40:5

Dimensions and Design of the Temple Area

13So he measured the temple, one [a]hun-
dred cubits long; and the separating courtyard with the building and its walls *was*
one hundred cubits long; 14also the width
of the eastern face of the temple, including
the separating courtyard, *was* one hundred
cubits. 15He measured the length of the
building behind it, facing the separating
courtyard, with its [a]galleries on the one side
and on the other side, one hundred cubits,
as well as the inner temple and the porches
of the court, 16their doorposts and [a]the beveled window frames. And the galleries all
around their three stories opposite the
threshold were paneled with [b]wood from
the ground to the windows—the windows
were covered— 17from the space above the
door, even to the inner room,[1] as well as
outside, and on every wall all around, inside and outside, by measure.

18And *it was* made [a]with cherubim and
[b]palm trees, a palm tree between cherub
and cherub. *Each* cherub had two faces, 19[a]so
that the face of a man *was* toward a palm
tree on one side, and the face of a young
lion toward a palm tree on the other side;
thus *it was* made throughout the temple all
around. 20From the floor to the space above
the door, and on the wall of the sanctuary,
cherubim and palm trees *were* carved.

21The [a]doorposts of the temple *were*
square, *as was* the front of the sanctuary;
their appearance was similar. 22[a]The altar *was* of wood, three cubits high, and its
length two cubits. Its corners, its length,
and its sides *were* of wood; and he said to
me, "This *is* [b]the table that *is* [c]before the
LORD."

23[a]The temple and the sanctuary had two
doors. 24The doors had two [a]panels *apiece,*
two folding panels: two *panels* for one door
and two panels for the other *door.* 25Cher-
ubim and palm trees *were* carved on the
doors of the temple just as they *were* carved
on the walls. A wooden canopy *was* on the
front of the vestibule outside. 26*There were*
[a]beveled window *frames* and palm trees on
one side and on the other, on the sides of
the vestibule—also on the side chambers
of the temple and on the canopies.

The Chambers for the Priests

42 Then he [a]brought me out into the
outer court, by the way toward
the [b]north; and he brought me into [c]the
chamber which *was* opposite the separating courtyard, and which *was* opposite
the building toward the north. 2Facing the
length, *which was* one hundred cubits (the
width was fifty cubits), was the north door.
3Opposite the inner court of twenty *cubits,*
and opposite the [a]pavement of the outer
court, *was* [b]gallery against gallery in three
stories. 4In front of the chambers, toward
the inside, *was* a walk ten cubits wide, at
a distance of one cubit; and their doors
faced north. 5Now the upper chambers *were*
shorter, because the galleries took away
space from them more than from the lower
and middle stories of the building. 6For
they *were* in three *stories* and did not have
pillars like the pillars of the courts; therefore *the upper level* was shortened more
than the lower and middle levels from the
ground up. 7And a wall which *was* outside
ran parallel to the chambers, at the front of
the chambers, toward the outer court; its
length *was* fifty cubits. 8The length of the
chambers toward the outer court *was* fifty
cubits, whereas that facing the temple *was*
one [a]hundred cubits. 9At the lower chambers *was* the entrance on the east side, as
one goes into them from the outer court.

10Also *there were* chambers in the thickness of the wall of the court toward the east,
opposite the separating courtyard and opposite the building. 11[a]*There was* a walk in
front of them also, and their appearance
was like the chambers which *were* toward
the north; they *were* as long and as wide as
the others, and all their exits and entrances
were according to plan. 12And corresponding to the doors of the chambers that *were*
facing south, as one enters them, *there was*
a door in front of the walk, the way directly
in front of the wall toward the east.

41:13 [a] Ezek. 40:47 41:15 [a] Ezek. 42:3, 5 41:16 [a] 1 Kin. 6:4; Ezek. 40:16, 25 [b] 1 Kin. 6:15 41:17 [1] Literally *house,* here *the Most Holy Place* 41:18 [a] 1 Kin. 6:29; 2 Chr. 3:7 [b] 2 Chr. 3:5; Ezek. 40:16 41:19 [a] Ezek. 1:10; 10:14 41:21 [a] 1 Kin. 6:33; Ezek. 40:9, 14, 16; 41:1 41:22 [a] Ex. 30:1–3; 1 Kin. 6:20; Rev. 8:3 [b] Ex. 25:23, 30; Lev. 24:6; Ezek. 23:41; 44:16; Mal. 1:7, 12 [c] Ex. 30:8 41:23 [a] 1 Kin. 6:31–35 41:24 [a] 1 Kin. 6:34 41:26 [a] Ezek. 40:16 42:1 [a] Ezek. 41:1 [b] Ezek. 40:20 [c] Ezek. 41:12, 15 42:3 [a] Ezek. 40:17 [b] Ezek. 41:15, 16; 42:5 42:8 [a] Ezek. 41:13, 14 42:11 [a] Ezek. 42:4

13 Then he said to me, "The north chambers *and* the south chambers, which *are* opposite the separating courtyard, *are* the holy chambers where the priests who approach the LORD [a]shall eat the most holy offerings. There they shall lay the most holy offerings—[b]the grain offering, the sin offering, and the trespass offering—for the place *is* holy. 14 [a]When the priests enter them, they shall not go out of the holy *chamber* into the outer court; but there they shall leave their garments in which they minister, for they *are* holy. They shall put on other garments; then they may approach *that* which *is* for the people."

Outer Dimensions of the Temple

15 Now when he had finished measuring the inner temple, he brought me out through the gateway that faces toward the [a]east, and measured it all around. 16 He measured the east side with the measuring rod,[1] five hundred rods by the measuring rod all around. 17 He measured the north side, five hundred rods by the measuring rod all around. 18 He measured the south side, five hundred rods by the measuring rod. 19 He came around to the west side *and* measured five hundred rods by the measuring rod. 20 He measured it on the four sides; [a]it had a wall all around, [b]five hundred *cubits* long and five hundred wide, to separate the holy areas from the common.

The Temple, the LORD's Dwelling Place

43 Afterward he brought me to the gate, the gate [a]that faces toward the east. 2 [a]And behold, the glory of the God of Israel came from the way of the east. [b]His voice *was* like the sound of many waters; [c]and the earth shone with His glory. 3 *It was* [a]like the appearance of the vision which I saw—like the vision which I saw when I[1] came [b]to destroy the city. The visions *were* like the vision which I saw [c]by the River Chebar; and I fell on my face. 4 [a]And the glory of the LORD came into the temple by way of the gate which faces toward the east. 5 [a]The Spirit lifted me up and brought me into the inner court; and behold, [b]the glory of the LORD filled the temple.

6 Then I heard *Him* speaking to me from the temple, while [a]a man stood beside me. 7 And He said to me, "Son of man, *this is* [a]the place of My throne and [b]the place of the soles of My feet, [c]where I will dwell in the midst of the children of Israel forever. [d]No more shall the house of Israel defile My holy name, they nor their kings, by their harlotry or with [e]the carcasses of their kings on their high places. 8 [a]When they set their threshold by My threshold, and their doorpost by My doorpost, with a wall between them and Me, they defiled My holy name by the abominations which they committed; therefore I have consumed them in My anger. 9 Now let them put their harlotry and the carcasses of their kings far away from Me, and I will dwell in their midst forever.

10 "Son of man, [a]describe the temple to the house of Israel, that they may be ashamed of their iniquities; and let them measure the pattern. 11 And if they are ashamed of all that they have done, make known to them the design of the temple and its arrangement, its exits and its entrances, its entire design and all its [a]ordinances, all its forms and all its laws. Write *it* down in their sight, so that they may keep its whole design and all its ordinances, and [b]perform them. 12 This *is* the law of the temple: The whole area surrounding [a]the mountaintop *is* most holy. Behold, this *is* the law of the temple.

Dimensions of the Altar

13 "These are the measurements of the [a]altar in cubits [b](the cubit *is* one cubit and a handbreadth): the base one cubit high and one cubit wide, with a rim all around its edge of one span. This *is* the height of the altar: 14 from the base on the ground to the lower ledge, two cubits; the width of the ledge, one cubit; from the smaller ledge to the larger ledge, four cubits; and the width

---

42:13 [a] Lev. 6:16, 26; 24:9; Ezek. 43:19 [b] Lev. 2:3, 10; 6:14, 17, 25 42:14 [a] Ezek. 44:19 42:15 [a] Ezek. 40:6; 43:1 42:16 [1] Compare 40:5 42:20 [a] [Is. 60:18]; Ezek. 40:5; Zech. 2:5 [b] Ezek. 45:2; Rev. 21:16 43:1 [a] Ezek. 10:19; 46:1 43:2 [a] Ezek. 11:23 [b] Ezek. 1:24; Rev. 1:15; 14:2 [c] Ezek. 10:4; Rev. 18:1 43:3 [a] Ezek. 1:4–28 [b] Jer. 1:10; Ezek. 9:1, 5; 32:18 [c] Ezek. 1:28; 3:23 [1] Some Hebrew manuscripts and Vulgate read *He*. 43:4 [a] Ezek. 10:19; 11:23 43:5 [a] Ezek. 3:12, 14; 8:3; 2 Cor. 12:2–4 [b] Ezek. 40:34; 1 Kin. 8:10, 11 43:6 [a] Ezek. 1:26; 40:3 43:7 [a] Ps. 99:1; Is. 60:13 [b] 1 Chr. 28:2; Ps. 99:5 [c] Ex. 29:45; Ps. 68:16; 132:14; Ezek. 37:26–28; Joel 3:17; [John 1:14; 2 Cor. 6:16] [d] Ezek. 39:7 [e] Lev. 26:30; Jer. 16:18; Ezek. 6:5, 13 43:8 [a] 2 Kin. 16:14; 21:4, 5, 7; Ezek. 8:3; 23:39; 44:7 43:10 [a] Ezek. 40:4 43:11 [a] Ezek. 44:5 [b] Ezek. 11:20 43:12 [a] Ezek. 40:2 43:13 [a] Ex. 27:1–8; 2 Chr. 4:1 [b] Ezek. 41:8

of the ledge, *one* cubit. 15The altar hearth *is*
four cubits high, with four [a]horns extending upward from the hearth. 16The altar
hearth *is* twelve *cubits* long, twelve wide,
[a]square at its four corners; 17the ledge, fourteen *cubits* long and fourteen wide on its
four sides, with a rim of half a cubit around
it; its base, one cubit all around; and [a]its
steps face toward the east."

Consecrating the Altar

18And He said to me, "Son of man, thus
says the Lord GOD: 'These *are* the ordinances for the altar on the day when it is
made, for sacrificing [a]burnt offerings on it,
and for [b]sprinkling blood on it. 19You shall
give [a]a young bull for a sin offering to [b]the
priests, the Levites, who are of the seed of
[c]Zadok, who approach Me to minister to
Me,' says the Lord GOD. 20'You shall take
some of its blood and put *it* on the four
horns of the altar, on the four corners of
the ledge, and on the rim around it; thus
you shall cleanse it and make atonement
for it. 21Then you shall also take the bull
of the sin offering, and [a]burn it in the appointed place of the temple, [b]outside the
sanctuary. 22On the second day you shall
offer a kid of the goats without blemish
for a sin offering; and they shall cleanse
the altar, as they cleansed *it* with the bull.
23When you have finished cleansing *it*, you
shall offer a young bull without blemish,
and a ram from the flock without blemish.
24When you offer them before the LORD,
[a]the priests shall throw salt on them, and
they will offer them up *as* a burnt offering
to the LORD. 25Every day for [a]seven days
you shall prepare a goat *for* a sin offering;
they shall also prepare a young bull and a
ram from the flock, both without blemish.
26Seven days they shall make atonement
for the altar and purify it, and so consecrate
it. 27[a]When these days are over it shall be,
on the eighth day and thereafter, that the
priests shall offer your burnt offerings and
your peace offerings on the altar; and I will
[b]accept you,' says the Lord GOD."

The East Gate and the Prince

44 Then He brought me back to the
outer gate of the sanctuary [a]which
faces toward the east, but it *was* shut. 2And
the LORD said to me, "This gate shall be
shut; it shall not be opened, and no man
shall enter by it, [a]because the LORD God of
Israel has entered by it; therefore it shall
be shut. 3*As for* the [a]prince, *because* he *is*
the prince, he may sit in it to [b]eat bread
before the LORD; he shall enter by way of
the vestibule of the gateway, and go out
the same way."

Those Admitted to the Temple

4Also He brought me by way of the north
gate to the front of the temple; so I looked,
and [a]behold, the glory of the LORD filled
the house of the LORD; [b]and I fell on my
face. 5And the LORD said to me, [a]"Son of
man, mark well, see with your eyes and
hear with your ears, all that I say to you
concerning all the [b]ordinances of the house
of the LORD and all its laws. Mark well who
may enter the house and all who go out
from the sanctuary.

6"Now say to the [a]rebellious, to the house
of Israel, 'Thus says the Lord GOD: "O house
of Israel, [b]let Us have no more of all your
abominations. 7[a]When you brought in [b]for-
eigners, [c]uncircumcised in heart and uncircumcised in flesh, to be in My sanctuary
to defile it—My house—and when you offered [d]My food, [e]the fat and the blood, then
they broke My covenant because of all your
abominations. 8And you have not [a]kept
charge of My holy things, but you have set
others to keep charge of My sanctuary for
you." 9Thus says the Lord GOD: [a]"No foreigner, uncircumcised in heart or uncircumcised in flesh, shall enter My sanctuary,
including any foreigner who *is* among the
children of Israel.

Laws Governing Priests

10[a]"And the Levites who went far from
Me, when Israel went astray, who strayed
away from Me after their idols, they shall

43:15 [a] Ex. 27:2; Lev. 9:9; 1 Kin. 1:50 43:16 [a] Ex. 27:1 43:17 [a] Ex. 20:26 43:18 [a] Ex. 40:29 [b] Lev. 1:5, 11; [Heb. 9:21, 22] 43:19 [a] Ex. 29:10; Lev. 8:14; Ezek. 45:18, 19 [b] Ezek. 44:15, 16 [c] 1 Kin. 2:35; Ezek. 40:46 43:21 [a] Ex. 29:14; Lev. 4:12 [b] Heb. 13:11 43:24 [a] Lev. 2:13; Num. 18:19; [Mark 9:49, 50; Col. 4:6] 43:25 [a] Ex. 29:35; Lev. 8:33 43:27 [a] Lev. 9:1–4 [b] Ezek. 20:40, 41; [Rom. 12:1; 1 Pet. 2:5] 44:1 [a] Ezek. 43:1 44:2 [a] Ezek. 43:2–4 44:3 [a] Gen. 31:54; Ex. 24:9–11; [1 Cor. 10:18] [b] Ezek. 46:2, 8 44:4 [a] Is. 6:3; Ezek. 3:23; 43:5 [b] Ezek. 1:28; 43:3 44:5 [a] Deut. 32:46; Ezek. 40:4 [b] Deut. 12:32; Ezek. 43:10, 11 44:6 [a] Ezek. 2:5 [b] Ezek. 45:9; 1 Pet. 4:3 44:7 [a] Ezek. 43:8; Acts 21:28 [b] Lev. 22:25 [c] Lev. 26:41; Deut. 10:16; Jer. 4:4; 9:26; [Acts 7:51] [d] Lev. 21:17 [e] Lev. 3:16 44:8 [a] Lev. 22:2; Num. 18:7 44:9 [a] Ezek. 44:7; Joel 3:17; Zech. 14:21 44:10 [a] 2 Kin. 23:8; Ezek. 48:11

bear their iniquity. 11Yet they shall be ministers in My sanctuary, [a]*as* gatekeepers of
the house and ministers of the house; [b]they
shall slay the burnt offering and the sacrifice for the people, and [c]they shall stand
before them to minister to them. 12Because
they ministered to them before their idols
and [a]caused the house of Israel to fall into
iniquity, therefore I have [b]raised My hand
in an oath against them," says the Lord
GOD, "that they shall bear their iniquity.
13[a]And they shall not come near Me to minister to Me as priest, nor come near any
of My holy things, nor into the Most Holy
Place; but they shall [b]bear their shame and
their abominations which they have committed. 14Nevertheless I will make them
[a]keep charge of the temple, for all its work,
and for all that has to be done in it.

15[a]"But the priests, the Levites, [b]the sons
of Zadok, who kept charge of My sanctuary
[c]when the children of Israel went astray
from Me, they shall come near Me to minister to Me; and they [d]shall stand before
Me to offer to Me the [e]fat and the blood,"
says the Lord GOD. 16"They shall [a]enter
My sanctuary, and they shall come near
[b]My table to minister to Me, and they shall
keep My charge. 17And it shall be, whenever
they enter the gates of the inner court, that
[a]they shall put on linen garments; no wool
shall come upon them while they minister
within the gates of the inner court or within
the house. 18[a]They shall have linen turbans
on their heads and linen trousers on their
bodies; they shall not clothe themselves
with *anything that causes* sweat. 19When
they go out to the outer court, to the outer
court to the people, [a]they shall take off their
garments in which they have ministered,
leave them in the holy chambers, and put
on other garments; and in their holy garments they shall [b]not sanctify the people.

20[a]"They shall neither shave their heads
nor let their hair grow [b]long, but they shall
keep their hair well trimmed. 21[a]No priest
shall drink wine when he enters the inner
court. 22They shall not take as wife a [a]widow
or a divorced woman, but take virgins of
the descendants of the house of Israel, or
widows of priests.

23"And [a]they shall teach My people *the
difference* between the holy and the unholy,
and cause them to [b]discern between the unclean and the clean. 24[a]In controversy they
shall stand as judges, *and* judge it according
to My judgments. They shall keep My laws
and My statutes in all My appointed meet-
ings, [b]and they shall hallow My Sabbaths.

25"They shall not defile *themselves* by
coming near a dead person. Only for father
or mother, for son or daughter, for brother
or unmarried sister may they defile themselves. 26[a]After he is cleansed, they shall
count seven days for him. 27And on the day
that he goes to the sanctuary to minister in
the sanctuary, [a]he must offer his sin offering [b]in the inner court," says the Lord GOD.

28"It shall be, in regard to their inheritance, *that* I [a]*am* their inheritance. You
shall give them no [b]possession in Israel,
for I *am* their possession. 29[a]They shall eat
the grain offering, the sin offering, and the
trespass offering; [b]every dedicated thing
in Israel shall be theirs. 30The [a]best of all
firstfruits of any kind, and every sacrifice
of any kind from all your sacrifices, shall be
the priest's; also you [b]shall give to the priest
the first of your ground meal, [c]to cause a
blessing to rest on your house. 31The priests
shall not eat anything, bird or beast, that
[a]died naturally or was torn *by wild beasts.*

The Holy District

45 "Moreover, when you [a]divide the
land by lot into inheritance, you
shall [b]set apart a district for the LORD, a
holy section of the land; its length *shall be*
twenty-five thousand *cubits,* and the width
ten thousand. It *shall be* holy throughout
its territory all around. 2Of this there shall
be a square plot for the sanctuary, [a]five

44:11 [a] 1 Chr. 26:1–19 [b] 2 Chr. 29:34; 30:17 [c] Num. 16:9 44:12 [a] Is. 9:16; Mal. 2:8 [b] Ps. 106:26 44:13 [a] Num. 18:3; 2 Kin. 23:9 [b] Ezek. 32:30 44:14 [a] Num. 18:4; 1 Chr. 23:28–32; Ezek. 44:11 44:15 [a] Ezek. 40:46 [b] [1 Sam. 2:35]; 2 Sam. 15:27; Ezek. 43:19; 48:11 [c] Ezek. 44:10 [d] Deut. 10:8 [e] Lev. 3:16, 17; 17:5, 6; Ezek. 44:7 44:16 [a] Num. 18:5, 7, 8 [b] Ezek. 41:22; Mal. 1:7, 12 44:17 [a] Ex. 28:39–43; 39:27–29; Rev. 19:8 44:18 [a] Ex. 28:40; 39:28; Is. 3:20; Ezek. 24:17, 23 44:19 [a] Lev. 6:10; 16:4, 23, 24; Ezek. 42:14 [b] Ex. 30:29; Lev. 6:27; Ezek. 46:20; [Matt. 23:17] 44:20 [a] Lev. 21:5 [b] Num. 6:5 44:21 [a] Lev. 10:9 44:22 [a] Lev. 21:7, 13, 14 44:23 [a] Lev. 10:10, 11; Ezek. 22:26; Hos. 4:6; Mic. 3:9–11; Zeph. 3:4; Hag. 2:11–13; Mal. 2:6–8 [b] Lev. 20:25 44:24 [a] Deut. 17:8, 9; 1 Chr. 23:4; 2 Chr. 19:8–10 [b] Ezek. 22:26 44:26 [a] Num. 6:10; 19:11, 13–19 44:27 [a] Lev. 5:3, 6; Num. 6:9–11 [b] Ezek. 44:17 44:28 [a] Num. 18:20; Deut. 10:9; 18:1, 2; Josh. 13:14, 33 [b] Ezek. 45:4 44:29 [a] Lev. 7:6 [b] Lev. 27:21, 28; Num. 18:14 44:30 [a] Ex. 13:2; 22:29; 23:19; Num. 3:13; 18:12 [b] Num. 15:20; Neh. 10:37 [c] Prov. 3:9; [Mal. 3:10] 44:31 [a] Ex. 22:31; Lev. 22:8; Deut. 14:21; Ezek. 4:14 45:1 [a] Num. 26:52–56; Ezek. 47:22 [b] Ezek. 48:8, 9 45:2 [a] Ezek. 42:20

hundred by five hundred *rods,* with fifty
cubits around it for an open space. 3So this
is the district you shall measure: twenty-
five thousand *cubits* long and ten thousand
wide; [a]in it shall be the sanctuary, the Most
Holy *Place.* 4It shall be [a]a holy *section* of the
land, belonging to the priests, the ministers
of the sanctuary, who come near to minister to the LORD; it shall be a place for their
houses and a holy place for the sanctuary. 5[a]*An area* twenty-five thousand *cubits*
long and ten thousand wide shall belong
to the Levites, the ministers of the temple; they shall have [b]twenty chambers as
a possession.[1]

Properties of the City and the Prince

6[a]"You shall appoint as the property of
the city *an area* five thousand *cubits* wide
and twenty-five thousand long, adjacent to
the district of the holy *section;* it shall belong to the whole house of Israel.

7[a]"The prince shall have *a section* on one
side and the other of the holy district and
the city's property; and bordering on the
holy district and the city's property, extending westward on the west side and eastward
on the east side, the length *shall be* side by
side with one of the *tribal* portions, from
the west border to the east border. 8The
land shall be his possession in Israel; and
[a]My princes shall no more oppress My people, but they shall give *the rest of* the land
to the house of Israel, according to their
tribes."

Laws Governing the Prince

9'Thus says the Lord GOD: [a]"Enough,
O princes of Israel! [b]Remove violence and
plundering, execute justice and righteousness, and stop dispossessing My people,"
says the Lord GOD. 10"You shall have [a]hon-
est scales, an honest ephah, and an honest bath. 11The ephah and the bath shall
be of the same measure, so that the bath
contains one-tenth of a homer, and the
ephah one-tenth of a homer; their measure shall be according to the homer. 12The
[a]shekel *shall be* twenty gerahs; twenty shekels, twenty-five shekels, *and* fifteen shekels
shall be your mina.

13"This *is* the offering which you shall
offer: you shall give one-sixth of an ephah
from a homer of wheat, and one-sixth of
an ephah from a homer of barley. 14The ordinance concerning oil, the bath of oil, *is*
one-tenth of a bath from a kor. *A kor is* a homer or ten baths, for ten baths *are* a homer.
15And one lamb shall be given from a flock
of two hundred, from the rich pastures of
Israel. These shall be for grain offerings,
burnt offerings, and peace offerings, [a]to
make atonement for them," says the Lord
GOD. 16"All the people of the land shall give
this offering for the prince in Israel. 17Then
it shall be the [a]prince's part *to give* burnt
offerings, grain offerings, and drink offerings, at the feasts, the New Moons, the
Sabbaths, and at all the appointed seasons
of the house of Israel. He shall prepare the
sin offering, the grain offering, the burnt
offering, and the peace offerings to make
atonement for the house of Israel."

Keeping the Feasts
(Ex. 12:1–20; Lev. 23:33–43)

18'Thus says the Lord GOD: "In the first
month, on the first *day* of the month, you
shall take a young bull without blemish and
[a]cleanse the sanctuary. 19[a]The priest shall
take some of the blood of the sin offering
and put *it* on the doorposts of the temple,
on the four corners of the ledge of the altar, and on the gateposts of the gate of the
inner court. 20And so you shall do on the
seventh *day* of the month [a]for everyone
who has sinned unintentionally or in ignorance. Thus you shall make atonement
for the temple.

21[a]"In the first *month,* on the fourteenth
day of the month, you shall observe the
Passover, a feast of seven days; unleavened
bread shall be eaten. 22And on that day the
prince shall prepare for himself and for all
the people of the land [a]a bull *for* a sin offering. 23On the [a]seven days of the feast he

45:3 [a] Ezek. 48:10 45:4 [a] Ezek. 48:10, 11 45:5 [a] Ezek. 48:13 [b] Ezek. 40:17 [1] Following Masoretic Text, Targum, and Vulgate; Septuagint reads *a possession, cities of dwelling.* 45:6 [a] Ezek. 48:15 45:7 [a] Ezek. 48:21 45:8 [a] [Is. 11:3–5]; Jer. 22:17; Ezek. 22:27 45:9 [a] Ezek. 44:6 [b] Jer. 22:3; Zech. 8:16 45:10 [a] Lev. 19:36; Deut. 25:15; Prov. 16:11; Amos 8:4–6; Mic. 6:10, 11 45:12 [a] Ex. 30:13; Lev. 27:25; Num. 3:47 45:15 [a] Lev. 1:4; 6:30 45:17 [a] Ezek. 46:4–12 45:18 [a] Lev. 16:16, 33; Ezek. 43:22, 26 45:19 [a] Lev. 16:18–20; Ezek. 43:20 45:20 [a] Lev. 4:27; Ps. 19:12 45:21 [a] Ex. 12:18; Lev. 23:5, 6; Num. 9:2, 3; 28:16, 17; Deut. 16:1 45:22 [a] Lev. 4:14 45:23 [a] Lev. 23:8

shall prepare a burnt offering to the LORD,
seven bulls and seven rams without blemish, daily for seven days, [b]and a kid of the
goats daily *for* a sin offering. 24[a]And he shall
prepare a grain offering of one ephah for
each bull and one ephah for each ram, together with a hin of oil for each ephah.
25"In the seventh *month,* on the fifteenth
day of the month, at the [a]feast, he shall do
likewise for seven days, according to the
sin offering, the burnt offering, the grain
offering, and the oil."

The Manner of Worship

46 'Thus says the Lord GOD: "The gateway of the inner court that faces toward the east shall be shut the six [a]working
days; but on the Sabbath it shall be opened,
and on the day of the New Moon it shall be
opened. 2[a]The prince shall enter by way of
the vestibule of the gateway from the outside, and stand by the gatepost. The priests
shall prepare his burnt offering and his
peace offerings. He shall worship at the
threshold of the gate. Then he shall go out,
but the gate shall not be shut until evening. 3Likewise the people of the land shall
worship at the entrance to this gateway
before the LORD on the Sabbaths and the
New Moons. 4The burnt offering that [a]the
prince offers to the LORD on the [b]Sabbath
day *shall be* six lambs without blemish, and
a ram without blemish; 5[a]and the grain offering *shall be one* ephah for a ram, and the
grain offering for the lambs, as much as he
wants to give, as well as a hin of oil with every ephah. 6On the day of the New Moon *it
shall be* a young bull without blemish, six
lambs, and a ram; they shall be without
blemish. 7He shall prepare a grain offering
of an ephah for a bull, an ephah for a ram,
as much as he wants to give for the lambs,
and a hin of oil with every ephah. 8[a]When
the prince enters, he shall go in by way of
the vestibule of the gateway, and go out
the same way.
9"But when the people of the land [a]come
before the LORD on the appointed feast
days, whoever enters by way of the north
[b]gate to worship shall go out by way of the
south gate; and whoever enters by way of
the south gate shall go out by way of the
north gate. He shall not return by way of
the gate through which he came, but shall
go out through the opposite gate. 10The
prince shall then be in their midst. When
they go in, he shall go in; and when they go
out, he shall go out. 11At the festivals and
the appointed feast days [a]the grain offering
shall be an ephah for a bull, an ephah for
a ram, as much as he wants to give for the
lambs, and a hin of oil with every ephah.
12"Now when the prince makes a voluntary burnt offering or voluntary peace
offering to the LORD, the gate that faces
toward the east [a]shall then be opened for
him; and he shall prepare his burnt offering and his peace offerings as he did on the
Sabbath day. Then he shall go out, and after
he goes out the gate shall be shut.
13[a]"You shall daily make a burnt offering to the LORD *of* a lamb of the first year
without blemish; you shall prepare it every
morning. 14And you shall prepare a grain
offering with it every morning, a sixth of an
ephah, and a third of a hin of oil to moisten
the fine flour. This grain offering is a perpetual ordinance, to be made regularly to
the LORD. 15Thus they shall prepare the
lamb, the grain offering, and the oil, *as* a
[a]regular burnt offering every morning."

The Prince and Inheritance Laws

16'Thus says the Lord GOD: "If the prince
gives a gift *of some* of his inheritance to any
of his sons, it shall belong to his sons; it is
their possession by inheritance. 17But if he
gives a gift of some of his inheritance to
one of his servants, it shall be his until [a]the
year of liberty, after which it shall return to
the prince. But his inheritance shall belong
to his sons; it shall become theirs. 18More-
over [a]the prince shall not take any of the
people's inheritance by evicting them from
their property; he shall provide an inheritance for his sons from his own property,
so that none of My people may be scattered
from his property."'"

45:23 [b] Num. 28:15, 22, 30; 29:5, 11, 16, 19 45:24 [a] Num. 28:12–15; Ezek. 46:5, 7 45:25 [a] Lev. 23:34; Num. 29:12; Deut. 16:13; 2 Chr. 5:3; 7:8, 10 46:1 [a] Ex. 20:9 46:2 [a] Ezek. 44:3 46:4 [a] Ezek. 45:17 [b] Num. 28:9, 10 46:5 [a] Num. 28:12; Ezek. 45:24; 46:7, 11 46:8 [a] Ezek. 44:3; 46:2 46:9 [a] Ex. 23:14–17; 34:23; Deut. 16:16, 17; Ps. 84:7; Mic. 6:6 [b] Ezek. 48:31, 33 46:11 [a] Ezek. 46:5, 7 46:12 [a] Ezek. 44:3; 46:1, 2, 8 46:13 [a] Ex. 29:38; Num. 28:3–5 46:15 [a] Ex. 29:42; Num. 28:6 46:17 [a] Lev. 25:10 46:18 [a] Ezek. 45:8

How the Offerings Were Prepared

19Now he brought me through the entrance, which *was* at the side of the gate,
into the holy [a]chambers of the priests
which face toward the north; and there a
place *was* situated at their extreme western
end. 20And he said to me, "This *is* the place
where the priests shall [a]boil the trespass offering and the sin offering, *and* where they
shall [b]bake the grain offering, so that they
do not bring *them* out into the outer court
[c]to sanctify the people."

21Then he brought me out into the outer
court and caused me to pass by the four
corners of the court; and in fact, in every corner of the court *there was another*
court. 22In the four corners of the court
were enclosed courts, forty *cubits* long and
thirty wide; all four corners *were* the same
size. 23*There was* a row *of building stones*
all around in them, all around the four of
them; and cooking hearths were made under the rows of stones all around. 24And he
said to me, "These *are* the kitchens where
the ministers of the temple shall [a]boil the
sacrifices of the people."

The Healing Waters and Trees

47 Then he brought me back to the door
of the temple; and there was [a]water,
flowing from under the threshold of the
temple toward the east, for the front of the
temple faced east; the water was flowing
from under the right side of the temple,
south of the altar. 2He brought me out by
way of the north gate, and led me around
on the outside to the outer gateway that
faces [a]east; and there was water, running
out on the right side.

3And when [a]the man went out to the
east with the line in his hand, he measured
one thousand cubits, and he brought me
through the waters; the water *came up to*
my ankles. 4Again he measured one thousand and brought me through the waters;
the water *came up to my* knees. Again he
measured one thousand and brought me
through; the water *came up to my* waist.
5Again he measured one thousand, *and*
it was a river that I could not cross; for
the water was too deep, water in which
one must swim, a river that could not be
crossed. 6He said to me, "Son of man, have
you seen *this?*" Then he brought me and returned me to the bank of the river.

7When I returned, there, along the bank
of the river, *were* very many [a]trees on one
side and the other. 8Then he said to me:
"This water flows toward the eastern region, goes down into the valley, and enters the sea. *When it* reaches the sea, *its*
waters are healed. 9And it shall be *that* every living thing that moves, wherever the
rivers go, will live. There will be a very great
multitude of fish, because these waters go
there; for they will be healed, and everything will live wherever the river goes. 10It
shall be *that* fishermen will stand by it from
En Gedi to En Eglaim; they will be *places*
for spreading their nets. Their fish will be
of the same kinds as the fish [a]of the Great
Sea, exceedingly many. 11But its swamps
and marshes will not be healed; they will
be given over to salt. 12[a]Along the bank of
the river, on this side and that, will grow all
kinds of trees used for food; [b]their leaves
will not wither, and their fruit will not fail.
They will bear fruit every month, because
their water flows from the sanctuary. Their
fruit will be for food, and their leaves for
[c]medicine."

Borders of the Land
(cf. Num. 34:1–12)

13Thus says the Lord GOD: "These *are* the
[a]borders by which you shall divide the land
as an inheritance among the twelve tribes
of Israel. [b]Joseph *shall have two* portions.
14You shall inherit it equally with one another; for I [a]raised My hand in an oath to
give it to your fathers, and this land shall
[b]fall to you as your inheritance.

15"This *shall be* the border of the land on
the north: from the Great Sea, *by* [a]the road
to Hethlon, as one goes to [b]Zedad, 16[a]Ha-
math, [b]Berothah, Sibraim (which *is* between
the border of Damascus and the border of
Hamath), to Hazar Hatticon (which *is* on

46:19 [a] Ezek. 42:13 **46:20** [a] 2 Chr. 35:13 [b] Lev. 2:4, 5, 7 [c] Ezek. 44:19 **46:24** [a] Ezek. 46:20 **47:1** [a] Ps. 46:4; Is. 30:25; 55:1; [Jer. 2:13]; Joel 3:18; Zech. 13:1; 14:8; [Rev. 22:1, 17] **47:2** [a] Ezek. 44:1, 2 **47:3** [a] Ezek. 40:3 **47:7** [a] [Is. 60:13, 21; 61:3; Ezek. 47:12; Rev. 22:2] **47:10** [a] Num. 34:3; Josh. 23:4; Ezek. 48:28 **47:12** [a] Ezek. 47:7; [Rev. 22:2] [b] Job 18:16; [Ps. 1:3; Jer. 17:8] [c] [Rev. 22:2] **47:13** [a] Num. 34:1–29 [b] Gen. 48:5; 1 Chr. 5:1; Ezek. 48:4, 5 **47:14** [a] Gen. 12:7; 13:15; 15:7; 17:8; 26:3; 28:13; Deut. 1:8; Ezek. 20:5, 6, 28, 42 [b] Ezek. 48:29 **47:15** [a] Ezek. 48:1 [b] Num. 34:7, 8 **47:16** [a] Num. 34:8 [b] 2 Sam. 8:8

the border of Hauran). 17Thus the boundary shall be from the Sea to [a]Hazar Enan, the border of Damascus; and as for the north, northward, it is the border of Hamath. *This is* the north side.

18"On the east side you shall mark out the border from between Hauran and Damascus, and between Gilead and the land of Israel, along the Jordan, and along the eastern side of the sea. *This is* the east side.

19"The south side, toward the South,[1] *shall be* from Tamar to [a]the waters of Meribah by Kadesh, along the brook to the Great Sea. *This is* the south side, toward the South.

20"The west side *shall be* the Great Sea, from the *southern* boundary until one comes to a point opposite Hamath. This *is* the west side.

21"Thus you shall [a]divide this land among yourselves according to the tribes of Israel. 22It shall be that you will divide it by [a]lot as an inheritance for yourselves, [b]and for the strangers who dwell among you and who bear children among you. [c]They shall be to you as native-born among the children of Israel; they shall have an inheritance with you among the tribes of Israel. 23And it shall be *that* in whatever tribe the stranger dwells, there you shall give *him* his inheritance," says the Lord GOD.

Division of the Land

48 "Now these *are* the names of the tribes: [a]From the northern border along the road to Hethlon at the entrance of Hamath, to Hazar Enan, the border of Damascus northward, in the direction of Hamath, *there shall be* one *section for* [b]Dan from its east to its west side; 2by the border of Dan, from the east side to the west, one *section for* [a]Asher; 3by the border of Asher, from the east side to the west, one *section for* [a]Naphtali; 4by the border of Naphtali, from the east side to the west, one *section for* [a]Manasseh; 5by the border of Manasseh, from the east side to the west, one *section for* [a]Ephraim; 6by the border of Ephraim, from the east side to the west, one *section for* [a]Reuben; 7by the border of Reuben, from the east side to the west, one *section for* [a]Judah; 8by the border of Judah, from the east side to the west, shall be [a]the district which you shall set apart, twenty-five thousand *cubits* in width, and *in* length the same as one of the *other* portions, from the east side to the west, with the [b]sanctuary in the center.

9"The district that you shall set apart for the LORD *shall be* twenty-five thousand *cubits* in length and ten thousand in width. 10To these—to the priests—the holy district shall belong: on the north twenty-five thousand *cubits in length,* on the west ten thousand in width, on the east ten thousand in width, and on the south twenty-five thousand in length. The sanctuary of the LORD shall be in the center. 11[a]*It shall be* for the priests of the sons of Zadok, who are sanctified, who have kept My charge, who did not go astray when the children of Israel went astray, [b]as the Levites went astray. 12And *this* district of land that is set apart shall be to them a thing most [a]holy by the border of the Levites.

13"Opposite the border of the priests, the [a]Levites *shall have an area* twenty-five thousand *cubits* in length and ten thousand in width; its entire length *shall be* twenty-five thousand and its width ten thousand. 14[a]And they shall not sell or exchange any of it; they may not alienate this best *part* of the land, for *it is* holy to the LORD.

15[a]"The five thousand *cubits* in width that remain, along the edge of the twenty-five thousand, shall be [b]for general use by the city, for dwellings and common-land; and the city shall be in the center. 16These *shall be* its measurements: the north side four thousand five hundred *cubits,* the south side four thousand five hundred, the east side four thousand five hundred, and the west side four thousand five hundred. 17The common-land of the city shall be: to the north two hundred and fifty *cubits,* to the south two hundred and fifty, to the east two hundred and fifty, and to the west two

47:17 [a] Num. 34:9; Ezek. 48:1 47:19 [a] Num. 20:13; Deut. 32:51; Ps. 81:7; Ezek. 48:28 [1] Hebrew *Negev*
47:21 [a] Ezek. 45:1 47:22 [a] Num. 26:55, 56 [b] [Eph. 3:6; Rev. 7:9, 10] [c] [Acts 11:18; 15:9; Gal. 3:28; Eph. 2:12–14; Col. 3:11]
48:1 [a] Ezek. 47:15 [b] Josh. 19:40–48 48:2 [a] Josh. 19:24–31 48:3 [a] Josh. 19:32–39 48:4 [a] Josh. 13:29–31; 17:1–11, 17, 18
48:5 [a] Josh. 16:5–10; 17:8–10, 14–18 48:6 [a] Josh. 13:15–23 48:7 [a] Josh. 15:1–63; 19:9 48:8 [a] Ezek. 45:1–6 [b] [Is. 12:6; 33:20–22]; Ezek. 45:3, 4 48:11 [a] Ezek. 40:46; 44:15 [b] Ezek. 44:10, 12 48:12 [a] Ezek. 45:4 48:13 [a] Ezek. 45:5
48:14 [a] Ex. 22:29; Lev. 27:10, 28, 33; Ezek. 44:30 48:15 [a] Ezek. 45:6 [b] Ezek. 42:20

hundred and fifty. 18The rest of the length,
alongside the district of the holy *section,*
shall be ten thousand *cubits* to the east and
ten thousand to the west. It shall be adjacent to the district of the holy *section,* and
its produce shall be food for the workers
of the city. 19[a]The workers of the city, from
all the tribes of Israel, shall cultivate it.
20The entire district *shall be* twenty-five
thousand *cubits* by twenty-five thousand
cubits, foursquare. You shall set apart the
holy district with the property of the city.

21[a]"The rest *shall belong* to the prince, on
one side and on the other of the holy district and of the city's property, next to the
twenty-five thousand *cubits* of the *holy* district as far as the eastern border, and westward next to the twenty-five thousand as
far as the western border, adjacent to the
tribal portions; *it shall belong* to the prince.
It shall be the holy district, [b]and the sanctuary of the temple *shall be* in the center.
22Moreover, apart from the possession of
the Levites and the possession of the city
which are in the midst of what *belongs* to
the prince, *the area* between the border of
Judah and the border of [a]Benjamin shall
belong to the prince.

23"As for the rest of the tribes, from the
east side to the west, Benjamin *shall have*
one *section;* 24by the border of Benjamin,
from the east side to the west, [a]Simeon *shall*
have one *section;* 25by the border of Simeon,
from the east side to the west, [a]Issachar
shall have one *section;* 26by the border of Issachar, from the east side to the west, [a]Zeb-
ulun *shall have* one *section;* 27by the border
of Zebulun, from the east side to the west,
[a]Gad *shall have* one *section;* 28by the border
of Gad, on the south side, toward the South,[1]
the border shall be from Tamar *to* [a]the waters of Meribah *by* Kadesh, along the brook
to the [b]Great Sea. 29[a]This *is* the land which
you shall divide by lot as an inheritance
among the tribes of Israel, and these *are*
their portions," says the Lord GOD.

The Gates of the City and Its Name

30"These *are* the exits of the city. On
the north side, measuring four thousand
five hundred *cubits* 31[a](the gates of the city
shall be named after the tribes of Israel), the
three gates northward: one gate for Reuben, one gate for Judah, and one gate for
Levi; 32on the east side, four thousand five
hundred *cubits,* three gates: one gate for Joseph, one gate for Benjamin, and one gate
for Dan; 33on the south side, measuring
four thousand five hundred *cubits,* three
gates: one gate for Simeon, one gate for
Issachar, and one gate for Zebulun; 34on
the west side, four thousand five hundred
cubits with their three gates: one gate for
Gad, one gate for Asher, and one gate for
Naphtali. 35All the way around *shall be* eighteen thousand *cubits;* [a]and the name of the
city from *that* day *shall be:* [b]THE LORD *IS*
THERE."[1]

48:19 [a] Ezek. 45:6 **48:21** [a] Ezek. 34:24; 45:7; 48:22 [b] Ezek. 48:8, 10 **48:22** [a] Josh. 18:21–28 **48:24** [a] Josh. 19:1–9 **48:25** [a] Josh. 19:17–23 **48:26** [a] Josh. 19:10–16 **48:27** [a] Josh. 13:24–28 **48:28** [a] Gen. 14:7; 2 Chr. 20:2; Ezek. 47:19 [b] Ezek. 47:10, 15, 19, 20 [1] Hebrew *Negev* **48:29** [a] Ezek. 47:14, 21, 22 **48:31** [a] [Rev. 21:10–14] **48:35** [a] Jer. 23:6; 33:16 [b] Is. 12:6; 14:32; 24:23; Jer. 3:17; 8:19; 14:9; Ezek. 35:10; Joel 3:21; Zech. 2:10; Rev. 21:3; 22:3 [1] Hebrew *YHWH Shammah*

THE BOOK OF DANIEL

OVERVIEW

The Book of Daniel is named after its author, the prophet Daniel, whose name means "God is my judge." Daniel was one of the major prophets of the Old Testament, and his message affirmed that God is the only true and living God who is sovereign over all.

Daniel was captured by the Babylonians in 605 BC and was appointed to serve in the court of King Nebuchadnezzar. The events covered in the Book of Daniel occurred between 605 and 536 BC. During this time Daniel served three additional kings: Belshazzar, Darius, and Cyrus. The Book of Daniel can be divided into two sections. The first section (chs. 1–6) is a historical account of the life and work of Daniel and his friends as servants to the Babylonian kings. The second section (chs. 7–12) describes Daniel's dreams and visions about the future.

The Book of Daniel opens with Nebuchadnezzar's capture of Jerusalem, some of the articles from the temple, and King Jehoiakim (see 1:1–2). In addition, Nebuchadnezzar instructed that "some of the children of Israel and some of the king's descendants and some of the nobles" (v. 3) be brought to Babylon "to serve in the king's palace" (v. 1:4). Daniel and three of his friends were among those chosen.

When Nebuchadnezzar had a troubling dream, he called for "the magicians, the astrologers, the sorcerers, and the Chaldeans" (2:2) to not only tell him his dream but also interpret it (see vv. 3–9). He became furious when none of them could tell him his dream. However, God revealed the dream and its meaning to Daniel in a vision, and Daniel, in turn, explained it to Nebuchadnezzar. The king declared, "Truly your God is the God of gods, the Lord of kings, and a revealer of secrets" (v. 47). As an act of gratitude, the king promoted Daniel "over all the wise men of Babylon" (v. 48), and his friends were placed "over the affairs of the province of Babylon" (v. 49).

One of the most popular biblical stories found in Daniel is that of Daniel's friends whom Nebuchadnezzar named Shadrach, Meshach, and Abed-Nego. Because of their refusal to worship a golden image of Nebuchadnezzar, the three were brought before the king (see 3:1–13). The king demanded that they "fall down and worship the image" that he had made (v. 15). Even though the penalty was to be thrown in a fiery furnace, they responded, "We have no need to answer you in this matter . . . Our God whom we serve is able to deliver us from the burning fiery furnace" (vv. 16–17). When they were thrown into the furnace, they were not harmed, and once they were released, they did not even smell of smoke. As a result, Nebuchadnezzar praised God and promoted Shadrach, Meshach and Abed-Nego (see vv. 19–30).

During the reign of King Darius, Daniel was elevated and set "over the whole realm" (6:3). Other governors became jealous and sought to destroy Daniel. They advised the king to decree that anyone who petitioned a god or man who was not the king would "be cast into the den of lions" (v. 7). Daniel prayed to the one true God anyway, and Darius was forced to cast him into the lions' den (see vv. 10–17). God saved Daniel, prompting Darius to decree that "men must tremble and fear before the God of Daniel" (v. 26).

Chapters 7–12 recount Daniel's visions and prophecies about coming events. The vision of the four beasts (see 7:1–28), the vision of the ram and goat (see 8:1–27), and the vision by the Tigris

River (see 10:1–21) are three of the most well-known visions. In chapter 9, we learn of Daniel's prayer for the Israelites when he asked that God's "fury be turned away" (v. 16) and that He would cause His "face to shine" upon them (v. 17). Chapter 11 tells of Israel's suffering between opposing armies, and chapter 12 details Daniel's prophecy of the end of time.

The Book of Daniel describes God's mighty works and His commitment to those who honor His covenant with them. Each time Daniel and his friends were ordered by pagan kings to go against God, they stood firmly on their belief in Him. In turn, God showed His commitment to them by demonstrating His power in such magnificent ways that nonbelievers were compelled to acknowledge Him as the only true God.

BREATHE IT IN

Daniel and his friends were taken into captivity and forced to live in a land with a different culture and different customs. Many of these customs contradicted the customs and laws of the Israelites. In Babylon, they were expected to eat differently and worship people and images rather than God. Instead of succumbing to the intense pressure to conform, they remained true to God's covenant. Often, they were punished and threatened with death, but God always protected them. The miracles He performed proved His sovereignty and His faithfulness to those who honor Him.

The prophet Daniel provides a powerful example of how to be faithful to God. This book reveals the attitude of heart that results in serving God, even when difficult situations arise or when everyone around us has succumbed to temptation and turned away from Him. Daniel was faithful, and God showed up to deliver him in every situation. Daniel remained hopeful, even though he was a captive in a foreign land.

We Christians often find ourselves in difficult situations and feel as if God has abandoned us. We cannot understand why things are not going well for us. We ask, "God, why did You let me lose my job?" or "How could You take my loved one away from me?" or "Lord, do You see how the enemy is treating me?" In these times, it is easy to lose sight of who God is and how He operates.

Every day we are impacted by laws and policies that do not reflect God's Word. We are bombarded with movies and music that promote idolatry and immorality. We are encouraged to participate in activities that contradict our relationship with God. Life dictates, and the Bible mandates, that we interact with those who do not believe in God at all, those who believe half-heartedly, and those who believe but are unwilling to be changed. It can be overwhelming living in the midst of the resulting turmoil.

Rest assured that God reigns amid turmoil. God is sovereign, meaning He has all authority and power. Thus, He is in control of everyone and everything on the earth. Nothing is outside of His purview. Remember that God is good. He does not just act good; He is all that is good, and nothing is good without Him. If we remember that, then we can always respond to our own questions by saying, "Yes, Lord, we trust You." We can follow Daniel's example and remain steadfast in our faith and live according to God's commandments.

Never be afraid to follow God when others turn their backs on Him. God knows all that is happening in the world and in our lives. If we stand up and speak up on His behalf, He will protect us and ultimately deliver us from hurt, harm, and danger. We should live our lives convinced that God is sovereign. Stand up for what is right and be an example of faithfulness to those around you.

THE BOOK OF

DANIEL

Daniel and His Friends Obey God
(cf. 2 Kin. 24:10–17)

1 In the third year of the reign of [a]Jehoi-
akim king of Judah, Nebuchadnezzar
king of Babylon came to Jerusalem and
besieged it. 2And the Lord gave Jehoiakim
king of Judah into his hand, with [a]some of
the articles of the house of God, which he
carried [b]into the land of Shinar to the house
of his god; [c]and he brought the articles into
the treasure house of his god.
3Then the king instructed Ashpenaz,
the master of his eunuchs, to bring [a]some
of the children of Israel and some of the
king's descendants and some of the nobles, 4young men [a]in whom *there was* no
blemish, but good-looking, gifted in all
wisdom, possessing knowledge and quick
to understand, who *had* ability to serve in
the king's palace, and [b]whom they might
teach the language and literature of the
Chaldeans. 5And the king appointed for
them a daily provision of the king's delicacies and of the wine which he drank, and
three years of training for them, so that at
the end of *that time* they might [a]serve before the king. 6Now from among those of
the sons of Judah were Daniel, Hananiah,
Mishael, and Azariah. 7[a]To them the chief
of the eunuchs gave names: [b]he gave Daniel *the name* Belteshazzar; to Hananiah,
Shadrach; to Mishael, Meshach; and to Azariah, Abed-Nego.
8But Daniel purposed in his heart that
he would not defile himself [a]with the portion of the king's delicacies, nor with the
wine which he drank; therefore he requested of the chief of the eunuchs that
he might not defile himself. 9Now [a]God had
brought Daniel into the favor and goodwill of the chief of the eunuchs. 10And the
chief of the eunuchs said to Daniel, "I fear
my lord the king, who has appointed your
food and drink. For why should he see your
faces looking worse than the young men
who *are* your age? Then you would endan-
ger my head before the king."
11So Daniel said to the steward[1] whom the
chief of the eunuchs had set over Daniel,
Hananiah, Mishael, and Azariah, 12"Please
test your servants for ten days, and let them
give us vegetables to eat and water to drink.
13Then let our appearance be examined before you, and the appearance of the young
men who eat the portion of the king's delicacies; and as you see fit, *so* deal with your
servants." 14So he consented with them in
this matter, and tested them ten days.

#OXYGEN

DANIEL 1:12

Elevate Your Way of Thinking

The way you think determines the altitude of your thinking. Focusing on God helps you pull your focus from the worldly to the holy. Do not settle for the treasures of the world when the riches of God can be yours.

Breathe and elevate your way of thinking.

1:1 [a] 2 Kin. 24:1, 2; 2 Chr. 36:5–7; Jer. 25:1; 52:12–30 1:2 [a] 2 Chr. 36:7; Jer. 27:19, 20; Dan. 5:2 [b] Gen. 10:10; 11:2; Is. 11:11; Zech. 5:11 [c] 2 Chr. 36:7 1:3 [a] 2 Kin. 20:17, 18; Is. 39:7 1:4 [a] Lev. 24:19, 20 [b] Acts 7:22 1:5 [a] Gen. 41:46; 1 Sam. 16:22; 1 Kin. 10:8; Dan. 1:19 1:7 [a] Gen. 41:45; 2 Kin. 24:17 [b] Dan. 2:26; 4:8; 5:12 1:8 [a] Lev. 11:47; Deut. 32:38; Ezek. 4:13; Hos. 9:3 1:9 [a] Gen. 39:21; 1 Kin. 8:50; [Job 5:15, 16]; Ps. 106:46; [Prov. 16:7]; Acts 7:10; 27:3 1:11 [1] Hebrew *Melzar*, also in verse 16

15And at the end of ten days their features appeared better and fatter in flesh
than all the young men who ate the portion
of the king's delicacies. 16Thus the steward
took away their portion of delicacies and
the wine that they were to drink, and gave
them vegetables.
17As for these four young men, [a]God gave
them [b]knowledge and skill in all literature
and wisdom; and Daniel had [c]understand-
ing in all visions and dreams.
18Now at the end of the days, when the
king had said that they should be brought
in, the chief of the eunuchs brought them in
before Nebuchadnezzar. 19Then the king in-
terviewed[1] them, and among them all none
was found like Daniel, Hananiah, Mishael,
and Azariah; therefore [a]they served before
the king. 20[a]And in all matters of wisdom
and understanding about which the king examined them, he found them ten times better than all the magicians *and* astrologers
who *were* in all his realm. 21[a]Thus Daniel
continued until the first year of King Cyrus.

Nebuchadnezzar's Dream

2 Now in the second year of Nebuchadnezzar's reign, Nebuchadnezzar had
dreams; [a]and his spirit was *so* troubled that
[b]his sleep left him. 2[a]Then the king gave the
command to call the magicians, the astrologers, the sorcerers, and the Chaldeans to
tell the king his dreams. So they came and
stood before the king. 3And the king said to
them, "I have had a dream, and my spirit
is anxious to know the dream."
4Then the Chaldeans spoke to the king
in Aramaic,[1] [a]"O king, live forever! Tell your
servants the dream, and we will give the
interpretation."
5The king answered and said to the Chaldeans, "My decision is firm: if you do not
make known the dream to me, and its interpretation, you shall be [a]cut in pieces, and
your houses shall be made an ash heap.
6[a]However, if you tell the dream and its
interpretation, you shall receive from me
gifts, rewards, and great honor. Therefore
tell me the dream and its interpretation."
7They answered again and said, "Let the
king tell his servants the dream, and we will
give its interpretation."
8The king answered and said, "I know for
certain that you would gain time, because
you see that my decision is firm: 9if you do
not make known the dream to me, *there
is only* one decree for you! For you have
agreed to speak lying and corrupt words
before me till the time has changed. Therefore tell me the dream, and I shall know
that you can give me its interpretation."
10The Chaldeans answered the king, and
said, "There is not a man on earth who can
tell the king's matter; therefore no king,
lord, or ruler has *ever* asked such things of
any magician, astrologer, or Chaldean. 11*It
is* a difficult thing that the king requests,
and there is no other who can tell it to the
king [a]except the gods, whose dwelling is
not with flesh."
12For this reason the king was angry and
very furious, and gave the command to destroy all the wise *men* of Babylon. 13So the
decree went out, and they began killing the
wise *men;* and they sought [a]Daniel and his
companions, to kill *them.*

God Reveals Nebuchadnezzar's Dream

14Then with counsel and wisdom Daniel
answered Arioch, the captain of the king's
guard, who had gone out to kill the wise
men of Babylon; 15he answered and said to
Arioch the king's captain, "Why is the decree from the king so urgent?" Then Arioch
made the decision known to Daniel.
16So Daniel went in and asked the king
to give him time, that he might tell the king
the interpretation. 17Then Daniel went to
his house, and made the decision known to
Hananiah, Mishael, and Azariah, his companions, 18[a]that they might seek mercies
from the God of heaven concerning this
secret, so that Daniel and his companions
might not perish with the rest of the wise
men of Babylon. 19Then the secret was revealed to Daniel [a]in a night vision. So Daniel blessed the God of heaven.

1:17 [a] 1 Kin. 3:12, 28; 2 Chr. 1:10–12; [Luke 21:15; James 1:5–7] [b] Acts 7:22 [c] Num. 12:6; 2 Chr. 26:5; Dan. 5:11, 12, 14; 10:1 1:19 [a] Gen. 41:46; [Prov. 22:29]; Dan. 1:5 [1] Literally *talked with them* 1:20 [a] 1 Kin. 10:1 1:21 [a] Dan. 6:28; 10:1 2:1 [a] Gen. 40:5–8; 41:1, 8; Job 33:15–17; Dan. 2:3; 4:5 [b] Esth. 6:1; Dan. 6:18 2:2 [a] Gen. 41:8; Ex. 7:11; Is. 47:12, 13; Dan. 1:20; 2:10, 27; 4:6; 5:7 2:4 [a] 1 Kin. 1:31; Dan. 3:9; 5:10; 6:6, 21 [1] The original language of Daniel 2:4b through 7:28 is Aramaic. 2:5 [a] 2 Kin. 10:27; Ezra 6:11; Dan. 3:29 2:6 [a] Dan. 5:16 2:11 [a] Gen. 41:39; Dan. 5:11 2:13 [a] Dan. 1:19, 20 2:18 [a] [Dan. 9:9; Matt. 18:19] 2:19 [a] Num. 12:6; Job 33:15; [Prov. 3:32]; Amos 3:7

20Daniel answered and said:

[a]"Blessed be the name of God
forever and ever,
[b]For wisdom and might are His.
21 And He changes [a]the times
and the seasons;
[b]He removes kings and raises up kings;
[c]He gives wisdom to the wise
And knowledge to those who
have understanding.
22 [a]He reveals deep and secret things;
[b]He knows what *is* in the darkness,
And [c]light dwells with Him.

23 "I thank You and praise You,
O God of my fathers;
You have given me wisdom and might,
And have now made known to
me what we [a]asked of You,
For You have made known to
us the king's demand."

Daniel Explains the Dream

24Therefore Daniel went to Arioch,
whom the king had appointed to destroy
the wise *men* of Babylon. He went and said
thus to him: "Do not destroy the wise *men*
of Babylon; take me before the king, and I
will tell the king the interpretation."
25Then Arioch quickly brought Daniel
before the king, and said thus to him, "I
have found a man of the captives[1] of Judah, who will make known to the king the
interpretation."
26The king answered and said to Daniel,
whose name *was* Belteshazzar, "Are you
able to make known to me the dream which
I have seen, and its interpretation?"
27Daniel answered in the presence of the
king, and said, "The secret which the king
has demanded, the wise *men,* the astrologers, the magicians, and the soothsayers
cannot declare to the king. 28[a]But there is
a God in heaven who reveals secrets, and
He has made known to King Nebuchadnezzar [b]what will be in the latter days. Your
dream, and the visions of your head upon
your bed, were these: 29As for you, O king,
thoughts came *to* your *mind while* on your
bed, *about* what would come to pass after
this; [a]and He who reveals secrets has made
known to you what will be. 30[a]But as for me,
this secret has not been revealed to me because I have more wisdom than anyone
living, but for *our* sakes who make known
the interpretation to the king, [b]and that
you may know the thoughts of your heart.
31"You, O king, were watching; and behold, a great image! This great image,
whose splendor *was* excellent, stood before you; and its form *was* awesome. 32[a]This
image's head *was* of fine gold, its chest
and arms of silver, its belly and thighs[1] of
bronze, 33its legs of iron, its feet partly of
iron and partly of clay.[1] 34You watched while
a stone was cut out [a]without hands, which
struck the image on its feet of iron and
clay, and broke them in pieces. 35[a]Then the
iron, the clay, the bronze, the silver, and
the gold were crushed together, and became [b]like chaff from the summer threshing floors; the wind carried them away so
that [c]no trace of them was found. And the
stone that struck the image [d]became a great
mountain [e]and filled the whole earth.
36"This *is* the dream. Now we will tell the
interpretation of it before the king. 37[a]You,
O king, *are* a king of kings. [b]For the God of
heaven has given you a kingdom, power,
strength, and glory; 38[a]and wherever the
children of men dwell, or the beasts of the
field and the birds of the heaven, He has
given *them* into your hand, and has made
you ruler over them all—[b]you *are* this head
of gold. 39But after you shall arise [a]another
kingdom [b]inferior to yours; then another, a
third kingdom of bronze, which shall rule
over all the earth. 40And [a]the fourth kingdom shall be as strong as iron, inasmuch
as iron breaks in pieces and shatters everything; and like iron that crushes, *that
kingdom* will break in pieces and crush all
the others. 41Whereas you saw the feet and

2:20 [a] Ps. 113:2 [b] [1 Chr. 29:11, 12; Job 12:13; Ps. 147:5; Jer. 32:19; Matt. 6:13; Rom. 11:33] **2:21** [a] Ps. 31:15; Esth. 1:13; Dan. 2:9; 7:25 [b] Job 12:18; [Ps. 75:6, 7; Jer. 27:5; Dan. 4:35] [c] 1 Kin. 3:9, 10; 4:29; [James 1:5] **2:22** [a] Job 12:22; Ps. 25:14; [Prov. 3:22] [b] Job 26:6; Ps. 139:12; [Is. 45:7; Jer. 23:24; Heb. 4:13] [c] [Ps. 36:9]; Dan. 5:11, 14; [1 Tim. 6:16; James 1:17; 1 John 1:5] **2:23** [a] Ps. 21:2, 4; Dan. 2:18, 29, 30 **2:25** [1] Literally *of the sons of the captivity* **2:28** [a] Gen. 40:8; Amos 4:13 [b] Gen. 49:1; Is. 2:2; Dan. 10:14; Mic. 4:1 **2:29** [a] [Dan. 2:22, 28] **2:30** [a] Acts 3:12 [b] Dan. 2:47 **2:32** [a] Dan. 2:38, 45 [1] Or *sides* **2:33** [1] Or *baked clay,* and so in verses 34, 35, and 42 **2:34** [a] Dan. 8:25; [Zech. 4:6]; 2 Cor. 5:1; Heb. 9:24 **2:35** [a] Dan. 7:23–27; [Rev. 16:14] [b] Ps. 1:4; Is. 17:13; 41:15, 16; Hos. 13:3 [c] Ps. 37:10, 36 [d] [Is. 2:2, 3]; Mic. 4:1 [e] Ps. 80:9 **2:37** [a] Ezra 7:12; Is. 47:5; Jer. 27:6, 7; Ezek. 26:7; Hos. 8:10 [b] Ezra 1:2 **2:38** [a] Ps. 50:10, 11; Jer. 27:6; Dan. 4:21, 22 [b] Dan. 2:32 **2:39** [a] Dan. 5:28, 31 [b] Dan. 2:32 **2:40** [a] Dan. 7:7, 23

toes, partly of potter's clay and partly of
iron, the kingdom shall be divided; yet the
strength of the iron shall be in it, just as you
saw the iron mixed with ceramic clay. 42And
as the toes of the feet *were* partly of iron
and partly of clay, [a]*so* the kingdom shall be
partly strong and partly fragile. 43As you
saw iron mixed with ceramic clay, they will
mingle with the seed of men; but they will
not adhere to one another, just as iron does
not mix with clay. 44And in the days of these
kings [a]the God of heaven will set up a kingdom [b]which shall never be destroyed; and
the kingdom shall not be left to other people; [c]it shall break in pieces and consume all
these kingdoms, and it shall stand forever.
45[a]Inasmuch as you saw that the stone was
cut out of the mountain without hands, and
that it broke in pieces the iron, the bronze,
the clay, the silver, and the gold—the great
God has made known to the king what will
come to pass after this. The dream is certain, and its interpretation is sure."

Daniel and His Friends Promoted

46[a]Then King Nebuchadnezzar fell on
his face, prostrate before Daniel, and
commanded that they should present an
offering [b]and incense to him. 47The king answered Daniel, and said, "Truly [a]your God
is the God of [b]gods, the Lord of kings, and
a revealer of secrets, since you could reveal this secret." 48[a]Then the king promoted
Daniel [b]and gave him many great gifts; and
he made him ruler over the whole province
of Babylon, and [c]chief administrator over
all the wise *men* of Babylon. 49Also Daniel
petitioned the king, [a]and he set Shadrach,
Meshach, and Abed-Nego over the affairs
of the province of Babylon; but Daniel [b]*sat*
in the gate[1] of the king.

The Image of Gold

3 Nebuchadnezzar the king made an image of gold, whose height *was* sixty cubits *and* its width six cubits. He set it up
in the plain of Dura, in the province of
Babylon. 2And King Nebuchadnezzar sent
word to gather together the satraps, the
administrators, the governors, the counselors, the treasurers, the judges, the magistrates, and all the officials of the provinces,
to come to the dedication of the image
which King Nebuchadnezzar had set up.
3So the satraps, the administrators, the governors, the counselors, the treasurers, the
judges, the magistrates, and all the officials
of the provinces gathered together for the
dedication of the image that King Nebuchadnezzar had set up; and they stood before the image that Nebuchadnezzar had
set up. 4Then a herald cried aloud: "To you
it is commanded, [a]O peoples, nations, and
languages, 5*that* at the time you hear the
sound of the horn, flute, harp, lyre, *and*
psaltery, in symphony with all kinds of music, you shall fall down and worship the
gold image that King Nebuchadnezzar has
set up; 6and whoever does not fall down
and worship shall [a]be cast immediately into
the midst of a burning fiery furnace."

7So at that time, when all the people
heard the sound of the horn, flute, harp,
and lyre, in symphony with all kinds of music, all the people, nations, and languages
fell down *and* worshiped the gold image
which King Nebuchadnezzar had set up.

Daniel's Friends Disobey the King

8Therefore at that time certain Chaldeans [a]came forward and accused the Jews.
9They spoke and said to King Nebuchadnezzar, [a]"O king, live forever! 10You, O king, have
made a decree that everyone who hears
the sound of the horn, flute, harp, lyre, *and*
psaltery, in symphony with all kinds of music, shall fall down and worship the gold
image; 11and whoever does not fall down
and worship shall be cast into the midst of
a burning fiery furnace. 12[a]There are certain
Jews whom you have set over the affairs
of the province of Babylon: Shadrach, Meshach, and Abed-Nego; these men, O king,
have [b]not paid due regard to you. They do
not serve your gods or worship the gold
image which you have set up."

13Then Nebuchadnezzar, in [a]rage and
fury, gave the command to bring Shadrach,

2:42 [a] Dan. 7:24 2:44 [a] Dan. 2:28, 37 [b] Is. 9:6, 7; Ezek. 37:25; Dan. 4:3, 34; 6:26; 7:14, 27; Mic. 4:7; [Luke 1:32, 33] [c] Ps. 2:9; Is. 60:12; Dan. 2:34, 35; [1 Cor. 15:24] 2:45 [a] Dan. 2:35; Is. 28:16 2:46 [a] Dan. 3:5, 7; Acts 10:25; 14:13; Rev. 19:10; 22:8 [b] Lev. 26:31; Ezra 6:10 2:47 [a] Dan. 3:28, 29; 4:34–37 [b] [Deut. 10:17] 2:48 [a] [Prov. 14:35; 21:1] [b] Dan. 2:6 [c] Dan. 4:9; 5:11 2:49 [a] Dan. 1:7; 3:12 [b] Esth. 2:19, 21; 3:2; Amos 5:15 [1] That is, the king's court 3:4 [a] Dan. 4:1; 6:25 3:6 [a] Jer. 29:22; Ezek. 22:18–22; Matt. 13:42, 50; Rev. 9:2; 13:15; 14:11 3:8 [a] Ezra 4:12–16; Esth. 3:8, 9; Dan. 6:12, 13 3:9 [a] Dan. 2:4; 5:10; 6:6, 21 3:12 [a] Dan. 2:49 [b] Dan. 1:8; 6:12, 13 3:13 [a] Dan. 2:12; 3:19

Meshach, and Abed-Nego. So they brought
these men before the king. 14Nebuchadnez-
zar spoke, saying to them, "*Is it* true, Shadrach, Meshach, and Abed-Nego, *that* you
do not serve my gods or worship the gold
image which I have set up? 15Now if you are
ready at the time you hear the sound of the
horn, flute, harp, lyre, *and* psaltery, in symphony with all kinds of music, and you fall
down and worship the image which I have
made, [a]*good!* But if you do not worship, you
shall be cast immediately into the midst of
a burning fiery furnace. [b]And who *is* the
god who will deliver you from my hands?"
16Shadrach, Meshach, and Abed-Nego
answered and said to the king, "O Nebuchadnezzar, [a]we have no need to answer
you in this matter. 17If that *is the case,* our
[a]God whom we serve is able to [b]deliver us
from the burning fiery furnace, and He will
deliver *us* from your hand, O king. 18But if
not, let it be known to you, O king, that we
do not serve your gods, nor will we [a]wor-
ship the gold image which you have set up."

#OXYGEN

DANIEL 3:17

Elevate Your Way of Thinking

Our God is righteous, powerful, and majestic beyond our imagining. We must not make Him less in our minds; we must not assign human traits to Him. Allow Him to reveal His awe-inspiring nature to you.

Know your identity, **breathe**, and **elevate your way of thinking.**

Saved in Fiery Trial

19Then Nebuchadnezzar was full of fury,
and the expression on his face changed toward Shadrach, Meshach, and Abed-Nego.
He spoke and commanded that they heat
the furnace seven times more than it was
usually heated. 20And he commanded
certain mighty men of valor who *were* in
his army to bind Shadrach, Meshach, and
Abed-Nego, *and* cast *them* into the burning
fiery furnace. 21Then these men were bound
in their coats, their trousers, their turbans,
and their *other* garments, and were cast
into the midst of the burning fiery furnace.
22Therefore, because the king's command
was urgent, and the furnace exceedingly
hot, the flame of the fire killed those men
who took up Shadrach, Meshach, and Abed-
Nego. 23And these three men, Shadrach,
Meshach, and Abed-Nego, fell down bound
into the midst of the burning fiery furnace.
24Then King Nebuchadnezzar was astonished; and he rose in haste *and* spoke,
saying to his counselors, "Did we not cast
three men bound into the midst of the fire?"
They answered and said to the king,
"True, O king."
25"Look!" he answered, "I see four men
loose, [a]walking in the midst of the fire;
and they are not hurt, and the form of the
fourth is like [b]the Son of God."[1]

Nebuchadnezzar Praises God

26Then Nebuchadnezzar went near the
mouth of the burning fiery furnace *and*
spoke, saying, "Shadrach, Meshach, and
Abed-Nego, servants of the [a]Most High God,
come out, and come *here.*" Then Shadrach,
Meshach, and Abed-Nego came from the
midst of the fire. 27And the satraps, administrators, governors, and the king's counselors gathered together, and they saw
these men [a]on whose bodies the fire had
no power; the hair of their head was not
singed nor were their garments affected,
and the smell of fire was not on them.
28Nebuchadnezzar spoke, saying,
"Blessed be the God of Shadrach, Meshach, and Abed-Nego, who sent His [a]An-
gel[1] and delivered His servants who trusted
in Him, and they have frustrated the king's
word, and yielded their bodies, that they
should not serve nor worship any god except their own God! 29[a]Therefore I make a
decree that any people, nation, or language
which speaks anything amiss against the
[b]God of Shadrach, Meshach, and Abed-Nego

3:15 [a] Ex. 32:32; Luke 13:9 [b] Ex. 5:2; 2 Kin. 18:35; Is. 36:18–20; Dan. 2:47 3:16 [a] [Matt. 10:19] 3:17 [a] Job 5:19; [Ps. 27:1, 2; Is. 26:3, 4]; Jer. 1:8; 15:20, 21; Dan. 6:19–22 [b] 1 Sam. 17:37; Jer. 1:8; 15:20, 21; 42:11; Dan. 6:16, 19–22; Mic. 7:7; 2 Cor. 1:10 3:18 [a] Job 13:15 3:25 [a] [Ps. 91:3–9]; Is. 43:2 [b] Job 1:6; 38:7; [Ps. 34:7]; Dan. 3:28 [1] Or *a son of the gods* 3:26 [a] [Dan. 4:2, 3, 17, 34, 35] 3:27 [a] [Is. 43:2]; Heb. 11:34 3:28 [a] [Ps. 34:7, 8]; Is. 37:36; [Jer. 17:7]; Dan. 6:22, 23; Acts 5:19; 12:7 [1] Or *angel* 3:29 [a] Dan. 6:26 [b] Dan. 2:46, 47; 4:34–37

shall be [c]cut in pieces, and their houses
shall be made an ash heap; [d]because there
is no other God who can deliver like this."
30 Then the king promoted Shadrach,
Meshach, and Abed-Nego in the province
of Babylon.

Nebuchadnezzar's Second Dream

4 Nebuchadnezzar the king,

[a]To all peoples, nations, and languages
that dwell in all the earth:

Peace be multiplied to you.

2 I thought it good to declare the signs
and wonders [a]that the Most High God
has worked for me.

3 [a]How great *are* His signs,
And how mighty His wonders!
His kingdom *is* [b]an
everlasting kingdom,
And His dominion *is* from
generation to generation.

4 I, Nebuchadnezzar, was at rest in my
house, and flourishing in my palace.
5 I saw a dream which made me afraid,
[a]and the thoughts on my bed and
the visions of my head [b]troubled me.
6 Therefore I issued a decree to bring in
all the wise *men* of Babylon before me,
that they might make known to me the
interpretation of the dream. 7 [a]Then
the magicians, the astrologers, the
Chaldeans, and the soothsayers came
in, and I told them the dream; but
they did not make known to me its
interpretation. 8 But at last Daniel came
before me [a](his name *is* Belteshazzar,
according to the name of my god; [b]in
him *is* the Spirit of the Holy God), and
I told the dream before him, *saying:*
9 "Belteshazzar, [a]chief of the magicians,
because I know that the Spirit of the
Holy God *is* in you, and no secret
troubles you, explain to me the visions
of my dream that I have seen, and its
interpretation.

10 "These *were* the visions of my head
while on my bed:

I was looking, and behold,
[a]A tree in the midst of the earth,
And its height was great.
11 The tree grew and became strong;
Its height reached to the heavens,
And it could be seen to the
ends of all the earth.
12 Its leaves *were* lovely,
Its fruit abundant,
And in it *was* food for all.
[a]The beasts of the field found
shade under it,
The birds of the heavens
dwelt in its branches,
And all flesh was fed from it.

13 "I saw in the visions of my head *while*
on my bed, and there was [a]a watcher,
[b]a holy one, coming down from
heaven. 14 He cried aloud and said thus:

[a]'Chop down the tree and
cut off its branches,
Strip off its leaves and scatter its fruit.
[b]Let the beasts get out from under it,
And the birds from its branches.
15 Nevertheless leave the stump
and roots in the earth,
Bound with a band of iron and bronze,
In the tender grass of the field.
Let it be wet with the dew of heaven,
And *let* him graze with the beasts
On the grass of the earth.
16 Let his heart be changed
from *that of* a man,
Let him be given the heart of a beast,
And let seven [a]times[1] pass over him.

17 'This decision *is* by the decree
of the watchers,
And the sentence by the
word of the holy ones,

3:29 [c] Ezra 6:11; Dan. 2:5 [d] Dan. 6:27 4:1 [a] Ezra 4:17; Dan. 3:4; 6:25 4:2 [a] Dan. 3:26 4:3 [a] 2 Sam. 7:16; Ps. 89:35–37; Dan. 6:27; 7:13, 14; [Luke 1:31–33] [b] [Dan. 2:44; 4:34; 6:26] 4:5 [a] Dan. 2:28, 29 [b] Dan. 2:1 4:7 [a] Dan. 2:2 4:8 [a] Dan. 1:7 [b] Is. 63:11; Dan. 2:11; 4:18; 5:11, 14 4:9 [a] Dan. 2:48; 5:11 4:10 [a] Ezek. 31:3; Dan. 4:20 4:12 [a] Jer. 27:6; Ezek. 17:23; 31:6; Lam. 4:20 4:13 [a] [Dan. 4:17, 23] [b] Deut. 33:2; Ps. 89:7; Dan. 8:13; Zech. 14:5; Jude 14 4:14 [a] Ezek. 31:10–14; Dan. 4:23; [Matt. 3:10; 7:19; Luke 13:7–9] [b] Ezek. 31:12, 13; Dan. 4:12 4:16 [a] Dan. 11:13; 12:7

[1] Possibly *seven years,* and so in verses 23, 25, and 32

In order [a]that the living may know
[b]That the Most High rules in
the kingdom of men,
[c]Gives it to whomever He will,
And sets over it the [d]lowest of men.'

18 "This dream I, King Nebuchadnezzar,
have seen. Now you, Belteshazzar,
declare its interpretation, [a]since all
the wise *men* of my kingdom are
not able to make known to me the
interpretation; but you *are* able, [b]for
the Spirit of the Holy God *is* in you."

Daniel Explains the Second Dream

19 Then Daniel, [a]whose name *was*
Belteshazzar, was astonished for a
time, and his thoughts [b]troubled
him. *So* the king spoke, and said,
"Belteshazzar, do not let the dream or
its interpretation trouble you."
Belteshazzar answered and
said, "My lord, *may* [c]the dream
concern those who hate you, and its
interpretation concern your enemies!

20 [a]"The tree that you saw, which grew and
became strong, whose height reached
to the heavens and which *could be*
seen by all the earth, 21whose leaves
were lovely and its fruit abundant, in
which *was* food for all, under which the
beasts of the field dwelt, and in whose
branches the birds of the heaven had
their home— 22[a]it *is* you, O king, who
have grown and become strong; for
your greatness has grown and reaches
to the heavens, [b]and your dominion to
the end of the earth.
23 [a]"And inasmuch as the king saw a
watcher, a holy one, coming down from
heaven and saying, 'Chop down the tree
and destroy it, but leave its stump and
roots in the earth, *bound* with a band
of iron and bronze in the tender grass
of the field; let it be wet with the dew
of heaven, [b]and let him graze with the
beasts of the field, till seven times pass
over him'; 24this is the interpretation,
O king, and this is the decree of the
Most High, which has come upon my
lord the king: 25They shall [a]drive you
from men, your dwelling shall be with
the beasts of the field, and they shall
make you [b]eat grass like oxen. They
shall wet you with the dew of heaven,
and seven times shall pass over you,
[c]till you know that the Most High rules
in the kingdom of men, and [d]gives it to
whomever He chooses.
26 "And inasmuch as they gave the
command to leave the stump *and* roots
of the tree, your kingdom shall be
assured to you, after you come to know
that [a]Heaven rules. 27Therefore, O king,
let my advice be acceptable to you;
[a]break off your sins by *being* righteous,
and your iniquities by showing mercy
to *the* poor. [b]Perhaps there may be [c]a
lengthening of your prosperity."

Nebuchadnezzar's Humiliation

28 All *this* came upon King Nebuchadnezzar.
29At the end of the twelve months he
was walking about the royal palace of
Babylon. 30The king [a]spoke, saying, "Is
not this great Babylon, that I have built
for a royal dwelling by my mighty power
and for the honor of my majesty?"
31 [a]While the word *was still* in the king's
mouth, [b]a voice fell from heaven:
"King Nebuchadnezzar, to you it is
spoken: the kingdom has departed
from you! 32And [a]they shall drive you
from men, and your dwelling *shall be*
with the beasts of the field. They shall
make you eat grass like oxen; and
seven times shall pass over you, until
you know that the Most High rules in
the kingdom of men, and gives it to
whomever He chooses."
33 That very hour the word was fulfilled
concerning Nebuchadnezzar; he was
driven from men and ate grass like
oxen; his body was wet with the dew
of heaven till his hair had grown like

4:17 [a] Ps. 9:16; 83:18 [b] Dan. 2:21; 4:25, 32; 5:21 [c] Jer. 27:5–7; Ezek. 29:18–20; Dan. 2:37; 5:18 [d] 1 Sam. 2:8; Dan. 11:21 **4:18** [a] Gen. 41:8, 15; Dan. 5:8, 15 [b] Dan. 4:8, 9; 5:11, 14 **4:19** [a] Dan. 4:8 [b] Jer. 4:19; Dan. 7:15, 28; 8:27 [c] 2 Sam. 18:32; Jer. 29:7; Dan. 4:24; 10:16 **4:20** [a] Dan. 4:10–12 **4:22** [a] Dan. 2:37, 38 [b] Jer. 27:6–8 **4:23** [a] Dan. 4:13–15 [b] Dan. 5:21 **4:25** [a] Dan. 4:32; 5:21 [b] Ps. 106:20 [c] Ps. 83:18; Dan. 4:2, 17, 32 [d] Jer. 27:5 **4:26** [a] Matt. 21:25; Luke 15:18 **4:27** [a] [Prov. 28:13]; Is. 55:7; Ezek. 18:21, 22; [Rom. 2:9–11; 1 Pet. 4:8] [b] [Ps. 41:1–3]; Is. 58:6, 7, 10 [c] 1 Kin. 21:29 **4:30** [a] Prov. 16:18; Is. 13:19; Dan. 5:20 **4:31** [a] Dan. 5:5; Luke 12:20 [b] Dan. 4:24 **4:32** [a] [Dan. 4:25]

eagles' *feathers* and his nails like birds' *claws.*

Nebuchadnezzar Praises God

34 And [a]at the end of the time[1] I,
Nebuchadnezzar, lifted my eyes
to heaven, and my understanding
returned to me; and I blessed the Most
High and praised and honored Him
[b]who lives forever:

For His dominion *is* [c]an
everlasting dominion,
And His kingdom *is* from
generation to generation.
35 [a]All the inhabitants of the earth
are reputed as nothing;
[b]He does according to His will
in the army of heaven
And *among* the inhabitants
of the earth.
[c]No one can restrain His hand
Or say to Him, [d]"What have You done?"
36 At the same time my reason returned
to me, [a]and for the glory of my
kingdom, my honor and splendor
returned to me. My counselors and
nobles resorted to me, I was [b]restored
to my kingdom, and excellent
majesty was [c]added to me. 37 Now I,
Nebuchadnezzar, [a]praise and extol
and honor the King of heaven, [b]all of
whose works *are* truth, and His ways

DANIEL 4:37

I AM NEBUCHADNEZZAR

Now I, Nebuchadnezzar, praise and extol and honor the King of heaven, all of whose works are truth, and His ways justice. And those who walk in pride He is able to put down. Daniel 4:37

I am Nebuchadnezzar, king of Babylon. I believed that I was a great king. I had overcome Jerusalem and taken the Hebrew people captive. In honor of my greatness, I erected a golden statue of myself and ordered all the people to bow down and worship it whenever they heard music. Everyone did as they were ordered except Shadrach, Meshach, and Abed-Nego, whom I had given positions of honor. So, I had them cast into a blazing furnace that had been made seven times hotter than normal. But when I looked into the furnace, there were *four* men walking around in the fire. The fourth man was like the Son of God! When I ordered Shadrach, Meshach, and Abed-Nego to be set free, they were untouched by the fire and did not even smell of smoke.

In response to what I had seen, I gave great praise and respect to their God who delivered them. I even decreed that no one could speak against their God, and I promoted Shadrach, Meshach, and Abed-Nego. I respected their God, but I did not accept Him as my God. It was because I continued to sin and would not show mercy to the poor that their God condemned me. Through a dream, He decreed that I would lose my mind and become like a beast in the field, eating grass like a wild ox for seven years.

At the end of this time, I lifted my eyes toward heaven and praised God. My mind was then returned to me. I resumed leading my nation, and I became more powerful than ever. For the rest of my days, I praised and exalted the one true God and acknowledged that His ways alone were right and just.

Like Nebuchadnezzar, each one of us must learn to humble ourselves before God. If we do not and we think that we are in charge of our lives, God will always demonstrate His sovereignty. We might then find ourselves living far beneath God's best for us.

4:34 [a] Dan. 4:26 [b] Ps. 102:24–27; Dan. 6:26; 12:7; [Rev. 4:10] [c] [Ps. 10:16]; Dan. 2:44; 7:14; Mic. 4:7; [Luke 1:33] [1] Literally *days*
4:35 [a] Ps. 39:5; Is. 40:15, 17 [b] Ps. 115:3; 135:6; Dan. 6:27 [c] Job 34:29; Is. 43:13 [d] Job 9:12; Is. 45:9; Jer. 18:6; Rom. 9:20; [1 Cor. 2:16]
4:36 [a] Dan. 4:26 [b] 2 Chr. 20:20 [c] Job 42:12; [Prov. 22:4; Matt. 6:33] 4:37 [a] Dan. 2:46, 47; 3:28, 29
[b] Deut. 32:4; [Ps. 33:4]; Is. 5:16; [Rev. 15:3]

justice. [c]And those who walk in pride
He is able to put down.

Belshazzar's Feast

5 Belshazzar the king [a]made a great feast
for a thousand of his lords, and drank
wine in the presence of the thousand.
2 While he tasted the wine, Belshazzar gave
the command to bring the gold and silver
vessels [a]which his father Nebuchadnezzar had taken from the temple which *had*
been in Jerusalem, that the king and his
lords, his wives, and his concubines might
drink from them. 3 Then they brought the
gold [a]vessels that had been taken from the
temple of the house of God which *had been*
in Jerusalem; and the king and his lords,
his wives, and his concubines drank from
them. 4 They drank wine, [a]and praised the
gods of gold and silver, bronze and iron,
wood and stone.

5 [a]In the same hour the fingers of a
man's hand appeared and wrote opposite
the lampstand on the plaster of the wall of
the king's palace; and the king saw the part
of the hand that wrote. 6 Then the king's
countenance changed, and his thoughts
troubled him, so that the joints of his hips
were loosened and his [a]knees knocked
against each other. 7 [a]The king cried aloud
to bring in [b]the astrologers, the Chaldeans,
and the soothsayers. The king spoke, saying to the wise *men* of Babylon, "Whoever
reads this writing, and tells me its interpretation, shall be clothed with purple and
have a chain of gold around his neck; [c]and
he shall be the third ruler in the kingdom."
8 Now all the king's wise *men* came, [a]but
they could not read the writing, or make
known to the king its interpretation. 9 Then
King Belshazzar was greatly [a]troubled, his
countenance was changed, and his lords
were astonished.

10 The queen, because of the words of
the king and his lords, came to the banquet hall. The queen spoke, saying, "O king,
live forever! Do not let your thoughts trouble you, nor let your countenance change.
11 [a]There is a man in your kingdom in whom
is the Spirit of the Holy God. And in the days
of your father, light and understanding and
wisdom, like the wisdom of the gods, were
found in him; and King Nebuchadnezzar
your father—your father the king—made
him chief of the magicians, astrologers,
Chaldeans, *and* soothsayers. 12 Inasmuch
as an excellent spirit, knowledge, understanding, interpreting dreams, solving rid-
dles, and explaining enigmas[1] were found
in this Daniel, [a]whom the king named Belteshazzar, now let Daniel be called, and he
will give the interpretation."

The Writing on the Wall Explained

13 Then Daniel was brought in before
the king. The king spoke, and said to Daniel, "*Are* you that Daniel who is one of the
captives[1] from Judah, whom my father the
king brought from Judah? 14 I have heard
of you, that [a]the Spirit of God *is* in you, and
that light and understanding and excellent
wisdom are found in you. 15 Now [a]the wise
men, the astrologers, have been brought
in before me, that they should read this
writing and make known to me its interpretation, but they could not give the interpretation of the thing. 16 And I have heard
of you, that you can give interpretations
and explain enigmas. [a]Now if you can read
the writing and make known to me its interpretation, you shall be clothed with purple and *have* a chain of gold around your
neck, and shall be the third ruler in the
kingdom."

17 Then Daniel answered, and said before
the king, "Let your gifts be for yourself, and
give your rewards to another; yet I will read
the writing to the king, and make known to
him the interpretation. 18 O king, [a]the Most
High God gave Nebuchadnezzar your father
a kingdom and majesty, glory and honor.
19 And because of the majesty that He gave
him, [a]all peoples, nations, and languages
trembled and feared before him. Whomever he wished, he [b]executed; whomever he
wished, he kept alive; whomever he wished,
he set up; and whomever he wished, he put
down. 20 [a]But when his heart was lifted up,

4:37 [c] Ex. 18:11; Job 40:11, 12; Dan. 5:20 5:1 [a] Esth. 1:3; Is. 22:12–14 5:2 [a] 2 Kin. 24:13; 25:15; Ezra 1:7–11; Jer. 52:19; Dan. 1:2 5:3 [a] 2 Chr. 36:10 5:4 [a] Is. 42:8; Dan. 5:23; Rev. 9:20 5:5 [a] Dan. 4:31 5:6 [a] Ezek. 7:17; 21:7 5:7 [a] Dan. 4:6, 7; 5:11, 15 [b] Is. 47:13 [c] Dan. 6:2, 3 5:8 [a] Gen. 41:8; Dan. 2:27; 4:7; 5:15 5:9 [a] Job 18:11; Is. 21:2–4; Jer. 6:24; Dan. 2:1; 5:6 5:11 [a] Dan. 2:48; 4:8, 9, 18 5:12 [a] Dan. 1:7; 4:8 [1] Literally *untying knots,* and so in verse 16 5:13 [1] Literally *of the sons of the captivity* 5:14 [a] Dan. 4:8, 9, 18; 5:11, 12 5:15 [a] Dan. 5:7, 8 5:16 [a] Dan. 5:7, 29 5:18 [a] Jer. 27:5–7; Dan. 2:37, 38; 4:17, 22, 25 5:19 [a] Jer. 27:7 [b] Dan. 2:12, 13; 3:6 5:20 [a] Ex. 9:17; Job 15:25; Is. 14:13–15; Dan. 4:30, 37

and his spirit was hardened in pride, he
was deposed from his kingly throne, and
they took his glory from him. 21Then he
was [a]driven from the sons of men, his heart
was made like the beasts, and his dwelling
was with the wild donkeys. They fed him
with grass like oxen, and his body was wet
with the dew of heaven, [b]till he knew that
the Most High God rules in the kingdom
of men, and appoints over it whomever
He chooses.

22"But you his son, Belshazzar, [a]have not
humbled your heart, although you knew
all this. 23[a]And you have lifted yourself
up against the Lord of heaven. They have
brought the [b]vessels of His house before
you, and you and your lords, your wives and
your concubines, have drunk wine from
them. And you have praised the gods of
silver and gold, bronze and iron, wood and
stone, [c]which do not see or hear or know;
and the God who *holds* your breath in His
hand [d]and owns all your ways, you have not
glorified. 24Then the fingers[1] of the hand
were sent from Him, and this writing was
written.

25"And this is the inscription that was
written:

MENE,[1] MENE, TEKEL,[2] UPHARSIN.[3]

26This *is* the interpretation of *each* word.
MENE: God has numbered your kingdom,
and finished it; 27TEKEL: [a]You have been
weighed in the balances, and found wanting; 28PERES: Your kingdom has been
divided, and given to the [a]Medes and [b]Per-
sians."[1] 29Then Belshazzar gave the command, and they clothed Daniel with purple
and *put* a chain of gold around his neck,
and made a proclamation concerning him
[a]that he should be the third ruler in the
kingdom.

Belshazzar's Fall

30[a]That very night Belshazzar, king of
the Chaldeans, was slain. 31[a]And Darius the
Mede received the kingdom, *being* about
sixty-two years old.

The Plot Against Daniel

6 It pleased Darius to set over the kingdom one hundred and twenty satraps,
to be over the whole kingdom; 2and over
these, three governors, of whom Daniel *was*
one, that the satraps might give account
to them, so that the king would suffer no
loss. 3Then this Daniel distinguished himself above the governors and satraps, [a]be-
cause an excellent spirit *was* in him; and
the king gave thought to setting him over
the whole realm. 4[a]So the governors and
satraps sought to find *some* charge against
Daniel concerning the kingdom; but they
could find no charge or fault, because he
was faithful; nor was there any error or
fault found in him. 5Then these men said,
"We shall not find any charge against this
Daniel unless we find *it* against him concerning the law of his God."

6So these governors and satraps
thronged before the king, and said thus to
him: [a]"King Darius, live forever! 7All the
governors of the kingdom, the administrators and satraps, the counselors and advi-
sors, have [a]consulted together to establish
a royal statute and to make a firm decree,
that whoever petitions any god or man for
thirty days, except you, O king, shall be cast
into the den of lions. 8Now, O king, establish
the decree and sign the writing, so that it
cannot be changed, according to the [a]law
of the Medes and Persians, which does not
alter." 9Therefore King Darius signed the
written decree.

Daniel in the Lions' Den

10Now when Daniel knew that the writing
was signed, he went home. And in his upper
room, with his windows open [a]toward Jerusalem, he knelt down on his knees [b]three
times that day, and prayed and gave thanks
before his God, as was his custom since
early days.

5:21 [a] Job 30:3–7; Dan. 4:32, 33 [b] Ex. 9:14–16; Ps. 83:17, 18; Ezek. 17:24; [Dan. 4:17, 34, 35] 5:22 [a] Ex. 10:3; 2 Chr. 33:23; 36:12 5:23 [a] Dan. 5:3, 4 [b] Ex. 40:9; Num. 18:3; Is. 52:11; Heb. 9:21 [c] Ps. 115:5, 6; Is. 37:19; Hab. 2:18, 19; Acts 17:24–26; Rom. 1:21 [d] Ps. 139:3; Prov. 20:24; [Jer. 10:23] 5:24 [1] Literally *palm* 5:25 [1] Literally *a mina* (50 shekels) from the verb "to number" [2] Literally *a shekel* from the verb "to weigh" [3] Literally *and half-shekels* from the verb "to divide" 5:27 [a] Job 31:6; Ps. 62:9; Jer. 6:30 5:28 [a] Is. 21:2; Dan. 5:31; 9:1 [b] Dan. 6:28; Acts 2:9 [1] Aramaic *Paras,* consonant with *Peres* 5:29 [a] Dan. 5:7, 16 5:30 [a] Jer. 51:31, 39, 57 5:31 [a] Dan. 2:39; 9:1 6:3 [a] Dan. 5:12 6:4 [a] Eccl. 4:4 6:6 [a] Neh. 2:3; Dan. 2:4; 6:21 6:7 [a] Ps. 59:3; 62:4; 64:2–6 6:8 [a] Esth. 1:19; 8:8; Dan. 6:12, 15 6:10 [a] 1 Kin. 8:29, 30, 46–48; Ps. 5:7; Jon. 2:4 [b] Ps. 55:17; Acts 2:1, 2, 15; [Phil. 4:6]; 1 Thess. 5:17, 18

RELEASE // ELEVATE YOUR WAY OF THINKING

Discernment of His Divine Assignment

Daniel 5:29 // Then Belshazzar gave the command, and they clothed Daniel with purple and put a chain of gold around his neck, and made a proclamation concerning him that he should be the third ruler in the kingdom.

Summary Message // A popular phrase that speaks of a sure outcome is "the handwriting is on the wall." We get this saying from the Book of Daniel. When the prophet Daniel was in captivity in Babylon, he became known and trusted by the nation's kings. The second king Daniel served, Belshazzar, threw a party and used vessels that had been stolen from the temple in Jerusalem to serve his guests. In front of the king and all the guests, the fingers of a hand appeared and wrote on the wall the unintelligible words "MENE, MENE, TEKEL, UPHARSIN" (Dan. 5:25). The meaning of the words was a complete mystery, so the king called on astrologers, soothsayers, and others to interpret them. No one could, though. Finally, he called Daniel, who told him the writing revealed that Belshazzar's reign was about to end. The Persian army overtook Babylon that very night, and Belshazzar was killed.

Practical Application // Have you ever asked, "Why am I here?" or "Why did God let this happen to me?" Many of us have wrestled with knowing our purpose while contemplating quitting a job, packing up and moving across the country, or even trying to learn and understand our place in this world. Daniel was a young man when the Babylonians exiled the people of God. Though a captive, he was admired by the king and given responsibilities, but Daniel remained committed to God.

Daniel was an unlikely revolutionary. His actions did not inspire war or result in freedom from his captors. Instead, God used him to openly defy the power of his captors. This was no small feat and was otherwise impossible without mental fortitude coupled with divine revelation. This generation of Jews were captives not because of anything they had done but because of King Hezekiah's actions many years before (see Is. 39:5–8).

Because of Daniel's excellent spirit and pure heart, God used him mightily during the reigns of Nebuchadnezzar and his successor, Belshazzar. God upheld Daniel in his captivity, to the point that Daniel actually prospered under the reigns of four kings (see Dan. 6:28). Daniel's safety and prosperity throughout their reigns was not by chance but because He chose to serve God in a strange land amid strange circumstances. He did not bemoan his circumstances but elevated his thinking to a place of submission and obedience to God, no matter what his life held.

Let us do as Daniel did and elevate our way of thinking despite our strange circumstances. Let us change "Why am I here?" to "Lord, what shall I do for You in this place?" Let us ask "Lord, what am I to accomplish in these circumstances?" rather than "Why did this happen to me?"

Fervent Prayer // Father, we confess that we do not always seek to understand why You allow us to experience dire circumstances. Help us stand strong in the faith wherever You place us. When we are tempted to quit or turn our backs on Your will, strengthen our resolve. Help us remember that You are with us wherever we go and You will never leave us or forsake us. Renew our spirits and keep Your manifold promises on our hearts and minds so that we do not faint in times of trouble and trials. In Jesus' name we pray. Amen.

11Then these men assembled and found
Daniel praying and making supplication
before his God. 12[a]And they went before
the king, and spoke concerning the king's
decree: "Have you not signed a decree that
every man who petitions any god or man
within thirty days, except you, O king, shall
be cast into the den of lions?"

The king answered and said, "The thing
is true, [b]according to the law of the Medes
and Persians, which does not alter."

13So they answered and said before the

6:12 [a] Dan. 3:8–12; Acts 16:19–21 [b] Esth. 1:19; Dan. 6:8, 15

ELEVATE YOUR WAY OF THINKING

INHALE

I have got an idea for a business; however, I'm a bit intimidated to go out on my own. A bunch of pressure comes with that. I'm not sure if I can take a gamble on my family's well-being. What if I fail? I have prayed and fasted and done everything else I can think of. How can I be sure about what I'm supposed to do? If I'm supposed to step out in this new business, how can I grow my faith to take that big step?

EXHALE

Entrepreneurship has made this country what it is today, and small businesses are the backbone of communities and the very lifeline of our nation. You can make a real difference for your family and community by starting your own business. But, as you are feeling, doing that also comes with plenty of anxiety and apprehension. This is normal. You aren't alone.

Remember, though, that while we are to have faith, it isn't blind faith. As you weigh this decision, there are several things you can do to help you determine if you should pursue this venture. For example, is there anyone who has started and successfully operated a business you can meet with? A wise mentor can either be a source of encouragement and give you reasons to go forward or provide some warnings and red flags to consider. Either way, this mentor can give you peace in whichever path you take.

Critical thinking and focus on details are also keys to whether you can pull it off. It's important to put a business plan together and have someone vet it from top to bottom. Think through all the steps you will need to take to launch your business—do you have a plan in place to do each?

But, as you suggest, still the most crucial thing you will need to do is to keep your faith strong. Faith will always be an element as you step out in any endeavor, no matter how well you have planned and how much wisdom you have received from others. Know that if you go forward with this business, that same faith will not only help launch it but make it successful. Daniel 6:3 says, "Then this Daniel distinguished himself above the governors and satraps, because an excellent spirit was in him; and the king gave thought to setting him over the whole realm." Faith set Daniel apart and made him successful. It will for you too. Take appropriate steps and just go!

king, "That Daniel, [a]who is one of the captives[1] from Judah, [b]does not show due regard for you, O king, or for the decree that
you have signed, but makes his petition
three times a day."
14And the king, when he heard *these*
words, [a]was greatly displeased with himself, and set *his* heart on Daniel to deliver
him; and he labored till the going down of
the sun to deliver him. 15Then these men
approached the king, and said to the king,
"Know, O king, that *it is* [a]the law of the Medes
and Persians that no decree or statute which
the king establishes may be changed."

16So the king gave the command, and they
brought Daniel and cast *him* into the den of
lions. *But* the king spoke, saying to Daniel,
"Your God, whom you serve continually, He
will deliver you." 17[a]Then a stone was brought
and laid on the mouth of the den, [b]and the
king sealed it with his own signet ring and
with the signets of his lords, that the purpose
concerning Daniel might not be changed.

Daniel Saved from the Lions

18Now the king went to his palace and
spent the night fasting; and no musicians[1]
were brought before him. [a]Also his sleep

6:13 [a] Dan. 1:6; 5:13 [b] Esth. 3:8; Dan. 3:12; Acts 5:29 [1] Literally *of the sons of the captivity* 6:14 [a] Mark 6:26 6:15 [a] Esth. 8:8; Ps. 94:20, 21; Dan. 6:8, 12 6:17 [a] Lam. 3:53 [b] Matt. 27:66 6:18 [a] Esth. 6:1; Ps. 77:4; Dan. 2:1 [1] Exact meaning unknown

went from him. 19 Then the [a]king arose very
early in the morning and went in haste to
the den of lions. 20 And when he came to
the den, he cried out with a lamenting voice
to Daniel. The king spoke, saying to Daniel, "Daniel, servant of the living God, [a]has
your God, whom you serve continually,
been able to deliver you from the lions?"
21 Then Daniel said to the king, [a]"O king,
live forever! 22 [a]My God sent His angel and
[b]shut the lions' mouths, so that they have
not hurt me, because I was found innocent
before Him; and also, O king, I have done
no wrong before you."
23 Now the king was exceedingly glad for
him, and commanded that they should take
Daniel up out of the den. So Daniel was
taken up out of the den, and no injury whatever was found on him, [a]because he believed in his God.

Darius Honors God

24 And the king gave the command, [a]and
they brought those men who had accused
Daniel, and they cast *them* into the den
of lions—them, [b]their children, and their
wives; and the lions overpowered them,
and broke all their bones in pieces before
they ever came to the bottom of the den.
25 [a]Then King Darius wrote:

To all peoples, nations, and languages
that dwell in all the earth:

Peace be multiplied to you.

26 [a]I make a decree that in every
dominion of my kingdom *men must*
[b]tremble and fear before the God of
Daniel.

[c]For He *is* the living God,
And steadfast forever;
His kingdom *is the one* which
shall not be [d]destroyed,
And His dominion *shall*
endure to the end.
27 He delivers and rescues,
[a]And He works signs and
wonders
In heaven and on earth,
Who has delivered Daniel from
the power of the lions.

28 So this Daniel prospered in the reign
of Darius [a]and in the reign of [b]Cyrus the
Persian.

Vision of the Four Beasts

7 In the first year of Belshazzar king of
Babylon, [a]Daniel had a dream and [b]vi-
sions of his head *while* on his bed. Then he
wrote down the dream, telling the main
facts.[1]
2 Daniel spoke, saying, "I saw in my vision by night, and behold, the four winds
of heaven were stirring up the Great Sea.
3 And four great beasts [a]came up from the
sea, each different from the other. 4 The first
was [a]like a lion, and had eagle's wings. I
watched till its wings were plucked off; and
it was lifted up from the earth and made to
stand on two feet like a man, and a [b]man's
heart was given to it.
5 [a]"And suddenly another beast, a second, like a bear. It was raised up on one
side, and *had* three ribs in its mouth between its teeth. And they said thus to it:
'Arise, devour much flesh!'
6 "After this I looked, and there was another, like a leopard, which had on its back
four wings of a bird. The beast also had
[a]four heads, and dominion was given to it.
7 "After this I saw in the night visions, and
behold, [a]a fourth beast, dreadful and terrible, exceedingly strong. It had huge iron
teeth; it was devouring, breaking in pieces,
and trampling the residue with its feet. It
was different from all the beasts that *were*
before it, [b]and it had ten horns. 8 I was considering the horns, and [a]there was another
horn, a little one, coming up among them,
before whom three of the first horns were
plucked out by the roots. And there, in this
horn, *were* eyes like the eyes [b]of a man, [c]and
a mouth speaking pompous words.

6:19 [a] Dan. 3:24 6:20 [a] Gen. 18:14; Num. 11:23; Jer. 32:17; Dan. 3:17; [Luke 1:37] 6:21 [a] Dan. 2:4; 6:6 6:22 [a] Num. 20:16; Is. 63:9; Dan. 3:28; Acts 12:11; [Heb. 1:14] [b] Ps. 91:11–13; 2 Tim. 4:17; Heb. 11:33 6:23 [a] Heb. 11:33 6:24 [a] Deut. 19:18, 19; Esth. 7:10 [b] Deut. 24:16; 2 Kin. 14:6; Esth. 9:10 6:25 [a] Ezra 1:1, 2; Esth. 3:12; 8:9; Dan. 4:1 6:26 [a] Ezra 6:8–12; 7:13; Dan. 3:29 [b] Ps. 99:1 [c] Dan. 4:34; 6:20; Hos. 1:10; Rom. 9:26 [d] Dan. 2:44; 4:3; 7:14, 27; [Luke 1:33] 6:27 [a] Dan. 4:2, 3 6:28 [a] Dan. 1:21 [b] Ezra 1:1, 2 7:1 [a] Num. 12:6; [Amos 3:7] [b] [Dan. 2:28] [1] Literally *the head* (or *chief*) *of the words* 7:3 [a] Dan. 7:17; Rev. 13:1; 17:8 7:4 [a] Deut. 28:49; 2 Sam. 1:23; Jer. 48:40; Ezek. 17:3; Hab. 1:8 [b] Dan. 4:16, 34 7:5 [a] Dan. 2:39 7:6 [a] Dan. 8:8, 22 7:7 [a] Dan. 2:40 [b] Dan. 2:41; Rev. 12:3; 13:1 7:8 [a] Dan. 8:9 [b] Rev. 9:7 [c] Ps. 12:3; Rev. 13:5, 6

Vision of the Ancient of Days

9 "I[a] watched till thrones
were put in place,
And [b]the Ancient of Days was seated;
[c]His garment *was* white as snow,
And the hair of His head
was like pure wool.
His throne *was* a fiery flame,
[d]Its wheels a burning fire;
10 [a]A fiery stream issued
And came forth from before Him.
[b]A thousand thousands
ministered to Him;
Ten thousand times ten thousand
stood before Him.
[c]The court[1] was seated,
And the books were opened.

11 "I watched then because of the sound
of the pompous words which the horn
was speaking; [a]I watched till the beast was
slain, and its body destroyed and given to
the burning flame.
12 As for the rest of the
beasts, they had their dominion taken away,
yet their lives were prolonged for a season
and a time.

13 "I was watching in the night visions,
And behold, [a]*One* like the Son of Man,
Coming with the clouds of heaven!
He came to the Ancient of Days,
And they brought Him
near before Him.
14 [a]Then to Him was given dominion
and glory and a kingdom,
That all [b]peoples, nations, and
languages should serve Him.
His dominion *is* [c]an
everlasting dominion,
Which shall not pass away,
And His kingdom *the one*
Which shall not be destroyed.

Daniel's Visions Interpreted

15 "I, Daniel, was grieved in my spirit
within *my* body, and the visions of my head
troubled me.
16 I came near to one of those
who stood by, and asked him the truth of
all this. So he told me and made known
to me the interpretation of these things:
17 'Those great beasts, which are four, *are*
four kings[1] *which* arise out of the earth.
18 But [a]the saints of the Most High shall receive the kingdom, and possess the kingdom forever, even forever and ever.'

19 "Then I wished to know the truth about
the fourth beast, which was different from
all the others, exceedingly dreadful, *with* its
teeth of iron and its nails of bronze, *which*
devoured, broke in pieces, and trampled
the residue with its feet;
20 and the ten
horns that *were* on its head, and the other
horn which came up, before which three
fell, namely, that horn which had eyes and a
mouth which spoke pompous words, whose
appearance *was* greater than his fellows.

21 "I was watching; [a]and the same horn
was making war against the saints, and pre-
vailing against them,
22 until the Ancient of
Days came, [a]and a judgment was made *in
favor* of the saints of the Most High, and
the time came for the saints to possess the
kingdom.

23 "Thus he said:

'The fourth beast shall be
[a]A fourth kingdom on earth,
Which shall be different from
all *other* kingdoms,
And shall devour the whole earth,
Trample it and break it in pieces.
24 [a]The ten horns *are* ten kings
Who shall arise from this kingdom.
And another shall rise after them;
He shall be different from
the first *ones,*
And shall subdue three kings.
25 [a]He shall speak *pompous* words
against the Most High,
Shall [b]persecute[1] the saints
of the Most High,
And shall [c]intend to change
times and law.
Then [d]*the saints* shall be
given into his hand
[e]For a time and times and half a time.

7:9 [a] [Rev. 20:4] [b] Ps. 90:2 [c] Ps. 104:2; Rev. 1:14 [d] Ezek. 1:15 7:10 [a] Ps. 50:3; Is. 30:33; 66:15 [b] Deut. 33:2; 1 Kin. 22:19; Ps. 68:17; Rev. 5:11 [c] Dan. 12:1; [Rev. 20:11–15] [1] Or *judgment* 7:11 [a] [Rev. 19:20; 20:10] 7:13 [a] Ezek. 1:26; [Matt. 24:30; 26:64; Mark 13:26; 14:62; Luke 21:27; Rev. 1:7, 13; 14:14] 7:14 [a] Ps. 2:6–8; Dan. 7:27; [Matt. 28:18; John 3:35, 36; 1 Cor. 15:27; Eph. 1:22; Phil. 2:9–11; Rev. 1:6; 11:15] [b] Dan. 3:4 [c] Ps. 145:13; Mic. 4:7; [Luke 1:33]; John 12:34; Heb. 12:28 7:17 [1] Representing their kingdoms (compare verse 23) 7:18 [a] Ps. 149:5–9; Is. 60:12–14; Dan. 7:14; [2 Tim. 2:11; Rev. 2:26, 27; 20:4; 22:5] 7:21 [a] Rev. 11:7; 13:7; 17:14 7:22 [a] [Rev. 1:6] 7:23 [a] Dan. 2:40 7:24 [a] Dan. 7:7; Rev. 13:1; 17:12 7:25 [a] Is. 37:23; Dan. 11:36; Rev. 13:1–6 [b] Rev. 17:6 [c] Dan. 2:21 [d] Rev. 13:7; 18:24 [e] Dan. 12:7; Rev. 12:14 [1] Literally *wear out*

26 'But[a] the court shall be seated,
And they shall [b]take away
his dominion,
To consume and destroy *it* forever.
27 Then the [a]kingdom and dominion,
And the greatness of the kingdoms
under the whole heaven,
Shall be given to the people, the
saints of the Most High.
[b]His kingdom *is* an
everlasting kingdom,
[c]And all dominions shall
serve and obey Him.'

28 "This *is* the end of the account.[1] As for
me, Daniel, [a]my thoughts greatly troubled
me, and my countenance changed; but I
[b]kept the matter in my heart."

Vision of a Ram and a Goat

8 In the third year of the reign of King
Belshazzar a vision appeared *to* me—to
me, Daniel—after the one that appeared
to me [a]the first time. 2 I saw in the vision,
and it so happened while I was looking,
that I *was* in [a]Shushan, the citadel, which
is in the province of Elam; and I saw in the
vision that I was by the River Ulai. 3 Then
I lifted my eyes and saw, and there, standing beside the river, was a ram which had
two horns, and the two horns *were* high;
but one *was* [a]higher than the other, and
the higher *one* came up last. 4 I saw the ram
pushing westward, northward, and southward, so that no animal could withstand
him; nor *was there any* that could deliver
from his hand, [a]but he did according to his
will and became great.

5 And as I was considering, suddenly a
male goat came from the west, across the
surface of the whole earth, without touching the ground; and the goat *had* a notable
[a]horn between his eyes. 6 Then he came to
the ram that had two horns, which I had
seen standing beside the river, and ran at
him with furious power. 7 And I saw him
confronting the ram; he was moved with
rage against him, attacked the ram, and
broke his two horns. There was no power
in the ram to withstand him, but he cast
him down to the ground and trampled him;
and there was no one that could deliver the
ram from his hand.

8 Therefore the male goat grew very
great; but when he became strong, the large
horn was broken, and in place of it [a]four notable ones came up toward the four winds
of heaven. 9 [a]And out of one of them came
a little horn which grew exceedingly great
toward the south, [b]toward the east, and toward the [c]Glorious *Land.* 10 [a]And it grew up
to [b]the host of heaven; and [c]it cast down
some of the host and *some* of the stars to
the ground, and trampled them. 11 [a]He even
exalted *himself* as high as [b]the Prince of the
host; [c]and by him [d]the daily *sacrifices* were
taken away, and the place of His sanctuary was cast down. 12 Because of transgression, [a]an army was given over *to the horn*
to oppose the daily *sacrifices;* and he cast
[b]truth down to the ground. He [c]did *all this*
and prospered.

13 Then I heard [a]a holy one speaking; and
another holy one said to that certain *one*
who was speaking, "How long *will* the vision *be, concerning* the daily *sacrifices* and
the transgression of desolation, the giving
of both the sanctuary and the host to be
trampled underfoot?"

14 And he said to me, "For two thousand
three hundred days;[1] then the sanctuary
shall be cleansed."

Gabriel Interprets the Vision

15 Then it happened, when I, Daniel,
had seen the vision and [a]was seeking the
meaning, that suddenly there stood before me [b]one having the appearance of a
man. 16 And I heard a man's voice [a]between
the banks of the Ulai, who called, and said,
[b]"Gabriel, make this *man* understand the
vision." 17 So he came near where I stood,
and when he came I was afraid and [a]fell on
my face; but he said to me, "Understand,
son of man, that the vision *refers* to the
time of the end."

7:26 [a] [Dan. 2:35; 7:10, 22] [b] Rev. 19:20 **7:27** [a] Is. 54:3; Dan. 7:14, 18, 22; Rev. 20:4 [b] 2 Sam. 7:16; Ps. 89:35–37; Is. 9:7; Dan. 2:44; 4:34; 7:14; [Luke 1:33, 34]; John 12:34; [Rev. 11:15; 22:5] [c] Ps. 2:6–12; 22:27; 72:11; 86:9; Is. 60:12; Rev. 11:1 **7:28** [a] Dan. 8:27 [b] Luke 2:19, 51 [1] Literally *the word* **8:1** [a] Dan. 7:1 **8:2** [a] Neh. 1:1; Esth. 1:2; 2:8 **8:3** [a] Dan. 7:5 **8:4** [a] Dan. 5:19 **8:5** [a] Dan. 8:8, 21; 11:3 **8:8** [a] Dan. 7:6; 8:22; 11:4 **8:9** [a] Dan. 11:21 [b] Dan. 11:25 [c] Ps. 48:2 **8:10** [a] Dan. 11:28 [b] Is. 14:13; Jer. 48:26 [c] Rev. 12:4 **8:11** [a] 2 Kin. 19:22, 23; 2 Chr. 32:15–17; Is. 37:23; Dan. 8:25; 11:36, 37 [b] Josh. 5:14 [c] Ezek. 46:14; Dan. 11:31; 12:11 [d] Ex. 29:38 **8:12** [a] Dan. 11:31 [b] Ps. 119:43; Is. 59:14 [c] Dan. 8:4; 11:36 **8:13** [a] Dan. 4:13, 23; 1 Pet. 1:12 **8:14** [1] Literally *evening-mornings* **8:15** [a] 1 Pet. 1:10 [b] Ezek. 1:26 **8:16** [a] Dan. 12:6, 7 [b] Dan. 9:21; Luke 1:19, 26 **8:17** [a] Ezek. 1:28; 44:4; Dan. 2:46; Rev. 1:17

18[a]Now, as he was speaking with me, I was
in a deep sleep with my face to the ground;
[b]but he touched me, and stood me upright.
19And he said, "Look, I am making known to
you what shall happen in the latter time of
the indignation; [a]for at the appointed time
the end *shall be.* 20The ram which you saw,
having the two horns—*they are* the kings
of Media and Persia. 21And the male goat *is*
the kingdom[1] of Greece. The large horn that
is between its eyes [a]*is* the first king. 22[a]As
for the broken *horn* and the four that stood
up in its place, four kingdoms shall arise
out of that nation, but not with its power.

23 "And in the latter time of
their kingdom,
When the transgressors have
reached their fullness,
A king shall arise,
[a]Having fierce features,
Who understands sinister schemes.
24 His power shall be mighty, [a]but
not by his own power;
He shall destroy fearfully,
[b]And shall prosper and thrive;
[c]He shall destroy the mighty,
and *also* the holy people.

25 "Through[a] his cunning
He shall cause deceit to
prosper under his rule;[1]
[b]And he shall exalt *himself* in his heart.
He shall destroy many in
their prosperity.
[c]He shall even rise against
the Prince of princes;
But he shall be [d]broken
without *human* means.[2]

26 "And the vision of the evenings
and mornings
Which was told is true;
[a]Therefore seal up the vision,
For *it refers* to many days *in the future.*"

27[a]And I, Daniel, fainted and was sick for
days; afterward I arose and went about the
king's business. I was astonished by the vision, but no one understood it.

Daniel's Prayer for the People

9 In the first year [a]of Darius the son of
Ahasuerus, of the lineage of the Medes,
who was made king over the realm of the
Chaldeans— 2in the first year of his reign I,
Daniel, understood by the books the num-
ber of the years *specified* by the word of the
LORD through [a]Jeremiah the prophet, that
He would accomplish seventy years in the
desolations of Jerusalem.

3[a]Then I set my face toward the Lord
God to make request by prayer and supplications, with fasting, sackcloth, and ashes.
4And I prayed to the LORD my God, and
made confession, and said, "O [a]Lord, great
and awesome God, who keeps His covenant
and mercy with those who love Him, and
with those who keep His commandments,
5[a]we have sinned and committed iniquity,
we have done wickedly and rebelled, even
by departing from Your precepts and Your
judgments. 6[a]Neither have we heeded Your
servants the prophets, who spoke in Your
name to our kings and our princes, to
our fathers and all the people of the land.
7O Lord, [a]righteousness *belongs* to You, but
to us shame of face, as *it is* this day—to the
men of Judah, to the inhabitants of Jerusalem and all Israel, those near and those far
off in all the countries to which You have
driven them, because of the unfaithfulness
which they have committed against You.

8"O Lord, to us *belongs* shame of face,
to our kings, our princes, and our fathers,
because we have sinned against You. 9[a]To
the Lord our God *belong* mercy and forgiveness, though we have rebelled against
Him. 10We have not obeyed the voice of the
LORD our God, to walk in His laws, which
He set before us by His servants the prophets. 11Yes, [a]all Israel has transgressed Your
law, and has departed so as not to obey
Your voice; therefore the curse and the
oath written in the [b]Law of Moses the servant of God have been poured out on us,

---

8:18 [a] Dan. 10:9; Luke 9:32 [b] Ezek. 2:2; Dan. 10:10, 16, 18 **8:19** [a] Hab. 2:3 **8:21** [a] Dan. 11:3 [1] Literally *king,* representing his kingdom (compare 7:17, 23) **8:22** [a] Dan. 11:4 **8:23** [a] Deut. 28:50 **8:24** [a] Rev. 17:13 [b] Dan. 11:36 [c] Dan. 7:25 **8:25** [a] Dan. 11:21 [b] Dan. 8:11–13; 11:36; 12:7 [c] Dan. 11:36; Rev. 19:19, 20 [d] Job 34:20; Lam. 4:6 [1] Literally *hand* [2] Literally *hand* **8:26** [a] Ezek. 12:27; Dan. 12:4, 9; Rev. 22:10 **8:27** [a] Dan. 7:28; 8:17; Hab. 3:16 **9:1** [a] Dan. 1:21 **9:2** [a] 2 Chr. 36:21; Ezra 1:1; Jer. 25:11, 12; 29:10; Zech. 7:5 **9:3** [a] Neh. 1:4; Dan. 6:10; 10:15 **9:4** [a] Ex. 20:6 **9:5** [a] 1 Kin. 8:47, 48; Neh. 9:33; Ps. 106:6; Is. 64:5–7; Jer. 14:7 **9:6** [a] 2 Chr. 36:15; Jer. 44:4, 5 **9:7** [a] Neh. 9:33 **9:9** [a] [Neh. 9:17; Ps. 130:4, 7] **9:11** [a] Is. 1:3–6; Jer. 8:5–10 [b] Lev. 26:14; Neh. 1:6; Ps. 106:6

because we have sinned against Him. 12And
He has [a]confirmed His words, which He
spoke against us and against our judges
who judged us, by bringing upon us a great
disaster; [b]for under the whole heaven such
has never been done as what has been done
to Jerusalem.
13[a]"As *it is* written in the Law of Moses,
all this disaster has come upon us; [b]yet
we have not made our prayer before the
LORD our God, that we might turn from
our iniquities and understand Your truth.
14Therefore the LORD has [a]kept the disaster in mind, and brought it upon us; for
[b]the LORD our God *is* righteous in all the
works which He does, though we have not
obeyed His voice. 15And now, O Lord our
God, [a]who brought Your people out of the
land of Egypt with a mighty hand, and
made Yourself [b]a name, as *it is* this day—we
have sinned, we have done wickedly!
16"O Lord, [a]according to all Your righteousness, I pray, let Your anger and Your
fury be turned away from Your city Jerusalem, [b]Your holy mountain; because for our
sins, [c]and for the iniquities of our fathers,
[d]Jerusalem and Your people [e]*are* a reproach
to all *those* around us. 17Now therefore, our
God, hear the prayer of Your servant, and
his supplications, [a]and [b]for the Lord's sake
cause Your face to shine on Your sanctuary, [c]which is desolate. 18[a]O my God, incline
Your ear and hear; open Your eyes [b]and
see our desolations, and the city [c]which is
called by Your name; for we do not present
our supplications before You because of
our righteous deeds, but because of Your
great mercies. 19O Lord, hear! O Lord, forgive! O Lord, listen and act! Do not delay
for Your own sake, my God, for Your city
and Your people are called by Your name."

The Seventy-Weeks Prophecy

20Now while I *was* speaking, praying, and
confessing my sin and the sin of my people Israel, and presenting my supplication
before the LORD my God for the holy mountain of my God, 21yes, while I *was* speaking
in prayer, the man [a]Gabriel, whom I had
seen in the vision at the beginning, being
caused to fly swiftly, reached me about the
time of the evening offering. 22And he informed *me,* and talked with me, and said,
"O Daniel, I have now come forth to give
you skill to understand. 23At the beginning
of your supplications the command went
out, and I have come to tell *you,* for you *are*
greatly [a]beloved; therefore [b]consider the
matter, and understand the vision:

24"Seventy weeks[1] are determined
For your people and for your holy city,
To finish the transgression,
To make an end of[2] sins,
[a]To make reconciliation for iniquity,
[b]To bring in everlasting righteousness,
To seal up vision and prophecy,
[c]And to anoint the Most Holy.

25"Know therefore and understand,
That from the going forth
of the command
To restore and build Jerusalem
Until [a]Messiah [b]the Prince,
There shall be seven weeks
and sixty-two weeks;
The street[1] shall be built
again, and the wall,[2]
Even in troublesome times.

26"And after the sixty-two weeks
[a]Messiah shall be cut off,
[b]but not for Himself;
And [c]the people of the prince
who is to come
[d]Shall destroy the city and
the sanctuary.
The end of it *shall be* with a flood,
And till the end of the war
desolations are determined.
27 Then he shall confirm [a]a covenant
with [b]many for one week;

9:12 [a] Is. 44:26; Jer. 44:2–6; Lam. 2:17; Zech. 1:6 [b] Lam. 1:12; 2:13; Ezek. 5:9; [Amos 3:2] **9:13** [a] Lev. 26:14–45; Deut. 28:15–68; Lam. 2:17 [b] Job 36:13; Is. 9:13; Jer. 2:30; Hos. 7:7 **9:14** [a] Jer. 31:28; 44:27 [b] Neh. 9:33 **9:15** [a] Ex. 32:11; 1 Kin. 8:51; Neh. 1:10 [b] Ex. 14:18; Neh. 9:10; Jer. 32:20 **9:16** [a] 1 Sam. 12:7; Ps. 31:1; Mic. 6:4, 5 [b] Ps. 87:1–3; Dan. 9:20; Joel 3:17; Zech. 8:3 [c] Ex. 20:5 [d] Ps. 122:6; Jer. 29:7; Lam. 2:16 [e] Ps. 79:4 **9:17** [a] Num. 6:24–26; Ps. 80:3, 7, 19 [b] Lam. 5:18 [c] [John 16:24] **9:18** [a] Is. 37:17 [b] Ex. 3:7 [c] Jer. 25:29 **9:21** [a] Dan. 8:16; Luke 1:19, 26 **9:23** [a] Dan. 10:11, 19 [b] Matt. 24:15 **9:24** [a] 2 Chr. 29:24; [Is. 53:10]; Acts 10:43; [Rom. 5:10]; Heb. 9:12, 14 [b] Rev. 14:6 [c] Ps. 45:7 [1] Literally *sevens,* and so throughout the chapter [2] Following Qere, Septuagint, Syriac, and Vulgate; Kethib and Theodotion read *To seal up.* **9:25** [a] Luke 2:1, 2; John 1:41; 4:25 [b] Is. 55:4 [1] Or *open square* [2] Or *moat* **9:26** [a] [Is. 53:8]; Matt. 27:50; Mark 9:12; 15:37; [Luke 23:46; 24:26]; John 19:30; Acts 8:32 [b] [1 Pet. 2:21] [c] Matt. 22:7 [d] Matt. 24:2; Mark 13:2; Luke 19:43, 44 **9:27** [a] Is. 42:6 [b] [Matt. 26:28]

But in the middle of the week
He shall bring an end to
sacrifice and offering.
And on the wing of abominations
shall be one who makes desolate,
[c]Even until the consummation,
which is determined,
Is poured out on the desolate."

Vision of the Glorious Man

10 In the third year of Cyrus king of Persia a message was revealed to Daniel, whose [a]name was called Belteshazzar.
The message *was* true, but the appointed
time *was* long;[1] and he understood the
message, and had understanding of the
vision. 2In those days I, Daniel, was mourning three full weeks. 3I ate no pleasant food,
no meat or wine came into my mouth, nor
did I anoint myself at all, till three whole
weeks were fulfilled.
4Now on the twenty-fourth day of the
first month, as I was by the side of the great
river, that *is,* the Tigris,[1] 5I lifted my eyes and
looked, and behold, a certain man clothed
in [a]linen, whose waist *was* [b]girded with gold
of Uphaz! 6His body *was* like beryl, his face
like the appearance of lightning, his eyes
like torches of fire, his arms and feet like
burnished bronze in color, [a]and the sound
of his words like the voice of a multitude.
7And I, Daniel, alone saw the vision, for
the men who were with me did not see the
vision; but a great terror fell upon them, so
that they fled to hide themselves. 8There-
fore I was left alone when I saw this great
vision, and no strength remained in me;
for my vigor was turned to frailty in me,
and I retained no strength. 9Yet I heard the
sound of his words; and while I heard the
sound of his words I was in a deep sleep on
my face, with my face to the ground.

Prophecies Concerning Persia and Greece

10[a]Suddenly, a hand touched me, which
made me tremble on my knees and *on*
the palms of my hands. 11And he said to
me, "O Daniel, [a]man greatly beloved,
understand the words that I speak to you,
and stand upright, for I have now been sent
to you." While he was speaking this word
to me, I stood trembling.
12Then he said to me, [a]"Do not fear, Daniel, for from the first day that you set your
heart to understand, and to humble yourself
before your God, [b]your words were heard;
and I have come because of your words.
13[a]But the prince of the kingdom of Persia
withstood me twenty-one days; and behold,
[b]Michael, one of the chief princes, came to
help me, for I had been left alone there with
the kings of Persia. 14Now I have come to
make you understand what will happen to
your people [a]in the latter days, [b]for the vision *refers* to *many* days yet *to come.*"
15When he had spoken such words to
me, [a]I turned my face toward the ground
and became speechless. 16And suddenly,
[a]*one* having the likeness of the sons[1] of men
[b]touched my lips; then I opened my mouth
and spoke, saying to him who stood before me, "My lord, because of the vision
[c]my sorrows have overwhelmed me, and
I have retained no strength. 17For how can
this servant of my lord talk with you, my
lord? As for me, no strength remains in me
now, nor is any breath left in me."
18Then again, *the one* having the likeness
of a man touched me and strengthened
me. 19[a]And he said, "O man greatly beloved,
[b]fear not! Peace *be* to you; be strong, yes,
be strong!"
So when he spoke to me I was strengthened, and said, "Let my lord speak, for you
have strengthened me."
20Then he said, "Do you know why I have
come to you? And now I must return to
fight [a]with the prince of Persia; and when
I have gone forth, indeed the prince of
Greece will come. 21But I will tell you what
is noted in the Scripture of Truth. (No one
upholds me against these, [a]except Michael
your prince.

11 "Also [a]in the first year of [b]Darius
the Mede, I, *even* I, stood up to confirm and strengthen him.) 2And now I

9:27 [c] Dan. 11:36 10:1 [a] Dan. 1:7 [1] Or *and of great conflict* 10:4 [1] Hebrew *Hiddekel* 10:5 [a] Ezek. 9:2; 10:2 [b] Rev. 1:13; 15:6
10:6 [a] [Rev. 1:15] 10:10 [a] Dan. 9:21 10:11 [a] Dan. 9:23 10:12 [a] Rev. 1:17 [b] Dan. 9:3, 4, 22, 23; Acts 10:4
10:13 [a] Dan. 10:20 [b] Dan. 10:21; 12:1; Jude 9; [Rev. 12:7] 10:14 [a] Gen. 49:1; Deut. 31:29; Dan. 2:28 [b] Dan. 8:26; 10:1
10:15 [a] Dan. 8:18; 10:9 10:16 [a] Dan. 8:15 [b] Jer. 1:9; Dan. 10:10 [c] Dan. 10:8, 9 [1] Theodotion and Vulgate read *the son;* Septuagint reads *a hand.* 10:19 [a] Dan. 10:11 [b] Judg. 6:23; Is. 43:1; Dan. 10:12 10:20 [a] Dan. 10:13
10:21 [a] Dan. 10:13; Jude 9; [Rev. 12:7] 11:1 [a] Dan. 9:1 [b] Dan. 5:31

will tell you the truth: Behold, three more
kings will arise in Persia, and the fourth
shall be far richer than *them* all; by his
strength, through his riches, he shall stir
up all against the realm of Greece. 3Then [a]a
mighty king shall arise, who shall rule with
great dominion, and [b]do according to his
will. 4And when he has arisen, [a]his kingdom
shall be broken up and divided toward the
four winds of heaven, but not among his
posterity [b]nor according to his dominion
with which he ruled; for his kingdom shall
be uprooted, even for others besides these.

Warring Kings of North and South

5"Also the king of the South shall become strong, as well as *one* of his princes;
and he shall gain power over him and have
dominion. His dominion *shall be* a great
dominion. 6And at the end of *some* years
they shall join forces, for the daughter of
the king of the South shall go to the king of
the North to make an agreement; but she
shall not retain the power of her authority,[1] and neither he nor his authority[2] shall
stand; but she shall be given up, with those
who brought her, and with him who begot
her, and with him who strengthened her
in *those* times. 7But from a branch of her
roots *one* shall arise in his place, who shall
come with an army, enter the fortress of the
king of the North, and deal with them and
prevail. 8And he shall also carry their gods
captive to Egypt, with their princes[1] *and*
their precious articles of silver and gold;
and he shall continue *more* years than the
king of the North.

9"Also *the king of the North* shall come
to the kingdom of the king of the South,
but shall return to his own land. 10However
his sons shall stir up strife, and assemble
a multitude of great forces; and *one* shall
certainly come [a]and overwhelm and pass
through; then he shall return [b]to his fortress and stir up strife.

11"And the king of the South shall be
[a]moved with rage, and go out and fight with
him, with the king of the North, who shall
muster a great multitude; but the [b]mul-
titude shall be given into the hand of his
enemy. 12When he has taken away the multitude, his heart will be lifted up; and he
will cast down tens of thousands, but he
will not prevail. 13For the king of the North
will return and muster a multitude greater
than the former, and shall certainly come
at the end of some years with a great army
and much equipment.

14"Now in those times many shall rise up
against the king of the South. Also, violent
men[1] of your people shall exalt themselves
in fulfillment of the vision, but they shall
[a]fall. 15So the king of the North shall come
and [a]build a siege mound, and take a fortified city; and the forces[1] of the South shall
not withstand *him*. Even his choice troops
shall have no strength to resist. 16But he
who comes against him [a]shall do according to his own will, and [b]no one shall stand
against him. He shall stand in the Glorious
Land with destruction in his power.[1]

17"He shall also [a]set his face to enter with
the strength of his whole kingdom, and upright ones[1] with him; thus shall he do. And
he shall give him the daughter of women to
destroy it; but she shall not stand *with him,*
[b]or be for him. 18After this he shall turn his
face to the coastlands, and shall take many.
But a ruler shall bring the reproach against
them to an end; and with the reproach removed, he shall turn back on him. 19Then
he shall turn his face toward the fortress
of his own land; but he shall [a]stumble and
fall, [b]and not be found.

20"There shall arise in his place one who
imposes taxes *on* the glorious kingdom; but
within a few days he shall be destroyed, but
not in anger or in battle. 21And in his place
[a]shall arise a vile person, to whom they will
not give the honor of royalty; but he shall
come in peaceably, and seize the kingdom
by intrigue. 22With the force[1] of a [a]flood
they shall be swept away from before him
and be broken, [b]and also the prince of the
covenant. 23And after the league *is made*
with him [a]he shall act deceitfully, for he

11:3 [a] Dan. 7:6; 8:5 [b] Dan. 8:4; 11:16, 36 11:4 [a] Jer. 49:36; Ezek. 37:9; Dan. 7:2; 8:8; Zech. 2:6; Rev. 7:1 [b] Dan. 8:22 11:6 [1] Literally *arm* [2] Literally *arm* 11:8 [1] Or *molded images* 11:10 [a] Is. 8:8; Jer. 46:7, 8; 51:42; Dan. 9:26; 11:26, 40 [b] Dan. 11:7 11:11 [a] Prov. 16:14 [b] [Ps. 33:10, 16] 11:14 [a] Job 9:13 [1] Or *robbers,* literally *sons of breakage* 11:15 [a] Jer. 6:6; Ezek. 4:2; 17:17 [1] Literally *arms* 11:16 [a] Dan. 8:4, 7 [b] Josh. 1:5 [1] Literally *hand* 11:17 [a] 2 Kin. 12:17; 2 Chr. 20:3; Ezek. 4:3, 7 [b] Dan. 9:26 [1] Or *bring equitable terms* 11:19 [a] Ps. 27:2; Jer. 46:6 [b] Job 20:8; Ps. 37:36; Ezek. 26:21 11:21 [a] Dan. 7:8 11:22 [a] Dan. 9:26 [b] Dan. 8:10, 11 [1] Literally *arms* 11:23 [a] Dan. 8:25

shall come up and become strong with a small *number of* people. 24He shall enter peaceably, even into the richest places of the province; and he shall do *what* his fathers have not done, nor his forefathers: he shall disperse among them the plunder, spoil, and riches; and he shall devise his plans against the strongholds, but *only* for a time.

25"He shall stir up his power and his courage against the king of the South with a great army. And the king of the South shall be stirred up to battle with a very great and mighty army; but he shall not stand, for they shall devise plans against him. 26Yes, those who eat of the portion of his delicacies shall destroy him; his army shall be swept away, and many shall fall down slain. 27Both these kings' hearts *shall be* bent on evil, and they shall speak lies at the same table; but it shall not prosper, for the end *will* still *be* at the [a]appointed time. 28While returning to his land with great riches, his heart shall be *moved* against the holy covenant; so he shall do *damage* and return to his own land.

The Northern King's Blasphemies

29"At the appointed time he shall return and go toward the south; but it shall not be like the former or the latter. 30[a]For ships from Cyprus[1] shall come against him; therefore he shall be grieved, and return in rage against the holy covenant, and do *damage.*

"So he shall return and show regard for those who forsake the holy covenant. 31And forces[1] shall be mustered by him, [a]and they shall defile the sanctuary fortress; then they shall take away the daily *sacrifices,* and place *there* the abomination of desolation. 32Those who do wickedly against the covenant he shall corrupt with flattery; but the people who know their God shall be strong, and carry out *great exploits.* 33And those of the people who understand shall instruct many; yet *for many* days they shall fall by sword and flame, by captivity and plundering. 34Now when they fall, they shall be aided with a little help; but many shall join with them by intrigue. 35And *some* of those of understanding shall fall, [a]to refine them, purify *them,* and make *them* white, *until* the time of the end; because *it is* still for the appointed time.

36"Then the king shall do according to his own will: he shall [a]exalt and magnify himself above every god, shall speak blasphemies against the God of gods, and shall prosper till the wrath has been accomplished; for what has been determined shall be done. 37He shall regard neither the God[1] of his fathers nor the desire of women, [a]nor regard any god; for he shall exalt himself above *them* all. 38But in their place he shall honor a god of fortresses; and a god which his fathers did not know he shall honor with gold and silver, with precious stones and pleasant things. 39Thus he shall act against the strongest fortresses with a foreign god, which he shall acknowledge, *and* advance *its* glory; and he shall cause them to rule over many, and divide the land for gain.

The Northern King's Conquests

40"At the [a]time of the end the king of the South shall attack him; and the king of the North shall come against him [b]like a whirlwind, with chariots, [c]horsemen, and with many ships; and he shall enter the countries, overwhelm *them,* and pass through. 41He shall also enter the Glorious Land, and many *countries* shall be overthrown; but these shall escape from his hand: [a]Edom, Moab, and the prominent people of Ammon. 42He shall stretch out his hand against the countries, and the land of [a]Egypt shall not escape. 43He shall have power over the treasures of gold and silver, and over all the precious things of Egypt; also the Libyans and Ethiopians *shall follow* [a]at his heels. 44But news from the east and the north shall trouble him; therefore he shall go out with great fury to destroy and annihilate many. 45And he shall plant the tents of his palace between the seas and [a]the glorious holy mountain; [b]yet he shall come to his end, and no one will help him.

11:27 [a] Dan. 8:19; Hab. 2:3 **11:30** [a] Gen. 10:4; Num. 24:24; Is. 23:1, 12; Jer. 2:10 [1] Hebrew *Kittim,* western lands, especially Cyprus **11:31** [a] Dan. 8:11–13; 12:11 [1] Literally *arms* **11:35** [a] [Deut. 8:16; Prov. 17:3]; Dan. 12:10; Zech. 13:9; Mal. 3:2, 3 **11:36** [a] Dan. 7:8, 25 **11:37** [a] Is. 14:13; 2 Thess. 2:4 [1] Or *gods* **11:40** [a] Dan. 11:27, 35; 12:4, 9 [b] Is. 21:1 [c] Ezek. 38:4; Rev. 9:16 **11:41** [a] Is. 11:14 **11:42** [a] Joel 3:19 **11:43** [a] Ex. 11:8 **11:45** [a] Ps. 48:2 [b] Rev. 19:20

Prophecy of the End Time

12 "At that time Michael
shall stand up,
The great prince who stands *watch*
over the sons of your people;
[a]And there shall be a time
of trouble,
Such as never was since
there was a nation,
Even to that time.
And at that time your people
[b]shall be delivered,
Every one who is found
[c]written in the book.
2 And many of those who sleep
in the dust of the earth shall
awake,
[a]Some to everlasting life,
Some to shame [b]*and*
everlasting contempt.

DANIEL 12:4

I AM DANIEL

"But you, Daniel, shut up the words, and seal the book until the time of the end; many shall run to and fro, and knowledge shall increase." Daniel 12:4

I am Daniel, a Jew living in exile. I was brought to Babylon, given the Babylonian name of Belteshazzar, and trained into the trusted service of King Nebuchadnezzar. Training me in the ways of the Babylonians took three years.

In time, the king had two dreams that no one could interpret. I used the gift that God gave me to interpret the dreams and won favor with the king. So, he put me in charge of his wise men.

As the years passed, King Nebuchadnezzar was replaced by a new king of Babylon, King Belshazzar. One night, he was giving a banquet and brought out the golden goblets that Nebuchadnezzar had taken from the temple of God in Jerusalem. He and his guests drank wine from them and praised the pagan gods of gold and silver, bronze and iron, wood and stone. Just then, mysterious fingers began to write on the wall. No one could tell the king what the writing meant, so I was called to give an interpretation. The writing meant that Belshazzar's kingdom would be taken from him, and he would perish because he mocked the God of Israel.

King Darius, who favored me and made me a governor, succeeded King Belshazzar. The other governors jealously plotted against me. Knowing that my faith was in God, they convinced the king to decree that for a period of thirty days no one could petition any god. Only prayers and petitions to the king were allowed. Anyone defying the decree would be cast into a lions' den. Because I continued to petition the Lord, I was thrown into a den filled with hungry lions. That night I prayed and fasted before the Lord, and He delivered me from the mouths of the lions! The next day King Darius released me.

Then I had my own dreams, but I did not know what they meant. So I asked a bystander in my dream, and he interpreted the dreams for me. I continued to pray and fast as the Lord gave me vivid visions of the future. It is ironic that I could not interpret the visions for myself but those in my visions gave me the interpretations.

Some things only happen with prayer and fasting. We should petition God to remove whatever blocks our righteous path, even if it is a ferocious lion. We should ask for wisdom and understanding, as Daniel did. Our God is able to deliver us from and equip us for whatever we face, but we must ask Him for what we need.

12:1 [a] Is. 26:20; Jer. 30:7; Ezek. 5:9; Dan. 9:12; Matt. 24:21; Mark 13:19 [b] Rom. 11:26 [c] Ex. 32:32; Ps. 56:8
12:2 [a] [Matt. 25:46; John 5:28, 29; Acts 24:15] [b] [Is. 66:24; Rom. 9:21]

3 Those who are wise shall [a]shine
Like the brightness of the firmament,
[b]And those who turn many
to righteousness
[c]Like the stars forever and ever.

4"But you, Daniel, [a]shut up the words,
and seal the book until the time of the end;
many shall [b]run to and fro, and knowledge
shall increase."
5Then I, Daniel, looked; and there stood
two others, one on this riverbank and the
other on that [a]riverbank. 6And *one* said to
the man clothed in [a]linen, who *was* above
the waters of the river, [b]"How long shall the
fulfillment of these wonders *be?*"
7Then I heard the man clothed in linen,
who *was* above the waters of the river, when
he [a]held up his right hand and his left hand
to heaven, and swore by Him [b]who lives forever, [c]that *it shall be* for a time, times, and
half *a time;* [d]and when the power of [e]the
holy people has been completely shattered,
all these *things* shall be finished.
8Although I heard, I did not understand.
Then I said, "My lord, what *shall be* the end
of these *things?*"
9And he said, "Go *your way,* Daniel, for
the words *are* closed up and sealed till the
time of the end. 10[a]Many shall be purified,
made white, and refined, [b]but the wicked
shall do wickedly; and none of the wicked
shall understand, but [c]the wise shall understand.
11"And from the time *that* the daily *sacrifice* is taken away, and the abomination
of desolation is set up, *there shall be* one
thousand two hundred and ninety days.
12Blessed *is* he who waits, and comes to the
one thousand three hundred and thirty-
five days.
13"But you, go *your way* till the end; [a]for
you shall rest, [b]and will arise to your inheritance at the end of the days."

12:3 [a] Prov. 3:35; Dan. 11:33, 35; Matt. 13:43 [b] Prov. 11:30; [James 5:19, 20] [c] 1 Cor. 15:41 12:4 [a] Is. 8:16; Dan. 12:9; Rev. 22:10 [b] Amos 8:12 12:5 [a] Dan. 10:4 12:6 [a] Ezek. 9:2; Dan. 10:5 [b] Dan. 8:13; 12:8; Matt. 24:3; Mark 13:4 12:7 [a] Deut. 32:40 [b] Dan. 4:34 [c] Dan. 7:25; Rev. 12:14 [d] Luke 21:24 [e] Dan. 8:24 12:10 [a] Zech. 13:9 [b] Is. 32:6, 7; Rev. 22:11 [c] Dan. 12:3; Hos. 14:9; John 7:17; 8:47 12:13 [a] Is. 57:2; Rev. 14:13 [b] Ps. 1:5

THE BOOK OF

HOSEA

OVERVIEW

The Book of Hosea was written by the prophet Hosea, whose name means "salvation." He is considered one of the twelve minor prophets of the Old Testament. Hosea's prophecies warned the Israelites of the judgment they would endure because of their betrayal of God.

Hosea's prophecies regarded the kings of Israel and Judah. The first four—Uzziah, Jotham, Ahaz, and Hezekiah—reigned over the southern kingdom of Judah from 792 BC to 686 BC. Jeroboam II ruled the northern kingdom of Israel from 793 BC to 753 BC. Hosea lived during the rule of the last six kings of Israel who came after Jeroboam and was a contemporary of the prophets Isaiah and Micah.

During Hosea's ministry, Israel was in spiritual and political decline. Jeroboam had instituted idolatry, and the Israelites were unfaithful to God's covenant. They had embraced pagan idols and engaged in immoral practices. Instead of seeking God's protection against their enemies, the nation formed alliances with other nations, such as Egypt and Assyria.

In the first three chapters, God used Hosea's personal life as an example of His relationship with Israel. Hosea was commanded by God to take "a wife of harlotry and children of harlotry, for the land has committed great harlotry by departing from the LORD" (Hos. 1:2). Thus, Hosea married a harlot named Gomer, and she bore him three children—two sons and a daughter (see vv. 3–9). God used Gomer's unfaithfulness and the names He instructed the prophet to give his children to send specific messages to the people of Israel. These messages described the Israelites' rebelliousness and God's disappointment and mercy. The pinnacle of this section is when God tells Hosea to buy his wife back and reconcile their marriage, a stark picture of what God would do for His people.

The remaining chapters of Hosea (4–14) warn of God's judgment. God judged the Israelites because there was "no truth or mercy or knowledge of God in the land" (4:1). The people were "swearing and lying, killing and stealing and committing adultery" (v. 2). They engaged in willful idolatry and rebelled against God. Ultimately, the Lord held the priests and the leaders responsible for not keeping the law (see 4:4—5:15).

Chapters 6–8 describe the specific sins of the Israelites, including prostitution (see 6:10), theft (see 7:1), adultery (see 7:4), and idolatry (see 8:6). As punishment for these sins, God planned to disperse the people, cause bareness, and send destruction (chs. 9–13). In the final chapter, Hosea encouraged the Israelites to "return to the LORD" (14:1).

In the Book of Hosea, God used Hosea and his life experiences to demonstrate the Israelites' unfaithfulness and to encourage them to turn away from their wickedness and back to Him. God desired for them to honor the Law and His covenant with them. When they refused, Hosea prophesied the destruction that would come due to their disobedience. But God also promised He would show mercy to them at the end of the coming period of judgment.

BREATHE IT IN

The Israelites broke their covenant with God in the time of Hosea by engaging in a multitude of sins, including idolatry and immorality. Hosea spent decades calling on them to repent, but they refused.

Throughout the Bible, God's relationship with His people is compared to a marriage between a husband and wife. In Hosea, God instructed the prophet to marry Gomer, a woman He knew would be unfaithful to Hosea. Gomer's behavior in the marriage was God's way of giving an earthly analogy of the Israelites' behavior toward Him.

Gomer was openly unfaithful to Hosea, often engaging in extramarital affairs. Her wandering ways led her into bondage, but Hosea paid to have her released. After a brief period of disciplining Gomer, Hosea forgave her and restored her as his wife. Regardless of Gomer's behavior, Hosea remained committed to his vows to her as her husband.

Just as Gomer was openly unfaithful to Hosea in their marriage, the Israelites were openly unfaithful to God and their covenant with Him. Their unfaithfulness led to their bondage to sin and God disciplining them through judgment. But God promised to restore them later.

Marriage is a sacred covenant relationship built on a foundation of love, trust, and faithfulness. As Christians, when we enter into marriage, our whole lives should change, and we should be wholly committed to this relationship. We must die to our selfish desires and learn to put our spouses first. We should not engage in any other romantic or sexual relationships; a married couple should cling to one another only. Recognizing that no one is without sin, we should also practice repentance and forgiveness often.

Like the picture in Hosea, the marital relationship reflects our relationship with God. The foundation of our relationship with God is His love for us and our love for Him. The substance is our trust in God, our confession of faith, and God's plan of salvation. Our whole lives change when we encounter Christ as our Savior. We should be totally committed to Him and put Him first in our lives. We should have no other gods, clinging only to Him as our source of everything. Even when we sin and fall short (which will happen often), we must repent and experience His forgiveness.

Does this describe your relationship with God and with your spouse if you are married? Are you actively present and committed in these relationships? Are you demonstrating love and putting God's will and your spouse's needs first? Are you remaining faithful to God's covenant with you and your covenant with your spouse? Do you acknowledge your sins and failings? Do you readily ask for and offer forgiveness?

Our relationships, especially our marital relationship, should reflect God's relationship with His children. Demonstrate God's traits in your marriage. Be loving, faithful, and forgiving. Show mercy and grace. Never take your partner for granted. Never turn away from your spouse and seek solace in others. Show your appreciation for his or her presence in your life. Always remain committed to the covenant you have made to each other.

†

THE BOOK OF

HOSEA

1 The word of the LORD that came to Hosea the son of Beeri, in the days of [a]Uz-
ziah, [b]Jotham, [c]Ahaz, *and* [d]Hezekiah, kings
of Judah, and in the days of [e]Jeroboam the
son of Joash, king of Israel.

The Family of Hosea

2 When the LORD began to speak by Hosea,
the LORD said to Hosea:

[a]"Go, take yourself a wife of harlotry
And children of harlotry,
For [b]the land has committed
great harlotry
By departing from the LORD."

3 So he went and took Gomer the daughter
of Diblaim, and she conceived and bore
him a son. 4 Then the LORD said to him:

"Call his name Jezreel,
For in a little *while*
[a]I will avenge the bloodshed of
Jezreel on the house of Jehu,
[b]And bring an end to the kingdom
of the house of Israel.
5 [a]It shall come to pass in that day
That I will break the bow of Israel
in the Valley of Jezreel."

6 And she conceived again and bore a
daughter. Then *God* said to him:

"Call her name Lo-Ruhamah,[1]
[a]For I will no longer have mercy
on the house of Israel,
But I will utterly take them away.[2]
7 [a]Yet I will have mercy on
the house of Judah,
Will save them by the LORD their God,
And [b]will not save them by bow,
Nor by sword or battle,
By horses or horsemen."

8 Now when she had weaned Lo-Ruhamah, she conceived and bore a son. 9 Then
God said:

"Call his name Lo-Ammi,[1]
For you *are* not My people,
And I will not be your *God.*

The Restoration of Israel

10 "Yet [a]the number of the
children of Israel
Shall be as the sand of the sea,
Which cannot be measured
or numbered.
[b]And it shall come to pass
In the place where it was said to them,
'You *are* not My [c]people,'[1]
There it shall be said to them,
'*You are* [d]sons of the living God.'
11 [a]Then the children of Judah and
the children of Israel
Shall be gathered together,
And appoint for themselves one head;
And they shall come up
out of the land,
For great *will be* the day of Jezreel!

2 Say to your brethren, 'My people,'[1]
And to your sisters, 'Mercy[2] *is shown.*'

1:1 [a] 2 Chr. 26; Is. 1:1; Amos 1:1 [b] 2 Kin. 15:5, 7, 32–38; 2 Chr. 27; Mic. 1:1 [c] 2 Kin. 16:1–20; 2 Chr. 28 [d] 2 Kin. 18—20; 2 Chr. 29:1—32:33; Mic. 1:1 [e] 2 Kin. 13:13; 14:23–29; Amos 1:1 1:2 [a] Hos. 3:1 [b] Deut. 31:16; Judg. 2:17; Ps. 73:27; Jer. 2:13; Ezek. 16:1–59; 23:1–49 1:4 [a] 2 Kin. 10:11 [b] 2 Kin. 15:8–10; 17:6, 23; 18:11 1:5 [a] 2 Kin. 15:29 1:6 [a] 2 Kin. 17:6 [1] Literally *No-Mercy* [2] Or *That I may forgive them at all* 1:7 [a] 2 Kin. 19:29–35; Is. 30:18; 37:36, 37 [b] Ps. 44:3–7; [Zech. 4:6] 1:9 [1] Literally *Not-My-People* 1:10 [a] Gen. 22:17; 32:12; Jer. 33:22 [b] 1 Pet. 2:10 [c] Rom. 9:26 [d] Is. 63:16; 64:8; [John 1:12] [1] Hebrew *lo-ammi* (compare verse 9) 1:11 [a] Is. 11:11–13; Jer. 3:18; 50:4; [Ezek. 34:23; 37:15–28] 2:1 [1] Hebrew *Ammi* (compare 1:9, 10) [2] Hebrew *Ruhamah* (compare 1:6)

God's Unfaithful People

2 "Bring charges against your
mother, bring charges;
For [a]she *is* not My wife, nor
am I her Husband!
Let her put away her [b]harlotries
from her sight,
And her adulteries from
between her breasts;
3 Lest [a]I strip her naked
And expose her, as in the
day she was [b]born,
And make her like a wilderness,
And set her like a dry land,
And slay her with [c]thirst.

4 "I will not have mercy on her children,
For they *are* the [a]children of harlotry.
5 For their mother has played the
harlot;
She who conceived them has
behaved shamefully.
For she said, 'I will go after my lovers,
[a]Who give *me* my bread and my water,
My wool and my linen,
My oil and my drink.'

6 "Therefore, behold,
[a]I will hedge up your way with thorns,
And wall her in,
So that she cannot find her paths.
7 She will chase her lovers,
But not overtake them;
Yes, she will seek them,
but not find *them.*
Then she will say,
[a]'I will go and return to my
[b]first husband,
For then *it was* better for
me than now.'
8 For she did not [a]know
That I gave her grain, new
wine, and oil,
And multiplied her silver and gold—
Which they prepared for Baal.

9 "Therefore I will return and take
away
My grain in its time
And My new wine in its season,
And will take back My
wool and My linen,
Given to cover her nakedness.
10 Now [a]I will uncover her lewdness
in the sight of her lovers,
And no one shall deliver
her from My hand.
11 [a]I will also cause all her mirth to cease,
Her feast days,
Her New Moons,
Her Sabbaths—
All her appointed feasts.

12 "And I will destroy her vines
and her fig trees,
Of which she has said,
'These *are* my wages that my
lovers have given me.'
So I will make them a forest,
And the beasts of the field
shall eat them.
13 I will punish her
For the days of the Baals to
which she burned incense.
She decked herself with her
earrings and jewelry,
And went after her lovers;
But Me she forgot," says the LORD.

God's Mercy on His People

14 "Therefore, behold, I will allure her,
Will bring her into the wilderness,
And speak comfort to her.
15 I will give her her vineyards
from there,
And [a]the Valley of Achor
as a door of hope;
She shall sing there,
As in [b]the days of her youth,
[c]As in the day when she came up
from the land of Egypt.

16 "And it shall be, in that day,"
Says the LORD,
"*That* you will call Me 'My Husband,'[1]
And no longer call Me 'My Master,'[2]
17 For [a]I will take from her mouth
the names of the Baals,
And they shall be remembered
by their name no more.

2:2 [a] Is. 50:1 [b] Ezek. 16:25 2:3 [a] Jer. 13:22, 26; Ezek. 16:37–39 [b] Ezek. 16:4–7, 22 [c] Jer. 14:3; Amos 8:11–13 2:4 [a] John 8:41 2:5 [a] Ezek. 23:5; Hos. 2:8, 12 2:6 [a] Job 19:8; Lam. 3:7, 9 2:7 [a] Luke 15:17, 18 [b] Is. 54:5–8; Jer. 2:2; 3:1; Ezek. 16:8; 23:4 2:8 [a] Is. 1:3; Ezek. 16:19 2:10 [a] Ezek. 16:37 2:11 [a] Jer. 7:34; 16:9; Hos. 3:4; Amos 5:21; 8:10 2:15 [a] Josh. 7:26 [b] Jer. 2:1–3; Ezek. 16:8–14 [c] Ex. 15:1 2:16 [1] Hebrew *Ishi* [2] Hebrew *Baali* 2:17 [a] Ex. 23:13; Josh. 23:7; Ps. 16:4

18 In that day I will make a
[a]covenant for them
With the beasts of the field,
With the birds of the air,
And *with* the creeping
things of the ground.
Bow and sword of battle [b]I will
shatter from the earth,
To make them [c]lie down safely.

19 "I will betroth you to Me forever;
Yes, I will betroth you to Me
In righteousness and justice,
In lovingkindness and mercy;
20 I will betroth you to Me in faithfulness,
And [a]you shall know the LORD.

21 "It shall come to pass in that day
That [a]I will answer," says the LORD;
"I will answer the heavens,
And they shall answer the earth.
22 The earth shall answer
With grain,
With new wine,
And with oil;
They shall answer Jezreel.[1]
23 Then [a]I will sow her for
Myself in the earth,
[b]And I will have mercy on *her who
had* not obtained mercy;[1]
Then [c]I will say to *those who
were* not My people,[2]
'You *are* My people!'
And they shall say, '*You are* my God!' "

Israel Will Return to God

3 Then the LORD said to me, "Go again,
love a woman *who is* loved by a [a]lover[1]
and is committing adultery, just like the
love of the LORD for the children of Israel,
who look to other gods and love *the* raisin
cakes *of the pagans.*"

2 So I bought her for myself for fifteen
shekels of silver, and one and one-half hom-
ers of barley. 3 And I said to her, "You shall
[a]stay with me many days; you shall not play
the harlot, nor shall you have a man—so,
too, *will* I *be* toward you."

4 For the children of Israel shall abide
many days [a]without king or prince, without
sacrifice or *sacred* pillar, without [b]ephod or
[c]teraphim. 5 Afterward the children of Israel shall return and [a]seek the LORD their
God and [b]David their king. They shall fear
the LORD and His goodness in the [c]latter
days.

God's Charge Against Israel

4 Hear the word of the LORD,
You children of Israel,
For the LORD *brings* a [a]charge against
the inhabitants of the land:

"There is no truth or mercy
Or [b]knowledge of God in the land.
2 *By* swearing and lying,
Killing and stealing and
committing adultery,
They break all restraint,
With bloodshed upon bloodshed.
3 Therefore [a]the land will mourn;
And [b]everyone who dwells
there will waste away
With the beasts of the field
And the birds of the air;
Even the fish of the sea
will be taken away.

4 "Now let no man contend,
or rebuke another;
For your people *are* like those
[a]who contend with the priest.
5 Therefore you shall stumble
[a]in the day;
The prophet also shall stumble
with you in the night;
And I will destroy your mother.
6 [a]My people are destroyed for
lack of knowledge.
Because you have rejected
knowledge,
I also will reject you from
being priest for Me;
[b]Because you have forgotten
the law of your God,
I also will forget your children.

2:18 [a] Job 5:23; Is. 11:6–9; Ezek. 34:25 [b] Is. 2:4; Ezek. 39:1–10 [c] Lev. 26:5; Is. 32:18; Jer. 23:6; Ezek. 34:25 2:20 [a] [Jer. 31:33, 34]; Hos. 6:6; 13:4; [John 17:3] 2:21 [a] Is. 55:10; Zech. 8:12; [Mal. 3:10, 11] 2:22 [1] Literally *God Will Sow* 2:23 [a] Jer. 31:27; Amos 9:15 [b] Hos. 1:6 [c] Hos. 1:10; Zech. 13:9; Rom. 9:25, 26; [Eph. 2:11–22]; 1 Pet. 2:10 [1] Hebrew *lo-ruhamah* [2] Hebrew *lo-ammi* 3:1 [a] Jer. 3:20 [1] Literally *friend* or *husband* 3:3 [a] Deut. 21:13 3:4 [a] Hos. 10:3 [b] Ex. 28:4–12; 1 Sam. 23:9–12 [c] Gen. 31:19, 34; Judg. 17:5; 18:14, 17; [1 Sam. 15:23] 3:5 [a] Jer. 50:4 [b] Jer. 30:9; Ezek. 34:24 [c] [Is. 2:2, 3]; Jer. 31:9 4:1 [a] Is. 1:18; Hos. 12:2; Mic. 6:2 [b] Jer. 4:22 4:3 [a] Is. 24:4; 33:9; Jer. 4:28; 12:4; Amos 5:16; 8:8 [b] Zeph. 1:3 4:4 [a] Deut. 17:12 4:5 [a] Jer. 15:8; Hos. 2:2, 5 4:6 [a] Is. 5:13 [b] Ezek. 22:26

#OXYGEN
HOSEA 4:6

Believe in Forgiveness

Nothing can be more destructive to our lives than unforgiveness. It's like a poison within us that slowly pollutes every aspect of our lives. God's Word tells us we must forgive. We fail to do so at our own peril!

Turn your cheek, **breathe**, and **believe in forgiveness.**

7 "The more they increased,
The more they sinned against Me;
[a]I will change[1] their glory[2] into shame.
8 They eat up the sin of My people;
They set their heart on their iniquity.
9 And it shall be: [a]like people, like priest.
So I will punish them for their ways,
And reward them for their deeds.
10 For [a]they shall eat, but
not have enough;
They shall commit harlotry,
but not increase;
Because they have ceased
obeying the LORD.

The Idolatry of Israel

11 "Harlotry, wine, and new wine
[a]enslave the heart.
12 My people ask counsel from
their [a]wooden *idols,*
And their staff informs them.
For [b]the spirit of harlotry has
caused *them* to stray,
And they have played the
harlot against their God.
13 [a]They offer sacrifices on
the mountaintops,
And burn incense on the hills,
Under oaks, poplars, and terebinths,
Because their shade *is* good.
[b]Therefore your daughters
commit harlotry,
And your brides commit adultery.

14 "I will not punish your daughters
when they commit harlotry,
Nor your brides when they
commit adultery;
For *the men* themselves go
apart with harlots,
And offer sacrifices with
a [a]ritual harlot.[1]
Therefore people *who* do not
understand will be trampled.

15 "Though you, Israel, play the harlot,
Let not Judah offend.
[a]Do not come up to Gilgal,
Nor go up to [b]Beth Aven,
[c]Nor swear an oath, *saying,*
'As the LORD lives'—

16 "For Israel [a]is stubborn
Like a stubborn calf;
Now the LORD will let them forage
Like a lamb in open country.

17 "Ephraim *is* joined to idols,
[a]Let him alone.
18 Their drink is rebellion,
They commit harlotry continually.
[a]Her rulers dearly[1] love dishonor.
19 [a]The wind has wrapped her
up in its wings,
And [b]they shall be ashamed
because of their sacrifices.

Impending Judgment on Israel and Judah

5 "Hear this, O priests!
Take heed, O house of Israel!
Give ear, O house of the king!
For yours *is* the judgment,
Because [a]you have been a
snare to Mizpah
And a net spread on Tabor.
2 The revolters are [a]deeply
involved in slaughter,

4:7 [a] 1 Sam. 2:30; Mal. 2:9 [1] Following Masoretic Text, Septuagint, and Vulgate; scribal tradition, Syriac, and Targum read *They will change.* [2] Following Masoretic Text, Septuagint, Syriac, Targum, and Vulgate; scribal tradition reads *My glory.* 4:9 [a] Is. 24:2; Jer. 5:30, 31; 2 Tim. 4:3, 4 4:10 [a] Lev. 26:26; Is. 65:13; Mic. 6:14; Hag. 1:6 4:11 [a] Prov. 20:1; Is. 5:12; 28:7 4:12 [a] Jer. 2:27 [b] Is. 44:19, 20 4:13 [a] Is. 1:29; 57:5, 7; Jer. 2:20; Ezek. 6:13; 20:28 [b] Amos 7:17; [Rom. 1:28–32] 4:14 [a] Deut. 23:18 [1] Compare Deuteronomy 23:18 4:15 [a] Hos. 9:15; 12:11 [b] 1 Kin. 12:29; Josh. 7:2; Hos. 10:8 [c] Jer. 5:2; 44:26; Amos 8:14 4:16 [a] Jer. 3:6; 7:24; 8:5; Zech. 7:11 4:17 [a] Matt. 15:14 4:18 [a] Mic. 3:11 [1] Hebrew is difficult; a Jewish tradition reads *Her rulers shamefully love, 'Give!'* 4:19 [a] Jer. 51:1 [b] Is. 1:29 5:1 [a] Hos. 6:9 5:2 [a] Is. 29:15; Hos. 4:2; 6:9

Though I rebuke them all.
3 [a]I know Ephraim,
And Israel is not hidden from Me;
For now, O Ephraim, [b]you
commit harlotry;
Israel is defiled.

4 "They do not direct their deeds
Toward turning to their God,
For [a]the spirit of harlotry
is in their midst,
And they do not know the LORD.
5 The [a]pride of Israel testifies to his face;
Therefore Israel and Ephraim
stumble in their iniquity;
Judah also stumbles with them.

6 "With their flocks and herds
[a]They shall go to seek the LORD,
But they will not find *Him;*
He has withdrawn Himself from them.
7 They have [a]dealt treacherously
with the LORD,
For they have begotten
pagan children.
Now a New Moon shall devour
them and their heritage.

8 "Blow[a] the ram's horn in Gibeah,
The trumpet in Ramah!
[b]Cry aloud *at* [c]Beth Aven,
'*Look* behind you, O Benjamin!'
9 Ephraim shall be desolate
in the day of rebuke;
Among the tribes of Israel I
make known what is sure.

10 "The princes of Judah are like those
who [a]remove a landmark;
I will pour out My wrath
on them like water.
11 Ephraim is [a]oppressed *and*
broken in judgment,
Because he willingly walked
by [b]*human* precept.
12 Therefore I *will be* to
Ephraim like a moth,
And to the house of Judah
[a]like rottenness.

13 "When Ephraim saw his sickness,
And Judah *saw* his [a]wound,
Then Ephraim went [b]to Assyria
And sent to King Jareb;
Yet he cannot cure you,
Nor heal you of your wound.
14 For [a]I *will be* like a lion to Ephraim,
And like a young lion to
the house of Judah.
[b]I, *even* I, will tear *them* and go away;
I will take *them* away, and
no one shall rescue.
15 I will return again to My place
Till they acknowledge their offense.
Then they will seek My face;
In their affliction they will
earnestly seek Me."

A Call to Repentance

6 Come,[a] and let us return to the LORD;
For [b]He has torn, but [c]He will heal us;
He has stricken, but He will bind us up.
2 [a]After two days He will revive us;
On the third day He will raise us up,
That we may live in His sight.
3 [a]Let us know,
Let us pursue the knowledge
of the LORD.
His going forth is established
[b]as the morning;
[c]He will come to us [d]like the rain,
Like the latter *and* former
rain to the earth.

Impenitence of Israel and Judah

4 "O Ephraim, what shall I do to you?
O Judah, what shall I do to you?
For your faithfulness is like
a morning cloud,
And like the early dew it goes away.
5 Therefore I have hewn *them*
by the prophets,
I have slain them by [a]the
words of My mouth;
And your judgments *are like*
light *that* goes forth.
6 For I desire [a]mercy and [b]not sacrifice,
And the [c]knowledge of God more
than burnt offerings.

5:3 [a] Amos 3:2; 5:12 [b] Hos. 4:17 5:4 [a] Hos. 4:12 5:5 [a] Hos. 7:10 5:6 [a] Prov. 1:28; Is. 1:15; Jer. 11:11; Ezek. 8:18; Mic. 3:4; John 7:34 5:7 [a] Is. 48:8; Jer. 3:20; Hos. 6:7 5:8 [a] Hos. 8:1; Joel 2:1 [b] Is. 10:30 [c] Josh. 7:2 5:10 [a] Deut. 19:14; 27:17 5:11 [a] Deut. 28:33 [b] Mic. 6:16 5:12 [a] Prov. 12:4 5:13 [a] Jer. 30:12–15 [b] 2 Kin. 15:19; Hos. 7:11; 10:6 5:14 [a] Ps. 7:2; Lam. 3:10; Hos. 13:7, 8 [b] Ps. 50:22 6:1 [a] Is. 1:18; Acts 10:43 [b] Deut. 32:39; Hos. 5:14 [c] Jer. 30:17; Hos. 14:4 6:2 [a] Luke 24:46; Acts 10:40; [1 Cor. 15:4] 6:3 [a] Is. 54:13 [b] 2 Sam. 23:4 [c] Ps. 72:6; Joel 2:23 [d] Job 29:23 6:5 [a] [Jer. 23:29] 6:6 [a] Matt. 9:13; 12:7 [b] Is. 1:12, 13; [Mic. 6:6–8] [c] [John 17:3]

BELIEVE IN FORGIVENESS

INHALE

"Shopping while Black" is a real thing. It has happened to me and my friends too many times to count. Having your dignity stripped by a store clerk or security guard who follows you around or watches you intensely is unforgivable. When I see others with a different skin color getting to shop freely, while I am falsely accused of stealing, it's just too much to forgive. How can I turn the other cheek when people are wrongfully dying and I personally know the weight of injustice? What does it mean to believe in forgiveness, and why should I?

EXHALE

No one is saying turning the other cheek is easy, but it is biblical. It doesn't mean those who commit such atrocities are given a pass either. But there is always a better way and a more just way than seeking revenge. Forgiving someone for their wrongdoing doesn't mean he or she won't face consequences or punishment, but forgiveness is more for the forgiver than the forgiven. Forgiveness frees you from the prison of anger and vengeance so you can live again.

Over two thousand years ago, the highest example of forgiveness took place through the person of Jesus Christ. You talk about injustice; well, what was done to Jesus was the ultimate injustice. Not only was Jesus dehumanized, but He also died from how He was treated. I love the words Jesus spoke from the cross: "Father, forgive them, for they do not know what they do" (Luke 23:34). How about that! While being abused, the sinless One sought forgiveness for His wrongdoers. If He, who is the Son of God, modeled forgiveness, then how can we do otherwise?

God gives us the capacity to forgive. It doesn't come from us. Hosea 6:1 says, "Come, and let us return to the LORD; for He has torn, but He will heal us; He has stricken, but He will bind us up." What we cannot do, God can.

7 "But like men[1] they transgressed
the covenant;
There they dealt treacherously
with Me.
8 [a]Gilead *is* a city of evildoers
And defiled with blood.
9 As bands of robbers lie in
wait for a man,
So the company of [a]priests [b]murder
on the way to Shechem;
Surely they commit [c]lewdness.
10 I have seen a horrible thing
in the house of Israel:
There *is* the harlotry of
Ephraim;
Israel is defiled.
11 Also, O Judah, a harvest is
appointed for you,
When I return the captives
of My people.

7 "When I would have healed Israel,
Then the iniquity of Ephraim
was uncovered,
And the wickedness of Samaria.
For [a]they have committed fraud;
A thief comes in;
A band of robbers takes spoil
outside.
2 They do not consider in their hearts
That [a]I remember all their
wickedness;
Now their own deeds have
surrounded them;
They are before My face.
3 They make a [a]king glad with
their wickedness,
And princes [b]with their lies.
4 "They[a] *are* all adulterers.
Like an oven heated by a baker—

6:7 [1] Or *like Adam* 6:8 [a] Hos. 12:11 6:9 [a] Hos. 5:1 [b] Jer. 7:9, 10; Hos. 4:2 [c] Ezek. 22:9; 23:27; Hos. 2:10 7:1 [a] Ezek. 23:4–8; Hos. 5:1
7:2 [a] Ps. 25:7; Jer. 14:10; 17:1; Hos. 8:13; 9:9; Amos 8:7 7:3 [a] Hos. 1:1 [b] Mic. 7:3; [Rom. 1:32] 7:4 [a] Jer. 9:2; 23:10

He ceases stirring *the fire* after
kneading the dough,
Until it is leavened.
5 In the day of our king
Princes have made *him* sick,
inflamed with [a]wine;
He stretched out his hand
with scoffers.
6 They prepare their heart like an oven,
While they lie in wait;
Their baker[1] sleeps all night;
In the morning it burns
like a flaming fire.
7 They are all hot, like an oven,
And have devoured their judges;
All their kings have fallen.
[a]None among them calls upon Me.

8 "Ephraim [a]has mixed himself
among the peoples;
Ephraim is a cake unturned.
9 [a]Aliens have devoured his strength,
But he does not know *it;*
Yes, gray hairs are here
and there on him,
Yet he does not know *it.*
10 And the [a]pride of Israel
testifies to his face,
But [b]they do not return to
the LORD their God,
Nor seek Him for all this.

Futile Reliance on the Nations

11 "Ephraim[a] also is like a silly
dove, without sense—
[b]They call to Egypt,
They go to [c]Assyria.
12 Wherever they go, I will
[a]spread My net on them;
I will bring them down like
birds of the air;
I will chastise them
[b]According to what their
congregation has heard.

13 "Woe to them, for they have
fled from Me!
Destruction to them,
Because they have transgressed
against Me!
Though [a]I redeemed them,
Yet they have spoken lies against Me.
14 [a]They did not cry out to Me
with their heart
When they wailed upon their beds.

"They assemble together for[1]
grain and new [b]wine,
They rebel against Me;[2]
15 Though I disciplined *and*
strengthened their arms,
Yet they devise evil against Me;
16 They return, *but* not to the Most High;[1]
[a]They are like a treacherous bow.
Their princes shall fall by the sword
For the [b]cursings of their tongue.
This *shall be* their derision
[c]in the land of Egypt.

The Apostasy of Israel

8 "*Set* the trumpet[1] to your mouth!
He shall come [a]like an eagle against
the house of the LORD,
Because they have transgressed
My covenant
And rebelled against My law.
2 [a]Israel will cry to Me,
'My God, [b]we know You!'
3 Israel has rejected the good;
The enemy will pursue him.

4 "They[a] set up kings, but not by Me;
They made princes, but I did
not acknowledge *them.*
From their silver and gold
They made idols for themselves—
That they might be cut off.
5 Your calf is rejected, O Samaria!
My anger is aroused against them—
[a]How long until they attain
to innocence?
6 For from Israel *is* even this:
A [a]workman made it, and it
is not God;

7:5 [a] Is. 28:1, 7 7:6 [1] Following Masoretic Text and Vulgate; Syriac and Targum read *Their anger;* Septuagint reads *Ephraim.* 7:7 [a] Is. 64:7 7:8 [a] Ps. 106:35 7:9 [a] Is. 1:7; 42:25; Hos. 8:7 7:10 [a] Hos. 5:5 [b] Is. 9:13 7:11 [a] Hos. 11:11 [b] Is. 30:3 [c] Hos. 5:13; 8:9 7:12 [a] Ezek. 12:13 [b] Lev. 26:14; Deut. 28:15; 2 Kin. 17:13 7:13 [a] Ex. 18:8; Mic. 6:4 7:14 [a] Job 35:9, 10; Ps. 78:36; Jer. 3:10; Zech. 7:5 [b] Judg. 9:27; Amos 2:8 [1] Following Masoretic Text and Targum; Vulgate reads *thought upon;* Septuagint reads *slashed themselves for* (compare 1 Kings 18:28). [2] Following Masoretic Text, Syriac, and Targum; Septuagint omits *They rebel against Me;* Vulgate reads *They departed from Me.* 7:16 [a] Ps. 78:57 [b] Ps. 73:9; Dan. 7:25; Mal. 3:13, 14 [c] Deut. 28:68; Ezek. 23:32; Hos. 8:13; 9:3 [1] Or *upward* 8:1 [a] Deut. 28:49; Jer. 4:13 [1] Hebrew *shophar,* ram's horn 8:2 [a] Ps. 78:34; Hos. 5:15; 7:14 [b] Titus 1:16 8:4 [a] 1 Kin. 12:20; 2 Kin. 15:23, 25; Hos. 13:10, 11 8:5 [a] Ps. 19:13; Jer. 13:27 8:6 [a] Is. 40:19

But the calf of Samaria shall
be broken to pieces.

7 "They[a] sow the wind,
And reap the whirlwind.
The stalk has no bud;
It shall never produce meal.
If it should produce,
[b]Aliens would swallow it up.
8 [a]Israel is swallowed up;
Now they are among the Gentiles
[b]Like a vessel in which *is* no
pleasure.
9 For they have gone up to Assyria,
Like [a]a wild donkey alone
by itself;
Ephraim [b]has hired lovers.
10 Yes, though they have hired
among the nations,
Now [a]I will gather them;
And they shall sorrow a little,[1]
Because of the burden[2] of
[b]the king of princes.

11 "Because Ephraim has made
many altars for sin,
They have become for him
altars for sinning.
12 I have written for him [a]the
great things of My law,
But they were considered
a strange thing.
13 *For* the sacrifices of My offerings
[a]they sacrifice flesh and eat *it,*
[b]*But* the LORD does not accept
them.
[c]Now He will remember their
iniquity and punish their sins.
They shall return to Egypt.

14 "For[a] Israel has forgotten [b]his
Maker,
And has built temples;[1]
Judah also has multiplied
[c]fortified cities;
But [d]I will send fire upon his
cities,
And it shall devour his palaces."

Judgment of Israel's Sin

9 Do[a] not rejoice, O Israel, with
joy like *other* peoples,
For you have played the harlot
against your God.
You have made love *for* [b]hire
on every threshing floor.
2 The threshing floor and the
winepress
Shall not feed them,
And the new wine shall fail in her.

3 They shall not dwell in
[a]the LORD's land,
[b]But Ephraim shall return to Egypt,
And [c]shall eat unclean
things in Assyria.
4 They shall not offer wine
offerings to the LORD,
Nor [a]shall their [b]sacrifices
be pleasing to Him.
It shall be like bread of
mourners to them;
All who eat it shall be defiled.
For their bread *shall be*
for their *own* life;
It shall not come into the
house of the LORD.

5 What will you do in the appointed
day,
And in the day of the feast
of the LORD?
6 For indeed they are gone
because of destruction.
Egypt shall gather them up;
Memphis shall bury them.
[a]Nettles shall possess their
valuables of silver;
Thorns *shall be* in their tents.

7 The [a]days of punishment have come;
The days of recompense have come.
Israel knows!
The prophet *is* a [b]fool,
[c]The spiritual man *is* insane,
Because of the greatness of your
iniquity and great enmity.

8:7 [a] Prov. 22:8 [b] Hos. 7:9 8:8 [a] 2 Kin. 17:6; Jer. 51:34 [b] Jer. 22:28; 25:34 8:9 [a] Hos. 7:11; 12:1; Jer. 2:24 [b] Ezek. 16:33, 34 8:10 [a] Ezek. 16:37; 22:20 [b] Is. 10:8; Ezek. 26:7; Dan. 2:37 [1] Or *begin to diminish* [2] Or *oracle* 8:12 [a] [Deut. 4:6–8]; Ps. 119:18; 147:19, 20 8:13 [a] Zech. 7:6 [b] Jer. 14:10; Hos. 6:6; 9:4; 1 Cor. 4:5 [c] Hos. 9:9; Amos 8:7; Luke 12:2 8:14 [a] Deut. 32:18; [Hos. 2:13; 4:6; 13:6] [b] Is. 29:23 [c] Num. 32:17; 2 Kin. 18:13 [d] Jer. 17:27 [1] Or *palaces* 9:1 [a] Is. 22:12, 13; Hos. 10:5 [b] Jer. 44:17 9:3 [a] [Lev. 25:23]; Jer. 2:7 [b] Hos. 7:16; 8:13 [c] Ezek. 4:13 9:4 [a] Jer. 6:20 [b] Hos. 8:13; Amos 5:22 9:6 [a] Is. 5:6; 7:23; Hos. 10:8 9:7 [a] Is. 10:3; Jer. 10:15; Mic. 7:4; Luke 21:22 [b] Lam. 2:14; [Ezek. 13:3, 10] [c] Mic. 2:11

8 The [a]watchman of Ephraim
is with my God;
But the prophet *is* a fowler's[1]
snare in all his ways—
Enmity in the house of his God.
9 [a]They are deeply corrupted,
As in the days of [b]Gibeah.
He will remember their iniquity;
He will punish their sins.

10 "I found Israel
Like grapes in the [a]wilderness;
I saw your fathers
As the [b]firstfruits on the fig
tree in its first season.
But they went to [c]Baal Peor,
And separated themselves
to that shame;
[d]They became an abomination
like the thing they loved.
11 *As for* Ephraim, their glory shall
fly away like a bird—
No birth, no pregnancy,
and no conception!
12 Though they bring up their
children,
Yet I will bereave them to the last man.
Yes, [a]woe to them when I
depart from them!
13 Just [a]as I saw Ephraim like Tyre,
planted in a pleasant place,
So Ephraim will bring out his
children to the murderer."

14 Give them, O LORD—
What will You give?
Give them [a]a miscarrying womb
And dry breasts!

15 "All their wickedness *is* in [a]Gilgal,
For there I hated them.
Because of the evil of their deeds
I will drive them from My house;
I will love them no more.
[b]All their princes *are* rebellious.
16 Ephraim is [a]stricken,
Their root is dried up;
They shall bear no fruit.
Yes, were they to bear children,
I would kill the darlings
of their womb."

17 My God will [a]cast them away,
Because they did not obey Him;
And they shall be [b]wanderers
among the nations.

Israel's Sin and Captivity

10 Israel [a]empties *his* vine;
He brings forth fruit for himself.
According to the multitude of his fruit
[b]He has increased the altars;
According to the bounty of his land
They have embellished
his sacred pillars.
2 Their heart is [a]divided;
Now they are held guilty.
He will break down their altars;
He will ruin their *sacred* pillars.

3 For now they say,
"We have no king,
Because we did not fear the LORD.
And as for a king, what
would he do for us?"
4 They have spoken words,
Swearing falsely in making a covenant.
Thus judgment springs up [a]like
hemlock in the furrows of the field.

5 The inhabitants of Samaria fear
Because of the [a]calf[1] of Beth Aven.
For its people mourn for it,
And its priests shriek for it—
Because its [b]glory has
departed from it.
6 *The idol* also shall be carried
to Assyria
As a present for King [a]Jareb.
Ephraim shall receive shame,
And Israel shall be ashamed
of his own counsel.

7 *As for* Samaria, her king is cut off
Like a twig on the water.
8 Also the [a]high places of Aven,
[b]the sin of Israel,
Shall be destroyed.

9:8 [a] Jer. 6:17; 31:6; Ezek. 3:17; 33:7 [1] That is, one who catches birds in a trap or snare 9:9 [a] Hos. 10:9 [b] Judg. 19:22 9:10 [a] Jer. 2:2 [b] Is. 28:4; Mic. 7:1 [c] Num. 25:3; Ps. 106:28 [d] Ps. 81:12 9:12 [a] Deut. 31:17; Hos. 7:13 9:13 [a] Ezek. 26—28 9:14 [a] Luke 23:29 9:15 [a] Hos. 4:15; 12:11 [b] Is. 1:23; Hos. 5:2 9:16 [a] Hos. 5:11 9:17 [a] 2 Kin. 17:20; [Zech. 10:6] [b] Lev. 26:33 10:1 [a] Nah. 2:2 [b] Jer. 2:28; Hos. 8:11; 12:11 10:2 [a] 1 Kin. 18:21; Zeph. 1:5; [Matt. 6:24] 10:4 [a] Deut. 31:16, 17; 2 Kin. 17:3, 4; Amos 5:7 10:5 [a] 1 Kin. 12:28, 29; Hos. 8:5, 6; 13:2 [b] Hos. 9:11 [1] Literally *calves* 10:6 [a] Hos. 5:13 10:8 [a] Hos. 4:15 [b] Deut. 9:21; 1 Kin. 13:34

The thorn and thistle shall
grow on their altars;
[c]They shall say to the
mountains, "Cover us!"
And to the hills, "Fall on us!"

9 "O Israel, you have sinned from
the days of [a]Gibeah;
There they stood.
The [b]battle in Gibeah against
the children of iniquity[1]
Did not overtake them.
10 When *it is* My desire, I will
chasten them.
[a]Peoples shall be gathered
against them
When I bind them for their
two transgressions.[1]
11 Ephraim *is* [a]a trained heifer
That loves to thresh *grain;*
But I harnessed her fair neck,
I will make Ephraim pull *a plow.*
Judah shall plow;
Jacob shall break his clods."

12 Sow for yourselves righteousness;
Reap in mercy;
[a]Break up your fallow ground,
For *it is* time to seek the LORD,
Till He [b]comes and rains
righteousness on you.
13 [a]You have plowed wickedness;
You have reaped iniquity.
You have eaten the fruit of lies,
Because you trusted in your own way,
In the multitude of your mighty men.
14 Therefore tumult shall arise
among your people,
And all your fortresses
shall be plundered
As Shalman plundered Beth
Arbel in the day of battle—
A mother dashed in pieces
upon *her* children.
15 Thus it shall be done to you, O Bethel,
Because of your great wickedness.
At dawn the king of Israel
Shall be cut off utterly.

God's Continuing Love for Israel

11 "When Israel *was* a child,
I loved him,
And out of Egypt [a]I called My [b]son.
2 *As* they called them,[1]
So they [a]went from them;[2]
They sacrificed to the Baals,
And burned incense to carved images.

3 "I[a] taught Ephraim to walk,
Taking them by their arms;[1]
But they did not know that
[b]I healed them.
4 I drew them with gentle cords,[1]
With bands of love,
And [a]I was to them as those who
take the yoke from their neck.[2]
[b]I stooped *and* fed them.

5 "He shall not return to the
land of Egypt;
But the Assyrian shall be his king,
Because they refused to repent.
6 And the sword shall slash in his cities,
Devour his districts,
And consume *them,*
Because of their own counsels.
7 My people are bent on
[a]backsliding from Me.
Though they call to the Most High,[1]
None at all exalt *Him.*

8 "How[a] can I give you up, Ephraim?
How can I hand you over, Israel?
How can I make you like [b]Admah?
How can I set you like Zeboiim?
My heart churns within Me;
My sympathy is stirred.
9 I will not execute the
fierceness of My anger;
I will not again destroy Ephraim.
[a]For I *am* God, and not man,
The Holy One in your midst;
And I will not come with terror.[1]

10:8 [c] Is. 2:19; Luke 23:30; Rev. 6:16 10:9 [a] Hos. 9:9 [b] Judg. 20 [1] So read many Hebrew manuscripts, Septuagint, and Vulgate; Masoretic Text reads *unruliness.* 10:10 [a] Jer. 16:16 [1] Or *in their two habitations* 10:11 [a] [Jer. 50:11; Hos. 4:16; Mic. 4:13] 10:12 [a] Jer. 4:3 [b] Hos. 6:3 10:13 [a] [Job 4:8; Prov. 22:8; Gal. 6:7, 8] 11:1 [a] Matt. 2:15 [b] Ex. 4:22, 23 11:2 [a] 2 Kin. 17:13–15 [1] Following Masoretic Text and Vulgate; Septuagint reads *Just as I called them;* Targum interprets as *I sent prophets to a thousand of them.* [2] Following Masoretic Text, Targum, and Vulgate; Septuagint reads *from My face.* 11:3 [a] Deut. 1:31; 32:10, 11 [b] Ex. 15:26 [1] Some Hebrew manuscripts, Septuagint, Syriac, and Vulgate read *My arms.* 11:4 [a] Lev. 26:13 [b] Ex. 16:32; Ps. 78:25 [1] Literally *cords of a man* [2] Literally *jaws* 11:7 [a] Jer. 3:6, 7; 8:5 [1] Or *upward* 11:8 [a] Jer. 9:7 [b] Gen. 14:8; 19:24, 25; Deut. 29:23 11:9 [a] Num. 23:19 [1] Or *I will not enter a city*

#OXYGEN

HOSEA 11:8

Believe in Forgiveness

Are you perfect? Of course not. No one is. That is why you need others to cut you slack. But be just as quick to grant the grace to others that God has granted to you.

Release the offense, **breathe**, and **believe in forgiveness**.

10 “They shall walk after the LORD.
[a]He will roar like a lion.
When He roars,
Then *His* sons shall come
trembling from the west;
11 They shall come trembling
like a bird from Egypt,
[a]Like a dove from the land of Assyria.
[b]And I will let them dwell
in their houses,”
Says the LORD.

God’s Charge Against Ephraim

12 “Ephraim has encircled Me with lies,
And the house of Israel with deceit;
But Judah still walks with God,
Even with the Holy One[1]
who is faithful.

12

“Ephraim [a]feeds on the wind,
And pursues the east wind;
He daily increases lies and
desolation.
[b]Also they make a covenant
with the Assyrians,
And [c]oil is carried to Egypt.

2 “The[a] LORD also *brings* a
charge against Judah,
And will punish Jacob
according to his ways;
According to his deeds He
will recompense him.
3 He took his brother [a]by the
heel in the womb,
And in his strength he
[b]struggled with God.[1]
4 Yes, he struggled with the
Angel and prevailed;
He wept, and sought favor from Him.
He found Him *in* [a]Bethel,
And there He spoke to us—
5 That is, the LORD God of hosts.
The LORD *is* His [a]memorable name.
6 [a]So you, by *the help of* your God, return;
Observe mercy and justice,
And wait on your God continually.

7 “A cunning Canaanite!
[a]Deceitful scales *are* in his hand;
He loves to oppress.
8 And Ephraim said,
[a]‘Surely I have become rich,
I have found wealth for myself;
In all my labors
They shall find in me no
iniquity that *is* sin.’

9 “But I *am* the LORD your God,
Ever since the land of Egypt;
[a]I will again make you dwell in tents,
As in the days of the appointed feast.
10 [a]I have also spoken by the prophets,
And have multiplied visions;
I have given symbols through the
witness of the prophets.”

11 Though [a]Gilead *has* idols—
Surely they are vanity—
Though they sacrifice bulls in [b]Gilgal,
Indeed their altars *shall be* heaps
in the furrows of the field.

12 Jacob [a]fled to the country of Syria;
[b]Israel served for a spouse,
And for a wife he tended *sheep.*
13 [a]By a prophet the LORD brought
Israel out of Egypt,
And by a prophet he was
preserved.

11:10 [a] Is. 31:4; [Joel 3:16]; Amos 1:2 **11:11** [a] Is. 11:11; 60:8; Hos. 7:11 [b] Ezek. 28:25, 26; 34:27, 28 **11:12** [1] Or *holy ones* **12:1** [a] Job 15:2, 3; Hos. 8:7 [b] 2 Kin. 17:4; Hos. 8:9 [c] Is. 30:6 **12:2** [a] Hos. 4:1; Mic. 6:2 **12:3** [a] Gen. 25:26 [b] Gen. 32:24–28 [1] Compare Genesis 32:28 **12:4** [a] [Gen. 28:12–19; 35:9–15] **12:5** [a] Ex. 3:15 **12:6** [a] Hos. 14:1; Mic. 6:8 **12:7** [a] Prov. 11:1; Amos 8:5; Mic. 6:11 **12:8** [a] Ps. 62:10; Hos. 13:6; Rev. 3:17 **12:9** [a] Lev. 23:42 **12:10** [a] 2 Kin. 17:13; Jer. 7:25 **12:11** [a] Hos. 6:8 [b] Hos. 9:15 **12:12** [a] Gen. 28:5; Deut. 26:5 [b] Gen. 29:20, 28 **12:13** [a] Ex. 12:50, 51; 13:3; Ps. 77:20; Is. 63:11, 12; Mic. 6:4

LIFE SUPPORT

BE PATIENT: WAIT ON THE LORD

So you, by the help of your God, return; observe mercy and justice, and wait on your God continually. Hosea 12:6

LIFE: Be Patient

It is often said that God is an on-time God. We might know this is true, but it does not always feel that way. However, it is important that we accept the patience given to us by the Holy Spirit because God will often place us in times of waiting. Because He wants the best for us, He will take the time to make sure we are properly equipped to handle the blessing or ordeal that is coming and to align everything to work for His glory and our good and not against us. Many times, the Enemy will make us think that our wait means nothing is going to happen. However, we should wait in expectation, knowing God never goes back on His word.

If God has us waiting, it is for our own good. Why do you think the Enemy targets our patience while waiting? Why do you think he tries to encourage us to go in the opposite direction or give up? It is because he knows that what we are waiting for will change our lives for the better. Remember, the Enemy opposes God's will for us. When God is saying "wait" and the Enemy is saying "go," it is because the Enemy wants us to forfeit all that God has planned for us.

SUPPORT: Wait on the Lord

What a stance! Waiting on the Lord can be incredibly difficult. Our society has spoiled us. Everything is superfast. Food is cooked in a microwave. Online purchases sometimes show up at our doors within hours. Fast is not always bad. There are times when God answers us or provides what we desire right away. However, we must understand that His timing is never off. His answers and provision will arrive at exactly the right time, even if that is slower than we might want.

We need to trust God. We need to stand quietly, controlling our thoughts of doubt and impatience and knowing God's actions in our lives are worth the wait. When God moves, mountains move. Our lives can change for the better when we allow the Lord to mold us and our lives into all He desires. When we pause and allow Him to do His work, we can thrive.

SUPPORT EXAMPLE: Stand still, fast, and pray.

14 Ephraim [a]provoked *Him* to
anger most bitterly;
Therefore his Lord will leave the
guilt of his bloodshed upon him,
[b]And return his reproach upon him.

Relentless Judgment on Israel

13 When Ephraim spoke, trembling,
He exalted *himself* in Israel;
But when he offended through
Baal *worship*, he died.
2 Now they sin more and more,
And have made for themselves
molded images,
Idols of their silver, according
to their skill;
All of it *is* the work of craftsmen.
They say of them,
"Let the men who sacrifice[1]
kiss the calves!"
3 Therefore they shall be like
the morning cloud
And like the early dew
that passes away,

12:14 [a] Ezek. 18:10–13 [b] Dan. 11:18; Mic. 6:16 13:2 [1] Or *those who offer human sacrifice*

[a]Like chaff blown off from
a threshing floor
And like smoke from a chimney.

4 "Yet [a]I *am* the LORD your God
Ever since the land of Egypt,
And you shall know no God but Me;
For [b]*there is* no savior besides Me.
5 [a]I knew you in the wilderness,
[b]In the land of great drought.
6 [a]When they had pasture,
they were filled;
They were filled and their
heart was exalted;
Therefore they forgot Me.

7 "So [a]I will be to them like a lion;
Like [b]a leopard by the road I will lurk;
8 I will meet them [a]like a bear
deprived *of her cubs;*
I will tear open their rib cage,
And there I will devour
them like a lion.
The wild beast shall tear them.

9 "O Israel, you are destroyed,[1]
But your help[2] *is* from Me.
10 I will be your King;[1]
[a]Where *is any other,*
That he may save you in all your cities?
And your judges to whom [b]you said,
'Give me a king and princes'?
11 [a]I gave you a king in My anger,
And took *him* away in My wrath.

12 "The[a] iniquity of Ephraim *is* bound up;
His sin *is* stored up.
13 [a]The sorrows of a woman in
childbirth shall come upon him.
He *is* an unwise son,
For he should not stay long
where children are born.

14 "I will ransom them from the
power of the grave;[1]
I will redeem them from death.
[a]O Death, I will be your plagues![2]
O Grave,[3] I will be your destruction![4]
[b]Pity is hidden from My eyes."

15 Though he is fruitful among
his brethren,
[a]An east wind shall come;
The wind of the LORD shall come
up from the wilderness.
Then his spring shall become dry,
And his fountain shall be dried up.
He shall plunder the treasury
of every desirable prize.
16 Samaria is held guilty,[1]
For she has [a]rebelled against her God.
They shall fall by the sword,
Their infants shall be dashed in pieces,
And their women with
child [b]ripped open.

Israel Restored at Last

14 O Israel, [a]return to the LORD
your God,
For you have stumbled because
of your iniquity;
2 Take words with you,
And return to the LORD.
Say to Him,
"Take away all iniquity;
Receive *us* graciously,
For we will offer the
[a]sacrifices[1] of our lips.
3 Assyria shall [a]not save us,
[b]We will not ride on horses,
Nor will we say anymore to the work
of our hands, '*You are* our gods.'
[c]For in You the fatherless finds mercy."

4 "I will heal their [a]backsliding,
I will [b]love them freely,
For My anger has turned
away from him.
5 I will be like the [a]dew to Israel;
He shall grow like the lily,
And lengthen his roots like Lebanon.
6 His branches shall spread;
[a]His beauty shall be like an olive tree,
And [b]his fragrance like Lebanon.

13:3 [a] Ps. 1:4; Is. 17:13; Dan. 2:35 13:4 [a] Is. 43:11 [b] Is. 43:11; 45:21, 22; [1 Tim. 2:5] 13:5 [a] Deut. 2:7; 32:10 [b] Deut. 8:15 13:6 [a] Deut. 8:12, 14; 32:13–15; Jer. 5:7 13:7 [a] Lam. 3:10; Hos. 5:14 [b] Jer. 5:6 13:8 [a] 2 Sam. 17:8; Prov. 17:12 13:9 [1] Literally *it* or *he destroyed you* [2] Literally *in your help* 13:10 [a] Deut. 32:38 [b] 1 Sam. 8:5, 6 [1] Septuagint, Syriac, Targum, and Vulgate read *Where is your king?* 13:11 [a] 1 Sam. 8:7; 10:17–24 13:12 [a] Deut. 32:34, 35; Job 14:17; [Rom. 2:5] 13:13 [a] Is. 13:8; Mic. 4:9, 10 13:14 [a] [1 Cor. 15:54, 55] [b] Jer. 15:6 [1] Or *Sheol* [2] Septuagint reads *where is your punishment?* [3] Or *Sheol* [4] Septuagint reads *where is your sting?* 13:15 [a] Gen. 41:6; Jer. 4:11, 12; Ezek. 17:10; 19:12 13:16 [a] 2 Kin. 18:12 [b] 2 Kin. 15:16 [1] Septuagint reads *shall be disfigured* 14:1 [a] Hos. 12:6; [Joel 2:13] 14:2 [a] [Ps. 51:16, 17; Hos. 6:6; Heb. 13:15] [1] Literally *bull calves;* Septuagint reads *fruit.* 14:3 [a] Hos. 7:11; 10:13; 12:1 [b] [Ps. 33:17]; Is. 31:1 [c] Ps. 10:14; 68:5 14:4 [a] Jer. 14:7 [b] [Eph. 1:6] 14:5 [a] Job 29:19; Prov. 19:12; Is. 26:19 14:6 [a] Ps. 52:8; 128:3 [b] Gen. 27:27

RELEASE // BELIEVE IN FORGIVENESS

Making the Tough Choice

Hosea 14:4 // "I will heal their backsliding, I will love them freely, for My anger has turned away from him."

Summary Message // It can be difficult to forgive ourselves and those who have hurt us. Seeking forgiveness when we are in the wrong can also be challenging. Yet, Scripture reminds us that forgiveness is central to God's redemptive and restorative agenda. In Hosea 14, God models forgiveness (even when it is undeserved) and demonstrates that it is often the means to freeing ourselves and others from the burdens of guilt, shame, anger, and revenge. So, the question is, what are we holding on to that God desires us to release and forgive?

Practical Application // Think of the times you asked for forgiveness from someone for something you did. Now, consider when you have been asked to forgive others for something they did. Most likely, requesting forgiveness was easier than extending forgiveness. This is because it is natural for us to desire a quick release from the guilt and shame we often carry when we have done something wrong. However, releasing others from a wrong committed against us can be just as natural if we allow ourselves to be guided by the Holy Spirit and not the stubbornness of our flesh.

In Hosea 14 we find a stark picture of how forgiveness looks from God's perspective. The kingdom of Israel had split into two separate kingdoms: Judah in the south and Israel in the north. During the writings of Hosea, the northern portion faced several challenges, brought on by God because of their continued idolatry. Notably, when threatened by increased aggression from the Assyrians, the leadership of Israel did not repent and turn to God. Instead, they requested help from their neighbors and sought assistance from anywhere and everywhere else. In doing so, God's people chose to continue in their sin, justifying God's wrath. However, as we see throughout the Old Testament, God's forgiveness was never withheld when people asked for forgiveness. Hosea called the people of Israel to come back to God (see Hos. 14:1). What would God's response be? "I will heal their backsliding, I will love them freely, for My anger has turned away from him" (Hos. 14:4). What does this mean for us?

- Forgiveness is not dependent on deservedness. In God's kingdom, forgiveness is not conditional—it is not based on whether we deserve it. Rather, God pours out His forgiveness according to His infinite mercy and grace.
- Forgiveness is for both the forgiver and the forgiven. Forgiving others removes the burden of bitterness and revenge that we might carry and leaves the door open to rebuild relationship.
- Forgiveness is a redemptive and restorative action that enables healing and reconciliation to overcome the broken, fallen, human condition (e.g., broken relationship, broken spirit).

Forgiveness is not easy, but its power is freeing and life-giving. It enables us to breathe even when the world around us can feel suffocating. From Genesis to Revelation, we are treated to an ongoing account of God modeling forgiveness by redeeming and restoring an undeserving, fallen creation full of broken people. May we be those who live out God's example so others can experience the redemptive, restorative, breath-giving power of forgiveness too.

Fervent Prayer // Father, we are imperfect and have made mistakes. Those who have hurt and wronged us are no different. Yet, we have been carrying these burdens of guilt and shame, anger and bitterness for far too long. Thank You for reminding us that Your forgiveness is freely available to all. Help us not only to forgive those who have wronged us but also to seek forgiveness from those we have wronged. Today, we want to rest in the release of Your forgiveness. We ask this in Jesus' name. Amen.

7 [a]Those who dwell under his
shadow shall return;
They shall be revived *like* grain,
And grow like a vine.
Their scent[1] *shall be* like the
wine of Lebanon.

8 "Ephraim *shall say,* 'What have I
to do anymore with idols?'
I have heard and observed him.
I *am* like a green cypress tree;
[a]Your fruit is found in Me."

9 Who *is* wise?
Let him understand these things.
Who is prudent?
Let him know them.
For [a]the ways of the LORD *are* right;
The righteous walk in them,
But transgressors stumble in them.

14:7 [a] Dan. 4:12 [1] Literally *remembrance* 14:8 [a] [John 15:4] 14:9 [a] [Ps. 111:7, 8; Prov. 10:29]; Zeph. 3:5

THE BOOK OF

JOEL

OVERVIEW

The prophet Joel, whose name means "Yahweh is God," is considered one of the twelve minor prophets of the Old Testament. Joel's prophecies proclaimed that the calamities brought upon the Israelites were God's judgment against them because of their sin.

Most scholars believe that Joel was a well-educated priest. They believe he was a resident of Jerusalem. No specific references to dates appear in the book, but scholars believe it was written during the reign of King Joash, who ruled between 835 and 796 BC.

During Joel's ministry, Israel experienced several disasters. The book opens with a description of a plague of locusts (see Joel 1:1–12). The devastation was catastrophic, as this description reflects: "What the chewing locust left, the swarming locust has eaten; what the swarming locust left, the crawling locust has eaten; and what the crawling locust left, the consuming locust has eaten" (v. 4). The vines, trees, fields, and grains were all ruined (see vv. 7–12). In response, the suffering priests and the distressed people were instructed to repent (see vv. 13–14).

Chapter 2 speaks of a coming people "great and strong, the like of whom has never been; nor will there ever be any such after them" (v. 2). They are described as "the noise of a flaming fire that devours the stubble" and "a strong people set in battle array" (v. 5). Joel calls for repentance "with fasting, with weeping, and with mourning" (v. 12). He declared the Lord's response should they repent: "Then the LORD will be zealous for His land, and pity His people" (v. 18). He promised that repentance would result in them no longer being "a reproach among the nations" (v. 19).

God's promises of salvation and the Holy Spirit appear in Joel. He declared that He would "pour out [His] Spirit on all flesh" (v. 28). He proclaimed, "Your sons and your daughters shall prophesy, your old men shall dream dreams, your young men shall see visions" (v. 28). God pledged that "whoever calls on the name of the LORD shall be saved" (v. 32). Peter would later reference this passage in his Pentecost sermon (see Acts 2:14–21).

The final chapter of Joel speaks of God's judgment of nations who have scattered His people and divided His land (see 3:2). He warns them to "prepare for war" (v. 9) while promising to "be a shelter for His people, and the strength of the children of Israel" (v. 16). The book ends with God's plan to bless their land (see v. 18) and "acquit" (v. 21) the Israelites of their guilt.

BREATHE IT IN

The Book of Joel describes a catastrophic locust swarm and a severe drought, both of which were God's judgment against the sins of the Israelites. The land was devastated, and Joel called upon the people to repent. God promised salvation to those who believed in Him, declaring that He would send His Spirit to abide within His people.

As soon as a person professes faith in Christ as Savior and Lord, the Holy Spirit takes up residence within him or her. Christians are fortunate to have the Holy Spirit leading and guiding us

in our daily lives. But the most important role He has is transforming us and making us more like Christ. For such a transformation to take place, however, we must be willing to change.

Even as believers, we each continue to have sins and issues to address. When we confess our sins, God reminds us of the forgiveness we have found in Christ. When we yield to the Holy Spirit, He teaches us how to live in a manner that is holy and acceptable to God so that we find ourselves sinning less often. He also renews our minds to become ever more like the mind of Christ so that we see sin and obedience for what they truly are.

When our minds are renewed, we think and act differently. We recognize sin when the Holy Spirit convicts us, and we willingly repent. Through the process of conviction and repentance, we learn more about ourselves and about God's grace and mercy and His expectations of us as Christians.

The Holy Spirit also teaches us through the Word of God, which helps us grow as Christians. It is often difficult to understand the Bible; however, we can gain true understanding through revelation from the Holy Spirit. When we have spiritual eyes and ears, Scripture takes on a deeper, more profound meaning. The Holy Spirit convicts us of sinful acts and attitudes and teaches us how to do what is right. Through the Scriptures, the Holy Spirit encourages us to separate ourselves from ungodly behaviors and people, while increasing our desire for holiness and godliness so that we become more like Christ.

Unfortunately, some Christians resist the Holy Spirit, preventing Him from working in their lives as God intended. This leads only to harm for believers. God intended for the Spirit to serve as our guide, showing us the direction we need to go. The Spirit of God will never leave us confused. He will always reveal God's best purpose for our lives. If you have not allowed the Holy Spirit to operate in your life, now is the time to do so.

Seek to know the Holy Spirit fully. Open your heart and mind to receive His guidance and His power. Let Him reveal God's plan for your life. Repent when He convicts you. Allow Him to transform you into the image of Christ so that your life becomes a walking demonstration of the fruit of the Spirit: love, joy, peace, longsuffering (patience), kindness, goodness, faithfulness, gentleness, and self-control (see Gal. 5:22–23).

THE BOOK OF

JOEL

1 The word of the LORD that came to [a]Joel the son of Pethuel.

The Land Laid Waste
(Ex. 10:1–20)

2 Hear this, you elders,
And give ear, all you
inhabitants of the land!
[a]Has *anything like* this
happened in your days,
Or even in the days of your fathers?
3 [a]Tell your children about it,
Let your children *tell* their children,
And their children another
generation.

4 [a]What the chewing locust[1] left, the
[b]swarming locust has eaten;
What the swarming locust left, the
crawling locust has eaten;
And what the crawling locust left,
the consuming locust has eaten.

5 Awake, you [a]drunkards, and weep;
And wail, all you drinkers of wine,
Because of the new wine,
[b]For it has been cut off
from your mouth.
6 For [a]a nation has come up
against My land,
Strong, and without number;
[b]His teeth *are* the teeth of a lion,
And he has the fangs of a fierce lion.
7 He has [a]laid waste My vine,
And ruined My fig tree;
He has stripped it bare and
thrown *it* away;
Its branches are made white.
8 [a]Lament like a virgin girded
with sackcloth
For [b]the husband of her youth.
9 [a]The grain offering and
the drink offering
Have been cut off from the
house of the LORD;
The priests [b]mourn, who
minister to the LORD.
10 The field is wasted,
[a]The land mourns;
For the grain is ruined,
[b]The new wine is dried up,
The oil fails.

11 [a]Be ashamed, you farmers,
Wail, you vinedressers,
For the wheat and the barley;
Because the harvest of the
field has perished.
12 [a]The vine has dried up,
And the fig tree has withered;
The pomegranate tree,
The palm tree also,
And the apple tree—
All the trees of the field are withered;
Surely [b]joy has withered away
from the sons of men.

Mourning for the Land

13 [a]Gird yourselves and lament,
you priests;
Wail, you who minister
before the altar;
Come, lie all night in sackcloth,
You who minister to my God;
For the grain offering and
the drink offering

1:1 [a] Acts 2:16 1:2 [a] Jer. 30:7; Joel 2:2 1:3 [a] Ex. 10:2; Ps. 78:4; Is. 38:19 1:4 [a] Deut. 28:38; Joel 2:25; Amos 4:9 [b] Is. 33:4 [1] Exact identity of these locusts is unknown. 1:5 [a] Is. 5:11; 28:1; Hos. 7:5 [b] Is. 32:10 1:6 [a] Prov. 30:25; Joel 2:2, 11, 25 [b] Rev. 9:8 1:7 [a] Is. 5:6; Amos 4:9 1:8 [a] Is. 22:12 [b] Prov. 2:17; Jer. 3:4 1:9 [a] Hos. 9:4; Joel 1:13; 2:14 [b] Joel 2:17 1:10 [a] Jer. 12:11; Hos. 3:4 [b] Is. 24:7 1:11 [a] Jer. 14:3, 4; Amos 5:16 1:12 [a] Joel 1:10; Hab. 3:17 [b] Is. 16:10; 24:11; Jer. 48:33 1:13 [a] Jer. 4:8; Ezek. 7:18

Are withheld from the
house of your God.
14 [a]Consecrate a fast,
Call [b]a sacred assembly;
Gather the elders
And [c]all the inhabitants of the land
Into the house of the LORD your God,
And cry out to the LORD.

15 [a]Alas for the day!
For [b]the day of the LORD *is* at hand;
It shall come as destruction
from the Almighty.
16 Is not the food [a]cut off before
our eyes,
[b]Joy and gladness from the
house of our God?
17 The seed shrivels under the clods,
Storehouses are in shambles;
Barns are broken down,
For the grain has withered.
18 How [a]the animals groan!
The herds of cattle are restless,
Because they have no pasture;
Even the flocks of sheep
suffer punishment.[1]

19 O LORD, [a]to You I cry out;
For [b]fire has devoured the
open pastures,
And a flame has burned all
the trees of the field.
20 The beasts of the field also
[a]cry out to You,
For [b]the water brooks are
dried up,
And fire has devoured the
open pastures.

JOEL 1:1

I AM JOEL

The word of the LORD that came to Joel the son of Pethuel. Joel 1:1

I am the prophet Joel, son of Pethuel. During my day, a plague of locusts was devastating the land of Israel, bringing the threat of famine. This plague was brought on because the people had turned away from God. He told me to warn them that He would bring an army against them in the hope that they would repent. Should they repent of their sinfulness, God said He would restore their crops and give them back what the locusts had eaten.

Then the Lord showed me times in the future when He would pour out His Spirit on all flesh and sons and daughters would prophesy, old men would dream dreams, and young men would see visions. He showed me the coming day of judgment followed by the day of decision when God would bless those who love Him.

My message was not one of despair but one of hope. It was God's will for the people to turn from their wicked ways. The God of Israel was ready to embrace His people and forgive them because He is gracious and merciful. He said that one day all the nations would be judged, and Jerusalem would once again be a holy place where the Lord dwells. He spoke with authority that everyone who called on His name would be saved.

†

In the busyness of our lives and as we strive for more of what the world has to offer, we cannot forget that this is a dying world that cannot provide life. Only the Word of God can give us direction, and only the goodness of God can afford what we truly need. If you turn your back on God, you will never see His face. But if you humble yourself before Him, you will forever be in His presence.

1:14 [a] 2 Chr. 20:3; Joel 2:15, 16 [b] Lev. 23:36 [c] 2 Chr. 20:13 1:15 [a] [Is. 13:9; Jer. 30:7]; Amos 5:16 [b] Is. 13:6; Ezek. 7:2–12 1:16 [a] Is. 3:1; Amos 4:6 [b] Deut. 12:7; Ps. 43:4 1:18 [a] 1 Kin. 8:5; Jer. 12:4; 14:5, 6; Hos. 4:3 [1] Septuagint and Vulgate read *are made desolate.* 1:19 [a] [Ps. 50:15]; Mic. 7:7 [b] Jer. 9:10; Amos 7:4 1:20 [a] Job 38:41; Ps. 104:21; 147:9; Joel 1:18 [b] 1 Kin. 17:7; 18:5

The Day of the LORD

2 Blow [a]the trumpet in Zion,
And [b]sound an alarm in
My holy mountain!
Let all the inhabitants of
the land tremble;
For [c]the day of the LORD is coming,
For it is at hand:
2 [a]A day of darkness and gloominess,
A day of clouds and thick darkness,
Like the morning *clouds* spread
over the mountains.
[b]A people *come,* great and strong,
[c]The like of whom has never been;
Nor will there ever be any
such after them,
Even for many successive generations.

3 A fire devours before them,
And behind them a flame burns;
The land *is* like [a]the Garden
of Eden before them,
[b]And behind them a desolate
wilderness;
Surely nothing shall escape them.
4 [a]Their appearance is like the
appearance of horses;
And like swift steeds, so they run.
5 [a]With a noise like chariots
Over mountaintops they leap,
Like the noise of a flaming fire
that devours the stubble,
Like a strong people set in battle array.

6 Before them the people writhe
in pain;
[a]All faces are drained of color.[1]
7 They run like mighty men,
They climb the wall like men of war;
Every one marches in formation,
And they do not break [a]ranks.
8 They do not push one another;
Every one marches in his
own column.[1]
Though they lunge between
the weapons,
They are not cut down.[2]
9 They run to and fro in the city,
They run on the wall;
They climb into the houses,
They [a]enter at the windows
[b]like a thief.

10 [a]The earth quakes before them,
The heavens tremble;
[b]The sun and moon grow dark,
And the stars diminish
their brightness.
11 [a]The LORD gives voice before
His army,
For His camp is very great;
[b]For strong *is the One* who
executes His word.
For the [c]day of the LORD *is*
great and very terrible;
[d]Who can endure it?

A Call to Repentance

12 "Now, therefore," says the LORD,
[a]"Turn to Me with all your heart,
With fasting, with weeping,
and with mourning."
13 So [a]rend your heart, and
not [b]your garments;
Return to the LORD your God,
For He *is* [c]gracious and merciful,
Slow to anger, and of great kindness;
And He relents from doing harm.
14 [a]Who knows *if* He will turn and
relent,
And leave [b]a blessing behind
Him—
[c]A grain offering and a drink
offering
For the LORD your God?

15 [a]Blow the trumpet in Zion,
[b]Consecrate a fast,
Call a sacred assembly;
16 Gather the people,
[a]Sanctify the congregation,
Assemble the elders,

2:1 [a] Jer. 4:5; Joel 2:15; Zeph. 1:16 [b] Num. 10:5 [c] Joel 1:15; 2:11, 31; 3:14; [Obad. 15]; Zeph. 1:14 **2:2** [a] Joel 2:10, 31; Amos 5:18; Zeph. 1:15 [b] Joel 1:6; 2:11, 25 [c] Ex. 10:14; Lam. 1:12; Dan. 9:12; 12:1; Joel 1:2 **2:3** [a] Gen. 2:8; Is. 51:3; Ezek. 36:35 [b] Ex. 10:5, 15; Ps. 105:34, 35; Zech. 7:14 **2:4** [a] Rev. 9:7 **2:5** [a] Rev. 9:9 **2:6** [a] Is. 13:8; Jer. 8:21; Lam. 4:8; Nah. 2:10 [1] Septuagint, Targum, and Vulgate read *gather blackness.* **2:7** [a] Prov. 30:27 **2:8** [1] Literally *his own highway* [2] That is, they are not halted by losses **2:9** [a] Jer. 9:21 [b] John 10:1 **2:10** [a] Ps. 18:7; Joel 3:16; Nah. 1:5 [b] Is. 13:10; 34:4; Jer. 4:23; Ezek. 32:7, 8; Joel 2:31; 3:15; Matt. 24:29; Rev. 8:12 **2:11** [a] Jer. 25:30; Joel 3:16; Amos 1:2 [b] Jer. 50:34; Rev. 18:8 [c] Jer. 30:7; Amos 5:18; Zeph. 1:15 [d] [Mal. 3:2] **2:12** [a] [Deut. 4:29]; Jer. 4:1; Ezek. 33:11; Hos. 12:6; 14:1 **2:13** [a] [Ps. 34:18; 51:17; Is. 57:15] [b] Gen. 37:34; 2 Sam. 1:11; Job 1:20; Jer. 41:5 [c] [Ex. 34:6] **2:14** [a] Josh. 14:12; 2 Sam. 12:22; 2 Kin. 19:4; Jer. 26:3; Jon. 3:9 [b] Hag. 2:19 [c] Joel 1:9, 13 **2:15** [a] Num. 10:3; 2 Kin. 10:20 [b] Joel 1:14 **2:16** [a] Ex. 19:10

RELEASE // RECONCILE SEPARATION WITH REUNION

Reunited and I Feel So Good

Joel 2:12 // "Now, therefore," says the LORD, "turn to Me with all your heart, with fasting, with weeping, and with mourning."

Summary Message // The prophet Joel spoke on behalf of God when he called the people to "turn to" God. Joel understood that turning toward the answer is required in a disastrous or trying situation. However, we must take care to turn toward the right answer. We must understand that God is our omniscient Creator and only He knows the proper course for us to follow. He can and will give you the power to turn away from the pressures of life and toward that which will cause you to rise up and conquer evil. However, your heart must turn first. You must believe that God is the source of all that is right and good.

Practical Application // Amid chaos or pressure, some of us may turn uncharacteristically from the normal things and people in our everyday lives to the unfamiliar, unusual, and even unthinkable. This, of course, only causes more chaos in our lives and leaves those around us wondering what happened to us or what we were thinking. There are real evil forces in this world that look for every opportunity to turn us in the wrong direction. This evil comes to destroy the divine purpose and destiny of God's people. But evil has no power over you because you have been saved, sanctified, and redeemed by the blood of Jesus, which washes over you.

Be careful, though, because you will be tried and tempted to give in to evil. Do not put yourself in situations where the Enemy can get a foothold. First Peter 5:8 says, "Be sober, be vigilant; because your adversary the devil walks about like a roaring lion, seeking whom he may devour." This means we must watch out for the schemes of the Enemy as he tries to twist the truth and walk us into sinful behavior. Our safeguards are to meditate daily on the Word of God, pray continually, and always lift up His name. We should also surround ourselves with others who love the Lord and live for Him. The Lord can use these brothers and sisters as tools that help keep us on the path of His will.

But if we should fall, we must turn away from sin and turn toward God in true repentance. God is faithful to forgive us, and we can take our rightful position of abiding in Him once more. How much better it is to return to Him instead of drinking, drugging, thinking depressing thoughts, or engaging in wrong relationships to ease the pressure. The reunion with God returns us to fellowship with Him and restores our right standing with Him. God promises to do marvelous things in our lives when we reunite with Him. He will return to us what the devourer attempted to steal. We may fall empty, but we will rise with plenty.

Fervent Prayer // God, we are sorry that we have left Your side. We pray Your Spirit will draw us nearer to You every day. We will allow ourselves to be vulnerable in Your presence so we can be cleansed and reunited with You. We turn from our ways to Your ways. You love us more than anyone else does. Thank You for the provision and comfort You will give to us because we have returned to You. Thank You for receiving us once again. It feels so good. Draw us nearer every day by Your Spirit. In Jesus' name we pray. Amen.

Gather the children and
nursing babes;
[b]Let the bridegroom go out
from his chamber,
And the bride from her dressing room.
17 Let the priests, who minister
to the LORD,
Weep [a]between the porch
and the altar;
Let them say, [b]"Spare Your
people, O LORD,
And do not give Your
heritage to reproach,
That the nations should
rule over them.
[c]Why should they say
among the peoples,
'Where *is* their God?' "

2:16[b] Ps. 19:5 2:17[a] Matt. 23:35 [b] Ex. 32:11, 12; [Is. 37:20]; Amos 7:2, 5 [c] Ps. 42:10

The Land Refreshed
(Acts 2:17)

18 Then the LORD will [a]be
zealous for His land,
And pity His people.
19 The LORD will answer and
say to His people,
"Behold, I will send you [a]grain
and new wine and oil,
And you will be satisfied by them;
I will no longer make you a
reproach among the nations.

20 "But [a]I will remove far from
you [b]the northern *army,*
And will drive him away into a
barren and desolate land,
With his face toward the eastern sea
And his back [c]toward the western sea;
His stench will come up,
And his foul odor will rise,
Because he has done
monstrous things."

21 Fear not, O land;
Be glad and rejoice,
For the LORD has done
marvelous things!
22 Do not be afraid, you
beasts of the field;
For [a]the open pastures
are springing up,
And the tree bears its fruit;
The fig tree and the vine
yield their strength.
23 Be glad then, you children of Zion,
And [a]rejoice in the LORD your God;
For He has given you the
former rain faithfully,[1]
And He [b]will cause the rain to
come down for you—
The former rain,
And the latter rain in the first
month.
24 The threshing floors shall
be full of wheat,
And the vats shall overflow
with new wine and oil.

25 "So I will restore to you the years [a]that
the swarming locust has eaten,
The crawling locust,
The consuming locust,
And the chewing locust,[1]
My great army which I
sent among you.
26 You shall [a]eat in plenty
and be satisfied,
And praise the name of the
LORD your God,
Who has dealt wondrously with you;
And My people shall never
be put to [b]shame.
27 Then you shall know that I *am*
[a]in the midst of Israel:
[b]I *am* the LORD your God
And there is no other.
My people shall never be put to shame.

God's Spirit Poured Out

28 "And[a] it shall come to pass afterward
That [b]I will pour out My
Spirit on all flesh;
[c]Your sons and your [d]daughters
shall prophesy,
Your old men shall dream dreams,
Your young men shall see visions.
29 And also on *My* [a]menservants
and on *My* maidservants
I will pour out My Spirit in those days.

30 "And [a]I will show wonders in the
heavens and in the earth:
Blood and fire and pillars of smoke.
31 [a]The sun shall be turned into darkness,
And the moon into blood,
[b]Before the coming of the great and
awesome day of the LORD.
32 And it shall come to pass
That [a]whoever calls on the
name of the LORD
Shall be saved.
For [b]in Mount Zion and in Jerusalem
there shall be deliverance,
As the LORD has said,
Among [c]the remnant whom
the LORD calls.

2:18 [a] [Is. 60:10; 63:9, 15] **2:19** [a] Jer. 31:12; Hos. 2:21, 22; Joel 1:10; [Mal. 3:10] **2:20** [a] Ex. 10:19 [b] Jer. 1:14, 15 [c] Deut. 11:24 **2:22** [a] Joel 1:19 **2:23** [a] Deut. 11:14; Is. 41:16; Jer. 5:24; Hab. 3:18; Zech. 10:7 [b] Lev. 26:4; Hos. 6:3; Zech. 10:1; James 5:7 [1] Or *the teacher of righteousness* **2:25** [a] Joel 1:4–7; 2:2–11 [1] Compare 1:4 **2:26** [a] Lev. 26:5; Deut. 11:15; Is. 62:9 [b] Is. 45:17 **2:27** [a] Lev. 26:11, 12; [Joel 3:17, 21] [b] [Is. 45:5, 6] **2:28** [a] Ezek. 39:29; Acts 2:17–21 [b] Zech. 12:10 [c] Is. 54:13 [d] Acts 21:9 **2:29** [a] [1 Cor. 12:13; Gal. 3:28] **2:30** [a] Matt. 24:29; Mark 13:24, 25; Luke 21:11, 25, 26; Acts 2:19 **2:31** [a] Is. 13:9, 10; 34:4; Joel 2:10; 3:15; Matt. 24:29; Mark 13:24; Luke 21:25; Acts 2:20; Rev. 6:12, 13 [b] Is. 13:9; Zeph. 1:14–16; [Mal. 4:1, 5, 6] **2:32** [a] Jer. 33:3; Acts 2:21; Rom. 10:13 [b] Is. 46:13; [Rom. 11:26] [c] Is. 11:11; Jer. 31:7; [Mic. 4:7]; Rom. 9:27

God Judges the Nations

3 "For behold, [a]in those days
and at that time,
When I bring back the captives
of Judah and Jerusalem,
2 [a]I will also gather all nations,
And bring them down to the
Valley of Jehoshaphat;
And I [b]will enter into judgment
with them there
On account of My people,
My heritage Israel,
Whom they have scattered
among the nations;
They have also divided up My land.
3 They have [a]cast lots for My people,
Have given a boy *as payment*
for a harlot,
And sold a girl for wine,
that they may drink.

4 "Indeed, what have you to do with Me,
[a]O Tyre and Sidon, and all the
coasts of Philistia?
Will you retaliate against Me?
But if you retaliate against Me,
Swiftly and speedily I will return your
retaliation upon your own head;
5 Because you have taken My
silver and My gold,
And have carried into your temples
My prized possessions.
6 Also the people of Judah and
the people of Jerusalem
You have sold to the Greeks,
That you may remove them
far from their borders.

7 "Behold, [a]I will raise them
Out of the place to which
you have sold them,
And will return your retaliation
upon your own head.
8 I will sell your sons and
your daughters
Into the hand of the people of Judah,
And they will sell them
to the [a]Sabeans,[1]
To a people [b]far off;
For the LORD has spoken."

9 [a]Proclaim this among the nations:
"Prepare for war!
Wake up the mighty men,
Let all the men of war draw near,
Let them come up.
10 [a]Beat your plowshares into swords
And your pruning hooks into spears;
[b]Let the weak say, 'I *am* strong.'"
11 Assemble and come, all you nations,
And gather together all around.
Cause [a]Your mighty ones to
go down there, O LORD.

#OXYGEN

JOEL 3:11

Reconcile Separation with Reunion

God is the God of all nations and all people. God loves you, so love others. Turn to God to help you overcome your judgments and prejudices so you, too, can accept all.

Forgive, **breathe**, and **reconcile separation with reunion**.

12 "Let the nations be wakened,
and come up to the Valley
of Jehoshaphat;
For there I will sit to [a]judge all
the surrounding nations.
13 [a]Put in the sickle, for [b]the
harvest is ripe.
Come, go down;
For the [c]winepress is full,
The vats overflow—
For their wickedness *is* great."

14 Multitudes, multitudes in
the valley of decision!
For [a]the day of the LORD *is* near
in the valley of decision.

3:1 [a] Jer. 30:3; Ezek. 38:14 3:2 [a] Is. 66:18; Mic. 4:12; Zech. 14:2 [b] Is. 66:16; Jer. 25:31; Ezek. 38:22 3:3 [a] Obad. 11; Nah. 3:10 3:4 [a] Is. 14:29–31; Jer. 47:1–7; Ezek. 25:15–17; Amos 1:6–8; Zech. 9:5–7 3:7 [a] Is. 43:5, 6; Jer. 23:8; Zech. 9:13 3:8 [a] Ezek. 23:42 [b] Jer. 6:20 [1] Literally *Shebaites* (compare Isaiah 60:6 and Ezekiel 27:22) 3:9 [a] Jer. 6:4; Ezek. 38:7; Mic. 3:5 3:10 [a] [Is. 2:4; Mic. 4:3] [b] Zech. 12:8 3:11 [a] Ps. 103:20; Is. 13:3 3:12 [a] [Ps. 96:13]; Is. 2:4 3:13 [a] [Matt. 13:39]; Rev. 14:15 [b] Jer. 51:33; Hos. 6:11 [c] [Is. 63:3]; Lam. 1:5; Rev. 14:19 3:14 [a] Joel 2:1

15 The sun and moon will grow dark,
And the stars will diminish
their brightness.
16 The LORD also will roar from Zion,
And utter His voice from Jerusalem;
The heavens and earth will shake;
[a]But the LORD will be a shelter
for His people,
And the strength of the
children of Israel.

17 "So you shall know that I *am*
the LORD your God,
Dwelling in Zion My [a]holy mountain.
Then Jerusalem shall be holy,
And no aliens shall ever pass
through her again."

God Blesses His People

18 And it will come to pass in that day
That the mountains shall
drip with new wine,
The hills shall flow with milk,
And all the brooks of Judah shall
be flooded with water;
A [a]fountain shall flow from
the house of the LORD
And water the Valley
of Acacias.

19 "Egypt shall be a desolation,
And Edom a desolate
wilderness,
Because of violence *against*
the people of Judah,
For they have shed innocent
blood in their land.
20 But Judah shall abide forever,
And Jerusalem from generation
to generation.
21 For I will [a]acquit them of the
guilt of bloodshed, whom
I had not acquitted;
For the LORD dwells in Zion."

3:16 [a] [Is. 51:5, 6] 3:17 [a] Obad. 16; Zech. 8:3 3:18 [a] Ps. 46:4; Ezek. 47:1; Zech. 14:8; [Rev. 22:1] 3:21 [a] Is. 4:4

THE BOOK OF

AMOS

OVERVIEW

The Book of Amos bears the name of its author, the prophet Amos. His name means "burdened" in Hebrew. He is considered one of the twelve minor prophets of the Old Testament. Amos's prophecies were delivered to the northern kingdom of Israel. He announced a day of judgment for the Israelites, which he called "the day of the LORD" (Amos 5:18–20).

Amos lived in the southern kingdom of Judah, but God called him to minister in the northern kingdom of Israel. A sheep breeder and tender of sycamore fruit by trade, Amos left everything behind to answer the call of God to deliver His messages to the Israelites. He prophesied during a particularly prosperous time for Israel and Judah. Both nations considered their prosperity a sign of God's favor. As much as their societies prospered materially, though, their spiritual lives were profoundly displeasing to God. The people had become content and had forgotten about God. Instead of worshiping Him, they idolized pagan gods. Instead of caring for one another, the strong and wealthy took advantage of the weak and poor. Through Amos, God declared His plans for judgment on the surrounding nations and on His people.

Amos outlined God's judgment on several nations. Damascus was judged because it "threshed Gilead" (1:3). Gaza was judged for carrying away "captive the whole captivity" (v. 6), and Tyre was judged because it "delivered up the whole captivity to Edom" (v. 9). God also passed judgment on Edom, Ammon, Moab, and Judah (see 1:11—2:5).

Amos strongly declared God's judgment on the Israelites for their injustices (see 2:6–8). He described God's relationship with Israel (see vv. 9–12) and outlined the consequences of the people's disobedience (see 2:13—3:15). He reminded Israel of its past transgressions and refusal to accept correction (see 4:1–13). The Israelites were condemned for abusing the poor (see v. 1) and being dishonest in their worship (see vv. 4–5). After each reminder, God lamented, "Yet you have not returned to Me" (vv. 6, 8–11). The Israelites were urged to repent, and God called on them to "seek" Him so they could live (5:4). Amos warned that those who did not seek God would be judged (see vv. 16–27).

God gave Amos visions of the judgment that would befall the Israelites (see 7:1—9:10). He had a vision of locusts (see 7:1–3), fire (see 7:4–6), a plumb line (see 7:7–9), summer fruit (see 8:1–14), and "the Lord standing by the altar" (9:1; see 9:1–10).

The final verses in the book present God's promise to restore Israel. He will "raise up the tabernacle of David" (9:11) and "plant" the Israelites "in their land, and no longer shall they be pulled up from the land" (v. 15), which He gave them.

Amos, at God's command, strongly admonished the Israelites for their mistreatment of the poor, false pride, and insincere worship. He reminded them of their past transgressions and the consequences they had suffered because of them. He then shared with them the visions God gave him, detailing the judgment that would come. The Israelites were encouraged to repent, and God's promise to restore them was made clear.

BREATHE IT IN

The Book of Amos describes a people who had become comfortable and complacent with God's blessings. During this period, the Israelites were not at war with other nations, and they experienced prosperity. But instead of turning toward God in gratitude, they turned from God and worshiped pagan idols. They also established a class system with the rich being of more value than the poor. The lower class was not treated well. The Israelites were only concerned about themselves and not their neighbors. Not pleased with their behavior, God sent the prophet Amos to declare His judgment on Israel and the other nations. But He also promised to restore them when they repented and returned to Him.

In today's world, injustices are everywhere. We hear about, witness, or even experience social, racial, political, and economic injustices almost daily. Unfortunately, far too often the victims of these injustices are people of color. As we see in the Book of Amos, though, injustice is not new. Much of it is deeply rooted in history. As a result, injustice may even be systemic, having been designed purposely to deny equal and equitable access to goods, services, rights, and privileges by those who do not operate according to God's Word and way.

Some who profess Christ do not notice the mistreatment and suffering of others, while some even perpetuate it. Neither of these positions align with God's expectations of His people. The Book of Amos reminds us that God cares deeply about how His people treat others. Having a right relationship with Him is impossible if we fail to live in right relationship with each other. We should not be concerned only about those in our circles, our families, and our friends. We must note what is happening in the world around us and determine how we can be of service to those who are less fortunate than we are.

God often blesses His people with personal success. However, many consume themselves with their well-being, bragging and boasting about what they have accomplished and accumulated. We must never allow worldly success to lead us astray. When the Israelites experienced success, they became arrogant and materialistic. They turned from the Lord and worshiped other gods. No matter how prosperous we may be, we must always remember the source. Every good and perfect thing in our lives comes from God (see James 1:17).

Do not let success go to your head. We have an obligation to help those around us. Do your part to counteract injustice. God has called us to be in relationship with Him and those around us. Nurture all of these relationships. We must do all we can to meet the needs of others without causing feelings of inferiority or shame. God will hold us accountable for our actions and our motives.

What have you done to help those less fortunate than you? What have you done to combat the injustices in society? Have you thought about the plight of others, or have you been consumed with your own prosperity and desires? Do you look the other way when you see the homeless and hungry? Would you turn your head if you witnessed police brutality or racism?

While it may seem the world's problems are too big for you to tackle, remember that you are not alone. You are a member of God's army. Your contributions matter, and God wants you to do your part. Start in your community. Identify an issue that you want to address. There are plenty from which to choose. Talk to people. Determine how you can be of service. Then roll up your sleeves and get to work!

†

THE BOOK OF

AMOS

1 The words of Amos, who was among
the [a]sheepbreeders[1] of [b]Tekoa, which he
saw concerning Israel in the days of [c]Uz-
ziah king of Judah, and in the days of [d]Jer-
oboam the son of Joash, king of Israel, two
years before the [e]earthquake.
2 And he said:

"The LORD [a]roars from Zion,
And utters His voice from
Jerusalem;
The pastures of the shepherds
mourn,
And the top of [b]Carmel withers."

Judgment on the Nations

3 Thus says the LORD:

"For three transgressions of
[a]Damascus, and for four,
I will not turn away its *punishment,*
Because they have [b]threshed
Gilead with implements
of iron.
4 [a]But I will send a fire into
the house of Hazael,
Which shall devour the
palaces of [b]Ben-Hadad.
5 I will also break the *gate*
[a]bar of Damascus,
And cut off the inhabitant
from the Valley of Aven,
And the one who holds the
scepter from Beth Eden.
The people of Syria shall
go captive to Kir,"
Says the LORD.

6 Thus says the LORD:

"For three transgressions of
[a]Gaza, and for four,
I will not turn away its *punishment,*
Because they took captive
the whole captivity
To deliver *them* up to Edom.
7 [a]But I will send a fire upon
the wall of Gaza,
Which shall devour its palaces.
8 I will cut off the inhabitant
[a]from Ashdod,
And the one who holds the
scepter from Ashkelon;
I will [b]turn My hand against Ekron,
And [c]the remnant of the
Philistines shall perish,"
Says the Lord GOD.

9 Thus says the LORD:

"For three transgressions of
[a]Tyre, and for four,
I will not turn away its *punishment,*
Because they delivered up the
whole captivity to Edom,
And did not remember the
covenant of brotherhood.
10 But I will send a fire upon
the wall of Tyre,
Which shall devour its palaces."

11 Thus says the LORD:

"For three transgressions of
[a]Edom, and for four,

1:1 [a] 2 Kin. 3:4; Amos 7:14 [b] 2 Sam. 14:2; Jer. 6:1 [c] 2 Kin. 15:1–7; 2 Chr. 26:1–23; Is. 1:1; Hos. 1:1 [d] 2 Kin. 14:23–29; Amos 7:10 [e] Zech. 14:5
[1] Compare 2 Kings 3:4 1:2 [a] Is. 42:13; Jer. 25:30; Joel 3:16 [b] 1 Sam. 25:2; Is. 33:9 1:3 [a] Is. 8:4; 17:1–3; Jer. 49:23–27; Zech. 9:1
[b] 2 Kin. 10:32, 33 1:4 [a] Jer. 49:27; 51:30 [b] 1 Kin. 20:1; 2 Kin. 6:24 1:5 [a] 2 Kin. 14:28; Is. 8:4; Jer. 51:30; Lam. 2:9 1:6 [a] 1 Sam. 6:17;
Jer. 47:1, 5; Zeph. 2:4 1:7 [a] Jer. 47:1 1:8 [a] Jer. 47:5; Zeph. 2:4 [b] Ps. 81:14 [c] Is. 14:29–31; Jer. 47:1–7; Ezek. 25:16; Joel 3:4–8; Zeph. 2:4–7;
Zech. 9:5–7 1:9 [a] Is. 23:1–18; Jer. 25:22; Ezek. 26:2–4; Joel 3:4–8 1:11 [a] Is. 21:11; Jer. 49:8; Ezek. 25:12–14; Mal. 1:2–5

I will not turn away its *punishment,*
Because he pursued his
[b]brother with the sword,
And cast off all pity;
His anger tore perpetually,
And he kept his wrath forever.
12 But [a]I will send a fire upon
Teman,
Which shall devour the
palaces of Bozrah."

13 Thus says the LORD:

"For three transgressions of [a]the
people of Ammon, and for four,
I will not turn away its *punishment,*
Because they ripped open the
women with child in Gilead,
That they might enlarge their
territory.
14 But I will kindle a fire in
the wall of [a]Rabbah,
And it shall devour its palaces,
[b]Amid shouting in the day of battle,
And a tempest in the day
of the whirlwind.
15 [a]Their king shall go into captivity,
He and his princes together,"
Says the LORD.

2 Thus says the LORD:

[a]"For three transgressions of
Moab, and for four,
I will not turn away its *punishment,*
Because he [b]burned the bones of
the king of Edom to lime.
2 But I will send a fire upon Moab,
And it shall devour the
palaces of [a]Kerioth;
Moab shall die with tumult,
With shouting *and* trumpet
sound.
3 And I will cut off [a]the judge
from its midst,
And slay all its princes with him,"
Says the LORD.

Judgment on Judah

4 Thus says the LORD:

"For three transgressions of
[a]Judah, and for four,
I will not turn away its *punishment,*
[b]Because they have despised
the law of the LORD,
And have not kept His
commandments.
[c]Their lies lead them astray,
Lies [d]which their fathers followed.
5 [a]But I will send a fire upon Judah,
And it shall devour the
palaces of Jerusalem."

Judgment on Israel

6 Thus says the LORD:

"For three transgressions of
[a]Israel, and for four,
I will not turn away its *punishment,*
Because [b]they sell the
righteous for silver,
And the [c]poor for a pair of sandals.
7 They pant after[1] the dust of the earth
which is on the head of the poor,
And [a]pervert the way of the humble.
[b]A man and his father go
in to the *same* girl,
[c]To defile My holy name.
8 They lie down [a]by every altar on
clothes [b]taken in pledge,
And drink the wine of the condemned
in the house of their god.

9 "Yet *it was* I *who* destroyed the
[a]Amorite before them,
Whose height *was* like the
[b]height of the cedars,
And he *was as* strong as the oaks;
Yet I [c]destroyed his fruit above
And his roots beneath.
10 Also *it was* [a]I *who* brought you
up from the land of Egypt,
And [b]led you forty years
through the wilderness,

1:11 [b] Num. 20:14–21; 2 Chr. 28:17; Obad. 10–12 **1:12** [a] Jer. 49:7, 20; Obad. 9, 10 **1:13** [a] Jer. 49:1; Ezek. 25:2; Zeph. 2:8, 9 **1:14** [a] Deut. 3:11; 1 Chr. 20:1; Jer. 49:2 [b] Ezek. 21:22; Amos 2:2 **1:15** [a] Jer. 49:3 **2:1** [a] Is. 16:1–6; Jer. 25:21; Ezek. 25:8–11; Zeph. 2:8–11 [b] 2 Kin. 3:26, 27 **2:2** [a] Jer. 48:24, 41 **2:3** [a] Num. 24:17; Jer. 48:7 **2:4** [a] 2 Kin. 17:19; Hos. 12:2; Amos 3:2 [b] Lev. 26:14 [c] Is. 9:15, 16; 28:15; Jer. 16:19; Hab. 2:18 [d] Jer. 9:14; 16:11, 12; Ezek. 20:13, 16, 18 **2:5** [a] Jer. 17:27; Hos. 8:14 **2:6** [a] Judg. 2:17–20; 2 Kin. 17:7–18; 18:12; Ezek. 22:1–13, 23–29 [b] Is. 29:21 [c] Joel 3:3; Amos 4:1; 5:11; 8:6; Mic. 2:2; 3:3 **2:7** [a] Amos 5:12 [b] Lev. 18:6–8; Ezek. 22:11 [c] Lev. 20:3; Ezek. 36:20–22 [1] Or *trample on* **2:8** [a] 1 Cor. 8:10 [b] Ex. 22:26 **2:9** [a] Gen. 15:16; Num. 21:25; Deut. 2:31; Josh. 10:12 [b] Ezek. 31:3 [c] Is. 5:24; Ezek. 17:9; [Mal. 4:1] **2:10** [a] Ex. 12:51; Amos 3:1; 9:7 [b] Deut. 2:7

To possess the land of the Amorite.
11 I raised up some of your
sons as [a]prophets,
And some of your young
men as [b]Nazirites.
Is it not so, O you children of Israel?"
Says the LORD.
12 "But you gave the Nazirites
wine to drink,
And commanded the
prophets [a]saying,
'Do not prophesy!'

13 "Behold,[a] I am weighed down by you,
As a cart full of sheaves is
weighed down.
14 [a]Therefore flight shall perish
from the swift,
The strong shall not
strengthen his power,
[b]Nor shall the mighty deliver himself;
15 He shall not stand who
handles the bow,
The swift of foot shall not escape,
Nor shall he who rides a
horse deliver himself.
16 The most courageous men of might
Shall flee naked in that day,"
Says the LORD.

Authority of the Prophet's Message

3 Hear this word that the LORD has spoken against you, O children of Israel, against the whole family which I brought up from the land of Egypt, saying:

2 "You[a] only have I known of all
the families of the earth;
[b]Therefore I will punish you
for all your iniquities."

3 Can two walk together, unless
they are agreed?
4 Will a lion roar in the forest,
when he has no prey?
Will a young lion cry out of his
den, if he has caught nothing?
5 Will a bird fall into a snare on the
earth, where there is no trap for it?
Will a snare spring up from
the earth, if it has caught
nothing at all?
6 If a trumpet is blown in a city, will
not the people be afraid?
[a]If there is calamity in a city, will
not the LORD have done *it?*

7 Surely the Lord GOD does
nothing,
Unless [a]He reveals His secret to
His servants the prophets.
8 A lion has roared!
Who will not fear?
The Lord GOD has spoken!
[a]Who can but prophesy?

Punishment of Israel's Sins

9 "Proclaim in the palaces at Ashdod,[1]
And in the palaces in the land
of Egypt, and say:
'Assemble on the mountains
of Samaria;
See great tumults in her midst,
And the oppressed within her.
10 For they [a]do not know to do right,'
Says the LORD,
'Who store up violence and
robbery in their palaces.'"

11 Therefore thus says the Lord GOD:

"An adversary *shall be* all
around the land;
He shall sap your strength
from you,
And your palaces shall be
plundered."

12 Thus says the LORD:

"As a shepherd takes from
the mouth of a lion
Two legs or a piece of an ear,
So shall the children of
Israel be taken out
Who dwell in Samaria—
In the corner of a bed and on
the edge[1] of a couch!

2:11 [a] Num. 12:6 [b] Num. 6:2, 3; Judg. 13:5 2:12 [a] Is. 30:10; Jer. 11:21; Amos 7:13, 16; Mic. 2:6 2:13 [a] Is. 1:14 2:14 [a] Jer. 46:6 [b] Ps. 33:16; Jer. 9:23 3:2 [a] [Gen. 18:19; Ex. 19:5, 6; Deut. 7:6; Ps. 147:19] [b] Jer. 14:10; Ezek. 20:36; Dan. 9:12; Matt. 11:22; [Rom. 2:9] 3:6 [a] Is. 45:7 3:7 [a] Gen. 6:13; 18:17; [Jer. 23:22]; Dan. 9:22; [John 15:15] 3:8 [a] Jer. 20:9; [Mic. 3:8]; Acts 4:20; 1 Cor. 9:16 3:9 [1] Following Masoretic Text; Septuagint reads *Assyria.* 3:10 [a] Ps. 14:4; Jer. 4:22; Amos 5:7; 6:12 3:12 [1] The Hebrew is uncertain.

13 Hear and testify against the
house of Jacob,"
Says the Lord GOD, the God of hosts,
14 "That in the day I punish Israel
for their transgressions,
I will also visit *destruction* on
the altars of [a]Bethel;
And the horns of the altar
shall be cut off
And fall to the ground.
15 I will destroy [a]the winter house
along with [b]the summer house;
The [c]houses of ivory shall perish,
And the great houses shall
have an end,"
Says the LORD.

4 Hear this word, you [a]cows of
Bashan, who *are* on the
mountain of Samaria,
Who oppress the [b]poor,
Who crush the needy,
Who say to your husbands,[1]
"Bring *wine,* let us [c]drink!"
2 [a]The Lord GOD has sworn
by His holiness:
"Behold, the days shall come upon you
When He will take you away
[b]with fishhooks,
And your posterity with fishhooks.
3 [a]You will go out *through* broken
walls,
Each one straight ahead of her,

AMOS 3:1

I AM AMOS

Hear this word that the LORD has spoken against you, O children of Israel, against the whole family which I brought up from the land of Egypt. Amos 3:1

I am the prophet Amos. I spoke boldly and harshly to Israel because their love for the Lord had grown cold. They continued to forget the kindness and mercy God had shown them for generations. I warned God's people that God would judge the nations of idolaters who have never known Him, but He would judge Israel and Judah much more harshly. God's love and protection had been toward them, but they had turned away and rejected Him. God had chosen them and given them His law, which they passed down from generation to generation. But because they were prosperous, they thought they no longer needed the God of their ancestors. For this, God disciplined Israel, just as He disciplined their neighbors. None escaped His wrath.

I warned the people, but they did not listen. Even as God sent disasters upon them, they refused to listen. Some put on a show of faith, but it was not real. Their hearts were turned from God. They stood by while justice was absent and the poor were oppressed. They considered themselves safe from God's judgment for their lack of involvement, but God judged their complacency.

I faithfully delivered God's messages, but Amaziah, the priest, ordered me to stop prophesying because he did not like the message of judgment. Amaziah told Jeroboam, king of Israel, that I was just a troublemaker who sought to start a conspiracy against the king.

But the judgment of the Lord will come whether I speak it or not, for our Lord is a God of justice and moral righteousness. However, God is merciful. He will one day restore the house of David.

†

Standing by, watching, and doing nothing as injustice and oppression thrive will not save you from the judgment of God. Dr. Martin Luther King Jr. quoted Amos 5:24 in his famous "I Have a Dream" speech. His point was that we cannot stand still. We must act in ways that glorify God in our quest to achieve a world in which all people are free from oppression.

3:14 [a] 2 Kin. 23:15; Hos. 10:5–8, 14, 15; Amos 4:4 3:15 [a] Jer. 36:22 [b] Judg. 3:20 [c] 1 Kin. 22:39; Ps. 45:8
4:1 [a] Ps. 22:12; Ezek. 39:18 [b] Amos 2:6 [c] Prov. 23:20 [1] Literally *their lords* or *their masters*
4:2 [a] Ps. 89:35 [b] Jer. 16:16; Ezek. 29:4; Hab. 1:15 4:3 [a] Ezek. 12:5

And you will be cast into Harmon,"
Says the LORD.

4 "Come[a] to Bethel and transgress,
At [b]Gilgal multiply transgression;
[c]Bring your sacrifices every morning,
[d]Your tithes every three days.[1]
5 [a]Offer a sacrifice of thanksgiving
with leaven,
Proclaim *and* announce [b]the
freewill offerings;
For this you love,
You children of Israel!"
Says the Lord GOD.

Israel Did Not Accept Correction

6 "Also I gave you cleanness of
teeth in all your cities,
And lack of bread in all your places;
[a]Yet you have not returned to Me,"
Says the LORD.

7 "I also withheld rain from you,
When *there were* still three
months to the harvest.
I made it rain on one city,
I withheld rain from another city.
One part was rained upon,
And where it did not rain
the part withered.
8 So two *or* three cities wandered to
another city to drink water,
But they were not satisfied;
Yet you have not returned to Me,"
Says the LORD.

9 "I[a] blasted you with blight and
mildew.
When your gardens increased,
Your vineyards,
Your fig trees,
And your olive trees,
[b]The locust devoured *them;*
Yet you have not returned to Me,"
Says the LORD.

10 "I sent among you a plague [a]after
the manner of Egypt;
Your young men I killed with a sword,
Along with your captive horses;
I made the stench of your camps
come up into your nostrils;
Yet you have not returned to Me,"
Says the LORD.

11 "I overthrew *some* of you,
As God overthrew [a]Sodom
and Gomorrah,
And you were like a firebrand
plucked from the burning;
Yet you have not returned to Me,"
Says the LORD.

12 "Therefore thus will I do
to you, O Israel;
Because I will do this to you,
[a]Prepare to meet your God,
O Israel!"

13 For behold,
He who forms mountains,
And creates the wind,
[a]Who declares to man what
his[1] thought *is,*
And makes the morning darkness,
[b]Who treads the high places
of the earth—
[c]The LORD God of hosts
is His name.

A Lament for Israel

5 Hear this word which I [a]take up against
you, a lamentation, O house of Israel:

2 The virgin of Israel has fallen;
She will rise no more.
She lies forsaken on her land;
There is no one to raise her up.

3For thus says the Lord GOD:

"The city that goes out by
a thousand
Shall have a hundred left,
And that which goes out by
a hundred
Shall have ten left to the
house of Israel."

4:4 [a] Ezek. 20:39; Amos 3:14 [b] Hos. 4:15 [c] Num. 28:3; Amos 5:21, 22 [d] Deut. 14:28 [1] Or *years* (compare Deuteronomy 14:28)
4:5 [a] Lev. 7:13 [b] Lev. 22:18; Deut. 12:6 4:6 [a] 2 Chr. 28:22; Is. 26:11; Jer. 5:3; Hag. 2:17 4:9 [a] Deut. 28:22; Hag. 2:17 [b] Joel 1:4, 7; Amos 7:1, 2 4:10 [a] Ex. 9:3, 6; Lev. 26:25; Deut. 28:27, 60; Ps. 78:50 4:11 [a] Gen. 19:24, 25; Deut. 29:23; Is. 13:19; Jer. 49:18; Lam. 4:6 4:12 [a] Jer. 5:22 4:13 [a] Ps. 139:2; Dan. 2:28 [b] Mic. 1:3 [c] Is. 47:4; Jer. 10:16 [1] Or *His* 5:1 [a] Jer. 7:29; 9:10, 17; Ezek. 19:1

A Call to Repentance

4For thus says the LORD to the house of Israel:

[a]"Seek Me [b]and live;
5 But do not seek [a]Bethel,
Nor enter Gilgal,
Nor pass over to [b]Beersheba;
For Gilgal shall surely go into
captivity,
And [c]Bethel shall come to nothing.
6 [a]Seek the LORD and live,
Lest He break out like fire *in*
the house of Joseph,
And devour *it*,
With no one to quench *it* in Bethel—
7 You who [a]turn justice to wormwood,
And lay righteousness to
rest in the earth!"

8 He made the [a]Pleiades and Orion;
He turns the shadow of
death into morning
[b]And makes the day dark as night;
He [c]calls for the waters of the sea
And pours them out on the
face of the earth;
[d]The LORD *is* His name.
9 He rains ruin upon the strong,
So that fury comes upon the fortress.

10 [a]They hate the one who
rebukes in the gate,
And they [b]abhor the one
who speaks uprightly.
11 [a]Therefore, because you
tread down the poor
And take grain taxes from him,
Though [b]you have built
houses of hewn stone,
Yet you shall not dwell in them;
You have planted pleasant vineyards,
But you shall not drink
wine from them.
12 For I [a]know your manifold
transgressions
And your mighty sins:
[b]Afflicting the just *and* taking bribes;
[c]Diverting the poor *from*
justice at the gate.
13 Therefore [a]the prudent keep
silent at that time,
For it *is* an evil time.

14 Seek good and not evil,
That you may live;
So the LORD God of hosts
will be with you,
[a]As you have spoken.
15 [a]Hate evil, love good;
Establish justice in the gate.
[b]It may be that the LORD God
of hosts
Will be gracious to the
remnant of Joseph.

The Day of the LORD

16Therefore the LORD God of hosts, the Lord, says this:

"*There shall be* wailing in all streets,
And they shall say in all the highways,
'Alas! Alas!'
They shall call the farmer
to mourning,
[a]And skillful lamenters to wailing.
17 In all vineyards *there shall be*
wailing,
For [a]I will pass through you,"
Says the LORD.

18 [a]Woe to you who desire the
day of the LORD!
For what good *is* [b]the day
of the LORD to you?
It *will be* darkness, and not light.
19 It *will be* [a]as though a man
fled from a lion,
And a bear met him!
Or *as though* he went into the house,
Leaned his hand on the wall,
And a serpent bit him!
20 *Is* not the day of the LORD
darkness, and not light?
Is it not very dark, with no
brightness in it?

5:4 [a] [Deut. 4:29; 2 Chr. 15:2; Jer. 29:13] [b] [Is. 55:3] 5:5 [a] 1 Kin. 12:28, 29; Amos 4:4 [b] Gen. 21:31–33; Amos 8:14 [c] Hos. 4:15 5:6 [a] [Is. 55:3, 6, 7; Amos 5:14] 5:7 [a] Amos 6:12 5:8 [a] Job 9:9; 38:31 [b] Ps. 104:20 [c] Job 38:34 [d] [Amos 4:13] 5:10 [a] Is. 29:21; 66:5; Amos 5:15 [b] 1 Kin. 22:8; Is. 59:15; Jer. 17:16–18 5:11 [a] Amos 2:6 [b] Deut. 28:30, 38, 39; Mic. 6:15; Zeph. 1:13; Hag. 1:6 5:12 [a] Hos. 5:3 [b] Is. 1:23; 5:23; Amos 2:6 [c] Is. 29:21 5:13 [a] Amos 6:10 5:14 [a] Mic. 3:11 5:15 [a] Ps. 97:10; Rom. 12:9 [b] Joel 2:14 5:16 [a] 2 Chr. 35:25; Jer. 9:17 5:17 [a] Ex. 12:12 5:18 [a] Is. 5:19; Jer. 17:15; Joel 1:15; 2:1, 11, 31 [b] Is. 5:30; Joel 2:2 5:19 [a] Job 20:24; Is. 24:17, 18; Jer. 48:44

21 "I[a] hate, I despise your feast days,
And [b]I do not savor your
sacred assemblies.
22 [a]Though you offer Me burnt offerings
and your grain offerings,
I will not accept *them,*
Nor will I regard your fattened
peace offerings.
23 Take away from Me the
noise of your songs,
For I will not hear the melody of
your stringed instruments.
24 [a]But let justice run down like
water,
And righteousness like a
mighty stream.

#OXYGEN

AMOS 5:24

Reconcile Separation with Reunion

Demand justice, but walk in righteousness. Stand with others and honor the humanity of everyone.

You just need to **breathe** and **reconcile separation with reunion.**

25 "Did[a] you offer Me sacrifices
and offerings
In the wilderness forty years,
O house of Israel?
26 You also carried Sikkuth[1] [a]your
king[2]
And Chiun,[3] your idols,
The star of your gods,
Which you made for yourselves.
27 Therefore I will send you into
captivity [a]beyond Damascus,"
Says the LORD, [b]whose name
is the God of hosts.

Warnings to Zion and Samaria

6 Woe [a]to you *who are* at [b]ease in Zion,
And [c]trust in Mount Samaria,
Notable persons in the [d]chief nation,
To whom the house of Israel comes!
2 [a]Go over to [b]Calneh and see;
And from there go to
[c]Hamath the great;
Then go down to Gath of
the Philistines.
[d]*Are you* better than these kingdoms?
Or is their territory greater
than your territory?

3 *Woe to* you who [a]put far off
the day of [b]doom,
[c]Who cause [d]the seat of
violence to come near;
4 Who lie on beds of ivory,
Stretch out on your couches,
Eat lambs from the flock
And calves from the midst of the stall;
5 [a]Who sing idly to the sound of
stringed instruments,
And invent for yourselves [b]musical
instruments [c]like David;
6 Who [a]drink wine from bowls,
And anoint yourselves with
the best ointments,
[b]But are not grieved for the
affliction of Joseph.
7 Therefore they shall now go [a]captive
as the first of the captives,
And those who recline at
banquets shall be removed.

8 [a]The Lord GOD has sworn by Himself,
The LORD God of hosts says:
"I abhor [b]the pride of Jacob,
And hate his palaces;
Therefore I will deliver up *the* city
And all that is in it."

9Then it shall come to pass, that if ten
men remain in one house, they shall die.
10And when a relative *of the dead,* with one
who will burn *the bodies,* picks up the bodies[1] to take them out of the house, he will

5:21 [a] Is. 1:11–16; Amos 4:4, 5; 8:10 [b] Lev. 26:31; Jer. 14:12; Hos. 5:6 5:22 [a] Is. 66:3; Mic. 6:6, 7 5:24 [a] Jer. 22:3; Ezek. 45:9; Hos. 6:6; Mic. 6:8 5:25 [a] Deut. 32:17; Josh. 24:14; Neh. 9:18–21; Acts 7:42, 43 5:26 [a] 1 Kin. 11:33 [1] A pagan deity [2] Septuagint and Vulgate read *tabernacle of Moloch.* [3] A pagan deity 5:27 [a] 2 Kin. 17:6; Amos 7:11, 17; Mic. 4:10 [b] Amos 4:13 6:1 [a] Luke 6:24 [b] Ps. 123:4; Is. 32:9–11; Zeph. 1:12 [c] Is. 31:1; Jer. 49:4 [d] Ex. 19:5; Amos 3:2 6:2 [a] Jer. 2:10 [b] Gen. 10:10; Is. 10:9 [c] 1 Kin. 8:65; 2 Kin. 18:34 [d] Nah. 3:8 6:3 [a] Is. 56:12; Ezek. 12:27; Amos 9:10; Matt. 24:37–39 [b] Amos 5:18 [c] Amos 5:12 [d] Ps. 94:20 6:5 [a] Is. 5:12; Amos 5:23 [b] 1 Chr. 15:16; 16:42 [c] 1 Chr. 23:5 6:6 [a] Amos 2:8; 4:1 [b] Gen. 37:25 6:7 [a] Amos 5:27 6:8 [a] Gen. 22:16; Jer. 51:14; Amos 4:2; 8:7; Heb. 6:13–17 [b] Ps. 47:4; Ezek. 24:21; Amos 8:7 6:10 [1] Literally *bones*

say to one inside the house, "*Are there* any
more with you?"
Then someone will say, "None."
And he will say, [a]"Hold your tongue!
[b]For we dare not mention the name of the
LORD."

11 For behold, [a]the LORD
gives a command:
[b]He will break the great house into bits,
And the little house into pieces.

12 Do horses run on rocks?
Does *one* plow *there* with oxen?
Yet [a]you have turned justice into gall,
And the fruit of righteousness
into wormwood,
13 You who rejoice over Lo Debar,[1]
Who say, "Have we not taken
Karnaim[2] for ourselves
By our own strength?"

14 "But, behold, [a]I will raise up
a nation against you,
O house of Israel,"
Says the LORD God of hosts;
"And they will afflict you from
the [b]entrance of Hamath
To the Valley of the Arabah."

Vision of the Locusts

7 Thus the Lord GOD showed me: Behold,
He formed locust swarms at the beginning of the late crop; indeed *it was* the late
crop after the king's mowings. 2And so it
was, when they had finished eating the
grass of the land, that I said:

"O Lord GOD, forgive, I pray!
[a]Oh, that Jacob may stand,
For he *is* small!"
3 *So* [a]the LORD relented concerning this.
"It shall not be," said the LORD.

Vision of the Fire

4Thus the Lord GOD showed me: Behold,
the Lord GOD called for conflict by fire, and
it consumed the great deep and devoured
the territory. 5Then I said:

"O Lord GOD, cease, I pray!
[a]Oh, that Jacob may stand,
For he *is* small!"
6 *So* the LORD relented concerning
this.
"This also shall not be,"
said the Lord GOD.

Vision of the Plumb Line

7Thus He showed me: Behold, the Lord
stood on a wall *made* with a plumb line,
with a plumb line in His hand. 8And the
LORD said to me, "Amos, what do you see?"
And I said, "A plumb line."
Then the Lord said:

"Behold, [a]I am setting a plumb line
In the midst of My people Israel;
[b]I will not pass by them anymore.
9 [a]The high places of Isaac
shall be desolate,
And the sanctuaries of Israel
shall be laid waste.
[b]I will rise with the sword against
the house of Jeroboam."

Amaziah's Complaint

10Then Amaziah the [a]priest of [b]Bethel
sent to [c]Jeroboam king of Israel, saying,
"Amos has conspired against you in the
midst of the house of Israel. The land is
not able to bear all his words. 11For thus
Amos has said:

'Jeroboam shall die by the sword,
And Israel shall surely be
led away [a]captive
From their own land.'"

12Then Amaziah said to Amos:

"Go, you seer!
Flee to the land of Judah.
There eat bread,
And there prophesy.
13 But [a]never again prophesy
at Bethel,
[b]For it *is* the king's sanctuary,
And it *is* the royal residence."

6:10 [a] Amos 5:13 [b] Amos 8:3 6:11 [a] Is. 55:11 [b] 2 Kin. 25:9; Amos 3:15 6:12 [a] 1 Kin. 21:7–13; Is. 59:13, 14; Hos. 10:4; Amos 5:7, 11, 12
6:13 [1] Literally *Nothing* [2] Literally *Horns,* symbol of strength 6:14 [a] Jer. 5:15 [b] Num. 34:7, 8; 1 Kin. 8:65; 2 Kin. 14:25 7:2 [a] Is. 51:19
7:3 [a] Deut. 32:36; Jer. 26:19; Hos. 11:8; Amos 5:15; Jon. 3:10; [James 5:16] 7:5 [a] Amos 7:2, 3 7:8 [a] 2 Kin. 21:13; Is. 28:17; 34:11; Lam. 2:8
[b] Mic. 7:18 7:9 [a] Gen. 46:1; Hos. 10:8; Mic. 1:5 [b] 2 Kin. 15:8–10; Amos 7:11 7:10 [a] 1 Kin. 12:31, 32; 13:33 [b] 1 Kin. 13:32;
Amos 4:4 [c] 2 Kin. 14:23 7:11 [a] Amos 5:27; 6:7 7:13 [a] Amos 2:12; Acts 4:18 [b] 1 Kin. 12:29, 32; Amos 7:9

14Then Amos answered, and said to Amaziah:

"I *was* no prophet,
Nor *was* I [a]a son of a prophet,
But I *was* a [b]sheepbreeder[1]
And a tender of sycamore fruit.
15 Then the LORD took me as
I followed the flock,
And the LORD said to me,
'Go, [a]prophesy to My people Israel.'
16 Now therefore, hear the
word of the LORD:
You say, 'Do not prophesy against Israel,
And [a]do not spout against
the house of Isaac.'

17"Therefore[a] thus says the LORD:

[b]'Your wife shall be a harlot in the city;
Your sons and daughters
shall fall by the sword;
Your land shall be divided
by *survey* line;
You shall die in a [c]defiled land;
And Israel shall surely be
led away captive
From his own land.'"

Vision of the Summer Fruit

8 Thus the Lord GOD showed me: Behold,
a basket of summer fruit. 2And He said,
"Amos, what do you see?"
So I said, "A basket of summer fruit."
Then the LORD said to me:

[a]"The end has come upon My people Israel;
[b]I will not pass by them anymore.
3 And [a]the songs of the temple
Shall be wailing in that day,"
Says the Lord GOD—
"Many dead bodies everywhere,
[b]They shall be thrown out in silence."

4 Hear this, you who swallow
up[1] the needy,
And make the poor of the land fail,

5Saying:

"When will the New Moon be past,
That we may sell grain?
And [a]the Sabbath,
That we may trade wheat?
[b]Making the ephah small
and the shekel large,
Falsifying the scales by [c]deceit,
6 That we may buy the poor for [a]silver,
And the needy for a pair of sandals—
Even sell the bad wheat?"

7 The LORD has sworn by
[a]the pride of Jacob:
"Surely [b]I will never forget
any of their works.
8 [a]Shall the land not tremble for this,
And everyone mourn who dwells in it?
All of it shall swell like the River,[1]
Heave and subside
[b]Like the River of Egypt.

9 "And it shall come to pass in that
day," says the Lord GOD,
[a]"That I will make the sun
go down at noon,
And I will darken the earth
in broad daylight;
10 I will turn your feasts into
[a]mourning,
[b]And all your songs into lamentation;
[c]I will bring sackcloth on every
waist,
And baldness on every head;
I will make it like mourning
for an only *son,*
And its end like a bitter day.

11 "Behold, the days are coming,"
says the Lord GOD,
"That I will send a famine on the land,
Not a famine of bread,
Nor a thirst for water,
But [a]of hearing the words of the LORD.
12 They shall wander from sea to sea,
And from north to east;

7:14 [a] 1 Kin. 20:35; 2 Kin. 2:5; 2 Chr. 19:2 [b] 2 Kin. 3:4; Amos 1:1; Zech. 13:5 [1] Compare 2 Kings 3:4 7:15 [a] Amos 3:8 7:16 [a] Deut. 32:2; Ezek. 21:2; Mic. 2:6 7:17 [a] Jer. 28:12; 29:21, 32 [b] Is. 13:16; Lam. 5:11; Hos. 4:13; Zech. 14:2 [c] 2 Kin. 17:6; Ezek. 4:13; Hos. 9:3 8:2 [a] Ezek. 7:2 [b] Amos 7:8 8:3 [a] Amos 5:23 [b] Amos 6:9, 10 8:4 [1] Or *trample on* (compare 2:7) 8:5 [a] Ex. 31:13–17; Neh. 13:15 [b] Mic. 6:10, 11 [c] Lev. 19:35, 36; Deut. 25:13–15 8:6 [a] Amos 2:6 8:7 [a] Deut. 33:26, 29; Ps. 68:34; Amos 6:8 [b] Ps. 10:11; Hos. 7:2; 8:13 8:8 [a] Hos. 4:3 [b] Jer. 46:7, 8; Amos 9:5 [1] That is, the Nile; some Hebrew manuscripts, Septuagint, Syriac, Targum, and Vulgate read *River;* Masoretic Text reads *the light.* 8:9 [a] Job 5:14; Is. 13:10; 59:9, 10; Jer. 15:9; [Mic. 3:6]; Matt. 27:45; Mark 15:33; Luke 23:44 8:10 [a] Lam. 5:15; Ezek. 7:18 [b] Is. 15:2, 3; Jer. 48:37; Ezek. 27:31 [c] Jer. 6:26; [Zech. 12:10] 8:11 [a] 1 Sam. 3:1; 2 Chr. 15:3; Ps. 74:9; Ezek. 7:26; Mic. 3:6

RECONCILE SEPARATION WITH REUNION

INHALE

This is a hard week. I am burying too many. I lost a parent to a disease. I lost a friend to gun violence. A coworker took his own life. I am a believer, but I'm just not sure of what happens after we die. I want to believe I'll see them again. There's an old song that says, "When we all get to heaven, what a day of rejoicing that will be." Will it, though?

EXHALE

There's no way to put into words the hurt that we feel when we lose people we love. The pain is real and strikes us to our core. It is a powerful grief that seems never to go away. However, know that God gives us peace even in the midst of the storm.

While the Bible can be challenging to understand at times, one thing is clear: believers are in the presence of God when we die. Second Corinthians 5:8 says, "We are confident, yes, well pleased rather to be absent from the body and to be present with the Lord." Jesus told the thief on the cross that he would be with Him that day (see Luke 23:43). So, this we can know for sure. But the Bible also teaches another important truth about what happens after we die: believers will be together. The Old Testament talks about believers who died as being "gathered" to their people (Gen. 49:33), and Revelation describes large gatherings of believers (see 7:9). Now, we might not know the exact details about heaven, but we know the most important details of us being with God and one another and that there will be plenty of celebration and no more tears (see Rev. 4:1—5:14; 21:1–4). That old hymn is surely right!

The Bible can sometimes leave us with questions, but remember that God gave us the Bible to provide what we need to know. There are six words in the Book of Amos that give great guidance and comfort. Amos 7:4 says, "Thus the Lord GOD showed me." That is all we need to know. The Lord God will show us all that we need to know and much of what we want to know.

They shall run to and fro, seeking
the word of the LORD,
But shall [a]not find *it.*

13 "In that day the fair virgins
And strong young men
Shall faint from thirst.
14 Those who [a]swear by [b]the
sin[1] of Samaria,
Who say,
'As your god lives, O Dan!'
And, 'As the way of [c]Beersheba lives!'
They shall fall and never rise again."

The Destruction of Israel

9 I saw the Lord standing by the altar, and He said:

"Strike the doorposts, that the
thresholds may shake,
And [a]break them on the
heads of them all.
I will slay the last of them
with the sword.
[b]He who flees from them
shall not get away,
And he who escapes from them
shall not be delivered.

2 "Though[a] they dig into hell,[1]
From there My hand shall take
them;
[b]Though they climb up to heaven,
From there I will bring them down;
3 And though they [a]hide themselves
on top of Carmel,
From there I will search
and take them;
Though they hide from My sight
at the bottom of the sea,

8:12 [a] Hos. 5:6 8:14 [a] Hos. 4:15 [b] Deut. 9:21 [c] Amos 5:5 [1] Or *Ashima,* a Syrian goddess 9:1 [a] Ps. 68:21; Hab. 3:13 [b] Amos 2:14
9:2 [a] Ps. 139:8; Jer. 23:24 [b] Job 20:6; Jer. 51:53; Obad. 4; Matt. 11:23 [1] Or *Sheol* 9:3 [a] Jer. 23:24

From there I will command the
serpent, and it shall bite them;
4 Though they go into captivity
before their enemies,
From there [a]I will command
the sword,
And it shall slay them.
[b]I will set My eyes on them for
harm and not for good."

5 The Lord GOD of hosts,
He who touches the earth
and it [a]melts,
[b]And all who dwell there mourn;
All of it shall swell like the River,[1]
And subside like the River of Egypt.
6 He who builds His [a]layers in the sky,
And has founded His
strata in the earth;
Who [b]calls for the waters of the sea,
And pours them out on the
face of the earth—
[c]The LORD *is* His name.

7 "*Are* you not like the people
of Ethiopia to Me,
O children of Israel?" says the LORD.
"Did I not bring up Israel from
the land of Egypt,
The [a]Philistines from [b]Caphtor,
And the Syrians from [c]Kir?

8 "Behold, [a]the eyes of the Lord GOD
are on the sinful kingdom,
And I [b]will destroy it from
the face of the earth;
Yet I will not utterly destroy
the house of Jacob,"
Says the LORD.

9 "For surely I will command,
And will sift the house of Israel
among all nations,
As *grain* is sifted in a sieve;
[a]Yet not the smallest grain
shall fall to the ground.
10 All the sinners of My people
shall die by the sword,
[a]Who say, 'The calamity shall not
overtake nor confront us.'

Israel Will Be Restored

11 "On[a] that day I will raise up
The tabernacle[1] of David,
which has fallen down,
And repair its damages;
I will raise up its ruins,
And rebuild it as in the days of old;
12 [a]That they may possess the
remnant of [b]Edom,[1]
And all the Gentiles who are
called by My name,"
Says the LORD who does this thing.

13 "Behold, [a]the days are coming,"
says the LORD,
"When the plowman shall
overtake the reaper,
And the treader of grapes
him who sows seed;
[b]The mountains shall drip
with sweet wine,
And all the hills shall flow *with it.*
14 [a]I will bring back the captives
of My people Israel;
[b]They shall build the waste
cities and inhabit *them;*
They shall plant vineyards and
drink wine from them;
They shall also make gardens
and eat fruit from them.
15 I will plant them in their land,
[a]And no longer shall they be
pulled up
From the land I have given them,"
Says the LORD your God.

9:4 [a] Lev. 26:33 [b] Lev. 17:10; Jer. 21:10; 39:16; 44:11 9:5 [a] Ps. 104:32; 144:5; Is. 64:1; Mic. 1:4 [b] Amos 8:8 [1] That is, the Nile 9:6 [a] Ps. 104:3, 13 [b] Amos 5:8 [c] Amos 4:13; 5:27 9:7 [a] Jer. 47:4 [b] Deut. 2:23 [c] Amos 1:5 9:8 [a] Jer. 44:27; Amos 9:4 [b] Jer. 5:10; 30:11; [Joel 2:32]; Amos 3:12; [Obad. 16, 17] 9:9 [a] [Is. 65:8–16] 9:10 [a] [Is. 28:15]; Jer. 5:12; Amos 6:3 9:11 [a] Acts 15:16–18 [1] Literally *booth,* figure of a deposed dynasty 9:12 [a] Obad. 19 [b] Num. 24:18; Is. 11:14 [1] Septuagint reads *mankind.* 9:13 [a] Lev. 26:5 [b] Joel 3:18 9:14 [a] Ps. 53:6; Is. 60:4; Jer. 30:3, 18 [b] Is. 61:4 9:15 [a] Is. 60:21; Ezek. 34:28; 37:25

THE BOOK OF

OBADIAH

OVERVIEW

The Book of Obadiah bears the name of its author. His name means "servant or worshiper of the Lord" in Hebrew. The author is considered one of the twelve minor prophets of the Old Testament. However, because several men in the Old Testament were named Obadiah, the author cannot be identified from among them with certainty. The shortest book in the Old Testament, Obadiah proclaims God's judgment on Edom for conspiring against the Israelites and promises God's future blessings for His people. The inhabitants of Edom were descendants of Esau, and the Israelites were descendants of Jacob. God viewed the nations as brothers.

There is no specific date associated with Obadiah. Based on biblical references, scholars believe the book was written after King Nebuchadnezzar's destruction of Jerusalem in 586 BC. Edom aided in that attack, looted the city, and prevented the Israelites from fleeing.

The primary message in Obadiah is God's judgment of Edom. This makes the book rather unique because even when the prophets spoke of judgment on the nations, they also addressed God's judgment on Israel. Only three prophets (Obadiah, Nahum, and Habakkuk) spoke predominately of judgment on other nations. Other books of the Bible also include references to God's judgment of Edom and other nations. However, Obadiah's focus on Edom signals God's utter displeasure with the nation for opposing His people.

Obadiah opens with a vison from God concerning Edom (see v. 1). God criticized the Edomites for being prideful and thinking they could withstand an attack (see vv. 2–4). He promised to destroy them and turn their families against them (see vv. 5–9).

God revealed that His anger against Edom resulted from their treatment of the Israelites (see vv. 10–11). When the Israelites were attacked, Edom "rejoiced over the children of Judah in the day of their destruction" (v. 12) and "cut off those among them who escaped" (v. 14). God was not pleased. He promised the Edomites would "be cut off forever" (v. 10).

Obadiah concludes with God promising Edom, "As you have done, it shall be done to you" (v. 15). He declared that the descendants of Jacob and Joseph would "devour them, and no survivor shall remain of the house of Esau" (v. 18). The final verses promise that God would destroy all the enemies of the Israelites (see vv. 19–21).

The Book of Obadiah speaks of God's anger toward Edom for going against its brother nation during a time of suffering. God judged Edom and promised to destroy the nation forever. Obadiah demonstrates that God will avenge His people and judge those who mistreat them.

BREATHE IT IN

In the Book of Obadiah, Edom is guilty of being prideful. The nation did not believe its enemies could destroy it. They thought so highly of themselves that they believed they could harm the chosen people of God, the Israelites. In response, God sent Obadiah to declare His power and His judgment against Edom for what they had done to His people.

Pride is an overly grand perception of one's abilities, worldly possessions, accomplishments, and status in life. It is a particularly detestable sin (see Prov. 6:16–19) because haughty, prideful people are preoccupied with their own importance. The proud give themselves the honor and esteem that is only due to God. Pride is sin because it does not acknowledge God's sovereignty and His preeminent role in everything that occurs.

The Bible offers many examples of individuals who suffered because of their pride. Lucifer fell because of pride (see Is. 14:12–15). God took the kingdom from Nebuchadnezzar because of pride (see Dan. 4:30–31). Because of his pride, Haman was put to death by King Ahasuerus (see Esth. 7:10).

Not only does the Bible give examples of prideful individuals, but it also speaks to how God feels about pride and how He deals with prideful people: "For the day of the LORD of hosts shall come upon everything proud and lofty, upon everything lifted up—and it shall be brought low" (Is. 2:12). "The wicked in his proud countenance does not seek God; God is in none of his thoughts" (Ps. 10:4). "Everyone proud in heart is an abomination to the LORD; though they join forces, none will go unpunished" (Prov. 16:5). "Pride goes before destruction, and a haughty spirit before a fall" (Prov. 16:18). "When pride comes, then comes shame; but with the humble is wisdom" (Prov. 11:2).

The opposite of sinful pride is godly humility, which is to be the character of all Christians. Without God, we would be nothing. All that we have and all that we are comes from His saving grace and His favor in our lives. Who are we to think ourselves worthy of praise? God is the source of all good things; we have nothing without Him.

Christians who are prideful often do not recognize this trait within them or view it as sin. Therefore, they do not realize their need to repent. But repentance is surely needed. When we operate in pride, we turn away from God and focus on ourselves, which is a form of idolatry. We erroneously believe our accomplishments are due to our efforts. This could not be further from the truth.

To rid ourselves of the spirit of pride, we must first acknowledge it and repent. Ask God to purge pride from your mind and heart and restore your relationship with Him. Learn, instead, to practice humility. Never consider yourself better than those around you. Be grateful for all God has given you. Instead of attempting to draw all attention to yourself, direct it all toward God. Let people see His goodness through the work He does in your life. Remember, pride points to self. Humility points to God.

†

THE BOOK OF

OBADIAH

The Coming Judgment on Edom

The vision of Obadiah.

Thus says the Lord GOD
[a]concerning Edom
[b](We have heard a report
from the LORD,
And a messenger has been sent
among the nations, *saying,*
"Arise, and let us rise up
against her for battle"):

2 "Behold, I will make you small
among the nations;
You shall be greatly despised.
3 The [a]pride of your heart
has deceived you,
You who dwell in the clefts
of the rock,
Whose habitation is high;
[b]*You* who say in your heart, 'Who will
bring me down to the ground?'
4 [a]Though you ascend *as*
high as the eagle,
And though you [b]set your
nest among the stars,
From there I will bring you
down," says the LORD.

5 "If [a]thieves had come to you,
If robbers by night—
Oh, how you will be cut off!—
Would they not have stolen
till they had enough?
If grape-gatherers had come
to you,
[b]Would they not have left
some gleanings?

#OXYGEN
OBADIAH VV. 2-4
Exalt His Splendid Omnipotence

God's power is everywhere, always working in us and in our world to bring about His plan for humanity. He will do what is right and good in His sight to bring us closer to Him. Let us give Him the glory for His greatness.

Breathe and **exalt His splendid omnipotence**.

6 "Oh, how Esau shall be searched
out!
How his hidden treasures
shall be sought after!
7 All the men in your confederacy
Shall force you to the border;
[a]The men at peace with you
Shall deceive you *and*
prevail against you.
Those who eat your bread
shall lay a trap[1] for you.
[b]No one is aware of it.

8 "Will[a] I not in that day," says
the LORD,
"Even destroy the wise
men from Edom,
And understanding from the
mountains of Esau?
9 Then your [a]mighty men, O [b]Teman,
shall be dismayed,

---

1 [a] Is. 21:11; Ezek. 25:12; Joel 3:19; Mal. 1:3 [b] Jer. 49:14–16; Obad. 1–4 3 [a] Is. 16:6; Jer. 49:16 [b] Is. 14:13–15; Rev. 18:7 4 [a] Job 20:6 [b] Hab. 2:9; Mal. 1:4 5 [a] Jer. 49:9 [b] Deut. 24:21 7 [a] Jer. 38:22 [b] Is. 19:11; Jer. 49:7 [1] Or *wound,* or *plot* 8 [a] [Job 5:12–14]; Is. 29:14 9 [a] Ps. 76:5 [b] Gen. 36:11; 1 Chr. 1:45; Job 2:11; Jer. 49:7

RELEASE // EXALT HIS SPLENDID OMNIPOTENCE

Good Will Win

Obadiah vv. 17–18 //"But on Mount Zion there shall be deliverance, and there shall be holiness; the house of Jacob shall possess their possessions. The house of Jacob shall be a fire, and the house of Joseph a flame; but the house of Esau shall be stubble; they shall kindle them and devour them, and no survivor shall remain of the house of Esau," for the LORD has spoken.

Summary Message //Our world is broken. At times, it can feel like the good side is losing and the bad side is winning by a wide margin. It can be discouraging to watch evil people around us seem to win. But looks can be deceiving, and their worldly success is only temporary. Let us remember that God has unlimited power. Nothing is impossible for Him.

Obadiah is the shortest book in the Old Testament, consisting of only one chapter. But inside its twenty-one verses we see our Creator's omnipotence on display. Obadiah's prophetic vision shares the fall of the nation of Edom, relatives of Israel accused of sinful pride and poor treatment of God's people. The Edomites thought they were greater than they really were. As a result, they mocked, stole from, and harmed God's chosen people. This book ends with a promise of redemption for the people of Israel and destruction for the prideful Edomites.

Practical Application //God sent Obadiah, whose name meant "worshiper of Yahweh," to warn the Edomites of their destructive pride. We love stories like this in which we see oppressors get a taste of their own medicine. But let us put the spotlight on ourselves for a minute. The Edomites' sin started with pride, and we have all struggled with pride at some point too. Pridefully, we might think we are more talented than our coworkers, smarter than our family members, better looking than our friends, or stronger than everyone else in the gym. Pride creeps up in little ways and can soon become a beast. This account of the Edomites reminds us of the consequences of living in a self-serving way—following our feelings and desires without thinking about their effect on those around us.

Many of us have experienced some injustice or know someone who has. This story encourages us that divine justice is coming. God cares for His people when they suffer. Throughout Scripture, God warns that eventual judgment is coming for those who persecute His people. God will give victory to His faithful ones. At the same time, we can learn from this book that we should not take joy in the downfall of our enemies. God's judgment is intended to bring repentance because He cares for all people. We still need to show love to all, including those we consider undeserving.

Fervent Prayer //Heavenly Father, thank You for Your unlimited power that can turn any situation around. Forgive us for the moments we have doubted Your strength. We are sorry for the times we have been prideful and celebrated the losses of our enemies. Help us to learn to trust You and Your divine timing and justice. Give us new vision to see situations through Your eyes. In Jesus' name we pray. Amen.

To the end that everyone from
the mountains of Esau
May be cut off by slaughter.

Edom Mistreated His Brother

10 "For [a]violence against your
brother Jacob,
Shame shall cover you,
And [b]you shall be cut off
forever.

11 In the day that you [a]stood
on the other side—
In the day that strangers carried
captive his forces,
When foreigners entered his gates
And [b]cast lots for Jerusalem—
Even you *were* as one of them.

12 "But you should not have [a]gazed
on the day of your brother

10 [a] Gen. 27:41; Ezek. 25:12; Amos 1:11 [b] Ezek. 35:9; Joel 3:19 11 [a] Ps. 83:5–8; Amos 1:6, 9 [b] Joel 3:3; Nah. 3:10
12 [a] Mic. 4:11; 7:10

In the day of his captivity;[1]
Nor should you have [b]rejoiced
over the children of Judah
In the day of their destruction;
Nor should you have spoken proudly
In the day of distress.
13 You should not have entered
the gate of My people
In the day of their calamity.
Indeed, you should not have
gazed on their affliction
In the day of their calamity,
Nor laid *hands* on their substance
In the day of their calamity.
14 You should not have stood
at the crossroads
To cut off those among
them who escaped;
Nor should you have delivered up
those among them who remained
In the day of distress.

15 "For[a] the day of the LORD upon
all the nations *is* near;
[b]As you have done, it shall
be done to you;
Your reprisal shall return
upon your own head.
16 [a]For as you drank on My
holy mountain,
So shall all the nations
drink continually;
Yes, they shall drink, and swallow,
And they shall be as though
they had never been.

Israel's Final Triumph

17 "But on Mount Zion there
[a]shall be deliverance,
And there shall be holiness;
The house of Jacob shall possess
their possessions.
18 The house of Jacob shall be a fire,
And the house of Joseph [a]a flame;
But the house of Esau *shall be* stubble;
They shall kindle them
and devour them,
And no survivor shall *remain*
of the house of Esau,"
For the LORD has spoken.

19 The South[1] [a]shall possess the
mountains of Esau,
[b]And the Lowland shall
possess Philistia.
They shall possess the
fields of Ephraim
And the fields of Samaria.
Benjamin *shall possess* Gilead.
20 And the captives of this host
of the children of Israel
Shall possess the land of the Canaanites
As [a]far as Zarephath.
The captives of Jerusalem
who are in Sepharad
[b]Shall possess the cities of the South.[1]
21 Then [a]saviors[1] shall come
to Mount Zion
To judge the mountains of Esau,
And the [b]kingdom shall be
the LORD's.

---

12 [b] [Prov. 17:5]; Ezek. 35:15; 36:5 [1] Literally *On the day he became a foreigner* 15 [a] Ezek. 30:3; [Joel 1:15; 2:1, 11, 31; Amos 5:18, 20] [b] Jer. 50:29; 51:56; Hab. 2:8 16 [a] Joel 3:17 17 [a] Is. 14:1, 2; Joel 2:32; Amos 9:8 18 [a] Is. 5:24; 9:18, 19; Zech. 12:6 19 [a] Is. 11:14; Amos 9:12 [b] Zeph. 2:7 [1] Hebrew *Negev* 20 [a] 1 Kin. 17:9; Luke 4:26 [b] Jer. 32:44 [1] Hebrew *Negev* 21 [a] [James 5:20] [b] Ps. 22:28; [Dan. 2:44; 7:14; Zech. 14:9; Rev. 11:15] [1] Or *deliverers*

THE BOOK OF

JONAH

OVERVIEW

The Book of Jonah does not identify its author, but it bears the name of its subject, the prophet Jonah. The name Jonah means "dove" in Hebrew. As one of the minor prophets, Jonah was called by God to deliver a message to the city of Nineveh, the capital of Assyria and enemy of Israel. Jonah was active in ministry between 800 and 750 BC.

The popular story of Jonah centers largely on the theme of obedience. When the book opens, God commands Jonah to go to Nineveh to deliver a message from Him (see Jon. 1:1–2). Instead of doing as he was instructed, "Jonah arose to flee to Tarshish from the presence of the LORD" (v. 3). He boarded a ship heading the opposite direction from Nineveh, but God sent a storm to stop him. Afraid for their safety, the ship's crew questioned Jonah. When he revealed that he was a prophet running from God, they were troubled. To remain safe from the storm, they threw Jonah overboard by his instruction (see vv. 4–13). At once, "the sea ceased from its raging" (v. 15).

Having been thrown overboard in the raging seas, Jonah would have died had God not sent a fish to swallow Jonah to preserve his life. The wayward prophet then spent three days and three nights "in the belly of the fish" (v. 17). During this time, Jonah prayed to God asking for mercy (see 2:1–9). God spoke to the fish, and "it vomited Jonah onto dry land" (v. 10). In the New Testament, Jesus notes that Jonah's three-day experience in the belly of the fish was a foreshadowing of the three days He would spend in the grave before His resurrection (see Matt. 12:39–41).

After the fish released Jonah, God commanded Jonah a second time to preach to the people of Nineveh. This time, Jonah obeyed (see Jon. 3:1–3). When he arrived, he proclaimed that the nation would be overthrown in forty days (see v. 4). The people of Nineveh believed the prophecy. They "turned from their evil way; and God relented from the disaster" He had planned (v. 10). Jonah, however, became angry because God did not punish the enemies of the Israelites (see 4:1). He pleaded with God to take his life, and God chastised Jonah (see vv. 3–4). God told Jonah that He had a right to "pity Nineveh" (v. 11).

In the Book of Jonah, the prophet was displeased with God's decision to extend mercy to a nation other than Israel. Jonah disobediently fled in an effort to avoid delivering the message. God made his journey difficult, and Jonah eventually delivered the message God sent to the Assyrians. After he delivered it, Jonah became angry that God withheld His judgment and spared the people. God reminded Jonah of His sovereignty, demonstrating that He is the God of all people, and He can extend grace to whomever He chooses. The Book of Jonah is a reminder that God shows compassion to all people.

BREATHE IT IN

The prophet Jonah dared to disobey God's instructions to preach to the people of Nineveh. But his disobedience did not get him very far, and he eventually delivered God's message of destruction in Nineveh. When the people received the word and repented, God spared them. This angered Jonah, who did not understand why God would show mercy to Israel's enemies.

Jonah's angry response to God extending mercy to the Assyrians was selfish. He wanted God to be the God of the Israelites only. He wanted to preach and prophesy mercy and grace only to the Israelites. Out of anger, Jonah even wished death upon himself when God spared the people of Nineveh. He wanted to keep God all to himself and his people.

God, though, desires that all people repent and receive salvation. He created all humanity and is no respecter of persons. God extends His mercy to all who are willing to receive it. Salvation is by faith, not by works. Now, like in Jonah's day, God continues to extend mercy and grace to all. His salvation is free to all who confess their sins, believe in Jesus' sacrifice, and trust in Him.

Have you ever been angered by what God is doing in the lives of those around you? Have you questioned why God blessed others in a particular way and not you? Have you compared yourself to them and determined yourself worthier of the blessing? Have you treated them begrudgingly or talked negatively about them? Have you become angry with God and refused to follow His instruction because of your displeasure?

Hopefully, the answer to these questions is no. As Christians, we should rejoice and celebrate along with others who receive God's blessings and to whom He extends His mercy. We should be excited for them and keep encouraging them. We should not covet God's favor only for ourselves; we should be glad that God blesses all. Instead of questioning God about why and how He chooses to operate in others' lives, we should look at our own lives. We must ask if we pull away from God when our desires do not match His instructions. We must admit when we let our desires get the best of us and disobey Him.

When Jonah followed his plan instead of the plan God set before him, he was caught in the middle of a storm. What storms has God sent into your life to get you back on track? Did the storms blow on your family or your finances? Did they toss and turn your relationships? Did they uproot the anger and jealousy in your life?

Whenever you find yourself in a storm, consider what its source might be. Reflect on your thoughts, words, and deeds. Repent of any sins. Tell God you are willing for Him to use you in whatever way He sees fit. Align your desires with His plans. Have a humble heart. Do not resist His instruction. No matter what He commands, your response to Him should always be, "Here I am, Lord, send me!"

†

THE BOOK OF

JONAH

Jonah's Disobedience

1 Now the word of the LORD came to [a]Jo-
nah the son of Amittai, saying, 2“Arise,
go to [a]Nineveh, that [b]great city, and cry out
against it; for [c]their wickedness has come
up before Me.” 3But Jonah arose to flee to
Tarshish from the presence of the LORD.
He went down to [a]Joppa, and found a ship
going to Tarshish; so he paid the fare, and
went down into it, to go with them to [b]Tar-
shish [c]from the presence of the LORD.

The Storm at Sea

4But [a]the LORD sent out a great wind on
the sea, and there was a mighty tempest
on the sea, so that the ship was about to
be broken up.
5Then the mariners were afraid; and every man cried out to his god, and threw the
cargo that *was* in the ship into the sea, to
lighten the load.[1] But Jonah had gone down
[a]into the lowest parts of the ship, had lain
down, and was fast asleep.
6So the captain came to him, and said
to him, “What do you mean, sleeper? Arise,
[a]call on your God; [b]perhaps your God will
consider us, so that we may not perish.”
7And they said to one another, “Come, let
us [a]cast lots, that we may know for whose
cause this trouble *has come* upon us.” So
they cast lots, and the lot fell on Jonah.
8Then they said to him, [a]“Please tell us!
For whose cause *is* this trouble upon us?
What is your occupation? And where do you
come from? What is your country? And of
what people are you?”
9So he said to them, “I *am* a Hebrew; and
I fear the LORD, the God of heaven, [a]who
made the sea and the dry *land*.”

Jonah Thrown into the Sea

10Then the men were exceedingly afraid,
and said to him, “Why have you done this?”
For the men knew that he fled from the
presence of the LORD, because he had told
them. 11Then they said to him, “What shall
we do to you that the sea may be calm for
us?”—for the sea was growing more tempestuous.
12And he said to them, [a]“Pick me up and
throw me into the sea; then the sea will
become calm for you. For I know that this
great tempest *is* because of me.”
13Nevertheless the men rowed hard to
return to land, [a]but they could not, for the
sea continued to grow more tempestuous
against them. 14Therefore they cried out
to the LORD and said, “We pray, O LORD,
please do not let us perish for this man's
life, and [a]do not charge us with innocent blood; for You, O LORD, [b]have done
as it pleased You.” 15So they picked up
Jonah and threw him into the sea, [a]and
the sea ceased from its raging. 16Then
the men [a]feared the LORD exceedingly,
and offered a sacrifice to the LORD and
took vows.

Jonah's Prayer and Deliverance

17Now the LORD had prepared a great fish
to swallow Jonah. And [a]Jonah was in the
belly of the fish three days and three nights.
2 Then Jonah prayed to the LORD his God
from the fish's belly. 2And he said:

1:1 [a] 2 Kin. 14:25; Matt. 12:39–41; 16:4; Luke 11:29, 30, 32 1:2 [a] Is. 37:37 [b] Gen. 10:11, 12; 2 Kin. 19:36; Jon. 4:11; Nah. 1:1; Zeph. 2:13 [c] Gen. 18:20; Hos. 7:2 1:3 [a] Josh. 19:46; 2 Chr. 2:16; Ezra 3:7; Acts 9:36, 43 [b] Is. 23:1 [c] Gen. 4:16; Job 1:12; 2:7 1:4 [a] Ps. 107:25 1:5 [a] 1 Sam. 24:3 [1] Literally *from upon them* 1:6 [a] Ps. 107:28 [b] Joel 2:14 1:7 [a] Josh. 7:14; 1 Sam. 14:41, 42; Prov. 16:33 1:8 [a] Josh. 7:19; 1 Sam. 14:43 1:9 [a] [Neh. 9:6]; Ps. 146:6; Acts 17:24 1:12 [a] John 11:50 1:13 [a] [Prov. 21:30] 1:14 [a] Deut. 21:8 [b] Ps. 115:3; [Dan. 4:35] 1:15 [a] [Ps. 89:9; 107:29]; Luke 8:24 1:16 [a] Mark 4:41; Acts 5:11 1:17 [a] [Matt. 12:40; Luke 11:30]

"I [a]cried out to the LORD
because of my affliction,
[b]And He answered me.

"Out of the belly of Sheol I cried,
And You heard my voice.
3 [a]For You cast me into the deep,
Into the heart of the seas,
And the floods surrounded me;
[b]All Your billows and Your
waves passed over me.
4 [a]Then I said, 'I have been cast
out of Your sight;
Yet I will look again [b]toward
Your holy temple.'
5 The [a]waters surrounded
me, *even* to my soul;
The deep closed around me;
Weeds were wrapped around my head.
6 I went down to the moorings
of the mountains;
The earth with its bars *closed*
behind me forever;
Yet You have brought up my
[a]life from the pit,
O LORD, my God.

7 "When my soul fainted within me,
I remembered the LORD;
[a]And my prayer went *up* to You,
Into Your holy temple.

8 "Those who regard [a]worthless idols
Forsake their own Mercy.
9 But I will [a]sacrifice to You
With the voice of thanksgiving;
I will pay what I have [b]vowed.
[c]Salvation *is* of the [d]LORD."

10So the LORD spoke to the fish, and it
vomited Jonah onto dry *land*.

Jonah Preaches at Nineveh

3 Now the word of the LORD came to Jonah the second time, saying, 2"Arise,
go to Nineveh, that great city, and preach
to it the message that I tell you." 3So Jonah
arose and went to Nineveh, according to
the word of the LORD. Now Nineveh was an
exceedingly great city, a three-day journey[1]
in extent. 4And Jonah began to enter the
city on the first day's walk. Then [a]he cried
out and said, "Yet forty days, and Nineveh
shall be overthrown!"

The People of Nineveh Believe

5So the [a]people of Nineveh believed God,
proclaimed a fast, and put on sackcloth,
from the greatest to the least of them. 6Then
word came to the king of Nineveh; and he
arose from his throne and laid aside his robe,
covered *himself* with sackcloth [a]and sat in
ashes. 7[a]And he caused *it* to be proclaimed
and published throughout Nineveh by the
decree of the king and his nobles, saying,

Let neither man nor beast, herd nor
flock, taste anything; do not let them
eat, or drink water. 8But let man and
beast be covered with sackcloth, and
cry mightily to God; yes, [a]let every one
turn from his evil way and from [b]the
violence that is in his hands. 9[a]Who can
tell *if* God will turn and relent, and turn
away from His fierce anger, so that we
may not perish?

10[a]Then God saw their works, that they
turned from their evil way; and God relented
from the disaster that He had said He would
bring upon them, and He did not do it.

#OXYGEN

JONAH 3:10

Exalt His Splendid Omnipotence

Even when it may seem like others deserve adversity, trust God's unlimited power to right all wrongs. Our God is not limited in His ability to turn hearts and alter situations. Trust Him to change other people. You are called to love them.

Breathe and exalt His splendid omnipotence.

2:2 [a] 1 Sam. 30:6; Ps. 120:1; Lam. 3:55 [b] Ps. 65:2 2:3 [a] Ps. 88:6 [b] Ps. 42:7 2:4 [a] Ps. 31:22; Jer. 7:15 [b] 1 Kin. 8:38; 2 Chr. 6:38; Ps. 5:7 2:5 [a] Ps. 69:1; Lam. 3:54 2:6 [a] Job 33:28; [Ps. 16:10; Is. 38:17] 2:7 [a] 2 Chr. 30:27; Ps. 18:6 2:8 [a] 2 Kin. 17:15; Ps. 31:6; Jer. 10:8 2:9 [a] Ps. 50:14, 23; Jer. 33:11; Hos. 14:2 [b] Job 22:27; [Eccl. 5:4, 5] [c] Ps. 3:8; [Is. 45:17] [d] [Jer. 3:23] 3:3 [1] Exact meaning unknown 3:4 [a] [Deut. 18:22] 3:5 [a] [Matt. 12:41; Luke 11:32] 3:6 [a] Job 2:8 3:7 [a] 2 Chr. 20:3; Dan. 3:29; Joel 2:15 3:8 [a] Is. 58:6 [b] Is. 59:6 3:9 [a] 2 Sam. 12:22; Joel 2:14; Amos 5:15 3:10 [a] Ex. 32:14; Jer. 18:8; Amos 7:3, 6

EXALT HIS SPLENDID OMNIPOTENCE

INHALE

I believe God can do anything except fail. I haven't seen proof of it in my life, though. It seems that my people and I face continual issues without answers. If God's power is complete, then Black and Brown people should not have to struggle as they do. I struggle with being judged by the color of my skin instead of the content of my character. If God is all-powerful, then why was slavery a thing? Why are we no better off all these years later? How can I believe God is omnipotent when He doesn't end the inequity?

EXHALE

These are legitimate, fair questions regarding racial inequality. There are obviously many things in the world that either don't make sense or are just downright unfair. Understanding the lot of humanity has always kept the human race up at night. But we must find a way to rest.

God is indeed all-powerful. He can do anything that does not go against who He is. So, you're right that He cannot fail. He cannot sin either. But He has limitless power to do all that He pleases. That doesn't mean, though, that He pleases to do everything. Much of what He can do, He chooses not to do. We might not be able to understand why, but this much we know.

Just as God's power is limitless, His mind is a mystery and so much greater than our limited understanding can ever grasp. Even if we cannot understand situations in the world, we can rest assured that God is working all things for our good. The fact that we cannot understand doesn't negate this truth. Nothing in this life is an accident. All is a part of the plan and purpose of God. In the Old Testament, God's people, Israel, went through very difficult and hideously unfair treatment. God was not powerless or careless about His people, though. And in Scripture, we see how God brought Israel through their difficulties and how they refined them. Sometimes, like Israel, we will be able to see why our all-powerful God let us go through adversity. Other times, we will not. But either way, we persevere and trust.

The story of Jonah can help us as we strive to understand. Jonah found himself in the midst of a raging sea. There seemed no way for him to avoid death, but God saved Jonah through the belly of a fish. Our omnipotent God sent a fish to save a man! Jonah 2:10 says, "So the LORD spoke to the fish, and it vomited Jonah onto dry land." That is the power of God. Even in our raging sea of life God can protect us and place us on dry land.

Jonah's Anger and God's Kindness

4 But it displeased Jonah exceedingly,
and he became angry. 2So he prayed to
the LORD, and said, "Ah, LORD, was not this
what I said when I was still in my country?
Therefore I [a]fled previously to Tarshish; for
I know that You *are* a [b]gracious and merciful God, slow to anger and abundant in
lovingkindness, One who relents from doing harm. 3[a]Therefore now, O LORD, please
take my life from me, for [b]*it is* better for me
to die than to live!"
4Then the LORD said, "*Is it* right for you
to be angry?"
5So Jonah went out of the city and sat
on the east side of the city. There he made
himself a shelter and sat under it in the
shade, till he might see what would become
of the city. 6And the LORD God prepared a
plant[1] and made it come up over Jonah,
that it might be shade for his head to deliver him from his misery. So Jonah was
very grateful for the plant. 7But as morning dawned the next day God prepared a
worm, and it *so* damaged the plant that it
withered. 8And it happened, when the sun
arose, that God prepared a vehement east
wind; and the sun beat on Jonah's head, so

4:2 [a] Jon. 1:3 [b] Ex. 34:6; Num. 14:18; Ps. 86:5, 15; Joel 2:13 4:3 [a] 1 Kin. 19:4; Job 6:8, 9 [b] Jon. 4:8
4:6 [1] Hebrew *kikayon*, exact identity unknown

that he grew faint. Then he wished death
for himself, and said, [a]"*It is* better for me
to die than to live."
9Then God said to Jonah, "*Is it* right for
you to be angry about the plant?"
And he said, "*It is* right for me to be angry, even to death!"
10But the LORD said, "You have had pity
on the plant for which you have not labored, nor made it grow, which came up
in a night and perished in a night. 11And
should I not pity Nineveh, [a]that great city,
in which are more than one hundred and
twenty thousand persons [b]who cannot discern between their right hand and their
left—and much livestock?"

JONAH 4:1

I AM JONAH

But it displeased Jonah exceedingly, and he became angry. Jonah 4:1

I am the prophet Jonah, son of Amittai. I tried to run from God because I did not want to deliver the word He gave me for the wicked people of Nineveh. I boarded a boat and headed away from Nineveh to avoid God's call. But a great wind arose on the sea and the boat nearly broke apart. The sailors cast lots to find out who was responsible for this calamity. When the lot fell to me, the sailors began to question me, and I had to admit that I was running from God. They asked me what needed to be done to make the sea calm. I told them to throw me overboard, but they did not want to be accountable for my death, so they tried to row to shore. The storm grew wilder, so they asked my God's forgiveness and threw me overboard. Immediately the sea grew calm, and the sailors fearfully made vows to God.

I was swallowed by a big fish and remained in his belly, praying for three days and three nights. Finally, the fish vomited me onto the shore. Then the Lord gave me the same command He had before: go to Nineveh and preach against the people because of their wicked ways. This time I obeyed the Lord. I began proclaiming that disaster would come upon them in forty days. All the people immediately repented, fasted, and put on sackcloth. Even the king of Nineveh put on sackcloth and sat down in the dust.

When the Lord saw that they repented and gave up their evil ways, He did not bring punishment upon them. I was angry with God because He had simply forgiven them. I argued with Him. But God showed me that He answers the prayers of those who call upon Him, just as He answered my prayers to be saved from the belly of the fish after I had disobeyed Him.

†

Sometimes, we want to see others punished for their wrongdoing or the wrongdoing of their family members or ancestors. But continued condemnation should be replaced with forgiveness, particularly if they are truly repentant and taking steps to live differently. Consider where you would be if God did not have such a great capacity for forgiveness toward all.

4:8 [a] Jon. 4:3 4:11 [a] Jon. 1:2; 3:2, 3 [b] Deut. 1:39; Is. 7:16

THE BOOK OF

MICAH

OVERVIEW

The Book of Micah bears the name of its author. Micah is a shortened version of the name Micaiah, a Hebrew name that means "Who is like Yahweh?" Micah was a minor prophet whose ministry covered several years between 740 and 696 BC. (He is not to be confused with the prophet Micaiah who prophesied in the northern kingdom during the rule of King Ahab. See 1 Kin. 22 and 2 Chr. 18.) Scholars believe Micah was written between 735 and 701 BC. His message declared judgment on the Israelites for combining their worship of God with the worship of idols.

Micah prophesied during the period when the Assyrians invaded Israel and Judah. His ministry covered the reigns of Jotham (750–735 BC), Ahaz (735–715 BC), and Hezekiah (715–686 BC). His contemporaries were the prophets Isaiah, Amos, and Hosea. Micah prophesied to the people of Judah and its leaders.

The book opens with the announcement of God's judgment upon Israel (see Mic. 1:2–7). The prophet mourned for the people because of God's inevitable judgment (see vv. 8–16), and he called out the evildoers, "those who devise iniquity" (2:1) and "covet fields and take them by violence" (v. 2). He declared that God was "devising disaster" against them (v. 3). Micah promised that God would protect a remnant and restore His people after judgment (see v. 12).

Chapter 3 details God's plans to deal with wicked rulers and prophets. Micah accused the rulers of mistreating the people (see vv. 1–4) and taking bribes (see vv. 8–12). He accused the prophets of lying to people for financial gain and declared God's plan to strip them of their prophetic calling (see vv. 5–7).

In addition to delivering the message of judgment, Micah offered a message of hope. He declared, "It shall come to pass in the latter days that the mountain of the LORD's house shall be established" (4:1) and that God would "redeem" His people from the hand of their enemies (v. 10).

The Book of Micah contains a detailed prophecy of Jesus Christ, identifying Bethlehem as His birthplace (see 5:2). Micah identifies Jesus as the King under whose power the Israelites would experience safety and peace (see vv. 3–5).

Chapter 6 begins with a reminder of God's faithfulness to the Israelites (see vv. 1–5). Micah outlines that God requires His people "to do justly, to love mercy, and to walk humbly" with Him (v. 8). In the last chapter, Micah prays for God's protection and rejoices in His plan for salvation (see 7:14–20).

The Book of Micah describes God's disdain of spiritual and social corruption. The prophet Micah chastised the priests and the prophets for charging to perform their religious duties and condemned the rich for oppressing the poor. He declared God's judgment on the people and encouraged them to repent and follow God's requirements of living with justice, mercy, and humility. Micah foretold the birth of Jesus and reminded the Israelites of God's promise of restoration and blessings.

BREATHE IT IN

The prophet Micah prophesied to the people of Judah concerning their corrupt practices. Instead of living according to God's covenant, they practiced idolatry. The priests and the prophets charged the people to perform their spiritual duties, and the society denied justice to the poor. God was not pleased with their actions, so He sent Micah to declare His judgment and call for them to repent.

No man or woman is perfect, including Christians. We are all imperfect creatures who serve a perfect God who loves us and continuously forgives us of our sins in Christ. Just because we stand forgiven in Christ, though, does not mean we can take our sins lightly. Such an attitude reveals a lack of understanding and appreciation of the gospel. Instead, we are to confess our sins continually and desire to sin no more.

Our hearts reveal our motives. When God searches our hearts, they reveal why we think and act in certain ways. There is nothing hidden from God. He knows the good, the bad, and the ugly. He sees our deepest desires. He knows our pain and fears. He is privy to our thoughts about others. He knows our intentions.

When God sent Micah to prophesy to Judah, the people's intentions were not pure. They purposely mistreated the poor and greedily charged the people for access to religious observances. They knew this was wrong, but they did it anyway. They had no intention to repent; this had become a way of life for them. This behavior placed a wedge between them and God.

In Micah 3:4, the prophet declares, "Then they will cry to the LORD, but He will not hear them; He will even hide His face from them at that time, because they have been evil in their deeds." In this verse, God made it clear that He is separated from evil. Therefore, because of the Israelites' intentional evil practices, He would not hear from them. They were no longer in a position to call on Him and be heard because they had turned away from what is right and just.

As Christians, if we intentionally practice evil and ignore our covenant with God, our positioning with God shifts. Even though He hears our prayers at those times, He may not be moved because He knows what is in our hearts. To get back into the right position with God, we must confess our sins. We must come to Him through Jesus, who paid the price for all our sins. Through Jesus, we can start anew with a clean heart whenever we sin against God.

What does God see in your heart? Do you consider your motives and intentions before acting? If not, in all you do, your intent should be to honor God, who does not judge based on outward appearances. He judges based on what is in the hearts of His people.

Ask God to give you a clean heart, a heart that seeks after Him. If you are sincere, He will hear you and encourage you. When you are in right position with God but your intentions are misguided, He will correct you. Fill your heart with love, mercy, and humility, for "He has shown you, O man, what is good; and what . . . the LORD [requires] of you" (6:8).

†

THE BOOK OF

MICAH

1 The word of the LORD that came to [a]Micah of Moresheth in the days of [b]Jotham, Ahaz, *and* Hezekiah, kings of Judah, which he saw concerning Samaria and Jerusalem.

The Coming Judgment on Israel

2 Hear, all you peoples!
Listen, O earth, and all that is in it!
Let the Lord GOD be a
witness against you,
The Lord from [a]His holy temple.

3 For behold, the LORD is coming
out of His place;
He will come down
And tread on the high
places of the earth.
4 [a]The mountains will melt under Him,
And the valleys will split
Like wax before the fire,
Like waters poured down
a steep place.
5 All this is for the transgression
of Jacob
And for the sins of the house of Israel.
What *is* the transgression of Jacob?
Is it not Samaria?
And what *are* the [a]high
places of Judah?
Are they not Jerusalem?

6 "Therefore I will make Samaria [a]a
heap of ruins in the field,
Places for planting a vineyard;
I will pour down her stones
into the valley,
And I will [b]uncover her foundations.
7 All her carved images shall
be beaten to pieces,
And all her [a]pay as a harlot shall
be burned with the fire;
All her idols I will lay desolate,
For she gathered *it* from
the pay of a harlot,
And they shall return to the
[b]pay of a harlot."

Mourning for Israel and Judah

8 Therefore I will wail and howl,
I will go stripped and naked;
[a]I will make a wailing like the jackals
And a mourning like the ostriches,
9 For her wounds *are* incurable.
For [a]it has come to Judah;
It has come to the gate of My people—
To Jerusalem.

10 [a]Tell *it* not in Gath,
Weep not at all;
In Beth Aphrah[1]
Roll yourself in the dust.
11 Pass by in naked shame, you
inhabitant of Shaphir;
The inhabitant of Zaanan[1]
does not go out.
Beth Ezel mourns;
Its place to stand is taken
away from you.

12 For the inhabitant of Maroth
pined[1] for good,
But [a]disaster came down
from the LORD
To the gate of Jerusalem.

1:1 [a] [2 Pet. 1:21]; Jer. 26:18 [b] 2 Kin. 15:5, 7, 32–38; 2 Chr. 27:1–9; Is. 1:1; Hos. 1:1 1:2 [a] [Ps. 11:4] 1:4 [a] Amos 9:5 1:5 [a] Deut. 32:13; 33:29; Amos 4:13 1:6 [a] 2 Kin. 19:25; Mic. 3:12 [b] Ezek. 13:14 1:7 [a] Hos. 2:5 [b] Deut. 23:18; Is. 23:17 1:8 [a] Ps. 102:6 1:9 [a] 2 Kin. 18:13; Is. 8:7, 8 1:10 [a] 2 Sam. 1:20 [1] Literally *House of Dust* 1:11 [1] Literally *Going Out* 1:12 [a] Is. 59:9–11; Jer. 14:19; Amos 3:6 [1] Literally *was sick*

13 O inhabitant of [a]Lachish,
Harness the chariot to the swift
steeds
(She *was* the beginning of sin
to the daughter of Zion),
For the transgressions of Israel
were [b]found in you.

14 Therefore you shall [a]give presents
to Moresheth Gath;[1]
The houses of [b]Achzib[2] *shall be*
a lie to the kings of Israel.
15 I will yet bring an heir to you,
O inhabitant of [a]Mareshah;[1]
The glory of Israel shall
come to [b]Adullam.
16 Make yourself [a]bald and
cut off your hair,
Because of your [b]precious
children;
Enlarge your baldness like an eagle,
For they shall go from you
into [c]captivity.

Woe to Evildoers

2 Woe to those who devise iniquity,
And work out evil on their beds!
At [a]morning light they practice it,
Because it is in the power
of their hand.
2 They [a]covet fields and take
them by violence,
Also houses, and seize *them*.
So they oppress a man and
his house,
A man and his inheritance.

3 Therefore thus says the LORD:

"Behold, against this [a]family I
am devising [b]disaster,
From which you cannot
remove your necks;
Nor shall you walk haughtily,
For this *is* an evil time.
4 In that day *one* shall take up
a proverb against you,

MICAH 1:2

I AM MICAH

Hear, all you peoples! Listen, O earth, and all that is in it! Let the Lord GOD be a witness against you, the Lord from His holy temple. Micah 1:2

I am the prophet Micah. After the death of King Solomon, Israel was divided into two kingdoms: Judah and Israel. Jerusalem was the capital of Judah, and Samaria was the capital of Israel. The word I brought to both kingdoms was that God's judgment was upon them for worshiping other gods, abhorring justice, oppressing the poor and widows, and acting with general lawlessness. I proclaimed that both Samaria and Jerusalem would be destroyed. Even as I spoke God's judgment, I assured His people that their enemies would not be able to gloat. The time would come when they would repent, and God would save them in honor of His promise to Abraham. I told them that an everlasting ruler would rise up in Israel who would be due all honor and praise. Hundreds of years later it came to pass when Jesus Christ was born.

†

Like Micah, we should examine the world around us and speak out when it is out of line with the heart of God. Just as in Micah's time, there is rampant lawlessness, injustice, oppression, and persecution of God's people today. Though this is the state of our world, we are citizens of another kingdom and should not behave as this world does. Instead, we are ambassadors of Christ. Our calling is to do justly, to love mercy, and to walk humbly with our God.

1:13 [a] Josh. 10:3; 2 Kin. 14:19; 18:14; Is. 36:2 [b] Ezek. 23:11 1:14 [a] 2 Sam. 8:2 [b] Josh. 15:44 [1] Literally *Possession of Gath* [2] Literally *Lie*
1:15 [a] Josh. 15:44 [b] 2 Chr. 11:7 [1] Literally *Inheritance* 1:16 [a] Job 1:20 [b] Lam. 4:5 [c] 2 Kin. 17:6; Amos 7:11, 17; [Mic. 4:10]
2:1 [a] Hos. 7:6, 7 2:2 [a] Is. 5:8 2:3 [a] Ex. 20:5; Jer. 8:3; Amos 3:1, 2 [b] Amos 5:13

And [a]lament with a bitter
lamentation, saying:
'We are utterly destroyed!
He has changed the heritage
of my people;
How He has removed *it* from me!
To a turncoat He has
divided our fields.'"
5 Therefore you will have no one to
determine boundaries[1] by lot
In the assembly of the LORD.

Lying Prophets

6 "Do not prattle," *you say to
those* who prophesy.
So they shall not prophesy to you;[1]
They shall not return insult for insult.[2]
7 *You who are* named the house of Jacob:
"Is the Spirit of the LORD restricted?
Are these His doings?
Do not My words do good
To him who walks uprightly?

8 "Lately My people have risen
up as an enemy—
You pull off the robe with the garment
From those who trust *you,*
as they pass by,
Like men returned from war.
9 The women of My people you cast out
From their pleasant houses;
From their children
You have taken away My glory forever.

10 "Arise and depart,
For this *is* not *your* [a]rest;
Because it is [b]defiled, it shall destroy,
Yes, with utter destruction.
11 If a man should walk in a false spirit
And speak a lie, *saying,*
'I will prophesy to you of
wine and drink,'
Even he would be the [a]prattler
of this people.

Israel Restored

12 "I[a] will surely assemble all
of you, O Jacob,
I will surely gather the
remnant of Israel;
I will put them together [b]like
sheep of the fold,[1]
Like a flock in the midst
of their pasture;
[c]They shall make a loud noise
because of *so many* people.
13 The one who breaks open will
come up before them;
They will break out,
Pass through the gate,
And go out by it;
[a]Their king will pass before them,
[b]With the LORD at their head."

Wicked Rulers and Prophets

3 And I said:

"Hear now, O heads of Jacob,
And you [a]rulers of the house
of Israel:
[b]*Is it* not for you to know justice?
2 You who hate good and love evil;
Who strip the skin from My people,[1]
And the flesh from their bones;
3 Who also [a]eat the flesh of My people,
Flay their skin from them,
Break their bones,
And chop *them* in pieces
Like *meat* for the pot,
[b]Like flesh in the caldron."

4 Then [a]they will cry to the LORD,
But He will not hear them;
He will even hide His face
from them at that time,
Because they have been
evil in their deeds.

5 Thus says the LORD [a]concerning
the prophets
Who make my people stray;
Who chant "Peace"
While they [b]chew with their teeth,
But who prepare war against him
[c]Who puts nothing into their mouths:
6 "Therefore[a] you shall have
night without vision,

2:4 [a] 2 Sam. 1:17 2:5 [1] Literally *one casting a surveyor's line* 2:6 [1] Literally *to these* [2] Vulgate reads *He shall not take shame.*
2:10 [a] Deut. 12:9 [b] Lev. 18:25 2:11 [a] Is. 30:10; Jer. 5:30, 31; 2 Tim. 4:3, 4 2:12 [a] [Mic. 4:6, 7] [b] Jer. 31:10 [c] Ezek. 33:22; 36:37 [1] Hebrew *Bozrah* 2:13 [a] [Hos. 3:5] [b] Is. 52:12 3:1 [a] Ezek. 22:27 [b] Ps. 82:1–5; Jer. 5:4, 5 3:2 [1] Literally *them* 3:3 [a] Ps. 14:4; 27:2; Zeph. 3:3 [b] Ezek. 11:3, 6, 7 3:4 [a] Ps. 18:41; Prov. 1:28; Is. 1:15; Jer. 11:11 3:5 [a] Is. 56:10, 11; Jer. 6:13; Ezek. 13:10, 19 [b] Matt. 7:15 [c] Ezek. 13:18 3:6 [a] Is. 8:20–22; 29:10–12

ACT AS HE DOES

INHALE

What would Jesus do? I try to live my life based on the answer to that question and let the Holy Spirit lead me daily. I try not to hold grudges. I try to see life through His eyes and be an agent for change. However, I'm truly frustrated with this world we live in. It seems people want to cause division rather than come together. Even God's people. How can I live like Jesus to make a difference in this area? How can I help bring people together who do not seem to want to be together?

EXHALE

To be led by Christ is to live exactly as God wants us to live. When we consider Christ before we take any step in life, we show the world what it is to be a true disciple of Christ—a literal Christ follower.

It certainly seems that everywhere you turn, someone or something is trying to divide us. But there is nothing like the gospel of Jesus Christ to bring people together. There is no divide too wide for Christ to bridge. There might be practical steps we can take to work toward unity, but none will be lasting unless it is anchored to the gospel. So, the answer to your question is the question you ask yourself: What would Jesus do? We all need to ask ourselves that day by day and minute by minute.

Division often happens quickly, but unity often happens slowly. One word or action can tear people apart. But bringing them back together can often take dozens, hundreds, or thousands of words and actions. Do not stop being a peacemaker and attempting to unite people. Do not allow the frustration to turn you from what you know God would have you do. Micah 3:8 says, "But truly I am full of power by the Spirit of the LORD, and of justice and might." The same is true of us as followers of Christ. So be led by the Holy Spirit in everything you do. Listen to the prompting of the Holy Spirit and be ready to move, but be patient.

It is never our way we seek. It is always God's way. And His way can be frustratingly slow at times! You are doing well. Keep it up! There is no other way to live.

And you shall have darkness
without divination;
The sun shall go down
on the prophets,
And the day shall be dark for [b]them.
7 So the seers shall be ashamed,
And the diviners abashed;
Indeed they shall all cover their lips;
[a]For *there is* no answer from God."

8 But truly I am full of power by
the Spirit of the LORD,
And of justice and might,
[a]To declare to Jacob his transgression
And to Israel his sin.
9 Now hear this,
You heads of the house of Jacob
And rulers of the house of Israel,
Who abhor justice
And pervert all equity,
10 [a]Who build up Zion with [b]bloodshed
And Jerusalem with iniquity:
11 [a]Her heads judge for a bribe,
[b]Her priests teach for pay,
And her prophets divine for
money.
[c]Yet they lean on the LORD, and say,
"Is not the LORD among us?
No harm can come upon us."
12 Therefore because of you
Zion shall be [a]plowed *like* a field,
[b]Jerusalem shall become
heaps of ruins,
And [c]the mountain of the
temple[1]
Like the bare hills of the forest.

3:6 [b] Is. 29:10; [Jer. 23:33–40]; Ezek. 13:23 3:7 [a] Amos 8:11 3:8 [a] Is. 58:1 3:10 [a] Jer. 22:13, 17 [b] Ezek. 22:27; Hab. 2:12 3:11 [a] Is. 1:23; Mic. 7:3 [b] Jer. 6:13 [c] Is. 48:2; Jer. 7:4 3:12 [a] Jer. 26:18 [b] Ps. 79:1; Jer. 9:11 [c] Mic. 4:1, 2 [1] Literally *house*

The LORD's Reign in Zion
(cf. Is. 2:2–4)

4 Now [a]it shall come to pass
in the latter days
That the mountain of the
LORD's house
Shall be established on the
top of the mountains,
And shall be exalted above the hills;
And peoples shall flow to it.
2 Many nations shall come and say,
"Come, and let us go up to the
mountain of the LORD,
To the house of the God of Jacob;
He will teach us His ways,
And we shall walk in His paths."
For out of Zion the law shall go forth,
And the word of the LORD
from Jerusalem.

#OXYGEN
MICAH 4:2
Act as He Does

The more we seek after God, the closer we will walk with Him. The closer we walk with Him, the more we will grow to resemble Him. May we daily become more like the God we serve.

Just **breathe** and **act as He does.**

3 He shall judge between many peoples,
And rebuke strong nations afar off;
They shall beat their swords
into [a]plowshares,
And their spears into pruning hooks;
Nation shall not lift up sword
against nation,
[b]Neither shall they learn war anymore.[1]
4 [a]But everyone shall sit under his
vine and under his fig tree,
And no one shall make *them* afraid;
For the mouth of the LORD
of hosts has spoken.
5 For all people walk each in
the name of his god,
But [a]we will walk in the name
of the LORD our God
Forever and ever.

Zion's Future Triumph

6 "In that day," says the LORD,
[a]"I will assemble the lame,
[b]I will gather the outcast
And those whom I have afflicted;
7 I will make the lame [a]a remnant,
And the outcast a strong nation;
So the LORD [b]will reign over
them in Mount Zion
From now on, even forever.
8 And you, O tower of the flock,
The stronghold of the
daughter of Zion,
To you shall it come,
Even the former dominion
shall come,
The kingdom of the daughter
of Jerusalem."

9 Now why do you cry aloud?
[a]*Is there* no king in your midst?
Has your counselor perished?
For [b]pangs have seized you
like a woman in labor.
10 Be in pain, and labor to bring forth,
O daughter of Zion,
Like a woman in birth pangs.
For now you shall go forth
from the city,
You shall dwell in the field,
And to [a]Babylon you shall go.
There you shall be delivered;
There the [b]LORD will [c]redeem you
From the hand of your enemies.

11 [a]Now also many nations have
gathered against you,
Who say, "Let her be defiled,
And let our eye [b]look upon Zion."
12 But they do not know [a]the
thoughts of the LORD,
Nor do they understand His counsel;

4:1 [a] Is. 2:2–4; Ezek. 17:22; Dan. 2:28; 10:14; Hos. 3:5 4:3 [a] Is. 2:4; Joel 3:10 [b] Ps. 72:7 [1] Compare Isaiah 2:2–4 4:4 [a] 1 Kin. 4:25; Zech. 3:10 4:5 [a] Zech. 10:12 4:6 [a] Ezek. 34:16 [b] Ps. 147:2 4:7 [a] Mic. 2:12 [b] [Is. 9:6; 24:23; Luke 1:33; Rev. 11:15] 4:9 [a] Jer. 8:19 [b] Is. 13:8; Jer. 30:6 4:10 [a] 2 Chr. 36:20; Amos 5:27 [b] [Is. 45:13; Mic. 7:8–12] [c] Ezra 1:1–3; 2:1; Ps. 18:17 4:11 [a] Lam. 2:16 [b] Obad. 12 4:12 [a] [Is. 55:8, 9]

For He will gather them [b]like
sheaves to the threshing floor.

13 "Arise[a] and [b]thresh, O daughter of Zion;
For I will make your horn iron,
And I will make your hooves bronze;
You shall [c]beat in pieces
many peoples;
[d]I will consecrate their
gain to the LORD,
And their substance to [e]the
Lord of the whole earth."

5 Now gather yourself in troops,
O daughter of troops;
He has laid siege against us;
They will [a]strike the judge of Israel
with a rod on the cheek.

The Coming Messiah

2 "But you, [a]Bethlehem [b]Ephrathah,
Though you are little [c]among
the [d]thousands of Judah,
Yet out of you shall come forth to Me
The One to be [e]Ruler in Israel,
[f]Whose goings forth *are* from of old,
From everlasting."

3 Therefore He shall give them up,
Until the time *that* [a]she who is
in labor has given birth;
Then [b]the remnant of His brethren
Shall return to the children of Israel.
4 And He shall stand and [a]feed
His flock
In the strength of the LORD,
In the majesty of the name
of the LORD His God;
And they shall abide,
For now He [b]shall be great
To the ends of the earth;
5 And this *One* [a]shall be peace.

Judgment on Israel's Enemies

When the Assyrian comes
into our land,
And when he treads in our palaces,
Then we will raise against him
Seven shepherds and eight
princely men.
6 They shall waste with the sword
the land of Assyria,
And the land of [a]Nimrod
at its entrances;
Thus He shall [b]deliver *us*
from the Assyrian,
When he comes into our land
And when he treads within our borders.

7 Then [a]the remnant of Jacob
Shall be in the midst of many peoples,
[b]Like dew from the LORD,
Like showers on the grass,
That tarry for no man
Nor wait for the sons of men.
8 And the remnant of Jacob
Shall be among the Gentiles,
In the midst of many peoples,
Like a [a]lion among the
beasts of the forest,
Like a young lion among
flocks of sheep,
Who, if he passes through,
Both treads down and tears in pieces,
And none can deliver.
9 Your hand shall be lifted
against your adversaries,
And all your enemies shall be cut off.

10 "And it shall be in that day,"
says the LORD,
"That I will [a]cut off your [b]horses
from your midst
And destroy your [c]chariots.
11 I will cut off the cities of your land
And throw down all your strongholds.
12 I will cut off sorceries from your hand,
And you shall have no [a]soothsayers.
13 [a]Your carved images I will also cut off,
And your *sacred* pillars
from your midst;
You shall [b]no more worship
the work of your hands;
14 I will pluck your wooden
images[1] from your midst;
Thus I will destroy your cities.

4:12 [b] Is. 21:10 4:13 [a] Jer. 51:33; [Zech. 12:1–8; 14:14] [b] Is. 41:15 [c] Dan. 2:44 [d] Is. 18:7 [e] Zech. 4:14 5:1 [a] 1 Kin. 22:24; Job 16:10; Lam. 3:30; Matt. 27:30; Mark 15:19 5:2 [a] Is. 11:1; Matt. 2:6; Luke 2:4, 11; John 7:42 [b] Gen. 35:19; 48:7; Ruth 4:11 [c] 1 Sam. 23:23 [d] Ex. 18:25 [e] [Gen. 49:10; Is. 9:6] [f] Ps. 90:2; [John 1:1] 5:3 [a] Hos. 11:8; Mic. 4:10 [b] Mic. 4:7; 7:18 5:4 [a] [Is. 40:11; 49:9; Ezek. 34:13–15, 23, 24]; Mic. 7:14 [b] Ps. 72:8; Is. 52:13; Zech. 9:10; [Luke 1:32] 5:5 [a] [Is. 9:6]; Luke 2:14; [Eph. 2:14; Col. 1:20] 5:6 [a] Gen. 10:8–11 [b] Is. 14:25; Luke 1:71 5:7 [a] Mic. 5:3 [b] Gen. 27:28; Deut. 32:2; Ps. 72:6; Hos. 14:5 5:8 [a] Gen. 49:9; Num. 24:9 5:10 [a] Zech. 9:10 [b] Deut. 17:16 [c] Is. 2:7; 22:18; Hos. 14:3 5:12 [a] Deut. 18:10–12; Is. 2:6 5:13 [a] Zech. 13:2 [b] Is. 2:8 5:14 [1] Hebrew *Asherim,* Canaanite deities

15 And I will [a]execute vengeance
in anger and fury
On the nations that have not heard."[1]

God Pleads with Israel

6 Hear now what the LORD says:

"Arise, plead your case before
the mountains,
And let the hills hear your voice.
2 [a]Hear, O you mountains, [b]the
LORD's complaint,
And you strong foundations
of the earth;
For [c]the LORD has a complaint
against His people,
And He will contend with Israel.

3 "O My people, what [a]have I done to you?
And how have I [b]wearied you?
Testify against Me.
4 [a]For I brought you up from
the land of Egypt,
I redeemed you from the
house of bondage;
And I sent before you Moses,
Aaron, and Miriam.
5 O My people, remember now
What [a]Balak king of Moab counseled,
And what Balaam the son of
Beor answered him,
From Acacia Grove[1] to Gilgal,
That you may know [b]the
righteousness of the LORD."

6 With what shall I come
before the LORD,
And bow myself before the High God?
Shall I come before Him
with burnt offerings,
With calves a year old?
7 [a]Will the LORD be pleased with
thousands of rams,
Ten thousand [b]rivers of oil?
[c]Shall I give my firstborn *for*
my transgression,
The fruit of my body *for*
the sin of my soul?
8 He has [a]shown you, O man,
what *is* good;
And what does the LORD
require of you
But [b]to do justly,
To love mercy,
And to walk humbly with your God?

Punishment of Israel's Injustice

9 The LORD's voice cries to the city—
Wisdom shall see Your name:

"Hear the rod!
Who has appointed it?
10 Are there yet the treasures
of wickedness
In the house of the wicked,
And the short measure *that*
is an abomination?
11 Shall I count pure *those* with
[a]the wicked scales,
And with the bag of deceitful weights?
12 For her rich men are full of [a]violence,
Her inhabitants have spoken lies,
And [b]their tongue is deceitful
in their mouth.

13 "Therefore I will also [a]make
you sick by striking you,
By making *you* desolate
because of your sins.
14 [a]You shall eat, but not be satisfied;
Hunger[1] *shall be* in your midst.
You may carry *some* away,[2]
but shall not save *them;*
And what you do rescue I will
give over to the sword.

15 "You shall [a]sow, but not reap;
You shall tread the olives, but not
anoint yourselves with oil;
And *make* sweet wine, but
not drink wine.
16 For the statutes of [a]Omri are [b]kept;
All the works of Ahab's house *are done;*
And you walk in their counsels,
That I may make you a desolation,
And your inhabitants a hissing.

5:15 [a] [2 Thess. 1:8] [1] Or *obeyed* 6:2 [a] Ps. 50:1, 4 [b] [Is. 1:18]; Hos. 12:2 [c] [Is. 1:18] 6:3 [a] Is. 5:4; Jer. 2:5, 31 [b] Is. 43:22, 23; Mal. 1:13 6:4 [a] [Deut. 4:20] 6:5 [a] Num. 22:5, 6; Josh. 24:9 [b] Judg. 5:11 [1] Hebrew *Shittim* (compare Numbers 25:1; Joshua 2:1; 3:1) 6:7 [a] Ps. 50:9; Is. 1:11 [b] Job 29:6 [c] Lev. 18:21; 20:1–5; 2 Kin. 16:3; Jer. 7:31; Ezek. 23:37 6:8 [a] [Deut. 10:12; 1 Sam. 15:22]; Hos. 6:6; 12:6 [b] Gen. 18:19; Is. 1:17 6:11 [a] Lev. 19:36; Hos. 12:7 6:12 [a] Is. 1:23; 5:7; Amos 6:3, 4; Mic. 2:1, 2 [b] Jer. 9:2–6, 8; Hos. 7:13; Amos 2:4 6:13 [a] Lev. 26:16; Ps. 107:17 6:14 [a] Lev. 26:26 [1] Or *Emptiness* or *Humiliation* [2] Targum and Vulgate read *You shall take hold.* 6:15 [a] Deut. 28:38–40; Amos 5:11; Zeph. 1:13; Hag. 1:6 6:16 [a] 1 Kin. 16:25, 26 [b] 1 Kin. 16:30; 21:25, 26; 2 Kin. 21:3; Hos. 5:11

RELEASE // ACT AS HE DOES

Justice and Mercy

Micah 6:8 //He has shown you, O man, what is good; and what does the LORD require of you but to do justly, to love mercy, and to walk humbly with your God?

Summary Message //The Book of Micah is a sequence of prophecies alternating between judgment and the hope of restoration. On the one hand, these prophecies proclaim judgment upon Israel for injustice, dishonesty, and idolatry. On the other hand, Micah announces the nation's restoration, transformation, and rise after their destruction. It appears that Israel prospered outwardly but disintegrated inwardly. Political and economic corruption was widespread, and ethical and moral violations were pervasive. The nation had wandered so far from God that they could not tell the difference between good and evil.

Micah 6 is the climax of Micah's prophecy. In this chapter, he blew the whistle on Israel's hypocrisy, showing them the error of their ways and contrasting their actions with what pleases the Lord. God wanted the people to understand that He wants His people to act as He does. He reminded them that He is not interested in futile religious rituals or empty worship. Micah summed up the prophecy in Micah 6:8 with how Israel could imitate God by acting justly, loving mercy, and walking humbly with Him.

Practical Application //We may imagine that imitating God is impossibly difficult. Micah, however, gives us direction that seems almost too simple: act justly, love mercy, and walk humbly.

To act justly means to do the right thing according to God's Word. We are constantly faced with opportunities to do the right thing or not. When we see injustice, will we do something about it, or will we ignore it? To act justly may mean being a whistleblower on unethical and discriminatory practices, confronting racial jokes and slurs, or defending the poor and marginalized.

We also act as God does by loving mercy. This can be as simple as serving at a homeless shelter, helping a needy family during a financial crisis, or taking a meal to the sick. But it can also be as difficult as showing undeserved kindness or treating people better than their behavior merits.

Justice and mercy affect our relationships with others, but the third quality Micah advocates focuses on our relationship with God. To walk humbly with God is to put Him at the center of our lives. It means we take ourselves out of first place and put Him there. Then God becomes first in our relationships, homes, and attitudes, as well as in our decisions about how we use time, spend money, and handle problems. In other words, we will constantly submit our wills and our ways to His will and His ways. Now that we know what pleases God and how to act as He does, let's do it!

Fervent Prayer //Heavenly Father, thank You for showing us what pleases You so that we can act as You do. Give us a heart and the wisdom to recognize and oppose injustice whenever we have the opportunity. Help us to grow in our love for mercy so that we can extend undeserved kindness to others. Please remind us to seek Your guidance and Your will through daily prayer, obedience, and worship. In Jesus' name we pray. Amen.

Therefore you shall bear the
[c]reproach of My people."[1]

Sorrow for Israel's Sins

7 Woe is me!
For I am like those who
gather summer fruits,
Like those who [a]glean vintage grapes;
There is no cluster to eat
Of the first-ripe fruit *which*
[b]my soul desires.
2 The [a]faithful *man* has perished
from the earth,
And *there is* no one upright
among men.
They all lie in wait for blood;
[b]Every man hunts his
brother with a net.

6:16 [c] Is. 25:8 [1] Following Masoretic Text, Targum, and Vulgate; Septuagint reads *of nations.*
7:1 [a] Is. 17:6 [b] Is. 28:4; Hos. 9:10 7:2 [a] Ps. 12:1; Is. 57:1 [b] Hab. 1:15

3 That they may successfully do
evil with both hands—
The prince asks *for gifts,*
The judge *seeks* a [a]bribe,
And the great *man* utters
his evil desire;
So they scheme together.
4 The best of them *is* [a]like a brier;
The most upright *is sharper*
than a thorn hedge;
The day of your watchman and
your punishment comes;
Now shall be their perplexity.

5 [a]Do not trust in a friend;
Do not put your confidence
in a companion;
Guard the doors of your mouth
From her who lies in your [b]bosom.
6 For [a]son dishonors father,
Daughter rises against her
mother,
Daughter-in-law against
her mother-in-law;
A man's enemies *are* the men
of his own household.
7 Therefore I will look to the LORD;
I will [a]wait for the God of my
salvation;
My God will hear me.

#OXYGEN
MICAH 7:7
Act as He Does

In the 1990s there was a popular wristband with the letters *WWJD* on it. Those letters stood for "What Would Jesus Do?" Imagine you are wearing that band. Before making any move or reacting to a situation, what if you asked yourself, "What would Jesus do?"

Breathe and act as He does.

Israel's Confession and Comfort

8 [a]Do not rejoice over me, my enemy;
[b]When I fall, I will arise;
When I sit in darkness,
The LORD *will be* a light to me.
9 [a]I will bear the indignation
of the LORD,
Because I have sinned against Him,
Until He pleads my [b]case
And executes justice for me.
He will bring me forth to the light;
I will see His righteousness.
10 Then *she who is* my enemy will see,
And [a]shame will cover her
who said to me,
[b]"Where is the LORD your God?"
My eyes will see her;
Now she will be trampled down
Like mud in the streets.

11 *In* the day when your [a]walls
are to be built,
In that day the decree shall
go far and wide.[1]
12 *In* that day [a]they[1] shall come to you
From Assyria and the fortified
cities,[2]
From the fortress[3] to the River,[4]
From sea to sea,
And mountain *to* mountain.
13 Yet the land shall be desolate
Because of those who dwell in it,
And [a]for the fruit of their deeds.

God Will Forgive Israel

14 Shepherd Your people with Your staff,
The flock of Your heritage,
Who dwell solitarily *in* a [a]woodland,
In the midst of Carmel;
Let them feed *in* Bashan and Gilead,
As in days of old.

15 "As[a] in the days when you came
out of the land of Egypt,
I will show them[1] [b]wonders."

16 The nations [a]shall see and be
ashamed of all their might;

7:3 [a] Amos 5:12; Mic. 3:11 7:4 [a] Is. 55:13; Ezek. 2:6 7:5 [a] Jer. 9:4 [b] Deut. 28:56 7:6 [a] Matt. 10:36; Mark 3:21; Luke 8:19; John 7:5 7:7 [a] Ps. 130:5; Is. 25:9; Lam. 3:24, 25 7:8 [a] Prov. 24:17; Obad. 12; [Acts 10:43] [b] Ps. 37:24; [Prov. 24:16]; 2 Cor. 4:9 7:9 [a] Lam. 3:39, 40; [2 Cor. 5:21] [b] Jer. 50:34 7:10 [a] Ps. 35:26 [b] Ps. 42:3 7:11 [a] Is. 54:11; [Amos 9:11] [1] Or *the boundary shall be extended* 7:12 [a] [Is. 11:16; 19:23–25] [1] Literally *he,* collective of the captives [2] Hebrew *arey mazor,* possibly *cities of Egypt* [3] Hebrew *mazor,* possibly *Egypt* [4] That is, the Euphrates 7:13 [a] Jer. 21:14 7:14 [a] Is. 37:24 7:15 [a] Ps. 68:22; 78:12 [b] Ex. 34:10 [1] Literally *him,* collective for the captives 7:16 [a] Is. 26:11

[b]They shall put *their* hand
over *their* mouth;
Their ears shall be deaf.
17 They shall lick the [a]dust like a serpent;
[b]They shall crawl from their holes
like snakes of the earth.
[c]They shall be afraid of the
LORD our God,
And shall fear because of You.
18 [a]Who *is* a God like You,
[b]Pardoning iniquity
And passing over the transgression
of [c]the remnant of His heritage?
[d]He does not retain His anger forever,
Because He delights *in* [e]mercy.
19 He will again have compassion
on us,
And will subdue our iniquities.

You will cast all our[1] sins
Into the depths of the sea.
20 [a]You will give truth to Jacob
And mercy to Abraham,
[b]Which You have sworn to
our fathers
From days of old.

7:16 [b] Job 21:5 7:17 [a] Ps. 72:9; [Is. 49:23] [b] Ps. 18:45 [c] Jer. 33:9 7:18 [a] Ex. 15:11 [b] Ex. 34:6, 7, 9; Is. 43:25; Jer. 50:20 [c] Mic. 4:7 [d] Ps. 103:8, 9, 13; [Is. 57:16] [e] [Ezek. 33:11] 7:19 [1] Literally *their* 7:20 [a] Luke 1:72, 73 [b] Ps. 105:9

THE BOOK OF

NAHUM

OVERVIEW

The Book of Nahum bears the name of its author. Nahum means "comfort" in Hebrew. Nahum was a minor prophet in the Old Testament who scholars believe wrote this book between 663 and 612 BC. Nahum's message declared judgment on the city of Nineveh, the capital of the Assyrian Empire. He preached during the reign of King Manasseh.

Nahum was not the first prophet to preach about Nineveh. God sent Jonah there over a century before Nahum delivered his message. After receiving God's prophecy from Jonah, the people of Nineveh repented. However, they eventually returned to their wicked ways. Nahum declared the destruction of Nineveh to the people of Judah to reassure them that God would destroy their enemies in due time. The Assyrian Empire fell in 612 BC.

The Book of Nahum opens with the declaration of God's wrath on His enemies. He promised that "the LORD will take vengeance on His adversaries" (Nah. 1:2) and "will not at all acquit the wicked" (v. 3). God was angry that the people of Nineveh had returned to their evil ways after they had repented and been spared His earlier judgment. As a result, He promised Judah that the Assyrians would be "utterly cut off" (v. 15).

Chapter 2 describes the planned destruction of Nineveh in detail. The city would come under siege with spoils taken. God promised to leave the city "empty" and "desolate" (v. 10). Its inhabitants would "flee away" (v. 8), allowing others to take silver and gold and "wealth of every desirable prize" (v. 9).

God's plan to destroy Nineveh gave hope to the people of Judah. Nahum encouraged them to keep their "appointed feasts" and remain faithful to God (1:15).

The final chapter of Nahum reveals that the people of Nineveh believed they were invincible because of their great military power. The prophet used the fall of other great cities as evidence that even powerful cities can be overtaken by enemies (see 3:1–17). In fulfillment of Nahum's prophecy, the leaders of Nineveh would be killed and the people would flee the city at a future invasion. The surrounding nations applauded its destruction (see vv. 18–19).

The Book of Nahum promised the people of Judah that God would destroy the Assyrian Empire, which had oppressed them. The prophet Nahum shared the simple, yet profound, truth that God will always judge those who practice wickedness and refuse to offer true repentance. Though the people of Nineveh repented after the message from Jonah, they returned to their wicked ways, causing God to carry out His judgment. Nahum teaches that God is loyal to His people and will avenge them against their enemies.

BREATHE IT IN

The prophet Nahum prophesied God's judgment on Nineveh, the capital city of the Assyrian Empire. Years prior, when God sent Jonah to deliver a prophecy, the people repented and God spared them. Instead of honoring the commitment they made to God after Jonah's prophecy to them, they returned to their evil ways, including oppressing the Israelites. God's eventual

judgment of Nineveh as declared by Nahum is evidence that He forgives those who turn away from sin but judges those who do not. It also serves as a reminder of God's sovereignty and reveals that God cares about how others treat His chosen people.

As Christians, we often find ourselves confused by the ways of the Lord. We do not understand how wicked people sometimes prosper while righteous people suffer. We often feel oppressed by the leaders and the systems that govern us. We wonder why we seem to be stuck at the bottom watching others pass us by as they rise to top. In moments of confusion, we sometimes question God's commitment to us individually and collectively.

Be assured that God is always with us. Even when our circumstances do not match our desires or expectations, He is working behind the scenes for our good. The Israelites could not understand why God allowed the Assyrians to oppress them or why He withheld judgment from them. God sent the prophet Nahum to reveal His plan. God's deliverance was on His schedule, not theirs. The same is true for us. God works in His timing and according to His ways, not ours. We are to just wait on God.

Waiting does not mean we are to sit idly and do nothing, though. With the grace given us through the gospel of Jesus Christ, we are to set our hands to "good works, which God prepared beforehand that we should walk in them" (Eph. 2:10). We are to "be rich in good works, ready to give, willing to share" (1 Tim. 6:18).

†

THE BOOK OF

NAHUM

1 The burden[1] [a]against Nineveh. The book
of the vision of Nahum the Elkoshite.

God's Wrath on His Enemies

2 God *is* [a]jealous, and the LORD avenges;
The LORD avenges and *is* furious.
The LORD will take vengeance
on His adversaries,
And He reserves *wrath*
for His enemies;
3 The LORD *is* [a]slow to anger
and [b]great in power,
And will not at all acquit *the wicked.*

[c]The LORD has His way
In the whirlwind and in the storm,
And the clouds *are* the dust of His feet.
4 [a]He rebukes the sea and makes it dry,
And dries up all the rivers.
[b]Bashan and Carmel wither,
And the flower of Lebanon wilts.
5 The mountains quake before Him,
The hills melt,
And the earth heaves[1] at His presence,
Yes, the world and all who dwell in it.

6 Who can stand before
His indignation?
And [a]who can endure the
fierceness of His anger?
His fury is poured out like fire,
And the rocks are thrown
down by Him.

7 [a]The LORD *is* good,
A stronghold in the day of trouble;
And [b]He knows those
who trust in Him.

#OXYGEN

NAHUM 1:7

Trust in His Wisdom

Choose faith over fear. Choose godly decisions over worldly thinking. God is with you in your troubles, and He will help you face your storms. Trust and be steadfast.

Breathe and **trust in His wisdom**.

8 But with an overflowing flood
He will make an utter end of its place,
And darkness will pursue His enemies.

9 [a]What do you conspire
against the LORD?
[b]He will make an utter end *of it.*
Affliction will not rise up a second time.
10 For while tangled [a]*like* thorns,
[b]And while drunken *like* drunkards,
[c]They shall be devoured like
stubble fully dried.
11 From you comes forth *one*
Who plots evil against the LORD,
A wicked counselor.

12 Thus says the LORD:

"Though *they are* safe, and
likewise many,

1:1 [a] 2 Kin. 19:36; Jon. 1:2; Nah. 2:8; Zeph. 2:13 [1] Or *oracle* 1:2 [a] Ex. 20:5; Josh. 24:19 1:3 [a] Ex. 34:6, 7; Neh. 9:17; Ps. 103:8 [b] [Job 9:4] [c] Ps. 18:17 1:4 [a] Josh. 3:15, 16; Ps. 106:9; Is. 50:2; Matt. 8:26 [b] Is. 33:9 1:5 [1] Targum reads *burns.* 1:6 [a] Jer. 10:10; [Mal. 3:2] 1:7 [a] Ps. 25:8; 37:39, 40; 100:5; [Jer. 33:11]; Lam. 3:25 [b] Ps. 1:6; John 10:14; 2 Tim. 2:19 1:9 [a] Ps. 2:1; Nah. 1:11 [b] 1 Sam. 3:12 1:10 [a] 2 Sam. 23:6; Mic. 7:4 [b] Is. 56:12; Nah. 3:11 [c] Is. 5:24; 10:17; Mal. 4:1

Yet in this manner they
will be [a]cut down
When he passes through.
Though I have afflicted you,
I will afflict you no more;
13 For now I will break off his
yoke from you,
And burst your bonds apart."

14 The LORD has given a command
concerning you:
"Your name shall be
perpetuated no longer.
Out of the house of your gods
I will cut off the carved image
and the molded image.
I will dig your [a]grave,
For you are [b]vile."

15 Behold, on the mountains
The [a]feet of him who brings
good tidings,
Who proclaims peace!
O Judah, keep your appointed feasts,
Perform your vows.
For the wicked one shall no
more pass through you;
He is [b]utterly cut off.

The Destruction of Nineveh

2 He who scatters[1] has come
up before your face.
Man the fort!
Watch the road!
Strengthen *your* flanks!
Fortify *your* power mightily.

2 For the LORD will restore the
excellence of Jacob
Like the excellence of Israel,
For the emptiers have
emptied them out
And ruined their vine branches.

3 The shields of his mighty
men *are* made red,
The valiant men *are* in scarlet.
The chariots *come* with
flaming torches
In the day of his preparation,
And the spears are brandished.[1]
4 The chariots rage in the streets,
They jostle one another in
the broad roads;
They seem like torches,
They run like lightning.

5 He remembers his nobles;
They stumble in their walk;
They make haste to her walls,
And the defense is prepared.
6 The gates of the rivers are opened,
And the palace is dissolved.
7 It is decreed:[1]
She shall be led away captive,
She shall be brought up;
And her maidservants shall lead
her as with the voice of doves,
Beating their breasts.

8 Though Nineveh of old *was*
like a pool of water,
Now they flee away.
"Halt! Halt!" *they cry;*
But no one turns back.
9 Take spoil of silver!
Take spoil of [a]gold!
There is no end of treasure,
Or wealth of every desirable prize.
10 She is empty, desolate, and waste!
The heart melts, and the knees shake;
Much pain *is* in every side,
And all their faces are
drained of color.[1]

11 Where *is* the dwelling of the [a]lions,
And the feeding place of
the young lions,
Where the lion walked, the
lioness *and* lion's cub,
And no one made *them* afraid?
12 The lion tore in pieces
enough for his cubs,
Killed for his lionesses,
[a]Filled his caves with prey,
And his dens with flesh.

13 "Behold, [a]I *am* against you," says the
LORD of hosts, "I will burn your[1] chariots
in smoke, and the sword shall devour your

1:12 [a] [Is. 10:16–19, 33, 34] 1:14 [a] Ezek. 32:22, 23 [b] Nah. 3:6 1:15 [a] Is. 40:9; 52:7; Rom. 10:15 [b] Is. 29:7, 8 2:1 [1] Vulgate reads *He who destroys.* 2:3 [1] Literally *the cypresses are shaken;* Septuagint and Syriac read *the horses rush about;* Vulgate reads *the drivers are stupefied.* 2:7 [1] Hebrew *Huzzab* 2:9 [a] Ezek. 7:19; Zeph. 1:18 2:10 [1] Compare Joel 2:6 2:11 [a] Job 4:10, 11; Ezek. 19:2–7 2:12 [a] Is. 10:6; Jer. 51:34 2:13 [a] Jer. 21:13; Ezek. 5:8; Nah. 3:5 [1] Literally *her*

young lions; I will cut off your prey from
the earth, and the voice of your [b]messen-
gers shall be heard no more."

The Woe of Nineveh

3 Woe to the [a]bloody city!
It *is* all full of lies *and* robbery.
Its victim never departs.
2 The noise of a whip
And the noise of rattling wheels,
Of galloping horses,
Of clattering chariots!
3 Horsemen charge with bright
sword and glittering spear.
There is a multitude of slain,
A great number of bodies,
Countless corpses—
They stumble over the corpses—
4 Because of the multitude of harlotries
of the seductive harlot,
[a]The mistress of sorceries,
Who sells nations through
her harlotries,
And families through her sorceries.

5 "Behold, I *am* [a]against you,"
says the LORD of hosts;
[b]"I will lift your skirts over your face,
I will show the nations
your nakedness,
And the kingdoms your shame.
6 I will cast abominable filth upon you,
Make you [a]vile,
And make you [b]a spectacle.
7 It shall come to pass *that* all
who look upon you
[a]Will flee from you, and say,
[b]'Nineveh is laid waste!
[c]Who will bemoan her?'
Where shall I seek
comforters for you?"

8 [a]Are you better than [b]No Amon[1]
That was situated by the River,[2]
That had the waters around her,
Whose rampart *was* the sea,
Whose wall *was* the sea?
9 Ethiopia and Egypt *were* her strength,
And *it was* boundless;
[a]Put and Lubim were your[1] helpers.
10 Yet she *was* carried away,
She went into captivity;
[a]Her young children also
were dashed to pieces
[b]At the head of every street;
They [c]cast lots for her honorable men,
And all her great men were
bound in chains.
11 You also will be [a]drunk;
You will be hidden;
You also will seek refuge
from the enemy.

12 All your strongholds *are* [a]fig
trees with ripened figs:
If they are shaken,
They fall into the mouth
of the eater.
13 Surely, [a]your people in your
midst *are* women!
The gates of your land are wide
open for your enemies;
Fire shall devour the [b]bars
of your *gates*.

14 Draw your water for the siege!
[a]Fortify your strongholds!
Go into the clay and tread the
mortar!
Make strong the brick kiln!
15 There the fire will devour you,
The sword will cut you off;
It will eat you up like a [a]locust.

Make yourself many—like the
locust!
Make yourself many—like
the *swarming* locusts!
16 You have multiplied your
[a]merchants more than
the stars of heaven.
The locust plunders and flies away.
17 [a]Your commanders *are* like
swarming locusts,
And your generals like
great grasshoppers,

2:13 [b] 2 Kin. 18:17–25; 19:9–13, 23 3:1 [a] Ezek. 22:2, 3; 24:6–9; Hab. 2:12 3:4 [a] Is. 47:9–12; Rev. 18:2, 3 3:5 [a] Jer. 50:31; Ezek. 26:3; Nah. 2:13 [b] Is. 47:2, 3; Jer. 13:26 3:6 [a] Nah. 1:14 [b] Heb. 10:33 3:7 [a] Rev. 18:10 [b] Jon. 3:3; 4:11 [c] Is. 51:19; Jer. 15:5 3:8 [a] Amos 6:2 [b] Jer. 46:25; Ezek. 30:14–16 [1] That is, ancient Thebes; Targum and Vulgate read *populous Alexandria.* [2] Literally *rivers,* that is, the Nile and the surrounding canals 3:9 [a] Gen. 10:6; Jer. 46:9; Ezek. 27:10 [1] Septuagint reads *her.* 3:10 [a] Ps. 137:9; Is. 13:16; Hos. 13:16 [b] Lam. 2:19 [c] Joel 3:3; Obad. 11 3:11 [a] Is. 49:26; Jer. 25:27; Nah. 1:10 3:12 [a] Rev. 6:12, 13 3:13 [a] Is. 19:16; Jer. 50:37; 51:30 [b] Ps. 147:13; Jer. 51:30 3:14 [a] Nah. 2:1 3:15 [a] Joel 1:4 3:16 [a] Rev. 18:3, 11–19 3:17 [a] Rev. 9:7

Which camp in the hedges
on a cold day;
When the sun rises they flee
away,
And the place where they
are is not known.

18 [a]Your shepherds slumber,
O [b]king of Assyria;
Your nobles rest *in the dust.*
Your people are [c]scattered
on the mountains,
And no one gathers them.
19 Your injury *has* no healing,
[a]Your wound is severe.
[b]All who hear news of you
Will clap *their* hands over you,
For upon whom has not your
wickedness passed
continually?

3:18 [a] Ex. 15:16; Ps. 76:5, 6; Is. 56:10; Jer. 51:57 [b] Jer. 50:18; Ezek. 31:3 [c] 1 Kin. 22:17; Is. 13:14
3:19 [a] Jer. 46:11; Mic. 1:9 [b] Job 27:23; Lam. 2:15; Zeph. 2:15

THE BOOK OF

HABAKKUK

OVERVIEW

The Book of Habakkuk is named after its author, a minor prophet whose name in Hebrew means "embrace." His ministry is dated somewhere between 612 and 586 BC. Scholars believe the book was written before the destruction of Jerusalem by the Babylonians, dating it between 625 and 587 BC. The message in Habakkuk is one of hope and comfort for the Israelites. Jeremiah, Nahum, and Zephaniah were all Habakkuk's contemporaries.

Habakkuk preached during the reign of Josiah, the last good king to reign over Judah. Josiah became king at the age of eight and turned the people back to God. He restored the temple, and when a copy of the Law was discovered, he had Huldah, a prophet, read to the people. But when Josiah died, the people turned away from the one true God and returned to worshiping false gods.

In the beginning of the Book of Habakkuk, the prophet questioned God about His lack of action against Judah's wickedness. He reported the "plundering and violence," as well as the "strife, and contention" (1:3). Habakkuk saw "the wicked surround the righteous" and "perverse judgment" proceed (v. 4). He asked God, "How long shall I cry, and You will not hear?" (v. 2).

God promised Habakkuk that He would "work a work" that he "would not believe" (v. 5). He reminded the prophet that His ways of handling situations differ from those of people. He also informed Habakkuk that He would raise up the Chaldeans, a nation that was arrogant and powerful in battle, to discipline His people (see vv. 6–11).

Habakkuk continued to question God's lack of response "when the wicked devours a person more righteous than he" and why He withheld justice "on those who deal treacherously" (v. 13). God answered with the details of His plans for the Babylonians, which included punishment for embezzlers (see 2:6–8), extortionists (see vv. 9–11), tyrants (see vv. 12–14), drunkards (see vv. 15–17), and idolaters (see vv. 18–20). He instructed Habakkuk to "write the vision and make it plain" (v. 2), assuring him that it would come to pass at "an appointed time" (v. 3).

With knowledge of the pending judgment, Habakkuk prayed for God to show mercy to His people. He reminded God of His faithfulness in delivering the Hebrews from Egypt (see 3:1–15) and closed his prayer with a hymn of praise, promising to "rejoice in the LORD" and "joy in the God of [his] salvation" (v. 18).

The Book of Habakkuk confirms that even the faithful can become weary and question God. Habakkuk was dismayed by what he believed to be God's failure to respond to the wickedness of Judah. God reminded Habakkuk of His power and outlined His plan for judgment. He also used the prophet to share His plan with the people by charging him to write it down on stone tablets, assuring him that all would come to pass in God's timing.

BREATHE IT IN

The Book of Habakkuk gives readers a firsthand account of a conversation between God and one of His prophets. The prophet Habakkuk questioned God because He allowed the people

of Judah to operate in wickedness without incurring judgment. He did not realize that God planned for judgment to come against Judah at an appointed time. Once Habakkuk understood God's plan, he prayed for the people of Judah and praised God for His faithfulness.

Life can be difficult. However, as Christians, we should not focus on the difficulties we experience. Rather, we should direct our attention to how we respond to those difficulties. When Habakkuk witnessed the wickedness in the world, much of it perpetrated by God's own people, he questioned God about His silence. The moral and spiritual decline he witnessed troubled him. God assured Habakkuk that He had everything under control. Nothing escapes His notice or justice. Recognizing God's power and His plan, the prophet rejoiced.

We have a choice as to how we respond to the difficulties in our lives. The situations we experience should not determine our response. We should rejoice in every situation. Our attitude and happiness should not depend upon our circumstances. Many Christians, however, base their happiness on external factors while missing joy from trusting in God. They base their joy on whether they receive what they believe they need. They continually think, "If I get this, then better things would happen, and I will finally find happiness." What they long for could be anything from a spouse to a new car. Unfortunately, people who make statements such as these are confused about what it really means to rejoice.

We should all strive to have the attitude of rejoicing that Habakkuk had. He decided that despite what was happening in the world, he would rejoice in the Lord and be happy about his salvation. He did not fully understand God's plan, but He trusted Him. He realized the importance of living by faith and that, unlike shifting situations, God is ever-present and always good.

Are you content in whatever situation you find yourself in, or do you constantly seek fulfillment from the things and people around you? Do you say to yourself and others that you would be happy only *if* something particular happened—you achieved a certain goal or acquired a specific item? If you are waiting on someone or something to bring you joy, you will be waiting for a while. You will only find true joy when you focus on God.

The just live by faith. It is through faith that we realize our relationship with God is all that truly matters in life. The ability to rejoice during trials and troubles comes from having a solid relationship with God and an understanding of His power and might. God is our redeemer. God is our protection. God is our provider. God is our strength. God is all we need. Rejoice in the God of our salvation!

†

THE BOOK OF

HABAKKUK

1 The burden[1] which the prophet Habakkuk saw.

The Prophet's Question

2 O LORD, how long shall I cry,
[a]And You will not hear?
Even cry out to You, [b]"Violence!"
And You will [c]not save.
3 Why do You show me iniquity,
And cause *me* to see trouble?
For plundering and violence
are before me;
There is strife, and contention arises.
4 Therefore the law is powerless,
And justice never goes forth.
For the [a]wicked surround
the righteous;
Therefore perverse
judgment proceeds.

The LORD's Reply

5 "Look[a] among the nations and watch—
Be utterly astounded!
For *I will* work a work in your days
Which you would not believe,
though it were told *you*.
6 For indeed I am [a]raising
up the Chaldeans,
A bitter and hasty [b]nation
Which marches through the
breadth of the earth,
To possess dwelling places
that are not theirs.
7 They are terrible and dreadful;
Their judgment and their dignity
proceed from themselves.
8 Their horses also are [a]swifter
than leopards,
And more fierce than evening
wolves.
Their chargers charge ahead;
Their cavalry comes from afar;
They fly as the [b]eagle *that*
hastens to eat.
9 "They all come for violence;
Their faces are set *like* the east wind.
They gather captives like sand.
10 They scoff at kings,
And princes are scorned by them.
They deride every stronghold,
For they heap up earthen
mounds and seize it.
11 Then *his* mind[1] changes,
and he transgresses;
He commits offense,
[a]*Ascribing* this power to his god."

The Prophet's Second Question

12 Are You not [a]from everlasting,
O LORD my God, my Holy One?
We shall not die.
O LORD, [b]You have appointed
them for judgment;
O Rock, You have marked
them for [c]correction.
13 *You are* of purer eyes than
to behold evil,
And cannot look on wickedness.
Why do You look on those
who deal treacherously,
And hold Your tongue when
the wicked devours
A *person* more righteous than he?
14 *Why* do You make men
like fish of the sea,

1:1 [1] Or *oracle* 1:2 [a] Lam. 3:8 [b] Mic. 2:1, 2; 3:1–3 [c] [Job 21:5–16] 1:4 [a] Jer. 12:1 1:5 [a] Is. 29:14; Ezek. 12:22–28 1:6 [a] Deut. 28:49, 50; 2 Kin. 24:2; 2 Chr. 36:17; Jer. 4:11–13; Mic. 4:10 [b] Ezek. 7:24; 21:31 1:8 [a] Jer. 4:13 [b] Job 9:26; 39:29, 30; Lam. 4:19; Ezek. 17:3; Hos. 8:1; Matt. 24:28; Luke 17:37 1:11 [a] Dan. 5:4 [1] Literally *spirit* or *wind*
1:12 [a] Deut. 33:27; Ps. 90:2; 93:2; Mal. 3:6 [b] Is. 10:5–7; Mal. 3:5 [c] Jer. 25:9

Like creeping things *that have*
no ruler over them?

15 They take up all of them with a hook,
They catch them in their net,
And gather them in their dragnet.
Therefore they rejoice and are glad.
16 Therefore [a]they sacrifice
to their net,
And burn incense to their dragnet;
Because by them their
share *is* sumptuous
And their food plentiful.
17 Shall they therefore empty their net,
And continue to slay nations
without pity?

2 I will [a]stand my watch
And set myself on the rampart,
And watch to see what He
will say to me,
And what I will answer when
I am corrected.

The Just Live by Faith

2 Then the LORD answered me and said:

[a]"Write the vision
And make *it* plain on tablets,
That he may run who reads it.
3 For [a]the vision *is* yet for an
appointed time;
But at the end it will speak,
and it will [b]not lie.
Though it tarries, [c]wait for it;
Because it will [d]surely come,
It will not tarry.

4 "Behold the proud,
His soul is not upright in him;
But the [a]just shall live by his faith.

Woe to the Wicked

5 "Indeed, because he
transgresses by wine,
He is a proud man,
And he does not stay at home.

HABAKKUK 2:3

I AM HABAKKUK

"For the vision is yet for an appointed time; but at the end it will speak, and it will not lie. Though it tarries, wait for it; because it will surely come, it will not tarry." Habakkuk 2:3

I am Habakkuk, a prophet of God. I loved the Lord, but I did not understand why He did not do anything about the injustices that happened in Judah. The people had neglected God's law, and their leaders were corrupt. I complained to God about the violence and the lack of justice. He said that He would cause the evil and pagan nation of Babylonia to rise to bring Judah down. It was hard to understand why God would allow such an evil nation to win.

All I could do was to watch and wait for God's answers. I was a patient man, but I just could not see what He was doing. God, in His great mercy, answered my questions. He said that both the present and future Chaldeans (Babylonians) may appear to win, but He would bring justice to all things in His perfect timing.

Like Habakkuk we must learn to trust God even when it appears evil is winning. Just as with the Babylonians, the evil hearts of the nations will bring forth judgment, and justice will prevail. We should be careful not to second-guess God's promises or timing; rather, we should look to the answers He provides in His Word. They will not disappoint.

1:16 [a] Deut. 8:17 2:1 [a] Is. 21:8, 11 2:2 [a] Is. 8:1 2:3 [a] Dan. 8:17, 19; 10:14 [b] Ezek. 12:24, 25 [c] [Heb. 10:37, 38] [d] Ps. 27:13, 14; [James 5:7, 8; 2 Pet. 3:9] 2:4 [a] [John 3:36]; Rom. 1:17; Heb. 10:38

Because he [a]enlarges his
desire as hell,[1]
And he *is* like death, and
cannot be satisfied,
He gathers to himself all nations
And heaps up for himself all peoples.

6 "Will not all these [a]take up a
proverb against him,
And a taunting riddle
against him, and say,
'Woe to him who increases
What is not his—how long?
And to him who loads himself
with many pledges'?[1]
7 Will not your creditors[1]
rise up suddenly?
Will they not awaken who
oppress you?
And you will become their booty.
8 [a]Because you have plundered
many nations,
All the remnant of the people
shall plunder you,
Because of men's blood
And the violence of the
land *and* the city,
And of all who dwell in it.

9 "Woe to him who covets evil
gain for his house,
That he may [a]set his nest on high,
That he may be delivered from
the power of disaster!
10 You give shameful counsel
to your house,
Cutting off many peoples,
And sin *against* your soul.
11 For the stone will cry out
from the wall,
And the beam from the
timbers will answer it.

12 "Woe to him who builds a
town with bloodshed,
Who establishes a city by iniquity!
13 Behold, *is it* not of the LORD of hosts
That the peoples labor to feed the fire,[1]
And nations weary themselves in vain?
14 For the earth will be filled
With the knowledge of the
glory of the LORD,
As the waters cover the sea.

15 "Woe to him who gives drink
to his neighbor,
Pressing[1] *him to* your [a]bottle,
Even to make *him* drunk,
That you may look on his nakedness!
16 You are filled with shame
instead of glory.
You also—drink!
And be exposed as uncircumcised![1]
The cup of the LORD's right hand
will be turned against you,
And utter shame will be on your
glory.
17 For the violence *done to*
Lebanon will cover you,
And the plunder of beasts
which made them afraid,
Because of men's blood
And the violence of the
land *and* the city,
And of all who dwell in it.

18 "What profit is the image, that
its maker should carve it,
The molded image, a teacher of lies,
That the maker of its mold
should trust in it,
To make mute idols?
19 Woe to him who says to wood, 'Awake!'
To silent stone, 'Arise! It shall teach!'
Behold, it is overlaid with
gold and silver,
Yet in it there is no breath at all.

20 "But[a] the LORD is in His holy temple.
Let all the earth keep
silence before Him."

The Prophet's Prayer

3 A prayer of Habakkuk the prophet, on
Shigionoth.[1]

2 O LORD, I have heard Your
speech *and* was afraid;

2:5 [a] Prov. 27:20; 30:16; Is. 5:11–15 [1] Or *Sheol* **2:6** [a] Mic. 2:4 [1] Syriac and Vulgate read *thick clay.* **2:7** [1] Literally *those who bite you* **2:8** [a] Is. 33:1; Jer. 27:7; Ezek. 39:10; Zech. 2:8 **2:9** [a] Jer. 49:16; Obad. 4 **2:13** [1] Literally *for what satisfies fire,* that is, for what is of no lasting value **2:15** [a] Hos. 7:5 [1] Literally *Attaching* or *Joining* **2:16** [1] Dead Sea Scrolls and Septuagint read *And reel!;* Syriac and Vulgate read *And fall fast asleep!* **2:20** [a] Zeph. 1:7; Zech. 2:13 **3:1** [1] Exact meaning unknown

O LORD, revive Your work in
the midst of the years!
In the midst of the years
make *it* known;
In wrath remember mercy.

3 God came from Teman,
The Holy One from Mount
Paran. *Selah*

His glory covered the heavens,
And the earth was full of His praise.
4 *His* brightness was like the light;
He had rays *flashing* from His hand,
And there His power *was* hidden.
5 Before Him went pestilence,
And fever followed at His feet.
6 He stood and measured the earth;
He looked and startled the nations.
[a]And the everlasting mountains
were scattered,
The perpetual hills bowed.
His ways *are* everlasting.
7 I saw the tents of Cushan in affliction;
The curtains of the land of
Midian trembled.

8 O LORD, were *You* displeased
with the rivers,
Was Your anger against the rivers,
Was Your wrath against the sea,
That You rode on Your horses,
Your chariots of salvation?
9 Your bow was made quite ready;
Oaths were sworn over
Your arrows.[1] *Selah*

You divided the earth with rivers.
10 The mountains saw You *and* trembled;
The overflowing of the
water passed by.
The deep uttered its voice,
And [a]lifted its hands on high.
11 The [a]sun and moon stood still
in their habitation;
At the light of Your arrows they went,
At the shining of Your glittering spear.

12 You marched through the
land in indignation;
You trampled the nations in anger.
13 You went forth for the salvation
of Your people,
For salvation with Your Anointed.
You struck the head from the
house of the wicked,
By laying bare from foundation
to neck. *Selah*

14 You thrust through with
his own arrows
The head of his villages.
They came out like a whirlwind
to scatter me;
Their rejoicing was like feasting
on the poor in secret.
15 [a]You walked through the sea
with Your horses,
Through the heap of great waters.

16 When I heard, [a]my body trembled;
My lips quivered at *the* voice;
Rottenness entered my bones;
And I trembled in myself,
That I might rest in the day of trouble.
When he comes up to the people,
He will invade them with his troops.

A Hymn of Faith

17 Though the fig tree may not blossom,
Nor fruit be on the vines;
Though the labor of the olive may fail,
And the fields yield no food;
Though the flock may be
cut off from the fold,
And there be no herd in the stalls—
18 Yet I will [a]rejoice in the LORD,
I will joy in the God of my salvation.

19 The LORD God[1] is my strength;
He will make my feet like [a]deer's *feet*,
And He will make me [b]walk
on my high hills.

To the Chief Musician. With my stringed instruments.

3:6 [a] Nah. 1:5 3:9 [1] Literally *rods* or *tribes* (compare verse 14) 3:10 [a] Ex. 14:22 3:11 [a] Josh. 10:12–14 3:15 [a] Ps. 77:19; Hab. 3:8 3:16 [a] Ps. 119:120 3:18 [a] Is. 41:16; 61:10 3:19 [a] 2 Sam. 22:34; Ps. 18:33 [b] Deut. 32:13; 33:29 [1] Hebrew *YHWH Adonai*

THE BOOK OF

ZEPHANIAH

OVERVIEW

The Book of Zephaniah bears the name of its author. The name Zephaniah in Hebrew means "the Lord has hidden." Zephaniah was a minor prophet in the Old Testament and a direct descendant of King Hezekiah. Scholars believe he delivered his prophecies between 628 and 622 BC. The message in Zephaniah is the future judgment at "the day of the LORD" (Zeph. 1:7). This judgment will come upon the entire earth, including Judah and its enemies.

Zephaniah preached during the reign of Josiah, the last good king to reign over Judah. Josiah became king at the age of eight and later in his reign turned the people back to God. During Josiah's reign, Judah experienced a period of peace with Assyria, Babylon, and Egypt. The nation was recovering from the wickedness it engaged in under the rule of Ahaz, Manasseh, and Amon. When God sent Zephaniah to deliver His message, he broke a prophetic silence that had existed for over fifty years. Jeremiah was a contemporary of Zephaniah.

Zephaniah's record begins with his announcement of God's plan to "utterly consume everything from the face of the land" (1:2). God's anger with the people of Judah stemmed from their worship of idols and other gods. Zephaniah proclaimed the coming judgment as "the day of the LORD" (v. 7). He described that day as one of "trouble and distress," "devastation and desolation," and "wrath" (v. 15).

In chapter 2, Zephaniah called for repentance "before the LORD's fierce anger comes" (v. 2). He encouraged those who "upheld His justice" to "seek righteousness" and "humility" so that they "will be hidden in the day of the LORD's anger" (v. 3). Zephaniah then turned his attention to God's judgment on the nations around Judah for their threats against God's people (see vv. 4–15). Zephaniah chastised the people of God for their wickedness and their refusal to obey God, receive correction, and trust in the Lord (see 3:1–2). God proclaimed that all nations would worship Him following the devastation that was to come (see vv. 8–9). He revealed His plan to gather a faithful remnant, purify them, and return them to the land He promised (see vv. 10–20).

The Book of Zephaniah is an example of God's judgment against those who practice wickedness and worship other gods. Not only would God judge His chosen people, but He would also judge their enemies and the entire world. Zephaniah announced judgment to all on "the day of the LORD" (1:7). He prophesied that even in the midst of God's judgment, He will offer hope to a remnant of people who are faithful and honor His covenant with them.

BREATHE IT IN

The Book of Zephaniah is a message to the people of Judah about "the day of the LORD" when God will deliver judgment on the Israelites, their enemies, and the world (1:7). The prophet Zephaniah outlines the many transgressions that would lead to the coming judgment and identifies specific groups who have sinned against God. He promises that God will spare a faithful remnant of people who will become benefactors of the promises of God.

When Christians think of sin, we often think of the obvious ones, such as lying, stealing, cheating, adultery, and jealousy. However, there are many other behaviors and attitudes in which we can engage that God considers sin. One of those is complacency.

Complacency means that out of self-satisfaction, we fail to act. It is borne out of pride that we are "good" right where we are, and we do not need to do anything more than what we are doing now. Inherent in complacency is that everything will stay just as it is. But the hope of the faithful is that each day will bring fresh manna from the Lord.

Many of us have become complacent in our relationships with God at times. We go to church on Sunday and return to our regular routines on Monday, forgetting about God. Instead of working to grow in Christ, we focus on other things like growing our bank accounts, possessions, social media followers, and status in this world. We focus our attention on the demands of life, not the work of the Father. This often results in worship of gods instead of God.

In Zephaniah, God says that He will "punish the men who are settled in complacency" (1:12). Does this passage refer to you? Are you content and settled in where you are with God? Do you put the work of the Lord aside to promote your personal agenda and priorities? Judah did. They even questioned God's involvement in their lives, saying, "The LORD will not do good, nor will He do evil" (1:12). Because of their complacency and their questioning of God's sovereignty, God listed them among those whom He would judge.

With all that is going on in the world, it is easy to get lost and begin focusing only on the present and fail to think eternally. But just as we physically grow and mature, we should spiritually grow and mature, too, by continuing to concern ourselves with the things of God. Faith is a journey or, better yet, a pilgrimage. We have to keep moving through the process. Standing still with God while trusting only our worldly possessions and positions should not be an option. Instead, we must put on the armor of God every day and charge forward, following the path that the Lord has laid out before us. And we should never think, as Judah did, that God Himself is complacent and will not do what He has said He will do.

†

THE BOOK OF

ZEPHANIAH

1 The word of the LORD which came to
Zephaniah the son of Cushi, the son of
Gedaliah, the son of Amariah, the son of
Hezekiah, in the days of [a]Josiah the son of
Amon, king of Judah.

The Great Day of the LORD

2 "I will utterly consume everything
From the face of the land,"
Says the LORD;
3 "I[a] will consume man and beast;
I will consume the birds
of the heavens,
The fish of the sea,
And the stumbling blocks[1]
along with the wicked.
I will cut off man from the
face of the land,"
Says the LORD.

4 "I will stretch out My hand
against Judah,
And against all the inhabitants
of Jerusalem.
I will cut off every trace of
Baal from this place,
The names of the [a]idolatrous priests[1]
with the *pagan* priests—
5 Those [a]who worship the host of
heaven on the housetops;
Those who worship and swear
oaths by the LORD,
But who *also* swear [b]by Milcom;[1]
6 [a]Those who have turned back
from *following* the LORD,
And [b]have not sought the LORD,
nor inquired of Him."

7 [a]Be silent in the presence
of the Lord GOD;
[b]For the day of the LORD *is* at hand,
For [c]the LORD has prepared a sacrifice;
He has invited[1] His guests.

8 "And it shall be,
In the day of the LORD's sacrifice,
That I will punish [a]the princes
and the king's children,
And all such as are clothed
with foreign apparel.
9 In the same day I will punish
All those who [a]leap over
the threshold,[1]
Who fill their masters' houses
with violence and deceit.

10 "And there shall be on that
day," says the LORD,
"The sound of a mournful cry
from [a]the Fish Gate,
A wailing from the Second Quarter,
And a loud crashing from the hills.
11 [a]Wail, you inhabitants of Maktesh![1]
For all the merchant people
are cut down;
All those who handle
money are cut off.

12 "And it shall come to pass at that time
That I will search Jerusalem
with lamps,
And punish the men
Who are [a]settled in complacency,[1]
[b]Who say in their heart,
'The LORD will not do good,

1:1 [a] 2 Kin. 22:1, 2; 2 Chr. 34:1–33; Jer. 1:2; 22:11 1:3 [a] Hos. 4:3 [1] Figurative of idols 1:4 [a] 2 Kin. 23:5; Hos. 10:5 [1] Hebrew *chemarim* 1:5 [a] 2 Kin. 23:12; Jer. 19:13 [b] Josh. 23:7 [1] Or *Malcam,* an Ammonite god, also called *Molech* (compare Leviticus 18:21) 1:6 [a] Is. 1:4; Jer. 2:13 [b] Hos. 7:7 1:7 [a] Hab. 2:20; Zech. 2:13 [b] Is. 13:6 [c] Deut. 28:26; Is. 34:6; Jer. 46:10; Ezek. 39:17–19 [1] Literally *set apart, consecrated* 1:8 [a] Jer. 39:6 1:9 [a] 1 Sam. 5:5 [1] Compare 1 Samuel 5:5 1:10 [a] 2 Chr. 33:14; Neh. 3:3; 12:39 1:11 [a] James 5:1 [1] Literally *Mortar,* a market district of Jerusalem 1:12 [a] Jer. 48:11; Amos 6:1 [b] Ps. 94:7 [1] Literally *on their lees,* that is, settled like the dregs of wine

Nor will He do evil.'
13 Therefore their goods shall
become booty,
And their houses a desolation;
They shall build houses, but
not inhabit *them;*
They shall plant vineyards, but
[a]not drink their wine."

14 [a]The great day of the LORD *is* near;
It is near and hastens quickly.
The noise of the day of
the LORD is bitter;
There the mighty men shall cry out.
15 [a]That day *is* a day of wrath,
A day of trouble and distress,
A day of devastation and desolation,
A day of darkness and gloominess,
A day of clouds and thick darkness,
16 A day of [a]trumpet and alarm
Against the fortified cities
And against the high towers.

17 "I will bring distress upon men,
And they shall [a]walk like blind men,
Because they have sinned
against the LORD;
Their blood shall be poured
out like dust,
And their flesh like refuse."

18 [a]Neither their silver nor their gold
Shall be able to deliver them
In the day of the LORD's wrath;
But the whole land shall be
devoured
By the fire of His jealousy,
For He will make speedy riddance
Of all those who dwell in the land.

A Call to Repentance

2 Gather[a] yourselves together,
yes, gather together,
O undesirable[1] nation,
2 Before the decree is issued,
Or the day passes like chaff,
Before the LORD's fierce anger
comes upon you,
Before the day of the LORD's
anger comes upon you!

#OXYGEN
ZEPHANIAH 1:18
Trust in His Wisdom

You cannot buy your way into heaven. Money will not protect you on judgment day. Therefore, be wise with your resources. Uplift His kingdom here on earth. Live righteously.

Breathe and **trust in His wisdom.**

3 [a]Seek the LORD, [b]all you
meek of the earth,
Who have upheld His justice.
Seek righteousness, seek humility.
[c]It may be that you will be hidden
In the day of the LORD's anger.

Judgment on Nations

4 For [a]Gaza shall be forsaken,
And Ashkelon desolate;
They shall drive out Ashdod
[b]at noonday,
And Ekron shall be uprooted.
5 Woe to the inhabitants
of [a]the seacoast,
The nation of the Cherethites!
The word of the LORD *is* against you,
O [b]Canaan, land of the Philistines:
"I will destroy you;
So there shall be no inhabitant."

6 The seacoast shall be pastures,
With shelters[1] for shepherds
[a]and folds for flocks.
7 The coast shall be for [a]the remnant
of the house of Judah;
They shall feed *their* flocks there;
In the houses of Ashkelon they
shall lie down at evening.
For the LORD their God will
[b]intervene for them,
And [c]return their captives.

1:13 [a] Deut. 28:39 1:14 [a] Jer. 30:7; Joel 2:1, 11 1:15 [a] Is. 22:5 1:16 [a] Is. 27:13; Jer. 4:19 1:17 [a] Deut. 28:29 1:18 [a] Ezek. 7:19
2:1 [a] 2 Chr. 20:4; Joel 1:14; 2:16 [1] Or *shameless* 2:3 [a] Ps. 105:4; Amos 5:6 [b] Ps. 76:9 [c] Joel 2:14; Amos 5:14, 15 2:4 [a] Jer. 47:1, 5; Amos 1:7, 8; Zech. 9:5 [b] Jer. 6:4 2:5 [a] Ezek. 25:15–17 [b] Josh. 13:3 2:6 [a] Is. 17:2 [1] Literally *excavations,* either underground huts or cisterns 2:7 [a] [Mic. 5:7, 8] [b] Luke 1:68 [c] Jer. 29:14

8 "I[a] have heard the reproach
of Moab,
And [b]the insults of the
people of Ammon,
With which they have
reproached My people,
And [c]made arrogant threats
against their borders.
9 Therefore, as I live,"
Says the LORD of hosts,
the God of Israel,
"Surely [a]Moab shall be like Sodom,
And [b]the people of Ammon
like Gomorrah—
[c]Overrun with weeds and saltpits,
And a perpetual desolation.
The residue of My people
shall plunder them,
And the remnant of My people
shall possess them."
10 This they shall have [a]for their pride,
Because they have reproached
and made arrogant threats
Against the people of the
LORD of hosts.
11 The LORD *will be* awesome to them,
For He will reduce to nothing
all the gods of the earth;
[a]*People* shall worship Him,
Each one from his place,
Indeed all [b]the shores of the nations.

12 "You[a] Ethiopians also,
You shall be slain by [b]My sword."

13 And He will stretch out His
hand against the north,
[a]Destroy Assyria,
And make Nineveh a desolation,
As dry as the wilderness.

ZEPHANIAH 2:3

I AM ZEPHANIAH

Seek the LORD, all you meek of the earth, who have upheld His justice. Seek righteousness, seek humility. It may be that you will be hidden in the day of the LORD's anger. Zephaniah 2:3

I am Zephaniah, a prophet of God during the time Josiah was king of Judah. After a long period of kings who did evil in the sight of God, King Josiah honored Him. However, the people continued to practice idolatry. They did not even realize that their lost prosperity and destroyed cities were God's penalty for their sin. Even after the king found the lost Book of the Law that told them how to live as God desires, their hearts remained far from God. I supported King Josiah and warned the people of Judah and Israel about the army God was sending to bring His judgment if they did not repent and return to Him.

I prophesied that Judah would see the wrath of God and all nations will be judged. God will pour out His indignation with a fierce anger, and the earth will be devoured by the fire of God's jealousy in order to purify the nations. Out of this will come a remnant that God will restore with a pure language so they will call on the name of the Lord as one. God will restore Jerusalem, and the living God will live among His people.

†

The people of Judah lived immoral and godless lives. Although they professed to be people of God, they made a mockery of His law. Today, we live in the same kind of world. Zephaniah reminds us that God will not be mocked. God will bring to justice those who bring violence, injustice, and chaos to this world, but He will show love and kindness to those who humble themselves before Him. This is the hope of the world.

2:8 [a] Jer. 48:27; Amos 2:1–3 [b] Ezek. 25:3; Amos 1:13 [c] Jer. 49:1 2:9 [a] Is. 15:1–9; Jer. 48:1–47 [b] Amos 1:13 [c] Deut. 29:23 2:10 [a] Is. 16:6 2:11 [a] Mal. 1:11 [b] Gen. 10:5 2:12 [a] Is. 18:1–7; Ezek. 30:4, 5 [b] Ps. 17:13 2:13 [a] Is. 10:5–27; 14:24–27; Mic. 5:5, 6

14 The herds shall lie down in her midst,
[a]Every beast of the nation.
Both the [b]pelican and the bittern
Shall lodge on the capitals *of* her
pillars;
Their voice shall sing in the windows;
Desolation *shall be* at the threshold;
For He will lay bare the [c]cedar work.
15 This is the rejoicing city
[a]That dwelt securely,
[b]That said in her heart,
"I *am it,* and *there is* none besides me."
How has she become a desolation,
A place for beasts to lie down!
Everyone who passes by her
[c]Shall hiss and [d]shake his fist.

The Wickedness of Jerusalem

3 Woe to her who is rebellious
and polluted,
To the oppressing city!
2 She has not obeyed *His* voice,
She has not received correction;
She has not trusted in the LORD,
She has not drawn near to her God.

3 [a]Her princes in her midst
are roaring lions;
Her judges *are* [b]evening wolves
That leave not a bone till morning.
4 Her [a]prophets are insolent,
treacherous people;
Her priests have polluted the
sanctuary,
They have done [b]violence to the law.
5 The LORD *is* righteous in her midst,
He will do no unrighteousness.
Every morning He brings
His justice to light;
He never fails,
But [a]the unjust knows no shame.

6 "I have cut off nations,
Their fortresses are devastated;
I have made their streets desolate,
With none passing by.
Their cities are destroyed;
There is no one, no inhabitant.
7 [a]I said, 'Surely you will fear Me,
You will receive instruction'—
So that her dwelling would
not be cut off,
Despite everything for which
I punished her.
But they rose early and
[b]corrupted all their deeds.

A Faithful Remnant
(cf. Gen. 11:1–9; Acts 2:1–11)

8 "Therefore [a]wait for Me," says
the LORD,
"Until the day I rise up for
plunder;[1]
My determination *is* to
[b]gather the nations
To My assembly of kingdoms,
To pour on them My indignation,
All My fierce anger;
All the earth [c]shall be devoured
With the fire of My jealousy.

9 "For then I will restore to the
peoples [a]a pure language,
That they all may call on the
name of the LORD,
To serve Him with one accord.
10 [a]From beyond the rivers of Ethiopia
My worshipers,
The daughter of My dispersed ones,
Shall bring My offering.
11 In that day you shall not be
shamed for any of your deeds
In which you transgress against Me;
For then I will take away
from your midst
Those who [a]rejoice in your pride,
And you shall no longer be
haughty
In My holy mountain.
12 I will leave in your midst
[a]A meek and humble people,
And they shall trust in the
name of the LORD.
13 [a]The remnant of Israel [b]shall
do no unrighteousness
[c]And speak no lies,

2:14 [a] Is. 13:21 [b] Is. 14:23; 34:11 [c] Jer. 22:14 2:15 [a] Is. 47:8 [b] Rev. 18:7 [c] Lam. 2:15 [d] Nah. 3:19 3:3 [a] Ezek. 22:27 [b] Jer. 5:6; Hab. 1:8 3:4 [a] Hos. 9:7 [b] Ezek. 22:26; Mal. 2:7, 8 3:5 [a] Jer. 3:3 3:7 [a] Jer. 8:6 [b] Gen. 6:12 3:8 [a] Prov. 20:22; Mic. 7:7; Hab. 2:3 [b] Is. 66:18; Ezek. 38:14–23; Joel 3:2; Mic. 4:12; Matt. 25:32 [c] Zeph. 1:18 [1] Septuagint and Syriac read *for witness;* Targum reads *for the day of My revelation for judgment;* Vulgate reads *for the day of My resurrection that is to come.* 3:9 [a] Is. 19:18; 57:19 3:10 [a] Ps. 68:31; Is. 18:1; Acts 8:27 3:11 [a] Is. 2:12; 5:15; Matt. 3:9 3:12 [a] Is. 14:32; Zech. 13:8, 9 3:13 [a] Is. 10:20–22; [Mic. 4:7] [b] Is. 60:21 [c] Zech. 8:3, 16; Rev. 14:5

TRUST IN HIS WISDOM

INHALE

I want to trust God more in my life. I am in the Word, but honestly, it's tough to understand. How can I trust God more when I don't know how to understand Him and His ways by reading the Bible? What is the proper way to grow in my understanding of God through the Scriptures so that I can trust Him in my life?

EXHALE

There is nothing more frustrating than wanting to know something but nothing seems to get you there. Solomon, the wisest person who ever lived, advised, "In all your getting, get understanding" (Prov. 4:7). God delights in our honest desire to understand Him and grow in our faith. And the good news is that He doesn't want to be a mystery to us.

No one who comes to faith in Christ instantly understands all there is to know about the Bible. To be saved, knowing the gospel is enough, but once we are saved, we want to know far more than that. There are proper Bible study skills and techniques you can learn and develop to guide your time in the Word. The best way to learn those and also fuel growing in your faith is through the connections you make. First, we connect with God. Then, we connect with His people—the church. Plugging into a growing church where the Word of God is taught and lives are being changed is critical for your growth. Being part of a small group where you can learn more of how to apply God's Word to life is also important. When you make these connections, greater understanding can happen.

Know this: if seeking the Lord is your desire, you will find Him in the seeking; you will discover the One who promises, "The LORD your God in your midst, the Mighty One, will save; He will rejoice over you with gladness, He will quiet you with His love, He will rejoice over you with singing" (Zeph. 3:17). God wants you to understand Him.

Nor shall a deceitful tongue be
found in their mouth;
For [d]they shall feed *their*
flocks and lie down,
And no one shall make *them* afraid."

Joy in God's Faithfulness

14 [a]Sing, O daughter of Zion!
Shout, O Israel!
Be glad and rejoice with all *your*
heart,
O daughter of Jerusalem!
15 The LORD has taken away
your judgments,
He has cast out your enemy.
[a]The King of Israel, the LORD,
[b]*is* in your midst;
You shall see[1] disaster no more.
16 In that day [a]it shall be said
to Jerusalem:
"Do not fear;
Zion, [b]let not your hands be weak.
17 The LORD your God [a]in your midst,
The Mighty One, will save;
[b]He will rejoice over you with gladness,
He will quiet *you* with His love,
He will rejoice over you with singing."

18 "I will gather those who [a]sorrow
over the appointed assembly,
Who are among you,
To whom its reproach *is* a burden.
19 Behold, at that time
I will deal with all who afflict you;
I will save the [a]lame,
And gather those who were driven out;

3:13 [d] Ezek. 34:13–15, 28 3:14 [a] Is. 12:6 3:15 [a] [John 1:49] [b] Ezek. 48:35; [Rev. 7:15] [1] Some Hebrew manuscripts, Septuagint, and Bomberg read *see;* Masoretic Text and Vulgate read *fear.* 3:16 [a] Is. 35:3, 4 [b] Job 4:3; Heb. 12:12 3:17 [a] Zeph. 3:5, 15 [b] Deut. 30:9; Is. 62:5; 65:19; Jer. 32:41 3:18 [a] Lam. 2:6 3:19 [a] [Ezek. 34:16; Mic. 4:6, 7]

I will appoint them for
praise and fame
In every land where they
were put to shame.
20 At that time [a]I will bring you back,
Even at the time I gather you;
For I will give you fame and praise
Among all the peoples of the
earth,
When I return your captives
before your eyes,"
Says the LORD.

3:20 [a] Is. 11:12; Ezek. 28:25; Amos 9:14

THE BOOK OF

HAGGAI

OVERVIEW

The Book of Haggai is named for its author, and Haggai means "feast of Yahweh." The book covers the ministry of the minor prophet Haggai during a four-month span in 520 BC. Haggai's message announced renewed promises for the Israelites. His four messages were directed to Zerubbabel, the governor of Judah; Joshua, the high priest; and the people.

The Israelites began rebuilding the temple in 539 BC during the reign of King Cyrus of Persia, who allowed them to return to Jerusalem from captivity. Due to opposition from the Samaritans, the Israelites stopped the work on the temple after laying its foundation in 536 BC. In 520 BC, the work resumed during the reign of Darius I, who had brought stability to the land. Haggai instructed the people of Israel to resume building the temple of God.

In the beginning of Haggai's ministry, the prophet chastised the people for building houses for themselves and allowing God's "temple to lie in ruins" (Hag. 1:4). He told them their lack of attention to the temple had caused the failure of their crops and other economic issues. Haggai instructed the people to begin rebuilding the temple (see vv. 6–11). God promised that He would be with the people, and "they came and worked on the house of the LORD of hosts, their God" (v. 14).

In chapter 2, Haggai declared that the people should "not fear" (v. 5). He prophesied God's plan to "fill this temple with glory" (v. 7), promising "the glory of this latter temple shall be greater than the former" (v. 9). Haggai revealed God's plan to bless Israel and continue the throne of David in Jerusalem through Zerubbabel (see vv. 15–23).

The Book of Haggai is a reminder of the blessings that come with obedience. God sent Haggai to instruct the Israelites to complete the work of rebuilding His temple that had begun several years before. Haggai admonished them for focusing on building their own homes and neglecting God's. The people and the leaders responded positively to the message and began to rebuild the temple. God promised that His glory would dwell in the temple and among them. Because of their obedience, God kept His promise to continue the throne of David.

BREATHE IT IN

The Book of Haggai focuses on the importance of completing the work of the Lord, no matter what obstacles appear. When the Israelites first returned to Jerusalem after being captives in Babylon, they excitedly began the work of rebuilding the temple. However, when they faced opposition, they stopped the work. God sent Haggai to chastise the people for focusing on themselves and leaving His work undone. He promised future blessings once the temple was completed.

God has a purpose for each of our lives, and He has placed everything we need to fulfill that purpose within our reach. Periodically, He will give us specific assignments that are part of that purpose. We do not always understand the assignments, nor do we always feel comfortable completing them. However, it is our responsibility as Christians to do the work of the Lord when He calls upon us.

Most Christians are eager to receive an assignment from God. We often say in our prayers, "Here am I, Lord. Send me." We plead with God to use us in the kingdom. Yet, when He actually calls on us, we can be slow to answer. When He gives us an assignment, we do not always complete it in a timely manner. We procrastinate. Often fear and misplaced priorities are the factors underlying this procrastination.

When the Israelites returned to Jerusalem, they accepted the assignment of rebuilding the temple. They began the work with fervor but faced resistance from their enemies. They feared those who opposed them and allowed the resistance to hinder their progress. Somehow, they had forgotten the many times that God had given them the victory and defeated their enemies.

After completing only the foundation of the temple, they stopped the work and focused on themselves. Fear interfered with their assigned task and turned their eyes toward pursuits that were more appealing. Their comfort took precedence over the things of God. Their homes were a more pressing, appealing endeavor. They were not concerned with having a sacred place to commune with God. He was no longer first in their lives.

Have you ever procrastinated when God gave you an assignment? Were you afraid that you would not be able to complete the assignment? Were you uncomfortable carrying it out? Did you think it was too big for you? Did you question your skills and your worth? Did you allow your fear to turn your attention away from the assignment to your own personal projects? Is God still waiting for you to do what He called you to do?

Because the Israelites had not rebuilt the temple, God sent Haggai to remind them of their assignment. The Book of Haggai serves as a reminder to us of our assignment and the importance of completing it. Our assignment is a part of God's master plan.

Whenever God gives us an assignment, He ensures that we have everything we need to complete it. He puts the right people in place at the right time. He gives us the appropriate words to speak and the power to speak them. Do not be afraid. Ask God for direction. Keep God first. Follow His lead and finish your assignment.

THE BOOK OF

HAGGAI

The Command to Build God's House
(Ezra 5:1)

1 In [a]the second year of King Darius, in
the sixth month, on the first day of the
month, the word of the LORD came by
[b]Haggai the prophet to [c]Zerubbabel the
son of Shealtiel, governor of Judah, and
to [d]Joshua the son of [e]Jehozadak, the high
priest, saying, 2"Thus speaks the LORD of
hosts, saying: 'This people says, "The time
has not come, the time that the LORD's
house should be built." ' "
3Then the word of the LORD [a]came by
Haggai the prophet, saying, 4"*Is it* [a]time
for you yourselves to dwell in your paneled houses, and this temple[1] *to lie* in ruins?" 5Now therefore, thus says the LORD
of hosts: [a]"Consider your ways!

6 "You have [a]sown much,
And bring in little;
You eat, but do not have enough;
You drink, but you are not
filled with drink;
You clothe yourselves, but
no one is warm;
And [b]he who earns wages,
Earns wages *to put* into a
bag with holes."

7Thus says the LORD of hosts: "Consider
your ways! 8Go up to the [a]mountains and
bring wood and build the temple, that I
may take pleasure in it and be glorified,"
says the LORD. 9[a]"*You* looked for much,
but indeed *it came to* little; and when you
brought it home, [b]I blew it away. Why?" says
the LORD of hosts. "Because of My house
that *is in* ruins, while every one of you runs
to his own house. 10Therefore [a]the heavens above you withhold the dew, and the
earth withholds its fruit. 11For I [a]called for
a drought on the land and the mountains,
on the grain and the new wine and the oil,
on whatever the ground brings forth, on
men and livestock, and on [b]all the labor of
your hands."

The People's Obedience

12[a]Then Zerubbabel the son of Shealtiel,
and Joshua the son of Jehozadak, the high
priest, with all the remnant of the people,
obeyed the voice of the LORD their God,
and the words of Haggai the prophet, as the
LORD their God had sent him; and the people feared the presence of the LORD. 13Then
Haggai, the LORD's messenger, spoke the
LORD's message to the people, saying, [a]"I
am with you, says the LORD." 14So [a]the LORD
stirred up the spirit of Zerubbabel the son
of Shealtiel, [b]governor of Judah, and the
spirit of Joshua the son of Jehozadak, the
high priest, and the spirit of all the remnant
of the people; [c]and they came and worked
on the house of the LORD of hosts, their
God, 15on the twenty-fourth day of the sixth
month, in the second year of King Darius.

The Coming Glory of God's House

2 In the seventh *month,* on the twenty-
first of the month, the word of the
LORD came by Haggai the prophet, saying:
2"Speak now to Zerubbabel the son of Shealtiel, governor of Judah, and to Joshua the

---

1:1 [a] Ezra 4:24; Hag. 2:10; Zech. 1:1, 7 [b] Ezra 5:1; 6:14 [c] 1 Chr. 3:19; Ezra 2:2; Neh. 7:7; Zech. 4:6; Matt. 1:12, 13 [d] Ezra 5:2, 3; Zech. 6:11 [e] 1 Chr. 6:15 1:3 [a] Ezra 5:1 1:4 [a] 2 Sam. 7:2 [1] Literally *house,* and so in verse 8 1:5 [a] Lam. 3:40 1:6 [a] Deut. 28:38–40; Hos. 8:7; Hag. 1:9, 10; 2:16, 17 [b] Zech. 8:10 1:8 [a] Ezra 3:7 1:9 [a] Hag. 2:16 [b] Hag. 2:17 1:10 [a] Lev. 26:19; Deut. 28:23; 1 Kin. 8:35; Joel 1:18–20 1:11 [a] 1 Kin. 17:1; 2 Kin. 8:1 [b] Hag. 2:17 1:12 [a] Ezra 5:2 1:13 [a] [Matt. 28:20; Rom. 8:31] 1:14 [a] 2 Chr. 36:22; Ezra 1:1 [b] Hag. 2:21 [c] Ezra 5:2, 8; Neh. 4:6

son of Jehozadak, the high priest, and to
the remnant of the people, saying: 3[a]'Who
is left among you who saw this temple[1] in
its former glory? And how do you see it
now? In comparison with it, [b]*is this* not in
your eyes as nothing? 4Yet now [a]be strong,
Zerubbabel,' says the LORD; 'and be strong,
Joshua, son of Jehozadak, the high priest;
and be strong, all you people of the land,'
says the LORD, 'and work; for I *am* with you,'
says the LORD of hosts. 5[a]'*According to* the
word that I covenanted with you when you
came out of Egypt, so [b]My Spirit remains
among you; do not fear!'

6"For thus says the LORD of hosts: [a]'Once
more (it *is* a little while) [b]I will shake heaven
and earth, the sea and dry land; 7and I will
shake all nations, and they shall come to
[a]the Desire of All Nations,[1] and I will fill
this temple with [b]glory,' says the LORD of
hosts. 8'The silver *is* Mine, and the gold *is*
Mine,' says the LORD of hosts. 9[a]'The glory
of this latter temple shall be greater than
the former,' says the LORD of hosts. 'And in
this place I will give [b]peace,' says the LORD
of hosts."

The People Are Defiled

10On the twenty-fourth *day* of the ninth
month, in the second year of Darius, the
word of the LORD came by Haggai the
prophet, saying, 11"Thus says the LORD of
hosts: 'Now, [a]ask the priests *concerning the*
law, saying, 12"If one carries holy meat in
the fold of his garment, and with the edge
he touches bread or stew, wine or oil, or any
food, will it become holy?"'"

Then the priests answered and said,
"No."

13And Haggai said, "If *one who is* [a]unclean
because of a dead body touches any
of these, will it be unclean?"

So the priests answered and said, "It
shall be unclean."

14Then Haggai answered and said, [a]"'So
is this people, and so is this nation before
Me,' says the LORD, 'and so is every work
of their hands; and what they offer there
is unclean.

Promised Blessing

15'And now, carefully [a]consider from this
day forward: from before stone was laid
upon stone in the temple of the LORD—
16since those *days,* [a]when *one* came to a
heap of twenty ephahs, there were *but* ten;
when *one* came to the wine vat to draw
out fifty baths from the press, there were
but twenty. 17[a]I struck you with blight and
mildew and hail [b]in all the labors of your
hands; [c]yet you did not *turn* to Me,' says
the LORD. 18'Consider now from this day
forward, from the twenty-fourth day of
the ninth month, from [a]the day that the
foundation of the LORD's temple was laid—
consider it: 19[a]Is the seed still in the barn?
As yet the vine, the fig tree, the pomegranate,
and the olive tree have not yielded *fruit.*
But from this day I will [b]bless *you.*'"

Zerubbabel Chosen as a Signet

20And again the word of the LORD came
to Haggai on the twenty-fourth day of the
month, saying, 21"Speak to Zerubbabel,
[a]governor of Judah, saying:

[b]'I will shake heaven and earth.
22 [a]I will overthrow the throne
of kingdoms;
I will destroy the strength of
the Gentile kingdoms.
[b]I will overthrow the chariots
And those who ride in them;
The horses and their riders
shall come down,
Every one by the sword of his brother.

23'In that day,' says the LORD of hosts, 'I
will take you, Zerubbabel My servant, the
son of Shealtiel,' says the LORD, [a]'and will
make you like a signet *ring;* for [b]I have chosen
you,' says the LORD of hosts."

2:3 [a] Ezra 3:12, 13 [b] Zech. 4:10 [1] Literally *house,* and so in verses 7 and 9 2:4 [a] Deut. 31:23; 1 Chr. 22:13; 28:20; Zech. 8:9; Eph. 6:10 2:5 [a] Ex. 29:45, 46 [b] [Neh. 9:20]; Is. 63:11, 14 2:6 [a] Heb. 12:26 [b] [Joel 3:16] 2:7 [a] Gen. 49:10; Mal. 3:1 [b] 1 Kin. 8:11; Is. 60:7; Zech. 2:5 [1] Or *the desire of all nations* 2:9 [a] [John 1:14] [b] Ps. 85:8, 9; Luke 2:14; [Eph. 2:14] 2:11 [a] Lev. 10:10, 11; Deut. 33:10; Mal. 2:7 2:13 [a] Lev. 22:4–6; Num. 19:11, 22 2:14 [a] [Titus 1:15] 2:15 [a] Hag. 1:5, 7; 2:18 2:16 [a] Hag. 1:6, 9; Zech. 8:10 2:17 [a] Deut. 28:22; 1 Kin. 8:37; Amos 4:9 [b] Hag. 1:11 [c] Jer. 5:3; Amos 4:6–11 2:18 [a] Ezra 5:1, 2, 16; Zech. 8:9 2:19 [a] Zech. 8:12 [b] Ps. 128:1–6; Jer. 31:12, 14; [Mal. 3:10] 2:21 [a] Ezra 5:2; Hag. 1:1, 14; Zech. 4:6–10 [b] Hag. 2:6, 7; [Heb. 12:26, 27] 2:22 [a] [Dan. 2:44; Rev. 19:11–21] [b] Ps. 46:9; Ezek. 39:20; Mic. 5:10; Zech. 9:10 2:23 [a] Song 8:6; Jer. 22:24 [b] Is. 42:1; 43:10

THE BOOK OF
ZECHARIAH

OVERVIEW

Zechariah was an Old Testament minor prophet, and this book bears his name, which means "Yahweh remembers." Zechariah began his ministry calling for the Israelites to renew their relationship with God in 520 BC. Zechariah was a contemporary of Haggai, the prophet whose message precedes the Book of Zechariah.

Zechariah ministered to the Israelites who returned from Babylonian exile and to those who remained in Babylon. The people in Jerusalem had begun rebuilding the temple in response to a prophetic message, and God blessed them because of their obedience. Zechariah preached that the Israelites would have to live in obedience for God to continue blessing them. He encouraged the people to complete the work of rebuilding the temple.

In this book, the prophet warned the Israelites not to repeat the sins of their fathers, with whom God had been angry (see Zech. 1:2). God promised to return to them if they would return to Him (see v. 3).

Zechariah shared the details of eight symbolic visions he received from God, all in one night (1:7—6:15). In the visions, an angel interpreted their meanings. Zechariah had visions of horses, horns, a measuring line, the high priest, a lampstand and olive trees, a flying scroll, a woman in a basket, and four chariots. The visions spoke of God's commitment to His people (see 1:12–17), His plan to punish their enemies (see 1:18–21), and the future prosperity of Jerusalem (see 2:1–13). They also addressed completion of the temple and God's renewal of the priesthood (3:1—4:14), purification of the land (see 5:1–11), and the crowning of "a priest on His throne" (6:13; see 6:9–15).

After outlining the visions, Zechariah instructed the people to "execute true justice" and "show mercy and compassion" (7:9). He reminded them that disobedience had been the cause of their captivity and encouraged them to look to the future for God's restoration of Israel (ch. 8). He proclaimed that their restoration would include God's judgment of their enemies, the arrival of Jesus, and salvation for all through Him (chs. 9–11). The remaining chapters (12–14) describe the future deliverance of the Israelites and the coming of Jesus Christ.

The prophet Zechariah encouraged the Israelites to finish rebuilding the temple. God gave him visions of various moments in the nation's future. While the visions included judgment, they also addressed restoration and the coming of Christ, at which time God will rule the earth. The Book of Zechariah offered hope for the future to a people who had suffered great pain and loss. It is a reminder that God keeps His promises.

BREATHE IT IN

The Book of Zechariah encouraged the Israelites to continue building the temple and to renew their relationship with God. After returning from captivity, they needed reassurance that God was still on their side and that their work on the temple was not in vain. Zechariah provided that assurance by sharing God's plans for the future and the blessings that would follow restoration.

When the Israelites returned from captivity in Babylonia, they lacked encouragement. They were unsure of their standing with God. They had habitually performed sinful acts and disobeyed God. God's judgment had brought them captivity, famine, sickness, military defeat, and oppression. On occasion, they repented and turned back to God. But inevitably, they fell back into sin. Once they were set free from captivity, they were unsure of where they stood in the sight of God.

One of the laws of physics is that for every action there is an equal and opposite reaction. This law reaches beyond science and is a universal truth. It has been in operation for all of time, and it is evidenced through God's interactions with the Israelites during the Old Testament—their actions produced consequences. This law of equal but opposite reactions applies to our lives as Christians too. All our actions have consequences; some are positive, and some are negative.

God provides the help we need to live in alignment with His plans and purposes. The two most important of these helpers are the Bible and the Holy Spirit. The Bible serves as a handbook for Christians, providing instruction on God's expectations of us. It also warns of potential consequences of certain actions. The Holy Spirit serves as an internal helper who leads us in the right direction and guides our thoughts and actions. Yet, even with these powerful helpers available to us, we still sin, and there are consequences associated with those sins.

When we sin and suffer its consequences, many of us feel abandoned by God. We question whether He still loves us and wonder if He will keep His promises to us. We feel lost and alone. We might even consider giving up and throwing in the towel. In times like these, we need encouragement.

We cannot allow our sin to separate us from God. He knows we are human. He knows we will sin. This is the very reason He sent His Son, Jesus, to die for our sins and create a path to forgiveness and rebirth into God's kingdom. When we make sinful choices, we should not dwell on them or beat ourselves up. We need to turn from our sin, turn our gaze back toward Christ, and rest in His forgiveness. Then we stand back up and keep pushing forward.

Be encouraged by the fact that God is a forgiving God. Be reminded that trouble is not eternal. Know that our future will be much greater than our present or our past. Remember, God is with us always!

THE BOOK OF

ZECHARIAH

A Call to Repentance
(Ezra 5:1)

1 In the eighth month [a]of the second
year of Darius, the word of the LORD
came [b]to Zechariah the son of Berechiah,
the son of [c]Iddo the prophet, saying, 2"The
LORD has been very angry with your fathers. 3Therefore say to them, 'Thus says
the LORD of hosts: "Return [a]to Me," says the
LORD of hosts, "and I will return to you,"
says the LORD of hosts. 4"Do not be like
your fathers, [a]to whom the former prophets preached, saying, 'Thus says the LORD
of hosts: [b]"Turn now from your evil ways
and your evil deeds."' But they did not hear
nor heed Me," says the LORD.

5 "Your fathers, where *are* they?
And the prophets, do they live forever?
6 Yet surely [a]My words and My statutes,
Which I commanded My
servants the prophets,
Did they not overtake your fathers?

"So they returned and said:

[b]'Just as the LORD of hosts
determined to do to us,
According to our ways and
according to our deeds,
So He has dealt with us.'"'"

Vision of the Horses

7On the twenty-fourth day of the eleventh month, which is the month Shebat,
in the second year of Darius, the word of
the LORD came to Zechariah the son of
Berechiah, the son of Iddo the prophet: 8I
saw by night, and behold, [a]a man riding on
a red horse, and it stood among the myrtle
trees in the hollow; and behind him *were*
[b]horses: red, sorrel, and white. 9Then I said,
[a]"My lord, what *are* these?" So the angel
who talked with me said to me, "I will show
you what they *are*."
10And the man who stood among the
myrtle trees answered and said, [a]"These *are*
the ones whom the LORD has sent to walk
to and fro throughout the earth."
11[a]So they answered the Angel of the
LORD, who stood among the myrtle trees,
and said, "We have walked to and fro
throughout the earth, and behold, all the
earth is resting quietly."

The LORD Will Comfort Zion

12Then the Angel of the LORD answered
and said, "O LORD of hosts, [a]how long will
You not have mercy on Jerusalem and on
the cities of Judah, against which You were
angry [b]these seventy years?"
13And the LORD answered the angel who
talked to me, *with* [a]good *and* comforting
words. 14So the angel who spoke with me
said to me, "Proclaim, saying, 'Thus says
the LORD of hosts:

"I am [a]zealous for Jerusalem
And for Zion with great zeal.
15 I am exceedingly angry with
the nations at ease;
For [a]I was a little angry,
And they helped—*but* with
evil *intent*."

1:1 [a] Ezra 4:24; 6:15; Hag. 1:1; Zech. 7:1 [b] Ezra 5:1; 6:14; Zech. 7:1; Matt. 23:35; Luke 11:51 [c] Neh. 12:4, 16 1:3 [a] Is. 31:6; 44:22; [Mic. 7:19; Mal. 3:7–10; Luke 15:20; James 4:8] 1:4 [a] 2 Chr. 36:15, 16 [b] Is. 31:6; Jer. 3:12; 18:11; Ezek. 18:30; [Hos. 14:1] 1:6 [a] [Is. 55:11] [b] Lam. 1:18; 2:17 1:8 [a] Is. 55:13; Zech. 6:2; [Rev. 6:4] [b] [Zech. 6:2–7; Rev. 6:2] 1:9 [a] Zech. 4:4, 5, 13; 6:4 1:10 [a] [Heb. 1:14] 1:11 [a] [Ps. 103:20, 21] 1:12 [a] Ps. 74:10; Jer. 12:4; Hab. 1:2 [b] 2 Chr. 36:21; Jer. 25:11, 12; 29:10; Dan. 9:2; Zech. 7:5 1:13 [a] Jer. 29:10 1:14 [a] Joel 2:18; Zech. 8:2 1:15 [a] Is. 47:6

HOPE FOR TRUE JUDGMENTS

INHALE

I love the verses "'Vengeance is Mine, I will repay,' says the Lord" (Rom. 12:19) and "Whatever a man sows, that he will also reap" (Gal. 6:7). But I'm not seeing these verses being played out in real life today. Many people are not getting true judgments, and I'm angry about that. How can people get away with killing unarmed teenagers and children by claiming they acted in self-defense? How can sleeping people be gunned down and no one be brought to justice? How can I trust in God's judgment when time after time the wrongdoers are getting off?

EXHALE

The situations you mention seem to have terrible endings; however, they have not ended. God will have the final word on these matters. Justice on earth may have been denied, but God's true and greater justice is still coming. Humanity's justice is one thing, but God's justice is another. No one gets away with evil, even though it may appear they have. This is where trusting in God is so important. God's judgment is sure and certain. Isaiah 30:18 tells us that "the LORD is a God of justice." If it is written, you can count on it.

Let me add one more verse that may be of help: "Cease from anger, and forsake wrath; do not fret—it only causes harm" (Ps. 37:8). As we experience humanity's injustice and work to trust in God's justice, we must be careful not to become a people of revenge. That is what one of your favorite verses is about. Justice will never be found by any unjust act—even those that seem warranted. As we see in Psalm 37, revenge isn't just the wrong path to take; it harms us when we travel down it. This is a warning every believer must hear: injustices will not stop, and it will seem as if God is not in control. But all things are under the watchful eye of the great King Jesus, and He alone determines what is truly just. The next time terrible things happen, remember that God did not somehow fall asleep or miss what happened. God saw, and He will execute His justice in His way and time. Zechariah 1:6 says, "Just as the LORD of hosts determined to do to us, according to our ways and according to our deeds, so He has dealt with us." In God's court of law, we rest in knowing He will render the final verdict.

16 'Therefore thus says the LORD:

[a]"I am returning to Jerusalem
with mercy;
My [b]house [c]shall be built in it,"
says the LORD of hosts,
"And [d]a *surveyor's* line shall be
stretched out over Jerusalem."'

17 "Again proclaim, saying, 'Thus says the
LORD of hosts:

"My cities shall again spread
out through prosperity;
[a]The LORD will again comfort Zion,
And [b]will again choose Jerusalem."'"

Vision of the Horns

18 Then I raised my eyes and looked, and
there *were* four [a]horns. 19 And I said to the
angel who talked with me, "What *are* these?"
So he answered me, [a]"These *are* the
horns that have scattered Judah, Israel,
and Jerusalem."
20 Then the LORD showed me four craftsmen. 21 And I said, "What are these coming to do?"
So he said, "These *are* the [a]horns that
scattered Judah, so that no one could lift
up his head; but the craftsmen[1] are coming
to terrify them, to cast out the horns of the
nations that [b]lifted up *their* horn against
the land of Judah to scatter it."

1:16 [a] [Is. 12:1; 54:8; Zech. 2:10; 8:3] [b] Ezra 6:14, 15; Hag. 1:4; Zech. 4:9 [c] 2 Chr. 36:23; Ezra 1:2, 3; Is. 44:28 [d] Zech. 2:1–3 1:17 [a] [Is. 40:1, 2; 51:3] [b] Is. 14:1; Zech. 2:12 1:18 [a] [Lam. 2:17] 1:19 [a] Ezra 4:1, 4, 7 1:21 [a] [Ps. 75:10] [b] Ps. 75:4, 5 [1] Literally *these*

Vision of the Measuring Line

2 Then I raised my eyes and looked, and
behold, [a]a man with a measuring line in
his hand. 2So I said, "Where are you going?"
And he said to me, [a]"To measure Jerusalem, to see what *is* its width and what *is*
its length."
3And there *was* the angel who talked
with me, going out; and another angel was
coming out to meet him, 4who said to him,
"Run, speak to this young man, saying: [a]'Jerusalem shall be inhabited *as* towns without walls, because of the multitude of men
and livestock in it. 5For I,' says the LORD,
'will be [a]a wall of fire all around her, [b]and I
will be the glory in her midst.'"

#OXYGEN

ZECHARIAH 2:9–11

Hope for True Judgments

God is the righteous Judge. Racially biased policies, disproportionate gun violence in urban communities, and the like are not just. When public policy creates conditions that perpetuate injustice for the marginalized, we must be on the Lord's side. His justice will come. Participate in the political process, **breathe**, and **hope for true judgments**.

Future Joy of Zion and Many Nations

6"Up, up! Flee [a]from the land of the
north," says the LORD; "for I have [b]spread
you abroad like the four winds of heaven,"
says the LORD. 7"Up, Zion! [a]Escape, you who
dwell with the daughter of Babylon."
8For thus says the LORD of hosts: "He
sent Me after glory, to the nations which
plunder you; for he who [a]touches you
touches the apple of His eye. 9For surely
I will [a]shake My hand against them, and
they shall become spoil for their servants.
Then [b]you will know that the LORD of hosts
has sent Me.
10[a]"Sing and rejoice, O daughter of Zion!
For behold, I am coming and I [b]will dwell
in your midst," says the LORD. 11[a]"Many nations shall be joined to the LORD [b]in that
day, and they shall become [c]My people. And
I will dwell in your midst. Then [d]you will
know that the LORD of hosts has sent Me to
you. 12And the LORD will [a]take possession of
Judah as His inheritance in the Holy Land,
and will again choose Jerusalem. 13[a]Be silent, all flesh, before the LORD, for He is
aroused [b]from His holy habitation!"

Vision of the High Priest

3 Then he showed me [a]Joshua the high
priest standing before the Angel of
the LORD, and [b]Satan standing at his right
hand to oppose him. 2And the LORD said
to Satan, [a]"The LORD rebuke you, Satan!
The LORD who [b]has chosen Jerusalem rebuke you! [c]*Is* this not a brand plucked from
the fire?"
3Now Joshua was clothed with [a]filthy
garments, and was standing before the
Angel.
4Then He answered and spoke to those
who stood before Him, saying, "Take away
the filthy garments from him." And to him
He said, "See, I have removed your iniquity from you, [a]and I will clothe you with
rich robes."
5And I said, "Let them put a clean [a]tur-
ban on his head."
So they put a clean turban on his head,
and they put the clothes on him. And the
Angel of the LORD stood by.

The Coming Branch

6Then the Angel of the LORD admonished Joshua, saying, 7"Thus says the LORD
of hosts:

'If you will walk in My ways,
And if you will [a]keep My command,
Then you shall also [b]judge My house,
And likewise have charge of
  My courts;
I will give you places to walk
Among these who [c]stand here.

2:1 [a] Jer. 31:39; Ezek. 40:3; 47:3; Zech. 1:16 2:2 [a] Rev. 11:1 2:4 [a] Jer. 31:27 2:5 [a] [Is. 26:1] [b] [Is. 60:19] 2:6 [a] Is. 48:20 [b] Deut. 28:64 2:7 [a] Is. 48:20; Jer. 51:6; [Rev. 18:4] 2:8 [a] Deut. 32:10; Ps. 17:8 2:9 [a] Is. 19:16 [b] Zech. 4:9 2:10 [a] Is. 12:6 [b] [Lev. 26:12] 2:11 [a] [Is. 2:2, 3] [b] Zech. 3:10 [c] Ex. 12:49 [d] Ezek. 33:33 2:12 [a] [Deut. 32:9]; Ps. 33:12; Jer. 10:16 2:13 [a] Hab. 2:20; Zeph. 1:7 [b] Ps. 68:5 3:1 [a] Ezra 5:2; Hag. 1:1; Zech. 6:11 [b] 1 Chr. 21:1; Job 1:6; Ps. 109:6; [Rev. 12:9, 10] 3:2 [a] Mark 9:25; [Jude 9] [b] [Rom. 8:33] [c] Amos 4:11; Jude 23 3:3 [a] Ezra 9:15; Is. 64:6 3:4 [a] Gen. 3:21; Is. 61:10 3:5 [a] Ex. 29:6 3:7 [a] Lev. 8:35; Ezek. 44:16 [b] Deut. 17:9, 12 [c] Zech. 3:4

8 'Hear, O Joshua, the high priest,
You and your companions
who sit before you,
For they are [a]a wondrous sign;
For behold, I am bringing forth
[b]My Servant the [c]BRANCH.
9 For behold, the stone
That I have laid before Joshua:
[a]Upon the stone *are* [b]seven eyes.
Behold, I will engrave its inscription,'
Says the LORD of hosts,
'And [c]I will remove the iniquity
of that land in one day.
10 [a]In that day,' says the LORD of hosts,
'Everyone will invite his neighbor
[b]Under his vine and under his
fig tree.'"

Vision of the Lampstand and Olive Trees

4 Now [a]the angel who talked with me
came back and wakened me, [b]as a man
who is wakened out of his sleep. 2And he
said to me, "What do you see?"
So I said, "I am looking, and there *is* [a]a
lampstand of solid gold with a bowl on top
of it, [b]and on the *stand* seven lamps with
seven pipes to the seven lamps. 3[a]Two olive
trees *are* by it, one at the right of the bowl
and the other at its left." 4So I answered and
spoke to the angel who talked with me, saying, "What *are* these, my lord?"
5Then the angel who talked with me answered and said to me, "Do you not know
what these are?"
And I said, "No, my lord."
6So he answered and said to me:

"This *is* the word of the LORD
to [a]Zerubbabel:
[b]'Not by might nor by power,
but by My Spirit,'
Says the LORD of hosts.
7 'Who *are* you, [a]O great mountain?
Before Zerubbabel *you shall*
become a plain!
And he shall bring forth [b]the
capstone
[c]With shouts of "Grace, grace to it!"'"

8Moreover the word of the LORD came
to me, saying:

9 "The hands of Zerubbabel
[a]Have laid the foundation
of this temple;[1]
His hands [b]shall also finish *it*.
Then [c]you will know
That the [d]LORD of hosts
has sent Me to you.
10 For who has despised the
day of [a]small things?
For these seven rejoice
to see
The plumb line in the hand
of Zerubbabel.
[b]They are the eyes of the
LORD,
Which scan to and fro throughout
the whole earth."

11Then I answered and said to him, "What
are these [a]two olive trees—at the right of
the lampstand and at its left?" 12And I further answered and said to him, "What *are*
these two olive branches that *drip* into the
receptacles[1] of the two gold pipes from
which the golden *oil* drains?"
13Then he answered me and said, "Do
you not know what these *are?*"
And I said, "No, my lord."
14So he said, [a]"These *are* the two anointed
ones, [b]who stand beside the Lord of the
whole earth."

Vision of the Flying Scroll

5 Then I turned and raised my eyes, and
saw there a flying [a]scroll.
2And he said to me, "What do you see?"
So I answered, "I see a flying scroll. Its
length *is* twenty cubits and its width ten
cubits."
3Then he said to me, "This *is* the [a]curse
that goes out over the face of the whole
earth: 'Every thief shall be expelled,' according *to* this side of *the scroll;* and, 'Every perjurer shall be expelled,' according
to that side of it."

3:8 [a] Ps. 71:7 [b] Is. 42:1 [c] Is. 11:1; 53:2; Jer. 23:5; 33:15; Zech. 6:12 3:9 [a] [Zech. 4:10; Rev. 5:6] [b] Ps. 118:22 [c] Jer. 31:34; 50:20; Zech. 3:4 3:10 [a] Zech. 2:11 [b] 1 Kin. 4:25; Is. 36:16; Mic. 4:4 4:1 [a] Zech. 1:9; 2:3 [b] Dan. 8:18 4:2 [a] Rev. 1:12 [b] Ex. 25:37; [Rev. 4:5] 4:3 [a] Rev. 11:3, 4 4:6 [a] Hag. 1:1 [b] Is. 30:1; Hos. 1:7; Hag. 2:4, 5 4:7 [a] Ps. 114:4, 6; Is. 40:4; Jer. 51:25; Nah. 1:5; Zech. 14:4, 5; [Matt. 21:21] [b] Ps. 118:22 [c] Ezra 3:10, 11, 13; Ps. 84:11 4:9 [a] Ezra 3:8–10; 5:16; Hag. 2:18 [b] Ezra 6:14, 15; Zech. 6:12, 13 [c] Zech. 2:9, 11; 6:15 [d] [Is. 43:16]; Zech. 2:8 [1] Literally *house* 4:10 [a] Neh. 4:2–4; Amos 7:2, 5; Hag. 2:3 [b] 2 Chr. 16:9; Prov. 15:3; Zech. 3:9 4:11 [a] Zech. 4:3; Rev. 11:4 4:12 [1] Literally *into the hands of* 4:14 [a] Rev. 11:4 [b] Zech. 3:1–7 5:1 [a] Jer. 36:2; Ezek. 2:9; Rev. 5:1 5:3 [a] Mal. 4:6

RELEASE // TRUST IN HIS WISDOM

The Journey to Transformation

Zechariah 4:6 // So he answered and said to me: "This is the word of the LORD to Zerubbabel: 'Not by might nor by power, but by My Spirit,' says the LORD of hosts."

Summary Message // If we allow the Holy Spirit to complete His work in us, we will find the destination well worth the journey. We are saved by grace, but we still need to put in the work to live out our faith. By seeking the Lord, seeking righteousness, and seeking humility, we will find that the Holy Spirit will transform us from citizens of this world to citizens of the kingdom of God. Second Corinthians 3:18 says, "But we all, with unveiled face, beholding as in a mirror the glory of the Lord, are being transformed into the same image from glory to glory, just as by the Spirit of the Lord." If we stay rooted in God and walk with Him daily, we can count on our lives being a pilgrimage to eternity based upon faith, hope, and love.

But, unfortunately, many of us consider our own knowledge and abilities sufficient to direct our lives. Often, we find ourselves trying to figure things out based on our own limited previous interactions, failures, and accomplishments. As a result, we fail to seek God, and our spiritual journey to transformation can become stagnant. Is it any wonder that, so often, our perceptions of the world and the concepts of justice, righteousness, and humility are not in line with God's kingdom ways? Right thinking is not a worldly concept; it is a spiritual one when our understanding of all things comes from the Creator of all things and not from the created.

Practical Application // Reflection is a very powerful tool. It gives us the ability to look back over the course of our lives and see where we have made wrong choices and have strayed from God's way. But the past is not our blueprint for the future. God meets us where we are today and leaves the past behind. The beauty of this is that most of us have a very tangled past, like a spiderweb that is nearly impossible to untangle. But when the past is discarded and we start with God, right now, where we are, our lives will become what we have only dared to imagine. God "is able to do exceedingly abundantly above all that we ask or think, according to the power that works in us" (Eph. 3:20).

We do not want to relive the past, but it would be beneficial to take a moment and reflect on what God has done, how far He has brought us, and how He has used us. We may not understand it all, but we have to trust that God's hand has been in it all. From this day forward, we should make ourselves available to be His hands and feet and know that we have a role to play while we are purposed for this world. By seeking His face each day and knowing that God holds every tomorrow in His hands, we can take confident steps forward and trust in His plan.

Fervent Prayer // Heavenly Father, we seek You and long to find You. We want to know You and Your ways. There have been times in the past when we strayed from Your leading and did things on our own. There have been many times when we have applied our thoughts and opinions rather than seeking Your will regarding the situations of our lives. For these prideful acts, we ask for Your forgiveness. Father God, we trust in You. We trust in Your wisdom. We trust in Your power for our lives, and we believe that our future will be brighter because of what You have shown us. Teach us to seek You more fervently with each passing day. In Jesus' name we pray. Amen.

---

4 "I will send out *the curse,*" says
the LORD of hosts;
"It shall enter the house of the [a]thief
And the house of [b]the one who
swears falsely by My name.
It shall remain in the
midst of his house
And consume [c]it, with its
timber and stones."

Vision of the Woman in a Basket

5 Then the angel who talked with me
came out and said to me, "Lift your eyes
now, and see what this *is* that goes forth."
6 So I asked, "What *is* it?" And he said, "It
is a basket[1] that is going forth."
He also said, "This *is* their resemblance
throughout the earth: 7 Here *is* a lead disc
lifted up, and this *is* a woman sitting inside

5:4 [a] Ex. 20:15; Lev. 19:11 [b] Ex. 20:7; Lev. 19:12; Is. 48:1; Jer. 5:2; Zech. 8:17; Mal. 3:5 [c] Lev. 14:34, 35; Job 18:15
5:6 [1] Hebrew *ephah,* a measuring container, and so elsewhere

the basket"; 8then he said, "This *is* Wickedness!" And he thrust her down into the
basket, and threw the lead cover[1] over its
mouth. 9Then I raised my eyes and looked,
and there *were* two women, coming with
the wind in their wings; for they had wings
like the wings of a [a]stork, and they lifted
up the basket between earth and heaven.
10So I said to the [a]angel who talked with
me, "Where are they carrying the basket?"
11And he said to me, "To [a]build a house
for it in [b]the land of Shinar;[1] when it is ready,
the basket will be set there on its base."

Vision of the Four Chariots

6 Then I turned and raised my eyes and
looked, and behold, four chariots *were*
coming from between two mountains, and
the mountains *were* mountains of bronze.
2With the first chariot *were* [a]red horses,
with the second chariot [b]black horses, 3with
the third chariot white horses, and with
the fourth chariot dappled horses—strong
steeds. 4Then I answered [a]and said to the
angel who talked with me, "What *are* these,
my lord?"
5And the angel answered and said to me,
[a]"These *are* four spirits of heaven, who go
out from *their* [b]station before the Lord of all
the earth. 6The one with the black horses is
going to [a]the north country, the white are
going after them, and the dappled are going
toward the south country." 7Then the strong
steeds went out, eager to go, that they might
[a]walk to and fro throughout the earth. And
He said, "Go, walk to and fro throughout the
earth." So they walked to and fro throughout the earth. 8And He called to me, and
spoke to me, saying, "See, those who go
toward the north country have given rest
to My [a]Spirit in the north country."

The Command to Crown Joshua

9Then the word of the LORD came to
me, saying: 10"Receive *the gift* from the
captives—from Heldai, Tobijah, and Jedaiah, who have come from Babylon—and
go the same day and enter the house of
Josiah the son of Zephaniah. 11Take the silver and gold, make [a]an elaborate crown,
and set *it* on the head of [b]Joshua the son of
Jehozadak, the high priest. 12Then speak to
him, saying, 'Thus says the LORD of hosts,
saying:

"Behold, [a]the Man whose
name *is* the [b]BRANCH!
From His place He shall branch out,
[c]And He shall build the
temple of the LORD;
13 Yes, He shall build the
temple of the LORD.
He [a]shall bear the glory,
And shall sit and rule on His throne;
So [b]He shall be a priest on His throne,
And the counsel of peace shall
be between them both." '

14"Now the elaborate crown shall be [a]for
a memorial in the temple of the LORD for
Helem,[1] Tobijah, Jedaiah, and Hen the son
of Zephaniah. 15Even [a]those from afar shall
come and build the temple of the LORD.
Then you shall know that the LORD of hosts
has sent Me to you. And *this* shall come to
pass if you diligently obey the voice of the
LORD your God."

Obedience Better than Fasting

7 Now in the fourth year of King Darius it
came to pass *that* the word of the LORD
came to Zechariah, on the fourth *day* of the
ninth month, Chislev, 2when *the people*[1]
sent Sherezer,[2] with Regem-Melech and his
men, *to* the house of God,[3] to pray before
the LORD, 3*and* to [a]ask the priests who *were*
in the house of the LORD of hosts, and the
prophets, saying, "Should I weep in [b]the
fifth month and fast as I have done for so
many years?"
4Then the word of the LORD of hosts
came to me, saying, 5"Say to all the people
of the land, and to the priests: 'When you
[a]fasted and mourned in the fifth [b]and seventh *months* [c]during those seventy years,
did you really fast [d]for Me—for Me? 6[a]When

5:8 [1] Literally *stone* 5:9 [a] Lev. 11:13, 19; Ps. 104:17; Jer. 8:7 5:10 [a] Zech. 5:5 5:11 [a] Jer. 29:5, 28 [b] Gen. 10:10; Is. 11:11; Dan. 1:2 [1] That is, Babylon 6:2 [a] Zech. 1:8; Rev. 6:4 [b] Rev. 6:5 6:4 [a] Zech. 5:10 6:5 [a] [Ps. 104:4; Heb. 1:7, 14] [b] 1 Kin. 22:19; Dan. 7:10; Zech. 4:14; Luke 1:19 6:6 [a] Jer. 1:14; Ezek. 1:4 6:7 [a] Gen. 13:17; Zech. 1:10 6:8 [a] Eccl. 10:4 6:11 [a] Ex. 29:6 [b] Ezra 3:2; Hag. 1:1; Zech. 3:1 6:12 [a] John 1:45 [b] Is. 4:2; 11:1; Jer. 23:5; 33:15; Zech. 3:8 [c] [Matt. 16:18; Eph. 2:20; Heb. 3:3] 6:13 [a] Is. 22:24 [b] Ps. 110:4; [Heb. 3:1] 6:14 [a] Ex. 12:14; Mark 14:9 [1] Following Masoretic Text, Targum, and Vulgate; Syriac reads *for Heldai* (compare verse 10); Septuagint reads *for the patient ones.* 6:15 [a] Is. 57:19; [Eph. 2:13] 7:2 [1] Literally *they* (compare verse 5) [2] Or *Sar-Ezer* [3] Hebrew *Bethel* 7:3 [a] Deut. 17:9; Mal. 2:7 [b] Zech. 8:19 7:5 [a] [Is. 58:1–9] [b] Jer. 41:1 [c] Zech. 1:12 [d] [Rom. 14:6] 7:6 [a] Deut. 12:7; 14:26; 1 Chr. 29:22

you eat and when you drink, do you not
eat and drink *for yourselves?* 7 *Should you*
not *have obeyed* the words which the LORD
proclaimed through the [a]former prophets
when Jerusalem and the cities around it
were inhabited and prosperous, and [b]the
South[1] and the Lowland were inhabited?' "

Disobedience Resulted in Captivity

8 Then the word of the LORD came to
Zechariah, saying, 9 "Thus says the LORD
of hosts:

[a]'Execute true justice,
Show mercy and compassion
Everyone to his brother.
10 [a]Do not oppress the widow
or the fatherless,
The alien or the poor.
[b]Let none of you plan evil
in his heart
Against his brother.'

11 "But they refused to heed, [a]shrugged
their shoulders, and [b]stopped their ears so
that they could not hear. 12 Yes, they made
their [a]hearts like flint, [b]refusing to hear
the law and the words which the LORD of
hosts had sent by His Spirit through the
former prophets. [c]Thus great wrath came
from the LORD of hosts. 13 Therefore it happened, *that* just as He proclaimed and they
would not hear, so [a]they called out and I
would not listen," says the LORD of hosts.
14 "But [a]I scattered them with a whirlwind
among all the nations which they had not
known. Thus the land became desolate after them, so that no one passed through
or returned; for they made the pleasant
land desolate."

Jerusalem, Holy City of the Future

8 Again the word of the LORD of hosts
came, saying, 2 "Thus says the LORD of
hosts:

[a]'I am zealous for Zion with great zeal;
With great fervor I am zealous for her.'

3 "Thus says the LORD:

[a]'I will return to Zion,
And [b]dwell in the midst of Jerusalem.
Jerusalem [c]shall be called
the City of Truth,
[d]The Mountain of the LORD of hosts,
[e]The Holy Mountain.'

4 "Thus says the LORD of hosts:

[a]'Old men and old women shall again sit
In the streets of Jerusalem,
Each one with his staff in his hand
Because of great age.
5 The streets of the city
Shall be [a]full of boys and girls
Playing in its streets.'

6 "Thus says the LORD of hosts:

'If it is marvelous in the eyes
of the remnant of this
people in these days,
[a]Will it also be marvelous in My eyes?'
Says the LORD of hosts.

7 "Thus says the LORD of hosts:

'Behold, [a]I will save My people
from the land of the east
And from the land of the west;
8 I will [a]bring them *back*,
And they shall dwell in the
midst of Jerusalem.
[b]They shall be My people
And I will be their God,
[c]In truth and righteousness.'

9 "Thus says the LORD of hosts:

[a]'Let your hands be strong,
You who have been hearing
in these days
These words by the mouth
of [b]the prophets,
Who *spoke* in [c]the day the
foundation was laid

7:7 [a] Is. 1:16–20; Jer. 7:5, 23; Zech. 1:4 [b] Jer. 17:26 [1] Hebrew *Negev* 7:9 [a] Is. 58:6, 7; Jer. 7:28 7:10 [a] Ex. 22:22; Ps. 72:4; Is. 1:17; Jer. 5:28 [b] Ps. 36:4; Ezek. 38:10; 45:9; Mic. 2:1; Zech. 8:16, 17 7:11 [a] Neh. 9:29 [b] Jer. 17:23; Acts 7:57 7:12 [a] Ezek. 11:19 [b] Neh. 9:29, 30 [c] 2 Chr. 36:16; Dan. 9:11, 12 7:13 [a] Prov. 1:24–28; Is. 1:15; Jer. 11:11; Mic. 3:4 7:14 [a] Lev. 26:33; Deut. 4:27; 28:64; Neh. 1:8 8:2 [a] Joel 2:18; Nah. 1:2; Zech. 1:14 8:3 [a] Zech. 1:16 [b] Zech. 2:10, 11 [c] Is. 1:21 [d] [Is. 2:2, 3] [e] Jer. 31:23 8:4 [a] 1 Sam. 2:31; Is. 65:20 8:5 [a] Jer. 30:19, 20 8:6 [a] [Gen. 18:14; Luke 1:37] 8:7 [a] Ps. 107:3; Is. 11:11; Ezek. 37:21 8:8 [a] Zeph. 3:20; Zech. 10:10 [b] [Jer. 30:22; 31:1, 33; Zech. 13:9] [c] Jer. 4:2 8:9 [a] 1 Chr. 22:13; Is. 35:4; Hag. 2:4 [b] Ezra 5:1, 2; 6:14; Zech. 4:9 [c] Hag. 2:18

RELEASE // HOPE FOR TRUE JUDGMENTS

Hope for Justice for All

Zechariah 7:9 //"Thus says the LORD of hosts: 'Execute true justice, show mercy and compassion everyone to his brother.'"

Summary Message //God's message through Zechariah to the returning exiles was fairly simple and consistent: if they purified themselves, God would grant them prosperity in the land He gave to their forebears. Zechariah's faithfulness to report the word of the Lord steered His people toward living as He desired and fixing their broken justice system.

In Zechariah 7, God turned the prophet's focus to the issue of righteousness. At God's prompting, Zechariah told the people they could not engage in perfunctory rituals without extending justice toward others and obeying God. The exiles had been introduced to many different gods while in Babylon. Zechariah's message urged them to be faithful to the one true God who had delivered their ancestors from bondage and them from Babylonian exile. But to move forward with the assurance of peace and prosperity, they were required to return to the Lord.

Practical Application //Lady Justice is the icon of the American judicial system. Her eyes are covered to guard against appearance unduly influencing her. Her scales are completely balanced. Yet many people would argue that the American justice system is both biased and broken. Poor people and people of color often get the harsher sentences. Health care and needed prescription drugs are not affordable for many, and the gap between the wealthy and the poor grows wider. Seniors who have worked hard all their lives have to choose between medicine and heat. Parents try to decide whether working makes sense when childcare costs exceed their paychecks.

History has shown that human beings cannot execute true and equal justice, tempered by mercy, in an unbiased manner. Therefore, to whom can the marginalized turn? Is there a real hope for justice? How can we hope that mere sinful people can operate in true mercy and impartial justice? Our assurance of true judgment rests with God alone. God's law is not to be compromised while God's love leaves open the door of redemption through Christ.

Believers often define their faithfulness according to "thou shalt nots." God is indeed concerned about what believers are not doing, though not in the same way as they think. God is concerned when we are *not* showing mercy toward the poor or *not* seeking justice for the marginalized. Attending worship, singing hymns, uttering prayers, and dropping an offering in the collection plate are important but insufficient demonstrations of faithfulness. Alternatively, God challenges us to throw stale, dry worship in the trash and stand for those Jesus has dubbed "the least of these."

Fervent Prayer //Creator God, You call us to extend ourselves beyond our selfish desires to care for those who have no voice. Our hope is in You to guide our hearts and bend them toward dealing justly with all. May we love justice and show mercy as You have shown it to us. In Jesus' name we pray. Amen.

For the house of the LORD of hosts,
That the temple might be built.
10 For before these days
There were no [a]wages for man
nor any hire for beast;
There was no peace from the enemy
for whoever went out or
came in;
For I set all men, everyone,
against his neighbor.

11 [a]But now I *will* not *treat* the remnant of
this people as in the former days,' says the
LORD of hosts.

12 'For[a] the seed *shall be* prosperous,
The vine shall give its fruit,
[b]The ground shall give her increase,
And [c]the heavens shall
give their dew—
I will cause the remnant
of this people
To possess all these.
13 And it shall come to pass

8:10 [a] Hag. 1:6, 9 8:11 [a] [Ps. 103:9]; Is. 12:1; Hag. 2:15–19 8:12 [a] Joel 2:22 [b] Ps. 67:6 [c] Hag. 1:10

That just as you were [a]a curse
among the nations,
O house of Judah and house
of Israel,
So I will save you, and [b]you
shall be a blessing.
Do not fear,
Let your hands be strong.'

14 "For thus says the LORD of hosts:

[a]'Just as I determined to punish you
When your fathers provoked
Me to wrath,'
Says the LORD of hosts,
[b]'And I would not relent,
15 So again in these days
I am determined to do good
To Jerusalem and to the
house of Judah.
Do not fear.
16 These *are* the things you shall [a]do:
[b]Speak each man the truth
to his neighbor;
Give judgment in your gates for
truth, justice, and peace;
17 [a]Let none of you think evil in your[1]
heart against your neighbor;
And do not love a false oath.
For all these *are things* that I hate,'
Says the LORD."

18 Then the word of the LORD of hosts came to me, saying, 19 "Thus says the LORD of hosts:

[a]'The fast of the fourth *month*,
[b]The fast of the fifth,
[c]The fast of the seventh,
[d]And the fast of the tenth,
Shall be [e]joy and gladness
and cheerful feasts
For the house of Judah.
[f]Therefore love truth and peace.'

ZECHARIAH 8:8

I AM ZECHARIAH

"I will bring them back, and they shall dwell in the midst of Jerusalem. They shall be My people and I will be their God, in truth and righteousness." Zechariah 8:8

I am Zechariah, a prophet of God during the reign of King Darius. Darius ruled in Babylon after the Hebrew people who had been exiled during the reign of Nebuchadnezzar were allowed to return to their land. My focus was to encourage the people to rebuild the temple of God that had been destroyed by the Babylonians. I hoped this would encourage them to return to God. But the people had forgotten the cause of their exile—they had forgotten the God of our fathers. I urged them not to make God angry as their ancestors had done. I told them that if they returned to Him, He would return to them.

God gave me eight visions that brought knowledge and insight about the rebuilding of Jerusalem and the future coming of the Messiah. The people would be present to see the fulfillment of these visions only if they remained faithful to God. I encouraged the people to focus on the future and recognize all they would gain if they remained faithful to the covenant. As a people, they could enjoy a time of peace with Jerusalem as the center of the kingdom of God. If they would but look past all worldly things, at an appointed time, God would pour out His Spirit on them.

†

Zechariah tried to get the people to look ahead and to be God-focused instead of world-focused. We should do the same by looking above the chaos and keeping our eyes on the things of God that are eternal.

8:13 [a] Jer. 42:18 [b] Gen. 12:2; Ruth 4:11, 12; Is. 19:24, 25; Ezek. 34:26; [Zeph. 3:20] 8:14 [a] Jer. 31:28 [b] [2 Chr. 36:16] 8:16 [a] Zech. 7:9, 10 [b] Ps. 15:2; [Prov. 12:17–19]; Zech. 8:3; [Eph. 4:25] 8:17 [a] Prov. 3:29; Jer. 4:14; Zech. 7:10 [1] Literally *his* 8:19 [a] Jer. 52:6 [b] Jer. 52:12 [c] 2 Kin. 25:25; Jer. 41:1, 2 [d] Jer. 52:4 [e] Esth. 8:17 [f] Zech. 8:16; Luke 1:74, 75

20 "Thus says the LORD of hosts:

'Peoples shall yet come,
Inhabitants of many cities;
21 The inhabitants of one *city* shall
go to another, saying,
[a]"Let us continue to go and
pray before the LORD,
And seek the LORD of hosts.
I myself will go also."
22 Yes, [a]many peoples and strong
nations
Shall come to seek the LORD
of hosts in Jerusalem,
And to pray before the LORD.'

23 "Thus says the LORD of hosts: 'In those
days ten men [a]from every language of the
nations shall [b]grasp the sleeve of a Jewish
man, saying, "Let us go with you, for we
have heard [c]*that* God *is* with you." ' "

Israel Defended Against Enemies

9 The burden[1] of the word of the LORD
Against the land of Hadrach,
And [a]Damascus its resting place
(For [b]the eyes of men
And all the tribes of Israel
Are on the LORD);
2 Also *against* [a]Hamath,
which borders on it,
And *against* [b]Tyre and [c]Sidon,
though they are very [d]wise.

3 For Tyre built herself a tower,
Heaped up silver like the dust,
And gold like the mire of the streets.
4 Behold, [a]the Lord will cast her out;
He will destroy [b]her power
in the sea,
And she will be devoured by fire.

5 Ashkelon shall see *it* and fear;
Gaza also shall be very sorrowful;
And [a]Ekron, for He dried
up her expectation.
The king shall perish from Gaza,
And Ashkelon shall not be
inhabited.

6 "A mixed race shall settle [a]in Ashdod,
And I will cut off the pride
of the [b]Philistines.
7 I will take away the blood
from his mouth,
And the abominations from
between his teeth.
But he who remains, even he
shall be for our God,
And shall be like a leader in Judah,
And Ekron like a Jebusite.
8 [a]I will camp around My house
Because of the army,
Because of him who passes by
and him who returns.
No more shall an oppressor
pass through them,
For now I have seen with My eyes.

The Coming King
(Matt. 21:5; John 12:14, 15)

9 "Rejoice [a]greatly, O daughter of Zion!
Shout, O daughter of Jerusalem!
Behold, [b]your King is coming to you;
He *is* just and having salvation,
Lowly and riding on a donkey,
A colt, the foal of a donkey.
10 I [a]will cut off the chariot
from Ephraim
And the horse from Jerusalem;
The [b]battle bow shall be cut off.
He shall speak peace to the nations;
His dominion *shall be*
[c]'from sea to sea,
And from the River to the
ends of the earth.'[1]

God Will Save His People

11 "As for you also,
Because of the blood of your covenant,
I will set your [a]prisoners free
from the waterless pit.
12 Return to the stronghold,
[a]You prisoners of hope.
Even today I declare
That I will restore [b]double to you.
13 For I have bent Judah, My *bow*,
Fitted the bow with Ephraim,
And raised up your sons, O Zion,

8:21 [a] [Is. 2:2, 3; Mic. 4:1, 2] **8:22** [a] Is. 60:3; 66:23; [Zech. 14:16–21] **8:23** [a] Is. 3:6 [b] [Is. 45:14] [c] 1 Cor. 14:25 **9:1** [a] Is. 17:1; Jer. 23:33 [b] Amos 1:3–5 [1] Or *oracle* **9:2** [a] Jer. 49:23 [b] Is. 23; Jer. 25:22; 47:4; Ezek. 26; Amos 1:9, 10 [c] 1 Kin. 17:9 [d] Ezek. 28:3 **9:4** [a] Is. 23:1 [b] Ezek. 26:17 **9:5** [a] Zeph. 2:4, 5 **9:6** [a] Amos 1:8; Zeph. 2:4 [b] Ezek. 25:15–17 **9:8** [a] [Ps. 34:7] **9:9** [a] Zeph. 3:14, 15; Zech. 2:10 [b] [Ps. 110:1; Is. 9:6, 7; Jer. 23:5, 6]; Matt. 21:5; Mark 11:7, 9; Luke 19:38; John 12:15 **9:10** [a] Hos. 1:7; Mic. 5:10 [b] Ps. 46:9; Is. 2:4; Hos. 2:18; Mic. 4:3 [c] Ps. 72:8 [1] Psalm 72:8 **9:11** [a] Is. 42:7 **9:12** [a] Is. 49:9; Jer. 17:13; Heb. 6:18–20 [b] Is. 61:7

Against your sons, O Greece,
And made you like the sword
of a mighty man."

14 Then the LORD will be seen over them,
And [a]His arrow will go
forth like lightning.
The Lord GOD will blow the trumpet,
And go [b]with whirlwinds
from the south.
15 The LORD of hosts will [a]defend them;
They shall devour and subdue
with slingstones.
They shall drink *and* roar
as if with wine;
They shall be filled *with*
blood like basins,
Like the corners of the altar.
16 The LORD their God will [a]save
them in that day,
As the flock of His people.
For [b]they *shall be like* the
jewels of a crown,
[c]Lifted like a banner over His land—
17 For [a]how great is its[1] goodness
And how great its[2] [b]beauty!
[c]Grain shall make the
young men thrive,
And new wine the young women.

Restoration of Judah and Israel

10 Ask [a]the LORD for [b]rain
In [c]the time of the latter rain.[1]
The LORD will make flashing clouds;
He will give them showers of rain,
Grass in the field for everyone.

2 For the [a]idols[1] speak delusion;
The diviners envision [b]lies,
And tell false dreams;
They [c]comfort in vain.
Therefore *the people* wend
their way like [d]sheep;
They are in trouble [e]because
there is no shepherd.

3 "My anger is kindled against
the [a]shepherds,
[b]And I will punish the goatherds.
For the LORD of hosts [c]will
visit His flock,
The house of Judah,
And [d]will make them as His
royal horse in the battle.
4 From him comes [a]the cornerstone,
From him [b]the tent peg,
From him the battle bow,
From him every ruler[1] together.
5 They shall be like mighty men,
Who [a]tread down *their enemies*
In the mire of the streets in the battle.
They shall fight because the
LORD is with them,
And the riders on horses
shall be put to shame.

6 "I will strengthen the house of Judah,
And I will save the house of Joseph.
[a]I will bring them back,
Because I [b]have mercy on them.
They shall be as though I had
not cast them aside;
For I *am* the LORD their God,
And I [c]will hear them.
7 *Those of* Ephraim shall be
like a mighty man,
And their [a]heart shall rejoice
as if with wine.
Yes, their children shall
see *it* and be glad;
Their heart shall rejoice in the LORD.
8 I will [a]whistle for them
and gather them,
For I will redeem them;
[b]And they shall increase as
they once increased.

9 "I[a] will sow them among the peoples,
And they shall [b]remember
Me in far countries;
They shall live, together
with their children,
And they shall return.
10 [a]I will also bring them back
from the land of Egypt,
And gather them from Assyria.

9:14 [a] Ps. 18:14; Hab. 3:11 [b] Is. 21:1 9:15 [a] Is. 37:35; Zech. 12:8 9:16 [a] Jer. 31:10, 11 [b] Is. 62:3; Mal. 3:17 [c] Is. 11:12 9:17 [a] [Ps. 31:19] [b] [Ps. 45:1–16] [c] Joel 3:18 [1] Or *His* [2] Or *His* 10:1 [a] [Jer. 14:22] [b] [Deut. 11:13, 14] [c] [Joel 2:23] [1] That is, spring rain 10:2 [a] Jer. 10:8 [b] Jer. 27:9; [Ezek. 13] [c] Job 13:4 [d] Jer. 50:6, 17 [e] Ezek. 34:5–8; Matt. 9:36; Mark 6:34 [1] Hebrew *teraphim* 10:3 [a] Jer. 25:34–36; Ezek. 34:2; Zech. 11:17 [b] Ezek. 34:17 [c] Luke 1:68 [d] Song 1:9 10:4 [a] Is. 28:16 [b] Is. 22:23 [1] Or *despot* 10:5 [a] Ps. 18:42 10:6 [a] Jer. 3:18; Ezek. 37:21 [b] Hos. 1:7; Zech. 1:16 [c] Zech. 13:9 10:7 [a] Ps. 104:15 10:8 [a] Is. 5:26 [b] Is. 49:19; Ezek. 36:37; Zech. 2:4 10:9 [a] Hos. 2:23 [b] Deut. 30:1 10:10 [a] Is. 11:11; Hos. 11:11

ELEVATE THE STEPS YOU TAKE

INHALE

I have lived pretty much my entire life the wrong way. I have done whatever it takes to get ahead, or sometimes just to get by. But the quick hustles finally caught up to me. I took that road one too many times. But now, I have got another chance. Jesus has saved me, and I want to get my life in order for Him. How do I do that? I don't even know where to start.

EXHALE

You have started the right way. You own the wrong and harmful choices you have made in the past, and you have turned away from them toward following Jesus instead. That is exactly what the Bible means by repentance. So, first, learn to rest in the love, forgiveness, and acceptance you have been given in Christ. No matter what you do, none of that will ever change.

But while you have started well, you are far from finished. Your life is still full of choices ahead. Even as believers, sometimes we put ourselves in situations that make life more difficult. Left to our own devices, it is nearly impossible to know what is right. But here's more of God's good news to us—we do not have to make any decision on our own. Christ is always with us to guide us. No choice is too big or too small for Him. He will guide us through any of them, if we seek Him. And when we do, we begin to experience life the way God intends. Not completely, mind you. There is no life without challenges and problems. Our sin and the sin of others is still real and damaging. Nonetheless, God will be with us in the middle of all our situations. Keep forging ahead no matter what. Do not wait to seek ways to develop in your faith. Get in a church. Get in a Bible study. Get around other believers. This is how you step your game up. In you, the Lord can show His name to be great. Zechariah 10:1 says, "Ask the LORD for rain in the time of the latter rain. The LORD will make flashing clouds; He will give them showers of rain, grass in the field for everyone." Ask God for the rain of a life pleasing to Him and watch the showers come. Step up and continue getting to know Him!

I will bring them into the land
of Gilead and Lebanon,
[b]Until no *more room* is found
for them.
11 [a]He shall pass through the
sea with affliction,
And strike the waves of the sea:
All the depths of the River[1]
shall dry up.
Then [b]the pride of Assyria
shall be brought down,
And [c]the scepter of Egypt shall
depart.

12 "So I will strengthen them in the LORD,
And [a]they shall walk up and
down in His name,"
Says the LORD.

Desolation of Israel

11 Open [a]your doors, O Lebanon,
That fire may devour your cedars.
2 Wail, O cypress, for the
[a]cedar has fallen,
Because the mighty *trees* are ruined.
Wail, O oaks of Bashan,
[b]For the thick forest has come down.
3 *There is* the sound of
wailing [a]shepherds!
For their glory is in ruins.
There is the sound of roaring lions!
For the pride[1] of the Jordan is in ruins.

Prophecy of the Shepherds

4Thus says the LORD my God, "Feed the
flock for slaughter, 5whose owners slaughter them and [a]feel no guilt; those who sell

10:10 [b] Is. 49:19, 20 10:11 [a] Is. 11:15 [b] Is. 14:25; Zeph. 2:13 [c] Ezek. 30:13 [1] That is, the Nile 10:12 [a] Mic. 4:5 11:1 [a] Zech. 10:10 11:2 [a] Ezek. 31:3 [b] Is. 32:19 11:3 [a] Jer. 25:34–36 [1] Or *floodplain, thicket* 11:5 [a] [Jer. 2:3]; 50:7

them [b]say, 'Blessed be the LORD, for I am
rich'; and their shepherds do [c]not pity them.
6 For I will no longer pity the inhabitants of
the land," says the LORD. "But indeed I will
give everyone into his neighbor's hand and
into the hand of his king. They shall attack
the land, and I will not deliver *them* from
their hand."

7 So I fed the flock for slaughter, in particular [a]the poor of the flock.[1] I took for
myself two staffs: the one I called Beauty,[2]
and the other I called Bonds;[3] and I fed
the flock. 8 I dismissed the three shepherds
[a]in one month. My soul loathed them, and
their soul also abhorred me. 9 Then I said, "I
will not feed you. [a]Let what is dying die, and
what is perishing perish. Let those that are
left eat each other's flesh." 10 And I took my
staff, Beauty, and cut it in two, that I might
break the covenant which I had made with
all the peoples. 11 So it was broken on that
day. Thus [a]the poor[1] of the flock, who were
watching me, knew that it *was* the word
of the LORD. 12 Then I said to them, "If it is
agreeable to you, give *me* my wages; and if
not, refrain." So they [a]weighed out for my
wages thirty *pieces* of silver.

13 And the LORD said to me, "Throw it to
the [a]potter"—that princely price they set
on me. So I took the thirty *pieces* of silver
and threw them into the house of the LORD
for the potter. 14 Then I cut in two my other
staff, Bonds, that I might break the brotherhood between Judah and Israel.

15 And the LORD said to me, [a]"Next, take
for yourself the implements of a foolish
shepherd. 16 For indeed I will raise up a
shepherd in the land *who* will not care for
those who are cut off, nor seek the young,
nor heal those that are broken, nor feed
those that still stand. But he will eat the
flesh of the fat and tear their hooves in
[a]pieces.

17 "Woe[a] to the worthless shepherd,
Who leaves the flock!
A sword *shall be* against his arm
And against his right eye;
His arm shall completely wither,
And his right eye shall be
totally blinded."

The Coming Deliverance of Judah

12 The burden[1] of the word of the LORD
against Israel. Thus says the LORD,
[a]who stretches out the heavens, lays the
foundation of the earth, and [b]forms the
spirit of man within him: 2 "Behold, I will
make Jerusalem [a]a cup of drunkenness to
all the surrounding peoples, when they lay
siege against Judah and Jerusalem. 3 [a]And
it shall happen in that day that I will make
Jerusalem [b]a very heavy stone for all peoples; all who would heave it away will surely
be cut in pieces, though all nations of the
earth are gathered against it. 4 In that day,"
says the LORD, [a]"I will strike every horse
with confusion, and its rider with madness;
I will open My eyes on the house of Judah,
and will strike every horse of the peoples
with blindness. 5 And the governors of Judah shall say in their heart, 'The inhabitants
of Jerusalem *are* my strength in the LORD
of hosts, their God.' 6 In that day I will make
the governors of Judah [a]like a firepan in
the woodpile, and like a fiery torch in the
sheaves; they shall devour all the surrounding peoples on the right hand and on the
left, but Jerusalem shall be inhabited again
in her own place—Jerusalem.

7 "The LORD will save the tents of Judah
first, so that the glory of the house of David
and the glory of the inhabitants of Jerusalem shall not become greater than that of
Judah. 8 In that day the LORD will defend
the inhabitants of Jerusalem; the one who
is feeble among them in that day shall be
like David, and the house of David *shall
be* like God, like the Angel of the LORD before them. 9 It shall be in that day *that* I will
seek to [a]destroy all the nations that come
against Jerusalem.

Mourning for the Pierced One

10 [a]"And I will pour on the house of David and on the inhabitants of Jerusalem the

---

11:5 [b] Deut. 29:19; Hos. 12:8; 1 Tim. 6:9 [c] Ezek. 34:2, 3 11:7 [a] Jer. 39:10; Zeph. 3:12; Matt. 11:5 [1] Following Masoretic Text, Targum, and Vulgate; Septuagint reads *for the Canaanites.* [2] Or *Grace,* and so in verse 10 [3] Or *Unity,* and so in verse 14 11:8 [a] Hos. 5:7 11:9 [a] Jer. 15:2 11:11 [a] Zeph. 3:12; Matt. 27:50; Mark 15:37; Luke 23:46; Acts 8:32 [1] Following Masoretic Text, Targum, and Vulgate; Septuagint reads *the Canaanites.* 11:12 [a] Gen. 37:28; Ex. 21:32; Matt. 26:15; 27:9, 10 11:13 [a] Matt. 27:3–10; Acts 1:18, 19 11:15 [a] Is. 56:11; Ezek. 34:2 11:16 [a] Ezek. 34:1–10; Mic. 3:1–3 11:17 [a] Jer. 23:1; Ezek. 34:2; Zech. 10:2; 11:15; John 10:12, 13 12:1 [a] Is. 42:5; 44:24 [b] Num. 16:22; [Eccl. 12:7; Is. 57:16]; Heb. 12:9 [1] Or *oracle* 12:2 [a] Is. 51:17 12:3 [a] Zech. 12:4, 6, 8; 13:1 [b] Matt. 21:44 12:4 [a] Ps. 76:6; Ezek. 38:4 12:6 [a] Is. 10:17, 18; Obad. 18; Zech. 11:1 12:9 [a] Hag. 2:22 12:10 [a] Jer. 31:9; 50:4; Ezek. 39:29; [Joel 2:28, 29]

Spirit of grace and supplication; then they
will [b]look on Me whom they pierced. Yes,
they will mourn for Him [c]as one mourns
for *his* only *son,* and grieve for Him as one
grieves for a firstborn. 11 In that day there
shall be a great [a]mourning in Jerusalem,
[b]like the mourning at Hadad Rimmon in
the plain of Megiddo.[1] 12 [a]And the land shall
mourn, every family by itself: the family of
the house of David by itself, and their wives
by themselves; the family of the house of
[b]Nathan by itself, and their wives by themselves; 13 the family of the house of Levi by
itself, and their wives by themselves; the
family of Shimei by itself, and their wives
by themselves; 14 all the families that remain, every family by itself, and their wives
by themselves.

Idolatry Cut Off

13 "In that [a]day [b]a fountain shall be
opened for the house of David and
for the inhabitants of Jerusalem, for sin
and for [c]uncleanness.

2 "It shall be in that day," says the LORD
of hosts, "*that* I will [a]cut off the names of
the idols from the land, and they shall no
longer be remembered. I will also cause
[b]the prophets and the unclean spirit to
depart from the land. 3 It shall come to
pass *that* if anyone still prophesies, then
his father and mother who begot him will
say to him, 'You shall [a]not live, because
you have spoken lies in the name of the
LORD.' And his father and mother who begot him [b]shall thrust him through when
he prophesies.

4 "And it shall be in that day *that* [a]every
prophet will be ashamed of his vision when
he prophesies; they will not wear [b]a robe of
coarse hair to deceive. 5 [a]But he will say, 'I
am no prophet, I *am* a farmer; for a man
taught me to keep cattle from my youth.'
6 And *one* will say to him, 'What are these
wounds between your arms?'[1] Then he will
answer, '*Those* with which I was wounded
in the house of my friends.'

The Shepherd Savior

7 "Awake, O sword, against
[a]My Shepherd,
Against the Man [b]who is
My Companion,"
Says the LORD of hosts.
[c]"Strike the Shepherd,
And the sheep will be scattered;
Then I will turn My hand
against [d]the little ones.
8 And it shall come to pass
in all the land,"
Says the LORD,
"*That* [a]two-thirds in it shall
be cut off *and* die,
[b]But *one*-third shall be left in it:
9 I will bring the *one*-third
[a]through the fire,
Will [b]refine them as silver is refined,
And test them as gold is tested.
[c]They will call on My name,
And I will answer them.
[d]I will say, 'This *is* My people';
And each one will say, 'The
LORD *is* my God.'"

The Day of the LORD
(cf. Ezek. 38; 39; Mark 13; Rev. 20—22)

14 Behold, [a]the day of the LORD
is coming,
And your spoil will be divided
in your midst.
2 For [a]I will gather all the nations
to battle against Jerusalem;
The city shall be taken,
The houses rifled,
And the women ravished.
Half of the city shall go into captivity,
But the remnant of the people shall
not be cut off from the city.

3 Then the LORD will go forth
And fight against those nations,
As He fights in the day of battle.
4 And in that day His feet will stand
[a]on the Mount of Olives,
Which faces Jerusalem on the east.

12:10 [b] John 19:34, 37; 20:27; [Rev. 1:7] [c] Jer. 6:26; Amos 8:10 12:11 [a] [Matt. 24:30]; Acts 2:37; [Rev. 1:7] [b] 2 Kin. 23:29 [1] Hebrew *Megiddon* 12:12 [a] [Matt. 24:30; Rev. 1:7] [b] Luke 3:31 13:1 [a] Acts 10:43; [Rev. 21:6, 7] [b] Ps. 36:9; [Heb. 9:14; 1 John 1:7] [c] Num. 19:17; Is. 4:4; Ezek. 36:25 13:2 [a] Ex. 23:13; Hos. 2:17 [b] Jer. 23:14, 15; 2 Pet. 2:1 13:3 [a] Deut. 18:20; [Ezek. 14:9] [b] Deut. 13:6–11; [Matt. 10:37] 13:4 [a] Jer. 6:15; 8:9; [Mic. 3:6, 7] [b] 2 Kin. 1:8; Is. 20:2; Matt. 3:4 13:5 [a] Amos 7:14 13:6 [1] Or *hands* 13:7 [a] Is. 40:11; Ezek. 34:23, 24; 37:24; Mic. 5:2, 4 [b] [John 10:30] [c] Matt. 26:31, 56, 67; Mark 14:27; 1 Pet. 5:4; Rev. 7:16, 17 [d] Luke 12:32 13:8 [a] Is. 6:13; Ezek. 5:2, 4, 12 [b] [Rom. 11:5] 13:9 [a] Is. 48:10; Ezek. 20:38; Mal. 3:3 [b] 1 Pet. 1:6, 7 [c] Ps. 50:15; Zeph. 3:9; [Zech. 12:10] [d] Jer. 30:22; Hos. 2:23 14:1 [a] [Is. 13:6, 9; Joel 2:1; Mal. 4:1] 14:2 [a] Joel 3:2; Zech. 12:2, 3 14:4 [a] Ezek. 11:23; Acts 1:9–12

#OXYGEN

ZECHARIAH 14:1

Hope for True Judgments

Everything is going to be all right. The day is coming when King Jesus will execute judgment against the world and establish His kingdom on earth. This is the wellspring of hope for the spiritual redemption of all the saints.

Wait on the Lord, **breathe**, and **hope for true judgments**.

And the Mount of Olives
shall be split in two,
From east to west,
[b]*Making* a very large valley;
Half of the mountain shall
move toward the north
And half of it toward the south.

5 Then you shall flee *through*
My mountain valley,
For the mountain valley
shall reach to Azal.
Yes, you shall flee
As you fled from the [a]earthquake
In the days of Uzziah king of Judah.

[b]Thus the LORD my God will come,
And [c]all the saints with You.[1]

6 It shall come to pass in that day
That there will be no light;
The lights will diminish.
7 It shall be one day
[a]Which is known to the LORD—
Neither day nor night.
But at [b]evening time it shall
happen
That it will be light.

8 And in that day it shall be
That living [a]waters shall flow
from Jerusalem,
Half of them toward the eastern
sea
And half of them toward
the western sea;
In both summer and winter
it shall occur.
9 And the LORD shall be [a]King
over all the earth.
In that day it shall be—
[b]"The LORD *is* one,"[1]
And His name one.

10 All the land shall be turned into a plain
from Geba to Rimmon south of Jerusalem.
Jerusalem[1] shall be raised up and [a]inhab-
ited in her place from Benjamin's Gate to
the place of the First Gate and the Corner
Gate, [b]and *from* the Tower of Hananel to
the king's winepresses.

11 *The people* shall dwell in it;
And [a]no longer shall there
be utter destruction,
[b]But Jerusalem shall be
safely inhabited.

12 And this shall be the plague with which
the LORD will strike all the people who
fought against Jerusalem:

Their flesh shall dissolve while
they stand on their feet,
Their eyes shall dissolve
in their sockets,
And their tongues shall
dissolve in their mouths.

13 It shall come to pass in that day
That [a]a great panic from the
LORD will be among them.
Everyone will seize the hand
of his neighbor,
And raise [b]his hand against
his neighbor's hand;
14 Judah also will fight at Jerusalem.
[a]And the wealth of all the
surrounding nations
Shall be gathered together:
Gold, silver, and apparel in
great abundance.

14:4 [b] Joel 3:12 14:5 [a] Is. 29:6; Amos 1:1 [b] [Ps. 96:13]; Is. 66:15, 16; Matt. 24:30, 31; 25:31; Jude 14 [c] Joel 3:11 [1] Or *you;* Septuagint, Targum, and Vulgate read *Him.* 14:7 [a] Matt. 24:36 [b] Is. 30:26 14:8 [a] Ezek. 47:1–12; Joel 3:18; [John 7:38; Rev. 22:1, 2] 14:9 [a] [Jer. 23:5, 6; Rev. 11:15] [b] [Eph. 4:5, 6]; Deut. 6:4 [1] Compare Deuteronomy 6:4 14:10 [a] Jer. 30:18; Zech. 12:6 [b] Neh. 3:1; Jer. 31:38 [1] Literally *She* 14:11 [a] Jer. 31:40 [b] Jer. 23:6; Ezek. 34:25–28; Hos. 2:18 14:13 [a] 1 Sam. 14:15, 20 [b] Judg. 7:22; 2 Chr. 20:23; Ezek. 38:21 14:14 [a] Ezek. 39:10, 17

15 [a]Such also shall be the plague
On the horse *and* the mule,
On the camel and the donkey,
And on all the cattle that will
be in those camps.
So *shall* this plague *be.*

The Nations Worship the King

16 And it shall come to pass *that* everyone
who is left of all the nations which came
against Jerusalem shall [a]go up from year
to year to [b]worship the King, the LORD of
hosts, and to keep [c]the Feast of Tabernacles. 17 [a]And it shall be *that* whichever of
the families of the earth do not come up to
Jerusalem to worship the King, the LORD
of hosts, on them there will be no rain. 18 If
the family of [a]Egypt will not come up and
enter in, [b]they *shall have* no *rain;* they shall
receive the plague with which the LORD
strikes the nations who do not come up to
keep the Feast of Tabernacles. 19 This shall
be the punishment of Egypt and the punishment of all the nations that do not come
up to keep the Feast of Tabernacles.
20 In that day [a]"HOLINESS TO THE LORD"
shall be *engraved* on the bells of the horses.
The [b]pots in the LORD's house shall be like
the bowls before the altar. 21 Yes, every pot
in Jerusalem and Judah shall be holiness to
the LORD of hosts.[1] Everyone who sacrifices
shall come and take them and cook in them.
In that day there shall no longer be a [a]Ca-
naanite [b]in the house of the LORD of hosts.

14:15 [a] Zech. 14:12 14:16 [a] [Is. 2:2, 3; 60:6–9; 66:18–21; Mic. 4:1, 2] [b] Is. 27:13 [c] Lev. 23:34–44; Neh. 8:14; Hos. 12:9; John 7:2 14:17 [a] Is. 60:12 14:18 [a] Is. 19:21 [b] Deut. 11:10 14:20 [a] Ex. 28:36; 39:30; Is. 23:18; Jer. 2:3 [b] Ezek. 46:20 14:21 [a] Is. 35:8; Ezek. 44:9; Joel 3:17; Rev. 21:27; 22:15 [b] [Eph. 2:19–22] [1] Or *on every pot . . . shall be (engraved) "HOLINESS TO THE LORD OF HOSTS"*

THE BOOK OF MALACHI

OVERVIEW

The Book of Malachi bears the name of its author and is the last book of the Old Testament. Malachi means "messenger" in Hebrew. Malachi was a minor prophet whose ministry occurred around 450 BC. He called for the Israelites to renew their relationship with God and was the last Old Testament prophet God sent to the Israelites after their return from Babylonian captivity. Malachi called for the people to serve God faithfully.

When Malachi prophesied to the Israelites, it was over a century after they had returned from captivity. The people expected to receive all the blessings God had promised them. However, they did not focus on God. The priests were corrupt, and the people did not follow God's instructions. They had rebuilt the temple, but it was not being used as God intended.

The Book of Malachi was written in a question-and-answer format. First, Malachi proposed questions from God to Israel. Then, he gave a likely answer from the Israelites. Finally, he gave God's response.

As the Book of Malachi opens, the Israelites question God's love for them. They associated their struggles with God's lack of love instead of their sins. God reminded them that He chose Jacob, the father of Israel, because of His love for him (see Mal. 1:2). As evidence of His love, He outlined the destruction that would befall Edom, the land of Esau (see vv. 4–5).

God admonished the Israelites for not showing Him "honor" and "reverence" (1:6). He chastised them for presenting Him with unacceptable offerings that were "defiled" (v. 7). He declared that He would no longer accept offerings from them (see v. 10) and looked forward to the day when His name would "be great among the nations" (v. 11).

During this time, the priests were disobedient to God. But for them to lead the people, their relationships with God needed to be intact. God promised to curse them because they did not honor His covenant (see 2:1–2). He reminded the priests that they were to be messengers who the people could go to for knowledge (see vv. 7–8).

The Israelites' practice of marrying foreign women who worshiped other gods was also displeasing to God and a violation of His covenant (see vv. 10–12). The many divorces that took place within the Israelite community were an affront to Him as well (see vv. 13–16).

Chapter 3 opens with this announcement: "Behold, I send My messenger, and he will prepare the way before Me" (v. 1). God reminded the Israelites that He had "not consumed" them because He does not change His promises, even though they had not kept the covenant (vv. 6–7). He urged the Israelites to return to Him and stop robbing Him of tithes and offerings (see vv. 7–10).

Many of the Israelites complained about Malachi's message (3:13–15). But God responded by reminding them that He listens to those who fear Him "and who meditate on His name" (v. 16). He promised to "spare them as a man spares his own son who serves him" (v. 17).

Malachi concludes with a description of the destiny of the wicked (see 4:1) and the blessings of the righteous (see vv. 2–3). Malachi reminded the Israelites of the importance of the Law of Moses and spoke of the coming "day of the LORD" (v. 5).

The prophet Malachi reminded the Israelites of their repeated disobedience to God. He informed them that God would remain true to His promise despite their disobedience and the resulting judgment. He would save a remnant of the people and send His Son to fulfill all His promises. As the last prophet to speak before the coming of Christ, Malachi encouraged the Israelites to return to God. The Book of Malachi is a reminder that God is faithful to His people over the years and across generations.

BREATHE IT IN

The Book of Malachi stresses God's love for His people and His desire for them to honor His covenant with them. Malachi urged the Israelites to turn away from their disobedient ways and to return to God. He reminded them of their past sins and God's judgment over the years. Malachi confirmed that God does not change and remains true to His word no matter how His followers behave. God will always honor His promises, if only to a chosen few.

For hundreds of years, God expressed His love for the Israelites as His chosen people. He established a covenant with them that they broke across many generations. God was consistent with His warnings and His judgment of the Israelites. When they disobeyed and turned from Him, they suffered. When they obeyed and followed His lead, they prospered.

The Israelites lived in a cycle of disobedience. Yet, God continued to identify them as His chosen people. The history of the Israelites and their relationship with God is an example of how patient God is with His followers. He provides us opportunity after opportunity to connect with Him and to renew our relationship when we go astray. It does not matter what we do; nothing can separate us from the love of God. He is always ready to receive us back. God is there and willing to restore us when we repent.

Although God wants us to repent, He also grows weary when Christians continue to ignore His covenant with Him and follow the ways of the world instead. When we follow the world's ways of doing things, we suffer consequences. When we repent, God restores us. When we remain faithful to Him, He blesses us.

God is an unchanging God. He is true to His word. We can depend on Him to be faithful until the end, but why test God? Why would we willingly go against His will and His word? Why would we bring His judgment upon ourselves and suffer unnecessarily?

Despite our actions, God always offers us hope. His door is always open. The opportunity to seek restoration is always present. God wants us to learn from our past and make God-honoring decisions in the future. He wants us to enjoy a covenant relationship with Him forever.

Never question God's love for us. God loves us through every phase of our lives. He even loves us when we do not love ourselves. Remain faithful to your commitment to God. Strive to walk earnestly and according to His Word—the Bible. Honor Him and show reverence to Him. Never lose hope. Be confident in knowing that you are a child of the King.

THE BOOK OF

MALACHI

1 The burden[1] of the word of the LORD to
Israel by Malachi.

Israel Beloved of God

2 "I[a] have loved you," says the LORD.
"Yet you say, 'In what way
have You loved us?'
Was not Esau Jacob's brother?"
Says the LORD.
"Yet [b]Jacob I have loved;
3 But Esau I have hated,
And [a]laid waste his mountains
and his heritage
For the jackals of the wilderness."

4 Even though Edom has said,
"We have been impoverished,
But we will return and build
the desolate places,"

Thus says the LORD of hosts:

"They may build, but I will
[a]throw down;
They shall be called the
Territory of Wickedness,
And the people against whom the
LORD will have indignation forever.
5 Your eyes shall see,
And you shall say,
[a]'The LORD is magnified beyond
the border of Israel.'

Polluted Offerings

6 "A son [a]honors *his* father,
And a servant *his* master.
[b]If then I am the Father,
Where *is* My honor?
And if I *am* a Master,
Where *is* My reverence?
Says the LORD of hosts
To you priests who despise My name.
[c]Yet you say, 'In what way have
we despised Your name?'

7 "You offer [a]defiled food on My altar,
But say,
'In what way have we defiled You?'
By saying,
[b]'The table of the LORD is contemptible.'
8 And [a]when you offer the
blind as a sacrifice,
Is it not evil?
And when you offer the lame and sick,
Is it not evil?
Offer it then to your governor!
Would he be pleased with you?
Would he [b]accept you favorably?"
Says the LORD of hosts.

9 "But now entreat God's favor,
That He may be gracious to us.
[a]*While* this is being *done* by your
hands,
Will He accept you favorably?"
Says the LORD of hosts.

10 "Who *is there* even among you
who would shut the doors,
[a]So that you would not kindle
fire *on* My altar in vain?
I have no pleasure in you,"
Says the LORD of hosts,
[b]"Nor will I accept an offering
from your hands.
11 For [a]from the rising of the sun,
even to its going down,

1:1 [1] Or *oracle* 1:2 [a] Deut. 4:37; 7:8; 23:5; Is. 41:8, 9; [Jer. 31:3]; John 15:12 [b] Rom. 9:13 1:3 [a] Jer. 49:18; Ezek. 35:9, 15 1:4 [a] Jer. 49:16–18 1:5 [a] Ps. 35:27; Mic. 5:4 1:6 [a] [Ex. 20:12]; Prov. 30:11, 17; [Matt. 15:4–8; Eph. 6:2, 3] [b] [Is. 63:16; 64:8]; Jer. 31:9; Luke 6:46 [c] Mal. 2:14 1:7 [a] Deut. 15:21 [b] Ezek. 41:22 1:8 [a] Lev. 22:22; Deut. 15:19–23 [b] [Job 42:8] 1:9 [a] Hos. 13:9 1:10 [a] 1 Cor. 9:13 [b] Is. 1:11 1:11 [a] Is. 59:19

My name *shall be* great
[b]among the Gentiles;
[c]In every place [d]incense *shall*
be offered to My name,
And a pure offering;
[e]For My name shall be great
among the nations,"
Says the LORD of hosts.

#OXYGEN

MALACHI 1:11

Elevate the Steps You Take

When God's name is lifted high in your life, He will lead you and guide you in the way of truth. When worship toward Him flows from your heart, all the steps you take will be strengthened and empowered; our God inhabits the praise of His people.

Breathe and elevate the steps you take.

12 "But you profane it,
In that you say,
[a]'The table of the LORD[1] is defiled;
And its fruit, its food, *is* contemptible.'
13 You also say,
'Oh, what a [a]weariness!'
And you sneer at it,"
Says the LORD of hosts.
"And you bring the stolen, the
lame, and the sick;
Thus you bring an offering!
[b]Should I accept this from your hand?"
Says the LORD.
14 "But cursed *be* [a]the deceiver
Who has in his flock a male,
And takes a vow,
But sacrifices to the Lord
[b]what is blemished—
For [c]I *am* a great King,"
Says the LORD of hosts,
"And My name *is to be* feared
among the nations.

Corrupt Priests

2 "And now, O [a]priests, this
commandment is for you.
2 [a]If you will not hear,
And if you will not take *it* to heart,
To give glory to My name,"
Says the LORD of hosts,
"I will send a curse upon you,
And I will curse your blessings.
Yes, I have cursed them [b]already,
Because you do not take *it* to heart.

3 "Behold, I will rebuke your descendants
And spread [a]refuse on your faces,
The refuse of your solemn feasts;
And *one* will [b]take you away with it.
4 Then you shall know that I have
sent this commandment to you,
That My covenant with Levi
may continue,"
Says the LORD of hosts.
5 "My[a] covenant was with him,
one of life and peace,
And I gave them to him [b]*that*
he might fear *Me;*
So he feared Me
And was reverent before My name.
6 [a]The law of truth[1] was in his mouth,
And injustice was not
found on his lips.
He walked with Me in
peace and equity,
And [b]turned many away from iniquity.

7 "For[a] the lips of a priest should
keep knowledge,
And *people* should seek the
law from his mouth;
[b]For he is the messenger of
the LORD of hosts.
8 But you have departed from the way;
You [a]have caused many to
stumble at the law.
[b]You have corrupted the
covenant of Levi,"
Says the LORD of hosts.
9 "Therefore [a]I also have made you
contemptible and base
Before all the people,

1:11 [b] Is. 60:3, 5 [c] 1 Tim. 2:8 [d] Rev. 8:3 [e] Is. 66:18, 19 1:12 [a] Mal. 1:7 [1] Following Bomberg; Masoretic Text reads *Lord.* 1:13 [a] Is. 43:22 [b] Lev. 22:20 1:14 [a] Mal. 1:8 [b] Lev. 22:18–20 [c] Ps. 47:2 2:1 [a] Mal. 1:6 2:2 [a] [Lev. 26:14, 15; Deut. 28:15] [b] Mal. 3:9 2:3 [a] Ex. 29:14 [b] 1 Kin. 14:10 2:5 [a] Num. 25:12; Ezek. 34:25 [b] Deut. 33:9 2:6 [a] Deut. 33:10 [b] Jer. 23:22; [James 5:20] [1] Or *true instruction* 2:7 [a] Num. 27:21; Deut. 17:8–11; Jer. 18:18 [b] [Gal. 4:14] 2:8 [a] Jer. 18:15 [b] Num. 25:12, 13; Neh. 13:29; Ezek. 44:10 2:9 [a] 1 Sam. 2:30

Because you have not kept My ways
But have shown [b]partiality
in the law."

Treachery of Infidelity

10 [a]Have we not all one Father?
[b]Has not one God created us?
Why do we deal treacherously
with one another
By profaning the covenant
of the fathers?
11 Judah has dealt treacherously,
And an abomination has
been committed in Israel
and in Jerusalem,
For Judah has [a]profaned
The LORD's holy *institution*
which He loves:
He has married the daughter
of a foreign god.
12 May the LORD cut off from
the tents of Jacob
The man who does this, being
awake and aware,[1]
Yet [a]who brings an offering
to the LORD of hosts!

13 And this is the second thing you do:
You cover the altar of the
LORD with tears,
With weeping and crying;
So He does not regard the
offering anymore,
Nor receive *it* with goodwill
from your hands.
14 Yet you say, "For what reason?"
Because the LORD has been
witness
Between you and [a]the wife
of your youth,
With whom you have dealt
treacherously;
[b]Yet she is your companion
And your wife by covenant.

MALACHI 2:10

I AM MALACHI

Have we not all one Father? Has not one God created us? Why do we deal treacherously with one another by profaning the covenant of the fathers? Malachi 2:10

I am Malachi, a prophet of God. I brought the word of God's love to His people. But they could not see the overwhelming love that God had poured out on them, generation after generation. He loved them even when they did wrong and worshiped other gods and turned their backs on Him. He protected them and gave them victory. Even in His discipline, He loved them.

But now, there was corruption in Jerusalem among the people and even among the priests who were to preserve knowledge so that the people could hear God's law from their mouths. The Lord was losing His patience with the people's injustice and them calling evil good, as if it was approved by God. Who could stand up in this age and the one to come? There would be some who would be steadfast and endure. In that time, they will greet the Lord's coming with joy while the unfaithful will be accused.

†

There is no excuse for treating others as if they are not our brothers, even if they treat us badly. Remember who you are. Are you one whose faith will endure to the end? One who keeps God's ways as your own ways? One who does not go the way of the world? One who loves truth and despises corruption? When you hear the trumpet blast and you see Jesus returning in the clouds, will you have joy or despair?

2:9 [b] Deut. 1:17; Mic. 3:11; 1 Tim. 5:21 2:10 [a] Jer. 31:9; 1 Cor. 8:6; [Eph. 4:6] [b] Job 31:15 2:11 [a] Ezra 9:1, 2; Neh. 13:23 2:12 [a] Neh. 13:29 [1] Talmud and Vulgate read *teacher and student.* 2:14 [a] Prov. 5:18; Jer. 9:2; Mal. 3:5 [b] Prov. 2:17

15 But [a]did He not make *them* one,
Having a remnant of the Spirit?
And why one?
He seeks [b]godly offspring.
Therefore take heed to your spirit,
And let none deal treacherously
with the wife of his youth.

16 "For [a]the LORD God of Israel says
That He hates divorce,
For it covers one's garment
with violence,"
Says the LORD of hosts.
"Therefore take heed to your spirit,
That you do not deal treacherously."

17 [a]You have wearied the LORD
with your words;
Yet you say,
"In what way have we wearied *Him?*"
In that you say,
[b]"Everyone who does evil
Is good in the sight of the LORD,
And He delights in them,"
Or, "Where *is* the God of justice?"

The Coming Messenger

3 "Behold, [a]I send My messenger,
And he will [b]prepare the
way before Me.
And the Lord, whom you seek,
Will suddenly come to His temple,
[c]Even the Messenger of the covenant,
In whom you delight.
Behold, [d]He is coming,"
Says the LORD of hosts.

2 "But who can endure [a]the
day of His coming?
And [b]who can stand when He appears?
For [c]He *is* like a refiner's fire
And like launderers' soap.
3 [a]He will sit as a refiner and
a purifier of silver;
He will purify the sons of Levi,
And purge them as gold and silver,
That they may [b]offer to the LORD
An offering in righteousness.

4 "Then [a]the offering of Judah
and Jerusalem
Will be pleasant to the LORD,
As in the days of old,
As in former years.
5 And I will come near you
for judgment;
I will be a swift witness
Against sorcerers,
Against adulterers,
[a]Against perjurers,
Against those who [b]exploit wage
earners and [c]widows and orphans,
And against those who turn
away an alien—
Because they do not fear Me,"
Says the LORD of hosts.

6 "For I *am* the LORD, [a]I do not change;
[b]Therefore you are not consumed,
O sons of Jacob.
7 Yet from the days of [a]your fathers
You have gone away from
My ordinances
And have not kept *them*.
[b]Return to Me, and I will return
to you,"
Says the LORD of hosts.
[c]"But you said,
'In what way shall we return?'

Do Not Rob God

8 "Will a man rob God?
Yet you have robbed Me!
But you say,
'In what way have we robbed You?'
[a]In tithes and offerings.
9 You are cursed with a curse,
For you have robbed Me,
Even this whole nation.
10 [a]Bring all the tithes into
the [b]storehouse,
That there may be food in My house,
And try Me now in this,"
Says the LORD of hosts,
"If I will not open for you the
[c]windows of heaven
And [d]pour out for you *such* blessing

2:15 [a] Gen. 2:24; Matt. 19:4, 5 [b] Ezra 9:2; [1 Cor. 7:14] 2:16 [a] Deut. 24:1; [Matt. 5:31; 19:6–8] 2:17 [a] Is. 43:22, 24 [b] Is. 5:20; Zeph. 1:12 3:1 [a] Matt. 11:10; Mark 1:2; Luke 1:76; 7:27; John 1:23; 2:14, 15 [b] [Is. 40:3] [c] Is. 63:9 [d] Hab. 2:7 3:2 [a] Jer. 10:10; Joel 2:11; Nah. 1:6; [Mal. 4:1] [b] Is. 33:14; Ezek. 22:14; Rev. 6:17 [c] Is. 4:4; Zech. 13:9; [Matt. 3:10–12; 1 Cor. 3:13–15] 3:3 [a] Is. 1:25; Dan. 12:10; Zech. 13:9 [b] [1 Pet. 2:5] 3:4 [a] Mal. 1:11 3:5 [a] Lev. 19:12; Zech. 5:4; [James 5:12] [b] Lev. 19:13; James 5:4 [c] Ex. 22:22 3:6 [a] [Num. 23:19; Rom. 11:29; James 1:17] [b] [Lam. 3:22] 3:7 [a] Acts 7:51 [b] Zech. 1:3 [c] Mal. 1:6 3:8 [a] Neh. 13:10–12 3:10 [a] Prov. 3:9, 10 [b] 1 Chr. 26:20 [c] Gen. 7:11 [d] 2 Chr. 31:10

That *there will* not *be room*
enough *to receive it.*

11 "And I will rebuke [a]the devourer
for your sakes,
So that he will not destroy the
fruit of your ground,
Nor shall the vine fail to bear
fruit for you in the field,"
Says the LORD of hosts;
12 "And all nations will call you blessed,
For you will be [a]a delightful land,"
Says the LORD of hosts.

The People Complain Harshly

13 "Your[a] words have been
harsh against Me,"
Says the LORD,
"Yet you say,
'What have we spoken against You?'
14 [a]You have said,
'It is useless to serve God;
What profit *is it* that we have
kept His ordinance,
And that we have walked as
mourners
Before the LORD of hosts?
15 So now [a]we call the proud blessed,
For those who do wickedness
are raised up;
They even [b]tempt God and go free.'"

A Book of Remembrance

16 Then those [a]who feared the LORD
[b]spoke to one another,
And the LORD listened
and heard *them;*
So [c]a book of remembrance
was written before Him
For those who fear the LORD
And who meditate on His name.

17 "They[a] shall be Mine," says
the LORD of hosts,
"On the day that I make
them My [b]jewels.[1]
And [c]I will spare them
As a man spares his own son
who serves him."
18 [a]Then you shall again discern

#OXYGEN
MALACHI 3:17
Elevate the Steps You Take

A life lived with reverence and honor toward Almighty God is a life lived well. A proper attitude toward our sovereign King will inform our actions, decisions, and attitudes. Those who walk in honor to God will know blessing in this life and the next.

Breathe and elevate the steps you take.

Between the righteous and
the wicked,
Between one who serves God
And one who does not serve Him.

The Great Day of God

4 "For behold, [a]the day is coming,
Burning like an oven,
And all [b]the proud, yes, all who
do wickedly will be [c]stubble.
And the day which is coming
shall burn them up,"
Says the LORD of hosts,
"That will [d]leave them neither
root nor branch.
2 But to you who [a]fear My name
The [b]Sun of Righteousness
shall arise
With healing in His wings;
And you shall go out
And grow fat like stall-fed calves.
3 [a]You shall trample the wicked,
For they shall be ashes under
the soles of your feet
On the day that I do *this,"*
Says the LORD of hosts.

4 "Remember the [a]Law of
Moses, My servant,
Which I commanded him in
Horeb for all Israel,
With [b]*the* statutes and judgments.

3:11 [a] Amos 4:9 3:12 [a] Dan. 8:9 3:13 [a] Mal. 2:17 3:14 [a] Job 21:14 3:15 [a] Ps. 73:12 [b] Ps. 95:9 3:16 [a] Ps. 66:16 [b] Heb. 3:13 [c] Ps. 56:8 3:17 [a] Ex. 19:5; Deut. 7:6; Is. 43:21; [1 Pet. 2:9] [b] Is. 62:3 [c] Ps. 103:13 [1] Literally *special treasure* 3:18 [a] [Ps. 58:11] 4:1 [a] Ps. 21:9; [Nah. 1:5, 6; Mal. 3:2, 3; 2 Pet. 3:7] [b] Mal. 3:18 [c] Is. 5:24; Obad. 18 [d] Amos 2:9 4:2 [a] Mal. 3:16 [b] Matt. 4:16; Luke 1:78; Acts 10:43; 2 Cor. 4:6; Eph. 5:14 4:3 [a] Mic. 7:10 4:4 [a] Ex. 20:3 [b] Deut. 4:10

RELEASE // ELEVATE THE STEPS YOU TAKE

In the End, We Win!

Malachi 4:2 // "But to you who fear My name the Sun of Righteousness shall arise with healing in His wings; and you shall go out and grow fat like stall-fed calves."

Summary Message // As the last of the twelve minor prophets, Malachi was dedicated to the service of God in a time when God's people were not serving Him. Malachi spoke clearly about the sins of the people of Israel and about God's unchanging love and mercy toward them. Malachi had a great love for the people of Israel, and their drastic spiritual decline broke his heart.

Malachi spoke of the corruption of the priesthood through idolatry and infidelity. He rebuked the people for indifference toward the things of God. In the final chapter in this final book of the Old Testament, both cause for celebration and stern warning are put forth: justice will finally be served, but the people must remember the Law of Moses.

Practical Application // Malachi makes it clear that the wicked and proud will be utterly obliterated. This is just as true today, but we prefer never to see ourselves in either of those categories. Conversely, this prophet who loved the Lord and His people clearly stated to those who fear the name of the Lord: "You shall go out and grow fat like stall-fed calves. You shall trample the wicked, for they shall be ashes under the soles of your feet" (Mal. 4:2–3).

It sometimes seems as if evil will get its way forever and that the Lord has forgotten about the plight of His people. We often feel that doing good and living right is without benefit. Racism, classism, materialism, sexism, and ageism are problems that seem never to go away. But this word from the Lord to Malachi is a reminder that a great day is indeed coming. It will be a day when all that is right and good will triumph. Though it may take a while, do not get lost in the wait. This word from the Lord should strengthen the heart of the believer. This reminder is proof that, in the end, the Lord's righteous cause will emerge victorious. The Lord "will arise with healing in His wings" (Mal. 4:2). Through Him and by Him, all in the world will be healed. Simply put, in the end, we win! The Lord has always shown up for His people in His timing. This rising will be glorious for believers and treacherous for evildoers. It is our duty as believers to wait patiently for the salvation of the Lord and not fall into temptation and become like those to whom Malachi spoke judgment. The Scriptures call on all believers to live godly lives as we await the "Sun of Righteousness" who will one day arise. What a glorious day that will be!

Fervent Prayer // Father, we thank You for Your Word that reminds us of assured victory. We thank You for the "Sun of Righteousness [who] shall arise with healing in His wings." Lord, we place our hope in this great day when You will avenge all wrongs committed. We praise You for the promise that Your righteous children will trample evil under their feet. Now we ask for pure hearts and minds to keep us from the temptation to become like the unrighteous who will be destroyed on that great day. We know You are "not willing that any should perish but that all should come to repentance" (2 Pet. 3:9). While there is time, we ask that many would come to repentance and turn from their wicked ways. We love You and ask these things in Jesus' name. Amen.

---

5 Behold, I will send you
[a]Elijah the prophet
[b]Before the coming of the
great and dreadful day
of the LORD.
6 And [a]he will turn
The hearts of the fathers
to the children,
And the hearts of the children
to their fathers,
Lest I come and [b]strike the
earth with [c]a curse."

4:5 [a] [Matt. 11:14; 17:10–13; Mark 9:11–13; Luke 1:17]; John 1:21 [b] Joel 2:31 4:6 [a] Luke 1:17 [b] Zech. 14:12 [c] Zech. 5:3

NEW TESTAMENT

THE GOSPEL ACCORDING TO

MATTHEW

OVERVIEW

Gospel (which means "good news" or "good tidings") refers to the narrative containing the birth, life, ministry, death, and resurrection of Jesus Christ. This narrative is described in four books of the Bible told from the vantage point of four different witnesses: Matthew, Mark, Luke, and John. The Gospel of Matthew was written by a Hebrew man acquainted with the Old Testament teachings and customs. Matthew wrote his account predominantly to a Hebrew audience. Toward that end, Matthew's Gospel is presented as the fulfillment of Old Testament prophecy. Matthew means "gift of the Lord."

Matthew describes how the foundation of the Christian faith is built upon the events of a carpenter turned itinerant preacher, also known as Jesus of Nazareth. Jesus was born into obscurity, poverty, and a corrupt society. Yet, Jesus was no ordinary preacher. He was the Messiah, the anointed Savior of the entire world. Peter professed that Jesus is "the Christ, the Son of the living God" (Matt. 16:16).

The children of Israel had been anticipating a messiah for centuries. Old Testament prophets foreshadowed the arrival of this new king, a descendant of King David, who would restore the throne of Israel. Matthew's Gospel begins with a genealogy, listing a total of forty-two generations between Abraham and Jesus: "So all the generations from Abraham to David are fourteen generations, from David until the captivity in Babylon are fourteen generations, and from the captivity in Babylon until the Christ are fourteen generations" (1:17). Jesus was descended from the bloodline of King David from the tribe of Judah. The inclusion of this genealogy at the beginning of this Gospel shows Matthew's distinctly Jewish nature that distinguishes his witness from the other three Gospels.

Matthew was concerned about linking the ministry of Jesus Christ with the expectations of the Old Testament prophets. There are fifty-three Old Testament quotations within Matthew's Gospel, and fifteen times Jesus Christ is described as the fulfillment of the Old Testament prophecies. Jesus was, and is, the culmination of a divine plan for reconciliation and redemption.

BREATHE IT IN

Jesus and His half-siblings were raised to know their lineage and faith heritage. They knew they were of the tribe of Judah. They knew the bloodline of Israel's greatest king, David, raced through their veins. There was a cultural expectation that they would bring honor to their clan, their tribe, and their nation. Their experience tells us that what comes before us matters.

Family history matters because God uses families from generation to generation to accomplish His plan for human redemption. For example, the blessings of Abraham found in Genesis 12 and 17 include the flourishing of future generations. Although God's plan of salvation began long before Abraham, Matthew's focus on Jesus' earthly family started with Abraham and Sarah. Forty-two generations later, the baby Jesus was born to Mary and Joseph. As we breathe in the gospel according to Matthew, we should each learn more about our family lineages too. Knowing our family history can give us a profound understanding of who we are and where

we came from. It can reconnect us to the family ties that were purposefully severed under the institution of slavery.

Among the highest priorities of the newly emancipated, formerly enslaved people in the late 1800s was reuniting with family members who had been sold during slavery. They used newspaper classified ads to locate family members who had been separated by the brutal institution of slavery. Then in 1977, an eight-episode saga called *Roots* refueled a fire to reconstruct family trees and recapture the importance of legacy, faith, and dignity in African American families. Recognition of generational identity is important for establishing worth.

Although many people may find tracing their family history difficult, those who are descended from enslaved people will be hard-pressed to trace their family's journey from Africa, through the middle passage, and into the plantations of the Caribbean islands and the Americas apart from oral history or chattel records. It is worth the effort to discover and document your bloodline as best you can, though. Scripture is clear that family matters to God, so it should matter to us too.

Today, DNA testing can help you trace your origins. Search public records for your family's unique journey. Interview and record your elderly ancestors to document a family oral history. How did your family settle in the region where your history is most prominent? Are there any property records? Does your family have a military history? Did your family experience any migration? Does your family have a faith heritage or a church home? Is there a family Bible where births, deaths, and other historical events were recorded? What redemptive contributions have emerged from your bloodline? Most importantly, what kind of legacy will you leave behind for future generations?

God is working through history to redeem humanity. Be mindful that not every generation in Jesus' bloodline was remarkable. Some were outright regrettable. As you retrace your family's past, you might discover more cause to cringe than celebrate. Know that this history might have shaped you, but it does not define you. The gospel's message is one of transformation. In God's power, you can change the direction of your family for generations to come.

†

THE GOSPEL ACCORDING TO

MATTHEW

The Genealogy of Jesus Christ
(Ruth 4:18–22; 1 Chr. 2:1–15; Luke 3:23–38)

1 The book of the [a]genealogy of Jesus
Christ, [b]the Son of David, [c]the Son of
Abraham:
2 [a]Abraham begot Isaac, [b]Isaac begot
Jacob, and Jacob begot [c]Judah and his
brothers. 3 [a]Judah begot Perez and Zerah
by Tamar, [b]Perez begot Hezron, and Hezron begot Ram. 4 Ram begot Amminadab,
Amminadab begot Nahshon, and Nahshon
begot Salmon. 5 Salmon begot [a]Boaz by Rahab, Boaz begot Obed by Ruth, Obed begot
Jesse, 6 and [a]Jesse begot David the king.
[b]David the king begot Solomon by her
who had been the wife[1] of Uriah. 7 [a]Solomon
begot Rehoboam, Rehoboam begot [b]Abijah,
and Abijah begot Asa.[1] 8 Asa begot [a]Jehosha-
phat, Jehoshaphat begot Joram, and Joram
begot [b]Uzziah. 9 Uzziah begot Jotham, Jotham begot [a]Ahaz, and Ahaz begot Hezekiah.
10 [a]Hezekiah begot Manasseh, Manasseh begot Amon,[1] and Amon begot [b]Josiah. 11 [a]Jo-
siah begot Jeconiah and his brothers about
the time they were [b]carried away to Babylon.
12 And after they were brought to Babylon, [a]Jeconiah begot Shealtiel, and Shealtiel begot [b]Zerubbabel. 13 Zerubbabel begot
Abiud, Abiud begot Eliakim, and Eliakim
begot Azor. 14 Azor begot Zadok, Zadok begot Achim, and Achim begot Eliud. 15 Eliud
begot Eleazar, Eleazar begot Matthan, and
Matthan begot Jacob. 16 And Jacob begot Joseph the husband of [a]Mary, of whom was
born Jesus who is called Christ.
17 So all the generations from Abraham
to David *are* fourteen generations, from
David until the captivity in Babylon *are*
fourteen generations, and from the captivity in Babylon until the Christ *are* fourteen generations.

Christ Born of Mary
(Luke 2:1–7)

18 Now the [a]birth of Jesus Christ was as
follows: After His mother Mary was betrothed to Joseph, before they came together, she was found with child [b]of the
Holy Spirit. 19 Then Joseph her husband,
being a just *man,* and not wanting [a]to make
her a public example, was minded to put
her away secretly. 20 But while he thought
about these things, behold, an angel of the
Lord appeared to him in a dream, saying,
"Joseph, son of David, do not be afraid to
take to you Mary your wife, [a]for that which
is conceived in her is of the Holy Spirit.
21 [a]And she will bring forth a Son, and you
shall call His name JESUS, [b]for He will save
His people from their sins."
22 So all this was done that it might be
fulfilled which was spoken by the Lord
through the prophet, saying: 23 [a]"Behold,
the virgin shall be with child, and bear a
Son, and they shall call His name Immanuel,"[1] which is translated, "God with us."
24 Then Joseph, being aroused from
sleep, did as the angel of the Lord commanded him and took to him his wife,
25 and did not know her till she had brought

1:1 [a] Luke 3:23 [b] 2 Sam. 7:12–16; Ps. 132:11; Is. 9:6; 11:1; Jer. 23:5; [Matt. 1:18; Luke 3:23, 31]; John 7:42; Acts 2:30; [Rom. 1:3]; Rev. 22:16 [c] Gen. 12:3; 22:18; [Gal. 3:16] **1:2** [a] Gen. 21:2, 12 [b] Gen. 25:26; 28:14 [c] Gen. 29:35 **1:3** [a] Gen. 38:27; 49:10 [b] Ruth 4:18–22; 1 Chr. 2:1–15; Matt. 1:3–6 **1:5** [a] Ruth 2:1; 4:1–13 **1:6** [a] 1 Sam. 16:1; Is. 11:1, 10 [b] 2 Sam. 7:12; 12:24; Is. 9:7 [1] Words in italic type have been added for clarity. They are not found in the original Greek. **1:7** [a] 1 Kin. 11:43; 1 Chr. 3:10 [b] 2 Chr. 11:20 [1] NU-Text reads *Asaph.* **1:8** [a] 1 Chr. 3:10 [b] 2 Kin. 15:13 **1:9** [a] 2 Kin. 15:38 **1:10** [a] 2 Kin. 20:21 [b] 1 Kin. 13:2 [1] NU-Text reads *Amos.* **1:11** [a] 1 Chr. 3:15, 16 [b] 2 Kin. 24:14–16; Jer. 27:20; Matt. 1:17 **1:12** [a] 1 Chr. 3:17 [b] Ezra 3:2; Neh. 12:1; Hag. 1:1 **1:16** [a] Matt. 13:55; Mark 6:3 **1:18** [a] Matt. 12:46; Luke 1:27 [b] Is. 7:14; 49:5; Luke 1:35 **1:19** [a] Deut. 24:1; John 8:4, 5 **1:20** [a] Luke 1:35 **1:21** [a] [Is. 7:14; 9:6, 7]; Luke 1:31; 2:21 [b] Luke 2:11; John 1:29; [Acts 4:12; 5:31; 13:23, 38; Rom. 5:18, 19; Col. 1:20–23] **1:23** [a] Is. 7:14 [1] Isaiah 7:14

forth [a]her firstborn Son.[1] And he called His
name JESUS.

Wise Men from the East

2 Now after [a]Jesus was born in Bethlehem of Judea in the days of Herod the
king, behold, wise men [b]from the East came
to Jerusalem, 2saying, [a]"Where is He who
has been born King of the Jews? For we
have seen [b]His star in the East and have
come to worship Him."
3When Herod the king heard *this,* he
was troubled, and all Jerusalem with him.
4And when he had gathered all [a]the chief
priests and [b]scribes of the people together,
[c]he inquired of them where the Christ was
to be born.
5So they said to him, "In Bethlehem of
Judea, for thus it is written by the prophet:

6 'But[a] you, Bethlehem, *in*
the land of Judah,
Are not the least among
the rulers of Judah;
For out of you shall come a Ruler
[b]Who will shepherd My people
Israel.'"[1]

7Then Herod, when he had secretly
called the wise men, determined from
them what time the [a]star appeared. 8And
he sent them to Bethlehem and said, "Go
and search carefully for the young Child,
and when you have found *Him,* bring back
word to me, that I may come and worship
Him also."
9When they heard the king, they departed; and behold, the star which they
had seen in the East went before them, till
it came and stood over where the young
Child was. 10When they saw the star, they
rejoiced with exceedingly great joy. 11And
when they had come into the house, they
saw the young Child with Mary His mother,
and fell down and worshiped Him. And
when they had opened their treasures,
[a]they presented gifts to Him: gold, frankincense, and myrrh.
12Then, being divinely warned [a]in a
dream that they should not return to Herod,
they departed for their own country another way.

The Flight into Egypt

13Now when they had departed, behold,
an angel of the Lord appeared to Joseph
in a dream, saying, "Arise, take the young
Child and His mother, flee to Egypt, and
stay there until I bring you word; for Herod
will seek the young Child to destroy Him."
14When he arose, he took the young Child
and His mother by night and departed for
Egypt, 15and was there until the death of
Herod, that it might be fulfilled which was
spoken by the Lord through the prophet,
saying, [a]"Out of Egypt I called My Son."[1]

Massacre of the Innocents

16Then Herod, when he saw that he was
deceived by the wise men, was exceedingly
angry; and he sent forth and put to death all
the male children who were in Bethlehem
and in all its districts, from two years old
and under, according to the time which he
had determined from the wise men. 17Then
was fulfilled what was spoken by Jeremiah
the prophet, saying:

18 "A [a]voice was heard in Ramah,
Lamentation, weeping, and
great mourning,
Rachel weeping *for* her children,
Refusing to be comforted,
Because they are no more."[1]

The Home in Nazareth
(Luke 2:39)

19Now when Herod was dead, behold,
an angel of the Lord appeared in a dream
to Joseph in Egypt, 20[a]saying, "Arise, take
the young Child and His mother, and go to
the land of Israel, for those who [b]sought
the young Child's life are dead." 21Then
he arose, took the young Child and His
mother, and came into the land of Israel.
22But when he heard that Archelaus was
reigning over Judea instead of his father
Herod, he was afraid to go there. And being warned by God in a [a]dream, he turned
aside [b]into the region of Galilee. 23And he

1:25 [a] Ex. 13:2; Luke 2:7, 21 [1] NU-Text reads *a Son.* 2:1 [a] Mic. 5:2; Luke 2:4–7 [b] Gen. 25:6; 1 Kin. 4:30 2:2 [a] Luke 2:11 [b] [Num. 24:17; Is. 60:3] 2:4 [a] 2 Chr. 36:14 [b] 2 Chr. 34:13 [c] Mal. 2:7 2:6 [a] Mic. 5:2; John 7:42 [b] Gen. 49:10; [Rev. 2:27] [1] Micah 5:2 2:7 [a] Num. 24:17 2:11 [a] Ps. 72:10; Is. 60:6 2:12 [a] [Job 33:15, 16]; Matt. 1:20 2:15 [a] Num. 24:8; Hos. 11:1 [1] Hosea 11:1 2:18 [a] Jer. 31:15 [1] Jeremiah 31:15 2:20 [a] Luke 2:39 [b] Matt. 2:16 2:22 [a] Matt. 2:12, 13, 19 [b] Matt. 3:13; Luke 2:39

came and dwelt in a city called [a]Nazareth,
that it might be fulfilled [b]which was spoken by the prophets, "He shall be called a
Nazarene."

John the Baptist Prepares the Way

(Mark 1:2–8; Luke 3:1–20)

3 In those days [a]John the Baptist came
preaching [b]in the wilderness of Judea,
2and saying, "Repent, for [a]the kingdom of
heaven is at hand!" 3For this is he who was
spoken of by the prophet Isaiah, saying:

[a]"The voice of one crying in
the wilderness:
[b]'Prepare the way of the LORD;
Make His paths straight.'"[1]

4Now [a]John himself was clothed in camel's hair, with a leather belt around his
waist; and his food was [b]locusts and [c]wild
honey. 5[a]Then Jerusalem, all Judea, and
all the region around the Jordan went out
to him 6[a]and were baptized by him in the
Jordan, confessing their sins.

7But when he saw many of the Pharisees
and Sadducees coming to his baptism, he
said to them, [a]"Brood of vipers! Who warned
you to flee from [b]the wrath to come? 8There-
fore bear fruits worthy of repentance, 9and
do not think to say to yourselves, [a]'We have
Abraham as *our* father.' For I say to you that
God is able to raise up children to Abraham
from these stones. 10And even now the ax is
laid to the root of the trees. [a]Therefore every
tree which does not bear good fruit is cut
down and thrown into the fire. 11[a]I indeed
baptize you with water unto repentance,
but He who is coming after me is mightier than I, whose sandals I am not worthy
to carry. [b]He will baptize you with the Holy
Spirit and fire.[1] 12[a]His winnowing fan *is* in
His hand, and He will thoroughly clean out
His threshing floor, and gather His wheat
into the barn; but He will [b]burn up the chaff
with unquenchable fire."

John Baptizes Jesus

(Mark 1:9–11; Luke 3:21, 22; John 1:29–34)

13[a]Then Jesus came [b]from Galilee to John
at the Jordan to be baptized by him. 14And
John *tried to* prevent Him, saying, "I need
to be baptized by You, and are You coming to me?"

15But Jesus answered and said to him,
"Permit *it to be so* now, for thus it is fitting
for us to fulfill all righteousness." Then he
allowed Him.

16[a]When He had been baptized, Jesus
came up immediately from the water; and
behold, the heavens were opened to Him,
and He[1] saw [b]the Spirit of God descending
like a dove and alighting upon Him. 17[a]And
suddenly a voice *came* from heaven, saying, [b]"This is My beloved Son, in whom I
am well pleased."

Satan Tempts Jesus

(Mark 1:12, 13; Luke 4:1–13)

4 Then [a]Jesus was led up by [b]the Spirit
into the wilderness to be tempted by
the devil. 2And when He had fasted forty
days and forty nights, afterward He was
hungry. 3Now when the tempter came to
Him, he said, "If You are the Son of God,
command that these stones become bread."

4But He answered and said, "It is written, [a]'Man shall not live by bread alone,
but by every word that proceeds from the
mouth of God.'"[1]

5Then the devil took Him up [a]into the
holy city, set Him on the pinnacle of the temple, 6and said to Him, "If You are the Son of
God, throw Yourself down. For it is written:

[a]'He shall give His angels
charge over you,'

and,

[b]'In *their* hands they shall bear you up,
Lest you dash your foot
against a stone.'"[1]

2:23 [a] Luke 1:26; 2:39; John 1:45, 46 [b] Judg. 13:5 3:1 [a] Matt. 3:1–12; Mark 1:3–8; Luke 3:2–17; John 1:6–8, 19–28 [b] Josh. 14:10 3:2 [a] Dan. 2:44; Mal. 4:6; Matt. 4:17; Mark 1:15; Luke 1:17; 10:9; 11:20; 21:31 3:3 [a] Is. 40:3; Luke 3:4; John 1:23 [b] Luke 1:76 [1] Isaiah 40:3 3:4 [a] 2 Kin. 1:8; Zech. 13:4; Matt. 11:8; Mark 1:6 [b] Lev. 11:22 [c] 1 Sam. 14:25, 26 3:5 [a] Mark 1:5 3:6 [a] Acts 19:4, 18 3:7 [a] Matt. 12:34; Luke 3:7–9 [b] [Rom. 5:9; 1 Thess. 1:10] 3:9 [a] John 8:33; Acts 13:26; [Rom. 4:1, 11, 16; Gal. 3:29] 3:10 [a] [Ps. 92:12–14]; Matt. 7:19; Luke 13:7, 9; [John 15:6] 3:11 [a] Mark 1:4, 8; Luke 3:16; John 1:26; Acts 1:5 [b] [Is. 4:4; John 20:22; Acts 2:3, 4; 1 Cor. 12:13] [1] M-Text omits *and fire.* 3:12 [a] Mal. 3:3 [b] Mal. 4:1; Matt. 13:30 3:13 [a] Matt. 3:13–17; Mark 1:9–11; Luke 3:21, 22; John 1:31–34 [b] Matt. 2:22 3:16 [a] Mark 1:10 [b] [Is. 11:2]; Luke 3:22; John 1:32; Acts 7:56 [1] Or *he* 3:17 [a] John 12:28 [b] Ps. 2:7; Is. 42:1; Mark 1:11; Luke 1:35; 9:35; Col. 1:13 4:1 [a] Matt. 4:1–11; Mark 1:12; Luke 4:1 [b] Ezek. 3:14; Acts 8:39 4:4 [a] Deut. 8:3 [1] Deuteronomy 8:3 4:5 [a] Neh. 11:1, 18; Dan. 9:24; Matt. 27:53 4:6 [a] Ps. 91:11 [b] Ps. 91:12 [1] Psalm 91:11, 12

RELEASE // BELIEVE IN THE SON

That "It" Factor

Matthew 3:13–14 // Then Jesus came from Galilee to John at the Jordan to be baptized by him. And John tried to prevent Him, saying, "I need to be baptized by You, and are You coming to me?"

Summary Message // When the world around us seems to be falling apart and it is difficult to see where or how we will get through, God invites us to believe in His Son, Jesus. In Matthew 3, we find John the Baptist responding to that invitation. Despite the leaders of that day challenging and ridiculing his ministry, John still understood the assignment and believed in Jesus. His belief afforded him the opportunity to bear witness to God's mighty works. God extends the same invitation to each of us today. So, the question is, what is distracting you and preventing you from believing in God's Son?

Practical Application // Have you ever encountered a stranger and known immediately that they were someone special? Maybe you met a leader you admired or your future spouse. Whoever it was, for you, they had what some call the "it factor"—that swagger. Those encounters often leave a mark; some have forever changed lives.

John the Baptist had such an encounter. If you will recall, John was a respected prophet who preached that someone "mightier" than him would soon step on the scene (Matt. 3:11). Then one day, Jesus came to him to be baptized. In an instant, John recognized that he stood in the presence of greatness. His belief then enabled him to bear witness of the voice of God declaring His pleasure in His Son (see vv. 16–17). What does this mean for us?

- Our belief in the Son should prompt our obedience to God's calling on our lives. John was initially hesitant to baptize Jesus. However, in response to Jesus' prompting, John obediently fulfilled his purpose in God's grand plan. Our obedience to God's call will afford us opportunities to see God at work. Because John believed and was obedient, he was positioned to hear and witness God speaking over Jesus and the Holy Spirit descending as a dove (see Matt. 3:16–17).
- Our witness prompts us to share the Good News and invite others also to believe in the Son of God.

While we do not know if John the Baptist and this first-century community knew anything about "swagger," John demonstrates to us the freedom that belief in the Son affords us. It frees us from the shackles of the natural and positions us to experience the supernatural in a way that forever changes us. God's invitation to each of us is simply to believe—to set aside our doubts and trust that God's Son came to earth, took on human flesh, died, and was resurrected so that we might experience the abundant life God desires for each of us (see John 10:10).

Fervent Prayer // Lord Jesus, thank You! Thank You for loving us so much that You would leave Your throne in heaven, enter this broken world, and sacrifice everything for us. We are overwhelmed by the lengths to which You went so that we might have a relationship with You. All You ask is that we believe. Thank You for Your unconditional love. We ask that You help us in our unbelief when the things we experience day in and day out distract us from You. Help us keep our eyes trained on You so we might bear witness to the miracles, signs, and wonders that You are still doing in this world. In Jesus' name we pray. Amen.

---

7 Jesus said to him, "It is written again,
[a]'You shall not tempt the LORD your God.'"[1]
8 Again, the devil took Him up on an exceedingly high mountain, and [a]showed Him all the kingdoms of the world and their glory.
9 And he said to Him, "All these things I will give You if You will fall down and worship me."
10 Then Jesus said to him, "Away with you,[1] Satan! For it is written, [a]'You shall worship the LORD your God, and Him only you shall serve.'"[2]

4:7 [a] Deut. 6:16 [1] Deuteronomy 6:16 4:8 [a] [Matt. 16:26; 1 John 2:15–17] 4:10 [a] Deut. 6:13; 10:20; Josh. 24:14 [1] M-Text reads *Get behind Me.* [2] Deuteronomy 6:13

11Then the devil [a]left Him, and behold,
[b]angels came and ministered to Him.

Jesus Begins His Galilean Ministry
(Mark 1:14, 15; Luke 4:14, 15)

12[a]Now when Jesus heard that John had
been put in prison, He departed to Galilee.
13And leaving Nazareth, He came and dwelt
in Capernaum, which is by the sea, in the
regions of Zebulun and Naphtali, 14that it
might be fulfilled which was spoken by Isaiah the prophet, saying:

15 "The[a] land of Zebulun and
the land of Naphtali,
By the way of the sea,
beyond the Jordan,
Galilee of the Gentiles:
16 [a]The people who sat in
darkness have seen a
great light,
And upon those who sat in
the region and shadow
of death
Light has dawned."[1]

17[a]From that time Jesus began to preach
and to say, [b]"Repent, for the kingdom of
heaven is at hand."

Four Fishermen Called as Disciples
(Mark 1:16–20; Luke 5:1–11)

18[a]And Jesus, walking by the Sea of Galilee, saw two brothers, Simon [b]called Peter,
and Andrew his brother, casting a net into
the sea; for they were fishermen. 19Then He
said to them, "Follow Me, and [a]I will make
you fishers of men." 20[a]They immediately
left *their* nets and followed Him.

21[a]Going on from there, He saw two
other brothers, James *the son* of Zebedee,
and John his brother, in the boat with Zebedee their father, mending their nets. He
called them, 22and immediately they left
the boat and their father, and followed
Him.

Jesus Heals a Great Multitude
(Mark 1:35–39; Luke 4:44; 6:17–19)

23And Jesus went about all Galilee,
[a]teaching in their synagogues, preaching
[b]the gospel of the kingdom, [c]and healing all
kinds of sickness and all kinds of disease
among the people. 24Then His fame went
throughout all Syria; and they [a]brought to
Him all sick people who were afflicted with
various diseases and torments, and those
who were demon-possessed, epileptics, and
paralytics; and He healed them. 25[a]Great
multitudes followed Him—from Galilee,
and *from* Decapolis, Jerusalem, Judea, and
beyond the Jordan.

The Beatitudes
(Luke 6:20–26)

5 And seeing the multitudes, [a]He went
up on a mountain, and when He was
seated His disciples came to Him. 2Then
He opened His mouth and [a]taught them,
saying:

3 "Blessed[a] *are* the poor in spirit,
For theirs is the kingdom of heaven.
4 [a]Blessed *are* those who mourn,
For they shall be comforted.
5 [a]Blessed *are* the meek,
For [b]they shall inherit the earth.
6 Blessed *are* those who [a]hunger
and thirst for righteousness,
[b]For they shall be filled.
7 Blessed *are* the merciful,
[a]For they shall obtain mercy.
8 [a]Blessed *are* the pure in heart,
For [b]they shall see God.
9 Blessed *are* the peacemakers,
For they shall be called sons of God.
10 [a]Blessed *are* those who are persecuted
for righteousness' sake,
For theirs is the kingdom
of heaven.

11[a]Blessed are you when they revile and persecute you, and say all kinds of [b]evil against

4:11 [a] [James 4:7] [b] Matt. 26:53; Luke 22:43; [Heb. 1:14] 4:12 [a] Matt. 14:3; Mark 1:14; Luke 3:20; John 4:43 4:15 [a] Is. 9:1, 2 4:16 [a] Is. 42:7; Luke 2:32 [1] Isaiah 9:1, 2 4:17 [a] Mark 1:14, 15 [b] Matt. 3:2; 10:7 4:18 [a] Matt. 4:18–22; Mark 1:16–20; Luke 5:2–11; John 1:40–42 [b] Matt. 10:2; 16:18; John 1:40–42 4:19 [a] Luke 5:10 4:20 [a] Matt. 19:27; Mark 10:28 4:21 [a] Mark 1:19 4:23 [a] Ps. 22:22; Matt. 9:35; Mark 1:21; 6:2; 10:1; Luke 4:15; 6:6; 13:10; John 6:59; 18:20 [b] [Matt. 24:14]; Mark 1:14; Luke 4:43; 8:1; 16:16 [c] Mark 1:34; Luke 4:40; 7:21; Acts 10:38 4:24 [a] Mark 1:32, 33; Luke 4:40 4:25 [a] Matt. 5:1; 8:1, 18; Mark 3:7, 8 5:1 [a] Matt. 14:23; 15:29; 17:1; Mark 3:13; Luke 6:17; 9:28; John 6:3, 15 5:2 [a] [Matt. 7:29]; Mark 10:1; 12:35; John 8:2 5:3 [a] Prov. 16:19; Is. 66:2; Luke 6:20–23 5:4 [a] Is. 61:2, 3; Luke 6:21; [John 16:20]; Acts 16:34; [2 Cor. 1:7]; Rev. 21:4 5:5 [a] Ps. 37:11; Is. 29:19 [b] [Rom. 4:13] 5:6 [a] Luke 1:53; Acts 2:4 [b] [Is. 55:1; 65:13; John 4:14; 6:48; 7:37] 5:7 [a] Ps. 41:1; Mark 11:25 5:8 [a] Ps. 15:2; 24:4; Heb. 12:14 [b] Acts 7:55, 56; 1 Cor. 13:12 5:10 [a] [2 Cor. 4:17]; 1 Pet. 3:14 5:11 [a] Luke 6:22 [b] 1 Pet. 4:14

you falsely for My sake. 12 [a]Rejoice and be
exceedingly glad, for great *is* your reward in
heaven, for [b]so they persecuted the prophets who were before you.

Believers Are Salt and Light
(Mark 9:50; Luke 14:34, 35)

13 "You are the salt of the earth; [a]but if
the salt loses its flavor, how shall it be seasoned? It is then good for nothing but to
be thrown out and trampled underfoot by
men.

14 [a]"You are the light of the world. A city
that is set on a hill cannot be hidden. 15 Nor
do they [a]light a lamp and put it under a
basket, but on a lampstand, and it gives
light to all *who are* in the house. 16 Let your
light so shine before men, [a]that they may
see your good works and [b]glorify your Father in heaven.

Christ Fulfills the Law

17 [a]"Do not think that I came to destroy
the Law or the Prophets. I did not come to
destroy but to fulfill. 18 For assuredly, I say
to you, [a]till heaven and earth pass away, one
jot or one tittle will by no means pass from
the law till all is fulfilled. 19 [a]Whoever therefore breaks one of the least of these commandments, and teaches men so, shall be
called least in the kingdom of heaven; but
whoever does and teaches *them,* he shall
be called great in the kingdom of heaven.
20 For I say to you, that unless your righteousness exceeds [a]*the righteousness* of the
scribes and Pharisees, you will by no means
enter the kingdom of heaven.

Murder Begins in the Heart
(Luke 12:57–59)

21 "You have heard that it was said to
those of old, [a]'You shall not murder,[1] and
whoever murders will be in danger of the
judgment.' 22 But I say to you that [a]whoever
is angry with his brother without a cause[1]
shall be in danger of the judgment. And
whoever says to his brother, [b]'Raca!' shall
be in danger of the council. But whoever
says, 'You fool!' shall be in danger of hell
fire. 23 Therefore [a]if you bring your gift to
the altar, and there remember that your
brother has something against you, 24 [a]leave
your gift there before the altar, and go your
way. First be reconciled to your brother, and
then come and offer your gift. 25 [a]Agree with
your adversary quickly, [b]while you are on
the way with him, lest your adversary deliver you to the judge, the judge hand you
over to the officer, and you be thrown into
prison. 26 Assuredly, I say to you, you will
by no means get out of there till you have
paid the last penny.

Adultery in the Heart

27 "You have heard that it was said to
those of old,[1] [a]'You shall not commit adultery.'[2] 28 But I say to you that whoever [a]looks
at a woman to lust for her has already committed adultery with her in his heart. 29 [a]If
your right eye causes you to sin, [b]pluck it
out and cast *it* from you; for it is more profitable for you that one of your members
perish, than for your whole body to be cast
into hell. 30 And if your right hand causes
you to sin, cut it off and cast *it* from you;
for it is more profitable for you that one of
your members perish, than for your whole
body to be cast into hell.

Marriage Is Sacred and Binding
(Matt. 19:9; Mark 10:11, 12; Luke 16:18)

31 "Furthermore it has been said, [a]'Whoever divorces his wife, let him give her a
certificate of divorce.' 32 But I say to you
that [a]whoever divorces his wife for any
reason except sexual immorality[1] causes
her to commit adultery; and whoever marries a woman who is divorced commits
adultery.

Jesus Forbids Oaths

33 "Again you have heard that [a]it was said to
those of old, [b]'You shall not swear falsely, but
[c]shall perform your oaths to the Lord.' 34 But

5:12 [a] Luke 6:23; Acts 5:41; 1 Pet. 4:13, 14 [b] 2 Chr. 36:16; Neh. 9:26; Matt. 23:37; Acts 7:52; 1 Thess. 2:15; Heb. 11:35–37; James 5:10 5:13 [a] Mark 9:50; Luke 14:34 5:14 [a] [Prov. 4:18; John 8:12]; Phil. 2:15 5:15 [a] Mark 4:21; Luke 8:16; Phil. 2:15 5:16 [a] 1 Pet. 2:12 [b] [John 15:8]; 1 Cor. 14:25 5:17 [a] Rom. 10:4 5:18 [a] Matt. 24:35; Luke 16:17 5:19 [a] [James 2:10] 5:20 [a] [Rom. 10:3] 5:21 [a] Ex. 20:13; Deut. 5:17 [1] Exodus 20:13; Deuteronomy 5:17 5:22 [a] [1 John 3:15] [b] [James 2:20; 3:6] [1] NU-Text omits *without a cause.* 5:23 [a] Matt. 8:4 5:24 [a] [Job 42:8; 1 Tim. 2:8; 1 Pet. 3:7] 5:25 [a] [Prov. 25:8]; Luke 12:58, 59 [b] [Ps. 32:6; Is. 55:6] 5:27 [a] Ex. 20:14; Deut. 5:18 [1] NU-Text and M-Text omit *to those of old.* [2] Exodus 20:14; Deuteronomy 5:18 5:28 [a] 2 Sam. 11:2–5; Job 31:1; Prov. 6:25; [Matt. 15:19; James 1:14, 15] 5:29 [a] Mark 9:43 [b] [Col. 3:5] 5:31 [a] Deut. 24:1; [Jer. 3:1]; Mark 10:2 5:32 [a] [Matt. 19:9; Mark 10:11; Luke 16:18; Rom. 7:3]; 1 Cor. 7:11 [1] Or *fornication* 5:33 [a] Matt. 23:16 [b] [Ex. 20:7]; Lev. 19:12; Num. 30:2 [c] Deut. 23:23

I say to you, [a]do not swear at all: neither by
heaven, for it is [b]God's throne; 35 nor by the
earth, for it is His footstool; nor by Jerusalem,
for it is the city of [a]the great King. 36 Nor shall
you swear by your head, because you cannot
make one hair white or black. 37 [a]But let your
'Yes' be 'Yes,' and your 'No,' 'No.' For whatever
is more than these is from the evil one.

Go the Second Mile
(Luke 6:29–31)

38 "You have heard that it was said, [a]'An eye
for an eye and a tooth for a tooth.'[1] 39 [a]But I
tell you not to resist an evil person. [b]But whoever slaps you on your right cheek, turn the
other to him also. 40 If anyone wants to sue
you and take away your tunic, let him have
your cloak also. 41 And whoever [a]compels you
to go one mile, go with him two. 42 Give to
him who asks you, and [a]from him who wants
to borrow from you do not turn away.

Love Your Enemies
(Luke 6:27, 28, 32–36)

43 "You have heard that it was said, [a]'You
shall love your neighbor[1] [b]and hate your enemy.' 44 But I say to you, [a]love your enemies,
bless those who curse you, [b]do good to those
who hate you, and pray [c]for those who spitefully use you and persecute you,[1] 45 that you
may be sons of your Father in heaven; for
[a]He makes His sun rise on the evil and on
the good, and sends rain on the just and on
the unjust. 46 [a]For if you love those who love
you, what reward have you? Do not even
the tax collectors do the same? 47 And if you
greet your brethren[1] only, what do you do
more *than others?* Do not even the tax collectors[2] do so? 48 [a]Therefore you shall be perfect, just [b]as your Father in heaven is perfect.

Do Good to Please God

6 "Take heed that you do not do your
charitable deeds before men, to be seen
by them. Otherwise you have no reward
from your Father in heaven. 2 Therefore,
[a]when you do a charitable deed, do not
sound a trumpet before you as the hypocrites do in the synagogues and in the
streets, that they may have glory from men.
Assuredly, I say to you, they have their reward. 3 But when you do a charitable deed,
do not let your left hand know what your
right hand is doing, 4 that your charitable
deed may be in secret; and your Father
who sees in secret [a]will Himself reward
you openly.[1]

The Model Prayer
(Luke 11:2–4)

5 "And when you pray, you shall not be
like the hypocrites. For they love to pray
standing in the synagogues and on the corners of the streets, that they may be seen
by men. Assuredly, I say to you, they have
their reward. 6 But you, when you pray, [a]go
into your room, and when you have shut
your door, pray to your Father who *is* in the
secret *place;* and your Father who sees in
secret will reward you openly.[1] 7 And when
you pray, [a]do not use vain repetitions as the
heathen *do.* [b]For they think that they will
be heard for their many words.

8 "Therefore do not be like them. For
your Father [a]knows the things you have
need of before you ask Him. 9 In this [a]man-
ner, therefore, pray:

[b]Our Father in heaven,
Hallowed be Your [c]name.
10 Your kingdom come.
[a]Your will be done
On earth [b]as *it is* in heaven.
11 Give us this day our [a]daily bread.
12 And [a]forgive us our debts,
As we forgive our debtors.
13 [a]And do not lead us into
temptation,
But [b]deliver us from the
evil one.

5:34 [a] Matt. 23:16; James 5:12 [b] Is. 66:1 5:35 [a] Ps. 48:2; [Matt. 5:2, 19; 6:10] 5:37 [a] [Col. 4:6]; James 5:12 5:38 [a] Ex. 21:24; Lev. 24:20; Deut. 19:21 [1] Exodus 21:24; Leviticus 24:20; Deuteronomy 19:21 5:39 [a] [Prov. 20:22]; Luke 6:29; [Rom. 12:17; 1 Cor. 6:7; 1 Pet. 3:9] [b] Is. 50:6; Lam. 3:30 5:41 [a] Matt. 27:32 5:42 [a] Deut. 15:7–11; Luke 6:30–34; 1 Tim. 6:18 5:43 [a] Lev. 19:18 [b] Deut. 23:3–6; Ps. 41:10 [1] Compare Leviticus 19:18 5:44 [a] Luke 6:27; Rom. 12:14 [b] [Rom. 12:20] [c] Luke 23:34; Acts 7:60; 1 Cor. 4:12; 1 Pet. 2:23 [1] NU-Text omits three clauses from this verse, leaving, *"But I say to you, love your enemies and pray for those who persecute you."* 5:45 [a] Job 25:3; Ps. 65:9–13; Luke 12:16, 17; Acts 14:17 5:46 [a] Luke 6:32 5:47 [1] M-Text reads *friends.* [2] NU-Text reads *Gentiles.* 5:48 [a] Gen. 17:1; Lev. 11:44; 19:2; Luke 6:36; [Col. 1:28; 4:12]; James 1:4; 1 Pet. 1:15 [b] Eph. 5:1 6:2 [a] Rom. 12:8 6:4 [a] Luke 14:12–14 [1] NU-Text omits *openly.* 6:6 [a] 2 Kin. 4:33 [1] NU-Text omits *openly.* 6:7 [a] Eccl. 5:2 [b] 1 Kin. 18:26 6:8 [a] [Rom. 8:26, 27] 6:9 [a] Matt. 6:9–13; Luke 11:2–4; [John 16:24; Eph. 6:18; Jude 20] [b] [Matt. 5:9, 16] [c] Mal. 1:11 6:10 [a] Matt. 26:42; Luke 22:42; Acts 21:14 [b] Ps. 103:20 6:11 [a] [Job 23:12]; Prov. 30:8; Is. 33:16; Luke 11:3 6:12 [a] [Matt. 18:21, 22] 6:13 [a] [Matt. 26:41; 1 Cor. 10:31; 2 Pet. 2:9; Rev. 3:10] [b] John 17:15; [2 Thess. 3:3]; 2 Tim. 4:18; [1 John 5:18]

For Yours is the kingdom and the
power and the glory forever.
Amen.[1]

14[a]"For if you forgive men their trespasses, your heavenly Father will also forgive you. 15But [a]if you do not forgive men
their trespasses, neither will your Father
forgive your trespasses.

Fasting to Be Seen Only by God

16"Moreover, [a]when you fast, do not be
like the hypocrites, with a sad countenance.
For they disfigure their faces that they may
appear to men to be fasting. Assuredly, I
say to you, they have their reward. 17But
you, when you fast, [a]anoint your head and
wash your face, 18so that you do not appear
to men to be fasting, but to your Father
who *is* in the secret *place;* and your Father
who sees in secret will reward you openly.[1]

Lay Up Treasures in Heaven
(Luke 12:33, 34)

19[a]"Do not lay up for yourselves treasures
on earth, where moth and rust destroy and
where thieves break in and steal; 20[a]but
lay up for yourselves treasures in heaven,
where neither moth nor rust destroys and
where thieves do not break in and steal.
21For where your treasure is, there your
heart will be also.

The Lamp of the Body
(Luke 11:34–36)

22[a]"The lamp of the body is the eye. If
therefore your eye is good, your whole body
will be full of light. 23But if your eye is bad,
your whole body will be full of darkness.
If therefore the light that is in you is darkness, how great *is* that darkness!

You Cannot Serve God and Riches

24[a]"No one can serve two masters; for either he will hate the one and love the other,
or else he will be loyal to the one and despise the other. [b]You cannot serve God and
mammon.

Do Not Worry
(Luke 12:22–31)

25"Therefore I say to you, [a]do not worry
about your life, what you will eat or what
you will drink; nor about your body, what
you will put on. Is not life more than food
and the body more than clothing? 26[a]Look
at the birds of the air, for they neither sow
nor reap nor gather into barns; yet your
heavenly Father feeds them. Are you not
of more value than they? 27Which of you by
worrying can add one cubit to his stature?

28"So why do you worry about clothing?
Consider the lilies of the field, how they
grow: they neither toil nor spin; 29and yet I
say to you that even Solomon in all his glory
was not arrayed like one of these. 30Now if
God so clothes the grass of the field, which
today is, and tomorrow is thrown into the
oven, *will He* not much more *clothe* you,
O you of little faith?

31"Therefore do not worry, saying, 'What
shall we eat?' or 'What shall we drink?' or
'What shall we wear?' 32For after all these
things the Gentiles seek. For your heavenly Father knows that you need all these
things. 33But [a]seek first the kingdom of God
and His righteousness, and all these things
shall be added to you. 34Therefore do not
worry about tomorrow, for tomorrow will
worry about its own things. Sufficient for
the day *is* its own trouble.

Do Not Judge
(Luke 6:37–42)

7 "Judge [a]not, that you be not judged. 2For
with what judgment you judge, you will
be judged; [a]and with the measure you use, it
will be measured back to you. 3[a]And why do
you look at the speck in your brother's eye,
but do not consider the plank in your own
eye? 4Or how can you say to your brother,
'Let me remove the speck from your eye';
and look, a plank *is* in your own eye? 5Hyp-
ocrite! First remove the plank from your
own eye, and then you will see clearly to
remove the speck from your brother's eye.

6[a]"Do not give what is holy to the dogs;

6:13 [1] NU-Text omits *For Yours* through *Amen.* 6:14 [a] [Matt. 7:2]; Mark 11:25; [Eph. 4:32; Col. 3:13] 6:15 [a] Matt. 18:35; James 2:13 6:16 [a] Is. 58:3–7; Luke 18:12 6:17 [a] Ruth 3:3; 2 Sam. 12:20; Dan. 10:3 6:18 [1] NU-Text and M-Text omit *openly.* 6:19 [a] Prov. 23:4; [1 Tim. 6:17; Heb. 13:5]; James 5:1 6:20 [a] Matt. 19:21; Luke 12:33; 18:22; 1 Tim. 6:19; 1 Pet. 1:4 6:22 [a] Luke 11:34, 35 6:24 [a] Luke 16:9, 11, 13 [b] [Gal. 1:10; 1 Tim. 6:17; James 4:4; 1 John 2:15] 6:25 [a] [Ps. 55:22]; Luke 12:22; [Phil. 4:6; 1 Pet. 5:7] 6:26 [a] Job 38:41; Ps. 147:9; Matt. 10:29; Luke 12:24 6:33 [a] 1 Kin. 3:13; Luke 12:31; [1 Tim. 4:8] 7:1 [a] Matt. 7:1–5; Luke 6:37; Rom. 14:3; [1 Cor. 4:3, 4] 7:2 [a] Mark 4:24; Luke 6:38 7:3 [a] Luke 6:41 7:6 [a] Prov. 9:7, 8; Acts 13:45

BELIEVE IN THE SON

INHALE

The Bible tells of Jesus answering many requests and meeting many needs. He healed the sick, turned water to wine, fed five thousand people with only two fish and five loaves of bread, and above all, raised the dead! Well, I need Him to act in my life now. My mortgage has increased, but my income has not. On top of that, my parents are aging, and they always seem to need financial assistance. Now, my spouse has a chronic illness. I have saved for my kids' college fund, but I have had to dip into that just to live from day to day. In just a couple of months, I'm going to be flat broke. Does God still act in our lives and meet our urgent needs? If He does, why hasn't He shown up for me?

EXHALE

God is a need-meeting God. Notice that I did not say that He *was* a need-meeting God! He is unchanging. So, the same God who provided lunch for over five thousand people can provide for your needs too. The challenge for us, though, is that while God can grant any and all requests, He is not obligated to. We see this in the life of Jesus, don't we? He healed and fed many people—but there were still others who were sick and hungry in His day. Sometimes He walked on water. At other times, He rode in a boat.

The problem we often face is thinking that we can figure out the mind of God. Or that we know what He should do. We can't and we don't. But one thing we see clearly in the Bible is God's love for people. All of Jesus' miraculous actions were done for two key reasons. First, they revealed that He is the Son of God. He did what normal people cannot do. Second, though, His actions revealed His deep love for people. He had love and compassion for the sick and hungry. And He has that same love and compassion for us.

God knows every detail of our problems. It can seem like He disregards our problems, but that is simply not true. This is a fallen world, and we will still have difficulties. But God cares about everyone, and God will answer in the way that is best for us. Matthew 7:7 says, "Ask, and it will be given to you; seek, and you will find; knock, and it will be opened to you." Jesus cares for you.

nor cast your pearls before swine, lest they trample them under their feet, and turn and tear you in pieces.

Keep Asking, Seeking, Knocking *(Luke 11:9–13)*

7[a]"Ask, and it will be given to you; seek, and you will find; knock, and it will be opened to you. 8For [a]everyone who asks receives, and he who seeks finds, and to him who knocks it will be opened. 9[a]Or what man is there among you who, if his son asks for bread, will give him a stone? 10Or if he asks for a fish, will he give him a serpent? 11If you then, [a]being evil, know how to give good gifts to your children, how much more will your Father who is in heaven give good things to those who ask Him! 12Therefore, [a]whatever you want men to do to you, do also to them, for [b]this is the Law and the Prophets.

The Narrow Way *(Luke 13:24)*

13[a]"Enter by the narrow gate; for wide *is* the gate and broad *is* the way that leads to destruction, and there are many who go in by it. 14Because[1] narrow *is* the gate and difficult *is* the way which leads to life, and there are few who find it.

7:7 [a] [Matt. 21:22; Mark 11:24]; Luke 11:9–13; 18:1–8; [John 15:7; James 1:5, 6; 1 John 3:22] 7:8 [a] Prov. 8:17; Jer. 29:12 7:9 [a] Luke 11:11 7:11 [a] Gen. 6:5; 8:21; Ps. 84:11; Is. 63:7; [Rom. 8:32; James 1:17]; 1 John 3:1 7:12 [a] Luke 6:31 [b] Matt. 22:40; Rom. 13:8; Gal. 5:14; [1 Tim. 1:5] 7:13 [a] Luke 13:24 7:14 [1] NU-Text and M-Text read *How . . . !*

You Will Know Them by Their Fruits
(Matt. 12:33; Luke 6:43–45)

15[a]"Beware of false prophets, [b]who come
to you in sheep's clothing, but inwardly
they are ravenous wolves. 16[a]You will know
them by their fruits. [b]Do men gather grapes
from thornbushes or figs from thistles?
17Even so, [a]every good tree bears good fruit,
but a bad tree bears bad fruit. 18A good tree
cannot bear bad fruit, nor *can* a bad tree
bear good fruit. 19[a]Every tree that does not
bear good fruit is cut down and thrown into
the fire. 20Therefore by their fruits you will
know them.

I Never Knew You
(Luke 6:46; 13:26, 27)

21"Not everyone who says to Me, [a]'Lord,
Lord,' shall enter the kingdom of heaven,
but he who [b]does the will of My Father in
heaven. 22Many will say to Me in that day,
'Lord, Lord, have we [a]not prophesied in
Your name, cast out demons in Your name,
and done many wonders in Your name?'
23And [a]then I will declare to them, 'I never
knew you; [b]depart from Me, you who practice lawlessness!'

Build on the Rock
(Luke 6:47–49)

24"Therefore [a]whoever hears these sayings of Mine, and does them, I will liken
him to a wise man who built his house on
the rock: 25and the rain descended, the
floods came, and the winds blew and beat
on that house; and it did not fall, for it was
founded on the rock.

26"But everyone who hears these sayings
of Mine, and does not do them, will be like
a foolish man who built his house on the
sand: 27and the rain descended, the floods
came, and the winds blew and beat on that
house; and it fell. And great was its fall."

28And so it was, when Jesus had ended
these sayings, that [a]the people were astonished at His teaching, 29[a]for He taught
them as one having authority, and not as
the scribes.

Jesus Cleanses a Leper
(Mark 1:40–45; Luke 5:12–16)

8 When He had come down from the
mountain, great multitudes followed
Him. 2[a]And behold, a leper came and [b]wor-
shiped Him, saying, "Lord, if You are willing, You can make me clean."

3Then Jesus put out *His* hand and
touched him, saying, "I am willing; be
cleansed." Immediately his leprosy [a]was
cleansed.

4And Jesus said to him, [a]"See that you
tell no one; but go your way, show yourself
to the priest, and offer the gift that [b]Mo-
ses [c]commanded, as a testimony to them."

Jesus Heals a Centurion's Servant
(Luke 7:1–10)

5[a]Now when Jesus had entered Capernaum, a [b]centurion came to Him, pleading with Him, 6saying, "Lord, my servant
is lying at home paralyzed, dreadfully tormented."

7And Jesus said to him, "I will come and
heal him."

8The centurion answered and said,
"Lord, [a]I am not worthy that You should
come under my roof. But only [b]speak a
word, and my servant will be healed. 9For
I also am a man under authority, having
soldiers under me. And I say to this *one,*
'Go,' and he goes; and to another, 'Come,'
and he comes; and to my servant, 'Do this,'
and he does *it.*"

10When Jesus heard *it,* He marveled,
and said to those who followed, "Assuredly, I say to you, I have not found such
great faith, not even in Israel! 11And I say
to you that [a]many will come from east and
west, and sit down with Abraham, Isaac,
and Jacob in the kingdom of heaven. 12But
[a]the sons of the kingdom [b]will be cast out
into outer darkness. There will be weeping

7:15 [a] Deut. 13:3; Jer. 23:16; Ezek. 22:28; Mark 13:22; [Luke 6:26]; Rom. 16:17; Eph. 5:6; [Col. 2:8; 2 Pet. 2:1; 1 John 4:1–3] [b] Mic. 3:5 7:16 [a] Matt. 7:20; 12:33; Luke 6:44; James 3:12 [b] Luke 6:43 7:17 [a] Jer. 11:19; Matt. 12:33 7:19 [a] Matt. 3:10; Luke 3:9; [John 15:2, 6] 7:21 [a] Hos. 8:2; Matt. 25:11; Luke 6:46; Acts 19:13 [b] Rom. 2:13; James 1:22 7:22 [a] Num. 24:4 7:23 [a] Matt. 25:12; Luke 13:25; [2 Tim. 2:19] [b] Ps. 5:5; 6:8; [Matt. 25:41]; Luke 13:27 7:24 [a] Matt. 7:24–27; Luke 6:47–49 7:28 [a] Matt. 13:54; Mark 1:22; 6:2; Luke 4:32; John 7:46 7:29 [a] [John 7:46] 8:2 [a] Matt. 8:2–4; Mark 1:40–45; Luke 5:12–14 [b] Matt. 2:11; 9:18; 15:25; John 9:38; Acts 10:25 8:3 [a] Matt. 11:5; Luke 4:27 8:4 [a] Matt. 9:30; Mark 5:43; Luke 4:41; 8:56; 9:21 [b] Lev. 14:3, 4, 10; Mark 1:44; Luke 5:14 [c] Lev. 14:4–32; Deut. 24:8 8:5 [a] Luke 7:1–3 [b] Matt. 27:54; Acts 10:1 8:8 [a] Luke 15:19, 21 [b] Ps. 107:20 8:11 [a] [Gen. 12:3; Is. 2:2, 3; 11:10]; Mal. 1:11; Luke 13:29; [Acts 10:45; 11:18; 14:27; Rom. 15:9–13; Eph. 3:6] 8:12 [a] [Matt. 21:43] [b] Matt. 13:42, 50; 22:13; 24:51; 25:30; Luke 13:28; 2 Pet. 2:17; Jude 13

and gnashing of teeth." 13Then Jesus said to the centurion, "Go your way; and as you have believed, *so* let it be done for you." And his servant was healed that same hour.

Peter's Mother-in-Law Healed
(Mark 1:29–31; Luke 4:38, 39)

14[a]Now when Jesus had come into Peter's house, He saw [b]his wife's mother lying sick with a fever. 15So He touched her hand, and the fever left her. And she arose and served them.[1]

Many Healed in the Evening
(Mark 1:32–34; Luke 4:40, 41)

16[a]When evening had come, they brought to Him many who were demon-possessed. And He cast out the spirits with a word, and healed all who were sick, 17that it might be fulfilled which was spoken by Isaiah the prophet, saying:

[a]"He Himself took our infirmities
And bore *our* sicknesses."[1]

The Cost of Discipleship
(Luke 9:57–62)

18And when Jesus saw great multitudes about Him, He gave a command to depart to the other side. 19[a]Then a certain scribe came and said to Him, "Teacher, I will follow You wherever You go."

20And Jesus said to him, "Foxes have holes and birds of the air *have* nests, but the Son of Man has nowhere to lay *His* head."

21[a]Then another of His disciples said to Him, "Lord, [b]let me first go and bury my father."

22But Jesus said to him, "Follow Me, and let the dead bury their own dead."

Wind and Wave Obey Jesus
(Mark 4:35–41; Luke 8:22–25)

23Now when He got into a boat, His disciples followed Him. 24[a]And suddenly a great tempest arose on the sea, so that the boat was covered with the waves. But He was asleep. 25Then His disciples came to *Him* and awoke Him, saying, "Lord, save us! We are perishing!"

26But He said to them, "Why are you fearful, O you of little faith?" Then [a]He arose and rebuked the winds and the sea, and there was a great calm. 27So the men marveled, saying, "Who can this be, that even the winds and the sea obey Him?"

Two Demon-Possessed Men Healed
(Mark 5:1–20; Luke 8:26–39)

28[a]When He had come to the other side, to the country of the Gergesenes,[1] there met Him two demon-possessed *men*, coming out of the tombs, exceedingly fierce, so that no one could pass that way. 29And suddenly they cried out, saying, "What have we to do with You, Jesus, You Son of God? Have You come here to torment us before the time?"

30Now a good way off from them there was a herd of many swine feeding. 31So the demons begged Him, saying, "If You cast us out, permit us to go away[1] into the herd of swine."

32And He said to them, "Go." So when they had come out, they went into the herd of swine. And suddenly the whole herd of swine ran violently down the steep place into the sea, and perished in the water.

33Then those who kept *them* fled; and they went away into the city and told everything, including what *had happened* to the demon-possessed *men*. 34And behold, the whole city came out to meet Jesus. And when they saw Him, [a]they begged *Him* to depart from their region.

Jesus Forgives and Heals a Paralytic
(Mark 2:1–12; Luke 5:17–26)

9 So He got into a boat, crossed over, [a]and came to His own city. 2[a]Then behold, they brought to Him a paralytic lying on a bed. [b]When Jesus saw their faith, He said to the paralytic, "Son, be of good cheer; your sins are forgiven you."

3And at once some of the scribes said within themselves, "This Man blasphemes!"

4But Jesus, [a]knowing their thoughts, said, "Why do you think evil in your hearts?

8:14 [a] Matt. 8:14–16; Mark 1:29–31; Luke 4:38, 39 [b] 1 Cor. 9:5 8:15 [1] NU-Text and M-Text read *Him*. 8:16 [a] Mark 1:32–34; Luke 4:40, 41 8:17 [a] Is. 53:4; 1 Pet. 2:24 [1] Isaiah 53:4 8:19 [a] Matt. 8:19–22; Luke 9:57, 58 8:21 [a] Luke 9:59, 60 [b] 1 Kin. 19:20 8:24 [a] Mark 4:37; Luke 8:23–25 8:26 [a] Ps. 65:7; 89:9; 107:29 8:28 [a] Mark 5:1–4; Luke 8:26–33 [1] NU-Text reads *Gadarenes*. 8:31 [1] NU-Text reads *send us*. 8:34 [a] Deut. 5:25; 1 Kin. 17:18; Amos 7:12; Luke 5:8; Acts 16:39 9:1 [a] Matt. 4:13; 11:23; Mark 5:21 9:2 [a] Mark 2:3–12; Luke 5:18–26 [b] Matt. 8:10 9:4 [a] Ps. 139:2; Matt. 12:25; Mark 12:15; Luke 5:22; 6:8; 9:47; 11:17

5 For which is easier, to say, '*Your* sins are
forgiven you,' or to say, 'Arise and walk'?
6 But that you may know that the Son of
Man has power on earth to forgive sins"—
then He said to the paralytic, "Arise, take
up your bed, and go to your house." 7 And
he arose and departed to his house.
8 Now when the multitudes saw *it,* they
[a]marveled[1] and glorified God, who had
given such power to men.

Matthew the Tax Collector
(Mark 2:13–17; Luke 5:27–32)

9 [a]As Jesus passed on from there, He saw
a man named Matthew sitting at the tax office.
And He said to him, "Follow Me." So
he arose and followed Him.
10 [a]Now it happened, as Jesus sat at the
table in the house, *that* behold, many tax
collectors and sinners came and sat down
with Him and His disciples. 11 And when the
Pharisees saw *it,* they said to His disciples,
"Why does your Teacher eat with [a]tax collectors
and [b]sinners?"
12 When Jesus heard *that,* He said to
them, "Those who are well have no need of
a physician, but those who are sick. 13 But go
and learn what *this* means: [a]'I desire mercy
and not sacrifice.'[1] For I did not come to call
the righteous, [b]but sinners, to repentance."[2]

Jesus Is Questioned About Fasting
(Mark 2:18–22; Luke 5:33–39)

14 Then the disciples of John came to
Him, saying, [a]"Why do we and the Pharisees
fast often,[1] but Your disciples do not fast?"
15 And Jesus said to them, "Can [a]the
friends of the bridegroom mourn as long
as the bridegroom is with them? But the
days will come when the bridegroom will
be taken away from them, and [b]then they
will fast. 16 No one puts a piece of unshrunk
cloth on an old garment; for the patch pulls
away from the garment, and the tear is
made worse. 17 Nor do they put new wine
into old wineskins, or else the wineskins
break, the wine is spilled, and the wineskins
are ruined. But they put new wine into new
wineskins, and both are preserved."

A Girl Restored to Life and a Woman Healed
(Mark 5:21–43; Luke 8:40–56)

18 [a]While He spoke these things to them,
behold, a ruler came and worshiped Him,
saying, "My daughter has just died, but
come and lay Your hand on her and she
will live." 19 So Jesus arose and followed him,
and so *did* His [a]disciples.
20 [a]And suddenly, a woman who had a
flow of blood for twelve years came from
behind and [b]touched the hem of His garment.
21 For she said to herself, "If only I may
touch His garment, I shall be made well."
22 But Jesus turned around, and when He
saw her He said, "Be of good cheer, daughter;
[a]your faith has made you well." And
the woman was made well from that hour.
23 [a]When Jesus came into the ruler's
house, and saw [b]the flute players and the
noisy crowd wailing, 24 He said to them,
[a]"Make room, for the girl is not dead, but
sleeping." And they ridiculed Him. 25 But
when the crowd was put outside, He went
in and [a]took her by the hand, and the girl
arose. 26 And the [a]report of this went out
into all that land.

Two Blind Men Healed

27 When Jesus departed from there, [a]two
blind men followed Him, crying out and
saying, [b]"Son of David, have mercy on us!"
28 And when He had come into the
house, the blind men came to Him. And
Jesus said to them, "Do you believe that I
am able to do this?"
They said to Him, "Yes, Lord."
29 Then He touched their eyes, saying,
"According to your faith let it be to you."
30 And their eyes were opened. And Jesus
sternly warned them, saying, [a]"See *that* no
one knows *it.*" 31 [a]But when they had departed,
they spread the news about Him
in all that country.

9:8 [a] Matt. 8:27; John 7:15 [1] NU-Text reads *were afraid.* 9:9 [a] Mark 2:14; Luke 5:27 9:10 [a] Mark 2:15; Luke 5:29 9:11 [a] Matt. 11:19; Mark 2:16; Luke 5:30; 15:2 [b] [Gal. 2:15] 9:13 [a] Hos. 6:6; [Mic. 6:6–8]; Matt. 12:7 [b] Mark 2:17; Luke 5:32; 1 Tim. 1:15 [1] Hosea 6:6 [2] NU-Text omits *to repentance.* 9:14 [a] Mark 2:18; Luke 5:33–35; 18:12 [1] NU-Text brackets *often* as disputed. 9:15 [a] John 3:29 [b] Acts 13:2, 3; 14:23 9:18 [a] Mark 5:22–43; Luke 8:41–56 9:19 [a] Matt. 10:2–4 9:20 [a] Mark 5:25; Luke 8:43 [b] Num. 15:38; Deut. 22:12; Matt. 14:36; 23:5; Mark 6:56 9:22 [a] Matt. 9:29; 15:28; Mark 5:34; 10:52; Luke 7:50; 8:48; 17:19; 18:42 9:23 [a] Mark 5:38; Luke 8:51 [b] 2 Chr. 35:25; Jer. 9:17; 16:6; Ezek. 24:17 9:24 [a] John 11:3; Acts 20:10 9:25 [a] Matt. 8:3, 15; Mark 1:31 9:26 [a] Matt. 4:24; Mark 1:28, 45; Luke 4:14, 37; 5:15; 7:17 9:27 [a] Matt. 20:29–34 [b] Matt. 15:22; Mark 10:47; Luke 18:38, 39 9:30 [a] Matt. 8:4; Luke 5:14 9:31 [a] Mark 7:36

A Mute Man Speaks

32[a]As they went out, behold, they
brought to Him a man, mute and demon-
possessed. 33And when the demon was cast
out, the mute spoke. And the multitudes
marveled, saying, "It was never seen like
this in Israel!"
34But the Pharisees said, [a]"He casts out
demons by the ruler of the demons."

The Compassion of Jesus
(Luke 10:2, 3)

35Then Jesus went about all the cities
and villages, [a]teaching in their synagogues,
preaching the gospel of the kingdom, and
healing every sickness and every disease
among the people.[1] 36[a]But when He saw the
multitudes, He was moved with compassion for them, because they were weary[1] and
scattered, [b]like sheep having no shepherd.
37Then He said to His disciples, [a]"The harvest truly *is* plentiful, but the laborers *are*
few. 38[a]Therefore pray the Lord of the harvest to send out laborers into His harvest."

The Twelve Apostles
(Mark 3:13–19; Luke 6:12–16)

10 And [a]when He had called His twelve
disciples to *Him,* He gave them power
over unclean spirits, to cast them out, and
to heal all kinds of sickness and all kinds of
disease. 2Now the names of the twelve apostles are these: first, Simon, [a]who is called Peter, and Andrew his brother; James the *son*
of Zebedee, and John his brother; 3Philip
and Bartholomew; Thomas and Matthew
the tax collector; James the *son* of Alphaeus,
and Lebbaeus, whose surname was[1] Thaddaeus; 4[a]Simon the Cananite,[1] and Judas
[b]Iscariot, who also betrayed Him.

Sending Out the Twelve
(Mark 6:7–13; Luke 9:1–6)

5These twelve Jesus sent out and commanded them, saying: [a]"Do not go into the
way of the Gentiles, and do not enter a city
of [b]the Samaritans. 6[a]But go rather to the
[b]lost sheep of the house of Israel. 7[a]And as
you go, preach, saying, [b]'The kingdom of
heaven is at hand.' 8Heal the sick, cleanse
the lepers, raise the dead,[1] cast out demons.
[a]Freely you have received, freely give. 9[a]Pro-
vide neither gold nor silver nor [b]copper in
your money belts, 10nor bag for *your* journey, nor two tunics, nor sandals, nor staffs;
[a]for a worker is worthy of his food.
11[a]"Now whatever city or town you enter,
inquire who in it is worthy, and stay there
till you go out. 12And when you go into a
household, greet it. 13[a]If the household is
worthy, let your peace come upon it. [b]But
if it is not worthy, let your peace return to
you. 14[a]And whoever will not receive you
nor hear your words, when you depart from
that house or city, [b]shake off the dust from
your feet. 15Assuredly, I say to you, [a]it will
be more tolerable for the land of Sodom
and Gomorrah in the day of judgment than
for that city!

Persecutions Are Coming
(Mark 13:9–13; Luke 21:12–17)

16[a]"Behold, I send you out as sheep in
the midst of wolves. [b]Therefore be wise
as serpents and [c]harmless as doves. 17But
beware of men, for [a]they will deliver you
up to councils and [b]scourge you in their
synagogues. 18[a]You will be brought before
governors and kings for My sake, as a testimony to them and to the Gentiles. 19[a]But
when they deliver you up, do not worry
about how or what you should speak. For
[b]it will be given to you in that hour what
you should speak; 20[a]for it is not you who
speak, but the Spirit of your Father who
speaks in you.
21[a]"Now brother will deliver up brother
to death, and a father *his* child; and children will rise up against parents and cause
them to be put to death. 22And [a]you will be

9:32 [a] Matt. 12:22, 24; Luke 11:14 9:34 [a] Matt. 12:24; Mark 3:22; Luke 11:15; John 7:20 9:35 [a] Matt. 4:23 [1] NU-Text omits *among the people.* 9:36 [a] Mark 6:34 [b] Num. 27:17; 1 Kin. 22:17; Ezek. 34:5; Zech. 10:2; Mark 6:34 [1] NU-Text and M-Text read *harassed.* 9:37 [a] Luke 10:2; John 4:35 9:38 [a] [Matt. 28:19, 20; Eph. 4:11, 12]; 2 Thess. 3:1 10:1 [a] Mark 3:13; Luke 6:13 10:2 [a] John 1:42 10:3 [1] NU-Text omits *Lebbaeus, whose surname was.* 10:4 [a] Luke 6:15; Acts 1:13 [b] Matt. 26:14; Luke 22:3; John 13:2, 26 [1] NU-Text reads *Cananaean.* 10:5 [a] Matt. 4:15 [b] 2 Kin. 17:24; Luke 9:52; 10:33; 17:16; John 4:9 10:6 [a] Matt. 15:24; Acts 13:46 [b] Is. 53:6; Jer. 50:6 10:7 [a] Luke 9:2 [b] Matt. 3:2; Luke 10:9 10:8 [a] [Acts 8:18] [1] NU-Text reads *raise the dead, cleanse the lepers;* M-Text omits *raise the dead.* 10:9 [a] 1 Sam. 9:7; Mark 6:8 [b] Mark 6:8 10:10 [a] Luke 10:7; [1 Cor. 9:4–14]; 1 Tim. 5:18 10:11 [a] Luke 10:8 10:13 [a] Luke 10:5 [b] Ps. 35:13 10:14 [a] Mark 6:11; Luke 9:5 [b] Neh. 5:13; Luke 10:10, 11; Acts 13:51 10:15 [a] Matt. 11:22, 24 10:16 [a] Luke 10:3 [b] 2 Cor. 12:16; Eph. 5:15; Col. 4:5 [c] [Phil. 2:14–16] 10:17 [a] Matt. 23:34; Mark 13:9; Luke 12:11 [b] Acts 5:40; 22:19; 26:11 10:18 [a] Acts 12:1; 2 Tim. 4:16 10:19 [a] Mark 13:11; Luke 12:11, 12; 21:14, 15 [b] Ex. 4:12; Jer. 1:7 10:20 [a] 2 Sam. 23:2; [2 Tim. 4:17] 10:21 [a] Mic. 7:6; Luke 21:16 10:22 [a] Matt. 24:9; Luke 21:17; John 15:18

hated by all for My name's sake. [b]But he who endures to the end will be saved. 23 [a]When they persecute you in this city, flee to another. For assuredly, I say to you, you will not have [b]gone through the cities of Israel [c]before the Son of Man comes.

24 [a]"A disciple is not above *his* teacher, nor a servant above his master. 25 It is enough for a disciple that he be like his teacher, and a servant like his master. If [a]they have called the master of the house Beelzebub,[1] how much more *will they call* those of his household! 26 Therefore do not fear them. [a]For there is nothing covered that will not be revealed, and hidden that will not be known.

Jesus Teaches the Fear of God
(Luke 12:3–7)

27 "Whatever I tell you in the dark, [a]speak in the light; and what you hear in the ear, preach on the housetops. 28 [a]And do not fear those who kill the body but cannot kill the soul. But rather [b]fear Him who is able to destroy both soul and body in hell. 29 Are not two [a]sparrows sold for a copper coin? And not one of them falls to the ground apart from your Father's will. 30 [a]But the very hairs of your head are all numbered. 31 Do not fear therefore; you are of more value than many sparrows.

Confess Christ Before Men
(Luke 12:8, 9)

32 [a]"Therefore whoever confesses Me before men, [b]him I will also confess before My Father who is in heaven. 33 [a]But whoever denies Me before men, him I will also deny before My Father who is in heaven.

Christ Brings Division
(Luke 12:51–53; 14:26, 27)

34 [a]"Do not think that I came to bring peace on earth. I did not come to bring peace but a sword. 35 For I have come to [a]'set a man against his father, a daughter against her mother, and a daughter-in-law against her mother-in-law'; 36 and [a]'a man's enemies *will be* those of his *own* household.'[1] 37 [a]He who loves father or mother more than Me is not worthy of Me. And he who loves son or daughter more than Me is not worthy of Me. 38 [a]And he who does not take his cross and follow after Me is not worthy of Me. 39 [a]He who finds his life will lose it, and he who loses his life for My sake will find it.

A Cup of Cold Water
(Mark 9:41)

40 [a]"He who receives you receives Me, and he who receives Me receives Him who sent Me. 41 [a]He who receives a prophet in the name of a prophet shall receive a prophet's reward. And he who receives a righteous man in the name of a righteous man shall receive a righteous man's reward. 42 [a]And whoever gives one of these little ones only a cup of cold *water* in the name of a disciple, assuredly, I say to you, he shall by no means lose his reward."

John the Baptist Sends Messengers to Jesus
(Luke 7:18–35)

11 Now it came to pass, when Jesus finished commanding His twelve disciples, that He departed from there to [a]teach and to preach in their cities.

2 [a]And when John had heard [b]in prison about the works of Christ, he sent two of[1] his disciples 3 and said to Him, "Are You [a]the Coming One, or do we look for another?"

4 Jesus answered and said to them, "Go and tell John the things which you hear and see: 5 [a]*The* blind see and *the* lame walk; *the* lepers are cleansed and *the* deaf hear; *the* dead are raised up and [b]*the* poor have the gospel preached to them. 6 And blessed is he who is not [a]offended because of Me."

7 [a]As they departed, Jesus began to say to the multitudes concerning John: "What did you go out into the wilderness to see? [b]A reed shaken by the wind? 8 But what did you

---

10:22 [b] [Dan. 12:12]; Matt. 24:13; Mark 13:13 10:23 [a] Matt. 2:13; Acts 8:1 [b] [Matt. 24:14; Mark 13:10] [c] Matt. 16:28 10:24 [a] Luke 6:40; John 15:20 10:25 [a] Mark 3:22; Luke 11:15, 18, 19; John 8:48, 52 [1] NU-Text and M-Text read *Beelzebul.* 10:26 [a] Mark 4:22; Luke 8:17; 12:2, 3; [1 Cor. 4:5] 10:27 [a] Luke 12:3; Acts 5:20 10:28 [a] Luke 12:4; [1 Pet. 3:14] [b] Is. 8:13; Matt. 5:22; Luke 12:5 10:29 [a] Luke 12:6, 7 10:30 [a] 1 Sam. 14:45; 2 Sam. 14:11; 1 Kin. 1:52; Luke 21:18; Acts 27:34 10:32 [a] Ps. 119:46; Luke 12:8; [Rom. 10:9] [b] [Rev. 3:5] 10:33 [a] [Mark 8:38; Luke 9:26]; 2 Tim. 2:12 10:34 [a] [Luke 12:49] 10:35 [a] Mic. 7:6; Matt. 10:21; Luke 12:53 10:36 [a] Ps. 41:9; 55:13; John 13:18 [1] Micah 7:6 10:37 [a] Deut. 33:9; Luke 14:26 10:38 [a] [Matt. 16:24; Mark 8:34; Luke 9:23; 14:27] 10:39 [a] Matt. 16:25; Mark 8:35; Luke 9:24; 17:33; John 12:25 10:40 [a] Mark 9:37; Luke 9:48; John 12:44; Gal. 4:14 10:41 [a] 1 Kin. 17:10; 2 Kin. 4:8 10:42 [a] [Matt. 25:40]; Mark 9:41; Heb. 6:10 11:1 [a] Matt. 9:35; Luke 23:5 11:2 [a] Luke 7:18–35 [b] Matt. 4:12; 14:3; Mark 6:17; Luke 9:7 [1] NU-Text reads *by* for *two of.* 11:3 [a] Gen. 49:10; Num. 24:17; Deut. 18:15, 18; Dan. 9:24; John 6:14 11:5 [a] Is. 29:18; 35:4–6; John 2:23 [b] Ps. 22:26; Is. 61:1; Luke 4:18; James 2:5 11:6 [a] Is. 8:14, 15; [Rom. 9:32]; 1 Pet. 2:8 11:7 [a] Luke 7:24 [b] [Eph. 4:14]

go out to see? A man clothed in soft garments? Indeed, those who wear soft *clothing* are in kings' houses. 9 But what did you
go out to see? A prophet? Yes, I say to you,
[a]and more than a prophet. 10 For this is *he*
of whom it is written:

> [a]'Behold, I send My messenger
> before Your face,
> Who will prepare Your
> way before You.'[1]

11 "Assuredly, I say to you, among those
born of women there has not risen one
greater than John the Baptist; but he who
is least in the kingdom of heaven is greater
than he. 12 [a]And from the days of John the
Baptist until now the kingdom of heaven
suffers violence, and the violent take it by
force. 13 [a]For all the prophets and the law
prophesied until John. 14 And if you are willing to receive *it,* he is [a]Elijah who is to come.
15 [a]He who has ears to hear, let him hear!
16 [a]"But to what shall I liken this generation? It is like children sitting in the marketplaces and calling to their companions,
17 and saying:

> 'We played the flute for you,
> And you did not dance;
> We mourned to you,
> And you did not lament.'

18 For John came neither eating nor drinking, and they say, 'He has a demon.' 19 The
Son of Man came eating and drinking, and
they say, 'Look, a glutton and a winebibber,
[a]a friend of tax collectors and sinners!' [b]But
wisdom is justified by her children."[1]

Woe to the Impenitent Cities
(Gen. 19:12–14; Luke 10:13–15)

20 [a]Then He began to rebuke the cities in
which most of His mighty works had been
done, because they did not repent: 21 "Woe
to you, Chorazin! Woe to you, Bethsaida!
For if the mighty works which were done in
you had been done in Tyre and Sidon, they
would have repented long ago [a]in sackcloth
and ashes. 22 But I say to you, [a]it will be more
tolerable for Tyre and Sidon in the day of
judgment than for you. 23 And you, Capernaum, [a]who are exalted to heaven, will be[1]
brought down to Hades; for if the mighty
works which were done in you had been
done in Sodom, it would have remained
until this day. 24 But I say to you [a]that it shall
be more tolerable for the land of Sodom in
the day of judgment than for you."

Jesus Gives True Rest
(Luke 10:21, 22)

25 [a]At that time Jesus answered and said,
"I thank You, Father, Lord of heaven and
earth, that [b]You have hidden these things
from *the* wise and prudent [c]and have revealed them to babes. 26 Even so, Father, for
so it seemed good in Your sight. 27 [a]All things
have been delivered to Me by My Father, and
no one knows the Son except the Father.
[b]Nor does anyone know the Father except
the Son, and *the one* to whom the Son wills to
reveal *Him.* 28 Come to [a]Me, all *you* who labor
and are heavy laden, and I will give you rest.
29 Take My yoke upon you [a]and learn from
Me, for I am gentle and [b]lowly in heart, [c]and
you will find rest for your souls. 30 [a]For My
yoke *is* easy and My burden is light."

#OXYGEN
MATTHEW 11:28
Believe in the Son

You may be tired. You may be worn out.
You need to rest. But resting is giving
your burden to Christ, not stopping.
Find relief, but keep pressing on.

Breathe and **believe
in the Son.**

11:9 [a] Matt. 14:5; 21:26; Luke 1:76; 20:6 11:10 [a] Mal. 3:1; Mark 1:2; Luke 1:76 [1] Malachi 3:1 11:12 [a] Luke 16:16 11:13 [a] Mal. 4:4–6 11:14 [a] Mal. 4:5; Matt. 17:10–13; Mark 9:11–13; Luke 1:17; John 1:21 11:15 [a] Matt. 13:9; Luke 8:8; Rev. 2:7, 11, 17, 29; 3:6, 13 11:16 [a] Luke 7:31 11:19 [a] Matt. 9:10 [b] Luke 7:35; John 2:1–11 [1] NU-Text reads *works.* 11:20 [a] Luke 10:13–15, 18 11:21 [a] Jon. 3:6–8 11:22 [a] Matt. 10:15; 11:24 11:23 [a] Is. 14:13; Lam. 2:1; Ezek. 26:20; 31:14; 32:18, 24 [1] NU-Text reads *will you be exalted to heaven? No, you will be.* 11:24 [a] Matt. 10:15 11:25 [a] Luke 10:21, 22 [b] Ps. 8:2; 1 Cor. 1:19; [2 Cor. 3:14] [c] Matt. 16:17 11:27 [a] Matt. 28:18; Luke 10:22; John 3:35; 13:3; 1 Cor. 15:27 [b] John 1:18; 6:46; 10:15 11:28 [a] [John 6:35–37] 11:29 [a] [John 13:15]; Eph. 4:2; [Phil. 2:5; 1 Pet. 2:21; 1 John 2:6] [b] Zech. 9:9; [Phil. 2:7, 8] [c] Jer. 6:16 11:30 [a] [1 John 5:3]

Jesus Is Lord of the Sabbath
(Mark 2:23–28; Luke 6:1–5)

12 At that time [a]Jesus went through the
grainfields on the Sabbath. And His
disciples were hungry, and began to [b]pluck
heads of grain and to eat. 2And when the
Pharisees saw *it,* they said to Him, "Look,
Your disciples are doing what is not lawful
to do on the Sabbath!"

3But He said to them, "Have you not
read [a]what David did when he was hungry, he and those who were with him: 4how
he entered the house of God and ate [a]the
showbread which was not lawful for him
to eat, nor for those who were with him,
[b]but only for the priests? 5Or have you not
read in the [a]law that on the Sabbath the
priests in the temple profane the Sabbath,
and are blameless? 6Yet I say to you that
in this place there is [a]*One* greater than the
temple. 7But if you had known what *this*
means, [a]'I desire mercy and not sacrifice,'[1]
you would not have condemned the guiltless. 8For the Son of Man is Lord even[1] of
the Sabbath."

Healing on the Sabbath
(Mark 3:1–6; Luke 6:6–11)

9[a]Now when He had departed from
there, He went into their synagogue. 10And
behold, there was a man who had a withered hand. And they asked Him, saying,
[a]"Is it lawful to heal on the Sabbath?"—that
they might accuse Him.

11Then He said to them, "What man is
there among you who has one sheep, and
if it falls into a pit on the Sabbath, will
not lay hold of it and lift *it* out? 12Of how
much more value then is a man than a
sheep? Therefore it is lawful to do good on
the Sabbath." 13Then He said to the man,
"Stretch out your hand." And he stretched
it out, and it was restored as whole as the
other. 14Then [a]the Pharisees went out and
plotted against Him, how they might destroy Him.

Behold, My Servant

15But when Jesus knew *it,* [a]He withdrew
from there. [b]And great multitudes[1] followed Him, and He healed them all. 16Yet
He [a]warned them not to make Him known,
17that it might be fulfilled which was spoken by Isaiah the prophet, saying:

18 "Behold![a] My Servant whom
I have chosen,
My Beloved [b]in whom My
soul is well pleased!
I will put My Spirit upon Him,
And He will declare justice
to the Gentiles.
19 He will not quarrel nor cry out,
Nor will anyone hear His
voice in the streets.
20 A bruised reed He will not break,
And smoking flax He will not quench,
Till He sends forth justice
to victory;
21 And in His name Gentiles will
trust."[1]

A House Divided Cannot Stand
(Mark 3:22–27; Luke 11:14–23)

22[a]Then one was brought to Him who
was demon-possessed, blind and mute;
and He healed him, so that the blind and[1]
mute man both spoke and saw. 23And all the
multitudes were amazed and said, "Could
this be the [a]Son of David?"

24[a]Now when the Pharisees heard *it*
they said, "This *fellow* does not cast out
demons except by Beelzebub,[1] the ruler of
the demons."

25But Jesus [a]knew their thoughts, and
said to them: "Every kingdom divided
against itself is brought to desolation, and
every city or house divided against itself
will not stand. 26If Satan casts out Satan,
he is divided against himself. How then
will his kingdom stand? 27And if I cast out
demons by Beelzebub, by whom do your
sons cast *them* out? Therefore they shall

12:1 [a] Mark 2:23; Luke 6:1–5 [b] Deut. 23:25 12:3 [a] Ex. 31:15; 35:2; 1 Sam. 21:6 12:4 [a] Ex. 25:30; Lev. 24:5 [b] Ex. 29:32; Lev. 8:31; 24:9 12:5 [a] Num. 28:9; [John 7:22] 12:6 [a] [2 Chr. 6:18; Is. 66:1, 2; Mal. 3:1]; Matt. 12:41, 42 12:7 [a] [1 Sam. 15:22; Hos. 6:6; Mic. 6:6–8]; Matt. 9:13 [1] Hosea 6:6 12:8 [1] NU-Text and M-Text omit *even.* 12:9 [a] Mark 3:1–6; Luke 6:6–11 12:10 [a] Luke 13:14; 14:3; John 9:16 12:14 [a] Ps. 2:2; Matt. 27:1; Mark 3:6; [Luke 6:11]; John 5:18; 10:39; 11:53 12:15 [a] Matt. 10:23; Mark 3:7 [b] Matt. 19:2 [1] NU-Text brackets *multitudes* as disputed. 12:16 [a] Matt. 8:4; 9:30; 17:9 12:18 [a] Is. 42:1–4; 49:3 [b] Matt. 3:17; 17:5 12:21 [1] Isaiah 42:1–4 12:22 [a] Matt. 9:32; [Mark 3:11]; Luke 11:14, 15 [1] NU-Text omits *blind and.* 12:23 [a] Matt. 9:27; 21:9 12:24 [a] Matt. 9:34; Mark 3:22; Luke 11:15 [1] NU-Text and M-Text read *Beelzebul.* 12:25 [a] Matt. 9:4; John 2:25; Rev. 2:23

be your judges. 28But if I cast out demons
by the Spirit of God, [a]surely the kingdom
of God has come upon you. 29[a]Or how can
one enter a strong man's house and plunder
his goods, unless he first binds the strong
man? And then he will plunder his house.
30He who is not with Me is against Me, and
he who does not gather with Me scatters
abroad.

The Unpardonable Sin
(Mark 3:28–30)

31"Therefore I say to you, [a]every sin and
blasphemy will be forgiven men, [b]but the
blasphemy *against* the Spirit will not be forgiven men.
32Anyone who [a]speaks a word
against the Son of Man, [b]it will be forgiven
him; but whoever speaks against the Holy
Spirit, it will not be forgiven him, either in
this age or in the *age* to come.

A Tree Known by Its Fruit
(Matt. 7:15–20)

33"Either make the tree good and [a]its
fruit good, or else make the tree bad and
its fruit bad; for a tree is known by *its* fruit.
34[a]Brood of vipers! How can you, being evil,
speak good things? [b]For out of the abundance of the heart the mouth speaks.
35A
good man out of the good treasure of his
heart[1] brings forth good things, and an evil
man out of the evil treasure brings forth
evil things. 36But I say to you that for every
idle word men may speak, they will give
account of it in the day of judgment. 37For
by your words you will be justified, and by
your words you will be condemned."

The Scribes and Pharisees Ask for a Sign
(Luke 11:29–32)

38[a]Then some of the scribes and Pharisees answered, saying, "Teacher, we want
to see a sign from You."

39But He answered and said to them,
"An evil and [a]adulterous generation seeks
after a sign, and no sign will be given to
it except the sign of the prophet Jonah.
40[a]For as Jonah was three days and three
nights in the belly of the great fish, so will
the Son of Man be three days and three
nights in the heart of the earth. 41[a]The men
of Nineveh will rise up in the judgment
with this generation and [b]condemn it, [c]because they repented at the preaching of
Jonah; and indeed a greater than Jonah
is here. 42[a]The queen of the South will rise
up in the judgment with this generation
and condemn it, for she came from the
ends of the earth to hear the wisdom of
Solomon; and indeed a greater than Solomon *is* here.

An Unclean Spirit Returns
(Luke 11:24–26)

43[a]"When an unclean spirit goes out of
a man, [b]he goes through dry places, seeking rest, and finds none.
44Then he says,
'I will return to my house from which
I came.' And when he comes, he finds *it*
empty, swept, and put in order. 45Then he
goes and takes with him seven other spirits
more wicked than himself, and they enter
and dwell there; [a]and the last *state* of that
man is worse than the first. So shall it also
be with this wicked generation."

Jesus' Mother and Brothers Send for Him
(Mark 3:31–35; Luke 8:19–21)

46While He was still talking to the multitudes, [a]behold, His mother and [b]brothers
stood outside, seeking to speak with Him.
47Then one said to Him, "Look, [a]Your
mother and Your brothers are standing
outside, seeking to speak with You."

48But He answered and said to the one
who told Him, "Who is My mother and who
are My brothers?" 49And He stretched out
His hand toward His disciples and said,
"Here are My mother and My [a]brothers!
50For [a]whoever does the will of My Father
in heaven is My brother and sister and
mother."

12:28 [a] [Dan. 2:44; 7:14; Luke 1:33]; 11:20; [17:20, 21; 1 John 3:8] **12:29** [a] Is. 49:24; [Luke 11:21–23] **12:31** [a] Mark 3:28–30; Luke 12:10; [Heb. 6:4–6; 10:26, 29; 1 John 5:16] [b] Acts 7:51 **12:32** [a] Matt. 11:19; 13:55; John 7:12, 52 [b] 1 Tim. 1:13 **12:33** [a] Matt. 7:16–18; Luke 6:43, 44; [John 15:4–7] **12:34** [a] Matt. 3:7; 23:33; Luke 3:7 [b] 1 Sam. 24:13; Is. 32:6; [Matt. 15:18]; Luke 6:45; Eph. 4:29; [James 3:2–12] **12:35** [1] NU-Text and M-Text omit *of his heart.* **12:38** [a] Matt. 16:1; Mark 8:11; Luke 11:16; John 2:18; 1 Cor. 1:22 **12:39** [a] Is. 57:3; Matt. 16:4; Mark 8:38; [Luke 11:29–32]; John 4:48 **12:40** [a] Jon. 1:17; Luke 24:46; Acts 10:40; 1 Cor. 15:4 **12:41** [a] Jon. 3:5; Luke 11:32 [b] Jer. 3:11; Ezek. 16:51; [Rom. 2:27] [c] Jon. 3:5 **12:42** [a] 1 Kin. 10:1–13; 2 Chr. 9:1; Luke 11:31 **12:43** [a] Luke 11:24–26 [b] [Job 1:7; 1 Pet. 5:8] **12:45** [a] Mark 5:9; Luke 11:26; [Heb. 6:4–8; 10:26; 2 Pet. 2:20–22] **12:46** [a] Mark 3:31–35; Luke 8:19–21 [b] Matt. 13:55; Mark 6:3; John 2:12; 7:3, 5; Acts 1:14; 1 Cor. 9:5; Gal. 1:19 **12:47** [a] Matt. 13:55, 56; John 2:12; Acts 1:14 **12:49** [a] John 20:17; [Rom. 8:29] **12:50** [a] John 15:14; [Gal. 5:6; 6:15; Col. 3:11; Heb. 2:11]

The Parable of the Sower
(Mark 4:1–9; Luke 8:4–8)

13 On the same day Jesus went out of
the house [a]and sat by the sea. 2 [a]And
great multitudes were gathered together to
Him, so that [b]He got into a boat and sat; and
the whole multitude stood on the shore.
3 Then He spoke many things to them in
parables, saying: [a]"Behold, a sower went out
to sow. 4 And as he sowed, some *seed* fell by
the wayside; and the birds came and devoured them. 5 Some fell on stony places,
where they did not have much earth; and
they immediately sprang up because they
had no depth of earth. 6 But when the sun
was up they were scorched, and because
they had no root they withered away. 7 And
some fell among thorns, and the thorns
sprang up and choked them. 8 But others fell
on good ground and yielded a crop: some [a]a
hundredfold, some sixty, some thirty. 9 [a]He
who has ears to hear, let him hear!"

The Purpose of Parables
(Mark 4:10–12; Luke 8:9, 10)

10 And the disciples came and said to
Him, "Why do You speak to them in parables?"
11 He answered and said to them, "Because [a]it has been given to you to know the
mysteries of the kingdom of heaven, but
to them it has not been given. 12 [a]For whoever has, to him more will be given, and he
will have abundance; but whoever does not
have, even what he has will be taken away
from him. 13 Therefore I speak to them in
parables, because seeing they do not see,
and hearing they do not hear, nor do they
understand. 14 And in them the prophecy
of Isaiah is fulfilled, which says:

[a]'Hearing you will hear and
shall not understand,
And seeing you will see
and not [b]perceive;
15 For the hearts of this people
have grown dull.
Their ears [a]are hard of hearing,
And their eyes they have [b]closed,
Lest they should see with *their*
eyes and hear with *their* ears,
Lest they should understand
with *their* hearts and turn,
So that I should[1] [c]heal them.'[2]

16 But [a]blessed *are* your eyes for they see,
and your ears for they hear; 17 for assuredly,
I say to you [a]that many prophets and righteous *men* desired to see what you see, and
did not see *it,* and to hear what you hear,
and did not hear *it.*

The Parable of the Sower Explained
(Mark 4:13–20; Luke 8:11–15)

18 [a]"Therefore hear the parable of the
sower: 19 When anyone hears the word [a]of
the kingdom, and does not understand *it,*
then the wicked *one* comes and snatches
away what was sown in his heart. This is he
who received seed by the wayside. 20 But he
who received the seed on stony places, this
is he who hears the word and immediately
[a]receives it with joy; 21 yet he has no root in
himself, but endures only for a while. For
when [a]tribulation or persecution arises because of the word, immediately [b]he stumbles. 22 Now [a]he who received seed [b]among
the thorns is he who hears the word, and
the cares of this world and the deceitfulness of riches choke the word, and he becomes unfruitful. 23 But he who received
seed on the good ground is he who hears
the word and understands *it,* who indeed
bears [a]fruit and produces: some a hundredfold, some sixty, some thirty."

The Parable of the Wheat and the Tares

24 Another parable He put forth to them,
saying: "The kingdom of heaven is like a
man who sowed good seed in his field; 25 but
while men slept, his enemy came and sowed
tares among the wheat and went his way.
26 But when the grain had sprouted and produced a crop, then the tares also appeared.

13:1 [a] Matt. 13:1–15; Mark 4:1–12; Luke 8:4–10 13:2 [a] Luke 8:4 [b] Luke 5:3 13:3 [a] Luke 8:5 13:8 [a] Gen. 26:12; Matt. 13:23 13:9 [a] Matt. 11:15; Mark 4:9; Rev. 2:7, 11, 17, 29; 3:6, 13, 22 13:11 [a] [Matt. 11:25; 16:17]; Mark 4:10, 11; [John 6:65; 1 Cor. 2:10; Col. 1:27; 1 John 2:20, 27] 13:12 [a] Matt. 25:29; Mark 4:25; Luke 8:18; 19:26 13:14 [a] Is. 6:9, 10; Ezek. 12:2; Mark 4:12; Luke 8:10; John 12:40; Acts 28:26, 27; Rom. 11:8; [2 Cor. 3:14, 15] [b] [John 3:36] 13:15 [a] Ps. 119:70; Zech. 7:11; 2 Tim. 4:4; Heb. 5:11 [b] Luke 19:42 [c] Acts 28:26, 27 [1] NU-Text and M-Text read *would.* [2] Isaiah 6:9, 10 13:16 [a] [Prov. 20:12; Matt. 16:17]; Luke 10:23, 24; [John 20:29] 13:17 [a] John 8:56; Heb. 11:13; 1 Pet. 1:10, 11 13:18 [a] Mark 4:13–20; Luke 8:11–15 13:19 [a] Matt. 4:23 13:20 [a] Is. 58:2; Ezek. 33:31, 32; John 5:35 13:21 [a] [Acts 14:22] [b] Matt. 11:6; 2 Tim. 1:15 13:22 [a] Matt. 19:23; Mark 10:23; Luke 18:24; 1 Tim. 6:9; 2 Tim. 4:10 [b] Jer. 4:3 13:23 [a] [John 15:5]; Phil. 1:11; Col. 1:6

27So the servants of the owner came and
said to him, 'Sir, did you not sow good seed
in your field? How then does it have tares?'
28He said to them, 'An enemy has done this.'
The servants said to him, 'Do you want us
then to go and gather them up?' 29But he
said, 'No, lest while you gather up the tares
you also uproot the wheat with them. 30Let
both grow together until the harvest, and at
the time of harvest I will say to the reapers,
"First gather together the tares and bind
them in bundles to burn them, but [a]gather
the wheat into my barn."'"

The Parable of the Mustard Seed
(Mark 4:30–32; Luke 13:18, 19)

31Another parable He put forth to them,
saying: [a]"The kingdom of heaven is like a
mustard seed, which a man took and sowed
in his field, 32which indeed is the least of all
the seeds; but when it is grown it is greater
than the herbs and becomes a [a]tree, so that
the birds of the air come and nest in its
branches."

The Parable of the Leaven
(Luke 13:20, 21)

33[a]Another parable He spoke to them:
"The kingdom of heaven is like leaven,
which a woman took and hid in three measures[1] of meal till [b]it was all leavened."

Prophecy and the Parables

34[a]All these things Jesus spoke to the
multitude in parables; and without a parable He did not speak to them, 35that it
might be fulfilled which was spoken by the
prophet, saying:

[a]"I will open My mouth in parables;
[b]I will utter things kept secret from
the foundation of the world."[1]

The Parable of the Tares Explained

36Then Jesus sent the multitude away
and went into the house. And His disciples
came to Him, saying, "Explain to us the
parable of the tares of the field."

37He answered and said to them: "He
who sows the good seed is the Son of Man.
38[a]The field is the world, the good seeds
are the sons of the kingdom, but the tares
are [b]the sons of the wicked *one.* 39The enemy who sowed them is the devil, [a]the harvest is the end of the age, and the reapers
are the angels. 40Therefore as the tares are
gathered and burned in the fire, so it will
be at the end of this age. 41The Son of Man
will send out His angels, [a]and they will
gather out of His kingdom all things that
offend, and those who practice lawlessness,
42[a]and will cast them into the furnace of
fire. [b]There will be wailing and gnashing
of teeth. 43[a]Then the righteous will shine
forth as the sun in the kingdom of their Father. [b]He who has ears to hear, let him hear!

The Parable of the Hidden Treasure

44"Again, the kingdom of heaven is like
treasure hidden in a field, which a man
found and hid; and for joy over it he goes
and [a]sells all that he has and [b]buys that
field.

The Parable of the Pearl of Great Price

45"Again, the kingdom of heaven is
like a merchant seeking beautiful pearls,
46who, when he had found [a]one pearl of
great price, went and sold all that he had
and bought it.

The Parable of the Dragnet

47"Again, the kingdom of heaven is like
a dragnet that was cast into the sea and
[a]gathered some of every kind, 48which,
when it was full, they drew to shore; and
they sat down and gathered the good into
vessels, but threw the bad away. 49So it will
be at the end of the age. The angels will
come forth, [a]separate the wicked from
among the just, 50and cast them into the
furnace of fire. There will be wailing and
gnashing of teeth."

51Jesus said to them,[1] "Have you understood all these things?"
They said to Him, "Yes, Lord."[2]

13:30 [a] Matt. 3:12 13:31 [a] [Is. 2:2, 3; Mic. 4:1]; Mark 4:30; Luke 13:18, 19 13:32 [a] Ps. 104:12; Ezek. 17:22–24; 31:3–9; Dan. 4:12 13:33 [a] Luke 13:20, 21 [b] [1 Cor. 5:6; Gal. 5:9] [1] Greek *sata,* approximately two pecks in all 13:34 [a] Mark 4:33, 34; John 10:6; 16:25 13:35 [a] Ps. 78:2 [b] Rom. 16:25, 26; 1 Cor. 2:7; Eph. 3:9; Col. 1:26 [1] Psalm 78:2 13:38 [a] Matt. 24:14; 28:19; Mark 16:15; Luke 24:47; Rom. 10:18; Col. 1:6 [b] Gen. 3:15; John 8:44; Acts 13:10 13:39 [a] Joel 3:13; Rev. 14:15 13:41 [a] Matt. 18:7; 2 Pet. 2:1, 2 13:42 [a] Matt. 3:12; Rev. 19:20; 20:10 [b] Matt. 8:12; 13:50 13:43 [a] [Dan. 12:3; 1 Cor. 15:42, 43, 58] [b] Matt. 13:9 13:44 [a] Phil. 3:7, 8 [b] [Is. 55:1; Rev. 3:18] 13:46 [a] Prov. 2:4; 3:14, 15; 8:10, 19 13:47 [a] Matt. 22:9, 10 13:49 [a] Matt. 25:32
13:51 [1] NU-Text omits *Jesus said to them.* [2] NU-Text omits *Lord.*

52Then He said to them, "Therefore every scribe instructed concerning[1] the kingdom of heaven is like a householder who
brings out of his treasure [a]*things* new and
old."

Jesus Rejected at Nazareth
(Mark 6:1–6; Luke 4:16–30)

53Now it came to pass, when Jesus had
finished these parables, that He departed
from there. 54[a]When He had come to His
own country, He taught them in their synagogue, so that they were astonished and
said, "Where did this *Man* get this wisdom
and *these* mighty works? 55[a]Is this not the
carpenter's son? Is not His mother called
Mary? And [b]His brothers [c]James, Joses,[1]
Simon, and Judas? 56And His sisters, are
they not all with us? Where then did this
Man get all these things?" 57So they [a]were
offended at Him.

But Jesus said to them, [b]"A prophet is
not without honor except in his own country and in his own house." 58Now [a]He did
not do many mighty works there because
of their unbelief.

John the Baptist Beheaded
(Mark 6:14–29; Luke 9:7–9)

14 At that time [a]Herod the tetrarch
heard the report about Jesus 2and
said to his servants, "This is John the Baptist; he is risen from the dead, and therefore these powers are at work in him." 3[a]For
Herod had laid hold of John and bound
him, and put *him* in prison for the sake
of Herodias, his brother Philip's wife. 4Be-
cause John had said to him, [a]"It is not lawful for you to have her." 5And although he
wanted to put him to death, he feared the
multitude, [a]because they counted him as
a prophet.

6But when Herod's birthday was celebrated, the daughter of Herodias danced
before them and pleased Herod. 7There-
fore he promised with an oath to give her
whatever she might ask.

8So she, having been prompted by her
mother, said, "Give me John the Baptist's
head here on a platter."

9And the king was sorry; nevertheless,
because of the oaths and because of those
who sat with him, he commanded *it* to be
given to *her.* 10So he sent and had John
beheaded in prison. 11And his head was
brought on a platter and given to the girl,
and she brought *it* to her mother. 12Then his
disciples came and took away the body and
buried it, and went and told Jesus.

Feeding the Five Thousand
(Mark 6:30–44; Luke 9:10–17; John 6:1–14)

13[a]When Jesus heard *it,* He departed
from there by boat to a deserted place by
Himself. But when the multitudes heard it,
they followed Him on foot from the cities.
14And when Jesus went out He saw a great
multitude; and He [a]was moved with compassion for them, and healed their sick.
15[a]When it was evening, His disciples came
to Him, saying, "This is a deserted place,
and the hour is already late. Send the multitudes away, that they may go into the villages and buy themselves food."

16But Jesus said to them, "They do not
need to go away. You give them something
to eat."

17And they said to Him, "We have here
only five loaves and two fish."

18He said, "Bring them here to Me."
19Then He commanded the multitudes to
sit down on the grass. And He took the
five loaves and the two fish, and looking
up to heaven, [a]He blessed and broke and
gave the loaves to the disciples; and the
disciples gave to the multitudes. 20So they
all ate and were filled, and they took up
twelve baskets full of the fragments that
remained. 21Now those who had eaten were
about five thousand men, besides women
and children.

Jesus Walks on the Sea
(Mark 6:45–52; John 6:15–21)

22Immediately Jesus made His disciples get into the boat and go before Him

---

13:52 [a] Song 7:13 [1] Or *for* 13:54 [a] Ps. 22:22; Matt. 2:23; Mark 6:1; Luke 4:16; John 7:15 13:55 [a] Is. 49:7; Mark 6:3; [Luke 3:23]; John 6:42 [b] Matt. 12:46 [c] Mark 15:40 [1] NU-Text reads *Joseph.* 13:57 [a] Matt. 11:6; Mark 6:3, 4 [b] Luke 4:24; John 4:44 13:58 [a] Mark 6:5, 6; John 5:44, 46, 47 14:1 [a] Mark 6:14–29; Luke 9:7–9 14:3 [a] Matt. 4:12; Mark 6:17; Luke 3:19, 20 14:4 [a] Lev. 18:16; 20:21 14:5 [a] Matt. 21:26; Luke 20:6 14:13 [a] Matt. 10:23; 12:15; Mark 6:32–44; Luke 9:10–17; John 6:1, 2 14:14 [a] Matt. 9:36; Mark 6:34 14:15 [a] Mark 6:35; Luke 9:12 14:19 [a] 1 Sam. 9:13; Matt. 15:36; 26:26; Mark 6:41; 8:7; 14:22; Luke 24:30; Acts 27:35; [Rom. 14:6]

to the other side, while He sent the multitudes away. 23[a]And when He had sent
the multitudes away, He went up on the
mountain by Himself to pray. [b]Now when
evening came, He was alone there. 24But
the boat was now in the middle of the sea,[1]
tossed by the waves, for the wind was contrary.
25Now in the fourth watch of the night
Jesus went to them, walking on the sea.
26And when the disciples saw Him [a]walk-
ing on the sea, they were troubled, saying,
"It is a ghost!" And they cried out for fear.
27But immediately Jesus spoke to them,
saying, "Be of good [a]cheer! It is I; do not
be afraid."
28And Peter answered Him and said,
"Lord, if it is You, command me to come
to You on the water."
29So He said, "Come." And when Peter
had come down out of the boat, he walked
on the water to go to Jesus. 30But when he
saw that the wind *was* boisterous,[1] he was
afraid; and beginning to sink he cried out,
saying, "Lord, save me!"
31And immediately Jesus stretched out
His hand and caught him, and said to him,
"O you of [a]little faith, why did you doubt?"
32And when they got into the boat, the wind
ceased.
33Then those who were in the boat came
and[1] worshiped Him, saying, "Truly [a]You
are the Son of God."

Many Touch Him and Are Made Well
(Mark 6:53–56)

34[a]When they had crossed over, they
came to the land of[1] Gennesaret. 35And
when the men of that place recognized
Him, they sent out into all that surrounding region, brought to Him all who were
sick, 36and begged Him that they might
only [a]touch the hem of His garment. And
[b]as many as touched *it* were made perfectly
well.

Defilement Comes from Within
(Mark 7:1–23)

15 Then [a]the scribes and Pharisees who
were from Jerusalem came to Jesus,
saying, 2[a]"Why do Your disciples transgress
the tradition of the elders? For they do not
wash their hands when they eat bread."
3He answered and said to them, "Why
do you also transgress the commandment
of God because of your tradition? 4For God
commanded, saying, [a]'Honor your father
and your mother';[1] and, [b]'He who curses
father or mother, let him be put to death.'[2]
5But you say, 'Whoever says to his father or
mother, [a]"Whatever profit you might have
received from me *is* a gift *to God*"— 6then he
need not honor his father or mother.'[1] Thus
you have made the commandment[2] of God
of no effect by your tradition. 7[a]Hypocrites!
Well did Isaiah prophesy about you, saying:

8 'These[a] people draw near to
Me with their mouth,
And[1] honor Me with *their* lips,
But their heart is far from Me.
9 And in vain they worship Me,
[a]Teaching *as* doctrines the
commandments of men.'"[1]

10[a]When He had called the multitude to
Himself, He said to them, "Hear and understand: 11[a]Not what goes into the mouth defiles a man; but what comes out of the
mouth, this defiles a man."
12Then His disciples came and said to
Him, "Do You know that the Pharisees were
offended when they heard this saying?"
13But He answered and said, [a]"Every
plant which My heavenly Father has not
planted will be uprooted. 14Let them alone.
[a]They are blind leaders of the blind. And
if the blind leads the blind, both will fall
into a ditch."
15[a]Then Peter answered and said to Him,
"Explain this parable to us."

14:23 [a] Mark 6:46; Luke 9:28; John 6:15 [b] John 6:16 14:24 [1] NU-Text reads *many furlongs away from the land.* 14:26 [a] Job 9:8 14:27 [a] Acts 23:11; 27:22, 25, 36 14:30 [1] NU-Text brackets *that* and *boisterous* as disputed. 14:31 [a] Matt. 6:30; 8:26 14:33 [a] Ps. 2:7; Matt. 16:16; 26:63; Mark 1:1; Luke 4:41; John 1:49; 6:69; 11:27; Acts 8:37; Rom. 1:4 [1] NU-Text omits *came and.* 14:34 [a] Mark 6:53; Luke 5:1 [1] NU-Text reads *came to land at.* 14:36 [a] [Mark 5:24–34] [b] Matt. 9:20; Mark 3:10; [Luke 6:19]; Acts 19:12 15:1 [a] Mark 7:1; John 1:19; Acts 25:7 15:2 [a] Mark 7:5 15:4 [a] Ex. 20:1, 12; Lev. 19:3; [Deut. 5:16]; Prov. 23:22; [Eph. 6:2, 3] [b] Ex. 21:17; Lev. 20:9; Deut. 27:16; Prov. 20:20; 30:17 [1] Exodus 20:12; Deuteronomy 5:16 [2] Exodus 21:17 15:5 [a] Mark 7:11, 12 15:6 [1] NU-Text omits *or mother.* [2] NU-Text reads *word.* 15:7 [a] Mark 7:6 15:8 [a] Ps. 78:36; Is. 29:13; Ezek. 33:31 [1] NU-Text omits *draw near to Me with their mouth, And.* 15:9 [a] Is. 29:13; [Col. 2:18–22]; Titus 1:14 [1] Isaiah 29:13 15:10 [a] Mark 7:14 15:11 [a] [Acts 10:15; Rom. 14:14, 17, 20; 1 Tim. 4:4; Titus 1:15] 15:13 [a] [Is. 60:21; 61:3; John 15:2; 1 Cor. 3:12, 13] 15:14 [a] Is. 9:16; Mal. 2:8; Matt. 23:16, 24; Luke 6:39; Rom. 2:19 15:15 [a] Mark 7:17

16 So Jesus said, [a]"Are you also still without understanding? 17 Do you not yet understand that [a]whatever enters the mouth goes
into the stomach and is eliminated? 18 But
[a]those things which proceed out of the
mouth come from the heart, and they defile a man. 19 [a]For out of the heart proceed
evil thoughts, murders, adulteries, forni-
cations, thefts, false witness, blasphemies.
20 These are *the things* which defile a man,
but to eat with unwashed hands does not
defile a man."

A Gentile Shows Her Faith
(Mark 7:24–30)

21 [a]Then Jesus went out from there and
departed to the region of Tyre and Sidon.
22 And behold, a woman of Canaan came
from that region and cried out to Him,
saying, "Have mercy on me, O Lord, [a]Son
of David! My daughter is severely demon-
possessed."

23 But He answered her not a word.

And His disciples came and urged Him,
saying, "Send her away, for she cries out
after us."

24 But He answered and said, [a]"I was not
sent except to the lost sheep of the house
of Israel."

25 Then she came and worshiped Him,
saying, "Lord, help me!"

26 But He answered and said, "It is not
good to take the children's bread and throw
it to the little [a]dogs."

27 And she said, "Yes, Lord, yet even the
little dogs eat the crumbs which fall from
their masters' table."

28 Then Jesus answered and said to her,
"O woman, [a]great *is* your faith! Let it be to
you as you desire." And her daughter was
healed from that very hour.

Jesus Heals Great Multitudes
(Mark 7:31–37)

29 [a]Jesus departed from there, [b]skirted
the Sea of Galilee, and went up on the
mountain and sat down there. 30 [a]Then
great multitudes came to Him, having with
them *the* lame, blind, mute, maimed, and
many others; and they laid them down at
Jesus' [b]feet, and He healed them. 31 So the
multitude marveled when they saw *the*
mute speaking, *the* maimed made whole,
the lame walking, and *the* blind seeing; and
they [a]glorified the God of Israel.

Feeding the Four Thousand
(Mark 8:1–10)

32 [a]Now Jesus called His disciples to *Himself* and said, "I have compassion on the
multitude, because they have now continued with Me three days and have nothing to
eat. And I do not want to send them away
hungry, lest they faint on the way."

33 [a]Then His disciples said to Him,
"Where could we get enough bread in the
wilderness to fill such a great multitude?"

34 Jesus said to them, "How many loaves
do you have?"

And they said, "Seven, and a few little
fish."

35 So He commanded the multitude to
sit down on the ground. 36 And [a]He took the
seven loaves and the fish and [b]gave thanks,
broke *them* and gave *them* to His disciples;
and the disciples *gave* to the multitude.
37 So they all ate and were filled, and they
took up seven large baskets full of the fragments that were left. 38 Now those who ate
were four thousand men, besides women
and children. 39 [a]And He sent away the multitude, got into the boat, and came to the
region of Magdala.[1]

The Pharisees and Sadducees Seek a Sign
(Mark 8:11–13; Luke 12:54–56)

16 Then the [a]Pharisees and Sadducees
came, and testing Him asked that
He would show them a sign from heaven.
2 He answered and said to them, "When it
is evening you say, '*It will be* fair weather,
for the sky is red'; 3 and in the morning,
'*It will be* foul weather today, for the sky
is red and threatening.' Hypocrites![1] You
know how to discern the face of the sky,
but you cannot *discern* the signs of the

15:16 [a] Matt. 16:9; Mark 7:18 15:17 [a] [1 Cor. 6:13] 15:18 [a] [Matt. 12:34]; Mark 7:20; [James 3:6] 15:19 [a] Gen. 6:5; 8:21; Prov. 6:14; Jer. 17:9; Mark 7:21; [Rom. 1:29–32; Gal. 5:19–21] 15:21 [a] Mark 7:24–30 15:22 [a] Matt. 1:1; 22:41, 42 15:24 [a] Matt. 10:5, 6; [Rom. 15:8] 15:26 [a] Matt. 7:6; Phil. 3:2 15:28 [a] Luke 7:9 15:29 [a] Matt. 15:29–31; Mark 7:31–37 [b] Matt. 4:18 15:30 [a] Is. 35:5, 6; Matt. 11:5; Luke 7:22 [b] Mark 7:25; Luke 7:38; 8:41; 10:39 15:31 [a] Luke 5:25, 26; 19:37, 38 15:32 [a] Mark 8:1–10 15:33 [a] 2 Kin. 4:43 15:36 [a] Matt. 14:19; 26:27; Luke 22:17, 19; John 6:11, 23; Acts 27:35; [Rom. 14:6] [b] 1 Sam. 9:13; Luke 22:19 15:39 [a] Mark 8:10 [1] NU-Text reads *Magadan.* 16:1 [a] Matt. 12:38; Mark 8:11; Luke 11:16; 12:54–56; 1 Cor. 1:22 16:3 [1] NU-Text omits *Hypocrites.*

times. 4[a]A wicked and adulterous generation seeks after a sign, and no sign shall be
given to it except the sign of the prophet[1]
Jonah." And He left them and departed.

The Leaven of the Pharisees
and Sadducees
(Mark 8:14–21)

5Now [a]when His disciples had come to
the other side, they had forgotten to take
bread. 6Then Jesus said to them, [a]"Take
heed and beware of the leaven of the Pharisees and the Sadducees."
7And they reasoned among themselves,
saying, "*It is* because we have taken no
bread."
8But Jesus, being aware of *it,* said to
them, "O you of little faith, why do you
reason among yourselves because you
have brought no bread?[1] 9[a]Do you not yet
understand, or remember the five loaves
of the five thousand and how many baskets
you took up? 10[a]Nor the seven loaves of the
four thousand and how many large baskets
you took up? 11How is it you do not understand that I did not speak to you concerning bread?—*but* to beware of the leaven
of the Pharisees and Sadducees." 12Then
they understood that He did not tell *them*
to beware of the leaven of bread, but of the
doctrine of the Pharisees and Sadducees.

Peter Confesses Jesus as the Christ
(Mark 8:27–30; Luke 9:18–20)

13When Jesus came into the region of
Caesarea Philippi, He asked His disciples,
saying, [a]"Who do men say that I, the Son
of Man, am?"
14So they said, [a]"Some *say* John the Baptist, some Elijah, and others Jeremiah or
[b]one of the prophets."
15He said to them, "But who do [a]you say
that I am?"
16Simon Peter answered and said, [a]"You
are the Christ, the Son of the living God."
17Jesus answered and said to him,
"Blessed are you, Simon Bar-Jonah, [a]for
flesh and blood has not revealed *this* to you,
but [b]My Father who is in heaven. 18And I
also say to you that [a]you are Peter, and [b]on
this rock I will build My church, and [c]the
gates of Hades shall not prevail against it.
19[a]And I will give you the keys of the kingdom of heaven, and whatever you bind on
earth will be bound in heaven, and whatever you loose on earth will be loosed[1] in
heaven."
20[a]Then He commanded His disciples
that they should tell no one that He was
Jesus the Christ.

Jesus Predicts His Death
and Resurrection
(Mark 8:31–33; Luke 9:21, 22)

21From that time Jesus began [a]to show
to His disciples that He must go to Jerusalem, and suffer many things from the elders and chief priests and scribes, and be
killed, and be raised the third day.
22Then Peter took Him aside and began
to rebuke Him, saying, "Far be it from You,
Lord; this shall not happen to You!"
23But He turned and said to Peter, "Get
behind Me, [a]Satan! [b]You are an offense to
Me, for you are not mindful of the things
of God, but the things of men."

Take Up the Cross and Follow Him
(Mark 8:34–38; Luke 9:23–26)

24[a]Then Jesus said to His disciples, "If
anyone desires to come after Me, let him
deny himself, and take up his cross, and
[b]follow Me. 25For [a]whoever desires to save
his life will lose it, but whoever loses his life
for My sake will find it. 26For what [a]profit is
it to a man if he gains the whole world, and
loses his own soul? Or [b]what will a man give
in exchange for his soul? 27For [a]the Son of
Man will come in the glory of His Father
[b]with His angels, [c]and then He will reward
each according to his works. 28Assuredly,
I say to you, [a]there are some standing here

16:4 [a] Prov. 30:12; Matt. 12:39; Luke 11:29; 24:46 [1] NU-Text omits *the prophet.* 16:5 [a] Mark 8:14 16:6 [a] Mark 8:15; Luke 12:1 16:8 [1] NU-Text reads *you have no bread.* 16:9 [a] Matt. 14:15–21; Mark 6:30–44; Luke 9:10–17; John 6:1–14 16:10 [a] Matt. 15:32–38; Mark 8:1–9 16:13 [a] Mark 8:27; Luke 9:18 16:14 [a] Matt. 14:2; Luke 9:7–9 [b] Matt. 21:11 16:15 [a] John 6:67 16:16 [a] Matt. 14:33; Mark 8:29; Luke 9:20; John 6:69; 11:27; Acts 8:37; 9:20; Heb. 1:2, 5; 1 John 4:15 16:17 [a] [Eph. 2:8] [b] [Matt. 11:27; 1 Cor. 2:10]; Gal. 1:16 16:18 [a] John 1:42 [b] Acts 2:41; [Eph. 2:20; Rev. 21:14] [c] Job 33:17; Ps. 9:13; 107:18; Is. 38:10 16:19 [a] Matt. 18:18; John 20:23 [1] Or *will have been bound . . . will have been loosed* 16:20 [a] Matt. 17:9; Mark 8:30; Luke 9:21 16:21 [a] Matt. 20:17; Mark 8:31; 9:31; Luke 9:22; 18:31; 24:46; John 2:19 16:23 [a] Matt. 4:10 [b] [Rom. 8:7] 16:24 [a] Mark 8:34; Luke 9:23; [Acts 14:22; 2 Cor. 4:10, 11; 1 Thess. 3:3; 2 Tim. 3:12] [b] [1 Pet. 2:21] 16:25 [a] Luke 17:33; John 12:25 16:26 [a] Luke 12:20, 21 [b] Ps. 49:7, 8 16:27 [a] Matt. 26:64; Mark 8:38; Luke 9:26 [b] [Dan. 7:10]; Zech. 14:5 [c] Job 34:11; Ps. 62:12; Prov. 24:12; Rom. 2:6; 2 Cor. 5:10; 1 Pet. 1:17; Rev. 2:23 16:28 [a] Mark 9:1; Luke 9:27; Acts 7:55, 56; Rev. 19:11

who shall not taste death till they see the Son of Man coming in His kingdom."

Jesus Transfigured on the Mount
(Mark 9:1–13; Luke 9:27–36; 2 Pet. 1:16–18)

17 Now [a]after six days Jesus took Peter, James, and John his brother, led them up on a high mountain by themselves; 2and He was transfigured before them. His face shone like the sun, and His clothes became as white as the light. 3And behold, Moses and Elijah appeared to them, talking with Him. 4Then Peter answered and said to Jesus, "Lord, it is good for us to be here; if You wish, let us[1] make here three tabernacles: one for You, one for Moses, and one for Elijah."

5[a]While he was still speaking, behold, a bright cloud overshadowed them; and suddenly a voice came out of the cloud, saying, [b]"This is My beloved Son, [c]in whom I am well pleased. [d]Hear Him!" 6[a]And when the disciples heard *it,* they fell on their faces and were greatly afraid. 7But Jesus came and [a]touched them and said, "Arise, and do not be afraid." 8When they had lifted up their eyes, they saw no one but Jesus only.

9Now as they came down from the mountain, Jesus commanded them, saying, "Tell the vision to no one until the Son of Man is risen from the dead."

10And His disciples asked Him, saying, [a]"Why then do the scribes say that Elijah must come first?"

11Jesus answered and said to them, "Indeed, Elijah is coming first[1] and will [a]restore all things. 12[a]But I say to you that Elijah has come already, and they [b]did not know him but did to him whatever they wished. Likewise [c]the Son of Man is also about to suffer at their hands." 13[a]Then the disciples understood that He spoke to them of John the Baptist.

A Boy Is Healed
(Mark 9:14–29; Luke 9:37–42)

14[a]And when they had come to the multitude, a man came to Him, kneeling down to Him and saying, 15"Lord, have mercy on my son, for he is an epileptic[1] and suffers severely; for he often falls into the fire and often into the water. 16So I brought him to Your disciples, but they could not cure him."

17Then Jesus answered and said, "O faithless and [a]perverse generation, how long shall I be with you? How long shall I bear with you? Bring him here to Me." 18And Jesus [a]rebuked the demon, and it came out of him; and the child was cured from that very hour.

19Then the disciples came to Jesus privately and said, "Why could we not cast it out?"

20So Jesus said to them, "Because of your unbelief;[1] for assuredly, I say to you, [a]if you have faith as a mustard seed, you will say to this mountain, 'Move from here to there,' and it will move; and nothing will be impossible for you. 21However, this kind does not go out except by prayer and fasting."[1]

#OXYGEN

MATTHEW 17:20

Believe in the Son

You are ready for anything that gets in your way. You can go over, under, around, or even through because you know Jesus. Even small faith is more than enough.

Tell the mountain to move, **breathe,** and **believe in the Son.**

Jesus Again Predicts His Death and Resurrection
(Mark 9:30–32; Luke 9:43–45)

22[a]Now while they were staying[1] in Galilee, Jesus said to them, "The Son of Man is about to be betrayed into the hands of men, 23and they will kill Him, and the third

---

17:1 [a] Matt. 17:1–8; Mark 9:2–8; Luke 9:28–36 17:4 [1] NU-Text reads *I will.* 17:5 [a] 2 Pet. 1:17 [b] Ps. 2:7; Matt. 3:17; Mark 1:11; Luke 1:35; 3:22; [John 12:28–30] [c] Is. 42:1; Matt. 3:17; 12:18; 2 Pet. 1:17 [d] [Deut. 18:15, 19; Acts 3:22, 23] 17:6 [a] 2 Pet. 1:18 17:7 [a] Dan. 8:18 17:10 [a] Mal. 4:5; Matt. 11:14; 16:14; Mark 9:11 17:11 [a] [Mal. 4:6]; Luke 1:17 [1] NU-Text omits *first.* 17:12 [a] Matt. 11:14; Mark 9:12, 13 [b] Matt. 14:3, 10 [c] Matt. 16:21 17:13 [a] Matt. 11:14 17:14 [a] Matt. 17:14–19; Mark 9:14–28; Luke 9:37–42 17:15 [1] Literally *moonstruck* 17:17 [a] Deut. 32:5; Phil. 2:15 17:18 [a] Luke 4:41 17:20 [a] Matt. 21:21; Mark 11:23; Luke 17:6; [1 Cor. 12:9] [1] NU-Text reads *little faith.* 17:21 [1] NU-Text omits this verse. 17:22 [a] Matt. 16:21; 26:57; Mark 8:31; Luke 9:22, 44; John 18:12 [1] NU-Text reads *gathering together.*

day He will be raised up." And they were exceedingly [a]sorrowful.

Peter and His Master Pay Their Taxes

24 [a]When they had come to Capernaum,[1]
those who received the *temple* tax came to
Peter and said, "Does your Teacher not pay
the *temple* tax?"
25 He said, "Yes."
And when he had come into the house,
Jesus anticipated him, saying, "What do
you think, Simon? From whom do the kings
of the earth take customs or taxes, from
their sons or from [a]strangers?"
26 Peter said to Him, "From strangers."
Jesus said to him, "Then the sons are
free. 27 Nevertheless, lest we offend them,
go to the sea, cast in a hook, and take the
fish that comes up first. And when you have
opened its mouth, you will find a piece of
money;[1] take that and give it to them for
Me and you."

Who Is the Greatest?
(Mark 9:33–37; Luke 9:46–48)

18 At [a]that time the disciples came to
Jesus, saying, "Who then is greatest
in the kingdom of heaven?"
2 Then Jesus called a little [a]child to Him,
set him in the midst of them, 3 and said,
"Assuredly, I say to you, [a]unless you are
converted and become as little children,
you will by no means enter the kingdom
of heaven. 4 [a]Therefore whoever humbles
himself as this little child is the greatest
in the kingdom of heaven. 5 [a]Whoever receives one little child like this in My name
receives Me.

Jesus Warns of Offenses
(Mark 9:42–48; Luke 17:1, 2)

6 [a]"But whoever causes one of these little ones who believe in Me to sin, it would
be better for him if a millstone were hung
around his neck, and he were drowned
in the depth of the sea. 7 Woe to the world
because of offenses! For [a]offenses must
come, but [b]woe to that man by whom the
offense comes!
8 [a]"If your hand or foot causes you to sin,
cut it off and cast *it* from you. It is better
for you to enter into life lame or maimed,
rather than having two hands or two feet,
to be cast into the everlasting fire. 9 And if
your eye causes you to sin, pluck it out and
cast *it* from you. It is better for you to enter
into life with one eye, rather than having
two eyes, to be cast into hell fire.

The Parable of the Lost Sheep
(Luke 15:1–7)

10 "Take heed that you do not despise one
of these little ones, for I say to you that in
heaven [a]their angels always [b]see the face of
My Father who is in heaven. 11 [a]For the Son of
Man has come to save that which was lost.[1]
12 [a]"What do you think? If a man has
a hundred sheep, and one of them goes
astray, does he not leave the ninety-nine
and go to the mountains to seek the one
that is straying? 13 And if he should find it,
assuredly, I say to you, he rejoices more
over that *sheep* than over the ninety-nine
that did not go astray. 14 Even so it is not
the [a]will of your Father who is in heaven
that one of these little ones should perish.

Dealing with a Sinning Brother

15 "Moreover [a]if your brother sins against
you, go and tell him his fault between you
and him alone. If he hears you, [b]you have
gained your brother. 16 But if he will not hear,
take with you one or two more, that [a]'by the
mouth of two or three witnesses every word
may be established.'[1] 17 And if he refuses to
hear them, tell *it* to the church. But if he
refuses even to hear the church, let him be
to you like a [a]heathen and a tax collector.
18 "Assuredly, I say to you, [a]whatever you
bind on earth will be bound in heaven, and
whatever you loose on earth will be loosed
in heaven.

17:23 [a] Matt. 26:22; 27:50; Luke 23:46; 24:46; John 16:6; 19:30; Acts 10:40 **17:24** [a] Mark 9:33 [1] NU-Text reads *Capharnaum* (here and elsewhere). **17:25** [a] [Is. 60:10–17] **17:27** [1] Greek *stater,* the exact amount to pay the temple tax (didrachma) for two **18:1** [a] Mark 9:33–37; Luke 9:46–48; 22:24–27 **18:2** [a] Matt. 19:14; Mark 10:14; Luke 18:14–17 **18:3** [a] Ps. 131:2; Matt. 19:14; Mark 10:15; Luke 18:16; [1 Cor. 14:20; 1 Pet. 2:2] **18:4** [a] [Matt. 20:27; 23:11] **18:5** [a] [Matt. 10:42]; Luke 9:48 **18:6** [a] Mark 9:42; Luke 17:2; [1 Cor. 8:12] **18:7** [a] Luke 17:1; [1 Cor. 11:19]; 1 Tim. 4:1 [b] Matt. 26:24; 27:4, 5 **18:8** [a] Matt. 5:29, 30; Mark 9:43, 45 **18:10** [a] [Ps. 34:7]; Zech. 13:7; [Heb. 1:14] [b] Esth. 1:14; Luke 1:19; Acts 12:15; [Rev. 8:2] **18:11** [a] Luke 9:56; John 3:17 [1] NU-Text omits this verse. **18:12** [a] Matt. 18:12–14; Luke 15:4–7 **18:14** [a] [1 Tim. 2:4] **18:15** [a] Lev. 19:17; [Luke 17:3, 4; Gal. 6:1]; 2 Thess. 3:15; [James 5:19] [b] [James 5:20]; 1 Pet. 3:1 **18:16** [a] Deut. 17:6; 19:15; John 8:17; 2 Cor. 13:1; 1 Tim. 5:19; Heb. 10:28 [1] Deuteronomy 19:15 **18:17** [a] Rom. 16:17; 1 Cor. 5:9; [2 Thess. 3:6, 14; 2 John 10] **18:18** [a] Matt. 16:19; [John 20:22, 23; 1 Cor. 5:4]

19 [a]"Again I say[1] to you that if two of you agree on earth concerning anything that they ask, [b]it will be done for them by My Father in heaven. 20 For where two or three are gathered [a]together in My name, I am there in the midst of them."

The Parable of the Unforgiving Servant

21 Then Peter came to Him and said, "Lord, how often shall my brother sin against me, and I forgive him? [a]Up to seven times?"

22 Jesus said to him, "I do not say to you, [a]up to seven times, but up to seventy times seven. 23 Therefore the kingdom of heaven is like a certain king who wanted to settle accounts with his servants. 24 And when he had begun to settle accounts, one was brought to him who owed him ten thousand talents. 25 But as he was not able to pay, his master commanded [a]that he be sold, with his wife and children and all that he had, and that payment be made. 26 The servant therefore fell down before him, saying, 'Master, have patience with me, and I will pay you all.' 27 Then the master of that servant was moved with compassion, released him, and forgave him the debt.

28 "But that servant went out and found one of his fellow servants who owed him a hundred denarii; and he laid hands on him and took *him* by the throat, saying, 'Pay me what you owe!' 29 So his fellow servant fell down at his feet[1] and begged him, saying, 'Have patience with me, and I will pay you all.'[2] 30 And he would not, but went and threw him into prison till he should pay the debt. 31 So when his fellow servants saw what had been done, they were very grieved, and came and told their master all that had been done. 32 Then his master, after he had called him, said to him, 'You wicked servant! I forgave you [a]all that debt because you begged me. 33 Should you not also have had compassion on your fellow servant, just as I had pity on you?' 34 And his master was angry, and delivered him to the torturers until he should pay all that was due to him.

35 [a]"So My heavenly Father also will do to you if each of you, from his heart, does not forgive his brother his trespasses."[1]

Marriage and Divorce
(Mark 10:1–12)

19 Now it came to pass, [a]when Jesus had finished these sayings, *that* He departed from Galilee and came to the region of Judea beyond the Jordan. 2 [a]And great multitudes followed Him, and He healed them there.

3 The Pharisees also came to Him, testing Him, and saying to Him, "Is it lawful for a man to divorce his wife for *just* any reason?"

4 And He answered and said to them, "Have you not read that He who made[1] *them* at the beginning [a]'made them male and female,'[2] 5 and said, [a]'For this reason a man shall leave his father and mother and be joined to his wife, and [b]the two shall become one flesh'?[1] 6 So then, they are no longer two but one flesh. Therefore what God has joined together, let not man separate."

7 They said to Him, [a]"Why then did Moses command to give a certificate of divorce, and to put her away?"

8 He said to them, "Moses, because of the [a]hardness of your hearts, permitted you to divorce your [b]wives, but from the beginning it was not so. 9 [a]And I say to you, whoever divorces his wife, except for sexual immorality,[1] and marries another, commits adultery; and whoever marries her who is divorced commits adultery."

10 His disciples said to Him, [a]"If such is the case of the man with *his* wife, it is better not to marry."

Jesus Teaches on Celibacy

11 But He said to them, [a]"All cannot accept this saying, but only *those* to whom it has been given: 12 For there are eunuchs who were born thus from *their* mother's womb, and [a]there are eunuchs who were made eunuchs by men, and there are eunuchs

---

18:19 [a] [1 Cor. 1:10] [b] [1 John 3:22; 5:14] [1] NU-Text and M-Text read *Again, assuredly, I say.* 18:20 [a] Acts 20:7; 1 Cor. 14:26 18:21 [a] Luke 17:4 18:22 [a] [Matt. 6:14; Mark 11:25]; Col. 3:13 18:25 [a] Ex. 21:2; Lev. 25:39; 2 Kin. 4:1; Neh. 5:5, 8 18:29 [1] NU-Text omits *at his feet.* [2] NU-Text and M-Text omit *all.* 18:32 [a] Luke 7:41–43 18:35 [a] Prov. 21:13; Matt. 6:12; Mark 11:26; James 2:13 [1] NU-Text omits *his trespasses.* 19:1 [a] Matt. 19:1–9; Mark 10:1–12; John 10:40 19:2 [a] Matt. 12:15 19:4 [a] Gen. 1:27; 5:2; [Mal. 2:15] [1] NU-Text reads *created.* [2] Genesis 1:27; 5:2 19:5 [a] Gen. 2:24; Mark 10:5–9; Eph. 5:31 [b] [1 Cor. 6:16; 7:2] [1] Genesis 2:24 19:7 [a] Deut. 24:1–4; Matt. 5:31 19:8 [a] Heb. 3:15 [b] Mal. 2:16 19:9 [a] [Matt. 5:32]; Mark 10:11; Luke 16:18; 1 Cor. 7:10 [1] Or *fornication* 19:10 [a] [Prov. 21:19] 19:11 [a] [1 Cor. 7:2, 7, 9, 17] 19:12 [a] [1 Cor. 7:32]

who have made themselves eunuchs for
the kingdom of heaven's sake. He who is
able to accept *it,* let him accept *it.*"

Jesus Blesses Little Children
(Mark 10:13–16; Luke 18:15–17)

13[a]Then little children were brought to
Him that He might put *His* hands on them
and pray, but the disciples rebuked them.
14But Jesus said, "Let the little children
come to Me, and do not forbid them; for
[a]of such is the kingdom of heaven." 15And
He laid *His* hands on them and departed
from there.

Jesus Counsels the Rich Young Ruler
(Mark 10:17–22; Luke 18:18–23)

16[a]Now behold, one came and said to
Him, [b]"Good[1] Teacher, what good thing
shall I do that I may have eternal life?"
17So He said to him, "Why do you call
Me good?[1] No one *is* [a]good but One, *that
is,* God.[2] But if you want to enter into life,
[b]keep the commandments."
18He said to Him, "Which ones?"
Jesus said, [a]"'You shall not murder,' 'You
shall not commit adultery,' 'You shall not
steal,' 'You shall not bear false witness,'
19[a]'Honor your father and *your* mother,'[1]
and, [b]'You shall love your neighbor as yourself.'"[2]
20The young man said to Him, "All these
things I have [a]kept from my youth.[1] What
do I still lack?"
21Jesus said to him, "If you want to be
perfect, [a]go, sell what you have and give
to the poor, and you will have treasure in
heaven; and come, follow Me."
22But when the young man heard that
saying, he went away sorrowful, for he had
great possessions.

With God All Things Are Possible
(Mark 10:23–31; Luke 18:24–30)

23Then Jesus said to His disciples, "Assuredly, I say to you that [a]it is hard for a rich
man to enter the kingdom of heaven. 24And
again I say to you, it is easier for a camel
to go through the eye of a needle than for
a rich man to enter the kingdom of God."
25When His disciples heard *it,* they were
greatly astonished, saying, "Who then can
be saved?"
26But Jesus looked at *them* and said to
them, "With men this is impossible, but
[a]with God all things are possible."
27Then Peter answered and said to Him,
"See, [a]we have left all and followed You.
Therefore what shall we have?"
28So Jesus said to them, "Assuredly I say
to you, that in the regeneration, when the
Son of Man sits on the throne of His glory,
[a]you who have followed Me will also sit on
twelve thrones, judging the twelve tribes of
Israel. 29[a]And everyone who has left houses
or brothers or sisters or father or mother
or wife[1] or children or lands, for My name's
sake, shall receive a hundredfold, and inherit eternal life. 30[a]But many *who are* first
will be last, and the last first.

The Parable of the Workers in the Vineyard

20 "For the kingdom of heaven is like
a landowner who went out early in
the morning to hire laborers for his vineyard. 2Now when he had agreed with the
laborers for a denarius a day, he sent them
into his vineyard. 3And he went out about
the third hour and saw others standing idle
in the marketplace, 4and said to them, 'You
also go into the vineyard, and whatever is
right I will give you.' So they went. 5Again
he went out about the sixth and the ninth
hour, and did likewise. 6And about the eleventh hour he went out and found others
standing idle,[1] and said to them, 'Why have
you been standing here idle all day?' 7They
said to him, 'Because no one hired us.' He
said to them, 'You also go into the vineyard,
and whatever is right you will receive.'[1]
8"So when evening had come, the owner

19:13 [a] Matt. 20:31; Mark 10:13; Luke 18:15 19:14 [a] Matt. 18:3, 4; Mark 10:15; Luke 18:17; [1 Cor. 14:20; 1 Pet. 2:2] 19:16 [a] Matt. 19:16–29; Mark 10:17–30; Luke 18:18–30 [b] Luke 10:25 [1] NU-Text omits *Good.* 19:17 [a] Ps. 25:8; 34:8; Nah. 1:7; [Rom. 2:4] [b] Lev. 18:5; Deut. 4:40; 6:17; 7:11; 11:22; 28:9; Neh. 9:29; Ezek. 20:21; [Gal. 3:10] [1] NU-Text reads *Why do you ask Me about what is good?* [2] NU-Text reads *There is One who is good.* 19:18 [a] Ex. 20:13–16; Deut. 5:17–20 19:19 [a] Ex. 20:12–16; Deut. 5:16–20; Matt. 15:4 [b] Lev. 19:18; Matt. 22:39; [Rom. 13:9; Gal. 5:14; James 2:8] [1] Exodus 20:12–16; Deuteronomy 5:16–20 [2] Leviticus 19:18 19:20 [a] [Phil. 3:6, 7] [1] NU-Text omits *from my youth.* 19:21 [a] Matt. 6:20; Luke 12:33; Acts 2:45; 4:34, 35; 1 Tim. 6:18, 19 19:23 [a] [Matt. 13:22]; Mark 10:24; 1 Cor. 1:26; [1 Tim. 6:9] 19:26 [a] Gen. 18:14; Num. 11:23; Job 42:2; Is. 59:1; Jer. 32:17; Zech. 8:6; Luke 1:37 19:27 [a] Deut. 33:9; Matt. 4:20; Luke 5:11 19:28 [a] Matt. 20:21; Luke 22:28–30; [1 Cor. 6:2; Rev. 2:26] 19:29 [a] [Matt. 6:33]; Mark 10:29, 30; Luke 18:29, 30 [1] NU-Text omits *or wife.* 19:30 [a] [Matt. 20:16; 21:31, 32]; Mark 10:31; Luke 13:30 20:6 [1] NU-Text omits *idle.* 20:7 [1] NU-Text omits the last clause of this verse.

of the vineyard said to his steward, 'Call the
laborers and give them *their* wages, beginning with the last to the first.' 9And when
those came who *were hired* about the eleventh hour, they each received a denarius.
10But when the first came, they supposed
that they would receive more; and they
likewise received each a denarius. 11And
when they had received *it,* they complained
against the landowner, 12saying, 'These last
men have worked *only* one hour, and you
made them equal to us who have borne the
burden and the heat of the day.' 13But he answered one of them and said, 'Friend, I am
doing you no wrong. Did you not agree with
me for a denarius? 14Take *what is* yours and
go your way. I wish to give to this last man
the same as to you. 15[a]Is it not lawful for me
to do what I wish with my own things? Or
[b]is your eye evil because I am good?' 16[a]So
the last will be first, and the first last. [b]For
many are called, but few chosen."[1]

Jesus a Third Time Predicts His Death and Resurrection
(Mark 10:32–34; Luke 18:31–34)

17[a]Now Jesus, going up to Jerusalem,
took the twelve disciples aside on the road
and said to them, 18[a]"Behold, we are going up to Jerusalem, and the Son of Man
will be betrayed to the chief priests and to
the scribes; and they will condemn Him to
death, 19[a]and deliver Him to the Gentiles to
[b]mock and to [c]scourge and to [d]crucify. And
the third day He will [e]rise again."

Greatness Is Serving
(Mark 10:35–45)

20[a]Then the mother of [b]Zebedee's sons
came to Him with her sons, kneeling down
and asking something from Him.

21And He said to her, "What do you
wish?"

She said to Him, "Grant that these two
sons of mine [a]may sit, one on Your right
hand and the other on the left, in Your kingdom."

22But Jesus answered and said, "You
do not know what you ask. Are you able
to drink [a]the cup that I am about to drink,
and be baptized with [b]the baptism that I
am baptized with?"[1]

They said to Him, "We are able."

23So He said to them, [a]"You will indeed
drink My cup, and be baptized with the baptism that I am baptized with;[1] but to sit on
My right hand and on My left is not Mine
to give, but *it is for those* for whom it is prepared by My Father."

24[a]And when the ten heard *it,* they were
greatly displeased with the two brothers.
25But Jesus called them to *Himself* and said,
"You know that the rulers of the Gentiles
lord it over them, and those who are great
exercise authority over them. 26Yet [a]it shall
not be so among you; but [b]whoever desires
to become great among you, let him be
your servant. 27[a]And whoever desires to
be first among you, let him be your slave—
28[a]just as the [b]Son of Man did not come to
be served, [c]but to serve, and [d]to give His
life a ransom [e]for many."

Two Blind Men Receive Their Sight
(Mark 10:46–52; Luke 18:35–43)

29[a]Now as they went out of Jericho, a
great multitude followed Him. 30And behold, [a]two blind men sitting by the road,
when they heard that Jesus was passing
by, cried out, saying, "Have mercy on us,
O Lord, [b]Son of David!"

31Then the multitude [a]warned them that
they should be quiet; but they cried out
all the more, saying, "Have mercy on us,
O Lord, Son of David!"

32So Jesus stood still and called them,
and said, "What do you want Me to do for
you?"

20:15 [a] [Rom. 9:20, 21] [b] Deut. 15:9; Prov. 23:6; [Matt. 6:23]; Mark 7:22 **20:16** [a] Matt. 19:30; Mark 10:31; Luke 13:30 [b] Matt. 22:14 [1] NU-Text omits the last sentence of this verse. **20:17** [a] Matt. 20:17–19; Mark 10:32–34; Luke 18:31–33; John 12:12 **20:18** [a] Matt. 16:21; 26:47–57; Mark 14:42, 64; John 18:5; 19:7 **20:19** [a] Matt. 27:2; Mark 15:1, 16; Luke 23:1; John 18:28; Acts 3:13 [b] Matt. 26:67, 68; 27:29, 41; Mark 15:20, 31 [c] Matt. 27:26; Mark 15:15; John 19:1 [d] Matt. 27:35; Luke 23:33; Acts 3:13–15 [e] Matt. 28:5, 6; Mark 16:6, 9; Luke 24:5–8, 46; Acts 10:40; 1 Cor. 15:4 **20:20** [a] Mark 10:35–45 [b] Matt. 4:21; 10:2 **20:21** [a] [Matt. 19:28] **20:22** [a] Is. 51:17, 22; Jer. 49:12; Matt. 26:39, 42; Mark 14:36; Luke 22:42; John 18:11 [b] Luke 12:50 [1] NU-Text omits *and be baptized with the baptism that I am baptized with.* **20:23** [a] [Acts 12:2; Rom. 8:17; 2 Cor. 1:7; Rev. 1:9] [1] NU-Text omits *and be baptized with the baptism that I am baptized with.* **20:24** [a] Mark 10:41; Luke 22:24, 25 **20:26** [a] [1 Pet. 5:3] [b] Matt. 23:11; Mark 9:35; 10:43; Luke 22:26 **20:27** [a] [Matt. 18:4] **20:28** [a] John 13:4 [b] [Matt. 26:28; John 13:13; 2 Cor. 8:9; Phil. 2:6, 7; 1 Tim. 2:5, 6; Titus 2:14; Heb. 9:28; Rev. 1:5] [c] Luke 22:27; John 13:14 [d] [Is. 53:10, 11; Dan. 9:24, 26; John 11:51, 52; 1 Pet. 1:18, 19] [e] [Rom. 5:15, 19; Heb. 9:28] **20:29** [a] Mark 10:46–52; Luke 18:35–43 **20:30** [a] Matt. 9:27 [b] [2 Sam. 7:14–17; Ps. 89:3–5, 19–37; Is. 11:10–12; Ezek. 37:21–25]; Matt. 1:1; Luke 1:31, 32; [Acts 15:14–17] **20:31** [a] Matt. 19:13

33 They said to Him, "Lord, that our eyes
may be opened." 34 So Jesus had [a]compas-
sion and touched their eyes. And immediately their eyes received sight, and they
followed Him.

The Triumphal Entry
(Mark 11:1–10; Luke 19:28–40; John 12:12–19)

21 Now [a]when they drew near Jerusalem, and came to Bethphage,[1] at [b]the
Mount of Olives, then Jesus sent two disciples, 2 saying to them, "Go into the village opposite you, and immediately you
will find a donkey tied, and a colt with her.
Loose *them* and bring *them* to Me. 3 And if
anyone says anything to you, you shall say,
'The Lord has need of them,' and immediately he will send them."
4 All[1] this was done that it might be fulfilled which was spoken by the prophet,
saying:

5 "Tell[a] the daughter of Zion,
'Behold, your King is coming
to you,
Lowly, and sitting on a donkey,
A colt, the foal of a donkey.' "[1]

6 [a]So the disciples went and did as Jesus
commanded them. 7 They brought the donkey and the colt, [a]laid their clothes on them,
and set *Him*[1] on them. 8 And a very great
multitude spread their clothes on the road;
[a]others cut down branches from the trees
and spread *them* on the road. 9 Then the
multitudes who went before and those who
followed cried out, saying:

"Hosanna to the Son of David!
[a]'Blessed *is* He who comes in
the name of the LORD!'[1]
Hosanna in the highest!"

10 [a]And when He had come into Jerusalem, all the city was moved, saying, "Who
is this?"
11 So the multitudes said, "This is Jesus,
[a]the prophet from Nazareth of Galilee."

Jesus Cleanses the Temple
(Mark 11:15–19; Luke 19:45–48; John 2:13–22)

12 [a]Then Jesus went into the temple of
God[1] and drove out all those who bought
and sold in the temple, and overturned
the tables of the [b]money changers and the
seats of those who sold doves. 13 And He
said to them, "It is written, [a]'My house shall
be called a house of prayer,'[1] but you have
made it a [b]'den of thieves.' "[2]
14 Then *the* blind and *the* lame came to
Him in the temple, and He healed them.
15 But when the chief priests and scribes saw
the wonderful things that He did, and the
children crying out in the temple and saying, "Hosanna to the [a]Son of David!" they
were indignant 16 and said to Him, "Do You
hear what these are saying?"
And Jesus said to them, "Yes. Have you
never read,

[a]'Out of the mouth of babes
and nursing infants
You have perfected
praise'?"[1]

17 Then He left them and [a]went out of
the city to Bethany, and He lodged there.

The Fig Tree Withered
(Mark 11:12–14)

18 [a]Now in the morning, as He returned to
the city, He was hungry. 19 [a]And seeing a fig
tree by the road, He came to it and found
nothing on it but leaves, and said to it, "Let
no fruit grow on you ever again." Immediately the fig tree withered away.

The Lesson of the Withered Fig Tree
(Mark 11:20–24)

20 [a]And when the disciples saw *it*, they
marveled, saying, "How did the fig tree
wither away so soon?"
21 So Jesus answered and said to them,
"Assuredly, I say to you, [a]if you have faith
and [b]do not doubt, you will not only do
what was done to the fig tree, [c]but also if
you say to this mountain, 'Be removed and

20:34 [a] Matt. 9:36; 14:14; 15:32; 18:27 21:1 [a] Mark 11:1–10; Luke 19:29–38 [b] [Zech. 14:4] [1] M-Text reads *Bethsphage.* 21:4 [1] NU-Text omits *All.* 21:5 [a] Is. 62:11; Zech. 9:9; John 12:15 [1] Zechariah 9:9 21:6 [a] Mark 11:4 21:7 [a] 2 Kin. 9:13 [1] NU-Text reads *and He sat.* 21:8 [a] Lev. 23:40; John 12:13 21:9 [a] Ps. 118:26; Matt. 23:39 [1] Psalm 118:26 21:10 [a] John 2:13, 15 21:11 [a] [Deut. 18:15, 18]; Matt. 2:23; 16:14; Luke 4:16–29; John 6:14; 7:40; 9:17; [Acts 3:22, 23] 21:12 [a] Mal. 3:1; Mark 11:15–18; Luke 19:45–47; John 2:13–16 [b] Deut. 14:25 [1] NU-Text omits *of God.* 21:13 [a] Is. 56:7 [b] Jer. 7:11 [1] Isaiah 56:7 [2] Jeremiah 7:11 21:15 [a] Matt. 1:1; John 7:42 21:16 [a] Ps. 8:2; Matt. 11:25 [1] Psalm 8:2 21:17 [a] Matt. 26:6; Mark 11:1, 11, 12; 14:3; Luke 19:29; 24:50; John 11:1, 18; 12:1 21:18 [a] Mark 11:12–14, 20–24 21:19 [a] Mark 11:13 21:20 [a] Mark 11:20 21:21 [a] Matt. 17:20 [b] James 1:6 [c] 1 Cor. 13:2

be cast into the sea,' it will be done. 22And
[a]whatever things you ask in prayer, believing, you will receive."

Jesus' Authority Questioned
(Mark 11:27–33; Luke 20:1–8)

23[a]Now when He came into the temple,
the chief priests and the elders of the people confronted Him as He was teaching,
and [b]said, "By what authority are You doing these things? And who gave You this
authority?"
24But Jesus answered and said to them,
"I also will ask you one thing, which if you
tell Me, I likewise will tell you by what authority I do these things: 25The [a]baptism of
[b]John—where was it from? From heaven
or from men?"
And they reasoned among themselves,
saying, "If we say, 'From heaven,' He will say
to us, 'Why then did you not believe him?'
26But if we say, 'From men,' we [a]fear the
multitude, [b]for all count John as a prophet."
27So they answered Jesus and said, "We do
not know."
And He said to them, "Neither will I tell
you by what authority I do these things.

The Parable of the Two Sons

28"But what do you think? A man had
two sons, and he came to the first and said,
'Son, go, work today in my [a]vineyard.' 29He
answered and said, 'I will not,' but afterward he regretted it and went. 30Then he
came to the second and said likewise. And
he answered and said, 'I *go,* sir,' but he did
not go. 31Which of the two did the will of
his father?"
They said to Him, "The first."
Jesus said to them, [a]"Assuredly, I say
to you that tax collectors and harlots enter the kingdom of God before you. 32For
[a]John came to you in the way of righteousness, and you did not believe him; [b]but tax
collectors and harlots believed him; and
when you saw *it,* you did not afterward relent and believe him.

The Parable of the Wicked Vinedressers
(Mark 12:1–12; Luke 20:9–19)

33"Hear another parable: There was a
certain landowner [a]who planted a vineyard
and set a hedge around it, dug a winepress
in it and built a tower. And he leased it to
vinedressers and [b]went into a far country.
34Now when vintage-time drew near, he
sent his servants to the vinedressers, that
they might receive its fruit. 35[a]And the vinedressers took his servants, beat one, killed
one, and stoned another. 36Again he sent
other servants, more than the first, and
they did likewise to them. 37Then last of
all he sent his [a]son to them, saying, 'They
will respect my son.' 38But when the vinedressers saw the son, they said among
themselves, [a]'This is the heir. [b]Come, let
us kill him and seize his inheritance.' 39[a]So
they took him and cast *him* out of the vineyard and killed *him.*
40"Therefore, when the owner of the
vineyard comes, what will he do to those
vinedressers?"
41[a]They said to Him, [b]"He will destroy
those wicked men miserably, [c]and lease
his vineyard to other vinedressers who will
render to him the fruits in their seasons."
42Jesus said to them, "Have you never
read in the Scriptures:

> [a]'The stone which the builders rejected
> Has become the chief cornerstone.
> This was the LORD's doing,
> And it is marvelous in our eyes'?[1]

43"Therefore I say to you, [a]the kingdom
of God will be taken from you and given
to a nation bearing the fruits of it. 44And
[a]whoever falls on this stone will be broken;
but on whomever it falls, [b]it will grind him
to powder."
45Now when the chief priests and Pharisees heard His parables, they perceived
that He was speaking of them. 46But when
they sought to lay hands on Him, they

21:22 [a] Matt. 7:7–11; Mark 11:24; Luke 11:9; [John 15:7; James 5:16; 1 John 3:22; 5:14] 21:23 [a] Mark 11:27–33; Luke 20:1–8 [b] Ex. 2:14; Acts 4:7; 7:27 21:25 [a] [John 1:29–34] [b] John 1:15–28 21:26 [a] Matt. 14:5; 21:46; Luke 20:6 [b] Matt. 14:5; Mark 6:20 21:28 [a] Matt. 20:1; 21:33 21:31 [a] Luke 7:29, 37–50 21:32 [a] Luke 3:1–12; 7:29 [b] Luke 3:12, 13 21:33 [a] Ps. 80:9; Mark 12:1–12; Luke 20:9–19 [b] Matt. 25:14 21:35 [a] 2 Chr. 24:21; 36:16; [Matt. 23:34, 37; Acts 7:52; 1 Thess. 2:15]; Heb. 11:36, 37 21:37 [a] [John 3:16] 21:38 [a] [Ps. 2:8; Heb. 1:2] [b] [Ps. 2:2]; John 11:53; Acts 4:27 21:39 [a] [Matt. 26:50]; Mark 14:46; Luke 22:54; John 18:12; [Acts 2:23] 21:41 [a] Luke 20:16 [b] [Luke 21:24] [c] [Matt. 8:11; Acts 13:46; Rom. 9; 10] 21:42 [a] Ps. 118:22, 23; Is. 28:16; Mark 12:10; Luke 20:17; Acts 4:11; [Rom. 9:33]; Eph. 2:20; [1 Pet. 2:6, 7] [1] Psalm 118:22, 23 21:43 [a] [Matt. 8:12]; Acts 13:46 21:44 [a] Is. 8:14, 15; Zech. 12:3; Luke 20:18; [Rom. 9:33]; 1 Pet. 2:8 [b] [Is. 60:12; Dan. 2:44]

[a]feared the multitudes, because [b]they took
Him for a prophet.

The Parable of the Wedding Feast
(Luke 14:15–24)

22 And Jesus answered [a]and spoke to
them again by parables and said:
2"The kingdom of heaven is like a certain
king who arranged a marriage for his son,
3and sent out his servants to call those who
were invited to the wedding; and they were
not willing to come. 4Again, he sent out
other servants, saying, 'Tell those who are
invited, "See, I have prepared my dinner;
[a]my oxen and fatted cattle *are* killed, and
all things *are* ready. Come to the wedding."'
5But they made light of it and went their
ways, one to his own farm, another to his
business. 6And the rest seized his servants,
treated *them* spitefully, and killed *them.* 7But
when the king heard *about it,* he was furious. And he sent out [a]his armies, destroyed
those murderers, and burned up their city.
8Then he said to his servants, 'The wedding
is ready, but those who were invited were
not [a]worthy. 9Therefore go into the highways, and as many as you find, invite to
the wedding.' 10So those servants went out
into the highways and [a]gathered together
all whom they found, both bad and good.
And the wedding *hall* was filled with guests.

11"But when the king came in to see the
guests, he saw a man there [a]who did not
have on a wedding garment. 12So he said
to him, 'Friend, how did you come in here
without a wedding garment?' And he was
[a]speechless. 13Then the king said to the servants, 'Bind him hand and foot, take him
away, and[1] cast *him* [a]into outer darkness;
there will be weeping and gnashing of teeth.'

14[a]"For many are called, but few *are*
chosen."

The Pharisees: Is It Lawful to Pay Taxes to Caesar?
(Mark 12:13–17; Luke 20:20–26)

15[a]Then the Pharisees went and plotted
how they might entangle Him in *His* talk.
16And they sent to Him their disciples with
the [a]Herodians, saying, "Teacher, we know
that You are true, and teach the way of God
in truth; nor do You care about anyone, for
You do not regard the person of men. 17Tell
us, therefore, what do You think? Is it lawful to pay taxes to Caesar, or not?"

18But Jesus perceived their wickedness,
and said, "Why do you test Me, *you* hypocrites? 19Show Me the tax money."

So they brought Him a denarius.

20And He said to them, "Whose image
and inscription *is* this?"

21They said to Him, "Caesar's."

And He said to them, [a]"Render therefore
to Caesar the things that are [b]Caesar's, and
to God the things that are [c]God's." 22When
they had heard *these words,* they marveled,
and left Him and went their way.

The Sadducees: What About the Resurrection?
(Mark 12:18–27; Luke 20:27–40)

23[a]The same day the Sadducees, [b]who
say there is no resurrection, came to Him
and asked Him, 24saying: "Teacher, [a]Moses
said that if a man dies, having no children,
his brother shall marry his wife and raise
up offspring for his brother. 25Now there
were with us seven brothers. The first died
after he had married, and having no offspring, left his wife to his brother. 26Like-
wise the second also, and the third, even
to the seventh. 27Last of all the woman
died also. 28Therefore, in the resurrection,
whose wife of the seven will she be? For
they all had her."

29Jesus answered and said to them, "You
are mistaken, [a]not knowing the Scriptures
nor the power of God. 30For in the resurrection they neither marry nor are given
in marriage, but [a]are like angels of God[1] in
heaven. 31But concerning the resurrection
of the dead, have you not read what was
spoken to you by God, saying, 32[a]'I am the
God of Abraham, the God of Isaac, and
the God of Jacob'?[1] God is not the God of
the dead, but of the living." 33And when

21:46 [a] Matt. 21:26; Mark 11:18, 32 [b] Matt. 21:11; Luke 7:16; John 7:40 **22:1** [a] Luke 14:16; [Rev. 19:7–9] **22:4** [a] Prov. 9:2 **22:7** [a] [Dan. 9:26] **22:8** [a] Matt. 10:11 **22:10** [a] Matt. 13:38, 47, 48; [Acts 28:28] **22:11** [a] [2 Cor. 5:3; Eph. 4:24; Col. 3:10, 12; Rev. 3:4; 16:15; 19:8] **22:12** [a] [Rom. 3:19] **22:13** [a] Matt. 8:12; 25:30; Luke 13:28 [1] NU-Text omits *take him away, and.* **22:14** [a] Matt. 20:16 **22:15** [a] Mark 12:13–17; Luke 20:20–26 **22:16** [a] Mark 3:6; 8:15; 12:13 **22:21** [a] Matt. 17:25 [b] [Rom. 13:1–7; 1 Pet. 2:13–15] [c] [1 Cor. 3:23; 6:19, 20; 12:27] **22:23** [a] Mark 12:18–27; Luke 20:27–40 [b] Acts 23:8 **22:24** [a] Deut. 25:5 **22:29** [a] John 20:9 **22:30** [a] [1 John 3:2] [1] NU-Text omits *of God.* **22:32** [a] Gen. 17:7; 26:24; 28:21; Ex. 3:6, 15; Mark 12:26; Luke 20:37; Acts 7:32; [Heb. 11:16] [1] Exodus 3:6, 15

the multitudes heard *this,* [a]they were astonished at His teaching.

The Scribes: Which Is the First Commandment of All?
(Mark 12:28–34; Luke 10:25–28)

34 [a]But when the Pharisees heard that He had silenced the Sadducees, they gathered together. 35 Then one of them, [a]a lawyer, asked *Him a question,* testing Him, and saying, 36 "Teacher, which *is* the great commandment in the law?"

37 Jesus said to him, [a]" 'You shall love the LORD your God with all your heart, with all your soul, and with all your mind.'[1] 38 This is *the* first and great commandment. 39 And *the* second *is* like it: [a]'You shall love your neighbor as yourself.'[1] 40 [a]On these two commandments hang all the Law and the Prophets."

Jesus: How Can David Call His Descendant Lord?
(Mark 12:35–37; Luke 20:41–44)

41 [a]While the Pharisees were gathered together, Jesus asked them, 42 saying, "What do you think about the Christ? Whose Son is He?"

They said to Him, "*The* [a]*Son* of David."

43 He said to them, "How then does David in the Spirit call Him 'Lord,' saying:

44 'The[a] LORD said to my Lord,
"Sit at My right hand,
Till I make Your enemies
Your footstool" '?[1]

45 If David then calls Him 'Lord,' how is He his Son?" 46 [a]And no one was able to answer Him a word, [b]nor from that day on did anyone dare question Him anymore.

Woe to the Scribes and Pharisees
(Mark 12:38–40; Luke 20:45–47)

23 Then Jesus spoke to the multitudes and to His disciples, 2 saying: [a]"The scribes and the Pharisees sit in Moses' seat. 3 Therefore whatever they tell you to observe,[1] *that* observe and do, but do not do according to their works; for [a]they say, and do not do. 4 [a]For they bind heavy burdens, hard to bear, and lay *them* on men's shoulders; but they *themselves* will not move them with one of their fingers. 5 But all their works they do to [a]be seen by men. They make their phylacteries broad and enlarge the borders of their garments. 6 [a]They love the best places at feasts, the best seats in the synagogues, 7 greetings in the marketplaces, and to be called by men, 'Rabbi, Rabbi.' 8 [a]But you, do not be called 'Rabbi'; for One is your Teacher, the Christ,[1] and you are all brethren. 9 Do not call anyone on earth your father; [a]for One is your Father, He who is in heaven. 10 And do not be called teachers; for One is your Teacher, the Christ. 11 But [a]he who is greatest among you shall be your servant. 12 [a]And whoever exalts himself will be humbled, and he who humbles himself will be exalted.

13 "But [a]woe to you, scribes and Pharisees, hypocrites! For you shut up the kingdom of heaven against men; for you neither go in *yourselves,* nor do you allow those who are entering to go in. 14 Woe to you, scribes and Pharisees, hypocrites! [a]For you devour widows' houses, and for a pretense make long prayers. Therefore you will receive greater condemnation.[1]

15 "Woe to you, scribes and Pharisees, hypocrites! For you travel land and sea to win one proselyte, and when he is won, you make him twice as much a son of hell as yourselves.

16 "Woe to you, [a]blind guides, who say, [b]'Whoever swears by the temple, it is nothing; but whoever swears by the gold of the temple, he is obliged *to perform it.*' 17 Fools and blind! For which is greater, the gold [a]or the temple that sanctifies[1] the gold? 18 And, 'Whoever swears by the altar, it is nothing; but whoever swears by the gift that is on it, he is obliged *to perform it.*' 19 Fools

---

22:33 [a] Matt. 7:28 **22:34** [a] Mark 12:28–31; Luke 10:25–37 **22:35** [a] Luke 7:30; 10:25; 11:45, 46, 52; 14:3; Titus 3:13 **22:37** [a] Deut. 6:5; 10:12; 30:6 [1] Deuteronomy 6:5 **22:39** [a] Lev. 19:18; Matt. 19:19; Mark 12:31; Luke 10:27; [Rom. 13:9; Gal. 5:14; James 2:8] [1] Leviticus 19:18 **22:40** [a] [Matt. 7:12; Rom. 13:10; 1 Tim. 1:5] **22:41** [a] Mark 12:35–37; Luke 20:41–44 **22:42** [a] Matt. 1:1; 21:9 **22:44** [a] Ps. 110:1; [Matt. 26:64]; Mark 16:19; Acts 2:34; 1 Cor. 15:25; Heb. 1:13; 10:13 [1] Psalm 110:1 **22:46** [a] Luke 14:6 [b] Mark 12:34; Luke 20:40 **23:2** [a] Deut. 33:3; Ezra 7:6, 25; Neh. 8:4, 8; [Mal. 2:7]; Mark 12:38; Luke 20:45 **23:3** [a] [Rom. 2:19] [1] NU-Text omits *to observe.* **23:4** [a] [Matt. 11:29, 30]; Luke 11:46; Acts 15:10; Rom. 2:17–24; [Gal. 5:1; 6:13; Col. 2:16, 17] **23:5** [a] [Matt. 6:1–6, 16–18] **23:6** [a] Mark 12:38, 39; Luke 11:43; 20:46; 3 John 9 **23:8** [a] [2 Cor. 1:24; James 3:1; 1 Pet. 5:3] [1] NU-Text omits *the Christ.* **23:9** [a] [Mal. 1:6]; Matt. 5:16, 48; 6:1, 9, 14, 26, 32; 7:11 **23:11** [a] Matt. 20:26, 27 **23:12** [a] Job 22:29; Prov. 15:33; 29:23; Luke 14:11; 18:14; James 4:6; 1 Pet. 5:5 **23:13** [a] Luke 11:52 **23:14** [a] Mark 12:40; Luke 20:47; [2 Tim. 3:6; Titus 1:10, 11] [1] NU-Text omits this verse. **23:16** [a] Matt. 15:14; 23:24 [b] [Matt. 5:33, 34] **23:17** [a] Ex. 30:29 [1] NU-Text reads *sanctified.*

and blind! For which is greater, the gift [a]or
the altar that sanctifies the gift? 20 Therefore he who swears by the altar, swears by
it and by all things on it. 21 He who swears
by the temple, swears by it and by [a]Him
who dwells[1] in it. 22 And he who swears by
heaven, swears by [a]the throne of God and
by Him who sits on it.

23 "Woe to you, scribes and Pharisees,
hypocrites! [a]For you pay tithe of mint and
anise and cummin, and [b]have neglected
the weightier *matters* of the law: justice and
mercy and faith. These you ought to have
done, without leaving the others undone.
24 Blind guides, who strain out a gnat and
swallow a camel!

25 "Woe to you, scribes and Pharisees,
hypocrites! [a]For you cleanse the outside of
the cup and dish, but inside they are full
of extortion and self-indulgence.[1] 26 Blind
Pharisee, first cleanse the inside of the cup
and dish, that the outside of them may be
clean also.

27 "Woe to you, scribes and Pharisees,
hypocrites! [a]For you are like whitewashed
tombs which indeed appear beautiful outwardly, but inside are full of dead *men's*
bones and all uncleanness. 28 Even so you
also outwardly appear righteous to men,
but inside you are full of hypocrisy and
lawlessness.

29 [a]"Woe to you, scribes and Pharisees,
hypocrites! Because you build the tombs of
the prophets and adorn the monuments of
the righteous, 30 and say, 'If we had lived in
the days of our fathers, we would not have
been partakers with them in the blood of
the prophets.'

31 "Therefore you are witnesses against
yourselves that [a]you are sons of those who
murdered the prophets. 32 [a]Fill up, then, the
measure of your fathers' *guilt.* 33 Serpents,
[a]brood of vipers! How can you escape the
condemnation of hell? 34 [a]Therefore, indeed, I send you prophets, wise men, and
scribes: [b]*some* of them you will kill and
crucify, and [c]*some* of them you will scourge
in your synagogues and persecute from
city to city, 35 [a]that on you may come all the
righteous blood shed on the earth, [b]from
the blood of righteous Abel to [c]the blood
of Zechariah, son of Berechiah, whom you
murdered between the temple and the altar. 36 Assuredly, I say to you, all these things
will come upon this generation.

Jesus Laments over Jerusalem
(Luke 13:34, 35)

37 [a]"O Jerusalem, Jerusalem, the one who
kills the prophets [b]and stones those who are
sent to her! How often [c]I wanted to gather
your children together, as a hen gathers
her chicks [d]under *her* wings, but you were
not willing! 38 See! Your house is left to you
desolate; 39 for I say to you, you shall see Me
no more till you say, [a]'Blessed *is* He who
comes in the name of the LORD!'"[1]

Jesus Predicts the Destruction of the Temple
(Mark 13:1, 2; Luke 21:5, 6)

24 Then [a]Jesus went out and departed
from the temple, and His disciples
came up to show Him the buildings of the
temple. 2 And Jesus said to them, "Do you
not see all these things? Assuredly, I say to
you, [a]not *one* stone shall be left here upon
another, that shall not be thrown down."

The Signs of the Times and the End of the Age
(Mark 13:3–13; Luke 21:7–19)

3 Now as He sat on the Mount of Olives,
[a]the disciples came to Him privately, saying, [b]"Tell us, when will these things be?
And what *will be* the sign of Your coming,
and of the end of the age?"

4 And Jesus answered and said to them:
[a]"Take heed that no one deceives you. 5 For
[a]many will come in My name, saying, 'I am
the Christ,' [b]and will deceive many. 6 And
you will hear of [a]wars and rumors of wars.

23:19 [a] Ex. 29:37 23:21 [a] 1 Kin. 8:13; 2 Chr. 6:2; Ps. 26:8; 132:14 [1] M-Text reads *dwelt.* 23:22 [a] Ps. 11:4; Is. 66:1; Matt. 5:34; Acts 7:49 23:23 [a] Matt. 23:13; Luke 11:42; 18:12 [b] [1 Sam. 15:22; Hos. 6:6; Mic. 6:8]; Matt. 9:13; 12:7 23:25 [a] Mark 7:4; Luke 11:39 [1] M-Text reads *unrighteousness.* 23:27 [a] Luke 11:44; Acts 23:3 23:29 [a] Luke 11:47, 48 23:31 [a] Matt. 23:34, 37; [Acts 7:51, 52]; 1 Thess. 2:15 23:32 [a] Gen. 15:16; [1 Thess. 2:16] 23:33 [a] Matt. 3:7; 12:34; Luke 3:7 23:34 [a] Matt. 21:34, 35; Luke 11:49 [b] John 16:2; Acts 7:54–60; 22:19 [c] Matt. 10:17; Acts 5:40; 2 Cor. 11:24, 25 23:35 [a] Rev. 18:24 [b] Gen. 4:8; Heb. 11:4; 1 John 3:12 [c] 2 Chr. 24:20, 21 23:37 [a] Luke 13:34, 35 [b] 2 Chr. 24:20, 21; 36:15, 16; Neh. 9:26; Matt. 21:35, 36 [c] Deut. 32:11, 12; Matt. 11:28–30 [d] Ps. 17:8; 91:4; Is. 49:5 23:39 [a] Ps. 118:26; Matt. 21:9 [1] Psalm 118:26 24:1 [a] Mark 13:1; Luke 21:5–36 24:2 [a] 1 Kin. 9:7; Mic. 3:12; Luke 19:44 24:3 [a] Mark 13:3 [b] [Matt. 24:27, 37, 39; Luke 17:20–37; 1 Thess. 5:1–3] 24:4 [a] Eph. 5:6; [Col. 2:8, 18; 2 Thess. 2:3; 1 John 4:1–3] 24:5 [a] Jer. 14:14; John 5:43; Acts 5:36; [1 John 2:18; 4:3] [b] Matt. 24:11 24:6 [a] [Rev. 6:2–4]

See that you are not troubled; for all[1] *these things* must come to pass, but the end is not yet. 7For [a]nation will rise against nation, and kingdom against kingdom. And there will be [b]famines, pestilences,[1] and earthquakes in various places. 8All these *are* the beginning of sorrows.

9[a]"Then they will deliver you up to tribulation and kill you, and you will be hated by all nations for My name's sake. 10And then many will be offended, will betray one another, and will hate one another. 11Then [a]many false prophets will rise up and [b]deceive many. 12And because lawlessness will abound, the love of many will grow [a]cold. 13[a]But he who endures to the end shall be saved. 14And this [a]gospel of the kingdom [b]will be preached in all the world as a witness to all the nations, and then the end will come.

The Great Tribulation
(Mark 13:14–23; Luke 17:23, 24, 37; 21:20–24)

15[a]"Therefore when you see the [b]'abomination of desolation,'[1] spoken of by Daniel the prophet, standing in the holy place" [c](whoever reads, let him understand), 16"then let those who are in Judea flee to the mountains. 17Let him who is on the housetop not go down to take anything out of his house. 18And let him who is in the field not go back to get his clothes. 19But [a]woe to those who are pregnant and to those who are nursing babies in those days! 20And pray that your flight may not be in winter or on the Sabbath. 21For [a]then there will be great tribulation, such as has not been since the beginning of the world until this time, no, nor ever shall be. 22And unless those days were shortened, no flesh would be saved; [a]but for the elect's sake those days will be shortened.

23[a]"Then if anyone says to you, 'Look, here *is* the Christ!' or 'There!' do not believe *it.* 24For [a]false christs and false prophets will rise and show great signs and wonders to deceive, [b]if possible, even the elect. 25See, I have told you beforehand.

26"Therefore if they say to you, 'Look, He is in the desert!' do not go out; *or* 'Look, *He is* in the inner rooms!' do not believe *it.* 27[a]For as the lightning comes from the east and flashes to the west, so also will the coming of the Son of Man be. 28[a]For wherever the carcass is, there the eagles will be gathered together.

The Coming of the Son of Man
(Mark 13:24–27; Luke 21:25–28)

29[a]"Immediately after the tribulation of those days [b]the sun will be darkened, and the moon will not give its light; the stars will fall from heaven, and the powers of the heavens will be shaken. 30[a]Then the sign of the Son of Man will appear in heaven, [b]and then all the tribes of the earth will mourn, and they will see the Son of Man coming on the clouds of heaven with power and great glory. 31[a]And He will send His angels with a great sound of a trumpet, and they will gather together His elect from the four winds, from one end of heaven to the other.

The Parable of the Fig Tree
(Mark 13:28–31; Luke 21:29–33)

32"Now learn [a]this parable from the fig tree: When its branch has already become tender and puts forth leaves, you know that summer *is* near. 33So you also, when you see all these things, know [a]that it[1] is near—at the doors! 34Assuredly, I say to you, [a]this generation will by no means pass away till all these things take place. 35[a]Heaven and earth will pass away, but My words will by no means pass away.

No One Knows the Day or Hour
(Mark 13:32–37; Luke 17:26, 27, 34, 35; 21:34–36)

36[a]"But of that day and hour no one knows, not even the angels of heaven,[1]

24:6 [1] NU-Text omits *all.* **24:7** [a] 2 Chr. 15:6; Is. 19:2; Hag. 2:22; Zech. 14:13 [b] Acts 11:28; Rev. 6:5, 6 [1] NU-Text omits *pestilences.* **24:9** [a] Matt. 10:17; Luke 21:12; [John 16:2]; Acts 4:2, 3; Rev. 2:10 **24:11** [a] Acts 20:29; 2 Pet. 2:1; Rev. 13:11; 19:20 [b] [1 Tim. 4:1] **24:12** [a] [2 Thess. 2:3; 2 Tim. 3:1–3] **24:13** [a] Matt. 10:22; Mark 13:13 **24:14** [a] Matt. 4:23 [b] Rom. 10:18; Col. 1:6, 23 **24:15** [a] Mark 13:14; Luke 21:20; [John 11:48]; Acts 6:13; 21:28 [b] Dan. 9:27; 11:31; 12:11 [c] Dan. 9:23 [1] Daniel 11:31; 12:11 **24:19** [a] Luke 23:29 **24:21** [a] Dan. 9:26 **24:22** [a] Is. 65:8, 9; [Zech. 14:2] **24:23** [a] Mark 13:21; Luke 17:23 **24:24** [a] Deut. 13:1; John 4:48; [2 Thess. 2:9]; Rev. 13:13 [b] [John 6:37; Rom. 8:28; 2 Tim. 2:19] **24:27** [a] Luke 17:24 **24:28** [a] Job 39:30; Ezek. 39:17; Hab. 1:8; Luke 17:37 **24:29** [a] [Dan. 7:11] [b] Is. 13:10; 24:23; Ezek. 32:7; Joel 2:10, 31; 3:15; Amos 5:20; 8:9; Zeph. 1:15; Matt. 24:29–35; Acts 2:20; Rev. 6:12–17; 8:12 **24:30** [a] [Dan. 7:13, 14; Matt. 16:27; 24:3, 37, 39] [b] Zech. 12:12 **24:31** [a] Ex. 19:16; Deut. 30:4; Is. 27:13; Zech. 9:14; [1 Cor. 15:52; 1 Thess. 4:16]; Heb. 12:19; Rev. 8:2; 11:15 **24:32** [a] Luke 21:29 **24:33** [a] [James 5:9; Rev. 3:20] [1] Or *He* **24:34** [a] [Matt. 10:23; 16:28; 23:36] **24:35** [a] Ps. 102:25, 26; Is. 51:6; Mark 13:31; Luke 21:33; [1 Pet. 1:23–25; 2 Pet. 3:10] **24:36** [a] Mark 13:32; Acts 1:7; 1 Thess. 5:2; 2 Pet. 3:10 [1] NU-Text adds *nor the Son.*

[b]but My Father only. 37But as the days of
Noah *were,* so also will the coming of the
Son of Man be. 38[a]For as in the days before the flood, they were eating and drinking, marrying and giving in marriage, until
the day that Noah entered the ark, 39and
did not know until the flood came and
took them all away, so also will the coming of the Son of Man be. 40[a]Then two *men*
will be in the field: one will be taken and
the other left. 41Two *women will be* grinding at the mill: one will be taken and the
other left. 42[a]Watch therefore, for you do
not know what hour[1] your Lord is coming. 43[a]But know this, that if the master of
the house had known what hour the thief
would come, he would have watched and
not allowed his house to be broken into.
44[a]Therefore you also be ready, for the Son
of Man is coming at an hour you do not
expect.

The Faithful Servant and the Evil Servant
(Luke 12:41–48)

45[a]"Who then is a faithful and wise servant, whom his master made ruler over his
household, to give them food in due season? 46[a]Blessed *is* that servant whom his
master, when he comes, will find so doing. 47Assuredly, I say to you that [a]he will
make him ruler over all his goods. 48But if
that evil servant says in his heart, 'My master [a]is delaying his coming,'[1] 49and begins
to beat *his* fellow servants, and to eat and
drink with the drunkards, 50the master of
that servant will come on a day when he is
not looking for *him* and at an hour that he
is [a]not aware of, 51and will cut him in two
and appoint *him* his portion with the hypocrites. [a]There shall be weeping and gnashing of teeth.

The Parable of the Wise and Foolish Virgins

25 "Then the kingdom of heaven shall
be likened to ten virgins who took
their lamps and went out to meet [a]the
bridegroom. 2[a]Now five of them were wise,
and five *were* foolish. 3Those who *were* foolish took their lamps and took no oil with
them, 4but the wise took oil in their vessels with their lamps. 5But while the bridegroom was delayed, [a]they all slumbered
and slept.

6"And at midnight [a]a cry was *heard:* 'Behold, the bridegroom is coming;[1] go out to
meet him!' 7Then all those virgins arose
and [a]trimmed their lamps. 8And the foolish
said to the wise, 'Give us *some* of your oil,
for our lamps are going out.' 9But the wise
answered, saying, '*No,* lest there should not
be enough for us and you; but go rather
to those who sell, and buy for yourselves.'
10And while they went to buy, the bridegroom came, and those who were ready
went in with him to the wedding; and [a]the
door was shut.

11"Afterward the other virgins came also,
saying, [a]'Lord, Lord, open to us!' 12But he
answered and said, 'Assuredly, I say to you,
[a]I do not know you.'

13[a]"Watch therefore, for you [b]know neither the day nor the hour[1] in which the Son
of Man is coming.

The Parable of the Talents
(Luke 19:11–27)

14[a]"For *the kingdom of heaven is* [b]like a
man traveling to a far country, *who* called
his own servants and delivered his goods
to them. 15And to one he gave five talents,
to another two, and to another one, [a]to
each according to his own ability; and immediately he went on a journey. 16Then he
who had received the five talents went and
traded with them, and made another five
talents. 17And likewise he who *had received*
two gained two more also. 18But he who had
received one went and dug in the ground,
and hid his lord's money. 19After a long time
the lord of those servants came and settled
accounts with them.

20"So he who had received five talents came and brought five other talents,

---

24:36 [b] Zech. 14:7 24:38 [a] [Gen. 6:3–5]; Luke 17:26; [1 Pet. 3:20] 24:40 [a] Luke 17:34 24:42 [a] Matt. 25:13; Luke 21:36; 1 Thess. 5:6 [1] NU-Text reads *day.* 24:43 [a] Luke 12:39; 1 Thess. 5:2; Rev. 3:3 24:44 [a] Luke 12:35–40; [1 Thess. 5:6] 24:45 [a] Luke 12:42–46; [Acts 20:28] 24:46 [a] Rev. 16:15 24:47 [a] Matt. 25:21, 23; Luke 22:29 24:48 [a] [2 Pet. 3:4–9] [1] NU-Text omits *his coming.* 24:50 [a] Mark 13:32 24:51 [a] Matt. 8:12; 25:30 25:1 [a] [Eph. 5:29, 30; Rev. 19:7; 21:2, 9] 25:2 [a] Matt. 13:47; 22:10 25:5 [a] 1 Thess. 5:6 25:6 [a] [Matt. 24:31; 1 Thess. 4:16] [1] NU-Text omits *is coming.* 25:7 [a] Luke 12:35 25:10 [a] [Matt. 7:21]; Luke 13:25 25:11 [a] [Matt. 7:21–23; Luke 13:25–30] 25:12 [a] [Ps. 5:5; Hab. 1:13; John 9:31] 25:13 [a] Mark 13:35; [Luke 21:36]; 1 Thess. 5:6 [b] Matt. 24:36, 42 [1] NU-Text omits the rest of this verse. 25:14 [a] Luke 19:12–27 [b] Matt. 21:33 25:15 [a] [Rom. 12:6; 1 Cor. 12:7, 11, 29; Eph. 4:11]

saying, 'Lord, you delivered to me five talents; look, I have gained five more talents
besides them.' 21His lord said to him, 'Well
done, good and faithful servant; you were
[a]faithful over a few things, [b]I will make you
ruler over many things. Enter into [c]the joy
of your lord.' 22He also who had received
two talents came and said, 'Lord, you delivered to me two talents; look, I have gained
two more talents besides them.' 23His lord
said to him, [a]'Well *done,* good and faithful
servant; you have been faithful over a few
things, I will make you ruler over many
things. Enter into [b]the joy of your lord.'

24"Then he who had received the one
talent came and said, 'Lord, I knew you to
be a hard man, reaping where you have not
sown, and gathering where you have not
scattered seed. 25And I was afraid, and went
and hid your talent in the ground. Look,
there you have *what is* yours.'

26"But his lord answered and said to
him, 'You [a]wicked and lazy servant, you
knew that I reap where I have not sown, and
gather where I have not scattered seed. 27So
you ought to have deposited my money
with the bankers, and at my coming I would
have received back my own with interest.
28So take the talent from him, and give *it*
to him who has ten talents.

29[a]'For to everyone who has, more will
be given, and he will have abundance; but
from him who does not have, even what
he has will be taken away. 30And cast the
unprofitable servant [a]into the outer darkness. [b]There will be weeping and [c]gnash-
ing of teeth.'

The Son of Man Will Judge the Nations

31[a]"When the Son of Man comes in His
glory, and all the holy[1] angels with Him, then
He will sit on the throne of His glory. 32[a]All
the nations will be gathered before Him,
and [b]He will separate them one from another, as a shepherd divides *his* sheep from
the goats. 33And He will set the [a]sheep on
His right hand, but the goats on the left.
34Then the King will say to those on His right
hand, 'Come, you blessed of My Father, [a]in-
herit the kingdom [b]prepared for you from
the foundation of the world: 35[a]for I was
hungry and you gave Me food; I was thirsty
and you gave Me drink; [b]I was a stranger
and you took Me in; 36I *was* [a]naked and you
clothed Me; I was sick and you visited Me; [b]I
was in prison and you came to Me.'

37"Then the righteous will answer Him,
saying, 'Lord, when did we see You hungry
and feed *You,* or thirsty and give *You* drink?
38When did we see You a stranger and take
You in, or naked and clothe *You?* 39Or when
did we see You sick, or in prison, and come
to You?' 40And the King will answer and say
to them, 'Assuredly, I say to you, [a]inasmuch
as you did *it* to one of the least of these My
brethren, you did *it* to Me.'

41"Then He will also say to those on the left
hand, [a]'Depart from Me, you cursed, [b]into the
everlasting fire prepared for [c]the devil and
his angels: 42for I was hungry and you gave
Me no food; I was thirsty and you gave Me
no drink; 43I was a stranger and you did not
take Me in, naked and you did not clothe Me,
sick and in prison and you did not visit Me.'

44"Then they also will answer Him,[1] saying, 'Lord, when did we see You hungry or
thirsty or a stranger or naked or sick or in
prison, and did not minister to You?' 45Then
He will answer them, saying, 'Assuredly, I
say to you, [a]inasmuch as you did not do *it*
to one of the least of these, you did not do *it*
to Me.' 46And [a]these will go away into everlasting punishment, but the righteous into
eternal life."

The Plot to Kill Jesus
(Mark 14:1, 2; Luke 22:1, 2; John 11:45–53)

26 Now it came to pass, when Jesus
had finished all these sayings, *that*
He said to His disciples, 2[a]"You know that
after two days is the Passover, and the Son
of Man will be delivered up to be crucified."

25:21 [a] [Luke 16:10; 1 Cor. 4:2; 2 Tim. 4:7, 8] [b] [Matt. 24:47; 25:34, 46; Luke 12:44; 22:29, 30; Rev. 3:21; 21:7] [c] [2 Tim. 2:12; Heb. 12:2; 1 Pet. 1:8] 25:23 [a] Matt. 24:45, 47; 25:21 [b] [Ps. 16:11; John 15:10, 11] 25:26 [a] Matt. 18:32; Luke 19:22 25:29 [a] Matt. 13:12; Mark 4:25; Luke 8:18; [John 15:2] 25:30 [a] Matt. 8:12; 22:13; [Luke 13:28] [b] Matt. 7:23; 8:12; 24:51 [c] Ps. 112:10 25:31 [a] [Zech. 14:5]; Matt. 16:27; Mark 8:38; Acts 1:11; [1 Thess. 4:16]; 2 Thess. 1:7; [Jude 14]; Rev. 1:7 [1] NU-Text omits *holy.* 25:32 [a] [Rom. 14:10; 2 Cor. 5:10; Rev. 20:12] [b] Ezek. 20:38 25:33 [a] Ps. 79:13; 100:3; [John 10:11, 27, 28] 25:34 [a] [Rom. 8:17; 1 Pet. 1:4, 9; Rev. 21:7] [b] Matt. 20:23; Mark 10:40; 1 Cor. 2:9; Heb. 11:16 25:35 [a] Is. 58:7; Ezek. 18:7, 16; [James 1:27; 2:15, 16] [b] Job 31:32; [Heb. 13:2]; 3 John 5 25:36 [a] Is. 58:7; Ezek. 18:7, 16; [James 2:15, 16] [b] 2 Tim. 1:16 25:40 [a] Prov. 14:31; Matt. 10:42; Mark 9:41; Heb. 6:10 25:41 [a] Ps. 6:8; Matt. 7:23; Luke 13:27 [b] Matt. 13:40, 42 [c] [2 Pet. 2:4]; Jude 6 25:44 [1] NU-Text and M-Text omit *Him.* 25:45 [a] Prov. 14:31; Zech. 2:8; Acts 9:5 25:46 [a] [Dan. 12:2; John 5:29; Acts 24:15; Rom. 2:7] 26:2 [a] Matt. 27:35; Mark 14:1, 2; Luke 22:1, 2; John 13:1; 19:18

LIFE SUPPORT

BE A GIVER: OPEN YOUR HAND TO THE POOR

"And the King will answer and say to them, 'Assuredly, I say to you, inasmuch as you did it to one of the least of these My brethren, you did it to Me.'" Matthew 25:40

LIFE: Be a Giver

God is the greatest giver because He gave us the greatest gift: His only begotten Son. Jesus is our greatest gift, but far from our only one. The Bible shows us just how giving God is. Every good gift comes from God (see James 1:17). Every day is a gift from God. But beyond that, God gives us new mercies every day. God does this, in part, to show us the fundamentals of giving. Life is so much sweeter when we learn to give as God gives.

We are called to live as Jesus lived—to be His hands, feet, and voice to the world. The key is love. We cannot live the way He wants us to live if we do not love the way He wants us to love. Jesus made it clear that whatever we do for others, we do for Him. Thus, if we refuse to give to those in need, we have denied Jesus Himself.

SUPPORT: Open Your Hand to the Poor

What a cause! Give, serve, and care. Share what you have so that those less fortunate can be better because of your generosity. This is the example of our Lord and Savior. If we do not give when someone is in need, we fail to live in love. No one should go hungry while others have more than enough. As we profess our love for Christ, we should actively care for those in need.

To be poor is not only to lack food, clothing, or shelter. Some may be poor in spirit. Some may be brokenhearted. Some may be downtrodden. Some may be depressed. If others are thirsty, we must help them to the well. Christ's living water can fill their empty souls and allow them to rise above challenges and return to a healthy place. When we give to the poor, the Lord uses us to lift others and help them see His love for them.

SUPPORT EXAMPLE: Help feed and clothe the homeless.

3[a]Then the chief priests, the scribes,[1] and
the elders of the people assembled at the
palace of the high priest, who was called
Caiaphas, 4and [a]plotted to take Jesus by
trickery and kill *Him.* 5But they said, "Not
during the feast, lest there be an uproar
among the [a]people."

The Anointing at Bethany
(Mark 14:3–9; John 12:1–8)

6And when Jesus was in [a]Bethany at the
house of Simon the leper, 7a woman came to
Him having an alabaster flask of very costly
fragrant oil, and she poured *it* on His head as
He sat *at the table.* 8[a]But when His disciples
saw *it,* they were indignant, saying, "Why
this waste? 9For this fragrant oil might have
been sold for much and given to *the* poor."

10But when Jesus was aware of *it,* He said
to them, "Why do you trouble the woman?
For she has done a good work for Me. 11[a]For
you have the poor with you always, but [b]Me
you do not have always. 12For in pouring
this fragrant oil on My body, she did *it* for
My [a]burial. 13Assuredly, I say to you, wherever this gospel is preached in the whole
world, what this woman has done will also
be told as a memorial to her."

26:3 [a] Ps. 2:2; John 11:47; Acts 4:25 [1] NU-Text omits *the scribes.* 26:4 [a] John 11:47; Acts 4:25–28 26:5 [a] Matt. 21:26 26:6 [a] Matt. 8:2; Mark 14:3–9; Luke 7:37–39; John 11:1, 2; 12:1–8 26:8 [a] John 12:4 26:11 [a] [Deut. 15:11; Mark 14:7]; John 12:8 [b] [Matt. 18:20; 28:20; John 13:33; 14:19; 16:5, 28; 17:11] 26:12 [a] Matt. 27:60; Luke 23:53; John 19:38–42

Judas Agrees to Betray Jesus
(Mark 14:10, 11; Luke 22:3–6)

14 [a]Then one of the twelve, called [b]Judas Iscariot, went to the chief priests 15 and said, [a]"What are you willing to give me if I deliver Him to you?" And they counted out to him thirty pieces of silver. 16 So from that time he sought opportunity to betray Him.

Jesus Celebrates Passover with His Disciples
(Mark 14:12–21; Luke 22:7–13)

17 [a]Now on the first *day of the Feast* of the Unleavened Bread the disciples came to Jesus, saying to Him, "Where do You want us to prepare for You to eat the Passover?"

18 And He said, "Go into the city to a certain man, and say to him, 'The Teacher says, [a]"My time is at hand; I will keep the Passover at your house with My disciples."'"

19 So the disciples did as Jesus had directed them; and they prepared the Passover.

20 [a]When evening had come, He sat down with the twelve. 21 Now as they were eating, He said, "Assuredly, I say to you, one of you will [a]betray Me."

22 And they were exceedingly sorrowful, and each of them began to say to Him, "Lord, is it I?"

23 He answered and said, [a]"He who dipped *his* hand with Me in the dish will betray Me. 24 The Son of Man indeed goes just [a]as it is written of Him, but [b]woe to that man by whom the Son of Man is betrayed! [c]It would have been good for that man if he had not been born."

25 Then Judas, who was betraying Him, answered and said, "Rabbi, is it I?"

He said to him, "You have said it."

Jesus Institutes the Lord's Supper
(Mark 14:22–26; Luke 22:14–23; 1 Cor. 11:23–26)

26 [a]And as they were eating, [b]Jesus took bread, blessed[1] and broke *it,* and gave *it* to the disciples and said, "Take, eat; [c]this is My body."

27 Then He took the cup, and gave thanks, and gave *it* to them, saying, [a]"Drink from it, all of you. 28 For [a]this is My blood [b]of the new[1] covenant, which is shed [c]for many for the remission of sins. 29 But [a]I say to you, I will not drink of this fruit of the vine from now on [b]until that day when I drink it new with you in My Father's kingdom."

30 [a]And when they had sung a hymn, they went out to the Mount of Olives.

Jesus Predicts Peter's Denial
(Mark 14:27–31; Luke 22:31–34; John 13:36–38)

31 Then Jesus said to them, [a]"All of you will [b]be made to stumble because of Me this night, for it is written:

[c]'I will strike the Shepherd,
And the sheep of the flock
will be scattered.'[1]

32 But after I have been raised, [a]I will go before you to Galilee."

33 Peter answered and said to Him, "Even if all are made to stumble because of You, I will never be made to stumble."

34 Jesus said to him, [a]"Assuredly, I say to you that this night, before the rooster crows, you will deny Me three times."

35 Peter said to Him, "Even if I have to die with You, I will not deny You!"

And so said all the disciples.

The Prayer in the Garden
(Mark 14:32–42; Luke 22:39–46)

36 [a]Then Jesus came with them to a place called Gethsemane, and said to the disciples, "Sit here while I go and pray over there." 37 And He took with Him Peter and [a]the two sons of Zebedee, and He began to be sorrowful and deeply distressed. 38 Then He said to them, [a]"My soul is exceedingly sorrowful, even to death. Stay here and watch with Me."

26:14 [a] Mark 14:10, 11; Luke 22:3–6; John 13:2, 30 [b] Matt. 10:4 **26:15** [a] Ex. 21:32; Zech. 11:12; Matt. 27:3 **26:17** [a] Ex. 12:6, 18–20 **26:18** [a] Luke 9:51; John 12:23; 13:1; 17:1 **26:20** [a] Mark 14:17–21; Luke 22:14; John 13:21 **26:21** [a] Matt. 26:46; Mark 14:42; Luke 22:21–23; John 6:70, 71; 13:21 **26:23** [a] Ps. 41:9; Luke 22:21; John 13:18 **26:24** [a] Ps. 22; Dan. 9:26; Mark 9:12; Luke 24:25, 26, 46; Acts 17:2, 3; 26:22, 23; 1 Cor. 15:3 [b] Matt. 27:3–5; Luke 17:1; Acts 1:16–20 [c] John 17:12; Acts 1:25 **26:26** [a] Mark 14:22–25; Luke 22:17–20 [b] 1 Cor. 11:23–25 [c] [1 Pet. 2:24] [1] M-Text reads *gave thanks for.* **26:27** [a] Mark 14:23 **26:28** [a] [Ex. 24:8; Lev. 17:11; Heb. 9:20] [b] Jer. 31:31 [c] Matt. 20:28; [Rom. 5:15; Heb. 9:22] [1] NU-Text omits *new.* **26:29** [a] Mark 14:25; Luke 22:18 [b] Acts 10:41 **26:30** [a] Mark 14:26–31; Luke 22:31–34 **26:31** [a] Matt. 26:56; Mark 14:27; John 16:32 [b] [Matt. 11:6] [c] Zech. 13:7 [1] Zechariah 13:7 **26:32** [a] Matt. 28:7, 10, 16; Mark 14:28; 16:7; John 21:1 **26:34** [a] Matt. 26:74, 75; Mark 14:30; Luke 22:34; John 13:38 **26:36** [a] Mark 14:32–35; Luke 22:39, 40; John 18:1 **26:37** [a] Matt. 4:21; 17:1; Mark 5:37 **26:38** [a] John 12:27

39He went a little farther and fell on His
face, and [a]prayed, saying, [b]"O My Father, if
it is possible, [c]let this cup pass from Me;
nevertheless, [d]not as I will, but as You *will*."
40Then He came to the disciples and
found them sleeping, and said to Peter,
"What! Could you not watch with Me one
hour? 41[a]Watch and pray, lest you enter into
temptation. [b]The spirit indeed *is* willing,
but the flesh *is* weak."
42Again, a second time, He went away
and prayed, saying, "O My Father, if this
cup cannot pass away from Me unless[1] I
drink it, Your will be done." 43And He came
and found them asleep again, for their eyes
were heavy.
44So He left them, went away again, and
prayed the third time, saying the same
words. 45Then He came to His disciples
and said to them, "Are *you* still sleeping
and resting? Behold, the hour is at hand,
and the Son of Man is being [a]betrayed into
the hands of sinners. 46Rise, let us be going. See, My betrayer is at hand."

Betrayal and Arrest in Gethsemane

(Mark 14:43–52; Luke 22:47–53; John 18:1–11)

47And [a]while He was still speaking, behold, Judas, one of the twelve, with a great
multitude with swords and clubs, came
from the chief priests and elders of the
people.
48Now His betrayer had given them a
sign, saying, "Whomever I kiss, He is the
One; seize Him." 49Immediately he went
up to Jesus and said, "Greetings, Rabbi!"
[a]and kissed Him.
50But Jesus said to him, [a]"Friend, why
have you come?"
Then they came and laid hands on Jesus
and took Him. 51And suddenly, [a]one of
those *who were* with Jesus stretched out
his hand and drew his sword, struck the servant of the high priest, and cut off his ear.
52But Jesus said to him, "Put your sword
in its place, [a]for all who take the sword will
perish[1] by the sword. 53Or do you think that
I cannot now pray to My Father, and He will
provide Me with [a]more than twelve legions
of angels? 54How then could the Scriptures
be fulfilled, [a]that it must happen thus?"
55In that hour Jesus said to the multitudes, "Have you come out, as against a
robber, with swords and clubs to take Me?
I sat daily with you, teaching in the temple,
and you did not seize Me. 56But all this was
done that the [a]Scriptures of the prophets
might be fulfilled."
Then [b]all the disciples forsook Him and
fled.

Jesus Faces the Sanhedrin

(Mark 14:53–65; Luke 22:66–71; John 18:12–14, 19–24)

57[a]And those who had laid hold of Jesus
led *Him* away to Caiaphas the high priest,
where the scribes and the elders were assembled. 58But [a]Peter followed Him at a
distance to the high priest's courtyard. And
he went in and sat with the servants to see
the end.
59Now the chief priests, the elders,[1] and
all the council sought [a]false testimony
against Jesus to put Him to death, 60but
found none. Even though [a]many false witnesses came forward, they found none.[1] But
at last [b]two false witnesses[2] came forward
61and said, "This *fellow* said, [a]'I am able to
destroy the temple of God and to build it
in three days.'"
62[a]And the high priest arose and said to
Him, "Do You answer nothing? What *is it*
these men testify against You?" 63But [a]Jesus
kept silent. And the high priest answered
and said to Him, [b]"I put You under oath by
the living God: Tell us if You are the Christ,
the Son of God!"
64Jesus said to him, "*It is as* you said.
Nevertheless, I say to you, [a]hereafter you
will see the Son of Man [b]sitting at the right

26:39 [a] Mark 14:36; Luke 22:42; [Heb. 5:7–9] [b] John 12:27 [c] Matt. 20:22 [d] Ps. 40:8; Is. 50:5; John 5:30; 6:38; Phil. 2:8 **26:41** [a] Mark 13:33; 14:38; Luke 22:40, 46; [Eph. 6:18] [b] Ps. 103:14–16; [Rom. 7:15; 8:23; Gal. 5:17] **26:42** [1] NU-Text reads *if this may not pass away unless.* **26:45** [a] Matt. 17:22, 23; 20:18, 19 **26:47** [a] Mark 14:43–50; Luke 22:47–53; John 18:3–11; Acts 1:16 **26:49** [a] 2 Sam. 20:9; [Prov. 27:6] **26:50** [a] Ps. 41:9; 55:13 **26:51** [a] Mark 14:47; Luke 22:50; John 18:10 **26:52** [a] Gen. 9:6; Rev. 13:10 [1] M-Text reads *die.* **26:53** [a] 2 Kin. 6:17; Dan. 7:10 **26:54** [a] Is. 50:6; 53:2–11; Luke 24:25–27, 44–46; John 19:28; Acts 13:29; 17:3; 26:23 **26:56** [a] Lam. 4:20 [b] Zech. 13:7; Matt. 26:31; Mark 14:27; John 18:15 **26:57** [a] Matt. 17:22; Mark 14:53–65; Luke 22:54; John 18:12, 19–24 **26:58** [a] John 18:15, 16 **26:59** [a] Ex. 20:16; Ps. 35:11 [1] NU-Text omits *the elders.* **26:60** [a] Ps. 27:12; 35:11; Mark 14:55; Acts 6:13 [b] Deut. 19:15 [1] NU-Text puts a comma after *but found none,* does not capitalize *Even,* and omits *they found none.* [2] NU-Text omits *false witnesses.* **26:61** [a] Matt. 27:40; Mark 14:58; 15:29; John 2:19; Acts 6:14 **26:62** [a] Mark 14:60 **26:63** [a] Ps. 38:13, 14; Is. 53:7; Matt. 27:12, 14; Acts 8:32 [b] Lev. 5:1; 1 Sam. 14:24, 26; Luke 22:67–71 **26:64** [a] Dan. 7:13; Matt. 16:27; 24:30; 25:31; Luke 21:27; [John 1:51; Rom. 14:10; 1 Thess. 4:16]; Rev. 1:7 [b] Ps. 110:1; [Acts 7:55]

hand of the Power, and coming on the
clouds of heaven."
65[a]Then the high priest tore his clothes,
saying, "He has spoken blasphemy! What
further need do we have of witnesses?
Look, now you have heard His [b]blasphemy!
66What do you think?"
They answered and said, [a]"He is deserving of death."
67[a]Then they spat in His face and beat
Him; and [b]others struck *Him* with the
palms of their hands, 68saying, [a]"Prophesy to us, Christ! Who is the one who struck
You?"

Peter Denies Jesus, and Weeps Bitterly
(Mark 14:66–72; Luke 22:54–62; John 18:15–18, 25–27)

69[a]Now Peter sat outside in the courtyard. And a servant girl came to him, saying, "You also were with Jesus of Galilee."
70But he denied it before *them* all, saying, "I do not know what you are saying."
71And when he had gone out to the gateway, another *girl* saw him and said to those
who were there, "This *fellow* also was with
Jesus of Nazareth."
72But again he denied with an oath, "I
do not know the Man!"
73And a little later those who stood by
came up and said to Peter, "Surely you also
are *one* of them, for your [a]speech betrays
you."
74Then [a]he began to curse and swear,
saying, "I do not know the Man!"
Immediately a rooster crowed. 75And
Peter remembered the word of Jesus who
had said to him, [a]"Before the rooster crows,
you will deny Me three times." So he went
out and wept bitterly.

Jesus Handed Over to Pontius Pilate
(Mark 15:1; Luke 23:1; John 18:28)

27 When morning came, [a]all the chief
priests and elders of the people plotted against Jesus to put Him to death. 2And
when they had bound Him, they led Him
away and [a]delivered Him to Pontius[1] Pilate
the governor.

Judas Hangs Himself
(Acts 1:18, 19)

3[a]Then Judas, His betrayer, seeing that
He had been condemned, was remorseful
and brought back the thirty [b]pieces of silver
to the chief priests and elders, 4saying, "I
have sinned by betraying innocent blood."
And they said, "What *is that* to us? You
see *to it!*"
5Then he threw down the pieces of silver in the temple and [a]departed, and went
and hanged himself.
6But the chief priests took the silver
pieces and said, "It is not lawful to put them
into the treasury, because they are the price
of blood." 7And they consulted together
and bought with them the potter's field, to
bury strangers in. 8Therefore that field has
been called [a]the Field of Blood to this day.
9Then was fulfilled what was spoken by
Jeremiah the prophet, saying, [a]"And they
took the thirty pieces of silver, the value of
Him who was priced, whom they of the children of Israel priced, 10and [a]gave them for
the potter's field, as the LORD directed me."[1]

Jesus Faces Pilate
(Mark 15:2–5; Luke 23:2–5; John 18:29–38)

11Now Jesus stood before the governor.
[a]And the governor asked Him, saying, "Are
You the King of the Jews?"
Jesus said to him, [b]"*It is as* you say."
12And while He was being accused by the
chief priests and elders, [a]He answered
nothing.
13Then Pilate said to Him, [a]"Do You not
hear how many things they testify against
You?" 14But He answered him not one word,
so that the governor marveled greatly.

Taking the Place of Barabbas
(Mark 15:6–15; Luke 23:13–25; John 18:39, 40)

15[a]Now at the feast the governor was accustomed to releasing to the multitude one

---

26:65 [a] 2 Kin. 18:37 [b] John 10:30–36 **26:66** [a] Lev. 24:16; Matt. 20:18; John 19:7 **26:67** [a] Job 16:10; Is. 50:6; 53:3; Lam. 3:30; Matt. 27:30 [b] Mic. 5:1; Luke 22:63–65; John 19:3 **26:68** [a] Mark 14:65; Luke 22:64 **26:69** [a] Mark 14:66–72; Luke 22:55–62; John 18:16–18, 25–27 **26:73** [a] Mark 14:70; Luke 22:59; John 18:26 **26:74** [a] Matt. 26:34; Mark 14:71; Luke 22:34; John 13:38 **26:75** [a] Matt. 26:34; Luke 22:61; John 13:38 **27:1** [a] Ps. 2:2; Mark 15:1; Luke 22:66; 23:1; John 18:28 **27:2** [a] Matt. 20:19; Luke 18:32; Acts 3:13 [1] NU-Text omits *Pontius.* **27:3** [a] Matt. 26:14 [b] Matt. 26:15 **27:5** [a] 2 Sam. 17:23; Matt. 18:7; 26:24; John 17:12; Acts 1:18 **27:8** [a] Acts 1:19 **27:9** [a] Zech. 11:12 **27:10** [a] Jer. 32:6–9; Zech. 11:12, 13 [1] Jeremiah 32:6–9 **27:11** [a] Mark 15:2–5; Luke 23:2, 3; John 18:29–38 [b] John 18:37; 1 Tim. 6:13 **27:12** [a] Ps. 38:13, 14; Matt. 26:63; John 19:9 **27:13** [a] Matt. 26:62; John 19:10 **27:15** [a] Mark 15:6–15; Luke 23:17–25; John 18:39—19:16

prisoner whom they wished. 16And at that
time they had a notorious prisoner called
Barabbas.[1] 17Therefore, when they had gathered together, Pilate said to them, "Whom
do you want me to release to you? Barabbas, or Jesus who is called Christ?" 18For
he knew that they had handed Him over
because of [a]envy.

19While he was sitting on the judgment
seat, his wife sent to him, saying, "Have
nothing to do with that just Man, for I have
suffered many things today in a dream because of Him."

20[a]But the chief priests and elders persuaded the multitudes that they should ask
for Barabbas and destroy Jesus. 21The governor answered and said to them, "Which
of the two do you want me to release to
you?"

They said, [a]"Barabbas!"

22Pilate said to them, "What then shall I
do with Jesus who is called Christ?"

They all said to him, "Let Him be crucified!"

23Then the governor said, [a]"Why, what
evil has He done?"

But they cried out all the more, saying,
"Let Him be crucified!"

24When Pilate saw that he could not prevail at all, but rather *that* a tumult was rising, he [a]took water and washed *his* hands
before the multitude, saying, "I am innocent of the blood of this just Person.[1] You
see *to it.*"

25And all the people answered and said,
[a]"His blood *be* on us and on our children."

26Then he released Barabbas to them;
and when [a]he had scourged Jesus, he delivered *Him* to be crucified.

The Soldiers Mock Jesus
(Mark 15:16–20)

27[a]Then the soldiers of the governor took
Jesus into the Praetorium and gathered the
whole garrison around Him. 28And they
[a]stripped Him and [b]put a scarlet robe on
Him. 29[a]When they had twisted a crown
of thorns, they put *it* on His head, and a
reed in His right hand. And they bowed the
knee before Him and mocked Him, saying,
"Hail, King of the Jews!" 30Then [a]they spat
on Him, and took the reed and struck Him
on the head. 31And when they had mocked
Him, they took the robe off Him, put His
own clothes on Him, [a]and led Him away
to be crucified.

The King on a Cross
(Mark 15:21–32; Luke 23:26–43; John 19:17–27)

32[a]Now as they came out, [b]they found a
man of Cyrene, Simon by name. Him they
compelled to bear His cross. 33[a]And when
they had come to a place called Golgotha,
that is to say, Place of a Skull, 34[a]they gave
Him sour[1] wine mingled with gall to drink.
But when He had tasted *it,* He would not
drink.

35[a]Then they crucified Him, and divided
His garments, casting lots,[1] that it might be
fulfilled which was spoken by the prophet:

[b]"They divided My garments
among them,
And for My clothing they cast lots."[2]

36[a]Sitting down, they kept watch over Him
there. 37And they [a]put up over His head the
accusation written against Him:

THIS IS JESUS THE KING OF THE JEWS.

38[a]Then two robbers were crucified with
Him, one on the right and another on the
left.

39And [a]those who passed by blasphemed
Him, wagging their heads 40and saying,
[a]"You who destroy the temple and build *it*
in three days, save Yourself! [b]If You are the
Son of God, come down from the cross."

41Likewise the chief priests also, mocking with the scribes and elders,[1] said, 42"He

---

27:16 [1] NU Text reads *Jesus Barabbas.* **27:18** [a] Matt. 21:38; [John 15:22–25] **27:20** [a] Mark 15:11; Luke 23:18; John 18:40; Acts 3:14 **27:21** [a] Acts 3:14 **27:23** [a] Acts 3:13 **27:24** [a] Deut. 21:6–8 [1] NU-Text omits *just.* **27:25** [a] Deut. 19:10; Josh. 2:19; 2 Sam. 1:16; 1 Kin. 2:32; Acts 5:28 **27:26** [a] [Is. 50:6; 53:5]; Matt. 20:19; Mark 15:15; Luke 23:16, 24, 25; John 19:1, 16 **27:27** [a] Mark 15:16–20; John 19:2 **27:28** [a] Mark 15:17; John 19:2 [b] Luke 23:11 **27:29** [a] Ps. 69:19; Is. 53:3; Matt. 20:19; Mark 10:34; Luke 18:32 **27:30** [a] Is. 50:6; 52:14; Mic. 5:1; Matt. 26:67; Mark 10:34; 14:65; 15:19 **27:31** [a] Is. 53:7; Matt. 20:19 **27:32** [a] 1 Kin. 21:13; Acts 7:58; Heb. 13:12 [b] Mark 15:21; Luke 23:26; John 19:17 **27:33** [a] Mark 15:22–32; Luke 23:33–43; John 19:17 **27:34** [a] Ps. 69:21; Matt. 27:48 [1] NU-Text omits *sour.* **27:35** [a] Mark 15:24; Luke 23:34; John 19:24 [b] Ps. 22:18 [1] NU-Text and M-Text omit the rest of this verse. [2] Psalm 22:18 **27:36** [a] Ps. 22:17; Matt. 27:54 **27:37** [a] Mark 15:26; Luke 23:38; John 19:19 **27:38** [a] Is. 53:9, 12; Mark 15:27; Luke 23:32, 33; John 19:18 **27:39** [a] Job 16:4; Ps. 22:7; 109:25; Lam. 2:15; Mark 15:29; Luke 23:35 **27:40** [a] Matt. 26:61; John 2:19 [b] Matt. 26:63 **27:41** [1] M-Text reads *with the scribes, the Pharisees, and the elders.*

[a]saved others; Himself He cannot save. If
He is the King of Israel,[1] let Him now come
down from the cross, and we will believe
Him.[2] 43 [a]He trusted in God; let Him deliver
Him now if He will have Him; for He said,
'I am the Son of God.'"
44 [a]Even the robbers who were crucified
with Him reviled Him with the same thing.

Jesus Dies on the Cross
(Mark 15:33–41; Luke 23:44–49; John 19:28–30)

45 [a]Now from the sixth hour until the
ninth hour there was darkness over all the
land. 46 And about the ninth hour [a]Jesus
cried out with a loud voice, saying, "Eli, Eli,
lama sabachthani?" that is, [b]"My God, My
God, why have You forsaken Me?"[1]
47 Some of those who stood there, when
they heard *that,* said, "This Man is calling
for Elijah!" 48 Immediately one of them ran
and took a sponge, [a]filled *it* with sour wine
and put *it* on a reed, and offered it to Him
to drink.
49 The rest said, "Let Him alone; let us see
if Elijah will come to save Him."
50 And Jesus [a]cried out again with a loud
voice, and [b]yielded up His spirit.
51 Then, behold, [a]the veil of the temple
was torn in two from top to bottom; and
the earth quaked, and the rocks were split,
52 and the graves were opened; and many
bodies of the saints who had fallen asleep
were raised; 53 and coming out of the graves
after His resurrection, they went into the
holy city and appeared to many.
54 [a]So when the centurion and those with
him, who were guarding Jesus, saw the
earthquake and the things that had happened, they feared greatly, saying, [b]"Truly
this was the Son of God!"
55 And many women [a]who followed Jesus
from Galilee, ministering to Him, were
there looking on from afar, 56 [a]among whom

M A T T H E W 2 7 : 3 2

I AM SIMON OF CYRENE

Now as they came out, they found a man of Cyrene, Simon by name. Him they compelled to bear His cross. Matthew 27:32

I am Simon, a Jew from the North African country of Cyrene (now eastern Libya). My two sons, Alexander and Rufus, were Christian missionaries who, with Paul, spread the gospel. Paul even mentioned in his letters that my wife was like a mother to him.

Much earlier, I was in Jerusalem for the Passover and happened to pass by a procession of Romans leading some poor soul struggling to carry a cross. As the man began to fall under the weight of the cross, the centurion grabbed me and made me carry this man's heavy cross to a nearby hill called Golgotha. There, this man named Jesus was crucified.

✝

Nothing is ever by chance with God. Simon of Cyrene must have thought he was the unluckiest of men to have crossed the path of the centurions just as they needed someone to carry Jesus' cross. But this North African man will forever be remembered for that "unlucky" act and his participation in the crucifixion story. He had just a quick glimpse of Jesus, but perhaps that is all he needed. That one encounter likely led to his whole family coming to know Christ. One interaction may be all it takes for others to see Christ in you. We are never to be bystanders when we have the opportunity to help others have an encounter with the cross.

27:42 [a] [Matt. 18:11; John 3:14, 15] [1] NU-Text reads *He is the King of Israel!* [2] NU-Text and M-Text read *we will believe in Him.* **27:43** [a] Ps. 22:8 **27:44** [a] Mark 15:32; Luke 23:39–43 **27:45** [a] Amos 8:9; Mark 15:33–41; Luke 23:44–49 **27:46** [a] [Heb. 5:7] [b] Ps. 22:1 [1] Psalm 22:1 **27:48** [a] Ps. 69:21; Mark 15:36; Luke 23:36; John 19:29 **27:50** [a] Mark 15:37; Luke 23:46; John 19:30 [b] Dan. 9:26; Zech. 11:10, 11; Matt. 17:23; [John 10:18; 1 Cor. 15:3] **27:51** [a] Ex. 26:31; 2 Chr. 3:14; Zech. 11:10; Mark 15:38; Luke 23:45; Heb. 9:3 **27:54** [a] Mark 15:39; Luke 23:47 [b] Matt. 14:33 **27:55** [a] Mark 15:41; Luke 8:2, 3 **27:56** [a] Matt. 28:1; Mark 15:40, 47; 16:9; Luke 8:2; John 19:25; 20:1, 18

were Mary Magdalene, Mary the mother of James and Joses,[1] and the mother of Zebedee's sons.

Jesus Buried in Joseph's Tomb
(Mark 15:42–47; Luke 23:50–56; John 19:38–42)

57 Now [a]when evening had come, there came a rich man from Arimathea, named Joseph, who himself had also become a disciple of Jesus. 58 This man went to Pilate and asked for the body of Jesus. Then Pilate commanded the body to be given to him. 59 When Joseph had taken the body, he wrapped it in a clean linen cloth, 60 and [a]laid it in his new tomb which he had hewn out of the rock; and he rolled a large stone against the door of the tomb, and departed. 61 And Mary Magdalene was there, and the other Mary, sitting opposite the tomb.

Pilate Sets a Guard

62 On the next day, which followed the Day of Preparation, the chief priests and Pharisees gathered together to Pilate, 63 saying, "Sir, we remember, while He was still alive, how that deceiver said, [a]'After three days I will rise.' 64 Therefore command that the tomb be made secure until the third day, lest His disciples come by night[1] and steal Him *away,* and say to the people, 'He has risen from the dead.' So the last deception will be worse than the first."

65 Pilate said to them, "You have a guard; go your way, make *it* as secure as you know how." 66 So they went and made the tomb secure, [a]sealing the stone and setting the guard.

He Is Risen
(Mark 16:1–8; Luke 24:1–12; John 20:1–10)

28 Now [a]after the Sabbath, as the first *day* of the week began to dawn, Mary Magdalene [b]and the other Mary came to see the tomb. 2 And behold, there was a great earthquake; for [a]an angel of the Lord descended from heaven, and came and rolled back the stone from the door,[1] and sat on it. 3 [a]His countenance was like lightning, and his clothing as white as snow. 4 And the guards shook for fear of him, and became like [a]dead *men.*

5 But the angel answered and said to the women, "Do not be afraid, for I know that you seek Jesus who was crucified. 6 He is not here; for He is risen, [a]as He said. Come, see the place where the Lord lay. 7 And go quickly and tell His disciples that He is risen from the dead, and indeed [a]He is going before you into Galilee; there you will see Him. Behold, I have told you."

8 So they went out quickly from the tomb with fear and great joy, and ran to bring His disciples word.

The Women Worship the Risen Lord

9 And as they went to tell His disciples,[1] behold, [a]Jesus met them, saying, "Rejoice!" So they came and held Him by the feet and worshiped Him. 10 Then Jesus said to them, "Do not be afraid. Go *and* tell [a]My brethren to go to Galilee, and there they will see Me."

The Soldiers Are Bribed

11 Now while they were going, behold, some of the guard came into the city and reported to the chief priests all the things that had happened. 12 When they had assembled with the elders and consulted together, they gave a large sum of money to the soldiers, 13 saying, "Tell them, 'His disciples came at night and stole Him *away* while we slept.' 14 And if this comes to the governor's ears, we will appease him and make you secure." 15 So they took the money and did as they were instructed; and this saying is commonly reported among the Jews until this day.

The Great Commission
(Mark 16:14–18; Luke 24:36–49; John 20:19–23; Acts 1:6–8)

16 Then the eleven disciples went away into Galilee, to the mountain [a]which Jesus had appointed for them. 17 When they saw

27:56 [1] NU-Text reads *Joseph.* **27:57** [a] Mark 15:42–47; Luke 23:50–56; John 19:38–42 **27:60** [a] Is. 53:9; Matt. 26:12 **27:63** [a] Matt. 16:21; 17:23; 20:19; 26:61; Mark 8:31; 10:34; Luke 9:22; 13:33; 24:6, 7; John 2:19 **27:64** [1] NU-Text omits *by night.* **27:66** [a] Dan. 6:17 **28:1** [a] Mark 16:1–8; Luke 24:1–10; John 20:1–8 [b] Matt. 27:56, 61 **28:2** [a] Mark 16:5; Luke 24:4; John 20:12 [1] NU-Text omits *from the door.* **28:3** [a] Dan. 7:9; 10:6; Mark 9:3; John 20:12; Acts 1:10 **28:4** [a] Rev. 1:17 **28:6** [a] Hos. 6:2; Ps. 16:10; 49:15; Matt. 12:40; 16:21; 17:23; 20:19 **28:7** [a] Matt. 26:32; 28:10, 16; Mark 16:7 **28:9** [a] Mark 16:9; John 20:14 [1] NU-Text omits the first clause of this verse. **28:10** [a] Ps. 22:22; John 20:17; Rom. 8:29; [Heb. 2:11] **28:16** [a] Matt. 26:32; 28:7, 10; Mark 14:28; 15:41; 16:7

Him, they worshiped Him; but some
[a]doubted.
18And Jesus came and spoke to them,
saying, [a]"All authority has been given to
Me in heaven and on earth. 19[a]Go therefore[1] and [b]make disciples of all the nations,
baptizing them in the name of the Father
and of the Son and of the Holy Spirit,
20[a]teaching them to observe all things
that I have commanded you; and lo, I am
[b]with you always, *even* to the end of the
age." Amen.[1]

28:17 [a] John 20:24–29 28:18 [a] [Dan. 7:13, 14]; Matt. 11:27; Luke 1:32; 10:22; John 3:35; Acts 2:36; Rom. 14:9; 1 Cor. 15:27; [Eph. 1:10, 21]; Phil. 2:9, 10; [Heb. 1:2]; 1 Pet. 3:22 28:19 [a] Mark 16:15 [b] Is. 52:10; Luke 24:47; [Acts 2:38, 39]; Rom. 10:18; Col. 1:23 [1] M-Text omits *therefore.* 28:20 [a] [Acts 2:42] [b] [Acts 4:31; 18:10; 23:11] [1] NU-Text omits *Amen.*

THE GOSPEL ACCORDING TO

MARK

OVERVIEW

While the Gospel of Matthew appears first in the New Testament, the Gospel of Mark is often considered the oldest Gospel. Mark is the shortest of all four Gospels, and many scholars believe that Luke and Matthew used Mark's account as a primary source for their own. For this reason, given the stark similarities in the details and sequence of events, these Gospels are called the Synoptic Gospels. Only the Gospel according to John stands alone in its style, content, and sequence. The early church assigned a symbolic image to each of the four Gospels that personifies the unique contribution of each. Matthew is depicted by an angel, Luke by an ox, and John by an eagle. Mark's Gospel is depicted by a lion. Mark was written by the cousin of Barnabas and son of the woman in whose home the early church often gathered. He is also known as John Mark.

While Matthew's Gospel was written largely to a Hebrew audience, Mark's Gospel was intended for Gentiles living within the Roman Empire. As such, Mark seldom quoted the Old Testament and took time to describe Jewish customs that were likely unfamiliar to non-Jewish readers.

All four Gospels have similar themes, yet each has attributes clearly distinguishing it from the other accounts. In Mark's Gospel, Jesus is uniquely portrayed as a Suffering Servant who serves suffering people. Jesus Christ does two things in Mark's Gospel that epitomize this central theme. First, Christ commends service to His disciples. Second, He exemplifies service to His disciples.

When Jesus' disciples were angling for status and seats of power, Jesus instead advocated service as the highest ambition of His kingdom. Jesus expressed His way simply: "Whoever desires to become great among you shall be your servant" (Mark 10:43). Mark then proves that service is not just what Jesus demanded from His disciples but is an ethic that He embodies. Jesus exemplifies this notion of the selfless servant two verses later: "For even the Son of Man did not come to be served, but to serve, and to give His life a ransom for many" (v. 45).

While Mark is the shortest of the four Gospels, it includes the most miracles. These miracles are tangible demonstrations of the authority of Christ but also demonstrated His desire to serve humanity. While other Gospels record more content about the messages and discourse of Jesus, Mark clearly focuses more on the actions of Jesus, who did not stand by idly in the face of human suffering. Jesus always met human needs with compassion.

BREATHE IT IN

Many of us think that the suffering in the world is so enormous that there is nothing we can do about it. But there are many examples of one person's suffering, persistence, and advocacy making a significant impact on the suffering of others.

On August 31, 1997, the world was stunned at the news of the tragic death of Princess Diana of Wales, who succumbed to injuries suffered in a car accident. The entire world mourned the loss of a philanthropic, servant-minded member of the British monarchy. There is no way to sum up the enormity of the loss. Princess "Di" had used her prominence to raise money for, and bring international attention to, egregious human suffering. She had advocated for children, warned of the danger of land mines to civilian populations, brought to light the generational effects of poverty, championed HIV/AIDS research, and promoted care for people all around the globe.

Six days after the death of Princess Di, the world mourned yet another servant of humanity when Mother Teresa of Calcutta passed away. Her lifetime of Christian service took place among the most economically deprived regions of the world. She had led a cadre of initiatives that provided free health care, food, and shelter to the poorest of the poor. When asked about how she was able to bear all the suffering and death that she had witnessed in her lifetime, she said to her official biographer, "We are called upon not to be successful, but to be faithful."[1]

Dr. Martin Luther King Jr. urged every one of us to take action. He called on each person to create the "beloved community" by adopting nonviolent social change as a lifestyle and a blueprint to address the suffering of the world, brought about by the many sins of the world, including institutions of economic and social injustice, poverty, racism, and militarism.

So, we are not to be passive bystanders, which often happens in the face of suffering and injustice that everyone can see. No one acts because everyone believes that someone else will. But we live in a fallen world that is quickly declining. There is no time to sit back and wait for someone else to act. The someone must be us.

Princess Diana of Wales, Teresa of Calcutta, and Dr. Martin Luther King Jr. are all wonderful examples of Christ-inspired service. They refused to be bystanders. Children's Defense Fund founder and fellow believer Marian Wright Edelman encapsulates their love in action when she stated, "Service is the rent you pay for being. It is the very purpose of life and not something you do in your spare time."[2] We must pick up the mantle of service to the suffering. We can exercise our faith by addressing the suffering of the world, one person at a time, through acts of love. In our own suffering we must not quit but use it to affect the world around us for Christ. By doing so we share in Christ's suffering for the world and turn a bitter pill into something sweet.

So, we should ask ourselves, what is our response to human suffering? Are we guilty of being bystanders to human suffering in our communities? How does service as defined by the ministry of Jesus Christ manifest in our family life? How do we cultivate service among our friends, siblings, and children? We may not like some of the ways we answer these questions, but the good news is that we have the power to change our answers in the future. We can become more servantlike in our families, social circles, and communities.

First, list the greatest needs in your community. You might turn your attention toward the criminal justice or educational system. Maybe there is a lack of nutritional foods or foster parents in your community. Ask yourself where the most acute suffering exists around you. Then, consider what problems you are best equipped to address.

Second, discover who in your community is already working on the problems you have identified. Solving a problem that already has a solution or has one in motion is redundant. Be willing to partner and collaborate with other individuals, organizations, or churches that have a track record of making a difference.

Third, give. To attack the human suffering and racial and economic disparities of our time, contribute financially, as much as you are able. Giving of your time and talents is just as important. As you contribute, be sure to include your children. Remember, Jesus called for acts of service and modeled service to His disciples so that they would be better able to serve on their own. The same is true of those of us who are parents. When we involve our children, our efforts will continue well into the future through them.

†

[1] Navin Chawla, *Mother Teresa: The Authorized Biography* (Element Books, 1996).

[2] Marian Wright Edelman, *The Measure of Our Success: A Letter to My Children and Yours* (New York: Harper Perennial, 1993).

THE GOSPEL ACCORDING TO

MARK

John the Baptist Prepares the Way
(Matt. 3:1–12; Luke 3:1–20; John 1:19–28)

1 The [a]beginning of the gospel of Jesus Christ, [b]the Son of God. 2 As it is written in the Prophets:[1]

> [a]"Behold, I send My messenger
> before Your face,
> Who will prepare Your
> way before You."[2]

> 3 "The[a] voice of one crying
> in the wilderness:
> 'Prepare the way of the LORD;
> Make His paths straight.' "[1]

4 [a]John came baptizing in the wilderness and preaching a baptism of repentance for the remission of sins. 5 [a]Then all the land of Judea, and those from Jerusalem, went out to him and were all baptized by him in the Jordan River, confessing their sins. 6 Now John was [a]clothed with camel's hair and with a leather belt around his waist, and he ate locusts and wild honey. 7 And he preached, saying, [a]"There comes One after me who is mightier than I, whose sandal strap I am not worthy to stoop down and loose. 8 [a]I indeed baptized you with water, but He will baptize you [b]with the Holy Spirit."

John Baptizes Jesus
(Matt. 3:13–17; Luke 3:21, 22; John 1:29–34)

9 [a]It came to pass in those days *that* Jesus came from Nazareth of Galilee, and was baptized by John in the Jordan. 10 [a]And immediately, coming up from[1] the water, He saw the heavens parting and the Spirit [b]descending upon Him like a dove. 11 Then a voice came from heaven, [a]"You are My beloved Son, in whom I am well pleased."

Satan Tempts Jesus
(Matt. 4:1–11; Luke 4:1–13)

12 [a]Immediately the Spirit drove Him into the wilderness. 13 And He was there in the wilderness forty days, tempted by Satan, and was with the wild beasts; [a]and the angels ministered to Him.

Jesus Begins His Galilean Ministry
(Matt. 4:12–17; Luke 4:14, 15)

14 [a]Now after John was put in prison, Jesus came to Galilee, [b]preaching the gospel of the kingdom[1] of God, 15 and saying, [a]"The time is fulfilled, and [b]the kingdom of God is at hand. Repent, and believe in the gospel."

Four Fishermen Called as Disciples
(Matt. 4:18–22; Luke 5:1–11)

16 [a]And as He walked by the Sea of Galilee, He saw Simon and Andrew his brother casting a net into the sea; for they were fishermen. 17 Then Jesus said to them, "Follow Me, and I will make you become [a]fishers of men." 18 [a]They immediately left their nets and followed Him.

19 When He had gone a little farther from there, He saw James the *son* of Zebedee, and John his brother, who also *were* in the boat mending their nets. 20 And immediately He

---

1:1 [a] Matt. 1:1; 3:1; Luke 3:22 [b] Ps. 2:7; Matt. 14:33; Luke 1:35 1:2 [a] Mal. 3:1; Matt. 11:10; Luke 7:27 [1] NU-Text reads *Isaiah the prophet.* [2] Malachi 3:1 1:3 [a] Is. 40:3; Matt. 3:3; Luke 3:4; John 1:23 [1] Isaiah 40:3 1:4 [a] Mal. 4:6; Matt. 3:1; Luke 3:3 1:5 [a] Matt. 3:5 1:6 [a] Matt. 3:4 1:7 [a] Matt. 3:11; John 1:27; Acts 13:25 1:8 [a] Acts 1:5; 11:16 [b] Is. 44:3; John 20:22; [Acts 2:4; 10:45, 46; 1 Cor. 12:13] 1:9 [a] Matt. 3:13–17; Luke 3:21, 22 1:10 [a] Ezek. 1:1; Matt. 3:16; John 1:32 [b] Is. 11:2; 61:1; Acts 10:38 [1] NU-Text reads *out of.* 1:11 [a] [Ps. 2:7]; Is. 42:1; Matt. 3:17; 12:18; Mark 9:7; Luke 3:22 1:12 [a] Matt. 4:1–11; Luke 4:1–13 1:13 [a] Matt. 4:10, 11 1:14 [a] Matt. 4:12 [b] Matt. 4:23 [1] NU-Text omits *of the kingdom.* 1:15 [a] Dan. 9:25; [Gal. 4:4; Eph. 1:10; 1 Tim. 2:6]; Titus 1:3 [b] Matt. 3:2; 4:17; [Acts 20:21] 1:16 [a] Matt. 4:18–22; Luke 5:2–11; John 1:40–42 1:17 [a] Matt. 13:47, 48 1:18 [a] Matt. 19:27; [Luke 14:26]

called them, and they left their father Zebedee in the boat with the hired servants,
and went after Him.

Jesus Casts Out an Unclean Spirit
(Luke 4:31–37)

21 [a]Then they went into Capernaum, and
immediately on the Sabbath He entered the
[b]synagogue and taught. 22 [a]And they were
astonished at His teaching, for He taught
them as one having authority, and not as
the scribes.

23 Now there was a man in their synagogue with an [a]unclean spirit. And he cried
out, 24 saying, "Let *us* alone! [a]What have we
to do with You, Jesus of Nazareth? Did You
come to destroy us? I [b]know who You are—
the [c]Holy One of God!"

25 But Jesus [a]rebuked him, saying, "Be
quiet, and come out of him!" 26 And when
the unclean spirit [a]had convulsed him
and cried out with a loud voice, he came
out of him. 27 Then they were all amazed,
so that they questioned among themselves, saying, "What is this? What new
doctrine *is* this? For with authority[1] He
commands even the unclean spirits, and
they obey Him." 28 And immediately His
[a]fame spread throughout all the region
around Galilee.

Peter's Mother-in-Law Healed
(Matt. 8:14, 15; Luke 4:38, 39)

29 [a]Now as soon as they had come out of
the synagogue, they entered the house of
Simon and Andrew, with James and John.
30 But Simon's wife's mother lay sick with a
fever, and they told Him about her at once.
31 So He came and took her by the hand and
lifted her up, and immediately the fever left
her. And she served them.

Many Healed After Sabbath Sunset
(Matt. 8:16, 17; Luke 4:40, 41)

32 [a]At evening, when the sun had set,
they brought to Him all who were sick and
those who were demon-possessed. 33 And
the whole city was gathered together at the
door. 34 Then He healed many who were sick
with various diseases, and [a]cast out many
demons; and He [b]did not allow the demons
to speak, because they knew Him.

Preaching in Galilee
(Matt. 4:23–25; Luke 4:42–44)

35 Now [a]in the morning, having risen a
long while before daylight, He went out and
departed to a solitary place; and there He
[b]prayed. 36 And Simon and those *who were*
with Him searched for Him. 37 When they
found Him, they said to Him, [a]"Everyone
[b]is looking for You."

38 But He said to them, [a]"Let us go into
the next towns, that I may preach there
also, because [b]for this purpose I have come
forth."

39 [a]And He was preaching in their synagogues throughout all Galilee, and [b]cast-
ing out demons.

Jesus Cleanses a Leper
(Matt. 8:1–4; Luke 5:12–16)

40 [a]Now a leper came to Him, imploring
Him, kneeling down to Him and saying
to Him, "If You are willing, You can make
me clean."

41 Then Jesus, moved with [a]compas-
sion, stretched out *His* hand and touched
him, and said to him, "I am willing; be
cleansed." 42 As soon as He had spoken,
[a]immediately the leprosy left him, and he
was cleansed. 43 And He strictly warned
him and sent him away at once, 44 and said
to him, "See that you say nothing to anyone; but go your way, show yourself to the
priest, and offer for your cleansing those
things [a]which Moses commanded, as a testimony to them."

45 [a]However, he went out and began to
proclaim *it* freely, and to spread the matter, so that Jesus could no longer openly
enter the city, but was outside in deserted
places; [b]and they came to Him from every
direction.

1:21 [a] Matt. 4:13; Luke 4:31–37 [b] Ps. 22:22; Matt. 4:23; Luke 4:16; 13:10 **1:22** [a] Matt. 7:28, 29; 13:54 **1:23** [a] [Matt. 12:43]; Mark 5:2; 7:25; Luke 4:33 **1:24** [a] Matt. 8:28, 29; Mark 5:7, 8; Luke 8:28 [b] Mark 3:11; Luke 4:41; James 2:19 [c] Ps. 16:10 **1:25** [a] [Luke 4:39] **1:26** [a] Mark 9:20 **1:27** [1] NU-Text reads *What is this? A new doctrine with authority.* **1:28** [a] Matt. 4:24; 9:31 **1:29** [a] Matt. 8:14, 15; Luke 4:38, 39 **1:32** [a] Matt. 8:16, 17; Luke 4:40, 41 **1:34** [a] Matt. 9:33; Luke 13:32 [b] Mark 3:12; Luke 4:41; Acts 16:17, 18 **1:35** [a] Luke 4:42, 43 [b] Matt. 26:39, 44; Mark 6:46; Luke 5:16; 6:12; 9:28, 29; Heb. 5:7 **1:37** [a] Matt. 4:25; John 3:26; 12:19 [b] [Heb. 11:6] **1:38** [a] Luke 4:43 [b] [Is. 61:1, 2; Mark 10:45; John 16:28; 17:4, 8] **1:39** [a] Ps. 22:22; Matt. 4:23; 9:35; Mark 1:21; 3:1; Luke 4:44 [b] Mark 5:8, 13; 7:29, 30 **1:40** [a] Matt. 8:2–4; Luke 5:12–14 **1:41** [a] Luke 7:13 **1:42** [a] Matt. 15:28; Mark 5:29 **1:44** [a] Lev. 14:1–32 **1:45** [a] Matt. 28:15; Luke 5:15 [b] Mark 2:2, 13; 3:7; Luke 5:17; John 6:2

Jesus Forgives and Heals a Paralytic
(Matt. 9:2–8; Luke 5:17–26)

2 And again [a]He entered Capernaum after *some* days, and it was heard that
He was in the house. 2 Immediately[1] many
gathered together, so that there was no longer room to receive *them,* not even near the
door. And He preached the word to them.
3 Then they came to Him, bringing a [a]par-
alytic who was carried by four *men.* 4 And
when they could not come near Him because of the crowd, they uncovered the roof
where He was. So when they had broken
through, they let down the bed on which
the paralytic was lying.
5 When Jesus saw their faith, He said to
the paralytic, "Son, your sins are forgiven
you."
6 And some of the scribes were sitting
there and reasoning in their hearts, 7 "Why
does this *Man* speak blasphemies like this?
[a]Who can forgive sins but God alone?"
8 But immediately, when Jesus perceived
in His spirit that they reasoned thus within
themselves, He said to them, "Why do you
reason about these things in your hearts?
9 [a]Which is easier, to say to the paralytic,
'*Your* sins are forgiven you,' or to say, 'Arise,
take up your bed and walk'? 10 But that you
may know that the Son of Man has power
on earth to forgive sins"—He said to the
paralytic, 11 "I say to you, arise, take up your
bed, and go to your house." 12 Immediately
he arose, took up the bed, and went out in
the presence of them all, so that all were
amazed and [a]glorified God, saying, "We
never saw *anything* like this!"

Matthew the Tax Collector
(Matt. 9:9–13; Luke 5:27–32)

13 [a]Then He went out again by the sea;
and all the multitude came to Him, and
He taught them. 14 [a]As He passed by, He saw
Levi the *son* of Alphaeus sitting at the tax
office. And He said to him, [b]"Follow Me."
So he arose and [c]followed Him.
15 [a]Now it happened, as He was dining in
Levi's house, that many tax collectors and
sinners also sat together with Jesus and His
disciples; for there were many, and they
followed Him. 16 And when the scribes and[1]
Pharisees saw Him eating with the tax collectors and sinners, they said to His disciples, "How *is it* that He eats and drinks with
tax collectors and sinners?"
17 When Jesus heard *it,* He said to them,
[a]"Those who are well have no need of a physician, but those who are sick. I did not
come to call *the* righteous, but sinners, to
repentance."[1]

Jesus Is Questioned About Fasting
(Matt. 9:14–17; Luke 5:33–39)

18 [a]The disciples of John and of the Pharisees were fasting. Then they came and said
to Him, "Why do the disciples of John and
of the Pharisees fast, but Your disciples
do not fast?"
19 And Jesus said to them, "Can the
friends of the bridegroom fast while the
bridegroom is with them? As long as they
have the bridegroom with them they cannot fast. 20 But the days will come when the
bridegroom will be [a]taken away from them,
and then they will fast in those days. 21 No
one sews a piece of unshrunk cloth on an
old garment; or else the new piece pulls
away from the old, and the tear is made
worse. 22 And no one puts new wine into
old wineskins; or else the new wine bursts
the wineskins, the wine is spilled, and the
wineskins are ruined. But new wine must
be put into new wineskins."

Jesus Is Lord of the Sabbath
(Matt. 12:1–8; Luke 6:1–5)

23 [a]Now it happened that He went
through the grainfields on the Sabbath;
and as they went His disciples began [b]to
pluck the heads of grain. 24 And the Pharisees said to Him, "Look, why do they do
what is [a]not lawful on the Sabbath?"
25 But He said to them, "Have you never
read [a]what David did when he was in need
and hungry, he and those with him: 26 how
he went into the house of God *in the days* of
Abiathar the high priest, and ate the showbread, [a]which is not lawful to eat except for

---

2:1 [a] Matt. 9:1 **2:2** [1] NU-Text omits *Immediately.* **2:3** [a] Matt. 4:24; 8:6; Acts 8:7; 9:33 **2:7** [a] Job 14:4; Is. 43:25; Dan. 9:9 **2:9** [a] Matt. 9:5 **2:12** [a] Matt. 15:31; [Phil. 2:11] **2:13** [a] Matt. 9:9 **2:14** [a] Matt. 9:9–13; Luke 5:27–32 [b] Matt. 4:19; 8:22; 19:21; John 1:43; 12:26; 21:22 [c] Luke 18:28 **2:15** [a] Matt. 9:10 **2:16** [1] NU-Text reads *of the.* **2:17** [a] Matt. 9:12, 13; 18:11; Luke 5:31, 32; 19:10 [1] NU-Text omits *to repentance.* **2:18** [a] Matt. 9:14–17; Luke 5:33–38 **2:20** [a] Acts 1:9; 13:2, 3; 14:23 **2:23** [a] Matt. 12:1–8; Luke 6:1–5 [b] Deut. 23:25 **2:24** [a] Ex. 20:10; 31:15 **2:25** [a] 1 Sam. 21:1–6 **2:26** [a] Ex. 29:32, 33; Lev. 24:5–9

the priests, and also gave some to those who were with him?"

27And He said to them, "The Sabbath was made for man, and not man for the [a]Sabbath. 28Therefore [a]the Son of Man is also Lord of the Sabbath."

Healing on the Sabbath
(Matt. 12:9–14; Luke 6:6–11)

3 And [a]He entered the synagogue again, and a man was there who had a withered hand. 2So they [a]watched Him closely, whether He would [b]heal him on the Sabbath, so that they might accuse Him. 3And He said to the man who had the withered hand, "Step forward." 4Then He said to them, "Is it lawful on the Sabbath to do good or to do evil, to save life or to kill?" But they kept silent. 5And when He had looked around at them with anger, being grieved by the [a]hardness of their hearts, He said to the man, "Stretch out your hand." And he stretched *it* out, and his hand was restored as whole as the other.[1] 6[a]Then the Pharisees went out and immediately plotted with [b]the Herodians against Him, how they might destroy Him.

A Great Multitude Follows Jesus
(Matt. 12:15–21)

7But Jesus withdrew with His disciples to the sea. And a great multitude from Galilee followed Him, [a]and from Judea 8and Jerusalem and Idumea and beyond the Jordan; and those from Tyre and Sidon, a great multitude, when they heard how [a]many things He was doing, came to Him. 9So He told His disciples that a small boat should be kept ready for Him because of the multitude, lest they should crush Him. 10For He healed [a]many, so that as many as had afflictions pressed about Him to [b]touch Him. 11[a]And the unclean spirits, whenever they saw Him, fell down before Him and cried out, saying, [b]"You are the Son of God." 12But [a]He sternly warned them that they should not make Him known.

The Twelve Apostles
(Matt. 10:1–4; Luke 6:12–16)

13[a]And He went up on the mountain and called to *Him* those He Himself wanted. And they came to Him. 14Then He appointed twelve,[1] that they might be with Him and that He might send them out to preach, 15and to have power to heal sicknesses and[1] to cast out demons: 16Simon,[1] [a]to whom He gave the name Peter; 17James the *son* of Zebedee and John the brother of James, to whom He gave the name Boanerges, that is, "Sons of Thunder"; 18Andrew, Philip, Bartholomew, Matthew, Thomas, James the *son* of Alphaeus, Thaddaeus, Simon the Cananite; 19and Judas Iscariot, who also betrayed Him. And they went into a house.

A House Divided Cannot Stand
(Matt. 12:22–30; Luke 11:14–23)

20Then the multitude came together again, [a]so that they could not so much as eat bread. 21But when His [a]own people heard *about this,* they went out to lay hold of Him, [b]for they said, "He is out of His mind."

22And the scribes who came down from Jerusalem said, [a]"He has Beelzebub," and, "By the [b]ruler of the demons He casts out demons."

23[a]So He called them to *Himself* and said to them in parables: "How can Satan cast out Satan? 24If a kingdom is divided against itself, that kingdom cannot stand. 25And if a house is divided against itself, that house cannot stand. 26And if Satan has risen up against himself, and is divided, he cannot stand, but has an end. 27[a]No one can enter a strong man's house and plunder his goods, unless he first binds the strong man. And then he will plunder his house.

The Unpardonable Sin
(Matt. 12:31, 32; Luke 12:10)

28[a]"Assuredly, I say to you, all sins will be forgiven the sons of men, and whatever

---

2:27 [a] Gen. 2:3; Ex. 23:12; Deut. 5:14; Neh. 9:14; Ezek. 20:12 2:28 [a] Matt. 12:8 3:1 [a] Matt. 12:9–14; Luke 6:6–11 3:2 [a] [Ps. 37:32]; Luke 14:1; 20:20 [b] Luke 13:14 3:5 [a] Zech. 7:12 [1] NU-Text omits *as whole as the other.* 3:6 [a] Ps. 2:2; Mark 12:13 [b] Matt. 22:16 3:7 [a] Matt. 4:25; Luke 6:17 3:8 [a] Mark 5:19 3:10 [a] Mark 5:29, 34; Luke 7:21 [b] Matt. 9:21; 14:36; Mark 6:56; 8:22 3:11 [a] Mark 1:23, 24; Luke 4:41 [b] Matt. 8:29; 14:33; Mark 1:1; 5:7; Luke 8:28 3:12 [a] Matt. 12:16; Mark 1:25, 34 3:13 [a] Matt. 10:1; Mark 6:7; Luke 9:1 3:14 [1] NU-Text adds *whom He also named apostles.* 3:15 [1] NU-Text omits *to heal sicknesses and.* 3:16 [a] Matt. 16:18; John 1:42 [1] NU-Text reads *and He appointed the twelve: Simon . . . .* 3:20 [a] Mark 6:31 3:21 [a] Ps. 69:8; Matt. 13:55; Mark 6:3; John 2:12 [b] John 7:5; 10:20; Acts 26:24; [2 Cor. 5:13] 3:22 [a] Matt. 9:34; 10:25; Luke 11:15; John 7:20; 8:48, 52; 10:20 [b] [John 12:31; 14:30; 16:11; Eph. 2:2] 3:23 [a] Matt. 12:25–29; Luke 11:17–22 3:27 [a] [Is. 49:24, 25]; Matt. 12:29 3:28 [a] Matt. 12:31, 32; Luke 12:10; [1 John 5:16]

RECONCILE CHAOS WITH PEACE

INHALE

I have been married for five years, but I cannot see making it five more days. I would rather be anywhere but home. I would rather talk to anyone other than my spouse. Everything is an issue. If it isn't the bills, it's the kids. My spouse is never happy with anything. As bad as it all is right now, I want to fix things. I don't want to give up. But the problem is that I don't know how to fix anything. I don't even know where to start. Instead, it just seems that every day is worse than the one before. What do I do when peace seems like an impossible dream?

EXHALE

The marriage relationship can be one of the most rewarding of all. Unfortunately, it can also be one of the most difficult and devastating ones of all. As you know, marriage is hard. But also know that you are not alone. You aren't the only ones who struggle even to keep your heads above the waters. You aren't the only ones to feel like you're drowning in despair. But there is hope!

Many of the problems we experience in marriage are because of our differences. Perhaps the most important key to unity is to focus on Jesus. If you and your spouse are both growing to be more like Him, you will also be growing closer together. This one important aspect of marriage keeps you from being caught in irreconcilable division. Jesus said in Mark 3:25, "And if a house is divided against itself, that house cannot stand." Growing close to Jesus helps overcome your differences that can divide.

Communication is close behind in importance. You build the relationship over time. For so many, the problem begins when the communication stops. The same communication that helped create the relationship is needed to sustain it. Now is the time to reopen or ramp up those communication lines. Even if it doesn't go well at first, sit down and talk. Share and listen. Acknowledge your part in the problems. But seek solutions, not blame. You cannot live in unity if you don't know and seek to understand the thoughts and feelings of your spouse. Remember that Jesus wants your marriage to work. And He doesn't just want your house to stand; He wants it to be a home.

blasphemies they may utter; 29but he who
blasphemes against the Holy Spirit never
has forgiveness, but is subject to eternal
condemnation"— 30because they [a]said, "He
has an unclean spirit."

Jesus' Mother and Brothers Send for Him
(Matt. 12:46–50; Luke 8:19–21)

31[a]Then His brothers and His mother
came, and standing outside they sent to
Him, calling Him. 32And a multitude was
sitting around Him; and they said to Him,
"Look, Your mother and Your brothers[1] are
outside seeking You."
33But He answered them, saying, "Who
is My mother, or My brothers?" 34And He
looked around in a circle at those who sat
about Him, and said, "Here are My mother
and My brothers! 35For whoever does the
[a]will of God is My brother and My sister
and mother."

The Parable of the Sower
(Matt. 13:1–9; Luke 8:4–8)

4 And [a]again He began to teach by the
sea. And a great multitude was gathered to Him, so that He got into a boat and
sat *in it* on the sea; and the whole multitude was on the land facing the sea. 2Then
He taught them many things by parables,
[a]and said to them in His teaching:
3"Listen! Behold, a sower went out to

3:30 [a] Matt. 9:34; John 7:20; 8:48, 52; 10:20 3:31 [a] Matt. 12:46–50; Luke 8:19–21 3:32 [1] NU-Text and M-Text add *and Your sisters.* 3:35 [a] Eph. 6:6; Heb. 10:36; 1 Pet. 4:2; [1 John 2:17] 4:1 [a] Matt. 13:1–15; Luke 8:4–10 4:2 [a] Mark 12:38

sow. 4And it happened, as he sowed, *that*
some *seed* fell by the wayside; and the birds
of the air[1] came and devoured it. 5Some
fell on stony ground, where it did not have
much earth; and immediately it sprang
up because it had no depth of earth. 6But
when the sun was up it was scorched, and
because it had no root it withered away.
7And some *seed* fell among thorns; and
the thorns grew up and choked it, and it
yielded no crop. 8But other *seed* fell on
good ground and yielded a crop that sprang
up, increased and produced: some thir-
tyfold, some sixty, and some a hundred."
9And He said to them,[1] "He who has ears
to hear, let him hear!"

The Purpose of Parables
(Matt. 13:10–17; Luke 8:9, 10)

10[a]But when He was alone, those around
Him with the twelve asked Him about the
parable. 11And He said to them, "To you it
has been given to [a]know the mystery of the
kingdom of God; but to [b]those who are outside, all things come in parables, 12so that

[a]'Seeing they may see and not perceive,
And hearing they may hear
and not understand;
Lest they should turn,
And *their* sins be forgiven them.'"[1]

The Parable of the Sower Explained
(Matt. 13:18–23; Luke 8:11–15)

13And He said to them, "Do you not
understand this parable? How then will you
understand all the parables? 14[a]The sower
sows the word. 15And these are the ones by
the wayside where the word is sown. When
they hear, Satan comes immediately and
takes away the word that was sown in their
hearts. 16These likewise are the ones sown
on stony ground who, when they hear the
word, immediately receive it with gladness;
17and they have no root in themselves, and
so endure only for a time. Afterward, when
tribulation or persecution arises for the
word's sake, immediately they stumble.
18Now these are the ones sown among
thorns; *they are* the ones who hear the word,
19and the [a]cares of this world, [b]the deceitfulness of riches, and the desires for other
things entering in choke the word, and it becomes unfruitful. 20But these are the ones
sown on good ground, those who hear the
word, accept *it,* and bear [a]fruit: some thir-
tyfold, some sixty, and some a hundred."

Light Under a Basket
(Luke 8:16–18)

21[a]Also He said to them, "Is a lamp
brought to be put under a basket or under
a bed? Is it not to be set on a lampstand?
22[a]For there is nothing hidden which will
not be revealed, nor has anything been kept
secret but that it should come to light. 23[a]If
anyone has ears to hear, let him hear."
24Then He said to them, "Take heed what
you hear. [a]With the same measure you use,
it will be measured to you; and to you who
hear, more will be given. 25[a]For whoever
has, to him more will be given; but whoever does not have, even what he has will
be taken away from him."

The Parable of the Growing Seed

26And He said, [a]"The kingdom of God
is as if a man should scatter seed on the
ground, 27and should sleep by night and
rise by day, and the seed should sprout
and [a]grow, he himself does not know how.
28For the earth [a]yields crops by itself: first
the blade, then the head, after that the full
grain in the head. 29But when the grain
ripens, immediately [a]he puts in the sickle,
because the harvest has come."

The Parable of the Mustard Seed
(Matt. 13:31, 32; Luke 13:18, 19)

30Then He said, [a]"To what shall we liken
the kingdom of God? Or with what parable
shall we picture it? 31*It is* like a mustard seed
which, when it is sown on the ground, is
smaller than all the seeds on earth; 32but
when it is sown, it grows up and becomes
greater than all herbs, and shoots out large

4:4 [1] NU-Text and M-Text omit *of the air.* 4:9 [1] NU-Text and M-Text omit *to them.* 4:10 [a] Matt. 13:10; Luke 8:9 4:11 [a] [Matt. 11:25; 1 Cor. 2:10–16; 2 Cor. 4:6] [b] [1 Cor. 5:12, 13; Col. 4:5; 1 Thess. 4:12; 1 Tim. 3:7] 4:12 [a] Is. 6:9, 10; 43:8; Jer. 5:21; Ezek. 12:2; Matt. 13:14; Luke 8:10; John 12:40; Rom. 11:8 [1] Isaiah 6:9, 10 4:14 [a] Matt. 13:18–23; Luke 8:11–15 4:19 [a] Luke 21:34 [b] Prov. 23:5; Eccl. 5:13; Luke 18:24; 1 Tim. 6:9, 10, 17 4:20 [a] [John 15:2, 5; Rom. 7:4] 4:21 [a] Matt. 5:15; Luke 8:16; 11:33 4:22 [a] Eccl. 12:14; Matt. 10:26, 27; Luke 12:3; [1 Cor. 4:5] 4:23 [a] Matt. 11:15; 13:9, 43; Mark 4:9; Luke 8:8; 14:35; Rev. 3:6, 13, 22; 13:9 4:24 [a] Matt. 7:2; Luke 6:38; 2 Cor. 9:6 4:25 [a] Matt. 13:12; 25:29; Luke 8:18; 19:26 4:26 [a] [Matt. 13:24–30, 36–43]; Luke 8:1 4:27 [a] [2 Cor. 3:18; 2 Pet. 3:18] 4:28 [a] [John 12:24] 4:29 [a] [Matt. 13:30, 39]; Rev. 14:15 4:30 [a] Matt. 13:31, 32; Luke 13:18, 19; [Acts 2:41; 4:4; 5:14; 19:20]

branches, so that the birds of the air may
nest under its shade."

Jesus' Use of Parables

33[a]And with many such parables He
spoke the word to them as they were able to
hear *it*. 34But without a parable He did not
speak to them. And when they were alone,
[a]He explained all things to His disciples.

Wind and Wave Obey Jesus
(Matt. 8:23–27; Luke 8:22–25)

35[a]On the same day, when evening had
come, He said to them, "Let us cross over
to the other side." 36Now when they had left
the multitude, they took Him along in the
boat as He was. And other little boats were
also with Him. 37And a great windstorm
arose, and the waves beat into the boat,
so that it was already filling. 38But He was
in the stern, asleep on a pillow. And they
awoke Him and said to Him, [a]"Teacher, [b]do
You not care that we are perishing?"
39Then He arose and [a]rebuked the wind,
and said to the sea, [b]"Peace, be still!" And
the wind ceased and there was a great calm.
40But He said to them, "Why are you so
fearful? [a]How *is it* that you have no faith?"[1]
41And they feared exceedingly, and said to
one another, "Who can this be, that even
the wind and the sea obey Him!"

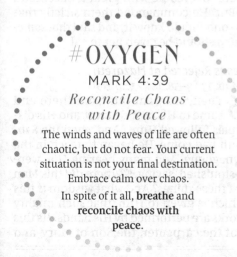

#OXYGEN
MARK 4:39
Reconcile Chaos with Peace
The winds and waves of life are often chaotic, but do not fear. Your current situation is not your final destination. Embrace calm over chaos.
In spite of it all, **breathe** and **reconcile chaos with peace.**

A Demon-Possessed Man Healed
(Matt. 8:28—9:1; Luke 8:26–39)

5 Then [a]they came to the other side of
the sea, to the country of the Gadarenes.[1] 2And when He had come out of the
boat, immediately there met Him out of
the tombs a man with an [a]unclean spirit,
3who had *his* dwelling among the tombs;
and no one could bind him,[1] not even with
chains, 4because he had often been bound
with shackles and chains. And the chains
had been pulled apart by him, and the
shackles broken in pieces; neither could
anyone tame him. 5And always, night and
day, he was in the mountains and in the
tombs, crying out and cutting himself with
stones.
6When he saw Jesus from afar, he ran
and worshiped Him. 7And he cried out with
a loud voice and said, "What have I to do
with You, Jesus, Son of the Most High God?
I [a]implore You by God that You do not torment me."
8For He said to him, [a]"Come out of the
man, unclean spirit!" 9Then He asked him,
"What *is* your name?"
And he answered, saying, "My name *is*
Legion; for we are many." 10Also he begged
Him earnestly that He would not send them
out of the country.
11Now a large herd of [a]swine was feeding there near the mountains. 12So all the
demons begged Him, saying, "Send us to
the swine, that we may enter them." 13And
at once Jesus[1] gave them permission. Then
the unclean spirits went out and entered
the swine (there were about two thousand);
and the herd ran violently down the steep
place into the sea, and drowned in the sea.
14So those who fed the swine fled, and
they told *it* in the city and in the country.
And they went out to see what it was that
had happened. 15Then they came to Jesus,
and saw the one *who had been* [a]demon-
possessed and had the legion, [b]sitting and
[c]clothed and in his right mind. And they
were afraid. 16And those who saw it told
them how it happened to him *who had been*
demon-possessed, and about the swine.

4:33 [a] Matt. 13:34, 35; [John 16:12] 4:34 [a] Luke 24:27, 45 4:35 [a] Matt. 8:18, 23–27; Luke 8:22, 25 4:38 [a] [Matt. 23:8–10] [b] Ps. 44:23 4:39 [a] Mark 9:25; Luke 4:39 [b] Ps. 65:7; 89:9; 93:4; 104:6, 7; Matt. 8:26; Luke 8:24 4:40 [a] Matt. 14:31, 32; Luke 8:25 [1] NU-Text reads *Have you still no faith?* 5:1 [a] Matt. 8:28–34; Luke 8:26–37 [1] NU-Text reads *Gerasenes.* 5:2 [a] Mark 1:23; 7:25; [Rev. 16:13, 14] 5:3 [1] NU-Text adds *anymore.* 5:7 [a] Matt. 26:63; Mark 1:24; Acts 19:13 5:8 [a] Mark 1:25; 9:25; [Acts 16:18] 5:11 [a] Lev. 11:7, 8; Deut. 14:8; Luke 15:15, 16 5:13 [1] NU-Text reads *And He gave.* 5:15 [a] Matt. 4:24; 8:16; Mark 1:32 [b] Luke 10:39 [c] [Is. 61:10]

17 Then [a]they began to plead with Him to
depart from their region.
18 And when He got into the boat, [a]he
who had been demon-possessed begged
Him that he might be with Him. 19 However, Jesus did not permit him, but said
to him, "Go home to your friends, and tell
them what great things the Lord has done
for you, and how He has had compassion
on you." 20 And he departed and began to
[a]proclaim in Decapolis all that Jesus had
done for him; and all [b]marveled.

A Girl Restored to Life and a Woman Healed

(Matt. 9:18–26; Luke 8:40–56)

21 [a]Now when Jesus had crossed over
again by boat to the other side, a great
multitude gathered to Him; and He was
by the sea. 22 [a]And behold, one of the rulers of the synagogue came, Jairus by name.
And when he saw Him, he fell at His feet
23 and begged Him earnestly, saying, "My
little daughter lies at the point of death.
Come and [a]lay Your hands on her, that she
may be healed, and she will live." 24 So *Jesus*
went with him, and a great multitude followed Him and thronged Him.
25 Now a certain woman [a]had a flow of
blood for twelve years, 26 and had suffered
many things from many physicians. She
had spent all that she had and was no better, but rather grew worse. 27 When she
heard about Jesus, she came behind *Him* in
the crowd and [a]touched His garment. 28 For
she said, "If only I may touch His clothes,
I shall be made well."
29 Immediately the fountain of her blood
was dried up, and she felt in *her* body that
she was healed of the affliction. 30 And
Jesus, immediately knowing in Himself
that [a]power had gone out of Him, turned
around in the crowd and said, "Who
touched My clothes?"
31 But His disciples said to Him, "You see
the multitude thronging You, and You say,
'Who touched Me?'"
32 And He looked around to see her who
had done this thing. 33 But the woman,
[a]fearing and trembling, knowing what had
happened to her, came and fell down before Him and told Him the whole truth.
34 And He said to her, "Daughter, [a]your faith
has made you well. [b]Go in peace, and be
healed of your affliction."
35 [a]While He was still speaking, *some*
came from the ruler of the synagogue's
house who said, "Your daughter is dead.
Why trouble the Teacher any further?"
36 As soon as Jesus heard the word that
was spoken, He said to the ruler of the synagogue, "Do not be afraid; only [a]believe."
37 And He permitted no one to follow Him
except Peter, James, and John the brother
of James. 38 Then He came to the house
of the ruler of the synagogue, and saw a
tumult and those who [a]wept and wailed
loudly. 39 When He came in, He said to
them, "Why make this commotion and
weep? The child is not dead, but [a]sleeping."
40 And they ridiculed Him. [a]But when He
had put them all outside, He took the father
and the mother of the child, and those *who*
were with Him, and entered where the child
was lying. 41 Then He took the child by the
hand, and said to her, "Talitha, cumi," which
is translated, "Little girl, I say to you, arise."
42 Immediately the girl arose and walked,
for she was twelve years *of age.* And they
were [a]overcome with great amazement.
43 But [a]He commanded them strictly that
no one should know it, and said that *some-*
thing should be given her to eat.

Jesus Rejected at Nazareth

(Matt. 13:53–58; Luke 4:16–30)

6 Then [a]He went out from there and
came to His own country, and His disciples followed Him. 2 And when the Sabbath had come, He began to teach in the
synagogue. And many hearing *Him* were
[a]astonished, saying, [b]"Where *did* this Man
get these things? And what wisdom *is* this
which is given to Him, that such mighty
works are performed by His hands! 3 Is this
not the carpenter, the Son of Mary, and

5:17 [a] Matt. 8:34; Acts 16:39 5:18 [a] Luke 8:38, 39 5:20 [a] Ex. 15:2; Ps. 66:16 [b] Matt. 9:8, 33; John 5:20; 7:21; Acts 3:12; 4:13
5:21 [a] Matt. 9:1; Luke 8:40 5:22 [a] Matt. 9:18–26; Luke 8:41–56; Acts 13:15 5:23 [a] Matt. 8:15; Mark 6:5; 7:32; 8:23, 25; 16:18;
Luke 4:40; Acts 9:17; 28:8 5:25 [a] Lev. 15:19, 25; Matt. 9:20 5:27 [a] Matt. 14:35, 36; Mark 3:10; 6:56 5:30 [a] Luke 6:19; 8:46
5:33 [a] [Ps. 89:7] 5:34 [a] Matt. 9:22; Mark 10:52; Acts 14:9 [b] 1 Sam. 1:17; 20:42; 2 Kin. 5:19; Luke 7:50; 8:48; Acts 16:36; [James 2:16]
5:35 [a] Luke 8:49 5:36 [a] [Mark 9:23; John 11:40] 5:38 [a] Mark 16:10; Acts 9:39 5:39 [a] John 11:4, 11 5:40 [a] Acts 9:40
5:42 [a] Mark 1:27; 7:37 5:43 [a] [Matt. 8:4; 12:16–19; 17:9]; Mark 3:12 6:1 [a] Matt. 13:54; Luke 4:16
6:2 [a] Matt. 7:28; Luke 4:32; Acts 4:13 [b] John 6:42

[a]brother of James, Joses, Judas, and Simon? And are not His sisters here with us?" So they [b]were offended at Him.

4 But Jesus said to them, [a]"A prophet is not without honor except in his own country, among his own relatives, and in his own house." 5 [a]Now He could do no mighty work there, except that He laid His hands on a few sick people and healed *them.* 6 And [a]He marveled because of their unbelief. [b]Then He went about the villages in a circuit, teaching.

Sending Out the Twelve
(Matt. 10:1, 5–15; Luke 9:1–6)

7 [a]And He called the twelve to *Himself,* and began to send them out [b]two *by* two, and gave them power over unclean spirits. 8 He commanded them to take nothing for the journey except a staff—no bag, no bread, no copper in *their* money belts— 9 but [a]to wear sandals, and not to put on two tunics.

10 [a]Also He said to them, "In whatever place you enter a house, stay there till you depart from that place. 11 [a]And whoever[1] will not receive you nor hear you, when you depart from there, [b]shake off the dust under your feet as a testimony against them.[2] Assuredly, I say to you, it will be more tolerable for Sodom and Gomorrah in the day of judgment than for that city!"

12 So they went out and preached that *people* should repent. 13 And they cast out many demons, [a]and anointed with oil many who were sick, and healed *them.*

John the Baptist Beheaded
(Matt. 14:1–12; Luke 9:7–9)

14 [a]Now King Herod heard *of Him,* for His name had become well known. And he said, "John the Baptist is risen from the dead, and therefore [b]these powers are at work in him."

15 [a]Others said, "It is Elijah."

And others said, "It is the Prophet, [b]or[1] like one of the prophets."

16 [a]But when Herod heard, he said, "This is John, whom I beheaded; he has been raised from the dead!" 17 For Herod himself had sent and laid hold of John, and bound him in prison for the sake of Herodias, his brother Philip's wife; for he had married her. 18 Because John had said to Herod, [a]"It is not lawful for you to have your brother's wife."

19 Therefore Herodias held it against him and wanted to kill him, but she could not; 20 for Herod [a]feared John, knowing that he *was* a just and holy man, and he protected him. And when he heard him, he did many things, and heard him gladly.

21 [a]Then an opportune day came when Herod [b]on his birthday gave a feast for his nobles, the high officers, and the chief *men* of Galilee. 22 And when Herodias' daughter herself came in and danced, and pleased Herod and those who sat with him, the king said to the girl, "Ask me whatever you want, and I will give *it* to you." 23 He also swore to her, [a]"Whatever you ask me, I will give you, up to half my kingdom."

24 So she went out and said to her mother, "What shall I ask?"

And she said, "The head of John the Baptist!"

25 Immediately she came in with haste to the king and asked, saying, "I want you to give me at once the head of John the Baptist on a platter."

26 [a]And the king was exceedingly sorry; *yet,* because of the oaths and because of those who sat with him, he did not want to refuse her. 27 Immediately the king sent an executioner and commanded his head to be brought. And he went and beheaded him in prison, 28 brought his head on a platter, and gave it to the girl; and the girl gave it to her mother. 29 When his disciples heard *of it,* they came and [a]took away his corpse and laid it in a tomb.

Feeding the Five Thousand
(Matt. 14:13–21; Luke 9:10–17; John 6:1–14)

30 [a]Then the apostles gathered to Jesus and told Him all things, both what they had done and what they had taught. 31 [a]And He said to them, "Come aside by yourselves

6:3 [a] Matt. 12:46; Gal. 1:19 [b] [Matt. 11:6] 6:4 [a] Matt. 13:57; Luke 4:24; John 4:44 6:5 [a] Gen. 19:22; 32:25; Matt. 13:58; [Mark 9:23] 6:6 [a] Is. 59:16; Matt. 17:17, 20; [Heb. 3:18, 19; 4:2] [b] Matt. 9:35; Luke 13:22; Acts 10:38; Eph. 2:17 6:7 [a] Matt. 10:1; 28:19, 20; Mark 3:13, 14; Luke 9:1 [b] [Eccl. 4:9, 10] 6:9 [a] [Eph. 6:15] 6:10 [a] Matt. 10:11; Luke 9:4; 10:7, 8 6:11 [a] Matt. 10:14; Luke 10:10 [b] Acts 13:51; 18:6 [1] NU-Text reads *whatever place.* [2] NU-Text omits the rest of this verse. 6:13 [a] [James 5:14] 6:14 [a] Matt. 14:1–12; Mark 6:14–16; Luke 9:7–9 [b] Luke 19:37 6:15 [a] Matt. 16:14; Mark 8:28; Luke 9:19 [b] Matt. 21:11 [1] NU-Text and M-Text omit *or.* 6:16 [a] Matt. 14:2; Luke 3:19 6:18 [a] Lev. 18:16; 20:21 6:20 [a] Matt. 14:5; 21:26 6:21 [a] Matt. 14:6 [b] Gen. 40:20 6:23 [a] Esth. 5:3, 6; 7:2 6:26 [a] Matt. 14:9 6:29 [a] 1 Kin. 13:29, 30; Matt. 27:58–61; Acts 8:2 6:30 [a] Luke 9:10 6:31 [a] Matt. 14:13

to a deserted place and rest a while." For
[b]there were many coming and going, and
they did not even have time to eat. 32[a]So
they departed to a deserted place in the
boat by themselves.

33But the multitudes[1] saw them departing, and many [a]knew Him and ran there on
foot from all the cities. They arrived before
them and came together to Him. 34[a]And
Jesus, when He came out, saw a great multitude and was moved with compassion
for them, because they were like [b]sheep
not having a shepherd. So [c]He began to
teach them many things. 35[a]When the day
was now far spent, His disciples came to
Him and said, "This is a deserted place,
and already the hour *is* late. 36Send them
away, that they may go into the surrounding country and villages and buy themselves bread;[1] for they have nothing to eat."

37But He answered and said to them,
"You give them something to eat."

And they said to Him, [a]"Shall we go and
buy two hundred denarii worth of bread
and give them *something* to eat?"

38But He said to them, "How many
loaves do you have? Go and see."

And when they found out they said,
[a]"Five, and two fish."

39Then He [a]commanded them to make
them all sit down in groups on the green
grass. 40So they sat down in ranks, in hundreds and in fifties. 41And when He had
taken the five loaves and the two fish, He
[a]looked up to heaven, [b]blessed and broke
the loaves, and gave *them* to His disciples
to set before them; and the two fish He divided among *them* all. 42So they all ate and
were filled. 43And they took up twelve baskets full of fragments and of the fish. 44Now
those who had eaten the loaves were about[1]
five thousand men.

Jesus Walks on the Sea
(Matt. 14:22–33; John 6:15–21)

45[a]Immediately He made His disciples
get into the boat and go before Him to the
other side, to Bethsaida, while He sent the
multitude away. 46And when He had sent
them away, He [a]departed to the mountain to pray. 47Now when evening came,
the boat was in the middle of the sea; and
He *was* alone on the land. 48Then He saw
them straining at rowing, for the wind was
against them. Now about the fourth watch
of the night He came to them, walking on
the sea, and [a]would have passed them by.
49And when they saw Him walking on the
sea, they supposed it was a [a]ghost, and
cried out; 50for they all saw Him and were
troubled. But immediately He talked with
them and said to them, [a]"Be of good cheer!
It is I; do not be [b]afraid." 51Then He went
up into the boat to them, and the wind
[a]ceased. And they were greatly [b]amazed
in themselves beyond measure, and marveled. 52For [a]they had not understood
about the loaves, because their [b]heart was
hardened.

Many Touch Him and Are Made Well
(Matt. 14:34–36)

53[a]When they had crossed over, they
came to the land of Gennesaret and anchored there. 54And when they came out
of the boat, immediately the people recognized Him, 55ran through that whole surrounding region, and began to carry about
on beds those who were sick to wherever
they heard He was. 56Wherever He entered,
into villages, cities, or the country, they laid
the sick in the marketplaces, and begged
Him that [a]they might just touch the [b]hem
of His garment. And as many as touched
Him were made well.

Defilement Comes from Within
(Matt. 15:1–20)

7 Then [a]the Pharisees and some of the
scribes came together to Him, having
come from Jerusalem. 2Now when[1] they
saw some of His disciples eat bread with
defiled, that is, with [a]unwashed hands,
they found fault. 3For the Pharisees and

6:31 [b] Mark 3:20 6:32 [a] Matt. 14:13–21; Luke 9:10–17; John 6:5–13 6:33 [a] [Col. 1:6] [1] NU-Text and M-Text read *they.*
6:34 [a] Matt. 9:36; 14:14; [Heb. 5:2] [b] Num. 27:17; 1 Kin. 22:17; 2 Chr. 18:16; Zech. 10:2 [c] [Is. 48:17; 61:1–3]; Luke 9:11 6:35 [a] Matt. 14:15;
Luke 9:12 6:36 [1] NU-Text reads *something to eat* and omits the rest of this verse. 6:37 [a] Num. 11:13, 22; 2 Kin. 4:43
6:38 [a] Matt. 14:17; Luke 9:13; John 6:9 6:39 [a] Matt. 15:35; Mark 8:6 6:41 [a] John 11:41, 42 [b] 1 Sam. 9:13; Matt. 15:36; 26:26;
Mark 8:7; Luke 24:30 6:44 [1] NU-Text and M-Text omit *about.* 6:45 [a] Matt. 14:22–32; John 6:15–21 6:46 [a] Mark 1:35; Luke 5:16
6:48 [a] Luke 24:28 6:49 [a] Matt. 14:26; Luke 24:37 6:50 [a] Matt. 9:2; John 16:33 [b] Is. 41:10 6:51 [a] Ps. 107:29 [b] Mark 1:27; 2:12;
5:42; 7:37 6:52 [a] Matt. 16:9–11; Mark 8:17, 18 [b] Is. 63:17; Mark 3:5; 16:14 6:53 [a] Matt. 14:34–36; John 6:24, 25 6:56 [a] Matt. 9:20;
Mark 5:27, 28; [Acts 19:12] [b] Num. 15:38, 39 7:1 [a] Matt. 15:1–20 7:2 [a] Matt. 15:20 [1] NU-Text omits *when* and *they found fault.*

all the Jews do not eat unless they wash
their hands in a special way, holding the
[a]tradition of the elders. 4*When they come*
from the marketplace, they do not eat unless they wash. And there are many other
things which they have received and hold,
like the washing of cups, pitchers, copper
vessels, and couches.
5[a]Then the Pharisees and scribes asked
Him, "Why do Your disciples not walk according to the tradition of the elders, but
eat bread with unwashed hands?"
6He answered and said to them, "Well
did Isaiah prophesy of you [a]hypocrites, as
it is written:

[b]'This people honors Me with *their* lips,
But their heart is far from Me.
7 And in vain they worship Me,
Teaching *as* doctrines the
commandments of men.'[1]

8For laying aside the commandment of
God, you hold the tradition of men[1]—the
washing of pitchers and cups, and many
other such things you do."
9He said to them, "*All too* well [a]you reject the commandment of God, that you
may keep your tradition. 10For Moses said,
[a]'Honor your father and your mother';[1] and,
[b]'He who curses father or mother, let him
be put to death.'[2] 11But you say, 'If a man
says to his father or mother, [a]"Whatever
profit you might have received from me
is Corban"—' (that is, a gift *to God*), 12then
you no longer let him do anything for his
father or his mother, 13making the word
of God of no effect through your tradition
which you have handed down. And many
such things you do."
14[a]When He had called all the multitude to *Himself,* He said to them, "Hear
Me, everyone, and [b]understand: 15There

MARK 7:7

I AM A JEWISH RELIGIOUS LEADER

"And in vain they worship Me, teaching as doctrines the commandments of men." Mark 7:7

I am one of the Jewish religious leaders during the time when Jesus ministered in Israel. We were all doing just fine. We had a good life. We were respected as leaders of the Jews, and we had eminence and power. Then, this Jesus came and began to tell the people something different from what we were telling them. Many of His parables spoke against us and condemned the way we were leading the people.

We saw what He was teaching as heresy because He and His followers claimed that He was the Messiah. But we knew His family and that His father was just a lowly carpenter from Nazareth. But we did not really care who He was; we just could not let Him mess things up with Rome for us. We had to silence Him and discredit Him with the people to prevent an uprising and Rome from stepping in and taking our power away. If we could, we sought to silence Him forever by killing Him.

†

Many of the religious leaders did not believe Jesus' message. Their hearts were hardened to hear any truth if it interfered with the benefits they had gained, both in prestige and possessions. These leaders claimed to live by the law, but they used the law to dominate the people, not to love them. They were chasing not the heart of God but the rules of people. We must have hearts that are open and ready to receive all that the Word of God says and not filter it through a selfish lens.

7:3 [a] Mark 7:5, 8, 9, 13; Gal. 1:14; 1 Pet. 1:18 7:5 [a] Matt. 15:2 7:6 [a] Matt. 23:13–29 [b] Is. 29:13 7:7 [1] Isaiah 29:13 7:8 [1] NU-Text omits the rest of this verse. 7:9 [a] Prov. 1:25; Is. 24:5; Jer. 7:23, 24 7:10 [a] Ex. 20:12; Deut. 5:16; Matt. 15:4 [b] Ex. 21:17; Lev. 20:9; Prov. 20:20 [1] Exodus 20:12; Deuteronomy 5:16 [2] Exodus 21:17 7:11 [a] Matt. 15:5; 23:18 7:14 [a] Matt. 15:10 [b] Matt. 16:9, 11, 12

is nothing that enters a man from outside
which can defile him; but the things which
come out of him, those are the things that
[a]defile a man. 16[a]If anyone has ears to hear,
let him hear!"[1]

17[a]When He had entered a house away
from the crowd, His disciples asked Him
concerning the parable. 18So He said to
them, [a]"Are you thus without understanding also? Do you not perceive that whatever enters a man from outside cannot
defile him, 19because it does not enter his
heart but his stomach, and is eliminated,
thus purifying all foods?"[1] 20And He said,
[a]"What comes out of a man, that defiles a
man. 21[a]For from within, out of the heart
of men, [b]proceed evil thoughts, [c]adulter-
ies, [d]fornications, murders, 22thefts, [a]cov-
etousness, wickedness, [b]deceit, [c]lewdness,
an evil eye, [d]blasphemy, [e]pride, foolishness.
23All these evil things come from within
and defile a man."

A Gentile Shows Her Faith
(Matt. 15:21–28)

24[a]From there He arose and went to the
region of Tyre and Sidon.[1] And He entered
a house and wanted no one to know *it,* but
He could not be [b]hidden. 25For a woman
whose young daughter had an unclean
spirit heard about Him, and she came and
[a]fell at His feet. 26The woman was a Greek,
a Syro-Phoenician by birth, and she kept
asking Him to cast the demon out of her
daughter. 27But Jesus said to her, "Let the
children be filled first, for it is not good to
take the children's bread and throw *it* to
the little dogs."

28And she answered and said to Him,
"Yes, Lord, yet even the little dogs under
the table eat from the children's crumbs."

29Then He said to her, "For this saying
go your way; the demon has gone out of
your daughter."

30And when she had come to her house,
she found the demon gone out, and her
daughter lying on the bed.

Jesus Heals a Deaf-Mute
(Matt. 15:29–31)

31[a]Again, departing from the region of
Tyre and Sidon, He came through the midst
of the region of Decapolis to the Sea of Galilee. 32Then [a]they brought to Him one who
was deaf and had an impediment in his
speech, and they begged Him to put His
hand on him. 33And He took him aside
from the multitude, and put His fingers
in his ears, and [a]He spat and touched his
tongue. 34Then, [a]looking up to heaven, [b]He
sighed, and said to him, "Ephphatha," that
is, "Be opened."

35[a]Immediately his ears were opened,
and the impediment of his tongue was
loosed, and he spoke plainly. 36Then [a]He
commanded them that they should tell no
one; but the more He commanded them,
the more widely they proclaimed *it.* 37And
they were [a]astonished beyond measure,
saying, "He has done all things well. He
[b]makes both the deaf to hear and the mute
to speak."

Feeding the Four Thousand
(Matt. 15:32–39)

8 In those days, [a]the multitude being
very great and having nothing to eat,
Jesus called His disciples *to Him* and said
to them, 2"I have [a]compassion on the multitude, because they have now continued
with Me three days and have nothing to
eat. 3And if I send them away hungry to
their own houses, they will faint on the
way; for some of them have come from
afar."

4Then His disciples answered Him,
"How can one satisfy these people with
bread here in the wilderness?"

5[a]He asked them, "How many loaves do
you have?"

And they said, "Seven."

6So He commanded the multitude
to sit down on the ground. And He took
the seven loaves and gave thanks, broke
them and gave *them* to His disciples to

7:15 [a] Is. 59:3; [Heb. 12:15] 7:16 [a] Matt. 11:15 [1] NU-Text omits this verse. 7:17 [a] Matt. 15:15 7:18 [a] [Is. 28:9–11; 1 Cor. 3:2; Heb. 5:11–14] 7:19 [1] NU-Text ends quotation with *eliminated,* setting off the final clause as Mark's comment that Jesus has declared all foods clean. 7:20 [a] Ps. 39:1; [Matt. 12:34–37; James 3:6] 7:21 [a] Gen. 6:5; 8:21; Prov. 6:18; Jer. 17:9; Matt. 15:19 [b] [Gal. 5:19–21] [c] 2 Pet. 2:14 [d] 1 Thess. 4:3 7:22 [a] Luke 12:15 [b] Rom. 1:28, 29 [c] 1 Pet. 4:3 [d] Rev. 2:9 [e] 1 John 2:16 7:24 [a] Matt. 15:21 [b] Mark 2:1, 2 [1] NU-Text omits *and Sidon.* 7:25 [a] Mark 5:22; John 11:32; Rev. 1:17 7:31 [a] Matt. 15:29; Mark 15:37; Luke 23:46; 24:46; Acts 10:40; 1 Cor. 15:4 7:32 [a] Matt. 9:32; Luke 11:14 7:33 [a] Mark 8:23; John 9:6 7:34 [a] Mark 6:41; John 11:41; 17:1 [b] John 11:33, 38 7:35 [a] Is. 35:5, 6 7:36 [a] Mark 5:43 7:37 [a] Mark 6:51; 10:26 [b] Matt. 12:22 8:1 [a] Matt. 15:32–39; Mark 6:34–44; Luke 9:12 8:2 [a] Matt. 9:36; 14:14; Mark 1:41; 6:34 8:5 [a] Matt. 15:34; Mark 6:38; John 6:9

set before *them;* and they set *them* before the multitude. 7They also had a few
small fish; and [a]having blessed them, He
said to set them also before *them.* 8So
they ate and were filled, and they took
up seven large baskets of leftover fragments. 9Now those who had eaten were
about four thousand. And He sent them
away, 10[a]immediately got into the boat
with His disciples, and came to the region of Dalmanutha.

The Pharisees Seek a Sign
(Matt. 16:1–4)

11[a]Then the Pharisees came out and began to dispute with Him, seeking from Him
a sign from heaven, testing Him. 12But He
[a]sighed deeply in His spirit, and said, "Why
does this generation seek a sign? Assuredly,
I say to you, [b]no sign shall be given to this
generation."

Beware of the Leaven of the Pharisees and Herod
(Matt. 16:5–12)

13And He left them, and getting into
the boat again, departed to the other side.
14[a]Now the disciples[1] had forgotten to take
bread, and they did not have more than
one loaf with them in the boat. 15[a]Then
He charged them, saying, "Take heed, beware of the leaven of the Pharisees and the
leaven of Herod."

16And they reasoned among themselves,
saying, "*It is* because we have no bread."
17But Jesus, being aware of *it,* said to
them, "Why do you reason because you
have no bread? [a]Do you not yet perceive
nor understand? Is your heart still[1] hardened? 18Having eyes, do you not see? And
having ears, do you not hear? And do you
not remember? 19[a]When I broke the five
loaves for the five thousand, how many
baskets full of fragments did you take up?"
They said to Him, "Twelve."
20"Also, [a]when I broke the seven for the
four thousand, how many large baskets full
of fragments did you take up?"
And they said, "Seven."
21So He said to them, "How *is it* [a]you do
not understand?"

A Blind Man Healed at Bethsaida

22Then He came to Bethsaida; and they
brought a [a]blind man to Him, and begged
Him to [b]touch him. 23So He took the blind
man by the hand and led him out of the
town. And when [a]He had spit on his eyes
and put His hands on him, He asked him
if he saw anything.
24And he looked up and said, "I see men
like trees, walking."
25Then He put *His* hands on his eyes
again and made him look up. And he was
restored and saw everyone clearly. 26Then
He sent him away to his house, saying,
"Neither go into the town, [a]nor tell anyone in the town."[1]

Peter Confesses Jesus as the Christ
(Matt. 16:13–20; Luke 9:18–20)

27[a]Now Jesus and His disciples went out
to the towns of Caesarea Philippi; and on
the road He asked His disciples, saying to
them, "Who do men say that I am?"
28So they answered, [a]"John the Baptist;
but some *say,* [b]Elijah; and others, one of
the prophets."
29He said to them, "But who do you say
that I am?"
Peter answered and said to Him, [a]"You
are the Christ."
30[a]Then He strictly warned them that
they should tell no one about Him.

Jesus Predicts His Death and Resurrection
(Matt. 16:21–23; Luke 9:21, 22)

31And [a]He began to teach them that the
Son of Man must suffer many things, and
be [b]rejected by the elders and chief priests
and scribes, and be [c]killed, and after three
days rise again. 32He spoke this word openly.
Then Peter took Him aside and began to rebuke Him. 33But when He had turned around
and looked at His disciples, He [a]rebuked

8:7 [a] Matt. 14:19; Mark 6:41 8:10 [a] Matt. 15:39 8:11 [a] Matt. 12:38; 16:1; Luke 11:16; John 2:18; 6:30; 1 Cor. 1:22 8:12 [a] Mark 7:34 [b] Matt. 12:39 8:14 [a] Matt. 16:5 [1] NU-Text and M-Text read *they.* 8:15 [a] Matt. 16:6; Luke 12:1 8:17 [a] Mark 6:52; 16:14 [1] NU-Text omits *still.* 8:19 [a] Matt. 14:20; Mark 6:43; Luke 9:17; John 6:13 8:20 [a] Matt. 15:37 8:21 [a] [Mark 6:52] 8:22 [a] Matt. 9:27; John 9:1 [b] Luke 18:15 8:23 [a] Mark 7:33 8:26 [a] Matt. 8:4; Mark 5:43; 7:36 [1] NU-Text reads *"Do not even go into the town."* 8:27 [a] Matt. 16:13–16; Luke 9:18–20 8:28 [a] Matt. 14:2 [b] Mark 6:14, 15; Luke 9:7, 8 8:29 [a] John 1:41; 4:42; 6:69; 11:27; Acts 2:36; 8:37; 9:20 8:30 [a] Matt. 8:4; 16:20; Luke 9:21 8:31 [a] [Is. 53:3–11]; Matt. 16:21; 20:19; Luke 18:31–33; 1 Pet. 1:11 [b] Mark 10:33 [c] Mark 9:31; 10:34 8:33 [a] Mark 16:14; [Rev. 3:19]

Peter, saying, "Get behind Me, Satan! For you are not mindful of the things of God, but the things of men."

Take Up the Cross and Follow Him

(Matt. 16:24–27; Luke 9:23–26)

34 When He had called the people to
Himself, with His disciples also, He said
to them, [a]"Whoever desires to come after Me, let him deny himself, and take
up his cross, and follow Me. 35 For [a]who-
ever desires to save his life will lose it, but
whoever loses his life for My sake and the
gospel's will save it. 36 For what will it profit
a man if he gains the whole world, and
loses his own soul? 37 Or what will a man
give in exchange for his soul? 38 [a]For whoever [b]is ashamed of Me and My words in
this adulterous and sinful generation, of
him the Son of Man also will be ashamed
when He comes in the glory of His Father
with the holy angels."

9 And He said to them, [a]"Assuredly, I say
to you that there are some standing
here who will not taste death till they see
[b]the kingdom of God present with power."

Jesus Transfigured on the Mount

(Matt. 16:28—17:13; Luke 9:27–36; 2 Pet. 1:16–18)

2 [a]Now after six days Jesus took Peter,
James, and John, and led them up on a high
mountain apart by themselves; and He was
transfigured before them. 3 His clothes
became shining, exceedingly [a]white, like
snow, such as no launderer on earth can
whiten them. 4 And Elijah appeared to them
with Moses, and they were talking with
Jesus. 5 Then Peter answered and said to
Jesus, "Rabbi, it is good for us to be here;
and let us make three tabernacles: one for
You, one for Moses, and one for Elijah"—
6 because he did not know what to say, for
they were greatly afraid.

7 And a [a]cloud came and overshadowed
them; and a voice came out of the cloud,
saying, "This is [b]My beloved Son. [c]Hear
Him!" 8 Suddenly, when they had looked
around, they saw no one anymore, but only
Jesus with themselves.

9 [a]Now as they came down from the
mountain, He commanded them that
they should tell no one the things they had
seen, till the Son of Man had risen from
the dead. 10 So they kept this word to themselves, questioning [a]what the rising from
the dead meant.

11 And they asked Him, saying, "Why
do the scribes say [a]that Elijah must come
first?"

12 Then He answered and told them, "Indeed, Elijah is coming first and restores all
things. And [a]how is it written concerning
the Son of Man, that He must suffer many
things and [b]be treated with contempt? 13 But
I say to you that [a]Elijah has also come, and
they did to him whatever they wished, as it
is written of him."

A Boy Is Healed

(Matt. 17:14–21; Luke 9:37–42)

14 [a]And when He came to the disciples,
He saw a great multitude around them,
and scribes disputing with them. 15 Immediately, when they saw Him, all the people
were greatly amazed, and running to *Him,*
greeted Him. 16 And He asked the scribes,
"What are you discussing with them?"

17 Then [a]one of the crowd answered and
said, "Teacher, I brought You my son, who
has a mute spirit. 18 And wherever it seizes
him, it throws him down; he foams at the
mouth, gnashes his teeth, and becomes
rigid. So I spoke to Your disciples, that
they should cast it out, but they could
not."

19 He answered him and said, "O [a]faith-
less generation, how long shall I be with
you? How long shall I bear with you? Bring
him to Me." 20 Then they brought him to
Him. And [a]when he saw Him, immediately
the spirit convulsed him, and he fell on
the ground and wallowed, foaming at the
mouth.

21 So He asked his father, "How long has
this been happening to him?"

8:34 [a] [Matt. 10:38]; Luke 14:27 8:35 [a] Matt. 10:39; Luke 17:33; John 12:25 8:38 [a] Matt. 10:33; Luke 9:26; 12:9 [b] Rom. 1:16; 2 Tim. 1:8, 9; 2:12 9:1 [a] Matt. 16:28; Mark 13:26; Luke 9:27; Acts 7:55, 56; Rev. 20:4 [b] [Matt. 24:30] 9:2 [a] Matt. 17:1–8; Luke 9:28–36 9:3 [a] Dan. 7:9; Matt. 28:3 9:7 [a] Ex. 40:34; 1 Kin. 8:10; Acts 1:9; Rev. 1:7 [b] Ps. 2:7; [Is. 42:1]; Matt. 3:17; Mark 1:11; Luke 1:35; 3:22; 2 Pet. 1:17 [c] Acts 3:22 9:9 [a] Matt. 17:9–13; Mark 16:6; Luke 24:6, 7, 46 9:10 [a] John 2:19–22 9:11 [a] Mal. 4:5; Matt. 17:10 9:12 [a] Ps. 22:6; Is. 53:3; Dan. 9:26 [b] Luke 23:11; Phil. 2:7 9:13 [a] Mal. 4:5; Matt. 11:14; 17:12; Luke 1:17 9:14 [a] Matt. 17:14–19; Luke 9:37–42 9:17 [a] Matt. 17:14; Luke 9:38 9:19 [a] John 4:48 9:20 [a] Mark 1:26; Luke 9:42

RELEASE // RECONCILE CHAOS WITH PEACE

Do Not Allow Unbelief to Steal Your Peace

Mark 9:23 // Jesus said to him, "If you can believe, all things are possible to him who believes."

Summary Message // A father brought his child who was suffering from convulsions to Jesus' disciples for them to heal him, but they could not. The father, in turn, told Jesus of his son's condition and what had happened with the disciples. Jesus' response was, "If you can believe, all things are possible to him who believes" (Mark 9:23). When the father believed, the son was healed.

Practical Application // Many of us have become well acquainted with crises in our lives, which often visit us without our invitation or compliance. The child in Mark 9 had a condition that wreaked havoc on his body and in his family. We will experience many issues—such as health challenges, job loss, death of loved ones, and divorce—that can overwhelm us and sometimes cause us to question God. We wonder, "God, if You want only good things for me, then why is this bad thing happening?" This question, and perhaps God's nonimmediate answer to it, can cause our faith to falter and the situation to overwhelm us. In these chaotic and overwhelming situations, like the father in Mark 9, our response should be to turn to the Lord in faith, knowing His will for us is good and He is able to see far beyond what we can know or understand. In the account of the child in need of healing, the father responded to Jesus' words by saying: "Lord, I believe; help my unbelief!" (Mark 9:24). The father had a mixture of belief and some level of doubt or unbelief. Consequently, he had no peace. He was as tortured as his son. When we find our lives in chaos and we need a touch from the Lord, we must turn to Jesus to help us build our faith. Unbelief will destroy our peace, but a piece of faith is more than enough for Jesus to work with and grow.

Fervent Prayer // Father, because You know all things, You know when our faith is weak. Please, help us today. Holy Spirit, please remind us that faith can move confusion and bewilderment out of our lives when chaotic situations descend. We ask You to enable us to speak peace over every chaotic situation we face. We trust the power You have given to us through simply believing. In Jesus' name we pray. Amen.

And he said, "From childhood. 22And
often he has thrown him both into the fire
and into the water to destroy him. But if
You can do anything, have compassion on
us and help us."
23Jesus said to him, [a]"If you can believe,[1]
all things *are* possible to him who believes."
24Immediately the father of the child
cried out and said with tears, "Lord, I believe; [a]help my unbelief!"
25When Jesus saw that the people came
running together, He [a]rebuked the unclean
spirit, saying to it, "Deaf and dumb spirit,
I command you, come out of him and enter him no more!" 26Then *the spirit* cried
out, convulsed him greatly, and came out
of him. And he became as one dead, so that
many said, "He is dead." 27But Jesus took
him by the hand and lifted him up, and he
arose.
28[a]And when He had come into the
house, His disciples asked Him privately,
"Why could we not cast it out?"
29So He said to them, "This kind can
come out by nothing but [a]prayer and
fasting."[1]

Jesus Again Predicts His Death and Resurrection

30Then they departed from there and
passed through Galilee, and He did not
want anyone to know *it.* 31[a]For He taught
His disciples and said to them, "The Son
of Man is being betrayed into the hands of
men, and they will [b]kill Him. And after He
is killed, He will [c]rise the third day." 32But

9:23 [a] Matt. 17:20; Mark 11:23; Luke 17:6; John 11:40 [1] NU-Text reads "*'If You can!' All things . . . .*" 9:24 [a] Luke 17:5 9:25 [a] Mark 1:25 9:28 [a] Matt. 17:19 9:29 [a] [James 5:16] [1] NU-Text omits *and fasting.* 9:31 [a] Matt. 17:22; Luke 9:44 [b] Matt. 16:21; 27:50; Luke 18:33; 23:46; Acts 2:23 [c] Matt. 20:19; Luke 24:46; Acts 10:40; 1 Cor. 15:4

they [a]did not understand this saying, and
were afraid to ask Him.

Who Is the Greatest?
(Matt. 18:1–5; Luke 9:46–48)

33 [a]Then He came to Capernaum. And
when He was in the house He asked them,
"What was it you disputed among yourselves on the road?" 34 But they kept silent,
for on the road they had [a]disputed among
themselves who *would be the* [b]greatest.
35 And He sat down, called the twelve, and
said to them, [a]"If anyone desires to be first,
he shall be last of all and servant of all."
36 Then [a]He took a little child and set him in
the midst of them. And when He had taken
him in His arms, He said to them, 37 "Whoever receives one of these little children in
My name receives Me; and [a]whoever receives Me, receives not Me but Him who
sent Me."

Jesus Forbids Sectarianism
(Matt. 10:40–42; Luke 9:49, 50)

38 [a]Now John answered Him, saying,
"Teacher, we saw someone who does not
follow us casting out demons in Your name,
and we forbade him because he does not
follow us."

39 But Jesus said, "Do not forbid him, [a]for
no one who works a miracle in My name
can soon afterward speak evil of Me. 40 For
[a]he who is not against us is on our[1] side.
41 [a]For whoever gives you a cup of water to
drink in My name, because you belong to
Christ, assuredly, I say to you, he will by no
means lose his reward.

Jesus Warns of Offenses
(Matt. 18:6–9; Luke 17:1, 2)

42 [a]"But whoever causes one of these little ones who believe in Me to stumble, it
would be better for him if a millstone were
hung around his neck, and he were thrown
into the sea. 43 [a]If your hand causes you to
sin, cut it off. It is better for you to enter
into life maimed, rather than having two
hands, to go to hell, into the fire that shall
never be quenched— 44 where

[a]'Their worm does not die
And the fire is not quenched.'[1]

45 And if your foot causes you to sin, cut it
off. It is better for you to enter life lame,
rather than having two feet, to be cast
into hell, into the fire that shall never be
quenched— 46 where

[a]'Their worm does not die
And the fire is not quenched.'[1]

47 And if your eye causes you to sin, pluck
it out. It is better for you to enter the kingdom of God with one eye, rather than
having two eyes, to be cast into hell fire—
48 where

[a]'Their worm does not die
And the [b]fire is not quenched.'[1]

Tasteless Salt Is Worthless

49 "For everyone will be [a]seasoned with
fire,[1] [b]and every sacrifice will be seasoned
with salt. 50 [a]Salt *is* good, but if the salt loses
its flavor, how will you season it? [b]Have salt
in yourselves, and [c]have peace with one
another."

Marriage and Divorce
(Matt. 19:1–9)

10 Then [a]He arose from there and came
to the region of Judea by the other
side of the Jordan. And multitudes gathered to Him again, and as He was accustomed, He taught them again.

2 [a]The Pharisees came and asked Him,
"Is it lawful for a man to divorce *his* wife?"
testing Him.

3 And He answered and said to them,
"What did Moses command you?"

4 They said, [a]"Moses permitted *a man*

9:32 [a] Luke 2:50; 18:34; John 12:16 9:33 [a] Matt. 18:1–5; Mark 14:53, 64; Luke 9:46–48; 22:24; John 18:12; 19:7 9:34 [a] [Prov. 13:10]; Mark 15:20, 31 [b] Matt. 18:4; [Mark 9:50]; 14:65; 15:15, 37; Luke 22:24; 23:46; 24:46 9:35 [a] Matt. 20:26, 27; 23:11; Mark 10:43, 44; Luke 22:26, 27 9:36 [a] Mark 10:13–16 9:37 [a] Matt. 10:40; Luke 10:16; John 13:20 9:38 [a] Num. 11:27–29; Luke 9:49 9:39 [a] 1 Cor. 12:3 9:40 [a] [Matt. 12:30]; Luke 11:23 [1] M-Text reads *against you is on your side.* 9:41 [a] Matt. 10:42 9:42 [a] Matt. 18:6; Luke 17:1, 2; [1 Cor. 8:12] 9:43 [a] [Deut. 13:6]; Matt. 5:29, 30; 18:8, 9 9:44 [a] Is. 66:24 [1] NU-Text omits this verse. 9:46 [a] Is. 66:24 [1] NU-Text omits the last clause of verse 45 and all of verse 46. 9:48 [a] Is. 66:24 [b] Jer. 7:20; [Rev. 21:8] [1] Isaiah 66:24 9:49 [a] [Matt. 3:11] [b] Lev. 2:13; Ezek. 43:24 [1] NU-Text omits the rest of this verse. 9:50 [a] Matt. 5:13; Luke 14:34 [b] [Eph. 4:29]; Col. 4:6 [c] Rom. 12:18; 14:19; 2 Cor. 13:11; 1 Thess. 5:13; Heb. 12:14 10:1 [a] Matt. 19:1–9; John 10:40; 11:7 10:2 [a] Matt. 19:3 10:4 [a] Deut. 24:1–4; Matt. 5:31; 19:7

to write a certificate of divorce, and to dismiss *her*."
5And Jesus answered and said to them,
"Because of the hardness of your heart he
wrote you this precept. 6But from the beginning of the creation, God [a]'made them
male and female.'[1] 7[a]'For this reason a man
shall leave his father and mother and be
joined to his wife, 8and the two shall become one flesh';[1] so then they are no longer two, but one flesh. 9Therefore what
God has joined together, let not man separate."
10In the house His disciples also asked
Him again about the same *matter*. 11So He
said to them, [a]"Whoever divorces his wife
and marries another commits adultery
against her. 12And if a woman divorces her
husband and marries another, she commits adultery."

Jesus Blesses Little Children
(Matt. 19:13–15; Luke 18:15–17)

13[a]Then they brought little children to
Him, that He might touch them; but the
disciples rebuked those who brought *them*.
14But when Jesus saw *it*, He was greatly displeased and said to them, "Let the little
children come to Me, and do not forbid
them; for [a]of such is the kingdom of God.
15Assuredly, I say to you, [a]whoever does
not receive the kingdom of God as a little
child will [b]by no means enter it." 16And He
took them up in His arms, laid *His* hands
on them, and blessed them.

Jesus Counsels the Rich Young Ruler
(Matt. 19:16–22; Luke 18:18–23)

17[a]Now as He was going out on the road,
one came running, knelt before Him, and
asked Him, "Good Teacher, what shall I [b]do
that I may inherit eternal life?"
18So Jesus said to him, "Why do you call
Me good? No one *is* good but One, *that is*,
[a]God. 19You know the commandments: [a]'Do
not commit adultery,' 'Do not murder,' 'Do
not steal,' 'Do not bear false witness,' 'Do
not defraud,' 'Honor your father and your
mother.'"[1]
20And he answered and said to Him,
"Teacher, all these things I have [a]kept from
my youth."
21Then Jesus, looking at him, loved him,
and said to him, "One thing you lack: Go
your way, [a]sell whatever you have and give
to the poor, and you will have [b]treasure in
heaven; and come, [c]take up the cross, and
follow Me."
22But he was sad at this word, and went
away sorrowful, for he had great possessions.

With God All Things Are Possible
(Matt. 19:23–30; Luke 18:24–30)

23[a]Then Jesus looked around and said
to His disciples, "How hard it is for those
who have riches to enter the kingdom
of God!" 24And the disciples were astonished at His words. But Jesus answered
again and said to them, "Children, how
hard it is for those [a]who trust in riches[1]
to enter the kingdom of God! 25It is easier for a camel to go through the eye of a
needle than for a [a]rich man to enter the
kingdom of God."
26And they were greatly astonished, saying among themselves, "Who then can be
saved?"
27But Jesus looked at them and said,
"With men *it is* impossible, but not [a]with
God; for with God all things are possible."
28[a]Then Peter began to say to Him, "See,
we have left all and followed You."
29So Jesus answered and said, "Assuredly, I say to you, there is no one who
has left house or brothers or sisters or
father or mother or wife[1] or children or
lands, for My sake and the gospel's, 30[a]who
shall not receive a hundredfold now in this
time—houses and brothers and sisters
and mothers and children and lands, with
[b]persecutions—and in the age to come,
eternal life. 31[a]But many *who are* first will
be last, and the last first."

10:6 [a] Gen. 1:27; 5:2 [1] Genesis 1:27; 5:2 10:7 [a] Gen. 2:24; [1 Cor. 6:16]; Eph. 5:31 10:8 [1] Genesis 2:24 10:11 [a] Ex. 20:14; [Matt. 5:32; 19:9]; Luke 16:18; [Rom. 7:3]; 1 Cor. 7:10, 11 10:13 [a] Matt. 19:13–15; Luke 18:15–17 10:14 [a] [1 Cor. 14:20; 1 Pet. 2:2] 10:15 [a] Matt. 18:3, 4; 19:14; Luke 18:17 [b] Luke 13:28 10:17 [a] Matt. 19:16–30; Luke 18:18–30 [b] John 6:28; Acts 2:37 10:18 [a] 1 Sam. 2:2 10:19 [a] Ex. 20:12–16; Deut. 5:16–20; [Rom. 13:9; James 2:10, 11] [1] Exodus 20:12–16; Deuteronomy 5:16–20 10:20 [a] Phil. 3:6 10:21 [a] [Luke 12:33; 16:9] [b] Matt. 6:19, 20; 19:21 [c] [Mark 8:34] 10:23 [a] Matt. 19:23; [Mark 4:19]; Luke 18:24 10:24 [a] Job 31:24; Ps. 52:7; 62:10; [Prov. 11:28; 1 Tim. 6:17] [1] NU-Text omits *for those who trust in riches.* 10:25 [a] [Matt. 13:22; 19:24] 10:27 [a] Job 42:2; Jer. 32:17; Matt. 19:26; Luke 1:37 10:28 [a] Matt. 19:27; Luke 18:28 10:29 [1] NU-Text omits *or wife.* 10:30 [a] 2 Chr. 25:9; Luke 18:29, 30 [b] 1 Thess. 3:3; 2 Tim. 3:12; [1 Pet. 4:12, 13] 10:31 [a] Matt. 19:30; 20:16; Luke 13:30

Jesus a Third Time Predicts His Death and Resurrection
(Matt. 20:17–19; Luke 18:31–34)

32[a]Now they were on the road, going
up to Jerusalem, and Jesus was going before them; and they were amazed. And as
they followed they were afraid. [b]Then He
took the twelve aside again and began to
tell them the things that would happen to
Him: 33"Behold, we are going up to Jerusalem, and the Son of Man will be betrayed
to the chief priests and to the scribes; and
they will condemn Him to death and deliver Him to the Gentiles; 34and they will
mock Him, and scourge Him, and spit on
Him, and kill Him. And the third day He
will rise again."

Greatness Is Serving
(Matt. 20:20–28)

35[a]Then James and John, the sons of
Zebedee, came to Him, saying, "Teacher,
we want You to do for us whatever we ask."
36And He said to them, "What do you
want Me to do for you?"
37They said to Him, "Grant us that we
may sit, one on Your right hand and the
other on Your left, in Your glory."
38But Jesus said to them, "You do not
know what you ask. Are you able to drink
the [a]cup that I drink, and be baptized with
the [b]baptism that I am baptized with?"
39They said to Him, "We are able."
So Jesus said to them, [a]"You will indeed
drink the cup that I drink, and with the baptism I am baptized with you will be baptized; 40but to sit on My right hand and on
My left is not Mine to give, but *it is for those*
[a]for whom it is prepared."
41[a]And when the ten heard *it,* they began
to be greatly displeased with James and
John. 42But Jesus called them to *Himself*
and said to them, [a]"You know that those
who are considered rulers over the Gentiles lord it over them, and their great ones
exercise authority over them. 43[a]Yet it shall
not be so among you; but whoever desires
to become great among you shall be your
servant. 44And whoever of you desires to
be first shall be slave of all. 45For even [a]the
Son of Man did not come to be served, but
to serve, and [b]to give His life a ransom for
many."

Jesus Heals Blind Bartimaeus
(Matt. 20:29–34; Luke 18:35–43)

46[a]Now they came to Jericho. As He went
out of Jericho with His disciples and a great
multitude, blind Bartimaeus, the son of Ti-
maeus, sat by the road begging. 47And when
he heard that it was Jesus of Nazareth, he
began to cry out and say, "Jesus, [a]Son of
David, [b]have mercy on me!"
48Then many warned him to be quiet;
but he cried out all the more, "Son of David, have mercy on me!"
49So Jesus stood still and commanded
him to be called.
Then they called the blind man, saying
to him, "Be of good cheer. Rise, He is calling you."
50And throwing aside his garment, he
rose and came to Jesus.
51So Jesus answered and said to him,
"What do you want Me to do for you?"
The blind man said to Him, "Rabboni,
that I may receive my sight."
52Then Jesus said to him, "Go your way;
[a]your faith has made you well." And immediately he received his sight and followed
Jesus on the road.

The Triumphal Entry
(Matt. 21:1–11; Luke 19:28–40; John 12:12–19)

11 Now [a]when they drew near Jerusalem, to Bethphage[1] and Bethany, at
the Mount of Olives, He sent two of His disciples; 2and He said to them, "Go into the
village opposite you; and as soon as you
have entered it you will find a colt tied, on
which no one has sat. Loose it and bring *it.*
3And if anyone says to you, 'Why are you
doing this?' say, 'The Lord has need of it,'
and immediately he will send it here."
4So they went their way, and found the[1]
colt tied by the door outside on the street,

10:32 [a] Matt. 20:17–19; Luke 18:31–33 [b] Mark 8:31; 9:31; Luke 9:22; 18:31 10:35 [a] [James 4:3] 10:38 [a] Matt. 26:39, 42; Mark 14:36; Luke 22:42; John 18:11 [b] Luke 12:50 10:39 [a] Matt. 10:17, 18, 21, 22; 24:9; John 16:33; Acts 12:2; Rev. 1:9 10:40 [a] [Matt. 25:34; John 17:2, 6, 24; Rom. 8:30; Heb. 11:16] 10:41 [a] Matt. 20:24 10:42 [a] Luke 22:25 10:43 [a] Matt. 20:26, 28; Mark 9:35; Luke 9:48 10:45 [a] Luke 22:27; John 13:14; [Phil. 2:7, 8] [b] Matt. 20:28; [2 Cor. 5:21; 1 Tim. 2:5, 6; Titus 2:14] 10:46 [a] Matt. 20:29–34; Luke 18:35–43 10:47 [a] Jer. 23:5; Matt. 22:42; Rom. 1:3, 4; Rev. 22:16 [b] Matt. 15:22; Luke 17:13 10:52 [a] Matt. 9:22; Mark 5:34 11:1 [a] Matt. 21:1–9; Luke 19:29; John 2:13 [1] M-Text reads *Bethsphage.* 11:4 [1] NU-Text and M-Text read *a.*

and they loosed it. 5But some of those who
stood there said to them, "What are you doing, loosing the colt?"

6And they spoke to them just as Jesus
had commanded. So they let them go.
7Then they brought the colt to Jesus and
threw their clothes on it, and He sat on it.
8[a]And many spread their clothes on the
road, and others cut down leafy branches
from the trees and spread *them* on the road.
9Then those who went before and those
who followed cried out, saying:

"Hosanna!
[a]'Blessed *is* He who comes in
the name of the LORD!'[1]
10 Blessed *is* the kingdom of
our father David
That comes in the name of the Lord![1]
[a]Hosanna in the highest!"

11[a]And Jesus went into Jerusalem and into
the temple. So when He had looked around
at all things, as the hour was already late,
He went out to Bethany with the twelve.

The Fig Tree Withered
(Matt. 21:18, 19)

12[a]Now the next day, when they had come
out from Bethany, He was hungry. 13[a]And
seeing from afar a fig tree having leaves, He
went to see if perhaps He would find something on it. When He came to it, He found
nothing but leaves, for it was not the season for figs. 14In response Jesus said to it,
"Let no one eat fruit from you ever again."

And His disciples heard *it*.

Jesus Cleanses the Temple
(Matt. 21:12–17; Luke 19:45–48; John 2:13–22)

15[a]So they came to Jerusalem. Then Jesus
went into the temple and began to drive out
those who bought and sold in the temple,
and overturned the tables of the money
changers and the seats of those who sold
[b]doves. 16And He would not allow anyone
to carry wares through the temple. 17Then
He taught, saying to them, "Is it not written,
[a]'My house shall be called a house of prayer
for all nations'?[1] But you have made it a
[b]'den of thieves.'"[2]

18And [a]the scribes and chief priests
heard it and sought how they might destroy Him; for they feared Him, because [b]all
the people were astonished at His teaching. 19When evening had come, He went
out of the city.

The Lesson of the Withered Fig Tree
(Matt. 21:20–22)

20[a]Now in the morning, as they passed
by, they saw the fig tree dried up from the
roots. 21And Peter, remembering, said to
Him, "Rabbi, look! The fig tree which You
cursed has withered away."

22So Jesus answered and said to them,
"Have faith in God. 23For [a]assuredly, I say
to you, whoever says to this mountain, 'Be
removed and be cast into the sea,' and does
not doubt in his heart, but believes that
those things he says will be done, he will
have whatever he says. 24Therefore I say
to you, [a]whatever things you ask when you
pray, believe that you receive *them*, and you
will have *them*.

Forgiveness and Prayer
(Matt. 6:14, 15)

25"And whenever you stand praying, [a]if
you have anything against anyone, forgive
him, that your Father in heaven may also
forgive you your trespasses. 26But [a]if you
do not forgive, neither will your Father in
heaven forgive your trespasses."[1]

Jesus' Authority Questioned
(Matt. 21:23–27; Luke 20:1–8)

27Then they came again to Jerusalem.
[a]And as He was walking in the temple,
the chief priests, the scribes, and the elders came to Him. 28And they said to Him,
"By what [a]authority are You doing these
things? And who gave You this authority
to do these things?"

29But Jesus answered and said to them, "I
also will ask you one question; then answer

11:8 [a] Matt. 21:8 **11:9** [a] Ps. 118:25, 26; Matt. 21:9 [1] Psalm 118:26 **11:10** [a] Ps. 148:1 [1] NU-Text omits *in the name of the Lord.* **11:11** [a] Matt. 21:12 **11:12** [a] Matt. 21:18–22 **11:13** [a] Matt. 21:19 **11:15** [a] Mal. 3:1; Matt. 21:12–16; Luke 19:45–47; John 2:13–16 [b] Lev. 14:22 **11:17** [a] Is. 56:7 [b] Jer. 7:11 [1] Isaiah 56:7 [2] Jeremiah 7:11 **11:18** [a] Ps. 2:2; Matt. 21:45, 46; Luke 19:47 [b] Matt. 7:28; Mark 1:22; 6:2; Luke 4:32 **11:20** [a] Matt. 21:19–22 **11:23** [a] Matt. 17:20; 21:21; Luke 17:6 **11:24** [a] Matt. 7:7; Luke 11:9; [John 14:13; 15:7; 16:24; James 1:5, 6] **11:25** [a] Matt. 6:14; 18:23–35; Eph. 4:32; [Col. 3:13] **11:26** [a] Matt. 6:15; 18:35 [1] NU-Text omits this verse. **11:27** [a] Matt. 21:23–27; Luke 20:1–8 **11:28** [a] John 5:27

Me, and I will tell you by what authority I do
these things: 30The [a]baptism of John—was
it from heaven or from men? Answer Me."
31And they reasoned among themselves,
saying, "If we say, 'From heaven,' He will
say, 'Why then did you not believe him?'
32But if we say, 'From men'"—they feared
the people, for [a]all counted John to have
been a prophet indeed. 33So they answered
and said to Jesus, "We do not know."

And Jesus answered and said to them,
"Neither will I tell you by what authority I
do these things."

The Parable of the Wicked Vinedressers
(Matt. 21:33–46; Luke 20:9–19)

12 Then [a]He began to speak to them in
parables: "A man planted a vineyard
and set a hedge around *it,* dug *a place for* the
wine vat and built a tower. And he leased it
to vinedressers and went into a far country.
2Now at vintage-time he sent a servant to the
vinedressers, that he might receive some
of the fruit of the vineyard from the vinedressers. 3And they took *him* and beat him
and sent *him* away empty-handed. 4Again
he sent them another servant, and at him
they threw stones,[1] wounded *him* in the head,
and sent *him* away shamefully treated. 5And
again he sent another, and him they killed;
and many others, [a]beating some and killing some. 6Therefore still having one son,
his beloved, he also sent him to them last,
saying, 'They will respect my son.' 7But those
vinedressers said among themselves, 'This
is the heir. Come, let us kill him, and the inheritance will be ours.' 8So they took him and
[a]killed *him* and cast *him* out of the vineyard.
9"Therefore what will the owner of the
vineyard do? He will come and destroy the
vinedressers, and give the vineyard to others. 10Have you not even read this Scripture:

[a]'The stone which the builders rejected
Has become the chief cornerstone.
11 This was the LORD's doing,
And it is marvelous in our eyes'?"[1]

12[a]And they sought to lay hands on Him,
but feared the multitude, for they knew He
had spoken the parable against them. So
they left Him and went away.

The Pharisees: Is It Lawful to Pay Taxes to Caesar?
(Matt. 22:15–22; Luke 20:20–26)

13[a]Then they sent to Him some of the
Pharisees and the Herodians, to catch Him
in *His* words. 14When they had come, they
said to Him, "Teacher, we know that You
are true, and care about no one; for You do
not regard the person of men, but teach
the [a]way of God in truth. Is it lawful to pay
taxes to Caesar, or not? 15Shall we pay, or
shall we not pay?"

But He, knowing their [a]hypocrisy, said
to them, "Why do you test Me? Bring Me
a denarius that I may see *it.*" 16So they
brought *it.*

And He said to them, "Whose image
and inscription *is* this?" They said to Him,
"Caesar's."

17And Jesus answered and said to them,
"Render to Caesar the things that are Caesar's, and to [a]God the things that are God's."

And they marveled at Him.

The Sadducees: What About the Resurrection?
(Matt. 22:23–33; Luke 20:27–40)

18[a]Then *some* Sadducees, [b]who say there
is no resurrection, came to Him; and they
asked Him, saying: 19"Teacher, [a]Moses wrote
to us that if a man's brother dies, and leaves
his wife behind, and leaves no children, his
brother should take his wife and raise up
offspring for his brother. 20Now there were
seven brothers. The first took a wife; and
dying, he left no offspring. 21And the second
took her, and he died; nor did he leave any
offspring. And the third likewise. 22So the
seven had her and left no offspring. Last of
all the woman died also. 23Therefore, in the
resurrection, when they rise, whose wife
will she be? For all seven had her as wife."

24Jesus answered and said to them,
"Are you not therefore mistaken, because
you do not know the Scriptures nor the
power of God? 25For when they rise from
the dead, they neither marry nor are given

11:30 [a] [Mark 1:4, 5, 8]; Luke 7:29, 30 11:32 [a] Matt. 3:5; 14:5; Mark 6:20 12:1 [a] Matt. 21:33–46; Luke 20:9–19 12:4 [1] NU-Text omits *and at him they threw stones.* 12:5 [a] 2 Chr. 36:16 12:8 [a] [Acts 2:23] 12:10 [a] Ps. 118:22, 23 12:11 [1] Psalm 118:22, 23 12:12 [a] Matt. 21:45, 46; Mark 11:18; John 7:25, 30, 44 12:13 [a] Matt. 22:15–22; Luke 20:20–26 12:14 [a] Acts 18:26 12:15 [a] Matt. 23:28; Luke 12:1 12:17 [a] [Eccl. 5:4, 5] 12:18 [a] Matt. 22:23–33; Luke 20:27–38 [b] Acts 23:8 12:19 [a] Deut. 25:5

in marriage, but [a]are like angels in heaven.
26 But concerning the dead, that they [a]rise,
have you not read in the book of Moses, in
the *burning* bush *passage,* how God spoke to
him, saying, [b]'I *am* the God of Abraham, the
God of Isaac, and the God of Jacob'?[1] 27 He is
not the God of the dead, but the God of the
living. You are therefore greatly mistaken."

The Scribes: Which Is the First Commandment of All?
(Matt. 22:34–40; Luke 10:25–28)

28 [a]Then one of the scribes came, and
having heard them reasoning together,
perceiving[1] that He had answered them
well, asked Him, "Which is the first commandment of all?"
29 Jesus answered him, "The first of all
the commandments *is:* [a]'Hear, O Israel, the
LORD our God, the LORD is one. 30 And you
shall [a]love the LORD your God with all your
heart, with all your soul, with all your mind,
and with all your strength.'[1] This *is* the first
commandment.[2] 31 And the second, like *it,*
is this: [a]'You shall love your neighbor as
yourself.'[1] There is no other commandment
greater than [b]these."
32 So the scribe said to Him, "Well *said,*
Teacher. You have spoken the truth, for
there is one God, [a]and there is no other but
He. 33 And to love Him with all the heart,
with all the understanding, with all the
soul,[1] and with all the strength, and to love
one's neighbor as oneself, [a]is more than all
the whole burnt offerings and sacrifices."
34 Now when Jesus saw that he answered
wisely, He said to him, "You are not far from
the kingdom of God."
[a]But after that no one dared question
Him.

Jesus: How Can David Call His Descendant Lord?
(Matt. 22:41–46; Luke 20:41–44)

35 [a]Then Jesus answered and said, while
He taught in the temple, "How *is it* that
the scribes say that the Christ is the Son
of David? 36 For David himself said [a]by the
Holy Spirit:

> [b]'The LORD said to my Lord,
> "Sit at My right hand,
> Till I make Your enemies
> Your footstool."'[1]

37 Therefore David himself calls Him 'Lord';
how is He *then* his [a]Son?"
And the common people heard Him
gladly.

Beware of the Scribes
(Matt. 23:1–7; Luke 20:45–47)

38 Then [a]He said to them in His teaching, [b]"Beware of the scribes, who desire to
go around in long robes, [c]*love* greetings in
the marketplaces, 39 the [a]best seats in the
synagogues, and the best places at feasts,
40 [a]who devour widows' houses, and for a
pretense make long prayers. These will receive greater condemnation."

The Widow's Two Mites
(Luke 21:1–4)

41 [a]Now Jesus sat opposite the treasury
and saw how the people put money [b]into
the treasury. And many *who were* rich put
in much. 42 Then one poor widow came
and threw in two mites,[1] which make a
quadrans. 43 So He called His disciples to
Himself and said to them, "Assuredly, I
say to you that [a]this poor widow has put
in more than all those who have given to
the treasury; 44 for they all put in out of their
abundance, but she out of her poverty put
in all that she had, [a]her whole livelihood."

Jesus Predicts the Destruction of the Temple
(Matt. 24:1, 2; Luke 21:5, 6)

13 Then [a]as He went out of the temple,
one of His disciples said to Him,
"Teacher, see what manner of stones and
what buildings *are here!*"
2 And Jesus answered and said to him,

12:25 [a] [1 Cor. 15:42, 49, 52] 12:26 [a] [John 5:25, 28, 29]; Acts 26:8; Rom. 4:17; [Rev. 20:12, 13] [b] Ex. 3:6, 15 [1] Exodus 3:6, 15
12:28 [a] Matt. 22:34–40; Luke 10:25–28; 20:39 [1] NU-Text reads *seeing.* 12:29 [a] Deut. 6:4, 5; Is. 44:8; 45:22; 46:9; 1 Cor. 8:6
12:30 [a] [Deut. 10:12; 30:6]; Luke 10:27 [1] Deuteronomy 6:4, 5 [2] NU-Text omits this sentence. 12:31 [a] Lev. 19:18; Matt. 22:39;
Gal. 5:14; James 2:8 [b] [Rom. 13:9] [1] Leviticus 19:18 12:32 [a] Deut. 4:39; Is. 45:6, 14; 46:9; [John 1:14, 17; 14:6] 12:33 [a] [1 Sam. 15:22;
Hos. 6:6; Mic. 6:6–8; Matt. 9:13; 12:7] [1] NU-Text omits *with all the soul.* 12:34 [a] Matt. 22:46 12:35 [a] Matt. 22:41–46; Luke 20:41–44
12:36 [a] 2 Sam. 23:2 [b] Ps. 110:1 [1] Psalm 110:1 12:37 [a] [Acts 2:29–31] 12:38 [a] Mark 4:2 [b] Matt. 23:1–7; Luke 20:45–47 [c] Matt. 23:7;
Luke 11:43 12:39 [a] Luke 14:7 12:40 [a] Matt. 23:14 12:41 [a] Luke 21:1–4 [b] 2 Kin. 12:9 12:42 [1] Greek *lepta,* very small copper coins
worth a fraction of a penny 12:43 [a] [2 Cor. 8:12] 12:44 [a] Deut. 24:6; [1 John 3:17] 13:1 [a] Matt. 24:1; Luke 21:5–36

"Do you see these great buildings? [a]Not *one*
stone shall be left upon another, that shall
not be thrown down."

The Signs of the Times and the End of the Age
(Matt. 24:3–14; Luke 21:7–19)

3 Now as He sat on the Mount of Olives
opposite the temple, [a]Peter, [b]James, [c]John,
and [d]Andrew asked Him privately, 4 [a]"Tell
us, when will these things be? And what *will
be* the sign when all these things will be fulfilled?"

5 And Jesus, answering them, began to say:
[a]"Take heed that no one deceives you. 6 For
many will come in My name, saying, 'I am
He,' and will deceive many. 7 But when you
hear of wars and rumors of wars, do not be
troubled; for *such things* must happen, but
the end *is* not yet. 8 For nation will rise against
nation, and [a]kingdom against kingdom. And
there will be earthquakes in various places,
and there will be famines and troubles.[1]
[b]These *are* the beginnings of sorrows.

9 "But [a]watch out for yourselves, for they
will deliver you up to councils, and you will
be beaten in the synagogues. You will be
brought[1] before rulers and kings for My
sake, for a testimony to them. 10 And [a]the
gospel must first be preached to all the nations.
11 [a]But when they arrest *you* and deliver
you up, do not worry beforehand, or
premeditate[1] what you will speak. But whatever
is given you in that hour, speak that;
for it is not you who speak, [b]but the Holy
Spirit. 12 Now [a]brother will betray brother to
death, and a father *his* child; and children
will rise up against parents and cause them
to be put to death. 13 [a]And you will be hated
by all for My name's sake. But [b]he who endures
to the end shall be saved.

The Great Tribulation
(Matt. 24:15–28; Luke 21:20–24)

14 [a]"So when you see the [b]'abomination
of desolation,'[1] spoken of by Daniel the
prophet,[2] standing where it ought not" (let
the reader understand), "then [c]let those
who are in Judea flee to the mountains.
15 Let him who is on the housetop not go
down into the house, nor enter to take anything
out of his house. 16 And let him who is
in the field not go back to get his clothes.
17 [a]But woe to those who are pregnant and
to those who are nursing babies in those
days! 18 And pray that your flight may not
be in winter. 19 [a]For *in* those days there will
be tribulation, such as has not been since
the beginning of the creation which God
created until this time, nor ever shall be.
20 And unless the Lord had shortened those
days, no flesh would be saved; but for the
elect's sake, whom He chose, He shortened
the days.

21 [a]"Then if anyone says to you, 'Look,
here *is* the Christ!' or, 'Look, *He is* there!'
do not believe it. 22 For false christs and
false prophets will rise and show signs and
[a]wonders to deceive, if possible, even the
elect. 23 But [a]take heed; see, I have told you
all things beforehand.

The Coming of the Son of Man
(Matt. 24:29–31; Luke 21:25–28)

24 [a]"But in those days, after that tribulation,
the sun will be darkened, and the
moon will not give its light; 25 the stars of
heaven will fall, and the powers in the heavens
will be [a]shaken. 26 [a]Then they will see
the Son of Man coming in the clouds with
great power and glory. 27 And then He will
send His angels, and gather together His
elect from the four winds, from the farthest
part of earth to the farthest part of heaven.

The Parable of the Fig Tree
(Matt. 24:32–35; Luke 21:29–33)

28 [a]"Now learn this parable from the fig
tree: When its branch has already become
tender, and puts forth leaves, you know
that summer is near. 29 So you also, when
you see these things happening, know that

13:2 [a] Luke 19:44 13:3 [a] Matt. 16:18; Mark 1:16 [b] Mark 1:19 [c] Mark 1:19 [d] John 1:40 13:4 [a] Matt. 24:3; Luke 21:7 13:5 [a] Jer. 29:8; Eph. 5:6; [Col. 2:8]; 1 Thess. 2:3; 2 Thess. 2:3 13:8 [a] Hag. 2:22 [b] Matt. 24:8 [1] NU-Text omits *and troubles.* 13:9 [a] Matt. 10:17, 18; 24:9; Acts 12:4; [Rev. 2:10] [1] NU-Text and M-Text read *will stand.* 13:10 [a] Matt. 24:14 13:11 [a] Matt. 10:19–22; Luke 12:11; 21:12–17 [b] Acts 2:4; 4:8, 31 [1] NU-Text omits *or premeditate.* 13:12 [a] Mic. 7:6; Matt. 10:21; 24:10; Luke 21:16 13:13 [a] Matt. 24:9; Luke 21:17; John 15:21 [b] Dan. 12:12; Matt. 10:22; 24:13; [Rev. 2:10] 13:14 [a] Matt. 24:15 [b] Dan. 9:27; 11:31; 12:11 [c] Luke 21:21 [1] Daniel 11:31; 12:11 [2] NU-Text omits *spoken of by Daniel the prophet.* 13:17 [a] Luke 21:23 13:19 [a] Dan. 9:26; 12:1; Joel 2:2; Matt. 24:21; Mark 10:6 13:21 [a] Matt. 24:23; Luke 17:23; 21:8 13:22 [a] Deut. 13:1–3; Rev. 13:13, 14 13:23 [a] John 16:1–4; [2 Pet. 3:17] 13:24 [a] Zeph. 1:15; Matt. 24:29 13:25 [a] Is. 13:10; 34:4; Heb. 12:26; Rev. 6:13 13:26 [a] [Dan. 7:13, 14; Matt. 16:27; 24:30]; Mark 14:62; Acts 1:11; [1 Thess. 4:16; 2 Thess. 1:7, 10]; Rev. 1:7 13:28 [a] Matt. 24:32; Luke 21:29

it[1] is near—at the doors! 30Assuredly, I say
to you, this generation will by no means
pass away till all these things take place.
31Heaven and earth will pass away, but [a]My
words will by no means pass away.

No One Knows the Day or Hour
(Matt. 24:36–44; Luke 21:34–36)

32"But of that day and hour [a]no one
knows, not even the angels in heaven, nor
the Son, but only the [b]Father. 33[a]Take heed,
watch and pray; for you do not know when
the time is. 34[a]*It is* like a man going to a
far country, who left his house and gave
[b]authority to his servants, and to each his
work, and commanded the doorkeeper
to watch. 35[a]Watch therefore, for you do
not know when the master of the house is
coming—in the evening, at midnight, at
the crowing of the rooster, or in the morning— 36lest, coming suddenly, he find you
sleeping. 37And what I say to you, I say to
all: Watch!"

The Plot to Kill Jesus
(Matt. 26:1–5; Luke 22:1, 2; John 11:45–53)

14 After [a]two days it was the Passover
and [b]*the Feast* of Unleavened Bread.
And the chief priests and the scribes sought
how they might take Him by trickery and
put *Him* to death. 2But they said, "Not
during the feast, lest there be an uproar
of the people."

The Anointing at Bethany
(Matt. 26:6–13; John 12:1–8)

3[a]And being in Bethany at the house
of Simon the leper, as He sat at the table,
a woman came having an alabaster flask
of very costly oil of spikenard. Then she
broke the flask and poured *it* on His head.
4But there were some who were indignant
among themselves, and said, "Why was this
fragrant oil wasted? 5For it might have been
sold for more than three hundred [a]denarii
and given to the poor." And they [b]criticized
her sharply.

6But Jesus said, "Let her alone. Why do
you trouble her? She has done a good work
for Me. 7[a]For you have the poor with you
always, and whenever you wish you may
do them good; [b]but Me you do not have
always. 8She has done what she could. She
has come beforehand to anoint My body
for burial. 9Assuredly, I say to you, wherever this gospel is [a]preached in the whole
world, what this woman has done will also
be told as a memorial to her."

#OXYGEN
MARK 14:6
Reconcile Chaos with Peace

Do not let the inconsistency of people wreak havoc on your worship. Your sacrifice matters to God. He will understand your sacrifice even when others do not.

Accept His peace, **breathe**, and **reconcile chaos with peace.**

Judas Agrees to Betray Jesus
(Matt. 26:14–16; Luke 22:3–6)

10[a]Then Judas Iscariot, one of the twelve,
went to the chief priests to betray Him to
them. 11And when they heard *it,* they were
glad, and promised to give him money. So
he sought how he might conveniently betray Him.

Jesus Celebrates the Passover with His Disciples
(Matt. 26:17–25; Luke 22:7–13; John 13:21–30)

12[a]Now on the first day of Unleavened
Bread, when they killed the Passover *lamb,*
His disciples said to Him, "Where do You
want us to go and prepare, that You may
eat the Passover?"

13And He sent out two of His disciples
and said to them, "Go into the city, and a
man will meet you carrying a pitcher of water; follow him. 14Wherever he goes in, say

13:29 [1] Or *He* 13:31 [a] Is. 40:8; [2 Pet. 3:7, 10, 12] 13:32 [a] Matt. 25:13 [b] Matt. 24:36; Acts 1:7 13:33 [a] Matt. 24:42; 25:13; Luke 12:40; 21:34; [Rom. 13:11]; 1 Thess. 5:6; 1 Pet. 4:7 13:34 [a] Matt. 24:45; 25:14 [b] [Matt. 16:19] 13:35 [a] Matt. 24:42, 44 14:1 [a] Matt. 26:2–5; Luke 22:1, 2; John 11:55; 13:1 [b] Ex. 12:1–27; Mark 14:12 14:3 [a] Matt. 26:6; Luke 7:37; John 12:1, 3 14:5 [a] Matt. 18:28; Mark 12:15 [b] Matt. 20:11; John 6:61 14:7 [a] Deut. 15:11; Matt. 26:11; John 12:8 [b] [John 7:33; 8:21; 14:2, 12; 16:10, 17, 28] 14:9 [a] Matt. 28:19, 20; Mark 16:15; Luke 24:47 14:10 [a] Ps. 41:9; 55:12–14; Matt. 10:2–4 14:12 [a] Ex. 12:8; Matt. 26:17–19; Luke 22:7–13

to the master of the house, 'The Teacher says, "Where is the guest room in which I may eat the Passover with My disciples?"'
15 Then he will show you a large upper room, furnished *and* prepared; there make ready for us."

16 So His disciples went out, and came into the city, and found it just as He had said to them; and they prepared the Passover.

17 [a]In the evening He came with the twelve. 18 Now as they sat and ate, Jesus said, "Assuredly, I say to you, [a]one of you who eats with Me will betray Me."

19 And they began to be sorrowful, and to say to Him one by one, "*Is* it I?" And another *said,* "*Is* it I?"[1]

20 He answered and said to them, "*It is* one of the twelve, who dips with Me in the dish. 21 [a]The Son of Man indeed goes just as it is written of Him, but woe to that man by whom the Son of Man is betrayed! It would have been good for that man if he had never been born."

Jesus Institutes the Lord's Supper

(Matt. 26:26–29; Luke 22:14–23; 1 Cor. 11:23–26)

22 [a]And as they were eating, Jesus took bread, blessed and broke *it,* and gave *it* to them and said, "Take, eat;[1] this is My [b]body."

23 Then He took the cup, and when He had given thanks He gave *it* to them, and they all drank from it. 24 And He said to them, "This is My blood of the new[1] covenant, which is shed for many. 25 Assuredly, I say to you, I will no longer drink of the fruit of the vine until that day when I drink it new in the kingdom of God."

26 [a]And when they had sung a hymn, they went out to the Mount of Olives.

Jesus Predicts Peter's Denial

(Matt. 26:31–35; Luke 22:31–34; John 13:36–38)

27 [a]Then Jesus said to them, "All of you will be made to stumble because of Me this night,[1] for it is written:

[b]'I will strike the Shepherd,
And the sheep will be scattered.'[2]

28 "But [a]after I have been raised, I will go before you to Galilee."

29 [a]Peter said to Him, "Even if all are made to stumble, yet I *will* not *be.*"

30 Jesus said to him, "Assuredly, I say to you that today, *even* this night, before the rooster crows twice, you will deny Me three times."

31 But he spoke more vehemently, "If I have to die with You, I will not deny You!"

And they all said likewise.

The Prayer in the Garden

(Matt. 26:36–46; Luke 22:39–46)

32 [a]Then they came to a place which was named Gethsemane; and He said to His disciples, "Sit here while I pray." 33 And He [a]took Peter, James, and John with Him, and He began to be troubled and deeply distressed. 34 Then He said to them, [a]"My soul is exceedingly sorrowful, *even* to death. Stay here and watch."

35 He went a little farther, and fell on the ground, and prayed that if it were possible, the hour might pass from Him. 36 And He said, [a]"Abba, Father, [b]all things *are* possible for You. Take this cup away from Me; [c]nevertheless, not what I will, but what You *will.*"

37 Then He came and found them sleeping, and said to Peter, "Simon, are you sleeping? Could you not watch one hour? 38 [a]Watch and pray, lest you enter into temptation. [b]The spirit indeed *is* willing, but the flesh *is* weak."

39 Again He went away and prayed, and spoke the same words. 40 And when He returned, He found them asleep again, for their eyes were heavy; and they did not know what to answer Him.

41 Then He came the third time and said to them, "Are you still sleeping and resting? It is enough! [a]The hour has come; behold, the Son of Man is being betrayed into the hands of sinners. 42 [a]Rise, let us be going. See, My betrayer is at hand."

14:17 [a] Matt. 26:20–24; Luke 22:14, 21–23 14:18 [a] Ps. 41:9; Matt. 26:46; Mark 14:42; John 6:70, 71; 13:18 14:19 [1] NU-Text omits this sentence. 14:21 [a] Matt. 26:24; Luke 22:22; Acts 1:16–20 14:22 [a] Matt. 26:26–29; Luke 22:17–20; 1 Cor. 11:23–25 [b] [1 Pet. 2:24] [1] NU-Text omits *eat.* 14:24 [1] NU-Text omits *new.* 14:26 [a] Matt. 26:30 14:27 [a] Matt. 26:31–35; Mark 14:50; John 16:32 [b] [Is. 53:5, 10]; Zech. 13:7 [1] NU-Text omits *because of Me this night.* [2] Zechariah 13:7 14:28 [a] Matt. 28:16; Mark 16:7; John 21:1 14:29 [a] Matt. 26:33, 34; Luke 22:33, 34; John 13:37, 38 14:32 [a] Matt. 26:36–46; Luke 22:40–46; John 18:1 14:33 [a] Mark 5:37; 9:2; 13:3 14:34 [a] Is. 53:3, 4; Matt. 26:38; John 12:27 14:36 [a] Rom. 8:15; Gal. 4:6 [b] [Heb. 5:7] [c] Is. 50:5; John 5:30; 6:38 14:38 [a] Luke 21:36 [b] [Rom. 7:18, 21–24; Gal. 5:17] 14:41 [a] John 13:1; 17:1 14:42 [a] Matt. 26:46; Mark 14:18; Luke 9:44; John 13:21; 18:1, 2

Betrayal and Arrest in Gethsemane
(Matt. 26:47–56; Luke 22:47–53; John 18:1–11)

43[a]And immediately, while He was still
speaking, Judas, one of the twelve, with
a great multitude with swords and clubs,
came from the chief priests and the scribes
and the elders. 44Now His betrayer had
given them a signal, saying, "Whomever
I [a]kiss, He is the One; seize Him and lead
Him away safely."

45As soon as he had come, immediately
he went up to Him and said to Him, "Rabbi,
Rabbi!" and kissed Him.

46Then they laid their hands on Him and
took Him. 47And one of those who stood by
drew his sword and struck the servant of
the high priest, and cut off his ear.

48[a]Then Jesus answered and said to
them, "Have you come out, as against a robber, with swords and clubs to take Me? 49I
was daily with you in the temple [a]teaching,
and you did not seize Me. But [b]the Scriptures must be fulfilled."

50[a]Then they all forsook Him and fled.

A Young Man Flees Naked

51Now a certain young man followed
Him, having a linen cloth thrown around
his naked *body.* And the young men laid
hold of him, 52and he left the linen cloth
and fled from them naked.

Jesus Faces the Sanhedrin
(Matt. 26:57–68; Luke 22:66–71; John 18:12–14, 19–24)

53[a]And they led Jesus away to the high
priest; and with him were [b]assembled
all the [c]chief priests, the elders, and the
scribes. 54But [a]Peter followed Him at a distance, right into the courtyard of the high
priest. And he sat with the servants and
warmed himself at the fire.

55[a]Now the chief priests and all the council sought testimony against Jesus to put
Him to death, but found none. 56For many
bore [a]false witness against Him, but their
testimonies did not agree.

57Then some rose up and bore false witness against Him, saying, 58"We heard Him
say, [a]'I will destroy this temple made with
hands, and within three days I will build
another made without hands.' " 59But not
even then did their testimony agree.

60[a]And the high priest stood up in the
midst and asked Jesus, saying, "Do You answer nothing? What *is it* these men testify
against You?" 61But [a]He kept silent and answered nothing.

[b]Again the high priest asked Him, saying to Him, "Are You the Christ, the Son of
the Blessed?"

62Jesus said, "I am. [a]And you will see
the Son of Man sitting at the right hand
of the Power, and coming with the clouds
of heaven."

63Then the high priest tore his clothes
and said, "What further need do we have
of witnesses? 64You have heard the [a]blas-
phemy! What do you think?"

And they all condemned Him to be deserving of [b]death.

65Then some began to [a]spit on Him, and
to blindfold Him, and to beat Him, and to
say to Him, "Prophesy!" And the officers
struck Him with the palms of their hands.[1]

Peter Denies Jesus, and Weeps
(Matt. 26:69–75; Luke 22:54–62; John 18:15–18, 25–27)

66[a]Now as Peter was below in the courtyard, one of the servant girls of the high
priest came. 67And when she saw Peter
warming himself, she looked at him and
said, "You also were with [a]Jesus of Nazareth."

68But he denied it, saying, "I neither
know nor understand what you are saying." And he went out on the porch, and a
rooster crowed.

69[a]And the servant girl saw him again,
and began to say to those who stood by,
"This is *one* of them." 70But he denied it
again.

[a]And a little later those who stood by said
to Peter again, "Surely you are *one* of them;

14:43 [a] Ps. 3:1; Matt. 26:47–56; Luke 22:47–53; John 18:3–11 14:44 [a] [Prov. 27:6] 14:48 [a] Matt. 26:55; Luke 22:52 14:49 [a] Matt. 21:23 [b] Ps. 22:6; Is. 53:7; Luke 22:37; 24:44 14:50 [a] Ps. 88:8; Zech. 13:7; Matt. 26:31; Mark 14:27 14:53 [a] Matt. 26:57–68; Mark 10:33; Luke 22:54; John 18:12, 13, 19–24 [b] Mark 15:1 [c] Matt. 16:21; 27:12; Luke 9:22; 23:23; John 7:32; 18:3; 19:6 14:54 [a] John 18:15 14:55 [a] Matt. 26:59 14:56 [a] Ex. 20:16; Ps. 27:12; 35:11; Prov. 6:16–19; 19:5 14:58 [a] Matt. 26:61; Mark 15:29; John 2:19; [2 Cor. 5:1] 14:60 [a] Matt. 26:62; Mark 15:3–5 14:61 [a] Is. 53:7; John 19:9; Acts 8:32; [1 Pet. 2:23] [b] Matt. 26:63; Luke 22:67–71 14:62 [a] Matt. 24:30; 26:64; Luke 22:69 14:64 [a] John 10:33, 36 [b] Matt. 20:18; Mark 10:33; John 19:7 14:65 [a] Job 16:10; Is. 50:6; 52:14; Lam. 3:30; Mark 10:34; Luke 18:32 [1] NU-Text reads *received Him with slaps.* 14:66 [a] Matt. 26:58, 69–75; Luke 22:55–62; John 18:16–18, 25–27 14:67 [a] Mark 10:47; John 1:45; Acts 10:38 14:69 [a] Matt. 26:71; Luke 22:58; John 18:25 14:70 [a] Matt. 26:73; Luke 22:59; John 18:26

[b]for you are a Galilean, and your speech
shows *it*."[1]
71 Then he began to curse and swear, "I
do not know this Man of whom you speak!"
72 [a]A second time *the* rooster crowed.
Then Peter called to mind the word that
Jesus had said to him, "Before the rooster
crows twice, you will deny Me three times."
And when he thought about it, he wept.

Jesus Faces Pilate

(Matt. 27:1, 2, 11–14; Luke 23:1–5; John 18:28–38)

15 Immediately, [a]in the morning, the
chief priests held a consultation with
the elders and scribes and the whole council; and they bound Jesus, led *Him* away,
and [b]delivered *Him* to Pilate. 2 [a]Then Pilate
asked Him, "Are You the King of the Jews?"
He answered and said to him, "*It is as*
you say."
3 And the chief priests accused Him of
many things, but He [a]answered nothing.
4 [a]Then Pilate asked Him again, saying, "Do
You answer nothing? See how many things
they testify against You!"[1] 5 [a]But Jesus still
answered nothing, so that Pilate marveled.

Taking the Place of Barabbas

(Matt. 27:15–26; Luke 23:17–25; John 18:39—19:16)

6 Now [a]at the feast he was accustomed
to releasing one prisoner to them, whomever they requested. 7 And there was one
named Barabbas, *who was* chained with his
fellow rebels; they had committed murder
in the rebellion. 8 Then the multitude, crying aloud,[1] began to ask *him to do* just as he
had always done for them. 9 But Pilate answered them, saying, "Do you want me to
release to you the King of the Jews?" 10 For
he knew that the chief priests had handed
Him over because of envy.
11 But [a]the chief priests stirred up the
crowd, so that he should rather release Barabbas to them. 12 Pilate answered and said
to them again, "What then do you want me
to do *with Him* whom you call the [a]King of
the Jews?"
13 So they cried out again, "Crucify Him!"
14 Then Pilate said to them, "Why, [a]what
evil has He done?"
But they cried out all the more, "Crucify Him!"
15 [a]So Pilate, wanting to gratify the crowd,
released Barabbas to them; and he delivered Jesus, after he had scourged *Him*, to
be [b]crucified.

The Soldiers Mock Jesus

(Matt. 27:27–31)

16 [a]Then the soldiers led Him away into
the hall called Praetorium, and they called
together the whole garrison. 17 And they
clothed Him with purple; and they twisted
a crown of thorns, put it on His *head*, 18 and
began to salute Him, "Hail, King of the
Jews!" 19 Then they [a]struck Him on the head
with a reed and spat on Him; and bowing
the knee, they worshiped Him. 20 And when
they had [a]mocked Him, they took the purple off Him, put His own clothes on Him,
and led Him out to crucify Him.

The King on a Cross

(Matt. 27:32–44; Luke 23:26–43; John 19:17–27)

21 [a]Then they compelled a certain man,
Simon a Cyrenian, the father of Alexander and Rufus, as he was coming out of the
country and passing by, to bear His cross.
22 [a]And they brought Him to the place Golgotha, which is translated, Place of a Skull.
23 [a]Then they gave Him wine mingled with
myrrh to drink, but He did not take *it*. 24 And
when they crucified Him, [a]they divided His
garments, casting lots for them *to determine* what every man should take.
25 Now [a]it was the third hour, and they
crucified Him. 26 And [a]the inscription of
His accusation was written above:

THE KING OF THE JEWS.

14:70 [b] Acts 2:7 [1] NU-Text omits *and your speech shows it.* 14:72 [a] Matt. 26:75; Mark 14:30; Luke 22:34; John 13:38 15:1 [a] Ps. 2:2; Matt. 27:1; Luke 22:66; 23:1; John 18:28; Acts 3:13; 4:26 [b] Luke 18:32; Acts 3:13 15:2 [a] Matt. 27:11–14; Luke 23:2, 3; John 18:29–38 15:3 [a] Is. 53:7; John 19:9; Acts 8:32 15:4 [a] Matt. 27:13 [1] NU-Text reads *of which they accuse You.* 15:5 [a] Ps. 38:13, 14; Is. 53:7; John 19:9 15:6 [a] Matt. 27:15–26; Luke 23:18–25; John 18:39—19:16 15:8 [1] NU-Text reads *going up.* 15:11 [a] Matt. 27:20; Acts 3:14 15:12 [a] Ps. 2:6; [Is. 9:7]; Jer. 23:5; 33:15; Mic. 5:2 15:14 [a] Is. 53:9; John 8:46; 1 Pet. 2:21–23 15:15 [a] Is. 50:6; Matt. 27:26; Mark 10:34; John 19:1, 16 [b] [Is. 53:8] 15:16 [a] Matt. 27:27–31 15:19 [a] [Is. 50:6; 52:14; 53:5]; Mic. 5:1; Mark 14:65 15:20 [a] Ps. 35:16; 69:19; Is. 53:3; Matt. 20:19; Mark 10:34; Luke 22:63; 23:11 15:21 [a] Matt. 27:32; Luke 23:26 15:22 [a] Matt. 27:33–44; Luke 23:33–43; John 19:17–24; Heb. 13:12 15:23 [a] Ps. 69:21; Matt. 27:34 15:24 [a] Ps. 22:18; Luke 23:34; John 19:23 15:25 [a] Matt. 27:45; Luke 23:44; John 19:14 15:26 [a] Matt. 27:37; John 19:19

27[a]With Him they also crucified two robbers, one on His right and the other on
His left. 28So the Scripture was fulfilled[1]
which says, [a]"And He was numbered with
the transgressors."[2]
29And [a]those who passed by blasphemed
Him, [b]wagging their heads and saying,
"Aha! [c]*You* who destroy the temple and
build *it* in three days, 30save Yourself, and
come down from the cross!"
31Likewise the chief priests also, [a]mock-
ing among themselves with the scribes,
said, "He saved [b]others; Himself He cannot save. 32Let the Christ, the King of Israel, descend now from the cross, that we
may see and believe."[1]
Even [a]those who were crucified with
Him reviled Him.

Jesus Dies on the Cross
(Matt. 27:45–56; Luke 23:44–49; John 19:28–30)

33Now [a]when the sixth hour had come,
there was darkness over the whole land
until the ninth hour. 34And at the ninth
hour Jesus cried out with a loud voice, saying, "Eloi, Eloi, lama sabachthani?" which
is translated, [a]"My God, My God, why have
You forsaken Me?"[1]
35Some of those who stood by, when they
heard *that*, said, "Look, He is calling for
Elijah!" 36Then [a]someone ran and filled a
sponge full of sour wine, put *it* on a reed,
and [b]offered *it* to Him to drink, saying, "Let
Him alone; let us see if Elijah will come to
take Him down."
37[a]And Jesus cried out with a loud voice,
and breathed His last.
38Then [a]the veil of the temple was torn
in two from top to bottom. 39So [a]when the
centurion, who stood opposite Him, saw
that He cried out like this and breathed
His last,[1] he said, "Truly this Man was the
Son of God!"
40[a]There were also women looking
on [b]from afar, among whom were Mary
Magdalene, Mary the mother of James the
Less and of Joses, and Salome, 41who also
[a]followed Him and ministered to Him when
He was in Galilee, and many other women
who came up with Him to Jerusalem.

Jesus Buried in Joseph's Tomb
(Matt. 27:57–61; Luke 23:50–56; John 19:38–42)

42[a]Now when evening had come, because
it was the Preparation Day, that is, the day
before the Sabbath, 43Joseph of Arimathea, a
prominent council member, who [a]was himself waiting for the kingdom of God, coming
and taking courage, went in to Pilate and
asked for the body of Jesus. 44Pilate marveled that He was already dead; and sum-
moning the centurion, he asked him if He
had been dead for some time. 45So when he
found out from the centurion, he granted
the body to Joseph. 46[a]Then he bought fine
linen, took Him down, and wrapped Him in
the linen. And he laid Him in a tomb which
had been hewn out of the rock, and rolled a
stone against the door of the tomb. 47And
Mary Magdalene and Mary *the mother* of Joses observed where He was laid.

He Is Risen
(Matt. 28:1–8; Luke 24:1–12; John 20:1–10)

16 Now [a]when the Sabbath was past,
Mary Magdalene, Mary *the mother*
of James, and Salome [b]bought spices, that
they might come and anoint Him. 2[a]Very
early in the morning, on the first *day* of
the week, they came to the tomb when the
sun had risen. 3And they said among themselves, "Who will roll away the stone from
the door of the tomb for us?" 4But when
they looked up, they saw that the stone had
been rolled away—for it was very large.
5[a]And entering the tomb, they saw a young
man clothed in a long white robe sitting
on the right side; and they were alarmed.
6[a]But he said to them, "Do not be
alarmed. You seek Jesus of Nazareth, who

15:27 [a] Is. 53:9, 12; Matt. 27:38; Luke 22:37 15:28 [a] Is. 53:12; Luke 22:37 [1] Isaiah 53:12 [2] NU-Text omits this verse. 15:29 [a] Ps. 22:6, 7; 69:7 [b] Ps. 109:25 [c] Mark 14:58; John 2:19–21 15:31 [a] Luke 18:32 [b] Luke 7:14, 15; John 11:43, 44 15:32 [a] Matt. 27:44; Luke 23:39 [1] M-Text reads *believe Him.* 15:33 [a] Amos 8:9; Matt. 27:45–56; Luke 23:44–49 15:34 [a] Ps. 22:1; Matt. 27:46 [1] Psalm 22:1 15:36 [a] Matt. 27:48; John 19:29 [b] Ps. 69:21 15:37 [a] Dan. 9:26; Zech. 11:10, 11; Matt. 27:50; Mark 8:31; Luke 23:46; John 19:30 15:38 [a] Ex. 26:31–33; Matt. 27:51; Luke 23:45 15:39 [a] Matt. 27:54; Luke 23:47 [1] NU-Text reads *that He thus breathed His last.* 15:40 [a] Matt. 27:55; Luke 23:49; John 19:25 [b] Ps. 38:11 15:41 [a] Luke 8:2, 3 15:42 [a] Matt. 27:57–61; Luke 23:50–56; John 19:38–42 15:43 [a] Matt. 27:57; Luke 2:25, 38; 23:51; John 19:38 15:46 [a] Is. 53:9; Matt. 27:59, 60; Luke 23:53; John 19:40 16:1 [a] Matt. 28:1–8; Luke 24:1–10; John 20:1–8 [b] Luke 23:56; John 19:39 16:2 [a] Luke 24:1; John 20:1 16:5 [a] Luke 24:3; John 20:11, 12 16:6 [a] Ps. 16:10; 49:15; Hos. 6:2; Matt. 28:6; Mark 9:31; Luke 24:6

was crucified. He is risen! He is not here.
See the place where they laid Him. 7But
go, tell His disciples—and Peter—that He
is going before you into Galilee; there you
will see Him, [a]as He said to you."
8So they went out quickly[1] and fled
from the tomb, for they trembled and were
amazed. [a]And they said nothing to anyone,
for they were afraid.

Mary Magdalene Sees the Risen Lord
(Matt. 28:9, 10; John 20:11–18)

9Now when *He* rose early on the first *day*
of the week, He appeared first to Mary Magdalene, [a]out of whom He had cast seven
demons. 10[a]She went and told those who
had been with Him, as they mourned and
wept. 11[a]And when they heard that He was
alive and had been seen by her, they did
not believe.

Jesus Appears to Two Disciples
(Luke 24:13–35)

12After that, He appeared in another
form [a]to two of them as they walked and
went into the country. 13And they went and
told *it* to the rest, *but* they did not believe
them either.

The Great Commission
(Matt. 28:16–20; Luke 24:44–49; Acts 1:6–8)

14[a]Later He appeared to the eleven as
they sat at the table; and He rebuked their
unbelief and hardness of heart, because
they did not believe those who had seen
Him after He had risen. 15[a]And He said to
them, "Go into all the world [b]and preach
the gospel to every creature. 16[a]He who believes and is baptized will be saved; [b]but he
who does not believe will be condemned.
17And these [a]signs will follow those who
believe: [b]In My name they will cast out demons; [c]they will speak with new tongues;
18[a]they[1] will take up serpents; and if they
drink anything deadly, it will by no means
hurt them; [b]they will lay hands on the sick,
and they will recover."

Christ Ascends to God's Right Hand
(Luke 24:50–53)

19So then, [a]after the Lord had spoken to
them, He was [b]received up into heaven, and
[c]sat down at the right hand of God. 20And
they went out and preached everywhere,
the Lord working with *them* [a]and confirming the word through the accompanying
signs. Amen.[1]

16:7 [a] Matt. 26:32; 28:16, 17; Mark 14:28 16:8 [a] Matt. 28:8 [1] NU-Text and M-Text omit *quickly.* 16:9 [a] Luke 8:2 16:10 [a] Luke 24:10 16:11 [a] Matt. 28:17; Luke 24:11, 41; John 20:25 16:12 [a] Luke 24:13–35 16:14 [a] Luke 24:36; John 20:19, 26; 1 Cor. 15:5 16:15 [a] Matt. 28:19; [John 15:16; Acts 1:8]; Col. 1:6 [b] [Col. 1:23] 16:16 [a] [John 3:18, 36; Acts 2:38; 16:30, 31; Rom. 10:8–10] [b] [John 12:48] 16:17 [a] Acts 5:12 [b] Mark 9:38; Luke 10:17; Acts 5:16; 8:7; 16:18; 19:12 [c] [Acts 2:4; 1 Cor. 12:10] 16:18 [a] [Luke 10:19]; Acts 28:3–6 [b] [Acts 5:15]; James 5:14 [1] NU-Text reads *and in their hands they will.* 16:19 [a] Acts 1:2, 3 [b] Ps. 68:18; Luke 9:51; 24:51; John 6:62; 20:17; Acts 1:2, 9–11; [1 Tim. 3:16; Rev. 4:2] [c] [Ps. 110:1]; Luke 22:69; [Acts 7:55]; 1 Pet. 3:22 16:20 [a] Acts 5:12; [1 Cor. 2:4, 5; Heb. 2:4] [1] Verses 9–20 are bracketed in NU-Text as not original. They are lacking in Codex Sinaiticus and Codex Vaticanus, although nearly all other manuscripts of Mark contain them.

THE GOSPEL ACCORDING TO

LUKE

OVERVIEW

The Gospel of Luke is the third New Testament book detailing the birth, life, death, resurrection, and ascension of Jesus Christ. It is the final book of the Synoptic Gospels (Matthew, Mark, and Luke). Luke begins his Gospel by addressing it to a recipient named Theophilus. Luke is believed to have been a doctor and companion of the apostle Paul, who often acknowledged him in his writings (e.g., Col. 4:14). Luke's authorship is supported by various church traditions and other extrabiblical resources. It is also believed that he authored the Book of Acts. These two chronicles of the early church make up more than a quarter of the New Testament.

The name Theophilus means "one who loves God," and the title "most excellent" (Luke 1:3) was often used for Roman officials, providing clues to who this recipient may have been. Because of the abrupt ending of Acts, some believe that Theophilus was Paul's attorney in Rome and that Luke provided him with his writings to aid in Paul's defense. It is important to understand, however, that a document addressed to an individual would also have had use for entire communities.

Luke's Gospel is intended for a Gentile, specifically a Greek, audience. Luke was a meticulous and diligent historian, perhaps stemming from his work as a doctor. He provided details that are unavailable in the other Gospel accounts. Luke alone described the blood relationship between Elizabeth, the mother of John the Baptist, and Mary, the mother of Jesus. He alone provided the narrative of Jesus' earliest encounter in the temple when He was presented for circumcision on the eighth day. Luke also emphasized prayer more than the previous two Gospels. He referred to the Spirit seventeen times, almost more than the other two Synoptic Gospels combined. Forty times, Luke gave definition to the "kingdom of God." Luke also used the phrase "Son of Man" twenty-six times to describe Jesus, establishing that Christ is fully God and fully human.

Luke wrote with the purpose of consolidation and correction. He sought to unite the witnesses of those who had firsthand accounts of Jesus. He also sought to discredit extrabiblical accounts that did not conform to the narrative of the primary witnesses. In sum, Luke provided the reader "an orderly account . . . that you may know the certainty of those things in which you were instructed" (Luke 1:3–4).

BREATHE IT IN

Luke asserts that his account of the gospel of Jesus Christ is one among many. While four Gospel narratives exist in the canon of the Holy Scriptures, there were other accounts that did not survive scrutiny and were determined not to have been written by the inspiration of God (see 2 Tim. 3:16–17). Early on, the authenticity of Luke's Gospel was questioned and debated. Yet, the credibility of Luke has now been affirmed for nearly two millennia. We are all the beneficiaries of Luke's integrity as a detailed truth teller.

Who are the truth tellers of our day? What sources do we find most credible? Have you struggled in recent times with your ability to trust institutions and individuals? In the age of "fake news," manipulation, and the mainstreaming of conspiracies being spread online by anonymous

sources at warp speed, many people are asking, "Who can we really trust?" This question along with countless more swirl through society, and nothing seems to be truly trustworthy. However, the veracity and authority of the Bible have been proven over a period exceeding two thousand years. When all else proves false, God's Word remains trustworthy and sure.

God has not given us His Word without basis; He has given us the witness of Scripture to serve as the foundation and grounding of our faith. There are two ways to read and study the Bible: as just *a* book or as *the* Book. Does the Bible have authority in your life to the degree that you are willing to allow it to reorganize your priorities and inform your worldview?

God's Word is the lens through which we should evaluate all claims of truth. First, do they reflect honor and love for God according to His Word? Second, but equally important, do they reflect love for all people also according to His Word? In loving all people, we must acknowledge that their varied experiences have value and have formulated their perspectives, which we should also value. But we cannot know what we do not stop to listen to and try to understand. In this age of selfish extremism, many of us only see life from our own viewpoint and do not care to see it from anyone else's. Many of us do not stop to listen to the perspectives of others and their experiences. But if we did, we would have more love and empathy for one another, allowing us to more closely adhere to the overwhelming truth of Christ's message to love our neighbor as ourselves.

THE GOSPEL ACCORDING TO

LUKE

Dedication to Theophilus

1 Inasmuch as many have taken in hand to set in order a narrative of those [a]things which have been fulfilled[1] among us, 2 just as those who [a]from the beginning were [b]eyewitnesses and ministers of the word [c]delivered them to us, 3 it seemed good to me also, having had perfect understanding of all things from the very first, to write to you an orderly account, [a]most excellent Theophilus, 4 [a]that you may know the certainty of those things in which you were instructed.

John's Birth Announced to Zacharias

5 There was [a]in the days of Herod, the king of Judea, a certain priest named Zacharias, [b]of the division of [c]Abijah. His [d]wife *was* of the daughters of Aaron, and her name *was* Elizabeth. 6 And they were both righteous before God, walking in all the commandments and ordinances of the Lord blameless. 7 But they had no child, because Elizabeth was barren, and they were both well advanced in years.

8 So it was, that while he was serving as priest before God in the order of his division, 9 according to the custom of the priesthood, his lot fell [a]to burn incense when he went into the temple of the Lord. 10 [a]And the whole multitude of the people was praying outside at the hour of incense. 11 Then an angel of the Lord appeared to him, standing on the right side of [a]the altar of incense. 12 And when Zacharias saw *him,* [a]he was troubled, and fear fell upon him.

13 But the angel said to him, "Do not be afraid, Zacharias, for your prayer is heard; and your wife Elizabeth will bear you a son, and [a]you shall call his name John. 14 And you will have joy and gladness, and [a]many will rejoice at his birth. 15 For he will be [a]great in the sight of the Lord, and [b]shall drink neither wine nor strong drink. He will also be filled with the Holy Spirit, [c]even from his mother's womb. 16 And he will turn many of the children of Israel to the Lord their God. 17 [a]He will also go before Him in the spirit and power of Elijah, 'to turn the hearts of the fathers to the children,'[1] and the disobedient to the wisdom of the just, to make ready a people prepared for the Lord."

18 And Zacharias said to the angel, [a]"How shall I know this? For I am an old man, and my wife is well advanced in years."

19 And the angel answered and said to him, "I am [a]Gabriel, who stands in the presence of God, and was sent to speak to you and bring you these glad [b]tidings. 20 But behold, [a]you will be mute and not able to speak until the day these things take place, because you did not believe my words which will be fulfilled in their own time."

21 And the people waited for Zacharias, and marveled that he lingered so long in the temple. 22 But when he came out, he could not speak to them; and they perceived that he had seen a vision in the temple, for he beckoned to them and remained speechless.

23 So it was, as soon as [a]the days of his service were completed, that he departed to his own house. 24 Now after those days his wife

---

1:1 [a] John 20:31 [1] Or *are most surely believed* 1:2 [a] Mark 1:1; John 15:27; Acts 1:21, 22 [b] Acts 1:2 [c] Acts 1:3; 10:39; Heb. 2:3; 1 Pet. 5:1; 2 Pet. 1:16; 1 John 1:1 1:3 [a] Acts 1:1 1:4 [a] [John 20:31] 1:5 [a] Matt. 2:1 [b] 1 Chr. 24:1, 10 [c] Neh. 12:4 [d] Lev. 21:13, 14 1:9 [a] Ex. 30:7, 8; 1 Chr. 23:13; 2 Chr. 29:11 1:10 [a] Lev. 16:17 1:11 [a] Ex. 30:1 1:12 [a] Judg. 6:22; Dan. 10:8; Luke 2:9; Acts 10:4; Rev. 1:17 1:13 [a] Luke 1:57, 60, 63 1:14 [a] Luke 1:58 1:15 [a] [Luke 7:24–28] [b] Num. 6:3; Judg. 13:4; Matt. 11:18 [c] Jer. 1:5; Gal. 1:15 1:17 [a] Mal. 4:5, 6; Matt. 3:2; 11:14; Mark 1:4; 9:12 [1] Malachi 4:5, 6 1:18 [a] Gen. 17:17 1:19 [a] Dan. 8:16; [Matt. 18:10]; Heb. 1:4 [b] Luke 2:10 1:20 [a] Ezek. 3:26; 24:27 1:23 [a] 2 Kin. 11:5; 1 Chr. 9:25

Elizabeth conceived; and she hid herself five
months, saying, 25 “Thus the Lord has dealt
with me, in the days when He looked on *me,*
to [a]take away my reproach among people.”

Christ’s Birth Announced to Mary

26 Now in the sixth month the angel Gabriel was sent by God to a city of Galilee
named Nazareth, 27 to a virgin [a]betrothed
to a man whose name was Joseph, of the
house of David. The virgin’s name *was* Mary.
28 And having come in, the angel said to her,
[a]“Rejoice, highly favored *one,* [b]the Lord *is*
with you; blessed *are* you among women!”[1]
29 But when she saw *him,*[1] [a]she was troubled at his saying, and considered what manner of greeting this was. 30 Then the angel
said to her, “Do not be afraid, Mary, for you
have found [a]favor with God. 31 [a]And behold,
you will conceive in your womb and bring
forth a Son, and [b]shall call His name JESUS.
32 He will be great, [a]and will be called the Son
of the Highest; and [b]the Lord God will give
Him the [c]throne of His [d]father David. 33 [a]And
He will reign over the house of Jacob forever,
and of His kingdom there will be no end.”
34 Then Mary said to the angel, “How can
this be, since I do not know a man?”
35 And the angel answered and said to
her, [a]“*The* Holy Spirit will come upon you,
and the power of the Highest will overshadow you; therefore, also, that Holy One
who is to be born will be called [b]the Son of
God. 36 Now indeed, Elizabeth your relative
has also conceived a son in her old age; and
this is now the sixth month for her who was
called barren. 37 For [a]with God nothing will
be impossible.”
38 Then Mary said, “Behold the maidservant of the Lord! Let it be to me according to your word.” And the angel departed
from her.

Mary Visits Elizabeth

39 Now Mary arose in those days and
went into the hill country with haste, [a]to
a city of Judah, 40 and entered the house
of Zacharias and greeted Elizabeth. 41 And
it happened, when Elizabeth heard the
greeting of Mary, that the babe leaped in
her womb; and Elizabeth was [a]filled with
the Holy Spirit. 42 Then she spoke out with
a loud voice and said, [a]“Blessed *are* you
among women, and blessed *is* the fruit of
your womb! 43 But why *is* this *granted* to me,
that the mother of my Lord should come
to me? 44 For indeed, as soon as the voice
of your greeting sounded in my ears, the
babe leaped in my womb for joy. 45 [a]Blessed
is she who believed, for there will be a fulfillment of those things which were told
her from the Lord.”

The Song of Mary

46 And Mary said:

[a]“My soul magnifies the Lord,
47 And my spirit has [a]rejoiced
in [b]God my Savior.
48 For [a]He has regarded the lowly
state of His maidservant;
For behold, henceforth [b]all
generations will call me blessed.
49 For He who is mighty [a]has done
great things for me,
And [b]holy *is* His name.
50 And [a]His mercy *is* on those
who fear Him
From generation to generation.
51 [a]He has shown strength with
His arm;
[b]He has scattered *the* proud in the
imagination of their hearts.
52 [a]He has put down the mighty
from *their* thrones,
And exalted *the* lowly.
53 He has [a]filled *the* hungry
with good things,
And *the* rich He has sent away
empty.
54 He has helped His [a]servant Israel,
[b]In remembrance of *His* mercy,

1:25 [a] Gen. 30:23; Is. 4:1; 54:1, 4 1:27 [a] Matt. 1:18; Luke 2:4, 5 1:28 [a] Dan. 9:23 [b] Judg. 6:12 [1] NU-Text omits *blessed are you among women.* 1:29 [a] Luke 1:12 [1] NU-Text omits *when she saw him.* 1:30 [a] Luke 2:52 1:31 [a] Is. 7:14; Matt. 1:21, 25; Gal. 4:4 [b] Luke 2:21; [Phil. 2:9–11] 1:32 [a] Matt. 3:17; 17:5; Mark 5:7; Luke 1:35, 76; 6:35; Acts 7:48 [b] 2 Sam. 7:12, 13, 16; Ps. 132:11; [Is. 9:6, 7; 16:5; Jer. 23:5] [c] 2 Sam. 7:14–17; Acts 2:33; 7:55 [d] Matt. 1:1 1:33 [a] [Dan. 2:44; Obad. 21; Mic. 4:7]; John 12:34; [Heb. 1:8]; 2 Pet. 1:11 1:35 [a] Matt. 1:20 [b] Ps. 2:7; Matt. 3:17; 14:33; 17:5; Mark 1:1; John 1:34; 20:31; Acts 8:37; [Rom. 1:1–4; Heb. 1:2, 8] 1:37 [a] Gen. 18:14; Jer. 32:17; Matt. 19:26; Mark 10:27; Rom. 4:21 1:39 [a] Josh. 21:9 1:41 [a] Acts 6:3 1:42 [a] Judg. 5:24 1:45 [a] John 20:29 1:46 [a] 1 Sam. 2:1–10; Ps. 34:2, 3; Hab. 3:18 1:47 [a] Ps. 35:9; Hab. 3:18 [b] 1 Tim. 1:1; 2:3; Titus 1:3; 2:10; 3:4; Jude 25 1:48 [a] 1 Sam. 1:11; Ps. 138:6 [b] Luke 11:27 1:49 [a] Ps. 71:19; 126:2, 3 [b] Ps. 111:9; Rev. 4:8 1:50 [a] Gen. 17:7; Ex. 20:6; 34:6, 7; Ps. 103:17 1:51 [a] Ps. 98:1; 118:15; Is. 40:10 [b] Ps. 33:10; [1 Pet. 5:5] 1:52 [a] 1 Sam. 2:7, 8 1:53 [a] [Matt. 5:6] 1:54 [a] Is. 41:8 [b] Ps. 98:3; [Jer. 31:3]

EXALT HIS IMMUTABILITY

INHALE

I have been the same all my life: a strong-willed person who has to protect my own. Now that I have given my life to Christ, I know I have to let go of my tough exterior and lean toward exerting grace. However, it is truly hard to want to change when I see so much injustice in the world. Just when I am able to get past one incident, another terrible ordeal happens. If God can change the hearts of people, why won't He change theirs? Why won't He change mine?

EXHALE

God is the God of change, yet He changes not. This is one of the greatest attributes of our great God. He is unchanging, and that includes His desire and work to change us from the inside out! There is no Christianity without change. We begin our walk with the Lord damaged by sin and its effect in our lives. He has to birth within us new hearts and minds so we can be freed from our old ways of acting and reacting.

Changes in your life and toward the things of God do not come from any power within you; rather, they come from the power that belongs to God alone. His creative power has been at work in creation since the very first moment. It has not changed, and His power has not decreased. He will remake you into the very image of His Son. It only requires your willingness and submission to His will.

God finds us where we are and works within us so we can become all we were meant to be. The secret of change is to let go and let God do it. Petition Him for the change you desire. Then look out—it's on the way. In Luke 1:35, we read what the angel explained to Mary, the mother of Jesus: "The Holy Spirit will come upon you, and the power of the Highest will overshadow you." That is what happens when God changes us. The Holy Spirit overshadows the person we were and brings new life into us—the abundant life Jesus brings frees us from our old ways of thinking and responding to life. Just as Mary submitted to God's will in her life, we must also allow Him to work in us to bring about new life.

55 [a]As He spoke to our [b]fathers,
To Abraham and to his [c]seed forever."

56And Mary remained with her about three months, and returned to her house.

Birth of John the Baptist

57Now Elizabeth's full time came for her to be delivered, and she brought forth a son. 58When her neighbors and relatives heard how the Lord had shown great mercy to her, they [a]rejoiced with her.

Circumcision of John the Baptist

59So it was, [a]on the eighth day, that they came to circumcise the child; and they would have called him by the name of his father, Zacharias. 60His mother answered and said, [a]"No; he shall be called John."

61But they said to her, "There is no one among your relatives who is called by this name." 62So they made signs to his father—what he would have him called.

63And he asked for a writing tablet, and wrote, saying, "His name is John." So they all marveled. 64Immediately his mouth was opened and his tongue *loosed,* and he spoke, praising God. 65Then fear came on all who dwelt around them; and all these sayings were discussed throughout all the hill country of Judea. 66And all those who heard *them* [a]kept *them* in their hearts, saying, "What kind of child will this be?" And [b]the hand of the Lord was with him.

1:55 [a] Gen. 17:19; Ps. 132:11; [Gal. 3:16] [b] [Rom. 11:28] [c] Gen. 17:7 1:58 [a] [Rom. 12:15] 1:59 [a] Gen. 17:12; Lev. 12:3; Luke 2:21; Phil. 3:5 1:60 [a] Luke 1:13, 63 1:66 [a] Luke 2:19 [b] Gen. 39:2; Acts 11:21

Zacharias' Prophecy

67Now his father Zacharias [a]was filled
with the Holy Spirit, and prophesied, saying:

68"Blessed[a] *is* the Lord God of Israel,
For [b]He has visited and
redeemed His people,
69 [a]And has raised up a horn
of salvation for us
In the house of His servant David,
70 [a]As He spoke by the mouth
of His holy prophets,
Who *have been* [b]since the world began,
71 That we should be saved
from our enemies
And from the hand of all who hate us,
72 [a]To perform the mercy
promised to our fathers
And to remember His holy covenant,
73 [a]The oath which He swore to
our father Abraham:
74 To grant us that we,
Being delivered from the
hand of our enemies,
Might [a]serve Him without fear,
75 [a]In holiness and righteousness before
Him all the days of our life.

76 "And you, child, will be called the
[a]prophet of the Highest;
For [b]you will go before the face of
the Lord to prepare His ways,
77 To give [a]knowledge of
salvation to His people
By the remission of their sins,
78 Through the tender mercy of our God,
With which the Dayspring from
on high has visited[1] us;
79 [a]To give light to those who sit in
darkness and the shadow of death,
To [b]guide our feet into the
way of peace."

80So [a]the child grew and became strong
in spirit, and [b]was in the deserts till the day
of his manifestation to Israel.

Christ Born of Mary

(Matt. 1:18–25)

2 And it came to pass in those days *that*
a decree went out from Caesar Augustus that all the world should be registered.
2[a]This census first took place while Quirin-
ius was governing Syria. 3So all went to be
registered, everyone to his own city.
4Joseph also went up from Galilee, out
of the city of Nazareth, into Judea, to [a]the
city of David, which is called Bethlehem,
[b]because he was of the house and lineage
of David, 5to be registered with Mary, [a]his
betrothed wife,[1] who was with child. 6So it
was, that while they were there, the days
were completed for her to be delivered.
7And [a]she brought forth her firstborn Son,
and wrapped Him in swaddling cloths, and
laid Him in a manger, because there was
no room for them in the inn.

Glory in the Highest

8Now there were in the same country
shepherds living out in the fields, keeping watch over their flock by night. 9And
behold,[1] an angel of the Lord stood before
them, and the glory of the Lord shone
around them, [a]and they were greatly afraid.
10Then the angel said to them, [a]"Do not be
afraid, for behold, I bring you good tidings of great joy [b]which will be to all people. 11[a]For there is born to you this day in
the city of David [b]a Savior, [c]who is Christ
the Lord. 12And this *will be* the sign to you:
You will find a Babe wrapped in swaddling
cloths, lying in a manger."
13[a]And suddenly there was with the angel
a multitude of the heavenly host praising
God and saying:

14 "Glory[a] to God in the highest,
And on earth [b]peace, [c]goodwill
toward men!"[1]

15So it was, when the angels had gone
away from them into heaven, that the

1:67 [a] Joel 2:28 **1:68** [a] 1 Kin. 1:48; Ps. 106:48 [b] Ex. 3:16 **1:69** [a] 2 Sam. 22:3; Ps. 132:17; Ezek. 29:21 **1:70** [a] Jer. 23:5; Rom. 1:2 [b] Acts 3:21 **1:72** [a] Lev. 26:42 **1:73** [a] Gen. 12:3; 22:16–18; [Heb. 6:13] **1:74** [a] [Rom. 6:18; Heb. 9:14] **1:75** [a] Jer. 32:39; [Eph. 4:24; 2 Thess. 2:13] **1:76** [a] Matt. 3:3; 11:9; Mark 3:2, 3; Luke 3:4; John 1:23 [b] Is. 40:3; Mal. 3:1; Matt. 11:10 **1:77** [a] [Jer. 31:34; Mark 1:4]; Luke 3:3 **1:78** [1] NU-Text reads *shall visit.* **1:79** [a] Is. 9:2; Matt. 4:16; [Acts 26:18; 2 Cor. 4:6; Eph. 5:14] [b] [John 10:4; 14:27; 16:33] **1:80** [a] Luke 2:40 [b] Matt. 3:1 **2:2** [a] Dan. 9:25; Acts 5:37 **2:4** [a] 1 Sam. 16:1; Mic. 5:2 [b] Matt. 1:16 **2:5** [a] [Matt. 1:18] [1] NU-Text omits *wife.* **2:7** [a] Matt. 1:25; Luke 1:31 **2:9** [a] Luke 1:12 [1] NU-Text omits *behold.* **2:10** [a] Luke 1:13, 30 [b] Gen. 12:3; Is. 49:6; [Matt. 28:19; Mark 1:15; Col. 1:23] **2:11** [a] Is. 9:6 [b] Matt. 1:21; John 4:42; [Acts 5:31] [c] Matt. 1:16; 16:16, 20; John 11:27; Acts 2:36; Phil. 2:11 **2:13** [a] Gen. 28:12; Ps. 103:20; 148:2; Dan. 7:10; [Heb. 1:14]; Rev. 5:11 **2:14** [a] Matt. 21:9; Luke 19:38; Eph. 1:6 [b] Is. 57:19; [Rom. 5:1]; Eph. 2:17; [Col. 1:20] [c] [John 3:16; Eph. 2:4, 7; 2 Thess. 2:16; 1 John 4:9] [1] NU-Text reads *toward men of goodwill.*

shepherds said to one another, "Let us now
go to Bethlehem and see this thing that has
come to pass, which the Lord has made
known to us." 16And they came with haste
and found Mary and Joseph, and the Babe
lying in a manger. 17Now when they had seen
Him, they made widely[1] known the saying
which was told them concerning this Child.
18And all those who heard *it* marveled at
those things which were told them by the
shepherds. 19[a]But Mary kept all these things
and pondered *them* in her heart. 20Then the
shepherds returned, glorifying and [a]prais-
ing God for all the things that they had heard
and seen, as it was told them.

Circumcision of Jesus

21[a]And when eight days were completed
for the circumcision of the Child,[1] His name
was called [b]JESUS, the name given by the angel [c]before He was conceived in the womb.

Jesus Presented in the Temple

22Now when [a]the days of her purification
according to the law of Moses were completed, they brought Him to Jerusalem to
present *Him* to the Lord 23[a](as it is written
in the law of the Lord, [b]"Every male who
opens the womb shall be called holy to the
LORD"),[1] 24and to offer a sacrifice according
to what is said in the law of the Lord, [a]"A
pair of turtledoves or two young pigeons."[1]

Simeon Sees God's Salvation

25And behold, there was a man in Jerusalem whose name *was* Simeon, and this
man *was* just and devout, [a]waiting for the
Consolation of Israel, and the Holy Spirit
was upon him. 26And it had been revealed
to him by the Holy Spirit that he would not
[a]see death before he had seen the Lord's
Christ. 27So he came [a]by the Spirit into the
temple. And when the parents brought in
the Child Jesus, to do for Him according to
the custom of the law, 28he took Him up in
his arms and blessed God and said:

29"Lord, [a]now You are letting Your
servant depart in peace,
According to Your word;
30 For my eyes [a]have seen Your salvation
31 Which You have prepared before
the face of all peoples,
32 [a]A light to *bring* revelation
to the Gentiles,
And the glory of Your people Israel."

33And Joseph and His mother[1] marveled
at those things which were spoken of Him.
34Then Simeon blessed them, and said to
Mary His mother, "Behold, this *Child* is destined for the [a]fall and rising of many in Israel, and for [b]a sign which will be spoken
against 35(yes, [a]a sword will pierce through
your own soul also), that the thoughts of
many hearts may be revealed."

Anna Bears Witness to the Redeemer

36Now there was one, Anna, a prophetess, the daughter of Phanuel, of the tribe
of [a]Asher. She was of a great age, and had
lived with a husband seven years from her
virginity; 37and this woman *was* a widow of
about eighty-four years,[1] who did not depart from the temple, but served *God* with
fastings and prayers [a]night and day. 38And
coming in that instant she gave thanks to
the Lord,[1] and spoke of Him to all those
who [a]looked for redemption in Jerusalem.

The Family Returns to Nazareth

39So when they had performed all things
according to the law of the Lord, they returned to Galilee, to their *own* city, Nazareth. 40[a]And the Child grew and became
strong in spirit,[1] filled with wisdom; and
the grace of God was upon Him.

The Boy Jesus Amazes the Scholars

41His parents went to [a]Jerusalem [b]ev-
ery year at the Feast of the Passover. 42And
when He was twelve years old, they went
up to Jerusalem according to the [a]custom

2:17 [1] NU-Text omits *widely.* 2:19 [a] Gen. 37:11; Luke 1:66 2:20 [a] Luke 19:37 2:21 [a] Gen. 17:12; Lev. 12:3 [b] [Matt. 1:21] [c] Luke 1:31 [1] NU-Text reads *for His circumcision.* 2:22 [a] Lev. 12:2–8 2:23 [a] Ex. 13:12; 22:29; Lev. 27:26; Deut. 18:4; Neh. 10:36 [b] Ex. 13:2, 12, 15; Num. 3:13; 8:17 [1] Exodus 13:2, 12, 15 2:24 [a] Lev. 12:2, 8 [1] Leviticus 12:8 2:25 [a] Is. 40:1; Mark 15:43; Luke 2:38; 23:51 2:26 [a] Ps. 89:48; [John 8:51; Heb. 11:5] 2:27 [a] Matt. 4:1 2:29 [a] Gen. 46:30; [Phil. 1:23] 2:30 [a] Ps. 119:166, 174; [Is. 52:10; Luke 3:6] 2:32 [a] Is. 9:2; 42:6; 49:6; 60:1–3; Matt. 4:16; Acts 10:45; 13:47; 28:28; [Rom. 9:24; Gal. 3:14] 2:33 [1] NU-Text reads *And His father and mother.* 2:34 [a] Is. 8:14; Hos. 14:9; Matt. 21:44; [Rom. 9:32]; 1 Cor. 1:23; [2 Cor. 2:16; 1 Pet. 2:7, 8] [b] Matt. 28:12–15; Acts 4:2; 17:32; 28:22; [1 Pet. 2:12; 4:14] 2:35 [a] Ps. 42:10; John 19:25 2:36 [a] Josh. 19:24 2:37 [a] Acts 26:7; 1 Tim. 5:5 [1] NU-Text reads *a widow until she was eighty-four.* 2:38 [a] Lam. 3:25, 26; Mark 15:43; Luke 24:21 [1] NU-Text reads *to God.* 2:40 [a] Luke 1:80; 2:52; [1 Cor. 1:24, 30] [1] NU-Text omits *in spirit.* 2:41 [a] John 4:20 [b] Ex. 23:15, 17; 34:23; Deut. 16:1, 16; Luke 22:15 2:42 [a] Ex. 23:14, 15

of the feast. 43When they had finished the
[a]days, as they returned, the Boy Jesus lingered behind in Jerusalem. And Joseph
and His mother[1] did not know *it;* 44but supposing Him to have been in the company,
they went a day's journey, and sought Him
among *their* relatives and acquaintances.
45So when they did not find Him, they returned to Jerusalem, seeking Him. 46Now
so it was *that* after three days they found
Him in the temple, sitting in the midst of
the teachers, both listening to them and
asking them questions. 47And [a]all who
heard Him were astonished at His understanding and answers. 48So when they saw
Him, they were amazed; and His mother
said to Him, "Son, why have You done this
to us? Look, Your father and I have sought
You anxiously."

49And He said to them, "Why did you
seek Me? Did you not know that I must be
[a]about [b]My Father's business?" 50But [a]they
did not understand the statement which
He spoke to them.

Jesus Advances in Wisdom and Favor

51Then He went down with them and
came to Nazareth, and was subject to them,
but His mother [a]kept all these things in
her heart. 52And Jesus [a]increased in wisdom and stature, [b]and in favor with God
and men.

John the Baptist Prepares the Way
(Matt. 3:1–6; Mark 1:2–6; John 1:19–23)

3 Now in the fifteenth year of the reign
of Tiberius Caesar, [a]Pontius Pilate
being governor of Judea, Herod being
tetrarch of Galilee, his brother Philip tetrarch of Iturea and the region of Tracho-
nitis, and Lysanias tetrarch of Abilene,
2while [a]Annas and Caiaphas were high
priests,[1] the word of God came to [b]John
the son of Zacharias in the wilderness.
3[a]And he went into all the region around
the Jordan, preaching a baptism of repentance [b]for the remission of sins, 4as it is
written in the book of the words of Isaiah
the prophet, saying:

[a]"The voice of one crying in
the wilderness:
'Prepare the way of the
LORD;
Make His paths straight.
5 Every valley shall be filled
And every mountain and
hill brought low;
The crooked places shall
be made straight
And the rough ways
smooth;
6 And [a]all flesh shall see the
salvation of God.'"[1]

John Preaches to the People
(Matt. 3:7–12; Mark 1:7, 8; John 1:24–28)

7Then he said to the multitudes that
came out to be baptized by him, [a]"Brood
of vipers! Who warned you to flee from
the wrath to come? 8Therefore bear fruits
[a]worthy of repentance, and do not begin
to say to yourselves, 'We have Abraham
as *our* father.' For I say to you that God is
able to raise up children to Abraham from
these stones. 9And even now the ax is laid
to the root of the trees. Therefore [a]every
tree which does not bear good fruit is cut
down and thrown into the fire."

10So the people asked him, saying,
[a]"What shall we do then?"

11He answered and said to them, [a]"He
who has two tunics, let him give to him
who has none; and he who has food, [b]let
him do likewise."

12Then [a]tax collectors also came to be
baptized, and said to him, "Teacher, what
shall we do?"

13And he said to them, [a]"Collect no more
than what is appointed for you."

14Likewise the soldiers asked him, saying, "And what shall we do?"

So he said to them, "Do not intimidate
anyone [a]or accuse falsely, and be content
with your wages."

2:43 [a] Ex. 12:15 [1] NU-Text reads *And His parents.* 2:47 [a] Matt. 7:28; 13:54; 22:33; Mark 1:22; 6:2; 11:18; Luke 4:32; John 7:15 2:49 [a] John 9:4 [b] [Mark 1:22; Luke 4:22, 32; John 4:34; 5:17, 36] 2:50 [a] Mark 9:32; Luke 9:45; 18:34; John 7:15, 46 2:51 [a] Dan. 7:28 2:52 [a] [Is. 11:2, 3; Col. 2:2, 3] [b] 1 Sam. 2:26; [Prov. 3:1–4] 3:1 [a] Matt. 27:2 3:2 [a] John 11:49; 18:13; Acts 4:6 [b] Luke 1:13 [1] NU-Text and M-Text read *in the high priesthood of Annas and Caiaphas.* 3:3 [a] Matt. 3:1; Mark 1:4 [b] Luke 1:77 3:4 [a] Is. 40:3–5; Matt. 3:3; Mark 1:3 3:6 [a] Ps. 98:2; Is. 52:10; Luke 2:10; [Rom. 10:8–18] [1] Isaiah 40:3–5 3:7 [a] Matt. 3:7; 12:34; 23:33 3:8 [a] [2 Cor. 7:9–11] 3:9 [a] Matt. 7:19; Luke 13:6–9 3:10 [a] Luke 3:12, 14; [Acts 2:37, 38; 16:30, 31] 3:11 [a] Luke 11:41; 2 Cor. 8:14; James 2:15, 16; [1 John 3:17; 4:20] [b] Is. 58:7; [1 Tim. 6:17, 18] 3:12 [a] Matt. 21:32; Luke 7:29 3:13 [a] Luke 19:8 3:14 [a] Ex. 20:16; 23:1; Lev. 19:11

15Now as the people were in expectation,
and all reasoned in their hearts about John,
whether he was the Christ *or* not, 16John
answered, saying to all, [a]"I indeed baptize
you with water; but One mightier than I is
coming, whose sandal strap I am not worthy to loose. He will [b]baptize you with the
Holy Spirit and fire. 17His winnowing fan *is*
in His hand, and He will thoroughly clean
out His threshing floor, and [a]gather the
wheat into His barn; but the chaff He will
burn with unquenchable fire."
18And with many other exhortations he
preached to the people. 19[a]But Herod the tetrarch, being rebuked by him concerning
Herodias, his brother Philip's wife,[1] and for
all the evils which Herod had done, 20also
added this, above all, that he shut John up
in prison.

John Baptizes Jesus

(Matt. 3:13–17; Mark 1:9–11; John 1:29–34)

21When all the people were baptized,
[a]it came to pass that Jesus also was baptized; and while He prayed, the heaven
was opened. 22And the Holy Spirit descended in bodily form like a dove upon
Him, and a voice came from heaven which
said, "You are My beloved Son; in You I am
[a]well pleased."

LUKE 3:4

I AM JOHN THE BAPTIST

As it is written in the book of the words of Isaiah the prophet, saying: "The voice of one crying in the wilderness: 'Prepare the way of the LORD; make His paths straight.'" Luke 3:4

I am John the Baptist. I am the one the prophets Isaiah and Malachi spoke of as the "one crying in the wilderness." My mother, Elizabeth, was a relative of Jesus' mother, Mary. Jesus and I were born only months apart.

As I grew into a man, I lived alone in the wilderness. My calling was to tell the people that the Messiah was coming and they should repent of their sins in preparation. People thought I was pretty strange. I wore clothes made of camel's hair and ate wild honey and locusts. Despite my appearance, many believed my message and demonstrated their repentance and acceptance of the coming Messiah by being baptized by me with water.

One day, as I was baptizing people in the Jordan River, Jesus came and asked me to baptize Him. I resisted because I was not fit even to untie His sandals. Jesus explained that it had to happen this way. As I baptized Jesus, the heavens opened, and the Holy Spirit descended like a dove. The Father spoke from heaven saying that this was His beloved Son in whom He is well pleased. This startling event should have been enough for me to be sure that He was the Holy One. But later when I was in prison and likely about to be executed, I sent messengers to ask Jesus if He was the One or if we should wait for another. Jesus told them to inform me of all they had seen Jesus do. Now I know that Jesus truly is the Messiah.

†

Jesus called John the Baptist the greatest prophet, but then He said, "But he who is least in the kingdom of God is greater than he" (Luke 7:28). John sacrificed much for the gospel and for his calling and was eventually beheaded. But Jesus wanted us to understand that the least are the greatest because they pour out all they have as servants of God and others. Dr. Martin L. King Jr. said that everybody can be great because anybody can serve. We were all born for greatness.

3:16 [a] Matt. 3:11, 12; Mark 1:7, 8 [b] John 7:39; 20:22; Acts 2:1–4 3:17 [a] Mic. 4:12; Matt. 13:24–30 3:19 [a] Matt. 14:3; Mark 6:17
[1] NU-Text reads *his brother's wife.* 3:21 [a] Matt. 3:13–17; John 1:32 3:22 [a] Ps. 2:7; [Is. 42:1];
Matt. 3:17; 17:5; Mark 1:11; Luke 1:35; 9:35; 2 Pet. 1:17

The Genealogy of Jesus Christ
(Gen. 5:1–32; 11:10–26; Ruth 4:18–22; 1 Chr.
1:1–4, 24–27, 34; 2:1–15; Matt. 1:2–16)

23 Now Jesus Himself began *His minis-*
try at [a]about thirty years of age, being (as
was supposed) [b]*the* son of Joseph, *the son*
of Heli, 24 *the son* of Matthat,[1] *the son* of Levi,
the son of Melchi, *the son* of Janna, *the son*
of Joseph, 25 *the son* of Mattathiah, *the son* of
Amos, *the son* of Nahum, *the son* of Esli, *the*
son of Naggai, 26 *the son* of Maath, *the son* of
Mattathiah, *the son* of Semei, *the son* of Joseph, *the son* of Judah, 27 *the son* of Joannas,
the son of Rhesa, *the son* of [a]Zerubbabel, *the*
son of Shealtiel, *the son* of Neri, 28 *the son* of
Melchi, *the son* of Addi, *the son* of Cosam,
the son of Elmodam, *the son* of Er, 29 *the son*
of Jose, *the son* of Eliezer, *the son* of Jorim,
the son of Matthat, *the son* of Levi, 30 *the son*
of Simeon, *the son* of Judah, *the son* of Joseph, *the son* of Jonan, *the son* of Eliakim,
31 *the son* of Melea, *the son* of Menan, *the son*
of Mattathah, *the son* of [a]Nathan, [b]*the son* of
David, 32 [a]*the son* of Jesse, *the son* of Obed,
the son of Boaz, *the son* of Salmon, *the son*
of Nahshon, 33 *the son* of Amminadab, *the*
son of Ram, *the son* of Hezron, *the son* of Perez, *the son* of Judah, 34 *the son* of Jacob, *the*
son of Isaac, *the son* of Abraham, [a]*the son* of
Terah, *the son* of Nahor, 35 *the son* of Serug,
the son of Reu, *the son* of Peleg, *the son* of
Eber, *the son* of Shelah, 36 [a]*the son* of Cainan,
the son of [b]Arphaxad, [c]*the son* of Shem, *the*
son of Noah, *the son* of Lamech, 37 *the son* of
Methuselah, *the son* of Enoch, *the son* of Jared, *the son* of Mahalalel, *the son* of Cainan,
38 *the son* of Enosh, *the son* of Seth, *the son* of
Adam, [a]*the son* of God.

Satan Tempts Jesus
(Matt. 4:1–11; Mark 1:12, 13)

4 Then [a]Jesus, being filled with the Holy
Spirit, returned from the Jordan and
[b]was led by the Spirit into[1] the wilderness,
2 being tempted for forty days by the devil.
And [a]in those days He ate nothing, and
afterward, when they had ended, He was
hungry.

3 And the devil said to Him, "If You are
[a]the Son of God, command this stone to
become bread."

4 But Jesus answered him, saying,[1] "It is
written, [a]'Man shall not live by bread alone,
but by every word of God.'"[2]

5 Then the devil, taking Him up on a high
mountain, showed Him[1] all the kingdoms
of the world in a moment of time. 6 And the
devil said to Him, "All this authority I will
give You, and their glory; for [a]*this* has been
delivered to me, and I give it to whomever I
wish. 7 Therefore, if You will worship before
me, all will be Yours."

8 And Jesus answered and said to him,
"Get behind Me, Satan![1] For[2] it is written,
[a]'You shall worship the LORD your God, and
Him only you shall serve.'"[3]

9 [a]Then he brought Him to Jerusalem, set
Him on the pinnacle of the temple, and said
to Him, "If You are the Son of God, throw
Yourself down from here. 10 For it is written:

[a]'He shall give His angels
charge over you,
To keep you,'

11 and,

[a]'In *their* hands they shall bear you up,
Lest you dash your foot
against a stone.'"[1]

12 And Jesus answered and said to him,
"It has been said, [a]'You shall not tempt the
LORD your God.'"[1]

13 Now when the devil had ended every
temptation, he departed from Him [a]until
an opportune time.

Jesus Begins His Galilean Ministry
(Matt. 4:12–17; Mark 1:14, 15)

14 [a]Then Jesus returned [b]in the power of
the Spirit to [c]Galilee, and [d]news of Him went

3:23 [a] [Num. 4:3, 35, 39, 43, 47] [b] Matt. 13:55; John 6:42 3:24 [1] This and several other names in the genealogy are spelled somewhat differently in the NU-Text. Since the New King James Version uses the Old Testament spelling for persons mentioned in the New Testament, these variations, which come from the Greek, have not been footnoted. 3:27 [a] Ezra 2:2; 3:8 3:31 [a] Zech. 12:12 [b] 2 Sam. 5:14; 7:12; 1 Chr. 3:5; 17:11; Is. 9:7; Jer. 23:5 3:32 [a] Ruth 4:18–22; 1 Chr. 2:10–12; Is. 11:1, 10 3:34 [a] Gen. 11:24, 26–30; 12:3; Num. 24:17; 1 Chr. 1:24–27 3:36 [a] Gen. 11:12 [b] Gen. 10:22, 24; 11:10–13; 1 Chr. 1:17, 18 [c] Gen. 5:6–32; 9:27; 11:10 3:38 [a] Gen. 5:1, 2 4:1 [a] [Is. 11:2; 61:1]; Matt. 4:1–11; Mark 1:12, 13 [b] Ezek. 3:12; Luke 2:27 [1] NU-Text reads *in.* 4:2 [a] Ex. 34:28; 1 Kin. 19:8 4:3 [a] Mark 3:11; John 20:31 4:4 [a] Deut. 8:3 [1] Deuteronomy 8:3 [2] NU-Text omits *but by every word of God.* 4:5 [1] NU-Text reads *And taking Him up, he showed Him.* 4:6 [a] [John 12:31; 14:30; Rev. 13:2, 7] 4:8 [a] Deut. 6:13; 10:20; Matt. 4:10 [1] NU-Text omits *Get behind Me, Satan.* [2] NU-Text and M-Text omit *For.* [3] Deuteronomy 6:13 4:9 [a] Matt. 4:5–7 4:10 [a] Ps. 91:11 4:11 [a] Ps. 91:12 [1] Psalm 91:11, 12 4:12 [a] Deut. 6:16 [1] Deuteronomy 6:16 4:13 [a] [John 14:30; Heb. 4:15; James 4:7] 4:14 [a] Matt. 4:12 [b] John 4:43 [c] Acts 10:37 [d] Matt. 4:24

out through all the surrounding region.
15And He [a]taught in their synagogues, [b]be-
ing glorified by all.

Jesus Rejected at Nazareth
(Matt. 13:54–58; Mark 6:1–6)

16So He came to [a]Nazareth, where He had
been brought up. And as His custom was,
[b]He went into the synagogue on the Sabbath day, and stood up to read. 17And He
was handed the book of the prophet Isaiah. And when He had opened the book,
He found the place where it was written:

18 "The[a] Spirit of the LORD *is* upon Me,
Because He has anointed Me
To preach the gospel to *the* poor;
He has sent Me to heal the
brokenhearted,[1]
To proclaim liberty to *the* captives
And recovery of sight to *the* blind,
To [b]set at liberty those who
are oppressed;
19 To proclaim the acceptable
year of the LORD."[1]

20Then He closed the book, and gave *it* back
to the attendant and sat down. And the eyes
of all who were in the synagogue were fixed
on Him. 21And He began to say to them,
"Today this Scripture is [a]fulfilled in your
hearing." 22So all bore witness to Him, and
[a]marveled at the gracious words which proceeded out of His mouth. And they said,
[b]"Is this not Joseph's son?"

23He said to them, "You will surely say
this proverb to Me, 'Physician, heal yourself! Whatever we have heard done in [a]Ca-
pernaum,[1] do also here in [b]Your country.'"
24Then He said, "Assuredly, I say to you, no
[a]prophet is accepted in his own country.
25But I tell you truly, [a]many widows were in
Israel in the days of Elijah, when the heaven
was shut up three years and six months,
and there was a great famine throughout all
the land; 26but to none of them was Elijah
sent except to Zarephath,[1] *in the region* of
Sidon, to a woman *who was* a widow. 27[a]And
many lepers were in Israel in the time of
Elisha the prophet, and none of them was
cleansed except Naaman the Syrian."

28So all those in the synagogue, when
they heard these things, were [a]filled with
wrath, 29[a]and rose up and thrust Him out
of the city; and they led Him to the brow of
the hill on which their city was built, that
they might throw Him down over the cliff.
30Then [a]passing through the midst of them,
He went His way.

Jesus Casts Out an Unclean Spirit
(Mark 1:21–28)

31Then [a]He went down to Capernaum, a
city of Galilee, and was teaching them on
the Sabbaths. 32And they were [a]astonished
at His teaching, [b]for His word was with authority. 33[a]Now in the synagogue there was
a man who had a spirit of an unclean demon. And he cried out with a loud voice,
34saying, "Let *us* alone! What have we to do
with You, Jesus of Nazareth? Did You come
to destroy us? [a]I know who You are—[b]the
Holy One of God!"

35But Jesus rebuked him, saying, "Be
quiet, and come out of him!" And when
the demon had thrown him in *their* midst,
it came out of him and did not hurt him.
36Then they were all amazed and spoke
among themselves, saying, "What a word
this *is!* For with authority and power He
commands the unclean spirits, and they
come out." 37And the report about Him
went out into every place in the surrounding region.

Peter's Mother-in-Law Healed
(Matt. 8:14, 15; Mark 1:29–31)

38[a]Now He arose from the synagogue
and entered Simon's house. But Simon's
wife's mother was sick with a high fever,
and they [b]made request of Him concerning
her. 39So He stood over her and [a]rebuked
the fever, and it left her. And immediately
she arose and served them.

4:15 [a] Ps. 22:22; Matt. 4:23 [b] Is. 52:13 4:16 [a] Matt. 2:23; 13:54; Mark 6:1 [b] Mark 1:21; John 18:20; Acts 13:14–16; 17:2 4:18 [a] Is. 49:8, 9; 61:1, 2; Matt. 11:5; 12:18; John 3:34 [b] [Dan. 9:24] [1] NU-Text omits *to heal the brokenhearted.* 4:19 [1] Isaiah 61:1, 2 4:21 [a] Matt. 1:22, 23; Acts 13:29 4:22 [a] [Ps. 45:2]; Matt. 13:54; Mark 6:2; Luke 2:47; [John 1:14, 17] [b] John 6:42 4:23 [a] Matt. 4:13; 11:23 [b] Matt. 13:54; Mark 6:1 [1] Here and elsewhere the NU-Text spelling is *Capharnaum.* 4:24 [a] Matt. 13:57; Mark 6:4; John 4:44 4:25 [a] 1 Kin. 17:9; James 5:17 4:26 [1] Greek *Sarepta* 4:27 [a] 2 Kin. 5:1–14 4:28 [a] Luke 6:11 4:29 [a] Luke 17:25; John 8:37; 10:31 4:30 [a] John 8:59; 10:39 4:31 [a] Is. 9:1; Matt. 4:13; Mark 1:21 4:32 [a] Matt. 7:28, 29 [b] Luke 4:36; [John 6:63; 7:46; 8:26, 28, 38, 47; 12:49, 50] 4:33 [a] Mark 1:23 4:34 [a] Luke 4:41 [b] Ps. 16:10; Is. 49:7; Dan. 9:24; Luke 1:35 4:38 [a] Matt. 8:14, 15; Mark 1:29–31 [b] Mark 5:23 4:39 [a] Luke 8:24

Many Healed After Sabbath Sunset
(Matt. 8:16, 17; Mark 1:32–34)

40[a]When the sun was setting, all those
who had any that were sick with various
diseases brought them to Him; and He
laid His hands on every one of them and
healed them. 41[a]And demons also came out
of many, crying out and saying, [b]"You are
the Christ,[1] the Son of God!"

And He, [c]rebuking *them,* did not allow
them to speak, for they knew that He was
the Christ.

Jesus Preaches in Galilee
(Matt. 4:23–25; Mark 1:35–39)

42[a]Now when it was day, He departed and
went into a deserted place. And the crowd
sought Him and came to Him, and tried to
keep Him from leaving them; 43but He said
to them, "I must [a]preach the kingdom of
God to the other cities also, because for this
purpose I have been sent." 44[a]And He was
preaching in the synagogues of Galilee.[1]

Four Fishermen Called as Disciples
(Matt. 4:18–22; Mark 1:16–20)

5 So [a]it was, as the multitude pressed
about Him to [b]hear the word of God,
that He stood by the Lake of Gennesaret,
2and saw two boats standing by the lake;
but the fishermen had gone from them
and were washing *their* nets. 3Then He got
into one of the boats, which was Simon's,
and asked him to put out a little from the
land. And He [a]sat down and taught the multitudes from the boat.

4When He had stopped speaking, He
said to Simon, [a]"Launch out into the deep
and let down your nets for a catch."

5But Simon answered and said to Him,
"Master, we have toiled all night and
caught [a]nothing; nevertheless [b]at Your
word I will let down the net." 6And when
they had done this, they caught a great
number of fish, and their net was breaking. 7So they signaled to *their* partners in
the other boat to come and help them.
And they came and filled both the boats,
so that they began to sink. 8When Simon
Peter saw *it,* he fell down at Jesus' knees,
saying, [a]"Depart from me, for I am a sinful man, O Lord!"

9For he and all who were with him were
[a]astonished at the catch of fish which they
had taken; 10and so also *were* James and
John, the sons of Zebedee, who were partners with Simon. And Jesus said to Simon,
"Do not be afraid. [a]From now on you will
catch men." 11So when they had brought
their boats to land, [a]they forsook all and
followed Him.

Jesus Cleanses a Leper
(Matt. 8:1–4; Mark 1:40–45)

12[a]And it happened when He was in a
certain city, that behold, a man who was
full of [b]leprosy saw Jesus; and he fell on
his face and implored Him, saying, "Lord,
if You are willing, You can make me clean."

13Then He put out *His* hand and touched
him, saying, "I am willing; be cleansed."
[a]Immediately the leprosy left him. 14[a]And
He charged him to tell no one, "But go and
show yourself to the priest, and make an
offering for your cleansing, as a testimony
to them, [b]just as Moses commanded."

15However, [a]the report went around concerning Him all the more; and [b]great multitudes came together to hear, and to be
healed by Him of their infirmities. 16[a]So He
Himself *often* withdrew into the wilderness
and [b]prayed.

Jesus Forgives and Heals a Paralytic
(Matt. 9:2–8; Mark 2:1–12)

17Now it happened on a certain day, as
He was teaching, that there were Pharisees and teachers of the law sitting by, who
had come out of every town of Galilee, Judea, and Jerusalem. And the power of the
Lord was *present* to heal them.[1] 18[a]Then
behold, men brought on a bed a man who
was paralyzed, whom they sought to bring

4:40 [a] Matt. 8:16, 17; Mark 1:32–34 4:41 [a] Mark 1:34; 3:11; Acts 8:7 [b] Mark 8:29 [c] Mark 1:25, 34; 3:11; Luke 4:34, 35 [1] NU-Text omits *the Christ.* 4:42 [a] Mark 1:35–38; Luke 9:10 4:43 [a] Mark 1:14; [John 9:4] 4:44 [a] Matt. 4:23; 9:35; Mark 1:39 [1] NU-Text reads *Judea.* 5:1 [a] Matt. 4:18–22; Mark 1:16–20; John 1:40–42 [b] Acts 13:44 5:3 [a] John 8:2 5:4 [a] John 21:6 5:5 [a] John 21:3 [b] Ps. 33:9 5:8 [a] 2 Sam. 6:9; 1 Kin. 17:18 5:9 [a] Mark 5:42; 10:24, 26 5:10 [a] Matt. 4:19; Mark 1:17 5:11 [a] Matt. 4:20; 19:27; [Mark 1:18; 8:34, 35; Luke 9:59–62]; John 12:26 5:12 [a] Matt. 8:2–4; Mark 1:40–44 [b] Lev. 13:14 5:13 [a] Matt. 20:34; Luke 8:44; John 5:9 5:14 [a] Matt. 8:4; Luke 17:14 [b] Lev. 13:1–3; 14:2–32 5:15 [a] Mark 1:45 [b] Matt. 4:25; Mark 3:7; John 6:2 5:16 [a] Luke 9:10 [b] Matt. 14:23; Mark 1:35; Luke 6:12; 9:18; 11:1 5:17 [1] NU-Text reads *present with Him to heal.* 5:18 [a] Matt. 9:2–8; Mark 2:3–12

in and lay before Him. 19 And when they
could not find how they might bring him
in, because of the crowd, they went up
on the housetop and let him down with
his bed through the tiling into the midst
[a]before Jesus.
20 When He saw their faith, He said to
him, "Man, your sins are forgiven you."
21 [a]And the scribes and the Pharisees began to reason, saying, "Who is this who
speaks blasphemies? [b]Who can forgive sins
but God alone?"
22 But when Jesus [a]perceived their
thoughts, He answered and said to them,
"Why are you reasoning in your hearts?
23 Which is easier, to say, 'Your sins are forgiven you,' or to say, 'Rise up and walk'?
24 But that you may know that the Son
of Man has power on earth to forgive
sins"—He said to the man who was paralyzed, [a]"I say to you, arise, take up your
bed, and go to your house."
25 Immediately he rose up before them,
took up what he had been lying on, and departed to his own house, [a]glorifying God.
26 And they were all amazed, and they [a]glo-
rified God and were filled with fear, saying,
"We have seen strange things today!"

Matthew the Tax Collector
(Matt. 9:9–13; Mark 2:13–17)

27 [a]After these things He went out and
saw a tax collector named Levi, sitting at
the tax office. And He said to him, [b]"Follow Me." 28 So he left all, rose up, and [a]fol-
lowed Him.
29 [a]Then Levi gave Him a great feast in
his own house. And [b]there were a great
number of tax collectors and others who
sat down with them. 30 And their scribes
and the Pharisees[1] complained against
His disciples, saying, [a]"Why do You eat
and drink with tax collectors and sinners?"
31 Jesus answered and said to them,
"Those who are well have no need of a physician, but those who are sick. 32 [a]I have not
come to call *the* righteous, but sinners, to
repentance."

Jesus Is Questioned About Fasting
(Matt. 9:14–17; Mark 2:18–22)

33 Then they said to Him, [a]"Why do[1]
the disciples of John fast often and make
prayers, and likewise those of the Pharisees, but Yours eat and drink?"
34 And He said to them, "Can you make
the friends of the bridegroom fast while
the [a]bridegroom is with them? 35 But the
days will come when the bridegroom will
be taken away from them; then they will
fast in those days."
36 [a]Then He spoke a parable to them: "No
one puts a piece from a new garment on an
old one;[1] otherwise the new makes a tear,
and also the piece that was *taken* out of
the new does not match the old. 37 And no
one puts new wine into old wineskins; or
else the new wine will burst the wineskins
and be spilled, and the wineskins will be
ruined. 38 But new wine must be put into
new wineskins, and both are preserved.[1]
39 And no one, having drunk old *wine,* immediately[1] desires new; for he says, 'The
old is better.' "[2]

Jesus Is Lord of the Sabbath
(Matt. 12:1–8; Mark 2:23–28)

6 Now [a]it happened on the second Sabbath after the first[1] that He went through
the grainfields. And His disciples plucked
the heads of grain and ate *them,* rubbing
them in *their* hands. 2 And some of the Pharisees said to them, "Why are you doing [a]what
is not lawful to do on the Sabbath?"
3 But Jesus answering them said, "Have
you not even read this, [a]what David did
when he was hungry, he and those who
were with him: 4 how he went into the house
of God, took and ate the showbread, and
also gave some to those with him, [a]which
is not lawful for any but the priests to eat?"
5 And He said to them, "The Son of Man is
also Lord of the Sabbath."

5:19 [a] Matt. 15:30 5:21 [a] Matt. 9:3; 26:65; Mark 2:6, 7; John 10:33 [b] Ps. 32:5; 130:4; Is. 43:25 5:22 [a] Luke 9:47; John 2:25 5:24 [a] Mark 2:11; 5:41; Luke 7:14 5:25 [a] Luke 17:15, 18; Acts 3:8 5:26 [a] Luke 1:65; 7:16 5:27 [a] Matt. 9:9–17; Mark 2:13–22 [b] [Mark 8:34]; Luke 9:59; John 12:26; 21:19, 22 5:28 [a] Matt. 4:22; 19:27; Mark 10:28 5:29 [a] Matt. 9:9, 10; Mark 2:15 [b] Luke 15:1 5:30 [a] Matt. 11:19; Luke 15:2; Acts 23:9 [1] NU-Text reads *But the Pharisees and their scribes.* 5:32 [a] Matt. 9:13; 1 Tim. 1:15 5:33 [a] Matt. 9:14; Mark 2:18; Luke 7:33 [1] NU-Text omits *Why do,* making the verse a statement. 5:34 [a] John 3:29 5:36 [a] Matt. 9:16, 17; Mark 2:21, 22 [1] NU-Text reads *No one tears a piece from a new garment and puts it on an old one.* 5:38 [1] NU-Text omits *and both are preserved.* 5:39 [1] NU-Text omits *immediately.* [2] NU-Text reads *good.* 6:1 [a] Matt. 12:1–8; Mark 2:23–28 [1] NU-Text reads *on a Sabbath.* 6:2 [a] Ex. 20:10 6:3 [a] 1 Sam. 21:6 6:4 [a] Lev. 24:9

Healing on the Sabbath
(Matt. 12:9–14; Mark 3:1–6)

6[a]Now it happened on another Sabbath,
also, that He entered the synagogue and
taught. And a man was there whose right
hand was withered. 7So the scribes and
Pharisees watched Him closely, whether
He would [a]heal on the Sabbath, that they
might find an [b]accusation against Him.
8But He [a]knew their thoughts, and said to
the man who had the withered hand, "Arise
and stand here." And he arose and stood.
9Then Jesus said to them, "I will ask you
one thing: [a]Is it lawful on the Sabbath to
do good or to do evil, to save life or to destroy?"[1] 10And when He had looked around
at them all, He said to the man,[1] "Stretch out
your hand." And he did so, and his hand was
restored as whole as the other.[2] 11But they
were filled with rage, and discussed with
one another what they might do to Jesus.

The Twelve Apostles
(Matt. 10:1–4; Mark 3:13–19)

12Now it came to pass in those days
that He went out to the mountain to pray,
and continued all night in [a]prayer to God.
13And when it was day, He called His disciples to *Himself;* [a]and from them He chose
[b]twelve whom He also named apostles:
14Simon, [a]whom He also named Peter,
and Andrew his brother; James and John;
Philip and Bartholomew; 15Matthew and
Thomas; James the *son* of Alphaeus, and
Simon called the Zealot; 16Judas [a]*the son*
of James, and [b]Judas Iscariot who also became a traitor.

Jesus Heals a Great Multitude
(cf. Matt. 4:24, 25; Mark 3:7–12)

17And He came down with them and
stood on a level place with a crowd of His
disciples [a]and a great multitude of people from all Judea and Jerusalem, and
from the seacoast of Tyre and Sidon, who
came to hear Him and be healed of their
diseases, 18as well as those who were tormented with unclean spirits. And they were
healed. 19And the whole multitude [a]sought
to [b]touch Him, for [c]power went out from
Him and healed *them* all.

The Beatitudes
(Matt. 5:1–12)

20Then He lifted up His eyes toward His
disciples, and said:

[a]"Blessed *are you* poor,
For yours is the kingdom of God.
21 [a]Blessed *are you* who hunger now,
For you shall be [b]filled.
[c]Blessed *are you* who weep now,
For you shall [d]laugh.
22 [a]Blessed are you when men hate you,
And when they [b]exclude you,
And revile *you,* and cast out
your name as evil,
For the Son of Man's sake.
23 [a]Rejoice in that day and leap for joy!
For indeed your reward
is great in heaven,
For [b]in like manner their
fathers did to the prophets.

Jesus Pronounces Woes

24"But[a] woe to you [b]who are rich,
For [c]you have received
your consolation.
25 [a]Woe to you who are full,
For you shall hunger.
[b]Woe to you who laugh now,
For you shall mourn and [c]weep.
26 [a]Woe to you[1] when all[2] men
speak well of you,
For so did their fathers to
the false prophets.

Love Your Enemies
(Matt. 5:38–48)

27[a]"But I say to you who hear: Love your
enemies, do good to those who hate you,
28[a]bless those who curse you, and [b]pray

6:6 [a] Matt. 12:9–14; Mark 3:1–6; Luke 13:14; 14:3; John 9:16 6:7 [a] Luke 13:14; 14:1–6 [b] Luke 20:20 6:8 [a] Matt. 9:4; John 2:24, 25 6:9 [a] John 7:23 [1] M-Text reads *to kill.* 6:10 [1] NU-Text and M-Text read *to him.* [2] NU-Text omits *as whole as the other.* 6:12 [a] Matt. 14:23; Mark 1:35; Luke 5:16; 9:18; 11:1 6:13 [a] John 6:70 [b] Matt. 10:1 6:14 [a] John 1:42 6:16 [a] Jude 1 [b] Luke 22:3–6 6:17 [a] Matt. 4:25; Mark 3:7, 8 6:19 [a] Matt. 9:21; 14:36; Mark 3:10 [b] Mark 5:27, 28; Luke 8:44–47 [c] Mark 5:30; Luke 8:46 6:20 [a] Matt. 5:3–12; [11:5]; Luke 6:20–23; [James 2:5] 6:21 [a] Is. 55:1; 65:13; Matt. 5:6 [b] [Rev. 7:16] [c] [Is. 61:3; Rev. 7:17] [d] Ps. 126:5 6:22 [a] Matt. 5:11; 1 Pet. 2:19; 3:14; 4:14 [b] [John 16:2] 6:23 [a] Matt. 5:12; Acts 5:41; [Col. 1:24]; James 1:2 [b] Acts 7:51 6:24 [a] Amos 6:1; Luke 12:21; James 5:1–6 [b] Luke 12:21 [c] Matt. 6:2, 5, 16; Luke 16:25 6:25 [a] [Is. 65:13] [b] [Prov. 14:13] [c] James 4:9 6:26 [a] [John 15:19; 1 John 4:5] [1] NU-Text and M-Text omit *to you.* [2] M-Text omits *all.* 6:27 [a] Ex. 23:4; Prov. 25:21; Matt. 5:44; Rom. 12:20 6:28 [a] Rom. 12:14 [b] Luke 23:24; Acts 7:60

for those who spitefully use you. 29[a]To him
who strikes you on the *one* cheek, offer the
other also. [b]And from him who takes away
your cloak, do not withhold *your* tunic either. 30[a]Give to everyone who asks of you.
And from him who takes away your goods
do not ask *them* back. 31[a]And just as you
want men to do to you, you also do to them
likewise.

32[a]"But if you love those who love you,
what credit is that to you? For even sinners
love those who love them. 33And if you do
good to those who do good to you, what
credit is that to you? For even sinners do
the same. 34[a]And if you lend *to those* from
whom you hope to receive back, what credit
is that to you? For even sinners lend to sinners to receive as much back. 35But [a]love
your enemies, [b]do good, and [c]lend, hoping
for nothing in return; and your reward will
be great, and [d]you will be sons of the Most
High. For He is kind to the unthankful and
evil. 36[a]Therefore be merciful, just as your
Father also is merciful.

Do Not Judge
(Matt. 7:1–5)

37[a]"Judge not, and you shall not be
judged. Condemn not, and you shall not
be condemned. [b]Forgive, and you will be
forgiven. 38[a]Give, and it will be given to you:
good measure, pressed down, shaken together, and running over will be put into
your [b]bosom. For [c]with the same measure
that you use, it will be measured back to
you."

39And He spoke a parable to them:
[a]"Can the blind lead the blind? Will they
not both fall into the ditch? 40[a]A disciple
is not above his teacher, but everyone who
is perfectly trained will be like his teacher.
41[a]And why do you look at the speck in your
brother's eye, but do not perceive the plank
in your own eye? 42Or how can you say to
your brother, 'Brother, let me remove the
speck that *is* in your eye,' when you yourself do not see the plank that *is* in your own
eye? Hypocrite! First remove the plank
from your own eye, and then you will see
clearly to remove the speck that is in your
brother's eye.

A Tree Is Known by Its Fruit
(Matt. 7:15–20)

43[a]"For a good tree does not bear bad
fruit, nor does a bad tree bear good fruit.
44For [a]every tree is known by its own fruit.
For *men* do not gather figs from thorns, nor
do they gather grapes from a bramble bush.
45[a]A good man out of the good treasure of
his heart brings forth good; and an evil
man out of the evil treasure of his heart[1]
brings forth evil. For out [b]of the abundance
of the heart his mouth speaks.

Build on the Rock
(Matt. 7:21–27)

46[a]"But why do you call Me 'Lord, Lord,'
and not do the things which I say? 47[a]Who-
ever comes to Me, and hears My sayings and
does them, I will show you whom he is like:
48He is like a man building a house, who dug
deep and laid the foundation on the rock.
And when the flood arose, the stream beat
vehemently against that house, and could
not shake it, for it was founded on the rock.[1]
49But he who heard and did nothing is like a
man who built a house on the earth without
a foundation, against which the stream beat
vehemently; and immediately it fell.[1] And
the ruin of that house was great."

Jesus Heals a Centurion's Servant
(Matt. 8:5–13)

7 Now when He concluded all His sayings in the hearing of the people, He
[a]entered Capernaum. 2And a certain centurion's servant, who was dear to him, was
sick and ready to die. 3So when he heard
about Jesus, he sent elders of the Jews to
Him, pleading with Him to come and heal
his servant. 4And when they came to Jesus,
they begged Him earnestly, saying that the
one for whom He should do this was deserving, 5"for he loves our nation, and has
built us a synagogue."

6:29 [a] Matt. 5:39–42 [b] [1 Cor. 6:7] 6:30 [a] Deut. 15:7, 8; Prov. 3:27; 21:26; Matt. 5:42 6:31 [a] Matt. 7:12 6:32 [a] Matt. 5:46 6:34 [a] Matt. 5:42 6:35 [a] [Rom. 13:10] [b] Heb. 13:16 [c] Lev. 25:35–37; Ps. 37:26 [d] Matt. 5:46 6:36 [a] Matt. 5:48; Eph. 4:32 6:37 [a] Matt. 7:1–5; Rom. 14:4; [1 Cor. 4:5] [b] Matt. 18:21–35 6:38 [a] [Prov. 19:17; 28:27] [b] Ps. 79:12; Is. 65:6, 7; Jer. 32:18 [c] Matt. 7:2; Mark 4:24; James 2:13 6:39 [a] Matt. 15:14; 23:16; Rom. 2:19 6:40 [a] Matt. 10:24; [John 13:16; 15:20] 6:41 [a] Matt. 7:3 6:43 [a] Matt. 7:16–18, 20 6:44 [a] Matt. 12:33 6:45 [a] Matt. 12:35 [b] Prov. 15:2, 28; 16:23; 18:21; Matt. 12:34 [1] NU-Text omits *treasure of his heart.* 6:46 [a] Mal. 1:6; Matt. 7:21; 25:11; Luke 13:25 6:47 [a] Matt. 7:24–27; [John 14:21]; James 1:22–25 6:48 [1] NU-Text reads *for it was well built.* 6:49 [1] NU-Text reads *collapsed.* 7:1 [a] Matt. 8:5–13

RELEASE // EXALT HIS IMMUTABILITY

God Will Not Change on You

Luke 6:46 // "But why do you call Me 'Lord, Lord,' and not do the things which I say?"

Summary Message // God is immutable. He will not change on you. It does not matter if there is a pandemic, an economic collapse, an uprising of injustice, or war. God does not change. He is the same God yesterday, today, and forever.

At the end of Luke 6, Jesus painted a powerful picture regarding the importance of building our lives on the unchanging foundation of God. He contrasted someone who calls Him "Lord," someone who recognizes His absolute authority but does not actually follow Him, with someone who genuinely follows Him by applying His teachings. Jesus shared an object lesson of two men building houses. One built his house on the rock. The other built his house on sand. A storm came and floodwaters, wind, and rain beat against both of their houses. The house built on the foundation of rock stood, while the house built on the sand was destroyed. If we build our spiritual houses on Christ, our rock, we can get through the rapidly changing storms of life.

Practical Application // One storm after another can hit our lives: a pandemic, racial injustice, economic upheaval, war, natural disasters. In these times, we can wonder what else could possibly be in store as we struggle to handle the present storm that batters us. In such troubled and chaotic times, our spiritual foundation matters more than ever. In the crucible of crisis, we can shed bad theology and practices and rebuild our faith in stronger, healthier, more biblical ways.

Many Christians, however, go through a deconstruction of their faith during these turbulent times. Many professing Christians can turn toward false religions and secular philosophies, causing them to lose their Christian faith altogether. Some turn toward negative politics and rhetoric, having more to say about them than the gospel, thereby turning others away from Christ and His church. It can be heartbreaking to watch. It is what Paul warned us against in Galatians 1:6–10. He cautioned that when we deviate from the gospel of Jesus Christ in any way and attempt to craft it to fit our own purposes, it is no longer the gospel of Jesus Christ at all.

This is why it is so important to build our spiritual houses on Jesus. We cannot build them on our finances, jobs, political affiliations, or pastors. All those things will inevitably let us down. When a major storm hits, they will not stand, let alone hold us up. Jesus warned us that many people will call Him "Lord," but they do not do the things He says. Do not be a house built on sand. Build your foundation on Jesus and truly make Him the leader of your life. He will sustain you and protect you in this rapidly changing world because He never changes.

Fervent Prayer // Heavenly Father, we declare You are the Lord of our lives; You are our leader. Expose the areas we still need to surrender to You and give us the courage to submit. We want to build the foundation of our lives on You. We pray for those who have fallen away from You during the storms of life. We pray that they will come back to their faith and submit to You in a deeper way than ever before. Use us to be lights to those who are drifting in darkness. Thank You for being our rock and for never changing. In Jesus' name we pray. Amen.

6Then Jesus went with them. And when
He was already not far from the house, the
centurion sent friends to Him, saying to
Him, "Lord, do not trouble Yourself, for I
am not worthy that You should enter under my roof. 7Therefore I did not even think
myself worthy to come to You. But [a]say the
word, and my servant will be healed. 8For
I also am a man placed under [a]authority,
having soldiers under me. And I say to one,
'Go,' and he goes; and to another, 'Come,'
and he comes; and to my servant, 'Do this,'
and he does *it*."
9When Jesus heard these things, He
marveled at him, and turned around and
said to the crowd that followed Him, "I say
to you, I have not found such great faith,
not even in Israel!" 10And those who were
sent, returning to the house, found the servant well who had been sick.[1]

7:7 [a] Ps. 33:9; 107:20 7:8 [a] [Mark 13:34] 7:10 [1] NU-Text omits *who had been sick.*

Jesus Raises the Son of the Widow of Nain

11Now it happened, the day after, *that* He
went into a city called Nain; and many of
His disciples went with Him, and a large
crowd. 12And when He came near the gate
of the city, behold, a dead man was being
carried out, the only son of his mother; and
she was a widow. And a large crowd from
the city was with her. 13When the Lord saw
her, He had [a]compassion on her and said
to her, [b]"Do not weep." 14Then He came and
touched the open coffin, and those who
carried *him* stood still. And He said, "Young
man, I say to you, [a]arise." 15So he who was
dead [a]sat up and began to speak. And He
[b]presented him to his mother.
16[a]Then fear came upon all, and they
[b]glorified God, saying, [c]"A great prophet
has risen up among us"; and, [d]"God has
visited His people." 17And this report about
Him went throughout all Judea and all the
surrounding region.

John the Baptist Sends Messengers to Jesus
(Matt. 11:2–19)

18[a]Then the disciples of John reported
to him concerning all these things. 19And
John, calling two of his disciples to *him,*
sent *them* to Jesus,[1] saying, "Are You [a]the
Coming One, or do we look for another?"
20When the men had come to Him, they
said, "John the Baptist has sent us to You,
saying, 'Are You the Coming One, or do we
look for another?'" 21And that very hour He
cured many of infirmities, afflictions, and
evil spirits; and to many blind He gave sight.
22[a]Jesus answered and said to them, "Go
and tell John the things you have seen and
heard: [b]that *the* blind [c]see, *the* lame [d]walk,
the lepers are [e]cleansed, *the* deaf [f]hear, *the*
dead are raised, [g]*the* poor have the gospel
preached to them. 23And blessed is *he* who
is not offended because of Me."
24[a]When the messengers of John had
departed, He began to speak to the multitudes
concerning John: "What did you
go out into the wilderness to see? A reed
shaken by the wind? 25But what did you
go out to see? A man clothed in soft garments?
Indeed those who are gorgeously
appareled and live in luxury are in kings'
courts. 26But what did you go out to see? A
prophet? Yes, I say to you, and more than a
prophet. 27This is *he* of whom it is written:

[a]'Behold, I send My messenger
before Your face,
Who will prepare Your
way before You.'[1]

28For I say to you, among those born of
women there is not a [a]greater prophet than
John the Baptist;[1] but he who is least in the
kingdom of God is greater than he."
29And when all the people heard *Him,*
even the tax collectors justified God, [a]having
been baptized with the baptism of John.
30But the Pharisees and lawyers rejected
[a]the will of God for themselves, not having
been baptized by him.
31And the Lord said,[1] [a]"To what then shall
I liken the men of this generation, and what
are they like? 32They are like children sitting
in the marketplace and calling to one
another, saying:

'We played the flute for you,
And you did not dance;
We mourned to you,
And you did not weep.'

33For [a]John the Baptist came [b]neither eating
bread nor drinking wine, and you say,
'He has a demon.' 34The Son of Man has
come [a]eating and drinking, and you say,
'Look, a glutton and a winebibber, a friend
of tax collectors and sinners!' 35[a]But wisdom
is justified by all her children."

A Sinful Woman Forgiven

36[a]Then one of the Pharisees asked Him
to eat with him. And He went to the Pharisee's
house, and sat down to eat. 37And behold,
a woman in the city who was a sinner,
when she knew that *Jesus* sat at the table in

7:13 [a] Lam. 3:32; John 11:35; [Heb. 4:15] [b] Luke 8:52 7:14 [a] Mark 5:41; Luke 8:54; John 11:43; Acts 9:40; [Rom. 4:17] 7:15 [a] Matt. 11:5; Luke 8:55; John 11:44 [b] 1 Kin. 17:23; 2 Kin. 4:36 7:16 [a] Luke 1:65 [b] Luke 5:26 [c] Luke 24:19; John 4:19; 6:14; 9:17 [d] Luke 1:68 7:18 [a] Matt. 11:2–19 7:19 [a] [Mic. 5:2; Zech. 9:9; Mal. 3:1–3] [1] NU-Text reads *the Lord.* 7:22 [a] Matt. 11:4 [b] Is. 35:5 [c] John 9:7 [d] Matt. 15:31 [e] Luke 17:12–14 [f] Mark 7:37 [g] [Is. 61:1–3; Luke 4:18] 7:24 [a] Matt. 11:7 7:27 [a] Is. 40:3; Mal. 3:1; Matt. 11:10; Mark 1:2 [1] Malachi 3:1 7:28 [a] [Luke 1:15] [1] NU-Text reads *there is none greater than John.* 7:29 [a] Matt. 3:5; Luke 3:12 7:30 [a] Acts 20:27 7:31 [a] Matt. 11:16 [1] NU-Text and M-Text omit *And the Lord said.* 7:33 [a] Matt. 3:1 [b] [Matt. 3:4]; Luke 1:15 7:34 [a] Luke 15:2 7:35 [a] Matt. 11:19 7:36 [a] Matt. 26:6; Mark 14:3; John 11:2

the Pharisee's house, brought an alabaster
flask of fragrant oil, 38and stood at His feet
behind *Him* weeping; and she began to wash
His feet with her tears, and wiped *them* with
the hair of her head; and she kissed His feet
and anointed *them* with the fragrant oil.
39Now when the Pharisee who had invited
Him saw *this,* he spoke to himself, saying,
[a]"This Man, if He were a prophet, would
know who and what manner of woman *this*
is who is touching Him, for she is a sinner."

40And Jesus answered and said to him,
"Simon, I have something to say to you."

So he said, "Teacher, say it."

41"There was a certain creditor who had
two debtors. One owed five hundred [a]de-
narii, and the other fifty. 42And when they
had nothing with which to repay, he freely
forgave them both. Tell Me, therefore,
which of them will love him more?"

43Simon answered and said, "I suppose
the *one* whom he forgave more."

And He said to him, "You have rightly
judged." 44Then He turned to the woman
and said to Simon, "Do you see this woman?
I entered your house; you gave Me no [a]wa-
ter for My feet, but she has washed My feet
with her tears and wiped *them* with the hair
of her head. 45You gave Me no [a]kiss, but this
woman has not ceased to kiss My feet since
the time I came in. 46[a]You did not anoint My
head with oil, but this woman has anointed
My feet with fragrant oil. 47[a]Therefore I say
to you, her sins, which *are* many, are forgiven, for she loved much. But to whom little is forgiven, *the same* loves little."

48Then He said to her, [a]"Your sins are
forgiven."

49And those who sat at the table with
Him began to say to themselves, [a]"Who is
this who even forgives sins?"

50Then He said to the woman, [a]"Your
faith has saved you. Go in peace."

Many Women Minister to Jesus

8 Now it came to pass, afterward, that He
went through every city and village,
preaching and bringing the glad tidings of
the kingdom of God. And the twelve *were*
with Him, 2and [a]certain women who had
been healed of evil spirits and infirmities—
Mary called Magdalene, [b]out of whom had
come seven demons, 3and Joanna the wife
of Chuza, Herod's steward, and Susanna,
and many others who provided for Him[1]
from their substance.

The Parable of the Sower
(Matt. 13:1–9; Mark 4:1–9)

4[a]And when a great multitude had gathered, and they had come to Him from every
city, He spoke by a parable: 5"A sower went
out to sow his seed. And as he sowed, some
fell by the wayside; and it was trampled
down, and the birds of the air devoured it.
6Some fell on rock; and as soon as it sprang
up, it withered away because it lacked moisture. 7And some fell among thorns, and the
thorns sprang up with it and choked it. 8But
others fell on good ground, sprang up, and
yielded a crop a hundredfold." When He
had said these things He cried, [a]"He who
has ears to hear, let him hear!"

The Purpose of Parables
(Matt. 13:10–17; Mark 4:10–12)

9[a]Then His disciples asked Him, saying,
"What does this parable mean?"

10And He said, "To you it has been given
to know the mysteries of the kingdom of
God, but to the rest *it is given* in parables,
that

[a]'Seeing they may not see,
And hearing they may
not understand.'[1]

The Parable of the Sower Explained
(Matt. 13:18–23; Mark 4:13–20)

11[a]"Now the parable is this: The seed is
the [b]word of God. 12Those by the wayside
are the ones who hear; then the devil comes
and takes away the word out of their hearts,
lest they should believe and be saved. 13But
the ones on the rock *are those* who, when
they hear, receive the word with joy; and

7:39 [a] Luke 15:2 7:41 [a] Matt. 18:28; Mark 6:37 7:44 [a] Gen. 18:4; 19:2; 43:24; Judg. 19:21; 1 Tim. 5:10 7:45 [a] Rom. 16:16 7:46 [a] 2 Sam. 12:20; Ps. 23:5; Eccl. 9:8; Dan. 10:3 7:47 [a] [1 Tim. 1:14] 7:48 [a] Matt. 9:2; Mark 2:5 7:49 [a] Matt. 9:3; [Mark 2:7]; Luke 5:21 7:50 [a] Matt. 9:22; Mark 5:34; 10:52; Luke 8:48; 18:42 8:2 [a] Matt. 27:55; Mark 15:40, 41; Luke 23:49, 55 [b] Matt. 27:56; Mark 16:9 8:3 [1] NU-Text and M-Text read *them.* 8:4 [a] Matt. 13:2–9; Mark 4:1–9 8:8 [a] Matt. 11:15; Mark 7:16; Luke 14:35; Rev. 2:7, 11, 17, 29; 3:6, 13, 22; 13:9 8:9 [a] Matt. 13:10–23; Mark 4:10–20 8:10 [a] Is. 6:9; Matt. 13:14; Acts 28:26 [1] Isaiah 6:9 8:11 [a] Matt. 13:18; Mark 4:14; [1 Pet. 1:23] [b] Luke 5:1; 11:28

these have no root, who believe for a while
and in time of temptation fall away. 14Now
the ones *that* fell among thorns are those
who, when they have heard, go out and are
choked with cares, [a]riches, and pleasures
of life, and bring no fruit to maturity. 15But
the ones *that* fell on the good ground are
those who, having heard the word with a
noble and good heart, keep *it* and bear fruit
with [a]patience.

The Parable of the Revealed Light
(Mark 4:21–25)

16[a]"No one, when he has lit a lamp, covers
it with a vessel or puts *it* under a bed, but
sets *it* on a lampstand, that those who enter may see the [b]light. 17[a]For nothing is secret that will not be [b]revealed, nor *anything*
hidden that will not be known and come to
light. 18Therefore take heed how you hear.
[a]For whoever has, to him *more* will be given;
and whoever does not have, even what he
seems to [b]have will be taken from him."

Jesus' Mother and Brothers Come to Him
(Matt. 12:46–50, Mark 3:31–35)

19[a]Then His mother and brothers came
to Him, and could not approach Him because of the crowd. 20And it was told Him
by some, who said, "Your mother and Your
brothers are standing outside, desiring to
see You."

21But He answered and said to them, "My
mother and My brothers are these who hear
the word of God and do it."

Wind and Wave Obey Jesus
(Matt. 8:23–27; Mark 4:35–41)

22[a]Now it happened, on a certain day,
that He got into a boat with His disciples.
And He said to them, "Let us cross over
to the other side of the lake." And they
launched out. 23But as they sailed He fell
asleep. And a windstorm came down on the
lake, and they were filling *with water,* and
were in jeopardy. 24And they came to Him
and awoke Him, saying, "Master, Master,
we are perishing!"

Then He arose and rebuked the wind and
the raging of the water. And they ceased,
and there was a calm. 25But He said to them,
[a]"Where is your faith?"

And they were afraid, and marveled, saying to one another, [b]"Who can this be? For
He commands even the winds and water,
and they obey Him!"

A Demon-Possessed Man Healed
(Matt. 8:28—9:1; Mark 5:1–20)

26[a]Then they sailed to the country of
the Gadarenes,[1] which is opposite Galilee. 27And when He stepped out on the
land, there met Him a certain man from
the city who had demons for a long time.
And he wore no clothes,[1] nor did he live in
a house but in the tombs. 28When he saw
Jesus, he [a]cried out, fell down before Him,
and with a loud voice said, [b]"What have I to
do with [c]You, Jesus, Son of the Most High
God? I beg You, do not torment me!" 29For
He had commanded the unclean spirit to
come out of the man. For it had often seized
him, and he was kept under guard, bound
with chains and shackles; and he broke the
bonds and was driven by the demon into
the wilderness.

30Jesus asked him, saying, "What is your
name?"

And he said, "Legion," because many demons had entered him. 31And they begged
Him that He would not command them to
go out [a]into the abyss.

32Now a herd of many [a]swine was feeding there on the mountain. So they begged
Him that He would permit them to enter
them. And He permitted them. 33Then the
demons went out of the man and entered
the swine, and the herd ran violently down
the steep place into the lake and drowned.

34When those who fed *them* saw what
had happened, they fled and told *it* in the
city and in the country. 35Then they went
out to see what had happened, and came to
Jesus, and found the man from whom the
demons had departed, [a]sitting at the [b]feet
of Jesus, clothed and in his [c]right mind.

8:14 [a] Matt. 19:23; 1 Tim. 6:9, 10 8:15 [a] [Rom. 2:7; Heb. 10:36–39; James 5:7, 8] 8:16 [a] Matt. 5:15; Mark 4:21; Luke 11:33 [b] Matt. 5:14
8:17 [a] Matt. 10:26; Luke 12:2; [1 Cor. 4:5] [b] [Eccl. 12:14; 2 Cor. 5:10] 8:18 [a] Matt. 25:29 [b] Matt. 13:12 8:19 [a] Ps. 69:8; Matt. 12:46–50; Mark 3:31–35 8:22 [a] Matt. 8:23–27; Mark 4:36–41 8:25 [a] Luke 9:41 [b] Luke 4:36; 5:26 8:26 [a] Matt. 8:28–34; Mark 5:1–17 [1] NU-Text reads *Gerasenes.* 8:27 [1] NU-Text reads *who had demons and for a long time wore no clothes.*
8:28 [a] Mark 1:26; 9:26 [b] Mark 1:23, 24 [c] Luke 4:41 8:31 [a] Rom. 10:7; [Rev. 20:1, 3] 8:32 [a] Lev. 11:7; Deut. 14:8
8:35 [a] [Matt. 11:28] [b] Matt. 28:9; Mark 7:25; Luke 10:39; 17:16; John 11:32 [c] [2 Tim. 1:7]

And they were afraid. 36 They also who had
seen *it* told them by what means he who
had been demon-possessed was healed.
37 [a]Then the whole multitude of the surrounding region of the Gadarenes[1] [b]asked
Him to [c]depart from them, for they were
seized with great [d]fear. And He got into the
boat and returned.

38 Now [a]the man from whom the demons
had departed begged Him that he might be
with Him. But Jesus sent him away, saying,
39 "Return to your own house, and tell what
great things God has done for you." And he
went his way and proclaimed throughout
the whole city what great things Jesus had
done for him.

A Girl Restored to Life and a Woman Healed

40 So it was, when Jesus returned, that
the multitude welcomed Him, for they
were all waiting for Him. 41 [a]And behold,
there came a man named Jairus, and he
was a ruler of the synagogue. And he fell
down at Jesus' feet and begged Him to
come to his house, 42 for he had an only
daughter about twelve years of age, and
she [a]was dying.

But as He went, the multitudes thronged
Him. 43 [a]Now a woman, having a [b]flow of
blood for twelve years, who had spent all
her livelihood on physicians and could not
be healed by any, 44 came from behind and
[a]touched the border of His garment. And
immediately her flow of blood stopped.

45 And Jesus said, "Who touched Me?"

When all denied it, Peter and those with
him[1] said, "Master, the multitudes throng
and press You, and You say, 'Who touched
Me?' "[2]

46 But Jesus said, "Somebody touched
Me, for I perceived [a]power going out from
Me." 47 Now when the woman saw that she
was not hidden, she came trembling; and
falling down before Him, she declared to
Him in the presence of all the people the
reason she had touched Him and how she
was healed immediately.

48 And He said to her, "Daughter, be of
good cheer;[1] [a]your faith has made you well.
[b]Go in peace."

49 [a]While He was still speaking, someone
came from the ruler of the synagogue's
house, saying to him, "Your daughter is
dead. Do not trouble the Teacher."[1]

50 But when Jesus heard *it,* He answered
him, saying, "Do not be afraid; [a]only believe, and she will be made well." 51 When He
came into the house, He permitted no one
to go in[1] except Peter, James, and John,[2]
and the father and mother of the girl. 52 Now
all wept and mourned for her; but He said,
[a]"Do not weep; she is not dead, [b]but sleeping." 53 And they ridiculed Him, knowing
that she was dead.

54 But He put them all outside,[1] took
her by the hand and called, saying, "Little girl, [a]arise." 55 Then her spirit returned,
and she arose immediately. And He commanded that she be given *something* to eat.
56 And her parents were astonished, but
[a]He charged them to tell no one what had
happened.

Sending Out the Twelve
(Matt. 10:5–15)

9 Then [a]He called His twelve disciples
together and [b]gave them power and
authority over all demons, and to cure diseases. 2 [a]He sent them to preach the kingdom of God and to heal the sick. 3 [a]And He
said to them, "Take nothing for the journey, neither staffs nor bag nor bread nor
money; and do not have two tunics apiece.

4 [a]"Whatever house you enter, stay there,
and from there depart. 5 [a]And whoever will
not receive you, when you go out of that
city, [b]shake off the very dust from your feet
as a testimony against them."

6 [a]So they departed and went through
the towns, preaching the gospel and healing everywhere.

8:37 [a] Matt. 8:34 [b] Mark 1:24; Luke 4:34 [c] Job 21:14; Acts 16:39 [d] Luke 5:26 [1] NU-Text reads *Gerasenes.* 8:38 [a] Mark 5:18–20
8:41 [a] Matt. 9:18–26; Mark 5:22–43 8:42 [a] Luke 7:2 8:43 [a] Matt. 9:20 [b] Luke 15:19–22 8:44 [a] Mark 6:56; Luke 5:13
8:45 [1] NU-Text omits *and those with him.* [2] NU-Text omits *and You say, 'Who touched Me?'* 8:46 [a] Mark 5:30; Luke 6:19
8:48 [a] Mark 5:34; Luke 7:50 [b] John 8:11 [1] NU-Text omits *be of good cheer.* 8:49 [a] Mark 5:35 [1] NU-Text adds *anymore.*
8:50 [a] [Mark 11:22–24] 8:51 [1] NU-Text adds *with Him.* [2] NU-Text and M-Text read *Peter, John, and James.* 8:52 [a] Luke 7:13
[b] [John 11:11, 13] 8:54 [a] Luke 7:14; John 11:43 [1] NU-Text omits *put them all outside.* 8:56 [a] Matt. 8:4; 9:30; Mark 5:43
9:1 [a] Matt. 10:1, 2; Mark 3:13; 6:7 [b] Mark 16:17, 18; [John 14:12] 9:2 [a] Matt. 10:7, 8; Mark 6:12; Luke 10:1, 9
9:3 [a] Matt. 10:9–15; Mark 6:8–11; Luke 10:4–12; 22:35 9:4 [a] Matt. 10:11; Mark 6:10
9:5 [a] Matt. 10:14 [b] Luke 10:11; Acts 13:51 9:6 [a] Mark 6:12; Luke 8:1

Herod Seeks to See Jesus
(Matt. 14:1–12; Mark 6:14–29)

7[a]Now Herod the tetrarch heard of all that was done by Him; and he was perplexed, because it was said by some that John had risen from the dead, 8and by some that Elijah had appeared, and by others that one of the old prophets had risen again. 9Herod said, "John I have beheaded, but who is this of whom I hear such things?" [a]So he sought to see Him.

Feeding the Five Thousand
(Matt. 14:13–21; Mark 6:30–44; John 6:1–15)

10[a]And the apostles, when they had returned, told Him all that they had done. [b]Then He took them and went aside privately into a deserted place belonging to the city called Bethsaida. 11But when the multitudes knew *it*, they followed Him; and He received them and spoke to them about the kingdom of God, and healed those who had need of healing. 12[a]When the day began to wear away, the twelve came and said to Him, "Send the multitude away, that they may go into the surrounding towns and country, and lodge and get provisions; for we are in a deserted place here."

13But He said to them, "You give them something to eat."

And they said, "We have no more than five loaves and two fish, unless we go and buy food for all these people." 14For there were about five thousand men.

Then He said to His disciples, "Make them sit down in groups of fifty." 15And they did so, and made them all sit down.

16Then He took the five loaves and the two fish, and looking up to heaven, He [a]blessed and broke them, and gave *them* to the disciples to set before the multitude. 17So they all ate and were filled, and twelve baskets of the leftover fragments were taken up by them.

Peter Confesses Jesus as the Christ
(Matt. 16:13–20; Mark 8:27–30)

18[a]And it happened, as He was alone praying, *that* His disciples joined Him, and He asked them, saying, "Who do the crowds say that I am?"

19So they answered and said, [a]"John the Baptist, but some *say* Elijah; and others *say* that one of the old prophets has risen again."

20He said to them, "But who do you say that I am?"

[a]Peter answered and said, "The Christ of God."

Jesus Predicts His Death and Resurrection
(Matt. 16:20–23; Mark 8:30–33)

21[a]And He strictly warned and commanded them to tell this to no one, 22saying, [a]"The Son of Man must suffer many things, and be rejected by the elders and chief priests and scribes, and be killed, and be raised the third day."

Take Up the Cross and Follow Him
(Matt. 16:24–27; Mark 8:34–38)

23[a]Then He said to *them* all, "If anyone desires to come after Me, let him deny himself, and take up his cross daily,[1] and follow Me. 24[a]For whoever desires to save his life will lose it, but whoever loses his life for My sake will save it. 25[a]For what profit is it to a man if he gains the whole world, and is himself destroyed or lost? 26[a]For whoever is ashamed of Me and My words, of him the Son of Man will be [b]ashamed when He comes in His *own* glory, and *in His* Father's, and of the holy angels. 27[a]But I tell you truly, there are some standing here who shall not taste death till they see the kingdom of God."

Jesus Transfigured on the Mount
(Matt. 16:28—17:9; Mark 9:2–10; 2 Pet. 1:16–18)

28[a]Now it came to pass, about eight days after these sayings, that He took Peter, John, and James and went up on the mountain to pray. 29As He prayed, the appearance of His face was altered, and His robe *became* white *and* glistening. 30And behold, two men talked with Him, who were

---

9:7 [a] Matt. 14:1, 2; Mark 6:14 9:9 [a] Luke 23:8 9:10 [a] Mark 6:30 [b] Matt. 14:13 9:12 [a] Matt. 14:15; Mark 6:35; John 6:1, 5 9:16 [a] Luke 22:19; 24:30 9:18 [a] Matt. 16:13–16; Mark 8:27–29 9:19 [a] Matt. 14:2 9:20 [a] Matt. 16:16; John 6:68, 69 9:21 [a] Matt. 8:4; 16:20; Mark 8:30 9:22 [a] Matt. 16:21; 17:22; Luke 18:31–33; 23:46; 24:46 9:23 [a] Matt. 10:38; 16:24; Mark 8:34; Luke 14:27 [1] M-Text omits *daily.* 9:24 [a] Matt. 10:39; Luke 17:33; [John 12:25] 9:25 [a] Matt. 16:26; Mark 8:36; [Luke 16:19–31]; Acts 1:18, 25 9:26 [a] [Rom. 1:16] [b] Matt. 10:33; Mark 8:38; Luke 12:9; 2 Tim. 2:12 9:27 [a] Matt. 16:28; Mark 9:1; Acts 7:55, 56; Rev. 20:4 9:28 [a] Matt. 17:1–8; Mark 9:2–8

[a]Moses and [b]Elijah, 31 who appeared in glory and spoke of His decease which He was about to accomplish at Jerusalem. 32 But Peter and those with him [a]were heavy with sleep; and when they were fully awake, they saw His glory and the two men who stood with Him. 33 Then it happened, as they were parting from Him, *that* Peter said to Jesus, "Master, it is good for us to be here; and let us make three tabernacles: one for You, one for Moses, and one for Elijah"—not knowing what he said.

34 While he was saying this, a cloud came and overshadowed them; and they were fearful as they entered the [a]cloud. 35 And a voice came out of the cloud, saying, [a]"This is My beloved Son.[1] [b]Hear Him!" 36 When the voice had ceased, Jesus was found alone. [a]But they kept quiet, and told no one in those days any of the things they had seen.

A Boy Is Healed

(Matt. 17:14–21; Mark 9:14–29)

37 [a]Now it happened on the next day, when they had come down from the mountain, that a great multitude met Him. 38 Suddenly a man from the multitude cried out, saying, "Teacher, I implore You, look on my son, for he is my only child. 39 And behold, a spirit seizes him, and he suddenly cries out; it convulses him so that he foams *at the mouth;* and it departs from him with great difficulty, bruising him. 40 So I implored Your disciples to cast it out, but they could not."

41 Then Jesus answered and said, "O faithless and perverse generation, how long shall I be with you and bear with you? Bring your son here." 42 And as he was still coming, the demon threw him down and convulsed *him.* Then Jesus rebuked the unclean spirit, healed the child, and gave him back to his father.

Jesus Again Predicts His Death

(Matt. 17:22, 23; Mark 9:30–32)

43 And they were all amazed at the majesty of God.

But while everyone marveled at all the things which Jesus did, He said to His disciples, 44 [a]"Let these words sink down into your ears, for the Son of Man is about to be betrayed into the hands of men." 45 [a]But they did not understand this saying, and it was hidden from them so that they did not perceive it; and they were afraid to ask Him about this saying.

Who Is the Greatest?

(Matt. 18:1–5; Mark 9:33–37)

46 [a]Then a dispute arose among them as to which of them would be greatest. 47 And Jesus, [a]perceiving the thought of their heart, took a [b]little child and set him by Him, 48 and said to them, [a]"Whoever receives this little child in My name receives Me; and [b]whoever receives Me [c]receives Him who sent Me. [d]For he who is least among you all will be great."

Jesus Forbids Sectarianism

(Mark 9:38–41)

49 [a]Now John answered and said, "Master, we saw someone casting out demons in Your name, and we forbade him because he does not follow with us."

50 But Jesus said to him, "Do not forbid *him,* for [a]he who is not against us[1] is on our[2] side."

A Samaritan Village Rejects the Savior

51 Now it came to pass, when the time had come for [a]Him to be received up, that He steadfastly set His face to go to Jerusalem, 52 and sent messengers before His face. And as they went, they entered a village of the Samaritans, to prepare for Him. 53 But [a]they did not receive Him, because His face was *set* for the journey to Jerusalem. 54 And when His disciples [a]James and John saw *this,* they said, "Lord, do You want us to command fire to come down from heaven and consume them, just as [b]Elijah did?"[1]

55 But He turned and rebuked them,[1] and said, "You do not know what manner of

---

9:30 [a] Heb. 11:23–29 [b] 2 Kin. 2:1–11 9:32 [a] Dan. 8:18; 10:9; Matt. 26:40, 43; Mark 14:40 9:34 [a] Ex. 13:21; Acts 1:9 9:35 [a] Ps. 2:7; [Is. 42:1; Matt. 3:17; 12:18]; Mark 1:11; Luke 3:22 [b] Acts 3:22 [1] NU-Text reads *This is My Son, the Chosen One.* 9:36 [a] Matt. 17:9; Mark 9:9 9:37 [a] Matt. 17:14–18; Mark 9:14–27 9:44 [a] Matt. 17:22; Mark 10:33; 14:53; Luke 22:54; John 18:12 9:45 [a] Mark 9:32; Luke 2:50; 18:34 9:46 [a] Matt. 18:1–5; Mark 9:33–37; Luke 22:24 9:47 [a] Matt. 9:4; John 2:24, 25 [b] Luke 18:17 9:48 [a] Matt. 18:5 [b] Matt. 10:40; Mark 9:37; John 12:44 [c] John 13:20 [d] [Matt. 23:11, 12]; 1 Cor. 15:9; Eph. 3:8 9:49 [a] Mark 9:38–40 9:50 [a] Matt. 12:30; Luke 11:23 [1] NU-Text reads *you.* [2] NU-Text reads *your.* 9:51 [a] Is. 50:7; Mark 16:19; Acts 1:2 9:53 [a] John 4:4, 9 9:54 [a] Mark 3:17 [b] 2 Kin. 1:10, 12 [1] NU-Text omits *just as Elijah did.* 9:55 [1] NU-Text omits the rest of this verse.

[a]spirit you are of. 56 For [a]the Son of Man did not come to destroy men's lives but to save *them*."[1] And they went to another village.

The Cost of Discipleship
(Matt. 8:18–22)

57 [a]Now it happened as they journeyed on the road, *that* someone said to Him, "Lord, I will follow You wherever You go."

58 And Jesus said to him, "Foxes have holes and birds of the air *have* nests, but the Son of Man [a]has nowhere to lay *His* head."

59 [a]Then He said to another, "Follow Me."

But he said, "Lord, let me first go and bury my father."

60 Jesus said to him, "Let the dead bury their own dead, but you go and preach the kingdom of God."

61 And another also said, "Lord, [a]I will follow You, but let me first go *and* bid them farewell who are at my house."

62 But Jesus said to him, "No one, having put his hand to the plow, and looking back, is [a]fit for the kingdom of God."

The Seventy Sent Out

10 After these things the Lord appointed seventy others also,[1] and [a]sent them two by two before His face into every city and place where He Himself was about to go. 2 Then He said to them, [a]"The harvest truly *is* great, but the laborers *are* few; therefore [b]pray the Lord of the harvest to send out laborers into His harvest. 3 Go your way; [a]behold, I send you out as lambs among wolves. 4 [a]Carry neither money bag, knapsack, nor sandals; and [b]greet no one along the road. 5 [a]But whatever house you enter, first say, 'Peace to this house.' 6 And if a son of peace is there, your peace will rest on it; if not, it will return to you. 7 [a]And remain in the same house, [b]eating and drinking such things as they give, for [c]the laborer is worthy of his wages. Do not go from house to house. 8 Whatever city you enter, and they receive you, eat such things as are set before you. 9 [a]And heal the sick there, and say to them, [b]'The kingdom of God has come near to you.' 10 But whatever city you enter, and they do not receive you, go out into its streets and say, 11 [a]'The very dust of your city which clings to us[1] we wipe off against you. Nevertheless know this, that the kingdom of God has come near you.' 12 But[1] I say to you that [a]it will be more tolerable in that Day for Sodom than for that city.

Woe to the Impenitent Cities
(Matt. 11:20–24)

13 [a]"Woe to you, Chorazin! Woe to you, Bethsaida! [b]For if the mighty works which were done in you had been done in Tyre and Sidon, they would have repented long ago, sitting in sackcloth and ashes. 14 But it will be more tolerable for Tyre and Sidon at the judgment than for you. 15 [a]And you, Capernaum, who are [b]exalted to heaven, [c]will be brought down to Hades.[1] 16 [a]He who hears you hears Me, [b]he who rejects you rejects Me, and [c]he who rejects Me rejects Him who sent Me."

The Seventy Return with Joy

17 Then [a]the seventy[1] returned with joy, saying, "Lord, even the demons are subject to us in Your name."

18 And He said to them, [a]"I saw Satan fall like lightning from heaven. 19 Behold, [a]I give you the authority to trample on serpents and scorpions, and over all the power of the enemy, and nothing shall by any means hurt you. 20 Nevertheless do not rejoice in this, that the spirits are subject to you, but rather[1] rejoice because [a]your names are written in heaven."

Jesus Rejoices in the Spirit
(Matt. 11:25–27)

21 [a]In that hour Jesus rejoiced in the Spirit and said, "I thank You, Father, Lord of heaven and earth, that You have hidden

---

9:55 [a] [Rom. 8:15; 2 Tim. 1:7] 9:56 [a] Luke 19:10; John 3:17; 12:47 [1] NU-Text omits the first sentence of this verse. 9:57 [a] Matt. 8:19–22 9:58 [a] Luke 2:7; 8:23 9:59 [a] Matt. 8:21, 22 9:61 [a] 1 Kin. 19:20 9:62 [a] 2 Tim. 4:10 10:1 [a] Matt. 10:1; Mark 6:7 [1] NU-Text reads *seventy-two others.* 10:2 [a] Matt. 9:37, 38; John 4:35 [b] [1 Cor. 3:9]; 2 Thess. 3:1 10:3 [a] Matt. 10:16 10:4 [a] Matt. 10:9–14; Mark 6:8–11; Luke 9:3–5 [b] 2 Kin. 4:29 10:5 [a] 1 Sam. 25:6; Matt. 10:12 10:7 [a] Matt. 10:11 [b] 1 Cor. 10:27 [c] [Matt. 10:10]; 1 Cor. 9:4–8; 1 Tim. 5:18 10:9 [a] Mark 3:15 [b] Matt. 3:2; 10:7; Luke 10:11 10:11 [a] Matt. 10:14; Mark 6:11; Luke 9:5; Acts 13:51 [1] NU-Text reads *our feet.* 10:12 [a] Gen. 19:24–28; Lam. 4:6; Matt. 10:15; 11:24; Mark 6:11 [1] NU-Text and M-Text omit *But.* 10:13 [a] Matt. 11:21–23 [b] Ezek. 3:6 10:15 [a] Matt. 11:23 [b] Gen. 11:4; Deut. 1:28; Is. 14:13–15; Jer. 51:53 [c] Ezek. 26:20 [1] NU-Text reads *will you be exalted to heaven? You will be thrust down to Hades!* 10:16 [a] Matt. 10:40; Mark 9:37; John 13:20; Gal. 4:14 [b] [John 12:48]; 1 Thess. 4:8 [c] John 5:23 10:17 [a] Luke 10:1 [1] NU-Text reads *seventy-two.* 10:18 [a] John 12:31; Rev. 9:1; 12:8, 9 10:19 [a] Ps. 91:13; Mark 16:18; Acts 28:5 10:20 [a] [Ex. 32:32, 33]; Ps. 69:28; Is. 4:3; Dan. 12:1; Phil. 4:3; Heb. 12:23; Rev. 13:8 [1] NU-Text and M-Text omit *rather.* 10:21 [a] Matt. 11:25–27

these things from *the* wise and prudent
and revealed them to babes. Even so, Father, for so it seemed good in Your sight.
22[a]All[1] things have been delivered to Me by
My Father, and [b]no one knows who the Son
is except the Father, and who the Father is
except the Son, and *the one* to whom the
Son wills to reveal *Him.*"

23Then He turned to *His* disciples and
said privately, [a]"Blessed *are* the eyes which
see the things you see; 24for I tell you [a]that
many prophets and kings have desired to
see what you see, and have not seen *it,*
and to hear what you hear, and have not
heard *it.*"

The Parable of the Good Samaritan
(Matt. 22:34–40; Mark 12:28–34)

25And behold, a certain lawyer stood up
and tested Him, saying, [a]"Teacher, what
shall I do to inherit eternal life?"

26He said to him, "What is written in the
law? What is your reading *of it?*"

27So he answered and said, [a]"'You shall
love the LORD your God with all your heart,
with all your soul, with all your strength,
and with all your mind,'[1] and [b]'your neighbor as yourself.'"[2]

28And He said to him, "You have answered rightly; do this and [a]you will live."

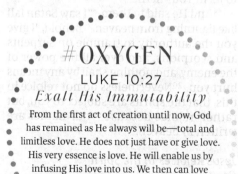

#OXYGEN
LUKE 10:27
Exalt His Immutability

From the first act of creation until now, God has remained as He always will be—total and limitless love. He does not just have or give love. His very essence is love. He will enable us by infusing His love into us. We then can love even the unlovely and endure anything in order to show the love of God.

Breathe and exalt His immutability.

29But he, wanting to [a]justify himself, said
to Jesus, "And who is my neighbor?"

30Then Jesus answered and said: "A
certain *man* went down from Jerusalem
to Jericho, and fell among thieves, who
stripped him of his clothing, wounded
him, and departed, leaving *him* half dead.
31Now by chance a certain priest came
down that road. And when he saw him,
[a]he passed by on the other side. 32Like-
wise a Levite, when he arrived at the place,
came and looked, and passed by on the
other side. 33But a certain [a]Samaritan, as
he journeyed, came where he was. And
when he saw him, he had [b]compassion.
34So he went to *him* and bandaged his
wounds, pouring on oil and wine; and he
set him on his own animal, brought him
to an inn, and took care of him. 35On the
next day, when he departed,[1] he took out
two [a]denarii, gave *them* to the innkeeper,
and said to him, 'Take care of him; and
whatever more you spend, when I come
again, I will repay you.' 36So which of these
three do you think was neighbor to him
who fell among the thieves?"

37And he said, "He who showed mercy
on him."

Then Jesus said to him, [a]"Go and do likewise."

Mary and Martha Worship and Serve

38Now it happened as they went that
He entered a certain village; and a certain
woman named [a]Martha welcomed Him
into her house. 39And she had a sister called
Mary, [a]who also [b]sat at Jesus'[1] feet and heard
His word. 40But Martha was distracted with
much serving, and she approached Him
and said, "Lord, do You not care that my
sister has left me to serve alone? Therefore
tell her to help me."

41And Jesus[1] answered and said to her,
"Martha, Martha, you are worried and troubled about many things. 42But [a]one thing
is needed, and Mary has chosen that good
part, which will not be taken away from
her."

10:22 [a] Matt. 28:18; John 3:35; 5:27; 17:2 [b] [John 1:18; 6:44, 46] [1] M-Text reads *And turning to the disciples He said, "All . . . .*
10:23 [a] Matt. 13:16, 17 10:24 [a] 1 Pet. 1:10, 11 10:25 [a] Matt. 19:16–19; 22:35 10:27 [a] Deut. 6:5 [b] Lev. 19:18; Matt. 19:19 [1] Deuteronomy 6:5 [2] Leviticus 19:18 10:28 [a] Lev. 18:5; Neh. 9:29; Ezek. 20:11, 13, 21; Matt. 19:17; Rom. 10:5 10:29 [a] Luke 16:15 10:31 [a] Ps. 38:11
10:33 [a] John 4:9 [b] Luke 15:20 10:35 [a] Matt. 20:2 [1] NU-Text omits *when he departed.* 10:37 [a] Prov. 14:21; [Matt. 9:13; 12:7]
10:38 [a] John 11:1; 12:2, 3 10:39 [a] [1 Cor. 7:32–40] [b] Luke 8:35; Acts 22:3 [1] NU-Text reads *the Lord's.*
10:41 [1] NU-Text reads *the Lord.* 10:42 [a] [Ps. 27:4; John 6:27]

The Model Prayer
(Matt. 6:9–15)

11 Now it came to pass, as He was praying in a certain place, when He ceased,
that one of His disciples said to Him, "Lord,
teach us to pray, as John also taught his
disciples."
2So He said to them, "When you pray,
say:

[a]Our Father in heaven,[1]
Hallowed be Your name.
Your kingdom come.[2]
Your will be done
On earth as *it is* in heaven.
3 Give us day by day our daily bread.
4 And [a]forgive us our sins,
For we also forgive everyone
who is indebted to us.
And do not lead us into temptation,
But deliver us from the evil one."[1]

A Friend Comes at Midnight

5And He said to them, "Which of you
shall have a friend, and go to him at midnight and say to him, 'Friend, lend me three
loaves; 6for a friend of mine has come to
me on his journey, and I have nothing to
set before him'; 7and he will answer from
within and say, 'Do not trouble me; the door
is now shut, and my children are with me
in bed; I cannot rise and give to you'? 8I say
to you, [a]though he will not rise and give to
him because he is his friend, yet because
of his persistence he will rise and give him
as many as he needs.

Keep Asking, Seeking, Knocking
(Matt. 7:7–11)

9[a]"So I say to you, ask, and it will be given
to you; [b]seek, and you will find; knock, and
it will be opened to you. 10For everyone who
asks receives, and he who seeks finds, and
to him who knocks it will be opened. 11[a]If a
son asks for bread[1] from any father among
you, will he give him a stone? Or if *he asks*
for a fish, will he give him a serpent instead
of a fish? 12Or if he asks for an egg, will he
offer him a scorpion? 13If you then, being
evil, know how to give [a]good gifts to your
children, how much more will *your* heavenly Father give the Holy Spirit to those
who ask Him!"

A House Divided Cannot Stand
(Matt. 12:22–30; Mark 3:22–27)

14[a]And He was casting out a demon, and
it was mute. So it was, when the demon had
gone out, that the mute spoke; and the multitudes marveled. 15But some of them said,
[a]"He casts out demons by Beelzebub,[1] the
ruler of the demons."
16Others, testing *Him*, [a]sought from Him
a sign from heaven. 17[a]But [b]He, knowing
their thoughts, said to them: "Every kingdom divided against itself is brought to
desolation, and a house *divided* against
a house falls. 18If Satan also is divided
against himself, how will his kingdom
stand? Because you say I cast out demons
by Beelzebub. 19And if I cast out demons by
Beelzebub, by whom do your sons cast *them*
out? Therefore they will be your judges.
20But if I cast out demons [a]with the finger of God, surely the kingdom of God has
come upon you. 21[a]When a strong man,
fully armed, guards his own palace, his
goods are in peace. 22But [a]when a stronger
than he comes upon him and overcomes
him, he takes from him all his armor in
which he trusted, and divides his spoils.
23[a]He who is not with Me is against Me, and
he who does not gather with Me scatters.

An Unclean Spirit Returns
(Matt. 12:43–45)

24[a]"When an unclean spirit goes out of
a man, he goes through dry places, seeking rest; and finding none, he says, 'I will
return to my house from which I came.'
25And when he comes, he finds *it* swept and
put in order. 26Then he goes and takes with
him seven other spirits more wicked than
himself, and they enter and dwell there;
and [a]the last *state* of that man is worse than
the first."

11:2 [a] Matt. 6:9–13 [1] NU-Text omits *Our* and *in heaven.* [2] NU-Text omits the rest of this verse. 11:4 [a] [Eph. 4:32] [1] NU-Text omits *But deliver us from the evil one.* 11:8 [a] [Luke 18:1–5] 11:9 [a] Ps. 50:14, 15; Jer. 33:3; [Matt. 7:7; 21:22; Mark 11:24; John 15:7; James 1:5, 6; 1 John 3:22; 5:14, 15] [b] Is. 55:6 11:11 [a] Matt. 7:9 [1] NU-Text omits the words from *bread* through *for* in the next sentence. 11:13 [a] James 1:17 11:14 [a] Matt. 9:32–34; 12:22, 24 11:15 [a] Matt. 9:34; 12:24 [1] NU-Text and M-Text read *Beelzebul.* 11:16 [a] Matt. 12:38; 16:1; Mark 8:11 11:17 [a] Matt. 12:25–29; Mark 3:23–27 [b] Matt. 9:4; John 2:25 11:20 [a] Ex. 8:19 11:21 [a] Matt. 12:29; Mark 3:27 11:22 [a] [Is. 53:12; Col. 2:15] 11:23 [a] Matt. 12:30; Mark 9:40 11:24 [a] Matt. 12:43–45; Mark 1:27; 3:11; 5:13; Acts 5:16; 8:7 11:26 [a] John 5:14; [Heb. 6:4–6; 10:26; 2 Pet. 2:20]

Keeping the Word

27 And it happened, as He spoke these
things, that a certain woman from the
crowd raised her voice and said to Him,
[a]"Blessed *is* the womb that bore You, and
the breasts which nursed You!"
28 But He said, [a]"More than that, blessed
are those who hear the word of God and
keep it!"

Seeking a Sign
(Matt. 12:38–42)

29 [a]And while the crowds were thickly
gathered together, He began to say, "This is
an evil generation. It seeks a [b]sign, and no
sign will be given to it except the sign of Jonah the prophet.[1] 30 For as [a]Jonah became a
sign to the Ninevites, so also the Son of Man
will be to this generation. 31 [a]The queen of the
South will rise up in the judgment with the
men of this generation and condemn them,
for she came from the ends of the earth to
hear the wisdom of Solomon; and indeed a
[b]greater than Solomon *is* here. 32 The men of
Nineveh will rise up in the judgment with
this generation and condemn it, for [a]they
repented at the preaching of Jonah; and indeed a greater than Jonah *is* here.

The Lamp of the Body
(Matt. 6:22, 23)

33 [a]"No one, when he has lit a lamp, puts
it in a secret place or under a [b]basket, but
on a lampstand, that those who come in
may see the light. 34 [a]The lamp of the body
is the eye. Therefore, when your eye is good,
your whole body also is full of light. But
when *your eye* is bad, your body also *is* full
of darkness. 35 Therefore take heed that the
light which is in you is not darkness. 36 If
then your whole body *is* full of light, having
no part dark, *the* whole *body* will be full of
light, as when the bright shining of a lamp
gives you light."

Woe to the Pharisees and Lawyers

37 And as He spoke, a certain Pharisee
asked Him to dine with him. So He went
in and sat down to eat. 38 [a]When the Pharisee saw *it,* he marveled that He had not
first washed before dinner.
39 [a]Then the Lord said to him, "Now you
Pharisees make the outside of the cup and
dish clean, but [b]your inward part is full of
greed and wickedness. 40 Foolish ones! Did
not [a]He who made the outside make the
inside also? 41 [a]But rather give alms of such
things as you have; then indeed all things
are clean to you.
42 [a]"But woe to you Pharisees! For you
tithe the mint and rue and all manner of herbs,
and [b]pass by justice and the [c]love of God.
These you ought to have done, without
leaving the others undone. 43 [a]Woe to you
Pharisees! For you love the best seats in
the synagogues and greetings in the marketplaces. 44 [a]Woe to you, scribes and Pharisees, hypocrites![1] [b]For you are like graves
which are not seen, and the men who walk
over *them* are not aware *of them."*
45 Then one of the lawyers answered
and said to Him, "Teacher, by saying these
things You reproach us also."
46 And He said, "Woe to you also, lawyers!
[a]For you load men with burdens hard to
bear, and you yourselves do not touch the
burdens with one of your fingers. 47 [a]Woe
to you! For you build the tombs of the
prophets, and your fathers killed them.
48 In fact, you bear witness that you approve
the deeds of your fathers; for they indeed
killed them, and you build their tombs.
49 Therefore the wisdom of God also said,
[a]'I will send them prophets and apostles,
and *some* of them they will kill and persecute,' 50 that the blood of all the prophets
which was shed from the foundation of the
world may be required of this generation,
51 [a]from the blood of Abel to [b]the blood of
Zechariah who perished between the altar
and the temple. Yes, I say to you, it shall be
required of this generation.
52 [a]"Woe to you lawyers! For you have
taken away the key of knowledge. You did
not enter in yourselves, and those who were
entering in you hindered."

11:27 [a] Luke 1:28, 48 11:28 [a] Ps. 1:1, 2; 112:1; 119:1, 2; Is. 48:17, 18; [Matt. 7:21; Luke 8:21]; James 1:25 11:29 [a] Matt. 12:38–42 [b] 1 Cor. 1:22 [1] NU-Text omits *the prophet.* 11:30 [a] Jon. 1:17; 2:10; 3:3–10; Luke 24:46; Acts 10:40; 1 Cor. 15:4 11:31 [a] 1 Kin. 10:1–9; 2 Chr. 9:1–8 [b] [Is. 9:6; Rom. 9:5] 11:32 [a] Jon. 3:5 11:33 [a] Matt. 5:15; Mark 4:21; Luke 8:16 [b] Matt. 5:15 11:34 [a] Matt. 6:22, 23 11:38 [a] Matt. 15:2; Mark 7:2, 3 11:39 [a] Matt. 23:25 [b] Gen. 6:5; Titus 1:15 11:40 [a] Gen. 1:26, 27 11:41 [a] Is. 58:7; Dan. 4:27; [Luke 12:33; 16:9] 11:42 [a] Matt. 23:23 [b] [Mic. 6:7, 8] [c] John 5:42 11:43 [a] Matt. 23:6; Mark 12:38, 39; Luke 14:7; 20:46 11:44 [a] Matt. 23:27 [b] Ps. 5:9 [1] NU-Text omits *scribes and Pharisees, hypocrites.* 11:46 [a] Matt. 23:4 11:47 [a] Matt. 23:29; Acts 7:52 11:49 [a] Prov. 1:20; Matt. 23:34 11:51 [a] Gen. 4:8; 2 Chr. 36:16 [b] 2 Chr. 24:20, 21 11:52 [a] Matt. 23:13

53 And as He said these things to them,[1] the scribes and the Pharisees began to assail *Him* vehemently, and to cross-examine Him about many things, 54 lying in wait for Him, and [a]seeking to catch Him in something He might say, that they might accuse Him.[1]

Beware of Hypocrisy
(Matt. 10:26, 27)

12 In [a]the meantime, when an innumerable multitude of people had gathered together, so that they trampled one another, He began to say to His disciples first *of all,* [b]"Beware of the leaven of the Pharisees, which is hypocrisy. 2 [a]For there is nothing covered that will not be revealed, nor hidden that will not be known. 3 Therefore whatever you have spoken in the dark will be heard in the light, and what you have spoken in the ear in inner rooms will be proclaimed on the housetops.

Jesus Teaches the Fear of God
(Matt. 10:8–31)

4 [a]"And I say to you, [b]My friends, do not be afraid of those who kill the body, and after that have no more that they can do. 5 But I will show you whom you should fear: Fear Him who, after He has killed, has power to cast into hell; yes, I say to you, [a]fear Him!

6 "Are not five sparrows sold for two copper coins?[1] And [a]not one of them is forgotten before God. 7 But the very hairs of your head are all numbered. Do not fear therefore; you are of more value than many sparrows.

Confess Christ Before Men
(Matt. 10:32, 33)

8 [a]"Also I say to you, whoever confesses Me [b]before men, him the Son of Man also will confess before the angels of God. 9 But he who [a]denies Me before men will be denied before the angels of God.

10 "And [a]anyone who speaks a word against the Son of Man, it will be forgiven him; but to him who blasphemes against the Holy Spirit, it will not be forgiven.

11 [a]"Now when they bring you to the synagogues and magistrates and authorities, do not worry about how or what you should answer, or what you should say. 12 For the Holy Spirit will [a]teach you in that very hour what you ought to say."

The Parable of the Rich Fool

13 Then one from the crowd said to Him, "Teacher, tell my brother to divide the inheritance with me."

14 But He said to him, [a]"Man, who made Me a judge or an arbitrator over you?" 15 And He said to them, [a]"Take heed and beware of covetousness,[1] for one's life does not consist in the abundance of the things he possesses."

16 Then He spoke a parable to them, saying: "The ground of a certain rich man yielded plentifully. 17 And he thought within himself, saying, 'What shall I do, since I have no room to store my crops?' 18 So he said, 'I will do this: I will pull down my barns and build greater, and there I will store all my crops and my goods. 19 And I will say to my soul, [a]"Soul, you have many goods laid up for many years; take your ease; [b]eat, drink, *and* be merry."' 20 But God said to him, 'Fool! This night [a]your soul will be required of you; [b]then whose will those things be which you have provided?'

21 "So *is* he who lays up treasure for himself, [a]and is not rich toward God."

Do Not Worry
(Matt. 6:19–21, 25–34)

22 Then He said to His disciples, "Therefore I say to you, [a]do not worry about your life, what you will eat; nor about the body, what you will put on. 23 Life is more than food, and the body *is more* than clothing. 24 Consider the ravens, for they neither sow nor reap, which have neither storehouse nor barn; and [a]God feeds them. Of how much more value are you than the birds?

11:53 [1] NU-Text reads *And when He left there.* 11:54 [a] Mark 12:13 [1] NU-Text omits *and seeking* and *that they might accuse Him.* 12:1 [a] Matt. 16:6; Mark 8:15 [b] Matt. 16:12; Luke 11:39 12:2 [a] Matt. 10:26; Mark 4:22; Luke 8:17; [1 Cor. 4:5] 12:4 [a] Is. 51:7, 8, 12, 13; Jer. 1:8; Matt. 10:28 [b] [John 15:13–15] 12:5 [a] Ps. 119:120 12:6 [a] Matt. 6:26 [1] Greek *assarion,* a coin of very small value 12:8 [a] 1 Sam. 2:30; Matt. 10:32; [Mark 8:38; Rom. 10:9; 2 Tim. 2:12; 1 John 2:23] [b] Ps. 119:46 12:9 [a] Matt. 10:33; [Mark 8:38; 2 Tim. 2:12] 12:10 [a] [Matt. 12:31, 32; Mark 3:28; 1 John 5:16] 12:11 [a] Matt. 6:25; 10:19; Mark 13:11 12:12 [a] [John 14:26] 12:14 [a] [John 18:36] 12:15 [a] [1 Tim. 6:6–10] [1] NU-Text reads *all covetousness.* 12:19 [a] Eccl. 11:9; 1 Cor. 15:32; James 5:5 [b] [Eccl. 2:24; 3:13; 5:18; 8:15] 12:20 [a] Job 27:8; Ps. 52:7; [James 4:14] [b] Ps. 39:6; Jer. 17:11 12:21 [a] [Matt. 6:20; Luke 12:33; 1 Tim. 6:18, 19; James 2:5; 5:1–5] 12:22 [a] Matt. 6:25–33 12:24 [a] Job 38:41; Ps. 147:9

25And which of you by worrying can add
one cubit to his stature? 26If you then are
not able to do *the* least, why are you anxious
for the rest? 27Consider the lilies, how they
grow: they neither toil nor spin; and yet I
say to you, even [a]Solomon in all his glory
was not arrayed like one of these. 28If then
God so clothes the grass, which today is in
the field and tomorrow is thrown into the
oven, how much more *will He clothe* you,
O *you* of [a]little faith?

29"And do not seek what you should
eat or what you should drink, nor have an
anxious mind. 30For all these things the
nations of the world seek after, and your
Father [a]knows that you need these things.
31[a]But seek the kingdom of God, and all
these things[1] shall be added to you.

32"Do not fear, little flock, for [a]it is your
Father's good pleasure to give you the kingdom. 33[a]Sell what you have and give [b]alms;
[c]provide yourselves money bags which do
not grow old, a treasure in the heavens that
does not fail, where no thief approaches
nor moth destroys. 34For where your treasure is, there your heart will be also.

The Faithful Servant and the Evil Servant
(Matt. 24:42–51)

35[a]"Let your waist be girded and [b]*your*
lamps burning; 36and you yourselves be
like men who wait for their master, when
he will return from the wedding, that when
he comes and knocks they may open to
him immediately. 37[a]Blessed *are* those servants whom the master, when he comes,
will find watching. Assuredly, I say to you
that he will gird himself and have them
sit down *to eat,* and will come and serve
them. 38And if he should come in the second watch, or come in the third watch,
and find *them* so, blessed are those servants. 39[a]But know this, that if the master
of the house had known what hour the
thief would come, he would have watched
and[1] not allowed his house to be broken
into. 40[a]Therefore you also be ready, for
the Son of Man is coming at an hour you
do not expect."

41Then Peter said to Him, "Lord, do You
speak this parable *only* to us, or to all *peo-*
ple?"

42And the Lord said, [a]"Who then is that
faithful and wise steward, whom *his* master
will make ruler over his household, to give
them their portion of food in due season?
43Blessed *is* that servant whom his master
will find so doing when he comes. 44[a]Truly,
I say to you that he will make him ruler
over all that he has. 45[a]But if that servant
says in his heart, 'My master is delaying his
coming,' and begins to beat the male and
female servants, and to eat and drink and
be drunk, 46the master of that servant will
come on a [a]day when he is not looking for
him, and at an hour when he is not aware,
and will cut him in two and appoint *him* his
portion with the unbelievers. 47And [a]that
servant who [b]knew his master's will, and
did not prepare *himself* or do according to
his will, shall be beaten with many *stripes.*
48[a]But he who did not know, yet committed
things deserving of stripes, shall be beaten
with few. For everyone to whom much is
given, from him much will be required;
and to whom much has been committed,
of him they will ask the more.

Christ Brings Division
(Matt. 10:34–39)

49[a]"I came to send fire on the earth, and
how I wish it were already kindled! 50But
[a]I have a baptism to be baptized with, and
how distressed I am till it is [b]accomplished!
51[a]Do *you* suppose that I came to give peace
on earth? I tell you, not at all, [b]but rather
division. 52[a]For from now on five in one
house will be divided: three against two,
and two against three. 53[a]Father will be divided against son and son against father,
mother against daughter and daughter
against mother, mother-in-law against
her daughter-in-law and daughter-in-law
against her mother-in-law."

12:27 [a] 1 Kin. 10:4–7; 2 Chr. 9:3–6 **12:28** [a] Matt. 6:30; 8:26; 14:31; 16:8 **12:30** [a] Matt. 6:31, 32 **12:31** [a] Matt. 6:33 [1] NU-Text reads *His kingdom, and these things.* **12:32** [a] [Dan. 7:18, 27]; Zech. 13:7; [Matt. 11:25, 26; Luke 22:29, 30] **12:33** [a] Matt. 19:21; Acts 2:45; 4:34 [b] Luke 11:41 [c] Matt. 6:20; Luke 16:9; [1 Tim. 6:19] **12:35** [a] [Eph. 6:14; 1 Pet. 1:13] [b] [Matt. 25:1–13] **12:37** [a] Matt. 24:46 **12:39** [a] Matt. 24:43; 1 Thess. 5:2; [2 Pet. 3:10]; Rev. 3:3; 16:15 [1] NU-Text reads *he would not have allowed.* **12:40** [a] Matt. 24:44; 25:13; Mark 13:33; [Luke 21:34, 36]; 1 Thess. 5:6; [2 Pet. 3:12] **12:42** [a] Matt. 24:45, 46; 25:21; [1 Cor. 4:2] **12:44** [a] Matt. 24:47; 25:21; [Rev. 3:21] **12:45** [a] Matt. 24:48; 2 Pet. 3:3, 4 **12:46** [a] 1 Thess. 5:3 **12:47** [a] Num. 15:30; Deut. 25:2; [John 9:41; 15:22; Acts 17:30] [b] [James 4:17] **12:48** [a] [Lev. 5:17]; Num. 15:29; [1 Tim. 1:13] **12:49** [a] Luke 12:51 **12:50** [a] Matt. 20:18, 22, 23; Mark 10:38 [b] John 12:27; 19:30 **12:51** [a] Matt. 10:34–36 [b] Mic. 7:6; John 7:43; 9:16; 10:19; Acts 14:4 **12:52** [a] Matt. 10:35; Mark 13:12 **12:53** [a] Matt. 10:21, 36

Discern the Time
(Matt. 16:1–4)
54Then He also said to the multitudes,
[a]"Whenever you see a cloud rising out of
the west, immediately you say, 'A shower is
coming'; and so it is. 55And when *you see*
the [a]south wind blow, you say, 'There will
be hot weather'; and there is. 56Hypocrites!
You can discern the face of the sky and of
the earth, but how *is it* you do not discern
[a]this time?

Make Peace with Your Adversary
57"Yes, and why, even of yourselves, do
you not judge what is right? 58[a]When you
go with your adversary to the magistrate,
make every effort [b]along the way to settle
with him, lest he drag you to the judge, the
judge deliver you to the officer, and the officer throw you into prison. 59I tell you, you
shall not depart from there till you have
paid the very last mite."

Repent or Perish
13 There were present at that season
some who told Him about the Galileans whose blood Pilate had mingled
with their sacrifices. 2And Jesus answered
and said to them, "Do you suppose that
these Galileans were worse sinners than
all *other* Galileans, because they suffered
such things? 3I tell you, no; but unless
you repent you will all likewise perish.
4Or those eighteen on whom the tower in
Siloam fell and killed them, do you think
that they were worse sinners than all *other*
men who dwelt in Jerusalem? 5I tell you,
no; but unless you repent you will all likewise perish."

The Parable of the Barren Fig Tree
6He also spoke this parable: [a]"A certain
man had a fig tree planted in his vineyard,
and he came seeking fruit on it and found
none. 7Then he said to the keeper of his
vineyard, 'Look, for three years I have come
seeking fruit on this fig tree and find none.
Cut it down; why does it use up the ground?'
8But he answered and said to him, 'Sir, let
it alone this year also, until I dig around it
and fertilize *it*. 9And if it bears fruit, *well*.
But if not, after that[1] you can [a]cut it down.'"

A Spirit of Infirmity
10Now He was teaching in one of the
synagogues on the Sabbath. 11And behold,
there was a woman who had a spirit of infirmity eighteen years, and was bent over
and could in no way raise *herself* up. 12But
when Jesus saw her, He called *her* to *Him*
and said to her, "Woman, you are loosed
from your [a]infirmity." 13[a]And He laid *His*
hands on her, and immediately she was
made straight, and glorified God.
14But the ruler of the synagogue answered with indignation, because Jesus
had [a]healed on the Sabbath; and he said
to the crowd, [b]"There are six days on which
men ought to work; therefore come and
be healed on them, and [c]not on the Sabbath day."
15The Lord then answered him and said,
"Hypocrite![1] [a]Does not each one of you on
the Sabbath loose his ox or donkey from the
stall, and lead *it* away to water it? 16So ought
not this woman, [a]being a daughter of Abraham, whom Satan has bound—think of
it—for eighteen years, be loosed from this
bond on the Sabbath?" 17And when He said
these things, all His adversaries were put to
shame; and all the multitude rejoiced for all
the glorious things that were [a]done by Him.

The Parable of the Mustard Seed
(Matt. 13:31, 32; Mark 4:30–32)
18[a]Then He said, "What is the kingdom
of God like? And to what shall I compare
it? 19It is like a mustard seed, which a man
took and put in his garden; and it grew and
became a large[1] tree, and the birds of the
air nested in its branches."

The Parable of the Leaven
(Matt. 13:33)
20And again He said, "To what shall I
liken the kingdom of God? 21It is like leaven,
which a woman took and hid in three [a]mea-
sures[1] of meal till it was all leavened."

12:54 [a] Matt. 16:2, 3   12:55 [a] Job 37:17   12:56 [a] Luke 19:41–44   12:58 [a] Prov. 25:8; Matt. 5:25, 26 [b] [Ps. 32:6; Is. 55:6]   13:6 [a] Is. 5:2; Matt. 21:19   13:9 [a] [John 15:2] [1] NU-Text reads *And if it bears fruit after that, well. But if not, you can cut it down.*   13:12 [a] Luke 7:21; 8:2   13:13 [a] Mark 16:18; Acts 9:17   13:14 [a] [Luke 6:6–11; 14:1–6]; John 5:16 [b] Ex. 20:9; 23:12 [c] Matt. 12:10; Mark 3:2; Luke 6:7; 14:3   13:15 [a] [Matt. 7:5; 23:13]; Luke 14:5 [1] NU-Text and M-Text read *Hypocrites.*   13:16 [a] Luke 19:9   13:17 [a] Mark 5:19, 20   13:18 [a] Matt. 13:31, 32; Mark 4:30–32   13:19 [1] NU-Text omits *large.*   13:21 [a] Matt. 13:33 [1] Greek *sata,* approximately two pecks in all

The Narrow Way
(Matt. 7:13, 14)

22[a]And He went through the cities and
villages, teaching, and journeying toward
Jerusalem. 23Then one said to Him, "Lord,
are there [a]few who are saved?"

And He said to them, 24[a]"Strive to enter
through the narrow gate, for [b]many, I say to
you, will seek to enter and will not be able.
25[a]When once the Master of the house has
risen up and [b]shut the door, and you begin
to stand outside and knock at the door, saying, [c]'Lord, Lord, open for us,' and He will
answer and say to you, [d]'I do not know you,
where you are from,' 26then you will begin
to say, 'We ate and drank in Your presence,
and You taught in our streets.' 27[a]But He will
say, 'I tell you I do not know you, where you
are from. [b]Depart from Me, all you workers
of iniquity.' 28[a]There will be weeping and
gnashing of teeth, [b]when you see Abraham
and Isaac and Jacob and all the prophets in
the kingdom of God, and yourselves thrust
out. 29They will come from the east and the
west, from the north and the south, and
sit down in the kingdom of God. 30[a]And
indeed there are last who will be first, and
there are first who will be last."

31On that very day[1] some Pharisees came,
saying to Him, "Get out and depart from
here, for Herod wants to kill You."

32And He said to them, "Go, tell that fox,
'Behold, I cast out demons and perform
cures today and tomorrow, and the third
day [a]I shall be perfected.' 33Nevertheless I
must journey today, tomorrow, and the *day*
following; for it cannot be that a prophet
should perish outside of Jerusalem.

Jesus Laments over Jerusalem
(Matt. 23:37–39)

34[a]"O Jerusalem, Jerusalem, the one who
kills the prophets and stones those who are
sent to her! How often I wanted to gather
your children together, as a hen *gathers*
her brood under *her* wings, but you were
not willing! 35See! [a]Your house is left to you
desolate; and assuredly,[1] I say to you, you
shall not see Me until *the time* comes when
you say, [b]'Blessed is He who comes in the
name of the LORD!' "[2]

A Man with Dropsy Healed
on the Sabbath

14 Now it happened, as He went into
the house of one of the rulers of the
Pharisees to eat bread on the Sabbath, that
they watched Him closely. 2And behold,
there was a certain man before Him who
had dropsy. 3And Jesus, answering, spoke
to the lawyers and Pharisees, saying, [a]"Is
it lawful to heal on the Sabbath?"[1]

4But they kept silent. And He took *him*
and healed him, and let him go. 5Then He
answered them, saying, [a]"Which of you,
having a donkey[1] or an ox that has fallen
into a pit, will not immediately pull him
out on the Sabbath day?" 6And they could
not answer Him regarding these things.

Take the Lowly Place

7So He told a parable to those who were
invited, when He noted how they chose the
best places, saying to them: 8"When you are
invited by anyone to a wedding feast, do not
sit down in the best place, lest one more
honorable than you be invited by him; 9and
he who invited you and him come and say
to you, 'Give place to this man,' and then
you begin with shame to take the lowest
place. 10[a]But when you are invited, go and
sit down in the lowest place, so that when
he who invited you comes he may say to
you, 'Friend, go up higher.' Then you will
have glory in the presence of those who sit
at the table with you. 11[a]For whoever exalts
himself will be humbled, and he who humbles himself will be exalted."

12Then He also said to him who invited
Him, "When you give a dinner or a supper,
do not ask your friends, your brothers, your
relatives, nor rich neighbors, lest they also
invite you back, and you be repaid. 13But
when you give a feast, invite [a]*the* poor, *the*

13:22 [a] Matt. 9:35; Mark 6:6 13:23 [a] [Matt. 7:14; 20:16] 13:24 [a] [Matt. 7:13] [b] [John 7:34; 8:21; 13:33; Rom. 9:31] 13:25 [a] [Ps. 32:6]; Is. 55:6 [b] Matt. 25:10; Rev. 22:11 [c] Luke 6:46 [d] Matt. 7:23; 25:12 13:27 [a] [Matt. 7:23; 25:41] [b] Ps. 6:8; [Matt. 25:41]; Titus 1:16 13:28 [a] Matt. 8:12; 13:42; 24:51 [b] Matt. 8:11 13:30 [a] [Matt. 19:30; 20:16]; Mark 10:31 13:31 [1] NU-Text reads *In that very hour.* 13:32 [a] Luke 24:46; Acts 10:40; 1 Cor. 15:4; [Heb. 2:10; 5:9; 7:28] 13:34 [a] Matt. 23:37–39; 2 Chr. 24:20, 21; 36:15, 16 13:35 [a] Lev. 26:31, 32; Ps. 69:25; Is. 1:7; Jer. 22:5; Dan. 9:27; Mic. 3:12 [b] Ps. 118:26; Matt. 21:9; Mark 11:10; Luke 19:38; John 12:13 [1] NU-Text and M-Text omit *assuredly.* [2] Psalm 118:26 14:3 [a] Matt. 12:10 [1] NU-Text adds *or not.* 14:5 [a] [Ex. 23:5; Deut. 22:4]; Luke 13:15 [1] NU-Text and M-Text read *son.* 14:10 [a] Prov. 25:6, 7 14:11 [a] Job 22:29; Ps. 18:27; Prov. 29:23; Matt. 23:12; Luke 18:14; James 4:6; [1 Pet. 5:5] 14:13 [a] Neh. 8:10, 12

maimed, *the* lame, *the* blind. 14And you will
be [a]blessed, because they cannot repay you;
for you shall be repaid at the resurrection
of the just."

The Parable of the Great Supper
(Matt. 22:1–14)

15Now when one of those who sat at the
table with Him heard these things, he said
to Him, [a]"Blessed *is* he who shall eat bread[1]
in the kingdom of God!"

16[a]Then He said to him, "A certain man
gave a great supper and invited many,
17and [a]sent his servant at supper time to
say to those who were invited, 'Come, for
all things are now ready.' 18But they all with
one *accord* began to make excuses. The
first said to him, 'I have bought a piece of
ground, and I must go and see it. I ask you
to have me excused.' 19And another said,
'I have bought five yoke of oxen, and I am
going to test them. I ask you to have me
excused.' 20Still another said, 'I have married a wife, and therefore I cannot come.'
21So that servant came and reported these
things to his master. Then the master of
the house, being angry, said to his servant,
'Go out quickly into the streets and lanes
of the city, and bring in here *the* poor and
the maimed and *the* lame and *the* blind.'
22And the servant said, 'Master, it is done
as you commanded, and still there is room.'
23Then the master said to the servant, 'Go
out into the highways and hedges, and
compel *them* to come in, that my house
may be filled. 24For I say to you [a]that none
of those men who were invited shall taste
my supper.'"

Leaving All to Follow Christ
(Matt. 10:34–39)

25Now great multitudes went with Him.
And He turned and said to them, 26[a]"If
anyone comes to Me [b]and does not hate
his father and mother, wife and children,
brothers and sisters, [c]yes, and his own life
also, he cannot be My disciple. 27And [a]who-
ever does not bear his cross and come after
Me cannot be My disciple. 28For [a]which of
you, intending to build a tower, does not sit
down first and count the cost, whether he
has *enough* to finish *it*— 29lest, after he has
laid the foundation, and is not able to finish,
all who see *it* begin to mock him, 30saying,
'This man began to build and was not able
to finish'? 31Or what king, going to make war
against another king, does not sit down first
and consider whether he is able with ten
thousand to meet him who comes against
him with twenty thousand? 32Or else, while
the other is still a great way off, he sends a
delegation and asks conditions of peace.
33So likewise, whoever of you [a]does not forsake all that he has cannot be My disciple.

Tasteless Salt Is Worthless
(Matt. 5:13; Mark 9:50)

34[a]"Salt *is* good; but if the salt has lost
its flavor, how shall it be seasoned? 35It is
neither fit for the land nor for the dunghill,
but men throw it out. He who has ears to
hear, let him hear!"

The Parable of the Lost Sheep
(Matt. 18:10–14)

15 Then [a]all the tax collectors and the
sinners drew near to Him to hear
Him. 2And the Pharisees and scribes complained, saying, "This Man receives sinners
[a]and eats with them." 3So He spoke this parable to them, saying:

4[a]"What man of you, having a hundred
sheep, if he loses one of them, does not
leave the ninety-nine in the wilderness,
and go after the one which is lost until he
finds it? 5And when he has found *it,* he lays
it on his shoulders, rejoicing. 6And when he
comes home, he calls together *his* friends
and neighbors, saying to them, [a]'Rejoice
with me, for I have found my sheep [b]which
was lost!' 7I say to you that likewise there
will be more joy in heaven over one sinner
who repents [a]than over ninety-nine just
persons who [b]need no repentance.

The Parable of the Lost Coin

8"Or what woman, having ten silver
coins,[1] if she loses one coin, does not light

14:14 [a] [Matt. 25:34–40] 14:15 [a] Rev. 19:9 [1] M-Text reads *dinner.* 14:16 [a] Matt. 22:2–14 14:17 [a] Prov. 9:2, 5 14:24 [a] [Matt. 21:43; 22:8; Acts 13:46] 14:26 [a] Deut. 13:6; 33:9; Matt. 10:37 [b] Rom. 9:13 [c] Rev. 12:11 14:27 [a] Matt. 16:24; Mark 8:34; Luke 9:23; [2 Tim. 3:12] 14:28 [a] Prov. 24:27 14:33 [a] Matt. 19:27 14:34 [a] Matt. 5:13; [Mark 9:50] 15:1 [a] [Matt. 9:10–13] 15:2 [a] Acts 11:3; Gal. 2:12 15:4 [a] Matt. 18:12–14; 1 Pet. 2:25 15:6 [a] [Rom. 12:15] [b] [Luke 19:10; 1 Pet. 2:10, 25] 15:7 [a] [Luke 5:32] [b] [Mark 2:17]
15:8 [1] Greek *drachma,* a valuable coin often worn in a ten-piece garland by married women

a lamp, sweep the house, and search carefully until she finds *it?* 9And when she has found *it,* she calls *her* friends and neighbors together, saying, 'Rejoice with me, for I have found the piece which I lost!' 10Likewise, I say to you, there is joy in the presence of the angels of God over one sinner who repents."

The Parable of the Lost Son

11Then He said: "A certain man had two sons. 12And the younger of them said to *his* father, 'Father, give me the portion of goods that falls *to me.*' So he divided to them [a]*his* livelihood. 13And not many days after, the younger son gathered all together, journeyed to a far country, and there wasted his possessions with prodigal living. 14But when he had spent all, there arose a severe famine in that land, and he began to be in want. 15Then he went and joined himself to a citizen of that country, and he sent him into his fields to feed swine. 16And he would gladly have filled his stomach with the pods that the swine ate, and no one gave him *anything.*

17"But when he came to himself, he said, 'How many of my father's hired servants have bread enough and to spare, and I perish with hunger! 18I will arise and go to my father, and will say to him, "Father, [a]I have sinned against heaven and before you, 19and I am no longer worthy to be called your son. Make me like one of your hired servants." '

20"And he arose and came to his father. But [a]when he was still a great way off, his father saw him and had compassion, and ran and fell on his neck and kissed him. 21And the son said to him, 'Father, I have sinned against heaven [a]and in your sight, and am no longer worthy to be called your son.'

22"But the father said to his servants, 'Bring[1] out the best robe and put *it* on him, and put a ring on his hand and sandals on *his* feet. 23And bring the fatted calf here and kill *it,* and let us eat and be merry; 24[a]for this my son was dead and is alive again; he was lost and is found.' And they began to be merry.

25"Now his older son was in the field. And as he came and drew near to the house, he heard music and dancing. 26So he called one of the servants and asked what these things meant. 27And he said to him, 'Your brother has come, and because he has received him safe and sound, your father has killed the fatted calf.'

28"But he was angry and would not go in. Therefore his father came out and pleaded with him. 29So he answered and said to *his* father, 'Lo, these many years I have been serving you; I never transgressed your commandment at any time; and yet you never gave me a young goat, that I might make merry with my friends. 30But as soon as this son of yours came, who has devoured your livelihood with harlots, you killed the fatted calf for him.'

31"And he said to him, 'Son, you are always with me, and all that I have is yours. 32It was right that we should make merry and be glad, [a]for your brother was dead and is alive again, and was lost and is found.' "

The Parable of the Unjust Steward

16 He also said to His disciples: "There was a certain rich man who had a steward, and an accusation was brought to him that this man was wasting his goods. 2So he called him and said to him, 'What is this I hear about you? Give an [a]account of your stewardship, for you can no longer be steward.'

3"Then the steward said within himself, 'What shall I do? For my master is taking the stewardship away from me. I cannot dig; I am ashamed to beg. 4I have resolved what to do, that when I am put out of the stewardship, they may receive me into their houses.'

5"So he called every one of his master's debtors to *him,* and said to the first, 'How much do you owe my master?' 6And he said, 'A hundred measures[1] of oil.' So he said to him, 'Take your bill, and sit down quickly and write fifty.' 7Then he said to another, 'And how much do you owe?' So he said, 'A hundred measures[1] of wheat.' And he said

---

15:12 [a] Mark 12:44 15:18 [a] Ex. 9:27; 10:16; Num. 22:34; Josh. 7:20; 1 Sam. 15:24, 30; 26:21; 2 Sam. 12:13; 24:10, 17; Ps. 51:4; Matt. 27:4 15:20 [a] [Jer. 3:12]; Matt. 9:36; [Acts 2:39; Eph. 2:13, 17] 15:21 [a] Ps. 51:4 15:22 [1] NU-Text reads *Quickly bring.* 15:24 [a] Matt. 8:22; Luke 9:60; 15:32; Rom. 11:15; [Eph. 2:1, 5; 5:14; Col. 2:13; 1 Tim. 5:6] 15:32 [a] Luke 15:24 16:2 [a] [Rom. 14:12; 2 Cor. 5:10; 1 Pet. 4:5, 6] 16:6 [1] Greek *batos,* eight or nine gallons each (Old Testament *bath*) 16:7 [1] Greek *koros,* ten or twelve bushels each (Old Testament *kor*)

to him, 'Take your bill, and write eighty.' 8So
the master commended the unjust steward
because he had dealt shrewdly. For the sons
of this world are more shrewd in their generation than [a]the sons of light.
9"And I say to you, [a]make friends for
yourselves by unrighteous mammon, that
when you fail,[1] they may receive you into an
everlasting home. 10[a]He who *is* faithful in
what is least is faithful also in much; and he
who is unjust in *what is* least is unjust also
in much. 11Therefore if you have not been
faithful in the unrighteous mammon, who
will commit to your trust the true *riches?*
12And if you have not been faithful in what
is another man's, who will give you what is
your [a]own?
13[a]"No servant can serve two masters;
for either he will hate the one and love the
other, or else he will be loyal to the one and
despise the other. You cannot serve God
and mammon."

The Law, the Prophets, and the Kingdom

14Now the Pharisees, [a]who were lovers
of money, also heard all these things, and
they derided Him. 15And He said to them,
"You are those who [a]justify yourselves [b]be-
fore men, but [c]God knows your hearts. For
[d]what is highly esteemed among men is an
abomination in the sight of God.
16[a]"The law and the prophets *were* until
John. Since that time the kingdom of God
has been preached, and everyone is pressing into it. 17[a]And it is easier for heaven and
earth to pass away than for one tittle of the
law to fail.
18[a]"Whoever divorces his wife and marries another commits adultery; and whoever marries her who is divorced from *her*
husband commits adultery.

The Rich Man and Lazarus

19"There was a certain rich man who was
clothed in purple and fine linen and fared
sumptuously every day. 20But there was a
certain beggar named Lazarus, full of sores,
who was laid at his gate, 21desiring to be fed
with the crumbs which fell[1] from the rich
man's table. Moreover the dogs came and
licked his sores. 22So it was that the beggar died, and was carried by the angels to
[a]Abraham's bosom. The rich man also died
and was buried. 23And being in torments in
Hades, he lifted up his eyes and saw Abraham afar off, and Lazarus in his bosom.
24"Then he cried and said, 'Father Abraham, have mercy on me, and send Lazarus that he may dip the tip of his finger in
water and [a]cool my tongue; for I [b]am tormented in this flame.' 25But Abraham said,
'Son, [a]remember that in your lifetime you
received your good things, and likewise
Lazarus evil things; but now he is comforted and you are tormented. 26And besides all this, between us and you there is
a great gulf fixed, so that those who want
to pass from here to you cannot, nor can
those from there pass to us.'
27"Then he said, 'I beg you therefore,
father, that you would send him to my father's house, 28for I have five brothers, that
he may testify to them, lest they also come
to this place of torment.' 29Abraham said to
him, [a]'They have Moses and the prophets;
let them hear them.' 30And he said, 'No, father Abraham; but if one goes to them from
the dead, they will repent.' 31But he said to
him, [a]'If they do not hear Moses and the
prophets, [b]neither will they be persuaded
though one rise from the dead.'"

Jesus Warns of Offenses
(Matt. 18:6, 7; Mark 9:42)

17 Then He said to the disciples, [a]"It is
impossible that no offenses should
come, but [b]woe *to him* through whom they
do come! 2It would be better for him if a
millstone were hung around his neck, and
he were thrown into the sea, than that he
should offend one of these little ones. 3Take
heed to yourselves. [a]If your brother sins
against you,[1] [b]rebuke him; and if he repents,
forgive him. 4And if he sins against you

16:8 [a] [John 12:36; Eph. 5:8]; 1 Thess. 5:5 **16:9** [a] Dan. 4:27; [Matt. 6:19; 19:21]; Luke 11:41; [1 Tim. 6:17–19] [1] NU-Text reads *it fails.* **16:10** [a] Matt. 25:21; Luke 19:17 **16:12** [a] [1 Pet. 1:3, 4] **16:13** [a] Matt. 6:24; Gal. 1:10 **16:14** [a] Matt. 23:14 **16:15** [a] Luke 10:29 [b] [Matt. 6:2, 5, 16] [c] 1 Chr. 28:9; 2 Chr. 6:30; Ps. 7:9; Prov. 15:11; Jer. 17:10 [d] 1 Sam. 16:7; Ps. 10:3; Prov. 6:16–19; 16:5 **16:16** [a] Matt. 3:1–12; 4:17; 11:12, 13; Luke 7:29 **16:17** [a] Ps. 102:26, 27; Is. 40:8; 51:6; Matt. 5:18; 1 Pet. 1:25 **16:18** [a] Matt. 5:32; 19:9; Mark 10:11; 1 Cor. 7:10, 11 **16:21** [1] NU-Text reads *with what fell.* **16:22** [a] Matt. 8:11 **16:24** [a] Zech. 14:12 [b] [Is. 66:24; Mark 9:42–48] **16:25** [a] Job 21:13; Luke 6:24; James 5:5 **16:29** [a] Is. 8:20; 34:16; [John 5:39, 45]; Acts 15:21; 17:11; [2 Tim. 3:15] **16:31** [a] [John 5:46] [b] John 12:10, 11 **17:1** [a] [1 Cor. 11:19] [b] Matt. 18:6, 7; 26:24; Mark 9:42; [2 Thess. 1:6]; Jude 11 **17:3** [a] [Matt. 18:15, 21] [b] Lev. 19:17; [Prov. 17:10; Gal. 6:1; James 5:19, 20] [1] NU-Text omits *against you.*

seven times in a day, and seven times in a
day returns to you,[1] saying, 'I repent,' you
shall forgive him."

Faith and Duty
(Matt. 17:19–21; Mark 9:28, 29)

5 And the apostles said to the Lord, "Increase our faith."

6 [a]So the Lord said, "If you have faith as
a mustard seed, you can say to this mulberry tree, 'Be pulled up by the roots and
be planted in the sea,' and it would obey
you. 7 And which of you, having a servant
plowing or tending sheep, will say to him
when he has come in from the field, 'Come
at once and sit down to eat'? 8 But will he not
rather say to him, 'Prepare something for
my supper, and gird yourself [a]and serve me
till I have eaten and drunk, and afterward
you will eat and drink'? 9 Does he thank that
servant because he did the things that were
commanded him? I think not.[1] 10 So likewise
you, when you have done all those things
which you are commanded, say, 'We are
[a]unprofitable servants. We have done what
was our duty to do.'"

Ten Lepers Cleansed

11 Now it happened [a]as He went to Jerusalem that He passed through the midst of
Samaria and Galilee. 12 Then as He entered
a certain village, there met Him ten men
who were lepers, [a]who stood afar off. 13 And
they lifted up *their* voices and said, "Jesus,
Master, have mercy on us!"

14 So when He saw *them,* He said to them,
[a]"Go, show yourselves to the priests." And so
it was that as they went, they were cleansed.

15 And one of them, when he saw that he
was healed, returned, and with a loud voice
[a]glorified God, 16 and fell down on *his* face
at His feet, giving Him thanks. And he was
a [a]Samaritan.

17 So Jesus answered and said, "Were
there not ten cleansed? But where *are*
the nine? 18 Were there not any found who
returned to give glory to God except this
foreigner?" 19 [a]And He said to him, "Arise,
go your way. Your faith has made you well."

The Coming of the Kingdom
(Gen. 6:5—8:22; 19:12–14)

20 Now when He was asked by the Pharisees when the kingdom of God would come,
He answered them and said, "The kingdom of God does not come with observation; 21 [a]nor will they say, 'See here!' or 'See
there!'[1] For indeed, [b]the kingdom of God
is within you."

22 Then He said to the disciples, [a]"The
days will come when you will desire to see
one of the days of the Son of Man, and you
will not see *it.* 23 [a]And they will say to you,
'Look here!' or 'Look there!'[1] Do not go after
them or follow *them.* 24 [a]For as the lightning
that flashes out of one *part* under heaven
shines to the other *part* under heaven, so
also the Son of Man will be in His day. 25 [a]But
first He must suffer many things and be
[b]rejected by this generation. 26 [a]And as it
[b]was in the [c]days of [d]Noah, so it will be also
in the days of the Son of Man: 27 They ate,
they drank, they married wives, they were
given in marriage, until the [a]day that Noah
entered the ark, and the flood came and
[b]destroyed them all. 28 [a]Likewise as it was
also in the days of Lot: They ate, they drank,
they bought, they sold, they planted, they
built; 29 but on [a]the day that Lot went out of
Sodom it rained fire and brimstone from
heaven and destroyed *them* all. 30 Even so
will it be in the day when the Son of Man
[a]is revealed.

31 "In that day, he [a]who is on the housetop, and his goods *are* in the house, let
him not come down to take them away.
And likewise the one who is in the field, let
him not turn back. 32 [a]Remember Lot's wife.
33 [a]Whoever seeks to save his life will lose it,
and whoever loses his life will preserve it.
34 [a]I tell you, in that night there will be two
men in one bed: the one will be taken and

17:4 [1] M-Text omits *to you.* 17:6 [a] Matt. 17:20; 21:21; [Mark 9:23; 11:23]; Luke 13:19 17:8 [a] [Luke 12:37] 17:9 [1] NU-Text ends verse with *commanded;* M-Text omits *him.* 17:10 [a] Job 22:3; 35:7; Ps. 16:2; Matt. 25:30; Rom. 3:12; 11:35; [1 Cor. 9:16, 17]; Philem. 11 17:11 [a] Luke 9:51, 52; John 4:4 17:12 [a] Lev. 13:46; Num. 5:2 17:14 [a] Lev. 13:1–59; 14:1–32; Matt. 8:4; Luke 5:14 17:15 [a] Luke 5:25; 18:43 17:16 [a] 2 Kin. 17:24; Luke 9:52, 53; John 4:9 17:19 [a] Matt. 9:22; Mark 5:34; 10:52; Luke 7:50; 8:48; 18:42 17:21 [a] Luke 17:23 [b] [Rom. 14:17] [1] NU-Text reverses *here* and *there.* 17:22 [a] Matt. 9:15; Mark 2:20; Luke 5:35; [John 17:12] 17:23 [a] Matt. 24:23; Mark 13:21; [Luke 21:8] [1] NU-Text reverses *here* and *there.* 17:24 [a] Matt. 24:27 17:25 [a] Matt. 26:67; 27:29–31; Mark 8:31; 9:31; 10:33 [b] Luke 9:22 17:26 [a] Matt. 24:37–39 [b] [Gen. 6:5–7] [c] [Gen. 6:8–13] [d] 1 Pet. 3:20 17:27 [a] Gen. 7:1–16 [b] Gen. 7:19–23 17:28 [a] Gen. 19 17:29 [a] Gen. 19:16, 24, 29; 2 Pet. 2:6, 7 17:30 [a] [Matt. 16:27]; 1 Cor. 1:7; [Col. 3:4; 2 Thess. 1:7]; 1 Pet. 1:7; 4:13; 1 John 2:28 17:31 [a] Matt. 24:17, 18; Mark 13:15 17:32 [a] Gen. 19:26 17:33 [a] Matt. 10:39; 16:25; Mark 8:35; Luke 9:24; John 12:25 17:34 [a] Matt. 24:40, 41; [1 Thess. 4:17]

the other will be left. 35[a]Two *women* will be
grinding together: the one will be taken and
the other left. 36Two *men* will be in the field:
the one will be taken and the other left."[1]

37And they answered and said to Him,
[a]"Where, Lord?"

So He said to them, "Wherever the body
is, there the eagles will be gathered together."

The Parable of the Persistent Widow

18 Then He spoke a parable to them,
that men [a]always ought to pray and
not lose heart, 2saying: "There was in a certain city a judge who did not fear God nor
regard man. 3Now there was a widow in
that city; and she came to him, saying, 'Get
justice for me from my adversary.' 4And he
would not for a while; but afterward he said
within himself, 'Though I do not fear God
nor regard man, 5[a]yet because this widow
troubles me I will avenge her, lest by her
continual coming she weary me.' "

6Then the Lord said, "Hear what the unjust judge said. 7And [a]shall God not avenge
His own elect who cry out day and night to
Him, though He bears long with them? 8I
tell you [a]that He will avenge them speedily.
Nevertheless, when the Son of Man comes,
will He really find faith on the earth?"

The Parable of the Pharisee and the Tax Collector

9Also He spoke this parable to some
[a]who trusted in themselves that they were
righteous, and despised others: 10"Two
men went up to the temple to pray, one
a Pharisee and the other a tax collector.
11The Pharisee [a]stood and prayed thus with
himself, [b]'God, I thank You that I am not
like other men—extortioners, unjust, adulterers, or even as this tax collector. 12I fast
twice a week; I give tithes of all that I possess.' 13And the tax collector, standing afar
off, would not so much as raise *his* eyes to
heaven, but beat his breast, saying, 'God,
be merciful to me a sinner!' 14I tell you,
this man went down to his house justified
rather than the other; [a]for everyone who
exalts himself will be humbled, and he who
humbles himself will be exalted."

Jesus Blesses Little Children
(Matt. 19:13–15; Mark 10:13–16)

15[a]Then they also brought infants to Him
that He might touch them; but when the
disciples saw *it,* they rebuked them. 16But
Jesus called them to *Him* and said, "Let
the little children come to Me, and do not
forbid them; for [a]of such is the kingdom
of God. 17[a]Assuredly, I say to you, whoever
does not receive the kingdom of God as a
little child will by no means enter it."

Jesus Counsels the Rich Young Ruler
(Matt. 19:16–22; Mark 10:17–22)

18[a]Now a certain ruler asked Him, saying, "Good Teacher, what shall I do to inherit eternal life?"

19So Jesus said to him, "Why do you call
Me good? No one *is* good but [a]One, *that*
is, God. 20You know the commandments:
[a]'Do not commit adultery,' 'Do not murder,'
'Do not steal,' 'Do not bear false witness,'
[b]'Honor your father and your mother.' "[1]

21And he said, "All [a]these things I have
kept from my youth."

22So when Jesus heard these things, He
said to him, "You still lack one thing. [a]Sell
all that you have and distribute to the poor,
and you will have treasure in heaven; and
come, follow Me."

23But when he heard this, he became
very sorrowful, for he was very rich.

With God All Things Are Possible
(Matt. 19:23–30; Mark 10:23–31)

24And when Jesus saw that he became
very sorrowful, He said, [a]"How hard it is for
those who have riches to enter the kingdom
of God! 25For it is easier for a camel to go
through the eye of a needle than for a rich
man to enter the kingdom of God."

26And those who heard it said, "Who
then can be saved?"

27But He said, [a]"The things which are

17:35 [a] Matt. 24:40, 41 17:36 [1] NU-Text and M-Text omit verse 36. 17:37 [a] Job 39:30; Matt. 24:28 18:1 [a] Luke 11:5–10; Rom. 12:12; [Eph. 6:18]; Col. 4:2; 1 Thess. 5:17 18:5 [a] Luke 11:8 18:7 [a] Rev. 6:10 18:8 [a] Heb. 10:37; [2 Pet. 3:8, 9] 18:9 [a] Prov. 30:12; Luke 10:29; 16:15 18:11 [a] Ps. 135:2 [b] Is. 1:15; 58:2; Rev. 3:17 18:14 [a] Job 22:29; Matt. 23:12; Luke 14:11; [James 4:6; 1 Pet. 5:5] 18:15 [a] Matt. 19:13–15; Mark 10:13–16 18:16 [a] Matt. 18:3; 1 Cor. 14:20; 1 Pet. 2:2 18:17 [a] Matt. 18:3; 19:14; Mark 10:15 18:18 [a] Matt. 19:16–29; Mark 10:17–30 18:19 [a] Ps. 86:5; 119:68 18:20 [a] Ex. 20:12–16; Deut. 5:16–20; Mark 10:19; Rom. 13:9 [b] Eph. 6:2; Col. 3:20 [1] Exodus 20:12–16; Deuteronomy 5:16–20 18:21 [a] Phil. 3:6 18:22 [a] Matt. 6:19, 20; 19:21; [1 Tim. 6:19] 18:24 [a] Prov. 11:28; Matt. 19:23; Mark 10:23 18:27 [a] Job 42:2; Jer. 32:17; Zech. 8:6; Matt. 19:26; Luke 1:37

impossible with men are possible with
God."
28[a]Then Peter said, "See, we have left all[1]
and followed You."
29So He said to them, "Assuredly, I say
to you, [a]there is no one who has left house
or parents or brothers or wife or children,
for the sake of the kingdom of God, 30[a]who
shall not receive many times more in this
present time, and in the age to come eternal life."

Jesus a Third Time Predicts His Death and Resurrection

(Matt. 20:17–19; Mark 10:32–34)

31[a]Then He took the twelve aside and
said to them, "Behold, we are going up to
Jerusalem, and all things [b]that are written
by the prophets concerning the Son of Man
will be accomplished. 32For [a]He will be delivered to the Gentiles and will be mocked
and insulted and spit upon. 33They will
scourge *Him* and kill Him. And the third
day He will rise again."
34[a]But they understood none of these
things; this saying was hidden from them,
and they did not know the things which
were spoken.

A Blind Man Receives His Sight

(Matt. 20:29–34; Mark 10:46–52)

35[a]Then it happened, as He was coming
near Jericho, that a certain blind man sat
by the road begging. 36And hearing a multitude passing by, he asked what it meant.
37So they told him that Jesus of Nazareth
was passing by. 38And he cried out, saying,
"Jesus, [a]Son of David, have mercy on me!"
39Then those who went before warned
him that he should be quiet; but he cried
out all the more, "Son of David, have mercy
on me!"
40So Jesus stood still and commanded
him to be brought to Him. And when he
had come near, He asked him, 41saying,
"What do you want Me to do for you?"
He said, "Lord, that I may receive my
sight."
42Then Jesus said to him, "Receive your

#OXYGEN

LUKE 18:38–39

Exalt His Immutability

The same God who had mercy on a blind man when no one else did continues to shower His mercy on us today. Though the world around us may be filled with hard-heartedness, cruelty, and inhumanity, we can know His mercy, grace, love, and peace are more powerful than any circumstance. Christ Jesus is still the source of all mercy, and He always will be.

Breathe and exalt His immutability.

sight; [a]your faith has made you well." 43And
immediately he received his sight, and followed Him, [a]glorifying God. And all the
people, when they saw *it,* gave praise to
God.

Jesus Comes to Zacchaeus' House

19 Then *Jesus* entered and passed
through [a]Jericho. 2Now behold, *there
was* a man named Zacchaeus who was a
chief tax collector, and he was rich. 3And he
sought to [a]see who Jesus was, but could not
because of the crowd, for he was of short
stature. 4So he ran ahead and climbed up
into a sycamore tree to see Him, for He was
going to pass that *way.* 5And when Jesus
came to the place, He looked up and saw
him,[1] and said to him, "Zacchaeus, make
haste and come down, for today I must
stay at your house." 6So he made haste and
came down, and received Him joyfully. 7But
when they saw *it,* they all complained, saying, [a]"He has gone to be a guest with a man
who is a sinner."
8Then Zacchaeus stood and said to the
Lord, "Look, Lord, I give half of my goods
to the [a]poor; and if I have taken anything
from anyone by [b]false accusation, [c]I restore
fourfold."
9And Jesus said to him, "Today salvation has come to this house, because [a]he

---

18:28 [a] Matt. 19:27 [1] NU-Text reads *our own.* 18:29 [a] Deut. 33:9 18:30 [a] Job 42:10 18:31 [a] Matt. 16:21; 17:22; 20:17; Mark 10:32; Luke 9:51 [b] Ps. 22; [Is. 53] 18:32 [a] Matt. 26:67; 27:2, 29, 41; Mark 14:65; 15:1, 19, 20, 31; Luke 23:1; John 18:28; Acts 3:13 18:34 [a] Mark 9:32; Luke 2:50; 9:45; [John 10:6; 12:16] 18:35 [a] Matt. 20:29–34; Mark 10:46–52 18:38 [a] Matt. 9:27 18:42 [a] Luke 17:19 18:43 [a] Luke 5:26; Acts 4:21; 11:18 19:1 [a] Josh. 6:26; 1 Kin. 16:34 19:3 [a] John 12:21 19:5 [1] NU-Text omits *and saw him.* 19:7 [a] Matt. 9:11; Luke 5:30; 15:2 19:8 [a] [Ps. 41:1] [b] Luke 3:14 [c] Ex. 22:1; Lev. 6:5; Num. 5:7; 1 Sam. 12:3; 2 Sam. 12:6 19:9 [a] Luke 3:8; 13:16; [Rom. 4:16; Gal. 3:7]

also is [b]a son of Abraham; 10[a]for the Son
of Man has come to seek and to save that
which was lost."

The Parable of the Minas
(Matt. 25:14–30)

11Now as they heard these things, He
spoke another parable, because He was
near Jerusalem and because [a]they thought
the kingdom of God would appear immediately. 12[a]Therefore He said: "A certain nobleman went into a far country to receive for
himself a kingdom and to return. 13So he
called ten of his servants, delivered to them
ten minas,[1] and said to them, 'Do business
till I come.' 14[a]But his citizens hated him,
and sent a delegation after him, saying,
'We will not have this *man* to reign over us.'

15"And so it was that when he returned,
having received the kingdom, he then commanded these servants, to whom he had
given the money, to be called to him, that
he might know how much every man had
gained by trading. 16Then came the first,
saying, 'Master, your mina has earned ten
minas.' 17And he said to him, [a]'Well *done,*
good servant; because you were [b]faithful
in a very little, have authority over ten cities.' 18And the second came, saying, 'Master,
your mina has earned five minas.' 19Likewise
he said to him, 'You also be over five cities.'

20"Then another came, saying, 'Master, here is your mina, which I have kept
put away in a handkerchief. 21[a]For I feared
you, because you are an austere man. You
collect what you did not deposit, and reap
what you did not sow.' 22And he said to him,
[a]'Out of your own mouth I will judge you,
you wicked servant. [b]You knew that I was
an austere man, collecting what I did not
deposit and reaping what I did not sow.
23Why then did you not put my money in
the bank, that at my coming I might have
collected it with interest?'

24"And he said to those who stood by,
'Take the mina from him, and give *it* to
him who has ten minas.' 25(But they said
to him, 'Master, he has ten minas.') 26'For I
say to you, [a]that to everyone who has will
be given; and from him who does not have,
even what he has will be taken away from
him. 27But bring here those enemies of
mine, who did not want me to reign over
them, and slay *them* before me.'"

The Triumphal Entry
(Matt. 21:1–11; Mark 11:1–11; John 12:12–19)

28When He had said this, [a]He went on
ahead, going up to Jerusalem. 29[a]And it
came to pass, when He drew near to Bethphage[1] and [b]Bethany, at the mountain
called [c]Olivet, *that* He sent two of His disciples, 30saying, "Go into the village opposite
you, where as you enter you will find a colt
tied, on which no one has ever sat. Loose it
and bring *it here.* 31And if anyone asks you,
'Why are you loosing *it?*' thus you shall say
to him, 'Because the Lord has need of it.'"

32So those who were sent went their way
and found *it* just [a]as He had said to them.
33But as they were loosing the colt, the owners of it said to them, "Why are you loosing the colt?"

34And they said, "The Lord has need of
him." 35Then they brought him to Jesus.
[a]And they threw their own clothes on the
colt, and they set Jesus on him. 36And as
He went, *many* spread their clothes on the
road.

37Then, as He was now drawing near the
descent of the Mount of Olives, the whole
multitude of the disciples began to [a]rejoice
and praise God with a loud voice for all the
mighty works they had seen, 38saying:

[a]" 'Blessed *is* the King who comes
in the name of the LORD!'[1]
[b]Peace in heaven and glory
in the highest!"

39And some of the Pharisees called to
Him from the crowd, "Teacher, rebuke Your
disciples."

40But He answered and said to them,
"I tell you that if these should keep silent,
[a]the stones would immediately cry out."

19:9 [b] [Luke 13:16] 19:10 [a] Matt. 18:11; [Luke 5:32; Rom. 5:8] 19:11 [a] Acts 1:6 19:12 [a] Matt. 25:14–30; Mark 13:34 19:13 [1] The *mina* (Greek *mna,* Hebrew *minah*) was worth about three months' salary. 19:14 [a] [John 1:11] 19:17 [a] Matt. 25:21, 23 [b] Luke 16:10 19:21 [a] Matt. 25:24 19:22 [a] 2 Sam. 1:16; Job 15:6; [Matt. 12:37] [b] Matt. 25:26 19:26 [a] Matt. 13:12; 25:29; Mark 4:25; Luke 8:18 19:28 [a] Mark 10:32 19:29 [a] Matt. 21:1; Mark 11:1 [b] Matt. 26:6; John 12:1 [c] John 8:1; Acts 1:12 [1] M-Text reads *Bethsphage.* 19:32 [a] Luke 22:13 19:35 [a] 2 Kin. 9:13; Matt. 21:7; Mark 11:7 19:37 [a] Luke 13:17; 18:43 19:38 [a] Ps. 118:26; Luke 13:35 [b] Luke 2:14; [Eph. 2:14] [1] Psalm 118:26 19:40 [a] Hab. 2:11

Jesus Weeps over Jerusalem

41Now as He drew near, He saw the city
and [a]wept over it, 42saying, "If you had
known, even you, especially in this [a]your
day, the things *that* [b]*make* for your [c]peace!
But now they are hidden from your eyes.
43For days will come upon you when your
enemies will [a]build an embankment
around you, surround you and close you
in on every side, 44[a]and level you, and your
children within you, to the ground; and
[b]they will not leave in you one stone upon
another, [c]because you did not know the
time of your visitation."

Jesus Cleanses the Temple
(Matt. 21:12–17; Mark 11:15–19; John 2:12–25)

45[a]Then He went into the temple and
began to drive out those who bought and
sold in it,[1] 46saying to them, "It is written,
[a]'My house is[1] a house of prayer,'[2] but you
have made it a [b]'den of thieves.'"[3]

47And He [a]was teaching daily in the temple. But [b]the chief priests, the scribes, and
the leaders of the people sought to destroy
Him, 48and were unable to do anything;
for all the people were very attentive to
[a]hear Him.

Jesus' Authority Questioned
(Matt. 21:23–27; Mark 11:27–33)

20 Now [a]it happened on one of those
days, as He taught the people in the
temple and preached the gospel, *that* the
chief priests and the scribes, together with
the elders, confronted *Him* 2and spoke to
Him, saying, "Tell us, [a]by what authority
are You doing these things? Or who is he
who gave You this authority?"

3But He answered and said to them, "I
also will ask you one thing, and answer Me:
4The [a]baptism of John—was it from heaven
or from men?"

5And they reasoned among themselves,
saying, "If we say, 'From heaven,' He will
say, 'Why then[1] did you not believe him?'
6But if we say, 'From men,' all the people
will stone us, [a]for they are persuaded that
John was a prophet." 7So they answered
that they did not know where *it was* from.

8And Jesus said to them, "Neither will I
tell you by what authority I do these things."

The Parable of the Wicked Vinedressers
(Matt. 21:33–46; Mark 12:1–12)

9Then He began to tell the people this
parable: [a]"A certain man planted a vineyard, leased it to vinedressers, and went
into a far country for a long time. 10Now
at vintage-time he [a]sent a servant to the
vinedressers, that they might give him
some of the fruit of the vineyard. But the
vinedressers beat him and sent *him* away
empty-handed. 11Again he sent another
servant; and they beat him also, treated
him shamefully, and sent *him* away empty-
handed. 12And again he sent a third; and
they wounded him also and cast *him* out.

13"Then the owner of the vineyard said,
'What shall I do? I will send my beloved
son. Probably they will respect *him* when
they see him.' 14But when the vinedressers
saw him, they reasoned among themselves,
saying, 'This is the [a]heir. Come, [b]let us kill
him, that the inheritance may be [c]ours.'
15So they cast him out of the vineyard and
[a]killed *him*. Therefore what will the owner
of the vineyard do to them? 16He will come
and destroy those vinedressers and give
the vineyard to [a]others."

And when they heard *it* they said, "Certainly not!"

17Then He looked at them and said,
"What then is this that is written:

[a]'The stone which the builders rejected
Has become the chief cornerstone'?[1]

18Whoever falls on that stone will be [a]bro-
ken; but [b]on whomever it falls, it will grind
him to powder."

19And the chief priests and the scribes

19:41 [a] Is. 53:3; John 11:35 19:42 [a] Ps. 95:7, 8; Heb. 3:13 [b] [Luke 1:77–79; Acts 10:36] [c] [Rom. 5:1] 19:43 [a] Is. 29:3, 4; Jer. 6:3, 6; Luke 21:20 19:44 [a] 1 Kin. 9:7, 8; Mic. 3:12 [b] Matt. 24:2; Mark 13:2; Luke 21:6 [c] [Dan. 9:24; Luke 1:68, 78; 1 Pet. 2:12] 19:45 [a] Mal. 3:1; Matt. 21:12, 13; Mark 11:11, 15–17; John 2:13–16 [1] NU-Text reads *those who were selling.* 19:46 [a] Is. 56:7 [b] Jer. 7:11 [1] NU-Text reads *shall be.* [2] Isaiah 56:7 [3] Jeremiah 7:11 19:47 [a] Luke 21:37; 22:53 [b] Mark 11:18; Luke 20:19; John 7:19; 8:37 19:48 [a] Luke 21:38 20:1 [a] Matt. 21:23–27; Mark 11:27–33 20:2 [a] Acts 4:7; 7:27 20:4 [a] John 1:26, 31 20:5 [1] NU-Text and M-Text omit *then.* 20:6 [a] Matt. 14:5; 21:26; Mark 6:20; Luke 7:24–30 20:9 [a] Ps. 80:8; Matt. 21:33–46; Mark 12:1–12 20:10 [a] 2 Kin. 17:13, 14; 2 Chr. 36:15, 16; [Acts 7:52; 1 Thess. 2:15] 20:14 [a] [Heb. 1:1–3] [b] Matt. 27:21–23 [c] John 11:47, 48 20:15 [a] Luke 23:33; Acts 2:22, 23; 3:15 20:16 [a] [John 1:11–13]; Rom. 11:1, 11; 1 Cor. 6:15; Gal. 2:17; 3:21; 6:14 20:17 [a] Ps. 118:22; Matt. 21:42; 1 Pet. 2:7, 8 [1] Psalm 118:22 20:18 [a] Is. 8:14, 15 [b] [Dan. 2:34, 35, 44, 45]; Matt. 21:44

that very hour sought to lay hands on Him,
but they feared the people[1]—for they knew
He had spoken this parable against them.

The Pharisees: Is It Lawful to Pay Taxes to Caesar?
(Matt. 22:15–22; Mark 12:13–17)

20[a]So they watched *Him,* and sent spies
who pretended to be righteous, that they
might seize on His words, in order to deliver Him to the power and the authority
of the governor.
21Then they asked Him, saying,
[a]"Teacher, we know that You say and teach
rightly, and You do not show personal favoritism, but teach the way of God in truth:
22Is it lawful for us to pay taxes to Caesar
or not?"
23But He perceived their craftiness, and
said to them, "Why do you test Me?[1] 24Show
Me a denarius. Whose image and inscription does it have?"
They answered and said, "Caesar's."
25And He said to them, [a]"Render therefore to Caesar the things that are Caesar's,
and to God the things that are God's."
26But they could not catch Him in His
words in the presence of the people. And
they marveled at His answer and kept silent.

The Sadducees: What About the Resurrection?
(Matt. 22:23–33; Mark 12:18–27)

27[a]Then some of the Sadducees, [b]who
deny that there is a resurrection, came to
Him and asked Him, 28saying: "Teacher,
Moses wrote to us *that* if a man's brother
dies, having a wife, and he dies without
children, his brother should take his wife
and raise up offspring for his brother.
29Now there were seven brothers. And the
first took a wife, and died without children.
30And the second[1] took her as wife, and he
died childless. 31Then the third took her,
and in like manner the seven also; and
they left no children,[1] and died. 32Last of
all the woman died also. 33Therefore, in the
resurrection, whose wife does she become?
For all seven had her as wife."
34Jesus answered and said to them,
"The sons of this age marry and are given
in marriage. 35But those who are [a]counted
worthy to attain that age, and the resurrection from the dead, neither marry nor are
given in marriage; 36nor can they die anymore, for [a]they are equal to the angels and
are sons of God, [b]being sons of the resurrection. 37But even Moses showed in the *burning* bush *passage* that the dead are raised,
when he called the Lord [a]'the God of Abraham, the God of Isaac, and the God of Jacob.'[1] 38For He is not the God of the dead
but of the living, for [a]all live to Him."
39Then some of the scribes answered
and said, "Teacher, You have spoken well."
40But after that they dared not question
Him anymore.

Jesus: How Can David Call His Descendant Lord?
(Matt. 22:41–46; Mark 12:35–37)

41And He said to them, [a]"How can they
say that the Christ is the Son of David?
42Now David himself said in the Book of
Psalms:

[a]'The LORD said to my Lord,
"Sit at My right hand,
43 Till I make Your enemies
Your footstool."'[1]

44Therefore David calls Him 'Lord'; [a]how is
He then his Son?"

Beware of the Scribes
(Matt. 23:1–7; Mark 12:38–40)

45[a]Then, in the hearing of all the people,
He said to His disciples, 46[a]"Beware of the
scribes, who desire to go around in long
robes, [b]love greetings in the marketplaces,
the best seats in the synagogues, and the
best places at feasts, 47[a]who devour widows' houses, and for a [b]pretense make long
prayers. These will receive greater condemnation."

20:19 [1] M-Text reads *but they were afraid.* 20:20 [a] Matt. 22:15 20:21 [a] Matt. 22:16; Mark 12:14 20:23 [1] NU-Text omits *Why do you test Me?* 20:25 [a] Matt. 17:24–27; Rom. 13:7; [1 Pet. 2:13–17] 20:27 [a] Matt. 22:23–33; Mark 12:18–27 [b] Acts 23:6, 8 20:30 [1] NU-Text ends verse 30 here. 20:31 [1] NU-Text and M-Text read *the seven also left no children.* 20:35 [a] Phil. 3:11 20:36 [a] [1 Cor. 15:42, 49, 52; 1 John 3:2] [b] Rom. 8:23 20:37 [a] Ex. 3:1–6, 15; Acts 7:30–32 [1] Exodus 3:6, 15 20:38 [a] [Rom. 6:10, 11; 14:8, 9; Heb. 11:16] 20:41 [a] Matt. 22:41–46; Mark 12:35–37 20:42 [a] Ps. 110:1; Acts 2:34, 35 20:43 [1] Psalm 110:1 20:44 [a] Acts 13:22, 23; Rom. 1:3; 9:4, 5 20:45 [a] Matt. 23:1–7; Mark 12:38–40 20:46 [a] Matt. 23:5 [b] Luke 11:43; 14:7 20:47 [a] Matt. 23:14 [b] [Matt. 6:5, 6]

The Widow's Two Mites
(Mark 12:41–44)

21 And He looked up [a]and saw the rich
putting their gifts into the treasury,
2 and He saw also a certain [a]poor widow
putting in two [b]mites. 3 So He said, "Truly
I say to you [a]that this poor widow has put
in more than all; 4 for all these out of their
abundance have put in offerings for God,[1]
but she out of her poverty put in [a]all the
livelihood that she had."

Jesus Predicts the Destruction of the Temple
(Matt. 24:1, 2; Mark 13:1, 2)

5 [a]Then, as some spoke of the temple,
how it was adorned with beautiful stones
and donations, He said, 6 "These things
which you see—the days will come in which
[a]not *one* stone shall be left upon another
that shall not be thrown down."

The Signs of the Times and the End of the Age
(Matt. 24:3–14; Mark 13:3–13)

7 So they asked Him, saying, "Teacher,
but when will these things be? And what
sign *will there be* when these things are
about to take place?"

8 And He said: [a]"Take heed that you
not be deceived. For many will come in
My name, saying, 'I am *He,*' and, 'The time
has drawn near.' Therefore[1] do not go after them. 9 But when you hear of [a]wars and
commotions, do not be terrified; for these
things must come to pass first, but the end
will not *come* immediately."

10 [a]Then He said to them, "Nation will
rise against nation, and kingdom against
kingdom. 11 And there will be great [a]earth-
quakes in various places, and famines and
pestilences; and there will be fearful sights
and great signs from heaven. 12 [a]But before
all these things, they will lay their hands
on you and persecute *you,* delivering *you*
up to the synagogues and [b]prisons. [c]You
will be brought before kings and rulers [d]for
My name's sake. 13 But [a]it will turn out for
you as an occasion for testimony. 14 [a]There-
fore settle *it* in your hearts not to meditate beforehand on what you will answer;
15 for I will give you a mouth and wisdom
[a]which all your adversaries will not be able
to contradict or resist. 16 [a]You will be betrayed even by parents and brothers, relatives and friends; and they will put [b]*some*
of you to death. 17 And [a]you will be hated by
all for My name's sake. 18 [a]But not a hair of
your head shall be lost. 19 By your patience
possess your souls.

The Destruction of Jerusalem
(Matt. 24:15–28; Mark 13:14–23)

20 [a]"But when you see Jerusalem surrounded by armies, then know that its desolation is near. 21 Then let those who are in
Judea flee to the mountains, let those who
are in the midst of her depart, and let not
those who are in the country enter her. 22 For
these are the days of vengeance, that [a]all
things which are written may be fulfilled.
23 [a]But woe to those who are pregnant and
to those who are nursing babies in those
days! For there will be great distress in the
land and wrath upon this people. 24 And they
will fall by the edge of the sword, and be led
away captive into all nations. And Jerusalem will be trampled by Gentiles [a]until the
times of the Gentiles are fulfilled.

The Coming of the Son of Man
(Matt. 24:29–31; Mark 13:24–27)

25 [a]"And there will be signs in the sun, in
the moon, and in the stars; and on the earth
distress of nations, with perplexity, the sea
and the waves roaring; 26 men's hearts failing them from fear and the expectation
of those things which are coming on the
earth, [a]for the powers of the heavens will
be shaken. 27 Then they will see the Son of
Man [a]coming in a cloud with power and
great glory. 28 Now when these things begin
to happen, look up and lift up your heads,
because [a]your redemption draws near."

21:1 [a] Mark 12:41–44 **21:2** [a] [2 Cor. 6:10] [b] Mark 12:42 **21:3** [a] [2 Cor. 8:12] **21:4** [a] [2 Cor. 8:12] [1] NU-Text omits *for God.* **21:5** [a] Matt. 24:1; Mark 13:1 **21:6** [a] Is. 64:10, 11; Lam. 2:6–9; Mic. 3:12; Luke 19:41–44 **21:8** [a] Matt. 24:4; Mark 13:5; Eph. 5:6; 2 Thess. 2:3; [1 John 4:1] [1] NU-Text omits *Therefore.* **21:9** [a] Rev. 6:4 **21:10** [a] Matt. 24:7 **21:11** [a] Rev. 6:12 **21:12** [a] Mark 13:9; John 16:2; [Rev. 2:10] [b] Acts 4:3; 5:18; 12:4; 16:24 [c] Acts 25:23 [d] 1 Pet. 2:13 **21:13** [a] [Phil. 1:12–14, 28; 2 Thess. 1:5] **21:14** [a] Matt. 10:19; Mark 13:11; Luke 12:11 **21:15** [a] Acts 6:10 **21:16** [a] Mic. 7:6; Mark 13:12 [b] Acts 7:59; 12:2 **21:17** [a] Matt. 10:22 **21:18** [a] Matt. 10:30; Luke 12:7 **21:20** [a] Matt. 24:15; Mark 13:14 **21:22** [a] Is. 63:4; [Dan. 9:24–27]; Hos. 9:7; [Zech. 11:1] **21:23** [a] Matt. 24:19 **21:24** [a] [Dan. 9:27; 12:7] **21:25** [a] Is. 13:9, 10, 13; Matt. 24:29; Mark 13:24; [2 Pet. 3:10–12] **21:26** [a] Matt. 24:29 **21:27** [a] Dan. 7:13; [Matt. 16:27; 24:30; 26:64]; Mark 13:26; Rev. 1:7; 14:14 **21:28** [a] [Rom. 8:19, 23]

The Parable of the Fig Tree
(Matt. 24:32–35; Mark 13:28–31)

29 [a]Then He spoke to them a parable:
"Look at the fig tree, and all the trees.
30 When they are already budding, you see
and know for yourselves that summer is
now near. 31 So you also, when you see these
things happening, know that the kingdom
of God is near. 32 Assuredly, I say to you, this
generation will by no means pass away till
all things take place. 33 [a]Heaven and earth
will pass away, but My [b]words will by no
means pass away.

The Importance of Watching
(Matt. 24:36–44; Mark 13:32–37)

34 "But [a]take heed to yourselves, lest
your hearts be weighed down with carousing, drunkenness, and [b]cares of this life,
and that Day come on you unexpectedly.
35 For [a]it will come as a snare on all those
who dwell on the face of the whole earth.
36 [a]Watch therefore, and [b]pray always that
you may be counted [c]worthy[1] to escape all
these things that will come to pass, and [d]to
stand before the Son of Man."

37 [a]And in the daytime He was teaching
in the temple, but [b]at night He went out
and stayed on the mountain called Olivet.
38 Then early in the morning all the people
came to Him in the temple to hear Him.

The Plot to Kill Jesus
(Matt. 26:1–5, 14–16; Mark 14:1, 2, 10, 11; John 11:45–53)

22 Now [a]the Feast of Unleavened Bread
drew near, which is called Passover.
2 And [a]the chief priests and the scribes
sought how they might kill Him, for they
feared the people.

3 [a]Then Satan entered Judas, surnamed
Iscariot, who was numbered among the
[b]twelve. 4 So he went his way and conferred
with the chief priests and captains, how
he might betray Him to them. 5 And they
were glad, and [a]agreed to give him money.
6 So he promised and sought opportunity
to [a]betray Him to them in the absence of
the multitude.

Jesus and His Disciples Prepare the Passover

7 [a]Then came the Day of Unleavened
Bread, when the Passover must be killed.
8 And He sent Peter and John, saying, "Go
and prepare the Passover for us, that we
may eat."

9 So they said to Him, "Where do You
want us to prepare?"

10 And He said to them, "Behold, when
you have entered the city, a man will meet
you carrying a pitcher of water; follow him
into the house which he enters. 11 Then you
shall say to the master of the house, 'The
Teacher says to you, "Where is the guest
room where I may eat the Passover with My
disciples?"' 12 Then he will show you a large,
furnished upper room; there make ready."

13 So they went and [a]found it just as He
had said to them, and they prepared the
Passover.

Jesus Institutes the Lord's Supper

14 [a]When the hour had come, He sat
down, and the twelve[1] apostles with Him.
15 Then He said to them, "With *fervent* desire I have desired to eat this Passover with
you before I suffer; 16 for I say to you, I will
no longer eat of it [a]until it is fulfilled in the
kingdom of God."

17 Then He took the cup, and gave thanks,
and said, "Take this and divide *it* among
yourselves; 18 for [a]I say to you,[1] I will not
drink of the fruit of the vine until the kingdom of God comes."

19 [a]And He took bread, gave thanks and
broke *it,* and gave *it* to them, saying, "This
is My [b]body which is given for you; [c]do this
in remembrance of Me."

20 Likewise He also *took* the cup after
supper, saying, [a]"This cup *is* the new covenant in My blood, which is shed for you.
21 [a]But behold, the hand of My betrayer *is*
with Me on the table. 22 [a]And truly the Son

21:29 [a] Matt. 24:32; Mark 13:28 21:33 [a] Is. 51:6; Matt. 24:35; Heb. 1:10, 11; [2 Pet. 3:7, 10, 12] [b] Is. 40:8; Luke 16:17; 1 Pet. 1:24, 25
21:34 [a] Matt. 24:42–44; Mark 4:19; Luke 12:40, 45; Rom. 13:13; 1 Thess. 5:6; 1 Pet. 4:7 [b] Luke 8:14 21:35 [a] 1 Thess. 5:2; [2 Pet. 3:10]; Rev. 3:3; 16:15 21:36 [a] Matt. 24:42; 25:13; Mark 13:33; Luke 12:40 [b] Luke 18:1; [Eph. 6:18]; Col. 4:2; 1 Thess. 5:17 [c] Luke 20:35 [d] Ps. 1:5; [Eph. 6:13]
[1] NU-Text reads *may have strength.* 21:37 [a] John 8:1, 2 [b] Luke 22:39 22:1 [a] Matt. 26:2–5; Mark 14:1, 2 22:2 [a] Ps. 2:2; John 11:47; Acts 4:27 22:3 [a] Matt. 26:14–16; Mark 14:10, 11; John 13:2, 27 [b] Matt. 10:2–4 22:5 [a] Zech. 11:12 22:6 [a] Ps. 41:9 22:7 [a] Matt. 26:17–19; Mark 14:12–16 22:13 [a] Luke 19:32 22:14 [a] Matt. 26:20; Mark 14:17 [1] NU-Text omits *twelve.* 22:16 [a] Luke 14:15; [Acts 10:41; Rev. 19:9]
22:18 [a] Matt. 26:29; Mark 14:25 [1] NU-Text adds *from now on.* 22:19 [a] Matt. 26:26; Mark 14:22 [b] [1 Pet. 2:24] [c] 1 Cor. 11:23–26
22:20 [a] 1 Cor. 10:16 22:21 [a] Ps. 41:9; Matt. 26:21, 23; Mark 14:18; Luke 22:48; John 13:21, 26, 27 22:22 [a] Matt. 26:24

of Man goes [b]as it has been determined, but
woe to that man by whom He is betrayed!"
23[a]Then they began to question among
themselves, which of them it was who
would do this thing.

The Disciples Argue About Greatness

24[a]Now there was also a dispute among
them, as to which of them should be considered the greatest. 25[a]And He said to
them, "The kings of the Gentiles exercise
lordship over them, and those who exercise authority over them are called 'benefactors.' 26[a]But not so *among* you; on the
contrary, [b]he who is greatest among you,
let him be as the younger, and he who gov-
erns as he who serves. 27[a]For who *is* greater,
he who sits at the table, or he who serves?
Is it not he who sits at the table? Yet [b]I am
among you as the One who serves.
28"But you are those who have continued with Me in [a]My trials. 29And [a]I bestow
upon you a kingdom, just as My Father bestowed *one* upon Me, 30that [a]you may eat and
drink at My table in My kingdom, [b]and sit on
thrones judging the twelve tribes of Israel."

Jesus Predicts Peter's Denial
(Matt. 26:31–35; Mark 14:27–31; John 13:36–38)

31And the Lord said,[1] "Simon, Simon! Indeed, [a]Satan has asked for you, that he may
[b]sift *you* as wheat. 32But [a]I have prayed for
you, that your faith should not fail; and
when you have returned to *Me,* [b]strengthen
your brethren."
33But he said to Him, "Lord, I am ready
to go with You, both to prison and to death."
34[a]Then He said, "I tell you, Peter, the
rooster shall not crow this day before you
will deny three times that you know Me."

Supplies for the Road

35[a]And He said to them, "When I sent
you without money bag, knapsack, and sandals, did you lack anything?"
So they said, "Nothing."
36Then He said to them, "But now, he
who has a money bag, let him take *it,* and
likewise a knapsack; and he who has no
sword, let him sell his garment and buy
one. 37For I say to you that this which is
written must still be accomplished in Me:
[a]'And He was numbered with the transgressors.'[1] For the things concerning Me
have an end."
38So they said, "Lord, look, here *are* two
swords."
And He said to them, "It is enough."

The Prayer in the Garden
(Matt. 26:36–46; Mark 14:32–42; John 18:1)

39[a]Coming out, [b]He went to the Mount
of Olives, as He was accustomed, and His
disciples also followed Him. 40[a]When He
came to the place, He said to them, "Pray
that you may not enter into temptation."
41[a]And He was withdrawn from them
about a stone's throw, and He knelt down
and prayed, 42saying, "Father, if it is Your
will, take this cup away from Me; nevertheless [a]not My will, but Yours, be done."
43Then [a]an angel appeared to Him from
heaven, strengthening Him. 44[a]And being
in agony, He prayed more earnestly. Then
His sweat became like great drops of blood
falling down to the ground.[1]
45When He rose up from prayer, and
had come to His disciples, He found them
sleeping from sorrow. 46Then He said to
them, "Why [a]do you sleep? Rise and [b]pray,
lest you enter into temptation."

Betrayal and Arrest in Gethsemane
(Matt. 26:47–56; Mark 14:43–52; John 18:1–11)

47And while He was still speaking, [a]be-
hold, a multitude; and he who was called
[b]Judas, one of the twelve, went before them
and drew near to Jesus to kiss Him. 48But
Jesus said to him, "Judas, are you betraying the Son of Man with a [a]kiss?"
49When those around Him saw what was

22:22 [b] John 17:12; Acts 2:23 **22:23** [a] Matt. 26:22; John 13:22, 25 **22:24** [a] Mark 9:34; Luke 9:46–48 **22:25** [a] [Matt. 20:25–28]; Mark 10:42–45 **22:26** [a] Matt. 20:26; [1 Pet. 5:3] [b] Luke 9:48 **22:27** [a] [Luke 12:37] [b] Matt. 20:28; John 13:13, 14; Phil. 2:7 **22:28** [a] [Heb. 2:18; 4:15] **22:29** [a] Matt. 24:47 **22:30** [a] [Matt. 8:11; Rev. 19:9] [b] Ps. 49:14; [Matt. 19:28; 1 Cor. 6:2; Rev. 3:21] **22:31** [a] 1 Pet. 5:8 [b] Amos 9:9 [1] NU-Text omits *And the Lord said.* **22:32** [a] [John 17:9, 11, 15] [b] John 21:15–17; Acts 1:15; 2:14; 2 Pet. 1:10–15 **22:34** [a] Matt. 26:33–35; Mark 14:29–31; Luke 22:61; John 13:37, 38 **22:35** [a] Matt. 10:9; Mark 6:8; Luke 9:3; 10:4 **22:37** [a] Is. 53:12; Matt. 27:38; Mark 15:28; Luke 22:32 [1] Isaiah 53:12 **22:39** [a] Matt. 26:36; John 18:1 [b] Luke 21:37 **22:40** [a] Matt. 26:36–46; Mark 14:32–42 **22:41** [a] Matt. 26:39; Mark 14:35; [Luke 18:11–14] **22:42** [a] Is. 50:5; John 4:34; 5:30; 6:38; 8:29 **22:43** [a] Matt. 4:11 **22:44** [a] John 12:27; [Heb. 5:7] [1] NU-Text brackets verses 43 and 44 as not in the original text. **22:46** [a] Luke 9:32 [b] 1 Chr. 16:11; Luke 22:40; [Eph. 6:18]; 1 Thess. 5:17 **22:47** [a] Matt. 26:47–56; Mark 14:43–50; John 18:3–11 [b] Ps. 41:9; Matt. 20:18; Luke 9:44; 22:21; Acts 1:16, 17 **22:48** [a] [Prov. 27:6]

going to happen, they said to Him, "Lord,
shall we strike with the sword?" 50 And [a]one
of them struck the servant of the high
priest and cut off his right ear.
51 But Jesus answered and said, "Permit
even this." And He touched his ear and
healed him.
52 [a]Then Jesus said to the chief priests,
captains of the temple, and the elders who
had come to Him, "Have you come out, as
against a [b]robber, with swords and clubs?
53 When I was with you daily in the [a]temple,
you did not try to seize Me. But this is your
[b]hour, and the power of darkness."

Peter Denies Jesus, and Weeps Bitterly
(Matt. 26:69–75; Mark 14:66–72; John 18:13–18, 25–27)

54 [a]Having arrested Him, they led *Him*
and brought Him into the high priest's
house. [b]But Peter followed at a distance.
55 [a]Now when they had kindled a fire in the
midst of the courtyard and sat down together, Peter sat among them. 56 And a certain servant girl, seeing him as he sat by the
fire, looked intently at him and said, "This
man was also with Him."
57 But he denied Him,[1] saying, "Woman,
I do not know Him."
58 [a]And after a little while another saw
him and said, "You also are of them."
But Peter said, "Man, I am not!"
59 [a]Then after about an hour had passed,
another confidently affirmed, saying,
"Surely this *fellow* also was with Him, for
he is a [b]Galilean."
60 But Peter said, "Man, I do not know
what you are saying!"
Immediately, while he was still speaking,
the rooster[1] crowed. 61 And the Lord turned
and looked at Peter. Then [a]Peter remembered the word of the Lord, how He had
said to him, [b]"Before the rooster crows,[1]
you will deny Me three times." 62 So Peter
went out and wept bitterly.

Jesus Mocked and Beaten
(Matt. 26:67, 68; Mark 14:65)

63 [a]Now the men who held Jesus mocked
Him and [b]beat Him. 64 And having blindfolded Him, they [a]struck Him on the face
and asked Him,[1] saying, "Prophesy! Who
is the one who struck You?" 65 And many
other things they blasphemously spoke
against Him.

Jesus Faces the Sanhedrin
(Matt. 26:57–68; Mark 14:61–64; John 18:12–14, 19–24)

66 [a]As soon as it was day, [b]the elders of
the people, both chief priests and scribes,
came together and led Him into their council, saying, 67 [a]"If You are the Christ, tell us."
But He said to them, "If I tell you, you
will [b]by no means believe. 68 And if I also
ask *you,* you will by no means answer Me or
let *Me* go.[1] 69 [a]Hereafter the Son of Man will
sit on the right hand of the power of God."
70 Then they all said, "Are You then the
Son of God?"
So He said to them, [a]"You *rightly* say that
I am."
71 [a]And they said, "What further testimony do we need? For we have heard it
ourselves from His own mouth."

Jesus Handed Over to Pontius Pilate
(Matt. 27:1, 2, 11–14; Mark 15:1–5; John 18:28–38)

23 Then [a]the whole multitude of them
arose and led Him to [b]Pilate. 2 And
they began to [a]accuse Him, saying, "We
found this *fellow* [b]perverting the[1] nation,
and [c]forbidding to pay taxes to Caesar, saying [d]that He Himself is Christ, a King."
3 [a]Then Pilate asked Him, saying, "Are
You the King of the Jews?"
He answered him and said, "*It is as* you
say."
4 So Pilate said to the chief priests and
the crowd, [a]"I find no fault in this Man."

22:50 [a] Matt. 26:51 **22:52** [a] Matt. 26:55 [b] Luke 23:32 **22:53** [a] Luke 19:47, 48 [b] [John 12:27] **22:54** [a] Is. 53:7, 8; Matt. 26:57; Mark 14:53; Luke 9:44; Acts 8:32 [b] Matt. 26:58; Mark 14:54; John 18:15 **22:55** [a] Matt. 26:69–75; Mark 14:66–72; John 18:15, 17, 18 **22:57** [1] NU-Text reads *denied it.* **22:58** [a] Matt. 26:71; Mark 14:69; John 18:25 **22:59** [a] Matt. 26:73; Mark 14:70; John 18:26 [b] Acts 1:11; 2:7 **22:60** [1] NU-Text and M-Text read *a rooster.* **22:61** [a] Matt. 26:75; Mark 14:72 [b] Matt. 26:34, 75; Mark 14:30; Luke 22:34; John 13:38 [1] NU-Text adds *today.* **22:63** [a] Ps. 69:1, 4, 7–9; Matt. 26:67, 68; Mark 14:65; John 18:22 [b] Job 16:10; Is. 50:6; Lam. 3:30 **22:64** [a] Zech. 13:7 [1] NU-Text reads *And having blindfolded Him, they asked Him.* **22:66** [a] Matt. 27:1; Mark 15:1 [b] Ps. 2:2; Acts 4:26 **22:67** [a] Matt. 26:63–66; Mark 14:61–63; Luke 22:67–71; John 18:19–21 [b] Luke 20:5–7 **22:68** [1] NU-Text omits *also* and *Me or let Me go.* **22:69** [a] [Ps. 110:1; Matt. 26:64; Mark 14:62; 16:19]; Acts 2:33; 7:55; Eph. 1:20; Col. 3:1; Heb. 1:3; 8:1 **22:70** [a] Matt. 26:64; 27:11; Mark 14:62; Luke 1:35 **22:71** [a] Matt. 26:65; Mark 14:63; John 19:7 **23:1** [a] Matt. 27:2; Mark 15:1; Luke 18:32; John 18:28 [b] Luke 3:1; 13:1 **23:2** [a] Acts 24:2 [b] Acts 17:7 [c] Matt. 17:27; Mark 12:17 [d] John 19:12 [1] NU-Text reads *our.* **23:3** [a] Matt. 27:11; 1 Tim. 6:13 **23:4** [a] Matt. 27:19; [1 Pet. 2:22]

5But they were the more fierce, saying, "He stirs up the people, teaching throughout all Judea, beginning from [a]Galilee to this place."

Jesus Faces Herod

6When Pilate heard of Galilee,[1] he asked if the Man were a Galilean. 7And as soon as he knew that He belonged to [a]Herod's jurisdiction, he sent Him to Herod, who was also in Jerusalem at that time. 8Now when Herod saw Jesus, [a]he was exceedingly glad; for he had desired for a long *time* to see Him, because [b]he had heard many things about Him, and he hoped to see some miracle done by Him. 9Then he questioned Him with many words, but He answered him [a]nothing. 10And the chief priests and scribes stood and vehemently accused Him. 11[a]Then Herod, with his men of war, treated Him with contempt and mocked *Him,* arrayed Him in a gorgeous robe, and sent Him back to Pilate. 12That very day [a]Pilate and Herod became friends with each other, for previously they had been at enmity with each other.

Taking the Place of Barabbas
(Matt. 27:15–26; Mark 15:6–15; John 18:38—19:16)

13[a]Then Pilate, when he had called together the chief priests, the rulers, and the people, 14said to them, [a]"You have brought this Man to me, as one who misleads the people. And indeed, [b]having examined *Him* in your presence, I have found no fault in this Man concerning those things of which you accuse Him; 15no, neither did Herod, for I sent you back to him;[1] and indeed nothing deserving of death has been done by Him. 16[a]I will therefore chastise Him and release *Him*" 17[a](for it was necessary for him to release one to them at the feast).[1]

18And [a]they all cried out at once, saying, "Away with this *Man,* and release to us Barabbas"— 19who had been thrown into prison for a certain rebellion made in the city, and for murder.

20Pilate, therefore, wishing to release Jesus, again called out to them. 21But they shouted, saying, "Crucify *Him,* crucify Him!"

22Then he said to them the third time, "Why, what evil has He done? I have found no reason for death in Him. I will therefore chastise Him and let *Him* go."

23But they were insistent, demanding with loud voices that He be crucified. And the voices of these men and of the chief priests prevailed.[1] 24So [a]Pilate gave sentence that it should be as they requested. 25[a]And he released to them[1] the one they requested, who for rebellion and murder had been thrown into prison; but he delivered Jesus to their will.

The King on a Cross
(Matt. 27:32–44; Mark 15:21–32; John 19:17–24)

26[a]Now as they led Him away, they laid hold of a certain man, Simon a Cyrenian, who was coming from the country, and on him they laid the cross that he might bear *it* after Jesus.

27And a great multitude of the people followed Him, and women who also mourned and lamented Him. 28But Jesus, turning to them, said, "Daughters of Jerusalem, do not weep for Me, but weep for yourselves and for your children. 29[a]For indeed the days are coming in which they will say, 'Blessed *are* the barren, wombs that never bore, and breasts which never nursed!' 30Then they will begin [a]'to say to the mountains, "Fall on us!" and to the hills, "Cover us!" '[1] 31[a]For if they do these things in the green wood, what will be done in the dry?"

32[a]There were also two others, criminals, led with Him to be put to death. 33And [a]when they had come to the place called Calvary, there they crucified Him, and the criminals, one on the right hand and the

23:5 [a] John 7:41 23:6 [1] NU-Text omits *of Galilee.* 23:7 [a] Matt. 14:1; Mark 6:14; Luke 3:1; 9:7; 13:31 23:8 [a] Luke 9:9 [b] Matt. 14:1; Mark 6:14 23:9 [a] Is. 53:7; Matt. 27:12, 14; Mark 15:5; John 19:9 23:11 [a] Is. 53:3 23:12 [a] Acts 4:26, 27 23:13 [a] Matt. 27:23; Mark 15:14; John 18:38 23:14 [a] Luke 23:1, 2 [b] Luke 23:4 23:15 [1] NU-Text reads *for he sent Him back to us.* 23:16 [a] Matt. 27:26; Mark 15:15; Luke 23:22; John 19:1; Acts 16:37 23:17 [a] Matt. 27:15; Mark 15:6; John 18:39 [1] NU-Text omits verse 17. 23:18 [a] Is. 53:3; Acts 3:13–15 23:23 [1] NU-Text omits *and of the chief priests.* 23:24 [a] Matt. 27:26; Mark 15:15; John 19:16 23:25 [a] Is. 53:8 [1] NU-Text and M-Text omit *to them.* 23:26 [a] Matt. 27:32; Mark 15:21; John 19:17 23:29 [a] Matt. 24:19; Luke 21:23 23:30 [a] Is. 2:19; Hos. 10:8; Rev. 6:16, 17; 9:6 [1] Hosea 10:8 23:31 [a] [Prov. 11:31; Jer. 25:29]; Ezek. 20:47; 21:3, 4; 1 Pet. 4:17 23:32 [a] Is. 53:9, 12; Matt. 27:38; Mark 15:27; John 19:18 23:33 [a] Ps. 22:16–18; Matt. 27:33–44; Mark 15:22–32; John 19:17–24

other on the left. 34 Then Jesus said, "Father, [a]forgive them, for [b]they do not know what they do."[1]

And [c]they divided His garments and cast lots. 35 And [a]the people stood looking on. But even the [b]rulers with them sneered, saying, "He saved others; let Him save Himself if He is the Christ, the chosen of God."

36 The soldiers also mocked Him, coming and offering Him [a]sour wine, 37 and saying, "If You are the King of the Jews, save Yourself."

38 [a]And an inscription also was written over Him in letters of Greek, Latin, and Hebrew:[1]

THIS IS THE KING OF THE JEWS.

39 [a]Then one of the criminals who were hanged blasphemed Him, saying, "If You are the Christ,[1] save Yourself and us."

40 But the other, answering, rebuked him, saying, "Do you not even fear God, seeing you are under the same condemnation? 41 And we indeed justly, for we receive the due reward of our deeds; but this Man has done [a]nothing wrong." 42 Then he said to Jesus, "Lord,[1] remember me when You come into Your kingdom."

43 And Jesus said to him, "Assuredly, I say to you, today you will be with Me in [a]Paradise."

Jesus Dies on the Cross
(Matt. 27:45–56; Mark 15:33–41; John 19:25–30)

44 [a]Now it was[1] about the sixth hour, and there was darkness over all the earth until the ninth hour. 45 Then the sun was darkened,[1] and [a]the veil of the temple was torn in two. 46 And when Jesus had cried out with a loud voice, He said, "Father, [a]'into Your hands I commit My spirit.'"[1] [b]Having said this, He breathed His last.

47 [a]So when the centurion saw what had happened, he glorified God, saying, "Certainly this was a righteous Man!"

48 And the whole crowd who came together to that sight, seeing what had been done, beat their breasts and returned. 49 [a]But all His acquaintances, and the women who followed Him from Galilee, stood at a distance, watching these things.

Jesus Buried in Joseph's Tomb
(Matt. 27:57–61; Mark 15:42–47; John 19:38–42)

50 [a]Now behold, *there was* a man named Joseph, a council member, a good and just man. 51 He had not consented to their decision and deed. *He was* from Arimathea, a city of the Jews, [a]who himself was also waiting[1] for the kingdom of God. 52 This man went to Pilate and asked for the body of Jesus. 53 [a]Then he took it down, wrapped it in linen, and laid it in a tomb *that was* hewn out of the rock, where no one had ever lain before. 54 That day was [a]the Preparation, and the Sabbath drew near.

55 And the women [a]who had come with Him from Galilee followed after, and [b]they observed the tomb and how His body was laid. 56 Then they returned and [a]prepared spices and fragrant oils. And they rested on the Sabbath [b]according to the commandment.

He Is Risen
(Matt. 28:1–10; Mark 16:1–8; John 20:1–10)

24 Now [a]on the first *day* of the week, very early in the morning, they, and certain *other women* with them,[1] came to the tomb [b]bringing the spices which they had prepared. 2 [a]But they found the stone rolled away from the tomb. 3 [a]Then they went in and did not find the body of the Lord Jesus. 4 And it happened, as they were greatly[1] perplexed about this, that

---

23:34 [a] Ps. 109:4; [Matt. 5:44]; Acts 7:60; 1 Cor. 4:12 [b] Acts 3:17 [c] Ps. 22:18; Matt. 27:35; Mark 15:24; John 19:23 [1] NU-Text brackets the first sentence as a later addition. 23:35 [a] Ps. 22:17; [Zech. 12:10] [b] Ps. 22:8; Matt. 27:39; Mark 15:29 23:36 [a] Ps. 69:21 23:38 [a] Matt. 27:37; Mark 15:26; John 19:19 [1] NU-Text omits *written* and *in letters of Greek, Latin, and Hebrew.* 23:39 [a] Matt. 27:44; Mark 15:32 [1] NU-Text reads *Are You not the Christ?* 23:41 [a] [2 Cor. 5:21; Heb. 7:26; 1 Pet. 2:21–24] 23:42 [1] NU-Text reads *And he said, "Jesus, remember me.* 23:43 [a] [2 Cor. 12:4; Eph. 4:8–10; Rev. 2:7] 23:44 [a] Amos 8:9; Matt. 27:45–56; Mark 15:33–41 [1] NU-Text adds *already.* 23:45 [a] Ex. 26:31–33; Zech. 11:10; Matt. 27:51; Mark 15:38; [Heb. 9:3; 10:19, 20] [1] NU-Text reads *obscured.* 23:46 [a] Ps. 31:5; 1 Pet. 2:23 [b] Dan. 9:26; Zech. 11:10, 11; Matt. 27:50; Mark 15:37; Luke 9:22; 18:33; John 19:30 [1] Psalm 31:5 23:47 [a] Matt. 27:54; Mark 15:39 23:49 [a] Ps. 38:11; Matt. 27:55; Mark 15:40; John 16:20–22; 19:25 23:50 [a] Matt. 27:57–61; Mark 15:42–47; John 19:38–42 23:51 [a] Mark 15:43; Luke 2:25, 38 [1] NU-Text reads *who was waiting.* 23:53 [a] Is. 53:9; Matt. 27:59; Mark 15:46 23:54 [a] Matt. 27:62; Mark 15:42 23:55 [a] Luke 8:2 [b] Mark 15:47 23:56 [a] Mark 16:1; Luke 24:1 [b] Ex. 20:10; Deut. 5:14 24:1 [a] Matt. 28:1–8; Mark 16:1–8; John 20:1–8 [b] Luke 23:56 [1] NU-Text omits *and certain other women with them.* 24:2 [a] Matt. 28:2; Mark 16:4 24:3 [a] Mark 16:5 24:4 [1] NU-Text omits *greatly.*

[a]behold, two men stood by them in shining garments. 5Then, as they were afraid
and bowed *their* faces to the earth, they
said to them, "Why do you seek the living
among the dead? 6He is not here, but is
risen! [a]Remember how He spoke to you
when He was still in Galilee, 7saying, 'The
Son of Man must be [a]delivered into the
hands of sinful men, and be crucified, and
the third day rise again.'"

8And [a]they remembered His words.
9[a]Then they returned from the tomb and
told all these things to the eleven and to all
the rest. 10It was Mary Magdalene, [a]Joanna,
Mary *the mother* of James, and the other
women with them, who told these things
to the apostles. 11[a]And their words seemed
to them like idle tales, and they did not
believe them. 12[a]But Peter arose and ran
to the tomb; and stooping down, he saw
the linen cloths lying[1] by themselves; and
he departed, marveling to himself at what
had happened.

The Road to Emmaus
(Mark 16:12, 13)

13[a]Now behold, two of them were traveling that same day to a village called
Emmaus, which was seven miles[1] from
Jerusalem. 14And they talked together
of all these things which had happened.
15So it was, while they conversed and reasoned, that [a]Jesus Himself drew near and
went with them. 16But [a]their eyes were restrained, so that they did not know Him.

17And He said to them, "What kind of
conversation *is* this that you have with one
another as you walk and are sad?"[1]

18Then the one [a]whose name was Cle-
opas answered and said to Him, "Are You
the only stranger in Jerusalem, and have
You not known the things which happened
there in these days?"

19And He said to them, "What things?"

So they said to Him, "The things concerning Jesus of Nazareth, [a]who was a
Prophet [b]mighty in deed and word before
God and all the people, 20[a]and how the chief
priests and our rulers delivered Him to be
condemned to death, and crucified Him.
21But we were hoping [a]that it was He who
was going to redeem Israel. Indeed, besides all this, today is the third day since
these things happened. 22Yes, and [a]certain
women of our company, who arrived at the
tomb early, astonished us. 23When they did
not find His body, they came saying that
they had also seen a vision of angels who
said He was alive. 24And [a]certain of those
who were with us went to the tomb and
found *it* just as the women had said; but
Him they did not see."

25Then He said to them, "O foolish ones,
and slow of heart to believe in all that the
prophets have spoken! 26[a]Ought not the
Christ to have suffered these things and
to enter into His [b]glory?" 27And beginning
at [a]Moses and [b]all the Prophets, He expounded to them in all the Scriptures the
things concerning Himself.

The Disciples' Eyes Opened

28Then they drew near to the village
where they were going, and [a]He indicated
that He would have gone farther. 29But
[a]they constrained Him, saying, [b]"Abide
with us, for it is toward evening, and the
day is far spent." And He went in to stay
with them.

30Now it came to pass, as [a]He sat at the
table with them, that He took bread, blessed
and broke *it,* and gave it to them. 31Then
their eyes were opened and they knew Him;
and He vanished from their sight.

32And they said to one another, "Did not
our heart burn within us while He talked
with us on the road, and while He opened
the Scriptures to us?" 33So they rose up that
very hour and returned to Jerusalem, and
found the eleven and those *who were* with
them gathered together, 34saying, "The
Lord is risen indeed, and [a]has appeared to
Simon!" 35And they told about the things
that had happened on the road, and how

24:4 [a] John 20:12; Acts 1:10 **24:6** [a] Matt. 16:21; Mark 8:31; Luke 9:22 **24:7** [a] Hos. 6:1, 2; Luke 9:44; 11:29, 30; 18:31–33 **24:8** [a] Luke 9:22, 44; John 2:19–22 **24:9** [a] Matt. 28:8; Mark 16:10 **24:10** [a] Luke 8:3 **24:11** [a] Luke 24:25 **24:12** [a] John 20:3–6 [1] NU-Text omits *lying.* **24:13** [a] Mark 16:12 [1] Literally *sixty stadia* **24:15** [a] [Matt. 18:20] **24:16** [a] John 20:14; 21:4 **24:17** [1] NU-Text reads *as you walk? And they stood still, looking sad.* **24:18** [a] John 19:25 **24:19** [a] Matt. 21:11; Luke 7:16; John 3:2; Acts 2:22 [b] Acts 7:22 **24:20** [a] Luke 23:1; Acts 13:27, 28 **24:21** [a] Luke 1:68; 2:38; [Acts 1:6] **24:22** [a] Matt. 28:8; Mark 16:10; Luke 24:9, 10 **24:24** [a] Luke 24:12 **24:26** [a] Acts 17:2, 3; [Heb. 2:9, 10] [b] [1 Pet. 1:10–12] **24:27** [a] [Gen. 3:15; 12:3; Num. 21:9; Deut. 18:15]; John 5:46 [b] [Ps. 16:9, 10; 22; 132:11; Is. 7:14; 9:6; Jer. 23:5; 33:14, 15; Ezek. 34:23; 37:25; Dan. 9:24]; Mic. 7:20; [Mal. 3:1; 4:2]; John 1:45; 5:39; [Rom. 1:1–6] **24:28** [a] Gen. 32:26; 42:7; Mark 6:48 **24:29** [a] Gen. 19:2, 3; Acts 16:15 [b] [John 14:23] **24:30** [a] Matt. 14:19; Mark 8:6; Luke 9:16 **24:34** [a] 1 Cor. 15:5

He was known to them in the breaking of
bread.

Jesus Appears to His Disciples
(John 20:19–23; Acts 1:3–5; 1 Cor. 15:5)

36[a]Now as they said these things, Jesus
Himself stood in the midst of them, and
said to them, "Peace to you." 37But they
were terrified and frightened, and supposed they had seen [a]a spirit. 38And He
said to them, "Why are you troubled? And
why do doubts arise in your hearts? 39Be-
hold My hands and My feet, that it is I Myself. [a]Handle Me and see, for a [b]spirit does
not have flesh and bones as you see I have."
40When He had said this, He showed
them His hands and His feet.[1] 41But while
they still did not believe [a]for joy, and marveled, He said to them, [b]"Have you any
food here?" 42So they gave Him a piece of a
broiled fish and some honeycomb.[1] 43[a]And
He took *it* and ate in their presence.

The Scriptures Opened

44Then He said to them, [a]"These *are* the
words which I spoke to you while I was still
with you, that all things must be fulfilled
which were written in the Law of Moses
and *the* Prophets and *the* Psalms concerning Me." 45And [a]He opened their understanding, that they might comprehend the
Scriptures.
46Then He said to them, [a]"Thus it is written, and thus it was necessary for the Christ
to suffer and to rise[1] from the dead the third
day, 47and that repentance and [a]remission
of sins should be preached in His name [b]to
all nations, beginning at Jerusalem. 48And
[a]you are witnesses of these things. 49[a]Be-
hold, I send the Promise of My Father upon
you; but tarry in the city of Jerusalem[1] until
you are endued with power from on high."

The Ascension
(Mark 16:19, 20; Acts 1:9)

50And He led them out [a]as far as Bethany, and He lifted up His hands and blessed
them. 51[a]Now it came to pass, while He
blessed them, that He was parted from
them and carried up into heaven. 52[a]And
they worshiped Him, and returned to Jerusalem with great joy, 53and were continually [a]in the temple praising and[1] blessing
God. Amen.[2]

24:36 [a] Mark 16:14; John 20:19; 1 Cor. 15:5 24:37 [a] Matt. 14:26; Mark 6:49 24:39 [a] John 20:20, 27; 1 John 1:1 [b] [1 Cor. 15:50] 24:40 [1] Some printed New Testaments omit this verse. It is found in nearly all Greek manuscripts. 24:41 [a] Gen. 45:26 [b] John 21:5 24:42 [1] NU-Text omits *and some honeycomb.* 24:43 [a] Acts 10:39–41 24:44 [a] Matt. 16:21; 17:22; 20:18; Mark 8:31; Luke 9:22; 18:31 24:45 [a] Acts 16:14; 1 John 5:20 24:46 [a] Ps. 22; Hos. 6:2; Luke 11:29, 30; Acts 17:3 [1] NU-Text reads *written, that the Christ should suffer and rise.* 24:47 [a] Dan. 9:24; Acts 5:31; 10:43; 13:38; 26:18 [b] [Ps. 22:27; Jer. 31:34; Mic. 4:2] 24:48 [a] [Acts 1:8]; 1 Pet. 5:1 24:49 [a] Is. 44:3; Joel 2:28; Acts 2:4 [1] NU-Text omits *of Jerusalem.* 24:50 [a] Matt. 21:17; Acts 1:12 24:51 [a] Ps. 68:18; 110:1; Mark 16:19; Acts 1:9–11 24:52 [a] Matt. 28:9 24:53 [a] Acts 2:46 [1] NU-Text omits *praising and.* [2] NU-Text omits *Amen.*

THE GOSPEL ACCORDING TO

JOHN

OVERVIEW

The final of the four Gospels carries the name of the apostle John, which in Hebrew means "Yahweh has been gracious." He is often referred to as the "disciple whom Jesus loved" (John 21:7, 20). Surely, Jesus loved each of His disciples, but there is certainly a special intimacy that characterized the relationship between this disciple and his Lord. John was originally a follower of John the Baptist before becoming a disciple of Jesus. He was likely a young man during Jesus' earthly ministry, eventually writing his Gospel, his epistles, and the Book of Revelation around AD 90.

Although it follows a different structure and has the most unique content, John's Gospel has many similar themes to the Synoptic Gospels in describing the person and ministry of Jesus. The divine nature of Jesus is the most definitive theme in John's Gospel.

The prologue of John's Gospel is a preview of all twenty-one chapters of the book. The author intentionally starts the Gospel with the same words used to start the Book of Genesis: "In the beginning." John wanted to establish that Jesus was present at the beginning of creation and then depict the life, ministry, death, and resurrection of Jesus as God's way of restoring what He had intended originally in Eden. As God created by the spoken word, Jesus is the Word or the Logos. He is the Word made flesh.

In the way John presented Jesus, he clarified the basis of the triune nature of the God. We serve one God in three persons: God the Father, God the Son, and God the Holy Spirit. In this way, John wanted to establish quickly and firmly the identity and nature of Christ for his readers: Christ is God (see John 1:1); Christ is the Word (see v. 1); Christ is Creator (see v. 3); Christ is life (see v. 4); Christ is the light that shines in darkness (see v. 5).

John continued to reveal the identity of Christ throughout the Gospel with the seven powerful "I am" statements of Jesus: "I am the bread of life" (6:35); "I am the light of the world" (8:12); "I am the door of the sheep" (10:7); "I am the good shepherd" (10:11); "I am the resurrection and the life" (11:25); "I am the way, the truth, and the life" (14:6); and "I am the true vine, and My Father is the vinedresser" (15:1). These metaphors underscore Jesus' divine nature and authority. In addition, John chose seven signs, or attesting miracles, to point to Christ's divine character: turning water into wine (see 2:1–10), healing a boy (see 4:46–54), healing a man with an infirmity (see 5:1–9), feeding more than five thousand people (see 6:1–14), walking on water (see 6:15–21), healing a blind man (see 9:1–38), and raising Lazarus (see 11:1–44).

John depicts that "the Word was God" (1:1) but also that "the Word became flesh" (1:14). John demonstrates the humanity of Jesus in His weariness (see 4:6), thirst (see 4:7), dependence (see 5:19), grief (see 11:35), troubled soul (see 12:27), and anguish and death (see 19:1–37).

BREATHE IT IN

There was a great deal of confusion during Jesus' lifetime about His identity, which John sought to clear up in his Gospel. A profound account found in Matthew, Mark, and Luke also speaks to this issue. Jesus asked His disciples who people said He was. They answered that some said

He was John the Baptist, others said Elijah, and some said He was Jeremiah or one of the other prophets. Jesus responded to their answer with a follow-up question about who *they* said He was. Peter affirmed that Jesus is the Christ, the Son of the living God. This is precisely what John wanted to bear witness to: Jesus is God wrapped in flesh.

The city of Jerusalem provides a stark reminder of our need to define who Jesus is clearly and carefully. Three of the world's largest religions all make a historic claim to the sanctity of Jerusalem in their faith tradition. In today's Jerusalem, there are Jewish, Muslim, and Christian residents. A Muslim temple rests on the site of the former Jewish temple. Hasidic Jews in traditional regalia pray at the Wailing Wall. And finally, the Church of the Holy Sepulchre stands on the approximate site where Jesus was crucified. People in Jerusalem from each of these religions are familiar with Jesus. However, not everyone in today's Jerusalem accepts Jesus as the King of kings and the Lord of lords. Each person must individually, clearly, and carefully decide who Jesus is.

Further still, people all over the world say nice things about Jesus. For example, Gandhi, although not a Christian, admired the moral teaching of the Sermon on the Mount. Like Gandhi, there are people who see Christ's example and teachings as helpful but stop short of affirming His divinity. For true believers in Christ, however, it is not enough to acknowledge Jesus as a teacher. It is not enough to define Jesus as a prophet. It is insufficient to regard Him as simply a moral example. As you read the Gospels, it is necessary to settle the issue of who Christ really is to you and not just who Christ is to the world. Who is Christ to you? How will you describe Christ to your children and the people you love?

THE GOSPEL ACCORDING TO

JOHN

The Eternal Word
(Gen. 1:1—2:3)

1 In the beginning [a]was the Word, and
the [b]Word was [c]with God, and the Word
was [d]God. 2 [a]He was in the beginning with
God. 3 [a]All things were made through Him,
and without Him nothing was made that
was made. 4 [a]In Him was life, and [b]the life
was the light of men. 5 And [a]the light shines
in the darkness, and the darkness did not
comprehend[1] it.

John's Witness: The True Light

6 There was a [a]man sent from God, whose
name *was* John. 7 This man came for a [a]wit-
ness, to bear witness of the Light, that all
through him might [b]believe. 8 He was not
that Light, but *was sent* to bear witness of
that [a]Light. 9 [a]That was the true Light which
gives light to every man coming into the
world.[1]

10 He was in the world, and the world was
made through Him, and [a]the world did not
know Him. 11 [a]He came to His own,[1] and His
own[2] did not receive Him. 12 But [a]as many
as received Him, to them He gave the right
to become children of God, to those who
believe in His name: 13 [a]who were born, not
of blood, nor of the will of the flesh, nor of
the will of man, but of God.

The Word Becomes Flesh

14 [a]And the Word [b]became [c]flesh and
dwelt among us, and [d]we beheld His glory,
the glory as of the only begotten of the Father, [e]full of grace and truth.

15 [a]John bore witness of Him and cried
out, saying, "This was He of whom I said,
[b]'He who comes after me is preferred before me, [c]for He was before me.'"

16 And[1] of His [a]fullness we have all received, and grace for grace. 17 For [a]the law
was given through Moses, *but* [b]grace and
[c]truth came through Jesus Christ. 18 [a]No one
has seen God at any time. [b]The only begotten Son,[1] who is in the bosom of the Father,
He has declared *Him*.

A Voice in the Wilderness
(Matt. 3:1–12; Mark 1:1–8; Luke 3:1–20)

19 Now this is [a]the testimony of John,
when the Jews sent priests and Levites
from Jerusalem to ask him, "Who are
you?"

20 [a]He confessed, and did not deny, but
confessed, "I am not the Christ."

21 And they asked him, "What then? Are
you Elijah?"

He said, "I am not."

"Are you [a]the Prophet?"

And he answered, "No."

22 Then they said to him, "Who are you,
that we may give an answer to those who
sent us? What do you say about yourself?"

23 He said: [a]"I *am*

[b]'The voice of one crying
in the wilderness:

1:1 [a] Gen. 1:1; [Col. 1:17]; 1 John 1:1 [b] [John 1:14]; Rev. 19:13 [c] [John 17:5; 1 John 1:2] [d] [1 John 5:20] **1:2** [a] Gen. 1:1 **1:3** [a] Ps. 33:6; [Eph. 3:9; Col. 1:16, 17; Heb. 1:2] **1:4** [a] [1 John 5:11] [b] John 8:12; 9:5; 12:46 **1:5** [a] [John 3:19] [1] Or *overcome* **1:6** [a] Mal. 3:1; Matt. 3:1–17; Mark 1:1–11; Luke 3:1–22 **1:7** [a] John 3:25–36; 5:33–35 [b] [John 3:16] **1:8** [a] Is. 9:2; 49:6 **1:9** [a] Is. 49:6 [1] Or *That was the true Light which, coming into the world, gives light to every man.* **1:10** [a] Acts 13:27; 1 Cor. 8:6; Col. 1:16; Heb. 1:2 **1:11** [a] Is. 53:3; [Luke 19:14] [1] That is, His own things or domain [2] That is, His own people **1:12** [a] [John 11:52]; Gal. 3:26 **1:13** [a] [John 3:5]; James 1:18; [1 Pet. 1:23; 1 John 2:29; 3:9] **1:14** [a] Matt. 1:16; Rev. 19:13 [b] Rom. 1:3; Gal. 4:4; Phil. 2:7; 1 Tim. 3:16; Heb. 2:14; 1 John 1:1; 4:2; 2 John 7 [c] Heb. 2:11 [d] Is. 40:5; 2 Pet. 1:16–18 [e] [John 8:32; 14:6; 18:37]; Col. 1:19 **1:15** [a] Mal. 3:1; John 3:32 [b] [Matt. 3:11] [c] [Col. 1:17] **1:16** [a] [Eph. 1:23; 3:19; 4:13; Col. 1:19; 2:9] [1] NU-Text reads *For.* **1:17** [a] [Ex. 20:1] [b] John 1:14; [Rom. 5:21; 6:14] [c] [John 8:32; 14:6; 18:37] **1:18** [a] Ex. 33:20; Matt. 11:27; 1 Tim. 6:16 [b] Ps. 2:7; John 3:16, 18; 1 John 4:9 [1] NU-Text reads *only begotten God.* **1:19** [a] John 5:33 **1:20** [a] Luke 3:15; John 3:28; Acts 13:25 **1:21** [a] Deut. 18:15, 18; Matt. 21:11; John 6:14; 7:40 **1:23** [a] Matt. 3:3 [b] Is. 40:3; Mal. 3:1

"Make straight the way
of the LORD,"'[1]
as the prophet Isaiah said."

24Now those who were sent were from
the Pharisees. 25And they asked him, saying, "Why then do you baptize if you are
not the Christ, nor Elijah, nor the Prophet?"

26John answered them, saying, [a]"I baptize with water, [b]but there stands One
among you whom you do not know. 27[a]It
is He who, coming after me, is preferred
before me, whose sandal strap I am not
worthy to loose."

28These things were done [a]in Bethabara[1]
beyond the Jordan, where John was baptizing.

The Lamb of God
(Matt. 3:13–17; Mark 1:9–11; Luke 3:21, 22)

29The next day John saw Jesus coming toward him, and said, "Behold! [a]The
Lamb of God [b]who takes away the sin of the
world! 30This is He of whom I said, 'After me
comes a Man who is preferred before me,
for He was before me.' 31I did not know Him;
but that He should be revealed to Israel,
[a]therefore I came baptizing with water."

32[a]And John bore witness, saying, "I saw
the Spirit descending from heaven like a
dove, and He remained upon Him. 33I did
not know Him, but He who sent me to baptize with water said to me, 'Upon whom you
see the Spirit descending, and remaining
on Him, [a]this is He who baptizes with the
Holy Spirit.' 34And I have seen and testified
that this is the [a]Son of God."

The First Disciples

35Again, the next day, John stood with
two of his disciples. 36And looking at Jesus
as He walked, he said, [a]"Behold the Lamb
of God!"

37The two disciples heard him speak,
and they [a]followed Jesus. 38Then Jesus
turned, and seeing them following, said
to them, "What do you seek?"

They said to Him, "Rabbi" (which is to
say, when translated, Teacher), "where are
You staying?"

39He said to them, "Come and see." They
came and saw where He was staying, and
remained with Him that day (now it was
about the tenth hour).

40One of the two who heard John *speak,*
and followed Him, was [a]Andrew, Simon
Peter's brother. 41He first found his own
brother Simon, and said to him, "We have
found the Messiah" (which is translated,
the Christ). 42And he brought him to Jesus.

Now when Jesus looked at him, He said,
"You are Simon the son of Jonah.[1] [a]You
shall be called Cephas" (which is translated, A Stone).

Philip and Nathanael

43The following day Jesus wanted to go
to Galilee, and He found [a]Philip and said to
him, "Follow Me." 44Now [a]Philip was from
Bethsaida, the city of Andrew and Peter.
45Philip found [a]Nathanael and said to him,
"We have found Him of whom [b]Moses in the
law, and also the [c]prophets, wrote—Jesus
[d]of Nazareth, the [e]son of Joseph."

46And Nathanael said to him, [a]"Can anything good come out of Nazareth?"

Philip said to him, "Come and see."

47Jesus saw Nathanael coming toward
Him, and said of him, "Behold, [a]an Israelite indeed, in whom is no deceit!"

48Nathanael said to Him, "How do You
know me?"

Jesus answered and said to him, "Before
Philip called you, when you were under the
fig tree, I saw you."

49Nathanael answered and said to Him,
"Rabbi, [a]You are the Son of God! You are
[b]the King of Israel!"

50Jesus answered and said to him, "Because I said to you, 'I saw you under the fig
tree,' do you believe? You will see greater
things than these." 51And He said to him,
"Most assuredly, I say to you, [a]hereafter[1]
you shall see heaven open, and the angels

1:23 [1] Isaiah 40:3 1:26 [a] Matt. 3:11; [Mark 1:8; Luke 3:16; Acts 1:5] [b] Mal. 3:1; John 4:10; 8:19; 9:30; Acts 13:27 1:27 [a] [John 3:31]; Acts 19:4; [Col. 1:17] 1:28 [a] Judg. 7:24 [1] NU-Text and M-Text read *Bethany.* 1:29 [a] [Ex. 12:3]; Acts 8:32; [1 Pet. 1:19]; Rev. 5:6–14 [b] [Is. 53:11; 1 Cor. 15:3; Gal. 1:4; 1 Pet. 2:24; 1 John 2:2; Rev. 1:5] 1:31 [a] Mal. 3:1; Matt. 3:6 1:32 [a] Is. 42:1; 61:1; Matt. 3:16; Mark 1:10; Luke 3:22 1:33 [a] Matt. 3:11; Mark 1:8; Luke 3:16; Acts 1:5 1:34 [a] Ps. 2:7; Luke 1:35; John 11:27 1:36 [a] John 1:29 1:37 [a] Matt. 4:20, 22 1:40 [a] Matt. 4:18; Mark 1:29; 13:3; John 6:8; 12:22 1:42 [a] Matt. 16:18 [1] NU-Text reads *John.* 1:43 [a] Matt. 10:3; John 6:5; 12:21, 22; 14:8, 9 1:44 [a] John 12:21 1:45 [a] John 21:2 [b] [Gen. 3:15; Deut. 18:18]; Luke 24:27 [c] [Is. 4:2; 7:14; 9:6; Mic. 5:2; Zech. 6:12]; Luke 24:27 [d] [Matt. 2:23]; Luke 2:4 [e] Luke 3:23 1:46 [a] John 7:41, 42, 52 1:47 [a] Ps. 32:2; 73:1 1:49 [a] Ps. 2:7; Matt. 14:33; Luke 1:35 [b] Matt. 21:5 1:51 [a] Gen. 28:12; [Luke 2:9, 13]; Acts 1:10; 7:55, 56 [1] NU-Text omits *hereafter.*

of God ascending and descending upon
the Son of Man."

Water Turned to Wine

2 On the third day there was a [a]wedding
in [b]Cana of Galilee, and the [c]mother of
Jesus was there. 2Now both Jesus and His
disciples were invited to the wedding. 3And
when they ran out of wine, the mother of
Jesus said to Him, "They have no wine."
4Jesus said to her, [a]"Woman, [b]what does
your concern have to do with Me? [c]My hour
has not yet come."
5His mother said to the servants, "Whatever He says to you, do *it*."
6Now there were set there six waterpots
of stone, [a]according to the manner of purification of the Jews, containing twenty or
thirty gallons apiece. 7Jesus said to them,
"Fill the waterpots with water." And they
filled them up to the brim. 8And He said to
them, "Draw *some* out now, and take *it* to
the master of the feast." And they took *it*.
9When the master of the feast had tasted
[a]the water that was made wine, and did not
know where it came from (but the servants
who had drawn the water knew), the master
of the feast called the bridegroom. 10And
he said to him, "Every man at the beginning sets out the good wine, and when the
guests have well drunk, then the inferior.
You have kept the good wine until now!"
11This [a]beginning of signs Jesus did in
Cana of Galilee, [b]and manifested His glory;
and His disciples believed in Him.
12After this He went down to [a]Caper-
naum, He, His mother, [b]His brothers, and
His disciples; and they did not stay there
many days.

Jesus Cleanses the Temple
(Matt. 21:12–17; Mark 11:15–19; Luke 19:45–48)

13[a]Now the Passover of the Jews was at
hand, and Jesus went up to Jerusalem.
14[a]And He found in the temple those who
sold oxen and sheep and doves, and the
money changers doing business. 15When
He had made a whip of cords, He drove
them all out of the temple, with the sheep
and the oxen, and poured out the changers'
money and overturned the tables. 16And He
said to those who sold doves, "Take these
things away! Do not make [a]My Father's
house a house of merchandise!" 17Then His
disciples remembered that it was written,
[a]"Zeal for Your house has eaten[1] Me up."[2]
18So the Jews answered and said to Him,
[a]"What sign do You show to us, since You
do these things?"
19Jesus answered and said to them, [a]"Destroy this temple, and in three days I will
raise it up."
20Then the Jews said, "It has taken forty-
six years to build this temple, and will You
raise it up in three days?"
21But He was speaking [a]of the temple of
His body. 22Therefore, when He had risen
from the dead, [a]His disciples remembered
that He had said this to them;[1] and they believed the Scripture and the word which
Jesus had said.

The Discerner of Hearts

23Now when He was in Jerusalem at the
Passover, during the feast, many believed
in His name when they saw the [a]signs which
He did. 24But Jesus did not commit Himself
to them, because He [a]knew all *men*, 25and
had no need that anyone should testify of
man, for [a]He knew what was in man.

The New Birth

3 There was a man of the Pharisees
named Nicodemus, a ruler of the Jews.
2[a]This man came to Jesus by night and
said to Him, "Rabbi, we know that You are
a teacher come from God; for [b]no one can
do these signs that You do unless [c]God is
with him."
3Jesus answered and said to him, "Most
assuredly, I say to you, [a]unless one is born
again, he cannot see the kingdom of God."
4Nicodemus said to Him, "How can a
man be born when he is old? Can he enter

2:1 [a] [Heb. 13:4] [b] John 4:46 [c] John 19:25 **2:4** [a] John 19:26 [b] 2 Sam. 16:10 [c] John 7:6, 8, 30; 8:20 **2:6** [a] Matt. 15:2; [Mark 7:3; Luke 11:39]; John 3:25 **2:9** [a] John 4:46 **2:11** [a] John 4:54 [b] [John 1:14] **2:12** [a] Matt. 4:13; John 4:46 [b] Matt. 12:46; 13:55 **2:13** [a] Ex. 12:14; Deut. 16:1–6; John 5:1; 6:4; 11:55 **2:14** [a] Mal. 3:1; Matt. 21:12; Mark 11:15, 17; Luke 19:45 **2:16** [a] Luke 2:49 **2:17** [a] Ps. 69:9 [1] NU-Text and M-Text read *will eat.* [2] Psalm 69:9 **2:18** [a] Matt. 12:38; John 6:30 **2:19** [a] Matt. 26:61; 27:40; [Mark 14:58; 15:29]; Luke 24:46; Acts 6:14; 10:40; 1 Cor. 15:4 **2:21** [a] [1 Cor. 3:16; 6:19; 2 Cor. 6:16; Col. 2:9; Heb. 8:2] **2:22** [a] Luke 24:8; John 2:17; 12:16; 14:26 [1] NU-Text and M-Text omit *to them.* **2:23** [a] [John 5:36; Acts 2:22] **2:24** [a] Matt. 9:4; John 16:30; Rev. 2:23 **2:25** [a] 1 Sam. 16:7; 1 Chr. 28:9; Matt. 9:4; [Mark 2:8]; John 6:64; 16:30; Acts 1:24; Rev. 2:23 **3:2** [a] John 7:50; 19:39 [b] John 9:16, 33; Acts 2:22 [c] [Acts 10:38] **3:3** [a] [John 1:13; Gal. 6:15; Titus 3:5; James 1:18; 1 Pet. 1:23; 1 John 3:9]

a second time into his mother's womb and
be born?"
5Jesus answered, "Most assuredly, I say
to you, [a]unless one is born of water and
the Spirit, he cannot enter the kingdom
of God. 6That which is born of the flesh is
[a]flesh, and that which is born of the Spirit
is spirit. 7Do not marvel that I said to you,
'You must be born again.' 8[a]The wind blows
where it wishes, and you hear the sound of
it, but cannot tell where it comes from and
where it goes. So is everyone who is born
of the Spirit."
9Nicodemus answered and said to Him,
[a]"How can these things be?"
10Jesus answered and said to him, "Are
you the teacher of Israel, and do not know
these things? 11[a]Most assuredly, I say to you,
We speak what We know and testify what
We have seen, and [b]you do not receive Our
witness. 12If I have told you earthly things
and you do not believe, how will you believe if I tell you heavenly things? 13[a]No one
has ascended to heaven but He who came
down from heaven, *that is,* the Son of Man
who is in heaven.[1] 14[a]And as Moses lifted
up the serpent in the wilderness, even so
[b]must the Son of Man be lifted up, 15that
whoever [a]believes in Him should not perish
but[1] [b]have eternal life. 16[a]For God so loved
the world that He gave His only begotten
[b]Son, that whoever believes in Him should
not perish but have everlasting life. 17[a]For
God did not send His Son into the world
to condemn the world, but that the world
through Him might be saved.
18[a]"He who believes in Him is not condemned; but he who does not believe is
condemned already, because he has not
believed in the name of the only begotten
Son of God. 19And this is the condemnation,
[a]that the light has come into the world, and
men loved darkness rather than light, because their deeds were evil. 20For [a]everyone
practicing evil hates the light and does not
come to the light, lest his deeds should be
exposed. 21But he who does the truth comes
to the light, that his deeds may be clearly
seen, that they have been [a]done in God."

John the Baptist Exalts Christ

22After these things Jesus and His disciples came into the land of Judea, and
there He remained with them [a]and baptized. 23Now John also was baptizing in Ae-
non near [a]Salim, because there was much
water there. [b]And they came and were baptized. 24For [a]John had not yet been thrown
into prison.
25Then there arose a dispute between
some of John's disciples and the Jews about
purification. 26And they came to John and
said to him, "Rabbi, He who was with you
beyond the Jordan, [a]to whom you have
testified—behold, He is baptizing, and all
[b]are coming to Him!"
27John answered and said, [a]"A man can
receive nothing unless it has been given
to him from heaven. 28You yourselves
bear me witness, that I said, [a]'I am not
the Christ,' but, [b]'I have been sent before
Him.' 29[a]He who has the bride is the bridegroom; but [b]the friend of the bridegroom,
who stands and hears him, rejoices greatly
because of the bridegroom's voice. Therefore this joy of mine is fulfilled. 30[a]He must
increase, but I *must* decrease. 31[a]He who
comes from above [b]is above all; [c]he who
is of the earth is earthly and speaks of the
earth. [d]He who comes from heaven is above
all. 32And [a]what He has seen and heard,
that He testifies; and no one receives His
testimony. 33He who has received His testimony [a]has certified that God is true. 34[a]For
He whom God has sent speaks the words
of God, for God does not give the Spirit [b]by
measure. 35[a]The Father loves the Son, and
has given all things into His hand. 36[a]He
who believes in the Son has everlasting life;
and he who does not believe the Son shall

3:5 [a] Mark 16:16; [Acts 2:38] **3:6** [a] John 1:13; 1 Cor. 15:50 **3:8** [a] Ps. 135:7; Eccl. 11:5; Ezek. 37:9; 1 Cor. 2:11 **3:9** [a] John 6:52, 60 **3:11** [a] [Matt. 11:27] [b] John 3:32; 8:14 **3:13** [a] Deut. 30:12; Prov. 30:4; Acts 2:34; Rom. 10:6; 1 Cor. 15:47; Eph. 4:9 [1] NU-Text omits *who is in heaven.* **3:14** [a] Num. 21:9 [b] Matt. 27:35; Mark 15:24; Luke 23:33; John 8:28; 12:34; 19:18 **3:15** [a] John 6:47 [b] John 3:36 [1] NU-Text omits *not perish but.* **3:16** [a] Rom. 5:8; Eph. 2:4; 2 Thess. 2:16; [1 John 4:9, 10; Rev. 1:5] [b] [Is. 9:6] **3:17** [a] Matt. 1:21; Luke 9:56; 1 John 4:14 **3:18** [a] John 5:24; 6:40, 47; 20:31; Rom. 8:1 **3:19** [a] [John 1:4, 9–11] **3:20** [a] Job 24:13; Eph. 5:11, 13 **3:21** [a] [John 15:4, 5]; 1 Cor. 15:10 **3:22** [a] John 4:1, 2 **3:23** [a] 1 Sam. 9:4 [b] Matt. 3:5, 6 **3:24** [a] Matt. 4:12; 14:3; Mark 6:17; Luke 3:20 **3:26** [a] John 1:7, 15, 27, 34 [b] Mark 2:2; 3:10; 5:24; Luke 8:19 **3:27** [a] [Rom. 12:5–8]; 1 Cor. 3:5, 6; 4:7; Heb. 5:4; [James 1:17; 1 Pet. 4:10, 11] **3:28** [a] John 1:19–27 [b] Mal. 3:1; Mark 1:2; [Luke 1:17] **3:29** [a] Matt. 22:2; [2 Cor. 11:2; Eph. 5:25, 27]; Rev. 21:9 [b] Song 5:1 **3:30** [a] [Is. 9:7] **3:31** [a] John 3:13; 8:23 [b] Matt. 28:18; John 1:15, 27; 13:13; Rom. 9:5; [Col. 1:17, 18] [c] 1 Cor. 15:47 [d] John 6:33; 1 Cor. 15:47; Eph. 1:21; Phil. 2:9 **3:32** [a] Is. 53:1, 3; John 3:11; 15:15 **3:33** [a] Rom. 3:4; 1 John 5:10 **3:34** [a] Deut. 18:18; John 7:16 [b] John 1:16 **3:35** [a] Matt. 11:27; Luke 10:22; John 5:20; [Heb. 2:8] **3:36** [a] John 3:16, 17; 6:47; Rom. 1:17; 1 John 5:10

not see life, but the [b]wrath of God abides
on him."

A Samaritan Woman Meets Her Messiah

4 Therefore, when the Lord knew that the
Pharisees had heard that Jesus made
and [a]baptized more disciples than John
2(though Jesus Himself did not baptize,
but His disciples), 3He left Judea and departed again to Galilee. 4But He needed to
go through Samaria.

5So He came to a city of Samaria which
is called Sychar, near the plot of ground
that [a]Jacob [b]gave to his son Joseph. 6Now
Jacob's well was there. Jesus therefore, being wearied from *His* journey, sat thus by
the well. It was about the sixth hour.

7A woman of Samaria came to draw water. Jesus said to her, "Give Me a drink." 8For
His disciples had gone away into the city
to buy food.

9Then the woman of Samaria said to
Him, "How is it that You, being a Jew, ask
a drink from me, a Samaritan woman?" For
[a]Jews have no dealings with [b]Samaritans.
10Jesus answered and said to her, "If you
knew the [a]gift of God, and who it is who says
to you, 'Give Me a drink,' you would have
asked Him, and He would have given you
[b]living water."

11The woman said to Him, "Sir, You have
nothing to draw with, and the well is deep.
Where then do You get that living water?
12Are You greater than our father Jacob, who
gave us the well, and drank from it himself,
as well as his sons and his livestock?"

13Jesus answered and said to her, "Whoever drinks of this water will thirst again,
14but [a]whoever drinks of the water that I
shall give him will never thirst. But the water that I shall give him [b]will become in
him a fountain of water springing up into
everlasting life."

15[a]The woman said to Him, "Sir, give me
this water, that I may not thirst, nor come
here to draw."

16Jesus said to her, "Go, call your husband, and come here."

17The woman answered and said, "I have
no husband."

Jesus said to her, "You have well said,
'I have no husband,' 18for you have had
five husbands, and the one whom you
now have is not your husband; in that you
spoke truly."

19The woman said to Him, "Sir, [a]I perceive that You are a prophet. 20Our fathers
worshiped on [a]this mountain, and you *Jews*
say that in [b]Jerusalem is the place where
one ought to worship."

21Jesus said to her, "Woman, believe Me,
the hour is coming [a]when you will neither
on this mountain, nor in Jerusalem, worship the Father. 22You worship [a]what you
do not know; we know what we worship,
for [b]salvation is of the Jews. 23But the hour
is coming, and now is, when the true worshipers will [a]worship the Father in [b]spirit
[c]and truth; for the Father is seeking such
to worship Him. 24[a]God *is* Spirit, and those
who worship Him must worship in spirit
and truth."

25The woman said to Him, "I know that
Messiah [a]is coming" (who is called Christ).
"When He comes, [b]He will tell us all things."

26Jesus said to her, [a]"I who speak to you
am *He*."

The Whitened Harvest

27And at this *point* His disciples came,
and they marveled that He talked with a
woman; yet no one said, "What do You
seek?" or, "Why are You talking with her?"

28The woman then left her waterpot,
went her way into the city, and said to the
men, 29"Come, see a Man [a]who told me all
things that I ever did. Could this be the
Christ?" 30Then they went out of the city
and came to Him.

31In the meantime His disciples urged
Him, saying, "Rabbi, eat."

32But He said to them, "I have food to
eat of which you do not know."

33Therefore the disciples said to one another, "Has anyone brought Him *anything*
to eat?"

3:36 [b] Rom. 1:18; Eph. 5:6; 1 Thess. 1:10 4:1 [a] John 3:22, 26; 1 Cor. 1:17 4:5 [a] Gen. 33:19; Josh. 24:32 [b] Gen. 48:22; Josh. 4:12 4:9 [a] Acts 10:28 [b] 2 Kin. 17:24; Matt. 10:5, 6; Luke 9:52; 10:33; 17:16; John 8:48 4:10 [a] [Rom. 5:15] [b] Is. 12:3; 44:3; Jer. 2:13; Zech. 13:1; 14:8; John 7:38 4:14 [a] [John 6:35, 58] [b] John 7:37, 38 4:15 [a] John 6:34, 35; 17:2, 3; [Rom. 6:23; 1 John 5:20] 4:19 [a] Matt. 21:11; Luke 7:16, 39; 24:19; John 6:14; 7:40; 9:17 4:20 [a] Gen. 12:6–8; 33:18, 20; Judg. 9:7 [b] Deut. 12:5, 11; 1 Kin. 9:3; 2 Chr. 7:12; Ps. 122:1–9 4:21 [a] [Mal. 1:11]; 1 Tim. 2:8 4:22 [a] [2 Kin. 17:28–41] [b] [Is. 2:3; Luke 24:47; Rom. 3:1; 9:4, 5] 4:23 [a] Matt. 18:20; [Heb. 13:10–14] [b] Phil. 3:3 [c] [John 1:17] 4:24 [a] 2 Cor. 3:17 4:25 [a] Deut. 18:15 [b] John 4:29, 39 4:26 [a] Dan. 9:25; Matt. 26:63, 64; Mark 14:61, 62 4:29 [a] John 4:25

34 Jesus said to them, [a]"My food is to do the will of Him who sent Me, and to [b]finish His work. 35 Do you not say, 'There are still four months and *then* comes [a]the harvest'? Behold, I say to you, lift up your eyes and look at the fields, [b]for they are already white for harvest! 36 [a]And he who reaps receives wages, and gathers fruit for eternal life, that [b]both he who sows and he who reaps may rejoice together. 37 For in this the saying is true: [a]'One sows and another reaps.' 38 I sent you to reap that for which you have not labored; [a]others have labored, and you have entered into their labors."

The Savior of the World

39 And many of the Samaritans of that city believed in Him [a]because of the word of the woman who testified, "He told me all that I *ever* did." 40 So when the Samaritans had come to Him, they urged Him to stay with them; and He stayed there two days. 41 And many more believed because of His own [a]word.

42 Then they said to the woman, "Now we believe, not because of what you said, for [a]we ourselves have heard *Him* and we know that this is indeed the Christ,[1] the Savior of the world."

Welcome at Galilee

43 Now after the two days He departed from there and went to Galilee. 44 For [a]Jesus Himself testified that a prophet has no honor in his own country. 45 So when He came to Galilee, the Galileans received Him, [a]having seen all the things He did in Jerusalem at the feast; [b]for they also had gone to the feast.

A Nobleman's Son Healed

46 So Jesus came again to Cana of Galilee [a]where He had made the water wine. And there was a certain nobleman whose son was sick at Capernaum. 47 When he heard that Jesus had come out of Judea into Galilee, he went to Him and implored Him to come down and heal his son, for he was at the point of death. 48 Then Jesus said to him, [a]"Unless you *people* see signs and wonders, you will by no means believe."

49 The nobleman said to Him, "Sir, come down before my child dies!"

50 Jesus said to him, "Go your way; your son lives." So the man believed the word that Jesus spoke to him, and he went his way. 51 And as he was now going down, his servants met him and told *him,* saying, "Your son lives!"

52 Then he inquired of them the hour when he got better. And they said to him, "Yesterday at the seventh hour the fever left him." 53 So the father knew that *it was* at the same hour in which Jesus said to him, "Your son lives." And he himself believed, and his whole household.

54 This again *is* the second sign Jesus did when He had come out of Judea into Galilee.

A Man Healed at the Pool of Bethesda

5 After [a]this there was a feast of the Jews, and Jesus [b]went up to Jerusalem. 2 Now there is in Jerusalem [a]by the Sheep *Gate* a pool, which is called in Hebrew, Bethesda,[1] having five porches. 3 In these lay a great multitude of sick people, blind, lame, paralyzed, waiting for the moving of the water. 4 For an angel went down at a certain time into the pool and stirred up the water; then whoever stepped in first, after the stirring of the water, was made well of whatever disease he had.[1] 5 Now a certain man was there who had an infirmity thirty-eight years. 6 When Jesus saw him lying there, and knew that he already had been *in that condition* a long time, He said to him, "Do you want to be made well?"

7 The sick man answered Him, "Sir, I have no man to put me into the pool when the water is stirred up; but while I am coming, another steps down before me."

8 Jesus said to him, [a]"Rise, take up your bed and walk." 9 And immediately the man was made well, took up his bed, and walked.

And [a]that day was the Sabbath. 10 The

4:34 [a] Ps. 40:7, 8; Heb. 10:9 [b] Job 23:12; [John 6:38; 17:4; 19:30] 4:35 [a] Gen. 8:22 [b] Matt. 9:37; Luke 10:2 4:36 [a] Dan. 12:3; Rom. 6:22 [b] 1 Thess. 2:19 4:37 [a] 1 Cor. 3:5–9 4:38 [a] Jer. 44:4; [1 Pet. 1:12] 4:39 [a] John 4:29 4:41 [a] Luke 4:32; [John 6:63] 4:42 [a] John 17:8; 1 John 4:14 [1] NU-Text omits *the Christ.* 4:44 [a] Matt. 13:57; Mark 6:4; Luke 4:24 4:45 [a] John 2:13, 23; 3:2 [b] Deut. 16:16 4:46 [a] John 2:1, 11 4:48 [a] John 6:30; Rom. 15:19; 1 Cor. 1:22; 2 Cor. 12:12; [2 Thess. 2:9]; Heb. 2:4 5:1 [a] Lev. 23:2; Deut. 16:16 [b] John 2:13 5:2 [a] Neh. 3:1, 32; 12:39 [1] NU-Text reads *Bethzatha.* 5:4 [1] NU-Text omits *waiting for the moving of the water* at the end of verse 3, and all of verse 4. 5:8 [a] Matt. 9:6; Mark 2:11; Luke 5:24 5:9 [a] John 9:14

Jews therefore said to him who was cured,
"It is the Sabbath; [a]it is not lawful for you
to carry your bed."
11He answered them, "He who made
me well said to me, 'Take up your bed and
walk.'"
12Then they asked him, "Who is the Man
who said to you, 'Take up your bed and
walk'?" 13But the one who was [a]healed did
not know who it was, for Jesus had withdrawn, a multitude being in *that* place. 14Af-
terward Jesus found him in the temple,
and said to him, "See, you have been made
well. [a]Sin no more, lest a worse thing come
upon you."
15The man departed and told the Jews
that it was Jesus who had made him well.

Honor the Father and the Son

16For this reason the Jews [a]persecuted
Jesus, and sought to kill Him,[1] because
He had done these things on the Sabbath.
17But Jesus answered them, [a]"My Father
has been working until now, and I have
been working."
18Therefore the Jews [a]sought all the
more to kill Him, because He not only
broke the Sabbath, but also said that God
was His Father, [b]making Himself equal
with God. 19Then Jesus answered and said
to them, "Most assuredly, I say to you, [a]the
Son can do nothing of Himself, but what
He sees the Father do; for whatever He
does, the Son also does in like manner.
20For [a]the Father loves the Son, and [b]shows
Him all things that He Himself does; and
He will show Him greater works than
these, that you may marvel. 21For as the
Father raises the dead and gives life to
them, [a]even so the Son gives life to whom
He will. 22For the Father judges no one,
but [a]has committed all judgment to the
Son, 23that all should honor the Son just
as they honor the Father. [a]He who does not
honor the Son does not honor the Father
who sent Him.

Life and Judgment Are Through the Son

24"Most assuredly, I say to you, [a]he who
hears My word and believes in Him who
sent Me has everlasting life, and shall not
come into judgment, [b]but has passed from
death into life. 25Most assuredly, I say to
you, the hour is coming, and now is, when
[a]the dead will hear the voice of the Son of
God; and those who hear will live. 26For
[a]as the Father has life in Himself, so He
has granted the Son to have [b]life in Himself, 27and [a]has given Him authority to execute judgment also, [b]because He is the
Son of Man. 28Do not marvel at this; for
the hour is coming in which all who are in
the graves will [a]hear His voice 29[a]and come
forth—[b]those who have done good, to the
resurrection of life, and those who have
done evil, to the resurrection of condemnation. 30[a]I can of Myself do nothing. As
I hear, I judge; and My judgment is righteous, because [b]I do not seek My own will
but the will of the Father who sent Me.

The Fourfold Witness

31[a]"If I bear witness of Myself, My witness is not true. 32[a]There is another who
bears witness of Me, and I know that the
witness which He witnesses of Me is true.
33You have sent to John, [a]and he has borne
witness to the truth. 34Yet I do not receive
testimony from man, but I say these things
that you may be saved. 35He was the burning and [a]shining lamp, and [b]you were willing for a time to rejoice in his light. 36But
[a]I have a greater witness than John's; for
[b]the works which the Father has given Me
to finish—the very [c]works that I do—bear
witness of Me, that the Father has sent Me.
37And the Father Himself, who sent Me,
[a]has testified of Me. You have neither heard
His voice at any time, [b]nor seen His form.
38But you do not have His word abiding in
you, because whom He sent, Him you do
not believe. 39[a]You search the Scriptures,
for in them you think you have eternal

5:10 [a] Ex. 20:10; Neh. 13:19; Jer. 17:21, 22; Matt. 12:2; Mark 2:24; Luke 6:2 **5:13** [a] Luke 13:14; 22:51 **5:14** [a] Matt. 12:45; [Mark 2:5]; John 8:11 **5:16** [a] Luke 4:29; John 8:37; 10:39 [1] NU-Text omits *and sought to kill Him.* **5:17** [a] [John 9:4; 17:4] **5:18** [a] John 7:1, 19 [b] John 10:30; Phil. 2:6 **5:19** [a] Matt. 26:39; John 5:30; 6:38; 8:28; 12:49; 14:10 **5:20** [a] Matt. 3:17; John 3:35; 2 Pet. 1:17 [b] [Matt. 11:27] **5:21** [a] Luke 7:14; 8:54; [John 11:25] **5:22** [a] Matt. 11:27; 28:18; [John 3:35; 17:2; Acts 17:31; 1 Pet. 4:5] **5:23** [a] Luke 10:16; 1 John 2:23 **5:24** [a] John 3:16, 18; 6:47 [b] [1 John 3:14] **5:25** [a] [Eph. 2:1, 5; Col. 2:13] **5:26** [a] Ps. 36:9 [b] [John 1:4; 14:6]; 1 Cor. 15:45 **5:27** [a] John 9:39; [Acts 10:42; 17:31] [b] Dan. 7:13 **5:28** [a] [1 Thess. 4:15–17] **5:29** [a] Is. 26:19; [1 Cor. 15:52] [b] Dan. 12:2; Matt. 25:46; Acts 24:15 **5:30** [a] John 5:19 [b] Matt. 26:39; John 4:34; 6:38 **5:31** [a] John 8:14; Rev. 3:14 **5:32** [a] [Matt. 3:17; John 8:18; 1 John 5:6] **5:33** [a] [John 1:15, 19, 27, 32] **5:35** [a] 2 Sam. 21:17; 2 Pet. 1:19 [b] Matt. 13:20; Mark 6:20 **5:36** [a] 1 John 5:9 [b] John 3:2; 10:25; 17:4 [c] John 9:16; 10:38 **5:37** [a] Matt. 3:17; John 6:27; 8:18 [b] Deut. 4:12; John 1:18; 1 Tim. 1:17; 1 John 4:12 **5:39** [a] Is. 8:20; 34:16; Luke 16:29; Acts 17:11

life; and [b]these are they which testify of
Me. 40[a]But you are not willing to come to
Me that you may have life.

41[a]"I do not receive honor from men.
42But I know you, that you do not have the
love of God in you. 43I have come in My Father's name, and you do not receive Me; if
another comes in his own name, him you
will receive. 44[a]How can you believe, who
receive honor from one another, and do
not seek [b]the honor that *comes* from the
only God? 45Do not think that I shall accuse you to the Father; [a]there is *one* who
accuses you—Moses, in whom you trust.
46For if you believed Moses, you would believe Me; [a]for he wrote about Me. 47But if
you [a]do not believe his writings, how will
you believe My words?"

Feeding the Five Thousand

(Matt. 14:13–21; Mark 6:30–44; Luke 9:10–17)

6 After [a]these things Jesus went over the
Sea of Galilee, which is *the Sea* of [b]Tibe-
rias. 2Then a great multitude followed Him,
because they saw His signs which He performed on those who were [a]diseased. 3And
Jesus went up on the mountain, and there
He sat with His disciples.

4[a]Now the Passover, a feast of the Jews,
was near. 5[a]Then Jesus lifted up *His* eyes,
and seeing a great multitude coming toward Him, He said to [b]Philip, "Where shall
we buy bread, that these may eat?" 6But this
He said to test him, for He Himself knew
what He would do.

7Philip answered Him, [a]"Two hundred
denarii worth of bread is not sufficient for
them, that every one of them may have a
little."

8One of His disciples, [a]Andrew, Simon
Peter's brother, said to Him, 9"There is a
lad here who has five barley loaves and
two small fish, [a]but what are they among
so many?"

10Then Jesus said, "Make the people sit
down." Now there was much grass in the
place. So the men sat down, in number
about five thousand. 11And Jesus took the
loaves, and when He had given thanks He
distributed *them* to the disciples, and the
disciples[1] to those sitting down; and likewise of the fish, as much as they wanted.
12So when they were filled, He said to His
disciples, "Gather up the fragments that remain, so that nothing is lost." 13Therefore
they gathered *them* up, and filled twelve
baskets with the fragments of the five barley loaves which were left over by those
who had eaten. 14Then those men, when
they had seen the sign that Jesus did, said,
"This is truly [a]the Prophet who is to come
into the world."

Jesus Walks on the Sea

(Matt. 14:22–33; Mark 6:45–52)

15Therefore when Jesus perceived that
they were about to come and take Him by
force to make Him [a]king, He departed again
to the mountain by Himself alone.

16[a]Now when evening came, His disciples
went down to the sea, 17got into the boat,
and went over the sea toward Capernaum.
And it was already dark, and Jesus had not
come to them. 18Then the sea arose because
a great wind was blowing. 19So when they
had rowed about three or four miles,[1] they
saw Jesus walking on the sea and drawing
near the boat; and they were [a]afraid. 20But
He said to them, [a]"It is I; do not be afraid."
21Then they willingly received Him into the
boat, and immediately the boat was at the
land where they were going.

The Bread from Heaven

22On the following day, when the people
who were standing on the other side of the
sea saw that there was no other boat there,
except that one which His disciples had entered,[1] and that Jesus had not entered the
boat with His disciples, but His disciples
had gone away alone— 23however, other
boats came from Tiberias, near the place
where they ate bread after the Lord had
given thanks— 24when the people therefore saw that Jesus was not there, nor His
disciples, they also got into boats and came

5:39 [b] Deut. 18:15, 18; Luke 24:27 5:40 [a] [John 1:11; 3:19] 5:41 [a] John 5:44; 7:18; 1 Thess. 2:6 5:44 [a] John 12:43 [b] [Rom. 2:29] 5:45 [a] Rom. 2:12 5:46 [a] [Gen. 3:15]; Deut. 18:15, 18; John 1:45; Acts 26:22 5:47 [a] Luke 16:29, 31 6:1 [a] Matt. 14:13; Mark 6:32; Luke 9:10, 12 [b] John 6:23; 21:1 6:2 [a] Matt. 4:23; 8:16; 9:35; 14:36; 15:30; 19:2 6:4 [a] Lev. 23:5, 7; Deut. 16:1; John 2:13 6:5 [a] Matt. 14:14; Mark 6:35; Luke 9:12 [b] John 1:43 6:7 [a] Num. 11:21, 22 6:8 [a] John 1:40 6:9 [a] 2 Kin. 4:43 6:11 [1] NU-Text omits *to the disciples, and the disciples.* 6:14 [a] Gen. 49:10; Deut. 18:15, 18; John 1:21; 7:40; Acts 3:22; 7:37 6:15 [a] [John 18:36] 6:16 [a] Matt. 14:23; Mark 6:47 6:19 [a] Matt. 17:6 [1] Literally *twenty-five or thirty stadia* 6:20 [a] Is. 43:1, 2 6:22 [1] NU-Text omits *that* and *which His disciples had entered.*

to Capernaum, [a]seeking Jesus. 25And when they found Him on the other side of the sea, they said to Him, "Rabbi, when did You come here?"

26Jesus answered them and said, "Most assuredly, I say to you, you seek Me, not because you saw the signs, but because you ate of the loaves and were filled. 27[a]Do not labor for the food which perishes, but [b]for the food which endures to everlasting life, which the Son of Man will give you, [c]because God the Father has set His seal on Him."

28Then they said to Him, "What shall we do, that we may work the works of God?"

29Jesus answered and said to them, [a]"This is the work of God, that you believe in Him whom He sent."

30Therefore they said to Him, [a]"What sign will You perform then, that we may see it and believe You? What work will You do? 31[a]Our fathers ate the manna in the desert; as it is written, [b]'He gave them bread from heaven to eat.'"[1]

32Then Jesus said to them, "Most assuredly, I say to you, Moses did not give you the bread from heaven, but [a]My Father gives you the true bread from heaven. 33For the bread of God is He who comes down from heaven and gives life to the world."

34[a]Then they said to Him, "Lord, give us this bread always."

35And Jesus said to them, [a]"I am the bread of life. [b]He who comes to Me shall never hunger, and he who believes in Me shall never [c]thirst. 36[a]But I said to you that you have seen Me and yet [b]do not believe. 37[a]All that the Father gives Me will come to Me, and [b]the one who comes to Me I will by no means cast out. 38For I have come down from heaven, [a]not to do My own will, [b]but the will of Him who sent Me. 39This is the will of the Father who sent Me, [a]that of all He has given Me I should lose nothing, but should raise it up at the last day. 40And this is the will of Him who sent Me, [a]that everyone who sees the Son and believes in Him may have everlasting life; and I will raise him up at the last day."

Rejected by His Own

41The Jews then complained about Him, because He said, "I am the bread which came down from heaven." 42And they said, [a]"Is not this Jesus, the son of Joseph, whose father and mother we know? How is it then that He says, 'I have come down from heaven'?"

43Jesus therefore answered and said to them, "Do not murmur among yourselves. 44[a]No one can come to Me unless the Father who sent Me [b]draws him; and I will raise him up at the last day. 45It is written in the prophets, [a]'And they shall all be taught by God.'[1] [b]Therefore everyone who has heard and learned[2] from the Father comes to Me. 46[a]Not that anyone has seen the Father, [b]except He who is from God; He has seen the Father. 47Most assuredly, I say to you, [a]he who believes in Me[1] has everlasting life. 48[a]I am the bread of life. 49[a]Your fathers ate the manna in the wilderness, and are dead. 50[a]This is the bread which comes down from heaven, that one may eat of it and not die. 51I am the living bread [a]which came down from heaven. If anyone eats of this bread, he will live forever; and [b]the bread that I shall give is My flesh, which I shall give for the life of the world."

52The Jews therefore [a]quarreled among themselves, saying, "How can this Man give us *His* flesh to eat?"

53Then Jesus said to them, "Most assuredly, I say to you, unless [a]you eat the flesh of the Son of Man and drink His blood, you have no life in you. 54[a]Whoever eats My flesh and drinks My blood has eternal life, and I will raise him up at the last day. 55For My flesh is food indeed,[1] and My blood is drink indeed. 56He who eats My flesh and drinks My blood [a]abides in Me, and I in him. 57As the living Father sent Me, and I live because of the Father, so he who feeds on Me will live because of Me. 58[a]This is the bread

---

6:24 [a] Mark 1:37; Luke 4:42 6:27 [a] Matt. 6:19 [b] John 4:14; [Eph. 2:8, 9] [c] Ps. 2:7; Is. 42:1; Matt. 3:17; 17:5; Mark 1:11; 9:7; Luke 3:22; 9:35; John 5:37; Acts 2:22; 2 Pet. 1:17 6:29 [a] 1 Thess. 1:3; James 2:22; [1 John 3:23]; Rev. 2:26 6:30 [a] Matt. 12:38; 16:1; Mark 8:11; 1 Cor. 1:22 6:31 [a] Ex. 16:15; Num. 11:7; 1 Cor. 10:3 [b] Ex. 16:4, 15; Neh. 9:15; Ps. 78:24 [1] Exodus 16:4; Nehemiah 9:15; Psalm 78:24 6:32 [a] John 3:13, 16 6:34 [a] John 4:15 6:35 [a] John 6:48, 58 [b] John 4:14; 7:37; Rev. 7:16 [c] Is. 55:1, 2 6:36 [a] John 6:26, 64; 15:24 [b] John 10:26 6:37 [a] John 6:45 [b] [Matt. 24:24; John 10:28, 29]; 2 Tim. 2:19; 1 John 2:19 6:38 [a] Matt. 26:39; John 5:30 [b] John 4:34 6:39 [a] John 10:28; 17:12; 18:9 6:40 [a] John 3:15, 16; 4:14; 6:27, 47, 54 6:42 [a] Matt. 13:55; Mark 6:3; Luke 4:22 6:44 [a] Song 1:4 [b] [Eph. 2:8, 9; Phil. 1:29; 2:12, 13] 6:45 [a] Is. 54:13; Jer. 31:34; Mic. 4:2; [Heb. 8:10] [b] John 6:37 [1] Isaiah 54:13 [2] M-Text reads *hears and has learned.* 6:46 [a] John 1:18 [b] Matt. 11:27; [Luke 10:22]; John 7:29 6:47 [a] [John 3:16, 18] [1] NU-Text omits *in Me.* 6:48 [a] John 6:33, 35; [Gal. 2:20; Col. 3:3, 4] 6:49 [a] John 6:31, 58 6:50 [a] John 6:51, 58 6:51 [a] John 3:13 [b] Heb. 10:5 6:52 [a] John 7:43; 9:16; 10:19 6:53 [a] Matt. 26:26 6:54 [a] John 4:14; 6:27, 40 6:55 [1] NU-Text reads *true food* and *true drink.* 6:56 [a] [1 John 3:24; 4:15, 16] 6:58 [a] John 6:49–51

RELEASE // ACT IN CONFIDENCE

Boosting Confidence

John 6:41 // The Jews then complained about Him, because He said, "I am the bread which came down from heaven."

Summary Message // The Gospel of John is unique in style, tone, and content from the other three Gospels—Matthew, Mark, and Luke. John's focus was on addressing the controversy surrounding the mystery of Jesus' divine nature—He is fully God and fully human. John 6 is a great example of this focus. Jesus had fed over five thousand people with a few loaves and fish, and He had walked across a stormy sea. Because of these miracles, crowds followed Him to seek the source of His power. So, with Jesus' assurance of His identity on full display, He confidently explained the meaning of His miracles. He told the crowd that He is the "bread of life" (John 6:48) from heaven and the source of the miracles they sought.

Jesus' proclamation caused some to turn on Him. They were offended and enraged at Jesus' claim that He was something other than an ordinary man. They knew His earthly parents and had watched Him grow up, so they questioned how He could make such claims.

Jesus had full confidence in His purpose. From where did He get His self-assurance? It came from His Father in heaven. Confidence in abilities can only come from God and our dependency on Jesus. If it is confidence in self, it is only ungodly pride.

Practical Application // How do we develop relationships with Jesus that are strong enough to enable us to act boldly as He leads? First, we must determine if our confidence rests in our abilities and accomplishments or in Jesus' work and abilities. It is a close, personal, dynamic relationship with Jesus that allows us to walk in His boldness and confidence. As children, our confidence was sure whenever our big brothers or sisters stood behind us. Jesus is our elder brother (see Rom. 8:29). Knowing He is always with us is vital to our ability to walk as bold and confident children of God. Second, just as children imitate those who care for them, we must imitate Jesus. Just as Jesus followed the Father's plans, we are, in turn, to follow in the ways of Jesus. True confidence is a fruit of our relationship with Jesus. The deeper the relationship, the more confidence we will have to do as our Lord leads.

As we learn more about Jesus, He will show us what He is doing. Knowledge of Him and His ways will enable us boldly to do as He does. We can conclude from watching Jesus' relationship with His Father that everything He did was according to God's will. Jesus could speak out against His critics and go to the cross for us because He trusted His Father's will. We can have the same confidence to surrender our lives to Jesus and boldly proclaim Him because we can trust Him to lead and guide us throughout every day.

Fervent Prayer // Heavenly Father, replace our confidence in our abilities and accomplishments with trust in You. Help us go deeper in our relationship with You. Teach us to reflect the confidence in You that Jesus displayed when He spoke out against His critics and boldly proclaimed His divine nature. Help us follow You boldly so that our obedience brings glory to Your name. Keep us constantly focused on Your kingdom and Your will in every situation. In Jesus' name we pray. Amen.

---

which came down from heaven—not [b]as
your fathers ate the manna, and are dead.
He who eats this bread will live forever."
59 These things He said in the synagogue
as He taught in Capernaum.

Many Disciples Turn Away

60 [a]Therefore many of His disciples,
when they heard *this,* said, "This is a hard
saying; who can understand it?"
61 When Jesus knew in Himself that His
disciples complained about this, He said to
them, "Does this offend you? 62 [a]*What* then
if you should see the Son of Man ascend
where He was before? 63 [a]It is the Spirit who
gives life; the [b]flesh profits nothing. The
[c]words that I speak to you are spirit, and
they are life. 64 But [a]there are some of you
who do not believe." For [b]Jesus knew from
the beginning who they were who did not

6:58 [b] Ex. 16:14–35 6:60 [a] Matt. 11:6; John 6:66 6:62 [a] Mark 16:19; John 3:13; Acts 1:9; 2:32, 33; Eph. 4:8 6:63 [a] Gen. 2:7; 2 Cor. 3:6 [b] John 3:6 [c] [John 6:68; 14:24] 6:64 [a] John 6:36 [b] John 2:24, 25; 13:11

believe, and who would betray Him. 65And
He said, "Therefore [a]I have said to you that
no one can come to Me unless it has been
granted to him by My Father."

66[a]From that *time* many of His disciples
went back and walked with Him no more.
67Then Jesus said to the twelve, "Do you
also want to go away?"

68But Simon Peter answered Him, "Lord,
to whom shall we go? You have [a]the words
of eternal life. 69[a]Also we have come to believe and know that You are the Christ, the
Son of the living God."[1]

70Jesus answered them, [a]"Did I not
choose you, the twelve, [b]and one of you is
a devil?" 71He spoke of [a]Judas Iscariot, *the
son* of Simon, for it was he who would [b]be-
tray Him, being one of the twelve.

Jesus' Brothers Disbelieve

7 After these things Jesus walked in Galilee; for He did not want to walk in Judea, [a]because the Jews[1] sought to kill Him.
2[a]Now the Jews' Feast of Tabernacles was at
hand. 3[a]His brothers therefore said to Him,
"Depart from here and go into Judea, that
Your disciples also may see the works that
You are doing. 4For no one does anything in
secret while he himself seeks to be known
openly. If You do these things, show Yourself to the world." 5For [a]even His [b]brothers
did not believe in Him.

6Then Jesus said to them, [a]"My time has
not yet come, but your time is always ready.
7[a]The world cannot hate you, but it hates
Me [b]because I testify of it that its works are
evil. 8You go up to this feast. I am not yet[1]
going up to this feast, [a]for My time has not
yet fully come." 9When He had said these
things to them, He remained in Galilee.

The Heavenly Scholar

10But when His brothers had gone up,
then He also went up to the feast, not
openly, but as it were in secret. 11Then [a]the
Jews sought Him at the feast, and said,
"Where is He?" 12And [a]there was much
complaining among the people concerning Him. [b]Some said, "He is good"; others
said, "No, on the contrary, He deceives the
people." 13However, no one spoke openly
of Him [a]for fear of the Jews.

14Now about the middle of the feast Jesus
went up into the temple and [a]taught. 15[a]And
the Jews marveled, saying, "How does this
Man know letters, having never studied?"

16Jesus[1] answered them and said, [a]"My
doctrine is not Mine, but His who sent Me.
17[a]If anyone wills to do His will, he shall
know concerning the doctrine, whether it
is from God or *whether* I speak on My own
authority. 18[a]He who speaks from himself
seeks his own glory; but He who [b]seeks the
glory of the One who sent Him is true, and
[c]no unrighteousness is in Him. 19[a]Did not
Moses give you the law, yet none of you
keeps the law? [b]Why do you seek to kill Me?"

20The people answered and said, [a]"You
have a demon. Who is seeking to kill You?"

21Jesus answered and said to them, "I
did one work, and you all marvel. 22[a]Moses
therefore gave you circumcision (not that it
is from Moses, [b]but from the fathers), and
you circumcise a man on the Sabbath. 23If
a man receives circumcision on the Sabbath, so that the law of Moses should not
be broken, are you angry with Me because
[a]I made a man completely well on the Sabbath? 24[a]Do not judge according to appearance, but judge with righteous judgment."

Could This Be the Christ?

25Now some of them from Jerusalem said,
"Is this not He whom they seek to [a]kill? 26But
look! He speaks boldly, and they say nothing to Him. [a]Do the rulers know indeed that
this is truly[1] the Christ? 27[a]However, we know
where this Man is from; but when the Christ
comes, no one knows where He is from."

28Then Jesus cried out, as He taught in

6:65 [a] John 6:37, 44, 45 **6:66** [a] Luke 9:62; John 6:60 **6:68** [a] Acts 5:20 **6:69** [a] Matt. 16:16; Mark 8:29; Luke 9:20; John 1:49; 11:27 [1] NU-Text reads *You are the Holy One of God.* **6:70** [a] Luke 6:13 [b] [John 13:27] **6:71** [a] John 12:4; 13:2, 26 [b] Matt. 26:14–16 **7:1** [a] Matt. 21:38; 26:4; John 5:18; 7:19, 25; 8:37, 40 [1] That is, the ruling authorities **7:2** [a] Lev. 23:34; Deut. 16:13–15; Neh. 8:14, 18; Zech. 14:16–19 **7:3** [a] Matt. 12:46; Mark 3:21; John 7:5, 10; Acts 1:14 **7:5** [a] Ps. 69:8; Mic. 7:6 [b] Matt. 12:46; 13:55; Mark 3:21; John 7:3, 10 **7:6** [a] John 2:4; 8:20 **7:7** [a] [John 15:19] [b] John 3:19 **7:8** [a] John 8:20 [1] NU-Text omits *yet.* **7:11** [a] John 11:56 **7:12** [a] John 9:16; 10:19 [b] Matt. 21:46; Luke 7:16; John 6:14; 7:40 **7:13** [a] [John 9:22; 12:42; 19:38] **7:14** [a] Ps. 22:22; Matt. 4:23; 5:2; 7:29; Mark 6:34; Luke 4:15; 5:3; John 8:2 **7:15** [a] Matt. 13:54; Mark 6:2; [Luke 4:22]; Acts 2:7 **7:16** [a] Deut. 18:15, 18, 19; John 3:11 [1] NU-Text and M-Text read *So Jesus.* **7:17** [a] Ps. 25:9, 14; Prov. 3:32; Dan. 12:10; John 3:21; 8:43 **7:18** [a] John 5:41 [b] John 8:50 [c] John 8:46; [2 Cor. 5:21; Heb. 4:15; 7:26; 1 Pet. 1:19; 2:22] **7:19** [a] Ex. 24:3; Deut. 33:4; Acts 7:38 [b] Matt. 12:14 **7:20** [a] John 8:48, 52 **7:22** [a] Lev. 12:3 [b] Gen. 17:9–14; Acts 7:8 **7:23** [a] John 5:8, 9, 16 **7:24** [a] Deut. 1:16; Prov. 24:23; John 8:15; James 2:1 **7:25** [a] Matt. 21:38; 26:4; Luke 22:2; John 5:18; 8:37, 40 **7:26** [a] John 7:48 [1] NU-Text omits *truly.* **7:27** [a] Matt. 13:55; Mark 6:3; Luke 4:22

the temple, saying, [a]"You both know Me,
and you know where I am from; and [b]I have
not come of Myself, but He who sent Me [c]is
true, [d]whom you do not know. 29But[1] [a]I know
Him, for I am from Him, and He sent Me."
30Therefore [a]they sought to take Him;
but [b]no one laid a hand on Him, because
His hour had not yet come. 31And [a]many
of the people believed in Him, and said,
"When the Christ comes, will He do more
signs than these which this *Man* has done?"

Jesus and the Religious Leaders

32The Pharisees heard the crowd murmuring these things concerning Him, and
the Pharisees and the chief priests sent
officers to take Him. 33Then Jesus said to
them,[1] [a]"I shall be with you a little while
longer, and *then* I [b]go to Him who sent Me.
34You [a]will seek Me and not find *Me,* and
where I am you [b]cannot come."
35Then the Jews said among themselves,
"Where does He intend to go that we shall
not find Him? Does He intend to go to [a]the
Dispersion among the Greeks and teach
the Greeks? 36What is this thing that He
said, 'You will seek Me and not find Me, and
where I am you cannot come'?"

The Promise of the Holy Spirit

37[a]On the last day, that great *day* of the
feast, Jesus stood and cried out, saying,
[b]"If anyone thirsts, let him come to Me
and drink. 38[a]He who believes in Me, as the
Scripture has said, [b]out of his heart will flow
rivers of living water." 39[a]But this He spoke
concerning the Spirit, whom those believing[1] in Him would receive; for the Holy[2]
Spirit was not yet *given,* because Jesus was
not yet [b]glorified.

Who Is He?

40Therefore many[1] from the crowd,
when they heard this saying, said, "Truly
this is [a]the Prophet." 41Others said, "This is
[a]the Christ."
But some said, "Will the Christ come
out of Galilee? 42[a]Has not the Scripture
said that the Christ comes from the seed
of David and from the town of Bethlehem,
[b]where David was?" 43So [a]there was a division among the people because of Him.
44Now [a]some of them wanted to take Him,
but no one laid hands on Him.

Rejected by the Authorities

45Then the officers came to the chief
priests and Pharisees, who said to them,
"Why have you not brought Him?"
46The officers answered, [a]"No man ever
spoke like this Man!"
47Then the Pharisees answered them,
"Are you also deceived? 48Have any of the
rulers or the Pharisees believed in Him?
49But this crowd that does not know the
law is accursed."
50Nicodemus [a](he who came to Jesus
by night,[1] being one of them) said to them,
51[a]"Does our law judge a man before it hears
him and knows what he is doing?"
52They answered and said to him, "Are
you also from Galilee? Search and look,
for [a]no prophet has arisen[1] out of Galilee."

An Adulteress Faces the Light of the World

53And everyone went to his *own* house.[1]
8 But Jesus went to the Mount of Olives.
2Now early[1] in the morning He came
again into the temple, and all the people came to Him; and He sat down and
[a]taught them. 3Then the scribes and Pharisees brought to Him a woman caught in
adultery. And when they had set her in the
midst, 4they said to Him, "Teacher, this
woman was caught[1] in [a]adultery, in the very
act. 5[a]Now Moses, in the law, commanded[1]
us that such should be stoned.[2] But what

7:28 [a] John 8:14 [b] John 5:43 [c] Rom. 3:4 [d] John 1:18; 8:55 7:29 [a] Matt. 11:27; John 8:55; 17:25 [1] NU-Text and M-Text omit *But.* 7:30 [a] Mark 11:18 [b] Matt. 21:46; John 7:32, 44; 8:20; 10:39 7:31 [a] Matt. 12:23 7:33 [a] John 13:33 [b] [Mark 16:19; Luke 24:51; Acts 1:9; Heb. 9:24; 1 Pet. 3:22] [1] NU-Text and M-Text omit *to them.* 7:34 [a] Hos. 5:6 [b] [Matt. 5:20; 1 Cor. 6:9; 15:50; Rev. 21:27] 7:35 [a] Ps. 147:2; [Is. 11:12; 56:8; Zeph. 3:10]; James 1:1; 1 Pet. 1:1 7:37 [a] Lev. 23:36; Num. 29:35; Neh. 8:18 [b] [Is. 55:1] 7:38 [a] Deut. 18:15 [b] Is. 12:3; 43:20; 44:3; 55:1; [John 6:35]; Rev. 21:6; 22:17 7:39 [a] Is. 44:3; [Joel 2:28]; John 1:33 [b] John 12:16; 13:31; 17:5 [1] NU-Text reads *who believed.* [2] NU-Text omits *Holy.* 7:40 [a] Deut. 18:15, 18 [1] NU-Text reads *some.* 7:41 [a] John 4:42; 6:69 7:42 [a] Ps. 132:11; Jer. 23:5; Mic. 5:2; Matt. 2:5; [Luke 2:4] [b] 1 Sam. 16:1, 4 7:43 [a] John 7:12 7:44 [a] John 7:30 7:46 [a] Matt. 13:54, 56; Luke 4:22 7:50 [a] John 3:1, 2; 19:39 [1] NU-Text reads *before.* 7:51 [a] Deut. 1:16, 17; 19:15 7:52 [a] [Is. 9:1, 2]; Matt. 4:15 [1] NU-Text reads *is to rise.* 7:53 [1] The words *And everyone* through *sin no more* (8:11) are bracketed by NU-Text as not original. They are present in over 900 manuscripts. 8:2 [a] John 8:20; 18:20 [1] M-Text reads *very early.* 8:4 [a] Ex. 20:14; [Matt. 5:27; 19:9; Rom. 7:3] [1] M-Text reads *we found this woman.* 8:5 [a] Lev. 20:10; Deut. 22:22–24 [1] M-Text reads *in our law Moses commanded.* [2] NU-Text and M-Text read *to stone such.*

do You say?"[3] 6This they said, testing Him, that they [a]might have *something* of which to accuse Him. But Jesus stooped down and wrote on the ground with *His* finger, as though He did not hear.[1]

7So when they continued asking Him, He raised Himself up[1] and said to them, [a]"He who is without sin among you, let him throw a stone at her first." 8And again He stooped down and wrote on the ground. 9Then those who heard *it,* [a]being convicted by *their* conscience,[1] went out one by one, beginning with the oldest *even* to the last. And Jesus was left alone, and the woman standing in the midst. 10When Jesus had raised Himself up and saw no one but the woman, He said to her,[1] "Woman, where are those accusers of yours?[2] Has no one condemned you?"

11She said, "No one, Lord."

And Jesus said to her, [a]"Neither do I condemn you; go and[1] [b]sin no more."

12Then Jesus spoke to them again, saying, [a]"I am the light of the world. He who [b]follows Me shall not walk in darkness, but have the light of life."

Jesus Defends His Self-Witness

13The Pharisees therefore said to Him, [a]"You bear witness of Yourself; Your witness is not true."

14Jesus answered and said to them, "Even if I bear witness of Myself, My witness is true, for I know where I came from and where I am going; but [a]you do not know where I come from and where I am going. 15[a]You judge according to the flesh; [b]I judge no one. 16And yet if I do judge, My judgment is true; for [a]I am not alone, but I *am* with the Father who sent Me. 17[a]It is also written in your law that the testimony of two men is true. 18I am One who bears witness of Myself, and [a]the Father who sent Me bears witness of Me."

19Then they said to Him, "Where is Your Father?"

Jesus answered, [a]"You know neither Me nor My Father. [b]If you had known Me, you would have known My Father also."

20These words Jesus spoke in [a]the treasury, as He taught in the temple; and [b]no one laid hands on Him, for [c]His hour had not yet come.

Jesus Predicts His Departure

21Then Jesus said to them again, "I am going away, and [a]you will seek Me, and [b]will die in your sin. Where I go you cannot come."

22So the Jews said, "Will He kill Himself, because He says, 'Where I go you cannot come'?"

23And He said to them, [a]"You are from beneath; I am from above. [b]You are of this world; I am not of this world. 24[a]Therefore I said to you that you will die in your sins; [b]for if you do not believe that I am *He,* you will die in your sins."

25Then they said to Him, "Who are You?"

And Jesus said to them, "Just what I [a]have been saying to you from the beginning. 26I have many things to say and to judge concerning you, but [a]He who sent Me is true; and [b]I speak to the world those things which I heard from Him."

27They did not understand that He spoke to them of the Father.

28Then Jesus said to them, "When you [a]lift up the Son of Man, [b]then you will know that I am *He,* and [c]*that* I do nothing of Myself; but [d]as My Father taught Me, I speak these things. 29And [a]He who sent Me is with Me. [b]The Father has not left Me alone, [c]for I always do those things that please Him." 30As He spoke these words, [a]many believed in Him.

The Truth Shall Make You Free

31Then Jesus said to those Jews who believed Him, "If you [a]abide in My word, you are My disciples indeed. 32And you shall know the [a]truth, and [b]the truth shall make you free."

8:5 [3] M-Text adds *about her.* **8:6** [a] Matt. 22:15 [1] NU-Text and M-Text omit *as though He did not hear.* **8:7** [a] Deut. 17:7; [Rom. 2:1] [1] M-Text reads *He looked up.* **8:9** [a] Rom. 2:22 [1] NU-Text and M-Text omit *being convicted by their conscience.* **8:10** [1] NU-Text omits *and saw no one but the woman;* M-Text reads *He saw her and said.* [2] NU-Text and M-Text omit *of yours.* **8:11** [a] [Luke 9:56; 12:14; John 3:17] [b] [John 5:14] [1] NU-Text and M-Text add *from now on.* **8:12** [a] Is. 9:2; Mal. 4:2; John 1:4; 9:5; 12:35; [2 Tim. 1:10] [b] 1 Thess. 5:5 **8:13** [a] John 5:31 **8:14** [a] John 7:28; 9:29 **8:15** [a] 1 Sam. 16:7; John 7:24 [b] [John 3:17; 12:47; 18:36] **8:16** [a] John 16:32 **8:17** [a] Deut. 17:6; 19:15; Matt. 18:16; 2 Cor. 13:1; Heb. 10:28 **8:18** [a] John 5:37; 1 John 5:9 **8:19** [a] John 16:3 [b] John 14:7 **8:20** [a] Mark 12:41, 43; Luke 21:1 [b] John 2:4; 7:30 [c] John 7:8 **8:21** [a] John 7:34; 13:33 [b] John 8:24 **8:23** [a] John 3:31 [b] John 15:19; 17:16; 1 John 4:5 **8:24** [a] John 8:21 [b] [Mark 16:16] **8:25** [a] John 4:26 **8:26** [a] John 7:28 [b] John 3:32; 15:15 **8:28** [a] Matt. 27:35; Mark 15:24; Luke 23:33; John 3:14; 12:32; 19:18 [b] [Rom. 1:4] [c] John 5:19, 30 [d] Deut. 18:15, 18, 19; John 3:11 **8:29** [a] John 14:10 [b] John 8:16; 16:32 [c] John 4:34; 5:30; 6:38 **8:30** [a] John 7:31; 10:42; 11:45 **8:31** [a] [John 14:15, 23] **8:32** [a] [John 1:14, 17; 14:6] [b] [Rom. 6:14, 18, 22; James 1:25; 2:12]

33They answered Him, [a]"We are Abraham's descendants, and have never been
in bondage to anyone. How *can* You say,
'You will be made free'?"

34Jesus answered them, "Most assuredly,
I say to you, [a]whoever commits sin is a slave
of sin. 35And [a]a slave does not abide in the
house forever, *but* a son abides forever.
36[a]Therefore if the Son makes you free, you
shall be free indeed.

Abraham's Seed and Satan's

37"I know that you are Abraham's descendants, but [a]you seek to kill Me, because
My word has no place in you. 38[a]I speak
what I have seen with My Father, and you
do what you have seen with[1] your father."

39They answered and said to Him,
[a]"Abraham is our father."

Jesus said to them, [b]"If you were Abraham's children, you would do the works of
Abraham. 40[a]But now you seek to kill Me,
a Man who has told you the truth [b]which I
heard from God. Abraham did not do this.
41You do the deeds of your father."

Then they said to Him, "We were not
born of fornication; [a]we have one Father—
God."

42Jesus said to them, [a]"If God were your
Father, you would love Me, for [b]I proceeded
forth and came from God; [c]nor have I come
of Myself, but He sent Me. 43[a]Why do you
not understand My speech? Because you
are not able to listen to My word. 44[a]You
are of *your* father the devil, and the [b]de-
sires of your father you want to [c]do. He
was a murderer from the beginning, and
[d]does not stand in the truth, because there
is no truth in him. When he speaks a lie, he
speaks from his own *resources,* for he is a
liar and the father of it. 45But because I tell
the truth, you do not believe Me. 46Which
of you convicts Me of sin? And if I tell the
truth, why do you not believe Me? 47[a]He who
is of God hears God's words; therefore you
do not hear, because you are not of God."

Before Abraham Was, I AM

48Then the Jews answered and said to
Him, "Do we not say rightly that You are a
Samaritan and [a]have a demon?"

49Jesus answered, "I do not have a demon; but I honor My Father, and [a]you dishonor Me. 50And [a]I do not seek My *own*
glory; there is One who seeks and judges.
51Most assuredly, I say to you, [a]if anyone
keeps My word he shall never see death."

52Then the Jews said to Him, "Now we
know that You [a]have a demon! [b]Abraham
is dead, and the prophets; and You say, 'If
anyone keeps My word he shall never taste
death.' 53Are You greater than our father
Abraham, who is dead? And the prophets
are dead. [a]Who do You make Yourself out
to be?"

54Jesus answered, [a]"If I honor Myself, My
honor is nothing. [b]It is My Father who honors Me, of whom you say that He is your[1]
God. 55Yet [a]you have not known Him, but I
know Him. And if I say, 'I do not know Him,'
I shall be a liar like you; but I do know Him
and [b]keep His word. 56Your father Abraham [a]rejoiced to see My day, [b]and he saw
it and was glad."

57Then the Jews said to Him, "You are
not yet fifty years old, and have You seen
Abraham?"

58Jesus said to them, "Most assuredly,
I say to you, [a]before Abraham was, [b]I AM."

59Then [a]they took up stones to throw at
Him; but Jesus hid Himself and went out
of the temple,[1] [b]going through the midst of
them, and so passed by.

A Man Born Blind Receives Sight

9 Now as *Jesus* passed by, He saw a man
who was blind from birth. 2And His
disciples asked Him, saying, "Rabbi, [a]who
sinned, this man or his parents, that he
was born blind?"

3Jesus answered, "Neither this man nor
his parents sinned, [a]but that the works of
God should be revealed in him. 4[a]I[1] must

8:33 [a] Lev. 25:42; [Matt. 3:9]; Luke 3:8 8:34 [a] Prov. 5:22; Rom. 6:16; 2 Pet. 2:19 8:35 [a] Gen. 21:10; Gal. 4:30 8:36 [a] [Rom. 8:2; 2 Cor. 3:17]; Gal. 5:1 8:37 [a] John 7:19 8:38 [a] [John 3:32; 5:19, 30; 14:10, 24] [1] NU-Text reads *heard from.* 8:39 [a] Matt. 3:9; John 8:37 [b] [Rom. 2:28; Gal. 3:7, 29] 8:40 [a] John 8:37 [b] John 8:26 8:41 [a] Deut. 32:6; Is. 63:16; Mal. 1:6 8:42 [a] 1 John 5:1 [b] John 16:27; 17:8, 25 [c] John 5:43; Gal. 4:4 8:43 [a] [John 7:17] 8:44 [a] Matt. 13:38; 1 John 3:8 [b] 1 John 2:16, 17 [c] [1 John 3:8–10, 15] [d] [Jude 6] 8:47 [a] Luke 8:15; John 10:26; 1 John 4:6 8:48 [a] John 7:20; 10:20 8:49 [a] John 5:41 8:50 [a] John 5:41; 7:18; [Phil. 2:6–8] 8:51 [a] John 5:24; 11:26 8:52 [a] John 7:20; 10:20 [b] Zech. 1:5; Heb. 11:13 8:53 [a] John 10:33; 19:7 8:54 [a] John 5:31, 32 [b] John 5:41; Acts 3:13 [1] NU-Text and M-Text read *our.* 8:55 [a] John 7:28, 29 [b] [John 15:10] 8:56 [a] Luke 10:24 [b] Matt. 13:17; Heb. 11:13 8:58 [a] Mic. 5:2; John 17:5; Heb. 7:3; Rev. 22:13 [b] Ex. 3:14; Is. 43:13; John 17:5, 24; Col. 1:17; Rev. 1:8 8:59 [a] John 10:31; 11:8 [b] Luke 4:30; John 10:39 [1] NU-Text omits the rest of this verse. 9:2 [a] Luke 13:2; John 9:34; Acts 28:4 9:3 [a] John 11:4 9:4 [a] [John 4:34; 5:19, 36; 17:4] [1] NU-Text reads *We.*

work the works of Him who sent Me while
it is [b]day; *the* night is coming when no one
can work. 5As long as I am in the world, [a]I
am the light of the world."

6When He had said these things, [a]He
spat on the ground and made clay with
the saliva; and He anointed the eyes of
the blind man with the clay. 7And He said
to him, "Go, wash [a]in the pool of Siloam"
(which is translated, Sent). So [b]he went and
washed, and came back seeing.

8Therefore the neighbors and those who
previously had seen that he was blind[1] said,
"Is not this he who sat and begged?"
9Some said, "This is he." Others *said,* "He
is like him."[1]

He said, "I am *he*."

10Therefore they said to him, "How were
your eyes opened?"

11He answered and said, [a]"A Man called
Jesus made clay and anointed my eyes and
said to me, 'Go to the pool of[1] Siloam and
wash.' So I went and washed, and I received
sight."

12Then they said to him, "Where is He?"

He said, "I do not know."

The Pharisees Excommunicate the Healed Man

13They brought him who formerly was
blind to the Pharisees. 14Now it was a Sabbath when Jesus made the clay and opened
his eyes. 15Then the Pharisees also asked
him again how he had received his sight.
He said to them, "He put clay on my eyes,
and I washed, and I see."

16Therefore some of the Pharisees said,
"This Man is not from God, because He does
not keep the Sabbath."

Others said, [a]"How can a man who is a
sinner do such signs?" And [b]there was a division among them.

17They said to the blind man again,
"What do you say about Him because He
opened your eyes?"

He said, [a]"He is a prophet."

18But the Jews did not believe concerning him, that he had been blind and
received his sight, until they called the
parents of him who had received his sight.
19And they asked them, saying, "Is this your
son, who you say was born blind? How then
does he now see?"

20His parents answered them and said,
"We know that this is our son, and that he
was born blind; 21but by what means he
now sees we do not know, or who opened
his eyes we do not know. He is of age; ask
him. He will speak for himself." 22His parents said these *things* because [a]they feared
the Jews, for the Jews had agreed already
that if anyone confessed *that* He *was* Christ,
he [b]would be put out of the synagogue.
23Therefore his parents said, "He is of age;
ask him."

24So they again called the man who was
blind, and said to him, [a]"Give God the glory!
[b]We know that this Man is a sinner."

25He answered and said, "Whether He is
a sinner *or not* I do not know. One thing I
know: that though I was blind, now I see."

#OXYGEN
JOHN 9:25
Act in Confidence

To have faith in Christ does not mean that we know all we might want to know; it means that we know all that we need to know. The gap in between is why we must live in faith. Our faith allows us to live with confidence, though, because it is rooted in the One we have come to know, Christ Jesus, and what He has done for us.

Breathe and act in confidence.

26Then they said to him again, "What did
He do to you? How did He open your eyes?"

27He answered them, "I told you already,
and you did not listen. Why do you want to
hear *it* again? Do you also want to become
His disciples?"

28Then they reviled him and said, "You
are His disciple, but we are Moses' disciples.

9:4 [b] John 11:9, 10; 12:35; Gal. 6:10 9:5 [a] [John 1:5, 9; 3:19; 8:12; 12:35, 46] 9:6 [a] Mark 7:33; 8:23 9:7 [a] Neh. 3:15; Is. 8:6; Luke 13:4; John 9:11 [b] 2 Kin. 5:14 9:8 [1] NU-Text reads *a beggar.* 9:9 [1] NU-Text reads *"No, but he is like him."* 9:11 [a] John 9:6, 7 [1] NU-Text omits *the pool of.* 9:16 [a] John 3:2; 9:33 [b] John 7:12, 43; 10:19 9:17 [a] [John 4:19; 6:14] 9:22 [a] John 7:13; 12:42; 19:38; Acts 5:13 [b] John 16:2 9:24 [a] Josh. 7:19; 1 Sam. 6:5; Ezra 10:11; Rev. 11:13 [b] John 9:16

29We know that God [a]spoke to [b]Moses; *as
for* this *fellow,* [c]we do not know where He
is from."

30The man answered and said to them,
[a]"Why, this is a marvelous thing, that you
do not know where He is from; yet He has
opened my eyes! 31Now we know that [a]God
does not hear sinners; but if anyone is a
worshiper of God and does His will, He
hears him. 32Since the world began it has
been unheard of that anyone opened the
eyes of one who was born blind. 33[a]If this
Man were not from God, He could do nothing."

34They answered and said to him, [a]"You
were completely born in sins, and are you
teaching us?" And they cast him out.

True Vision and True Blindness

35Jesus heard that they had cast him out;
and when He had [a]found him, He said to
him, "Do you [b]believe in [c]the Son of God?"[1]

36He answered and said, "Who is He,
Lord, that I may believe in Him?"

37And Jesus said to him, "You have both
seen Him and [a]it is He who is talking with
you."

38Then he said, "Lord, I believe!" And he
[a]worshiped Him.

39And Jesus said, [a]"For judgment I have
come into this world, [b]that those who do
not see may see, and that those who see
may be made blind."

40Then *some* of the Pharisees who were
with Him heard these words, [a]and said to
Him, "Are we blind also?"

41Jesus said to them, [a]"If you were blind,
you would have no sin; but now you say, 'We
see.' Therefore your sin remains.

Jesus the True Shepherd

10 "Most assuredly, I say to you, he who
does not enter the sheepfold by the
door, but climbs up some other way, the
same is a thief and a robber. 2But he who
enters by the door is the shepherd of the
sheep. 3To him the doorkeeper opens, and
the sheep hear his voice; and he calls his
own sheep by [a]name and leads them out.
4And when he brings out his own sheep,
he goes before them; and the sheep follow
him, for they know his voice. 5Yet they will
by no means follow a [a]stranger, but will flee
from him, for they do not know the voice of
strangers." 6Jesus used this illustration, but
they did not understand the things which
He spoke to them.

Jesus the Good Shepherd

7Then Jesus said to them again, "Most
assuredly, I say to you, I am the door of the
sheep. 8All who *ever* came before Me[1] are
thieves and robbers, but the sheep did not
hear them. 9[a]I am the door. If anyone enters
by Me, he will be saved, and will go in and
out and find pasture. 10The thief does not
come except to steal, and to kill, and to destroy. I have come that they may have life,
and that they may have *it* more abundantly.

11[a]"I am the good shepherd. The good
shepherd gives His life for the sheep. 12But
a hireling, *he who is* not the shepherd, one
who does not own the sheep, sees the wolf
coming and [a]leaves the sheep and flees;
and the wolf catches the sheep and scatters
them. 13The hireling flees because he is a
hireling and does not care about the sheep.
14I am the good shepherd; and [a]I know My
sheep, and [b]am known by My own. 15[a]As the
Father knows Me, even so I know the Father; [b]and I lay down My life for the sheep.
16And [a]other sheep I have which are not of
this fold; them also I must bring, and they
will hear My voice; [b]and there will be one
flock *and* one shepherd.

17"Therefore My Father [a]loves Me, [b]be-
cause I lay down My life that I may take it
again. 18No one takes it from Me, but I lay
it down of Myself. I [a]have power to lay it
down, and I have power to take it again.
[b]This command I have received from My
Father."

9:29 [a] Ex. 19:19, 20; 33:11; 34:29; Num. 12:6–8 [b] [John 5:45–47] [c] John 7:27, 28; 8:14 9:30 [a] John 3:10 9:31 [a] Job 27:9; 35:12; Ps. 18:41; Prov. 1:28; 15:29; 28:9; Is. 1:15; Jer. 11:11; 14:12; Ezek. 8:18; Mic. 3:4; Zech. 7:13; [James 5:16] 9:33 [a] John 3:2; 9:16 9:34 [a] Ps. 51:5; John 9:2 9:35 [a] John 5:14 [b] John 1:7; 16:31 [c] Matt. 14:33; 16:16; Mark 1:1; John 10:36; 1 John 5:13 [1] NU-Text reads *Son of Man.* 9:37 [a] John 4:26 9:38 [a] Matt. 8:2 9:39 [a] [John 3:17; 5:22, 27; 12:47] [b] Matt. 13:13; 15:14 9:40 [a] [Rom. 2:19] 9:41 [a] John 15:22, 24 10:3 [a] John 20:16 10:5 [a] [2 Cor. 11:13–15] 10:8 [1] M-Text omits *before Me.* 10:9 [a] [John 14:6; Eph. 2:18] 10:11 [a] Gen. 49:24; Is. 40:11; Ezek. 34:23; [Heb. 13:20]; 1 Pet. 2:25; 5:4; Rev. 7:17 10:12 [a] Zech. 11:16, 17 10:14 [a] Is. 40:11; Nah. 1:7; Zech. 13:7; John 6:64; 2 Tim. 2:19 [b] 2 Tim. 1:12 10:15 [a] Matt. 11:27 [b] Matt. 27:50; Mark 15:37; Luke 23:46; [John 15:13; 19:30]; 1 John 3:16 10:16 [a] Is. 42:6; 56:8; Acts 10:45; 11:18; 13:46 [b] Ezek. 37:22; John 11:52; 17:20; Eph. 2:13–18; 1 Pet. 2:25 10:17 [a] John 5:20 [b] [Is. 53:7, 8, 12; Heb. 2:9] 10:18 [a] Matt. 26:53; [John 2:19; 5:26] [b] [John 6:38; 14:31; 17:4; Acts 2:24, 32]

19Therefore [a]there was a division again
among the Jews because of these sayings. 20And many of them said, [a]"He has
a demon and is mad. Why do you listen
to Him?"

21Others said, "These are not the words
of one who has a demon. [a]Can a demon
[b]open the eyes of the blind?"

The Shepherd Knows His Sheep

22Now it was the Feast of Dedication in
Jerusalem, and it was winter. 23And Jesus
walked in the temple, [a]in Solomon's porch.
24Then the Jews surrounded Him and said
to Him, "How long do You keep us in doubt?
If You are the Christ, tell us plainly."

25Jesus answered them, "I told you, and
you do not believe. [a]The works that I do in
My Father's name, they [b]bear witness of
Me. 26But [a]you do not believe, because you
are not of My sheep, as I said to you.[1] 27[a]My
sheep hear My voice, and I know them, and
they follow Me. 28And I give them eternal
life, and they shall never perish; neither
shall anyone snatch them out of My hand.
29[a]My Father, [b]who has given *them* to Me,
is greater than all; and no one is able to
snatch *them* out of My Father's hand. 30[a]I
and *My* Father are one."

Renewed Efforts to Stone Jesus

31Then [a]the Jews took up stones again to
stone Him. 32Jesus answered them, "Many
good works I have shown you from My Father. For which of those works do you stone
Me?"

33The Jews answered Him, saying, "For
a good work we do not stone You, but for
[a]blasphemy, and because You, being a Man,
[b]make Yourself God."

34Jesus answered them, "Is it not written
in your law, [a]'I said, "You are gods"'?[1] 35If He
called them gods, [a]to whom the word of God
came (and the Scripture [b]cannot be broken), 36do you say of Him [a]whom the Father
sanctified and [b]sent into the world, 'You are
blaspheming,' [c]because I said, 'I am [d]the
Son of God'? 37[a]If I do not do the works of
My Father, do not believe Me; 38but if I do,
though you do not believe Me, [a]believe the
works, that you may know and believe[1] [b]that
the Father *is* in Me, and I in Him." 39[a]There-
fore they sought again to seize Him, but He
escaped out of their hand.

The Believers Beyond Jordan

40And He went away again beyond the
Jordan to the place [a]where John was baptizing at first, and there He stayed. 41Then
many came to Him and said, "John performed no sign, [a]but all the things that
John spoke about this Man were true."
42And many believed in Him there.

The Death of Lazarus

11 Now a certain *man* was sick, Lazarus
of Bethany, the town of [a]Mary and
her sister Martha. 2[a]It was *that* Mary who
anointed the Lord with fragrant oil and
wiped His feet with her hair, whose brother
Lazarus was sick. 3Therefore the sisters sent
to Him, saying, "Lord, behold, he whom
You love is sick."

4When Jesus heard *that*, He said, "This
sickness is not unto death, but for the glory
of God, that the Son of God may be glorified through it."

5Now Jesus loved Martha and her sister
and Lazarus. 6So, when He heard that he
was sick, [a]He stayed two more days in the
place where He was. 7Then after this He said
to *the* disciples, "Let us go to Judea again."

8*The* disciples said to Him, "Rabbi, lately
the Jews sought to [a]stone You, and are You
going there again?"

9Jesus answered, "Are there not twelve
hours in the day? [a]If anyone walks in the
day, he does not stumble, because he sees
the [b]light of this world. 10But [a]if one walks
in the night, he stumbles, because the light
is not in him." 11These things He said, and
after that He said to them, "Our friend
Lazarus [a]sleeps, but I go that I may wake
him up."

12Then His disciples said, "Lord, if he
sleeps he will get well." 13However, Jesus

10:19 [a] John 7:43; 9:16 10:20 [a] John 7:20 10:21 [a] [Ex. 4:11] [b] John 9:6, 7, 32, 33 10:23 [a] Acts 3:11; 5:12 10:25 [a] John 5:36; 10:38 [b] Matt. 11:4; John 2:11; 20:30 10:26 [a] [John 8:47] [1] NU-Text omits *as I said to you.* 10:27 [a] John 10:4, 14 10:29 [a] John 14:28 [b] [John 17:2, 6, 12, 24] 10:30 [a] John 17:11, 21–24 10:31 [a] John 8:59 10:33 [a] Matt. 9:3 [b] John 5:18 10:34 [a] Ps. 82:6 [1] Psalm 82:6 10:35 [a] Matt. 5:17, 18 [b] 1 Pet. 1:25 10:36 [a] John 6:27 [b] John 3:17 [c] John 5:17, 18 [d] Luke 1:35 10:37 [a] John 10:25; 15:24 10:38 [a] John 5:36 [b] John 14:10, 11 [1] NU-Text reads *understand.* 10:39 [a] John 7:30, 44 10:40 [a] John 1:28 10:41 [a] [John 1:29, 36; 3:28–36; 5:33] 11:1 [a] Luke 10:38, 39; John 11:5, 19 11:2 [a] Matt. 26:7 11:6 [a] John 10:40 11:8 [a] John 8:59; 10:31 11:9 [a] Luke 13:33; John 9:4; 12:35 [b] Is. 9:2 11:10 [a] John 12:35 11:11 [a] Deut. 31:16; [Dan. 12:2]; Matt. 9:24; Acts 7:60; [1 Cor. 15:18, 51]

spoke of his death, but they thought that He was speaking about taking rest in sleep.

14 Then Jesus said to them plainly, "Lazarus is dead. 15 And I am glad for your sakes that I was not there, that you may believe. Nevertheless let us go to him."

16 Then [a]Thomas, who is called the Twin, said to his fellow disciples, "Let us also go, that we may die with Him."

I Am the Resurrection and the Life

17 So when Jesus came, He found that he had already been in the tomb four days. 18 Now Bethany was near Jerusalem, about two miles[1] away. 19 And many of the Jews had joined the women around Martha and Mary, to comfort them concerning their brother.

20 Then Martha, as soon as she heard that Jesus was coming, went and met Him, but Mary was sitting in the house. 21 Now Martha said to Jesus, "Lord, if You had been here, my brother would not have died. 22 But even now I know that [a]whatever You ask of God, God will give You."

23 Jesus said to her, "Your brother will rise again."

24 Martha said to Him, [a]"I know that he will rise again in the resurrection at the last day."

25 Jesus said to her, "I am [a]the resurrection and the life. [b]He who believes in Me, though he may [c]die, he shall live. 26 And whoever lives and believes in Me shall never die. Do you believe this?"

27 She said to Him, "Yes, Lord, [a]I believe that You are the Christ, the Son of God, who is to come into the world."

Jesus and Death, the Last Enemy

28 And when she had said these things, she went her way and secretly called Mary her sister, saying, "The Teacher has come and is calling for you." 29 As soon as she heard *that,* she arose quickly and came to Him. 30 Now Jesus had not yet come into the town, but was[1] in the place where Martha met Him. 31 [a]Then the Jews who were with her in the house, and comforting her, when they saw that Mary rose up quickly and went out, followed her, saying, "She is going to the tomb to weep there."[1]

32 Then, when Mary came where Jesus was, and saw Him, she [a]fell down at His feet, saying to Him, [b]"Lord, if You had been here, my brother would not have died."

33 Therefore, when Jesus saw her weeping, and the Jews who came with her weeping, He groaned in the spirit and was troubled. 34 And He said, "Where have you laid him?"

They said to Him, "Lord, come and see."

35 [a]Jesus wept. 36 Then the Jews said, "See how He loved him!"

37 And some of them said, "Could not this Man, [a]who opened the eyes of the blind, also have kept this man from dying?"

Lazarus Raised from the Dead

38 Then Jesus, again groaning in Himself, came to the tomb. It was a cave, and a [a]stone lay against it. 39 Jesus said, "Take away the stone."

Martha, the sister of him who was dead, said to Him, "Lord, by this time there is a stench, for he has been *dead* four days."

40 Jesus said to her, "Did I not say to you that if you would believe you would [a]see the glory of God?" 41 Then they took away the stone *from the place* where the dead man was lying.[1] And Jesus lifted up *His* eyes and said, "Father, I thank You that You have heard Me. 42 And I know that You always hear Me, but [a]because of the people who are standing by I said *this,* that they may believe that You sent Me." 43 Now when He had said these things, He cried with a loud voice, "Lazarus, come forth!" 44 And he who had died came out bound hand and foot with [a]graveclothes, and [b]his face was wrapped with a cloth. Jesus said to them, "Loose him, and let him go."

The Plot to Kill Jesus
(Matt. 26:1–5; Mark 14:1, 2; Luke 22:1, 2)

45 Then many of the Jews who had come to Mary, [a]and had seen the things Jesus did, believed in Him. 46 But some of them went

---

11:16 [a] Matt. 10:3; Mark 3:18; Luke 6:15; John 14:5; 20:26–28; Acts 1:13 11:18 [1] Literally *fifteen stadia* 11:22 [a] [John 9:31; 11:41] 11:24 [a] [Luke 14:14; John 5:29] 11:25 [a] John 5:21; 6:39, 40, 44; [Rev. 1:18] [b] John 3:16, 36; 1 John 5:10 [c] 1 Cor. 15:22; [Heb. 9:27] 11:27 [a] Matt. 16:16; Luke 2:11; John 4:42; 6:14, 69 11:30 [1] NU-Text adds *still.* 11:31 [a] John 11:19, 33 [1] NU-Text reads *supposing that she was going to the tomb to weep there.* 11:32 [a] Mark 5:22; 7:25; Rev. 1:17 [b] John 11:21 11:35 [a] Luke 19:41 11:37 [a] John 9:6, 7 11:38 [a] Matt. 27:60, 66; Mark 15:46; Luke 24:2; John 20:1 11:40 [a] [John 11:4, 23] 11:41 [1] NU-Text omits *from the place where the dead man was lying.* 11:42 [a] John 12:30; 17:21 11:44 [a] John 19:40 [b] John 20:7 11:45 [a] John 2:23; 10:42; 12:11, 18

away to the Pharisees and [a]told them the
things Jesus did. 47[a]Then the chief priests
and the Pharisees gathered a council and
said, [b]"What shall we do? For this Man
works many signs. 48If we let Him alone
like this, everyone will believe in Him, and
the Romans will come and take away both
our place and nation."

49And one of them, [a]Caiaphas, being
high priest that year, said to them, "You
know nothing at all, 50[a]nor do you consider
that it is expedient for us[1] that one man
should die for the people, and not that the
whole nation should perish." 51Now this
he did not say on his own *authority;* but
being high priest that year he prophesied
that Jesus would die for the nation, 52and
[a]not for that nation only, but [b]also that He
would gather together in one the children
of God who were scattered abroad.

53Then, from that day on, they plotted
to [a]put Him to death. 54[a]Therefore Jesus no
longer walked openly among the Jews, but
went from there into the country near the
wilderness, to a city called [b]Ephraim, and
there remained with His disciples.

55[a]And the Passover of the Jews was near,
and many went from the country up to Jerusalem before the Passover, to [b]purify themselves. 56[a]Then they sought Jesus, and spoke
among themselves as they stood in the temple, "What do you think—that He will not
come to the feast?" 57Now both the chief
priests and the Pharisees had given a command, that if anyone knew where He was, he
should report *it,* that they might [a]seize Him.

The Anointing at Bethany
(Matt. 26:6–13; Mark 14:3–9)

12 Then, six days before the Passover,
Jesus came to Bethany, [a]where Lazarus was who had been dead,[1] whom He had
raised from the dead. 2[a]There they made
Him a supper; and Martha served, but Lazarus was one of those who sat at the table
with Him. 3Then [a]Mary took a pound of
very costly oil of [b]spikenard, anointed the
feet of Jesus, and wiped His feet with her
hair. And the house was filled with the fragrance of the oil.

4But one of His disciples, [a]Judas Iscariot, Simon's *son,* who would betray Him,
said, 5"Why was this fragrant oil not sold
for three hundred denarii[1] and given to the
poor?" 6This he said, not that he cared for
the poor, but because he was a thief, and
[a]had the money box; and he used to take
what was put in it.

7But Jesus said, "Let her alone; she has
kept[1] this for the day of My burial. 8For [a]the
poor you have with you always, but Me you
do not have always."

The Plot to Kill Lazarus

9Now a great many of the Jews knew that
He was there; and they came, not for Jesus'
sake only, but that they might also see Lazarus, [a]whom He had raised from the dead.
10[a]But the chief priests plotted to put Lazarus to death also, 11[a]because on account of
him many of the Jews went away and believed in Jesus.

The Triumphal Entry
(Matt. 21:1–11; Mark 11:1–11; Luke 19:28–40)

12[a]The next day a great multitude that
had come to the feast, when they heard
that Jesus was coming to Jerusalem, 13took
branches of palm trees and went out to
meet Him, and cried out:

"Hosanna!
[a]'Blessed *is* He who comes in
the name of the LORD!'[1]
The King of Israel!"

14[a]Then Jesus, when He had found a
young donkey, sat on it; as it is written:

15 "Fear[a] not, daughter of Zion;
Behold, your King is coming,
Sitting on a donkey's colt."[1]

11:46 [a] John 5:15 11:47 [a] Ps. 2:2; Matt. 26:3; Mark 14:1; Luke 22:2 [b] John 12:19; Acts 4:16 11:49 [a] Matt. 26:3; Luke 3:2; John 18:14; Acts 4:6 11:50 [a] John 18:14 [1] NU-Text reads *you.* 11:52 [a] Is. 49:6; Acts 10:45; 11:18; 13:46; [1 John 2:2] [b] Ps. 22:27; John 10:16; [Eph. 2:14–17] 11:53 [a] Matt. 26:4; Luke 6:11; 19:47; 22:2; John 5:16 11:54 [a] John 4:1, 3; 7:1 [b] 2 Chr. 13:19 11:55 [a] Matt. 26:1; Mark 14:1; Luke 22:1; John 2:13; 5:1; 6:4 [b] Num. 9:10, 13; 31:19, 20; 2 Chr. 30:17; Luke 2:22 11:56 [a] John 7:11 11:57 [a] Matt. 26:14–16 12:1 [a] Matt. 21:17; John 11:1, 43 [1] NU-Text omits *who had been dead.* 12:2 [a] Matt. 26:6; Mark 14:3; Luke 10:38–41 12:3 [a] Luke 10:38, 39; John 11:2 [b] Song 1:12 12:4 [a] John 13:26 12:5 [1] About one year's wages for a worker 12:6 [a] John 13:29 12:7 [1] NU-Text reads *that she may keep.* 12:8 [a] Deut. 15:11; Matt. 26:11; Mark 14:7; John 17:11 12:9 [a] John 11:43, 44 12:10 [a] Luke 16:31 12:11 [a] John 11:45; 12:18 12:12 [a] Matt. 21:4–9; Mark 11:7–10; Luke 19:35–38 12:13 [a] Ps. 118:25, 26 [1] Psalm 118:26 12:14 [a] Matt. 21:7 12:15 [a] Is. 40:9; Zech. 9:9 [1] Zechariah 9:9

16[a]His disciples did not understand these things at first; [b]but when Jesus was glorified, [c]then they remembered that these things were written about Him and *that* they had done these things to Him.

17Therefore the people, who were with Him when He called Lazarus out of his tomb and raised him from the dead, bore witness. 18[a]For this reason the people also met Him, because they heard that He had done this sign. 19The Pharisees therefore said among themselves, [a]"You see that you are accomplishing nothing. Look, the world has gone after Him!"

The Fruitful Grain of Wheat

20Now there [a]were certain Greeks among those [b]who came up to worship at the feast. 21Then they came to Philip, [a]who was from Bethsaida of Galilee, and asked him, saying, "Sir, we wish to see Jesus."

22Philip came and told Andrew, and in turn Andrew and Philip told Jesus.

23But Jesus answered them, saying, [a]"The hour has come that the Son of Man should be glorified. 24Most assuredly, I say to you, [a]unless a grain of wheat falls into the ground and dies, it remains alone; but if it dies, it produces much grain. 25[a]He who loves his life will lose it, and he who hates his life in this world will keep it for eternal life. 26If anyone serves Me, let him [a]follow Me; and [b]where I am, there My servant will be also. If anyone serves Me, him *My* Father will honor.

Jesus Predicts His Death on the Cross

27[a]"Now My soul is troubled, and what shall I say? 'Father, save Me from this hour'? [b]But for this purpose I came to this hour. 28Father, glorify Your name."

[a]Then a voice came from heaven, *saying,* "I have both glorified *it* and will glorify *it* again."

29Therefore the people who stood by and heard *it* said that it had thundered. Others said, "An angel has spoken to Him."

30Jesus answered and said, [a]"This voice did not come because of Me, but for your sake. 31Now is the judgment of this world; now [a]the ruler of this world will be cast out. 32And I, [a]if I am lifted up from the earth, will draw [b]all *peoples* to Myself." 33[a]This He said, signifying by what death He would die.

34The people answered Him, [a]"We have heard from the law that the Christ remains forever; and how *can* You say, 'The Son of Man must be lifted up'? Who is this Son of Man?"

35Then Jesus said to them, "A little while longer [a]the light is with you. [b]Walk while you have the light, lest darkness overtake you; [c]he who walks in darkness does not know where he is going. 36While you have the light, believe in the light, that you may become [a]sons of light." These things Jesus spoke, and departed, and [b]was hidden from them.

Who Has Believed Our Report?

37But although He had done so many [a]signs before them, they did not believe in Him, 38that the word of Isaiah the prophet might be fulfilled, which he spoke:

> [a]"Lord, who has believed our report?
> And to whom has the arm of
> the LORD been revealed?"[1]

39Therefore they could not believe, because Isaiah said again:

> 40"He[a] has blinded their eyes and
> hardened their hearts,
> [b]Lest they should see with *their* eyes,
> Lest they should understand
> with *their* hearts and turn,
> So that I should heal them."[1]

41[a]These things Isaiah said when[1] he saw His glory and spoke of Him.

Walk in the Light

42Nevertheless even among the rulers many believed in Him, but [a]because of the

---

12:16 [a] Luke 18:34 [b] John 7:39; 12:23 [c] [John 14:26] 12:18 [a] John 12:11 12:19 [a] John 11:47, 48 12:20 [a] Mark 7:26; Acts 17:4 [b] 1 Kin. 8:41, 42; Acts 8:27 12:21 [a] John 1:43, 44; 14:8–11 12:23 [a] Matt. 26:18, 45; John 13:32; Acts 3:13 12:24 [a] [Rom. 14:9]; 1 Cor. 15:36 12:25 [a] Matt. 10:39; Mark 8:35; Luke 9:24 12:26 [a] [Matt. 16:24] [b] John 14:3; 17:24; [1 Thess. 4:17] 12:27 [a] [Matt. 26:38, 39]; Mark 14:34; Luke 12:50; John 11:33 [b] Luke 22:53; John 18:37 12:28 [a] Matt. 3:17; 17:5; Mark 1:11; 9:7; Luke 3:22; 9:35 12:30 [a] John 11:42 12:31 [a] Matt. 12:29; Luke 10:18; [Acts 26:18; 2 Cor. 4:4] 12:32 [a] John 3:14; 8:28 [b] [Rom. 5:18; Heb. 2:9] 12:33 [a] John 18:32; 21:19 12:34 [a] Ps. 89:36, 37; Is. 9:6, 7; Mic. 4:7 12:35 [a] [John 1:9; 7:33; 8:12] [b] Jer. 13:16; [Gal. 6:10]; Eph. 5:8 [c] John 11:10; [1 John 2:9–11] 12:36 [a] Luke 16:8; John 8:12 [b] John 8:59 12:37 [a] John 11:47 12:38 [a] Is. 53:1; Rom. 10:16 [1] Isaiah 53:1 12:40 [a] Is. 6:9, 10 [b] Matt. 13:14 [1] Isaiah 6:10 12:41 [a] Is. 6:1 [1] NU-Text reads *because.* 12:42 [a] John 7:13; 9:22

Pharisees they did not confess *Him,* lest
they should be put out of the synagogue;
43[a]for they loved the praise of men more
than the praise of God.
44Then Jesus cried out and said, [a]"He
who believes in Me, [b]believes not in Me
[c]but in Him who sent Me. 45And [a]he who
sees Me sees Him who sent Me. 46[a]I have
come *as* a light into the world, that whoever
believes in Me should not abide in darkness. 47And if anyone hears My words and
does not believe,[1] [a]I do not judge him; for
[b]I did not come to judge the world but to
save the world. 48[a]He who rejects Me, and
does not receive My words, has that which
judges him—[b]the word that I have spoken
will judge him in the last day. 49For [a]I have
not spoken on My own *authority;* but the
Father who sent Me gave Me a command,
[b]what I should say and what I should speak.
50And I know that His command is everlasting life. Therefore, whatever I speak,
just as the Father has told Me, so I [a]speak."

Jesus Washes the Disciples' Feet

13 Now [a]before the Feast of the Passover, when Jesus knew that [b]His hour
had come that He should depart from this
world to the Father, having loved His own
who were in the world, He [c]loved them to
the end.
2And supper being ended,[1] [a]the devil having already put it into the heart of Judas Iscariot, Simon's *son,* to betray Him, 3Jesus,
knowing [a]that the Father had given all things
into His hands, and that He [b]had come from
God and [c]was going to God, 4[a]rose from supper and laid aside His garments, took a towel
and girded Himself. 5After that, He poured
water into a basin and began to wash the disciples' feet, and to wipe *them* with the towel
with which He was girded. 6Then He came to
Simon Peter. And *Peter* said to Him, [a]"Lord,
are You washing my feet?"
7Jesus answered and said to him, "What
I am doing you [a]do not understand now,
[b]but you will know after this."
8Peter said to Him, "You shall never
wash my feet!"
Jesus answered him, [a]"If I do not wash
you, you have no part with Me."
9Simon Peter said to Him, "Lord, not my
feet only, but also *my* hands and *my* head!"
10Jesus said to him, "He who is bathed
needs only to wash *his* feet, but is completely clean; and [a]you are clean, but not
all of you." 11For [a]He knew who would betray Him; therefore He said, "You are not
all clean."
12So when He had washed their feet,
taken His garments, and sat down again,
He said to them, "Do you know what I have
done to you? 13[a]You call Me Teacher and
Lord, and you say well, for *so* I am. 14[a]If I
then, *your* Lord and Teacher, have washed
your feet, [b]you also ought to wash one another's feet. 15For [a]I have given you an example, that you should do as I have done
to you. 16[a]Most assuredly, I say to you, a
servant is not greater than his master; nor
is he who is sent greater than he who sent
him. 17[a]If you know these things, blessed
are you if you do them.

Jesus Identifies His Betrayer
(Matt. 26:21–25; Mark 14:18, 19; Luke 22:21–23)

18"I do not speak concerning all of you.
I know whom I have chosen; but that the
[a]Scripture may be fulfilled, [b]'He who eats
bread with Me[1] has lifted up his heel against
Me.'[2] 19[a]Now I tell you before it comes, that
when it does come to pass, you may believe
that I am *He.* 20[a]Most assuredly, I say to you,
he who receives whomever I send receives
Me; and he who receives Me receives Him
who sent Me."
21[a]When Jesus had said these things, [b]He
was troubled in spirit, and testified and
said, "Most assuredly, I say to you, [c]one of

12:43 [a] John 5:41, 44 12:44 [a] Mark 9:37 [b] [John 3:16, 18, 36; 11:25, 26] [c] [John 5:24] 12:45 [a] [John 14:9] 12:46 [a] John 1:4, 5; 8:12; 12:35, 36 12:47 [a] John 5:45 [b] John 3:17 [1] NU-Text reads *keep them.* 12:48 [a] [Luke 10:16] [b] Deut. 18:18, 19; [John 5:45; 8:47] 12:49 [a] John 8:38 [b] Deut. 18:18 12:50 [a] John 5:19; 8:28 13:1 [a] Matt. 26:2 [b] John 12:23; 17:1 [c] John 15:9 13:2 [a] Luke 22:3 [1] NU-Text reads *And during supper.* 13:3 [a] Matt. 11:27; [John 5:20–23; 17:2]; Acts 2:36; 1 Cor. 15:27; [Heb. 2:8] [b] John 8:42; 16:28 [c] John 17:11; 20:17 13:4 [a] [Luke 22:27; Phil. 2:7, 8] 13:6 [a] Matt. 3:14 13:7 [a] John 12:16; 16:12 [b] John 13:19 13:8 [a] [Ps. 51:2, 7; Ezek. 36:25; Acts 22:16; 1 Cor. 6:11; Eph. 5:26; Titus 3:5; Heb. 10:22] 13:10 [a] [John 15:3; Eph. 5:26] 13:11 [a] John 6:64; 18:4 13:13 [a] Matt. 23:8, 10; Luke 6:46; [1 Cor. 8:6; 12:3]; Eph. 6:9; [Phil. 2:11] 13:14 [a] Luke 22:27 [b] [Rom. 12:10; Gal. 6:1, 2; 1 Pet. 5:5] 13:15 [a] Matt. 11:29; Phil. 2:5; [1 Pet. 2:21–24]; 1 John 2:6 13:16 [a] Matt. 10:24; [Luke 6:40]; John 15:20 13:17 [a] Matt. 7:24; Luke 11:28; [James 1:25] 13:18 [a] John 15:25; 17:12 [b] Ps. 41:9; Matt. 26:23 [1] NU-Text reads *My bread.* [2] Psalm 41:9 13:19 [a] John 14:29; 16:4 13:20 [a] Matt. 10:40; Mark 9:37; Luke 9:48; 10:16; Gal. 4:14 13:21 [a] Matt. 26:21; Mark 14:18; Luke 22:21 [b] John 12:27 [c] Ps. 41:9; Matt. 26:46; Mark 14:42; Luke 22:48; John 6:64; 18:5; Acts 1:17; 1 John 2:19

you will betray Me." 22Then the disciples
looked at one another, perplexed about
whom He spoke.
23Now [a]there was leaning on Jesus'
bosom one of His disciples, whom Jesus
loved. 24Simon Peter therefore motioned
to him to ask who it was of whom He spoke.
25Then, leaning back[1] on Jesus' breast,
he said to Him, "Lord, who is it?"
26Jesus answered, "It is he to whom I
shall give a piece of bread when I have
dipped *it.*" And having dipped the bread,
He gave *it* to [a]Judas Iscariot, *the son* of Simon. 27[a]Now after the piece of bread, Satan entered him. Then Jesus said to him,
"What you do, do quickly." 28But no one
at the table knew for what reason He said
this to him. 29For some thought, because
[a]Judas had the money box, that Jesus had
said to him, "Buy *those things* we need for
the feast," or that he should give something
to the poor.
30Having received the piece of bread,
he then went out immediately. And it was
night.

The New Commandment

31So, when he had gone out, Jesus said,
[a]"Now the Son of Man is glorified, and [b]God
is glorified in Him. 32If God is glorified in
Him, God will also glorify Him in Himself,
and [a]glorify Him immediately. 33Little children, I shall be with you a [a]little while longer.
You will seek Me; [b]and as I said to the Jews,
'Where I am going, you cannot come,' so
now I say to you. 34[a]A new commandment
I give to you, that you love one another; as
I have loved you, that you also love one another. 35[a]By this all will know that you are My
disciples, if you have love for one another."

Jesus Predicts Peter's Denial

36Simon Peter said to Him, "Lord, where
are You going?"
Jesus answered him, "Where I [a]am going
you cannot follow Me now, but [b]you shall
follow Me afterward."
37Peter said to Him, "Lord, why can I not
follow You now? I will [a]lay down my life for
Your sake."
38Jesus answered him, "Will you lay
down your life for My sake? Most assuredly,
I say to you, the rooster shall not [a]crow till
you have denied Me three times.

The Way, the Truth, and the Life

14 "Let [a]not your heart be troubled; you
believe in God, believe also in Me. 2In
My Father's house are many mansions;[1] if
it were not *so,* I would have told you. [a]I go
to prepare a place for you.[2] 3And if I go and
prepare a place for you, [a]I will come again
and receive you to Myself; that [b]where I am,
there you may be also. 4And where I go you
know, and the way you know."
5[a]Thomas said to Him, "Lord, we do not
know where You are going, and how can we
know the way?"
6Jesus said to him, "I am [a]the way, [b]the
truth, and [c]the life. [d]No one comes to the
Father [e]except through Me.

The Father Revealed

7[a]"If you had known Me, you would have
known My Father also; and from now on
you know Him and have seen Him."
8Philip said to Him, "Lord, show us the
Father, and it is sufficient for us."
9Jesus said to him, "Have I been with
you so long, and yet you have not known
Me, Philip? [a]He who has seen Me has seen
the Father; so how can you say, 'Show us
the Father'? 10Do you not believe that [a]I am
in the Father, and the Father in Me? The
words that I speak to you [b]I do not speak
on My own *authority;* but the Father who
dwells in Me does the works. 11Believe Me
that I *am* in the Father and the Father in
Me, [a]or else believe Me for the sake of the
works themselves.

13:23 [a] John 19:26; 20:2; 21:7, 20 13:25 [1] NU-Text and M-Text add *thus.* 13:26 [a] Matt. 10:4; John 6:70, 71; 12:4; Acts 1:16 13:27 [a] Luke 22:3 13:29 [a] John 12:6 13:31 [a] John 12:23; Acts 3:13 [b] [John 14:13; 17:4; 1 Pet. 4:11] 13:32 [a] John 12:23 13:33 [a] John 12:35; 14:19; 16:16–19 [b] Mark 16:19; [John 7:34; 8:21]; Acts 1:9 13:34 [a] Lev. 19:18; Eph. 5:2; 1 Thess. 4:9; James 2:8; 1 Pet. 1:22; 1 John 2:7 13:35 [a] 1 John 2:5 13:36 [a] John 13:33; 14:2; 16:5 [b] John 21:17; 2 Pet. 1:14 13:37 [a] Matt. 26:33–35; Mark 14:29–31; Luke 22:33, 34 13:38 [a] Matt. 26:74; Mark 14:30; Luke 22:61; John 18:25–27 14:1 [a] [John 14:27; 16:22, 24] 14:2 [a] Matt. 25:34; John 13:33, 36; Heb. 11:16 [1] Literally *dwellings* [2] NU-Text adds a word which would cause the text to read either *if it were not so, would I have told you that I go to prepare a place for you?* or *if it were not so I would have told you; for I go to prepare a place for you.* 14:3 [a] [Acts 1:11] [b] [John 12:26; 1 Thess. 4:17] 14:5 [a] Matt. 10:3; John 11:16; 20:24–29; 21:2 14:6 [a] [John 10:9; Rom. 5:2; Eph. 2:18; Heb. 9:8; 10:19, 20] [b] [John 1:14, 17; 8:32; 18:37] [c] [John 11:25] [d] 1 Tim. 2:5 [e] [John 10:7–9; Acts 4:12] 14:7 [a] John 8:19 14:9 [a] John 12:45; Col. 1:15; Heb. 1:3 14:10 [a] John 10:38; 14:11, 20 [b] Deut. 18:18; John 5:19; 14:24 14:11 [a] John 5:36; 10:38

ACT IN CONFIDENCE

INHALE

My relationship of four years abruptly ended. I am shattered as the self-blame game keeps creeping in. We went to college together and had planned to get married. But problems crept in, and isolation began pulling us apart. Now, I feel like I am not good enough to be loved by anyone. How do I move forward when I feel totally destroyed and love has left me so broken?

EXHALE

No matter how hard we try, our own expectations can lead to frustration and disappointment. Defeat will overtake us especially if we miss the key component to every relationship: Christ. He is there if your relationship survives, and Christ is there even if it does not. The most you can do is your best in any relationship.

If you find all your effort is in vain and you are broken, take heart! In John 14:1 Jesus says, "Let not your heart be troubled; you believe in God, believe also in Me." No matter the circumstance, whenever life holds trouble and sorrow, look to Christ, who gives strength and the will to move forward in faith no matter what.

A relationship with Jesus is one you can always depend on; you can truly believe Jesus will be there at every turn of life. Relationships can bring deep pain and even result in depression and defeat. This is not God's will for you. Jesus will be with you in every situation and provide the comfort you need as He walks you into healing and peace.

Most people profess to a belief in God. However, we must realize even the demons believe in Him. It was Jesus who brought connection between us and our heavenly Father. We must realize that because of Jesus' sacrifice for us, we are in a relationship with the One who created us and utterly knows us. He knows our pain and our need. Because of Jesus, we have complete access to God and His power to heal all our hurts. Turn to Him and find the cure for your brokenness.

The Answered Prayer

12[a]"Most assuredly, I say to you, he who
believes in Me, the works that I do he will do
also; and greater *works* than these he will
do, because I go to My Father. 13[a]And whatever you ask in My name, that I will do, that
the Father may be [b]glorified in the Son. 14If
you ask[1] anything in My name, I will do *it*.

Jesus Promises Another Helper

15[a]"If you love Me, keep[1] My commandments. 16And I will pray the Father, and [a]He
will give you another Helper, that He may
abide with you forever— 17[a]the Spirit of
truth, [b]whom the world cannot receive, because it neither sees Him nor knows Him;
but you know Him, for He dwells with you
[c]and will be in you. 18[a]I will not leave you
orphans; [b]I will come to you.

Indwelling of the Father and the Son

19"A little while longer and the world will
see Me no more, but [a]you will see Me. [b]Be-
cause I live, you will live also. 20At that day
you will know that [a]I *am* in My Father, and
you in Me, and I in you. 21[a]He who has My
commandments and keeps them, it is he
who loves Me. And he who loves Me will be
loved by My Father, and I will love him and
manifest Myself to him."

22[a]Judas (not Iscariot) said to Him,

14:12 [a] Matt. 21:21; Mark 16:17; Luke 10:17 14:13 [a] Matt. 7:7; [Mark 11:24]; Luke 11:9; John 15:16; 16:23, 24; [James 1:5–7; 1 John 3:22] [b] John 13:31 14:14 [1] NU-Text adds *Me*. 14:15 [a] 1 John 5:3 [1] NU-Text reads *you will keep*. 14:16 [a] [John 15:26; 20:22]; Acts 2:4, 33; Rom. 8:15 14:17 [a] [John 15:26; 16:13; 1 John 4:6; 5:7] [b] [1 Cor. 2:14] [c] [1 John 2:27] 14:18 [a] [Matt. 28:20] [b] [John 14:3, 28] 14:19 [a] John 16:16, 22 [b] [Rom. 5:10; 1 Cor. 15:20; 2 Cor. 4:10] 14:20 [a] John 10:38; 14:11 14:21 [a] 1 John 2:5 14:22 [a] Luke 6:16; Acts 1:13

"Lord, how is it that You will manifest Yourself to us, and not to the world?"
23 Jesus answered and said to him, "If
anyone loves Me, he will keep My word;
and My Father will love him, [a]and We will
come to him and make Our home with him.
24 He who does not love Me does not keep
My words; and [a]the word which you hear
is not Mine but the Father's who sent Me.

The Gift of His Peace

25 "These things I have spoken to you
while being present with you. 26 But [a]the
Helper, the Holy Spirit, whom the Father
will [b]send in My name, [c]He will teach you
all things, and bring to your [d]remembrance
all things that I said to you. 27 [a]Peace I leave
with you, My peace I give to you; not as the
world gives do I give to you. Let not your
heart be troubled, neither let it be afraid.
28 You have heard Me [a]say to you, 'I am going away and coming *back* to you.' If you
loved Me, you would rejoice because I said,[1]
[b]'I am going to the Father,' for [c]My Father
is greater than I.
29 "And [a]now I have told you before it
comes, that when it does come to pass, you
may believe. 30 I will no longer talk much
with you, [a]for the ruler of this world is coming, and he has [b]nothing in Me. 31 But that
the world may know that I love the Father,
and [a]as the Father gave Me commandment,
so I do. Arise, let us go from here.

The True Vine

15 "I am the true vine, and My Father is
the vinedresser. 2 [a]Every branch in Me
that does not bear fruit He takes away;[1] and
every *branch* that bears fruit He prunes,
that it may bear [b]more fruit. 3 [a]You are already clean because of the word which I
have spoken to you. 4 [a]Abide in Me, and I
in you. As the branch cannot bear fruit of
itself, unless it abides in the vine, neither
can you, unless you abide in Me.
5 "I am the vine, you *are* the branches. He
who abides in Me, and I in him, bears much
[a]fruit; for without Me you can do [b]nothing.
6 If anyone does not abide in Me, [a]he is cast
out as a branch and is withered; and they
gather them and throw *them* into the fire,
and they are burned. 7 If you abide in Me,
and My words [a]abide in you, [b]you will[1] ask
what you desire, and it shall be done for
you. 8 [a]By this My Father is glorified, that
you bear much fruit; [b]so you will be My
disciples.

Love and Joy Perfected

9 "As the Father [a]loved Me, I also have
loved you; abide in My love. 10 [a]If you keep
My commandments, you will abide in My
love, just as I have kept My Father's commandments and abide in His love.
11 "These things I have spoken to you,
that My joy may remain in you, and [a]*that*
your joy may be full. 12 [a]This is My [b]com-
mandment, that you love one another as I
have loved you. 13 [a]Greater love has no one
than this, than to lay down one's life for
his friends. 14 [a]You are My friends if you
do whatever I command you. 15 No longer
do I call you servants, for a servant does
not know what his master is doing; but
I have called you friends, [a]for all things
that I heard from My Father I have made
known to you. 16 [a]You did not choose Me,
but I chose you and [b]appointed you that
you should go and bear fruit, and *that* your
fruit should remain, that whatever you ask
the Father [c]in My name He may give you.
17 These things I command you, that you
love one another.

The World's Hatred

18 [a]"If the world hates you, you know that
it hated Me before *it hated* you. 19 [a]If you
were of the world, the world would love its
own. Yet [b]because you are not of the world,
but I chose you out of the world, therefore
the world hates you. 20 Remember the word
that I said to you, [a]'A servant is not greater

14:23 [a] 2 Cor. 6:16; Eph. 3:17; [1 John 2:24]; Rev. 3:20; 21:3 14:24 [a] John 5:19 14:26 [a] Luke 24:49 [b] John 15:26 [c] 1 Cor. 2:13 [d] John 2:22; 12:16; 1 John 2:20 14:27 [a] Luke 1:79; [John 16:33; 20:19; Phil. 4:7]; Col. 3:15 14:28 [a] John 14:3, 18 [b] John 16:16 [c] [John 5:18; Phil. 2:6] [1] NU-Text omits *I said.* 14:29 [a] John 13:19 14:30 [a] [John 12:31] [b] [John 8:46; 2 Cor. 5:21; Heb. 4:15; 1 Pet. 1:19; 2:22] 14:31 [a] Is. 50:5; John 10:18; Phil. 2:8 15:2 [a] Matt. 15:13 [b] [Matt. 13:12] [1] Or *lifts up* 15:3 [a] [John 13:10; 17:17]; Eph. 5:26 15:4 [a] John 17:23; Eph. 3:17; [Col. 1:23] 15:5 [a] Hos. 14:8; [Gal. 5:22, 23] [b] 2 Cor. 3:5 15:6 [a] Matt. 3:10 15:7 [a] 1 John 2:14 [b] John 14:13; 16:23 [1] NU-Text omits *you will.* 15:8 [a] Ps. 22:23; [Matt. 5:16]; John 13:31; 17:4; [Phil. 1:11]; 1 Pet. 4:11 [b] John 8:31 15:9 [a] John 5:20; 17:26 15:10 [a] John 14:15 15:11 [a] [John 16:24]; 1 John 1:4 15:12 [a] John 13:34; 1 John 3:11 [b] Rom. 12:9 15:13 [a] Eph. 5:2; 1 John 3:16 15:14 [a] [Matt. 12:50; 28:20]; John 14:15, 21; Acts 10:42; 1 John 3:23, 24 15:15 [a] Gen. 18:17 15:16 [a] John 6:70; 13:18; 15:19; 1 John 4:10 [b] [Matt. 28:19; Mark 16:15; Col. 1:6] [c] John 14:13; 16:23, 24 15:18 [a] John 7:7; 1 John 3:13 15:19 [a] 1 John 4:5 [b] John 17:14 15:20 [a] Matt. 10:24; John 13:16

than his master.' If they persecuted Me,
they will also persecute you. [b]If they kept
My word, they will keep yours also. 21 But
[a]all these things they will do to you for My
name's sake, because they do not know Him
who sent Me. 22 [a]If I had not come and spoken to them, they would have no sin, [b]but
now they have no excuse for their sin. 23 [a]He
who hates Me hates My Father also. 24 If
I had not done among them [a]the works
which no one else did, they would have
no sin; but now they have [b]seen and also
hated both Me and My Father. 25 But *this
happened* that the word might be fulfilled
which is written in their law, [a]'They hated
Me without a cause.'[1]

The Coming Rejection

26 [a]"But when the Helper comes, whom I
shall send to you from the Father, the Spirit
of truth who proceeds from the Father, [b]He
will testify of Me. 27 And [a]you also will bear
witness, because [b]you have been with Me
from the beginning.

16 "These things I have spoken to you,
that you [a]should not be made to
stumble. 2 [a]They will put you out of the synagogues; yes, the time is coming [b]that whoever kills you will think that he offers God
service. 3 And [a]these things they will do to
you[1] because they have not known the Father nor Me. 4 But these things I have told
you, that when the[1] time comes, you may
remember that I told you of them.
"And these things I did not say to you
at the beginning, because I was with you.

The Work of the Holy Spirit

5 "But now I [a]go away to Him who sent
Me, and none of you asks Me, 'Where are
You going?' 6 But because I have said these
things to you, [a]sorrow has filled your heart.
7 Nevertheless I tell you the truth. It is to
your advantage that I go away; for if I do
not go away, the Helper will not come to
you; but [a]if I depart, I will send Him to you.
8 And when He has [a]come, He will convict
the world of sin, and of righteousness, and
of judgment: 9 [a]of sin, because they do not
believe in Me; 10 [a]of righteousness, [b]because
I go to My Father and you see Me no more;
11 [a]of judgment, because [b]the ruler of this
world is judged.

12 "I still have many things to say to you,
[a]but you cannot bear *them* now. 13 However,
when He, [a]the Spirit of truth, has come, [b]He
will guide you into all truth; for He will not
speak on His own *authority,* but whatever
He hears He will speak; and He will tell you
things to come. 14 [a]He will glorify Me, for He
will take of what is Mine and declare *it* to
you. 15 [a]All things that the Father has are
Mine. Therefore I said that He will take of
Mine and declare *it* to you.[1]

Sorrow Will Turn to Joy

16 "A [a]little while, and you will not see Me;
and again a little while, and you will see Me,
[b]because I go to the Father."

17 Then *some* of His disciples said among
themselves, "What is this that He says to us,
'A little while, and you will not see Me; and
again a little while, and you will see Me';
and, 'because I go to the Father'?" 18 They
said therefore, "What is this that He says,
'A little while'? We do not know what He is
saying."

19 Now Jesus knew that they desired to
ask Him, and He said to them, "Are you
inquiring among yourselves about what
I said, 'A little while, and you will not see
Me; and again a little while, and you will
see Me'? 20 Most assuredly, I say to you that
you will weep and [a]lament, but the world
will rejoice; and you will be sorrowful, but
your sorrow will be turned into [b]joy. 21 [a]A
woman, when she is in labor, has sorrow
because her hour has come; but as soon as
she has given birth to the child, she no longer remembers the anguish, for joy that a
human being has been born into the world.
22 Therefore you now have sorrow; but I will

15:20 [b] Ezek. 3:7 15:21 [a] Matt. 10:22; 24:9; [1 Pet. 4:14]; Rev. 2:3 15:22 [a] John 9:41; 15:24 [b] [Rom. 1:20; James 4:17] 15:23 [a] 1 John 2:23 15:24 [a] John 3:2 [b] John 14:9 15:25 [a] Ps. 35:19; 69:4; 109:3–5 [1] Psalm 69:4 15:26 [a] Luke 24:49; [John 14:17]; Acts 2:4, 33 [b] 1 John 5:6 15:27 [a] Luke 24:48; 1 Pet. 5:1; 2 Pet. 1:16 [b] Matt. 3:14; Luke 1:2; 1 John 1:1 16:1 [a] Matt. 11:6 16:2 [a] John 9:22 [b] Acts 8:1 16:3 [a] John 8:19; 15:21; Acts 13:27; Rom. 10:2 [1] NU-Text and M-Text omit *to you.* 16:4 [1] NU-Text reads *their.* 16:5 [a] John 7:33; 13:33; 14:28; 17:11 16:6 [a] Matt. 17:23; [John 16:20, 22] 16:7 [a] Acts 2:33 16:8 [a] Acts 1:8; 2:1–4, 37 16:9 [a] Acts 2:22 16:10 [a] Acts 2:32 [b] John 5:32 16:11 [a] Acts 26:18 [b] [Luke 10:18] 16:12 [a] Mark 4:33 16:13 [a] [John 14:17] [b] John 14:26; Acts 11:28; Rev. 1:19 16:14 [a] John 15:26 16:15 [a] Matt. 11:27; John 3:35 [1] NU-Text and M-Text read *He takes of Mine and will declare it to you.* 16:16 [a] John 7:33; 12:35; 13:33; 14:19; 19:40–42; 20:19 [b] John 13:3 16:20 [a] Mark 16:10; Luke 23:48; 24:17 [b] Luke 24:32, 41 16:21 [a] Gen. 3:16; Is. 13:8; 26:17; 42:14; 1 Thess. 5:3

see you again and [a]your heart will rejoice,
and your joy no one will take from you.
23“And in that day you will ask Me nothing. [a]Most assuredly, I say to you, whatever
you ask the Father in My name He will give
you. 24Until now you have asked nothing in
My name. Ask, and you will receive, [a]that
your joy may be [b]full.

Jesus Christ Has Overcome the World

25“These things I have spoken to you in
figurative language; but the time is coming
when I will no longer speak to you in figurative language, but I will tell you [a]plainly
about the Father. 26In that day you will
ask in My name, and I do not say to you
that I shall pray the Father for you; 27[a]for
the Father Himself loves you, because you
have loved Me, and [b]have believed that
I came forth from God. 28[a]I came forth
from the Father and have come into the
world. Again, I leave the world and go to
the Father.”
29His disciples said to Him, “See, now
You are speaking plainly, and using no figure of speech! 30Now we are sure that [a]You
know all things, and have no need that anyone should question You. By this [b]we believe that You came forth from God.”
31Jesus answered them, “Do you now
believe? 32[a]Indeed the hour is coming, yes,
has now come, that you will be scattered,
[b]each to his own, and will leave Me alone.
And [c]yet I am not alone, because the Father
is with Me. 33These things I have spoken to
you, that [a]in Me you may have peace. [b]In
the world you will[1] have tribulation; but be
of good cheer, [c]I have overcome the world.”

Jesus Prays for Himself

17 Jesus spoke these words, lifted up His
eyes to heaven, and said: “Father, [a]the
hour has come. Glorify Your Son, that Your
Son also may glorify You, 2[a]as You have
given Him authority over all flesh, that He
should[1] give eternal life to as many [b]as You

#OXYGEN

JOHN 16:33

Act in Confidence

This present world is not as God intended it to be. When Jesus returns, however, all will become as it should have been. We don’t have to wait for that glorious day to have a taste of it now, though. By being born again, we have been connected to God according to His original design. We can have peace and joy today because Jesus has overcome the world. We can trust Him to lead and guide us.

Your life matters and you have a purpose, so **breathe and act in confidence**.

have given Him. 3And [a]this is eternal life,
that they may know You, [b]the only true God,
and Jesus Christ [c]whom You have sent. 4[a]I
have glorified You on the earth. [b]I have finished the work [c]which You have given Me to
do. 5And now, O Father, glorify Me together
with Yourself, with the glory [a]which I had
with You before the world was.

Jesus Prays for His Disciples

6[a]“I have manifested Your name to the
men [b]whom You have given Me out of the
world. [c]They were Yours, You gave them to
Me, and they have kept Your word. 7Now
they have known that all things which You
have given Me are from You. 8For I have
given to them the words [a]which You have
given Me; and they have received *them*,
[b]and have known surely that I came forth
from You; and they have believed that [c]You
sent Me.
9“I pray for them. [a]I do not pray for the
world but for those whom You have given
Me, for they are Yours. 10And all Mine are
Yours, and [a]Yours are Mine, and I am glorified in them. 11[a]Now I am no longer in
the world, but these are in the world, and
I come to You. Holy Father, [b]keep through

16:22 [a] Luke 24:41; John 14:1, 27; 20:20; Acts 2:46; 13:52; 1 Pet. 1:8 **16:23** [a] Matt. 7:7; [John 14:13; 15:16] **16:24** [a] John 17:13 [b] John 15:11 **16:25** [a] John 7:13 **16:27** [a] [John 14:21, 23] [b] John 3:13 **16:28** [a] John 13:1, 3; 16:5, 10, 17 **16:30** [a] John 21:17 [b] John 17:8 **16:32** [a] Zech. 13:7; Matt. 26:31, 56; Mark 14:27, 50; Acts 8:1 [b] John 20:10 [c] John 8:29 **16:33** [a] [Is. 9:6; Rom. 5:1; Eph. 2:14] [b] 2 Tim. 3:12 [c] Rom. 8:37; [1 John 4:4] [1] NU-Text and M-Text omit *will*. **17:1** [a] John 12:23 **17:2** [a] Dan. 7:14; Matt. 11:27; John 3:35; [Phil. 2:10; Heb. 2:8] [b] John 6:37, 39; 17:6, 9, 24 [1] M-Text reads *shall*. **17:3** [a] [Is. 53:11]; Jer. 9:23, 24 [b] 1 Cor. 8:4; 1 Thess. 1:9 [c] John 3:34 **17:4** [a] John 13:31 [b] [Dan. 9:24]; John 4:34; 19:30 [c] Is. 49:3; 50:5; John 14:31 **17:5** [a] Prov. 8:22–30; John 1:1, 2; Phil. 2:6; Col. 1:15; Heb. 1:3 **17:6** [a] Ps. 22:22 [b] John 6:37 [c] Ezek. 18:4; Rom. 14:8 **17:8** [a] John 8:28 [b] John 8:42; 16:27, 30 [c] Deut. 18:15, 18 **17:9** [a] [1 John 5:19] **17:10** [a] John 16:15 **17:11** [a] [Mark 16:19; Luke 24:51]; John 13:1; [Acts 1:9; Heb. 4:14; 9:24; 1 Pet. 3:22] [b] [1 Pet. 1:5]; Jude 1

Your name those whom You have given Me,[1]
that they may be one [c]as We *are.* 12While I
was with them in the world,[1] [a]I kept them
in Your name. Those whom You gave Me I
have kept;[2] and [b]none of them is lost [c]ex-
cept the son of perdition, [d]that the Scripture might be fulfilled. 13But now I come to
You, and these things I speak in the world,
that they may have My joy fulfilled in themselves. 14I have given them Your word; [a]and
the world has hated them because they are
not of the world, [b]just as I am not of the
world. 15I do not pray that You should take
them out of the world, but [a]that You should
keep them from the evil one. 16They are not
of the world, just as I am not of the world.
17[a]Sanctify them by Your truth. [b]Your word
is truth. 18[a]As You sent Me into the world, I
also have sent them into the world. 19And
[a]for their sakes I sanctify Myself, that they
also may be sanctified by the truth.

Jesus Prays for All Believers

20"I do not pray for these alone, but also
for those who will[1] believe in Me through
their word; 21[a]that they all may be one, as
[b]You, Father, *are* in Me, and I in You; that
they also may be one in Us, that the world
may believe that You sent Me. 22And the
[a]glory which You gave Me I have given
them, [b]that they may be one just as We are
one: 23I in them, and You in Me; [a]that they
may be made perfect in one, and that the
world may know that You have sent Me,
and have loved them as You have loved Me.
24[a]"Father, I desire that they also whom
You gave Me may be with Me where I am,
that they may behold My glory which You
have given Me; [b]for You loved Me before
the foundation of the world. 25O righteous
Father! [a]The world has not known You, but
[b]I have known You; and [c]these have known
that You sent Me. 26[a]And I have declared to
them Your name, and will declare *it,* that
the love [b]with which You loved Me may be
in them, and I in them."

Betrayal and Arrest in Gethsemane
(Matt. 26:47–56; Mark 14:43–52; Luke 22:47–53)

18 When Jesus had spoken these words,
[a]He went out with His disciples over
[b]the Brook Kidron, where there was a garden, which He and His disciples entered.
2And Judas, who betrayed Him, also knew
the place; [a]for Jesus often met there with
His disciples. 3[a]Then Judas, having received
a detachment *of troops,* and officers from
the chief priests and Pharisees, came there
with lanterns, torches, and weapons. 4Jesus
therefore, [a]knowing all things that would
come upon Him, went forward and said to
them, "Whom are you seeking?"

5They answered Him, [a]"Jesus of Nazareth."

Jesus said to them, "I am *He.*" And Judas, who [b]betrayed Him, also stood with
them. 6Now when He said to them, "I am
He," they drew back and fell to the ground.

7Then He asked them again, "Whom are
you seeking?"

And they said, "Jesus of Nazareth."

8Jesus answered, "I have told you that I
am *He.* Therefore, if you seek Me, let these
go their way," 9that the saying might be fulfilled which He spoke, [a]"Of those whom You
gave Me I have lost none."

10[a]Then Simon Peter, having a sword,
drew it and struck the high priest's servant,
and cut off his right ear. The servant's name
was Malchus.

11So Jesus said to Peter, "Put your sword
into the sheath. Shall I not drink [a]the cup
which My Father has given Me?"

Before the High Priest

12Then the detachment *of troops* and
the captain and the officers of the Jews

17:11 [c] John 10:30 [1] NU-Text and M-Text read *keep them through Your name which You have given Me.* 17:12 [a] Heb. 2:13 [b] [John 6:39; 18:9]; 1 John 2:19 [c] Matt. 27:4, 5; John 6:70; Acts 1:16–20 [d] Ps. 41:9; 109:8; John 13:18; Acts 1:20 [1] NU-Text omits *in the world.* [2] NU-Text reads *in Your name which You gave Me. And I guarded them;* (or *it;*). 17:14 [a] Matt. 24:9; Luke 6:22; 21:17; John 15:19; 1 John 3:13 [b] John 8:23 17:15 [a] Matt. 6:13; Gal. 1:4; 2 Thess. 3:3; [2 Tim. 4:18]; 2 Pet. 2:9; 1 John 5:18 17:17 [a] [Acts 15:9; Eph. 5:26; 1 Pet. 1:22] [b] Ps. 119:9, 142, 151 17:18 [a] John 4:38; 20:21 17:19 [a] 1 Cor. 1:2; 1 Thess. 4:7; [Heb. 10:10] 17:20 [1] NU-Text and M-Text omit *will.* 17:21 [a] [John 10:16; Rom. 12:5; Gal. 3:28]; Eph. 4:4, 6 [b] John 10:38; 17:11, 23 17:22 [a] John 14:20; 1 John 1:3 [b] [2 Cor. 3:18] 17:23 [a] [Col. 3:14] 17:24 [a] [John 12:26; 14:3; 1 Thess. 4:17] [b] Matt. 25:34; John 17:5 17:25 [a] John 15:21 [b] John 7:29; 8:55; 10:15 [c] John 3:17; 17:3, 8, 18, 21, 23 17:26 [a] Ex. 34:5–7; John 17:6 [b] John 15:9; [Eph. 3:17–19] 18:1 [a] Matt. 26:30, 36; Mark 14:26, 32; Luke 22:39 [b] 2 Sam. 15:23; 1 Kin. 2:37; 15:13; 2 Kin. 23:4, 6, 12; 2 Chr. 15:16; 29:16; 30:14; Jer. 31:40 18:2 [a] Luke 21:37; 22:39 18:3 [a] Matt. 26:47–56; Mark 14:43–50; Luke 22:47–53; Acts 1:16 18:4 [a] John 6:64; 13:1, 3; 19:28 18:5 [a] Matt. 21:11; Mark 1:24; 14:67; 16:6; Luke 18:37; 24:19 [b] Ps. 41:9; Matt. 20:18; 26:21; John 13:21 18:9 [a] [John 6:39; 17:12] 18:10 [a] Matt. 26:51; Mark 14:47; Luke 22:49, 50 18:11 [a] Matt. 20:22; 26:39; Mark 14:36; Luke 22:42

arrested Jesus and bound Him. 13And [a]they
led Him away to [b]Annas first, for he was the
father-in-law of [c]Caiaphas who was high
priest that year. 14[a]Now it was Caiaphas who
advised the Jews that it was expedient that
one man should die for the people.

Peter Denies Jesus
(Matt. 26:69–75; Mark 14:66–72;
Luke 22:54–62)

15[a]And Simon Peter followed Jesus, and
so *did* [b]another[1] disciple. Now that disciple
was known to the high priest, and went with
Jesus into the courtyard of the high priest.
16[a]But Peter stood at the door outside. Then
the other disciple, who was known to the
high priest, went out and spoke to her who
kept the door, and brought Peter in. 17Then
the servant girl who kept the door said to
Peter, "You are not also *one* of this Man's
disciples, are you?"
He said, "I am [a]not."
18Now the servants and officers who
had made a fire of coals stood there, for
it was cold, and they warmed themselves.
And Peter stood with them and warmed
himself.

Jesus Questioned by the High Priest

19The high priest then asked Jesus about
His disciples and His doctrine.
20Jesus answered him, [a]"I spoke openly
to the world. I always taught [b]in synagogues
and [c]in the temple, where the Jews always
meet,[1] and in secret I have said nothing.
21Why do you ask Me? Ask [a]those who have
heard Me what I said to them. Indeed they
know what I said."
22And when He had said these things,
one of the officers who stood by [a]struck
Jesus with the palm of his hand, saying,
"Do You answer the high priest like that?"
23Jesus answered him, "If I have spoken
evil, bear witness of the evil; but if well, why
do you strike Me?"
24[a]Then Annas sent Him bound to [b]Ca-
iaphas the high priest.

Peter Denies Twice More

25Now Simon Peter stood and warmed
himself. [a]Therefore they said to him, "You
are not also *one* of His disciples, are you?"
He denied *it* and said, "I am not!"
26One of the servants of the high priest,
a relative *of him* whose ear Peter cut off,
said, "Did I not see you in the garden with
Him?" 27Peter then denied again; and [a]im-
mediately a rooster crowed.

In Pilate's Court
(Matt. 27:1, 2, 11–14; Mark 15:1–5; Luke 23:1–5)

28[a]Then they led Jesus from Caiaphas to
the Praetorium, and it was early morning.
[b]But they themselves did not go into the
Praetorium, lest they should be defiled, but
that they might eat the Passover. 29[a]Pilate
then went out to them and said, "What accusation do you bring against this Man?"
30They answered and said to him, "If He
were not an evildoer, we would not have
delivered Him up to you."
31Then Pilate said to them, "You take
Him and judge Him according to your law."
Therefore the Jews said to him, "It is
not lawful for us to put anyone to death,"
32[a]that the saying of Jesus might be fulfilled
which He spoke, [b]signifying by what death
He would die.
33[a]Then Pilate entered the Praetorium
again, called Jesus, and said to Him, "Are
You the King of the Jews?"
34Jesus answered him, "Are you speaking for yourself about this, or did others
tell you this concerning Me?"
35Pilate answered, "Am I a Jew? Your
own nation and the chief priests have delivered You to me. What have You done?"
36[a]Jesus answered, [b]"My kingdom is not
of this world. If My kingdom were of this
world, My servants would fight, so that I
should not be delivered to the Jews; but
now My kingdom is not from here."
37Pilate therefore said to Him, "Are You
a king then?"
Jesus answered, "You say *rightly* that I

18:13 [a] Matt. 26:57 [b] Luke 3:2; John 18:24; Acts 4:6 [c] Matt. 26:3; John 11:49, 51 18:14 [a] John 11:50 18:15 [a] Matt. 26:58; Mark 14:54; Luke 22:54 [b] John 20:2–5 [1] M-Text reads *the other.* 18:16 [a] Matt. 26:69; Mark 14:66–68; Luke 22:55–57 18:17 [a] Matt. 26:34 18:20 [a] Matt. 26:55; Luke 4:15; John 8:26 [b] John 6:59 [c] Mark 14:49; John 7:14, 28 [1] NU-Text reads *where all the Jews meet.* 18:21 [a] Mark 12:37 18:22 [a] Job 16:10; Is. 50:6; Jer. 20:2; Lam. 3:30; Acts 23:2 18:24 [a] Matt. 26:57; Luke 3:2; Acts 4:6 [b] John 11:49 18:25 [a] Matt. 26:71–75; Mark 14:69–72; Luke 22:58–62 18:27 [a] Matt. 26:74; Mark 14:72; Luke 22:60; John 13:38 18:28 [a] Matt. 27:2; Mark 15:1; Luke 23:1; Acts 3:13 [b] John 11:55; Acts 10:28; 11:3 18:29 [a] Matt. 27:11–14; Mark 15:2–5; Luke 23:2, 3 18:32 [a] Matt. 20:17–19; 26:2; Mark 10:33; Luke 18:32 [b] John 3:14; 8:28; 12:32, 33 18:33 [a] Matt. 27:11 18:36 [a] 1 Tim. 6:13 [b] [Dan. 2:44; 7:14]; Luke 12:14; John 6:15; 8:15

am a king. For this cause I was born, and for
this cause I have come into the world, [a]that
I should bear [b]witness to the truth. Everyone who [c]is of the truth [d]hears My voice."
38Pilate said to Him, "What is truth?"
And when he had said this, he went out
again to the Jews, and said to them, [a]"I find
no fault in Him at all.

Taking the Place of Barabbas
(Matt. 27:15–23; Mark 15:6–14; Luke 23:13–23)

39[a]"But you have a custom that I should
release someone to you at the Passover. Do
you therefore want me to release to you the
King of the Jews?"
40[a]Then they all cried again, saying, "Not
this Man, but Barabbas!" [b]Now Barabbas
was a robber.

The Soldiers Mock Jesus
(Matt. 27:27–31; Mark 15:16–20)

19 So then [a]Pilate took Jesus and
scourged *Him.* 2And the soldiers
twisted a crown of thorns and put *it* on His
head, and they put on Him a purple robe.
3Then they said,[1] "Hail, King of the Jews!"
And they [a]struck Him with their hands.
4Pilate then went out again, and said
to them, "Behold, I am bringing Him out
to you, [a]that you may know that I find no
fault in Him."

Pilate's Decision

5Then Jesus came out, wearing the
crown of thorns and the purple robe. And
Pilate said to them, "Behold the Man!"
6[a]Therefore, when the chief priests and
officers saw Him, they cried out, saying,
"Crucify *Him,* crucify *Him!*"
Pilate said to them, "You take Him and
crucify *Him,* for I find no fault in Him."
7The Jews answered him, [a]"We have a law,
and according to our[1] law He ought to die,
because [b]He made Himself the Son of God."
8Therefore, when Pilate heard that saying, he was the more afraid, 9and went
again into the Praetorium, and said to
Jesus, "Where are You from?" [a]But Jesus
gave him no answer.
10Then Pilate said to Him, "Are You not
speaking to me? Do You not know that I
have power to crucify You, and power to
release You?"
11Jesus answered, [a]"You could have no
power at all against Me unless it had been
given you from above. Therefore [b]the one
who delivered Me to you has the greater sin."
12From then on Pilate sought to release
Him, but the Jews cried out, saying, "If you
let this Man go, you are not Caesar's friend.
[a]Whoever makes himself a king speaks
against Caesar."
13[a]When Pilate therefore heard that saying, he brought Jesus out and sat down in
the judgment seat in a place that is called
The Pavement, but in Hebrew, Gabbatha.
14Now [a]it was the Preparation Day of the
Passover, and about the sixth hour. And
he said to the Jews, "Behold your King!"
15But they cried out, "Away with *Him,*
away with *Him!* Crucify Him!"
Pilate said to them, "Shall I crucify your
King?"
The chief priests answered, [a]"We have
no king but Caesar!"
16[a]Then he delivered Him to them to
be crucified. Then they took Jesus and led
Him away.[1]

The King on a Cross
(Matt. 27:32–56; Mark 15:21–41;
Luke 23:26–49)

17[a]And He, bearing His cross, [b]went out
to a place called *the Place* of a Skull, which
is called in Hebrew, Golgotha, 18where they
crucified Him, and [a]two others with Him,
one on either side, and Jesus in the center.
19[a]Now Pilate wrote a title and put *it* on the
cross. And the writing was:

JESUS OF NAZARETH, THE
KING OF THE JEWS.

18:37 [a] [Matt. 5:17; 20:28; Luke 4:43; 12:49; 19:10; John 3:17; 9:39; 10:10; 12:47] [b] Is. 55:4; Rev. 1:5 [c] [John 14:6] [d] John 8:47; 10:27; [1 John 3:19; 4:6] 18:38 [a] Is. 53:9; Matt. 27:24; Luke 23:4; John 19:4, 6; 1 Pet. 2:22–24 18:39 [a] Matt. 27:15–26; Mark 15:6–15; Luke 23:17–25 18:40 [a] Is. 53:3; Acts 3:14 [b] Luke 23:19 19:1 [a] Matt. 20:19; 27:26; Mark 15:15; Luke 18:33 19:3 [a] Is. 50:6 [1] NU-Text reads *And they came up to Him and said.* 19:4 [a] Is. 53:9; John 18:33, 38; 1 Pet. 2:22–24 19:6 [a] Acts 3:13 19:7 [a] Lev. 24:16 [b] Matt. 26:63–66; John 5:18; 10:33 [1] NU-Text reads *the law.* 19:9 [a] Is. 53:7; Matt. 27:12, 14; Luke 23:9 19:11 [a] [Luke 22:53]; John 7:30 [b] John 3:27; Rom. 13:1 19:12 [a] Luke 23:2; John 18:33; Acts 17:7 19:13 [a] Deut. 1:17; 1 Sam. 15:24; Prov. 29:25; Is. 51:12; Acts 4:19 19:14 [a] Matt. 27:62; John 19:31, 42 19:15 [a] [Gen. 49:10] 19:16 [a] Matt. 27:26, 31; Mark 15:15; Luke 23:24 [1] NU-Text omits *and led Him away.* 19:17 [a] Matt. 27:31, 33; Mark 15:21, 22; Luke 23:26, 33 [b] Num. 15:36; Heb. 13:12 19:18 [a] Ps. 22:16–18; Is. 53:12; Matt. 20:19; 26:2 19:19 [a] Matt. 27:37; Mark 15:26; Luke 23:38

20 Then many of the Jews read this title, for the place where Jesus was crucified was near the city; and it was written in Hebrew, Greek, *and* Latin.

21 Therefore the chief priests of the Jews said to Pilate, "Do not write, 'The King of the Jews,' but, 'He said, "I am the King of the Jews." ' "

22 Pilate answered, "What I have written, I have written."

23 [a]Then the soldiers, when they had crucified Jesus, took His garments and made four parts, to each soldier a part, and also the tunic. Now the tunic was without seam, woven from the top in one piece. 24 They said therefore among themselves, "Let us not tear it, but cast lots for it, whose it shall be," that the Scripture might be fulfilled which says:

[a]"They divided My garments
among them,
And for My clothing they cast lots."[1]

Therefore the soldiers did these things.

Behold Your Mother

25 [a]Now there stood by the cross of Jesus His mother, and His mother's sister, Mary the *wife* of [b]Clopas, and Mary Magdalene. 26 When Jesus therefore saw His mother, and [a]the disciple whom He loved standing by, He said to His mother, [b]"Woman, behold your son!" 27 Then He said to the disciple, "Behold your mother!" And from that hour that disciple took her [a]to his own *home.*

It Is Finished

28 After this, Jesus, knowing[1] that all things were now accomplished, [a]that the Scripture might be fulfilled, said, "I thirst!" 29 Now a vessel full of sour wine was sitting there; and [a]they filled a sponge with sour wine, put *it* on hyssop, and put *it* to His mouth. 30 So when Jesus had received the sour wine, He said, [a]"It is finished!" And bowing His head, He gave up His spirit.

Jesus' Side Is Pierced

31 [a]Therefore, because it was the Preparation *Day,* [b]that the bodies should not remain on the cross on the Sabbath (for that Sabbath was a [c]high day), the Jews asked Pilate that their legs might be broken, and *that* they might be taken away. 32 Then the soldiers came and broke the legs of the first and of the other who was crucified with Him. 33 But when they came to Jesus and saw that He was already dead, they did not break His legs. 34 But one of the soldiers pierced His side with a spear, and immediately [a]blood and water came out. 35 And he who has seen has testified, and his testimony is [a]true; and he knows that he is telling the truth, so that you may [b]believe. 36 For these things were done that the Scripture should be fulfilled, [a]"Not *one* of His bones shall be broken."[1] 37 And again another Scripture says, [a]"They shall look on Him whom they pierced."[1]

Jesus Buried in Joseph's Tomb
(Matt. 27:57–61; Mark 15:42–47; Luke 23:50–56)

38 [a]After this, Joseph of Arimathea, being a disciple of Jesus, but secretly, [b]for fear of the Jews, asked Pilate that he might take away the body of Jesus; and Pilate gave *him* permission. So he came and took the body of Jesus. 39 And [a]Nicodemus, who at first came to Jesus by night, also came, bringing a mixture of [b]myrrh and aloes, about a hundred pounds. 40 Then they took the body of Jesus, and [a]bound it in strips of linen with the spices, as the custom of the Jews is to bury. 41 Now in the place where He was crucified there was a garden, and in the garden a new tomb in which no one had yet been laid. 42 So [a]there they laid Jesus, [b]because of the Jews' Preparation *Day,* for the tomb was nearby.

The Empty Tomb
(Matt. 28:1–10; Mark 16:1–8; Luke 24:1–12)

20 Now the [a]first *day* of the week Mary Magdalene went to the tomb early, while it was still dark, and saw *that*

19:23 [a] Matt. 27:35; Mark 15:24; Luke 23:34 19:24 [a] Ps. 22:18 [1] Psalm 22:18 19:25 [a] Matt. 27:55; Mark 15:40; Luke 2:35; 23:49 [b] Luke 24:18 19:26 [a] John 13:23; 20:2; 21:7, 20, 24 [b] John 2:4 19:27 [a] Luke 18:28; John 1:11; 16:32; Acts 21:6 19:28 [a] Ps. 22:15 [1] M-Text reads *seeing.* 19:29 [a] Ps. 69:21; Matt. 27:48, 50; Mark 15:36; Luke 23:36 19:30 [a] Dan. 9:26; Zech. 11:10, 11; John 17:4 19:31 [a] Matt. 27:62; Mark 15:42; Luke 23:54 [b] Deut. 21:23; Josh. 8:29; 10:26 [c] Ex. 12:16; Lev. 23:6, 7 19:34 [a] [1 John 5:6, 8] 19:35 [a] John 21:24 [b] [John 20:31] 19:36 [a] [Ex. 12:46; Num. 9:12]; Ps. 34:20 [1] Exodus 12:46; Numbers 9:12; Psalm 34:20 19:37 [a] Ps. 22:16, 17; Zech. 12:10; 13:6; Rev. 1:7 [1] Zechariah 12:10 19:38 [a] Matt. 27:57–61; Mark 15:42–47; Luke 23:50–56 [b] [John 7:13; 9:22; 12:42] 19:39 [a] John 3:1, 2; 7:50 [b] Ps. 45:8; Prov. 7:17; Song 4:14; Matt. 2:11 19:40 [a] Luke 24:12; John 20:5, 7; Acts 5:6 19:42 [a] Is. 53:9; Matt. 26:12; Mark 14:8 [b] John 19:14, 31 20:1 [a] Matt. 28:1–8; Mark 16:1–8; Luke 24:1–10; Acts 20:7; 1 Cor. 16:2

the [b]stone had been taken away from the
tomb. 2Then she ran and came to Simon
Peter, and to the [a]other disciple, [b]whom
Jesus loved, and said to them, "They have
taken away the Lord out of the tomb, and
we do not know where they have laid
Him."
3[a]Peter therefore went out, and the other
disciple, and were going to the tomb. 4So
they both ran together, and the other disciple outran Peter and came to the tomb
first. 5And he, stooping down and looking in, saw [a]the linen cloths lying *there;*
yet he did not go in. 6Then Simon Peter
came, following him, and went into the
tomb; and he saw the linen cloths lying
there, 7and [a]the handkerchief that had been
around His head, not lying with the linen
cloths, but folded together in a place by itself. 8Then the [a]other disciple, who came
to the tomb first, went in also; and he saw
and believed. 9For as yet they did not know
the [a]Scripture, that He must rise again from
the dead. 10Then the disciples went away
again to their own homes.

Mary Magdalene Sees the Risen Lord

11[a]But Mary stood outside by the tomb
weeping, and as she wept she stooped down
and looked into the tomb. 12And she saw
two angels in white sitting, one at the head
and the other at the feet, where the body
of Jesus had lain. 13Then they said to her,
"Woman, why are you weeping?"
She said to them, "Because they have
taken away my Lord, and I do not know
where they have laid Him."
14[a]Now when she had said this, she
turned around and saw Jesus standing
there, and [b]did not know that it was Jesus.
15Jesus said to her, "Woman, why are you
weeping? Whom are you seeking?"
She, supposing Him to be the gardener,
said to Him, "Sir, if You have carried Him

JOHN 20:1

I AM MARY MAGDALENE

Now the first day of the week Mary Magdalene went to the tomb early, while it was still dark, and saw that the stone had been taken away from the tomb. John 20:1

I am Mary of Magdala, often called Mary Magdalene. Jesus traveled to the town where I lived, bringing the good news of the kingdom of God. When I came to hear Him, He cast out of me seven demons that had long tormented me. From that time on, I followed Him. Along with some other women, I helped take care of Him and His disciples, financially supporting His ministry. I followed Jesus all the way through what seemed to be the end. I saw when they crucified my Lord. I followed as they carried His body away and watched to see where He was laid. After the Sabbath had passed, I came with the other Mary and Salome to anoint Jesus' body with spices. When we got to the tomb, the stone had been rolled away from the entrance and an angel of the Lord was inside. He told us that Jesus was not there; He had risen! Only a short time later, I was honored to be the first to see Jesus in His resurrected body.

†

It is interesting when people focus on who Mary Magdalene was before she met Jesus. Some think she may have been a prostitute. But the person she became after meeting Jesus is the reason we remember her two thousand years later. We remember Mary Magdalene because she was a steadfast, consistent, and faithful follower of Jesus. All of us have a past; however, none of us should be judged by our past once we have come to know the Lord. We have become brand-new creatures in Him.

20:1 [b] Matt. 27:60, 66; 28:2; Mark 15:46; 16:4; Luke 24:2; John 11:38 20:2 [a] John 21:23, 24 [b] John 13:23; 19:26; 21:7, 20, 24 20:3 [a] Luke 24:12 20:5 [a] John 19:40 20:7 [a] John 11:44 20:8 [a] John 21:23, 24 20:9 [a] Ps. 16:10; Acts 2:25, 31; 13:34, 35 20:11 [a] Mark 16:5 20:14 [a] Matt. 28:9; Mark 16:9 [b] [Luke 24:16, 31]; John 21:4

away, tell me where You have laid Him, and
I will take Him away."
16 Jesus said to her, [a]"Mary!"
She turned and said to Him,[1] "Rabboni!"
(which is to say, Teacher).
17 Jesus said to her, "Do not cling to Me,
for I have not yet [a]ascended to My Father;
but go to [b]My brethren and say to them, [c]'I
am ascending to My Father and your Father, and *to* [d]My God and your God.'"
18 [a]Mary Magdalene came and told the
disciples that she had seen the Lord,[1] and
that He had spoken these things to her.

The Apostles Commissioned
(Luke 24:36–43; 1 Cor. 15:5)

19 [a]Then, the same day at evening, being
the first *day* of the week, when the doors
were shut where the disciples were assembled,[1] for [b]fear of the Jews, Jesus came
and stood in the midst, and said to them,
[c]"Peace *be* with you." 20 When He had said
this, He [a]showed them *His* hands and His
side. [b]Then the disciples were glad when
they saw the Lord.
21 So Jesus said to them again, "Peace
to you! [a]As the Father has sent Me, I also
send you." 22 And when He had said this, He
breathed on *them,* and said to them, "Receive the Holy Spirit. 23 [a]If you forgive the
sins of any, they are forgiven them; if you
retain the *sins* of any, they are retained."

Seeing and Believing

24 Now Thomas, [a]called the Twin, one of
the twelve, was not with them when Jesus
came. 25 The other disciples therefore said
to him, "We have seen the Lord."
So he said to them, "Unless I see in His
hands the print of the nails, and put my
finger into the print of the nails, and put
my hand into His side, I will not believe."
26 And after eight days His disciples were
again inside, and Thomas with them. Jesus
came, the doors being shut, and stood in
the midst, and said, "Peace to you!" 27 Then
He said to Thomas, "Reach your finger here,
and look at My hands; and [a]reach your hand
here, and put *it* into My side. Do not be [b]un-
believing, but believing."
28 And Thomas answered and said to
Him, "My Lord and my God!"
29 Jesus said to him, "Thomas,[1] because
you have seen Me, you have believed.
[a]Blessed *are* those who have not seen and
yet have believed."

That You May Believe

30 And [a]truly Jesus did many other signs
in the presence of His disciples, which are
not written in this book; 31 [a]but these are
written that [b]you may believe that Jesus
[c]is the Christ, the Son of God, [d]and that
believing you may have life in His name.

Breakfast by the Sea

21 After these things Jesus showed
Himself again to the disciples at the
[a]Sea of Tiberias, and in this way He showed
Himself: 2 Simon Peter, [a]Thomas called the
Twin, [b]Nathanael of [c]Cana in Galilee, [d]the
sons of Zebedee, and two others of His disciples were together. 3 Simon Peter said to
them, "I am going fishing."
They said to him, "We are going with you
also." They went out and immediately[1] got
into the boat, and that night they caught
nothing. 4 But when the morning had now
come, Jesus stood on the shore; yet the
disciples [a]did not know that it was Jesus.
5 Then [a]Jesus said to them, "Children, have
you any food?"
They answered Him, "No."
6 And He said to them, [a]"Cast the net on
the right side of the boat, and you will find
some." So they cast, and now they were not
able to draw it in because of the multitude
of fish.
7 Therefore [a]that disciple whom Jesus
loved said to Peter, "It is the Lord!" Now
when Simon Peter heard that it was the
Lord, he put on *his* outer garment (for he had

20:16 [a] John 10:3 [1] NU-Text adds *in Hebrew.* 20:17 [a] Mark 16:19; Luke 24:5; Acts 1:9; 2:34–36; Eph. 4:8–10; Heb. 4:14 [b] Ps. 22:22; Matt. 18:10; Rom. 8:29; Heb. 2:11 [c] John 16:28; 17:11 [d] Eph. 1:17 20:18 [a] Matt. 28:10; Luke 24:10, 23 [1] NU-Text reads *disciples, "I have seen the Lord,"* . . . . 20:19 [a] Mark 16:14; Luke 24:36; John 14:27; 1 Cor. 15:5 [b] John 9:22; 19:38 [c] John 14:27; 16:33; Eph. 2:17 [1] NU-Text omits *assembled.* 20:20 [a] Acts 1:3 [b] John 16:20, 22 20:21 [a] [Matt. 28:18–20]; John 17:18, 19; [2 Tim. 2:2]; Heb. 3:1 20:23 [a] Matt. 16:19; 18:18 20:24 [a] John 11:16 20:27 [a] Ps. 22:16; Zech. 12:10; 13:6; 1 John 1:1 [b] Mark 16:14 20:29 [a] 2 Cor. 5:7; 1 Pet. 1:8 [1] NU-Text and M-Text omit *Thomas.* 20:30 [a] John 21:25 20:31 [a] Luke 1:4 [b] John 19:35; 1 John 5:13 [c] Luke 2:11; 1 John 5:1 [d] John 3:15, 16; 5:24; [1 Pet. 1:8, 9] 21:1 [a] Matt. 26:32; Mark 14:28; John 6:1 21:2 [a] John 20:24 [b] John 1:45–51 [c] John 2:1 [d] Matt. 4:21; Mark 1:19; Luke 5:10 21:3 [1] NU-Text omits *immediately.* 21:4 [a] Luke 24:16; John 20:14 21:5 [a] Luke 24:41 21:6 [a] Luke 5:4, 6, 7 21:7 [a] John 13:23; 20:2

removed it), and plunged into the sea. 8 But
the other disciples came in the little boat (for
they were not far from land, but about two
hundred cubits), dragging the net with fish.
9 Then, as soon as they had come to land,
they saw a fire of coals there, and fish laid
on it, and bread. 10 Jesus said to them, "Bring
some of the fish which you have just caught."

11 Simon Peter went up and dragged the
net to land, full of large fish, one hundred
and fifty-three; and although there were
so many, the net was not broken. 12 Jesus
said to them, [a]"Come *and* eat breakfast."
Yet none of the disciples dared ask Him,
"Who are You?"—knowing that it was the
Lord. 13 Jesus then came and took the bread
and gave it to them, and likewise the fish.

14 This *is* now [a]the third time Jesus
showed Himself to His disciples after He
was raised from the dead.

Jesus Restores Peter

15 So when they had eaten breakfast,
Jesus said to Simon Peter, "Simon, *son* of
Jonah,[1] do you love Me more than these?"

He said to Him, "Yes, Lord; You know
that I love You."

He said to him, [a]"Feed My lambs."

16 He said to him again a second time,
"Simon, *son* of Jonah,[1] do you love Me?"

He said to Him, "Yes, Lord; You know
that I love You."

[a]He said to him, "Tend My [b]sheep."

17 He said to him the third time, "Simon,
son of Jonah,[1] do you love Me?" Peter was
grieved because He said to him the third
time, "Do you love Me?"

And he said to Him, "Lord, [a]You know all
things; You know that I love You."

Jesus said to him, "Feed My sheep.
18 [a]Most assuredly, I say to you, when you
were younger, you girded yourself and
walked where you wished; but when you
are old, you will stretch out your hands, and
another will gird you and carry *you* where
you do not wish." 19 This He spoke, signifying [a]by what death he would glorify God.
And when He had spoken this, He said to
him, [b]"Follow Me."

The Beloved Disciple and His Book

20 Then Peter, turning around, saw
the disciple [a]whom Jesus loved following, [b]who also had leaned on His breast
at the supper, and said, "Lord, who is the
one who betrays You?" 21 Peter, seeing him,
said to Jesus, "But Lord, what *about* this
man?"

22 Jesus said to him, "If I will that he remain [a]till I come, what *is that* to you? You
follow Me."

23 Then this saying went out among the
brethren that this disciple would not die.
Yet Jesus did not say to him that he would
not die, but, "If I will that he remain till I
come, what *is that* to you?"

24 This is the disciple who [a]testifies of
these things, and wrote these things; and
we know that his testimony is true.

25 [a]And there are also many other things
that Jesus did, which if they were written
one by one, [b]I suppose that even the world
itself could not contain the books that
would be written. Amen.

21:12 [a] Acts 10:41 **21:14** [a] John 20:19, 26 **21:15** [a] Acts 20:28; 1 Tim. 4:6; 1 Pet. 5:2 [1] NU-Text reads *John.* **21:16** [a] Matt. 2:6; Acts 20:28; Heb. 13:20; 1 Pet. 2:25; 5:2, 4 [b] Ps. 79:13; Matt. 10:16; 15:24; 25:33; 26:31 [1] NU-Text reads *John.* **21:17** [a] John 2:24, 25; 16:30 [1] NU-Text reads *John.* **21:18** [a] John 13:36; Acts 12:3, 4 **21:19** [a] 2 Pet. 1:13, 14 [b] [Matt. 4:19; 16:24]; John 21:22 **21:20** [a] John 13:23; 20:2 [b] John 13:25 **21:22** [a] [Matt. 16:27, 28; 25:31; 1 Cor. 4:5; 11:26; Rev. 2:25; 3:11; 22:7, 20] **21:24** [a] John 19:35; 3 John 12 **21:25** [a] John 20:30 [b] Amos 7:10

THE

ACTS

OF THE APOSTLES

OVERVIEW

Each of the four Gospels ends with Jesus commissioning His followers to go into the world and make Him known (see Matt. 28:18–20; Mark 16:14–18; Luke 24:46–49; John 20:21–23, 30–31). Likewise, the Acts of the Apostles begins with a similar commission by Jesus (see Acts 1:8), tying it together with the Gospels' record. That Luke addressed Acts to the same Theophilus mentioned in his Gospel further ties the genres together. The Gospels begin the story of Jesus; Acts continues it. Acts, therefore, is the history of how Christ's disciples worked against astounding odds, persecution and violence, and incarceration to carry out Jesus' final command.

The Book of Acts begins with the ascension of Jesus Christ and the birth of the New Testament church. Early on, Acts focuses primarily on Peter but then turns its attention to the apostle Paul and his missionary journeys that spread the gospel throughout the known world. Acts records the journey toward church unity with conflict, schism, persecution, and martyrdom on one hand, and miracles, emerging leadership, and expansion of the church on the other.

The miraculous founding of the church on the day of Pentecost (see 2:1–4) is dated around AD 33. For nearly two thousand years now, the church has been the institutional representation of Christ on the earth. The term *church* comes from the Greek *ekklēsia*, which means "the called-out ones." Acts 2 describes not only the church's founding but also how it was intended to function. Acts 2 provides six pillars that constitute a functional and fruitful church. The first pillar is worship (see vv. 1–11). The church was birthed in the context of Christ-centered, Spirit-filled worship. The second pillar is Christian education and discipleship (see vv. 12–36). The phenomena of the Holy Spirit's arrival required immediate explanation and interpretation. The third pillar is evangelism (see vv. 37–41), which includes sharing the faith and inviting others to repent of their sins and trust in Christ. The fourth pillar of the church is connection, or fellowship (see vv. 42–47). To be part of the church is to experience the benefits of community. The fifth pillar is stewardship (see vv. 42–47) as the new followers of Christ pooled their resources as needed and had everything in common. The final pillar is service (see vv. 42–47). The church is compelled by the power of the Holy Spirit to meet needs within its community. Each of these pillars is expressed by the early church throughout the rest of Acts.

BREATHE IT IN

Acts 8:26–40 records an account of an African official from the Ethiopian government becoming a follower of Christ. The official had visited Jerusalem to participate in a Jewish corporate worship service. While returning south to Ethiopia, the official was perplexed as he read from the Book of Isaiah. Philip, sent by the Holy Spirit, provided insight for this official that illuminated the finished work of Jesus Christ. The encounter concluded with the Ethiopian official professing faith in Christ and being baptized. Worship, education/discipleship, and evangelism all played a role in this Ethiopian coming to Christ.

This account serves as a helpful example of strategic evangelism. When the gospel was shared with this Ethiopian official, it was then effectively shared within the highest levels of Ethiopian royalty and governance. Church tradition contends that this lone believer was the progenitor of the Ethiopian Coptic Church. Christianity eventually became the state religion of Ethiopia around AD 300, some fifty years before Christianity became the official religion of the Roman Empire in Europe and Asia. Why is this significant?

Many Christians see the Bible and Christianity as a European phenomenon because biblical figures have often been portrayed in art as being Caucasian. But Christianity is not the primary, or even exclusively, white religion that the Sistine Chapel and many other places of worship, including many predominantly Black churches, depict. In reality, the majority of individuals in the Bible were Near Eastern and African, with only some coming from Europe. Furthermore, as we see in the account in Acts 8, it is important to understand that Christianity initially spread faster in Africa than it did in Europe. This continues to be true even now.

When we realize that Africa is no stranger to Jesus Christ and the people of Palestine are largely Afro-Asiatic people, it liberates us from a limited or false interpretation of Scripture and the Christian faith. Contrary to the missionaries who justified slavery as a means of evangelizing the "dark continent" of Africa, enslaved people kidnapped from Africa never needed to be sold into slavery and pulled from Africa in order to be converted to Christianity. Christianity was already there. Acts 8 reminds us that we are to appreciate that the Bible is not limited to the racial categories that burden our contemporary worldview. Racial discrimination was not the order of the day during the biblical age, and neither should it be today.

How have social constructs of race in America affected your understanding of a biblical worldview and culture and biblical characters? Consider the fact that the categories of black and white had no value during biblical times. Consider that no one nation or continent has a greater claim on Christianity than any other. God's heart always has been, and always will be, for all to hear the gospel and trust in Christ for salvation. He made each of us distinct and unique in many ways, including race. Race was never meant to divide us; it was designed to give us each a role in the beautiful, diverse, united body of Christ. And it is Christ who makes us one. Remember, on the day of Pentecost people came from Asia, Africa, and Europe, and the Holy Spirit allowed them *all* to share in the revelation of Jesus Christ.

THE ACTS OF THE APOSTLES

Prologue

1 The former account I made, O [a]Theoph-
ilus, of all that Jesus began both to do
and teach, 2[a]until the day in which He was
taken up, after He through the Holy Spirit
[b]had given commandments to the apostles
whom He had chosen, 3[a]to whom He also
presented Himself alive after His suffering
by many infallible proofs, being seen by
them during forty days and speaking of the
things pertaining to the kingdom of God.

The Holy Spirit Promised

4[a]And being assembled together with
them, He commanded them not to depart
from Jerusalem, but to wait for the Promise of the Father, "which," *He said,* "you have
[b]heard from Me; 5[a]for John truly baptized
with water, [b]but you shall be baptized with
the Holy Spirit not many days from now."
6Therefore, when they had come together,
they asked Him, saying, "Lord, will You at
this time restore the kingdom to Israel?"
7And He said to them, [a]"It is not for you
to [b]know times or seasons which the Father has put in His own authority. 8[a]But you
shall receive power [b]when the Holy Spirit
has come upon you; and [c]you shall be witnesses to Me[1] in Jerusalem, and in all Judea
and [d]Samaria, and to the [e]end of the earth."

Jesus Ascends to Heaven
(Mark 16:19, 20; Luke 24:50–53)

9[a]Now when He had spoken these things,
while they watched, [b]He was taken up, and
a cloud received Him out of their sight.
10And while they looked steadfastly toward
heaven as He went up, behold, two men
stood by them [a]in white apparel, 11who also
said, "Men of Galilee, why do you stand gazing up into heaven? This *same* Jesus, who
was taken up from you into heaven, [a]will
so come in like manner as you saw Him go
into heaven."

The Upper Room Prayer Meeting

12[a]Then they returned to Jerusalem from
the mount called Olivet, which is near Jerusalem, a Sabbath day's journey. 13And
when they had entered, they went up [a]into
the upper room where they were staying:
[b]Peter, James, John, and Andrew; Philip
and Thomas; Bartholomew and Matthew;
James *the son* of Alphaeus and [c]Simon
the Zealot; and [d]Judas *the son* of James.
14[a]These all continued with one accord in
prayer and supplication,[1] with [b]the women
and Mary the mother of Jesus, and with
[c]His brothers.

Matthias Chosen
(cf. Ps. 109:8; Matt. 27:7, 8)

15And in those days Peter stood up in
the midst of the disciples[1] (altogether the
number [a]of names was about a hundred
and twenty), and said, 16"Men *and* brethren,
this Scripture had to be fulfilled, [a]which
the Holy Spirit spoke before by the mouth
of David concerning Judas, [b]who became
a guide to those who arrested Jesus; 17for

1:1 [a] Luke 1:3 1:2 [a] Mark 16:19; Acts 1:9, 11, 22 [b] Matt. 28:19; Mark 16:15; John 20:21; Acts 10:42 1:3 [a] Matt. 28:17; Mark 16:12, 14; Luke 24:34, 36; John 20:19, 26; 21:1, 14; 1 Cor. 15:5–7 1:4 [a] Luke 24:49 [b] [John 14:16, 17, 26; 15:26]; Acts 2:33 1:5 [a] Matt. 3:11; Mark 1:8; Luke 3:16; John 1:33; Acts 11:16 [b] [Joel 2:28] 1:7 [a] 1 Thess. 5:1 [b] Matt. 24:36; Mark 13:32 1:8 [a] [Acts 2:1, 4] [b] Luke 24:49 [c] Luke 24:48; John 15:27 [d] Acts 8:1, 5, 14 [e] Matt. 28:19; Mark 16:15; Rom. 10:18; Col. 1:23; [Rev. 14:6] [1] NU-Text reads *My witnesses.* 1:9 [a] Luke 24:50, 51 [b] Ps. 68:18; 110:1; Mark 16:19; Luke 23:43; John 20:17; Acts 1:2; [Heb. 4:14; 9:24; 1 Pet. 3:22] 1:10 [a] Matt. 28:3; Mark 16:5; Luke 24:4; John 20:12; Acts 10:3, 30 1:11 [a] Dan. 7:13; Mark 13:26; Luke 21:27; [John 14:3]; 2 Thess. 1:10; Rev. 1:7 1:12 [a] Luke 24:52 1:13 [a] Mark 14:15; Luke 22:12; Acts 9:37, 39; 20:8 [b] Matt. 10:2–4 [c] Luke 6:15 [d] Jude 1 1:14 [a] Acts 2:1, 46 [b] Luke 23:49, 55 [c] Matt. 13:55 [1] NU-Text omits *and supplication.* 1:15 [a] Luke 22:32; Rev. 3:4 [1] NU-Text reads *brethren.* 1:16 [a] Ps. 41:9 [b] Matt. 26:47; Mark 14:43; Luke 22:47; John 18:3

[a]he was numbered with us and obtained a
part in [b]this ministry."
18 [a](Now this man purchased a field with
[b]the wages of iniquity; and falling headlong, he burst open in the middle and all
his entrails gushed out. 19 And it became
known to all those dwelling in Jerusalem;
so that field is called in their own language,
Akel Dama, that is, Field of Blood.)
20 "For it is written in the Book of Psalms:

[a]'Let his dwelling place be desolate,
And let no one live in it';[1]

and,

[b]'Let[2] another take his office.'[3]

21 "Therefore, of these men who have accompanied us all the time that the Lord
Jesus went in and out among us, 22 beginning from the baptism of John to that day
when [a]He was taken up from us, one of
these must [b]become a witness with us of
His resurrection."
23 And they proposed two: Joseph called
[a]Barsabas, who was surnamed Justus, and
Matthias. 24 And they prayed and said, "You,
O Lord, [a]who know the hearts of all, show
which of these two You have chosen 25 [a]to
take part in this ministry and apostleship
from which Judas by transgression fell, that
he might go to his own place." 26 And they cast
their lots, and the lot fell on Matthias. And
he was numbered with the eleven apostles.

Coming of the Holy Spirit

2 When [a]the Day of Pentecost had fully
come, [b]they were all with one accord[1]
in one place. 2 And suddenly there came a
sound from heaven, as of a rushing mighty
wind, and [a]it filled the whole house where
they were sitting. 3 Then there appeared to
them divided tongues, as of fire, and *one*
sat upon each of them. 4 And [a]they were
all filled with the Holy Spirit and began
[b]to speak with other tongues, as the Spirit
gave them utterance.

The Crowd's Response

5 And there were dwelling in Jerusalem
Jews, [a]devout men, from every nation under heaven. 6 And when this sound occurred, the [a]multitude came together, and
were confused, because everyone heard
them speak in his own language. 7 Then
they were all amazed and marveled, saying to one another, "Look, are not all these
who speak [a]Galileans? 8 And how *is it that*
we hear, each in our own language in which
we were born? 9 Parthians and Medes and
Elamites, those dwelling in Mesopotamia,
Judea and [a]Cappadocia, Pontus and Asia,
10 Phrygia and Pamphylia, Egypt and the
parts of Libya adjoining Cyrene, visitors
from Rome, both Jews and proselytes, 11 Cretans and Arabs—we hear them speaking in
our own tongues the wonderful works of
God." 12 So they were all amazed and perplexed, saying to one another, "Whatever
could this mean?"
13 Others mocking said, "They are full of
new wine."

Peter's Sermon
(Joel 2:28–32)

14 But Peter, standing up with the eleven,
raised his voice and said to them, "Men of
Judea and all who dwell in Jerusalem, let
this be known to you, and heed my words.
15 For these are not drunk, as you suppose,
[a]since it is *only* the third hour of the day.
16 But this is what was spoken by the prophet
Joel:

17 'And[a] it shall come to pass in
the last days, says God,
[b]That I will pour out of My
Spirit on all flesh;
Your sons and [c]your daughters
shall prophesy,
Your young men shall see visions,
Your old men shall dream dreams.
18 And on My menservants and
on My maidservants
I will pour out My Spirit in those days;
[a]And they shall prophesy.

1:17 [a] Matt. 10:4 [b] Acts 1:25 1:18 [a] Matt. 27:3–10 [b] Matt. 18:7; 26:14, 15, 24; Mark 14:21; Luke 22:22; John 17:12 1:20 [a] Ps. 69:25 [b] Ps. 109:8 [1] Psalm 69:25 [2] Psalm 109:8 [3] Greek *episkopen,* position of overseer 1:22 [a] Acts 1:9 [b] Acts 1:8; 2:32 1:23 [a] Acts 15:22 1:24 [a] 1 Sam. 16:7; Jer. 17:10; Acts 1:2 1:25 [a] Acts 1:17 2:1 [a] Lev. 23:15; Deut. 16:9; Acts 20:16; 1 Cor. 16:8 [b] Acts 1:14 [1] NU-Text reads *together.* 2:2 [a] Acts 4:31 2:4 [a] Matt. 3:11; 5:6; 10:20; Luke 3:16; John 14:16; 16:7–15; Acts 1:5 [b] Mark 16:17; Acts 10:46; 19:6; [1 Cor. 12:10, 28, 30; 13:1] 2:5 [a] Luke 2:25; Acts 8:2 2:6 [a] Acts 4:32 2:7 [a] Matt. 26:73; Acts 1:11 2:9 [a] 1 Pet. 1:1 2:15 [a] 1 Thess. 5:7 2:17 [a] Is. 44:3; Ezek. 11:19; Joel 2:28–32; [Zech. 12:10; John 7:38] [b] Acts 10:45 [c] Acts 21:9 2:18 [a] Acts 21:4, 9; 1 Cor. 12:10

19 [a]I will show wonders in heaven above
And signs in the earth beneath:
Blood and fire and vapor of smoke.
20 [a]The sun shall be turned into darkness,
And the moon into blood,
Before the coming of the great and
awesome day of the LORD.
21 And it shall come to pass
That [a]whoever calls on the
name of the LORD
Shall be saved.'[1]

22"Men of Israel, hear these words: Jesus
of Nazareth, a Man attested by God to you
[a]by miracles, wonders, and signs which
God did through Him in your midst, as
you yourselves also know— 23Him, [a]be-
ing delivered by the determined purpose
and foreknowledge of God, [b]you have taken[1]
by lawless hands, have crucified, and put
to death; 24[a]whom God raised up, having
loosed the pains of death, because it was
not possible that He should be held by it.
25For David says concerning Him:

[a]'I foresaw the LORD always
before my face,
For He is at my right hand, that
I may not be shaken.
26 Therefore my heart rejoiced,
and my tongue was glad;
Moreover my flesh also
will rest in hope.
27 For You will not leave my
soul in Hades,
Nor will You allow Your Holy
One to see [a]corruption.
28 You have made known to
me the ways of life;
You will make me full of joy
in Your presence.'[1]

29"Men *and* brethren, let *me* speak freely
to you [a]of the patriarch David, that he is
both dead and buried, and his tomb is with
us to this day. 30Therefore, being a prophet,
[a]and knowing that God had sworn with an
oath to him that of the fruit of his body, according to the flesh, He would raise up the
Christ to sit on his throne,[1] 31he, foreseeing
this, spoke concerning the resurrection
of the Christ, [a]that His soul was not left in
Hades, nor did His flesh see corruption.
32[a]This Jesus God has raised up, [b]of which
we are all witnesses. 33Therefore [a]being exalted to [b]the right hand of God, and [c]having
received from the Father the promise of the
Holy Spirit, He [d]poured out this which you
now see and hear.

34"For David did not ascend into the
heavens, but he says himself:

[a]'The LORD said to my Lord,
"Sit at My right hand,
35 Till I make Your enemies
Your footstool."'[1]

36"Therefore let all the house of Israel
know assuredly that God has made this
Jesus, whom you crucified, both Lord and
Christ."

37Now when they heard *this,* [a]they were
cut to the heart, and said to Peter and the
rest of the apostles, "Men *and* brethren,
what shall we do?"

38Then Peter said to them, [a]"Repent,
and let every one of you be baptized in the
name of Jesus Christ for the remission of
sins; and you shall receive the gift of the
Holy Spirit. 39For the promise is to you and
[a]to your children, and [b]to all who are afar
off, as many as the Lord our God will call."

A Vital Church Grows

40And with many other words he testified and exhorted them, saying, "Be saved
from this perverse generation." 41Then
those who gladly[1] received his word were
baptized; and that day about three thousand souls were added *to them.* 42[a]And they
continued steadfastly in the apostles' doctrine and fellowship, in the breaking of

2:19 [a] Joel 2:30 **2:20** [a] Is. 13:10; Ezek. 32:7; Matt. 24:29; Mark 13:24, 25; Luke 21:25; Rev. 6:12 **2:21** [a] Rom. 10:13 [1] Joel 2:28–32 **2:22** [a] Is. 50:5; John 3:2; 5:6; Acts 10:38 **2:23** [a] Matt. 26:4; Luke 22:22; Acts 3:18; 4:28; [1 Pet. 1:20] [b] Acts 5:30 [1] NU-Text omits *have taken.* **2:24** [a] [Rom. 8:11; 1 Cor. 6:14; 2 Cor. 4:14; Eph. 1:20; Col. 2:12]; 1 Thess. 1:10; Heb. 13:20 **2:25** [a] Ps. 16:8–11 **2:27** [a] Acts 13:30–37 **2:28** [1] Psalm 16:8–11 **2:29** [a] Acts 13:36 **2:30** [a] 2 Sam. 7:12; Ps. 132:11; Luke 1:32; Rom. 1:3; 2 Tim. 2:8 [1] NU-Text omits *according to the flesh, He would raise up the Christ* and completes the verse with *He would seat one on his throne.* **2:31** [a] Ps. 16:10; Is. 50:8; 53:10 **2:32** [a] Acts 2:24 [b] Acts 1:8; 3:15 **2:33** [a] Ps. 68:18; [Acts 5:31]; Phil. 2:9 [b] Ps. 110:1; Mark 16:19; [Heb. 10:12] [c] Luke 24:49; [John 14:26] [d] Matt. 3:11; 5:6; Luke 3:16; 22:69; John 14:16; 16:7–15; Acts 2:1–11, 17; 10:45; Eph. 4:8 **2:34** [a] Ps. 68:18; 110:1; Matt. 22:44; Luke 23:43; John 20:17; 1 Cor. 15:25; Eph. 1:20; Heb. 1:13 **2:35** [1] Psalm 110:1 **2:37** [a] [Zech. 12:10]; Luke 3:10, 12, 14; John 16:8 **2:38** [a] Luke 24:47 **2:39** [a] Joel 2:28, 32 [b] Acts 11:15, 18; Eph. 2:13 **2:41** [1] NU-Text omits *gladly.* **2:42** [a] Acts 1:14; Rom. 12:12; Eph. 6:18; Col. 4:2; Heb. 10:25

RELEASE // TRUST IN HIS WONDER

Wonders and Signs

Acts 2:43 // Then fear came upon every soul, and many wonders and signs were done through the apostles.

Summary Message // The wonders of God are evident and attainable for all to access. We know from the account of the early church in Acts that "signs and wonders" were a part of their fellowship and life of faith. They trusted in God to reveal Himself to hearts turned faithfully toward Him. They were dedicated to being a people who represented the living God who touches humanity through faith. That is a wonder in itself.

Practical Application // When we give our lives to the worship of the Lord and join with others of faith, it is amazing what can happen. There are no bounds or boundaries. Nothing is impossible, even the supernatural. Do you know the word *supernatural* does not appear in the Bible? That is because with God every miracle and wonder He does is natural for Him, even if unbelievable to us. How, for example, does a huge, luscious, green tree grow from a tiny seed and then produce fruit that can nourish our bodies? How does a mother make milk that has just the right nutrients to feed her baby, and how is it that a baby's field of eyesight at birth is the exact distance to the mother's face when the baby is being nursed? We have taken these things for granted because they happen all around us, but they are truly wonders.

But the wonders talked about in Acts 2:43 are the kind that our sinful nature is not accustomed to, things that come only from God when His people are walking in harmony with Him and with their sisters and brothers. Ask most anyone who is devoted to Christ if they have experienced such wonders in their lives and they will tell you that they have.

Fervent Prayer // Heavenly Father, we trust in Your wondrous love and bask in the beauty of Your presence. Lord, our eyes are open to a new perspective in You. We find our identity in becoming the people You called us to be. Help us be effective people of faith who are impressed only by Your amazing glory and how You see us and others. We thank You for Your wondrous love, grace, and mercy. In Jesus' name we pray. Amen.

---

bread, and in prayers. [43]Then fear came
upon every soul, and [a]many wonders and
signs were done through the apostles.
[44]Now all who believed were together, and
[a]had all things in common, [45]and sold their
possessions and goods, and [a]divided them
among all, as anyone had need.

[46][a]So continuing daily with one accord
[b]in the temple, and [c]breaking bread from
house to house, they ate their food with
gladness and simplicity of heart, [47]praising
God and having favor with all the people.
And [a]the Lord added to the church[1] daily
those who were being saved.

A Lame Man Healed

3 Now Peter and John went up together
[a]to the temple at the hour of prayer,
[b]the ninth *hour.* [2]And [a]a certain man lame
from his mother's womb was carried,
whom they laid daily at the gate of the
temple which is called Beautiful, [b]to ask
alms from those who entered the temple;
[3]who, seeing Peter and John about to go
into the temple, asked for alms. [4]And fixing his eyes on him, with John, Peter said,
"Look at us." [5]So he gave them his atten-
tion, expecting to receive something from
them. [6]Then Peter said, "Silver and gold
I do not have, but what I do have I give
you: [a]In the name of Jesus Christ of Nazareth, rise up and walk." [7]And he took him
by the right hand and lifted *him* up, and
immediately his feet and ankle bones received strength. [8]So he, [a]leaping up, stood
and walked and entered the temple with
them—walking, leaping, and praising God.
[9][a]And all the people saw him walking and
praising God. [10]Then they knew that it was
he who [a]sat begging alms at the Beautiful

2:43 [a] Mark 16:17; Acts 2:22 2:44 [a] Acts 4:32, 34, 37; 5:2 2:45 [a] Is. 58:7 2:46 [a] Acts 1:14 [b] Luke 24:53 [c] Luke 24:30; Acts 2:42; 20:7; [1 Cor. 10:16] 2:47 [a] Acts 5:14 [1] NU-Text omits *to the church.* 3:1 [a] Acts 2:46 [b] Ps. 55:17; Matt. 27:45; Acts 10:30 3:2 [a] Acts 14:8 [b] John 9:8; Acts 3:10 3:6 [a] Acts 4:10 3:8 [a] Is. 35:6 3:9 [a] Acts 4:16, 21 3:10 [a] John 9:8; Acts 3:2

Gate of the temple; and they were filled with wonder and amazement at what had happened to him.

Preaching in Solomon's Portico

11Now as the lame man who was healed held on to Peter and John, all the people ran together to them in the porch [a]which is called Solomon's, greatly amazed. 12So when Peter saw *it,* he responded to the people: "Men of Israel, why do you marvel at this? Or why look so intently at us, as though by our own power or godliness we had made this man walk? 13[a]The God of Abraham, Isaac, and Jacob, the God of our fathers, [b]glorified His Servant Jesus, whom you [c]delivered up and [d]denied in the presence of Pilate, when he was determined to let *Him* go. 14But you denied [a]the Holy One [b]and the Just, and [c]asked for a murderer to be granted to you, 15and killed the Prince of life, [a]whom God raised from the dead, [b]of which we are witnesses. 16[a]And His name, through faith in His name, has made this man strong, whom you see and know. Yes, the faith which *comes* through Him has given him this perfect soundness in the presence of you all.

17"Yet now, brethren, I know that [a]you did *it* in ignorance, as *did* also your rulers. 18But [a]those things which God foretold [b]by the mouth of all His prophets, that the Christ would suffer, He has thus fulfilled. 19[a]Repent therefore and be converted, that your sins may be blotted out, so that times of refreshing may come from the presence of the Lord, 20and that He may send Jesus Christ, who was preached to you before,[1] 21[a]whom heaven must receive until the times of [b]restoration of all things, [c]which God has spoken by the mouth of all His holy prophets since the world began. 22For Moses truly said to the fathers, [a]'The LORD your God will raise up for you a Prophet like me from your brethren. Him you shall hear in all things, whatever He says to you. 23And it shall be *that* every soul who will not hear that Prophet shall be utterly destroyed from among the people.'[1] 24Yes, and [a]all the prophets, from Samuel and those who follow, as many as have spoken, have also foretold[1] these days. 25[a]You are sons of the prophets, and of the covenant which God made with our fathers, saying to Abraham, [b]'And in your seed all the families of the earth shall be blessed.'[1] 26To you [a]first, God, having raised up His Servant Jesus, sent Him to bless you, [b]in turning away every one *of you* from your iniquities."

Peter and John Arrested

4 Now as they spoke to the people, the priests, the captain of the temple, and the [a]Sadducees came upon them, 2being greatly disturbed that they taught the people and preached in Jesus the resurrection from the dead. 3And they laid hands on them, and put *them* in custody until the next day, for it was already evening. 4However, many of those who heard the word believed; and the number of the men came to be about five thousand.

Addressing the Sanhedrin

5And it came to pass, on the next day, that their rulers, elders, and scribes, 6as well as [a]Annas the high priest, Caiaphas, John, and Alexander, and as many as were of the family of the high priest, were gathered together at Jerusalem. 7And when they had set them in the midst, they asked, [a]"By what power or by what name have you done this?"

8[a]Then Peter, filled with the Holy Spirit, said to them, "Rulers of the people and elders of Israel: 9If we this day are judged for a good deed *done* to a helpless man, by what means he has been made well, 10let it be known to you all, and to all the people of Israel, [a]that by the name of Jesus Christ of Nazareth, whom you crucified, [b]whom God raised from the dead, by Him this man

---

3:11 [a] John 10:23; Acts 5:12 3:13 [a] John 5:30 [b] Is. 49:3; John 7:39; 12:23; 13:31 [c] Matt. 27:2 [d] Matt. 27:20; Mark 15:11; Luke 23:18; John 18:40; Acts 13:28 3:14 [a] Ps. 16:10; Mark 1:24; Luke 1:35 [b] Acts 7:52; 2 Cor. 5:21 [c] John 18:40 3:15 [a] Acts 2:24 [b] Acts 2:32 3:16 [a] Matt. 9:22; Acts 4:10; 14:9 3:17 [a] Luke 23:34; John 16:3; [Acts 13:27; 17:30]; 1 Cor. 2:8; 1 Tim. 1:13 3:18 [a] Luke 24:44; Acts 26:22 [b] Ps. 22; Is. 50:6; 53:5; Dan. 9:26; Hos. 6:1; Zech. 13:6; 1 Pet. 1:10 3:19 [a] [Acts 2:38; 26:20] 3:20 [1] NU-Text and M-Text read *Christ Jesus, who was ordained for you before.* 3:21 [a] Acts 1:11 [b] Matt. 17:11; [Rom. 8:21] [c] Luke 1:70 3:22 [a] Deut. 18:15, 18, 19; Acts 7:37 3:23 [1] Deuteronomy 18:15, 18, 19 3:24 [a] 2 Sam. 7:12; Luke 24:25 [1] NU-Text and M-Text read *proclaimed.* 3:25 [a] Acts 2:39; [Rom. 9:4, 8; Gal. 3:26] [b] Gen. 12:3; 18:18; 22:18; 26:4; 28:14 [1] Genesis 22:18; 26:4; 28:14 3:26 [a] Matt. 15:24; John 4:22; Acts 13:46; [Rom. 1:16; 2:9] [b] Is. 42:1; Matt. 1:21 4:1 [a] Matt. 22:23 4:6 [a] Luke 3:2; John 11:49; 18:13 4:7 [a] Ex. 2:14; Matt. 21:23; Acts 7:27 4:8 [a] Luke 12:11, 12 4:10 [a] Acts 2:22; 3:6, 16 [b] Acts 2:24

stands here before you whole. 11This is the
[a]'stone which was rejected by you builders,
which has become the chief cornerstone.'[1]
12[a]Nor is there salvation in any other, for
there is no other name under heaven given
among men by which we must be saved."

The Name of Jesus Forbidden

13Now when they saw the boldness of
Peter and John, [a]and perceived that they
were uneducated and untrained men, they
marveled. And they realized that they had
been with Jesus. 14And seeing the man who
had been healed [a]standing with them, they
could say nothing against it. 15But when
they had commanded them to go aside out
of the council, they conferred among themselves, 16saying, [a]"What shall we do to these
men? For, indeed, that a notable miracle
has been done through them *is* [b]evident to
all who dwell in Jerusalem, and we cannot
deny *it.* 17But so that it spreads no further
among the people, let us severely threaten
them, that from now on they speak to no
man in this name."

18[a]So they called them and commanded
them not to speak at all nor teach in the
name of Jesus. 19But Peter and John answered and said to them, [a]"Whether it is
right in the sight of God to listen to you
more than to God, you judge. 20[a]For we cannot but speak the things which [b]we have
seen and heard." 21So when they had further
threatened them, they let them go, finding no way of punishing them, [a]because
of the people, since they all [b]glorified God
for [c]what had been done. 22For the man was
over forty years old on whom this miracle
of healing had been performed.

Prayer for Boldness
(cf. Ps. 2:1, 2)

23And being let go, [a]they went to their
own *companions* and reported all that the
chief priests and elders had said to them.
24So when they heard that, they raised their
voice to God with one accord and said:
"Lord, [a]You *are* God, who made heaven and
earth and the sea, and all that is in them,
25who by the mouth of Your servant David[1] have said:

[a]'Why did the nations rage,
And the people plot vain things?
26 The kings of the earth took their stand,
And the rulers were gathered together
Against the LORD and
against His Christ.'[1]

27"For [a]truly against [b]Your holy Servant
Jesus, [c]whom You anointed, both Herod
and Pontius Pilate, with the Gentiles and
the people of Israel, were gathered together
28[a]to do whatever Your hand and Your purpose determined before to be done. 29Now,
Lord, look on their threats, and grant to
Your servants [a]that with all boldness they
may speak Your word, 30by stretching out
Your hand to heal, [a]and that signs and wonders may be done [b]through the name of
[c]Your holy Servant Jesus."

31And when they had prayed, [a]the place
where they were assembled together was
shaken; and they were all filled with the
Holy Spirit, [b]and they spoke the word of
God with boldness.

Sharing in All Things

32Now the multitude of those who believed [a]were of one heart and one soul; [b]nei-
ther did anyone say that any of the things
he possessed was his own, but they had all
things in common. 33And with [a]great power
the apostles gave [b]witness to the resurrection of the Lord Jesus. And [c]great grace
was upon them all. 34Nor was there anyone
among them who lacked; [a]for all who were
possessors of lands or houses sold them,
and brought the proceeds of the things that
were sold, 35[a]and laid *them* at the apostles'
feet; [b]and they distributed to each as anyone had need.

4:11 [a] Ps. 118:22; Is. 28:16; Matt. 21:42 [1] Psalm 118:22 4:12 [a] Is. 42:1, 6, 7; 53:11; Dan. 9:24; [Matt. 1:21; John 14:6; Acts 10:43; 1 Tim. 2:5, 6] 4:13 [a] Matt. 11:25; [1 Cor. 1:27] 4:14 [a] Acts 3:11 4:16 [a] John 11:47 [b] Acts 3:7–10 4:18 [a] Acts 5:28, 40 4:19 [a] Acts 5:29 4:20 [a] Acts 1:8; 2:32 [b] Acts 22:15; [1 John 1:1, 3] 4:21 [a] Matt. 21:26; Luke 20:6, 19; 22:2; Acts 5:26 [b] Matt. 15:31 [c] Acts 3:7, 8 4:23 [a] Acts 2:44–46; 12:12 4:24 [a] Ex. 20:11; 2 Kin. 19:15; Neh. 9:6; Ps. 146:6 4:25 [a] Ps. 2:1, 2 [1] NU-Text reads *who through the Holy Spirit, by the mouth of our father, Your servant David.* 4:26 [1] Psalm 2:1, 2 4:27 [a] Matt. 26:3; Luke 22:2; 23:1, 8 [b] [Luke 1:35] [c] Luke 4:18; John 10:36 4:28 [a] Acts 2:23; 3:18 4:29 [a] Acts 4:13, 31; 9:27; 13:46; 14:3; 19:8; 26:26; Eph. 6:19 4:30 [a] Acts 2:43; 5:12 [b] Acts 3:6, 16 [c] Acts 4:27 4:31 [a] Matt. 5:6; Acts 2:2, 4; 16:26 [b] Acts 4:29 4:32 [a] Acts 5:12; Rom. 15:5, 6; 2 Cor. 13:11; Phil. 1:27; 2:2; 1 Pet. 3:8 [b] Acts 2:44 4:33 [a] [Acts 1:8] [b] Acts 1:22 [c] Rom. 6:15 4:34 [a] [Matt. 19:21]; Acts 2:45 4:35 [a] Acts 4:37; 5:2 [b] Acts 2:45; 6:1

36And Joses,[1] who was also named Barnabas by the apostles (which is translated
Son of Encouragement), a Levite of the
country of Cyprus, 37[a]having land, sold *it,*
and brought the money and laid *it* at the
apostles' feet.

Lying to the Holy Spirit

5 But a certain man named Ananias, with
Sapphira his wife, sold a possession.
2And he kept back *part* of the proceeds, his
wife also being aware *of it,* and brought a
certain part and laid *it* at the apostles' feet.
3[a]But Peter said, "Ananias, why has [b]Satan
filled your heart to lie to the Holy Spirit
and keep back *part* of the price of the land
for yourself? 4While it remained, was it not
your own? And after it was sold, was it not
in your own control? Why have you conceived this thing in your heart? You have
not lied to men but to God."

5Then Ananias, hearing these words,
[a]fell down and breathed his last. So great
fear came upon all those who heard these
things. 6And the young men arose and
[a]wrapped him up, carried *him* out, and
buried *him.*

7Now it was about three hours later when
his wife came in, not knowing what had
happened. 8And Peter answered her, "Tell
me whether you sold the land for so much?"

She said, "Yes, for so much."

9Then Peter said to her, "How is it that
you have agreed together [a]to test the Spirit
of the Lord? Look, the feet of those who
have buried your husband *are* at the door,
and they will carry you out." 10[a]Then immediately she fell down at his feet and
breathed her last. And the young men came
in and found her dead, and carrying *her*
out, buried *her* by her husband. 11[a]So great
fear came upon all the church and upon
all who heard these things.

Continuing Power in the Church

12And [a]through the hands of the apostles many signs and wonders were done
among the people. [b]And they were all with
one accord in Solomon's Porch. 13Yet [a]none
of the rest dared join them, [b]but the people esteemed them highly. 14And believers
were increasingly added to the Lord, multitudes of both men and women, 15so that
they brought the sick out into the streets
and laid *them* on beds and couches, [a]that at
least the shadow of Peter passing by might
fall on some of them. 16Also a multitude
gathered from the surrounding cities to
Jerusalem, bringing [a]sick people and those
who were tormented by unclean spirits,
and they were all healed.

Imprisoned Apostles Freed

17[a]Then the high priest rose up, and all
those who *were* with him (which is the sect
of the Sadducees), and they were filled
with indignation, 18[a]and laid their hands
on the apostles and put them in the common prison. 19But at night [a]an angel of the
Lord opened the prison doors and brought
them out, and said, 20"Go, stand in the temple and speak to the people [a]all the words
of this life."

21And when they heard *that,* they entered the temple early in the morning and
taught. [a]But the high priest and those with
him came and called the council together,
with all the elders of the children of Israel, and sent to the prison to have them
brought.

Apostles on Trial Again

22But when the officers came and did
not find them in the prison, they returned
and reported, 23saying, "Indeed we found
the prison shut securely, and the guards
standing outside[1] before the doors; but
when we opened them, we found no one
inside!" 24Now when the high priest,[1] [a]the
captain of the temple, and the chief priests
heard these things, they wondered what
the outcome would be. 25So one came and
told them, saying,[1] "Look, the men whom
you put in prison are standing in the temple and teaching the people!"

26Then the captain went with the officers

4:36 [1] NU-Text reads *Joseph.* 4:37 [a] Acts 4:34, 35; 5:1, 2 5:3 [a] Num. 30:2; Deut. 23:21; Eccl. 5:4 [b] Matt. 4:10; Luke 22:3; John 13:2, 27 5:5 [a] Ezek. 11:13; Acts 5:10, 11 5:6 [a] John 19:40 5:9 [a] Matt. 4:7; Acts 5:3, 4 5:10 [a] Ezek. 11:13; Acts 5:5 5:11 [a] Acts 2:43; 5:5; 19:17 5:12 [a] Acts 2:43; 4:30; 6:8; 14:3; 15:12; [Rom. 15:19]; 2 Cor. 12:12; Heb. 2:4 [b] Acts 3:11; 4:32 5:13 [a] John 9:22 [b] Acts 2:47; 4:21 5:15 [a] Matt. 9:21; 14:36; Acts 19:12 5:16 [a] Mark 16:17, 18; [John 14:12] 5:17 [a] Matt. 3:7; Acts 4:1, 2, 6 5:18 [a] Luke 21:12; Acts 4:3; 16:37 5:19 [a] Matt. 1:20, 24; 2:13, 19; 28:2; Luke 1:11; 2:9; Acts 12:7; 16:26 5:20 [a] [John 6:63, 68; 17:3; 1 John 5:11] 5:21 [a] Acts 4:5, 6 5:23 [1] NU-Text and M-Text omit *outside.* 5:24 [a] Luke 22:4; Acts 4:1; 5:26 [1] NU-Text omits *the high priest.* 5:25 [1] NU-Text and M-Text omit *saying.*

and brought them without violence, [a]for
they feared the people, lest they should be
stoned. 27And when they had brought them,
they set *them* before the council. And the
high priest asked them, 28saying, [a]"Did we
not strictly command you not to teach in
this name? And look, you have filled Jerusalem with your doctrine, [b]and intend to
bring this Man's [c]blood on us!"

29But Peter and the *other* apostles answered and said: [a]"We ought to obey God
rather than men. 30[a]The God of our fathers
raised up Jesus whom you murdered by
[b]hanging on a tree. 31[a]Him God has exalted
to His right hand *to be* [b]Prince and [c]Savior,
[d]to give repentance to Israel and forgiveness of sins. 32And [a]we are His witnesses to
these things, and *so* also *is* the Holy Spirit
[b]whom God has given to those who obey
Him."

Gamaliel's Advice

33When they heard *this,* they were [a]fu-
rious and plotted to kill them. 34Then one
in the council stood up, a Pharisee named
[a]Gamaliel, a teacher of the law held in respect by all the people, and commanded
them to put the apostles outside for a little
while. 35And he said to them: "Men of Israel, take heed to yourselves what you intend to do regarding these men. 36For some
time ago Theudas rose up, claiming to be
somebody. A number of men, about four
hundred, joined him. He was slain, and all
who obeyed him were scattered and came
to nothing. 37After this man, Judas of Galilee rose up in the days of the census, and
drew away many people after him. He also
perished, and all who obeyed him were dispersed. 38And now I say to you, keep away
from these men and let them alone; for if
this plan or this work is of men, it will come
to nothing; 39[a]but if it is of God, you cannot overthrow it—lest you even be found
[b]to fight against God."

40And they agreed with him, and when
they had [a]called for the apostles [b]and
beaten *them,* they commanded that they
should not speak in the name of Jesus, and
let them go. 41So they departed from the
presence of the council, [a]rejoicing that they
were counted worthy to suffer shame for
His[1] name. 42And daily [a]in the temple, and
in every house, [b]they did not cease teaching
and preaching Jesus *as* the Christ.

Seven Chosen to Serve

6 Now in those days, [a]when *the number*
of the disciples was multiplying, there
arose a complaint against the Hebrews
by the [b]Hellenists,[1] because their widows
were neglected [c]in the daily distribution.
2Then the twelve summoned the multitude of the disciples and said, [a]"It is not
desirable that we should leave the word
of God and serve tables. 3Therefore, brethren, [a]seek out from among you seven men
of *good* reputation, full of the Holy Spirit
and wisdom, whom we may appoint over
this [b]business; 4but we [a]will give ourselves
continually to prayer and to the ministry
of the word."

5And the saying pleased the whole multitude. And they chose Stephen, [a]a man full
of faith and the Holy Spirit, and [b]Philip,
Prochorus, Nicanor, Timon, Parmenas, and
[c]Nicolas, a proselyte from Antioch, 6whom
they set before the apostles; and [a]when they
had prayed, [b]they laid hands on them.

7Then [a]the word of God spread, and the
number of the disciples multiplied greatly
in Jerusalem, and a great many [b]of the
priests were obedient to the faith.

Stephen Accused of Blasphemy

8And Stephen, full of faith[1] and power,
did great [a]wonders and signs among the
people. 9Then there arose some from what
is called the Synagogue of the Freedmen
(Cyrenians, Alexandrians, and those from
Cilicia and Asia), disputing with Stephen.
10And [a]they were not able to resist the

5:26 [a] Matt. 21:26 5:28 [a] Acts 4:17, 18 [b] Acts 2:23, 36 [c] Matt. 23:35 5:29 [a] Acts 4:19 5:30 [a] Acts 3:13, 15 [b] Acts 10:39; 13:29; [Gal. 3:13; 1 Pet. 2:24] 5:31 [a] Mark 16:19; [Acts 2:33, 36; Phil. 2:9–11] [b] Acts 3:15; Rev. 1:5 [c] Matt. 1:21 [d] Luke 24:47; [Eph. 1:7; Col. 1:14] 5:32 [a] John 15:26, 27; Acts 15:28; Rom. 8:16; Heb. 2:4 [b] Acts 2:4; 10:44 5:33 [a] Acts 2:37; 7:54 5:34 [a] Acts 22:3 5:39 [a] Luke 21:15; 1 Cor. 1:25 [b] Acts 7:51; 9:5 5:40 [a] Acts 4:18 [b] Matt. 10:17; Mark 13:9; Acts 16:22, 23; 21:32; 2 Cor. 11:25 5:41 [a] Matt. 5:10–12; Rom. 5:3; 2 Cor. 12:10; Heb. 10:34; [James 1:2; 1 Pet. 4:13–16] [1] NU-Text reads *the name;* M-Text reads *the name of Jesus.* 5:42 [a] Acts 2:46 [b] Acts 4:20, 29 6:1 [a] Acts 2:41; 4:4 [b] Acts 9:29; 11:20 [c] Acts 4:35; 11:29 [1] That is, Greek-speaking Jews 6:2 [a] Ex. 18:17 6:3 [a] Deut. 1:13; 1 Tim. 3:7 [b] Phil. 1:1; 1 Tim. 3:8–13 6:4 [a] Acts 2:42 6:5 [a] Acts 6:3; 11:24 [b] Acts 8:5, 26; 21:8 [c] Rev. 2:6, 15 6:6 [a] Acts 1:24 [b] Num. 8:10; 27:18; Deut. 34:9; [Mark 5:23; Acts 8:17; 9:17; 13:3; 19:6; 1 Tim. 4:14; 2 Tim. 1:6]; Heb. 6:2 6:7 [a] Acts 12:24; Col. 1:6 [b] John 12:42 6:8 [a] Acts 2:43; 5:12; 8:15; 14:3 [1] NU-Text reads *grace.* 6:10 [a] Ex. 4:12; Is. 54:17; Luke 21:15

wisdom and the Spirit by which he spoke.
11[a]Then they secretly induced men to say,
"We have heard him speak blasphemous
words against Moses and God." 12And they
stirred up the people, the elders, and the
scribes; and they came upon *him,* seized
him, and brought *him* to the council. 13They
also set up false witnesses who said, "This
man does not cease to speak blasphemous[1]
words against this holy place and the law;
14[a]for we have heard him say that this Jesus
of Nazareth will destroy this place and
change the customs which Moses delivered to us." 15And all who sat in the council, looking steadfastly at him, saw his face
as the face of an angel.

Stephen's Address: The Call of Abraham

7 Then the high priest said, "Are these
things so?"
2And he said, [a]"Brethren and fathers,
listen: The [b]God of glory appeared to our
father Abraham when he was in Mesopotamia, before he dwelt in [c]Haran, 3and said
to him, [a]'Get out of your country and from
your relatives, and come to a land that I will
show you.'[1] 4Then [a]he came out of the land
of the Chaldeans and dwelt in Haran. And
from there, when his father was [b]dead, He
moved him to this land in which you now
dwell. 5And *God* gave him no inheritance
in it, not even *enough* to set his foot on.
But even when *Abraham* had no child, [a]He
promised to give it to him for a possession,
and to his descendants after him. 6But God
spoke in this way: [a]that his descendants
would dwell in a foreign land, and that they
would bring them into [b]bondage and oppress *them* four hundred years. 7[a]'And the
nation to whom they will be in bondage I
will [b]judge,'[1] said God, [c]'and after that they
shall come out and serve Me in this place.'[2]
8[a]Then He gave him the covenant of circumcision; [b]and so *Abraham* begot Isaac
and circumcised him on the eighth day;
[c]and Isaac *begot* Jacob, and [d]Jacob *begot*
the twelve patriarchs.

The Patriarchs in Egypt

9[a]"And the patriarchs, becoming envious, [b]sold Joseph into Egypt. [c]But God
was with him 10and delivered him out of
all his troubles, [a]and gave him favor and
wisdom in the presence of Pharaoh, king
of Egypt; and he made him governor over
Egypt and all his house. 11[a]Now a famine
and great trouble came over all the land of
Egypt and Canaan, and our fathers found
no sustenance. 12[a]But when Jacob heard
that there was grain in Egypt, he sent out
our fathers first. 13And the [a]second *time*
Joseph was made known to his brothers,
and Joseph's family became known to the
Pharaoh. 14[a]Then Joseph sent and called his
father Jacob and [b]all his relatives to *him,*
seventy-five[1] people. 15[a]So Jacob went down
to Egypt; [b]and he died, he and our fathers.
16And [a]they were carried back to Shechem
and laid in [b]the tomb that Abraham bought
for a sum of money from the sons of Hamor, *the father* of Shechem.

God Delivers Israel by Moses

17"But when [a]the time of the promise
drew near which God had sworn to Abraham, [b]the people grew and multiplied in
Egypt 18till another king [a]arose who did not
know Joseph. 19This man dealt treacherously with our people, and oppressed our
forefathers, [a]making them expose their
babies, so that they might not live. 20[a]At
this time Moses was born, and [b]was well
pleasing to God; and he was brought up in
his father's house for three months. 21But
[a]when he was set out, [b]Pharaoh's daughter took him away and brought him up as
her own son. 22And Moses was learned in
all the wisdom of the Egyptians, and was
[a]mighty in words and deeds.
23[a]"Now when he was forty years old, it
came into his heart to visit his brethren, the
children of Israel. 24And seeing one of *them*
suffer wrong, he defended and avenged
him who was oppressed, and struck down
the Egyptian. 25For he supposed that his

6:11 [a] 1 Kin. 21:10, 13; Matt. 26:59, 60 6:13 [1] NU-Text omits *blasphemous.* 6:14 [a] Acts 10:38; 25:8 7:2 [a] Acts 22:1 [b] Ps. 29:3; 1 Cor. 2:8 [c] Gen. 11:31, 32 7:3 [a] Gen. 12:1 [1] Genesis 12:1 7:4 [a] Gen. 11:31; 15:7; Heb. 11:8–10 [b] Gen. 11:32 7:5 [a] Gen. 12:7; 13:15; 15:3, 18; 17:8; 26:3 7:6 [a] Gen. 15:13, 14, 16; 47:11, 12 [b] Ex. 1:8–14; 12:40, 41; Gal. 3:17 7:7 [a] Gen. 15:14 [b] Ex. 14:13–31 [c] Ex. 3:12; Josh. 3:1–17 [1] Genesis 15:14 [2] Exodus 3:12 7:8 [a] Gen. 17:9–14 [b] Gen. 21:1–5 [c] Gen. 25:21–26 [d] Gen. 29:31—30:24; 35:18, 22–26 7:9 [a] Gen. 37:4, 11, 28; Ps. 105:17 [b] Gen. 37:28 [c] Gen. 39:2, 21, 23 7:10 [a] Gen. 41:38–44 7:11 [a] Gen. 41:54; 42:5 7:12 [a] Gen. 42:1, 2 7:13 [a] Gen. 45:4, 16 7:14 [a] Gen. 45:9, 27 [b] Gen. 46:26, 27; Deut. 10:22 [1] Or *seventy* (compare Exodus 1:5) 7:15 [a] Gen. 46:1–7 [b] Gen. 49:33; Ex. 1:6 7:16 [a] Gen. 50:13; Ex. 13:19; Josh. 24:32 [b] Gen. 23:16 7:17 [a] Gen. 15:13; Ex. 2:23–25; Acts 7:6, 7 [b] Ex. 1:7–9; Ps. 105:24, 25 7:18 [a] Ex. 1:8 7:19 [a] Ex. 1:22 7:20 [a] Ex. 2:1, 2 [b] Heb. 11:23 7:21 [a] Ex. 2:3, 4 [b] Ex. 2:5–10 7:22 [a] Luke 24:19 7:23 [a] Ex. 2:11, 12; Heb. 11:24–26

brethren would have understood that God
would deliver them by his hand, but they
did not understand. 26 And the next day he
appeared to *two of* them as they were fighting, and *tried to* reconcile them, saying,
'Men, you are brethren; why do you wrong
one another?' 27 But he who did his neighbor wrong pushed him away, saying, [a]'Who
made you a ruler and a judge over us? 28 Do
you want to kill me as you did the Egyptian
yesterday?'[1] 29 [a]Then, at this saying, Moses
fled and became a dweller in the land of
Midian, where he [b]had two sons.

30 [a]"And when forty years had passed,
an Angel of the Lord[1] appeared to him in a
flame of fire in a bush, in the wilderness of
Mount Sinai. 31 When Moses saw *it,* he marveled at the sight; and as he drew near to
observe, the voice of the Lord came to him,
32 *saying,* [a]'I *am* the God of your fathers—
the God of Abraham, the God of Isaac, and
the God of Jacob.'[1] And Moses trembled and
dared not look. 33 [a]'Then the LORD said to
him, "Take your sandals off your feet, for
the place where you stand is holy ground.
34 I have surely [a]seen the oppression of My
people who are in Egypt; I have heard their
groaning and have come down to deliver
them. And now come, I will [b]send you to
Egypt."'[1]

35 "This Moses whom they rejected, saying, [a]'Who made you a ruler and a judge?'[1]
is the one God sent *to be* a ruler and a deliverer [b]by the hand of the Angel who appeared to him in the bush. 36 [a]He brought
them out, after he had [b]shown wonders
and signs in the land of Egypt, [c]and in the
Red Sea, [d]and in the wilderness forty years.

Israel Rebels Against God

37 "This is that Moses who said to the children of Israel,[1] [a]'The LORD your God will
raise up for you a Prophet like me from
your brethren. [b]Him you shall hear.'[2]

38 [a]"This is he who was in the congregation in the wilderness with [b]the Angel who
spoke to him on Mount Sinai, and *with* our
fathers, [c]the one who received the living
[d]oracles to give to us, 39 whom our fathers
[a]would not obey, but rejected. And in their
hearts they turned back to Egypt, 40 [a]say-
ing to Aaron, 'Make us gods to go before
us; *as for* this Moses who brought us out
of the land of Egypt, we do not know what
has become of him.'[1] 41 [a]And they made a
calf in those days, offered sacrifices to the
idol, and [b]rejoiced in the works of their own
hands. 42 Then [a]God turned and gave them
up to worship [b]the host of heaven, as it is
written in the book of the Prophets:

[c]'Did you offer Me slaughtered
animals and sacrifices *during*
forty years in the wilderness,
O house of Israel?
43 You also took up the
tabernacle of Moloch,
And the star of your god Remphan,
Images which you made
to worship;
And [a]I will carry you away
beyond Babylon.'[1]

God's True Tabernacle

44 "Our fathers had the tabernacle of witness in the wilderness, as He appointed,
instructing Moses [a]to make it according
to the pattern that he had seen, 45 [a]which
our fathers, having received it in turn, also
brought with Joshua into the land possessed by the Gentiles, [b]whom God drove
out before the face of our fathers until the
[c]days of David, 46 [a]who found favor before
God and [b]asked to find a dwelling for the
God of Jacob. 47 [a]But Solomon built Him
a house.

48 "However, [a]the Most High does not
dwell in temples made with hands, as the
prophet says:

49 'Heaven[a] *is* My throne,
And earth *is* My footstool.

7:27 [a] Ex. 2:14; Luke 12:14; Acts 7:35 7:28 [1] Exodus 2:14 7:29 [a] Heb. 11:27 [b] Ex. 2:15, 21, 22; 4:20; 18:3 7:30 [a] Ex. 3:1–10; Is. 63:9 [1] NU-Text omits *of the Lord.* 7:32 [a] Ex. 3:6, 15; [Matt. 22:32]; Heb. 11:16 [1] Exodus 3:6, 15 7:33 [a] Ex. 3:5, 7, 8, 10 7:34 [a] Ex. 2:24, 25 [b] Ps. 105:26 [1] Exodus 3:5, 7, 8, 10 7:35 [a] Ex. 2:14; Acts 7:27 [b] Ex. 14:21 [1] Exodus 2:14 7:36 [a] Ex. 12:41; 33:1; Deut. 6:21, 23; Heb. 8:9 [b] Ex. 7:8, 9; Deut. 6:22; Ps. 105:27; John 4:48 [c] Ex. 14:21 [d] Ex. 16:1, 35; Num. 14:33; Ps. 95:8–10; Acts 7:42; 13:18; Heb. 3:8 7:37 [a] Deut. 18:15, 18, 19; Acts 3:22 [b] Matt. 17:5 [1] Deuteronomy 18:15 [2] NU-Text and M-Text omit *Him you shall hear.* 7:38 [a] Ex. 19:3 [b] Is. 63:9; Gal. 3:19; Heb. 2:2 [c] Ex. 21:1; Deut. 5:27; John 1:17 [d] Rom. 3:2; Heb. 5:12; 1 Pet. 4:11 7:39 [a] Ps. 95:8–11 7:40 [a] Ex. 32:1, 23 [1] Exodus 32:1, 23 7:41 [a] Ex. 32:2–4; Deut. 9:16; Ps. 106:19 [b] Ex. 32:6, 18, 19 7:42 [a] Ps. 81:12; [2 Thess. 2:11] [b] Deut. 4:19; 2 Kin. 21:3 [c] Amos 5:25–27 7:43 [a] 2 Chr. 36:11–21; Jer. 25:9–12 [1] Amos 5:25–27 7:44 [a] Ex. 25:40; [Heb. 8:5] 7:45 [a] Deut. 32:49; Josh. 3:14; 18:1; 23:9 [b] Neh. 9:24; Ps. 44:2 [c] 2 Sam. 6:2–15 7:46 [a] 2 Sam. 7:1–13; 1 Kin. 8:17 [b] 1 Chr. 22:7; Ps. 132:4, 5 7:47 [a] 1 Kin. 6:1–38; 8:20, 21; 2 Chr. 3:1–17 7:48 [a] 1 Kin. 8:27; 2 Chr. 2:6; Acts 17:24 7:49 [a] Is. 66:1, 2; Matt. 5:34

What house will you build
for Me? says the LORD,
Or what *is* the place of My rest?
50 Has My hand not [a]made
all these things?’[1]

Israel Resists the Holy Spirit

51“*You* [a]stiff-necked and [b]uncircumcised
in heart and ears! You always resist the
Holy Spirit; as your fathers *did,* so *do* you.
52[a]Which of the prophets did your fathers
not persecute? And they killed those who
foretold the coming of [b]the Just One, of
whom you now have become the betray-
ers and murderers, 53[a]who have received
the law by the direction of angels and have
not kept *it.*”

Stephen the Martyr

54[a]When they heard these things they
were cut to the heart, and they gnashed at
him with *their* teeth. 55But he, [a]being full of
the Holy Spirit, gazed into heaven and saw
the [b]glory of God, and Jesus standing at the
right hand of God, 56and said, “Look! [a]I see
the heavens opened and the [b]Son of Man
standing at the right hand of God!”

57Then they cried out with a loud voice,
stopped their ears, and ran at him with one
accord; 58and they cast *him* out of the city
and stoned *him.* And [a]the witnesses laid
down their clothes at the feet of a young
man named Saul. 59And they stoned Stephen as he was calling on *God* and saying,
“Lord Jesus, [a]receive my spirit.” 60Then he
knelt down and cried out with a loud voice,
[a]“Lord, do not charge them with this sin.”
And when he had said this, he fell asleep.

Saul Persecutes the Church

8 Now Saul was consenting to his death.
At that time a great persecution arose
against the church which was at Jerusalem;
and [a]they were all scattered throughout
the regions of Judea and Samaria, except
the apostles. 2And devout men carried Stephen *to his burial,* and [a]made great lamentation over him.

3As for Saul, [a]he made havoc of the
church, entering every house, and dragging off men and women, committing *them*
to prison.

Christ Is Preached in Samaria

4Therefore [a]those who were scattered
went everywhere preaching the word.
5Then [a]Philip went down to the[1] city of Samaria and preached Christ to them. 6And
the multitudes with one accord heeded the
things spoken by Philip, hearing and seeing
the miracles which he did. 7For [a]unclean
spirits, crying with a loud voice, came out
of many who were possessed; and many
who were paralyzed and lame were healed.
8And there was great joy in that city.

The Sorcerer’s Profession of Faith

9But there was a certain man called Simon, who previously [a]practiced sorcery in
the city and [b]astonished the people of Samaria, claiming that he was someone great,
10to whom they all gave heed, from the least
to the greatest, saying, “This man is the
great power of God.” 11And they heeded him
because he had astonished them with his
sorceries for a long time. 12But when they
believed Philip as he preached the things
[a]concerning the kingdom of God and the
name of Jesus Christ, both men and women
were baptized. 13Then Simon himself also
believed; and when he was baptized he continued with Philip, and was amazed, seeing
the miracles and signs which were done.

The Sorcerer’s Sin

14Now when the [a]apostles who were at Jerusalem heard that Samaria had received
the word of God, they sent Peter and John
to them, 15who, when they had come down,
prayed for them [a]that they might receive
the Holy Spirit. 16For [a]as yet He had fallen
upon none of them. [b]They had only been
baptized in [c]the name of the Lord Jesus.
17Then [a]they laid hands on them, and they
received the Holy Spirit.

18And when Simon saw that through the

7:50 [a] Ps. 102:25 [1] Isaiah 66:1, 2 7:51 [a] Ex. 32:9; Is. 6:10 [b] Lev. 26:41 7:52 [a] 2 Chr. 36:16; Matt. 21:35; 23:35; 1 Thess. 2:15 [b] Acts 3:14; 22:14; 1 John 2:1 7:53 [a] Ex. 20:1; Deut. 33:2; Acts 7:38; Gal. 3:19; Heb. 2:2 7:54 [a] Acts 5:33 7:55 [a] Matt. 5:8; 16:28; Mark 9:1; Luke 9:27; Acts 6:5 [b] [Ex. 24:17] 7:56 [a] Matt. 3:16 [b] Dan. 7:13 7:58 [a] Acts 22:20 7:59 [a] Ps. 31:5 7:60 [a] Matt. 5:44; Luke 23:34 8:1 [a] John 16:2; Acts 8:4; 11:19 8:2 [a] Gen. 23:2 8:3 [a] Acts 7:58; 1 Cor. 15:9; Gal. 1:13; Phil. 3:6; 1 Tim. 1:13 8:4 [a] Matt. 10:23 8:5 [a] Acts 6:5; 8:26, 30 [1] Or *a* 8:7 [a] Mark 16:17 8:9 [a] Acts 8:11; 13:6 [b] Acts 5:36 8:12 [a] Acts 1:3; 8:4 8:14 [a] Acts 5:12, 29, 40 8:15 [a] Acts 2:38; 19:2 8:16 [a] Acts 19:2 [b] Matt. 28:19; Acts 2:38 [c] Acts 10:48; 19:5 8:17 [a] Acts 6:6; 19:6; Heb. 6:2

laying on of the apostles' hands the Holy
Spirit was given, he offered them money,
19 saying, "Give me this power also, that anyone on whom I lay hands may receive the
Holy Spirit."

20 But Peter said to him, "Your money
perish with you, because [a]you thought that
[b]the gift of God could be purchased with
money! 21 You have neither part nor portion
in this matter, for your [a]heart is not right in
the sight of God. 22 Repent therefore of this
your wickedness, and pray God [a]if perhaps
the thought of your heart may be forgiven
you. 23 For I see that you are [a]poisoned by
bitterness and bound by iniquity."

24 Then Simon answered and said,
[a]"Pray to the Lord for me, that none of the
things which you have spoken may come
upon me."

25 So when they had testified and
preached the word of the Lord, they returned to Jerusalem, preaching the gospel
in many villages of the Samaritans.

Christ Is Preached to an Ethiopian
(cf. Is. 53:7, 8)

26 Now an angel of the Lord spoke to
[a]Philip, saying, "Arise and go toward the
south along the road which goes down from
Jerusalem to Gaza." This is desert. 27 So he
arose and went. And behold, [a]a man of Ethiopia, a eunuch of great authority under Can-
dace the queen of the Ethiopians, who had
charge of all her treasury, and [b]had come
to Jerusalem to worship, 28 was returning.
And sitting in his chariot, he was reading
Isaiah the prophet. 29 Then the Spirit said to
Philip, "Go near and overtake this chariot."
30 So Philip ran to him, and heard him
reading the prophet Isaiah, and said, "Do
you understand what you are reading?"
31 And he said, "How can I, unless someone guides me?" And he asked Philip to
come up and sit with him. 32 The place in
the Scripture which he read was this:

[a]"He was led as a sheep to the
slaughter;
And as a lamb before its
shearer *is* silent,
[b]So He opened not His mouth.
33 In His humiliation His [a]justice
was taken away,
And who will declare His generation?
For His life is [b]taken from
the earth."[1]

34 So the eunuch answered Philip and
said, "I ask you, of whom does the prophet
say this, of himself or of some other man?"
35 Then Philip opened his mouth, [a]and beginning at this Scripture, preached Jesus
to him. 36 Now as they went down the road,
they came to some water. And the eunuch
said, "See, *here is* water. [a]What hinders me
from being baptized?"

37 Then Philip said, [a]"If you believe with
all your heart, you may."

And he answered and said, [b]"I believe
that Jesus Christ is the Son of God."[1]

38 So he commanded the chariot to stand
still. And both Philip and the eunuch went
down into the water, and he baptized him.
39 Now when they came up out of the water,
[a]the Spirit of the Lord caught Philip away,
so that the eunuch saw him no more; and
he went on his way rejoicing. 40 But Philip
was found at Azotus. And passing through,
he preached in all the cities till he came to
[a]Caesarea.

The Damascus Road: Saul Converted
(Acts 22:6–16; 26:12–18)

9 Then [a]Saul, still breathing threats and
murder against the disciples of the
Lord, went to the high priest 2 and asked
[a]letters from him to the synagogues of Damascus, so that if he found any who were of
the Way, whether men or women, he might
bring them bound to Jerusalem.

3 [a]As he journeyed he came near Damascus, and suddenly a light shone around him
from heaven. 4 Then he fell to the ground,
and heard a voice saying to him, "Saul, Saul,
[a]why are you persecuting Me?"

5 And he said, "Who are You, Lord?"

8:20 [a] 2 Kin. 5:16; Is. 55:1; Dan. 5:17; [Matt. 10:8] [b] [Acts 2:38; 10:45; 11:17] **8:21** [a] Jer. 17:9 **8:22** [a] Dan. 4:27; 2 Tim. 2:25 **8:23** [a] Heb. 12:15 **8:24** [a] Gen. 20:7, 17; Ex. 8:8; Num. 21:7; 1 Kin. 13:6; Job 42:8; James 5:16 **8:26** [a] Acts 6:5 **8:27** [a] Ps. 68:31; 87:4; Is. 56:3; Zeph. 3:10 [b] 1 Kin. 8:41, 42; John 12:20 **8:32** [a] Is. 53:7, 8 [b] Matt. 26:62, 63; 27:12, 14; John 19:9 **8:33** [a] Luke 23:1–25 [b] Luke 23:33–46 [1] Isaiah 53:7, 8 **8:35** [a] Luke 24:27; Acts 17:2; 18:28; 28:23 **8:36** [a] Acts 10:47; 16:33 **8:37** [a] Matt. 28:19; [Mark 16:16; Rom. 10:9, 10] [b] Matt. 16:16; John 6:69; 9:35, 38; 11:27 [1] NU-Text and M-Text omit this verse. It is found in Western texts, including the Latin tradition. **8:39** [a] 1 Kin. 18:12; 2 Kin. 2:16; Ezek. 3:12, 14; 2 Cor. 12:2 **8:40** [a] Acts 21:8 **9:1** [a] Acts 7:57; 8:1, 3; 26:10, 11; Gal. 1:13; 1 Tim. 1:13 **9:2** [a] Acts 22:5 **9:3** [a] Acts 22:6; 26:12, 13; 1 Cor. 15:8 **9:4** [a] [Matt. 25:40]

Then the Lord said, "I am Jesus, whom
you are persecuting.[1] It *is* hard for you to
kick against the goads."
6So he, trembling and astonished, said,
"Lord, what do You want me to do?"
Then the Lord *said* to him, "Arise and
go into the city, and you will be told what
you must do."
7And [a]the men who journeyed with
him stood speechless, hearing a voice but
seeing no one. 8Then Saul arose from the
ground, and when his eyes were opened he
saw no one. But they led him by the hand
and brought *him* into Damascus. 9And he
was three days without sight, and neither
ate nor drank.

Ananias Baptizes Saul

10Now there was a certain disciple at Damascus [a]named Ananias; and to him the
Lord said in a vision, "Ananias."
And he said, "Here I am, Lord."
11So the Lord *said* to him, "Arise and go
to the street called Straight, and inquire at
the house of Judas for *one* called Saul [a]of
Tarsus, for behold, he is praying. 12And in
a vision he has seen a man named Ananias
coming in and putting *his* hand on him, so
that he might receive his sight."
13Then Ananias answered, "Lord, I have
heard from many about this man, [a]how
much harm he has done to Your saints in
Jerusalem. 14And here he has authority
from the chief priests to bind all [a]who call
on Your name."
15But the Lord said to him, "Go, for [a]he is
a chosen vessel of Mine to bear My name
before [b]Gentiles, [c]kings, and the [d]children
of Israel. 16For [a]I will show him how many
things he must suffer for My [b]name's sake."
17[a]And Ananias went his way and entered
the house; and [b]laying his hands on him he
said, "Brother Saul, the Lord Jesus,[1] who
appeared to you on the road as you came,
has sent me that you may receive your sight
and [c]be filled with the Holy Spirit." 18Imme-
diately there fell from his eyes *something*
like scales, and he received his sight at
once; and he arose and was baptized.
19So when he had received food, he was
strengthened. [a]Then Saul spent some days
with the disciples at Damascus.

Saul Preaches Christ

20Immediately he preached the Christ[1]
in the synagogues, that He is the Son of
God.
21Then all who heard were amazed, and
said, [a]"Is this not he who destroyed those
who called on this name in Jerusalem, and
has come here for that purpose, so that
he might bring them bound to the chief
priests?"
22But Saul increased all the more in
strength, [a]and confounded the Jews who
dwelt in Damascus, proving that this *Jesus*
is the Christ.

Saul Escapes Death

23Now after many days were past, [a]the
Jews plotted to kill him. 24[a]But their plot
became known to Saul. And they watched
the gates day and night, to kill him. 25Then
the disciples took him by night and [a]let
him down through the wall in a large
basket.

Saul at Jerusalem

26And [a]when Saul had come to Jerusalem, he tried to join the disciples; but they
were all afraid of him, and did not believe
that he was a disciple. 27[a]But Barnabas took
him and brought *him* to the apostles. And
he declared to them how he had seen the
Lord on the road, and that He had spoken
to him, [b]and how he had preached boldly
at Damascus in the name of Jesus. 28So
[a]he was with them at Jerusalem, coming
in and going out. 29And he spoke boldly in
the name of the Lord Jesus and disputed
against the [a]Hellenists, [b]but they attempted
to kill him. 30When the brethren found out,
they brought him down to Caesarea and
sent him out to Tarsus.

9:5 [1] NU-Text and M-Text omit the last sentence of verse 5 and begin verse 6 with *But arise and go.* 9:7 [a] Dan. 10:7; John 12:29; [Acts 22:9; 26:13] 9:10 [a] Acts 22:12 9:11 [a] Acts 21:39; 22:3 9:13 [a] Acts 9:1 9:14 [a] Acts 7:59; 9:2, 21; 1 Cor. 1:2; 2 Tim. 2:22 9:15 [a] Acts 13:2; 22:21; Rom. 1:1; 1 Cor. 15:10; Gal. 1:15; Eph. 3:7, 8; 1 Tim. 2:7; 2 Tim. 1:11 [b] Rom. 1:5; 11:13; Gal. 2:7, 8 [c] Acts 25:22, 23; 26:1 [d] Acts 21:40; Rom. 1:16; 9:1–5 9:16 [a] Acts 20:23; 2 Cor. 11:23–28; 12:7–10; Gal. 6:17; Phil. 1:29, 30 [b] 2 Cor. 4:11 9:17 [a] Acts 22:12, 13 [b] Acts 8:17 [c] Acts 2:4; 4:31; 8:17; 13:52 [1] M-Text omits *Jesus.* 9:19 [a] Acts 26:20 9:20 [1] NU-Text reads *Jesus.* 9:21 [a] Acts 8:3; 9:13; Gal. 1:13, 23 9:22 [a] Acts 18:28 9:23 [a] Acts 23:12; 2 Cor. 11:26 9:24 [a] 2 Cor. 11:32 9:25 [a] Josh. 2:15; 1 Sam. 19:12 9:26 [a] Acts 22:17–20; 26:20; Gal. 1:17, 18 9:27 [a] Acts 4:36; 13:2 [b] Acts 9:20, 22 9:28 [a] Gal. 1:18 9:29 [a] Acts 6:1; 11:20 [b] Acts 9:23; 2 Cor. 11:26

The Church Prospers

31[a]Then the churches[1] throughout all Judea, Galilee, and Samaria had peace and
were [b]edified. And walking in the [c]fear of
the Lord and in the [d]comfort of the Holy
Spirit, they were [e]multiplied.

Aeneas Healed

32Now it came to pass, as Peter went
[a]through all *parts of the country,* that he
also came down to the saints who dwelt
in Lydda. 33There he found a certain man
named Aeneas, who had been bedridden
eight years and was paralyzed. 34And Peter said to him, "Aeneas, [a]Jesus the Christ
heals you. Arise and make your bed." Then
he arose immediately. 35So all who dwelt at
Lydda and [a]Sharon saw him and [b]turned
to the Lord.

Dorcas Restored to Life

36At Joppa there was a certain disciple
named Tabitha, which is translated Dorcas. This woman was full [a]of good works
and charitable deeds which she did. 37But
it happened in those days that she became
sick and died. When they had washed her,
they laid *her* in [a]an upper room. 38And since
Lydda was near Joppa, and the disciples
had heard that Peter was there, they sent
two men to him, imploring *him* not to delay in coming to them. 39Then Peter arose
and went with them. When he had come,
they brought *him* to the upper room. And
all the widows stood by him weeping, showing the tunics and garments which Dorcas
had made while she was with them. 40But
Peter [a]put them all out, and [b]knelt down
and prayed. And turning to the body he
[c]said, "Tabitha, arise." And she opened her
eyes, and when she saw Peter she sat up.
41Then he gave her *his* hand and lifted her
up; and when he had called the saints and
widows, he presented her alive. 42And it
became known throughout all Joppa, [a]and
many believed on the Lord. 43So it was that
he stayed many days in Joppa with [a]Simon,
a tanner.

#OXYGEN

ACTS 9:40–41

Trust in His Wonder

God is still in the miracle-working business. He breathes life into dead situations. Take comfort in knowing He understands you and He will help you rise. Marvel at His power.

Breathe and **trust** in **His wonder.**

Cornelius Sends a Delegation

10 There was a certain man in [a]Caes-
area called Cornelius, a centurion
of what was called the Italian Regiment,
2[a]a devout *man* and one who [b]feared God
with all his household, who gave alms generously to the people, and prayed to God
always. 3About the ninth hour of the day
[a]he saw clearly in a vision an angel of God
coming in and saying to him, "Cornelius!"
4And when he observed him, he was
afraid, and said, "What is it, lord?"

So he said to him, "Your prayers and
your alms have come up for a memorial
before God. 5Now [a]send men to Joppa,
and send for Simon whose surname is Peter. 6He is lodging with [a]Simon, a tanner,
whose house is by the sea.[1] [b]He will tell you
what you must do." 7And when the angel
who spoke to him had departed, Cornelius
called two of his household servants and
a devout soldier from among those who
waited on him continually. 8So when he
had explained all *these* things to them, he
sent them to Joppa.

Peter's Vision

9The next day, as they went on their journey and drew near the city, [a]Peter went up
on the housetop to pray, about the sixth

9:31 [a] Acts 5:11; 8:1; 16:5 [b] [Eph. 4:16, 29] [c] Ps. 34:9 [d] John 14:16 [e] Acts 16:5 [1] NU-Text reads *church . . . was edified.* 9:32 [a] Acts 8:14 9:34 [a] [Acts 3:6, 16; 4:10] 9:35 [a] 1 Chr. 5:16; 27:29; Is. 33:9; 35:2; 65:10 [b] Acts 11:21; 15:19 9:36 [a] 1 Tim. 2:10; Titus 3:8 9:37 [a] Acts 1:13; 9:39 9:40 [a] Matt. 9:25 [b] Luke 22:41; Acts 7:60 [c] Mark 5:41, 42; John 11:43 9:42 [a] John 11:45 9:43 [a] Acts 10:6 10:1 [a] Acts 8:40; 23:23 10:2 [a] Acts 8:2; 9:22; 22:12 [b] [Acts 10:22, 35; 13:16, 26] 10:3 [a] Acts 10:30; 11:13 10:5 [a] Acts 11:13, 14 10:6 [a] Acts 9:43 [b] Acts 11:14 [1] NU-Text and M-Text omit the last sentence of this verse. 10:9 [a] Acts 10:9–32; 11:5–14

hour. 10Then he became very hungry and
wanted to eat; but while they made ready,
he fell into a trance 11and [a]saw heaven
opened and an object like a great sheet
bound at the four corners, descending
to him and let down to the earth. 12In it
were all kinds of four-footed animals of
the earth, wild beasts, creeping things, and
birds of the air. 13And a voice came to him,
"Rise, Peter; kill and eat."

14But Peter said, "Not so, Lord! [a]For I
have never eaten anything common or
unclean."

15And a voice *spoke* to him again the second time, [a]"What God has cleansed you
must not call common." 16This was done
three times. And the object was taken up
into heaven again.

Summoned to Caesarea

17Now while Peter wondered within himself what this vision which he had seen
meant, behold, the men who had been
sent from Cornelius had made inquiry for
Simon's house, and stood before the gate.
18And they called and asked whether Simon, whose surname was Peter, was lodging there.

19While Peter thought about the vision,
[a]the Spirit said to him, "Behold, three men
are seeking you. 20[a]Arise therefore, go
down and go with them, doubting nothing; for I have sent them."

21Then Peter went down to the men who
had been sent to him from Cornelius,[1] and
said, "Yes, I am he whom you seek. For what
reason have you come?"

22And they said, "Cornelius *the* centurion, a just man, one who fears God and
[a]has a good reputation among all the nation of the Jews, was divinely instructed by
a holy angel to summon you to his house,
and to hear words from you." 23Then he invited them in and lodged *them.*

On the next day Peter went away with
them, [a]and some brethren from Joppa accompanied him.

Peter Meets Cornelius

24And the following day they entered
Caesarea. Now Cornelius was waiting for
them, and had called together his relatives
and close friends. 25As Peter was coming
in, Cornelius met him and fell down at his
feet and worshiped *him.* 26But Peter lifted
him up, saying, [a]"Stand up; I myself am
also a man." 27And as he talked with him, he
went in and found many who had come together. 28Then he said to them, "You know
how [a]unlawful it is for a Jewish man to keep
company with or go to one of another nation. But [b]God has shown me that I should
not call any man common or unclean.
29Therefore I came without objection as
soon as I was sent for. I ask, then, for what
reason have you sent for me?"

30So Cornelius said, "Four days ago I was
fasting until this hour; and at the ninth
hour[1] I prayed in my house, and behold, [a]a
man stood before me [b]in bright clothing,
31and said, 'Cornelius, [a]your prayer has been
heard, and [b]your alms are remembered in
the sight of God. 32Send therefore to Joppa
and call Simon here, whose surname is Peter. He is lodging in the house of Simon, a
tanner, by the sea.[1] When he comes, he will
speak to you.' 33So I sent to you immediately, and you have done well to come. Now
therefore, we are all present before God, to
hear all the things commanded you by God."

Preaching to Cornelius' Household

34Then Peter opened *his* mouth and
said: [a]"In truth I perceive that God shows
no partiality. 35But [a]in every nation whoever fears Him and works righteousness is
[b]accepted by Him. 36The word which *God*
sent to the children of Israel, [a]preaching
peace through Jesus Christ—[b]He is Lord
of all— 37that word you know, which was
proclaimed throughout all Judea, and [a]be-
gan from Galilee after the baptism which
John preached: 38how [a]God anointed Jesus
of Nazareth with the Holy Spirit and with
power, who [b]went about doing good and

10:11 [a] Ezek. 1:1; Matt. 3:16; Acts 7:56; Rev. 4:1; 19:11 **10:14** [a] Lev. 11:4; 20:25; Deut. 14:3, 7; Ezek. 4:14 **10:15** [a] [Matt. 15:11; Mark 7:19]; Acts 10:28; [Rom. 14:14]; 1 Cor. 10:25; [1 Tim. 4:4; Titus 1:15] **10:19** [a] Acts 11:12 **10:20** [a] Acts 15:7–9 **10:21** [1] NU-Text and M-Text omit *who had been sent to him from Cornelius.* **10:22** [a] Acts 22:12 **10:23** [a] Acts 10:45; 11:12 **10:26** [a] Acts 14:14, 15; Rev. 19:10; 22:8 **10:28** [a] John 4:9; 18:28; Acts 11:3; Gal. 2:12 [b] [Acts 10:14, 35; 15:8, 9] **10:30** [a] Acts 1:10 [b] Matt. 28:3; Mark 16:5 [1] NU-Text reads *Four days ago to this hour, at the ninth hour.* **10:31** [a] Dan. 10:12 [b] Heb. 6:10 **10:32** [1] NU-Text omits the last sentence of this verse. **10:34** [a] Deut. 10:17; 2 Chr. 19:7; Rom. 2:11; Gal. 2:6; Eph. 6:9 **10:35** [a] Acts 15:9; [1 Cor. 12; 13; Eph. 2:13] [b] Ps. 15:1, 2 **10:36** [a] Is. 57:19; Eph. 2:14; [Col. 1:20] [b] Matt. 28:18; Acts 2:36; Rom. 10:12; 1 Cor. 15:27 **10:37** [a] Luke 4:14 **10:38** [a] Is. 61:1–3; Luke 4:18 [b] Matt. 4:23

healing all who were oppressed by the
devil, [c]for God was with Him. 39And we
are [a]witnesses of all things which He did
both in the land of the Jews and in Jerusalem, whom they[1] [b]killed by hanging on
a tree. 40Him [a]God raised up on the third
day, and showed Him openly, 41[a]not to all
the people, but to witnesses chosen before
by God, *even* to us [b]who ate and drank with
Him after He arose from the dead. 42And
[a]He commanded us to preach to the people, and to testify [b]that it is He who was
ordained by God *to be* Judge [c]of the living
and the dead. 43[a]To Him all the prophets
witness that, through His name, [b]whoever
believes in Him will receive [c]remission
of sins."

The Holy Spirit Falls on the Gentiles

44While Peter was still speaking these
words, [a]the Holy Spirit fell upon all those
who heard the word. 45[a]And those of the circumcision who believed were astonished,
as many as came with Peter, [b]because the
gift of the Holy Spirit had been poured out
on the Gentiles also. 46For they heard them
speak with tongues and magnify God.

Then Peter answered, 47"Can anyone forbid water, that these should not be baptized
who have received the Holy Spirit [a]just as
we *have?*" 48[a]And he commanded them to
be baptized [b]in the name of the Lord. Then
they asked him to stay a few days.

Peter Defends God's Grace

11 Now the apostles and brethren who
were in Judea heard that the Gentiles
had also received the word of God. 2And
when Peter came up to Jerusalem, [a]those
of the circumcision contended with him,
3saying, [a]"You went in to uncircumcised
men [b]and ate with them!"

4But Peter explained *it* to them [a]in order
from the beginning, saying: 5[a]"I was in the
city of Joppa praying; and in a trance I saw
a vision, an object descending like a great
sheet, let down from heaven by four corners; and it came to me. 6When I observed
it intently and considered, I saw four-footed
animals of the earth, wild beasts, creeping
things, and birds of the air. 7And I heard a
voice saying to me, 'Rise, Peter; kill and eat.'
8But I said, 'Not so, Lord! For nothing common or unclean has at any time entered my
mouth.' 9But the voice answered me again
from heaven, 'What God has cleansed you
must not call common.' 10Now this was
done three times, and all were drawn up
again into heaven. 11At that very moment,
three men stood before the house where
I was, having been sent to me from Caesarea. 12Then [a]the Spirit told me to go with
them, doubting nothing. Moreover [b]these
six brethren accompanied me, and we entered the man's house. 13[a]And he told us
how he had seen an angel standing in his
house, who said to him, 'Send men to Joppa,
and call for Simon whose surname is Peter,
14who will tell you words by which you and
all your household will be saved.' 15And as
I began to speak, the Holy Spirit fell upon
them, [a]as upon us at the beginning. 16Then
I remembered the word of the Lord, how He
said, [a]'John indeed baptized with water, but
[b]you shall be baptized with the Holy Spirit.'
17[a]If therefore God gave them the same gift
as *He gave* us when we believed on the Lord
Jesus Christ, [b]who was I that I could withstand God?"

18When they heard these things they became silent; and they glorified God, saying,
[a]"Then God has also granted to the Gentiles
repentance to life."

Barnabas and Saul at Antioch

19[a]Now those who were scattered after
the persecution that arose over Stephen
traveled as far as Phoenicia, Cyprus, and
Antioch, preaching the word to no one but
the Jews only. 20But some of them were
men from Cyprus and Cyrene, who, when
they had come to Antioch, spoke to [a]the

10:38 [c] John 3:2; 8:29 10:39 [a] Acts 1:8 [b] Acts 2:23 [1] NU-Text and M-Text add *also.* 10:40 [a] Hos. 6:2; Matt. 12:39, 40; 16:4; 20:19; John 2:19–21; Acts 2:24 10:41 [a] [John 14:17, 19, 22; 15:27] [b] Luke 24:30, 41–43 10:42 [a] Matt. 28:19 [b] John 5:22, 27; Acts 17:31 [c] Rom. 14:9; 2 Tim. 4:1; 1 Pet. 4:5 10:43 [a] [Is. 42:1; 53:11; 61:1]; Jer. 31:34; Dan. 9:24; Hos. 6:1–3; Mic. 7:18; Zech. 13:1; Mal. 4:2 [b] [John 3:16, 18; Acts 26:18]; Rom. 10:11; Gal. 3:22 [c] Acts 13:38, 39 10:44 [a] Acts 4:31 10:45 [a] Acts 10:23 [b] Is. 42:1, 6; 49:6; Luke 2:32; John 11:52; Acts 11:18 10:47 [a] Acts 2:4; 10:44; 11:17; 15:8 10:48 [a] 1 Cor. 1:14–17 [b] Acts 2:38; 8:16; 19:5 11:2 [a] Acts 10:45 11:3 [a] Matt. 9:11; Acts 10:28 [b] Gal. 2:12 11:4 [a] Luke 1:3 11:5 [a] Acts 10:9 11:12 [a] [John 16:13]; Acts 10:19; 15:7 [b] Acts 10:23 11:13 [a] Acts 10:30 11:15 [a] Acts 2:1–4; 15:7–9 11:16 [a] Matt. 3:11; Mark 1:8; John 1:26, 33; Acts 1:5; 19:4 [b] Is. 44:3 11:17 [a] [Acts 15:8, 9] [b] Acts 10:47 11:18 [a] Is. 42:1, 6; 49:6; Luke 2:32; John 11:52; Rom. 10:12, 13; 15:9, 16 11:19 [a] Acts 8:1, 4 11:20 [a] Acts 6:1; 9:29

Hellenists, preaching the Lord Jesus. 21And
[a]the hand of the Lord was with them, and
a great number believed and [b]turned to
the Lord.

22Then news of these things came to the
ears of the church in Jerusalem, and they
sent out [a]Barnabas to go as far as Antioch.
23When he came and had seen the grace of
God, he was glad, and [a]encouraged them
all that with purpose of heart they should
continue with the Lord. 24For he was a good
man, [a]full of the Holy Spirit and of faith.
[b]And a great many people were added to
the Lord.

25Then Barnabas departed for [a]Tarsus to
seek Saul. 26And when he had found him,
he brought him to Antioch. So it was that
for a whole year they assembled with the
church and taught a great many people.
And the disciples were first called Christians in Antioch.

Relief to Judea

27And in these days [a]prophets came
from Jerusalem to Antioch. 28Then one
of them, named [a]Agabus, stood up and
showed by the Spirit that there was going to
be a great famine throughout all the world,
which also happened in the days of [b]Clau-
dius Caesar. 29Then the disciples, each according to his ability, determined to send
[a]relief to the brethren dwelling in Judea.
30[a]This they also did, and sent it to the elders by the hands of Barnabas and Saul.

Herod's Violence to the Church

12 Now about that time Herod the
king stretched out *his* hand to harass some from the church. 2Then he killed
James [a]the brother of John with the sword.
3And because he saw that it pleased the
Jews, he proceeded further to seize Peter
also. Now it was *during* [a]the Days of Unleavened Bread. 4So [a]when he had arrested
him, he put *him* in prison, and delivered
him to four squads of soldiers to keep him,
intending to bring him before the people
after Passover.

Peter Freed from Prison

5Peter was therefore kept in prison, but
constant[1] prayer was offered to God for
him by the church. 6And when Herod was
about to bring him out, that night Peter was
sleeping, bound with two chains between
two soldiers; and the guards before the
door were keeping the prison. 7Now behold,
[a]an angel of the Lord stood by *him,* and a
light shone in the prison; and he struck Peter on the side and raised him up, saying,
"Arise quickly!" And his chains fell off *his*
hands. 8Then the angel said to him, "Gird
yourself and tie on your sandals"; and so he
did. And he said to him, "Put on your garment and follow me." 9So he went out and
followed him, and [a]did not know that what
was done by the angel was real, but thought
[b]he was seeing a vision. 10When they were
past the first and the second guard posts,
they came to the iron gate that leads to
the city, [a]which opened to them of its own
accord; and they went out and went down
one street, and immediately the angel departed from him.

11And when Peter had come to himself,
he said, "Now I know for certain that [a]the
Lord has sent His angel, and [b]has delivered
me from the hand of Herod and *from* all the
expectation of the Jewish people."

12So, when he had considered *this,* [a]he
came to the house of Mary, the mother of
[b]John whose surname was Mark, where
many were gathered together [c]praying.
13And as Peter knocked at the door of the
gate, a girl named Rhoda came to answer.
14When she recognized Peter's voice, because of *her* gladness she did not open the
gate, but ran in and announced that Peter stood before the gate. 15But they said
to her, "You are beside yourself!" Yet she
kept insisting that it was so. So they said,
[a]"It is his angel."

16Now Peter continued knocking; and
when they opened *the door* and saw him,
they were astonished. 17But [a]motioning to
them with his hand to keep silent, he declared to them how the Lord had brought

---

11:21 [a] Luke 1:66; Acts 2:47 [b] Acts 9:35; 14:1 **11:22** [a] Acts 4:36; 9:27 **11:23** [a] Acts 13:43; 14:22 **11:24** [a] Acts 6:5 [b] Acts 5:14; 11:21 **11:25** [a] Acts 9:11, 30 **11:27** [a] Acts 2:17; 13:1; 15:32; 21:9; 1 Cor. 12:28; Eph. 4:11 **11:28** [a] John 16:13; Acts 21:10 [b] Acts 18:2 **11:29** [a] Rom. 15:26; 1 Cor. 16:1; 2 Cor. 9:1 **11:30** [a] Acts 12:25 **12:2** [a] Matt. 4:21; 20:23 **12:3** [a] Ex. 12:15; 23:15; Acts 20:6 **12:4** [a] John 21:18 **12:5** [1] NU-Text reads *constantly* (or *earnestly*). **12:7** [a] Acts 5:19 **12:9** [a] Ps. 126:1 [b] Acts 10:3, 17; 11:5 **12:10** [a] Acts 5:19; 16:26 **12:11** [a] [Ps. 34:7]; Dan. 3:28; 6:22; [Heb. 1:14] [b] Job 5:19; [Ps. 33:18, 19; 34:22; 41:2]; 2 Cor. 1:10; [2 Pet. 2:9] **12:12** [a] Acts 4:23 [b] Acts 13:5, 13; 15:37; 2 Tim. 4:11; Philem. 24; 1 Pet. 5:13 [c] Acts 12:5 **12:15** [a] Gen. 48:16; [Matt. 18:10] **12:17** [a] Acts 13:16; 19:33; 21:40

him out of the prison. And he said, "Go,
tell these things to James and to the brethren." And he departed and went to another
place.
18Then, as soon as it was day, there was
no small stir among the soldiers about what
had become of Peter. 19But when Herod had
searched for him and not found him, he examined the guards and commanded that
they should be put to death.
And he went down from Judea to Caesarea, and stayed *there.*

Herod's Violent Death

20Now Herod had been very angry with
the people of [a]Tyre and Sidon; but they
came to him with one accord, and having made Blastus the king's personal aide
their friend, they asked for peace, because
[b]their country was supplied with food by
the king's *country.*
21So on a set day Herod, arrayed in royal
apparel, sat on his throne and gave an ora-
tion to them. 22And the people kept shouting, "The voice of a god and not of a man!"
23Then immediately an angel of the Lord
[a]struck him, because [b]he did not give glory
to God. And he was eaten by worms and
died.
24But [a]the word of God grew and multiplied.

Barnabas and Saul Appointed

25And [a]Barnabas and Saul returned
from[1] Jerusalem when they had [b]fulfilled
their ministry, and they also [c]took with
them [d]John whose surname was Mark.

13 Now [a]in the church that was at Antioch there were certain prophets
and teachers: [b]Barnabas, Simeon who was
called Niger, [c]Lucius of Cyrene, Manaen
who had been brought up with Herod the
tetrarch, and Saul. 2As they ministered to
the Lord and fasted, the Holy Spirit said,
[a]"Now separate to Me Barnabas and Saul
for the work [b]to which I have called them."
3Then, [a]having fasted and prayed, and laid
hands on them, they sent *them* away.

Preaching in Cyprus

4So, being sent out by the Holy Spirit,
they went down to Seleucia, and from there
they sailed to [a]Cyprus. 5And when they arrived in Salamis, [a]they preached the word
of God in the synagogues of the Jews. They
also had [b]John as *their* assistant.
6Now when they had gone through the
island[1] to Paphos, they found [a]a certain sorcerer, a false prophet, a Jew whose name
was Bar-Jesus, 7who was with the proconsul, Sergius Paulus, an intelligent man.
This man called for Barnabas and Saul and
sought to hear the word of God. 8But [a]Ely-
mas the sorcerer (for so his name is translated) withstood them, seeking to turn the
proconsul away from the faith. 9Then Saul,
who also *is called* Paul, [a]filled with the Holy
Spirit, looked intently at him 10and said,
"O full of all deceit and all fraud, [a]*you* son
of the devil, *you* enemy of all righteousness,
will you not cease perverting the straight
ways of the Lord? 11And now, indeed, [a]the
hand of the Lord *is* upon you, and you shall
be blind, not seeing the sun for a time."
And immediately a dark mist fell on
him, and he went around seeking someone to lead him by the hand. 12Then the
proconsul believed, when he saw what had
been done, being astonished at the teaching of the Lord.

At Antioch in Pisidia

13Now when Paul and his party set sail
from Paphos, they came to Perga in Pamphylia; and [a]John, departing from them,
returned to Jerusalem. 14But when they
departed from Perga, they came to Antioch in Pisidia, and [a]went into the synagogue on the Sabbath day and sat down.
15And [a]after the reading of the Law and
the Prophets, the rulers of the synagogue
sent to them, saying, "Men *and* brethren,
if you have [b]any word of exhortation for
the people, say on."
16Then Paul stood up, and motioning
with *his* hand said, "Men of Israel, and
[a]you who fear God, listen: 17The God of

12:20 [a] Matt. 11:21 [b] 1 Kin. 5:11; Ezra 3:7; Ezek. 27:17 12:23 [a] 1 Sam. 25:38; 2 Sam. 24:16, 17; 2 Kin. 19:35; Acts 5:19 [b] Ps. 115:1 12:24 [a] Is. 55:11; Acts 6:7; 19:20 12:25 [a] Acts 11:30 [b] Acts 11:30 [c] Acts 13:5, 13 [d] Acts 12:12; 15:37 [1] NU-Text and M-Text read *to.* 13:1 [a] Acts 14:26 [b] Acts 11:22 [c] Rom. 16:21 13:2 [a] Num. 8:14; Acts 9:15; 22:21; Rom. 1:1; Gal. 1:15; 2:9 [b] Matt. 9:38; Acts 14:26; Rom. 10:15; Eph. 3:7, 8; 1 Tim. 2:7; 2 Tim. 1:11; Heb. 5:4 13:3 [a] Matt. 9:15; Mark 2:20; Luke 5:35; Acts 6:6 13:4 [a] Acts 4:36 13:5 [a] [Acts 13:46] [b] Acts 12:25; 15:37 13:6 [a] Acts 8:9 [1] NU-Text reads *the whole island.* 13:8 [a] Ex. 7:11; 2 Tim. 3:8 13:9 [a] Acts 2:4; 4:8 13:10 [a] Matt. 13:38; John 8:44; [1 John 3:8] 13:11 [a] Ex. 9:3; 1 Sam. 5:6; Job 19:21; Ps. 32:4; Heb. 10:31 13:13 [a] Acts 15:38 13:14 [a] Acts 16:13 13:15 [a] Luke 4:16 [b] Heb. 13:22 13:16 [a] Acts 10:35

this people Israel[1] [a]chose our fathers, and
exalted the people [b]when they dwelt as
strangers in the land of Egypt, and with
an uplifted arm He [c]brought them out of
it. 18Now [a]for a time of about forty years He
put up with their ways in the wilderness.
19And when He had destroyed [a]seven nations in the land of Canaan, [b]He distributed
their land to them by allotment.

20"After that [a]He gave *them* judges for
about four hundred and fifty years, [b]until
Samuel the prophet. 21[a]And afterward they
asked for a king; so God gave them [b]Saul
the son of Kish, a man of the tribe of Benjamin, for forty years. 22And [a]when He had
removed him, [b]He raised up for them David
as king, to whom also He gave testimony and
said, [c]'I have found David[1] the *son* of Jesse,
[d]a man after My *own* heart, who will do all
My will.'[2] 23[a]From this man's seed, according [b]to *the* promise, God raised up for Israel
[c]a Savior—Jesus—[1] 24[a]after John had first
preached, before His coming, the baptism of
repentance to all the people of Israel. 25And
as John was finishing his course, he said,
[a]'Who do you think I am? I am not *He.* But
behold, [b]there comes One after me, the sandals of whose feet I am not worthy to loose.'

26"Men *and* brethren, sons of the family
of Abraham, and [a]those among you who
fear God, [b]to you the word of this salvation has been sent. 27For those who dwell
in Jerusalem, and their rulers, [a]because
they did not know Him, nor even the voices
of the Prophets which are read every Sabbath, have fulfilled *them* in condemning
Him. 28[a]And though they found no cause
for death *in Him,* they asked Pilate that He
should be put to death. 29[a]Now when they
had fulfilled all that was written concerning Him, [b]they took *Him* down from the
tree and laid *Him* in a tomb. 30[a]But God
raised Him from the dead. 31[a]He was seen
for many days by those who came up with
Him from Galilee to Jerusalem, who are His
witnesses to the people. 32And we declare
to you glad tidings—[a]that promise which
was made to the fathers. 33God has fulfilled
this for us their children, in that He has
raised up Jesus. As it is also written in the
second Psalm:

> [a]'You are My Son,
> Today I have begotten You.'[1]

34And that He raised Him from the dead,
no more to return to corruption, He has
spoken thus:

> [a]'I will give you the sure
> mercies of David.'[1]

35Therefore He also says in another *Psalm:*

> [a]'You will not allow Your Holy
> One to see corruption.'[1]

36"For David, after he had served his own
generation by the will of God, [a]fell asleep,
was buried with his fathers, and saw corruption; 37but He whom God raised up saw
no corruption. 38Therefore let it be known
to you, brethren, that [a]through this Man
is preached to you the forgiveness of sins;
39and [a]by Him everyone who believes is justified from all things from which you could
not be justified by the law of Moses. 40Be-
ware therefore, lest what has been spoken
in the prophets come upon you:

> 41 'Behold,[a] you despisers,
> Marvel and perish!
> For I work a work in your days,
> A work which you will by
> no means believe,
> Though one were to
> declare it to you.'"[1]

Blessing and Conflict at Antioch

42So when the Jews went out of the synagogue,[1] the Gentiles begged that these
words might be preached to them the next

13:17 [a] Ex. 6:1, 6; 13:14, 16; Deut. 7:6–8 [b] Acts 7:17 [c] Ex. 14:8 [1] M-Text omits *Israel.* **13:18** [a] Ex. 16:35; Num. 14:34; Acts 7:36 **13:19** [a] Deut. 7:1 [b] Josh. 14:1, 2; 19:51; Ps. 78:55 **13:20** [a] Judg. 2:16; 1 Sam. 4:18; 7:15 [b] 1 Sam. 3:20; Acts 3:24 **13:21** [a] 1 Sam. 8:5 [b] 1 Sam. 10:20–24 **13:22** [a] 1 Sam. 15:23, 26, 28 [b] 1 Sam. 16:1, 12, 13 [c] Ps. 89:20 [d] 1 Sam. 13:14 [1] Psalm 89:20 [2] 1 Samuel 13:14 **13:23** [a] Is. 11:1 [b] Ps. 132:11 [c] [Matt. 1:21] [1] M-Text reads *for Israel salvation.* **13:24** [a] Matt. 3:1; [Luke 3:3] **13:25** [a] Matt. 3:11; Mark 1:7; Luke 3:16 [b] John 1:20, 27 **13:26** [a] Ps. 66:16 [b] Matt. 10:6 **13:27** [a] Luke 23:34 **13:28** [a] Matt. 27:22, 23; Mark 15:13, 14; Luke 23:21–23; John 19:15; Acts 3:14; [2 Cor. 5:21; Heb. 4:15]; 1 Pet. 2:22 **13:29** [a] Luke 18:31 [b] Matt. 27:57–61; Mark 15:42–47; Luke 23:50–56; John 19:38–42 **13:30** [a] Ps. 16:10, 11; Hos. 6:2; Matt. 12:39, 40; 28:6 **13:31** [a] Matt. 28:16; Acts 1:3, 11; 1 Cor. 15:5–8 **13:32** [a] [Gen. 3:15] **13:33** [a] Ps. 2:7; Heb. 1:5 [1] Psalm 2:7 **13:34** [a] Is. 55:3 [1] Isaiah 55:3 **13:35** [a] Ps. 16:10; Acts 2:27 [1] Psalm 16:10 **13:36** [a] Acts 2:29 **13:38** [a] Jer. 31:34 **13:39** [a] [Is. 53:11; John 3:16] **13:41** [a] Hab. 1:5 [1] Habakkuk 1:5 **13:42** [1] Or *And when they went out of the synagogue of the Jews;* NU-Text reads *And when they went out, they begged.*

Sabbath. 43Now when the congregation had
broken up, many of the Jews and devout
proselytes followed Paul and Barnabas,
who, speaking to them, [a]persuaded them
to continue in [b]the grace of God.
44On the next Sabbath almost the whole
city came together to hear the word of God.
45But when the Jews saw the multitudes,
they were filled with envy; and contradicting and blaspheming, they [a]opposed the
things spoken by Paul. 46Then Paul and
Barnabas grew bold and said, [a]"It was necessary that the word of God should be spoken to you first; but [b]since you reject it, and
judge yourselves unworthy of everlasting
life, behold, [c]we turn to the Gentiles. 47For
so the Lord has commanded us:

> [a]'I have set you as a light to the Gentiles,
> That you should be for salvation
> to the ends of the earth.'"[1]

48Now when the Gentiles heard this,
they were glad and glorified the word of
the Lord. [a]And as many as had been appointed to eternal life believed.
49And the word of the Lord was being
spread throughout all the region. 50But
the Jews stirred up the devout and prominent women and the chief men of the city,
[a]raised up persecution against Paul and
Barnabas, and expelled them from their
region. 51[a]But they shook off the dust from
their feet against them, and came to Iconium. 52And the disciples [a]were filled with
joy and [b]with the Holy Spirit.

At Iconium

14 Now it happened in Iconium that
they went together to the synagogue
of the Jews, and so spoke that a great multitude both of the Jews and of the [a]Greeks
believed. 2But the unbelieving Jews stirred
up the Gentiles and poisoned their minds
against the brethren. 3Therefore they
stayed there a long time, speaking boldly
in the Lord, [a]who was bearing witness to
the word of His grace, granting signs and
[b]wonders to be done by their hands.
4But the multitude of the city was [a]di-
vided: part sided with the Jews, and part
with the [b]apostles. 5And when a violent attempt was made by both the Gentiles and
Jews, with their rulers, [a]to abuse and stone
them, 6they became aware of it and [a]fled
to Lystra and Derbe, cities of Lycaonia, and
to the surrounding region. 7And they were
preaching the gospel there.

Idolatry at Lystra

8[a]And in Lystra a certain man without
strength in his feet was sitting, a cripple
from his mother's womb, who had never
walked. 9*This* man heard Paul speaking.
Paul, observing him intently and seeing
that he had faith to be healed, 10said with a
loud voice, [a]"Stand up straight on your feet!"
And he leaped and walked. 11Now when the
people saw what Paul had done, they raised
their voices, saying in the Lycaonian *language,* [a]"The gods have come down to us in
the likeness of men!" 12And Barnabas they
called Zeus, and Paul, Hermes, because he
was the chief speaker. 13Then the priest of
Zeus, whose temple was in front of their
city, brought oxen and garlands to the gates,
[a]intending to sacrifice with the multitudes.
14But when the apostles Barnabas and
Paul heard this, [a]they tore their clothes
and ran in among the multitude, crying
out 15and saying, "Men, [a]why are you doing
these things? [b]We also are men with the
same nature as you, and preach to you that
you should turn from [c]these useless things
[d]to the living God, [e]who made the heaven,
the earth, the sea, and all things that are in
them, 16[a]who in bygone generations allowed
all nations to walk in their own ways. 17[a]Nev-
ertheless He did not leave Himself without
witness, in that He did good, [b]gave us rain
from heaven and fruitful seasons, filling our
hearts with [c]food and gladness." 18And with
these sayings they could scarcely restrain
the multitudes from sacrificing to them.

13:43 [a] Acts 11:23 [b] Titus 2:11; Heb. 12:15; 1 Pet. 5:12 13:45 [a] Acts 18:6; 1 Pet. 4:4; Jude 10 13:46 [a] Matt. 10:6; Acts 3:26; Rom. 1:16 [b] Ex. 32:10; Deut. 32:21; Is. 55:5; Matt. 21:43; Rom. 10:19 [c] Acts 18:6 13:47 [a] Is. 42:6; 49:6; Luke 2:32 [1] Isaiah 49:6 13:48 [a] [Acts 2:47] 13:50 [a] Acts 7:52; 2 Tim. 3:11 13:51 [a] Matt. 10:14; Mark 6:11; [Luke 9:5] 13:52 [a] Matt. 5:12; John 16:22 [b] Acts 2:4; 4:8, 31; 13:9 14:1 [a] John 7:35; Acts 18:4; Rom. 1:14, 16; 1 Cor. 1:22 14:3 [a] Mark 16:20; Acts 4:29; 20:32; Heb. 2:4 [b] Acts 5:12 14:4 [a] Luke 12:51 [b] Acts 13:2, 3 14:5 [a] 2 Tim. 3:11 14:6 [a] Matt. 10:23 14:8 [a] Acts 3:2 14:10 [a] [Is. 35:6] 14:11 [a] Acts 8:10; 28:6 14:13 [a] Dan. 2:46 14:14 [a] Num. 14:6; Matt. 26:65; Mark 14:63 14:15 [a] Acts 10:26 [b] James 5:17 [c] 1 Sam. 12:21; Jer. 8:19; 14:22; Amos 2:4; 1 Cor. 8:4 [d] 1 Thess. 1:9 [e] Gen. 1:1; Ex. 20:11; Ps. 146:6; Acts 4:24; 17:24; Rev. 14:7 14:16 [a] Ps. 81:12; Mic. 4:5; 1 Pet. 4:3 14:17 [a] Acts 17:24–27; Rom. 1:19, 20 [b] Lev. 26:4; Deut. 11:14; [Matt. 5:45] [c] Ps. 145:16

Stoning, Escape to Derbe

19[a]Then Jews from Antioch and Iconium
came there; and having persuaded the multitudes, [b]they stoned Paul *and* dragged *him*
out of the city, supposing him to be [c]dead.
20However, when the disciples gathered
around him, he rose up and went into the
city. And the next day he departed with Barnabas to Derbe.

Strengthening the Converts

21And when they had preached the gospel to that city [a]and made many disciples,
they returned to Lystra, Iconium, and Antioch, 22strengthening the souls of the disciples, [a]exhorting *them* to continue in the
faith, and *saying,* [b]"We must through many
tribulations enter the kingdom of God." 23So
when they had [a]appointed elders in every
church, and prayed with fasting, they commended them to the Lord in whom they
had believed. 24And after they had passed
through Pisidia, they came to Pamphylia.
25Now when they had preached the word in
Perga, they went down to Attalia. 26From
there they sailed to Antioch, where they
had been commended to the grace of God
for the work which they had completed.

27Now when they had come and gathered the church together, [a]they reported
all that God had done with them, and that
He had [b]opened the door of faith to the
Gentiles. 28So they stayed there a long time
with the disciples.

Conflict over Circumcision

15 And [a]certain *men* came down from
Judea and taught the brethren, [b]"Unless you are circumcised according to the
custom of Moses, you cannot be saved."
2Therefore, when Paul and Barnabas had
no small dissension and dispute with them,
they determined that [a]Paul and Barnabas
and certain others of them should go up
to Jerusalem, to the apostles and elders,
about this question.

3So, [a]being sent on their way by the
church, they passed through Phoenicia
and Samaria, [b]describing the conversion
of the Gentiles; and they caused great joy
to all the brethren. 4And when they had
come to Jerusalem, they were received by
the church and the apostles and the elders;
and they reported all things that God had
done with them. 5But some of the sect of
the Pharisees who believed rose up, saying,
"It is necessary to circumcise them, and to
command *them* to keep the law of Moses."

The Jerusalem Council

6Now the apostles and elders came together to consider this matter. 7And when
there had been much dispute, Peter rose
up *and* said to them: [a]"Men *and* brethren,
you know that a good while ago God chose
among us, that by my mouth the Gentiles
should hear the word of the gospel and believe. 8So God, [a]who knows the heart, acknowledged them by [b]giving them the Holy
Spirit, just as *He did* to us, 9[a]and made no
distinction between us and them, [b]purifying their hearts by faith. 10Now therefore,
why do you test God [a]by putting a yoke on
the neck of the disciples which neither our
fathers nor we were able to bear? 11But [a]we
believe that through the grace of the Lord
Jesus Christ[1] we shall be saved in the same
manner as they."

12Then all the multitude kept silent and
listened to Barnabas and Paul declaring
how many miracles and wonders God had
[a]worked through them among the Gentiles.
13And after they had become silent, [a]James
answered, saying, "Men *and* brethren, listen to me: 14[a]Simon has declared how God
at the first visited the Gentiles to take out
of them a people for His name. 15And with
this the words of the prophets agree, just
as it is written:

16 'After[a] this I will return
And will rebuild the tabernacle
of David, which has fallen
down;
I will rebuild its ruins,
And I will set it up;

14:19 [a] Acts 13:45, 50; 14:2–5; 1 Thess. 2:14 [b] Acts 14:5; 2 Cor. 11:25; 2 Tim. 3:11 [c] [2 Cor. 12:1–4] 14:21 [a] Matt. 28:19 14:22 [a] Acts 11:23 [b] Matt. 10:38; Luke 22:28; [Rom. 8:17; 2 Tim. 2:12; 3:12] 14:23 [a] Matt. 9:15; Mark 2:20; Luke 5:35; 2 Cor. 8:19; Titus 1:5 14:27 [a] Acts 15:4, 12 [b] 1 Cor. 16:9; 2 Cor. 2:12; Col. 4:3; Rev. 3:8 15:1 [a] Gal. 2:12 [b] John 7:22; Acts 15:5; Gal. 5:2; Phil. 3:2; [Col. 2:8, 11, 16] 15:2 [a] Gal. 2:1 15:3 [a] Acts 20:38; 21:5; Rom. 15:24; 1 Cor. 16:6, 11; 2 Cor. 1:16; Titus 3:13; 3 John 6 [b] Acts 14:27; 15:4, 12 15:7 [a] Acts 10:20 15:8 [a] 1 Chr. 28:9; Acts 1:24 [b] Acts 2:4; 10:44, 47 15:9 [a] Rom. 10:12 [b] Acts 10:15, 28 15:10 [a] Matt. 23:4; Gal. 5:1 15:11 [a] Rom. 3:4; 5:15; 2 Cor. 13:14; [Eph. 2:5–8; Titus 2:11] [1] NU-Text and M-Text omit *Christ.* 15:12 [a] Acts 14:27; 15:3, 4 15:13 [a] Acts 12:17 15:14 [a] Acts 15:7; 2 Pet. 1:1 15:16 [a] Amos 9:11, 12

17 So that the rest of mankind
may seek the LORD,
Even all the Gentiles who are
called by My name,
Says the LORD who does
all these things.'[1]

18"Known to God from eternity are all
His works.[1] 19Therefore [a]I judge that we
should not trouble those from among the
Gentiles who [b]are turning to God, 20but that
we [a]write to them to abstain [b]from things
polluted by idols, [c]*from* sexual immorality,[1] [d]*from* things strangled, and *from* blood.
21For Moses has had throughout many generations those who preach him in every
city, [a]being read in the synagogues every
Sabbath."

The Jerusalem Decree

22Then it pleased the apostles and elders, with the whole church, to send chosen
men of their own company to Antioch with
Paul and Barnabas, *namely,* Judas who was
also named [a]Barsabas,[1] and Silas, leading
men among the brethren.
23They wrote this *letter* by them:

The apostles, the elders, and the
brethren,

To the brethren who are of the
Gentiles in Antioch, Syria, and Cilicia:

Greetings.

24 Since we have heard that [a]some who
went out from us have troubled you
with words, [b]unsettling your souls,
saying, "*You must* be circumcised and
keep the law"[1]—to whom we gave no
such commandment— 25it seemed
good to us, being assembled with
one accord, to send chosen men to
you with our beloved Barnabas and
Paul, 26[a]men who have risked their
lives for the name of our Lord Jesus
Christ. 27We have therefore sent
Judas and Silas, who will also report
the same things by word of mouth.
28For it seemed good to the Holy
Spirit, and to us, to lay upon you no
greater burden than these necessary
things: 29[a]that you abstain from things
offered to idols, [b]from blood, from
things strangled, and from [c]sexual
immorality.[1] If you keep yourselves
from these, you will do well.

Farewell.

Continuing Ministry in Syria

30So when they were sent off, they came
to Antioch; and when they had gathered the
multitude together, they delivered the letter. 31When they had read it, they rejoiced
over its encouragement. 32Now Judas and
Silas, themselves being [a]prophets also, [b]ex-
horted and strengthened the brethren with
many words. 33And after they had stayed
there for a time, they were [a]sent back with
greetings from the brethren to the apostles.[1]
34However, it seemed good to Silas to
remain there.[1] 35[a]Paul and Barnabas also
remained in Antioch, teaching and preaching the word of the Lord, with many others also.

Division over John Mark

36Then after some days Paul said to
Barnabas, "Let us now go back and visit
our brethren in every city where we have
preached the word of the Lord, *and see* how
they are doing." 37Now Barnabas was determined to take with them [a]John called Mark.
38But Paul insisted that they should not
take with them [a]the one who had departed
from them in Pamphylia, and had not gone
with them to the work. 39Then the contention became so sharp that they parted from
one another. And so Barnabas took Mark
and sailed to [a]Cyprus; 40but Paul chose Silas

15:17 [1] Amos 9:11, 12 15:18 [1] NU-Text (combining with verse 17) reads *Says the Lord, who makes these things known from eternity (of old).* 15:19 [a] Acts 15:28; 21:25 [b] 1 Thess. 1:9 15:20 [a] Acts 21:25 [b] Gen. 35:2; Ex. 20:3, 23; Ezek. 20:30; [1 Cor. 8:1; 10:20, 28]; Rev. 2:14 [c] [1 Cor. 6:9]; Gal. 5:19; Eph. 5:3; Col. 3:5; 1 Thess. 4:3; 1 Pet. 4:3 [d] Gen. 9:4; Lev. 3:17; Deut. 12:16; 1 Sam. 14:33 [1] Or *fornication* 15:21 [a] Acts 13:15, 27; 2 Cor. 3:14 15:22 [a] Acts 1:23 [1] NU-Text and M-Text read *Barsabbas.* 15:24 [a] Acts 15:1; Gal. 2:4; 5:12; Titus 1:10, 11 [b] Gal. 1:7; 5:10 [1] NU-Text omits *saying, "You must be circumcised and keep the law."* 15:26 [a] Acts 13:50; 14:19; 1 Cor. 15:30; 2 Cor. 11:23–26 15:29 [a] Acts 15:20; 21:25; Rev. 2:14, 20 [b] Lev. 17:14 [c] 1 Cor. 5:1; 6:18; 7:2; Col. 3:5; 1 Thess. 4:3 [1] Or *fornication* 15:32 [a] Acts 11:27; 1 Cor. 12:28; Eph. 4:11; Rev. 18:20 [b] Acts 14:22; 18:23 15:33 [a] Mark 5:34; Acts 16:36; 1 Cor. 16:11; Heb. 11:31 [1] NU-Text reads *to those who had sent them.* 15:34 [1] NU-Text and M-Text omit this verse. 15:35 [a] Acts 13:1 15:37 [a] Acts 12:12, 25; Col. 4:10; 2 Tim. 4:11; Philem. 24 15:38 [a] Acts 13:13 15:39 [a] Acts 4:36; 13:4

and departed, [a]being commended by the brethren to the grace of God. 41And he went through Syria and Cilicia, [a]strengthening the churches.

Timothy Joins Paul and Silas

16 Then he came to [a]Derbe and Lystra. And behold, a certain disciple was there, [b]named Timothy, [c]*the* son of a certain Jewish woman who believed, but his father *was* Greek. 2He was well spoken of by the brethren who were at Lystra and Iconium. 3Paul wanted to have him go on with him. And he [a]took *him* and circumcised him because of the Jews who were in that region, for they all knew that his father was Greek. 4And as they went through the cities, they delivered to them the [a]decrees to keep, [b]which were determined by the apostles and elders at Jerusalem. 5[a]So the churches were strengthened in the faith, and increased in number daily.

The Macedonian Call

6Now when they had gone through Phrygia and the region of [a]Galatia, they were forbidden by the Holy Spirit to preach the word in Asia. 7After they had come to Mysia, they tried to go into Bithynia, but the Spirit[1] did not permit them. 8So passing by Mysia, they [a]came down to Troas. 9And a vision appeared to Paul in the night. A [a]man of Macedonia stood and pleaded with him, saying, "Come over to Macedonia and help us." 10Now after he had seen the vision, immediately we sought to go [a]to Macedonia, concluding that the Lord had called us to preach the gospel to them.

Lydia Baptized at Philippi

11Therefore, sailing from Troas, we ran a straight course to Samothrace, and the next *day* came to Neapolis, 12and from there to [a]Philippi, which is the foremost city of that part of Macedonia, a colony. And we were staying in that city for some days. 13And on the Sabbath day we went out of the city to the riverside, where prayer was customarily made; and we sat down and spoke to the women who met *there.* 14Now a certain woman named Lydia heard *us.* She was a seller of purple from the city of [a]Thyatira, who worshiped God. [b]The Lord opened her heart to heed the things spoken by Paul. 15And when she and her household were baptized, she begged *us,* saying, "If you have judged me to be faithful to the Lord, come to my house and stay." So [a]she persuaded us.

Paul and Silas Imprisoned

16Now it happened, as we went to prayer, that a certain slave girl [a]possessed with a spirit of divination met us, who brought her masters [b]much profit by fortune-telling. 17This girl followed Paul and us, and cried out, saying, "These men are the servants of the Most High God, who proclaim to us the way of salvation." 18And this she did for many days.

But Paul, [a]greatly annoyed, turned and said to the spirit, "I command you in the name of Jesus Christ to come out of her." [b]And he came out that very hour. 19But [a]when her masters saw that their hope of profit was gone, they seized Paul and Silas and [b]dragged *them* into the marketplace to the authorities.

20And they brought them to the magistrates, and said, "These men, being Jews, [a]exceedingly trouble our city; 21and they teach customs which are not lawful for us, being Romans, to receive or observe." 22Then the multitude rose up together against them; and the magistrates tore off their clothes [a]and commanded *them* to be beaten with rods. 23And when they had laid many stripes on them, they threw *them* into prison, commanding the jailer to keep them securely. 24Having received such a charge, he put them into the inner prison and fastened their feet in the stocks.

The Philippian Jailer Saved

25But at midnight Paul and Silas were praying and singing hymns to God, and the

15:40 [a] Acts 11:23; 14:26 15:41 [a] Acts 16:5 16:1 [a] Acts 14:6 [b] Acts 19:22; Rom. 16:21; 1 Cor. 4:17; 16:10; Phil. 1:1; 2:19; 1 Thess. 3:2; 2 Tim. 1:2 [c] 2 Tim. 1:5; 3:15 16:3 [a] [1 Cor. 9:20; Gal. 2:3; 5:2] 16:4 [a] Acts 15:19–21 [b] Acts 15:28, 29 16:5 [a] Acts 2:47; 15:41 16:6 [a] Acts 18:23; Gal. 1:1, 2 16:7 [1] NU-Text adds *of Jesus.* 16:8 [a] Acts 16:11; 20:5; 2 Cor. 2:12; 2 Tim. 4:13 16:9 [a] Acts 10:30 16:10 [a] 2 Cor. 2:13 16:12 [a] Acts 20:6; Phil. 1:1; 1 Thess. 2:2 16:14 [a] Rev. 1:11; 2:18, 24 [b] Luke 24:45 16:15 [a] Gen. 19:3; 33:11; Judg. 19:21; Luke 24:29; [Heb. 13:2] 16:16 [a] Lev. 19:31; 20:6, 27; Deut. 18:11; 1 Sam. 28:3, 7; 2 Kin. 21:6; 1 Chr. 10:13; Is. 8:19 [b] Acts 19:24 16:18 [a] Mark 1:25, 34 [b] Mark 16:17 16:19 [a] Acts 16:16; 19:25, 26 [b] Matt. 10:18 16:20 [a] 1 Kin. 18:17; Acts 17:8 16:22 [a] 2 Cor. 6:5; 11:23, 25; 1 Thess. 2:2

prisoners were listening to them. 26[a]Suddenly there was a great earthquake, so that the foundations of the prison were shaken; and immediately [b]all the doors were opened and everyone's chains were loosed. 27And the keeper of the prison, awaking from sleep and seeing the prison doors open, supposing the prisoners had fled, drew his sword and was about to kill himself. 28But Paul called with a loud voice, saying, "Do yourself no harm, for we are all here."

29Then he called for a light, ran in, and fell down trembling before Paul and Silas. 30And he brought them out and said, [a]"Sirs, what must I do to be saved?"

31So they said, [a]"Believe on the Lord Jesus Christ, and you will be saved, you and your household." 32Then they spoke the word of the Lord to him and to all who were in his house. 33And he took them the same hour of the night and washed *their* stripes. And immediately he and all his *family* were baptized. 34Now when he had brought them into his house, [a]he set food before them; and he rejoiced, having believed in God with all his household.

Paul Refuses to Depart Secretly

35And when it was day, the magistrates sent the officers, saying, "Let those men go."

36So the keeper of the prison reported these words to Paul, saying, "The magistrates have sent to let you go. Now therefore depart, and go in peace."

37But Paul said to them, "They have beaten us openly, uncondemned [a]Romans, *and* have thrown *us* into prison. And now do they put us out secretly? No indeed! Let them come themselves and get us out."

38And the officers told these words to the magistrates, and they were afraid

ACTS 16:37

I AM PAUL

But Paul said to them, "They have beaten us openly, uncondemned Romans, and have thrown us into prison. And now do they put us out secretly? No indeed! Let them come themselves and get us out." Acts 16:37

I am Paul from Tarsus. I also go by Saul. I was a persecutor of Christians and was on my way to Damascus to round up more when I encountered Jesus. I was surrounded by a light, and the Lord said to me, "Saul, Saul, why are you persecuting Me?" I fell before the Lord and asked what He wanted of me. I then did as I was instructed. I repented of my sins, was soon baptized, and began teaching and proclaiming Jesus as Lord. This surprised many and angered some. The religious leaders plotted against me because of my testimony of being changed through faith in Jesus. But I was undeterred; I had dedicated and sacrificed my life for the call of the kingdom of God. I traveled as a missionary. I started churches and wrote letters to help those churches understand the ways of kingdom life. Over a dozen of those letters are now books in the New Testament.

Although I was stripped and publicly beaten and jailed based upon mob rule, I stood strongly for righteousness and for justice. As a Roman citizen, I was entitled to a trial as required by law before my punishment, but my rights were denied. It was important that I not accept such unjust treatment, so I demanded my right to appear before Caesar.

†

Like Paul, we should stand for righteousness and justice, no matter what. It is a matter of integrity and the consistency of our faith. We should stand up for ourselves when our rights are threatened and do the same for others, no matter who they are.

16:26 [a] Acts 4:31 [b] Acts 5:19; 12:7, 10 16:30 [a] Luke 3:10; Acts 2:37; 9:6; 22:10 16:31 [a] [John 3:16, 36; 6:47; Acts 13:38, 39; Rom. 10:9–11; 1 John 5:10] 16:34 [a] Matt. 5:4; Luke 5:29; 19:6 16:37 [a] Acts 22:25–29

when they heard that they were Romans.
39 Then they came and pleaded with them
and brought *them* out, and [a]asked *them* to
depart from the city. 40 So they went out of
the prison [a]and entered *the house of* Lydia;
and when they had seen the brethren, they
encouraged them and departed.

Preaching Christ at Thessalonica

17 Now when they had passed through
Amphipolis and Apollonia, they came
to [a]Thessalonica, where there was a synagogue of the Jews. 2 Then Paul, as his custom
was, [a]went in to them, and for three Sabbaths [b]reasoned with them from the Scriptures, 3 explaining and demonstrating [a]that
the Christ had to suffer and rise again from
the dead, and *saying,* "This Jesus whom I
preach to you is the Christ." 4 [a]And some of
them were persuaded; and a great multitude of the devout Greeks, and not a few of
the leading women, joined Paul and [b]Silas.

Assault on Jason's House

5 But the Jews who were not persuaded,
becoming [a]envious,[1] took some of the evil
men from the marketplace, and gathering
a mob, set all the city in an uproar and attacked the house of [b]Jason, and sought to
bring them out to the people. 6 But when
they did not find them, they dragged Jason and some brethren to the rulers of the
city, crying out, [a]"These who have turned
the world upside down have come here too.
7 Jason has harbored them, and these are
all acting contrary to the decrees of Caesar,
[a]saying there is another king—Jesus." 8 And
they troubled the crowd and the rulers of
the city when they heard these things. 9 So
when they had taken security from Jason
and the rest, they let them go.

Ministering at Berea

10 Then [a]the brethren immediately sent
Paul and Silas away by night to Berea. When
they arrived, they went into the synagogue
of the Jews. 11 These were more fair-minded
than those in Thessalonica, in that they
received the word with all readiness, and
[a]searched the Scriptures daily *to find out*
whether these things were so. 12 Therefore
many of them believed, and also not a few
of the Greeks, prominent women as well
as men. 13 But when the Jews from Thessalonica learned that the word of God was
preached by Paul at Berea, they came there
also and stirred up the crowds. 14 [a]Then immediately the brethren sent Paul away, to
go to the sea; but both Silas and Timothy
remained there. 15 So those who conducted
Paul brought him to Athens; and [a]receiv-
ing a command for Silas and Timothy to
come to him with all speed, they departed.

The Philosophers at Athens

16 Now while Paul waited for them at Athens, [a]his spirit was provoked within him
when he saw that the city was given over to
idols. 17 Therefore he reasoned in the synagogue with the Jews and with the *Gentile*
worshipers, and in the marketplace daily
with those who happened to be there.
18 Then[1] certain Epicurean and Stoic philosophers encountered him. And some
said, "What does this babbler want to say?"

Others said, "He seems to be a proclaimer of foreign gods," because he
preached to them [a]Jesus and the resurrection.

19 And they took him and brought him
to the Areopagus, saying, "May we know
what this new doctrine *is* of which you
speak? 20 For you are bringing some strange
things to our ears. Therefore we want to
know what these things mean." 21 For all
the Athenians and the foreigners who were
there spent their time in nothing else but
either to tell or to hear some new thing.

Addressing the Areopagus

22 Then Paul stood in the midst of the
Areopagus and said, "Men of Athens, I perceive that in all things you are very religious; 23 for as I was passing through and
considering the objects of your worship, I
even found an altar with this inscription:

TO THE UNKNOWN GOD.

16:39 [a] Matt. 8:34 16:40 [a] Acts 16:14 17:1 [a] Acts 17:11, 13; 20:4; 27:2; Phil. 4:16; 1 Thess. 1:1; 2 Thess. 1:1; 2 Tim. 4:10 17:2 [a] Luke 4:16; Acts 9:20; 13:5, 14; 14:1; 16:13; 19:8 [b] 1 Thess. 2:1–16 17:3 [a] Luke 24:26, 46; Acts 18:5, 28; Gal. 3:1 17:4 [a] Acts 28:24 [b] Acts 15:22, 27, 32, 40 17:5 [a] Acts 13:45 [b] Acts 17:6, 7, 9; Rom. 16:21 [1] NU-Text omits *who were not persuaded;* M-Text omits *becoming envious.* 17:6 [a] [Acts 16:20] 17:7 [a] Luke 23:2; John 19:12; 1 Pet. 2:13 17:10 [a] Acts 9:25; 17:14 17:11 [a] Is. 34:16; Luke 16:29; John 5:39 17:14 [a] Matt. 10:23 17:15 [a] Acts 18:5 17:16 [a] 2 Pet. 2:8 17:18 [a] 1 Cor. 15:12 [1] NU-Text and M-Text add *also.*

Therefore, the One whom you worship without knowing, Him I proclaim to you: 24 [a]God, who made the world and everything in it, since He is [b]Lord of heaven and earth, [c]does not dwell in temples made with hands. 25 Nor is He worshiped with men's hands, as though He needed anything, since He [a]gives to all life, breath, and all things. 26 And He has made from one blood[1] every nation of men to dwell on all the face of the earth, and has determined their preappointed times and [a]the boundaries of their dwellings, 27 [a]so that they should seek the Lord, in the hope that they might grope for Him and find Him, [b]though He is not far from each one of us; 28 for [a]in Him we live and move and have our being, [b]as also some of your own poets have said, 'For we are also His offspring.' 29 Therefore, since we are the offspring of God, [a]we ought not to think that the Divine Nature is like gold or silver or stone, something shaped by art and man's devising. 30 Truly, [a]these times of ignorance God overlooked, but [b]now commands all men everywhere to repent, 31 because He has appointed a day on which [a]He will judge the world in righteousness by the Man whom He has ordained. He has given assurance of this to all by [b]raising Him from the dead."

32 And when they heard of the resurrection of the dead, some mocked, while others said, "We will hear you again on this *matter.*" 33 So Paul departed from among them. 34 However, some men joined him and believed, among them Dionysius the Areopagite, a woman named Damaris, and others with them.

Ministering at Corinth

18 After these things Paul departed from Athens and went to Corinth. 2 And he found a certain Jew named [a]Aquila, born in Pontus, who had recently come from Italy with his wife Priscilla (because Claudius had commanded all the Jews to depart from Rome); and he came to them. 3 So, because he was of the same trade, he stayed with them [a]and worked; for by occupation they were tentmakers. 4 [a]And he reasoned in the synagogue every Sabbath, and persuaded both Jews and Greeks.

5 [a]When Silas and Timothy had come from Macedonia, Paul was [b]compelled by the Spirit, and testified to the Jews *that* Jesus *is* the Christ. 6 But [a]when they opposed him and blasphemed, [b]he shook *his* garments and said to them, [c]"Your blood *be* upon your *own* heads; [d]I *am* clean. [e]From now on I will go to the Gentiles." 7 And he departed from there and entered the house of a certain *man* named Justus,[1] *one* who worshiped God, whose house was next door to the synagogue. 8 [a]Then Crispus, the ruler of the synagogue, believed on the Lord with all his household. And many of the Corinthians, hearing, believed and were baptized.

9 Now [a]the Lord spoke to Paul in the night by a vision, "Do not be afraid, but speak, and do not keep silent; 10 [a]for I am with you, and no one will attack you to hurt you; for I have many people in this city." 11 And he continued *there* a year and six months, teaching the word of God among them.

12 When Gallio was proconsul of Achaia, the Jews with one accord rose up against Paul and brought him to the judgment seat, 13 saying, "This *fellow* persuades men to worship God contrary to the law."

14 And when Paul was about to open *his* mouth, Gallio said to the Jews, "If it were a matter of wrongdoing or wicked crimes, O Jews, there would be reason why I should bear with you. 15 But if it is a [a]question of words and names and your own law, look *to it* yourselves; for I do not want to be a judge of such *matters.*" 16 And he drove them from the judgment seat. 17 Then all the Greeks[1] took [a]Sosthenes, the ruler of the synagogue, and beat *him* before the judgment seat. But Gallio took no notice of these things.

17:24 [a] Is. 42:5; Acts 14:15 [b] Deut. 10:14; Ps. 115:16; Matt. 11:25 [c] 1 Kin. 8:27; Acts 7:48–50 **17:25** [a] Gen. 2:7; Is. 42:5; Dan. 5:23 **17:26** [a] Deut. 32:8; Job 12:23; Dan. 4:35 [1] NU-Text omits *blood.* **17:27** [a] [Rom. 1:20] [b] Deut. 4:7; Ps. 139:7, 10; Jer. 23:23, 24; [Acts 14:17] **17:28** [a] [Col. 1:17; Heb. 1:3] [b] Titus 1:12 **17:29** [a] Ps. 115:4–7; Is. 40:18, 19; Rom. 1:23 **17:30** [a] Acts 14:16; [Rom. 3:25] [b] Luke 24:47; Acts 26:20; [Titus 2:11, 12]; 1 Pet. 1:14; 4:3 **17:31** [a] Ps. 9:8; 96:13; 98:9; John 5:22, 27; Acts 10:42; Rom. 2:16 [b] Acts 2:24 **18:2** [a] Rom. 16:3; 1 Cor. 16:19; 2 Tim. 4:19 **18:3** [a] Acts 20:34; 1 Cor. 4:12; 9:14; 2 Cor. 11:7; 12:13; 1 Thess. 2:9; 4:11; 2 Thess. 3:8 **18:4** [a] Acts 17:2 **18:5** [a] Acts 17:14, 15 [b] Acts 18:28 **18:6** [a] Acts 13:45 [b] Neh. 5:13; Matt. 10:14; Acts 13:51 [c] Lev. 20:9, 11, 12; 2 Sam. 1:16; 1 Kin. 2:33; Ezek. 18:13; 33:4, 6, 8; Matt. 27:25; Acts 20:26 [d] [Ezek. 3:18, 19] [e] Acts 13:46–48; 28:28 **18:7** [1] NU-Text reads *Titius Justus.* **18:8** [a] 1 Cor. 1:14 **18:9** [a] Acts 23:11 **18:10** [a] Jer. 1:18, 19 **18:15** [a] Acts 23:29; 25:19 **18:17** [a] 1 Cor. 1:1 [1] NU-Text reads *they all.*

Paul Returns to Antioch

18 So Paul still remained a good while.
Then he took leave of the brethren and
sailed for Syria, and Priscilla and Aquila
were with him. [a]He had *his* hair cut off at
[b]Cenchrea, for he had taken a vow. 19 And
he came to Ephesus, and left them there;
but he himself entered the synagogue and
reasoned with the Jews. 20 When they asked
him to stay a longer time with them, he did
not consent, 21 but took leave of them, saying, [a]"I must by all means keep this coming feast in Jerusalem;[1] but I will return
again to you, [b]God willing." And he sailed
from Ephesus.

22 And when he had landed at [a]Caesarea,
and gone up and greeted the church, he
went down to Antioch. 23 After he had spent
some time *there,* he departed and went over
the region of [a]Galatia and Phrygia in order,
[b]strengthening all the disciples.

Ministry of Apollos

24 [a]Now a certain Jew named Apollos,
born at Alexandria, an eloquent man *and*
mighty in the Scriptures, came to Ephesus.
25 This man had been instructed in the way
of the Lord; and being [a]fervent in spirit, he
spoke and taught accurately the things of
the Lord, [b]though he knew only the baptism of John. 26 So he began to speak boldly
in the synagogue. When Aquila and Priscilla heard him, they took him aside and
explained to him the way of God more accurately. 27 And when he desired to cross
to Achaia, the brethren wrote, exhorting
the disciples to receive him; and when he
arrived, [a]he greatly helped those who had
believed through grace; 28 for he vigorously
refuted the Jews publicly, [a]showing from
the Scriptures that Jesus is the Christ.

Paul at Ephesus

19 And it happened, while [a]Apollos was
at Corinth, that Paul, having passed
through [b]the upper regions, came to Ephesus. And finding some disciples 2 he said
to them, "Did you receive the Holy Spirit
when you believed?"

So they said to him, [a]"We have not so
much as heard whether there is a Holy
Spirit."

3 And he said to them, "Into what then
were you baptized?"

So they said, [a]"Into John's baptism."

4 Then Paul said, [a]"John indeed baptized with a baptism of repentance, saying to the people that they should believe
on Him who would come after him, that is,
on Christ Jesus."

5 When they heard *this,* they were baptized [a]in the name of the Lord Jesus. 6 And
when Paul had [a]laid hands on them, the
Holy Spirit came upon them, and [b]they
spoke with tongues and prophesied. 7 Now
the men were about twelve in all.

8 [a]And he went into the synagogue and
spoke boldly for three months, reasoning
and persuading [b]concerning the things of
the kingdom of God. 9 But [a]when some were
hardened and did not believe, but spoke
evil [b]of the Way before the multitude, he
departed from them and withdrew the disciples, reasoning daily in the school of Ty-
rannus. 10 And [a]this continued for two years,
so that all who dwelt in Asia heard the word
of the Lord Jesus, both Jews and Greeks.

Miracles Glorify Christ

11 Now [a]God worked unusual miracles by
the hands of Paul, 12 [a]so that even hand-
kerchiefs or aprons were brought from
his body to the sick, and the diseases left
them and the evil spirits went out of them.
13 [a]Then some of the itinerant Jewish exor-
cists [b]took it upon themselves to call the
name of the Lord Jesus over those who had
evil spirits, saying, "We[1] exorcise you by the
Jesus whom Paul [c]preaches." 14 Also there
were seven sons of Sceva, a Jewish chief
priest, who did so.

15 And the evil spirit answered and said,
"Jesus I know, and Paul I know; but who
are you?"

18:18 [a] Num. 6:2, 5, 9, 18; Acts 21:24 [b] Rom. 16:1 18:21 [a] Acts 19:21; 20:16 [b] 1 Cor. 4:19; Heb. 6:3; James 4:15 [1] NU-Text omits *I must through Jerusalem.* 18:22 [a] Acts 8:40 18:23 [a] Gal. 1:2 [b] Acts 14:22; 15:32, 41 18:24 [a] Acts 19:1; 1 Cor. 1:12; 3:4; 16:12; Titus 3:13 18:25 [a] Rom. 12:11 [b] [Matt. 3:1–11; Mark 1:7, 8; Luke 3:16, 17; 7:29; John 1:26, 33]; Acts 19:3 18:27 [a] 1 Cor. 3:6 18:28 [a] Acts 9:22; 17:3; 18:5 19:1 [a] 1 Cor. 1:12; 3:5, 6; Titus 3:13 [b] Acts 18:23 19:2 [a] 1 Sam. 3:7; Acts 8:16 19:3 [a] Luke 7:29; Acts 18:25 19:4 [a] Matt. 3:11; Mark 1:4, 7, 8; Luke 3:16; [John 1:15, 26, 27]; Acts 13:24 19:5 [a] Matt. 28:19; Acts 8:12, 16; 10:48 19:6 [a] Acts 6:6; 8:17 [b] Mark 16:17; Acts 2:4; 10:46 19:8 [a] Acts 17:2; 18:4 [b] Acts 1:3; 28:23 19:9 [a] 2 Tim. 1:15; 2 Pet. 2:2; Jude 10 [b] Acts 9:2; 19:23; 22:4; 24:14 19:10 [a] Acts 19:8; 20:31 19:11 [a] Mark 16:20; Acts 14:3 19:12 [a] 2 Kin. 4:29; Acts 5:15 19:13 [a] Matt. 12:27; Luke 11:19 [b] Mark 9:38; Luke 9:49 [c] 1 Cor. 1:23; 2:2 [1] NU-Text reads *I.*

16 Then the man in whom the evil spirit was leaped on them, overpowered[1] them, and prevailed against them,[2] so that they fled out of that house naked and wounded. 17 This became known both to all Jews and Greeks dwelling in Ephesus; and [a]fear fell on them all, and the name of the Lord Jesus was magnified. 18 And many who had believed came [a]confessing and telling their deeds. 19 Also, many of those who had practiced magic brought their books together and burned *them* in the sight of all. And they counted up the value of them, and *it* totaled fifty thousand *pieces* of silver. 20 [a]So the word of the Lord grew mightily and prevailed.

The Riot at Ephesus

21 [a]When these things were accomplished, Paul [b]purposed in the Spirit, when he had passed through [c]Macedonia and Achaia, to go to Jerusalem, saying, "After I have been there, [d]I must also see Rome." 22 So he sent into Macedonia two of those who ministered to him, [a]Timothy and [b]Erastus, but he himself stayed in Asia for a time.

23 And [a]about that time there arose a great commotion about [b]the Way. 24 For a certain man named Demetrius, a silversmith, who made silver shrines of Diana,[1] brought [a]no small profit to the craftsmen. 25 He called them together with the workers of similar occupation, and said: "Men, you know that we have our prosperity by this trade. 26 Moreover you see and hear that not only at Ephesus, but throughout almost all Asia, this Paul has persuaded and turned away many people, saying that [a]they are not gods which are made with hands. 27 So not only is this trade of ours in danger of falling into disrepute, but also the temple of the great goddess Diana may be despised and her magnificence destroyed,[1] whom all Asia and the world worship."

28 Now when they heard *this,* they were full of wrath and cried out, saying, "Great *is* Diana of the Ephesians!" 29 So the whole city was filled with confusion, and rushed into the theater with one accord, having seized [a]Gaius and [b]Aristarchus, Macedonians, Paul's travel companions. 30 And when Paul wanted to go in to the people, the disciples would not allow him. 31 Then some of the officials of Asia, who were his friends, sent to him pleading that he would not venture into the theater. 32 Some therefore cried one thing and some another, for the assembly was confused, and most of them did not know why they had come together. 33 And they drew Alexander out of the multitude, the Jews putting him forward. And [a]Alexander [b]motioned with his hand, and wanted to make his defense to the people. 34 But when they found out that he was a Jew, all with one voice cried out for about two hours, "Great *is* Diana of the Ephesians!"

35 And when the city clerk had quieted the crowd, he said: "Men of Ephesus, what man is there who does not know that the city of the Ephesians is temple guardian of the great goddess Diana, and of the *image* which fell down from Zeus? 36 Therefore, since these things cannot be denied, you ought to be quiet and do nothing rashly. 37 For you have brought these men here who are neither robbers of temples nor blasphemers of your[1] goddess. 38 Therefore, if Demetrius and his fellow craftsmen have a case against anyone, the courts are open and there are proconsuls. Let them bring charges against one another. 39 But if you have any other inquiry to make, it shall be determined in the lawful assembly. 40 For we are in danger of being called in question for today's uproar, there being no reason which we may give to account for this disorderly gathering." 41 And when he had said these things, he dismissed the assembly.

Journeys in Greece

20 After the uproar had ceased, Paul called the disciples to *himself,* embraced *them,* and [a]departed to go to Macedonia. 2 Now when he had gone over that

---

19:16 [1] M-Text reads *and they overpowered.* [2] NU-Text reads *both of them.* 19:17 [a] Luke 1:65; 7:16; Acts 2:43; 5:5, 11
19:18 [a] Matt. 3:6 19:20 [a] Acts 6:7; 12:24 19:21 [a] Rom. 15:25; Gal. 2:1 [b] Acts 20:22; 2 Cor. 1:16 [c] Acts 20:1; 1 Cor. 16:5 [d] Acts 18:21; 23:11; Rom. 1:13; 15:22–29 19:22 [a] 1 Tim. 1:2 [b] Rom. 16:23; 2 Tim. 4:20 19:23 [a] 2 Cor. 1:8 [b] Acts 9:2 19:24 [a] Acts 16:16, 19 [1] Greek *Artemis*
19:26 [a] Deut. 4:28; Ps. 115:4; Is. 44:10–20; Jer. 10:3; Acts 17:29; 1 Cor. 8:4; 10:19; Rev. 9:20 19:27 [1] NU-Text reads *she be deposed from her magnificence.* 19:29 [a] Acts 20:4; Rom. 16:23; 1 Cor. 1:14; 3 John 1 [b] Acts 20:4; 27:2; Col. 4:10; Philem. 24
19:33 [a] 1 Tim. 1:20; 2 Tim. 4:14 [b] Acts 12:17 19:37 [1] NU-Text reads *our.* 20:1 [a] 1 Cor. 16:5; 1 Tim. 1:3

region and encouraged them with many
words, he came to [a]Greece 3and stayed
three months. And [a]when the Jews plotted against him as he was about to sail to
Syria, he decided to return through Macedonia. 4And Sopater of Berea accompanied him to Asia—also [a]Aristarchus and
Secundus of the Thessalonians, and [b]Ga-
ius of Derbe, and [c]Timothy, and [d]Tychicus
and [e]Trophimus of Asia. 5These men, going ahead, waited for us at [a]Troas. 6But we
sailed away from Philippi after [a]the Days of
Unleavened Bread, and in five days joined
them [b]at Troas, where we stayed seven days.

Ministering at Troas

7Now on [a]the first *day* of the week, when
the disciples came together [b]to break bread,
Paul, ready to depart the next day, spoke
to them and continued his message until midnight. 8There were many lamps [a]in
the upper room where they[1] were gathered together. 9And in a window sat a certain young man named Eutychus, who was
sinking into a deep sleep. He was overcome
by sleep; and as Paul continued speaking,
he fell down from the third story and was
taken up dead. 10But Paul went down, [a]fell
on him, and embracing *him* said, [b]"Do not
trouble yourselves, for his life is in him."
11Now when he had come up, had broken
bread and eaten, and talked a long while,
even till daybreak, he departed. 12And they
brought the young man in alive, and they
were not a little comforted.

From Troas to Miletus

13Then we went ahead to the ship and
sailed to Assos, there intending to take Paul
on board; for so he had given orders, intending himself to go on foot. 14And when
he met us at Assos, we took him on board
and came to Mitylene. 15We sailed from
there, and the next *day* came opposite
Chios. The following *day* we arrived at Samos and stayed at Trogyllium. The next
day we came to Miletus. 16For Paul had decided to sail past Ephesus, so that he would
not have to spend time in Asia; for [a]he was
hurrying [b]to be at Jerusalem, if possible, on
[c]the Day of Pentecost.

The Ephesian Elders Exhorted

17From Miletus he sent to Ephesus and
called for the elders of the church. 18And
when they had come to him, he said to
them: "You know, [a]from the first day that
I came to Asia, in what manner I always
lived among you, 19serving the Lord with
all humility, with many tears and trials
which happened to me [a]by the plotting
of the Jews; 20how [a]I kept back nothing
that was helpful, but proclaimed it to you,
and taught you publicly and from house
to house, 21[a]testifying to Jews, and also to
Greeks, [b]repentance toward God and faith
toward our Lord Jesus Christ. 22And see,
now [a]I go bound in the spirit to Jerusalem,
not knowing the things that will happen
to me there, 23except that [a]the Holy Spirit
testifies in every city, saying that chains
and tribulations await me. 24But [a]none of
these things move me; nor do I count my
life dear to myself,[1] [b]so that I may finish
my race with joy, [c]and the ministry [d]which
I received from the Lord Jesus, to testify to
the gospel of the grace of God.

25"And indeed, now I know that you all,
among whom I have gone preaching the
kingdom of God, will see my face no more.
26Therefore I testify to you this day that I
am [a]innocent of the blood of all *men.* 27For
I have not shunned to declare to you [a]the
whole counsel of God. 28[a]Therefore take
heed to yourselves and to all the flock,
among which the Holy Spirit [b]has made you
overseers, to shepherd the church of God[1]
[c]which He purchased [d]with His own blood.
29For I know this, that after my departure
[a]savage wolves will come in among you,
not sparing the flock. 30Also [a]from among
yourselves men will rise up, speaking

20:2 [a] Acts 17:15; 18:1 **20:3** [a] Acts 9:23; 23:12; 25:3; 2 Cor. 11:26 **20:4** [a] Acts 19:29; Col. 4:10 [b] Acts 19:29 [c] Acts 16:1 [d] Eph. 6:21; Col. 4:7; 2 Tim. 4:12; Titus 3:12 [e] Acts 21:29; 2 Tim. 4:20 **20:5** [a] 2 Cor. 2:12; 2 Tim. 4:13 **20:6** [a] Ex. 12:14, 15 [b] Acts 16:8; 2 Cor. 2:12; 2 Tim. 4:13 **20:7** [a] 1 Cor. 16:2; Rev. 1:10 [b] Acts 2:42, 46; 20:11; 1 Cor. 10:16 **20:8** [a] Acts 1:13 [1] NU-Text and M-Text read *we.* **20:10** [a] 1 Kin. 17:21; 2 Kin. 4:34 [b] Matt. 9:23, 24; Mark 5:39 **20:16** [a] Acts 18:21; 19:21; 21:4 [b] Acts 24:17 [c] Acts 2:1; 1 Cor. 16:8 **20:18** [a] Acts 18:19; 19:1, 10; 20:4, 16 **20:19** [a] Acts 20:3 **20:20** [a] Acts 20:27 **20:21** [a] Acts 18:5; 19:10 [b] Mark 1:15 **20:22** [a] Acts 19:21 **20:23** [a] Acts 21:4, 11 **20:24** [a] Acts 21:13 [b] Acts 13:25; 2 Tim. 4:7 [c] Acts 1:17 [d] Gal. 1:1 [1] NU-Text reads *But I do not count my life of any value or dear to myself.* **20:26** [a] Acts 18:6; 2 Cor. 7:2 **20:27** [a] Luke 7:30; John 15:15; Eph. 1:11 **20:28** [a] Luke 12:32; John 21:15–17; Acts 20:29; [1 Tim. 4:16]; 1 Pet. 5:2 [b] 1 Cor. 12:28 [c] Eph. 1:7, 14; Col. 1:14; Titus 2:14; Heb. 9:12; [1 Pet. 1:19]; Rev. 5:9 [d] Heb. 9:14 [1] M-Text reads *of the Lord and God.* **20:29** [a] Ezek. 22:27; Matt. 7:15 **20:30** [a] 1 Tim. 1:20; 2 Tim. 1:15

perverse things, to draw away the disciples after themselves. 31Therefore watch,
and remember that [a]for three years I did
not cease to warn everyone night and day
with tears.

32"So now, brethren, I commend you to
God and [a]to the word of His grace, which is
able [b]to build you up and give you [c]an inheritance among all those who are sanctified. 33I have coveted no one's silver or
gold or apparel. 34Yes,[1] you yourselves know
[a]that these hands have provided for my
necessities, and for those who were with
me. 35I have shown you in every way, [a]by
laboring like this, that you must support
the weak. And remember the words of the
Lord Jesus, that He said, 'It is more blessed
to give than to receive.'"

36And when he had said these things,
he knelt down and prayed with them all.
37Then they all [a]wept freely, and [b]fell on
Paul's neck and kissed him, 38sorrowing
most of all for the words which he spoke,
that they would see his face no more. And
they accompanied him to the ship.

Warnings on the Journey to Jerusalem

21 Now it came to pass, that when we
had departed from them and set
sail, running a straight course we came
to Cos, the following *day* to Rhodes, and
from there to Patara. 2And finding a ship
sailing over to Phoenicia, we went aboard
and set sail. 3When we had sighted Cyprus,
we passed it on the left, sailed to Syria, and
landed at Tyre; for there the ship was to
unload her cargo. 4And finding disciples,[1]
we stayed there seven days. [a]They told Paul
through the Spirit not to go up to Jerusalem. 5When we had come to the end of
those days, we departed and went on our
way; and they all accompanied us, with
wives and children, till *we were* out of the
city. And [a]we knelt down on the shore and
prayed. 6When we had taken our leave of
one another, we boarded the ship, and they
returned [a]home.

7And when we had finished *our* voyage
from Tyre, we came to Ptolemais, greeted
the brethren, and stayed with them one day.
8On the next *day* we who were Paul's companions[1] departed and came to [a]Caesarea,
and entered the house of Philip [b]the evangelist, [c]who was *one* of the seven, and stayed
with him. 9Now this man had four virgin
daughters [a]who prophesied. 10And as we
stayed many days, a certain prophet named
[a]Agabus came down from Judea. 11When he
had come to us, he took Paul's belt, bound
his *own* hands and feet, and said, "Thus says
the Holy Spirit, [a]'So shall the Jews at Jerusalem bind the man who owns this belt, and
deliver *him* into the hands of the Gentiles.'"

12Now when we heard these things, both
we and those from that place pleaded with
him not to go up to Jerusalem. 13Then Paul
answered, [a]"What do you mean by weeping
and breaking my heart? For I am ready not
only to be bound, but also to die at Jerusalem for the name of the Lord Jesus."

14So when he would not be persuaded,
we ceased, saying, [a]"The will of the Lord
be done."

Paul Urged to Make Peace

15And after those days we packed and
went up to Jerusalem. 16Also some of the
disciples from Caesarea went with us and
brought with them a certain Mnason of
Cyprus, an early disciple, with whom we
were to lodge.

17[a]And when we had come to Jerusalem,
the brethren received us gladly. 18On the following *day* Paul went in with us to [a]James,
and all the elders were present. 19When he
had greeted them, [a]he told in detail those
things which God had done among the Gentiles [b]through his ministry. 20And when
they heard *it,* they glorified the Lord. And
they said to him, "You see, brother, how
many myriads of Jews there are who have
believed, and they are all [a]zealous for the
law; 21but they have been informed about
you that you teach all the Jews who are
among the Gentiles to forsake Moses, saying that they ought not to circumcise *their*

20:31 [a] Acts 19:8, 10; 24:17 20:32 [a] Heb. 13:9 [b] Acts 9:31 [c] Acts 26:18; Eph. 1:14, 18; 5:5; Col. 1:12; 3:24; [Heb. 9:15; 1 Pet. 1:4] 20:34 [a] Acts 18:3; 1 Cor. 4:12; 1 Thess. 2:9; 2 Thess. 3:8 [1] NU-Text and M-Text omit *Yes.* 20:35 [a] Rom. 15:1; 1 Cor. 9:12; 2 Cor. 11:9, 12; Eph. 4:28; 1 Thess. 4:11; 2 Thess. 3:8 20:37 [a] Acts 21:13 [b] Gen. 45:14 21:4 [a] [Acts 20:23; 21:12] [1] NU-Text reads *the disciples.* 21:5 [a] Luke 22:41; Acts 9:40; 20:36 21:6 [a] John 1:11 21:8 [a] Acts 8:40; 21:16 [b] Acts 8:5, 26, 40; Eph. 4:11; 2 Tim. 4:5 [c] Acts 6:5 [1] NU-Text omits *who were Paul's companions.* 21:9 [a] Joel 2:28; Acts 2:17 21:10 [a] Acts 11:28 21:11 [a] Acts 20:23; 21:33; 22:25 21:13 [a] Acts 20:24, 37 21:14 [a] Matt. 6:10; 26:42; Luke 11:2; 22:42 21:17 [a] Acts 15:4 21:18 [a] Acts 15:13; Gal. 1:19; 2:9 21:19 [a] Acts 15:4, 12; Rom. 15:18, 19 [b] Acts 1:17; 20:24; 1 Tim. 2:7 21:20 [a] Acts 15:1; 22:3; [Rom. 10:2]; Gal. 1:14

children nor to walk according to the customs. 22What then? The assembly must certainly meet, for they will[1] hear that you have come. 23Therefore do what we tell you: We have four men who have taken a vow. 24Take them and be purified with them, and pay their expenses so that they may [a]shave *their* heads, and that all may know that those things of which they were informed concerning you are nothing, but *that* you yourself also walk orderly and keep the law. 25But concerning the Gentiles who believe, [a]we have written *and* decided that they should observe no such thing, except[1] that they should keep themselves from *things* offered to idols, from blood, from things strangled, and from sexual immorality."

Arrested in the Temple

26Then Paul took the men, and the next day, having been purified with them, [a]entered the temple [b]to announce the expiration of the days of purification, at which time an offering should be made for each one of them.

27Now when the seven days were almost ended, [a]the Jews from Asia, seeing him in the temple, stirred up the whole crowd and [b]laid hands on him, 28crying out, "Men of Israel, help! This is the man [a]who teaches all *men* everywhere against the people, the law, and this place; and furthermore he also brought Greeks into the temple and has defiled this holy place." 29(For they had previously[1] seen [a]Trophimus the Ephesian with him in the city, whom they supposed that Paul had brought into the temple.)

30And [a]all the city was disturbed; and the people ran together, seized Paul, and dragged him out of the temple; and immediately the doors were shut. 31Now as they were [a]seeking to kill him, news came to the commander of the garrison that all Jerusalem was in an uproar. 32[a]He immediately took soldiers and centurions, and ran down to them. And when they saw the commander and the soldiers, they stopped beating Paul. 33Then the [a]commander came near and took him, and [b]commanded *him* to be bound with two chains; and he asked who he was and what he had done. 34And some among the multitude cried one thing and some another.

So when he could not ascertain the truth because of the tumult, he commanded him to be taken into the barracks. 35When he reached the stairs, he had to be carried by the soldiers because of the violence of the mob. 36For the multitude of the people followed after, crying out, [a]"Away with him!"

Addressing the Jerusalem Mob
(Acts 9:1–19; 26:12–18)

37Then as Paul was about to be led into the barracks, he said to the commander, "May I speak to you?"

He replied, "Can you speak Greek? 38[a]Are you not the Egyptian who some time ago stirred up a rebellion and led the four thousand assassins out into the wilderness?"

39But Paul said, [a]"I am a Jew from Tarsus, in Cilicia, a citizen of no mean city; and I implore you, permit me to speak to the people."

40So when he had given him permission, Paul stood on the stairs and [a]motioned with his hand to the people. And when there was a great silence, he spoke to *them* in the [b]Hebrew language, saying,

22 "Brethren[a] and fathers, hear my defense before you now." 2And when they heard that he spoke to them in the [a]Hebrew language, they kept all the more silent.

Then he said: 3[a]"I am indeed a Jew, born in Tarsus of Cilicia, but brought up in this city [b]at the feet of [c]Gamaliel, taught [d]according to the strictness of our fathers' law, and [e]was zealous toward God [f]as you all are today. 4[a]I persecuted this Way to the death, binding and delivering into prisons both men and women, 5as also the high priest bears me witness, and [a]all the council of the elders, [b]from whom I also received letters

---

21:22 [1] NU-Text reads *What then is to be done? They will certainly.* **21:24** [a] Num. 6:2, 13, 18; Acts 18:18 **21:25** [a] Acts 15:19, 20, 29 [1] NU-Text omits *that they should observe no such thing, except.* **21:26** [a] John 11:55; Acts 21:24; 24:18 [b] Num. 6:13; Acts 24:18 **21:27** [a] Acts 20:19; 24:18 [b] Acts 26:21 **21:28** [a] [Matt. 24:15]; Acts 6:13; 24:6 **21:29** [a] Acts 20:4 [1] M-Text omits *previously.* **21:30** [a] 2 Kin. 11:15; Acts 16:19; 26:21 **21:31** [a] 2 Cor. 11:23 **21:32** [a] Acts 23:27; 24:7 **21:33** [a] Acts 24:7 [b] Acts 20:23; 21:11; Eph. 6:20; 2 Tim. 1:16; 2:9 **21:36** [a] Luke 23:18; John 19:15; Acts 22:22 **21:38** [a] Acts 5:36 **21:39** [a] Acts 9:11; 22:3; 2 Cor. 11:22; Phil. 3:4–6 **21:40** [a] Acts 12:17 [b] John 5:2; Acts 22:2 **22:1** [a] Acts 7:2 **22:2** [a] Acts 21:40 **22:3** [a] Acts 21:39; 2 Cor. 11:22 [b] Deut. 33:3 [c] Acts 5:34 [d] Acts 23:6; 26:5; Phil. 3:6 [e] Acts 21:20; Gal. 1:14 [f] [Rom. 10:2] **22:4** [a] Acts 8:3; 26:9–11; Phil. 3:6; 1 Tim. 1:13 **22:5** [a] Acts 23:14; 24:1; 25:15 [b] Luke 22:66; Acts 4:5; 1 Tim. 4:14

to the brethren, and went to Damascus [c]to
bring in chains even those who were there
to Jerusalem to be punished.
6"Now [a]it happened, as I journeyed and
came near Damascus at about noon, suddenly a great light from heaven shone
around me. 7And I fell to the ground and
heard a voice saying to me, 'Saul, Saul, why
are you persecuting Me?' 8So I answered,
'Who are You, Lord?' And He said to me, 'I
am Jesus of Nazareth, whom you are persecuting.'
9"And [a]those who were with me indeed
saw the light and were afraid,[1] but they did
not hear the voice of Him who spoke to me.
10So I said, 'What shall I do, Lord?' And the
Lord said to me, 'Arise and go into Damascus, and there you will be told all things
which are appointed for you to do.' 11And
since I could not see for the glory of that
light, being led by the hand of those who
were with me, I came into Damascus.
12"Then [a]a certain Ananias, a devout man
according to the law, [b]having a good testimony with all the [c]Jews who dwelt *there,*
13came to me; and he stood and said to me,
'Brother Saul, receive your sight.' And at
that same hour I looked up at him. 14Then
he said, [a]'The God of our fathers [b]has chosen you that you should [c]know His will, and
[d]see the Just One, [e]and hear the voice of His
mouth. 15[a]For you will be His witness to all
men of [b]what you have seen and heard.
16And now why are you waiting? Arise and
be baptized, [a]and wash away your sins, [b]call-
ing on the name of the Lord.'
17"Now [a]it happened, when I returned to
Jerusalem and was praying in the temple,
that I was in a trance 18and [a]saw Him saying to me, [b]'Make haste and get out of Jerusalem quickly, for they will not receive
your testimony concerning Me.' 19So I said,
'Lord, [a]they know that in every synagogue I
imprisoned and [b]beat those who believe on
You. 20[a]And when the blood of Your martyr Stephen was shed, I also was standing
by [b]consenting to his death,[1] and guarding
the clothes of those who were killing him.'

#OXYGEN
ACTS 22:14-15
Trust in His Wonder

Tests are the prerequisite to testimonies. God's goodness often manifests in the struggle. You can be sure that God has a purpose in your trials and that He will make a way out of no way. Be ready for God to work as you get to work telling the story you will have to tell.

Breathe and trust in His wonder.

21Then He said to me, 'Depart, [a]for I will
send you far from here to the Gentiles.'"

Paul's Roman Citizenship

22And they listened to him until this
word, and *then* they raised their voices and
said, [a]"Away with such a *fellow* from the
earth, for [b]he is not fit to live!" 23Then, as
they cried out and tore off *their* clothes and
threw dust into the air, 24the commander
ordered him to be brought into the barracks, and said that he should be examined
under scourging, so that he might know
why they shouted so against him. 25And as
they bound him with thongs, Paul said to
the centurion who stood by, [a]"Is it lawful
for you to scourge a man who is a Roman,
and uncondemned?"
26When the centurion heard *that,* he
went and told the commander, saying,
"Take care what you do, for this man is a
Roman."
27Then the commander came and said
to him, "Tell me, are you a Roman?"
He said, "Yes."
28The commander answered, "With a
large sum I obtained this citizenship."
And Paul said, "But I was born *a citizen.*"
29Then immediately those who were
about to examine him withdrew from him;

22:5 [c] Acts 9:2 22:6 [a] Acts 9:3; 26:12, 13 22:9 [a] Dan. 10:7; Acts 9:7 [1] NU-Text omits *and were afraid.* 22:12 [a] Acts 9:17 [b] Acts 10:22 [c] 1 Tim. 3:7 22:14 [a] Acts 3:13; 5:30 [b] Acts 9:15; 26:16; Gal. 1:15 [c] Acts 3:14; 7:52 [d] Acts 9:17; 26:16; 1 Cor. 9:1; 15:8 [e] 1 Cor. 11:23; Gal. 1:12 22:15 [a] Acts 23:11 [b] Acts 4:20; 26:16 22:16 [a] Acts 2:38; 1 Cor. 6:11; [Eph. 5:26]; Heb. 10:22 [b] Acts 9:14; Rom. 10:13 22:17 [a] Acts 9:26; 26:20; 2 Cor. 12:2 22:18 [a] Acts 22:14 [b] Matt. 10:14 22:19 [a] Acts 8:3; 22:4 [b] Matt. 10:17; Acts 26:11 22:20 [a] Acts 7:54—8:1 [b] Luke 11:48 [1] NU-Text omits *to his death.* 22:21 [a] Acts 9:15; Rom. 1:5; 11:13; Gal. 2:7, 8; Eph. 3:7, 8; 1 Tim. 2:7; 2 Tim. 1:11 22:22 [a] Acts 21:36; 1 Thess. 2:16 [b] Acts 25:24 22:25 [a] Acts 16:37

and the commander was also afraid after
he found out that he was a Roman, and because he had bound him.

The Sanhedrin Divided

30The next day, because he wanted to
know for certain why he was accused by
the Jews, he released him from *his* bonds,
and commanded the chief priests and all
their council to appear, and brought Paul
down and set him before them.

23 Then Paul, looking earnestly at the
council, said, "Men *and* brethren,
[a]I have lived in all good conscience before
God until this day." 2And the high priest
Ananias commanded those who stood by
him [a]to strike him on the mouth. 3Then
Paul said to him, "God will strike you, *you*
whitewashed wall! For you sit to judge me
according to the law, and [a]do you command
me to be struck contrary to the law?"
4And those who stood by said, "Do you
revile God's high priest?"
5Then Paul said, [a]"I did not know, brethren, that he was the high priest; for it is
written, [b]'You shall not speak evil of a ruler
of your people.'"[1]
6But when Paul perceived that one part
were Sadducees and the other Pharisees, he
cried out in the council, "Men *and* brethren, [a]I am a Pharisee, the son of a Pharisee;
[b]concerning the hope and resurrection of
the dead I am being judged!"
7And when he had said this, a dissension arose between the Pharisees and
the Sadducees; and the assembly was divided. 8[a]For Sadducees say that there is no
resurrection—and no angel or spirit; but
the Pharisees confess both. 9Then there
arose a loud outcry. And the scribes of the
Pharisees' party arose and protested, saying, [a]"We find no evil in this man; but [b]if a
spirit or an angel has spoken to him, [c]let
us not fight against God."[1]
10Now when there arose a great dissension, the commander, fearing lest Paul
might be pulled to pieces by them, commanded the soldiers to go down and take
him by force from among them, and bring
him into the barracks.

The Plot Against Paul

11But [a]the following night the Lord stood
by him and said, "Be of good cheer, Paul; for
as you have testified for Me in [b]Jerusalem,
so you must also bear witness at [c]Rome."
12And when it was day, [a]some of the Jews
banded together and bound themselves
under an oath, saying that they would neither eat nor drink till they had [b]killed Paul.
13Now there were more than forty who had
formed this conspiracy. 14They came to the
chief priests and [a]elders, and said, "We have
bound ourselves under a great oath that we
will eat nothing until we have killed Paul.
15Now you, therefore, together with the
council, suggest to the commander that
he be brought down to you tomorrow,[1] as
though you were going to make further in-
quiries concerning him; but we are ready
to kill him before he comes near."
16So when Paul's sister's son heard
of their ambush, he went and entered
the barracks and told Paul. 17Then Paul
called one of the centurions to *him* and
said, "Take this young man to the commander, for he has something to tell him."
18So he took him and brought *him* to the
commander and said, "Paul the prisoner
called me to *him* and asked *me* to bring
this young man to you. He has something
to say to you."
19Then the commander took him by
the hand, went aside, and asked privately,
"What is it that you have to tell me?"
20And he said, [a]"The Jews have agreed to
ask that you bring Paul down to the council tomorrow, as though they were going to
inquire more fully about him. 21But do not
yield to them, for more than forty of them
lie in wait for him, men who have bound
themselves by an oath that they will neither
eat nor drink till they have killed him; and
now they are ready, waiting for the promise from you."
22So the commander let the young man

23:1 [a] Acts 24:16; 1 Cor. 4:4; 2 Cor. 1:12; 4:2; 2 Tim. 1:3; Heb. 13:18 **23:2** [a] 1 Kin. 22:24; Jer. 20:2; John 18:22 **23:3** [a] Lev. 19:35; Deut. 25:1, 2; John 7:51 **23:5** [a] Lev. 5:17, 18 [b] Ex. 22:28; Eccl. 10:20; 2 Pet. 2:10 [1] Exodus 22:28 **23:6** [a] Acts 26:5; Phil. 3:5 [b] Acts 24:15, 21; 26:6; 28:20 **23:8** [a] Matt. 22:23; Mark 12:18; Luke 20:27 **23:9** [a] Acts 25:25; 26:31 [b] John 12:29; Acts 22:6, 7, 17, 18 [c] Acts 5:39 [1] NU-Text omits last clause and reads *what if a spirit or an angel has spoken to him?* **23:11** [a] Acts 18:9; 27:23, 24 [b] Acts 21:18, 19; 22:1–21 [c] Acts 28:16, 17, 23 **23:12** [a] Acts 23:21, 30; 25:3 [b] Acts 9:23, 24; 25:3; 26:21; 27:42; 1 Thess. 2:15 **23:14** [a] Acts 4:5, 23; 6:12; 22:5; 24:1; 25:15 **23:15** [1] NU-Text omits *tomorrow.* **23:20** [a] Acts 23:12

depart, and commanded *him,* "Tell no one
that you have revealed these things to me."

Sent to Felix

23And he called for two centurions, saying, "Prepare two hundred soldiers, seventy
horsemen, and two hundred spearmen to
go to [a]Caesarea at the third hour of the
night; 24and provide mounts to set Paul
on, and bring *him* safely to Felix the governor." 25He wrote a letter in the following
manner:

26 Claudius Lysias,

To the most excellent governor Felix:

Greetings.

27 [a]This man was seized by the Jews
and was about to be killed by them.
Coming with the troops I rescued
him, having learned that he was a
Roman. 28[a]And when I wanted to
know the reason they accused him,
I brought him before their council.
29I found out that he was accused
[a]concerning questions of their law,
[b]but had nothing charged against
him deserving of death or chains.
30And [a]when it was told me that the
Jews lay in wait for the man,[1] I sent
him immediately to you, and [b]also
commanded his accusers to state
before you the charges against him.

Farewell.

31Then the soldiers, as they were commanded, took Paul and brought *him* by
night to Antipatris. 32The next day they left
the horsemen to go on with him, and returned to the barracks. 33When they came
to [a]Caesarea and had delivered the [b]letter
to the governor, they also presented Paul
to him. 34And when the governor had read
it, he asked what province he was from.
And when he understood that *he was* from
[a]Cilicia, 35he said, [a]"I will hear you when
your accusers also have come." And he
commanded him to be kept in [b]Herod's
Praetorium.

Accused of Sedition

24 Now after [a]five days [b]Ananias the
high priest came down with the elders and a certain orator *named* Tertul-
lus. These gave evidence to the governor
against Paul.

2And when he was called upon, Tertul-
lus began his accusation, saying: "Seeing
that through you we enjoy great peace,
and prosperity is being brought to this
nation by your foresight, 3we accept *it* always and in all places, most noble Felix,
with all thankfulness. 4Nevertheless, not
to be tedious to you any further, I beg you
to hear, by your courtesy, a few words from
us. 5[a]For we have found this man a plague,
a creator of dissension among all the Jews
throughout the world, and a ringleader of
the sect of the Nazarenes. 6[a]He even tried
to profane the temple, and we seized him,[1]
and wanted [b]to judge him according to our
law. 7[a]But the commander Lysias came by
and with great violence took *him* out of our
hands, 8[a]commanding his accusers to come
to you. By examining him yourself you may
ascertain all these things of which we accuse him." 9And the Jews also assented,[1]
maintaining that these things were so.

The Defense Before Felix

10Then Paul, after the governor had
nodded to him to speak, answered: "Inasmuch as I know that you have been for
many years a judge of this nation, I do the
more cheerfully answer for myself, 11be-
cause you may ascertain that it is no more
than twelve days since I went up to Jerusalem [a]to worship. 12[a]And they neither found
me in the temple disputing with anyone
nor inciting the crowd, either in the synagogues or in the city. 13Nor can they prove
the things of which they now accuse me.
14But this I confess to you, that according

23:23 [a] Acts 8:40; 23:33 23:27 [a] Acts 21:30, 33; 24:7 23:28 [a] Acts 22:30 23:29 [a] Acts 18:15; 25:19 [b] Acts 25:25; 26:31 23:30 [a] Acts 23:20 [b] Acts 24:8; 25:6 [1] NU-Text reads *there would be a plot against the man.* 23:33 [a] Acts 8:40 [b] Acts 23:26–30 23:34 [a] Acts 6:9; 21:39 23:35 [a] Acts 24:1, 10; 25:16 [b] Matt. 27:27 24:1 [a] Acts 21:27 [b] Acts 23:2, 30, 35; 25:2 24:5 [a] Luke 23:2; Acts 6:13; 16:20; 17:6; 21:28; 1 Pet. 2:12, 15 24:6 [a] Acts 21:28 [b] John 18:31 [1] NU-Text ends the sentence here and omits the rest of verse 6, all of verse 7, and the first clause of verse 8. 24:7 [a] Acts 21:33; 23:10 24:8 [a] Acts 23:30 24:9 [1] NU-Text and M-Text read *joined the attack.* 24:11 [a] Acts 21:15, 18, 26, 27; 24:17 24:12 [a] Acts 25:8; 28:17

TRUST IN HIS WONDER

INHALE

God has been so good to me. When I was down, He lifted me. When I needed His grace, He forgave me even though I did not deserve His pardon. Now, I feel the urgency to share who He is with others. However, when I share about God's goodness, they laugh. Many feel that if there was a God who really cared, then they would not be struggling. How can I get them to see God how I see Him?

EXHALE

People can never understand the goodness of God when they do not have a personal relationship with Jesus. To them, the gospel is a foreign language, completely unintelligible. But it doesn't always have to be that way for them. Through our faithfulness and the Holy Spirit's work, they can come to see and love God as you do. When Paul was on trial for his faith near the end of Acts, he knew that he faced an uphill battle. Securing his freedom was unlikely because of the hardened hearts of those around him. But notice how he felt: "I do the more cheerfully answer for myself" (Acts 24:10). The reason was because Paul knew his job wasn't to convince anyone of the gospel he shared. Ultimately, it is the Spirit who draws people to the Father.

That drawing begins when people first recognize that they are in need. They must realize their sin has separated them from the God who created them. They must acknowledge that they need Jesus to bridge the gap between holy God and sinful humanity. After understanding, they need to cry to God for forgiveness found only through Jesus. When they do, Christ enters their lives.

You are Christ's ambassador. You represent Him to your friends so that they can come to see Him for themselves. Trust God, follow Him, and keep telling others about the amazing gift of salvation He has for them. Leave the rest to Him.

to [a]the Way which they call a sect, so I worship the [b]God of my fathers, believing all
things which are written in [c]the Law and in
the Prophets. 15 [a]I have hope in God, which
they themselves also accept, [b]that there will
be a resurrection of *the* dead,[1] both of *the*
just and *the* unjust. 16 [a]This *being* so, I myself
always strive to have a conscience without
offense toward God and men.
17 "Now after many years [a]I came to bring
alms and offerings to my nation, 18 [a]in the
midst of which some Jews from Asia found
me [b]purified in the temple, neither with a
mob nor with tumult. 19 [a]They ought to have
been here before you to object if they had
anything against me. 20 Or else let those
who are *here* themselves say if they found
any wrongdoing[1] in me while I stood before the council, 21 unless *it is* for this one
statement which I cried out, standing
among them, [a]'Concerning the resurrection of the dead I am being judged by you
this day.'"

Felix Procrastinates

22 But when Felix heard these things,
having more accurate knowledge of *the*
[a]Way, he adjourned the proceedings and
said, "When [b]Lysias the commander comes
down, I will make a decision on your case."
23 So he commanded the centurion to keep
Paul and to let *him* have liberty, and [a]told
him not to forbid any of his friends to provide for or visit him.
24 And after some days, when Felix came
with his wife Drusilla, who was Jewish, he
sent for Paul and heard him concerning
the [a]faith in Christ. 25 Now as he reasoned

24:14 [a] Amos 8:14; Acts 9:2; 24:22 [b] 2 Tim. 1:3 [c] Acts 26:22; 28:23 **24:15** [a] Acts 23:6; 26:6, 7; 28:20 [b] [Dan. 12:2; John 5:28, 29; 11:24] [1] NU-Text omits *of the dead.* **24:16** [a] Acts 23:1 **24:17** [a] Acts 11:29, 30; Rom. 15:25–28; 1 Cor. 16:1–4; 2 Cor. 8:1–4; 9:1, 2, 12; Gal. 2:10 **24:18** [a] Acts 21:27; 26:21 [b] Acts 21:26 **24:19** [a] [Acts 23:30; 25:16] **24:20** [1] NU-Text and M-Text read *say what wrongdoing they found.* **24:21** [a] [Acts 23:6; 24:15; 28:20] **24:22** [a] Acts 9:2; 18:26; 19:9, 23; 22:4 [b] Acts 23:26; 24:7 **24:23** [a] Acts 23:16; 27:3; 28:16 **24:24** [a] [John 3:15; 5:24; 11:25; 12:46; 20:31; Rom. 10:9]

about righteousness, self-control, and the
judgment to come, Felix was afraid and answered, "Go away for now; when I have a
convenient time I will call for you." 26Mean-
while he also hoped that [a]money would be
given him by Paul, that he might release
him.[1] Therefore he sent for him more often and conversed with him.
27But after two years Porcius Festus succeeded Felix; and Felix, [a]wanting to do the
Jews a favor, left Paul bound.

Paul Appeals to Caesar

25 Now when Festus had come to the
province, after three days he went
up from [a]Caesarea to Jerusalem. 2[a]Then the
high priest[1] and the chief men of the Jews
informed him against Paul; and they petitioned him, 3asking a favor against him,
that he would summon him to Jerusalem—[a]while *they* lay in ambush along the
road to kill him. 4But Festus answered that
Paul should be kept at Caesarea, and that
he himself was going *there* shortly. 5"Therefore," he said, "let those who have authority
among you go down with *me* and accuse
this man, to see [a]if there is any fault in him."
6And when he had remained among
them more than ten days, he went down
to Caesarea. And the next day, sitting on
the judgment seat, he commanded Paul to
be brought. 7When he had come, the Jews
who had come down from Jerusalem stood
about [a]and laid many serious complaints
against Paul, which they could not prove,
8while he answered for himself, [a]"Neither
against the law of the Jews, nor against the
temple, nor against Caesar have I offended
in anything at all."
9But Festus, [a]wanting to do the Jews a
favor, answered Paul and said, [b]"Are you
willing to go up to Jerusalem and there
be judged before me concerning these
things?"
10So Paul said, "I stand at Caesar's judgment seat, where I ought to be judged. To
the Jews I have done no wrong, as you very
well know. 11[a]For if I am an offender, or have
committed anything deserving of death, I
do not object to dying; but if there is nothing in these things of which these men accuse me, no one can deliver me to them.
[b]I appeal to Caesar."
12Then Festus, when he had conferred
with the council, answered, "You have appealed to Caesar? To Caesar you shall go!"

Paul Before Agrippa

13And after some days King Agrippa and
Bernice came to Caesarea to greet Festus.
14When they had been there many days,
Festus laid Paul's case before the king, saying: [a]"There is a certain man left a prisoner
by Felix, 15[a]about whom the chief priests
and the elders of the Jews informed *me*,
when I was in Jerusalem, asking for a judgment against him. 16[a]To them I answered,
'It is not the custom of the Romans to deliver any man to destruction[1] before the accused meets the accusers face to face, and
has opportunity to answer for himself concerning the charge against him.' 17There-
fore when they had come together, [a]without
any delay, the next day I sat on the judgment seat and commanded the man to be
brought in. 18When the accusers stood up,
they brought no accusation against him of
such things as I supposed, 19[a]but had some
questions against him about their own religion and about a certain Jesus, who had
died, whom Paul affirmed to be alive. 20And
because I was uncertain of such questions,
I asked whether he was willing to go to Jerusalem and there be judged concerning
these matters. 21But when Paul [a]appealed
to be reserved for the decision of Augustus, I commanded him to be kept till I could
send him to Caesar."
22Then [a]Agrippa said to Festus, "I also
would like to hear the man myself."
"Tomorrow," he said, "you shall hear
him."
23So the next day, when Agrippa and
Bernice had come with great pomp, and
had entered the auditorium with the commanders and the prominent men of the
city, at Festus' command [a]Paul was brought
in. 24And Festus said: "King Agrippa and

24:26 [a] Ex. 23:8 [1] NU-Text omits *that he might release him.* 24:27 [a] Ex. 23:2; Acts 12:3; 23:35; 25:9, 14 25:1 [a] Acts 8:40; 25:4, 6, 13 25:2 [a] Acts 24:1; 25:15 [1] NU-Text reads *chief priests.* 25:3 [a] Acts 23:12, 15 25:5 [a] Acts 18:14; 25:18 25:7 [a] Mark 15:3; Luke 23:2, 10; Acts 24:5, 13 25:8 [a] Acts 6:13; 24:12; 28:17 25:9 [a] Acts 12:2; 24:27 [b] Acts 25:20 25:11 [a] Acts 18:14; 23:29; 25:25; 26:31 [b] Acts 26:32; 28:19 25:14 [a] Acts 24:27 25:15 [a] Acts 24:1; 25:2, 3 25:16 [a] Acts 25:4, 5 [1] NU-Text omits *to destruction,* although it is implied. 25:17 [a] Matt. 27:19; Acts 25:6, 10 25:19 [a] Acts 18:14, 15; 23:29 25:21 [a] Acts 25:11, 12 25:22 [a] Acts 9:15 25:23 [a] Acts 9:15

all the men who are here present with us, you see this man about whom [a]the whole assembly of the Jews petitioned me, both at Jerusalem and here, crying out that he was [b]not fit to live any longer. 25But when I found that [a]he had committed nothing deserving of death, [b]and that he himself had appealed to Augustus, I decided to send him. 26I have nothing certain to write to my lord concerning him. Therefore I have brought him out before you, and especially before you, King Agrippa, so that after the examination has taken place I may have something to write. 27For it seems to me unreasonable to send a prisoner and not to specify the charges against him."

Paul's Early Life

26 Then Agrippa said to Paul, "You are permitted to speak for yourself."

So Paul stretched out his hand and answered for himself: 2"I think myself [a]happy, King Agrippa, because today I shall answer [b]for myself before you concerning all the things of which I am [c]accused by the Jews, 3especially because you are expert in all customs and questions which have to do with the Jews. Therefore I beg you to hear me patiently.

4"My manner of life from my youth, which was spent from the beginning among my own nation at Jerusalem, all the Jews know. 5They knew me from the first, if they were willing to testify, that according to [a]the strictest sect of our religion I lived a Pharisee. 6[a]And now I stand and am judged for the hope of [b]the promise made by God to our fathers. 7To this *promise* [a]our twelve tribes, earnestly serving *God* [b]night and day, [c]hope to attain. For this hope's sake, King Agrippa, I am accused by the Jews. 8Why should it be thought incredible by you that God raises the dead?

9[a]"Indeed, I myself thought I must do many things contrary to the name of [b]Jesus of Nazareth. 10[a]This I also did in Jerusalem, and many of the saints I shut up in prison, having received authority [b]from the chief priests; and when they were put to death, I cast my vote against *them.* 11[a]And I punished them often in every synagogue and compelled *them* to blaspheme; and being exceedingly enraged against them, I persecuted *them* even to foreign cities.

Paul Recounts His Conversion
(Acts 9:1–19; 22:6–16)

12[a]"While thus occupied, as I journeyed to Damascus with authority and commission from the chief priests, 13at midday, O king, along the road I saw a light from heaven, brighter than the sun, shining around me and those who journeyed with me. 14And when we all had fallen to the ground, I heard a voice speaking to me and saying in the Hebrew language, 'Saul, Saul, why are you persecuting Me? *It is* hard for you to kick against the goads.' 15So I said, 'Who are You, Lord?' And He said, 'I am Jesus, whom you are persecuting. 16But rise and stand on your feet; for I have appeared to you for this purpose, [a]to make you a minister and a witness both of the things which you have seen and of the things which I will yet reveal to you. 17I will deliver you from the *Jewish* people, as well as *from* the Gentiles, [a]to whom I now[1] send you, 18[a]to open their eyes, *in order* [b]to turn *them* from darkness to light, and *from* the power of Satan to God, [c]that they may receive forgiveness of sins and [d]an inheritance among those who are [e]sanctified by faith in Me.'

Paul's Post-Conversion Life

19"Therefore, King Agrippa, I was not disobedient to the heavenly vision, 20but [a]declared first to those in Damascus and in Jerusalem, and throughout all the region of Judea, and *then* to the Gentiles, that they should repent, turn to God, and do [b]works befitting repentance. 21For these reasons the Jews seized me in the temple and tried to kill *me.* 22Therefore, having obtained

---

25:24 [a] Acts 25:2, 3, 7 [b] Acts 21:36; 22:22 **25:25** [a] Acts 23:9, 29; 26:31 [b] Acts 25:11, 12 **26:2** [a] [1 Pet. 3:14; 4:14] [b] [1 Pet. 3:15, 16] [c] Acts 21:28; 24:5, 6 **26:5** [a] [Acts 22:3; 23:6; 24:15, 21]; Phil. 3:5 **26:6** [a] Acts 23:6 [b] [Gen. 3:15; 22:18; 26:4; 49:10; Deut. 18:15; 2 Sam. 7:12; Ps. 132:11; Is. 4:2; 7:14; 9:6; 40:10; Jer. 23:5; 33:14–16; Ezek. 34:23; 37:24; Dan. 9:24]; Acts 13:32; Rom. 15:8; [Titus 2:13] **26:7** [a] James 1:1 [b] Luke 2:37; 1 Thess. 3:10; 1 Tim. 5:5 [c] Phil. 3:11 **26:9** [a] John 16:2; 1 Cor. 15:9; 1 Tim. 1:12, 13 [b] Acts 2:22; 10:38 **26:10** [a] Acts 8:1–3; 9:13; Gal. 1:13 [b] Acts 9:14 **26:11** [a] Matt. 10:17; Acts 22:19 **26:12** [a] Acts 9:3–8; 22:6–11; 26:12–18 **26:16** [a] Acts 22:15; Eph. 3:6–8 **26:17** [a] Acts 22:21 [1] NU-Text and M-Text omit *now.* **26:18** [a] Is. 35:5; 42:7, 16; Luke 1:79; [John 8:12; 2 Cor. 4:4]; Eph. 1:18; 1 Thess. 5:5 [b] 2 Cor. 6:14; Eph. 4:18; 5:8; [Col. 1:13]; 1 Pet. 2:9 [c] Luke 1:77 [d] Eph. 1:11; Col. 1:12 [e] Acts 20:32 **26:20** [a] Acts 9:19, 20, 22; 11:26 [b] Matt. 3:8; Luke 3:8

help from God, to this day I stand, witnessing both to small and great, saying no
other things than those [a]which the prophets and [b]Moses said would come— 23[a]that
the Christ would suffer, [b]that He would be
the first to rise from the dead, and [c]would
proclaim light to the *Jewish* people and to
the Gentiles."

Agrippa Parries Paul's Challenge

24Now as he thus made his defense, Festus said with a loud voice, "Paul, [a]you are
beside yourself! Much learning is driving
you mad!"
25But he said, "I am not mad, most noble Festus, but speak the words of truth
and reason. 26For the king, before whom I
also speak freely, [a]knows these things; for
I am convinced that none of these things
escapes his attention, since this thing was
not done in a corner. 27King Agrippa, do
you believe the prophets? I know that you
do believe."
28Then Agrippa said to Paul, "You almost persuade me to become a Christian."
29And Paul said, [a]"I would to God that
not only you, but also all who hear me today, might become both almost and altogether such as I am, except for these
chains."
30When he had said these things, the
king stood up, as well as the governor and
Bernice and those who sat with them;
31and when they had gone aside, they
talked among themselves, saying, [a]"This
man is doing nothing deserving of death
or chains."
32Then Agrippa said to Festus, "This man
might have been set [a]free [b]if he had not appealed to Caesar."

The Voyage to Rome Begins

27 And when [a]it was decided that we
should sail to Italy, they delivered
Paul and some other prisoners to *one*
named Julius, a centurion of the Augus-
tan Regiment. 2So, entering a ship of Ad-
ramyttium, we put to sea, meaning to sail
along the coasts of Asia. [a]Aristarchus, a
Macedonian of Thessalonica, was with us.
3And the next *day* we landed at Sidon. And
Julius [a]treated Paul kindly and gave *him* liberty to go to his friends and receive care.
4When we had put to sea from there, we
sailed under *the shelter of* Cyprus, because
the winds were contrary. 5And when we
had sailed over the sea which is off Cilicia
and Pamphylia, we came to Myra, *a city* of
Lycia. 6There the centurion found [a]an Alexandrian ship sailing to Italy, and he put
us on board.
7When we had sailed slowly many days,
and arrived with difficulty off Cnidus, the
wind not permitting us to proceed, we
sailed under *the shelter of* [a]Crete off Salmone. 8Passing it with difficulty, we came
to a place called Fair Havens, near the city
of Lasea.

Paul's Warning Ignored

9Now when much time had been spent,
and sailing was now dangerous [a]because
the Fast was already over, Paul advised
them, 10saying, "Men, I perceive that this
voyage will end with disaster and much
loss, not only of the cargo and ship, but also
our lives." 11Nevertheless the centurion was
more persuaded by the helmsman and the
owner of the ship than by the things spoken by Paul. 12And because the harbor was
not suitable to winter in, the majority advised to set sail from there also, if by any
means they could reach Phoenix, a harbor
of Crete opening toward the southwest and
northwest, *and* winter *there.*

In the Tempest

13When the south wind blew softly, supposing that they had obtained *their* desire, putting out to sea, they sailed close
by Crete. 14But not long after, a tempestuous head wind arose, called Euroclydon.[1]
15So when the ship was caught, and could
not head into the wind, we let *her* drive.
16And running under *the shelter of* an island called Clauda,[1] we secured the skiff
with difficulty. 17When they had taken it
on board, they used cables to undergird

26:22 [a] Luke 24:27; Acts 24:14; 28:23; Rom. 3:21 [b] John 5:46 26:23 [a] Luke 24:26 [b] 1 Cor. 15:20, 23; Col. 1:18; Rev. 1:5 [c] Is. 42:6; 49:6; Luke 2:32; 2 Cor. 4:4 26:24 [a] 2 Kin. 9:11; John 10:20; [1 Cor. 1:23; 2:13, 14; 4:10] 26:26 [a] Acts 26:3 26:29 [a] 1 Cor. 7:7 26:31 [a] Acts 23:9, 29; 25:25 26:32 [a] Acts 28:18 [b] Acts 25:11 27:1 [a] Acts 25:12, 25 27:2 [a] Acts 19:29 27:3 [a] Acts 24:23; 28:16 27:6 [a] Acts 28:11 27:7 [a] Acts 2:11; 27:12, 21; Titus 1:5, 12 27:9 [a] Lev. 16:29–31; 23:27–29; Num. 29:7
27:14 [1] NU-Text reads *Euraquilon.* 27:16 [1] NU-Text reads *Cauda.*

the ship; and fearing lest they should run
aground on the Syrtis[1] *Sands,* they struck
sail and so were driven. 18And because we
were exceedingly tempest-tossed, the next
day they lightened the ship. 19On the third
day [a]we threw the ship's tackle overboard
with our own hands. 20Now when neither
sun nor stars appeared for many days, and
no small tempest beat on *us,* all hope that
we would be saved was finally given up.

21But after long abstinence from food,
then Paul stood in the midst of them and
said, "Men, you should have listened to
me, and not have sailed from Crete and
incurred this disaster and loss. 22And now
I urge you to take heart, for there will be
no loss of life among you, but only of the
ship. 23[a]For there stood by me this night
an angel of the God to whom I belong and
[b]whom I serve, 24saying, 'Do not be afraid,
Paul; you must be brought before Caesar;
and indeed God has granted you all those
who sail with you.' 25Therefore take heart,
men, [a]for I believe God that it will be just
as it was told me. 26However, [a]we must run
aground on a certain island."

27Now when the fourteenth night had
come, as we were driven up and down in
the Adriatic *Sea,* about midnight the sailors
sensed that they were drawing near some
land. 28And they took soundings and found
it to be twenty fathoms; and when they had
gone a little farther, they took soundings
again and found *it* to be fifteen fathoms.
29Then, fearing lest we should run aground
on the rocks, they dropped four anchors
from the stern, and prayed for day to come.
30And as the sailors were seeking to escape
from the ship, when they had let down the
skiff into the sea, under pretense of putting out anchors from the prow, 31Paul said
to the centurion and the soldiers, "Unless
these men stay in the ship, you cannot be
saved." 32Then the soldiers cut away the
ropes of the skiff and let it fall off.

33And as day was about to dawn, Paul
implored *them* all to take food, saying, "Today is the fourteenth day you have waited
and continued without food, and eaten
nothing. 34Therefore I urge you to take
nourishment, for this is for your survival,
[a]since not a hair will fall from the head of
any of you." 35And when he had said these
things, he took bread and [a]gave thanks to
God in the presence of them all; and when
he had broken *it* he began to eat. 36Then
they were all encouraged, and also took
food themselves. 37And in all we were two
hundred and seventy-six [a]persons on the
ship. 38So when they had eaten enough,
they lightened the ship and threw out the
wheat into the sea.

Shipwrecked on Malta

39When it was day, they did not recognize the land; but they observed a bay with
a beach, onto which they planned to run
the ship if possible. 40And they let go the
anchors and left *them* in the sea, meanwhile loosing the rudder ropes; and they
hoisted the mainsail to the wind and made
for shore. 41But striking a place where two
seas met, [a]they ran the ship aground; and
the prow stuck fast and remained immovable, but the stern was being broken up by
the violence of the waves.

42And the soldiers' plan was to kill the
prisoners, lest any of them should swim
away and escape. 43But the centurion,
wanting to save Paul, kept them from *their*
purpose, and commanded that those who
could swim should jump *overboard* first
and get to land, 44and the rest, some on
boards and some on *parts* of the ship. And
so it was [a]that they all escaped safely to
land.

Paul's Ministry on Malta

28 Now when they had escaped, they
then found out that [a]the island was
called Malta. 2And the [a]natives showed us
unusual kindness; for they kindled a fire
and made us all welcome, because of the
rain that was falling and because of the
cold. 3But when Paul had gathered a bundle of sticks and laid *them* on the fire, a
viper came out because of the heat, and
fastened on his hand. 4So when the natives
saw the creature hanging from his hand,
they said to one another, "No doubt this

27:17 [1] M-Text reads *Syrtes.* 27:19 [a] Jon. 1:5 27:23 [a] Acts 18:9; 23:11; 2 Tim. 4:17 [b] Dan. 6:16; Rom. 1:9; 2 Tim. 1:3 27:25 [a] Luke 1:45; Rom. 4:20, 21; 2 Tim. 1:12 27:26 [a] Acts 28:1 27:34 [a] 1 Kin. 1:52; [Matt. 10:30; Luke 12:7; 21:18] 27:35 [a] 1 Sam. 9:13; Matt. 15:36; Mark 8:6; John 6:11; [1 Tim. 4:3, 4] 27:37 [a] Acts 2:41; 7:14; Rom. 13:1; 1 Pet. 3:20 27:41 [a] 2 Cor. 11:25 27:44 [a] Acts 27:22, 31 28:1 [a] Acts 27:26 28:2 [a] Acts 28:4; Rom. 1:14; 1 Cor. 14:11; Col. 3:11

man is a murderer, whom, though he has
escaped the sea, yet justice does not allow
to live." 5 But he shook off the creature into
the fire and [a]suffered no harm. 6 However,
they were expecting that he would swell
up or suddenly fall down dead. But after
they had looked for a long time and saw
no harm come to him, they changed their
minds and [a]said that he was a god.

7 In that region there was an estate of the
leading citizen of the island, whose name
was Publius, who received us and entertained us courteously for three days. 8 And
it happened that the father of Publius lay
sick of a fever and dysentery. Paul went in
to him and [a]prayed, and [b]he laid his hands
on him and healed him. 9 So when this was
done, the rest of those on the island who
had diseases also came and were healed.
10 They also honored us in many [a]ways; and
when we departed, they provided such
things as were [b]necessary.

Arrival at Rome

11 After three months we sailed in [a]an
Alexandrian ship whose figurehead was
the Twin Brothers, which had wintered at
the island. 12 And landing at Syracuse, we
stayed three days. 13 From there we circled
round and reached Rhegium. And after
one day the south wind blew; and the next
day we came to Puteoli, 14 where we found
[a]brethren, and were invited to stay with
them seven days. And so we went toward
Rome. 15 And from there, when the brethren heard about us, they came to meet
us as far as Appii Forum and Three Inns.
When Paul saw them, he thanked God and
took courage.

16 Now when we came to Rome, the centurion delivered the prisoners to the captain of the guard; but [a]Paul was permitted
to dwell by himself with the soldier who
guarded him.

Paul's Ministry at Rome

17 And it came to pass after three days
that Paul called the leaders of the Jews
together. So when they had come together,
he said to them: "Men *and* brethren,
[a]though I have done nothing against our
people or the customs of our fathers, yet
[b]I was delivered as a prisoner from Jerusalem into the hands of the Romans, 18 who,
[a]when they had examined me, wanted to
let *me* go, because there was no cause for
putting me to death. 19 But when the Jews[1]
spoke against *it,* [a]I was compelled to appeal to Caesar, not that I had anything
of which to accuse my nation. 20 For this
reason therefore I have called for you, to
see *you* and speak with *you,* because [a]for
the hope of Israel I am bound with [b]this
chain."

21 Then they said to him, "We neither received letters from Judea concerning you,
nor have any of the brethren who came reported or spoken any evil of you. 22 But we
desire to hear from you what you think;
for concerning this sect, we know that [a]it
is spoken against everywhere."

23 So when they had appointed him a day,
many came to him at *his* lodging, [a]to whom
he explained and solemnly testified of the
kingdom of God, persuading them concerning Jesus [b]from both the Law of Moses and the Prophets, from morning till
evening. 24 And [a]some were persuaded by
the things which were spoken, and some
disbelieved. 25 So when they did not agree
among themselves, they departed after
Paul had said one word: "The Holy Spirit
spoke rightly through Isaiah the prophet
to our[1] fathers, 26 saying,

[a]'Go to this people and say:
"Hearing you will hear, and
shall not understand;
And seeing you will see,
and not perceive;
27 For the hearts of this people
have grown dull.
Their ears are hard of hearing,
And their eyes they have closed,
Lest they should see with *their*
eyes and hear with *their* ears,

28:5 [a] Mark 16:18; Luke 10:19 28:6 [a] Acts 12:22; 14:11 28:8 [a] Acts 9:40; [James 5:14, 15] [b] Matt. 9:18; Mark 5:23; 6:5; 7:32; 16:18; Luke 4:40; Acts 19:11, 12; [1 Cor. 12:9, 28] 28:10 [a] Matt. 15:6; 1 Tim. 5:17 [b] [Phil. 4:19] 28:11 [a] Acts 27:6 28:14 [a] Rom. 1:8 28:16 [a] Acts 23:11; 24:25; 27:3 28:17 [a] Acts 23:29; 24:12, 13; 26:31 [b] Acts 21:33 28:18 [a] Acts 22:24; 24:10; 25:8; 26:32 28:19 [a] Acts 25:11, 21, 25 [1] That is, the ruling authorities 28:20 [a] Acts 26:6, 7 [b] Acts 26:29; Eph. 3:1; 4:1; 6:20; 2 Tim. 1:8, 16; Philem. 10, 13 28:22 [a] Luke 2:34; Acts 24:5, 14; [1 Pet. 2:12; 3:16; 4:14, 16] 28:23 [a] Luke 24:27; [Acts 17:3; 19:8] [b] Acts 26:6, 22 28:24 [a] Acts 14:4; 19:9 28:25 [1] NU-Text reads *your.* 28:26 [a] Is. 6:9, 10; Jer. 5:21; Ezek. 12:2; Matt. 13:14, 15; Mark 4:12; Luke 8:10; John 12:40, 41; Rom. 11:8

Lest they should understand
with *their* hearts and turn,
So that I should heal them."'[1]

28"Therefore let it be known to you that
the salvation of God has been sent [a]to
the Gentiles, and they will hear it!" 29And
when he had said these words, the Jews
departed and had a great dispute among
themselves.[1]

30Then Paul dwelt two whole years in
his own rented house, and received all who
came to him, 31[a]preaching the kingdom of
God and teaching the things which concern
the Lord Jesus Christ with all confidence,
no one forbidding him.

28:27 [1] Isaiah 6:9, 10 28:28 [a] Is. 42:1, 6; 49:6; Matt. 21:41; Luke 2:32; Rom. 11:11
28:29 [1] NU-Text omits this verse. 28:31 [a] Acts 4:31; Eph. 6:19

THE EPISTLE OF PAUL TO THE

ROMANS

OVERVIEW

Acts 2:10 establishes that "visitors from Rome" were present at the birth of the church on the day of Pentecost. These new Christians likely returned and laid the foundation for the early church in Rome. In time, the church grew, requiring the need to meet in several places (see Rom. 16:1–16). A growing church, however, is not always a healthy church. Paul wrote this letter, the longest of all the epistles, to the church at Rome while he ministered to the church at Corinth to ensure that the Roman church was being built on the right foundation of the gospel. Paul recognized that a healthy ministry in the center of the Roman Empire was essential for the spread of the gospel, the growth of the church, and the fulfillment of the Great Commission (see Matt. 28:16–20).

In Romans, Paul presents the most systematic presentation of the doctrine of salvation in Scripture. As such, several of its key verses are often used by evangelists and in evangelism materials, such as the "Romans Road to Salvation."

Romans 3:23 tells us that "all have sinned and fall short of the glory of God." The sins we have committed by our actions (commission) and the sins we have committed by our inactions (omission) separate us as creatures from our Creator.

Romans 6:23 explains the effect of sin on all humanity: "For the wages of sin is death, but the gift of God is eternal life in Christ Jesus our Lord." Sin has created an infinitely wide barrier between us and God that we cannot cross and that has condemned us to eternal separation from Him. Sin also has more immediate direct and indirect consequences, such as suffering, sickness, pain, and death. But this verse also hints at a solution found only in Jesus Christ.

Romans 5:8 says, "But God demonstrates His own love toward us, in that while we were still sinners, Christ died for us." There is a price, a penalty, that must be paid to atone for sin. The wrong of sin must be righted. Christianity, therefore, makes little sense to people who do not value forgiveness. The atonement theology of the Old and New Testaments establishes that there is no forgiveness of sin without the shedding of blood (see Lev. 16; Heb. 9:22). But we are incapable of cleansing ourselves from sin; we cannot save ourselves. Thus, in the Old Testament, the sacrifice of a spotless lamb was required for the forgiveness of sin. Then, when Jesus became the "Lamb of God who takes away the sin of the world" (John 1:29), He settled the account once and for all. Jesus Christ is God's answer to the separation of humanity from God caused by sin.

Romans then explains that "if you confess with your mouth the Lord Jesus and believe in your heart that God has raised Him from the dead, you will be saved . . . For 'whoever calls on the name of the LORD shall be saved'" (10:9, 13). From this, we see that salvation requires confession of sin and the profession that Jesus is both Savior and Lord.

BREATHE IT IN

For generations, the Pew Research Center has conducted an annual survey that measures the religious attitudes of Americans. Based on its findings, there is no question that we are wit-

nesses to the secularization of our nation and world. Adults who self-identify as Christians dropped from 78 percent in 2007 to 63 percent in 2021. In that same decade, 29 percent of adults surveyed identified as religiously unaffiliated, up from 16 percent.[1] Christian values, it seems, are being abandoned and redefined with each generation. *Sin* has become a word without definition by the world. Lifestyles and behaviors deemed unacceptable by nearly every society less than a generation ago are now conventional. Consider your own definition of *sin* and what you base it upon.

Sin is not a term often used in everyday life. It means "transgression of divine law." Although the world has attempted to redefine or even nullify the concept of sin, its meaning is solely based upon whether one desires to obey God. If a person does not, then he or she will live according to self-rule but will have to answer for this one day. If a person does, though, then the issue of sin must first be addressed. A person seeking the heart of God will find it, and by God's grace, his or her sins will be covered by the blood of Christ. Only upon repentance of sin and trusting in Christ can someone live within the grace of God.

Unlike the world that has an abundance of moral compass options, as a believer set Jesus as your sole moral compass. Even though the gospel makes it clear that salvation is not by our works but only by grace, that does not mean that Christians are not required to work out their faith. Jesus provides us with the boundaries we need to ensure our works are done in obedience to God. These boundaries, however, do not exist simply to prevent us from sinning. These boundaries also exist to protect us. Secularization is trending. Religion is declining. But as believers, we have an increasing opportunity to show the beauty and fragrant aroma of Christ in how we live.

†

[1] Gregory A. Smith, "About Three-in-Ten U.S. Adults Are Now Religiously Unaffiliated," Pew Research Center, December 14, 2021, https://www.pewresearch.org/religion/2021/12/14/about-three-in-ten-u-s-adults-are-now-religiously-unaffiliated/.

THE EPISTLE OF PAUL TO THE

ROMANS

Greeting

1 Paul, a bondservant of Jesus Christ,
[a]called *to be* an apostle, [b]separated to the
gospel of God 2[a]which He promised before
[b]through His prophets in the Holy Scriptures, 3concerning His Son Jesus Christ our
Lord, who was [a]born of the seed of David
according to the flesh, 4*and* [a]declared *to be*
the Son of God with power according [b]to
the Spirit of holiness, by the resurrection
from the dead. 5Through Him [a]we have
received grace and apostleship for [b]obe-
dience to the faith among all nations [c]for
His name, 6among whom you also are the
called of Jesus Christ;

7To all who are in Rome, beloved of God,
[a]called *to be* saints:

[b]Grace to you and peace from God our
Father and the Lord Jesus Christ.

Desire to Visit Rome

8First, [a]I thank my God through Jesus
Christ for you all, that [b]your faith is spoken of throughout the whole world. 9For
[a]God is my witness, [b]whom I serve with my
spirit in the gospel of His Son, that [c]without
ceasing I make mention of you always in
my prayers, 10making request if, by some
means, now at last I may find a way in the
will of God to come to you. 11For I long to see
you, that [a]I may impart to you some spiritual gift, so that you may be established—
12that is, that I may be encouraged together
with you by [a]the mutual faith both of you
and me.

13Now I do not want you to be unaware,
brethren, that I often planned to come to
you (but [a]was hindered until now), that I
might have some [b]fruit among you also,
just as among the other Gentiles. 14I am a
debtor both to Greeks and to barbarians,
both to wise and to unwise. 15So, as much
as is in me, *I am* ready to preach the gospel
to you who are in Rome also.

The Just Live by Faith

16For [a]I am not ashamed of the gospel
of Christ,[1] for [b]it is the power of God to salvation for everyone who believes, [c]for the
Jew first and also for the Greek. 17For [a]in it
the righteousness of God is revealed from
faith to faith; as it is written, [b]"The just shall
live by faith."[1]

God's Wrath on Unrighteousness

18[a]For the wrath of God is revealed from
heaven against all ungodliness and [b]un-
righteousness of men, who suppress the
truth in unrighteousness, 19because [a]what
may be known of God is manifest in them,
for [b]God has shown *it* to them. 20For since
the creation of the world [a]His invisible *attributes* are clearly seen, being understood by
the things that are made, *even* His eternal
power and Godhead, so that they are without excuse, 21because, although they knew
God, they did not glorify *Him* as God, nor
were thankful, but [a]became futile in their

1:1 [a] 1 Cor. 1:1; 9:1; 15:9; 2 Cor. 1:1; 1 Tim. 1:11 [b] Acts 9:15; 13:2; [Gal. 1:15] 1:2 [a] Acts 26:6 [b] Gal. 3:8 1:3 [a] 2 Sam. 7:12; 1 Chr. 17:11; Is. 9:7; Jer. 23:5; Gal. 4:4 1:4 [a] Ps. 2:7; Acts 9:20; 13:33; Heb. 1:2 [b] Ps. 16:10; [Heb. 9:14] 1:5 [a] Eph. 3:8 [b] Acts 6:7; Rom. 16:26 [c] Acts 9:15 1:7 [a] Acts 9:13; Rom. 8:28; 1 Cor. 1:2, 24 [b] Num. 6:25; 1 Cor. 1:3; 2 Cor. 1:2; Gal. 1:3; Eph. 1:2; Phil. 1:2; Col. 1:2; 1 Thess. 1:1; 2 Thess. 1:2 1:8 [a] 1 Cor. 1:4; Eph. 1:15; Phil. 1:3; Col. 1:3; 1 Thess. 1:2; 2:13 [b] Acts 28:22; Rom. 16:19 1:9 [a] Rom. 9:1 [b] Acts 27:23 [c] 1 Thess. 3:10 1:11 [a] Rom. 15:29 1:12 [a] Titus 1:4 1:13 [a] [1 Thess. 2:18] [b] Phil. 4:17 1:16 [a] Ps. 40:9, 10 [b] 1 Cor. 1:18, 24 [c] Luke 2:30; Acts 3:26; Rom. 2:9 [1] NU-Text omits *of Christ.* 1:17 [a] Rom. 3:21; 9:30; Phil. 3:9 [b] Hab. 2:4; Gal. 3:11; Heb. 10:38 [1] Habakkuk 2:4 1:18 [a] [Acts 17:30] [b] Rom. 6:13; 2 Thess. 2:10; 2 Pet. 2:13; 1 John 5:17 1:19 [a] [Acts 14:17; 17:24] [b] [John 1:9] 1:20 [a] Job 12:7–9; Ps. 19:1–6; Jer. 5:22 1:21 [a] 2 Kin. 17:15; Jer. 2:5; Eph. 4:17

thoughts, and their foolish hearts were
darkened. 22[a]Professing to be wise, they
became fools, 23and changed the glory of
the [a]incorruptible [b]God into an image made
like corruptible man—and birds and four-
footed animals and creeping things.
24[a]Therefore God also gave them up to
uncleanness, in the lusts of their hearts, [b]to
dishonor their bodies [c]among themselves,
25who exchanged [a]the truth of God [b]for the
lie, and worshiped and served the creature
rather than the Creator, who is blessed forever. Amen.
26For this reason God gave them up to
[a]vile passions. For even their women exchanged the natural use for what is against
nature. 27Likewise also the men, leaving
the natural use of the woman, burned in
their lust for one another, men with men
committing what is shameful, and receiving in themselves the penalty of their error
which was due.
28And even as they did not like to retain God in *their* knowledge, God gave
them over to a debased mind, to do those
things [a]which are not fitting; 29being filled
with all unrighteousness, sexual immorality,[1] wickedness, covetousness, malicious-
ness; full of envy, murder, strife, deceit,
evil-mindedness; *they are* whisperers,
30backbiters, haters of God, violent, proud,
boasters, inventors of evil things, disobedient to parents, 31undiscerning, untrustworthy, unloving, unforgiving,[1] unmerciful;
32who, [a]knowing the righteous judgment of
God, that those who practice such things
[b]are deserving of death, not only do the
same but also [c]approve of those who practice them.

God's Righteous Judgment

2 Therefore you are [a]inexcusable, O man,
whoever you are who judge, [b]for in
whatever you judge another you condemn yourself; for you who judge practice the same things. 2But we know that
the judgment of God is according to truth
against those who practice such things.
3And do you think this, O man, you who
judge those practicing such things, and
doing the same, that you will escape the
judgment of God? 4Or do you despise [a]the
riches of His goodness, [b]forbearance, and
[c]longsuffering, [d]not knowing that the goodness of God leads you to repentance? 5But
in accordance with your hardness and your
impenitent heart [a]you are treasuring up for
yourself wrath in the day of wrath and revelation of the righteous judgment of God,
6who [a]"will render to each one according
to his deeds":[1] 7eternal life to those who by
patient continuance in doing good seek
for glory, honor, and immortality; 8but
to those who are self-seeking and [a]do not
obey the truth, but obey unrighteousness—
indignation and wrath, 9tribulation and
anguish, on every soul of man who does
evil, of the Jew [a]first and also of the Greek;
10[a]but glory, honor, and peace to everyone
who works what is good, to the Jew first and
also to the Greek. 11For [a]there is no partiality with God.
12For as many as have sinned without law
will also perish without law, and as many
as have sinned in the law will be judged by
the law 13(for [a]not the hearers of the law
are just in the sight of God, but the doers
of the law will be justified; 14for when Gentiles, who do not have the law, by nature do
the things in the law, these, although not
having the law, are a law to themselves,
15who show the [a]work of the law written in
their hearts, their [b]conscience also bearing witness, and between themselves *their*
thoughts accusing or else excusing *them*)
16[a]in the day when God will judge the secrets of men [b]by Jesus Christ, [c]according
to my gospel.

The Jews Guilty as the Gentiles

17Indeed[1] [a]you are called a Jew, and [b]rest
on the law, [c]and make your boast in God,

1:22 [a] Jer. 10:14; [1 Cor. 1:20] **1:23** [a] 1 Tim. 1:17; 6:15, 16 [b] Deut. 4:16–18; Ps. 106:20; Jer. 2:11; Acts 17:29 **1:24** [a] Ps. 81:12; Acts 7:42; Eph. 4:18, 19 [b] 1 Cor. 6:18 [c] Lev. 18:22 **1:25** [a] 1 Thess. 1:9 [b] Is. 44:20; Jer. 10:14; 13:25; 16:19 **1:26** [a] Lev. 18:22; Eph. 5:12 **1:28** [a] Eph. 5:4 **1:29** [1] NU-Text omits *sexual immorality.* **1:31** [1] NU-Text omits *unforgiving.* **1:32** [a] [Rom. 2:2] [b] [Rom. 6:21] [c] [Ps. 50:18]; Hos. 7:3 **2:1** [a] [Rom. 1:20] [b] 2 Sam. 12:5–7; [Matt. 7:1–5; Luke 6:37]; John 8:9; Rom. 14:22 **2:4** [a] Rom. 9:23; 11:33; [2 Cor. 8:2; Eph. 1:7, 18; 2:7; Phil. 4:19; Col. 1:27; 2:2; Titus 3:6] [b] [Rom. 3:25] [c] Ex. 34:6; [Rom. 9:22; 1 Tim. 1:16]; 1 Pet. 3:20 [d] Is. 30:18; [2 Pet. 3:9, 15] **2:5** [a] [Deut. 32:34]; Prov. 1:18; James 5:3 **2:6** [a] [Job 34:11]; Ps. 62:12; Prov. 24:12; Jer. 17:10; [2 Cor. 5:10; Rev. 20:12, 13] [1] Psalm 62:12; Proverbs 24:12 **2:8** [a] Job 24:13; [2 Thess. 1:8] **2:9** [a] Amos 3:2; Luke 12:47; Acts 3:26; Rom. 1:16; 1 Pet. 4:17 **2:10** [a] Rom. 2:7; Heb. 2:7; [1 Pet. 1:7] **2:11** [a] Deut. 10:17; [Job 34:19]; Acts 10:34; [Eph. 6:9] **2:13** [a] Matt. 7:21, 22; John 13:17; [James 1:22, 25; 1 John 3:7] **2:15** [a] 1 Cor. 5:1 [b] Acts 24:25 **2:16** [a] Eccl. 12:14; [Matt. 25:31]; Rev. 20:12 [b] John 5:22; Acts 10:42; 17:31; Rom. 3:6; 14:10 [c] 1 Tim. 1:11 **2:17** [a] [Matt. 3:9]; John 8:33 [b] Mic. 3:11; John 5:45; Rom. 2:23; 9:4 [c] Is. 48:1, 2 [1] NU-Text reads *But if.*

18and [a]know *His* will, and [b]approve the
things that are excellent, being instructed
out of the law, 19and [a]are confident that you
yourself are a guide to the blind, a light to
those who are in darkness, 20an instructor of the foolish, a teacher of babes, [a]hav-
ing the form of knowledge and truth in
the law. 21[a]You, therefore, who teach another, do you not teach yourself? You who
preach that a man should not steal, do you
steal? 22You who say, "Do not commit adultery," do you commit adultery? You who abhor idols, [a]do you rob temples? 23You who
[a]make your boast in the law, do you dishonor God through breaking the law? 24For
[a]"the name of God is [b]blasphemed among
the Gentiles because of you,"[1] as it is written.

Circumcision of No Avail

25[a]For circumcision is indeed profitable if you keep the law; but if you are a
breaker of the law, your circumcision has
become uncircumcision. 26Therefore, [a]if
an uncircumcised man keeps the righteous
requirements of the law, will not his uncircumcision be counted as circumcision?
27And will not the physically uncircumcised, if he fulfills the law, [a]judge you who,
even with *your* written *code* and circumcision, *are* a transgressor of the law? 28For
[a]he is not a Jew who *is one* outwardly, nor *is*
circumcision that which *is* outward in the
flesh; 29but *he is* a Jew [a]who *is one* inwardly;
and [b]circumcision *is that* of the heart, [c]in
the Spirit, not in the letter; [d]whose praise
is not from men but from God.

God's Judgment Defended

3 What advantage then has the Jew, or
what *is* the profit of circumcision?
2Much in every way! Chiefly because [a]to
them were committed the oracles of God.
3For what if [a]some did not believe? [b]Will
their unbelief make the faithfulness of God
without effect? 4[a]Certainly not! Indeed, let
[b]God be true but [c]every man a liar. As it is
written:

[d]"That You may be justified
in Your words,
And may overcome when
You are judged."[1]

5But if our unrighteousness demonstrates the righteousness of God, what
shall we say? *Is* God unjust who inflicts
wrath? [a](I speak as a man.) 6Certainly not!
For then [a]how will God judge the world?
7For if the truth of God has increased
through my lie to His glory, why am I also
still judged as a sinner? 8And *why* not *say*,
[a]"Let us do evil that good may come"?—as
we are slanderously reported and as some
affirm that we say. Their condemnation
is just.

All Have Sinned
(Ps. 14:1–3; 53:1–4)

9What then? Are we better *than they?* Not
at all. For we have previously charged both
Jews and Greeks that [a]they are all under sin.
10As it is written:

[a]"There is none righteous, no, not one;
11 There is none who understands;
There is none who seeks after God.
12 They have all turned aside;
They have together become
unprofitable;
There is none who does
good, no, not one."[1]
13 "Their[a] throat *is* an open tomb;
With their tongues they have
practiced deceit";[1]
[b]"The poison of asps *is*
under their lips";[2]
14 "Whose[a] mouth *is* full of
cursing and bitterness."[1]
15 "Their[a] feet *are* swift to shed blood;
16 Destruction and misery
are in their ways;
17 And the way of peace they
have not known."[1]
18 "There[a] is no fear of God
before their eyes."[1]

2:18 [a] Deut. 4:8 [b] Phil. 1:10 **2:19** [a] Matt. 15:14; John 9:34 **2:20** [a] [2 Tim. 3:5] **2:21** [a] Ps. 50:16; Matt. 23:3 **2:22** [a] Mal. 3:8 **2:23** [a] Mic. 3:11; John 5:45; Rom. 2:17; 9:4 **2:24** [a] Ezek. 16:27 [b] 2 Sam. 12:14; Is. 52:5; Ezek. 36:22 [1] Isaiah 52:5; Ezekiel 36:22 **2:25** [a] Gen. 17:10–14; [Gal. 5:3] **2:26** [a] [Acts 10:34] **2:27** [a] Matt. 12:41 **2:28** [a] [Matt. 3:9]; John 8:39; Rom. 2:17; 9:6; [Gal. 6:15] **2:29** [a] [1 Pet. 3:4] [b] Phil. 3:3; Col. 2:11 [c] Deut. 30:6; Rom. 2:27; 7:6; [2 Cor. 3:6] [d] John 5:44; 12:43; [1 Cor. 4:5; 2 Cor. 10:18]; 1 Thess. 2:4 **3:2** [a] Deut. 4:5–8; Ps. 147:19; Rom. 9:4 **3:3** [a] Rom. 10:16; Heb. 4:2 [b] Num. 23:19; [2 Tim. 2:13] **3:4** [a] Job 40:8 [b] [John 3:33] [c] Ps. 62:9 [d] Ps. 51:4 [1] Psalm 51:4 **3:5** [a] Rom. 6:19; 1 Cor. 9:8; 15:32; Gal. 3:15 **3:6** [a] [Gen. 18:25] **3:8** [a] Rom. 5:20 **3:9** [a] Rom. 3:19, 23; 11:32; Gal. 3:22 **3:10** [a] Ps. 14:1–3; 53:1–3; Eccl. 7:20 **3:12** [1] Psalms 14:1–3; 53:1–3; Ecclesiastes 7:20 **3:13** [a] Ps. 5:9 [b] Ps. 140:3 [1] Psalm 5:9 [2] Psalm 140:3 **3:14** [a] Ps. 10:7 [1] Psalm 10:7 **3:15** [a] Prov. 1:16; Is. 59:7, 8 **3:17** [1] Isaiah 59:7, 8 **3:18** [a] Ps. 36:1 [1] Psalm 36:1

19 Now we know that whatever [a]the law
says, it says to those who are under the law,
that [b]every mouth may be stopped, and all
the world may become guilty before God.
20 Therefore [a]by the deeds of the law no
flesh will be justified in His sight, for by
the law *is* the knowledge of sin.

God's Righteousness Through Faith

21 But now [a]the righteousness of God
apart from the law is revealed, [b]being witnessed by the Law [c]and the Prophets, 22 even
the righteousness of God, through faith
in Jesus Christ, to all and on all[1] who believe. For [a]there is no difference; 23 for [a]all
have sinned and fall short of the glory of
God, 24 being justified freely [a]by His grace
[b]through the redemption that is in Christ
Jesus, 25 whom God set forth [a]*as* a propitiation [b]by His blood, through faith, to demonstrate His righteousness, because in His
forbearance God had passed over [c]the sins
that were previously committed, 26 to demonstrate at the present time His righteousness, that He might be just and the justifier
of the one who has faith in Jesus.

Boasting Excluded

27 [a]Where *is* boasting then? It is excluded.
By what law? Of works? No, but by the law of
faith. 28 Therefore we conclude [a]that a man
is justified by faith apart from the deeds of
the law. 29 Or *is He* the God of the Jews only?
Is He not also the God of the Gentiles? Yes,
of the Gentiles also, 30 since [a]*there is* one
God who will justify the circumcised by
faith and the uncircumcised through faith.
31 Do we then make void the law through
faith? Certainly not! On the contrary, we
establish the law.

Abraham Justified by Faith
(Gen. 17:10)

4 What then shall we say that [a]Abraham
our [b]father has found according to the
flesh?[1] 2 For if Abraham was [a]justified by
works, he has *something* to boast about, but
not before God. 3 For what does the Scripture say? [a]"Abraham believed God, and it
was accounted to him for righteousness."[1]
4 Now [a]to him who works, the wages are not
counted as grace but as debt.

David Celebrates the Same Truth

5 But to him who [a]does not work but believes on Him who justifies [b]the ungodly,
his faith is accounted for righteousness,
6 just as David also [a]describes the blessedness of the man to whom God imputes
righteousness apart from works:

7 "Blessed[a] *are those* whose lawless
deeds are forgiven,
And whose sins are covered;
8 Blessed *is the* man to whom the
LORD shall not impute sin."[1]

Abraham Justified Before Circumcision

9 *Does* this blessedness then *come* upon
the circumcised *only,* or upon the uncircumcised also? For we say that faith was
accounted to Abraham for righteousness.
10 How then was it accounted? While he was
circumcised, or uncircumcised? Not while
circumcised, but while uncircumcised.
11 And [a]he received the sign of circumcision, a seal of the righteousness of the faith
which *he had while still* uncircumcised, that
[b]he might be the father of all those who believe, though they are uncircumcised, that
righteousness might be imputed to them
also, 12 and the father of circumcision to
those who not only *are* of the circumcision,
but who also walk in the steps of the faith
which our father [a]Abraham *had while still*
uncircumcised.

The Promise Granted Through Faith

13 For the promise that he would be the
[a]heir of the world *was* not to Abraham or
to his seed through the law, but through
the righteousness of faith. 14 For [a]if those
who are of the law *are* heirs, faith is made
void and the promise made of no effect,

3:19 [a] John 10:34 [b] Job 5:16; Ps. 107:42 **3:20** [a] Ps. 143:2; [Acts 13:39; Gal. 2:16] **3:21** [a] Acts 15:11 [b] John 5:46 [c] 1 Pet. 1:10 **3:22** [a] Rom. 10:12; [Gal. 3:28; Col. 3:11] [1] NU-Text omits *and on all.* **3:23** [a] Gal. 3:22 **3:24** [a] Rom. 4:4, 16; [Eph. 2:8; Titus 3:5, 7] [b] [Matt. 20:28; Eph. 1:7; Col. 1:14; 1 Tim. 2:6; Heb. 9:12, 15; 1 Pet. 1:18, 19] **3:25** [a] Lev. 16:15 [b] Col. 1:20 [c] Acts 14:16; 17:30; [Rom. 2:4] **3:27** [a] Rom. 2:17, 23; [1 Cor. 1:29]; Eph. 2:9 **3:28** [a] Gal. 2:16 **3:30** [a] Rom. 10:12; [Gal. 3:8, 20] **4:1** [a] Gen. 11:27—25:9; Is. 51:2; [Matt. 3:9]; John 8:33 [b] [Luke 3:8]; John 8:53; James 2:21 [1] Or *Abraham our (fore)father according to the flesh has found?* **4:2** [a] Rom. 3:20, 27 **4:3** [a] Gen. 15:6; Rom. 4:9, 22; Gal. 3:6; James 2:23 [1] Genesis 15:6 **4:4** [a] Rom. 11:6 **4:5** [a] [Gal. 2:16; Eph. 2:8, 9] [b] Josh. 24:2 **4:6** [a] Ps. 32:1, 2 **4:7** [a] Ps. 32:1, 2 **4:8** [1] Psalm 32:1, 2 **4:11** [a] Gen. 17:10 [b] Luke 19:9; Rom. 4:16 **4:12** [a] Rom. 4:18–22 **4:13** [a] Gen. 17:4–6; 22:17 **4:14** [a] Gal. 3:18

15because [a]the law brings about wrath; for
where there is no law *there is* no transgression.

16Therefore *it is* of faith that *it might be*
[a]according to grace, [b]so that the promise
might be sure to all the seed, not only to
those who are of the law, but also to those
who are of the faith of Abraham, [c]who is
the father of us all 17(as it is written, [a]"I have
made you a father of many nations"[1]) in
the presence of Him whom he believed—
God, [b]who gives life to the dead and calls
those [c]things which do not exist as though
they did; 18who, contrary to hope, in hope
believed, so that he became the father of
many nations, according to what was spoken, [a]"So shall your descendants be."[1] 19And
not being weak in faith, [a]he did not consider his own body, already dead (since he
was about a hundred years old), [b]and the
deadness of Sarah's womb. 20He did not
waver at the promise of God through unbelief, but was strengthened in faith, giving
glory to God, 21and being fully convinced
that what He had promised [a]He was also
able to perform. 22And therefore [a]"it was
accounted to him for righteousness."[1]

23Now [a]it was not written for his sake
alone that it was imputed to him, 24but also
for us. It shall be imputed to us who believe
[a]in Him who raised up Jesus our Lord from
the dead, 25[a]who was delivered up because
of our offenses, and [b]was raised because of
our justification.

Faith Triumphs in Trouble

5 Therefore, [a]having been justified by
faith, we have[1] [b]peace with God through
our Lord Jesus Christ, 2[a]through whom also
we have access by faith into this grace [b]in
which we stand, and [c]rejoice in hope of
the glory of God. 3And not only *that,* but
[a]we also glory in tribulations, [b]knowing
that tribulation produces perseverance;
4[a]and perseverance, character; and character, hope. 5[a]Now hope does not disappoint,
[b]because the love of God has been poured
out in our hearts by the Holy Spirit who
was given to us.

Christ in Our Place

6For when we were still without strength,
in due time [a]Christ died for the ungodly.
7For scarcely for a righteous man will one
die; yet perhaps for a good man someone
would even dare to die. 8But [a]God demonstrates His own love toward us, in that
while we were still sinners, Christ died for
us. 9Much more then, having now been
justified [a]by His blood, we shall be saved
[b]from wrath through Him. 10For [a]if when
we were enemies [b]we were reconciled to
God through the death of His Son, much
more, having been reconciled, we shall be
saved [c]by His life. 11And not only *that,* but
we also [a]rejoice in God through our Lord
Jesus Christ, through whom we have now
received the reconciliation.

Death in Adam, Life in Christ
(Gen. 3:1–19)

12Therefore, just as [a]through one man
sin entered the world, and [b]death through
sin, and thus death spread to all men, because all sinned— 13(For until the law sin
was in the world, but [a]sin is not imputed
when there is no law. 14Nevertheless death
reigned from Adam to Moses, even over
those who had not sinned according to the
likeness of the transgression of Adam, [a]who
is a type of Him who was to come. 15But the
free gift *is* not like the offense. For if by the
one man's offense many died, much more
the grace of God and the gift by the grace
of the one Man, Jesus Christ, abounded [a]to
many. 16And the gift *is* not like *that which
came* through the one who sinned. For the
judgment *which came* from one *offense resulted* in condemnation, but the free gift
which came from many offenses *resulted*
in justification. 17For if by the one man's
offense death reigned through the one,

4:15 [a] Rom. 3:20 4:16 [a] [Rom. 3:24] [b] [Gal. 3:22] [c] Is. 51:2 4:17 [a] Gen. 17:5 [b] [Rom. 8:11] [c] Rom. 9:26 [1] Genesis 17:5 4:18 [a] Gen. 15:5 [1] Genesis 15:5 4:19 [a] Gen. 17:17 [b] Heb. 11:11 4:21 [a] Gen. 18:14; [Ps. 115:3; Luke 1:37; Heb. 11:19] 4:22 [a] Gen. 15:6 [1] Genesis 15:6 4:23 [a] Rom. 15:4; 1 Cor. 10:6 4:24 [a] Acts 2:24 4:25 [a] Is. 53:4, 5; [Rom. 5:6, 8; 8:32; Gal. 2:20; Eph. 5:2; Heb. 9:28] [b] [Rom. 5:18; 1 Cor. 15:17; 2 Cor. 5:15] 5:1 [a] Is. 32:17; John 16:33 [b] [Is. 53:5]; Acts 10:36; [Eph. 2:14] [1] Another ancient reading is, *let us have peace.* 5:2 [a] [John 10:9; Eph. 2:18; 3:12; Heb. 10:19; 1 Pet. 3:18] [b] 1 Cor. 15:1 [c] Heb. 3:6 5:3 [a] Matt. 5:11, 12; [John 16:33; Acts 5:41; 2 Cor. 12:9]; James 1:2 [b] James 1:3 5:4 [a] Phil. 2:22; [James 1:12] 5:5 [a] Phil. 1:20 [b] 2 Cor. 1:22; Eph. 1:13 5:6 [a] Is. 53:5; [Rom. 4:25; 5:8; 8:32; Gal. 2:20; Eph. 5:2] 5:8 [a] [John 3:16; 15:13; Rom. 8:39] 5:9 [a] Eph. 2:13; [1 John 1:7] [b] Rom. 1:18; 1 Thess. 1:10 5:10 [a] [Rom. 8:32] [b] Rom. 11:28; 2 Cor. 5:18; [Eph. 2:5, 6]; Col. 1:21 [c] John 14:19 5:11 [a] [Gal. 4:9] 5:12 [a] Gen. 2:17; 3:6, 19; [Rom. 5:15–17; 1 Cor. 15:21] [b] Gen. 2:17 5:13 [a] 1 John 3:4 5:14 [a] [1 Cor. 15:21, 22] 5:15 [a] [Is. 53:11]

HOPE FOR DELIVERANCE

INHALE

Since I was a teen, I have had a problem with drugs. I haven't always wanted to admit it to myself, but God knows. I know that I am on a path toward destruction, and I don't want to go down it another step. Before I lose my family, my job, and my home, I need to make a change and turn this all around. I know this will not be easy, but I truly have hope that the Lord can deliver me. Is hope enough though?

EXHALE

Without hope life would be even more difficult than it already is. Hope is about our future. It is defined by our trust that God is good, He has planned a good future for us, and the good future He planned will come to be. In this case, you need hope in a future that is drug-free. So, hope is what God gives us, but our part is to be patient and to persevere in continuing to believe that God can deliver us from all troubles and sin through Jesus.

Perseverance also includes you pushing through with practical steps like getting the medical help you need. Taking action like that is not failing to trust in God. He often works in our lives through other people and the knowledge He has provided them.

But don't make the mistake of putting your hope only in medicine or other things for deliverance. Don't leave God out of it. God can give you the strength you need to do whatever is needed for you to be wherever He wants you to be. Even if God uses something else to deliver you, that deliverance always begins with belief in Him and ends with that same belief in Him. Hoping in His power for deliverance and taking action steps can move you from where you are to where you want to be.

The Book of Romans has a lot to say about hope. Romans 5:3–5 says, "We also glory in tribulations, knowing that tribulation produces perseverance; and perseverance, character; and character, hope. Now hope does not disappoint, because the love of God has been poured out in our hearts by the Holy Spirit who was given to us." Hope is important, even necessary. But you must put your hope in the right place: in God and in His desire for you to be all He made you to be.

much more those who receive abundance
of grace and of the gift of righteousness will
reign in life through the One, Jesus Christ.)
18Therefore, as through one man's offense *judgment came* to all men, resulting
in condemnation, even so through [a]one
Man's righteous act *the free gift came* [b]to
all men, resulting in justification of life.
19For as by one man's disobedience many
were made sinners, so also by [a]one Man's
obedience many will be made righteous.
20Moreover [a]the law entered that the
offense might abound. But where sin
abounded, grace [b]abounded much more,
21so that as sin reigned in death, even so
grace might reign through righteousness to
eternal life through Jesus Christ our Lord.

Dead to Sin, Alive to God

6 What shall we say then? [a]Shall we continue in sin that grace may abound?
2Certainly not! How shall we who [a]died to
sin live any longer in it? 3Or do you not
know that [a]as many of us as were baptized
into Christ Jesus [b]were baptized into His
death? 4Therefore we were [a]buried with
Him through baptism into death, that [b]just
as Christ was raised from the dead by [c]the
glory of the Father, [d]even so we also should
walk in newness of life.

5:18 [a] [1 Cor. 15:21, 45] [b] Matt. 1:21; [John 12:32] 5:19 [a] Is. 53:11, 12; [Phil. 2:8] 5:20 [a] John 15:22 [b] Luke 7:47; Rom. 6:1; 1 Tim. 1:14 6:1 [a] Rom. 3:8; 6:15 6:2 [a] [Rom. 6:11; 7:4, 6; Gal. 2:19; Col. 2:20; 3:3]; 1 Pet. 2:24 6:3 [a] Acts 2:38; 8:16; 19:5; [Gal. 3:27]; Col. 2:12 [b] [1 Cor. 15:29] 6:4 [a] Col. 2:12 [b] 1 Cor. 6:14 [c] John 2:11 [d] Rom. 7:6; [2 Cor. 5:17; Gal. 6:15; Eph. 4:23; Col. 3:10]

5[a]For if we have been united together
in the likeness of His death, certainly we
also shall be *in the likeness* of *His* resurrection, 6knowing this, that [a]our old man was
crucified with *Him,* that [b]the body of sin
might be done away with, that we should
no longer be slaves of sin. 7For [a]he who has
died has been freed from sin. 8Now [a]if we
died with Christ, we believe that we shall
also live with Him, 9knowing that [a]Christ,
having been raised from the dead, dies no
more. Death no longer has dominion over
Him. 10For *the death* that He died, [a]He died
to sin once for all; but *the life* that He lives,
[b]He lives to God. 11Likewise you also, reckon
yourselves to be [a]dead indeed to sin, but
[b]alive to God in Christ Jesus our Lord.
12[a]Therefore do not let sin reign in your
mortal body, that you should obey it in its
lusts. 13And do not present your [a]members
as instruments of unrighteousness to sin,
but [b]present yourselves to God as being
alive from the dead, and your members *as*
instruments of righteousness to God. 14For
[a]sin shall not have dominion over you, for
you are not under law but under grace.

From Slaves of Sin to Slaves of God

15What then? Shall we sin [a]because we
are not under law but under grace? Certainly not! 16Do you not know that [a]to whom
you present yourselves slaves to obey,
you are that one's slaves whom you obey,
whether of sin *leading* to death, or of obedience *leading* to righteousness? 17But God be
thanked that *though* you were slaves of sin,
yet you obeyed from the heart [a]that form
of doctrine to which you were delivered.
18And [a]having been set free from sin, you
became slaves of righteousness. 19I speak
in human *terms* because of the weakness of
your flesh. For just as you presented your
members *as* slaves of uncleanness, and of
lawlessness *leading* to *more* lawlessness,
so now present your members *as* slaves *of*
righteousness for holiness.
20For when you were [a]slaves of sin,
you were free in regard to righteousness.
21[a]What fruit did you have then in the
things of which you are now ashamed? For
[b]the end of those things *is* death. 22But now
[a]having been set free from sin, and having
become slaves of God, you have your fruit
to holiness, and the end, everlasting life.
23For [a]the wages of sin *is* death, but [b]the
gift of God *is* eternal life in Christ Jesus
our Lord.

Freed from the Law

7 Or do you not know, brethren (for I
speak to those who know the law), that
the law has dominion over a man as long
as he lives? 2For [a]the woman who has a husband is bound by the law to *her* husband
as long as he lives. But if the husband dies,
she is released from the law of *her* husband.
3So then [a]if, while *her* husband lives, she
marries another man, she will be called an
adulteress; but if her husband dies, she is
free from that law, so that she is no adulteress, though she has married another
man. 4Therefore, my brethren, you also
have become [a]dead to the law through the
body of Christ, that you may be married
to another—to Him who was raised from
the dead, that we should [b]bear fruit to God.
5For when we were in the flesh, the sinful
passions which were aroused by the law
[a]were at work in our members [b]to bear fruit
to death. 6But now we have been delivered
from the law, having died to what we were
held by, so that we should serve [a]in the newness of the Spirit and not *in* the oldness of
the letter.

Sin's Advantage in the Law

7What shall we say then? *Is* the law sin?
Certainly not! On the contrary, [a]I would not
have known sin except through the law. For
I would not have known covetousness unless the law had said, [b]"You shall not covet."[1]
8But [a]sin, taking opportunity by the commandment, produced in me all *manner*
of evil desire. For [b]apart from the law sin

6:5 [a] 2 Cor. 4:10; Phil. 3:10; Col. 2:12; 3:1 6:6 [a] Gal. 2:20; 5:24; 6:14 [b] Col. 2:11 6:7 [a] 1 Pet. 4:1 6:8 [a] Rom. 6:4; 2 Cor. 4:10; 2 Tim. 2:11 6:9 [a] Rev. 1:18 6:10 [a] Heb. 9:27 [b] Luke 20:38 6:11 [a] [Rom. 6:2; 7:4, 6] [b] [Gal. 2:19; Col. 2:20; 3:3]; 1 Pet. 2:24 6:12 [a] Ps. 19:13 6:13 [a] Rom. 6:16, 19; 7:5; Col. 3:5; James 4:1 [b] Rom. 12:1; 2 Cor. 5:14; 1 Pet. 2:24; 4:2 6:14 [a] [Rom. 7:4, 6; 8:2; Gal. 5:18] 6:15 [a] 1 Cor. 9:21 6:16 [a] Prov. 5:22; [Matt. 6:24]; John 8:34; 2 Pet. 2:19 6:17 [a] 2 Tim. 1:13 6:18 [a] John 8:32; Rom. 6:22; 8:2; 1 Cor. 7:22; Gal. 5:1; 1 Pet. 2:16 6:20 [a] John 8:34 6:21 [a] Jer. 12:13; Ezek. 16:63; Rom. 7:5 [b] Rom. 1:32; Gal. 6:8 6:22 [a] [John 8:32]; Rom. 6:18; 8:2 6:23 [a] Gen. 2:17 [b] Rom. 2:7; 1 Pet. 1:4 7:2 [a] 1 Cor. 7:39 7:3 [a] [Matt. 5:32] 7:4 [a] Rom. 8:2; Gal. 2:19; 5:18; [Col. 2:14] [b] Gal. 5:22 7:5 [a] Rom. 6:13 [b] Rom. 6:21; Gal. 5:19; James 1:15 7:6 [a] Rom. 2:29; 2 Cor. 3:6 7:7 [a] Rom. 3:20 [b] Ex. 20:17; Deut. 5:21; Acts 20:33 [1] Exodus 20:17; Deuteronomy 5:21 7:8 [a] Rom. 4:15 [b] 1 Cor. 15:56

was dead. 9I was alive once without the
law, but when the commandment came,
sin revived and I died. 10And the commandment, [a]which *was* to *bring* life, I found to
bring death. 11For sin, taking occasion by
the commandment, deceived me, and by it
killed *me.* 12Therefore [a]the law *is* holy, and
the commandment holy and just and good.

Law Cannot Save from Sin

13Has then what is good become death
to me? Certainly not! But sin, that it might
appear sin, was producing death in me
through what is good, so that sin through
the commandment might become exceedingly sinful. 14For we know that the law is
spiritual, but I am carnal, [a]sold under sin.
15For what I am doing, I do not understand.
[a]For what I will to do, that I do not practice;
but what I hate, that I do. 16If, then, I do what
I will not to do, I agree with the law that *it is*
good. 17But now, *it is* no longer I who do it,
but sin that dwells in me. 18For I know that
[a]in me (that is, in my flesh) nothing good
dwells; for to will is present with me, but
how to perform what is good I do not find.
19For the good that I will *to do,* I do not do;
but the evil I will not *to do,* that I practice.
20Now if I do what I will not *to do,* it is no
longer I who do it, but sin that dwells in me.
21I find then a law, that evil is present
with me, the one who wills to do good. 22For
I [a]delight in the law of God according to
[b]the inward man. 23But [a]I see another law
in [b]my members, warring against the law
of my mind, and bringing me into captivity to the law of sin which is in my members. 24O wretched man that I am! Who will
deliver me [a]from this body of death? 25[a]I
thank God—through Jesus Christ our Lord!
So then, with the mind I myself serve the
law of God, but with the flesh the law of sin.

#OXYGEN

ROMANS 7:24–25

Hope for Deliverance

We see our sinfulness to the degree we perceive God's holiness. When we see Him as He is, we will be brought to our knees. When we are wronged, we will respond in ways that please Him. Thanks be to God that Jesus has delivered us from sin.

Receive and extend forgiveness, **breathe**, and **hope for deliverance.**

Free from Indwelling Sin

8 *There is* therefore now no condemnation to those who are in Christ Jesus,[1]
[a]who do not walk according to the flesh,
but according to the Spirit. 2For [a]the law of
[b]the Spirit of life in Christ Jesus has made
me free from [c]the law of sin and death. 3For
[a]what the law could not do in that it was
weak through the flesh, [b]God *did* by sending
His own Son in the likeness of sinful flesh,
on account of sin: He condemned sin in the
flesh, 4that the righteous requirement of
the law might be fulfilled in us who [a]do not
walk according to the flesh but according
to the Spirit. 5For [a]those who live according
to the flesh set their minds on the things
of the flesh, but those *who live* according
to the Spirit, [b]the things of the Spirit. 6For
[a]to be carnally minded *is* death, but to be
spiritually minded *is* life and peace. 7Be-
cause [a]the carnal mind *is* enmity against
God; for it is not subject to the law of God,
[b]nor indeed can be. 8So then, those who are
in the flesh cannot please God.
9But you are not in the flesh but in the
Spirit, if indeed the Spirit of God dwells in
you. Now if anyone does not have the Spirit
of Christ, he is not His. 10And if Christ *is* in
you, the body *is* dead because of sin, but
the Spirit *is* life because of righteousness.
11But if the Spirit of [a]Him who raised Jesus
from the dead dwells in you, [b]He who raised
Christ from the dead will also give life to
your mortal bodies through His Spirit who
dwells in you.

7:10 [a] Lev. 18:5; Ezek. 20:11, 13, 21; Luke 10:28; Rom. 10:5; 2 Cor. 3:7; Gal. 3:12 7:12 [a] Ps. 19:8 7:14 [a] 1 Kin. 21:20, 25; 2 Kin. 17:17; Rom. 6:16 7:15 [a] Rom. 7:19; [Gal. 5:17] 7:18 [a] [Gen. 6:5; 8:21] 7:22 [a] Ps. 1:2 [b] [2 Cor. 4:16; Eph. 3:16; 1 Pet. 3:4] 7:23 [a] Rom. 6:19; [Gal. 5:17]; James 4:1; 1 Pet. 2:11 [b] Rom. 6:13, 19 7:24 [a] [Rom. 8:11; 1 Cor. 15:51, 52; 1 Thess. 4:14–17] 7:25 [a] 1 Cor. 15:57 8:1 [a] Gal. 5:16 [1] NU-Text omits the rest of this verse. 8:2 [a] Rom. 6:18, 22 [b] [1 Cor. 15:45] [c] Rom. 7:24, 25 8:3 [a] Acts 13:39; [Heb. 7:18] [b] [2 Cor. 5:21; Gal. 3:13] 8:4 [a] [Rom. 6:4; 2 Cor. 5:7]; Gal. 5:16, 25; Eph. 4:1; 5:2, 15; [1 John 1:7; 2:6] 8:5 [a] John 3:6 [b] [Gal. 5:22–25] 8:6 [a] Gal. 6:8 8:7 [a] James 4:4 [b] 1 Cor. 2:14 8:11 [a] Acts 2:24; Rom. 6:4 [b] 1 Cor. 6:14

Sonship Through the Spirit

12[a]Therefore, brethren, we are debtors—
not to the flesh, to live according to the
flesh. 13For [a]if you live according to the flesh
you will die; but if by the Spirit you [b]put to
death the deeds of the body, you will live.
14For [a]as many as are led by the Spirit of
God, these are sons of God. 15For [a]you did
not receive the spirit of bondage again [b]to
fear, but you received the [c]Spirit of adoption by whom we cry out, [d]"Abba, Father."
16[a]The Spirit Himself bears witness with
our spirit that we are children of God, 17and
if children, then [a]heirs—heirs of God and
joint heirs with Christ, [b]if indeed we suffer with *Him,* that we may also be glorified together.

From Suffering to Glory

18For I consider that [a]the sufferings of
this present time are not worthy *to be compared* with the glory which shall be revealed
in us. 19For [a]the earnest expectation of the
creation eagerly waits for the revealing of
the sons of God. 20For [a]the creation was
subjected to futility, not willingly, but because of Him who subjected *it* in hope;
21because the creation itself also will be
delivered from the bondage of corruption
into the glorious [a]liberty of the children
of God. 22For we know that the whole creation [a]groans and labors with birth pangs
together until now. 23Not only *that,* but we
also who have [a]the firstfruits of the Spirit,
[b]even we ourselves groan [c]within ourselves,
eagerly waiting for the adoption, the [d]re-
demption of our body. 24For we were saved
in this hope, but [a]hope that is seen is not
hope; for why does one still hope for what
he sees? 25But if we hope for what we do
not see, we eagerly wait for *it* with perseverance.

26Likewise the Spirit also helps in our
weaknesses. For [a]we do not know what we
should pray for as we ought, but [b]the Spirit
Himself makes intercession for us[1] with
groanings which cannot be uttered. 27Now
[a]He who searches the hearts knows what
the mind of the Spirit *is,* because He makes
intercession for the saints [b]according to
the will of God.

28And we know that all things work together for good to those who love God, to
those [a]who are the called according to *His*
purpose. 29For whom [a]He foreknew, [b]He
also predestined [c]*to be* conformed to the
image of His Son, [d]that He might be the
firstborn among many brethren. 30More-
over whom He predestined, these He also
[a]called; whom He called, these He also [b]jus-
tified; and whom He justified, these He also
[c]glorified.

God's Everlasting Love

31What then shall we say to these things?
[a]If God *is* for us, who *can be* against us?
32[a]He who did not spare His own Son, but
[b]delivered Him up for us all, how shall He
not with Him also freely give us all things?
33Who shall bring a charge against God's
elect? [a]*It is* God who justifies. 34[a]Who *is* he
who condemns? *It is* Christ who died, and
furthermore is also risen, [b]who is even at
the right hand of God, [c]who also makes
intercession for us. 35Who shall separate
us from the love of Christ? *Shall* tribulation, or distress, or persecution, or famine, or nakedness, or peril, or sword? 36As
it is written:

> [a]"For Your sake we are killed
> all day long;
> We are accounted as sheep
> for the slaughter."[1]

37[a]Yet in all these things we are more
than conquerors through Him who loved
us. 38For I am persuaded that neither death
nor life, nor angels nor [a]principalities nor
powers, nor things present nor things to
come, 39nor height nor depth, nor any other
created thing, shall be able to separate us

8:12 [a] [Rom. 6:7, 14] **8:13** [a] Gal. 6:8 [b] Eph. 4:22; [Col. 3:5–10] **8:14** [a] [Gal. 5:18] **8:15** [a] [1 Cor. 2:12]; Heb. 2:15 [b] 2 Tim. 1:7 [c] [Is. 56:5] [d] Mark 14:36; Gal. 4:6 **8:16** [a] Eph. 1:13 **8:17** [a] Acts 26:18 [b] Phil. 1:29 **8:18** [a] 2 Cor. 4:17; [1 Pet. 1:6; 4:13] **8:19** [a] [2 Pet. 3:13] **8:20** [a] Gen. 3:17–19 **8:21** [a] [2 Cor. 3:17]; Gal. 5:1, 13 **8:22** [a] Jer. 12:4, 11 **8:23** [a] 2 Cor. 5:5; Eph. 1:14 [b] 2 Cor. 5:2, 4 [c] [Luke 20:36] [d] Luke 21:28; Eph. 1:14; 4:30; [Phil. 3:20, 21] **8:24** [a] Rom. 4:18; 2 Cor. 5:7; Heb. 11:1 **8:26** [a] Matt. 20:22; 2 Cor. 12:8 [b] John 14:16; Rom. 8:15; Eph. 6:18 [1] NU-Text omits *for us.* **8:27** [a] 1 Chr. 28:9 [b] 1 John 5:14 **8:28** [a] 2 Tim. 1:9 **8:29** [a] 2 Tim. 2:19 [b] Rom. 9:23; 1 Cor. 2:7; Eph. 1:5, 11 [c] [2 Cor. 3:18] [d] [Col. 1:15, 18]; Heb. 1:6 **8:30** [a] Rom. 8:28; 9:24; 1 Cor. 1:9; Gal. 1:6, 15; 5:8; Eph. 1:11; 3:11; 2 Thess. 2:14; [Heb. 9:15; 1 Pet. 2:9; 3:9] [b] 1 Cor. 6:11; [Gal. 2:16] [c] John 17:22; Rom. 8:21 **8:31** [a] Num. 14:9 **8:32** [a] Rom. 5:6, 10 [b] [Rom. 4:25] **8:33** [a] Is. 50:8, 9; Rev. 12:10 **8:34** [a] John 3:18 [b] Mark 16:19; Col. 3:1; Heb. 1:3 [c] Heb. 7:25; 9:24 **8:36** [a] Ps. 44:22; Acts 20:24; 1 Cor. 4:9; 15:30; [2 Cor. 1:9; 4:10; 6:9; 11:23] [1] Psalm 44:22 **8:37** [a] John 16:33; 1 Cor. 15:57; 2 Cor. 2:14; 1 John 5:4 **8:38** [a] [1 Cor. 15:24; Eph. 1:21; 1 Pet. 3:22]

from the love of God which is in Christ
Jesus our Lord.

Israel's Rejection of Christ

9 I [a]tell the truth in Christ, I am not lying,
my conscience also bearing me wit-
ness in the Holy Spirit, 2[a]that I have great
sorrow and continual grief in my heart.
3For [a]I could wish that I myself were accursed from Christ for my brethren, my
countrymen[1] according to the flesh, 4who
are Israelites, [a]to whom *pertain* the adoption, [b]the glory, [c]the covenants, [d]the giving of the law, [e]the service *of God,* and [f]the
promises; 5[a]of whom *are* the fathers and
from [b]whom, according to the flesh, Christ
came, [c]who is over all, *the* eternally blessed
God. Amen.

Israel's Rejection and God's Purpose
(Gen. 25:19–23)

6[a]But it is not that the word of God has
taken no effect. For [b]they *are* not all Israel
who *are* of Israel, 7[a]nor *are they* all children
because they are the seed of Abraham; but,
[b]"In Isaac your seed shall be called."[1] 8That
is, those who *are* the children of the flesh,
these *are* not the children of God; but [a]the
children of the promise are counted as the
seed. 9For this *is* the word of promise: [a]"At
this time I will come and Sarah shall have
a son."[1]

10And not only *this,* but when [a]Rebecca
also had conceived by one man, *even* by our
father Isaac 11(for *the children* not yet being
born, nor having done any good or evil, that
the purpose of God according to election
might stand, not of works but of [a]Him who
calls), 12it was said to her, [a]"The older shall
serve the younger."[1] 13As it is written, [a]"Jacob I have loved, but Esau I have hated."[1]

Israel's Rejection and God's Justice

14What shall we say then? [a]*Is there* unrighteousness with God? Certainly not!
15For He says to Moses, [a]"I will have mercy
on whomever I will have mercy, and I will
have compassion on whomever I will have
compassion."[1] 16So then *it is* not of him who
wills, nor of him who runs, but of God who
shows mercy. 17For [a]the Scripture says to
the Pharaoh, [b]"For this very purpose I have
raised you up, that I may show My power
in you, and that My name may be declared
in all the earth."[1] 18Therefore He has mercy
on whom He wills, and whom He wills He
[a]hardens.

19You will say to me then, "Why does He
still find fault? For [a]who has resisted His
will?" 20But indeed, O man, who are you to
reply against God? [a]Will the thing formed
say to him who formed *it,* "Why have you
made me like this?" 21Does not the [a]potter
have power over the clay, from the same
lump to make [b]one vessel for honor and
another for dishonor?

22*What* if God, wanting to show *His* wrath
and to make His power known, endured
with much longsuffering [a]the vessels of
wrath [b]prepared for destruction, 23and that
He might make known [a]the riches of His
glory on the vessels of mercy, which He had
[b]prepared beforehand for glory, 24even us
whom He [a]called, [b]not of the Jews only, but
also of the Gentiles?

25As He says also in Hosea:

[a]"I will call them My people, who
were not My people,
And her beloved, who was
not beloved."[1]
26 "And[a] it shall come to pass in the
place where it was said to them,
'You *are* not My people,'
There they shall be called
sons of the living God."[1]

27Isaiah also cries out concerning Israel:[1]

[a]"Though the number of the children
of Israel be as the sand of the sea,
[b]The remnant will be saved.

9:1 [a] 2 Cor. 1:23 **9:2** [a] Rom. 10:1 **9:3** [a] Ex. 32:32 [1] Or *relatives* **9:4** [a] Ex. 4:22; [Rom. 8:15] [b] 1 Sam. 4:21 [c] Gen. 17:2; Deut. 29:14; Luke 1:72; Acts 3:25 [d] Deut. 4:13; Ps. 147:19 [e] Heb. 9:1, 6 [f] [Acts 2:39; 13:32; Eph. 2:12] **9:5** [a] Deut. 10:15 [b] [Luke 1:34, 35; 3:23] [c] Jer. 23:6 **9:6** [a] Num. 23:19 [b] [John 8:39; Gal. 6:16] **9:7** [a] [John 8:33, 39; Gal. 4:23] [b] Gen. 21:12; Heb. 11:18 [1] Genesis 21:12 **9:8** [a] Gal. 4:28 **9:9** [a] Gen. 18:10, 14; Heb. 11:11 [1] Genesis 18:10, 14 **9:10** [a] Gen. 25:21 **9:11** [a] [Rom. 4:17; 8:28] **9:12** [a] Gen. 25:23 [1] Genesis 25:23 **9:13** [a] Mal. 1:2, 3 [1] Malachi 1:2, 3 **9:14** [a] Deut. 32:4 **9:15** [a] Ex. 33:19 [1] Exodus 33:19 **9:17** [a] Gal. 3:8 [b] Ex. 9:16 [1] Exodus 9:16 **9:18** [a] Ex. 4:21; Deut. 2:30; Josh. 11:20; John 12:40; Rom. 11:7, 25 **9:19** [a] 2 Chr. 20:6; Job 9:12; Dan. 4:35 **9:20** [a] Is. 29:16; Jer. 18:6; Rom. 9:22; 2 Tim. 2:20 **9:21** [a] Prov. 16:4 [b] 2 Tim. 2:20 **9:22** [a] [1 Thess. 5:9] [b] Prov. 16:4; [1 Pet. 2:8] **9:23** [a] [Col. 1:27] [b] [Rom. 8:28–30] **9:24** [a] [Rom. 8:28] [b] Is. 42:6, 7; 49:6; Luke 2:32; Rom. 3:29 **9:25** [a] Hos. 2:23; 1 Pet. 2:10 [1] Hosea 2:23 **9:26** [a] Hos. 1:10 [1] Hosea 1:10 **9:27** [a] Is. 10:22, 23 [b] Rom. 11:5 [1] Isaiah 10:22, 23

28 For He will finish the work and
cut *it* short in righteousness,
[a]Because the LORD will make a
short work upon the earth."[1]

29 And as Isaiah said before:

[a]"Unless the LORD of Sabaoth[1]
had left us a seed,
[b]We would have become like Sodom,
And we would have been
made like Gomorrah."[2]

Present Condition of Israel

30 What shall we say then? [a]That Gentiles, who did not pursue righteousness,
have attained to righteousness, [b]even the
righteousness of faith; 31 but Israel, [a]pursu-
ing the law of righteousness, [b]has not attained to the law of righteousness.[1] 32 Why?
Because *they did* not *seek it* by faith, but as
it were, by the works of the law.[1] For [a]they
stumbled at that stumbling stone. 33 As it
is written:

[a]"Behold, I lay in Zion a stumbling
stone and rock of offense,
And [b]whoever believes on Him
will not be put to shame."[1]

Israel Needs the Gospel

10 Brethren, my heart's desire and
prayer to God for Israel[1] is that they
may be saved. 2 For I bear them witness
[a]that they have a zeal for God, but not according to knowledge. 3 For they being ignorant of [a]God's righteousness, and seeking
to establish their own [b]righteousness, have
not submitted to the righteousness of God.
4 For [a]Christ *is* the end of the law for righteousness to everyone who believes.
5 For Moses writes about the righteousness which is of the law, [a]"The man who
does those things shall live by them."[1] 6 But
the righteousness of faith speaks in this
way, [a]"Do not say in your heart, 'Who will
ascend into heaven?'"[1] (that is, to bring
Christ down *from above*) 7 or, [a]"'Who will
descend into the abyss?'"[1] (that is, to bring
Christ up from the dead). 8 But what does it
say? [a]"The word is near you, in your mouth
and in your heart"[1] (that is, the word of faith
which we preach): 9 that [a]if you confess with
your mouth the Lord Jesus and believe in
your heart that God has raised Him from
the dead, you will be saved. 10 For with the
heart one believes unto righteousness, and
with the mouth confession is made unto
salvation. 11 For the Scripture says, [a]"Whoever believes on Him will not be put to
shame."[1] 12 For [a]there is no distinction between Jew and Greek, for [b]the same Lord
over all [c]is rich to all who call upon Him.
13 For [a]"whoever calls [b]on the name of the
LORD shall be saved."[1]

Israel Rejects the Gospel

14 How then shall they call on Him in
whom they have not believed? And how
shall they believe in Him of whom they
have not heard? And how shall they hear
[a]without a preacher? 15 And how shall they
preach unless they are sent? As it is written:

[a]"How beautiful are the feet of those
who preach the gospel of peace,[1]
Who bring glad tidings
of good things!"[2]

16 But they have not all obeyed the gospel.
For Isaiah says, [a]"LORD, who has believed
our report?"[1] 17 So then faith *comes* by hearing, and hearing by the word of God.
18 But I say, have they not heard? Yes indeed:

[a]"Their sound has gone out
to all the earth,
And their words to the
ends of the world."[1]

9:28 [a] Is. 10:23; 28:22 [1] NU-Text reads *For the LORD will finish the work and cut it short upon the earth.* 9:29 [a] Is. 1:9 [b] Deut. 29:23; Is. 13:19; Jer. 49:18; 50:40; Amos 4:11 [1] Literally, in Hebrew, *Hosts* [2] Isaiah 1:9 9:30 [a] Rom. 4:11 [b] Rom. 1:17; 3:21; 10:6; [Gal. 2:16; 3:24; Phil. 3:9]; Heb. 11:7 9:31 [a] [Rom. 10:2–4] [b] [Gal. 5:4] [1] NU-Text omits *of righteousness.* 9:32 [a] [Luke 2:34; 1 Cor. 1:23] [1] NU-Text reads *by works.* 9:33 [a] [Ps. 118:22]; Is. 8:14; 28:16; [Matt. 21:42; 1 Pet. 2:6–8] [b] Rom. 5:5; 10:11 [1] Isaiah 8:14; 28:16 10:1 [1] NU-Text reads *them.* 10:2 [a] Acts 21:20; Gal. 1:14 10:3 [a] [Rom. 1:17] [b] [Phil. 3:9] 10:4 [a] Matt. 5:17; [Rom. 7:1–4; Gal. 3:24; 4:5] 10:5 [a] Lev. 18:5; Neh. 9:29; Ezek. 20:11, 13, 21; Rom. 7:10; Gal. 3:12 [1] Leviticus 18:5 10:6 [a] Deut. 30:12–14 [1] Deuteronomy 30:12 10:7 [a] Deut. 30:13 [1] Deuteronomy 30:13 10:8 [a] Deut. 30:14 [1] Deuteronomy 30:14 10:9 [a] Matt. 10:32; Luke 12:8; Acts 8:37; Rom. 14:9; [1 Cor. 12:3]; Phil. 2:11 10:11 [a] Is. 28:16; Jer. 17:7; Rom. 9:33 [1] Isaiah 28:16 10:12 [a] Acts 15:9; Rom. 3:22, 29; Gal. 3:28 [b] Acts 10:36; 1 Tim. 2:5 [c] Eph. 1:7 10:13 [a] Joel 2:32; Acts 2:21 [b] Acts 9:14 [1] Joel 2:32 10:14 [a] Acts 8:31; Titus 1:3 10:15 [a] Is. 52:7; Nah. 1:15 [1] NU-Text omits *preach the gospel of peace, Who.* [2] Isaiah 52:7; Nahum 1:15 10:16 [a] Is. 53:1; John 12:38 [1] Isaiah 53:1 10:18 [a] Ps. 19:4; Matt. 24:14; Mark 16:15; Rom. 1:8; Col. 1:6, 23; 1 Thess. 1:8 [1] Psalm 19:4

19 But I say, did Israel not know? First Moses says:

[a]"I will provoke you to jealousy by
those who are not a nation,
I will move you to anger by
a [b]foolish nation."[1]

20 But Isaiah is very bold and says:

[a]"I was found by those who
did not seek Me;
I was made manifest to those
who did not ask for Me."[1]

21 But to Israel he says:

[a]"All day long I have stretched
out My hands
To a disobedient and contrary people."[1]

Israel's Rejection Not Total

11 I say then, [a]has God cast away His people? [b]Certainly not! For [c]I also am an
Israelite, of the seed of Abraham, *of* the
tribe of Benjamin. 2 God has not cast away
His people whom [a]He foreknew. Or do you
not know what the Scripture says of Elijah,
how he pleads with God against Israel, saying, 3 [a]"LORD, they have killed Your prophets and torn down Your altars, and I alone
am left, and they seek my life"?[1] 4 But what
does the divine response say to him? [a]"I
have reserved for Myself seven thousand
men who have not bowed the knee to Baal."[1]
5 [a]Even so then, at this present time there
is a remnant according to the election of
grace. 6 And [a]if by grace, then *it is* no longer of works; otherwise grace is no longer
grace.[1] But if *it is* of works, it is no longer
grace; otherwise work is no longer work.
7 What then? [a]Israel has not obtained
what it seeks; but the elect have obtained
it, and the rest were [b]blinded. 8 Just as it is
written:

[a]"God has given them a spirit of stupor,
[b]Eyes that they should not see
And ears that they should not hear,
To this very day."[1]

9 And David says:

[a]"Let their table become a
snare and a trap,
A stumbling block and a
recompense to them.
10 Let their eyes be darkened, so
that they do not see,
And bow down their back
always."[1]

Israel's Rejection Not Final

11 I say then, have they stumbled that they
should fall? Certainly not! But [a]through
their fall, to provoke them to [b]jealousy, salvation *has come* to the Gentiles. 12 Now if
their fall *is* riches for the world, and their
failure riches for the Gentiles, how much
more their fullness!
13 For I speak to you Gentiles; inasmuch
as [a]I am an apostle to the Gentiles, I magnify my ministry, 14 if by any means I may
provoke to jealousy *those who are* my flesh
and [a]save some of them. 15 For if their being
cast away *is* the reconciling of the world,
what *will* their acceptance *be* [a]but life from
the dead?
16 For if [a]the firstfruit *is* holy, the lump *is*
also *holy;* and if the root *is* holy, so *are* the
branches. 17 And if [a]some of the branches
were broken off, [b]and you, being a wild olive tree, were grafted in among them, and
with them became a partaker of the root
and fatness of the olive tree, 18 [a]do not boast
against the branches. But if you do boast,
remember that you do not support the root,
but the root *supports* you.
19 You will say then, "Branches were broken off that I might be grafted in." 20 Well
said. Because of [a]unbelief they were broken off, and you stand by faith. Do not be
haughty, but fear. 21 For if God did not spare
the natural branches, He may not spare
you either. 22 Therefore consider the goodness and severity of God: on those who fell,

10:19 [a] Deut. 32:21; Rom. 11:11 [b] Titus 3:3 [1] Deuteronomy 32:21 10:20 [a] Is. 65:1; Rom. 9:30 [1] Isaiah 65:1 10:21 [a] Is. 65:2 [1] Isaiah 65:2
11:1 [a] Ps. 94:14; Jer. 46:28 [b] 1 Sam. 12:22; Jer. 31:37 [c] 2 Cor. 11:22; Phil. 3:5 11:2 [a] [Rom. 8:29] 11:3 [a] 1 Kin. 19:10, 14 [1] 1 Kings 19:10, 14
11:4 [a] 1 Kin. 19:18 [1] 1 Kings 19:18 11:5 [a] 2 Kin. 19:4; Rom. 9:27 11:6 [a] Rom. 4:4 [1] NU-Text omits the rest of this verse. 11:7 [a] Rom. 9:31
[b] Mark 6:52; Rom. 9:18; 11:25; 2 Cor. 3:14 11:8 [a] Is. 29:10, 13 [b] Deut. 29:3, 4; Is. 6:9; Matt. 13:13, 14; John 12:40; Acts 28:26, 27
[1] Deuteronomy 29:4; Isaiah 29:10 11:9 [a] Ps. 69:22, 23 11:10 [1] Psalm 69:22, 23 11:11 [a] Is. 42:6, 7; Acts 28:28 [b] Deut. 32:21; Acts 13:46;
Rom. 10:19 11:13 [a] Acts 9:15; 22:21; Gal. 1:16; 2:7–9; Eph. 3:8 11:14 [a] 1 Cor. 9:22; 1 Tim. 4:16; James 5:20 11:15 [a] [Is. 26:16–19]
11:16 [a] Lev. 23:10; [James 1:18] 11:17 [a] Jer. 11:16; [John 15:2] [b] Acts 2:39; [Eph. 2:12] 11:18 [a] [1 Cor. 10:12] 11:20 [a] Heb. 3:19

severity; but toward you, goodness,[1] [a]if you
continue in *His* goodness. Otherwise [b]you
also will be cut off. 23And they also, [a]if they
do not continue in unbelief, will be grafted
in, for God is able to graft them in again.
24For if you were cut out of the olive tree
which is wild by nature, and were grafted
contrary to nature into a cultivated olive
tree, how much more will these, who *are*
natural *branches,* be grafted into their own
olive tree?

25For I do not desire, brethren, that you
should be ignorant of this mystery, lest you
should be [a]wise in your own opinion, that
[b]blindness in part has happened to Israel
[c]until the fullness of the Gentiles has come
in. 26And so all Israel will be saved,[1] as it
is written:

[a]"The Deliverer will come out of Zion,
And He will turn away
ungodliness from Jacob;
27 For [a]this *is* My covenant with
them,
When I take away their sins."[1]

28Concerning the gospel *they are* enemies for your sake, but concerning the
election *they are* [a]beloved for the sake of
the fathers. 29For the gifts and the calling
of God *are* [a]irrevocable. 30For as you [a]were
once disobedient to God, yet have now obtained mercy through their disobedience,
31even so these also have now been disobedient, that through the mercy shown you
they also may obtain mercy. 32For God has
committed them [a]all to disobedience, that
He might have mercy on all.

33Oh, the depth of the riches both of the
wisdom and knowledge of God! How unsearchable *are* His judgments and His ways
past finding out!

34 "For who has known the
[a]mind of the LORD?
Or [b]who has become His counselor?"[1]
35 "Or[a] who has first given to Him
And it shall be repaid to him?"[1]

36For [a]of Him and through Him and to
Him *are* all things, [b]to whom *be* glory forever. Amen.

Living Sacrifices to God

12 I [a]beseech you therefore, brethren, by
the mercies of God, that you present
your bodies [b]a living sacrifice, holy, acceptable to God, *which is* your reasonable service.
2And [a]do not be conformed to this world, but
[b]be transformed by the renewing of your
mind, that you may [c]prove what *is* that good
and acceptable and perfect will of God.

Serve God with Spiritual Gifts

3For I say, [a]through the grace given to
me, to everyone who is among you, [b]not to
think *of himself* more highly than he ought
to think, but to think soberly, as God has
dealt [c]to each one a measure of faith. 4For
[a]as we have many members in one body,
but all the members do not have the same
function, 5so [a]we, *being* many, are one body
in Christ, and individually members of one
another. 6Having then gifts differing according to the grace that is [a]given to us, *let
us use them:* if prophecy, *let us* [b]*prophesy* in
proportion to our faith; 7or ministry, *let us
use it* in *our* ministering; [a]he who teaches,
in teaching; 8[a]he who exhorts, in exhortation; [b]he who gives, with liberality; [c]he who
leads, with diligence; he who shows mercy,
[d]with cheerfulness.

Behave Like a Christian

9[a]*Let* love *be* without hypocrisy. [b]Abhor
what is evil. Cling to what is good. 10[a]*Be*
kindly affectionate to one another with
brotherly love, [b]in honor giving preference
to one another; 11not lagging in diligence,
fervent in spirit, serving the Lord; 12[a]rejoic-
ing in hope, [b]patient in tribulation, [c]con-
tinuing steadfastly in prayer; 13[a]distributing

11:22 [a] 1 Cor. 15:2; Heb. 3:6, 14 [b] [John 15:2] [1] NU-Text adds *of God.* **11:23** [a] [2 Cor. 3:16] **11:25** [a] Rom. 12:16 [b] 2 Cor. 3:14 [c] Luke 21:24; John 10:16; Rom. 11:12 **11:26** [a] Ps. 14:7; Is. 59:20, 21 [1] Or *delivered* **11:27** [a] Is. 27:9; Heb. 8:12 [1] Isaiah 59:20, 21 **11:28** [a] Deut. 7:8; 10:15; Rom. 9:5 **11:29** [a] Num. 23:19 **11:30** [a] [Eph. 2:2] **11:32** [a] Rom. 3:9; [Gal. 3:22] **11:34** [a] Is. 40:13; Jer. 23:18; 1 Cor. 2:16 [b] Job 36:22 [1] Isaiah 40:13; Jeremiah 23:18 **11:35** [a] Job 41:11 [1] Job 41:11 **11:36** [a] [1 Cor. 8:6; 11:12]; Col. 1:16; Heb. 2:10 [b] Heb. 13:21 **12:1** [a] 1 Cor. 1:10; 2 Cor. 10:1–4 [b] Phil. 4:18; Heb. 10:18, 20 **12:2** [a] Matt. 13:22; Gal. 1:4; 1 John 2:15 [b] Eph. 4:23; [Titus 3:5] [c] [1 Thess. 4:3] **12:3** [a] Rom. 1:5; 15:15; 1 Cor. 3:10; 15:10; Gal. 2:9; Eph. 3:7 [b] Prov. 25:27 [c] [Eph. 4:7] **12:4** [a] 1 Cor. 12:12–14; [Eph. 4:4, 16] **12:5** [a] [1 Cor. 10:17]; Gal. 3:28 **12:6** [a] [John 3:27] [b] Acts 11:27 **12:7** [a] Eph. 4:11 **12:8** [a] Acts 15:32 [b] [Matt. 6:1–3] [c] [Acts 20:28] [d] 2 Cor. 9:7 **12:9** [a] 2 Cor. 6:6; 1 Tim. 1:5 [b] Ps. 34:14 **12:10** [a] John 13:34; 1 Thess. 4:9; Heb. 13:1; 2 Pet. 1:7 [b] Rom. 13:7; Phil. 2:3; [1 Pet. 2:17] **12:12** [a] Luke 10:20 [b] Luke 21:19 [c] Luke 18:1 **12:13** [a] 1 Cor. 16:1; Heb. 13:16; 1 Pet. 4:9

RELEASE // HOPE FOR DELIVERANCE

Give It to God

Romans 12:19 // Beloved, do not avenge yourselves, but rather give place to wrath; for it is written, "Vengeance is Mine, I will repay," says the Lord.

Summary Message // Paul wrote the Book of Romans as a letter sent to the church in Rome, the capital city of the Roman Empire. This congregation likely had a high profile and the capacity to influence large numbers of people well beyond that city. Paul, therefore, knew it was essential for this church to be grounded in the gospel.

Paul's letter addresses several broad themes related to discipleship. He offered a series of exhortations in chapter 12, including verses 14–21 focusing on overcoming evil by doing good. Paul likely wanted the church to be prepared to face persecution for their faith. The apostle did not want their energies for serving Christ to be consumed by thoughts or acts of revenge that could dissuade nonbelievers from believing their message.

Practical Application // Revenge is a seductive entrapment that can consume our thoughts. It is hard to turn the other cheek in response to an offense. But this is what we are called to do. Paul wanted the church in Rome and us to understand that God will take care of an offender in due time. If Paul wrote his letter today, he may have put it this way: "Leave it alone. Justice is God's job." But God's timing is not our timing. We normally desire more immediate results.

When we are scarred by another's misdeeds, the unchecked urge for payback rises until it builds a prison that confines us. Thirst for retaliation has resulted in the deaths of too many people. Revenge causes children and families to suffer when they are caught in the middle of feuds and vindictive actions.

In due time, God will deal with every unjust act. God's Word assures us in a myriad of ways, warning us that we will reap what we sow (e.g., Gal. 6:7). This reciprocal principle includes deeds that prompt desire for retaliation. Therefore, revenge is not our weight to bear. Paul's words are God's invitation for us to live free from the burden of seeking revenge.

Fervent Prayer // Father, You are a God of justice. When we are hurt, our first reaction, though, is to return hurt with equal force. We do not always react toward people with Your love. We do not immediately extend compassion when we feel we have been wronged. We turn those feelings over to You. We cannot see the whole story, and we know You are the One to bring justice in every situation. We ask to be relieved of the burden of justice that we have placed on ourselves. We long for the freedom that comes through meeting injustice with love and hatefulness with compassion. In Jesus' name we pray. Amen.

---

to the needs of the saints, [b]given to hospitality.
14 [a]Bless those who persecute you; bless
and do not curse. 15 [a]Rejoice with those who
rejoice, and weep with those who weep.
16 [a]Be of the same mind toward one another.
[b]Do not set your mind on high things, but
associate with the humble. Do not be wise
in your own opinion.
17 [a]Repay no one evil for evil. [b]Have regard for good things in the sight of all men.
18 If it is possible, as much as depends on
you, [a]live peaceably with all men. 19 Beloved,
[a]do not avenge yourselves, but *rather* give
place to wrath; for it is written, [b]"Vengeance *is* Mine, I will repay,"[1] says the Lord.
20 Therefore

[a]"If your enemy is hungry,
feed him;
If he is thirsty, give him a drink;
For in so doing you will heap
coals of fire on his head."[1]

21 Do not be overcome by evil, but [a]over-
come evil with good.

12:13 [b] Matt. 25:35; 1 Tim. 3:2 12:14 [a] [Matt. 5:44]; Luke 6:28; 1 Cor. 4:12 12:15 [a] [1 Cor. 12:26] 12:16 [a] Rom. 15:5; 2 Cor. 13:11; [Phil. 2:2; 4:2]; 1 Pet. 3:8 [b] Jer. 45:5 12:17 [a] [Matt. 5:39]; 1 Pet. 3:9 [b] 2 Cor. 8:21 12:18 [a] Heb. 12:14 12:19 [a] Lev. 19:18 [b] Deut. 32:35; Ps. 94:1; 1 Thess. 4:6; Heb. 10:30 [1] Deuteronomy 32:35 12:20 [a] 2 Kin. 6:22; Prov. 25:21, 22; [Matt. 5:44]; Luke 6:27 [1] Proverbs 25:21, 22 12:21 [a] [Rom. 12:1, 2]

Submit to Government

13 Let every soul be [a]subject to the governing authorities. For there is no
authority except from God, and the authorities that exist are appointed by God.
2Therefore whoever resists [a]the authority resists the ordinance of God, and those
who resist will bring judgment on themselves. 3For rulers are not a terror to good
works, but to evil. Do you want to be unafraid of the authority? [a]Do what is good,
and you will have praise from the same.
4For he is God's minister to you for good.
But if you do evil, be afraid; for he does not
bear the sword in vain; for he is God's minister, an avenger to *execute* wrath on him
who practices evil. 5Therefore [a]*you* must
be subject, not only because of wrath [b]but
also for conscience' sake. 6For because of
this you also pay taxes, for they are God's
ministers attending continually to this very
thing. 7[a]Render therefore to all their due:
taxes to whom taxes *are due,* customs to
whom customs, fear to whom fear, honor
to whom honor.

Love Your Neighbor
(cf. Mark 12:31; James 2:8)

8Owe no one anything except to love
one another, for [a]he who loves another has
fulfilled the law. 9For the commandments,
[a]"You shall not commit adultery," "You shall
not murder," "You shall not steal," "You
shall not bear false witness,"[1] "You shall not
covet,"[2] and if *there is* any other commandment, are *all* summed up in this saying,
namely, [b]"You shall love your neighbor as
yourself."[3] 10Love does no harm to a neighbor; therefore [a]love *is* the fulfillment of
the law.

Put on Christ

11And *do* this, knowing the time, that now
it is high time [a]to awake out of sleep; for
now our salvation *is* nearer than when we
first believed. 12The night is far spent, the
day is at hand. [a]Therefore let us cast off the
works of darkness, and [b]let us put on the
armor of light. 13[a]Let us walk properly, as in
the day, [b]not in revelry and drunkenness,
[c]not in lewdness and lust, [d]not in strife and
envy. 14But [a]put on the Lord Jesus Christ,
and [b]make no provision for the flesh, to
fulfill its lusts.

The Law of Liberty

14 Receive[a] one who is weak in the faith,
but not to disputes over doubtful
things. 2For one believes he [a]may eat all
things, but he who is weak eats *only* vegetables. 3Let not him who eats despise him
who does not eat, and [a]let not him who
does not eat judge him who eats; for God
has received him. 4[a]Who are you to judge
another's servant? To his own master he
stands or falls. Indeed, he will be made to
stand, for God is able to make him stand.
5[a]One person esteems *one* day above another; another esteems every day *alike.* Let
each be fully convinced in his own mind.
6He who [a]observes the day, observes *it* to
the Lord;[1] and he who does not observe
the day, to the Lord he does not observe *it.*
He who eats, eats to the Lord, for [b]he gives
God thanks; and he who does not eat, to the
Lord he does not eat, and gives God thanks.
7For [a]none of us lives to himself, and no one
dies to himself. 8For if we [a]live, we live to
the Lord; and if we die, we die to the Lord.
Therefore, whether we live or die, we are
the Lord's. 9For [a]to this end Christ died
and rose[1] and lived again, that He might be
[b]Lord of both the dead and the living. 10But
why do you judge your brother? Or why do
you show contempt for your brother? For
[a]we shall all stand before the judgment seat
of Christ.[1] 11For it is written:

[a]"*As* I live, says the LORD,
Every knee shall bow to Me,
And every tongue shall
confess to God."[1]

13:1 [a] Titus 3:1; 1 Pet. 2:13 13:2 [a] [Titus 3:1] 13:3 [a] 1 Pet. 2:14 13:5 [a] Eccl. 8:2 [b] Acts 24:16; [1 Pet. 2:13, 19] 13:7 [a] Matt. 22:21; Mark 12:17; Luke 20:25 13:8 [a] [Matt. 7:12; 22:39; John 13:34; Rom. 13:10; Gal. 5:13, 14; 1 Tim. 1:5; James 2:8] 13:9 [a] Ex. 20:13–17; Deut. 5:17–21; Matt. 19:18 [b] Lev. 19:18; Mark 12:31; James 2:8 [1] NU-Text omits *"You shall not bear false witness."* [2] Exodus 20:13–15, 17; Deuteronomy 5:17–19, 21 [3] Leviticus 19:18 13:10 [a] [Matt. 7:12; 22:39, 40; John 13:34]; Rom. 13:8; Gal. 5:14; James 2:8 13:11 [a] Mark 13:37; [1 Cor. 15:34; Eph. 5:14]; 1 Thess. 5:6 13:12 [a] Eph. 5:11 [b] [2 Cor. 6:7; 10:4; Eph. 6:11, 13; 1 Thess. 5:8] 13:13 [a] Phil. 4:8 [b] Prov. 23:20 [c] [1 Cor. 6:9] [d] James 3:14 13:14 [a] Job 29:14; Gal. 3:27; [Eph. 4:24; Col. 3:10, 12] [b] [Gal. 5:16]; 1 Pet. 2:11 14:1 [a] [Rom. 14:2; 15:1; 1 Cor. 8:9; 9:22] 14:2 [a] 1 Cor. 10:25; [Titus 1:15] 14:3 [a] [Rom. 14:10, 13; Col. 2:16] 14:4 [a] Rom. 9:20; James 4:11, 12 14:5 [a] Gal. 4:10 14:6 [a] Gal. 4:10 [b] Matt. 14:19; 15:36; [1 Cor. 10:31; 1 Tim. 4:3] [1] NU-Text omits the rest of this sentence. 14:7 [a] [1 Cor. 6:19; Gal. 2:20]; 1 Thess. 5:10; [1 Pet. 4:2] 14:8 [a] 2 Cor. 5:14, 15 14:9 [a] 2 Cor. 5:15 [b] Acts 10:36 [1] NU-Text omits *and rose.* 14:10 [a] Rom. 2:16; 2 Cor. 5:10 [1] NU-Text reads *of God.* 14:11 [a] Is. 45:23; [Phil. 2:10, 11] [1] Isaiah 45:23

12 So then [a]each of us shall give account
of himself to God. 13 Therefore let us not
judge one another anymore, but rather resolve this, [a]not to put a stumbling block or
a cause to fall in *our* brother's way.

The Law of Love

14 I know and am convinced by the Lord
Jesus [a]that *there is* nothing unclean of itself; but to him who considers anything
to be unclean, to him *it is* unclean. 15 Yet
if your brother is grieved because of *your*
food, you are no longer walking in love.
[a]Do not destroy with your food the one for
whom Christ died. 16 [a]Therefore do not let
your good be spoken of as evil; 17 [a]for the
kingdom of God is not eating and drinking,
but righteousness and [b]peace and joy in
the Holy Spirit. 18 For he who serves Christ
in these things[1] [a]*is* acceptable to God and
approved by men.

19 [a]Therefore let us pursue the things
which make for peace and the things by
which [b]one may edify another. 20 [a]Do not
destroy the work of God for the sake of
food. [b]All things indeed *are* pure, [c]but *it*
is evil for the man who eats with offense.
21 *It is* good neither to eat [a]meat nor drink
wine nor *do anything* by which your brother
stumbles or is offended or is made weak.[1]
22 Do you have faith? Have[1] *it* to yourself before God. [a]Happy *is* he who does not condemn himself in what he approves. 23 But
he who doubts is condemned if he eats, because *he does* not *eat* from faith; for [a]what-
ever *is* not from faith is sin.[1]

Bearing Others' Burdens

15 We [a]then who are strong ought to
bear with the scruples of the weak,
and not to please ourselves. 2 [a]Let each of
us please *his* neighbor for *his* good, leading to edification. 3 [a]For even Christ did not
please Himself; but as it is written, [b]"The reproaches of those who reproached You fell
on Me."[1] 4 For [a]whatever things were written
before were written for our learning, that
we through the patience and comfort of
the Scriptures might have hope. 5 [a]Now may
the God of patience and comfort grant you
to be like-minded toward one another, according to Christ Jesus, 6 that you may [a]with
one mind *and* one mouth glorify the God
and Father of our Lord Jesus Christ.

Glorify God Together

7 Therefore [a]receive one another, just [b]as
Christ also received us,[1] to the glory of God.
8 Now I say that [a]Jesus Christ has become
a servant to the circumcision for the truth
of God, [b]to confirm the promises *made* to
the fathers, 9 and [a]that the Gentiles might
glorify God for *His* mercy, as it is written:

[b]"For this reason I will confess to
You among the Gentiles,
And sing to Your name."[1]

10 And again he says:

[a]"Rejoice, O Gentiles, with His people!"[1]

11 And again:

[a]"Praise the LORD, all you Gentiles!
Laud Him, all you peoples!"[1]

12 And again, Isaiah says:

[a]"There shall be a root of Jesse;
And He who shall rise to reign
over the Gentiles,
In Him the Gentiles shall hope."[1]

13 Now may the God of hope fill you with
all [a]joy and peace in believing, that you may
abound in hope by the power of the Holy
Spirit.

From Jerusalem to Illyricum

14 Now [a]I myself am confident concerning you, my brethren, that you also are full

---

14:12 [a] Matt. 12:36; 16:27; [Gal. 6:5]; 1 Pet. 4:5 14:13 [a] 1 Cor. 8:9 14:14 [a] 1 Cor. 10:25 14:15 [a] Rom. 14:20; 1 Cor. 8:11 14:16 [a] [Rom. 12:17] 14:17 [a] 1 Cor. 8:8 [b] [Rom. 8:6] 14:18 [a] 2 Cor. 8:21; Phil. 4:8; 1 Pet. 2:12 [1] NU-Text reads *this*. 14:19 [a] Ps. 34:14; Rom. 12:18; 1 Cor. 7:15; 2 Tim. 2:22; Heb. 12:14 [b] 1 Cor. 14:12; 1 Thess. 5:11 14:20 [a] Rom. 14:15 [b] Acts 10:15 [c] 1 Cor. 8:9–12 14:21 [a] 1 Cor. 8:13 [1] NU-Text omits *or is offended or is made weak*. 14:22 [a] [1 John 3:21] [1] NU-Text reads *The faith which you have—have*. 14:23 [a] Titus 1:15 [1] M-Text puts Romans 16:25–27 here. 15:1 [a] Rom. 14:1; [Gal. 6:1, 2]; 1 Thess. 5:14 15:2 [a] 1 Cor. 9:22; 10:24, 33; 2 Cor. 13:9 15:3 [a] Matt. 26:39; [Phil. 2:5–8] [b] Ps. 69:9 [1] Psalm 69:9 15:4 [a] Rom. 4:23, 24; 1 Cor. 10:11; 2 Tim. 3:16, 17 15:5 [a] 1 Cor. 1:10; Phil. 1:27 15:6 [a] Acts 4:24 15:7 [a] Rom. 14:1, 3 [b] Rom. 5:2 [1] NU-Text and M-Text read *you*. 15:8 [a] Matt. 15:24; Acts 3:26 [b] [Rom. 4:16]; 2 Cor. 1:20 15:9 [a] John 10:16 [b] 2 Sam. 22:50; Ps. 18:49 [1] 2 Samuel 22:50; Psalm 18:49 15:10 [a] Deut. 32:43 [1] Deuteronomy 32:43 15:11 [a] Ps. 117:1 [1] Psalm 117:1 15:12 [a] Is. 11:1, 10 [1] Isaiah 11:10 15:13 [a] Rom. 12:12; 14:17 15:14 [a] 2 Pet. 1:12

of goodness, [b]filled with all knowledge, able
also to admonish one another.[1] 15Neverthe-
less, brethren, I have written more boldly
to you on *some* points, as reminding you,
[a]because of the grace given to me by God,
16that [a]I might be a minister of Jesus Christ
to the Gentiles, ministering the gospel of
God, that the [b]offering of the Gentiles might
be acceptable, sanctified by the Holy Spirit.
17Therefore I have reason to glory in Christ
Jesus [a]in the things *which pertain* to God.
18For I will not dare to speak of any of those
things [a]which Christ has not accomplished
through me, in word and deed, [b]to make the
Gentiles obedient— 19[a]in mighty signs and
wonders, by the power of the Spirit of God,
so that from Jerusalem and round about
to Illyricum I have fully preached the gospel of Christ. 20And so I have made it my
aim to preach the gospel, not where Christ
was named, [a]lest I should build on another
man's foundation, 21but as it is written:

[a]"To whom He was not announced,
they shall see;
And those who have not heard
shall understand."[1]

Plan to Visit Rome

22For this reason [a]I also have been much
hindered from coming to you. 23But now
no longer having a place in these parts, and
[a]having a great desire these many years to
come to you, 24whenever I journey to Spain,
I shall come to you.[1] For I hope to see you
on my journey, [a]and to be helped on my
way there by you, if first I may [b]enjoy your
company for a while. 25But now [a]I am going to Jerusalem to minister to the saints.
26For [a]it pleased those from Macedonia and
Achaia to make a certain contribution for
the poor among the saints who are in Jerusalem. 27It pleased them indeed, and they
are their debtors. For [a]if the Gentiles have
been partakers of their spiritual things,
[b]their duty is also to minister to them in
material things. 28Therefore, when I have
performed this and have sealed to them
[a]this fruit, I shall go by way of you to Spain.
29[a]But I know that when I come to you, I
shall come in the fullness of the blessing
of the gospel[1] of Christ.

30Now I beg you, brethren, through the
Lord Jesus Christ, and [a]through the love
of the Spirit, [b]that you strive together with
me in prayers to God for me, 31[a]that I may
be delivered from those in Judea who do
not believe, and that [b]my service for Jerusalem may be acceptable to the saints,
32[a]that I may come to you with joy [b]by the
will of God, and may [c]be refreshed together
with you. 33Now [a]the God of peace *be* with
you all. Amen.

#OXYGEN

ROMANS 15:31–32

Hope for Deliverance

You are worthy of love and belonging. The people who support you will be there for you. When you encounter others who do not believe in your worth, just pray. God will be an umbrella of protection over you. Renew your mind, **breathe**, and **hope for deliverance.**

Sister Phoebe Commended

16 I commend to you Phoebe our sister, who is a servant of the church in
[a]Cenchrea, 2[a]that you may receive her in
the Lord [b]in a manner worthy of the saints,
and assist her in whatever business she
has need of you; for indeed she has been a
helper of many and of myself also.

Greeting Roman Saints

3Greet [a]Priscilla and Aquila, my fellow
workers in Christ Jesus, 4who risked their

15:14 [b] 1 Cor. 1:5; 8:1, 7, 10 [1] M-Text reads *others.* 15:15 [a] Rom. 1:5; 12:3 15:16 [a] Acts 9:15; Rom. 11:13 [b] [Is. 66:20] 15:17 [a] Heb. 2:17; 5:1 15:18 [a] Acts 15:12; 21:19; 2 Cor. 3:5; Gal. 2:8 [b] Rom. 1:5 15:19 [a] Acts 19:11 15:20 [a] 1 Cor. 3:10; [2 Cor. 10:13, 15, 16] 15:21 [a] Is. 52:15 [1] Isaiah 52:15 15:22 [a] Rom. 1:13; 1 Thess. 2:17, 18 15:23 [a] Acts 19:21; 23:11; Rom. 1:10, 11 15:24 [a] Acts 15:3 [b] Rom. 1:12 [1] NU-Text omits *I shall come to you* (and joins *Spain* with the next sentence). 15:25 [a] Acts 19:21 15:26 [a] 1 Cor. 16:1; 2 Cor. 8:1–15 15:27 [a] Rom. 11:17 [b] 1 Cor. 9:11 15:28 [a] Phil. 4:17 15:29 [a] [Rom. 1:11] [1] NU-Text omits *of the gospel.* 15:30 [a] Phil. 2:1 [b] 2 Cor. 1:11; Col. 4:12 15:31 [a] 2 Tim. 3:11; 4:17 [b] 2 Cor. 8:4 15:32 [a] Rom. 1:10 [b] Acts 18:21 [c] 1 Cor. 16:18 15:33 [a] Rom. 16:20; 1 Cor. 14:33; 2 Cor. 13:11; Phil. 4:9; [1 Thess. 5:23]; 2 Thess. 3:16; Heb. 13:20 16:1 [a] Acts 18:18 16:2 [a] Phil. 2:29 [b] Phil. 1:27 16:3 [a] Acts 18:2, 18, 26; 1 Cor. 16:19; 2 Tim. 4:19

own necks for my life, to whom not only I give thanks, but also all the churches of the Gentiles. 5Likewise *greet* [a]the church that is in their house.

Greet my beloved Epaenetus, who is [b]the firstfruits of Achaia[1] to Christ. 6Greet Mary, who labored much for us. 7Greet Andronicus and Junia, my countrymen and my fellow prisoners, who are of note among the [a]apostles, who also [b]were in Christ before me.

8Greet Amplias, my beloved in the Lord. 9Greet Urbanus, our fellow worker in Christ, and Stachys, my beloved. 10Greet Apelles, approved in Christ. Greet those who are of the *household* of Aristobulus. 11Greet Herodion, my countryman.[1] Greet those who are of the *household* of Narcissus who are in the Lord.

12Greet Tryphena and Tryphosa, who have labored in the Lord. Greet the beloved Persis, who labored much in the Lord. 13Greet Rufus, [a]chosen in the Lord, and his mother and mine. 14Greet Asyncritus, Phlegon, Hermas, Patrobas, Hermes, and the brethren who are with them. 15Greet Philologus and Julia, Nereus and his sister, and Olympas, and all the saints who are with them.

16[a]Greet one another with a holy kiss. The[1] churches of Christ greet you.

Avoid Divisive Persons

17Now I urge you, brethren, note those [a]who cause divisions and offenses, contrary to the doctrine which you learned, and [b]avoid them. 18For those who are such do not serve our Lord Jesus[1] Christ, but [a]their own belly, and [b]by smooth words and flattering speech deceive the hearts of the simple. 19For [a]your obedience has become known to all. Therefore I am glad on your behalf; but I want you to be [b]wise in what is good, and simple concerning evil. 20And [a]the God of peace [b]will crush Satan under your feet shortly.

[c]The grace of our Lord Jesus Christ *be* with you. Amen.

Greetings from Paul's Friends

21[a]Timothy, my fellow worker, and [b]Lucius, [c]Jason, and [d]Sosipater, my countrymen, greet you.

22I, Tertius, who wrote *this* epistle, greet you in the Lord.

23[a]Gaius, my host and *the host* of the whole church, greets you. [b]Erastus, the treasurer of the city, greets you, and Quartus, a brother. 24[a]The grace of our Lord Jesus Christ *be* with you all. Amen.[1]

Benediction

25Now [a]to Him who is able to establish you [b]according to my gospel and the preaching of Jesus Christ, [c]according to the revelation of the mystery [d]kept secret since the world began 26but [a]now made manifest, and by the prophetic Scriptures made known to all nations, according to the commandment of the everlasting God, for [b]obedience to the faith— 27to [a]God, alone wise, *be* glory through Jesus Christ forever. Amen.[1]

16:5 [a] 1 Cor. 16:19; Col. 4:15; Philem. 2 [b] 1 Cor. 16:15 [1] NU-Text reads *Asia.* 16:7 [a] Acts 1:13, 26 [b] Rom. 8:11; 16:3, 9, 10; 2 Cor. 5:17; 12:2; Gal. 1:22 16:11 [1] Or *relative* 16:13 [a] 2 John 1 16:16 [a] 1 Cor. 16:20; 2 Cor. 13:12; 1 Thess. 5:26; 1 Pet. 5:14 [1] NU-Text reads *All the churches.* 16:17 [a] [Acts 15:1] [b] [1 Cor. 5:9] 16:18 [a] Phil. 3:19 [b] Col. 2:4; 2 Pet. 2:3 [1] NU-Text and M-Text omit *Jesus.* 16:19 [a] Rom. 1:8 [b] Jer. 4:22; Matt. 10:16; 1 Cor. 14:20 16:20 [a] Rom. 15:33 [b] Gen. 3:15 [c] 1 Cor. 16:23; 2 Cor. 13:14; Gal. 6:18; Phil. 4:23; 1 Thess. 5:28; 2 Thess. 3:18; Rev. 22:21 16:21 [a] Acts 16:1; Heb. 13:23 [b] Acts 13:1 [c] Acts 17:5 [d] Acts 20:4 16:23 [a] 1 Cor. 1:14 [b] Acts 19:22; 2 Tim. 4:20 16:24 [a] 1 Thess. 5:28 [1] NU-Text omits this verse. 16:25 [a] [Eph. 3:20; Jude 24] [b] Rom. 2:16 [c] Matt. 13:35; Rom. 11:25; 1 Cor. 2:1, 7; 4:1; Eph. 1:9 [d] Col. 1:26; 2:2; 4:3; [1 Tim. 3:16] 16:26 [a] Eph. 1:9 [b] [Acts 6:7]; Rom. 1:5 16:27 [a] Jude 25 [1] M-Text puts Romans 16:25–27 after Romans 14:23.

THE FIRST EPISTLE OF PAUL TO THE

CORINTHIANS

OVERVIEW

At the conclusion of the Gospels, Jesus Christ instructed His followers to go and "make disciples of all the nations" (Matt. 28:19). The apostle Paul was not present the day Jesus spoke these words; however, no biblical figure likely logged more miles in service to the Great Commission than he did. Over approximately fifteen years, Paul traveled the Mediterranean region establishing and equipping churches on four separate missionary journeys. On his second and third journeys, Paul traveled through modern-day Turkey, including the coastal city of Corinth. He spent eighteen months there and founded its church.

Paul's letters to the church in Corinth must be understood within the cultural context of this diverse city. When Paul arrived in AD 50, Corinth already had a one-thousand-year history and was a thriving society in many ways:

- **Economics**
  Corinth was a coastal city sandwiched between an eastern and western harbor, allowing it to facilitate brisk commerce and generate broad wealth. Corinthian water canals were used to distribute goods throughout the surrounding areas, generating further wealth through taxes and fees. Corinth was both an economic and a political center with several Roman officials inhabiting the city. Paul spent his days as a local tentmaker during his residency.
- **Population**
  Corinth had both a Greek and Roman history. The official language was Latin, but many of its residents continued to speak Greek after the Roman Empire took control. Approximately two hundred thousand people lived within the city's borders at the time of Paul's initial visit.
- **Culture**
  Corinth was the host city for an annual athletic competition that rivaled the more widely known Olympic Games. The administration of these games was conducted by citizens of Corinth, attesting to the city's ability to accommodate large crowds.
- **Religion**
  Corinth was notorious for sexual immorality and promiscuity. Being the site of many pagan temples, religious pluralism was widespread throughout the city. These pagan and hybrid faiths presented unique challenges that were often the focus of Paul's writings to the church there. Paul also contended with rejection by Jewish Corinthians. He was attacked and dragged before the Roman ruler for allegedly contradicting Jewish law (see Acts 18:12–13).

As with all of Paul's writings, he addressed several themes in this letter to the Corinthians, including controversies and conflicts among believers. In addressing these concerns, Paul provides the most comprehensive description of the unconditional agape love of God that believers are to express toward one another too. Paul concluded his treatise on godly love with these words: "And now abide faith, hope, love, these three; but the greatest of these is love" (1 Cor. 13:13).

BREATHE IT IN

Churches in New Testament days were generally identified, or named, by the city in which they were located. Most often, churches did not meet in a large, central location. Instead, small groups met in various homes. As mentioned in the Overview, the city of Corinth was notorious for indulgence, sexual promiscuity, debauchery, and lewd behavior. In fact, the word *corinthianize* was used as a synonym for practicing this ungodly behavior. According to our contemporary standard, to name or brand a church by using "Corinth" would be wholly unacceptable. Corinth represented everything the church did *not* want to be associated with.

Similarly, our contemporary use of a cross as the most recognized Christian symbol was not present during biblical times. Instead, the cross was a symbol of punishment, humiliation, and death by crucifixion. The cross that we incorporate into our jewelry, clothing, Bible covers, and buildings was the mark of society's worst criminals. This means that Jesus' manner of death was especially heinous (see Phil. 2:8). But when Jesus rose from the dead on the third day, everything changed. Paul wrote about the impact of that day, proclaiming that "death is swallowed up in victory" (1 Cor. 15:54). The cross no longer represented death; it was transformed into a symbol of victory. Even the salacious name "Corinth" could therefore be transformed by the blood of Jesus. The Corinthian church had the opportunity to create a reputation of godliness from one that was marked by godlessness.

Is there anything about your family history, your family's reputation, or your personal track record that needs to be transformed? Have you ever been insultingly accused of being just like your father? Do you come from a history of failure or shame? Are there any patterns that need to be broken? Even if your family has suffered from major strongholds of sin for generations, the resurrection brings reconciliation, redemption, and renewal. You are no longer bound to any burden that exists in your bloodline by the power of the blood of Jesus! Like the Corinthian church, you can go forward and allow God to make your name great as you make His name great.

†

THE FIRST EPISTLE OF PAUL TO THE

CORINTHIANS

Greeting

1 Paul, [a]called *to be* an apostle of Jesus Christ [b]through the will of God, and [c]Sosthenes *our* brother,

2 To the church of God which is at Corinth, to those who [a]are sanctified in Christ Jesus, [b]called *to be* saints, with all who in every place call on the name of Jesus Christ [c]our Lord, [d]both theirs and ours:

3 [a]Grace to you and peace from God our Father and the Lord Jesus Christ.

Spiritual Gifts at Corinth

4 [a]I thank my God always concerning you for the grace of God which was given to you by Christ Jesus, 5 that you were enriched in everything by Him [a]in all utterance and all knowledge, 6 even as [a]the testimony of Christ was confirmed in you, 7 so that you come short in no gift, eagerly [a]waiting for the revelation of our Lord Jesus Christ, 8 [a]who will also confirm you to the end, [b]*that you may be* blameless in the day of our Lord Jesus Christ. 9 [a]God *is* faithful, by whom you were called into [b]the fellowship of His Son, Jesus Christ our Lord.

Sectarianism Is Sin

10 Now I plead with you, brethren, by the name of our Lord Jesus Christ, [a]that you all speak the same thing, and *that* there be no divisions among you, but *that* you be perfectly joined together in the same mind and in the same judgment. 11 For it has been declared to me concerning you, my brethren, by those of Chloe's *household,* that there are contentions among you. 12 Now I say this, that [a]each of you says, "I am of Paul," or "I am of [b]Apollos," or "I am of [c]Cephas," or "I am of Christ." 13 [a]Is Christ divided? Was Paul crucified for you? Or were you baptized in the name of Paul?

14 I thank God that I baptized [a]none of you except [b]Crispus and [c]Gaius, 15 lest anyone should say that I had baptized in my own name. 16 Yes, I also baptized the household of [a]Stephanas. Besides, I do not know whether I baptized any other. 17 For Christ did not send me to baptize, but to preach the gospel, [a]not with wisdom of words, lest the cross of Christ should be made of no effect.

Christ the Power and Wisdom of God (cf. Is. 29:14)

18 For the message of the cross is [a]foolishness to [b]those who are perishing, but to us [c]who are being saved it is the [d]power of God. 19 For it is written:

[a]"I will destroy the wisdom of the wise,
And bring to nothing the
understanding of the prudent."[1]

20 [a]Where *is* the wise? Where *is* the scribe? Where *is* the disputer of this age? [b]Has not God made foolish the wisdom of this world? 21 For since, in the [a]wisdom of God, the world through wisdom did not know God, it pleased God through the

---

1:1 [a] Rom. 1:1 [b] 2 Cor. 1:1 [c] Acts 18:17 1:2 [a] [Acts 15:9] [b] Rom. 1:7; Eph. 4:1; 1 Thess. 2:12 [c] [1 Cor. 8:6] [d] [Rom. 3:22] 1:3 [a] Rom. 1:7 1:4 [a] Rom. 1:8 1:5 [a] [1 Cor. 12:8] 1:6 [a] 2 Thess. 1:10; 1 Tim. 2:6; 2 Tim. 1:8; Rev. 1:2 1:7 [a] Luke 17:30; Rom. 8:19, 23; Phil. 3:20; Titus 2:13; [2 Pet. 3:12] 1:8 [a] 1 Thess. 3:13; 5:23 [b] Phil. 1:6; Col. 1:22; 2:7 1:9 [a] Deut. 7:9; Is. 49:7; 1 Cor. 10:13; 2 Cor. 1:18; 1 Thess. 5:24; 2 Thess. 3:3 [b] [John 15:4] 1:10 [a] 2 Cor. 13:11; 1 Pet. 3:8 1:12 [a] Matt. 3:8–10; 1 Cor. 3:4 [b] Acts 18:24; 1 Cor. 3:22 [c] John 1:42; 1 Cor. 3:22; 9:5; 15:5 1:13 [a] 2 Cor. 11:4 1:14 [a] John 4:2 [b] Acts 18:8 [c] Rom. 16:23 1:16 [a] 1 Cor. 16:15, 17 1:17 [a] [1 Cor. 2:1, 4, 13] 1:18 [a] 1 Cor. 2:14 [b] 2 Cor. 2:15 [c] [1 Cor. 15:2] [d] Rom. 1:16; 1 Cor. 1:24 1:19 [a] Is. 29:14 [1] Isaiah 29:14 1:20 [a] Is. 19:12; 33:18 [b] Job 12:17; Matt. 13:22; 1 Cor. 2:6, 8; 3:18, 19 1:21 [a] Dan. 2:20; [Rom. 11:33]

foolishness of the message preached to
save those who believe. 22For [a]Jews request
a sign, and Greeks seek after wisdom; 23but
we preach Christ crucified, [a]to the Jews a
stumbling block and to the Greeks[1] [b]fool-
ishness, 24but to those who are called, both
Jews and Greeks, Christ [a]the power of God
and [b]the wisdom of God. 25Because the foolishness of God is wiser than men, and the
weakness of God is stronger than men.

Glory Only in the Lord

26For you see your calling, brethren, [a]that
not many wise according to the flesh, not
many mighty, not many noble, *are called.*
27But [a]God has chosen the foolish things of
the world to put to shame the wise, and God
has chosen the weak things of the world to
put to shame the things which are mighty;
28and the base things of the world and the
things which are despised God has chosen, and the things which are not, to bring
to nothing the things that are, 29that no
flesh should glory in His presence. 30But of
Him you are in Christ Jesus, who became
for us wisdom from God—and [a]righteous-
ness and sanctification and redemption—
31that, as it is written, [a]"He who glories, let
him glory in the LORD."[1]

Christ Crucified

2 And I, brethren, when I came to you, did
not come with excellence of speech or
of wisdom declaring to you the testimony[1]
of God. 2For I determined not to know anything among you [a]except Jesus Christ and
Him crucified. 3[a]I was with you [b]in weakness, in fear, and in much trembling. 4And
my speech and my preaching [a]*were* not with
persuasive words of human[1] wisdom, [b]but
in demonstration of the Spirit and of power,
5that your faith should not be in the wisdom
of men but in the [a]power of God.

Spiritual Wisdom

6However, we speak wisdom among
those who are mature, yet not the wisdom
of this age, nor of the rulers of this age,
who are coming to nothing. 7But we speak
the wisdom of God in a mystery, the hidden *wisdom* which God ordained before the
ages for our glory, 8which none of the rulers
of this age knew; for [a]had they known, they
would not have [b]crucified the Lord of glory.
9But as it is written:

[a]"Eye has not seen, nor ear heard,
Nor have entered into
the heart of man
The things which God has prepared
for those who love Him."[1]

10But [a]God has revealed *them* to us through
His Spirit. For the Spirit searches all things,
yes, the deep things of God. 11For what man
knows the things of a man except the [a]spirit
of the man which is in him? [b]Even so no
one knows the things of God except the
Spirit of God. 12Now we have received, not
the spirit of the world, but [a]the Spirit who
is from God, that we might know the things
that have been freely given to us by God.
13These things we also speak, not in
words which man's wisdom teaches but
which the Holy[1] Spirit teaches, comparing
spiritual things with spiritual. 14[a]But the
natural man does not receive the things
of the Spirit of God, for they are foolishness to him; nor can he know *them,* because they are spiritually discerned. 15But
he who is spiritual judges all things, yet he
himself is *rightly* judged by no one. 16For
[a]"who has known the mind of the LORD
that he may instruct Him?"[1] [b]But we have
the mind of Christ.

Sectarianism Is Carnal

3 And I, brethren, could not speak to you
as to spiritual *people* but as to carnal, as
to [a]babes in Christ. 2I fed you with [a]milk and
not with solid food; [b]for until now you were
not able *to receive it,* and even now you are
still not able; 3for you are still carnal. For
where *there are* envy, strife, and divisions
among you, are you not carnal and behaving like *mere* men? 4For when one says, "I

1:22 [a] Matt. 12:38; Mark 8:11; John 2:18; 4:48 **1:23** [a] Is. 8:14; Luke 2:34; John 6:60; Gal. 5:11; [1 Pet. 2:8] [b] [1 Cor. 2:14] [1] NU-Text reads *Gentiles.* **1:24** [a] [Rom. 1:4] [b] Col. 2:3 **1:26** [a] John 7:48 **1:27** [a] Ps. 8:2; Matt. 11:25 **1:30** [a] Jer. 23:5; 33:16; [2 Cor. 5:21; Phil. 3:9] **1:31** [a] Jer. 9:23, 24; 2 Cor. 10:17 [1] Jeremiah 9:24 **2:1** [1] NU-Text reads *mystery.* **2:2** [a] 1 Cor. 1:23; Gal. 6:14 **2:3** [a] Acts 18:1 [b] [2 Cor. 4:7] **2:4** [a] 2 Pet. 1:16 [b] Rom. 15:19; 1 Cor. 4:20 [1] NU-Text omits *human.* **2:5** [a] Rom. 1:16; 1 Thess. 1:5 **2:8** [a] Luke 23:34 [b] Matt. 27:33–50 **2:9** [a] [Is. 64:4; 65:17] [1] Isaiah 64:4 **2:10** [a] Matt. 11:25; 13:11; 16:17; [Gal. 1:12; Eph. 3:3, 5] **2:11** [a] Job 32:8; Eccl. 12:7; [1 Cor. 6:20; James 2:26] [b] Rom. 11:33 **2:12** [a] [Rom. 8:15] **2:13** [1] NU-Text omits *Holy.* **2:14** [a] Matt. 16:23 **2:16** [a] Job 15:8; Is. 40:13; Rom. 11:34 [b] [John 15:15] [1] Isaiah 40:13 **3:1** [a] 1 Cor. 2:6; Eph. 4:14; Heb. 5:13 **3:2** [a] Heb. 5:12; 1 Pet. 2:2 [b] John 16:12

ELEVATE YOUR IDENTITY

INHALE

To those in my circle, I am looked on as the deadweight. I am the only one in our neighborhood who is not a US citizen. People never come out and say not being born in America makes me less than, but I have overheard the discussions about my accent and culture. How can I believe in myself when the way others see me makes me doubt my worth? If my identity is in Christ and I know He loves me, why doesn't He help me feel good about who He made me to be?

EXHALE

The secret to answering your question is no secret at all. You are not less than anyone else because you weren't born a US citizen. Being a citizen of a nation matters, but it is far from what matters most. The problem here is that there are people who are unable to see and treat others with respect, particularly those who don't look or sound like them. Unfortunately, the world is filled with people like this.

The key, then, is not to focus on the problem of others but to focus instead on the problem of how you might not see yourself rightly. Your identity and sense of value are not found in what others say or think about you. Instead, true worth is found in what God says about you. He created you. He crafted and designed you to be who you are. And He never makes mistakes. Developing a strong and proper sense of who you are—and whose you are—will empower you to see the truth and untruth of any statement made about you or others who look and sound like you.

Remember, God is not the author of you feeling bad about yourself. The Enemy is. He delights in destroying peace and confidence in God's people. And to do that, he will often use the world's systems and thinking to attack us. Know who is ultimately speaking these negative things to you and why. What you are being told is just not true. In 1 Corinthians 2:13, Paul contrasts the world's thinking with ours: "These things we also speak, not in words which man's wisdom teaches but which the Holy Spirit teaches, comparing spiritual things with spiritual." The world's wisdom is that your value is found in the things of the world. But none of that is true. Know that there are people who accept you just the way you are and, most importantly, that in Christ God does!

am of Paul," and another, "I *am* of Apollos,"
are you not carnal?

Watering, Working, Warning

5 Who then is Paul, and who *is* Apollos,
but [a]ministers through whom you believed,
as the Lord gave to each one? 6 [a]I planted,
[b]Apollos watered, [c]but God gave the increase. 7 So then [a]neither he who plants is
anything, nor he who waters, but God who
gives the increase. 8 Now he who plants and
he who waters are one, [a]and each one will
receive his own reward according to his
own labor.
9 For [a]we are God's fellow workers; you
are God's field, *you are* [b]God's building.
10 [a]According to the grace of God which was
given to me, as a wise master builder I have
laid [b]the foundation, and another builds
on it. But let each one take heed how he
builds on it. 11 For no other foundation can
anyone lay than [a]that which is laid, [b]which
is Jesus Christ. 12 Now if anyone builds on
this foundation *with* gold, silver, precious
stones, wood, hay, straw, 13 each one's work
will become clear; for the Day [a]will declare
it, because [b]it will be revealed by fire; and
the fire will test each one's work, of what
sort it is. 14 If anyone's work which he has
built on *it* endures, he will receive a reward.

3:5 [a] Rom. 15:16; 2 Cor. 3:3, 6; 4:1; 5:18; 6:4; Eph. 3:7; Col. 1:25; 1 Tim. 1:12 3:6 [a] Acts 18:4; 1 Cor. 4:15; 9:1; 15:1; 2 Cor. 10:14 [b] Acts 18:24–27; 1 Cor. 1:12 [c] [2 Cor. 3:5] 3:7 [a] 2 Cor. 12:11; [Gal. 6:3] 3:8 [a] Ps. 62:12; Rom. 2:6 3:9 [a] Mark 16:20; Acts 15:4; 2 Cor. 6:1 [b] [1 Cor. 3:16; Eph. 2:20–22]; Col. 2:7; Heb. 3:3, 4; [1 Pet. 2:5] 3:10 [a] Rom. 1:5 [b] 1 Cor. 4:15 3:11 [a] Is. 28:16; Matt. 16:18; 2 Cor. 11:4 [b] Eph. 2:20; 1 Pet. 2:4 3:13 [a] 1 Pet. 1:7 [b] Mal. 3:1–3; Luke 2:35

15If anyone's work is burned, he will suffer loss; but he himself will be saved, yet so as through fire.

16[a]Do you not know that you are the temple of God and *that* the Spirit of God dwells in you? 17If anyone defiles the temple of God, God will destroy him. For the temple of God is holy, which *temple* you are.

Avoid Worldly Wisdom

18[a]Let no one deceive himself. If anyone among you seems to be wise in this age, let him become a fool that he may become wise. 19For the wisdom of this world is foolishness with God. For it is written, [a]"He catches the wise in their *own* craftiness";[1] 20and again, [a]"The LORD knows the thoughts of the wise, that they are futile."[1] 21Therefore let no one boast in men. For [a]all things are yours: 22whether Paul or Apollos or Cephas, or the world or life or death, or things present or things to come—all are yours. 23And [a]you *are* Christ's, and Christ *is* God's.

Stewards of the Mysteries of God

4 Let a man so consider us, as [a]servants of Christ [b]and stewards of the mysteries of God. 2Moreover it is required in stewards that one be found faithful. 3But with me it is a very small thing that I should be judged by you or by a human court.[1] In fact, I do not even judge myself. 4For I know of nothing against myself, yet I am not justified by this; but He who judges me is the Lord. 5[a]Therefore judge nothing before the time, until the Lord comes, who will both bring to [b]light the hidden things of darkness and [c]reveal the counsels of the hearts. [d]Then each one's praise will come from God.

Fools for Christ's Sake

6Now these things, brethren, I have figuratively transferred to myself and Apollos for your sakes, that you may learn in us not to think beyond what is written, that none of you may be puffed up on behalf of one against the other. 7For who makes you differ *from another?* And [a]what do you have that you did not receive? Now if you did indeed receive *it,* why do you boast as if you had not received *it?*

8You are already full! [a]You are already rich! You have reigned as kings without us—and indeed I could wish you did reign, that we also might reign with you! 9For I think that God has displayed us, the apostles, last, as men condemned to death; for we have been made a [a]spectacle to the world, both to angels and to men. 10We *are* [a]fools for Christ's sake, but you *are* wise in Christ! [b]We *are* weak, but you *are* strong! You *are* distinguished, but we *are* dishonored! 11To the present hour we both hunger and thirst, and we are poorly clothed, and beaten, and homeless. 12[a]And we labor, working with our own hands. [b]Being reviled, we bless; being persecuted, we endure; 13being defamed, we entreat. [a]We have been made as the filth of the world, the offscouring of all things until now.

Paul's Paternal Care

14I do not write these things to shame you, but [a]as my beloved children I warn *you.* 15For though you might have ten thousand instructors in Christ, yet *you do* not *have* many fathers; for [a]in Christ Jesus I have

> ## #OXYGEN
> 1 CORINTHIANS 4:4
>
> ***Elevate Your Identity***
>
> When you please God, it does not matter who you displease. Wear no mask to hide the real you. Follow the standards He sets for your life. Be proud of your faith.
>
> **Breathe** and **elevate your identity**.

3:16 [a] Rom. 8:9; 1 Cor. 6:19; 2 Cor. 6:16; Eph. 2:21 3:18 [a] Prov. 3:7 3:19 [a] Job 5:13 [1] Job 5:13 3:20 [a] Ps. 94:11 [1] Psalm 94:11 3:21 [a] [2 Cor. 4:5] 3:23 [a] [Rom. 14:8]; 1 Cor. 15:23; 2 Cor. 10:7; [Gal. 3:29] 4:1 [a] Matt. 24:45; Rom. 13:6; 2 Cor. 3:6; Col. 1:25 [b] Luke 12:42; 1 Cor. 9:17; Titus 1:7; 1 Pet. 4:10 4:3 [1] Literally *day* 4:5 [a] Matt. 7:1; Rom. 2:1; [Rev. 20:12] [b] Matt. 10:26 [c] 1 Cor. 3:13 [d] Rom. 2:29; 1 Cor. 3:8; [2 Cor. 5:10] 4:7 [a] John 3:27; Rom. 12:3, 6; 1 Pet. 4:10 4:8 [a] Rev. 3:17 4:9 [a] Heb. 10:33 4:10 [a] Acts 17:18; 26:24; 1 Cor. 1:18 [b] 1 Cor. 2:3; 2 Cor. 13:9 4:12 [a] Acts 18:3; 20:34 [b] Matt. 5:44 4:13 [a] Lam. 3:45 4:14 [a] 2 Cor. 6:13; 12:14; 1 Thess. 2:11; 1 John 2:1; 3 John 4 4:15 [a] Num. 11:12; Acts 18:11; 1 Cor. 3:8; Gal. 4:19; Philem. 10

begotten you through the gospel. 16There-
fore I urge you, [a]imitate me. 17For this reason I have sent [a]Timothy to you, [b]who is my
beloved and faithful son in the Lord, who
will [c]remind you of my ways in Christ, as I
[d]teach everywhere [e]in every church.
18[a]Now some are puffed up, as though I
were not coming to you. 19[a]But I will come
to you shortly, [b]if the Lord wills, and I will
know, not the word of those who are puffed
up, but the power. 20For [a]the kingdom of
God *is* not in word but in [b]power. 21What
do you want? [a]Shall I come to you with a
rod, or in love and a spirit of gentleness?

Immorality Defiles the Church

5 It is actually reported *that there is* sexual
immorality among you, and such sexual
immorality as is not even named[1] among
the Gentiles—that a man has his father's
[a]wife! 2[a]And you are puffed up, and have not
rather [b]mourned, that he who has done this
deed might be taken away from among you.
3[a]For I indeed, as absent in body but present in spirit, have already judged (as though
I were present) him who has so done this
deed. 4In the [a]name of our Lord Jesus Christ,
when you are gathered together, along with
my spirit, [b]with the power of our Lord Jesus
Christ, 5[a]deliver such a one to [b]Satan for the
destruction of the flesh, that his spirit may
be saved in the day of the Lord Jesus.[1]
6[a]Your glorying *is* not good. Do you not
know that [b]a little leaven leavens the whole
lump? 7Therefore purge out the old leaven,
that you may be a new lump, since you truly
are unleavened. For indeed [a]Christ, our
[b]Passover, was sacrificed for us.[1] 8There-
fore [a]let us keep the feast, [b]not with old
leaven, nor [c]with the leaven of malice and
wickedness, but with the unleavened *bread*
of sincerity and truth.

Immorality Must Be Judged

9I wrote to you in my epistle [a]not to keep
company with sexually immoral people.
10Yet *I* certainly *did* not *mean* with the sexually immoral people of this world, or with
the covetous, or extortioners, or idolaters,
since then you would need to go [a]out of the
world. 11But now I have written to you not
to keep company [a]with anyone named a
brother, who is sexually immoral, or covetous, or an idolater, or a reviler, or a drunkard, or an extortioner—[b]not even to eat
with such a person.
12For what *have* I *to do* with judging those
also who are outside? Do you not judge
those who are inside? 13But those who are
outside God judges. Therefore [a]"put away
from yourselves the evil person."[1]

Do Not Sue the Brethren

6 Dare any of you, having a matter against
another, go to law before the unrighteous, and not before the [a]saints? 2Do you
not know that [a]the saints will judge the
world? And if the world will be judged by
you, are you unworthy to judge the smallest matters? 3Do you not know that we shall
[a]judge angels? How much more, things that
pertain to this life? 4If then you have judgments concerning things pertaining to this
life, do you appoint those who are least esteemed by the church to judge? 5I say this
to your shame. Is it so, that there is not a
wise man among you, not even one, who
will be able to judge between his brethren?
6But brother goes to law against brother,
and that before unbelievers!
7Now therefore, it is already an utter failure for you that you go to law against one
another. [a]Why do you not rather accept
wrong? Why do you not rather *let yourselves*
be cheated? 8No, you yourselves do wrong
and cheat, and *you do* these things *to your*
brethren! 9Do you not know that the unrighteous will not inherit the kingdom of
God? Do not be deceived. [a]Neither fornicators, nor idolaters, nor adulterers, nor homosexuals,[1] nor sodomites, 10nor thieves,
nor covetous, nor drunkards, nor revilers,

4:16 [a] [1 Cor. 11:1]; Phil. 3:17; 4:9; [1 Thess. 1:6]; 2 Thess. 3:9 4:17 [a] Acts 19:22; Phil. 2:19 [b] 1 Cor. 4:14; 1 Tim. 1:2, 18; 2 Tim. 1:2 [c] 1 Cor. 11:2 [d] 1 Cor. 7:17; Titus 1:5 [e] 1 Cor. 14:33 4:18 [a] 1 Cor. 5:2 4:19 [a] Acts 19:21; 20:2; 1 Cor. 11:34; 16:5, 7–9; 2 Cor. 1:15 [b] Acts 18:21; Heb. 6:3; James 4:15 4:20 [a] 1 Thess. 1:5 [b] 1 Cor. 2:4 4:21 [a] 2 Cor. 10:2 5:1 [a] Lev. 18:6–8; Deut. 22:30; 27:20 [1] NU-Text omits *named.* 5:2 [a] 1 Cor. 4:18 [b] 2 Cor. 7:7–10 5:3 [a] Col. 2:5; 1 Thess. 2:17 5:4 [a] [Matt. 18:20] [b] [Matt. 16:19; John 20:23]; 2 Cor. 12:9 5:5 [a] Ps. 109:6; Prov. 23:14; Luke 22:31; 1 Tim. 1:20 [b] [Acts 26:18] [1] NU-Text omits *Jesus.* 5:6 [a] 1 Cor. 3:21 [b] Hos. 7:4; Matt. 16:6, 12; Gal. 5:9; 2 Tim. 2:17 5:7 [a] Is. 53:7 [b] John 19:14 [1] NU-Text omits *for us.* 5:8 [a] Ex. 12:15 [b] Deut. 16:3 [c] Matt. 16:6 5:9 [a] 2 Cor. 6:14; Eph. 5:11; 2 Thess. 3:6 5:10 [a] John 17:15 5:11 [a] Matt. 18:17 [b] Gal. 2:12 5:13 [a] Deut. 13:5; 17:7, 12; 19:19; 21:21; 22:21, 24; 24:7; 1 Cor. 5:2 [1] Deuteronomy 17:7; 19:19; 22:21, 24; 24:7 6:1 [a] Dan. 7:22; Matt. 19:28 6:2 [a] Ps. 49:14 6:3 [a] 2 Pet. 2:4 6:7 [a] [Prov. 20:22] 6:9 [a] Acts 20:32; [1 Cor. 15:50]; Gal. 5:21; Eph. 5:5; 1 Tim. 1:9 [1] That is, catamites

nor extortioners will inherit the kingdom of God. 11And such were [a]some of you. [b]But you were washed, but you were sanctified, but you were justified in the name of the Lord Jesus and by the Spirit of our God.

Glorify God in Body and Spirit

12[a]All things are lawful for me, but all things are not helpful. All things are lawful for me, but I will not be brought under the power of any. 13[a]Foods for the stomach and the stomach for foods, but God will destroy both it and them. Now the body *is* not for [b]sexual immorality but [c]for the Lord, [d]and the Lord for the body. 14And [a]God both raised up the Lord and will also raise us up [b]by His power.

15Do you not know that [a]your bodies are members of Christ? Shall I then take the members of Christ and make *them* members of a harlot? Certainly not! 16Or do you not know that he who is joined to a harlot is one body *with her?* For [a]"the two," He says, "shall become one flesh."[1] 17[a]But he who is joined to the Lord is one spirit *with Him.*

18[a]Flee sexual immorality. Every sin that a man does is outside the body, but he who commits sexual immorality sins [b]against his own body. 19Or [a]do you not know that your body is the temple of the Holy Spirit *who is* in you, whom you have from God, [b]and you are not your own? 20For [a]you were bought at a price; therefore glorify God in your body[1] and in your spirit, which are God's.

Principles of Marriage

7 Now concerning the things of which you wrote to me:

[a]*It is* good for a man not to touch a woman. 2Nevertheless, because of sexual immorality, let each man have his own wife, and let each woman have her own husband. 3[a]Let the husband render to his wife the affection due her, and likewise also the wife to her husband. 4The wife does not have authority over her own body, but the husband *does.* And likewise the husband does not have authority over his own body, but the wife *does.* 5[a]Do not deprive one another except with consent for a time, that you may give yourselves to fasting and prayer; and come together again so that [b]Satan does not tempt you because of your lack of self-control. 6But I say this as a concession, [a]not as a commandment. 7For [a]I wish that all men were even as I myself. But each one has his own gift from God, one in this manner and another in that.

8But I say to the unmarried and to the widows: [a]It is good for them if they remain even as I am; 9but [a]if they cannot exercise self-control, let them marry. For it is better to marry than to burn *with passion.*

Keep Your Marriage Vows

10Now to the married I command, *yet* not I but the [a]Lord: [b]A wife is not to depart from *her* husband. 11But even if she does depart, let her remain unmarried or be reconciled to *her* husband. And a husband is not to divorce *his* wife.

12But to the rest I, not the Lord, say: If any brother has a wife who does not believe, and she is willing to live with him, let him not divorce her. 13And a woman who has a husband who does not believe, if he is willing to live with her, let her not divorce him. 14For the unbelieving husband is sanctified by the wife, and the unbelieving wife is sanctified by the husband; otherwise [a]your children would be unclean, but now they are holy. 15But if the unbeliever departs, let him depart; a brother or a sister is not under bondage in such *cases.* But God has called us [a]to peace. 16For how do you know, O wife, whether you will [a]save *your* husband? Or how do you know, O husband, whether you will save *your* wife?

Live as You Are Called

17But as God has distributed to each one, as the Lord has called each one, so let him walk. And [a]so I ordain in all the churches.

6:11 [a] [1 Cor. 12:2; Col. 3:5–7; Titus 3:3–7] [b] Heb. 10:22 **6:12** [a] 1 Cor. 10:23 **6:13** [a] Matt. 15:17; [Rom. 14:17]; Col. 2:22 [b] 1 Cor. 5:1; Gal. 5:19; Eph. 5:3; Col. 3:5; 1 Thess. 4:3 [c] 1 Thess. 4:3 [d] [Eph. 5:23] **6:14** [a] Rom. 6:5, 8; 2 Cor. 4:14 [b] Eph. 1:19 **6:15** [a] Rom. 12:5; 1 Cor. 6:13; 12:27; Eph. 5:30 **6:16** [a] Gen. 2:24; Matt. 19:5; Mark 10:8; Eph. 5:31 [1] Genesis 2:24 **6:17** [a] [John 17:21–23; Rom. 8:9–11]; 1 Cor. 6:15; [Gal. 2:20]; Eph. 4:4 **6:18** [a] Rom. 6:12; 1 Cor. 6:9; 2 Cor. 12:21; Eph. 5:3; Col. 3:5; Heb. 13:4 [b] Rom. 1:24; 1 Thess. 4:4 **6:19** [a] John 2:21; 1 Cor. 3:16; 2 Cor. 6:16 [b] Rom. 14:7 **6:20** [a] Acts 20:28; 1 Cor. 7:23; Gal. 3:13; 1 Pet. 1:18; 2 Pet. 2:1; Rev. 5:9 [1] NU-Text ends the verse at *body.* **7:1** [a] 1 Cor. 7:8, 26 **7:3** [a] Ex. 21:10 **7:5** [a] Joel 2:16 [b] 1 Thess. 3:5 **7:6** [a] 2 Cor. 8:8 **7:7** [a] Acts 26:29 **7:8** [a] 1 Cor. 7:1, 26 **7:9** [a] 1 Tim. 5:14 **7:10** [a] Mark 10:6–10 [b] Mal. 2:14; [Matt. 5:32] **7:14** [a] Ezra 9:2; Mal. 2:15 **7:15** [a] Rom. 12:18 **7:16** [a] Rom. 11:14; 1 Pet. 3:1 **7:17** [a] 1 Cor. 4:17

RELEASE // ELEVATE YOUR IDENTITY

From Sinners to Servants

1 Corinthians 7:17 // But as God has distributed to each one, as the Lord has called each one, so let him walk.

Summary Message // Paul's instructions to the church at Corinth were weighty because he sought to deliver the believers from continuing to act according to their pagan past. As a result, his words were direct and unflinching. But they were also rooted in Christian love, as he told the Corinthian believers what they should do and what they should not do for their own good. Paul carefully answered their questions and corrected their problematic behavior. He wanted them to understand that life in Christ was far better than anything they had ever experienced; it was nothing like the worship of dead, pagan gods.

Paul gave clear direction to the Corinthian Christians that they were to live in the Lord faithfully, in all ways. A believer should walk as Jesus walked, not according to the ways around them.

Practical Application // "Who am I?" That question is as old as time but can be answered in such different ways. In 1 Corinthians 7, Paul answered the question for believers: "You were bought at a price" (v. 23). Just prior, in verses 21–22, Paul made it clear that Christians are to be known not by any worldly status but as servants of God. Biblical slavery, indentured servanthood, and chattel slavery are difficult subjects to examine. However, in this letter Paul uses this illustration to tell believers in Corinth that living in service to God is the highest of callings.

We live in a time when identity matters more than ever. Millions have chosen identities for themselves based on their feelings, past traumas, or sociopolitical leanings. But as Solomon said, there is nothing new under the sun. This tendency to allow the world to define us is as old as time. As Christians, our identity is connected to the work of Christ and the calling of God. We are to live in love and obedience because everything flows from there.

We have made identities of race, gender, financial status, heritage, and other worldly issues, but in Christ, we are servants. The greatest identity of all is being a servant of Christ Jesus. Regardless of our situation as believers, this call to God's service is paramount. We should ask ourselves, "How do I serve the cause of Christ in this situation?" Many of us will find the answer to why we face the circumstances we face when we see life through the lens of serving God with our lives.

Fervent Prayer // Father, we thank You for calling us to holiness. You have called us out of darkness into Your eternal light, and we ask that You help us serve You in all we do. Whether married, single, free, or bound, we are to serve You with our lives in every circumstance. We ask You to keep us ever mindful that we are Your servants and we live to glorify You. Remind us that we are bought with a price and our lives are no longer our own. Help us serve You with gladness and live in obedience to all You have commanded. Finally, Lord, help us elevate our identities by embracing the truth that being Your servants is the highest call we could ever receive. Cause us to set our sights on service for the glory of Your name in every place. In Jesus' name we pray. Amen.

---

18 Was anyone called while circumcised?
Let him not become uncircumcised. Was
anyone called while uncircumcised? [a]Let
him not be circumcised. 19 [a]Circumcision
is nothing and uncircumcision is nothing, but [b]keeping the commandments of
God *is what matters.* 20 Let each one remain in the same calling in which he was
called. 21 Were you called *while* a slave?
Do not be concerned about it; but if you
can be made free, rather use *it.* 22 For he
who is called in the Lord *while* a slave is
[a]the Lord's freedman. Likewise he who is
called *while* free is [b]Christ's slave. 23 [a]You
were bought at a price; do not become
slaves of men. 24 Brethren, let each one
remain with [a]God in that *state* in which
he was called.

7:18 [a] Acts 15:1 7:19 [a] [Rom. 2:27, 29; Gal. 3:28; 5:6; 6:15; Col. 3:11] [b] [John 15:14] 7:22 [a] [John 8:36]; Rom. 6:18; Philem. 16 [b] [1 Cor. 9:21; Gal. 5:13]; Eph. 6:6; Col. 3:24; 1 Pet. 2:16 7:23 [a] Lev. 25:42; 1 Cor. 6:20; 1 Pet. 1:18, 19; Rev. 5:9 7:24 [a] [Eph. 6:5–8; Col. 3:22–24]

To the Unmarried and Widows
25Now concerning virgins: [a]I have no
commandment from the Lord; yet I give
judgment as one [b]whom the Lord in His
mercy has made [c]trustworthy. 26I suppose
therefore that this is good because of the
present distress—[a]that *it is* good for a man
to remain as he is: 27Are you bound to a
wife? Do not seek to be loosed. Are you
loosed from a wife? Do not seek a wife.
28But even if you do marry, you have not
sinned; and if a virgin marries, she has not
sinned. Nevertheless such will have trouble
in the flesh, but I would spare you.
29But [a]this I say, brethren, the time *is*
short, so that from now on even those who
have wives should be as though they had
none, 30those who weep as though they did
not weep, those who rejoice as though they
did not rejoice, those who buy as though
they did not possess, 31and those who use
this world as not [a]misusing *it.* For [b]the form
of this world is passing away.
32But I want you to be without care. [a]He
who is unmarried cares for the things of
the Lord—how he may please the Lord.
33But he who is married cares about the
things of the world—how he may please
his wife. 34There is[1] a difference between a
wife and a virgin. The unmarried woman
[a]cares about the things of the Lord, that she
may be holy both in body and in spirit. But
she who is married cares about the things
of the world—how she may please *her* husband. 35And this I say for your own profit,
not that I may put a leash on you, but for
what is proper, and that you may serve the
Lord without distraction.
36But if any man thinks he is behaving
improperly toward his virgin, if she is past
the flower of youth, and thus it must be,
let him do what he wishes. He does not
sin; let them marry. 37Nevertheless he who
stands steadfast in his heart, having no
necessity, but has power over his own will,
and has so determined in his heart that he
will keep his virgin,[1] does well. 38[a]So then
he who gives *her*[1] in marriage does well,
but he who does not give *her* in marriage
does better.
39[a]A wife is bound by law as long as her
husband lives; but if her husband dies,
she is at liberty to be married to whom
she wishes, [b]only in the Lord. 40But she is
happier if she remains as she is, [a]according
to my judgment—and [b]I think I also have
the Spirit of God.

Be Sensitive to Conscience
8 Now [a]concerning things offered to
idols: We know that we all have [b]knowl-
edge. [c]Knowledge puffs up, but love edifies.
2And [a]if anyone thinks that he knows anything, he knows nothing yet as he ought to
know. 3But if anyone loves God, this one is
known by Him.
4Therefore concerning the eating of
things offered to idols, we know that [a]an
idol *is* nothing in the world, [b]and that *there*
is no other God but one. 5For even if there
are [a]so-called gods, whether in heaven or
on earth (as there are many gods and many
lords), 6yet [a]for us *there is* one God, the Father, [b]of whom *are* all things, and we for
Him; and [c]one Lord Jesus Christ, [d]through
whom *are* all things, and [e]through whom
we *live.*
7However, *there is* not in everyone that
knowledge; for some, [a]with consciousness
of the idol, until now eat *it* as a thing offered to an idol; and their conscience, being weak, is [b]defiled. 8But [a]food does not
commend us to God; for neither if we eat
are we the better, nor if we do not eat are
we the worse.
9But [a]beware lest somehow this liberty of yours become [b]a stumbling block
to those who are weak. 10For if anyone
sees you who have knowledge eating in
an idol's temple, will not [a]the conscience
of him who is weak be emboldened to eat
those things offered to idols? 11And [a]be-
cause of your knowledge shall the weak
brother perish, for whom Christ died? 12But
[a]when you thus sin against the brethren,
and wound their weak conscience, you sin

7:25 [a] 2 Cor. 8:8 [b] 2 Cor. 4:1; 1 Tim. 1:13, 16 [c] 1 Tim. 1:12 **7:26** [a] 1 Cor. 7:1, 8 **7:29** [a] [Rom. 13:11]; 1 Cor. 7:31; 1 Pet. 4:7; [2 Pet. 3:8, 9] **7:31** [a] 1 Cor. 9:18 [b] Ps. 39:6; 1 Cor. 7:29; James 1:10; 4:14; 1 Pet. 1:24; 4:7; [1 John 2:17] **7:32** [a] 1 Tim. 5:5 **7:34** [a] Luke 10:40 [1] M-Text adds *also.* **7:37** [1] Or *virgin daughter* **7:38** [a] Heb. 13:4 [1] NU-Text reads *his own virgin.* **7:39** [a] Rom. 7:2 [b] 2 Cor. 6:14 **7:40** [a] 1 Cor. 7:6, 25 [b] 1 Thess. 4:8 **8:1** [a] Acts 15:20; 1 Cor. 8:4, 7, 10 [b] Rom. 14:14 [c] Rom. 14:3 **8:2** [a] [1 Cor. 13:8–12]; Gal. 6:3; [1 Tim. 6:4] **8:4** [a] Is. 41:24 [b] Deut. 4:35, 39; 6:4; 1 Cor. 8:6 **8:5** [a] [John 10:34] **8:6** [a] Mal. 2:10; Eph. 4:6 [b] Acts 17:28 [c] John 13:13; 1 Cor. 1:2; Eph. 4:5; [1 Tim. 2:5] [d] John 1:3; [Col. 1:16, 17]; Heb. 1:2 [e] Rom. 5:11; Rev. 4:11; 5:9, 10 **8:7** [a] [1 Cor. 10:28] [b] Rom. 14:14, 22 **8:8** [a] [Rom. 14:17] **8:9** [a] Gal. 5:13 [b] Rom. 14:13, 21; 1 Cor. 10:28 **8:10** [a] 1 Cor. 10:28 **8:11** [a] Rom. 14:15, 20 **8:12** [a] Matt. 25:40

against Christ. 13Therefore, [a]if food makes
my brother stumble, I will never again eat
meat, lest I make my brother stumble.

A Pattern of Self-Denial

9 Am [a]I not an apostle? Am I not free?
[b]Have I not seen Jesus Christ our Lord?
[c]Are you not my work in the Lord? 2If I am
not an apostle to others, yet doubtless I am
to you. For you are [a]the seal of my apostleship in the Lord.
3My defense to those who examine me is
this: 4[a]Do we have no right to eat and drink?
5Do we have no right to take along a believing wife, as *do* also the other apostles, [a]the
brothers of the Lord, and [b]Cephas? 6Or *is*
it only Barnabas and I [a]*who* have no right
to refrain from working? 7Who ever [a]goes
to war at his own expense? Who [b]plants a
vineyard and does not eat of its fruit? Or
who [c]tends a flock and does not drink of
the milk of the flock?
8Do I say these things as a *mere* man? Or
does not the law say the same also? 9For it
is written in the law of Moses, [a]"You shall
not muzzle an ox while it treads out the
grain."[1] Is it oxen God is concerned about?
10Or does He say *it* altogether for our sakes?
For our sakes, no doubt, *this* is written, that
[a]he who plows should plow in hope, and he
who threshes in hope should be partaker of
his hope. 11[a]If we have sown spiritual things
for you, *is it* a great thing if we reap your
material things? 12If others are partakers of
this right over you, *are* we not even more?
[a]Nevertheless we have not used this
right, but endure all things [b]lest we hinder the gospel of Christ. 13[a]Do you not know
that those who minister the holy things eat
of the things of the [b]temple, and those who
serve at the altar partake of *the offerings*
of the altar? 14Even so [a]the Lord has commanded [b]that those who preach the gospel
should live from the gospel.
15But [a]I have used none of these things,
nor have I written these things that it
should be done so to me; for [b]it *would*
be better for me to die than that anyone
should make my boasting void. 16For if I
preach the gospel, I have nothing to boast
of, for [a]necessity is laid upon me; yes, woe
is me if I do not preach the gospel! 17For
if I do this willingly, [a]I have a reward; but
if against my will, [b]I have been entrusted
with a stewardship. 18What is my reward
then? That [a]when I preach the gospel, I
may present the gospel of Christ[1] without
charge, that I [b]may not abuse my authority in the gospel.

Serving All Men

19For though I am [a]free from all *men,* [b]I
have made myself a servant to all, [c]that I
might win the more; 20and [a]to the Jews I
became as a Jew, that I might win Jews; to
those *who are* under the law, as under the
law,[1] that I might win those *who are* under
the law; 21[a]to [b]those *who are* without law, as
without law [c](not being without law toward
God,[1] but under law toward Christ[2]), that I
might win those *who are* without law; 22[a]to
the weak I became as[1] weak, that I might
win the weak. [b]I have become all things
to all *men,* [c]that I might by all means save
some. 23Now this I do for the gospel's sake,
that I may be partaker of it with *you.*

Striving for a Crown

24Do you not know that those who run
in a race all run, but one receives the prize?
[a]Run in such a way that you may obtain *it.*
25And everyone who competes *for the prize*
is temperate in all things. Now they *do it* to
obtain a perishable crown, but we *for* [a]an
imperishable *crown.* 26Therefore I run thus:
[a]not with uncertainty. Thus I fight: not as
one who beats the air. 27[a]But I discipline
my body and [b]bring *it* into subjection, lest,
when I have preached to others, I myself
should become [c]disqualified.

8:13 [a] Rom. 14:21; 1 Cor. 10:32; 2 Cor. 6:3; 11:29 9:1 [a] Acts 9:15; 2 Cor. 12:12 [b] Acts 9:3, 17; 18:9; 22:14, 18; 23:11; 1 Cor. 15:8 [c] 1 Cor. 3:6; 4:15 9:2 [a] 2 Cor. 12:12 9:4 [a] 1 Cor. 9:14; [1 Thess. 2:6, 9]; 2 Thess. 3:8 9:5 [a] Matt. 13:55 [b] Matt. 8:14; John 1:42 9:6 [a] Acts 4:36; [2 Thess. 3:8] 9:7 [a] 2 Cor. 10:4; 1 Tim. 1:18; 2 Tim. 2:3 [b] Deut. 20:6; Prov. 27:18; 1 Cor. 3:6, 8 [c] John 21:15 9:9 [a] Deut. 25:4; 1 Tim. 5:18 [1] Deuteronomy 25:4 9:10 [a] 2 Tim. 2:6 9:11 [a] Rom. 15:27; 1 Cor. 9:14 9:12 [a] [Acts 18:3; 20:33]; 1 Cor. 9:15, 18 [b] 2 Cor. 11:12 9:13 [a] Lev. 6:16, 26; 7:6, 31 [b] Num. 18:8–31; Deut. 18:1 9:14 [a] Matt. 10:10; Luke 10:7, 8; 1 Tim. 5:18 [b] Rom. 10:15 9:15 [a] Acts 18:3; 20:33; 1 Cor. 9:12, 18 [b] 2 Cor. 11:10 9:16 [a] Acts 9:15; [Rom. 1:14] 9:17 [a] John 4:36; 1 Cor. 3:8, 14; 9:18 [b] 1 Cor. 4:1; Gal. 2:7; Eph. 3:2; Col. 1:25 9:18 [a] 1 Cor. 10:33 [b] 1 Cor. 7:31; 9:12 [1] NU-Text omits *of Christ.* 9:19 [a] 1 Cor. 9:1 [b] 2 Cor. 4:5; Gal. 5:13 [c] Matt. 18:15; 1 Pet. 3:1 9:20 [a] Acts 16:3; 21:23–26; Rom. 11:14 [1] NU-Text adds *though not being myself under the law.* 9:21 [a] [Gal. 2:3; 3:2] [b] [Rom. 2:12, 14] [c] [1 Cor. 7:22; Gal. 6:2] [1] NU-Text reads *God's law.* [2] NU-Text reads *Christ's law.* 9:22 [a] Rom. 14:1; 15:1; 2 Cor. 11:29 [b] 1 Cor. 10:33 [c] Rom. 11:14 [1] NU-Text omits *as.* 9:24 [a] Gal. 2:2; 2 Tim. 4:7; Heb. 12:1 9:25 [a] 2 Tim. 4:8; James 1:12; [1 Pet. 5:4; Rev. 2:10; 3:11] 9:26 [a] 2 Tim. 2:5 9:27 [a] [Rom. 8:13] [b] [Rom. 6:18] [c] Jer. 6:30; 2 Cor. 13:5

Old Testament Examples

10 Moreover, brethren, I do not want
you to be unaware that all our fathers were under [a]the cloud, all passed
through [b]the sea, 2all were baptized into
Moses in the cloud and in the sea, 3all ate
the same [a]spiritual food, 4and all drank
the same [a]spiritual drink. For they drank
of that spiritual Rock that followed them,
and that Rock was Christ. 5But with most
of them God was not well pleased, for *their*
bodies [a]were scattered in the wilderness.
6Now these things became our examples, to the intent that we should not lust
after evil things as [a]they also lusted. 7[a]And
do not become idolaters as *were* some of
them. As it is written, [b]"The people sat down
to eat and drink, and rose up to play."[1] 8[a]Nor
let us commit sexual immorality, as [b]some
of them did, and [c]in one day twenty-three
thousand fell; 9nor let us tempt Christ, as
[a]some of them also tempted, and [b]were
destroyed by serpents; 10nor complain,
as [a]some of them also complained, and
[b]were destroyed by [c]the destroyer. 11Now
all[1] these things happened to them as examples, and [a]they were written for our admonition, [b]upon whom the ends of the ages
have come.
12Therefore [a]let him who thinks he
stands take heed lest he fall. 13No temptation has overtaken you except such as is
common to man; but [a]God *is* faithful, [b]who
will not allow you to be tempted beyond
what you are able, but with the temptation
will also make the way of escape, that you
may be able to bear *it.*

Flee from Idolatry

14Therefore, my beloved, [a]flee from idolatry. 15I speak as to [a]wise men; judge for
yourselves what I say. 16[a]The cup of blessing
which we bless, is it not the communion of
the blood of Christ? [b]The bread which we
break, is it not the communion of the body
of Christ? 17For [a]we, *though* many, are one
bread *and* one body; for we all partake of
that one bread.
18Observe [a]Israel [b]after the flesh: [c]Are not
those who eat of the sacrifices partakers of
the altar? 19What am I saying then? [a]That an
idol is anything, or what is offered to idols
is anything? 20Rather, that the things which
the Gentiles [a]sacrifice [b]they sacrifice to demons and not to God, and I do not want
you to have fellowship with demons. 21[a]You
cannot drink the cup of the Lord and [b]the
cup of demons; you cannot partake of the
[c]Lord's table and of the table of demons.
22Or do we [a]provoke the Lord to jealousy?
[b]Are we stronger than He?

All to the Glory of God
(cf. Ps. 24:1)

23All things are lawful for me,[1] but not
all things are [a]helpful; all things are lawful
for me,[2] but not all things edify. 24Let no
one seek his own, but each one [a]the other's *well-being.*
25[a]Eat whatever is sold in the meat market, asking no questions for conscience'
sake; 26for [a]"the earth *is* the LORD's, and
all its fullness."[1]
27If any of those who do not believe invites you *to dinner,* and you desire to go,
[a]eat whatever is set before you, asking no
question for conscience' sake. 28But if anyone says to you, "This was offered to idols,"
do not eat it [a]for the sake of the one who
told you, and for conscience' sake;[1] for [b]"the
earth *is* the LORD's, and all its fullness."[2]
29"Conscience," I say, not your own, but that
of the other. For [a]why is my liberty judged
by another *man's* conscience? 30But if I partake with thanks, why am I evil spoken of
for *the food* [a]over which I give thanks?
31[a]Therefore, whether you eat or drink,
or whatever you do, do all to the glory of
God. 32[a]Give no offense, either to the Jews
or to the Greeks or to the church of God,

10:1 [a] Ex. 13:21, 22; Ps. 105:39 [b] Ex. 14:21, 22, 29; Neh. 9:11; Ps. 66:6 10:3 [a] Ex. 16:4, 15, 35; Deut. 8:3; Neh. 9:15, 20; Ps. 78:24; John 6:31 10:4 [a] Ex. 17:5–7; Num. 20:11; Ps. 78:15 10:5 [a] Num. 14:29, 37; 26:65; Heb. 3:17; Jude 5 10:6 [a] Num. 11:4, 34; Ps. 106:14 10:7 [a] Ex. 32:4; 1 Cor. 5:11; 10:14 [b] Ex. 32:6; 1 Cor. 15:32 [1] Exodus 32:6 10:8 [a] Rev. 2:14 [b] Num. 25:1–9 [c] Ps. 106:29 10:9 [a] Ex. 17:2, 7 [b] Num. 21:6–9 10:10 [a] Ex. 16:2 [b] Num. 14:37 [c] Ex. 12:23; 2 Sam. 24:16; 1 Chr. 21:15; Heb. 11:28 10:11 [a] Rom. 15:4 [b] Phil. 4:5 [1] NU-Text omits *all.* 10:12 [a] Rom. 11:20 10:13 [a] 1 Cor. 1:9 [b] Ps. 125:3 10:14 [a] 2 Cor. 6:17 10:15 [a] 1 Cor. 8:1 10:16 [a] Matt. 26:26–28; Mark 14:23; Luke 22:20; 1 Cor. 11:25 [b] Matt. 26:26; Luke 22:19; Acts 2:42; 1 Cor. 11:23 10:17 [a] Rom. 12:5; 1 Cor. 12:12, 27; Eph. 4:4, 16; Col. 3:15 10:18 [a] Rom. 4:12 [b] Rom. 4:1 [c] Lev. 3:3; 7:6, 14; Deut. 12:17 10:19 [a] 1 Cor. 8:4 10:20 [a] Lev. 17:7 [b] Deut. 32:17; Ps. 106:37; Gal. 4:8; Rev. 9:20 10:21 [a] 2 Cor. 6:15, 16 [b] Deut. 32:38 [c] [1 Cor. 11:23–29] 10:22 [a] Deut. 32:21 [b] Ezek. 22:14 10:23 [a] 1 Cor. 6:12 [1] NU-Text omits *for me.* [2] NU-Text omits *for me.* 10:24 [a] Phil. 2:4 10:25 [a] [1 Tim. 4:4] 10:26 [a] Ex. 19:5; Ps. 24:1; 50:12; 1 Tim. 4:4 [1] Psalm 24:1 10:27 [a] Luke 10:7, 8 10:28 [a] [1 Cor. 8:7, 10, 12] [b] Deut. 10:14; Ps. 24:1 [1] NU-Text omits the rest of this verse. [2] Psalm 24:1 10:29 [a] Rom. 14:16; [1 Cor. 9:19] 10:30 [a] Rom. 14:6 10:31 [a] Col. 3:17; 1 Pet. 4:11 10:32 [a] Rom. 14:13

33just [a]as I also please all *men* in all *things,*
not seeking my own profit, but the *profit*
of many, that they may be saved.

11 Imitate[a] me, just as I also *imitate*
Christ.

Head Coverings

2Now I praise you, brethren, that you remember me in all things and keep the traditions just as I delivered *them* to you. 3But
I want you to know that [a]the head of every
man is Christ, [b]the head of woman *is* man,
and [c]the head of Christ *is* God. 4Every man
praying or [a]prophesying, having *his* head
covered, dishonors his head. 5But every
woman who prays or prophesies with *her*
head uncovered dishonors her head, for
that is one and the same as if her head were
[a]shaved. 6For if a woman is not covered, let
her also be shorn. But if it is [a]shameful for a
woman to be shorn or shaved, let her be covered. 7For a man indeed ought not to cover
his head, since [a]he is the image and glory of
God; but woman is the glory of man. 8For
man is not from woman, but woman [a]from
man. 9Nor was man created for the woman,
but woman [a]for the man. 10For this reason
the woman ought to have *a symbol of* authority on *her* head, because of the angels.
11Nevertheless, [a]neither *is* man independent
of woman, nor woman independent of man,
in the Lord. 12For as woman *came* from man,
even so man also *comes* through woman;
but all things are from God.
13Judge among yourselves. Is it proper
for a woman to pray to God with her head
uncovered? 14Does not even nature itself
teach you that if a man has long hair, it is
a dishonor to him? 15But if a woman has
long hair, it is a glory to her; for *her* hair is
given to her[1] for a covering. 16But [a]if anyone seems to be contentious, we have no
such custom, [b]nor *do* the churches of God.

Conduct at the Lord's Supper

17Now in giving these instructions I do
not praise *you,* since you come together not
for the better but for the worse. 18For first
of all, when you come together as a church,
[a]I hear that there are divisions among you,
and in part I believe it. 19For [a]there must
also be factions among you, [b]that those who
are approved may be recognized among
you. 20Therefore when you come together
in one place, it is not to eat the Lord's Supper. 21For in eating, each one takes his own
supper ahead of *others;* and one is hungry and [a]another is drunk. 22What! Do you
not have houses to eat and drink in? Or do
you despise [a]the church of God and [b]shame
those who have nothing? What shall I say
to you? Shall I praise you in this? I do not
praise *you.*

Institution of the Lord's Supper
(Matt. 26:26–29; Mark 14:22–25; Luke 22:14–23)

23For [a]I received from the Lord that
which I also delivered to you: [b]that the Lord
Jesus on the *same* night in which He was
betrayed took bread; 24and when He had
given thanks, He broke *it* and said, "Take,
eat;[1] this is My body which is broken[2] for
you; do this in remembrance of Me." 25In
the same manner *He* also *took* the cup after supper, saying, "This cup is the new covenant in My blood. This do, as often as you
drink *it,* in remembrance of Me."
26For as often as you eat this bread and
drink this cup, you proclaim the Lord's
death [a]till He comes.

Examine Yourself

27Therefore whoever eats [a]this bread or
drinks *this* cup of the Lord in an unworthy manner will be guilty of the body and
blood[1] of the Lord. 28But [a]let a man examine himself, and so let him eat of the bread
and drink of the cup. 29For he who eats and
drinks in an unworthy manner[1] eats and
drinks judgment to himself, not discerning the Lord's[2] body. 30For this reason many
are weak and sick among you, and many
sleep. 31For [a]if we would judge ourselves,

10:33 [a] Rom. 15:2; 1 Cor. 9:22; [Gal. 1:10] **11:1** [a] Eph. 5:1 **11:3** [a] Eph. 1:22; 4:15; 5:23; Col. 1:18; 2:19 [b] Gen. 3:16; [Eph. 5:23] [c] John 14:28 **11:4** [a] 1 Cor. 12:10 **11:5** [a] Deut. 21:12 **11:6** [a] Num. 5:18 **11:7** [a] Gen. 1:26, 27; 5:1; 9:6; James 3:9 **11:8** [a] Gen. 2:21–23; 1 Tim. 2:13 **11:9** [a] Gen. 2:18 **11:11** [a] [Gal. 3:28] **11:15** [1] M-Text omits *to her.* **11:16** [a] 1 Tim. 6:4 [b] 1 Cor. 7:17 **11:18** [a] 1 Cor. 1:10–12; 3:3 **11:19** [a] Matt. 18:7; Luke 17:1; 1 Tim. 4:1; 2 Pet. 2:1 [b] [Deut. 13:3]; Luke 2:35; 1 John 2:19 **11:21** [a] 2 Pet. 2:13; Jude 12 **11:22** [a] 1 Cor. 10:32 [b] James 2:6 **11:23** [a] 1 Cor. 15:3; Gal. 1:12; Col. 3:24 [b] Matt. 26:26–28; Mark 14:22–24; Luke 22:17–20; 1 Cor. 10:16 **11:24** [1] NU-Text omits *Take, eat.* [2] NU-Text omits *broken.* **11:26** [a] John 14:3; [Acts 1:11] **11:27** [a] [John 6:51] [1] NU-Text and M-Text read *the blood.* **11:28** [a] Matt. 26:22; 2 Cor. 13:5; Gal. 6:4 **11:29** [1] NU-Text omits *in an unworthy manner.* [2] NU-Text omits *Lord's.* **11:31** [a] [Ps. 32:5; 1 John 1:9]

we would not be judged. 32But when we are
judged, [a]we are chastened by the Lord, that
we may not be condemned with the world.
33Therefore, my brethren, when you
[a]come together to eat, wait for one another. 34But if anyone is hungry, let him
eat at home, lest you come together for
judgment. And the rest I will set in order
when I come.

Spiritual Gifts: Unity in Diversity

12 Now [a]concerning spiritual *gifts,*
brethren, I do not want you to be
ignorant: 2You know [a]that[1] you were Gentiles, carried away to these [b]dumb idols,
however you were led. 3Therefore I make
known to you that no one speaking by the
Spirit of God calls Jesus accursed, and [a]no
one can say that Jesus is Lord except by
the Holy Spirit.
4[a]There are diversities of gifts, but [b]the
same Spirit. 5[a]There are differences of ministries, but the same Lord. 6And there are
diversities of activities, but it is the same
God [a]who works all in all. 7But the manifestation of the Spirit is given to each one
for the profit *of all:* 8for to one is given [a]the
word of wisdom through the Spirit, to another [b]the word of knowledge through the
same Spirit, 9[a]to another faith by the same
Spirit, to another [b]gifts of healings by the
same[1] Spirit, 10[a]to another the working of
miracles, to another [b]prophecy, to another
[c]discerning of spirits, to another [d]*different*
kinds of tongues, to another the interpretation of tongues. 11But one and the same
Spirit works all these things, [a]distributing
to each one individually [b]as He wills.

Unity and Diversity in One Body
(cf. Eph. 4:1–16)

12For [a]as the body is one and has many
members, but all the members of that one
body, being many, are one body, [b]so also
is Christ. 13For [a]by one Spirit we were all
baptized into one body—[b]whether Jews or
Greeks, whether slaves or free—and [c]have all
been made to drink into[1] one Spirit. 14For in
fact the body is not one member but many.
15If the foot should say, "Because I am
not a hand, I am not of the body," is it therefore not of the body? 16And if the ear should
say, "Because I am not an eye, I am not of
the body," is it therefore not of the body? 17If
the whole body *were* an eye, where *would
be* the hearing? If the whole *were* hearing, where *would be* the smelling? 18But
now [a]God has set the members, each one
of them, in the body [b]just as He pleased.
19And if they were all one member, where
would the body *be?*
20But now indeed *there are* many members, yet one body. 21And the eye cannot say
to the hand, "I have no need of you"; nor
again the head to the feet, "I have no need
of you." 22No, much rather, those members of the body which seem to be weaker
are necessary. 23And those *members* of the
body which we think to be less honorable,
on these we bestow greater honor; and our
unpresentable *parts* have greater modesty,
24but our presentable *parts* have no need.
But God composed the body, having given
greater honor to that *part* which lacks it,
25that there should be no schism in the
body, but *that* the members should have
the same care for one another. 26And if
one member suffers, all the members suffer with *it;* or if one member is honored, all
the members rejoice with *it.*
27Now [a]you are the body of Christ, and
[b]members individually. 28And [a]God has appointed these in the church: first [b]apostles,
second [c]prophets, third teachers, after that
[d]miracles, then [e]gifts of healings, [f]helps,
[g]administrations, varieties of tongues.
29*Are* all apostles? *Are* all prophets? *Are* all
teachers? *Are* all workers of miracles? 30Do
all have gifts of healings? Do all speak with
tongues? Do all interpret? 31But [a]earnestly
desire the best[1] gifts. And yet I show you a
more excellent way.

11:32 [a] 2 Sam. 7:14; Ps. 94:12; [Heb. 12:5–10; Rev. 3:19] **11:33** [a] 1 Cor. 14:26 **12:1** [a] 1 Cor. 12:4; 14:1, 37 **12:2** [a] 1 Cor. 6:11; Eph. 2:11; 1 Pet. 4:3 [b] Ps. 115:5; Is. 46:7; Jer. 10:5; Hab. 2:18 [1] NU-Text and M-Text add *when.* **12:3** [a] Matt. 16:17 **12:4** [a] Rom. 12:3–8; 1 Cor. 12:11; Eph. 4:4, 11; Heb. 2:4 [b] Eph. 4:4 **12:5** [a] Rom. 12:6 **12:6** [a] 1 Cor. 15:28; Eph. 1:23; 4:6 **12:8** [a] 1 Cor. 2:6, 7; 2 Cor. 1:12 [b] Rom. 15:14; [1 Cor. 2:11, 16]; 2 Cor. 8:7 **12:9** [a] Matt. 17:19; [1 Cor. 13:2]; 2 Cor. 4:13 [b] Matt. 10:1; Mark 3:15; 16:18; James 5:14 [1] NU-Text reads *one.* **12:10** [a] Mark 16:17 [b] Rom. 12:6 [c] 1 John 4:1 [d] Acts 2:4–11 **12:11** [a] Rom. 12:6; 2 Cor. 10:13 [b] [John 3:8] **12:12** [a] Rom. 12:4, 5; 1 Cor. 10:17; Eph. 4:4 [b] [Gal. 3:16] **12:13** [a] [Rom. 6:5] [b] Rom. 3:22; Gal. 3:28; [Eph. 2:13–18]; Col. 3:11 [c] [John 7:37–39] [1] NU-Text omits *into.* **12:18** [a] 1 Cor. 12:28 [b] Rom. 12:3 **12:27** [a] Rom. 12:5; Eph. 1:23; 4:12; 5:23, 30; Col. 1:24 [b] Eph. 5:30 **12:28** [a] Eph. 4:11 [b] [Eph. 2:20; 3:5] [c] Acts 13:1; Rom. 12:6 [d] 1 Cor. 12:10, 29; Gal. 3:5 [e] Mark 16:18; 1 Cor. 12:9, 30 [f] Num. 11:17 [g] Rom. 12:8; 1 Tim. 5:17; Heb. 13:17, 24 **12:31** [a] 1 Cor. 14:1, 39 [1] NU-Text reads *greater.*

The Greatest Gift

13 Though I speak with the tongues
of men and of angels, but have not
love, I have become sounding brass or
a clanging cymbal. 2And though I have
the gift of [a]prophecy, and understand all
mysteries and all knowledge, and though
I have all faith, [b]so that I could remove
mountains, but have not love, I am nothing. 3And [a]though I bestow all my goods to
feed *the poor,* and though I give my body
to be burned,[1] but have not love, it profits
me nothing.

4[a]Love suffers long *and* is [b]kind; love
[c]does not envy; love does not parade itself,
is not puffed up; 5does not behave rudely,
[a]does not seek its own, is not provoked,
thinks no evil; 6[a]does not rejoice in iniquity, but [b]rejoices in the truth; 7[a]bears all
things, believes all things, hopes all things,
endures all things.

8Love never fails. But whether *there are*
prophecies, they will fail; whether *there*
are tongues, they will cease; whether *there*
is knowledge, it will vanish away. 9[a]For we
know in part and we prophesy in part. 10But
when that which is perfect has come, then
that which is in part will be done away.

11When I was a child, I spoke as a child, I
understood as a child, I thought as a child;
but when I became a man, I put away child-
ish things. 12For [a]now we see in a mirror,
dimly, but then [b]face to face. Now I know
in part, but then I shall know just as I also
am known.

13And now abide faith, hope, love, these
three; but the greatest of these *is* love.

Prophecy and Tongues

14 Pursue love, and [a]desire spiritual
gifts, [b]but especially that you may
prophesy. 2For he who [a]speaks in a tongue
does not speak to men but to God, for no
one understands *him;* however, in the spirit
he speaks mysteries. 3But he who prophesies speaks [a]edification and [b]exhorta-
tion and comfort to men. 4He who speaks
in a tongue edifies himself, but he who
prophesies edifies the church. 5I wish you
all spoke with tongues, but even more that
you prophesied; for[1] he who prophesies *is*
greater than he who speaks with tongues,
unless indeed he interprets, that the church
may receive edification.

Tongues Must Be Interpreted

6But now, brethren, if I come to you
speaking with tongues, what shall I profit
you unless I speak to you either by [a]rev-
elation, by knowledge, by prophesying,
or by teaching? 7Even things without life,
whether flute or harp, when they make a
sound, unless they make a distinction in
the sounds, how will it be known what is
piped or played? 8For if the trumpet makes
an uncertain sound, who will prepare for
battle? 9So likewise you, unless you utter
by the tongue words easy to understand,
how will it be known what is spoken? For
you will be speaking into the air. 10There
are, it may be, so many kinds of languages
in the world, and none of them *is* without
significance. 11Therefore, if I do not know
the meaning of the language, I shall be a
foreigner to him who speaks, and he who
speaks *will be* a foreigner to me. 12Even so
you, since you are zealous for spiritual *gifts,*
let it be for the edification of the church *that*
you seek to excel.

13Therefore let him who speaks in a
tongue pray that he may [a]interpret. 14For
if I pray in a tongue, my spirit prays, but my
understanding is unfruitful. 15What is *the*
conclusion then? I will pray with the spirit,
and I will also pray with the understanding. [a]I will sing with the spirit, and I will also
sing [b]with the understanding. 16Otherwise,
if you bless with the spirit, how will he who
occupies the place of the uninformed say
"Amen" [a]at your giving of thanks, since he
does not understand what you say? 17For
you indeed give thanks well, but the other
is not edified.

18I thank my God I speak with tongues
more than you all; 19yet in the church I
would rather speak five words with my

13:2 [a] Matt. 7:22; 1 Cor. 12:8–10, 28; 14:1 [b] Matt. 17:20; 21:21; Mark 11:23; Luke 17:6 13:3 [a] Matt. 6:1, 2 [1] NU-Text reads *so I may boast.* 13:4 [a] Prov. 10:12; 17:9; 1 Thess. 5:14; [1 Pet. 4:8] [b] Eph. 4:32 [c] Gal. 5:26 13:5 [a] 1 Cor. 10:24; Phil. 2:4 13:6 [a] Ps. 10:3; Rom. 1:32 [b] 2 John 4; 3 John 3 13:7 [a] Rom. 15:1; Gal. 6:2; 2 Tim. 2:24 13:9 [a] 1 Cor. 8:2; 13:12 13:12 [a] [2 Cor. 3:18; 5:7]; Phil. 3:12; James 1:23 [b] Gen. 32:30; Num. 12:8; Matt. 18:10; [1 John 3:2] 14:1 [a] 1 Cor. 12:31; 14:39 [b] Num. 11:25, 29 14:2 [a] Acts 2:4; 10:46 14:3 [a] Rom. 14:19; 15:2; 2 Cor. 10:8; 12:19; Eph. 4:12, 29 [b] 1 Tim. 4:13; 2 Tim. 4:2; Titus 1:9; 2:15; Heb. 3:13; 10:25 14:5 [1] NU-Text reads *and.* 14:6 [a] 1 Cor. 14:26; Eph. 1:17 14:13 [a] 1 Cor. 12:10 14:15 [a] Eph. 5:19; Col. 3:16 [b] Ps. 47:7 14:16 [a] Deut. 27:15–26; 1 Chr. 16:36; Neh. 5:13; 8:6; Ps. 106:48; Jer. 11:5; 28:6; 1 Cor. 11:24; Rev. 5:14; 7:12

understanding, that I may teach others
also, than ten thousand words in a tongue.

Tongues a Sign to Unbelievers

20 Brethren, [a]do not be children in understanding; however, in malice [b]be babes, but
in understanding be mature.
21 [a]In the law it is written:

[b]"With *men of* other tongues
and other lips
I will speak to this people;
And yet, for all that, they
will not hear Me,"[1]

says the Lord.
22 Therefore tongues are for a [a]sign, not
to those who believe but to unbelievers; but
prophesying is not for unbelievers but for
those who believe. 23 Therefore if the whole
church comes together in one place, and
all speak with tongues, and there come in
those who are uninformed or unbelievers,
[a]will they not say that you are out of your
mind? 24 But if all prophesy, and an unbeliever or an uninformed person comes in,
he is convinced by all, he is convicted by
all. 25 And thus[1] the secrets of his heart are
revealed; and so, falling down on *his* face,
he will worship God and report [a]that God
is truly among you.

Order in Church Meetings

26 How is it then, brethren? Whenever
you come together, each of you has a
psalm, [a]has a teaching, has a tongue, has
a revelation, has an interpretation. [b]Let all
things be done for edification. 27 If anyone
speaks in a tongue, *let there be* two or at
the most three, *each* in turn, and let one
interpret. 28 But if there is no interpreter,
let him keep silent in church, and let him
speak to himself and to God. 29 Let two or
three prophets speak, and [a]let the others
judge. 30 But if *anything* is revealed to another who sits by, [a]let the first keep silent.
31 For you can all prophesy one by one, that
all may learn and all may be encouraged.
32 And [a]the spirits of the prophets are subject to the prophets. 33 For God is not *the
author* of confusion but of peace, [a]as in all
the churches of the saints.
34 [a]Let your[1] women keep silent in the
churches, for they are not permitted to
speak; but *they are* to be submissive, as
the [b]law also says. 35 And if they want to
learn something, let them ask their own
husbands at home; for it is shameful for
women to speak in church.
36 Or did the word of God come *originally* from you? Or *was it* you only that it
reached? 37 [a]If anyone thinks himself to be
a prophet or spiritual, let him acknowledge
that the things which I write to you are the
commandments of the Lord. 38 But if anyone is ignorant, let him be ignorant.[1]
39 Therefore, brethren, [a]desire earnestly
to prophesy, and do not forbid to speak
with tongues. 40 [a]Let all things be done decently and in order.

The Risen Christ, Faith's Reality
(cf. Mark 16:9–20)

15 Moreover, brethren, I declare to
you the gospel [a]which I preached to
you, which also you received and [b]in which
you stand, 2 [a]by which also you are saved, if
you hold fast that word which I preached
to you—unless [b]you believed in vain.
3 For [a]I delivered to you first of all that
[b]which I also received: that Christ died for
our sins [c]according to the Scriptures, 4 and
that He was buried, and that He rose again
the third day [a]according to the Scriptures,
5 [a]and that He was seen by Cephas, then [b]by
the twelve. 6 After that He was seen by over
five hundred brethren at once, of whom
the greater part remain to the present, but
some have fallen asleep. 7 After that He was
seen by James, then [a]by all the apostles.
8 [a]Then last of all He was seen by me also,
as by one born out of due time.

14:20 [a] Ps. 131:2; [Matt. 11:25; 18:3; 19:14]; Rom. 16:19; 1 Cor. 3:1; Eph. 4:14; Heb. 5:12, 13 [b] [Matt. 18:3; 1 Pet. 2:2] 14:21 [a] John 10:34; 1 Cor. 14:34 [b] Is. 28:11, 12 [1] Isaiah 28:11, 12 14:22 [a] Mark 16:17 14:23 [a] Acts 2:13 14:25 [a] Is. 45:14; Dan. 2:47; Zech. 8:23; Acts 4:13 [1] NU-Text omits *And thus.* 14:26 [a] 1 Cor. 12:8–10; 14:6 [b] 1 Cor. 12:7; [2 Cor. 12:19] 14:29 [a] 1 Cor. 12:10 14:30 [a] [1 Thess. 5:19, 20] 14:32 [a] 1 John 4:1 14:33 [a] 1 Cor. 11:16 14:34 [a] 1 Tim. 2:11; 1 Pet. 3:1 [b] Gen. 3:16 [1] NU-Text omits *your.* 14:37 [a] 2 Cor. 10:7; [1 John 4:6] 14:38 [1] NU-Text reads *if anyone does not recognize this, he is not recognized.* 14:39 [a] 1 Cor. 12:31; 1 Thess. 5:20 14:40 [a] 1 Cor. 14:33 15:1 [a] Rom. 2:16; [Gal. 1:11] [b] [Rom. 5:2; 11:20; 2 Cor. 1:24] 15:2 [a] Rom. 1:16; 1 Cor. 1:21 [b] Gal. 3:4 15:3 [a] 1 Cor. 11:2, 23 [b] [Gal. 1:12] [c] Ps. 22:15; Is. 53:5–12; Acts 3:18; 1 Pet. 1:11 15:4 [a] Gen. 1:9–13; 2 Kin. 20:8; Ps. 16:9–11; 68:18; 110:1; Is. 53:10; Hos. 6:2; Jon. 1:17; 2:10; Matt. 12:39, 40; Mark 8:31; Luke 11:29, 30; 24:26; John 2:19–21; Acts 2:25 15:5 [a] Luke 24:34 [b] Matt. 28:17 15:7 [a] Luke 24:50; Acts 1:3, 4 15:8 [a] [Acts 9:3–8; 22:6–11; 26:12–18]; 1 Cor. 9:1

9For I am [a]the least of the apostles, who
am not worthy to be called an apostle, because [b]I persecuted the church of God. 10But
[a]by the grace of God I am what I am, and
His grace toward me was not in vain; but I
labored more abundantly than they all, [b]yet
not I, but the grace of God *which was* with
me. 11Therefore, whether *it was* I or they, so
we preach and so you believed.

The Risen Christ, Our Hope
(cf. 1 Thess. 4:13–18)

12Now if Christ is preached that He has
been raised from the dead, how do some
among you say that there is no resurrection of the dead? 13But if there is no resurrection of the dead, [a]then Christ is not
risen. 14And if Christ is not risen, then our
preaching *is* empty and your faith *is* also
empty. 15Yes, and we are found false witnesses of God, because [a]we have testified of
God that He raised up Christ, whom He did
not raise up—if in fact the dead do not rise.
16For if *the* dead do not rise, then Christ is
not risen. 17And if Christ is not risen, your
faith *is* futile; [a]you are still in your sins!
18Then also those who have fallen [a]asleep
in Christ have perished. 19[a]If in this life only
we have hope in Christ, we are of all men
the most pitiable.

The Last Enemy Destroyed

20But now [a]Christ is risen from the dead,
and has become [b]the firstfruits of those
who have fallen asleep. 21For [a]since by man
came death, [b]by Man also *came* the resurrection of the dead. 22For as in Adam all
die, even so in Christ all shall [a]be made
alive. 23But [a]each one in his own order:
Christ the firstfruits, afterward those *who
are* Christ's at His coming. 24Then *comes*
the end, when He delivers [a]the kingdom
to God the Father, when He puts an end to
all rule and all authority and power. 25For
He must reign [a]till He has put all enemies
under His feet. 26[a]The last enemy *that* will
be destroyed *is* death. 27For [a]"He has put all
things under His feet."[1] But when He says
"all things are put under *Him," it is* evident
that He who put all things under Him is ex-
cepted. 28[a]Now when all things are made
subject to Him, then [b]the Son Himself will
also be subject to Him who put all things
under Him, that God may be all in all.

Effects of Denying the Resurrection

29Otherwise, what will they do who are
baptized for the dead, if the dead do not rise
at all? Why then are they baptized for the
dead? 30And [a]why do we stand in jeopardy
every hour? 31I affirm, by [a]the boasting in
you which I have in Christ Jesus our Lord, [b]I
die daily. 32If, in the manner of men, [a]I have
fought with beasts at Ephesus, what advantage *is it* to me? If *the* dead do not rise, [b]"Let
us eat and drink, for tomorrow we die!"[1]
33Do not be deceived: [a]"Evil company
corrupts good habits." 34[a]Awake to righteousness, and do not sin; [b]for some do
not have the knowledge of God. [c]I speak
this to your shame.

A Glorious Body

35But someone will say, [a]"How are the
dead raised up? And with what body do they
come?" 36Foolish one, [a]what you sow is not
made alive unless it dies. 37And what you
sow, you do not sow that body that shall be,
but mere grain—perhaps wheat or some
other *grain.* 38But God gives it a body as
He pleases, and to each seed its own body.
39All flesh *is* not the same flesh, but *there
is* one *kind of* flesh[1] of men, another flesh
of animals, another of fish, *and* another
of birds.
40*There are* also celestial bodies and terrestrial bodies; but the glory of the celestial *is* one, and the *glory* of the terrestrial
is another. 41*There is* one glory of the sun,
another glory of the moon, and another
glory of the stars; for *one* star differs from
another star in glory.
42[a]So also *is* the resurrection of the dead.
The body is sown in corruption, it is raised

15:9 [a] 2 Cor. 12:11; Eph. 3:8; 1 Tim. 1:15 [b] Acts 8:3 15:10 [a] Eph. 3:7, 8 [b] Matt. 10:20; Rom. 15:18; Gal. 2:8; Phil. 2:13 15:13 [a] [1 Thess. 4:14] 15:15 [a] Acts 2:24 15:17 [a] [Rom. 4:25] 15:18 [a] Job 14:12; Ps. 13:3 15:19 [a] 1 Cor. 4:9; 2 Tim. 3:12 15:20 [a] Acts 2:24; 1 Pet. 1:3 [b] Acts 26:23; 1 Cor. 15:23; Rev. 1:5 15:21 [a] Gen. 3:19; Ezek. 18:4; Rom. 5:12; 6:23; Heb. 9:27 [b] John 11:25 15:22 [a] [John 5:28, 29] 15:23 [a] [1 Thess. 4:15–17] 15:24 [a] [Dan. 2:44; 7:14, 27; 2 Pet. 1:11] 15:25 [a] Ps. 110:1; Matt. 22:44 15:26 [a] [2 Tim. 1:10; Rev. 20:14; 21:4] 15:27 [a] Ps. 8:6 [1] Psalm 8:6 15:28 [a] [Phil. 3:21] [b] 1 Cor. 3:23; 11:3; 12:6 15:30 [a] 2 Cor. 11:26 15:31 [a] 1 Thess. 2:19 [b] Rom. 8:36 15:32 [a] 2 Cor. 1:8 [b] Eccl. 2:24; Is. 22:13; 56:12; Luke 12:19 [1] Isaiah 22:13 15:33 [a] [1 Cor. 5:6] 15:34 [a] Rom. 13:11; Eph. 5:14 [b] [1 Thess. 4:5] [c] 1 Cor. 6:5 15:35 [a] Ezek. 37:3 15:36 [a] John 12:24 15:39 [1] NU-Text and M-Text omit *of flesh.* 15:42 [a] [Dan. 12:3; Matt. 13:43]

in incorruption. 43[a]It is sown in dishonor,
it is raised in glory. It is sown in weakness,
it is raised in power. 44It is sown a natural
body, it is raised a spiritual body. There is a
natural body, and there is a spiritual body.
45And so it is written, [a]"The first man Adam
became a living being."[1] [b]The last Adam *became* [c]a life-giving spirit.

46However, the spiritual is not first, but
the natural, and afterward the spiritual.
47[a]The first man *was* of the earth, [b]*made*
of dust; the second Man *is* the Lord[1] [c]from
heaven. 48As *was* the *man* of dust, so also
are those *who are made* of dust; [a]and as *is*
the heavenly *Man,* so also *are* those *who are*
heavenly. 49And [a]as we have borne the image of the *man* of dust, [b]we shall also bear[1]
the image of the heavenly *Man.*

Our Final Victory

50Now this I say, brethren, that [a]flesh and
blood cannot inherit the kingdom of God;
nor does corruption inherit incorruption.
51Behold, I tell you a mystery: [a]We shall not
all sleep, [b]but we shall all be changed— 52in
a moment, in the twinkling of an eye, at the
last trumpet. [a]For the trumpet will sound,
and the dead will be raised incorruptible,
and we shall be changed. 53For this corruptible must put on incorruption, and [a]this
mortal *must* put on immortality. 54So when
this corruptible has put on incorruption,
and this mortal has put on immortality, then
shall be brought to pass the saying that is
written: [a]"Death is swallowed up in victory."[1]

55 "O[a] Death, where *is* your sting?[1]
O Hades, where *is* your victory?"[2]

56The sting of death *is* sin, and [a]the strength
of sin *is* the law. 57[a]But thanks *be* to God,
who gives us [b]the victory through our Lord
Jesus Christ.

58[a]Therefore, my beloved brethren, be
steadfast, immovable, always abounding
in the work of the Lord, knowing [b]that your
labor is not in vain in the Lord.

Collection for the Saints

16 Now concerning [a]the collection for
the saints, as I have given orders to
the churches of Galatia, so you must do also:
2[a]On the first *day* of the week let each one
of you lay something aside, storing up as he
may prosper, that there be no collections
when I come. 3And when I come, [a]whom-
ever you approve by *your* letters I will send
to bear your gift to Jerusalem. 4[a]But if it is
fitting that I go also, they will go with me.

Personal Plans
(cf. Acts 19:21)

5Now I will come to you [a]when I pass
through Macedonia (for I am passing
through Macedonia). 6And it may be that
I will remain, or even spend the winter with
you, that you may [a]send me on my journey,
wherever I go. 7For I do not wish to see you
now on the way; but I hope to stay a while
with you, [a]if the Lord permits.

8But I will tarry in Ephesus until [a]Pen-
tecost. 9For [a]a great and effective door has
opened to me, and [b]*there are* many adversaries.

10And [a]if Timothy comes, see that he may
be with you without fear; for [b]he does the
work of the Lord, as I also *do.* 11[a]Therefore
let no one despise him. But send him on his
journey [b]in peace, that he may come to me;
for I am waiting for him with the brethren.

12Now concerning *our* brother [a]Apollos,
I strongly urged him to come to you with
the brethren, but he was quite unwilling to
come at this time; however, he will come
when he has a convenient time.

Final Exhortations

13[a]Watch, [b]stand fast in the faith, be
brave, [c]be strong. 14[a]Let all *that* you *do* be
done with love.

15:43 [a] [Phil. 3:21; Col. 3:4] 15:45 [a] Gen. 2:7 [b] [Rom. 5:14] [c] John 5:21; 6:57; [Rom. 8:2; Phil. 3:21; Col. 3:4] [1] Genesis 2:7
15:47 [a] John 3:31 [b] Gen. 2:7; 3:19 [c] John 3:13 [1] NU-Text omits *the Lord.* 15:48 [a] Phil. 3:20 15:49 [a] Gen. 5:3 [b] Rom. 8:29;
[2 Cor. 3:18; Phil. 3:21; 1 John 3:2] [1] M-Text reads *let us also bear.* 15:50 [a] Matt. 16:17; [John 3:3, 5] 15:51 [a] [1 Thess. 4:15]
[b] [Phil. 3:21] 15:52 [a] Zech. 9:14; Matt. 24:31; John 5:25 15:53 [a] 2 Cor. 5:4 15:54 [a] Is. 25:8; [Rev. 20:14] [1] Isaiah 25:8
15:55 [a] Hos. 13:14 [1] Hosea 13:14 [2] NU-Text reads *O Death, where is your victory? O Death, where is your sting?* 15:56 [a] [Rom. 3:20;
4:15; 7:8] 15:57 [a] [Rom. 7:25]; 2 Cor. 2:14 [b] Rom. 8:37; [Heb. 2:14; 1 John 5:4]; Rev. 21:4 15:58 [a] 2 Pet. 3:14 [b] [1 Cor. 3:8]
16:1 [a] Acts 11:29; Gal. 2:10 16:2 [a] Acts 20:7 16:3 [a] 2 Cor. 3:1; 8:18 16:4 [a] 2 Cor. 8:4, 19 16:5 [a] Acts 19:21; 2 Cor. 1:15, 16
16:6 [a] Acts 15:3; Rom. 15:24; 1 Cor. 16:11 16:7 [a] Acts 18:21; James 4:15 16:8 [a] Lev. 23:15–22 16:9 [a] Acts 14:27; 2 Cor. 2:12; Col. 4:3
[b] Acts 19:9 16:10 [a] Acts 19:22; 2 Tim. 1:2 [b] Phil. 2:20; 1 Thess. 3:2 16:11 [a] 1 Tim. 4:12; Titus 2:15 [b] Acts 15:33 16:12 [a] Acts 18:24;
1 Cor. 1:12; 3:5 16:13 [a] Matt. 24:42 [b] 1 Cor. 15:1; Gal. 5:1; Phil. 1:27; 4:1; 1 Thess. 3:8; 2 Thess. 2:15
[c] [Ps. 31:24; Eph. 3:16; 6:10; Col. 1:11] 16:14 [a] [1 Pet. 4:8]

#OXYGEN

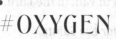

1 CORINTHIANS 16:13–14

Elevate Your Identity

Your character speaks volumes. Let your actions show your faith. Stand for Christ and allow Him to refine you every day. Allow your identity in Christ to show.

Breathe and elevate your identity.

15I urge you, brethren—you know [a]the
household of Stephanas, that it is [b]the firstfruits of Achaia, and *that* they have devoted themselves to [c]the ministry of the
saints— 16[a]that you also submit to such, and
to everyone who works and [b]labors with *us.*
17I am glad about the coming of Stephanas, Fortunatus, and Achaicus, [a]for what
was lacking on your part they supplied.
18[a]For they refreshed my spirit and yours.
Therefore [b]acknowledge such men.

Greetings and a Solemn Farewell

19The churches of Asia greet you. Aquila
and Priscilla greet you heartily in the Lord,
[a]with the church that is in their house. 20All
the brethren greet you.
[a]Greet one another with a holy kiss.
21[a]The salutation with my own hand—
Paul's.
22If anyone [a]does not love the Lord
Jesus Christ, [b]let him be accursed.[1] [c]O Lord,
come![2]
23[a]The grace of our Lord Jesus Christ *be*
with you. 24My love *be* with you all in Christ
Jesus. Amen.

16:15 [a] 1 Cor. 1:16 [b] Rom. 16:5 [c] 2 Cor. 8:4 16:16 [a] Eph. 5:21; 1 Thess. 5:12; Heb. 13:17 [b] [Heb. 6:10] 16:17 [a] 2 Cor. 11:9; Phil. 2:30 16:18 [a] Col. 4:8 [b] Phil. 2:29 16:19 [a] Rom. 16:5 16:20 [a] Rom. 16:16 16:21 [a] Rom. 16:22; Gal. 6:11; Col. 4:18; 2 Thess. 3:17; Philem. 19 16:22 [a] Eph. 6:24 [b] Gal. 1:8, 9 [c] Jude 14, 15 [1] Greek *anathema* [2] Aramaic *Maranatha* 16:23 [a] Rom. 16:20

THE SECOND EPISTLE OF PAUL TO THE

CORINTHIANS

OVERVIEW

Since Paul's first letter to the Corinthian church, false teachers had swayed the believers and stirred the people against Paul. They claimed Paul was fickle, arrogant, unimpressive in appearance and speech, and unqualified to be an apostle of Jesus Christ. Paul paid an unpleasant visit to the church (see 2 Cor. 2:1–4). He then sent another letter to them (see 7:8–12), a letter that has since been lost. Paul then sent Titus to Corinth to deal with these difficulties, and upon Titus's return, the apostle rejoiced to hear of the Corinthians' change of heart. Paul wrote 2 Corinthians to express his thanksgiving for the repentant majority and appeal to the rebellious minority to accept his authority.

The church, though, was still in crisis. Numerous controversies had created significant structural and theological fissures that would affect the future of the church if left unaddressed. This extremely pagan city could continue to influence human behavior negatively, even that of a believer. The church desperately needed to distinguish itself from the larger culture. Yet, the remaining issues Paul addressed in 2 Corinthians were largely internal conflicts. Rival factions, teachers, and apostles continued to challenge Paul's authority in his absence.

Paul's experiences with the church in Corinth were fraught with many conflicts that needed to be addressed. However, 2 Corinthians is not simply a repudiation of church conflicts and controversies; Paul also provides a remedy. He wrote in exhortation, "Now all things are of God, who has reconciled us to Himself through Jesus Christ, and has given us the ministry of reconciliation, that is, that God was in Christ reconciling the world to Himself, not imputing their trespasses to them, and has committed to us the word of reconciliation" (5:18–19). Whenever the church over the last nearly two thousand years has been guilty of losing sight of its mission and drifting from its foundations, Paul's words have reminded believers that we have both a "ministry of reconciliation" and "word of reconciliation."

BREATHE IT IN

Perhaps there is nothing more discouraging than conflict among Christians who are supposed to exhibit the love of Jesus Christ. Yet, conflict among Christians has proven to be as vicious as disputes between non-Christians. Divorce statistics among Christians and non-Christians are in lockstep with each other. Despite the existence of thriving Christian communities, violence, particularly family violence, continues to threaten our society. When we are bogged down by the divisions and schisms of our day, we must remember that even while people are the center of the problem, God empowers us also to be used in the solution. Believers must play the role given to us by Christ and performed in His power in the process of reconciliation and resolving conflict. There is a reason Jesus asks us to pray for enemies.

Unfortunately, church conflict is nothing new. As we see in Paul's two letters to the Corinthians, the early church had many conflicts. Yet, often these disputes, conflicts, or problems resulted in the church's advancement. In Acts 6, for example, non-Jewish widows in the church were being mistreated by fellow believers. This controversy, however, resulted in the formation of the New

Testament position of deacon. It was the deacons who were to ensure that the needs of all were met and that there was order in the church. Additionally, a dispute between Paul and John Mark resulted in the exponential growth of the church (see Acts 15:36–41). What would have become one missionary journey became two. While we always should seek to avoid conflict, when it occurs, it does not have to be the end of a ministry, marriage, job, or relationship. Conflict can actually be the impetus for growth.

Are you experiencing any unresolved conflicts with your siblings, parents, children, or extended family? Has conflict soured your involvement within a church community? Second Corinthians reminds us that we who confess Christ have both a ministry and a word of reconciliation. Practice this ministry of reconciliation by either seeking or extending forgiveness. Work through conflict in a humble, godly way, and then see how you can grow from the experience.

Put the Word of God to the test. Identify those areas in your life where you need to apply conflict resolution skills. Talk with your children about how to resolve conflicts among their friends. Remember, God often gives His greatest gifts through relationships. God often uses others to bless you. But God also wants to use you to bless others. Jesus said that the two greatest commands were to "love the LORD your God with all your heart, with all your soul, and with all your mind" and to "love your neighbor as yourself" (Matt. 22:37, 39). Spiritual maturity compels us to understand that claiming to love God and failing to love the people He loves is hypocrisy.

†

THE SECOND EPISTLE OF PAUL TO THE

CORINTHIANS

Greeting

1 Paul, [a]an apostle of Jesus Christ by the
will of God, and [b]Timothy *our* brother,

To the church of God which is at Corinth,
[c]with all the saints who are in all Achaia:

2 [a]Grace to you and peace from God our
Father and the Lord Jesus Christ.

Comfort in Suffering

3 [a]Blessed *be* the God and Father of our
Lord Jesus Christ, the Father of mercies
and God of all comfort, 4 who [a]comforts us
in all our tribulation, that we may be able to
comfort those who are in any trouble, with
the comfort with which we ourselves are
comforted by God. 5 For as [a]the sufferings
of Christ abound in us, so our consolation
also abounds through Christ. 6 Now if we
are afflicted, [a]*it is* for your consolation and
salvation, which is effective for enduring
the same sufferings which we also suffer.
Or if we are comforted, *it is* for your consolation and salvation. 7 And our hope for
you *is* steadfast, because we know that [a]as
you are partakers of the sufferings, so also
you will partake of the consolation.

Delivered from Suffering

8 For we do not want you to be ignorant,
brethren, of [a]our trouble which came to
us in Asia: that we were burdened beyond
measure, above strength, so that we despaired even of life. 9 Yes, we had the sentence of death in ourselves, that we should
[a]not trust in ourselves but in God who
raises the dead, 10 [a]who delivered us from
so great a death, and does[1] deliver us; in
whom we trust that He will still deliver *us,*
11 you also [a]helping together in prayer for
us, that thanks may be given by many persons on our[1] behalf [b]for the gift *granted* to
us through many.

Paul's Sincerity

12 For our boasting is this: the testimony
of our conscience that we conducted ourselves in the world in simplicity and [a]godly
sincerity, [b]not with fleshly wisdom but by
the grace of God, and more abundantly
toward you. 13 For we are not writing any
other things to you than what you read or
understand. Now I trust you will understand, even to the end 14 (as also you have
understood us in part), [a]that we are your
boast as [b]you also *are* ours, in the day of
the Lord Jesus.

Sparing the Church

15 And in this confidence [a]I intended to
come to you before, that you might have [b]a
second benefit— 16 to pass by way of you to
Macedonia, [a]to come again from Macedonia to you, and be helped by you on my way
to Judea. 17 Therefore, when I was planning
this, did I do it lightly? Or the things I plan,
do I plan [a]according to the flesh, that with
me there should be Yes, Yes, and No, No?
18 But *as* God *is* [a]faithful, our word to you
was not Yes and No. 19 For [a]the Son of God,
Jesus Christ, who was preached among you

1:1 [a] 1 Cor. 1:1; Eph. 1:1; Col. 1:1; 1 Tim. 1:1; 2 Tim. 1:1 [b] Acts 16:1; 1 Cor. 16:10 [c] Phil. 1:1; Col. 1:2 1:2 [a] Rom. 1:7 1:3 [a] Eph. 1:3; 1 Pet. 1:3 1:4 [a] Is. 51:12; 66:13; 2 Cor. 7:6, 7, 13 1:5 [a] [Acts 9:4]; 2 Cor. 4:10; Phil. 3:10; Col. 1:24 1:6 [a] 2 Cor. 4:15; 12:15; Eph. 3:1, 13; 2 Tim. 2:10 1:7 [a] [Rom. 8:17; 2 Tim. 2:12] 1:8 [a] Acts 19:23; 1 Cor. 15:32; 16:9 1:9 [a] Jer. 17:5, 7 1:10 [a] [2 Pet. 2:9] [1] NU-Text reads *shall.* 1:11 [a] Rom. 15:30; Phil. 1:19; Philem. 22 [b] 2 Cor. 4:15; 9:11 [1] M-Text reads *your behalf.* 1:12 [a] 2 Cor. 2:17 [b] [1 Cor. 2:4] 1:14 [a] 2 Cor. 5:12 [b] Phil. 2:16; 1 Thess. 2:19 1:15 [a] 1 Cor. 4:19 [b] Rom. 1:11; 15:29 1:16 [a] Acts 19:21; 1 Cor. 16:3–6 1:17 [a] 2 Cor. 10:2; 11:18 1:18 [a] 1 John 5:20 1:19 [a] Mark 1:1; Luke 1:35; John 1:34; 20:31; 1 John 5:5, 20

BELIEVE IN THE RESURRECTION LIFE

INHALE

I'm going to be honest; things are not easy right now. I cannot help my parents. I cannot help my friends. I cannot even buy a pet for my kids because I can barely make ends meet. I live from paycheck to paycheck. I feel so defeated and depressed. I love the Lord, and I know His mercies are new every day, but I feel like a failure. I believe in the resurrection life so much that I want to end it all now. Can God give me grace if I commit suicide? Will I go to heaven if I take my own life?

EXHALE

First, let me tell you how sorry I am that you are going through such a difficult time and that you are feeling defeated and depressed. I'm truly sorry. Second, I want to encourage you to talk with a counselor or therapist about what you are experiencing if you haven't done that already. There is nothing wrong with what you are feeling and thinking. There's no shame in getting help from someone who understands and can help you process your thoughts and emotions.

With that said, I can now answer the question you posed. Nowhere in the Bible does it tell us that God saves and forgives us *except* if we commit suicide. What the Bible does tell us, though, is that salvation is by grace through faith and that those in Christ are forgiven of all their sins and will live forever with God.

The Bible also tells us that God's heart is for us right where we are today. He wants us to experience joyful, abundant living here and now. He cares for us and wants to help us through whatever we face. When we think we can't make it through, it is the perfect time to remember that God can do what we feel we cannot do. God can help us through. Second Corinthians 1:10 says that Christ "delivered us from so great a death, and does deliver us; in whom we trust that He will still deliver us." Jesus can deliver us from anything. He can deliver you. I want you to fight to believe that. You are not the first person to be where you are. Trust me. You are not alone. God is with you, and He has also provided others to come alongside you and help. Turn to Jesus in this time of need and turn to others who He has provided to help you. You are cared for and loved, and you matter to the God of the universe who fully accepts you.

by us—by me, [b]Silvanus, and [c]Timothy—
was not Yes and No, [d]but in Him was Yes.
20 [a]For all the promises of God in Him *are*
Yes, and in Him Amen, to the glory of God
through us. 21 Now He who establishes us
with you in Christ and [a]has anointed us *is*
God, 22 who [a]also has sealed us and [b]given
us the Spirit in our hearts as a guarantee.
23 Moreover [a]I call God as witness against
my soul, [b]that to spare you I came no more
to Corinth. 24 Not [a]that we have dominion
over your faith, but are fellow workers for
your joy; for [b]by faith you stand.

2 But I determined this within myself,
[a]that I would not come again to you in
sorrow. 2 For if I make you [a]sorrowful, then
who is he who makes me glad but the one
who is made sorrowful by me?

Forgive the Offender

3 And I wrote this very thing to you,
lest, when I came, [a]I should have sorrow
over those from whom I ought to have joy,
[b]having confidence in you all that my joy
is *the joy* of you all. 4 For out of much affliction and anguish of heart I wrote to you,
with many tears, [a]not that you should be
grieved, but that you might know the love
which I have so abundantly for you.
5 But [a]if anyone has caused grief, he has

1:19 [b] 1 Thess. 1:1; 2 Thess. 1:1; 1 Pet. 5:12 [c] Acts 18:5; 2 Cor. 1:1 [d] [Heb. 13:8] 1:20 [a] [Rom. 15:8, 9] 1:21 [a] [1 John 2:20, 27] 1:22 [a] [Eph. 4:30] [b] Rom. 8:16; 2 Cor. 5:5; [Eph. 1:14] 1:23 [a] Rom. 1:9; Gal. 1:20; Phil. 1:8 [b] 1 Cor. 4:21; 2 Cor. 2:3; 12:20 1:24 [a] 1 Cor. 3:5; 2 Cor. 4:5; 11:20; [1 Pet. 5:3] [b] Rom. 11:20; 1 Cor. 15:1 2:1 [a] 2 Cor. 1:23 2:2 [a] 2 Cor. 7:8 2:3 [a] 1 Cor. 4:21; 2 Cor. 12:21 [b] 2 Cor. 8:22; Gal. 5:10; 2 Thess. 3:4; Philem. 21 2:4 [a] [2 Cor. 2:9; 7:8, 12] 2:5 [a] [1 Cor. 5:1]

not [b]grieved me, but all of you to some
extent—not to be too severe. 6This punishment which *was inflicted* [a]by the majority *is* sufficient for such a man, 7[a]so that,
on the contrary, you *ought* rather to forgive
and comfort *him*, lest perhaps such a one
be swallowed up with too much sorrow.
8Therefore I urge you to reaffirm *your* love
to him. 9For to this end I also wrote, that
I might put you to the test, whether you
are [a]obedient in all things. 10Now whom
you forgive anything, I also *forgive*. For
if indeed I have forgiven anything, I have
forgiven that one[1] for your sakes in the
presence of Christ, 11lest Satan should take
advantage of us; for we are not ignorant of
his devices.

Triumph in Christ

12Furthermore, [a]when I came to Troas
to *preach* Christ's gospel, and [b]a door was
opened to me by the Lord, 13[a]I had no rest
in my spirit, because I did not find Titus
my brother; but taking my leave of them,
I departed for Macedonia.
14Now thanks *be* to God who always leads
us in triumph in Christ, and through us dif-
fuses the fragrance of His knowledge in every place. 15For we are to God the fragrance
of Christ [a]among those who are being saved
and [b]among those who are perishing. 16[a]To
the one *we are* the aroma of death *leading*
to death, and to the other the aroma of life
leading to life. And [b]who *is* sufficient for
these things? 17For we are not, as so many,[1]
[a]peddling the word of God; but as [b]of sincerity, but as from God, we speak in the sight
of God in Christ.

Christ's Epistle
(cf. Jer. 31:31–34)

3 Do [a]we begin again to commend ourselves? Or do we need, as some *others*,
[b]epistles of commendation to you or *letters*
of commendation from you? 2[a]You are our
epistle written in our hearts, known and
read by all men; 3clearly you are an epistle of Christ, [a]ministered by us, written not
with ink but by the Spirit of the living God,
not [b]on tablets of stone but [c]on tablets of
flesh, *that is*, of the heart.

The Spirit, Not the Letter

4And we have such trust through Christ
toward God. 5[a]Not that we are sufficient
of ourselves to think of anything as *being*
from ourselves, but [b]our sufficiency *is* from
God, 6who also made us sufficient as [a]min-
isters of [b]the new covenant, not [c]of the letter but of the Spirit;[1] for [d]the letter kills, [e]but
the Spirit gives life.

Glory of the New Covenant

7But if [a]the ministry of death, [b]written
and engraved on stones, was glorious, [c]so
that the children of Israel could not look
steadily at the face of Moses because of the
glory of his countenance, which *glory* was
passing away, 8how will [a]the ministry of
the Spirit not be more glorious? 9For if the
ministry of condemnation *had* glory, the
ministry [a]of righteousness exceeds much
more in glory. 10For even what was made
glorious had no glory in this respect, because of the glory that excels. 11For if what
is passing away *was* glorious, what remains
is much more glorious.
12Therefore, since we have such hope,
[a]we use great boldness of speech— 13un-
like Moses, [a]*who* put a veil over his face so
that the children of Israel could not look
steadily at [b]the end of what was passing
away. 14But [a]their minds were blinded. For
until this day the same veil remains un-
lifted in the reading of the Old Testament,
because the *veil* is taken away in Christ.
15But even to this day, when Moses is read,
a veil lies on their heart. 16Nevertheless
[a]when one turns to the Lord, [b]the veil is
taken away. 17Now [a]the Lord is the Spirit;
and where the Spirit of the Lord *is*, there
is [b]liberty. 18But we all, with unveiled face,

2:5 [b] Gal. 4:12 **2:6** [a] 1 Cor. 5:4, 5; 2 Cor. 7:11; 1 Tim. 5:20 **2:7** [a] Gal. 6:1; Eph. 4:32 **2:9** [a] 2 Cor. 7:15; 10:6 **2:10** [1] NU-Text reads *For indeed, what I have forgiven, if I have forgiven anything, I did it.* **2:12** [a] Acts 16:8 [b] 1 Cor. 16:9 **2:13** [a] 2 Cor. 7:6, 13; 8:6; Gal. 2:1, 3; 2 Tim. 4:10; Titus 1:4 **2:15** [a] [1 Cor. 1:18] [b] [2 Cor. 4:3] **2:16** [a] Luke 2:34; [John 9:39; 1 Pet. 2:7] [b] [1 Cor. 15:10] **2:17** [a] 2 Pet. 2:3 [b] 1 Cor. 5:8; 2 Cor. 1:12; 1 Thess. 2:4; 1 Pet. 4:11 [1] M-Text reads *the rest.* **3:1** [a] 2 Cor. 5:12; 10:12, 18; 12:11 [b] Acts 18:27 **3:2** [a] 1 Cor. 9:2 **3:3** [a] 1 Cor. 3:5 [b] Ex. 24:12; 31:18; 32:15; 2 Cor. 3:7 [c] Ps. 40:8 **3:5** [a] [John 15:5] [b] 1 Cor. 15:10 **3:6** [a] 1 Cor. 3:5; Eph. 3:7 [b] Jer. 31:31; Matt. 26:28; Luke 22:20 [c] Rom. 2:27 [d] [Rom. 3:20]; Gal. 3:10 [e] John 6:63; Rom. 8:2 [1] Or *spirit* **3:7** [a] Rom. 7:10 [b] Ex. 34:1; Deut. 10:1 [c] Ex. 34:29 **3:8** [a] [Gal. 3:5] **3:9** [a] [Rom. 1:17; 3:21] **3:12** [a] Acts 4:13, 29; 2 Cor. 7:4; Eph. 6:19 **3:13** [a] Ex. 34:33–35; 2 Cor. 3:7 [b] Rom. 10:4; [Gal. 3:23] **3:14** [a] Is. 6:10; 29:10; Acts 28:26; Rom. 11:7, 8; 2 Cor. 4:4 **3:16** [a] Ex. 34:34; Rom. 11:23 [b] Is. 25:7 **3:17** [a] [1 Cor. 15:45] [b] John 8:32; Gal. 5:1, 13

beholding [a]as in a mirror [b]the glory of the
Lord, [c]are being transformed into the same
image from glory to glory, just as by the
Spirit of the Lord.

The Light of Christ's Gospel

4 Therefore, since we have this ministry, [a]as we have received mercy, we [b]do
not lose heart. 2 But we have renounced
the hidden things of shame, not walking in
craftiness nor handling the word of God deceitfully, but by manifestation of the truth
[a]commending ourselves to every man's
conscience in the sight of God. 3 But even
if our gospel is veiled, [a]it is veiled to those
who are perishing, 4 whose minds [a]the god
of this age [b]has blinded, who do not believe,
lest [c]the light of the gospel of the glory of
Christ, [d]who is the image of God, should
shine on them. 5 [a]For we do not preach ourselves, but Christ Jesus the Lord, and [b]our-
selves your bondservants for Jesus' sake.
6 For it is the God [a]who commanded light
to shine out of darkness, who has [b]shone
in our hearts to *give* the light of the knowledge of the glory of God in the face of Jesus
Christ.

Cast Down but Unconquered

7 But we have this treasure in earthen
vessels, [a]that the excellence of the power
may be of God and not of us. 8 *We are* [a]hard-
pressed on every side, yet not crushed; *we
are* perplexed, but not in despair; 9 persecuted, but not [a]forsaken; [b]struck down, but
not destroyed— 10 [a]always carrying about in
the body the dying of the Lord Jesus, [b]that
the life of Jesus also may be manifested
in our body. 11 For we who live [a]are always
delivered to death for Jesus' sake, that the
life of Jesus also may be manifested in our
mortal flesh. 12 So then death is working in
us, but life in you.

13 And since we have [a]the same spirit of
faith, according to what is written, [b]"I believed and therefore I spoke,"[1] we also believe and therefore speak, 14 knowing that
[a]He who raised up the Lord Jesus will also
raise us up with Jesus, and will present *us*
with you. 15 For [a]all things *are* for your sakes,
that [b]grace, having spread through the
many, may cause thanksgiving to abound
to the glory of God.

Seeing the Invisible

16 Therefore we [a]do not lose heart. Even
though our outward man is perishing,
yet the inward *man* is [b]being renewed day
by day. 17 For [a]our light affliction, which
is but for a moment, is working for us a
far more exceeding *and* eternal weight of
glory, 18 [a]while we do not look at the things
which are seen, but at the things which are
not seen. For the things which are seen *are*
temporary, but the things which are not
seen *are* eternal.

Assurance of the Resurrection

5 For we know that if [a]our earthly house,
this tent, is destroyed, we have a building from God, a house [b]not made with
hands, eternal in the heavens. 2 For in this
[a]we groan, earnestly desiring to be clothed
with our habitation which is from heaven,
3 if indeed, [a]having been clothed, we shall
not be found naked. 4 For we who are in *this*
tent groan, being burdened, not because we
want to be unclothed, [a]but further clothed,
that mortality may be swallowed up by life.
5 Now He who has prepared us for this very
thing *is* God, who also [a]has given us the
Spirit as a guarantee.

6 So *we are* always confident, knowing
that while we are at home in the body we
are absent from the Lord. 7 For [a]we walk by
faith, not by sight. 8 We are confident, yes,
[a]well pleased rather to be absent from the
body and to be present with the Lord.

The Judgment Seat of Christ

9 Therefore we make it our aim, whether
present or absent, to be well pleasing to
Him. 10 [a]For we must all appear before the
judgment seat of Christ, [b]that each one may

3:18 [a] 1 Cor. 13:12 [b] [2 Cor. 4:4, 6] [c] [Rom. 8:29, 30] 4:1 [a] 1 Cor. 7:25 [b] Luke 18:1; 2 Cor. 4:16; Gal. 6:9; Eph. 3:13; 2 Thess. 3:13 4:2 [a] 2 Cor. 5:11 4:3 [a] [1 Cor. 1:18]; 2 Cor. 2:15 4:4 [a] John 12:31; [Eph. 6:12] [b] John 12:40 [c] [2 Cor. 3:8, 9] [d] [John 1:18]; Phil. 2:6; Col. 1:15; Heb. 1:3 4:5 [a] 1 Cor. 1:13 [b] 1 Cor. 9:19 4:6 [a] Gen. 1:3 [b] Is. 9:2; Mal. 4:2; Luke 1:78; 2 Pet. 1:19 4:7 [a] Judg. 7:2; 1 Cor. 2:5 4:8 [a] 2 Cor. 1:8; 7:5 4:9 [a] Ps. 129:2; [Heb. 13:5] [b] Ps. 37:24 4:10 [a] Phil. 3:10 [b] Rom. 8:17 4:11 [a] Rom. 8:36 4:13 [a] 2 Pet. 1:1 [b] Ps. 116:10 [1] Psalm 116:10 4:14 [a] [Rom. 8:11] 4:15 [a] Col. 1:24 [b] 1 Cor. 9:19; 2 Cor. 1:11 4:16 [a] 2 Cor. 4:1; Gal. 6:9 [b] [Is. 40:29, 31; Col. 3:10] 4:17 [a] Matt. 5:12; Rom. 8:18; 1 Pet. 1:6 4:18 [a] Rom. 8:24; [2 Cor. 5:7; Heb. 11:1, 13] 5:1 [a] Job 4:19; 1 Cor. 15:47; 2 Cor. 4:7 [b] Mark 14:58; Acts 7:48; Heb. 9:11, 24 5:2 [a] Rom. 8:23; 2 Cor. 5:4 5:3 [a] Rev. 3:18 5:4 [a] 1 Cor. 15:53 5:5 [a] Rom. 8:23; [2 Cor. 1:22]; Eph. 1:14 5:7 [a] Rom. 8:24; Heb. 11:1 5:8 [a] Phil. 1:23 5:10 [a] Matt. 16:27; Acts 10:42; Rom. 2:16; 14:10, 12 [b] Gal. 6:7; Eph. 6:8

RELEASE // BELIEVE IN THE RESURRECTION LIFE

Dying to Live

2 Corinthians 4:11 // For we who live are always delivered to death for Jesus' sake, that the life of Jesus also may be manifested in our mortal flesh.

Summary Message // When we trust in Christ as our Lord and Savior, spiritually we are a new creation; we are saved but striving to understand who we are in Christ. This is a process, so we do not automatically stop sinning. Rather, we work at living out the new resurrection life day by day. In 2 Corinthians 4, we are reminded that we will find freedom only in embracing the resurrection life, knowing what we seek to achieve is not grounded in the fleeting things of this world (wealth, fame, status, etc.). Rather, the resurrection life grounds our hope in Jesus and what awaits us beyond this present world. So, the question is, what do you hold to that you need to put to death so that you might live more freely?

Practical Application // Throughout Scripture, we are repeatedly pointed to a truth: our acceptance of Christ as Lord changes us. Once we confess Jesus as Lord, we start a new life—the resurrection life made possible through Christ's sacrifice. As we pursue a relationship with Jesus we will continually be changed. What is our responsibility? In what ways are we to live differently? What does it mean to live the resurrection life?

In 2 Corinthians 4, the apostle Paul provided guidance to the church of Corinth as they wrestled with similar questions. Paul exhorted the Corinthians that living in pursuit of Christ is not easy or comfortable. On the contrary, it is a life marked by sacrifice, resilience, hope, and humility. More importantly, it is a life dedicated to ensuring others experience Christ's unending, unconditional, undeserved love through us. What does this mean for us?

- The resurrection life is one of action and impact. We are called to live out our faith in ways that invite others to experience the transformative power of Christ.
- The resurrection life is about setting our agendas aside and picking up the cause of Christ. Wealth and prosperity are what the world uses to define success. However, the resurrection life flips that model on its head and defines success as our service to others.
- The resurrection life is a hopeful life. It is a life that is freed by the belief in what is to come. It is a life that understands that the afflictions of today are insignificant compared to the "far more exceeding and eternal weight of glory" (2 Cor. 4:17) that awaits us in the hereafter.

Before resurrection, there must be death. In the case of a Christ follower, this means setting aside living according to our thoughts, desires, worldviews, and emotions. Simply put, by embracing a belief in the resurrection life, the weight and burdens of this world begin to fall away. We are freed to breathe deeply as we live out our faith, trusting that what we are working toward is far greater than anything we will experience this side of eternity.

Fervent Prayer // Heavenly Father, You never promised us that following You would be easy. However, You invite us to experience a freedom that comes from a hope grounded in Your eternal promise. With war and famine, death and destruction increasing everywhere we look, placing our hope in the things of this world seems more and more pointless. However, through the resurrection life made possible through Jesus' sacrifice, You have made a way for us to ground our hopes and dreams in something that is steadfast and never changing. Thank You. Help us live out the resurrection life daily so we might breathe easily, confidently trusting in Your promise. In Jesus' name we pray. Amen.

receive the things *done* in the body, according to what he has done, whether good or bad. [11]Knowing, therefore, [a]the terror of the Lord, we persuade men; but we are well known to God, and I also trust are well known in your consciences.

5:11 [a] [Heb. 10:31; 12:29; Jude 23]

Be Reconciled to God

12For [a]we do not commend ourselves
again to you, but give you opportunity [b]to
boast on our behalf, that you may have *an*
answer for those who boast in appearance
and not in heart. 13For [a]if we are beside ourselves, *it is* for God; or if we are of sound
mind, *it is* for you. 14For the love of Christ
compels us, because we judge thus: that
[a]if One died for all, then all died; 15and He
died for all, [a]that those who live should live
no longer for themselves, but for Him who
died for them and rose again.

16[a]Therefore, from now on, we regard no
one according to the flesh. Even though
we have known Christ according to the
flesh, [b]yet now we know *Him thus* no longer. 17Therefore, if anyone [a]*is* in Christ, *he*
is [b]a new creation; [c]old things have passed
away; behold, all things have become [d]new.
18Now all things *are* of God, [a]who has reconciled us to Himself through Jesus Christ,
and has given us the ministry of reconciliation, 19that is, that [a]God was in Christ reconciling the world to Himself, not imputing
their trespasses to them, and has committed to us the word of reconciliation.

20Now then, we are [a]ambassadors for
Christ, as though God were pleading through
us: we implore *you* on Christ's behalf, be reconciled to God. 21For [a]He made Him who
knew no sin *to be* sin for us, that we might
become [b]the righteousness of God in Him.

Marks of the Ministry

6 We then, *as* [a]workers together *with Him*
also [b]plead with *you* not to receive the
grace of God in vain. 2For He says:

> [a]"In an acceptable time I
> have heard you,
> And in the day of salvation
> I have helped you."[1]

Behold, now *is* the accepted time; behold,
now *is* the day of salvation.

3[a]We give no offense in anything, that
our ministry may not be blamed. 4But in
all *things* we commend ourselves [a]as ministers of God: in much patience, in tribulations, in needs, in distresses, 5[a]in stripes,
in imprisonments, in tumults, in labors,
in sleeplessness, in fastings; 6by purity, by
knowledge, by longsuffering, by kindness,
by the Holy Spirit, by sincere love, 7[a]by the
word of truth, by [b]the power of God, by [c]the
armor of righteousness on the right hand
and on the left, 8by honor and dishonor, by
evil report and good report; as deceivers,
and *yet* true; 9as unknown, and [a]*yet* well
known; [b]as dying, and behold we live; [c]as
chastened, and *yet* not killed; 10as sorrowful, yet always rejoicing; as poor, yet making many [a]rich; as having nothing, and *yet*
possessing all things.

Be Holy

11O Corinthians! We have spoken openly
to you, [a]our heart is wide open. 12You are
not restricted by us, but [a]you are restricted
by your *own* affections. 13Now in return for
the same [a](I speak as to children), you also
be open.

14[a]Do not be unequally yoked together
with unbelievers. For [b]what fellowship has
righteousness with lawlessness? And what
communion has light with darkness? 15And
what accord has Christ with Belial? Or what
part has a believer with an unbeliever?
16And what agreement has the temple of
God with idols? For [a]you[1] are the temple of
the living God. As God has said:

> [b]"I will dwell in them
> And walk among *them*.
> I will be their God,
> And they shall be My people."[2]

17Therefore

> [a]"Come out from among them
> And be separate, says the Lord.

5:12 [a] 2 Cor. 3:1 [b] 2 Cor. 1:14; Phil. 1:26 5:13 [a] Mark 3:21; 2 Cor. 11:1, 16; 12:11 5:14 [a] [Rom. 5:15; 6:6; Gal. 2:20; Col. 3:3] 5:15 [a] [Rom. 6:11] 5:16 [a] 2 Cor. 10:3 [b] [Matt. 12:50] 5:17 [a] [John 6:63] [b] [Rom. 8:9] [c] Is. 43:18; 65:17; [Eph. 4:24]; Rev. 21:4 [d] [Rom. 6:3–10; Col. 3:3] 5:18 [a] Rom. 5:10; [Eph. 2:16; Col. 1:20] 5:19 [a] [Rom. 3:24] 5:20 [a] Mal. 2:7; Eph. 6:20 5:21 [a] Is. 53:6, 9 [b] [Rom. 1:17; 3:21]; 1 Cor. 1:30 6:1 [a] 1 Cor. 3:9 [b] 2 Cor. 5:20 6:2 [a] Is. 49:8 [1] Isaiah 49:8 6:3 [a] Rom. 14:13 6:4 [a] 1 Cor. 4:1 6:5 [a] 2 Cor. 11:23 6:7 [a] 2 Cor. 7:14 [b] 1 Cor. 2:4 [c] Rom. 13:12; 2 Cor. 10:4 6:9 [a] 2 Cor. 4:2; 5:11 [b] 1 Cor. 4:9, 11 [c] Ps. 118:18 6:10 [a] 1 Cor. 1:5; [2 Cor. 8:9] 6:11 [a] Is. 60:5; 2 Cor. 7:3 6:12 [a] 2 Cor. 12:15 6:13 [a] 1 Cor. 4:14 6:14 [a] Deut. 7:2, 3; 22:10; 1 Cor. 5:9 [b] 1 Sam. 5:2, 3; 1 Kin. 18:21; Eph. 5:6, 7, 11; 1 John 1:6 6:16 [a] [1 Cor. 3:16, 17; 6:19]; Eph. 2:21; [Heb. 3:6] [b] Ex. 29:45; Lev. 26:12; Jer. 31:33; 32:38; Ezek. 37:26, 27; Zech. 8:8 [1] NU-Text reads *we*. [2] Leviticus 26:12; Jeremiah 32:38; Ezekiel 37:27 6:17 [a] Num. 33:51–56; Is. 52:11; Rev. 18:4

LIFE SUPPORT

BE HOLY: REGARD OTHERS FROM AN ETERNAL PERSPECTIVE

Therefore, from now on, we regard no one according to the flesh. Even though we have known Christ according to the flesh, yet now we know Him thus no longer. 2 Corinthians 5:16

LIFE: Be Holy

Being holy is important to God because as His image bearers, we are earthly vessels God uses to show and display His characteristics to others. We are to be His ambassadors of righteousness and holiness. We are to be His hands and feet to others because God wants no soul to be lost.

God wants us, His children, to show the world that where we will spend eternity is what matters most. But beware: the Enemy will attempt to divert our attention toward fulfilling fleshly desires instead. We cease to be a light for the world when we allow the Enemy to darken our lives. This does not have to occur, though. James 4:7 tells you to "resist the devil and he will flee from you." When the Enemy tries to tempt you with temporary pleasures, have a Holy Spirit attitude that declares, "God has better for me!" The devil will always offer a counterfeit of what God desires to give. But we must not listen to the Enemy. Instead, we should listen to God, who says, "Be holy, for I am holy" (Lev. 11:45).

SUPPORT: Regard Others from an Eternal Perspective

What an attitude! Caring for others from an eternal perspective means that their salvation matters most. As believers, we have the eternal purpose of being used by God to bring the good news of His saving love to all whose lives we touch. We are called to bring the reality of heaven to earth. God wants us to lift His name so that He draws all people to Himself.

As believers, we must understand the urgency of our mission to be part of the salvation of the lost. This is the hour in which God wants us to fulfill our true calling. He wants us to be our brothers' and sisters' keepers and share our faith. Even in the small things, we represent Him. Every time we bless someone, every time we do not complain, every time we turn the other cheek and stop our tongues from speaking evil, we are being Christlike and showing people what it looks like to live for Him. Allow God to use you to win souls for Him and help others discover the true riches of God's kingdom.

SUPPORT EXAMPLE: **Ask people: "How can I pray for you?"**

Do not touch what is
unclean,
And I will receive you."[1]
18 "I [a]will be a Father to you,
And you shall be My [b]sons
and daughters,
Says the LORD Almighty."[1]

7 Therefore,[a] having these promises, beloved, let us cleanse ourselves from all filthiness of the flesh and spirit, perfecting holiness in the fear of God.

The Corinthians' Repentance

2 Open *your hearts* to us. We have wronged no one, we have corrupted no one,
[a]we have cheated no one. 3 I do not say *this*
to condemn; for [a]I have said before that
you are in our hearts, to die together and
to live together. 4 [a]Great *is* my boldness of

6:17 [1] Isaiah 52:11; Ezekiel 20:34, 41 6:18 [a] 2 Sam. 7:14; Jer. 31:1, 9; [Rev. 21:7] [b] [John 1:12; Rom. 8:14; Gal. 4:5–7]; Phil. 2:15; 1 John 3:1 [1] 2 Samuel 7:14 7:1 [a] [1 John 3:3] 7:2 [a] Acts 20:33 7:3 [a] 2 Cor. 6:11, 12 7:4 [a] 2 Cor. 3:12

speech toward you, [b]great *is* my boasting
on your behalf. [c]I am filled with comfort. I
am exceedingly joyful in all our tribulation.
5For indeed, [a]when we came to Macedonia, our bodies had no rest, but [b]we were
troubled on every side. [c]Outside *were* conflicts, inside *were* fears. 6Nevertheless [a]God,
who comforts the downcast, comforted us
by [b]the coming of Titus, 7and not only by his
coming, but also by the consolation with
which he was comforted in you, when he
told us of your earnest desire, your mourning, your zeal for me, so that I rejoiced even
more.
8For even if I made you [a]sorry with my
letter, I do not regret it; [b]though I did regret it. For I perceive that the same epistle
made you sorry, though only for a while.
9Now I rejoice, not that you were made
sorry, but that your sorrow led to repentance. For you were made sorry in a godly
manner, that you might suffer loss from us
in nothing. 10For [a]godly sorrow produces
repentance *leading* to salvation, not to be
regretted; [b]but the sorrow of the world
produces death. 11For observe this very
thing, that you sorrowed in a godly manner: What diligence it produced in you,
what [a]clearing *of yourselves, what* indignation, *what* fear, *what* vehement desire,
what zeal, *what* vindication! In all *things*
you proved yourselves to be [b]clear in this
matter. 12Therefore, although I wrote to
you, *I did* not *do it* for the sake of him who

2 CORINTHIANS 7:9

WE ARE THE CHURCH AT CORINTH

Now I rejoice, not that you were made sorry, but that your sorrow led to repentance. For you were made sorry in a godly manner, that you might suffer loss from us in nothing. 2 Corinthians 7:9

We are the church at Corinth. Paul came to Corinth to share the message of Jesus. He stayed with a man named Justus who lived next door to the synagogue. Justus believed Paul's message. Then Crispus, who was the ruler of the synagogue, and his household also believed. Because these two respected leaders became followers of Jesus, many Corinthians believed and were baptized during the time Paul stayed with us.

As our church grew, it was clear that God had greatly blessed us and given us every spiritual gift. But we were far from perfect. We boasted about whose teaching we followed: some claimed to follow Paul; others, Apollos; others, Cephas; and still others, Jesus. This resulted in our body being divided, contrary to the command that the body of Christ be one. So, Paul addressed this in a letter to all of us. Along with the division, he also spoke against other areas of sin in our congregation: sexual immorality, arguments over the freedom to eat certain foods, disorderly gatherings, and disagreements about whether the resurrection of Jesus was real or important to the gospel. Most of us were sorrowful and convicted by Paul's words; we repented and returned to the teachings of Christ.

†

The founding of the church in Corinth demonstrates that faith is not something we are meant to keep to ourselves. We are to pass the message of salvation to our neighbors, families, and communities, that all might be saved. In addition, every issue that Paul addressed in the church at Corinth regarded their failure to love God and one another. This divine love must override the love of fleshly things and the lure of idle arguments. The church in Corinth warns us that there can be no division in the body of Christ.

7:4 [b] 1 Cor. 1:4 [c] Phil. 2:17; Col. 1:24 7:5 [a] Rom. 15:26; 2 Cor. 2:13 [b] 2 Cor. 4:8 [c] Deut. 32:25 7:6 [a] Is. 49:13; 2 Cor. 1:3, 4 [b] 2 Cor. 2:13; 7:13 7:8 [a] 2 Cor. 2:2 [b] 2 Cor. 2:4 7:10 [a] 2 Sam. 12:13; Ps. 32:10; Matt. 26:75 [b] Prov. 17:22 7:11 [a] Eph. 5:11 [b] 2 Cor. 2:5–11

had done the wrong, nor for the sake of
him who suffered wrong, [a]but that our care
for you in the sight of God might appear
to you.

The Joy of Titus

13Therefore we have been comforted in
your comfort. And we rejoiced exceedingly
more for the joy of Titus, because his spirit
[a]has been refreshed by you all. 14For if in
anything I have boasted to him about you, I
am not ashamed. But as we spoke all things
to you in truth, even so our boasting to Titus was found true. 15And his affections
are greater for you as he remembers [a]the
obedience of you all, how with fear and
trembling you received him. 16Therefore
I rejoice that [a]I have confidence in you in
everything.

Excel in Giving

8 Moreover, brethren, we make known
to you the grace of God bestowed on
the churches of Macedonia: 2that in a great
trial of affliction the abundance of their joy
and [a]their deep poverty abounded in the
riches of their liberality. 3For I bear witness
that according to *their* ability, yes, and beyond *their* ability, *they were* freely willing,
4imploring us with much urgency that we
would receive[1] the gift and [a]the fellowship
of the ministering to the saints. 5And not
only as we had hoped, but they first [a]gave
themselves to the Lord, and *then* to us by
the [b]will of God. 6So [a]we urged Titus, that
as he had begun, so he would also complete this grace in you as well. 7But as [a]you
abound in everything—in faith, in speech,
in knowledge, in all diligence, and in your
love for us—*see* [b]that you abound in this
grace also.

Christ Our Pattern

8[a]I speak not by commandment, but I
am testing the sincerity of your love by
the diligence of others. 9For you know the
grace of our Lord Jesus Christ, [a]that though
He was rich, yet for your sakes He became
poor, that you through His poverty might
become [b]rich.

10And in this [a]I give advice: [b]It is to your
advantage not only to be doing what you
began and [c]were desiring to do a year ago;
11but now you also must complete the doing *of it;* that as *there was* a readiness to desire *it,* so *there* also *may be* a completion
out of what *you* have. 12For [a]if there is first
a willing mind, *it is* accepted according to
what one has, *and* not according to what
he does not have.

13For *I do* not *mean* that others should be
eased and you burdened; 14but by an equality, *that* now at this time your abundance
may supply their lack, that their abundance
also may *supply* your lack—that there may
be equality. 15As it is written, [a]"He who *gathered* much had nothing left over, and he
who *gathered* little had no lack."[1]

Collection for the Judean Saints

16But thanks *be* to God who puts[1] the
same earnest care for you into the heart
of Titus. 17For he not only accepted the
exhortation, but being more diligent, he
went to you of his own accord. 18And we
have sent with him [a]the brother whose
praise *is* in the gospel throughout all the
churches, 19and not only *that,* but who was
also [a]chosen by the churches to travel with
us with this gift, which is administered by
us [b]to the glory of the Lord Himself and
to show your ready mind, 20avoiding this:
that anyone should blame us in this lavish
gift which is administered by us— 21[a]pro-
viding honorable things, not only in the
sight of the Lord, but also in the sight of
men.

22And we have sent with them our
brother whom we have often proved diligent in many things, but now much more
diligent, because of the great confidence
which *we have* in you. 23If *anyone inquires* about [a]Titus, *he is* my partner and
fellow worker concerning you. Or if our

7:12 [a] 2 Cor. 2:4 7:13 [a] Rom. 15:32 7:15 [a] 2 Cor. 2:9; Phil. 2:12 7:16 [a] 2 Cor. 2:3; 8:22; 2 Thess. 3:4; Philem. 8, 21 8:2 [a] Mark 12:44 8:4 [a] Acts 11:29; 24:17; Rom. 15:25, 26; 1 Cor. 16:1, 3, 4; 2 Cor. 9:1 [1] NU-Text and M-Text omit *that we would receive,* thus changing text to *urgency for the favor and fellowship* . . . . 8:5 [a] [Rom. 12:1, 2] [b] [Eph. 6:6] 8:6 [a] 2 Cor. 8:17; 12:18 8:7 [a] [1 Cor. 1:5; 12:13] [b] 2 Cor. 9:8 8:8 [a] 1 Cor. 7:6 8:9 [a] Matt. 8:20; Luke 9:58; Phil. 2:6, 7 [b] Rom. 9:23; [Eph. 1:7; Rev. 3:18] 8:10 [a] 1 Cor. 7:25, 40 [b] [Prov. 19:17; Matt. 10:42; 1 Tim. 6:18, 19; Heb. 13:16] [c] 1 Cor. 16:2; 2 Cor. 9:2 8:12 [a] Mark 12:43, 44; Luke 21:3, 4; 2 Cor. 9:7 8:15 [a] Ex. 16:18 [1] Exodus 16:18 8:16 [1] NU-Text reads *has put.* 8:18 [a] 1 Cor. 16:3; 2 Cor. 12:18 8:19 [a] Acts 14:23; 1 Cor. 16:3, 4 [b] 2 Cor. 4:15 8:21 [a] Rom. 12:17; Phil. 4:8; 1 Pet. 2:12 8:23 [a] 2 Cor. 7:13, 14

brethren *are inquired about, they are* [b]messengers of the churches, the glory of Christ. 24 Therefore show to them, and[1] before the churches, the proof of your love and of our [a]boasting on your behalf.

Administering the Gift

9 Now concerning [a]the ministering to the saints, it is superfluous for me to write to you; 2 for I know your willingness, about which I boast of you to the Macedonians, that Achaia was ready a [a]year ago; and your zeal has stirred up the majority. 3 [a]Yet I have sent the brethren, lest our boasting of you should be in vain in this respect, that, as I said, you may be ready; 4 lest if *some* Macedonians come with me and find you unprepared, we (not to mention you!) should be ashamed of this confident boasting.[1] 5 Therefore I thought it necessary to exhort the brethren to go to you ahead of time, and prepare your generous gift beforehand, which *you had* previously promised, that it may be ready as *a matter of* generosity and not as a grudging obligation.

The Cheerful Giver

6 [a]But this *I say:* He who sows sparingly will also reap sparingly, and he who sows bountifully will also reap bountifully. 7 *So let* each one *give* as he purposes in his heart, [a]not grudgingly or of necessity; for [b]God loves a cheerful giver. 8 [a]And God *is* able to make all grace abound toward you, that you, always having all sufficiency in all *things,* may have an abundance for every good work. 9 As it is written:

[a]"He has dispersed abroad,
He has given to the poor;
His righteousness endures
forever."[1]

10 Now may[1] He who [a]supplies seed to the sower, and bread for food, supply and multiply the seed you have *sown* and increase the fruits of your [b]righteousness, 11 while *you are* enriched in everything for all liberality, [a]which causes thanksgiving through us to God. 12 For the administration of this service not only [a]supplies the needs of the saints, but also is abounding through many thanksgivings to God, 13 while, through the proof of this ministry, they [a]glorify God for the obedience of your confession to the gospel of Christ, and for *your* liberal [b]sharing with them and all *men,* 14 and by their prayer for you, who long for you because of the exceeding [a]grace of God in you. 15 Thanks *be* to God [a]for His indescribable gift!

The Spiritual War

10 Now [a]I, Paul, myself am pleading with you by the meekness and gentleness of Christ—[b]who in presence *am* lowly among you, but being absent am bold toward you. 2 But I beg *you* [a]that when I am present I may not be bold with that confidence by which I intend to be bold against some, who think of us as if we walked according to the flesh. 3 For though we walk in the flesh, we do not war according to the flesh. 4 [a]For the weapons [b]of our warfare *are* not carnal but [c]mighty in God [d]for pulling down strongholds, 5 [a]casting down arguments and every high thing that exalts itself against the knowledge of God, bringing every thought into captivity to the obedience of Christ, 6 [a]and being ready to punish all disobedience when [b]your obedience is fulfilled.

Reality of Paul's Authority

7 [a]Do you look at things according to the outward appearance? [b]If anyone is convinced in himself that he is Christ's, let him again consider this in himself, that just as he *is* Christ's, even so [c]we *are* Christ's.[1] 8 For even if I should boast somewhat more [a]about our authority, which the Lord gave

---

8:23 [b] [John 13:16]; Phil. 2:25 8:24 [a] 2 Cor. 7:4, 14; 9:2 [1] NU-Text and M-Text omit *and.* 9:1 [a] Acts 11:29; Rom. 15:26; 1 Cor. 16:1; 2 Cor. 8:4; Gal. 2:10 9:2 [a] 2 Cor. 8:10 9:3 [a] 2 Cor. 8:6, 17 9:4 [1] NU-Text reads *this confidence.* 9:6 [a] Prov. 11:24; 22:9; Gal. 6:7, 9 9:7 [a] Deut. 15:7 [b] Deut. 15:10; 1 Chr. 29:17; [Prov. 11:25]; Rom. 12:8; [2 Cor. 8:12] 9:8 [a] [Prov. 11:24] 9:9 [a] Ps. 112:9 [1] Psalm 112:9 9:10 [a] Is. 55:10 [b] Hos. 10:12 [1] NU-Text reads *Now He who supplies . . . will supply . . . .* 9:11 [a] 2 Cor. 1:11 9:12 [a] 2 Cor. 8:14 9:13 [a] [Matt. 5:16] [b] [Heb. 13:16] 9:14 [a] 2 Cor. 8:1 9:15 [a] [John 3:16; 4:10; Rom. 6:23; 8:32; Eph. 2:8; James 1:17] 10:1 [a] Rom. 12:1 [b] 1 Thess. 2:7 10:2 [a] 1 Cor. 4:21; 2 Cor. 13:2, 10 10:4 [a] Eph. 6:13 [b] 1 Cor. 9:7; [2 Cor. 6:7]; 1 Tim. 1:18 [c] Acts 7:22 [d] Jer. 1:10; [2 Cor. 10:8; 13:10] 10:5 [a] 1 Cor. 1:19 10:6 [a] 2 Cor. 13:2, 10 [b] 2 Cor. 7:15 10:7 [a] [John 7:24]; 2 Cor. 5:12 [b] 1 Cor. 1:12; 14:37 [c] [Rom. 14:8]; 1 Cor. 3:23 [1] NU-Text reads *even as we are.* 10:8 [a] 2 Cor. 13:10

us[1] for edification and not for your destruction, [b]I shall not be ashamed— 9lest
I seem to terrify you by letters. 10"For *his*
letters," they say, "*are* weighty and powerful, but [a]*his* bodily presence *is* weak, and *his*
[b]speech contemptible." 11Let such a person
consider this, that what we are in word by
letters when we are absent, such *we will*
also *be* in deed when we are present.

Limits of Paul's Authority

12[a]For we dare not class ourselves or
compare ourselves with those who commend themselves. But they, measuring
themselves by themselves, and comparing themselves among themselves, are
not wise. 13[a]We, however, will not boast beyond measure, but within the limits of the
sphere which God appointed us—a sphere
which especially includes you. 14For we are
not overextending ourselves (as though
our authority did not extend to you), [a]for
it was to you that we came with the gospel
of Christ; 15not boasting of things beyond
measure, *that is,* [a]in other men's labors,
but having hope, *that* as your faith is increased, we shall be greatly enlarged by
you in our sphere, 16to preach the gospel in the *regions* beyond you, *and* not to
boast in another man's sphere of accom-
plishment.

17But [a]"he who glories, let him glory in
the LORD."[1] 18For [a]not he who commends
himself is approved, but [b]whom the Lord
commends.

Concern for Their Faithfulness

11 Oh, that you would bear with me in a
little [a]folly—and indeed you do bear
with me. 2For I am [a]jealous for you with
godly jealousy. For [b]I have betrothed you
to one husband, [c]that I may present *you* [d]*as* a
chaste virgin to Christ. 3But I fear, lest somehow, as [a]the serpent deceived Eve by his
craftiness, so your minds [b]may be corrupted
from the simplicity[1] that is in Christ. 4For
if he who comes preaches another Jesus
whom we have not preached, or *if* you receive a different spirit which you have not
received, or a [a]different gospel which you
have not accepted—you may well put up
with it!

Paul and False Apostles

5For I consider that [a]I am not at all inferior to the most eminent apostles. 6Even
though [a]*I am* untrained in speech, yet *I*
am not [b]in knowledge. But [c]we have been
thoroughly manifested[1] among you in all
things.

7Did I commit sin in humbling myself that you might be exalted, because I
preached the gospel of God to you [a]free
of charge? 8I robbed other churches, taking wages *from them* to minister to you.
9And when I was present with you, and in
need, [a]I was a burden to no one, for what
I lacked [b]the brethren who came from
Macedonia supplied. And in everything
I kept myself from being burdensome to
you, and so I will keep *myself.* 10[a]As the
truth of Christ is in me, [b]no one shall stop
me from this boasting in the regions of
Achaia. 11Why? [a]Because I do not love you?
God knows!

12But what I do, I will also continue to
do, [a]that I may cut off the opportunity
from those who desire an opportunity to
be regarded just as we are in the things
of which they boast. 13For such [a]*are* false
apostles, [b]deceitful workers, transforming
themselves into apostles of Christ. 14And
no wonder! For Satan himself transforms
himself into [a]an angel of light. 15Therefore
it is no great thing if his ministers also
transform themselves into ministers of
righteousness, [a]whose end will be according to their works.

Reluctant Boasting

16I say again, let no one think me a fool.
If otherwise, at least receive me as a fool,

10:8 [b] 2 Cor. 7:14 [1] NU-Text omits *us.* **10:10** [a] 1 Cor. 2:3, 4; 2 Cor. 12:7; Gal. 4:13 [b] [1 Cor. 1:17]; 2 Cor. 11:6 **10:12** [a] 2 Cor. 5:12 **10:13** [a] 2 Cor. 10:15 **10:14** [a] 1 Cor. 3:5, 6 **10:15** [a] Rom. 15:20 **10:17** [a] Is. 65:16; Jer. 9:24; 1 Cor. 1:31 [1] Jeremiah 9:24 **10:18** [a] Prov. 27:2 [b] Rom. 2:29; [1 Cor. 4:5] **11:1** [a] Matt. 17:17; 2 Cor. 11:4, 16, 19 **11:2** [a] Gal. 4:17 [b] Hos. 2:19; [Eph. 5:26] [c] Col. 1:28 [d] Lev. 21:13 **11:3** [a] Gen. 3:4, 13; John 8:44; 1 Thess. 3:5; 1 Tim. 2:14; [Rev. 12:9, 15] [b] Eph. 6:24 [1] NU-Text adds *and purity.* **11:4** [a] Gal. 1:6–8 **11:5** [a] [1 Cor. 15:10]; 2 Cor. 12:11; Gal. 2:6 **11:6** [a] [1 Cor. 1:17] [b] [1 Cor. 12:8; Eph. 3:4] [c] [2 Cor. 12:12] [1] NU-Text omits *been.* **11:7** [a] Acts 18:3; 1 Cor. 9:18; 2 Cor. 12:13 **11:9** [a] Acts 20:33 [b] Phil. 4:10 **11:10** [a] Rom. 1:9; 9:1; 2 Cor. 1:23; [Gal. 2:20] [b] 1 Cor. 9:15 **11:11** [a] 2 Cor. 6:11; 12:15 **11:12** [a] 1 Cor. 9:12 **11:13** [a] Acts 15:24; Rom. 16:18; Gal. 1:7; Phil. 1:15; 2 Pet. 2:1; Rev. 2:2 [b] Phil. 3:2; Titus 1:10 **11:14** [a] Gal. 1:8 **11:15** [a] [Phil. 3:19]

that I also may boast a little. 17 What I speak, [a]I speak not according to the Lord, but as it were, foolishly, in this confidence of boasting. 18 Seeing that many boast according to the flesh, I also will boast. 19 For you put up with fools gladly, [a]since you *yourselves* are wise! 20 For you put up with it [a]if one brings you into bondage, if one devours *you,* if one takes *from you,* if one exalts himself, if one strikes you on the face. 21 To *our* shame [a]I say that we were too weak for that! But [b]in whatever anyone is bold—I speak foolishly—I am bold also.

Suffering for Christ

22 Are they [a]Hebrews? So *am* I. Are they Israelites? So *am* I. Are they the seed of Abraham? So *am* I. 23 Are they ministers of Christ?—I speak as a fool—I *am* more: [a]in labors more abundant, [b]in stripes above measure, in prisons more frequently, [c]in deaths often. 24 From the Jews five times I received [a]forty [b]*stripes* minus one. 25 Three times I was [a]beaten with rods; [b]once I was stoned; three times I [c]was shipwrecked; a night and a day I have been in the deep; 26 *in* journeys often, *in* perils of waters, *in* perils of robbers, [a]*in* perils of *my own* countrymen, [b]*in* perils of the Gentiles, *in* perils in the city, *in* perils in the wilderness, *in* perils in the sea, *in* perils among false brethren; 27 in weariness and toil, [a]in sleeplessness often, [b]in hunger and thirst, in [c]fastings often, in cold and nakedness— 28 besides the other things, what comes upon me daily: [a]my deep concern for all the churches. 29 [a]Who is weak, and I am not weak? Who is made to stumble, and I do not burn *with indignation?*

30 If I must boast, [a]I will boast in the things which concern my infirmity. 31 [a]The God and Father of our Lord Jesus Christ, [b]who is blessed forever, knows that I am not lying. 32 [a]In Damascus the governor, under Aretas the king, was guarding the city of the Damascenes with a garrison, desiring to arrest me; 33 but I was let down in a basket through a window in the wall, and escaped from his hands.

#OXYGEN

2 CORINTHIANS 11:23–28

Believe in the Resurrection Life

We are not in this world to stay. Why would we want to when what is in store for us as believers is better than we can imagine? There is no need to fear death. Jesus has conquered it. Merely **breathe** and **believe in the resurrection life.**

The Vision of Paradise

12 It is doubtless[1] not profitable for me to boast. I will come to [a]visions and [b]revelations of the Lord: 2 I know a man [a]in Christ who fourteen years ago—whether in the body I do not know, or whether out of the body I do not know, God knows—such a one [b]was caught up to the third heaven. 3 And I know such a man—whether in the body or out of the body I do not know, God knows— 4 how he was caught up into [a]Paradise and heard inexpressible words, which it is not lawful for a man to utter. 5 Of such a one I will boast; yet of myself I will not [a]boast, except in my infirmities. 6 For though I might desire to boast, I will not be a fool; for I will speak the truth. But I refrain, lest anyone should think of me above what he sees me *to be* or hears from me.

The Thorn in the Flesh

7 And lest I should be exalted above measure by the abundance of the revelations, a [a]thorn in the flesh was given to me, [b]a messenger of Satan to buffet me, lest I be exalted above measure. 8 [a]Concerning this

---

11:17 [a] 1 Cor. 7:6 **11:19** [a] 1 Cor. 4:10 **11:20** [a] 2 Cor. 1:24; [Gal. 2:4; 4:3, 9; 5:1] **11:21** [a] 2 Cor. 10:10 [b] Phil. 3:4 **11:22** [a] Acts 22:3; Rom. 11:1; Phil. 3:4–6 **11:23** [a] 1 Cor. 15:10 [b] Acts 9:16 [c] 1 Cor. 15:30 **11:24** [a] Deut. 25:3 [b] 2 Cor. 6:5 **11:25** [a] Acts 16:22, 23; 21:32 [b] Acts 14:5, 19 [c] Acts 27:1–44 **11:26** [a] Acts 9:23, 24; 13:45, 50; 17:5, 13; 1 Thess. 2:15 [b] Acts 14:5, 19; 19:23; 27:42 **11:27** [a] Acts 20:31 [b] 1 Cor. 4:11; Phil. 4:12 [c] Acts 9:9; 13:2, 3; 14:23 **11:28** [a] Acts 20:18; [Rom. 1:14]; 2 Cor. 7:12; 12:20; Gal. 4:11; 1 Thess. 3:10 **11:29** [a] [1 Cor. 8:9, 13; 9:22] **11:30** [a] [2 Cor. 12:5, 9, 10] **11:31** [a] Rom. 1:9; Gal. 1:20; 1 Thess. 2:5 [b] Rom. 9:5 **11:32** [a] Acts 9:19–25 **12:1** [a] Acts 16:9; 18:9; 22:17, 18; 23:11; 26:13–15; 27:23 [b] Acts 9:3–6; 1 Cor. 14:6; 2 Cor. 12:7; [Gal. 1:12; 2:2; Eph. 3:3–6] [1] NU-Text reads *necessary, though not profitable, to boast.* **12:2** [a] Rom. 16:7; Gal. 1:22 [b] Acts 22:17 **12:4** [a] Luke 23:43; [Rev. 2:7] **12:5** [a] 2 Cor. 11:30 **12:7** [a] Num. 33:55; Ezek. 28:24; Hos. 2:6; Gal. 4:13, 14 [b] Job 2:7; Matt. 4:10; Luke 13:16; [1 Cor. 5:5] **12:8** [a] Deut. 3:23; Matt. 26:44

thing I pleaded with the Lord three times
that it might depart from me. 9And He
said to me, "My grace is sufficient for you,
for My strength is made perfect in weakness." Therefore most gladly [a]I will rather
boast in my infirmities, [b]that the power of
Christ may rest upon me. 10Therefore [a]I
take pleasure in infirmities, in reproaches,
in needs, in persecutions, in distresses, for
Christ's sake. [b]For when I am weak, then I
am strong.

Signs of an Apostle

11I have become [a]a fool in boasting;[1] you
have compelled me. For I ought to have
been commended by you; for [b]in nothing
was I behind the most eminent apostles,
though [c]I am nothing. 12[a]Truly the signs of
an apostle were accomplished among you
with all perseverance, in signs and [b]won-
ders and mighty [c]deeds. 13For what is it in
which you were inferior to other churches,
except that I myself was not burdensome
to you? Forgive me this wrong!

Love for the Church

14[a]Now *for* the third time I am ready to
come to you. And I will not be burdensome
to you; for [b]I do not seek yours, but you. [c]For
the children ought not to lay up for the parents, but the parents for the children. 15And
I will very gladly spend and be spent [a]for
your souls; though [b]the more abundantly
I love you, the less I am loved.

16But be that *as it may,* [a]I did not burden
you. Nevertheless, being crafty, I caught
you by cunning! 17Did I take advantage of
you by any of those whom I sent to you?
18I urged Titus, and sent our [a]brother with
him. Did Titus take advantage of you? Did
we not walk in the same spirit? Did *we* not
walk in the same steps?

19[a]Again, do you think[1] that we excuse
ourselves to you? [b]We speak before God in
Christ. [c]But *we do* all things, beloved, for
your edification. 20For I fear lest, when I
come, I shall not find you such as I wish,
and *that* [a]I shall be found by you such as
you do not wish; lest *there be* contentions,
jealousies, outbursts of wrath, selfish ambitions, backbitings, whisperings, conceits,
tumults; 21lest, when I come again, my God
[a]will humble me among you, and I shall
mourn for many [b]who have sinned before
and have not repented of the uncleanness,
[c]fornication, and lewdness which they have
practiced.

Coming with Authority

13 This *will be* [a]the third *time* I am coming to you. [b]"By the mouth of two or
three witnesses every word shall be established."[1] 2[a]I have told you before, and fore-
tell as if I were present the second time,
and now being absent I write[1] to those [b]who
have sinned before, and to all the rest, that
if I come again [c]I will not spare— 3since
you seek a proof of Christ [a]speaking in me,
who is not weak toward you, but mighty [b]in
you. 4[a]For though He was crucified in weakness, yet [b]He lives by the power of God. For
[c]we also are weak in Him, but we shall live
with Him by the power of God toward you.

5Examine yourselves *as to* whether you
are in the faith. Test yourselves. Do you
not know yourselves, [a]that Jesus Christ is
in you?—unless indeed you are [b]disquali-
fied. 6But I trust that you will know that we
are not disqualified.

Paul Prefers Gentleness

7Now I[1] pray to God that you do no evil,
not that we should appear approved, but
that you should do what is honorable,
though [a]we may seem disqualified. 8For we
can do nothing against the truth, but for the
truth. 9For we are glad [a]when we are weak
and you are strong. And this also we pray,
[b]that you may be made complete. 10[a]There-
fore I write these things being absent, lest

12:9 [a] 2 Cor. 11:30 [b] [1 Pet. 4:14] **12:10** [a] [Rom. 5:3; 8:35] [b] 2 Cor. 13:4 **12:11** [a] 2 Cor. 5:13; 11:1, 16; 12:6 [b] 1 Cor. 15:10; 2 Cor. 11:5 [c] 1 Cor. 3:7; 13:2; 15:9 [1] NU-Text omits *in boasting.* **12:12** [a] Acts 14:3; Rom. 15:18 [b] Acts 15:12 [c] Acts 14:8–10; 16:16–18; 19:11, 12; 20:6–12; 28:1–10 **12:14** [a] 2 Cor. 1:15; 13:1, 2 [b] Acts 20:33; [1 Cor. 10:24–33] [c] 1 Cor. 4:14; Gal. 4:19 **12:15** [a] John 10:11; Rom. 9:3; 2 Cor. 1:6; Phil. 2:17; Col. 1:24; 1 Thess. 2:8; [2 Tim. 2:10] [b] 2 Cor. 6:12, 13 **12:16** [a] 2 Cor. 11:9 **12:18** [a] 2 Cor. 8:18 **12:19** [a] 2 Cor. 5:12 [b] [Rom. 9:1, 2]; 2 Cor. 11:31 [c] 1 Cor. 10:33 [1] NU-Text reads *You have been thinking for a long time . . . .* **12:20** [a] 1 Cor. 4:21; 2 Cor. 13:2, 10 **12:21** [a] 2 Cor. 2:1, 4 [b] 2 Cor. 13:2 [c] 1 Cor. 5:1 **13:1** [a] 2 Cor. 12:14 [b] Num. 35:30; Deut. 17:6; 19:15; Matt. 18:16; John 8:17; Heb. 10:28 [1] Deuteronomy 19:15 **13:2** [a] 2 Cor. 10:2 [b] 2 Cor. 12:21 [c] 2 Cor. 1:23; 10:11 [1] NU-Text omits *I write.* **13:3** [a] Matt. 10:20; [1 Cor. 5:4; 7:40] [b] [1 Cor. 9:2] **13:4** [a] Phil. 2:7, 8; [1 Pet. 3:18] [b] [Rom. 1:4; 6:4; 1 Cor. 6:14] [c] [2 Cor. 10:3, 4] **13:5** [a] Rom. 8:10; [Gal. 4:19] [b] 1 Cor. 9:27 **13:7** [a] 2 Cor. 6:9 [1] NU-Text reads *we.* **13:9** [a] 1 Cor. 4:10 [b] 1 Cor. 1:10; 2 Cor. 13:11; Eph. 4:12; [1 Thess. 3:10] **13:10** [a] 1 Cor. 4:21

being present I should use sharpness, according to the [b]authority which the Lord
has given me for edification and not for
destruction.

Greetings and Benediction

11Finally, brethren, farewell. Become
complete. [a]Be of good comfort, be of one
mind, live in peace; and the God of love
[b]and peace will be with you.
12[a]Greet one another with a holy kiss.
13All the saints greet you.
14[a]The grace of the Lord Jesus Christ, and
the love of God, and [b]the communion of the
Holy Spirit *be* with you all. Amen.

#OXYGEN

2 CORINTHIANS 13:11

Believe in the Resurrection Life

The Word says God is with you. This is true both on this side of eternity and the next. Even in the tough times when death separates you from a loved one, God is there. Pain might be present in the moment, but a day of rejoicing awaits.

Breathe and believe in the resurrection life.

13:10 [b] 1 Cor. 5:4; 2 Cor. 10:8 13:11 [a] Rom. 12:16, 18 [b] Rom. 15:33; Eph. 6:23 13:12 [a] Rom. 16:16
13:14 [a] Rom. 16:24 [b] Phil. 2:1

THE EPISTLE OF PAUL TO THE

GALATIANS

OVERVIEW

Galatia was a region in Asia Minor (modern-day Turkey) that included Iconium, Lystra, and Derbe. It is believed that Paul addressed this epistle to all the churches he helped found during his missionary journeys within this Galatian region (Acts 14:20–22).

Paul's epistle to the Galatians is considered one of his earliest writings and contains several of the most profound verses in Scripture. The Galatians were facing a crisis involving the central aspect of the gospel. At issue was whether righteousness comes by faith in Christ or by works in compliance with the Mosaic law. Many early Jewish Christians called Judaizers felt it was essential for non-Jewish Christians to observe Old Testament customs, diets, and laws. These Judaizers had constructed many legalistic hurdles for new believers. Paul began Galatians, then, by warning that nothing can be added to or subtracted from the gospel of Jesus Christ or it becomes no gospel at all. There is only one gospel, and it is the one revealed by Christ.

In this epistle, Paul organized his arguments around the supremacy of Christ's authority. Paul establishes that Jesus was the fulfillment of God's covenant with Abraham and the Mosaic law. Divine reconciliation, therefore, is accomplished only by the acceptance of Christ. Paul wrote, "There is neither Jew nor Greek, there is neither slave nor free, there is neither male nor female; for you are all one in Christ Jesus. And if you are Christ's, then you are Abraham's seed, and heirs according to the promise" (Gal. 3:28–29). Here, Paul made it clear that there is no differentiation between a Jewish Christian and a Gentile Christian. Salvation is found only in Christ, and all in Christ are one and on equal footing.

Christ's authority and grace were, thus, game changers. Jewish believers could claim no greater righteousness than Gentiles. The same salvation, the same forgiveness, the same authority, the same righteousness, and the same status were available to all, regardless of ethnic and religious background, socio-economic class, or gender. Everything that God promised the children of Abraham's seed is now available to those who accept Christ as Savior and Lord. In Christ, there is acceptance for the Gentiles, liberation for the enslaved, and inclusion for women. Therefore, Paul's central message to the Galatians was that false teachers could not place a burden on the Gentile believers that required them to live under the law when Christ set all free by His grace. With this epistle, Paul attempted to bring harmony to the churches of Galatia by clearly asserting that justification comes by faith in Christ and cannot be earned by pedigree or piety.

BREATHE IT IN

The United States is one of the richest nations the world has ever known. Like in many other cultures, in America, prosperity is most often measured by the accumulation of wealth and property. This commercially focused society always encourages us to spend, upgrade, and replace. To maintain our social status, many of us have been all too willing to pay whatever price our culture wishes to extract.

A by-product of such rampant consumerism has been a widening wealth gap that in turn produces an increasingly unstable economic system. The result is a problem not only for the poor

but ultimately for all of society. God did not intend a world of inequities, but He knew the poor would always be with us. Therefore, He commands us to share what we have and to take care of the poor so that no one goes without. Without giving and sharing, we may be financially prosperous, but we will also be spiritually bankrupt. In addition, wealth does not exempt us from sickness, brokenness, pain, mental health crises, or other struggles.

In Galatians, the apostle Paul paints a better picture of prosperity for us. Prosperity is to be found not in accumulating physical possessions but in possessing the fruit of the Spirit: love, joy, peace, longsuffering, kindness, goodness, faithfulness, gentleness, and self-control (see 5:22–23). Love is the greatest gift of all (see 1 Cor. 13). Joy is unspeakable. Peace is priceless. And that still leaves six other amazing gifts from God. When Jesus considered the tension between pursuing the wealth of the world or the gifts of God, He asked a critical question: "For what will it profit a man if he gains the whole world, and loses his own soul?" (Mark 8:36).

Your net worth is the accumulation of your debts subtracted from the accumulation of your assets. This is important, as it determines the measure of what your children will inherit. But the greatest inheritance you can pass on to your children is their witnessing of the fruit of the Spirit in you. How will you ensure that your children inherit what truly matters?

THE EPISTLE OF PAUL TO THE

GALATIANS

Greeting

1 Paul, an apostle (not from men nor
through man, but [a]through Jesus Christ
and God the Father [b]who raised Him from
the dead), 2and all the brethren who are
with me,

To the churches of Galatia:

3Grace to you and peace from God the
Father and our Lord Jesus Christ, 4[a]who
gave Himself for our sins, that He might
deliver us [b]from this present evil age, according to the will of our God and Father,
5to whom *be* glory forever and ever. Amen.

Only One Gospel

6I marvel that you are turning away so
soon [a]from Him who called you in the grace
of Christ, to a different gospel, 7[a]which is
not another; but there are some [b]who trouble you and want to [c]pervert the gospel of
Christ. 8But even if [a]we, or an angel from
heaven, preach any other gospel to you
than what we have preached to you, let him
be accursed. 9As we have said before, so
now I say again, if anyone preaches any
other gospel to you [a]than what you have
received, let him be accursed.

10For [a]do I now [b]persuade men, or God?
Or [c]do I seek to please men? For if I still
pleased men, I would not be a bondservant
of Christ.

Call to Apostleship
(cf. Acts 9:1–25)

11[a]But I make known to you, brethren,
that the gospel which was preached by me
is not according to man. 12For [a]I neither received it from man, nor was I taught *it,* but
it came [b]through the revelation of Jesus
Christ.

13For you have heard of my former conduct in Judaism, how [a]I persecuted the
church of God beyond measure and [b]*tried
to* destroy it. 14And I advanced in Judaism
beyond many of my contemporaries in my
own nation, [a]being more exceedingly zealous [b]for the traditions of my fathers.

15But when it pleased God, [a]who separated me from my mother's womb and
called *me* through His grace, 16[a]to reveal
His Son in me, that [b]I might preach Him
among the Gentiles, I did not immediately
confer with [c]flesh and blood, 17nor did I go
up to Jerusalem to those *who were* apostles before me; but I went to Arabia, and
returned again to Damascus.

#OXYGEN

GALATIANS 1:10

Reconcile Sins with Righteousness

Your sins are forgiven by God. Your righteousness is determined by God. Therefore, what purpose is there in trying to please people who are not trying to please God?

Trust God, **breathe**, and **reconcile sins with righteousness.**

1:1 [a] Acts 9:6 [b] Acts 2:24 1:4 [a] [Matt. 20:28] [b] Heb. 2:5 1:6 [a] [Rom. 8:28]; Gal. 1:15; 5:8 1:7 [a] 2 Cor. 11:4 [b] Acts 15:1; Gal. 5:10, 12 [c] 2 Cor. 2:17 1:8 [a] 1 Cor. 16:22 1:9 [a] Deut. 4:2 1:10 [a] [1 Cor. 10:33]; 1 Thess. 2:4 [b] 1 Sam. 24:7 [c] 1 Thess. 2:4 1:11 [a] [Rom. 2:16]; 1 Cor. 15:1 1:12 [a] 1 Cor. 15:1 [b] [Eph. 3:3–5] 1:13 [a] Acts 9:1 [b] Acts 8:3; 22:4, 5 1:14 [a] Acts 26:9; Phil. 3:6 [b] Jer. 9:14; Matt. 15:2; Mark 7:3; [Col. 2:8] 1:15 [a] Is. 49:1, 5; Jer. 1:5; Acts 9:15; Rom. 1:1; Gal. 1:6 1:16 [a] [2 Cor. 4:5–7] [b] Acts 9:15; Gal. 2:9 [c] Matt. 16:17

Contacts at Jerusalem
(cf. Acts 9:26–31)

18 Then after three years [a]I went up to Jerusalem to see Peter,[1] and remained with
him fifteen days. 19 But [a]I saw none of the
other apostles except [b]James, the Lord's
brother. 20 (Now *concerning* the things
which I write to you, indeed, before God,
I do not lie.)

21 [a]Afterward I went into the regions of
Syria and Cilicia. 22 And I was unknown by
face to the churches of Judea which [a]*were*
in Christ. 23 But they were [a]hearing only, "He
who formerly [b]persecuted us now preaches
the faith which he once *tried to* destroy."
24 And they [a]glorified God in me.

Defending the Gospel
(cf. Acts 15:1–21)

2 Then after fourteen years [a]I went up
again to Jerusalem with Barnabas,
and also took Titus with *me.* 2 And I went
up by revelation, and communicated to
them that gospel which I preach among the
Gentiles, but [a]privately to those who were
of reputation, lest by any means [b]I might
run, or had run, in vain. 3 Yet not even Titus who *was* with me, being a Greek, was
compelled to be circumcised. 4 And *this occurred* because of [a]false brethren secretly
brought in (who came in by stealth to spy
out our [b]liberty which we have in Christ
Jesus, [c]that they might bring us into bondage), 5 to whom we did not yield submission
even for an hour, that [a]the truth of the gospel might continue with you.

6 But from those [a]who seemed to be
something—whatever they were, it makes
no difference to me; [b]God shows personal
favoritism to no man—for those who
seemed *to be something* [c]added nothing
to me. 7 But on the contrary, [a]when they
saw that the gospel for the uncircumcised
[b]had been committed to me, as *the gospel* for the circumcised *was* to Peter 8 (for
He who worked effectively in Peter for
the apostleship to the [a]circumcised [b]also
[c]worked effectively in me toward the Gentiles), 9 and when James, Cephas, and John,
who seemed to be [a]pillars, perceived [b]the
grace that had been given to me, they gave
me and Barnabas the right hand of fellowship, [c]that we *should go* to the Gentiles and
they to the circumcised. 10 *They desired* only
that we should remember the poor, [a]the
very thing which I also was eager to do.

No Return to the Law

11 [a]Now when Peter[1] had come to Antioch, I withstood him to his face, because
he was to be blamed; 12 for before certain
men came from James, [a]he would eat with
the Gentiles; but when they came, he withdrew and separated himself, fearing those
who were of the circumcision. 13 And the
rest of the Jews also played the hypocrite
with him, so that even Barnabas was carried away with their hypocrisy.

14 But when I saw that they were not
straightforward about [a]the truth of the
gospel, I said to Peter [b]before *them* all,
[c]"If you, being a Jew, live in the manner of
Gentiles and not as the Jews, why do you[1]
compel Gentiles to live as Jews?[2] 15 [a]We *who
are* Jews by nature, and not [b]sinners of the
Gentiles, 16 [a]knowing that a man is not justified by the works of the law but [b]by faith
in Jesus Christ, even we have believed in
Christ Jesus, that we might be justified by
faith in Christ and not [c]by the works of the
law; for by the works of the law no flesh
shall be justified.

17 "But if, while we seek to be justified by
Christ, we ourselves also are found [a]sin-
ners, *is* Christ therefore a minister of sin?
Certainly not! 18 For if I build again those
things which I destroyed, I make myself
a transgressor. 19 For I [a]through the law
[b]died to the law that I might [c]live to God.
20 I have been [a]crucified with Christ; it is
no longer I who live, but Christ lives in me;
and the *life* which I now live in the flesh [b]I

1:18 [a] Acts 9:26 [1] NU-Text reads *Cephas.* 1:19 [a] 1 Cor. 9:5 [b] Matt. 13:55 1:21 [a] Acts 9:30 1:22 [a] Rom. 16:7 1:23 [a] Acts 9:20, 21 [b] Acts 8:3 1:24 [a] Acts 11:18 2:1 [a] Acts 15:2 2:2 [a] Acts 15:1–4 [b] [Rom. 9:16; 1 Cor. 9:24]; Gal. 5:7; Phil. 2:16; 1 Thess. 3:5; 2 Tim. 4:7; Heb. 12:1 2:4 [a] Acts 15:1, 24; 2 Cor. 11:13, 26; Gal. 1:7 [b] Gal. 3:25; 5:1, 13; [James 1:25] [c] Gal. 4:3, 9 2:5 [a] [Gal. 1:6; 2:14; 3:1]; Col. 1:5 2:6 [a] Gal. 2:9; 6:3 [b] Acts 10:34; Rom. 2:11 [c] 2 Cor. 11:5; 12:11 2:7 [a] Acts 9:15; 13:46; 22:21; Rom. 11:13 [b] 1 Cor. 9:17; 1 Thess. 2:4; 1 Tim. 1:11 2:8 [a] 1 Pet. 1:1 [b] Acts 9:15 [c] [Gal. 3:5] 2:9 [a] Matt. 16:18 [b] Rom. 1:5 [c] Acts 13:3 2:10 [a] Acts 11:30 2:11 [a] Acts 15:35 [1] NU-Text reads *Cephas.* 2:12 [a] [Acts 10:28; 11:2, 3] 2:14 [a] Gal. 1:6; 2:5; Col. 1:5 [b] 1 Tim. 5:20 [c] [Acts 10:28]; Gal. 2:12 [1] NU-Text reads *how can you.* [2] Some interpreters stop the quotation here. 2:15 [a] [Acts 15:10] [b] Matt. 9:11 2:16 [a] Acts 13:38, 39; Gal. 3:11 [b] Rom. 1:17 [c] Ps. 143:2; Rom. 3:20 2:17 [a] [1 John 3:8] 2:19 [a] Rom. 8:2 [b] [Rom. 6:2, 14; 7:4]; 1 Cor. 9:20 [c] [Rom. 6:11] 2:20 [a] [Rom. 6:6; Gal. 5:24; 6:14] [b] Rom. 6:8–11; 2 Cor. 5:15; [Eph. 2:4–6; Col. 3:1–4]

live by faith in the Son of God, [c]who loved
me and gave Himself for me. 21 I do not set
aside the grace of God; for [a]if righteousness *comes* through the law, then Christ
died in vain."

Justification by Faith
(cf. Rom. 4:1–25)

3 O foolish Galatians! Who has bewitched
you that you should not obey the truth,[1]
before whose eyes Jesus Christ was clearly
portrayed among you[2] as crucified? 2 This
only I want to learn from you: Did you receive the Spirit by the works of the law, [a]or
by the hearing of faith? 3 Are you so foolish?
[a]Having begun in the Spirit, are you now
being made perfect by [b]the flesh? 4 [a]Have
you suffered so many things in vain—if
indeed *it was* in vain?
5 Therefore He who supplies the Spirit
to you and works miracles among you,
does He do it by the works of the law, or by

GALATIANS 2:1

I AM BARNABAS

Then after fourteen years I went up again to Jerusalem with Barnabas, and also took Titus with me. Galatians 2:1

I am Barnabas, a Levite from Cyprus, an island in the Mediterranean Sea. My name at birth was Joses, but because of my gifting and character, the apostles called me Barnabas, which means "Son of Encouragement." I was honored that some described me as "a good man, full of the Holy Spirit and of faith" (Acts 11:24).

When Paul became a follower of Jesus, many people did not believe his conversion and the disciples would not let him join them. But I believed that Paul had met the Lord as he traveled to Damascus. I knew Paul had been changed after I heard him speak boldly for Christ. I presented him to the apostles and vouched for him and his sincerity.

After Stephen was martyred for the faith, many believers scattered in fear. I was sent as far as Antioch to assist them. I was glad and encouraged that the church in Antioch had continued in the Lord. Paul joined me in Antioch, and we taught the church about Jesus and His kingdom for an entire year. The church in Antioch was very multicultural, and no one was excluded. It was here that believers were first called Christians.

Paul and I desired to continue our mission to lead the Jews to faith in Christ. However, many rejected our message. We were then led by God to bring the Good News to the Gentiles. We traveled to many cities preaching the gospel, and many Gentiles came into the kingdom of God.

After some time, Paul and I disagreed about whether to bring John Mark with us on our travels. Rather than continue in disagreement, Paul and I went our separate ways. Although our disagreement caused a break in our relationship, separating from one another resulted in the two of us being able to reach more people with the message of Christ. Fourteen years passed before Paul and I reunited for another missionary journey.

†

Barnabas was known to be an encourager. Although he could have boasted about his accomplishments in serving the churches, he chose to lift others up. He did not draw attention to himself but instead served the needs of the people and gave them the gospel of Jesus Christ. Serving the Lord is not about being out front and being seen and approved by people; it is about doing as God leads, regardless of who sees. Be assured, God sees, and His approval is what counts.

2:20 [c] Is. 53:12; Eph. 5:2 2:21 [a] Heb. 7:11 3:1 [1] NU-Text omits *that you should not obey the truth.* [2] NU-Text omits *among you.*
3:2 [a] Rom. 10:16, 17 3:3 [a] [Gal. 4:9] [b] Heb. 7:16 3:4 [a] Heb. 10:35

the hearing of faith?— 6just as Abraham [a]"believed God, and it was accounted to him for righteousness."[1] 7Therefore know that *only* [a]those who are of faith are sons of Abraham. 8And [a]the Scripture, foreseeing that God would justify the Gentiles by faith, preached the gospel to Abraham beforehand, *saying,* [b]"In you all the nations shall be blessed."[1] 9So then those who *are* of faith are blessed with believing Abraham.

The Law Brings a Curse

10For as many as are of the works of the law are under the curse; for it is written, [a]"Cursed *is* everyone who does not continue in all things which are written in the book of the law, to do them."[1] 11But that no one is justified by the law in the sight of God *is* evident, for [a]"the just shall live by faith."[1] 12Yet [a]the law is not of faith, but [b]"the man who does them shall live by them."[1]

13[a]Christ has redeemed us from the curse of the law, having become a curse for us (for it is written, [b]"Cursed *is* everyone who hangs on a tree"[1]), 14[a]that the blessing of Abraham might come upon the [b]Gentiles in Christ Jesus, that we might receive [c]the promise of the Spirit through faith.

The Changeless Promise
(cf. Gen. 12:1–3)

15Brethren, I speak in the manner of men: [a]Though *it is* only a man's covenant, yet *if it is* confirmed, no one annuls or adds to it. 16Now to Abraham and his Seed were the promises made. He does not say, "And to seeds," as of many, but as of [a]one, [b]"And to your Seed,"[1] who is [c]Christ. 17And this I say, *that* the law, [a]which was four hundred and thirty years later, cannot annul the covenant that was confirmed before by God in Christ,[1] [b]that it should make the promise of no effect. 18For if [a]the inheritance *is* of the law, [b]*it is* no longer of promise; but God gave *it* to Abraham by promise.

Purpose of the Law

19What purpose then *does* the law *serve?* [a]It was added because of transgressions, till the [b]Seed should come to whom the promise was made; *and it was* [c]appointed through angels by the hand [d]of a mediator. 20Now a mediator does not *mediate* for one *only,* [a]but God is one.

21*Is* the law then against the promises of God? Certainly not! For if there had been a law given which could have given life, truly righteousness would have been by the law. 22But the Scripture has confined [a]all under sin, [b]that the promise by faith in Jesus Christ might be given to those who believe. 23But before faith came, we were kept under guard by the law, kept for the faith which would afterward be revealed. 24Therefore [a]the law was our tutor *to bring us* to Christ, [b]that we might be justified by faith. 25But after faith has come, we are no longer under a tutor.

Sons and Heirs

26For you [a]are all sons of God through faith in Christ Jesus. 27For [a]as many of you as were baptized into Christ [b]have put on Christ. 28[a]There is neither Jew nor Greek, [b]there is neither slave nor free, there is neither male nor female; for you are all [c]one in Christ Jesus. 29And [a]if you *are* Christ's, then you are Abraham's [b]seed, and [c]heirs according to the promise.

4 Now I say *that* the heir, as long as he is a child, does not differ at all from a slave, though he is master of all, 2but is under guardians and stewards until the time appointed by the father. 3Even so we, when we were children, [a]were in bondage under the elements of the world. 4But [a]when the fullness of the time had come, God sent forth His Son, [b]born[1] [c]of a woman, [d]born under the law, 5[a]to redeem those who were under the law, [b]that we might receive the adoption as sons.

3:6 [a] Gen. 15:6 [1] Genesis 15:6 **3:7** [a] John 8:39 **3:8** [a] Rom. 9:17 [b] Gen. 12:3; 18:18; 22:18; 26:4; 28:14 [1] Genesis 12:3; 18:18; 22:18; 26:4; 28:14 **3:10** [a] Deut. 27:26 [1] Deuteronomy 27:26 **3:11** [a] Hab. 2:4; Rom. 1:17; Heb. 10:38 [1] Habakkuk 2:4 **3:12** [a] Rom. 4:4, 5 [b] Lev. 18:5; Rom. 10:5 [1] Leviticus 18:5 **3:13** [a] [Rom. 8:3] [b] Deut. 21:23 [1] Deuteronomy 21:23 **3:14** [a] [Rom. 4:1–5, 9, 16; Gal. 3:28] [b] Is. 42:1, 6; 49:6; Luke 2:32; Rom. 3:29, 30 [c] Is. 32:15 **3:15** [a] Heb. 9:17 **3:16** [a] Gen. 22:18 [b] Gen. 12:3, 7; 13:15; 24:7 [c] [1 Cor. 12:12] [1] Genesis 12:7; 13:15; 24:7 **3:17** [a] Gen. 15:13; Ex. 12:40; Acts 7:6 [b] [Rom. 4:13] [1] NU-Text omits *in Christ.* **3:18** [a] [Rom. 8:17] [b] Rom. 4:14 **3:19** [a] John 15:22 [b] Gal. 4:4 [c] Acts 7:53 [d] Ex. 20:19; Deut. 5:5 **3:20** [a] [Rom. 3:29] **3:22** [a] Rom. 11:32 [b] Rom. 4:11 **3:24** [a] Rom. 10:4 [b] Acts 13:39 **3:26** [a] John 1:12 **3:27** [a] Matt. 28:19; [Rom. 6:3]; 1 Cor. 10:2 [b] Rom. 10:12; 13:14 **3:28** [a] [John 10:16]; Rom. 3:22; 10:12; [Eph. 2:14]; Col. 3:11 [b] [1 Cor. 12:13] [c] John 17:11; [1 Cor. 12:13; Eph. 2:15, 16] **3:29** [a] Gen. 21:10; Heb. 11:18 [b] Rom. 4:11; Gal. 3:7 [c] Gen. 12:3; 18:18; Rom. 8:17 **4:3** [a] Gal. 4:9; Col. 2:8, 20; Heb. 5:12; 9:10 **4:4** [a] [Gen. 49:10] [b] [John 1:14]; Rom. 1:3; 8:3; [Phil. 2:7] [c] Gen. 3:15; [Is. 7:14; Matt. 1:25] [d] [Matt. 5:17]; Luke 2:21, 27 [1] Or *made* **4:5** [a] [Matt. 20:28; Gal. 3:13] [b] [John 1:12]

RECONCILE SINS WITH RIGHTEOUSNESS

INHALE

I was exposed to pornography at a young age when an older cousin showed me and some other cousins some websites at a family party. Ever since then, I have continued to look at it, even after getting married. My spouse has never really had much of a sexual appetite, so porn helps satisfy mine, and because of that, I'm faithful in my marriage. So, is that a sin then? I feel like as long as what I'm doing keeps me into my spouse, it can't be wrong, right?

EXHALE

We cannot always trust our feelings. They can lead us astray at times. Think of it this way: A train has an engine and a caboose. The engine of the train is "fact," and the caboose is "feeling." Can the engine operate without the caboose? Yes, it can. The caboose has a role to play, but it isn't the main one. Can the caboose operate without the engine, though? Not at all. So, feelings matter, but they should never lead our way. That you feel that pornography is helpful isn't where this conversation should begin. Instead, we need to think about what God says about pornography.

Frequent visits to pornographic sites cannot be justified or explained away. Actions that require either justification or explanation are rarely, if ever, the right ones. Being into your spouse alone should have been settled a long time ago. So yes, sin has crept into your mind and heart! Your eyes should be only for your mate, period. If something takes the place of the one you've committed fidelity to, you have entered into sin.

Galatians 4:8–9 says: "But then, indeed, when you did not know God, you served those which by nature are not gods. But now after you have known God, or rather are known by God, how is it that you turn again to the weak and beggarly elements, to which you desire again to be in bondage?" Once allegiance is vowed to God and to your spouse, it should not be withdrawn, certainly not for convenience or self-fulfillment. You are trading God's wonderful gift of marriage for a god of pornography that is keeping you in bondage. There is no explanation or justification that will free you from the Lord's call to obedience. Let go of those things that do not lead to godliness and focus on the gift God has given you in your spouse.

6And because you are sons, God has sent
forth [a]the Spirit of His Son into your hearts,
crying out, "Abba, Father!" 7Therefore you
are no longer a slave but a son, [a]and if a
son, then an heir of[1] God through Christ.

Fears for the Church

8But then, indeed, [a]when you did not
know God, [b]you served those which by nature are not gods. 9But now [a]after you have
known God, or rather are known by God,
[b]how *is it that* you turn again to [c]the weak
and beggarly elements, to which you desire again to be in bondage? 10[a]You observe
days and months and seasons and years.
11I am afraid for you, [a]lest I have labored
for you in vain.

12Brethren, I urge you to become like me,
for I *became* like you. [a]You have not injured
me at all. 13You know that [a]because of physical infirmity I preached the gospel to you
at the first. 14And my trial which was in my
flesh you did not despise or reject, but you
received me [a]as an angel of God, [b]*even* as
Christ Jesus. 15What[1] then was the blessing
you *enjoyed?* For I bear you witness that, if
possible, you would have plucked out your
own eyes and given them to me. 16Have I
therefore become your enemy because I
tell you the truth?

4:6 [a] [Acts 16:7; Rom. 5:5; 8:9, 15, 16; 2 Cor. 3:17] 4:7 [a] [Rom. 8:16, 17] [1] NU-Text reads *through God* and omits *through Christ.* 4:8 [a] 1 Cor. 1:21; Eph. 2:12; 1 Thess. 4:5; 2 Thess. 1:8 [b] Rom. 1:25 4:9 [a] [1 Cor. 8:3] [b] Gal. 3:1–3; Col. 2:20 [c] Heb. 7:18 4:10 [a] Rom. 14:5; Col. 2:16 4:11 [a] 1 Thess. 3:5 4:12 [a] 2 Cor. 2:5 4:13 [a] 1 Cor. 2:3 4:14 [a] Mal. 2:7 [b] [Luke 10:16] 4:15 [1] NU-Text reads *Where.*

17They [a]zealously court you, *but* for no good; yes, they want to exclude you, that you may be zealous for them. 18But it is good to be zealous in a good thing always, and not only when I am present with you. 19[a]My little children, for whom I labor in birth again until Christ is formed in you, 20I would like to be present with you now and to change my tone; for I have doubts about you.

Two Covenants
(Gen. 21:8–21; Is. 54:1)

21Tell me, you who desire to be under the law, do you not hear the law? 22For it is written that Abraham had two sons: [a]the one by a bondwoman, [b]the other by a freewoman. 23But he *who was* of the bondwoman [a]was born according to the flesh, [b]and he of the freewoman through promise, 24which things are symbolic. For these are the[1] two covenants: the one from Mount [a]Sinai which gives birth to bondage, which is Hagar— 25for this Hagar is Mount Sinai in Arabia, and corresponds to Jerusalem which now is, and is in bondage with her children— 26but the [a]Jerusalem above is free, which is the mother of us all. 27For it is written:

[a]"Rejoice, O barren,
You who do not bear!
Break forth and shout,
You who are not in labor!
For the desolate has many
more children
Than she who has a husband."[1]

28Now [a]we, brethren, as Isaac *was,* are [b]children of promise. 29But, as [a]he who was born according to the flesh then persecuted him *who was born* according to the Spirit, [b]even so *it is* now. 30Nevertheless what does [a]the Scripture say? [b]"Cast out the bondwoman and her son, for [c]the son of the bondwoman shall not be heir with the son of the freewoman."[1] 31So then, brethren, we are not children of the bondwoman but of the free.

Christian Liberty

5 [a]Stand fast therefore in the liberty by which Christ has made us free,[1] and do not be entangled again with a [b]yoke of bondage. 2Indeed I, Paul, say to you that [a]if you become circumcised, Christ will profit you nothing. 3And I testify again to every man who becomes circumcised [a]that he is a debtor to keep the whole law. 4[a]You have become estranged from Christ, you who *attempt to* be justified by law; [b]you have fallen from grace. 5For we through the Spirit eagerly [a]wait for the hope of righteousness by faith. 6For [a]in Christ Jesus neither circumcision nor uncircumcision avails anything, but [b]faith working through love.

Love Fulfills the Law

7You [a]ran well. Who hindered you from obeying the truth? 8This persuasion does not *come* from Him who calls you. 9[a]A little leaven leavens the whole lump. 10I have confidence in you, in the Lord, that you will have no other mind; but he who troubles you shall bear his judgment, whoever he is.

11And I, brethren, if I still preach circumcision, [a]why do I still suffer persecution? Then [b]the offense of the cross has ceased. 12[a]I could wish that those [b]who trouble you would even cut themselves off!

13For you, brethren, have been called to liberty; only [a]do not *use* liberty as an [b]opportunity for the flesh, but [c]through love serve one another. 14For [a]all the law is fulfilled in one word, *even* in this: [b]"You shall love your neighbor as yourself."[1] 15But if you bite and devour one another, beware lest you be consumed by one another!

Walking in the Spirit

16I say then: [a]Walk in the Spirit, and you shall not fulfill the lust of the flesh. 17For

---

4:17 [a] Rom. 10:2 4:19 [a] 1 Cor. 4:15 4:22 [a] Gen. 16:15 [b] Gen. 21:2 4:23 [a] Rom. 9:7, 8; Gal. 4:29 [b] Gen. 16:15; 17:15–19; 18:10; 21:1; Gal. 4:28; Heb. 11:11 4:24 [a] Ex. 24:6–8; Deut. 33:2 [1] NU-Text and M-Text omit *the.* 4:26 [a] [Is. 2:2] 4:27 [a] Is. 54:1 [1] Isaiah 54:1 4:28 [a] Rom. 9:7, 8; Gal. 3:29 [b] Acts 3:25 4:29 [a] Gen. 21:9 [b] Gal. 5:11 4:30 [a] [Gal. 3:8, 22] [b] Gen. 21:10, 12 [c] [John 8:35] [1] Genesis 21:10 5:1 [a] Phil. 4:1 [b] Acts 15:10; Gal. 2:4 [1] NU-Text reads *For freedom Christ has made us free; stand fast therefore.* 5:2 [a] Acts 15:1; Gal. 5:3, 6, 11 5:3 [a] [Deut. 27:26; Rom. 2:25; Gal. 3:10] 5:4 [a] [Rom. 9:31] [b] Heb. 12:15; 2 Pet. 3:17 5:5 [a] Rom. 8:24 5:6 [a] [1 Cor. 7:19; Gal. 6:15; Col. 3:11] [b] Col. 1:4; 1 Thess. 1:3; [James 2:18, 20, 22] 5:7 [a] 1 Cor. 9:24 5:9 [a] 1 Cor. 5:6 5:11 [a] 1 Cor. 15:30 [b] Rom. 9:33; [1 Cor. 1:23] 5:12 [a] Josh. 7:25 [b] Acts 15:1, 2 5:13 [a] [Rom. 8:2]; 1 Cor. 8:9; Gal. 5:1 [b] Rom. 6:1; 1 Pet. 2:16 [c] 1 Cor. 9:19; Eph. 5:21 5:14 [a] Matt. 7:12; 22:40; Rom. 13:8, 10; Gal. 6:2 [b] Lev. 19:18; Matt. 22:39; Rom. 13:9 [1] Leviticus 19:18 5:16 [a] Rom. 6:12

RELEASE // RECONCILE SINS WITH RIGHTEOUSNESS

We Must Love Others

Galatians 5:14 // For all the law is fulfilled in one word, even in this: "You shall love your neighbor as yourself."

Summary Message // Galatians 5 is a much-needed refresher course in today's society. It reminds us that laws and government should be based on true care and concern for the people under those laws and governments. We have freedom, but the freedom we enjoy should not infringe upon another's freedom or be practiced to their detriment. Galatians 5:14–15 tells us that we must learn to love our neighbors as ourselves or we will "devour one another." When there is no love, there is no real life. Something must change in the world if we are to live out the principles we claim to believe.

Practical Application // It may sound obvious, but we must each realize that we are not on this earth alone. As such, we are to care for those around us. In contrast, a self-centered worldview creates hate, violence, racism, and injustice. Because too many people share that worldview, we see these in action far too often.

When we raise children with a love for the church and teach them to love others, their lives are shaped by these lessons. This upbringing creates good citizens of God's kingdom and earthly society who possess godly values and stand against the unfair treatment of anyone. Those who have faith as a foundation grow up with a desire to live moral, godly lives. The Holy Spirit enlivens God's love in their hearts and actions.

Destructive behaviors such as racism, police brutality, and murder are strong indicators that the love of Jesus Christ is not in control of those who practice them, and the Spirit of God is not leading our society. As a society, we have become vicious and mean-spirited. We who understand how God's love through Jesus can change a person must share our testimonies and live as ambassadors of Christ. When we walk after the Spirit, we will not fulfill our base desire to destroy others. Instead, we will want the best for all. In this way, we will preserve ourselves and our world.

Fervent Prayer // Father, You displayed Your greatest act of love when You gave Your only begotten Son, Jesus Christ, to die for our sin. You said whoever believes that Jesus is the Son of God will be saved from their sins and from those things that destroy them and those around them. Please, save our nation today. Take out stony hearts and replace them with hearts of flesh that are open to You and Your love. You have a beautiful plan for us. Let us all look to You, we pray, to learn how to love, protect, and empower one another. In Jesus' name we pray. Amen.

---

[a]the flesh lusts against the Spirit, and the
Spirit against the flesh; and these are contrary to one another, [b]so that you do not do
the things that you wish. 18But [a]if you are
led by the Spirit, you are not under the law.
19Now [a]the works of the flesh are evident, which are: adultery,[1] fornication, uncleanness, lewdness, 20idolatry, sorcery,
hatred, contentions, jealousies, outbursts
of wrath, selfish ambitions, dissensions,
heresies, 21envy, murders,[1] drunkenness,
revelries, and the like; of which I tell you
beforehand, just as I also told *you* in time
past, that [a]those who practice such things
will not inherit the kingdom of God.
22But [a]the fruit of the Spirit is [b]love, joy,
peace, longsuffering, kindness, [c]goodness,
[d]faithfulness, 23gentleness, self-control.
[a]Against such there is no law. 24And those
who are Christ's [a]have crucified the flesh
with its passions and desires. 25[a]If we live
in the Spirit, let us also walk in the Spirit.
26[a]Let us not become conceited, provoking
one another, envying one another.

5:17 [a] Rom. 7:18, 22, 23; 8:5 [b] Rom. 7:15 5:18 [a] [Rom. 6:14; 7:4; 8:14; 1 Tim. 1:9] 5:19 [a] Rom. 1:26–31; Eph. 5:3, 11; 2 Tim. 3:2–4 [1] NU-Text omits *adultery.* 5:21 [a] 1 Cor. 6:9, 10 [1] NU-Text omits *murders.* 5:22 [a] [John 15:2] [b] [Rom. 5:1–5; 1 Cor. 13:4; Col. 3:12–15] [c] Rom. 15:14 [d] 1 Cor. 13:7 5:23 [a] 1 Tim. 1:9 5:24 [a] Rom. 6:6; [Gal. 2:20; 6:14] 5:25 [a] [Rom. 8:4, 5] 5:26 [a] Phil. 2:3

Bear and Share Burdens

6 Brethren, if a man is overtaken in any
trespass, you who *are* spiritual restore
such a one in a spirit of [a]gentleness, considering yourself lest you also be tempted.
2[a]Bear one another's burdens, and so fulfill
[b]the law of Christ. 3For [a]if anyone thinks himself to be something, when [b]he is nothing,
he deceives himself. 4But [a]let each one examine his own work, and then he will have
rejoicing in himself alone, and [b]not in another. 5For [a]each one shall bear his own load.

Be Generous and Do Good

6[a]Let him who is taught the word share
in all good things with him who teaches.
7Do not be deceived, God is not mocked;
for [a]whatever a man sows, that he will also
reap. 8For he who sows to his flesh will of
the flesh reap corruption, but he who sows
to the Spirit will of the Spirit reap [a]everlast-
ing life. 9And [a]let us not grow weary while
doing good, for in due season we shall reap
[b]if we do not lose heart. 10[a]Therefore, as we
have opportunity, [b]let us do good to all,
[c]especially to those who are of the household of faith.

Glory Only in the Cross

11See with what large letters I have written to you with my own hand! 12As many
as desire to make a good showing in the
flesh, these *would* compel you to be circumcised, [a]only that they may not suffer
persecution for the cross of Christ. 13For
not even those who are circumcised keep
the law, but they desire to have you circumcised that they may boast in your flesh.
14But God forbid that I should boast except
in the [a]cross of our Lord Jesus Christ, by
whom[1] the world has been crucified to me,
and [b]I to the world. 15For [a]in Christ Jesus
neither circumcision nor uncircumcision
avails anything, but a new creation.

Blessing and a Plea

16And as many as walk according to this
rule, peace and mercy *be* upon them, and
upon the Israel of God.
17From now on let no one trouble me,
for I bear in my body the marks of the Lord
Jesus.
18Brethren, the grace of our Lord Jesus
Christ *be* with your spirit. Amen.

#OXYGEN

GALATIANS 6:10

Reconcile Sins with Righteousness

Sin separates and righteousness restores. Doing good is restorative work. Therefore, do not give up on doing the right thing just because it is not immediately recognized or rewarded. Hold fast!

Breathe and **reconcile sins with righteousness.**

6:1 [a] Eph. 4:2 6:2 [a] Acts 20:35; Rom. 15:1; 1 Thess. 5:14 [b] [James 2:8] 6:3 [a] Rom. 12:3 [b] [2 Cor. 3:5; James 1:22] 6:4 [a] 1 Cor. 11:28 [b] Luke 18:11 6:5 [a] [Rom. 2:6] 6:6 [a] 1 Cor. 9:11, 14 6:7 [a] [Rom. 2:6] 6:8 [a] [Rom. 6:8] 6:9 [a] 1 Cor. 15:58; 2 Cor. 4:1; 2 Thess. 3:13 [b] [Matt. 24:13]; Heb. 12:3, 5; [James 5:7, 8] 6:10 [a] Prov. 3:27; [John 9:4; 12:35] [b] Titus 3:8 [c] Rom. 12:13 6:12 [a] Gal. 5:11; Phil. 3:8 6:14 [a] [1 Cor. 1:18] [b] [Gal. 2:20]; Col. 2:20 [1] Or *by which* (the cross) 6:15 [a] [Rom. 2:26, 28]; 1 Cor. 7:19; [Gal. 5:6]

THE EPISTLE OF PAUL TO THE

EPHESIANS

OVERVIEW

When Paul the Pharisee (also known as Saul) is introduced in Acts 6, he is involved in violent, systematic persecution of the church. By the time Paul the apostle wrote to the church in Ephesus, he was a prisoner because of the same unjust system for which he once was an agent. The apostle Paul wrote four books of the Bible while an "ambassador in chains" (Eph. 6:20): Philippians, Ephesians, Colossians, and Philemon. These letters contain the testimony of a man whose life had gone full circle—from persecutor to persecuted. Despite the adversity caused by his incarceration, Paul's passion for sharing the gospel only increased.

Paul visited the church at Ephesus on his second and third missionary journeys. During his third missionary journey, he spent three years in Ephesus, his longest residency of any missionary journey. Why was Ephesus so important to the Great Commission?

- **Economics**
  Ephesus was a coastal city on the Mediterranean Sea. Three continents line the Mediterranean, making Ephesus a convenient distribution center for goods and services. Trade was also augmented by the Cayster River that connected Ephesus to other inland cities. These two natural resources accommodated one of the most active seaports for trading and transportation in that day.
- **Population**
  Ephesus was home to approximately three hundred thousand residents during the height of its popularity, making it a major metropolis. The city boasted a robust infrastructure that included housing, sanitation, education, recreation, a legal system, security, engineering, and city planning.
- **Culture**
  Ephesus was a cultural center with a central library, theater, and music. It boasted a twenty-five-thousand-seat arena and the Library of Celsus that stored approximately twelve thousand scrolls.
- **Religion**
  Religion in Ephesus was extremely popular. The Temple of Diana (Artemis) was located nearby. The mythological Diana was worshiped as the twin sister of Apollo and the daughter of Zeus. She was the moon goddess of nature and sexual immorality. The temple, a tourist destination, was one of the seven wonders of the ancient world. It boasted 127 pillars that were nearly 200 feet tall, the equivalent of a 20-story building. The city's main religious expression was an unholy alliance between spirituality and public sexuality. This pagan temple teaching was so entrenched in Ephesus that the seductive image of Diana was minted into its currency.

For the Great Commission to penetrate this metropolitan area, a Christian church had to be established. Successful acceptance of the gospel in Ephesus could be a breakthrough for the world. Years after Paul's investment in Ephesus began, a strong Christian church emerged.

Paul wrote this letter as he sat in jail with the expectation of sharing the gospel of Jesus Christ with the Roman emperor. Many consider this letter Paul's magnum opus. The central themes of Ephesians are of great importance to life within the family of faith. The authority of Jesus

Christ as the head of the church is presented. The victorious Christ as the conquering hero who descends from heaven—"He who descended is also the One who ascended far above all the heavens, that He might fill all things" (4:10)—is found in this letter. Paul upheld the sanctity of marriage as he wrote, "Husbands, love your wives, just as Christ also loved the church" (5:25).

Inclusion is a familiar theme in Paul's writing that he also addresses in his letter to the Ephesians: "Now, therefore, you are no longer strangers and foreigners, but fellow citizens with the saints and members of the household of God" (2:19) and "the Gentiles should be fellow heirs, of the same body, and partakers of His promise in Christ through the gospel" (3:6). Paul clarified the leadership roles within the church: "And He Himself gave some to be apostles, some prophets, some evangelists, and some pastors and teachers, for the equipping of the saints for the work of ministry, for the edifying of the body of Christ, till we all come to the unity of the faith and of the knowledge of the Son of God" (4:11–13). He also prepared the church for spiritual warfare through the use of a powerful analogy of the "whole armor of God" (6:11; see 6:10–20).

BREATHE IT IN

The apostle Paul was controversial among early Judeo-Christians because his ministry was almost exclusively to the Gentiles while the focus of the other apostles was on the Jews. Some argued that Christians should conform to the legal requirements of the Old Testament, including circumcision and dietary restrictions. But Paul made it clear that Gentile Christians are "no longer strangers and foreigners, but fellow citizens with the saints and members of the household of God" (2:19). Who better to deliver this message than Paul, who was both Jewish and a Roman citizen? As a result, Paul cultivated a church where all were welcome. He argued that God had always intended to make Gentiles "fellow heirs" with the children of Israel (3:5–6), even from the time of the Old Testament prophets. Jesus Christ widened the circle of inclusion; whether you were a Jew like Nicodemus (see John 3) or a Gentile like the Syro-Phoenician woman (see Mark 7), His sacrifice was unrestricted by race, culture, or social acceptance. Christ offered equal access to salvation for all when He said, "For God so loved the world that He gave His only begotten Son, that whoever believes in Him should not perish but have everlasting life" (John 3:16). Christ made it known that everybody is included in His promises when they accept the gift of salvation in Him.

Inclusion is a big issue in the world today. Everyone wants a group or tribe to give them a sense of belonging. Being included is a good thing until it means that we exclude others. Throughout history, exclusion has existed for various reasons such as family, land, or religion. Only in the modern age has race become a motive for exclusion. When a person or group of people is excluded, they have to create their own place of belonging.

Such was the case even in the American church in 1787. Instead of continuing to worship in a segregated church, Rev. Richard Allen led free Black worshipers out of the St. George Methodist Episcopal Church in Philadelphia, Pennsylvania. In 1794, the parishioners began the African Methodist Episcopal Church, an independent denomination dedicated to the spiritual formation of free Blacks and slaves. People of color needed a church where they could belong. The same was true of Black colleges and universities that were institutions that uplifted the African American family and community. When you belong, you are more likely to excel.

Being excluded from society, organizations, churches, and even families is hurtful and can cause damage for generations. While being an agent of change within an exclusionary society is critical, everyone has to find relationships and places that feed their souls while still living within this context. We were never meant to be alone or lonely; we were meant to be part of a body of believers and in relationship with one another. Find a body of believers that fits you and where you feel welcome. If one church does not fit, try another. Do not give up on church because one church does not feel right for you. God may just be leading you to the right church that you can finally call home.

THE EPISTLE OF PAUL TO THE

EPHESIANS

Greeting

1 Paul, an apostle of Jesus Christ by the
will of God,

To the saints who are in Ephesus, and
faithful in Christ Jesus:

2 Grace to you and peace from God our
Father and the Lord Jesus Christ.

Redemption in Christ

3[a]Blessed *be* the God and Father of our
Lord Jesus Christ, who has blessed us with
every spiritual blessing in the heavenly
places in Christ, 4 just as [a]He chose us in
Him [b]before the foundation of the world,
that we should [c]be holy and without blame
before Him in love, 5[a]having predestined
us to [b]adoption as sons by Jesus Christ to
Himself, [c]according to the good pleasure
of His will, 6 to the praise of the glory of His
grace, [a]by which He made us accepted in
[b]the Beloved.

7[a]In Him we have redemption through
His blood, the forgiveness of sins, according to [b]the riches of His grace 8 which He
made to abound toward us in all wisdom
and prudence, 9[a]having made known to us
the mystery of His will, according to His
good pleasure [b]which He purposed in Himself, 10 that in the dispensation of [a]the fullness of the times [b]He might gather together
in one [c]all things in Christ, both[1] which are
in heaven and which are on earth—in Him.
11[a]In Him also we have obtained an inheritance, being predestined according to [b]the
purpose of Him who works all things according to the counsel of His will, 12[a]that
we [b]who first trusted in Christ should be to
the praise of His glory.

13 In Him you also *trusted,* after you
heard [a]the word of truth, the gospel of your
salvation; in whom also, having believed,
[b]you were sealed with the Holy Spirit of
promise, 14[a]who[1] is the guarantee of our
inheritance [b]until the redemption of [c]the
purchased possession, [d]to the praise of
His glory.

Prayer for Spiritual Wisdom

15 Therefore I also, [a]after I heard of your
faith in the Lord Jesus and your love for all
the saints, 16[a]do not cease to give thanks
for you, making mention of you in my
prayers: 17 that [a]the God of our Lord Jesus
Christ, the Father of glory, [b]may give to
you the spirit of wisdom and revelation in
the knowledge of Him, 18[a]the eyes of your
understanding[1] being enlightened; that
you may know what is [b]the hope of His
calling, what are the riches of the glory of
His inheritance in the saints, 19 and what
is the exceeding greatness of His power
toward us who believe, [a]according to the
working of His mighty power 20 which He
worked in Christ when [a]He raised Him
from the dead and [b]seated *Him* at His right
hand in the heavenly *places,* 21[a]far above
all [b]principality and power and might and
dominion, and every name that is named,
not only in this age but also in that which
is to come.

1:3 [a] 2 Cor. 1:3 1:4 [a] Rom. 8:28 [b] 1 Pet. 1:2 [c] Luke 1:75 1:5 [a] Acts 13:48; [Rom. 8:29] [b] John 1:12 [c] [1 Cor. 1:21] 1:6 [a] [Rom. 3:24] [b] Matt. 3:17 1:7 [a] [Heb. 9:12] [b] [Rom. 3:24, 25] 1:9 [a] [Rom. 16:25] [b] [2 Tim. 1:9] 1:10 [a] Gal. 4:4 [b] 1 Cor. 3:22 [c] Eph. 3:15; [Phil. 2:9; Col. 1:16, 20] [1] NU-Text and M-Text omit *both.* 1:11 [a] Rom. 8:17 [b] Is. 46:10 1:12 [a] 2 Thess. 2:13 [b] James 1:18 1:13 [a] John 1:17 [b] [2 Cor. 1:22] 1:14 [a] 2 Cor. 5:5 [b] Rom. 8:23 [c] [Acts 20:28] [d] 1 Pet. 2:9 [1] NU-Text reads *which.* 1:15 [a] Col. 1:4; Philem. 5 1:16 [a] Rom. 1:9 1:17 [a] John 20:17; Rom. 15:6 [b] Is. 11:2; Col. 1:9 1:18 [a] Acts 26:18; 2 Cor. 4:6; Heb. 6:4 [b] Eph. 2:12 [1] NU-Text and M-Text read *hearts.* 1:19 [a] Col. 2:12 1:20 [a] Acts 2:24 [b] Ps. 110:1 1:21 [a] Is. 9:6, 7; Luke 1:32, 33; Phil. 2:9, 10; Rev. 19:12 [b] [Rom. 8:38, 39]

LIFE SUPPORT

BE A LEADER: UNIFY THE BODY OF CHRIST

Blessed be the God and Father of our Lord Jesus Christ, who has blessed us with every spiritual blessing in the heavenly places in Christ, just as He chose us in Him before the foundation of the world, that we should be holy and without blame before Him in love, having predestined us to adoption as sons by Jesus Christ to Himself, according to the good pleasure of His will, to the praise of the glory of His grace, by which He made us accepted in the Beloved. Ephesians 1:3–6

LIFE: Be a Leader

Being a leader means more than just having a title. Real leadership is handling whatever position you hold in a godly manner and being an example of living according to God's ways. A real leader leads by example. That means taking biblical principles and living them out. Scripture speaks many times about the importance of uniting God's people and moving forward together, leaving no one behind. We are all one people, united in Christ and with Christ. So, a leader will take the initiative to bring all of God's people forward, together.

No one is perfect, and no one gets it right every time. However, we are always to make sure we do things God's way. Whoever we are and whatever our role, people follow, watch, and look up to us.

There are numerous books on leadership, but the best lessons can be found in the Bible. Jesus is the greatest leader ever. The disciples followed Him because He was trustworthy, He modeled what He taught, and He always obeyed God the Father. We must follow Jesus as others follow us to the foot of His cross.

SUPPORT: Unify the Body of Christ

What a task! Every believer is given the same Spirit, so we are joined as one body—the body of Christ. Sometimes our human nature wins, though, and we find ourselves focusing on differences among God's people rather than our similarities. This causes divisions in the church and separates us from one another. While we have different opinions, cultures, backgrounds, and denominations, we should collaborate on being about our Father's business—fulfilling the Great Commission by telling others about the one and only true gospel of Jesus Christ. There is no other.

Let us come together to build up the body of Christ. It is only through our unity that we can truly flourish in accomplishing our role of making disciples for our Lord. While the world dies and decays, as was prophesied regarding the last days, it is time for us to join hands and collectively show others the way to Jesus Christ. We must set our sights on strengthening the church by loving each other and being welcoming to all. We are all heading to live in God's house. Therefore, let us appreciate one another now and be instruments of healing and grace to those around us.

SUPPORT EXAMPLE: Break bread with those of different cultures and denominations.

22And [a]He put all *things* under His feet,
and gave Him [b]*to be* head over all *things* to
the church, 23[a]which is His body, [b]the fullness of Him [c]who fills all in all.

By Grace Through Faith

2 And [a]you *He made alive,* [b]who were
dead in trespasses and sins, 2[a]in which
you once walked according to the course of

1:22 [a] Ps. 8:6; 110:1; Matt. 28:18; 1 Cor. 15:27 [b] Heb. 2:7 1:23 [a] Rom. 12:5 [b] Col. 2:9 [c] [1 Cor. 12:6]
2:1 [a] Eph. 2:5; Col. 2:13 [b] Eph. 4:18 2:2 [a] Col. 1:21

this world, according to [b]the prince of the
power of the air, the spirit who now works
in [c]the sons of disobedience, 3[a]among
whom also we all once conducted ourselves in [b]the lusts of our flesh, fulfilling
the desires of the flesh and of the mind,
and [c]were by nature children of wrath, just
as the others.

4But God, [a]who is rich in mercy, because
of His [b]great love with which He loved us,
5[a]even when we were dead in trespasses,
[b]made us alive together with Christ (by
grace you have been saved), 6and raised
us up together, and made *us* sit together
[a]in the heavenly *places* in Christ Jesus, 7that
in the ages to come He might show the exceeding riches of His grace in [a]*His* kindness
toward us in Christ Jesus. 8[a]For by grace
you have been saved [b]through faith, and
that not of yourselves; [c]*it is* the gift of God,
9not of [a]works, lest anyone should [b]boast.
10For we are [a]His workmanship, created
in Christ Jesus for good works, which God
prepared beforehand that we should walk
in them.

#OXYGEN

EPHESIANS 2:10

Elevate the Love You Share

The central theme of the gospel is the ability to love God and your neighbor as yourself. Love, though, is never authenticated until it is given away. Love is an action that we are to walk in. Be selfless. Be loving.

Breathe and elevate the love you share.

Brought Near by His Blood

11Therefore remember that you, once
Gentiles in the flesh—who are called
Uncircumcision by what is called [a]the
Circumcision made in the flesh by hands—
12that at that time you were without Christ,
being aliens from the commonwealth of Israel and strangers from the covenants of
promise, having no hope and without God
in the world. 13But now in Christ Jesus you
who once were far off have been brought
near by the blood of Christ.

Christ Our Peace

14For He Himself is our peace, who has
made both one, and has broken down the
middle wall of separation, 15having abolished in His flesh the enmity, *that is,* the
law of commandments *contained* in ordinances, so as to create in Himself one
[a]new man *from* the two, *thus* making peace,
16and that He might [a]reconcile them both
to God in one body through the cross,
thereby [b]putting to death the enmity. 17And
He came and preached peace to you who
were afar off and to those who were near.
18For [a]through Him we both have access
[b]by one Spirit to the Father.

Christ Our Cornerstone

19Now, therefore, you are no longer
strangers and foreigners, but fellow citizens with the saints and members of the
household of God, 20having been [a]built [b]on
the foundation of the [c]apostles and prophets, Jesus Christ Himself being [d]the chief
corner*stone,* 21in whom the whole building,
being fitted together, grows into [a]a holy
temple in the Lord, 22[a]in whom you also are
being built together for a [b]dwelling place
of God in the Spirit.

The Mystery Revealed

3 For this reason I, Paul, the prisoner of
Christ Jesus for you Gentiles— 2if indeed you have heard of the dispensation
of the grace of God [a]which was given to me
for you, 3[a]how that by revelation [b]He made
known to me the mystery (as I have briefly
written already, 4by which, when you read,
you may understand my knowledge in the
mystery of Christ), 5which in other ages

2:2 [b] [John 12:31]; Eph. 6:12 [c] Col. 3:6 **2:3** [a] 1 Pet. 4:3 [b] Gal. 5:16 [c] [Ps. 51:5] **2:4** [a] Ps. 103:8–11; Rom. 10:12 [b] John 3:16; 1 John 4:9, 10 **2:5** [a] Rom. 5:6, 8 [b] [Rom. 6:4, 5] **2:6** [a] Eph. 1:20 **2:7** [a] Titus 3:4 **2:8** [a] [2 Tim. 1:9] [b] Rom. 4:16 [c] [John 1:12, 13] **2:9** [a] Rom. 4:4, 5; 11:6 [b] Rom. 3:27 **2:10** [a] Is. 19:25 **2:11** [a] [Rom. 2:28; Col. 2:11] **2:15** [a] Gal. 6:15 **2:16** [a] 2 Cor. 5:18; [Col. 1:20–22] [b] [Rom. 6:6] **2:18** [a] John 10:9 [b] 1 Cor. 12:13; Eph. 4:4 **2:20** [a] 1 Pet. 2:4 [b] Matt. 16:18; 1 Cor. 3:10, 11; Rev. 21:14 [c] 1 Cor. 12:28; Eph. 3:5 [d] Ps. 118:22; Luke 20:17 **2:21** [a] 1 Cor. 3:16, 17 **2:22** [a] 1 Pet. 2:5 [b] John 17:23 **3:2** [a] Acts 9:15 **3:3** [a] Acts 22:17, 21; 26:16 [b] [Rom. 11:25; 16:25; Eph. 3:4, 9; 6:19]; Col. 1:26; 4:3

ELEVATE THE LOVE YOU SHARE

INHALE

My spouse wants me to be more romantic. It's not that I don't feel love or want to give love. I guess I just show love differently. To me, being loving is about serving. It's about doing dishes, keeping gas in the cars, and that sort of everyday thing. I understand what my spouse would like, but it feels like I wouldn't be true to who I am and would just be faking it. What am I supposed to do? Do I compromise who I am to make my spouse happy, or should my spouse compromise with me instead?

EXHALE

Marriage is a relationship that requires love and understanding flowing from both people in both directions. Within a marriage relationship, things are not just about you. (And if children enter the picture, it will become even less about you.) Just as Jesus came to serve, we are to live likewise, especially in marriage. Meeting the needs of our spouse is the most important thing. But as you put your spouse's needs first, your spouse should be putting yours first. So, in the end, both of you have your needs met, but in a Christlike, beautiful, selfless way, rather than a selfish way.

So, sit down together and have those hard conversations. Talk through what each of you needs and how each of you can work toward selflessly seeking to meet those needs. Be more intentional about doing all you can to meet your spouse's needs. This doesn't mean you have to change who you are and the way you are wired completely. But it does mean that you need to focus on giving rather than getting. But that isn't a bad thing. It is what marriage is about—two people becoming more like Jesus and drawing closer to each other.

Ephesians 3:17 tells us our goal of living should be "that Christ may dwell in [our] hearts through faith" and that we are "rooted and grounded in love." That's God's wonderful plan for all our relationships, especially our marriages (see Eph. 5:25). Recognize your frustration as an important warning sign that something is going on that could separate you. Keep your eyes open and see the big picture. There is a role and responsibility for both the husband and the wife becoming one. Take great pride in these roles and God's design, and watch how your marriage flourishes.

was not made known to the sons of men,
as it has now been revealed by the Spirit
to His holy apostles and prophets: 6that
the Gentiles [a]should be fellow heirs, of the
same body, and partakers of His promise
in Christ through the gospel, 7[a]of which I
became a minister [b]according to the gift of
the grace of God given to me by [c]the effective working of His power.

Purpose of the Mystery

8To me, [a]who am less than the least of
all the saints, this grace was given, that I
should preach among the Gentiles [b]the unsearchable riches of Christ, 9and to make all
see what *is* the fellowship[1] of the mystery,
which from the beginning of the ages has
been hidden in God who [a]created all things
through Jesus Christ;[2] 10[a]to the intent that
now [b]the manifold wisdom of God might be
made known by the church [c]to the principalities and powers in the heavenly *places,*
11[a]according to the eternal purpose which He
accomplished in Christ Jesus our Lord, 12in
whom we have boldness and access [a]with
confidence through faith in Him. 13[a]Therefore I ask that you do not lose heart at my
tribulations for you, [b]which is your glory.

Appreciation of the Mystery

14For this reason I bow my knees to the
[a]Father of our Lord Jesus Christ,[1] 15from

3:6 [a] Gal. 3:28, 29 3:7 [a] Rom. 15:16 [b] Rom. 1:5 [c] Rom. 15:18 3:8 [a] [1 Cor. 15:9] [b] [Col. 1:27; 2:2, 3] 3:9 [a] John 1:3; Col. 1:16; Heb. 1:2 [1] NU-Text and M-Text read *stewardship* (dispensation). [2] NU-Text omits *through Jesus Christ.* 3:10 [a] 1 Pet. 1:12 [b] [1 Tim. 3:16] [c] Eph. 1:21; 6:12; Col. 1:16; 2:10, 15 3:11 [a] [Eph. 1:4, 11] 3:12 [a] 2 Cor. 3:4; Heb. 4:16; 10:19, 35; [1 John 2:28; 3:21] 3:13 [a] Phil. 1:14 [b] 2 Cor. 1:6 3:14 [a] Eph. 1:3 [1] NU-Text omits *of our Lord Jesus Christ.*

whom the whole family in heaven and
earth is named, 16that He would grant
you, [a]according to the riches of His glory,
[b]to be strengthened with might through
His Spirit in [c]the inner man, 17[a]that Christ
may dwell in your hearts through faith;
that you, [b]being rooted and grounded in
love, 18[a]may be able to comprehend with
all the saints [b]what *is* the width and length
and depth and height— 19to know the love
of Christ which passes knowledge; that
you may be filled [a]with all the fullness
of God.

20Now [a]to Him who is able to do exceedingly abundantly [b]above all that we ask or
think, [c]according to the power that works
in us, 21[a]to Him *be* glory in the church by
Christ Jesus to all generations, forever and
ever. Amen.

Walk in Unity

4 I, therefore, the prisoner of the Lord,
beseech you to [a]walk worthy of the calling with which you were called, 2with all
lowliness and gentleness, with longsuffering, bearing with one another in love, 3en-
deavoring to keep the unity of the Spirit
[a]in the bond of peace. 4[a]*There is* one body
and one Spirit, just as you were called in
one hope of your calling; 5[a]one Lord, [b]one
faith, [c]one baptism; 6[a]one God and Father
of all, who *is* above all, and [b]through all,
and in you[1] all.

Spiritual Gifts

7But [a]to each one of us grace was given
according to the measure of Christ's gift.
8Therefore He says:

[a]"When He ascended on high,
He led captivity captive,
And gave gifts to men."[1]

9[a](Now this, "He ascended"—what does
it mean but that He also first[1] descended
into the lower parts of the earth? 10He who
descended is also the One [a]who ascended
far above all the heavens, [b]that He might
fill all things.)

11And He Himself gave some *to be* apostles, some prophets, some evangelists, and
some pastors and teachers, 12for the equipping of the saints for the work of ministry,
[a]for the edifying of [b]the body of Christ, 13till
we all come to the unity of the faith [a]and
of the knowledge of the Son of God, to [b]a
perfect man, to the measure of the stature
of the fullness of Christ; 14that we should
no longer be [a]children, tossed to and fro
and carried about with every wind of doctrine, by the trickery of men, in the cunning craftiness of [b]deceitful plotting, 15but,
speaking the truth in love, may grow up
in all things into Him who is the [a]head—
Christ— 16[a]from whom the whole body,
joined and knit together by what every
joint supplies, according to the effective
working by which every part does its share,
causes growth of the body for the edifying
of itself in love.

The New Man

17This I say, therefore, and testify in the
Lord, that you should [a]no longer walk as
the rest of[1] the Gentiles walk, in the futility of their mind, 18having their understanding darkened, being alienated from
the life of God, because of the ignorance
that is in them, because of the [a]blindness
of their heart; 19[a]who, being past feeling,
[b]have given themselves over to lewdness,
to work all uncleanness with greediness.

20But you have not so learned Christ,
21if indeed you have heard Him and have
been taught by Him, as the truth is in Jesus:
22that you [a]put off, concerning your former
conduct, the old man which grows corrupt
according to the deceitful lusts, 23and [a]be
renewed in the spirit of your mind, 24and
that you [a]put on the new man which was
created according to God, in true righteousness and holiness.

3:16 [a] [Eph. 1:7; 2:4; Phil. 4:19] [b] 1 Cor. 16:13; Phil. 4:13; Col. 1:11 [c] Rom. 7:22 3:17 [a] John 14:23; Rom. 8:9; 2 Cor. 13:5; [Eph. 2:22] [b] Col. 1:23 3:18 [a] Eph. 1:18 [b] Rom. 8:39 3:19 [a] Eph. 1:23 3:20 [a] Rom. 16:25 [b] 1 Cor. 2:9 [c] Col. 1:29 3:21 [a] Rom. 11:36 4:1 [a] Eph. 2:10; [Col. 1:10; 2:6]; 1 Thess. 2:12 4:3 [a] Col. 3:14 4:4 [a] Rom. 12:5 4:5 [a] 1 Cor. 1:13 [b] [1 Cor. 15:1–8]; Jude 3 [c] 1 Cor. 12:12, 13; [Heb. 6:6] 4:6 [a] Mal. 2:10; 1 Cor. 8:6; 12:6 [b] Rom. 11:36 [1] NU-Text omits *you;* M-Text reads *us.* 4:7 [a] [1 Cor. 12:7, 11] 4:8 [a] Ps. 68:18; [Col. 2:15] [1] Psalm 68:18 4:9 [a] Luke 23:43; John 3:13; 20:17; [1 Pet. 3:19, 20] [1] NU-Text omits *first.* 4:10 [a] Acts 1:9 [b] [Acts 2:33; Eph. 1:23] 4:12 [a] 1 Cor. 14:26 [b] Col. 1:24 4:13 [a] Col. 2:2 [b] 1 Cor. 14:20; Col. 1:28; Heb. 5:14 4:14 [a] 1 Cor. 14:20 [b] Rom. 16:18 4:15 [a] Eph. 1:22 4:16 [a] [Rom. 12:4]; Col. 2:19 4:17 [a] Eph. 2:2; 4:22 [1] NU-Text omits *the rest of.* 4:18 [a] Rom. 1:21 4:19 [a] 1 Tim. 4:2 [b] 1 Pet. 4:3 4:22 [a] Col. 3:8 4:23 [a] [Rom. 12:2; Col. 3:10] 4:24 [a] [Rom. 6:4; 7:6; 12:2; 2 Cor. 5:17; Col. 3:10]

RELEASE // ELEVATE THE LOVE YOU SHARE

Shine Your Light with Love

Ephesians 4:1–3 // Walk worthy of the calling with which you were called, with all lowliness and gentleness, with longsuffering, bearing with one another in love, endeavoring to keep the unity of the Spirit in the bond of peace.

Summary Message // The apostle Paul wrote to the church in Ephesus from a Roman prison. In this letter, he spoke eloquently of how the church is Christ's body and a powerful instrument in the hands of God to defeat the Enemy. His message of living together in love stressed the importance of being unified in the Lord and in the faith.

Love is needed among believers now more than ever. Sharp divisions have arisen within the church. Though the gates of hell will never prevail against the church, division may have stagnated her mission. We must realize the importance of unity. Without it, we risk losing our witness to the world of the love and sacrifice of Jesus.

Practical Application // How do you get one from many? Generally, we would think of our need to subtract or divide to end up with such a result, but in Christ, many can become one a different way: unity through the Spirit. Although we have created different denominations, the Bible describes the church as being made up of many nations, tribes, and tongues that become one in heart and mind as we serve the Lord together. As such, addition and multiplication continue to make one. There is one hope of our calling, one Lord, one faith, one baptism, and one God. In these, Christ's body should be completely united. It is not just about one person or one group of people moving forward and maturing their faith. It is also about leaving no one behind.

Distractions, though, often cause us to lose focus and, ultimately, the vision of following Christ in unity. When we stop looking toward Jesus, we also stop seeing our neighbors as one with us. Instead, we focus on what they look like, what they have, or where they come from, and we begin to see them as different. The result is that one becomes many again. Unity quickly becomes disunity.

Society's turn from the ways of the Lord is seen in the replacement of Christian identity with political affiliation, sound doctrine with unsound interpretations of Scripture, pursuit of God with financial pursuits, and allegiance to our Lord with faithful adherence to sinful systems. Recent history is littered with believers who have lost unity with their brothers and sisters in the faith because they have drifted into these murky waters of a different gospel than the one that Jesus taught. Still, we are called not just to love them but to run after them so Christ might rescue them from the present evil age (see Gal. 1:4–6). This is spiritual love—a love that takes its cues from Jesus and does its best to maintain the bond of peace that helps us preserve the spirit of unity. Peace should not only hold us together as the body of Christ, but it should also draw us closer to one another as we endeavor to walk out our faith for the world to see.

Fervent Prayer // Lord, we thank You for calling us to Yourself and for our family of faith. We confess that we have allowed race, class, riches, and other cares of the world to choke out our love for each other. We now seek a singleness of mind and vision that causes us to see You as You are: God, the Creator of all. Help us see You in ourselves so that we might see You in others and serve each other in the bonds of peace and love. In Jesus' name we pray. Amen.

Do Not Grieve the Spirit

25 Therefore, putting away lying, [a]"*Let*
each one *of you* speak truth with his neighbor,"[1] for [b]we are members of one another.
26 [a]"Be angry, and do not sin":[1] do not let
the sun go down on your wrath, 27 [a]nor give
place to the devil. 28 Let him who stole steal
no longer, but rather [a]let him labor, working with *his* hands what is good, that he
may have something [b]to give him who
has need. 29 [a]Let no corrupt word proceed
out of your mouth, but [b]what is good for
necessary edification, [c]that it may impart
grace to the hearers. 30 And [a]do not grieve

4:25 [a] Zech. 8:16; Eph. 4:15; Col. 3:9 [b] Rom. 12:5 [1] Zechariah 8:16 4:26 [a] Ps. 4:4; 37:8 [1] Psalm 4:4 4:27 [a] [Rom. 12:19; James 4:7]; 1 Pet. 5:9 4:28 [a] Acts 20:35; 1 Cor. 4:12; Gal. 6:10 [b] Luke 3:11; 1 Thess. 4:12 4:29 [a] Matt. 12:34; Eph. 5:4; Col. 3:8 [b] 1 Thess. 5:11 [c] Col. 3:16 4:30 [a] Is. 7:13

the Holy Spirit of God, by whom you were
sealed for the day of redemption. 31[a]Let
all bitterness, wrath, anger, clamor, and
[b]evil speaking be put away from you, [c]with
all malice. 32And [a]be kind to one another,
tenderhearted, [b]forgiving one another,
even as God in Christ forgave you.

Walk in Love

5 Therefore[a] be imitators of God as dear
[b]children. 2And [a]walk in love, [b]as Christ
also has loved us and given Himself for
us, an offering and a sacrifice to God [c]for a
sweet-smelling aroma.

#OXYGEN

EPHESIANS 5:2

Elevate the Love You Share

Love is to be sincere, coming from a heart devoted to Christ. Tenderhearted, kind love is essential in the building of the family, the body of Christ, and the community. Love positions us to truly thrive.

Breathe and **elevate the love you share.**

3But fornication and all [a]uncleanness
or [b]covetousness, let it not even be named
among you, as is fitting for saints; 4[a]neither
filthiness, nor [b]foolish talking, nor coarse
jesting, [c]which are not fitting, but rather
[d]giving of thanks. 5For this you know,[1] that
no fornicator, unclean person, nor covetous man, who is an idolater, has any [a]inher-
itance in the kingdom of Christ and God.
6Let no one deceive you with empty words,
for because of these things the wrath of
God comes upon the sons of disobedience.
7Therefore do not be [a]partakers with them.

Walk in Light

8For you were once darkness, but now
you are [a]light in the Lord. Walk as children of light 9(for [a]the fruit of the Spirit[1] *is*
in all goodness, righteousness, and truth),
10[a]finding out what is acceptable to the Lord.
11And have [a]no fellowship with the unfruitful works of darkness, but rather expose
them. 12[a]For it is shameful even to speak of
those things which are done by them in secret. 13But [a]all things that are exposed are
made manifest by the light, for whatever
makes manifest is light. 14Therefore He says:

[a]"Awake, you who sleep,
Arise from the dead,
And Christ will give you light."

Walk in Wisdom

15[a]See then that you walk circumspectly,
not as fools but as wise, 16[a]redeeming the
time, [b]because the days are evil.
17[a]Therefore do not be unwise, but
[b]understand [c]what the will of the Lord *is.*
18And [a]do not be drunk with wine, in which
is dissipation; but be filled with the Spirit,
19speaking to one another [a]in psalms and
hymns and spiritual songs, singing and
making [b]melody in your heart to the Lord,
20[a]giving thanks always for all things to God
the Father [b]in the name of our Lord Jesus
Christ, 21[a]submitting to one another in the
fear of God.[1]

Marriage—Christ and the Church
(cf. Col. 3:18, 19)

22Wives, [a]submit to your own husbands,
as to the Lord. 23For [a]the husband is head
of the wife, as also [b]Christ is head of the
church; and He is the Savior of the body.
24Therefore, just as the church is subject
to Christ, so *let* the wives *be* to their own
husbands [a]in everything.
25[a]Husbands, love your wives, just as
Christ also loved the church and [b]gave Himself for her, 26that He might sanctify and

4:31 [a] Rom. 3:14; Col. 3:8, 19 [b] James 4:11 [c] Titus 3:3 **4:32** [a] [Matt. 6:14]; 2 Cor. 6:10 [b] [Mark 11:25; Luke 6:37] **5:1** [a] [Matt. 5:48]; Luke 6:36; Eph. 4:32 [b] 1 Pet. 1:14–16 **5:2** [a] 1 Thess. 4:9 [b] John 15:9; Gal. 1:4; 1 John 3:16 [c] Ex. 29:18, 25; 2 Cor. 2:14, 15 **5:3** [a] Col. 3:5–7 [b] [Luke 12:15] **5:4** [a] Matt. 12:34, 35; Eph. 4:29; Col. 3:8; James 1:21 [b] Titus 3:9 [c] Rom. 1:28 [d] Phil. 4:6; Col. 3:17; [1 Thess. 5:18] **5:5** [a] 1 Cor. 6:9, 10; Col. 3:5 [1] NU-Text reads *For know this.* **5:7** [a] 1 Tim. 5:22 **5:8** [a] 1 Thess. 5:5 **5:9** [a] Gal. 5:22 [1] NU-Text reads *light.* **5:10** [a] [Rom. 12:1, 2] **5:11** [a] 1 Cor. 5:9; 2 Cor. 6:14 **5:12** [a] Rom. 1:24 **5:13** [a] [John 3:20, 21] **5:14** [a] [Is. 26:19; 60:1; Rom. 13:11] **5:15** [a] Col. 4:5 **5:16** [a] Col. 4:5 [b] Eccl. 11:2 **5:17** [a] Col. 4:5 [b] [Rom. 12:2]; Col. 1:9 [c] 1 Thess. 4:3 **5:18** [a] Prov. 20:1; 23:31; Rom. 13:13; 1 Cor. 5:11; 1 Thess. 5:7 **5:19** [a] Acts 16:25 [b] James 5:13 **5:20** [a] Ps. 34:1 [b] [1 Pet. 2:5] **5:21** [a] [Phil. 2:3]; 1 Pet. 5:5 [1] NU-Text reads *Christ.* **5:22** [a] Eph. 5:22—6:9; Col. 3:18—4:1; 1 Pet. 3:1–6 **5:23** [a] [1 Cor. 11:3] [b] Col. 1:18 **5:24** [a] Titus 2:4, 5 **5:25** [a] Eph. 5:28, 33; Col. 3:19; [1 Pet. 3:7] [b] Acts 20:28

ACT WITH SELF-CONTROL

INHALE

People make me angry! Sometimes, I want to go off on my coworkers when they talk about poor folks. Being poor is not always a mindset. Being poor is not always a choice. Getting out of the projects isn't easy. I see a system that promotes some and locks others out. When you are the last hired and the first fired, that is a system that locks many out of financial freedom. I am fed up with most of the people I work with wrongly talking about situations they do not know. How do I educate without speaking in anger?

EXHALE

The hard reality is that these types of statements and conversations are going on all the time. Those of us who have experienced such a difficult set of circumstances are even more sensitive to these types of insensitive remarks. But really, even if we are not from these experiences, we should not allow this mindset to go unchallenged. Speak when you feel it will be productive, but as you recognize, do it in a respectful and decent manner.

Life is hard enough as it is, which is why we all need to show more empathy. But that does not mean that there is not a time to confront and correct. At times, speaking up is the right thing to do, and you should not be criticized if you do it. Know that even if you do it in the right way, that still could happen. Stereotyping someone as an angry Black person isn't appropriate and certainly should be addressed, but do what you can to not give credence to this false narrative. We may not ever see the day when everyone sees others fairly, but you can be a change agent to help make things better. That is what it's about: doing things to help those who are in difficult situations improve their lives.

You got one major thing right for sure: we all fall short in this life. If you think you don't, then keep living, and you will soon come to realize that you surely do. However, God's Word gives us encouragement. Ephesians 6:12 says, "For we do not wrestle against flesh and blood, but against principalities, against powers, against the rulers of the darkness of this age, against spiritual hosts of wickedness in the heavenly places." People are never our enemies. They might frustrate us. They might even be against us. But we should never be against them. In times when you could be rightfully angry, remember the Lord wants you to exude love and grace.

cleanse her [a]with the washing of water [b]by
the word, 27 [a]that He might present her to
Himself a glorious church, [b]not having spot
or wrinkle or any such thing, but that she
should be holy and without blemish. 28 So
husbands ought to love their own wives
as their own bodies; he who loves his wife
loves himself. 29 For no one ever hated his
own flesh, but nourishes and cherishes it,
just as the Lord *does* the church. 30 For [a]we
are members of His body,[1] of His flesh and
of His bones. 31 [a]"For this reason a man shall
leave his father and mother and be joined
to his wife, and the [b]two shall become one
flesh."[1] 32 This is a great mystery, but I speak
concerning Christ and the church. 33 Nevertheless [a]let each one of you in particular
so love his own wife as himself, and let the
wife *see* that she [b]respects *her* husband.

Children and Parents
(Ex. 20:12; Deut. 5:16)

6 Children, [a]obey your parents in the
Lord, for this is right. 2 [a]"Honor your
father and mother," which is the first commandment with promise: 3 "that it may be

5:26 [a] John 3:5 [b] [John 15:3; 17:17; Rom. 10:8; Eph. 6:17] 5:27 [a] [2 Cor. 4:14; 11:2]; Col. 1:22 [b] Song 4:7 5:30 [a] Gen. 2:23 [1] NU-Text omits the rest of this verse. 5:31 [a] Gen. 2:24; Matt. 19:5; Mark 10:7 [b] [1 Cor. 6:16] [1] Genesis 2:24 5:33 [a] Col. 3:19 [b] 1 Pet. 3:1, 6 6:1 [a] Prov. 6:20; 23:22; Col. 3:20 6:2 [a] Ex. 20:12; Deut. 5:16

well with you and you may live long on the
earth."[1]
4 And [a]you, fathers, do not provoke your
children to wrath, but [b]bring them up in
the training and admonition of the Lord.

Bondservants and Masters

5 [a]Bondservants, be obedient to those
who are your masters according to the
flesh, [b]with fear and trembling, [c]in sincerity
of heart, as to Christ; 6 [a]not with eyeservice,
as men-pleasers, but as bondservants of
Christ, doing the will of God from the heart,
7 with goodwill doing service, as to the Lord,
and not to men, 8 [a]knowing that whatever
good anyone does, he will receive the same
from the Lord, whether *he is* a slave or free.
9 And you, masters, do the same things
to them, giving up threatening, knowing
that your own [a]Master also[1] is in heaven,
and [b]there is no partiality with Him.

The Whole Armor of God

10 Finally, my brethren, be strong in the
Lord and in the power of His might. 11 [a]Put
on the whole armor of God, that you may be
able to stand against the wiles of the devil.
12 For we do not wrestle against flesh and
blood, but against [a]principalities, against
powers, against [b]the rulers of the darkness
of this age,[1] against spiritual *hosts* of wickedness in the heavenly *places.* 13 [a]Therefore
take up the whole armor of God, that you
may be able to withstand [b]in the evil day,
and having done all, to stand.
14 Stand therefore, [a]having girded your
waist with truth, [b]having put on the breastplate of righteousness, 15 [a]and having shod
your feet with the preparation of the gospel
of peace; 16 above all, taking [a]the shield of
faith with which you will be able to quench
all the fiery darts of the wicked one. 17 And
[a]take the helmet of salvation, and [b]the
sword of the Spirit, which is the word of
God; 18 [a]praying always with all prayer and
supplication in the Spirit, [b]being watchful
to this end with all perseverance and [c]sup-
plication for all the saints— 19 and for me,
that utterance may be given to me, [a]that I
may open my mouth boldly to make known
the mystery of the gospel, 20 for which [a]I am
an ambassador in chains; that in it I may
speak boldly, as I ought to speak.

A Gracious Greeting

21 But that you also may know my affairs
and how I am doing, [a]Tychicus, a beloved
brother and [b]faithful minister in the Lord,
will make all things known to you; 22 [a]whom
I have sent to you for this very purpose, that
you may know our affairs, and *that* he may
[b]comfort your hearts.
23 Peace to the brethren, and love with
faith, from God the Father and the Lord
Jesus Christ. 24 Grace *be* with all those who
love our Lord Jesus Christ in sincerity. Amen.

6:3 [1] Deuteronomy 5:16 6:4 [a] Col. 3:21 [b] Gen. 18:19; Deut. 6:7; 11:19; Ps. 78:4; Prov. 22:6; 2 Tim. 3:15 6:5 [a] Col. 3:22; [1 Tim. 6:1]; Titus 2:9; 1 Pet. 2:18 [b] 2 Cor. 7:15 [c] 1 Chr. 29:17 6:6 [a] Col. 3:22 6:8 [a] Rom. 2:6 6:9 [a] Job 31:13; John 13:13; Col. 4:1 [b] Deut. 10:17; Acts 10:34; Rom. 2:11; Col. 3:25 [1] NU-Text reads *He who is both their Master and yours.* 6:11 [a] [2 Cor. 6:7] 6:12 [a] Rom. 8:38 [b] Luke 22:53 [1] NU-Text reads *rulers of this darkness.* 6:13 [a] [2 Cor. 10:4] [b] Eph. 5:16 6:14 [a] Is. 11:5; Luke 12:35; 1 Pet. 1:13 [b] Is. 59:17; Rom. 13:12; Eph. 6:13; 1 Thess. 5:8 6:15 [a] Is. 52:7; Rom. 10:15 6:16 [a] 1 John 5:4 6:17 [a] 1 Thess. 5:8 [b] Is. 49:2; Hos. 6:5; [Heb. 4:12] 6:18 [a] Luke 18:1; Col. 1:3; 4:2; 1 Thess. 5:17 [b] [Matt. 26:41] [c] Phil. 1:4 6:19 [a] Acts 4:29; Col. 4:3 6:20 [a] 2 Cor. 5:20; Philem. 9 6:21 [a] Acts 20:4; 2 Tim. 4:12; Titus 3:12 [b] 1 Cor. 4:1, 2 6:22 [a] Col. 4:8 [b] 2 Cor. 1:6

THE EPISTLE OF PAUL TO THE

PHILIPPIANS

OVERVIEW

The origin of the church at Philippi is recorded in Acts 16. Believed to be the first church in Europe, three major biblical events surrounded its founding. First, the church began in the home of a businesswoman named Lydia, a wealthy convert who manufactured clothing with purple dye, a highly prized commodity. Only the noble class could afford to wear purple because the process to extract it from shellfish was difficult and tedious. This is why purple is most often associated with nobility and royalty.

Second, Paul and Silas were imprisoned in Philippi for emancipating an enslaved girl. By liberating the girl from exploitation, Paul disrupted her captor's ability to profit from her abilities, leading to Silas's and his imprisonment.

Paul and Silas's brief imprisonment led to the third remarkable event. During a time of prayer and praise, the pair were supernaturally released from prison by an earthquake. Fearing the prisoners had escaped, the prison guard was prepared to kill himself. Paul, though, reassured him that they were still there and shared the gospel with him. As a result, the guard's entire family was saved.

Philippi was a Roman city with a diverse population at the time of Paul's ministry. It was the capital city of Macedonia and located approximately ten miles inland and surrounded by mountains on three sides. Paul embarked on his initial journey to Philippi as the result of a dream (see Acts 16:9). This epistle—along with Ephesians, Galatians, and Philemon—was written when Paul was a prisoner in Rome.

Even though Paul wrote from prison, he expressed his joy and gratitude toward the church at Philippi: "I thank my God upon every remembrance of you, always in every prayer of mine making request for you all with joy, for your fellowship in the gospel from the first day until now" (Phil. 1:3–5). Paul had received a glowing progress report about the church and proudly wrote about the unique perspective of witnessing the church at its inception and its progress in the twelve intervening years. He also applauded the benevolence of the church at a vulnerable time in his ministry.

Paul's letters were often prompted by the need of correction and reproof in response to controversy within a church. In Philippians, however, his goal was to express his gratitude while also inspiring the church to continue its progress. The centrality of Jesus Christ was at the heart of his discourse. He urged the church to remain committed to the mission of Christ as he had done when he said, "Not that I have already attained, or am already perfected; but I press on, that I may lay hold of that for which Christ Jesus has also laid hold of me" (3:12).

BREATHE IT IN

Paul included many assurances and promises in his letter to the church at Philippi. The first and last promises are God's "bookend promises." The first promise found in Philippians 1:6 assures the church that God was not finished with this sacred community. Paul encouraged the twelve-

year-old church to continue to be faithful so the church might flourish. Paul's final promise is another widely quoted passage that encourages many: "I can do all things through Christ who strengthens me" (4:13). Paul assured the church that he remained confident in Christ, who strengthened him to complete his assignment in Rome, no matter the circumstances.

In these bookend promises we find enthusiasm and confidence both for what Christ wants to do with the institution of the church and how Christ empowers us individually during our challenges. Your kingdom contribution can have an amazing multifaceted effect. You can be a mentor and encourage a younger generation or serve an older generation as a companion. If you are able, you can hire those who are jobless to help feed the homeless. You could mow the grass and house-sit for your neighbor who needs to travel for long periods to help care for an elderly parent. Whatever you choose, the unity of the church should motivate you. We live in a time when individual believers are abandoning the church. Many young people see the value of believing but reject the value of belonging. Take measures to ensure that your contribution to sharing the gospel with people like Lydia, the enslaved girl, and the distraught jailor is rivaled only by your commitment to the church—the body of Christ. Find a church that is committed to uplifting the community and get involved.

†

THE EPISTLE OF PAUL TO THE

PHILIPPIANS

Greeting

1 Paul and Timothy, bondservants of
Jesus Christ,

To all the saints in Christ Jesus who are
in Philippi, with the bishops[1] and [a]deacons:

2Grace to you and peace from God our
Father and the Lord Jesus Christ.

Thankfulness and Prayer

3[a]I thank my God upon every remembrance of you, 4always in [a]every prayer of
mine making request for you all with joy,
5[a]for your fellowship in the gospel from the
first day until now, 6being confident of this
very thing, that He who has begun [a]a good
work in you will complete *it* until the day of
Jesus Christ; 7just as it is right for me to think
this of you all, because I have you in my
heart, inasmuch as both in my chains and
in the defense and confirmation of the gospel, you all are partakers with me of grace.
8For God is my witness, how greatly I long
for you all with the affection of Jesus Christ.
9And this I pray, that your love may
abound still more and more in knowledge
and all discernment, 10that you may approve the things that are excellent, that you
may be sincere and without offense till the
day of Christ, 11being filled with the fruits of
righteousness [a]which *are* by Jesus Christ,
[b]to the glory and praise of God.

Christ Is Preached

12But I want you to know, brethren, that
the things *which happened* to me have actually turned out for the furtherance of the
gospel, 13so that it has become evident [a]to
the whole palace guard, and to all the rest,
that my chains are in Christ; 14and most of
the brethren in the Lord, having become
confident by my chains, are much more
bold to speak the word without fear.
15Some indeed preach Christ even from
envy and strife, and some also from goodwill: 16The former[1] preach Christ from selfish ambition, not sincerely, supposing to
add affliction to my chains; 17but the latter
out of love, knowing that I am appointed
for the defense of the gospel. 18What then?
Only *that* in every way, whether in pretense
or in truth, Christ is preached; and in this
I rejoice, yes, and will rejoice.

To Live Is Christ

19For I know that [a]this will turn out for
my deliverance through your prayer and
the supply of the Spirit of Jesus Christ,
20according to my earnest expectation and
hope that in nothing I shall be ashamed,
but [a]with all boldness, as always, so now
also Christ will be magnified in my body,
whether by life [b]or by death. 21For to me,
to live *is* Christ, and to die *is* gain. 22But if *I*
live on in the flesh, this *will mean* fruit from
my labor; yet what I shall choose I cannot
tell. 23For[1] I am hard-pressed between the
two, having a [a]desire to depart and be with
Christ, *which is* [b]far better. 24Nevertheless to
remain in the flesh *is* more needful for you.
25And being confident of this, I know that I
shall remain and continue with you all for
your progress and joy of faith, 26that [a]your
rejoicing for me may be more abundant in
Jesus Christ by my coming to you again.

1:1 [a] [1 Tim. 3:8–13] [1] Literally *overseers* 1:3 [a] 1 Cor. 1:4 1:4 [a] Eph. 1:16; 1 Thess. 1:2 1:5 [a] [Rom. 12:13] 1:6 [a] [John 6:29] 1:11 [a] [Eph. 2:10]; Col. 1:6 [b] John 15:8 1:13 [a] Phil. 4:22 1:16 [1] NU-Text reverses the contents of verses 16 and 17. 1:19 [a] Job 13:16, LXX 1:20 [a] Eph. 6:19, 20 [b] [Rom. 14:8] 1:23 [a] [2 Cor. 5:2, 8]; 2 Tim. 4:6 [b] [Ps. 16:11] [1] NU-Text and M-Text read *But.* 1:26 [a] 2 Cor. 1:14

Striving and Suffering for Christ

27Only [a]let your conduct be worthy of
the gospel of Christ, so that whether I come
and see you or am absent, I may hear of
your affairs, that you stand fast in one
spirit, [b]with one mind [c]striving together
for the faith of the gospel, 28and not in any
way terrified by your adversaries, which is
to them a proof of perdition, but to you of
salvation,[1] and that from God. 29For to you
[a]it has been granted on behalf of Christ,
[b]not only to believe in Him, but also to [c]suf-
fer for His sake, 30[a]having the same conflict [b]which you saw in me and now hear
is in me.

#OXYGEN

PHILIPPIANS 1:27

Act with Self-Control

Life has a way of teaching us many lessons. One lesson in particular is that we must learn to deal with our emotions, or our emotions will deal with us.

Shift your focus, **breathe**, and **act with self-control**.

Unity Through Humility

2 Therefore if *there is* any consolation
in Christ, if any comfort of love, if any
fellowship of the Spirit, if any [a]affection
and mercy, 2[a]fulfill my joy [b]by being like-
minded, having the same love, *being* of [c]one
accord, of one mind. 3[a]*Let* nothing *be done*
through selfish ambition or conceit, but [b]in
lowliness of mind let each esteem others
better than himself. 4[a]Let each of you look
out not only for his own interests, but also
for the interests of [b]others.

The Humbled and Exalted Christ

5[a]Let this mind be in you which was also
in Christ Jesus, 6who, [a]being in the form of
God, did not consider it robbery to be equal
with God, 7[a]but made Himself of no reputation, taking the form [b]of a bondservant,
and [c]coming in the likeness of men. 8And
being found in appearance as a man, He
humbled Himself and [a]became [b]obedient
to *the point of* death, even the death of the
cross. 9[a]Therefore God also [b]has highly exalted Him and [c]given Him the name which
is above every name, 10[a]that at the name of
Jesus every knee should bow, of those in
heaven, and of those on earth, and of those
under the earth, 11and [a]*that* every tongue
should confess that Jesus Christ *is* Lord,
to the glory of God the Father.

Light Bearers

12Therefore, my beloved, [a]as you have
always obeyed, not as in my presence only,
but now much more in my absence, [b]work
out your own salvation with [c]fear and trembling; 13for [a]it is God who works in you both
to will and to do [b]for *His* good pleasure.

14Do all things [a]without complaining and
[b]disputing, 15that you may become blameless and harmless, children of God without
fault in the midst of a crooked and perverse generation, among whom you shine
as [a]lights in the world, 16holding fast the
word of life, so that [a]I may rejoice in the
day of Christ that [b]I have not run in vain
or labored in [c]vain.

17Yes, and if [a]I am being poured out *as a*
drink offering on the sacrifice [b]and service
of your faith, [c]I am glad and rejoice with
you all. 18For the same reason you also be
glad and rejoice with me.

Timothy Commended

19But I trust in the Lord Jesus to send
[a]Timothy to you shortly, that I also may
be encouraged when I know your state.
20For I have no one [a]like-minded, who will

1:27 [a] Eph. 4:1; 1 Thess. 2:12 [b] 1 Cor. 1:10; Eph. 4:3 [c] Jude 3 **1:28** [1] NU-Text reads *of your salvation.* **1:29** [a] [Matt. 5:11, 12; Acts 5:41; Rom. 5:3] [b] Eph. 2:8 [c] [2 Tim. 3:12] **1:30** [a] Col. 1:29; 2:1; 1 Thess. 2:2; 1 Tim. 6:12; 2 Tim. 4:7; Heb. 10:32; 12:1 [b] Acts 16:19–40; Phil. 1:13; 1 Thess. 2:2 **2:1** [a] Col. 3:12 **2:2** [a] John 3:29 [b] Rom. 12:16 [c] Phil. 4:2 **2:3** [a] Gal. 5:26; James 3:14 [b] Rom. 12:10; Eph. 5:21 **2:4** [a] 1 Cor. 13:5 [b] Rom. 15:1, 2 **2:5** [a] [Matt. 11:29]; Rom. 15:3 **2:6** [a] 2 Cor. 4:4 **2:7** [a] Ps. 22:6 [b] Is. 42:1 [c] [John 1:14]; Rom. 8:3; Gal. 4:4; [Heb. 2:17] **2:8** [a] Ps. 40:6–8; Matt. 26:39; John 10:18; [Rom. 5:19] [b] Heb. 5:8 **2:9** [a] [Matt. 28:18]; Heb. 2:9 [b] Ps. 68:18; 110:1; Is. 52:13; Acts 2:33 [c] Is. 9:6; Luke 1:32; Eph. 1:21 **2:10** [a] Is. 45:23; Rom. 14:11; Rev. 5:13 **2:11** [a] John 13:13; [Rom. 10:9; 14:9] **2:12** [a] Phil. 1:5, 6; 4:15 [b] John 6:27, 29; 2 Pet. 1:10 [c] Eph. 6:5 **2:13** [a] Rom. 12:3; 1 Cor. 12:6; 15:10; 2 Cor. 3:5; Heb. 13:20, 21 [b] Eph. 1:5 **2:14** [a] 1 Cor. 10:10; 1 Pet. 4:9 [b] Rom. 14:1 **2:15** [a] Matt. 5:15, 16 **2:16** [a] 2 Cor. 1:14 [b] Gal. 2:2 [c] Is. 49:4; Gal. 4:11; 1 Thess. 3:5 **2:17** [a] 2 Cor. 12:15; 2 Tim. 4:6 [b] Num. 28:6, 7; Rom. 15:16 [c] 2 Cor. 7:4 **2:19** [a] Rom. 16:21 **2:20** [a] 1 Cor. 16:10; 2 Tim. 3:10

RELEASE // ACT WITH SELF-CONTROL

Winning Inward Battles

Philippians 2:5 // Let this mind be in you which was also in Christ Jesus.

Summary Message // Philippians is Paul's discourse on living the Christian life, written from a Roman prison cell. In this epistle, he emphasized the importance of mindset or attitude and how it affects the lives and faith of Christ followers. He encouraged the Philippians to think in the way Jesus did. Specifically, Paul was talking about how Jesus willingly left His heavenly home, entered time and space, allowed Himself to be clothed in human flesh, and came to earth to go to the cross for us. Humility, therefore, is a fundamental and necessary aspect of the Christian life. Christ had a heart and mind of submission, humility, and commitment to the Father. We are to conform to Jesus' image, so we must also seek to possess the mind and attitude He had that resulted in His total commitment to the will of the Father. Jesus was the perfect example of what it means to act with self-control even when faced with all that is not of God.

Practical Application // Whether we want to admit it or not, most of our struggles originate within our minds. Choosing to respond to life with self-control is perhaps the hardest of these mental struggles because it is multifaceted, involving actions, motives, and emotions. Self-control is precisely what is needed, though, in the battle between following sinful urges and doing what is Christlike. Spending quiet time in prayer every day is a good way of transforming our minds so that we are better able to pursue self-control. Instead of getting upset about something, we can turn it over to God and exhale, reflecting on what we can control and moving on from what we cannot. Through self-control, we find the ability to control our behaviors and yield good fruit that brings God glory.

Through the power of the Holy Spirit, we can overcome our impulses and learn to embody the fruit of self-control (see Gal. 5:22–23). As with any fruit, we must choose it. Just as an apple will not jump from a tree into a waiting mouth, so the fruit of self-control must be chosen and used. Acting with self-control allows you to keep your mind focused on God while avoiding the temptation of selfish desires.

As we seek the kingdom of God, pray, and study God's Word, we embark on a pathway to use the fruit of self-control that the Spirit produces within us. In these ways, we become more in tune with the Lord and the prompting of His Spirit. We will also be able to accept Spirit-given self-control more readily.

If we wish to operate in Spirit-led self-control, we must pursue the mind of Christ and never give up.

Fervent Prayer // Heavenly Father, we want the mind of Your Son, Jesus, to be in us and guide us. Therefore, help us act with self-control. Help us choose the fruit of the Spirit so we will not be prone to fits of anger, pride, envy, greed, lust, worry, overindulgence, or any unethical decisions. Thank You for Your kingdom. May it always be a priority in our lives so that the fruit of our lives brings You glory. In Jesus' name we pray. Amen.

---

sincerely care for your state. 21For all seek
their own, not the things which are of Christ
Jesus. 22But you know his proven character, [a]that as a son with *his* father he served
with me in the gospel. 23Therefore I hope
to send him at once, as soon as I see how it
goes with me. 24But I trust in the Lord that
I myself shall also come shortly.

Epaphroditus Praised

25Yet I considered it necessary to send
to you [a]Epaphroditus, my brother, fellow
worker, and [b]fellow soldier, [c]but your messenger and [d]the one who ministered to my
need; 26[a]since he was longing for you all,
and was distressed because you had heard
that he was sick. 27For indeed he was sick
almost unto death; but God had mercy on
him, and not only on him but on me also,
lest I should have sorrow upon sorrow.
28Therefore I sent him the more eagerly,
that when you see him again you may rejoice, and I may be less sorrowful. 29Re-
ceive him therefore in the Lord with all

2:22 [a] 1 Cor. 4:17 2:25 [a] Phil. 4:18 [b] Philem. 2 [c] John 13:16; 2 Cor. 8:23 [d] 2 Cor. 11:9 2:26 [a] Phil. 1:8

gladness, and hold such men in esteem;
30because for the work of Christ he came
close to death, not regarding his life, [a]to
supply what was lacking in your service
toward me.

All for Christ

3 Finally, my brethren, [a]rejoice in the
Lord. For me to write the same things
to you *is* not tedious, but for you *it is* safe.
2[a]Beware of dogs, beware of [b]evil workers, [c]beware of the mutilation! 3For we
are [a]the circumcision, [b]who worship God
in the Spirit,[1] rejoice in Christ Jesus, and
have no confidence in the flesh, 4though
[a]I also might have confidence in the flesh.
If anyone else thinks he may have confidence in the flesh, I [b]more so: 5circum-
cised the eighth day, of the stock of Israel,
[a]*of* the tribe of Benjamin, [b]a Hebrew of the
Hebrews; concerning the law, [c]a Pharisee;
6concerning zeal, [a]persecuting the church;
concerning the righteousness which is in
the law, blameless.
7But [a]what things were gain to me, these
I have counted loss for Christ. 8Yet indeed
I also count all things loss [a]for the excellence of the knowledge of Christ Jesus my
Lord, for whom I have suffered the loss
of all things, and count them as rubbish,
that I may gain Christ 9and be found in
Him, not having [a]my own righteousness,
which *is* from the law, but [b]that which *is*
through faith in Christ, the righteousness
which is from God by faith; 10that I may
know Him and the [a]power of His resurrection, and [b]the fellowship of His sufferings,
being conformed to His death, 11if, by any
means, I may [a]attain to the resurrection
from the dead.

Pressing Toward the Goal

12Not that I have already [a]attained, or
am already [b]perfected; but I press on, that I
may lay hold of that for which Christ Jesus
has also laid hold of me. 13Brethren, I do not
count myself to have apprehended; but one
thing *I do,* [a]forgetting those things which
are behind and [b]reaching forward to those

#OXYGEN

PHILIPPIANS 3:13

Act with Self-Control

How many times have you allowed anger to cause you to make decisions you later regretted? You cannot rewrite your past, but you can improve your future. Change is not easy. However, God is giving you the strength to do better.

Breathe and act with self-control.

things which are ahead, 14[a]I press toward
the goal for the prize of [b]the upward call of
God in Christ Jesus.
15Therefore let us, as many as are [a]ma-
ture, [b]have this mind; and if in anything
you think otherwise, [c]God will reveal even
this to you. 16Nevertheless, to *the degree*
that we have already attained, [a]let us walk
[b]by the same rule,[1] let us be of the same
mind.

Our Citizenship in Heaven

17Brethren, [a]join in following my example, and note those who so walk, as [b]you
have us for a pattern. 18For many walk, of
whom I have told you often, and now tell
you even weeping, *that they are* [a]the enemies of the cross of Christ: 19[a]whose end *is*
destruction, [b]whose god *is their* belly, and
[c]*whose* glory *is* in their shame—[d]who set
their mind on earthly things. 20For [a]our
citizenship is in heaven, [b]from which we
also [c]eagerly wait for the Savior, the Lord
Jesus Christ, 21[a]who will transform our

2:30 [a] 1 Cor. 16:17; Phil. 4:10 3:1 [a] 1 Thess. 5:16 3:2 [a] Ps. 22:16, 20; Gal. 5:15; Rev. 22:15 [b] Ps. 119:115 [c] Rom. 2:28 3:3 [a] Deut. 30:6; Rom. 2:28, 29; 9:6; [Gal. 6:15] [b] John 4:24; Rom. 7:6 [1] NU-Text and M-Text read *who worship in the Spirit of God.* 3:4 [a] 2 Cor. 5:16; 11:18 [b] 2 Cor. 11:22, 23 3:5 [a] Rom. 11:1 [b] 2 Cor. 11:22 [c] Acts 23:6 3:6 [a] Acts 8:3; 22:4, 5; 26:9–11 3:7 [a] Matt. 13:44 3:8 [a] Is. 53:11; Jer. 9:23; John 17:3; 1 Cor. 2:2; [Eph. 4:13] 3:9 [a] Rom. 10:3 [b] Rom. 1:17 3:10 [a] Eph. 1:19, 20 [b] [Rom. 6:3–5]; 2 Cor. 1:5; 1 Pet. 4:13 3:11 [a] Acts 26:6–8; [1 Cor. 15:23; Rev. 20:5] 3:12 [a] 1 Cor. 9:24; [1 Tim. 6:12, 19] [b] Heb. 12:23 3:13 [a] Luke 9:62 [b] Heb. 6:1 3:14 [a] 2 Tim. 4:7 [b] Heb. 3:1 3:15 [a] Matt. 5:48; 1 Cor. 2:6 [b] Gal. 5:10 [c] Hos. 6:3; James 1:5 3:16 [a] Gal. 6:16 [b] Rom. 12:16; 15:5 [1] NU-Text omits *rule* and the rest of the verse. 3:17 [a] [1 Cor. 4:16; 11:1]; Phil. 4:9 [b] Titus 2:7, 8; 1 Pet. 5:3 3:18 [a] Gal. 1:7 3:19 [a] 2 Cor. 11:15 [b] 1 Tim. 6:5 [c] Hos. 4:7 [d] Rom. 8:5; Col. 3:2 3:20 [a] Eph. 2:6, 19; Phil. 1:27; [Col. 3:1; Heb. 12:22] [b] Acts 1:11 [c] 1 Cor. 1:7 3:21 [a] [1 Cor. 15:43–53]

lowly body that it may be [b]conformed to
His glorious body, [c]according to the working by which He is able even to [d]subdue all
things to Himself.

4 Therefore, my beloved and [a]longed-for
brethren, [b]my joy and crown, so [c]stand
fast in the Lord, beloved.

Be United, Joyful, and in Prayer

2I implore Euodia and I implore Syntyche [a]to be of the same mind in the Lord.
3And[1] I urge you also, true companion, help
these women who [a]labored with me in the
gospel, with Clement also, and the rest of
my fellow workers, whose names *are* in [b]the
Book of Life.

4[a]Rejoice in the Lord always. Again I will
say, rejoice!

5Let your gentleness be known to all
men. [a]The Lord *is* at hand.

6[a]Be anxious for nothing, but in everything by prayer and supplication,
with [b]thanksgiving, let your requests be
made known to God; 7and [a]the peace of
God, which surpasses all understanding,
will guard your hearts and minds through
Christ Jesus.

Meditate on These Things

8Finally, brethren, whatever things are
[a]true, whatever things *are* [b]noble, whatever
things *are* [c]just, [d]whatever things *are* pure,
whatever things *are* [e]lovely, whatever things
are of good report, if *there is* any virtue and if
there is anything praiseworthy—meditate on
these things. 9The things which you learned
and received and heard and saw in me, these
do, and [a]the God of peace will be with you.

Philippian Generosity

10But I rejoiced in the Lord greatly that
now at last [a]your care for me has flourished
again; though you surely did care, but you
lacked opportunity. 11Not that I speak in regard to need, for I have learned in whatever
state I am, [a]to be content: 12[a]I know how

PHILIPPIANS 4:2

WE ARE EUODIA AND SYNTYCHE

I implore Euodia and I implore Syntyche to be of the same mind in the Lord. Philippians 4:2

We are the two women Paul addressed in his letter to the Philippian church, Euodia and Syntyche. We were both members of the Philippian church and co-laborers with Paul.

Although we were sisters in Christ and coworkers in the gospel, the two of us were at odds with one another. This situation was reported to Paul, and he considered it serious enough to address in his letter to the church. He implored us to be of one mind in the Lord. He also invited another member of our church to intervene and help us to come into agreement.

†

We are compelled by Scripture to be in unity as the body of Christ. How do we achieve this when the inevitable disagreements arise? Paul teaches us that the only way to be of one mind in the Lord is to humble ourselves. This means we sacrifice our right to be right and put others first. We should try to see from the perspective of the one we contend against. We must actively love the other person more than we love the position we have taken. As Paul directs, if we make every sincere effort to be reconciled and still cannot come into agreement, we should bring in another mutually respected member of the body of Christ to mediate. Unity in the body of Christ is of utmost importance.

3:21 [b] 1 John 3:2 [c] Eph. 1:19 [d] [1 Cor. 15:28] 4:1 [a] Phil. 1:8 [b] 2 Cor. 1:14 [c] 1 Cor. 16:13; Phil. 1:27 4:2 [a] Phil. 2:2; 3:16 4:3 [a] Rom. 16:3 [b] Ex. 32:32; Luke 10:20 [1] NU-Text and M-Text read *Yes.* 4:4 [a] Rom. 12:12 4:5 [a] 1 Cor. 16:22; Heb. 10:25, 37; [James 5:7–9]; Rev. 22:7, 20 4:6 [a] Ps. 55:22; Matt. 6:25; 1 Pet. 5:7 [b] [1 Thess. 5:17, 18] 4:7 [a] [Is. 26:3; John 14:27]; Phil. 4:9; Col. 3:15 4:8 [a] Eph. 4:25 [b] 2 Cor. 8:21 [c] Deut. 16:20 [d] 1 Thess. 5:22; James 3:17 [e] 1 Cor. 13:4–7 4:9 [a] Rom. 15:33; Heb. 13:20 4:10 [a] 2 Cor. 11:9; Phil. 2:30 4:11 [a] 2 Cor. 9:8; 1 Tim. 6:6, 8; Heb. 13:5 4:12 [a] 1 Cor. 4:11

to be abased, and I know how to abound. Everywhere and in all things I have learned both to be full and to be hungry, both to abound and to suffer need. 13I can do all things [a]through Christ[1] who strengthens me.

14Nevertheless you have done well that [a]you shared in my distress. 15Now you Philippians know also that in the beginning of the gospel, when I departed from Macedonia, [a]no church shared with me concerning giving and receiving but you only. 16For even in Thessalonica you sent *aid* once and again for my necessities. 17Not that I seek the gift, but I seek [a]the fruit that abounds to your account. 18Indeed I have all and abound. I am full, having received from [a]Epaphroditus the things *sent* from you, [b]a sweet-smelling aroma, [c]an acceptable sacrifice, well pleasing to God. 19And my God [a]shall supply all your need according to His riches in glory by Christ Jesus. 20[a]Now to our God and Father *be* glory forever and ever. Amen.

Greeting and Blessing

21Greet every saint in Christ Jesus. The brethren [a]who are with me greet you. 22All the saints greet you, but especially those who are of Caesar's household.

23The grace of our Lord Jesus Christ be with you all.[1] Amen.

4:13 [a] John 15:5 [1] NU-Text reads *Him who.* 4:14 [a] Phil. 1:7 4:15 [a] 2 Cor. 11:8, 9 4:17 [a] Titus 3:14 4:18 [a] Phil. 2:25 [b] Heb. 13:16 [c] Rom. 12:1; 2 Cor. 9:12 4:19 [a] Ps. 23:1; 2 Cor. 9:8 4:20 [a] Rom. 16:27 4:21 [a] Gal. 1:2 4:23 [1] NU-Text reads *your spirit.*

THE EPISTLE OF PAUL TO THE

COLOSSIANS

OVERVIEW

Paul wrote the letter to the church at Colosse during his incarceration in Rome. Colosse was a commercial center with both Jewish and Gentile residents. The church there was founded by a ministry partnership between Paul and Epaphras, who was a resident of Colosse. Epaphras had met Paul in Ephesus, approximately 120 miles from Colosse. Despite Paul's inability to meet the Colossian church face-to-face right away (see Col. 2:1), the church at Colosse was a direct result of his missionary work. Paul wrote to the Colossians before visiting them in person and acknowledged the labor of Epaphras. Paul stated that they "learned from Epaphras" (1:7).

Paul's purpose in writing this letter was to help the believers in Colosse contend with the teachings of Gnosticism that had infiltrated the church. Gnosticism was a hybrid teaching that combined Christian theology, the legal practices of the Jewish law, and pagan practices. This hybrid, rival religion was extremely unsettling in that it had the appearance of Christian truth and discipline but failed to acknowledge the divinity of Christ. Gnosticism produced adherence to legalistic practices that Paul criticized as merely human in origin.

In response to denouncing Gnosticism, Paul affirmed the supremacy of Christ: "For in Him dwells all the fullness of the Godhead bodily; and you are complete in Him, who is the head of all principality and power" (2:9–10). Paul also firmly upheld Christ's authority over the church: "All things were created through Him and for Him. And He is before all things, and in Him all things consist. And He is the head of the body, the church, who is the beginning, the firstborn from the dead, that in all things He may have the preeminence" (1:16–18).

BREATHE IT IN

Cancer begins when uncontrolled cell duplication invades normal tissues and overtakes healthy organs and systems. It damages cells, tissue, and major organs, leading to severe illness and often death.

In many ways, it is a miracle that the early church survived the cancer of false teachings that threatened its existence. In answer to the many theological cancers that threatened the integrity of the church at Colosse, Paul's letter provided a meticulous treatment: the promise that Christ "is before all things, and in Him all things consist" (1:17).

What "cancers" are at work in your understanding of the faith and how you live it out? In what ways have you added other things to the gospel of Jesus Christ? "I believe in Jesus, but I also believe in . . ." or "I believe in Jesus, but I do not believe what the Bible says about . . ." There is only one true gospel, and to add or subtract from it will erode your understanding of the one true God and the one true gospel of Jesus.

Consider taking the time to write a credo, a personal faith statement. You do not have to be a trained theologian. Just write a list of the things you believe. Then ask yourself if each sentence of your belief system is in line with Christ and the Word of God. Doing so will help you guard your faith against any "cancers" that might be at work, whether you realize them or not.

Christ is to be the center of our faith and the cornerstone of the church. Do not allow any other teaching to challenge or replace Christ as your Christian foundation. Whenever you stand on the supremacy of Christ, you surgically remove these "cancers" from your faith. There is only one gospel, the gospel of Jesus Christ. It cannot be cherry-picked, modified, or abridged—if it is, then it is no gospel at all (see Gal. 1:6–7).

THE EPISTLE OF PAUL TO THE

COLOSSIANS

Greeting

1 Paul, [a]an apostle of Jesus Christ by the
will of God, and Timothy our brother,

2To the saints [a]and faithful brethren in
Christ *who are* in Colosse:

[b]Grace to you and peace from God our
Father and the Lord Jesus Christ.[1]

Their Faith in Christ

3[a]We give thanks to the God and Father
of our Lord Jesus Christ, praying always
for you, 4[a]since we heard of your faith in
Christ Jesus and of [b]your love for all the
saints; 5because of the hope [a]which is laid
up for you in heaven, of which you heard
before in the word of the truth of the gospel, 6which has come to you, [a]as *it has* also
in all the world, and [b]is bringing forth fruit,[1]
as *it is* also among you since the day you
heard and knew [c]the grace of God in truth;
7as you also learned from [a]Epaphras, our
dear fellow servant, who is [b]a faithful minister of Christ on your behalf, 8who also declared to us your [a]love in the Spirit.

Preeminence of Christ

9[a]For this reason we also, since the day
we heard it, do not cease to pray for you,
and to ask [b]that you may be filled with [c]the
knowledge of His will [d]in all wisdom and
spiritual understanding; 10[a]that you may
walk worthy of the Lord, [b]fully pleasing
Him, [c]being fruitful in every good work
and increasing in the [d]knowledge of God;
11[a]strengthened with all might, according
to His glorious power, [b]for all patience and
longsuffering [c]with joy; 12[a]giving thanks to
the Father who has qualified us to be partakers of [b]the inheritance of the saints in
the light. 13He has delivered us from [a]the
power of darkness [b]and conveyed *us* into
the kingdom of the Son of His love, 14[a]in
whom we have redemption through His
blood,[1] the forgiveness of sins.
15He is [a]the image of the invisible God,
[b]the firstborn over all creation. 16For [a]by
Him all things were created that are in
heaven and that are on earth, visible and
invisible, whether thrones or [b]dominions
or principalities or powers. All things were
created [c]through Him and for Him. 17[a]And
He is before all things, and in Him [b]all
things consist. 18And [a]He is the head of the
body, the church, who is the beginning, [b]the
firstborn from the dead, that in all things
He may have the preeminence.

Reconciled in Christ

19For it pleased *the Father that* [a]in Him
all the fullness should dwell, 20and [a]by
Him to reconcile [b]all things to Himself, by
Him, whether things on earth or things in
heaven, [c]having made peace through the
blood of His cross.

21And you, [a]who once were alienated and
enemies in your mind [b]by wicked works,
yet now He has [c]reconciled 22[a]in the body
of His flesh through death, [b]to present you

1:1 [a] Eph. 1:1 **1:2** [a] 1 Cor. 4:17 [b] Gal. 1:3 [1] NU-Text omits *and the Lord Jesus Christ.* **1:3** [a] 1 Cor. 1:4; Eph. 1:16; Phil. 1:3 **1:4** [a] Eph. 1:15 [b] [Heb. 6:10] **1:5** [a] [1 Pet. 1:4] **1:6** [a] Matt. 24:14 [b] John 15:16 [c] Eph. 3:2 [1] NU-Text and M-Text add *and growing.* **1:7** [a] Col. 4:12; Philem. 23 [b] 1 Cor. 4:1, 2; 2 Cor. 11:23 **1:8** [a] Rom. 15:30 **1:9** [a] Eph. 1:15–17 [b] 1 Cor. 1:5 [c] [Rom. 12:2]; Eph. 5:17 [d] Eph. 1:8 **1:10** [a] Eph. 4:1; Phil. 1:27; 1 Thess. 2:12 [b] 1 Thess. 4:1 [c] Heb. 13:21 [d] 2 Pet. 3:18 **1:11** [a] [Eph. 3:16; 6:10] [b] Eph. 4:2 [c] [Acts 5:41]; 2 Cor. 8:2; [Heb. 10:34] **1:12** [a] [Eph. 5:20] [b] Eph. 1:11 **1:13** [a] Eph. 6:12 [b] 2 Pet. 1:11 **1:14** [a] Eph. 1:7 [1] NU-Text and M-Text omit *through His blood.* **1:15** [a] 2 Cor. 4:4; Heb. 1:3 [b] Ps. 89:27; Rev. 3:14 **1:16** [a] John 1:3; Heb. 1:2, 3 [b] [Eph. 1:20, 21; Col. 2:15] [c] John 1:3; Rom. 11:36; 1 Cor. 8:6; Heb. 2:10 **1:17** [a] [John 17:5] [b] Heb. 1:3 **1:18** [a] 1 Cor. 11:3; Eph. 1:22 [b] Rev. 1:5 **1:19** [a] John 1:16 **1:20** [a] Rom. 5:1; Eph. 2:14 [b] 2 Cor. 5:18 [c] Eph. 1:10 **1:21** [a] [Eph. 2:1] [b] Titus 1:15 [c] 2 Cor. 5:18, 19 **1:22** [a] 2 Cor. 5:18; [Eph. 2:14–16] [b] [Eph. 5:27]; Col. 1:28

RELEASE // TRUST IN HIS WARMTH

The Only Place of Comfort

Colossians 1:13 // He has delivered us from the power of darkness and conveyed us into the kingdom of the Son of His love.

Summary Message // Paul wrote Colossians in the middle of his suffering, but you would not know it. He so basked in the sweetness of his calling that he did not take on the mantle of that suffering. The words he prayed in Colossians 1:9–12 are profound and so real that they are palpable. How heartwarming it is to know that the Father has already qualified us to share in the inheritance of grace administered to His holy people through the authority of Jesus Christ. This assurance brings comfort and peace to our daily lives and should provide the foundation of stability in our hearts. To trust in God's warmth is to know that He has revealed the mystery of Christ to us. In Christ, He has hidden all the treasures of wisdom and knowledge. God has brought us out of darkness and into the warmth of His light. We just need to believe it. This is our birthright: to live as a people who trust in the loving arms of our Father and bask in His presence. In Him we now live and find the very essence of life. What a glorious place of calm and comfort.

Practical Application // Do you trust in your heavenly Father? Have you received His comfort? Do you trust in His warmth? Have you reclined in the arms of your Father? Many times, we can get lost in the issues of life and forget to take a moment and allow ourselves to just sit and be in the presence of God. To be still, and know that He is God (see Ps. 46:10). How glorious it is simply to trust in the warmth of His Word.

Let us try an exercise of faith. Repeat these words: "I believe, and I receive. I believe, and I receive." These words bring a sense of dependency and hope to our souls and acknowledge that we cannot do life on our own. His strength and provision are there to bring the very peace we desire.

Fervent Prayer // Heavenly Father, we trust in the warmth of Your love. Our hearts are filled with compassion as we ponder this new way of living—this new way of becoming people who are comforted by the satisfaction of Your grace. To know that You see us from a place of patience and strength magnifies our desire to be in Your presence. Lord, we marvel at who You are and how You see us and others. We thank You for Your wondrous love, grace, and mercy. We appreciate all You have done, and will do, in our lives. We are thankful and grateful that You are leading and guiding us into every positive possibility. We are excited to see what will happen next. In Jesus' name we pray. Amen.

---

holy, and blameless, and above reproach in
His sight— 23if indeed you continue [a]in the
faith, grounded and steadfast, and are [b]not
moved away from the hope of the gospel
which you heard, [c]which was preached to
every creature under heaven, [d]of which I,
Paul, became a minister.

Sacrificial Service for Christ

24[a]I now rejoice in my sufferings [b]for you,
and fill up in my flesh [c]what is lacking in the
afflictions of Christ, for [d]the sake of His body,
which is the church, 25of which I became
a minister according to [a]the stewardship
from God which was given to me for you,
to fulfill the word of God, 26[a]the mystery
which has been hidden from ages and from
generations, [b]but now has been revealed to
His saints. 27[a]To them God willed to make
known what are [b]the riches of the glory of
this mystery among the Gentiles: which[1] is
[c]Christ in you, [d]the hope of glory. 28Him we
preach, [a]warning every man and teaching
every man in all wisdom, [b]that we may present every man perfect in Christ Jesus. 29To
this *end* I also labor, striving according to
His working which works in me [a]mightily.

Not Philosophy but Christ

2 For I want you to know what a great
[a]conflict I have for you and those in
Laodicea, and *for* as many as have not seen

1:23 [a] Eph. 3:17; Col. 2:7 [b] [John 15:6]; 1 Cor. 15:58 [c] Mark 16:15; Acts 2:5; Rom. 10:18; Col. 1:6 [d] Acts 1:17; Eph. 3:7; Col. 1:25
1:24 [a] 2 Cor. 7:4 [b] Eph. 3:1, 13 [c] [Rom. 8:17; 2 Cor. 1:5; 12:15]; Phil. 2:17 [d] Eph. 1:23 1:25 [a] Gal. 2:7 1:26 [a] [1 Cor. 2:7] [b] [2 Tim. 1:10]
1:27 [a] 2 Cor. 2:14 [b] Rom. 9:23 [c] [Rom. 8:10, 11] [d] 1 Tim. 1:1 [1] M-Text reads *who.* 1:28 [a] Acts 20:20 [b] Eph. 5:27
1:29 [a] Eph. 3:7 2:1 [a] Phil. 1:30; Col. 1:29; 4:12; 1 Thess. 2:2

my face in the flesh, 2that their hearts may
be encouraged, being knit together in love,
and *attaining* to all riches of the full assurance of understanding, to the knowledge
of the mystery of God, both of the Father
and[1] of Christ, 3[a]in whom are hidden all
the treasures of wisdom and knowledge.
4Now this I say [a]lest anyone should deceive
you with persuasive words. 5For [a]though I
am absent in the flesh, yet I am with you in
spirit, rejoicing to see [b]your *good* order and
the [c]steadfastness of your faith in Christ.
6[a]As you therefore have received Christ
Jesus the Lord, so walk in Him, 7[a]rooted
and built up in Him and established in the
faith, as you have been taught, abounding
in it[1] with thanksgiving.

#OXYGEN
COLOSSIANS 2:6–7

Trust in His Warmth

Be filled with faith. Allow God to breathe life into your heart and mind. When your heart feels cold, only God can warm your soul. He is faithful to bring the warmth of His love and life whenever you need it.

Breathe and trust in His warmth.

8Beware lest anyone cheat you through
philosophy and empty deceit, according
to [a]the tradition of men, according to the
[b]basic principles of the world, and not according to Christ. 9For [a]in Him dwells all
the fullness of the Godhead bodily; 10and
you are complete in Him, who is the [a]head
of all principality and power.

Not Legalism but Christ

11In Him you were also [a]circumcised with
the circumcision made without hands, by
[b]putting off the body of the sins[1] of the flesh,
by the circumcision of Christ, 12[a]buried with
Him in baptism, in which you also were
raised with *Him* through [b]faith in the working of God, [c]who raised Him from the dead.
13And you, being dead in your trespasses
and the uncircumcision of your flesh, He
has made alive together with Him, having
forgiven you all trespasses, 14[a]having wiped
out the handwriting of requirements that
was against us, which was contrary to us.
And He has taken it out of the way, having
nailed it to the cross. 15[a]Having disarmed
[b]principalities and powers, He made a public spectacle of them, triumphing over them
in it.
16So let no one [a]judge you in food or in
drink, or regarding a festival or a new moon
or sabbaths, 17[a]which are a shadow of things
to come, but the substance is of Christ. 18Let
no one cheat you of your reward, taking
delight in *false* humility and worship of
angels, intruding into those things which
he has not[1] seen, vainly puffed up by his
fleshly mind, 19and not holding fast to [a]the
Head, from whom all the body, nourished
and knit together by joints and ligaments,
[b]grows with the increase *that is* from God.
20Therefore,[1] if you [a]died with Christ
from the basic principles of the world, [b]why,
as *though* living in the world, do you subject yourselves to regulations— 21[a]"Do not
touch, do not taste, do not handle," 22which
all concern things which perish with the
using—[a]according to the commandments
and doctrines of men? 23[a]These things indeed have an appearance of wisdom in
self-imposed religion, *false* humility, and
neglect of the body, *but are* of no value
against the indulgence of the flesh.

Not Carnality but Christ

3 If then you were [a]raised with Christ,
seek those things which are above,
[b]where Christ is, sitting at the right hand
of God. 2Set your mind on things above,
not on things on the [a]earth. 3[a]For you died,
[b]and your life is hidden with Christ in God.

2:2 [1] NU-Text omits *both of the Father and.* 2:3 [a] 1 Cor. 1:24, 30 2:4 [a] Rom. 16:18; 2 Cor. 11:13; Eph. 4:14; 5:6 2:5 [a] 1 Thess. 2:17 [b] 1 Cor. 14:40 [c] 1 Pet. 5:9 2:6 [a] 1 Thess. 4:1 2:7 [a] Eph. 2:21 [1] NU-Text omits *in it.* 2:8 [a] Gal. 1:14 [b] Gal. 4:3, 9, 10; Col. 2:20 2:9 [a] [John 1:14]; Col. 1:19 2:10 [a] [Eph. 1:20, 21; 1 Pet. 3:22] 2:11 [a] Deut. 10:16 [b] Rom. 6:6; 7:24; Gal. 5:24; Col. 3:5 [1] NU-Text omits *of the sins.* 2:12 [a] Rom. 6:4 [b] Eph. 1:19, 20 [c] Acts 2:24 2:14 [a] [Eph. 2:15, 16]; Col. 2:20 2:15 [a] [Is. 53:12; Heb. 2:14] [b] Eph. 6:12 2:16 [a] Rom. 14:3 2:17 [a] Heb. 8:5; 10:1 2:18 [1] NU-Text omits *not.* 2:19 [a] Eph. 4:15 [b] Eph. 1:23; 4:16 2:20 [a] Rom. 6:2–5 [b] Gal. 4:3, 9 [1] NU-Text and M-Text omit *Therefore.* 2:21 [a] 1 Tim. 4:3 2:22 [a] Is. 29:13; Matt. 15:9; Titus 1:14 2:23 [a] Rom. 13:14; 1 Tim. 4:8 3:1 [a] Rom. 6:5; Eph. 2:6; Col. 2:12 [b] Ps. 68:18; 110:1; [Rom. 8:34]; Eph. 1:20 3:2 [a] [Matt. 6:19–21] 3:3 [a] [Rom. 6:2; 2 Cor. 5:14; Gal. 2:20]; Col. 2:20 [b] [2 Cor. 5:7]

4[a]When Christ *who is* [b]our life appears, then
you also will appear with Him in [c]glory.
5[a]Therefore put to death [b]your members
which are on the earth: [c]fornication, uncleanness, passion, evil desire, and covetousness, [d]which is idolatry. 6[a]Because of these
things the wrath of God is coming upon [b]the
sons of disobedience, 7[a]in which you yourselves once walked when you lived in them.
8[a]But now you yourselves are to put off
all these: anger, wrath, malice, blasphemy,
filthy language out of your mouth. 9Do not
lie to one another, since you have put off
the old man with his deeds, 10and have put
on the new *man* who [a]is renewed in knowledge [b]according to the image of Him who
[c]created him, 11where there is neither [a]Greek
nor Jew, circumcised nor uncircumcised,
barbarian, Scythian, slave *nor* free, [b]but
Christ *is* all and in all.

Character of the New Man

12Therefore, [a]as *the* elect of God, holy and
beloved, [b]put on tender mercies, kindness,
humility, meekness, longsuffering; 13[a]bear-
ing with one another, and forgiving one
another, if anyone has a complaint against
another; even as Christ forgave you, so you
also *must do.* 14[a]But above all these things
[b]put on love, which is the [c]bond of perfection. 15And let [a]the peace of God rule in your
hearts, [b]to which also you were called [c]in
one body; and [d]be thankful. 16Let the word
of Christ dwell in you richly in all wisdom,
teaching and admonishing one another
[a]in psalms and hymns and spiritual songs,
singing with grace in your hearts to the
Lord. 17And [a]whatever you do in word or
deed, *do* all in the name of the Lord Jesus,
giving thanks to God the Father through
Him.

The Christian Home
(cf. Eph. 5:21—6:9)

18[a]Wives, submit to your own husbands,
[b]as is fitting in the Lord.

#OXYGEN

COLOSSIANS 3:16

Trust in His Warmth

Though life can get cold from the chaos, God cares. His Word can fire you up. Allow the flame of the Holy Spirit to kindle godliness within you. Remember His burning love for you.

Breathe and **trust in His warmth.**

19[a]Husbands, love your wives and do not
be [b]bitter toward them.
20[a]Children, obey your parents [b]in all
things, for this is well pleasing to the Lord.
21[a]Fathers, do not provoke your children,
lest they become discouraged.
22[a]Bondservants, obey in all things your
masters according to the flesh, not with
eyeservice, as men-pleasers, but in sincerity of heart, fearing God. 23[a]And whatever
you do, do it heartily, as to the Lord and not
to men, 24[a]knowing that from the Lord you
will receive the reward of the inheritance;
[b]for[1] you serve the Lord Christ. 25But he who
does wrong will be repaid for what he has
done, and [a]there is no partiality.

4 Masters,[a] give your bondservants what
is just and fair, knowing that you also
have a Master in heaven.

Christian Graces

2[a]Continue earnestly in prayer, being
vigilant in it [b]with thanksgiving; 3[a]mean-
while praying also for us, that God would
[b]open to us a door for the word, to speak
[c]the mystery of Christ, [d]for which I am also
in chains, 4that I may make it manifest, as
I ought to speak.

3:4 [a] [1 John 3:2] [b] John 14:6 [c] 1 Cor. 15:43 3:5 [a] [Rom. 8:13] [b] [Rom. 6:13] [c] Eph. 5:3 [d] Mark 7:21; 1 Cor. 6:9, 18; 2 Cor. 12:21; Gal. 5:19; Eph. 4:19; 5:3, 5 3:6 [a] Rom. 1:18; Eph. 5:6; Rev. 22:15 [b] [Eph. 2:2] 3:7 [a] 1 Cor. 6:11; [Eph. 2:2]; Titus 3:3 3:8 [a] Eph. 4:22; 1 Pet. 2:1 3:10 [a] Rom. 12:2; 2 Cor. 4:16 [b] [Rom. 8:29] [c] [Eph. 2:10] 3:11 [a] Rom. 10:12; [1 Cor. 12:13]; Gal. 3:27, 28 [b] Eph. 1:23 3:12 [a] [1 Pet. 1:2] [b] Luke 1:78; Phil. 2:1; 1 John 3:17 3:13 [a] [Mark 11:25] 3:14 [a] 1 Pet. 4:8 [b] [1 Cor. 13] [c] Eph. 4:3 3:15 [a] [John 14:27; Phil. 4:7] [b] 1 Cor. 7:15 [c] Eph. 4:4 [d] [1 Thess. 5:18] 3:16 [a] Eph. 5:19 3:17 [a] 1 Cor. 10:31 3:18 [a] 1 Pet. 3:1 [b] [Col. 3:18—4:1; Eph. 5:22—6:9] 3:19 [a] [Eph. 5:25; 1 Pet. 3:7] [b] Eph. 4:31 3:20 [a] Eph. 6:1 [b] Eph. 5:24 3:21 [a] Eph. 6:4 3:22 [a] Eph. 6:5; [1 Tim. 6:1]; Titus 2:9; 1 Pet. 2:18 3:23 [a] [Eccl. 9:10] 3:24 [a] Eph. 6:8 [b] 1 Cor. 7:22 [1] NU-Text omits *for.* 3:25 [a] Rom. 2:11 4:1 [a] Eph. 6:9 4:2 [a] Luke 18:1 [b] Col. 2:7 4:3 [a] Eph. 6:19 [b] 1 Cor. 16:9 [c] Eph. 3:3, 4; 6:19 [d] Eph. 6:20

TRUST IN HIS WARMTH

INHALE

I really don't have anything to give. People around me, though, only seem to care about what I can give to them. It's extremely difficult to care and be warm when I know the feelings of others are not genuine. I'm not a fake and I'm not phony. I have learned the hard way that being nice gets you nowhere but left back and counted out. Can I trust God to soften the hearts of others? If not, what will I gain from turning the other cheek?

EXHALE

The business of softening a person's heart is God's. We cannot soften a heart, but God can. This doesn't mean that God will always do that. Remember in the Book of Exodus, God actually hardened Pharaoh's heart (see Ex. 7:3–4). But He had a good reason to do that. And He has a good reason for the times when He chooses not to soften a person's heart. But even when He does soften a heart, sometimes He breaks up the hardened soil over time. God's actions are mysterious, but He knows exactly what He is doing, when is best to do it, and why. People don't frustrate God, causing Him to react out of character. This is why turning your frustrations over to Him instead of wanting God to respond the way you think He should is the right direction to take.

We cannot allow others to change who we are or dictate the way we go about doing our business. If we allow this focus to remain, it will continue to be a stumbling block and not a stepping stone in our lives. I get it. People can frustrate you, but keep in mind that you have a God who can take on your frustration and turn it into joy.

It says in Colossians 4:5 that we should "walk in wisdom toward those who are outside, redeeming the time." So, gratefully accept each opportunity to show character and draw others to your God of love.

5[a]Walk in [b]wisdom toward those *who*
are outside, [c]redeeming the time. 6*Let*
your speech always *be* [a]with grace, [b]sea-
soned with salt, [c]that you may know how
you ought to answer each one.

Final Greetings
(cf. Eph. 6:21, 22)

7[a]Tychicus, a beloved brother, faithful
minister, and fellow servant in the Lord,
will tell you all the news about me. 8[a]I am
sending him to you for this very purpose,
that he[1] may know your circumstances and
comfort your hearts, 9with [a]Onesimus, a
faithful and beloved brother, who is *one* of
you. They will make known to you all things
which *are happening* here.

10[a]Aristarchus my fellow prisoner greets
you, with [b]Mark the cousin of Barnabas
(about whom you received instructions: if
he comes to you, welcome him), 11and Jesus
who is called Justus. These *are my* only fellow workers for the kingdom of God who
are of the circumcision; they have proved
to be a comfort to me.

12[a]Epaphras, who is *one* of you, a bondservant of Christ, greets you, always [b]la-
boring fervently for you in prayers, that
you may stand [c]perfect and complete[1] in
all the will of God. 13For I bear him witness
that he has a great zeal[1] for you, and those
who are in Laodicea, and those in Hierap-
olis. 14[a]Luke the beloved physician and [b]De-
mas greet you. 15Greet the brethren who are

4:5 [a] Eph. 5:15 [b] [Matt. 10:16] [c] Eph. 5:16 4:6 [a] Eccl. 10:12 [b] Mark 9:50 [c] 1 Pet. 3:15 4:7 [a] Acts 20:4; Eph. 6:21; 2 Tim. 4:12; Titus 3:12 4:8 [a] Eph. 6:22 [1] NU-Text reads *you may know our circumstances and he may.* 4:9 [a] Philem. 10
4:10 [a] Acts 19:29; 20:4; 27:2; Philem. 24 [b] Acts 15:37; 2 Tim. 4:11 4:12 [a] Col. 1:7; Philem. 23 [b] Rom. 15:30
[c] Matt. 5:48; 1 Cor. 2:6 [1] NU-Text reads *fully assured.* 4:13 [1] NU-Text reads *concern.*
4:14 [a] 2 Tim. 4:11; Philem. 24 [b] 2 Tim. 4:10

in Laodicea, and Nymphas and [a]the church
that *is* in his[1] house.

Closing Exhortations and Blessing

16Now when [a]this epistle is read among
you, see that it is read also in the church
of the Laodiceans, and that you likewise
read the *epistle* from Laodicea. 17And say
to [a]Archippus, "Take heed to [b]the ministry
which you have received in the Lord, that
you may fulfill it."

18[a]This salutation by my own hand—
Paul. [b]Remember my chains. Grace *be* with
you. Amen.

4:15 [a] Rom. 16:5; 1 Cor. 16:19 [1] NU-Text reads *Nympha . . . her house.* 4:16 [a] 1 Thess. 5:27; 2 Thess. 3:14 4:17 [a] Philem. 2 [b] 1 Tim. 4:6; 2 Tim. 4:5 4:18 [a] 1 Cor. 16:21; 2 Thess. 3:17 [b] Heb. 13:3

THE FIRST EPISTLE OF PAUL TO THE

THESSALONIANS

OVERVIEW

The response to the early church was volatile. Though the church was considered just one more emerging cultlike belief system, it was received with hostility by both Jews and Gentiles alike. For the Gentiles, the church became the target of fierce and violent persecution as it stood in opposition to the paganism and polytheism at the center of so much of the Greco-Roman world. Meanwhile, the message that Jesus was the long-awaited, prophesied Messiah was extremely controversial and disruptive to the Judaic belief system. As a result, many of the apostles and church leaders were martyred, suffering violent deaths.

Paul's visit to the city of Thessalonica is recorded in Acts 17. When entering a new city, it was Paul's custom to visit the local synagogue to establish a base of operation in proclaiming the gospel. As happened in many cities, Paul's preaching in Thessalonica was threatening to the local religious leaders, who met him with anger and strong resistance. The Jewish leaders of Thessalonica were so hostile, they chased Paul out of town. When they learned that he was ministering in the synagogue of the nearby town of Berea, they even sent men there to disrupt his ministry. Overall, Paul's visit to Thessalonica ended much sooner than he had hoped.

Paul's first letter to the church at Thessalonica was an instruction manual for the church that survived after his abrupt departure. In this letter, Paul refuted the charges that had been leveled against him, encouraged the new believers to be faithful to their leadership and teaching, and provided clarity about the Parousia—the second coming of Jesus Christ.

BREATHE IT IN

Paul wrote to the church at Thessalonica to equip, encourage, and empower a congregation of young, new Christians. Nearly two thousand years later, equipping, encouraging, and empowering new Christians continue to be high priorities of the church.

The Thessalonians had misunderstood Paul's teaching and believed that the return of Christ was imminent. In their zeal, the new Christians in Thessalonica quit their jobs to focus solely on Jesus' return. Although living in anticipation of Christ's return is understandable and proper, idleness discouraged the believers as they waited. At the same time, seeing some fellow believers die prompted questions and concerns about them missing Christ's return.

In this life, so many things can shake us to our core. If you have ever mourned the death of someone you cared about deeply, you can relate with the emotional state of the Thessalonians. Nothing challenges our understanding of God like death. What do you do when your faithful enthusiasm is met with this frustrating reality, or some other one? How do you rebound when your expectations do not come to fruition?

Paul's response to the grieving and frustrated believers in Thessalonica was to comfort them with the truth of the gospel: "But I do not want you to be ignorant, brethren, concerning those who have fallen asleep, lest you sorrow as others who have no hope. For if we believe that Jesus died and rose again, even so God will bring with Him those who sleep in Jesus. For this we say to you by the word of the Lord, that we who are alive and remain until the coming of the Lord

will by no means precede those who are asleep" (1 Thess. 4:13–15). Paul gave the Thessalonians hope that death is not the end. Death might separate believers for a time, but not forever. Those who die in Christ are with Christ, and we will all be together again one day.

First Thessalonians reminds us that we must be familiar with the promises of God. Faith built on the solid foundation of the Word will endure. We cannot know the exact time or date for the return of Jesus Christ; we actually have no idea of the timing of any event in our lives. But we have absolute confidence that He will return and that He holds our lives in the palm of His hand. How much of your frustration with God has to do with timing? Refuse to put God on a deadline. Remember that patience is a fruit of the Holy Spirit. God will fulfill all He promises in His perfect timing. Wait patiently but not idly.

†

THE FIRST EPISTLE OF PAUL TO THE

THESSALONIANS

Greeting

1 Paul, [a]Silvanus, and Timothy,

To the church of the [b]Thessalonians in
God the Father and the Lord Jesus Christ:

Grace to you and peace from God our
Father and the Lord Jesus Christ.[1]

Their Good Example

2 [a]We give thanks to God always for you
all, making mention of you in our prayers,
3 remembering without ceasing [a]your work
of faith, [b]labor of love, and patience of hope
in our Lord Jesus Christ in the sight of our
God and Father, 4 knowing, beloved brethren, [a]your election by God. 5 For [a]our gospel did not come to you in word only, but
also in power, [b]and in the Holy Spirit [c]and
in much assurance, as you know what kind
of men we were among you for your sake.
6 And [a]you became followers of us and
of the Lord, having received the word
in much affliction, [b]with joy of the Holy
Spirit, 7 so that you became examples to
all in Macedonia and Achaia who believe.
8 For from you the word of the Lord [a]has
sounded forth, not only in Macedonia and
Achaia, but also [b]in every place. Your faith
toward God has gone out, so that we do
not need to say anything. 9 For they themselves declare concerning us [a]what manner of entry we had to you, [b]and how you
turned to God from idols to serve the living and true God, 10 and [a]to wait for His
Son from heaven, whom He raised from
the dead, *even* Jesus who delivers us [b]from
the wrath to come.

Paul's Conduct
(cf. Acts 17:1–9)

2 For you yourselves know, brethren, that
our coming to you was not in vain. 2 But
even[1] after we had suffered before and were
spitefully treated at [a]Philippi, as you know,
we were [b]bold in our God to speak to you
the gospel of God in much conflict. 3 [a]For
our exhortation *did* not *come* from error or
uncleanness, nor *was it* in deceit.
4 But as [a]we have been approved by God
[b]to be entrusted with the gospel, even so we
speak, [c]not as pleasing men, but God [d]who
tests our hearts. 5 For [a]neither at any time
did we use flattering words, as you know,
nor a cloak for covetousness—[b]God *is* witness. 6 [a]Nor did we seek glory from men,
either from you or from others, when [b]we
might have [c]made demands [d]as apostles
of Christ. 7 But [a]we were gentle among you,
just as a nursing *mother* cherishes her own
children. 8 So, affectionately longing for
you, we were well pleased [a]to impart to you
not only the gospel of God, but also [b]our
own lives, because you had become dear
to us. 9 For you remember, brethren, our
[a]labor and toil; for laboring night and day,
[b]that we might not be a burden to any of
you, we preached to you the gospel of God.
10 [a]You *are* witnesses, and God *also,* [b]how
devoutly and justly and blamelessly we
behaved ourselves among you who believe; 11 as you know how we exhorted, and

---

1:1 [a] 1 Pet. 5:12 [b] Acts 17:1–9 [1] NU-Text omits *from God our Father and the Lord Jesus Christ.* **1:2** [a] Rom. 1:8; 2 Thess. 1:3 **1:3** [a] John 6:29 [b] Rom. 16:6 **1:4** [a] Col. 3:12 **1:5** [a] Mark 16:20 [b] 2 Cor. 6:6 [c] Heb. 2:3 **1:6** [a] 1 Cor. 4:16; 11:1 [b] Acts 5:41; 13:52; 2 Cor. 6:10; Gal. 5:22 **1:8** [a] Rom. 10:18 [b] Rom. 1:8; 16:19; 2 Cor. 2:14; 2 Thess. 1:4 **1:9** [a] 1 Thess. 2:1 [b] 1 Cor. 12:2 **1:10** [a] [Rom. 2:7] [b] Matt. 3:7; Rom. 5:9 **2:2** [a] Acts 14:5; 16:19–24; Phil. 1:30 [b] Acts 17:1–9 [1] NU-Text and M-Text omit *even.* **2:3** [a] 2 Cor. 7:2 **2:4** [a] 1 Cor. 7:25 [b] Titus 1:3 [c] Gal. 1:10 [d] Prov. 17:3 **2:5** [a] 2 Cor. 2:17 [b] Rom. 1:9; 1 Thess. 2:10 **2:6** [a] 1 Tim. 5:17 [b] 1 Cor. 9:4 [c] 2 Cor. 11:9 [d] 1 Cor. 9:1 **2:7** [a] 1 Cor. 2:3 **2:8** [a] Rom. 1:11 [b] 2 Cor. 12:15; 1 John 3:16 **2:9** [a] Acts 18:3; 20:34, 35; 1 Cor. 4:12; 2 Thess. 3:7, 8 [b] 2 Cor. 12:13 **2:10** [a] 2 Cor. 1:12; 1 Thess. 1:5 [b] 2 Cor. 7:2

comforted, and charged[1] every one of you,
as a father *does* his own children, 12[a]that you
would walk worthy of God [b]who calls you
into His own kingdom and glory.

Their Conversion

13For this reason we also thank God
[a]without ceasing, because when you [b]re-
ceived the word of God which you heard
from us, you welcomed *it* [c]not *as* the word
of men, but as it is in truth, the word of God,
which also effectively [d]works in you who
believe. 14For you, brethren, became imitators [a]of the churches of God which are in
Judea in Christ Jesus. For [b]you also suffered
the same things from your own countrymen, just as they *did* from the Judeans,
15[a]who killed both the Lord Jesus and [b]their
own prophets, and have persecuted us; and
they do not please God [c]and are contrary
to all men, 16[a]forbidding us to speak to the
Gentiles that they may be saved, so as always [b]to fill up *the measure of* their sins;
[c]but wrath has come upon them to the uttermost.

Longing to See Them

17But we, brethren, having been taken
away from you for a short time [a]in presence, not in heart, endeavored more eagerly to see your face with great desire.
18Therefore we wanted to come to you—
even I, Paul, time and again—but [a]Satan
hindered us. 19For [a]what *is* our hope, or joy,

1 THESSALONIANS 1:1

I AM SILAS

Paul, Silvanus, and Timothy, to the church of the Thessalonians in God the Father and the Lord Jesus Christ: Grace to you and peace from God our Father and the Lord Jesus Christ. 1 Thessalonians 1:1

I am Silas. I have been honored to serve the Lord Jesus Christ, even at risk of my life for His name. The apostles sent me to deliver a letter of encouragement to Paul and Barnabas in Antioch. I stayed there with them for a while. When Paul and Barnabas parted ways, I went with Paul to visit the cities where the gospel had already been preached to see how believers in each were doing. When we visited Derbe and Lystra, a young man named Timothy joined us.

One night, we cast out a demon from a young slave girl. Her masters made money using her divination powers, so they were unhappy about what we had done and reported us to the magistrates. In punishment, we were beaten with rods and thrown into prison. About midnight, we sat on the prison floor praying and singing hymns. Suddenly, there was a great earthquake and the doors of the jail opened and our chains fell away. The guard was overtaken by fear that all the prisoners had escaped. He knew he would be killed for failing in his duties, so he thought to take his own life. However, for his sake, we remained inside the prison. The guard was so amazed that we remained that his heart was softened. He asked what he must do to be saved. He and his whole family were saved and baptized because the display of God's power and love through us bore witness to the truth of the gospel.

†

Silas and Paul practiced integrity by remaining in their jail cells even when they could have walked right out. They knew the jailer would be held responsible for their escape and would likely pay with his life. As a result of such kindness, the door was opened for the jailer to hear the gospel. Sometimes acts of kindness and meeting the needs of others can soften their hearts so they can hear from God through us.

2:11 [1] NU-Text and M-Text read *implored.* 2:12 [a] Eph. 4:1; Col. 1:10 [b] Rom. 8:28; 1 Cor. 1:9; 1 Thess. 5:24; 2 Thess. 2:14; [2 Tim. 1:9] 2:13 [a] Rom. 1:8; 1 Thess. 1:2, 3 [b] Mark 4:20 [c] [Matt. 10:20; Gal. 4:14] [d] [1 Pet. 1:23] 2:14 [a] Gal. 1:22 [b] Acts 17:5; 1 Thess. 3:4; 2 Thess. 1:4 2:15 [a] Luke 24:20; Acts 2:23 [b] Jer. 2:30; Matt. 5:12; 23:34, 35; Acts 7:52 [c] Esth. 3:8 2:16 [a] Luke 11:52 [b] Gen. 15:16; Dan. 8:23; Matt. 23:32 [c] Matt. 24:6 2:17 [a] 1 Cor. 5:3 2:18 [a] Rom. 1:13; 15:22 2:19 [a] 2 Cor. 1:14

#OXYGEN

1 THESSALONIANS 2:18

Hope for What We Do Not See

Using your God-given gifts for God's glory is your ministry. Even if you are hindered and even if you do not see the fruit of your labor, trust God and keep working. God sees. And that is what matters most. You are a blessing, so **breathe** and **hope for what we do not see.**

or [b]crown of rejoicing? *Is it* not even you
in the [c]presence of our Lord Jesus Christ
[d]at His coming? 20 For you are our glory
and joy.

Concern for Their Faith

3 Therefore, when we could no longer
endure it, we thought it good to be left
in Athens alone, 2 and sent [a]Timothy, our
brother and minister of God, and our fellow
laborer in the gospel of Christ, to establish
you and encourage you concerning your
faith, 3 [a]that no one should be shaken by
these afflictions; for you yourselves know
that [b]we are appointed to this. 4 [a]For, in fact,
we told you before when we were with you
that we would suffer tribulation, just as it
happened, and you know. 5 For this reason,
when I could no longer endure it, I sent to
know your faith, [a]lest by some means the
tempter had tempted you, and [b]our labor
might be in vain.

Encouraged by Timothy

6 [a]But now that Timothy has come to us
from you, and brought us good news of
your faith and love, and that you always
have good remembrance of us, greatly desiring to see us, [b]as we also *to see* you—
7 therefore, brethren, in all our affliction
and distress [a]we were comforted concerning you by your faith. 8 For now we live, if
you [a]stand fast in the Lord.
9 For what thanks can we render to God
for you, for all the joy with which we rejoice for your sake before our God, 10 night
and day praying exceedingly that we may
see your face [a]and perfect what is lacking
in your faith?

Prayer for the Church

11 Now may our God and Father Himself,
and our Lord Jesus Christ, [a]direct our way
to you. 12 And may the Lord make you increase and [a]abound in love to one another
and to all, just as we *do* to you, 13 so that He
may establish [a]your hearts blameless in
holiness before our God and Father at the
coming of our Lord Jesus Christ with all
His saints.

Plea for Purity

4 Finally then, brethren, we urge and exhort in the Lord Jesus [a]that you should
abound more and more, [b]just as you received from us how you ought to walk and
to please God; 2 for you know what commandments we gave you through the Lord
Jesus.
3 For this is [a]the will of God, [b]your sanctification: [c]that you should abstain from sexual immorality; 4 [a]that each of you should
know how to possess his own vessel in
sanctification and honor, 5 [a]not in passion
of lust, [b]like the Gentiles [c]who do not know
God; 6 that no one should take advantage of
and defraud his brother in this matter, because the Lord [a]*is* the avenger of all such, as
we also forewarned you and testified. 7 For
God did not call us to uncleanness, [a]but in
holiness. 8 [a]Therefore he who rejects *this*
does not reject man, but God, [b]who has also
given[1] us His Holy Spirit.

A Brotherly and Orderly Life

9 But concerning brotherly love you have
no need that I should write to you, for [a]you
yourselves are taught by God [b]to love one

2:19 [b] Prov. 16:31 [c] Jude 24 [d] 1 Cor. 15:23 3:2 [a] Rom. 16:21 3:3 [a] Eph. 3:13 [b] John 16:2; Acts 9:16; 14:22; 1 Cor. 4:9; 2 Tim. 3:12; 1 Pet. 2:21 3:4 [a] Acts 20:24 3:5 [a] 1 Cor. 7:5 [b] Gal. 2:2 3:6 [a] Acts 18:5 [b] Phil. 1:8 3:7 [a] 2 Cor. 1:4 3:8 [a] [Eph. 6:13, 14]; Phil. 4:1 3:10 [a] 2 Cor. 13:9; Col. 4:12 3:11 [a] Mark 1:3 3:12 [a] Phil. 1:9; 1 Thess. 4:1, 10; 2 Thess. 1:3 3:13 [a] 2 Thess. 2:17 4:1 [a] 1 Cor. 15:58 [b] Phil. 1:27; Col. 1:10 4:3 [a] [Rom. 12:2] [b] Eph. 5:27 [c] [1 Cor. 6:15–20; Col. 3:5] 4:4 [a] Rom. 6:19 4:5 [a] Col. 3:5 [b] Eph. 4:17, 18 [c] 1 Cor. 15:34 4:6 [a] 2 Thess. 1:8 4:7 [a] Lev. 11:44; [Heb. 12:14]; 1 Pet. 1:14–16 4:8 [a] Luke 10:16 [b] 1 Cor. 2:10 [1] NU-Text reads *who also gives.* 4:9 [a] [Jer. 31:33, 34]; John 6:45; 15:12, 17; [1 John 2:27] [b] Matt. 22:39

another; 10 and indeed you do so toward all
the brethren who are in all Macedonia. But
we urge you, brethren, [a]that you increase
more and more; 11 that you also aspire to
lead a quiet life, [a]to mind your own business, and [b]to work with your own hands, as
we commanded you, 12 [a]that you may walk
properly toward those who are outside, and
that you may lack nothing.

The Comfort of Christ's Coming

13 But I do not want you to be ignorant,
brethren, concerning those who have fallen
asleep, lest you sorrow [a]as others [b]who have
no hope. 14 For [a]if we believe that Jesus died
and rose again, even so God will bring with
Him [b]those who sleep in Jesus.[1]

15 For this we say to you [a]by the word of
the Lord, that [b]we who are alive *and* remain until the coming of the Lord will by
no means precede those who are asleep.
16 For [a]the Lord Himself will descend from
heaven with a shout, with the voice of an
archangel, and with [b]the trumpet of God.
[c]And the dead in Christ will rise first. 17 [a]Then
we who are alive *and* remain shall be caught
up together with them [b]in the clouds to
meet the Lord in the air. And thus [c]we shall
always be with the Lord. 18 [a]Therefore comfort one another with these words.

The Day of the Lord

5 But concerning [a]the times and the seasons, brethren, you have no need that
I should write to you. 2 For you yourselves
know perfectly that [a]the day of the Lord so
comes as a thief in the night. 3 For when they
say, "Peace and safety!" then [a]sudden destruction comes upon them, [b]as labor pains
upon a pregnant woman. And they shall
not escape. 4 [a]But you, brethren, are not in
darkness, so that this Day should overtake
you as a thief. 5 You are all [a]sons of light and
sons of the day. We are not of the night nor
of darkness. 6 [a]Therefore let us not sleep, as
others *do,* but [b]let us watch and be sober.
7 For [a]those who sleep, sleep at night, and
those who get drunk [b]are drunk at night.
8 But let us who are of the day be sober, [a]put-
ting on the breastplate of faith and love, and
as a helmet the hope of salvation. 9 For [a]God
did not appoint us to wrath, [b]but to obtain
salvation through our Lord Jesus Christ,
10 [a]who died for us, that whether we wake
or sleep, we should live together with Him.

11 Therefore comfort each other and edify one another, just as you also are doing.

Various Exhortations

12 And we urge you, brethren, [a]to recognize those who labor among you, and are
over you in the Lord and admonish you,
13 and to esteem them very highly in love
for their work's sake. [a]Be at peace among
yourselves.

14 Now we exhort you, brethren, [a]warn
those who are unruly, [b]comfort the fainthearted, [c]uphold the weak, [d]be patient with
all. 15 [a]See that no one renders evil for evil
to anyone, but always [b]pursue what is good
both for yourselves and for all.

16 [a]Rejoice always, 17 [a]pray without ceasing, 18 in everything give thanks; for this is
the will of God in Christ Jesus for you.

19 [a]Do not quench the Spirit. 20 [a]Do not
despise prophecies. 21 [a]Test all things; [b]hold
fast what is good. 22 Abstain from every
form of evil.

Blessing and Admonition

23 Now may [a]the God of peace Himself
[b]sanctify you completely; and may your
whole spirit, soul, and body [c]be preserved
blameless at the coming of our Lord Jesus
Christ. 24 He who calls you *is* [a]faithful, who
also will [b]do *it.*

25 Brethren, pray for us.

26 Greet all the brethren with a holy kiss.

27 I charge you by the Lord that this epistle be read to all the holy[1] brethren.

28 The grace of our Lord Jesus Christ *be*
with you. Amen.

4:10 [a] 1 Thess. 3:12 **4:11** [a] 2 Thess. 3:11; 1 Pet. 4:15 [b] Acts 20:35 **4:12** [a] Rom. 13:13; Col. 4:5; [1 Pet. 2:12] **4:13** [a] Lev. 19:28 [b] [Eph. 2:12] **4:14** [a] 1 Cor. 15:13 [b] 1 Cor. 15:20, 23 [1] Or *those who through Jesus sleep* **4:15** [a] 1 Kin. 13:17; 20:35; 2 Cor. 12:1; Gal. 1:12 [b] 1 Cor. 15:51, 52; 1 Thess. 5:10 **4:16** [a] [Matt. 24:30, 31] [b] [1 Cor. 15:52] [c] [1 Cor. 15:23]; 2 Thess. 2:1; Rev. 14:13; 20:6 **4:17** [a] [1 Cor. 15:51–53]; 1 Thess. 5:10 [b] Dan. 7:13; Acts 1:9; Rev. 11:12 [c] John 14:3; 17:24 **4:18** [a] 1 Thess. 5:11 **5:1** [a] Matt. 24:3 **5:2** [a] Luke 21:34; 1 Thess. 5:4; [2 Pet. 3:10]; Rev. 3:3; 16:15 **5:3** [a] Is. 13:6–9 [b] Hos. 13:13 **5:4** [a] [Acts 26:18]; Rom. 13:12; Eph. 5:8; 1 John 2:8 **5:5** [a] Eph. 5:8 **5:6** [a] Matt. 25:5 [b] Matt. 25:13; Mark 13:35; [1 Pet. 5:8] **5:7** [a] [Luke 21:34] [b] Acts 2:15; 2 Pet. 2:13 **5:8** [a] Is. 59:17; Eph. 6:14 **5:9** [a] Rom. 9:22 [b] [2 Thess. 2:13] **5:10** [a] 2 Cor. 5:15 **5:12** [a] 1 Cor. 16:18; 1 Tim. 5:17; Heb. 13:7, 17 **5:13** [a] Mark 9:50 **5:14** [a] 2 Thess. 3:6, 7, 11 [b] Heb. 12:12 [c] Rom. 14:1; 15:1; 1 Cor. 8:7 [d] Gal. 5:22 **5:15** [a] Lev. 19:18 [b] Rom. 12:9; Gal. 6:10; 1 Thess. 5:21 **5:16** [a] [2 Cor. 6:10] **5:17** [a] Eph. 6:18 **5:19** [a] Eph. 4:30 **5:20** [a] Acts 13:1; 1 Cor. 14:1, 31 **5:21** [a] 1 Cor. 14:29; 1 John 4:1 [b] Phil. 4:8 **5:23** [a] Phil. 4:9 [b] 1 Thess. 3:13 [c] 1 Cor. 1:8, 9 **5:24** [a] [1 Cor. 10:13]; 2 Thess. 3:3 [b] Phil. 1:6 **5:27** [1] NU-Text omits *holy.*

RELEASE //

HOPE FOR WHAT WE DO NOT SEE

A Failure Is Not a Fatality

1 Thessalonians 5:16–18 // Rejoice always, pray without ceasing, in everything give thanks; for this is the will of God in Christ Jesus for you.

Summary Message // In this first letter to the Thessalonian believers, the apostle Paul recalled how he had been badly beaten in Philippi before coming to Thessalonica. There, he ended up hiding from a mob attempting to stone him and Silas. The two escaped the Thessalonian mob under the cloak of darkness and headed to Berea, only to encounter the mob a second time.

Paul was not doing anything wrong; he was preaching the gospel and planting churches to make a difference for Christ in the world. He was living out God's calling on his life that began when he met Christ on the road to Damascus (see Acts 9:3–22). Yet many times, his sincere efforts did not yield his intended result. Paul experienced the sad fact that change is always disruptive, even when it is good.

At times, Paul suffered great bodily harm for his determination to preach the gospel. Despite his sufferings, the apostle closed this letter to the believers in Thessalonica on a hopeful note. He encouraged them never to stop rejoicing, praying, or thanking God.

Practical Application // Most of us strive to make a difference in the world. Even though we labor for God's good and seek to better the world or our families, sometimes our efforts fail. Like Paul's labors in Philippi and Thessalonica, sometimes what we hope, pray, and work for with all our might never materializes.

Failure is painful, especially when we feel we have given God our best and our all. It can also be embarrassing, mainly because we tend to associate a failed deed with a failed self. To protect our fragile egos, we try to avoid the appearance of failure at all costs. However, at some point, our life experiences push us off the roller coaster of perfectionism to the realization that a failure is not necessarily a bad thing. In God's hands, failure can bring forth incredible growth. The Bible demonstrates that what is deemed a failure in the eyes of the world is not necessarily a failure in the eyes of God.

Has an apparent failure caused you to lose hope? Instead of wallowing in your failures, pray that God's redemptive power will turn your decline toward disaster into dancing in delight.

Fervent Prayer // O Lord, when we feel like a failure, comfort us and assure us that there is more to our situation than we can see. When we cannot see a positive end, help us keep on rejoicing and praying. Help us keep on thanking You because You have already determined our future. You know the plans You have for us, plans to prosper us and not to harm us. You have plans to give us hope and a future. Grant us strength to keep moving according to Your will and Your way, even when opposition, discouragement, and despair come to attack us. Our hope is built on nothing less than Jesus' blood and righteousness. In Jesus' name we pray. Amen.

THE SECOND EPISTLE OF PAUL TO THE

THESSALONIANS

OVERVIEW

Thessalonica was a major city with a population of approximately two hundred thousand people during the New Testament era. The citizenry of this port city on the Aegean Sea included Romans, Greeks, and Asians. A seven-hundred-mile stretch of road called the Egnatian Way that had been constructed by the Romans ran through Thessalonica, making it a major commercial distribution hub. Acts 17 indicates an influential Jewish community was located there as well, one in which Paul had a successful ministry for three consecutive Sabbaths.

First and Second Thessalonians are two of Paul's earliest letters. Within a year after writing and delivering the first letter to the church at Thessalonica, Paul wrote a second letter to the young church that sought to thrive within a pagan culture and endure persecution from the Jewish synagogue.

It is believed that the messenger who delivered Paul's first letter returned with a mixed report on the condition of the church. The church remained faithful, as Paul noted in his follow-up letter: "We ourselves boast of you among the churches of God for your patience and faith in all your persecutions and tribulations that you endure" (2 Thess. 1:4). However, we also read about Paul's concern that some believers struggled to hold to sound doctrine (see 2:1–15) and live in obedience (see 3:6–15). Primarily, confusion regarding the day of Christ's return persisted. Believers earnestly desired the return of the Lord, but their single-focused outlook gave room for lawlessness.

The remedy to the threat of deception was to stand firm in established doctrine: "Therefore, brethren, stand fast and hold the traditions which you were taught, whether by word or our epistle" (2:15). In chapter 3, Paul addressed the ongoing problem of idleness as believers did not work in anticipation of the second coming of Christ. Paul made it clear that the church was not obligated to care for able-bodied people who would not support themselves when he asserted that "if anyone will not work, neither shall he eat" (v. 10). As in 1 Thessalonians, Paul's point was clear: believers are to expect Christ's return at any time and yet wait patiently for it, all while continuing to be hard at work.

BREATHE IT IN

The issue of discipline and correction within the church was a prominent theme in Paul's writing. More than once, he wrote about insubordination causing separation among members. The church was constantly threatened by false teaching and corrupt practices, which placed great strain upon it. Rogue behavior within the body of Christ was a source of added turmoil, confusion, and poor morale.

It seems the church today is not much different. Some churches are notorious for intolerant, judgmental behavior. We cannot control the behavior of others, but neither can we turn a blind eye to the hypocritical and ungodly behavior of those who claim the name of Christ. We might not be able to prevent others from engaging in sinful conduct, but we can surely control who we let into our lives. Consider how you might need to regulate your environment to be selective

in who you share time and space with. Are there places that are best for you to avoid? Are there social media platforms to withdraw from or accounts to block?

But we also must be honest about our behavior. Are we ever guilty of behaving in glaring contrast to biblical teaching? Is there any behavior or speech that we permit in our homes that we should not? Conversely, what are the godly, nonnegotiable values and behaviors you hold to and model in your home? Has your list changed over time? Why? Were the changes for the better or the worse?

Establishing and holding boundaries is difficult, especially as a young Christian. Family, friends, and longtime acquaintances may behave in ways that conflict with your Christian values. Paul writes that for some, separation from those closest to you may be necessary to maintain a life of obedience to Christ. Ministering to others means that we live by example, showing Christ to them. At times, however, we might be unable to do so without being compromised ourselves. Separation—partial or full, for a time or for good—may be what is needed. In other words, how far away do we need to be from some of the people in our lives in order to love them with the love of Jesus? Living from a biblical worldview is a challenge, but it is what our Savior demands.

†

THE SECOND EPISTLE OF PAUL TO THE

THESSALONIANS

Greeting

1 Paul, Silvanus, and Timothy,

To the church of the Thessalonians in
God our Father and the Lord Jesus Christ:

2[a]Grace to you and peace from God our
Father and the Lord Jesus Christ.

God's Final Judgment and Glory

3We are bound to thank God always for
you, brethren, as it is fitting, because your
faith grows exceedingly, and the love of every
one of you all abounds toward each other, 4so
that [a]we ourselves boast of you among the
churches of God [b]for your patience and faith
[c]in all your persecutions and tribulations
that you endure, 5*which is* [a]manifest evidence of the righteous judgment of God, that
you may be counted worthy of the kingdom
of God, [b]for which you also suffer; 6[a]since *it*
is a righteous thing with God to repay with
tribulation those who trouble you, 7and to
give you who are troubled [a]rest with us when
[b]the Lord Jesus is revealed from heaven with
His mighty angels, 8in flaming fire taking
vengeance on those who do not know God,
and on those who do not obey the gospel of
our Lord Jesus Christ. 9[a]These shall be punished with everlasting destruction from the
presence of the Lord and [b]from the glory of
His power, 10when He comes, in that Day, [a]to
be [b]glorified in His saints and to be admired
among all those who believe,[1] because our
testimony among you was believed.
11Therefore we also pray always for you
that our God would [a]count you worthy of

#OXYGEN

2 THESSALONIANS 1:7–8

Hope for What We Do Not See

The hope we need to live today is anchored on both yesterday and tomorrow. We find hope in what Christ has done for us in the past and in what He has promised to do for us in the future. One day, Jesus will return. We don't know when, but we know He will. And when the unseen becomes seen on that day, He will make all things right.

Breathe and **hope for what we do not see.**

this calling, and fulfill all the good pleasure
of *His* goodness and [b]the work of faith with
power, 12[a]that the name of our Lord Jesus
Christ may be glorified in you, and you in
Him, according to the grace of our God and
the Lord Jesus Christ.

The Great Apostasy

2 Now, brethren, [a]concerning the coming
of our Lord Jesus Christ [b]and our gathering together to Him, we ask you, 2[a]not to be
soon shaken in mind or troubled, either by
spirit or by word or by letter, as if from us, as
though the day of Christ[1] had come. 3Let no
one deceive you by any means; for *that Day*
will not come [a]unless the falling away comes
first, and [b]the man of sin[1] is revealed, [c]the
son of perdition, 4who opposes and [a]exalts
himself [b]above all that is called God or that is

1:2 [a] 1 Cor. 1:3 **1:4** [a] 2 Cor. 7:4; [1 Thess. 2:19] [b] 1 Thess. 1:3 [c] 1 Thess. 2:14 **1:5** [a] Phil. 1:28 [b] 1 Thess. 2:14 **1:6** [a] Rev. 6:10 **1:7** [a] Rev. 14:13 [b] [1 Thess. 4:16]; Jude 14 **1:9** [a] Phil. 3:19; 1 Thess. 5:3 [b] Deut. 33:2 **1:10** [a] Matt. 25:31 [b] Is. 49:3; John 17:10; 1 Thess. 2:12 [1] NU-Text and M-Text read *have believed.* **1:11** [a] Col. 1:12 [b] 1 Thess. 1:3 **1:12** [a] [Col. 3:17] **2:1** [a] Mark 13:26; [1 Thess. 4:15–17] [b] Matt. 24:31 **2:2** [a] Matt. 24:4 [1] NU-Text reads *the Lord.* **2:3** [a] 1 Tim. 4:1 [b] Dan. 7:25; 8:25; 11:36; 2 Thess. 2:8; Rev. 13:5 [c] John 17:12 [1] NU-Text reads *lawlessness.* **2:4** [a] Is. 14:13, 14; Ezek. 28:2 [b] 1 Cor. 8:5

worshiped, so that he sits as God[1] in the temple of God, showing himself that he is God.
5Do you not remember that when I was
still with you I told you these things? 6And
now you know what is restraining, that he
may be revealed in his own time. 7For [a]the
mystery of lawlessness is already at work;
only He[1] who now restrains *will do so* until He[2] is taken out of the way. 8And then
the lawless one will be revealed, [a]whom
the Lord will consume [b]with the breath of
His mouth and destroy [c]with the brightness of His coming. 9The coming of the
lawless one is [a]according to the working of
Satan, with all power, [b]signs, and lying wonders, 10and with all unrighteous deception
among [a]those who perish, because they did
not receive [b]the love of the truth, that they
might be saved. 11And [a]for this reason God
will send them strong delusion, [b]that they
should believe the lie, 12that they all may be
condemned who did not believe the truth
but [a]had pleasure in unrighteousness.

Stand Fast

13But we are bound to give thanks to God
always for you, brethren beloved by the
Lord, because God [a]from the beginning
[b]chose you for salvation [c]through sanctification by the Spirit and belief in the truth,
14to which He called you by our gospel, for
[a]the obtaining of the glory of our Lord Jesus
Christ. 15Therefore, brethren, [a]stand fast
and hold [b]the traditions which you were
taught, whether by word or our epistle.
16Now may our Lord Jesus Christ Himself, and our God and Father, [a]who has
loved us and given *us* everlasting consolation and [b]good hope by grace, 17comfort
your hearts [a]and establish you in every
good word and work.

Pray for Us

3 Finally, brethren, [a]pray for us, that the
word of the Lord may run *swiftly* and be
glorified, just as *it is* with you, 2and [a]that we
may be delivered from unreasonable and
wicked men; [b]for not all have faith.
3But [a]the Lord is faithful, who will establish you and [b]guard *you* from the evil one.
4And [a]we have confidence in the Lord concerning you, both that you do and will do
the things we command you.
5Now may [a]the Lord direct your hearts
into the love of God and into the patience
of Christ.

Warning Against Idleness

6But we command you, brethren, in the
name of our Lord Jesus Christ, [a]that you
withdraw [b]from every brother who walks
[c]disorderly and not according to the tradition which he[1] received from us. 7For you
yourselves know how you ought to follow us, for we were not disorderly among
you; 8nor did we eat anyone's bread free
of charge, but worked with [a]labor and toil
night and day, that we might not be a burden to any of you, 9not because we do not
have [a]authority, but to make ourselves an
example of how you should follow us.
10For even when we were with you, we
commanded you this: If anyone will not
work, neither shall he eat. 11For we hear that
there are some who walk among you in a
disorderly manner, not working at all, but
are [a]busybodies. 12Now those who are such
we command and exhort through our Lord
Jesus Christ [a]that they work in quietness and
eat their own bread.
13But *as for* you, brethren, [a]do not grow
weary *in* doing good. 14And if anyone does not
obey our word in this epistle, note that person
and [a]do not keep company with him, that he
may be ashamed. 15[a]Yet do not count *him* as
an enemy, [b]but admonish *him* as a brother.

Benediction

16Now may [a]the Lord of peace Himself
give you peace always in every way. The Lord
be with you all.
17[a]The salutation of Paul with my own
hand, which is a sign in every epistle; so I
write.
18[a]The grace of our Lord Jesus Christ *be*
with you all. Amen.

2:4 [1] NU-Text omits *as God.* 2:7 [a] 1 John 2:18 [1] Or *he* [2] Or *he* 2:8 [a] Dan. 7:10 [b] Is. 11:4; Rev. 2:16; 19:15 [c] Heb. 10:27 2:9 [a] John 8:41 [b] Deut. 13:1 2:10 [a] 2 Cor. 2:15 [b] 1 Cor. 16:22 2:11 [a] Rom. 1:28 [b] 1 Tim. 4:1 2:12 [a] Rom. 1:32; 1 Cor. 13:6 2:13 [a] Eph. 1:4 [b] 1 Thess. 1:4 [c] 1 Thess. 4:7; [1 Pet. 1:2] 2:14 [a] 1 Pet. 5:10 2:15 [a] 1 Cor. 16:13 [b] Rom. 6:17; 1 Cor. 11:2; 2 Thess. 3:6; Jude 3 2:16 [a] [Rev. 1:5] [b] Titus 3:7; 1 Pet. 1:3 2:17 [a] 1 Cor. 1:8 3:1 [a] Eph. 6:19 3:2 [a] Rom. 15:31 [b] Acts 28:24 3:3 [a] 1 Cor. 1:9; 1 Thess. 5:24 [b] John 17:15 3:4 [a] 2 Cor. 7:16 3:5 [a] 1 Chr. 29:18 3:6 [a] Rom. 16:17 [b] 1 Cor. 5:1 [c] 1 Thess. 4:11 [1] NU-Text and M-Text read *they.* 3:8 [a] 1 Thess. 2:9 3:9 [a] 1 Cor. 9:4, 6–14 3:11 [a] 1 Tim. 5:13; 1 Pet. 4:15 3:12 [a] Eph. 4:28; 1 Thess. 4:11, 12 3:13 [a] 2 Cor. 4:1; Gal. 6:9 3:14 [a] Matt. 18:17 3:15 [a] Lev. 19:17 [b] Titus 3:10 3:16 [a] John 14:27; Rom. 15:33; Phil. 4:9 3:17 [a] 1 Cor. 16:21 3:18 [a] Rom. 16:20, 24; 1 Thess. 5:28

HOPE FOR WHAT WE DO NOT SEE

INHALE

I want to see justice under the law. I share Dr. Martin Luther King Jr.'s dream of a future in which "the sons of former slaves and the sons of former slave owners" can "sit down together at the table of brotherhood." I long for a future in which my children are judged not "by the color of their skin but by the content of their character." How can I have hope that God will bring change?

EXHALE

There are many injustices in the world that can hurt to the very core of our being. In a fallen world, all manner of injustices happen. But be reminded that God also "happens." In loud and powerful ways, God "happens." His power is on display in an evangelistic rally where thousands of people come to hear the gospel of salvation and peace. He makes His power known in a hospital where unexplained healing occurs. He also "happens" in subtle ways—in a song that He has guided someone to write and perform that prompts someone to forgive and forget. Or, at a dinner table where a prayer of thankfulness unites and strengthens a family.

God "happens" every single day of our lives. It's not an impossible hope, then, that He will "happen" in a way that will change how people are treated. He can and will continue to "happen" in this world. Believe it or not, He's "happening" in just such ways, even right now. He is "happening" in ways that are seen and unseen, and He is bringing change. Injustice will not reign forever. Your hope for change will someday be realized. In the meantime, don't stop believing that it can come at any moment and in any place.

Second Thessalonians 3:13 says, "But as for you, brethren, do not grow weary in doing good." Keep doing what is good in God's sight, even though it is hard to do. Don't give in to hate and fear. Keep the faith in all that you do.

THE FIRST EPISTLE OF PAUL TO

TIMOTHY

OVERVIEW

Paul's letters to Timothy and Titus are often called the Pastoral Epistles. These three epistles contain Paul's instruction and encouragement to two pastors who were helping establish leadership infrastructure in the early church. Timothy, a young convert from Paul's visit to the city of Lystra, was Paul's "true son of the faith" (1 Tim. 1:2). This young man became a trusted member of Paul's missionary work. His name is mentioned in many of Paul's epistles, as well as in Acts 16:1–3, where it is reported that Paul circumcised his young apprentice so Timothy would be accepted among the Jewish Christians. Timothy joined Paul and Silas on their second and third missionary journeys and was present for Paul's first incarceration in Rome. When writing the Prison Epistles, Paul acknowledged the presence of Timothy in three of the four letters (see Phil. 1:1; Col. 1:1; Philem. v. 1).

Paul commended Timothy with glowing words to the church at Philippi: "But I trust in the Lord Jesus to send Timothy to you shortly, that I also may be encouraged when I know your state. For I have no one like-minded, who will sincerely care for your state. For all seek their own, not the things which are of Christ Jesus. But you know his proven character, that as a son with his father he served with me in the gospel" (Phil. 2:19–22). The relationship between Paul and Timothy serves as a contemporary model for training by clergy and mentors.

Paul invested a great deal of time in Ephesus because the church was threatened by false teaching. He entrusted Timothy to oversee the church when he wrote to him, "As I urged you when I went into Macedonia—remain in Ephesus that you may charge some that they teach no other doctrine" (1 Tim. 1:3). Timothy's assignment was to challenge false doctrine and cleanse the church of false teachers. Paul's two letters to Timothy were his attempts to encourage Timothy during this challenging assignment. Apparently, Timothy's youth was an issue as he provided leadership to older people. Paul wrote, "Let no one despise your youth, but be an example to the believers in word, in conduct, in love, in spirit, in faith, in purity" (4:12). The letters to Timothy included clear instructions for establishing church order and resolving church disputes.

BREATHE IT IN

The relationship between Paul and Timothy was intimate and emotional. Paul and Timothy traveled together and served together, but what tied them together most closely was that Paul was Timothy's spiritual father. Whether this meant that Paul led Timothy to Christ is unknown. Clearly, though, it meant at least that Paul was his primary discipler. Paul believed that God had placed a unique calling on Timothy's life and had given him a distinct work to complete (see 1 Tim. 1:18). This belief seemed to have driven much of the apostle's interactions with the young pastor. Paul had a fatherly affection and ambition for Timothy.

We know little about Timothy's father, other than he was likely Greek based on Timothy not being circumcised as a child in accordance with the Law. When Paul entered Timothy's life, he seems to have fulfilled a role that was vacant. Paul spoke of this important role as it related to his fatherly affection for the Corinthian believers also: "For though you might have ten thou-

sand instructors in Christ, yet you do not have many fathers; for in Christ Jesus I have begotten you through the gospel" (1 Cor. 4:15). Paul provides a reminder of both the family-like relationship between believers and the importance of earthly fathers.

According to the Pew Research Center, the United States of America has the highest occurrence of single-parent homes in the world, with more than 130 countries included in this study. Almost a quarter of US children under the age of eighteen live with one parent and no other adult (23 percent), more than three times the share of children around the world who do so (7 percent). In the United States, 8 percent of children live with relatives, such as aunts and grandparents, compared with 38 percent of children globally.[1] Among single parents, 28 percent are Black. Although there are many historical, systematic, and individual reasons for this data, the fact remains that there are many Black children who have a gap left by a missing parent in the household. This presents an opportunity for members of the community to step up to surround these children—and all children—with love and support.

These staggering statistics mandate that people, like Paul, who invest time and energy in counseling, encouraging, motivating, and influencing children and teenagers should be celebrated and emulated. Many successful people in America can tell you the story of how someone took a special interest in their development. There are young people in your family, community, and church who need your encouragement, advice, and wisdom. Find at least one young person to walk alongside and mentor. Connect on a weekly phone call to listen to their concerns. Schedule monthly lunches to challenge them face-to-face. Often, the greatest contribution that a parent, teacher, mentor, coach, or pastor can provide to a young person is to believe in them, even when they do not believe in themselves. Be the difference maker in someone's life.

[1] "Almost a Quarter of U.S. Children Live in Single-Parent Homes, More Than in Any Other Country," Pew Research Center, accessed July 21, 2022, https://www.pewresearch.org/wp-content/uploads/2019/12/FT_19.12.12_USsingleParents_map.png?w=640.

THE FIRST EPISTLE OF PAUL TO

TIMOTHY

Greeting

1 Paul, an apostle of Jesus Christ, by the commandment of God our Savior and the Lord Jesus Christ, our hope,

2 To Timothy, a [a]true son in the faith:

[b]Grace, mercy, *and* peace from God our Father and Jesus Christ our Lord.

No Other Doctrine

3 As I urged you [a]when I went into Macedonia—remain in Ephesus that you may charge some [b]that they teach no other doctrine, 4 [a]nor give heed to fables and endless genealogies, which cause disputes rather than godly edification which is in faith. 5 Now [a]the purpose of the commandment is love [b]from a pure heart, *from* a good conscience, and *from* sincere faith, 6 from which some, having strayed, have turned aside to [a]idle talk, 7 desiring to be teachers of the law, understanding neither what they say nor the things which they affirm.

8 But we know that the law *is* [a]good if one uses it lawfully, 9 knowing this: that the law is not made for a righteous person, but for *the* lawless and insubordinate, for *the* ungodly and for sinners, for *the* unholy and profane, for murderers of fathers and murderers of mothers, for manslayers, 10 for fornicators, for sodomites, for kidnappers, for liars, for perjurers, and if there is any other thing that is contrary to sound doctrine, 11 according to the glorious gospel of the [a]blessed God which was [b]committed to my trust.

Glory to God for His Grace

(cf. Acts 8:1–3; 9:1–19)

12 And I thank Christ Jesus our Lord who has [a]enabled me, [b]because He counted me faithful, [c]putting *me* into the ministry, 13 although [a]I was formerly a blasphemer, a persecutor, and an insolent man; but I obtained mercy because [b]I did *it* ignorantly in unbelief. 14 [a]And the grace of our Lord was exceedingly abundant, [b]with faith and love which are in Christ Jesus. 15 [a]This *is* a faithful saying and worthy of all acceptance, that [b]Christ Jesus came into the world to save sinners, of whom I am chief. 16 However, for this reason I obtained mercy, that in me first Jesus Christ might show all longsuffering, as a pattern to those who are going to believe on Him for everlasting life. 17 Now to [a]the King eternal, [b]immortal, [c]invisible, to God [d]who alone is wise,[1] [e]*be* honor and glory forever and ever. Amen.

Fight the Good Fight

18 This charge I commit to you, son Timothy, according to the prophecies previously made concerning you, that by them you may wage the good warfare, 19 having faith and a good conscience, which some having rejected, concerning the faith have suffered shipwreck, 20 of whom are [a]Hymenaeus and [b]Alexander, whom I delivered to Satan that they may learn not to [c]blaspheme.

1:2 [a] Acts 16:1, 2; Rom. 1:7; 2 Tim. 1:2; Titus 1:4 [b] Gal. 1:3 1:3 [a] Acts 20:1, 3 [b] Rom. 16:17; 2 Cor. 11:4; Gal. 1:6, 7; 1 Tim. 6:3 1:4 [a] 1 Tim. 6:3, 4, 20; Titus 1:14 1:5 [a] Rom. 13:8–10; Gal. 5:14 [b] Eph. 6:24 1:6 [a] 1 Tim. 6:4, 20 1:8 [a] Rom. 7:12, 16 1:11 [a] 1 Tim. 6:15 [b] 1 Cor. 9:17 1:12 [a] 1 Cor. 15:10 [b] 1 Cor. 7:25 [c] Col. 1:25 1:13 [a] Acts 8:3; 1 Cor. 15:9 [b] John 4:21 1:14 [a] Rom. 5:20; 1 Cor. 3:10; 2 Cor. 4:15; Gal. 1:13–16 [b] 1 Thess. 1:3; 1 Tim. 2:15; 4:12; 6:11; 2 Tim. 1:13; 2:22; Titus 2:2 1:15 [a] 1 Tim. 3:1; 4:9; 2 Tim. 2:11; Titus 3:8 [b] Is. 53:5; 61:1; Hos. 6:1–3; Matt. 1:21; 9:13 1:17 [a] Ps. 10:16 [b] Rom. 1:23 [c] Heb. 11:27 [d] Rom. 16:27 [e] 1 Chr. 29:11 [1] NU-Text reads *to the only God.* 1:20 [a] 2 Tim. 2:17, 18 [b] 2 Tim. 4:14 [c] Acts 13:45

EXALT HIS MIGHTY NAME

INHALE

I need to work long hours to make ends meet. The time it takes for me to get involved with the church, I could be working more hours, and I certainly can't afford to give 10 percent of my money to the church. I have bills to pay. How can I lift God up with my time and money when it's hard to stand on my own two feet?

EXHALE

Know that you are not alone. There are many others who are struggling to make ends meet every day. But let's not lose sight of who we are and who God is. We have our lives and our breath because of Him. Let us not forget that jobs and opportunities come from God. They are ours only by God's grace.

God wants us to trust that He will take care of us and that our lives are safe in Him. He is so far beyond our usual perception of Him. We cannot buy His favor with time or money. We have it in Christ. If we truly recognize that God is greater than we can conceive and more loving than our finite minds can grasp, then we can trust Him with our entire lives—time, money, and all else is safe in His hands. When this mindset leads us, we grow incredibly in our faith.

You might feel down about your situation right now, but God is the lifter of our heads. When God lifts us up, we stay up! Your situations may not change, but your attitude and outlook will rise heavenward when you contemplate just who God is and how good He is to you. First Timothy 1:17 says, "Now to the King eternal, immortal, invisible, to God who alone is wise, be honor and glory forever and ever. Amen." These are words we can live by! God is outside time and space—He sees all things in proper perspective. His Word says He will care for us at all times, so He will. He always acts perfectly based on His unlimited wisdom. He will never fail to honor His promises. His glory will be revealed in our lives when we trust Him. Put nothing ahead of God! When all else is considered, there is still nothing left but God. Keep Him first place in all things.

Pray for All Men

2 Therefore I exhort first of all that supplications, prayers, intercessions, *and*
giving of thanks be made for all men, 2[a]for
kings and [b]all who are in authority, that we
may lead a quiet and peaceable life in all
godliness and reverence. 3For this *is* [a]good
and acceptable in the sight [b]of God our Savior, 4[a]who desires all men to be saved [b]and
to come to the knowledge of the truth. 5[a]For
there is one God and [b]one Mediator between God and men, *the* Man Christ Jesus,
6[a]who gave Himself a ransom for all, to
be testified in due time, 7[a]for which I was
appointed a preacher and an apostle—I
am speaking the truth in Christ[1] *and* not
lying—[b]a teacher of the Gentiles in faith
and truth.

Men and Women in the Church

8I desire therefore that the men pray
[a]everywhere, [b]lifting up holy hands, without wrath and doubting; 9in like manner
also, that the [a]women adorn themselves in
modest apparel, with propriety and moderation, not with braided hair or gold or
pearls or costly clothing, 10[a]but, which is
proper for women professing godliness,
with good works. 11Let a woman learn in silence with all submission. 12And [a]I do not
permit a woman to teach or to have authority over a man, but to be in silence. 13For

2:2 [a] Ezra 6:10 [b] [Rom. 13:1] 2:3 [a] Rom. 12:2 [b] 2 Tim. 1:9 2:4 [a] Ezek. 18:23, 32; John 3:17; 1 Tim. 4:10; Titus 2:11; 2 Pet. 3:9 [b] [John 17:3] 2:5 [a] 1 Cor. 8:6; Gal. 3:20 [b] [Heb. 9:15] 2:6 [a] Mark 10:45 2:7 [a] Eph. 3:7, 8; 1 Tim. 1:11; 2 Tim. 1:11 [b] [Gal. 1:15, 16] [1] NU-Text omits *in Christ.* 2:8 [a] Luke 23:34 [b] Ps. 134:2 2:9 [a] 1 Pet. 3:3 2:10 [a] 1 Pet. 3:4 2:12 [a] 1 Cor. 14:34; Titus 2:5

#OXYGEN
1 TIMOTHY 2:3-5
Exalt His Mighty Name

Although life can get heavy, stay focused on what is really important. God's heart is for all people to be saved and experience abundant life in Christ. This is what matters. This is ample cause to exalt God and praise His name no matter what life throws our way.

Breathe and **exalt His mighty name.**

Adam was formed first, then Eve. 14And
Adam was not deceived, but the woman being deceived, fell into transgression. 15Nev-
ertheless she will be saved in childbearing
if they continue in faith, love, and holiness,
with self-control.

Qualifications of Overseers

3 This *is* a faithful saying: If a man desires the position of a bishop,[1] he desires a good work. 2A bishop then must be
blameless, the husband of one wife, temperate, sober-minded, of good behavior,
hospitable, able to teach; 3not given to
wine, not violent, not greedy for money,[1]
but gentle, not quarrelsome, not covetous;
4one who rules his own house well, having
his children in submission with all reverence 5(for if a man does not know how to
rule his own house, how will he take care
of the church of God?); 6not a novice, lest
being puffed up with pride he fall into the
same condemnation as the devil. 7More-
over he must have a good testimony among
those who are outside, lest he fall into reproach and the [a]snare of the devil.

Qualifications of Deacons

8Likewise deacons *must be* reverent, not
double-tongued, [a]not given to much wine,
not greedy for money, 9holding the mystery
of the faith with a pure conscience. 10But
let these also first be tested; then let them
serve as deacons, being *found* blameless.
11Likewise, *their* wives *must be* reverent, not
slanderers, temperate, faithful in all things.
12Let deacons be the husbands of one wife,
ruling *their* children and their own houses
well. 13For those who have served well as
deacons [a]obtain for themselves a good
standing and great boldness in the faith
which is in Christ Jesus.

The Great Mystery

14These things I write to you, though I
hope to come to you shortly; 15but if I am
delayed, *I write* so that you may know how
you ought to conduct yourself in the house
of God, which is the church of the living
God, the pillar and ground of the truth.
16And without controversy great is the mystery of godliness:

[a]God[1] was manifested in the flesh,
[b]Justified in the Spirit,
[c]Seen by angels,
[d]Preached among the Gentiles,
[e]Believed on in the world,
[f]Received up in glory.

The Great Apostasy

4 Now the Spirit expressly says that in
latter times some will depart from
the faith, giving heed [a]to deceiving spirits and doctrines of demons, 2[a]speaking
lies in hypocrisy, having their own conscience [b]seared with a hot iron, 3forbidding
to marry, *and commanding* to abstain from
foods which God created to be received
with thanksgiving by those who believe
and know the truth. 4For every creature of
God *is* good, and nothing is to be refused
if it is received with thanksgiving; 5for it is
sanctified by the word of God and prayer.

A Good Servant of Jesus Christ

6If you instruct the brethren in these
things, you will be a good minister of Jesus
Christ, [a]nourished in the words of faith and
of the good doctrine which you have carefully followed. 7But [a]reject profane and old
wives' fables, and [b]exercise yourself toward

3:1 [1] Literally *overseer* 3:3 [1] NU-Text omits *not greedy for money.* 3:7 [a] 1 Tim. 6:9; 2 Tim. 2:26 3:8 [a] Ezek. 44:21 3:13 [a] Matt. 25:21 3:16 [a] [John 1:14; 1 Pet. 1:20; 1 John 1:2; 3:5, 8] [b] [Matt. 3:16; Rom. 1:4] [c] Matt. 28:2 [d] Acts 10:34; Rom. 10:18 [e] Rom. 16:26; 2 Cor. 1:19; Col. 1:6, 23 [f] Luke 24:51 [1] NU-Text reads *Who.* 4:1 [a] 2 Tim. 3:13; Rev. 16:14 4:2 [a] Matt. 7:15 [b] Eph. 4:19 4:6 [a] 2 Tim. 3:14 4:7 [a] 2 Tim. 2:16; Titus 1:14 [b] Heb. 5:14

godliness. 8For [a]bodily exercise profits a little, but godliness is profitable for all things,
[b]having promise of the life that now is and
of that which is to come. 9This *is* a faithful saying and worthy of all acceptance.
10For to this *end* we both labor and suffer
reproach,[1] because we trust in the living
God, [a]who is *the* Savior of all men, especially of those who believe. 11These things
command and teach.

Take Heed to Your Ministry

12Let no one despise your youth, but be
an [a]example to the believers in word, in
conduct, in love, in spirit,[1] in faith, in purity. 13Till I come, give attention to reading, to exhortation, to doctrine. 14[a]Do not
neglect the gift that is in you, which was
given to you by prophecy [b]with the laying
on of the hands of the eldership. 15Meditate
on these things; give yourself entirely to
them, that your progress may be evident
to all. 16Take heed to yourself and to the
doctrine. Continue in them, for in doing
this you will save both yourself and those
who hear you.

Treatment of Church Members

5 Do not rebuke an older man, but exhort *him* as a father, younger men
as brothers, 2older women as mothers,
younger women as sisters, with all purity.

Honor True Widows

3Honor widows who are really widows.
4But if any widow has children or grandchildren, let them first learn to show piety
at home and [a]to repay their parents; for
this is good and[1] acceptable before God.
5Now she who is really a widow, and left

---

1 TIMOTHY 4:12

I AM TIMOTHY

Let no one despise your youth, but be an example to the believers in word, in conduct, in love, in spirit, in faith, in purity. 1 Timothy 4:12

I am Timothy. I was a Greek man brought up in the faith of Jesus Christ by my Jewish mother, Eunice, and grandmother, Lois. I became pastor of the church at Ephesus.

As a young man, I traveled with Paul and Silas on some of their many journeys. Like them, I was committed to bringing the message of Jesus Christ to everyone. To give no opportunity for offense to those I ministered to, I allowed myself to be circumcised. As a result, the religious leaders were more likely to accept me as a teacher to the Jews.

Paul later sent me in his place to Thessalonica to establish the church there and encourage the believers in their faith. I was exceedingly blessed that he referred to me as his son in the Lord and wrote two letters to me that are now included in the New Testament. He taught me many things; he taught me that maturity in Christ is not based on age, assuring me that I should not hold back from teaching others because of my youth. He also warned me to expect hardships in my pursuit of being a good soldier for Christ. He faithfully taught me so that I would be adequately prepared for the calling God had placed on my life.

†

Paul and Timothy are the biblical model of mentorship. If at all possible, everyone should be both a mentor and a mentee to another sister or brother. God has placed in all our lives someone from whom we can learn, as well as someone who can learn from us. In addition, every Christian would benefit from having at least one study partner with whom they can dig into the Word of God. The study of God's Word should be a priority focus on a daily basis.

4:8 [a] 1 Cor. 8:8 [b] Ps. 37:9 4:10 [a] Ps. 36:6 [1] NU-Text reads *we labor and strive.* 4:12 [a] Phil. 3:17; Titus 2:7; 1 Pet. 5:3 [1] NU-Text omits *in spirit.* 4:14 [a] 2 Tim. 1:6 [b] Acts 6:6; 1 Tim. 5:22 5:4 [a] Gen. 45:10 [1] NU-Text and M-Text omit *good and.*

alone, trusts in God and continues in supplications and prayers [a]night and day. 6But
she who lives in pleasure is dead while she
lives. 7And these things command, that
they may be blameless. 8But if anyone does
not provide for his own, [a]and especially
for those of his household, [b]he has denied
the faith [c]and is worse than an unbeliever.
9Do not let a widow under sixty years old
be taken into the number, *and not unless*
she has been the wife of one man, 10well reported for good works: if she has brought
up children, if she has lodged strangers, if
she has washed the saints' feet, if she has
relieved the afflicted, if she has diligently
followed every good work.

#OXYGEN

1 TIMOTHY 5:6

Exalt His Mighty Name

The world offers many things that claim to bring us to an exalted state. However, no worldly gain has any eternal worth, and many lead to death. Only the things of God's kingdom are everlasting and life-giving. Only He can fill our senses and enable us to find true satisfaction. Only He should be lifted high in our hearts and minds.

Breathe and exalt His mighty name.

11But refuse *the* younger widows; for
when they have begun to grow wanton
against Christ, they desire to marry, 12hav-
ing condemnation because they have cast
off their first faith. 13And besides they learn
to be idle, wandering about from house
to house, and not only idle but also gos-
sips and busybodies, saying things which
they ought not. 14Therefore I desire that
the younger *widows* marry, bear children,
manage the house, give no opportunity to
the adversary to speak reproachfully. 15For
some have already turned aside after Satan. 16If any believing man or[1] woman has
widows, let them relieve them, and do not
let the church be burdened, that it may relieve those who are really widows.

Honor the Elders

17Let the elders who rule well be counted
worthy of double honor, especially those
who labor in the word and doctrine. 18For
the Scripture says, [a]"You shall not muzzle
an ox while it treads out the grain,"[1] and,
[b]"The laborer *is* worthy of his wages."[2] 19Do
not receive an accusation against an elder except [a]from two or three witnesses.
20Those who are sinning rebuke in the presence of all, that the rest also may fear.
21I charge *you* before God and the Lord
Jesus Christ and the elect angels that you
observe these things without [a]prejudice,
doing nothing with partiality. 22Do not
lay hands on anyone hastily, nor [a]share
in other people's sins; keep yourself pure.
23No longer drink only water, but use a
little wine for your stomach's sake and your
frequent infirmities.
24Some men's sins are [a]clearly evident,
preceding *them* to judgment, but those of
some *men* follow later. 25Likewise, the good
works *of some* are clearly evident, and those
that are otherwise cannot be hidden.

Honor Masters

6 Let as many [a]bondservants as are under the yoke count their own masters
worthy of all honor, so that the name of
God and *His* doctrine may not be blasphemed. 2And those who have believing
masters, let them not despise *them* because they are brethren, but rather serve
them because those who are benefited are
believers and beloved. Teach and exhort
these things.

Error and Greed

3If anyone teaches otherwise and does
not consent to [a]wholesome words, *even* the
words of our Lord Jesus Christ, [b]and to the
doctrine which accords with godliness, 4he
is proud, knowing nothing, but is obsessed
with disputes and arguments over words,
from which come envy, strife, reviling, evil
suspicions, 5useless wranglings[1] of men of

5:5 [a] Acts 26:7 5:8 [a] Is. 58:7; 2 Cor. 12:14 [b] 2 Tim. 3:5 [c] Matt. 18:17 5:16 [1] NU-Text omits *man or.* 5:18 [a] Deut. 25:4; 1 Cor. 9:7–9 [b] Lev. 19:13; Deut. 24:15; Matt. 10:10; Luke 10:7; 1 Cor. 9:14 [1] Deuteronomy 25:4 [2] Luke 10:7 5:19 [a] Deut. 17:6; 19:15; Matt. 18:16 5:21 [a] Deut. 1:17 5:22 [a] Eph. 5:6, 7; 2 John 11 5:24 [a] Gal. 5:19–21 6:1 [a] Eph. 6:5; Titus 2:9; 1 Pet. 2:18 6:3 [a] 2 Tim. 1:13 [b] Titus 1:1 6:5 [1] NU-Text and M-Text read *constant friction.*

RELEASE // EXALT HIS MIGHTY NAME

God over Money

1 Timothy 6:17 // Command those who are rich in this present age not to be haughty, nor to trust in uncertain riches but in the living God, who gives us richly all things to enjoy.

Summary Message // It is easy to claim that God is Lord over our money, but it is not as easy to live it out. We live in a consumeristic culture where new possessions are constantly pushed on us as what we need or will make us successful and happy. If we look at our bank accounts and how we spend our money, we might find that God is not Lord over our money but that our money might be our god.

First Timothy 6 makes it clear, though, that if we exalt God over our money and possessions, we will have the life of truth, purpose, and contentment that we long for. Paul's words encourage us to find these things in godliness, not in the world's riches. He reminds us that we brought nothing into this world, and we will not take anything with us out of it. He warns us that chasing after riches can bring us all kinds of trouble. Money is not mighty. God is. Our money can let us down and quickly disappear. We cannot trust it, although we so often want to try. Even the dollars themselves remind us of this truth, though, with the words "In God We Trust" printed on each bill.

Practical Application // You are rich. It might not seem that way, but you are most likely in the top 10 percent of the wealthiest people on this planet. You likely have amenities that billions of people do not: heat, running water, Wi-Fi, a vehicle. You probably ate at a restaurant recently. You likely have multiple sets of clothing, perhaps some items you have not worn in years. These are all luxuries we take for granted. Most of the people on the planet, though, do without them. Knowing this might reframe how you read 1 Timothy 6:17. This verse actually speaks to us when it refers to those who are rich in this present day. It warns us not to trust in our money because it is uncertain. Our economy fluctuates frequently. We watch as the value of stocks, cryptocurrency, real estate, and assets prove vulnerable to inflation. If you put your hope in your bank account, you are always one economic downturn away from disappointment. But even if you have a healthy bank account that can withstand economic fluctuations, this does not mean you will be content. There will always be more expensive toys you can buy. Someone will always have more than you do. And even if you have all you want, you will find that none of it provides true joy.

God wants us to enjoy what He has given us, but He also wants us to learn to trust Him and live generously. First Timothy 6:18 tells us to do good works with our resources, giving to, sharing with, and loving our neighbors. This will give us an eternal return on investment (ROI) that is much greater than any earthly investment could yield. Do a personal audit and determine if God is really Lord over your money.

Fervent Prayer // Heavenly Father, we thank You for all Your blessings. Forgive us for the times we take for granted the resources and opportunities You have given us. Your Word tells us that when much is given, much is required. Help us to be good managers of the money You allow us to hold. Teach us not to hold on too tightly and always to remember our possessions are temporary. Give us wisdom to use our resources in ways that best serve Your eternal purposes. Help us develop true contentment in every season, whether we have a little or an overflow. In Jesus' name we pray. Amen.

corrupt minds and destitute of the truth,
who suppose that godliness is a *means of*
gain. From [a]such withdraw yourself.[2]
6Now godliness with [a]contentment
is great gain. 7For we brought nothing
into *this* world, *and it is* [a]certain[1] we can
carry nothing out. 8And having food and
clothing, with these we shall be [a]content.
9But those who desire to be rich fall into
temptation and a snare, and *into* many
foolish and harmful lusts which drown
men in destruction and perdition. 10For
the love of money is a root of all *kinds of*
evil, for which some have strayed from the

6:5 [a] 2 Tim. 3:5 [2] NU-Text omits this sentence. 6:6 [a] Phil. 4:11; Heb. 13:5 6:7 [a] Job 1:21; Ps. 49:17; Eccl. 5:15 [1] NU-Text omits *and it is certain.* 6:8 [a] Prov. 30:8, 9

faith in their greediness, and pierced themselves through with many sorrows.

The Good Confession

11But you, O man of God, flee these things
and pursue righteousness, godliness, faith,
love, patience, gentleness. 12Fight the good
fight of faith, lay hold on eternal life, to
which you were also called and have confessed the good confession in the presence
of many witnesses. 13I urge you in the sight
of God who gives life to all things, and *be-*
fore Christ Jesus [a]who witnessed the good
confession before Pontius Pilate, 14that
you keep *this* commandment without spot,
blameless until our Lord Jesus Christ's appearing, 15which He will manifest in His
own time, *He who is* the blessed and only
Potentate, the King of kings and Lord of
lords, 16who alone has immortality, dwelling in [a]unapproachable light, [b]whom no
man has seen or can see, to whom *be* honor
and everlasting power. Amen.

Instructions to the Rich

17Command those who are rich in this
present age not to be haughty, nor to trust
in uncertain [a]riches but in the living God,
who gives us richly all things [b]to enjoy.
18*Let them* do good, that they be rich in
good works, ready to give, willing to share,
19[a]storing up for themselves a good foundation for the time to come, that they may
lay hold on eternal life.

Guard the Faith

20O Timothy! [a]Guard what was committed to your trust, [b]avoiding the profane *and*
idle babblings and contradictions of what is
falsely called knowledge— 21by professing
it some have strayed concerning the faith.

Grace *be* with you. Amen.

6:13 [a] Matt. 27:2; John 18:36, 37 6:16 [a] Dan. 2:22 [b] John 6:46 6:17 [a] Jer. 9:23; 48:7 [b] Eccl. 5:18, 19 6:19 [a] [Matt. 6:20, 21; 19:21] 6:20 [a] [2 Tim. 1:12, 14] [b] Titus 1:14

THE SECOND EPISTLE OF PAUL TO

TIMOTHY

OVERVIEW

Paul wrote 1 Timothy shortly after being released from his first Roman incarceration and while the young pastor was serving the church at Ephesus. A few years later, he wrote this second letter to his young protégé under more dire circumstances.

Paul was again a prisoner of Rome, but his condition was worse than during his initial confinement. Under Emperor Nero, Christian persecution had become more prevalent and brutal. Paul now anticipated his death and martyrdom, indicated by what he wrote to Timothy: "For I am already being poured out as a drink offering, and the time of my departure is at hand. I have fought the good fight, I have finished the race, I have kept the faith" (2 Tim. 4:6–7). Meanwhile, Timothy had been replaced as the overseer of the church at Ephesus, yet he had remained in the area. Paul wanted to see Timothy, so he sent Tychicus to Ephesus (see 4:9, 12). With Tychicus in the region, Timothy was free to come to Paul's aid in Rome, where he had been abandoned by Demas. Only Luke remained by the aged apostle's side.

In what appeared to be the waning moments of their close relationship on earth, Paul urged Timothy to continue in the faith. He used this occasion to address Timothy's anxiety and urged him to press forward despite the hindrances and suffering caused by each of their circumstances. Paul appealed to Timothy's inner character: "I call to remembrance the genuine faith that is in you, which dwelt first in your grandmother Lois and your mother Eunice, and I am persuaded is in you also. Therefore, I remind you to stir up the gift of God which is in you through the laying on of my hands" (1:5–6). Because of this great faith heritage enjoyed first by his mother, Eunice, Timothy had what was needed to forge ahead with the ministry of Jesus Christ.

Many people had abandoned "sound doctrine" (4:3) during this time of persecution and widespread false teaching. But Paul told Timothy to "hold fast the pattern of sound words which you have heard from me, in faith and love which are in Christ Jesus. That good thing which was committed to you, keep by the Holy Spirit who dwells in us" (1:13–14). Sound doctrine would carry Timothy through any time of difficulty.

BREATHE IT IN

In Paul's final letter to Timothy, he recalled their pained farewell the last time they had seen each other (see 1:4). When Paul had departed from Timothy and some others, "they all wept freely, and fell on Paul's neck and kissed him, sorrowing most of all for the words which he spoke, that they would see his face no more" (Acts 20:37–38). Though the future was fraught with turmoil, uncertainty, and danger, Paul encouraged Timothy to move forward with courage: "For God has not given us a spirit of fear, but of power and of love and of a sound mind" (2 Tim. 1:7). Sorrow is a heartfelt emotion, but we must not let it be a barrier to kingdom service. One can grieve with hope, strength, and determination.

Yet, fear and anxiety can be overwhelming emotions that stifle us from acting in the way God intends. When they prevent us from acting in faith, we will not realize the power of love and of

a strong mind that God has given us. As such, fear and anxiety can cripple our walk with God and our service to Him, harming not only us but others.

When confronted by overwhelming fear and anxiety, we can respond with either cowardice or courage. Cowardice is considering oneself above all else. A coward is one who acts disgracefully in the presence of fear, motivated by an intense sense of self-preservation. Courage, on the other hand, is strength in the face of threat, pain, or grief. It is the ability to act with valor despite fear, difficulty, and danger.

Paul and Timothy were as close as spiritual father and son. For Timothy to lose his father figure and his spiritual mentor must have been traumatic. But Timothy, with Paul's admonishment, knew that his ministry and calling must continue and that it was ultimately not Paul that he was following; it was Christ's calling. It is important to note that Paul did not puff up his role in Timothy's success but encouraged his absence as an opportunity for Timothy to rise to all he was meant to be. It takes courage to acknowledge that we are obsolete and pass all that we worked for on to the next generation. Remember that David set his son Solomon up for success in building the temple to the Lord even though it was David's dream to build the temple himself.

As believers, we have the ability to muster such courage because we know that Christ is with us, guiding us and strengthening us, and because we know that all we are and have is because of Christ. There is a point in our lives when we should turn our focus and actions toward setting up the next generation for success. But we can only do that when we recognize that we are not the only valuable piece of the puzzle that God has created.

THE SECOND EPISTLE OF PAUL TO

TIMOTHY

Greeting

1 Paul, an apostle of Jesus Christ[1] by the
will of God, according to the [a]promise
of life which is in Christ Jesus,

2To Timothy, a [a]beloved son:

Grace, mercy, *and* peace from God the
Father and Christ Jesus our Lord.

Timothy's Faith and Heritage

3I thank God, whom I serve with a pure
conscience, as *my* [a]forefathers *did,* as without ceasing I remember you in my prayers
night and day, 4greatly desiring to see you,
being mindful of your tears, that I may
be filled with joy, 5when I call to remembrance [a]the genuine faith that is in you,
which dwelt first in your grandmother Lois
and [b]your mother Eunice, and I am persuaded is in you also. 6Therefore I remind
you [a]to stir up the gift of God which is in
you through the laying on of my hands.
7For [a]God has not given us a spirit of fear,
[b]but of power and of love and of a sound
mind.

Not Ashamed of the Gospel

8[a]Therefore do not be ashamed of [b]the
testimony of our Lord, nor of me [c]His
prisoner, but share with me in the sufferings for the gospel according to the power
of God, 9who has saved us and called *us*
with a holy calling, [a]not according to our
works, but [b]according to His own purpose
and grace which was given to us in Christ
Jesus [c]before time began, 10but [a]has now
been revealed by the appearing of our
Savior Jesus Christ, *who* has abolished
death and brought life and immortality
to light through the gospel, 11[a]to which I
was appointed a preacher, an apostle, and
a teacher of the Gentiles.[1] 12For this reason
I also suffer these things; nevertheless I
am not ashamed, [a]for I know whom I have
believed and am persuaded that He is able
to keep what I have committed to Him until that Day.

Be Loyal to the Faith

13[a]Hold fast [b]the pattern of [c]sound words
which you have heard from me, in faith and
love which are in Christ Jesus. 14That good
thing which was committed to you, keep by
the Holy Spirit who dwells in us.

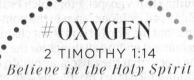

#OXYGEN

2 TIMOTHY 1:14

Believe in the Holy Spirit

The Holy Spirit was given to us as a comforter, helper, guide, and reminder of every teaching of Jesus. He dwells within those who call Jesus Savior. He is closer than your next breath and will never fail to lead you closer to the Father's heart. Only listen and believe.

Breathe and **believe in the Holy Spirit.**

1:1 [a] Titus 1:2 [1] NU-Text and M-Text read *Christ Jesus.* 1:2 [a] 1 Tim. 1:2; 2 Tim. 2:1; Titus 1:4 1:3 [a] Acts 24:14 1:5 [a] 1 Tim. 1:5; 4:6 [b] Acts 16:1 1:6 [a] 1 Tim. 4:14 1:7 [a] John 14:27; Rom. 8:15; 1 John 4:18 [b] [Acts 1:8] 1:8 [a] [Mark 8:38; Luke 9:26; Rom. 1:16]; 2 Tim. 1:12, 16 [b] 1 Tim. 2:6 [c] Eph. 3:1; 2 Tim. 1:16 1:9 [a] [Rom. 3:20]; Eph. 2:8, 9 [b] Rom. 8:28 [c] Rom. 16:25; Eph. 1:4; Titus 1:2 1:10 [a] Eph. 1:9 1:11 [a] Acts 9:15 [1] NU-Text omits *of the Gentiles.* 1:12 [a] 1 Pet. 4:19 1:13 [a] 2 Tim. 3:14; Titus 1:9 [b] Rom. 2:20; 6:17 [c] 1 Tim. 6:3

15 This you know, that all those in Asia
have turned away from me, among whom
are Phygellus and Hermogenes. 16 The Lord
grant mercy to the [a]household of Onesiph-
orus, for he often refreshed me, and was
not ashamed of my chain; 17 but when he
arrived in Rome, he sought me out very
zealously and found *me.* 18 The Lord [a]grant
to him that he may find mercy from the
Lord [b]in that Day—and you know very well
how many ways he [c]ministered *to me*[1] at
Ephesus.

Be Strong in Grace

2 You therefore, [a]my son, [b]be strong in
the grace that is in Christ Jesus. 2 And
the things that you have heard from me
among many witnesses, commit these
to faithful men who will be able to teach
others also. 3 You therefore must [a]endure[1]
hardship [b]as a good soldier of Jesus Christ.
4 [a]No one engaged in warfare entangles
himself with the affairs of *this* life, that
he may please him who enlisted him as a
soldier. 5 And also [a]if anyone competes in
athletics, he is not crowned unless he competes according to the rules. 6 The hard-
working farmer must be first to partake of
the crops. 7 Consider what I say, and may[1]
the Lord [a]give you understanding in all
things.

8 Remember that Jesus Christ, [a]of the
seed of David, [b]was raised from the dead
[c]according to my gospel, 9 [a]for which I suffer
trouble as an evildoer, [b]*even* to the point of
chains; [c]but the word of God is not chained.
10 Therefore [a]I endure all things for the sake
of the elect, [b]that they also may obtain the
salvation which is in Christ Jesus with eternal glory.

11 *This is* a faithful saying:

For [a]if we died with *Him,*
We shall also live with *Him.*
12 [a]If we endure,
We shall also reign with *Him.*
[b]If we deny *Him,*
He also will deny us.
13 If we are faithless,
He remains faithful;
He [a]cannot deny Himself.

Approved and Disapproved Workers

14 Remind *them* of these things, [a]charging
them before the Lord not to strive about
words to no profit, to the ruin of the hearers. 15 [a]Be diligent to present yourself approved to God, a worker who does not need
to be ashamed, rightly dividing the word
of truth. 16 But shun profane *and* idle babblings, for they will increase to more ungodliness. 17 And their message will spread
like cancer. [a]Hymenaeus and Philetus are
of this sort, 18 who have strayed concerning
the truth, [a]saying that the resurrection is
already past; and they overthrow the faith
of some. 19 Nevertheless [a]the solid foundation of God stands, having this seal: "The
Lord [b]knows those who are His," and, "Let
everyone who names the name of Christ[1]
depart from iniquity."

20 But in a great house there are not
only [a]vessels of gold and silver, but also
of wood and clay, some for honor and
some for dishonor. 21 Therefore if anyone cleanses himself from the latter, he
will be a vessel for honor, sanctified and
useful for the Master, [a]prepared for every
good work. 22 [a]Flee also youthful lusts; but
pursue righteousness, faith, love, peace
with those who call on the Lord out of a
pure heart. 23 But avoid foolish and ignorant disputes, knowing that they generate
strife. 24 And [a]a servant of the Lord must
not quarrel but be gentle to all, [b]able to
teach, [c]patient, 25 [a]in humility correcting
those who are in opposition, [b]if God perhaps will grant them repentance, [c]so that
they may know the truth, 26 and *that* they
may come to their senses *and* [a]*escape* the
snare of the devil, having been taken captive by him to *do* his will.

1:16 [a] 2 Tim. 4:19 **1:18** [a] Matt. 6:4; Mark 9:41 [b] 2 Thess. 1:10 [c] Heb. 6:10 [1] *To me* is from the Vulgate and a few Greek manuscripts. **2:1** [a] 1 Tim. 1:2 [b] Eph. 6:10 **2:3** [a] 2 Tim. 4:5 [b] 1 Cor. 9:7; 1 Tim. 1:18 [1] NU-Text reads *You must share.* **2:4** [a] [2 Pet. 2:20] **2:5** [a] [1 Cor. 9:25] **2:7** [a] Prov. 2:6 [1] NU-Text reads *the Lord will give you.* **2:8** [a] Rom. 1:3, 4 [b] 1 Cor. 15:4 [c] Rom. 2:16 **2:9** [a] Acts 9:16 [b] Eph. 3:1 [c] Acts 28:31; [2 Tim. 4:17] **2:10** [a] Eph. 3:13 [b] 2 Cor. 1:6; 1 Thess. 5:9 **2:11** [a] Rom. 6:5, 8; 1 Thess. 5:10 **2:12** [a] [Matt. 19:28]; Luke 22:29; [Rom. 5:17; 8:17] [b] Matt. 10:33; Luke 12:9; 1 Tim. 5:8 **2:13** [a] Num. 23:19; Titus 1:2 **2:14** [a] 1 Tim. 5:21; 6:4; 2 Tim. 2:23; Titus 3:9 **2:15** [a] 1 Tim. 4:13; 2 Pet. 1:10 **2:17** [a] 1 Tim. 1:20 **2:18** [a] 1 Cor. 15:12 **2:19** [a] Matt. 24:24; [1 Cor. 3:11] [b] Num. 16:5; [Nah. 1:7]; John 10:14, 27 [1] NU-Text and M-Text read *the Lord.* **2:20** [a] Rom. 9:21 **2:21** [a] 2 Cor. 9:8; [Eph. 2:10]; 2 Tim. 3:17 **2:22** [a] 1 Tim. 6:11 **2:24** [a] Titus 3:2 [b] Titus 1:9 [c] 1 Tim. 3:3; Titus 1:7 **2:25** [a] Gal. 6:1; Titus 3:2; 1 Pet. 3:15 [b] Acts 8:22 [c] 1 Tim. 2:4 **2:26** [a] 1 Tim. 3:7

RELEASE // BELIEVE IN THE HOLY SPIRIT

Never Alone

2 Timothy 3:14–15 // But you must continue in the things which you have learned and been assured of, knowing from whom you have learned them, and that from childhood you have known the Holy Scriptures, which are able to make you wise for salvation through faith which is in Christ Jesus.

Summary Message // God giving us someone with a desire to help us live according to His desires is truly a blessing. In 2 Timothy, the apostle Paul reminded Timothy that God had first given him his grandmother and mother (see 1:5) to fulfill this role. Now, Paul helped fill this role for Timothy, a young leader who oversaw a challenging ministry. But beyond even these good provisions, God had given Timothy the ever-present Holy Spirit (see 1:14) and the Holy Scriptures. Paul wanted his friend and co-laborer in the gospel to know that he was not alone. He encouraged Timothy to remember that the obstacles awaiting him in the future were no match for the power, love, and wisdom God makes available to him through the Holy Spirit and His Word. The same is true for us. So, the question is, will we rely on our own abilities, or will we embrace the gift of the Holy Spirit to achieve even greater things?

Practical Application // Have you ever faced what felt like an insurmountable task? Maybe it was a job or project you felt insecure or ill-prepared to complete. The fear we feel in these moments can be paralyzing. However, Scripture reveals that God never leaves us alone. He surrounds us with fellow believers to encourage us. He has given us His perfect Scriptures to guide us. And He has given us the "Helper," the Holy Spirit, who will help us overcome even the most insurmountable of obstacles (John 14:26–27; 16:7–8). It is by the power of the Holy Spirit that we can understand the Scriptures and recognize godly encouragement from others. And it is by the power of the Holy Spirit that God has made peace, power, and perspective supernaturally available to us—if we would only believe.

The Book of 2 Timothy was a letter written by the apostle Paul to a dear friend and young colleague. Paul understood the obstacles Timothy would undoubtedly face in the weeks, months, and years ahead of him. As encouragement, Paul reminded Timothy that he was not alone in the fight. Even though Paul would not be there in person to support him, Timothy had someone even greater on his side who would help him face and get through any seeming impossibility: the Holy Spirit. What does this mean for us?

- We are never alone. Even though Christ is not here with us in the flesh, He sent us the Holy Spirit, who makes Christ's heart and desires known to us as He also comforts us in our times of need (see 2 Cor. 1:3–4).
- The Holy Spirit is our enabler and advocate (see Rom. 8:26). Put another way, the Holy Spirit is our bridge to align with God's will and tap into God's power even when the odds seem to be stacked against us.
- The Holy Spirit frees us from fear and empowers us to face our greatest challenges confidently, knowing that God's power, love, and wisdom are greater than anything we will encounter in this life.

We do not have to go it alone! In fact, we should not. Living in our own strength is actually weakness because we should be leaning on God's strength instead. The burden of shouldering the responsibility of being successful is not ours to carry. We can breathe easier as we embrace the Holy Spirit's invitation to lean on Him especially when things are beyond our abilities.

Fervent Prayer // God, we thank You for being so intentional. You knew that we would need help to live as Jesus has called us to through His ultimate sacrifice. We confess that we can sometimes be easily distracted, both by the situations we face and our abilities to achieve and overcome them. We ask You to continue reminding us, especially when we feel stuck and unable to move forward, that the Holy Spirit is with us. Indeed, You have not left us or forsaken us, nor will You ever. Thank You. In Jesus' name we pray. Amen.

Perilous Times and Perilous Men

3 But know this, that [a]in the last days perilous times will come: 2For men will
be lovers of themselves, lovers of money,
boasters, proud, blasphemers, disobedient to parents, unthankful, unholy, 3un-
loving, unforgiving, slanderers, without
self-control, brutal, despisers of good,
4[a]traitors, headstrong, haughty, lovers of
pleasure rather than lovers of God, 5[a]hav-
ing a form of godliness but [b]denying its
power. And [c]from such people turn away!
6For [a]of this sort are those who creep into
households and make captives of gullible
women loaded down with sins, led away by
various lusts, 7always learning and never
able [a]to come to the knowledge of the truth.
8[a]Now as Jannes and Jambres resisted Moses, so do these also resist the truth: [b]men
of corrupt minds, [c]disapproved concerning the faith; 9but they will progress no
further, for their folly will be manifest to
all, [a]as theirs also was.

The Man of God and the Word of God

10[a]But you have carefully followed my
doctrine, manner of life, purpose, faith,
longsuffering, love, perseverance, 11per-
secutions, afflictions, which happened to
me [a]at Antioch, [b]at Iconium, [c]at Lystra—
what persecutions I endured. And [d]out
of *them* all the Lord delivered me. 12Yes,
and [a]all who desire to live godly in Christ
Jesus will suffer persecution. 13[a]But evil
men and impostors will grow worse and
worse, deceiving and being deceived. 14But
you must [a]continue in the things which you
have learned and been assured of, knowing
from whom you have learned *them,* 15and
that from childhood you have known [a]the
Holy Scriptures, which are able to make
you wise for salvation through faith which
is in Christ Jesus.
16[a]All Scripture *is* given by inspiration
of God, [b]and *is* profitable for doctrine, for
reproof, for correction, for instruction in
righteousness, 17[a]that the man of God may
be complete, [b]thoroughly equipped for every good work.

Preach the Word

4 I [a]charge *you* therefore before God and
the Lord Jesus Christ, [b]who will judge
the living and the dead at[1] His appearing
and His kingdom: 2Preach the word! Be
ready in season *and* out of season. [a]Con-
vince, [b]rebuke, [c]exhort, with all longsuffering and teaching. 3[a]For the time will come
when they will not endure [b]sound doctrine, [c]but according to their own desires,
because they have itching ears, they will
heap up for themselves teachers; 4and they
will turn *their* ears away from the truth,
and [a]be turned aside to fables. 5But you
be watchful in all things, [a]endure afflictions, do the work of [b]an evangelist, fulfill
your ministry.

Paul's Valedictory

6For [a]I am already being poured out as
a drink offering, and the time of [b]my departure is at hand. 7[a]I have fought the good
fight, I have finished the race, I have kept
the faith. 8Finally, there is laid up for me
[a]the crown of righteousness, which the
Lord, the righteous [b]Judge, will give to me
[c]on that Day, and not to me only but also to
all who have loved His appearing.

The Abandoned Apostle

9Be diligent to come to me quickly; 10for
[a]Demas has forsaken me, [b]having loved this
present world, and has departed for Thessalonica—Crescens for Galatia, Titus for
Dalmatia. 11Only Luke is with me. Get [a]Mark
and bring him with you, for he is useful to
me for ministry. 12And [a]Tychicus I have sent
to Ephesus. 13Bring the cloak that I left with
Carpus at Troas when you come—and the
books, especially the parchments.
14[a]Alexander the coppersmith did me
much harm. May the Lord repay him

3:1 [a] 1 Tim. 4:1; 2 Pet. 3:3; 1 John 2:18; Jude 17, 18 3:4 [a] 2 Pet. 2:10 3:5 [a] Titus 1:16 [b] 1 Tim. 5:8 [c] Matt. 23:3; 2 Thess. 3:6; 1 Tim. 6:5 3:6 [a] Matt. 23:14; Titus 1:11 3:7 [a] 1 Tim. 2:4 3:8 [a] Ex. 7:11, 12, 22; 8:7; 9:11 [b] 1 Tim. 6:5 [c] Rom. 1:28 3:9 [a] Ex. 7:11, 12; 8:18; 9:11 3:10 [a] Phil. 2:20, 22; 1 Tim. 4:6 3:11 [a] Acts 13:44–52 [b] Acts 14:1–6, 19 [c] Acts 14:8–20 [d] Ps. 34:19 3:12 [a] [Ps. 34:19] 3:13 [a] 2 Thess. 2:11 3:14 [a] 2 Tim. 1:13; Titus 1:9 3:15 [a] Ps. 119:97–104; John 5:39 3:16 [a] [2 Pet. 1:20] [b] Rom. 4:23; 15:4 3:17 [a] 1 Tim. 6:11 [b] 2 Tim. 2:21; Heb. 13:21 4:1 [a] 1 Tim. 5:21; 2 Tim. 4:1 [b] Acts 10:42 [1] NU-Text omits *therefore* and reads *and by* for *at.* 4:2 [a] Titus 2:15 [b] 1 Tim. 5:20; Titus 1:13; 2:15 [c] 1 Tim. 4:13 4:3 [a] 2 Tim. 3:1 [b] 1 Tim. 1:10; 2 Tim. 1:13 [c] Is. 30:9–11; Jer. 5:30, 31; 2 Tim. 3:6 4:4 [a] 1 Tim. 1:4 4:5 [a] 2 Tim. 1:8 [b] Acts 21:8 4:6 [a] Phil. 2:17 [b] [Phil. 1:23]; 2 Pet. 1:14 4:7 [a] 1 Cor. 9:24–27; Phil. 3:13, 14 4:8 [a] [1 Cor. 9:25; 2 Tim. 2:5]; James 1:12 [b] John 5:22 [c] 2 Tim. 1:12 4:10 [a] Col. 4:14; Philem. 24 [b] 1 John 2:15 4:11 [a] Acts 12:12, 25; 15:37–39; Col. 4:10 4:12 [a] Acts 20:4; Eph. 6:21, 22; Col. 4:7; Titus 3:12 4:14 [a] Acts 19:33; 1 Tim. 1:20

according to his works. 15You also must
beware of him, for he has greatly resisted
our words.

16At my first defense no one stood with
me, but all forsook me. [a]May it not be
charged against them.

The Lord Is Faithful

17[a]But the Lord stood with me and
strengthened me, [b]so that the message
might be preached fully through me,
and *that* all the Gentiles might hear. Also
I was delivered [c]out of the mouth of the
lion. 18[a]And the Lord will deliver me from
every evil work and preserve *me* for His
heavenly kingdom. [b]To Him *be* glory forever and ever. Amen!

Come Before Winter

19Greet [a]Prisca and Aquila, and the
household of [b]Onesiphorus. 20[a]Erastus
stayed in Corinth, but [b]Trophimus I have
left in Miletus sick.

21Do your utmost to come before winter.
Eubulus greets you, as well as Pudens,
Linus, Claudia, and all the brethren.

Farewell

22The Lord Jesus Christ[1] be with your
spirit. Grace be with you. Amen.

---

2 TIMOTHY 4:10

I AM TITUS

For Demas has forsaken me, having loved this present world, and has departed for Thessalonica—Crescens for Galatia, Titus for Dalmatia. 2 Timothy 4:10

I am Titus, a Greek Christian who ministered alongside Paul. A good part of my ministry focused on the churches at Corinth and Crete.

While traveling with Paul, we found ourselves on Crete, a large island off the coast of Greece. Paul assigned me to this area because there was trouble with disorder and dissension in the church. The Cretan people were attached to the Greek gods that were part of their culture. Often, it seemed the church attempted to merge those gods and teachings of their old culture with the deity and teachings of Jesus. Many of the leaders of the church in Crete were corrupt—only interested in what they could gain through their positions. My tasks were to spread the message of hope through the Messiah, Jesus Christ, separate His message from those of the Greek gods, and appoint godly leaders. We knew that once the Cretans saw true Christianity in action through lives of integrity, kindness, and love, they would turn from their false gods and sinful ways to the Lord.

†

How we live as Christians matters. We are ambassadors of Christ. This means we represent Him to the world; we are called to be His hands and feet wherever we go. When the world sees us, they should see Him. What we do to benefit the world will be credited to Him. If we live and love like Jesus, the world will know who He is.

4:16 [a] Acts 7:60; [1 Cor. 13:5] 4:17 [a] Deut. 31:6; Acts 23:11 [b] Acts 9:15; Phil. 1:12 [c] 1 Sam. 17:37; Ps. 22:21 4:18 [a] Ps. 121:7; [2 Pet. 2:9] [b] Rom. 11:36; Gal. 1:5; Heb. 13:21; 2 Pet. 3:18 4:19 [a] Acts 18:2; Rom. 16:3 [b] 2 Tim. 1:16 4:20 [a] Acts 19:22; Rom. 16:23 [b] Acts 20:4; 21:29 4:22 [1] NU-Text omits *Jesus Christ.*

THE EPISTLE OF PAUL TO

TITUS

OVERVIEW

Paul described Titus, like Timothy, as "a true son in our common faith" (Titus 1:4). At various times in the ministry, Titus was entrusted to deliver offerings and letters on behalf of the Corinthian church and Paul, respectively. He was also a trusted and reliable ministry partner of the apostle Paul to the people on the island of Crete.

The island location of Crete proved a natural barrier that hampered but did not prevent the spread of the gospel. It is unclear if Paul ever traveled to Crete, where pagan religions ran rampant. However, we know Paul appointed his trusted son in the ministry, Titus, as the overseer of the church in Crete. Paul had given Titus a challenging assignment in serving the church in Corinth (see 2 Cor. 2:13), and now the apostle was giving the pastor more challenging work to do: "You should set in order the things that are lacking, and appoint elders in every city as I commanded you" (Titus 1:5).

Paul provided a brutal critique of the Cretan people. He wrote, "One of them, a prophet of their own, said, 'Cretans are always liars, evil beasts, lazy gluttons'" (1:12–13). Serving in such a community would have made for a difficult assignment for any church leader, so Paul sent a letter to Titus providing guidance. Paul made it clear that the church in Crete needed to be rebuked and corrected when he said, "They profess to know God, but in works they deny Him, being abominable, disobedient, and disqualified for every good work" (1:16). What this church needed most was godly leadership, which is what Paul assigned Titus to establish. Godly leadership provides godly teaching, which leads to godly behavior.

Acts 14:23 makes it clear that appointing leaders chosen by God was imperative to the success of the early church: "So when they had appointed elders in every church, and prayed with fasting, they commended them to the Lord in whom they had believed." But identifying and appointing qualified church leaders is no small task. Establishing church leadership required more than merely choosing those who were most prominent in the church or community. Leaders needed to be those who lived discernible godly lives. As such, Paul began his letter by listing the qualifications of church elders and specifying their duties. The church needed stable, qualified leadership then, and it still does today.

BREATHE IT IN

When Jesus made His triumphal entry into Jerusalem in advance of His crucifixion and resurrection, the temple was the first place He visited. He could have visited the palace, the praetorium, the courts, or the military quarters. Yet, Jesus prioritized the spiritual center of Jerusalem and immediately began to clean house. The Gospel of Matthew records, "Then Jesus went into the temple of God and drove out all those who bought and sold in the temple, and overturned the tables of the money changers and the seats of those who sold doves. And He said to them, 'It is written, "My house shall be called a house of prayer," but you have made it a den of thieves'" (Matt. 21:12–13). The leaders of the temple had allowed its activities to stray far off course. Jesus

not only wanted to correct the temple practices, but He also wanted the future church to raise its standards to preserve its mission.

Raising and holding high standards was a recurring theme in the early church. When the apostles moved to replace Judas, who had betrayed Jesus, they were diligent to specify lofty standards of those who would be eligible as an apostle (see Acts 1:15–26). In his letters to Timothy and Titus, Paul set clear and high standards for being ordained as an elder or deacon. High standards are necessary because they are preventative. They prevent unqualified leaders from serving, thereby also preventing Satan from getting a foothold within the church. Being a leader in the church, therefore, is not a right to enjoy but a privilege to steward. As Paul says, we "press toward the goal for the prize of the upward call of God in Christ Jesus" (Phil. 3:14). The deeper our dedication to Christ, the higher we should raise our standards.

Airplane pilots have high standards. Captains of cruise ships and military vessels must meet the most demanding standards. Physicians and engineers face rigorous testing and must maintain high standards. Teachers and principals must meet exacting standards and qualifications before they can teach our children. We not only tolerate all these standards, but we are grateful for them and require them. Why? Because we know what is at stake. How much more, then, should the church maintain the highest of standards for its leadership? But it does not stop there. Examine how you might need to raise your standards as a spouse, parent, caregiver, employee or employer, or disciple of Jesus Christ.

†

THE EPISTLE OF PAUL TO

TITUS

Greeting

1 Paul, a bondservant of God and an apostle
of Jesus Christ, according to the faith of
God's elect and [a]the acknowledgment of the
truth [b]which accords with godliness, 2in hope
of eternal life which God, who [a]cannot lie,
promised before time began, 3but has in due
time manifested His word through preaching, which was committed to me according
to the commandment of God our Savior;

4To [a]Titus, a true son in *our* common
faith:

Grace, mercy, *and* peace from God the
Father and the Lord Jesus Christ[1] our Savior.

Qualified Elders

5For this reason I left you in Crete, that
you should [a]set in order the things that are
lacking, and appoint elders in every city as
I commanded you— 6if a man is blameless,
the husband of one wife, [a]having faithful
children not accused of dissipation or insubordination. 7For a bishop[1] must be blameless, as a steward of God, not self-willed, not
quick-tempered, [a]not given to wine, not violent, not greedy for money, 8but hospitable,
a lover of what is good, sober-minded, just,
holy, self-controlled, 9holding fast the faithful word as he has been taught, that he may
be able, by sound doctrine, both to exhort
and convict those who contradict.

The Elders' Task

10For there are many insubordinate, both
idle [a]talkers and deceivers, especially those
of the circumcision, 11whose mouths must
be stopped, who subvert whole households,
teaching things which they ought not, [a]for
the sake of dishonest gain. 12[a]One of them,
a prophet of their own, said, "Cretans *are*
always liars, evil beasts, lazy gluttons."
13This testimony is true. [a]Therefore rebuke
them sharply, that they may be sound in
the faith, 14not giving heed to Jewish fables and [a]commandments of men who turn
from the truth. 15[a]To the pure all things are
pure, but to those who are defiled and unbelieving nothing is pure; but even their
mind and conscience are defiled. 16They
profess to [a]know God, but [b]in works they
deny *Him,* being abominable, disobedient, [c]and disqualified for every good work.

Qualities of a Sound Church

2 But as for you, speak the things which
are proper for sound doctrine: 2that
the older men be sober, reverent, temperate, sound in faith, in love, in patience; 3the
older women likewise, that they be reverent in behavior, not slanderers, not given
to much wine, teachers of good things—
4that they admonish the young women to
love their husbands, to love their children,
5*to be* discreet, chaste, [a]homemakers, good,
[b]obedient to their own husbands, [c]that the
word of God may not be blasphemed.

6Likewise, exhort the young men to
be sober-minded, 7in all things showing
yourself *to be* [a]a pattern of good works; in
doctrine *showing* integrity, reverence, [b]in-
corruptibility,[1] 8sound speech that cannot be condemned, that one who is an

---

1:1 [a] 2 Tim. 2:25 [b] [1 Tim. 3:16] 1:2 [a] Num. 23:19 1:4 [a] 2 Cor. 2:13; 8:23; Gal. 2:3; 2 Tim. 4:10 [1] NU-Text reads *and Christ Jesus.* 1:5 [a] 1 Cor. 11:34 1:6 [a] 1 Tim. 3:2–4; Titus 1:6–8 1:7 [a] Lev. 10:9 [1] Literally *overseer* 1:10 [a] James 1:26 1:11 [a] 1 Tim. 6:5 1:12 [a] Acts 17:28 1:13 [a] 2 Cor. 13:10; 2 Tim. 4:2 1:14 [a] Is. 29:13 1:15 [a] Luke 11:41; Rom. 14:14, 20; 1 Cor. 6:12 1:16 [a] Matt. 7:20–23; 25:12; 1 John 2:4 [b] [2 Tim. 3:5, 7] [c] Rom. 1:28 2:5 [a] 1 Tim. 5:14 [b] 1 Cor. 14:34; 1 Tim. 2:11 [c] Rom. 2:24 2:7 [a] Phil. 3:17; 1 Tim. 4:12 [b] Eph. 6:24 2:7 [1] NU-Text omits *incorruptibility.*

BELIEVE IN THE HOLY SPIRIT

INHALE

I haven't been a believer for long, but I thought I would see the Holy Spirit guiding my thoughts and actions more by now. I want to be a light for God. I want to make godly choices in all I do. I want to make the Lord proud. However, my flesh is still ruling more than I would like to admit. If the Holy Spirit is supposed to be living in me, why don't I recognize Him and see His work? How come I still mess up?

EXHALE

First, let's not use *if* to qualify the presence of the Holy Spirit. It's not a matter of *if*. The day you gave your life to Jesus Christ you became a child of God. In that moment, the Holy Spirit entered your life, and He will be with you until the end of the age. The way you know that is first and foremost based on the promises of God's Word. It's what God has promised that matters and nothing else.

The Bible teaches us in Acts 2:38, Ephesians 1:13, and other places that the instant you trust in Christ, God forgives you and gives you the Holy Spirit. This is one of the greatest promises in all the Bible. The Holy Spirit changes you, causing you to desire the things of God. We will never desire the things of God apart from the Holy Spirit giving us the awareness that is so important and never leads us astray. But allowing the Holy Spirit to lead is a process that can be especially slow at first.

Messing up is a product of the fallen nature we all have. We will all make mistakes along the way, even as believers, but they are not to be considered final. You see, God has the final word. Titus 3:5 says, "Not by works of righteousness which we have done, but according to His mercy He saved us, through the washing of regeneration and renewing of the Holy Spirit." We see here that we were not saved by any of our works; we were saved by the work of Jesus and the washing of the Holy Spirit. And nothing we do can undo what He has done. As long as you are in your flesh, you will make mistakes, but as you yield more to the Holy Spirit within you, you will find yourself thinking and acting like Christ.

opponent may be ashamed, having nothing evil to say of you.[1]
9*Exhort* [a]bondservants to be obedient
to their own masters, to be well pleasing
in all *things,* not answering back, 10not pil-
fering, but showing all good fidelity, that
they may adorn the doctrine of God our
Savior in all things.

Trained by Saving Grace

11For [a]the grace of God that brings salvation has appeared to all men, 12teaching
us that, denying ungodliness and worldly
lusts, we should live soberly, righteously,
and godly in the present age, 13[a]looking for
the blessed [b]hope and glorious appearing
of our great God and Savior Jesus Christ,
14[a]who gave Himself for us, that He might
redeem us from every lawless deed [b]and
purify for Himself [c]*His* own special people,
zealous for good works.
15Speak these things, [a]exhort, and rebuke with all authority. Let no one despise
you.

Graces of the Heirs of Grace

3 Remind them [a]to be subject to rulers
and authorities, to obey, [b]to be ready for
every good work, 2to speak evil of no one,
to be peaceable, gentle, showing all humility to all men. 3For [a]we ourselves were also
once foolish, disobedient, deceived, serving various lusts and pleasures, living in
malice and envy, hateful and hating one

2:8 [1] NU-Text and M-Text read *us.* 2:9 [a] Eph. 6:5; 1 Tim. 6:1 2:11 [a] [Rom. 5:15] 2:13 [a] 1 Cor. 1:7 [b] [Col. 3:4] 2:14 [a] Is. 53:12; Gal. 1:4 [b] Ezek. 37:23; [Heb. 1:3; 9:14; 1 John 1:7] [c] Ex. 15:16 2:15 [a] 1 Tim. 4:13; 5:20; 2 Tim. 4:2 3:1 [a] [Rom. 13:1]; 1 Pet. 2:13 [b] Col. 1:10 3:3 [a] 1 Cor. 6:11; 1 Pet. 4:3

another. 4But when [a]the kindness and the
love of [b]God our Savior toward man appeared, 5[a]not by works of righteousness
which we have done, but according to His
mercy He saved us, through [b]the washing of regeneration and renewing of the
Holy Spirit, 6[a]whom He poured out on us
abundantly through Jesus Christ our Savior, 7that having been justified by His grace
[a]we should become heirs according to the
hope of eternal life.

#OXYGEN

TITUS 3:5

Believe in the Holy Spirit

God left you a gift you did not earn or deserve. He is a gift sent to help you day by day. Be wise and allow the Holy Spirit to daily renew you.

Trust, **breathe**, and **believe in the Holy Spirit**.

8[a]This is a faithful saying, and these
things I want you to affirm constantly, that
those who have believed in God should be
careful to maintain good works. These
things are good and profitable to men.

Avoid Dissension

9But [a]avoid foolish disputes, genealogies, contentions, and strivings about the
law; for they are unprofitable and useless.
10[a]Reject a divisive man after the first and
second admonition, 11knowing that such a
person is warped and sinning, being self-
condemned.

Final Messages

12When I send Artemas to you, or [a]Tych-
icus, be diligent to come to me at Nicopo-
lis, for I have decided to spend the winter
there. 13Send Zenas the lawyer and [a]Apol-
los on their journey with haste, that they
may lack nothing. 14And let our *people* also
learn to maintain good works, to *meet* urgent needs, that they may not be unfruitful.

Farewell

15All who *are* with me greet you. Greet
those who love us in the faith.
Grace *be* with you all. Amen.

3:4 [a] Titus 2:11 [b] 1 Tim. 2:3 3:5 [a] [Rom. 3:20]; Eph. 2:4–9 [b] John 3:3 3:6 [a] Ezek. 36:26 3:7 [a] [Matt. 25:34]; Mark 10:17; [Rom. 8:17, 23, 24; Titus 1:2] 3:8 [a] 1 Tim. 1:15 3:9 [a] 1 Tim. 1:4; 2 Tim. 2:23 3:10 [a] Matt. 18:17 3:12 [a] Acts 20:4; Eph. 6:21; Col. 4:7; 2 Tim. 4:12 3:13 [a] Acts 18:24; 1 Cor. 16:12

THE EPISTLE OF PAUL TO

PHILEMON

OVERVIEW

Paul's purpose for writing to Philemon, a member of the Colossian church and possible host to it meeting in his home, was to discuss a runaway, enslaved man named Onesimus. Onesimus had escaped from Philemon and traveled to Rome, where he met the apostle Paul and became a servant of Christ. By law, Onesimus could have been put to death for his insubordination to a legal system that accommodated slavery. Paul, however, also recognized that Onesimus's departure had potentially created a problem between the two. Now that Onesimus was a believer, any divide between believers could be dangerous.

In his letter to Philemon, Paul made a twofold appeal to the slave master on behalf of the escaped slave. First, the man who was returning to Philemon was not the man who had left. The Onesimus who left Philemon was a runaway slave. Paul urged Philemon to understand, however, that the Onesimus who returned carrying this letter was a fellow member of the body of Christ. Therefore, Paul pleaded with him to welcome Onesimus "no longer as a slave but more than a slave—a beloved brother" (Philem. v. 16). Paul implored Philemon to celebrate the redemption of Onesimus as is befitting a follower of Christ and, as a result, to recognize that their relationship had fundamentally changed. At issue was restoration. Paul wanted Philemon to see Onesimus for who he truly was—an image bearer of God who had been saved by Christ—and to treat him accordingly.

Second, Paul sent Onesimus back to the man who defined him as property because it was the only pathway for his liberation. Onesimus could not be free while he remained a fugitive slave. The only path to complete restoration, then, was to appeal to Philemon to receive him as an equal and afford him freedom on earth. In doing so, Paul was willing to pay any restitution to reimburse any expenses accrued by Philemon since Onesimus's escape (see vv. 17–19). Paul reminded Philemon of their loving history, compelling him to rise above the label of his socioeconomic reality. He asked Philemon to put the love of Christ and his love of people above a system that enslaved people for profit.

We do not know how Onesimus was received by Philemon, but we might anticipate he did precisely what Paul expected of him (see v. 21). Hopefully, Philemon was capable of seeing an enslaved person as a Christian brother whom Christ had set free and do the same.

BREATHE IT IN

When many people think of slavery, they might not realize that there have been several iterations of institutional slavery throughout history. Historian David Blight lists five distinct slave societies: Ancient Greece, Ancient Rome, Brazil, the Caribbean, and the American South.[1] Roman slavery is depicted in Philemon. This early form of slavery involved enslaving prisoners of war and debtors. American slavery, known as chattel slavery because the slaves were considered as property belonging to the slave owner, was unique in that it was racially determined, intergenerational, and lifelong. Unlike what had come before it, chattel slavery in the Americas

[1] David Blight, "A Southern World View: The Old South and Proslavery Ideology," Brewminate.com, January 22, 2008, https://brewminate.com/the-civil-war-southern-and-northern-world-views/.

dehumanized a race of people and doomed their descendants to perpetual slavery with little to no hope of an ending. Slavery in all its forms is evidence of moral deficiency and denies the important doctrine of all people being image bearers of God.

When we read about slavery in the Bible, we can often view it through the eyes of the race-based American chattel slavery. We envision all the slave masters, like Philemon, as white people and all the slaves, such as Onesimus, as Black people. Like in all cases, however, we must resist reading the Bible through the lens of our contemporary attitudes and associations. When Paul instructed "bondservants" to "obey in all things [their] masters" (Col. 3:22), he was not endorsing American slavery. Furthermore, in Philemon, Paul seems to condemn slavery as being incompatible with Christianity. But this did not prevent some American theologians and churches from using the Bible to endorse chattel slavery.

Paul's epistle to Philemon paints a vivid picture of our true identity. He stated that none of us, no matter our lot in life, should be defined by our worldly status. Instead, each of us should be welcomed as a brother or sister in Christ. Paul wrote to Philemon, "Perhaps [Onesimus] departed . . . that you might receive him forever, no longer as a slave but more than a slave—a beloved brother, especially to me but how much more to you, both in the flesh and in the Lord" (Philem. vv. 15–16).

In the present day, it is tempting to think that the impact of slavery is a thing of the past in America. But there are forty million descendants of the four million slaves who were emancipated in 1863. Their history and connection to their origins is a broken path because of this dehumanizing institution. It is undeniable that dehumanizing racial practices and racial animus continue to exist. So, the central message of the Book of Philemon continues to be needed today. God has never intended any person to see others or himself or herself as less than or more than.

It is also tempting to think that the very practice of slavery is a thing of the past, but this is also a fallacy. Human trafficking of the vulnerable continues to be a worldwide tragedy. Trafficking of women and children into the sex industry is becoming more prevalent the world over, and it often occurs closer to us than we might think. The vulnerable of all races are considered prey to the base instincts of perverted men and women who are devoid of love, compassion, and basic humanity. This is the condition of the soul that results in the callous enslavement of others. As Solomon said, "There is nothing new under the sun" (Eccl. 1:9).

As you breathe in the epistle to Philemon, consider how you and your family can celebrate and thank God for the emancipation of four million men, women, and children and their forty million descendants from American slavery. African American emancipation is often celebrated in two key ways. Watch Night services are held each December 31 to commemorate the Emancipation Proclamation that liberated the enslaved people at midnight on January 1, 1863. Then, June 19, called Juneteenth, is set aside to celebrate the liberation of enslaved people in Texas during June of 1865. If your family or church does not celebrate these, doing so can be a helpful step to remember and celebrate God-given freedom on earth as well as Christ-provided freedom throughout eternity.

†

THE EPISTLE OF PAUL TO

PHILEMON

Greeting

Paul, a [a]prisoner of Christ Jesus, and Timothy *our* brother,

To Philemon our beloved *friend* and
fellow laborer, 2to the beloved[1] Apphia,
[a]Archippus our fellow soldier, and to the
church in your house:

3Grace to you and peace from God our
Father and the Lord Jesus Christ.

Philemon's Love and Faith

4[a]I thank my God, making mention of
you always in my prayers, 5[a]hearing of your
love and faith which you have toward the
Lord Jesus and toward all the saints, 6that
the sharing of your faith may become effective [a]by the acknowledgment of [b]every
good thing which is in you[1] in Christ Jesus.
7For we have[1] great joy[2] and consolation in
your love, because the hearts of the saints
have been refreshed by you, brother.

The Plea for Onesimus

8Therefore, though I might be very bold
in Christ to command you what is fitting,
9*yet* for love's sake I rather appeal *to you*—
being such a one as Paul, the aged, and now
also a prisoner of Jesus Christ— 10I appeal
to you for my son [a]Onesimus, whom I have
begotten *while* in my chains, 11who once was
unprofitable to you, but now is profitable
to you and to me.

12I am sending him back.[1] You therefore
receive him, that is, my own heart, 13whom
I wished to keep with me, that on your behalf he might minister to me in my chains
for the gospel. 14But without your consent I
wanted to do nothing, [a]that your good deed
might not be by compulsion, as it were, but
voluntary.

15For perhaps he departed for a while for
this *purpose,* that you might receive him
forever, 16no longer as a slave but more than
a slave—a beloved brother, especially to
me but how much more to you, both in the
[a]flesh and in the Lord.

Philemon's Obedience Encouraged

17If then you count me as a partner, receive him as *you would* me. 18But if he has
wronged you or owes anything, put that on
my account. 19I, Paul, am writing with my
own [a]hand. I will repay—not to mention
to you that you owe me even your own self
besides. 20Yes, brother, let me have joy from
you in the Lord; refresh my heart in the Lord.

21[a]Having confidence in your obedience,
I write to you, knowing that you will do
even more than I say. 22But, meanwhile,
also prepare a guest room for me, for [a]I
trust that [b]through your prayers I shall be
granted to you.

Farewell

23[a]Epaphras, my fellow prisoner in
Christ Jesus, greets you, 24*as do* [a]Mark,
[b]Aristarchus, [c]Demas, [d]Luke, my fellow laborers.

25[a]The grace of our Lord Jesus Christ *be*
with your spirit. Amen.

---

1 [a] Eph. 3:1 2 [a] Col. 4:17 [1] NU-Text reads *to our sister Apphia.* 4 [a] Eph. 1:16; 1 Thess. 1:2; 2 Thess. 1:3 5 [a] Eph. 1:15; Col. 1:4; 1 Thess. 3:6 6 [a] Phil. 1:9; [Col. 1:9; 3:10; James 2:14–17] [b] [1 Thess. 5:18] [1] NU-Text and M-Text read *us.* 7 [1] NU-Text reads *had.* [2] M-Text reads *thanksgiving.* 10 [a] Col. 4:9 12 [1] NU-Text reads *back to you in person, that is, my own heart.* 14 [a] 2 Cor. 9:7; 1 Pet. 5:2 16 [a] Eph. 6:5; Col. 3:22 19 [a] 1 Cor. 16:21; Gal. 6:11; 2 Thess. 3:17 21 [a] 2 Cor. 7:16 22 [a] Phil. 1:25; 2:24 [b] 2 Cor. 1:11 23 [a] Col. 1:7; 4:12 24 [a] Acts 12:12, 25; 15:37–39; Col. 4:10 [b] Acts 19:29; 27:2; Col. 4:10 [c] Col. 4:14; 2 Tim. 4:10 [d] 2 Tim. 4:11 25 [a] 2 Tim. 4:22

PHILEMON VV. 15-16

I AM ONESIMUS

For perhaps he departed for a while for this purpose, that you might receive him forever, no longer as a slave but more than a slave—a beloved brother, especially to me but how much more to you, both in the flesh and in the Lord. Philemon vv. 15–16

I am Onesimus. I was a slave of Philemon and became a free man in Christ. Paul called me "a faithful and beloved brother" and his "son."

I had run away from my master, Philemon, and ended up in Rome, where I met Paul. Paul led me to faith in Christ from his Roman jail cell. Paul wanted me to stay with him in Rome to help him, but he knew that my relationship with Philemon needed to be restored. So, he wrote to Philemon, telling him that he was sending me back to him. He asked Philemon to receive me as graciously as he would have welcomed Paul. He urged Philemon to see me no longer as a slave but as a brother, both in the flesh and in the Lord. Paul even told Philemon that he would repay any debt I might have owed.

The story of Philemon is a message of reconciliation and God's view that all are equal in His eyes. Paul became the mediator and central point of the reconciliation between Philemon, Onesimus, and the heart of God. Paul further presented a picture of Christ when he volunteered to take on any of Onesimus's debts against Philemon. Like Philemon, we are also called to treat one another as equals. We should never keep another in bondage or see anyone else beneath us. Instead, we are to treat everyone with the respect and dignity we would grant to a brother or sister.

THE EPISTLE TO THE

HEBREWS

OVERVIEW

While the original readers of the Book of Hebrews knew the writer (see Heb. 13:18–24), its authorship has been lost to us. One school of thought attributes authorship to the apostle Paul. However, the grammar and syntax are not typical of Paul's other writings. The greeting of the letter is inconsistent with Paul's epistles, but the closing does mirror them. Other potential authors include Barnabas, Luke, Apollos, Silas, Philip, and Clement of Rome.

Despite the difficulty in determining authorship, the intended audience of this letter is somewhat easier to identify. Based on the frequent references to Jewish worship practices, the assumed understanding of many Old Testament people and events, and the absence of any mention of Gentiles, the intended readers were surely Jewish believers, either those remaining in Palestine or those who had scattered throughout Asia, Africa, and Europe.

The purpose of Hebrews is to establish the sufficiency of Christ and to implore the readers to hold fast to the faith and pursue spiritual maturity. Spiritual stagnation was as much a threat to the early church as false teaching was. The author expected disciples to progress in their faith, according to the metaphor of a toddler moving from a milk-based diet to a more substantive diet. This author wanted his readers to understand that maturing is more than just aging. It requires the ability "to discern both good and evil" (5:14). Obedience to Christ is essential in placing the believer on the journey toward spiritual maturity. The author explained this expectation as the reasonable response to the atonement provided by Christ, who was, is, and will always be our "great High Priest" (4:14).

But while obedience is essential for growth, the author also stressed the truth that faith in Jesus is greater than obedience to the law. The author quoted Habakkuk 2:4 when he stated that "the just shall live by faith" (Heb. 10:38). Faith has always been the impetus for salvation and obedience; thus, it is an essential part of maturity as well. Our pursuit of spiritual maturity is not a legal requirement; it is a voluntary response to God's benevolence in granting us forgiveness and salvation.

BREATHE IT IN

Two sets of children from two different families waited for the dentist in the office waiting room. The pediatric dentist provided toys, books, and magazines for patients as they waited. When the first family was called, the children returned their books to the shelf and put away the toys without any urging from the parents or staff. When the second set of children was called, they left magazines, trash, and toys everywhere. From this brief encounter, we could safely conclude that the first set of children was being raised with clear expectations for how to conduct themselves in public. The second set of children, however, had not been exposed to this form of discipline.

We often think negatively of discipline. Even when it is administered correctly and for the right reasons, it is not pleasant or enjoyable. Then there are times when discipline is done

incorrectly and even abusively. But the Bible says that God disciplines those whom He loves. Divine discipline from God, then, is a good thing. To be treated as God's son or daughter is to accept the discipline that comes with this relationship. We are not the parents in our story of salvation; God is. We are the children who should live with a teachable and correctable spirit. Do you have trouble accepting correction? Are you overly defensive in the face of criticism? Do you stay away from environments where your behavior is scrutinized? How do you handle performance reviews on your job? Who are the people in your life from whom you refuse to take correction and why?

We all need people in our lives who we give permission to rate and measure our progress. God has invested a great deal in His children. Your spiritual growth and progress are the returns on that investment. Students need teachers. Athletes need coaches. Professionals need mentors. Congregations need pastors. Sheep need shepherds. Find someone to hold you accountable for your development as a believer and as a professional, spouse, parent, sibling, friend—whatever roles you fill each day.

THE EPISTLE TO THE

HEBREWS

God's Supreme Revelation
(cf. John 1:1–4)

1 God, who at various times and [a]in various ways spoke in time past to the fathers by the prophets, 2 has in these last
days spoken to us by *His* Son, whom He
has appointed heir of all things, through
whom also He made the worlds; 3 [a]who being the brightness of *His* glory and the express [b]image of His person, and [c]upholding
all things by the word of His power, [d]when
He had by Himself[1] purged our[2] sins, [e]sat
down at the right hand of the Majesty on
high, 4 having become so much better than
the angels, as [a]He has by inheritance obtained a more excellent name than they.

The Son Exalted Above Angels

5 For to which of the angels did He ever
say:

[a]"You are My Son,
Today I have begotten You"?[1]

And again:

[b]"I will be to Him a Father,
And He shall be to Me a Son"?[2]

6 But when He again brings [a]the firstborn
into the world, He says:

[b]"Let all the angels of God
worship Him."[1]

7 And of the angels He says:

[a]"Who makes His angels spirits
And His ministers a flame of fire."[1]

8 But to the Son *He says:*

[a]"Your throne, O God, *is*
forever and ever;
A scepter of righteousness *is* the
scepter of Your kingdom.
9 You have loved righteousness
and hated lawlessness;
Therefore God, Your God,
[a]has anointed You
With the oil of gladness more
than Your companions."[1]

10 And:

[a]"You, LORD, in the beginning laid
the foundation of the earth,
And the heavens are the
work of Your hands.
11 [a]They will perish, but You remain;
And [b]they will all grow old
like a garment;
12 Like a cloak You will fold them up,
And they will be changed.
But You are the [a]same,
And Your years will not fail."[1]

13 But to which of the angels has He ever
said:

[a]"Sit at My right hand,
Till I make Your enemies
Your footstool"?[1]

1:1 [a] Num. 12:6, 8; Joel 2:28 1:3 [a] John 1:14 [b] 2 Cor. 4:4; Col. 1:15 [c] Col. 1:17 [d] [Heb. 7:27] [e] Ps. 110:1 [1] NU-Text omits *by Himself.* [2] NU-Text omits *our.* 1:4 [a] Is. 9:6, 7; Luke 1:32, 33; [Phil. 2:9, 10] 1:5 [a] Ps. 2:7; Acts 13:33; Heb. 5:5 [b] 2 Sam. 7:14 [1] Psalm 2:7 [2] 2 Samuel 7:14 1:6 [a] Ps. 89:27; [Rom. 8:29] [b] Deut. 32:43, LXX, DSS; Ps. 97:7; 1 Pet. 3:22; Rev. 5:11–13 [1] Deuteronomy 32:43 (Septuagint, Dead Sea Scrolls); Psalm 97:7 1:7 [a] Ps. 104:4 [1] Psalm 104:4 1:8 [a] Ps. 45:6, 7 1:9 [a] Is. 61:1, 3 [1] Psalm 45:6, 7 1:10 [a] Ps. 102:25–27 1:11 [a] [Is. 34:4] [b] Is. 50:9; 51:6; Heb. 8:13 1:12 [a] Heb. 13:8 [1] Psalm 102:25–27 1:13 [a] Ps. 110:1; Matt. 22:44; Heb. 1:3 [1] Psalm 110:1

14[a]Are they not all ministering spirits sent
forth to minister for those who will [b]in-
herit salvation?

Do Not Neglect Salvation

2 Therefore we must give the more earnest heed to the things we have heard,
lest we drift away. 2For if the word [a]spo-
ken through angels proved steadfast, and
[b]every transgression and disobedience received a just reward, 3[a]how shall we escape
if we neglect so great a salvation, [b]which at
the first began to be spoken by the Lord,
and was [c]confirmed to us by those who
heard *Him,* 4[a]God also bearing witness
[b]both with signs and wonders, with various miracles, and [c]gifts of the Holy Spirit,
[d]according to His own will?

The Son Made Lower than Angels
(cf. Ps. 8:1–9)

5For He has not put [a]the world to come,
of which we speak, in subjection to angels. 6But one testified in a certain place,
saying:

[a]"What is man that You are
mindful of him,
Or the son of man that You
take care of him?
7 You have made him a little
lower than the angels;
You have crowned him with
glory and honor,[1]
And set him over the works
of Your hands.
8 [a]You have put all things
in subjection under
his feet."[1]

For in that He put all in subjection under
him, He left nothing *that is* not put under
him. But now [b]we do not yet see all things
put under him. 9But we see Jesus, [a]who was
made a little lower than the angels, for the
suffering of death [b]crowned with glory and
honor, that He, by the grace of God, might
taste death [c]for everyone.

#OXYGEN
HEBREWS 2:9
Reconcile Darkness with Light

Jesus came to be the light of the world, but that light could only be experienced in full through the dark hours of the cross. But that darkness would not last. Light burst forth once more, more brilliantly than ever. Likewise, when we place the needs of others above our own, we become bearers of the light of God. Light will always dispel the darkness, no matter how intense it may be.

Just be open, **breathe**, and **reconcile darkness with light.**

Bringing Many Sons to Glory

10For it was fitting for Him, [a]for whom
are all things and by whom *are* all things,
in bringing many sons to glory, to make the
captain of their salvation [b]perfect through
sufferings. 11For [a]both He who sanctifies
and those who are being sanctified [b]*are* all
of one, for which reason [c]He is not ashamed
to call them brethren, 12saying:

[a]"I will declare Your name
to My brethren;
In the midst of the assembly I
will sing praise to You."[1]

13And again:

[a]"I will put My trust in Him."[1]

And again:

[b]"Here am I and the children
whom God has given Me."[2]

14Inasmuch then as the children have
partaken of flesh and blood, He [a]Himself
likewise shared in the same, [b]that through
death He might destroy him who had the
power of [c]death, that is, the devil, 15and
release those who [a]through fear of death

1:14 [a] Ps. 103:20; Dan. 7:10 [b] Rom. 8:17 2:2 [a] Deut. 33:2; Acts 7:53; Gal. 3:19 [b] Num. 15:30 2:3 [a] Heb. 10:28 [b] Matt. 4:17 [c] Mark 16:20; Luke 1:2; 1 John 1:1 2:4 [a] Mark 16:20 [b] Acts 2:22, 43; 2 Cor. 12:2 [c] 1 Cor. 12:4, 7, 11; Eph. 4:7 [d] Eph. 1:5, 9 2:5 [a] [2 Pet. 3:13] 2:6 [a] Job 7:17; Ps. 8:4–6 2:7 [1] NU-Text and M-Text omit the rest of verse 7. 2:8 [a] Matt. 28:18 [b] Ps. 8:6; 1 Cor. 15:25, 27 [1] Psalm 8:4–6 2:9 [a] Phil. 2:7–9; Heb. 1:9 [b] Acts 2:33; 3:13; 1 Pet. 1:21 [c] Is. 53:12; [John 3:16] 2:10 [a] Col. 1:16 [b] Heb. 5:8, 9; 7:28 2:11 [a] Heb. 10:10 [b] Acts 17:26 [c] Matt. 28:10 2:12 [a] Ps. 22:22 [1] Psalm 22:22 2:13 [a] 2 Sam. 22:3; Is. 8:17 [b] Is. 8:18 [1] 2 Samuel 22:3; Isaiah 8:17 [2] Isaiah 8:18 2:14 [a] John 1:14 [b] Col. 2:15 [c] [1 Cor. 15:54–57]; 2 Tim. 1:10 2:15 [a] Ps. 68:18; Is. 42:7; 45:13; 49:9; 61:1; [Luke 1:74]

were all their lifetime subject to bondage.
16For indeed He does not give aid to angels,
but He does give aid to the seed of Abraham. 17Therefore, in all things He had [a]to
be made like *His* brethren, that He might
be [b]a merciful and faithful High Priest in
things *pertaining* to God, to make propitiation for the sins of the people. 18[a]For in that
He Himself has suffered, being tempted,
He is able to aid those who are tempted.

The Son Was Faithful

3 Therefore, holy brethren, partakers
of the heavenly calling, consider the
Apostle and High Priest of our confession, Christ Jesus, 2who was faithful to
Him who appointed Him, as [a]Moses also
was faithful in all His house. 3For this One
has been counted worthy of more glory
than Moses, inasmuch as [a]He who built
the house has more honor than the house.
4For every house is built by someone, but
[a]He who built all things *is* God. 5[a]And Moses indeed *was* faithful in all His house
as [b]a servant, [c]for a testimony of those
things which would be spoken *afterward,*
6but Christ as [a]a Son over His own house,
[b]whose house we are [c]if we hold fast the
confidence and the rejoicing of the hope
firm to the end.[1]

Be Faithful
(Ps. 95:7–11)

7Therefore, as [a]the Holy Spirit says:

[b]"Today, if you will hear His voice,
8 Do not harden your hearts
as in the rebellion,
In the day of trial in the wilderness,
9 Where your fathers tested
Me, tried Me,
And saw My works forty years.
10 Therefore I was angry with
that generation,
And said, 'They always go
astray in *their* heart,
And they have not known My ways.'
11 So I swore in My wrath,
'They shall not enter My rest.'"[1]

12Beware, brethren, lest there be in any
of you an evil heart of unbelief in departing
from the living God; 13but exhort one another daily, while it is called "Today," lest any
of you be hardened through the deceitfulness of sin. 14For we have become partakers
of Christ if we hold the beginning of our confidence steadfast to the end, 15while it is said:

[a]"Today, if you will hear His voice,
Do not harden your hearts
as in the rebellion."[1]

Failure of the Wilderness Wanderers

16[a]For who, having heard, rebelled? Indeed, *was it* not all who came out of Egypt,
led by Moses? 17Now with whom was He angry forty years? *Was it* not with those who
sinned, [a]whose corpses fell in the wilderness? 18And [a]to whom did He swear that
they would not enter His rest, but to those
who did not obey? 19So we see that they
could not enter in because of [a]unbelief.

The Promise of Rest

4 Therefore, since a promise remains of
entering His rest, [a]let us fear lest any
of you seem to have come short of it. 2For
indeed the gospel was preached to us as
well as to them; but the word which they
heard did not profit them,[1] not being mixed
with faith in those who heard *it.* 3For we
who have believed do enter that rest, as
He has said:

[a]"So I swore in My wrath,
'They shall not enter My rest,'"[1]

although the works were finished from the
foundation of the world. 4For He has spoken in a certain place of the seventh *day*
in this way: [a]"And God rested on the seventh day from all His works";[1] 5and again in
this *place:* [a]"They shall not enter My rest."[1]

2:17 [a] Phil. 2:7; Heb. 2:14 [b] [Heb. 4:15; 5:1–10] 2:18 [a] [Heb. 4:15, 16] 3:2 [a] Ex. 40:16; Num. 12:7; Heb. 3:5 3:3 [a] Zech. 6:12, 13 3:4 [a] [Eph. 2:10] 3:5 [a] Ex. 40:16; Num. 12:7; Heb. 3:2 [b] Ex. 14:31; Num. 12:7 [c] Deut. 18:15, 18, 19 3:6 [a] Ps. 2:7; 110:4; Heb. 1:2 [b] [1 Cor. 3:16]; 1 Tim. 3:15 [c] [Matt. 10:22] [1] NU-Text omits *firm to the end.* 3:7 [a] Acts 1:16 [b] Ps. 95:7–11; Heb. 3:15; 4:7 3:11 [1] Psalm 95:7–11 3:15 [a] Ps. 95:7, 8 [1] Psalm 95:7, 8 3:16 [a] Num. 14:2, 11, 30; Deut. 1:35, 36, 38 3:17 [a] Num. 14:22, 23 3:18 [a] Num. 14:30 3:19 [a] Num. 14:1–39; 1 Cor. 10:11, 12 4:1 [a] 2 Cor. 6:1; [Gal. 5:4]; Heb. 12:15 4:2 [1] NU-Text and M-Text read *profit them, since they were not united by faith with those who heeded it.* 4:3 [a] Ps. 95:11; Heb. 3:11 [1] Psalm 95:11 4:4 [a] Gen. 2:2; Ex. 20:11; 31:17 [1] Genesis 2:2 4:5 [a] Ps. 95:11 [1] Psalm 95:11

RECONCILE DARKNESS WITH LIGHT

INHALE

People say that I'm part of the group, but they don't act like it. They talk about me behind my back, and I am never invited to their social functions. I think that many of my so-called friends really want me to fail. It's really a negative situation. What can I do to create more positive and truthful relationships with people who treat me badly?

EXHALE

We are all sinners. Only when we allow the Lord to lead us, though, can we see the sin in our lives. It is in that very illuminating situation that we see how blind we really are. Ironically, blindness is what we need to see. It's blindness that drives this sinful behavior that is affecting you, and the sooner others realize they are blind, the sooner they can see their need to see.

While only God can bring sight to spiritually blind eyes, He can give you the gift of a bridge that reaches to someone who desperately needs this spiritual sight. When He gives you this opportunity, run with it! It starts with having open and honest conversations about how you feel about these relationships. This could be difficult, but it is needed. Being treated badly is not a healthy or comfortable way to exist, and anyone fostering this behavior needs to know about it. This isn't about being confrontational, but instead it's about being conversational. Go ahead and take the lead and see who follows.

Know that God allows difficult and dark situations in our lives for a reason. It's up to us to be used by the Father to illuminate goodness. Loving those who make it difficult requires more than we have within ourselves, though. Hebrews 3:12–13 warns us: "Beware, brethren, lest there be in any of you an evil heart of unbelief in departing from the living God; but exhort one another daily, while it is called 'Today,' lest any of you be hardened through the deceitfulness of sin." Guard your heart and turn to the Lord and ask Him to love through you. Don't shy away when a moment like this appears. Trust in the One who makes a way where there is no way. He will enable you to love without it being returned; He will enable you to love without limit and without cause.

6 Since therefore it remains that some
must enter it, and those to whom it was first
preached did not enter because of disobedience, 7 again He designates a certain day,
saying in David, "Today," after such a long
time, as it has been said:

[a]"Today, if you will hear
His voice,
Do not harden your hearts."[1]

8 For if Joshua had [a]given them rest, then
He would not afterward have spoken of another day. 9 There remains therefore a rest
for the people of God. 10 For he who has entered His rest has himself also ceased from
his works as God *did* from His.

The Word Discovers Our Condition

11 [a]Let us therefore be diligent to enter
that rest, lest anyone fall according to the
same example of disobedience. 12 For the
word of God *is* [a]living and powerful, and
[b]sharper than any [c]two-edged sword, piercing even to the division of soul and spirit,
and of joints and marrow, and is [d]a discerner of the thoughts and intents of the
heart. 13 [a]And there is no creature hidden
from His sight, but all things *are* [b]naked
and open to the eyes of Him to whom we
must give account.

Our Compassionate High Priest

14 Seeing then that we have a great [a]High
Priest who has passed through the heavens,

4:7 [a] Ps. 95:7, 8 [1] Psalm 95:7, 8 4:8 [a] Josh. 22:4 4:11 [a] 2 Pet. 1:10 4:12 [a] Ps. 147:15 [b] Is. 49:2 [c] Eph. 6:17; Rev. 2:12 [d] [John 12:48]; 1 Cor. 14:24, 25 4:13 [a] 2 Chr. 16:9; Ps. 33:13–15; 90:8 [b] Job 26:6; Prov. 15:11 4:14 [a] Heb. 2:17; 7:26

Jesus the Son of God, [b]let us hold fast *our*
confession. 15For [a]we do not have a High
Priest who cannot sympathize with our
weaknesses, but [b]was in all *points* tempted
as *we are,* [c]*yet* without sin. 16[a]Let us therefore come boldly to the throne of grace,
that we may obtain mercy and find grace
to help in time of need.

Qualifications for High Priesthood

5 For every high priest taken from among
men [a]is appointed for men in things
pertaining to God, that he may offer both
gifts and sacrifices for sins. 2He can have
compassion on those who are ignorant and
going astray, since he himself is also subject to [a]weakness. 3Because of this he is
required as for the people, so also for [a]him-
self, to offer *sacrifices* for sins. 4And no man
takes this honor to himself, but he who is
called by God, just as [a]Aaron *was.*

A Priest Forever

5[a]So also Christ did not glorify Himself
to become High Priest, but *it was* He who
said to Him:

[b]"You are My Son,
Today I have begotten You."[1]

6As *He* also says in another *place:*

[a]"You *are* a priest forever
According to the order of
Melchizedek";[1]

7who, in the days of His flesh, when He
had [a]offered up prayers and supplications, [b]with vehement cries and tears to
Him [c]who was able to save Him from death,
and was heard [d]because of His godly fear,
8though He was a Son, *yet* He learned [a]obe-
dience by the things which He suffered.
9And [a]having been perfected, He became
the author of eternal salvation to all who
obey Him, 10called by God as High Priest
[a]"according to the order of Melchizedek,"
11of whom [a]we have much to say, and hard
to explain, since you have become [b]dull
of hearing.

Spiritual Immaturity

12For though by this time you ought to
be teachers, you need *someone* to teach
you again the first principles of the oracles of God; and you have come to need
[a]milk and not solid food. 13For everyone
who partakes *only* of milk *is* unskilled in
the word of righteousness, for he is [a]a babe.
14But solid food belongs to those who are
of full age, *that is,* those who by reason of
use have their senses exercised [a]to discern
both good and evil.

The Peril of Not Progressing

6 Therefore, [a]leaving the discussion of
the elementary *principles* of Christ, let
us go on to perfection, not laying again
the foundation of repentance from [b]dead
works and of faith toward God, 2[a]of the doctrine of baptisms, [b]of laying on of hands,
[c]of resurrection of the dead, [d]and of eternal judgment. 3And this we will[1] do if God
permits.
4For *it is* impossible for those who were
once enlightened, and have tasted [a]the
heavenly gift, and [b]have become partakers of the Holy Spirit, 5and have tasted the
good word of God and the powers of the age
to come, 6if they fall away,[1] to renew them
again to repentance, [a]since they crucify
again for themselves the Son of God, and
put *Him* to an open shame.
7For the earth which drinks in the rain
that often comes upon it, and bears herbs
useful for those by whom it is cultivated,
[a]receives blessing from God; 8[a]but if it bears
thorns and briers, *it is* rejected and near to
being cursed, whose end *is* to be burned.

A Better Estimate

9But, beloved, we are confident of better things concerning you, yes, things that
accompany salvation, though we speak in
this manner. 10For [a]God *is* not unjust to
forget [b]your work and labor of[1] love which

4:14 [b] Heb. 10:23 4:15 [a] Is. 53:3–5 [b] Luke 22:28 [c] 2 Cor. 5:21; Heb. 7:26 4:16 [a] [Eph. 2:18; Heb. 10:19, 22] 5:1 [a] Heb. 2:17; 8:3 5:2 [a] Heb. 7:28 5:3 [a] Lev. 9:7; 16:6; [Heb. 7:27; 9:7] 5:4 [a] Ex. 28:1; Num. 16:40; 1 Chr. 23:13 5:5 [a] John 8:54 [b] Ps. 2:7 [1] Psalm 2:7 5:6 [a] Ps. 110:4; Heb. 7:17 [1] Psalm 110:4 5:7 [a] Matt. 26:39, 42, 44; Mark 14:36, 39; Luke 22:41, 44 [b] Ps. 22:1 [c] Matt. 26:53 [d] Matt. 26:39 5:8 [a] Phil. 2:8 5:9 [a] Heb. 2:10 5:10 [a] Ps. 110:4 5:11 [a] [John 16:12]; Heb. 7:1–22 [b] [Matt. 13:15] 5:12 [a] 1 Cor. 3:1–3; 1 Pet. 2:2 5:13 [a] Eph. 4:14 5:14 [a] Is. 7:15; Phil. 1:9 6:1 [a] Heb. 5:12 [b] [Heb. 9:14] 6:2 [a] John 3:25; Acts 19:3–5 [b] [Acts 8:17] [c] Acts 17:31 [d] Acts 24:25 6:3 [1] M-Text reads *let us do.* 6:4 [a] [John 4:10]; Eph. 2:8 [b] [Gal. 3:2, 5]; Heb. 2:4 6:6 [a] Heb. 10:29 [1] Or *and have fallen away* 6:7 [a] Ps. 65:10 6:8 [a] Is. 5:6 6:10 [a] Rom. 3:4 [b] 1 Thess. 1:3 [1] NU-Text omits *labor of*

RELEASE // RECONCILE FAITH WITH MATURITY

Maturing in Christ

Hebrews 6:1 // Therefore, leaving the discussion of the elementary principles of Christ, let us go on to perfection, not laying again the foundation of repentance from dead works and of faith toward God.

Summary Message // Faith is a gift from God. When we first accept Christ, we are like little children. We know we need Him, but we have not yet learned much of who He is or how He acts, and we certainly do not know who we are in Him. But as things happen in our lives, the Lord shows up every time. Through His faithfulness we come to understand that He is reliable and trustworthy, and that He and His Word do not change. We get our footing, and He becomes the full rock on which we stand. But this process of maturing in Christ is not automatic. We have to strive to achieve what is necessary to grow in Christ. Luke 13 says that the purpose of the fig tree is to produce fruit. If it does not produce fruit, what good is it?

Practical Application // So many changes have happened that continue to upset our lives and the world. Natural disasters, elections, wars, rumors of wars, sickness, and financial trials have been unleashed with frequency and fierceness. However, God does not change. So, He becomes our life preserver that we can cling to when everything around us is unstable. His counsel is immutable, and His guidance is sure. The reason God never changes is because He cannot change. But we can and must as we continue to grow our faith in Him by reading the Word, praying, being teachable, and progressing in discernment. As we do these things, we will reap the many benefits of maturity in Christ:

- Hearing and experiencing God
- Growing in God's wisdom
- Experiencing the mysteries of God
- Bearing fruit in our lives

As believers, we desire to mature in our faith so that what our eyes perceive no longer destroys our confidence in God. We believe that God holds our hope in His trustworthy hands and is the anchor that will never fail. Then we can walk through every trial to the end. God will give us all that He has promised in His perfect and divine time.

Fervent Prayer // Father God, help us to see past our problems to Your promises. Help us learn to allow Your Holy Spirit to teach us Your Word, Your will, and Your way. We pray that our growth in You becomes paramount in our lives. We want to learn Your Word so we become steadfast in our hope in You. The things around us will change, but You never change. You are eternally the same. In Jesus' name we pray. Amen.

---

you have shown toward His name, *in that*
you have [c]ministered to the saints, and do
minister. 11 And we desire that each one of
you show the same diligence [a]to the full
assurance of hope until the end, 12 that you
do not become sluggish, but imitate those
who through faith and patience [a]inherit
the promises.

God's Infallible Purpose in Christ

13 For when God made a promise to
Abraham, because He could swear by no
one greater, [a]He swore by Himself, 14 saying, [a]"Surely blessing I will bless you, and
multiplying I will multiply you."[1] 15 And so,
after he had patiently endured, he obtained
the [a]promise. 16 For men indeed swear by
the greater, and [a]an oath for confirmation
is for them an end of all dispute. 17 Thus God,
determining to show more abundantly to
[a]the heirs of promise [b]the immutability
of His counsel, confirmed *it* by an oath,
18 that by two immutable things, in which it
is impossible for God to [a]lie, we might[1] have
strong consolation, who have fled for refuge to lay hold of the hope [b]set before *us.*
19 This *hope* we have as an anchor of
the soul, both sure and steadfast, [a]and

6:10 [c] Rom. 15:25; Heb. 10:32–34. 6:11 [a] Col. 2:2 6:12 [a] Heb. 10:36 6:13 [a] Gen. 22:16, 17; Luke 1:73 6:14 [a] Gen. 22:16, 17 [1] Genesis 22:17 6:15 [a] Gen. 12:4; 21:5 6:16 [a] Ex. 22:11 6:17 [a] Rom. 8:17; Heb. 11:9 [b] Rom. 11:29 6:18 [a] Num. 23:19; 1 Sam. 15:29; Titus 1:2 [b] [Col. 1:5]; Heb. 3:6; 7:19; 12:1 [1] M-Text omits *might.* 6:19 [a] Lev. 16:2, 15; Heb. 9:3, 7

which enters the *Presence* behind the veil,
20[a]where the forerunner has entered for us,
even Jesus, [b]having become High Priest forever according to the order of Melchizedek.

The King of Righteousness
(Gen. 14:17–20)

7 For this [a]Melchizedek, king of Salem,
priest of the Most High God, who met
Abraham returning from the slaughter
of the kings and blessed him, 2to whom
also Abraham gave a tenth part of all, first
being translated "king of righteousness,"
and then also king of Salem, meaning
"king of peace," 3without father, without
mother, without genealogy, having neither beginning of days nor end of life, but
made like the Son of God, remains a priest
continually.

4Now consider how great this man *was,*
to whom even the patriarch Abraham gave
a tenth of the spoils. 5And indeed [a]those
who are of the sons of Levi, who receive
the priesthood, have a commandment
to receive tithes from the people according to the law, that is, from their brethren,
though they have come from the loins of
Abraham; 6but he whose genealogy is not
derived from them received tithes from
Abraham [a]and blessed [b]him who had the
promises. 7Now beyond all contradiction
the lesser is blessed by the better. 8Here
mortal men receive tithes, but there he *receives them,* [a]of whom it is witnessed that
he lives. 9Even Levi, who receives tithes,
paid tithes through Abraham, so to speak,
10for he was still in the loins of his father
when Melchizedek met him.

Need for a New Priesthood
(Ps. 110:4)

11[a]Therefore, if perfection were through
the Levitical priesthood (for under it the
people received the law), what further
need *was there* that another priest should
rise according to the order of Melchizedek, and not be called according to the order of Aaron? 12For the priesthood being
changed, of necessity there is also a change
of the law. 13For He of whom these things
are spoken belongs to another tribe, from
which no man has officiated at the altar.

14For *it is* evident that [a]our Lord arose
from [b]Judah, of which tribe Moses spoke
nothing concerning priesthood.[1] 15And it is
yet far more evident if, in the likeness of
Melchizedek, there arises another priest
16who has come, not according to the law
of a fleshly commandment, but according to the power of an endless life. 17For
He testifies:[1]

> [a]"You *are* a priest forever
> According to the order of
> Melchizedek."[2]

18For on the one hand there is an annul-
ling of the former commandment because
of [a]its weakness and unprofitableness,
19for [a]the law made nothing perfect; on
the other hand, *there is the* bringing in of
[b]a better hope, through which [c]we draw
near to God.

Greatness of the New Priest

20And inasmuch as *He was* not *made
priest* without an oath 21(for they have become priests without an oath, but He with
an oath by Him who said to Him:

> [a]"The LORD has sworn
> And will not relent,
> 'You *are* a priest forever[1]
> According to the order of
> Melchizedek'"),[2]

22by so much more Jesus has become a
surety of a [a]better covenant.

23Also there were many priests, because
they were prevented by death from continuing. 24But He, because He continues
forever, has an unchangeable priesthood.
25Therefore He is also [a]able to save to the
uttermost those who come to God through
Him, since He always lives [b]to make intercession for them.

6:20 [a] [John 14:2; Heb. 4:14] [b] Gen. 14:17–19; Ps. 110:4; Heb. 3:1; 5:10, 11 7:1 [a] Gen. 14:18–20; Heb. 7:6 7:5 [a] Num. 18:21–26; 2 Chr. 31:4 7:6 [a] Gen. 14:19, 20 [b] [Rom. 4:13] 7:8 [a] Heb. 5:6; 6:20; [Rev. 1:18] 7:11 [a] [Rom. 7:7–14]; Gal. 2:21; Heb. 7:18; 8:7 7:14 [a] Gen. 49:8–10; Num. 24:17; Is. 1:1; Mic. 5:2; Matt. 1:3; 2:6; Rev. 5:5 [b] Matt. 1:2 [1] NU-Text reads *priests.* 7:17 [a] Ps. 110:4; Heb. 5:6; 6:20; 7:21 [1] NU-Text reads *it is testified.* [2] Psalm 110:4 7:18 [a] [Rom. 8:3]; Gal. 3:21; Heb. 7:11 7:19 [a] [Acts 13:39]; Rom. 3:20; 7:7; Gal. 2:16; 3:21; Heb. 9:9; 10:1 [b] Heb. 6:18, 19 [c] Lam. 3:57; Rom. 5:2; [Eph. 2:18]; Heb. 4:16; James 4:8 7:21 [a] Ps. 110:4; Heb. 5:6; 7:17 [1] NU-Text ends the quotation here. [2] Psalm 110:4 7:22 [a] Heb. 8:6 7:25 [a] Jude 24 [b] Rom. 8:34; 1 Tim. 2:5; Heb. 9:24; 1 John 2:1

26For such a High Priest was fitting for us, [a]*who is* holy, harmless, undefiled, separate from sinners, [b]and has become higher than the heavens; 27who does not need daily, as those high priests, to offer up sacrifices, first for His [a]own sins and then for the people's, for this He did once for all when He offered up Himself. 28For the law appoints as high priests men who have weakness, but the word of the oath, which came after the law, *appoints* the Son who has been perfected forever.

The New Priestly Service

8 Now *this is* the main point of the things we are saying: We have such a High Priest, [a]who is seated at the right hand of the throne of the Majesty in the heavens, 2a Minister of [a]the sanctuary and of [b]the true tabernacle which the Lord erected, and not man.

3For [a]every high priest is appointed to offer both gifts and sacrifices. Therefore [b]*it is* necessary that this One also have something to offer. 4For if He were on earth, He would not be a priest, since there are priests who offer the gifts according to the law; 5who serve [a]the copy and [b]shadow of the heavenly things, as Moses was divinely instructed when he was about to make the tabernacle. For He said, [c]"See *that* you make all things according to the pattern shown you on the mountain."[1] 6But now [a]He has obtained a more excellent ministry, inasmuch as He is also Mediator of a [b]better covenant, which was established on better promises.

A New Covenant
(Jer. 31:31–34)

7For if that [a]first *covenant* had been faultless, then no place would have been sought for a second. 8Because finding fault with them, He says: [a]"Behold, the days are coming, says the LORD, when I will make a new covenant with the house of Israel and with the house of Judah— 9not according to the covenant that I made with their fathers in the day when I took them by the hand to lead them out of the land of Egypt; because they did not continue in My covenant, and I disregarded them, says the LORD. 10For this *is* the covenant that I will make with the house of Israel after those days, says the [a]LORD: I will put My laws in their mind and write them on their hearts; and [b]I will be their God, and they shall be My people. 11[a]None of them shall teach his neighbor, and none his brother, saying, 'Know the [b]LORD,' for all shall know Me, from the least of them to the greatest of them. 12For I will be merciful to their unrighteousness, [a]and their sins and their lawless deeds[1] I will remember no more."[2]

13[a]In that He says, "A new *covenant,*" He has made the first obsolete. Now what is becoming obsolete and growing old is ready to vanish away.

The Earthly Sanctuary
(cf. Ex. 25:10–40)

9 Then indeed, even the first *covenant* had ordinances of divine service and [a]the earthly sanctuary. 2For a tabernacle was prepared: the first *part,* in which *was* the lampstand, the table, and the showbread, which is called the sanctuary; 3[a]and behind the second veil, the part of the tabernacle which is called the Holiest of All, 4which had the [a]golden censer and [b]the ark of the covenant overlaid on all sides with gold, in which *were* [c]the golden pot that had the manna, [d]Aaron's rod that budded, and [e]the tablets of the covenant; 5and [a]above it were the cherubim of glory overshadowing the mercy seat. Of these things we cannot now speak in detail.

Limitations of the Earthly Service

6Now when these things had been thus prepared, [a]the priests always went into the first part of the tabernacle, performing the services. 7But into the second part the high priest *went* alone [a]once a year, not without blood, which he offered for [b]himself and *for* the people's sins *committed* in ignorance; 8the Holy Spirit indicating this, that

---

7:26 [a] [2 Cor. 5:21]; Heb. 4:15 [b] Eph. 1:20 7:27 [a] Lev. 9:7; 16:6; Heb. 5:3 8:1 [a] Ps. 68:18; 110:1; Eph. 1:20; Col. 3:1; Heb. 2:17; 3:1; 10:12 8:2 [a] Heb. 9:8, 12 [b] Heb. 9:11, 24 8:3 [a] [Rom. 4:25; 5:6, 8; Gal. 2:20; Eph. 5:2]; Heb. 5:1; 8:4 [b] [Eph. 5:2; Heb. 9:14] 8:5 [a] Heb. 9:23, 24 [b] Col. 2:17; Heb. 10:1 [c] Ex. 25:40 [1] Exodus 25:40 8:6 [a] [2 Cor. 3:6–8] [b] [Luke 22:20]; Heb. 7:22 8:7 [a] Ex. 3:8; 19:5 8:8 [a] Jer. 31:31–34 8:10 [a] Jer. 31:33; Rom. 11:27; Heb. 10:16 [b] Zech. 8:8 8:11 [a] Is. 54:13; John 6:45; [1 John 2:27] [b] Jer. 31:34 8:12 [a] Rom. 11:27 [1] NU-Text omits *and their lawless deeds.* [2] Jeremiah 31:31–34 8:13 [a] [2 Cor. 5:17]; Heb. 1:11 9:1 [a] Ex. 25:8; [Heb. 8:2; 9:11, 24] 9:3 [a] Ex. 26:31–35; 40:3 9:4 [a] Lev. 16:12 [b] Ex. 25:10 [c] Ex. 16:33 [d] Num. 17:1–10 [e] Ex. 25:16; 34:29; Deut. 10:2–5 9:5 [a] Ex. 25:17, 20; Lev. 16:2; 1 Kin. 8:7 9:6 [a] Num. 18:2–6; 28:3 9:7 [a] Ex. 30:10; Lev. 16:34; Heb. 10:3 [b] Heb. 5:3

[a]the way into the Holiest of All was not yet
made manifest while the first tabernacle
was still standing. 9It *was* symbolic for the
present time in which both gifts and sacrifices are offered [a]which cannot make him
who performed the service perfect in regard to the conscience— 10*concerned* only
with [a]foods and drinks, [b]various washings,
[c]and fleshly ordinances imposed until the
time of reformation.

The Heavenly Sanctuary

11But Christ came *as* High Priest of [a]the
good things to come,[1] with the greater and
more perfect tabernacle not made with
hands, that is, not of this creation. 12Not
[a]with the blood of goats and calves, but
[b]with His own blood He entered the Most
Holy Place [c]once for all, [d]having obtained
eternal redemption. 13For if [a]the blood of
bulls and goats and [b]the ashes of a heifer,
sprinkling the unclean, sanctifies for the
purifying of the flesh, 14how much more
shall the blood of Christ, who through
the eternal Spirit offered Himself without spot to God, [a]cleanse your conscience
from [b]dead works [c]to serve the living God?
15And for this reason [a]He is the Mediator
of the new covenant, by means of death,
for the redemption of the transgressions
under the first covenant, that [b]those who
are called may receive the promise of the
eternal inheritance.

The Mediator's Death Necessary

16For where there *is* a testament, there
must also of necessity be the death of the
testator. 17For [a]a testament *is* in force after
men are dead, since it has no power at all
while the testator lives. 18[a]Therefore not
even the first *covenant* was dedicated without blood. 19For when Moses had spoken
every precept to all the people according
to the law, [a]he took the blood of calves and
goats, [b]with water, scarlet wool, and hyssop,
and sprinkled both the book itself and all
the people, 20saying, [a]"This *is* the [b]blood of
the covenant which God has commanded
you."[1] 21Then likewise [a]he sprinkled with
blood both the tabernacle and all the vessels of the ministry. 22And according to
the law almost all things are purified with
blood, and [a]without shedding of blood
there is no remission.

Greatness of Christ's Sacrifice

23Therefore *it was* necessary that [a]the
copies of the things in the heavens should
be purified with these, but the heavenly
things themselves with better sacrifices
than these. 24For [a]Christ has not entered
the holy places made with hands, *which*
are copies of [b]the true, but into heaven itself, now [c]to appear in the presence of God
for us; 25not that He should offer Himself
often, as [a]the high priest enters the Most
Holy Place every year with blood of another— 26He then would have had to suffer often since the foundation of the world; but
now, once at the end of the ages, He has appeared to put away sin by the sacrifice of
Himself. 27[a]And as it is appointed for men
to die once, [b]but after this the judgment,
28so [a]Christ was [b]offered once to bear the
sins [c]of many. To those who [d]eagerly wait
for Him He will appear a second time, apart
from sin, for salvation.

Animal Sacrifices Insufficient

10 For the law, having a [a]shadow of the
good things to come, *and* not the
very image of the things, [b]can never with
these same sacrifices, which they offer continually year by year, make those who approach perfect. 2For then would they not
have ceased to be offered? For the worshipers, once purified, would have had no
more consciousness of sins. 3But in those
sacrifices there is a reminder of sins every
year. 4For [a]*it is* not possible that the blood
of bulls and goats could take away sins.

Christ's Death Fulfills God's Will
(cf. Ps. 40:6–8)

5Therefore, when He came into the
world, He said:

9:8 [a] [John 14:6; Heb. 10:20] 9:9 [a] [Gal. 3:21]; Heb. 7:19 9:10 [a] Lev. 11:2; Col. 2:16 [b] Num. 19:7 [c] Eph. 2:15 9:11 [a] [Eph. 1:3–11]; Heb. 10:1 [1] NU-Text reads *that have come.* 9:12 [a] Heb. 10:4 [b] Is. 53:12; Eph. 1:7 [c] Zech. 3:9 [d] [Dan. 9:24] 9:13 [a] Lev. 16:14, 15; Heb. 9:19; 10:4 [b] Num. 19:2 9:14 [a] 1 John 1:7 [b] Heb. 6:1 [c] Luke 1:74 9:15 [a] Rom. 3:25 [b] Heb. 3:1 9:17 [a] Gal. 3:15 9:18 [a] Ex. 24:6 9:19 [a] Ex. 24:5, 6 [b] Lev. 14:4, 7; Num. 19:6, 18 9:20 [a] [Matt. 26:28] [b] Ex. 24:3–8 [1] Exodus 24:8 9:21 [a] Ex. 29:12, 36 9:22 [a] Lev. 17:11 9:23 [a] Heb. 8:5 9:24 [a] Heb. 6:20 [b] Heb. 8:2 [c] Rom. 8:34 9:25 [a] Heb. 9:7 9:27 [a] Gen. 3:19; Eccl. 3:20 [b] [2 Cor. 5:10]; 1 John 4:17 9:28 [a] Rom. 6:10 [b] Is. 53:12; 1 Pet. 2:24 [c] Matt. 26:28 [d] 1 Cor. 1:7; Titus 2:13 10:1 [a] Heb. 8:5 [b] Heb. 7:19; 9:9 10:4 [a] Mic. 6:6, 7

[a]"Sacrifice and offering You
did not desire,
But a body You have prepared for Me.
6 In burnt offerings and *sacrifices*
for sin
You had no pleasure.
7 Then I said, 'Behold, I have come—
In the volume of the book
it is written of Me—
To do Your will, O God.'"[1]

8 Previously saying, "Sacrifice and offering,
burnt offerings, and *offerings* for sin You
did not desire, nor had pleasure *in them*"
(which are offered according to the law),
9 then He said, "Behold, I have come to do
Your will, O God."[1] He takes away the first
that He may establish the second. 10 [a]By that
will we have been sanctified [b]through the
offering of the body of Jesus Christ once
for all.

Christ's Death Perfects the Sanctified

11 And every priest stands [a]ministering
daily and offering repeatedly the same
sacrifices, which can never take away sins.
12 [a]But this Man, after He had offered one
sacrifice for sins forever, sat down [b]at the
right hand of God, 13 from that time waiting
[a]till His enemies are made His footstool.
14 For by one offering He has perfected forever those who are being sanctified.

15 But the Holy Spirit also witnesses to
us; for after He had said before,

16 [a]"This *is* the covenant that I will make
with them after those days, says the LORD:
I will put My laws into their hearts, and in
their minds I will write them,"[1] 17 *then He
adds,* [a]"Their sins and their lawless deeds
I will remember no more."[1] 18 Now where
there is remission of these, *there is* no longer an offering for sin.

Hold Fast Your Confession

19 Therefore, brethren, having [a]boldness
to enter [b]the Holiest by the blood of Jesus,
20 by a new and [a]living way which He consecrated for us, through the veil, that is,
His flesh, 21 and *having* a High Priest over
the house of God, 22 let us [a]draw near with
a true heart [b]in full assurance of faith, having our hearts sprinkled from an evil conscience and our bodies washed with pure
water. 23 Let us hold fast the confession of
our hope without wavering, for [a]He who
promised *is* faithful. 24 And let us consider
one another in order to stir up love and
good works, 25 [a]not forsaking the assembling of ourselves together, as *is* the manner of some, but exhorting *one another,*
and [b]so much the more as you see [c]the Day
approaching.

The Just Live by Faith

26 For [a]if we sin willfully [b]after we have
received the knowledge of the truth, there
[c]no longer remains a sacrifice for sins,
27 but a certain fearful expectation of judgment, and [a]fiery indignation which will devour the adversaries. 28 Anyone who has
rejected Moses' law dies without mercy on
the testimony of two or three [a]witnesses.
29 [a]Of how much worse punishment, do
you suppose, will he be thought worthy
who has trampled the Son of God underfoot, [b]counted the blood of the covenant by
which he was sanctified a common thing,
[c]and insulted the Spirit of grace? 30 For we
know Him who said, [a]"Vengeance is Mine,
I will repay,"[1] says the Lord.[2] And again,
[b]"The LORD will judge His people."[3] 31 [a]It
is a fearful thing to fall into the hands of
the living God.

32 But [a]recall the former days in which,
after you were illuminated, you endured
a great struggle with sufferings: 33 partly
while you were made [a]a spectacle both by
reproaches and tribulations, and partly
while [b]you became companions of those
who were so treated; 34 for you had compassion on me[1] [a]in my chains, and [b]joyfully
accepted the plundering of your goods,

10:5 [a] Ps. 40:6–8 10:7 [1] Psalm 40:6–8 10:9 [1] NU-Text and M-Text omit *O God.* 10:10 [a] John 17:19; [Eph. 5:26; Heb. 2:11; 10:14, 29; 13:12] [b] [Heb. 9:12] 10:11 [a] Num. 28:3 10:12 [a] Col. 3:1; Heb. 1:3 [b] Ps. 110:1 10:13 [a] Ps. 110:1; Heb. 1:13 10:16 [a] Jer. 31:33, 34; Heb. 8:10 [1] Jeremiah 31:33 10:17 [a] Jer. 31:34 [1] Jeremiah 31:34 10:19 [a] [Eph. 2:18]; Heb. 4:16 [b] Heb. 9:8, 12 10:20 [a] John 14:6; [Heb. 7:24, 25] 10:22 [a] Heb. 7:19; 10:1 [b] Eph. 3:12 10:23 [a] 1 Cor. 1:9; 10:13; 1 Thess. 5:24; Heb. 11:11 10:25 [a] Acts 2:42 [b] Rom. 13:11 [c] Phil. 4:5 10:26 [a] Num. 15:30 [b] 2 Pet. 2:20 [c] Heb. 6:6 10:27 [a] Zeph. 1:18 10:28 [a] Deut. 17:2–6; 19:15; Matt. 18:16; Heb. 2:2 10:29 [a] [Heb. 2:3] [b] 1 Cor. 11:29 [c] [Matt. 12:31] 10:30 [a] Deut. 32:35; Rom. 12:19 [b] Deut. 32:36 [1] Deuteronomy 32:35 [2] NU-Text omits *says the Lord.* [3] Deuteronomy 32:36 10:31 [a] [Luke 12:5] 10:32 [a] Gal. 3:4; Heb. 6:9, 10 10:33 [a] 1 Cor. 4:9; Heb. 12:4 [b] Phil. 1:7 10:34 [a] 2 Tim. 1:16 [b] Matt. 5:12
[1] NU-Text reads *the prisoners* instead of *me in my chains.*

LIFE SUPPORT

BE UNMOVABLE: STICK WITH GOD'S PLAN IN THE MIDST OF SUFFERING

Let us hold fast the confession of our hope without wavering, for He who promised is faithful. Hebrews 10:23

LIFE: Be Unmovable

When you are in a tough place, imagine God soothing you by declaring the truth of Romans 8:18 over you: "I will never allow the intensity of the suffering to be greater than the intensity of My glory." We must know that when we suffer, although it can be intense and difficult, God will never allow our pain to overshadow His power. He will never allow our struggles to overshadow His strength. He will never allow the warfare against us to overshadow His will for us. God has promised that He will work all things for our good if we love Him (see Rom. 8:28). We cannot let our circumstances become louder than God's Word over us. We cannot let our issues become more important than what God has promised us.

There will be days when we feel as though all our strength is gone. Remember, where we are weak, He is strong. Before He will let us fall, He will carry us. Before He will let us give up, He will strengthen us. Whatever we go through is always subject to God's Word because His Word is always final and guaranteed. We cannot know the future, but God does. He has a plan and purpose for each of our lives, and He will bring about His best in our tomorrows, no matter how fierce today's trials might be.

SUPPORT: Stick with God's Plan in the Midst of Suffering

What a viewpoint! To stick with God in the midst of our suffering, it is good first to know that He sees, knows, and cares about what we are going through. As we go through pain, God wants us to go to Him. Then we can rest in knowing He will bring comfort amid the chaos.

In dark times, we should spend time in God's Word. By meditating on His Word, we learn about the characteristics of God. On the pages of the Bible, we find that God does not faint. He never gets weary. We might, but He does not. The Almighty also gives us power through the Holy Spirit to endure. Being connected to God, then, increases our strength. When the wind tosses us to and fro and tough circumstances bring chaos, we can stick with God and allow Him to give us peace in the midst of our storms. He is unchanging and He is faithful. Even in the trials, we can know His power, love, and peace.

SUPPORT EXAMPLE: **Offer to do household chores for someone in the hospital or recovering at home.**

knowing that [c]you have a better and an enduring possession for yourselves in heaven.[2] 35Therefore do not cast away your confidence, [a]which has great reward. 36[a]For you have need of endurance, so that after you have done the will of God, [b]you may receive the promise:

37 "For [a]yet a little while,
And [b]He[1] who is coming will
come and will not tarry.
38 Now [a]the[1] just shall live by faith;
But if *anyone* draws back,
My soul has no pleasure
in him."[2]

10:34 [c] Matt. 6:20 [2] NU-Text omits *in heaven.* 10:35 [a] Matt. 5:12 10:36 [a] Luke 21:19; Heb. 12:1 [b] [Col. 3:24] 10:37 [a] Luke 18:8 [b] Hab. 2:3, 4; Heb. 10:25; Rev. 22:20 [1] Or *that which* 10:38 [a] Hab. 2:3, 4; Rom. 1:17; Gal. 3:11 [1] NU-Text reads *My just one.* [2] Habakkuk 2:3, 4

39But we are not of those [a]who draw back
to perdition, but of those who [b]believe to
the saving of the soul.

By Faith We Understand

11 Now faith is the substance of things
hoped for, the evidence [a]of things not
seen. 2For by it the elders obtained a *good*
testimony.

3By faith we understand that [a]the worlds
were framed by the word of God, so that
the things which are seen were not made
of things which are visible.

Faith at the Dawn of History

(Gen. 4:1–16; 5:18–24; 6:5—8:22)

4By faith [a]Abel offered to God a more excellent sacrifice than Cain, through which
he obtained witness that he was righteous,
God testifying of his gifts; and through it
he being dead still [b]speaks.

5By faith Enoch was taken away so that
he did not see death, [a]"and was not found,
because God had taken him";[1] for before
he was taken he had this testimony, that
he pleased God. 6But without faith *it is* impossible to please *Him,* for he who comes to
God must believe that He is, and *that* He is a
rewarder of those who diligently seek Him.

7By faith [a]Noah, being divinely warned
of things not yet seen, moved with godly
fear, [b]prepared an ark for the saving of his
household, by which he condemned the
world and became heir of [c]the righteousness which is according to faith.

Faithful Abraham

(Gen. 15:1–6; 21:1–7)

8By faith [a]Abraham obeyed when he was
called to go out to the place which he would
receive as an inheritance. And he went out,
not knowing where he was going. 9By faith
he dwelt in the land of promise as *in* a foreign country, [a]dwelling in tents with Isaac
and Jacob, [b]the heirs with him of the same
promise; 10for he waited for [a]the city which
has foundations, [b]whose builder and maker
is God.

11By faith [a]Sarah herself also received
strength to conceive seed, and [b]she bore
a child[1] when she was past the age, because she judged Him [c]faithful who had
promised. 12Therefore from one man, and
him as good as [a]dead, were born *as many*
as the [b]stars of the sky in multitude—
innumerable as the sand which is by the
seashore.

The Heavenly Hope

13These all died in faith, [a]not having received the [b]promises, but [c]having seen them
afar off were assured of them,[1] embraced
them and [d]confessed that they were strangers and pilgrims on the earth. 14For those
who say such things [a]declare plainly that
they seek a homeland. 15And truly if they
had called to mind [a]that *country* from which
they had come out, they would have had opportunity to return. 16But now they desire
a better, that is, a heavenly *country.* Therefore God is not ashamed [a]to be called their
God, for He has [b]prepared a city for them.

The Faith of the Patriarchs

(Gen. 22:1–14; 48:8–16; 50:22–25)

17By faith Abraham, [a]when he was tested,
offered up Isaac, and he who had received
the promises offered up his only begotten
son, 18of whom it was said, [a]"In Isaac your
seed shall be called,"[1] 19concluding that God
[a]*was* able to raise *him* up, even from the
dead, from which he also received him in
a figurative sense.

20By faith [a]Isaac blessed Jacob and Esau
concerning things to come.

21By faith Jacob, when he was dying,
[a]blessed each of the sons of Joseph, and
worshiped, *leaning* on the top of his staff.

22By faith [a]Joseph, when he was dying,
made mention of the departure of the children of Israel, and gave instructions concerning his bones.

10:39 [a] 2 Pet. 2:20 [b] Acts 16:31 11:1 [a] Rom. 8:24; [2 Cor. 4:18; 5:7]; Heb. 11:7, 27 11:3 [a] Gen. 1:1; Ps. 33:6; [John 1:3]; 2 Pet. 3:5
11:4 [a] Gen. 4:3–5; Matt. 23:35; 1 John 3:12 [b] Gen. 4:8–10; Heb. 12:24 11:5 [a] Gen. 5:21–24 [1] Genesis 5:24 11:7 [a] Gen. 6:13–22
[b] 1 Pet. 3:20 [c] Rom. 3:22 11:8 [a] Gen. 12:1–4; Acts 7:2–4 11:9 [a] Gen. 12:8; 13:3, 18; 18:1, 9 [b] Heb. 6:17 11:10 [a] [Heb. 12:22; 13:14]
[b] [Rev. 21:10] 11:11 [a] Gen. 17:19; 18:11–14; 21:1, 2 [b] Luke 1:36 [c] Heb. 10:23 [1] NU-Text omits *she bore a child.*
11:12 [a] Rom. 4:19 [b] Gen. 15:5; 22:17; 32:12 11:13 [a] Heb. 11:39 [b] Gen. 12:7 [c] John 8:56; Heb. 11:27 [d] Gen. 23:4; 47:9; 1 Chr. 29:15;
Ps. 39:12; Eph. 2:19; 1 Pet. 1:17; 2:11 [1] NU-Text and M-Text omit *were assured of them.* 11:14 [a] Heb. 13:14 11:15 [a] Gen. 11:31
11:16 [a] Gen. 26:24; 28:13; Ex. 3:6, 15; 4:5 [b] [John 14:2]; Heb. 11:10; [Rev. 21:2] 11:17 [a] Gen. 22:1–14; James 2:21
11:18 [a] Gen. 21:12; Rom. 9:7 [1] Genesis 21:12 11:19 [a] Rom. 4:17 11:20 [a] Gen. 27:26–40
11:21 [a] Gen. 48:1, 5, 16, 20 11:22 [a] Gen. 50:24, 25; Ex. 13:19

The Faith of Moses
(Ex. 2:1–10; 12:31–51)

23By faith [a]Moses, when he was born,
was hidden three months by his parents,
because they saw *he was* a beautiful child;
and they were not afraid of the king's [b]com-
mand.
24By faith [a]Moses, when he became of
age, refused to be called the son of Pharaoh's daughter, 25choosing rather to suffer
affliction with the people of God than to enjoy the passing pleasures of sin, 26esteem-
ing [a]the reproach of Christ greater riches
than the treasures in[1] Egypt; for he looked
to the [b]reward.
27By faith [a]he forsook Egypt, not fearing the wrath of the king; for he endured
as seeing Him who is invisible. 28By faith
[a]he kept the Passover and the sprinkling of
blood, lest he who destroyed the firstborn
should touch them.
29By faith [a]they passed through the Red
Sea as by dry *land, whereas* the Egyptians,
attempting to do so, were drowned.

By Faith They Overcame

30By faith [a]the walls of Jericho fell down
after they were encircled for seven days.
31By faith [a]the harlot Rahab did not perish
with those who did not believe, when [b]she
had received the spies with peace.
32And what more shall I say? For the
time would fail me to tell of [a]Gideon and
[b]Barak and [c]Samson and [d]Jephthah, also
of [e]David and [f]Samuel and the prophets:
33who through faith subdued kingdoms,
worked righteousness, obtained promises,
[a]stopped the mouths of lions, 34[a]quenched
the violence of fire, escaped the edge of the
sword, out of weakness were made strong,
became valiant in battle, turned to flight
the armies of the aliens. 35[a]Women received
their dead raised to life again.
Others were [b]tortured, not accepting deliverance, that they might obtain a better resurrection. 36Still others
had trial of mockings and scourgings,
yes, and [a]of chains and imprisonment.
37[a]They were stoned, they were sawn in
two, were tempted,[1] were slain with the
sword. [b]They wandered about [c]in sheep-
skins and goatskins, being destitute, afflicted, tormented— 38of whom the world
was not worthy. They wandered in deserts and mountains, [a]*in* dens and caves
of the earth.
39And all these, [a]having obtained a good
testimony through faith, did not receive
the promise, 40God having provided something better for us, that they should not be
[a]made perfect apart from us.

The Race of Faith

12 Therefore we also, since we are surrounded by so great a cloud of witnesses, [a]let us lay aside every weight, and
the sin which so easily ensnares *us*, and [b]let
us run [c]with endurance the race that is set
before us, 2looking unto Jesus, the author
and finisher of *our* faith, [a]who for the joy
that was set before Him [b]endured the cross,
despising the shame, and [c]has sat down at
the right hand of the throne of God.

The Discipline of God
(Prov. 3:11, 12)

3[a]For consider Him who endured such
hostility from sinners against Himself, [b]lest
you become weary and discouraged in your
souls. 4[a]You have not yet resisted to bloodshed, striving against sin. 5And you have
forgotten the exhortation which speaks to
you as to sons:

[a]"My son, do not despise the
chastening of the LORD,
Nor be discouraged when you
are rebuked by Him;
6 For [a]whom the LORD loves
He chastens,
And scourges every son
whom He receives."[1]

11:23 [a] Ex. 2:1–3 [b] Ex. 1:16, 22 11:24 [a] Ex. 2:11–15 11:26 [a] Heb. 13:13 [b] Rom. 8:18; 2 Cor. 4:17 [1] NU-Text and M-Text read *of*. 11:27 [a] Ex. 10:28 11:28 [a] Ex. 12:21 11:29 [a] Ex. 14:22–29; Jude 5 11:30 [a] Josh. 6:20 11:31 [a] Josh. 2:9; 6:23; James 2:25 [b] Josh. 2:1 11:32 [a] Judg. 6:11; 7:1–25 [b] Judg. 4:6–24 [c] Judg. 13:24—16:31 [d] Judg. 11:1–29; 12:1–7 [e] 1 Sam. 16; 17 [f] 1 Sam. 7:9–14 11:33 [a] Judg. 14:6; 1 Sam. 17:34; Dan. 6:22 11:34 [a] Dan. 3:23–28 11:35 [a] 1 Kin. 17:22; 2 Kin. 4:35–37 [b] Acts 22:25 11:36 [a] Gen. 39:20; 1 Kin. 22:27; 2 Chr. 18:26; Jer. 20:2; 37:15 11:37 [a] 1 Kin. 21:13; 2 Chr. 24:21; Acts 7:58 [b] 2 Kin. 1:8; Matt. 3:4 [c] 1 Kin. 19:13, 19; 2 Kin. 2:8, 13; Zech. 13:4 [1] NU-Text omits *were tempted*. 11:38 [a] 1 Kin. 18:4, 13; 19:9 11:39 [a] Heb. 11:2, 13 11:40 [a] Heb. 5:9 12:1 [a] Col. 3:8 [b] 1 Cor. 9:24; Gal. 2:2; Heb. 10:39 [c] Rom. 12:12; Heb. 10:36 12:2 [a] Luke 24:26 [b] Ps. 69:7, 19; Phil. 2:8; [Heb. 2:9] [c] Ps. 110:1 12:3 [a] Matt. 10:24 [b] Gal. 6:9; Heb. 12:5 12:4 [a] [1 Cor. 10:13] 12:5 [a] Job 5:17; Prov. 3:11, 12 12:6 [a] Ps. 94:12; Rev. 3:19 [1] Proverbs 3:11, 12

7[a]If[1] you endure chastening, God deals
with you as with sons; for what [b]son is there
whom a father does not chasten? 8But if
you are without chastening, [a]of which all
have become partakers, then you are illegitimate and not sons. 9Furthermore, we
have had human fathers who corrected
us, and we paid *them* respect. Shall we not
much more readily be in subjection to [a]the
Father of spirits and live? 10For they indeed for a few days chastened *us* as seemed
best to them, but He for *our* profit, [a]that *we*
may be partakers of His holiness. 11Now no
chastening seems to be joyful for the present, but painful; nevertheless, afterward
it yields [a]the peaceable fruit of righteousness to those who have been trained by it.

#OXYGEN
HEBREWS 12:11
Reconcile Darkness with Light

We often equate darkness with being frustrated by life. However, God works within our circumstances to train and strengthen us. Be careful that you do not attribute the training tactics of the Lord to the Enemy. Remember, God works all things for good for the ones who love Him.

Be patient, **breathe,** and **reconcile darkness with light.**

Renew Your Spiritual Vitality
(Gen. 25:29–34; 27:30–40)

12Therefore [a]strengthen the hands which
hang down, and the feeble knees, 13and
make straight paths for your feet, so that
what is lame may not be dislocated, but
rather be healed.
14[a]Pursue peace with all *people,* and holiness, [b]without which no one will see the
Lord: 15looking carefully lest anyone [a]fall
short of the grace of God; lest any [b]root of
bitterness springing up cause trouble, and
by this many become defiled; 16lest there
be any [a]fornicator or profane person like
Esau, [b]who for one morsel of food sold his
birthright. 17For you know that afterward,
when he wanted to inherit the blessing,
he was [a]rejected, for he found no place for
repentance, though he sought it diligently
with tears.

The Glorious Company

18For you have not come to [a]the mountain that[1] may be touched and that burned
with fire, and to blackness and darkness[2]
and tempest, 19and the sound of a trumpet
and the voice of words, so that those who
heard *it* [a]begged that the word should not
be spoken to them anymore. 20(For they
could not endure what was commanded:
[a]"And if so much as a beast touches the
mountain, it shall be stoned[1] or shot with
an arrow."[2] 21And so terrifying was the sight
that Moses said, [a]"I am exceedingly afraid
and trembling."[1])
22But you have come to Mount Zion and
to the city of the living God, the heavenly
Jerusalem, to an innumerable company
of angels, 23to the general assembly and
church of [a]the firstborn [b]*who are* registered
in heaven, to God [c]the Judge of all, to the
spirits of just men [d]made perfect, 24to Jesus
[a]the Mediator of the new covenant, and to
[b]the blood of sprinkling that speaks better
things [c]than *that of* Abel.

Hear the Heavenly Voice

25See that you do not refuse Him who
speaks. For [a]if they did not escape who refused Him who spoke on earth, much more
shall we not escape if we turn away from
Him who *speaks* from heaven, 26whose
voice then shook the earth; but now He
has promised, saying, [a]"Yet once more I
shake[1] not only the earth, but also heaven."[2]
27Now this, "Yet once more," indicates the
[a]removal of those things that are being
shaken, as of things that are made, that

12:7 [a] Deut. 8:5; 2 Sam. 7:14 [b] Prov. 13:24; 19:18; 23:13 [1] NU-Text and M-Text read *It is for discipline that you endure; God. . . .* **12:8** [a] 1 Pet. 5:9 **12:9** [a] [Job 12:10] **12:10** [a] Lev. 11:44 **12:11** [a] Is. 32:17; 2 Tim. 4:8; James 3:17, 18 **12:12** [a] Is. 35:3 **12:14** [a] Ps. 34:14 [b] Matt. 5:8; [Heb. 9:28] **12:15** [a] 2 Cor. 6:1; Gal. 5:4; Heb. 4:1 [b] Deut. 29:18 **12:16** [a] [1 Cor. 6:13–18] [b] Gen. 25:33 **12:17** [a] Gen. 27:30–40 **12:18** [a] Ex. 19:12, 16; 20:18; Deut. 4:11; 5:22 [1] NU-Text reads *to that which.* [2] NU-Text reads *gloom.* **12:19** [a] Ex. 20:18–26; Deut. 5:25; 18:16 **12:20** [a] Ex. 19:12, 13 [1] NU-Text and M-Text omit the rest of this verse. [2] Exodus 19:12, 13 **12:21** [a] Deut. 9:19 [1] Deuteronomy 9:19 **12:23** [a] [James 1:18] [b] Luke 10:20 [c] Gen. 18:25; Ps. 50:6; 94:2 [d] [Phil. 3:12] **12:24** [a] 1 Tim. 2:5; Heb. 8:6; 9:15 [b] Ex. 24:8 [c] Gen. 4:10; Heb. 11:4 **12:25** [a] Heb. 2:2, 3 **12:26** [a] Hag. 2:6 [1] NU-Text reads *will shake.* [2] Haggai 2:6 **12:27** [a] [Is. 34:4; 54:10; 65:17; Rom. 8:19, 21]; 1 Cor. 7:31; Heb. 1:10

the things which cannot be shaken may
remain.
28Therefore, since we are receiving a
kingdom which cannot be shaken, let us
have grace, by which we may[1] [a]serve God
acceptably with reverence and godly fear.
29For [a]our God *is* a consuming fire.

Concluding Moral Directions

13 Let [a]brotherly love continue. 2[a]Do
not forget to entertain strangers, for
by so *doing* [b]some have unwittingly entertained angels. 3[a]Remember the prisoners
as if chained with them—those who are
mistreated—since you yourselves are in
the body also.
4[a]Marriage *is* honorable among all, and
the bed undefiled; [b]but fornicators and
adulterers God will judge.
5*Let your* conduct *be* without covetousness; *be* content with such things as you
have. For He Himself has said, [a]"I will never
leave you nor forsake you."[1] 6So we may
boldly say:

[a]"The LORD *is* my helper;
I will not fear.
What can man do to me?"[1]

Concluding Religious Directions

7Remember those who rule over you,
who have spoken the word of God to you,
whose faith follow, considering the outcome of *their* conduct. 8Jesus Christ *is* [a]the
same yesterday, today, and forever. 9Do not
be carried about[1] with various and strange
doctrines. For *it is* good that the heart be
established by grace, not with foods which
have not profited those who have been occupied with them.
10We have an altar from which those who
serve the tabernacle have no right to eat.
11For the bodies of those animals, whose
blood is brought into the sanctuary by the
high priest for sin, are burned outside the
camp. 12Therefore Jesus also, that He might
sanctify the people with His own blood, suffered outside the gate. 13Therefore let us go
forth to Him, outside the camp, bearing
[a]His reproach. 14For here we have no continuing city, but we seek the one to come.
15[a]Therefore by Him let us continually offer
[b]the sacrifice of praise to God, that is, [c]the
fruit of *our* lips, giving thanks to His name.
16[a]But do not forget to do good and to share,
for [b]with such sacrifices God is well pleased.
17[a]Obey those who rule over you, and be
submissive, for [b]they watch out for your
souls, as those who must give account. Let
them do so with joy and not with grief, for
that would be unprofitable for you.

Prayer Requested

18[a]Pray for us; for we are confident that
we have [b]a good conscience, in all things
desiring to live honorably. 19But I especially
urge *you* to do this, that I may be restored
to you the sooner.

Benediction, Final Exhortation, Farewell

20Now may [a]the God of peace [b]who
brought up our Lord Jesus from the dead,
[c]that great Shepherd of the sheep, [d]through
the blood of the everlasting covenant,
21make you complete in every good work
to do His will, [a]working in you[1] what is well
pleasing in His sight, through Jesus Christ,
to whom *be* glory forever and ever. Amen.
22And I appeal to you, brethren, bear
with the word of exhortation, for I have
written to you in few words. 23Know that
our brother Timothy has been set free, with
whom I shall see you if he comes shortly.
24Greet all those who rule over you, and
all the saints. Those from Italy greet you.
25Grace *be* with you all. Amen.

12:28 [a] Heb. 13:15, 21 [1] M-Text omits *may*. **12:29** [a] Ex. 24:17 **13:1** [a] Rom. 12:10 **13:2** [a] Matt. 25:35; Rom. 12:13 [b] Gen. 18:1–22; 19:1 **13:3** [a] Matt. 25:36; Heb. 10:34 **13:4** [a] Prov. 5:18, 19 [b] 1 Cor. 6:9; Gal. 5:19, 21; 1 Thess. 4:6 **13:5** [a] Gen. 28:15; Deut. 31:6, 8; Josh. 1:5 [1] Deuteronomy 31:6, 8; Joshua 1:5 **13:6** [a] Ps. 27:1; 118:6 [1] Psalm 118:6 **13:8** [a] [John 8:58]; 2 Cor. 1:19; Heb. 1:12 **13:9** [1] NU-Text and M-Text read *away*. **13:13** [a] 1 Pet. 4:14 **13:15** [a] Eph. 5:20 [b] Lev. 7:12 [c] Is. 57:19; Hos. 14:2 **13:16** [a] Rom. 12:13 [b] 2 Cor. 9:12; Phil. 4:18 **13:17** [a] Phil. 2:29 [b] Is. 62:6; Ezek. 3:17; Acts 20:28 **13:18** [a] Eph. 6:19 [b] Acts 23:1 **13:20** [a] Rom. 5:1, 2, 10; 15:33 [b] Ps. 16:10, 11; Hos. 6:2; Rom. 4:24 [c] Ps. 23:1; Is. 40:11; 63:11; John 10:11; 1 Pet. 2:25; 5:4 [d] Zech. 9:11; Heb. 10:29 **13:21** [a] Phil. 2:13 [1] NU-Text and M-Text read *us*.

THE EPISTLE OF

JAMES

OVERVIEW

Tradition maintains that James, Jesus' brother, played a major role in the early church (see Acts 12:17; 15:13). Although James had not believed in Jesus during Christ's earthly ministry (see John 7:5), he later came to faith through a special postresurrection encounter (see 1 Cor. 15:7). James's main contribution to the early church focused on Christian conduct. Like the Epistle to the Hebrews, James's letter was written to Jewish Christians who were struggling to understand their new faith in Christ and its implications on how they were to live. James wrote to these Jewish Christians who lived throughout the Roman Empire (see James 1:1) with a clear message: "Faith without works is dead" (2:26). Grace does not mean that a Christian has no work to do; rather, it means that the Christian can finally complete the work God has given.

Historians agree that James's letter is older than any of Paul's epistles; thus his subject matter must be understood from an earlier context of the church. Lacking Paul's later writings expanding on the gospel, many early Jewish believers struggled with casting aside works, associating them with the old way of trying to live under the Law. James wrote: "But be doers of the word, and not hearers only, deceiving yourselves. For if anyone is a hearer of the word and not a doer, he is like a man observing his natural face in a mirror; for he observes himself, goes away, and immediately forgets what kind of man he was" (1:22–24). James made it clear that faith is a call to action when he also said that "faith by itself, if it does not have works, is dead" (2:17). James's argument that true faith must result in works comes from his perspective of addressing believers. Paul, on the other hand, often addressed faith and works from the opposite perspective, from that of the unbeliever. While Paul and James are sometimes seen in disagreement, in reality they are not.

James addressed the church from two perspectives. First, he wanted to help them endure external threats such as persecution and poverty. Second, he wanted to help them manage internal threats such as sin, false teaching, and idleness. Both issues required the active faith he stressed in the letter. The believers' faith was to prompt them to meet the needs of others. From the inception of the church recorded in Acts 2, there was an expectation of faithful service within it and beyond it. James recognized that neglecting the physical and spiritual needs of the church body was to give a foothold to sin. He wrote to the believers to set that expectation: "Is anyone among you suffering? Let him pray. Is anyone cheerful? Let him sing psalms. Is anyone among you sick? Let him call for the elders of the church, and let them pray over him, anointing him with oil in the name of the Lord. And the prayer of faith will save the sick, and the Lord will raise him up. And if he has committed sins, he will be forgiven" (5:13–15). Good thoughts were not enough, even with the best of intentions. Active faith was needed.

BREATHE IT IN

James addressed a Jewish Christian community that was not the biggest, richest, or most influential. The faithful were scattered and suffering. But James recognized the potential for growth as well as the possibility of decline. The early church was in a make-it-or-break-it situation that would destroy them or deliver them, eliminate them or elevate them.

With his community scattered and suffering, James believed that he could summon them back together through his epistle. He knew the Word is sufficient to restore a community, even one that is going through tribulation.

No one wants to endure hardships, but the stamina to persevere is activated in these conditions, which is what James led his letter with (see 1:2–8). The trial presents an opportunity to build endurance. The word *endurance* comes from the Greek word *hypomonē*, which means "perseverance, patience, tolerance, and forbearance." Endurance is not escape; it is bearing up. Endurance is not static; it is always in a state of flux. If you are not building it, you are losing it. Moreover, endurance takes longer to build than it does to lose, meaning it is essential to stay vigilant.

There is an even greater benefit of trials than building endurance, though. As James told the scattered early church: "Blessed is the man who endures temptation; for when he has been approved, he will receive the crown of life which the Lord has promised to those who love Him" (1:12). We have access to a crown that will affect life now on earth and last throughout eternity. With this in mind, breathe in James's call to change your perspective of adversity. You cannot control the circumstances you face, but you can control your responses. Endure and see the will of God anew.

THE EPISTLE OF

JAMES

Greeting to the Twelve Tribes

1 James, [a]a bondservant of God and of the
Lord Jesus Christ,

To the twelve tribes which are scattered
abroad:

Greetings.

Profiting from Trials

2My brethren, [a]count it all joy [b]when you
fall into various trials, 3[a]knowing that the
testing of your faith produces patience.
4But let patience have *its* perfect work, that
you may be perfect and complete, lacking
nothing. 5[a]If any of you lacks wisdom, [b]let
him ask of God, who gives to all liberally
and without reproach, and [c]it will be given
to him. 6[a]But let him ask in faith, with no
doubting, for he who doubts is like a wave
of the sea driven and tossed by the wind.
7For let not that man suppose that he will
receive anything from the Lord; 8*he is* [a]a
double-minded man, unstable in all his
ways.

The Perspective of Rich and Poor

9Let the lowly brother glory in his exaltation, 10but the rich in his humiliation,
because [a]as a flower of the field he will pass
away. 11For no sooner has the sun risen with
a burning heat than it withers the grass; its
flower falls, and its beautiful appearance
perishes. So the rich man also will fade
away in his pursuits.

Loving God Under Trials

12[a]Blessed *is* the man who endures temptation; for when he has been approved,
he will receive [b]the crown of life [c]which
the Lord has promised to those who love
Him. 13Let no one say when he is tempted,
"I am tempted by God"; for God cannot be
tempted by evil, nor does He Himself tempt
anyone. 14But each one is tempted when he
is drawn away by his own desires and enticed. 15Then, [a]when desire has conceived,
it gives birth to sin; and sin, when it is full-
grown, [b]brings forth death.

16Do not be deceived, my beloved brethren. 17[a]Every good gift and every perfect gift
is from above, and comes down from the
Father of lights, [b]with whom there is no
variation or shadow of turning. 18[a]Of His
own will He brought us forth by the [b]word
of truth, [c]that we might be a kind of firstfruits of His creatures.

Qualities Needed in Trials

19So then,[1] my beloved brethren, let every man be swift to hear, [a]slow to speak,
[b]slow to wrath; 20for the wrath of man does
not produce the righteousness of God.

Doers—Not Hearers Only

21Therefore [a]lay aside all filthiness and
overflow of wickedness, and receive with
meekness the implanted word, [b]which is
able to save your souls.

22But [a]be doers of the word, and not
hearers only, deceiving yourselves. 23For

1:1 [a] Acts 12:17 1:2 [a] Acts 5:41 [b] 1 Pet. 1:6 1:3 [a] Rom. 5:3–5 1:5 [a] 1 Kin. 3:9; James 3:17 [b] Prov. 2:3–6; Matt. 7:7 [c] Jer. 29:12
1:6 [a] [Mark 11:23, 24]; Acts 10:20 1:8 [a] James 4:8 1:10 [a] Job 14:2 1:12 [a] Job 5:17; Luke 6:22; Heb. 10:36; James 5:11; [1 Pet. 3:14; 4:14]
[b] [1 Cor. 9:25] [c] Matt. 10:22 1:15 [a] Job 15:35; Ps. 7:14; Is. 59:4 [b] [Rom. 5:12; 6:23] 1:17 [a] John 3:27 [b] Num. 23:19 1:18 [a] John 1:13
[b] 2 Cor. 6:7; 1 Thess. 2:13; 2 Tim. 2:15; [1 Pet. 1:3, 23] [c] [Eph. 1:12, 13]; Heb. 12:23; Rev. 14:4 1:19 [a] Prov. 10:19; 17:27 [b] Prov. 14:17; 16:32;
Eccl. 7:9 [1] NU-Text reads *Know this* or *This you know.* 1:21 [a] Col. 3:8 [b] Acts 13:26 1:22 [a] Matt. 7:21–28;
Luke 6:46–49; [Rom. 2:13; James 1:22–25; 2:14–20]

RELEASE // EXALT HIS SPLENDID OMNISCIENCE

God's Plan

James 1:5 // If any of you lacks wisdom, let him ask of God, who gives to all liberally and without reproach, and it will be given to him.

Summary Message // God knows all. He is the source of all wisdom. His Word assures us of this fact, and we are further encouraged to ask Him for His wisdom. There are moments, and sometimes even seasons, when we think we know everything we need to know. But then when we get hit with trials, transition, trouble, or tension, we realize we do not know much at all.

As James opened his epistle, he described trials and how we can benefit from them. Trials test our faith and produce patience, which in turn produces maturity. If we are to benefit from trials, then, we cannot rush to escape them too quickly. Instead, we must endure them with patience, getting all that God intended us to get from them. But if we do not know what we are to learn during a trial, then we only need to ask God, trusting that He will answer.

James also warns us how fast our worldly pursuits can dry up and fade away. This first chapter is full of challenging instructions about temptation, listening, anger, and controlling our tongues. He encourages us to apply these words, follow God's plan for our lives, and not let the world corrupt us.

Practical Application // Many of us have prayed for wisdom holding on to James 1:5 but forget about the verse that follows: "But let him ask in faith, with no doubting, for he who doubts is like a wave of the sea driven and tossed by the wind." Many of us struggle with lacking faith. The reason is that we have been conditioned to doubt. People and circumstances have let us down, and it is easy for us to connect these failures to God and think He has let us down. Many of us also have prayers that were not answered the way we wanted. Sometimes, God heals and provides, and other times He does not. The Bible does not promise that God will answer a prayer that lacks faith, but it is clear that He always loves us and has our best interests in mind. We must approach every request, then, with faith and hope.

We must trust God and remember that He is all-knowing. He has more information and wisdom than we can imagine. We cannot fathom His thoughts and plans. When James tells us to "count it all joy" during trials (James 1:2), he does not mean we are to find happiness in the trial itself. He is not saying to be joyful about a flat tire, sick family member, or conflict at work. Rather, we find joy knowing there can be a positive outcome, lesson, or blessing when the trial ends. The next time a drama jumps into your path, remind yourself that God could be up to something. If you walk through trials the right way, you will ultimately discover that God has a plan.

Fervent Prayer // Heavenly Father, forgive us for the times when we doubt Your wisdom. We admit we do not know everything, and we acknowledge that You do. Help us to learn to trust You through the trials of life and seek You for wisdom. Bless us with patience and endurance. Use our struggles and stories to bless others. Help us not only to be hearers of Your instructions but to become people who live according to Your leading all day, every day. In Jesus' name we pray. Amen.

---

[a]if anyone is a hearer of the word and not a
doer, he is like a man observing his natural
face in a mirror; 24for he observes himself,
goes away, and immediately forgets what
kind of man he was. 25But [a]he who looks
into the perfect law of liberty and continues *in it,* and is not a forgetful hearer but a
doer of the work, [b]this one will be blessed
in what he does.

26If anyone among you[1] thinks he is religious, and [a]does not bridle his tongue but
deceives his own heart, this one's religion
is useless. 27[a]Pure and undefiled religion
before God and the Father is this: [b]to visit

1:23 [a] Luke 6:47 1:25 [a] [John 8:32; Rom. 8:2; 2 Cor. 3:17]; Gal. 2:4; 6:2; James 2:12; 1 Pet. 2:16 [b] John 13:17
1:26 [a] Ps. 34:13 [1] NU-Text omits *among you.* 1:27 [a] Matt. 25:34–36 [b] Is. 1:17

orphans and widows in their trouble, [c]*and* to keep oneself unspotted from the world.

Beware of Personal Favoritism

2 My brethren, do not hold the faith of our Lord Jesus Christ, [a]*the Lord* of glory, with [b]partiality. 2 For if there should come into your assembly a man with gold rings, in fine apparel, and there should also come in a poor man in filthy clothes, 3 and you pay attention to the one wearing the fine clothes and say to him, "You sit here in a good place," and say to the poor man, "You stand there," or, "Sit here at my footstool," 4 have you not shown partiality among yourselves, and become judges with evil thoughts?

5 Listen, my beloved brethren: [a]Has God not chosen the poor of this world *to be* [b]rich in faith and heirs of the kingdom [c]which He promised to those who love Him? 6 But [a]you have dishonored the poor man. Do not the rich oppress you [b]and drag you into the courts? 7 Do they not blaspheme that noble name by which you are [a]called?

8 If you really fulfill *the* royal law according to the Scripture, [a]"You shall love your neighbor as yourself,"[1] you do well; 9 but if you show partiality, you commit sin, and are convicted by the law as [a]transgressors. 10 For whoever shall keep the whole law, and yet [a]stumble in one *point,* [b]he is guilty of all. 11 For He who said, [a]"Do not commit adultery,"[1] also said, [b]"Do not murder."[2] Now if you do not commit adultery, but you do murder, you have become a transgressor of the law. 12 So speak and so do as those who will be judged by [a]the law of liberty. 13 For [a]judgment is without mercy to the one who has shown [b]no [c]mercy. [d]Mercy triumphs over judgment.

Faith Without Works Is Dead

(cf. Gen. 22; Josh. 2)

14 [a]What *does it* profit, my brethren, if someone says he has faith but does not have works? Can faith save him? 15 [a]If a brother or sister is naked and destitute of daily food, 16 and [a]one of you says to them, "Depart in peace, be warmed and filled," but you do not give them the things which are needed for the body, what *does it* profit? 17 Thus also faith by itself, if it does not have works, is dead.

18 But someone will say, "You have faith, and I have works." [a]Show me your faith without your[1] works, [b]and I will show you my faith by my[2] works. 19 You believe that there is one God. You do well. Even the demons believe—and tremble! 20 But do you want to know, O foolish man, that faith without works is dead?[1] 21 Was not Abraham our father justified by works [a]when he offered Isaac his son on the altar? 22 Do you see [a]that faith was working together with his works, and by [b]works faith was made perfect? 23 And the Scripture was fulfilled which says, [a]"Abraham believed God, and it was accounted to him for righteousness."[1] And he was called [b]the friend of God. 24 You see then that a man is justified by works, and not by faith only.

25 Likewise, [a]was not Rahab the harlot also justified by works when she received the messengers and sent *them* out another way?

26 For as the body without the spirit is dead, so faith without works is dead also.

The Untamable Tongue

3 My brethren, [a]let not many of you become teachers, [b]knowing that we shall receive a stricter judgment. 2 For [a]we all stumble in many things. [b]If anyone does not stumble in word, [c]he *is* a perfect man, able also to bridle the whole body. 3 Indeed,[1] [a]we put bits in horses' mouths that they may obey us, and we turn their whole body. 4 Look also at ships: although they are so large and are driven by fierce winds, they are turned by a very small rudder wherever the pilot desires. 5 Even so

---

1:27 [c] [Rom. 12:2] 2:1 [a] Acts 7:2; 1 Cor. 2:8 [b] Lev. 19:15 2:5 [a] Job 34:19; John 7:48; 1 Cor. 1:27 [b] Luke 12:21; 1 Tim. 6:18; Rev. 2:9 [c] Ex. 20:6 2:6 [a] 1 Cor. 11:22 [b] Acts 13:50 2:7 [a] Acts 11:26; 1 Pet. 4:16 2:8 [a] Lev. 19:18 [1] Leviticus 19:18 2:9 [a] Lev. 19:15; Deut. 1:17 2:10 [a] Gal. 3:10 [b] Deut. 27:26 2:11 [a] Ex. 20:14; Deut. 5:18 [b] Ex. 20:13; Deut. 5:17 [1] Exodus 20:14; Deuteronomy 5:18 [2] Exodus 20:13; Deuteronomy 5:17 2:12 [a] James 1:25 2:13 [a] Job 22:6 [b] Prov. 21:13; Matt. 18:32–35; [Luke 6:37] [c] Mic. 7:18; [Matt. 5:7] [d] Rom. 12:8 2:14 [a] Matt. 7:21–23, 26; 21:28–32 2:15 [a] Matt. 25:35; Luke 3:11 2:16 [a] [1 John 3:17, 18] 2:18 [a] Col. 1:6; 1 Thess. 1:3; Heb. 6:10 [b] [Gal. 5:6]; James 3:13 [1] NU-Text omits *your.* [2] NU-Text omits *my.* 2:20 [1] NU-Text reads *useless.* 2:21 [a] Gen. 22:9, 10, 12, 16–18 2:22 [a] [John 6:29]; Heb. 11:17 [b] John 8:39 2:23 [a] Gen. 15:6; Rom. 4:3 [b] 2 Chr. 20:7; Is. 41:8 [1] Genesis 15:6 2:25 [a] Heb. 11:31 3:1 [a] [Matt. 23:8]; Rom. 2:21; 1 Tim. 1:7 [b] Luke 6:37 3:2 [a] 1 Kin. 8:46 [b] Ps. 34:13 [c] [Matt. 12:34–37; James 3:2–12] 3:3 [a] Ps. 32:9 [1] NU-Text reads *Now if.*

EXALT HIS SPLENDID OMNISCIENCE

INHALE

To say I'm worried for my children is an understatement. I'm a believer and know I need not fear, but hatred still persists, and I'm afraid for my children. If God is everywhere and is aware of everything, why won't He stop the violence? When will He fix the hearts of people?

EXHALE

Beginning with Adam and Eve, humankind has had the option of choosing to love and obey God or to disobey and withhold love. The choice to disobey God was the sin committed by Adam and Eve, and all people since have been held captive by sin and its result. We only need to look around us to see the destructive consequence of sin. No one is safe from its violent, hateful ways.

Yet, God was not taken by surprise by Adam and Eve's choice, just as He is not shocked by the choices made today. Because He is omniscient, His plan to free us from sin's power began even before He formed the world. He told His people throughout the Old Testament that He would send a Savior who would free His people from sin and death. Jesus is the Promised One who has conquered sin and now offers a new heart, mind, and life to all who will receive.

We can never forget that God is all-knowing. Whatever happens in this universe happens under His watchful eye. We know from His Word that He is even mindful of every sparrow and has numbered the hairs on our heads. God is not unaware of the hateful acts committed in this world or the consequences of those acts. However, God has given each of us the ability to choose a better way, to choose obedience and love, which James 2:8 describes as the "royal law." But love cannot be coerced. And as long as people can choose to love, they can choose not to love. They can choose to hate instead. But when we love our neighbors as ourselves, we show the way of love and we support the message of love we have to share—the gospel. God is at work fixing the hearts of people, and He does that, in part, through our loving obedience.

[a]the tongue is a little member and [b]boasts
great things.
See how great a forest a little fire kindles! 6And [a]the tongue *is* a fire, a world of
iniquity. The tongue is so set among our
members that it [b]defiles the whole body,
and sets on fire the course of nature; and
it is set on fire by hell. 7For every kind of
beast and bird, of reptile and creature of the
sea, is tamed and has been tamed by mankind. 8But no man can tame the tongue.
It is an unruly evil, [a]full of deadly poison.
9With it we bless our God and Father, and
with it we curse men, who have been made
[a]in the similitude of God. 10Out of the same
mouth proceed blessing and cursing. My
brethren, these things ought not to be so.
11Does a spring send forth fresh *water* and
bitter from the same opening? 12Can a [a]fig
tree, my brethren, bear olives, or a grapevine bear figs? Thus no spring yields both
salt water and fresh.[1]

Heavenly Versus Demonic Wisdom

13[a]Who *is* wise and understanding
among you? Let him show by good conduct *that* his works *are done* in the meekness of wisdom. 14But if you have [a]bitter
envy and self-seeking in your hearts, [b]do
not boast and lie against the truth. 15[a]This
wisdom does not descend from above, but
is earthly, sensual, demonic. 16For [a]where
envy and self-seeking *exist,* confusion and
every evil thing *are* there. 17But [a]the wisdom that is from above is first pure, then
peaceable, gentle, willing to yield, full of

3:5 [a] Prov. 12:18; 15:2; James 1:26 [b] Ps. 12:3; 73:8 3:6 [a] Ps. 120:2, 3; Prov. 16:27 [b] [Matt. 12:36; 15:11, 18] 3:8 [a] Ps. 140:3; Eccl. 10:11; Rom. 3:13 3:9 [a] Gen. 1:26; 5:1; 9:6; 1 Cor. 11:7 3:12 [a] Matt. 7:16–20 [1] NU-Text reads *Neither can a salty spring produce fresh water.* 3:13 [a] Gal. 6:4 3:14 [a] Rom. 13:13 [b] Rom. 2:17 3:15 [a] Phil. 3:19 3:16 [a] 1 Cor. 3:3 3:17 [a] 1 Cor. 2:6, 7

#OXYGEN
JAMES 3:17

Exalt His Splendid Omniscience

The Father truly knows us through and through. He has handcrafted circumstances in our lives that will produce everlasting fruit if we endure. But He also stands ready to pour out His wisdom on us so that we can endure. Even when it seems we are stuck, He has given us access to all we need. Hallelujah!

Breathe and **exalt His splendid omniscience.**

mercy and good fruits, [b]without partiality [c]and without hypocrisy. 18 [a]Now the fruit of righteousness is sown in peace by those who make peace.

Pride Promotes Strife

4 Where do wars and fights *come* from among you? Do *they* not *come* from your *desires for* pleasure [a]that war in your members? 2 You lust and do not have. You murder and covet and cannot obtain. You fight and war. Yet[1] you do not have because you do not ask. 3 [a]You ask and do not receive, [b]because you ask amiss, that you may spend *it* on your pleasures. 4 Adulterers and[1] adulteresses! Do you not know that [a]friendship with the world is enmity with God? [b]Whoever therefore wants to be a friend of the world makes himself an enemy of God. 5 Or do you think that the Scripture says in vain, [a]"The Spirit who dwells in us yearns jealously"?

6 But He gives more grace. Therefore He says:

> [a]"God resists the proud,
> But gives grace to the
> humble."[1]

Humility Cures Worldliness

7 Therefore submit to God. [a]Resist the devil and he will flee from you. 8 [a]Draw near to God and He will draw near to you. [b]Cleanse *your* hands, *you* sinners; and [c]purify *your* hearts, *you* double-minded. 9 [a]Lament and mourn and weep! Let your laughter be turned to mourning and *your* joy to gloom. 10 [a]Humble yourselves in the sight of the Lord, and He will lift you up.

Do Not Judge a Brother

11 [a]Do not speak evil of one another, brethren. He who speaks evil of a brother [b]and judges his brother, speaks evil of the law and judges the law. But if you judge the law, you are not a doer of the law but a judge. 12 There is one Lawgiver,[1] [a]who is able to save and to destroy. [b]Who[2] are you to judge another?[3]

Do Not Boast About Tomorrow

13 Come now, you who say, "Today or tomorrow we will[1] go to such and such a city, spend a year there, buy and sell, and make a profit"; 14 whereas you do not know what *will happen* tomorrow. For what *is* your life? [a]It is even a vapor that appears for a little time and then vanishes away. 15 Instead you *ought* to say, [a]"If the Lord wills, we shall live and do this or that." 16 But now you boast in your arrogance. [a]All such boasting is evil.

17 Therefore, [a]to him who knows to do good and does not do *it*, to him it is sin.

Rich Oppressors Will Be Judged

5 Come now, *you* [a]rich, weep and howl for your miseries that are coming upon *you!* 2 Your [a]riches are corrupted, and [b]your garments are moth-eaten. 3 Your gold and silver are corroded, and their corrosion will be a witness against you and will eat your flesh like fire. [a]You have heaped up treasure in the last days. 4 Indeed [a]the wages of the laborers who mowed your fields, which

3:17 [b] James 2:1 [c] Rom. 12:9; 2 Cor. 6:6; 1 Pet. 1:22 3:18 [a] Prov. 11:18; Is. 32:17; Hos. 10:12; Amos 6:12; [Gal. 6:8; Phil. 1:11] 4:1 [a] Rom. 7:23; [Gal. 5:17]; 1 Pet. 2:11 4:2 [1] NU-Text and M-Text omit *Yet.* 4:3 [a] Job 27:8, 9 [b] [Ps. 66:18] 4:4 [a] Rom. 8:7; 1 John 2:15 [b] Gal. 1:4 [1] NU-Text omits *Adulterers and.* 4:5 [a] Gen. 6:5 4:6 [a] Job 22:29; Ps. 138:6; Prov. 3:34; Matt. 23:12; 1 Pet. 5:5 [1] Proverbs 3:34 4:7 [a] [Eph. 4:27; 6:11]; 1 Pet. 5:8 4:8 [a] 2 Chr. 15:2; Zech. 1:3; Mal. 3:7; Heb. 7:19 [b] Job 17:9; Is. 1:16; 1 Tim. 2:8 [c] Jer. 4:14; James 3:17; 1 Pet. 1:22; 1 John 3:3 4:9 [a] Matt. 5:4 4:10 [a] Job 22:29; Luke 14:11; 18:14; 1 Pet. 5:6 4:11 [a] 2 Cor. 12:20; Eph. 4:31; James 5:9; 1 Pet. 2:1–3 [b] [Matt. 7:1–5]; Rom. 14:4 4:12 [a] [Matt. 10:28] [b] Rom. 14:4 [1] NU-Text adds *and Judge.* [2] NU-Text and M-Text read *But who.* [3] NU-Text reads *a neighbor.* 4:13 [1] M-Text reads *let us.* 4:14 [a] Job 7:7; Ps. 102:3; 1 Pet. 1:24 4:15 [a] Acts 18:21; 1 Cor. 4:19 4:16 [a] 1 Cor. 5:6 4:17 [a] [Luke 12:47]; John 9:41; 2 Pet. 2:21 5:1 [a] Prov. 11:28; [Luke 6:24; 1 Tim. 6:9] 5:2 [a] Jer. 17:11; Matt. 6:19 [b] Job 13:28 5:3 [a] Rom. 2:5 5:4 [a] Lev. 19:13; Job 24:10; Jer. 22:13; Mal. 3:5

you kept back by fraud, cry out; and [b]the
cries of the reapers have reached the ears
of the Lord of Sabaoth.[1] 5You have lived on
the earth in pleasure and luxury; you have
fattened your hearts as[1] in a day of slaughter. 6You have condemned, you have murdered the just; he does not resist you.

Be Patient and Persevering

7Therefore be patient, brethren, until
the coming of the Lord. See *how* the farmer
waits for the precious fruit of the earth,
waiting patiently for it until it receives the
early and latter rain. 8You also be patient.
Establish your hearts, for the coming of the
Lord is at hand.

9Do not grumble against one another,
brethren, lest you be condemned.[1] Behold,
the Judge is standing at the door! 10[a]My
brethren, take the prophets, who spoke in
the name of the Lord, as an example of suffering and [b]patience. 11Indeed [a]we count
them blessed who [b]endure. You have heard
of [c]the perseverance of Job and seen [d]the
end *intended by* the Lord—that [e]the Lord is
very compassionate and merciful.

12But above all, my brethren, [a]do not
swear, either by heaven or by earth or with
any other oath. But let your "Yes" be "Yes,"
and *your* "No," "No," lest you fall into judgment.[1]

Meeting Specific Needs
(cf. 1 Kin. 18:41–46)

13Is anyone among you suffering? Let
him [a]pray. Is anyone cheerful? [b]Let him
sing psalms. 14Is anyone among you sick?
Let him call for the elders of the church,
and let them pray over him, [a]anointing him
with oil in the name of the Lord. 15And the
prayer of faith will save the sick, and the
Lord will raise him up. [a]And if he has committed sins, he will be forgiven. 16Confess
your trespasses[1] to one another, and pray
for one another, that you may be healed.
[a]The effective, fervent prayer of a righteous

JAMES 4:10

I AM JAMES

Humble yourselves in the sight of the Lord, and He will lift you up. James 4:10

I am James, the son of Mary and Joseph and the younger, half brother of Jesus. Along with my other brothers, I thought Jesus was out of His mind when He started teaching such profound truths with authority. Soon, He started making bizarre claims of deity too. As a result, none of us believed Him during His earthly ministry.

After Jesus rose from the dead as He said He would, He appeared to me, and I could no longer deny His identity. I placed my faith in Jesus not as my half brother but as my Lord and Savior. I soon became a leader in His church and wrote an epistle that challenges Christians to live out their faith in practical ways according to God's wisdom and love. At the end of my life, I was martyred because I would not denounce Jesus as the Messiah. I had denied Him while He was on earth, but how could I deny Him when I was a witness to the risen Christ!

†

Familiarity can convince us that the people closest to us are not unique or special. This seems to have happened within Jesus' earthly family. Most of them thought He was a lunatic. Instead of discounting those around us, we should be looking for their unique gifts and talents and encouraging those gifts with love.

5:4[b] Ex. 2:23; Deut. 24:15; Job 31:38 [1] Literally, in Hebrew, *Hosts* 5:5 [1] NU-Text omits *as.* 5:9 [1] NU-Text and M-Text read *judged.*
5:10 [a] Matt. 5:12 [b] Heb. 10:36 5:11 [a] [Ps. 94:12; Matt. 5:10]; James 1:2 [b] [James 1:12] [c] Job 1:21, 22; 2:10 [d] Job 42:10 [e] Num. 14:18
5:12 [a] Matt. 5:34–37 [1] M-Text reads *hypocrisy.* 5:13 [a] Ps. 50:14, 15 [b] Eph. 5:19 5:14 [a] Mark 6:13; 16:18 5:15 [a] Is. 33:24
5:16 [a] Num. 11:2 [1] NU-Text reads *Therefore confess your sins.*

man avails much. 17Elijah was a man [a]with
a nature like ours, and [b]he prayed earnestly
that it would not rain; and it did not rain
on the land for three years and six months.
18And he prayed [a]again, and the heaven
gave rain, and the earth produced its fruit.

Bring Back the Erring One

19Brethren, if anyone among you wanders from the truth, and someone [a]turns
him back, 20let him know that he who turns
a sinner from the error of his way [a]will save
a soul[1] from death and [b]cover a multitude
of sins.

#OXYGEN
JAMES 5:12

Exalt His Splendid Omniscience

The small moments of life sometimes speed by and we barely notice. Hasty words disappear from our memory. Yet, if we give our word, even thoughtlessly, we dishonor our Lord when we fail to follow through. Every word that comes from our mouths should serve to glorify our Lord.

Breathe and exalt His splendid omniscience.

5:17 [a] Acts 14:15 [b] 1 Kin. 17:1; 18:1 5:18 [a] 1 Kin. 18:1, 42 5:19 [a] Matt. 18:15; Gal. 6:1 5:20 [a] Rom. 11:14; 1 Cor. 1:21; James 1:21 [b] Prov. 10:12; [1 Pet. 4:8] [1] NU-Text reads *his soul.*

THE FIRST EPISTLE OF

PETER

OVERVIEW

Simon Peter was a fisherman on the Sea of Galilee (see Mark 1:18), which is where he first met Jesus. He became one of Jesus' closest followers and a key leader in the early church. More than three decades later, Peter, who was likely imprisoned in Rome, wrote a letter to the scattered Jewish believers. His reference likening Rome to Babylon (see 1 Pet. 5:13), the place of Israel's captivity in the latter part of the Old Testament, would not have been missed by a Jewish community.

At the time of Peter's letters, the Roman emperor Nero was violently persecuting Christians. Nero's campaign to crush the church began in Rome around AD 64 and spread throughout the Roman provinces. Peter spoke plainly to the church about this "fiery trial" that was plaguing them (4:12). Peter's letter was intended to be an encouragement for the suffering, persecuted churches. He told them persecution was a testing of their faith when he wrote, "In this you greatly rejoice, though now for a little while, if need be, you have been grieved by various trials, that the genuineness of your faith, being much more precious than gold that perishes, though it is tested by fire, may be found to praise, honor, and glory at the revelation of Jesus Christ" (1:6–7). Peter wanted the church to understand they needed to remain faithful despite the suffering. The suffering was real—he in no way intended to minimize it—but it was also temporary, and God can bring good even through great evil.

Peter wanted to place the suffering of the church in its proper context. He shared: "Beloved, do not think it strange concerning the fiery trial which is to try you, as though some strange thing happened to you; but rejoice to the extent that you partake of Christ's sufferings, that when His glory is revealed, you may also be glad with exceeding joy" (4:12–14). Suffering is temporary, but the glory of God is eternal. Peter informed the church that their suffering would result in them being strengthened, perfected, and firmly established (see 5:10–11). The suffering of Jesus Christ on the cross served as the foremost example of suffering and provided inspiration for the early church as they endured persecution.

BREATHE IT IN

Peter wrote to the early church to equip believers to endure the suffering of their day. Likewise, we must all be prepared to endure the "fiery trials" of our day. There will always be a new crisis or tragedy, and the Enemy will always put obstacles in our paths. Living today with a fallen, human body may mean physical suffering. God has not promised to protect His own from pain and suffering in the present age. What are we to do, then, when suffering comes to us or our loved ones? If your suffering comes from persecution because you stood up for what is right according to the gospel, 1 Peter tells us to count it as a blessing (see 3:14). We should rejoice because we have become partakers of Christ's suffering (see 4:13). He was crucified for our sins, and we can now choose to suffer on His account. For this, to God be the glory (see 4:16).

If your suffering comes from the sin of the world or by physical or mental illness, the wisdom and comfort of 1 Peter still apply. If God has allowed suffering in your life, He is still a good,

good God. We must commit our souls to Him, our faithful Creator, for He is always good (see 4:19). Each breath of our lives has purpose and meaning. We can bless and serve others, even as they see us praising God and blessing His name amid our troubles. In doing so, we have the opportunity to show them Christ through us.

Do not forget that your relationship with Christ also gives you open access to the Father, who is there to comfort you in the midst of all your storms. Peter's encouragement to the early church resonates still today: that you should live "casting all your care upon Him, for He cares for you" (5:7).

THE FIRST EPISTLE OF

PETER

Greeting to the Elect Pilgrims

1 Peter, an apostle of Jesus Christ,

To the pilgrims [a]of the Dispersion in
Pontus, Galatia, Cappadocia, Asia, and Bithynia, 2 [a]elect [b]according to the foreknowledge of God the Father, [c]in sanctification of
the Spirit, for [d]obedience and [e]sprinkling
of the blood of Jesus Christ:

[f]Grace to you and peace be multiplied.

A Heavenly Inheritance

3 [a]Blessed *be* the God and Father of our
Lord Jesus Christ, who [b]according to His
abundant mercy [c]has begotten us again to
a living hope [d]through the resurrection of
Jesus Christ from the dead, 4 to an inheritance incorruptible and undefiled and that
does not fade away, [a]reserved in heaven for
you, 5 [a]who are kept by the power of God
through faith for salvation ready to be revealed in the last time.
6 [a]In this you greatly rejoice, though now
[b]for a little while, if need be, [c]you have been
grieved by various trials, 7 that [a]the genuineness of your faith, *being* much more
precious than gold that perishes, though
[b]it is tested by fire, [c]may be found to praise,
honor, and glory at the revelation of Jesus
Christ, 8 [a]whom having not seen[1] you love.
[b]Though now you do not see *Him,* yet believing, you rejoice with joy inexpressible
and full of glory, 9 receiving the end of your
faith—the salvation of *your* souls.
10 Of this salvation the prophets have inquired and searched carefully, who prophesied of the grace *that would come* to you,
11 searching what, or what manner of time,
[a]the Spirit of Christ who was in them was
indicating when He testified beforehand
the sufferings of Christ and the glories that
would follow. 12 To them it was revealed
that, not to themselves, but to us[1] they
were ministering the things which now
have been reported to you through those
who have preached the gospel to you by
the Holy Spirit sent from heaven—things
which [a]angels desire to look into.

Living Before God Our Father

13 Therefore gird up the loins of your
mind, be sober, and rest *your* hope fully
upon the grace that is to be brought to you
at the revelation of Jesus Christ; 14 as obedient children, not [a]conforming yourselves
to the former lusts, *as* in your ignorance;
15 [a]but as He who called you *is* holy, you also

#OXYGEN

1 PETER 1:3

Act Like His Chosen

You may be dealing with much. You may be on the verge of giving up on life because you feel all hope is gone. Hold on! Tell yourself, "God has not forgotten me. I have a living hope; His name is Jesus."

Then **breathe** and **act like His chosen**.

1:1 [a] John 7:35; James 1:1 1:2 [a] Eph. 1:4 [b] [Rom. 8:29]; 1 Pet. 1:20 [c] 2 Thess. 2:13 [d] Rom. 1:5 [e] Is. 52:15; Heb. 10:22; 12:24 [f] Rom. 1:7
1:3 [a] Eph. 1:3 [b] Gal. 6:16; Titus 3:5 [c] [John 3:3, 5] [d] 1 Cor. 15:20; 1 Pet. 3:21 1:4 [a] Col. 1:5 1:5 [a] John 10:28; [Phil. 4:7] 1:6 [a] Matt. 5:12
[b] 2 Cor. 4:17 [c] James 1:2; 1 Pet. 4:12 1:7 [a] James 1:3 [b] Job 23:10 [c] [Rom. 2:7] 1:8 [a] 1 John 4:20 [b] John 20:29 [1] M-Text reads *known.*
1:11 [a] 2 Pet. 1:21 1:12 [a] Eph. 3:10 [1] NU-Text and M-Text read *you.* 1:14 [a] [Rom. 12:2]; 1 Pet. 4:2 1:15 [a] [2 Cor. 7:1]

be holy in all *your* conduct, [16]because it is
written, [a]"Be holy, for I am holy."[1]
[17]And if you call on the Father, who
[a]without partiality judges according to each
one's work, conduct yourselves throughout
the time of your stay *here* in fear; [18]know-
ing that you were not redeemed with corruptible things, *like* silver or gold, from
your aimless conduct *received* by tradition from your fathers, [19]but [a]with the precious blood of Christ, [b]as of a lamb without
blemish and without spot. [20][a]He indeed
was foreordained before the foundation of
the world, but was manifest [b]in these last
times for you [21]who through Him believe
in God, [a]who raised Him from the dead
and [b]gave Him glory, so that your faith and
hope are in God.

The Enduring Word

[22]Since you [a]have purified your souls
in obeying the truth through the Spirit[1] in
sincere [b]love of the brethren, love one another fervently with a pure heart, [23][a]hav-
ing been born again, not of corruptible
seed but incorruptible, [b]through the word
of God which lives and abides forever,[1]
[24]because

[a]"All flesh *is* as grass,
And all the glory of man[1]
as the flower of the
grass.
The grass withers,
And its flower falls away,
[25] [a]But the word of the LORD
endures forever."[1]

[b]Now this is the word which by the gospel
was preached to you.

2 Therefore, [a]laying aside all malice, all
deceit, hypocrisy, envy, and all evil
speaking, [2][a]as newborn babes, desire the
pure [b]milk of the word, that you may grow
thereby,[1] [3]if indeed you have [a]tasted that
the Lord *is* gracious.

The Chosen Stone and His Chosen People
(Ps. 118:22; Is. 28:16)

[4]Coming to Him *as to* a living stone, [a]re-
jected indeed by men, but chosen by God
and precious, [5]you also, as living stones,
are being built up a spiritual house, a
holy priesthood, to offer up spiritual sacrifices acceptable to God through Jesus
Christ. [6]Therefore it is also contained in
the Scripture,

[a]"Behold, I lay in Zion
A chief cornerstone, elect,
precious,
And he who believes on Him
will by no means be put
to shame."[1]

[7]Therefore, to you who believe, *He is* precious; but to those who are disobedient,[1]

[a]"The stone which the builders rejected
Has become the chief cornerstone,"[2]

[8]and

[a]"A stone of stumbling
And a rock of offense."[1]

[b]They stumble, being disobedient to the
word, [c]to which they also were appointed.
[9]But you *are* a chosen generation, a royal
priesthood, a holy nation, His own special
people, that you may proclaim the praises
of Him who called you out of [a]darkness into
His marvelous light; [10][a]who once *were* not a
people but *are* now the people of God, who
had not obtained mercy but now have obtained mercy.

Living Before the World

[11]Beloved, I beg *you* as sojourners and
pilgrims, abstain from fleshly lusts [a]which
war against the soul, [12][a]having your conduct honorable among the Gentiles, that
when they speak against you as evildoers,

1:16 [a] Lev. 11:44, 45; 19:2; 20:7 [1] Leviticus 11:44, 45; 19:2; 20:7 **1:17** [a] Acts 10:34 **1:19** [a] Acts 20:28; 1 Pet. 1:2 [b] Ex. 12:5; Is. 53:7 **1:20** [a] Rom. 3:25 [b] Gal. 4:4 **1:21** [a] Acts 2:24 [b] Acts 2:33 **1:22** [a] Acts 15:9 [b] John 13:34; Rom. 12:10; Heb. 13:1; 1 Pet. 2:17; 3:8 [1] NU-Text omits *through the Spirit.* **1:23** [a] John 1:13 [b] 1 Thess. 2:13; James 1:18 [1] NU-Text omits *forever.* **1:24** [a] Is. 40:6–8; James 1:10 [1] NU-Text reads *all its glory.* **1:25** [a] Is. 40:8 [b] [John 1:1] [1] Isaiah 40:6–8 **2:1** [a] Heb. 12:1 **2:2** [a] [Matt. 18:3; 19:14; Mark 10:15; Luke 18:17]; 1 Cor. 14:20 [b] 1 Cor. 3:2 [1] NU-Text adds *up to salvation.* **2:3** [a] Ps. 34:8; Titus 3:4; Heb. 6:5 **2:4** [a] Ps. 118:22 **2:6** [a] Is. 28:16; Rom. 9:32, 33; 10:11; 1 Pet. 2:8 [1] Isaiah 28:16 **2:7** [a] Ps. 118:22; Matt. 21:42; Luke 2:34 [1] NU-Text reads *to those who disbelieve.* [2] Psalm 118:22 **2:8** [a] Is. 8:14 [b] 1 Cor. 1:23; Gal. 5:11 [c] Rom. 9:22 [1] Isaiah 8:14 **2:9** [a] Is. 9:2; 42:16; [Acts 26:18; 2 Cor. 4:6] **2:10** [a] Hos. 1:9, 10; 2:23; Rom. 9:25; 10:19 **2:11** [a] [Rom. 8:13]; Gal. 5:17; James 4:1 **2:12** [a] 2 Cor. 8:21; Phil. 2:15; Titus 2:8; 1 Pet. 2:15; 3:16

RELEASE // ACT LIKE HIS CHOSEN

Spiritual Identity

1 Peter 2:9 // But you are a chosen generation, a royal priesthood, a holy nation, His own special people, that you may proclaim the praises of Him who called you out of darkness into His marvelous light.

Summary Message // The apostle Peter wrote the Book of 1 Peter to comfort believers and encourage them to stay strong amid persecution. This letter was written thirty years after the resurrection of Jesus when the Roman Empire was persecuting Christ's followers under the ruthless leader Nero. Peter understood how important it was that these besieged believers realize who they were in Christ. He reminded them why God calls believers to live differently from those in the world.

In 1 Peter 2:9, Peter called the followers of Christ "a chosen generation, a royal priesthood," and "a holy nation." He wanted them to realize they were redeemed and possessed by God for a glorious new purpose. Peter gave the believers insight into their value and purpose from God's perspective. He even used language from the Old Testament that describes God's special relationship with Israel—a chosen race. But unlike Israel, Christians are not a race in the sense of our ethnicity, skin color, or country of origin. Instead, we are a spiritual race of people in Christ, sharing the same spiritual Father. We are a "holy nation"—a unique group called out and set apart from others to act according to God-given purpose and identity.

Practical Application // Self-worth is a misleading concept. It is a worldly notion that presupposes we will find our true worth somewhere within. This is not the case. Our worth is found within, but not in a way natural to who we are. It is found only in Christ within us. When we rightly define our value based on God's Word, we shift from a worldly to a spiritual identity. Our recognition of our identity affects the goals we pursue. It is essential to redefine our identities based on God's perspective. How do we make this change?

First, we are to know what God thinks about us from His Word, starting with 1 Peter 2:9. Read this verse until it is ingrained in your mind and heart. Next, look in a mirror and personalize it: "*I* am chosen." "*I* am a royal priest." "*I* am a citizen of a holy nation." Recite this list aloud at least once a day. Your words are powerful, and you can use them to help you change from a false, worldly perspective to God's view of you and your identity in Him. The more you recognize that only God can truly define you, the more you will act like who you are in Christ.

Second, we must identify a God-given characteristic about ourselves that is not appearance-related but is Christlike. It can be related to your personality, a positive attitude, or a work ethic. As negative thoughts about yourself come during the day, stop and thank God for the positive attribute He has given you. Just as in any other relationship, if you do not have anything good to say about yourself, then say nothing. When you begin to see yourself as God sees you, you will develop a positive and healthy outlook on life and weather any storm.

Fervent Prayer // Heavenly Father, thank You for giving us Your perspective on identity and worth. Thank You for Jesus, in whom we are made worthy. When tempted to feel valueless, remind us of Your thoughts toward us. Help us keep our minds and hearts focused on Your plans. May we always remember that we are who You say we are. In Jesus' name we pray. Amen.

---

[b]they may, by *your* good works which
they observe, glorify God in the day of
visitation.

Submission to Government
(cf. Rom. 13:1–5)

13 [a]Therefore submit yourselves to every ordinance of man for the Lord's sake,
whether to the king as supreme, 14 or to
governors, as to those who are sent by him
for the punishment of evildoers and *for
the* praise of those who do good. 15 For this
is the will of God, that by doing good you
may put to silence the ignorance of foolish
men— 16 [a]as free, yet not [b]using liberty as a
cloak for vice, but as bondservants of God.
17 Honor all *people.* Love the brotherhood.
Fear [a]God. Honor the king.

2:12 [b] Matt. 5:16; 9:8; John 13:31; 1 Pet. 4:11, 16 2:13 [a] Matt. 22:21 2:16 [a] Rom. 6:14, 20, 22; 1 Cor. 7:22; [Gal. 5:1] [b] Gal. 5:13 2:17 [a] Prov. 24:21

ACT LIKE HIS CHOSEN

INHALE

Years ago, a friend of mine asked me to join his business. I had a young family, so the time wasn't right. He has asked me again, and now I want to say yes. I know God made me strong and I have gifts and talents to succeed, but I must admit I'm a bit fearful to take this step. How can God help me to step into the unknown?

EXHALE

Taking a chance in the things of life has no guaranteed outcome. You can only do as you feel God leading you to do. He is a God who wants to speak to us at all times, and His ability to do that is not hampered at all. If we want to hear from Him, we will. He never fails to lead His people when we desire to follow Him.

The Bible says that God has not given us as believers "a spirit of fear" or timidity; instead, He has given us a spirit "of power and of love and of a sound mind" (2 Tim. 1:7). A sound mind is a powerful thing. In redeeming you and giving you such a mind, God has given you the capacity to process information and make wise decisions. Trust God's leading and the mind He has given you. He assures us that we are His sheep and that His sheep hear His voice. Step forward in the way you discern He is leading, and listen close to Him with each step you take.

First Peter 2:9 tells us that we are a "chosen generation" and a "special people." This doesn't mean God will prosper every move we make or give favor to every step we take. This means He has chosen us as His own. Regardless of which paths we follow and whether we hear His voice leading us, God will never leave us alone. He will never abandon His chosen people or forget His special ones. He will see us through whatever is before us. We didn't do a single thing to deserve His loyalty and love, but there is absolutely nothing we can do to lose either. He is as close as your next breath. Pray, listen, and then do as you believe God is leading. Place your trust in the One who considers you chosen, royal, and special enough to have His ear anytime and all the time.

Submission to Masters
(Is. 53:7–9)

18[a]Servants, *be* submissive to *your* masters with all fear, not only to the good and
gentle, but also to the harsh. 19For this *is*
[a]commendable, if because of conscience
toward God one endures grief, suffering
wrongfully. 20For [a]what credit *is it* if, when
you are beaten for your faults, you take it
patiently? But when you do good and suffer,
if you take it patiently, this *is* commendable
before God. 21For [a]to this you were called,
because Christ also suffered for us,[1] [b]leav-
ing us[2] an example, that you should follow His steps:

22"Who[a] committed no sin,
Nor was deceit found in His
mouth";[1]

23[a]who, when He was reviled, did not revile in return; when He suffered, He did
not threaten, but [b]committed *Himself* to
Him who judges righteously; 24[a]who Himself bore our sins in His own body on the
tree, [b]that we, having died to sins, might
live for righteousness—[c]by whose stripes
you were healed. 25For [a]you were like
sheep going astray, but have now returned
[b]to the Shepherd and Overseer[1] of your
souls.

2:18 [a] Eph. 6:5–8 2:19 [a] Matt. 5:10 2:20 [a] Luke 6:32–34 2:21 [a] Matt. 16:24; 1 Thess. 3:3, 4 [b] [1 John 2:6] [1] NU-Text reads *you.* [2] NU-Text and M-Text read *you.* 2:22 [a] Is. 53:9; 2 Cor. 5:21 [1] Isaiah 53:9 2:23 [a] Is. 53:7; Heb. 12:3; 1 Pet. 3:9 [b] Luke 23:46 2:24 [a] Is. 53:4, 11; 1 Cor. 15:3; [Heb. 9:28] [b] Rom. 7:6 [c] Is. 53:5 2:25 [a] Is. 53:5, 6 [b] Is. 40:11; [Ezek. 34:23]; Zech. 13:7 [1] Greek *Episkopos*

Submission to Husbands

3 Wives, likewise, *be* [a]submissive to your
own husbands, that even if some do
not obey the word, [b]they, without a word,
may [c]be won by the conduct of their wives,
2 [a]when they observe your chaste conduct
accompanied by fear. 3 [a]Do not let your
adornment be *merely* outward—arranging
the hair, wearing gold, or putting on *fine* apparel— 4 rather *let it be* [a]the hidden person
of the heart, with the incorruptible *beauty*
of a gentle and quiet spirit, which is very
precious in the sight of God. 5 For in this
manner, in former times, the holy women
who trusted in God also adorned themselves, being submissive to their own husbands, 6 as Sarah obeyed Abraham, [a]calling
him lord, whose daughters you are if you
do good and are not afraid with any terror.

A Word to Husbands

7 [a]Husbands, likewise, dwell with *them*
with understanding, giving honor to the
wife, [b]as to the weaker vessel, and as *being*
heirs together of the grace of life, [c]that your
prayers may not be hindered.

Called to Blessing

8 Finally, all *of you be* of one mind, having compassion for one another; love as
brothers, *be* tenderhearted, *be* courteous;[1]
9 [a]not returning evil for evil or reviling for
reviling, but on the contrary [b]blessing,
knowing that you were called to this, [c]that
you may inherit a blessing. 10 For

[a]"He who would love life
And see good days,
[b]Let him refrain his tongue from evil,
And his lips from speaking deceit.
11 Let him [a]turn away from
evil and do good;
[b]Let him seek peace and pursue it.
12 For the eyes of the LORD *are*
on the righteous,
[a]And His ears *are open* to their prayers;
But the face of the LORD *is*
against those who do evil."[1]

#OXYGEN

1 PETER 3:8

Act Like His Chosen

One of the hardest things to do is to show love when you do not know how love looks. Jesus is the greatest example of love. You are made in His image and likeness. You are loved. Now love in kind.

Breathe and **act like His chosen**.

Suffering for Right and Wrong

13 [a]And who *is* he who will harm you if
you become followers of what is good?
14 [a]But even if you should suffer for righteousness' sake, *you are* blessed. [b]"And do
not be afraid of their threats, nor be troubled."[1] 15 But sanctify the Lord God[1] in your
hearts, and always [a]*be* ready to *give* a defense to everyone who asks you a reason
for the [b]hope that is in you, with meekness
and fear; 16 [a]having a good conscience, that
when they defame you as evildoers, those
who revile your good conduct in Christ may
be ashamed. 17 For *it is* better, if it is the will
of God, to suffer for doing good than for
doing evil.

Christ's Suffering and Ours

18 For Christ also suffered once for sins,
the just for the unjust, that He might bring
us[1] to God, being put to death in the flesh
but made alive by the Spirit, 19 by whom
also He went and preached to the spirits in
prison, 20 who formerly were disobedient,
when once the Divine longsuffering waited[1]
in the days of Noah, while *the* ark was being prepared, in which a few, that is, eight
souls, were saved through water. 21 [a]There
is also an antitype which now saves us—
baptism [b](not the removal of the filth of the

3:1 [a] Gen. 3:16; 1 Cor. 14:34; Eph. 5:22; Col. 3:18 [b] 1 Cor. 7:16 [c] Matt. 18:15 3:2 [a] 1 Pet. 2:12; 3:6 3:3 [a] Is. 3:18; 1 Tim. 2:9 3:4 [a] Rom. 2:29 3:6 [a] Gen. 18:12 3:7 [a] 1 Cor. 7:3; [Eph. 5:25]; Col. 3:19 [b] 1 Cor. 12:23 [c] Job 42:8 3:8 [1] NU-Text reads *humble.* 3:9 [a] [Prov. 17:13] [b] Matt. 5:44 [c] Matt. 25:34 3:10 [a] Ps. 34:12–16 [b] James 1:26 3:11 [a] Ps. 37:27 [b] Rom. 12:18 3:12 [a] John 9:31 [1] Psalm 34:12–16 3:13 [a] Prov. 16:7 3:14 [a] James 1:12 [b] Is. 8:12 [1] Isaiah 8:12 3:15 [a] Ps. 119:46 [b] [Titus 3:7] [1] NU-Text reads *Christ as Lord.* 3:16 [a] 1 Tim. 1:5; Heb. 13:18; 1 Pet. 3:21 3:18 [1] NU-Text and M-Text read *you.* 3:20 [1] NU-Text and M-Text read *when the longsuffering of God waited patiently.* 3:21 [a] Acts 16:33; Eph. 5:26 [b] [Titus 3:5]

flesh, [c]but the answer of a good conscience toward God), through the resurrection of Jesus Christ, 22who has gone into heaven and [a]is at the right hand of God, [b]angels and authorities and powers having been made subject to Him.

4 Therefore, since Christ suffered for us[1] in the flesh, arm yourselves also with the same mind, for he who has suffered in the flesh has ceased from sin, 2that he no longer should live the rest of *his* time in the flesh for the lusts of men, [a]but for the will of God. 3For we *have spent* enough of our past lifetime[1] in doing the will of the Gentiles—when we walked in lewdness, lusts, drunkenness, revelries, drinking parties, and abominable idolatries. 4In regard to these, they think it strange that you do not run with *them* in the same flood of dissipation, speaking evil of *you.* 5They will give an account to Him who is ready [a]to judge the living and the dead. 6For this reason [a]the gospel was preached also to those who are dead, that they might be judged according to men in the flesh, but [b]live according to God in the spirit.

Serving for God's Glory

7But [a]the end of all things is at hand; therefore be serious and watchful in your prayers. 8And above all things have fervent love for one another, for [a]"love will cover a multitude of sins."[1] 9[a]*Be* hospitable to one another [b]without grumbling. 10[a]As each one has received a gift, minister it to one another, [b]as good stewards of [c]the manifold grace of God. 11[a]If anyone speaks, *let him speak* as the oracles of God. If anyone ministers, *let him do it* as with the ability which God supplies, that [b]in all things God may be glorified through Jesus Christ, to whom belong the glory and the dominion forever and ever. Amen.

Suffering for God's Glory

12Beloved, do not think it strange concerning the fiery trial which is to try you, as though some strange thing happened to you; 13but rejoice [a]to the extent that you partake of Christ's sufferings, that [b]when His glory is revealed, you may also be glad with exceeding joy. 14If you are reproached for the name of Christ, [a]blessed *are you,* for the Spirit of glory and of God rests upon you.[1] On their part He is blasphemed, [b]but on your part He is glorified. 15But let none of you suffer as a murderer, a thief, an evildoer, or as a busybody in other people's matters. 16Yet if *anyone suffers* as a Christian, let him not be ashamed, but let him glorify God in this matter.[1]

17For the time *has come* [a]for judgment to begin at the house of God; and if *it begins* with us first, [b]what will *be* the end of those who do not obey the gospel of God? 18Now

[a]"If the righteous one is scarcely saved,
Where will the ungodly and
the sinner appear?"[1]

19Therefore let those who suffer according to the will of God [a]commit their souls *to Him* in doing good, as to a faithful Creator.

Shepherd the Flock

5 The elders who are among you I exhort, I who am a fellow elder and a [a]witness of the sufferings of Christ, and also a partaker of the [b]glory that will be revealed: 2[a]Shepherd the flock of God which is among you, serving as overseers, [b]not by compulsion but willingly,[1] [c]not for dishonest gain but eagerly; 3nor as [a]being lords over [b]those entrusted to you, but [c]being examples to the flock; 4and when [a]the Chief Shepherd appears, you will receive [b]the crown of glory that does not fade away.

Submit to God, Resist the Devil

5Likewise you younger people, submit yourselves to *your* elders. Yes, [a]all of *you* be submissive to one another, and be clothed with humility, for

---

3:21 [c] [Rom. 10:10] 3:22 [a] Ps. 110:1 [b] Rom. 8:38; Heb. 1:6 4:1 [1] NU-Text omits *for us.* 4:2 [a] John 1:13 4:3 [1] NU-Text reads *time.* 4:5 [a] Acts 10:42; Rom. 14:9; 2 Tim. 4:1 4:6 [a] 1 Pet. 1:12; 3:19 [b] [Rom. 8:9, 13]; Gal. 5:25 4:7 [a] Rom. 13:11; Heb. 9:26; James 5:8, 9; 1 John 2:18 4:8 [a] [Prov. 10:12]; 1 Cor. 13:4; James 5:20 [1] Proverbs 10:12 4:9 [a] 1 Tim. 3:2; Heb. 13:2 [b] 2 Cor. 9:7 4:10 [a] Rom. 12:6–8 [b] Matt. 24:45; 1 Cor. 4:1, 2 [c] [1 Cor. 12:4] 4:11 [a] Eph. 4:29 [b] [1 Cor. 10:31]; Eph. 5:20 4:13 [a] James 1:2 [b] 2 Tim. 2:12 4:14 [a] Matt. 5:11; Luke 6:22; Acts 5:41 [b] Matt. 5:16 [1] NU-Text omits the rest of this verse. 4:16 [1] NU-Text reads *name.* 4:17 [a] Is. 10:12 [b] Luke 10:12 4:18 [a] Prov. 11:31 [1] Proverbs 11:31 4:19 [a] Ps. 37:5–7; 2 Tim. 1:12 5:1 [a] Matt. 26:37 [b] Rom. 8:17, 18 5:2 [a] John 21:16; Acts 20:28 [b] 1 Cor. 9:17 [c] 1 Tim. 3:3 [1] NU-Text adds *according to God.* 5:3 [a] Ezek. 34:4; Matt. 20:25 [b] Ps. 33:12 [c] John 13:15; Phil. 3:17; 1 Thess. 1:7; 2 Thess. 3:9; 1 Tim. 4:12; Titus 2:7 5:4 [a] Is. 40:11; Zech. 13:7; Heb. 13:20; 1 Pet. 2:25 [b] 2 Tim. 4:8 5:5 [a] Rom. 12:10; Eph. 5:21

[b]"God resists the proud,
But [c]gives grace to the humble."[1]

6Therefore humble yourselves under the
mighty hand of God, that He may exalt you
in due time, 7casting all your care upon
Him, for He cares for you.
8Be sober, be vigilant; because[1] your adversary the devil walks about like a roaring
lion, seeking whom he may devour. 9Re-
sist him, steadfast in the faith, knowing
that the same sufferings are experienced
by your brotherhood in the world. 10But
may[1] the God of all grace, [a]who called us[2]
to His eternal glory by Christ Jesus, after
you have suffered a while, perfect, establish, strengthen, and settle *you*. 11[a]To Him
be the glory and the dominion forever and
ever. Amen.

Farewell and Peace

12By [a]Silvanus, our faithful brother as I
consider him, I have written to you briefly,
exhorting and testifying [b]that this is the
true grace of God in which you stand.
13She who is in Babylon, elect together
with *you*, greets you; and *so does* [a]Mark my
son. 14Greet one another with a kiss of love.
Peace to you all who are in Christ Jesus.
Amen.

1 PETER 5:1

I AM PETER

The elders who are among you I exhort, I who am a fellow elder and a witness of the sufferings of Christ, and also a partaker of the glory that will be revealed. 1 Peter 5:1

I am Peter, one of the fishermen Jesus called as apostles. Jesus once asked me who I believed He was, and I responded, "You are the Christ, the Son of the living God." He called me "blessed" and said that such faith was the rock upon which He would build His church.

I was passionate in following Christ, but I was not always faithful. I firmly declared to Jesus that I would not deny Him, even if it meant dying with Him. Then, as He followed the cruel path to the cross, I denied Him three times. I was repentant and wept bitterly, but the painful, ugly truth plagued me. After Jesus rose from death, He restored me and freed me of the painful regret. He assured me of His continued love and commissioned me to feed His sheep.

Before Jesus ascended to heaven, He promised to send the Holy Spirit. Forty days later, 120 of Jesus' followers sat in an upper room, waiting as He instructed. Suddenly, with signs of fire and wind, the Holy Spirit fell upon us all. After that, I boldly spoke the message of repentance and performed miracles in the name of Jesus. The Spirit of God led me to preach the same message to the Gentiles. As I spoke, the Holy Spirit fell on all those who heard the gospel, and they began to speak with tongues and magnify God. God had granted His grace to the Gentiles.

†

How unlikely that a fisherman would be given such power and authority in the church. But none of us knows what God has in store for us. We only know that whatever He has for us is for our good and for His glory. Like Peter, we have to grow into our purpose, and we may get it wrong at times. Peter was impetuous and immature at first; however, in time and with growing faith, perseverance, and integrity, Peter became the man we know him to be. Like Peter, we must grow into the shoes Jesus will place upon our feet at just the right time.

5:5 [b] Prov. 3:34; James 4:6 [c] Is. 57:15 [1] Proverbs 3:34 5:8 [1] NU-Text and M-Text omit *because.* 5:10 [a] 1 Cor. 1:9; 1 Thess. 2:12 [1] NU-Text reads *But the God of all grace . . . will perfect, establish, strengthen, and settle you.* [2] NU-Text and M-Text read *you.* 5:11 [a] Rev. 1:6 5:12 [a] 2 Cor. 1:19; 1 Thess. 1:1; 2 Thess. 1:1 [b] Acts 20:24 5:13 [a] Acts 12:12, 25; 15:37, 39; Col. 4:10; Philem. 24

THE SECOND EPISTLE OF

PETER

OVERVIEW

When Peter met Jesus, he answered to the name Simon, which means "hearing." Jesus would later change his name to Peter, which means "rock" (Matt. 16:18). Peter was with Jesus during some of the most critical moments in Christ's ministry. When the daughter of Jairus was restored to life, Peter, James, and John were the only witnesses (see Mark 5:37). When Jesus was transfigured, He took only Peter, James, and John with Him (see Luke 9:28). When the sorrow of the impending crucifixion traumatized Jesus, He took Peter, James, and John to the Garden of Gethsemane for prayer (see Matt. 26:37). Peter played a key role in Jesus' ministry in the Gospels and then beyond as the initial key leader of the church (see Matt. 16:17–18; Acts 2:14–39).

Peter had been a follower of Jesus Christ for more than thirty years when he wrote this second epistle to the Jewish Christians scattered throughout Asia. The faithfulness that he witnessed in Jesus was the faithfulness he encouraged the early church to duplicate during a time of extreme persecution and public hostility. Peter urged the church to grow its faith using these words: "But also for this very reason, giving all diligence, add to your faith virtue, to virtue knowledge, to knowledge self-control, to self-control perseverance, to perseverance godliness, to godliness brotherly kindness, and to brotherly kindness love" (2 Pet. 1:5–7). In his first letter, Peter addressed the need for such robust faith to fend off threats from outside the church. Here, in 2 Peter, he turned his attention to false teachers and threats within the church. The same faith was necessary to see the church through this challenge too.

BREATHE IT IN

Jesus designated the apostle Peter to be the "rock" of the church (Matt. 16:17–18). Jesus chose Peter to help lay the foundation of the acceptance of the Good News and establish the church. The Book of Acts and Peter's two epistles show that Peter was faithful to this assignment and worked until his final breath. According to reliable tradition, Peter's life ended as his Savior's did, in crucifixion. However, tradition also holds that Peter refused to die exactly as Christ did and demanded to be crucified upside down. As we consider the tremendous sacrifices of the apostle Peter, it is also important to remember he was an imperfect witness.

Even though Peter was declared the "rock" of the church, he had some regrettable moments with Jesus. When Jesus foretold His impending crucifixion, Peter refused to accept His claim and rebuked Him. Jesus responded to Peter by saying, "Get behind Me, Satan! You are an offense to Me, for you are not mindful of the things of God, but the things of men" (Matt. 16:23). To be clear, Jesus named Peter the "rock" in Matthew 16:18 just after praising Peter's words as being given by God. Five verses later, in the subsequent discourse, He referred to Peter as "Satan."

When Jesus brought Peter, James, and John to the Mount of Transfiguration, Peter tried to remain on the mountain instead of accepting Jesus' fate—the cross. When Jesus brought Peter, James, and John to the Garden of Gethsemane, the group failed three times to remain awake to pray with Christ. When Jesus was arrested in the Garden of Gethsemane, Peter resorted to violence and cut off the ear of a man standing near him. Most egregious of all, after Jesus was

arrested and brought into the courtyard for trial before the elders and chief priests, Peter denied knowing Him three times. Peter then hid when Jesus was hanging from the cross; he was an absentee disciple.

Peter's failures are numerous, but on the day of Pentecost—the day of the church's birth—Peter was called upon to deliver the sermon. Jesus never expected a perfect Peter; Jesus only wanted a faithful Peter.

Chances are that you are far from perfect too. Perhaps you have matured enough to identify the flaws in your character and history. Be assured that your failures are not fatal. Be faithful, knowing that God still uses flawed vessels just as He did on the day the church was born.

THE SECOND EPISTLE OF

PETER

Greeting the Faithful

1 Simon Peter, a bondservant and [a]apos-
tle of Jesus Christ,

To those who have obtained [b]like precious faith with us by the righteousness of
our God and Savior Jesus Christ:

2 [a]Grace and peace be multiplied to you
in the knowledge of God and of Jesus our
Lord, 3 as His [a]divine power has given to us
all things that *pertain* to life and godliness,
through the knowledge of Him [b]who called
us by glory and virtue, 4 [a]by which have been
given to us exceedingly great and precious
promises, that through these you may be
[b]partakers of the divine nature, having escaped the corruption *that is* in the world
through lust.

Fruitful Growth in the Faith

5 But also for this very reason, [a]giving all
diligence, add to your faith virtue, to virtue
[b]knowledge, 6 to knowledge self-control, to
self-control perseverance, to perseverance
godliness, 7 to godliness brotherly kindness, and [a]to brotherly kindness love. 8 For
if these things are yours and abound, *you*
will be neither barren [a]nor unfruitful in the
knowledge of our Lord Jesus Christ. 9 For
he who lacks these things is [a]shortsighted,
even to blindness, and has forgotten that
he was cleansed from his old sins.

10 Therefore, brethren, be even more diligent [a]to make your call and election sure,
for if you do these things you will never
stumble; 11 for so an entrance will be supplied to you abundantly into the everlasting kingdom of our Lord and Savior Jesus
Christ.

Peter's Approaching Death

12 For this reason [a]I will not be negligent to remind you always of these things,
[b]though you know and are established in
the present truth. 13 Yes, I think it is right,
[a]as long as I am in this tent, [b]to stir you up
by reminding *you*, 14 [a]knowing that shortly
I *must* put off my tent, just as [b]our Lord
Jesus Christ showed me. 15 Moreover I will
be careful to ensure that you always have a
reminder of these things after my decease.

The Trustworthy Prophetic Word
(Matt. 17:5; Mark 9:7; Luke 9:35)

16 For we did not follow [a]cunningly devised fables when we made known to you
the [b]power and [c]coming of our Lord Jesus
Christ, but were [d]eyewitnesses of His majesty. 17 For He received from God the Father
honor and glory when such a voice came to
Him from the Excellent Glory: [a]"This is My
beloved Son, in whom I am well pleased."
18 And we heard this voice which came from
heaven when we were with Him on [a]the
holy mountain.

19 And so we have the prophetic word
confirmed,[1] which you do well to heed as
a [a]light that shines in a dark place, [b]un-
til [c]the day dawns and the morning star
rises in your [d]hearts; 20 knowing this first,
that [a]no prophecy of Scripture is of any

1:1 [a] Gal. 2:8 [b] Eph. 4:5 1:2 [a] Dan. 4:1 1:3 [a] 1 Pet. 1:5 [b] 1 Thess. 2:12; 2 Thess. 2:14; 1 Pet. 5:10 1:4 [a] 2 Cor. 1:20; 7:1 [b] [2 Cor. 3:18] 1:5 [a] 2 Pet. 3:18 [b] 2 Pet. 1:2 1:7 [a] Gal. 6:10 1:8 [a] [John 15:2] 1:9 [a] 1 John 2:9–11 1:10 [a] 2 Cor. 13:5; 1 John 3:19 1:12 [a] Phil. 3:1; 1 John 2:21; Jude 5 [b] 1 Pet. 5:12 1:13 [a] [2 Cor. 5:1, 4]; 2 Pet. 1:14 [b] 2 Pet. 3:1 1:14 [a] [2 Cor. 5:1; 2 Tim. 4:6] [b] John 13:36; 21:18, 19 1:16 [a] 1 Cor. 1:17 [b] [Matt. 28:18; Eph. 1:19–22] [c] [1 Pet. 5:4] [d] Matt. 17:1–5; Luke 1:2 1:17 [a] Ps. 2:7; Is. 42:1; Matt. 17:5; Mark 9:7; Luke 1:35; 9:35 1:18 [a] Matt. 17:1 1:19 [a] [John 1:4, 5, 9] [b] Prov. 4:18 [c] Rev. 2:28; 22:16 [d] [2 Cor. 4:5–7]

[1] Or *We also have the more sure prophetic word.* 1:20 [a] [Rom. 12:6]

RELEASE // TRUST IN HIS WORLD

Live from Another Place

2 Peter 1:3 // As His divine power has given to us all things that pertain to life and godliness, through the knowledge of Him who called us by glory and virtue.

Summary Message // When Jesus was here on earth, those who followed Him sat at His feet in order to grow in their faith and understanding. When Jesus went to be with the Father, He sent the Holy Spirit to guide us into all truth. So, our spiritual development does not come from the world, or even from other believers. It comes straight from the Father revealed to us through the Spirit of truth.

Therefore, we live from a higher standard that can often be difficult to grasp. The Holy Spirit directs us to live in such a way that our current state of being no longer determines our future position. We find that the goal of our hearts is no longer to please the world but to be changed from glory to glory. We put our trust in God's kingdom ways and live within that trust, hour by hour. As servants of God and of the Lord Jesus Christ, our commitment finds expression. In this place, we see from a higher plane and can respond to all things and act from a place of confidence in God.

Practical Application // God's Spirit lives within His children. When we are led by the Holy Spirit, everything we do will be blessed by God and be according to His will. The Holy Spirit will never lead us astray. We are the temples of His Spirit and are called to be examples of His character to the world. We represent Him to everyone our lives touch. Take a moment and ask yourself this: Am I living according to His ways or mine? Am I being led by the Holy Spirit or by my flesh?

Our hearts deceive us; they lead toward personal satisfaction rather than spiritual fulfillment. Every day—moment by moment—we should seek the will of the Father, revealed to us through the Spirit who dwells within us. Trust in His ways and you will be blessed. Life makes much more sense from the place where His kingdom comes and His will is done (see Matt. 6:10).

Fervent Prayer // Heavenly Father, we trust You and Your redemption for us. We thank You that we can now live from a place of grace and mercy. Our worldview has changed because of the enlightenment that comes from being in Your presence. Our world is nothing compared to Yours, and we are so overwhelmed with the satisfaction of living this new life in You. Lord, we marvel at who You are and how You see us and others. We are in awe of You and all You have done for us. In Jesus' name we pray. Amen.

---

private interpretation,[1] 21for [a]prophecy
never came by the will of man, [b]but holy
men of God[1] spoke *as they were* moved by
the Holy Spirit.

Destructive Doctrines

2 But there were also false prophets
among the people, even as there will
be [a]false teachers among you, who will secretly bring in destructive heresies, even
denying the Lord who bought them, *and*
bring on themselves swift destruction.
2And many will follow their destructive
ways, because of whom the way of truth
will be blasphemed. 3By covetousness
they will exploit you with deceptive words;
for a long time their judgment has not
been idle, and their destruction does[1] not
slumber.

Doom of False Teachers

4For if God did not spare the angels who
sinned, but cast *them* down to hell and delivered *them* into chains of darkness, to
be reserved for judgment; 5and did not
spare the ancient world, but saved Noah,
one of eight *people,* a preacher of righteousness, bringing in the flood on the world
of the ungodly; 6and turning the cities of
[a]Sodom and Gomorrah into ashes, condemned *them* to destruction, making *them*
an example to those who afterward would

1:20 [1] Or *origin* 1:21 [a] Jer. 23:26; [2 Tim. 3:16] [b] 2 Sam. 23:2; Luke 1:70; Acts 1:16; 3:18; 1 Pet. 1:11 [1] NU-Text reads *but men spoke from God.* 2:1 [a] Matt. 24:5, 24; 1 Tim. 4:1, 2 2:3 [1] M-Text reads *will not.* 2:6 [a] Gen. 19:1–26; Jude 7

live ungodly; 7and [a]delivered righteous Lot,
who was oppressed by the filthy conduct
of the wicked 8(for that righteous man,
dwelling among them, [a]tormented *his* righteous soul from day to day by seeing and
hearing *their* lawless deeds)— 9*then* [a]the
Lord knows how to deliver the godly out of
temptations and to reserve the unjust under punishment for the day of judgment,
10and especially [a]those who walk according to the flesh in the lust of uncleanness
and despise authority. [b]*They are* presumptuous, self-willed. They are not afraid to
speak evil of dignitaries, 11whereas [a]angels,
who are greater in power and might, do not
bring a reviling accusation against them
before the Lord.

#OXYGEN

2 PETER 2:9

Trust in His World

Follow God's pathway and make wise choices. Do not fall to temptations and sin. He will deliver you. God's blessings are great when you live in His world—the kingdom of His Son. Let God set you apart.

Just breathe and trust in His world.

Depravity of False Teachers

12But these, [a]like natural brute beasts
made to be caught and destroyed, speak
evil of the things they do not understand,
and will utterly perish in their own corruption, 13[a]*and* will receive the wages of
unrighteousness, *as* those who count it
pleasure [b]to carouse in the daytime. [c]*They*
are spots and blemishes, carousing in their
own deceptions while [d]they feast with you,
14having eyes full of adultery and that
cannot cease from sin, enticing unstable
souls. [a]They have a heart trained in covetous practices, *and are* accursed children. 15They have forsaken the right way
and gone astray, following the way of [a]Ba-
laam the *son* of Beor, who loved the wages
of unrighteousness; 16but he was rebuked
for his iniquity: a dumb donkey speaking
with a man's voice restrained the madness
of the prophet.

17[a]These are wells without water, clouds[1]
carried by a tempest, for whom is reserved
the blackness of darkness forever.[2]

Deceptions of False Teachers

18For when they speak great swelling
words of emptiness, they allure through
the lusts of the flesh, through lewdness,
the ones who have actually escaped[1] from
those who live in error. 19While they promise them liberty, they themselves are slaves
of corruption; [a]for by whom a person is
overcome, by him also he is brought into
bondage. 20For if, after they [a]have escaped
the pollutions of the world through the
knowledge of the Lord and Savior Jesus
Christ, they are [b]again entangled in them
and overcome, the latter end is worse for
them than the beginning. 21For [a]it would
have been better for them not to have
known the way of righteousness, than having known *it,* to turn from the holy commandment delivered to them. 22But it has
happened to them according to the true
proverb: [a]"A dog returns to his own vomit,"[1]
and, "a sow, having washed, to her wallowing in the mire."

God's Promise Is Not Slack
(Gen. 6:5—8:22)

3 Beloved, I now write to you this second epistle (in *both of* which [a]I stir up
your pure minds by way of reminder), 2that
you may be mindful of the words [a]which
were spoken before by the holy prophets,
[b]and of the commandment of us,[1] the apostles of the Lord and Savior, 3knowing this
first: that scoffers will come in the last days,
[a]walking according to their own lusts, 4and

2:7 [a] Gen. 19:16, 29 2:8 [a] Ps. 119:139 2:9 [a] Ps. 34:15–19; 1 Cor. 10:13; Rev. 3:10 2:10 [a] Jude 4, 7, 8 [b] Ex. 22:28; Jude 8 2:11 [a] Jude 9 2:12 [a] Jude 10 2:13 [a] Phil. 3:19 [b] Rom. 13:13 [c] Jude 12 [d] 1 Cor. 11:20, 21 2:14 [a] Jude 11 2:15 [a] Num. 22:5, 7; Deut. 23:4; Neh. 13:2; Jude 11; Rev. 2:14 2:17 [a] Jude 12, 13 [1] NU-Text reads *and mists.* [2] NU-Text omits *forever.* 2:18 [1] NU-Text reads *are barely escaping.* 2:19 [a] John 8:34; Rom. 6:16 2:20 [a] Matt. 12:45 [b] Luke 11:26; [Heb. 6:4–6] 2:21 [a] Luke 12:47 2:22 [a] Prov. 26:11 [1] Proverbs 26:11 3:1 [a] 2 Pet. 1:13 3:2 [a] 2 Pet. 1:21 [b] Jude 17 [1] NU-Text and M-Text read *commandment of the apostles of your Lord and Savior* or *commandment of your apostles of the Lord and Savior.* 3:3 [a] 2 Pet. 2:10

saying, "Where is the promise of His coming? For since the fathers fell asleep, all
things continue as *they were* from the beginning of [a]creation." 5For this they willfully
forget: that [a]by the word of God the heavens were of old, and the earth [b]standing
out of water and in the water, 6[a]by which
the world *that* then existed perished, being flooded with water. 7But [a]the heavens
and the earth *which* are now preserved by
the same word, are reserved for [b]fire until
the day of judgment and perdition of ungodly men.
8But, beloved, do not forget this one
thing, that with the Lord one day *is* as a
thousand years, and [a]a thousand years as
one day. 9[a]The Lord is not slack concerning *His* promise, as some count slackness,
but [b]is longsuffering toward us,[1] [c]not willing
that any should perish but [d]that all should
come to repentance.

The Day of the Lord

10But [a]the day of the Lord will come as
a thief in the night, in which [b]the heavens
will pass away with a great noise, and the
elements will melt with fervent heat; both
the earth and the works that are in it will
be burned up.[1] 11Therefore, since all these
things will be dissolved, what manner *of*
persons ought you to be [a]in holy conduct
and godliness, 12[a]looking for and hastening
the coming of the day of God, because of
which the heavens will [b]be dissolved, being
on fire, and the elements will [c]melt with
fervent heat? 13Nevertheless we, according to His promise, look for [a]new heavens
and a [b]new earth in which righteousness
dwells.

#OXYGEN
2 PETER 3:9
Trust in His World

God keeps His promises. The Lord has not forgotten you. Grow to trust God's timing and stay on the course He sets. Persevere. God's kingdom will one day be established on earth.

Breathe and **trust in His world.**

Be Steadfast

14Therefore, beloved, looking forward
to these things, be diligent [a]to be found
by Him in peace, without spot and blameless; 15and consider *that* [a]the longsuffering
of our Lord *is* salvation—as also our beloved brother Paul, according to the wisdom given to him, has written to you, 16as
also in all his [a]epistles, speaking in them of
these things, in which are some things hard
to understand, which untaught and unstable *people* twist to their own destruction,
as *they do* also the [b]rest of the Scriptures.
17You therefore, beloved, [a]since you
know *this* beforehand, [b]beware lest you
also fall from your own steadfastness, being led away with the error of the wicked;
18[a]but grow in the grace and knowledge of
our Lord and Savior Jesus Christ.
[b]To Him *be* the glory both now and forever. Amen.

3:4 [a] Gen. 6:1–7 3:5 [a] Gen. 1:6, 9; Heb. 11:3 [b] Ps. 24:2; 136:6 3:6 [a] Gen. 7:11, 12, 21–23; Matt. 24:37–39; Luke 17:26, 27; 2 Pet. 2:5 3:7 [a] 2 Pet. 3:10, 12 [b] Matt. 25:41; [2 Thess. 1:8] 3:8 [a] Ps. 90:4 3:9 [a] Hab. 2:3; Rom. 13:11; Heb. 10:37 [b] Ps. 86:15; Is. 30:18 [c] Ezek. 33:11 [d] Matt. 20:28; [Rom. 2:4] [1] NU-Text reads *you.* 3:10 [a] Matt. 24:42, 43; Luke 12:39; 1 Thess. 5:2; Rev. 3:3; 16:15 [b] Gen. 1:6–8; Ps. 102:25, 26; Is. 51:6; Rev. 20:11 [1] NU-Text reads *laid bare* (literally *found*). 3:11 [a] 1 Pet. 1:15 3:12 [a] 1 Cor. 1:7, 8; Titus 2:13–15 [b] Ps. 50:3 [c] Is. 24:19; 34:4; Mic. 1:4 3:13 [a] Is. 65:17; 66:22 [b] [Rom. 8:21]; Rev. 21:1 3:14 [a] 1 Cor. 1:8; 15:58; [1 Thess. 3:12, 13; 5:23] 3:15 [a] Ps. 86:15; Rom. 2:4; 1 Pet. 3:20 3:16 [a] Rom. 8:19; 1 Cor. 15:24; 1 Thess. 4:15; 2 Thess. 1:10 [b] 2 Tim. 3:16 3:17 [a] Mark 13:23 [b] Eph. 4:14 3:18 [a] Eph. 4:15 [b] Rom. 11:36; 2 Tim. 4:18; Rev. 1:6

THE FIRST EPISTLE OF

JOHN

OVERVIEW

On Resurrection Sunday morning, Mary Magdalene discovered that the burial tomb of Jesus was empty. She shared the news about the vacant tomb with Peter and the "other disciple, whom Jesus loved" (John 20:2), the moniker for the apostle John. The two disciples then sprinted to the empty tomb to investigate. John arrived first and looked inside. Then Peter arrived and entered the tomb. The Gospel of John records: "Then the other disciple, who came to the tomb first, went in also; and he saw and believed" (John 20:8). The Bible allows us to read the very moment when John believed in the resurrection of Jesus Christ. The two runners on Resurrection Sunday, Peter and John, kept "running" decades afterward. Peter and John, collectively, wrote six of the final seven books of the Bible.

John was one of the sons of Zebedee who was compelled by Christ to drop his nets and follow Him. John, along with his brother James, immediately left all and followed Jesus (see Mark 1:19–20). John also wrote the Gospel of John and Revelation. In his Gospel, John shared what Jesus Christ did for humanity. In his epistles, John described how it looks when Jesus Christ lives within each believer and clarified the process of sanctification.

John clearly provided the fourfold purpose for his first epistle: (1) "that you also may have fellowship with us" (1 John 1:3); (2) "that your joy may be full" (1:4); (3) "that you may not sin" (2:1); and (4) "that you may know that you have eternal life" (5:13).

The context of this epistle was false teachers confusing and deceiving the church (see 2:26). These false teachers seemed to have caused some in the church to doubt their salvation. John wrote to comfort and clarify.

The most familiar theme of John's letters is love. Here, he clearly explains the nature of love: "Beloved, let us love one another, for love is of God; and everyone who loves is born of God and knows God. He who does not love does not know God, for God is love" (4:7–8). He presents love as the basis of fellowship: "If someone says, 'I love God,' and hates his brother, he is a liar; for he who does not love his brother whom he has seen, how can he love God whom he has not seen? And this commandment we have from Him: that he who loves God must love his brother also" (vv. 20–21). The love that Jesus had lavished upon John had left an indelible mark.

BREATHE IT IN

Being sanctified, meaning "to be set apart," is a major theme within the Black church. Although it may connote something different in other cultures, it was first introduced to the Black church in the Pentecostal or Holiness movement of faith, but then it appeared in many other Black denominations. Specifically, sanctification here is belief in the Holy Spirit and His power in your life and in your actions that sets you apart from those who have not been likewise moved. When we are filled with the Holy Spirit, we are sanctified in Him as we sing, dance, worship, and exalt God in our own way. This is what we call being sanctified.

God did not make us to be like everyone else. As society called for Black people to assimilate, it was the Black church that called for us to maintain our African cultural identity. We embraced

for ourselves that we were set apart, both as a form of church doctrine and as a distinct culture that sought to reclaim the identity and purpose that were separated from us in slavery.

Think of how important gospel music has become as a cultural bridge. We are able to preserve our culture through our unique musical expression of faith. In this way, God has sanctified us and set us apart. He rescued us from sin and guilt, and He keeps us from being polluted by the ways of the world that so often seek to keep us in an inferior position. Conversely, God seeks to protect us as a holy people. In that, by the grace of God, we are more than conquerors. It was also God's grace that helped Black people to view themselves as more than slaves at a time when society told them that was all they were.

As we breathe in the first epistle of John, also consider how the church itself has served as a cultural bridge from generation to generation. Reflect on how the church has defined and supported communities. Imagine the void that would exist without Christ and Christ's church. The Jewish practice of reciting the history of the Hebrews' deliverance from slavery in Egypt to the establishment of the nation of Israel enriched generations who memorized it. We should consider doing the same with our children.

As we consider the concept of sanctification, we acknowledge that God has done a new thing in each of us. The new thing will not look the same from one culture to another or from one person to another. But each of us should know God chose us for salvation by the Spirit of truth so that we might be set apart for His purposes. Recognize that you are someone special to God. You have unique qualities and gifts that God has given you to use for His glory.

†

THE FIRST EPISTLE OF

JOHN

What Was Heard, Seen, and Touched
(John 1:1–5)

1 That [a]which was from the beginning,
which we have heard, which we have
[b]seen with our eyes, [c]which we have looked
upon, and [d]our hands have handled, concerning the [e]Word of life— 2 [a]the life [b]was
manifested, and we have seen, [c]and bear
witness, and declare to you that eternal
life which was [d]with the Father and was
manifested to us— 3 that which we have
seen and heard we declare to you, that
you also may have fellowship with us;
and truly our fellowship *is* [a]with the Father and with His Son Jesus Christ. 4 And
these things we write to you [a]that your[1]
joy may be full.

Fellowship with Him and One Another

5 [a]This is the message which we have
heard from Him and declare to you, that
[b]God is light and in Him is no darkness at
all. 6 [a]If we say that we have fellowship with
Him, and walk in darkness, we lie and do
not practice the truth. 7 But if we [a]walk in
the light as He is in the light, we have fellowship with one another, and [b]the blood
of Jesus Christ His Son cleanses us from
all sin.

8 If we say that we have no sin, we deceive ourselves, and the truth is not in us.
9 If we [a]confess our sins, He is [b]faithful and
just to forgive us *our* sins and to [c]cleanse us
from all unrighteousness. 10 If we say that
we have not sinned, we [a]make Him a liar,
and His word is not in us.

2 My little children, these things I write
to you, so that you may not sin. And
if anyone sins, [a]we have an Advocate with
the Father, Jesus Christ the righteous. 2 And
[a]He Himself is the propitiation for our sins,
and not for ours only but [b]also for the whole
world.

The Test of Knowing Him

3 Now by this we know that we know Him,
if we keep His commandments. 4 He who
says, "I know Him," and does not keep His
commandments, is a [a]liar, and the truth is
not in him. 5 But [a]whoever keeps His word,
truly the love of God is perfected [b]in him.
By this we know that we are in Him. 6 [a]He
who says he abides in Him [b]ought himself
also to walk just as He walked.

7 Brethren,[1] I write no new commandment to you, but an old commandment
which you have had [a]from the beginning.
The old commandment is the word which
you heard from the beginning.[2] 8 Again, [a]a
new commandment I write to you, which
thing is true in Him and in you, [b]because
the darkness is passing away, and [c]the true
light is already shining.

9 [a]He who says he is in the light, and
hates his brother, is in darkness until now.
10 [a]He who loves his brother abides in the
light, and [b]there is no cause for stumbling
in him. 11 But he who [a]hates his brother is

1:1 [a] [John 1:1]; 1 John 2:13, 14 [b] Luke 1:2; John 1:14 [c] 2 Pet. 1:16 [d] Luke 24:39; John 20:27 [e] [John 1:1, 4, 14] 1:2 [a] John 1:4; [1 John 3:5, 8; 5:20] [b] Rom. 16:26; 1 Tim. 3:16 [c] John 21:24 [d] [John 1:1, 18; 16:28] 1:3 [a] John 17:21; 1 Cor. 1:9; 1 John 2:24 1:4 [a] John 15:11; 16:24; 1 Pet. 1:8 [1] NU-Text and M-Text read *our.* 1:5 [a] John 1:19; 1 John 3:11 [b] [1 Tim. 6:16]; James 1:17 1:6 [a] [John 8:12]; 2 Cor. 6:14; [1 John 2:9–11] 1:7 [a] Is. 2:5 [b] [1 Cor. 6:11] 1:9 [a] Ps. 32:5; Prov. 28:13 [b] [Rom. 3:24–26] [c] Ps. 51:2 1:10 [a] John 3:33; 1 John 5:10 2:1 [a] Rom. 8:34; 1 Tim. 2:5; Heb. 7:25; 9:24 2:2 [a] [Rom. 3:25]; Heb. 2:17; 1 John 4:10 [b] John 1:29 2:4 [a] Rom. 3:4 2:5 [a] John 14:21, 23 [b] [1 John 4:12] 2:6 [a] John 15:4 [b] Matt. 11:29; John 13:15; 15:10; 1 Pet. 2:21 2:7 [a] John 13:34; 1 John 3:11, 23; 4:21; 2 John 5 [1] NU-Text reads *Beloved.* [2] NU-Text omits *from the beginning.* 2:8 [a] John 13:34; 15:12 [b] Rom. 13:12; Eph. 5:8; 1 Thess. 5:4 [c] [John 1:9; 8:12; 12:35] 2:9 [a] [1 Cor. 13:2]; 1 John 3:14 2:10 [a] [1 John 3:14] [b] 2 Pet. 1:10 2:11 [a] [1 John 2:9; 3:15; 4:20]

TRUST IN HIS WORLD

INHALE

I'm focused on God and want Him to be a friend like no other. But how do I focus on Him when the world has gone crazy? Wars, pandemics, and social challenges make it tough to focus on anything, let alone God. Where is God in all of this? Why should I have faith anchored in Him when the world I live in breaks me so?

EXHALE

None of the things happening in our world surprise God. He is all-knowing about every detail, person, and event throughout human history. He has said there will be wars and rumors of wars, diseases, and many other things that will upend the earth. These things must come to pass, or God's Word is a lie. And we know God's Word is not a lie. The truth we find in the Bible can be difficult to accept; however, the Word of God is accurate by every measure.

But God isn't just aware of what is going on; He is active in bringing good. God uses people and events to bring about His plans and purposes. When God says it, He always gets it done! Where is God in all of this, you ask? He is directly in the middle of it. That is where God wants to be. Why? Because that's where the action is. God lives within the action and is not intimidated by any of it. The more you read His Word and get a grasp of the plans of God and how those plans affect the world, the more it will make sense. God is not a God of confusion but a God of understanding and peace.

First John 2:17 says, "The world is passing away . . . but he who does the will of God abides forever." That is the Word and will of God. Whatever this world throws at us will not last. But we have staying power! He wants us to hold fast, standing firm against the sinful ways of the world as we cling to hope that Jesus is returning to make all things right. What God speaks will come to pass. Only God can make such a claim.

in darkness and [b]walks in darkness, and does not know where he is going, because the darkness has blinded his eyes.

Their Spiritual State

12 I write to you, little children,
Because [a]your sins are forgiven
you for His name's sake.
13 I write to you, fathers,
Because you have known Him
who is [a]from the beginning.
I write to you, young men,
Because you have overcome
the wicked one.
I write to you, little children,
Because you have [b]known
the Father.
14 I have written to you, fathers,
Because you have known Him
who is from the beginning.
I have written to you, young men,
Because [a]you are strong, and the
word of God abides in you,
And you have overcome
the wicked one.

Do Not Love the World

15 [a]Do not love the world or the things in the world. [b]If anyone loves the world, the love of the Father is not in him. 16 For all that *is* in the world—the lust of the flesh, [a]the lust of the eyes, and the pride of life—is not of the Father but is of the world. 17 And [a]the world is passing away, and the lust of it; but he who does the will of God abides forever.

2:11 [b] John 12:35; 1 John 1:6 2:12 [a] [1 Cor. 6:11] 2:13 [a] John 1:1; Rev. 22:13 [b] [Rom. 8:15–17; Gal. 4:6] 2:14 [a] Eph. 6:10
2:15 [a] [Rom. 12:2]; Gal. 1:4; James 1:27 [b] Matt. 6:24; James 4:4 2:16 [a] [Eccl. 5:10, 11] 2:17 [a] 1 Cor. 7:31; 1 Pet. 1:24

Deceptions of the Last Hour

18[a]Little children, [b]it is the last hour; and
as you have heard that [c]the[1] Antichrist is
coming, [d]even now many antichrists have
come, by which we know [e]that it is the last
hour. 19[a]They went out from us, but they
were not of us; for [b]if they had been of us,
they would have continued with us; but
they went out [c]that they might be made
manifest, that none of them were of us.
20But [a]you have an anointing [b]from the
Holy One, and [c]you know all things.[1] 21I have
not written to you because you do not know
the truth, but because you know it, and that
no lie is of the truth.
22[a]Who is a liar but he who denies that
[b]Jesus is the Christ? He is antichrist who
denies the Father and the Son. 23[a]Whoever
denies the Son does not have the [b]Father
either; [c]he who acknowledges the Son has
the Father also.

Let Truth Abide in You

24Therefore let that abide in you [a]which
you heard from the beginning. If what you
heard from the beginning abides in you,
[b]you also will abide in the Son and in the
Father. 25[a]And this is the promise that He
has promised us—eternal life.
26These things I have written to you
concerning those who *try to* deceive you.
27But the [a]anointing which you have received from Him abides in you, and [b]you
do not need that anyone teach you; but
as the same anointing [c]teaches you concerning all things, and is true, and is not a
lie, and just as it has taught you, you will[1]
abide in Him.

The Children of God

28And now, little children, abide in Him,
that when[1] He appears, we may have [a]con-
fidence and not be ashamed before Him at
His coming. 29[a]If you know that He is righteous, you know that [b]everyone who practices righteousness is born of Him.

3 Behold [a]what manner of love the Father
has bestowed on us, that [b]we should
be called children of God![1] Therefore the
world does not know us,[2] [c]because it did not
know Him. 2Beloved, [a]now we are children
of God; and [b]it has not yet been revealed
what we shall be, but we know that when
He is revealed, [c]we shall be like Him, for
[d]we shall see Him as He is. 3[a]And everyone
who has this hope in Him purifies himself,
just as He is pure.

#OXYGEN

1 JOHN 3:3

Hope for the Lord

Since you become what you behold, focus on Jesus. Meditating daily on His likeness will begin to transform your behavior until the day He returns and your desire to be like Him will be reality.

Focus, **breathe**, and **hope for the Lord.**

Sin and the Child of God

4Whoever commits sin also commits
lawlessness, and [a]sin is lawlessness. 5And
you know [a]that He was manifested [b]to take
away our sins, and [c]in Him there is no sin.
6Whoever abides in Him does not sin. Whoever sins has neither seen Him nor known
Him.
7Little children, let no one deceive you.
He who practices righteousness is righteous, just as He is righteous. 8[a]He who sins
is of the devil, for the devil has sinned from
the beginning. For this purpose the Son of
God was manifested, [b]that He might destroy the works of the devil. 9Whoever has
been [a]born of God does not sin, for [b]His

2:18 [a] John 21:5 [b] Rom. 13:11; 1 Tim. 4:1; Heb. 1:2; 1 Pet. 4:7 [c] 2 Thess. 2:3 [d] Matt. 24:5, 24; 1 John 2:22; 4:3; 2 John 7 [e] 1 Tim. 4:1 [1] NU-Text omits *the.* **2:19** [a] Deut. 13:13 [b] Matt. 24:24 [c] 1 Cor. 11:19 **2:20** [a] 2 Cor. 1:21; Heb. 1:9; 1 John 2:27 [b] Acts 3:14 [c] Prov. 28:5; [John 16:13]; 1 Cor. 2:15, 16 [1] NU-Text reads *you all know.* **2:22** [a] 2 John 7 [b] 1 John 4:3 **2:23** [a] John 15:23 [b] John 5:23 [c] 1 John 4:15; 5:1; 2 John 9 **2:24** [a] 2 John 5, 6 [b] John 14:23; 1 John 1:3; 2 John 9 **2:25** [a] John 3:14–16; 6:40; 17:2, 3; 1 John 1:2 **2:27** [a] [John 14:16; 16:13]; 1 John 2:20 [b] [Jer. 31:33] [c] [John 14:16; 1 Cor. 2:12]; 1 Thess. 4:9 [1] NU-Text reads *you abide.* **2:28** [a] Eph. 3:12; 1 John 3:21; 4:17; 5:14 [1] NU-Text reads *if.* **2:29** [a] Acts 22:14 [b] John 7:18; 1 John 3:7, 10 **3:1** [a] [John 3:16; Eph. 2:4–7; 1 John 4:10] [b] [John 1:12] [c] John 15:18, 21; 16:3 [1] NU-Text adds *And we are.* [2] M-Text reads *you.* **3:2** [a] [Is. 56:5; Rom. 8:15, 16] [b] [Rom. 8:18, 19, 23] [c] Rom. 8:29; 2 Pet. 1:4 [d] [Ps. 16:11] **3:3** [a] 1 John 4:17 **3:4** [a] Rom. 4:15; 1 John 5:17 **3:5** [a] 1 John 1:2; 3:8 [b] [Is. 53:5, 6]; John 1:29; [2 Cor. 5:21; Heb. 9:26] [c] [2 Cor. 5:21]; 1 John 2:29 **3:8** [a] Matt. 13:38; John 8:44; 1 John 3:10 [b] Luke 10:18; [Heb. 2:14] **3:9** [a] John 1:3; 3:3; [1 John 2:29; 4:7; 5:1, 4, 18]; 3 John 11 [b] 1 Pet. 1:23

seed remains in him; and he cannot sin, because he has been born of God.

The Imperative of Love
(Matt. 22:39)

10In this the children of God and the children of the devil are manifest: Whoever does not practice righteousness is not of God, nor *is* he who does not love his brother. 11For this is the message that you heard from the beginning, [a]that we should love one another, 12not as [a]Cain *who* was of the wicked one and murdered his brother. And why did he murder him? Because his works were evil and his brother's righteous.

13Do not marvel, my brethren, if [a]the world hates you. 14We know that we have passed from death to life, because we love the brethren. He who does not love *his* brother[1] abides in death. 15[a]Whoever hates his brother is a murderer, and you know that [b]no murderer has eternal life abiding in him.

The Outworking of Love

16[a]By this we know love, [b]because He laid down His life for us. And we also ought to lay down *our* lives for the brethren. 17But [a]whoever has this world's goods, and sees his brother in need, and shuts up his heart from him, how does the love of God abide in him?

18My little children, [a]let us not love in word or in tongue, but in deed and in truth. 19And by this we know[1] [a]that we are of the truth, and shall assure our hearts before Him. 20[a]For if our heart condemns us, God is greater than our heart, and knows all things. 21Beloved, if our heart does not condemn us, [a]we have confidence toward God. 22And [a]whatever we ask we receive from Him, because we keep His commandments [b]and do those things that are pleasing in His sight. 23And this is His commandment: that we should believe on the name of His Son Jesus Christ [a]and love one another, as He gave us[1] commandment.

The Spirit of Truth and the Spirit of Error

24Now [a]he who keeps His commandments [b]abides in Him, and He in him. And [c]by this we know that He abides in us, by the Spirit whom He has given us.

4 Beloved, do not believe every spirit, but [a]test the spirits, whether they are of God; because [b]many false prophets have gone out into the world. 2By this you know the Spirit of God: [a]Every spirit that confesses that Jesus Christ has come in the flesh is of God, 3and every spirit that does not confess that[1] Jesus Christ has come in the flesh is not of God. And this is the *spirit* of the Antichrist, which you have heard was coming, and is now already in the world.

4You are of God, little children, and have overcome them, because He who is in you is greater than [a]he who is in the world. 5[a]They are of the world. Therefore they speak *as* of the world, and [b]the world hears them. 6We are of God. He who knows God hears us; he who is not of God does not hear us. [a]By this we know the spirit of truth and the spirit of error.

Knowing God Through Love
(cf. John 3:16)

7[a]Beloved, let us love one another, for love is of God; and everyone who [b]loves is born of God and knows God. 8He who does not love does not know God, for God is love. 9[a]In this the love of God was manifested toward us, that God has sent His only begotten [b]Son into the world, that we might live through Him. 10In this is love, [a]not that we loved God, but that He loved us and sent His Son [b]*to be* the propitiation for our sins. 11Beloved, [a]if God so loved us, we also ought to love one another.

Seeing God Through Love

12[a]No one has seen God at any time. If we love one another, God abides in us, and His love has been perfected in us. 13[a]By this we know that we abide in Him, and He in

---

3:11 [a] [John 13:34; 15:12]; 1 John 4:7, 11, 21; 2 John 5 3:12 [a] Gen. 4:4, 8 3:13 [a] [John 15:18; 17:14] 3:14 [1] NU-Text omits *his brother.* 3:15 [a] Matt. 5:21; John 8:44 [b] [Gal. 5:20, 21; Rev. 21:8] 3:16 [a] [John 3:16] [b] John 10:11; 15:13; Gal. 2:20 3:17 [a] Deut. 15:7 3:18 [a] Ezek. 33:31 3:19 [a] John 18:37 [1] NU-Text reads *we shall know.* 3:20 [a] [1 Cor. 4:4, 5] 3:21 [a] [Heb. 10:22; 1 John 2:28; 5:14] 3:22 [a] Ps. 34:15; [John 15:7]; 1 John 5:14, 15 [b] John 8:29; Heb. 13:21 3:23 [a] Matt. 22:39 [1] M-Text omits *us.* 3:24 [a] John 14:23 [b] John 14:21; 17:21 [c] John 14:17; Rom. 8:9, 14, 16; 1 Thess. 4:8; 1 John 4:13 4:1 [a] 1 Cor. 14:29 [b] Matt. 24:5 4:2 [a] [Rom. 10:8–10]; 1 Cor. 12:3; 1 John 5:1 4:3 [1] NU-Text omits *that* and *Christ has come in the flesh.* 4:4 [a] John 14:30; 16:11 4:5 [a] John 3:31 [b] John 15:19; 17:14 4:6 [a] [1 Cor. 2:12–16] 4:7 [a] 1 John 3:10, 11, 23 [b] 1 Thess. 4:9; [1 John 3:14] 4:9 [a] Rom. 5:8 [b] Is. 9:6, 7; John 3:16 4:10 [a] Titus 3:5 [b] 1 John 2:2 4:11 [a] Matt. 18:33 4:12 [a] John 1:18; 1 Tim. 6:16; 1 John 4:20 4:13 [a] John 14:20

RELEASE // HOPE FOR THE LORD

God's Love Has "Receipts"

1 John 4:17 // Love has been perfected among us in this: that we may have boldness in the day of judgment; because as He is, so are we in this world.

Summary Message // John's first letter to the church encourages believers to show the kind of love that will identify them as children of God. Since all love comes from God, our loving actions are proof that we are God's children. If we show love for Christians and non-Christians, others can see that we are aligned with God.

God is love. Because God loved us first, we have the capacity to love God and others (see 1 John 4:19). Just as God's love is personal and tangible, our expressions of love must extend beyond mere words. As we continue to exhibit godly love, our love becomes more like God's. John tells us that when believers possess mature love, we can have confidence regarding the day of judgment. We can live securely in God's love without any fear of the divine punishment coming.

Practical Application // Not long ago, growing up in many Black families meant that you had to behave a certain way in public; you had to demonstrate "home training." It was expected that you had a respectful attitude toward elders and the attitude of servanthood toward others. It was a cultural expectation.

The same can be said of God's children and showing love to others. When we demonstrate love toward God's creatures, we prove that we belong to God, know God, and are learning how to love like God. We cannot, however, do the latter apart from the former. We cannot claim to love God while treating others with disregard. If we are living a closed, miserly existence, only helping those who can help us in return, John says we have no love.

In John 13:35, Jesus said: "By this all will know that you are My disciples, if you have love for one another." People will not know we are Christ followers because we go to church every Sunday or because we carry a huge Bible. What gives credibility to God's love is evidence of that love among God's people. Love is an action word. It is up to God's people to reflect His love through what we do. This includes loving those who are hard to love and those who may never return our love. Loving them does not give them permission to disrespect us, but it does give us permission to deny ourselves the right to be offended. Expressing godly love when it is difficult allows us to grow in our confidence regarding our relationship with God. Then others will come to know the reality of God's love because they can see it being demonstrated by Christians. As we are admonished in Psalm 37:34: "Wait on the LORD, and keep His way."

Fervent Prayer // Loving God, because of Your perfect love, we do not have to live in fear. You are our hope. Your perfect expression of love teaches us how to show love toward all humanity. We celebrate the love You gave us before we even knew You. Every day, help us devote ourselves to loving others as You love us. With intentionality, we want to be an expression of Your love toward others every day, especially toward those who are hurting most. In Jesus' name we pray. Amen.

---

us, because He has given us of His Spirit.
14And [a]we have seen and testify that [b]the
Father has sent the Son *as* Savior of the
world. 15[a]Whoever confesses that Jesus is
the Son of God, God abides in him, and he
in God. 16And we have known and believed
the love that God has for us. God is love,
and [a]he who abides in love abides in God,
and God [b]in him.

The Consummation of Love

17Love has been perfected among us in
this: that [a]we may have boldness in the day
of judgment; because as He is, so are we in
this world. 18There is no fear in love; but
perfect love casts out fear, because fear in-
volves torment. But he who fears has not
been made perfect in love. 19[a]We love Him[1]
because He first loved us.

4:14 [a] John 1:14 [b] John 3:17; 4:42; 1 John 2:2 4:15 [a] [Rom. 10:9]; 1 John 3:23; 4:2; 5:1, 5
4:16 [a] [1 John 3:24] [b] [John 14:23] 4:17 [a] [James 2:13]; 1 John 2:28
4:19 [a] 1 John 4:10 [1] NU-Text omits *Him*.

Obedience by Faith

20[a]If someone says, “I love God,” and
hates his brother, he is a liar; for he who
does not love his brother whom he has
seen, how can[1] he love God [b]whom he has
not seen? 21And [a]this commandment we
have from Him: that he who loves God *must*
love his brother also.

5 Whoever believes that [a]Jesus is the
Christ is [b]born of God, and everyone
who loves Him who begot also loves him
who is begotten of Him. 2By this we know
that we love the children of God, when we
love God and [a]keep His commandments.
3[a]For this is the love of God, that we keep
His commandments. And [b]His commandments are not burdensome. 4For [a]whatever
is born of God overcomes the world. And
this is the victory that [b]has overcome the
world—our[1] faith. 5Who is he who overcomes the world, but [a]he who believes that
Jesus is the Son of God?

The Certainty of God’s Witness

6This is He who came [a]by water and
blood—Jesus Christ; not only by water, but
by water and blood. [b]And it is the Spirit who
bears witness, because the Spirit is truth.
7For there are three that bear witness in
heaven: the Father, [a]the Word, and the Holy
Spirit; [b]and these three are one. 8And there
are three that bear witness on earth:[1] [a]the
Spirit, the water, and the blood; and these
three agree as one.

9If we receive [a]the witness of men, the
witness of God is greater; [b]for this is the
witness of God which[1] He has testified of
His Son. 10He who believes in the Son of
God [a]has the witness in himself; he who
does not believe God [b]has made Him a liar,
because he has not believed the testimony
that God has given of His Son. 11And this is
the testimony: that God has given us eternal life, and this life is in His Son. 12[a]He who
has the Son has life; he who does not have
the Son of God does not have life. 13These
things I have written to you who believe in
the name of the Son of God, that you may
know that you have eternal life,[1] and that
you may *continue to* believe in the name
of the Son of God.

Confidence and Compassion in Prayer

14Now this is the confidence that we
have in Him, that [a]if we ask anything according to His will, He hears us. 15And if
we know that He hears us, whatever we ask,
we know that we have the petitions that we
have asked of Him.

16If anyone sees his brother sinning a
sin *which does* not *lead* to death, he will
ask, and [a]He will give him life for those who
commit sin not *leading* to death. [b]There
is sin *leading* to death. [c]I do not say that
he should pray about that. 17[a]All unrighteousness is sin, and there is sin not *leading* to death.

Knowing the True—Rejecting the False

18We know that [a]whoever is born of God
does not sin; but he who has been born of
God [b]keeps himself,[1] and the wicked one
does not touch him.

19We know that we are of God, and [a]the

#OXYGEN

1 JOHN 5:21

Hope for the Lord

We are inundated all day, every day by our televisions, radios, and smartphones suggesting ways for us to be better, look better, and do better. But the world’s philosophy pales in comparison to the wisdom of God’s plan for our lives.

Believe, **breathe**, and **hope for the Lord**.

4:20 [a] [1 John 2:4] [b] 1 Pet. 1:8; 1 John 4:12 [1] NU-Text reads *he cannot.* 4:21 [a] Lev. 19:18; [Matt. 5:43, 44; 22:39]; John 13:34
5:1 [a] 1 John 2:22; 4:2, 15 [b] John 1:13 5:2 [a] John 15:10; 2 John 6 5:3 [a] John 14:15; 2 John 6 [b] Mic. 6:8; Matt. 11:30; 23:4
5:4 [a] John 16:33 [b] 1 John 2:13; 4:4 [1] M-Text reads *your.* 5:5 [a] 1 Cor. 15:57 5:6 [a] John 1:31–34; [Eph. 5:26, 27] [b] [John 14:17]
5:7 [a] [John 1:1] [b] John 10:30 5:8 [a] John 15:26 [1] NU-Text and M-Text omit the words from *in heaven* (verse 7) through *on earth* (verse 8). Only four or five very late manuscripts contain these words in Greek. 5:9 [a] John 5:34, 37; 8:17, 18 [b] [Matt. 3:16, 17]; John 5:32, 37 [1] NU-Text reads *God, that.* 5:10 [a] [Rom. 8:16]; Gal. 4:6; Rev. 12:17 [b] John 3:18, 33; 1 John 1:10 5:12 [a] [John 3:15, 36; 6:47; 17:2, 3] 5:13 [1] NU-Text omits the rest of this verse. 5:14 [a] [1 John 2:28; 3:21, 22] 5:16 [a] Job 42:8 [b] [Matt. 12:31] [c] Jer. 7:16; 14:11 5:17 [a] 1 John 3:4 5:18 [a] [1 Pet. 1:23]; 1 John 3:9 [b] James 1:27 [1] NU-Text reads *him.*
5:19 [a] John 12:31; 17:15; Gal. 1:4

whole world lies *under the sway of* the
wicked one.
20And we know that the [a]Son of God has
come and [b]has given us an understanding,
[c]that we may know Him who is true;
and we are in Him who is true, in His Son
Jesus Christ. [d]This is the true God [e]and eternal life.
21Little children, keep yourselves from
idols. Amen.

5:20 [a] 1 John 4:2 [b] Luke 24:45 [c] John 17:3; Rev. 3:7 [d] Is. 9:6 [e] 1 John 5:11, 12

THE SECOND EPISTLE OF

JOHN

OVERVIEW

John's three epistles were written in the later stages of his life and ministry. Christ's resurrection and the birth of the church occurred in about AD 33. John's letters were written around AD 95. In his epistles, John gave us a portrait of discipleship at multiple stages of maturation. In the first epistle of John, the apostle wrote to the church about love as the primary identifier of followers of Christ. In the shorter epistles of 2 John and 3 John, the apostle wrote to individuals.

Second John was addressed to a mother in the church and her children, which may have been a literal woman and her children or a figurative description of the church's leaders and its members. In any case, the unnamed woman was distinguished by her love and desire for truth. The purpose of the short letter was to acknowledge and encourage the alignment of truth with life practices.

It seems the lady in question was a seasoned believer and may even have been an officer of the church. John had no new commandment to share or lesson to teach her. Rather, he implored her to continue to walk in the commandment of God's love, demonstrating the love of God by abiding in the Word of God: "And now I plead with you, lady, not as though I wrote a new commandment to you, but that which we have had from the beginning: that we love one another. This is love, that we walk according to His commandments. This is the commandment, that as you have heard from the beginning, you should walk in it" (2 John vv. 5–6).

John then issued a warning about deceivers who denied Christ's humanity. He called the deceptive, false teacher "an antichrist" (vv. 7–8). The truth and the church were under attack, and John wrote this brief letter to commend the practice of the church to protect that truth. He warned the beloved mother about potential infiltration: "If anyone comes to you and does not bring this doctrine, do not receive him into your house nor greet him" (v. 10). John's love was expressed in his warnings to remain vigilant in the faith.

BREATHE IT IN

Mamie Till-Mobley is one the most underappreciated figures in American history. On August 28, 1955, her only son was kidnapped and lynched for allegedly whistling suggestively at a white woman in Mississippi. More than fifty years later, that same white woman admitted that those allegations were false. What Mamie Till-Mobley did after the lynching of her son, though, is what changed the course of human history. Recognizing that there would be no justice for her only son, she elected to invite the world to view his mutilated body in an open casket. Pictures of the brutality were seen all over the world.

Mamie Till-Mobley lived forty-seven years after the death of her son. She earned an undergraduate and graduate degree and worked in public education for more than two decades, becoming a tireless advocate for children living in poverty. She spoke out publicly against lynching. She loved Jesus and was a pillar in her local church. Mamie Till-Mobley passed away in 2003. The epitaph inscribed on her tombstone reads: "Her Pain United a Nation."

Parenting is not a competitive sport. There is no need to determine whether fatherhood is more important than motherhood or vice versa. According to God's design, the two roles are interdependent. There are scriptures that refer to God as Father and others that liken God to a nurturer, like a mother. What bears consideration as we breathe in 2 John is how much the Bible in general, and the early church in particular, relied on the strength of mothers to provide, proclaim, and protect the message of the gospel.

You cannot talk about the contributions of Abraham, Isaac, and Jacob without considering Sarah, Rebekah, Leah, and Rachel. Without the Old Testament mothers like Hannah and Ruth there would have been no Samuel or David. Elizabeth and Mary were needed to provide the world with John the Baptist and the baby Jesus.

In Jesus' infancy, Mary was warned of what her son would endure. It was prophesied to her that "a sword will pierce through [her] own soul" (Luke 2:35). Mamie's pain united a nation; Mary's pain united the world. Mothers are the foundation of the family, and mothers have traditionally been the foundation of the church. This is certainly the case for the unnamed mother addressed in 2 John.

An American sociologist, Dr. Andrew Billingsley, invested his scholarship into tracing the lineage of African American families to their origins in Africa. He discovered that the value of African American families cannot be measured by their conformity to the nuclear family model. Every family has value. But what is consistent in most models is the nurturing role of the mother. Spiritual formation and moral worldviews are initially delivered maternally.

Consider the mothers in your life and the difference they have made. How much did honoring your mother's sacrifices play a role in your spiritual formation, professional development, and personal relationships? How does your personal relationship with your mother affect your relationships with your spouse and children? As you explore your own maternal relationship, recognize that you can prosper by the example of a godly woman.

†

THE SECOND EPISTLE OF

JOHN

Greeting the Elect Lady

The Elder,

To the elect lady and her children, whom
I love in truth, and not only I, but also all
those who have known [a]the truth, 2because
of the truth which abides in us and will be
with us forever:

3[a]Grace, mercy, *and* peace will be with
you[1] from God the Father and from the
Lord Jesus Christ, the Son of the Father,
in truth and love.

Walk in Christ's Commandments

4I [a]rejoiced greatly that I have found
some of your children walking in truth, as
we received commandment from the Father. 5And now I plead with you, lady, not
as though I wrote a new commandment
to you, but that which we have had from
the beginning: [a]that we love one another.

HOPE FOR THE LORD

INHALE

My faith is in action. I volunteer at the food pantry. I'm there for my family. I'm a hardworking business owner who employs many people. I always pitch in to help wherever I see a need. But the more I help, the more I see people who need help. I'm not tired of trying and giving my all, but sometimes I lose hope that the human condition will ever get better. When will the need to hope for the Lord to fix things be over? When will that hope be realized?

EXHALE

In Matthew 26:11, Jesus said the poor will always be with us. That isn't because God ordained that to be but because the sin of the world will always be with us. So, there will always be the need to help others. And the most important part of helping others is the desire to do so. God will use that desire and turn it into opportunity to change someone's life.

This lack and want of this world will never be over until Christ returns. He is the only eternal answer to the fallen state of humanity. We do our best to put a bandage on the problem, but we cannot heal the problem. God has the cure. This is the hope and optimism we need to keep in front of us. No matter how difficult the task is before us, God can give us what we need to hold up beneath it. We cannot lose our passion for people and meeting their needs. In a world filled with lack, nothing is more important than love and support. This world is difficult, and trouble continues to land on the doorsteps of many. But we get to be the ambassadors of Christ for people who need help and hope.

Second John verse 3 says, "Grace, mercy, and peace will be with you from God the Father and from the Lord Jesus Christ, the Son of the Father, in truth and love." Wow! What a passage to hang your hat on, no matter what you are going through.

1 [a] Col. 1:5 3 [a] Rom. 1:7; 1 Tim. 1:2 [1] NU-Text and M-Text read *us*. 4 [a] 1 Thess. 2:19, 20; 3 John 3, 4 5 [a] [John 13:34, 35; 15:12, 17]; 1 John 3:11; 4:7, 11

6[a]This is love, that we walk according to His
commandments. This is the command-
ment, that [b]as you have heard from the
beginning, you should walk in it.

Beware of Antichrist Deceivers

7For [a]many deceivers have gone out
into the world [b]who do not confess Jesus
Christ *as* coming in the flesh. [c]This is a deceiver and an antichrist. 8[a]Look to yourselves, [b]that we[1] do not lose those things
we worked for, but *that* we[2] may receive
a full reward.

9[a]Whoever transgresses[1] and does
not abide in the doctrine of Christ does
not have God. He who abides in the doctrine of Christ has both the Father and
the Son. 10If anyone comes to you and
[a]does not bring this doctrine, do not receive him into your house nor greet him;
11for he who greets him shares in his evil
deeds.

John's Farewell Greeting

12[a]Having many things to write to you,
I did not wish *to do so* with paper and ink;
but I hope to come to you and speak face
to face, [b]that our joy may be full.

13[a]The children of your elect sister greet
you. Amen.

---

6 [a] John 14:15; 1 John 2:5; 5:3 [b] 1 John 2:24 7 [a] 1 John 2:19; 4:1 [b] 1 John 4:2 [c] 1 John 2:22 8 [a] Mark 13:9 [b] Gal. 3:4 [1] NU-Text reads *you.* [2] NU-Text reads *you.* 9 [a] John 7:16; 8:31; 1 John 2:19, 23, 24 [1] NU-Text reads *goes ahead.* 10 [a] 1 Kin. 13:16; Rom. 16:17; 2 Thess. 3:6, 14; Titus 3:10 12 [a] 3 John 13, 14 [b] John 17:13 13 [a] 1 Pet. 5:13

THE THIRD EPISTLE OF

JOHN

OVERVIEW

John's final letter in the trilogy of epistles that bear his name was addressed to Gaius, a member of the church. Gaius was likely of financial means and provided hospitality for traveling evangelists. John may have been the recipient of his benevolence in the past. In his writing, John expressed concern for Gaius's physical and spiritual health, addressing him as a servant whose "soul prospers" (3 John v. 2).

John urged Gaius to continue his support of other believers because the church was fortified by his efforts. He also addressed two others in the early church, Diotrephes and Demetrius. Diotrephes was a church leader who had undermined the authority of the apostle John. He also denied hospitality to other believers and prevented others from showing hospitality under the threat of putting them out of the church. Diotrephes abused his authority, and John sought to end that abuse. He urged Gaius, "Do not imitate what is evil, but what is good" (v. 11).

In contrast, John had heard good reports about Demetrius (see v. 12). Unlike Diotrephes, Demetrius earned a worthy reputation for walking in the truth.

John's leadership endorsement was critical and empowered Gaius to provide an alternative to the misguided leadership of Diotrephes. John's scathing critique was that Diotrephes "loves to have the preeminence" (v. 9). The church needed leaders who prioritized the church above self-interest. John was so concerned about this division in leadership that he vowed in his final words to visit "face to face" to bring resolution to the issues (v. 14).

BREATHE IT IN

John's final letter was to Gaius, who had proven to be a reliable, stable contributor to the early church. John was an old man when he penned this letter. In encouraging the church to value Gaius, John continued a pattern throughout Scripture of mentoring others and passing the torch of leadership.

John encouraged Gaius in his strengths and warned him of the pitfalls ahead. That is what a good mentor does; they give to others the benefit of their knowledge, wisdom, and experience so that those who follow will be successful and not repeat the mistakes of the past. This is also what Paul did with Timothy; he taught him what he knew and encouraged him in the Lord.

Many great ideas, businesses, and ministries die with the originator because the originator made no plans to pass them along. This may occur because they thought they were the only ones who could make it all work because they alone were the visionaries, or because they refused to accept their own mortality. Either way, they did not acknowledge that God is the originator of all good things.

When wise people have children or age or own something of value, they make a definitive plan about what will happen to their children and possessions when they go to be with the Lord. What could be more urgent to protect and steward than the precious things of God?

Every business, church, and ministry should have a succession plan from the beginning. If God gave you something to accomplish, it is good stewardship to prepare for it to continue in your absence. What is it that God has given you? Have you planned for what will happen to it when the Lord calls you home?

THE THIRD EPISTLE OF

JOHN

Greeting to Gaius

The Elder,

To the beloved Gaius, [a]whom I love in truth:

2Beloved, I pray that you may prosper in all things and be in health, just as your soul prospers. 3For I [a]rejoiced greatly when brethren came and testified of the truth *that is* in you, just as you walk in the truth. 4I have no greater [a]joy than to hear that [b]my children walk in truth.[1]

Gaius Commended for Generosity

5Beloved, you do faithfully whatever you do for the brethren and[1] for strangers, 6who have borne witness of your love before the church. *If* you send them forward on their journey in a manner worthy of God, you will do well, 7because they went forth for His name's sake, [a]taking nothing from the Gentiles. 8We therefore ought to [a]receive[1] such, that we may become fellow workers for the truth.

Diotrephes and Demetrius

9I wrote to the church, but Diotrephes, who loves to have the preeminence among them, does not receive us. 10Therefore, if I come, I will call to mind his deeds which he does, [a]prating against us with malicious words. And not content with that, he himself does not receive the brethren, and forbids those who wish to, putting *them* out of the church.

11Beloved, [a]do not imitate what is evil, but what is good. [b]He who does good is of God, but[1] he who does evil has not seen [c]God.

12Demetrius [a]has a *good* testimony from all, and from the truth itself. And we also bear witness, [b]and you know that our testimony is true.

Farewell Greeting

13[a]I had many things to write, but I do not wish to write to you with pen and ink; 14but I hope to see you shortly, and we shall speak face to face.

Peace to you. Our friends greet you. Greet the friends by name.

---

1 [a] 2 John 1 3 [a] 2 John 4 4 [a] 1 Thess. 2:19, 20; 2 John 4 [b] [1 Cor. 4:15] [1] NU-Text reads *the truth.* 5 [1] NU-Text adds *especially.* 7 [a] 1 Cor. 9:12, 15 8 [a] Matt. 10:40; Rom. 12:13; Heb. 13:2; 1 Pet. 4:9 [1] NU-Text reads *support.* 10 [a] Prov. 10:8, 10 11 [a] Ps. 34:14; 37:27; Rom. 14:19; 1 Thess. 5:15; 1 Tim. 6:11; 2 Tim. 2:22 [b] [1 John 2:29; 3:10] [c] [1 John 3:10] [1] NU-Text and M-Text omit *but.* 12 [a] Acts 6:3; 1 Tim. 3:7 [b] John 19:35; 21:24 13 [a] 2 John 12

THE EPISTLE OF

JUDE

OVERVIEW

Jude (also called Judas) was the half brother of Jesus (see Mark 6:3) and the author of the Epistle of Jude. Notice, however, that Jude was not interested in gaining credibility as Christ's brother. Instead, he referred to himself as "a bondservant of Jesus Christ" (Jude v. 1).

As the early church grew, they were initially called "the Way" (Acts 9:2). They "were first called Christians in Antioch" (Acts 11:26). The Christian community spread rapidly and required leadership and infrastructure to sustain and support it. Such leadership and infrastructure could then provide for continuity in doctrine and practice, defending the church against its greatest threat of false teaching. Because false teaching could erode the church's foundation of the gospel, the apostles Paul and Peter wrote extensively to identify and counteract it. Jude had desired to write about something else but ended up addressing this heinous threat as well (see Jude v. 3). Jude's letter became a diagnosis and a remedy for false teaching.

Jude defined the problem in these words: "For certain men have crept in unnoticed, who long ago were marked out for this condemnation, ungodly men, who turn the grace of our God into lewdness and deny the only Lord God and our Lord Jesus Christ" (v. 4). His rallying cry was for believers to "contend earnestly for the faith" (v. 3). He then offered examples to prove that God's judgment always comes against those who reject truth:

1. The Israelites delivered out of Egypt who did not believe (see v. 5)
2. Fallen angels who did not keep their proper domain (see v. 6)
3. The people of Sodom and Gomorrah for their wickedness (see v. 7)
4. Cain, Balaam, and Korah (see v. 11)

Jude warned that ungodly sinners continue to follow their own evil desires and cautioned that such people would try to pervert the grace of God. He wanted believers to understand that when this happens, the gospel of Jesus Christ becomes no gospel at all (see Gal. 1:7). These attempts by false teachers not only pervert the gospel but also divide the church.

Jude ended his letter by encouraging the readers to be rooted in faith by praying and staying in God's love, and to be merciful to those who doubt and who are not saved (see Jude vv. 20–23). His final words give glory to the God who can keep us from stumbling (see vv. 24–25).

BREATHE IT IN

Jude was the half brother of Jesus who became His servant. After dismissing Jesus as the Son of God during His earthly ministry, Jude later came to have faith in Him. He would end up writing this letter urging the early church to contend for the faith that he had resisted at first and imploring them to take a stand and fight against the threat of false teachers. Jude urged the church forward as a unified family of faith.

The extended Black family and their church family have traditionally been one and the same. They have survived slavery and its resulting, ongoing discrimination because of the viability

of the faith and the adaptability of the family. Faith has held the family together just as it has held the church together.

Within our biological and church families, we are to continue that tradition of standing for the true gospel of Jesus Christ and not allowing scoffers and unbelievers to divide us. From Jude, we learn that we can prevent disunity from happening if we pray and stay close to God through His Word. We must be diligent in this, but we cannot stop there. We must also chase after those family members who are lost and have mercy on them as we reveal the gospel to them.

For many of us, ministering to our families is met with mixed results. In some families, faith is a subject of open discussion. These families are also often involved in Sunday school, Wednesday Bible study, vacation Bible school, church picnics, and many other faith family events. But some families have gone the way of the world, and discussion of faith or Christianity is off limits.

As we breathe in Jude, consider whether you are rooted in your faith deeply enough to be unmoved by false teaching. Consider also whether you have taken responsibility for being the Lord's instrument in sharing the gospel with those family members who do not know Christ. Even if they resist, it is worth the effort to point them to Christ "with fear, pulling them out of the fire" (v. 23).

THE EPISTLE OF

JUDE

Greeting to the Called

Jude, a bondservant of Jesus Christ, and
[a]brother of James,

To those who are [b]called, sanctified[1] by
God the Father, and [c]preserved in Jesus
Christ:

2Mercy, [a]peace, and love be multiplied
to you.

Contend for the Faith

3Beloved, while I was very diligent to
write to you [a]concerning our common salvation, I found it necessary to write to you
exhorting [b]you to contend earnestly for the
faith which was once for all delivered to the
saints. 4For certain men have crept in unnoticed, who long ago were marked out for this
condemnation, ungodly men, who turn the
grace of our God into lewdness and deny the
only Lord God[1] and our Lord Jesus Christ.

Old and New Apostates

5But I want to remind you, though you
once knew this, that [a]the Lord, having saved
the people out of the land of Egypt, afterward destroyed those who did not believe.
6And the angels who did not keep their
proper domain, but left their own abode,
He has reserved in everlasting chains under darkness for the judgment of the great
day; 7as [a]Sodom and Gomorrah, and the
cities around them in a similar manner
to these, having given themselves over to
sexual immorality and gone after strange
flesh, are set forth as an example, suffering the vengeance of eternal fire.
8[a]Likewise also these dreamers defile
the flesh, reject authority, and [b]speak evil
of dignitaries. 9Yet Michael the archangel,
in contending with the devil, when he disputed about the body of Moses, dared not
bring against him a reviling accusation,
but said, [a]"The Lord rebuke you!" 10[a]But
these speak evil of whatever they do not
know; and whatever they know naturally,
like brute beasts, in these things they corrupt themselves. 11Woe to them! For they
have gone in the way [a]of Cain, [b]have run
greedily in the error of Balaam for profit,
and perished [c]in the rebellion of Korah.

Apostates Depraved and Doomed

12These are spots in your love feasts,
while they feast with you without fear,
serving *only* themselves. *They are* clouds
without water, carried about[1] by the winds;
late autumn trees without fruit, twice dead,
pulled up by the roots; 13[a]raging waves of
the sea, [b]foaming up their own shame;
wandering stars [c]for whom is reserved the
blackness of darkness forever.

14Now Enoch, the seventh from Adam,
prophesied about these men also, saying,
"Behold, the Lord comes with ten thousands of His saints, 15to execute judgment
on all, to convict all who are ungodly among
them of all their ungodly deeds which they
have committed in an ungodly way, and of
all the [a]harsh things which ungodly sinners
have spoken against Him."

Apostates Predicted

16These are grumblers, complainers,
walking according to their own lusts; and

---

1 [a] Acts 1:13 [b] Rom. 1:7 [c] John 17:11, 12 [1] NU-Text reads *beloved.* 2 [a] 1 Pet. 1:2; 2 Pet. 1:2 3 [a] Titus 1:4 [b] Phil. 1:27 4 [1] NU-Text omits *God.* 5 [a] Ex. 12:51; 1 Cor. 10:5–10; Heb. 3:16 7 [a] Gen. 19:24; 2 Pet. 2:6 8 [a] 2 Pet. 2:10 [b] Ex. 22:28 9 [a] Zech. 3:2 10 [a] 2 Pet. 2:12 11 [a] Gen. 4:3–8; Heb. 11:4; 1 John 3:12 [b] Num. 31:16; 2 Pet. 2:15; Rev. 2:14 [c] Num. 16:1–3, 31–35 12 [1] NU-Text and M-Text read *along.* 13 [a] Is. 57:20 [b] [Phil. 3:19] [c] 2 Pet. 2:17; Jude 6 15 [a] 1 Sam. 2:3

they [a]mouth great swelling *words*, [b]flat-
tering people to gain advantage. 17 [a]But
you, beloved, remember the words which
were spoken before by the apostles of our
Lord Jesus Christ: 18 how they told you that
[a]there would be mockers in the last time
who would walk according to their own
ungodly lusts. 19 These are sensual persons, who cause divisions, not having the
Spirit.

Maintain Your Life with God

20 But you, beloved, [a]building yourselves
up on your most holy faith, [b]praying in the
Holy Spirit, 21 keep yourselves in the love
of God, [a]looking for the mercy of our Lord
Jesus Christ unto eternal life.

22 And on some have compassion, mak-
ing a distinction;[1] 23 but [a]others save with
fear, [b]pulling *them* out of the fire,[1] hating
even [c]the garment defiled by the flesh.

Glory to God

24 [a]Now to Him who is able to keep
you[1] from stumbling,
And [b]to present *you* faultless
Before the presence of His
glory with exceeding joy,
25 To God our Savior,[1]
Who alone is wise,[2]
Be glory and majesty,
Dominion and power,[3]
Both now and forever.
Amen.

JUDE V. 4

I AM A FALSE TEACHER

For certain men have crept in unnoticed, who long ago were marked out for this condemnation, ungodly men, who turn the grace of our God into lewdness and deny the only Lord God and our Lord Jesus Christ. Jude v. 4

I am one of the false teachers who deceive many. My kind comes in many forms, but we all have evil and malicious intentions. Some deny the one true God. They challenge faith by making it seem worthless. Others come for selfish gain. They say whatever is expeditious in getting what they want. Beware of those of us who come as wolves in sheep's clothes, pretending to be true prophets with great signs and wonders but spewing lies on behalf of the evil one. In every case, it is the purpose of my king to lead astray any who are not steadfast in their faith and not careful to watch for our deceptions. Even the very elect of God need to be vigilant and watchful. God has dealt with evil in the past by casting out the angels who sinned, flooding the world (but saving Noah and his family), and obliterating Sodom and Gomorrah for their wicked and lawless deeds.

We false teachers are brute beasts who will utterly perish in our corruption and will receive the wages of unrighteousness because we entice unstable souls. We are destructive, doomed, depraved, and deceived. But try as we might, we cannot deceive the ones who build themselves up in their faith, praying in the Holy Spirit, keeping themselves in the love of God, and looking for the mercy of their Lord Jesus Christ unto eternal life.

It is not biblical to trust everyone because everyone is not trustworthy. We should place our trust only in Jesus Christ and the living Word of God. Not all who say "Lord, Lord" belong to Jesus. We are to contend for our faith and stand guard over it. We are to serve others, but we must guard ourselves from ungodly teaching and the temptation to listen to foolishness that flows from the hearts of evil people.

16 [a] 2 Pet. 2:18 [b] Prov. 28:21 17 [a] 2 Pet. 3:2 18 [a] Acts 20:29; [1 Tim. 4:1]; 2 Tim. 3:1; 4:3; 2 Pet. 3:3 20 [a] Col. 2:7; 1 Thess. 5:11 [b] [Rom. 8:26] 21 [a] Titus 2:13; Heb. 9:28; 2 Pet. 3:12 22 [1] NU-Text reads *who are doubting* (or *making distinctions*). 23 [a] Rom. 11:14 [b] Amos 4:11; Zech. 3:2; 1 Cor. 3:15 [c] [Zech. 3:4, 5]; Rev. 3:4 [1] NU-Text adds *and on some have mercy with fear* and omits *with fear* in first clause. 24 [a] [Eph. 3:20] [b] Col. 1:22 [1] M-Text reads *them.* 25 [1] NU-Text reads *To the only God our Savior.* [2] NU-Text omits *Who . . . is wise* and adds *Through Jesus Christ our Lord.* [3] NU-Text adds *Before all time.*

THE

REVELATION

OF JESUS CHRIST

OVERVIEW

John "the beloved disciple," is the author of Revelation, a vision describing events surrounding the end of the age. This vision was recorded during the elderly John's time of confinement on a sixty-square-mile island off the coast of Asia Minor called Patmos. This island was a place of banishment for political prisoners, criminals, and those who, like John, were the targets of religious persecution.

While confined, isolated, and persecuted on Patmos, John proved that faithful people can still be productive and hear from God no matter their circumstance. Christ appeared to His friend John and revealed a view of the events all creation presses toward. Through this revelation, John was able to look beyond his confinement toward a vision of future hope for him and all believers.

Revelation is classified as apocalyptic literature—an account of the end times. It is addressed to the seven churches of Asia Minor, which are examined in chapters 2 and 3. Chapters 4–22, then, focus on what will happen in the end times, culminating in the return of Christ (chs. 19–20) and the establishment of the new heavens and earth (chs. 21–22).

John wrote of the time when Babylon, representing the world system, will be completely destroyed. He also told of how Satan and his demons will be thrown into the fiery pit. John further told of a time when Jesus will rule and reign on earth for one thousand years. In the end, all generations will rejoice that Jesus is triumphant and that "God will wipe away every tear from their eyes; there shall be no more death, nor sorrow, nor crying. There shall be no more pain, for the former things have passed away" (Rev. 21:4).

Revelation is replete with signs, symbols, and numbers that often lead to confusion. But the book's singular, clear focus is on revealing the ultimate victory of Jesus Christ. When this world is over, Jesus will be on the throne in a new heaven and earth, and worship will be the order of the day. Everyone—all nations, tribes, peoples, and tongues—will praise Him (see 7:9–12). Oh, what a glorious day that will be!

BREATHE IT IN

End-times theology is an important part of our beliefs and final hope. It reminds us that God has an end game. We must be mindful that the Bible begins in Genesis 1–2 with the creation of the perfect heavens and the earth and ends in Revelation 21–22 with perfect heaven coming down upon a renewed earth. The first petition that Jesus prays in the Lord's Prayer is "Your kingdom come. Your will be done on earth as it is in heaven" (Matt. 6:10). The ultimate fulfillment of this prayer will be accomplished when the New Jerusalem comes down out of heaven.

These final two chapters of the Bible, then, give us great hope. We live in a world where very little is as it should be, causing us to lose even our ability to breathe at times. But a day is coming when the King of kings will come back and fix everything that is broken. He will make each and

every crooked line straight. He will right every wrong, reward the faithful, and bring judgment to the unrighteous. This is not to say that God does not reign now or that there is no justice today. But we must remember that what we experience right now is veiled. It foreshadows what Jesus will bring in fullness one day. And it is in this truth that we can find the hope we need to carry us through even one more day. Knowing that this day is coming can lift our heads and give us just enough courage to carry on. Remembering that Jesus is returning and bringing full victory with Him is to be the oxygen we gasp for. Revelation 21–22 is life-giving.

As we draw a direct line from the Bible's first chapter to its final chapter, we must also consider the sanctity and significance of the earth. Christians are called to value and nurture the earth (see Gen. 1:25–27). The earth is God's creation, and we are the chief stewards of our present home. It is imperative, therefore, that we care for the earth.

Throughout the pages of this Bible, you have been encouraged to "breathe." We cannot do this practically, though, without breathable air, drinkable water, agricultural infrastructure, and renewable energy. Caring for the earth is part of the creation mandate God has given to us. We are to care for not just the souls of people but also the world in which we all live. The United States National Oceanic and Atmospheric Administration lists ten ways we all can preserve the earth:

1. Reduce, reuse, and recycle.
2. Volunteer for cleanups in your community.
3. Educate others in how to preserve natural resources.
4. Conserve water and thereby reduce runoff into our natural bodies of water.
5. Choose sustainable food.
6. Commit to reusable bags and other means of reducing use of plastics.
7. Switch to long-lasting, energy-efficient light bulbs.
8. Plant trees to help save energy, have healthier air, and combat climate change.
9. Use only nontoxic chemicals in your home and yard.
10. Reduce your reliance on gasoline by carpooling, biking, walking, or investing in electric transportation technology.[1]

Through these steps and others, we can commit to being good stewards over this great gift of God we call earth while we wait for the return of His Son.

†

[1] "Protecting Our Planet Starts with You: Ten Simple Choices for a Healthier Planet," National Ocean Service, National Oceanic and Atmospheric Administration, accessed July 21, 2022, https://oceanservice.noaa.gov/ocean/earthday.html.

THE REVELATION OF JESUS CHRIST

Introduction and Benediction

1 The Revelation of Jesus Christ, [a]which
God gave Him to show His servants—
things which must shortly take place. And
[b]He sent and signified *it* by His angel to His
servant John, 2 [a]who bore witness to the
word of God, and to the testimony of Jesus
Christ, to all things [b]that he saw. 3 [a]Blessed
is he who reads and those who hear the
words of this prophecy, and keep those
things which are written in it; for [b]the time
is near.

Greeting the Seven Churches

4 John, to the seven churches which are
in Asia:

Grace to you and peace from Him [a]who
is and [b]who was and who is to come, [c]and
from the seven Spirits who are before
His throne, 5 and from Jesus Christ, [a]the
faithful [b]witness, the [c]firstborn from the
dead, and [d]the ruler over the kings of the
earth.

To Him [e]who loved us [f]and washed[1] us
from our sins in His own blood, 6 and has
[a]made us kings[1] and priests to His God and
Father, [b]to Him *be* glory and dominion forever and ever. Amen.

7 Behold, He is coming with [a]clouds, and
every eye will see Him, even [b]they who
pierced Him. And all the tribes of the earth
will mourn because of Him. Even so, Amen.

8 [a]"I am the Alpha and the Omega, *the*
Beginning and *the* End,"[1] says the Lord,[2]
[b]"who is and who was and who is to come,
the [c]Almighty."

Vision of the Son of Man

9 I, John, both[1] your brother and [a]com-
panion in the tribulation and [b]kingdom
and patience of Jesus Christ, was on the
island that is called Patmos for the word of
God and for the testimony of Jesus Christ.
10 [a]I was in the Spirit on [b]the Lord's Day,
and I heard behind me [c]a loud voice, as of
a trumpet, 11 saying, "I am the Alpha and
the Omega, the First and the Last," and,[1]
"What you see, write in a book and send *it*
to the seven churches which are in Asia:[2]
to Ephesus, to Smyrna, to Pergamos, to
Thyatira, to Sardis, to Philadelphia, and
to Laodicea."

12 Then I turned to see the voice that
spoke with me. And having turned [a]I saw
seven golden lampstands, 13 [a]and in the
midst of the seven lampstands [b]*One* like
the Son of Man, [c]clothed with a garment
down to the feet and [d]girded about the
chest with a golden band. 14 His head and
[a]hair *were* white like wool, as white as snow,
and [b]His eyes like a flame of fire; 15 [a]His feet
were like fine brass, as if refined in a furnace, and [b]His voice as the sound of many
waters; 16 [a]He had in His right hand seven
stars, [b]out of His mouth went a sharp two-
edged sword, [c]and His countenance *was*
like the sun shining in its strength. 17 And

1:1 [a] John 3:32 [b] Rev. 22:6 1:2 [a] 1 Cor. 1:6 [b] 1 John 1:1 1:3 [a] Luke 11:28; Rev. 22:7 [b] James 5:8; Rev. 22:10 1:4 [a] Ex. 3:14 [b] John 1:1 [c] [Is. 11:2]; Zech. 3:9; Rev. 3:1; 4:5; 5:6 1:5 [a] John 8:14; Prov. 14:5 [b] Is. 55:4 [c] Ps. 89:27; 1 Cor. 15:20; [Col. 1:18] [d] Rev. 17:14 [e] John 13:34 [f] Heb. 9:14 [1] NU-Text reads *loves us and freed;* M-Text reads *loves us and washed.* 1:6 [a] 1 Pet. 2:5, 9 [b] 1 Tim. 6:16 [1] NU-Text and M-Text read *a kingdom.* 1:7 [a] Matt. 24:30 [b] Zech. 12:10–14; John 19:37 1:8 [a] Is. 41:4; Rev. 21:6; 22:13 [b] Rev. 4:8; 11:17 [c] Is. 9:6 [1] NU-Text and M-Text omit *the Beginning and the End.* [2] NU-Text and M-Text add *God.* 1:9 [a] Phil. 1:7 [b] [Rom. 8:17; 2 Tim. 2:12] [1] NU-Text and M-Text omit *both.* 1:10 [a] Acts 10:10 [b] Acts 20:7 [c] Rev. 4:1 1:11 [1] NU-Text and M-Text omit *I am* through third *and.* [2] NU-Text and M-Text omit *which are in Asia.* 1:12 [a] Ex. 25:37; Zech. 4:2; Rev. 1:20; 2:1 1:13 [a] Rev. 2:1 [b] Ezek. 1:26; Dan. 7:13; 10:16; Rev. 14:14 [c] Dan. 10:5 [d] Rev. 15:6 1:14 [a] Dan. 7:9 [b] Dan. 10:6; Rev. 2:18; 19:12 1:15 [a] Ezek. 1:7; Dan. 10:6; Rev. 2:18 [b] Ezek. 1:24; 43:2; Rev. 14:2; 19:6 1:16 [a] Rev. 1:20; 2:1; 3:1 [b] Is. 49:2; [Heb. 4:12]; Rev. 2:12, 16; 19:15 [c] Matt. 17:2; Acts 26:13; Rev. 10:1

ELEVATE YOUR TIME WITH HIM

INHALE

I've read through the Bible, and walking with God has blessed my soul. I'm still learning, and I want to be better for Him. How can my time with Him be maximized so that I'm better for Him? What does God want me to learn from my time with Him?

EXHALE

One thing needs to be clear: it really isn't a matter of striving to be "better for Him." The Bible tells us that God is the one who works within us and changes us. We are totally incapable of changing ourselves. We also learn that in Christ, we are fully accepted by God. He changed us completely and made us new creatures (see 2 Cor. 5:17). So, it really isn't a matter of "being" better; it's a matter of "living" better—living our new, true identity in Jesus.

With that said, you are right to want to live in a more godly way. The wonderful news is that God has provided all we need to grow closer to Him and into the people we were created to be. First and foremost is the Word of God. Every word of Scripture will lead us into righteousness and equip us to follow our Lord closely and share His truth with others. God's Word will teach us who He is and who we are in Christ, and it will train us in His ways. It will correct us when we veer from the path God desires and, even better, prevent us from doing that. This is why reading the Bible should be seen not as a chore or assignment but more as a gift. Even a few minutes can go a long way, and there's never a bad time to be with God and in His Word. Think of the apostle John. Even when he was an elderly man exiled as a prisoner on Patmos, he still spent regular time with the Lord (see Rev. 1:9–10). John could not get enough of Jesus. And we shouldn't either.

Furthermore, God has promised to be with us at all times. Jesus said He would send the "Helper" to help us live according to God's will and to remind us of every word Jesus ever spoke (see John 14–16). This "Helper" is the Holy Spirit. Jesus said He will live within us and enable us to grow into the people God designed us to be. Each of us has a plan and purpose, assigned by God from the foundation of the world. God's Word says He will complete the work He has begun in us. Just trust Him, seek Him, and submit to Him. This is God's will for each of us.

[a]when I saw Him, I fell at His feet as dead.
But [b]He laid His right hand on me, saying
to me,[1] "Do not be afraid; [c]I am the First
and the Last. 18 [a]I *am* He who lives, and
was dead, and behold, [b]I am alive forevermore. Amen. And [c]I have the keys of Hades and of Death. 19 Write[1] the things which
you have [a]seen, [b]and the things which are,
[c]and the things which will take place after this. 20 The mystery of the seven stars
which you saw in My right hand, and the
seven golden lampstands: The seven stars
are [a]the angels of the seven churches, and
[b]the seven lampstands which you saw[1] are
the seven churches.

The Loveless Church

2 "To the angel of the church of Ephesus write,
'These things says [a]He who holds the
seven stars in His right hand, [b]who walks in
the midst of the seven golden lampstands:
2 [a]"I know your works, your labor, your patience, and that you cannot bear those who
are evil. And [b]you have tested those [c]who
say they are apostles and are not, and have
found them liars; 3 and you have persevered
and have patience, and have labored for My
name's sake and have [a]not become weary.
4 Nevertheless I have *this* against you, that
you have left your first love. 5 Remember

1:17 [a] Ezek. 1:28 [b] Dan. 8:18; 10:10, 12 [c] Is. 41:4; 44:6; 48:12; Rev. 2:8; 22:13 [1] NU-Text and M-Text omit *to me.* 1:18 [a] Rom. 6:9; Rev. 2:8; 10:6; 15:7 [b] Rev. 4:9 [c] Ps. 68:20 1:19 [a] Rev. 1:9–18 [b] Rev. 2:1 [c] John 16:13; Rev. 4:1 [1] NU-Text and M-Text read *Therefore, write.* 1:20 [a] Mal. 2:7; Rev. 2:1 [b] Ex. 25:37; 37:23; Zech. 4:2; Matt. 5:15; Phil. 2:15 [1] NU-Text and M-Text omit *which you saw.* 2:1 [a] Rev. 1:16 [b] Rev. 1:13 2:2 [a] Ps. 1:6 [b] John 6:6; 1 John 4:1 [c] 2 Cor. 11:13 2:3 [a] Gal. 6:9; Heb. 12:3, 5

therefore from where you have fallen; repent and do the first works, [a]or else I will
come to you quickly and remove your
lampstand from its place—unless you repent. 6 But this you have, that you hate the
deeds of the Nicolaitans, which I also hate.
7 [a]"He who has an ear, let him hear what
the Spirit says to the churches. To him who
overcomes I will give [b]to eat from [c]the tree
of life, which is in the midst of the Paradise of God."'

The Persecuted Church

8 "And to the angel of the church in
Smyrna write,
'These things says [a]the First and the Last,
who was dead, and came to life: 9 "I know
your works, tribulation, and poverty (but
you are [a]rich); and *I know* the blasphemy
of [b]those who say they are Jews and are
not, [c]but *are* a synagogue of Satan. 10 [a]Do
not fear any of those things which you are
about to suffer. Indeed, the devil is about
to throw *some* of you into prison, that you
may be tested, and you will have tribulation ten days. [b]Be faithful until death, and
I will give you [c]the crown of life.
11 [a]"He who has an ear, let him hear what
the Spirit says to the churches. He who
overcomes shall not be hurt by [b]the second death."'

The Compromising Church

12 "And to the angel of the church in Pergamos write,
'These things says [a]He who has the sharp
two-edged sword: 13 "I know your works,
and where you dwell, where Satan's throne
is. And you hold fast to My name, and did
not deny My faith even in the days in which
Antipas *was* My faithful martyr, who was
killed among you, where Satan dwells. 14 But
I have a few things against you, because
you have there those who hold the doctrine of [a]Balaam, who taught Balak to put
a stumbling block before the children of
Israel, [b]to eat things sacrificed to idols, [c]and
to commit sexual immorality. 15 Thus you
also have those who hold the doctrine of
the Nicolaitans, which thing I hate.[1] 16 Repent, or else I will come to you quickly and
[a]will fight against them with the sword of
My mouth.
17 "He who has an ear, let him hear what
the Spirit says to the churches. To him who
overcomes I will give some of the hidden
[a]manna to eat. And I will give him a white
stone, and on the stone [b]a new name written which no one knows except him who
receives *it*."'

The Corrupt Church

18 "And to the angel of the church in Thyatira write,
'These things says the Son of God, [a]who
has eyes like a flame of fire, and His feet
like fine brass: 19 [a]"I know your works, love,
service, faith,[1] and your patience; and *as* for
your works, the last *are* more than the first.
20 Nevertheless I have a few things against
you, because you allow[1] that woman[2] [a]Jeze-
bel, who calls herself a prophetess, to teach
and seduce[3] My servants [b]to commit sexual immorality and eat things sacrificed
to idols. 21 And I gave her time [a]to repent
of her sexual immorality, and she did not
repent.[1] 22 Indeed I will cast her into a sickbed, and those who commit adultery with
her into great tribulation, unless they repent of their[1] deeds. 23 I will kill her children
with death, and all the churches shall know
that I am He who [a]searches the minds and
hearts. And I will give to each one of you
according to your works.
24 "Now to you I say, and[1] to the rest in
Thyatira, as many as do not have this doctrine, who have not known the [a]depths of
Satan, as they say, [b]I will[2] put on you no
other burden. 25 But hold fast [a]what you
have till I come. 26 And he who overcomes,
and keeps [a]My works until the end, [b]to him
I will give power over the nations—

2:5 [a] Matt. 21:41 2:7 [a] Matt. 11:15; Rev. 2:11, 17; 3:6, 13, 22; 13:9 [b] [Rev. 22:2, 14] [c] [Gen. 2:9; 3:22] 2:8 [a] Rev. 1:8, 17, 18 2:9 [a] Luke 12:21 [b] Rom. 2:17 [c] Rev. 3:9 2:10 [a] Matt. 10:22 [b] Matt. 24:13 [c] James 1:12 2:11 [a] Rev. 13:9 [b] [Rev. 20:6, 14; 21:8] 2:12 [a] Is. 49:2; Rev. 1:16; 2:16 2:14 [a] Num. 31:16 [b] Num. 25; Acts 15:29; [1 Cor. 10:20]; Rev. 2:20 [c] 1 Cor. 6:13 2:15 [1] NU-Text and M-Text read *likewise for which thing I hate.* 2:16 [a] Is. 11:4; 2 Thess. 2:8; Rev. 19:15 2:17 [a] Ex. 16:33, 34; [John 6:49, 51] [b] Is. 56:5; 62:2; 65:15; Rev. 3:12 2:18 [a] Rev. 1:14, 15 2:19 [a] Rev. 2:2 [1] NU-Text and M-Text read *faith, service.* 2:20 [a] 1 Kin. 16:31; 21:25; 2 Kin. 9:7, 22, 30 [b] Ex. 34:15 [1] NU-Text and M-Text read *I have against you that you tolerate.* [2] M-Text reads *your wife Jezebel.* [3] NU-Text and M-Text read *and teaches and seduces.* 2:21 [a] Rom. 2:5; Rev. 9:20; 16:9, 11 [1] NU-Text and M-Text read *time to repent, and she does not want to repent of her sexual immorality.* 2:22 [1] NU-Text and M-Text read *her.* 2:23 [a] Ps. 7:9; 26:2; 139:1; Jer. 11:20; 17:10; Matt. 16:27; Luke 16:15; Acts 1:24; Rom. 8:27 2:24 [a] 2 Tim. 3:1–9 [b] Acts 15:28 [1] NU-Text and M-Text omit *and.* [2] NU-Text and M-Text omit *will.* 2:25 [a] Rev. 3:11 2:26 [a] [John 6:29] [b] [Matt. 19:28]

27 'He[a] shall rule them with a rod of iron;
They shall be dashed to pieces
like the potter's vessels'[1]—

as I also have received from My Father;
28 and I will give him [a]the morning star.
29 "He who has an ear, let him hear what
the Spirit says to the churches." '

The Dead Church

3 "And to the angel of the church in Sardis write,
'These things says He who [a]has the seven
Spirits of God and the seven stars: "I know
your works, that you have a name that you
are alive, but you are dead. 2 Be watchful,
and strengthen the things which remain,
that are ready to die, for I have not found
your works perfect before God.[1] 3 [a]Remem-
ber therefore how you have received and
heard; hold fast and [b]repent. [c]Therefore if
you will not watch, I will come upon you
[d]as a thief, and you will not know what hour
I will come upon you. 4 You[1] have [a]a few
names even in Sardis who have not [b]defiled
their garments; and they shall walk with Me
[c]in white, for they are worthy. 5 He who overcomes [a]shall be clothed in white garments,
and I will not [b]blot out his name from the
[c]Book of Life; but [d]I will confess his name
before My Father and before His angels.
6 [a]"He who has an ear, let him hear what
the Spirit says to the churches." '

The Faithful Church

7 "And to the angel of the church in Philadelphia write,
'These things says [a]He who is holy, [b]He
who is true, [c]"He who has the key of David, [d]He who opens and no one shuts, and
[e]shuts and no one opens":[1] 8 [a]"I know your
works. See, I have set before you [b]an open
door, and no one can shut it;[1] for you have a
little strength, have kept My word, and have
not denied My name. 9 Indeed I will make
[a]*those* of the synagogue of Satan, who say
they are Jews and are not, but lie—indeed
[b]I will make them come and worship before
your feet, and to know that I have loved
you. 10 Because you have kept My command
to persevere, [a]I also will keep you from the
hour of trial which shall come upon [b]the
whole world, to test those who dwell [c]on
the earth. 11 Behold,[1] [a]I am coming quickly!
[b]Hold fast what you have, that no one may
take [c]your crown. 12 He who overcomes, I
will make him [a]a pillar in the temple of My
God, and he shall [b]go out no more. [c]I will
write on him the name of My God and the
name of the city of My God, the [d]New Jerusalem, which [e]comes down out of heaven
from My God. [f]And *I will write on him* My
new name.
13 [a]"He who has an ear, let him hear what
the Spirit says to the churches." '

The Lukewarm Church

14 "And to the angel of the church of the
Laodiceans[1] write,
[a]'These things says the Amen, [b]the Faithful and True Witness, [c]the Beginning of the
creation of God: 15 [a]"I know your works, that
you are neither cold nor hot. I could wish
you were cold or hot. 16 So then, because you
are lukewarm, and neither cold nor hot,[1] I
will vomit you out of My mouth. 17 Because
you say, [a]'I am rich, have become wealthy,
and have need of nothing'—and do not
know that you are wretched, miserable,
poor, blind, and naked— 18 I counsel you
[a]to buy from Me gold refined in the fire,
that you may be rich; and [b]white garments,
that you may be clothed, *that* the shame of
your nakedness may not be revealed; and
anoint your eyes with eye salve, that you
may see. 19 [a]As many as I love, I rebuke and
[b]chasten. Therefore be zealous and repent.
20 Behold, [a]I stand at the door and knock. [b]If
anyone hears My voice and opens the door,
[c]I will come in to him and dine with him,

2:27 [a] Ps. 2:8, 9; Rev. 12:5; 19:15 [1] Psalm 2:9 2:28 [a] 2 Pet. 1:19; Rev. 22:16 3:1 [a] Rev. 1:4, 16 3:2 [1] NU-Text and M-Text read *My God.* 3:3 [a] 1 Tim. 6:20 [b] Rev. 3:19 [c] Matt. 24:42, 43; Luke 12:39 [d] 1 Thess. 5:2; [2 Pet. 3:10; Rev. 16:15] 3:4 [a] Acts 1:15 [b] [Jude 23] [c] Rev. 4:4; 6:11 [1] NU-Text and M-Text read *Nevertheless you have a few names in Sardis.* 3:5 [a] [Rev. 19:8] [b] Ex. 32:32; Ps. 69:28; Luke 10:20; [Rev. 13:8; 17:8; 20:12, 15; 21:27] [c] Phil. 4:3 [d] Matt. 10:32; Luke 12:8 3:6 [a] Rev. 2:7 3:7 [a] Acts 3:14 [b] John 14:6; 1 John 5:20; Rev. 3:14; 19:11 [c] Is. 9:7; 22:22; Jer. 23:5 [d] [Matt. 16:19; Rev. 1:18] [e] Job 12:14 [1] Isaiah 22:22 3:8 [a] Rev. 3:1 [b] 1 Cor. 16:9 [1] NU-Text and M-Text read *which no one can shut.* 3:9 [a] Rev. 2:9 [b] Is. 45:14; 49:23; 60:14 3:10 [a] 2 Tim. 2:12; 2 Pet. 2:9 [b] Luke 2:1 [c] Is. 24:17 3:11 [a] Phil. 4:5 [b] Rev. 2:25 [c] [Rev. 2:10] [1] NU-Text and M-Text omit *Behold.* 3:12 [a] 1 Kin. 7:21; Jer. 1:18; Gal. 2:9 [b] Ps. 23:6 [c] [Rev. 14:1; 22:4] [d] [Heb. 12:22] [e] Rev. 21:2 [f] [Rev. 2:17; 22:4] 3:13 [a] Rev. 2:7 3:14 [a] Is. 65:16; 2 Cor. 1:20 [b] Rev. 1:5; 3:7; 19:11 [c] [Col. 1:15] [1] NU-Text and M-Text read *in Laodicea.* 3:15 [a] Rev. 3:1 3:16 [1] NU-Text and M-Text read *hot nor cold.* 3:17 [a] Hos. 12:8; Zech. 11:5; [Matt. 5:3]; 1 Cor. 4:8 3:18 [a] Is. 55:1; Matt. 13:44 [b] 2 Cor. 5:3 3:19 [a] Job 5:17 [b] Prov. 3:12; [2 Cor. 11:32]; Heb. 12:6 3:20 [a] Song 5:2 [b] Luke 12:36, 37; John 10:3 [c] [John 14:23]

#OXYGEN

REVELATION 3:20

Elevate Your Time with Him

To grow your spiritual life, start every day with a quiet time. Pray, meditate, and read the Word. Commit to a good nurturing church and find a Bible study group. Be intentional about your walk.

Breathe and elevate your time with Him.

and he with Me. 21To him who overcomes
[a]I will grant to sit with Me on My throne,
as I also overcame and sat down with My
Father on His throne.
22[a]"He who has an ear, let him hear what
the Spirit says to the churches." '

The Throne Room of Heaven
(Is. 6:1–3)

4 After these things I looked, and behold,
a door *standing* [a]open in heaven. And
the first voice which I heard *was* like a
[b]trumpet speaking with me, saying, "Come
up here, and I will show you things which
must take place after this."
2Immediately [a]I was in the Spirit; and
behold, [b]a throne set in heaven, and *One*
sat on the throne. 3And He who sat there
was[1] [a]like a jasper and a sardius stone in
appearance; [b]and *there was* a rainbow
around the throne, in appearance like
an emerald. 4[a]Around the throne *were*
twenty-four thrones, and on the thrones
I saw twenty-four elders sitting, [b]clothed
in white robes; and they had crowns[1] of
gold on their heads. 5And from the throne
proceeded [a]lightnings, thunderings, and
voices.[1] [b]Seven lamps of fire *were* burning
before the throne, which are [c]the[2] seven
Spirits of God.
6Before the throne *there was*[1] [a]a sea of
glass, like crystal. [b]And in the midst of the
throne, and around the throne, *were* four
living creatures full of eyes in front and in
back. 7[a]The first living creature *was* like a
lion, the second living creature like a calf,
the third living creature had a face like a
man, and the fourth living creature *was*
like a flying eagle. 8*The* four living creatures, each having [a]six wings, were full of
eyes around and within. And they do not
rest day or night, saying:

[b]"Holy, holy, holy,[1]
[c]Lord God Almighty,
[d]Who was and is and is to come!"

9Whenever the living creatures give
glory and honor and thanks to Him who
sits on the throne, [a]who lives forever and
ever, 10[a]the twenty-four elders fall down before Him who sits on the throne and worship Him who lives forever and ever, and
cast their crowns before the throne, saying:

11 "You[a] are worthy, O Lord,[1]
To receive glory and honor and power;
[b]For You created all things,
And by [c]Your will they exist[2]
and were created."

The Lamb Takes the Scroll

5 And I saw in the right *hand* of Him who
sat on the throne [a]a scroll written inside and on the back, [b]sealed with seven
seals. 2Then I saw a strong angel proclaiming with a loud voice, [a]"Who is worthy to
open the scroll and to loose its seals?" 3And
no one in heaven or on the earth or under
the earth was able to open the scroll, or to
look at it.
4So I wept much, because no one was
found worthy to open and read[1] the scroll,
or to look at it. 5But one of the elders said

3:21 [a] Matt. 19:28; 2 Tim. 2:12; [Rev. 2:26; 20:4] 3:22 [a] Rev. 2:7 4:1 [a] Ezek. 1:1; Rev. 19:11 [b] Rev. 1:10 4:2 [a] Rev. 1:10 [b] 1 Kin. 22:19; Is. 6:1; Ezek. 1:26; Dan. 7:9; Rev. 3:21; 4:9 4:3 [a] Matt. 5:8; Rev. 21:11 [b] Gen. 9:13–17; Ezek. 1:28; Rev. 10:1 [1] M-Text omits *And He who sat there was* (which makes the description in verse 3 modify the throne rather than God). 4:4 [a] Rev. 11:16 [b] Rev. 3:4, 5 [1] NU-Text and M-Text read *robes, with crowns.* 4:5 [a] Gen. 49:9, 10; Ex. 19:16; Rev. 8:5; 11:19; 16:18 [b] Ex. 37:23 [c] 2 Sam. 7:12; [Rev. 1:4] [1] NU-Text and M-Text read *voices, and thunderings.* [2] M-Text omits *the.* 4:6 [a] Ex. 38:8; Ezek. 1:22; Rev. 15:2 [b] Ezek. 1:5; Rev. 4:8; 5:6; 6:1, 6; 7:11; 14:3; 15:7; 19:4 [1] NU-Text and M-Text add *something like.* 4:7 [a] Ezek. 1:10; 10:14 4:8 [a] Is. 6:2 [b] Is. 6:3 [c] Rev. 1:8 [d] Rev. 1:4 [1] M-Text has *holy* nine times. 4:9 [a] Rev. 1:18 4:10 [a] Rev. 5:8, 14; 7:11; 11:16; 19:4 4:11 [a] Rev. 1:6; 5:12 [b] Gen. 1:1; John 1:3 [c] Col. 1:16 [1] NU-Text and M-Text read *our Lord and God.* [2] NU-Text and M-Text read *existed.* 5:1 [a] Ezek. 2:9, 10 [b] Is. 29:11; Dan. 12:4 5:2 [a] Rev. 4:11; 5:9 5:4 [1] NU-Text and M-Text omit *and read.*

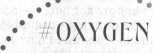

to me, "Do not weep. Behold, [a]the Lion of the tribe of [b]Judah, [c]the Root of David, has [d]prevailed to open the scroll [e]and to loose[1] its seven seals."

6And I looked, and behold,[1] in the midst of the throne and of the four living creatures, and in the midst of the elders, stood [a]a Lamb as though it had been slain, having seven horns and [b]seven eyes, which are [c]the seven Spirits of God sent out into all the earth. 7Then He came and took the scroll out of the right hand [a]of Him who sat on the throne.

Worthy Is the Lamb

8Now when He had taken the scroll, [a]the four living creatures and the twenty-four elders fell down before the Lamb, each having a harp, and golden bowls full of incense, which are the [b]prayers of the saints. 9And [a]they sang a new song, saying:

[b]"You are worthy to take the scroll,
And to open its seals;
For You were slain,
And [c]have redeemed us to
God [d]by Your blood
Out of every tribe and tongue
and people and nation,
10 And have made us[1] [a]kings[2]
and [b]priests to our God;
And we[3] shall reign on the earth."

11Then I looked, and I heard the voice of many angels around the throne, the living creatures, and the elders; and the number of them was ten thousand times ten thousand, and thousands of thousands, 12saying with a loud voice:

"Worthy is the Lamb who was slain
To receive power and
riches and wisdom,
And strength and honor and
glory and blessing!"

13And [a]every creature which is in heaven and on the earth and under the earth and such as are in the sea, and all that are in them, I heard saying:

[b]"Blessing and honor and
glory and power
Be to Him [c]who sits on the throne,
And to the Lamb, forever
and ever!"[1]

14Then the four living creatures said, "Amen!" And the twenty-four[1] elders fell down and worshiped Him who lives forever and ever.[2]

First Seal: The Conqueror

6 Now [a]I saw when the Lamb opened one of the seals;[1] and I heard [b]one of the four living creatures saying with a voice like thunder, "Come and see." 2And I looked, and behold, [a]a white horse. [b]He who sat on it had a bow; [c]and a crown was given to him, and he went out [d]conquering and to conquer.

Second Seal: Conflict on Earth

3When He opened the second seal, [a]I heard the second living creature saying, "Come and see."[1] 4[a]Another horse, fiery red, went out. And it was granted to the one who sat on it to [b]take peace from the earth, and that *people* should kill one another; and there was given to him a great sword.

Third Seal: Scarcity on Earth

5When He opened the third seal, [a]I heard the third living creature say, "Come and see." So I looked, and behold, [b]a black horse, and he who sat on it had a pair of [c]scales in his hand. 6And I heard a voice in the midst of the four living creatures saying, "A quart[1] of wheat for a denarius,[2] and three quarts of barley for a denarius; and [a]do not harm the oil and the wine."

5:5 [a] Gen. 49:9 [b] Heb. 7:14 [c] Is. 11:1, 10; Rom. 15:12; Rev. 22:16 [d] Rev. 3:21 [e] Rev. 6:1 [1] NU-Text and M-Text omit *to loose.* 5:6 [a] Is. 53:7; [John 1:29; 1 Pet. 1:19] [b] Zech. 3:9; 4:10 [c] Rev. 1:4; 3:1; 4:5 [1] NU-Text and M-Text read *I saw in the midst . . . a Lamb standing.* 5:7 [a] Rev. 4:2 5:8 [a] Rev. 4:8–10; 19:4 [b] Ps. 141:2; Rev. 8:3 5:9 [a] Rev. 14:3 [b] Rev. 4:11 [c] John 1:29 [d] [Heb. 9:12; 1 Pet. 1:18, 19] 5:10 [a] Ex. 19:6 [b] Is. 61:6 [1] NU-Text and M-Text read *them.* [2] NU-Text reads *a kingdom.* [3] NU-Text and M-Text read *they.* 5:13 [a] Phil. 2:10; Rev. 5:3 [b] 1 Chr. 29:11; Rom. 9:5; 1 Tim. 6:16; 1 Pet. 4:11 [c] Rev. 4:2, 3; 6:16; 20:11 [1] M-Text adds *Amen.* 5:14 [1] NU-Text and M-Text omit *twenty-four.* [2] NU-Text and M-Text omit *Him who lives forever and ever.* 6:1 [a] Is. 53:7; [John 1:29; Rev. 5:5–7, 12; 13:8] [b] Rev. 4:7 [1] NU-Text and M-Text read *seven seals.* 6:2 [a] Zech. 1:8; 6:3 [b] Ps. 45:4, 5, LXX [c] Zech. 6:11; Rev. 9:7; 14:14; 19:12 [d] Matt. 24:5; Rev. 3:21 6:3 [a] Rev. 4:7 [1] NU-Text and M-Text omit *and see.* 6:4 [a] Zech. 1:8; 6:2 [b] Matt. 24:6, 7 6:5 [a] Rev. 4:7 [b] Zech. 6:2, 6 [c] Matt. 24:7 6:6 [a] Rev. 7:3; 9:4 [1] Greek *choinix;* that is, approximately one quart [2] This was approximately one day's wage for a worker.

Fourth Seal: Widespread Death on Earth

7When He opened the fourth seal, [a]I
heard the voice of the fourth living creature saying, "Come and see." 8[a]So I looked,
and behold, a pale horse. And the name of
him who sat on it was Death, and Hades
followed with him. And power was given
to them over a fourth of the earth, [b]to kill
with sword, with hunger, with death, [c]and
by the beasts of the earth.

Fifth Seal: The Cry of the Martyrs

9When He opened the fifth seal, I saw
under [a]the altar [b]the souls of those who
had been slain [c]for the word of God and for
[d]the testimony which they held. 10And they
cried with a loud voice, saying, [a]"How long,
O Lord, [b]holy and true, [c]until You judge and
avenge our blood on those who dwell on
the earth?" 11Then a [a]white robe was given
to each of them; and it was said to them
[b]that they should rest a little while longer,
until both *the number of* their fellow servants and their brethren, who would be
killed as they *were,* was completed.

Sixth Seal: Cosmic Disturbances

12I looked when He opened the sixth
seal, [a]and behold,[1] there was a great earthquake; and [b]the sun became black as sackcloth of hair, and the moon[2] became like
blood. 13[a]And the stars of heaven fell to the
earth, as a fig tree drops its late figs when it
is shaken by a mighty wind. 14[a]Then the sky
receded as a scroll when it is rolled up, and
[b]every mountain and island was moved out
of its place. 15And the [a]kings of the earth,
the great men, the rich men, the commanders,[1] the mighty men, every slave and every free man, [b]hid themselves in the caves
and in the rocks of the mountains, 16[a]and
said to the mountains and rocks, "Fall on
us and hide us from the face of Him who
[b]sits on the throne and from the wrath of
the Lamb! 17For the great day of His wrath
has come, [a]and who is able to stand?"

The Sealed of Israel

7 After these things I saw four angels standing at the four corners of
the earth, [a]holding the four winds of the
earth, [b]that the wind should not blow on
the earth, on the sea, or on any tree. 2Then I
saw another angel ascending from the east,
having the seal of the living God. And he
cried with a loud voice to the four angels to
whom it was granted to harm the earth and
the sea, 3saying, [a]"Do not harm the earth,
the sea, or the trees till we have sealed the
servants of our God [b]on their foreheads."
4[a]And I heard the number of those who
were sealed. [b]One hundred *and* forty-four
thousand [c]of all the tribes of the children
of Israel *were* sealed:

5 of the tribe of Judah twelve
thousand *were* sealed;[1]
of the tribe of Reuben twelve
thousand *were* sealed;
of the tribe of Gad twelve
thousand *were* sealed;
6 of the tribe of Asher twelve
thousand *were* sealed;
of the tribe of Naphtali twelve
thousand *were* sealed;
of the tribe of Manasseh twelve
thousand *were* sealed;
7 of the tribe of Simeon twelve
thousand *were* sealed;
of the tribe of Levi twelve
thousand *were* sealed;
of the tribe of Issachar twelve
thousand *were* sealed;
8 of the tribe of Zebulun twelve
thousand *were* sealed;
of the tribe of Joseph twelve
thousand *were* sealed;
of the tribe of Benjamin twelve
thousand *were* sealed.

A Multitude from the Great Tribulation

9After these things I looked, and behold, [a]a great multitude which no one could

---

6:7 [a] Rev. 4:7 6:8 [a] Zech. 6:3 [b] Jer. 14:12; 15:2; 24:10; 29:17; Ezek. 5:12, 17; 14:21; 29:5; Matt. 24:9 [c] Lev. 26:22 6:9 [a] Rev. 8:3 [b] [Rev. 20:4] [c] Rev. 1:2, 9 [d] 2 Tim. 1:8 6:10 [a] Ps. 13:1–6; Zech. 1:12 [b] Rev. 3:7 [c] Rev. 11:18 6:11 [a] Rev. 3:4, 5; 7:9 [b] Heb. 11:40 6:12 [a] Matt. 24:7; Rev. 8:5; 11:13; 16:18 [b] Is. 13:10; Joel 2:10, 31; 3:15; Matt. 24:29; Mark 13:24 [1] NU-Text and M-Text omit *behold.* [2] NU-Text and M-Text read *the whole moon.* 6:13 [a] Matt. 24:29; Mark 13:25; Rev. 8:10; 9:1 6:14 [a] Ps. 102:26; Is. 34:4; [2 Pet. 3:10]; Rev. 20:11; 21:1 [b] Jer. 3:23; Rev. 16:20 6:15 [a] Ps. 2:2–4 [b] Is. 2:10, 19, 21; 24:21; Rev. 19:18 [1] NU-Text and M-Text read *the commanders, the rich men.* 6:16 [a] Hos. 10:8; Luke 23:29, 30; Rev. 9:6 [b] Rev. 20:11 6:17 [a] Is. 63:4; Jer. 30:7; Joel 1:15; 2:1, 11, 31; Zeph. 1:14; Rev. 16:14 7:1 [a] Jer. 49:36; Dan. 7:2; Zech. 6:5; Matt. 24:31 [b] Rev. 7:3; 8:7; 9:4 7:3 [a] Rev. 6:6 [b] Ezek. 9:4, 6; Rev. 22:4 7:4 [a] Rev. 9:16 [b] Rev. 14:1, 3 [c] Gen. 49:1–27 7:5 [1] In NU-Text and M-Text *were sealed* is stated only in verses 5a and 8c; the words are understood in the remainder of the passage. 7:9 [a] Is. 60:1–5; Rom. 11:25

LIFE SUPPORT

BE OPEN: LIFT EVERY NATION, TRIBE, AND TONGUE

After these things I looked, and behold, a great multitude which no one could number, of all nations, tribes, peoples, and tongues, standing before the throne and before the Lamb, clothed with white robes, with palm branches in their hands. Revelation 7:9

LIFE: Be Open

God loves people from every nation on every continent and every tribe within those nations. Conversely, so many people love God that we cannot even begin to number them. We are commanded as His people to be united in worship of Him. We are called to fight together and thrive together. There is no ethnicity or nation that is better than any other. God loves us all the same. We are all His favorites. It pleases God when we put our differences aside to help each other and come together to serve and worship Him. As a human parent equally loves multiple children, though they are different, God loves each of us the same.

We are not created to look the same or sound the same. Our differences are not errors or weaknesses or incidental aspects of who we are, only to be ignored. God's glory is seen in our unified diversity. We have diverse ways of worship, but it is all a pleasing sound to God. We have different kingdom assignments, but each is a way we spread God's love and the good news of Jesus. It is not God's will for us to allow anything on this earth to separate the members of the body of Christ. We can do some amazing things when we are unified, but unity requires postures of receptivity and acceptance.

SUPPORT: Lift Every Nation, Tribe, and Tongue

What a glorious diversity! Different does not mean wrong. God loves us all. He made us all. We all have value. Appreciate the worth in every individual and be about building each person up.

We can start by using our words to encourage others in their uniqueness. There is power in the tongue. With our words we can help those who may feel out of place to feel at home. When we speak life, we can help those who do not see the beauty in their uniqueness to find their confidence. When we speak unity, we help others to see that we are all God's children and that each of us is fearfully and wonderfully made in His image. See the unique skills and talents in others and tell them of their treasures. Pouring affirmations into others makes us all better. By building others up, we are channels of God's love, and His love flowing through us changes us.

SUPPORT EXAMPLE: Volunteer in a community other than your own.

number, [b]of all nations, tribes, peoples, and
tongues, standing before the throne and
before the Lamb, [c]clothed with white robes,
with palm branches in their hands, 10 and
crying out with a loud voice, saying, [a]"Salvation *belongs* to our God [b]who sits on the
throne, and to the Lamb!" 11 [a]All the angels
stood around the throne and the elders and
the four living creatures, and fell on their
faces before the throne and [b]worshiped
God, 12 [a]saying:

"Amen! Blessing and glory
and wisdom,
Thanksgiving and honor and
power and might,

7:9 [b] Rev. 5:9 [c] Rev. 3:5, 18; 4:4; 6:11 7:10 [a] Ps. 3:8; Is. 43:11; Jer. 3:23; Hos. 13:4; Rev. 19:1 [b] Rev. 5:13
7:11 [a] Rev. 4:6 [b] Rev. 4:11; 5:9, 12, 14; 11:16 7:12 [a] Rev. 5:13, 14

Be to our God forever and ever.
Amen."

13Then one of the elders answered, saying to me, "Who are these arrayed in [a]white
robes, and where did they come from?"
14And I said to him, "Sir,[1] you know."
So he said to me, [a]"These are the ones
who come out of the great tribulation, and
[b]washed their robes and made them white
in the blood of the Lamb. 15Therefore they
are before the throne of God, and serve
Him day and night in His temple. And He
who sits on the throne will [a]dwell among
them. 16[a]They shall neither hunger anymore nor thirst anymore; [b]the sun shall not
strike them, nor any heat; 17for the Lamb
who is in the midst of the throne [a]will shepherd them and lead them to living fountains of waters.[1] [b]And God will wipe away
every tear from their eyes."

Seventh Seal: Prelude to the Seven Trumpets

8 When[a] He opened the seventh seal,
there was silence in heaven for about
half an hour. 2[a]And I saw the seven angels
who stand before God, [b]and to them were
given seven trumpets. 3Then another angel,
having a golden censer, came and stood at
the altar. He was given much incense, that
he should offer *it* with [a]the prayers of all
the saints upon [b]the golden altar which was
before the throne. 4And [a]the smoke of the
incense, with the prayers of the saints, ascended before God from the angel's hand.
5Then the angel took the censer, filled it
with fire from the altar, and threw *it* to the
earth. And [a]there were noises, thunderings,
[b]lightnings, [c]and an earthquake.
6So the seven angels who had the seven
trumpets prepared themselves to sound.

First Trumpet: Vegetation Struck

7The first angel sounded: [a]And hail and
fire followed, mingled with blood, and they
were thrown [b]to the earth.[1] And a third [c]of
the trees were burned up, and all green
grass was burned up.

Second Trumpet: The Seas Struck

8Then the second angel sounded: [a]And
something like a great mountain burning
with fire was thrown into the sea, [b]and a
third of the sea [c]became blood. 9[a]And a
third of the living creatures in the sea died,
and a third of the ships were destroyed.

Third Trumpet: The Waters Struck

10Then the third angel sounded: [a]And a
great star fell from heaven, burning like a
torch, [b]and it fell on a third of the rivers and
on the springs of water. 11[a]The name of the
star is Wormwood. [b]A third of the waters
became wormwood, and many men died
from the water, because it was made bitter.

Fourth Trumpet: The Heavens Struck

12[a]Then the fourth angel sounded: And
a third of the sun was struck, a third of the
moon, and a third of the stars, so that a
third of them were darkened. A third of the
day did not shine, and likewise the night.
13And I looked, [a]and I heard an angel[1]
flying through the midst of heaven, saying
with a loud voice, [b]"Woe, woe, woe to the
inhabitants of the earth, because of the remaining blasts of the trumpet of the three
angels who are about to sound!"

Fifth Trumpet: The Locusts from the Bottomless Pit

9 Then the fifth angel sounded: [a]And I
saw a star fallen from heaven to the
earth. To him was given the key to [b]the bottomless pit. 2And he opened the bottomless pit, and smoke arose out of the pit like
the smoke of a great furnace. So the [a]sun
and the air were darkened because of the
smoke of the pit. 3Then out of the smoke
locusts came upon the earth. And to them
was given power, [a]as the scorpions of the

7:13 [a] Rev. 7:9 7:14 [a] Rev. 6:9 [b] Is. 1:18; Zech. 3:3–5; [Heb. 9:14] [1] NU-Text and M-Text read *My lord.* 7:15 [a] Is. 4:5, 6; Rev. 21:3 7:16 [a] Ps. 121:5; Is. 49:10 [b] Ps. 121:6; Rev. 21:4 7:17 [a] Ps. 23:1; Matt. 2:6; [John 10:11, 14] [b] Is. 25:8; Matt. 5:4; Rev. 21:4 [1] NU-Text and M-Text read *to fountains of the waters of life.* 8:1 [a] Rev. 6:1 8:2 [a] [Matt. 18:10]; Luke 1:19 [b] 2 Chr. 29:25–28 8:3 [a] Rev. 5:8 [b] Ex. 30:1; Rev. 8:3 8:4 [a] Ps. 141:2; Luke 1:10 8:5 [a] Ex. 19:16; Rev. 11:19; 16:18 [b] Rev. 4:5 [c] 2 Sam. 22:8; 1 Kin. 19:11; Acts 4:31 8:7 [a] Ex. 9:23; Is. 28:2; Ezek. 38:22; Joel 2:30 [b] Rev. 16:2 [c] Is. 2:13; Rev. 9:4, 15–18 [1] NU-Text and M-Text add *and a third of the earth was burned up.* 8:8 [a] Jer. 51:25; Amos 7:4 [b] Ex. 7:17; Rev. 11:6; 16:3 [c] Ezek. 14:19 8:9 [a] Rev. 16:3 8:10 [a] Is. 14:12; Rev. 6:13; 9:1 [b] Rev. 14:7; 16:4 8:11 [a] Ruth 1:20 [b] Ex. 15:23 8:12 [a] Is. 13:10; Joel 2:31; Amos 8:9; Matt. 24:29; Rev. 6:12 8:13 [a] Rev. 14:6; 19:17 [b] Rev. 9:12; 11:14; 12:12 [1] NU-Text and M-Text read *eagle.* 9:1 [a] Luke 10:18; Rev. 8:10 [b] Luke 8:31; Rev. 9:2, 11; 17:8 9:2 [a] Joel 2:2, 10 9:3 [a] Ex. 10:4; Judg. 7:12

earth have power. 4They were commanded
[a]not to harm [b]the grass of the earth, or any
green thing, or any tree, but only those men
who do not have [c]the seal of God on their
foreheads. 5And they were not given *authority* to kill them, [a]but to torment them
for five months. Their torment *was* like
the torment of a scorpion when it strikes
a man. 6In those days [a]men will seek death
and will not find it; they will desire to die,
and death will flee from them.

7[a]The shape of the locusts was like horses
prepared for battle. [b]On their heads were
crowns of something like gold, [c]and their
faces *were* like the faces of men. 8They had
hair like women's hair, and [a]their teeth were
like lions' *teeth.* 9And they had breastplates
like breastplates of iron, and the sound of
their wings *was* [a]like the sound of chariots with many horses running into battle.
10They had tails like scorpions, and there
were stings in their tails. Their power *was*
to hurt men five months. 11And they had as
king over them [a]the angel of the bottomless
pit, whose name in Hebrew *is* Abaddon, but
in Greek he has the name Apollyon.

12[a]One woe is past. Behold, still two more
woes are coming after these things.

Sixth Trumpet: The Angels from the Euphrates

13Then the sixth angel sounded: And I
heard a voice from the four horns of the
[a]golden altar which is before God, 14saying
to the sixth angel who had the trumpet,
"Release the four angels who are bound [a]at
the great river Euphrates." 15So the four angels, who had been prepared for the hour
and day and month and year, were released
to kill a [a]third of mankind. 16Now [a]the number of the army [b]of the horsemen *was* two
hundred million; [c]I heard the number of
them. 17And thus I saw the horses in the
vision: those who sat on them had breastplates of fiery red, hyacinth blue, and sul-
fur yellow; [a]and the heads of the horses
were like the heads of lions; and out of their
mouths came fire, smoke, and brimstone.
18By these three *plagues* a third of mankind was killed—by the fire and the smoke
and the brimstone which came out of their
mouths. 19For their power[1] is in their mouth
and in their tails; [a]for their tails *are* like serpents, having heads; and with them they
do harm.

20But the rest of mankind, who were not
killed by these plagues, [a]did not repent of
the works of their hands, that they should
not worship [b]demons, [c]and idols of gold,
silver, brass, stone, and wood, which can
neither see nor hear nor walk. 21And they
did not repent of their murders [a]or their
sorceries[1] or their sexual immorality or
their thefts.

The Mighty Angel with the Little Book

10 I saw still another mighty angel coming down from heaven, clothed with
a cloud. [a]And a rainbow *was* on [b]his head,
his face *was* like the sun, and [c]his feet like
pillars of fire. 2He had a little book open
in his hand. [a]And he set his right foot on
the sea and *his* left *foot* on the land, 3and
cried with a loud voice, as *when* a lion roars.
When he cried out, [a]seven thunders uttered
their voices. 4Now when the seven thunders
uttered their voices,[1] I was about to write;
but I heard a voice from heaven saying to
me,[2] [a]"Seal up the things which the seven
thunders uttered, and do not write them."

5The angel whom I saw standing on the
sea and on the land [a]raised up his hand[1] to
heaven 6and swore by Him who lives forever and ever, [a]who created heaven and
the things that are in it, the earth and the
things that are in it, and the sea and the
things that are in it, [b]that there should be
delay no longer, 7but [a]in the days of the
sounding of the seventh angel, when he is
about to sound, the mystery of God would
be finished, as He declared to His servants
the prophets.

9:4 [a] Rev. 6:6 [b] Rev. 8:7 [c] Ex. 12:23; Ezek. 9:4; Rev. 7:2, 3 9:5 [a] [Rev. 9:10; 11:7] 9:6 [a] Job 3:21; 7:15; Is. 2:19; Jer. 8:3; Rev. 6:16 9:7 [a] Joel 2:4 [b] Nah. 3:17 [c] Dan. 7:8 9:8 [a] Joel 1:6 9:9 [a] Jer. 47:3; Joel 2:5–7 9:11 [a] Eph. 2:2 9:12 [a] Rev. 8:13; 11:14 9:13 [a] Rev. 8:3 9:14 [a] Gen. 15:18; Deut. 1:7; Josh. 1:4; Rev. 16:12 9:15 [a] Rev. 8:7–9; 9:18 9:16 [a] Ps. 68:17; Dan. 7:10 [b] Ezek. 38:4 [c] Rev. 7:4 9:17 [a] 1 Chr. 12:8; Is. 5:28, 29 9:19 [a] Is. 9:15 [1] NU-Text and M-Text read *the power of the horses.* 9:20 [a] Deut. 31:29 [b] Lev. 17:7; Deut. 32:17; Ps. 106:37; 1 Cor. 10:20 [c] Ps. 115:4–7; 135:15–17; Dan. 5:23 9:21 [a] Rev. 21:8; 22:15 [1] NU-Text and M-Text read *drugs.* 10:1 [a] Ezek. 1:26–28; Rev. 4:3 [b] Matt. 17:2; Rev. 1:16 [c] Rev. 1:15 10:2 [a] Ps. 95:5; Matt. 28:18 10:3 [a] Ps. 29:3–9; Rev. 4:5; 8:5 10:4 [a] Dan. 8:26; 12:4, 9; Rev. 22:10 [1] NU-Text and M-Text read *sounded.* [2] NU-Text and M-Text omit *to me.* 10:5 [a] Ex. 6:8; Deut. 32:40; Dan. 12:7 [1] NU-Text and M-Text read *right hand.* 10:6 [a] Gen. 1:1; Ex. 20:11; Neh. 9:6; Rev. 4:11 [b] Dan. 12:7; Rev. 16:17 10:7 [a] Rev. 11:15

John Eats the Little Book

8 Then the voice which I heard from
heaven spoke to me again and said, "Go,
take the little book which is open in the
hand of the angel who stands on the sea
and on the earth."

9 So I went to the angel and said to him,
"Give me the little book."

And he said to me, [a]"Take and eat it; and
it will make your stomach bitter, but it will
be as sweet as honey in your mouth."

10 Then I took the little book out of the
angel's hand and ate it, [a]and it was as sweet
as honey in my mouth. But when I had
eaten it, [b]my stomach became bitter. 11 And
he[1] said to me, "You must prophesy again
about many peoples, nations, tongues, and
kings."

The Two Witnesses

11 Then I was given [a]a reed like a measuring rod. And the angel stood,[1] saying, [b]"Rise and measure the temple of God,
the altar, and those who worship there. 2 But
leave out [a]the court which is outside the
temple, and do not measure it, [b]for it has
been given to the Gentiles. And they will
[c]tread the holy city underfoot *for* [d]forty-two
months. 3 And I will give *power* to my two
[a]witnesses, [b]and they will prophesy [c]one
thousand two hundred and sixty days,
clothed in sackcloth."

4 These are the [a]two olive trees and the
two lampstands standing before the God[1]
of the earth. 5 And if anyone wants to harm
them, [a]fire proceeds from their mouth and
devours their enemies. [b]And if anyone
wants to harm them, he must be killed in
this manner. 6 These [a]have power to shut
heaven, so that no rain falls in the days
of their prophecy; and they have power
over waters to turn them to blood, and to
strike the earth with all plagues, as often
as they desire.

The Witnesses Killed

7 When they [a]finish their testimony, [b]the
beast that ascends [c]out of the bottomless
pit [d]will make war against them, overcome
them, and kill them. 8 And their dead bodies *will lie* in the street of [a]the great city
which spiritually is called Sodom and
Egypt, [b]where also our[1] Lord was crucified. 9 [a]Then *those* from the peoples, tribes,
tongues, and nations will see their dead
bodies three-and-a-half days, [b]and not allow[1] their dead bodies to be put into graves.
10 [a]And those who dwell on the earth will
rejoice over them, make merry, [b]and send
gifts to one another, [c]because these two
prophets tormented those who dwell on
the earth.

The Witnesses Resurrected

11 [a]Now after the three-and-a-half days
[b]the breath of life from God entered them,
and they stood on their feet, and great fear
fell on those who saw them. 12 And they[1]
heard a loud voice from heaven saying to
them, "Come up here." [a]And they ascended
to heaven [b]in a cloud, [c]and their enemies
saw them. 13 In the same hour [a]there was a
great earthquake, [b]and a tenth of the city
fell. In the earthquake seven thousand people were killed, and the rest were afraid
[c]and gave glory to the God of heaven.

14 [a]The second woe is past. Behold, the
third woe is coming quickly.

Seventh Trumpet: The Kingdom Proclaimed

15 Then [a]the seventh angel sounded: [b]And
there were loud voices in heaven, saying,
[c]"The kingdoms[1] of this world have become
the kingdoms of our Lord and of His Christ,
[d]and He shall reign forever and ever!" 16 And
[a]the twenty-four elders who sat before God
on their thrones fell on their faces and
[b]worshiped God, 17 saying:

10:9 [a] Jer. 15:16; Ezek. 2:8; 3:1–3 10:10 [a] Ezek. 3:3 [b] Ezek. 2:10 10:11 [1] NU-Text and M-Text read *they.* 11:1 [a] Ezek. 40:3—42:20; Zech. 2:1; Rev. 21:15 [b] Num. 23:18 [1] NU-Text and M-Text omit *And the angel stood.* 11:2 [a] Ezek. 40:17, 20 [b] Ps. 79:1; Luke 21:24 [c] Dan. 8:10 [d] Dan. 7:25; 12:7; Rev. 12:6; 13:5 11:3 [a] Deut. 17:6; Rev. 20:4 [b] Rev. 19:10 [c] Rev. 12:6 11:4 [a] Ps. 52:8; Jer. 11:16; Zech. 4:2, 3, 11, 14 [1] NU-Text and M-Text read *Lord.* 11:5 [a] 2 Kin. 1:10–12; Jer. 1:10; 5:14; Ezek. 43:3; Hos. 6:5; Rev. 9:17 [b] Num. 16:29 11:6 [a] 1 Kin. 17:1; Luke 4:25; [James 5:16, 17] 11:7 [a] Luke 13:32 [b] Rev. 13:1, 11; 17:8 [c] Rev. 9:1, 2 [d] Dan. 7:21; Rev. 13:7 11:8 [a] Rev. 14:8 [b] Heb. 13:12 [1] NU-Text and M-Text read *their.* 11:9 [a] Rev. 17:15 [b] 1 Kin. 13:22; Ps. 79:2, 3 [1] NU-Text and M-Text read *nations see . . . and will not allow.* 11:10 [a] Rev. 12:12 [b] Neh. 8:10, 12; Esth. 9:19, 22 [c] Rev. 16:10 11:11 [a] Rev. 11:9 [b] Ezek. 37:5, 9, 10 11:12 [a] Is. 14:13 [b] Is. 60:8; Acts 1:9 [c] 2 Kin. 2:11, 12 [1] M-Text reads *I.* 11:13 [a] Rev. 6:12; 8:5; 11:19; 16:18 [b] Rev. 16:19 [c] Josh. 7:19; John 9:24; Rev. 14:7; 16:9; 19:7 11:14 [a] Rev. 8:13; 9:12 11:15 [a] Rev. 8:2; 10:7 [b] Is. 27:13 [c] Rev. 12:10 [d] Ex. 15:18; Dan. 2:44; 7:14, 27; Luke 1:33 [1] NU-Text and M-Text read *kingdom . . . has become.* 11:16 [a] Matt. 19:28; Rev. 4:4 [b] Rev. 4:11; 5:9, 12, 14; 7:11

"We give You thanks, O Lord
God Almighty,
The One [a]who is and who was
and who is to come,[1]
Because You have taken Your
great power [b]and reigned.
18 The nations were [a]angry, and
Your wrath has come,
And the time of the [b]dead,
that they should be
judged,
And that You should reward
Your servants the prophets
and the saints,
And those who fear Your
name, small and great,

REVELATION 10:11

I AM JOHN

And he said to me, "You must prophesy again about many peoples, nations, tongues, and kings." Revelation 10:11

I am John the apostle. I was a young man working with my father in the family fishing business when I met Jesus. One day, my brother, James, and I were fishing. Jesus came by our boat and invited us to follow Him. We immediately left everything and never looked back.

Like the other apostles, we made our share of mistakes with Jesus. On one occasion, our mother asked Jesus to give us the seats on either side of Him in glory. He asked us if we were able to suffer as He would suffer, and in our arrogance, we foolishly said that we were. Jesus taught us that we must be servants if we want to be first. We must be slaves to all because even He came not to be served but to serve. This lesson set the course for the rest of my life as a slave to the gospel of Jesus Christ.

When Jesus was on the cross, He looked down at His mother and me and told her, "Woman, behold your son!" Jesus entrusted me to look after His mother and ensure she was cared for.

After Jesus' ascension, the Holy Spirit fell on me and the others, and I shared about Jesus' resurrection from the dead and performed miracles in His name. One day in particular, Peter and I spoke to a massive crowd and about five thousand men believed in the Lord Jesus. The Sadducees arrested us for speaking about Jesus, a name they feared. The next day the Sadducees told us we could no longer speak or teach in the name of Jesus. We told them we were compelled to speak about what we had seen and heard. We were a bit intimidated by such resistance, so we gathered with the others and asked the Lord for boldness. In that moment, we were empowered by the Holy Spirit to speak fearlessly about our Lord. I never stopped speaking and writing about the divine and eternal nature of Jesus Christ and how much God loves us all. What an honor God bestowed on me on the island of Patmos when He gave me divine revelations through visions and dreams.

†

John is known as the beloved apostle or the "disciple whom Jesus loved." He had a special relationship with Jesus—a true friendship. John was steadfast and a committed believer. It is believed that he is the John that God entrusted with the dreams and visions of the Book of Revelation. He was the only one of the apostles who was present at the crucifixion. Even though Mary, Jesus' mother, had other sons, John was the man Jesus trusted to look after her. Jesus surrounded Himself with those who believed in Him and whom He could trust. We should do the same by cultivating deep relationships with other believers who will be there to do the hard work during the hard times and who we can freely share our lives and ministry with.

11:17 [a] Rev. 16:5 [b] Rev. 19:6 [1] NU-Text and M-Text omit *and who is to come.*
11:18 [a] Ps. 2:1 [b] Dan. 7:10; [Rev. 20:12, 13]

And should destroy those
who destroy the earth."

19 Then [a]the temple of God was opened
in heaven, and the ark of His covenant[1] was
seen in His temple. And [b]there were lightnings, noises, thunderings, an earthquake,
[c]and great hail.

The Woman, the Child, and the Dragon

12 Now a great sign appeared in heaven:
a woman clothed with the sun, with
the moon under her feet, and on her head
a garland of twelve stars. 2 Then being with
child, she cried out [a]in labor and in pain to
give birth.

3 And another sign appeared in heaven:
behold, [a]a great, fiery red dragon having
seven heads and ten horns, and seven diadems on his heads. 4 [a]His tail drew a third
[b]of the stars of heaven [c]and threw them to
the earth. And the dragon stood [d]before the
woman who was ready to give birth, [e]to devour her Child as soon as it was born. 5 She
bore a male Child [a]who was to rule all nations with a rod of iron. And her Child was
[b]caught up to God and His throne. 6 Then
[a]the woman fled into the wilderness, where
she has a place prepared by God, that they
should feed her there [b]one thousand two
hundred and sixty days.

Satan Thrown Out of Heaven

7 And war broke out in heaven: [a]Michael
and his angels fought [b]with the dragon; and
the dragon and his angels fought, 8 but they
did not prevail, nor was a place found for
them[1] in heaven any longer. 9 So [a]the great
dragon was cast out, [b]that serpent of old,
called the Devil and Satan, [c]who deceives
the whole world; [d]he was cast to the earth,
and his angels were cast out with him.

10 Then I heard a loud voice saying in
heaven, [a]"Now salvation, and strength, and
the kingdom of our God, and the power of
His Christ have come, for the accuser of
our brethren, [b]who accused them before
our God day and night, has been cast down.
11 And [a]they overcame him by the blood of
the Lamb and by the word of their testimony, [b]and they did not love their lives to
the death. 12 Therefore [a]rejoice, O heavens,
and you who dwell in them! [b]Woe to the
inhabitants of the earth and the sea! For
the devil has come down to you, having
great wrath, [c]because he knows that he has
a short time."

The Woman Persecuted

13 Now when the dragon saw that he had
been cast to the earth, he persecuted [a]the
woman who gave birth to the male *Child.*
14 [a]But the woman was given two wings of a
great eagle, [b]that she might fly [c]into the wilderness to her place, where she is nourished
[d]for a time and times and half a time, from
the presence of the serpent. 15 So the serpent
[a]spewed water out of his mouth like a flood
after the woman, that he might cause her to
be carried away by the flood. 16 But the earth
helped the woman, and the earth opened its
mouth and swallowed up the flood which the
dragon had spewed out of his mouth. 17 And
the dragon was enraged with the woman,
and he went to make war with the rest of her
offspring, who keep the commandments of
God and have the testimony of Jesus Christ.[1]

The Beast from the Sea

13 Then I[1] stood on the sand of the
sea. And I saw [a]a beast rising up out
of the sea, [b]having seven heads and ten
horns,[2] and on his horns ten crowns, and
on his heads a [c]blasphemous name. 2 Now
the beast which I saw was like a leopard,
his feet were like *the feet of* a bear, and his
mouth like the mouth of a lion. The [a]dragon
gave him his power, his throne, and great
authority. 3 And I saw one of his heads [a]as
if it had been mortally wounded, and his
deadly wound was healed. And [b]all the
world marveled and followed the beast.
4 So they worshiped the dragon who gave
authority to the beast; and they worshiped

11:19 [a] Rev. 4:1; 15:5, 8 [b] Rev. 8:5 [c] Rev. 16:21 [1] M-Text reads *the covenant of the Lord.* 12:2 [a] Is. 26:17; 66:6–9; Mic. 4:9; Gal. 4:19 12:3 [a] Rev. 13:1; 17:3, 7, 9 12:4 [a] Rev. 9:10, 19 [b] Rev. 8:7, 12 [c] Dan. 8:10 [d] Rev. 12:2 [e] Ex. 1:16; Matt. 2:16 12:5 [a] Ps. 2:9; Is. 7:14; 9:6; Rev. 2:27; 19:15 [b] Luke 24:51; Acts 1:9–11 12:6 [a] Rev. 12:4, 14 [b] Rev. 11:3; 13:5 12:7 [a] Dan. 10:13, 21; 12:1; Jude 9 [b] Rev. 20:2 12:8 [1] M-Text reads *him.* 12:9 [a] Luke 10:18; John 12:31 [b] Gen. 3:1, 4; 2 Cor. 11:3; Rev. 12:15; 20:2 [c] Rev. 20:3 [d] Rev. 9:1 12:10 [a] Rev. 11:15 [b] Job 1:9, 11; 2:5; Zech. 3:1 12:11 [a] Rom. 16:20 [b] Luke 14:26; [Rev. 2:10] 12:12 [a] Ps. 96:11; Is. 44:23; Rev. 18:20 [b] Rev. 8:13 [c] Rev. 10:6 12:13 [a] Rev. 12:5 12:14 [a] Ex. 19:4; Deut. 32:11; Is. 40:31 [b] Rev. 12:6 [c] Rev. 17:3 [d] Dan. 7:25; 12:7 12:15 [a] Is. 59:19 12:17 [1] NU-Text and M-Text omit *Christ.* 13:1 [a] Dan. 7:2, 7 [b] Rev. 12:3 [c] Dan. 7:8; 11:36; Rev. 17:3 [1] NU-Text reads *he.* [2] NU-Text and M-Text read *ten horns and seven heads.* 13:2 [a] Rev. 12:3, 9; 13:4, 12 13:3 [a] Rev. 13:12, 14 [b] Rev. 17:8

the beast, saying, [a]"Who *is* like the beast?
Who is able to make war with him?"
5 And he was given [a]a mouth speaking
great things and blasphemies, and he was
given authority to continue[1] for [b]forty-two
months. 6 Then he opened his mouth in
blasphemy against God, to blaspheme His
name, [a]His tabernacle, and those who dwell
in heaven. 7 It was granted to him [a]to make
war with the saints and to overcome them.
And [b]authority was given him over every
tribe,[1] tongue, and nation. 8 All who dwell on
the earth will worship him, [a]whose names
have not been written in the Book of Life
of the Lamb slain [b]from the foundation of
the world.
9 [a]If anyone has an ear, let him hear.
10 [a]He who leads into captivity shall go into
captivity; [b]he who kills with the sword must
be killed with the sword. [c]Here is the patience and the faith of the saints.

The Beast from the Earth

11 Then I saw another beast [a]coming up
out of the earth, and he had two horns like
a lamb and spoke like a dragon. 12 And he
exercises all the authority of the first beast
in his presence, and causes the earth and
those who dwell in it to worship the first
beast, [a]whose deadly wound was healed.
13 [a]He performs great signs, [b]so that he even
makes fire come down from heaven on the
earth in the sight of men. 14 [a]And he deceives those[1] who dwell on the earth [b]by
those signs which he was granted to do
in the sight of the beast, telling those who
dwell on the earth to make an image to the
beast who was wounded by the sword [c]and
lived. 15 He was granted *power* to give breath
to the image of the beast, that the image
of the beast should both speak [a]and cause
as many as would not worship the image
of the beast to be killed. 16 He causes all,
both small and great, rich and poor, free
and slave, [a]to receive a mark on their right
hand or on their foreheads, 17 and that no
one may buy or sell except one who has
the mark or[1] [a]the name of the beast, [b]or the
number of his name.
18 [a]Here is wisdom. Let him who has
[b]understanding calculate [c]the number of
the beast, [d]for it is the number of a man:
His number *is* 666.

The Lamb and the 144,000

14 Then I looked, and behold, a[1] [a]Lamb
standing on Mount Zion, and with
Him [b]one hundred *and* forty-four thousand,
having[2] His Father's name [c]written on their
foreheads. 2 And I heard a voice from heaven,
[a]like the voice of many waters, and like the
voice of loud thunder. And I heard the sound
of [b]harpists playing their harps. 3 They sang
as it were a new song before the throne, before the four living creatures, and the elders;
and no one could learn that song [a]except
the hundred *and* forty-four thousand who
were redeemed from the earth. 4 These are
the ones who were not defiled with women,
[a]for they are virgins. These are the ones [b]who
follow the Lamb wherever He goes. These
[c]were redeemed[1] from *among* men, [d]*being*
firstfruits to God and to the Lamb. 5 And [a]in
their mouth was found no deceit,[1] for [b]they
are without fault before the throne of God.[2]

The Proclamations of Three Angels

6 Then I saw another angel [a]flying in the
midst of heaven, [b]having the everlasting
gospel to preach to those who dwell on the
earth—[c]to every nation, tribe, tongue, and
people— 7 saying with a loud voice, [a]"Fear
God and give glory to Him, for the hour of
His judgment has come; [b]and worship Him
who made heaven and earth, the sea and
springs of water."
8 And another angel followed, saying,
[a]"Babylon[1] is fallen, is fallen, that great city,

13:4 [a] Ex. 15:11; Is. 46:5; Rev. 18:18 13:5 [a] Dan. 7:8, 11, 20, 25; 11:36; 2 Thess. 2:3 [b] Rev. 11:2 [1] M-Text reads *make war.* 13:6 [a] [John 1:14; Col. 2:9] 13:7 [a] Dan. 7:21; Rev. 11:7 [b] Rev. 11:18 [1] NU-Text and M-Text add *and people.* 13:8 [a] Ex. 32:32; [Rev. 20:12–15] [b] Matt. 25:34; Rev. 17:8 13:9 [a] Rev. 2:7 13:10 [a] Is. 33:1; Jer. 15:2; 43:11 [b] Gen. 9:6; Matt. 26:52; Rev. 11:18 13:10 [c] Heb. 6:12; Rev. 14:12 13:11 [a] Rev. 11:7 13:12 [a] Rev. 13:3, 4 13:13 [a] Deut. 13:1; Matt. 24:24; 2 Thess. 2:9; Rev. 16:14 [b] 1 Kin. 18:38; 2 Kin. 1:10; Luke 9:54; Rev. 11:5; 20:9 13:14 [a] Rev. 12:9 [b] 2 Thess. 2:9 [c] 2 Kin. 20:7 [1] M-Text reads *my own people.* 13:15 [a] Rev. 16:2 13:16 [a] Gal. 6:17; Rev. 7:3; 14:9; 20:4 13:17 [a] Rev. 14:9–11 [b] Rev. 15:2 [1] NU-Text and M-Text omit *or.* 13:18 [a] Rev. 17:9 [b] [1 Cor. 2:14] [c] Rev. 15:2 [d] Rev. 21:17 14:1 [a] Rev. 5:6 [b] Rev. 7:4; 14:3 [c] Ezek. 9:4; Rev. 7:3; 22:4 [1] NU-Text and M-Text read *the.* [2] NU-Text and M-Text add *His name and.* 14:2 [a] Rev. 1:15; 19:6 [b] Rev. 5:8 14:3 [a] Rev. 5:9 14:4 [a] [Matt. 19:12; 2 Cor. 11:2; Eph. 5:27] [b] Rev. 3:4; 7:17 [c] Rev. 5:9 [d] Heb. 12:23; James 1:18 [1] M-Text adds *by Jesus.* 14:5 [a] Ps. 32:2; Zeph. 3:13; Mal. 2:6; John 1:47; 1 Pet. 2:22 [b] Eph. 5:27 [1] NU-Text and M-Text read *falsehood.* [2] NU-Text and M-Text omit *before the throne of God.* 14:6 [a] Rev. 8:13 [b] Eph. 3:9 [c] Rev. 13:7 14:7 [a] Rev. 11:18 [b] Neh. 9:6 14:8 [a] Is. 21:9; Jer. 51:8; Rev. 18:2 [1] NU-Text reads *Babylon the great is fallen, is fallen, which has made;* M-Text reads *Babylon the great is fallen. She has made.*

because [b]she has made all nations drink of
the wine of the wrath of her fornication."
9 Then a third angel followed them, saying with a loud voice, [a]"If anyone worships
the beast and his image, and receives *his*
[b]mark on his forehead or on his hand, 10 he
himself [a]shall also drink of the wine of the
wrath of God, which is [b]poured out full
strength into [c]the cup of His indignation.
[d]He shall be tormented with [e]fire and brimstone in the presence of the holy angels
and in the presence of the Lamb. 11 And [a]the
smoke of their torment ascends forever and
ever; and they have no rest day or night,
who worship the beast and his image, and
whoever receives the mark of his name."

#OXYGEN
REVELATION 14:12
Elevate Your Time with Him

The Christian journey is not a sprint, ending in a short time. This journey is more of a marathon and not for the faint of heart. Start now. Be in it for the long haul.

Breathe and elevate your time with Him.

12 [a]Here is the patience of the saints;
[b]here *are* those[1] who keep the commandments of God and the faith of Jesus.
13 Then I heard a voice from heaven saying to me,[1] "Write: [a]'Blessed *are* the dead
[b]who die in the Lord from now on.'"
"Yes," says the Spirit, [c]"that they may rest
from their labors, and their works follow
[d]them."

Reaping the Earth's Harvest

14 Then I looked, and behold, a white
cloud, and on the cloud sat *One* like the
Son of Man, having on His head a golden
crown, and in His hand a sharp sickle. 15 And
another angel [a]came out of the temple, crying with a loud voice to Him who sat on the
cloud, [b]"Thrust in Your sickle and reap, for
the time has come for You[1] to reap, for the
harvest [c]of the earth is ripe." 16 So He who
sat on the cloud thrust in His sickle on the
earth, and the earth was reaped.

Reaping the Grapes of Wrath

17 Then another angel came out of the
temple which is in heaven, he also having
a sharp sickle.
18 And another angel came out from
the altar, [a]who had power over fire, and
he cried with a loud cry to him who had
the sharp sickle, saying, [b]"Thrust in your
sharp sickle and gather the clusters of the
vine of the earth, for her grapes are fully
ripe." 19 So the angel thrust his sickle into
the earth and gathered the vine of the
earth, and threw *it* into [a]the great winepress of the wrath of God. 20 And [a]the winepress was trampled [b]outside the city, and
blood came out of the winepress, [c]up to
the horses' bridles, for one thousand six
hundred furlongs.

Prelude to the Bowl Judgments

15 Then [a]I saw another sign in heaven,
great and marvelous: [b]seven angels
having the seven last plagues, [c]for in them
the wrath of God is complete.
2 And I saw *something* like [a]a sea of glass
[b]mingled with fire, and those who have the
victory over the beast, [c]over his image and
over his mark[1] *and* over the [d]number of his
name, standing on the sea of glass, [e]hav-
ing harps of God. 3 They sing [a]the song of
Moses, the servant of God, and the song of
the [b]Lamb, saying:

[c]"Great and marvelous *are*
Your works,
Lord God Almighty!
[d]Just and true *are* Your ways,
O King of the saints![1]

14:8 [b] Jer. 51:7; Rev. 17:2 14:9 [a] Rev. 13:14, 15; 14:11 [b] Rev. 13:16 14:10 [a] Ps. 75:8 [b] Rev. 18:6 [c] Rev. 16:19 [d] Rev. 20:10 [e] Gen. 19:24; Ezek. 38:22; 2 Thess. 1:7; Rev. 19:20 14:11 [a] Is. 34:8–10; Rev. 18:9, 18; 19:3 14:12 [a] Rev. 13:10 [b] Rev. 12:17 [1] NU-Text and M-Text omit *here are those.* 14:13 [a] Eccl. 4:1, 2 [b] 1 Cor. 15:18; [1 Thess. 4:16] [c] 2 Thess. 1:7; Heb. 4:9, 10; Rev. 6:11 [d] [1 Cor. 3:11–15; 15:58] [1] NU-Text and M-Text omit *to me.* 14:15 [a] Rev. 16:17 [b] Joel 3:13; Mark 4:29; Rev. 14:18 [c] Jer. 51:33; [Matt. 13:39–41] [1] NU-Text and M-Text omit *for You.* 14:18 [a] Rev. 16:8 [b] Joel 3:13; Mark 4:29; Rev. 14:15 14:19 [a] Is. 63:2; Rev. 19:15 14:20 [a] Is. 63:3; Lam. 1:15; Rev. 19:15 [b] Heb. 13:12; Rev. 11:8 [c] Is. 34:3 15:1 [a] Rev. 12:1, 3 [b] Rev. 21:9 [c] Rev. 14:10 15:2 [a] Rev. 4:6 [b] [Matt. 3:11] [c] Rev. 13:14, 15 [d] Rev. 13:17 [e] Rev. 5:8 [1] NU-Text and M-Text omit *over his mark.* 15:3 [a] Ex. 15:1–21 [b] Rev. 15:3 [c] Deut. 32:3, 4; Ps. 92:5; Rom. 11:33 [d] Ps. 145:17; Rev. 16:7 [1] NU-Text and M-Text read *nations.*

4 [a]Who shall not fear You, O Lord,
and glorify Your name?
For *You* alone *are* [b]holy.
For [c]all nations shall come and
worship before You,
For Your judgments have
been manifested."

5After these things I looked, and behold,[1] [a]the temple of the tabernacle of the
testimony in heaven was opened. 6And
out of the temple came the seven angels
having the seven plagues, [a]clothed in
pure bright linen, and having their chests
girded with golden bands. 7[a]Then one of
the four living creatures gave to the seven
angels seven golden bowls full of the wrath
of God [b]who lives forever and ever. 8[a]The
temple was filled with smoke [b]from the
glory of God and from His power, and no
one was able to enter the temple till the
seven plagues of the seven angels were
completed.

16 Then I heard a loud voice from the
temple saying [a]to the seven angels,
"Go and pour out the bowls[1] [b]of the wrath
of God on the earth."

First Bowl: Loathsome Sores

2So the first went and poured out his
bowl [a]upon the earth, and a foul and [b]loath-
some sore came upon the men [c]who had
the mark of the beast and those [d]who worshiped his image.

Second Bowl: The Sea Turns to Blood

3Then the second angel poured out his
bowl [a]on the sea, and [b]it became blood as
of a dead *man;* [c]and every living creature
in the sea died.

Third Bowl: The Waters Turn to Blood

4Then the third angel poured out his
bowl [a]on the rivers and springs of water,
[b]and they became blood. 5And I heard the
angel of the waters saying:

[a]"You are righteous, O Lord,[1]
The One [b]who is and who
was and who is to be,[2]
Because You have judged these
things.
6 For [a]they have shed the blood
[b]of saints and prophets,
[c]And You have given them
blood to drink.
For[1] it is their just due."

7And I heard another from[1] the altar saying, "Even so, [a]Lord God Almighty, [b]true
and righteous *are* Your judgments."

Fourth Bowl: Men Are Scorched

8Then the fourth angel poured out his
bowl [a]on the sun, [b]and power was given
to him to scorch men with fire. 9And men
were scorched with great heat, and they
[a]blasphemed the name of God who has
power over these plagues; [b]and they did
not repent [c]and give Him glory.

Fifth Bowl: Darkness and Pain

10Then the fifth angel poured out his
bowl [a]on the throne of the beast, [b]and his
kingdom became full of darkness; [c]and
they gnawed their tongues because of the
pain. 11They blasphemed the God of heaven
because of their pains and their sores, and
did not repent of their deeds.

Sixth Bowl: Euphrates Dried Up

12Then the sixth angel poured out his
bowl [a]on the great river Euphrates, [b]and
its water was dried up, [c]so that the way of
the kings from the east might be prepared.
13And I saw three unclean [a]spirits like frogs
coming out of the mouth of [b]the dragon,
out of the mouth of the beast, and out of
the mouth of [c]the false prophet. 14For they
are spirits of demons, [a]performing signs,
which go out to the kings of the earth and[1]
of [b]the whole world, to gather them to [c]the
battle of that great day of God Almighty.

15:4 [a] Ex. 15:14 [b] Lev. 11:44; 1 Pet. 1:16; Rev. 4:8 [c] Ps. 86:9; Is. 66:23 15:5 [a] Ex. 38:21; Num. 1:50; Heb. 8:5; Rev. 13:6 [1] NU-Text and M-Text omit *behold.* 15:6 [a] Ex. 28:6 15:7 [a] Rev. 4:6 [b] 1 Thess. 1:9 15:8 [a] Ex. 19:18; 40:34; Lev. 16:2; 1 Kin. 8:10; 2 Chr. 5:13; Is. 6:4 [b] 2 Thess. 1:9 16:1 [a] Rev. 15:1 [b] Rev. 14:10 [1] NU-Text and M-Text read *seven bowls.* 16:2 [a] Rev. 8:7 [b] Ex. 9:9–11; Deut. 28:35; Rev. 16:11 [c] Rev. 13:15–17; 14:9 [d] Rev. 13:14 16:3 [a] Rev. 8:8; 11:6 [b] Ex. 7:17–21 [c] Rev. 8:9 16:4 [a] Rev. 8:10 [b] Ex. 7:17–20; Ps. 78:44; Rev. 11:6 16:5 [a] Rev. 15:3, 4 [b] Rev. 1:4, 8 [1] NU-Text and M-Text omit *O Lord.* [2] NU-Text and M-Text read *who was, the Holy One.* 16:6 [a] Matt. 23:34 [b] Rev. 11:18 [c] Is. 49:26; Luke 11:49–51 [1] NU-Text and M-Text omit *For.* 16:7 [a] Rev. 15:3 [b] Rev. 13:10; 19:2 [1] NU-Text and M-Text omit *another from.* 16:8 [a] Rev. 8:12 [b] Rev. 9:17, 18 16:9 [a] Rev. 16:11 [b] Dan. 5:22 [c] Rev. 11:13 16:10 [a] Rev. 13:2 [b] Ex. 10:21; Is. 8:22; Rev. 8:12; 9:2 [c] Rev. 11:10 16:12 [a] Rev. 9:14 [b] Jer. 50:38 [c] Is. 41:2, 25; 46:11 16:13 [a] 1 John 4:1 [b] Rev. 12:3, 9 [c] Rev. 13:11, 14; 19:20; 20:10 16:14 [a] 2 Thess. 2:9 [b] Luke 2:1 [c] 1 Kin. 22:21–23; Rev. 17:14; 19:19; 20:8 [1] NU-Text and M-Text omit *of the earth and.*

15[a]"Behold, I am coming as a thief.
Blessed *is* he who watches, and keeps his
garments, [b]lest he walk naked and they see
his shame."
16[a]And they gathered them together to
the place called in Hebrew, Armageddon.[1]

Seventh Bowl: The Earth Utterly Shaken

17Then the seventh angel poured out his
bowl into the air, and a loud voice came
out of the temple of heaven, from the
throne, saying, [a]"It is done!" 18And [a]there
were noises and thunderings and lightnings; [b]and there was a great earthquake,
such a mighty and great earthquake [c]as
had not occurred since men were on the
earth. 19Now [a]the great city was divided
into three parts, and the cities of the nations fell. And [b]great Babylon [c]was remembered before God, [d]to give her the cup of
the wine of the fierceness of His wrath.
20Then [a]every island fled away, and the
mountains were not found. 21And great
hail from heaven fell upon men, *each hail-
stone* about the weight of a talent. Men
blasphemed God because of the plague
of the hail, since that plague was exceedingly great.

The Scarlet Woman and the Scarlet Beast

17 Then [a]one of the seven angels who
had the seven bowls came and talked
with me, saying to me,[1] "Come, [b]I will show
you the judgment of [c]the great harlot [d]who
sits on many waters, 2[a]with whom the kings
of the earth committed fornication, and
[b]the inhabitants of the earth were made
drunk with the wine of her fornication."
3So he carried me away in the Spirit [a]into
the wilderness. And I saw a woman sitting
[b]on a scarlet beast *which was* full of [c]names
of blasphemy, having seven heads and ten
horns. 4The woman [a]was arrayed in purple
and scarlet, [b]and adorned with gold and
precious stones and pearls, [c]having in her
hand a golden cup [d]full of abominations
and the filthiness of her fornication.[1] 5And
on her forehead a name *was* written:

[a]MYSTERY, BABYLON THE GREAT,
THE MOTHER OF HARLOTS
AND OF THE ABOMINATIONS
OF THE EARTH.

6I saw [a]the woman, drunk [b]with the blood of
the saints and with the blood of [c]the martyrs of Jesus. And when I saw her, I marveled with great amazement.

The Meaning of the Woman and the Beast

7But the angel said to me, "Why did you
marvel? I will tell you the mystery of the
woman and of the beast that carries her,
which has the seven heads and the ten
horns. 8The beast that you saw was, and
is not, and [a]will ascend out of the bottomless pit and [b]go to perdition. And those who
[c]dwell on the earth [d]will marvel, [e]whose
names are not written in the Book of Life
from the foundation of the world, when
they see the beast that was, and is not, and
yet is.[1]
9[a]"Here *is* the mind which has wisdom:
[b]The seven heads are seven mountains
on which the woman sits. 10There are also
seven kings. Five have fallen, one is, *and*
the other has not yet come. And when he
comes, he must [a]continue a short time.
11The [a]beast that was, and is not, is himself
also the eighth, and is of the seven, and is
going to perdition.
12[a]"The ten horns which you saw are ten
kings who have received no kingdom as
yet, but they receive authority for one hour
as kings with the beast. 13These are of one
mind, and they will give their power and
authority to the beast. 14[a]These will make
war with the Lamb, and the Lamb will [b]over-
come them, [c]for He is Lord of lords and
King of kings; [d]and those *who are* with Him
are called, chosen, and faithful."

16:15 [a] Matt. 24:43; Luke 12:39; Rev. 3:3, 11 [b] 2 Cor. 5:3 16:16 [a] Rev. 19:19 [1] M-Text reads *Megiddo.* 16:17 [a] Rev. 10:6; 21:6 16:18 [a] Rev. 4:5 [b] Rev. 11:13 [c] Dan. 12:1; Matt. 24:21 16:19 [a] Rev. 14:8 [b] Rev. 17:5, 18 [c] Rev. 14:8; 18:5 [d] Is. 51:17; Rev. 14:10 16:20 [a] Rev. 6:14; 20:11 17:1 [a] Rev. 1:1; 21:9 [b] Rev. 16:19 [c] Is. 1:21; Jer. 2:20; Nah. 3:4; Rev. 17:5, 15; 19:2 [d] Jer. 51:13; Rev. 17:15 [1] NU-Text and M-Text omit *to me.* 17:2 [a] Rev. 2:22; 18:3, 9 [b] Jer. 51:7; Rev. 14:8 17:3 [a] Rev. 12:6, 14; 21:10 [b] Rev. 12:3 [c] Rev. 13:1 17:4 [a] Ezek. 28:13; Rev. 18:12, 16 [b] Dan. 11:38 [c] Jer. 51:7; Rev. 18:6 [d] Rev. 14:8 [1] M-Text reads *the filthiness of the fornication of the earth.* 17:5 [a] 2 Thess. 2:7; Rev. 1:20; 17:7 17:6 [a] Rev. 18:24 [b] Rev. 13:15 [c] Rev. 6:9, 10 17:8 [a] Rev. 11:7 [b] Rev. 13:10; 17:11 [c] Rev. 3:10 [d] Rev. 13:3 [e] Matt. 25:34; Rev. 13:8 [1] NU-Text and M-Text read *and shall be present.* 17:9 [a] Rev. 13:18 [b] Rev. 13:1 17:10 [a] Rev. 13:5 17:11 [a] Rev. 13:3, 12, 14; 17:8 17:12 [a] Dan. 7:20 17:14 [a] Rev. 16:14; 19:19 [b] Rev. 19:20 [c] Deut. 10:17; 1 Tim. 6:15; Rev. 19:16 [d] Jer. 50:44

15Then he said to me, [a]"The waters which
you saw, where the harlot sits, [b]are peoples,
multitudes, nations, and tongues. 16And
the ten horns which you saw on[1] the beast,
[a]these will hate the harlot, make her [b]des-
olate [c]and naked, eat her flesh and [d]burn
her with fire. 17[a]For God has put it into their
hearts to fulfill His purpose, to be of one
mind, and to give their kingdom to the
beast, [b]until the words of God are fulfilled.
18And the woman whom you saw [a]is that
great city [b]which reigns over the kings of
the earth."

The Fall of Babylon the Great

18 After[a] these things I saw another
angel coming down from heaven,
having great authority, [b]and the earth
was illuminated with his glory. 2And he
cried mightily[1] with a loud voice, saying,
[a]"Babylon the great is fallen, is fallen, and
[b]has become a dwelling place of demons,
a prison for every foul spirit, and [c]a cage
for every unclean and hated bird! 3For all
the nations [a]have drunk of the wine of the
wrath of her fornication, the kings of the
earth have committed fornication with her,
[b]and the merchants of the earth have become rich through the abundance of her
luxury."

4And I heard another voice from heaven
saying, [a]"Come out of her, my people, lest
you share in her sins, and lest you receive
of her plagues. 5[a]For her sins have reached[1]
to heaven, and [b]God has remembered her
iniquities. 6[a]Render to her just as she rendered to you,[1] and repay her double according to her works; [b]in the cup which she has
mixed, [c]mix double for her. 7[a]In the measure that she glorified herself and lived
luxuriously, in the same measure give her
torment and sorrow; for she says in her
heart, 'I sit *as* [b]queen, and am no widow,
and will not see sorrow.' 8Therefore her
plagues will come [a]in one day—death and
mourning and famine. And [b]she will be
utterly burned with fire, [c]for strong *is* the
Lord God who judges[1] her.

The World Mourns Babylon's Fall

9[a]"The kings of the earth who committed
fornication and lived luxuriously with her
[b]will weep and lament for her, [c]when they
see the smoke of her burning, 10standing
at a distance for fear of her torment, saying, [a]'Alas, alas, that great city Babylon, that
mighty city! [b]For in one hour your judgment has come.'

11"And [a]the merchants of the earth will
weep and mourn over her, for no one buys
their merchandise anymore: 12[a]merchan-
dise of gold and silver, precious stones and
pearls, fine linen and purple, silk and scarlet, every kind of citron wood, every kind of
object of ivory, every kind of object of most
precious wood, bronze, iron, and marble;
13and cinnamon and incense, fragrant oil
and frankincense, wine and oil, fine flour
and wheat, cattle and sheep, horses and
chariots, and bodies and [a]souls of men. 14The
fruit that your soul longed for has gone from
you, and all the things which are rich and
splendid have gone from you,[1] and you shall
find them no more at all. 15The merchants
of these things, who became rich by her, will
stand at a distance for fear of her torment,
weeping and wailing, 16and saying, 'Alas,
alas, [a]that great city [b]that was clothed in fine
linen, purple, and scarlet, and adorned with
gold and precious stones and pearls! 17[a]For
in one hour such great riches came to nothing.' [b]Every shipmaster, all who travel by
ship, sailors, and as many as trade on the
sea, stood at a distance 18[a]and cried out when
they saw the smoke of her burning, saying,
[b]'What *is* like this great city?'

19[a]"They threw dust on their heads and
cried out, weeping and wailing, and saying, 'Alas, alas, that great city, in which all
who had ships on the sea became rich by
her wealth! [b]For in one hour she is made
desolate.'

17:15 [a] Is. 8:7; Jer. 47:2; Rev. 17:1 [b] Rev. 13:7 17:16 [a] Jer. 50:41 [b] Rev. 18:17, 19 [c] Ezek. 16:37, 39 [d] Rev. 18:8 [1] NU-Text and M-Text read *saw, and the beast.* 17:17 [a] 2 Thess. 2:11 [b] Rev. 10:7 17:18 [a] Rev. 11:8; 16:19 [b] Rev. 12:4 18:1 [a] Rev. 17:1, 7 [b] Ezek. 43:2 18:2 [a] Is. 13:19; 21:9; Jer. 51:8; Rev. 14:8 [b] Is. 13:21; 34:11, 13–15; Jer. 50:39; 51:37; Zeph. 2:14 [c] Is. 14:23 [1] NU-Text and M-Text omit *mightily.* 18:3 [a] Jer. 51:7; Rev. 14:8 [b] Is. 47:15 18:4 [a] Is. 48:20 18:5 [a] Gen. 18:20 [b] Rev. 16:19 [1] NU-Text and M-Text read *have been heaped up.* 18:6 [a] Ps. 137:8; Jer. 50:15, 29 [b] Rev. 14:10 [c] Rev. 16:19 [1] NU-Text and M-Text omit *to you.* 18:7 [a] Ezek. 28:2–8 [b] Is. 47:7, 8; Zeph. 2:15 18:8 [a] Is. 47:9; Jer. 50:31; Rev. 18:10 [b] Rev. 17:16 [c] Jer. 50:34; Heb. 10:31; Rev. 11:17 [1] NU-Text and M-Text read *has judged.* 18:9 [a] Ezek. 26:16; 27:35 [b] Jer. 50:46; Rev. 17:2; 18:3 [c] Rev. 19:3 18:10 [a] Is. 21:9 [b] Rev. 18:17, 19 18:11 [a] Ezek. 27:27–34 18:12 [a] Ezek. 27:12–22; Rev. 17:4 18:13 [a] 1 Chr. 5:21; Ezek. 27:13 18:14 [1] NU-Text and M-Text read *been lost to you.* 18:16 [a] Rev. 17:18 [b] Rev. 17:4 18:17 [a] Rev. 18:10 [b] Is. 23:14 18:18 [a] Ezek. 27:30 [b] Rev. 13:4 18:19 [a] Josh. 7:6; Job 2:12; Lam. 2:10; Ezek. 27:30 [b] Rev. 18:8

20[a]“Rejoice over her, O heaven, and *you*
holy apostles[1] and prophets, for [b]God has
avenged you on her!”

Finality of Babylon’s Fall

21Then a mighty angel took up a stone
like a great millstone and threw *it* into
the sea, saying, [a]“Thus with violence the
great city Babylon shall be thrown down,
and [b]shall not be found anymore. 22[a]The
sound of harpists, musicians, flutists, and
trumpeters shall not be heard in you anymore. No craftsman of any craft shall be
found in you anymore, and the sound of
a millstone shall not be heard in you anymore. 23[a]The light of a lamp shall not shine
in you anymore, [b]and the voice of bridegroom and bride shall not be heard in you
anymore. For [c]your merchants were the
great men of the earth, [d]for by your sorcery all the nations were deceived. 24And
[a]in her was found the blood of prophets
and saints, and of all who [b]were slain on
the earth.”

Heaven Exults over Babylon

19 After these things [a]I heard[1] a loud
voice of a great multitude in heaven,
saying, “Alleluia! [b]Salvation and glory and
honor and power *belong* to the Lord[2] our
God! 2For [a]true and righteous *are* His judgments, because He has judged the great
harlot who corrupted the earth with her
fornication; and He [b]has avenged on her the
blood of His servants *shed* by her.” 3Again
they said, “Alleluia! [a]Her smoke rises up
forever and ever!” 4And [a]the twenty-four elders and the four living creatures fell down
and worshiped God who sat on the throne,
saying, [b]“Amen! Alleluia!” 5Then a voice
came from the throne, saying, [a]“Praise our
God, all you His servants and those who
fear Him, [b]both[1] small and great!”
6[a]And I heard, as it were, the voice of
a great multitude, as the sound of many
waters and as the sound of mighty thunderings, saying, “Alleluia! For [b]the[1] Lord
God Omnipotent reigns! 7Let us be glad
and rejoice and give Him glory, for [a]the
marriage of the Lamb has come, and His
wife has made herself ready.” 8And [a]to her
it was granted to be arrayed in fine linen,
clean and bright, [b]for the fine linen is the
righteous acts of the saints.
9Then he said to me, “Write: [a]‘Blessed
are those who are called to the marriage
supper of the Lamb!’” And he said to me,
[b]“These are the true sayings of God.” 10And
[a]I fell at his feet to worship him. But he said
to me, [b]“See *that you do* not *do that!* I am
your [c]fellow servant, and of your brethren
[d]who have the testimony of Jesus. Worship
God! For the [e]testimony of Jesus is the spirit
of prophecy.”

Christ on a White Horse

11[a]Now I saw heaven opened, and behold,
[b]a white horse. And He who sat on him
was called [c]Faithful and True, and [d]in righteousness He judges and makes war. 12[a]His
eyes *were* like a flame of fire, and on His
head *were* many crowns. [b]He had[1] a name
written that no one knew except Himself.
13[a]He *was* clothed with a robe dipped in
blood, and His name is called [b]The Word of
God. 14[a]And the armies in heaven, [b]clothed
in fine linen, white and clean,[1] followed
Him on white horses. 15Now [a]out of His
mouth goes a sharp[1] sword, that with it He
should strike the nations. And [b]He Himself will rule them with a rod of iron. [c]He
Himself treads the winepress of the fierceness and wrath of Almighty God. 16And [a]He
has on *His* robe and on His thigh a name
written:

[b]KING OF KINGS AND
LORD OF LORDS.

18:20 [a] Is. 44:23; 49:13; Jer. 51:48; Rev. 12:12 [b] Luke 11:49; Rev. 19:2 [1] NU-Text and M-Text read *saints and apostles.* 18:21 [a] Jer. 51:63, 64 [b] Rev. 12:8; 16:20 18:22 [a] Eccl. 12:4; Jer. 7:34; 16:9; 25:10; Rev. 14:1–3 18:23 [a] Jer. 25:10 [b] Jer. 7:34; 16:9 [c] Is. 23:8; Rev. 6:15; 18:3 [d] 2 Kin. 9:22 18:24 [a] Rev. 16:6; 17:6 [b] Jer. 51:49 19:1 [a] Jer. 51:48; Rev. 11:15; 19:6 [b] Rev. 4:11 [1] NU-Text and M-Text add *something like.* [2] NU-Text and M-Text omit *the Lord.* 19:2 [a] Rev. 15:3; 16:7 [b] Deut. 32:43; 2 Kin. 9:7; Luke 18:7, 8; Rev. 6:10 19:3 [a] Is. 34:10; Rev. 14:11 19:4 [a] Rev. 4:4, 6, 10 [b] 1 Chr. 16:36 19:5 [a] Ps. 134:1 [b] Rev. 11:18 [1] NU-Text and M-Text omit *both.* 19:6 [a] Ezek. 1:24; Rev. 1:15; 14:2 [b] Rev. 11:15 [1] NU-Text and M-Text read *our.* 19:7 [a] [Matt. 22:2; 25:10]; Luke 12:36; John 3:29; [2 Cor. 11:2]; Eph. 5:23, 32; Rev. 19:9 19:8 [a] Ps. 45:13; Ezek. 16:10 [b] Ps. 132:9 19:9 [a] Matt. 22:2; Luke 14:15 [b] Rev. 22:6 19:10 [a] Rev. 22:8 [b] Acts 10:26; Rev. 22:9 [c] [Heb. 1:14] [d] 1 John 5:10 [e] Luke 24:27; John 5:39 19:11 [a] Rev. 15:5 [b] Ps. 45:3, 4; Rev. 6:2; 19:19, 21 [c] Rev. 3:7, 14 [d] Ps. 96:13; Is. 11:4 19:12 [a] Dan. 10:6; Rev. 1:14 [b] Rev. 2:17; 19:16 [1] M-Text adds *names written, and.* 19:13 [a] Is. 63:2, 3 [b] [John 1:1, 14] 19:14 [a] Rev. 14:20 [b] Matt. 28:3 [1] NU-Text and M-Text read *pure white linen.* 19:15 [a] Is. 11:4; 2 Thess. 2:8; Rev. 1:16 [b] Ps. 2:8, 9 [c] Is. 63:3–6; Rev. 14:20 [1] M-Text adds *two-edged.* 19:16 [a] Rev. 2:17; 19:12 [b] Dan. 2:47

The Beast and His Armies Defeated

17 Then I saw an angel standing in the
sun; and he cried with a loud voice, saying to all the birds that fly in the midst of
heaven, [a]"Come and gather together for
the supper of the great God,[1] 18 [a]that you
may eat the flesh of kings, the flesh of captains, the flesh of mighty men, the flesh of
horses and of those who sit on them, and
the flesh of all *people,* free[1] and slave, both
small and great."
19 [a]And I saw the beast, the kings of the
earth, and their armies, gathered together
to make war against Him who sat on the
horse and against His army. 20 [a]Then the
beast was captured, and with him the false
prophet who worked signs in his presence,
by which he deceived those who received
the mark of the beast and [b]those who worshiped his image. [c]These two were cast alive
into the lake of fire [d]burning with brimstone. 21 And the rest [a]were killed with the
sword which proceeded from the mouth
of Him who sat on the horse. [b]And all the
birds [c]were filled with their flesh.

Satan Bound 1,000 Years

20 Then I saw an angel coming down
from heaven, [a]having the key to the
bottomless pit and a great chain in his hand.
2 He laid hold of [a]the dragon, that serpent of
old, who is *the* Devil and Satan, and bound
him for a thousand years; 3 and he cast him
into the bottomless pit, and shut him up,
and [a]set a seal on him, [b]so that he should
deceive the nations no more till the thousand years were finished. But after these
things he must be released for a little while.

The Saints Reign with Christ 1,000 Years

4 And I saw [a]thrones, and they sat on
them, and [b]judgment was committed to
them. Then *I saw* [c]the souls of those who
had been beheaded for their witness to
Jesus and for the word of God, [d]who had not
worshiped the beast [e]or his image, and had
not received *his* mark on their foreheads or
on their hands. And they [f]lived and [g]reigned
with Christ for a[1] thousand years. 5 But the
rest of the dead did not live again until the
thousand years were finished. This *is* the
first resurrection. 6 Blessed and holy *is* he
who has part in the first resurrection. Over
such [a]the second death has no power, but
they shall be [b]priests of God and of Christ,
[c]and shall reign with Him a thousand years.

Satanic Rebellion Crushed (cf. Ezek. 38; 39)

7 Now when the thousand years have
expired, Satan will be released from his
prison 8 and will go out [a]to deceive the nations which are in the four corners of the
earth, [b]Gog and Magog, [c]to gather them
together to battle, whose number *is* as
the sand of the sea. 9 [a]They went up on
the breadth of the earth and surrounded
the camp of the saints and the beloved
city. And fire came down from God out of
heaven and devoured them. 10 The devil,
who deceived them, was cast into the lake
of fire and brimstone [a]where[1] the beast and
the false prophet *are.* And they [b]will be tormented day and night forever and ever.

The Great White Throne Judgment

11 Then I saw a great white throne and
Him who sat on it, from whose face [a]the
earth and the heaven fled away. [b]And there
was found no place for them. 12 And I saw
the dead, [a]small and great, standing before God,[1] [b]and books were opened. And
another [c]book was opened, which is *the
Book* of Life. And the dead were judged [d]ac-
cording to their works, by the things which
were written in the books. 13 The sea gave
up the dead who were in it, [a]and Death and
Hades delivered up the dead who were in
them. [b]And they were judged, each one according to his works. 14 Then [a]Death and

---

19:17 [a] 1 Sam. 17:44; Jer. 12:9; Ezek. 39:17 [1] NU-Text and M-Text read *the great supper of God.* 19:18 [a] Ezek. 39:18–20 [1] NU-Text and M-Text read *both free.* 19:19 [a] Rev. 16:13–16 19:20 [a] Rev. 16:13 [b] Rev. 13:8, 12, 13 [c] Is. 30:33; Dan. 7:11 [d] Rev. 14:10 19:21 [a] Rev. 19:15 [b] Rev. 19:17, 18 [c] Rev. 17:16 20:1 [a] Rev. 1:18; 9:1 20:2 [a] Is. 24:22; 2 Pet. 2:4; Jude 6 20:3 [a] Dan. 6:17; Matt. 27:66 [b] Rev. 12:9; 20:8, 10 20:4 [a] Dan. 7:9; Matt. 19:28; Luke 22:30 [b] Dan. 7:22; [1 Cor. 6:2, 3] [c] Rev. 6:9 [d] Rev. 13:12 [e] Rev. 13:15 [f] John 14:19 [g] Rom. 8:17; 2 Tim. 2:12 [1] M-Text reads *the.* 20:6 [a] [Rev. 2:11; 20:14] [b] Is. 61:6; 1 Pet. 2:9; Rev. 1:6 [c] Rev. 20:4 20:8 [a] Rev. 12:9; 20:3, 10 [b] Ezek. 38:2; 39:1, 6 [c] Rev. 16:14 20:9 [a] Is. 8:8; Ezek. 38:9, 16 20:10 [a] Rev. 19:20; 20:14, 15 [b] Rev. 14:10 [1] NU-Text and M-Text add *also.* 20:11 [a] 2 Pet. 3:7; Rev. 21:1 [b] Dan. 2:35; Rev. 12:8 20:12 [a] Rev. 19:5 [b] Dan. 7:10 [c] Ps. 69:28; Dan. 12:1; Phil. 4:3; Rev. 3:5 [d] Jer. 17:10; Matt. 16:27; Rom. 2:6; Rev. 2:23; 20:12 [1] NU-Text and M-Text read *the throne.* 20:13 [a] 1 Cor. 15:26; Rev. 1:18; 6:8; 21:4 [b] Matt. 16:27; Rev. 2:23; 20:12 20:14 [a] 1 Cor. 15:26; Rev. 1:18; 6:8; 21:4

Hades were cast into the lake of fire. [b]This is the second death.[1] 15 And anyone not found written in the Book of Life [a]was cast into the lake of fire.

All Things Made New

21 Now [a]I saw a new heaven and a new earth, [b]for the first heaven and the first earth had passed away. Also there was no more sea. 2 Then I, John,[1] saw [a]the holy city, New Jerusalem, coming down out of heaven from God, prepared [b]as a bride adorned for her husband. 3 And I heard a loud voice from heaven saying, "Behold, [a]the tabernacle of God *is* with men, and He will dwell with them, and they shall be His people. God Himself will be with them *and be* their God. 4 [a]And God will wipe away every tear from their eyes; [b]there shall be no more death, [c]nor sorrow, nor crying. There shall be no more pain, for the former things have passed away."

5 Then [a]He who sat on the throne said, [b]"Behold, I make all things new." And He said to me,[1] "Write, for [c]these words are true and faithful."

6 And He said to me, [a]"It is done![1] [b]I am the Alpha and the Omega, the Beginning and the End. [c]I will give of the fountain of the water of life freely to him who thirsts. 7 He who overcomes shall inherit all things,[1] and [a]I will be his God and he shall be My son. 8 [a]But the cowardly, unbelieving,[1] abominable, murderers, sexually immoral, sorcerers, idolaters, and all liars shall have their part in [b]the lake which burns with fire and brimstone, which is the second death."

The New Jerusalem
(cf. Ezek. 48:30–35)

9 Then one of [a]the seven angels who had the seven bowls filled with the seven last plagues came to me[1] and talked with me, saying, "Come, I will show you [b]the bride, the Lamb's wife."[2] 10 And he carried me away [a]in the Spirit to a great and high mountain, and showed me [b]the great city, the holy[1] Jerusalem, descending out of heaven from God, 11 [a]having the glory of God. Her light *was* like a most precious stone, like a jasper stone, clear as crystal. 12 Also she had a great and high wall with [a]twelve gates, and twelve angels at the gates, and names written on them, which are *the names* of the twelve tribes of the children of Israel: 13 [a]three gates on the east, three gates on the north, three gates on the south, and three gates on the west.

14 Now the wall of the city had twelve foundations, and [a]on them were the names[1] of the twelve apostles of the Lamb. 15 And he who talked with me [a]had a gold reed to measure the city, its gates, and its wall. 16 The city is laid out as a square; its length is as great as its breadth. And he measured the city with the reed: twelve thousand furlongs. Its length, breadth, and height are equal. 17 Then he measured its wall: one hundred *and* forty-four cubits, *according* to the measure of a man, that is, of an angel. 18 The construction of its wall was *of* jasper; and the city *was* pure gold, like clear glass. 19 [a]The foundations of the wall of the city *were* adorned with all kinds of precious stones: the first foundation *was* jasper, the second sapphire, the third chalcedony, the fourth emerald, 20 the fifth sardonyx, the sixth sardius, the seventh chrysolite, the eighth beryl, the ninth topaz, the tenth chrysoprase, the eleventh jacinth, and the twelfth amethyst. 21 The twelve gates *were* twelve [a]pearls: each individual gate was of one pearl. [b]And the street of the city *was* pure gold, like transparent glass.

The Glory of the New Jerusalem

22 [a]But I saw no temple in it, for the Lord God Almighty and the Lamb are its temple. 23 [a]The city had no need of the sun or

---

20:14 [b] Rev. 21:8 [1] NU-Text and M-Text add *the lake of fire.* **20:15** [a] Rev. 19:20 **21:1** [a] Is. 65:17; 66:22; [2 Pet. 3:13] [b] [2 Pet. 3:10]; Rev. 20:11 **21:2** [a] Is. 52:1; [Gal. 4:26]; Heb. 11:10 [b] Is. 54:5; 2 Cor. 11:2 [1] NU-Text and M-Text omit *John.* **21:3** [a] Lev. 26:11; Ezek. 43:7; 2 Cor. 6:16 **21:4** [a] Is. 25:8; Rev. 7:17 [b] 1 Cor. 15:26; Rev. 20:14 [c] Is. 35:10; 51:11; 65:19 **21:5** [a] Rev. 4:2, 9; 20:11 [b] Is. 43:19; 2 Cor. 5:17 [c] Rev. 19:9; 22:6 [1] NU-Text and M-Text omit *to me.* **21:6** [a] Rev. 10:6; 16:17 [b] Rev. 1:8; 22:13 [c] Is. 12:3; 55:1; John 4:10; Rev. 7:17; 22:17 [1] M-Text omits *It is done.* **21:7** [a] Zech. 8:8; Heb. 8:10 [1] M-Text reads *overcomes, I shall give him these things.* **21:8** [a] 1 Cor. 6:9; Gal. 5:19; Eph. 5:5; 1 Tim. 1:9; [Heb. 12:14] [b] Rev. 20:14 [1] M-Text adds *and sinners.* **21:9** [a] Rev. 15:1 [b] Rev. 19:7; 21:2 [1] NU-Text and M-Text omit *to me.* [2] M-Text reads *I will show you the woman, the Lamb's bride.* **21:10** [a] Rev. 1:10 [b] Ezek. 48 [1] NU-Text and M-Text omit *the great* and read *the holy city, Jerusalem.* **21:11** [a] Is. 60:1; Ezek. 43:2; Rev. 15:8; 21:23; 22:5 **21:12** [a] Ezek. 48:31–34 **21:13** [a] Ezek. 48:31–34 **21:14** [a] Matt. 16:18; Luke 22:29, 30; Gal. 2:9; Eph. 2:20 [1] NU-Text and M-Text read *twelve names.* **21:15** [a] Ezek. 40:3; Zech. 2:1; Rev. 11:1 **21:19** [a] Ex. 28:17–20; Is. 54:11; Ezek. 28:13 **21:21** [a] Matt. 13:45, 46 [b] Rev. 22:2 **21:22** [a] Matt. 24:2; John 4:21, 23 **21:23** [a] Is. 24:23; 60:19, 20; Rev. 21:25; 22:5

RELEASE // ELEVATE YOUR TIME WITH HIM

Accept the Invitation

Revelation 22:17 // And the Spirit and the bride say, "Come!" And let him who hears say, "Come!" And let him who thirsts come. Whoever desires, let him take the water of life freely.

Summary Message // In this final chapter of the Bible, the Lord invites us to fellowship with Him. It is an invitation that extends beyond the here and now; it encompasses all eternity. Our Lord has intervened on behalf of His people and died for us so that we can live eternally with Him. Jesus is coming quickly, and His reward is with Him. This invitation is extended to those who are servants of God and of the Lord Jesus Christ. Only they are allowed inside the gates and have gained access to that beautiful, holy city described at the end of Revelation. Outside the gates of the New Jerusalem are those who love wickedness.

Practical Application // Here is a sad truth to consider: many will get their first, true glimpse of Christ on the day He returns. And then, it will be too late for them. This will not be because they have never had access to the gospel. It will be because they never took advantage of the opportunities they were given. Likewise, for us as believers, each day provides an opportunity to get to know Christ better and to make Him known. As we struggle to see Him as He truly is, we have opportunities to draw closer to Him as He draws closer to us.

David said that he rose early in the morning to seek God (see Ps. 63:1). Such was his desire to spend time with the Lord that sleep was set aside for the pure joy of beholding Him. The fruit of this devotion is found in the beauty and depth of the psalms he wrote.

What about you? Will you meet the Lord for the first time at the end of this age or now, while you have time? Salvation is available to you right now. It is the joyous beginning of a relationship with the Lord that has no end. Revelation 22 invites you to fellowship with God on a higher plane in a greater dimension of the fullness of joy.

For those of us in Christ, we should spend our time with the Lord preparing for the day when our fellowship will finally be unfettered and unhindered. But again, this everlasting fellowship will be ours only if we commit our lives to Him now. You can do this by elevating the time you spend with the Savior, today.

Jesus is coming to give every person the reward He has prepared (see Rev. 22:12). Our reward will be reflective of our obedience and the quality of our fellowship with Him.

Fervent Prayer // Lord, we look with anticipation toward an eternity with You. We look forward to entering through the gates of that beautiful, holy city we will never have to leave. We know there are many struggles that interfere with our fellowship with You on earth, but we commit to seeking You and increasing quality time in Your presence. We joyfully anticipate fellowship with You forever in Your kingdom. Help us steadfastly to focus our minds on heavenly things. Help us not to forsake the fellowship You have given us to enjoy on earth as we look forward to that great day when Your reward is in our hands. We pray for deeper fellowship with You until that great day. In Jesus' name we pray. Amen.

---

of the moon to shine in it,[1] for the glory[2]
of God illuminated it. The Lamb *is* its light.
24[a]And the nations of those who are saved[1]
shall walk in its light, and the kings of the
earth bring their glory and honor into it.[2]
25[a]Its gates shall not be shut at all by day
[b](there shall be no night there). 26[a]And they
shall bring the glory and the honor of the
nations into it.[1] 27But [a]there shall by no
means enter it anything that defiles, or
causes[1] an abomination or a lie, but only
those who are written in the Lamb's [b]Book
of Life.

The River of Life

22 And he showed me [a]a pure[1] river of
water of life, clear as crystal, proceeding from the throne of God and of the

---

21:23 [1] NU-Text and M-Text omit *in it.* [2] M-Text reads *the very glory.* 21:24 [a] Is. 60:3, 5; 66:12 [1] NU-Text and M-Text omit *of those who are saved.* [2] M-Text reads *the glory and honor of the nations to Him.* 21:25 [a] Is. 60:11 [b] Is. 60:20; Zech. 14:7 21:26 [a] Rev. 21:24 [1] M-Text adds *that they may enter in.* 21:27 [a] Is. 35:8; Joel 3:17 [b] Phil. 4:3 [1] NU-Text and M-Text read *anything profane, nor one who causes.* 22:1 [a] Ps. 46:4; Ezek. 47:1; [Zech. 14:8] [1] NU-Text and M-Text omit *pure.*

Lamb. 2[a]In the middle of its street, and on
either side of the river, *was* [b]the tree of life,
which bore twelve fruits, each *tree* yielding its fruit every month. The leaves of the
tree *were* [c]for the healing of the nations.
3And [a]there shall be no more curse, [b]but
the throne of God and of the Lamb shall
be in it, and His [c]servants shall serve Him.
4[a]They shall see His face, and [b]His name
shall be on their foreheads. 5[a]There shall
be no night there: They need no lamp nor
[b]light of the sun, for [c]the Lord God gives
them light. [d]And they shall reign forever
and ever.

The Time Is Near

6Then he said to me, [a]"These words *are*
faithful and true." And the Lord God of the
holy[1] prophets [b]sent His angel to show His
servants the things which must [c]shortly
take place.

7[a]"Behold, I am coming quickly! [b]Blessed
is he who keeps the words of the prophecy
of this book."

8Now I, John, saw and heard[1] these
things. And when I heard and saw, [a]I fell
down to worship before the feet of the angel who showed me these things.

9Then he said to me, [a]"See *that you do*
not *do that.* For[1] I am your fellow servant,
and of your brethren the prophets, and
of those who keep the words of this book.
Worship God." 10[a]And he said to me, "Do not
seal the words of the prophecy of this book,
[b]for the time is at hand. 11He who is unjust,
let him be unjust still; he who is filthy, let
him be filthy still; he who is righteous, let
him be righteous[1] still; he who is holy, let
him be holy still."

Jesus Testifies to the Churches

12"And behold, I am coming quickly, and
[a]My reward *is* with Me, [b]to give to every one
according to his work. 13[a]I am the Alpha and
the Omega, *the* Beginning and *the* End, the
First and the Last."[1]

14[a]Blessed *are* those who do His commandments,[1] that they may have the right
[b]to the tree of life, [c]and may enter through
the gates into the city. 15But[1] [a]outside *are*
[b]dogs and sorcerers and sexually immoral
and murderers and idolaters, and whoever
loves and practices a lie.

16[a]"I, Jesus, have sent My angel to testify
to you these things in the churches. [b]I am
the Root and the Offspring of David, [c]the
Bright and Morning Star."

17And the Spirit and [a]the bride say,
"Come!" And let him who hears say, "Come!"
[b]And let him who thirsts come. Whoever
desires, let him take the water of life freely.

A Warning

18For[1] I testify to everyone who hears
the words of the prophecy of this book: [a]If
anyone adds to these things, God will add[2]
to him the plagues that are written in this
book; 19and if anyone takes away from the
words of the book of this prophecy, [a]God
shall take away[1] his part from the Book[2] of
Life, from the holy city, and *from* the things
which are written in this book.

I Am Coming Quickly

20He who testifies to these things says,
"Surely I am coming quickly."

Amen. Even so, come, Lord Jesus!

21The grace of our Lord Jesus Christ *be*
with you all.[1] Amen.

22:2 [a] Ezek. 47:12 [b] Gen. 2:9; [Rev. 2:7; 22:14, 19] [c] Rev. 21:24 **22:3** [a] Zech. 14:11 [b] Ezek. 48:35 [c] Rev. 7:15 **22:4** [a] [Ps. 17:15; 42:2; Matt. 5:8; 1 Cor. 13:12; 1 John 3:2] [b] Rev. 14:1 **22:5** [a] Is. 60:19; Rev. 21:23 [b] Rev. 7:15 [c] Ps. 36:9 [d] Dan. 7:18, 27; Matt. 19:28; [Rom. 5:17]; 2 Tim. 2:12; Rev. 20:4 **22:6** [a] Rev. 19:9 [b] Rev. 1:1 [c] Heb. 10:37 [1] NU-Text and M-Text read *spirits of the prophets.* **22:7** [a] [Rev. 3:11] [b] Rev. 1:3 **22:8** [a] Rev. 19:10 [1] NU-Text and M-Text read *am the one who heard and saw.* **22:9** [a] Rev. 19:10 [1] NU-Text and M-Text omit *For.* **22:10** [a] Dan. 8:26; Rev. 10:4 [b] Rev. 1:3 **22:11** [1] NU-Text and M-Text read *do right.* **22:12** [a] Is. 40:10; 62:11 [b] Rev. 20:12 **22:13** [a] Is. 41:4 [1] NU-Text and M-Text read *the First and the Last, the Beginning and the End.* **22:14** [a] Dan. 12:12; [1 John 3:24] [b] [Prov. 11:30]; Rev. 2:7 [c] Rev. 21:27 [1] NU-Text reads *wash their robes.* **22:15** [a] Matt. 8:12; 1 Cor. 6:9; Gal. 5:19; Col. 3:6; Rev. 21:8 [b] Deut. 23:18; Matt. 7:6; Phil. 3:2 [1] NU-Text and M-Text omit *But.* **22:16** [a] Rev. 1:1 [b] 2 Sam. 7:12; Is. 9:7; Jer. 23:5; Rev. 5:5 [c] Num. 24:17; Luke 1:78; 2 Pet. 1:19 **22:17** [a] [Rev. 21:2, 9] [b] Is. 55:1; Rev. 21:6 **22:18** [a] Deut. 4:2; 12:32; Prov. 30:6 [1] NU-Text and M-Text omit *For.* [2] M-Text reads *may God add.* **22:19** [a] Ex. 32:33 [1] M-Text reads *may God take away.* [2] NU-Text and M-Text read *tree of life.* **22:21** [1] NU-Text reads *with all;* M-Text reads *with all the saints.*

CONTRIBUTOR BIOGRAPHIES

Jekalyn Carr

Jekalyn Carr is a Grammy Award nominee and GMA Dove Award–winning independent recording artist. She's a profound speaker, entrepreneur, actress, and author who has spent half a decade at the helm of gospel music charts. As a top-selling recording artist, Carr earned eight career Billboard number ones before the age of twenty-one. These include her hit singles "You're Bigger" and "You Will Win." Carr debuted with a featured role on the Oprah Winfrey Network (OWN) series *Greenleaf* and expanded her acting experience in the feature film *Never Heard.* Her entry into the literary marketplace was heralded by her debut release *You Will Win! Inspirational Strategies to Help You Overcome*, which was released in conjunction with the number-one Billboard song of the same title and premise.

Michele Clark Jenkins

Michele Clark Jenkins, cofounder of the Sisters in Faith brand, published by Thomas Nelson Publishers, is the author and editor of *She Speaks* and a contributing writer and coeditor of *The Sisters in Faith Bible* and *Real: The Complete New Testament* (Biblezine). She is also a contributing writer and editor of the *Children of Color Storybook Bible* and a contributing writer for the *Women of Color Devotional Bible* and the *Wisdom and Grace Devotional Bible*. Clark Jenkins is the Senior Director of the Consulting Group for Griffin & Strong, P.C., which specializes in disparity research. Previously she was the General Manager of the estate of Dr. Martin Luther King Jr., Vice President of Programming for the Black Family Channel, President and COO of the BET/Tim Reid Production Company, United Image Entertainment, and Director of Business Affairs at Home Box Office. Clark Jenkins is a graduate of Princeton University and New York Law School. She and her husband, Kym, are elders at Liberty Church in Marietta, Georgia, and have three daughters.

Dr. Thelma T. Daley

Thelma Thomas Daley is the President of the National Council of Negro Women. She is an American Counseling Association fellow and a National Board–Certified counselor. Daley completed a long, successful tenure with the Baltimore County Public Schools, where she directed the counseling program for 163 schools. At Loyola University (MD), she served as Assistant Professor in the graduate school and as Coordinator of Clinical Experiences. She was an adjunct professor at George Washington University and served as an instructor at the Harvard University Summer Institute for Counselors. Daley was appointed to the National Advisory Council on Career Education under the aegis of the Secretary of Education and became the first woman to chair the council. She is a graduate of Bowie State University, New York University, and George Washington University. Daley served as the sixteenth National President of Delta Sigma Theta Sorority, Incorporated. She lives in Maryland.

Dr. Charrita Danley Quimby

Charrita Danley Quimby is an author, an educator, and a communication strategist. As the founder of CDQ Consulting, she provides communication and education services to a broad range of clients and conducts presentations and trainings on various topics. Committed to impacting the lives of others through educational access, Quimby serves as the Director of Institutional Partnerships at Ed Advancement, an organization that strengthens the capacity of historically Black colleges and universities. Before this role, she served as Vice President and Chief of Staff at Hampton University. A member of Delta Sigma Theta Sorority, Inc., Quimby holds a BA, an MA, and a PhD in English. She is married to Dr. Ronald Quimby, and their family includes one son and two daughters.

Rev. Dr. Helen Delaney

Helen Delaney was a nuclear engineer and technical writer in the Ballistic Missile Division of the former TRW, Inc. Currently, she is on the speaking team at Liberty Church in Marietta, Georgia, where she uses her analytical skills and doctor of ministry to bring the Bible alive through her relevant, thought-provoking, systematic teachings and writings. Delaney is an international speaker and loves to see lives changed for God's kingdom and His glory. She is also the director of Blake's House of Independence, a nonprofit for adults with special needs. Delaney has written a Bible study guide titled *Advancing the Kingdom of God*. She is also a co-contributor to the *Sisters in Faith Bible*, having written the overview and personal insight for each book of the New Testament. Delaney is a wife to George, a mother to their daughter, and a grandmother of three.

Elder De'Leice R. Drane

De'Leice R. Drane is the Vice President of Operations for First Kingdom Management, Inc., in Atlanta, Georgia, and a King Center trainer. She is a business leader and an inspirational speaker. Her interpersonal relationship skills and expertise with Fortune 500 companies in contract negotiations for endorsement deals, event productions, intellectual property, and trademarks, as well as her global speaker management experience, have propelled her to make acquaintances with world leaders such as former presidents Barack Obama and George W. Bush, Nelson Mandela, and media icon Oprah Winfrey. Drane is a member of the Vatican Covid-19 Task Force commissioned by Pope Francis. She is the founder of YOUnique Legacies, LLC, formed to educate, equip, and empower others in managing and protecting intellectual property. Drane is the author of a daily devotional book, *Life Is*. She is a graduate of Memphis State University with a bachelor of science degree in criminal justice. She lives in the Greater Atlanta area.

S. James Guitard

S. James Guitard is Senior Vice President of Global Policy and Strategic Development for the Diaspora

Education Foundation (La Fundación Educativa de la Diáspora), a Christian ministry foundation, think tank, and philanthropic fund specializing in educational programs, global humanitarian projects, and evangelism, and has been instrumental in sponsoring and coordinating education events and health and community revitalization initiatives in different parts of the world. He is also author and editor of the national best-selling Christian anthology *Blessed Assurance: Inspirational Short Stories Full of Hope and Strength for Life's Journey*. His first best-selling book was *Chocolate Thoughts*, and he has also written several best-selling Christian novels, including *Delilah's Revenge*, *A Hot Mess*, and *Mocha Love*. Guitard actively serves in several ministries at Kingdom Fellowship African Methodist Episcopal Church. He splits time living in the Washington, D.C., area and abroad in Cartagena, Colombia.

Derrick Johnson

Derrick Johnson serves as President and CEO of the NAACP, where he has also served as Vice Chairman of the National Board of Directors and President for the Mississippi State Conference. He also continues to be on the frontlines of some of the most pressing civil rights issues of our time. Born in Detroit, Michigan, Johnson attended Tougaloo College in Jackson, Mississippi. He then received a juris doctor degree from the South Texas College of Law in Houston. Johnson has also furthered his training through fellowships with the Congressional Black Caucus Foundation, the George Washington University School of Political Management, and the Massachusetts Institute of Technology. He has served as an annual guest lecturer at Harvard Law School and as an adjunct professor at Tougaloo College in Mississippi. He is a member of Omega Psi Phi Fraternity, Inc., and lives in Mississippi with his wife and children.

Rev. Dr. Walter L. Kimbrough

Walter L. Kimbrough is a United Methodist Church (UMC) minister who served over fifty years providing evangelism, pastoral care, teaching, preaching, and community service. He has provided leadership at all levels of the United Methodist Church in both Northern Illinois and North Georgia. He successfully led Chicago congregations through racial transition in 1974. Then, he was appointed to the Cascade UMC in Atlanta, where his expertise was needed. He moved Cascade from less than one hundred members to more than seven thousand members. He retired from this pastorate but was called out of retirement and successfully rebuilt the Columbia Drive UMC and Cliftondale UMC. He retired again in 2020. Kimbrough is a member of Alpha Phi Alpha Fraternity, Inc. He has received numerous honors and awards and served on local and national boards and agencies. He and his wife, Marjorie, have two sons and two grandchildren.

Rev. Dr. Bernice A. King

Rev. Dr. Bernice A. King is a global thought leader, a strategist, a solutionist, an orator, a peace advocate, and the CEO of the Martin Luther King Jr. Center for Nonviolent Social Change. She is the youngest child of Martin Luther King Jr. and Coretta Scott King and is an international civil rights leader. King received a BA in psychology from Spelman College and an MDiv and a JD from Emory University. She became a member of the Georgia bar and was later given an Honorary Doctor of Divinity by Wesley College. She is a member of Alpha Kappa Alpha Sorority, Inc. King is the author of *Hard Questions, Heart Answers: Sermons and Speeches* and coauthor of *It Starts with Me*. Her oratorical talents have drawn comparisons to her father's and have made her a sought-after speaker. She lives in Atlanta, Georgia.

Pastor Tommy Kyllonen

Pastor Tommy "Urban D." Kyllonen has been in ministry for over twenty years at Crossover Church in Tampa, Florida, where he has been the Lead Pastor for the past fifteen years. This multiethnic, multigenerational, multiclass church has become a model for churches all over. Kyllonen is an internationally known hip-hop artist who has released nine full-length albums and several remix projects. He holds a bachelor of arts in pastoral theology with a concentration in youth ministry and has completed master's level church leadership coursework from Southeastern University. Kyllonen has authored five books and is the publisher of the urban lifestyle magazine *S.O.U.L.MAG*. With a passion to help other leaders win, he founded the Flavor Fest Urban Leadership Conference, which has trained over five thousand leaders. Kyllonen serves as the Vice-Chair of the Uptown Tampa Innovation Partnership board. He lives in Tampa with his wife, Lucy, and two daughters.

Rev. Dr. Eric W. Lee

Eric Wendel Lee Sr. serves as the Senior Pastor of the Springfield Baptist Church (SBC) in Covington and Conyers, Georgia. He is a third-generation pastor and has overseen the growth of the SBC membership from hundreds to more than ten thousand. Lee is an honors graduate of Morehouse College, where he earned a BA in history. As the Kelly Miller Smith Scholar, he earned an MDiv from Vanderbilt University, focusing on ethics, religion, and society. Lee earned a DMin in redemptive leadership from the Gordon-Conwell Theological School. Lee has served as a board member on several community and civic organizations. He has been honored and recognized by several city, county, state, and national organizations, colleges and universities, businesses and legislatures. Lee is married to Meik L. Lee, and they are the parents of five children. The Lees live in Georgia.

Jamell Meeks

Jamell Meeks is the Director of Women's Ministries for the Salem Baptist Church of Chicago, Illinois, under the leadership of her husband, Reverend James T. Meeks. This ministry, Women of Influence, serves over four thousand women. She is the National Chair for First Ladies Health Initiative and leader of a national pastors' wives prayer group. Meeks has been featured in several national publications for her work with entrepreneurship, women, and health. She is a certified John Maxwell speaker and addresses hundreds of women annually. She developed the nationally recognized A.R.I.S.E Entrepreneur Program in 2004, which has helped over one thousand people start and grow their small businesses. Meeks' mission is to inspire women of all ages to live a life grounded by faith, guided by purpose, and motivated by infinite possibilities. She lives in Chicago with her husband and is the mother of four children and grandmother of four.

Minister Derrick Moore

Derrick Moore is a former NFL running back, drafted by the Atlanta Falcons in 1992 and played with the Detroit Lions, Arizona Cardinals, and Carolina Panthers. As the starting back for the Panthers, Derrick set the expansion rushing record. Moore is the Executive Director for Player and Character Development

for the University of South Carolina. He was also the team chaplain and developmental coach for Georgia Institute of Technology for twenty years. Moore inspiringly infuses sports with faith as a motivational speaker for churches, corporations, and pro sports teams. He is also a voice-over artist. Moore is the author of *The Great Adventure, It's Possible, Raise Him Up*, and three book series for youth. He is a contributor to the *Men of Color Bible*, the *Young Men of Color Bible*, and the *Real* Biblezine. Derrick and his wife, Stephanie, have three children.

Stephanie Perry Moore
Stephanie Perry Moore is a Christian novelist who has written over seventy-five titles for children and adults. She is the trailblazing author of the Payton Skky Series, the first African American Christian teen series. Her newest series is Magic Strong. In addition to writing her own titles, Moore is the general editor for *Urban Spirit* and the editor of several Bible products, including the *Men of Color Study Bible*, the *Strength and Honor Bible*, the *Women of Color Devotional Bible*, the *Women of Color Cookbook*, and the *Wisdom and Grace Devotional Bible*. She is the coeditor of *REAL*, an urban Biblezine published by Thomas Nelson, and the cofounder of the Sisters in Faith brand. Moore speaks in schools across the nation, uplifting youth. She is a member of Springfield Baptist Church and lives in Columbia, South Carolina, with her husband, Derrick. They have three young adult children.

Pastor Debra B. Morton
Debra B. Morton is the much-admired and beloved Pastor Emeritus of Greater St. Stephen Full Gospel Baptist Church in New Orleans, Louisiana, and was co-pastor at Changing a Generation Full Gospel Baptist Church in Atlanta, Georgia. She is married to Bishop Paul S. Morton Sr., founder of the Full Gospel Baptist Church Fellowship International, where she served as General Overseer of the women's division, Daughters of the Promise. She serves on the MICAH board, a faith-based organization comprised of clergy who desire to see change in the Greater New Orleans community and initiate efforts that support this vision for change. Morton is also the founder of the DBM Arts and Entertainment Summer Camp and is currently rebuilding a parent-child center that was destroyed in Hurricane Katrina. Morton takes the greatest pride in her personal relationship with Jesus Christ and her roles as wife, mother, and grandmother.

Bishop Vashti Murphy McKenzie
Vashti Murphy McKenzie is the Interim President and General Secretary for the National Council of Churches. She has also served as the 117th elected and consecrated bishop of the African Methodist Episcopal Church and as presiding bishop in Southern Africa—Botswana, Swaziland, Mozambique, and Lesotho—and in the United States in Tennessee, Kentucky, and Texas. McKenzie is a graduate of the University of Maryland, College Park, and the Howard University School of Religion. She also has an earned doctorate from United Theological Seminary. McKenzie has been active in social justice issues for over three decades and in 2009 was appointed by President Barack Obama to be on the inaugural White House Commission of Faith-Based and Neighborhood Partnerships. This group worked on behalf of Americans committed to improving their communities, no matter their religious or political beliefs. She is the National Chaplain for Delta Sigma Theta Sorority, Inc., an author, and a mother.

Dr. Franklin Perry
Franklin Perry Sr. is Superintendent of Schools in Liberty County, Georgia. He is an Army veteran, ex-business leader, and former band director. Perry is Vice-Chair of the Professional Standards Commission for the state of Georgia. He has also held positions as Superintendent of Schools for Sumpter and Twiggs Counties of Georgia, teacher, vocational supervisor, high school assistant principal, middle and high school principal, and assistant superintendent of a large school system. In his successful career, Perry has developed effective means of closing achievement gaps, improving student achievement, improving student discipline, and increasing parental/community involvement. He is a contributor to the *Men of Color Bible* and is the coauthor of a motivational curriculum, *Operation Reach Every Attainable Dream*. He is a member of Springfield Baptist Church in Conyers, Georgia, and Omega Psi Phi Fraternity, Inc. He and his wife, Shirley, have two children and four grandchildren.

Antonio Neal Phelon
Antonio Neal Phelon is a Grammy-nominated, Stellar Award–winning, and Dove Award–winning gospel music producer. He is a former artist, writer, and producer for EMI Gospel and has published hundreds of songs. Phelon is also a published writer with Thomas Nelson on the *Revolve Spin* project. He loves traveling, taking pictures, and enjoying as much of life as possible. He lives in Texas.

Bishop Marvin Sapp
Marvin L. Sapp is a gospel music legend, cofounder of Lighthouse Full Life Center Church in Grand Rapids, Michigan, Senior Pastor of The Chosen Vessel Cathedral in Fort Worth, Texas, and a Metropolitan Bishop who oversees more than one hundred churches in the Central Deanery of Global United Fellowship. Sapp is a multiplatinum-selling artist who has enjoyed a decorated music career, receiving thirteen Grammy nominations, twenty-four Stellar Awards, two Soul Train Music Awards, two BET Awards, three Dove Awards, eight BMI songwriter's awards for sales, a Black Music Honors Gospel Music Icon Award, and many other accolades and honors from national, regional, and local institutions. He is an author of eight books and is also an entrepreneur. Sapp is the father of three and lives in Texas.

Dr. Arthur Satterwhite
Arthur L. Satterwhite III is a recognized voice on diversity and leadership. He received a doctorate in strategic leadership, a master's degree in religious education, and a bachelor's degree in business/marketing. As a consultant and speaker, he has helped communities around the world through inspiration, training, and strategic, consultative support. Satterwhite currently serves as the Vice President of Diversity, Belonging, and Strategy at Young Life and as an adjunct professor at Regent University. Additionally, he serves on boards and advisory committees for several local and global organizations, including Christian Leadership Alliance and Young Life's Northeast Division. Satterwhite and his wife, Safiyah, live in the New York area.

Pastor Tommy Stevenson
Tommy Stevenson is the Pastor of Deep Waters Community Church in Marietta, Georgia, a teacher, and a motivational speaker who has been ministering for over fifteen years in the Atlanta metropolitan area. Stevenson has also served as assistant Worship

Pastor and Youth Pastor at Liberty Church Marietta, Georgia. He earned a degree in telecommunications and music from Oral Roberts University in Tulsa, Oklahoma. He and his wife, Brandy, have three daughters and three grandsons. They live in Georgia.

Bishop Kenneth C. Ulmer

Kenneth C. Ulmer is the Pastor of Faith Central Bible Church in Inglewood, California. He received a BA in broadcasting and music from the University of Illinois. Ulmer has also studied at Pepperdine University, Hebrew Union College, the University of Judaism and Christ Church, and Wadham College at Oxford University. He received a doctor of philosophy from Grace Graduate School of Theology in Long Beach, California, an honorary doctor of divinity from Southern California School of Ministry, and a doctor of ministry from United Theological Seminary in Dayton, Ohio. Ulmer was consecrated Bishop of Christian Education of the Full Gospel Baptist Church Fellowship and is currently the Presiding Bishop over Macedonia International Bible Fellowship based in Johannesburg, South Africa. He is the author of several books. Ulmer and his wife live in Los Angeles, California, and have two daughters, one son, and five grandchildren.

Bishop Hezekiah Walker

Hezekiah Walker is a Grammy Award–winning gospel music artist and Pastor of Love Fellowship Tabernacle, a prominent Brooklyn, New York, Pentecostal megachurch. Walker has released several albums on Benson Records and Verity Records as Hezekiah Walker & The Love Fellowship Crusade Choir. He attended Long Island University, majoring in sociology; Hugee Theological Institute in New York; and the New York School of the Bible. Walker became a bishop in the Church of Our Lord Jesus Christ of the Apostolic Faith in 2008, and he transferred to the Pentecostal Churches of Jesus Christ later that year. He became the Presiding Prelate of the Pentecostal Churches of Jesus Christ in 2010. He lives in New York.

Dr. LaKeesha Walrond

LaKeesha Walrond is the President of New York Theological Seminary. She earned an undergraduate degree from Spelman College in Atlanta, Georgia, a master of divinity from Union Theological Seminary in New York, and a master of arts in teaching, master in school administration, and doctor of philosophy from the University of North Carolina at Chapel Hill. She has worked in public and charter schools, the United Church of Christ, and Baptist churches. Walrond is a dynamic speaker who has addressed national and international audiences; she has spoken in South Africa, Canada, the Bahamas, South Korea, and India. She has also launched the Getting to Greatness Women's Conference and is the author of the Let's Talk About It series. Walrond serves as the Executive Pastor at First Corinthian Baptist Church in New York alongside her husband, Michael A. Walrond Jr., the Senior Pastor. Walrond has two children and lives in New York.

Dr. Lakeba Hibbler Williams

Lakeba Hibbler Williams is a Licensed Professional Counselor and a National Certified Counselor with a bachelor of science degree in social work from Southern University A&M College in Baton Rouge, Louisiana, and both a master of education in community agency counseling and a doctor of philosophy in adult education from Auburn University in Auburn, Alabama. She is the Owner/Director of Fresh Hope Counseling Center and also works part-time with the City of Atlanta's Psychological Services/Employee Assistance Program as a Behavioral Health Specialist. An author, an educator, and a consultant with over twenty-five years of experience, Williams is a speaker and workshop leader at regional, national, and global events for universities, churches, and corporations on a variety of topics, including mental health and wellness, healthy relationships, and leadership. She is a member of Alpha Kappa Alpha Sorority, Inc., and lives in Decatur, Georgia, with her family.

Rev. Matthew Wesley Williams

Matthew Wesley Williams serves as President of the Interdenominational Theological Center (ITC) in Atlanta, Georgia. He has also served as a member of the senior leadership team and Vice President of Strategic Initiatives for the Forum for Theological Exploration (FTE), a national leadership incubator that cultivates wise, faithful, and courageous leaders who make a difference in the world through the church and academy. Before FTE, Williams served at the National Black Leadership Initiative on Cancer at the Morehouse School of Medicine in Atlanta, Georgia. He holds a master of divinity degree from the ITC and bachelor's degrees in psychology and philosophy and religion from Florida A&M University. Williams is an ordained ruling elder in the Presbyterian Church (USA). He is the coauthor of *Another Way: Living and Leading Change on Purpose*. He resides in the Atlanta area with his wife, Alexis, and children.

Ambassador Andrew Young

Andrew Young is a civil rights icon, an American politician, a diplomat, and an activist. Beginning his career as a pastor, Young was an early leader in the civil rights movement, serving as executive director of the Southern Christian Leadership Conference and a close confidant to Martin Luther King Jr. Young later became active in politics, serving as a United States Congressman from Georgia, United States Ambassador to the United Nations in the Carter Administration, and the fifty-fifth Mayor of Atlanta, Georgia. Since leaving office, Young has founded or served in many organizations, working on issues of public policy and political lobbying. He is the author of several books and lives in Atlanta with his family.

INDEX TO ARTICLES

Inhale-Exhale

Believe in the Promise .... Gen. 22:16
Reconcile Hurt with Healing .... Ex. 1:8
Exalt His Guiding Light .... Lev. 1:1
Act in Faith .... Num. 1:2
Trust in His Word .... Deut. 11:13
Hope for Today .... Josh. 10:42
Elevate the Stands You Take .... Judg. 21:25

Believe in Prayer .... 1 Sam. 9:15
Reconcile Weaknesses with Strength .... 2 Sam. 2:1
Exalt His Amazing Omnipresence .... 1 Kin. 1:29
Act When He Calls .... 2 Kin. 6:17
Trust in His Will .... 1 Chr. 1:1
Hope for Peace .... 2 Chr. 6:3
Exalt His Awesome Mercy .... Esth. 5:1

Believe in the Father .... Job 42:2
Reconcile Wrongs with Rights .... Ps. 13:2
Elevate How You Serve Others .... Prov. 3:5
Act out of Selflessness .... Is. 12:2
Trust in His Ways .... Jer. 12:1
Hope for the Salvation of the Lost .... Ezek. 8:1
Elevate Your Way of Thinking .... Dan. 6:3

Believe in Forgiveness .... Hos. 6:1
Reconcile Separation with Reunion .... Amos 7:4
Exalt His Splendid Omnipotence .... Jon. 2:10
Act as He Does .... Mic. 3:8
Trust in His Wisdom .... Zeph. 3:17
Hope for True Judgments .... Zech. 1:6
Elevate the Steps You Take .... Zech. 10:1

Believe in the Son .... Matt. 7:7
Reconcile Chaos with Peace .... Mark 3:25
Exalt His Immutability .... Luke 1:35
Act in Confidence .... John 14:1
Trust in His Wonder .... Acts 24:10
Hope for Deliverance .... Rom. 5:5
Elevate Your Identity .... 1 Cor. 2:13

Believe in the Resurrection Life .... 2 Cor. 1:10
Reconcile Sins with Righteousness .... Gal. 4:8
Elevate the Love You Share .... Eph. 3:17
Act with Self-Control .... Eph. 6:12
Trust in His Warmth .... Col. 4:5
Hope for What We Do Not See .... 2 Thess. 3:13
Exalt His Mighty Name .... 1 Tim. 1:17

Believe in the Holy Spirit .... Titus 3:5
Reconcile Darkness with Light .... Heb. 3:12
Exalt His Splendid Omniscience .... James 2:8
Act Like His Chosen .... 1 Pet. 2:9
Trust in His World .... 1 John 2:17
Hope for the Lord .... 2 John 1:3
Elevate Your Time with Him .... Rev. 1:9

Life Support

Be Devoted: Believe God.......Deut. 28:1
Be Righteous: Pursue Righteousness and Justice.......Ps. 89:14
Be Persistent: Chase After God.......Eccl. 1:14
Be Caring: Have a Heart for Others.......Lam. 2:11
Be Patient: Wait on the Lord.......Hos. 12:6
Be a Giver: Open Your Hand to the Poor.......Matt. 25:40
Be Holy: Regard Others from an Eternal Perspective.......2 Cor. 5:16
Be a Leader: Unify the Body of Christ.......Eph. 1:3
Be Unmovable: Stick with God's Plan in the Midst of Suffering.......Heb. 10:23
Be Open: Lift Every Nation, Tribe, and Tongue.......Rev. 7:9

#Oxygen

Believe in the Promise.......Gen. 1:3; 39:2
Reconcile Hurt with Healing.......Ex. 2:7; 23:25
Exalt His Guiding Light.......Lev. 22:32; 26:3
Act in Faith.......Num. 9:19; 23:19
Trust in His Word.......Deut. 5:32; 31:6
Hope for Today.......Josh. 4:23; 21:45
Elevate the Stands You Take.......Judg. 16:30; Ruth 2:12

Believe in Prayer.......1 Sam. 1:10; 12:15
Reconcile Weaknesses with Strength.......2 Sam. 6:14; 21:10
Exalt His Amazing Omnipresence.......1 Kin. 11:4; 18:37
Act When He Calls.......2 Kin. 1:15; 19:6
Trust in His Will.......1 Chr. 4:10; 28:20
Hope for Peace.......2 Chr. 15:15; 20:17
Exalt His Awesome Mercy.......Neh. 1:11; 13:2

Believe in the Father.......Job 2:9; 13:15
Reconcile Wrongs with Rights.......Pss. 41:5; 91:9
Elevate How You Serve Others.......Prov. 22:9; Eccl. 4:12
Act out of Selflessness.......Is. 41:6; 58:7
Trust in His Ways.......Jer. 17:7; 29:11
Hope for the Salvation of the Lost.......Ezek. 18:31; 34:11
Elevate Your Way of Thinking.......Dan. 1:12; 3:17

Believe in Forgiveness.......Hos. 4:6; 11:8
Reconcile Separation with Reunion.......Joel 3:11; Amos 5:24
Exalt His Splendid Omnipotence.......Obad. 1:2; Jon. 3:10
Act as He Does.......Mic. 4:2; 7:7
Trust in His Wisdom.......Nah. 1:7; Zeph. 1:18
Hope for True Judgments.......Zech. 2:9; 14:1
Elevate the Steps You Take.......Mal. 1:11; 3:17

Believe in the Son.......Matt. 11:28; 17:20
Reconcile Chaos with Peace.......Mark 4:39; 14:6
Exalt His Immutability.......Luke 10:27; 18:38
Act in Confidence.......John 9:25; 16:33
Trust in His Wonder.......Acts 9:40; 22:14
Hope for Deliverance.......Rom. 7:24; 15:31
Elevate Your Identity.......1 Cor. 4:4; 16:13

Believe in the Resurrection Life.......2 Cor. 11:23; 13:11
Reconcile Sins with Righteousness.......Gal. 1:10; 6:10
Elevate the Love You Share.......Eph. 2:10; 5:2
Act with Self-Control.......Phil. 1:27; 3:13
Trust in His Warmth.......Col. 2:6; 3:16
Hope for What We Do Not See.......1 Thess. 2:18; 2 Thess. 1:7
Exalt His Mighty Name.......1 Tim. 2:3; 5:6

Believe in the Holy Spirit.......2 Tim. 1:14; Titus 3:5
Reconcile Darkness with Light.......Heb. 2:9; 12:11
Exalt His Splendid Omniscience.......James 3:17; 5:12
Act Like His Chosen.......1 Pet. 1:3; 3:8
Trust in His World.......2 Pet. 2:9; 3:9

Hope for the Lord .... 1 John 3:3; 5:21
Elevate Your Time with Him .... Rev. 3:20; 14:12

Release
Believe in the Promise: *The Gift of Belief* .... Gen. 15:5
Reconcile Hurt with Healing: *From Hurt to Healing* .... Ex. 15:23
Exalt His Guiding Light: *Love Our City* .... Lev. 19:15
Act in Faith: *Carrying Out Assignments* .... Num. 4:15
Trust in His Word: *Ever-Increasing Faith* .... Deut. 1:32
Hope for Today: *Trust the Process* .... Josh. 1:9
Elevate the Stands You Take: *Faithfulness for the Fight* .... Judg. 4:23

Believe in Prayer: *Simple, Yet Powerful* .... 1 Sam. 7:7
Reconcile Weaknesses with Strength: *Victory over Weaknesses* .... 2 Sam. 7:18
Exalt His Amazing Omnipresence: *God Sees You* .... 1 Kin. 9:3
Act When He Calls: *The Importance of Obedience* .... 2 Kin. 17:15
Trust in His Will: *My Future in Him* .... 1 Chr. 17:8
Hope for Peace: *The Wisdom of Shalom* .... 2 Chr. 1:10
Exalt His Awesome Mercy: *Breaking the Patterns* .... Neh. 9:30

Believe in the Father: *Our Sustaining Father* .... Job 8:8
Reconcile Wrongs with Rights: *Let's Settle It* .... Ps. 33:5
Elevate How You Serve Others: *Service with Your Scepter* .... Prov. 31:8
Act out of Selflessness: *Develop a Servant's Heart* .... Is. 42:2
Trust in His Ways: *His Ways Are Higher* .... Is. 55:9
Hope for the Salvation of the Lost: *Salvation Is Our Hope* .... Ezek. 16:49
Elevate Your Way of Thinking: *Discernment of His Divine Assignment* .... Dan. 5:29

Believe in Forgiveness: *Making the Tough Choice* .... Hos. 14:4
Reconcile Separation with Reunion: *Reunited and I Feel So Good* .... Joel 2:12
Exalt His Splendid Omnipotence: *Good Will Win* .... Obad. 1:17
Act as He Does: *Justice and Mercy* .... Mic. 6:8
Trust in His Wisdom: *The Journey to Transformation* .... Zech. 4:6
Hope for True Judgments: *Hope for Justice for All* .... Zech. 7:9
Elevate the Steps You Take: *In the End, We Win!* .... Mal. 4:2

Believe in the Son: *That "It" Factor* .... Matt. 3:13
Reconcile Chaos with Peace: *Do Not Allow Unbelief to Steal Your Peace* .... Mark 9:23
Exalt His Immutability: *God Will Not Change on You* .... Luke 6:46
Act in Confidence: *Boosting Confidence* .... John 6:41
Trust in His Wonder: *Wonders and Signs* .... Acts 2:43
Hope for Deliverance: *Give It to God* .... Rom. 12:19
Elevate Your Identity: *From Sinners to Servants* .... 1 Cor. 7:17

Believe in the Resurrection Life: *Dying to Live* .... 2 Cor. 4:11
Reconcile Sins with Righteousness: *We Must Love Others* .... Gal. 5:14
Elevate the Love You Share: *Shine Your Light with Love* .... Eph. 4:1
Act with Self-Control: *Winning Inward Battles* .... Phil. 2:5
Trust in His Warmth: *The Only Place of Comfort* .... Col. 1:13
Hope for What We Do Not See: *A Failure Is Not a Fatality* .... 1 Thess. 5:16
Exalt His Mighty Name: *God over Money* .... 1 Tim. 6:17

Believe in the Holy Spirit: *Never Alone* .... 2 Tim. 3:14
Reconcile Faith with Maturity: *Maturing in Christ* .... Heb. 6:1
Exalt His Splendid Omniscience: *God's Plan* .... James 1:5
Act Like His Chosen: *Spiritual Identity* .... 1 Pet. 2:9
Trust in His World: *Live from Another Place* .... 2 Pet. 1:3
Hope for the Lord: *God's Love Has "Receipts"* .... 1 John 4:17
Elevate Your Time with Him: *Accept the Invitation* .... Rev. 22:17

We Speak
I Am Canaan .... Gen. 10:15
I Am Joseph .... Gen. 45:5
I Am Moses .... Ex. 10:3
I Am Aaron .... Lev. 8:12
I Am Miriam .... Num. 12:1
I Am Joshua .... Josh. 3:7

I Am Gideon . . . . . Judg. 6:13
I Am Ruth . . . . . Ruth 1:16
I Am Samuel. . . . . 1 Sam. 8:19
I Am Nathan. . . . . 2 Sam. 12:13
I Am Joab . . . . . 1 Kin. 2:5
I Am Elijah . . . . . 2 Kin. 2:9
I Am David . . . . . 1 Chr. 14:2
I Am the Queen of Sheba . . . . . 2 Chr. 9:1
I Am Cyrus . . . . . Ezra 1:2
I Am Nehemiah. . . . . Neh. 2:17
I Am Mordecai. . . . . Esth. 4:14
I Am Job . . . . . Job 1:21
I Am Solomon . . . . . Prov. 1:7
I Am the Shulamite Woman . . . . . Song 4:7
I Am Isaiah . . . . . Is. 1:17
I Am Ebed-Melech . . . . . Jer. 39:17
I Am Ezekiel . . . . . Ezek. 33:8
I Am Nebuchadnezzar. . . . . Dan. 4:37
I Am Daniel. . . . . Dan. 12:4
I Am Joel . . . . . Joel 1:1
I Am Amos . . . . . Amos 3:1
I Am Jonah . . . . . Jon. 4:1
I Am Micah . . . . . Mic. 1:2
I Am Habakkuk . . . . . Hab. 2:3
I Am Zephaniah. . . . . Zeph. 2:3
I Am Zechariah . . . . . Zech. 8:8
I Am Malachi . . . . . Mal. 2:10
I Am Simon of Cyrene . . . . . Matt. 27:32
I Am a Jewish Religious Leader . . . . . Mark 7:7
I Am John the Baptist . . . . . Luke 3:4
I Am Mary Magdalene. . . . . John 20:1
I Am Paul. . . . . Acts 16:37
We Are the Church at Corinth . . . . . 2 Cor. 7:9
I Am Barnabas. . . . . Gal. 2:1
We Are Euodia and Syntyche. . . . . Phil. 4:2
I Am Silas . . . . . 1 Thess. 1:1
I Am Timothy. . . . . 1 Tim. 4:12
I Am Titus . . . . . 2 Tim. 4:10
I Am Onesimus . . . . . Philem. 1:15
I Am James. . . . . James 4:10
I Am Peter. . . . . 1 Pet. 5:1
I Am a False Teacher . . . . . Jude 1:4
I Am John . . . . . Rev. 10:11

TABLE OF MONIES, WEIGHTS, AND MEASURES

The Hebrews probably first used coins in the Persian period (500–350 BC). However, minting began around 700 BC in other nations. Prior to this, precious metals were weighed, not counted as money. Thus, some units appear as both measures of money and measures of weights with the naming of these coins deriving from their weight. For example, the shekel was a weight long before it became the name of a coin. It is helpful to relate biblical monies to current values, but exact equivalents cannot be made. The fluctuating value of money's purchasing power is difficult to determine in our own day. It is even harder to evaluate currencies used two- to three-thousand years ago. Therefore, it is best to choose a value meaningful over time, such as a common laborer's daily wage. One day's wage corresponds to the ancient Jewish system (a silver shekel is four days' wages) as well as to the Greek and Roman systems (the drachma and the denarius were each coins representing a day's wage). The monies chart below takes a current day's wage as thirty-two dollars. Though there are differences of economies and standards of living, this measure will help us apply meaningful values to the monetary units in the chart and in the biblical text.

MONIES

UNIT	MONETARY VALUE	EQUIVALENTS	TRANSLATIONS
JEWISH			
Talent	gold—$5,760,000[1] silver—$384,000	3,000 shekels; 6,000 bekas	talent
Shekel	gold—$1,920 silver—$128	4 days' wages; 2 bekas; 20 gerahs	shekel
Beka	gold—$960 silver—$64	1/2 shekel; 10 gerahs	bekah
Gerah	gold—$96 silver—$6.40	1/20 shekel	gerah
PERSIAN			
Daric	gold—$1,280[2] silver—$64	2 days' wages; 1/2 Jewish silver shekel	daric, drachma
GREEK			
Tetradrachma (Stater)	$128	4 drachmas	piece of money
Didrachma	$64	2 drachmas	tribute
Drachma	$32	1 day's wage	piece of silver, coin
Lepton	$.25	1/2 of a Roman kodrantes	mite
ROMAN			
Aureus	$800	25 denarii	gold
Denarius	$32	1 day's wage	denarius
Assarius	$2	1/16 of a denarius	copper coin
Kodrantes	$0.50	1/4 of an assarius	penny

[1] Value of gold is fifteen times the value of silver. [2] Value of gold is twenty times the value of silver.

WEIGHTS

UNIT	WEIGHT	EQUIVALENTS	TRANSLATIONS
JEWISH			
Talent	c. 75 pounds for common talent, c. 150 pounds for royal talent	60 minas; 3,000 shekels	talent
Mina	1.25 pounds	50 shekels	mina

WEIGHTS *continued*

Unit	Weight	Equivalents	Translations
Shekel	c. 0.4 ounce (11.4 grams) for common shekel, c. 0.8 ounce for royal shekel	2 bekas; 20 gerahs	shekel
Beka	c. 0.2 ounce (5.7 grams)	½ shekel; 10 gerahs	half a shekel
Gerah	c. .02 ounce (0.57 grams)	1/20 shekel	gerah
Roman			
Litra	12 ounces		pound

MEASURES OF LENGTH

Unit	Length	Equivalents	Translations
Day's journey	c. 20 miles		day's journey
Roman mile	4,854 feet	8 stadia	mile
Sabbath day's journey	3,637 feet	6 stadia	Sabbath day's journey
Stadion	606 feet	⅛ Roman mile	furlong
Rod	9 feet (10.5 feet in Ezekiel)	3 paces; 6 cubits	measuring reed, reed
Fathom	6 feet	4 cubits	fathom
Pace	3 feet	⅓ rod; 2 cubits	pace
Cubit	18 inches	½ pace; 2 spans	cubit
Span	9 inches	½ cubit; 3 handbreadths	span
Handbreadth	3 inches	⅓ span; 4 fingers	handbreadth
Finger	0.75 inches	¼ handbreadth	finger

DRY MEASURES

Unit	Measure	Equivalents	Translations
Homer	6.52 bushels	10 ephahs	homer
Kor	6.52 bushels	1 homer; 10 ephahs	kor, measure
Lethech	3.26 bushels	½ kor	half homer
Ephah	0.65 bushel, 20.8 quarts	1/10 homer	ephah
Modius	7.68 quarts		bushel
Seah	7 quarts	⅓ ephah	measure
Omer	2.08 quarts	1/10 ephah; 1 4/5 kab	omer
Kab	1.16 quarts	4 logs	kab
Choenix	1 quart		measure
Xestes	1 1/16 pints		pot
Log	0.58 pint	¼ kab	log

LIQUID MEASURES

Unit	Measure	Equivalents	Translations
Kor	60 gallons	10 baths	kor
Metretes	10.2 gallons		gallon
Bath	6 gallons	6 hins	measure, bath
Hin	1 gallon	2 kabs	hin
Kab	2 quarts	4 logs	kab
Log	1 pint	¼ kab	log

THE PARABLES OF JESUS CHRIST

PARABLE	MATTHEW	MARK	LUKE
1. Lamp Under a Basket	5:14–16	4:21–22	8:16–17, 11:33–36
2. A Wise Man Builds on Rock and a Foolish Man Builds on Sand	7:24–27		6:47–49
3. Unshrunk (New) Cloth on an Old Garment	9:16	2:21	5:36
4. New Wine in Old Wineskins	9:17	2:22	5:37–38
5. The Sower	13:3–23	4:2–20	8:4–15
6. The Tares (Weeds)	13:24–30		
7. The Mustard Seed	13:31–32	4:30–32	13:18–19
8. The Leaven	13:33		13:20–21
9. The Hidden Treasure	13:44		
10. The Pearl of Great Price	13:45–46		
11. The Dragnet	13:47–50		
12. The Lost Sheep	18:12–14		15:3–7
13. The Unforgiving Servant	18:23–35		
14. The Laborers in the Vineyard	20:1–16		
15. The Two Sons	21:28–32		
16. The Wicked Vinedressers	21:33–45	12:1–12	20:9–19
17. The Wedding Feast	22:2–14		
18. The Fig Tree	24:32–44	13:28–32	21:29–33
19. The Wise and Foolish Virgins	25:1–13		
20. The Talents	25:14–30		
21. The Growing Seed		4:26–29	
22. The Absent Householder		13:33–37	
23. The Creditor and Two Debtors			7:41–43
24. The Good Samaritan			10:30–37
25. A Friend in Need			11:5–13
26. The Rich Fool			12:16–21
27. The Faithful Servant and the Evil Servant			12:35–40
28. Faithful and Wise Steward			12:42–48
29. The Barren Fig Tree			13:6–9
30. The Great Supper			14:16–24
31. Building a Tower and a King Making War			14:25–35
32. The Lost Coin			15:8–10
33. The Prodigal Son			15:11–32
34. The Unjust Steward			16:1–13
35. The Rich Man and Lazarus			16:19–31
36. Unprofitable Servants			17:7–10
37. The Persistent Widow			18:1–8
38. The Pharisee and the Tax Collector			18:9–14
39. The Minas (Pounds)			19:11–27

THE MIRACLES OF JESUS CHRIST

MIRACLE	MATTHEW	MARK	LUKE	JOHN
1. Leper cleansed	8:2–3	1:40–42	5:12–13	
2. Centurion's servant healed from sickness	8:5–6, 13		7:2–3, 10	
3. Peter's mother-in-law healed from fever	8:14–15	1:30–31	4:38–39	
4. Demons cast out and sick healed	8:16	1:32–34	4:40	
5. Storm calmed	8:26	4:39	8:24	
6. Demons cast out of a man and into a herd of swine	8:31–32	5:12–13	8:32–33	
7. Paralyzed man healed	9:6–7	2:11–12	5:24–25	
8. Ruler's daughter raised back to life	9:25	5:41–42	8:54–55	
9. Woman with a flow of blood healed	9:20–22	5:27–29	8:43–44	
10. Two blind men healed	9:27–30			
11. Demon-possessed, mute man healed	9:32–33			
12. Man with a withered hand healed	12:13	3:5	6:10	
13. Demon-possessed, blind, mute man healed	12:22		11:14	
14. Over five thousand fed	14:19–21	6:41–44	9:16–17	6:11–14
15. Walks on water and calms a storm	14:25, 32	6:48, 51		6:19
16. Gentile's demon-possessed daughter healed	15:28	7:29–30		
17. Over four thousand fed	15:36–38	8:6–9		
18. Demon-possessed boy healed	17:18	9:25–27	9:42	
19. Temple tax in the fish's mouth	17:27			
20. Two blind men healed	20:33–34	10:52	18:42–43	
21. Fig tree withers	21:19	11:13–14		
22. Demon cast out of a man		1:25–26	4:35	
23. Deaf, mute man healed		7:35		
24. Blind man healed		8:25		
25. Passes through crowd			4:30	
26. Great catch of fish			5:6	
27. Widow's son raised to life			7:14–15	
28. Infirm woman with bad back healed			13:12–13	
29. Man with dropsy healed			14:4	
30. Ten lepers cleansed			17:14–15	
31. Servant's severed ear restored			22:51	
32. Water turns into wine				2:7–9
33. Nobleman's son healed				4:50–51
34. Infirm man healed				5:8–9
35. Man born blind healed				9:6–7
36. Lazarus is raised to life				11:43–44
37. Great catch of fish				21:6

PRAYERS OF THE BIBLE

Abandonment
Jesus—by the Father .... Matt. 27:46

Blessing
Priests and Levites—of God's people .... 2 Chr. 30:27
Paul—in Romans .... Rom. 12:33–36
Paul—in Romans .... Rom. 16:25–27
Paul—in Ephesians .... Eph. 3:20–21
Paul—in Philippians .... Phil. 4:20
Writer—in Hebrews .... Heb. 13:20–21
Peter—in 1 Peter .... 1 Peter 5:10–11
Peter—in 2 Peter .... 2 Peter 3:18
Jude—in Jude .... Jude 1:24–25

Children
Abraham—because of barrenness .... Gen. 15:2–3
Abraham—for Ishmael .... Gen. 17:18–21
Isaac—because of barrenness .... Gen. 25:21
Hannah—because of barrenness .... 1 Sam. 1:10–17
Zechariah—because of barrenness .... Luke 1:13

Confession
Ezra—of the people's sin of intermarriage .... Ezra 9:6–15
Priests and Levites—of the people's history of sins .... Neh. 9:4–38
David—of his sins against Bathsheba and Uriah .... Ps 51:1–19
Daniel—of the people's sin of rebellion .... Dan. 9:3–19

Deliverance
Jacob—from Esau .... Gen. 32:9–12
Israelites—from captivity .... Ex. 2:23–25; 3:7–10
Moses—of Egypt from plague .... Ex. 8:9–13
Samuel—from the Philistines .... 1 Sam. 7:5–8
Jehoahaz—from the Syrians .... 2 Kin. 13:4–5
Hezekiah—from the Assyrians .... 2 Kin. 19:15–19
Jehoshaphat—from several enemies .... 2 Chr. 20:5–12
Manasseh—from the Assyrians .... 2 Chr. 33:12–13
Isaiah—from affliction .... Is. 33:1–9
Isaiah—from adversaries .... Is. 64:1–12
Daniel and his companions—from execution .... Dan. 2:16–18
Jonah—from the fish .... Jon. 2:1–10
Habakkuk—from invasion .... Hab. 3:1–16
Jesus—from the cup .... Matt. 26:39, 42, 44
Church—of Peter from prison .... Acts 12:5
Corinthians—of Paul from suffering .... 2 Cor. 1:9–11
Paul—from the thorn in the flesh .... 2 Cor. 12:7–9

Forgiveness
David—of his sin .... Ps. 25:1–22
Isaiah—of the people's straying .... Is. 63:15–19
Jesus—of those who crucified Him .... Luke 23:34
Stephen—of those stoning him .... Acts 7:60
Paul—of Israel for salvation .... Rom. 10:1

God's Glory
Moses—to see it .... Ex. 33:18
Elijah—to be known .... 1 Kin. 18:36–38
Jesus—to be known .... John 12:28
Jesus—to be experienced .... John 17:1–5

Guidance

Abraham's servant—in finding Isaac's bride .... Gen. 24:12–14
Moses—in God's leading .... Ex. 33:15–17
Gideon—in proving his calling .... Judg. 6:36–40
Manoah—in raising Samson .... Judg. 13:8
David—in going to Hebron .... 2 Sam. 2:1
Jeremiah—in how the people are to live .... Jer. 42:4
Cornelius—in sending for Peter .... Acts 10:1–5
Peter—in going to Cornelius .... Acts 10:9, 19–20

Healing

Moses—for Miriam .... Num. 12:11–13
Hezekiah—for himself .... 2 Kin. 20:2–3
Leper—for himself .... Matt. 8:2–3
Paul—for Publius's father .... Acts 28:8

Justice

David—for the wicked .... Ps. 9:17–20
Jeremiah—for his oppressors .... Is. 20:7–18
Habakkuk—for the wicked .... Hab. 1:1–4

Mercy

Cain—after killing Abel .... Gen. 4:13–15
Abraham—for Sodom .... Gen. 18:20–32
Abimelech—after taking Sarah .... Gen. 20:3–5
Abraham—for Abimelech .... Gen. 20:17
Moses—for Israel after the gold calf .... Ex. 32:31–32
Moses—for Israel after not entering Canaan .... Num. 14:11–19
Joshua—after defeat at Ai .... Josh. 7:6–9
Jeremiah—in coming judgment .... Jer. 14:7–10
Habakkuk—in coming judgment .... Hab. 3:2
Tax collector—in a parable about humility .... Luke 18:13

Provisions and Requests

Hagar—for water .... Gen. 21:14–20
Moses—for water .... Ex. 15:24–25
Moses—a successor .... Num. 27:15–17
Moses—to see the Promised Land .... Deut. 3:23–25
Joshua—for the sun to stand still .... Josh. 10:12–13
Samson—for water .... Judg. 15:18–19
Elijah—for death .... 1 Kin. 19:4
Elisha—for blindness and sight .... 2 Kin. 6:17–23
Jabez—for prosperity .... 1 Chr. 4:10
Jews—for protection on a journey .... Ezra 8:21, 23
Nehemiah—for success before the king .... Neh. 1:4–11
Ezekiel—for undefilement .... Ezek. 4:12–15
Disciples—for boldness .... Acts 4:24–31
Paul—to see the church in Rome .... Rom. 1:8–12
Elijah—for drought and rain .... James 5:17–18
John—for the church to prosper .... 3 John 1:2

Resurrection

Elijah—of the widow's son .... 1 Kin. 17:20–23
Peter—of Dorcas .... Acts 9:40

Spiritual Maturity

Jesus—for sanctification of the disciples .... John 17:6–19
Jesus—for unity of all believers .... John 17:6–19
Holy Spirit—for Christians in prayer .... Rom. 8:26–27
Paul—for the Corinthians to do no evil .... 2 Cor. 13:7–9
Paul—for the Ephesians' spiritual wisdom .... Eph. 1:8–21
Paul—for the Ephesians' spiritual growth .... Eph. 3:14–21
Paul—for the Philippians' spiritual growth .... Phil. 1:9–11
Paul—for the Colossians' spiritual understanding .... Col. 1:3–14
Paul—for the Thessalonians' love .... 1 Thess. 3:11–13

Submission

Solomon—to God's covenant .... 1 Kin. 8:22–53

People of Judah—to God's covenant ... 2 Chr. 15:14–15
Jesus—of His life ... Luke 23:46
Stephen—of His life ... Acts 7:59

Teachings On

Jesus—in secret ... Matt. 6:6
Jesus—with sincerity ... Matt. 6:7
Jesus—properly ... Matt. 6:9–13
Jesus—in faith ... Matt. 21:22; Mark 11:24
Jesus—to escape temptation ... Matt. 26:41
Jesus—for enemies ... Luke 6:27–28
Jesus—not to lose heart ... Luke 18:1–8
Paul—through the Spirit ... Rom. 8:26
Paul—without ceasing ... Rom. 12:12; Eph. 6:18; 1 Thess. 5:17
Paul—with supplication ... Eph. 6:18; 1 Tim. 2:1–4
Paul—for others ... Eph. 6:18; 1 Tim. 2:1–4
Paul—for all things ... Phil. 4:6
Paul—with Thanksgiving ... Phil. 4:6; Col 4:2; 1 Tim. 2:1–4
Paul—steadfastly ... Col. 4:2
Paul—for kings in authority ... 1 Tim. 2:1–2
John—according to God's will ... 1 John 5:14–15
James—for the suffering ... James 5:13
James—to confess sin ... James 5:16
James—in power ... James 5:16

Thanksgiving

Moses and Israel—for God's deliverance ... Ex. 15:1–18
Hannah—for providing a son ... 1 Sam. 2:1–10
David—for God's covenant ... 2 Sam. 7:18–29
David—for deliverance ... 2 Sam. 22:1–51
David—for temple provisions ... 1 Chr. 29:10–20
Simeon—for seeing salvation ... Luke 2:29–32
Jesus—for the Father's hearing ... John 11:41–42
Paul—for the Corinthians ... 1 Cor. 1:4–9
Paul—for the Thessalonians ... 1 Thess. 1:2–3
Paul—for the Thessalonians ... 2 Thess. 1:3
Paul—for Timothy ... 2 Tim. 1:3–4
Paul—for Philemon ... Philem. 1:4–6

Victory

Reubenites—over the Hagrites ... 1 Chr. 5:18–20
Abijah's army—over the Israelites ... 2 Chr. 13:14
Asa—over the Ethiopians ... 2 Chr. 14:11
Jehoshaphat—over the Israelites ... 2 Chr. 18:31

Wisdom and Knowledge

Rebekah—concerning her pregnancy ... Gen. 25:22–23
David—concerning a threat ... 1 Sam. 23:10–13
Solomon—concerning how to lead ... 1 Kin. 3:6–9
Daniel—concerning interpreting a dream ... Dan. 2:20–23
Jesus—concerning His teachings ... Matt. 11:25–26

NKJV CONCORDANCE

This concordance indexes over 3,500 words with over 9,200 context lines from verses in which they are used in the NKJV. Words are referenced with Scripture quotations, in which the first letter of the word, bolded and italicized, stands for the entire word. The first number in parenthesis following each heading indicates the times that word appears in the Bible. The second number indicates the number of verses in which it appears.

A

ABASED (1/1)
I know how to be ***a***. . . . . .Phil. 4:12
ABBA (3/3)
And He said, "***A***. . . . . .Mark 14:36
by whom we cry out, "***A*** . . . . .Rom. 8:15
ABHOR (21/20)
Therefore I ***a*** myself . . . . Job 42:6
ABHORRED (12/12)
a His own inheritance . . . . .Ps. 106:40
ABIDE (36/32)
LORD, who may ***a*** . . . . .Ps. 15:1
"If you ***a*** in My word . . . . John 8:31
If you ***a*** in Me. . . . . John 15:7
a in My love . . . . John 15:9
ABIDES (26/24)
He who ***a*** in Me. . . . . John 15:5
will of God ***a*** forever . . . . 1 John 2:17
ABIDING (2/2)
not have His word ***a***. . . . . .John 5:38
ABILITY (11/10)
according to his own ***a*** . . . . Matt. 25:15
a which God supplies . . . . 1 Pet. 4:11
ABLE (167/163)
For who is ***a*** to judge . . . . .1 Kin. 3:9
God whom we serve is ***a*** . . . . .Dan. 3:17
God is ***a*** to raise up . . . . .Matt. 3:9
fear Him who is ***a***. . . . . .Matt. 10:28
Are you ***a*** to drink the. . . . . Matt. 20:22
persuaded that He is ***a*** . . . . 2 Tim. 1:12
learning and never ***a***. . . . . .2 Tim. 3:7
that God was ***a*** to . . . . .Heb. 11:19
ABOLISHED (4/4)
having ***a*** in His flesh . . . . .Eph. 2:15
Christ, who has ***a*** . . . . 2 Tim. 1:10
ABOMINABLE (21/21)
they deny Him, being ***a*** . . . . Titus 1:16
unbelieving, ***a***, murderers. . . . . . . Rev. 21:8
ABOMINATION (78/71)
yes, seven are an ***a***. . . . . .Prov. 6:16
even his prayer is an ***a*** . . . . .Prov. 28:9
and place there the ***a***. . . . . .Dan. 11:31
the ***a*** of desolation. . . . . .Dan. 12:11
the '***a*** of desolation,' . . . . Matt. 24:15
ABOMINATIONS (75/73)
delights in their ***a***. . . . . Is. 66:3
a golden cup full of ***a***. . . . . Rev. 17:4
ABOUND (21/19)
the offense might ***a*** . . . . Rom. 5:20
sin that grace may ***a*** . . . . Rom. 6:1
to make all grace ***a***. . . . . 2 Cor. 9:8
and I know how to ***a*** . . . . .Phil. 4:12
ABOUNDED (6/5)
But where sin ***a***. . . . . Rom. 5:20
ABOUNDING (6/6)
immovable, always ***a***. . . . . .1 Cor. 15:58
ABOVE (234/221)
that is in heaven ***a*** . . . . .Ex. 20:4
A it stood seraphim. . . . . Is. 6:2
He who comes from ***a***. . . . . John 3:31
beneath; I am from ***a*** . . . . .John 8:23
been given you from ***a*** . . . . .John 19:11
things which are ***a*** . . . . Col. 3:1
perfect gift is from ***a*** . . . . James 1:17
ABSENT (11/11)
in the body we are ***a***. . . . . 2 Cor. 5:6
ABSTAIN (8/8)
we write to them to ***a***. . . . . .Acts 15:20
A from every form . . . . 1 Thess. 5:22
ABUNDANCE (79/77)
put in out of their ***a*** . . . . Mark 12:44
not consist in the ***a*** . . . . .Luke 12:15
ABUNDANT (23/23)
in labors more ***a***. . . . . .2 Cor. 11:23
ABUNDANTLY (23/23)
a satisfied with the. . . . . .Ps. 36:8
may have it more ***a*** . . . . John 10:10
to do exceedingly ***a*** . . . . Eph. 3:20
ACCEPT (35/33)
offering, I will not ***a***. . . . . .Jer. 14:12
Should I ***a*** this from . . . . Mal. 1:13
ACCEPTABLE (24/24)
a time I have heard . . . . Is. 49:8
proclaim the ***a*** year . . . . .Is. 61:2
proclaim the ***a*** year . . . . Luke 4:19
is that good and ***a***. . . . . .Rom. 12:2
ACCEPTABLY (1/1)
we may serve God ***a***. . . . . Heb. 12:28
ACCEPTED (26/26)
Behold, now is the ***a*** . . . . 2 Cor. 6:2
by which He made us ***a***. . . . . .Eph. 1:6
ACCESS (4/4)
we have ***a*** by faith. . . . . .Rom. 5:2
ACCOMPLISHED (16/16)
all things were now ***a***. . . . . John 19:28
ACCORD (22/22)
continued with one ***a*** . . . . Acts 1:14
ACCOUNT (28/28)
they will give ***a*** of it . . . . .Matt. 12:36
put that on my ***a***. . . . . .Philem. 1:18
ACCOUNTED (14/14)
and He ***a*** it to him . . . . .Gen. 15:6
his faith is ***a*** for. . . . . .Rom. 4:5
and it was ***a*** to him. . . . . Gal. 3:6
and it was ***a*** to him. . . . . .James 2:23
ACCURSED (24/20)
not know the law is ***a***. . . . . .John 7:49
calls Jesus ***a***, and no . . . . .1 Cor. 12:3
let him be ***a*** . . . . Gal. 1:8
ACCUSATION (12/12)
over His head the ***a*** . . . . .Matt. 27:37
they might find an ***a*** . . . . Luke 6:7
ACCUSE (13/13)
they began to ***a*** Him . . . . Luke 23:2
ACCUSED (13/13)
while He was being ***a***. . . . . Matt. 27:12
ACCUSER (2/2)
a of our brethren . . . . Rev. 12:10
ACCUSING (1/1)
their thoughts ***a*** or else . . . . Rom. 2:15
ACKNOWLEDGE (15/15)
a my transgressions . . . . Ps. 51:3
in all your ways ***a*** . . . . Prov. 3:6
ACKNOWLEDGES (3/3)
he who ***a*** the Son has. . . . . .1 John 2:23
ACQUAINT (1/1)
a yourself with Him. . . . . Job 22:21
ACQUAINTED (2/2)
a Man of sorrows and ***a*** . . . . Is. 53:3
ACQUIT (3/3)
at all ***a*** the wicked. . . . . .Nah. 1:3
ACT (24/23)
adultery, in the very ***a***. . . . . .John 8:4
ACTIONS (1/1)
by Him ***a*** are weighed. . . . . .1 Sam. 2:3
ACTS (74/72)
of Your awesome ***a***. . . . . Ps. 145:6
ADD (34/34)
Do not ***a*** to His words . . . . .Prov. 30:6
ADDED (19/19)
And the Lord ***a*** to the . . . . .Acts 2:47
It was ***a*** because of. . . . . Gal. 3:19
ADMONISH (5/5)
a him as a brother . . . . 2 Thess. 3:15
ADMONITION (3/3)
were written for our ***a***. . . . . 1 Cor. 10:11
in the training and ***a*** . . . . Eph. 6:4
ADOPTION (5/5)
received the Spirit of ***a*** . . . . .Rom. 8:15
waiting for the ***a***. . . . . Rom. 8:23
to whom pertain the ***a*** . . . . .Rom. 9:4
ADORN (5/5)
also, that the women ***a*** . . . . 1 Tim. 2:9
ADORNED (13/13)
also ***a*** themselves. . . . . .1 Pet. 3:5
prepared as a bride ***a***. . . . . Rev. 21:2
ADRIFT (1/1)
A among the dead . . . . Ps. 88:5
ADULTERER (3/3)
The eye of the ***a***. . . . . .Job 24:15
ADULTERERS (9/9)
nor idolaters, nor ***a*** . . . . .1 Cor. 6:9
a God will judge . . . . .Heb. 13:4
ADULTEROUS (6/6)
evil and ***a*** generation . . . . .Matt. 12:39
ADULTERY (40/33)
You shall not commit ***a*** . . . . .Ex. 20:14
already committed ***a***. . . . . .Matt. 5:28
is divorced commits ***a*** . . . . .Matt. 5:32
another commits ***a*** . . . . Mark 10:11
those who commit ***a*** . . . . .Rev. 2:22
ADVANTAGE (11/11)
a that I go away. . . . . John 16:7
Satan should take ***a*** . . . . 2 Cor. 2:11
ADVERSARIES (35/35)
and there are many ***a*** . . . . .1 Cor. 16:9
terrified by your ***a*** . . . . .Phil. 1:28
ADVERSARY (21/20)
Agree with your ***a***. . . . . .Matt. 5:25
opportunity to the ***a*** . . . . 1 Tim. 5:14
your ***a*** the devil walks . . . . .1 Pet. 5:8
ADVERSITY (20/20)
I shall never be in ***a*** . . . . Ps. 10:6
the day of ***a*** consider. . . . . .Eccl. 7:14
ADVICE (29/26)
in this I give my ***a***. . . . . 2 Cor. 8:10
ADVOCATE (1/1)
we have an ***A*** with the . . . . .1 John 2:1
AFAR (54/54)
and not a God ***a***. . . . . Jer. 23:23
to you who were ***a*** . . . . .Eph. 2:17
but having seen them ***a*** . . . . Heb. 11:13
AFFAIRS (9/9)
himself with the ***a*** . . . . 2 Tim. 2:4
AFFECTION (4/4)
to his wife the ***a***. . . . . .1 Cor. 7:3
AFFECTIONATE (1/1)
Be kindly ***a*** to one . . . . Rom. 12:10
AFFIRM (4/4)
you to ***a*** constantly . . . . Titus 3:8
AFFLICT (31/30)
a Your heritage . . . . Ps. 94:5
For He does not ***a***. . . . . Lam. 3:33
AFFLICTED (49/48)
To him who is ***a***. . . . . .Job 6:14
hears the cry of the ***a***. . . . . Job 34:28
days of the ***a*** are evil . . . . Prov. 15:15
Smitten by God, and ***a***. . . . . Is. 53:4
oppressed and He was ***a***. . . . . .Is. 53:7
"O you ***a*** one, tossed . . . . Is. 54:11
being destitute, ***a*** . . . . .Heb. 11:37
AFFLICTING (1/1)
A the just and taking. . . . . Amos 5:12
AFFLICTION (68/66)
the bread of ***a*** . . . . .Deut. 16:3
a take hold of me . . . . Job 30:16
and it is an evil ***a***. . . . . Eccl. 6:2
For our light ***a*** . . . . .2 Cor. 4:17
supposing to add ***a*** . . . . Phil. 1:16
AFRAID (216/212)
garden, and I was ***a*** . . . . .Gen. 3:10
saying, "Do not be ***a***. . . . . Gen. 15:1
none will make you ***a*** . . . . .Lev. 26:6
ungodliness made me ***a***. . . . . Ps. 18:4
Whenever I am ***a*** . . . . Ps. 56:3
no one will make them ***a*** . . . . .Is. 17:2
dream which made me ***a*** . . . . Dan. 4:5
It is I; do not be ***a*** . . . . Matt. 14:27
if you do evil, be ***a*** . . . . .Rom. 13:4
do good and are not ***a***. . . . . .1 Pet. 3:6

AFTERWARD (86/86)
a receive me to glory ... Ps. 73:24
you shall follow Me *a* ... John 13:36

AGAIN (428/412)
'You must be born *a* ... John 3:7
having been born *a* ... 1 Pet. 1:23

AGAINST (1,615/1,341)
come to 'set a man *a* ... Matt. 10:35
or house divided *a* ... Matt. 12:25
not with Me is *a* Me ... Matt. 12:30
blasphemy *a* the Spirit ... Matt. 12:31
lifted up his heel *a* ... John 13:18
LORD and *a* His Christ ... Acts 4:26
to kick *a* the goads ... Acts 9:5
a the promises of God ... Gal. 3:21
we do not wrestle *a* ... Eph. 6:12
I have a few things *a* ... Rev. 2:20

AGE (63/60)
the grave at a full *a* ... Job 5:26
and in the *a* to come ... Mark 10:30

AGED (9/9)
a one as Paul, the *a* ... Philem. 1:9

AGES (7/7)
ordained before the *a* ... 1 Cor. 2:7

AGONY (2/2)
And being in *a* ... Luke 22:44

AGREE (9/9)
that if two of you *a* ... Matt. 18:19

AGREED (11/11)
unless they are *a* ... Amos 3:3

AGREEMENT (12/11)
what *a* has the temple ... 2 Cor. 6:16

AIR (43/43)
the birds of the *a* ... Gen. 1:26
of the *a* have nests ... Luke 9:58
of the power of the *a* ... Eph. 2:2
the Lord in the *a* ... 1 Thess. 4:17

ALIENATED (7/6)
darkened, being *a* ... Eph. 4:18
you, who once were *a* ... Col. 1:21

ALIENS (17/17)
A have devoured his ... Hos. 7:9
without Christ, being *a* ... Eph. 2:12

ALIKE (14/14)
esteems every day *a* ... Rom. 14:5

ALIVE (91/89)
I kill and I make *a* ... Deut. 32:39
son was dead and is *a* ... Luke 15:24
presented Himself *a* ... Acts 1:3
dead indeed to sin, but *a* ... Rom. 6:11
all shall be made *a* ... 1 Cor. 15:22
that we who are *a* ... 1 Thess. 4:15
and behold, I am *a* ... Rev. 1:18
These two were cast *a* ... Rev. 19:20

ALLELUIA (4/4)
Again they said, "*A* ... Rev. 19:3

ALLOW (28/28)
a Your Holy One ... Ps. 16:10
a My faithfulness ... Ps. 89:33
a Your Holy One ... Acts 2:27

ALLURE (3/3)
they *a* through the lusts ... 2 Pet. 2:18

ALMOND (9/7)
a tree blossoms ... Eccl. 12:5

ALMOST (10/10)
a persuade me to ... Acts 26:28

ALOES (5/5)
mixture of myrrh and *a* ... John 19:39

ALPHA (4/4)
I am the *A* and the ... Rev. 1:8
I am the *A* and the ... Rev. 22:13

ALTAR (378/322)
Then Noah built an *a* ... Gen. 8:20
An *a* of earth you ... Ex. 20:24
it to you upon the *a* ... Lev. 17:11
your gift to the *a* ... Matt. 5:23
swears by the *a* ... Matt. 23:18
I even found an *a* ... Acts 17:23
We have an *a* from ... Heb. 13:10

ALTARS (63/52)
Even Your *a*, O LORD ... Ps. 84:3
and torn down Your *a* ... Rom. 11:3

ALTERED (2/2)
of His face was *a* ... Luke 9:29

ALWAYS (94/89)
delight, rejoicing *a* ... Prov. 8:30
the poor with you *a* ... Matt. 26:11
lo, I am with you *a* ... Matt. 28:20
men *a* ought to pray ... Luke 18:1
immovable, *a* abounding ... 1 Cor. 15:58
Rejoice in the Lord *a* ... Phil. 4:4
thus we shall *a* ... 1 Thess. 4:17
a be ready to give a ... 1 Pet. 3:15

AM (909/835)
to Moses, "I *A* WHO I *A* ... Ex. 3:14
First and I *a* the Last ... Is. 44:6
in My name, I *a* there ... Matt. 18:20
I *a* the bread of life ... John 6:35
I *a* the light of the ... John 8:12
I *a* from above ... John 8:23
Abraham was, I *A* ... John 8:58
I *a* the door ... John 10:9
I *a* the good shepherd ... John 10:11
I *a* the resurrection ... John 11:25
to him, "I *a* the way ... John 14:6
of God I *a* what I *a* ... 1 Cor. 15:10

AMBASSADOR (3/3)
for which I am an *a* ... Eph. 6:20

AMBASSADORS (7/7)
we are *a* for Christ ... 2 Cor. 5:20

AMBITION (2/2)
Christ from selfish *a* ... Phil. 1:16

AMEN (77/72)
are Yes, and in Him *A* ... 2 Cor. 1:20
creatures said, "*A* ... Rev. 5:14

ANCHOR (1/1)
hope we have as an *a* ... Heb. 6:19

ANCIENT (23/23)
Do not remove the *a* ... Prov. 23:10
until the *A* of Days ... Dan. 7:22

ANGEL (199/190)
"Behold, I send an *A* ... Ex. 23:20
the *A* of His Presence ... Is. 63:9
things, behold, an *a* ... Matt. 1:20
for an *a* of the Lord ... Matt. 28:2
Then an *a* of the Lord ... Luke 1:11
And behold, an *a* ... Luke 2:9
a appeared to Him from ... Luke 22:43
For an *a* went down at ... John 5:4
a has spoken to Him ... John 12:29
But at night an *a* ... Acts 5:19
A who appeared to him ... Acts 7:35
Then immediately an *a* ... Acts 12:23
himself into an *a* ... 2 Cor. 11:14
even if we, or an *a* ... Gal. 1:8
Then I saw a strong *a* ... Rev. 5:2
Jesus, have sent My *a* ... Rev. 22:16

ANGELS (92/90)
If He charges His *a* ... Job 4:18
lower than the *a* ... Ps. 8:5
He shall give His *a* ... Ps. 91:11
He shall give His *a* ... Matt. 4:6
not even the *a* of heaven ... Matt. 24:36
and all the holy *a* ... Matt. 25:31
twelve legions of *a* ... Matt. 26:53
And she saw two *a* ... John 20:12
and worship of *a* ... Col. 2:18
much better than the *a* ... Heb. 1:4
unwittingly entertained *a* ... Heb. 13:2
things which *a* desire ... 1 Pet. 1:12
did not spare the *a* ... 2 Pet. 2:4
a who did not keep ... Jude 1:6

ANGER (233/228)
For His *a* is but for a ... Ps. 30:5
gracious, slow to *a* ... Ps. 103:8
Nor will He keep His *a* ... Ps. 103:9
around at them with *a* ... Mark 3:5
bitterness, wrath, *a* ... Eph. 4:31

ANGRY (92/89)
Cain, "Why are you *a* ... Gen. 4:6
"Let not the LORD be *a* ... Gen. 18:30
the Son, lest He be *a* ... Ps. 2:12
a man stirs up strife ... Prov. 29:22
right for you to be *a* ... Jon. 4:4
you that whoever is *a* ... Matt. 5:22
"Be *a*, and do not sin" ... Eph. 4:26

ANGUISH (25/25)
longer remembers the *a* ... John 16:21
tribulation and *a* ... Rom. 2:9

ANIMAL (45/37)
of every clean *a* ... Gen. 7:2
set him on his own *a* ... Luke 10:34

ANIMALS (39/35)
of *a* after their kind ... Gen. 6:20
of four-footed *a* ... Acts 10:12

ANNUL (3/3)
years later, cannot *a* ... Gal. 3:17

ANNULS (1/1)
is confirmed, no one *a* ... Gal. 3:15

ANOINT (35/34)
a my head with oil ... Ps. 23:5
when you fast, *a* ... Matt. 6:17
a My body for burial ... Mark 14:8
a your eyes with eye ... Rev. 3:18

ANOINTED (101/99)
"Surely the LORD's *a* ... 1 Sam. 16:6
destroy the LORD's *a* ... 2 Sam. 1:14
"Do not touch My *a* ... 1 Chr. 16:22
Because He has *a* ... Luke 4:18
but this woman has *a* ... Luke 7:46
a the eyes of the ... John 9:6
It was that Mary who *a* ... John 11:2
Jesus, whom You *a* ... Acts 4:27
and has *a* us is God ... 2 Cor. 1:21

ANOINTING (27/25)
But you have an *a* ... 1 John 2:20

ANOTHER (442/401)
that you love one *a* ... John 13:34

ANSWER (148/145)
Call, and I will *a* ... Job 13:22
how shall I *a* Him ... Job 31:14
the day that I call, *a* ... Ps. 102:2
In Your faithfulness *a* ... Ps. 143:1
a turns away wrath ... Prov. 15:1
a a fool according ... Prov. 26:4
or what you should *a* ... Luke 12:11
you may have an *a* ... 2 Cor. 5:12

ANT (1/1)
Go to the *a*, you sluggard ... Prov. 6:6

ANTICHRIST (4/4)
heard that the *A* ... 1 John 2:18
a who denies the ... 1 John 2:22
is a deceiver and an *a* ... 2 John 1:7

ANTITYPE (1/1)
a which now saves us ... 1 Pet. 3:21

ANXIETIES (2/2)
the multitude of my *a* ... Ps. 94:19

ANXIETY (4/4)
A in the heart of man ... Prov. 12:25

ANXIOUS (7/7)
Be *a* for nothing ... Phil. 4:6

APART (40/39)
justified by faith *a* ... Rom. 3:28

APOSTLE (19/19)
called to be an *a* ... Rom. 1:1
consider the *A* and High ... Heb. 3:1

APOSTLES (55/54)
names of the twelve *a* ... Matt. 10:2
whom He also named *a* ... Luke 6:13
am the least of the *a* ... 1 Cor. 15:9
none of the other *a* ... Gal. 1:19
gave some to be *a* ... Eph. 4:11

APOSTLESHIP (4/4)
in this ministry and *a* ... Acts 1:25
are the seal of my *a* ... 1 Cor. 9:2

APPAREL (23/22)
gold rings, in fine *a* ... James 2:2
or putting on fine *a* ... 1 Pet. 3:3

APPEAL (6/6)
love's sake I rather *a* ... Philem. 1:9

APPEAR (40/39)
and let the dry land *a* ... Gen. 1:9
also outwardly *a* ... Matt. 23:28
kingdom of God would *a* ... Luke 19:11
For we must all *a* ... 2 Cor. 5:10

APPEARANCE (54/39)
Do not look at his *a* ... 1 Sam. 16:7
judge according to *a* ... John 7:24
those who boast in *a* ... 2 Cor. 5:12
found in *a* as a man ... Phil. 2:8

APPEARED (76/73)
an angel of the Lord *a* ... Luke 1:11
who *a* in glory and ... Luke 9:31
brings salvation has *a* ... Titus 2:11
of the ages, He has *a* ... Heb. 9:26

APPEARING (5/5)
Lord Jesus Christ's *a* ... 1 Tim. 6:14
and the dead at His *a* ... 2 Tim. 4:1
who have loved His *a* ... 2 Tim. 4:8

APPEARS (15/15)
can stand when He *a* ... Mal. 3:2
who is our life *a* ... Col. 3:4
the Chief Shepherd *a* ... 1 Pet. 5:4
in Him, that when He *a* ... 1 John 2:28

APPETITE (2/2)
are a man given to *a* ... Prov. 23:2

APPLE (7/7)
And my law as the *a* ... Prov. 7:2

APPLES (3/3)
fitly spoken is like *a* ... Prov. 25:11

APPLIED (4/4)
a my heart to know ... Eccl. 7:25

APPOINT (40/39)
For God did not *a* ... 1 Thess. 5:9

APPOINTED (152/150)
And as it is *a* for men ... Heb. 9:27

APPROACH (21/20)
year, make those who *a* ... Heb. 10:1

APPROACHING (2/2)
as you see the Day *a* ... Heb. 10:25

APPROVE (7/7)
do the same but also *a* ... Rom. 1:32

APPROVED (9/9)
to God and *a* by men ... Rom. 14:18
to present yourself *a* ... 2 Tim. 2:15

ARBITRATOR (1/1)
a judge or an *a* over ... Luke 12:14

ARCHANGEL (2/2)
with the voice of an *a* ... 1 Thess. 4:16

ARGUMENTS (3/3)
casting down *a* and ... 2 Cor. 10:5

ARISE (142/141)
A, shine; for your light ... Is. 60:1
But the LORD will *a* ... Is. 60:2
you who sleep, *a* ... Eph. 5:14

ARK (229/199)
Make yourself an *a* ... Gen. 6:14
she took an *a* of bulrushes ... Ex. 2:3
Bezalel made the *a* ... Ex. 37:1
of Noah, while the *a* ... 1 Pet. 3:20

ARM (67/62)
with an outstretched *a* ... Ex. 6:6
Have you an *a* like God ... Job 40:9
strength with His *a* ... Luke 1:51

a yourselves also with... 1 Pet. 4:1
ARMED (33/33)
a strong man, fully **a**... Luke 11:21
ARMIES (52/52)
And he sent out his **a**... Matt. 22:7
surrounded by **a**... Luke 21:20
And the **a** in heaven... Rev. 19:14
the earth, and their **a**... Rev. 19:19
ARMOR (30/30)
Put on the whole **a**... Eph. 6:11
ARMS (33/31)
are the everlasting **a**... Deut. 33:27
took Him up in his **a**... Luke 2:28
AROMA (46/45)
To the one we are the **a**... 2 Cor. 2:16
for a sweet-smelling **a**... Eph. 5:2
AROUSED (42/41)
the LORD was greatly **a**... Num. 11:10
Then Joseph, being **a**... Matt. 1:24
ARRAYED (9/9)
his glory was not **a**... Matt. 6:29
"Who are these **a**... Rev. 7:13
ARROGANCE (6/6)
Pride and **a** and the... Prov. 8:13
ARROW (20/18)
a that flies by day... Ps. 91:5
ARROWS (43/41)
a pierce me deeply... Ps. 38:2
Like **a** in the hand of... Ps. 127:4
ASCEND (19/19)
Who may **a** into the... Ps. 24:3
If I **a** into heaven... Ps. 139:8
'I will **a** into heaven... Is. 14:13
see the Son of Man **a**... John 6:62
ASCENDED (17/17)
You have **a** on high... Ps. 68:18
No one has **a** to heaven... John 3:13
"When He **a** on high... Eph. 4:8
ASCENDING (6/6)
the angels of God **a**... John 1:51
ASCRIBE (3/3)
A strength to God... Ps. 68:34
ASHAMED (117/105)
Let me not be **a**... Ps. 25:2
And Israel shall be **a**... Hos. 10:6
For whoever is **a**... Mark 8:38
am not **a** of the gospel... Rom. 1:16
Therefore God is not **a**... Heb. 11:16
ASHES (43/41)
become like dust and **a**... Job 30:19
in sackcloth and **a**... Luke 10:13
ASIDE (101/94)
lay something **a**, storing... 1 Cor. 16:2
lay **a** all filthiness... James 1:21
Therefore, laying **a**... 1 Pet. 2:1
ASK (119/113)
when your children **a**... Josh. 4:6
"**A** a sign for yourself... Is. 7:11
whatever things you **a**... Matt. 21:22
a, and it will be... Luke 11:9
that whatever You **a**... John 11:22
a anything in My... John 14:14
in that day you will **a**... John 16:23
above all that we **a**... Eph. 3:20
wisdom, let him **a**... James 1:5
But let him **a** in faith... James 1:6
because you do not **a**... James 4:2
ASKS (18/17)
For everyone who **a**... Matt. 7:8
if his son **a** for bread... Matt. 7:9
Or if he **a** for a fish... Luke 11:11
ASLEEP (19/19)
But He was **a**... Matt. 8:24
but some have fallen **a**... 1 Cor. 15:6
those who are **a**... 1 Thess. 4:15
ASSEMBLING (1/1)
not forsaking the **a**... Heb. 10:25
ASSEMBLY (132/125)
a I will praise You... Ps. 22:22
fast, call a sacred **a**... Joel 1:14
a I will sing praise... Heb. 2:12
to the general **a**... Heb. 12:23
ASSURANCE (7/7)
riches of the full **a**... Col. 2:2
Spirit and in much **a**... 1 Thess. 1:5
to the full **a** of hope... Heb. 6:11
ASSURE (1/1)
a our hearts before... 1 John 3:19
ASSURED (4/4)
learned and been **a**... 2 Tim. 3:14
ASTONISHED (46/46)
Just as many were **a**... Is. 52:14
who heard Him were **a**... Luke 2:47
ASTRAY (32/30)
and one of them goes **a**... Matt. 18:12
like sheep going **a**... 1 Pet. 2:25
ATONEMENT (99/86)
the blood that makes **a**... Lev. 17:11
for it is the Day of **A**... Lev. 23:28
there will be no **a**... Is. 22:14
ATTAIN (10/10)
It is high, I cannot **a**... Ps. 139:6
worthy to **a** that age... Luke 20:35
by any means, I may **a**... Phil. 3:11
ATTENTION (12/12)
My son, give **a** to my... Prov. 4:20
ATTENTIVE (8/8)
Let Your ears be **a**... Ps. 130:2
ATTESTED (1/1)
a Man **a** by God to you... Acts 2:22
AUSTERE (2/2)
because you are an **a**... Luke 19:21
AUTHOR (3/3)
For God is not the **a**... 1 Cor. 14:33
unto Jesus, the **a**... Heb. 12:2
AUTHORITIES (6/5)
a that exist are... Rom. 13:1
AUTHORITY (90/85)
them as one having **a**... Matt. 7:29
"All **a** has been given... Matt. 28:18
a I will give You... Luke 4:6
and has given Him **a**... John 5:27
You have given Him **a**... John 17:2
defile the flesh, reject **a**... Jude 1:8
AUTUMN (1/1)
a trees without fruit... Jude 1:12
AVAILS (4/4)
of a righteous man **a**... James 5:16
AVENGE (14/14)
Beloved, do not **a**... Rom. 12:19
a our blood on those... Rev. 6:10
AVENGER (17/16)
the Lord is the **a**... 1 Thess. 4:6
AWAKE (42/34)
be satisfied when I **a**... Ps. 17:15
it is high time to **a**... Rom. 13:11
A to righteousness... 1 Cor. 15:34
AWAY (888/832)
the wind drives **a**... Ps. 1:4
Do not cast me **a**... Ps. 51:11
A time to cast **a**... Eccl. 3:5
fair one, and come **a**... Song 2:10
minded to put her **a**... Matt. 1:19
and earth will pass **a**... Matt. 24:35
"I am going **a**, and you... John 8:21
they cried out, "**A**... John 19:15
unless the falling **a**... 2 Thess. 2:3
in Asia have turned **a**... 2 Tim. 1:15
heard, lest we drift **a**... Heb. 2:1
if they fall **a**, to renew... Heb. 6:6
which can never take **a**... Heb. 10:11
the world is passing **a**... 1 John 2:17
if anyone takes **a**... Rev. 22:19
AWESOME (38/38)
How **a** is this place... Gen. 28:17
God, the great and **a**... Deut. 7:21
By **a** deeds in... Ps. 65:5
O God, You are more **a**... Ps. 68:35
Your great and **a** name... Ps. 99:3
AWL (2/2)
his ear with an **a**... Ex. 21:6
AX (10/10)
If the **a** is dull, and one... Eccl. 10:10
And even now the **a**... Matt. 3:10

B

BABBLER (2/2)
"What does this **b**... Acts 17:18
BABBLINGS (2/2)
the profane and idle **b**... 1 Tim. 6:20
BABE (5/5)
the **b** leaped in my... Luke 1:44
You will find a **B**... Luke 2:12
righteousness, for he is a **b**... Heb. 5:13
BABES (11/11)
Out of the mouth of **b**... Ps. 8:2
revealed them to **b**... Matt. 11:25
'Out of the mouth of **b**... Matt. 21:16
as to carnal, as to **b**... 1 Cor. 3:1
as newborn **b**, desire... 1 Pet. 2:2
BACK (408/396)
a rod for the fool's **b**... Prov. 26:3
I gave My **b** to those... Is. 50:6
plow, and looking **b**... Luke 9:62
of those who draw **b**... Heb. 10:39
someone turns him **b**... James 5:19
BACKBITERS (1/1)
b, haters of God... Rom. 1:30
BACKBITING (1/1)
b tongue an angry... Prov. 25:23
BACKSLIDER (12/12)
The **b** in heart will be... Prov. 14:14
BACKSLIDINGS (4/4)
And I will heal your **b**... Jer. 3:22
BACKWARD (14/14)
shadow ten degrees **b**... 2 Kin. 20:11
BAD (44/35)
b tree bears **b** fruit... Matt. 7:17
BAG (15/15)
nor **b** for your journey... Matt. 10:10
BAKED (16/16)
b unleavened cakes... Ex. 12:39
BAKER (9/9)
the butler and the **b**... Gen. 40:1
BALANCES (1/1)
weighed in the **b**... Dan. 5:27
BALD (14/10)
every head shall be **b**... Jer. 48:37
BALDHEAD (2/1)
Go up, you **b**... 2 Kin. 2:23
BALM (6/6)
Is there no **b** in Gilead... Jer. 8:22
BANDAGED (2/2)
him, and **b** his wounds... Luke 10:34
BANKERS (1/1)
my money with the **b**... Matt. 25:27
BANNERS (4/4)
we will set up our **b**... Ps. 20:5
as an army with **b**... Song 6:4
BANQUET (12/12)
b that I have prepared... Esth. 5:4
BANQUETING (1/1)
He brought me to the **b**... Song 2:4
BAPTISM (22/22)
coming to his **b**... Matt. 3:7
b that I am baptized... Matt. 20:22
But I have a **b** to be... Luke 12:50
said, "Into John's **b**... Acts 19:3
Lord, one faith, one **b**... Eph. 4:5
buried with Him in **b**... Col. 2:12
BAPTISMS (1/1)
of the doctrine of **b**... Heb. 6:2
BAPTIZE (10/8)
I indeed **b** you with... Matt. 3:11
Himself did not **b**... John 4:2
BAPTIZED (59/49)
and is **b** will be saved... Mark 16:16
every one of you be **b**... Acts 2:38
all his family were **b**... Acts 16:33
Arise and be **b**, and wash... Acts 22:16
were **b** into Christ... Rom. 6:3
I thank God that I **b**... 1 Cor. 1:14
Spirit we were all **b**... 1 Cor. 12:13
BAPTIZING (7/7)
b them in the name of... Matt. 28:19
BARBARIAN (1/1)
nor uncircumcised, **b**... Col. 3:11
BARLEY (36/35)
who has five **b** loaves... John 6:9
BARN (5/5)
the wheat into my **b**... Matt. 13:30
BARNS (5/5)
reap nor gather into **b**... Matt. 6:26
I will pull down my **b**... Luke 12:18
BARREN (24/24)
But Sarai was **b**... Gen. 11:30
"Sing, O **b**, you who have... Is. 54:1
BASE (26/26)
and the **b** things of... 1 Cor. 1:28
BASIN (3/2)
poured water into a **b**... John 13:5
BASKET (32/29)
and put it under a **b**... Matt. 5:15
I was let down in a **b**... 2 Cor. 11:33
BASKETS (15/15)
they took up twelve **b**... Matt. 14:20
BATHED (4/4)
to him, "He who is **b**... John 13:10
BATS (1/1)
To the moles and **b**... Is. 2:20
BATTLE (184/171)
b is the LORD's... 1 Sam. 17:47
became valiant in **b**... Heb. 11:34
BEAR (225/215)
greater than I can **b**... Gen. 4:13
whom Sarah shall **b**... Gen. 17:21
not **b** false witness... Ex. 20:16
b their iniquities... Is. 53:11
child, and **b** a Son... Matt. 1:23
A good tree cannot **b**... Matt. 7:18
how long shall I **b**... Matt. 17:17
by, to **b** His cross... Mark 15:21
And whoever does not **b**... Luke 14:27
are strong ought to **b**... Rom. 15:1
B one another's... Gal. 6:2
b the sins of many... Heb. 9:28
BEARD (15/14)
the edges of your **b**... Lev. 19:27
Running down on the **b**... Ps. 133:2
BEARING (25/25)
goes forth weeping, **b**... Ps. 126:6
And He, **b** His cross... John 19:17
the camp, **b** His reproach... Heb. 13:13
BEARS (27/25)
Every branch that **b**... John 15:2
BEAST (127/117)
You preserve man and **b**... Ps. 36:6
And I saw a **b** rising... Rev. 13:1
the mark of the **b**... Rev. 19:20
BEASTS (100/97)
naturally, like brute **b**... Jude 1:10
BEAT (40/40)
b their swords into... Is. 2:4

spat in His face and *b* ... Matt. 26:67
BEATEN (27/26)
Three times I was *b* ... 2 Cor. 11:25
BEAUTIFUL (53/53)
B in elevation, the joy ... Ps. 48:2
has made everything *b* ... Eccl. 3:11
my love, you are as *b* ... Song 6:4
How *b* upon the ... Is. 52:7
indeed appear *b* ... Matt. 23:27
BEAUTIFY (4/4)
b the place of My ... Is. 60:13
BEAUTY (49/49)
"The *b* of Israel is ... 2 Sam. 1:19
To behold the *b* ... Ps. 27:4
see the King in His *b* ... Is. 33:17
no *b* that we should ... Is. 53:2
BECAME (269/263)
man *b* a living being ... Gen. 2:7
to the Jews I *b* as a Jew ... 1 Cor. 9:20
BED (89/87)
I remember You on my *b* ... Ps. 63:6
if I make my *b* in hell ... Ps. 139:8
"Arise, take up your *b* ... Matt. 9:6
be two men in one *b* ... Luke 17:34
and the *b* undefiled ... Heb. 13:4
BEDS (10/10)
sing aloud on their *b* ... Ps. 149:5
BEFOREHAND (13/13)
do not worry *b* ... Mark 13:11
told you all things *b* ... Mark 13:23
when He testified *b* ... 1 Pet. 1:11
BEG (16/16)
b you as sojourners ... 1 Pet. 2:11
BEGAN (131/129)
since the world *b* ... Luke 1:70
BEGGAR (3/3)
there was a certain *b* ... Luke 16:20
BEGGARLY (1/1)
weak and *b* elements ... Gal. 4:9
BEGINNING (105/103)
b God created the ... Gen. 1:1
In the *b* was the Word ... John 1:1
a murderer from the *b* ... John 8:44
True Witness, the *B* ... Rev. 3:14
and the Omega, the *B* ... Rev. 21:6
BEGOTTEN (18/18)
today I have *b* You ... Ps. 2:7
glory as of the only *b* ... John 1:14
loves him who is *b* ... 1 John 5:1
BEGUN (13/13)
Having *b* in the Spirit ... Gal. 3:3
BEHALF (24/24)
you on Christ's *b* ... 2 Cor. 5:20
BEHAVE (6/6)
does not *b* rudely ... 1 Cor. 13:5
BEHAVED (10/10)
and blamelessly we *b* ... 1 Thess. 2:10
BEHAVIOR (11/11)
of good *b*, hospitable ... 1 Tim. 3:2
BEHEADED (6/6)
he sent and had John *b* ... Matt. 14:10
BEHOLD (593/581)
B, the virgin shall ... Is. 7:14
Judah, "*B* your God ... Is. 40:9
B the Lamb of God ... John 1:36
to them, "*B* the Man ... John 19:5
B what manner of love ... 1 John 3:1
BEHOLDING (1/1)
with unveiled face, *b* ... 2 Cor. 3:18
BEING (243/235)
move and have our *b* ... Acts 17:28
who, *b* in the form of ... Phil. 2:6
BELIEVE (178/163)
tears, "Lord, I *b* ... Mark 9:24
have no root, who *b* ... Luke 8:13
and slow of heart to *b* ... Luke 24:25
to those who *b* ... John 1:12
this, that they may *b* ... John 11:42
written that you may *b* ... John 20:31
the Lord Jesus and *b* ... Rom. 10:9
Christ, not only to *b* ... Phil. 1:29
comes to God must *b* ... Heb. 11:6
Even the demons *b* ... James 2:19
BELIEVED (82/80)
And he *b* in the LORD ... Gen. 15:6
Who has *b* our report ... Is. 53:1
seen Me, you have *b* ... John 20:29
"Abraham *b* God ... Rom. 4:3
I know whom I have *b* ... 2 Tim. 1:12
BELIEVERS (3/3)
be an example to the *b* ... 1 Tim. 4:12
BELIEVES (34/33)
The simple *b* every ... Prov. 14:15
that whoever *b* in Him ... John 3:16
He who *b* in the Son ... John 3:36
with the heart one *b* ... Rom. 10:10
BELIEVING (11/11)
you ask in prayer, *b* ... Matt. 21:22
BELLY (18/18)
On your *b* you shall go ... Gen. 3:14
And Jonah was in the *b* ... Jon. 1:17

whose god is their *b* ... Phil. 3:19
BELOVED (122/110)
so He gives His *b* ... Ps. 127:2
My *b* is mine, and I am ... Song 2:16
"This is My *b* Son ... Matt. 3:17
us accepted in the *B* ... Eph. 1:6
Luke the *b* physician ... Col. 4:14
"This is My *b* Son ... 2 Pet. 1:17
BELT (17/15)
with a leather *b* ... Matt. 3:4
BEND (8/8)
The wicked *b* their bow ... Ps. 11:2
BENEATH (16/16)
"You are from *b* ... John 8:23
BENEFACTORS (1/1)
them are called '*b* ... Luke 22:25
BENEFIT (5/4)
might have a second *b* ... 2 Cor. 1:15
BESEECH (3/3)
b you therefore ... Rom. 12:1
BESIDE (65/64)
He leads me *b* the ... Ps. 23:2
"Paul, you are *b* ... Acts 26:24
BEST (49/44)
earnestly desire the *b* ... 1 Cor. 12:31
BESTOWED (8/7)
love the Father has *b* ... 1 John 3:1
BETRAY (18/18)
you, one of you will *b* ... Matt. 26:21
BETRAYED (16/16)
Man is about to be *b* ... Matt. 17:22
BETRAYER (6/6)
See, My *b* is at hand ... Matt. 26:46
BETRAYING (3/3)
"Judas, are you *b* ... Luke 22:48
BETRAYS (2/2)
who is the one who *b* ... John 21:20
BETROTH (4/3)
"I will *b* you to Me ... Hos. 2:19
BETROTHED (14/14)
to a virgin *b* to a man ... Luke 1:27
BETTER (122/119)
obey is *b* than sacrifice ... 1 Sam. 15:22
It is *b* to trust in ... Ps. 118:8
For it is *b* to marry ... 1 Cor. 7:9
Christ, which is far *b* ... Phil. 1:23
b than the angels ... Heb. 1:4
b things concerning ... Heb. 6:9
BEWARE (30/28)
"*B* of false prophets ... Matt. 7:15
BEWITCHED (1/1)
b you that you should ... Gal. 3:1
BEYOND (83/80)
advanced in Judaism *b* ... Gal. 1:14
BILLOWS (2/2)
b have gone over me ... Ps. 42:7
BIND (37/37)
and whatever you *b* ... Matt. 16:19
'*B* him hand and foot ... Matt. 22:13
BIRD (44/38)
soul, "Flee as a *b* ... Ps. 11:1
BIRDS (87/85)
b make their nests ... Ps. 104:17
Look at the *b* of the air ... Matt. 6:26
"Foxes have holes and *b* ... Matt. 8:20
BIRTH (48/46)
the day of one's *b* ... Eccl. 7:1
Now the *b* of Jesus ... Matt. 1:18
will rejoice at his *b* ... Luke 1:14
conceived, it gives *b* ... James 1:15
BIRTHDAY (3/3)
which was Pharaoh's *b* ... Gen. 40:20
BIRTHRIGHT (10/9)
Esau despised his *b* ... Gen. 25:34
BISHOP (3/3)
the position of a *b* ... 1 Tim. 3:1
b must be blameless ... Titus 1:7
BIT (3/3)
and they *b* the people ... Num. 21:6
BITE (4/4)
A serpent may *b* ... Eccl. 10:11
But if you *b* and ... Gal. 5:15
BITTER (43/41)
b herbs they shall eat it ... Ex. 12:8
and do not be *b* ... Col. 3:19
But if you have *b* ... James 3:14
BITTERLY (20/20)
And Hezekiah wept *b* ... 2 Kin. 20:3
he went out and wept *b* ... Matt. 26:75
BITTERNESS (21/21)
you are poisoned by *b* ... Acts 8:23
b springing up cause ... Heb. 12:15
BLACK (16/15)
one hair white or *b* ... Matt. 5:36
a *b* horse and he who sat ... Rev. 6:5
and the sun became *b* ... Rev. 6:12
BLACKNESS (6/6)
whom is reserved the *b* ... Jude 1:13
BLACKSMITH (3/3)
I have created the *b* ... Is. 54:16
BLADE (4/3)
first the *b*, then the head ... Mark 4:28

BLAME (4/4)
be holy and without *b* ... Eph. 1:4
BLAMELESS (47/45)
and that man was *b* ... Job 1:1
body be preserved *b* ... 1 Thess. 5:23
BLAMELESSLY (2/2)
b we behaved ... 1 Thess. 2:10
BLASPHEME (6/6)
b Your name forever ... Ps. 74:10
compelled them to *b* ... Acts 26:11
b that noble name ... James 2:7
BLASPHEMED (23/23)
who passed by *b* Him ... Matt. 27:39
great heat, and they *b* ... Rev. 16:9
BLASPHEMER (1/1)
I was formerly a *b* ... 1 Tim. 1:13
BLASPHEMES (5/4)
b the name of the LORD ... Lev. 24:16
"This Man *b*!" ... Matt. 9:3
BLASPHEMIES (7/7)
is this who speaks *b* ... Luke 5:21
BLASPHEMY (13/11)
but the *b* against ... Matt. 12:31
was full of names of *b* ... Rev. 17:3
BLEATING (1/1)
"What then is this *b* ... 1 Sam. 15:14
BLEMISH (56/50)
be holy and without *b* ... Eph. 5:27
as of a lamb without *b* ... 1 Pet. 1:19
BLEMISHED (1/1)
to the Lord what is *b* ... Mal. 1:14
BLESS (133/123)
b those who *b* you ... Gen. 12:3
You go unless You *b* ... Gen. 32:26
"The LORD *b* you and ... Num. 6:24
b the LORD at all ... Ps. 34:1
b You while I live ... Ps. 63:4
b His holy name ... Ps. 103:1
b those who curse ... Luke 6:28
B those who persecute ... Rom. 12:14
Being reviled, we *b* ... 1 Cor. 4:12
BLESSED (303/287)
B is the man who walks ... Ps. 1:1
B is the man to whom ... Ps. 32:2
B is the nation whose ... Ps. 33:12
B is he who comes ... Ps. 118:26
rise up and call her *b* ... Prov. 31:28
B are the poor in ... Matt. 5:3
B are those who mourn ... Matt. 5:4
B are the meek ... Matt. 5:5
B are those who hunger ... Matt. 5:6
B are the merciful ... Matt. 5:7
B are the pure in ... Matt. 5:8
B are the peacemakers ... Matt. 5:9
B are those who are ... Matt. 5:10
B is He who comes ... Matt. 21:9
'It is more *b* to give ... Acts 20:35
B be the God and ... Eph. 1:3
'*B* are the dead who ... Rev. 14:13
BLESSING (67/64)
and you shall be a *b* ... Gen. 12:2
before you today a *b* ... Deut. 11:26
shall be showers of *b* ... Ezek. 34:26
and you shall be a *b* ... Zech. 8:13
that the *b* of Abraham ... Gal. 3:14
with every spiritual *b* ... Eph. 1:3
BLIND (82/73)
To open *b* eyes ... Is. 42:7
His watchmen are *b* ... Is. 56:10
if the *b* leads the *b* ... Matt. 15:14
to Him, "Are we *b* ... John 9:40
miserable, poor, *b* ... Rev. 3:17
BLINDED (6/6)
and the rest were *b* ... Rom. 11:7
BLINDS (2/2)
a bribe, for a bribe *b* ... Deut. 16:19
BLOOD (424/357)
of your brother's *b* ... Gen. 4:10
b shall be shed ... Gen. 9:6
b that makes atonement ... Lev. 17:11
hands are full of *b* ... Is. 1:15
And the moon into *b* ... Joel 2:31
For this is My *b* ... Matt. 26:28
betraying innocent *b* ... Matt. 27:4
new covenant in My *b* ... Luke 22:20
were born, not of *b* ... John 1:13
b has eternal life ... John 6:54
with His own *b* ... Acts 20:28
propitiation by His *b* ... Rom. 3:25
justified by His *b* ... Rom. 5:9
redemption through His *b* ... Eph. 1:7
brought near by the *b* ... Eph. 2:13
against flesh and *b* ... Eph. 6:12
peace through the *b* ... Col. 1:20
with the precious *b* ... 1 Pet. 1:19
b of Jesus Christ His ... 1 John 1:7
our sins in His own *b* ... Rev. 1:5
us to God by Your *b* ... Rev. 5:9
them white in the *b* ... Rev. 7:14
overcame him by the *b* ... Rev. 12:11

a robe dipped in *b* ... Rev. 19:13
BLOODSHED (24/23)
me from the guilt of *b* ... Ps. 51:14
BLOODTHIRSTY (9/9)
The LORD abhors the *b* ... Ps. 5:6
BLOSSOM (9/9)
and *b* as the rose ... Is. 35:1
BLOT (11/11)
from my sins, and *b* ... Ps. 51:9
and I will not *b* ... Rev. 3:5
BLOTTED (8/8)
your sins may be *b* ... Acts 3:19
BLOW (35/34)
with a very severe *b* ... Jer. 14:17
BLOWS (13/12)
The wind *b* where it ... John 3:8
BOAST (46/41)
puts on his armor *b* ... 1 Kin. 20:11
and make your *b* ... Rom. 2:17
lest anyone should *b* ... Eph. 2:9
BOASTERS (2/2)
God, violent, proud, *b* ... Rom. 1:30
BOASTING (14/14)
Where is *b* then ... Rom. 3:27
BODIES (38/35)
b a living sacrifice ... Rom. 12:1
not know that your *b* ... 1 Cor. 6:15
wives as their own *b* ... Eph. 5:28
BODILY (4/4)
b form like a dove ... Luke 3:22
of the Godhead *b* ... Col. 2:9
BODY (224/196)
of the *b* is the eye ... Matt. 6:22
those who kill the *b* ... Matt. 10:28
Take, eat; this is My *b* ... Matt. 26:26
of the temple of His *b* ... John 2:21
deliver me from this *b* ... Rom. 7:24
redemption of our *b* ... Rom. 8:23
members in one *b* ... Rom. 12:4
But I discipline my *b* ... 1 Cor. 9:27
b which is broken ... 1 Cor. 11:24
baptized into one *b* ... 1 Cor. 12:13
are the *b* of Christ ... 1 Cor. 12:27
though I give my *b* ... 1 Cor. 13:3
It is sown a natural *b* ... 1 Cor. 15:44
in the *b* of His flesh ... Col. 1:22
our sins in His own *b* ... 1 Pet. 2:24
BOILS (7/6)
Job with painful *b* ... Job 2:7
BOLDLY (12/12)
therefore come *b* ... Heb. 4:16
BOLDNESS (12/12)
in whom we have *b* ... Eph. 3:12
that we may have *b* ... 1 John 4:17
BOND (9/9)
love, which is the *b* ... Col. 3:14
BONDAGE (42/41)
out of the house of *b* ... Ex. 13:14
again with a yoke of *b* ... Gal. 5:1
BONDS (17/17)
"Let us break Their *b* ... Ps. 2:3
BONDSERVANTS (9/9)
B, be obedient to ... Eph. 6:5
Masters, give your *b* ... Col. 4:1
BONDWOMAN (9/7)
the one by a *b* ... Gal. 4:22
BONE (16/15)
b clings to my skin ... Job 19:20
BONES (94/81)
I can count all My *b* ... Ps. 22:17
and my *b* waste away ... Ps. 31:10
I kept silent, my *b* ... Ps. 32:3
the wind, or how the *b* ... Eccl. 11:5
say to them, 'O dry *b* ... Ezek. 37:4
of dead men's *b* ... Matt. 23:27
b shall be broken ... John 19:36
BOOK (178/165)
are written in the *b* ... Gal. 3:10
in the Lamb's *B* ... Rev. 21:27
the prophecy of this *b* ... Rev. 22:18
BOOKS (8/7)
b there is no end ... Eccl. 12:12
not contain the *b* ... John 21:25
God, and *b* were opened ... Rev. 20:12
BOOTH (2/2)
of Zion is left as a *b* ... Is. 1:8
BORDERS (22/22)
and enlarge the *b* ... Matt. 23:5
BORE (148/143)
And to Sarah who *b* ... Is. 51:2
b the sin of many ... Is. 53:12
b our sicknesses ... Matt. 8:17
who Himself *b* our sins ... 1 Pet. 2:24
b a male Child who was ... Rev. 12:5
BORN (144/138)
A time to be *b* ... Eccl. 3:2
unto us a Child is *b* ... Is. 9:6
b Jesus who is called ... Matt. 1:16
unless one is *b* again ... John 3:3
That which is *b* ... John 3:6
having been *b* again ... 1 Pet. 1:23

who loves is *b* of God ... 1 John 4:7
BORROWER (2/2)
b is servant to the ... Prov. 22:7
BORROWS (2/2)
The wicked *b* and does ... Ps. 37:21
BOSOM (35/31)
angels to Abraham's *b* ... Luke 16:22
Son, who is in the *b* ... John 1:18
BOTTOMLESS (7/7)
ascend out of the *b* ... Rev. 17:8
the key to the *b* ... Rev. 20:1
BOUGHT (44/44)
b the threshing floor ... 2 Sam. 24:24
all that he had and *b* ... Matt. 13:46
For you were *b* at a ... 1 Cor. 6:20
denying the Lord who *b* ... 2 Pet. 2:1
BOUND (91/89)
on earth will be *b* ... Matt. 16:19
And see, now I go *b* ... Acts 20:22
who has a husband is *b* ... Rom. 7:2
Are you *b* to a wife ... 1 Cor. 7:27
Devil and Satan, and *b* ... Rev. 20:2
BOUNTIFULLY (8/7)
and he who sows *b* ... 2 Cor. 9:6
BOW (98/94)
You shall not *b* ... Ex. 23:24
let us worship and *b* ... Ps. 95:6
who sat on it had a *b* ... Rev. 6:2
BOWED (75/73)
stood all around and *b* ... Gen. 37:7
And they *b* the knee ... Matt. 27:29
BOWL (31/30)
and poured out his *b* ... Rev. 16:2
BOWLS (32/29)
Go and pour out the *b* ... Rev. 16:1
BOX (4/4)
Judas had the money *b* ... John 13:29
BOYS (3/3)
Shall be full of *b* ... Zech. 8:5
BRAIDED (9/8)
not with *b* hair or ... 1 Tim. 2:9
BRANCH (34/30)
raise to David a *B* ... Jer. 23:5
forth My Servant the *B* ... Zech. 3:8
b that bears fruit He ... John 15:2
BRANCHES (84/67)
vine, you are the *b* ... John 15:5
BRASS (4/4)
become sounding *b* ... 1 Cor. 13:1
BRAVE (1/1)
in the faith, be *b* ... 1 Cor. 16:13
BREAD (346/315)
of Salem brought out *b* ... Gen. 14:18
shall eat unleavened *b* ... Ex. 23:15
not live by *b* alone ... Deut. 8:3
b eaten in secret is ... Prov. 9:17
B gained by deceit is ... Prov. 20:17
Cast your *b* upon the ... Eccl. 11:1
for what is not *b* ... Is. 55:2
these stones become *b* ... Matt. 4:3
not live by *b* alone ... Matt. 4:4
this day our daily *b* ... Matt. 6:11
eating, Jesus took *b* ... Matt. 26:26
I am the *b* of life ... John 6:48
He was betrayed took *b* ... 1 Cor. 11:23
BREADTH (7/6)
is as great as its *b* ... Rev. 21:16
BREAK (138/131)
covenant I will not *b* ... Ps. 89:34
together to *b* bread ... Acts 20:7
BREAKING (20/20)
in the *b* of bread ... Acts 2:42
b bread from house to ... Acts 2:46
BREAKS (31/31)
Until the day *b* ... Song 2:17
BREAST (16/15)
back on Jesus' *b* ... John 13:25
BREASTPLATE (28/24)
righteousness as a *b* ... Is. 59:17
having put on the *b* ... Eph. 6:14
BREASTS (27/27)
Your two *b* are like ... Song 4:5
b which nursed You ... Luke 11:27
BREATH (54/51)
nostrils the *b* of life ... Gen. 2:7
that there was no *b* ... 1 Kin. 17:17
Man is like a *b* ... Ps. 144:4
everything that has *b* ... Ps. 150:6
"Surely I will cause *b* ... Ezek. 37:5
gives to all life, *b* ... Acts 17:25
power to give *b* ... Rev. 13:15
BREATHES (2/2)
indeed he *b* his last ... Job 14:10
BRETHREN (398/389)
and you are all *b* ... Matt. 23:8
least of these My *b* ... Matt. 25:40
firstborn among many *b* ... Rom. 8:29
thus sin against the *b* ... 1 Cor. 8:12
over five hundred *b* ... 1 Cor. 15:6
perils among false *b* ... 2 Cor. 11:26
sincere love of the *b* ... 1 Pet. 1:22

because we love the *b* ... 1 John 3:14
our lives for the *b* ... 1 John 3:16
BRIBE (15/13)
you shall take no *b* ... Ex. 23:8
b blinds the eyes ... Deut. 16:19
BRIBES (9/9)
hand is full of *b* ... Ps. 26:10
BRICK (9/9)
people straw to make *b* ... Ex. 5:7
BRICKS (5/5)
"Come, let us make *b* ... Gen. 11:3
BRIDE (14/14)
I will show you the *b* ... Rev. 21:9
the Spirit and the *b* ... Rev. 22:17
BRIDEGROOM (26/20)
and as the *b* rejoices ... Is. 62:5
mourn as long as the *b* ... Matt. 9:15
went out to meet the *b* ... Matt. 25:1
the friend of the *b* ... John 3:29
BRIDLE (8/8)
b the whole body ... James 3:2
BRIER (3/3)
b shall come up the ... Is. 55:13
BRIERS (11/11)
there shall come up *b* ... Is. 5:6
BRIGHTER (4/4)
a light from heaven, *b* ... Acts 26:13
BRIGHTNESS (19/19)
and kings to the *b* ... Is. 60:3
who being the *b* ... Heb. 1:3
BRIMSTONE (14/14)
the lake of fire and *b* ... Rev. 20:10
BRING (710/677)
b back his soul ... Job 33:30
b My righteousness ... Is. 46:13
Who shall *b* a charge ... Rom. 8:33
b Christ down from ... Rom. 10:6
even so God will *b* ... 1 Thess. 4:14
BROAD (16/16)
b is the way that ... Matt. 7:13
BROKE (79/76)
b them at the foot of ... Ex. 32:19
He blessed and *b* ... Matt. 14:19
b the legs of the ... John 19:32
BROKEN (166/160)
this stone will be *b* ... Matt. 21:44
Scripture cannot be *b* ... John 10:35
is My body which is *b* ... 1 Cor. 11:24
BROKENHEARTED (3/3)
He heals the *b* and ... Ps. 147:3
BRONZE (161/138)
So Moses made a *b* ... Num. 21:9
b walls against the ... Jer. 1:18
a third kingdom of *b* ... Dan. 2:39
BROOD (8/8)
B of vipers ... Matt. 12:34
hen gathers her *b* ... Luke 13:34
BROOK (50/47)
disciples over the *B* ... John 18:1
BROOKS (14/14)
for the water *b* ... Ps. 42:1
BROTHER (357/322)
"Where is Abel your *b* ... Gen. 4:9
b offended is harder ... Prov. 18:19
b will deliver up ... Matt. 10:21
how often shall my *b* ... Matt. 18:21
b will rise again ... John 11:23
b goes to law against ... 1 Cor. 6:6
Whoever hates his *b* ... 1 John 3:15
BROTHERHOOD (4/4)
Love the *b* ... 1 Pet. 2:17
BROTHERLY (5/4)
b love continue ... Heb. 13:1
BROTHER'S (34/30)
Am I my *b* keeper ... Gen. 4:9
at the speck in your *b* ... Matt. 7:3
BROTHERS (173/164)
is My mother, or My *b* ... Mark 3:33
b are these who hear ... Luke 8:21
BRUISE (4/3)
He shall *b* your head ... Gen. 3:15
the LORD to *b* Him ... Is. 53:10
BRUISED (4/4)
He was *b* for our ... Is. 53:5
b reed He will not ... Matt. 12:20
BUCKLER (4/4)
be your shield and *b* ... Ps. 91:4
BUFFET (1/1)
of Satan to *b* me ... 2 Cor. 12:7
BUILD (161/153)
b ourselves a city ... Gen. 11:4
"Would you *b* a house ... 2 Sam. 7:5
labor in vain who *b* ... Ps. 127:1
down, and a time to *b* ... Eccl. 3:3
'This man began to *b* ... Luke 14:30
What house will you *b* ... Acts 7:49
For if I *b* again ... Gal. 2:18
BUILDER (2/2)
foundations, whose *b* ... Heb. 11:10
BUILDING (31/30)
in whom the whole *b* ... Eph. 2:21

BUILDS (12/11)
one take heed how he **b** ... 1 Cor. 3:10
BUILT (214/197)
Wisdom has **b** her house ... Prov. 9:1
to a wise man who **b** ... Matt. 7:24
having been **b** on the ... Eph. 2:20
BULLS (59/56)
For if the blood of **b** ... Heb. 9:13
BULWARKS (2/2)
Mark well her **b** ... Ps. 48:13
BUNDLE (4/4)
each man's **b** of money ... Gen. 42:35
BURDEN (56/56)
Cast your **b** on the ... Ps. 55:22
easy and My **b** is light ... Matt. 11:30
we might not be a **b** ... 1 Thess. 2:9
on you no other **b** ... Rev. 2:24
BURDENS (19/18)
For they bind heavy **b** ... Matt. 23:4
Bear one another's **b** ... Gal. 6:2
BURDENSOME (9/9)
I myself was not **b** ... 2 Cor. 12:13
commandments are not **b** ... 1 John 5:3
BURIAL (17/16)
she did it for My **b** ... Matt. 26:12
for the day of My **b** ... John 12:7
BURIED (104/101)
Therefore we were **b** ... Rom. 6:4
and that He was **b** ... 1 Cor. 15:4
b with Him in baptism ... Col. 2:12
BURN (144/137)
the bush does not **b** ... Ex. 3:3
"Did not our heart **b** ... Luke 24:32
BURNED (167/159)
If anyone's work is **b** ... 1 Cor. 3:15
my body to be **b** ... 1 Cor. 13:3
BURNING (58/55)
b torch that passed ... Gen. 15:17
b fire shut up in my ... Jer. 20:9
plucked from the **b** ... Amos 4:11
BURNT (294/267)
lamb for a **b** offering ... Gen. 22:7
delight in **b** offering ... Ps. 51:16
BURST (10/10)
the new wine will **b** ... Luke 5:37
BURY (39/36)
and let the dead **b** ... Matt. 8:22
BUSH (11/9)
from the midst of a **b** ... Ex. 3:2
BUSINESS (20/19)
about My Father's **b** ... Luke 2:49
BUSYBODIES (2/2)
at all, but are **b** ... 2 Thess. 3:11
BUTLER (9/9)
b did not remember ... Gen. 40:23
BUTTER (3/3)
were smoother than **b** ... Ps. 55:21
BUY (58/53)
Yes, come, **b** wine and ... Is. 55:1
I counsel you to **b** ... Rev. 3:18
and that no one may **b** ... Rev. 13:17
BUYS (4/4)
has and **b** that field ... Matt. 13:44
BYWORD (10/10)
But He has made me a **b** ... Job 17:6

C

CAGE (4/4)
foul spirit, and a **c** ... Rev. 18:2
CAKE (13/12)
Ephraim is a **c** ... Hos. 7:8
CALAMITY (49/46)
will laugh at your **c** ... Prov. 1:26
CALCULATED (1/1)
c the dust of the ... Is. 40:12
CALDRON (5/5)
this city is the **c** ... Ezek. 11:3
CALF (31/31)
and made a molded **c** ... Ex. 32:4
And bring the fatted **c** ... Luke 15:23
CALL (187/182)
c upon Him while He ... Is. 55:6
c His name Jesus ... Matt. 1:21
c the righteous ... Matt. 9:13
Lord our God will **c** ... Acts 2:39
you must not **c** common ... Acts 10:15
c and election sure ... 2 Pet. 1:10
CALLED (619/593)
c the light Day ... Gen. 1:5
c his wife's name Eve ... Gen. 3:20
I have **c** you by your ... Is. 43:1
"Out of Egypt I **c** ... Matt. 2:15
a city **c** Nazareth ... Matt. 2:23
For many are **c** ... Matt. 20:16
to those who are the **c** ... Rom. 8:28
these He also **c** ... Rom. 8:30
c children of God ... 1 John 3:1
CALLING (29/29)
the gifts and the **c** ... Rom. 11:29
For you see your **c** ... 1 Cor. 1:26
remain in the same **c** ... 1 Cor. 7:20

CALLS (33/32)
c them all by name ... Ps. 147:4
David himself **c** ... Mark 12:37
c his own sheep ... John 10:3
CALM (6/6)
there was a great **c** ... Matt. 8:26
CAMEL (9/9)
it is easier for a **c** ... Matt. 19:24
CAMP (181/164)
to Him, outside the **c** ... Heb. 13:13
CAN (344/309)
I **c** do all things ... Phil. 4:13
CANCER (1/1)
will spread like **c** ... 2 Tim. 2:17
CANOPY (4/4)
His **c** around Him was ... Ps. 18:11
CAPSTONE (1/1)
bring forth the **c** ... Zech. 4:7
CAPTAIN (72/71)
which, having no **c** ... Prov. 6:7
CAPTIVE (88/82)
and be led away **c** ... Luke 21:24
He led captivity **c** ... Eph. 4:8
CAPTIVES (54/49)
make **c** of gullible women ... 2 Tim. 3:6
CAPTIVITY (106/98)
every thought into **c** ... 2 Cor. 10:5
CARCASS (20/16)
For wherever the **c** ... Matt. 24:28
CARE (32/30)
"Lord, do You not **c** ... Luke 10:40
how will he take **c** ... 1 Tim. 3:5
CARED (3/3)
he said, not that he **c** ... John 12:6
CAREFULLY (26/26)
I shall walk **c** all my ... Is. 38:15
CARELESS (2/2)
but he who is **c** ... Prov. 19:16
CARES (11/10)
no one **c** for my soul ... Ps. 142:4
for He **c** for you ... 1 Pet. 5:7
CARNAL (7/6)
c mind is enmity ... Rom. 8:7
CARNALLY (6/6)
c minded is death ... Rom. 8:6
CAROUSE (1/1)
count it pleasure to **c** ... 2 Pet. 2:13
CARPENTER (1/1)
Is this not the **c** ... Mark 6:3
CARRIED (153/141)
and **c** our sorrows ... Is. 53:4
CARRY (80/77)
for you to **c** your bed ... John 5:10
it is certain we can **c** ... 1 Tim. 6:7
CARRYING (17/15)
a man will meet you **c** ... Mark 14:13
CASE (34/33)
Festus laid Paul's **c** ... Acts 25:14
CASSIA (3/3)
myrrh and aloes and **c** ... Ps. 45:8
CAST (323/307)
Why are you **c** down ... Ps. 42:5
whole body to be **c** ... Matt. 5:29
In My name they will **c** ... Mark 16:17
by no means **c** out ... John 6:37
c their crowns before ... Rev. 4:10
the great dragon was **c** ... Rev. 12:9
CASTING (15/15)
c down arguments ... 2 Cor. 10:5
c all your care ... 1 Pet. 5:7
CASTS (12/12)
perfect love **c** out ... 1 John 4:18
CATCH (17/17)
c Him in His words ... Mark 12:13
From now on you will **c** ... Luke 5:10
CATCHES (6/6)
and the wolf **c** the ... John 10:12
c the wise in their ... 1 Cor. 3:19
CAUGHT (44/44)
behind him was a ram **c** ... Gen. 22:13
her Child was **c** up ... Rev. 12:5
CAUSE (219/210)
hated Me without a **c** ... John 15:25
For this **c** I was born ... John 18:37
CAVES (8/8)
in dens and **c** of the ... Heb. 11:38
CEASE (72/72)
and night shall not **c** ... Gen. 8:22
He makes wars **c** ... Ps. 46:9
tongues, they will **c** ... 1 Cor. 13:8
CEDAR (52/49)
dwell in a house of **c** ... 2 Sam. 7:2
CEDARS (22/21)
the LORD breaks the **c** ... Ps. 29:5
CELESTIAL (2/1)
but the glory of the **c** ... 1 Cor. 15:40
CENSER (12/10)
Aaron, each took his **c** ... Lev. 10:1
CERTAINTY (3/3)
you may know the **c** ... Luke 1:4
CERTIFICATE (7/7)
a man to write a **c** ... Mark 10:4

CHAFF (15/15)
be chased like the **c** ... Is. 17:13
He will burn up the **c** ... Matt. 3:12
CHAIN (10/10)
pit and a great **c** ... Rev. 20:1
CHAINED (3/3)
of God is not **c** ... 2 Tim. 2:9
CHAINS (49/47)
And his **c** fell off ... Acts 12:7
am, except for these **c** ... Acts 26:29
CHAMBERS (58/48)
brought me into his **c** ... Song 1:4
CHAMPION (3/3)
And a **c** went out from ... 1 Sam. 17:4
CHANGE (23/23)
now and to **c** my tone ... Gal. 4:20
there is also a **c** ... Heb. 7:12
CHANGED (37/36)
c the glory of the ... Rom. 1:23
but we shall all be **c** ... 1 Cor. 15:51
CHANGERS' (1/1)
and poured out the **c** ... John 2:15
CHANGES (12/11)
c the times and the ... Dan. 2:21
CHANNELS (4/4)
c of the sea were seen ... Ps. 18:15
CHARIOT (62/54)
that suddenly a **c** ... 2 Kin. 2:11
CHARIOTS (110/101)
Some trust in **c** ... Ps. 20:7
CHARITABLE (5/5)
you do not do your **c** ... Matt. 6:1
c deeds which she ... Acts 9:36
CHARM (1/1)
C is deceitful and ... Prov. 31:30
CHARMS (4/4)
who sew magic **c** ... Ezek. 13:18
CHASE (6/6)
Five of you shall **c** ... Lev. 26:8
CHASTE (3/3)
may present you as a **c** ... 2 Cor. 11:2
CHASTEN (7/7)
a father does not **c** ... Heb. 12:7
I love, I rebuke and **c** ... Rev. 3:19
CHASTENED (9/9)
c us as seemed best ... Heb. 12:10
CHASTENING (9/9)
do not despise the **c** ... Job 5:17
Now no **c** seems to be ... Heb. 12:11
CHASTENS (3/2)
the LORD loves He **c** ... Heb. 12:6
CHASTISEMENT (2/2)
the **c** for our peace ... Is. 53:5
CHATTER (1/1)
c leads only to poverty ... Prov. 14:23
CHEAT (4/4)
Beware lest anyone **c** ... Col. 2:8
CHEATED (4/4)
let yourselves be **c** ... 1 Cor. 6:7
CHEEK (7/7)
on your right **c** ... Matt. 5:39
CHEEKBONE (1/1)
my enemies on the **c** ... Ps. 3:7
CHEEKS (5/5)
His **c** are like a bed ... Song 5:13
CHEER (9/9)
"Son, be of good **c** ... Matt. 9:2
CHEERFUL (6/6)
for God loves a **c** ... 2 Cor. 9:7
CHEERFULNESS (1/1)
shows mercy, with **c** ... Rom. 12:8
CHEESE (2/2)
and curdle me like **c** ... Job 10:10
CHERISHES (2/2)
but nourishes and **c** ... Eph. 5:29
CHERUBIM (66/58)
above it were the **c** ... Heb. 9:5
CHIEF (271/238)
of whom I am **c** ... 1 Tim. 1:15
Zion a **c** cornerstone ... 1 Pet. 2:6
CHILD (181/160)
Train up a **c** in the ... Prov. 22:6
For unto us a **C** ... Is. 9:6
virgin shall be with **c** ... Matt. 1:23
of God as a little **c** ... Mark 10:15
So the **c** grew and ... Luke 1:80
When I was a **c** ... 1 Cor. 13:11
She bore a male **C** ... Rev. 12:5
CHILDBEARING (2/2)
she will be saved in **c** ... 1 Tim. 2:15
CHILDBIRTH (4/4)
pain as a woman in **c** ... Is. 13:8
CHILDHOOD (5/5)
c you have known ... 2 Tim. 3:15
CHILDLESS (7/6)
give me, seeing I go **c** ... Gen. 15:2
this man down as **c** ... Jer. 22:30
CHILDREN (1,350/1,186)
c are a heritage ... Ps. 127:3
c rise up and call her ... Prov. 31:28
and become as little **c** ... Matt. 18:3

"Let the little *c*............... Matt. 19:14
the right to become *c* .... John 1:12
now we are *c* of God............1 John 3:2
CHOOSE (39/39)
therefore *c* life............... Deut. 30:19
You did not *c* Me, but I .... John 15:16
CHOSE (35/35)
just as He *c* us in Him ....Eph. 1:4
CHOSEN (108/105)
servant whom I have *c* .... Is. 43:10
I know whom I have *c* .... John 13:18
c the foolish things ....1 Cor. 1:27
Has God not *c* the poor...........James 2:5
CHRIST (554/521)
Jesus who is called *C* .... Matt. 1:16
"You are the *C* .... Matt. 16:16
a Savior, who is *C* ....Luke 2:11
It is *C* who died ....Rom. 8:34
to be justified by *C* ....Gal. 2:17
been crucified with *C*............Gal. 2:20
C is head of the church......... Eph. 5:23
to me, to live is *C*................Phil. 1:21
which is *C* in you.................Col. 1:27
C who is our life...................Col. 3:4
Jesus *C* is the same .... Heb. 13:8
C His Son cleanses us ....1 John 1:7
that Jesus is the *C*..............1 John 5:1
CHRISTIAN (2/2)
anyone suffers as a *C*..........1 Pet. 4:16
CHRISTIANS (1/1)
were first called *C*.............. Acts 11:26
CHRISTS (2/2)
For false *c* and...................Matt. 24:24
CHURCH (74/73)
rock I will build My *c*.......... Matt. 16:18
c daily those who were ....Acts 2:47
Himself a glorious *c* ....Eph. 5:27
as the Lord does the *c*.......... Eph. 5:29
body, which is the *c* .... Col. 1:24
general assembly and *c* .... Heb. 12:23
CHURCHES (36/35)
these things in the *c* ....Rev. 22:16
CIRCLE (7/7)
who sits above the *c*.................Is. 40:22
CIRCUMCISE (8/8)
is necessary to *c* them.............Acts 15:5
CIRCUMCISED (48/42)
among you shall be *c*...........Gen. 17:10
who will justify the *c* .... Rom. 3:30
if you become *c*................... Gal. 5:2
CIRCUMCISION (29/26)
c is that of the heart........... Rom. 2:29
C is nothing and ....1 Cor. 7:19
Christ Jesus neither *c* .... Gal. 5:6
CIRCUMSPECTLY (1/1)
then that you walk *c*...............Eph. 5:15
CISTERN (5/5)
from your own *c*................. Prov. 5:15
CITIES (440/388)
He overthrew those *c* ....Gen. 19:25
three parts, and the *c* .... Rev. 16:19
CITIZEN (4/4)
But I was born a *c*............. Acts 22:28
CITIZENS (2/2)
but fellow *c* with the ....Eph. 2:19
CITIZENSHIP (2/2)
For our *c* is in heaven .... Phil. 3:20
CITY (851/765)
shall make glad the *c*.............Ps. 46:4
c has become a harlot..............Is. 1:21
How lonely sits the *c* ....Lam. 1:1
c that is set on a ....Matt. 5:14
He has prepared a *c*..............Heb. 11:16
have no continuing *c*...........Heb. 13:14
John, saw the holy *c*...............Rev. 21:2
CLAP (6/6)
of the field shall *c*..................Is. 55:12
CLAY (35/32)
pit, out of the miry *c* ....Ps. 40:2
We are the *c*, and You .... Is. 64:8
blind man with the *c*...............John 9:6
have power over the *c*..........Rom. 9:21
CLEAN (114/99)
He who has *c* hands and.......... Ps. 24:4
make yourselves *c* ....Is. 1:16
c out His threshing .... Matt. 3:12
You can make me *c* ....Matt. 8:2
"You are not all *c*...............John 13:11
You are already *c* .... John 15:3
CLEANSE (38/38)
C me from secret .... Ps. 19:12
and *c* me from my sin............ Ps. 51:2
How can a young man *c* .... Ps. 119:9
might sanctify and *c* .... Eph. 5:26
us our sins and to *c* ....1 John 1:9
CLEANSED (41/38)
"Were there not ten *c*............Luke 17:17
CLEANSES (2/2)
Jesus Christ His Son *c*......... 1 John 1:7
CLEAR (16/16)
of life, *c* as crystal.............. Rev. 22:1

CLIFF (3/3)
secret places of the *c* .... Song 2:14
CLIMBS (2/2)
c up some other way .... John 10:1
CLING (15/15)
C to what is good...............Rom. 12:9
CLINGS (9/9)
and My tongue *c* .... Ps. 22:15
CLOAK (8/8)
let him have your *c* ....Matt. 5:40
using liberty as a *c* ....1 Pet. 2:16
CLODS (5/5)
The *c* of the valley .... Job 21:33
CLOSE (33/32)
c friends abhor me.............Job 19:19
CLOSED (17/17)
the deep *c* around me .... Jon. 2:5
CLOTH (18/18)
a piece of unshrunk *c* .... Matt. 9:16
CLOTHE (21/21)
He not much more *c* .... Matt. 6:30
CLOTHED (76/73)
of skin, and *c* them..............Gen. 3:21
A man *c* in soft .... Matt. 11:8
I was naked and you *c*.........Matt. 25:36
legion, sitting and *c*............ Mark 5:15
desiring to be *c* .... 2 Cor. 5:2
that you may be *c* .... Rev. 3:18
CLOTHES (115/112)
c became shining ....Mark 9:3
many spread their *c*............ Luke 19:36
a poor man in filthy *c* ....James 2:2
CLOTHING (49/49)
c they cast lots.................. Ps. 22:18
do you worry about *c*...........Matt. 6:28
to you in sheep's *c* .... Matt. 7:15
c they cast lots................. John 19:24
CLOTHS (7/7)
wrapped in swaddling *c* .... Luke 2:12
CLOUD (108/96)
My rainbow in the *c*.............Gen. 9:13
day in a pillar of *c*................ Ex. 13:21
He led them with the *c* .... Ps. 78:14
behold, a bright *c* .... Matt. 17:5
of Man coming in a *c*.......... Luke 21:27
c received Him out of .... Acts 1:9
by so great a *c* .... Heb. 12:1
CLOUDS (56/53)
of Man coming on the *c* ...... Matt. 24:30
with them in the *c* ....1 Thess. 4:17
are *c* without water ....Jude 1:12
He is coming with *c*............... Rev. 1:7
CLOUDY (3/3)
them by day with a *c* ....Neh. 9:12
CLOVEN (10/8)
chew the cud or have *c* .... Deut. 14:7
CLUSTER (6/6)
beloved is to me a *c*............. Song 1:14
COAL (2/2)
in his hand a live *c*.................. Is. 6:6
COALS (23/23)
doing you will heap *c* ....Rom. 12:20
COBRA (3/3)
the lion and the *c* .... Ps. 91:13
COBRA'S (1/1)
shall play by the *c*.................. Is. 11:8
COFFIN (3/3)
and he was put in a *c*.......... Gen. 50:26
touched the open *c* .... Luke 7:14
COIN (2/2)
if she loses one *c*................. Luke 15:8
COLD (17/16)
and harvest, *c* and .... Gen. 8:22
of many will grow *c* .... Matt. 24:12
that you are neither *c* .... Rev. 3:15
COLLECTION (4/4)
concerning the *c*..............1 Cor. 16:1
COLT (15/14)
on a donkey, a *c*...................Zech. 9:9
on a donkey, a *c*.................. Matt. 21:5
COME (1,702/1,588)
He will *c* and save you............ Is. 35:4
who have no money, *C* ....Is. 55:1
Your kingdom *c* ....Matt. 6:10
C to Me.............................. Matt. 11:28
I have *c* in My.....................John 5:43
and I have not *c* ....John 7:28
thirsts, let him *c* .... John 7:37
c as a light into the.............John 12:46
O Lord, *c*...........................1 Cor. 16:22
the door, I will *c* ....Rev. 3:20
COMELINESS (1/1)
He has no form or *c*.................. Is. 53:2
COMES (272/257)
Lord's death till He *c* ....1 Cor. 11:26
COMFORT (59/55)
and Your staff, they *c*............. Ps. 23:4
yes, *c* My people ....Is. 40:1
c each other and edify........ 1 Thess. 5:11
COMFORTED (31/31)
So Isaac was *c* after .... Gen. 24:67

refusing to be *c*...................Jer. 31:15
COMFORTER (4/3)
She had no *c*..................... Lam. 1:9
COMFORTS (10/10)
I, even I, am He who *c*............Is. 51:12
COMING (260/254)
see the Son of Man *c* ....Mark 13:26
mightier than I is *c*............... Luke 3:16
are Christ's at His *c*............1 Cor. 15:23
Behold, I am *c* .... Rev. 3:11
"Surely I am *c* .... Rev. 22:20
COMMAND (202/195)
c I have received............... John 10:18
And I know that His *c* .... John 12:50
if you do whatever I *c* .... John 15:14
COMMANDED (450/437)
not endure what was *c* .... Heb. 12:20
COMMANDMENT (112/108)
c of the LORD is pure............. Ps. 19:8
which is the great *c* ....Matt. 22:36
A new *c* I give to .... John 13:34
which is the first *c* .... Eph. 6:2
And this is His *c* ....1 John 3:23
COMMANDMENTS (159/156)
covenant, the Ten *C* .... Ex. 34:28
as doctrines the *c* .... Matt. 15:9
c hang all the Law........... Matt. 22:40
He who has My *c*............... John 14:21
COMMANDS (20/20)
with authority He *c* .... Mark 1:27
COMMEND (7/7)
But food does not *c* ....1 Cor. 8:8
COMMENDABLE (2/2)
patiently, this is *c* ....1 Pet. 2:20
COMMENDED (8/8)
c the unjust steward .... Luke 16:8
COMMENDS (2/1)
but whom the Lord *c*..........2 Cor. 10:18
COMMIT (65/60)
"You shall not *c*.................Ex. 20:14
into Your hands I *c*............Luke 23:46
COMMITS (30/26)
sin also *c* lawlessness ....1 John 3:4
COMMITTED (112/106)
c Himself to Him who..........1 Pet. 2:23
COMMON (28/28)
c people heard Him........... Mark 12:37
had all things in *c*................Acts 2:44
concerning our *c* .... Jude 1:3
COMMOTION (3/3)
there arose a great *c* ....Acts 19:23
COMMUNED (1/1)
I *c* with my heart.................Eccl. 1:16
COMMUNION (4/3)
c of the Holy Spirit............2 Cor. 13:14
COMPANION (25/25)
a man my equal, My *c* .... Ps. 55:13
COMPANY (51/47)
great was the *c*................... Ps. 68:11
to an innumerable *c* .... Heb. 12:22
COMPARE (6/6)
c ourselves with those.........2 Cor. 10:12
COMPARED (4/4)
are not worthy to be *c* ....Rom. 8:18
COMPASSION (47/44)
are a God full of *c* .... Ps. 86:15
He was moved with *c*...........Matt. 9:36
whomever I will have *c*.........Rom. 9:15
He can have *c* on those........... Heb. 5:2
COMPASSIONATE (2/2)
the Lord is very *c* .... James 5:11
COMPASSIONS (1/1)
because His *c* fail not ....Lam. 3:22
COMPEL (4/4)
c them to come in .... Luke 14:23
COMPELS (3/3)
the love of Christ *c*.............2 Cor. 5:14
COMPLAINED (19/19)
some of them also *c*..............1 Cor. 10:10
COMPLAINERS (1/1)
These are grumblers, *c*..........Jude 1:16
COMPLAINING (2/2)
all things without *c* ....Phil. 2:14
COMPLAINT (13/12)
for the LORD has a *c*..............Mic. 6:2
COMPLETE (20/19)
work in you will *c* ....Phil. 1:6
and you are *c* in Him............ Col. 2:10
of God may be *c*.................2 Tim. 3:17
COMPLETELY (27/27)
Himself sanctify you *c* ...... 1 Thess. 5:23
COMPOSED (1/1)
But God *c* the body............1 Cor. 12:24
COMPREHEND (5/5)
which we cannot *c* .... Job 37:5
the darkness did not *c*............. John 1:5
CONCEAL (8/8)
of God to *c* a matter .... Prov. 25:2
CONCEALED (5/5)
than love carefully *c* .... Prov. 27:5
CONCEIT (1/1)
selfish ambition or *c* .... Phil. 2:3

CONCEITED (1/1)
Let us not become *c*............ Gal. 5:26
CONCEIVE (13/13)
the virgin shall *c*.................Is. 7:14
And behold, you will *c*..........Luke 1:31
CONCEIVED (46/45)
in sin my mother *c*................ Ps. 51:5
CONCERN (10/9)
Neither do I *c* myself............Ps. 131:1
CONCERNED (6/6)
Is it oxen God is *c*...............1 Cor. 9:9
CONCESSION (1/1)
But I say this as a *c*.............1 Cor. 7:6
CONCLUSION (2/2)
Let us hear the *c*..................Eccl. 12:13
CONDEMN (25/25)
world to *c* the world........... John 3:17
CONDEMNATION (16/16)
can you escape the *c*.........Matt. 23:33
And this is the *c*.................John 3:19
Their *c* is just......................Rom. 3:8
therefore now no *c*................Rom. 8:1
CONDEMNED (26/25)
does not believe is *c*............ John 3:18
c sin in the flesh ....Rom. 8:3
CONDEMNS (5/5)
Who is he who *c* ....Rom. 8:34
CONDUCT (24/23)
from your aimless *c*.................1 Pet. 1:18
may be won by the *c* .... 1 Pet. 3:1
CONFESS (25/25)
c my transgressions.............Ps. 32:5
that if you *c* with..............Rom. 10:9
every tongue shall *c*........... Rom. 14:11
If we *c* our sins ....1 John 1:9
CONFESSED (7/6)
c that He was Christ...........John 9:22
CONFESSES (5/5)
c that Jesus is the ....1 John 4:15
CONFESSION (11/11)
with the mouth *c* ....Rom. 10:10
High Priest of our *c*...............Heb. 3:1
let us hold fast our *c* ....Heb. 4:14
CONFIDENCE (36/35)
c shall be your.................... Is. 30:15
Jesus, and have no *c* .... Phil. 3:3
CONFINED (10/10)
the Scripture has *c*............... Gal. 3:22
CONFIRM (11/11)
who will also *c*.....................1 Cor. 1:8
CONFIRMED (15/15)
covenant that was *c*...............Gal. 3:17
c it by an oath ....Heb. 6:17
CONFIRMING (1/1)
c the word through the........Mark 16:20
CONFLICT (4/4)
to know what a great *c* .... Col. 2:1
CONFLICTS (1/1)
Outside were *c*....................2 Cor. 7:5
CONFORMED (4/4)
predestined to be *c* .... Rom. 8:29
And do not be *c*....................Rom. 12:2
CONFUSE (1/1)
c their language .... Gen. 11:7
CONFUSED (6/6)
the assembly was *c*...............Acts 19:32
CONGREGATION (139/131)
Nor sinners in the *c* .... Ps. 1:5
God stands in the *c*................. Ps. 82:1
CONQUER (2/2)
conquering and to *c*...............Rev. 6:2
CONQUERORS (1/1)
we are more than *c* ....Rom. 8:37
CONSCIENCE (25/24)
convicted by their *c* ....John 8:9
strive to have a *c*..................Acts 24:16
CONSECRATED (37/33)
c this house which you ....1 Kin. 9:3
CONSENT (15/15)
and does not *c* to ....1 Tim. 6:3
CONSENTED (3/3)
He had not *c* to their .... Luke 23:51
CONSENTING (2/2)
Now Saul was *c* to his..............Acts 8:1
CONSIDER (84/83)
When I *c* Your heavens.............Ps. 8:3
My people do not *c*...................Is. 1:3
C the lilies of the....................Matt. 6:28
C the ravens .... Luke 12:24
c Him who endured.................Heb. 12:3
CONSIST (2/2)
in Him all things *c* ....Col. 1:17
CONSOLATION (14/13)
if there is any *c* ....Phil. 2:1
given us everlasting *c* .... 2 Thess. 2:16
CONSOLE (2/2)
c those who mourn ....Is. 61:3
CONSTANT (1/1)
c prayer was offered..............Acts 12:5
CONSUME (41/39)
whom the Lord will *c*......... 2 Thess. 2:8

CONSUMED (74/73)
but the bush was not *c* ....Ex. 3:2
mercies we are not *c* ....Lam. 3:22
beware lest you be *c*............... Gal. 5:15
CONSUMING (8/8)
our God is a *c* fire .... Heb. 12:29
CONTAIN (4/4)
of heavens cannot *c*............ 2 Chr. 2:6
c the books that................John 21:25
CONTEMPT (14/14)
and be treated with *c*...........Mark 9:12
CONTEMPTIBLE (4/4)
and his speech *c*................2 Cor. 10:10
CONTEND (21/20)
c earnestly for the .... Jude 1:3
CONTENT (10/10)
state I am, to be *c*...............Phil. 4:11
covetousness; be *c*...............Heb. 13:5
CONTENTIONS (8/8)
sorcery, hatred, *c* ....Gal. 5:20
CONTENTIOUS (6/6)
anyone seems to be *c* .... 1 Cor. 11:16
CONTENTMENT (1/1)
c is great gain......................1 Tim. 6:6
CONTINUAL (10/10)
a merry heart has a *c*.......... Prov. 15:15
c coming she weary me .... Luke 18:5
CONTINUALLY (75/75)
heart was only evil *c* ....Gen. 6:5
will give ourselves *c*................Acts 6:4
remains a priest *c*.................Heb. 7:3
CONTINUE (46/45)
Shall we *c* in sin that ....Rom. 6:1
C earnestly in prayer .... Col. 4:2
Let brotherly love *c* ....Heb. 13:1
CONTINUED (37/37)
c steadfastly in the.................Acts 2:42
CONTRADICTIONS (1/1)
idle babblings and *c*............1 Tim. 6:20
CONTRARY (29/29)
to worship God *c*.................Acts 18:13
CONTRIBUTION (2/2)
to make a certain *c*...............Rom. 15:26
CONTRITE (5/4)
a broken and a *c* ....Ps. 51:17
poor and of a *c* spirit .... Is. 66:2
CONTROVERSY (6/6)
For the LORD has a *c* ....Jer. 25:31
CONVERSION (1/1)
describing the *c* ....Acts 15:3
CONVERTED (3/3)
unless you are *c* ....Matt. 18:3
CONVICT (3/3)
He has come, He will *c* .... John 16:8
CONVICTS (1/1)
Which of you *c*.....................John 8:46
CONVINCED (7/7)
Let each be fully *c*................Rom. 14:5
COOKED (3/3)
c their own children .... Lam. 4:10
COOL (4/4)
and *c* my tongue................ Luke 16:24
COPIES (2/2)
necessary that the *c*.............. Heb. 9:23
COPPER (7/7)
sold for two *c* coins .... Luke 12:6
COPPERSMITH (1/1)
c did me much harm.......... 2 Tim. 4:14
COPY (10/10)
who serve the *c*....................... Heb. 8:5
CORD (11/11)
this line of scarlet *c* ....Josh. 2:18
And a threefold *c* ....Eccl. 4:12
before the silver *c*................ Eccl. 12:6
CORDS (24/24)
had made a whip of *c*............. John 2:15
CORNER (23/21)
was not done in a *c* .... Acts 26:26
CORNERSTONE (11/11)
become the chief *c*............Matt. 21:42
in Zion a chief *c*.....................1 Pet. 2:6
CORRECT (9/9)
C your son, and he will .... Prov. 29:17
CORRECTED (3/3)
human fathers who *c* .... Heb. 12:9
CORRECTION (18/18)
Do not withhold *c*............. Prov. 23:13
for reproof, for *c*................2 Tim. 3:16
CORRECTS (5/5)
the LORD loves He *c*............Prov. 3:12
CORRODED (1/1)
and silver are *c* ....James 5:3
CORRUPT (20/19)
in these things they *c* ....Jude 1:10
CORRUPTED (12/12)
for all flesh had *c* ....Gen. 6:12
Your riches are *c*....................James 5:2
CORRUPTIBLE (5/5)
redeemed with *c* things .... 1 Pet. 1:18
CORRUPTION (18/18)
Your Holy One to see *c* .... Ps. 16:10

c inherit incorruption.........1 Cor. 15:50
having escaped the *c*.............2 Pet. 1:4
COST (4/4)
and count the *c*.................Luke 14:28
COULD (230/218)
c remove mountains............1 Cor. 13:2
which no one *c* number ....Rev. 7:9
COUNCILS (2/2)
deliver you up to *c* ....Mark 13:9
COUNSEL (90/89)
who walks not in the *c*...............Ps. 1:1
We took sweet *c*..................Ps. 55:14
guide me with Your *c*...............Ps. 73:24
according to the *c*.................Eph. 1:11
immutability of His *c* ....Heb. 6:17
I *c* you to buy from................Rev. 3:18
COUNSELOR (12/12)
be called Wonderful, *C* .... Is. 9:6
COUNSELORS (21/21)
c there is safety....................Prov. 11:14
COUNT (42/40)
c my life dear to .... Acts 20:24
His promise, as some *c*..........2 Pet. 3:9
COUNTED (35/35)
Even a fool is *c*...................Prov. 17:28
who rule well be *c*...................1 Tim. 5:17
COUNTENANCE (39/38)
The LORD lift up His *c*............ Num. 6:26
hypocrites, with a sad *c* .... Matt. 6:16
His *c* was like ....Matt. 28:3
of the glory of his *c* ....2 Cor. 3:7
COUNTRY (159/155)
"Get out of your *c* ....Gen. 12:1
that is, a heavenly *c* .... Heb. 11:16
COUNTRYMEN (8/8)
for my brethren, my *c*.............Rom. 9:3
COURAGE (22/22)
strong and of good *c* ....Deut. 31:6
COURT (131/108)
They zealously *c* you ....Gal. 4:17
COURTEOUS (1/1)
be tenderhearted, be *c* ....1 Pet. 3:8
COURTS (26/26)
and into His *c* ....Ps. 100:4
COVENANT (313/293)
I will establish My *c*...............Gen. 6:18
the LORD made a *c*.................Gen. 15:18
will show them His *c*................ Ps. 25:14
sons will keep My *c* .... Ps. 132:12
I will make a new *c*.................Jer. 31:31
the Messenger of the *c* .... Mal. 3:1
cup is the new *c*.....................Luke 22:20
He says, "A new *c* .... Heb. 8:13
Mediator of the new *c* .... Heb. 12:24
of the everlasting *c*............ Heb. 13:20
COVENANTS (3/3)
the glory, the *c*......................Rom. 9:4
COVER (73/72)
He shall *c* you with.................. Ps. 91:4
c a multitude of sins .... James 5:20
COVERED (99/95)
Whose sin is *c* .... Ps. 32:1
You have *c* all their sin .... Ps. 85:2
For there is nothing *c* ....Matt. 10:26
COVERING (43/38)
spread a cloud for a *c* ....Ps. 105:39
COVERINGS (2/2)
and made themselves *c* ....Gen. 3:7
COVET (10/9)
"You shall not *c*.....................Ex. 20:17
COVETED (2/2)
c no one's silver.................. Acts 20:33
COVETOUS (6/6)
nor thieves, nor *c* ....1 Cor. 6:10
COVETOUSNESS (17/17)
heed and beware of *c*..............Luke 12:15
COWARDLY (1/1)
the *c*, unbelieving.................. Rev. 21:8
CRAFTINESS (6/6)
not walking in *c*.................... 2 Cor. 4:2
in the cunning *c* ....Eph. 4:14
CRAFTSMAN (10/10)
instructor of every *c* .... Gen. 4:22
CRAFTY (7/7)
the devices of the *c* ....Job 5:12
Nevertheless, being *c* ....2 Cor. 12:16
CREAM (3/3)
were bathed with *c*....................Job 29:6
CREATE (11/9)
peace and *c* calamity.................Is. 45:7
CREATED (46/40)
So God *c* man in His ....Gen. 1:27
Has not one God *c* ....Mal. 2:10
c in Christ Jesus .... Eph. 2:10
new man which was *c* .... Eph. 4:24
CREATION (13/13)
know that the whole *c*......... Rom. 8:22
Christ, he is a new *c* .... 2 Cor. 5:17
anything, but a new *c* .... Gal. 6:15
CREATOR (7/7)
Remember now your *C*.......... Eccl. 12:1

God, the LORD, the **C** .... Is. 40:28
rather than the **C** .... Rom. 1:25
CREATURE (30/26)
the gospel to every **c** .... Mark 16:15
CREATURES (30/28)
firstfruits of His **c** .... James 1:18
CREDIT (4/4)
For what **c** is it if .... 1 Pet. 2:20
CREDITOR (5/5)
There was a certain **c** .... Luke 7:41
CREEP (7/7)
sort are those who **c** .... 2 Tim. 3:6
CREEPING (26/26)
c thing and beast of .... Gen. 1:24
CREPT (1/1)
For certain men have **c** .... Jude 1:4
CRIED (174/172)
the poor who **c** out .... Job 29:12
of the depths I have **c** .... Ps. 130:1
CRIES (18/18)
your brother's blood **c** .... Gen. 4:10
CRIMES (2/2)
land is filled with **c** .... Ezek. 7:23
CRIMINALS (3/3)
also two others, **c** .... Luke 23:32
CROOKED (13/13)
c places shall be made .... Is. 40:4
in the midst of a **c** .... Phil. 2:15
CROSS (85/84)
does not take his **c** .... Matt. 10:38
compelled to bear His **c** .... Matt. 27:32
down from the **c** .... Matt. 27:40
lest the **c** of Christ .... 1 Cor. 1:17
boast except in the **c** .... Gal. 6:14
the enemies of the **c** .... Phil. 3:18
Him endured the **c** .... Heb. 12:2
CROWD (31/31)
shall not follow a **c** .... Ex. 23:2
CROWN (60/59)
c the year with Your .... Ps. 65:11
they had twisted a **c** .... Matt. 27:29
obtain a perishable **c** .... 1 Cor. 9:25
laid up for me the **c** .... 2 Tim. 4:8
on His head a golden **c** .... Rev. 14:14
CROWNED (6/6)
angels, and You have **c** .... Ps. 8:5
athletics, he is not **c** .... 2 Tim. 2:5
CROWNS (8/8)
His head were many **c** .... Rev. 19:12
CRUCIFIED (39/39)
"Let Him be **c** .... Matt. 27:22
Calvary, there they **c** .... Luke 23:33
lawless hands, have **c** .... Acts 2:23
that our old man was **c** .... Rom. 6:6
Jesus Christ and Him **c** .... 1 Cor. 2:2
I have been **c** with Christ .... Gal. 2:20
CRUCIFY (14/10)
out again, "**C** Him .... Mark 15:13
CRUEL (19/19)
hate me with **c** hatred .... Ps. 25:19
CRUELTY (3/3)
the haunts of **c** .... Ps. 74:20
CRUSH (10/10)
of peace will **c** .... Rom. 16:20
CRUSHED (19/19)
every side, yet not **c** .... 2 Cor. 4:8
CRUST (1/1)
man is reduced to a **c** .... Prov. 6:26
CRY (172/160)
and their **c** came up to .... Ex. 2:23
Does not wisdom **c** .... Prov. 8:1
at midnight a **c** .... Matt. 25:6
His own elect who **c** .... Luke 18:7
CRYING (26/26)
nor sorrow, nor **c** .... Rev. 21:4
CRYSTAL (6/6)
a sea of glass, like **c** .... Rev. 4:6
CUBIT (42/27)
can add one **c** .... Matt. 6:27
CUNNING (6/6)
the serpent was more **c** .... Gen. 3:1
c craftiness of deceitful .... Eph. 4:14
CUP (69/60)
My **c** runs over .... Ps. 23:5
Then He took the **c** .... Matt. 26:27
possible, let this **c** .... Matt. 26:39
c is the new covenant .... Luke 22:20
cannot drink the **c** .... 1 Cor. 10:21
c is the new covenant .... 1 Cor. 11:25
CURE (4/4)
and to **c** diseases .... Luke 9:1
CURES (1/1)
and perform **c** .... Luke 13:32
CURSE (104/93)
c the ground for man's .... Gen. 8:21
C God and die .... Job 2:9
"I will send a **c** .... Mal. 2:2
law are under the **c** .... Gal. 3:10
CURSED (66/63)
c more than all cattle .... Gen. 3:14
'Depart from Me, you **c** .... Matt. 25:41
CURSES (18/18)
I will curse him who **c** .... Gen. 12:3
CURTAIN (25/14)
the heavens like a **c** .... Ps. 104:2
CUSTOM (27/27)
according to the **c** .... Acts 15:1
CUT (330/315)
evildoers shall be **c** .... Ps. 37:9
the wicked will be **c** .... Prov. 2:22
CYMBAL (1/1)
or a clanging **c** .... 1 Cor. 13:1

D

DAILY (58/57)
Give us this day our **d** .... Matt. 6:11
take up his cross **d** .... Luke 9:23
the Scriptures **d** .... Acts 17:11
DANCE (9/9)
mourn, and a time to **d** .... Eccl. 3:4
and you did not **d** .... Matt. 11:17
DANCED (5/5)
Then David **d** before .... 2 Sam. 6:14
DANCING (6/6)
saw the calf and the **d** .... Ex. 32:19
he heard music and **d** .... Luke 15:25
DARE (8/8)
someone would even **d** .... Rom. 5:7
DARK (44/44)
I tell you in the **d** .... Matt. 10:27
shines in a **d** place .... 2 Pet. 1:19
DARKENED (15/15)
their understanding **d** .... Eph. 4:18
DARKNESS (161/141)
d He called Night .... Gen. 1:5
Those who sat in **d** .... Ps. 107:10
d have seen a great light .... Is. 9:2
and deep **d** the people .... Is. 60:2
body will be full of **d** .... Matt. 6:23
cast out into outer **d** .... Matt. 8:12
d rather than light .... John 3:19
For you were once **d** .... Eph. 5:8
called you out of **d** .... 1 Pet. 2:9
blackness of **d** forever .... 2 Pet. 2:17
and in Him is no **d** .... 1 John 1:5
d is passing away .... 1 John 2:8
DARTS (2/2)
quench all the fiery **d** .... Eph. 6:16
DASH (8/8)
You shall **d** them to .... Ps. 2:9
lest you **d** your foot .... Matt. 4:6
DASHED (7/7)
infants shall be **d** .... Hos. 13:16
DAUGHTER (302/272)
"Rejoice greatly, O **d** .... Zech. 9:9
"Fear not, **d** of Zion .... John 12:15
the son of Pharaoh's **d** .... Heb. 11:24
DAUGHTERS (253/220)
of God saw the **d** .... Gen. 6:2
d shall prophesy .... Acts 2:17
DAY (1,563/1,390)
God called the light **D** .... Gen. 1:5
and **d** and night .... Gen. 8:22
Remember the Sabbath **d** .... Ex. 20:8
For a **d** in Your courts .... Ps. 84:10
d the LORD has made .... Ps. 118:24
not strike you by **d** .... Ps. 121:6
For the **d** of the LORD .... Joel 2:11
who can endure the **d** .... Mal. 3:2
d our daily bread .... Matt. 6:11
sent Me while it is **d** .... John 9:4
person esteems one **d** .... Rom. 14:5
D will declare it .... 1 Cor. 3:13
again the third **d** .... 1 Cor. 15:4
with the Lord one **d** .... 2 Pet. 3:8
DAYS (854/782)
d are swifter than a .... Job 7:6
of woman is of few **d** .... Job 14:1
The **d** of our lives are .... Ps. 90:10
Before the difficult **d** .... Eccl. 12:1
had shortened those **d** .... Mark 13:20
raise it up in three **d** .... John 2:20
DAYSPRING (1/1)
with which the **D** .... Luke 1:78
DEACONS (5/5)
with the bishops and **d** .... Phil. 1:1
d must be reverent .... 1 Tim. 3:8
d be the husbands .... 1 Tim. 3:12
DEAD (320/288)
But the **d** know nothing .... Eccl. 9:5
d bury their own **d** .... Matt. 8:22
not the God of the **d** .... Matt. 22:32
for this my son was **d** .... Luke 15:24
d will hear the voice .... John 5:25
was raised from the **d** .... Rom. 6:4
yourselves to be **d** .... Rom. 6:11
be Lord of both the **d** .... Rom. 14:9
resurrection of the **d** .... 1 Cor. 15:12
And the **d** in Christ .... 1 Thess. 4:16
without works is **d** .... James 2:26
And the **d** were judged .... Rev. 20:12
DEADLY (8/8)
they drink anything **d** .... Mark 16:18
evil, full of **d** poison .... James 3:8
DEADNESS (1/1)
the **d** of Sarah's womb .... Rom. 4:19
DEAF (15/15)
d shall be unstopped .... Is. 35:5
are cleansed and the **d** .... Matt. 11:5
DEAL (50/49)
My Servant shall **d** .... Is. 52:13
DEATH (395/360)
d parts you and me .... Ruth 1:17
and the shadow of **d** .... Job 10:21
I sleep the sleep of **d** .... Ps. 13:3
of the shadow of **d** .... Ps. 23:4
house leads down to **d** .... Prov. 2:18
who hate me love **d** .... Prov. 8:36
swallow up **d** forever .... Is. 25:8
no pleasure in the **d** .... Ezek. 18:32
who shall not taste **d** .... Matt. 16:28
but has passed from **d** .... John 5:24
Nevertheless **d** reigned .... Rom. 5:14
D no longer has .... Rom. 6:9
the wages of sin is **d** .... Rom. 6:23
proclaim the Lord's **d** .... 1 Cor. 11:26
since by man came **d** .... 1 Cor. 15:21
D is swallowed up in .... 1 Cor. 15:54
The sting of **d** is sin .... 1 Cor. 15:56
is sin leading to **d** .... 1 John 5:16
Be faithful until **d** .... Rev. 2:10
shall be no more **d** .... Rev. 21:4
which is the second **d** .... Rev. 21:8
DEBTOR (4/4)
I am a **d** both to .... Rom. 1:14
that he is a **d** to keep .... Gal. 5:3
DEBTORS (5/5)
as we forgive our **d** .... Matt. 6:12
of his master's **d** .... Luke 16:5
brethren, we are **d** .... Rom. 8:12
DECEIT (41/40)
Nor was any **d** in His .... Is. 53:9
philosophy and empty **d** .... Col. 2:8
no sin, nor was **d** .... 1 Pet. 2:22
mouth was found no **d** .... Rev. 14:5
DECEITFUL (24/24)
deliver me from the **d** .... Ps. 43:1
"The heart is **d** .... Jer. 17:9
are false apostles, **d** .... 2 Cor. 11:13
DECEITFULLY (10/10)
an idol, nor sworn **d** .... Ps. 24:4
the word of God **d** .... 2 Cor. 4:2
DECEITFULNESS (3/3)
this world and the **d** .... Matt. 13:22
DECEIVE (28/28)
rise up and **d** many .... Matt. 24:11
Let no one **d** you with .... Eph. 5:6
we have no sin, we **d** .... 1 John 1:8
DECEIVED (32/31)
"The serpent **d** .... Gen. 3:13
by the commandment, **d** .... Rom. 7:11
deceiving and being **d** .... 2 Tim. 3:13
DECEIVER (5/5)
how that **d** said .... Matt. 27:63
This is a **d** and an .... 2 John 1:7
DECEIVES (8/8)
heed that no one **d** .... Matt. 24:4
DECENTLY (1/1)
all things be done **d** .... 1 Cor. 14:40
DECEPTIVE (4/4)
you with **d** words .... 2 Pet. 2:3
DECISION (12/11)
in the valley of **d** .... Joel 3:14
DECLARE (90/90)
The heavens **d** the .... Ps. 19:1
d Your name to My .... Ps. 22:22
seen and heard we **d** .... 1 John 1:3
DECLARED (39/39)
and **d** to be the Son of .... Rom. 1:4
DECREE (50/49)
"I will declare the **d** .... Ps. 2:7
in those days that a **d** .... Luke 2:1
DEDICATION (13/12)
it was the Feast of **D** .... John 10:22
DEED (27/25)
you do in word or **d** .... Col. 3:17
DEEDS (79/79)
because their **d** .... John 3:19
You do the **d** of your .... John 8:41
one according to his **d** .... Rom. 2:6
you put to death the **d** .... Rom. 8:13
DEEP (74/72)
LORD God caused a **d** .... Gen. 2:21
d uttered its voice .... Hab. 3:10
"Launch out into the **d** .... Luke 5:4
I have been in the **d** .... 2 Cor. 11:25
DEEPER (11/11)
D than Sheol .... Job 11:8
DEEPLY (14/14)
But He sighed **d** .... Mark 8:12
DEER (17/16)
As the **d** pants for the .... Ps. 42:1
shall leap like a **d** .... Is. 35:6
DEFEATED (61/60)
and Israel was **d** .... 1 Sam. 4:10

DEFEND (15/15)
d the fatherless ... Is. 1:17
DEFENSE (25/24)
For wisdom is a *d* ... Eccl. 7:12
am appointed for the *d* ... Phil. 1:17
be ready to give a *d* ... 1 Pet. 3:15
DEFILE (47/42)
also these dreamers *d* ... Jude 1:8
DEFILED (84/80)
lest they should be *d* ... John 18:28
and conscience are *d* ... Titus 1:15
DEFILES (11/10)
mouth, this *d* a man ... Matt. 15:11
it anything that *d* ... Rev. 21:27
DEFRAUD (2/2)
d his brother in this ... 1 Thess. 4:6
DEGREES (8/5)
go forward ten *d* ... 2 Kin. 20:9
DELICACIES (11/11)
of the king's *d* ... Dan. 1:5
DELICATE (4/4)
a lovely and *d* woman ... Jer. 6:2
DELIGHT (62/60)
But his *d* is in the ... Ps. 1:2
I *d* to do Your will ... Ps. 40:8
And I was daily His *d* ... Prov. 8:30
And let your soul *d* ... Is. 55:2
call the Sabbath a *d* ... Is. 58:13
For I *d* in the law of ... Rom. 7:22
DELIGHTS (18/17)
For the LORD *d* in you ... Is. 62:4
DELIVER (264/253)
Let Him *d* Him ... Ps. 22:8
I will *d* him and honor ... Ps. 91:15
into temptation, but *d* ... Matt. 6:13
let Him *d* Him now if ... Matt. 27:43
And the Lord will *d* ... 2 Tim. 4:18
d the godly out of ... 2 Pet. 2:9
DELIVERANCE (17/16)
not accepting *d* ... Heb. 11:35
DELIVERED (246/244)
who was *d* up because ... Rom. 4:25
was once for all *d* ... Jude 1:3
DELIVERER (12/12)
D will come out of ... Rom. 11:26
DELIVERS (22/22)
even Jesus who *d* ... 1 Thess. 1:10
DELUSION (2/2)
send them strong *d* ... 2 Thess. 2:11
DEMON (20/18)
Jesus rebuked the *d* ... Matt. 17:18
and have a *d* ... John 8:48
DEMONIC (1/1)
is earthly, sensual, *d* ... James 3:15
DEMONS (49/42)
authority over all *d* ... Luke 9:1
the *d* are subject ... Luke 10:17
Even the *d* believe ... James 2:19
DEMONSTRATE (2/2)
faith, to *d* His ... Rom. 3:25
DEMONSTRATES (2/2)
d His own love toward ... Rom. 5:8
DEN (19/17)
cast him into the *d* ... Dan. 6:16
it a '*d* of thieves ... Matt. 21:13
DENARIUS (9/8)
the laborers for a *d* ... Matt. 20:2
DENIED (17/17)
before men will be *d* ... Luke 12:9
Peter then *d* again ... John 18:27
d the Holy One and the ... Acts 3:14
things cannot be *d* ... Acts 19:36
household, he has *d* ... 1 Tim. 5:8
DENIES (5/4)
But whoever *d* Me ... Matt. 10:33
d that Jesus is the ... 1 John 2:22
DENY (26/25)
let him *d* himself ... Matt. 16:24
He cannot *d* Himself ... 2 Tim. 2:13
DENYING (3/3)
but *d* its power ... 2 Tim. 3:5
d the Lord who bought ... 2 Pet. 2:1
DEPART (125/122)
scepter shall not *d* ... Gen. 49:10
on the left hand, '*D* ... Matt. 25:41
will *d* from the faith ... 1 Tim. 4:1
DEPARTING (8/8)
heart of unbelief in *d* ... Heb. 3:12
DEPARTURE (4/4)
d savage wolves will ... Acts 20:29
and the time of my *d* ... 2 Tim. 4:6
DEPRESSION (1/1)
of man causes *d* ... Prov. 12:25
DEPTH (9/9)
nor height nor *d* ... Rom. 8:39
Oh, the *d* of the ... Rom. 11:33
DEPTHS (31/31)
our sins into the *d* ... Mic. 7:19
DERISION (12/12)
shall hold them in *d* ... Ps. 2:4
DESCEND (10/10)
d now from the cross ... Mark 15:32
Lord Himself will *d* ... 1 Thess. 4:16
DESCENDANTS (157/143)
"We are Abraham's *d* ... John 8:33
DESCENDED (19/18)
He who *d* is also the ... Eph. 4:10
DESCENDING (11/11)
God ascending and *d* ... John 1:51
the holy Jerusalem, *d* ... Rev. 21:10
DESERT (28/28)
and rivers in the *d* ... Is. 43:19
'Look, He is in the *d* ... Matt. 24:26
DESERTED (15/15)
d place by Himself ... Matt. 14:13
DESERTS (6/6)
They wandered in *d* ... Heb. 11:38
DESIGN (11/9)
with an artistic *d* ... Ex. 26:31
DESIRABLE (9/9)
the eyes, and a tree *d* ... Gen. 3:6
DESIRE (122/121)
d shall be for your ... Gen. 3:16
Behold, You *d* truth in ... Ps. 51:6
"Father, I *d* that ... John 17:24
all manner of evil *d* ... Rom. 7:8
Brethren, my heart's *d* ... Rom. 10:1
d the best gifts ... 1 Cor. 12:31
the two, having a *d* ... Phil. 1:23
DESIRED (28/28)
d are they than gold ... Ps. 19:10
One thing I have *d* ... Ps. 27:4
DESIRES (43/41)
shall give you the *d* ... Ps. 37:4
the devil, and the *d* ... John 8:44
not come from your *d* ... James 4:1
DESOLATE (147/132)
any more be termed *D* ... Is. 62:4
house is left to you *d* ... Matt. 23:38
DESOLATION (45/45)
the 'abomination of *d* ... Matt. 24:15
DESPAIRED (2/2)
strength, so that we *d* ... 2 Cor. 1:8
DESPISE (40/40)
one and *d* the other ... Matt. 6:24
d the riches of His ... Rom. 2:4
DESPISED (58/57)
He is *d* and rejected ... Is. 53:3
the things which are *d* ... 1 Cor. 1:28
DESPISES (12/12)
d his neighbor sins ... Prov. 14:21
DESPISING (1/1)
the cross, *d* the shame ... Heb. 12:2
DESTITUTE (7/7)
of corrupt minds and *d* ... 1 Tim. 6:5
DESTROY (270/252)
Why should you *d* ... Eccl. 7:16
shall not hurt nor *d* ... Is. 11:9
I did not come to *d* ... Matt. 5:17
Him who is able to *d* ... Matt. 10:28
Barabbas and *d* Jesus ... Matt. 27:20
to save life or to *d* ... Luke 6:9
d men's lives but to ... Luke 9:56
d the wisdom of the ... 1 Cor. 1:19
able to save and to *d* ... James 4:12
DESTROYED (171/166)
d all living things ... Gen. 7:23
house, this tent, is *d* ... 2 Cor. 5:1
DESTRUCTION (108/106)
You turn man to *d* ... Ps. 90:3
d that lays waste ... Ps. 91:6
your life from *d* ... Ps. 103:4
Pride goes before *d* ... Prov. 16:18
whose end is *d* ... Phil. 3:19
with everlasting *d* ... 2 Thess. 1:9
DESTRUCTIVE (2/2)
bring in *d* heresies ... 2 Pet. 2:1
DETERMINED (41/41)
d their preappointed ... Acts 17:26
For I *d* not to know ... 1 Cor. 2:2
DEVICE (1/1)
there is no work or *d* ... Eccl. 9:10
DEVICES (3/3)
not ignorant of his *d* ... 2 Cor. 2:11
DEVIL (35/33)
to be tempted by the *d* ... Matt. 4:1
prepared for the *d* ... Matt. 25:41
of your father the *d* ... John 8:44
give place to the *d* ... Eph. 4:27
the snare of the *d* ... 2 Tim. 2:26
the works of the *d* ... 1 John 3:8
DEVIOUS (3/3)
crooked, and who are *d* ... Prov. 2:15
DEVISES (9/9)
d wickedness on his ... Ps. 36:4
But a generous man *d* ... Is. 32:8
DEVOID (6/6)
He who is *d* of wisdom ... Prov. 11:12
DEVOTED (7/6)
Your servant, who is *d* ... Ps. 119:38
DEVOUR (66/65)
For you *d* widows' ... Matt. 23:14
bite and *d* one another ... Gal. 5:15
seeking whom he may *d* ... 1 Pet. 5:8
d her Child as ... Rev. 12:4
DEVOURED (50/49)
Some wild beast has *d* ... Gen. 37:20
birds came and *d* them ... Matt. 13:4
of heaven and *d* them ... Rev. 20:9
DEVOUT (9/9)
man was just and *d* ... Luke 2:25
d soldier from among ... Acts 10:7
DEW (37/36)
God give you of the *d* ... Gen. 27:28
DIADEMS (1/1)
ten horns, and seven *d* ... Rev. 12:3
DIAMOND (4/4)
d it is engraved ... Jer. 17:1
DICTATES (9/9)
according to the *d* ... Jer. 23:17
DIE (290/271)
it you shall surely *d* ... Gen. 2:17
I shall not *d*, but live ... Ps. 118:17
born, and a time to *d* ... Eccl. 3:2
eat of it and not *d* ... John 6:50
to you that you will *d* ... John 8:24
though he may *d* ... John 11:25
that one man should *d* ... John 11:50
the flesh you will *d* ... Rom. 8:13
For as in Adam all *d* ... 1 Cor. 15:22
and to *d* is gain ... Phil. 1:21
for men to *d* once ... Heb. 9:27
are the dead who *d* ... Rev. 14:13
DIED (229/216)
And all flesh *d* ... Gen. 7:21
in due time Christ *d* ... Rom. 5:6
Christ *d* for us ... Rom. 5:8
Now if we *d* with ... Rom. 6:8
and He *d* for all ... 2 Cor. 5:15
for if we *d* with Him ... 2 Tim. 2:11
DIES (56/49)
made alive unless it *d* ... 1 Cor. 15:36
DIFFERS (1/1)
for one star *d* from ... 1 Cor. 15:41
DILIGENCE (9/9)
d it produced in you ... 2 Cor. 7:11
DILIGENT (17/16)
hand of the *d* makes rich ... Prov. 10:4
DILIGENTLY (23/23)
he sought it *d* with tears ... Heb. 12:17
DIM (10/10)
His eyes were not *d* ... Deut. 34:7
DIMLY (1/1)
we see in a mirror, *d* ... 1 Cor. 13:12
DINE (4/4)
come in to him and *d* ... Rev. 3:20
DINNER (5/5)
invites you to *d* ... 1 Cor. 10:27
DIP (10/10)
d your piece of bread ... Ruth 2:14
DIPPED (10/9)
clothed with a robe *d* ... Rev. 19:13
DIRECT (12/12)
Now may the Lord *d* ... 2 Thess. 3:5
DIRT (4/4)
cast up mire and *d* ... Is. 57:20
DISARMED (1/1)
d principalities ... Col. 2:15
DISASTER (39/37)
voyage will end with *d* ... Acts 27:10
DISCERN (15/13)
d the face of the sky ... Matt. 16:3
senses exercised to *d* ... Heb. 5:14
DISCERNED (1/1)
they are spiritually *d* ... 1 Cor. 2:14
DISCERNER (1/1)
d of the thoughts ... Heb. 4:12
DISCERNS (1/1)
a wise man's heart *d* ... Eccl. 8:5
DISCIPLE (29/27)
he cannot be My *d* ... Luke 14:26
d whom Jesus loved ... John 21:7
DISCIPLES (245/234)
My word, you are My *d* ... John 8:31
but we are Moses' *d* ... John 9:28
DISCIPLINES (1/1)
but he who loves him *d* ... Prov. 13:24
DISCORD (2/2)
and one who sows *d* ... Prov. 6:19
DISCOURAGED (8/8)
lest they become *d* ... Col. 3:21
you become weary and *d* ... Heb. 12:3
DISCRETION (9/9)
D will preserve you ... Prov. 2:11
DISFIGURE (2/2)
d their faces that ... Matt. 6:16
DISGUISES (2/2)
and he *d* his face ... Job 24:15
DISHONOR (19/19)
d their bodies among ... Rom. 1:24
It is sown in *d* ... 1 Cor. 15:43
DISHONORED (2/2)
But you have *d* the ... James 2:6
DISHONORS (3/3)
For son *d* father ... Mic. 7:6

DISOBEDIENT (14/14)
out My hands to a *d* .... Rom. 10:21
DISORDERLY (4/4)
for this *d* gathering ....Acts 19:40
DISPENSATION (2/2)
d of the fullness of............. Eph. 1:10
DISPERSION (2/2)
the pilgrims of the *D*..............1 Pet. 1:1
DISPLEASE (4/4)
LORD see it, and it *d*.......... Prov. 24:18
DISPLEASED (18/18)
they were greatly *d*........... Matt. 20:24
it, He was greatly *d*.......... Mark 10:14
DISPUTE (13/13)
Now there was also a *d* .... Luke 22:24
DISPUTER (1/1)
Where is the *d* of this ....1 Cor. 1:20
DISPUTES (6/6)
But avoid foolish *d*.............Titus 3:9
DISQUALIFIED (5/5)
myself should become *d* ....1 Cor. 9:27
DISQUIETED (3/3)
And why are you *d* .... Ps. 42:5
DISSENSION (4/4)
had no small *d* and ....Acts 15:2
DISSIPATION (3/3)
not accused of *d*............... Titus 1:6
DISSOLVED (6/6)
the heavens will be *d*..........2 Pet. 3:12
DISTINCTION (4/4)
compassion, making a *d* .... Jude 1:22
DISTRESS (44/44)
d them in His deep................. Ps. 2:5
tribulation, or *d* ....Rom. 8:35
DISTRESSED (18/18)
troubled and deeply *d*........Mark 14:33
DISTRESSES (7/7)
bring me out of my *d*........... Ps. 25:17
DISTRIBUTED (9/9)
and they *d* to each as...........Acts 4:35
DISTRIBUTING (2/2)
d to the needs of the .... Rom. 12:13
DITCH (3/3)
will fall into a *d*.............. Matt. 15:14
DIVERSITIES (2/2)
There are *d* of gifts.............1 Cor. 12:4
DIVIDE (45/43)
d the spoil with the .... Prov. 16:19
"Take this and *d* .... Luke 22:17
DIVIDED (72/69)
and the waters were *d*.......... Ex. 14:21
death they were not *d*........2 Sam. 1:23
"Every kingdom *d* .... Matt. 12:25
Is Christ *d*? Was Paul........... 1 Cor. 1:13
DIVIDES (7/7)
at home *d* the spoil .... Ps. 68:12
DIVIDING (5/5)
rightly *d* the word of.......... 2 Tim. 2:15
DIVINATION (15/15)
shall you practice *d*........... Lev. 19:26
a spirit of *d* met us............Acts 16:16
DIVINE (9/9)
d service and the ....Heb. 9:1
DIVISION (27/24)
So there was a *d* .... John 7:43
DIVISIONS (41/37)
note those who cause *d* .... Rom. 16:17
persons, who cause *d* ....Jude 1:19
DIVISIVE (1/1)
Reject a *d* man after............ Titus 3:10
DIVORCE (16/16)
her a certificate of *d*.......... Deut. 24:1
a certificate of *d* ....Mark 10:4
DO (2,574/2,243)
men to *d* to you, *d* .... Matt. 7:12
He sees the Father *d* .... John 5:19
without Me you can *d* .... John 15:5
"Sirs, what must I *d*............ Acts 16:30
d evil that good may ....Rom. 3:8
or whatever you *d*, *d* ....1 Cor. 10:31
DOCTRINE (37/36)
What new *d* is this .... Mark 1:27
"My *d* is not Mine .... John 7:16
with every wind of *d* ....Eph. 4:14
is contrary to sound *d*...........1 Tim. 1:10
is profitable for *d* ....2 Tim. 3:16
not endure sound *d*............2 Tim. 4:3
DOCTRINES (5/5)
the commandments and *d* ...... Col. 2:22
various and strange *d*.......... Heb. 13:9
DOERS (2/2)
But be *d* of the word ....James 1:22
DOG (15/15)
d is better than a................ Eccl. 9:4
d returns to his own .... 2 Pet. 2:22
DOGS (24/23)
what is holy to the *d*............Matt. 7:6
d eat the crumbs which .... Matt. 15:27
But outside are *d* .... Rev. 22:15
DOMINION (56/50)
let them have *d*................Gen. 1:26

d is an everlasting .... Dan. 4:34
sin shall not have *d* ....Rom. 6:14
glory and majesty, *d* .... Jude 1:25
DONKEY (84/75)
d its master's crib................Is. 1:3
and riding on a *d* ....Zech. 9:9
colt, the foal of a *d* .... Matt. 21:5
d speaking with a................2 Pet. 2:16
DOOM (15/15)
for the day of *d* .... Prov. 16:4
DOOR (163/155)
stone against the *d*...........Matt. 27:60
to you, I am the *d* .... John 10:7
before you an open *d* ....Rev. 3:8
I stand at the *d* ....Rev. 3:20
DOORKEEPER (3/3)
I would rather be a *d*........... Ps. 84:10
DOORPOSTS (17/17)
write them on the *d*........... Deut. 6:9
DOORS (70/67)
up, you everlasting *d*............ Ps. 24:7
DOUBLE (24/22)
from the LORD's hand *d* .... Is. 40:2
worthy of *d* honor ....1 Tim. 5:17
DOUBLE-MINDED (3/3)
he is a *d* man .... James 1:8
DOUBT (9/9)
faith, why did you *d* .... Matt. 14:31
DOUBTING (4/4)
in faith, with no *d*............... James 1:6
DOUBTS (4/4)
And why do *d* arise in .... Luke 24:38
for I have *d* about you.......... Gal. 4:20
DOVE (20/20)
d found no resting.............. Gen. 8:9
descending like a *d* .... Matt. 3:16
DOVES (10/10)
and harmless as *d* .... Matt. 10:16
DOWNCAST (1/1)
who comforts the *d* ....2 Cor. 7:6
DRAGNET (3/3)
d that was cast................. Matt. 13:47
DRAGON (13/12)
they worshiped the *d*............ Rev. 13:4
He laid hold of the *d* ....Rev. 20:2
DRAINED (6/6)
all faces are *d*....................Joel 2:6
DRANK (47/46)
them, and they all *d*.......... Mark 14:23
DRAW (65/64)
d honey from the rock ....Deut. 32:13
me to *d* near to God............ Ps. 73:28
and the years *d* .... Eccl. 12:1
will *d* all peoples............. John 12:32
D near to God and He ....James 4:8
DRAWS (12/12)
your redemption *d*............. Luke 21:28
DREAM (72/59)
Now Joseph had a *d*.............Gen. 37:5
your old men shall *d* ....Joel 2:28
to Joseph in a *d*................. Matt. 2:13
things today in a *d* .... Matt. 27:19
DREAMERS (2/2)
d defile the flesh................ Jude 1:8
DREAMS (26/25)
Nebuchadnezzar had *d*............Dan. 2:1
DRIED (36/35)
of her blood was *d* ....Mark 5:29
saw the fig tree *d*..............Mark 11:20
DRIFT (1/1)
have heard, lest we *d*............Heb. 2:1
DRINK (347/307)
gave me vinegar to *d*............ Ps. 69:21
lest they *d* and forget .... Prov. 31:5
follow intoxicating *d*.............Is. 5:11
d the milk of the.................. Is. 60:16
bosom, that you may *d*.............Is. 66:11
"Bring wine, let us *d*........... Amos 4:1
that day when I *d* .... Matt. 26:29
mingled with gall to *d*.........Matt. 27:34
with myrrh to *d*.................Mark 15:23
to her, "Give Me a *d* .... John 4:7
him come to Me and *d* .... John 7:37
do, as often as you *d* .... 1 Cor. 11:25
No longer *d* only water ....1 Tim. 5:23
DRINKS (21/20)
to her, "Whoever *d*............ John 4:13
d My blood has eternal ....John 6:54
For he who eats and *d*..........1 Cor. 11:29
DRIPPING (4/4)
His lips are lilies, *d*............ Song 5:13
DROSS (8/7)
purge away your *d* ....Is. 1:25
DROUGHT (9/9)
in the year of *d* ....Jer. 17:8
For I called for a *d* .... Hag. 1:11
DROVE (37/37)
So He *d* out the man .... Gen. 3:24
temple of God and *d* .... Matt. 21:12
DROWN (2/2)
nor can the floods *d*............ Song 8:7

harmful lusts which *d*..........1 Tim. 6:9
DROWSINESS (1/1)
d will clothe a.................. Prov. 23:21
DRUNK (48/46)
of the wine and was *d* ....Gen. 9:21
the guests have well *d*.......... John 2:10
For these are not *d*............... Acts 2:15
and another is *d* .... 1 Cor. 11:21
I saw the woman, *d* .... Rev. 17:6
DRUNKARD (6/6)
to and fro like a *d* .... Is. 24:20
or a reviler, or a *d* .... 1 Cor. 5:11
DRUNKEN (5/5)
I am like a *d* man .... Jer. 23:9
DRUNKENNESS (8/8)
will be filled with *d*...........Ezek. 23:33
not in revelry and *d* .... Rom. 13:13
envy, murders, *d*.................. Gal. 5:21
DRY (75/70)
place, and let the *d*................Gen. 1:9
made the sea into *d* .... Ex. 14:21
It was *d* on the fleece............ Judg. 6:40
will be done in the *d* .... Luke 23:31
DUE (38/35)
pay all that was *d* .... Matt. 18:34
d time Christ died...................Rom. 5:6
d season we shall .... Gal. 6:9
exalt you in *d* time..............1 Pet. 5:6
DULL (6/6)
heart of this people *d* .... Is. 6:10
people have grown *d*............ Matt. 13:15
DUMB (5/5)
the tongue of the *d*................. Is. 35:6
DUST (114/107)
formed man of the *d*...............Gen. 2:7
d you shall return..................Gen. 3:19
and repent in *d* .... Job 42:6
remembers that we are *d*........ Ps. 103:14
counted as the small *d* .... Is. 40:15
city, shake off the *d* .... Matt. 10:14
image of the man of *d*..........1 Cor. 15:49
DUTY (20/16)
done what was our *d* ....Luke 17:10
DWELL (369/343)
Who may *d* in Your holy............Ps. 15:1
"I will *d* in them ....2 Cor. 6:16
that Christ may *d* ....Eph. 3:17
men, and He will *d*............... Rev. 21:3
DWELLING (109/109)
built together for a *d* .... Eph. 2:22
a foreign country, *d*............... Heb. 11:9
DWELLS (68/66)
He who *d* in the secret ....Ps. 91:1
but the Father who *d*........... John 14:10
d all the fullness .... Col. 2:9
which righteousness *d* ....2 Pet. 3:13
you, where Satan *d*............... Rev. 2:13
DWELT (220/212)
became flesh and *d* .... John 1:14
By faith he *d* in the.............Heb. 11:9
DYING (13/13)
in the body the *d*..................2 Cor. 4:10

E

EAGLE (21/21)
fly away like an *e*.................Prov. 23:5
The way of an *e* ....Prov. 30:19
like a flying *e* .... Rev. 4:7
EAGLES (7/7)
up with wings like *e*............... Is. 40:31
e will be gathered.............Matt. 24:28
EAGLES' (2/2)
how I bore you on *e* .... Ex. 19:4
EAR (112/111)
shall pierce his *e*...................Ex. 21:6
And the *e* of the wise.......... Prov. 18:15
e is uncircumcised.................. Jer. 6:10
what you hear in the *e*........ Matt. 10:27
cut off his right *e* .... John 18:10
not seen, nor *e* heard.............1 Cor. 2:9
He who has an *e* .... Rev. 2:7
EARLY (83/82)
Very *e* in the morning........... Mark 16:2
arrived at the tomb *e*.......... Luke 24:22
EARNESTLY (24/24)
He prayed more *e*............... Luke 22:44
e that it would not .... James 5:17
you to contend *e*.................... Jude 1:3
EARS (86/83)
And hear with their *e*................ Is. 6:10
He who has *e* ....Matt. 11:15
they have itching *e*..............2 Tim. 4:3
EARTH (941/863)
coming to judge the *e* ....1 Chr. 16:33
foundations of the *e* .... Job 38:4
e is the LORD's.......................Ps. 24:1
You had formed the *e* ....Ps. 90:2
there was ever an *e*.............Prov. 8:23
e abides forever....................Eccl. 1:4
for the meek of the *e*..............Is. 11:4
e is My footstool ....Is. 66:1

I will darken the *e* ... Amos 8:9
shall inherit the *e* ... Matt. 5:5
heaven and *e* pass away ... Matt. 5:18
e as it is in heaven ... Matt. 6:10
treasures on *e*, where ... Matt. 6:19
then shook the *e* ... Heb. 12:26
new heaven and a new *e* ... Rev. 21:1
EARTHLY (6/6)
If I have told you *e* ... John 3:12
that if our *e* house ... 2 Cor. 5:1
their mind on *e* things ... Phil. 3:19
from above, but is *e* ... James 3:15
EARTHQUAKE (17/14)
LORD was not in the *e* ... 1 Kin. 19:11
there was a great *e* ... Matt. 28:2
EARTHQUAKES (3/3)
And there will be *e* ... Mark 13:8
EASIER (8/8)
Which is *e*, to say ... Mark 2:9
It is *e* for a camel ... Mark 10:25
EAST (169/161)
goes toward the *e* ... Gen. 2:14
wise men from the *E* ... Matt. 2:1
many will come from *e* ... Matt. 8:11
will come from the *e* ... Luke 13:29
EAT (554/494)
you may freely *e* ... Gen. 2:16
'You shall not *e* ... Gen. 3:17
e this scroll ... Ezek. 3:1
life, what you will *e* ... Matt. 6:25
give us His flesh to *e* ... John 6:52
one believes he may *e* ... Rom. 14:2
e meat nor drink wine ... Rom. 14:21
I will never again *e* ... 1 Cor. 8:13
neither shall he *e* ... 2 Thess. 3:10
EATEN (96/90)
Have you *e* from the ... Gen. 3:11
And he was *e* by worms ... Acts 12:23
EATS (47/42)
receives sinners and *e* ... Luke 15:2
Whoever *e* My flesh ... John 6:54
e this bread will live ... John 6:58
He who *e*, *e* to the ... Rom. 14:6
an unworthy manner *e* ... 1 Cor. 11:29
EDIFICATION (10/10)
has given me for *e* ... 2 Cor. 13:10
rather than godly *e* ... 1 Tim. 1:4
EDIFIES (3/2)
puffs up, but love *e* ... 1 Cor. 8:1
EDIFY (3/3)
but not all things *e* ... 1 Cor. 10:23
EDIFYING (2/2)
of the body for the *e* ... Eph. 4:16
ELDER (12/12)
against an *e* except ... 1 Tim. 5:19
ELDERS (199/194)
the tradition of the *e* ... Matt. 15:2
be rejected by the *e* ... Luke 9:22
they had appointed *e* ... Acts 14:23
e who rule well be ... 1 Tim. 5:17
lacking, and appoint *e* ... Titus 1:5
e obtained a good ... Heb. 11:2
e who are among you I ... 1 Pet. 5:1
I saw twenty-four *e* ... Rev. 4:4
ELDERSHIP (1/1)
of the hands of the *e* ... 1 Tim. 4:14
ELECT (20/20)
gather together His *e* ... Matt. 24:31
e have obtained it ... Rom. 11:7
e according to the ... 1 Pet. 1:2
a chief cornerstone, *e* ... 1 Pet. 2:6
ELECTION (5/5)
call and *e* sure ... 2 Pet. 1:10
ELEMENTS (4/4)
weak and beggarly *e* ... Gal. 4:9
e will melt with ... 2 Pet. 3:10
ELEVEN (24/24)
numbered with the *e* ... Acts 1:26
ELOQUENT (2/2)
an *e* man and mighty ... Acts 18:24
EMBALM (1/1)
to *e* his father ... Gen. 50:2
ENCOURAGED (14/14)
is, that I may be *e* ... Rom. 1:12
and all may be *e* ... 1 Cor. 14:31
END (256/239)
make me to know my *e* ... Ps. 39:4
shall keep it to the *e* ... Ps. 119:33
e is the way of death ... Prov. 14:12
There was no *e* of all ... Eccl. 4:16
Declaring the *e* ... Is. 46:10
what shall be the *e* ... Dan. 12:8
the harvest is the *e* ... Matt. 13:39
always, even to the *e* ... Matt. 28:20
He loved them to the *e* ... John 13:1
For Christ is the *e* ... Rom. 10:4
But the *e* of all ... 1 Pet. 4:7
the latter *e* is worse ... 2 Pet. 2:20
My works until the *e* ... Rev. 2:26
Beginning and the *E* ... Rev. 22:13
ENDLESS (2/2)
and *e* genealogies ... 1 Tim. 1:4

to the power of an *e* ... Heb. 7:16
ENDURANCE (2/2)
run with *e* the race that ... Heb. 12:1
ENDURE (42/40)
as the sun and moon *e* ... Ps. 72:5
His name shall *e* ... Ps. 72:17
persecuted, we *e* ... 1 Cor. 4:12
ENDURED (7/7)
he had patiently *e* ... Heb. 6:15
e as seeing Him who ... Heb. 11:27
For consider Him who *e* ... Heb. 12:3
ENDURES (64/64)
And His truth *e* ... Ps. 100:5
For His mercy *e* ... Ps. 136:1
But he who *e* to the ... Matt. 10:22
e only for a while ... Matt. 13:21
for the food which *e* ... John 6:27
he has built on it *e* ... 1 Cor. 3:14
hopes all things, *e* ... 1 Cor. 13:7
word of the LORD *e* ... 1 Pet. 1:25
ENDURING (7/7)
the LORD is clean, *e* ... Ps. 19:9
ENEMIES (267/260)
the presence of my *e* ... Ps. 23:5
e will lick the dust ... Ps. 72:9
to you, love your *e* ... Matt. 5:44
a man's *e* will be those ... Matt. 10:36
e we were reconciled ... Rom. 5:10
till He has put all *e* ... 1 Cor. 15:25
were alienated and *e* ... Col. 1:21
His *e* are made His ... Heb. 10:13
ENEMY (110/109)
If your *e* is hungry ... Prov. 25:21
rejoice over me, my *e* ... Mic. 7:8
and hate your *e* ... Matt. 5:43
last *e* that will be ... 1 Cor. 15:26
become your *e* because ... Gal. 4:16
not count him as an *e* ... 2 Thess. 3:15
makes himself an *e* ... James 4:4
ENJOY (13/12)
richly all things to *e* ... 1 Tim. 6:17
than to *e* the passing ... Heb. 11:25
ENJOYMENT (3/3)
So I commended *e* ... Eccl. 8:15
ENLIGHTEN (4/4)
E my eyes, lest I sleep ... Ps. 13:3
ENLIGHTENED (3/3)
those who were once *e* ... Heb. 6:4
ENMITY (10/10)
And I will put *e* ... Gen. 3:15
the carnal mind is *e* ... Rom. 8:7
in His flesh the *e* ... Eph. 2:15
ENRAPTURED (2/2)
And always be *e* ... Prov. 5:19
ENRICHED (4/4)
while you are *e* ... 2 Cor. 9:11
ENSNARED (3/3)
The wicked is *e* ... Prov. 12:13
ENSNARES (1/1)
sin which so easily *e* ... Heb. 12:1
ENTER (155/149)
E into His gates ... Ps. 100:4
you will by no means *e* ... Matt. 5:20
"*E* by the narrow ... Matt. 7:13
e the kingdom of God ... Matt. 19:24
E into the joy of your ... Matt. 25:21
and pray, lest you *e* ... Matt. 26:41
"Strive to *e* through ... Luke 13:24
who have believed do *e* ... Heb. 4:3
e the temple till the ... Rev. 15:8
ENTERED (99/98)
Then Satan *e* Judas ... Luke 22:3
through one man sin *e* ... Rom. 5:12
ear heard, nor have *e* ... 1 Cor. 2:9
the forerunner has *e* ... Heb. 6:20
e the Most Holy Place ... Heb. 9:12
ENTERS (20/19)
If anyone *e* by Me ... John 10:9
ENTHRONED (2/2)
You are holy, *e* in ... Ps. 22:3
ENTIRELY (4/4)
give yourself *e* to them ... 1 Tim. 4:15
ENTREAT (9/9)
being defamed, we *e* ... 1 Cor. 4:13
ENTREATED (6/6)
e our God for this ... Ezra 8:23
ENVIOUS (6/6)
patriarchs, becoming *e* ... Acts 7:9
ENVY (24/23)
e slays a simple ... Job 5:2
e is rottenness ... Prov. 14:30
full of *e*, murder ... Rom. 1:29
not in strife and *e* ... Rom. 13:13
love does not *e* ... 1 Cor. 13:4
e, murders, drunkenness ... Gal. 5:21
living in malice and *e* ... Titus 3:3
EPISTLE (12/11)
You are our *e* written ... 2 Cor. 3:2
EPISTLES (2/2)
as also in all his *e* ... 2 Pet. 3:16
ERR (7/7)
My people Israel to *e* ... Jer. 23:13

ERROR (14/14)
a sinner from the *e* ... James 5:20
led away with the *e* ... 2 Pet. 3:17
run greedily in the *e* ... Jude 1:11
ERRORS (3/3)
can understand his *e* ... Ps. 19:12
ESCAPE (65/61)
e all these things ... Luke 21:36
same, that you will *e* ... Rom. 2:3
also make the way of *e* ... 1 Cor. 10:13
how shall we *e* if we ... Heb. 2:3
ESCAPED (56/54)
after they have *e* ... 2 Pet. 2:20
ESTABLISH (56/55)
seeking to *e* their own ... Rom. 10:3
faithful, who will *e* ... 2 Thess. 3:3
E your hearts ... James 5:8
a while, perfect, *e* ... 1 Pet. 5:10
ESTABLISHED (89/87)
Your throne is *e* ... Ps. 93:2
let all your ways be *e* ... Prov. 4:26
built up in Him and *e* ... Col. 2:7
covenant, which was *e* ... Heb. 8:6
ESTEEM (6/6)
and we did not *e* ... Is. 53:3
e others better than ... Phil. 2:3
ESTEEMED (11/11)
For what is highly *e* ... Luke 16:15
ESTEEMS (2/1)
One person *e* one day ... Rom. 14:5
ETERNAL (50/50)
e God is your refuge ... Deut. 33:27
For man goes to his *e* ... Eccl. 12:5
and inherit *e* life ... Matt. 19:29
in the age to come, *e* ... Mark 10:30
not perish but have *e* ... John 3:15
you think you have *e* ... John 5:39
And I give them *e* life ... John 10:28
And this is *e* life ... John 17:3
the gift of God is *e* ... Rom. 6:23
are not seen are *e* ... 2 Cor. 4:18
lay hold on *e* life ... 1 Tim. 6:12
e life which was ... 1 John 1:2
ETERNITY (3/3)
Also He has put *e* ... Eccl. 3:11
One who inhabits *e* ... Is. 57:15
EUNUCH (10/10)
of Ethiopia, a *e* ... Acts 8:27
EUNUCHS (29/25)
have made themselves *e* ... Matt. 19:12
EVANGELIST (2/2)
house of Philip the *e* ... Acts 21:8
do the work of an *e* ... 2 Tim. 4:5
EVANGELISTS (1/1)
some prophets, some *e* ... Eph. 4:11
EVERLASTING (100/93)
from *E* is Your name ... Is. 63:16
awake, some to *e* life ... Dan. 12:2
not perish but have *e* ... John 3:16
Him who sent Me has *e* ... John 5:24
endures to *e* life ... John 6:27
in Him may have *e* ... John 6:40
believes in Me has *e* ... John 6:47
e destruction from the ... 2 Thess. 1:9
EVIDENCE (6/6)
e of things not seen ... Heb. 11:1
EVIDENT (10/10)
e that our Lord arose ... Heb. 7:14
EVIL (482/454)
knowledge of good and *e* ... Gen. 2:9
knowing good and *e* ... Gen. 3:5
his heart was only *e* ... Gen. 6:5
I will fear no *e* ... Ps. 23:4
e more than good ... Ps. 52:3
To do *e* is like sport ... Prov. 10:23
e will bow before the ... Prov. 14:19
Keeping watch on the *e* ... Prov. 15:3
e all the days of her ... Prov. 31:12
to those who call *e* ... Is. 5:20
of peace and not of *e* ... Jer. 29:11
Seek good and not *e* ... Amos 5:14
deliver us from the *e* ... Matt. 6:13
If you then, being *e* ... Matt. 7:11
e treasure brings ... Matt. 12:35
everyone practicing *e* ... John 3:20
done any good or *e* ... Rom. 9:11
Repay no one *e* for ... Rom. 12:17
provoked, thinks no *e* ... 1 Cor. 13:5
EVILDOER (6/6)
"If He were not an *e* ... John 18:30
suffer trouble as an *e* ... 2 Tim. 2:9
EVILDOERS (17/17)
e shall be cut off ... Ps. 37:9
Depart from me, you *e* ... Ps. 119:115
iniquity, a brood of *e* ... Is. 1:4
against you as *e* ... 1 Pet. 2:12
EXALT (34/34)
e His name together ... Ps. 34:3
E the humble ... Ezek. 21:26
and he shall *e* himself ... Dan. 8:25
EXALTATION (4/4)
who rejoice in My *e* ... Is. 13:3

brother glory in his *e*........... James 1:9
EXALTED (81/79)
Let God be *e*.............. 2 Sam. 22:47
I will be *e* among the........... Ps. 46:10
You are *e* far above.............. Ps. 97:9
His name alone is *e*............ Ps. 148:13
valley shall be *e*................. Is. 40:4
Him God has *e*................. Acts 5:31
And lest I should be *e*......... 2 Cor. 12:7
also has highly *e*............... Phil. 2:9
EXALTS (10/10)
Righteousness *e*............ Prov. 14:34
high thing that *e*............ 2 Cor. 10:5
e himself above all........... 2 Thess. 2:4
EXAMINE (29/27)
But let a man *e*.............. 1 Cor. 11:28
But let each one *e*............... Gal. 6:4
EXAMPLE (10/10)
to make her a public *e*............ Matt. 1:19
I have given you an *e*.......... John 13:15
youth, but be an *e*.............. 1 Tim. 4:12
us, leaving us an *e*............ 1 Pet. 2:21
are set forth as an *e*............. Jude 1:7
EXAMPLES (4/4)
happened to them as *e*......... 1 Cor. 10:11
to you, but being *e*.............. 1 Pet. 5:3
EXCHANGE (8/7)
give in *e* for his soul.......... Matt. 16:26
EXCHANGED (5/5)
Nor can it be *e*................. Job 28:17
e the truth of God for.......... Rom. 1:25
EXCUSE (4/4)
but now they have no *e*.......... John 15:22
they are without *e*............... Rom. 1:20
EXCUSES (1/1)
began to make *e*............. Luke 14:18
EXECUTE (40/40)
e judgment also .... John 5:27
e wrath on him who............ Rom. 13:4
EXECUTES (7/7)
e justice for me .... Mic. 7:9
EXERCISE (8/7)
e yourself toward .... 1 Tim. 4:7
EXHORT (14/14)
e him as a father.................. 1 Tim. 5:1
Speak these things, *e*........... Titus 2:15
e one another .... Heb. 3:13
EXHORTATION (8/8)
he who exhorts, in *e*.............. Rom. 12:8
to reading, to *e* .... 1 Tim. 4:13
EXHORTED (4/4)
as you know how we *e*......... 1 Thess. 2:11
EXIST (5/5)
by Your will they *e* .... Rev. 4:11
EXPECT (2/2)
an hour you do not *e*.......... Luke 12:40
EXPECTATION (14/14)
the people were in *e*............ Luke 3:15
a certain fearful *e*............. Heb. 10:27
EXPLAIN (16/16)
was no one who could *e*.......... Gen. 41:24
"*E* this parable to us........... Matt. 15:15
to say, and hard to *e*............. Heb. 5:11
EXPLAINED (11/10)
He *e* all things to His........... Mark 4:34
EXPOSED (6/6)
his deeds should be *e* .... John 3:20
EXPOUNDED (1/1)
He *e* to them in all .... Luke 24:27
EXPRESS (2/2)
of His glory and the *e* .... Heb. 1:3
EXTORTION (3/3)
they are full of *e*............... Matt. 23:25
EXTORTIONERS (3/3)
nor *e* will inherit............... 1 Cor. 6:10
EYE (108/85)
the ear, but now my *e* .... Job 42:5
guide you with My *e*.............. Ps. 32:8
e is not satisfied .... Eccl. 1:8
the apple of His *e* .... Zech. 2:8
If your right *e* causes............ Matt. 5:29
it was said, 'An *e* .... Matt. 5:38
plank in your own *e*................ Matt. 7:3
e causes you to sin............... Matt. 18:9
Or is your *e* evil................ Matt. 20:15
the *e* of a needle .... Luke 18:25
the twinkling of an *e* .... 1 Cor. 15:52
every *e* will see Him............... Rev. 1:7
your eyes with *e* salve.............. Rev. 3:18
EYES (501/481)
e will be opened .... Gen. 3:5
And my *e* shall behold .... Job 19:27
e are ever toward the............. Ps. 25:15
The *e* of the LORD are .... Ps. 34:15
I will lift up my *e*................ Ps. 121:1
but the *e* of a fool .... Prov. 17:24
be wise in his own *e*.............. Prov. 26:5
You have dove's *e*................ Song 1:15
e have seen the King .... Is. 6:5
Who have *e* and see................ Jer. 5:21
rims were full of *e*................ Ezek. 1:18
You are of purer *e*................ Hab. 1:13
But blessed are your *e*.......... Matt. 13:16
"He put clay on my *e*............ John 9:15
e they have closed .... Acts 28:27
e that they should not.......... Rom. 11:8
have seen with our *e* .... 1 John 1:1
the lust of the *e*................ 1 John 2:16
as snow, and His *e* .... Rev. 1:14
creatures full of *e* .... Rev. 4:6
horns and seven *e* .... Rev. 5:6
EYESERVICE (2/2)
not with *e*, as .... Eph. 6:6
EYEWITNESSES (2/2)
the beginning were *e*............. Luke 1:2
e of His majesty .... 2 Pet. 1:16

F

FABLES (5/5)
nor give heed to *f* .... 1 Tim. 1:4
cunningly devised *f*............ 2 Pet. 1:16
FACE (390/351)
"For I have seen God *f*......... Gen. 32:30
f shone while he .... Ex. 34:29
sins have hidden His *f*............ Is. 59:2
f shone like the sun .... Matt. 17:2
dimly, but then *f* .... 1 Cor. 13:12
with unveiled *f* .... 2 Cor. 3:18
withstood him to his *f*............ Gal. 2:11
They shall see His *f* .... Rev. 22:4
FADE (7/7)
we all *f* as a leaf .... Is. 64:6
rich man also will *f*............... James 1:11
and that does not *f*............... 1 Pet. 1:4
FADES (6/5)
withers, the flower *f*............. Is. 40:7
FAIL (52/52)
tittle of the law to *f*............ Luke 16:17
faith should not *f* .... Luke 22:32
prophecies, they will *f*......... 1 Cor. 13:8
Your years will not *f*............. Heb. 1:12
FAILING (3/3)
men's hearts *f* .... Luke 21:26
FAILS (14/14)
Love never *f*.................. 1 Cor. 13:8
FAINT (23/23)
shall walk and not *f* .... Is. 40:31
FAINTS (4/4)
My soul *f* for Your............... Ps. 119:81
And the whole heart *f* .... Is. 1:5
the earth, neither *f*.............. Is. 40:28
FAITH (245/229)
shall live by his *f*.................. Hab. 2:4
you, O you of little *f*........... Matt. 6:30
not found such great *f*.......... Matt. 8:10
that you have no *f*............... Mark 4:40
"Increase our *f*.................. Luke 17:5
will He really find *f*............. Luke 18:8
are sanctified by *f*............... Acts 26:18
God is revealed from *f*........... Rom. 1:17
f apart from the deeds .... Rom. 3:28
his *f* is accounted for............ Rom. 4:5
those who are of the *f*............. Rom. 4:16
f which we preach................ Rom. 10:8
f comes by hearing............. Rom. 10:17
and you stand by *f* .... Rom. 11:20
in proportion to our *f* .... Rom. 12:6
Do you have *f*................... Rom. 14:22
though I have all *f* .... 1 Cor. 13:2
And now abide *f* .... 1 Cor. 13:13
For we walk by *f*................ 2 Cor. 5:7
the flesh I live by *f* .... Gal. 2:20
f are sons of Abraham.............. Gal. 3:7
But after *f* has come.............. Gal. 3:25
of the household of *f*.............. Gal. 6:10
been saved through *f*.............. Eph. 2:8
one Lord, one *f* .... Eph. 4:5
taking the shield of *f* .... Eph. 6:16
your work of *f* .... 1 Thess. 1:3
for not all have *f* .... 2 Thess. 3:2
the mystery of the *f*.............. 1 Tim. 3:9
I have kept the *f* .... 2 Tim. 4:7
in our common *f*................... Titus 1:4
not being mixed with *f* .... Heb. 4:2
f is the substance .... Heb. 11:1
without *f* it is .... Heb. 11:6
someone says he has *f* .... James 2:14
Show me your *f*................... James 2:18
and not by *f* only................ James 2:24
f will save the sick............... James 5:15
add to your *f* virtue .... 2 Pet. 1:5
the patience and the *f*........... Rev. 13:10
FAITHFUL (85/81)
God, He is God, the *f*.............. Deut. 7:9
LORD preserves the *f*.............. Ps. 31:23
eyes shall be on the *f*.............. Ps. 101:6
But who can find a *f*............. Prov. 20:6
the Holy One who is *f* .... Hos. 11:12
"Who then is a *f*................. Matt. 24:45
good and *f* servant............... Matt. 25:23
He who is *f* in what.............. Luke 16:10
have judged me to be *f* .... Acts 16:15
God is *f*, by whom .... 1 Cor. 1:9
is my beloved and *f* .... 1 Cor. 4:17
But as God is *f* .... 2 Cor. 1:18
f brethren in Christ .... Col. 1:2
He who calls you is *f* .... 1 Thess. 5:24
This is a *f* saying and........... 1 Tim. 1:15
f High Priest in .... Heb. 2:17
He who promised is *f* .... Heb. 10:23
He is *f* and just to .... 1 John 1:9
Be *f* until death .... Rev. 2:10
words are true and *f*............... Rev. 21:5
FAITHFULNESS (27/27)
I have declared Your *f*........... Ps. 40:10
Your *f* also surrounds .... Ps. 89:8
f endures to all .... Ps. 119:90
great is Your *f*.................... Lam. 3:23
unbelief make the *f*............... Rom. 3:3
FAITHLESS (5/5)
"O *f* generation .... Mark 9:19
If we are *f*, He remains .... 2 Tim. 2:13
FALL (225/213)
a deep sleep to *f* .... Gen. 2:21
Let them *f* by their .... Ps. 5:10
but the wicked shall *f*........... Prov. 24:16
the blind, both will *f*........... Matt. 15:14
the stars will *f* .... Matt. 24:29
"I saw Satan *f*................... Luke 10:18
that they should *f*............... Rom. 11:11
take heed lest he *f*............. 1 Cor. 10:12
if they *f* away .... Heb. 6:6
lest anyone *f* short of............. Heb. 12:15
and rocks, "*F* on us.............. Rev. 6:16
FALLEN (80/77)
"Babylon is *f*....................... Is. 21:9
you have *f* from grace .... Gal. 5:4
"Babylon is *f*....................... Rev. 14:8
FALLING (10/10)
great drops of blood *f* .... Luke 22:44
f away comes first............ 2 Thess. 2:3
FALSE (68/63)
"You shall not bear *f* .... Ex. 20:16
I hate every *f* way .... Ps. 119:104
f witness shall perish........... Prov. 21:28
"Beware of *f* prophets .... Matt. 7:15
f christs and *f*.................. Matt. 24:24
and we are found *f*............. 1 Cor. 15:15
of *f* brethren secretly.............. Gal. 2:4
f prophets have gone........... 1 John 4:1
mouth of the *f* prophet.......... Rev. 16:13
FALSEHOOD (17/17)
For their deceit is *f*............ Ps. 119:118
offspring of *f* .... Is. 57:4
FALSELY (23/23)
of evil against you *f* .... Matt. 5:11
f called knowledge .... 1 Tim. 6:20
FAMILIES (176/167)
in you all the *f*.................... Gen. 12:3
the God of all the *f* .... Jer. 31:1
in your seed all the *f* .... Acts 3:25
FAMILY (145/99)
shall mourn, every *f*............ Zech. 12:12
f were baptized .... Acts 16:33
FAMINES (3/3)
And there will be *f* .... Matt. 24:7
FAMISH (1/1)
righteous soul to *f* .... Prov. 10:3
FAMISHED (2/2)
honorable men are *f*............... Is. 5:13
FAR (293/280)
Your judgments are *f*............... Ps. 10:5
Be not *f* from Me.................. Ps. 22:11
The LORD is *f* from the .... Prov. 15:29
their heart is *f* from............. Matt. 15:8
going to a *f* country............. Mark 13:34
though He is not *f*............... Acts 17:27
you who once were *f* .... Eph. 2:13
FARMER (6/6)
The hard-working *f* .... 2 Tim. 2:6
See how the *f* waits............. James 5:7
FASHIONED (7/7)
have made me and *f* .... Job 10:8
FASHIONS (3/3)
He *f* their hearts .... Ps. 33:15
FAST (81/72)
of your *f* you find pleasure......... Is. 58:3
f that I have chosen .... Is. 58:5
"Moreover, when you *f* .... Matt. 6:16
disciples do not *f* .... Matt. 9:14
I *f* twice a week .... Luke 18:12
FASTED (15/15)
'When you *f* and .... Zech. 7:5
And when He had *f* .... Matt. 4:2
FASTING (20/20)
except by prayer and *f*.......... Matt. 17:21
give yourselves to *f* .... 1 Cor. 7:5
FASTINGS (3/3)
in sleeplessness, in *f* .... 2 Cor. 6:5
FAT (110/85)
and you will eat the *f*........... Gen. 45:18
f is the LORD's .... Lev. 3:16
FATHER (943/820)
man shall leave his *f* .... Gen. 2:24

and you shall be a f ... Gen. 17:4
I was a f to the poor ... Job 29:16
A f of the fatherless ... Ps. 68:5
f pities his children ... Ps. 103:13
God, Everlasting F ... Is. 9:6
You, O LORD, are our F ... Is. 63:16
time cry to Me, My F ... Jer. 3:4
for I am a F to Israel ... Jer. 31:9
"A son honors his f ... Mal. 1:6
Have we not all one F ... Mal. 2:10
your F who sees in secret ... Matt. 6:4
He who loves f ... Matt. 10:37
does anyone know the F ... Matt. 11:27
'He who curses f ... Matt. 15:4
for One is your F ... Matt. 23:9
F will be divided ... Luke 12:53
F loves the Son ... John 3:35
F raises the dead ... John 5:21
F judges no one ... John 5:22
He has seen the F ... John 6:46
F who sent Me bears ... John 8:18
we have one F ... John 8:41
he is a liar and the f of it ... John 8:44
I and My F are one ... John 10:30
'I am going to the F ... John 14:28
came forth from the F ... John 16:28
that he might be the f ... Rom. 4:11
one God and F of all ... Eph. 4:6
"I will be to Him a F ... Heb. 1:5
comes down from the F ... James 1:17
if you call on the F ... 1 Pet. 1:17
and testify that the F ... 1 John 4:14

FATHERLESS (40/40)
the helper of the f ... Ps. 10:14
He relieves the f ... Ps. 146:9
do not defend the f ... Is. 1:23
they may rob the f ... Is. 10:2
You the f finds mercy ... Hos. 14:3

FATHER'S (166/157)
you in My F kingdom ... Matt. 26:29
I must be about My F ... Luke 2:49
F house are many ... John 14:2
that a man has his f ... 1 Cor. 5:1

FATHERS (435/411)
the LORD God of our f ... Ezra 7:27
f trusted in You ... Ps. 22:4
our ears, O God, our f ... Ps. 44:1
f ate the manna ... John 6:31
of whom are the f ... Rom. 9:5
unaware that all our f ... 1 Cor. 10:1

FATNESS (9/9)
of the root and f ... Rom. 11:17

FAULT (18/17)
I have found no f ... Luke 23:14
does He still find f ... Rom. 9:19
of God without f ... Phil. 2:15

FAULTLESS (2/2)
covenant had been f ... Heb. 8:7
to present you f ... Jude 1:24

FAULTS (3/3)
"I remember my f ... Gen. 41:9
me from secret f ... Ps. 19:12

FAVOR (96/96)
granted me life and f ... Job 10:12
His f is for life ... Ps. 30:5
A good man obtains f ... Prov. 12:2
and stature, and in f ... Luke 2:52
God and having f ... Acts 2:47

FAVORED (4/4)
"Rejoice, highly f ... Luke 1:28

FAVORITISM (2/2)
do not show personal f ... Luke 20:21
God shows personal f ... Gal. 2:6

FEAR (366/353)
this and live, for I f God ... Gen. 42:18
to put the dread and f ... Deut. 2:25
said, "Does Job f ... Job 1:9
Yes, you cast off f ... Job 15:4
of death, I will f ... Ps. 23:4
whom shall I f ... Ps. 27:1
Oh, f the LORD ... Ps. 34:9
there is no f of God ... Ps. 36:1
The f of man brings a ... Prov. 29:25
F God and keep His ... Eccl. 12:13
let Him be your f ... Is. 8:13
"Be strong, do not f ... Is. 35:4
who would not f ... Jer. 10:7
f Him who is able ... Matt. 10:28
"Do not f, little flock ... Luke 12:32
"Do you not even f ... Luke 23:40
given us a spirit of f ... 2 Tim. 1:7
those who through f ... Heb. 2:15
because of His godly f ... Heb. 5:7
F God. Honor the king ... 1 Pet. 2:17
love casts out f ... 1 John 4:18

FEARED (60/59)
He is also to be f ... 1 Chr. 16:25
f God more than ... Neh. 7:2
Yourself, are to be f ... Ps. 76:7
Then those who f ... Mal. 3:16

FEARFUL (9/9)
It is a f thing to ... Heb. 10:31

FEARFULLY (2/2)
f and wonderfully made ... Ps. 139:14

FEARING (9/9)
sincerity of heart, f ... Col. 3:22
forsook Egypt, not f ... Heb. 11:27

FEARS (19/19)
upright man, one who f ... Job 1:8
me from all my f ... Ps. 34:4
every nation whoever f ... Acts 10:35
f has not been made ... 1 John 4:18

FEAST (136/122)
and you shall keep a f ... Num. 29:12
hate, I despise your f ... Amos 5:21
every year at the F ... Luke 2:41
when you give a f ... Luke 14:13
Now the Passover, a f ... John 6:4
great day of the f ... John 7:37

FEASTING (9/9)
go to the house of f ... Eccl. 7:2

FEASTS (32/31)
the best places at f ... Luke 20:46
spots in your love f ... Jude 1:12

FED (26/25)
and f you with manna ... Deut. 8:3
f you with milk and ... 1 Cor. 3:2

FEEBLE (18/18)
strengthened the f ... Job 4:4
And there was none f ... Ps. 105:37
And my flesh is f ... Ps. 109:24
hang down, and the f ... Heb. 12:12

FEED (71/68)
ravens to f you there ... 1 Kin. 17:4
and f your flocks ... Is. 61:5
to him, "F My lambs ... John 21:15
your enemy hungers, f ... Rom. 12:20
my goods to f the poor ... 1 Cor. 13:3

FEEDS (10/10)
your heavenly Father f ... Matt. 6:26

FEET (243/227)
all things under his f ... Ps. 8:6
He makes my f like the ... Ps. 18:33
You have set my f ... Ps. 31:8
For their f run to ... Prov. 1:16
Her f go down to death ... Prov. 5:5
mountains are the f ... Is. 52:7
place of My f glorious ... Is. 60:13
in that day His f ... Zech. 14:4
two hands or two f ... Matt. 18:8
began to wash His f ... Luke 7:38
wash the disciples' f ... John 13:5
f are swift to shed ... Rom. 3:15
beautiful are the f ... Rom. 10:15
all things under His f ... 1 Cor. 15:27
and having shod your f ... Eph. 6:15
fell at His f as dead ... Rev. 1:17

FELLOW (48/46)
begins to beat his f ... Matt. 24:49
f citizens with the ... Eph. 2:19
Gentiles should be f ... Eph. 3:6
I am your f servant ... Rev. 19:10

FELLOWSHIP (16/15)
doctrine and f ... Acts 2:42
were called into the f ... 1 Cor. 1:9
f has righteousness ... 2 Cor. 6:14
the right hand of f ... Gal. 2:9
And have no f with the ... Eph. 5:11
of love, if any f ... Phil. 2:1
and the f of His ... Phil. 3:10
we say that we have f ... 1 John 1:6
the light, we have f ... 1 John 1:7

FERVENT (8/8)
f prayer of a ... James 5:16
will melt with f ... 2 Pet. 3:10

FERVENTLY (2/2)
love one another f ... 1 Pet. 1:22

FEW (61/59)
let your words be f ... Eccl. 5:2
there are f who find it ... Matt. 7:14
but the laborers are f ... Matt. 9:37
called, but f chosen ... Matt. 20:16
"Lord, are there f ... Luke 13:23

FIDELITY (1/1)
but showing all good f ... Titus 2:10

FIELD (290/263)
Let the f be joyful ... Ps. 96:12
The f is the world ... Matt. 13:38
and buys that f ... Matt. 13:44
you are God's f ... 1 Cor. 3:9

FIERY (28/28)
the LORD sent f serpents ... Num. 21:6
shall make them as a f ... Ps. 21:9
burning f furnace ... Dan. 3:6
concerning the f trial ... 1 Pet. 4:12

FIG (40/39)
f leaves together ... Gen. 3:7
fruit on this f ... Luke 13:7
'I saw you under the f ... John 1:50

FIGHT (102/98)
The LORD will f for you ... Ex. 14:14
Our God will f for us ... Neh. 4:20
My servants would f ... John 18:36
to him, let us not f ... Acts 23:9
F the good f ... 1 Tim. 6:12
have fought the good f ... 2 Tim. 4:7

FIGHTS (6/6)
your God is He who f ... Josh. 23:10
because my lord f ... 1 Sam. 25:28
f come from among ... James 4:1

FIGS (25/22)
from thornbushes or f ... Matt. 7:16
or a grapevine bear f ... James 3:12

FILL (52/52)
f the earth and subdue ... Gen. 1:28
"Do I not f heaven ... Jer. 23:24
f this temple with ... Hag. 2:7
"F the waterpots ... John 2:7
that He might f ... Eph. 4:10

FILLED (159/157)
the whole earth be f ... Ps. 72:19
for they shall be f ... Matt. 5:6
"Let the children be f ... Mark 7:27
he would gladly have f ... Luke 15:16
being f with all ... Rom. 1:29
but be f with the Spirit ... Eph. 5:18
peace, be warmed and f ... James 2:16

FILTHY (9/8)
with f garments ... Zech. 3:3
poor man in f clothes ... James 2:2
oppressed by the f ... 2 Pet. 2:7
let him be f ... Rev. 22:11

FIND (171/164)
sure your sin will f ... Num. 32:23
that no one can f ... Eccl. 3:11
seek, and you will f ... Matt. 7:7
f a Babe wrapped ... Luke 2:12
f no fault in this Man ... Luke 23:4
f grace to help in ... Heb. 4:16

FINDS (30/28)
whoever f me f life ... Prov. 8:35
f a wife f a good ... Prov. 18:22
and he who seeks f ... Matt. 7:8
f his life will lose ... Matt. 10:39
and he who seeks f ... Luke 11:10

FINGER (26/24)
written with the f ... Ex. 31:18
dip the tip of his f ... Luke 16:24
"Reach your f ... John 20:27

FINISH (15/15)
he has enough to f ... Luke 14:28
has given Me to f ... John 5:36

FINISHED (90/89)
f the work which You ... John 17:4
He said, "It is f ... John 19:30
I have f the race ... 2 Tim. 4:7

FIRE (543/503)
rained brimstone and f ... Gen. 19:24
to him in a flame of f ... Ex. 3:2
God, who answers by f ... 1 Kin. 18:24
LORD was not in the f ... 1 Kin. 19:12
we went through f ... Ps. 66:12
f goes before Him ... Ps. 97:3
burns as the f ... Is. 9:18
you walk through the f ... Is. 43:2
f that burns all the ... Is. 65:5
He break out like f ... Amos 5:6
for conflict by f ... Amos 7:4
like a refiner's f ... Mal. 3:2
the Holy Spirit and f ... Matt. 3:11
f is not quenched ... Mark 9:44
"I came to send f ... Luke 12:49
tongues, as of f ... Acts 2:3
f taking vengeance ... 2 Thess. 1:8
and that burned with f ... Heb. 12:18
And the tongue is a f ... James 3:6
vengeance of eternal f ... Jude 1:7
into the lake of f ... Rev. 20:14

FIRM (13/13)
of the hope f to the ... Heb. 3:6

FIRMAMENT (17/15)
Thus God made the f ... Gen. 1:7
f shows His handiwork ... Ps. 19:1

FIRST (443/415)
f father sinned ... Is. 43:27
desires to be f ... Matt. 20:27
f shall be slave ... Mark 10:44
And the gospel must f ... Mark 13:10
evil, of the Jew f ... Rom. 2:9
f man Adam became a ... 1 Cor. 15:45
that we who f trusted ... Eph. 1:12
love Him because He f ... 1 John 4:19
I am the F and the ... Rev. 1:17
you have left your f ... Rev. 2:4
is the f resurrection ... Rev. 20:5

FIRSTBORN (141/114)
LORD struck all the f ... Ex. 12:29
brought forth her f ... Matt. 1:25
that He might be the f ... Rom. 8:29
invisible God, the f ... Col. 1:15
the beginning, the f ... Col. 1:18
witness, the f from ... Rev. 1:5

FIRSTFRUITS (33/31)
also who have the f ... Rom. 8:23

and has become the *f* ... 1 Cor. 15:20
order: Christ the *f* ... 1 Cor. 15:23

FISH (61/56)
had prepared a great *f* ... Jon. 1:17
belly of the great *f* ... Matt. 12:40
five loaves and two *f* ... Matt. 14:17
and likewise the *f* ... John 21:13

FISHERS (2/2)
and I will make you *f* ... Matt. 4:19

FIVE (256/194)
f smooth stones ... 1 Sam. 17:40
about *f* thousand men ... Matt. 14:21
and *f* were foolish ... Matt. 25:2

FIXED (6/6)
is a great gulf *f* ... Luke 16:26

FLAME (32/31)
f will dry out his ... Job 15:30
am tormented in this *f* ... Luke 16:24
and His ministers a *f* ... Heb. 1:7
and His eyes like a *f* ... Rev. 1:14

FLAMES (5/4)
the LORD divides the *f* ... Ps. 29:7

FLAMING (8/8)
f sword which turned ... Gen. 3:24
in *f* fire taking ... 2 Thess. 1:8

FLATTER (3/3)
They *f* with their ... Ps. 5:9

FLATTERED (1/1)
Nevertheless they *f* ... Ps. 78:36

FLATTERING (9/9)
f speech deceive ... Rom. 16:18
swelling words, *f* ... Jude 1:16

FLATTERS (6/6)
f his neighbor spreads ... Prov. 29:5

FLATTERY (2/2)
shall corrupt with *f* ... Dan. 11:32

FLAVOR (3/3)
the salt loses its *f* ... Matt. 5:13

FLAX (9/8)
f He will not quench ... Matt. 12:20

FLEE (100/95)
Or where can I *f* ... Ps. 139:7
And the shadows *f* ... Song 2:17
who are in Judea *f* ... Matt. 24:16
F sexual immorality ... 1 Cor. 6:18
f these things and ... 1 Tim. 6:11
devil and he will *f* ... James 4:7

FLESH (337/300)
bone of my bones and *f* ... Gen. 2:23
shall become one *f* ... Gen. 2:24
f had corrupted their ... Gen. 6:12
f I shall see God ... Job 19:26
My *f* also will rest in ... Ps. 16:9
is wearisome to the *f* ... Eccl. 12:12
And all *f* shall see it ... Is. 40:5
"All *f* is grass ... Is. 40:6
out My Spirit on all *f* ... Joel 2:28
two shall become one *f* ... Matt. 19:5
were shortened, no *f* ... Matt. 24:22
shall become one *f* ... Mark 10:8
And the Word became *f* ... John 1:14
I shall give is My *f* ... John 6:51
unless you eat the *f* ... John 6:53
of God, but with the *f* ... Rom. 7:25
on the things of the *f* ... Rom. 8:5
to the *f* you will die ... Rom. 8:13
f should glory in His ... 1 Cor. 1:29
"shall become one *f* ... 1 Cor. 6:16
For the *f* lusts ... Gal. 5:17
have crucified the *f* ... Gal. 5:24
may boast in your *f* ... Gal. 6:13
the lust of the *f* ... 1 John 2:16
has come in the *f* ... 1 John 4:2

FLESHLY (6/6)
f wisdom but by the ... 2 Cor. 1:12
f lusts which war against ... 1 Pet. 2:11

FLIES (15/13)
Dead *f* putrefy the ... Eccl. 10:1

FLOAT (2/2)
and he made the iron *f* ... 2 Kin. 6:6

FLOCK (121/108)
lead Joseph like a *f* ... Ps. 80:1
He will feed His *f* ... Is. 40:11
you do not feed the *f* ... Ezek. 34:3
my God, "Feed the *f* ... Zech. 11:4
sheep of the *f* will be ... Matt. 26:31
"Do not fear, little *f* ... Luke 12:32
there will be one *f* ... John 10:16
Shepherd the *f* of God ... 1 Pet. 5:2
examples to the *f* ... 1 Pet. 5:3

FLOOD (33/31)
the waters of the *f* ... Gen. 7:10
them away like a *f* ... Ps. 90:5
the days before the *f* ... Matt. 24:38
bringing in the *f* ... 2 Pet. 2:5
of his mouth like a *f* ... Rev. 12:15

FLOODS (12/10)
me, and the *f* of ... Ps. 18:4
f on the dry ground ... Is. 44:3
rain descended, the *f* ... Matt. 7:25

FLOURISH (12/12)
the righteous shall *f* ... Ps. 72:7

FLOW (26/24)
of his heart will *f* ... John 7:38

FLOWER (21/18)
as a *f* of the field ... Ps. 103:15
beauty is a fading *f* ... Is. 28:4
grass withers, the *f* ... Is. 40:7
of man as the *f* ... 1 Pet. 1:24

FLOWERS (10/10)
f appear on the earth ... Song 2:12

FLOWING (27/26)
'a land *f* with milk ... Deut. 6:3
the Gentiles like a *f* ... Is. 66:12

FLUTE (14/14)
play the harp and *f* ... Gen. 4:21

FLUTES (5/4)
instruments and *f* ... Ps. 150:4

FLUTISTS (1/1)
harpists, musicians, *f* ... Rev. 18:22

FLY (17/17)
soon cut off, and we *f* ... Ps. 90:10

FOLLOW (95/92)
f You wherever You go ... Matt. 8:19
He said to him, "*F* ... Matt. 9:9
up his cross, and *f* ... Mark 8:34
will by no means *f* ... John 10:5
serves Me, let him *f* ... John 12:26
that you should *f* ... 1 Pet. 2:21
f the Lamb wherever He ... Rev. 14:4
and their works *f* ... Rev. 14:13

FOLLOWED (117/115)
f the LORD my God ... Josh. 14:8
we have left all and *f* ... Mark 10:28

FOLLOWS (14/14)
f Me shall not walk ... John 8:12

FOLLY (28/28)
taken much notice of *f* ... Job 35:15
not turn back to *f* ... Ps. 85:8
F is joy to him who is ... Prov. 15:21
F is set in great ... Eccl. 10:6

FOOD (212/196)
you it shall be for *f* ... Gen. 1:29
that lives shall be *f* ... Gen. 9:3
f which you eat shall ... Ezek. 4:10
the fields yield no *f* ... Hab. 3:17
that there may be *f* ... Mal. 3:10
to give them *f* in due ... Matt. 24:45
and you gave Me *f* ... Matt. 25:35
and he who has *f* ... Luke 3:11
have you any *f* ... John 21:5
they ate their *f* ... Acts 2:46
our hearts with *f* ... Acts 14:17
destroy with your *f* ... Rom. 14:15
f makes my brother ... 1 Cor. 8:13
the same spiritual *f* ... 1 Cor. 10:3
sower, and bread for *f* ... 2 Cor. 9:10
And having *f* and ... 1 Tim. 6:8
and not solid *f* ... Heb. 5:12
But solid *f* belongs to ... Heb. 5:14
of *f* sold his birthright ... Heb. 12:16
destitute of daily *f* ... James 2:15

FOODS (6/5)
f which God created ... 1 Tim. 4:3

FOOL (68/65)
f has said in his ... Ps. 14:1
is like sport to a *f* ... Prov. 10:23
f is right in his own ... Prov. 12:15
is too lofty for a *f* ... Prov. 24:7
whoever says, 'You *f* ... Matt. 5:22
I have become a *f* ... 2 Cor. 12:11

FOOLISH (54/53)
I was so *f* and ... Ps. 73:22
f pulls it down with ... Prov. 14:1
f man squanders it ... Prov. 21:20
Has not God made *f* ... 1 Cor. 1:20
O *f* Galatians ... Gal. 3:1
were also once *f* ... Titus 3:3
But avoid *f* disputes ... Titus 3:9

FOOLISHLY (9/9)
I speak *f*—I am bold ... 2 Cor. 11:21

FOOLISHNESS (23/23)
F is bound up in the ... Prov. 22:15
devising of *f* is sin ... Prov. 24:9
of the cross is *f* ... 1 Cor. 1:18
Because the *f* of God ... 1 Cor. 1:25

FOOLS (40/40)
f despise wisdom ... Prov. 1:7
folly of *f* is deceit ... Prov. 14:8
F mock at sin ... Prov. 14:9
We are *f* for Christ's ... 1 Cor. 4:10

FOOT (93/89)
will not allow your *f* ... Ps. 121:3
f will not stumble ... Prov. 3:23
From the sole of the *f* ... Is. 1:6
you turn away your *f* ... Is. 58:13
f causes you to sin ... Matt. 18:8
you dash your *f* ... Luke 4:11
If the *f* should say ... 1 Cor. 12:15

FOOTSTOOL (16/16)
Your enemies Your *f* ... Ps. 110:1
Your enemies Your *f* ... Matt. 22:44

FORBID (13/13)
said, "Do not *f* him ... Mark 9:39
"Can anyone *f* water ... Acts 10:47
f that I should boast ... Gal. 6:14

FORBIDDING (4/4)
f to marry ... 1 Tim. 4:3

FOREFATHERS (4/4)
conscience, as my *f* ... 2 Tim. 1:3

FOREHEADS (8/8)
put a mark on the *f* ... Ezek. 9:4
seal of God on their *f* ... Rev. 9:4
his mark on their *f* ... Rev. 20:4

FOREIGNER (26/24)
"I am a *f* and a ... Gen. 23:4
of me, since I am a *f* ... Ruth 2:10
to God except this *f* ... Luke 17:18

FOREIGNERS (18/18)
f who were there ... Acts 17:21
longer strangers and *f* ... Eph. 2:19

FOREKNEW (2/2)
For whom He *f* ... Rom. 8:29
His people whom He *f* ... Rom. 11:2

FOREKNOWLEDGE (2/2)
purpose and *f* of God ... Acts 2:23

FOREORDAINED (1/1)
He indeed was *f* ... 1 Pet. 1:20

FORESAW (1/1)
'I *f* the LORD ... Acts 2:25

FORESEEING (2/2)
f that God would ... Gal. 3:8

FORESEES (2/2)
A prudent man *f* ... Prov. 22:3

FORETOLD (3/3)
have also *f* these days ... Acts 3:24
killed those who *f* ... Acts 7:52

FOREVER (393/382)
and eat, and live *f* ... Gen. 3:22
to our children *f* ... Deut. 29:29
LORD sits as King *f* ... Ps. 29:10
Do not cast us off *f* ... Ps. 44:23
throne, O God, is *f* ... Ps. 45:6
"You are a priest *f* ... Ps. 110:4
His mercy endures *f* ... Ps. 136:1
of our God stands *f* ... Is. 40:8
My salvation will be *f* ... Is. 51:6
will not cast off *f* ... Lam. 3:31
Like the stars *f* ... Dan. 12:3
and the glory *f* ... Matt. 6:13
the Christ remains *f* ... John 12:34
who is blessed *f* ... 2 Cor. 11:31
to whom be glory *f* ... Gal. 1:5
generation, *f* and ever ... Eph. 3:21
and Father be glory *f* ... Phil. 4:20
throne, O God, is *f* ... Heb. 1:8
lives and abides *f* ... 1 Pet. 1:23
blackness of darkness *f* ... Jude 1:13
power, both now and *f* ... Jude 1:25
And they shall reign *f* ... Rev. 22:5

FOREVERMORE (18/18)
Blessed be the LORD *f* ... Ps. 89:52
this time forth and *f* ... Ps. 113:2
behold, I am alive *f* ... Rev. 1:18

FORGAVE (8/8)
to repay, he freely *f* ... Luke 7:42
God in Christ *f* ... Eph. 4:32
even as Christ *f* ... Col. 3:13

FORGET (60/57)
f the LORD who brought ... Deut. 6:12
I will not *f* Your word ... Ps. 119:16
If I *f* you, O Jerusalem ... Ps. 137:5
My son, do not *f* ... Prov. 3:1
f the LORD your Maker ... Is. 51:13
f your work and labor ... Heb. 6:10

FORGETFULNESS (1/1)
in the land of *f* ... Ps. 88:12

FORGETS (4/4)
and immediately *f* ... James 1:24

FORGETTING (1/1)
f those things which ... Phil. 3:13

FORGIVE (53/45)
f their sin and heal ... 2 Chr. 7:14
good, and ready to *f* ... Ps. 86:5
And *f* us our debts ... Matt. 6:12
Father will also *f* ... Matt. 6:14
his heart, does not *f* ... Matt. 18:35
Who can *f* sins but God ... Mark 2:7
f the sins of any ... John 20:23
you ought rather to *f* ... 2 Cor. 2:7
F me this wrong ... 2 Cor. 12:13
f us our sins and to ... 1 John 1:9

FORGIVEN (43/38)
sins be *f* them ... Mark 4:12
to whom little is *f* ... Luke 7:47
f you all trespasses ... Col. 2:13
your sins are *f* ... 1 John 2:12

FORGIVENESS (8/8)
But there is *f* with ... Ps. 130:4
preached to you the *f* ... Acts 13:38
they may receive *f* ... Acts 26:18
His blood, the *f* ... Eph. 1:7

FORGIVES (2/2)
f all your iniquities ... Ps. 103:3
"Who is this who even *f* ... Luke 7:49

FORGIVING (4/4)
tenderhearted, *f* ... Eph. 4:32
and *f* one another ... Col. 3:13
FORGOT (9/9)
remember Joseph, but *f* ... Gen. 40:23
They soon *f* His works ... Ps. 106:13
FORGOTTEN (45/45)
f the God who fathered ... Deut. 32:18
not one of them is *f* ... Luke 12:6
f the exhortation ... Heb. 12:5
f that he was cleansed ... 2 Pet. 1:9
FORM (33/33)
earth was without *f* ... Gen. 1:2
Who would *f* a god or ... Is. 44:10
f the light and create ... Is. 45:7
descended in bodily *f* ... Luke 3:22
time, nor seen His *f* ... John 5:37
For the *f* of this ... 1 Cor. 7:31
who, being in the *f* ... Phil. 2:6
having a *f* of godliness ... 2 Tim. 3:5
FORMED (38/35)
And the LORD God *f* ... Gen. 2:7
f my inward parts ... Ps. 139:13
say of him who *f* ... Is. 29:16
"Before I *f* you in ... Jer. 1:5
Will the thing *f* say to ... Rom. 9:20
until Christ is *f* ... Gal. 4:19
FORMER (60/57)
f days better than ... Eccl. 7:10
f rain to the earth ... Hos. 6:3
f prophets preached ... Zech. 1:4
your *f* conduct, the old ... Eph. 4:22
f things have passed ... Rev. 21:4
FORMS (6/6)
clay say to him who *f* ... Is. 45:9
f the spirit of man ... Zech. 12:1
FORNICATION (14/12)
"We were not born of *f* ... John 8:41
of the wrath of her *f* ... Rev. 14:8
FORNICATOR (2/2)
you know, that no *f* ... Eph. 5:5
lest there be any *f* ... Heb. 12:16
FORNICATORS (3/3)
but *f* and adulterers ... Heb. 13:4
FORSAKE (64/63)
But I did not *f* Your ... Ps. 119:87
father, and do not *f* ... Prov. 1:8
of you does not *f* ... Luke 14:33
never leave you nor *f* ... Heb. 13:5
FORSAKEN (75/73)
My God, why have You *f* ... Ps. 22:1
seen the righteous *f* ... Ps. 37:25
My God, why have You *f* ... Matt. 27:46
persecuted, but not *f* ... 2 Cor. 4:9
for Demas has *f* ... 2 Tim. 4:10
FORSAKING (1/1)
f the assembling ... Heb. 10:25
FORSOOK (16/16)
f God who made him ... Deut. 32:15
all the disciples *f* ... Matt. 26:56
with me, but all *f* ... 2 Tim. 4:16
FORTRESS (20/20)
LORD is my rock, my *f* ... 2 Sam. 22:2
my rock of refuge, a *f* ... Ps. 31:2
FOUND (398/384)
f a helper comparable ... Gen. 2:20
a thousand I have *f* ... Eccl. 7:28
LORD while He may be *f* ... Is. 55:6
fruit on it and *f* none ... Luke 13:6
he was lost and is *f* ... Luke 15:24
f the Messiah" (which ... John 1:41
and be *f* in Him ... Phil. 3:9
FOUNDATION (56/55)
Of old You laid the *f* ... Ps. 102:25
the earth without a *f* ... Luke 6:49
loved Me before the *f* ... John 17:24
I have laid the *f* ... 1 Cor. 3:10
f can anyone lay than ... 1 Cor. 3:11
us in Him before the *f* ... Eph. 1:4
not laying again the *f* ... Heb. 6:1
Lamb slain from the *f* ... Rev. 13:8
FOUNDATIONS (32/32)
when I laid the *f* ... Job 38:4
The *f* of the wall ... Rev. 21:19
FOUNTAIN (26/26)
will become in him a *f* ... John 4:14
FOUNTAINS (8/8)
on that day all the *f* ... Gen. 7:11
lead them to living *f* ... Rev. 7:17
FRAGRANCE (11/10)
was filled with the *f* ... John 12:3
we are to God the *f* ... 2 Cor. 2:15
FREE (73/71)
'You will be made *f* ... John 8:33
And having been set *f* ... Rom. 6:18
Jesus has made me *f* ... Rom. 8:2
is neither slave nor *f* ... Gal. 3:28
Christ has made us *f* ... Gal. 5:1
he is a slave or *f* ... Eph. 6:8
FREED (3/3)
has died has been *f* ... Rom. 6:7
FREEDMAN (1/1)
slave is the Lord's *f* ... 1 Cor. 7:22
FREELY (22/21)
the garden you may *f* ... Gen. 2:16
F you have received ... Matt. 10:8
f give us all things ... Rom. 8:32
the water of life *f* ... Rev. 22:17
FRIEND (55/51)
of Abraham Your *f* ... 2 Chr. 20:7
a *f* of tax collectors ... Matt. 11:19
of you shall have a *f* ... Luke 11:5
f Lazarus sleeps ... John 11:11
he was called the *f* ... James 2:23
wants to be a *f* ... James 4:4
FRIENDS (56/55)
My *f* scorn me ... Job 16:20
the rich has many *f* ... Prov. 14:20
one's life for his *f* ... John 15:13
I have called you *f* ... John 15:15
to forbid any of his *f* ... Acts 24:23
FROGS (14/14)
your territory with *f* ... Ex. 8:2
f coming out of the ... Rev. 16:13
FRUIT (189/175)
and showed them the *f* ... Num. 13:26
brings forth its *f* ... Ps. 1:3
f is better than gold ... Prov. 8:19
with good by the *f* ... Prov. 12:14
like the first *f* ... Is. 28:4
does not bear good *f* ... Matt. 3:10
good tree bears good *f* ... Matt. 7:17
not drink of this *f* ... Matt. 26:29
and blessed is the *f* ... Luke 1:42
life, and bring no *f* ... Luke 8:14
and he came seeking *f* ... Luke 13:6
And if it bears *f* ... Luke 13:9
branch that bears *f* ... John 15:2
that you bear much *f* ... John 15:8
should go and bear *f* ... John 15:16
God, you have your *f* ... Rom. 6:22
that we should bear *f* ... Rom. 7:4
But the *f* of the Spirit is ... Gal. 5:22
yields the peaceable *f* ... Heb. 12:11
Now the *f* of ... James 3:18
autumn trees without *f* ... Jude 1:12
tree yielding its *f* ... Rev. 22:2
FRUITFUL (37/34)
them, saying, "Be *f* ... Gen. 1:22
wife shall be like a *f* ... Ps. 128:3
pleasing Him, being *f* ... Col. 1:10
FRUITS (20/20)
Therefore bear *f* ... Matt. 3:8
know them by their *f* ... Matt. 7:16
of mercy and good *f* ... James 3:17
which bore twelve *f* ... Rev. 22:2
FULFILL (34/33)
for us to *f* all ... Matt. 3:15
f the law of Christ ... Gal. 6:2
f my joy by being ... Phil. 2:2
and *f* all the good ... 2 Thess. 1:11
If you really *f* ... James 2:8
FULFILLED (75/75)
the law till all is *f* ... Matt. 5:18
of the Gentiles are *f* ... Luke 21:24
all things must be *f* ... Luke 24:44
of the law might be *f* ... Rom. 8:4
loves another has *f* ... Rom. 13:8
For all the law is *f* ... Gal. 5:14
FULFILLMENT (6/6)
love is the *f* of the ... Rom. 13:10
FULL (242/234)
and it was *f* of bones ... Ezek. 37:1

G

GAIN (33/32)
and to die is *g* ... Phil. 1:21
rubbish, that I may *g* ... Phil. 3:8
is a means of *g* ... 1 Tim. 6:5
contentment is great *g* ... 1 Tim. 6:6
for dishonest *g* ... 1 Pet. 5:2
GAINED (19/18)
g five more talents ... Matt. 25:20
GAINS (5/5)
g the whole world ... Matt. 16:26
GALL (10/10)
They also gave me *g* ... Ps. 69:21
wine mingled with *g* ... Matt. 27:34
GAP (2/2)
and stand in the *g* ... Ezek. 22:30
GARDEN (54/49)
LORD God planted a *g* ... Gen. 2:8
g enclosed is my ... Song 4:12
Eden, the *g* of God ... Ezek. 28:13
where there was a *g* ... John 18:1
in the *g* a new tomb ... John 19:41
GARMENT (90/85)
the hem of His *g* ... Matt. 9:20
have on a wedding *g* ... Matt. 22:11
cloth on an old *g* ... Mark 2:21
all grow old like a *g* ... Heb. 1:11
hating even the *g* ... Jude 1:23
GARMENTS (118/97)
g did not wear out on ... Deut. 8:4
They divide My *g* ... Ps. 22:18
from Edom, with dyed *g* ... Is. 63:1
Take away the filthy *g* ... Zech. 3:4
man clothed in soft *g* ... Matt. 11:8
and divided His *g* ... Matt. 27:35
by them in shining *g* ... Luke 24:4
g are moth-eaten ... James 5:2
be clothed in white *g* ... Rev. 3:5
GATE (252/207)
by the narrow *g* ... Matt. 7:13
by the Sheep *G* a pool ... John 5:2
laid daily at the *g* ... Acts 3:2
suffered outside the *g* ... Heb. 13:12
GATES (139/128)
up your heads, O you *g* ... Ps. 24:7
The LORD loves the *g* ... Ps. 87:2
is known in the *g* ... Prov. 31:23
go through the *g* ... Is. 62:10
and the *g* of Hades ... Matt. 16:18
wall with twelve *g* ... Rev. 21:12
g were twelve pearls ... Rev. 21:21
g shall not be shut ... Rev. 21:25
GATHER (168/162)
and a time to *g* stones ... Eccl. 3:5
g the lambs with His ... Is. 40:11
g His wheat into the ... Matt. 3:12
sow nor reap nor *g* ... Matt. 6:26
Do men *g* grapes from ... Matt. 7:16
g where I have not ... Matt. 25:26
g together His elect ... Mark 13:27
GATHERED (259/248)
g some of every kind ... Matt. 13:47
the nations will be *g* ... Matt. 25:32
GATHERING (15/15)
g together of the waters ... Gen. 1:10
g together to Him ... 2 Thess. 2:1
GATHERS (18/17)
The Lord GOD, who *g* ... Is. 56:8
together, as a hen *g* ... Matt. 23:37
GAVE (496/463)
to be with me, she *g* ... Gen. 3:12
g You this authority ... Matt. 21:23
that He *g* His only ... John 3:16
Those whom You *g* ... John 17:12
but God *g* the increase ... 1 Cor. 3:6
who *g* for our sins ... Gal. 1:4
who loved me and *g* ... Gal. 2:20
loved the church and *g* ... Eph. 5:25
GENERATION (100/85)
One *g* passes away ... Eccl. 1:4
who will declare His *g* ... Is. 53:8
and adulterous *g* ... Matt. 12:39
this *g* will by no ... Matt. 24:34
from this perverse *g* ... Acts 2:40
But you are a chosen *g* ... 1 Pet. 2:9
GENERATIONS (97/94)
be remembered in all *g* ... Ps. 45:17
g will call me blessed ... Luke 1:48
GENEROUS (7/6)
no longer be called *g* ... Is. 32:5
GENTILES (149/141)
G were separated ... Gen. 10:5
as a light to the *G* ... Is. 42:6
G shall come to your ... Is. 60:3
all these things the *G* ... Matt. 6:32
into the way of the *G* ... Matt. 10:5
revelation to the *G* ... Luke 2:32
times of the *G* are ... Luke 21:24
bear My name before *G* ... Acts 9:15
poured out on the *G* ... Acts 10:45
a light to the *G* ... Acts 13:47
also the God of the *G* ... Rom. 3:29
mystery among the *G* ... Col. 1:27
a teacher of the *G* ... 1 Tim. 2:7
GENTLE (11/11)
from Me, for I am *g* ... Matt. 11:29
But we were *g* among ... 1 Thess. 2:7
to be peaceable, *g* ... Titus 3:2
only to the good and *g* ... 1 Pet. 2:18
ornament of a *g* and quiet ... 1 Pet. 3:4
GENTLENESS (9/9)
love and a spirit of *g* ... 1 Cor. 4:21
g, self-control ... Gal. 5:23
all lowliness and *g* ... Eph. 4:2
Let your *g* be known to ... Phil. 4:5
love, patience, *g* ... 1 Tim. 6:11
GHOST (2/2)
supposed it was a *g* ... Mark 6:49
GIFT (59/54)
it is the *g* of God ... Eccl. 3:13
"If you knew the *g* ... John 4:10
but the *g* of God is ... Rom. 6:23
each one has his own *g* ... 1 Cor. 7:7
though I have the *g* ... 1 Cor. 13:2
it is the *g* of God ... Eph. 2:8
Do not neglect the *g* ... 1 Tim. 4:14
you to stir up the *g* ... 2 Tim. 1:6
tasted the heavenly *g* ... Heb. 6:4
Every good *g* and every ... James 1:17

GIFTS (44/44)
You have received g ... Ps. 68:18
and Seba will offer g ... Ps. 72:10
how to give good g ... Matt. 7:11
rich putting their g ... Luke 21:1
Having then g differing ... Rom. 12:6
are diversities of g ... 1 Cor. 12:4
and desire spiritual g ... 1 Cor. 14:1
captive, and gave g ... Eph. 4:8

GIRD (19/18)
G Your sword upon Your ... Ps. 45:3
and another will g ... John 21:18
Therefore g up the ... 1 Pet. 1:13

GIRDED (22/20)
a towel and g Himself ... John 13:4

GIVE (865/795)
g you the desires ... Ps. 37:4
Yes, the LORD will g ... Ps. 85:12
G me understanding ... Ps. 119:34
G to him who asks ... Matt. 5:42
G us this day our ... Matt. 6:11
what you have and g ... Matt. 19:21
authority I will g ... Luke 4:6
g them eternal life ... John 10:28
new commandment I g ... John 13:34
but what I do have I g ... Acts 3:6
g us all things ... Rom. 8:32
G no offense ... 1 Cor. 10:32
g him who has need ... Eph. 4:28
g thanks to God ... 2 Thess. 2:13
g yourself entirely ... 1 Tim. 4:15

GIVEN (503/487)
to him more will be g ... Matt. 13:12
has, more will be g ... Matt. 25:29
to whom much is g ... Luke 12:48
g Me I should lose ... John 6:39
Spirit was not yet g ... John 7:39

GIVES (111/105)
g life to the world ... John 6:33
All that the Father g ... John 6:37
The good shepherd g ... John 10:11
not as the world g ... John 14:27
g us richly all things ... 1 Tim. 6:17
who g to all liberally ... James 1:5
g grace to the humble ... James 4:6

GLAD (91/91)
streams shall make g ... Ps. 46:4
I was g when they said ... Ps. 122:1
make merry and be g ... Luke 15:32
he saw it and was g ... John 8:56

GLADNESS (48/48)
me hear joy and g ... Ps. 51:8
Serve the LORD with g ... Ps. 100:2

GLORIFIED (48/47)
and they g the God of ... Matt. 15:31
Jesus was not yet g ... John 7:39
when Jesus was g ... John 12:16
By this My Father is g ... John 15:8
I have g You on the ... John 17:4
g His Servant Jesus ... Acts 3:13
these He also g ... Rom. 8:30
things God may be g ... 1 Pet. 4:11

GLORIFY (27/24)
g your Father in ... Matt. 5:16
"Father, g Your name ... John 12:28
He will g Me ... John 16:14
And now, O Father, g ... John 17:5
what death he would g ... John 21:19
therefore g God in ... 1 Cor. 6:20
also Christ did not g ... Heb. 5:5
ashamed, but let him g ... 1 Pet. 4:16

GLORIOUS (48/47)
G things are spoken ... Ps. 87:3
habitation, holy and g ... Is. 63:15
it to Himself a g ... Eph. 5:27
be conformed to His g ... Phil. 3:21
g appearing of our ... Titus 2:13

GLORY (379/351)
"Please, show me Your g ... Ex. 33:18
g has departed from ... 1 Sam. 4:21
Who is this King of g ... Ps. 24:8
Your power and Your g ... Ps. 63:2
wise shall inherit g ... Prov. 3:35
It is the g of God to ... Prov. 25:2
g I will not give ... Is. 42:8
that they may have g ... Matt. 6:2
the power and the g ... Matt. 6:13
g was not arrayed ... Matt. 6:29
Man will come in the g ... Matt. 16:27
with power and great g ... Matt. 24:30
"G to God in the ... Luke 2:14
and we beheld His g ... John 1:14
and manifested His g ... John 2:11
I do not seek My own g ... John 8:50
"Give God the g ... John 9:24
g which I had with You ... John 17:5
g which You gave Me I ... John 17:22
he did not give g ... Acts 12:23
doing good seek for g ... Rom. 2:7
in faith, giving g ... Rom. 4:20
the adoption, the g ... Rom. 9:4
the riches of His g ... Rom. 9:23
God, alone wise, be g ... Rom. 16:27
who glories, let him g ... 1 Cor. 1:31
to His riches in g ... Phil. 4:19
appear with Him in g ... Col. 3:4
For you are our g ... 1 Thess. 2:20
many sons to g ... Heb. 2:10
grass, and all the g ... 1 Pet. 1:24
to whom belong the g ... 1 Pet. 4:11
for the Spirit of g ... 1 Pet. 4:14
the presence of His g ... Jude 1:24
O Lord, to receive g ... Rev. 4:11

GLORYING (1/1)
Your g is not good ... 1 Cor. 5:6

GLUTTON (4/4)
you say, 'Look, a g ... Luke 7:34

GLUTTONS (2/2)
companion of g shames ... Prov. 28:7
evil beasts, lazy g ... Titus 1:12

GNASHING (7/7)
will be weeping and g ... Matt. 8:12

GO (1,487/1,358)
'Let My people g ... Ex. 5:1
for wherever you g ... Ruth 1:16
Those who g down to ... Ps. 107:23
Where can I g from ... Ps. 139:7
to whom shall we g ... John 6:68
g you cannot come ... John 8:21
I g to prepare a place ... John 14:2
and he shall g out no more ... Rev. 3:12

GOADS (4/4)
to kick against the g ... Acts 9:5

GOAL (1/1)
I press toward the g ... Phil. 3:14

GOATS (52/48)
his sheep from the g ... Matt. 25:32
with the blood of g ... Heb. 9:12
g could take away ... Heb. 10:4

GOD (4,393/3,841)
G created the heavens ... Gen. 1:1
Abram of G Most High ... Gen. 14:19
and I will be their G ... Gen. 17:8
"I am the LORD your G ... Ex. 20:2
G is a consuming fire ... Deut. 4:24
If the LORD is G ... 1 Kin. 18:21
G is greater than all ... 2 Chr. 2:5
You have been My G ... Ps. 22:10
G is our refuge ... Ps. 46:1
G is in the midst of ... Ps. 46:5
me a clean heart, O G ... Ps. 51:10
Our G is the G ... Ps. 68:20
Who is so great a G ... Ps. 77:13
Restore us, O G ... Ps. 80:7
You alone are G ... Ps. 86:10
Exalt the LORD our G ... Ps. 99:9
Yes, our G is merciful ... Ps. 116:5
For G is in heaven ... Eccl. 5:2
Counselor, Mighty G ... Is. 9:6
G is my salvation ... Is. 12:2
stricken, smitten by G ... Is. 53:4
translated, "G with us." ... Matt. 1:23
in G my Savior ... Luke 1:47
the Word was with G ... John 1:1
For G so loved the ... John 3:16
G is Spirit, and those ... John 4:24
"My Lord and my G ... John 20:28
Christ is the Son of G ... Acts 8:37
Indeed, let G be true ... Rom. 3:4
If G is for us ... Rom. 8:31
G is faithful ... 1 Cor. 1:9
G shall supply all ... Phil. 4:19
and I will be their G ... Heb. 8:10
G is a consuming fire ... Heb. 12:29
for G is love ... 1 John 4:8
No one has seen G ... 1 John 4:12
G Himself will be ... Rev. 21:3
and I will be his G ... Rev. 21:7

GODDESS (5/5)
after Ashtoreth the g ... 1 Kin. 11:5
of the great g Diana ... Acts 19:35

GODHEAD (2/2)
eternal power and G ... Rom. 1:20
the fullness of the G ... Col. 2:9

GODLINESS (16/16)
is the mystery of g ... 1 Tim. 3:16
Now g with contentment ... 1 Tim. 6:6
having a form of g ... 2 Tim. 3:5
to perseverance g ... 2 Pet. 1:6

GODLY (16/16)
who desire to live g ... 2 Tim. 3:12
reverence and g fear ... Heb. 12:28
to deliver the g ... 2 Pet. 2:9

GODS (235/207)
your God is God of g ... Deut. 10:17
I said, "You are g ... Ps. 82:6
yourselves with g ... Is. 57:5
If He called them g ... John 10:35
g have come down to ... Acts 14:11

GOLD (452/394)
g I do not have ... Acts 3:6
with braided hair or g ... 1 Tim. 2:9
a man with g rings ... James 2:2
Your g and silver are ... James 5:3
more precious than g ... 1 Pet. 1:7
like silver or g ... 1 Pet. 1:18
of the city was pure g ... Rev. 21:21

GONE (221/217)
like sheep have g ... Is. 53:6

GOOD (700/643)
God saw that it was g ... Gen. 1:10
but God meant it for g ... Gen. 50:20
Shall we indeed accept g ... Job 2:10
is none who does g ... Ps. 14:1
Truly God is g to ... Ps. 73:1
g word makes it glad ... Prov. 12:25
on the evil and the g ... Prov. 15:3
A merry heart does g ... Prov. 17:22
learn to do g ... Is. 1:17
talked to me, with g ... Zech. 1:13
A g man out of the ... Matt. 12:35
No one is g but One ... Matt. 19:17
For she has done a g ... Matt. 26:10
who went about doing g ... Acts 10:38
g man someone would ... Rom. 5:7
in my flesh) nothing g ... Rom. 7:18
overcome evil with g ... Rom. 12:21
fruitful in every g ... Col. 1:10
know that the law is g ... 1 Tim. 1:8
For this is g and ... 1 Tim. 2:3
bishop, he desires a g ... 1 Tim. 3:1
for this is g and ... 1 Tim. 5:4
prepared for every g ... 2 Tim. 2:21
Every g gift and every ... James 1:17

GOODNESS (45/42)
"I will make all My g ... Ex. 33:19
and abounding in g ... Ex. 34:6
"You are my Lord, my g ... Ps. 16:2
Surely g and mercy ... Ps. 23:6
that I would see the g ... Ps. 27:13
the riches of His g ... Rom. 2:4
kindness, g ... Gal. 5:22

GOSPEL (100/94)
The beginning of the g ... Mark 1:1
and believe in the g ... Mark 1:15
g must first be preached ... Mark 13:10
to testify to the g ... Acts 20:24
separated to the g ... Rom. 1:1
not ashamed of the g ... Rom. 1:16
to a different g ... Gal. 1:6
the everlasting g ... Rev. 14:6

GOVERNMENT (2/2)
and the g will be upon ... Is. 9:6

GRACE (148/137)
But Noah found g ... Gen. 6:8
G is poured upon Your ... Ps. 45:2
The LORD will give g ... Ps. 84:11
the Spirit of g ... Zech. 12:10
and the g of God was ... Luke 2:40
g and truth came ... John 1:17
And great g was upon ... Acts 4:33
receive abundance of g ... Rom. 5:17
g is no longer g ... Rom. 11:6
For you know the g ... 2 Cor. 8:9
"My g is sufficient ... 2 Cor. 12:9
The g of the Lord ... 2 Cor. 13:14
you have fallen from g ... Gal. 5:4
to the riches of His g ... Eph. 1:7
g you have been saved ... Eph. 2:8
g was given according ... Eph. 4:7
G be with all those ... Eph. 6:24
shaken, let us have g ... Heb. 12:28
But He gives more g ... James 4:6
but grow in the g ... 2 Pet. 3:18

GRACIOUS (32/31)
he said, "God be g ... Gen. 43:29
I will be g to whom I ... Ex. 33:19
at the g words which ... Luke 4:22
that the Lord is g ... 1 Pet. 2:3

GRAFTED (5/4)
in unbelief, will be g ... Rom. 11:23

GRAIN (251/229)
it treads out the g ... Deut. 25:4
be revived like g ... Hos. 14:7
to pluck heads of g ... Matt. 12:1
unless a g of wheat ... John 12:24

GRAPES (38/35)
brought forth wild g ... Is. 5:2
have eaten sour g ... Ezek. 18:2
Do men gather g ... Matt. 7:16
g are fully ripe ... Rev. 14:18

GRASS (63/56)
The g withers ... Is. 40:7
so clothes the g ... Matt. 6:30
"All flesh is as g ... 1 Pet. 1:24

GRAVE (53/50)
my soul up from the g ... Ps. 30:3
And they made His g ... Is. 53:9
the power of the g ... Hos. 13:14

GRAVES (19/17)
and the g were opened ... Matt. 27:52
g which are not ... Luke 11:44
g will hear His voice ... John 5:28

GRAY (10/10)
the man of *g* hairs ... Deut. 32:25
GREAT (837/803)
and make your name *g* ... Gen. 12:2
For the LORD is *g* ... 1 Chr. 16:25
Who does *g* things ... Job 5:9
g is the Holy One ... Is. 12:6
g is Your faithfulness ... Lam. 3:23
he shall be called *g* ... Matt. 5:19
one pearl of *g* price ... Matt. 13:46
desires to become *g* ... Matt. 20:26
g drops of blood ... Luke 22:44
appearing of our *g* ... Titus 2:13
g men, the rich men ... Rev. 6:15
Babylon the *G* ... Rev. 17:5
the dead, small and *g* ... Rev. 20:12
GREATER (82/78)
kingdom of heaven is *g* ... Matt. 11:11
place there is One *g* ... Matt. 12:6
g than Jonah is here ... Matt. 12:41
g than Solomon is here ... Matt. 12:42
a servant is not *g* ... John 13:16
G love has no one ... John 15:13
'A servant is not *g* ... John 15:20
he who prophesies is *g* ... 1 Cor. 14:5
condemns us, God is *g* ... 1 John 3:20
witness of God is *g* ... 1 John 5:9
GREATEST (21/21)
little child is the *g* ... Matt. 18:4
but the *g* of these is ... 1 Cor. 13:13
GREATNESS (31/31)
is the exceeding *g* ... Eph. 1:19
GREED (1/1)
part is full of *g* ... Luke 11:39
GREEDINESS (2/2)
all uncleanness with *g* ... Eph. 4:19
GREEDY (7/7)
of everyone who is *g* ... Prov. 1:19
not violent, not *g* ... 1 Tim. 3:3
GREEK (14/14)
written in Hebrew, *G* ... John 19:20
and also for the *G* ... Rom. 1:16
is neither Jew nor *G* ... Gal. 3:28
GREEN (39/38)
lie down in *g* pastures ... Ps. 23:2
GRIEF (28/28)
and acquainted with *g* ... Is. 53:3
joy and not with *g* ... Heb. 13:17
GRIEVE (4/4)
g the children of men ... Lam. 3:33
g the Holy Spirit ... Eph. 4:30
GRIEVED (34/34)
earth, and He was *g* ... Gen. 6:6
g His Holy Spirit ... Is. 63:10
with anger, being *g* ... Mark 3:5
GROAN (9/9)
even we ourselves *g* ... Rom. 8:23
who are in this tent *g* ... 2 Cor. 5:4
GROANING (12/12)
I am weary with my *g* ... Ps. 6:6
Then Jesus, again *g* ... John 11:38
GROANINGS (3/3)
g which cannot ... Rom. 8:26
GROUND (217/213)
"Cursed is the *g* ... Gen. 3:17
you stand is holy *g* ... Ex. 3:5
up your fallow *g* ... Jer. 4:3
others fell on good *g* ... Matt. 13:8
bought a piece of *g* ... Luke 14:18
God, the pillar and *g* ... 1 Tim. 3:15
GROUNDED (2/2)
being rooted and *g* ... Eph. 3:17
GROW (56/56)
truth in love, may *g* ... Eph. 4:15
but *g* in the grace and ... 2 Pet. 3:18
GRUDGINGLY (1/1)
in his heart, not *g* ... 2 Cor. 9:7
GUARANTEE (3/3)
in our hearts as a *g* ... 2 Cor. 1:22
us the Spirit as a *g* ... 2 Cor. 5:5
who is the *g* of our ... Eph. 1:14
GUIDE (16/16)
He will be our *g* ... Ps. 48:14
g our feet into the ... Luke 1:79
has come, He will *g* ... John 16:13
GUIDES (6/6)
Woe to you, blind *g* ... Matt. 23:16
GUILT (40/38)
of your fathers' *g* ... Matt. 23:32
GUILTLESS (8/8)
g who takes His name ... Ex. 20:7
have condemned the *g* ... Matt. 12:7
GUILTY (32/32)
"We are truly *g* ... Gen. 42:21
the world may become *g* ... Rom. 3:19
in one point, he is *g* ... James 2:10
GULF (1/1)
you there is a great *g* ... Luke 16:26

H

HABITATION (16/16)
Is God in His holy *h* ... Ps. 68:5
in a peaceful *h* ... Is. 32:18
from His holy *h* ... Zech. 2:13
be clothed with our *h* ... 2 Cor. 5:2
HADES (11/11)
be brought down to *H* ... Matt. 11:23
H shall not prevail ... Matt. 16:18
being in torments in *H* ... Luke 16:23
not leave my soul in *H* ... Acts 2:27
I have the keys of *H* ... Rev. 1:18
H were cast into the ... Rev. 20:14
HAIL (34/30)
of the plague of the *h* ... Rev. 16:21
HAIR (77/72)
you cannot make one *h* ... Matt. 5:36
But not a *h* of your ... Luke 21:18
not with braided *h* ... 1 Tim. 2:9
h like women's *h* ... Rev. 9:8
HAIRS (9/9)
But the very *h* ... Matt. 10:30
HALLOWED (15/15)
the Sabbath day and *h* ... Ex. 20:11
who is holy shall be *h* ... Is. 5:16
heaven, *h* be Your name ... Matt. 6:9
HAND (1,367/1,210)
My times are in Your *h* ... Ps. 31:15
"Sit at My right *h* ... Ps. 110:1
heart is in the *h* ... Prov. 21:1
Whatever your *h* finds ... Eccl. 9:10
is at his right *h* ... Eccl. 10:2
do not withhold your *h* ... Eccl. 11:6
My *h* has laid the ... Is. 48:13
Behold, the LORD's *h* ... Is. 59:1
are the work of Your *h* ... Is. 64:8
Am I a God near at *h* ... Jer. 23:23
of heaven is at *h* ... Matt. 3:2
if your right *h* causes ... Matt. 5:30
do not let your left *h* ... Matt. 6:3
h causes you to sin ... Mark 9:43
sitting at the right *h* ... Mark 14:62
at the right *h* of God ... Acts 7:55
The Lord is at *h* ... Phil. 4:5
"Sit at My right *h* ... Heb. 1:13
down at the right *h* ... Heb. 10:12
HANDIWORK (2/2)
firmament shows His *h* ... Ps. 19:1
HANDLE (11/10)
H Me and see ... Luke 24:39
do not taste, do not *h* ... Col. 2:21
HANDLED (2/2)
and our hands have *h* ... 1 John 1:1
HANDS (456/434)
took his life in his *h* ... 1 Sam. 19:5
but His *h* make whole ... Job 5:18
They pierced My *h* ... Ps. 22:16
h formed the dry land ... Ps. 95:5
than having two *h* ... Matt. 18:8
Behold My *h* and My ... Luke 24:39
h the print of the ... John 20:25
his *h* what is good ... Eph. 4:28
the laying on of the *h* ... 1 Tim. 4:14
to fall into the *h* ... Heb. 10:31
HANDWRITING (1/1)
having wiped out the *h* ... Col. 2:14
HANGED (19/19)
went and *h* himself ... Matt. 27:5
HANGS (2/2)
h the earth on nothing ... Job 26:7
is everyone who *h* ... Gal. 3:13
HAPPY (24/21)
H is the man who has ... Ps. 127:5
HARD (54/53)
I knew you to be a *h* ... Matt. 25:24
"This is a *h* saying ... John 6:60
are some things *h* ... 2 Pet. 3:16
HARDEN (12/12)
But I will *h* his heart ... Ex. 4:21
h your hearts as ... Heb. 3:8
HARDENED (22/22)
But Pharaoh *h* his ... Ex. 8:32
their heart was *h* ... Mark 6:52
eyes and *h* their hearts ... John 12:40
lest any of you be *h* ... Heb. 3:13
HARDENS (5/5)
whom He wills He *h* ... Rom. 9:18
HARLOT (76/71)
of a *h* named Rahab ... Josh. 2:1
h is one body with ... 1 Cor. 6:16
of the great *h* who ... Rev. 17:1
HARLOTRIES (5/4)
Let her put away her *h* ... Hos. 2:2
HARLOTRY (50/44)
are the children of *h* ... Hos. 2:4
for the spirit of *h* ... Hos. 5:4
HARLOTS (9/9)
h enter the kingdom ... Matt. 21:31
Great, The Mother of *H* ... Rev. 17:5
HARP (34/33)
Lamb, each having a *h* ... Rev. 5:8
HARPS (19/19)
We hung our *h* upon the ... Ps. 137:2
HARVEST (68/58)
seedtime and *h* ... Gen. 8:22
"The *h* is past ... Jer. 8:20
h truly is plentiful ... Matt. 9:37
sickle, because the *h* ... Mark 4:29
already white for *h* ... John 4:35
HASTENS (8/8)
and he sins who *h* ... Prov. 19:2
HASTILY (5/5)
utter anything *h* ... Eccl. 5:2
HASTY (4/4)
Do you see a man *h* ... Prov. 29:20
HATE (86/83)
love the LORD, *h* evil ... Ps. 97:10
h every false way ... Ps. 119:104
h the double-minded ... Ps. 119:113
I *h* and abhor lying ... Ps. 119:163
love, and a time to *h* ... Eccl. 3:8
You who *h* good and ... Mic. 3:2
either he will *h* the one ... Matt. 6:24
HATED (53/51)
but Esau I have *h* ... Mal. 1:3
And you will be *h* ... Matt. 10:22
have seen and also *h* ... John 15:24
but Esau I have *h* ... Rom. 9:13
For no one ever *h* ... Eph. 5:29
HATEFUL (2/2)
h woman when she is ... Prov. 30:23
in malice and envy, *h* ... Titus 3:3
HATERS (2/2)
backbiters, *h* of God ... Rom. 1:30
HATES (37/36)
six things the LORD *h* ... Prov. 6:16
lose it, and he who *h* ... John 12:25
"If the world *h* ... John 15:18
h his brother is ... 1 John 2:11
HAUGHTY (18/18)
bring down *h* looks ... Ps. 18:27
my heart is not *h* ... Ps. 131:1
h spirit before a fall ... Prov. 16:18
HEAD (361/331)
He shall bruise your *h* ... Gen. 3:15
you swear by your *h* ... Matt. 5:36
and gave Him to be *h* ... Eph. 1:22
For the husband is *h* ... Eph. 5:23
HEAL (46/45)
O LORD, *h* me ... Ps. 6:2
h your backslidings ... Jer. 3:22
torn, but He will *h* ... Hos. 6:1
H the sick, cleanse ... Matt. 10:8
so that I should *h* ... Matt. 13:15
sent Me to *h* the ... Luke 4:18
Physician, *h* yourself ... Luke 4:23
HEALED (78/76)
And return and be *h* ... Is. 6:10
His stripes we are *h* ... Is. 53:5
When I would have *h* ... Hos. 7:1
and He *h* them ... Matt. 4:24
that you may be *h* ... James 5:16
his deadly wound was *h* ... Rev. 13:3
HEALING (15/14)
shall arise with *h* ... Mal. 4:2
and *h* all kinds of ... Matt. 4:23
tree were for the *h* ... Rev. 22:2
HEALINGS (3/3)
to another gifts of *h* ... 1 Cor. 12:9
HEALS (5/5)
h all your diseases ... Ps. 103:3
Jesus the Christ *h* ... Acts 9:34
HEALTH (13/13)
all things and be in *h* ... 3 John 1:2
HEAR (537/504)
"*H*, O Israel: The LORD ... Deut. 6:4
Him you shall *h* ... Deut. 18:15
H me when I call ... Ps. 4:1
O You who *h* prayer ... Ps. 65:2
ear, shall He not *h* ... Ps. 94:9
h rather than to give ... Eccl. 5:1
'Hearing you will *h* ... Matt. 13:14
"Take heed what you *h* ... Mark 4:24
that God does not *h* ... John 9:31
And how shall they *h* ... Rom. 10:14
man be swift to *h* ... James 1:19
h what the Spirit says ... Rev. 2:7
HEARD (632/611)
h their cry because of ... Ex. 3:7
that they will be *h* ... Matt. 6:7
h the word believed ... Acts 4:4
not seen, nor ear *h* ... 1 Cor. 2:9
things that you have *h* ... 2 Tim. 2:2
the word which they *h* ... Heb. 4:2
which we have *h* ... 1 John 1:1
Lord's Day, and I *h* ... Rev. 1:10
HEARER (2/2)
if anyone is a *h* ... James 1:23
HEARERS (4/4)
for not the *h* of the ... Rom. 2:13
of the word, and not *h* ... James 1:22
HEARING (91/84)
'Keep on *h*, but do not ... Is. 6:9
h they do not ... Matt. 13:13
h they may hear ... Mark 4:12
or by the *h* of faith ... Gal. 3:2

HEARS (58/56)
out, and the LORD *h*............. Ps. 34:17
of God *h* God's words........... John 8:47
And if anyone *h* .... John 12:47
who is of the truth *h* .... John 18:37
He who knows God *h*........... 1 John 4:6
And let him who *h* .... Rev. 22:17
HEART (833/772)
h was only evil................. Gen. 6:5
h rejoices in the LORD............ 1 Sam. 2:1
God gave him another *h*....... 1 Sam. 10:9
LORD looks at the *h* .... 1 Sam. 16:7
his wives turned his *h*.......... 1 Kin. 11:4
He pierces my *h* ....Job 16:13
My *h* also instructs me .... Ps. 16:7
h is overflowing .... Ps. 45:1
h shall depart from me.......... Ps. 101:4
look and a proud *h*............. Ps. 101:5
with my whole *h*................. Ps. 111:1
as he thinks in his *h*........... Prov. 23:7
h reveals the man............. Prov. 27:19
trusts in his own *h*............Prov. 28:26
The *h* of the wise is.............. Eccl. 7:4
and a wise man's *h*.............. Eccl. 8:5
h yearned for him .... Song 5:4
and the whole *h* .... Is. 1:5
the yearning of Your *h* ....Is. 63:15
h is deceitful above .... Jer. 17:9
I will give them a *h*.............. Jer. 24:7
and take the stony *h* .... Ezek. 11:19
get yourselves a new *h* .... Ezek. 18:31
are the pure in *h*................ Matt. 5:8
is, there your *h* .... Matt. 6:21
of the *h* proceed evil .... Matt. 15:19
h will flow rivers................. John 7:38
"Let not your *h* .... John 14:1
Satan filled your *h* .... Acts 5:3
h that God has raised........... Rom. 10:9
refresh my *h* in the.......... Philem. 1:20
and shuts up his *h* .... 1 John 3:17
HEARTILY (2/2)
you do, do it *h* .... Col. 3:23
HEARTS (142/135)
God tests the *h*.................... Ps. 7:9
And he will turn the *h*............Mal. 4:6
h failing them from........... Luke 21:26
will guard your *h* ....Phil. 4:7
of God rule in your *h* .... Col. 3:15
HEATHEN (2/2)
repetitions as the *h* .... Matt. 6:7
HEAVEN (532/502)
called the firmament *H* .... Gen. 1:8
LORD looks down from *h* .... Ps. 14:2
word is settled in *h*............. Ps. 119:89
For God is in *h* .... Eccl. 5:2
"*H* is My throne.................. Is. 66:1
for the kingdom of *h*............ Matt. 3:2
your Father in *h* .... Matt. 5:16
on earth as it is in *h*........... Matt. 6:10
H and earth will .... Matt. 24:35
from Him a sign from *h* .... Mark 8:11
have sinned against *h*.......... Luke 15:18
you shall see *h* open .... John 1:51
one has ascended to *h*........... John 3:13
the true bread from *h* .... John 6:32
a voice came from *h* .... John 12:28
sheet, let down from *h* .... Acts 11:5
laid up for you in *h*................Col. 1:5
there was silence in *h* .... Rev. 8:1
Now I saw a new *h* .... Rev. 21:1
HEAVENLY (24/23)
h host praising God .... Luke 2:13
if I tell you *h* things .... John 3:12
blessing in the *h*................... Eph. 1:3
a better, that is, a *h*............. Heb. 11:16
the living God, the *h* .... Heb. 12:22
HEAVENS (171/166)
and the highest *h*............ Deut. 10:14
h cannot contain .... 1 Kin. 8:27
h declare the glory................Ps. 19:1
For as the *h* are high .... Ps. 103:11
behold, I create new *h*............Is. 65:17
and behold, the *h*.............. Matt. 3:16
h will be shaken .... Matt. 24:29
h are the work of Your......... Heb. 1:10
h will pass away................ 2 Pet. 3:10
HEEDS (4/4)
h counsel is wise............. Prov. 12:15
HEEL (6/6)
you shall bruise His *h* ....Gen. 3:15
has lifted up his *h*................ Ps. 41:9
Me has lifted up his *h* .... John 13:18
HEIGHT (65/60)
nor *h* nor depth.............. Rom. 8:39
length and depth and *h* ....Eph. 3:18
HEIR (21/19)
He has appointed *h* ....Heb. 1:2
the world and became *h*......... Heb. 11:7
HEIRS (13/11)
of God and joint *h*............. Rom. 8:17
should be fellow *h* .... Eph. 3:6
HELL (32/32)
shall be turned into *h* .... Ps. 9:17
go down alive into *h* .... Ps. 55:15
H and Destruction are ....Prov. 27:20
be in danger of *h* fire........... Matt. 5:22
to be cast into *h*................ Matt. 18:9
the condemnation of *h*.........Matt. 23:33
power to cast into *h*.............. Luke 12:5
HELMET (10/10)
And take the *h* of ....Eph. 6:17
and love, and as a *h* ....1 Thess. 5:8
HELP (137/129)
May He send you *h*................Ps. 20:2
A very present *h* .... Ps. 46:1
He is their *h* and .... Ps. 115:9
Our *h* is in the name .... Ps. 124:8
h my unbelief ....Mark 9:24
and find grace to *h*..............Heb. 4:16
HELPED (30/30)
fall, but the LORD *h* ....Ps. 118:13
of salvation I have *h* .... Is. 49:8
h His servant Israel .... Luke 1:54
HELPER (16/16)
I will make him a *h*...............Gen. 2:18
Behold, God is my *h*............... Ps. 54:4
give you another *H* .... John 14:16
"But when the *H*.............. John 15:26
"The LORD is my *h* .... Heb. 13:6
HELPFUL (3/3)
all things are not *h*............... 1 Cor. 6:12
HELPS (4/4)
the Spirit also *h*............... Rom. 8:26
HEM (9/8)
and touched the *h* ....Matt. 9:20
HERE (303/284)
Then I said, "*H* am I.............. Is. 6:8
HERESIES (2/2)
dissensions, *h* .... Gal. 5:20
HERITAGE (36/35)
for that is his *h* .... Eccl. 3:22
This is the *h* of the .... Is. 54:17
of My people, My *h*................Joel 3:2
The flock of Your *h*............... Mic. 7:14
HIDDEN (98/96)
and my sins are not *h* .... Ps. 69:5
Your word I have *h*.............. Ps. 119:11
h that will not ....Matt. 10:26
the *h* wisdom which God ....1 Cor. 2:7
bring to light the *h*.............1 Cor. 4:5
have renounced the *h*.......... 2 Cor. 4:2
rather let it be the *h*............ 1 Pet. 3:4
give some of the *h* .... Rev. 2:17
HIDE (85/82)
H me under the shadow.......... Ps. 17:8
You shall *h* them in .... Ps. 31:20
You *h* Your face................ Ps. 104:29
darkness shall not *h* .... Ps. 139:12
You are God, who *h* ....Is. 45:15
"Fall on us and *h*................ Rev. 6:16
HIDES (10/10)
He *h* His face ....Ps. 10:11
HIDING (10/10)
You are my *h* place.............. Ps. 32:7
HIGH (376/357)
priest of God Most *H*........... Gen. 14:18
For the LORD Most *H*............. Ps. 47:2
"I dwell in the *h*..................Is. 57:15
know that the Most *H* ....Dan. 4:17
up on a *h* mountain by ....Matt. 17:1
your mind on *h* things .... Rom. 12:16
h thing that exalts ....2 Cor. 10:5
and faithful *H* Priest ....Heb. 2:17
HIGHER (14/11)
you, 'Friend, go up *h* .... Luke 14:10
HIGHWAY (23/21)
in the desert a *h* .... Is. 40:3
HIGHWAYS (11/11)
h shall be elevated ....Is. 49:11
go into the *h*....................Matt. 22:9
HILL (60/58)
My King on My holy *h*............. Ps. 2:6
h cannot be hidden .... Matt. 5:14
and *h* brought low .... Luke 3:5
HILLS (63/63)
of the everlasting *h* .... Gen. 49:26
of the *h* are His also.............. Ps. 95:4
up my eyes to the *h* .... Ps. 121:1
HINDER (5/5)
all things lest we *h* .... 1 Cor. 9:12
HINDERED (8/8)
Who *h* you from obeying......... Gal. 5:7
prayers may not be *h*............. 1 Pet. 3:7
HOLD (135/134)
right hand shall *h*.............. Ps. 139:10
h fast that word................. 1 Cor. 15:2
h fast and repent .... Rev. 3:3
HOLIER (1/1)
near me, for I am *h* .... Is. 65:5
HOLIEST (3/3)
the way into the *H* .... Heb. 9:8
HOLINESS (32/32)
You, glorious in *h*.................Ex. 15:11
I have sworn by My *h*............Ps. 89:35
h adorns Your house .... Ps. 93:5
the Highway of *H* .... Is. 35:8
to the Spirit of *h* .... Rom. 1:4
spirit, perfecting *h*.............. 2 Cor. 7:1
uncleanness, but in *h* .... 1 Thess. 4:7
be partakers of His *h*............Heb. 12:10
HOLY (637/567)
where you stand is *h* .... Ex. 3:5
day, to keep it *h*.................. Ex. 20:8
the LORD your God am *h* .... Lev. 19:2
h seed is mixed .... Ezra 9:2
God sits on His *h*................... Ps. 47:8
God, in His *h* mountain .... Ps. 48:1
"*H*, *h*, *h* is the LORD .... Is. 6:3
if the firstfruit is *h* .... Rom. 11:16
one another with a *h* .... Rom. 16:16
that we should be *h* ....Eph. 1:4
has not entered the *h* .... Heb. 9:24
it is written, "Be *h*............... 1 Pet. 1:16
says He who is *h* .... Rev. 3:7
For You alone are *h* .... Rev. 15:4
is *h*, let him be *h*................ Rev. 22:11
HOLY SPIRIT (97/96)
not take Your *H* from me.......... Ps. 51:11
found with child of the *H*....... Matt. 1:18
baptize you with the *H* .... Matt. 3:11
speaks against the *H*, it........ Matt. 12:32
of the Son and of the *H*........Matt. 28:19
who speak, but the *H*.......... Mark 13:11
And the *H* descended in......... Luke 3:22
Father give the *H* .... Luke 11:13
the *H* was not yet given........... John 7:39
"But the Helper, the *H*......... John 14:26
to them, "Receive the *H* ....John 20:22
receive power when the *H*.......... Acts 1:8
were all filled with the *H* ....Acts 2:4
Peter, filled with the *H* ....Acts 4:8
were forbidden by the *H* ....Acts 16:6
peace and joy in the *H* .... Rom. 14:17
but which the *H* teaches.......... 1 Cor. 2:13
were sealed with the *H* of......... Eph. 1:13
And do not grieve the *H*......... Eph. 4:30
and renewing of the *H* .... Titus 3:5
HOME (67/66)
sparrow has found a *h*............ Ps. 84:3
to his eternal *h* ....Eccl. 12:5
that while we are at *h*............ 2 Cor. 5:6
to show piety at *h*.............. 1 Tim. 5:4
HOMEMAKERS (1/1)
be discreet, chaste, *h*............ Titus 2:5
HONEY (57/57)
and with *h* from the............... Ps. 81:16
was locusts and wild *h* ....Matt. 3:4
HONEYCOMB (8/8)
than honey and the *h* .... Ps. 19:10
fish and some *h* .... Luke 24:42
HONOR (144/132)
H your father and your..........Ex. 20:12
will deliver him and *h*............ Ps. 91:15
H and majesty are ....Ps. 96:6
H the LORD with your .... Prov. 3:9
before *h* is humility............. Prov. 15:33
spirit will retain *h*.............Prov. 29:23
Father, where is My *h*............. Mal. 1:6
is not without *h*.............. Matt. 13:57
H your father and your......... Matt. 15:4
h the Son just as they .... John 5:23
"I do not receive *h* .... John 5:41
but I *h* My Father .... John 8:49
"If I *h* Myself ....John 8:54
him My Father will *h*.......... John 12:26
make one vessel for *h*............Rom. 9:21
to whom fear, *h*................. Rom. 13:7
sanctification and *h*........... 1 Thess. 4:4
alone is wise, be *h*................ 1 Tim. 1:17
and clay, some for *h*.......... 2 Tim. 2:20
no man takes this *h* .... Heb. 5:4
from God the Father *h* .... 2 Pet. 1:17
give glory and *h* .... Rev. 4:9
HONORABLE (25/25)
His work is *h* and ....Ps. 111:3
holy day of the LORD *h* ....Is. 58:13
providing *h* things..............2 Cor. 8:21
Marriage is *h* among.............Heb. 13:4
having your conduct *h* .... 1 Pet. 2:12
HONORS (8/8)
'This people *h* Me................ Mark 7:6
It is My Father who *h*............John 8:54
HOPE (142/134)
h He has uprooted ....Job 19:10
also will rest in *h*.................. Ps. 16:9
My *h* is in You .... Ps. 39:7
For You are my *h*.................. Ps. 71:5
I *h* in Your word .... Ps. 119:147
good that one should *h*......... Lam. 3:26
to *h*, in *h* believed.............. Rom. 4:18
h does not disappoint............. Rom. 5:5
h that is seen is ....Rom. 8:24
And now abide faith, *h* .... 1 Cor. 13:13
life only we have *h* .... 1 Cor. 15:19

may know what is the *h* .... Eph. 1:18
were called in one *h* .... Eph. 4:4
Christ in you, the *h* .... Col. 1:27
Jesus Christ, our *h* .... 1 Tim. 1:1
for the blessed *h* .... Titus 2:13
to lay hold of the *h* .... Heb. 6:18
of a better *h* .... Heb. 7:19
who has this *h* in Him .... 1 John 3:3

HOPED (8/8)
substance of things *h* .... Heb. 11:1

HORSE (40/38)
and behold, a white *h* .... Rev. 6:2
and behold, a white *h* .... Rev. 19:11

HOSANNA (6/5)
H in the highest .... Matt. 21:9

HOSPITABLE (3/3)
Be *h* to one another .... 1 Pet. 4:9

HOSTS (289/277)
The LORD of *h* is with .... Ps. 46:7
word of the LORD of *h* .... Is. 39:5
against spiritual *h* .... Eph. 6:12

HOUR (97/89)
Man is coming at an *h* .... Matt. 24:44
But the *h* is coming .... John 4:23
save Me from this *h* .... John 12:27
keep you from the *h* .... Rev. 3:10

HOUSE (1,739/1,490)
But as for me and my *h* .... Josh. 24:15
Through wisdom a *h* .... Prov. 24:3
better to go to the *h* .... Eccl. 7:2
h was filled with .... Is. 6:4
h divided against .... Matt. 12:25
h shall be called a .... Matt. 21:13
make My Father's *h* .... John 2:16
h are many mansions .... John 14:2
publicly and from *h* .... Acts 20:20
who rules his own *h* .... 1 Tim. 3:4
the church in your *h* .... Philem. 1:2
For every *h* is built .... Heb. 3:4
His own *h*, whose *h* .... Heb. 3:6

HOUSEHOLD (104/103)
over the ways of her *h* .... Prov. 31:27
be those of his own *h* .... Matt. 10:36
h were baptized .... Acts 16:15
saved, you and your *h* .... Acts 16:31
who are of Caesar's *h* .... Phil. 4:22

HOUSEHOLDER (1/1)
h who brings out of .... Matt. 13:52

HOUSES (187/172)
H and riches are an .... Prov. 19:14
who has left *h* or .... Matt. 19:29
you devour widows' *h* .... Matt. 23:14

HOVERING (1/1)
Spirit of God was *h* .... Gen. 1:2

HUMBLE (43/40)
man Moses was very *h* .... Num. 12:3
the cry of the *h* .... Ps. 9:12
h shall hear of it and .... Ps. 34:2
contrite and *h* spirit .... Is. 57:15
a meek and *h* people .... Zeph. 3:12
associate with the *h* .... Rom. 12:16
gives grace to the *h* .... James 4:6
H yourselves in the .... James 4:10
gives grace to the *h* .... 1 Pet. 5:5
h yourselves under the .... 1 Pet. 5:6

HUMBLED (30/26)
as a man, He *h* Himself .... Phil. 2:8

HUMBLES (6/6)
h Himself to behold .... Ps. 113:6

HUMILITY (12/12)
the Lord with all *h* .... Acts 20:19
delight in false *h* .... Col. 2:18
mercies, kindness, *h* .... Col. 3:12
h correcting those .... 2 Tim. 2:25
gentle, showing all *h* .... Titus 3:2
and be clothed with *h* .... 1 Pet. 5:5

HUNGER (23/23)
They shall neither *h* .... Is. 49:10
are those who *h* .... Matt. 5:6
for you shall *h* .... Luke 6:25
to Me shall never *h* .... John 6:35
present hour we both *h* .... 1 Cor. 4:11
They shall neither *h* .... Rev. 7:16

HUNGRY (46/45)
and fills the *h* .... Ps. 107:9
gives food to the *h* .... Ps. 146:7
for I was *h* and you .... Matt. 25:35
when did we see You *h* .... Matt. 25:37
to be full and to be *h* .... Phil. 4:12

HUNTER (4/3)
Nimrod the mighty *h* .... Gen. 10:9
Esau was a skillful *h* .... Gen. 25:27

HURT (39/38)
h a woman with child .... Ex. 21:22
but I was not *h* .... Prov. 23:35
another to his own *h* .... Eccl. 8:9
They shall not *h* .... Is. 11:9
it will by no means *h* .... Mark 16:18
shall not be *h* by the .... Rev. 2:11

HUSBAND (119/103)
She also gave to her *h* .... Gen. 3:6
h safely trusts her .... Prov. 31:11
your Maker is your *h* .... Is. 54:5
now have is not your *h* .... John 4:18
you will save your *h* .... 1 Cor. 7:16
the *h* of one wife .... 1 Tim. 3:2

HUSBANDS (21/21)
H, love your wives .... Eph. 5:25
Let deacons be the *h* .... 1 Tim. 3:12

HYMN (2/2)
they had sung a *h* .... Matt. 26:30

HYMNS (3/3)
praying and singing *h* .... Acts 16:25
in psalms and *h* .... Eph. 5:19

HYPOCRISY (8/8)
you are full of *h* .... Matt. 23:28
Pharisees, which is *h* .... Luke 12:1
Let love be without *h* .... Rom. 12:9
away with their *h* .... Gal. 2:13
and without *h* .... James 3:17
malice, all deceit, *h* .... 1 Pet. 2:1

HYPOCRITE (12/12)
and the joy of the *h* .... Job 20:5
for everyone is a *h* .... Is. 9:17
also played the *h* .... Gal. 2:13

HYPOCRITES (22/22)
not be like the *h* .... Matt. 6:5
do you test Me, you *h* .... Matt. 22:18
and Pharisees, *h* .... Matt. 23:13

I

IDLE (17/14)
i person will suffer .... Prov. 19:15
i word men may speak .... Matt. 12:36
saw others standing *i* .... Matt. 20:3
they learn to be *i* .... 1 Tim. 5:13

IDOL (14/13)
thing offered to an *i* .... 1 Cor. 8:7
That an *i* is anything .... 1 Cor. 10:19

IDOLATER (2/2)
or covetous, or an *i* .... 1 Cor. 5:11

IDOLATERS (7/7)
fornicators, nor *i* .... 1 Cor. 6:9
and murderers and *i* .... Rev. 22:15

IDOLATRIES (1/1)
and abominable *i* .... 1 Pet. 4:3

IDOLATRY (4/4)
beloved, flee from *i* .... 1 Cor. 10:14
i, sorcery, hatred .... Gal. 5:20

IDOLS (124/118)
land is also full of *i* .... Is. 2:8
in the room of his *i* .... Ezek. 8:12
who regard worthless *i* .... Jon. 2:8
You who abhor *i* .... Rom. 2:22
keep yourselves from *i* .... 1 John 5:21
worship demons, and *i* .... Rev. 9:20

IGNORANCE (8/8)
that you did it in *i* .... Acts 3:17
i God overlooked .... Acts 17:30
sins committed in *i* .... Heb. 9:7

IGNORANTLY (1/1)
because I did it *i* .... 1 Tim. 1:13

ILLUMINATED (3/3)
after you were *i* .... Heb. 10:32
and the earth was *i* .... Rev. 18:1
for the glory of God *i* .... Rev. 21:23

IMAGE (110/91)
Us make man in Our *i* .... Gen. 1:26
since he is the *i* .... 1 Cor. 11:7
He is the *i* of the .... Col. 1:15
and not the very *i* .... Heb. 10:1
the beast and his *i* .... Rev. 14:9

IMAGINATION (2/2)
the proud in the *i* .... Luke 1:51

IMITATE (5/4)
as I also *i* Christ .... 1 Cor. 11:1

IMMANUEL (3/3)
shall call His name *I* .... Is. 7:14
shall call His name *I* .... Matt. 1:23

IMMORAL (10/10)
murderers, sexually *i* .... Rev. 21:8

IMMORALITY (21/19)
except sexual *i* .... Matt. 5:32
abstain from sexual *i* .... 1 Thess. 4:3

IMMORTAL (1/1)
to the King eternal, *i* .... 1 Tim. 1:17

IMMORTALITY (5/5)
mortal must put on *i* .... 1 Cor. 15:53
who alone has *i* .... 1 Tim. 6:16

IMMOVABLE (2/2)
be steadfast, *i* .... 1 Cor. 15:58

IMMUTABLE (1/1)
that by two *i* things .... Heb. 6:18

IMPART (3/3)
that it may *i* grace .... Eph. 4:29

IMPENITENT (1/1)
i heart you are .... Rom. 2:5

IMPOSSIBLE (9/9)
God nothing will be *i* .... Luke 1:37
without faith it is *i* .... Heb. 11:6

IMPUTE (4/4)
the LORD does not *i* .... Ps. 32:2

IMPUTED (6/6)
might be *i* to them .... Rom. 4:11
but sin is not *i* .... Rom. 5:13

IMPUTES (1/1)
i righteousness apart .... Rom. 4:6

INCORRUPTIBLE (5/5)
the glory of the *i* .... Rom. 1:23
dead will be raised *i* .... 1 Cor. 15:52
to an inheritance *i* .... 1 Pet. 1:4

INCORRUPTION (4/4)
corruption inherit *i* .... 1 Cor. 15:50

INCREASE (67/64)
Of the *i* of His .... Is. 9:7
Lord, "*I* our faith .... Luke 17:5
He must *i*, but I must .... John 3:30
but God gave the *i* .... 1 Cor. 3:6

INCREASES (13/12)
who have no might He *i* .... Is. 40:29

INCURABLE (6/6)
Your sorrow is *i* .... Jer. 30:15

INDIGNATION (36/36)
i which will devour .... Heb. 10:27
into the cup of His *i* .... Rev. 14:10

INEXCUSABLE (1/1)
Therefore you are *i* .... Rom. 2:1

INEXPRESSIBLE (2/2)
Paradise and heard *i* .... 2 Cor. 12:4
you rejoice with joy *i* .... 1 Pet. 1:8

INFALLIBLE (1/1)
suffering by many *i* .... Acts 1:3

INFIRMITIES (8/8)
"He Himself took our *i* .... Matt. 8:17

INHERIT (62/61)
love me to *i* wealth .... Prov. 8:21
i the kingdom prepared .... Matt. 25:34
unrighteous will not *i* .... 1 Cor. 6:9
who overcomes shall *i* .... Rev. 21:7

INHERITANCE (246/210)
"You shall have no *i* .... Num. 18:20
is the place of His *i* .... Deut. 32:9
the portion of my *i* .... Ps. 16:5
i shall be forever .... Ps. 37:18
He will choose our *i* .... Ps. 47:4
will arise to your *i* .... Dan. 12:13
And God gave him no *i* .... Acts 7:5
and give you an *i* .... Acts 20:32
For if the *i* is of the .... Gal. 3:18
we have obtained an *i* .... Eph. 1:11
be partakers of the *i* .... Col. 1:12
receive as an *i* .... Heb. 11:8
to an *i* incorruptible .... 1 Pet. 1:4

INIQUITIES (53/52)
i have overtaken me .... Ps. 40:12
forgives all your *i* .... Ps. 103:3
LORD, should mark *i* .... Ps. 130:3
was bruised for our *i* .... Is. 53:5
He shall bear their *i* .... Is. 53:11
i have separated you .... Is. 59:2

INIQUITY (241/229)
God, visiting the *i* of the .... Ex. 20:5
was brought forth in *i* .... Ps. 51:5
If I regard *i* in my .... Ps. 66:18
let no *i* have dominion .... Ps. 119:133
i will reap sorrow .... Prov. 22:8
a people laden with *i* .... Is. 1:4
i is taken away .... Is. 6:7
has laid on Him the *i* .... Is. 53:6
will remember their *i* .... Hos. 9:9
to those who devise *i* .... Mic. 2:1
like You, pardoning *i* .... Mic. 7:18
all you workers of *i* .... Luke 13:27
a fire, a world of *i* .... James 3:6

INJUSTICE (9/9)
i have your fathers .... Jer. 2:5

INN (2/2)
room for them in the *i* .... Luke 2:7
brought him to an *i* .... Luke 10:34

INNOCENCE (4/4)
washed my hands in *i* .... Ps. 73:13

INNOCENT (39/38)
because I was found *i* .... Dan. 6:22
saying, "I am *i* .... Matt. 27:24
this day that I am *i* .... Acts 20:26

INQUIRED (28/27)
Therefore David *i* .... 1 Sam. 23:2
the prophets have *i* .... 1 Pet. 1:10

INQUIRY (6/6)
shall make careful *i* .... Deut. 19:18

INSANE (3/3)
images, and they are *i* .... Jer. 50:38

INSPIRATION (1/1)
is given by *i* of God .... 2 Tim. 3:16

INSTRUCT (9/9)
I will *i* you and teach .... Ps. 32:8
the LORD that he may *i* .... 1 Cor. 2:16

INSTRUCTED (22/22)
This man had been *i* .... Acts 18:25
are excellent, being *i* .... Rom. 2:18
Moses was divinely *i* .... Heb. 8:5

INSTRUCTION (40/39)
seeing you hate *i* .... Ps. 50:17

Hear *i* and be wise ... Prov. 8:33
Give *i* to a wise man ... Prov. 9:9
for correction, for *i* ... 2 Tim. 3:16
INSTRUCTS (3/3)
My heart also *i* ... Ps. 16:7
INSTRUMENTS (47/43)
i of unrighteousness ... Rom. 6:13
INSUBORDINATE (2/2)
for the lawless and *i* ... 1 Tim. 1:9
INSUBORDINATION (1/1)
of dissipation or *i* ... Titus 1:6
INSULTED (2/2)
will be mocked and *i* ... Luke 18:32
i the Spirit of grace ... Heb. 10:29
INSULTS (2/2)
nor be afraid of their *i* ... Is. 51:7
INTEGRITY (20/20)
In the *i* of my heart ... Gen. 20:5
in doctrine showing *i* ... Titus 2:7
INTERCEDE (4/4)
the LORD, who will *i* ... 1 Sam. 2:25
INTERCESSION (7/7)
of many, and made *i* ... Is. 53:12
Spirit Himself makes *i* ... Rom. 8:26
always lives to make *i* ... Heb. 7:25
INTERCESSOR (1/1)
that there was no *i* ... Is. 59:16
INTEREST (11/7)
collected it with *i* ... Luke 19:23
INTERPRET (6/5)
Do all *i* ... 1 Cor. 12:30
pray that he may *i* ... 1 Cor. 14:13
INTERPRETATION (40/36)
to another the *i* ... 1 Cor. 12:10
of any private *i* ... 2 Pet. 1:20
INTERPRETATIONS (2/2)
Do not *i* belong to God ... Gen. 40:8
INVISIBLE (5/5)
of the world His *i* ... Rom. 1:20
is the image of the *i* ... Col. 1:15
eternal, immortal, *i* ... 1 Tim. 1:17
as seeing Him who is *i* ... Heb. 11:27
INWARD (12/12)
You have formed my *i* ... Ps. 139:13
God according to the *i* ... Rom. 7:22
i man is being renewed ... 2 Cor. 4:16
INWARDLY (3/3)
i they are ravenous ... Matt. 7:15
is a Jew who is one *i* ... Rom. 2:29
IRON (99/87)
i sharpens *i* ... Prov. 27:17
its feet partly of *i* ... Dan. 2:33
ISRAEL (2,567/2,294)
"Hear, O *I*: The LORD ... Deut. 6:4
For they are not all *I* ... Rom. 9:6
and upon the *I* of God ... Gal. 6:16
ITCHING (1/1)
they have *i* ears ... 2 Tim. 4:3

J

JEALOUS (13/11)
your God, am a *j* God ... Ex. 20:5
a consuming fire, *j* ... Deut. 4:24
For I am *j* for you ... 2 Cor. 11:2
JEALOUSY (33/30)
They provoked Him to *j* ... Deut. 32:16
as strong as death, *j* ... Song 8:6
for you with godly *j* ... 2 Cor. 11:2
JEOPARDY (4/4)
stand in *j* every hour ... 1 Cor. 15:30
JESTING (1/1)
talking, nor coarse *j* ... Eph. 5:4
JESUS (971/934)
birth of *J* Christ was as ... Matt. 1:18
shall call His name *J* ... Matt. 1:21
J was led up by the ... Matt. 4:1
and laid hands on *J* ... Matt. 26:50
Barabbas and destroy *J* ... Matt. 27:20
J withdrew with His ... Mark 3:7
J went into Jerusalem ... Mark 11:11
as they were eating, *J* ... Mark 14:22
and he delivered *J* ... Mark 15:15
truth came through *J* ... John 1:17
J lifted up His eyes ... John 6:5
J wept ... John 11:35
J was crucified ... John 19:20
This *J* God has raised ... Acts 2:32
of Your holy Servant *J* ... Acts 4:30
believed on the Lord *J* ... Acts 11:17
your mouth the Lord *J* ... Rom. 10:9
among you except *J* ... 1 Cor. 2:2
perfect in Christ *J* ... Col. 1:28
But we see *J*, who was ... Heb. 2:9
Revelation of *J* Christ ... Rev. 1:1
Even so, come, Lord *J* ... Rev. 22:20
JOIN (15/15)
of the rest dared *j* ... Acts 5:13
JOINED (43/42)
and mother and be *j* ... Gen. 2:24
what God has *j* ... Matt. 19:6
the whole body, *j* ... Eph. 4:16
JOINT (5/5)
j as He wrestled ... Gen. 32:25
My bones are out of *j* ... Ps. 22:14
j heirs with Christ ... Rom. 8:17
JOINTS (6/6)
and knit together by *j* ... Col. 2:19
and spirit, and of *j* ... Heb. 4:12
JOT (1/1)
one *j* or one tittle ... Matt. 5:18
JOY (158/150)
presence is fullness of *j* ... Ps. 16:11
j comes in the morning ... Ps. 30:5
You according to the *j* ... Is. 9:3
ashes, the oil of *j* ... Is. 61:3
shall sing for *j* ... Is. 65:14
receives it with *j* ... Matt. 13:20
Enter into the *j* ... Matt. 25:21
in my womb for *j* ... Luke 1:44
there will be more *j* ... Luke 15:7
did not believe for *j* ... Luke 24:41
My *j* may remain in ... John 15:11
they may have My *j* ... John 17:13
the Spirit is love, *j* ... Gal. 5:22
are our glory and *j* ... 1 Thess. 2:20
j that was set before ... Heb. 12:2
count it all *j* ... James 1:2
with exceeding *j* ... 1 Pet. 4:13
JOYFUL (23/23)
Make a *j* shout to the ... Ps. 100:1
and make them *j* ... Is. 56:7
JUDGE (188/170)
The LORD *j* between ... Gen. 16:5
coming to *j* the earth ... 1 Chr. 16:33
sword the LORD will *j* ... Is. 66:16
deliver you to the *j* ... Matt. 5:25
"*J* not, that you be not ... Matt. 7:1
"Man, who made Me a *j* ... Luke 12:14
j who did not fear God ... Luke 18:2
As I hear, I *j* ... John 5:30
Do not *j* according ... John 7:24
I *j* no one ... John 8:15
j the world but to ... John 12:47
this, O man, you who *j* ... Rom. 2:3
Therefore let us not *j* ... Rom. 14:13
Christ, who will *j* ... 2 Tim. 4:1
are you to *j* another ... James 4:12
JUDGES (69/67)
He makes the *j* of the ... Is. 40:23
For the Father *j* ... John 5:22
he who is spiritual *j* ... 1 Cor. 2:15
j me is the Lord ... 1 Cor. 4:4
Him who *j* righteously ... 1 Pet. 2:23
JUDGMENT (190/186)
Teach me good *j* ... Ps. 119:66
from prison and from *j* ... Is. 53:8
be in danger of the *j* ... Matt. 5:21
shall not come into *j* ... John 5:24
and My *j* is righteous ... John 5:30
if I do judge, My *j* ... John 8:16
Now is the *j* of this ... John 12:31
the righteous *j* of God ... Rom. 1:32
j which came from one ... Rom. 5:16
appear before the *j* ... 2 Cor. 5:10
after this the *j* ... Heb. 9:27
time has come for *j* ... 1 Pet. 4:17
a long time their *j* ... 2 Pet. 2:3
darkness for the *j* ... Jude 1:6
JUDGMENTS (122/120)
I dread, for Your *j* ... Ps. 119:39
unsearchable are His *j* ... Rom. 11:33
JUST (262/256)
Noah was a *j* man ... Gen. 6:9
j man who perishes ... Eccl. 7:15
j shall live by his ... Hab. 2:4
her husband, being a *j* ... Matt. 1:19
resurrection of the *j* ... Luke 14:14
j persons who need no ... Luke 15:7
the Holy One and the *J* ... Acts 3:14
dead, both of the *j* ... Acts 24:15
j shall live by faith ... Rom. 1:17
that He might be *j* ... Rom. 3:26
j men made perfect ... Heb. 12:23
have murdered the *j* ... James 5:6
He is faithful and *j* ... 1 John 1:9
JUSTICE (130/129)
j as the noonday ... Ps. 37:6
and Your poor with *j* ... Ps. 72:2
j the measuring line ... Is. 28:17
the LORD is a God of *j* ... Is. 30:18
He will bring forth *j* ... Is. 42:1
J is turned back ... Is. 59:14
I, the LORD, love *j* ... Is. 61:8
truth, and His ways *j* ... Dan. 4:37
'Execute true *j* ... Zech. 7:9
"Where is the God of *j* ... Mal. 2:17
And He will declare *j* ... Matt. 12:18
His humiliation His *j* ... Acts 8:33
JUSTIFICATION (3/3)
because of our *j* ... Rom. 4:25
offenses resulted in *j* ... Rom. 5:16
JUSTIFIED (37/33)
Me that you may be *j* ... Job 40:8
words you will be *j* ... Matt. 12:37
But wisdom is *j* ... Luke 7:35
j rather than the ... Luke 18:14
who believes is *j* ... Acts 13:39
"That You may be *j* ... Rom. 3:4
law no flesh will be *j* ... Rom. 3:20
j freely by His grace ... Rom. 3:24
having been *j* by ... Rom. 5:1
these He also *j* ... Rom. 8:30
that we might be *j* ... Gal. 2:16
the harlot also *j* ... James 2:25
JUSTIFIES (4/4)
He who *j* the wicked ... Prov. 17:15
It is God who *j* ... Rom. 8:33
JUSTIFY (9/9)
wanting to *j* himself ... Luke 10:29
"You are those who *j* ... Luke 16:15
is one God who will *j* ... Rom. 3:30

K

KEEP (371/362)
k you wherever you ... Gen. 28:15
day, to *k* it holy ... Ex. 20:8
Let all the earth *k* ... Hab. 2:20
k the commandments ... Matt. 19:17
If you love Me, *k* ... John 14:15
k through Your name ... John 17:11
orderly and *k* the law ... Acts 21:24
k the unity of the ... Eph. 4:3
k His commandments ... 1 John 2:3
KEEPER (19/19)
Am I my brother's *k* ... Gen. 4:9
The LORD is your *k* ... Ps. 121:5
KEEPS (42/40)
k truth forever ... Ps. 146:6
k the commandment ... Prov. 19:16
none of you *k* the law ... John 7:19
born of God *k* himself ... 1 John 5:18
and *k* his garments ... Rev. 16:15
KEPT (170/165)
For I have *k* the ways ... 2 Sam. 22:22
these things I have *k* ... Matt. 19:20
love, just as I have *k* ... John 15:10
k back part of the ... Acts 5:2
I have *k* the faith ... 2 Tim. 4:7
who are *k* by the power ... 1 Pet. 1:5
KEY (6/6)
have taken away the *k* ... Luke 11:52
"He who has the *k* ... Rev. 3:7
KEYS (2/2)
I will give you the *k* ... Matt. 16:19
And I have the *k* ... Rev. 1:18
KILL (196/184)
k the Passover lamb ... Ex. 12:21
I *k* and I make alive ... Deut. 32:39
"Am I God, to *k* ... 2 Kin. 5:7
a time to *k* ... Eccl. 3:3
of them they will *k* ... Luke 11:49
afraid of those who *k* ... Luke 12:4
Why do you seek to *k* ... John 7:19
"Rise, Peter; *k* and eat ... Acts 10:13
KILLED (266/246)
Abel his brother and *k* ... Gen. 4:8
for Your sake we are *k* ... Ps. 44:22
and scribes, and be *k* ... Matt. 16:21
Siloam fell and *k* them ... Luke 13:4
k the Prince of life ... Acts 3:15
"For Your sake we are *k* ... Rom. 8:36
who *k* both the Lord ... 1 Thess. 2:15
KILLS (29/27)
the one who *k* the ... Matt. 23:37
for the letter *k* ... 2 Cor. 3:6
KIND (65/46)
animals after their *k* ... Gen. 6:20
k can come out by ... Mark 9:29
suffers long and is *k* ... 1 Cor. 13:4
And be *k* to one ... Eph. 4:32
KINDLY (16/16)
Julius treated Paul *k* ... Acts 27:3
k affectionate to one ... Rom. 12:10
KINDNESS (46/41)
For His merciful *k* ... Ps. 117:2
k shall not depart ... Is. 54:10
I remember you, the *k* ... Jer. 2:2
by longsuffering, by *k* ... 2 Cor. 6:6
longsuffering, *k* ... Gal. 5:22
and to brotherly *k* ... 2 Pet. 1:7
KING (2,337/1,801)
Yet I have set My *K* ... Ps. 2:6
The LORD is *K* forever ... Ps. 10:16
And the *K* of glory ... Ps. 24:7
For God is my *K* ... Ps. 74:12
when your *k* is a child ... Eccl. 10:16
and the everlasting *K* ... Jer. 10:10
the LORD shall be *K* ... Zech. 14:9
He who has been born *K* ... Matt. 2:2
This is Jesus the *K* ... Matt. 27:37
"Behold your *K* ... John 19:14
Now to the *K* eternal ... 1 Tim. 1:17
only Potentate, the *K* ... 1 Tim. 6:15
this Melchizedek, *k* ... Heb. 7:1

K OF KINGS AND LORD OF ... Rev. 19:16
KINGDOM (333/308)
Yours is the *k* ... 1 Chr. 29:11
k is the LORD's ... Ps. 22:28
the scepter of Your *k* ... Ps. 45:6
is an everlasting *k* ... Ps. 145:13
k which shall never be ... Dan. 2:44
High rules in the *k* ... Dan. 4:17
for Yours is the *k* ... Matt. 6:13
are the sons of the *k* ... Matt. 13:38
up to half of my *k* ... Mark 6:23
against nation, and *k* ... Luke 21:10
he cannot enter the *k* ... John 3:5
If My *k* were of this ... John 18:36
the scepter of Your *k* ... Heb. 1:8
we are receiving a *k* ... Heb. 12:28
KINGDOMS (58/56)
the *k* were moved ... Ps. 46:6
showed Him all the *k* ... Matt. 4:8
have become the *k* ... Rev. 11:15
KINGS (326/302)
The *k* of the earth set ... Ps. 2:2
By me *k* reign ... Prov. 8:15
before governors and *k* ... Matt. 10:18
k have desired to see ... Luke 10:24
You have reigned as *k* ... 1 Cor. 4:8
and has made us *k* ... Rev. 1:6
that the way of the *k* ... Rev. 16:12
KISS (20/19)
K the Son, lest He be ... Ps. 2:12
You gave Me no *k* ... Luke 7:45
one another with a *k* ... 1 Pet. 5:14
KISSED (25/25)
they *k* one another ... 1 Sam. 20:41
Rabbi!" and *k* Him ... Matt. 26:49
and she *k* His feet and ... Luke 7:38
KNEE (8/8)
that to Me every *k* ... Is. 45:23
have not bowed the *k* ... Rom. 11:4
of Jesus every *k* ... Phil. 2:10
KNEES (29/29)
make firm the feeble *k* ... Is. 35:3
this reason I bow my *k* ... Eph. 3:14
and the feeble *k* ... Heb. 12:12
KNEW (98/98)
in the womb I *k* ... Jer. 1:5
to them, 'I never *k* ... Matt. 7:23
k what was in man ... John 2:25
For He made Him who *k* ... 2 Cor. 5:21
KNIT (6/6)
be encouraged, being *k* ... Col. 2:2
KNOCK (5/5)
k, and it will be ... Matt. 7:7
at the door and *k* ... Rev. 3:20
KNOW (964/904)
k good and evil ... Gen. 3:22
k that I am the LORD ... Ex. 6:7
'*k* that my Redeemer ... Job 19:25
make me to *k* wisdom ... Ps. 51:6
Who can *k* it ... Jer. 17:9
saying, '*K* the LORD ... Jer. 31:34
k what hour your Lord ... Matt. 24:42
an oath, "I do not *k* ... Matt. 26:72
the world did not *k* ... John 1:10
We speak what We *k* ... John 3:11
k that You are the Christ ... John 6:69
hear My voice, and I *k* ... John 10:27
If you *k* these things ... John 13:17
k whom I have chosen ... John 13:18
we are sure that You *k* ... John 16:30
k that I love You ... John 21:15
k times or seasons ... Acts 1:7
and said, "Jesus I *k* ... Acts 19:15
wisdom did not *k* ... 1 Cor. 1:21
nor can he *k* them ... 1 Cor. 2:14
For we *k* in part and ... 1 Cor. 13:9
k the love of Christ ... Eph. 3:19
k whom I have believed ... 2 Tim. 1:12
this we *k* that we *k* Him ... 1 John 2:3
and you *k* all things ... 1 John 2:20
By this we *k* love ... 1 John 3:16
k that He abides ... 1 John 3:24
k that we are of God ... 1 John 5:19
"I *k* your works ... Rev. 2:2
KNOWLEDGE (164/161)
and the tree of the *k* ... Gen. 2:9
unto night reveals *k* ... Ps. 19:2
k is too wonderful ... Ps. 139:6
Wise people store up *k* ... Prov. 10:14
k spares his words ... Prov. 17:27
and he who increases *k* ... Eccl. 1:18
k is that wisdom ... Eccl. 7:12
k shall increase ... Dan. 12:4
having more accurate *k* ... Acts 24:22
having the form of *k* ... Rom. 2:20
by the law is the *k* of sin ... Rom. 3:20
whether there is *k* ... 1 Cor. 13:8
Christ which passes *k* ... Eph. 3:19
is falsely called *k* ... 1 Tim. 6:20
in the grace and *k* ... 2 Pet. 3:18
KNOWN (229/218)
If you had *k* Me ... John 8:19
My sheep, and am *k* ... John 10:14
The world has not *k* ... John 17:25
peace they have not *k* ... Rom. 3:17
"For who has *k* ... Rom. 11:34
after you have *k* ... Gal. 4:9
requests be made *k* ... Phil. 4:6
k the Holy Scriptures ... 2 Tim. 3:15
KNOWS (82/80)
For God *k* that in ... Gen. 3:5
k what is in the ... Dan. 2:22
k the things you have ... Matt. 6:8
and hour no one *k* ... Matt. 24:36
but God *k* your hearts ... Luke 16:15
searches the hearts *k* ... Rom. 8:27
k the things of God ... 1 Cor. 2:11
k those who are His ... 2 Tim. 2:19
to him who *k* to do ... James 4:17
and *k* all things ... 1 John 3:20

L

LABOR (109/105)
Six days you shall *l* ... Ex. 20:9
things are full of *l* ... Eccl. 1:8
has man for all his *l* ... Eccl. 2:22
He shall see the *l* ... Is. 53:11
to Me, all you who *l* ... Matt. 11:28
Do not *l* for the ... John 6:27
knowing that your *l* ... 1 Cor. 15:58
but rather let him *l* ... Eph. 4:28
mean fruit from my *l* ... Phil. 1:22
your work of faith, *l* ... 1 Thess. 1:3
forget your work and *l* ... Heb. 6:10
your works, your *l* ... Rev. 2:2
LABORED (24/22)
l more abundantly than ... 1 Cor. 15:10
for you, lest I have *l* ... Gal. 4:11
LABORERS (13/12)
but the *l* are few ... Matt. 9:37
LABORING (4/4)
l night and day ... 1 Thess. 2:9
LABORS (18/16)
entered into their *l* ... John 4:38
creation groans and *l* ... Rom. 8:22
l more abundant ... 2 Cor. 11:23
may rest from their *l* ... Rev. 14:13
LACK (39/37)
What do I still *l* ... Matt. 19:20
"One thing you *l* ... Mark 10:21
LADDER (1/1)
and behold, a *l* ... Gen. 28:12
LAID (211/206)
the place where they *l* ... Mark 16:6
"Where have you *l* ... John 11:34
LAKE (10/10)
cast alive into the *l* ... Rev. 19:20
LAMB (102/95)
but where is the *l* ... Gen. 22:7
He was led as a *l* ... Is. 53:7
The *L* of God who takes ... John 1:29
the elders, stood a *L* ... Rev. 5:6
"Worthy is the *L* ... Rev. 5:12
by the blood of the *L* ... Rev. 12:11
LAME (34/32)
l shall leap like a ... Is. 35:6
blind see and the *l* ... Matt. 11:5
And a certain man *l* ... Acts 3:2
LAMENTATION (24/23)
was heard in Ramah, *l* ... Matt. 2:18
and made great *l* ... Acts 8:2
LAMP (34/34)
Your word is a *l* ... Ps. 119:105
the *l* of the wicked ... Prov. 13:9
his *l* will be put out ... Prov. 20:20
Nor do they light a *l* ... Matt. 5:15
"The *l* of the body ... Matt. 6:22
when he has lit a *l* ... Luke 8:16
l gives you light ... Luke 11:36
does not light a *l* ... Luke 15:8
burning and shining *l* ... John 5:35
LAMPS (35/29)
he made its seven *l* ... Ex. 37:23
and trimmed their *l* ... Matt. 25:7
LAMPSTAND (41/34)
branches of the *l* ... Ex. 25:32
a basket, but on a *l* ... Matt. 5:15
and remove your *l* ... Rev. 2:5
LAND (1,745/1,511)
l that I will show you ... Gen. 12:1
l flowing with milk ... Ex. 3:8
they will see the *l* ... Is. 33:17
Bethlehem, in the *l* ... Matt. 2:6
LANGUAGE (38/33)
whole earth had one *l* ... Gen. 11:1
speak in his own *l* ... Acts 2:6
blasphemy, filthy *l* ... Col. 3:8
LANGUAGES (9/9)
according to their *l* ... Gen. 10:20
LAST (107/101)
He shall stand at *l* ... Job 19:25
First and I am the *L* ... Is. 44:6
l will be first ... Matt. 20:16
the First and the *L* ... Rev. 1:11
LATTER (40/39)
l times some will ... 1 Tim. 4:1
LAUGH (15/13)
Why did Sarah *l* ... Gen. 18:13
Woe to you who *l* ... Luke 6:25
LAUGHS (4/4)
The Lord *l* at him ... Ps. 37:13
LAUGHTER (7/7)
your *l* be turned to ... James 4:9
LAW (441/388)
stones a copy of the *l* ... Josh. 8:32
The *l* of the LORD is ... Ps. 19:7
I delight in Your *l* ... Ps. 119:70
The *l* of Your mouth is ... Ps. 119:72
Oh, how I love Your *l* ... Ps. 119:97
And Your *l* is truth ... Ps. 119:142
l will proceed from Me ... Is. 51:4
in whose heart is My *l* ... Is. 51:7
the *L* is no more ... Lam. 2:9
The *l* of truth was in ... Mal. 2:6
to destroy the *L* ... Matt. 5:17
for this is the *L* ... Matt. 7:12
hang all the *L* and the ... Matt. 22:40
one tittle of the *l* to fail ... Luke 16:17
l was given through ... John 1:17
"Does our *l* judge a ... John 7:51
l is the knowledge ... Rom. 3:20
because the *l* brings ... Rom. 4:15
when there is no *l* ... Rom. 5:13
you are not under *l* ... Rom. 6:14
For what the *l* could ... Rom. 8:3
l that I might live ... Gal. 2:19
under guard by the *l* ... Gal. 3:23
l is fulfilled in one ... Gal. 5:14
into the perfect *l* ... James 1:25
fulfill the royal *l* ... James 2:8
LAWFUL (38/36)
Is it *l* to pay taxes ... Matt. 22:17
All things are *l* ... 1 Cor. 6:12
LAWGIVER (6/6)
There is one *L* ... James 4:12
LAWLESS (9/9)
l one will be revealed ... 2 Thess. 2:8
LAWLESSNESS (11/9)
Me, you who practice *l* ... Matt. 7:23
l is already at work ... 2 Thess. 2:7
LAWYERS (5/5)
Woe to you also, *l* ... Luke 11:46
LAY (203/196)
nowhere to *l* His head ... Matt. 8:20
l hands may receive ... Acts 8:19
LAZINESS (2/2)
l the building decays ... Eccl. 10:18
LAZY (16/16)
l man will be put to ... Prov. 12:24
wicked and *l* servant ... Matt. 25:26
liars, evil beasts, *l* ... Titus 1:12
LEAD (62/62)
L me in Your truth and ... Ps. 25:5
And do not *l* us into ... Matt. 6:13
"Can the blind *l* ... Luke 6:39
LEADS (22/22)
He *l* me in the paths ... Ps. 23:3
And if the blind *l* ... Matt. 15:14
LEAF (9/9)
plucked olive *l* ... Gen. 8:11
LEAN (6/6)
all your heart, and *l* ... Prov. 3:5
LEAP (9/9)
Then the lame shall *l* ... Is. 35:6
LEARN (35/35)
l to do good ... Is. 1:17
My yoke upon you and *l* ... Matt. 11:29
LEARNED (21/19)
Me the tongue of the *l* ... Is. 50:4
have not so *l* Christ ... Eph. 4:20
in all things I have *l* ... Phil. 4:12
LEARNING (7/7)
l is driving you mad ... Acts 26:24
LEAST (42/40)
so, shall be called *l* ... Matt. 5:19
LEAVE (107/106)
a man shall *l* his ... Gen. 2:24
For You will not *l* ... Ps. 16:10
"I will never *l* ... Heb. 13:5
LEAVEN (24/21)
of heaven is like *l* ... Matt. 13:33
l leavens the whole ... Gal. 5:9
LEAVES (23/20)
and they sewed fig *l* ... Gen. 3:7
The *l* of the tree ... Rev. 22:2
LED (89/89)
l them forth by the ... Ps. 107:7
For as many as are *l* ... Rom. 8:14
LEFT (335/324)
l hand know what your ... Matt. 6:3
LEND (15/12)
And if you *l* to those ... Luke 6:34
LENDER (2/2)
is servant to the *l* ... Prov. 22:7

LENDS (3/3)
ever merciful, and *l* .... Ps. 37:26
LENGTH (73/69)
is your life and the *l* .... Deut. 30:20
LEOPARD (6/6)
or the *l* its spots.................. Jer. 13:23
LEPERS (6/6)
And many *l* were in .... Luke 4:27
LET (1,557/1,272)
"*L* there be light".................. Gen. 1:3
LETTER (38/36)
for the *l* kills..................... 2 Cor. 3:6
or by word or by *l* .... 2 Thess. 2:2
LETTERS (34/32)
does this Man know *l*............. John 7:15
LEVIATHAN (6/5)
"Can you draw out *L*............... Job 41:1
LEVITE (28/28)
Likewise a *L*, when he .... Luke 10:32
LEWDNESS (23/22)
wickedness, deceit, *l* .... Mark 7:22
LIAR (12/12)
for he is a *l* and the............. John 8:44
but every man a *l* .... Rom. 3:4
we make Him a *l* .... 1 John 1:10
his brother, he is a *l* .... 1 John 4:20
LIARS (5/5)
"All men are *l*..................... Ps. 116:11
l shall have their.................. Rev. 21:8
LIBERALITY (3/3)
he who gives, with *l* .... Rom. 12:8
LIBERALLY (2/2)
who gives to all *l* .... James 1:5
LIBERTY (26/23)
year, and proclaim *l*.............. Lev. 25:10
to proclaim *l* to the .... Luke 4:18
into the glorious *l*................ Rom. 8:21
Lord is, there is *l*............... 2 Cor. 3:17
therefore in the *l*.................. Gal. 5:1
LIE (151/149)
Do not *l* to one...................... Col. 3:9
God, who cannot *l*.................. Titus 1:2
an abomination or a *l* .... Rev. 21:27
LIED (4/4)
You have not *l* to men............. Acts 5:4
LIES (121/115)
sin *l* at the door..................... Gen. 4:7
speaking *l* in hypocrisy.......... 1 Tim. 4:2
LIFE (495/449)
the breath of *l* .... Gen. 2:7
For the *l* of the..................... Lev. 17:11
before you today *l*.............. Deut. 30:15
He will redeem their *l* .... Ps. 72:14
word has given me *l*............. Ps. 119:50
She is a tree of *l*................... Prov. 3:18
finds me finds *l*................... Prov. 8:35
L is more than food .... Luke 12:23
l was the light......................... John 1:4
so the Son gives *l* .... John 5:21
spirit, and they are *l*............ John 6:63
have the light of *l* .... John 8:12
and I lay down My *l* .... John 10:15
resurrection and the *l* .... John 11:25
you lay down your *l* .... John 13:38
l which I now live .... Gal. 2:20
l is hidden with .... Col. 3:3
For what is your *l* .... James 4:14
l was manifested.................. 1 John 1:2
and the pride of *l* .... 1 John 2:16
has given us eternal *l*.......... 1 John 5:11
the Lamb's Book of *L*........... Rev. 21:27
right to the tree of *l* .... Rev. 22:14
the water of *l* freely .... Rev. 22:17
from the Book of *L*.............. Rev. 22:19
LIFT (94/91)
I will *l* up my eyes to .... Ps. 121:1
Lord, and He will *l* .... James 4:10
LIFTED (133/128)
your heart is *l* up .... Ezek. 28:2
in Hades, he *l* up his .... Luke 16:23
the Son of Man be *l* .... John 3:14
And I, if I am *l* .... John 12:32
LIGHT (253/221)
"Let there be *l* .... Gen. 1:3
The LORD is my *l*...................... Ps. 27:1
and a *l* to my path............... Ps. 119:105
The *l* of the righteous .... Prov. 13:9
The LORD gives *l*................. Prov. 29:13
Truly the *l* is sweet................ Eccl. 11:7
let us walk in the *l*.................... Is. 2:5
l shall break forth.................... Is. 58:8
"You are the *l*..................... Matt. 5:14
Let your *l* so shine .... Matt. 5:16
than the sons of *l* .... Luke 16:8
and the life was the *l* .... John 1:4
darkness rather than *l*........... John 3:19
saying, "I am the *l*................ John 8:12
God who commanded *l*........... 2 Cor. 4:6
Walk as children of *l* .... Eph. 5:8
You are all sons of *l* .... 1 Thess. 5:5
into His marvelous *l* .... 1 Pet. 2:9
to you, that God is *l* .... 1 John 1:5
l as He is in the .... 1 John 1:7
says he is in the *l*................. 1 John 2:9
The Lamb is its *l* .... Rev. 21:23
LIGHTNING (18/18)
For as the *l* comes................ Matt. 24:27
countenance was like *l* .... Matt. 28:3
LIGHTNINGS (10/10)
the throne proceeded *l*.............. Rev. 4:5
LIGHTS (10/10)
"Let there be *l* .... Gen. 1:14
whom you shine as *l* .... Phil. 2:15
LIKENESS (36/30)
according to Our *l*.................. Gen. 1:26
carved image—any *l* .... Ex. 20:4
when I awake in Your *l* .... Ps. 17:15
and coming in the *l* .... Phil. 2:7
LILY (6/6)
the *l* of the valleys .... Song 2:1
LIMIT (6/6)
to the sea its *l*.................... Prov. 8:29
LINE (42/33)
upon precept, *l* upon *l*............ Is. 28:10
I am setting a plumb *l*............ Amos 7:8
LINEN (105/93)
wrapped Him in the *l* .... Mark 15:46
LINGER (3/3)
salvation shall not *l*.............. Is. 46:13
LION (97/82)
l shall eat straw .... Is. 11:7
LIONS (43/39)
the mouths of *l* .... Heb. 11:33
LIPS (118/117)
off all flattering *l*.................... Ps. 12:3
The *l* of the righteous .... Prov. 10:21
but the *l* of knowledge .... Prov. 20:15
am a man of unclean *l* .... Is. 6:5
other *l* I will speak .... 1 Cor. 14:21
from evil, and his *l*.............. 1 Pet. 3:10
LISTEN (112/109)
you are not able to *l*............... John 8:43
you who fear God, *l* .... Acts 13:16
LISTENS (4/4)
but whoever *l* to me............. Prov. 1:33
LITTLE (231/215)
though you are *l* .... Mic. 5:2
l ones only a cup................. Matt. 10:42
"O you of *l* faith................. Matt. 14:31
to whom *l* is forgiven.............. Luke 7:47
faithful in a very *l*............... Luke 19:17
LIVE (272/254)
eat, and *l* forever................. Gen. 3:22
a man does, he shall *l* .... Lev. 18:5
"Seek Me and *l*....................... Amos 5:4
but the just shall *l*................. Hab. 2:4
l by bread alone...................... Matt. 4:4
for in Him we *l*.................... Acts 17:28
l peaceably with all.............. Rom. 12:18
the life which I now *l*.............. Gal. 2:20
If we *l* in the Spirit .... Gal. 5:25
to me, to *l* is Christ................. Phil. 1:21
LIVED (65/65)
died and rose and *l*............... Rom. 14:9
And they *l* and reigned........... Rev. 20:4
LIVES (138/125)
but man *l* by every .... Deut. 8:3
but Christ *l* in me .... Gal. 2:20
to lay down our *l*................ 1 John 3:16
I am He who *l*......................... Rev. 1:18
LIVING (179/168)
and man became a *l*................. Gen. 2:7
in the light of the *l* .... Ps. 56:13
the dead, but of the *l* .... Matt. 22:32
Why do you seek the *l* .... Luke 24:5
the word of God is *l* .... Heb. 4:12
l creature was like a .... Rev. 4:7
LOATHSOME (4/4)
but a wicked man is *l*.......... Prov. 13:5
LOAVES (32/30)
have here only five *l*........... Matt. 14:17
you ate of the *l*.................... John 6:26
LOCUST (22/12)
What the chewing *l* .... Joel 1:4
LOCUSTS (24/22)
and his food was *l*................... Matt. 3:4
LOFTY (10/10)
Wisdom is too *l* .... Prov. 24:7
LONG (236/227)
your days may be *l*.............. Deut. 5:16
who *l* for death .... Job 3:21
I *l* for Your salvation .... Ps. 119:174
go around in *l* robes............. Mark 12:38
LONGSUFFERING (16/16)
is love, joy, peace, *l*.............. Gal. 5:22
and gentleness, with *l*............ Eph. 4:2
for all patience and *l* .... Col. 1:11
might show all *l*................... 1 Tim. 1:16
when once the Divine *l*.......... 1 Pet. 3:20
and consider that the *l* .... 2 Pet. 3:15
LOOK (295/287)
A proud *l*, a lying .... Prov. 6:17
"*L* to Me, and be saved............ Is. 45:22
l on Me whom they............... Zech. 12:10
say to you, '*L* here............... Luke 17:23
while we do not *l*.................. 2 Cor. 4:18
LOOKED (146/144)
For He *l* down from the .... Ps. 102:19
He *l* for justice.......................... Is. 5:7
the Lord turned and *l* .... Luke 22:61
for he *l* to the reward........... Heb. 11:26
LOOKING (41/35)
the plow, and *l* back .... Luke 9:62
l for the blessed hope .... Titus 2:13
l unto Jesus, the author .... Heb. 12:2
l carefully lest .... Heb. 12:15
l for the mercy of .... Jude 1:21
LOOKS (27/26)
The lofty *l* of man...................... Is. 2:11
to you that whoever *l*............. Matt. 5:28
LOOSE (27/27)
and whatever you *l*............... Matt. 16:19
said to them, "*L* him .... John 11:44
LOOSED (18/17)
the silver cord is *l*................. Eccl. 12:6
LORD (7,773/6,614)
L is my strength .... Ex. 15:2
L our God, the *L*..................... Deut. 6:4
You alone are the *L* .... Neh. 9:6
The *L* of hosts .... Ps. 24:10
Gracious is the *L*.................... Ps. 116:5
L surrounds His people .... Ps. 125:2
The *L* is righteous.................. Ps. 129:4
L is near to all who .... Ps. 145:18
L is a God of justice .... Is. 30:18
L Our Righteousness............. Jer. 23:6
"The *L* is one .... Zech. 14:9
shall not tempt the *L*............... Matt. 4:7
shall worship the *L*................. Matt. 4:10
Son of Man is also *L*.............. Mark 2:28
who is Christ the *L* .... Luke 2:11
L is risen indeed .... Luke 24:34
call Me Teacher and *L* .... John 13:13
He is *L* of all .... Acts 10:36
with your mouth the *L* .... Rom. 10:9
say that Jesus is *L*................. 1 Cor. 12:3
second Man is the *L*............ 1 Cor. 15:47
the Spirit of the *L* .... 2 Cor. 3:17
that Jesus Christ is *L* .... Phil. 2:11
and deny the only *L* .... Jude 1:4
L God Omnipotent................. Rev. 19:6
LORDS (40/38)
for He is Lord of *l* .... Rev. 17:14
LOSE (18/18)
save his life will *l*............... Matt. 16:25
LOSES (11/11)
but if the salt *l* .... Matt. 5:13
and *l* his own soul .... Matt. 16:26
LOSS (15/14)
count all things *l*..................... Phil. 3:8
LOST (34/33)
save that which was *l*............ Matt. 18:11
and none of them is *l* .... John 17:12
You gave Me I have *l* .... John 18:9
LOTS (25/22)
garments, casting *l*.............. Mark 15:24
And they cast their *l*.............. Acts 1:26
LOUD (72/72)
cried out with a *l*................ Matt. 27:46
I heard behind me a *l* .... Rev. 1:10
LOVE (361/322)
l your neighbor as .... Lev. 19:18
l the LORD your God.............. Deut. 6:5
Oh, *l* the LORD .... Ps. 31:23
he has set his *l*...................... Ps. 91:14
Oh, how I *l* Your law............. Ps. 119:97
l covers all sins .... Prov. 10:12
a time to *l* .... Eccl. 3:8
banner over me was *l* .... Song 2:4
l is as strong as death .... Song 8:6
do justly, to *l* mercy .... Mic. 6:8
to you, *l* your enemies............ Matt. 5:44
which of them will *l*................ Luke 7:42
you do not have the *l*.............. John 5:42
if you have *l* for one............. John 13:35
"If you *l* Me, keep My............ John 14:15
and My Father will *l* .... John 14:23
l one another as I .... John 15:12
l has no one than this .... John 15:13
because the *l* of God............... Rom. 5:5
to *l* one another .... Rom. 13:8
greatest of these is *l*........... 1 Cor. 13:13
For the *l* of Christ.............. 2 Cor. 5:14
of the Spirit is *l* .... Gal. 5:22
Husbands, *l* your wives.......... Eph. 5:25
the commandment is *l*............. 1 Tim. 1:5
For the *l* of money is .... 1 Tim. 6:10
Let brotherly *l* .... Heb. 13:1
having not seen you *l* .... 1 Pet. 1:8
for "*l* will cover a.................. 1 Pet. 4:8
brotherly kindness *l* .... 2 Pet. 1:7
By this we know *l* .... 1 John 3:16
Beloved, let us *l*................. 1 John 4:7

know God, for God is *l* .... 1 John 4:8
There is no fear in *l* .... 1 John 4:18
l Him because He first .... 1 John 4:19
who loves God must *l* .... 1 John 4:21
For this is the *l* .... 1 John 5:3
have left your first *l* .... Rev. 2:4
LOVED (96/86)
L one and friend You .... Ps. 88:18
Yet Jacob I have *l* .... Mal. 1:2
forgiven, for she *l* .... Luke 7:47
so *l* the world that .... John 3:16
whom Jesus *l* .... John 13:23
"As the Father *l* .... John 15:9
l them as You have .... John 17:23
the Son of God, who *l* .... Gal. 2:20
l the church and gave .... Eph. 5:25
Beloved, if God so *l* .... 1 John 4:11
To Him who *l* us and .... Rev. 1:5
LOVELY (19/19)
he is altogether *l* .... Song 5:16
whatever things are *l* .... Phil. 4:8
LOVES (65/57)
He who *l* father or .... Matt. 10:37
l his life will lose .... John 12:25
l Me will be loved .... John 14:21
l a cheerful giver .... 2 Cor. 9:7
If anyone *l* the world .... 1 John 2:15
l God must love his .... 1 John 4:21
LOVINGKINDNESS (29/29)
to declare Your *l* .... Ps. 92:2
LOWER (29/28)
made him a little *l* .... Heb. 2:7
LOWLINESS (2/2)
with all *l* and .... Eph. 4:2
LOWLY (14/14)
for I am gentle and *l* .... Matt. 11:29
in presence am *l* .... 2 Cor. 10:1
l brother glory .... James 1:9
LUKEWARM (1/1)
because you are *l* .... Rev. 3:16
LUST (15/14)
looks at a woman to *l* .... Matt. 5:28
not fulfill the *l* .... Gal. 5:16
You *l* and do not have .... James 4:2
the *l* of the flesh .... 1 John 2:16
LUSTS (19/19)
to fulfill its *l* .... Rom. 13:14
also youthful *l* .... 2 Tim. 2:22
and worldly *l* .... Titus 2:12
to the former *l* .... 1 Pet. 1:14
abstain from fleshly *l* .... 1 Pet. 2:11
to their own ungodly *l* .... Jude 1:18
LUTE (6/6)
Praise Him with the *l* .... Ps. 150:3
LUXURY (8/8)
in pleasure and *l* .... James 5:5
the abundance of her *l* .... Rev. 18:3
LYING (76/76)
I hate and abhor *l* .... Ps. 119:163
righteous man hates *l* .... Prov. 13:5
not trust in these *l* .... Jer. 7:4
signs, and *l* wonders .... 2 Thess. 2:9

M

MADE (1,316/1,236)
m the stars also .... Gen. 1:16
things My hand has *m* .... Is. 66:2
All things were *m* .... John 1:3
MADNESS (11/11)
m is in their hearts .... Eccl. 9:3
MAGIC (3/3)
m brought their books .... Acts 19:19
MAGNIFIED (9/9)
So let Your name be *m* .... 2 Sam. 7:26
the Lord Jesus was *m* .... Acts 19:17
also Christ will be *m* .... Phil. 1:20
MAGNIFIES (1/1)
"My soul *m* the Lord .... Luke 1:46
MAGNIFY (7/7)
m the LORD with me .... Ps. 34:3
MAIDSERVANT (40/35)
"Behold the *m* .... Luke 1:38
MAIDSERVANTS (13/12)
m I will pour out My .... Acts 2:18
MAJESTY (32/32)
right hand of the *M* .... Heb. 1:3
eyewitnesses of His *m* .... 2 Pet. 1:16
wise, be glory and *m* .... Jude 1:25
MAKE (1,012/947)
"Let Us *m* man in Our .... Gen. 1:26
m you a great nation .... Gen. 12:2
"You shall not *m* .... Ex. 20:4
m Our home with him .... John 14:23
MAKER (22/21)
M is your husband .... Is. 54:5
has forgotten his *M* .... Hos. 8:14
builder and *m* is God .... Heb. 11:10
MALICE (6/6)
in *m* be babes .... 1 Cor. 14:20
laying aside all *m* .... 1 Pet. 2:1
MAN (2,081/1,872)
"Let Us make *m* .... Gen. 1:26
m that You are mindful .... Ps. 8:4
coming of the Son of *M* .... Matt. 24:27
"Behold the *M* .... John 19:5
since by *m* came death .... 1 Cor. 15:21
though our outward *m* .... 2 Cor. 4:16
that the *m* of God may .... 2 Tim. 3:17
is the number of a *m* .... Rev. 13:18
MANGER (4/4)
and laid Him in a *m* .... Luke 2:7
MANIFEST (15/14)
m Myself to him .... John 14:21
MANIFESTATION (3/3)
But the *m* of the .... 1 Cor. 12:7
MANIFESTED (13/12)
"I have *m* Your name .... John 17:6
God was *m* in the flesh .... 1 Tim. 3:16
the life was *m* .... 1 John 1:2
MANIFOLD (5/5)
the *m* wisdom of God .... Eph. 3:10
MANNA (18/16)
of Israel ate *m* .... Ex. 16:35
Our fathers ate the *m* .... John 6:31
MANNER (94/91)
Is this the *m* of man .... 2 Sam. 7:19
in an unworthy *m* .... 1 Cor. 11:27
Behold what *m* of love .... 1 John 3:1
MANSIONS (1/1)
house are many *m* .... John 14:2
MANTLE (7/7)
Then he took the *m* .... 2 Kin. 2:14
MARK (24/23)
And the LORD set a *m* .... Gen. 4:15
whoever receives the *m* .... Rev. 14:11
MARRED (3/3)
so His visage was *m* .... Is. 52:14
MARRIAGE (17/16)
M is honorable among .... Heb. 13:4
MARRIED (32/31)
But he who is *m* .... 1 Cor. 7:33
MARRY (21/19)
they neither *m* nor are .... Matt. 22:30
forbidding to *m* .... 1 Tim. 4:3
MARRYING (2/2)
and drinking, *m* .... Matt. 24:38
MARTYRS (1/1)
the blood of the *m* .... Rev. 17:6
MARVELED (34/34)
Jesus heard it, He *m* .... Matt. 8:10
so that Pilate *m* .... Mark 15:5
MARVELOUS (21/19)
It is *m* in our eyes .... Ps. 118:23
of darkness into His *m* .... 1 Pet. 2:9
MASTER (159/148)
a servant like his *m* .... Matt. 10:25
greater than his *m* .... John 15:20
and useful for the *M* .... 2 Tim. 2:21
MASTERS (17/16)
can serve two *m* .... Luke 16:13
who have believing *m* .... 1 Tim. 6:2
MATTERS (21/20)
the weightier *m* .... Matt. 23:23
MATURE (3/3)
understanding be *m* .... 1 Cor. 14:20
us, as many as are *m* .... Phil. 3:15
MEANT (6/5)
but God *m* it for good .... Gen. 50:20
MEASURE (57/53)
a perfect and just *m* .... Deut. 25:15
give the Spirit by *m* .... John 3:34
to each one a *m* .... Rom. 12:3
MEASURED (52/49)
m heaven with a span .... Is. 40:12
you use, it will be *m* .... Matt. 7:2
MEASURES (9/9)
your house differing *m* .... Deut. 25:14
MEASURING (17/16)
behold, a man with a *m* .... Zech. 2:1
m themselves by .... 2 Cor. 10:12
MEAT (56/47)
will never again eat *m* .... 1 Cor. 8:13
MEDIATOR (8/8)
by the hand of a *m* .... Gal. 3:19
is one God and one *M* .... 1 Tim. 2:5
to Jesus the *M* of the .... Heb. 12:24
MEDICINE (2/2)
does good, like *m* .... Prov. 17:22
MEDICINES (2/2)
you will use many *m* .... Jer. 46:11
MEDITATE (18/18)
but you shall *m* .... Josh. 1:8
M within your heart on .... Ps. 4:4
I will *m* on Your .... Ps. 119:15
m beforehand on what .... Luke 21:14
m on these things .... Phil. 4:8
MEDITATES (2/2)
in His law he *m* .... Ps. 1:2
MEDITATION (9/9)
O LORD, consider my *m* .... Ps. 5:1
It is my *m* all the day .... Ps. 119:97
MEDIUM (5/4)
a woman who is a *m* .... Lev. 20:27
MEDIUM'S (1/1)
shall be like a *m* .... Is. 29:4
MEDIUMS (9/9)
"Seek those who are *m* .... Is. 8:19
MEEK (5/5)
with equity for the *m* .... Is. 11:4
Blessed are the *m* .... Matt. 5:5
MEEKNESS (5/5)
are done in the *m* .... James 3:13
MEET (115/111)
prepare to *m* your God .... Amos 4:12
m the Lord in the air .... 1 Thess. 4:17
MELODY (5/5)
singing and making *m* .... Eph. 5:19
MELT (16/15)
the elements will *m* .... 2 Pet. 3:10
MEMBER (8/7)
body is not one *m* .... 1 Cor. 12:14
MEMBERS (32/24)
you that one of your *m* .... Matt. 5:29
do not present your *m* .... Rom. 6:13
neighbor, for we are *m* .... Eph. 4:25
MEMORIAL (26/25)
and this is My *m* .... Ex. 3:15
also be told as a *m* .... Matt. 26:13
MEMORY (9/9)
The *m* of the righteous .... Prov. 10:7
MEN (1,592/1,428)
m began to call on the .... Gen. 4:26
make you fishers of *m* .... Matt. 4:19
goodwill toward *m* .... Luke 2:14
from heaven or from *m* .... Luke 20:4
Likewise also the *m* .... Rom. 1:27
the Lord, and not to *m* .... Eph. 6:7
between God and *m* .... 1 Tim. 2:5
MENSERVANTS (2/2)
And also on My *m* .... Joel 2:29
And on My *m* and on My .... Acts 2:18
MERCHANDISE (14/14)
house a house of *m* .... John 2:16
MERCIES (35/35)
give you the sure *m* .... Acts 13:34
MERCIFUL (39/35)
LORD, the LORD God, *m* .... Ex. 34:6
He is ever *m* .... Ps. 37:26
Blessed are the *m* .... Matt. 5:7
saying, 'God be *m* .... Luke 18:13
For I will be *m* .... Heb. 8:12
MERCY (282/269)
but showing *m* to .... Ex. 20:6
and abundant in *m* .... Num. 14:18
m endures forever .... 1 Chr. 16:34
M and truth have met .... Ps. 85:10
m is everlasting .... Ps. 100:5
Let not *m* and truth .... Prov. 3:3
For I desire *m* and not .... Hos. 6:6
do justly, to love *m* .... Mic. 6:8
'I desire *m* and not .... Matt. 9:13
And His *m* is on those .... Luke 1:50
"I will have *m* .... Rom. 9:15
that He might have *m* .... Rom. 11:32
m has made trustworthy .... 1 Cor. 7:25
God, who is rich in *m* .... Eph. 2:4
but I obtained *m* .... 1 Tim. 1:13
that he may find *m* .... 2 Tim. 1:18
to His *m* He saved us .... Titus 3:5
that we may obtain *m* .... Heb. 4:16
MERRY (21/21)
m heart makes a .... Prov. 15:13
we should make *m* .... Luke 15:32
MESSENGER (35/33)
"Behold, I send My *m* .... Mal. 3:1
'Behold, I send My *m* .... Matt. 11:10
MESSIAH (4/4)
until *M* the Prince .... Dan. 9:25
"We have found the *M* .... John 1:41
MIDST (313/302)
God is in the *m* .... Ps. 46:5
I am there in the *m* .... Matt. 18:20
MIGHT (364/343)
'My power and the *m* .... Deut. 8:17
'Not by *m* nor by .... Zech. 4:6
in the power of His *m* .... Eph. 6:10
honor and power and *m* .... Rev. 7:12
MIGHTIER (13/13)
coming after me is *m* .... Matt. 3:11
MIGHTY (286/278)
He was a *m* hunter .... Gen. 10:9
How the *m* have fallen .... 2 Sam. 1:19
The LORD *m* in battle .... Ps. 24:8
their Redeemer is *m* .... Prov. 23:11
m has done great .... Luke 1:49
the flesh, not many *m* .... 1 Cor. 1:26
the working of His *m* .... Eph. 1:19
MILK (51/50)
come, buy wine and *m* .... Is. 55:1
shall flow with *m* .... Joel 3:18
have come to need *m* .... Heb. 5:12
desire the pure *m* .... 1 Pet. 2:2
MILLSTONE (9/9)
m were hung around his .... Matt. 18:6

a stone like a great *m* .... Rev. 18:21
MIND (90/88)
put wisdom in the *m*........... Job 38:36
perfect peace, whose *m* .... Is. 26:3
nor have an anxious *m*........ Luke 12:29
m I myself serve the .... Rom. 7:25
who has known the *m*......... Rom. 11:34
Be of the same *m* .... Rom. 12:16
convinced in his own *m*........ Rom. 14:5
have the *m* of Christ .... 1 Cor. 2:16
you are out of your *m*......... 1 Cor. 14:23
Let this *m* be in you............. Phil. 2:5
love and of a sound *m*......... 2 Tim. 1:7
MINDFUL (11/11)
is man that You are *m*............ Ps. 8:4
for you are not *m* .... Matt. 16:23
is man that You are *m*........... Heb. 2:6
MINDS (19/19)
put My law in their *m* .... Jer. 31:33
I stir up your pure *m*............ 2 Pet. 3:1
MINISTER (75/72)
for he is God's *m*.............. Rom. 13:4
you will be a good *m* .... 1 Tim. 4:6
MINISTERS (21/19)
for they are God's *m*........... Rom. 13:6
If anyone *m* .... 1 Pet. 4:11
MINISTRY (30/29)
But if the *m* of death .... 2 Cor. 3:7
since we have this *m* .... 2 Cor. 4:1
and has given us the *m*......... 2 Cor. 5:18
for the work of *m* .... Eph. 4:12
fulfill your *m* .... 2 Tim. 4:5
a more excellent *m* .... Heb. 8:6
MIRACLE (5/5)
no one who works a *m* .... Mark 9:39
MIRACLES (11/11)
God worked unusual *m*.......... Acts 19:11
the working of *m* .... 1 Cor. 12:10
MISERY (9/9)
and remember his *m*........... Prov. 31:7
MITES (2/2)
widow putting in two *m* .... Luke 21:2
MOCK (11/11)
Fools *m* at sin .... Prov. 14:9
to the Gentiles to *m*........... Matt. 20:19
MOCKED (20/20)
at noon, that Elijah *m*.......... 1 Kin. 18:27
deceived, God is not *m* .... Gal. 6:7
MOCKER (1/1)
Wine is a *m*.......................... Prov. 20:1
MOCKS (5/5)
He who *m* the poor .... Prov. 17:5
MODERATION (1/1)
with propriety and *m* .... 1 Tim. 2:9
MOMENT (24/24)
In a *m* they die .... Job 34:20
m, in the twinkling.............. 1 Cor. 15:52
MONEY (148/131)
be redeemed without *m*.............. Is. 52:3
and you who have no *m* .... Is. 55:1
and hid his lord's *m*............ Matt. 25:18
promised to give him *m*........... Mark 14:11
Carry neither *m* .... Luke 10:4
I sent you without *m*............ Luke 22:35
be purchased with *m*............ Acts 8:20
not greedy for *m*.................. 1 Tim. 3:3
m is a root of all .... 1 Tim. 6:10
MOON (52/51)
until the *m* is no more .... Ps. 72:7
m will not give its.............. Mark 13:24
MORNING (231/218)
Evening and *m* and at............ Ps. 55:17
Lucifer, son of the *m* .... Is. 14:12
very early in the *m*.............. Luke 24:1
the Bright and *M* Star .... Rev. 22:16
MORTAL (9/9)
sin reign in your *m* .... Rom. 6:12
and this *m* must put .... 1 Cor. 15:53
MORTALITY (1/1)
m may be swallowed .... 2 Cor. 5:4
MOTH (9/9)
where *m* and rust.............. Matt. 6:19
MOTHER (240/225)
because she was the *m*......... Gen. 3:20
leave his father and *m*.......... Matt. 19:5
"Behold your *m*..................... John 19:27
The *M* of Harlots................. Rev. 17:5
MOUNT (154/148)
come up to *M* Sinai .... Ex. 19:23
they shall *m* up with .... Is. 40:31
MOUNTAIN (208/181)
to Horeb, the *m*.................... Ex. 3:1
let us go up to the *m* .... Is. 2:3
image became a great *m* .... Dan. 2:35
Who are you, O great *m* .... Zech. 4:7
you will say to this *m*.......... Matt. 17:20
with Him on the holy *m*.......... 2 Pet. 1:18
MOUNTAINS (235/221)
m were brought forth .... Ps. 90:2
m shall depart and the .... Is. 54:10
in Judea flee to the *m*......... Matt. 24:16

that I could remove *m* .... 1 Cor. 13:2
MOURN (46/45)
a time to *m*....................... Eccl. 3:4
are those who *m* .... Matt. 5:4
of the earth will *m* .... Rev. 1:7
MOURNED (24/24)
and have not rather *m* .... 1 Cor. 5:2
MOURNING (52/48)
shall be a great *m* .... Zech. 12:11
be turned to *m* and .... James 4:9
MOUTH (394/374)
"Who has made man's *m* .... Ex. 4:11
Out of the *m* of babes .... Ps. 8:2
knowledge, but the *m*.......... Prov. 10:14
The *m* of an immoral .... Prov. 22:14
and a flattering *m*............... Prov. 26:28
m speaking pompous .... Dan. 7:8
m defiles a man .... Matt. 15:11
m I will judge you.............. Luke 19:22
I will give you a *m* .... Luke 21:15
m confession is made......... Rom. 10:10
m great swelling words.......... Jude 1:16
vomit you out of My *m* .... Rev. 3:16
MOVED (92/91)
she shall not be *m* .... Ps. 46:5
spoke as they were *m* .... 2 Pet. 1:21
MUCH (218/208)
m study is wearisome.......... Eccl. 12:12
to whom *m* is given .... Luke 12:48
MULTIPLIED (43/42)
of the disciples *m*................ Acts 6:7
word of God grew and *m* .... Acts 12:24
MULTIPLY (48/44)
"Be fruitful and *m* .... Gen. 1:22
m the descendants............... Jer. 33:22
MULTITUDE (222/215)
stars of heaven in *m* .... Deut. 1:10
In the *m* of words sin .... Prov. 10:19
compassion on the *m*............ Matt. 15:32
with the angel a *m* .... Luke 2:13
"love will cover a *m* .... 1 Pet. 4:8
and behold, a great *m* .... Rev. 7:9
MURDER (21/20)
"You shall not *m*..................... Ex. 20:13
'You shall not *m* .... Matt. 5:21
You *m* and covet and............. James 4:2
MURDERED (13/13)
Jesus whom you *m* .... Acts 5:30
MURDERER (21/16)
He was a *m* from the .... John 8:44
his brother is a *m*............... 1 John 3:15
MURDERERS (9/8)
and profane, for *m*............... 1 Tim. 1:9
abominable, *m* .... Rev. 21:8
MURDERS (6/6)
evil thoughts, *m* .... Matt. 15:19
MUSING (1/1)
while I was *m*, the fire............ Ps. 39:3
MUTILATION (2/2)
beware of the *m* .... Phil. 3:2
MUZZLE (4/4)
"You shall not *m*................. 1 Tim. 5:18
MYSTERIES (5/5)
to you to know the *m*.......... Matt. 13:11
and understand all *m* .... 1 Cor. 13:2
MYSTERY (22/22)
given to know the *m* .... Mark 4:11
wisdom of God in a *m*........... 1 Cor. 2:7
Behold, I tell you a *m* .... 1 Cor. 15:51
made known to us the *m* .... Eph. 1:9
the *m* of godliness .... 1 Tim. 3:16

N

NAILED (1/1)
n it to the cross .... Col. 2:14
NAKED (41/40)
And they were both *n* .... Gen. 2:25
knew that they were *n*........... Gen. 3:7
"*N* I came from my .... Job 1:21
I was *n* and you................. Matt. 25:36
but all things are *n*............... Heb. 4:13
brother or sister is *n* .... James 2:15
poor, blind, and *n*.................. Rev. 3:17
NAKEDNESS (57/43)
or famine, or *n* .... Rom. 8:35
n may not be revealed............ Rev. 3:18
NAME (930/835)
Abram called on the *n* .... Gen. 13:4
This is My *n* forever .... Ex. 3:15
shall not take the *n* .... Ex. 20:7
glorious and awesome *n* ...... Deut. 28:58
excellent is Your *n* .... Ps. 8:1
n will put their trust.............. Ps. 9:10
be His glorious *n* .... Ps. 72:19
do not call on Your *n*.............. Ps. 79:6
to Your *n* give glory .... Ps. 115:1
above all Your *n* .... Ps. 138:2
A good *n* is to be .... Prov. 22:1
what is His Son's *n*............... Prov. 30:4
be called by a new *n*............... Is. 62:2
Everlasting is Your *n* .... Is. 63:16

They will call on My *n* .... Zech. 13:9
to you who fear My *n*............. Mal. 4:2
hallowed be Your *n* .... Matt. 6:9
prophesied in Your *n*........... Matt. 7:22
n Gentiles will trust .... Matt. 12:21
together in My *n* .... Matt. 18:20
will come in My *n*................ Matt. 24:5
who believe in His *n* .... John 1:12
comes in his own *n* .... John 5:43
his own sheep by *n*............. John 10:3
through faith in His *n*............ Acts 3:16
there is no other *n* .... Acts 4:12
which is above every *n* .... Phil. 2:9
deed, do all in the *n* .... Col. 3:17
a more excellent *n* .... Heb. 1:4
you hold fast to My *n*............ Rev. 2:13
n that you are alive .... Rev. 3:1
having His Father's *n* .... Rev. 14:1
and glorify Your *n* .... Rev. 15:4
n written that no one........... Rev. 19:12
NAME'S (29/29)
saved them for His *n*............. Ps. 106:8
NARROW (8/8)
"Enter by the *n* gate............ Matt. 7:13
NATION (151/132)
make you a great *n*.............. Gen. 12:2
Righteousness exalts a *n* ...... Prov. 14:34
n that was not called .... Is. 65:1
I will make them one *n*......... Ezek. 37:22
since there was a *n*............... Dan. 12:1
n will rise against .... Matt. 24:7
for he loves our *n* .... Luke 7:5
those who are not a *n* .... Rom. 10:19
tribe, tongue, and *n* .... Rev. 13:7
NATIONS (445/426)
Why do the *n* rage .... Ps. 2:1
I will give You the *n* .... Ps. 2:8
n shall serve Him................... Ps. 72:11
disciples of all the *n*........... Matt. 28:19
who was to rule all *n* .... Rev. 12:5
the healing of the *n* .... Rev. 22:2
NATURAL (11/10)
women exchanged the *n* .... Rom. 1:26
the men, leaving the *n* .... Rom. 1:27
did not spare the *n*............... Rom. 11:21
n man does not receive .... 1 Cor. 2:14
It is sown a *n* body .... 1 Cor. 15:44
NATURE (13/12)
We who are Jews by *n* .... Gal. 2:15
by *n* children of wrath........... Eph. 2:3
of the divine *n*..................... 2 Pet. 1:4
NEAR (309/295)
But the word is very *n*......... Deut. 30:14
upon Him while He is *n* .... Is. 55:6
know that it is *n* .... Matt. 24:33
kingdom of God is *n* .... Luke 21:31
"The word is *n*..................... Rom. 10:8
to those who were *n*............... Eph. 2:17
for the time is *n*.................... Rev. 1:3
NEARER (1/1)
now our salvation is *n*......... Rom. 13:11
NEED (72/70)
the things you have *n* .... Matt. 6:8
supply all your *n*.................. Phil. 4:19
to help in time of *n* .... Heb. 4:16
NEGLECT (5/5)
if we *n* so great a .... Heb. 2:3
NEGLECTED (2/2)
n the weightier .... Matt. 23:23
NEIGHBOR (100/95)
you shall love your *n*............ Lev. 19:18
'You shall love your *n* .... Matt. 5:43
"And who is my *n* .... Luke 10:29
"You shall love your *n*........... Rom. 13:9
NEVER (123/114)
in Me shall *n* thirst.............. John 6:35
in Me shall *n* die .... John 11:26
Love *n* fails...................... 1 Cor. 13:8
n take away sins .... Heb. 10:11
"I will *n* leave you............... Heb. 13:5
prophecy *n* came by .... 2 Pet. 1:21
NEW (173/153)
and there is nothing *n* .... Eccl. 1:9
For behold, I create *n* .... Is. 65:17
n every morning.................. Lam. 3:23
wine into *n* wineskins........... Matt. 9:17
of the *n* covenant .... Matt. 26:28
n commandment I give .... John 13:34
he is a *n* creation .... 2 Cor. 5:17
when I will make a *n* .... Heb. 8:8
n heavens and a *n*............... 2 Pet. 3:13
n name written which........... Rev. 2:17
And they sang a *n*................. Rev. 5:9
And I saw a *n* heaven............ Rev. 21:1
I make all things *n* .... Rev. 21:5
NEWNESS (2/2)
also should walk in *n*............ Rom. 6:4
NIGHT (305/293)
darkness He called *N*............. Gen. 1:5
It is a *n* of solemn................ Ex. 12:42
pillar of fire by *n*................ Ex. 13:22

gives songs in the *n* .... Job 35:10
and continued all *n* .... Luke 6:12
man came to Jesus by *n* .... John 3:2
n is coming when no .... John 9:4
came to Jesus by *n* .... John 19:39
as a thief in the *n* .... 1 Thess. 5:2
there shall be no *n* .... Rev. 21:25

NINETY-NINE (6/6)
he not leave the *n* .... Matt. 18:12

NOTHING (286/280)
I can of Myself do *n* .... John 5:30
Me you can do *n* .... John 15:5
men, it will come to *n* .... Acts 5:38
have not love, I am *n* .... 1 Cor. 13:2
Be anxious for *n* .... Phil. 4:6
For we brought *n* .... 1 Tim. 6:7

NOURISHED (6/6)
"I have *n* and .... Is. 1:2

NOURISHES (2/2)
n and cherishes it .... Eph. 5:29

NUMBER (174/162)
if a man could *n* .... Gen. 13:16
teach us to *n* our days .... Ps. 90:12
which no one could *n* .... Rev. 7:9
His *n* is 666 .... Rev. 13:18

O

OATH (100/92)
for the sake of your *o* .... Eccl. 8:2
he denied with an *o* .... Matt. 26:72
o which He swore .... Luke 1:73

OATHS (8/8)
shall perform your *o* .... Matt. 5:33

OBEDIENCE (14/14)
o many will be made .... Rom. 5:19
captivity to the *o* .... 2 Cor. 10:5
for *o* and sprinkling .... 1 Pet. 1:2

OBEDIENT (14/14)
you are willing and *o* .... Is. 1:19
of the priests were *o* .... Acts 6:7
make the Gentiles *o* .... Rom. 15:18
Himself and became *o* .... Phil. 2:8
as *o* children .... 1 Pet. 1:14

OBEY (108/104)
God and *o* His voice .... Deut. 4:30
His voice we will *o* .... Josh. 24:24
o is better than .... 1 Sam. 15:22
o God rather than men .... Acts 5:29
and do not *o* the truth .... Rom. 2:8
yourselves slaves to *o* .... Rom. 6:16
o your parents in all .... Col. 3:20
Bondservants, *o* in all .... Col. 3:22
on those who do not *o* .... 2 Thess. 1:8
O those who rule .... Heb. 13:17

OBEYED (43/43)
of sin, yet you *o* .... Rom. 6:17
they have not all *o* .... Rom. 10:16
By faith Abraham *o* .... Heb. 11:8

OBSERVATION (1/1)
does not come with *o* .... Luke 17:20

OBSERVE (85/81)
teaching them to *o* all .... Matt. 28:20

OBTAIN (13/13)
they also may *o* mercy .... Rom. 11:31
o salvation through .... 1 Thess. 5:9

OBTAINED (27/25)
o a part in this .... Acts 1:17
yet have now *o* mercy .... Rom. 11:30
endured, he *o* the .... Heb. 6:15

OBTAINS (3/3)
o favor from the LORD .... Prov. 8:35

OFFEND (7/7)
lest we *o* them .... Matt. 17:27
than that he should *o* .... Luke 17:2
them, "Does this *o* .... John 6:61

OFFENDED (15/15)
So they were *o* at Him .... Matt. 13:57

OFFENSE (21/20)
and a rock of *o* .... Is. 8:14
You are an *o* to Me .... Matt. 16:23
by the one man's *o* .... Rom. 5:17
the *o* of the cross .... Gal. 5:11
sincere and without *o* .... Phil. 1:10
and a rock of *o* .... 1 Pet. 2:8

OFFENSES (8/7)
For *o* must come .... Matt. 18:7
impossible that no *o* .... Luke 17:1

OFFER (217/196)
come and *o* your gift .... Matt. 5:24
let us continually *o* .... Heb. 13:15

OFFERED (129/123)
to eat those things *o* .... 1 Cor. 8:10
so Christ was *o* .... Heb. 9:28
o one sacrifice .... Heb. 10:12

OFFERING (803/547)
o You did not require .... Ps. 40:6
You make His soul an *o* .... Is. 53:10
Himself for us, an *o* .... Eph. 5:2
o You did not .... Heb. 10:5
o He has perfected .... Heb. 10:14

OFFERINGS (279/210)
and offered burnt *o* .... Gen. 8:20
In burnt *o* and .... Heb. 10:6

OFFICE (11/11)
sitting at the tax *o* .... Matt. 9:9

OFFSPRING (41/41)
wife and raise up *o* .... Matt. 22:24
For we are also His *o* .... Acts 17:28
am the Root and the *O* .... Rev. 22:16

OFTEN (33/31)
o I wanted to gather .... Luke 13:34
as *o* as you eat this .... 1 Cor. 11:26

OIL (222/204)
a bin, and a little *o* .... 1 Kin. 17:12
very costly fragrant *o* .... Matt. 26:7
anointing him with *o* .... James 5:14
and do not harm the *o* .... Rev. 6:6

OLD (339/310)
young, and now am *o* .... Ps. 37:25
was said to those of *o* .... Matt. 5:21
but when you are *o* .... John 21:18
Your *o* men shall dream .... Acts 2:17
o man was crucified .... Rom. 6:6
o things have passed .... 2 Cor. 5:17
have put off the *o* man .... Col. 3:9
that serpent of *o* .... Rev. 20:2

OLDER (16/16)
o shall serve the .... Gen. 25:23
not rebuke an *o* man .... 1 Tim. 5:1

OLDEST (9/9)
beginning with the *o* .... John 8:9

OLIVE (41/38)
a freshly plucked *o* .... Gen. 8:11
o tree which is wild .... Rom. 11:24

OMNIPOTENT (1/1)
For the Lord God *O* .... Rev. 19:6

ONCE (83/81)
died, He died to sin *o* .... Rom. 6:10
for this He did *o* for all .... Heb. 7:27
also suffered *o* .... 1 Pet. 3:18

ONE (2,611/2,242)
"*O* thing you lack .... Mark 10:21
o thing is needed .... Luke 10:42
I and My Father are *o* .... John 10:30
Me, that they may be *o* .... John 17:11
o accord in the temple .... Acts 2:46
for you are all *o* .... Gal. 3:28
to create in Himself *o* .... Eph. 2:15
o Lord, *o* faith, *o* .... Eph. 4:5
o God and Father of .... Eph. 4:6
O Mediator between God .... 1 Tim. 2:5
a thousand years as *o* .... 2 Pet. 3:8

OPENED (128/122)
o not His mouth .... Is. 53:7
o the Scriptures .... Luke 24:32
o their understanding .... Luke 24:45
Now I saw heaven *o* .... Rev. 19:11

OPENS (18/17)
him the doorkeeper *o* .... John 10:3
and shuts and no one *o* .... Rev. 3:7

OPINION (5/5)
be wise in your own *o* .... Rom. 11:25

OPINIONS (1/1)
falter between two *o* .... 1 Kin. 18:21

OPPORTUNITY (13/12)
But sin, taking *o* .... Rom. 7:8
as we have *o* .... Gal. 6:10
but you lacked *o* .... Phil. 4:10

OPPRESS (27/27)
he loves to *o* .... Hos. 12:7
o the widow or the .... Zech. 7:10
Do not the rich *o* .... James 2:6

OPPRESSED (44/44)
for all who are *o* .... Ps. 103:6
The tears of the *o* .... Eccl. 4:1
He was *o* and He was .... Is. 53:7
healing all who were *o* .... Acts 10:38

OPPRESSES (5/5)
o the poor reproaches .... Prov. 14:31

OPPRESSION (27/27)
have surely seen the *o* .... Ex. 3:7
their life from *o* .... Ps. 72:14
brought low through *o* .... Ps. 107:39
Redeem me from the *o* .... Ps. 119:134
considered all the *o* .... Eccl. 4:1
o destroys a wise .... Eccl. 7:7
justice, but behold, *o* .... Is. 5:7
surely seen the *o* .... Acts 7:34

ORACLES (5/5)
received the living *o* .... Acts 7:38
were committed the *o* .... Rom. 3:2
principles of the *o* .... Heb. 5:12

ORDAINED (10/10)
o you a prophet .... Jer. 1:5
the Man whom He has *o* .... Acts 17:31

ORDER (73/72)
done decently and in *o* .... 1 Cor. 14:40

ORDERS (6/6)
o his conduct aright I .... Ps. 50:23

ORDINANCE (42/41)
resists the *o* of God .... Rom. 13:2

ORDINANCES (29/28)
and fleshly *o* imposed .... Heb. 9:10

ORPHANS (4/4)
I will not leave you *o* .... John 14:18
to visit *o* and widows .... James 1:27

OUGHT (52/52)
These you *o* to have .... Matt. 23:23
pray for as we *o* .... Rom. 8:26
persons *o* you to be .... 2 Pet. 3:11

OUTCAST (3/3)
they called you an *o* .... Jer. 30:17

OUTCASTS (7/7)
will assemble the *o* .... Is. 11:12

OUTRAN (2/2)
the other disciple *o* .... John 20:4

OUTSIDE (138/136)
and dish, that the *o* .... Matt. 23:26
Pharisees make the *o* .... Luke 11:39
toward those who are *o* .... Col. 4:5
to Him, *o* the camp .... Heb. 13:13
But *o* are dogs and .... Rev. 22:15

OUTSTRETCHED (18/18)
and with an *o* arm .... Deut. 26:8

OUTWARD (6/6)
at the *o* appearance .... 1 Sam. 16:7
adornment be merely *o* .... 1 Pet. 3:3

OUTWARDLY (3/3)
not a Jew who is one *o* .... Rom. 2:28

OVERCAME (2/2)
My throne, as I also *o* .... Rev. 3:21
And they *o* him by .... Rev. 12:11

OVERCOME (21/20)
good cheer, I have *o* .... John 16:33
and the Lamb will *o* .... Rev. 17:14

OVERCOMES (11/11)
of God *o* the world .... 1 John 5:4
o I will give to eat .... Rev. 2:7
o shall not be hurt .... Rev. 2:11
o shall inherit all .... Rev. 21:7

OVERSEER (8/8)
to the Shepherd and *O* .... 1 Pet. 2:25

OVERSEERS (8/8)
you, serving as *o* .... 1 Pet. 5:2

OVERSHADOW (1/1)
of the Highest will *o* .... Luke 1:35

OVERTHREW (11/10)
As God *o* Sodom and .... Jer. 50:40

OVERTHROW (17/16)
o the faith of some .... 2 Tim. 2:18

OVERTHROWN (16/14)
and Nineveh shall be *o* .... Jon. 3:4

OVERTHROWS (5/5)
and *o* the mighty .... Job 12:19
o them in the night .... Job 34:25
o the words of the .... Prov. 22:12

OVERWHELM (4/4)
o the fatherless .... Job 6:27

OVERWHELMED (10/10)
and my spirit was *o* .... Ps. 77:3
my spirit is *o* within .... Ps. 143:4

OVERWORK (1/1)
Do not *o* to be rich .... Prov. 23:4

OWE (5/5)
O no one anything .... Rom. 13:8

OWED (4/4)
o him ten thousand .... Matt. 18:24

OWN (652/591)
He came to His *o* .... John 1:11
having loved His *o* .... John 13:1
world would love its *o* .... John 15:19
and you are not your *o* .... 1 Cor. 6:19
But each one has his *o* .... 1 Cor. 7:7
For all seek their *o* .... Phil. 2:21
from our sins in His *o* .... Rev. 1:5

OX (68/58)
shall not muzzle an *o* .... Deut. 25:4
o knows its owner .... Is. 1:3
Sabbath loose his *o* .... Luke 13:15
shall not muzzle an *o* .... 1 Cor. 9:9

P

PACIFIES (2/2)
A gift in secret *p* .... Prov. 21:14

PAIN (28/27)
p you shall bring .... Gen. 3:16
p as a woman in .... Is. 13:8
Why is my *p* perpetual .... Jer. 15:18
shall be no more *p* .... Rev. 21:4

PAINED (2/2)
My heart is severely *p* .... Ps. 55:4
I am *p* in my very .... Jer. 4:19

PAINFUL (4/4)
for the present, but *p* .... Heb. 12:11

PAINS (6/6)
The *p* of death .... Ps. 116:3
having loosed the *p* .... Acts 2:24

PAINT (2/2)
your eyes with *p* .... Jer. 4:30

PALACE (32/32)
enter the King's *p* .... Ps. 45:15
guards his own *p* .... Luke 11:21
evident to the whole *p* .... Phil. 1:13

PALACES (30/29)
out of the ivory *p* .... Ps. 45:8

PALE (3/3)
behold, a *p* horse ... Rev. 6:8
PALM (39/35)
p branches in their ... Rev. 7:9
PALMS (8/8)
struck Him with the *p* ... Matt. 26:67
PAMPERS (1/1)
p his servant from ... Prov. 29:21
PANGS (16/15)
The *p* of death ... Ps. 18:4
labors with birth *p* ... Rom. 8:22
PARABLE (35/35)
do You speak this *p* ... Luke 12:41
PARABLES (16/16)
rest it is given in *p* ... Luke 8:10
PARADISE (3/3)
will be with Me in *P* ... Luke 23:43
in the midst of the *P* ... Rev. 2:7
PARDON (15/14)
He will abundantly *p* ... Is. 55:7
p all their iniquities ... Jer. 33:8
PARDONING (1/1)
is a God like You, *p* ... Mic. 7:18
PARENTS (21/20)
will rise up against *p* ... Matt. 10:21
has left house or *p* ... Luke 18:29
disobedient to *p* ... Rom. 1:30
PART (88/79)
has chosen that good *p* ... Luke 10:42
you, you have no *p* ... John 13:8
For we know in *p* ... 1 Cor. 13:9
shall take away his *p* ... Rev. 22:19
PARTAKE (8/8)
for we all *p* of that ... 1 Cor. 10:17
PARTAKER (5/5)
in hope should be *p* ... 1 Cor. 9:10
Christ, and also a *p* ... 1 Pet. 5:1
PARTAKERS (15/15)
Gentiles have been *p* ... Rom. 15:27
know that as you are *p* ... 2 Cor. 1:7
qualified us to be *p* ... Col. 1:12
PARTIAL (2/2)
You shall not be *p* ... Lev. 19:15
PARTIALITY (24/24)
that God shows no *p* ... Acts 10:34
doing nothing with *p* ... 1 Tim. 5:21
good fruits, without *p* ... James 3:17
PASS (426/410)
I will *p* over you ... Ex. 12:13
When you *p* through the ... Is. 43:2
and earth will *p* ... Matt. 24:35
PASSED (113/105)
forbearance God had *p* ... Rom. 3:25
High Priest who has *p* ... Heb. 4:14
know that we have *p* ... 1 John 3:14
PASSES (29/29)
of Christ which *p* ... Eph. 3:19
PASSION (3/3)
uncleanness, *p*, evil ... Col. 3:5
PASSIONS (3/3)
gave them up to vile *p* ... Rom. 1:26
PASSOVER (79/73)
It is the LORD's *P* ... Ex. 12:11
I will keep the *P* ... Matt. 26:18
indeed Christ, our *P* ... 1 Cor. 5:7
By faith he kept the *P* ... Heb. 11:28
PASTORS (1/1)
and some *p* and ... Eph. 4:11
PASTURE (24/22)
the sheep of Your *p* ... Ps. 74:1
in and out and find *p* ... John 10:9
PASTURES (14/14)
to lie down in green *p* ... Ps. 23:2
PATH (28/28)
You will show me the *p* ... Ps. 16:11
PATHS (41/41)
He leads me in the *p* ... Ps. 23:3
Make His *p* straight ... Matt. 3:3
and make straight *p* ... Heb. 12:13
PATIENCE (25/25)
'Master, have *p* ... Matt. 18:26
and bear fruit with *p* ... Luke 8:15
labor of love, and *p* ... 1 Thess. 1:3
faith, love, *p* ... 1 Tim. 6:11
your faith produces *p* ... James 1:3
p have its perfect ... James 1:4
in the kingdom and *p* ... Rev. 1:9
PATIENT (7/7)
rejoicing in hope, *p* ... Rom. 12:12
uphold the weak, be *p* ... 1 Thess. 5:14
PATIENTLY (7/6)
if you take it *p* ... 1 Pet. 2:20
PATRIARCHS (2/2)
begot the twelve *p* ... Acts 7:8
PATTERN (13/12)
p which you were ... Ex. 26:30
as you have us for a *p* ... Phil. 3:17
p shown you on the ... Heb. 8:5
PEACE (396/368)
you, and give you *p* ... Num. 6:26
both lie down in *p* ... Ps. 4:8
p have those who ... Ps. 119:165
I am for *p* ... Ps. 120:7
war, and a time of *p* ... Eccl. 3:8
Father, Prince of *P* ... Is. 9:6
keep him in perfect *p* ... Is. 26:3
p they have not ... Is. 59:8
slightly, saying, '*P* ... Jer. 6:14
place I will give *p* ... Hag. 2:9
is worthy, let your *p* ... Matt. 10:13
that I came to bring *p* ... Matt. 10:34
and on earth *p* ... Luke 2:14
if a son of *p* is there ... Luke 10:6
that make for your *p* ... Luke 19:42
I leave with you, My *p* ... John 14:27
in Me you may have *p* ... John 16:33
Grace to you and *p* ... Rom. 1:7
by faith, we have *p* ... Rom. 5:1
God has called us to *p* ... 1 Cor. 7:15
p will be with you ... 2 Cor. 13:11
Spirit is love, joy, *p* ... Gal. 5:22
He Himself is our *p* ... Eph. 2:14
and the *p* of God ... Phil. 4:7
And let the *p* of God ... Col. 3:15
faith, love, *p* ... 2 Tim. 2:22
meaning "king of *p*," ... Heb. 7:2
PEACEABLE (5/5)
is first pure, then *p* ... James 3:17
PEACEABLY (11/10)
on you, live *p* ... Rom. 12:18
PEACEFUL (4/4)
in a *p* habitation ... Is. 32:18
PEACEMAKERS (1/1)
Blessed are the *p* ... Matt. 5:9
PEARL (2/2)
had found one *p* ... Matt. 13:46
PEARLS (7/7)
nor cast your *p* ... Matt. 7:6
gates were twelve *p* ... Rev. 21:21
PENTECOST (3/3)
P had fully come ... Acts 2:1
PEOPLE (2,136/1,908)
will take you as My *p* ... Ex. 6:7
p shall be my *p* ... Ruth 1:16
p who know the joyful ... Ps. 89:15
We are His *p* and the ... Ps. 100:3
"Blessed is Egypt My *p* ... Is. 19:25
to make ready a *p* ... Luke 1:17
take out of them a *p* ... Acts 15:14
who were not My *p* ... Rom. 9:25
and they shall be My *p* ... 2 Cor. 6:16
LORD will judge His *p* ... Heb. 10:30
but are now the *p* ... 1 Pet. 2:10
tribe and tongue and *p* ... Rev. 5:9
they shall be His *p* ... Rev. 21:3
PERCEIVE (23/23)
seeing, but do not *p* ... Is. 6:9
may see and not *p* ... Mark 4:12
PERDITION (8/8)
except the son of *p* ... John 17:12
revealed, the son of *p* ... 2 Thess. 2:3
who draw back to *p* ... Heb. 10:39
PERFECT (61/56)
Noah was a just man, *p* ... Gen. 6:9
Father in heaven is *p* ... Matt. 5:48
they may be made *p* ... John 17:23
and *p* will of God ... Rom. 12:2
when that which is *p* ... 1 Cor. 13:10
present every man *p* ... Col. 1:28
good gift and every *p* ... James 1:17
in word, he is a *p* ... James 3:2
p love casts out fear ... 1 John 4:18
PERFECTED (11/11)
third day I shall be *p* ... Luke 13:32
or am already *p* ... Phil. 3:12
the Son who has been *p* ... Heb. 7:28
PERFECTION (7/7)
let us go on to *p* ... Heb. 6:1
PERISH (110/108)
so that we may not *p* ... Jon. 1:6
little ones should *p* ... Matt. 18:14
in Him should not *p* ... John 3:16
they shall never *p* ... John 10:28
among those who *p* ... 2 Thess. 2:10
that any should *p* ... 2 Pet. 3:9
PERISHABLE (1/1)
do it to obtain a *p* ... 1 Cor. 9:25
PERISHED (28/28)
Truth has *p* and has ... Jer. 7:28
PERISHING (11/11)
We are *p* ... Matt. 8:25
PERMIT (14/14)
I do not *p* a woman ... 1 Tim. 2:12
PERMITS (2/2)
we will do if God *p* ... Heb. 6:3
PERMITTED (12/12)
p no one to do them ... Ps. 105:14
PERSECUTE (19/19)
when they revile and *p* ... Matt. 5:11
PERSECUTED (18/18)
If they *p* Me ... John 15:20
p, but not forsaken ... 2 Cor. 4:9
PERSECUTES (1/1)
wicked in his pride *p* ... Ps. 10:2
PERSECUTION (9/9)
p arises because of ... Matt. 13:21
At that time a great *p* ... Acts 8:1
do I still suffer *p* ... Gal. 5:11
PERSECUTOR (1/1)
a blasphemer, a *p* ... 1 Tim. 1:13
PERSEVERANCE (9/8)
tribulation produces *p* ... Rom. 5:3
PERSEVERE (1/1)
kept My command to *p* ... Rev. 3:10
PERSISTENCE (1/1)
p he will rise and ... Luke 11:8
PERSON (100/94)
do not regard the *p* ... Matt. 22:16
express image of His *p* ... Heb. 1:3
PERSUADE (14/14)
"You almost *p* me ... Acts 26:28
PERSUADED (21/21)
neither will they be *p* ... Luke 16:31
p that He is able ... 2 Tim. 1:12
PERSUASIVE (2/2)
p words of human ... 1 Cor. 2:4
PERVERSE (33/33)
your way is *p* ... Num. 22:32
p man sows strife ... Prov. 16:28
from this *p* generation ... Acts 2:40
PERVERT (11/11)
You shall not *p* ... Deut. 16:19
p the gospel of Christ ... Gal. 1:7
PERVERTING (2/2)
will you not cease *p* ... Acts 13:10
PERVERTS (3/3)
p his ways will become ... Prov. 10:9
PESTILENCE (42/41)
from the perilous *p* ... Ps. 91:3
Before Him went *p* ... Hab. 3:5
PESTILENCES (2/2)
will be famines, *p* ... Matt. 24:7
PETITIONS (4/4)
p that we have asked ... 1 John 5:15
PHARISEE (11/10)
temple to pray, one a *P* ... Luke 18:10
PHILOSOPHERS (1/1)
p encountered him ... Acts 17:18
PHILOSOPHY (1/1)
cheat you through *p* ... Col. 2:8
PHYSICIAN (6/6)
have no need of a *p* ... Matt. 9:12
PHYSICIANS (6/5)
her livelihood on *p* ... Luke 8:43
PIECES (118/107)
they took the thirty *p* ... Matt. 27:9
PIERCE (9/9)
a sword will *p* ... Luke 2:35
PIERCED (9/9)
p My hands and My feet ... Ps. 22:16
Me whom they have *p* ... Zech. 12:10
of the soldiers *p* ... John 19:34
p themselves through ... 1 Tim. 6:10
and they also who *p* ... Rev. 1:7
PIERCING (1/1)
p even to the division ... Heb. 4:12
PILGRIMAGE (5/4)
heart is set on *p* ... Ps. 84:5
In the house of my *p* ... Ps. 119:54
PILGRIMS (4/4)
we are aliens and *p* ... 1 Chr. 29:15
were strangers and *p* ... Heb. 11:13
PILLAR (51/39)
and she became a *p* ... Gen. 19:26
and by night in a *p* ... Ex. 13:21
the living God, the *p* ... 1 Tim. 3:15
PILLARS (105/90)
break their sacred *p* ... Ex. 34:13
blood and fire and *p* ... Joel 2:30
and his feet like *p* ... Rev. 10:1
PIT (89/81)
who go down to the *p* ... Ps. 28:1
a harlot is a deep *p* ... Prov. 23:27
my life in the *p* ... Lam. 3:53
up my life from the *p* ... Jon. 2:6
into the bottomless *p* ... Rev. 20:3
PITIABLE (1/1)
of all men the most *p* ... 1 Cor. 15:19
PITS (6/6)
The proud have dug *p* ... Ps. 119:85
PITY (33/32)
for someone to take *p* ... Ps. 69:20
p He redeemed them ... Is. 63:9
just as I had *p* ... Matt. 18:33
PLACE (845/798)
Come, see the *p* ... Matt. 28:6
My word has no *p* ... John 8:37
I go to prepare a *p* ... John 14:2
might go to his own *p* ... Acts 1:25
PLACES (196/183)
and the rough *p* ... Is. 40:4
They love the best *p* ... Matt. 23:6
in the heavenly *p* ... Eph. 1:3

PLAGUE (75/64)
bring yet one more *p*. Ex. 11:1
PLAGUES (22/21)
p that are written Rev. 22:18
PLANK (6/5)
First remove the *p* Matt. 7:5
PLANS (22/22)
He makes the *p* of the Ps. 33:10
that devises wicked *p* Prov. 6:18
PLANT (50/48)
A time to *p* Eccl. 3:2
Him as a tender *p* Is. 53:2
p of an alien vine Jer. 2:21
p which My heavenly Matt. 15:13
PLANTED (41/41)
shall be like a tree *p* Ps. 1:3
by the roots and be *p* Luke 17:6
I *p*, Apollos watered 1 Cor. 3:6
PLANTS (12/12)
neither he who *p* 1 Cor. 3:7
PLATTER (17/17)
head here on a *p* Matt. 14:8
PLEASANT (47/47)
food, that it was *p* Gen. 3:6
they despised the *p* Ps. 106:24
PLEASANTNESS (1/1)
Her ways are ways of *p* Prov. 3:17
PLEASE (220/214)
in the flesh cannot *p* Rom. 8:8
p his neighbor for his Rom. 15:2
how he may *p* the Lord 1 Cor. 7:32
is impossible to *p* Him Heb. 11:6
PLEASED (60/59)
Then You shall be *p* Ps. 51:19
in whom I am well *p* Matt. 3:17
God was not well *p* 1 Cor. 10:5
testimony, that he *p* Heb. 11:5
PLEASES (23/23)
Whatever the LORD *p* Ps. 135:6
PLEASURE (55/54)
Do good in Your good *p* Ps. 51:18
p will be a poor man Prov. 21:17
shall perform all My *p* Is. 44:28
your Father's good *p* Luke 12:32
to the good *p* of His Eph. 1:5
for sin You had no *p* Heb. 10:6
back, My soul has no *p* Heb. 10:38
p that war in your James 4:1
PLEASURES (8/8)
Your right hand are *p* Ps. 16:11
cares, riches, and *p* Luke 8:14
to enjoy the passing *p* Heb. 11:25
PLOW (10/9)
put his hand to the *p* Luke 9:62
PLOWED (6/6)
You have *p* wickedness Hos. 10:13
PLOWMAN (2/2)
p shall overtake the Amos 9:13
PLUCK (22/21)
p the heads of grain Mark 2:23
PLUCKED (14/14)
cheeks to those who *p* Is. 50:6
And His disciples *p* Luke 6:1
you would have *p* Gal. 4:15
PLUNDER (71/61)
p the Egyptians Ex. 3:22
The *p* of the poor is Is. 3:14
house and *p* his goods Matt. 12:29
PLUNDERED (39/36)
a people robbed and *p* Is. 42:22
"And when you are *p* Jer. 4:30
PLUNDERING (9/9)
me because of the *p* Is. 22:4
accepted the *p* of your Heb. 10:34
POETS (1/1)
some of your own *p* Acts 17:28
POISON (9/8)
"The *p* of asps is Rom. 3:13
POISONED (2/2)
p by bitterness Acts 8:23
POLLUTIONS (1/1)
have escaped the *p* 2 Pet. 2:20
POMP (5/5)
had come with great *p* Acts 25:23
POMPOUS (4/4)
and a mouth speaking *p* Dan. 7:8
PONDER (2/2)
P the path of your Prov. 4:26
PONDERED (2/2)
p them in her heart Luke 2:19
PONDERS (1/1)
p all his paths Prov. 5:21
POOR (201/194)
p will never cease Deut. 15:11
So the *p* have hope Job 5:16
I delivered the *p* Job 29:12
p shall eat and be Ps. 22:26
But I am *p* and needy Ps. 40:17
Let the *p* and needy Ps. 74:21
He raises the *p* Ps. 113:7
a slack hand becomes *p* Prov. 10:4
p man is hated even Prov. 14:20
p reproaches his Maker Prov. 17:5
remembered that same *p* Eccl. 9:15
the alien or the *p* Zech. 7:10
"Blessed are the *p* Matt. 5:3
p have the gospel Matt. 11:5
For you have the *p* Matt. 26:11
your sakes He became *p* 2 Cor. 8:9
should remember the *p* Gal. 2:10
God not chosen the *p* James 2:5
wretched, miserable, *p* Rev. 3:17
PORTION (64/61)
O LORD, You are the *p* Ps. 16:5
heart and my *p* forever Ps. 73:26
You are my *p* Ps. 119:57
I will divide Him a *p* Is. 53:12
rejoice in their *p* Is. 61:7
The *P* of Jacob is not Jer. 10:16
"The LORD is my *p* Lam. 3:24
and appoint him his *p* Matt. 24:51
to give them their *p* Luke 12:42
give me the *p* Luke 15:12
POSSESS (101/92)
descendants shall *p* Gen. 22:17
p the land which Josh. 1:11
By your patience *p* Luke 21:19
p his own vessel 1 Thess. 4:4
POSSESSED (14/14)
"The LORD *p* me at Prov. 8:22
POSSESSING (2/2)
and yet *p* all things 2 Cor. 6:10
POSSESSION (105/94)
as an everlasting *p* Gen. 17:8
and an enduring *p* Heb. 10:34
POSSESSIONS (39/38)
and sold their *p* Acts 2:45
POSSIBLE (15/15)
God all things are *p* Matt. 19:26
p that the blood Heb. 10:4
POUR (67/66)
p My Spirit on your Is. 44:3
P out Your fury Jer. 10:25
that I will *p* out My Joel 2:28
"And I will *p* Zech. 12:10
angels, "Go and *p* Rev. 16:1
POURED (86/82)
I am *p* out like water Ps. 22:14
grace is *p* upon Your Ps. 45:2
strong, because He *p* Is. 53:12
and My fury will be *p* Jer. 7:20
broke the flask and *p* Mark 14:3
I am already being *p* 2 Tim. 4:6
whom He *p* out on us Titus 3:6
POVERTY (21/21)
leads only to *p* Prov. 14:23
p put in all the Luke 21:4
and their deep *p* 2 Cor. 8:2
p might become rich 2 Cor. 8:9
tribulation, and *p* Rev. 2:9
POWER (245/237)
that I may show My *p* Ex. 9:16
him who is without *p* Job 26:2
p who can understand Job 26:14
p belongs to God Ps. 62:11
p Your enemies shall Ps. 66:3
gives strength and *p* Ps. 68:35
a king is, there is *p* Eccl. 8:4
No one has *p* over the Eccl. 8:8
'Not by might nor by *p* Zech. 4:6
the kingdom and the *p* Matt. 6:13
the Son of Man has *p* Matt. 9:6
Scriptures nor the *p* Matt. 22:29
p went out from Him Luke 6:19
you are endued with *p* Luke 24:49
I have *p* to lay it John 10:18
"You could have no *p* John 19:11
you shall receive *p* Acts 1:8
as though by our own *p* Acts 3:12
man is the great *p* Acts 8:10
"Give me this *p* Acts 8:19
for it is the *p* Rom. 1:16
saved it is the *p* 1 Cor. 1:18
Greeks, Christ the *p* 1 Cor. 1:24
that the *p* of Christ 2 Cor. 12:9
greatness of His *p* Eph. 1:19
the Lord and in the *p* Eph. 6:10
to His glorious *p* Col. 1:11
the glory of His *p* 2 Thess. 1:9
of fear, but of *p* 2 Tim. 1:7
by the word of His *p* Heb. 1:3
p of death, that Heb. 2:14
as His divine *p* 2 Pet. 1:3
dominion and *p* Jude 1:25
to him I will give *p* Rev. 2:26
honor and glory and *p* Rev. 5:13
POWERFUL (6/6)
of the LORD is *p* Ps. 29:4
of God is living and *p* Heb. 4:12
POWERS (13/13)
principalities and *p* Col. 2:15
word of God and the *p* Heb. 6:5
PRAISE (236/205)
p shall be of You in Ps. 22:25
the people shall *p* Ps. 45:17
P is awaiting You Ps. 65:1
let all the peoples *p* Ps. 67:3
p shall be continually Ps. 71:6
And the heavens will *p* Ps. 89:5
Seven times a day I *p* Ps. 119:164
that has breath *p* Ps. 150:6
Let another man *p* Prov. 27:2
let her own works *p* Prov. 31:31
And your gates *P* Is. 60:18
He makes Jerusalem a *p* Is. 62:7
For You are my *p* Jer. 17:14
Me a name of joy, a *p* Jer. 33:9
give you fame and *p* Zeph. 3:20
You have perfected *p* Matt. 21:16
of men more than the *p* John 12:43
p is not from men but Rom. 2:29
Then each one's *p* 1 Cor. 4:5
should be to the *p* Eph. 1:12
to the glory and *p* Phil. 1:11
I will sing *p* to You Heb. 2:12
the sacrifice of *p* Heb. 13:15
and for the *p* of those 1 Pet. 2:14
saying, "*P* our God Rev. 19:5
PRAISED (24/24)
daily He shall be *p* Ps. 72:15
LORD's name is to be *p* Ps. 113:3
and greatly to be *p* Ps. 145:3
the Most High and *p* Dan. 4:34
PRAISES (36/32)
it is good to sing *p* Ps. 147:1
and he *p* her Prov. 31:28
PRAISEWORTHY (1/1)
if there is anything *p* Phil. 4:8
PRAISING (11/11)
they will still be *p* Ps. 84:4
of the heavenly host *p* Luke 2:13
in the temple *p* Luke 24:53
PRAY (146/139)
at noon I will *p* Ps. 55:17
who hate you, and *p* Matt. 5:44
"And when you *p* Matt. 6:5
manner, therefore, *p* Matt. 6:9
Watch and *p* Matt. 26:41
"Lord, teach us to *p* Luke 11:1
And I will *p* John 14:16
I do not *p* for the John 17:9
"I do not *p* for John 17:20
p without ceasing 1 Thess. 5:17
Brethren, *p* for us 1 Thess. 5:25
Let him *p* James 5:13
to one another, and *p* James 5:16
say that he should *p* 1 John 5:16
PRAYED (59/59)
p more earnestly Luke 22:44
p earnestly that it James 5:17
PRAYER (113/108)
p made in this place 2 Chr. 7:15
And my *p* is pure Job 16:17
A *p* to the God of my Ps. 42:8
P also will be made Ps. 72:15
He shall regard the *p* Ps. 102:17
to the LORD, but the *p* Prov. 15:8
not go out except by *p* Matt. 17:21
all night in *p* to God Luke 6:12
continually to *p* Acts 6:4
where *p* was Acts 16:13
steadfastly in *p* Rom. 12:12
to fasting and *p* 1 Cor. 7:5
always with all *p* Eph. 6:18
but in everything by *p* Phil. 4:6
the word of God and *p* 1 Tim. 4:5
And the *p* of faith James 5:15
PRAYERS (27/27)
though you make many *p* Is. 1:15
pretense make long *p* Matt. 23:14
fervently for you in *p* Col. 4:12
p may not be hindered 1 Pet. 3:7
which are the *p* Rev. 5:8
PREACH (47/45)
time Jesus began to *p* Matt. 4:17
you hear in the ear, *p* Matt. 10:27
P the gospel to the Luke 4:18
And how shall they *p* Rom. 10:15
p Christ crucified 1 Cor. 1:23
I or they, so we *p* 1 Cor. 15:11
P the word 2 Tim. 4:2
PREACHED (59/59)
out and *p* everywhere Mark 16:20
of sins should be *p* Luke 24:47
p Christ to them Acts 8:5
lest, when I have *p* 1 Cor. 9:27
than what we have *p* Gal. 1:8
the gospel was *p* Heb. 4:2
also He went and *p* 1 Pet. 3:19
PREACHER (11/11)
they hear without a *p* Rom. 10:14
I was appointed a *p* 1 Tim. 2:7
PREACHES (4/4)
the Jesus whom Paul *p* Acts 19:13

p another Jesus whom .... 2 Cor. 11:4
p any other gospel .... Gal. 1:9
p the faith which he .... Gal. 1:23
PREACHING (26/26)
p Jesus as the .... Acts 5:42
not risen, then our *p* .... 1 Cor. 15:14
PRECEPTS (25/25)
all His *p* are sure .... Ps. 111:7
how I love Your *p* .... Ps. 119:159
PRECIOUS (77/75)
P in the sight of the .... Ps. 116:15
She is more *p* than .... Prov. 3:15
p things shall not .... Is. 44:9
if you take out the *p* .... Jer. 15:19
farmer waits for the *p* .... James 5:7
more *p* than gold .... 1 Pet. 1:7
who believe, He is *p* .... 1 Pet. 2:7
p in the sight of .... 1 Pet. 3:4
PREDESTINED (4/4)
He foreknew, He also *p* .... Rom. 8:29
having *p* us to .... Eph. 1:5
inheritance, being *p* .... Eph. 1:11
PREEMINENCE (2/2)
He may have the *p* .... Col. 1:18
loves to have the *p* .... 3 John 1:9
PREFERENCE (2/2)
in honor giving *p* .... Rom. 12:10
PREJUDICE (1/1)
these things without *p* .... 1 Tim. 5:21
PREMEDITATE (1/1)
p what you will .... Mark 13:11
PREPARATION (11/10)
Now it was the *P* .... John 19:14
your feet with the *p* .... Eph. 6:15
PREPARE (97/96)
p a table before me in .... Ps. 23:5
P the way of the LORD .... Mark 1:3
p a place for you .... John 14:2
PREPARED (109/107)
for whom it is *p* .... Matt. 20:23
which You have *p* .... Luke 2:31
mercy, which He had *p* .... Rom. 9:23
things which God has *p* .... 1 Cor. 2:9
Now He who has *p* .... 2 Cor. 5:5
p beforehand that we .... Eph. 2:10
God, for He has *p* .... Heb. 11:16
PRESENCE (156/147)
themselves from the *p* .... Gen. 3:8
went out from the *p* .... Gen. 4:16
P will go with you .... Ex. 33:14
afraid in any man's *p* .... Deut. 1:17
p is fullness of joy .... Ps. 16:11
shall dwell in Your *p* .... Ps. 140:13
not tremble at My *p* .... Jer. 5:22
shall shake at My *p* .... Ezek. 38:20
and drank in Your *p* .... Luke 13:26
full of joy in Your *p* .... Acts 2:28
but his bodily *p* .... 2 Cor. 10:10
obeyed, not as in my *p* .... Phil. 2:12
PRESENT (130/127)
we are all *p* before .... Acts 10:33
evil is *p* with me .... Rom. 7:21
p your bodies a living .... Rom. 12:1
or death, or things *p* .... 1 Cor. 3:22
absent in body but *p* .... 1 Cor. 5:3
that He might *p* .... Eph. 5:27
p you faultless .... Jude 1:24
PRESERVE (35/34)
He shall *p* your soul .... Ps. 121:7
The LORD shall *p* .... Ps. 121:8
loses his life will *p* .... Luke 17:33
every evil work and *p* .... 2 Tim. 4:18
PRESERVED (16/16)
soul, and body be *p* .... 1 Thess. 5:23
PRESERVES (8/8)
For the LORD *p* the .... Ps. 31:23
p the souls of His .... Ps. 97:10
he who keeps his way *p* .... Prov. 16:17
PRETENSE (6/6)
p make long prayers .... Matt. 23:14
PRICE (26/25)
one pearl of great *p* .... Matt. 13:46
you were bought at a *p* .... 1 Cor. 6:20
PRIDE (51/48)
p serves as their necklace .... Ps. 73:6
By *p* comes nothing .... Prov. 13:10
P goes before .... Prov. 16:18
and her daughter had *p* .... Ezek. 16:49
was hardened in *p* .... Dan. 5:20
For the *p* of the .... Zech. 11:3
evil eye, blasphemy, *p* .... Mark 7:22
p he fall into the .... 1 Tim. 3:6
eyes, and the *p* of life .... 1 John 2:16
PRIEST (510/456)
he was the *p* of God .... Gen. 14:18
p forever according .... Ps. 110:4
So He shall be a *p* .... Zech. 6:13
and faithful High *P* .... Heb. 2:17
we have a great High *P* .... Heb. 4:14
p forever according .... Heb. 5:6
Christ came as High *P* .... Heb. 9:11
PRIESTHOOD (21/19)
p being changed .... Heb. 7:12
has an unchangeable *p* .... Heb. 7:24
generation, a royal *p* .... 1 Pet. 2:9
PRIESTS (409/383)
to Me a kingdom of *p* .... Ex. 19:6
her *p* teach for pay .... Mic. 3:11
made us kings and *p* .... Rev. 1:6
PRINCE (54/50)
is the house of the *p* .... Job 21:28
Everlasting Father, *P* .... Is. 9:6
until Messiah the *P* .... Dan. 9:25
days without king or *p* .... Hos. 3:4
p asks for gifts .... Mic. 7:3
and killed the *P* .... Acts 3:15
His right hand to be *P* .... Acts 5:31
the *p* of the power .... Eph. 2:2
PRINCES (173/161)
to put confidence in *p* .... Ps. 118:9
He brings the *p* .... Is. 40:23
PRISON (93/87)
and put him into the *p* .... Gen. 39:20
Bring my soul out of *p* .... Ps. 142:7
in darkness from the *p* .... Is. 42:7
the opening of the *p* .... Is. 61:1
John had heard in *p* .... Matt. 11:2
I was in *p* and you .... Matt. 25:36
PRIZE (9/9)
the goal for the *p* .... Phil. 3:14
PROCEED (17/17)
of the same mouth *p* .... James 3:10
PROCEEDED (8/8)
for I *p* forth .... John 8:42
PROCEEDS (12/12)
by every word that *p* .... Deut. 8:3
by every word that *p* .... Matt. 4:4
Spirit of truth who *p* .... John 15:26
PROCLAIM (54/52)
began to *p* it freely .... Mark 1:45
knowing, Him I *p* .... Acts 17:23
drink this cup, you *p* .... 1 Cor. 11:26
PROCLAIMED (33/32)
p the good news .... Ps. 40:9
he went his way and *p* .... Luke 8:39
PROCLAIMER (1/1)
"He seems to be a *p* .... Acts 17:18
PROCLAIMS (5/4)
good news, who *p* .... Is. 52:7
PRODIGAL (1/1)
with *p* living .... Luke 15:13
PROFANE (36/36)
and priest are *p* .... Jer. 23:11
tried to *p* the temple .... Acts 24:6
But reject *p* and old .... 1 Tim. 4:7
PROFANED (25/23)
and *p* My Sabbaths .... Ezek. 22:8
PROFANENESS (1/1)
of Jerusalem *p* has .... Jer. 23:15
PROFANING (2/2)
p the covenant of the .... Mal. 2:10
PROFESS (1/1)
They *p* to know God .... Titus 1:16
PROFIT (53/52)
For what *p* is it to .... Matt. 16:26
For what will it *p* .... Mark 8:36
For what *p* is it to .... Luke 9:25
her masters much *p* .... Acts 16:16
brought no small *p* .... Acts 19:24
what is the *p* of .... Rom. 3:1
not seeking my own *p* .... 1 Cor. 10:33
Christ will *p* you .... Gal. 5:2
about words to no *p* .... 2 Tim. 2:14
them, but He for our *p* .... Heb. 12:10
What does it *p* .... James 2:14
and sell, and make a *p* .... James 4:13
PROFITABLE (13/12)
It is doubtless not *p* .... 2 Cor. 12:1
of God, and is *p* .... 2 Tim. 3:16
PROFITS (7/7)
have not love, it *p* .... 1 Cor. 13:3
PROMISE (53/50)
Behold, I send the *P* .... Luke 24:49
but to wait for the *P* .... Acts 1:4
For the *p* is to you .... Acts 2:39
for the hope of the *p* .... Acts 26:6
p might be sure .... Rom. 4:16
Therefore, since a *p* .... Heb. 4:1
to the heirs of *p* .... Heb. 6:17
did not receive the *p* .... Heb. 11:39
PROMISED (51/50)
Him faithful who had *p* .... Heb. 11:11
PROMISES (13/13)
For all the *p* of God .... 2 Cor. 1:20
his Seed were the *p* .... Gal. 3:16
having received the *p* .... Heb. 11:13
great and precious *p* .... 2 Pet. 1:4
PROPER (13/13)
you, but for what is *p* .... 1 Cor. 7:35
but, which is *p* .... 1 Tim. 2:10
PROPERLY (2/2)
Let us walk *p* .... Rom. 13:13
PROPHECY (18/18)
miracles, to another *p* .... 1 Cor. 12:10
for *p* never came by .... 2 Pet. 1:21
is the spirit of *p* .... Rev. 19:10
of the book of this *p* .... Rev. 22:19
PROPHESIED (47/44)
Lord, have we not *p* .... Matt. 7:22
prophets and the law *p* .... Matt. 11:13
PROPHESIES (10/9)
p edifies the church .... 1 Cor. 14:4
PROPHESY (86/75)
prophets, "Do not *p* .... Is. 30:10
The prophets *p* falsely .... Jer. 5:31
your daughters shall *p* .... Joel 2:28
Who can but *p* .... Amos 3:8
saying, "*P* to us .... Matt. 26:68
your daughters shall *p* .... Acts 2:17
know in part and we *p* .... 1 Cor. 13:9
PROPHET (242/227)
raise up for you a *P* .... Deut. 18:15
"I alone am left a *p* .... 1 Kin. 18:22
I ordained you a *p* .... Jer. 1:5
The *p* is a fool .... Hos. 9:7
nor was I a son of a *p* .... Amos 7:14
send you Elijah the *p* .... Mal. 4:5
p shall receive a .... Matt. 10:41
p is not without honor .... Matt. 13:57
by Daniel the *p* .... Mark 13:14
is not a greater *p* .... Luke 7:28
it cannot be that a *p* .... Luke 13:33
Nazareth, who was a *P* .... Luke 24:19
"Are you the *P* .... John 1:21
"This is truly the *P* .... John 6:14
with him the false *p* .... Rev. 19:20
PROPHETIC (2/2)
p word confirmed .... 2 Pet. 1:19
PROPHETS (237/225)
the Law or the *P* .... Matt. 5:17
is the Law and the *P* .... Matt. 7:12
or one of the *p* .... Matt. 16:14
the tombs of the *p* .... Matt. 23:29
indeed, I send you *p* .... Matt. 23:34
one who kills the *p* .... Matt. 23:37
Then many false *p* .... Matt. 24:11
have Moses and the *p* .... Luke 16:29
You are sons of the *p* .... Acts 3:25
p did your fathers not .... Acts 7:52
To Him all the *p* .... Acts 10:43
do you believe the *p* .... Acts 26:27
by the Law and the *P* .... Rom. 3:21
have killed Your *p* .... Rom. 11:3
to be apostles, some *p* .... Eph. 4:11
this salvation the *p* .... 1 Pet. 1:10
because many false *p* .... 1 John 4:1
found the blood of *p* .... Rev. 18:24
PROPITIATION (4/4)
set forth as a *p* .... Rom. 3:25
to God, to make *p* .... Heb. 2:17
He Himself is the *p* .... 1 John 2:2
His Son to be the *p* .... 1 John 4:10
PROPRIETY (1/1)
modest apparel, with *p* .... 1 Tim. 2:9
PROSPER (49/48)
they *p* who love you .... Ps. 122:6
of the LORD shall *p* .... Is. 53:10
against you shall *p* .... Is. 54:17
storing up as he may *p* .... 1 Cor. 16:2
I pray that you may *p* .... 3 John 1:2
PROSPERED (12/12)
since the LORD has *p* .... Gen. 24:56
PROSPERING (2/2)
His ways are always *p* .... Ps. 10:5
PROSPERITY (24/24)
p all your days .... Deut. 23:6
p the destroyer .... Job 15:21
Now in my *p* I said .... Ps. 30:6
has pleasure in the *p* .... Ps. 35:27
When I saw the *p* .... Ps. 73:3
I pray, send now *p* .... Ps. 118:25
that we have our *p* .... Acts 19:25
PROSPEROUS (8/8)
will make your way *p* .... Josh. 1:8
PROSPERS (5/5)
just as your soul *p* .... 3 John 1:2
PROUD (47/47)
tongue that speaks *p* .... Ps. 12:3
and fully repays the *p* .... Ps. 31:23
does not respect the *p* .... Ps. 40:4
a haughty look and a *p* .... Ps. 101:5
p He knows from afar .... Ps. 138:6
Everyone *p* in heart .... Prov. 16:5
by wine, he is a *p* .... Hab. 2:5
He has scattered the *p* .... Luke 1:51
"God resists the *p* .... 1 Pet. 5:5
PROVERB (21/20)
of a drunkard is a *p* .... Prov. 26:9
one shall take up a *p* .... Mic. 2:4
to the true *p* .... 2 Pet. 2:22
PROVERBS (8/8)
spoke three thousand *p* .... 1 Kin. 4:32
in order many *p* .... Eccl. 12:9

PROVIDE (30/29)
“My son, God will *p* ... Gen. 22:8
P neither gold nor ... Matt. 10:9
if anyone does not *p* ... 1 Tim. 5:8
PROVIDED (21/21)
these hands have *p* ... Acts 20:34
p something better ... Heb. 11:40
PROVISION (9/9)
no *p* for the flesh ... Rom. 13:14
PROVOKE (37/36)
Do they *p* Me to ... Jer. 7:19
you, fathers, do not *p* ... Eph. 6:4
PROVOKED (30/29)
p the Most High ... Ps. 78:56
his spirit was *p* ... Acts 17:16
seek its own, is not *p* ... 1 Cor. 13:5
PRUDENCE (7/7)
To give *p* to the ... Prov. 1:4
wisdom, dwell with *p* ... Prov. 8:12
us in all wisdom and *p* ... Eph. 1:8
PRUDENT (22/22)
p man covers shame ... Prov. 12:16
A *p* man conceals ... Prov. 12:23
The wisdom of the *p* ... Prov. 14:8
p considers well ... Prov. 14:15
heart will be called *p* ... Prov. 16:21
p man foresees evil ... Prov. 22:3
Therefore the *p* ... Amos 5:13
from the wise and *p* ... Matt. 11:25
PRUDENTLY (2/2)
Servant shall deal *p* ... Is. 52:13
PRUNES (1/1)
that bears fruit He *p* ... John 15:2
PSALM (83/83)
each of you has a *p* ... 1 Cor. 14:26
PSALMIST (1/1)
And the sweet *p* ... 2 Sam. 23:1
PSALMS (10/10)
to one another in *p* ... Eph. 5:19
Let him sing *p* ... James 5:13
PUNISH (47/47)
p the righteous is ... Prov. 17:26
Shall I not *p* them for ... Jer. 5:9
PUNISHED (19/19)
p them often in every ... Acts 26:11
These shall be *p* ... 2 Thess. 1:9
PUNISHES (2/2)
will you say when He *p* ... Jer. 13:21
PUNISHMENT (46/42)
p is greater than I ... Gen. 4:13
you do in the day of *p* ... Is. 10:3
p they shall perish ... Jer. 10:15
not turn away its *p* ... Amos 1:3
into everlasting *p* ... Matt. 25:46
p which was inflicted ... 2 Cor. 2:6
Of how much worse *p* ... Heb. 10:29
sent by him for the *p* ... 1 Pet. 2:14
the unjust under *p* ... 2 Pet. 2:9
PURE (102/97)
a mercy seat of *p* gold ... Ex. 25:17
‘My doctrine is *p* ... Job 11:4
that he could be *p* ... Job 15:14
of the LORD are *p* ... Ps. 12:6
ways of a man are *p* ... Prov. 16:2
a generation that is *p* ... Prov. 30:12
things indeed are *p* ... Rom. 14:20
whatever things are *p* ... Phil. 4:8
keep yourself *p* ... 1 Tim. 5:22
p all things are *p* ... Titus 1:15
above is first *p* ... James 3:17
babes, desire the *p* ... 1 Pet. 2:2
just as He is *p* ... 1 John 3:3
PURER (1/1)
p eyes than to behold ... Hab. 1:13
PURGE (6/6)
P me with hyssop ... Ps. 51:7
PURGED (4/4)
away, and your sin *p* ... Is. 6:7
PURIFICATION (18/16)
with the water of *p* ... Num. 31:23
PURIFIED (15/14)
all things are *p* ... Heb. 9:22
Since you have *p* ... 1 Pet. 1:22
PURIFIES (1/1)
hope in Him *p* himself ... 1 John 3:3
PURIFY (15/14)
and *p* your hearts ... James 4:8
PURIFYING (5/5)
p their hearts by ... Acts 15:9
sanctifies for the *p* ... Heb. 9:13
PURIM (5/5)
called these days *P* ... Esth. 9:26
PURITY (5/5)
spirit, in faith, in *p* ... 1 Tim. 4:12
PURPOSE (39/39)
A time for every *p* ... Eccl. 3:1
But for this *p* I came ... John 12:27
by the determined *p* ... Acts 2:23
to fulfill His *p* ... Rev. 17:17
PURSUE (48/46)
p righteousness ... Rom. 9:30
P love, and desire ... 1 Cor. 14:1
PURSUES (9/8)
flee when no one *p* ... Prov. 28:1

Q

QUAIL (3/3)
and it brought *q* ... Num. 11:31
QUARREL (7/7)
He will not *q* nor cry ... Matt. 12:19
of the Lord must not *q* ... 2 Tim. 2:24
QUARRELSOME (1/1)
but gentle, not *q* ... 1 Tim. 3:3
QUEEN (53/52)
heart, ‘I sit as *q* ... Rev. 18:7
QUENCH (11/11)
Many waters cannot *q* ... Song 8:7
flax He will not *q* ... Matt. 12:20
q all the fiery ... Eph. 6:16
Do not *q* the Spirit ... 1 Thess. 5:19
QUENCHED (17/17)
that shall never be *q* ... Mark 9:43
QUESTIONS (10/10)
and asking them *q* ... Luke 2:46
QUICKLY (59/57)
with your adversary *q* ... Matt. 5:25
“Surely I am coming *q* ... Rev. 22:20
QUIET (36/36)
aspire to lead a *q* ... 1 Thess. 4:11
a gentle and *q* spirit ... 1 Pet. 3:4
QUIETNESS (8/8)
a handful with *q* ... Eccl. 4:6
in *q* and confidence ... Is. 30:15
of righteousness, *q* ... Is. 32:17
that they work in *q* ... 2 Thess. 3:12

R

RABBI (17/15)
be called by men, ‘*R* ... Matt. 23:7
RACA (1/1)
to his brother, ‘*R* ... Matt. 5:22
RACE (7/7)
man to run its *r* ... Ps. 19:5
r is not to the swift ... Eccl. 9:11
I have finished the *r* ... 2 Tim. 4:7
with endurance the *r* ... Heb. 12:1
RAGE (19/19)
Why do the nations *r* ... Ps. 2:1
‘Why did the nations *r* ... Acts 4:25
RAGES (3/3)
he *r* against all wise ... Prov. 18:1
RAIN (105/89)
had not caused it to *r* ... Gen. 2:5
And the *r* was on the ... Gen. 7:12
I will *r* down on him ... Ezek. 38:22
given you the former *r* ... Joel 2:23
the good, and sends *r* ... Matt. 5:45
and the *r* descended ... Matt. 7:25
r that often comes ... Heb. 6:7
that it would not *r* ... James 5:17
RAINBOW (6/6)
I set My *r* in the ... Gen. 9:13
and there was a *r* ... Rev. 4:3
RAINED (7/7)
r fire and brimstone ... Luke 17:29
RAINS (3/3)
r righteousness ... Hos. 10:12
RAISE (63/62)
third day He will *r* ... Hos. 6:2
in three days I will *r* ... John 2:19
and I will *r* him up at ... John 6:40
and the Lord will *r* ... James 5:15
RAISED (132/127)
be killed, and be *r* ... Matt. 16:21
just as Christ was *r* ... Rom. 6:4
Spirit of Him who *r* ... Rom. 8:11
“How are the dead *r* ... 1 Cor. 15:35
and the dead will be *r* ... 1 Cor. 15:52
and *r* us up together ... Eph. 2:6
RAISES (11/11)
For as the Father *r* ... John 5:21
but in God who *r* ... 2 Cor. 1:9
RANSOM (13/13)
to give His life a *r* ... Mark 10:45
who gave Himself a *r* ... 1 Tim. 2:6
RANSOMED (3/3)
and the *r* of the LORD ... Is. 35:10
redeemed Jacob, and *r* ... Jer. 31:11
RASH (4/4)
Do not be *r* with your ... Eccl. 5:2
RASHLY (3/3)
and do nothing *r* ... Acts 19:36
RAVENOUS (3/3)
inwardly they are *r* ... Matt. 7:15
RAVENS (5/5)
Consider the *r* ... Luke 12:24
REACHING (1/1)
r forward to those ... Phil. 3:13
READ (67/63)
day, and stood up to *r* ... Luke 4:16
hearts, known and *r* ... 2 Cor. 3:2
READER (1/1)
let the *r* understand ... Mark 13:14
READINESS (2/2)
the word with all *r* ... Acts 17:11
READING (10/9)
r the prophet Isaiah ... Acts 8:30
READS (4/4)
Blessed is he who *r* ... Rev. 1:3
READY (84/82)
and those who were *r* ... Matt. 25:10
“Lord, I am *r* ... Luke 22:33
Be *r* in season and out ... 2 Tim. 4:2
and always be *r* ... 1 Pet. 3:15
REAP (34/28)
they neither sow nor *r* ... Matt. 6:26
you knew that I *r* ... Matt. 25:26
REAPED (4/4)
you have *r* iniquity ... Hos. 10:13
REAPERS (10/10)
r are the angels ... Matt. 13:39
REAPING (3/3)
r what I did not ... Luke 19:22
REAPS (4/3)
One sows and another *r* ... John 4:37
REASON (67/67)
Come now, and let us *r* ... Is. 1:18
who asks you a *r* ... 1 Pet. 3:15
REASONED (14/14)
for three Sabbaths *r* ... Acts 17:2
REBEL (18/17)
if you refuse and *r* ... Is. 1:20
REBELLING (1/1)
more against Him by *r* ... Ps. 78:17
REBELLION (23/23)
hearts as in the *r* ... Heb. 3:8
REBELLIOUS (40/38)
day long to a *r* people ... Is. 65:2
REBUILD (8/7)
God, to *r* its ruins ... Ezra 9:9
r it as in the days of ... Amos 9:11
REBUKE (70/69)
Turn at my *r* ... Prov. 1:23
r a wise man ... Prov. 9:8
r is better than love ... Prov. 27:5
sins against you, *r* ... Luke 17:3
Do not *r* an older man ... 1 Tim. 5:1
who are sinning *r* ... 1 Tim. 5:20
“The Lord *r* you ... Jude 1:9
As many as I love, I *r* ... Rev. 3:19
REBUKED (31/31)
r the winds and the ... Matt. 8:26
r their unbelief ... Mark 16:14
but he was *r* for his ... 2 Pet. 2:16
REBUKES (9/9)
ear that hears the *r* ... Prov. 15:31
RECEIVE (173/167)
believing, you will *r* ... Matt. 21:22
and His own did not *r* ... John 1:11
will come again and *r* ... John 14:3
the world cannot *r* ... John 14:17
Ask, and you will *r* ... John 16:24
“*R* the Holy Spirit ... John 20:22
“Lord Jesus, *r* ... Acts 7:59
r the Holy Spirit ... Acts 19:2
R one who is weak ... Rom. 14:1
r the Spirit by the ... Gal. 3:2
suppose that he will *r* ... James 1:7
RECEIVED (155/153)
But as many as *r* ... John 1:12
for God has *r* him ... Rom. 14:3
For I *r* from the Lord ... 1 Cor. 11:23
have *r* Christ Jesus ... Col. 2:6
r up in glory ... 1 Tim. 3:16
RECEIVES (42/28)
r you *r* Me ... Matt. 10:40
and whoever *r* Me ... Mark 9:37
RECONCILE (4/4)
and that He might *r* ... Eph. 2:16
RECONCILED (7/6)
First be *r* to your ... Matt. 5:24
were enemies we were *r* ... Rom. 5:10
Christ’s behalf, be *r* ... 2 Cor. 5:20
RECONCILIATION (4/4)
now received the *r* ... Rom. 5:11
to us the word of *r* ... 2 Cor. 5:19
RECONCILING (2/2)
cast away is the *r* ... Rom. 11:15
God was in Christ *r* ... 2 Cor. 5:19
REDEEM (62/46)
But God will *r* my soul ... Ps. 49:15
r their life from ... Ps. 72:14
was going to *r* Israel ... Luke 24:21
r those who were ... Gal. 4:5
us, that He might *r* ... Titus 2:14
REDEEMED (60/59)
Let the *r* of the LORD ... Ps. 107:2
r shall walk there ... Is. 35:9
sea a road for the *r* ... Is. 51:10
and you shall be *r* ... Is. 52:3
and *r* His people ... Luke 1:68
Christ has *r* us from ... Gal. 3:13
that you were not *r* ... 1 Pet. 1:18
were slain, and have *r* ... Rev. 5:9

REDEEMER (18/18)
For I know that my *R*... Job 19:25
our *R* from Everlasting... Is. 63:16
REDEEMING (4/4)
r the time... Eph. 5:16
REDEMPTION (23/23)
those who looked for *r*... Luke 2:38
your *r* draws near... Luke 21:28
grace through the *r*... Rom. 3:24
the adoption, the *r*... Rom. 8:23
sanctification and *r*... 1 Cor. 1:30
In Him we have *r*... Eph. 1:7
for the day of *r*... Eph. 4:30
obtained eternal *r*... Heb. 9:12
REED (18/18)
r He will not break... Is. 42:3
r shaken by the wind... Matt. 11:7
REFINED (11/10)
us as silver is *r*... Ps. 66:10
REFINER (1/1)
He will sit as a *r*... Mal. 3:3
REFORMATION (1/1)
until the time of *r*... Heb. 9:10
REFRESH (6/6)
r my heart in the Lord... Philem. 1:20
REFRESHED (9/9)
his spirit has been *r*... 2 Cor. 7:13
for he often *r*... 2 Tim. 1:16
REFRESHES (1/1)
r the soul of his... Prov. 25:13
REFRESHING (2/2)
r may come from the... Acts 3:19
REFUGE (61/60)
eternal God is your *r*... Deut. 33:27
God is our *r* and... Ps. 46:1
who have fled for *r*... Heb. 6:18
REGARD (47/46)
r iniquity in my heart... Ps. 66:18
did not fear God nor *r*... Luke 18:2
REGARDED (13/13)
my hand and no one *r*... Prov. 1:24
r the lowly state... Luke 1:48
REGARDS (7/7)
r a rebuke will be... Prov. 13:18
REGENERATION (2/2)
to you, that in the *r*... Matt. 19:28
the washing of *r*... Titus 3:5
REGISTERED (10/10)
So all went to be *r*... Luke 2:3
REGRETTED (3/3)
but afterward he *r*... Matt. 21:29
REGULATIONS (2/2)
yourselves to *r*... Col. 2:20
REIGN (102/97)
And He will *r*... Luke 1:33
righteousness will *r*... Rom. 5:17
so grace might *r*... Rom. 5:21
do not let sin *r*... Rom. 6:12
For He must *r* till He... 1 Cor. 15:25
of Christ, and shall *r*... Rev. 20:6
REIGNED (177/164)
so that as sin *r*... Rom. 5:21
You have *r* as kings... 1 Cor. 4:8
And they lived and *r*... Rev. 20:4
REIGNS (12/12)
to Zion, "Your God *r*... Is. 52:7
Lord God Omnipotent *r*... Rev. 19:6
REJECT (10/10)
"All too well you *r*... Mark 7:9
R a divisive man... Titus 3:10
REJECTED (48/44)
He is despised and *r*... Is. 53:3
r has become the chief... Matt. 21:42
many things and be *r*... Luke 17:25
This Moses whom they *r*... Acts 7:35
to a living stone, *r*... 1 Pet. 2:4
REJECTION (1/1)
you shall know My *r*... Num. 14:34
REJECTS (6/3)
he who *r* Me *r*... Luke 10:16
REJOICE (199/187)
R in the LORD... Ps. 33:1
of Your wings I will *r*... Ps. 63:7
Let them *r* before God... Ps. 68:3
Let the heavens *r*... Ps. 96:11
Let the earth *r*... Ps. 97:1
we will *r* and be glad... Ps. 118:24
she shall *r* in time to... Prov. 31:25
R, O young man... Eccl. 11:9
your heart shall *r*... Is. 66:14
Do not *r* over me... Mic. 7:8
do not *r* in this... Luke 10:20
loved Me, you would *r*... John 14:28
but the world will *r*... John 16:20
and your heart will *r*... John 16:22
R with those who... Rom. 12:15
and in this I *r*... Phil. 1:18
faith, I am glad and *r*... Phil. 2:17
R in the Lord always... Phil. 4:4
R always... 1 Thess. 5:16
yet believing, you *r*... 1 Pet. 1:8
REJOICED (44/42)
and my spirit has *r*... Luke 1:47
In that hour Jesus *r*... Luke 10:21
Your father Abraham *r*... John 8:56
REJOICES (15/15)
glad, and my glory *r*... Ps. 16:9
but *r* in the truth... 1 Cor. 13:6
REJOICING (29/29)
come again with *r*... Ps. 126:6
he went on his way *r*... Acts 8:39
confidence and the *r*... Heb. 3:6
RELENT (17/16)
sworn and will not *r*... Ps. 110:4
sworn and will not *r*... Heb. 7:21
RELENTED (8/8)
and God *r* from the... Jon. 3:10
RELENTING (1/1)
I am weary of *r*... Jer. 15:6
RELIGION (5/5)
in self-imposed *r*... Col. 2:23
and undefiled *r*... James 1:27
RELIGIOUS (2/2)
things you are very *r*... Acts 17:22
REMAIN (111/108)
you, that My joy may *r*... John 15:11
your fruit should *r*... John 15:16
"If I will that he *r*... John 21:22
the greater part *r*... 1 Cor. 15:6
we who are alive and *r*... 1 Thess. 4:15
the things which *r*... Rev. 3:2
REMAINS (48/47)
"While the earth *r*... Gen. 8:22
Therefore your sin *r*... John 9:41
There *r* therefore a... Heb. 4:9
REMEMBER (164/160)
R the Sabbath day... Ex. 20:8
but we will *r* the name... Ps. 20:7
r Your name in the... Ps. 119:55
R now your Creator... Eccl. 12:1
r the former things... Is. 43:18
and their sin I will *r*... Jer. 31:34
in wrath *r* mercy... Hab. 3:2
and to *r* His holy... Luke 1:72
R Lot's wife... Luke 17:32
r the words of the... Acts 20:35
R that Jesus Christ... 2 Tim. 2:8
R those who rule... Heb. 13:7
REMEMBERED (51/51)
Then God *r* Noah... Gen. 8:1
r His covenant with... Ex. 2:24
yea, we wept when we *r*... Ps. 137:1
And Peter *r* the word... Matt. 26:75
r the word of the Lord... Acts 11:16
REMEMBRANCE (33/32)
I call to *r* my song... Ps. 77:6
Put Me in *r*... Is. 43:26
do this in *r* of Me... Luke 22:19
do this in *r* of Me... 1 Cor. 11:24
REMISSION (9/9)
repentance for the *r*... Mark 1:4
Jesus Christ for the *r*... Acts 2:38
where there is *r*... Heb. 10:18
REMNANT (85/83)
The *r* will return... Is. 10:21
time there is a *r*... Rom. 11:5
REMORSEFUL (1/1)
been condemned, was *r*... Matt. 27:3
REMOVE (56/53)
r your lampstand... Rev. 2:5
REMOVED (63/60)
Though the earth be *r*... Ps. 46:2
and the hills be *r*... Is. 54:10
this mountain, 'Be *r*... Matt. 21:21
REND (2/2)
So *r* your heart... Joel 2:13
RENDER (22/22)
What shall I *r* to the... Ps. 116:12
"*R* therefore to Caesar... Matt. 22:21
RENEW (8/8)
r a steadfast spirit... Ps. 51:10
on the LORD shall *r*... Is. 40:31
RENEWED (5/5)
that your youth is *r*... Ps. 103:5
inward man is being *r*... 2 Cor. 4:16
and be *r* in the spirit... Eph. 4:23
RENEWING (2/2)
transformed by the *r*... Rom. 12:2
RENOWN (6/6)
were of old, men of *r*... Gen. 6:4
REPAID (11/11)
Shall evil be *r*... Jer. 18:20
REPAY (47/45)
again, I will *r*... Luke 10:35
because they cannot *r*... Luke 14:14
R no one evil for evil... Rom. 12:17
is Mine, I will *r*... Rom. 12:19
r their parents... 1 Tim. 5:4
REPAYS (6/6)
the LORD, who fully *r*... Is. 66:6
REPENT (34/32)
I abhor myself, and *r*... Job 42:6
"*R*, for the kingdom... Matt. 3:2
you *r* you will all... Luke 13:3
said to them, "*R*... Acts 2:38
men everywhere to *r*... Acts 17:30
be zealous and *r*... Rev. 3:19
REPENTANCE (24/24)
you with water unto *r*... Matt. 3:11
a baptism of *r* for the... Mark 1:4
persons who need no *r*... Luke 15:7
renew them again to *r*... Heb. 6:6
found no place for *r*... Heb. 12:17
all should come to *r*... 2 Pet. 3:9
REPENTED (7/7)
it, because they *r*... Matt. 12:41
REPETITIONS (1/1)
r as the heathen do... Matt. 6:7
REPORT (41/38)
Who has believed our *r*... Is. 53:1
things are of good *r*... Phil. 4:8
REPROACH (89/87)
R has broken my heart... Ps. 69:20
with dishonor comes *r*... Prov. 18:3
not remember the *r*... Is. 54:4
because I bore the *r*... Jer. 31:19
these things You *r*... Luke 11:45
lest he fall into *r*... 1 Tim. 3:7
esteeming the *r*... Heb. 11:26
and without *r*... James 1:5
REPROACHED (13/12)
If you are *r* for the... 1 Pet. 4:14
REPROACHES (14/14)
is not an enemy who *r*... Ps. 55:12
in infirmities, in *r*... 2 Cor. 12:10
REPROOF (1/1)
for doctrine, for *r*... 2 Tim. 3:16
REPROOFS (1/1)
R of instruction are... Prov. 6:23
REPUTATION (5/5)
seven men of good *r*... Acts 6:3
made Himself of no *r*... Phil. 2:7
REQUEST (26/26)
He gave them their *r*... Ps. 106:15
For Jews *r* a sign... 1 Cor. 1:22
REQUESTS (2/2)
r be made known... Phil. 4:6
REQUIRE (26/25)
offering You did not *r*... Ps. 40:6
what does the LORD *r*... Mic. 6:8
REQUIRED (18/17)
your soul will be *r*... Luke 12:20
him much will be *r*... Luke 12:48
REQUIREMENTS (2/2)
keeps the righteous *r*... Rom. 2:26
r that was against us... Col. 2:14
RESERVED (15/15)
"I have *r* for Myself... Rom. 11:4
r in heaven for you... 1 Pet. 1:4
habitation, He has *r*... Jude 1:6
RESIST (10/10)
r an evil person... Matt. 5:39
r the Holy Spirit... Acts 7:51
R the devil and he... James 4:7
RESISTED (4/4)
For who has *r* His will... Rom. 9:19
for he has greatly *r*... 2 Tim. 4:15
You have not yet *r*... Heb. 12:4
RESISTS (4/3)
"God *r* the proud... James 4:6
for "God *r* the proud... 1 Pet. 5:5
RESPECT (17/17)
of the law held in *r*... Acts 5:34
and we paid them *r*... Heb. 12:9
RESPECTED (4/4)
And the LORD *r* Abel... Gen. 4:4
REST (305/295)
is the Sabbath of *r*... Ex. 31:15
to build a house of *r*... 1 Chr. 28:2
R in the LORD... Ps. 37:7
fly away and be at *r*... Ps. 55:6
"This is the *r*... Is. 28:12
is the place of My *r*... Is. 66:1
and I will give you *r*... Matt. 11:28
shall not enter My *r*... Heb. 3:11
remains therefore a *r*... Heb. 4:9
that they should *r*... Rev. 6:11
"that they may *r*... Rev. 14:13
But the *r* of the dead... Rev. 20:5
RESTED (55/55)
He had done, and He *r*... Gen. 2:2
"And God *r* on the... Heb. 4:4
RESTORATION (1/1)
until the times of *r*... Acts 3:21
RESTORE (56/55)
R to me the joy... Ps. 51:12
"So I will *r* to you... Joel 2:25
and will *r* all things... Matt. 17:11
You at this time *r*... Acts 1:6
who are spiritual *r*... Gal. 6:1
RESTORES (4/4)
He *r* my soul... Ps. 23:3
RESTRAINS (5/4)
only He who now *r*... 2 Thess. 2:7

RESTRAINT (4/4)
they break all *r* .... Hos. 4:2
RESTS (5/5)
r quietly in the heart .... Prov. 14:33
RESURRECTION (41/40)
to her, "I am the *r*.......... John 11:25
them Jesus and the *r*.......... Acts 17:18
the likeness of His *r*............Rom. 6:5
say that there is no *r* .... 1 Cor. 15:12
and the power of His *r* .... Phil. 3:10
obtain a better *r* ....Heb. 11:35
This is the first *r*................Rev. 20:5
RETAIN (9/9)
r the sins of any ....John 20:23
RETURN (282/258)
womb, naked shall he *r*..........Eccl. 5:15
let him *r* to the LORD..............Is. 55:7
me, and I will *r* ....Jer. 31:18
"*R* to Me," says the LORD.........Zech. 1:3
he says, 'I will *r* ....Matt. 12:44
RETURNED (187/185)
astray, but have now *r*..........1 Pet. 2:25
RETURNING (9/9)
r evil for evil or ....1 Pet. 3:9
RETURNS (6/6)
As a dog *r* to his own.......... Prov. 26:11
"A dog *r* to his own............ 2 Pet. 2:22
REVEAL (12/12)
the Son wills to *r* Him .... Matt. 11:27
r His Son in me.....................Gal. 1:16
REVEALED (58/57)
things which are *r* .... Deut. 29:29
righteousness to be *r*..............Is. 56:1
the Son of Man is *r*............ Luke 17:30
the wrath of God is *r* .... Rom. 1:18
glory which shall be *r* ....Rom. 8:18
the Lord Jesus is *r* ....2 Thess. 1:7
lawless one will be *r*........... 2 Thess. 2:8
ready to be *r* in the............. 1 Pet. 1:5
when His glory is *r*.................1 Pet. 4:13
r what we shall be..............1 John 3:2
REVEALER (1/1)
Lord of kings, and a *r* .... Dan. 2:47
REVEALING (1/1)
waits for the *r* ....Rom. 8:19
REVEALS (11/10)
as a talebearer *r* ....Prov. 20:19
r His secret to His............... Amos 3:7
REVELATION (15/15)
Where there is no *r* ....Prov. 29:18
it came through the *r* ....Gal. 1:12
spirit of wisdom and *r*........... Eph. 1:17
r He made known to .... Eph. 3:3
and glory at the *r* .... 1 Pet. 1:7
REVERENCE (9/9)
and *r* My sanctuary ....Lev. 19:30
God acceptably with *r* .... Heb. 12:28
REVERENT (6/6)
man who is always *r* ....Prov. 28:14
their wives must be *r*...........1 Tim. 3:11
REVILE (7/7)
are you when they *r*............ Matt. 5:11
r God's high priest ....Acts 23:4
REVILED (6/6)
crucified with Him *r* ....Mark 15:32
who, when He was *r*.............1 Pet. 2:23
REVIVAL (1/1)
give us a measure of *r*.......... Ezra 9:8
REVIVE (20/19)
Will You not *r* us.....................Ps. 85:6
two days He will *r*................ Hos. 6:2
REVIVED (6/6)
came, sin *r* and I died ....Rom. 7:9
REWARD (55/54)
exceedingly great *r* .... Gen. 15:1
look, and see the *r* .... Ps. 91:8
behold, His *r* is with............. Is. 40:10
for great is your *r*................ Matt. 5:12
you, they have their *r*...........Matt. 6:2
by no means lose his *r* ....Matt. 10:42
we receive the due *r*............ Luke 23:41
will receive his own *r*............1 Cor. 3:8
cheat you of your *r*............. Col. 2:18
for he looked to the *r*...........Heb. 11:26
quickly, and My *r* ....Rev. 22:12
REWARDS (4/4)
Whoever *r* evil for ....Prov. 17:13
and follows after *r* ....Is. 1:23
RICH (94/93)
Abram was very *r*.................Gen. 13:2
The *r* and the poor...............Prov. 22:2
r rules over the poor ....Prov. 22:7
r man is wise in his .... Prov. 28:11
do not curse the *r*............. Eccl. 10:20
it is hard for a *r*.................Matt. 19:23
to you who are *r* .... Luke 6:24
from the *r* man's table............ Luke 16:21
for he was very *r*.................. Luke 18:23
You are already *r* ....1 Cor. 4:8
though He was *r* .... 2 Cor. 8:9
who desire to be *r*................ 1 Tim. 6:9
of this world to be *r* ....James 2:5
you say, 'I am *r* .... Rev. 3:17
RICHES (92/89)
R and honor are .... Prov. 8:18
R do not profit......................Prov. 11:4
in his *r* will fall.................. Prov. 11:28
of the wise is their *r*........... Prov. 14:24
Houses and *r* are an........... Prov. 19:14
of the LORD are *r*................Prov. 22:4
r are not forever ....Prov. 27:24
do you despise the *r* ....Rom. 2:4
might make known the *r* ...... Rom. 9:23
what are the *r* ....Eph. 1:18
show the exceeding *r*..............Eph. 2:7
the unsearchable *r*................. Eph. 3:8
r than the treasures...............Heb. 11:26
to receive power and *r* .... Rev. 5:12
RICHLY (2/2)
Christ dwell in you *r* .... Col. 3:16
God, who gives us *r* .... 1 Tim. 6:17
RIGHT (358/329)
the *r* of the firstborn .... Deut. 21:17
"Is your heart *r* ....2 Kin. 10:15
Lord, "Sit at My *r*...................Ps. 110:1
is a way which seems *r* .... Prov. 14:12
clothed and in his *r* .... Mark 5:15
to them He gave the *r* .... John 1:12
your heart is not *r* ....Acts 8:21
seven stars in His *r* .... Rev. 2:1
RIGHTEOUS (262/248)
also destroy the *r* ....Gen. 18:23
and they justify the *r*........... Deut. 25:1
that he could be *r*..................Job 15:14
"The *r* see it and .... Job 22:19
r shows mercy and................. Ps. 37:21
I have not seen the *r* .... Ps. 37:25
the LORD loves the *r* .... Ps. 146:8
r is a well of life.................Prov. 10:11
r will be gladness ....Prov. 10:28
r will be delivered...............Prov. 11:21
r will be recompensed ....Prov. 11:31
the prayer of the *r* .... Prov. 15:29
r are bold as a lion .... Prov. 28:1
r considers the cause .... Prov. 29:7
Do not be overly *r* ....Eccl. 7:16
event happens to the *r* .... Eccl. 9:2
with My *r* right hand..............Is. 41:10
By His knowledge My *r*............ Is. 53:11
The *r* perishes .... Is. 57:1
they sell the *r*...................... Amos 2:6
not come to call the *r* .... Matt. 9:13
r men desired to see .... Matt. 13:17
r will shine forth as .... Matt. 13:43
that they were *r*................... Luke 18:9
"Certainly this was a *r*......... Luke 23:47
"There is none *r* ....Rom. 3:10
r man will one die .... Rom. 5:7
Jesus Christ the *r* .... 1 John 2:1
RIGHTEOUSLY (8/8)
should live soberly, *r*............ Titus 2:12
to Him who judges *r* ....1 Pet. 2:23
RIGHTEOUSNESS (311/292)
it to him for *r*.......................Gen. 15:6
I put on *r*............................ Job 29:14
I call, O God of my *r*............... Ps. 4:1
from the LORD, and *r*............... Ps. 24:5
shall speak of Your *r* ....Ps. 35:28
the good news of *r* ....Ps. 40:9
heavens declare His *r* ....Ps. 50:6
r and peace have..................... Ps. 85:10
R will go before Him .... Ps. 85:13
r endures forever .... Ps. 111:3
r delivers from death .... Prov. 10:2
The *r* of the blameless............Prov. 11:5
the way of *r* is life .... Prov. 12:28
R exalts a nation.................. Prov. 14:34
He who follows *r*.................. Prov. 21:21
r lodged in it .... Is. 1:21
r He shall judge...................... Is. 11:4
in the LORD I have *r*................. Is. 45:24
r will be forever........................Is. 51:8
I will declare your *r* ....Is. 57:12
r as a breastplate ....Is. 59:17
r goes forth as ....Is. 62:1
THE LORD OUR *R*.....................Jer. 23:6
to David a Branch of *r*............Jer. 33:15
The *r* of the righteous ....Ezek. 18:20
who turn many to *r* ....Dan. 12:3
to fulfill all *r*.......................Matt. 3:15
exceeds the *r* of the ....Matt. 5:20
to you in the way of *r*..........Matt. 21:32
For in it the *r* .... Rom. 1:17
even the *r* of God ....Rom. 3:22
accounted to him for *r* ....Rom. 4:22
r will reign in life .... Rom. 5:17
might reign through *r*............ Rom. 5:21
ignorant of God's *r*.................Rom. 10:3
we might become the *r*..........2 Cor. 5:21
the breastplate of *r*...................Eph. 6:14
not having my own *r*............ Phil. 3:9
r which we have .... Titus 3:5
does not produce the *r*.........James 1:20
a preacher of *r*........................2 Pet. 2:5
a new earth in which *r*...........2 Pet. 3:13
who practices *r* ....1 John 2:29
He who practices *r*..............1 John 3:7
RIGHTLY (13/13)
wise uses knowledge *r* .... Prov. 15:2
r dividing the word ....2 Tim. 2:15
RISE (154/152)
for He makes His sun *r*.......... Matt. 5:45
third day He will *r*.................Matt. 20:19
third day He will *r*................ Luke 18:33
be the first to *r*.....................Acts 26:23
in Christ will *r* ....1 Thess. 4:16
RISEN (42/42)
women there has not *r*......... Matt. 11:11
disciples that He is *r* ....Matt. 28:7
"The Lord is *r*........................Luke 24:34
then Christ is not *r*.............1 Cor. 15:13
if Christ is not *r*..................1 Cor. 15:17
But now Christ is *r*..............1 Cor. 15:20
RIVER (164/138)
peace to her like a *r* .... Is. 66:12
he showed me a pure *r* .... Rev. 22:1
RIVERS (67/62)
By the *r* of Babylon ....Ps. 137:1
All the *r* run into the ....Eccl. 1:7
his heart will flow *r* ....John 7:38
ROAR (21/19)
The LORD also will *r*............... Joel 3:16
ROARING (14/14)
and the waves *r*.................. Luke 21:25
walks about like a *r* ....1 Pet. 5:8
ROARS (6/6)
"The LORD *r* from.................. Amos 1:2
as when a lion *r*......................Rev. 10:3
ROB (8/7)
"Will a man *r* God....................Mal. 3:8
ROBBED (14/13)
r other churches.................2 Cor. 11:8
ROBBER (6/6)
is a thief and a *r* .... John 10:1
Barabbas was a *r*.................John 18:40
ROBBERS (12/12)
also crucified two *r* .... Mark 15:27
Me are thieves and *r* .... John 10:8
ROBBERY (7/7)
did not consider it *r*................ Phil. 2:6
ROBE (49/48)
'Bring out the best *r*........... Luke 15:22
on Him a purple *r*.................. John 19:2
Then a white *r* was .... Rev. 6:11
ROBES (17/17)
have stained all My *r*............... Is. 63:3
go around in long *r* ....Luke 20:46
clothed with white *r*................ Rev. 7:9
ROCK (123/111)
you shall strike the *r* .... Ex. 17:6
and struck the *r*.....................Num. 20:11
For their *r* is not ....Deut. 32:31
And who is a *r* .... 2 Sam. 22:32
Blessed be my *R* .... 2 Sam. 22:47
For You are my *r*..................... Ps. 31:3
r that is higher than................. Ps. 61:2
been mindful of the *R*................. Is. 17:10
shadow of a great *r*................. Is. 32:2
his house on the *r* .... Matt. 7:24
r I will build My.................. Matt. 16:18
stumbling stone and *r* .... Rom. 9:33
R that followed them............1 Cor. 10:4
ROD (93/83)
Your *r* and Your staff.................Ps. 23:4
shall come forth a *R* .... Is. 11:1
rule them with a *r*................... Rev. 2:27
ROOM (53/52)
you a large upper *r*.............. Mark 14:15
no *r* for them in the............... Luke 2:7
into the upper *r*.................... Acts 1:13
ROOT (36/35)
day there shall be a *R* .... Is. 11:10
because they had no *r*............Matt. 13:6
of money is a *r*.....................1 Tim. 6:10
lest any *r* of.............................Heb. 12:15
I am the *R* and the ....Rev. 22:16
ROOTED (3/3)
r and built up in Him .... Col. 2:7
ROSE (100/99)
end Christ died and *r*............Rom. 14:9
buried, and that He *r*............. 1 Cor. 15:4
that Jesus died and *r*.........1 Thess. 4:14
RULE (61/58)
and he shall *r*.........................Gen. 3:16
puts an end to all *r*.............1 Cor. 15:24
let the peace of God *r* .... Col. 3:15
Let the elders who *r*.............1 Tim. 5:17
Remember those who *r* ....Heb. 13:7
RULER (77/75)
to Me the One to be *r*................Mic. 5:2
by Beelzebub, the *r*............. Matt. 12:24
the *r* of this world.................. John 12:31
'Who made you a *r*................Acts 7:27

RULERS (81/73)
and the *r* take counsel............. Ps. 2:2
"You know that the *r*......... Matt. 20:25
which none of the *r*............1 Cor. 2:8
powers, against the *r*...........Eph. 6:12
RULES (16/16)
that the Most High *r*...........Dan. 4:17
that the Most High *r*.......... Dan. 4:32
r his own house well.........1 Tim. 3:4
RULING (4/4)
r their children...............1 Tim. 3:12
RUMORS (3/3)
hear of wars and *r*............Matt. 24:6
RUN (73/67)
r and not be weary............ Is. 40:31
us, and let us *r*...............Heb. 12:1

S

SABAOTH (2/2)
S had left us a............... Rom. 9:29
ears of the Lord of *S*...........James 5:4
SABBATH (132/111)
"Remember the *S*.............. Ex. 20:8
S was made for man ....Mark 2:27
SABBATHS (37/35)
S you shall keep .... Ex. 31:13
SACRIFICE (185/175)
to the LORD than *s*............ Prov. 21:3
For the LORD has a *s*............ Is. 34:6
of My offerings they *s*............Hos. 8:13
LORD has prepared a *s*.......... Zeph. 1:7
desire mercy and not *s*........ Matt. 9:13
an offering and a *s*............... Eph. 5:2
put away sin by the *s*............ Heb. 9:26
no longer remains a *s*......... Heb. 10:26
offer the *s* of praise ....Heb. 13:15
SACRIFICED (35/35)
s their sons and their........... Ps. 106:37
SACRIFICES (106/103)
The *s* of God are a...............Ps. 51:17
multitude of your *s*................ Is. 1:11
priests, to offer up *s*............Heb. 7:27
s God is well pleased...........Heb. 13:16
SAFE (12/12)
he has received him *s*........ Luke 15:27
SAFELY (28/28)
make them lie down *s*............Hos. 2:18
SAFETY (18/18)
say, "Peace and *s*...............1 Thess. 5:3
SAINTS (94/92)
s who are on the earth........... Ps. 16:3
does not forsake His *s*.............Ps. 37:28
is the death of His *s*..............Ps. 116:15
war against the *s*...................Dan. 7:21
Jesus, called to be *s*............1 Cor. 1:2
the least of all the *s*............ Eph. 3:8
be glorified in His *s*.........2 Thess. 1:10
all delivered to the *s*.............. Jude 1:3
shed the blood of *s*..............Rev. 16:6
SALT (42/36)
shall season with *s*................ Lev. 2:13
"You are the *s*.................. Matt. 5:13
s loses its flavor................ Mark 9:50
SALVATION (162/156)
still, and see the *s*................ Ex. 14:13
S belongs to the LORD.............. Ps. 3:8
is my light and my *s*................ Ps. 27:1
God is the God of *s*................Ps. 68:20
joy in the God of my *s*............ Hab. 3:18
raised up a horn of *s*............... Luke 1:69
Nor is there *s* in any...............Acts 4:12
the power of God to *s*............Rom. 1:16
now is the day of *s*.............. 2 Cor. 6:2
work out your own *s*..............Phil. 2:12
chose you for *s*............... 2 Thess. 2:13
neglect so great a *s*............... Heb. 2:3
SAMARITAN (4/4)
a drink from me, a *S*.............John 4:9
SANCTIFICATION (5/5)
will of God, your *s*..............1 Thess. 4:3
SANCTIFIED (38/37)
they also may be *s*...............John 17:19
washed, but you were *s*.......... 1 Cor. 6:11
for it is *s* by the .... 1 Tim. 4:5
SANCTIFIES (8/8)
For both He who *s*...............Heb. 2:11
SANCTIFY (36/34)
s My great name.............. Ezek. 36:23
S them by Your.................John 17:17
that He might *s*...................Eph. 5:26
SANCTUARY (158/153)
let them make Me a *s*..............Ex. 25:8
and the earthly *s*...................Heb. 9:1
SAND (31/29)
descendants as the *s*...........Gen. 32:12
innumerable as the *s*............ Heb. 11:12
SAT (175/165)
into heaven, and *s*............. Mark 16:19
And He who *s* there was..........Rev. 4:3
SATAN (54/48)
before the LORD, and *S*.............Job 1:6
"Away with you, *S*...................Matt. 4:10
"Get behind Me, *S*................Matt. 16:23
"How can *S* cast out............Mark 3:23
S has asked for you .... Luke 22:31
to the working of *S*.............2 Thess. 2:9
known the depths of *S*...........Rev. 2:24
years have expired, *S*..............Rev. 20:7
SATIATED (2/2)
s the weary soul ....Jer. 31:25
SATISFIED (50/50)
I shall be *s* when I....................Ps. 17:15
that are never *s*.................. Prov. 30:15
of His soul, and be *s*................ Is. 53:11
SATISFIES (2/2)
s the longing soul.................. Ps. 107:9
SATISFY (13/13)
s us early with Your .... Ps. 90:14
long life I will *s*.................... Ps. 91:16
for what does not *s*.................. Is. 55:2
SAVE (160/156)
Oh, *s* me for Your..................... Ps. 6:4
s the children of the............... Ps. 72:4
s the souls of the................. Ps. 72:13
that it cannot *s*........................Is. 59:1
s you and deliver you ....Jer. 15:20
other, That he may *s*............Hos. 13:10
Jesus, for He will *s*.............. Matt. 1:21
s his life will lose it...............Matt. 16:25
s that which was ....Matt. 18:11
let Him *s* Himself if................Luke 23:35
but to *s* the world.................John 12:47
the world to *s* sinners...........1 Tim. 1:15
SAVED (101/101)
"He *s* others....................Matt. 27:42
That we should be *s*...............Luke 1:71
"Your faith has *s*....................Luke 7:50
through Him might be *s*........ John 3:17
them, saying, "Be *s*.................. Acts 2:40
what must I do to be *s*......... Acts 16:30
which also you are *s*............ 1 Cor. 15:2
grace you have been *s*............. Eph. 2:8
to His mercy He *s*.................. Titus 3:5
of those who are *s*.................Rev. 21:24
SAVES (6/6)
antitype which now *s*..........1 Pet. 3:21
SAVIOR (36/36)
I, the LORD, am your *S*............. Is. 60:16
rejoiced in God my *S*............. Luke 1:47
the city of David a *S*..............Luke 2:11
up for Israel a *S*......................Acts 13:23
God, who is the *S*.................1 Tim. 4:10
God and *S* Jesus Christ .... Titus 2:13
SAWN (1/1)
stoned, they were *s*.............. Heb. 11:37
SAY (1,052/999)
But I *s* to you that............... Matt. 5:22
"But who do you *s*............... Matt. 16:15
SAYING (1,430/1,396)
This is a faithful *s*...............1 Tim. 1:15
SAYINGS (19/19)
whoever hears these *s*............ Matt. 7:24
SCALES (27/26)
on it had a pair of *s*................Rev. 6:5
SCARLET (49/49)
your sins are like *s*..................Is. 1:18
SCATTER (36/36)
I will *s* you among the.........Lev. 26:33
SCATTERED (77/75)
"Israel is like *s* sheep...........Jer. 50:17
the sheep will be *s*............. Mark 14:27
SCATTERS (10/10)
not gather with Me *s*..........Matt. 12:30
SCEPTER (19/15)
s shall not depart .... Gen. 49:10
SCHEMER (2/2)
will be called a *s*................ Prov. 24:8
SCHEMES (9/9)
sought out many *s*.................. Eccl. 7:29
SCHISM (1/1)
there should be no *s*..........1 Cor. 12:25
SCHOOL (1/1)
daily in the *s* of......................Acts 19:9
SCOFF (3/3)
They *s* at kings.........................Hab. 1:10
SCOFFER (11/11)
"He who corrects a *s*............. Prov. 9:7
s is an abomination...............Prov. 24:9
SCOFFERS (4/4)
s will come in the ....2 Pet. 3:3
SCORCHED (4/4)
And men were *s* with.............. Rev. 16:9
SCORN (9/9)
My friends *s* me....................... Job 16:20
SCORNS (5/5)
He *s* the scornful ....Prov. 3:34
SCORPIONS (5/5)
on serpents and *s*.................. Luke 10:19
They had tails like *s*................ Rev. 9:10
SCOURGE (11/11)
will mock Him, and *s*..............Mark 10:34
SCOURGES (6/6)
s every son whom.................. Heb. 12:6
SCRIBES (67/67)
"Beware of the *s*.................Mark 12:38
SCRIPTURE (32/32)
S cannot be broken ....John 10:35
All *S* is given by......................2 Tim. 3:16
SCRIPTURES (21/21)
S must be fulfilled ....Mark 14:49
SCROLL (35/33)
eat this *s*, and go..................... Ezek. 3:1
the sky receded as a *s*.............. Rev. 6:14
SEA (390/340)
drowned in the Red *S*.............. Ex. 15:4
who go down to the *s*............... Ps. 107:23
and the *s* obey Him.................Matt. 8:27
throne there was a *s*..................Rev. 4:6
there was no more *s*................ Rev. 21:1
SEAL (29/28)
stands, having this *s*............ 2 Tim. 2:19
SEALED (34/24)
by whom you were *s*............. Eph. 4:30
SEAM (3/3)
tunic was without *s*.............John 19:23
SÉANCE (1/1)
"Please conduct a *s*............1 Sam. 28:8
SEARCH (48/46)
glory of kings is to *s*.............. Prov. 25:2
s the Scriptures......................John 5:39
SEARCHED (21/21)
s the Scriptures.......................Acts 17:11
SEARCHES (8/8)
For the Spirit *s*.....................1 Cor. 2:10
SEASON (31/30)
Be ready in *s* and out............2 Tim. 4:2
SEASONED (5/4)
how shall it be *s*.................... Matt. 5:13
SEASONS (10/10)
the times and the *s*...............1 Thess. 5:1
SEAT (62/56)
shall make a mercy *s*.............. Ex. 25:17
before the judgment *s*...........2 Cor. 5:10
SEATS (6/6)
at feasts, the best *s*...............Matt. 23:6
SECRET (59/56)
s things belong .... Deut. 29:29
in the *s* place of His.................. Ps. 27:5
Father who is in the *s* ....Matt. 6:6
SECRETLY (34/34)
He lies in wait *s*....................... Ps. 10:9
SECRETS (9/9)
For He knows the *s*..................... Ps. 44:21
God will judge the *s*..............Rom. 2:16
SECT (6/6)
to the strictest *s*................... Acts 26:5
SECURELY (10/10)
nation that dwells *s*............... Jer. 49:31
SEDUCED (5/5)
flattering lips she *s*.............. Prov. 7:21
SEE (705/662)
in my flesh I shall *s*.............. Job 19:26
for they shall *s* God ....Matt. 5:8
seeing they do not *s*............. Matt. 13:13
rejoiced to *s* My day..................John 8:56
They shall *s* His face ....Rev. 22:4
SEED (113/103)
He shall see His *s*................... Is. 53:10
S were the promises................ Gal. 3:16
you are Abraham's *s*............... Gal. 3:29
SEEDS (5/5)
the good *s* are the...................Matt. 13:38
SEEK (243/229)
pray and *s* My face..................2 Chr. 7:14
Yet they *s* Me daily...................... Is. 58:2
s, and you will find.....................Matt. 7:7
of Man has come to *s*.............. Luke 19:10
You will *s* Me and ....John 7:34
For all *s* their own.....................Phil. 2:21
s those things which .... Col. 3:1
SEEKING (38/38)
like a roaring lion, *s*.................1 Pet. 5:8
SEEKS (41/38)
There is none who *s*............ Rom. 3:11
SEEMS (36/34)
There is a way which *s*......... Prov. 14:12
SEEN (274/259)
s God face to face .... Gen. 32:30
No one has *s* God at .... John 1:18
s Me has *s* the........................ John 14:9
things which are not *s*..............2 Cor. 4:18
SEES (55/53)
s his brother in need.............1 John 3:17
SELF-CONFIDENT (1/1)
a fool rages and is *s*............. Prov. 14:16
SELF-CONTROL (8/7)
gentleness, *s*........................... Gal. 5:23
to knowledge *s*........................2 Pet. 1:6
SELF-CONTROLLED (1/1)
just, holy, *s*............................. Titus 1:8
SELF-SEEKING (3/3)
envy and *s* exist.....................James 3:16
SELL (32/31)
s whatever you have..............Mark 10:21

SEND (231/222)
"Behold, I *s* you out . . . . Matt. 10:16
has sent Me, I also *s* . . . . John 20:21
SENSES (2/2)
of use have their *s* . . . . Heb. 5:14
SENSIBLY (1/1)
who can answer *s* . . . . Prov. 26:16
SENSUAL (2/2)
but is earthly, *s* . . . . James 3:15
SENT (688/665)
unless they are *s* . . . . Rom. 10:15
SEPARATED (33/33)
it pleased God, who *s* . . . . Gal. 1:15
SEPARATES (4/4)
who repeats a matter *s* . . . . Prov. 17:9
SEPARATION (10/8)
the middle wall of *s* . . . . Eph. 2:14
SERAPHIM (2/2)
Above it stood *s* . . . . Is. 6:2
SERIOUS (7/7)
therefore be *s* and . . . . 1 Pet. 4:7
SERPENT (42/39)
s was more cunning . . . . Gen. 3:1
"Make a fiery *s* . . . . Num. 21:8
Moses lifted up the *s* . . . . John 3:14
SERPENTS (14/14)
be wise as *s* . . . . Matt. 10:16
SERVANT (508/462)
s will rule over a son . . . . Prov. 17:2
good and faithful *s* . . . . Matt. 25:21
SERVANTS (464/430)
are unprofitable *s* . . . . Luke 17:10
SERVE (214/201)
to be served, but to *s* . . . . Matt. 20:28
but through love *s* . . . . Gal. 5:13
SERVES (10/8)
If anyone *s* Me . . . . John 12:26
SERVICE (105/96)
is your reasonable *s* . . . . Rom. 12:1
with goodwill doing *s* . . . . Eph. 6:7
SERVING (20/20)
fervent in spirit, *s* . . . . Rom. 12:11
SET (619/596)
"See, I have *s* . . . . Deut. 30:15
s aside the grace . . . . Gal. 2:21
SETTLE (11/11)
Therefore *s* it in . . . . Luke 21:14
SETTLED (15/15)
O LORD, Your word is *s* . . . . Ps. 119:89
SEVEN (433/365)
s churches which are . . . . Rev. 1:4
SEVENTY (67/66)
S weeks are . . . . Dan. 9:24
SEVERE (29/29)
not to be too *s* . . . . 2 Cor. 2:5
SEVERITY (2/1)
the goodness and *s* . . . . Rom. 11:22
SHADE (12/12)
may nest under its *s* . . . . Mark 4:32
SHADOW (60/58)
In the *s* of His hand . . . . Is. 49:2
the law, having a *s* . . . . Heb. 10:1
SHAKE (40/40)
s the earth . . . . Is. 2:19
I will *s* all nations . . . . Hag. 2:7
SHAKEN (32/31)
not to be soon *s* . . . . 2 Thess. 2:2
SHAKES (7/6)
s the Wilderness . . . . Ps. 29:8
SHAME (115/109)
never be put to *s* . . . . Joel 2:26
to put to *s* the wise . . . . 1 Cor. 1:27
glory is in their *s* . . . . Phil. 3:19
SHAMEFUL (8/8)
For it is *s* even to . . . . Eph. 5:12
SHARE (20/19)
to do good and to *s* . . . . Heb. 13:16
SHARING (3/3)
for your liberal *s* . . . . 2 Cor. 9:13
SHARP (23/21)
S as a two-edged sword . . . . Prov. 5:4
SHARPEN (5/5)
s their tongue like a . . . . Ps. 64:3
SHARPNESS (1/1)
I should use *s* . . . . 2 Cor. 13:10
SHEATH (8/8)
your sword into the *s* . . . . John 18:11
SHEAVES (11/10)
bringing his *s* . . . . Ps. 126:6
gather them like *s* . . . . Mic. 4:12
SHED (44/42)
which is *s* for many . . . . Matt. 26:28
SHEDDING (2/2)
blood, and without *s* . . . . Heb. 9:22
SHEEP (193/182)
s will be scattered . . . . Zech. 13:7
having a hundred *s* . . . . Luke 15:4
and I know My *s* . . . . John 10:14
"He was led as a *s* . . . . Acts 8:32
SHEEPFOLDS (6/6)
lie down among the *s* . . . . Ps. 68:13

SHEET (2/2)
object like a great *s* . . . . Acts 10:11
SHELTER (13/13)
the LORD will be a *s* . . . . Joel 3:16
SHELTERS (2/2)
s him all the day long . . . . Deut. 33:12
SHEOL (18/18)
not leave my soul in *S* . . . . Ps. 16:10
the belly of *S* I cried . . . . Jon. 2:2
SHEPHERD (55/52)
The LORD is my *s* . . . . Ps. 23:1
His flock like a *s* . . . . Is. 40:11
'I will strike the *S* . . . . Matt. 26:31
"I am the good *s* . . . . John 10:11
the dead, that great *S* . . . . Heb. 13:20
S the flock of God . . . . 1 Pet. 5:2
when the Chief *S* . . . . 1 Pet. 5:4
SHEPHERDS (43/38)
And I will give you *s* . . . . Jer. 3:15
s have led them astray . . . . Jer. 50:6
SHIELD (51/50)
I am your *s* . . . . Gen. 15:1
truth shall be your *s* . . . . Ps. 91:4
all, taking the *s* . . . . Eph. 6:16
SHINE (29/29)
LORD make His face *s* . . . . Num. 6:25
among whom you *s* . . . . Phil. 2:15
SHINED (1/1)
them a light has *s* . . . . Is. 9:2
SHINES (6/6)
And the light *s* . . . . John 1:5
SHINING (13/13)
light is already *s* . . . . 1 John 2:8
SHIPS (37/33)
down to the sea in *s* . . . . Ps. 107:23
SHIPWRECK (1/1)
faith have suffered *s* . . . . 1 Tim. 1:19
SHOOT (19/18)
they *s* out the lip . . . . Ps. 22:7
SHORT (18/17)
have sinned and fall *s* . . . . Rom. 3:23
SHORTENED (12/10)
those days were *s* . . . . Matt. 24:22
SHOUT (48/43)
from heaven with a *s* . . . . 1 Thess. 4:16
SHOW (163/155)
a land that I will *s* . . . . Gen. 12:1
s Him greater works . . . . John 5:20
SHOWBREAD (19/18)
s which was not lawful . . . . Matt. 12:4
SHOWERS (10/9)
make it soft with *s* . . . . Ps. 65:10
SHREWDLY (2/2)
because he had dealt *s* . . . . Luke 16:8
SHRINES (7/7)
who made silver *s* . . . . Acts 19:24
SHUFFLES (1/1)
with his eyes, he *s* . . . . Prov. 6:13
SHUNNED (2/2)
feared God and *s* evil . . . . Job 1:1
SHUT (82/80)
For you *s* up the . . . . Matt. 23:13
SHUTS (8/7)
s his eyes from seeing . . . . Is. 33:15
who opens and no one *s* . . . . Rev. 3:7
SICK (78/78)
I was *s* and you . . . . Matt. 25:36
faith will save the *s* . . . . James 5:15
SICKLE (13/12)
"Thrust in Your *s* . . . . Rev. 14:15
SICKNESS (17/17)
will sustain him in *s* . . . . Prov. 18:14
"This *s* is not unto . . . . John 11:4
SICKNESSES (4/4)
And bore our *s* . . . . Matt. 8:17
SIDE (396/310)
The LORD is on my *s* . . . . Ps. 118:6
SIFT (3/3)
s the nations with the . . . . Is. 30:28
SIGH (9/8)
our years like a *s* . . . . Ps. 90:9
SIGHING (10/10)
For my *s* comes before . . . . Job 3:24
SIGHT (318/304)
and see this great *s* . . . . Ex. 3:3
by faith, not by *s* . . . . 2 Cor. 5:7
SIGN (92/83)
will give you a *s* . . . . Is. 7:14
seeks after a *s* . . . . Matt. 12:39
For Jews request a *s* . . . . 1 Cor. 1:22
SIGNS (73/72)
and let them be for *s* . . . . Gen. 1:14
cannot discern the *s* . . . . Matt. 16:3
Jesus did many other *s* . . . . John 20:30
SILENCE (24/24)
that You may *s* . . . . Ps. 8:2
seal, there was *s* . . . . Rev. 8:1
SILENT (46/45)
season, and am not *s* . . . . Ps. 22:2
SILK (3/3)
and covered you with *s* . . . . Ezek. 16:10

SILVER (320/283)
may buy the poor for *s* . . . . Amos 8:6
him thirty pieces of *s* . . . . Matt. 26:15
SIMILITUDE (1/1)
been made in the *s* . . . . James 3:9
SIMPLE (21/21)
making wise the *s* . . . . Ps. 19:7
SIMPLICITY (4/4)
corrupted from the *s* . . . . 2 Cor. 11:3
SIN (446/393)
and be sure your *s* . . . . Num. 32:23
Be angry, and do not *s* . . . . Ps. 4:4
s is always before me . . . . Ps. 51:3
soul an offering for *s* . . . . Is. 53:10
And He bore the *s* . . . . Is. 53:12
who takes away the *s* . . . . John 1:29
"He who is without *s* . . . . John 8:7
convict the world of *s* . . . . John 16:8
s entered the world . . . . Rom. 5:12
s is not imputed . . . . Rom. 5:13
s shall not have . . . . Rom. 6:14
Shall we *s* because we . . . . Rom. 6:15
Him who knew no *s* . . . . 2 Cor. 5:21
man of *s* is revealed . . . . 2 Thess. 2:3
we are, yet without *s* . . . . Heb. 4:15
do it, to him it is *s* . . . . James 4:17
say that we have no *s* . . . . 1 John 1:8
and he cannot *s* . . . . 1 John 3:9
SINCERE (4/4)
and from *s* faith . . . . 1 Tim. 1:5
SINCERITY (10/10)
simplicity and godly *s* . . . . 2 Cor. 1:12
SINFUL (10/10)
from me, for I am a *s* . . . . Luke 5:8
become exceedingly *s* . . . . Rom. 7:13
SING (116/99)
Let him *s* psalms . . . . James 5:13
SINGERS (38/37)
The *s* went before . . . . Ps. 68:25
SINGING (27/25)
His presence with *s* . . . . Ps. 100:2
and spiritual songs, *s* . . . . Eph. 5:19
SINISTER (2/2)
who understands *s* . . . . Dan. 8:23
SINK (6/6)
I *s* in deep mire . . . . Ps. 69:2
to *s* he cried out . . . . Matt. 14:30
SINNED (110/106)
You only, have I *s* . . . . Ps. 51:4
"Father, I have *s* . . . . Luke 15:18
for all have *s* and . . . . Rom. 3:23
say that we have not *s* . . . . 1 John 1:10
for the devil has *s* . . . . 1 John 3:8
SINNER (21/21)
s who repents than . . . . Luke 15:7
the ungodly and the *s* . . . . 1 Pet. 4:18
SINNERS (46/44)
in the path of *s* . . . . Ps. 1:1
the righteous, but *s* . . . . Matt. 9:13
while we were still *s* . . . . Rom. 5:8
many were made *s* . . . . Rom. 5:19
the world to save *s* . . . . 1 Tim. 1:15
such hostility from *s* . . . . Heb. 12:3
SINS (197/190)
from presumptuous *s* . . . . Ps. 19:13
You, our secret *s* . . . . Ps. 90:8
the soul who *s* shall . . . . Ezek. 18:4
if your brother *s* . . . . Matt. 18:15
s according to the . . . . 1 Cor. 15:3
the forgiveness of *s* . . . . Eph. 1:7
If we confess our *s* . . . . 1 John 1:9
propitiation for our *s* . . . . 1 John 2:2
SISTER (105/101)
is My brother and *s* . . . . Matt. 12:50
SIT (122/119)
but to *s* on My right . . . . Matt. 20:23
"*S* at My right hand . . . . Heb. 1:13
I will grant to *s* . . . . Rev. 3:21
SITS (36/35)
It is He who *s* above . . . . Is. 40:22
so that he *s* as God . . . . 2 Thess. 2:4
SITTING (64/63)
where Christ is, *s* . . . . Col. 3:1
SKILL (11/11)
hand forget its *s* . . . . Ps. 137:5
SKILLFULNESS (1/1)
guided them by the *s* . . . . Ps. 78:72
SKIN (75/67)
God made tunics of *s* . . . . Gen. 3:21
LORD and said, "*S* . . . . Job 2:4
Ethiopian change his *s* . . . . Jer. 13:23
SKIP (1/1)
He makes them also *s* . . . . Ps. 29:6
SKIPPING (1/1)
upon the mountains, *s* . . . . Song 2:8
SKULL (5/5)
to say, Place of a *S* . . . . Matt. 27:33
SKY (9/8)
s receded as a scroll . . . . Rev. 6:14
SLACK (3/3)
The Lord is not *s* . . . . 2 Pet. 3:9

SLAIN (106/97)
is the Lamb who was *s*. . . . . Rev. 5:12
SLANDER (4/4)
and whoever spreads *s* . . . . . Prov. 10:18
SLANDERERS (5/5)
be reverent, not *s* . . . . . 1 Tim. 3:11
SLANDEROUSLY (1/1)
as we are *s* reported. . . . . Rom. 3:8
SLAUGHTER (60/59)
led as a lamb to the *s*. . . . . Is. 53:7
as sheep for the *s* . . . . . Rom. 8:36
SLAVE (33/31)
commits sin is a *s*. . . . . John 8:34
SLAVES (39/32)
should no longer be *s* . . . . . Rom. 6:6
SLAY (39/39)
s the righteous . . . . . Gen. 18:25
SLEEP (73/65)
God caused a deep *s*. . . . . Gen. 2:21
neither slumber nor *s*. . . . . Ps. 121:4
He gives His beloved *s* . . . . . Ps. 127:2
among you, and many *s*. . . . . 1 Cor. 11:30
We shall not all *s*. . . . . 1 Cor. 15:51
SLEEPERS (1/1)
gently the lips of *s* . . . . . Song 7:9
SLEEPING (13/12)
"Are you still *s* . . . . . Matt. 26:45
SLEEPLESSNESS (2/2)
in labors, in *s*. . . . . 2 Cor. 6:5
SLEEPS (4/4)
"Our friend Lazarus *s* . . . . . John 11:11
SLEPT (9/9)
I lay down and *s* . . . . . Ps. 3:5
SLIGHTED (1/1)
is the one who is *s* . . . . . Prov. 12:9
SLING (6/5)
he had, and his *s*. . . . . 1 Sam. 17:40
SLIP (7/7)
their foot shall *s* . . . . . Deut. 32:35
SLIPPERY (3/3)
set them in *s* places . . . . . Ps. 73:18
SLOOPS (1/1)
all the beautiful *s* . . . . . Is. 2:16
SLOW (15/13)
hear, *s* to speak, *s* . . . . . James 1:19
SLUGGARD (2/2)
will you slumber, O *s*. . . . . Prov. 6:9
SLUMBERING (1/1)
upon men, while *s* . . . . . Job 33:15
SMALL (87/87)
And I saw the dead, *s*. . . . . Rev. 20:12
SMELL (10/8)
and he smelled the *s*. . . . . Gen. 27:27
SMELLS (1/1)
s the battle from afar. . . . . Job 39:25
SMITTEN (1/1)
Him stricken, *s* . . . . . Is. 53:4
SMOKE (45/39)
was filled with *s*. . . . . Rev. 15:8
SMOOTH (11/11)
And the rough places *s*. . . . . Is. 40:4
SMOOTH-SKINNED (1/1)
man, and I am a *s*. . . . . Gen. 27:11
SNARE (46/44)
is a fowler's *s* . . . . . Hos. 9:8
it will come as a *s* . . . . . Luke 21:35
and escape the *s* . . . . . 2 Tim. 2:26
SNARED (8/8)
all of them are *s* . . . . . Is. 42:22
SNARES (14/14)
who seek my life lay *s* . . . . . Ps. 38:12
SNATCH (4/4)
neither shall anyone *s*. . . . . John 10:28
SNATCHES (2/2)
s away what was . . . . . Matt. 13:19
SNEER (1/1)
and you *s* at it . . . . . Mal. 1:13
SNIFFED (1/1)
they *s* at the wind . . . . . Jer. 14:6
SNORTING (2/2)
s strikes terror. . . . . Job 39:20
SNOW (21/21)
shall be whiter than *s* . . . . . Ps. 51:7
shall be as white as *s* . . . . . Is. 1:18
SOAKED (1/1)
their land shall be *s* . . . . . Is. 34:7
SOAP (3/3)
lye, and use much *s* . . . . . Jer. 2:22
SOBER (6/6)
the older men be *s* . . . . . Titus 2:2
SOBERLY (2/2)
think, but to think *s* . . . . . Rom. 12:3
SODA (1/1)
and like vinegar on *s* . . . . . Prov. 25:20
SODOMITES (2/2)
nor homosexuals, nor *s* . . . . . 1 Cor. 6:9
SOJOURNER (8/7)
But no *s* had to lodge. . . . . Job 31:32
SOJOURNERS (5/5)
are strangers and *s*. . . . . Lev. 25:23

SOLD (79/72)
s his birthright . . . . . Gen. 25:33
s all that he had. . . . . Matt. 13:46
but I am carnal, *s* . . . . . Rom. 7:14
SOLDIER (7/7)
hardship as a good *s* . . . . . 2 Tim. 2:3
SOLDIERS (35/34)
s twisted a crown . . . . . John 19:2
SOLITARILY (1/1)
heritage, who dwell *s*. . . . . Mic. 7:14
SOLITARY (1/1)
God sets the *s* in . . . . . Ps. 68:6
SOMEBODY (2/2)
up, claiming to be *s* . . . . . Acts 5:36
SOMETHING (52/49)
thinks himself to be *s* . . . . . Gal. 6:3
SON (2,363/1,776)
Me, 'You are My *S* . . . . . Ps. 2:7
is born, unto us a *S*. . . . . Is. 9:6
will bring forth a *S* . . . . . Matt. 1:21
"This is My beloved *S*. . . . . Matt. 3:17
are the Christ, the *S* . . . . . Matt. 16:16
Whose *S* is He . . . . . Matt. 22:42
of the *S* of Man . . . . . Matt. 24:37
'I am the *S* of God. . . . . Matt. 27:43
of Jesus Christ, the *S* . . . . . Mark 1:1
out, the only *s* . . . . . Luke 7:12
The only begotten *S*. . . . . John 1:18
gave His only begotten *S* . . . . . John 3:16
S can do nothing. . . . . John 5:19
s abides forever. . . . . John 8:35
"Woman, behold your *s* . . . . . John 19:26
Jesus Christ is the *S*. . . . . Acts 8:37
by sending His own *S* . . . . . Rom. 8:3
not spare His own *S*. . . . . Rom. 8:32
God sent forth His *S*. . . . . Gal. 4:4
"You are My *S*. . . . . Heb. 1:5
though He was a *S* . . . . . Heb. 5:8
Whoever denies the *S* . . . . . 1 John 2:23
SONG (80/77)
Sing to Him a new *s*. . . . . Ps. 33:3
He has put a new *s* . . . . . Ps. 40:3
I will sing a new *s*. . . . . Ps. 144:9
They sang a new *s*. . . . . Rev. 5:9
SONGS (19/19)
my Maker, who gives *s* . . . . . Job 35:10
and spiritual *s*. . . . . Eph. 5:19
SONS (1,327/1,122)
s shall come from afar . . . . . Is. 60:4
He will purify the *s*. . . . . Mal. 3:3
that you may become *s*. . . . . John 12:36
who are of faith are *s*. . . . . Gal. 3:7
the adoption as *s* . . . . . Gal. 4:5
in bringing many *s*. . . . . Heb. 2:10
speaks to you as to *s* . . . . . Heb. 12:5
SOON (65/64)
for it is *s* cut off. . . . . Ps. 90:10
SOOTHED (1/1)
or bound up, or *s* . . . . . Is. 1:6
SORCERER (3/3)
But Elymas the *s*. . . . . Acts 13:8
SORCERERS (7/7)
outside are dogs and *s* . . . . . Rev. 22:15
SORCERESS (2/2)
shall not permit a *s* . . . . . Ex. 22:18
SORCERY (6/6)
idolatry, *s* . . . . . Gal. 5:20
SORES (6/6)
and putrefying *s*. . . . . Is. 1:6
SORROW (70/66)
multiply your *s* . . . . . Gen. 3:16
s is continually . . . . . Ps. 38:17
And He adds no *s* . . . . . Prov. 10:22
Your *s* is incurable . . . . . Jer. 30:15
them sleeping from *s* . . . . . Luke 22:45
s will be turned . . . . . John 16:20
s produces repentance . . . . . 2 Cor. 7:10
s as others who have . . . . . 1 Thess. 4:13
no more death, nor *s*. . . . . Rev. 21:4
SORROWFUL (20/19)
But I am poor and *s*. . . . . Ps. 69:29
saying, he went away *s* . . . . . Matt. 19:22
soul is exceedingly *s* . . . . . Matt. 26:38
and I may be less *s*. . . . . Phil. 2:28
SORROWS (16/16)
s shall be multiplied . . . . . Ps. 16:4
by men, a Man of *s*. . . . . Is. 53:3
are the beginning of *s*. . . . . Matt. 24:8
SORRY (10/8)
s that He had made man . . . . . Gen. 6:6
For you were made *s* . . . . . 2 Cor. 7:9
SOUGHT (111/107)
I *s* the LORD . . . . . Ps. 34:4
s what was lost. . . . . Ezek. 34:4
SOUL (321/302)
with all your *s* . . . . . Deut. 6:5
"My *s* loathes my life . . . . . Job 10:1
s draws near the Pit . . . . . Job 33:22
will not leave my *s* . . . . . Ps. 16:10
converting the *s* . . . . . Ps. 19:7
He restores my *s*. . . . . Ps. 23:3
you cast down, O my *s*. . . . . Ps. 42:5

Let my *s* live. . . . . Ps. 119:175
No one cares for my *s* . . . . . Ps. 142:4
me wrongs his own *s*. . . . . Prov. 8:36
When You make His *s*. . . . . Is. 53:10
s delight itself . . . . . Is. 55:2
the *s* of the father as . . . . . Ezek. 18:4
able to destroy both *s* . . . . . Matt. 10:28
and loses his own *s* . . . . . Matt. 16:26
with all your *s* . . . . . Matt. 22:37
your whole spirit, *s*. . . . . 1 Thess. 5:23
to the saving of the *s*. . . . . Heb. 10:39
his way will save a *s* . . . . . James 5:20
health, just as your *s* . . . . . 3 John 1:2
SOULS (44/41)
and will save the *s* . . . . . Ps. 72:13
and he who wins *s* . . . . . Prov. 11:30
unsettling your *s*. . . . . Acts 15:24
is able to save your *s* . . . . . James 1:21
SOUND (121/112)
voice was like the *s*. . . . . Ezek. 43:2
s an alarm in My holy . . . . . Joel 2:1
do not *s* a trumpet . . . . . Matt. 6:2
s words which you . . . . . 2 Tim. 1:13
SOUNDNESS (4/4)
him this perfect *s*. . . . . Acts 3:16
SOUNDS (3/3)
a distinction in the *s* . . . . . 1 Cor. 14:7
SOW (42/41)
s trouble reap . . . . . Job 4:8
Those who *s* in tears . . . . . Ps. 126:5
Blessed are you who *s*. . . . . Is. 32:20
"They *s* the wind. . . . . Hos. 8:7
s is not made alive . . . . . 1 Cor. 15:36
SOWER (8/8)
"Behold, a *s* went . . . . . Matt. 13:3
SOWN (31/29)
s spiritual things. . . . . 1 Cor. 9:11
of righteousness is *s* . . . . . James 3:18
SOWS (15/13)
s the good seed is the . . . . . Matt. 13:37
'One *s* and another. . . . . John 4:37
for whatever a man *s*. . . . . Gal. 6:7
SPARE (43/42)
He who did not *s*. . . . . Rom. 8:32
if God did not *s* . . . . . 2 Pet. 2:4
SPARES (4/4)
s his rod hates his. . . . . Prov. 13:24
SPARK (1/1)
the work of it as a *s*. . . . . Is. 1:31
SPARKLES (1/1)
it is red, when it *s* . . . . . Prov. 23:31
SPARKS (4/3)
to trouble, as the *s* . . . . . Job 5:7
SPARROW (3/3)
s has found a home . . . . . Ps. 84:3
SPARROWS (4/4)
more value than many *s*. . . . . Matt. 10:31
SPAT (5/5)
Then they *s* on Him. . . . . Matt. 27:30
SPEAK (509/483)
only the word that I *s* . . . . . Num. 22:35
oh, that God would *s* . . . . . Job 11:5
and a time to *s*. . . . . Eccl. 3:7
s anymore in His name . . . . . Jer. 20:9
or what you should *s*. . . . . Matt. 10:19
to you when all men *s*. . . . . Luke 6:26
s what I have seen . . . . . John 8:38
He hears He will *s*. . . . . John 16:13
Spirit and began to *s* . . . . . Acts 2:4
SPEAKING (90/89)
envy, and all evil *s* . . . . . 1 Pet. 2:1
SPEAKS (79/72)
to face, as a man *s*. . . . . Ex. 33:11
He whom God has sent *s* . . . . . John 3:34
When he *s* a lie . . . . . John 8:44
he being dead still *s*. . . . . Heb. 11:4
of sprinkling that *s*. . . . . Heb. 12:24
SPEAR (50/43)
His side with a *s* . . . . . John 19:34
SPEARS (18/18)
and their *s* into . . . . . Is. 2:4
SPECK (6/5)
do you look at the *s* . . . . . Matt. 7:3
SPECTACLE (4/4)
you were made a *s* . . . . . Heb. 10:33
SPEECH (43/42)
one language and one *s* . . . . . Gen. 11:1
and his *s* contemptible . . . . . 2 Cor. 10:10
s always be with grace. . . . . Col. 4:6
SPEECHLESS (5/5)
your mouth for the *s*. . . . . Prov. 31:8
SPEED (3/3)
they shall come with *s*. . . . . Is. 5:26
SPEEDILY (14/14)
I call, answer me *s* . . . . . Ps. 102:2
SPEND (26/25)
Why do you *s* money for. . . . . Is. 55:2
amiss, that you may *s* . . . . . James 4:3
SPENT (23/22)
"But when he had *s* . . . . . Luke 15:14
SPIDER (1/1)
s skillfully grasps . . . . . Prov. 30:28

SPIES (16/16)
men who had been *s* .... Josh. 6:23
SPIN (2/2)
neither toil nor *s*.......... Matt. 6:28
SPINDLE (1/1)
her hand holds the *s* .... Prov. 31:19
SPIRIT (576/523)
S shall not strive.......... Gen. 6:3
S that is upon you.......... Num. 11:17
portion of your *s*.......... 2 Kin. 2:9
Then a *s* passed before .... Job 4:15
hand I commit my *s* .... Ps. 31:5
The *s* of a man is the .... Prov. 20:27
s will return to God .... Eccl. 12:7
S has gathered them .... Is. 34:16
I have put My *S* .... Is. 42:1
S entered me when He .... Ezek. 2:2
new heart and a new *s*.......... Ezek. 18:31
I will put My *S* .... Ezek. 36:27
walk in a false *s*.......... Mic. 2:11
I will put My *S* .... Matt. 12:18
S descending upon Him.......... Mark 1:10
s indeed is willing.......... Mark 14:38
go before Him in the *s* .... Luke 1:17
manner of *s* you are of .... Luke 9:55
hands I commit My *s*.......... Luke 23:46
they had seen a *s*.......... Luke 24:37
God is *S* .... John 4:24
I speak to you are *s* .... John 6:63
but if a *s* or an angel.......... Acts 23:9
the flesh but in the *S*.......... Rom. 8:9
s that we are children .... Rom. 8:16
what the mind of the *S* .... Rom. 8:27
to us through His *S* .... 1 Cor. 2:10
gifts, but the same *S*.......... 1 Cor. 12:4
but the *S* gives life .... 2 Cor. 3:6
Now the Lord is the *S*.......... 2 Cor. 3:17
Having begun in the *S*.......... Gal. 3:3
has sent forth the *S* .... Gal. 4:6
with the Holy *S* .... Eph. 1:13
the unity of the *S* .... Eph. 4:3
stand fast in one *s* .... Phil. 1:27
S expressly says that .... 1 Tim. 4:1
S who dwells in us .... James 4:5
made alive by the *S* .... 1 Pet. 3:18
do not believe every *s* .... 1 John 4:1
has given us of His *S* .... 1 John 4:13
S who bears witness.......... 1 John 5:6
not having the *S* .... Jude 1:19
I was in the *S* on the.......... Rev. 1:10
him hear what the *S*.......... Rev. 2:7
And the *S* and the.......... Rev. 22:17
SPIRITS (41/41)
who makes His angels *s* .... Ps. 104:4
heed to deceiving *s* .... 1 Tim. 4:1
SPIRITUAL (28/23)
s judges all things.......... 1 Cor. 2:15
However, the *s* is not .... 1 Cor. 15:46
s restore such a one.......... Gal. 6:1
SPIRITUALLY (3/3)
s minded is life .... Rom. 8:6
SPITEFULLY (4/4)
for those who *s* .... Matt. 5:44
SPITTING (1/1)
face from shame and *s* .... Is. 50:6
SPLENDOR (13/13)
on the glorious *s*.......... Ps. 145:5
SPOIL (57/53)
He shall divide the *s* .... Is. 53:12
SPOILER (2/2)
I have created the *s* .... Is. 54:16
SPOKE (554/548)
"No man ever *s* .... John 7:46
I was a child, I *s*.......... 1 Cor. 13:11
in various ways *s*.......... Heb. 1:1
s as they were moved .... 2 Pet. 1:21
SPOKEN (286/280)
I have not *s* in secret .... Is. 45:19
why am I evil *s*.......... 1 Cor. 10:30
SPOKESMAN (2/2)
So he shall be your *s* .... Ex. 4:16
SPONGE (3/3)
them ran and took a *s*.......... Matt. 27:48
SPOT (20/20)
church, not having *s* .... Eph. 5:27
Himself without *s*.......... Heb. 9:14
SPOTS (6/5)
These are *s* in your.......... Jude 1:12
SPREAD (106/103)
Then the word of God *s*.......... Acts 6:7
SPREADS (13/13)
s them out like a tent.......... Is. 40:22
SPRING (35/33)
Truth shall *s* out of.......... Ps. 85:11
s send forth fresh .... James 3:11
SPRINGING (4/4)
a fountain of water *s* .... John 4:14
SPRINGS (26/22)
and the thirsty land *s* .... Is. 35:7
SPRINKLE (29/28)
Then I will *s* .... Ezek. 36:25
SPRINKLED (23/20)
having our hearts *s* .... Heb. 10:22
SPRINKLING (5/5)
s that speaks .... Heb. 12:24
SPROUT (2/2)
and the seed should *s* .... Mark 4:27
SQUARES (2/2)
voice in the open *s*.......... Prov. 1:20
STAFF (34/33)
this Jordan with my *s* .... Gen. 32:10
Your rod and Your *s*.......... Ps. 23:4
on the top of his *s*.......... Heb. 11:21
STAGGER (4/4)
they will drink and *s* .... Jer. 25:16
STAGGERS (1/1)
as a drunken man *s* .... Is. 19:14
STAKES (2/2)
s will ever be removed .... Is. 33:20
STALLS (4/4)
be no herd in the *s*.......... Hab. 3:17
STAMMERERS (1/1)
s will be ready .... Is. 32:4
STAMMERING (2/2)
s tongue that you .... Is. 33:19
STAMPING (1/1)
At the noise of the *s*.......... Jer. 47:3
STAND (249/241)
one shall be able to *s*.......... Deut. 7:24
lives, and He shall *s* .... Job 19:25
ungodly shall not *s*.......... Ps. 1:5
not lack a man to *s*.......... Jer. 35:19
And who can *s* when He .... Mal. 3:2
that kingdom cannot *s* .... Mark 3:24
he will be made to *s*.......... Rom. 14:4
Watch, *s* fast in the.......... 1 Cor. 16:13
for by faith you *s*.......... 2 Cor. 1:24
having done all, to *s*.......... Eph. 6:13
S therefore .... Eph. 6:14
of God in which you *s* .... 1 Pet. 5:12
Behold, I *s* at the.......... Rev. 3:20
STANDARD (18/18)
LORD will lift up a *s* .... Is. 59:19
STANDING (81/77)
they love to pray *s* .... Matt. 6:5
and the Son of Man *s*.......... Acts 7:56
STANDS (36/35)
him who thinks he *s* .... 1 Cor. 10:12
STAR (15/14)
For we have seen His *s* .... Matt. 2:2
Bright and Morning *S*.......... Rev. 22:16
STARS (50/49)
He made the *s* also.......... Gen. 1:16
born as many as the *s* .... Heb. 11:12
STATE (16/14)
learned in whatever *s* .... Phil. 4:11
STATURE (16/16)
in wisdom and *s* .... Luke 2:52
STATUTE (35/35)
shall be a perpetual *s*.......... Lev. 3:17
STATUTES (134/133)
the *s* of the LORD are.......... Ps. 19:8
Teach me Your *s* .... Ps. 119:12
STAY (53/53)
S here and watch with.......... Matt. 26:38
STEADFAST (17/16)
brethren, be *s*.......... 1 Cor. 15:58
soul, both sure and *s* .... Heb. 6:19
Resist him, *s* in the.......... 1 Pet. 5:9
STEADFASTLY (5/5)
s set His face to go .... Luke 9:51
And they continued *s* .... Acts 2:42
STEADFASTNESS (2/2)
good order and the *s*.......... Col. 2:5
STEADILY (2/2)
could not look *s* .... 2 Cor. 3:13
STEADY (1/1)
and his hands were *s*.......... Ex. 17:12
STEAL (21/20)
"You shall not *s*.......... Ex. 20:15
thieves break in and *s*.......... Matt. 6:19
night and *s* Him away .... Matt. 27:64
STEM (1/1)
forth a Rod from the *s*.......... Is. 11:1
STENCH (5/5)
there will be a *s*.......... Is. 3:24
this time there is a *s*.......... John 11:39
STEP (3/3)
s has turned from the .... Job 31:7
STEPS (45/45)
The *s* of a good man.......... Ps. 37:23
and established my *s*.......... Ps. 40:2
the LORD directs his *s* .... Prov. 16:9
should follow His *s*.......... 1 Pet. 2:21
STEWARD (16/16)
be blameless, as a *s* .... Titus 1:7
STEWARDS (5/5)
of Christ and *s*.......... 1 Cor. 4:1
STEWARDSHIP (5/5)
entrusted with a *s*.......... 1 Cor. 9:17
STICK (14/9)
'For Joseph, the *s* .... Ezek. 37:16
STICKS (8/8)
a man gathering *s* .... Num. 15:32
STIFF (3/3)
rebellion and your *s*.......... Deut. 31:27
STIFF-NECKED (7/7)
"You *s* and uncircumcised.......... Acts 7:51
STILL (225/216)
When I awake, I am *s*.......... Ps. 139:18
sea, "Peace, be *s*.......... Mark 4:39
STILLBORN (3/3)
burial, I say that a *s* .... Eccl. 6:3
STINGS (2/2)
like a serpent, and *s*.......... Prov. 23:32
STIR (20/19)
I remind you to *s* .... 2 Tim. 1:6
STIRRED (24/24)
So the LORD *s* up the.......... Hag. 1:14
STIRS (11/11)
it *s* up the dead for.......... Is. 14:9
STOCKS (7/7)
s that were in the .... Jer. 20:2
STOIC (1/1)
and *S* philosophers .... Acts 17:18
STOMACH (20/19)
Foods for the *s*.......... 1 Cor. 6:13
STOMACH'S (1/1)
little wine for your *s*.......... 1 Tim. 5:23
STONE (187/175)
him, a pillar of *s* .... Gen. 35:14
s shall be a witness.......... Josh. 24:27
s which the builders.......... Ps. 118:22
I lay in Zion a *s* .... Is. 28:16
take the heart of *s*.......... Ezek. 36:26
will give him a *s* .... Matt. 7:9
s will be broken .... Matt. 21:44
s which the builders.......... Luke 20:17
those works do you *s*.......... John 10:32
Him as to a living *s*.......... 1 Pet. 2:4
STONED (23/22)
s Stephen as he was.......... Acts 7:59
They were *s*.......... Heb. 11:37
STONES (164/147)
Abraham from these *s* .... Matt. 3:9
command that these *s* .... Matt. 4:3
STONY (5/5)
Some fell on *s* ground.......... Mark 4:5
STOOPED (6/6)
And again He *s* down .... John 8:8
STOPPED (33/33)
her flow of blood *s* .... Luke 8:44
STORE (11/11)
no room to *s* my crops .... Luke 12:17
STORK (5/5)
s has her home in the .... Ps. 104:17
STORM (15/14)
He calms the *s*.......... Ps. 107:29
for a shelter from *s*.......... Is. 4:6
STRAIGHT (32/32)
make *s* in the desert a.......... Is. 40:3
and make *s* paths for.......... Heb. 12:13
STRAIGHTFORWARD (1/1)
that they were not *s* .... Gal. 2:14
STRAIN (1/1)
Blind guides, who *s* .... Matt. 23:24
STRAITS (4/4)
and desperate *s*.......... Deut. 28:53
STRANGE (13/12)
s thing happened .... 1 Pet. 4:12
STRANGER (82/78)
and loves the *s*.......... Deut. 10:18
I was a *s* and you took .... Matt. 25:35
STRANGERS (1/1)
know the voice of *s*.......... John 10:5
you are no longer *s* .... Eph. 2:19
STRANGLING (1/1)
that my soul chooses *s* .... Job 7:15
STRAP (5/5)
than I, whose sandal *s*.......... Mark 1:7
STRAW (19/18)
stones, wood, hay, *s* .... 1 Cor. 3:12
STRAY (8/8)
who make my people *s*.......... Mic. 3:5
STRAYED (6/6)
yet I have not *s* .... Ps. 119:110
for which some have *s*.......... 1 Tim. 6:10
STREAM (11/11)
like a flowing *s*.......... Is. 66:12
STREAMS (17/17)
He also brought *s*.......... Ps. 78:16
STREET (21/21)
In the middle of its *s* .... Rev. 22:2
STREETS (61/59)
You taught in our *s*.......... Luke 13:26
STRENGTH (230/223)
s no man shall.......... 1 Sam. 2:9
The LORD is the *s* .... Ps. 27:1
is our refuge and *s* .... Ps. 46:1
They go from *s* to .... Ps. 84:7
S and honor are her.......... Prov. 31:25
might He increases *s*.......... Is. 40:29
O LORD, my *s* and my.......... Jer. 16:19

were still without *s*. . . . . .Rom. 5:6
s is made perfect. . . . . .2 Cor. 12:9
STRENGTHEN (37/37)
and He shall *s* . . . . Ps. 27:14
S the weak hands . . . . Is. 35:3
s your brethren . . . . Luke 22:32
s the things. . . . . .Rev. 3:2
STRENGTHENED (37/36)
unbelief, but was *s* . . . . Rom. 4:20
stood with me and *s*. . . . . 2 Tim. 4:17
STRENGTHENING (5/5)
s the souls of the. . . . . .Acts 14:22
STRENGTHENS (4/4)
through Christ who *s*. . . . . .Phil. 4:13
STRETCH (49/49)
are old, you will *s* . . . . John 21:18
STRETCHED (66/64)
I have *s* out my hands. . . . . .Ps. 88:9
"All day long I have *s*. . . . . Rom. 10:21
STRETCHES (9/9)
For he *s* out his hand. . . . . .Job 15:25
STRICKEN (13/13)
of My people He was *s*. . . . . Is. 53:8
STRIFE (31/30)
man stirs up *s* . . . . Prov. 15:18
even from envy and *s* . . . . Phil. 1:15
which come envy, *s* . . . . 1 Tim. 6:4
STRIKE (86/81)
"*S* the Shepherd . . . . Zech. 13:7
'I will *s* the Shepherd. . . . . Matt. 26:31
STRINGED (27/27)
of your *s* instruments . . . . Amos 5:23
STRIP (9/9)
S yourselves. . . . . Is. 32:11
STRIPES (11/11)
s we are healed . . . . Is. 53:5
s you were healed. . . . . 1 Pet. 2:24
STRIVE (11/11)
"My Spirit shall not *s*. . . . . Gen. 6:3
"*S* to enter through . . . . Luke 13:24
the Lord not to *s* . . . . 2 Tim. 2:14
STRIVING (5/5)
for a man to stop *s*. . . . . .Prov. 20:3
STROKE (6/6)
with a mighty *s* . . . . Jer. 14:17
STRONG (195/184)
The LORD *s* and mighty . . . . Ps. 24:8
s is Your hand . . . . Ps. 89:13
When a *s* man . . . . Luke 11:21
We then who are *s* . . . . Rom. 15:1
I am weak, then I am *s* . . . . 2 Cor. 12:10
my brethren, be *s* . . . . Eph. 6:10
weakness were made *s* . . . . .Heb. 11:34
STRONGHOLD (28/27)
of my salvation, my *s*. . . . . Ps. 18:2
STRUCK (173/163)
s the rock twice. . . . . Num. 20:11
the hand of God has *s* . . . . .Job 19:21
Behold, He *s* the rock . . . . Ps. 78:20
in My wrath I *s*. . . . . Is. 60:10
s the head from the . . . . Hab. 3:13
took the reed and *s* . . . . .Matt. 27:30
STUBBLE (14/14)
do wickedly will be *s* . . . . Mal. 4:1
STUBBORN (10/9)
If a man has a *s*. . . . . .Deut. 21:18
STUBBORN-HEARTED (1/1)
"Listen to Me, you *s* . . . . Is. 46:12
STUBBORNNESS (2/2)
do not look on the *s*. . . . . .Deut. 9:27
STUDIED (2/2)
having never *s*. . . . . John 7:15
STUMBLE (48/44)
have caused many to *s* . . . . .Mal. 2:8
you will be made to *s*. . . . . .Matt. 26:31
immediately they *s* . . . . Mark 4:17
who believe in Me to *s*. . . . . .Mark 9:42
For we all *s* in many. . . . . .James 3:2
STUMBLED (10/10)
s that they should. . . . . .Rom. 11:11
STUMBLES (5/5)
word, immediately he *s* . . . . Matt. 13:21
STUMBLING (20/20)
the deaf, nor put a *s*. . . . . Lev. 19:14
but a stone of *s* . . . . .Is. 8:14
Behold, I will lay *s*. . . . . Jer. 6:21
I lay in Zion a *s* . . . . Rom. 9:33
this, not to put a *s*. . . . . .Rom. 14:13
of yours become a *s*. . . . . 1 Cor. 8:9
and "A stone of *s*. . . . . 1 Pet. 2:8
to keep you from *s* . . . . Jude 1:24
STUPID (3/3)
who hates correction is *s* . . . . Prov. 12:1
SUBDUE (9/9)
s all things to . . . . .Phil. 3:21
SUBJECT (17/16)
for it is not *s*. . . . . .Rom. 8:7
Let every soul be *s* . . . . Rom. 13:1
all their lifetime *s* . . . . .Heb. 2:15
SUBJECTED (2/1)
because of Him who *s*. . . . . Rom. 8:20

SUBJECTION (8/7)
put all things in *s* . . . . Heb. 2:8
SUBMISSION (4/4)
his children in *s* . . . . 1 Tim. 3:4
SUBMISSIVE (6/6)
Yes, all of you be *s*. . . . . 1 Pet. 5:5
SUBMIT (11/11)
Therefore *s* to God . . . . James 4:7
s yourselves to every. . . . . 1 Pet. 2:13
SUBSIDED (4/4)
and the waters *s* . . . . .Gen. 8:1
SUBSTANCE (12/12)
Bless his *s*. Deut. 33:11
SUCCESS (5/5)
please give me *s* . . . . .Gen. 24:12
but wisdom brings *s* . . . . Eccl. 10:10
SUCCESSFUL (1/1)
Joseph, and he was a *s* . . . . Gen. 39:2
SUDDENLY (72/71)
s there was with the. . . . . Luke 2:13
SUE (1/1)
s you and take away. . . . . .Matt. 5:40
SUFFER (46/46)
for the Christ to *s* . . . . .Luke 24:46
Christ, if indeed we *s*. . . . . Rom. 8:17
in Him, but also to *s*. . . . . .Phil. 1:29
SUFFERED (21/20)
s these things and to . . . . .Luke 24:26
for whom I have *s*. . . . . .Phil. 3:8
after you have *s* . . . . 1 Pet. 5:10
SUFFERING (7/7)
Is anyone among you *s*. . . . . James 5:13
SUFFERINGS (14/14)
I consider that the *s*. . . . . .Rom. 8:18
perfect through *s* . . . . Heb. 2:10
SUFFERS (5/5)
Love *s* long and is. . . . . 1 Cor. 13:4
SUFFICIENCY (2/2)
but our *s* is from God. . . . . 2 Cor. 3:5
SUFFICIENT (15/14)
S for the day is its . . . . .Matt. 6:34
SUM (9/9)
How great is the *s*. . . . . Ps. 139:17
SUMMER (25/25)
and heat, winter and *s*. . . . . Gen. 8:22
SUMPTUOUSLY (1/1)
fine linen and fared *s* . . . . Luke 16:19
SUN (161/153)
So the *s* stood still . . . . Josh. 10:13
s shall not strike you . . . . Ps. 121:6
s returned ten degrees . . . . Is. 38:8
the *s* and moon grow. . . . . .Joel 2:10
s shall go down on the . . . . .Mic. 3:6
for He makes His *s*. . . . . .Matt. 5:45
the *s* was darkened. . . . . Luke 23:45
do not let the *s*. Eph. 4:26
s became black as. . . . . Rev. 6:12
had no need of the *s* . . . . Rev. 21:23
SUPPER (15/15)
to eat the Lord's *S*. . . . . 1 Cor. 11:20
took the cup after *s* . . . . 1 Cor. 11:25
together for the *s* . . . . Rev. 19:17
SUPPLICATION (35/33)
by prayer and *s* . . . . Phil. 4:6
SUPPLIES (11/11)
by what every joint *s* . . . . .Eph. 4:16
SUPPLY (18/16)
And my God shall *s* . . . . .Phil. 4:19
SUPPORT (13/13)
this, that you must *s* . . . . Acts 20:35
SUPREME (1/1)
to the king as *s*. . . . . 1 Pet. 2:13
SURE (26/26)
s your sin will find . . . . Num. 32:23
call and election *s*. . . . . 2 Pet. 1:10
SURETY (12/10)
Be *s* for Your servant. . . . . Ps. 119:122
Jesus has become a *s*. . . . . Heb. 7:22
SURROUND (17/17)
LORD, mercy shall *s* . . . . Ps. 32:10
SURROUNDED (35/34)
also, since we are *s*. . . . . .Heb. 12:1
SURVIVOR (4/4)
was no refugee or *s* . . . . Lam. 2:22
SUSPICIONS (1/1)
reviling, evil *s* . . . . 1 Tim. 6:4
SUSTAIN (4/4)
S me with cakes of . . . . Song 2:5
SWADDLING (4/4)
Him in *s* cloths . . . . Luke 2:7
SWALLOW (21/21)
a gnat and *s* a camel . . . . .Matt. 23:24
SWEAR (48/46)
'You shall not *s* .Matt. 5:33
began to curse and *s* . . . . Matt. 26:74
SWEARING (2/2)
By *s* and lying . . . . Hos. 4:2
SWEARS (18/13)
but whoever *s* by the . . . . .Matt. 23:18
SWEAT (3/3)
Then His *s* became like. . . . . Luke 22:44

SWEET (94/91)
s are Your words . . . . Ps. 119:103
but it will be as *s* . . . . Rev. 10:9
SWEETNESS (5/5)
mouth like honey in *s* . . . . .Ezek. 3:3
SWELLING (10/9)
they speak great *s*. . . . . 2 Pet. 2:18
SWIFT (22/21)
let every man be *s* . . . . James 1:19
SWIM (5/5)
night I make my bed *s*. . . . . Ps. 6:6
SWOON (1/1)
as they *s* like the . . . . Lam. 2:12
SWORD (422/382)
s which turned every. . . . . Gen. 3:24
The *s* of the LORD is. . . . . Is. 34:6
'A *s*, a *s* is sharpened . . . . Ezek. 21:9
Bow and *s* of battle I . . . . .Hos. 2:18
to bring peace but a *s* . . . . Matt. 10:34
for all who take the *s* . . . . Matt. 26:52
the *s* of the Spirit . . . . Eph. 6:17
than any two-edged *s* . . . . Heb. 4:12
mouth goes a sharp *s* . . . . Rev. 19:15
SWORDS (27/27)
shall beat their *s*. . . . . Is. 2:4
SWORE (76/76)
So I *s* in My wrath. . . . . Heb. 3:11
SWORN (47/46)
"By Myself I have *s*. . . . . Gen. 22:16
"The LORD has *s* . . . . Heb. 7:21
SYMBOLIC (2/2)
which things are *s* . . . . Gal. 4:24
SYMPATHIZE (1/1)
Priest who cannot *s* . . . . Heb. 4:15
SYMPATHY (1/1)
My *s* is stirred . . . . Hos. 11:8
SYNAGOGUE (41/41)
but are a *s* of Satan. Rev. 2:9

T

TABERNACLE (320/286)
t He shall hide me . . . . Ps. 27:5
I will abide in Your *t*. . . . . Ps. 61:4
and will rebuild the *t*. . . . . Acts 15:16
and more perfect *t*. . . . . Heb. 9:11
TABERNACLES (13/13)
Feast of *T* was at hand. . . . . John 7:2
TABLE (79/75)
prepare a *t* before me . . . . Ps. 23:5
dogs under the *t*. . . . . .Mark 7:28
of the Lord's *t*. . . . . 1 Cor. 10:21
TABLES (18/13)
and overturned the *t*. . . . . Matt. 21:12
TABLET (6/6)
is engraved on the *t*. Jer. 17:1
TAIL (15/14)
t drew a third of the. . . . . Rev. 12:4
TAKE (894/848)
t Your Holy Spirit . . . . Ps. 51:11
T My yoke upon . . . . Matt. 11:29
and *t* up his cross. . . . . Mark 8:34
My life that I may *t*. John 10:17
TAKEN (286/274)
He was *t* from prison. . . . . Is. 53:8
one will be *t* and the . . . . Matt. 24:40
until He is *t* out of . . . . 2 Thess. 2:7
TALEBEARER (6/6)
t reveals secrets . . . . Prov. 11:13
TALENT (13/13)
went and hid your *t*. . . . . Matt. 25:25
TALK (25/25)
shall *t* of them when . . . . Deut. 6:7
TALKED (41/41)
within us while He *t*. . . . . Luke 24:32
TALKERS (2/2)
both idle *t* and. . . . . Titus 1:10
TAMBOURINE (4/4)
The mirth of the *t*. . . . . Is. 24:8
TARES (8/8)
the *t* also appeared . . . . Matt. 13:26
TARGET (4/4)
You set me as Your *t* . . . . Job 7:20
TARRY (7/7)
come and will not *t* . . . . Heb. 10:37
TASK (6/6)
this burdensome *t* . . . . Eccl. 1:13
TASTE (21/20)
Oh, *t* and see that the . . . . Ps. 34:8
might *t* death for . . . . Heb. 2:9
TASTED (9/9)
t the heavenly gift . . . . Heb. 6:4
TAUGHT (74/72)
as His counselor has *t*. Is. 40:13
from man, nor was I *t* . . . . Gal. 1:12
TAUNT (2/2)
and a byword, a *t* . . . . Jer. 24:9
TAX (33/30)
t collectors do the. . . . . Matt. 5:46
TAXES (12/11)
t to whom *t*. . . . . Rom. 13:7
TEACH (106/104)
"Can anyone *t* . . . . Job 21:22

t me Your paths.......Ps. 25:4
t you the fear of the.......Ps. 34:11
t transgressors Your.......Ps. 51:13
So *t* us to number our.......Ps. 90:12
t you again the first.......Heb. 5:12
TEACHER (55/54)
for One is your *T*.......Matt. 23:8
know that You are a *t*.......John 3:2
named Gamaliel, a *t*.......Acts 5:34
a *t* of the Gentiles in.......1 Tim. 2:7
TEACHERS (17/16)
than all my *t*.......Ps. 119:99
prophets, third *t*.......1 Cor. 12:28
and some pastors and *t*.......Eph. 4:11
desiring to be *t*.......1 Tim. 1:7
there will be false *t*.......2 Pet. 2:1
TEACHES (21/19)
the Holy Spirit *t*.......1 Cor. 2:13
the same anointing *t*.......1 John 2:27
TEACHING (42/42)
t them to observe all.......Matt. 28:20
t every man in all.......Col. 1:28
TEAR (35/34)
I, even I, will *t*.......Hos. 5:14
will wipe away every *t*.......Rev. 21:4
TEARS (37/36)
my couch with my *t*.......Ps. 6:6
mindful of your *t*.......2 Tim. 1:4
it diligently with *t*.......Heb. 12:17
TEETH (45/43)
You have broken the *t*.......Ps. 3:7
TELL (263/256)
Who can *t* if God.......Jon. 3:9
whatever they *t*.......Matt. 23:3
He comes, He will *t*.......John 4:25
TEMPERATE (4/4)
for the prize is *t* in all.......1 Cor. 9:25
husband of one wife, *t*.......1 Tim. 3:2
TEMPEST (16/16)
And suddenly a great *t*.......Matt. 8:24
TEMPLE (371/326)
So Solomon built the *t*.......1 Kin. 6:14
LORD is in His holy *t*.......Ps. 11:4
One greater than the *t*.......Matt. 12:6
"Destroy this *t*.......John 2:19
your body is the *t*.......1 Cor. 6:19
grows into a holy *t*.......Eph. 2:21
sits as God in the *t*.......2 Thess. 2:4
and the Lamb are its *t*.......Rev. 21:22
TEMPLES (8/8)
t made with hands.......Acts 7:48
TEMPORARY (1/1)
which are seen are *t*.......2 Cor. 4:18
TEMPT (8/8)
t the LORD your God.......Matt. 4:7
TEMPTATION (12/11)
do not lead us into *t*.......Matt. 6:13
the man who endures *t*.......James 1:12
TEMPTED (18/15)
forty days, *t* by Satan.......Mark 1:13
lest you also be *t*.......Gal. 6:1
in all points *t*.......Heb. 4:15
TEMPTER (2/2)
Now when the *t* came.......Matt. 4:3
TENDER (33/33)
your heart was *t*.......2 Kin. 22:19
TENDERHEARTED (2/2)
to one another, *t*.......Eph. 4:32
TENDS (2/2)
t a flock and does not.......1 Cor. 9:7
TENT (112/101)
earthly house, this *t*.......2 Cor. 5:1
TENTMAKERS (1/1)
occupation they were *t*.......Acts 18:3
TENTS (69/66)
than dwell in the *t*.......Ps. 84:10
TERRESTRIAL (2/1)
bodies and *t* bodies.......1 Cor. 15:40
TERRIBLE (23/23)
is great and very *t*.......Joel 2:11
TERRIFIED (11/11)
and not in any way *t*.......Phil. 1:28
TERRIFY (6/6)
me with dreams and *t*.......Job 7:14
TERRIFYING (1/1)
t was the sight.......Heb. 12:21
TERROR (39/39)
are nothing, you see *t*.......Job 6:21
not be afraid of the *t*.......Ps. 91:5
TERRORS (15/15)
consumed with *t*.......Ps. 73:19
TEST (37/37)
said, "Why do you *t*.......Matt. 22:18
T all things.......1 Thess. 5:21
but *t* the spirits.......1 John 4:1
TESTAMENT (3/3)
where there is a *t*.......Heb. 9:16
TESTED (27/26)
that God *t* Abraham.......Gen. 22:1
Where your fathers *t*.......Heb. 3:9
though it is *t* by fire.......1 Pet. 1:7
TESTIFIED (29/29)
he who has seen has *t*.......John 19:35
of God which He has *t*.......1 John 5:9
TESTIFIES (7/7)
that the Holy Spirit *t*.......Acts 20:23
TESTIFY (30/30)
t what We have.......John 3:11
t that the Father.......1 John 4:14
TESTIFYING (3/3)
was righteous, God *t*.......Heb. 11:4
TESTIMONIES (37/37)
those who keep His *t*.......Ps. 119:2
t are my meditation.......Ps. 119:99
TESTIMONY (96/90)
two tablets of the *T*.......Ex. 31:18
under your feet as a *t*.......Mark 6:11
no one receives His *t*.......John 3:32
not believed the *t*.......1 John 5:10
For the *t* of Jesus is.......Rev. 19:10
TESTING (12/12)
came to Him, *t* Him.......Matt. 19:3
TESTS (6/6)
men, but God who *t*.......1 Thess. 2:4
THANK (25/24)
"I *t* You, Father.......Matt. 11:25
t You that I am not.......Luke 18:11
THANKFUL (3/3)
Him as God, nor were *t*.......Rom. 1:21
THANKFULNESS (1/1)
Felix, with all *t*.......Acts 24:3
THANKS (75/72)
the cup, and gave *t*.......Matt. 26:27
T be to God for His.......2 Cor. 9:15
THANKSGIVING (32/31)
His presence with *t*.......Ps. 95:2
into His gates with *t*.......Ps. 100:4
supplication, with *t*.......Phil. 4:6
THEATER (2/2)
and rushed into the *t*.......Acts 19:29
THIEF (25/25)
do not despise a *t*.......Prov. 6:30
because he was a *t*.......John 12:6
Lord will come as a *t*.......2 Pet. 3:10
THIEVES (14/14)
And companions of *t*.......Is. 1:23
THINGS (302/290)
in heaven give good *t*.......Matt. 7:11
kept all these *t*.......Luke 2:51
share in all good *t*.......Gal. 6:6
THINK (59/57)
t you have eternal.......John 5:39
not to *t* of himself.......Rom. 12:3
THINKS (10/10)
yet the LORD *t* upon me.......Ps. 40:17
for as he *t* in his.......Prov. 23:7
t he stands take heed.......1 Cor. 10:12
THIRST (29/29)
those who hunger and *t*.......Matt. 5:6
in Me shall never *t*.......John 6:35
anymore nor *t* anymore.......Rev. 7:16
THIRSTS (6/6)
My soul *t* for God.......Ps. 42:2
saying, "If anyone *t*.......John 7:37
freely to him who *t*.......Rev. 21:6
THIRSTY (21/21)
I was *t* and you gave.......Matt. 25:35
THISTLES (3/3)
or figs from *t*.......Matt. 7:16
THORN (6/6)
a *t* in the flesh was.......2 Cor. 12:7
THORNBUSHES (1/1)
gather grapes from *t*.......Matt. 7:16
THORNS (48/45)
Both *t* and thistles it.......Gen. 3:18
And some fell among *t*.......Matt. 13:7
wearing the crown of *t*.......John 19:5
THOUGHT (51/51)
You understand my *t*.......Ps. 139:2
I *t* as a child.......1 Cor. 13:11
THOUGHTS (52/48)
The LORD knows the *t*.......Ps. 94:11
unrighteous man his *t*.......Is. 55:7
For My *t* are not your.......Is. 55:8
Jesus, knowing their *t*.......Matt. 9:4
heart proceed evil *t*.......Matt. 15:19
The LORD knows the *t*.......1 Cor. 3:20
THREAT (3/2)
shall flee at the *t*.......Is. 30:17
THREATEN (2/2)
suffered, He did not *t*.......1 Pet. 2:23
THREATENING (2/2)
to them, giving up *t*.......Eph. 6:9
THREATS (6/6)
still breathing *t*.......Acts 9:1
THREE (444/390)
hope, love, these *t*.......1 Cor. 13:13
THRESH (6/6)
it is time to *t* her.......Jer. 51:33
THRESHING (48/48)
t shall last till the.......Lev. 26:5
THROAT (7/7)
t is an open tomb.......Rom. 3:13
THRONE (175/159)
Your *t*, O God, is.......Ps. 45:6
Lord sitting on a *t*.......Is. 6:1
"Heaven is My *t*.......Is. 66:1
for it is God's *t*.......Matt. 5:34
will give Him the *t*.......Luke 1:32
"Your *t*, O God, is.......Heb. 1:8
come boldly to the *t*.......Heb. 4:16
My Father on His *t*.......Rev. 3:21
I saw a great white *t*.......Rev. 20:11
THRONES (13/11)
invisible, whether *t*.......Col. 1:16
THRONG (3/3)
house of God in the *t*.......Ps. 55:14
THROW (37/37)
t Yourself down.......Matt. 4:6
THROWN (41/41)
neck, and he were *t*.......Mark 9:42
THRUST (31/29)
and rose up and *t*.......Luke 4:29
THUNDER (22/22)
The voice of Your *t*.......Ps. 77:18
the voice of loud *t*.......Rev. 14:2
THUNDERED (4/4)
"The LORD *t* from.......2 Sam. 22:14
THUNDERINGS (7/7)
the sound of mighty *t*.......Rev. 19:6
THUNDERS (6/5)
The God of glory *t*.......Ps. 29:3
TIDINGS (12/11)
I bring you good *t*.......Luke 2:10
TILL (150/145)
no man to *t* the ground.......Gen. 2:5
TILLER (1/1)
but Cain was a *t*.......Gen. 4:2
TILLS (2/2)
t his land will have.......Prov. 28:19
TIME (609/551)
pray to You in a *t*.......Ps. 32:6
for the *t* is near.......Rev. 1:3
TIMES (159/152)
the signs of the *t*.......Matt. 16:3
not for you to know *t*.......Acts 1:7
last days perilous *t*.......2 Tim. 3:1
TITHE (17/16)
And he gave him a *t*.......Gen. 14:20
For you pay *t* of mint.......Matt. 23:23
TITHES (23/20)
and to bring the *t*.......Neh. 10:37
Bring all the *t*.......Mal. 3:10
TITHING (1/1)
the year of *t*.......Deut. 26:12
TITLE (2/2)
Now Pilate wrote a *t*.......John 19:19
TITTLE (2/2)
away, one jot or one *t*.......Matt. 5:18
TODAY (161/147)
t I have begotten You.......Ps. 2:7
t you will be with Me.......Luke 23:43
"*T*, if you will hear.......Heb. 3:7
the same yesterday, *t*.......Heb. 13:8
TOIL (11/11)
t you shall eat of.......Gen. 3:17
TOILED (6/6)
"Master, we have *t*.......Luke 5:5
TOLD (286/280)
Behold, I have *t*.......Matt. 28:7
so, I would have *t*.......John 14:2
TOLERABLE (6/6)
you, it will be more *t*.......Matt. 10:15
TOMB (61/57)
in the garden a new *t*.......John 19:41
TOMBS (20/19)
like whitewashed *t*.......Matt. 23:27
TOMORROW (58/57)
drink, for *t* we die.......Is. 22:13
do not worry about *t*.......Matt. 6:34
what will happen *t*.......James 4:14
TONGUE (114/113)
remember you, let my *t*.......Ps. 137:6
forever, but a lying *t*.......Prov. 12:19
t breaks a bone.......Prov. 25:15
t should confess that.......Phil. 2:11
does not bridle his *t*.......James 1:26
no man can tame the *t*.......James 3:8
every nation, tribe, *t*.......Rev. 14:6
TONGUES (35/33)
From the strife of *t*.......Ps. 31:20
speak with new *t*.......Mark 16:17
to them divided *t*, as of fire.......Acts 2:3
I speak with the *t*.......1 Cor. 13:1
TOOTH (11/6)
eye for an eye and a *t*.......Matt. 5:38
TOPHET (9/8)
the high places of *T*.......Jer. 7:31
TORCH (4/4)
and like a fiery *t*.......Zech. 12:6
TORCHES (9/9)
When he had set the *t*.......Judg. 15:5
come with flaming *t*.......Nah. 2:3
TORMENT (15/13)
You come here to *t*.......Matt. 8:29

t ascends forever ... Rev. 14:11
TORMENTED (10/10)
And they will be *t* ... Rev. 20:10
TORMENTS (2/2)
And being in *t* ... Luke 16:23
TORN (44/42)
of the temple was *t* ... Matt. 27:51
TORTURED (1/1)
Others were *t* ... Heb. 11:35
TOSSED (4/4)
t to and fro and ... Eph. 4:14
TOTTER (4/4)
drunkard, and shall *t* ... Is. 24:20
TOUCH (39/39)
"If only I may *t* ... Matt. 9:21
TOUCHED (48/44)
t my mouth with it ... Is. 6:7
TOUCHES (46/44)
He *t* the hills ... Ps. 104:32
TOWER (40/35)
t whose top is in the ... Gen. 11:4
a watchman in the *t* ... Is. 21:5
TRACKED (1/1)
t our steps so that we ... Lam. 4:18
TRADERS (7/7)
are princes, whose *t* ... Is. 23:8
TRADITION (11/11)
transgress the *t* ... Matt. 15:2
according to the *t* ... Col. 2:8
TRAIN (2/2)
T up a child in the ... Prov. 22:6
TRAINED (6/6)
those who have been *t* ... Heb. 12:11
TRAINING (2/2)
bring them up in the *t* ... Eph. 6:4
TRAITOR (1/1)
also became a *t* ... Luke 6:16
TRAITORS (1/1)
t, headstrong ... 2 Tim. 3:4
TRAMPLE (9/9)
serpent you shall *t* ... Ps. 91:13
swine, lest they *t* ... Matt. 7:6
TRAMPLED (28/26)
t the Son of God ... Heb. 10:29
the winepress was *t* ... Rev. 14:20
TRANCE (3/3)
t I saw a vision ... Acts 11:5
TRANSFIGURED (2/2)
and was *t* before them ... Matt. 17:2
TRANSFORMED (2/2)
this world, but be *t* ... Rom. 12:2
TRANSGRESS (14/14)
do Your disciples *t* ... Matt. 15:2
TRANSGRESSED (29/29)
Yes, all Israel has *t* ... Dan. 9:11
t your commandment ... Luke 15:29
TRANSGRESSES (3/3)
Whoever *t* and does not ... 2 John 1:9
TRANSGRESSION (44/43)
no law there is no *t* ... Rom. 4:15
deceived, fell into *t* ... 1 Tim. 2:14
TRANSGRESSIONS (50/49)
mercies, blot out my *t* ... Ps. 51:1
For I acknowledge my *t* ... Ps. 51:3
was wounded for our *t* ... Is. 53:5
for the *t* of My people ... Is. 53:8
TRANSGRESSOR (5/5)
I make myself a *t* ... Gal. 2:18
TRANSGRESSORS (12/11)
Then I will teach *t* ... Ps. 51:13
numbered with the *t* ... Is. 53:12
TRAP (7/7)
of Israel, as a *t* ... Is. 8:14
TRAPS (3/3)
for me, and from the *t* ... Ps. 141:9
TRAVEL (8/8)
For you *t* land and sea ... Matt. 23:15
TRAVELER (4/4)
t who turns aside ... Jer. 14:8
TREACHEROUS (11/10)
are insolent, *t* ... Zeph. 3:4
TREACHEROUSLY (26/21)
This man dealt *t* ... Acts 7:19
TREAD (22/22)
You shall *t* upon the ... Ps. 91:13
TREADS (12/12)
an ox while it *t* ... 1 Tim. 5:18
t the winepress ... Rev. 19:15
TREASURE (34/32)
and you will have *t* ... Matt. 19:21
So is he who lays up *t* ... Luke 12:21
But we have this *t* ... 2 Cor. 4:7
TREASURED (2/2)
t the words of His ... Job 23:12
TREASURER (2/2)
Erastus, the *t* of the ... Rom. 16:23
TREASURES (44/38)
it more than hidden *t* ... Job 3:21
I will give you the *t* ... Is. 45:3
for yourselves *t* ... Matt. 6:19
are hidden all the *t* ... Col. 2:3
riches than the *t* ... Heb. 11:26
TREATY (8/5)
Now Solomon made a *t* ... 1 Kin. 3:1
TREE (202/172)
you eaten from the *t* ... Gen. 3:11
t planted by the ... Ps. 1:3
like a native green *t* ... Ps. 37:35
t bears good fruit ... Matt. 7:17
His own body on the *t* ... 1 Pet. 2:24
to eat from the *t* ... Rev. 2:7
have the right to the *t* ... Rev. 22:14
TREES (146/134)
late autumn *t* without ... Jude 1:12
the sea, or the *t* ... Rev. 7:3
TREMBLE (31/31)
That the nations may *t* ... Is. 64:2
they shall fear and *t* ... Jer. 33:9
TREMBLED (23/22)
Then everyone who *t* ... Ezra 9:4
the earth shook and *t* ... Ps. 18:7
and indeed they *t* ... Jer. 4:24
TREMBLING (28/27)
in fear, and in much *t* ... 1 Cor. 2:3
t you received ... 2 Cor. 7:15
flesh, with fear and *t* ... Eph. 6:5
TRENCH (3/3)
and he made a *t* ... 1 Kin. 18:32
TRESPASSES (14/12)
forgive men their *t* ... Matt. 6:14
not imputing their *t* ... 2 Cor. 5:19
who were dead in *t* ... Eph. 2:1
TRIAL (7/7)
concerning the fiery *t* ... 1 Pet. 4:12
TRIBE (236/200)
the Lion of the *t* ... Rev. 5:5
blood out of every *t* ... Rev. 5:9
TRIBES (109/107)
t which are scattered ... James 1:1
TRIBULATION (22/22)
there will be great *t* ... Matt. 24:21
world you will have *t* ... John 16:33
with her into great *t* ... Rev. 2:22
out of the great *t* ... Rev. 7:14
TRIBULATIONS (8/8)
t enter the kingdom ... Acts 14:22
but we also glory in *t* ... Rom. 5:3
t that you endure ... 2 Thess. 1:4
TRIED (18/18)
a *t* stone, a precious ... Is. 28:16
TRIMMED (4/4)
and *t* their lamps ... Matt. 25:7
TRIUMPH (12/12)
always leads us in *t* ... 2 Cor. 2:14
TRIUMPHED (2/2)
the LORD, for He has *t* ... Ex. 15:1
TRODDEN (8/7)
t the winepress alone ... Is. 63:3
TROUBLE (143/143)
few days and full of *t* ... Job 14:1
t He shall hide me ... Ps. 27:5
not in *t* as other men ... Ps. 73:5
will be with him in *t* ... Ps. 91:15
Savior in time of *t* ... Jer. 14:8
there are some who *t* ... Gal. 1:7
TROUBLED (62/62)
You are worried and *t* ... Luke 10:41
shaken in mind or *t* ... 2 Thess. 2:2
TROUBLES (22/22)
out of all their *t* ... Ps. 25:22
will be famines and *t* ... Mark 13:8
him out of all his *t* ... Acts 7:10
TROUBLING (4/4)
wicked cease from *t* ... Job 3:17
TRUE (80/77)
He who sent Me is *t* ... John 7:28
Indeed, let God be *t* ... Rom. 3:4
whatever things are *t* ... Phil. 4:8
may know Him who is *t* ... 1 John 5:20
for these words are *t* ... Rev. 21:5
TRUMPET (60/58)
deed, do not sound a *t* ... Matt. 6:2
t makes an uncertain ... 1 Cor. 14:8
For the *t* will sound ... 1 Cor. 15:52
TRUST (125/125)
t also in Him, and He shall ... Ps. 37:5
T in the LORD with all ... Prov. 3:5
Do not *t* in a friend ... Mic. 7:5
those who *t* in riches ... Mark 10:24
TRUSTED (32/31)
"He *t* in the LORD ... Ps. 22:8
He *t* in God ... Matt. 27:43
TRUSTS (19/19)
But he who *t* in the ... Ps. 32:10
TRUTH (223/210)
led me in the way of *t* ... Gen. 24:48
Behold, You desire *t* ... Ps. 51:6
t shall be your shield ... Ps. 91:4
and Your law is *t* ... Ps. 119:142
t is fallen in the ... Is. 59:14
called the City of *T* ... Zech. 8:3
you shall know the *t* ... John 8:32
"I am the way, the *t* ... John 14:6
He, the Spirit of *t* ... John 16:13
to Him, "What is *t* ... John 18:38
who suppress the *t* ... Rom. 1:18
but, speaking the *t* ... Eph. 4:15
your waist with *t* ... Eph. 6:14
I am speaking the *t* ... 1 Tim. 2:7
they may know the *t* ... 2 Tim. 2:25
the knowledge of the *t* ... 2 Tim. 3:7
that we are of the *t* ... 1 John 3:19
the Spirit is *t* ... 1 John 5:6
TRY (10/10)
which is to *t* you ... 1 Pet. 4:12
TUMULT (20/20)
Your enemies make a *t* ... Ps. 83:2
TUNIC (17/13)
Also he made him a *t* ... Gen. 37:3
TUNICS (12/12)
the LORD God made *t* ... Gen. 3:21
TURBAN (16/12)
"Remove the *t* ... Ezek. 21:26
TURN (288/277)
you shall not *t* ... Deut. 17:11
"Repent, *t* away from ... Ezek. 14:6
on your right cheek, *t* ... Matt. 5:39
t them from darkness ... Acts 26:18
TURNED (259/253)
The wicked shall be *t* ... Ps. 9:17
of Israel, they have *t* ... Is. 1:4
and how you *t* to God ... 1 Thess. 1:9
TURNING (14/14)
marvel that you are *t* ... Gal. 1:6
or shadow of *t* ... James 1:17
TURNS (40/40)
A soft answer *t* ... Prov. 15:1
that he who *t* ... James 5:20
TURTLEDOVE (5/5)
t is heard in our land ... Song 2:12
TUTOR (2/2)
the law was our *t* ... Gal. 3:24
TWIST (2/2)
unstable people *t* to ... 2 Pet. 3:16
TWO (759/647)
T are better than one ... Eccl. 4:9
t shall become one ... Matt. 19:5
new man from the *t* ... Eph. 2:15
TYPE (1/1)
of Adam, who is a *t* ... Rom. 5:14

U

UNAFRAID (1/1)
Do you want to be *u* ... Rom. 13:3
UNBELIEF (12/12)
because of their *u* ... Matt. 13:58
help my *u* ... Mark 9:24
did it ignorantly in *u* ... 1 Tim. 1:13
enter in because of *u* ... Heb. 3:19
UNBELIEVERS (6/5)
yoked together with *u* ... 2 Cor. 6:14
UNBELIEVING (6/5)
Do not be *u* ... John 20:27
u nothing is pure ... Titus 1:15
But the cowardly, *u* ... Rev. 21:8
UNCIRCUMCISED (54/47)
not the physically *u* ... Rom. 2:27
UNCLEAN (208/167)
I am a man of *u* lips ... Is. 6:5
any man common or *u* ... Acts 10:28
there is nothing *u* ... Rom. 14:14
that no fornicator, *u* ... Eph. 5:5
UNCLEANNESS (34/30)
men's bones and all *u* ... Matt. 23:27
flesh in the lust of *u* ... 2 Pet. 2:10
UNCLOTHED (1/1)
we want to be *u* ... 2 Cor. 5:4
UNCOVERS (3/3)
u deep things out of ... Job 12:22
UNDEFILED (5/5)
incorruptible and *u* ... 1 Pet. 1:4
UNDERMINE (1/1)
And you *u* your friend ... Job 6:27
UNDERSTAND (121/116)
if there are any who *u* ... Ps. 14:2
hearing, but do not *u* ... Is. 6:9
Why do you not *u* ... John 8:43
lest they should *u* ... Acts 28:27
some things hard to *u* ... 2 Pet. 3:16
UNDERSTANDING (155/151)
His *u* is infinite ... Ps. 147:5
lean not on your own *u* ... Prov. 3:5
u will find good ... Prov. 19:8
His *u* is unsearchable ... Is. 40:28
also still without *u* ... Matt. 15:16
also pray with the *u* ... 1 Cor. 14:15
the Lord give you *u* ... 2 Tim. 2:7
Who is wise and *u* ... James 3:13
UNDERSTANDS (10/10)
there is none who *u* ... Rom. 3:11
UNDERSTOOD (24/24)
Then I *u* their end ... Ps. 73:17
clearly seen, being *u* ... Rom. 1:20

UNDESIRABLE (1/1)
gather together, O *u*............ Zeph. 2:1
UNDIGNIFIED (1/1)
I will be even more *u*......... 2 Sam. 6:22
UNDISCERNING (1/1)
u, untrustworthy .... Rom. 1:31
UNDONE (5/5)
"Woe is me, for I am *u*............ Is. 6:5
UNEDUCATED (1/1)
that they were *u* .... Acts 4:13
UNFAITHFUL (16/16)
way of the *u* is hard .... Prov. 13:15
UNFAITHFULLY (3/3)
back and acted *u*................ Ps. 78:57
UNFORGIVING (2/2)
unloving, *u*..................... Rom. 1:31
UNFORMED (1/1)
substance, being yet *u*......... Ps. 139:16
UNFRUITFUL (6/6)
and it becomes *u* .... Mark 4:19
UNGODLINESS (7/7)
heaven against all *u*............ Rom. 1:18
UNGODLY (25/22)
u shall not stand.................. Ps. 1:5
Christ died for the *u*.............Rom. 5:6
UNHOLY (5/5)
the holy and *u*.............. Ezek. 22:26
UNINFORMED (3/3)
the place of the *u* .... 1 Cor. 14:16
UNINTENTIONALLY (18/17)
kills his neighbor *u* ....Deut. 4:42
UNITE (1/1)
U my heart to fear .... Ps. 86:11
UNITY (4/4)
to dwell together in *u* .... Ps. 133:1
to keep the *u* of the .... Eph. 4:3
UNJUST (17/15)
commended the *u* .... Luke 16:8
of the just and the *u*..............Acts 24:15
For God is not *u*................ Heb. 6:10
UNJUSTLY (2/2)
long will you judge *u*.............Ps. 82:2
UNKNOWN (6/6)
To The *U* God.................. Acts 17:23
UNLEAVENED (61/50)
the Feast of *U* Bread .... Mark 14:1
UNLOVING (2/2)
untrustworthy, *u*............... Rom. 1:31
UNMERCIFUL (1/1)
unforgiving, *u*................. Rom. 1:31
UNPREPARED (1/1)
with me and find you *u*......... 2 Cor. 9:4
UNPRESENTABLE (1/1)
u parts have greater...........1 Cor. 12:23
UNPROFITABLE (8/8)
'We are *u* servants ....Luke 17:10
for that would be *u*.............Heb. 13:17
UNPUNISHED (12/10)
wicked will not go *u*............Prov. 11:21
UNQUENCHABLE (2/2)
up the chaff with *u*............ Matt. 3:12
UNRESTRAINED (1/1)
that the people were *u* ....Ex. 32:25
UNRIGHTEOUS (10/10)
u man his thoughts............... Is. 55:7
u will not inherit the............1 Cor. 6:9
UNRIGHTEOUSNESS (18/17)
all ungodliness and *u* .... Rom. 1:18
cleanse us from all *u*............1 John 1:9
All *u* is sin.................... 1 John 5:17
UNRULY (2/2)
those who are *u*.............1 Thess. 5:14
UNSEARCHABLE (6/6)
u are His judgments .... Rom. 11:33
UNSKILLED (1/1)
only of milk is *u* ....Heb. 5:13
UNSPOTTED (1/1)
to keep oneself *u* .... James 1:27
UNSTABLE (6/6)
U as water.................... Gen. 49:4
UNSTOPPED (1/1)
of the deaf shall be *u*............ Is. 35:5
UNTAUGHT (1/1)
which *u* and unstable ....2 Pet. 3:16
UNTRUSTWORTHY (1/1)
undiscerning, *u*............... Rom. 1:31
UNWASHED (3/3)
eat bread with *u* hands......... Mark 7:5
UNWISE (4/4)
Therefore do not be *u*...........Eph. 5:17
UNWORTHY (4/4)
u manner will be............ 1 Cor. 11:27
UPHOLD (11/11)
U me according to ....Ps. 119:116
UPHOLDING (1/1)
u all things by the...............Heb. 1:3
UPHOLDS (6/6)
LORD *u* all who fall............ Ps. 145:14
UPRIGHT (66/66)
u is His delight .... Prov. 15:8
UPRIGHTNESS (17/16)
princes for their *u* .... Prov. 17:26
UPROOT (4/4)
u the wheat with.............Matt. 13:29
URIM (7/7)
Thummim and Your *U* .... Deut. 33:8
US (1,447/1,095)
"God with *u*................... Matt. 1:23
If God is for *u*.................Rom. 8:31
They went out from *u* ....1 John 2:19
USE (39/39)
who spitefully *u* you .... Matt. 5:44
u liberty as an .... Gal. 5:13
USELESS (10/10)
one's religion is *u* ....James 1:26
USING (7/7)
u liberty as a...................1 Pet. 2:16
USURY (10/10)
Take no *u* or....................Lev. 25:36
UTTER (28/28)
u dark sayings of old............. Ps. 78:2
UTTERANCE (13/11)
the Spirit gave them *u*............Acts 2:4
UTTERED (14/13)
which cannot be *u* .... Rom. 8:26
UTTERMOST (3/3)
u those who come .... Heb. 7:25
UTTERS (5/5)
Day unto day *u* speech .... Ps. 19:2

V

VAGABOND (2/2)
v you shall be on the............Gen. 4:12
VAIN (59/53)
the people plot a *v*................ Ps. 2:1
you believed in *v* .... 1 Cor. 15:2
VALIANT (31/29)
They are not *v* for the .... Jer. 9:3
VALIANTLY (5/5)
God we will do *v* .... Ps. 60:12
VALLEY (145/129)
v shall be exalted .... Is. 40:4
VALOR (39/39)
a mighty man of *v* .... 1 Sam. 16:18
VALUE (15/13)
of more *v* than they...........Matt. 6:26
VALUED (6/5)
It cannot be *v* in the .... Job 28:16
VANISH (6/5)
knowledge, it will *v* ....1 Cor. 13:8
VANISHED (2/2)
and He *v* from their............ Luke 24:31
VANITY (35/31)
of vanities, all is *v*................Eccl. 1:2
VAPOR (6/5)
best state is but *v* .... Ps. 39:5
It is even a *v* that .... James 4:14
VARIATION (1/1)
whom there is no *v* .... James 1:17
VEGETABLES (3/3)
and let them give us *v*...........Dan. 1:12
is weak eats only *v* ....Rom. 14:2
VEHEMENT (4/4)
of fire, a most *v*...................Song 8:6
VEIL (48/45)
v of the temple was .... Matt. 27:51
Presence behind the *v* .... Heb. 6:19
VENGEANCE (51/45)
V is Mine................... Deut. 32:35
VENOM (2/2)
It becomes cobra *v*............ Job 20:14
VESSEL (38/34)
like a potter's *v* .... Ps. 2:9
for he is a chosen *v* .... Acts 9:15
VESSELS (50/47)
treasure in earthen *v*............2 Cor. 4:7
VEXED (2/2)
grieved, and I was *v*............. Ps. 73:21
VICE (1/1)
as a cloak for *v*.................1 Pet. 2:16
VICTIM (4/4)
and plucked the *v*.................Job 29:17
VICTORY (14/14)
v that has overcome ....1 John 5:4
VIEW (3/3)
"Go, *v* the land.................. Josh. 2:1
VIGILANT (2/2)
Be sober, be *v*....................1 Pet. 5:8
VIGOR (4/4)
nor his natural *v*...............Deut. 34:7
VILE (11/11)
them up to *v* passions..........Rom. 1:26
VINDICATED (2/2)
know that I shall be *v* ....Job 13:18
VINDICATION (3/3)
Let my *v* come from .... Ps. 17:2
VINE (60/55)
"I am the true *v*..................John 15:1
VINEDRESSER (1/1)
and My Father is the *v*...........John 15:1
VINEGAR (6/5)
As *v* to the teeth and ....Prov. 10:26
VINES (12/11)
foxes that spoil the *v*........... Song 2:15
VINEYARD (70/60)
Who plants a *v* and ....1 Cor. 9:7
VIOLENCE (60/59)
was filled with *v* ....Gen. 6:11
of heaven suffers *v*.............Matt. 11:12
VIOLENT (16/16)
haters of God, *v*................Rom. 1:30
VIPER (6/6)
and stings like a *v*.............Prov. 23:32
VIPERS (5/5)
to them, "Brood of *v* .... Matt. 3:7
VIRGIN (44/44)
v shall conceive.................... Is. 7:14
"Behold, the *v* shall .... Matt. 1:23
VIRGINS (21/21)
v who took their lamps......... Matt. 25:1
women, for they are *v*............. Rev. 14:4
VIRTUE (4/3)
to your faith *v* ....2 Pet. 1:5
VISAGE (1/1)
v was marred more than ....Is. 52:14
VISIBLE (2/2)
that are on earth, *v*...............Col. 1:16
VISION (77/71)
in a trance I saw a *v*............. Acts 11:5
v appeared to Paul in ....Acts 16:9
VISIONS (27/27)
young men shall see *v* ....Joel 2:28
VISIT (27/26)
v orphans and widows ....James 1:27
VISITATION (2/2)
God in the day of *v*..............1 Pet. 2:12
VISITED (17/17)
Israel, for He has *v*.............. Luke 1:68
VISITING (4/4)
v the iniquity of the fathers.......Ex. 20:5
VISITOR (1/1)
am a foreigner and a *v* .... Gen. 23:4
VITALITY (1/1)
v was turned into the ....Ps. 32:4
VOICE (458/422)
fire a still small *v* ....1 Kin. 19:12
if you will hear His *v* .... Ps. 95:7
"The *v* of one crying ....Matt. 3:3
And suddenly a *v* .... Matt. 3:17
for they know his *v*.............. John 10:4
the truth hears My *v* .... John 18:37
If anyone hears My *v*.............Rev. 3:20
VOICES (21/19)
And there were loud *v*...........Rev. 11:15
VOID (15/14)
they are a nation *v*........... Deut. 32:28
heirs, faith is made *v*........... Rom. 4:14
VOLUME (2/2)
in the *v* of the book ....Heb. 10:7
VOLUNTEERS (1/1)
Your people shall be *v*........... Ps. 110:3
VOMIT (11/11)
returns to his own *v*........... 2 Pet. 2:22
VOW (36/35)
for he had taken a *v*............ Acts 18:18
VOWS (28/26)
to reconsider his *v* ....Prov. 20:25

W

WAGE (4/4)
w the good warfare ....1 Tim. 1:18
WAGES (40/37)
For the *w* of sin is............ Rom. 6:23
Indeed the *w* of the ....James 5:4
WAIL (31/28)
"Son of man, *w* ....Ezek. 32:18
WAILING (24/22)
There will be *w* .... Matt. 13:42
WAIT (94/91)
w patiently for Him.............. Ps. 37:7
w shall renew their .... Is. 40:31
To those who eagerly *w* .... Heb. 9:28
WAITED (28/27)
w patiently for the............... Ps. 40:1
Divine longsuffering *w* ....1 Pet. 3:20
WAITING (15/15)
ourselves, eagerly *w* .... Rom. 8:23
from that time *w* ....Heb. 10:13
WAITS (11/11)
the creation eagerly *w* ....Rom. 8:19
WAKE (4/4)
us, that whether we *w*........1 Thess. 5:10
WALK (230/220)
w before Me and be............. Gen. 17:1
Yea, though I *w*.................. Ps. 23:4
W prudently when you...........Eccl. 5:1
"This is the way, *w* .... Is. 30:21
be weary, they shall *w*.......... Is. 40:31
w humbly with your God ....Mic. 6:8
W while you have the .... John 12:35
so we also should *w*..............Rom. 6:4
For we *w* by faith ....2 Cor. 5:7
W in the Spirit.................. Gal. 5:16
And *w* in love .... Eph. 5:2
that you may *w* worthy...........Col. 1:10

and they shall *w* ... Rev. 3:4
WALKED (103/102)
Enoch *w* with God ... Gen. 5:22
The people who *w* ... Is. 9:2
in which you once *w* ... Eph. 2:2
WALKING (32/32)
not *w* in craftiness ... 2 Cor. 4:2
WALKS (41/40)
the LORD your God *w* ... Deut. 23:14
is the man who *w* ... Ps. 1:1
he who *w* in darkness ... John 12:35
adversary the devil *w* ... 1 Pet. 5:8
WALL (179/163)
then the *w* of the city ... Josh. 6:5
you, you whitewashed *w* ... Acts 23:3
a window in the *w* ... 2 Cor. 11:33
Now the *w* of the city ... Rev. 21:14
WALLS (69/67)
By faith the *w* of ... Heb. 11:30
WANDER (16/16)
they have loved to *w* ... Jer. 14:10
WANDERED (10/10)
They *w* in deserts and ... Heb. 11:38
WANDERERS (1/1)
And they shall be *w* ... Hos. 9:17
WANDERING (6/6)
w stars for whom is ... Jude 1:13
WANDERS (5/4)
if anyone among you *w* ... James 5:19
WANT (71/70)
I shall not *w* ... Ps. 23:1
WANTING (8/8)
balances, and found *w* ... Dan. 5:27
WANTON (2/2)
have begun to grow *w* ... 1 Tim. 5:11
WAR (232/227)
"There is a noise of *w* ... Ex. 32:17
w may rise against ... Ps. 27:3
shall they learn *w* ... Is. 2:4
king, going to make *w* ... Luke 14:31
You fight and *w* ... James 4:2
fleshly lusts which *w* ... 1 Pet. 2:11
He judges and makes *w* ... Rev. 19:11
WARFARE (4/4)
to her, that her *w* ... Is. 40:2
w entangles ... 2 Tim. 2:4
WARMED (7/6)
Depart in peace, be *w* ... James 2:16
WARMING (1/1)
when she saw Peter *w* ... Mark 14:67
WARMS (2/2)
He even *w* himself and ... Is. 44:16
WARN (12/12)
w those who are ... 1 Thess. 5:14
WARNED (21/21)
Then, being divinely *w* ... Matt. 2:12
Who *w* you to flee ... Matt. 3:7
WARNING (9/8)
w every man and ... Col. 1:28
WARPED (2/2)
such a person is *w* ... Titus 3:11
WARRING (3/3)
w against the law of ... Rom. 7:23
WARRIOR (5/5)
He runs at me like a *w* ... Job 16:14
WARS (14/12)
And you will hear of *w* ... Matt. 24:6
Where do *w* and fights ... James 4:1
WASH (85/78)
w myself with snow ... Job 9:30
W me thoroughly ... Ps. 51:2
w His feet with her ... Luke 7:38
said to him, "Go, *w* ... John 9:7
w the disciples' ... John 13:5
w away your sins ... Acts 22:16
WASHED (42/41)
w his hands before the ... Matt. 27:24
But you were *w* ... 1 Cor. 6:11
Him who loved us and *w* ... Rev. 1:5
WASHING (12/12)
us, through the *w* ... Titus 3:5
WASHINGS (1/1)
and drinks, various *w* ... Heb. 9:10
WASTE (67/64)
the cities are laid *w* ... Is. 6:11
"Why this *w* ... Matt. 26:8
WASTED (7/7)
this fragrant oil *w* ... Mark 14:4
WASTELAND (4/4)
w shall be glad ... Is. 35:1
WASTING (4/4)
that this man was *w* ... Luke 16:1
WATCH (65/61)
is past, and like a *w* ... Ps. 90:4
W therefore, for you ... Matt. 24:42
WATCHED (21/20)
come, he would have *w* ... Matt. 24:43
WATCHES (9/9)
Blessed is he who *w* ... Rev. 16:15
WATCHFUL (5/5)
But you be *w* in all ... 2 Tim. 4:5

WATCHING (12/11)
he comes, will find *w* ... Luke 12:37
WATCHMAN (23/20)
I have made you a *w* ... Ezek. 3:17
WATCHMEN (9/9)
I have set *w* on your ... Is. 62:6
WATER (460/416)
Eden to *w* the garden ... Gen. 2:10
I am poured out like *w* ... Ps. 22:14
For I will pour *w* ... Is. 44:3
given you living *w* ... John 4:10
rivers of living *w* ... John 7:38
can yield both salt *w* ... James 3:12
the Spirit, the *w* ... 1 John 5:8
are clouds without *w* ... Jude 1:12
let him take the *w* ... Rev. 22:17
WATERED (10/10)
I planted, Apollos *w* ... 1 Cor. 3:6
WATERS (229/209)
me beside the still *w* ... Ps. 23:2
though its *w* roar and ... Ps. 46:3
your bread upon the *w* ... Eccl. 11:1
thirsts, come to the *w* ... Is. 55:1
fountain of living *w* ... Jer. 2:13
living fountains of *w* ... Rev. 7:17
WAVE (39/30)
Its fruit shall *w* ... Ps. 72:16
WAVER (1/1)
He did not *w* at the ... Rom. 4:20
WAVERING (1/1)
of our hope without *w* ... Heb. 10:23
WAVES (27/27)
sea, tossed by the *w* ... Matt. 14:24
WAX (4/4)
My heart is like *w* ... Ps. 22:14
WAY (557/516)
As for God, His *w* ... 2 Sam. 22:31
the LORD knows the *w* ... Ps. 1:6
Teach me Your *w* ... Ps. 27:11
in the *w* everlasting ... Ps. 139:24
w that seems right ... Prov. 14:12
The *w* of the just is ... Is. 26:7
wicked forsake his *w* ... Is. 55:7
and pervert the *w* ... Amos 2:7
he will prepare the *w* ... Mal. 3:1
and broad is the *w* ... Matt. 7:13
will prepare Your *w* ... Matt. 11:10
to him, "I am the *w* ... John 14:6
explained to him the *w* ... Acts 18:26
to have known the *w* ... 2 Pet. 2:21
WAYS (196/188)
for all His *w* are ... Deut. 32:4
transgressors Your *w* ... Ps. 51:13
w please the LORD ... Prov. 16:7
"Stand in the *w* ... Jer. 6:16
and owns all your *w* ... Dan. 5:23
w are everlasting ... Hab. 3:6
unstable in all his *w* ... James 1:8
and true are Your *w* ... Rev. 15:3
WEAK (52/49)
gives power to the *w* ... Is. 40:29
knee will be as *w* ... Ezek. 7:17
but the flesh is *w* ... Matt. 26:41
Receive one who is *w* ... Rom. 14:1
God has chosen the *w* ... 1 Cor. 1:27
We are *w*, but you are ... 1 Cor. 4:10
to the *w* I became as *w* ... 1 Cor. 9:22
For when I am *w* ... 2 Cor. 12:10
WEAKENED (3/3)
w my strength in the ... Ps. 102:23
WEAKENS (1/1)
w the hands of the men ... Jer. 38:4
WEAKER (4/3)
the wife, as to the *w* ... 1 Pet. 3:7
WEAKNESS (10/10)
w were made strong ... Heb. 11:34
WEAKNESSES (2/2)
also helps in our *w* ... Rom. 8:26
WEALTH (37/37)
W gained by dishonesty ... Prov. 13:11
WEALTHY (3/3)
rich, have become *w* ... Rev. 3:17
WEANED (12/9)
w child shall put his ... Is. 11:8
WEAPON (7/7)
w formed against you ... Is. 54:17
WEAPONS (28/28)
For the *w* of our ... 2 Cor. 10:4
WEAR (15/15)
'What shall we *w* ... Matt. 6:31
WEARIED (10/8)
you have *w* Me with ... Is. 43:24
therefore, being *w* ... John 4:6
WEARINESS (2/2)
say, 'Oh, what a *w* ... Mal. 1:13
WEARISOME (2/2)
and much study is *w* ... Eccl. 12:12
WEARY (53/52)
shall run and not be *w* ... Is. 40:31
And let us not grow *w* ... Gal. 6:9
do not grow *w* in ... 2 Thess. 3:13

WEATHER (4/4)
'It will be fair *w* ... Matt. 16:2
WEDDING (13/13)
day there was a *w* ... John 2:1
WEEK (13/12)
the first day of the *w* ... Matt. 28:1
WEEKS (15/13)
w are determined ... Dan. 9:24
WEEP (49/44)
Hannah, why do you *w* ... 1 Sam. 1:8
a time to *w* ... Eccl. 3:4
you shall *w* no more ... Is. 30:19
Blessed are you who *w* ... Luke 6:21
of Jerusalem, do not *w* ... Luke 23:28
w with those who *w* ... Rom. 12:15
WEEPING (51/48)
the noise of the *w* ... Ezra 3:13
They shall come with *w* ... Jer. 31:9
There will be *w* ... Matt. 8:12
outside by the tomb *w* ... John 20:11
WEIGH (7/7)
O Most Upright, You *w* ... Is. 26:7
WEIGHED (23/20)
You have been *w* ... Dan. 5:27
WEIGHS (4/4)
eyes, but the LORD *w* ... Prov. 16:2
WEIGHT (45/40)
us lay aside every *w* ... Heb. 12:1
WEIGHTIER (1/1)
have neglected the *w* ... Matt. 23:23
WELFARE (2/2)
does not seek the *w* ... Jer. 38:4
WELL (267/255)
daughters have done *w* ... Prov. 31:29
wheel broken at the *w* ... Eccl. 12:6
"Those who are *w* ... Matt. 9:12
said to him, "*W* done ... Matt. 25:21
WELLS (12/11)
These are *w* without ... 2 Pet. 2:17
WENT (1,406/1,295)
They *w* out from us ... 1 John 2:19
out and *w* bitterly ... Matt. 26:75
He saw the city and *w* ... Luke 19:41
Jesus *w* ... John 11:35
WET (6/6)
his body was *w* with ... Dan. 4:33
WHEAT (49/49)
w falls into the ... John 12:24
WHEELS (29/22)
noise of rattling *w* ... Nah. 3:2
WHERE (546/497)
not knowing *w* he was ... Heb. 11:8
WHIP (3/3)
A *w* for the horse ... Prov. 26:3
WHIRLWIND (27/25)
Job out of the *w* ... Job 38:1
has His way in the *w* ... Nah. 1:3
WHISPER (5/5)
my ear received a *w* ... Job 4:12
WHISPERER (1/1)
w separates the best ... Prov. 16:28
WHISPERERS (1/1)
they are *w* ... Rom. 1:29
WHISPERINGS (1/1)
backbitings, *w* ... 2 Cor. 12:20
WHITE (71/64)
clothed in *w* garments ... Rev. 3:5
behold, a *w* horse ... Rev. 6:2
and made them *w* ... Rev. 7:14
WHOLE (237/232)
w body were an eye ... 1 Cor. 12:17
WHOLESOME (2/2)
not consent to *w* words ... 1 Tim. 6:3
WHOLLY (17/17)
w followed the LORD ... Deut. 1:36
WICKED (342/324)
w shall be silent ... 1 Sam. 2:9
w shall be no more ... Ps. 37:10
if there is any *w* ... Ps. 139:24
w forsake his way ... Is. 55:7
and desperately *w* ... Jer. 17:9
the sway of the *w* ... 1 John 5:19
WICKEDLY (21/21)
God will never do *w* ... Job 34:12
WICKEDNESS (128/121)
LORD saw that the *w* ... Gen. 6:5
in the tents of *w* ... Ps. 84:10
man repented of his *w* ... Jer. 8:6
is full of greed and *w* ... Luke 11:39
sexual immorality, *w* ... Rom. 1:29
and overflow of *w* ... James 1:21
WIDE (47/43)
shall open your hand *w* ... Deut. 15:8
w is the gate and ... Matt. 7:13
to you, our heart is *w* ... 2 Cor. 6:11
WIDOW (56/56)
the fatherless and *w* ... Ps. 146:9
How like a *w* is she ... Lam. 1:1
Then one poor *w* ... Mark 12:42
w has children or ... 1 Tim. 5:4
WIDOW'S (4/4)
and I caused the *w* ... Job 29:13

WIDOWS (26/24)
w were neglected ... Acts 6:1
to visit orphans and *w* ... James 1:27
WIFE (389/357)
and be joined to his *w* ... Gen. 2:24
w finds a good thing ... Prov. 18:22
but a prudent *w* ... Prov. 19:14
"Go, take yourself a *w* ... Hos. 1:2
divorces his *w* ... Mark 10:11
'I have married a *w* ... Luke 14:20
Remember Lot's *w* ... Luke 17:32
so love his own *w* ... Eph. 5:33
the husband of one *w* ... Titus 1:6
WILD (59/56)
olive tree which is *w* ... Rom. 11:24
WILDERNESS (306/293)
I will make the *w* ... Is. 41:18
of one crying in the *w* ... Matt. 3:3
the serpent in the *w* ... John 3:14
WILES (1/1)
to stand against the *w* ... Eph. 6:11
WILL (105/98)
w be done on earth as ... Matt. 6:10
but he who does the *w* ... Matt. 7:21
nevertheless not My *w* ... Luke 22:42
flesh, nor of the *w* ... John 1:13
not to do My own *w* ... John 6:38
w is present with me ... Rom. 7:18
acceptable and perfect *w* ... Rom. 12:2
works in you both to *w* ... Phil. 2:13
according to His own *w* ... Heb. 2:4
good work to do His *w* ... Heb. 13:21
WILLFULLY (2/2)
For if we sin *w* ... Heb. 10:26
For this they *w* ... 2 Pet. 3:5
WILLING (41/41)
If you are *w* and ... Is. 1:19
The spirit indeed is *w* ... Matt. 26:41
w that any should ... 2 Pet. 3:9
WILLINGLY (22/20)
by compulsion but *w* ... 1 Pet. 5:2
WILLOWS (5/5)
our harps upon the *w* ... Ps. 137:2
WILLS (9/8)
to whom the Son *w* ... Matt. 11:27
it is not of him who *w* ... Rom. 9:16
say, "If the Lord *w* ... James 4:15
WIN (8/7)
to all, that I might *w* ... 1 Cor. 9:19
WIND (131/122)
the chaff which the *w* ... Ps. 1:4
A reed shaken by the *w* ... Matt. 11:7
The *w* blows where ... John 3:8
of a rushing mighty *w* ... Acts 2:2
WINDOWS (24/22)
not open for you the *w* ... Mal. 3:10
WINDS (23/22)
be, that even the *w* ... Matt. 8:27
WINDSTORM (2/2)
And a great *w* arose ... Mark 4:37
WINE (235/214)
W is a mocker ... Prov. 20:1
love is better than *w* ... Song 1:2
Yes, come, buy *w* ... Is. 55:1
they gave Him sour *w* ... Matt. 27:34
do not be drunk with *w* ... Eph. 5:18
not given to much *w* ... Titus 2:3
WINEBIBBERS (1/1)
Do not mix with *w* ... Prov. 23:20
WINEPRESS (18/17)
"I have trodden the *w* ... Is. 63:3
into the great *w* ... Rev. 14:19
Himself treads the *w* ... Rev. 19:15
WINESKINS (15/7)
new wine into old *w* ... Matt. 9:17
WING (15/8)
One *w* of the cherub ... 1 Kin. 6:24
WINGS (75/63)
the shadow of Your *w* ... Ps. 36:7
with healing in His *w* ... Mal. 4:2
WINNOW (3/3)
You shall *w* them ... Is. 41:16
WINS (1/1)
w souls is wise ... Prov. 11:30
WINTER (16/15)
For lo, the *w* is past ... Song 2:11
flight may not be in *w* ... Matt. 24:20
WIPE (7/7)
w away every tear ... Rev. 21:4
WISDOM (227/215)
for this is your *w* ... Deut. 4:6
is the man who finds *w* ... Prov. 3:13
Get *w*! Get understanding! ... Prov. 4:5
is the beginning of *w* ... Prov. 9:10
w is justified by her ... Matt. 11:19
Jesus increased in *w* ... Luke 2:52
riches both of the *w* ... Rom. 11:33
the gospel, not with *w* ... 1 Cor. 1:17
For the *w* of this world ... 1 Cor. 3:19
not with fleshly *w* ... 2 Cor. 1:12
all the treasures of *w* ... Col. 2:3
If any of you lacks *w* ... James 1:5
power and riches and *w* ... Rev. 5:12
WISE (207/197)
Do not be *w* in your ... Prov. 3:7
he who wins souls is *w* ... Prov. 11:30
Therefore be *w* as ... Matt. 10:16
five of them were *w* ... Matt. 25:2
to God, alone *w* ... Rom. 16:27
Where is the *w* ... 1 Cor. 1:20
not as fools but as *w* ... Eph. 5:15
are able to make you *w* ... 2 Tim. 3:15
WISER (7/7)
he was *w* than all men ... 1 Kin. 4:31
of God is *w* than men ... 1 Cor. 1:25
WISH (32/31)
w it were already ... Luke 12:49
WISHED (14/11)
Then he *w* death for ... Jon. 4:8
WITCHCRAFT (6/6)
is as the sin of *w* ... 1 Sam. 15:23
WITHDRAW (10/10)
From such *w* yourself ... 1 Tim. 6:5
WITHER (15/13)
also shall not *w* ... Ps. 1:3
WITHERS (9/9)
The grass *w* ... Is. 40:7
The grass *w* ... 1 Pet. 1:24
WITHHELD (15/14)
and your sins have *w* ... Jer. 5:25
WITHHOLD (13/13)
good thing will He *w* ... Ps. 84:11
WITHOUT (302/267)
pray *w* ceasing ... 1 Thess. 5:17
w works is dead ... James 2:26
WITHSTAND (13/13)
you may be able to *w* ... Eph. 6:13
WITHSTOOD (4/4)
I *w* him to his face ... Gal. 2:11
WITNESS (137/119)
all the world as a *w* ... Matt. 24:14
This man came for a *w* ... John 1:7
do not receive Our *w* ... John 3:11
Christ, the faithful *w* ... Rev. 1:5
beheaded for their *w* ... Rev. 20:4
WITNESSED (5/5)
is revealed, being *w* ... Rom. 3:21
WITNESSES (51/49)
"You are My *w* ... Is. 43:10
the presence of many *w* ... 1 Tim. 6:12
so great a cloud of *w* ... Heb. 12:1
WIVES (134/123)
Husbands, love your *w* ... Eph. 5:25
w must be reverent ... 1 Tim. 3:11
WOLF (6/5)
The *w* and the lamb ... Is. 65:25
WOLVES (7/7)
out as lambs among *w* ... Luke 10:3
savage *w* will come in ... Acts 20:29
WOMAN (395/367)
she shall be called *W* ... Gen. 2:23
whoever looks at a *w* ... Matt. 5:28
Then the *w* of Samaria ... John 4:9
"*W*, behold your ... John 19:26
natural use of the *w* ... Rom. 1:27
His Son, born of a *w* ... Gal. 4:4
w being deceived ... 1 Tim. 2:14
w clothed with the sun ... Rev. 12:1
WOMB (75/73)
nations are in your *w* ... Gen. 25:23
in the *w* I knew you ... Jer. 1:5
is the fruit of your *w* ... Luke 1:42
WOMEN (190/180)
O fairest among *w* ... Song 1:8
w will be grinding ... Matt. 24:41
are you among *w* ... Luke 1:28
admonish the young *w* ... Titus 2:4
times, the holy *w* ... 1 Pet. 3:5
WONDER (11/11)
marvelous work and a *w* ... Is. 29:14
WONDERFUL (20/20)
things too *w* for me ... Job 42:3
name will be called *W* ... Is. 9:6
WONDERFULLY (1/1)
fearfully and *w* made ... Ps. 139:14
WONDERS (58/58)
"And I will show *w* ... Joel 2:30
signs, and lying *w* ... 2 Thess. 2:9
WONDROUS (16/16)
w works declare that ... Ps. 75:1
WONDROUSLY (1/1)
God, who has dealt *w* ... Joel 2:26
WOOD (128/119)
precious stones, *w* ... 1 Cor. 3:12
WOODCUTTERS (3/3)
but let them be *w* ... Josh. 9:21
WOOL (19/19)
they shall be as *w* ... Is. 1:18
hair were white like *w* ... Rev. 1:14
WORD (733/707)
w is very near you ... Deut. 30:14
w I have hidden ... Ps. 119:11
w is a lamp to my feet ... Ps. 119:105
the *w* of our God ... Is. 40:8
for every idle *w* ... Matt. 12:36
beginning was the *W* ... John 1:1
W became flesh and ... John 1:14
Your *w* is truth ... John 17:17
Let the *w* of Christ ... Col. 3:16
come to you in *w* only ... 1 Thess. 1:5
by the *w* of His power ... Heb. 1:3
w which they heard did ... Heb. 4:2
does not stumble in *w* ... James 3:2
let us not love in *w* ... 1 John 3:18
His name is called The *W* ... Rev. 19:13
WORDS (568/543)
Let the *w* of my mouth ... Ps. 19:14
The *w* of the wise are ... Eccl. 12:11
pass away, but My *w* ... Matt. 24:35
You have the *w* of ... John 6:68
not with wisdom of *w* ... 1 Cor. 1:17
those who hear the *w* ... Rev. 1:3
WORK (402/374)
day God ended His *w* ... Gen. 2:2
people had a mind to *w* ... Neh. 4:6
the *w* of Your fingers ... Ps. 8:3
Man goes out to his *w* ... Ps. 104:23
w is honorable and ... Ps. 111:3
God will bring every *w* ... Eccl. 12:14
For I will *w* a *w* ... Hab. 1:5
could do no mighty *w* ... Mark 6:5
"This is the *w* of God ... John 6:29
I must *w* the works ... John 9:4
w which You have given ... John 17:4
know that all things *w* ... Rom. 8:28
w is no longer *w* ... Rom. 11:6
Do not destroy the *w* ... Rom. 14:20
abounding in the *w* ... 1 Cor. 15:58
If anyone will not *w* ... 2 Thess. 3:10
but a doer of the *w* ... James 1:25
WORKED (32/30)
which He *w* in Christ ... Eph. 1:20
WORKER (8/8)
w is worthy of his ... Matt. 10:10
w who does not need ... 2 Tim. 2:15
WORKERS (35/35)
we are God's fellow *w* ... 1 Cor. 3:9
WORKING (27/26)
My Father has been *w* ... John 5:17
through faith in the *w* ... Col. 2:12
WORKMANSHIP (16/15)
For we are His *w* ... Eph. 2:10
WORKS (250/235)
are Your wonderful *w* ... Ps. 40:5
and let her own *w* ... Prov. 31:31
"For I know their *w* ... Is. 66:18
show Him greater *w* ... John 5:20
w that I do he will do ... John 14:12
might stand, not of *w* ... Rom. 9:11
is the same God who *w* ... 1 Cor. 12:6
Now the *w* of the flesh ... Gal. 5:19
not of *w*, lest anyone ... Eph. 2:9
for it is God who *w* ... Phil. 2:13
but does not have *w* ... James 2:14
also justified by *w* ... James 2:25
"I know your *w* ... Rev. 2:2
their *w* follow them ... Rev. 14:13
according to their *w* ... Rev. 20:12
WORLD (252/217)
The field is the *w* ... Matt. 13:38
He was in the *w* ... John 1:10
For God so loved the *w* ... John 3:16
His Son into the *w* ... John 3:17
w cannot hate you ... John 7:7
You are of this *w* ... John 8:23
I have overcome the *w* ... John 16:33
w may become guilty ... Rom. 3:19
be conformed to this *w* ... Rom. 12:2
loved this present *w* ... 2 Tim. 4:10
Do not love the *w* ... 1 John 2:15
w is passing away ... 1 John 2:17
WORLDS (2/2)
also He made the *w* ... Heb. 1:2
WORM (11/11)
But I am a *w* ... Ps. 22:6
w does not die and the ... Mark 9:44
WORMS (7/7)
And he was eaten by *w* ... Acts 12:23
WORMWOOD (10/9)
of the star is *W* ... Rev. 8:11
WORRY (9/8)
to you, do not *w* ... Matt. 6:25
WORRYING (3/3)
by *w* can add one cubit ... Matt. 6:27
WORSE (23/22)
w than their fathers ... Jer. 7:26
WORSHIP (112/105)
and have come to *w* Him ... Matt. 2:2
w what you do not know ... John 4:22
the angels of God *w* ... Heb. 1:6
WORSHIPED (67/66)
on their faces and *w* ... Rev. 11:16
WORSHIPER (1/1)
if anyone is a *w* ... John 9:31

WORTH (12/12)
and make my speech *w* . . . . Job 24:25
WORTHLESS (18/18)
Indeed they are all *w*. . . . . .Is. 41:29
WORTHLESSNESS (2/2)
long will you love *w*. . . . . Ps. 4:2
WORTHY (52/50)
present time are not *w* . . . . .Rom. 8:18
to walk *w* of the calling. . . . . .Eph. 4:1
the world was not *w*. . . . . .Heb. 11:38
"*W* is the Lamb who. . . . . Rev. 5:12
WOUND (20/17)
and my *w* incurable. . . . . .Jer. 15:18
and his deadly *w*. . . . . Rev. 13:3
WOUNDED (34/34)
But He was *w* for our. . . . . Is. 53:5
WOUNDING (1/1)
killed a man for *w* . . . . Gen. 4:23
WOUNDS (16/16)
Faithful are the *w*. . . . . .Prov. 27:6
WRANGLINGS (1/1)
useless *w* of men of. . . . . 1 Tim. 6:5
WRATH (198/194)
speak to them in His *w*. . . . . Ps. 2:5
Surely the *w* of man . . . . Ps. 76:10
So I swore in My *w*. . . . . Ps. 95:11
W is cruel and anger a. . . . . Prov. 27:4
in My *w* I struck you . . . . Is. 60:10
w remember mercy. . . . . Hab. 3:2
For the *w* of God is. . . . . Rom. 1:18
up for yourself *w* . . . . Rom. 2:5
nature children of *w*. . . . . Eph. 2:3
sun go down on your *w* . . . . Eph. 4:26
Let all bitterness, *w* . . . . .Eph. 4:31
not fearing the *w*. . . . . Heb. 11:27
for the *w* of man does. . . . . James 1:20
of the wine of the *w*. . . . . Rev. 14:8
for in them the *w*. . . . . Rev. 15:1
fierceness of His *w* . . . . Rev. 16:19
WRATHFUL (2/2)
w man stirs up strife. . . . . Prov. 15:18
WRESTLE (1/1)
For we do not *w* . . . . .Eph. 6:12
WRETCHED (2/2)
w man that I am. . . . . .Rom. 7:24
know that you are *w* . . . . Rev. 3:17
WRETCHEDNESS (1/1)
do not let me see my *w*. . . . . Num. 11:15
WRINKLE (1/1)
not having spot or *w*. . . . . .Eph. 5:27
WRITE (89/81)
w them on their hearts. . . . . Heb. 8:10
WRITING (22/21)
the *w* was the *w* . . . . .Ex. 32:16
WRITINGS (1/1)
do not believe his *w*. . . . . John 5:47
WRITTEN (280/272)
tablets of stone, *w* . . . . Ex. 31:18
your names are *w*. . . . . .Luke 10:20
"What I have *w* . . . . .John 19:22
WRONG (31/29)
has done nothing *w*. . . . . Luke 23:41
But he who does *w*. . . . . Col. 3:25
WRONGED (8/8)
We have *w* no one . . . . .2 Cor. 7:2
WRONGS (1/1)
me *w* his own soul. . . . . .Prov. 8:36
WROTE (62/61)
stooped down and *w*. . . . . .John 8:6
WROUGHT (2/2)
And skillfully *w*. . . . . Ps. 139:15

Y

YEAR (366/320)
the acceptable *y* . . . . .Is. 61:2
of sins every *y* . . . . Heb. 10:3
YEARS (528/445)
lives are seventy *y* . . . . Ps. 90:10
when He was twelve *y*. . . . . Luke 2:42
with Him a thousand *y*. . . . . Rev. 20:6
YES (209/204)
let your '*Y*' be '*Y*,'. . . . . Matt. 5:37
YESTERDAY (9/9)
For we were born *y*. . . . . Job 8:9
YOKE (56/50)
Take My *y* upon you . . . . Matt. 11:29
YOKED (2/2)
Do not be unequally *y*. . . . . .2 Cor. 6:14
YOUNG (370/350)
I have been *y* . . . . Ps. 37:25
she may lay her *y* . . . . Ps. 84:3
I write to you, *y*. . . . . 1 John 2:13
YOUNGER (32/32)
Likewise you *y* people. . . . . 1 Pet. 5:5
YOURS (73/65)
the battle is not *y* . . . . 2 Chr. 20:15
Y is the kingdom . . . . Matt. 6:13
And all Mine are *Y* . . . . John 17:10
for I do not seek *y* . . . . 2 Cor. 12:14
YOUTH (70/67)
the sins of my *y*. Ps. 25:7
in the days of your *y* . . . . Eccl. 11:9
I have kept from my *y*. . . . . .Matt. 19:20
YOUTHFUL (4/4)
Flee also *y* lusts. . . . . .2 Tim. 2:22

Z

ZEAL (22/21)
The *z* of the LORD of . . . . .2 Kin. 19:31
"*Z* for Your house has . . . . John 2:17
that they have a *z* . . . . .Rom. 10:2
ZEALOUS (18/17)
z for good works. . . . . Titus 2:14

A Note Regarding the Type

This Bible was set in the Thomas Nelson NKJV Typeface, commissioned by Thomas Nelson Publishers and designed in Aarhus by Klaus Krogh and Heidi Rand Sørensen of 2K/DENMARK. The letter forms take inspiration from a distinctive typeface found in an early Thomas Nelson *Novum Testamentum*, printed in 1844 in Edinburgh—which in turn reflects the Scotch Roman typefaces created by the celebrated English punchcutter Richard Austin for the type foundry of William Miller, circa 1808–1813.

Just as the NKJV translation inherits the tradition and literary beauty of the King James Bible while updating the language for today's readers, so Thomas Nelson's custom NKJV font family builds on classic letter forms of the past while reflecting cutting-edge typographical design. The result is a type design that is at once beautiful and efficient, traditional and modern—ideal for presenting the sacred words of ancient Scripture to readers today.

WORLD OF THE PATRIARCHS

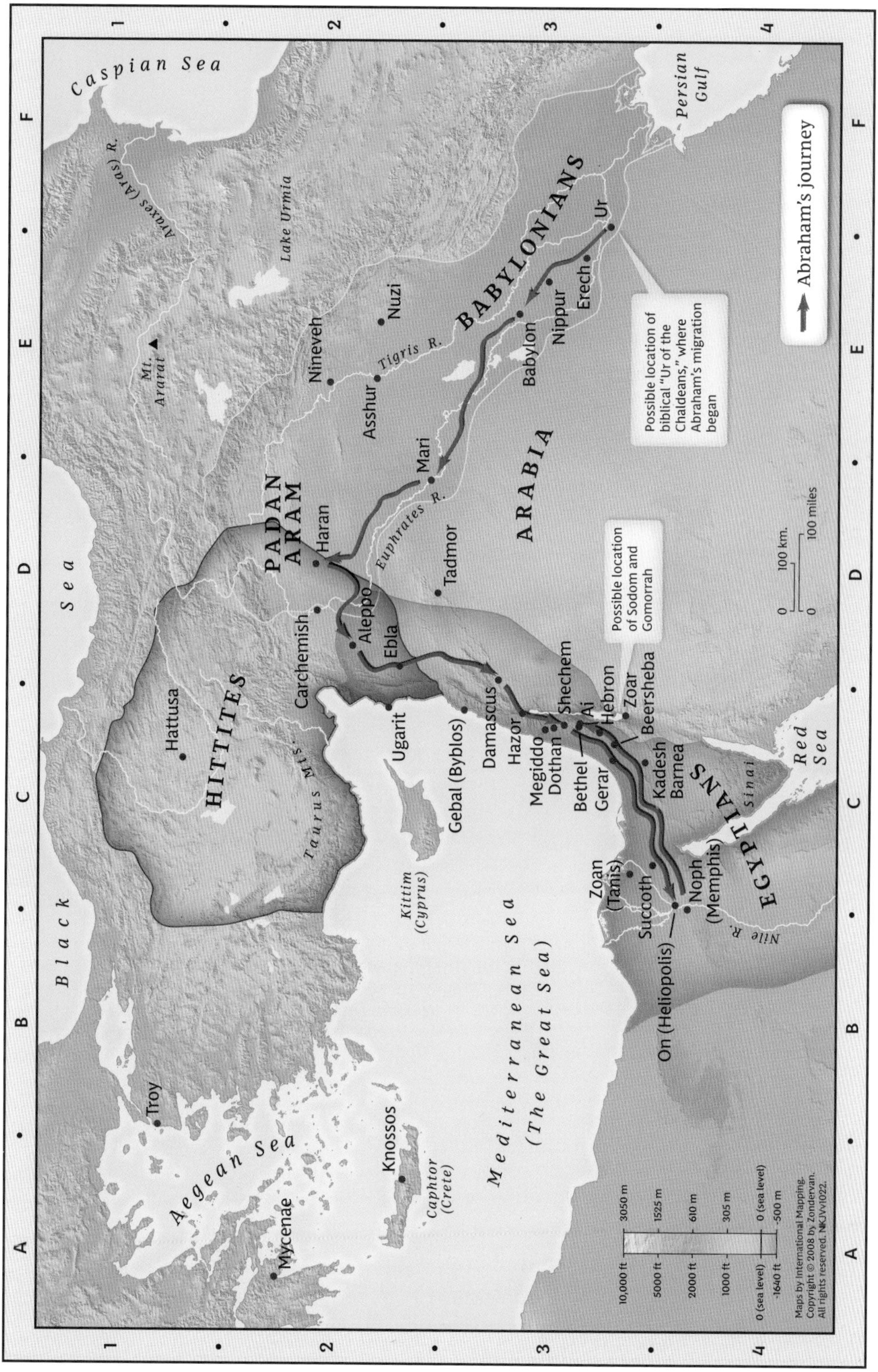

Caspian Sea
Black Sea
Aegean Sea
Mediterranean Sea
(The Great Sea)
Persian Gulf
Red Sea
Lake Urmia
Araxes (Aras) R.
Tigris R.
Euphrates R.
Nile R.
Mt. Ararat
Taurus Mts.
Sinai
HITTITES
PADAN ARAM
BABYLONIANS
ARABIA
EGYPTIANS
Troy
Mycenae
Knossos
Caphtor (Crete)
Kittim (Cyprus)
Hattusa
Carchemish
Haran
Aleppo
Ebla
Ugarit
Mari
Tadmor
Nineveh
Asshur
Nuzi
Babylon
Nippur
Erech
Ur
Gebal (Byblos)
Damascus
Hazor
Megiddo
Dothan
Shechem
Bethel
Ai
Hebron
Gerar
Beersheba
Zoar
Kadesh Barnea
Zoan (Tanis)
Succoth
On (Heliopolis)
Noph (Memphis)
Possible location of biblical "Ur of the Chaldeans," where Abraham's migration began
Possible location of Sodom and Gomorrah
Abraham's journey
0 100 km.
0 100 miles
10,000 ft 3050 m
5000 ft 1525 m
2000 ft 610 m
1000 ft 305 m
0 (sea level) 0 (sea level)
-1640 ft -500 m
A B C D E F
1 2 3 4

EXODUS AND CONQUEST OF CANAAN

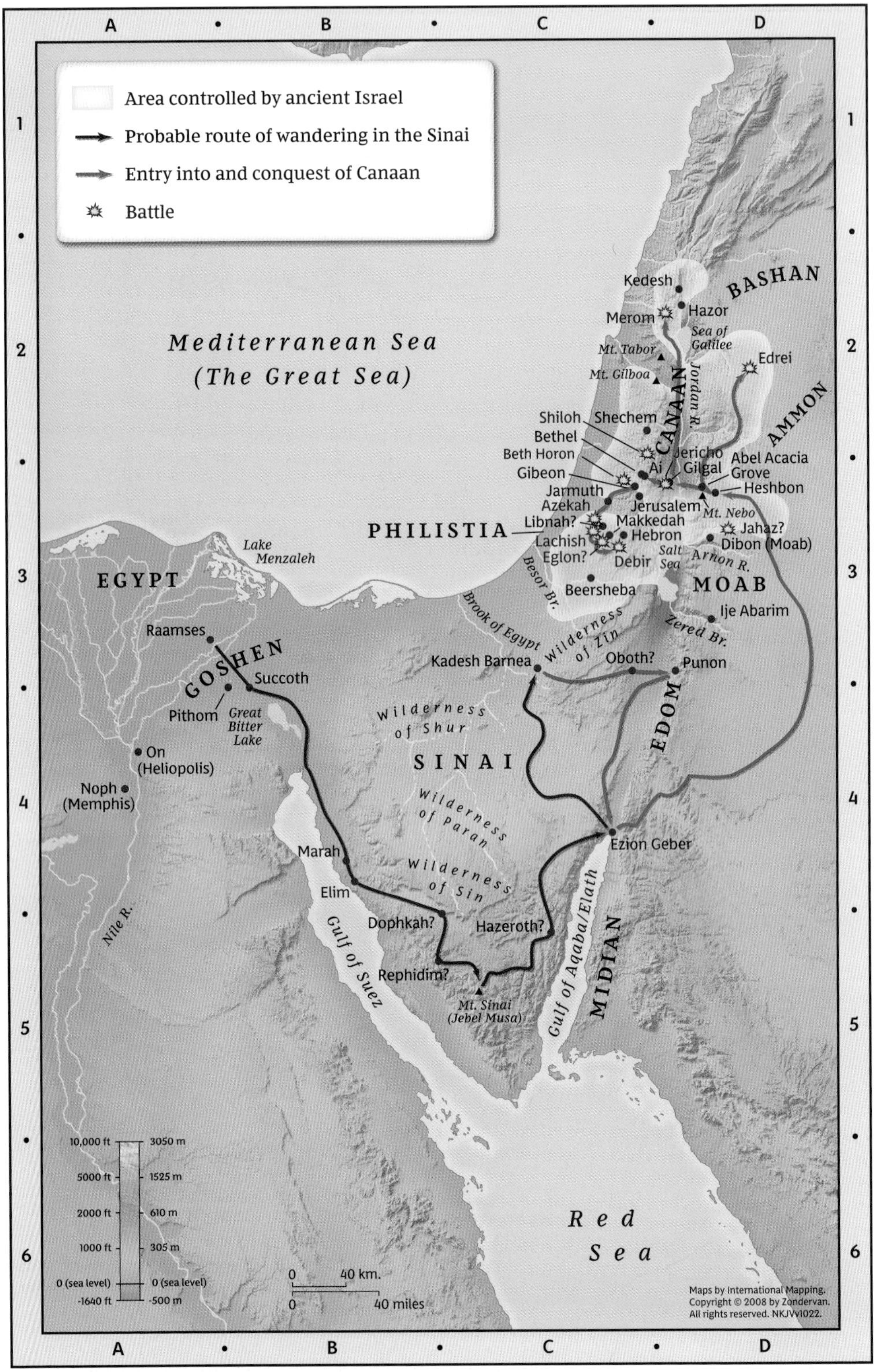

A
B
C
D
1
2
3
4
5
6
Area controlled by ancient Israel
Probable route of wandering in the Sinai
Entry into and conquest of Canaan
Battle
Mediterranean Sea
(The Great Sea)
Kedesh
BASHAN
Hazor
Merom
Sea of Galilee
Mt. Tabor
Mt. Gilboa
Jordan R.
Edrei
CANAAN
AMMON
Shiloh
Shechem
Bethel
Beth Horon
Jericho
Ai
Gilgal
Abel Acacia Grove
Gibeon
Heshbon
Jarmuth
Azekah
Jerusalem
Mt. Nebo
Libnah?
Makkedah
PHILISTIA
Hebron
Jahaz?
Lachish
Dibon (Moab)
Eglon?
Debir
Salt Sea
Arnon R.
Lake Menzaleh
EGYPT
Besor Br.
Beersheba
MOAB
Brook of Egypt
Wilderness of Zin
Ije Abarim
Zered Br.
Raamses
GOSHEN
Kadesh Barnea
Oboth?
Punon
Succoth
Pithom
Great Bitter Lake
Wilderness of Shur
EDOM
On (Heliopolis)
SINAI
Noph (Memphis)
Wilderness of Paran
Ezion Geber
Marah
Wilderness of Sin
Elim
Nile R.
Gulf of Suez
Dophkah?
Hazeroth?
Gulf of Aqaba/Elath
MIDIAN
Rephidim?
Mt. Sinai (Jebel Musa)
10,000 ft
3050 m
5000 ft
1525 m
2000 ft
610 m
1000 ft
305 m
0 (sea level)
0 (sea level)
-1640 ft
-500 m
0
40 km.
0
40 miles
Red Sea

LAND OF THE TWELVE TRIBES

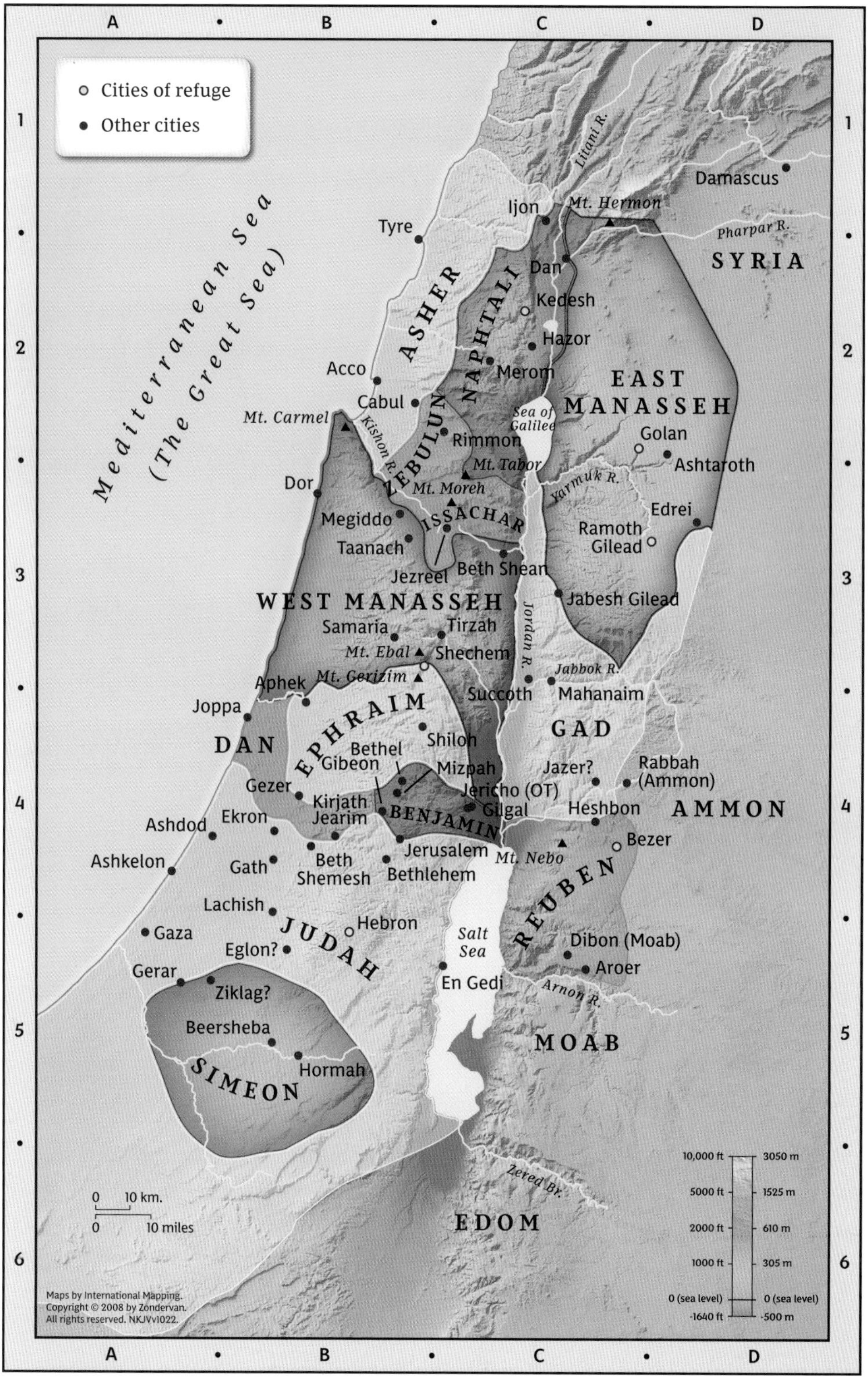

KINGDOM OF DAVID AND SOLOMON

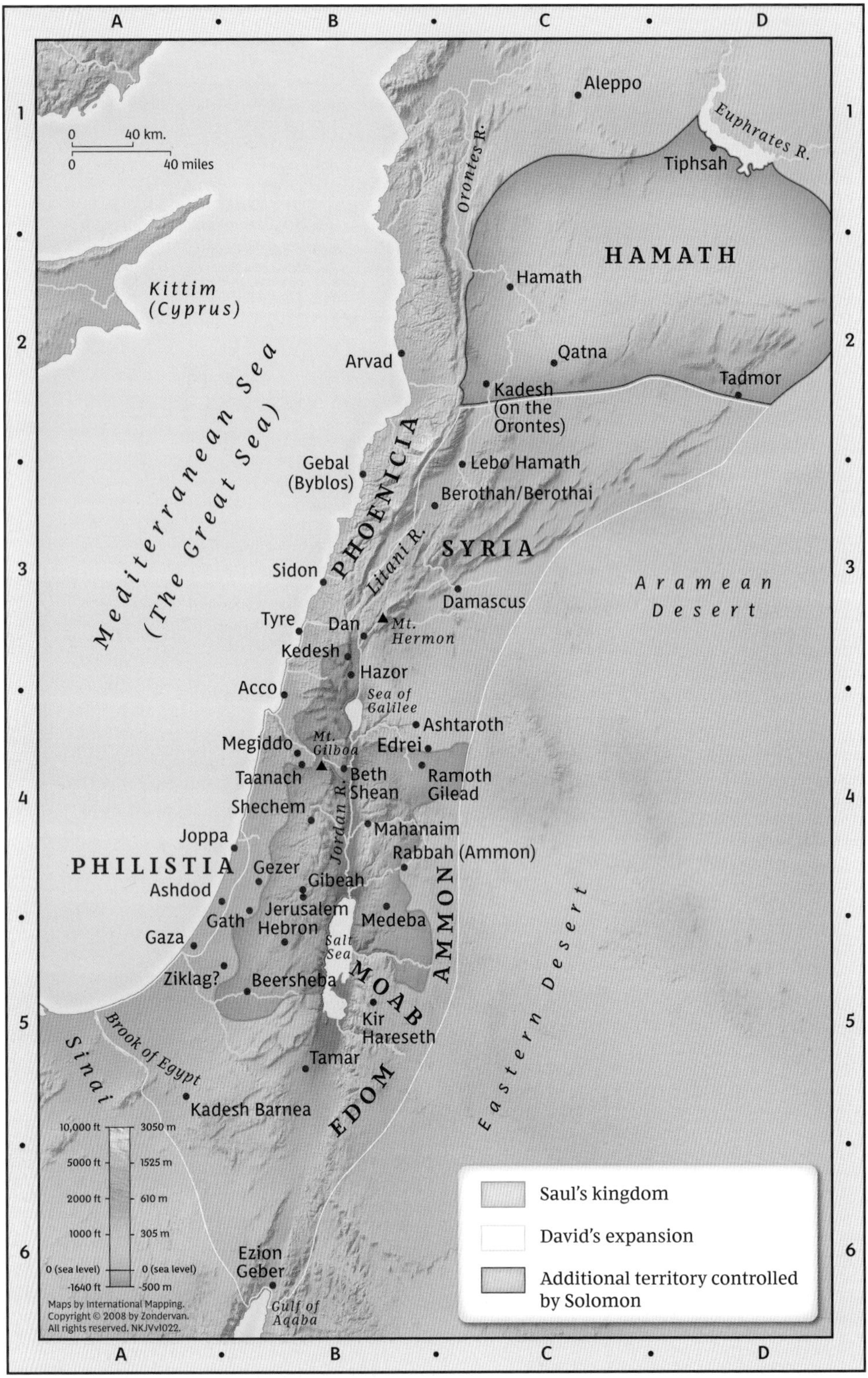
A
B
C
D
1
2
3
4
5
6
0 40 km.
0 40 miles
Aleppo
Euphrates R.
Tiphsah
Orontes R.
HAMATH
Hamath
Kittim
(Cyprus)
Qatna
Arvad
Mediterranean Sea
(The Great Sea)
Kadesh
(on the
Orontes)
Tadmor
PHOENICIA
Gebal
(Byblos)
Lebo Hamath
Berothah/Berothai
Litani R.
SYRIA
Sidon
Aramean
Desert
Damascus
Tyre
Dan
Mt.
Hermon
Kedesh
Hazor
Acco
Sea of
Galilee
Ashtaroth
Megiddo
Mt.
Gilboa
Edrei
Taanach
Beth
Shean
Ramoth
Gilead
Shechem
Jordan R.
Mahanaim
Joppa
Rabbah (Ammon)
PHILISTIA
Gezer
Gibeah
Ashdod
Jerusalem
Gath
Hebron
Medeba
AMMON
Gaza
Salt
Sea
Eastern Desert
Ziklag?
Beersheba
MOAB
Kir
Hareseth
Brook of Egypt
Sinai
Tamar
EDOM
Kadesh Barnea
10,000 ft
3050 m
5000 ft
1525 m
2000 ft
610 m
1000 ft
305 m
0 (sea level)
0 (sea level)
-1640 ft
-500 m
Ezion
Geber
Gulf of
Aqaba
Saul's kingdom
David's expansion
Additional territory controlled
by Solomon

JESUS' MINISTRY

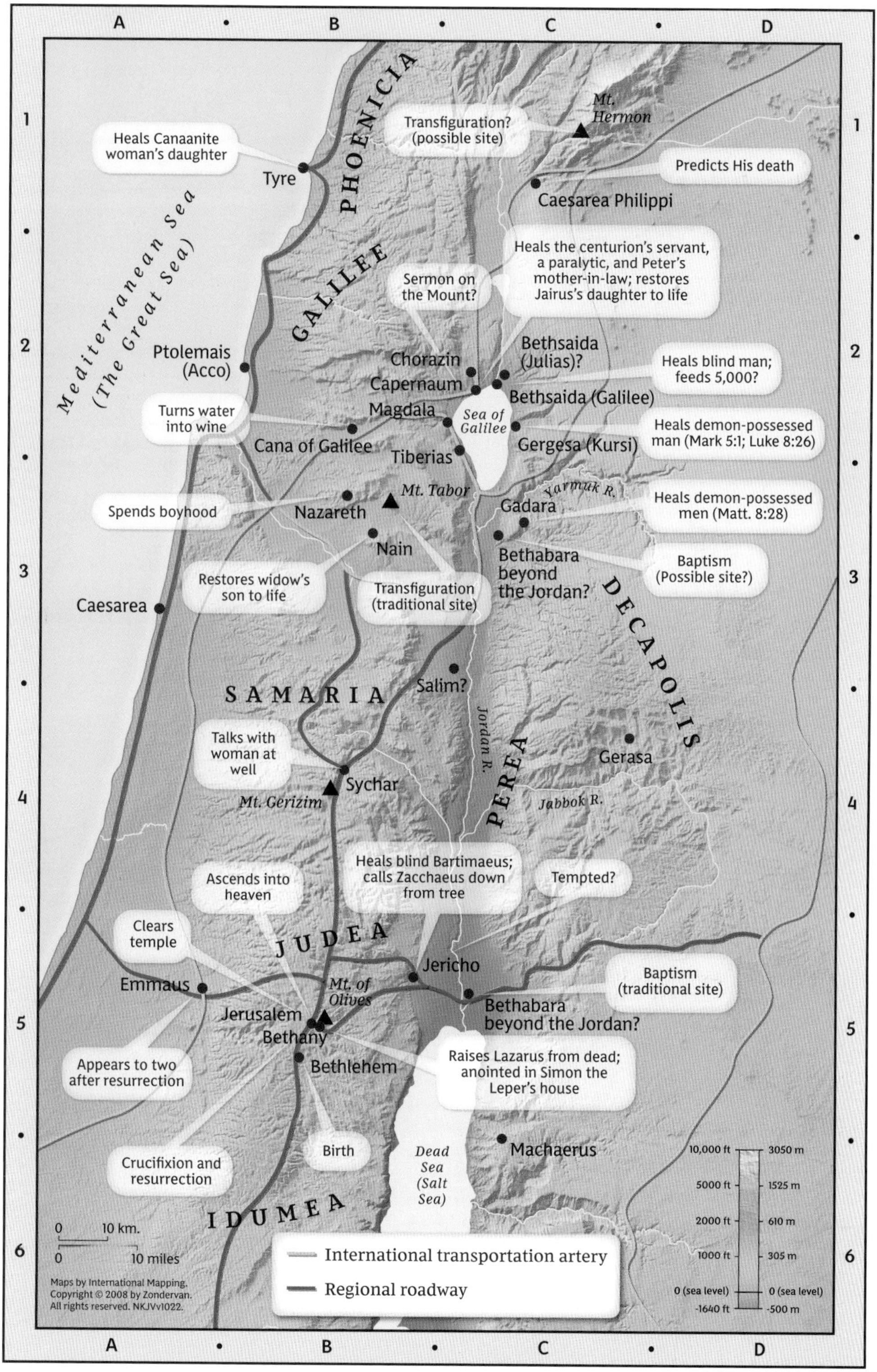

A
B
C
D
1
2
3
4
5
6
PHOENICIA
GALILEE
SAMARIA
JUDEA
IDUMEA
PEREA
DECAPOLIS
Mediterranean Sea
(The Great Sea)
Heals Canaanite woman's daughter
Tyre
Transfiguration? (possible site)
Mt. Hermon
Predicts His death
Caesarea Philippi
Heals the centurion's servant, a paralytic, and Peter's mother-in-law; restores Jairus's daughter to life
Sermon on the Mount?
Chorazin
Capernaum
Bethsaida (Julias)?
Heals blind man; feeds 5,000?
Bethsaida (Galilee)
Ptolemais (Acco)
Turns water into wine
Magdala
Sea of Galilee
Cana of Galilee
Tiberias
Gergesa (Kursi)
Heals demon-possessed man (Mark 5:1; Luke 8:26)
Mt. Tabor
Yarmuk R.
Spends boyhood
Nazareth
Gadara
Heals demon-possessed men (Matt. 8:28)
Nain
Bethabara beyond the Jordan?
Baptism (Possible site?)
Restores widow's son to life
Transfiguration (traditional site)
Caesarea
Salim?
Jordan R.
Talks with woman at well
Sychar
Mt. Gerizim
Gerasa
Jabbok R.
Heals blind Bartimaeus; calls Zacchaeus down from tree
Ascends into heaven
Tempted?
Clears temple
Jericho
Baptism (traditional site)
Emmaus
Mt. of Olives
Jerusalem
Bethany
Bethabara beyond the Jordan?
Raises Lazarus from dead; anointed in Simon the Leper's house
Appears to two after resurrection
Bethlehem
Birth
Crucifixion and resurrection
Machaerus
Dead Sea (Salt Sea)
0 10 km.
0 10 miles
International transportation artery
Regional roadway
10,000 ft 3050 m
5000 ft 1525 m
2000 ft 610 m
1000 ft 305 m
0 (sea level) 0 (sea level)
-1640 ft -500 m

PAUL'S MISSIONARY JOURNEYS

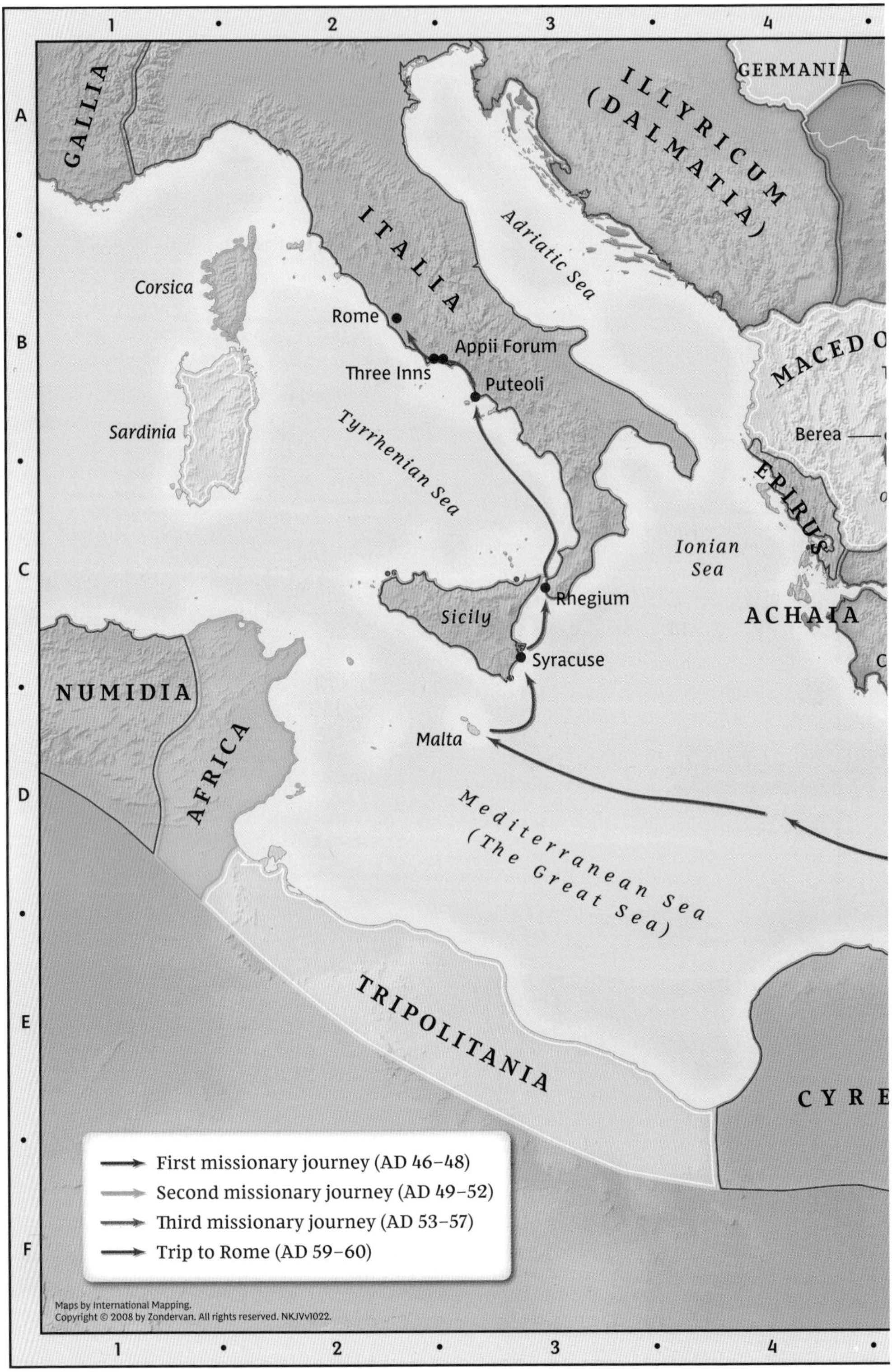

DACIA
MOESIA
THRACE
Black Sea
10,000 ft
5000 ft
2000 ft
1000 ft
0 (sea level)
-1640 ft
3050 m
1525 m
610 m
305 m
0 (sea level)
-500 m
DONIA
Amphipolis
Philippi
Thessalonica
Neapolis
Samothrace
Apollonia?
BITHYNIA & PONTUS
Mt. Olympus
Aegean Sea
Troas
MYSIA
Assos
ASIA
GALATIA
CAPPADOCIA
Mitylene
Pergamos
Thyatira
Chios
LYDIA
Sardis
LYCAONIA
Delphi
Smyrna
PISIDIA
Antioch in Pisidia
COMMAGENE
Athens
Ephesus
Philadelphia
Iconium
Samos
Laodicea
PAMPHYLIA
Euphrates R.
Cenchrea
Colosse
Derbe
Corinth
Miletus
Lystra
CILICIA
Sparta
Patmos
LYCIA
Tarsus
Issus
Attalia
SYRIA
Cos
Cnidus
Seleucia Pieria
Patara
Aleppo
Crete
Myra
Antioch
Rhodes
Perga
Cyprus
Phoenix
Salmone
Lasea
Salamis
Claudа
Fair Havens
Paphos
ABILENE
PHOENICIA
Mediterranean Sea
(The Great Sea)
Sidon
Tyre
Damascus
Ptolemais
Caesarea
JUDEA
Jordan R.
Jerusalem
Dead Sea
ENAICA
ARABIA
EGYPT
Nile R.
0
200 km.
0
200 miles
Red Sea
5
6
7
8
A
B
C
D
E
F

JERUSALEM IN THE TIME OF JESUS

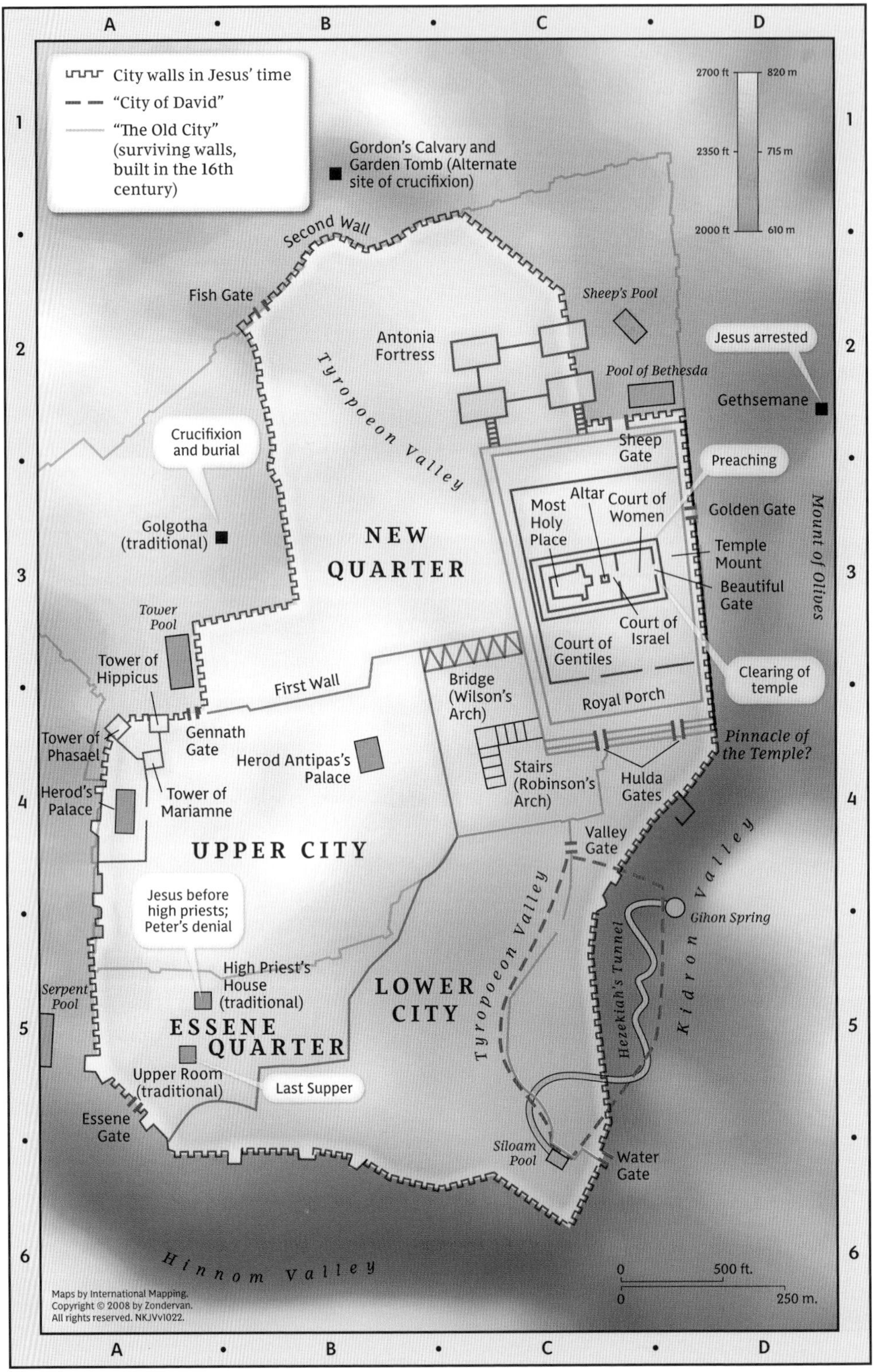

A
B
C
D
1
2
3
4
5
6
City walls in Jesus' time
"City of David"
"The Old City" (surviving walls, built in the 16th century)
2700 ft
820 m
2350 ft
715 m
2000 ft
610 m
Gordon's Calvary and Garden Tomb (Alternate site of crucifixion)
Second Wall
Fish Gate
Sheep's Pool
Antonia Fortress
Jesus arrested
Pool of Bethesda
Gethsemane
Tyropoeon Valley
Crucifixion and burial
Sheep Gate
Preaching
Altar
Most Holy Place
Court of Women
Golden Gate
Mount of Olives
Golgotha (traditional)
NEW QUARTER
Temple Mount
Beautiful Gate
Court of Israel
Court of Gentiles
Tower Pool
Tower of Hippicus
First Wall
Bridge (Wilson's Arch)
Clearing of temple
Royal Porch
Tower of Phasael
Gennath Gate
Herod Antipas's Palace
Pinnacle of the Temple?
Stairs (Robinson's Arch)
Hulda Gates
Herod's Palace
Tower of Mariamne
UPPER CITY
Valley Gate
Kidron Valley
Jesus before high priests; Peter's denial
Gihon Spring
Tyropoeon Valley
Hezekiah's Tunnel
High Priest's House (traditional)
Serpent Pool
LOWER CITY
ESSENE QUARTER
Upper Room (traditional)
Last Supper
Essene Gate
Siloam Pool
Water Gate
Hinnom Valley
0
500 ft.
0
250 m.